GALE DIRECTORY OF PUBLICATIONS AND BROADCAST MEDIA

ISSN 1048-7972

153rd Edition

Published annually since 1869

GALE DIRECTORY OF PUBLICATIONS AND BROADCAST MEDIA

(Formerly *Ayer Directory of Publications*)

An annual Guide to Publications and Broadcasting Stations
Including Newspapers, Magazines, Journals, Radio Stations,
Television Stations, and Cable Systems

Volume 1

U.S. and Canada

Alabama-New Hampshire

Entries 1-21147

GALE
CENGAGE Learning

Farmington Hills, Mich • San Francisco • New York • Waterville, Maine
Meriden, Conn • Mason, Ohio • Chicago

Gale Directory of Publications and Broadcast Media, 153rd Edition

Project Editors: Donna Batten

Editorial Support Services: Emmanuel T. Barrido

Composition and Electronic Prepress: Gary Leach

Manufacturing: Rita Wimberley

For product information and technology assistance, contact us at
Gale Customer Support, 1-800-877-4253.
For permission to use material from this text or product,
submit all requests online at **www.cengage.com/permissions.**
Further permissions questions can be emailed to
permissionrequest@cengage.com

While every effort has been made to ensure the reliability of the information presented in this publication, Gale, a part of Cengage Learning, does not guarantee the accuracy of the data contained herein. Gale accepts no payment for listing; and inclusion in the publication of any organization, agency, institution, publication, service, or individual does not imply endorsement of the editors or publisher. Errors brought to the attention of the publisher and verified to the satisfaction of the publisher will be corrected in future editions.

EDITORIAL DATA PRIVACY POLICY. Does this publication contain information about you as an individual? If so, for more information about our editorial data privacy policies, please see our Privacy Statement at www.gale.com.

Gale
27500 Drake Rd.
Farmington Hills, MI 48331-3535

ISBN-13: 978-1-4144-8808-0 (Set)
ISBN-13: 978-1-4144-8809-7 (Volume 1)
ISBN-13: 978-1-4144-8810-3 (Volume 2)
ISBN-13: 978-1-4144-8811-0 (Volume 3)
ISBN-13: 978-1-4144-8812-7 (Volume 4)
ISBN-13: 978-1-4144-8813-4 (Volume 5)

ISSN 1048-7972

This title is also available as an e-book
ISBN-13: 978-1-4144-8782-3
Contact your Gale, Cengage Learning, sales representative for ordering information.

Printed in the United States of America
1 2 3 4 5 6 7 20 19 18 17 16

Contents

Introduction

The Gale Directory of Publications and Broadcast Media (GDPBM) has been the definitive media source since its inception in 1869. Formerly the *Ayer Directory of Publications*, and now in its 153rd edition, *GDPBM* has grown with U.S., Canadian, and international media, and increased its scope to include the most current communication technologies. *GDPBM* now covers over 53,000 newspapers, magazines, journals, and other periodicals, as well as radio, television, and cable stations and systems. Organized to help users find facts fast, *GDPBM* covers the whole media picture—ad rates, circulation statistics, local programming, names of key personnel, and other useful, accurate information. In addition, *GDPBM* offers a geographic arrangement that provides easy access to listings. Only *GDPBM* presents print/online and broadcast entries in one geographic sort, then alphabetically within state, province, territory, region, or country; city; and media category (Print/online or Broadcast).

Highlights of this Edition

The 153rd Edition of *Gale Directory of Publications and Broadcast Media* features approximately 1000 new listings.

Scope and Preparation

The following categories of publications are **excluded** from the *Gale Directory of Publications and Broadcast Media*'s coverage of the U.S., Canadian, and international print/online and broadcast arenas:

- newsletters and pamphlets
- directories

Information provided in *GDPBM* is obtained primarily through research of publication and publisher websites. Other published sources are used to verify some information, such as the audited circulation data in publication listings.

Organizations identified as defunct are removed from the main body of entries and listed in the Master Name and Keyword Index as “Ceased.” The same procedure is followed for listings that cannot be located; these entries are listed in the Master Index as “Unable to locate.” Efforts to clarify the status of "unable to locate" organizations are ongoing.

Acknowledgments

The editors are grateful to the many media professionals who generously responded to our requests for updated information, and helped in the shaping of this edition with their comments and suggestions throughout the year.

Available in Electronic Formats

Online. *Gale Directory of Publications and Broadcast Media* is accessible through Dialog online services. *GDPBM* (along with *Directories In Print*) is available as File 469 through Dialog. For more information, contact Dialog, 2250 Perimeter Park Dr., Ste. 300, Morrisville, North Carolina 27560; phone: (919)804-6400; toll-free: 800-3-DIALOG.

GDPBM is also available through InfoTrac as part of the *Gale Directory Library*. For more information, call 1-800-877-GALE.

Comments and Suggestions Welcome

If you have questions, concerns, or comments about *Gale Directory of Publications and Broadcast Media* please contact:

Project Editor
Gale Directory of Publications and Broadcast Media
Gale
27500 Drake Rd.
Farmington Hills, MI 48331-3535
Phone: (248) 699-4253
Toll-free: 800-877-4253
Fax: (248) 699-8075
URL: http://www.gale.cengage.com
Email: donna.batten@cengage.com

Gale Directory of Publications and Broadcast Media comprises five volumes:

- Volume 1 includes U.S. entries from Alabama to New Hampshire.
- Volume 2 encompasses U.S. listings from New Jersey to Wyoming and Canadian entries.
- Volume 3 contains U.S. and Canadian broadcast & cable networks, news & feature syndicates, and 21 indexes.
- Volume 4 contains the U.S. and Canadian regional market index.
- Volume 5 includes entries from Afghanistan to Zimbabwe and 17 indexes to International listings.

The samples and notes below offer more details on specific content and how to use the *Directory's* listings and indexes. Please note that entry information appearing in this section has been fabricated.

Sample Entries

In the fabricated samples that follow, each numbered section designates information that might appear in a *GDPBM* listing. The numbered items are explained in the descriptive paragraphs following each sample.

Sample Publication Listing

▮1▮ 222 ▪ ▮2▮ American Computer Review: ▮3▮ The Programmer's Friend.
▮4▮ Jane Doe Publishing Company, Inc.
▮5▮ 199 E. 49th St.
PO Box 724866
Salem, NY 10528-5555
▮6▮ Phone: (518)555-9277
▮7▮ Fax: (518)555-9288
▮8▮ Free: 800-555-5432
▮9▮ Publication E-mail: acr@jdpci.com
▮10▮ Publisher E-mail: jdpci@jdpci.com
▮11▮ Magazine for users of Super Software Plus products. **▮12▮ Founded:** June 1979. **▮13▮ Freq:** Monthly (combined issue July/Aug.). **▮14▮ Print Method:** Offset. **▮15▮ Trim Size:** 8/12 x 11. **▮16▮ Cols./Page:** 3. **▮17▮ Col. Width:** 24 nonpareils. **▮18▮ Col. Depth:** 294 agate lines. **▮19▮ Key Personnel:** Ian Smith, Editor, phone (518)555-1201, fax (518)555-1202, ismith@jdpci.com; James Newman, Publisher; Steve Jones Jr., Advertising Mgr. **▮20▮ ISSN:** 0042-062X (print); **EISSN:** 1756-1221 (electronic). **▮21▮ Subscription Rates:** $25; $30 Canada; $2.50 single issue. **▮22▮ Online:** Lexis-Nexis **▮23▮ Alternate Format(s):** Braille; CD-ROM; Microform. **▮24▮ Formerly:** Computer Software Review (Dec. 13, 1986). **▮25▮ Feature Editors:** Ann Walker, *Consumer Affairs, Editorials,* phone (518)555-2306, fax (518)555-2307, aw@jdpci.com. **▮26▮ URL:** http://www.acrmagazine.com. **▮27▮ Mailing Address:** PO Box 601, New York, NY 10016. **▮28▮ Ad Rates:** BW: $850, PCI: $.75. **▮29▮ Remarks:** Color advertising not accepted. **▮30▮ Circulation:** 25,000

Description of Numbered Elements

▮1▮ Entry Number. Entries are numbered sequentially. Entry numbers, rather than page numbers, are used to refer to listings.

▮2▮ Publication Title. Publication names are listed *as they appear on the masthead or title page.*

▮3▮ Subtitle. Included if applicable.

▮4▮ Publishing Company. The name of the commercial publishing organization, association, or academic institution, as provided by respondents.

▮5▮ Address. Full mailing address information is provided wherever possible. This may include: street address; post office box; city; state or province; and ZIP or postal code. ZIP plus-four numbers are provided when known.

▮6▮ Phone. Phone numbers listed in this section are usually the publisher's switchboard number.

▮7▮ Fax. Facsimile numbers are listed when available.

▮8▮ Free. Toll-free numbers are listed when available.

▮9▮ Publication E-mail. Electronic mail addresses for the publication are included when available.

▮10▮ Publisher E-mail: Electronic mail addresses for the publishing company are included when available.

▮11▮ Description. Includes the type of publication (i.e., newspaper, magazine) as well as a brief statement of purpose, intended audience, or other relevant remarks.

▮12▮ Founded. Date the periodical was first published.

▮13▮ Frequency. Indicates how often the publication is issued—daily, weekly, monthly, quarterly, etc. Explanatory remarks sometimes accompany this information (e.g., for weekly titles, the day of issuance; for collegiate titles, whether publication is limited to the academic year; whether certain issues are combined.)

▮14▮ Print Method. Though offset is most common, other methods are listed as provided.

▮15▮ Trim Size. Presented in inches unless otherwise noted.

▮16▮ Number of Columns Per Page. Usually one figure, but some publications list two or more, indicating a variation in style.

▮17▮ Column Width. Column sizes can be in inches, picas (6 picas to an inch), nonpareils (each 6 points, 72 points to an inch), or agate lines (14 to an inch).

▮18▮ Column Depth. Column sizes can be in inches, picas (6 picas to an inch), nonpareils (each 6 points, 72 points to an inch), or agate lines (14 to an inch).

▮19▮ Key Personnel. Presents the names and titles of contacts for each publication. May include phone, fax, and e-mail addresses if different than those for the publication and company.

▮20▮ International Standard Serial Number (ISSN). Included for print and electronic when available. Occasionally, United States Publications Serial (USPS) numbers are reported rather than ISSNs.

▮21▮ Subscription Rates. Unless otherwise stated, prices shown in this section are the individual annual subscription rate. Other rates are listed when known, including multiyear rates, prices outside the United States, discount rates, library/institution rates, and single copy prices.

▮22▮ Online. If a publication is accessible online, that information is listed here. If the publication is available online but the details of the URL or vendor are not known, the notation "Available Online" will be listed.

▮23▮ Alternate Format(s). Lists additional mediums in which a publication may be available (other than online), including CD-ROM and microform.

▮24▮ Variant Name(s). Lists former or variant names of the publication, including the year the change took place, when known.

▮25▮ Feature Editors. Lists the names and beats of any feature editors employed by the publication.

▮26▮ URL: Internet access to the publication.

▮27▮ Mailing Address. Includes mailing address when different from the editorial/publisher address.

▮28▮ Ad Rates. Respondents may provide non-contract (open) rates in any of six categories:

GLR = general line rate

BW = one-time black & white page rate

4C = one-time four-color page rate

SAU = standard advertising unit rate

CNU = Canadian newspaper advertising unit rate

PCI = per column inch rate

Occasionally, explanatory information about other types of advertising appears in the Remarks section of the entry.

▮29▮ Remarks. Information listed in this section further explains the Ad Rates.

▮30▮ Circulation. Figures represent various circulation numbers; the figures are accompanied by a symbol (except for sworn and estimated figures). Following are explanations of the eight circulation classifications used by *GDPBM,* the corresponding symbols, if any, are listed at the bottom of each right hand page. All circulation figures *except* publisher's reports and estimated figures appear in boldface type.

These audit bureaus are independent, nonprofit organizations (with the exception of VAC, which is for-profit) that verify circulation rates. Interested users may contact the association for more information.

- **AAM:** Alliance for Audited Media, formerly Audit Bureau of Circulations, 48 W. Seegers Rd. Arlington Heights, IL 60005-3913; (224)366-6939. http://auditedmedia.com
- **CAC:** Certified Audit of Circulations, Inc., 155 Willowbrook Blvd., Wayne, NJ 07470; (973)785-3000. http://www.certifiedaudit.com
- **BPA:** BPA Worldwide, absorbed Canadian Circulations Audit Board, 100 Beard Sawmill Rd., 6th Fl., Shelton, CT 06484; (203)447-2900. http://www.bpaww.com
- **VAC:** Verified Audit Circulation, 900 Larkspur Landing Cir. #230, Larkspur, CA 94939; (415)461-6006. htttp://www.verifiedaudit.com
- **Post Office Statement:** These figures were verified from a U.S. Post Office form.
- **Publisher's Statement:** These figures were accompanied by the signature of the editor, publisher, or other officer.
- **Sworn Statement:** These figures, which appear in **boldface** without a symbol, were accompanied by the notarized signature of the editor, publisher, or other officer of the publication.
- **Estimated Figures:** These figures, which are shown in lightface without a symbol, are the unverified report of the publisher.

The footer on every odd-numbered page contains a key to circulation and entry type symbols, as well as advertising abbreviations.

Sample Broadcast Listing

▮1▮ 111 ▪ ▮2▮ WCAF-AM—1530
▮3▮ 199 E. 49th St.
PO Box 724866
Salem, NY 10528-5555
▮4▮ Phone: (518)555-9277
▮5▮ Fax: (518)555-9288
▮6▮ Free: 800-555-5432
▮7▮ E-mail: wcaf@wcaf.com
▮8▮ Format: Classical. **▮9▮ Simulcasts:** WCAF-FM. **▮10▮ Network(s):** Westwood One Radio; ABC. **▮11▮ Owner: Affici Communications, Inc., at above address. ▮12▮ Founded:** 1996. **▮13▮ Formerly:** WCAH-AM (1992). **▮14▮ Operating Hours:** Continuous; 90% local, 10% network. **▮15▮ ADI:** Elmira, NY. **▮16▮ Key Personnel:** James Smith, General Mgr., phone (518)555-1002, fax (518)555-1010, jsmith@wcaf.com; Don White, Program Dir. **▮17▮ Cities Served:** Salem, NY. **▮18▮ Postal Areas Served:** 10528; 10529. **▮19▮ Local Programs:** Who's Beethoven? Clement Goebel, Contact, (518)555-1301, fax (518)555-1320. **▮20▮ Wattage:** 5000. **▮21▮ Ad Rates:** Underwriting available. $10-15 for 30 seconds; $30-35 for 60

seconds. Combined advertising rates available with WCAF-FM. **▌22▌ URL:** http://www.wcaf.com. **▌23▌ Mailing Address:** PO Box 555, Elmira, NY, 10529.

Description of Numbered Elements

▌1▌ Entry Number. Entries are numbered sequentially. Entry numbers (rather than page numbers) are used to refer to listings.

▌2▌ Call Letters and Frequency/Channel or **Cable Company Name.**

▌3▌ Address. Location and studio addresses. If known, alternate addresses are listed in the Mailing Address section of the entries (see item 23 below).

▌4▌ Phone. Telephone numbers are listed when available.

▌5▌ Fax. Facsimile numbers are listed when available.

▌6▌ Free. Toll-free numbers are listed when available.

▌7▌ E-mail. Electronic mail addresses are included when available.

▌8▌ Format. For television station entries, this subheading indicates whether the station is commercial or public. Radio station entries contain industry-defined (and, in some cases, station-defined) formats.

▌9▌ Simulcasts. Lists stations that provide simulcasting.

▌10▌ Network(s). Notes national and regional networks with which a station is affiliated.

▌11▌ Owner. Lists the name of an individual or company, supplemented by the address and telephone number, when available. If the address is the same as that of the station or company, the notation "at above address" is used, referring to the station or cable company address.

▌12▌ Founded. In most cases, the year the station/company began operating, regardless of changes in call letters/names and ownership.

▌13▌ Variant Name(s). For radio and television stations, former call letters and the years in which there were changes are presented. Former cable company names and the years in which they were changed are also noted when available.

▌14▌ Operating Hours. Lists on-air hours and often includes percentages of network and local programming.

▌15▌ ADI (Area of Dominant Influence). The Area of Dominant Influence is a standard market region defined by the Arbitron Ratings Company for U.S. television stations. Some respondents also list radio stations as having ADIs.

▌16▌ Key Personnel. Presents the names and titles of contacts at each station or cable company.

▌17▌ Cities Served. This heading is primarily found in cable system entries and provides information on channels and the number of subscribers.

▌18▌ Postal Areas Served. This heading is primarily found in cable system entries and provides information on the postal (zip) codes served by the system.

▌19▌ Local Programs. Lists names, air times, and contact personnel of locally-produced television and radio shows.

▌20▌ Wattage. Applicable to radio stations, the wattage may differ for day and night in the case of AM stations. Occasionally a station's ERP (effective radiated power) is given in addition to, or instead of, actual licensed wattage.

▌21▌ Ad Rates. Includes rates for 10, 15, 30, and 60 seconds as provided by respondents. Some stations price advertisement spots "per unit" regardless of length; these units vary.

▌22▌ URL: Internet access to the broadcast organization.

▌23▌ Mailing Address: Includes mailing address when different from the station, owner, or company address.

Index Notes

Volumes 3 and 5 of the *Gale Directory of Publications and Broadcast Media* each feature a publishers index, referring to main section listings by entry number. Both volumes also include an index to subject terms, multiple subject indexes, and a master name and keyword index. These indexes refer to main section listings in Volumes 1 and 2 (U.S. and Canada) and Volume 5 (International) by entry number and geographic location. Volume 4 features a regional market index to all U.S. and Canadian listings, divided by publication or broadcast type. This index also refers back to main section listings in the first two volumes by entry number.

Publishers Index The Publishers Indexes in Volumes 3 (U.S. and Canada) and 5 (International) provide an alphabetical listing of the more than 18,000 publishers whose publications are listed in *GDPBM*. Entries in these indexes include publisher name, address, phone and fax numbers, email, URL and periodicals published. Multiple addresses for publishers are listed geographically by state, province, or country.

Index to Subject Terms The Index to Subject Terms is a consolidated alphabetical listing of the nearly 1,000 subject terms appearing in the Subject Indexes. Terms listed in this index are followed by page numbers in the appropriate subject index. Multiple page number citations indicate repeated uses of the terms. Additionally, "see" and "see also" references are provided.

Subject Indexes Eighteen indexes in Volume 3 (U.S. and Canada) and Fifteen indexes in Volume 5 (International) group listings by broad type or subject. These indexes have been arranged under several major categories with bleed tabs to facilitate use. Citations are presented in one of two formats:

- geographically, by states, provinces, and countries
- by subject, and within subject, geographically

Major categories are noted in the Table of Contents. Subcategories, shown as subheadings in the indexes, are listed alphabetically in the Index to Subject Terms.

Citations in the indexes refer to entry number, and for publications, provide circulation figures. (Circulation symbols are explained in footnotes on odd-numbered pages.) Additionally, the Daily Newspapers Indexes provide complete address and telephone information.

Master Index The two Master Indexes provide comprehensive listings of all entries and keywords, both print/online and broadcast, included in Volumes 1 and 2 (U.S. and Canada) and Volume 5 (International) of *GDPBM*. Citations in these indexes are interfiled alphabetically throughout, regardless of media type.

Publication citations include the following:

- titles
- keywords within titles
- former titles
- alternate titles

Broadcast media citations include the following:

- station call letters
- cable company names (U.S. and Canada)
- former call letters
- former cable company names (U.S. and Canada)
- radio, television, and cable company cessations

Indexing is word-by-word rather than letter-by-letter. Thus, "New York" is listed before "News." Current listings in the Index include geographic information and entry number. Former names, whether publication or broadcast, are indicated by an * and do not include a geographic designation.

Regional Market Index Volume 4 of the *Gale Directory of Publications and Broadcast Media* (*GDPBM*) features a regional market index, referring to main section entries in Volumes 1 and 2 (U.S. and Canada) by entry number. This index is divided into five sections:

- Newspaper Index
- Periodical Index
- Cable Index
- Radio Index
- Television Index

Each section is arranged geographically by region and then sorted by circulation, number of subscribing households, or Area of Dominant Influence (ADI). *[Note: Occasionally an ADI will appear under a region other than that listed. This is the result of an ADI designation which covers multiple neighboring states and will be represented multiple times.]* Newspaper and Periodical Index citations include publication title, entry number (given in parentheses immediately following the title), publisher name, address, phone and fax numbers, publication subject, and circulation figures. Cable Index citations include cable company name, entry number (given in parentheses immediately following the title), address, phone and fax numbers, cities served and number of subscribing households. Radio and Television Index citations include station call letters, entry number (given in parentheses immediately following the title), address, phone and fax numbers, and station format.

The regions have been defined as follows:

Great Lakes States

Illinois
Indiana
Michigan
Minnesota
Ohio
Wisconsin

Great Plains States

Iowa
Kansas
Missouri
Nebraska
North Dakota
South Dakota

Middle Atlantic States

Delaware
District of Columbia
Maryland
Virginia
West Virginia

Northeastern States

Connecticut
Maine
Massachusetts
New Hampshire
New Jersey
New York
Pennsylvania
Rhode Island
Vermont

South Central States

Arkansas
Louisiana
Oklahoma
Texas
New Mexico

Southern States

Alabama
Florida
Georgia
Kentucky
Mississippi
North Carolina
Puerto Rico
South Carolina
Tennessee

Western States

Alaska
Arizona
California

Colorado
Hawaii
Idaho
Montana
Nevada
Oregon
Utah
Washington
Wyoming

Central Canadian Provinces

Ontario
Manitoba
Saskatchewan

Eastern Canadian Provinces

Newfoundland and Labrador
Prince Edward Island
Nova Scotia
New Brunswick
Quebec

Northern Canadian Territories

Northern Territories
Nunavut
Yukon Territory

Western Canadian Provinces

British Columbia
Alberta

Geographic Abbreviations

U.S. State and Territory Postal Codes

AK Alaska
AL Alabama
AR Arkansas
AS American Samoa
AZ Arizona
CA California
CO Colorado
CT Connecticut
DC District of Columbia
DE Delaware
FL Florida
GA Georgia
GU Guam
HI Hawaii
IA Iowa
ID Idaho
IL Illinois
IN Indiana
KS Kansas
KY Kentucky
LA Louisiana
MA Massachusetts
MD Maryland
ME Maine
MI Michigan
MN Minnesota
MO Missouri
MS Mississippi
MT Montana
NC North Carolina
ND North Dakota
NE Nebraska
NH New Hampshire
NJ New Jersey
NM New Mexico
NV Nevada
NY New York
OH Ohio
OK Oklahoma
OR Oregon
PA Pennsylvania
PR Puerto Rico
RI Rhode Island
SC South Carolina
SD South Dakota
TN Tennessee
TX Texas
UT Utah
VA Virginia
VI Virgin Islands
VT Vermont
WA Washington
WI Wisconsin
WV West Virginia
WY Wyoming

Canadian Province and Territory Postal Codes

AB Alberta
BC British Columbia
MB Manitoba
NB New Brunswick
NL Newfoundland and Labrador
NS Nova Scotia
NT Northwest Territories
NU Nunavut
ON Ontario
PE Prince Edward Island
QC Quebec
SK Saskatchewan
YT Yukon Territory

Australian State and Territory Codes

ACT Australian Capitol Territory
NSW New South Wales
NT Northern Territory
QLD Queensland
SA South Australia
TAS Tasmania
VIC Victoria
WA Western Australia

Chinese Province and Region Codes

AN Anhui
FJ Fujian
GS Gansu
GD Guangdong
GZ Guangxi Zhuangzu
GH Guizhou
HB Hebei
HL Heilongjiang
HN Henan
HU Hubei
HA Hunan
JS Jiangsu
JX Jiangxi
JI Jilin
LI Liaoning
NM Nei Monggol Zizhiqu
NH Ningxia Huizu
QI Qinghai
SH Shaanxi
SD Shandong
SX Shanxi
SI Sichuan
XU Xinjiang Uygur Zizhigu
XZ Xizang
YU Yunnan
ZH Zhejiang

Indian State and Territory Codes

AN Andaman and Nicobar
AP Andhra Pradesh
AR Arunachal Pradesh
AS Assam
BH Bihar
CH Chandigarh
DN Dadra and Nagar Haveli
DH Delhi
GD Goa Daman and Diu
GJ Gujarat
HY Haryana
HP Himachal Pradesh
JK Jammu and Kashmir
KA Karnataka
KE Kerala
LC Laccadive Minicoy and Amindivi
MP Madhya Pradesh

MH Maharashtra
MN Manipur
MG Meghalaya
MZ Mizoram
MY Mysore
NG Nagaland
OR Orissa
PN Pondicherry
PJ Punjab
RJ Rajasthan
SK Sikkim
TN Tamil Nadu
TR Tripura
UP Uttar Pradesh
WB West Bengal (W. Bengal)

Irish County Codes

CV Cavan
CA Carlow
CL Clare
CK Cork
DO Donegal
DU Dublin
GL Galway
KR Kerry
KL Kildare
KK Kilkenny
LA Laoighis
LE Leitrim
LI Limerick
LO Longford
LU Louth
MA Mayo
ME Meath
MO Monaghan
OF Offaly
RO Roscommon
SL Sligo
TP Tipperary
WA Waterford
WE Westmeath
WX Wexford
WI Wicklow

Mexican State Codes

AG Aguascalientes
BN Baja California Norte
BS Baja California Sur
CM Campeche
CP Chiapas
CH Chihuahua
CO Coahuila
CL Colima
DF Distrito Federal
DU Durango
GJ Guanajuato
GU Guerrero
HD Hidalgo
JA Jalisco
ME Mexico
MI Michoacan
MO Morelos
NY Nayarit
NL Nuevo Leon
OX Oaxaca
PU Puebla
QT Queretaro
QR Quintana Roo
SP San Luis Potosi
SN Sinaloa
SR Sonora
TB Tabasco
TM Tamaulipas
TL Tlaxcala
VC Veracruz
YU Yucatan
ZA Zacatecas

Nigerian States

AN Anambra
BA Bauchi
BE Bendel
BN Benue
BR Borno
CR Cross River
GO Gongola
IM Imo
KD Kaduna
KN Kano
KW Kwara
LG Lagos
NG Niger
OG Ogun
ON Ondo
OY Oyo
PL Plateau
RV Rivers
SK Sokoto

Country Abbreviations

For England, Northern Ireland, Scotland, and Wales, please see United Kingdom (GBR).

AFG Afghanistan
ALB Albania
ALG Algeria
ANG Angola
AIA Anguilla
ATG Antigua-Barbuda
ARG Argentina
AMA Armenia
ARU Aruba
AUS Australia
AUT Austria
AJN Azerbaijan
AZO Azores
BHS Bahamas
BHR Bahrain
BGD Bangladesh
BRB Barbados
BLR Belarus
BEL Belgium
BLZ Belize
BEN Benin
BMU Bermuda
BTN Bhutan
BOL Bolivia
HBO Bosnia-Hercegovina
BWA Botswana
BRZ Brazil
BRN Brunei Darussalam
BUL Bulgaria
BFA Burkina Faso
BDI Burundi
CMB Cambodia
CMR Cameroon
CYM Cayman Islands
CHL Chile
CHN People's Republic of China
COL Colombia
CRI Costa Rica
COT Cote d'Ivoire
CTA Croatia
CUB Cuba
CYP Cyprus
CZE Czech Republic
DEN Denmark
DMA Dominica
DOM Dominican Republic
ECU Ecuador
EGY Egypt
ELS El Salvador
EST Estonia
ETH Ethiopia
FAR Faroe Islands
FIJ Fiji
FIN Finland
FRA France
FGN French Guiana
GAB Gabon
GMB Gambia
GRG Georgia
GER Germany
GHA Ghana
GIB Gibraltar
GRC Greece
GTM Guatemala
GIN Guinea
GUY Guyana
HTI Haiti
HND Honduras
HUN Hungary
ICE Iceland
IND India
IDN Indonesia
IRN Iran
IRQ Iraq
IRL Ireland
ISR Israel
ITA Italy

JAM	Jamaica
JPN	Japan
JOR	Jordan
KAZ	Kazakhstan
KEN	Kenya
KGA	Kirgizstan
KOD	Korea, Democratic People's Republic of
KOR	Republic of Korea
KWT	Kuwait
LAO	Lao People's Democratic Republic
LAT	Latvia
LBN	Lebanon
LES	Lesotho
LIT	Lithuania
LUX	Luxembourg
MEC	Macedonia
MDG	Madagascar
MWI	Malawi
MYS	Malaysia
MDV	Maldives
MLI	Mali
MAL	Malta
MTQ	Martinique
MUS	Mauritius
MEX	Mexico
MDI	Moldova
MCO	Monaco
MNG	Mongolia
MON	Montenegro
MOR	Morocco
MOZ	Mozambique
MYA	Myanmar
NAM	Namibia
NPL	Nepal
NLD	Netherlands
NAT	Netherlands Antilles
NCL	New Caledonia
NZL	New Zealand
NCG	Nicaragua
NER	Niger
NGA	Nigeria
NOR	Norway
OMN	Oman
PAK	Pakistan
PAN	Panama
PNG	Papua New Guinea
PAR	Paraguay
PER	Peru
PHL	Philippines
POL	Poland
PRT	Portugal
QAT	Qatar
ROM	Romania
RUS	Russia
RWA	Rwanda
SKN	St. Kitts and Nevis
SLC	St. Lucia
SMR	San Marino
SAU	Saudi Arabia
SEN	Senegal
SER	Serbia
SYC	Seychelles
SLE	Sierra Leone
SGP	Singapore
SLK	Slovakia
SVA	Slovenia
SLM	Solomon Islands
SAF	Republic of South Africa
SPA	Spain
SRI	Sri Lanka
SDN	Sudan
SWZ	Swaziland
SWE	Sweden
SWI	Switzerland
SYR	Syrian Arab Republic
TWN	Taiwan
TDN	Tajikistan
TZA	United Republic of Tanzania
THA	Thailand
TGO	Togo
TGA	Tonga
TTO	Trinidad and Tobago
TUN	Tunisia
TUR	Turkey
TUK	Turkmenistan
UGA	Uganda
URE	Ukraine
UAE	United Arab Emirates
GBR	United Kingdom
URY	Uruguay
UZN	Uzbekistan
VAT	Vatican City
VEN	Venezuela
VNM	Vietnam
BVI	British Virgin Islands
WIN	West Indies
YEM	Yemen
ZMB	Zambia
ZWE	Zimbabwe

Miscellaneous Abbreviations

&	And
4C	One-Time Four Color Page Rate
ABC	Audit Bureau of Circulations
Acad.	Academy
Act.	Acting
Adm.	Administrative, Administration
Admin.	Administrator
AFB	Air Force Base
AM	Amplitude Modulation
Amer.	American
APO	Army Post Office
Apt.	Apartment
Assn.	Association
Assoc.	Associate
Asst.	Assistant
Ave.	Avenue
Bldg.	Building
Blvd.	Boulevard
boul.	boulevard
BPA	Business Publications Audit of Circulations
BTA	Best Time Available
BW	One-time Black & White Page Rate
C	Central
CAC	Certified Audit of Circulations
CCAB	Canadian Circulations Audit Board
CEO	Chief Executive Officer
Chm.	Chairman
Chwm.	Chairwoman
CNU	Canadian Newspaper Advertising Unit Rate
c/o	Care of
Col.	Column
Coll.	College
Comm.	Committee
Co.	Company
COO	Chief Operating Officer
Coord.	Coordinator
Corp.	Corporation
Coun.	Council
CP	case postale
Ct.	Court
Dept.	Department
Dir.	Director
Div.	Division
Dr.	Doctor, Drive
E.	East
EC	East Central
ENE	East Northeast
ERP	Effective Radiated Power
ESE	East Southeast
Eve.	Evening
Exec.	Executive
Expy.	Expressway
Fed.	Federation
Fl.	Floor
FM	Frequency Modulation
FPO	Fleet Post Office
Fri.	Friday
Fwy.	Freeway
Gen.	General
GLR	General Line Rate
Hd.	Head
Hwy.	Highway
Inc.	Incorporated
Info.	Information
Inst.	Institute
Intl.	International
ISSN	International Standard Serial Number
Jr.	Junior
Libn.	Librarian

Ln.	Lane
Ltd.	Limited
Mgr.	Manager
mi.	miles
Mktg.	Marketing
Mng.	Managing
Mon.	Monday
Morn.	Morning
N.	North
NAS	Naval Air Station
Natl.	National
NC	North Central
NE	Northeast
NNE	North Northeast
NNW	North Northwest
No.	Number
NW	Northwest
Orgn.	Organization
PCI	Per Column Inch Rate
Pkwy.	Parkway
Pl.	Place
PO	Post Office
Pres.	President
Prof.	Professor
Rd.	Road
RFD	Rural Free Delivery
Rm.	Room
ROS	Run of Schedule
RR	Rural Route
Rte.	Route
S.	South
Sat.	Saturday
SAU	Standard Advertising Unit Rate
SC	South Central
SE	Southeast
Sec.	Secretary
Soc.	Society
Sq.	Square
Sr.	Senior
SSE	South Southeast
SSW	South Southwest
St.	Saint, Street
Sta.	Station
Ste.	Sainte, Suite
Sun.	Sunday
Supt.	Superintendent
SW	Southwest
Terr.	Terrace
Thurs.	Thursday
Tpke.	Turnpike
Treas.	Treasurer
Tues.	Tuesday
Univ.	University
USPS	United States Publications Serial
VAC	Verified Audit Circulation
VP	Vice President
W.	West
WC	West Central
Wed.	Wednesday
WNW	West Northwest
WSW	West Southwest
x/month	Times per Month
x/week	Times per Week
x/year	Times per Year

ALBERTVILLE

N. AL. Marshall Co. 21 mi. NW of Gadsen. Manufactures cottonseed products, woven fabrics, lumber, electric heaters, mobile homes, aluminum awnings. Hatcheries. Hardwood timber. Agriculture. Poultry, cotton, corn.

1 ■ The Sand Mountain Reporter
Sand Mountain Reporter
1603 Progress Dr.
Albertville, AL 35950
Phone: (256)840-3000
Fax: (256)840-2987
Publisher's E-mail: support@sandmountainreporter.com
Community newspaper. **Freq:** Tuesday, Thursday and Saturday. **Print Method:** Offset. **Trim Size:** 12.5 x 22.5. **Cols./Page:** 6. **Col. Width:** 1 3/4 inches. **Col. Depth:** 21 1/2 inches. **Key Personnel:** Jonathan Stinson, Publisher. **Subscription Rates:** $14 Individuals 3 months (Marshall, DeKalb, Etowah, Blount County); $65 Out of state; $39 Out of state 6 months; $24 Individuals 6 months (Marshall, DeKalb, Etowah, Blount County); $42 Individuals Marshall, DeKalb, Etowah, Blount County. **URL:** http://www.sandmountainreporter.com. **Mailing address:** PO Box 1729, Albertville, AL 35950. **Remarks:** Accepts classified advertising. **Circ:** Paid 10000.

2 ■ WAVU-AM - 630
PO Box 190
Albertville, AL 35950
Phone: (256)878-8575
Fax: (256)878-1051
Email: wqsb@aol.com
Format: Southern Gospel. **Networks:** AP. **Founded:** 1948. **Operating Hours:** Continuous. **Wattage:** 1,000 Day; 028 Night. **Ad Rates:** $8 for 30 seconds; $10 for 60 seconds. WQSB, WKXX. **URL:** http://www.wavuam.com/.

3 ■ WEYY-FM - 92.7
455 AL Hwy 75 N
Albertville, AL 35950
Phone: (256)878-8333
Fax: (256)878-7999
Format: Country. **Networks:** ABC. **Owner:** Jacobs Broadcast Group, Inc., at above address, Ph: (205)362-9041. **Founded:** 1972. **Formerly:** WHTB-FM. **Operating Hours:** Sunrise-Sunset Monday - Friday, 6:00 a.m. - 1:00 p.m. Saturday, 6:00 a.m. - 10:00 p.m. Sunday. **Key Personnel:** Jim Jacobs, President; Richard Yates, Sales Mgr.; Tom Kelley, Operations Mgr; Laura Jacobs, Contact. **Wattage:** 2,600 ERP. **Ad Rates:** $5.30-8.40 for 30 seconds; $7.05-11.10 for 60 seconds. **Mailing address:** PO Box 863, Albertville, AL 35950. **URL:** http://www.jeffbeckmedia.com.

4 ■ WKXX-FM - 102.9
PO Box 190
Albertville, AL 35950
Phone: (256)442-3944
Fax: (256)442-7287
Format: Adult Contemporary; Top 40. **Operating Hours:** Continuous. **Key Personnel:** Tommy Lee, Gen. Mgr., tommylee@wqsb.com; Dee Miller, Promotions Dir., deer@wqsb.com. **Wattage:** 1,100 ERP. **Ad Rates:** Advertising accepted; rates available upon request. **Mailing address:** PO Box 190, Albertville, AL 35950. **URL:** http://www.wkxx.com.

5 ■ WQSB-FM - 105.1
3770 US Highway 431
Albertville, AL 35951
Phone: (256)878-8575
Fax: (256)878-1051
Free: 800-233-1051
Email: production@wqsb.com
Format: Country. **Networks:** Independent. **Owner:** Sand Mountain Broadcasting Service Inc. **Founded:** 1949. **Key Personnel:** Ted McCreless, Sales Mgr., tedm@wqsb.com. **Wattage:** 2,700 ERP. **Ad Rates:** $44 for 30 seconds; $55 for 60 seconds. WKXX, WAVU. **URL:** http://www.wqsb.com.

ALEXANDER CITY

E. AL. Tallapoosa Co. 13 mi. NW of Dadeville. Residential.

6 ■ Alexander City Outlook
Alexander City Outlook Inc.
548 Cherokee Rd.
Alexander City, AL 35011
Phone: (205)234-4281
Fax: (205)234-6550
General newspaper. **Freq:** Tuesday through Saturday. **Print Method:** Offset. **Cols./Page:** 6. **Col. Width:** 25 nonpareils. **Col. Depth:** 301 agate lines. **Key Personnel:** Austin Nelson; Kenneth Boone, Publisher. **Subscription Rates:** $34 Individuals 3 months; $68 Individuals 6 months; $136 Individuals; $177.99 Out of area. **Mailing address:** PO Box 999, Alexander City, AL 35011. **Ad Rates:** SAU $6.50. **Remarks:** Advertising accepted; rates available upon request. **Circ:** (Not Reported).

7 ■ The Dadeville Record
Tallapoosa Publishers
548 Cherokee Rd.
Alexander City, AL 35011
Phone: (256)234-4281
Fax: (256)234-6550
Publisher's E-mail: newsroom@alexcityoutlook.com
Newspaper. **Freq:** Weekly (Thurs.). **Print Method:** Offset. **Cols./Page:** 6. **Col. Width:** 25 nonpareils. **Col. Depth:** 301 agate lines. **Key Personnel:** Kenneth Boone, Publisher; Dale Liesch, Editor; Lee Champion, Manager, Production; Virginia Spears, General Manager. **Subscription Rates:** $25 Individuals. **URL:** http://www.alexcityoutlook.com/category/dadeville. **Mailing address:** PO Box 999, Alexander City, AL 35011. **Ad Rates:** BW $451.50; 4C $691.50; SAU $3.50. **Remarks:** Accepts advertising. **Circ:** 1988.

8 ■ Charter Communications Inc.
1155 Cherokee Rd.
Alexander City, AL 35010
Free: 888-438-2427
Owner: Charter Communications Inc., 400 Atlantic St., Stamford, CT 06901, Ph: (203)905-7801. **Founded:** July 1964. **Key Personnel:** Christopher L. Winfrey, CFO, Exec. VP. **Cities Served:** subscribing households 16,000. **URL:** http://www.charter.com.

ANDALUSIA

S. AL. Covington Co. 85 mi. S. of Montgomery. Manufactures textiles, cardboard boxes, polypropolene fibers, caskets. Processes pecans, peanuts. Pine timber. Agriculture. Cattle, soybeans, cotton.

9 ■ The Andalusia Star News
The Andalusia Star News
207 Dunson St.
Andalusia, AL 36420
Phone: (334)222-2402
General newspaper. **Freq:** Tues.-Sat. (morning). **Print Method:** Offset. **Cols./Page:** 6. **Col. Width:** 24 nonpareils. **Col. Depth:** 301 agate lines. **Key Personnel:** Michele Gerlach, Publisher; Jeff Moore, Manager, Circulation; Ruck Ashworth, Manager, Advertising; Stephanie Nelson, Editor. **ISSN:** 0746--2115 (print). **Subscription Rates:** $104.54 Individuals in-county. **Ad Rates:** PCI $5.53. **Remarks:** Accepts advertising. **Circ:** ‡3400.

10 ■ TV Cable Co. of Andalusia Inc.
PO Box 34
Andalusia, AL 36420
Phone: (334)222-6464
Fax: (334)222-7226
Cities Served: Andalusia, Alabama; 68 channels. **URL:** http://www.andycable.com.

11 ■ WAAO-FM - 103.7
PO Box 987
Andalusia, AL 36420
Phone: (334)222-1166
Fax: (334)222-1167
Email: waao@waao.com
Format: Top 40; Country. **Owner:** Companion Broadcasting Service Inc. **Founded:** 1987. **Operating Hours:** Continuous. **Key Personnel:** Blaine Wilson, Gen. Mgr., Sales Mgr., Owner. **Wattage:** 3,000. **Ad Rates:** $6-9 for 30 seconds; $9-15 for 60 seconds. **URL:** http://www.waao.com.

12 ■ WFXX-FM - 107.7
1406 River Falls St.
Andalusia, AL 36420
Phone: (334)222-2222
Fax: (334)427-8888
Format: Oldies. **Owner:** Haynes Broadcasting Inc. **Key Personnel:** Billy Bimbo, Sales Mgr.; Jim Walker, Operations Mgr. **Ad Rates:** Noncommercial. **URL:** http://www.fox107.com.

13 ■ WKNI-AM - 620
14803 Pinewood Rd.
Andalusia, AL 36420
Format: Country. **Networks:** Satellite Music Network. **Founded:** 1982. **Formerly:** WWLX-AM. **Operating Hours:** Continuous; 80% network, 20% local. **ADI:** Huntsville-Decatur-Florence, AL. **Key Personnel:** Jerry Thompson, Contact. **Wattage:** 5,000. **Ad Rates:** $5 for 30 seconds; $10 for 60 seconds. **URL:** http://www.wkni.net.

Circulation: ★ = AAM; △ or • = BPA; ♦ = CAC; ❑ = VAC; ⊕ = PO Statement; ‡ = Publisher's Report; Boldface figures = sworn; Light figures = estimated.

14 ■ WKNI-TV - 25
26824 Hwy. 29 N
Andalusia, AL 36421
Founded: 2004. **Key Personnel:** Eddie Lewis, Gen. Mgr.; George Stringer, Ed.-in-Chief. **URL:** http://www.wkni.net.

ANNISTON

NE AL. Calhoun Co. 60 mi. NE of Birmingham. Manufacturing.

15 ■ The Cleburne News
Consolidated Publishing
PO Box 189
Anniston, AL 36202-0189
Publisher's E-mail: news@cleburnenews.com
Community newspaper. **Freq:** Weekly (Thurs.). **Print Method:** Offset. **Cols./Page:** 6. **Col. Width:** 21 nonpareils. **Col. Depth:** 290 agate lines. **Key Personnel:** Mickey Cook, General Manager; Wayne Ruple, Editor; Misty Pointer, Contact. **URL:** http://www.annistonstar.com/cleburne_news. **Ad Rates:** SAU $3. **Remarks:** Accepts advertising. **Circ:** Paid ‡3500.

16 ■ The Jacksonville News
Consolidating Publishing
4305 McClellan Blvd.
Anniston, AL 36202
Phone: (256)435-5021
Publisher's E-mail: news@jaxnews.com
Community newspaper. **Founded:** 1936. **Freq:** Weekly (Wed.). **Print Method:** Offset. **Trim Size:** 11.625 x 21.25. **Cols./Page:** 6. **Key Personnel:** Phillip A. Sanguinetti, Publisher; John Alred, Managing Editor; Shannon Martin, Manager, Advertising. **USPS:** 272-480. **Subscription Rates:** $27.50 Individuals in Calhoun County; $52.50 Two years in Calhoun County; $44 Out of area; $76 Out of area 2 years. **URL:** http://www.annistonstar.com/jacksonville_news. **Mailing address:** PO Box 189, Anniston, AL 36202. **Ad Rates:** BW $729.17; 4C $984.17; SAU $8.40; PCI $7.25. **Remarks:** Accepts advertising. **Circ:** Combined ‡3300.

17 ■ Longleaf Style
Consolidated Publishing
PO Box 189
Anniston, AL 36202-0189
Publisher's E-mail: news@cleburnenews.com
Magazine featuring the culture, regional development, and life in the south. **Freq:** Monthly. **Key Personnel:** Deirdre Long, Managing Editor; Josephine Ayers, Editor-in-Chief. **Subscription Rates:** $16.95 Individuals; $28.95 Individuals two years. **URL:** http://www.longleafstyle.com. **Remarks:** Accepts advertising. **Circ:** (Not Reported).

18 ■ The Piedmont Journal
Consolidated Publishing
4305 McClellan Blvd.
Anniston, AL 36202
Phone: (256)235-3553
Fax: (256)241-1991
Publisher's E-mail: news@cleburnenews.com
Newspaper covering Piedmont, Alabama. **Freq:** Weekly (Wed.). **Key Personnel:** John Alred, Publisher. **Subscription Rates:** $18 By mail in Piedmont; $33 By mail in Piedmont, 2 years; $30 By mail outside Piedmont; $58 By mail outside Piedmont, 2 years. **URL:** http://www.annistonstar.com/news_piedmont. **Mailing address:** PO Box 189, Anniston, AL 36202. **Remarks:** Accepts advertising. **Circ:** (Not Reported).

19 ■ Cable One
606 Noble S
Anniston, AL 36201
Phone: (256)236-7034
Email: terry.womack@cableone.net
Founded: 1960. **Formerly:** Anniston NewChannels; Time Warner Cable. **Key Personnel:** Becky Woods, Rep., Ad./Sales. **Cities Served:** Alexandria, Anniston, Eastaboga, Hobson City, Jacksonville, McClellan, Munford, Ohatchee, Oxford, Oxford, Weaver, Alabama: subscribing households 36,000; Saks, Bynum, Blue Mountain, Eastaboga; 188 channels; 1 community access channel. **URL:** http://www.cableone.net/li/pages/anniston-al.aspx.

20 ■ Infignos Media
600 Leighton Ave., Ste. C
Anniston, AL 36207
Phone: (236)405-4444
Format: Educational; News; Urban Contemporary; Oldies; Country; Talk; Gospel. **ADI:** Anniston, AL. **Ad Rates:** Advertising accepted; rates available upon request. **Mailing address:** PO Box 367, Anniston, AL 36202. **URL:** http://www.infignosmedia.com.

21 ■ WDNG-AM - 1450
1115 Leighton Ave.
Anniston, AL 36202
Phone: (256)236-8291
Fax: (256)237-8818
Format: Adult Contemporary. **Networks:** ABC. **Owner:** Infignos Media, 600 Leighton Ave., Ste. C, Anniston, AL 36207, Ph: (236)405-4444. **Founded:** 1957. **ADI:** Anniston, AL. **Key Personnel:** J.J. Dark, Gen. Mgr., Owner. **Wattage:** 1,000. **Ad Rates:** Noncommercial. **Mailing address:** PO Box 5, Anniston, AL 36202. **URL:** http://www.infignosmedia.com.

22 ■ WFMH-FM - 95.5
801 Noble St., 8th Fl., Ste. 30
Anniston, AL 36201
Phone: (205)935-3730
Fax: (205)935-3734
Email: 101fm@linkfast.netet
Format: Country. **Networks:** ABC. **Founded:** 1949. **Formerly:** WXXR-FM. **Operating Hours:** Continuous. **ADI:** Birmingham (Gadsden), AL. **Key Personnel:** Kerisa Walker, Mgr. **Wattage:** 006. **Ad Rates:** $10 for 30 seconds; $15 for 60 seconds. Combined advertising rates available with WFMH-AM, WXXR-AM, & WXXR-FM. **URL:** http://www.big955.com/.

23 ■ WFXO-FM - 104.9
PO Box 2552
Anniston, AL 36202
Phone: (601)423-6055
Email: fox@freedom2000net.com
Owner: Billy R. McLain, at above address. **Founded:** 1970. **Formerly:** WTIB-FM. **Wattage:** 50,000. **Ad Rates:** Accepts Advertising.

24 ■ WGRW-FM - 90.7
PO Box 2555
Anniston, AL 36202
Phone: (256)238-9990
Fax: (256)237-1102
Format: Contemporary Christian. **Networks:** Moody Broadcasting. **Owner:** Word Works, Inc., at above address, Boston, MA. **Founded:** 1999. **Operating Hours:** Continuous. **Key Personnel:** Jon Holder, Gen. Mgr., jon@graceradio.com. **Wattage:** 3,000. **Ad Rates:** Noncommercial. **URL:** http://www.graceradio.com.

25 ■ WHMA-AM
PO Box 2552
PO Box 278
Anniston, AL 36202
Phone: (256)237-8741
Fax: (256)231-9414
Format: Sports; Talk. **Owner:** Williams Communications, Inc., 5046 Tennessee Capital Blvd., Tallahassee, FL 32303, Ph: (850)385-1121, Fax: (850)575-0346, Free: 800-649-5783. **Founded:** 1938. **ADI:** Anniston, AL. **Key Personnel:** Tom Williams, Gen. Mgr., twilliams@internettport.net. **Wattage:** 5,000 Day; 1,000 Nig. **Ad Rates:** Advertising accepted; rates available upon request.

26 ■ WHMA-FM
PO Box 2552
801 Noble St.
Anniston, AL 36202
Phone: (256)237-8741
Fax: (256)231-9414
Free: 800-264-0902
Format: Country; Hot Country. **Networks:** NBC. **Owner:** Williams Communications, Inc., 5046 Tennessee Capital Blvd., Tallahassee, FL 32303, Ph: (850)385-1121, Fax: (850)575-0346, Free: 800-649-5783. **Founded:** 1947. **Key Personnel:** Shannon Smith, Office Mgr.; Stewart Young, News Dir.; Tom Williams, Gen. Mgr.; Larry James, Sales Mgr. **Wattage:** 400 ERP. **Ad Rates:** Advertising accepted; rates available upon request.

27 ■ WHOG-AM - 1120
1330 Noble St., Ste. 25
Anniston, AL 36201
Phone: (256)236-6484
Email: whog@whog1120.com
Format: Hip Hop; Blues.

WJXS-TV - See Gadsden

28 ■ WTXO-FM - 98.3
801 Noble St., 8th Fl., Ste. 30
Anniston, AL 36201
Phone: (256)444-7362
Fax: (256)231-9414
Format: Album-Oriented Rock (AOR). **Owner:** Williams Communications, Inc., 5046 Tennessee Capital Blvd., Tallahassee, FL 32303, Ph: (850)385-1121, Fax: (850)575-0346, Free: 800-649-5783. **Key Personnel:** Chris Wright, Contact, chris@rock1059.net; Chris Wright, Contact, chris@rock1059.net. **URL:** http://rock983.net.

29 ■ WZZX-AM
PO Box 2552
Anniston, AL 36202
Fax: (256)354-7224
Format: Country; Gospel; Talk. **Networks:** Satellite Music Network. **Owner:** Williams Communications, Inc., PO Box 343, Wedowee, AL 36278, Ph: (256)236-1880, Fax: (256)236-4480. **Founded:** 1967. **Formerly:** WANL-AM. **Key Personnel:** Walt Williams,, Jr., President. **Wattage:** 5,000 Day. **Ad Rates:** $8.24 for 30 seconds; $10.60 for 60 seconds.

ARAB

N. AL. Marshall Co. 60 mi. NE of Birmingham. Manufactures textiles, electronic components, plastics, chemicals. Nursery. Agriculture. Poultry, corn, cotton.

30 ■ WAFN-FM - 92.7
981 Brindlee Mountain Pkwy.
Arab, AL 35016
Phone: (256)586-9300
Format: Oldies. **Networks:** CNN Radio. **Owner:** Fun Media Group Inc. **Founded:** 1979. **Formerly:** WCRQ-FM. **Operating Hours:** Controlled. **ADI:** Huntsville-Decatur-Florence, AL. **Wattage:** 006 KW. **Ad Rates:** $10-40 per unit. **Mailing address:** PO Box 1297, Arab, AL 35016. **URL:** http://www.fun927.com.

31 ■ WRAB-AM
PO Box 625
Arab, AL 35016
Phone: (256)586-4123
Fax: (256)586-4124
Ad Rates: Accepts Advertising.

ASHLAND

C. AL. Clay Co. 26 mi. S. of Anniston. Cotton ginning.

32 ■ WCKF-FM - 100.7
518 Mountain View Rd.
Ashland, AL 36251n
Wattage: 1,700 ERP. **URL:** http://www.alabama1007fm.com/1.html.

ATHENS

N. AL. Limestone Co. 13 mi. N. of Decatur. Athens State College. Nuclear industry. Cotton gins, grist and saw mills. Pine, oak timber. Agriculture. Cotton, hay, corn, dairying.

33 ■ The News-Courier
Community Newspaper Holdings Inc.
410 W Green St.
Athens, AL 35611
Phone: (256)232-2720
Fax: (256)233-7753
Newspaper serving Athens, Alabama. **Freq:** Daily. **Key Personnel:** Budd McLaughlin, Managing Editor; Bill Morgan, Publisher; Katherine Miller, Director, Advertising; Antoinette Kauffman, Business Manager. **Subscription Rates:** $11.99 Individuals /month - print and online ; $9.99 Individuals /month - online only. **URL:** http://www.enewscourier.com. **Mailing address:** PO Box 670, Athens, AL 35611. **Remarks:** Advertising accepted; rates available upon request. **Circ:** Mon.-Sat. **★5990**, Sun. **★7247**.

34 ■ WHRP-FM - 94.1
1717 Hwy. 72 E
Athens, AL 35611
Phone: (256)830-8300
Fax: (256)232-6842
Free: 866-481-9477

Format: Gospel; Blues; Contemporary Christian; Jazz. **Owner:** Cumulus Broadcasting Inc., 3280 Peachtree Rd. NW, Ste. 2300, Atlanta, GA 30305-2447, Ph: (404)949-0700, Fax: (404)949-0740. **Operating Hours:** Continuous. **Wattage:** 710 ERP. **Ad Rates:** Advertising accepted; rates available upon request. **URL:** http://www.whrpfm.com.

35 ■ WKAC-AM - 1080
19245 Hwy. 127
Athens, AL 35614
Phone: (256)232-6827
Email: wkac@wkac1080.com
Format: Oldies. **Networks:** CNN Radio. **Founded:** 1964. **Operating Hours:** Sunrise-sunset; 7% network, 93% local. **Wattage:** 5,000 Day. **Ad Rates:** $4-7 for 30 seconds; $6-9 for 60 seconds. **URL:** http://www.wkac1080.com.

36 ■ W273AJ-FM - 102.5
PO Box 391
Twin Falls, ID 83303
Fax: (208)736-1958
Free: 800-357-4226
Format: Religious; Contemporary Christian. **Owner:** CSN International, PO Box 391, Twin Falls, ID 83303, Ph: (208)736-1958, Fax: (208)736-1958, Free: 800-357-4226. **URL:** http://www.csnradio.com.

37 ■ WUMP-AM - 730
1717 US Hwy., 72 E
Athens, AL 35611-4413
Phone: (256)830-8300
Fax: (256)232-6842
Free: 866-485-WUMP
Format: Sports; Talk. **Owner:** Cumulus Media Inc., 3280 Peachtree Rd. NW, Ste. 2300, Atlanta, GA 30305-2455, Ph: (404)949-0700, Fax: (404)949-0740. **Key Personnel:** Dave Kent, Dir. of Programs, dave.kent@cumulus.com. **Wattage:** 1,000. **Ad Rates:** Noncommercial. **URL:** http://www.730ump.com.

38 ■ WVNN-AM - 770
1717 US Highway 72 E
Athens, AL 35611-4413
Phone: (256)830-8300
Fax: (256)232-6842
Email: programdirector@wvnn.com
Format: Talk; News. **Networks:** ABC; CNN Radio. **Owner:** Cumulus Media Inc., 3280 Peachtree Rd. NW, Ste. 2300, Atlanta, GA 30305-2455, Ph: (404)949-0700, Fax: (404)949-0740. **Founded:** 1948. **ADI:** Atlanta (Athens & Rome), GA. **Key Personnel:** Dale Jackson, Contact, dale@wvnn.com. **Local Programs:** *The Schnitt Show*, Monday Tuesday Wednesday Thursday Friday 3:00 p.m. - 6:00 p.m.; *Rush Limbaugh*, Monday Tuesday Wednesday Thursday Friday Saturday Sunday 11:00 a.m. - 2:00 p.m. 12:00 p.m. - 3:00 p.m. 8:00 p.m. - 12:00 a.m. **Wattage:** 7,000 Day; 250 Night. **Ad Rates:** Advertising accepted; rates available upon request. $30-75 per unit. **URL:** http://wvnn.com.

39 ■ WXMR-FM - 93.3
1717 Hwy. 72 E
Athens, AL 35611
Free: 844-301-4933
Networks: Independent. **Owner:** Fortune Media Communications, at above address, Ph: (256)722-9649. **Founded:** 1970. **Formerly:** WKQD-FM; WHUK-FM. **Operating Hours:** Continuous; 100% local. **Key Personnel:** Bill Dunnavant, President, Contact; Mary Dunnavant, VP; Keith Parker, Sales Mgr.; Scott Holt, Dir. of Programs; Bill Dunnavant, Contact. **Wattage:** 14,500 ERP. **Ad Rates:** $40 for 30 seconds; $75 for 60 seconds. **URL:** http://www.933nashicon.com.

40 ■ WYZP-FM - 104.3
1717 Hwy. 72 E
Athens, AL 35611
Phone: (256)830-8300
Free: 866-476-1043
Format: News. **Networks:** Fox. **Owner:** Cumulus Broadcasting Inc., 3280 Peachtree Rd. NW, Ste. 2300, Atlanta, GA 30305-2447, Ph: (404)949-0700, Fax: (404)949-0740. **Operating Hours:** Continuous. **Wattage:** 100,000. **Ad Rates:** Advertising accepted; rates available upon request. **URL:** http://www.wzyp.com.

41 ■ WZYP-FM - 104.3
1717 Hwy. 72 E
Athens, AL 35611
Phone: (256)830-8300
Fax: (256)232-6842
Free: 866-476-1043
Format: Top 40; Contemporary Hit Radio (CHR). **Networks:** ABC. **Owner:** Cumulus Media Inc., 3280 Peachtree Rd. NW, Ste. 2300, Atlanta, GA 30305-2455, Ph: (404)949-0700, Fax: (404)949-0740. **Founded:** 1958. **Operating Hours:** Continuous. **Local Programs:** *The Mojo Radio Show*, Monday Tuesday Wednesday Thursday Friday 6:00 a.m. - 10:00 a.m. **Wattage:** 100,000 ERP. **URL:** http://www.wzyp.com.

ATMORE

SW AL. Escambia Co. 40 mi. NE of Mobile. Lumber milling, cotton ginning, and bottling. Agriculture. Corn, cotton, strawberries.

42 ■ Atmore Advance
Boone Newspapers Inc.
301 S Main St.
Atmore, AL 36502
Phone: (251)368-2123
Fax: (251)368-2124
Publication E-mail: newsroom@atmoreadvance.com
Local newspaper. **Freq:** Weekly (Wed.). **Print Method:** Offset. **Cols./Page:** 6. **Col. Width:** 12.5 picas. **Col. Depth:** 21 1/2 inches. **Key Personnel:** Allison Knowles, Manager, Circulation. **Subscription Rates:** $50 Individuals carrier delivery; $50 By mail; $45 Individuals senior citizen; $60 Out of area by mail; $65 Out of state by mail. **URL:** http://www.atmoreadvance.com; http://www.boonenewspapers.com. **Mailing address:** PO Box 28, Atmore, AL 36504. **Ad Rates:** BW $619; 4C $859; SAU $8.60; PCI $4.05. **Remarks:** Accepts advertising. **Circ:** 3300.

AUBURN

E. AL. Lee Co. 52 mi. NE of Montgomery. Auburn University. Manufactures door locks, wood products, power transmitting gears, laboratory furniture, pollution monitoring devices, greenhouses, signs, wire products, asphalt, drill bits, cutting tools. Agriculture. Livestock. Cotton.

43 ■ American Educational History Journal
Organization of Educational Historians
c/o Deborah L. Morowski, Executive Secretary
Department of Curriculum and Teaching
5022 Haley Ctr.
Auburn, AL 36849
Phone: (334)844-6796
Peer-reviewed covering the history of education in the United States. **Freq:** Annual. **Trim Size:** 8 1/2 x 11. **Key Personnel:** Donna M. Davis, Associate Editor; Dr. J. Wesley Null, Board Member. **ISSN:** 1535-0584 (print). **Subscription Rates:** $39.09 Individuals paperback - special price; $79.09 Individuals hardcover - special price; $45.99 Individuals paperback - regular price; $85.99 Individuals hardcover - regular price. **Alt. Formats:** E-book. **URL:** http://www.edhistorians.org/aehj-american-educational-history-journal.html; http://www.infoagepub.com/products/American-Educational-History-Journal-36. **Formerly:** Journal of the Midwest History of Education Society. **Remarks:** Advertising not accepted. **Circ:** Paid ‡110.

44 ■ Auburn Magazine
Auburn University Alumni Association
Auburn University
317 S College St.
Auburn, AL 36849
Phone: (334)844-2586
Magazine for college alumni. **Freq:** Biennial. **Print Method:** Offset. **Trim Size:** 9.25 x 11.125. **Cols./Page:** 3. **Col. Width:** 2.25 inches. **Col. Depth:** 10 inches. **Key Personnel:** Suzanne Johnson, Associate Editor, phone: (334)844-1164. **ISSN:** 1077--8640 (print). **URL:** http://www.alumni.auburn.edu/magazine. **Formerly:** The Auburn Alumnews. **Ad Rates:** BW $1750; 4C $2350. **Remarks:** Accepts advertising. **Circ:** 44000.

45 ■ The Auburn Plainsman
Auburn University
255 Heisman Dr., Ste. 1111
Auburn, AL 36849-5343
Phone: (334)844-9108
Publisher's E-mail: webmaster@auburn.edu
Collegiate newspaper. **Freq:** Weekly (Thurs.). **Print Method:** Offset. **Trim Size:** 13 x 21. **Cols./Page:** 6. **Col. Width:** 26 nonpareils. **Col. Depth:** 294 agate lines. **Key Personnel:** Becky Hardy, Editor-in-Chief. **Subscription Rates:** $40 Individuals. **URL:** http://www.theplainsman.com. **Remarks:** Accepts classified advertising. **Circ:** ‡9500.

46 ■ Career and Technical Education Research
Association for Career and Technical Education Research
c/o Dr. Leane Skinner, President
Dept. of Curriculum and Teaching
Auburn University
5040 Haley
Auburn, AL 36849-5212
Phone: (334)844-3823
Freq: 3/year. **ISSN:** 1554- 7558 (print). **Subscription Rates:** Included in membership. **Remarks:** Advertising not accepted. **Circ:** (Not Reported).

47 ■ Journal of STEM Education: Innovations and Research
Auburn University
Auburn, AL 36849
Phone: (334)844-4000
Publisher's E-mail: webmaster@auburn.edu
Journal for educators in Science, Technology, Engineering, and Mathematics (STEM) education. **Freq:** Semiannual. **Key Personnel:** P.K. Raju, Editor. **ISSN:** 1557--5284 (print). **URL:** http://ojs.jstem.org/index.php?journal=JSTEM. **Circ:** (Not Reported).

48 ■ Professional Educator
Auburn University
108 Ramsay Hall
Auburn, AL 36849
Phone: (334)844-4488
Fax: (334)844-0558
Publisher's E-mail: webmaster@auburn.edu
Trade journal covering issues in teacher education and professional development of teachers. **Founded:** 1976. **Freq:** Semiannual. **Cols./Page:** 2. **Col. Width:** 8 centimeters. **Col. Depth:** 20.2 centimeters. **Key Personnel:** Anna C. Weinstein, Editor; Cindy Reed, Ed.D., Executive Editor. **ISSN:** 0196-786X (print). **URL:** http://www.theprofessionaleducator.org. **Remarks:** Advertising not accepted. **Circ:** Combined 200.

49 ■ Southern Humanities Review
Auburn University
Auburn, AL 36849
Phone: (334)844-4000
Publisher's E-mail: webmaster@auburn.edu
Scholarly journal covering poetry, fiction, essays, and book reviews. **Founded:** 1967. **Freq:** Quarterly February, May, August and November. **Trim Size:** 6 x 9. **Key Personnel:** Chantel Acevedo, Editor. **ISSN:** 0038-4168 (print). **Subscription Rates:** $18 Individuals; $30 Two years; $23 Out of country; $39 Out of country two-year; $42 Individuals for 3 years; $55 Out of country for 3 years; $5 Individuals sample copy; $8 Out of country sample copy. **URL:** http://www.cla.auburn.edu/shr. **Ad Rates:** BW $100. **Remarks:** Accepts advertising. **Circ:** Combined 700.

50 ■ Transactions of the American Fisheries Society
American Fisheries Society
c/o Dr. Dennis R. DeVries, Editor
Dept. of Fisheries
Auburn University
Auburn, AL 36849
Phone: (334)844-9322
Fax: (334)844-9208
Publication E-mail: journals@fisheries.org
Fisheries science journal. **Freq:** 6/year. **Print Method:** Offset. **Trim Size:** 7 x 10. **Cols./Page:** 2. **Col. Width:** 32 nonpareils. **Col. Depth:** 114 agate lines. **Key Personnel:** Derek Aday, Editor; Churchill B. Grimes, Editor. **ISSN:** 0002--8487 (print); **EISSN:** 1548--8659 (electronic). **Subscription Rates:** $1501 Institutions online only; $1671 Institutions online only; $554 Institu-

Circulation: ★ = AAM; △ or • = BPA; ♦ = CAC; ❑ = VAC; ⊕ = PO Statement; ‡ = Publisher's Report; Boldface figures = sworn; Light figures = estimated.

tions online only (Fisheries Infobase); $1770 Institutions online only; $1956 Institutions online only (including Fisheries Magazine). **URL:** http://www.tandfonline.com/toc/utaf20/current#.VPOSyHyUdGY. **Remarks:** Accepts advertising. **Circ:** ‡3700, 4040.

51 ■ Transactions on Dielectrics and Electrical Insulation
IEEE - Dielectrics and Electrical Insulation Society
Auburn University
Electrical and Computer Engineering
200 Broun Hall
Auburn, AL 36849-5201
Phone: (334)844-1822
Fax: (334)844-1809
Journal publishing information on electrical insulation, electric and electronic circuits and distribution systems. **Freq:** 6/year. **ISSN:** 1070--9878 (print). **Subscription Rates:** Included in membership. **URL:** http://ieeexplore.ieee.org/xpl/RecentIssue.jsp?reload=true&punumber=94; http://sites.ieee.org/deis. **Remarks:** Advertising not accepted. **Circ:** (Not Reported).

52 ■ Tiger 93.9 FM WTGZ - 93.9
2415 S College St., Unit 105
Auburn, AL 36832
Phone: (334)887-9999
Fax: (334)826-9599
Free: 888-775-9595
Format: News; Album-Oriented Rock (AOR); Information. **Owner:** Tiger Communications Inc., 2514 S College St., Auburn, AL 36832. **Operating Hours:** Continuous. **Ad Rates:** Advertising accepted; rates available upon request. **URL:** http://www.thetiger.fm.

53 ■ WANI-AM - 1400
197 E University Dr.
Auburn, AL 36830
Phone: (334)826-2929
Fax: (334)826-9151
Format: Talk; News; Sports. **Networks:** Westwood One Radio. **Founded:** 1940. **Formerly:** WJHO-AM. **Operating Hours:** Continuous; 85% network, 15% local. **Key Personnel:** Mike Hubbard, President. **Local Programs:** *Auburn/Opelika This Morning*, Monday Tuesday Wednesday Thursday Friday 6:00 a.m. - 9:00 a.m. **Wattage:** 1,000. **Ad Rates:** $10-20 for 30 seconds; $12-25 for 60 seconds. Combined advertising rates available with WANI-AM. **Mailing address:** PO Box 950, Auburn, AL 36831-0950. **URL:** http://www.wani1400.com.

54 ■ WAUD-AM - 1230
2514 S College St.
Auburn, AL 36830
Phone: (334)887-3401
Fax: (334)826-9599
Format: Sports; Easy Listening; News. **Networks:** ABC; Alabama Radio (ALANET). **Owner:** Tiger Communications Inc., 2514 S College St., Auburn, AL 36832. **Founded:** 1947. **Operating Hours:** Continuous. **ADI:** Columbus, GA (Opelika, AL). **Key Personnel:** Bob Sanders, Contact. **Wattage:** 1,000. **Ad Rates:** $5.15-6 for 15 seconds; $8-9.25 for 30 seconds; $10-12 for 60 seconds. Combined advertising rates available with WTGT-FM.

55 ■ WEGL-FM - 91.1
255 Heisman Dr., Ste. 1105
Auburn, AL 36849
Phone: (334)844-4057
Fax: (334)844-4188
Format: Alternative/New Music/Progressive; Contemporary Hit Radio (CHR). **Networks:** CNN Radio. **Owner:** Auburn University, Auburn, AL 36849, Ph: (334)844-4000. **Founded:** 1971. **Operating Hours:** Continuous; 1% network, 99% local. **Wattage:** 3,000. **Ad Rates:** Noncommercial. **URL:** http://wegl.auburn.edu.

56 ■ WELL-FM - 88.7
PO Box 2208
Auburn, AL 36831
Phone: (334)705-8004
Fax: (334)705-8006
Format: Contemporary Christian. **Networks:** USA Radio. **Founded:** 1990. **Formerly:** WDVI-FM. **Operating Hours:** Continuous. **Key Personnel:** Jimmy Jarrell, President; Joe May, Dir. of Programs. **Wattage:** 100,000. **Ad Rates:** Noncommercial. **URL:** http://www.praise887.com.

57 ■ WGZZ-FM - 100.3
197 E University Dr.
Auburn, AL 36830
Phone: (334)826-2929
Fax: (334)826-9151
Format: Adult Contemporary. **Owner:** Auburn Network, PO Box 950, Auburn, AL 36831-0950. **Key Personnel:** Mike Hubbard, CEO, hubbard@aunetwork.com; Chris Hines, Sr. VP, hines@aunetwork.com; Drew McCracken, Traffic Mgr., dmccracken@aunetwork.com. **URL:** http://www.wingsfm.com.

58 ■ WJHO-FM - 89.7
PO Box 2208
Auburn, AL 36831
Phone: (256)234-4271
Fax: (256)234-4272
Format: Gospel. **Owner:** Jimmy Jarrell Communications Foundation, 908 Opelika Rd., Auburn, AL 36830-4024. **Key Personnel:** Gregg Hutchins, Contact; Cassie Keys, Contact; Gregg Hutchins, Contact.

59 ■ WQNR-FM - 99.9
2514 S College St.
Auburn, AL 36830
Phone: (334)887-9999
Fax: (334)826-9599
Format: Eighties; Oldies. **Owner:** Tiger Communications Inc., 2514 S College St., Auburn, AL 36832. **URL:** http://www.katefm.com.

WTRP-AM - See LaGrange, GA

BAY MINETTE

SW AL. Baldwin Co. 23 mi. NE of Mobile. Manufactures corrugated boxes, dental equipment, aluminum wire, lumber, furniture. Pine timber. Agriculture. Soybeans, hay, cattle.

60 ■ Baldwin Times
Gulf Coast Newspapers
329 Courthouse Sq.
Bay Minette, AL 36507
Phone: (251)937-2511
Fax: (251)937-1831
Community newspaper. **Freq:** Semiweekly (Wed. and Fri.). **Print Method:** Offset. **Cols./Page:** 6. **Col. Width:** 18 nonpareils. **Col. Depth:** 294 agate lines. **Key Personnel:** Jeanette Chandler, Advertising Representative; Cathy Higgins, Editor. **Subscription Rates:** $37.25 Individuals in county (print and online); $31.25 Individuals in county, senior (print and online); $39 Out of area print and online; $20 Individuals online (1 year). **URL:** http://www.gulfcoastnewstoday.com/baldwin-times. **Mailing address:** PO Box 519, Bay Minette, AL 36507. **Ad Rates:** GLR $.23. **Remarks:** Accepts advertising. **Circ:** ‡4800.

BIRMINGHAM

C. AL. Shelby Co. 90 mi. NW of Montgomery. Jefferson Co. (C). 90 m NW of Montgomery. Univ. of Alabama, Samford Univ., Birmingham Southern; Miles College. Coal mines. Limestone quarries. Telecommunications industry. Manufacturing. Major transportation distribution center. Retail, wholesale trade center. Medical center. Financial center.

61 ■ Acteens Leader
Woman's Missionary Union
100 Missionary Ridge
Birmingham, AL 35283-0010
Phone: (205)991-8100
Fax: (888)422-7032
Free: 800-968-7301
Publisher's E-mail: customer_service@wmu.org
Freq: 3/year. **Subscription Rates:** $21.99 Individuals. **URL:** http://www.wmustore.com/product.asp?sku=AL. **Mailing address:** PO Box 830010, Birmingham, AL 35283-0010. **Remarks:** Advertising not accepted. **Circ:** (Not Reported).

62 ■ Al-Arabiyya
American Association of Teachers of Arabic
3416 Primm Ln.
Birmingham, AL 35216
Phone: (205)822-6800
Fax: (205)823-2760
Publisher's E-mail: info@aataweb.org
Journal publishing articles in the fields of Arabic language, literature and linguistics. **Freq:** Annual. **ISSN:** 0889-8731 (print). **Subscription Rates:** Included in membership; $50 Individuals back issue; $15 Students back issue; $200 Institutions. **URL:** http://aataweb.org/alarabiyya. **Remarks:** Accepts advertising. **Circ:** 300.

63 ■ The Alabama Episcopalian
The Episcopal Diocese of Alabama
2156 Kent Way
Birmingham, AL 35226
Publisher's E-mail: rmorpeth@dioala.org
Newspaper (tabloid) for members of the Episcopal diocese of Alabama. **Freq:** Bimonthly. **Print Method:** Offset. **Trim Size:** 11 1/2 x 13 1/2. **Cols./Page:** 4. **Col. Width:** 2 1/2 inches. **Col. Depth:** 13 1/2 inches. **Key Personnel:** Norma E. McKittrick, Editor. **ISSN:** 1041-3316 (print). **USPS:** 070-910. **Alt. Formats:** PDF. **URL:** http://www.dioala.org/publications/the_apostle.html. **Formerly:** The Alabama Churchman; The Alabama Apostle; The Apostle. **Remarks:** Advertising not accepted. **Circ:** Non-paid ‡13000.

64 ■ American Journal of Trial Advocacy
Samford University Cumberland School of Law
800 Lakeshore Dr.
Birmingham, AL 35229
Phone: (205)726-2702
Free: 800-888-7213
Publisher's E-mail: lawadm@samford.edu
Journal covering studies dedicated to the advancement of trial advocacy. **Freq:** 3/year. **Subscription Rates:** $24 Individuals; $15 Single issue. **URL:** http://www.samford.edu/cumberlandlaw/american-journal-of-trial-advocacy. **Circ:** (Not Reported).

65 ■ American Nurseryman: Covering Commercial Horticulture Since 1904
Grand View Media Group Inc.
200 Croft St., Ste. 1
Birmingham, AL 35242
Phone: (205)408-3797
Fax: (205)408-3797
Free: 888-431-2877
Publication E-mail: editors@amerinursery.com
Trade magazine containing information on commercial horticulture: nursery, landscape and garden center management. **Freq:** Monthly. **Print Method:** Offset. **Trim Size:** 8 x 10 7/8. **Cols./Page:** 3. **Col. Width:** 13 picas. **Col. Depth:** 10 inches. **Key Personnel:** Korry Stagnito, Publisher; Stephanie Schartner, Associate Publisher. **ISSN:** 0003--0198 (print). **URL:** http://www.amerinursery.com. **Remarks:** Advertising accepted; rates available upon request. **Circ:** ‡13243.

66 ■ Archery Business: The Voice of the Archery Industry
Grand View Media Group Inc.
200 Croft St., Ste. 1
Birmingham, AL 35242
Phone: (205)408-3797
Fax: (205)408-3797
Free: 888-431-2877
Publisher's E-mail: webmaster@grandviewmedia.com
Trade magazine covering the business side of archery and bowhunting. **Freq:** Bimonthly 7/year. **Print Method:** Offset. Uses mats. **Trim Size:** 8 x 10 3/4. **Cols./Page:** 3. **Col. Width:** 27 nonpareils. **Col. Depth:** 140 agate lines. **Key Personnel:** Derrick Nawrocki, Publisher. **URL:** http://grandviewmedia.com/archery-business. **Formerly:** Archery Retailer. **Ad Rates:** BW $3300; 4C $4630. **Remarks:** Accepts advertising. **Circ:** Controlled ★11,099.

67 ■ Aura Literary/Arts Review
University of Alabama at Birmingham
1530 3rd Ave. S
Birmingham, AL 35294
Publication E-mail: uabaura@yahoo.com
Literary and arts magazine. **Freq:** Semiannual. **Print Method:** Offset. **Trim Size:** 6 x 9. **Key Personnel:** Molly Folse, Editor-in-Chief. **ISSN:** 0889--7433 (print). **Subscription Rates:** $6 Single issue + 2 for shipping. **URL:** http://studentaffairs.sass.uab.edu/aura. **Remarks:** Advertising accepted; rates available upon request. **Circ:** Non-paid ‡500.

68 ■ Birmingham Business Journal
American City Business Journals Inc.
2140 11th Ave. S, Ste. 205
Birmingham, AL 35205
Phone: (205)443-5600

Fax: (205)322-0040
Publication E-mail: birmingham@bizjournals.com
Local business newspaper. **Freq:** Weekly. **Key Personnel:** Joel Welker, Publisher, phone: (205)443-5617; Ty West, Managing Editor, phone: (205)443-5637; Cindy F. Crawford, Editor, phone: (205)443-5631. **Subscription Rates:** $92 Individuals print & digital or digital only. **Online:** American City Business Journals Inc. American City Business Journals Inc. **URL:** http://www.bizjournals.com/birmingham. **Ad Rates:** BW $4,665. **Remarks:** Accepts advertising. **Circ:** Paid 5402.

69 ■ Birmingham Home & Garden: Inspired Living for Birmingham and Beyond
PMT Publishing Company Inc.
2204 Lake Shore Dr., Ste. 120
Birmingham, AL 35209
Phone: (205)802-6363
Publisher's E-mail: wsorrell@pmtpublishing.com
Magazine featuring Birmingham's most beautiful homes and gardens. **Freq:** Bimonthly. **Trim Size:** 7 x 10. **Key Personnel:** Cathy Still McGowin, Editor; T.J. Potts, President, Publisher. **Subscription Rates:** $18.95 Individuals; $31.95 Two years; $43.95 Individuals three years. **URL:** http://birminghamhomeandgarden.com. **Ad Rates:** BW $2,632; 4C $2,685. **Remarks:** Accepts advertising. **Circ:** 13800.

70 ■ Birmingham Magazine: Smart Living, Savvy Business
Birmingham Regional Chamber of Commerce
505 20th St. N, Ste. 200
Birmingham, AL 35203
Phone: (205)324-2100
Fax: (205)324-2560
Magazine of the Birmingham Regional Chamber of Commerce. **Freq:** Monthly. **Print Method:** Offset. **Trim Size:** 8 1/2 x 11. **Cols./Page:** 3. **Col. Width:** 10 picas. **Col. Depth:** 10 inches. **Key Personnel:** Carla Jean Whitley, Managing Editor. **ISSN:** 0006--369X (print). **URL:** http://www.birminghamchamber.com/chamber/magazine.html. **Remarks:** Accepts advertising. **Circ:** (Not Reported).

71 ■ The Birmingham News
The Birmingham News
2201 4th Ave. N
Birmingham, AL 35202
Phone: (205)325-2444
General newspaper. **Freq:** Daily (morn.). **Print Method:** Offset. **Trim Size:** 10 x 10 7/8. **Cols./Page:** 5. **Col. Width:** 10.875 nonpareils. **Col. Depth:** 21 1/2 inches. **Key Personnel:** Tom Scarritt, Editor, phone: (205)325-2205, fax: (205)325-3278; Chuck Clark, Managing Editor, phone: (205)325-2148, fax: (205)325-2283. **Subscription Rates:** $143 Individuals. **URL:** http://www.alabamamediagroup.com/brands/news. **Feature Editors:** Jerry Underwood, *Financial/Business*, phone: (205)325-3250, fax: (205)325-3282, junderwood@bhamnews.com; Virginia Martin, *Political*, phone: (205)325-2483, fax: (205)325-2283, vmartin@bhamnews.com; Tom Arenberg, *Sports*, phone: (205)325-2433, fax: (205)325-2425, tarenberg@bhamnews.com; Alec Harvey, *Features*, phone: (205)325-2100, fax: (205)325-2494, aharvey@bhamnews.com. **Ad Rates:** BW $14047.02; 4C $15847.02; PCI $107.64. **Remarks:** Accepts advertising. **Circ:** Mon.-Fri. ★**147068**, Sun. ★**179872**.

72 ■ Birmingham Poetry Review
University of Alabama at Birmingham
1720 2nd Ave. S
Birmingham, AL 35294
Phone: (334)934-4011
Fax: (205)975-4691
Literary journal covering poetry. **Freq:** Annual in Spring. **Print Method:** Offset. **Trim Size:** 6 X 9. **Key Personnel:** Adam Vines, Editor. **ISSN:** 1047--2258 (print). **Subscription Rates:** $5 Individuals. **URL:** http://www.uab.edu/cas/englishpublications/birmingham-poetry-review. **Remarks:** Advertising not accepted. **Circ:** Paid 700.

73 ■ Birmingham Times
The Birmingham Times Publishing Co.
115 3rd Ave. W
Birmingham, AL 35204
Black community newspaper. **Freq:** Weekly. **Print Method:** Offset. **Cols./Page:** 6. **Col. Width:** 13 picas. **Col. Depth:** 21 inches. **URL:** http://www.birminghamtimes.com. **Remarks:** Advertising accepted; rates available upon request. **Circ:** Paid ‡10000, Free ‡350.

74 ■ BLiveTV.com
LoMo Magazine
228 Bayberry Rd.
Birmingham, AL 35214
Phone: (205)798-6061
Publication E-mail: bmoe@gobmoe.com
Consumer magazine covering local hip-hop, rock, reggae, gospel, and soul music. **Freq:** Monthly. **URL:** http://www.lomomag.com. **Formerly:** Lomo Magazine. **Circ:** (Not Reported).

75 ■ Bowhunting World: The Archery Equipment Authority
Grand View Media Group Inc.
200 Croft St., Ste. 1
Birmingham, AL 35242
Phone: (205)408-3797
Fax: (205)408-3797
Free: 888-431-2877
Publisher's E-mail: webmaster@grandviewmedia.com
Magazine for all-season bowhunters and competitive archers. **Freq:** 9/year. **Print Method:** Offset. **Trim Size:** 8 x 10 1/2. **Cols./Page:** 3. **Col. Width:** 27 nonpareils. **Col. Depth:** 140 agate lines. **Key Personnel:** Mike Strandlund, Editor; Derrick Nawrocki, Publisher, phone: (205)408-3732. **ISSN:** 1043--5492 (print). **Subscription Rates:** $12.97 Individuals; $21.97 Other countries. **URL:** http://grandviewmedia.com/bowhunting-world/overview. **Formerly:** Archery World. **Ad Rates:** BW $4795; 4C $6630. **Remarks:** Accepts advertising. **Circ:** ★**98420**.

76 ■ Cabela's Outfitter Journal
Grand View Media Group Inc.
200 Croft St., Ste. 1
Birmingham, AL 35242
Phone: (205)408-3797
Fax: (205)408-3797
Free: 888-431-2877
Publisher's E-mail: webmaster@grandviewmedia.com
Magazine for hunters and anglers. **Freq:** Bimonthly. **Trim Size:** 7.75 X 10.625. **Key Personnel:** Derrick Nowrocki, Publisher; Chuck Smock, Editor. **URL:** http://justmediakits.com/mediakit/1137-cabela_s_outfitter_journal.html. **Ad Rates:** BW $5250; 4C $6175. **Remarks:** Accepts advertising. **Circ:** 120000.

77 ■ Christian School Products: Purchasing solutions for religious education facilities
Valor Media Concepts
PO Box 36577
Birmingham, AL 35236
Fax: (205)979-1235
Free: 888-548-2567
Publication E-mail: info@cspmag.com
Magazine about products for Christian schools. Covers fundraisers, safe learning environments, playgrounds, and more. **Freq:** Monthly. **Trim Size:** 8 x 10.5. **Key Personnel:** Valarie Stiffler, Business Manager, phone: (205)979-1114; Loren A. Stiffler, Chief Executive Officer, Publisher; Jill Hasty, Managing Editor. **Subscription Rates:** Free. **URL:** http://www.christianschoolproducts.com. **Ad Rates:** 4C $3,590. **Remarks:** Accepts advertising. **Circ:** ‡20000.

78 ■ Civitan Magazine
Civitan International
PO Box 130744
Birmingham, AL 35213-0744
Phone: (205)591-8910
Publisher's E-mail: civitan@civitan.org
Magazine covering civic club activities and interests. **Freq:** Bimonthly. **Print Method:** Web. **Trim Size:** 8 1/8 x 10 7/8. **Cols./Page:** 4. **Col. Width:** 10 picas. **Col. Depth:** 57 picas. **ISSN:** 0914--5785 (print). **Subscription Rates:** $1 /copy; $2 for members in U.S. and Canada; $8 for members outside North America; $6 for nonmembers. **Alt. Formats:** PDF. **URL:** http://civitan.org/member-resource-center/pr-media/civitan-magazine. **Ad Rates:** BW $1000; 4C $1300. **Remarks:** Accepts advertising. **Circ:** ‡24000.

79 ■ Coastal Living: The Magazine for People who Love the Coast
Southern Progress Corp.
2100 Lakeshore Dr.
Birmingham, AL 35209-6721
Fax: (205)445-6700
Free: 800-366-4712
Publication E-mail: coastalliving@customersvc.com
Consumer magazine covering regional lifestyle, travel, and real estate. **Freq:** 10/year. **Trim Size:** 8 3/8 x 10 1/2. **Key Personnel:** Jamie Elliott, Manager, Production, phone: (212)522-7279; Peter Medwid, Publisher, phone: (212)522-5386; Tom Angelillo, Chief Executive Officer, President. **Subscription Rates:** $10 Individuals; C$18 Two years. **URL:** http://www.coastalliving.com. **Ad Rates:** BW $40,880; 4C $55,800. **Remarks:** Accepts classified advertising. **Circ:** Paid ★**661245**.

80 ■ Construction Business Owner: The business management resource for contractors
Cahaba Media Group
1900 28th Ave. S
Birmingham, AL 35209
Phone: (205)212-9402
Magazine that provides information for construction management and industry business information. **Freq:** Monthly. **Key Personnel:** Jeana Durst, Editor, phone: (205)314-8267; Kathy Wells, Editor, phone: (205)314-8268; Alecia Archibald, Senior Editor, phone: (205)278-2843. **Subscription Rates:** Free to qualified subscribers. **URL:** http://www.constructionbusinessowner.com. **Remarks:** Accepts advertising. **Circ:** Combined △**40050**.

81 ■ Cooking Light: Eat Smart Be Fit Live Well
Southern Progress Corp.
PO Box 1748
Birmingham, AL 35201
Phone: (205)445-6000
Fax: (205)445-6600
Publication E-mail: cookinglight@customersvc.com
The world's largest food and healthy lifestyle publication, devoted to helping readers eat smart, be fit and live well. Editorial covers food, entertaining, fitness, health, beauty, travel and home. **Freq:** 11/year. **Print Method:** Offset. **Trim Size:** 8 x 10 1/2. **Cols./Page:** 3. **Key Personnel:** Mary Kay Culpepper, Editor; Chris Allen, Publisher, Vice President, phone: (212)522-4305, fax: (212)522-4313. **ISSN:** 0886-4446 (print). **Subscription Rates:** $18 Individuals 1 year - 12 issues; $1.50 Single issue 1 year; $1 Single issue 2 years. **URL:** http://www.cookinglight.com; http://www.timeinc.com/brands/cooking-light. **Ad Rates:** 4C $154,700, full page; 4C $96,700, half page; BW $123,600, full page; BW $77,300, half page. **Remarks:** Accepts advertising. **Circ:** Paid ★**1750000**.

82 ■ Countdown
JDRF Alabama Chapter
2112 11th Ave. S, Ste. 520
Birmingham, AL 35205
Phone: (205)871-0333
Fax: (205)871-0355
Publisher's E-mail: alabama@jdrf.org
Magazine of the Juvenile Diabetes Research Foundation International, Alabama Chapter. **Freq:** Quarterly. **Key Personnel:** Sandra Puczynski, Contact. **URL:** http://www.jdrf.org/. **Circ:** (Not Reported).

83 ■ Doklady Earth Sciences
Springer Publishing Co.
Interperiodica
Birmingham, AL 35201-1831
Publisher's E-mail: cs@springerpub.com
Translation of research reports first published in the geophysics, seismology, tectonics, general and economic geology, lithology, mineralogy, petrography, geochemistry, paleontology, and oceanology sections of Transactions of the Soviet Academy of Sciences. **Freq:** 36/year. **Print Method:** Offset. **Cols./Page:** 1. **Col. Width:** 84 nonpareils. **Col. Depth:** 140 agate lines. **Key Personnel:** Irina V. Isavnina, Managing Editor; Vladimir E. Fortov, Editor-in-Chief; Yurii S. Osipov, Editor-in-Chief; Alexander F. Andreev, Board Member; Evgenii F. Mishenko, Editor-in-Chief; Alexander A. Boyarchuk, Board Member; Stanislav V. Emel'yanov, Board Member; Viktor A. Vasilev, Board Member; Vladimir M. Kotlyakov, Board Member. **ISSN:** 1028-334X (print); **EISSN:** 1531-8354 (electronic). **Subscription Rates:** €6753 Institutions print or online; €8104 Institutions print + enhanced access. **URL:** http://www.springer.com/earth+sciences+and+geography/journal/11471; http://www.maik.rssi.ru/journals/earthsci.htm. **Formerly:**

Circulation: ★ = AAM; △ or • = BPA; ♦ = CAC; ❑ = VAC; ⊕ = PO Statement; ‡ = Publisher's Report; Boldface figures = sworn; Light figures = estimated.

Transactions (Doklady) of the Russian Academy of Sciences. **Mailing address:** PO Box 1831, Birmingham, AL 35201-1831. **Remarks:** Accepts advertising. **Circ:** ‡500.

84 ■ Fertility and Sterility
American Society for Reproductive Medicine
1209 Montgomery Hwy.
Birmingham, AL 35216-2809
Phone: (205)978-5000
Fax: (205)978-5005
Publisher's E-mail: asrm@asrm.org
Medical journal covering all aspects of reproductive medicine. **Freq:** Monthly. **Print Method:** Offset. **Trim Size:** 8 1/4 x 10 7/8. **Cols./Page:** 2. **Col. Width:** 42 nonpareils. **Col. Depth:** 126 agate lines. **Key Personnel:** Craig Niederberger, MD, Editor-in-Chief; Eric Steinmehl, MD, Managing Editor; Antonio Pellicer, MD, Editor-in-Chief. **ISSN:** 0015--0282 (print). **Subscription Rates:** Included in membership. **URL:** http://www.asrm.org/FertilityAndSterility. **Ad Rates:** BW $1073; 4C $2198. **Remarks:** Accepts advertising. **Circ:** ‡15000, 14500.

85 ■ Flow Control: The Magazine of Fluid Handling Systems
Grand View Media Group Inc.
200 Croft St., Ste. 1
Birmingham, AL 35242
Phone: (205)408-3797
Fax: (205)408-3797
Free: 888-431-2877
Publication E-mail: flowcontrol@gvmg.com
Magazine for product and systems design engineers, managers, maintenance and repair specialists on fluid handling applications. **Freq:** Monthly. **Print Method:** Web offset. **Col. Width:** 7 inches. **Col. Depth:** 10 inches. **Key Personnel:** John P. Harris, Executive Director, phone: (205)408-3765. **URL:** http://www.flowcontrolnetwork.com. **Ad Rates:** BW $8,060; 4C $9,560. **Remarks:** Accepts advertising. **Circ:** (Not Reported).

86 ■ GA World
Woman's Missionary Union
100 Missionary Ridge
Birmingham, AL 35283-0010
Phone: (205)991-8100
Fax: (888)422-7032
Free: 800-968-7301
Publisher's E-mail: customer_service@wmu.org
Freq: Bimonthly. **Subscription Rates:** $16.99 Individuals. **URL:** http://www.wmustore.com/product.asp?sku=GAW. **Mailing address:** PO Box 830010, Birmingham, AL 35283-0010. **Remarks:** Advertising not accepted. **Circ:** (Not Reported).

87 ■ Geochemistry International
John Wiley & Sons Inc.
Interperiodica
Birmingham, AL 35201-1831
Publisher's E-mail: info@wiley.com
Translations of the principal Russian journal in geochemistry. Deals with composition of terrestrial and planetary rocks and atmospheres, plus all other aspects of geochemistry, mineral synthesis, spectroscopy, crystal chemistry, phase equilibria, petrology and geochronology. **Freq:** Monthly 13/yr. **Print Method:** Offset. **Cols./Page:** 1. **Col. Width:** 84 nonpareils. **Col. Depth:** 140 agate lines. **Key Personnel:** Evgenii B. Kurdyukov, Editor; Andrei V. Girnis, Editor; Igor D. Ryabchikov, Editor-in-Chief, Deputy; Oleg A. Bogatikov, Board Member; Prof. Claude J. Allegre, Board Member; Oleg Lukanin, Editor-in-Chief, Executive; Igor V. Chernyshev, Board Member; Dr. Arnold A. Kadik, Editor-in-Chief; Prof. Igor D. Ryabchikov, Editor-in-Chief; Oleg A. Lukanin, Editor-in-Chief; Vadim V. Ermakov, Board Member; Alexander T. Bazilevsky, Board Member; Erik M. Galimov, Editor-in-Chief; Claude J. Allegre, Board Member; Vadim S. Urusov, Board Member. **ISSN:** 0016--7029 (print); **EISSN:** 1556--1968 (electronic). **Subscription Rates:** €5937 Institutions print + online; €7124 Institutions print + enhanced access; $7196 Institutions print + online; $8635 Institutions print + enhanced access. **URL:** http://www.maik.rssi.ru/cgi-bin/journal.pl?name=geochem&page; http://www.maik.rssi.ru/cgi-bin/journal.pl?name=geochem&page=main; http://www.springer.com/earth+sciences+and+geography/geochemistry/journal/11476?cm_mmc=sgw-_-ps-_-journal-_-11476. **Mailing address:** PO Box 1831, Birmingham, AL 35201-1831. **Remarks:** Accepts advertising. **Circ:** 675.

88 ■ HomeCare
Cahaba Media Group
1900 28th Ave. S
Birmingham, AL 35209
Phone: (205)212-9402
Magazine for home medical equipment providers, publishing timely legislative, regulatory and business news, in-depth analysis of various market segments, emerging issues and trends, and practical how-to advice on business operations. **Freq:** Monthly. **Key Personnel:** Jane Longshore, Managing Editor; Wally Evans, Publisher, phone: (205)212-9402; Russ Willcutt, Editor. **Subscription Rates:** Free qualified U.S. readers; $48 U.S.; $125 Other countries. **URL:** http://homecaremag.com. **Ad Rates:** BW $4,290; 4C $5,240. **Remarks:** Accepts advertising. **Circ:** △**17091**.

89 ■ HomeCare Magazine: For Business Leaders in Home Medical Equipment
Cahaba Media Group
1900 28th Ave. S
Birmingham, AL 35209
Phone: (205)212-9402
Magazine serving home medical equipment suppliers, including independent and chain centers specializing in home care, pharmacies or chain drug stores with home care products, and joint-ventured hospital home health care businesses. Contains industry news and new product launches and marketing strategies. **Freq:** Monthly. **Print Method:** Offset. **Trim Size:** 7 3/4 x 10 3/4. **Cols./Page:** 3. **Col. Width:** 27 nonpareils. **Col. Depth:** 140 agate lines. **Key Personnel:** Jennifer Cox, Managing Editor. **ISSN:** 0882--2700 (print). **URL:** http://homecaremag.com. **Ad Rates:** BW $4290; 4C $5240. **Remarks:** Accepts advertising. **Circ:** △**17100**.

90 ■ JANA
American Nutraceutical Association
5120 Selkirk Dr., Ste. 100
Birmingham, AL 35242-4165
Phone: (205)980-5710
Fax: (205)991-9302
Free: 800-566-3622
Publisher's E-mail: info@ana-jana.org
Freq: Quarterly. **Subscription Rates:** $36 each. **Alt. Formats:** CD-ROM. **Remarks:** Advertising not accepted. **Circ:** (Not Reported).

91 ■ The Jewish Star: The Promised Land
The Jewish Star The Promised Land
PO Box 43706
Birmingham, AL 35243
Phone: (205)956-3929
Fax: (205)967-1417
Free: 888-261-STAR
Publisher's E-mail: rudolphhmail@aol.com
Jewish/Christian interest newspaper. **Freq:** Bimonthly. **Print Method:** Offset. **Cols./Page:** 6. **Col. Width:** 21 nonpareils. **Col. Depth:** 13 inches. **Key Personnel:** Margie Rudolph, Editor; Marvin Rudolph, Publisher. **Subscription Rates:** $10 Individuals; $15 Two years. **Ad Rates:** BW $600; 4C $850. **Remarks:** Accepts advertising. **Circ:** ‡8000.

92 ■ Journal of Addiction Nursing
International Nurses Society on Addictions
3416 Primm Ln.
Birmingham, AL 35216
Phone: (205)823-6106
Publisher's E-mail: intnsa@primemanagement.net
Journal containing peer reviewed original articles on current research, issues, practices and innovations as they relate to the field of addictions. **Freq:** Quarterly. **Key Personnel:** Louis Nadelson, Editor-in-Chief. **ISSN:** 1088--4602 (print); **EISSN:** 1548--7148 (electronic). **Subscription Rates:** $99 Individuals United States, Canada and Mexico; $827 Institutions United States, Canada and Mexico; $107 Individuals Other countries; $835 Institutions, other countries. **URL:** http://www.intnsa.org/publications/journal-of-addictions-nursing. **Remarks:** Advertising not accepted. **Circ:** (Not Reported).

93 ■ Journal of the American Pharmacists Association
APhA Academy of Pharmacy Practice and Management
PO Box 11806
Birmingham, AL 35202-1806
Fax: (205)995-1588
Free: 800-633-4931
Publisher's E-mail: infocenter@aphanet.org
Peer-reviewed journal for pharmacy professionals. **Freq:** Monthly Bimonthly. **Print Method:** Web offset. **Key Personnel:** Andy Stergachis, Editor. **ISSN:** 1544--3191 (print); **EISSN:** 1544--3450 (electronic). **Subscription Rates:** $450 Individuals print and online; $550 Other countries print and online. **URL:** http://www.japha.org. **Formerly:** American Pharmacy; Journal of the American Pharmaceutical Association. **Ad Rates:** BW $3640; 4C $1720. **Remarks:** Accepts advertising. **Circ:** Combined ‡44797.

94 ■ Journal of Continuing Education in the Health Professions
Society for Academic Continuing Medical Education
3416 Primm Ln.
Birmingham, AL 35216-5602
Phone: (205)978-7990
Fax: (205)823-2760
Publisher's E-mail: acehp@acehp.org
Journal covering information on health care performance through education, advocacy and collaboration. **Freq:** Quarterly. **Key Personnel:** Curtis Olson, PhD. **Subscription Rates:** $89.25 for nonmembers in U.S. and Canada (individual); $139.75 for nonmembers in U.S. and Canada (institution); $121.50 for nonmembers outside U.S. and Canada (individual); $177.40 for nonmembers outside U.S. and Canada (institution). **URL:** http://www.acehp.org/p/cm/ld/fid=10; http://www.sacme.org/Publications#JCEHP. **Remarks:** Advertising not accepted. **Circ:** (Not Reported).

95 ■ Journal of Neuro-Ophthalmology: Official Journal of the North American Neuro-Ophthamology Society
Lippincott Williams & Wilkins
c/o Lanning B. Kline, MD, Editor-in-Chief
University of Alabama School of Medicine
Dept. of Ophthalmology
700 S 18 St., Ste. 601
Birmingham, AL 35233
Phone: (205)325-8660
Fax: (205)325-8641
Publication E-mail: lkline@uabmc.edu
Peer-reviewed journal reporting on recent developments in diagnosing and treating ophthalmologic, neurologic, endocrinologic, inflammatory, and neoplastic conditions affecting the motor and the visual systems. **Freq:** Quarterly March, June, September, December. **Print Method:** Sheetfed Offset. **Trim Size:** 8 1/4 x 11. **Key Personnel:** David Myers, Publisher; Lanning B. Kline, MD, Editor-in-Chief. **ISSN:** 1070-8022 (print); **EISSN:** 1536-5166 (electronic). **Subscription Rates:** $566 Individuals; $1273 Institutions; $233 Individuals in-training; $1221 Institutions, other countries; $249 Other countries in-training; $582 Individuals international. **URL:** http://journals.lww.com/jneuro-ophthalmology/pages/default.aspx; http://www.lww.com/Product/1070-8022. **Ad Rates:** BW $1,115; 4C $1,285. **Remarks:** Accepts advertising. **Circ:** 856.

96 ■ Kaleidoscope
University of Alabama at Birmingham
1720 2nd Ave. S
Birmingham, AL 35294
Phone: (334)934-4011
Fax: (205)975-4691
Collegiate newspaper (broadsheet). **Founded:** 1967. **Freq:** Weekly (Tues.). **Print Method:** Offset. **Trim Size:** 13 x 21 1/2. **Cols./Page:** 6. **Col. Width:** 2 inches. **Col. Depth:** 21 1/2 inches. **URL:** http://www.uab.edu/kscope/. **Ad Rates:** GLR $12; 4C $375; PCI $8. **Remarks:** Accepts classified advertising. **Circ:** Combined 6000.

97 ■ The Land Report: The Magazine of The American Landowner
The Land Report
1 Perometer Pk. S, Ste. 100N
Birmingham, AL 35243
Phone: (205)915-5600
Publisher's E-mail: creative@sanmiguelpartners.com
Magazine providing news, information, and insight into America's land for existing and potential landowners. **Freq:** Quarterly. **Trim Size:** 8.75 x 10.75. **Key Personnel:** Eric O'Keefe, Editor. **Subscription Rates:** $59.99 Individuals 1 year; $69.99 Individuals 2 years. **URL:** http://landreport.com. **Ad Rates:** BW $7,060. **Remarks:** Accepts advertising. **Circ:** ‡50000.

98 ■ Louisiana Cookin'
Hoffman Media L.L.C.
1900 International Park Dr., Ste. 50
Birmingham, AL 35243-4244
Phone: (205)995-8860
Fax: (205)991-0071
Free: 888-411-8995
Publication E-mail: info@louisianacookin.com
Authentic Louisiana and southern recipes. **Freq:** 6/year. **Key Personnel:** Daniel Schumacher, Editor, phone: (504)648-2645; Aimee Abernathy, Director, Advertising and Sales. **Subscription Rates:** $19.98 Individuals; $4.99 Individuals cover price. **URL:** http://www.louisianacookin.com; http://www.hoffmanmedia.com/magazines. **Remarks:** Accepts advertising. **Circ:** (Not Reported).

99 ■ The MAG
Woman's Missionary Union
100 Missionary Ridge
Birmingham, AL 35283-0010
Phone: (205)991-8100
Fax: (888)422-7032
Free: 800-968-7301
Publisher's E-mail: customer_service@wmu.org
Freq: Bimonthly. **Subscription Rates:** $19.99 Individuals. **URL:** http://www.wmustore.com/product.asp?sku=AM; http://www.wmu.com/index.php?q=students/misc/mag-kaleidoscope-missions-awareness-and-growth. **Mailing address:** PO Box 830010, Birmingham, AL 35283-0010. **Remarks:** Advertising not accepted. **Circ:** (Not Reported).

100 ■ Mission Leader
Woman's Missionary Union
100 Missionary Ridge
Birmingham, AL 35283-0010
Phone: (205)991-8100
Fax: (888)422-7032
Free: 800-968-7301
Publisher's E-mail: customer_service@wmu.org
Freq: 3/year fall, spring, and summer. **ISSN:** 1062--6833 (print). **Subscription Rates:** $19.99 /year. **URL:** http://www.wmustore.com/product.asp?sku=MLC. **Mailing address:** PO Box 830010, Birmingham, AL 35283-0010. **Remarks:** Advertising not accepted. **Circ:** (Not Reported).

101 ■ Missions Leader
Woman's Missionary Union
100 Missionary Ridge
Birmingham, AL 35283-0010
Phone: (205)991-8100
Fax: (888)422-7032
Free: 800-968-7301
Publisher's E-mail: customer_service@wmu.org
Freq: 3/year fall, spring, and summer. **ISSN:** 0162--6825 (print). **Subscription Rates:** $19.99 Individuals. **URL:** http://www.wmustore.com/product.asp?sku=MLC. **Mailing address:** PO Box 830010, Birmingham, AL 35283-0010. **Remarks:** Advertising not accepted. **Circ:** (Not Reported).

102 ■ Missions Mosaic
Woman's Missionary Union
100 Missionary Ridge
Birmingham, AL 35283-0010
Phone: (205)991-8100
Fax: (888)422-7032
Free: 800-968-7301
Publisher's E-mail: customer_service@wmu.org
Freq: Monthly. **Print Method:** Offset. **Trim Size:** 8 x 10 1/2. **Cols./Page:** 3. **Col. Width:** 13 picas. **Col. Depth:** 50 picas. **Key Personnel:** Cindy Dake, Editor; Becky England, Assistant Editor; Janet Erwin, Editor; Sarah Hart, Editor. **ISSN:** 1083--3285 (print). **Subscription Rates:** $20.99 Individuals /year. **URL:** http://www.wmu.com/index.php?q=adults/misc/missions-mosaic; http://www.wmu.com/index.php?q=blog/adults/resources/adult-resources-missions-mosaic. **Formerly:** Royal Service. **Mailing address:** PO Box 830010, Birmingham, AL 35283-0010. **Remarks:** Accepts advertising. **Circ:** Paid 140500.

103 ■ Mitochondrion
Mitochondria Research and Medicine Society
PO Box 55322
Birmingham, AL 35255
Phone: (205)934-2735
Fax: (205)934-2766
Publisher's E-mail: info@mitoresearch.org
Journal containing topics on basic science of mitochondria from all organisms to reporting on pathology and clinical aspects of mitochondrial diseases. **Key Personnel:** Keshav K. Singh, Editor-in-Chief. **Subscription Rates:** Included in membership. **URL:** http://www.mitoresearch.org/publications.html. **Remarks:** Advertising not accepted. **Circ:** (Not Reported).

104 ■ Mitochondrion: Mitochondrion
RELX Group P.L.C.
Dept. of Genetics, School of Medicine
University of Alabama at Birmingham
Kaul Genetics Bldg., Ste. 620
720 20th St. S
Birmingham, AL 35294
Phone: (205)934-2750
Fax: (205)934-2766
Publisher's E-mail: amsterdam@relx.com
Journal that aims to report on basic science of mitochondria from all organisms and from basic research to pathology and clinical aspects of mitochondrial diseases. **Freq:** Bimonthly. **Key Personnel:** Keshav K. Singh, Editor-in-Chief; Anthony W. Linnane, Editor. **ISSN:** 1567-7249 (print). **Subscription Rates:** $585 Institutions online; $154 Individuals print; $585 Institutions print. **Circ:** (Not Reported).

105 ■ Nucleosides & Nucleotides & Nucleic Acids: An International Journal for Rapid Communication
Taylor & Francis Group Journals
c/o John A. Secrist, III, Exec. Ed.
Southern Research Institute
Birmingham, AL 35255-5305
Publisher's E-mail: customerservice@taylorandfrancis.com
Journal covering nucleosides & nucleotides. **Freq:** Monthly. **Trim Size:** 8 1/4 X 10 7/8. **Key Personnel:** John A. Secrist, III, Executive Editor. **ISSN:** 1525--7770 (print); **EISSN:** 1532--2335 (electronic). **Subscription Rates:** $830 Individuals print only; $3378 Institutions online only; $3861 Institutions print and online. **URL:** http://www.tandfonline.com/toc/lncn20/current#.Vd6_UCWqqko. **Formerly:** Nucleosides & Nucleotides. **Mailing address:** PO Box 55305, Birmingham, AL 35255-5305. **Ad Rates:** BW $890; 4C $1,935. **Remarks:** Accepts advertising. **Circ:** 400.

106 ■ PMS poemmemoirstory
University of Alabama at Birmingham
1720 2nd Ave. S
Birmingham, AL 35294
Phone: (334)934-4011
Fax: (205)975-4691
Publication E-mail: poememoirstory@gmail.com
Literary journal featuring the best work of women writers in the nation. **Freq:** Annual. **Key Personnel:** Kerry Madden, Editor-in-Chief. **Subscription Rates:** $10 Individuals; $15 Two years. **URL:** http://www.uab.edu/cas/englishpublications/pms-poemmemoirstory. **Circ:** (Not Reported).

107 ■ Predator Xtreme: Predator Xtreme
Grand View Media Group Inc.
200 Croft St., Ste. 1
Birmingham, AL 35242
Phone: (205)408-3797
Fax: (205)408-3797
Free: 888-431-2877
Publisher's E-mail: webmaster@grandviewmedia.com
Magazine that covers the newest in equipment, techniques and gear to hunt large predators. **Freq:** Bimonthly. **Key Personnel:** Bob Robb, Editor; Mike Kizzire, Publisher. **ISSN:** 1535--3982 (print). **URL:** http://grandviewmedia.com/predator-xtreme. **Ad Rates:** BW $5,130; 4C $6,040. **Remarks:** Accepts advertising. **Circ:** Combined ★**86530**.

108 ■ Pro Bull Rider: Official Magazine of the Professional Bull Riders
Grand View Media Group Inc.
200 Croft St., Ste. 1
Birmingham, AL 35242
Phone: (205)408-3797
Fax: (205)408-3797
Free: 888-431-2877
Publisher's E-mail: webmaster@grandviewmedia.com
Magazine featuring professional bull riding. **Freq:** Bimonthly. **Trim Size:** 7.75 x 10.625. **Key Personnel:** Jeff Jphnstone, Editor; Derrick Nawrocki, Publisher. **Subscription Rates:** $14.95 Individuals. **URL:** http://www.pbr.com. **Ad Rates:** BW $3,920; 4C $4,895. **Remarks:** Accepts advertising. **Circ:** (Not Reported).

109 ■ Progressive Farmer
Southern Progress Corp.
2100 Lakeshore Dr.
Birmingham, AL 35209-6721
Fax: (205)445-6700
Free: 800-366-4712
Agricultural magazine, published in 15 editions, for farmers and ranchers. **Founded:** 1886. **Freq:** Monthly. **Print Method:** Offset. **Trim Size:** 8 x 10 1/2. **Cols./Page:** 3. **Col. Width:** 2 1/4 inches. **Col. Depth:** 140 agate lines. **Key Personnel:** Gregg Hillyer, Editor-in-Chief; Dan Miller, Senior Editor; Victoria G. Myers, Senior Editor; Jim Patrico, Senior Editor; Jack Odle, Publisher. **ISSN:** 0033-0760 (print). **Subscription Rates:** $16 Individuals. **URL:** http://www.dtnprogressivefarmer.com/dtnag. **Ad Rates:** BW $56,129; 4C $77,206. **Circ:** 625000.

110 ■ Pumps & Systems
Cahaba Media Group
1900 28th Ave. S
Birmingham, AL 35209
Phone: (205)212-9402
Magazine covering pumps and related operations. **Freq:** Monthly. **Trim Size:** 7 7/8 x 10 1/2. **Key Personnel:** Amelia Messamore, Managing Editor; Savanna Gray, Managing Editor. **Subscription Rates:** Free for U.S. readers. **URL:** http://www.pumpsandsystems.com; http://www.cahabamedia.com/media-guides/pumps-and-systems. **Ad Rates:** 4C $7988. **Remarks:** Accepts advertising. **Circ:** △**42450**.

111 ■ Religious Product News: Religious Product News
Valor Media Concepts
PO Box 36577
Birmingham, AL 35236
Fax: (205)979-1235
Free: 888-548-2567
Publisher's E-mail: info@valormediaconcepts.com
Magazine covering church maintenance, construction, and technology. **Freq:** Monthly. **Key Personnel:** Loren A Stiffler, Chief Executive Officer, Publisher; Jill Hasty, Managing Editor. **Subscription Rates:** Free. **URL:** http://www.religiousproductnews.com. **Ad Rates:** 4C $4,720. **Remarks:** Accepts advertising. **Circ:** (Not Reported).

112 ■ Reviews in Medical Virology
John Wiley & Sons Inc.
c/o Dr. Richard R. Whitley, Editor
Department of Pediatrics
University of Alabama
1600 7th Ave. S
Birmingham, AL 35233
Publisher's E-mail: info@wiley.com
Journal focusing on current research and new information on all viruses of medical importance. **Freq:** Bimonthly. **Trim Size:** 11 3/4 x 8 1/4. **Key Personnel:** Prof. Paul Griffiths, Editor-in-Chief; Dr. Richard R. Whitley, Editor; Y.E. Cossart, Board Member; A.M. Arvin, Board Member; D.A. Clark, Board Member; Dr. Yiming Shao, Editor; N.J. Dimmock, Board Member; L. Corey, Board Member; Y. Koyanagi, Board Member; P. Minor, Board Member. **ISSN:** 1052--9276 (print); **EISSN:** 1099--1654 (electronic). **Subscription Rates:** $1785 Institutions online only - USA/Canada & Mexico/ROW; €1153 Institutions online only - Europe; £913 Institutions online only - UK. **URL:** http://onlinelibrary.wiley.com/journal/10.1002/(ISSN)1099-1654. **Ad Rates:** BW $720; 4C $2,020. **Remarks:** Advertising accepted; rates available upon request. **Circ:** Paid 3500.

113 ■ School Science and Mathematics
School Science and Mathematics Association
School of Education, EB 246B
University of Alabama Birmingham
Birmingham, AL 35233
Phone: (205)934-5067
Publication E-mail: ssmj@coe.tamu.edu
Science and mathematics education journal. **Freq:** Monthly. **Print Method:** Offset. **Trim Size:** 8 1/2 x 11. **Cols./Page:** 2. **Col. Width:** 3.25 inches. **Col. Depth:**

Circulation: ★ = AAM; △ or • = BPA; ♦ = CAC; ❑ = VAC; ⊕ = PO Statement; ‡ = Publisher's Report; Boldface figures = sworn; Light figures = estimated.

9.5 inches. **Key Personnel:** Heather Lee, Managing Editor; Gerald Kulm, Editor. **ISSN:** 0036-6803 (print). **Subscription Rates:** $308 U.S., Canada, and Mexico Institutions; £189 Institutions; €222 Institutions; $308 Institutions, other countries; $370 U.S., Canada, and Mexico Institutions, print and online; £227 Institutions print and online; €267 Institutions print and online; $370 Institutions, other countries print and online. **URL:** http://www.ssma.org/publications; http://onlinelibrary.wiley.com/journal/10.1111/(ISSN)1949-8594. **Ad Rates:** BW $160. **Remarks:** Accepts advertising. **Circ:** (Not Reported).

114 ■ Shock: Injury, Inflammation, and Sepsis: Laboratory and Clinical Approaches
Wolters Kluwer Health Inc.
c/o Dr. Irshad H. Chaudry, Ed.
University of Alabama at Birmingham, Ctr. for Surgical Research
1670 University Blvd.
Volker Hall - Rm. G094
Birmingham, AL 35294-0019
Peer-reviewed journal covering studies of novel therapeutic approaches, such as immunomodulation, gene therapy, nutrition, and others. **Freq:** Monthly. **Trim Size:** 8 1/8 x 10 7/8. **Key Personnel:** Naoki Aikawa, Board Member; Mayuki Aibiki, Board Member; Soheyl Bahrami, Board Member; Alfred Ayala, Board Member; Dr. Irshad H. Chaudry, PhD, Editor-in-Chief. **ISSN:** 1073--2322 (print); **EISSN:** 1540--0514 (electronic). **Subscription Rates:** $529 Individuals print; $2529 Institutions print; $716 Canada and Mexico print; $2766 Institutions, Canada and Mexico print; $746 Other countries print; $2796 Institutions, other countries print. **URL:** http://journals.lww.com/shockjournal/pages/default.aspx. **Ad Rates:** BW $740; 4C $880. **Remarks:** Accepts advertising. **Circ:** ‡473.

115 ■ The Southern Baptist Educator
International Association of Baptist Colleges and Universities
c/o Samford University
PO Box 293935
Birmingham, AL 35229
Phone: (205)726-2036
Journal covering the philosophy and methods of church-related higher education. Also includes Association of Southern Baptist Colleges and Schools campus reports. **Freq:** Quarterly. **Key Personnel:** Tim Fields, Managing Editor. **ISSN:** 0038--3848 (print). **Alt. Formats:** PDF. **URL:** http://www.baptistschools.org/the-baptist-educator. **Remarks:** Advertising not accepted. **Circ:** 11000.

116 ■ Southern Lady Magazine
Hoffman Media L.L.C.
1900 International Park Dr., Ste. 50
Birmingham, AL 35243-4244
Phone: (205)995-8860
Fax: (205)991-0071
Free: 888-411-8995
Magazine for the women of the Southern U.S. **Freq:** 7/year. **Print Method:** Offset. **Trim Size:** 8 x 10.875. **Cols./Page:** 3. **Col. Width:** 27 nonpareils. **Col. Depth:** 145 agate lines. **Key Personnel:** Andrea Fanning, Editor. **Subscription Rates:** $24.98 Individuals. **URL:** http://www.southernladymagazine.com; http://www.hoffmanmedia.com/magazines/southern-lady-magazine. **Remarks:** Advertising accepted; rates available upon request. **Circ:** Paid 500000.

117 ■ Southern Living Vacations: Family Vacations, Texas Vacations, Summer Vacations, Weekend Vacations
Southern Progress Corp.
2100 Lakeshore Dr.
Birmingham, AL 35209-6721
Fax: (205)445-6700
Free: 800-366-4712
Themed guides covering travel in the South. **Freq:** Monthly. **Print Method:** Offset. **Trim Size:** 8 x 10 7/8. **Cols./Page:** 3. **Col. Width:** 2 1/4 inches. **Col. Depth:** 10 inches. **ISSN:** 0891--8023 (print). **Subscription Rates:** $1.54 Single issue for 1 year; $1.35 Single issue for 2 years. **URL:** http://www.slvacations.com. **Formerly:** Southern Living Travel Guides; Southern Travel; Travel South. **Remarks:** Accepts advertising. **Circ:** (Not Reported).

118 ■ Southern Medical Journal
Southern Medical Association
35 W Lakeshore Dr., Ste. 201
Birmingham, AL 35209
Phone: (205)945-1840
Fax: (205)945-1830
Free: 800-423-4992
Publisher's E-mail: mbrsvc@sma.org
Freq: Monthly. **Trim Size:** 8 1/8 x 10 7/8. **Key Personnel:** G. Richard Holt, MD, Editor-in-Chief. **ISSN:** 0038--4348 (print); **EISSN:** 1541--8243 (electronic). **Subscription Rates:** $862 Institutions print; $993 Institutions, Canada and Mexico print; $1026 Institutions, other countries print. **URL:** http://www.lww.com/Product/0038-4348. **Ad Rates:** BW $3,750; 4C $3,015. **Remarks:** Accepts advertising. **Circ:** 9690, 30,000.

119 ■ TeaTime Magazine
Hoffman Media L.L.C.
1900 International Park Dr., Ste. 50
Birmingham, AL 35243-4244
Phone: (205)995-8860
Fax: (205)991-0071
Free: 888-411-8995
Magazine that offers information about tea and tea making. **Freq:** 6/year. **Trim Size:** 8 x 10 7/8. **Key Personnel:** Lorna Reeves, Editor. **Subscription Rates:** $19.98 Individuals. **URL:** http://www.teatimemagazine.com. **Ad Rates:** BW $3,130. **Remarks:** Accepts advertising. **Circ:** ‡65000.

120 ■ Technology Alabama
PMT Publishing Company Inc.
2204 Lake Shore Dr., Ste. 120
Birmingham, AL 35209
Phone: (205)802-6363
Publisher's E-mail: wsorrell@pmtpublishing.com
Journal covering broad spectrum of emerging technology. **Freq:** Quarterly. **Trim Size:** 7 x 10. **Key Personnel:** Erica West, Editor; Anita Miller, Manager, Circulation. **Ad Rates:** BW $1,570; 4C $1,972. **Remarks:** Accepts advertising. **Circ:** 7500.

121 ■ Tennis Industry
United States Racquet Stringers Association
310 Richard Arrington Jr. Blvd. N, Ste. 400
Birmingham, AL 35203
Phone: (760)536-1177
Fax: (760)536-1171
Publisher's E-mail: info@tennisindustry.org
Magazine covering the racquet sports industry. **Freq:** 10/year. **Subscription Rates:** $25 Individuals; $51 Other countries; $35 Canada; $40 Individuals Mexico. **URL:** http://www.tennisindustrymag.com. **Formerly:** Racquet Sports Industry. **Remarks:** Accepts advertising. **Circ:** (Not Reported).

122 ■ Victoria Magazine: Romantic Living, Homes, Gardens, Fashion, Beauty, Travel, Inspiring Warrier
Hoffman Media L.L.C.
1900 International Park Dr., Ste. 50
Birmingham, AL 35243-4244
Phone: (205)995-8860
Fax: (205)991-0071
Free: 888-411-8995
Lifestyle magazine for women. **Freq:** Bimonthly. **Print Method:** Web offset. **Trim Size:** 8 x 10 7/8. **Cols./Page:** 3. **Key Personnel:** Melissa Lester, Associate Editor. **ISSN:** 1040--6883 (print). **Subscription Rates:** $22.98 U.S. /year; $32.98 Canada /year; $42.98 Other countries /year. **URL:** http://www.victoriamag.com. **Remarks:** Accepts advertising. **Circ:** (Not Reported).

123 ■ Waterfowl & Retriever: Hunting Tactics, Retriever Training, Conservation
Grand View Media Group Inc.
200 Croft St., Ste. 1
Birmingham, AL 35242
Phone: (205)408-3797
Fax: (205)408-3797
Free: 888-431-2877
Publisher's E-mail: webmaster@grandviewmedia.com
Magazine for waterfowl hunters. Includes product reviews and hunting tips. **Freq:** Semiannual. **Key Personnel:** Hilary Dyer, Editor; Jared Pfeifer, Publisher. **URL:** http://www.grandviewoutdoors.com/duck-hunting. **Ad Rates:** BW $3,010; 4C $3,540. **Remarks:** Accepts advertising. **Circ:** (Not Reported).

124 ■ The Western Star
Alabama Press Association
Alabama Newspaper Advertising Service, Inc.
3324 Independence Dr., Ste. 200
Birmingham, AL 35209
Phone: (205)871-7737
Fax: (205)871-7740
Free: 800-264-7043
Newspaper and legal paper. **Founded:** 1900. **Freq:** Daily. **Print Method:** Offset. **Cols./Page:** 5. **Col. Width:** 1 inches. **Col. Depth:** 21 1/2 inches. **Key Personnel:** Shawn Woodford, General Manager, Publisher, phone: (709)637-4667; Troy Turner, Managing Editor, phone: (709)637-4668; Gladys Leonard, Business Manager, phone: (709)637-4654. **Subscription Rates:** $220.80 Individuals Daily-carrier delivery (print and digital); $232.57 Individuals motor route (print and digital); $2.75 Single issue. **URL:** http://www.thewesternstar.com/. **Formerly:** Bessemer Advertiser. **Ad Rates:** GLR $7.30; BW $7.30; 4C $50. **Remarks:** Advertising accepted; rates available upon request. **Circ:** ⊕10000.

125 ■ Whitetail Journal
Grand View Media Group Inc.
200 Croft St., Ste. 1
Birmingham, AL 35242
Phone: (205)408-3797
Fax: (205)408-3797
Free: 888-431-2877
Publisher's E-mail: webmaster@grandviewmedia.com
Magazine for hunters of white tailed deer. **Freq:** 5/year. **Key Personnel:** Bob Robb, Editor; Derrick Nawrocki, Vice President, Publisher. **URL:** http://grandviewmedia.com/whitetail-journal. **Remarks:** Accepts advertising. **Circ:** (Not Reported).

126 ■ Masada Corp.
2160 Highland Ave. S, Ste. 100.
Birmingham, AL 35205
Phone: (205)558-4688
Founded: 1978. **Key Personnel:** Terry Johnson, President; Daryl Harms, Contact; Joe Gibbs, Contact. **Cities Served:** subscribing households 62,139. **URL:** http://www.masada.com/.

127 ■ WABM-TV - 68
651 Beacon Pky. W, Ste. 105
Birmingham, AL 35209
Phone: (205)943-2168
Fax: (205)250-6788
Format: Commercial TV. **Networks:** United Paramount Network. **Owner:** Sinclair Broadcast Group Inc., 10706 Beaver Dam Rd., Hunt Valley, MD 21030, Ph: (410)568-1500, Fax: (410)568-1533. **Founded:** 1980. **Operating Hours:** Continuous; 50% network, 50% local. **ADI:** Birmingham (Gadsden), AL. **Local Programs:** *Cheaters*, Saturday Monday Tuesday Wednesday Thursday Friday 11:00 p.m. 3:00 a.m.; *Believers Voice of Victory with Kenneth & Gloria Copeland*; *Law & Order: Special Victims Unit*, Monday; *Everyday Life with Joyce Meyer*, Monday Tuesday Wednesday Thursday Friday 8:00 a.m.; *Mtn Dew's Thursday Night Lights*, Thursday. **Ad Rates:** Noncommercial. **URL:** http://www.wabm68.com.

128 ■ WAGG-AM - 610
2700 Corporate Dr., Ste. 115
Birmingham, AL 35242
Phone: (205)322-2987
Format: Gospel. **Owner:** Cox Radio Inc., 6205 Peachtree Dunwood Rd., Atlanta, GA 30328-4524, Ph: (678)645-0000, Fax: (678)645-5002. **ADI:** Birmingham (Gadsden), AL. **Wattage:** 5,000. **Ad Rates:** Advertising accepted; rates available upon request. **URL:** http://www.610wagg.com.

WAIQ-TV - See Montgomery

129 ■ WAPI-AM - 1070
244 Goodwin Crest Dr., Ste. 300
Birmingham, AL 35209
Phone: (205)945-4646
Fax: (205)945-3999
Free: 877-569-1005
Format: News; Talk. **Owner:** Citadel Broadcasting Corp., 7201 W Lake Mead Blvd., Ste. 400, Las Vegas, NV 89128-8366, Ph: (702)804-5200, Fax: (702)804-8250. **Founded:** 1922. **Operating Hours:** Continuous. **ADI:** Birmingham (Gadsden), AL. **Wattage:** 50,000 Day; 5,000 Ni. **Ad Rates:** Advertising accepted; rates available upon request. **URL:** http://www.1070wapi.com.

130 ■ WATV-AM - 900
960 Penn Ave., Ste. 200
Pittsburgh, PA 15222

Phone: (412)456-4000

Format: Oldies; Gospel. **Networks:** American Urban Radio; CBS. **Owner:** MCL/MCM Alabama, LLC, at above address. **Founded:** 1946. **ADI:** Birmingham (Gadsden), AL. **Key Personnel:** Sherri Stewart, Contact, spstewart@watv900.com. **Wattage:** 845 Daytime;158 Nigh. **Ad Rates:** Advertising accepted; rates available upon request. $30-50 for 30 seconds; $50-70 for 60 seconds. **URL:** http://www.900goldwatv.com/.

131 ■ WBFR-FM - 89.5
290 Hegenberger Rd.
Oakland, CA 94621
Free: 800-543-1495
Email: info@familyradio.org

Format: Religious. **Networks:** Family Stations Radio. **Owner:** Family Stations Inc., 290 Hegenberger Rd., Oakland, CA 94621, Free: 800-543-1495. **Founded:** 1973. **Operating Hours:** Continuous. **ADI:** Birmingham (Gadsden), AL. **Wattage:** 100. **Ad Rates:** Noncommercial. **URL:** http://www.familyradio.org.

132 ■ WBHJ-FM - 95.7
2700 Corporate Pkwy., Ste. 115
Birmingham, AL 35242
Phone: (205)322-2987
Free: 855-957-5269

Format: Hip Hop; Urban Contemporary. **Owner:** Cox Radio Inc., 6205 Peachtree Dunwood Rd., Atlanta, GA 30328-4524, Ph: (678)645-0000, Fax: (678)645-5002. **Ad Rates:** Noncommercial. **URL:** http://www.957jamz.com.

133 ■ WBHK-FM - 98.7
2700 Corporate Dr., Ste. 115
Birmingham, AL 35203

Format: Urban Contemporary; Adult Contemporary. **Networks:** ABC. **Owner:** Cox Radio Inc., 6205 Peachtree Dunwood Rd., Atlanta, GA 30328-4524, Ph: (678)645-0000, Fax: (678)645-5002. **Formerly:** WLBI-FM. **Operating Hours:** Continuous. **ADI:** Birmingham (Gadsden), AL. **Key Personnel:** Darryl Johnson, Dir. of Programs, darryl.johnson@coxradio.com; Kori White, Operations Mgr., kori.white@coxradio.com; David Dubose, Gen. Mgr., VP, david.dubose@coxradio.com. **Wattage:** 10,000. **URL:** http://www.987kiss.com.

134 ■ WBHM-FM - 90.3
650 11th St. S
Birmingham, AL 35294
Phone: (205)934-2606
Fax: (205)934-5075
Free: 800-444-9246
Email: underwriting@wbhm.org

Format: News; Classical. **Networks:** National Public Radio (NPR); Public Radio International (PRI). **Founded:** 1976. **Operating Hours:** Continuous. **Key Personnel:** Mike Morgan, Gen. Mgr., mike@wbhm.org; Patrick Dorriety, Operations Mgr., patrick@wbhm.org; Michael Krall, Promotions Dir., michael@wbhm.org; Scott E. Hanley, Prog. Dir. **Wattage:** 32,000. **Ad Rates:** Advertising accepted; rates available upon request. **URL:** http://www.wbhm.org.

135 ■ WBIQ-TV - 10
2112 11th Ave. S, Ste. 400
Birmingham, AL 35205
Phone: (205)328-8756
Fax: (205)251-2192
Email: w.wood@aptu.org

Format: Public TV. **Networks:** Public Broadcasting Service (PBS). **Owner:** Alabama Educational Television Commission, 2112 11th Ave. S, Ste. 400, Birmingham, AL 35205. **Founded:** 1955. **Key Personnel:** Phil Hutcheson, CFO, Dep. Dir. **Wattage:** 316,000 visual; 31,600 aural. **Ad Rates:** Accepts Advertising. **URL:** http://www.aptv.org.

136 ■ WBMA-TV - 33/40
PO Box 360039
Birmingham, AL 35236
Phone: (205)403-3340
Fax: (205)403-3329

Format: Commercial TV. **Networks:** ABC. **Owner:** TV Alabama, Inc., 800 Concourse Pkwy Ste 200, Hoover, AL 35244-1874, Ph: (205)403-3340. **Founded:** 1996. **Operating Hours:** 5:30 a.m.-2 a.m. weekdays; 6 a.m.-1 a.m. Sat.; 7 a.m.-1 a.m. Sun. **Ad Rates:** Noncommercial. **URL:** http://www.abc3340.com.

137 ■ WBRC-TV - 6
1720 Valley View Dr.
Birmingham, AL 35209
Phone: (205)322-6666
Fax: (205)583-4386
Free: 800-624-9272
Email: publicfile@myfoxal.com

Format: News. **Networks:** Fox. **Founded:** July 01, 1949. **Operating Hours:** 12 a.m. - 11:30 p.m. **Key Personnel:** Lou Kirchen, Gen. Mgr.; James Finch, News Dir., VP; Dave Duncan, Sales Mgr., dduncan@wbrc.com; Wayne Farrell, Contact, programming@gowbrc.com. **Wattage:** 100,000. **Ad Rates:** Advertising accepted; rates available upon request. **URL:** http://www.myfoxal.com.

138 ■ WCFT-TV - 33
PO Box 630039
Birmingham, AL 35236
Phone: (205)403-3340
Fax: (205)403-3329

Format: News. **Networks:** ABC. **Owner:** TV Alabama, Inc., 800 Concourse Pkwy Ste 200, Hoover, AL 35244-1874, Ph: (205)403-3340. **Founded:** 1996. **Operating Hours:** 6 a.m.-1:30 a.m.; 80% network, 20% local. **ADI:** Birmingham (Gadsden), AL. **Wattage:** 4,370 ERP. **Ad Rates:** $30-350 per unit. **URL:** http://www.abc3340.com.

WCIQ-TV - See Mount Cheaha

WDIQ-TV - See Dozier

139 ■ WDJC-FM - 93.7
120 Summit Pkwy., Ste. 200
Birmingham, AL 35209
Phone: (205)879-3324

Format: Religious; Contemporary Christian. **Owner:** Crawford Broadcasting Co., 2821 S Parker Rd., Ste. 1205, Denver, CO 80014, Ph: (303)433-5500, Fax: (303)433-1555. **Founded:** 1968. **Operating Hours:** Continuous; 100% local. **ADI:** Birmingham (Gadsden), AL. **Key Personnel:** Ronnie Bruce, Contact, ronniebruce@wdjconline.com. **Wattage:** 100,000. **Ad Rates:** Advertising accepted; rates available upon request. **URL:** http://www.wdjconline.com.

140 ■ WDXB-FM - 102.5
600 Beacon Pky. W, Ste. 400
Birmingham, AL 35209
Phone: (205)439-9600
Fax: (205)439-8390

Format: Country. **ADI:** Birmingham (Gadsden), AL. **Key Personnel:** Tom Hanrahan, Prog. Dir., tomhanrahan@clearchannel.com. **Wattage:** 83,000. **Ad Rates:** Noncommercial. **URL:** http://www.1025thebull.com.

141 ■ WERC-AM - 960
600 Beacon Pkwy. W, Ste. 400
Birmingham, AL 35209
Phone: (205)439-9600
Fax: (205)439-8390

Format: News; Talk. **Networks:** ABC. **Owner:** iHeartMedia Inc., 200 E Basse Rd., San Antonio, TX 78209, Ph: (210)832-3314. **Founded:** 1925. **Operating Hours:** Continuous. **Local Programs:** *The Go Natural Show*; *At Home with Gary Sullivan*, Saturday 9:00 a.m. - 10:00 a.m.; *Art Bell Somewhere in Time*, Monday Tuesday Wednesday Thursday Friday Saturday Sunday 12:00 a.m. - 5:00 a.m. 12:00 a.m. - 7:00 a.m. 9:00 p.m. - 12:00 a.m.; 12:00 a.m. - 7:00 a.m. 12:00 a.m. - 4:00 a.m. **Wattage:** 5,000. **Ad Rates:** Advertising accepted; rates available upon request. **URL:** http://www.wercfm.com//main.html.

WFIQ-TV - See Florence

142 ■ W46CY - 46
PO Box A
Santa Ana, CA 92711
Phone: (714)832-2950
Free: 888-731-1000
Email: comments@tbn.org

Owner: Trinity Broadcasting Network Inc., PO Box A, Santa Ana, CA 92711, Ph: (714)832-2950, Free: 888-731-1000. **URL:** http://www.tbn.org.

143 ■ WGIB-FM - 91.9
1137 10th Pl. S
Birmingham, AL 35205
Phone: (205)323-1516
Fax: (205)252-5432
Email: info@gleniris.net

Format: Religious. **Owner:** Glen Iris Baptist School, 1137 10th Pl. S, Birmingham, AL 35205, Ph: (205)323-1516. **Founded:** 1983. **Operating Hours:** Continuous. **Key Personnel:** Ron Haas, Contact, rhaas@gleniris.net; Paul Hancock, Director. **Wattage:** 3,500. **Ad Rates:** Noncommercial. **URL:** http://www.gleniris.net/GIBC.

WGIQ-TV - See Louisville

144 ■ WIAT-TV - 42
2075 Golden Crest Dr.
Birmingham, AL 35209
Phone: (205)322-4200
Fax: (205)320-2713
Email: feedback@wiat.com

Format: Commercial TV. **Networks:** CBS. **Owner:** New Vision Television, Inc., 11766 Wilshire Blvd., Ste. 405, Los Angeles, CA 90025, Ph: (310)478-3200, Fax: (310)478-3222. **Founded:** 1965. **Formerly:** WBMG-TV. **Operating Hours:** 5:30-4:59 a.m. weekdays; 6:30-3 a.m. Saturday and Sunday. **ADI:** Birmingham (Gadsden), AL. **Key Personnel:** Alison Lindsay, Dir. of Sales; Bill Payer, News Dir. **Ad Rates:** Noncommercial. **URL:** http://wiat.com.

WIIQ-TV - See Demopolis

145 ■ WIKX-FM - 106.9
3700 4th Ave. S
Birmingham, AL 35222
Phone: (205)595-1069

Format: Country. **Networks:** ABC. **Founded:** 1959. **Formerly:** WKXX-FM. **Operating Hours:** Continuous. **Key Personnel:** Ron Burgess, Mgr.; Zack Owen, Dir. of Programs; Olivia Lawrence, Sales Mgr. **Wattage:** 100,000.

146 ■ WJLD-AM - 1400
1449 Spaulding Ishkooda Rd.
Birmingham, AL 35211
Phone: (205)942-1776
Fax: (205)942-4814

Format: Oldies. **Networks:** CNN Radio; American Urban Radio. **Owner:** Richardson Broadcasting Corp. **Founded:** 1942. **Operating Hours:** Continuous; 50% network, 50% local. **ADI:** Birmingham (Gadsden), AL. **Wattage:** 1,000. **Ad Rates:** Noncommercial. **Mailing address:** PO Box 19123, Birmingham, AL 35211. **URL:** http://www.wjldradio.com.

147 ■ WJOX-FM - 94.5
244 Goodwin Crest Dr., Ste. 300
Birmingham, AL 35209
Phone: (205)945-4646
Fax: (205)945-3999
Free: 800-239-9569

Format: Sports; Talk. **Owner:** Citadel Broadcasting Corp., 7201 W Lake Mead Blvd., Ste. 400, Las Vegas, NV 89128-8366, Ph: (702)804-5200, Fax: (702)804-8250. **Founded:** 1993. **Operating Hours:** Continuous. **Key Personnel:** Bill Thomas, Gen. Mgr., bill.thomas@citcomm.com; Ryan Haney, Prog. Dir., ryan.haney@citcomm.com. **Wattage:** 100,000 ERP. **Ad Rates:** Advertising accepted; rates available upon request. **URL:** http://www.joxfm.com.

148 ■ WJSR-FM - 100.9
2601 Carson Rd.
Birmingham, AL 35215
Phone: (205)856-7702

Owner: Jefferson State Community College, 2601 Carson Rd., Birmingham, AL 35215-3098, Ph: (205)853-1200, Free: 800-239-5900. **Wattage:** 15,000 ERP. **Ad Rates:** Accepts Advertising.

149 ■ WJSU-TV - 40
PO Box 360039
Birmingham, AL 35236
Phone: (205)403-3340
Fax: (205)403-3329

Format: News. **Networks:** ABC. **Founded:** 1996. **Operating Hours:** Continuous. **Key Personnel:** Eric Gill, Chairman; Charles Steele, President; James Spann, Contact. **Local Programs:** *Good Morning America*, Sunday Monday Tuesday Wednesday Thursday Friday Saturday 7:00 a.m.; *Good Morning Alabama*, Monday Tuesday Wednesday Thursday Friday 4:30 a.m.; *Talk of Alabama*, Monday Tuesday Wednesday Thursday Friday 9:00 a.m.; *The View*, Monday Tuesday Wednesday Friday 10:00 a.m.; *One Life To Live*; *General Hospital*,

Circulation: ★ = AAM; △ or • = BPA; ♦ = CAC; ❑ = VAC; ⊕ = PO Statement; ‡ = Publisher's Report; Boldface figures = sworn; Light figures = estimated.

Monday Tuesday Wednesday Thursday Friday 2:00 p.m.; *Bonnie Hunt*; *The Oprah Winfrey Show*; *ABC 33/40 5pm News*, Sunday 5:00 p.m.; *News*; *Wheel of Fortune*; *Flash Forward*; *Grey's Anatomy*; *Private Practice*; *World News This Morning*, Sunday Monday Tuesday Wednesday Thursday 1:05 a.m. **Wattage**: 5,000 ERP. **Ad Rates:** Noncommercial. **URL:** http://www.abc3340.com.

150 ■ WLJR-FM - 88.5
2200 Briarwood Way
Birmingham, AL 35243
Phone: (205)776-5200
Fax: (205)776-5241
Email: info@briarwood.org
Format: Contemporary Christian. **Networks:** Moody Broadcasting. **Founded:** Feb. 1998. **Operating Hours**: Continuous. **Wattage**: 370. **Ad Rates:** Noncommercial. **URL:** http://www.briarwood.org.

151 ■ WMJJ-FM - 96.5
600 Beacon Pkwy. W, Ste. 400
Birmingham, AL 35209
Phone: (205)439-9600
Fax: (205)439-8390
Format: Adult Contemporary. **Founded:** 1982. **Operating Hours**: Continuous. **Wattage**: 100,000. **Ad Rates:** Noncommercial. **URL:** http://www.magic96.com//main.html.

152 ■ WODL-FM - 97.3
2700 Corporate Dr., Ste. 115
Birmingham, AL 35242
Phone: (205)322-2987
Format: Oldies. **Key Personnel:** Justin Case, Dir. of Programs, justin.case@coxradio.com; Ted Kinsler, Web Adm., ted.kinsler@coxradio.com; Justin Ragland, Promotions Dir., justin.ragland@coxradio.com; Meredith Hollingsworth, Dir. Cust. Serv., meredith.hollingsworth@coxradio.com; David Walls, Gen. Sales Mgr., david.walls@coxradio.com. **Wattage**: 640. **Ad Rates:** Advertising accepted; rates available upon request. **URL:** http://www.play973.com.

153 ■ WPXH-TV - 44
2085 Golden Crest Dr.
Birmingham, AL 35209
Phone: (205)870-4404
Fax: (205)870-0544
Format: Commercial TV. **Owner:** ION Media Networks Inc., 601 Clearwater Park Rd., West Palm Beach, FL 33401-6233, Ph: (561)659-4122, Fax: (561)659-4252. **Founded:** Apr. 12, 1986. **Operating Hours**: Continuous. **ADI**: Birmingham (Gadsden), AL. **Wattage**: 1,800,000. **Ad Rates:** Noncommercial. **URL:** http://www.ionmedianetworks.com.

154 ■ WPYA-FM
2700 Corporate Dr.
Birmingham, AL 35242
Phone: (205)916-1100
Fax: (205)290-1061
Format: Adult Contemporary; Contemporary Hit Radio (CHR). **Owner:** Sinclair Communications Inc., at above address. **Wattage**: 6,200 ERP. **Ad Rates:** Advertising accepted; rates available upon request.

155 ■ WQEM-FM - 101.5
1137 10th Pl. S
Birmingham, AL 35205
Phone: (205)323-1516
Email: info@gleniris.net
Format: Religious; Contemporary Christian. **Owner:** Glen Iris Baptist Church, 1137 10th Pl. S, Birmingham, AL 35205, Ph: (205)323-1516. **Operating Hours**: Continuous. **Key Personnel:** Paul Hancock, Director. **Ad Rates:** Noncommercial; underwriting available. **URL:** http://www.gleniris.net.

156 ■ WQEN-FM - 103.7
600 Beacon Pky. W, Ste. 400
Birmingham, AL 35209
Phone: (205)439-9600
Fax: (205)439-8390
Format: Contemporary Hit Radio (CHR). **Networks:** Unistar; ABC. **Founded:** 1976. **Operating Hours**: Continuous. **ADI**: Birmingham (Gadsden), AL. **Key Personnel:** Cyndi Collins, President, cynthiacollins@clearchannel.com. **Wattage**: 100,000. **Ad Rates:** Noncommercial. **URL:** http://www.1037theq.com//main.html.

157 ■ WRAX-FM - 107.7
244 Goodwin Crest Dr., Ste. 300
Birmingham, AL 35209
Phone: (205)942-1106
Fax: (205)942-3175
Format: Alternative/New Music/Progressive. **Owner:** Citadel Broadcasting Corp., 7201 W Lake Mead Blvd., Ste. 400, Las Vegas, NV 89128-8366, Ph: (702)804-5200, Fax: (702)804-8250. **Key Personnel:** Deano Yingian, Promotions Dir., deano@wrax.com; Davis Hawkins, Sales Mgr., davis.hawkins@citcomm.com. **Wattage**: 42,500. **Ad Rates:** Advertising accepted; rates available upon request. **URL:** http://www.wrax.com.

158 ■ WRRS-FM - 101.1
9340 Helena Rd., Ste. F-121
Birmingham, AL 35244-1747
Format: Contemporary Christian. **Owner:** AllWorship.com, at above address. **Founded:** 1998. **Operating Hours**: Continuous. **Key Personnel:** Bill Hardekopf, Gen. Mgr., billh@reality101.com. **Wattage**: 100,000. **Ad Rates:** Advertising accepted; rates available upon request. **URL:** http://www.reality101.com.

159 ■ WSPZ-AM - 690
244 Goowin Crest Dr., Ste. 300
Birmingham, AL 35209
Phone: (205)945-4646
Fax: (205)945-3999
Format: Sports. **Networks:** ESPN Radio; CBS. **Owner:** Citadel Broadcasting Corp., 7201 W Lake Mead Blvd., Ste. 400, Las Vegas, NV 89128-8366, Ph: (702)804-5200, Fax: (702)804-8250. **Founded:** 1947. **Formerly**: WVOK-AM; WJOX-AM. **Operating Hours**: Continuous. **ADI**: Birmingham (Gadsden), AL. **Key Personnel:** Ryan Haney, Dir. of Programs; Lenny Frisaro, Sales Mgr.; Jennifer Dickson, Promotions Dir. **Local Programs**: *The Opening Drive*, Monday 4:00 p.m. - 7:00 p.m.; *Fox Sports Radio*, Monday Wednesday Thursday Friday Tuesday Saturday Sunday 6:00 p.m. - 12:00 a.m. 7:00 p.m. - 12:00 a.m. 12:00 a.m. - 7:00 a.m.; 11:00 a.m. - 2:00 p.m.; 5:00 p.m. - 12:00 a.m. 12:00 a.m. - 11:00 a.m.; 2:00 p.m. - 12:00 a.m. **Wattage**: 50,000 Day 500 Night. **Ad Rates:** $50-125 per unit. **URL:** http://www.690thesportsanimal.com.

160 ■ WTTO-TV - 21
651 Beacon Pkwy. W, Ste. 105
Birmingham, AL 35209
Phone: (205)943-2168
Fax: (205)250-6788
Format: Commercial TV. **Networks:** Warner Brothers Studios. **Founded:** Apr. 21, 1982. **Operating Hours**: Continuous. **ADI**: Birmingham (Gadsden), AL. **Ad Rates:** Noncommercial. **URL:** http://www.wtto21.com.

161 ■ WVSU-FM - 91.1
800 Lakeshore Dr.
Birmingham, AL 35229
Phone: (205)726-2934
Fax: (205)726-4032
Email: wvsu@samford.edu
Format: Jazz. **Networks:** Independent. **Owner:** Samford University, 800 Lakeshore Dr., Birmingham, AL 35229, Ph: (205)726-2011. **Operating Hours**: 18 hours Daily; 100% local. **ADI**: Birmingham (Gadsden), AL. **Key Personnel:** Lauren Taylor, Director, lmtaylor@samford.edu; Andy Parrish, Gen. Mgr.; Nathan Troost, Sports Dir; Andy Jackson, Contact. **Wattage**: 125. **Ad Rates:** Noncommercial. **URL:** http://samford.edu/home.

162 ■ WVTM-TV - 13
1732 Valley View Dr.
Birmingham, AL 35209
Phone: (205)933-1313
Format: Commercial TV. **Networks:** NBC. **Formerly**: WAPI-TV. **Operating Hours**: Continuous. **ADI**: Birmingham (Gadsden), AL. **Ad Rates:** Advertising accepted; rates available upon request. **URL:** http://www2.alabamas13.com.

163 ■ WXJC-AM - 850
120 Summit Pkwy., Ste. 200
Birmingham, AL 35209
Phone: (205)879-3324
Format: Gospel. **Owner:** Crawford Broadcasting Co., 2821 S Parker Rd., Ste. 1205, Denver, CO 80014, Ph: (303)433-5500, Fax: (303)433-1555. **Key Personnel:** Wayne Wallace, Contact. **URL:** http://www.850wxjc.com.

164 ■ WXJC-FM - 92.5
120 Summit Pky., Ste. 200
Birmingham, AL 35209
Phone: (205)879-3324
Email: info@crawfordbroadcasting.com
Format: Southern Gospel; Talk. **Owner:** Crawford Broadcasting Co., 725 Skippack St., Ste. 210, Blue Bell, PA 19422. **Wattage**: 2,200. **URL:** http://www.crawfordbroadcasting.com.

165 ■ WYDE-AM - 1260
120 Summit Pky., Ste. 200
Birmingham, AL 35209
Phone: (205)942-8585
Fax: (205)942-1087
Free: 866-551-9933
Format: Big Band/Nostalgia; Oldies; Country. **Networks:** NBC. **Owner:** Crawford Broadcasting Co., 725 Skippack St., Ste. 210, Blue Bell, PA 19422; American General Media, 1400 Easton Dr., Ste. 144, Bakersfield, CA 93309, Ph: (661)328-1410, Fax: (661)328-0873. **Founded:** 1953. **Formerly**: WLGD-AM. **Operating Hours**: 24 Hrs. **ADI**: Birmingham (Gadsden), AL. **Key Personnel:** Leslie Edwards, Dir. of Programs; Jerry Voyles, Gen. Mgr. **Wattage**: 50,000. **Ad Rates:** $50; $25. **URL:** http://www.101wyde.com.

166 ■ WYDE-FM - 101.1
120 Summit Pkwy., Ste. 200
Birmingham, AL 35209
Phone: (205)941-1011
Free: 866-551-9933
Email: manager@101wyde.com
Format: Adult Contemporary. **Owner:** Crawford Broadcasting Co., 725 Skippack St., Ste. 210, Blue Bell, PA 19422. **Operating Hours**: Continuous. **Wattage**: 100,000. **Ad Rates:** Advertising accepted; rates available upon request. **URL:** http://www.101wyde.com.

167 ■ WYSF-FM - 94.5
244 Goodwin Crest Dr., Ste. 300
Birmingham, AL 35209
Phone: (205)945-4646
Fax: (205)945-3999
Free: 800-239-9569
Format: Country; Sports. **Networks:** Fox; CBS. **Owner:** Citadel Communications Corp., San Diego, CA, Ph: (505)767-6700, Fax: (505)767-6767. **Founded:** 1947. **Formerly**: WAPI-FM; WMXQ-FM. **Operating Hours**: Continuous. **ADI**: Birmingham (Gadsden), AL. **Key Personnel:** Gigi South, Gen. Mgr., VP, gigi.south@citcomm.com. **Wattage**: 100,000 ERP. **Ad Rates:** $35-350 per unit. **URL:** http://www.joxfm.com.

168 ■ WZRR-FM - 99.5
244 Goodwin Crest Dr., Ste. 300
Birmingham, AL 35209
Phone: (205)945-4646
Format: Classic Rock. **Owner:** Citadel Broadcasting Corp., 7201 W Lake Mead Blvd., Ste. 400, Las Vegas, NV 89128-8366, Ph: (702)804-5200, Fax: (702)804-8250. **Founded:** 1975. **Formerly**: WLTB-FM. **Operating Hours**: Continuous. **ADI**: Birmingham (Gadsden), AL. **Key Personnel:** Jason Mack, Dir. of Programs, jason.mack@citcomm.com; Laurence Salvary, Promotions Dir., sir.laurence@citcomm.com. **Wattage**: 100,000. **Ad Rates:** Advertising accepted; rates available upon request. **URL:** http://www.995nashicon.com.

169 ■ WZZK-AM
2700 Corporate Dr., Ste. 115.
Birmingham, AL 35242
Fax: (205)290-1061
Owner: CXR Holdings, LLC., Bridgeport, CT, Ph: (203)366-9321. **Founded:** 1927. **Ad Rates:** $40-325 per unit. **URL:** http://www.wzzk.com/contact-us/.

BOAZ

NE AL. Marshall Co. 15 mi. NW of Gadsden.

170 ■ WBSA-AM - 1300
1525 Wills Rd.
Boaz, AL 35957
Phone: (256)593-4264
Fax: (256)593-4265
Format: Gospel; Southern Gospel. **Owner:** Watkins Broadcasting Co., Inc, at above address. **Founded:** 1959. **Formerly**: WAVC-AM. **Key Personnel:** Roger Watkins, Gen. Mgr., Station Mgr., watkinsroger@bellsouth.net. **Wattage**: 1,000. **Ad Rates:** Advertising

accepted; rates available upon request. $5.00-7.00 for 30 seconds; $6.00-7.75 for 60 seconds. **URL:** http://www.wbsaam.com/.

BREWTON

S. AL. Escambia Co. 60 mi. N. of Pensacola, FL. Manufactures paper, textiles, lumber. Iron works. Timber. Agriculture. Cotton, livestock.

171 ■ The Brewton Standard
Brewton Newspapers Inc.
407 Saint Nicholas Ave.
Brewton, AL 36426
Phone: (251)867-4876
Fax: (251)867-4877
Publisher's E-mail: advertising@brewtonstandard.com
Community newspaper. **Freq:** Semiweekly (Wed. and Sun.). **Print Method:** Offset. **Cols./Page:** 6. **Col. Width:** 12 picas. **Col. Depth:** 301 agate lines. **Key Personnel:** Lisa Tindell, Editor; Kerry Whipple Bean, Publisher; Adam Robinson, Editor. **Subscription Rates:** $50 Individuals in Brewton area; $62.32 Out of area; $70.20 Out of state. **Formerly**: The Brewton Standard & The Plus. **Ad Rates:** BW $954.60; 4C $1154.66; SAU $8.30; PCI $8.30. **Remarks:** Accepts advertising. **Circ:** ‡4100.

172 ■ WEBJ-AM - 1240
301 Downing St.
Brewton, AL 36426
Phone: (251)867-5717
Format: News; Talk. **Networks:** Independent. **Owner:** Brewton Broadcasting Inc. **Founded:** 1947. **Operating Hours**: Continuous. **Wattage**: 1,000. **Ad Rates:** Noncommercial.

173 ■ WKNU-FM
Ridge Rd.
Rte. 6, Box 468
Brewton, AL 36427
Phone: (205)867-4824
Fax: (205)867-7003
Format: Country; Contemporary Country. **Networks:** ABC; Alabama Radio (ALANET). **Owner:** Carol Ellington, at above address. **Founded:** 1974. **Key Personnel:** Hugh Ellington, Sports Dir., Owner. **Wattage**: 3,800 ERP. **Ad Rates:** $5.25 for 30 seconds; $8.50 for 60 seconds.

BUTLER

SW AL. Choctaw Co. 35 mi. SE of Meridian, MS. Manufactures textiles, lumber. Pulpwood and timber.

174 ■ WHSL-FM
909 W Pushmataha S
Butler, AL 36904
Fax: (910)887-0104
Format: Hot Country. **Owner:** SFX Broadcasting, Inc., New York, NY, Ph: (212)980-4455, Fax: (212)735-3188. **Founded:** 1975. **Formerly**: WOJY-FM; WWWB-FM. **Key Personnel:** Metiza R. Royal, Contact. **Wattage**: 6,000 ERP.

CALERA

C. AL. Shelby Co. 20 mi. SE of Birmingham.

175 ■ WBYE-AM - 1370
PO Box 1727
Calera, AL 35040
Phone: (205)668-1370
Email: kingfkek@aol.com
Format: Gospel. **Networks:** Alabama Radio (ALANET). **Owner:** Progressive United Communications Inc. **Founded:** 1958. **Operating Hours**: 12 hours Daily; 10% network, 90% local. **Key Personnel:** Benjamin H. Franklin, Contact; Elizabeth Franklin, Contact. **Wattage**: 1,000. **Ad Rates:** $5 for 30 seconds; $10 for 60 seconds; $25-60 per unit.

CAMDEN

C. AL. Wilcox Co.

176 ■ WCOX-AM
PO Box 820
Camden, AL 36726
Phone: (205)682-9048
Fax: (205)682-4726
Format: Gospel; Religious; Talk. **Key Personnel:** Paul Johnson, Contact; Paul Johnson, Contact. **Wattage**: 1,000.

CARROLLTON

C. AL. Pickens Co. 30 mi. W. of Tuscaloosa. Lumber milling and cotton ginning.

177 ■ Pickens County Herald
Pickens County Herald
215 N Reform St.
Carrollton, AL 35447-0390
Phone: (205)367-2217
Fax: (205)367-2217
Publisher's E-mail: pickenscnty@centurytel.net
Community newspaper. **Freq:** Weekly. **Cols./Page:** 6. **Col. Width:** 1.83 inches. **Col. Depth:** 21 1/2 inches. **Key Personnel:** Doug Sanders, Jr., Editor; Ann Gates, Office Manager. **USPS:** 431-800. **Subscription Rates:** $29.50 Individuals /year in Pickens County; $33 Individuals /year adjoining county (Fayette, Greene, Tuscaloosa or Sumter Counties only); $22 Individuals /year for senior citizen; $40 Out of state 1 year; $18 Individuals /6 months in Pickens County; $21 Individuals /6 months adjoining county (Fayette, Greene, Tuscaloosa or Sumter Counties only); $14 Individuals /6 months for senior citizen; $24 Out of area 6 months. **Mailing address:** PO Box 390, Carrollton, AL 35447-0390. **Ad Rates:** PCI $7. **Remarks:** Accepts advertising. **Circ:** Paid ‡4300.

178 ■ WALN-FM - 89.3
PO Box 2440
Tupelo, MS 38803
Phone: (662)844-8888
Format: Religious. **Owner:** American Family Radio, at above address. **Ad Rates:** Noncommercial. **URL:** http://www.afa.net.

CENTRE

NE AL. Cherokee Co. 20 mi. S. of Fort Payne.

179 ■ Cherokee County Herald
News Publishing Co.
107 First Ave. W
Centre, AL 35960
Phone: (256)927-5037
Newspaper with a Democratic orientation. **Freq:** Weekly (Wed.). **Print Method:** Offset. **Trim Size:** 13 x 21 1/4. **Cols./Page:** 6. **Col. Width:** 12 picas. **Col. Depth:** 295 agate lines. **Key Personnel:** Terry Dean, Editor; Brenda Burger, Advisor; Vickie Robinson, Director, Advertising. **USPS:** 102-380. **URL:** http://www.northwestgeorgianews.com/cherokee_county. **Ad Rates:** GLR $6.80; BW $867; PCI $6.80. **Remarks:** Accepts advertising. **Circ:** (Not Reported).

180 ■ WEIS-AM - 990
PO Box 297
Centre, AL 35960
Phone: (256)927-4232
Fax: (256)927-6503
Email: weis@powernet.org
Format: Country; Southern Gospel. **Networks:** Arkansas Radio. **Owner:** Baker Enterprises Inc., 11112 Beaver Bridge Rd., Chesterfield, VA 23838, Ph: (804)640-6956. **Founded:** 1961. **Operating Hours**: Continuous; 5% network, 95% local. **ADI:** Birmingham (Gadsden), AL. **Key Personnel:** Jerry Baker, Owner, weis@powernet.org. **Local Programs**: *Weiss Lake fishing reports*, Monday Tuesday Wednesday Thursday Friday Saturday Sunday 6:45 a.m. **Wattage**: 1,000. **Ad Rates:** $10 for 30 seconds; $12-16 for 60 seconds.

CENTREVILLE

C. AL. Bibb Co. 34 mi. SE of Tuscaloosa. Lumber, grist mills; cotton gin. Manufactures wooden toys, pulpwood. Timber. Agriculture. Cotton, corn.

181 ■ Centreville Press
Bibb Publications
32 Ct. Sq. W
Centreville, AL 35042
Phone: (205)926-9769
Fax: (205)926-9760
Community newspaper. **Freq:** Weekly (Wed.). **Print Method:** Offset. Accepts mats. **Cols./Page:** 6. **Col. Width:** 24 nonpareils. **Col. Depth:** 301 agate lines. **Key Personnel:** Bob Tribble, President; Lorrie Rinehart, Publisher. **Subscription Rates:** $27.25 Individuals; $35.43 Out of area; $40 Out of state. **URL:** http://www.centrevillepress.com/images/index.html. **Mailing address:** PO Box 127, Centreville, AL 35042. **Ad Rates:** GLR $.28; BW $490.20; SAU $4.25; PCI $4. **Remarks:** Accepts advertising. **Circ:** 4200.

CHATOM

SW AL. Washington Co. 55 mi. N. of Mobile. Naval stores. Cotton-gins. Oil wells. Pine timber. Agriculture. Cotton, corn, poultry.

182 ■ Washington County News
Washington County Publications Inc.
PO Box 510
Chatom, AL 36518
Phone: (251)847-2599
Fax: (251)847-3847
Newspaper. **Founded:** 1892. **Freq:** Weekly (Wed.). **Print Method:** Offset. **Trim Size:** 14 x 23. **Cols./Page:** 6. **Col. Width:** 2 1/16 inches. **Col. Depth:** 21.5 picas. **Key Personnel:** Willie Gray, Owner, Publisher; Rhonda Gray, Owner, Publisher. **Subscription Rates:** $25 Individuals senior citizen; $30 Individuals; $35 Out of state; $25 Individuals online only. **URL:** http://www.washcountynews.com/v2/content.aspx?ID=7037&MemberID=1590. **Formerly**: Call-News Dispatch. **Ad Rates:** BW $1,083.60; 4C $1,283.60; SAU $8.40; PCI $5. **Remarks:** Accepts advertising. **Circ:** ‡4000, 6780.

CIDRA

183 ■ WBRQ-FM
828 20th St., S
Lanett, AL 36863
Phone: (809)720-7797
Fax: (809)746-6162
Format: Hispanic; Top 40. **Founded:** 1972. **Key Personnel:** Luis deLeon, Operations Mgr., lionkingpr@hotmail.com. **Wattage**: 1,000 ERP. **Ad Rates:** $18 for 15 seconds; $26 for 30 seconds; $44 for 60 seconds.

CITRONELLE

184 ■ WHXT-FM - 102.1
21615 Odom Rd.
Citronelle, AL 36522
Phone: (334)886-5454
Fax: (334)380-9029
Format: Country. **Founded:** 1989. **Formerly**: WKQR-FM. **Operating Hours**: 6 a.m. - 10 p.m. **Key Personnel:** Tom Wilson, Gen. Mgr.; Melisa Young, Office Mgr. **Wattage**: 25,000. **Ad Rates:** $5 for 30 seconds; $6 for 60 seconds. **Mailing address:** PO Box 127, Citronelle, AL 36522.

CLANTON

C. AL. Chilton Co. 40 mi. NW of Montgomery. Residential.

185 ■ Chilton County News
Chilton County News
PO Box 189
Clanton, AL 35046-0189
Phone: (205)755-0110
Publisher's E-mail: newscc@bellsouth.net
Community newspaper. **Freq:** Weekly (Thurs.). **Print Method:** Offset. **Trim Size:** 11 x 14. **Cols./Page:** 5. **Col. Width:** 2 1/16 inches. **Col. Depth:** 13 inches. **ISSN:** 0888--451X (print). **Subscription Rates:** $22.50 Individuals in Chilton; $30 Individuals in Alabama; $37.50 Out of state; $2 Individuals mailed copy. **URL:** http://www.beachbecky.com/index.html/index.html. **Ad Rates:** GLR $.31; BW $282.10; SAU $4.06; PCI $6.50. **Remarks:** Accepts advertising. **Circ:** Paid 2000.

186 ■ The Clanton Advertiser
Boone Newspapers Inc.
1109 7th St. N
Clanton, AL 35046
Phone: (205)755-5747
Publication E-mail: newsroom@clantonadvertiser.com
Community newspaper. **Freq:** Daily. **Print Method:** Offset. **Cols./Page:** 6. **Col. Width:** 26 nonpareils. **Col. Depth:** 301 agate lines. **Key Personnel:** Tim Prince, President, Publisher; Justin Averette, Managing Editor. **Subscription Rates:** $74.19 Individuals /year; $195 Out of area /year. **URL:** http://www.clantonadvertiser.com.

Circulation: ★ = AAM; △ or • = BPA; ♦ = CAC; ❑ = VAC; ⊕ = PO Statement; ‡ = Publisher's Report; Boldface figures = sworn; Light figures = estimated.

Formerly: Independent Advertiser. **Ad Rates:** PCI $5.81. **Remarks:** Accepts advertising. **Circ:** Paid ‡4000, Free ‡8500.

CLAYTON

SE AL. Barbour Co. 50 mi. Se of Montgomery. Residental.

187 ■ The Clayton Record
The Clayton Record
PO Box 69
Clayton, AL 36016
Phone: (334)775-3254
Fax: (334)775-8554
Local newspaper. **Freq:** Weekly (Thurs.). **Print Method:** Offset. **Cols./Page:** 6. **Col. Width:** 24 nonpareils. **Col. Depth:** 294 agate lines. **Key Personnel:** Rebecca Beasley, Editor. **USPS:** 116-960. **Subscription Rates:** $27 Individuals; $30 Out of state. **Ad Rates:** GLR $5.25; BW $300; SAU $5.25; PCI $4.50. **Remarks:** Accepts advertising. **Circ:** ‡2500.

COLLINSVILLE

188 ■ Collinsville TV Cable
PO Box 272
Collinsville, AL 35961
Cities Served: subscribing households 300. **URL:** http://www.collinsvillealabama.net.

COLUMBIANA

C. AL. Shelby Co. 30 mi. SE of Birmingham. Wire, foundry, textile mills. Timber. Diversified farming.

189 ■ Shelby County Reporter
Shelby County Newspapers Inc.
115 N Main St.
Columbiana, AL 35051
Phone: (205)669-3131
Fax: (205)669-4217
Community newspaper. **Freq:** Weekly (Wed.). **Print Method:** Offset. **Cols./Page:** 6. **Col. Width:** 22 nonpareils. **Col. Depth:** 280 agate lines. **Key Personnel:** Tim Prince, President, Publisher. **USPS:** 492-480. **Subscription Rates:** $45 By mail in county; $115 By mail out of county. **Mailing address:** PO Box 947, Columbiana, AL 35051. **Ad Rates:** 4C $1200; PCI $12.50. **Remarks:** Accepts advertising. **Circ:** Paid 9588.

CULLMAN

N. AL. Cullman Co. 34 mi. S. of Decatur. Manufactures lumber, cotton oil products, chrome trim, files, air conditioning compressors, missile components, truck wheels, cigars, boxes, textiles, fertilizer, headings, staves. Hatcheries. Pine, oak timber. Agriculture. Cotton, poultry.

190 ■ Community Shoppers Guide
Community Shopper's Guide Inc.
219 1st Ave., SW
Cullman, AL 35055
Phone: (256)734-1532
Fax: (256)734-1672
Shopper. **Freq:** Weekly (Wed.). **Print Method:** Offset. **Cols./Page:** 6. **Col. Width:** 19 nonpareils. **Col. Depth:** 210 agate lines. **Key Personnel:** Frances Cooper, Publisher. **Subscription Rates:** Free. **URL:** http://www.csgonline.com. **Ad Rates:** BW $597; 4C $849; PCI $11.50. **Remarks:** Accepts advertising. **Circ:** 35986.

191 ■ The Cullman Times
Cullman Times
300 4th Ave. SE
Cullman, AL 35055
Phone: (256)734-2131
Fax: (256)737-1006
Publisher's E-mail: editor@cullmantimes.com
General newspaper. **Founded:** 1901. **Freq:** Tues.-Fri.; Sun. **Print Method:** Offset. **Cols./Page:** 8. **Col. Width:** 25 nonpareils. **Col. Depth:** 301 agate lines. **Key Personnel:** Terry Connor, Publisher. **Subscription Rates:** $118 Individuals carrier or mail; in Cullman County. **URL:** http://www.cullmantimes.com/. **Ad Rates:** SAU $6.75. **Remarks:** Accepts advertising. **Circ:** Mon.-Sat. ★**10419**, Sun. ★**11020**.

192 ■ WFMH-AM - 1340
1707 Warnke Rd. NW
Cullman, AL 35055
Phone: (256)734-3271
Fax: (256)734-3622
Format: Southern Gospel; Gospel. **Founded:** 1950. **Operating Hours:** Continuous. **ADI:** Birmingham (Gadsden), AL. **Wattage:** 1,000. **Ad Rates:** $7.50 for 30 seconds; $10.50 for 60 seconds. Combined advertising rates available with WFMH-FM, WXXR-AM.

193 ■ WKUL-FM - 92.1
214 1st Ave. SE
Cullman, AL 35055
Phone: (256)734-0183
Fax: (256)739-2999
Format: Contemporary Country; Talk; Classic Rock; Alternative/New Music/Progressive; Contemporary Christian. **Networks:** ABC; Fox. **Founded:** 1967. **Operating Hours:** Continuous. **Key Personnel:** Ron Mosley, Jr., CEO, Founder, rcm@wkul.com. **Wattage:** 6,000 ERP. **Ad Rates:** Advertising accepted; rates available upon request. **URL:** http://wkul.com.

DALEVILLE

SE AL. Dale Co. 15 mi. S. of Ozark.

194 ■ WTKN-AM - 1560
PO Box 81
Daleville, AL 36322
Phone: (205)598-8810
Fax: (205)598-6506
Format: News; Talk. **Networks:** People's Network; Agrinet Farm Radio; USA Radio. **Owner:** News/Talk 1560, Inc., at above address. **Founded:** 1983. **Formerly:** WRDJ-AM. **Operating Hours:** 6 a.m.-8 p.m. 5% network, 95% local. **Key Personnel:** Wyatt Cox, Contact. **Wattage:** 5,000. **Ad Rates:** $5-10 for 30 seconds; $7.50-15 for 60 seconds.

DAPHNE

195 ■ Journal of Instructional Psychology
Project Innovation Inc.
109 Michocaun Cir.
Daphne, AL 36526-8031
Professional journal aimed at those interested in instructional and educational management. Bilingual and multicultural aspects are treated as well as technology and education. **Freq:** Quarterly. **Print Method:** Offset. **Trim Size:** 5 x 8. **ISSN:** 0094--1956 (print). **Subscription Rates:** $100 Institutions /year; $85 Individuals /year; $180 Institutions two years; $160 Individuals two years; $260 Institutions three years; $225 Individuals three years. **URL:** http://www.projectinnovation.biz/journal_of_instructional_psychology. **Remarks:** Advertising not accepted. **Circ:** ‡450.

DAUPHIN ISLAND

196 ■ Gulf of Mexico Science
Dauphin Island Sea Lab
101 Bienville Blvd.
Dauphin Island, AL 36528
Phone: (251)861-2141
Fax: (251)861-4646
Publication E-mail: goms@disl.org
Covering marine science in the Gulf of Mexico. **Founded:** Mar. 1996. **Freq:** Semiannual. **Trim Size:** 7 x 10. **Key Personnel:** Carolyn F. Wood, Assistant Editor, phone: (251)861-2215, fax: (251)861-7540; Kenneth L. Heck, Jr., Editor, phone: (251)861-2284, fax: (251)861-7540. **ISSN:** 1087-688X (print). **Subscription Rates:** $15 Individuals; $10 Students; $7.50 Individuals back issue. **URL:** http://goms.disl.org/. **Formerly:** Northeast Gulf Science; Journal of Marine Science. **Remarks:** Advertising not accepted. **Circ:** Paid 302, Non-paid 114.

DECATUR

N. AL. Morgan Co. On Tennessee River, 22 mi. SW of Huntsville. Manufactures cotton and cottonseed products, automobile parts, chemicals, tile,bridge steel, sheet metal, copper tubing, leather soles and belting, paper, air conditioners, refrigerators, boxes, baskets, gasoline tanks, fertilizer. Shipyard; meat packing, poultry processing plants, bottling works.

197 ■ Decatur Daily
Tennessee Valley Printing
201 1st Ave. SE
Decatur, AL 35609
Phone: (256)340-2410
Fax: (256)340-2411
Free: 888-353-4612
Publisher's E-mail: news@decaturdaily.com
Newspaper with a Democratic orientation. **Freq:** Daily (eve.), Sat. and Sun. (morn.). **Print Method:** Offset. **Cols./Page:** 6. **Col. Width:** 25 nonpareils. **Col. Depth:** 301 agate lines. **Key Personnel:** Clint Shelton, Publisher; Bruce McLellan, Managing Editor. **Subscription Rates:** $7 Individuals online only; $12 Individuals print subscription with EZ Pay. **Mailing address:** PO Box 2213, Decatur, AL 35609. **Ad Rates:** SAU $17; PCI $17. **Remarks:** Accepts advertising. **Circ:** Mon.-Sat. 20770, Sun. 22961.

198 ■ Journal of Content Area Reading
International Literacy Association
1533 Blackhall Ln. SE
Decatur, AL 35601
Phone: (256)351-8508
Fax: (256)351-9818
Publisher's E-mail: customerservice@reading.org
Journal that covers research and practice in content area reading for the purpose of promoting reading comprehension in all disciplines and at all grade levels. **Key Personnel:** Matthew Thomas, PhD, Board Member; Mary W. Spor, PhD, Editor. **ISSN:** 1539--4220 (print). **URL:** http://www.ucmo.edu/carsig/about. **Circ:** (Not Reported).

199 ■ WAZK-FM - 92.5
1102 4th Ave. SE, Ste. B
Decatur, AL 35601-4000
Phone: (205)355-4567
Fax: (205)355-4567
Format: Classic Rock. **Owner:** Brainerd Broadcasting, at above address. **Founded:** 1992. **Operating Hours:** Continuous. **Wattage:** 10,000. **Ad Rates:** $60 for 60 seconds.

200 ■ W33CM - 33
PO Box A
Santa Ana, CA 92711
Phone: (714)832-2950
Free: 888-731-1000
Owner: Trinity Broadcasting Network Inc., PO Box A, Santa Ana, CA 92711, Ph: (714)832-2950, Free: 888-731-1000. **URL:** http://www.tbn.org.

201 ■ WWTM-AM - 1400
1209 N Danville Rd. S
Decatur, AL 35601
Phone: (256)353-1400
Fax: (256)353-0363
Email: tarnold@wavd.com
Format: Sports. **Networks:** ESPN Radio. **Owner:** R & B Communications, Inc., 520 S Auburn St., Grass Valley, CA 95945, Ph: (530)478-1137. **Founded:** 1935. **Formerly:** WMSL-AM; WAVD-AM. **ADI:** Huntsville-Decatur-Florence, AL. **Key Personnel:** Brian Black, Contact, bblack1@1400theteam.com. **Local Programs:** *SVP & Russillo*, Monday Tuesday Wednesday Thursday Friday 1:00 p.m. - 4:00 p.m.; *The Pulse*, Saturday 1:00 p.m. - 4:00 p.m.; *Inside The Huddle*; *Baseball Show*, Tuesday Wednesday Thursday 4:00 p.m. - 6:30 p.m.; *Podcenter*, Thursday 7:00 p.m.; *The Herd*, Monday Tuesday Wednesday Thursday Friday 10:00 a.m. - 1:00 p.m.; *Sports Nation*, Monday Tuesday Wednesday Thursday Friday 3:00 p.m.; *All Night with Jason Smith*, Monday Tuesday Wednesday Thursday Friday 1:00 a.m. - 5:00 a.m.; *The V Show with Bobby Valvano*, Sunday 7:00 p.m.; *The Scott Van Pelt Show*, Monday Tuesday Wednesday Thursday Friday 1:00 p.m. - 4:00 p.m. **Wattage:** 1,000. **Ad Rates:** $5-7.50 for 30 seconds; $7.50-10 for 60 seconds. **URL:** http://espn1400.info/.

202 ■ WYFD-FM - 91.7
11530 Carmel Commons Blvd.
Charlotte, NC 28226
Phone: (704)523-5555
Free: 800-888-7077
Format: Religious; Educational. **Networks:** Bible Broadcasting. **Owner:** Bible Broadcasting Network Inc., 11530 Carmel Commons Blvd., Charlotte, NC 28226, Ph: (704)523-5555, Free: 800-888-7077. **Founded:** 1990. **Formerly:** WBQM-FM. **Operating Hours:**

Continuous. **ADI:** Huntsville-Decatur-Florence, AL. **Wattage:** 9,000. **Ad Rates:** Noncommercial. **Mailing address:** PO Box 7300, Charlotte, NC 28226. **URL:** http://www.bbnradio.org.

DEMOPOLIS

NW AL. Marengo Co. 48 mi. W. of Selma. Cotton, cattle, dairy farms, soybeans.

203 ■ Blackbelt Gazette
Boone Newspapers Inc.
315 E Jefferson St.
Demopolis, AL 36732
Phone: (334)289-4017
Fax: (334)289-4019
Newspaper covering community news. **URL:** http://www.demopolistimes.com/category/blackbelt-gazette. **Remarks:** Accepts advertising. **Circ:** (Not Reported).

204 ■ The Demopolis Times
Boone Newspapers Inc.
315 E Jefferson St.
Demopolis, AL 36732
Phone: (334)289-4017
Fax: (334)289-4019
Publication E-mail: news@demopolistimes.com
Community newspaper. **Freq:** Semiweekly (Wed. and Sat.). **Print Method:** Offset. **Cols./Page:** 6. **Col. Width:** 2 inches. **Col. Depth:** 21 1/2 inches. **USPS:** 153-520. **Subscription Rates:** $61 Individuals in Marengo, Greene, Hale, Sumter, and Perry County; $92 Out of area. **URL:** http://www.demopolistimes.com. **Remarks:** Accepts classified advertising. **Circ:** ‡2850.

205 ■ WIIQ-TV - 19
2112 11th Ave. S, Ste. 400
Birmingham, AL 35205
Phone: (205)328-8756
Fax: (205)251-2192
Free: 800-239-5233
Format: Public TV. **Simulcasts:** WBIQ-TV Birmingham, AL. **Networks:** Public Broadcasting Service (PBS). **Owner:** Alabama Public Television, 2112 11th Ave. S, Birmingham, AL 35205, Ph: (205)328-8756, Fax: (205)251-2192, Free: 800-239-5233. **Founded:** 1967. **Operating Hours:** Continuous. **ADI:** Birmingham (Gadsden), AL. **Key Personnel:** Jon Beans, Dir. Pub. Aff., News Dir., jbeans@aptv.org. **Local Programs:** *For the Record.* **Wattage:** 1,000. **Ad Rates:** Noncommercial. **URL:** http://www.aptv.org.

206 ■ WVFG-FM - 107.5
1502 East Hwy. 80
Demopolis, AL 36732
Phone: (334)628-2888
Fax: (334)628-6800
Email: chazjr@hotmail.com
Format: Blues. **Founded:** Jan. 1994. **Operating Hours:** Continuous. **Wattage:** 6,000. **Ad Rates:** Noncommercial. **URL:** http://wvfg1075.webs.com.

207 ■ WXAL-AM
PO Box 938
Demopolis, AL 36732
Phone: (334)289-1400
Fax: (334)289-2156
Format: Talk; Religious. **Networks:** USA Radio. **Owner:** Ross Communications, Inc., 919 Congress Ave., Ste. 1500, Austin, TX 78701. **Founded:** 1947. **Wattage:** 790. **Ad Rates:** $3.09-8.26 for 30 seconds; $4.28-9.26 for 60 seconds.

208 ■ WZNJ-FM - 106.5
1226 Jefferson Rd.
Demopolis, AL 36732
Phone: (206)774-1801
Format: Oldies. **Simulcasts:** WXAL-AM. **Networks:** Westwood One Radio; USA Radio. **Owner:** Ross Communications, Inc., 919 Congress Ave., Ste. 1500, Austin, TX 78701. **Founded:** 1975. **Formerly:** WNAN-FM. **Operating Hours:** Continuous; 80% network, 20% local. **Key Personnel:** Bill Jones, Gen. Mgr. **Wattage:** 25,000 Watts. **Ad Rates:** $7.50-12.00; $6.50-11.00 for 30 seconds; $4.28-12.70 for 60 seconds. **Mailing address:** PO Box 938, Demopolis, AL 36732.

DIXONS MILLS

209 ■ WMBV-FM - 91.9
10564 Marengo County Rd. 30
Dixons Mills, AL 36736
Free: 888-624-7234
Owner: The Moody Bible Institute of Chicago, 820 N Lasalle St., Chicago, IL 60610, Ph: (312)329-4000, Free: 800-356-6639. **Wattage:** 62,000. **Ad Rates:** Accepts Advertising. **Mailing address:** PO Box 91, Dixons Mills, AL 36736.

DOTHAN

SE AL. Houston Co. 110 mi. SE of Montgomery. Manufactures magnetic tapes, electric motors, peanut oil, latex products, furniture, pajamas, cigars, charcoal briquettes. Agriculture. Soybeans, peanuts.

210 ■ The Dothan Eagle
Eagle
227 N Oates St.
Dothan, AL 36302
Phone: (334)792-3141
Fax: (334)712-7979
Free: 800-779-2557
Publisher's E-mail: circulation@dothaneagle.com
General newspaper. **Freq:** Daily and Sun. (morn.). **Print Method:** Offset. **Cols./Page:** 6. **Col. Width:** 24 nonpareils. **Col. Depth:** 301 agate lines. **Key Personnel:** Ken Tuck, Managing Editor, phone: (334)712-7960; Jim Whittum, Publisher, phone: (334)712-7924, fax: (334)712-7992; Christie Kulavich, Editor, phone: (334)712-7966. **Subscription Rates:** $75 Individuals Daily; $1.50 Individuals Sunday. **Mailing address:** PO Box 1968, Dothan, AL 36302. **Ad Rates:** GLR $12.20; BW $4515; 4C $4890; SAU $11.22; PCI $35; 4C $375. **Remarks:** Accepts advertising. **Circ:** Mon.-Fri. ‡38000, Sun. ‡40000.

211 ■ The Dothan Progress
The Dothan Progress
PO Box 1968
Dothan, AL 36302
Phone: (334)792-3141
Fax: (334)712-7979
Free: 800-779-2557
Publisher's E-mail: news@dothaneagle.com
Community newspaper. **Freq:** Weekly (Thurs.). **Print Method:** Offset. **Cols./Page:** 6. **Col. Width:** 1.78 inches. **Col. Depth:** 21 1/2 inches. **Key Personnel:** Jim Whittum, Publisher, phone: (334)792-3141; Elaine Brackin, Managing Editor, phone: (334)712-7987. **Subscription Rates:** $15.45 Individuals Monday to Sunday (print + all access); $17.99 Individuals online only; $10.05 Individuals Monday to Sunday (print). **URL:** http://www.dothaneagle.com/news/dothan_progress. **Ad Rates:** GLR $10.92; BW $1408.68; 4C $1758.68; SAU $10.92. **Remarks:** Accepts advertising. **Circ:** Mon.-Fri. ‡38000, Sun. ‡40000.

212 ■ Time Warner
104 S Woodburn
Dothan, AL 36305
Phone: (334)793-1752
Fax: (334)793-5667
Formerly: Wometco Cable TV of Alabama; Cablevision Industries. **Key Personnel:** Alan Levy, Gen. Mgr. **Cities Served:** 60 channels.

213 ■ WAGF-AM - 1320
4106 Ross Clark Cir.
Dothan, AL 36303
Phone: (334)671-1753
Fax: (334)677-6923
Format: Urban Contemporary; Talk. **Owner:** Wilson Broadcasting Company Inc., at above address. **Key Personnel:** James Wilson, III, CEO, President. **Ad Rates:** Advertising accepted; rates available upon request. **URL:** http://www.wjjn.net.

214 ■ WAGF-FM - 101.3
4106 Ross Clark Cir.
Dothan, AL 36303
Phone: (334)671-1753
Fax: (334)677-6923
Format: Adult Contemporary; Gospel. **Owner:** Wilson Broadcasting Company Inc., at above address. **Key Personnel:** James R. Wilson, III, CEO, President. **Ad Rates:** Advertising accepted; rates available upon request. **URL:** http://www.wjjn.net/wagf_home.htm.

215 ■ WAQG-FM - 91.7
PO Box 3206
Tupelo, MS 38803
Format: Contemporary Christian; Religious. **Owner:** American Family Radio, at above address. **Ad Rates:** Noncommercial. **URL:** http://www.afa.net.

216 ■ WBBK-FM - 93.1
285 N Foster St., 8th Fl.
Dothan, AL 36303
Phone: (334)792-0047
Fax: (334)712-9346
Format: Urban Contemporary; Adult Contemporary. **Wattage:** 45,000. **Ad Rates:** Advertising accepted; rates available upon request.

217 ■ WDFX-TV - 34
2221 Ross Clark Cir.
Dothan, AL 36301
Phone: (334)794-3434
Format: Commercial TV. **Networks:** Fox. **Owner:** Waitt Broadcasting, Inc., at above address, Free: 877-943-6915. **Founded:** 1991. **Operating Hours:** Continuous. **ADI:** Dothan, AL. **Local Programs:** *FOX34*, Monday Tuesday Wednesday Thursday Friday Saturday Sunday 4:00 p.m. 9:00 p.m. **Wattage:** 1,100,000. **Ad Rates:** Advertising accepted; rates available upon request. **URL:** http://www.dothanconnect.revrocket.us.

218 ■ WDHN-TV - 18
PO Box 6237
Dothan, AL 36302
Phone: (334)793-1818
Fax: (334)793-2623
Format: Commercial TV. **Networks:** ABC. **Founded:** 1970. **Operating Hours:** 5:30 a.m.-midnight; 70% network, 30% local. **ADI:** Dothan, AL. **Key Personnel:** Ken Curtis, Dir. of Operations. **Ad Rates:** $35-800 per unit. **URL:** http://www.dothanfirst.com.

219 ■ WDJR-FM - 96.9
3245 Montgomery Hwy., Ste. 1
Dothan, AL 36303-2150
Format: Country. **Networks:** ABC. **Founded:** 1948. **Formerly:** WLHQ-FM. **Operating Hours:** Continuous. **ADI:** Dothan, AL. **Key Personnel:** Bill J. Moody, Sales Mgr., bill@wdjr.com; Brett Mason, Dir. of Programs, mason@wdjr.com; Ron Eubanks, Gen. Mgr., ron@wdjr.com. **Wattage:** 100,000. **Ad Rates:** Noncommercial. Combined advertising rates available with WBCD-FM & WESP-FM. **URL:** http://www.mix969.net.

220 ■ WDYF-FM - 90.3
381 Mendel Pkwy.
Montgomery, AL 36117
Phone: (334)271-8900
Fax: (334)260-8962
Free: 800-239-8900
Email: mail@faithradio.org
Format: Religious; Contemporary Christian. **Owner:** Faith Broadcasting Inc., 381 Mendel Pky. E, Montgomery, AL 36117, Ph: (334)271-8900, Fax: (334)260-8962, Free: 800-239-8900. **Operating Hours:** Continuous. **Key Personnel:** Russell Dean, Gen. Mgr. **Ad Rates:** Noncommercial. **URL:** http://www.faithradio.org.

221 ■ WESP-FM - 102.5
3245 Montgomery Hwy., Ste. 1
Dothan, AL 36303
Phone: (334)712-9233
Fax: (334)712-0374
Format: Classic Rock; Oldies. **Founded:** 1989. **Operating Hours:** Continuous. **ADI:** Dothan, AL. **Key Personnel:** David Sommers, Dir. of Programs, dsommers997@graceba.net; Ron Eubanks, Gen. Mgr., Owner, ron@wdjr.com; Bill Moody, Sales Mgr., bill@wdjr.com. **Wattage:** 25,000. **Ad Rates:** Advertising accepted; rates available upon request.

222 ■ WGTF-FM - 89.5
11530 Carmel Commons Blvd.
Charlotte, NC 28226
Phone: (704)523-5555
Fax: (800)888-7077
Email: bbn@bbnmedia.org
Format: Religious. **Networks:** Bible Broadcasting. **Owner:** Bible Broadcasting Network Inc., 11530 Carmel Commons Blvd., Charlotte, NC 28226, Ph: (704)523-5555, Free: 800-888-7077. **Founded:** 1988. **Operating**

Circulation: ★ = AAM; △ or • = BPA; ♦ = CAC; ❑ = VAC; ⊕ = PO Statement; ‡ = Publisher's Report; Boldface figures = sworn; Light figures = estimated.

Hours: Continuous. **ADI**: Dothan, AL. **Wattage**: 19,000. **URL**: http://www.bbnradio.org.

223 ■ WIZB-FM - 94.3
PO Box 8097
Dothan, AL 36304-0097
Phone: (334)699-5672
Fax: (334)699-5034
Free: 800-656-0111
Format: Contemporary Christian; Religious. **Owner:** RTN Family Station, PO Box 7217, Lakeland, FL 33807-7217, Ph: (863)644-3464, Fax: (863)646-5326, Free: 800-456-8910. **Operating Hours**: Continuous. **Key Personnel:** Russell Brooks, Dir. of Programs, russell@hisradio943.com; Johanna Antes, Director, johanna@rtn.cc; Earl Kelley, Account Mgr. **Wattage**: 19,500 ERP. **Ad Rates:** Noncommercial. **URL:** http://www.alabama.thejoyfm.com.

224 ■ WJJN-FM - 92.1
4106 Ross Clark Cir.
Dothan, AL 36303
Phone: (334)671-1753
Format: Hip Hop; News; Sports; Blues; Information. **Owner:** Wilson Broadcasting Company Inc., at above address. **Founded:** July 26, 1995. **Key Personnel:** James Wilson, III, CEO, President. **Wattage**: 2,550 ERP. **Ad Rates:** Advertising accepted; rates available upon request. **URL:** http://www.wjjn.net.

225 ■ WKMX-FM - 106.7
3245 Montgomery Hwy., Ste. 1
Dothan, AL 36303
Phone: (334)712-9233
Fax: (334)712-0374
Free: 855-251-1067
Format: Adult Contemporary. **Networks:** Independent. **Owner:** Magic Broadcasting L.L.C., 7106 Laird St., Panama City, FL 32408, Ph: (850)230-5855. **Founded:** 1974. **Operating Hours**: Continuous. **ADI**: Dothan, AL. **Wattage**: 100,000. **Ad Rates:** Advertising accepted; rates available upon request. **URL:** http://www.wkmx.com.

226 ■ WOOF-AM - 560
PO Box 1427
Dothan, AL 36302
Phone: (334)792-1149
Fax: (334)677-4612
Free: 888-793-2656
Format: Sports; Talk; News. **Owner:** WOOF Inc. **Founded:** 1947. **Operating Hours**: Continuous. **ADI**: Dothan, AL. **Wattage**: 5,000. **Ad Rates:** Advertising accepted; rates available upon request. **URL:** http://www.woofradio.com.

227 ■ WOOF-FM - 99.7
2518 Columbia Hwy.
Dothan, AL 36303
Phone: (334)792-1149
Fax: (334)677-4612
Free: 800-239-9663
Email: woof@ala.net
Format: Adult Contemporary. **Networks:** Standard Broadcast News. **Owner:** WOOF Inc. **Founded:** 1964. **Operating Hours**: Continuous; 1% network, 99% local. **ADI**: Dothan, AL. **Key Personnel:** Hal Edwards, Gen. Sales Mgr. **Wattage**: 100,000. **Ad Rates:** $33-50 for 30 seconds; $40-57 for 60 seconds. **Mailing address:** PO Box 1427, Dothan, AL 36303. **URL:** http://www.997wooffm.com.

228 ■ WQLS-FM - 103.9
3245 Montgomery Hwy., Ste. 1
Dothan, AL 36303
Phone: (334)712-9233
Format: Album-Oriented Rock (AOR). **Networks:** CNN Radio. **Founded:** 1974. **Operating Hours**: Continuous. **ADI**: Dothan, AL. **Key Personnel:** Ted Morgan, Gen. Mgr. **Wattage**: 25,000.

229 ■ WTVY-FM - 95.5
3245 Montgomery Highway Ste. 1
Dothan, AL 36301
Phone: (334)712-0374
Free: 855-599-9889
Format: Country; News. **Owner:** Magic Broadcasting L.L.C., 7106 Laird St., Panama City, FL 32408, Ph: (850)230-5855. **Operating Hours**: Continuous. **ADI**: Dothan, AL. **Key Personnel:** David Sommers, Prog. Dir., david@trpdothan.com. **Wattage**: 100,000 ERP. **Ad Rates:** $20-135 for 30 seconds; $30-145 for 60 seconds. **URL:** http://www.955wtvy.com.

230 ■ WTVY-TV - 4
285 N Foster St
Dothan, AL 36303
Phone: (334)792-3195
Fax: (334)793-3947
Email: news@wtvy.com
Format: Commercial TV. **Simulcasts:** WPAP-FM,WFSY-FM,WEBZ-FM. **Networks:** CBS. **Owner:** Gray Television Inc., 4370 Peachtree Rd. NE, No. 400, Atlanta, GA 30319-3054, Ph: (404)266-8333. **Operating Hours**: Continuous. **ADI**: Dothan, AL. **Key Personnel:** Tom Johnson, Chief Engineer, tom@wtvy.com; Wayne May, Div. Mgr.; David Paul, Officer, david.paul@wtvy.com. **Wattage**: 1,000,000 ERP. **Ad Rates:** Noncommercial; Advertising accepted; rates available upon request. **URL:** http://www.wtvy.com.

231 ■ WVOB-FM - 91.3
PO Box 1944
Dothan, AL 36302
Fax: (334)793-4344
Format: Southern Gospel; Contemporary Christian. **Networks:** USA Radio. **Owner:** Bethany Bible College and Bethany Theological Seminary, Inc., at above address. **Founded:** 1988. **Operating Hours**: Continuous. **ADI**: Dothan, AL. **Key Personnel:** Dr. H.D. Shuemake, Gen. Mgr., bethanybc@ala.net; Samuel Shuemake, Station Mgr., svshuemake@bethanybc.edu; Keith Brady, Dir. of Operations, kbrady@bethanybc.edu. **Wattage**: 2,500. **Ad Rates:** Noncommercial. **Mailing address:** PO Box 1944, Dothan, AL 36302. **URL:** http://www.bethanybc.edu.

232 ■ WWNT-AM - 1450
1733 Columbia Hwy.
Dothan, AL 36303
Phone: (334)671-0075
Email: info@wwntradio.com
Format: Religious; Talk; News. **Networks:** Independent. **Operating Hours**: 6 a.m.-10 p.m.; 10% network, 30% local. **ADI**: Dothan, AL. **Wattage**: 1,000. **Ad Rates:** Noncommercial. **URL:** http://www.wwntradio.com.

DOZIER

SC AL. Crenshaw Co. 50 mi. S. of Montgomery.

233 ■ WDIQ-TV - 2
2112 11th Ave. S, Ste. 400
2112 11th Ave. S, Ste. 400
Birmingham, AL 35205
Phone: (205)328-8756
Fax: (205)251-2192
Free: 800-239-5233
Format: Public TV. **Simulcasts:** WBIQ-TV. **Networks:** Public Broadcasting Service (PBS). **Owner:** Alabama Public Television, 2112 11th Ave. S, Birmingham, AL 35205, Ph: (205)328-8756, Fax: (205)251-2192, Free: 800-239-5233. **Founded:** Aug. 08, 1956. **Operating Hours**: Continuous. **ADI**: Birmingham (Gadsden), AL. **Key Personnel:** Kathie B. Martin, APR, Specialist, kmartin@aptv.org; Mike Mckenzie, Contact, mckenzie@aptv.org. **Wattage**: 100,000 ERP. **Ad Rates:** Noncommercial. **URL:** http://www.aptv.org.

EATONTON

234 ■ CommuniComm Services
PO Box 3310
Eatonton, AL 31024
Phone: (334)863-8112
Free: 800-239-5367
Cities Served: 61 channels. **URL:** http://www.netcommander.com.

ELBA

SE AL. Coffee Co. 40 mi. NW of Dothan. Manufactures truck trailers, fork lifts, textiles, lumber. Meat packing plant. Pine, oak timber. Diversified farming. Broilers, peanuts, livestock.

235 ■ The Elba Clipper
The Elba Clipper
PO Box 677
Elba, AL 36323-0677
Phone: (334)897-2823
Fax: (334)897-3434
Newspaper. **Freq:** Weekly (Thurs.). **Print Method:** Offset. **Cols./Page:** 6. **Col. Width:** 21 1/2 nonpareils. **Col. Depth:** 294 agate lines. **Key Personnel:** Ferrin Cox, Publisher; Linda Hodge, Editor; Heddy Cox, Business Manager. **Subscription Rates:** $21 Individuals 1 year subscription Coffee county and adjoining counties; $24 Out of area 1 year subscription; $27 Out of state 1 year subscription; $11 Individuals 6 months subscription Coffee County and Adjoining Counties; $13 Out of area 6 months subscription; $15 Out of state 6 months subscription. **Ad Rates:** GLR $.28; BW $549.54; 4C $774.54; SAU $3.88. **Remarks:** Advertising accepted; rates available upon request. **Circ:** 3200.

236 ■ WELB-AM
20334 Hwy. 87
Elba, AL 36323
Format: Oldies. **Owner:** Elba Radio Company, 100 Main Street N , Enterprise, AL 36330, Ph: (334)347-5621, Fax: (334)347.5631. **Founded:** 1958. **Key Personnel:** William D. Holderfield, Contact. **Wattage**: 1,000 Day; 044 Night.

ENTERPRISE

SE AL. Dale Co. 80 mi. S. of Montgomery. Manufactures weather and satellite radars, portable runway planking, flatbed trailers, forklifts, castings, door hinges, textiles. Poultry. Peanuts. Dairy farming.

237 ■ Enterprise Ledger
Enterprise Ledger
106 N Edwards St.
Enterprise, AL 36331
Publisher's E-mail: news@eprisenow.com
General newspaper. **Freq:** Daily and Sun. (eve.). **Print Method:** Offset. **Key Personnel:** Danny Lewis, Managing Editor; Jim Whittum, Publisher. **URL:** http://www.dothaneagle.com/enterprise_ledger. **Mailing address:** PO Box 311130, Enterprise, AL 36331. **Ad Rates:** 4C $230; SAU $9.45. **Remarks:** Accepts advertising. **Circ:** Mon.-Fri. ‡10000.

238 ■ WVVL-FM - 101.1
100 N Main St.
Enterprise, AL 36330
Phone: (334)347-5621
Fax: (334)347-5631
Email: wvvl@weevil101.com
Format: Country. **Owner:** Elba Radio Company, 100 Main Street N , Enterprise, AL 36330, Ph: (334)347-5621, Fax: (334)347.5631. **URL:** http://www.weevil101.com.

EUFAULA

SE AL. Barbour Co. On Chattahoochee River, 45 mi. S. of Columbus, GA. Manufactures cotton cloth and yarn, fishing lures, depth finders, textiles, cottonseed oil, shoes, carpet yarn, lumber, doors, paper, soft drinks, bricks. Pine timber. Agriculture. Cotton, peanuts, cattle.

239 ■ The Eufaula Tribune: locally-owned, independent, paid circulation newspaper
Tribune Publishing Co.
514 E Barbour St.
Eufaula, AL 36027
Phone: (334)687-3506
Fax: (334)687-3229
Community newspaper. **Freq:** Semiweekly (Wed. and Sun.). **Print Method:** Offset. **Cols./Page:** 6. **Col. Width:** 26 nonpareils. **Col. Depth:** 301 agate lines. **Key Personnel:** Ed Trainor, General Manager; Patrick Johnston, Managing Editor. **URL:** http://www.dothaneagle.com/eufaula_tribune. **Mailing address:** PO Box 628, Eufaula, AL 36027. **Ad Rates:** GLR $.32; SAU $4.27; PCI $7. **Remarks:** Accepts advertising. **Circ:** 6350.

240 ■ W30BD - 30
PO Box A
Santa Ana, CA 92711
Phone: (714)832-2950
Free: 888-731-1000
Owner: Trinity Broadcasting Network Inc., PO Box A, Santa Ana, CA 92711, Ph: (714)832-2950, Free: 888-731-1000. **URL:** http://www.tbn.org.

241 ■ WULA-AM
Hwy. 431 S
Eufaula, AL 36027

Phone: (334)688-2121
Fax: (334)688-2112
Format: News; Talk. **Networks:** People's Network. **Owner:** River Valley Media, LLC, at above address, Ph: (334)687-2066, Fax: (334)687-2067. **Founded:** 1948. **Key Personnel:** B. Smith, News Dir. **Wattage:** 600. **Ad Rates:** $4-25 per unit.

EUTAW

W. AL. Greene Co. 30 mi. SW of Tuscaloosa. Lumber mills; cotton gin; cattle market. Timber. Agriculture. Cotton, potatoes.

242 ■ Greene County Democrat
Greene County Newspaper Co.
206 Prairie Ave.
Eutaw, AL 35462
Phone: (205)372-3373
Fax: (205)372-2243
Black community newspaper. **Freq:** Weekly (Wed.). **Print Method:** Offset. **Cols./Page:** 6. **Col. Width:** 21 nonpareils. **Col. Depth:** 294 agate lines. **Key Personnel:** Laddi Jones, Manager, Advertising; Carol Zippert, Publisher; John Zippert, Publisher. **ISSN:** 0889--518X (print). **Subscription Rates:** $20 Individuals; $25 Out of area; $30 Out of state. **URL:** http://greenecountydemocrat.com. **Ad Rates:** BW $1,210; SAU $6; PCI $10. **Remarks:** Accepts advertising. **Circ:** ‡3500.

EVA

243 ■ WRJL-AM - 1170
5610 Hwy. 55 E
Eva, AL 35621-7927
Phone: (205)796-8000
Fax: (205)352-9787
Format: Gospel; Southern Gospel. **Networks:** USA Radio. **Founded:** 1986. **Formerly**: WHZI-AM. **Operating Hours**: Sunrise-sunset; 100% local. **Key Personnel:** Rolland French, Contact; Jo French, Contact. **Wattage**: 460.

FAIRHOPE

SW AL. Baldwin Co. 15 mi. SE of Mobile. Residential.

244 ■ Fairhope Courier
Gulf Coast Newspapers
325 Fairhope Ave.
Fairhope, AL 36532
Phone: (251)928-2321
Fax: (251)928-9963
Community newspaper. **Freq:** 104/yr. **Print Method:** Offset. **Cols./Page:** 6. **Col. Width:** 71 picas. **Col. Depth:** 21.5 agate lines. **Key Personnel:** Gabriel Tynes, Editor; Mike Odom, Writer. **Subscription Rates:** $2.75 Individuals in county, 1 month e-edition subscription; $20 Individuals in county, 1 year e-edition subscription; $.75 Individuals for 1 day. **URL:** http://www.gulfcoastnewstoday.com/the_fairhope_courier. **Formerly**: Eastern Shore Courier. **Ad Rates:** SAU $2.63. **Remarks:** Accepts advertising. **Circ:** ‡4400.

245 ■ Mediacom Communications Corp.
760 Middle St.
Fairhope, AL 36532
Free: 800-239-8411
Key Personnel: Mark E. Stephan, CFO. **Cities Served:** 80 channels. **Mailing address:** PO Box 1009, Fairhope, AL 36532. **URL:** http://www.mediacomcable.com.

246 ■ WABF-AM - 1220
PO Box 1220
Fairhope, AL 36533
Phone: (251)928-2384
Fax: (251)928-9229
Email: wabf@wabf1220.net
Format: Adult Contemporary. **Networks:** CNN Radio; Alabama Radio (ALANET). **Owner:** Gulf Coast Broadcasting Co. Inc., 2421 E 2nd St., Gulf Shores, AL 36542, Ph: (251)967-1057, Fax: (251)967-1050. **Founded:** 1961. **Operating Hours**: Continuous 80% net, 20% local. **ADI:** Mobile, AL-Pensacola, FL. **Key Personnel:** Lori DuBose, Gen. Mgr. **Wattage**: 1,000 Day 045 Night. **Ad Rates:** $8-10 for 30 seconds; $10-12 for 60 seconds. Combined advertising rates available with WCSN-FM, WPGG-GM, WIJK-AM. **URL:** http://www.wabf1220.net.

247 ■ W214BN-FM - 90.7
PO Box 391
Twin Falls, ID 83303
Fax: (208)736-1958
Free: 800-357-4226
Format: Religious; Contemporary Christian. **Owner:** CSN International, PO Box 391, Twin Falls, ID 83303, Ph: (208)736-1958, Fax: (208)736-1958, Free: 800-357-4226. **Key Personnel:** Don Mills, Div. Dir., Music Dir.; Kelly Carlson, Dir. of Engg.; Ray Gorney, Asst. Dir. **URL:** http://www.csnradio.com.

FAYETTE

C. AL. Fayette Co. 35 mi. NNW of Tuscaloosa.

248 ■ Cattle Today
Cattle Today Inc.
204 S Temple Ave.
Fayette, AL 35555
Phone: (205)932-8000
Fax: (205)932-4000
Publication E-mail: editor@cattletoday.com
Newspaper (tabloid) serving purebred and commercial cattle producers in the southeastern states. **Freq:** Semimonthly. **Key Personnel:** Belinda Ary, Editor. **Subscription Rates:** $15 Individuals; $25 Two years. **URL:** http://www.cattletoday.com. **Remarks:** Accepts classified advertising. **Circ:** 15000.

249 ■ West Alabama TV Cable Co.
213 2nd Ave. NE
Fayette, AL 35555
Phone: (205)932-4700
Founded: May 23, 1964. **Cities Served:** Belk, Brilliant, Fayette, Hamilton, Winfield, Alabama: subscribing households 6,775; 150 channels. **URL:** http://www.watvc.com.

250 ■ WLDX-AM - 990
733 Columbus St. E
Fayette, AL 35555
Phone: (205)932-3318
Fax: (205)932-3318
Email: wldx@wldx.com
Format: Contemporary Country. **Networks:** ABC. **Owner:** Dean Broadcasting Inc., 733 Columbus St. E, Fayette, AL 35555. **Founded:** 1949. **Formerly**: WWWF-AM. **Operating Hours**: Continuous. **Key Personnel:** Wiley J. Dean, President; Jill Dean, Gen. Mgr., VP, jilldean@wldx.com; Joe Jackson, Div. Dir., jredker@wldx.com; Steve Dean, VP, sdean@wldx.com; Jack Black, Gen. Mgr. **Wattage**: 1,000. **Ad Rates:** $8 for 15 seconds; $10 for 30 seconds; $12 for 60 seconds. **URL:** http://wldx.com.

FLORALA

SE AL. Covington Co. On Florida border. Sawmills.

251 ■ DeFuniak Herald
Woodham Family Publications
421 S 5th St.
Florala, AL 36442-1221
Phone: (334)858-3342
Community newspaper. **Freq:** Weekly (Thurs.). **Print Method:** Offset. **Cols./Page:** 6. **Col. Width:** 12 2/5 picas. **Col. Depth:** 21 inches. **Key Personnel:** Bruce Collier, Editor; Gary Woodham, Publisher. **USPS:** 149-900. **Subscription Rates:** $39 Individuals in Florida; $45 Out of area. **Formerly**: De Funiak Herald-Breeze. **Ad Rates:** PCI $3.50. **Remarks:** Advertising accepted; rates available upon request. **Circ:** 7500.

252 ■ WKWL-AM
PO Box 158
Florala, AL 36442
Phone: (334)858-6162
Fax: (334)858-6132
Email: wkwl@cyou.com
Format: Religious. **Owner:** Florala Broadcasting Co., Inc., at above address. **Founded:** 1979. **Key Personnel:** Robert Williamson, Gen. Mgr. **Wattage**: 1,000. **Ad Rates:** $4 for 30 seconds; $5 for 60 seconds.

FLORENCE

NW AL. Lauderdale Co. On Tennessee River, directly across the river from Sheffield. University of North Alabama. Manufactures chemicals, aluminum, corrugated containers, concrete blocks, pipe, chloride, caustic soda, fertilizer, nitrate, phosphate, boats. Machine shops, stove foundry; agriculture.

253 ■ American Journalism
University of North Alabama
1 Harrison Plz.
Florence, AL 35632
Phone: (256)765-4225
Free: 800-825-5862
Journal covering media history. **Freq:** Quarterly. **Key Personnel:** Barbara Friedman, Editor. **ISSN:** 0882--1127 (print); **EISSN:** 2326--2486 (electronic). **Subscription Rates:** $371 Institutions online; $424 Institutions print and online. **URL:** http://ajhaonline.org/journal.html; http://www.tandfonline.com/toc/uamj20/current#.VQdXsdKUfId. **Ad Rates:** BW $150. **Remarks:** Accepts advertising. **Circ:** Paid 800.

254 ■ BIOS
Beta Beta Beta
University of North Alabama
Math Bldg. M1 - A
1 Harrison Plz.
Florence, AL 35632
Phone: (256)765-6220
Fax: (256)765-6221
Publisher's E-mail: tribeta@una.edu
Journal covering biology for members. **Freq:** Quarterly. **Key Personnel:** Lori M. Kelman, Editor. **ISSN:** 0005--3155 (print). **Subscription Rates:** Included in membership. **URL:** http://tri-beta.org/bios.html. **Remarks:** Advertising accepted; rates available upon request. **Circ:** 11500, 11500.

255 ■ Courier Journal
Lake Street Publishing Co.
219 W Tennessee St.
Florence, AL 35630
Phone: (256)764-4268
Fax: (256)760-9618
Publication E-mail: editor@courierjournal.net
Newspaper. **Founded:** 1884. **Freq:** Weekly (Wed.). **Print Method:** Web offset. **Cols./Page:** 6. **Col. Width:** 24 nonpareils. **Col. Depth:** 301 agate lines. **Key Personnel:** Thomas V. Magazzu, Editor. **USPS:** 451-140. **Subscription Rates:** $20 Individuals; $24 Out of country Florida. **URL:** http://www.courierjournal.net. **Formerly**: Putnam County Courier Journal. **Ad Rates:** GLR $.29; BW $600; 4C $850; PCI $6.50. **Remarks:** Accepts advertising. **Circ:** 68200, 69403.

256 ■ The Flor-Ala
University of North Alabama
1 Harrison Plz.
Florence, AL 35632
Phone: (256)765-4225
Free: 800-825-5862
Publication E-mail: florala@una.edu
Collegiate newspaper. **Freq:** Weekly. **Print Method:** Offset. **Cols./Page:** 6. **Col. Width:** 1 7/8 inches. **Col. Depth:** 21 inches. **Subscription Rates:** $20 Members. **URL:** http://www.florala.net; http://www.una.edu/communications/registered-student-organizations.html#Flor-Ala. **Remarks:** Advertising accepted; rates available upon request. **Circ:** Paid 300, Non-paid 4700.

257 ■ TimesDaily
Tennessee Valley Printing Co.
219 W Tennessee St.
Florence, AL 35630-5440
Phone: (256)766-3434
Publisher's E-mail: online@timesdaily.com
General newspaper. **Freq:** Daily. **Print Method:** Offset. **Cols./Page:** 6. **Col. Width:** 25 nonpareils. **Col. Depth:** 301 agate lines. **Key Personnel:** Mike Goens, Managing Editor, phone: (256)740-5740; Darrell Sandlin, Publisher, phone: (205)740-4711. **Remarks:** Accepts advertising. **Circ:** Mon.-Fri. 29200, Sat. 27500, Sun. 29843.

258 ■ WBCF-TV - 1240; 3
525 E Tennessee St.
Florence, AL 35630
Phone: (205)764-8170
Format: News; Talk. **Networks:** Canadian Broadcasting Corporation (CBC)/Societe Radio-Canada (SRC); NBC; ABC; CBS; Fox. **Founded:** 1943. **Operating Hours**: Continuous; 80% network, 20% local. **ADI:** Huntsville-Decatur-Florence, AL. **Key Personnel:** Benji Carle, Dir. Pub. Aff., News Dir., news@wbcf.com; Benjy Carle, Gen.

Circulation: ★ = AAM; △ or • = BPA; ♦ = CAC; ❑ = VAC; ⊕ = PO Statement; ‡ = Publisher's Report; Boldface figures = sworn; Light figures = estimated.

Mgr., benji@wbcf.com. **Wattage**: 1,000. **Ad Rates:** $20-25 for 30 seconds; $30-35 for 60 seconds. Combined advertising rates available with WBCF-TV; WXFC-TV. **URL:** http://www.wbcf.com.

259 ■ W57BV - 57
PO Box A
Santa Ana, CA 92711
Phone: (714)832-2950
Free: 888-731-1000
Email: comments@tbn.org

Owner: Trinity Broadcasting Network Inc., PO Box A, Santa Ana, CA 92711, Ph: (714)832-2950, Free: 888-731-1000. **URL:** http://www.tbn.org.

260 ■ WFIQ-TV - 36
2112 11th Ave. S, Ste. 400
2112 11th Ave. S, Ste. 400
Birmingham, AL 35205
Phone: (205)328-8756
Fax: (205)251-2192
Free: 800-239-5233

Format: Public TV. **Simulcasts:** WBIQ-TV. **Networks:** Public Broadcasting Service (PBS). **Owner:** Alabama Public Television, 2112 11th Ave. S, Birmingham, AL 35205, Ph: (205)328-8756, Fax: (205)251-2192, Free: 800-239-5233. **Founded:** Aug. 16, 1967. **Operating Hours**: Continuous. **ADI**: Huntsville-Decatur-Florence, AL. **Key Personnel:** Jon Beans, Contact, jbeans@aptv.org; John Hardeman, Supervisor, jhardeman@aptv.org; Jon Beans, Contact, jbeans@aptv.org. **Wattage**: 851,000 ERP. **Ad Rates:** Noncommercial. **URL:** http://www.aptv.org.

261 ■ WFIX-FM - 91.3
113 N Seminary St.
Florence, AL 35630
Phone: (256)764-9964
Fax: (256)764-9154
Email: thescore@939thescore.com

Format: Contemporary Christian; Sports; Talk. **Networks:** ESPN Radio. **Owner:** Tri-State Inspirationl Broadcasting, ; Valley Broadcasting, Inc., at above address. **Founded:** July 01, 2001. **Operating Hours**: Continuous. **Wattage**: 6,000 ERP. **Ad Rates:** Noncommercial. **URL:** http://www.wfix.net.

262 ■ WQLT-FM - 107.3
624 Sam Phillips St.
Florence, AL 35630
Phone: (256)764-8121
Fax: (256)764-8169
Free: 800-239-6107

Format: Adult Contemporary. **Networks:** ABC; Unistar. **Owner:** Big River Broadcasting Corp., 624 Sam Phillips St., Florence, AL 35630. **Founded:** 1967. **Operating Hours**: Continuous; 100% local. **ADI**: Huntsville-Decatur-Florence, AL. **Wattage**: 100,000. **Ad Rates:** $32-50 for 30 seconds. Combined advertising rates available with WXFL-FM, WSBM-AM. **URL:** http://www.wqlt.com.

263 ■ WSBM-AM - 1340
624 Sam Phillips St.
Florence, AL 35630
Phone: (256)764-8121

Format: Sports. **Networks:** ABC. **Owner:** Big River Broadcasting Corp., 624 Sam Phillips St., Florence, AL 35630. **Founded:** 1946. **Formerly**: WJOI-AM. **Operating Hours:** Continuous; 100% network Mon.-Sat., 89% network, 11% local Sun. **ADI**: Huntsville-Decatur-Florence, AL. **Key Personnel:** Nick Martin, Gen. Mgr., nmartin@bigriverbroadcasting.com. **Wattage**: 1,000. **Ad Rates:** $10-22 for 30 seconds. Combined advertising rates available with WQLT-FM, WXFL-FM. **URL:** http://www.wsbm.com.

264 ■ WXFL-FM - 96.1
624 Sam Phillips St.
Florence, AL 35630
Phone: (256)764-8121

Format: Contemporary Country. **Networks:** ABC. **Owner:** Big River Broadcasting Corp., 624 Sam Phillips St., Florence, AL 35630. **Founded:** July 01, 1995. **Operating Hours:** Continuous. **Wattage**: 50,000. **Ad Rates:** Noncommercial. Combined advertising rates available with WQLT-FM, WSBM-AM. **URL:** http://www.kix96country.com.

265 ■ WXFL-TV - 5
525 E Tennessee St.
Florence, AL 35630
Phone: (256)764-8170
Email: news@wbcf.com

Founded: 1986. **URL:** http://www.wbcf.com.

FOLEY

SC AL. Baldwin Co. 30 mi. SE of Mobile. Fertilizer factory. Potatoes.

266 ■ Riviera Utilities Cable TV
413 E Laurel Ave.
Foley, AL 36535
Phone: (251)943-5001

Owner: Utilities Board of the City of Foley, 413 E Laurel Ave., Foley, AL 36535, Ph: (251)943-5001, Fax: (251)943-5275. **Founded:** 1982. **Cities Served:** subscribing households 6,675. **Mailing address:** PO Box 2050, Foley, AL 36536. **URL:** http://www.rivierautilities.com.

267 ■ WHEP-AM - 1310
PO Box 1747
Foley, AL 36536
Phone: (251)943-7131

Format: News; Sports; Talk. **Networks:** CNN Radio; Westwood One Radio. **Owner:** Stewart Broadcasting Co., Inc. **Founded:** May 31, 1953. **Operating Hours**: 6 a.m.-6 p.m.; 10% network, 90% local. **ADI**: Mobile, AL-Pensacola, FL. **Wattage**: 1,000. **Ad Rates:** $6.50-7 for 30 seconds; $6.75-7.15 for 60 seconds. **URL:** http://www.whep1310.com.

FORT PAYNE

NE AL. DeKalb Co. 32 mi. N. of Gadsden. Manufactures office furniture, steel fabricators. Pine timber. Agriculture. Poultry.

268 ■ Times-Journal
Fort Payne Newspapers Inc.
811 Greenhill Blvd. NW
Fort Payne, AL 35967
Phone: (256)845-2550
Fax: (256)845-7459
Publisher's E-mail: news@times-journal.com

Community newspaper. **Founded:** 1878. **Freq:** 5/week. **Print Method:** Offset. **Cols./Page:** 6. **Col. Width:** 26 nonpareils. **Col. Depth:** 301 agate lines. **Key Personnel:** David Clemons, President, Publisher. **Subscription Rates:** $98 By mail 1 year subscription; $120 Out of state 1 year subscription; $64.50 By mail 6 months subscription; $76.50 Out of state 6 months subscription; $35 By mail 3 months subscription; $54 Out of state 3 months subscription. **URL:** http://times-journal.com. **Formerly**: Northeast Alabamian Shopping News. **Ad Rates:** BW $1,161; 4C $1,351; PCI $9. **Remarks:** Accepts advertising. **Circ:** Combined ♦**4251**.

269 ■ WFPA-AM - 1400
204 6th St. SW
Fort Payne, AL 35967
Phone: (256)458-4028

Format: Public Radio. **Owner:** Dekalb Co. Community Radio, Inc., at above address. **Operating Hours:** Continuous. **Wattage:** 1,000. **Ad Rates:** , Advertising rate varies with different packages.

GADSDEN

NE AL. Etowah Co. On Coosa River, 60 mi. NE of Birmingham. Tourist attraction, Noccalula Falls. Hub of trade and healthcare for NE Alabama. Steel mill. High tech engineering, tooling, fabrication and manufacturing. Tire manufacturing.

270 ■ Gadsden Times
The Gadsden Times
401 Locust St.
Gadsden, AL 35901-3737
Phone: (256)549-2000
Fax: (256)549-2105
Publisher's E-mail: photo@gmnews.com

General newspaper. **Freq:** Daily (morn.). **Print Method:** Offset. **Cols./Page:** 6. **Col. Width:** 2 1/16 inches. **Col. Depth:** 21 1/2 inches. **Key Personnel:** Glen Porter, Publisher, phone: (205)549-2070; John Chapman, Manager, Circulation. **Subscription Rates:** $15.95 Individuals monthly, print and online; $6.95 Individuals monthly, online (Monday - Friday, weekend or Sunday-only print subscription, can add a digital subscription.); $9.95 Individuals monthly, online (Full access to websites, mobile sites and tablet apps). **URL:** http://www.gadsdentimes.com. **Mailing address:** PO Box 188, Gadsden, AL 35902. **Ad Rates:** BW $2322; 4C $2822; SAU $18. **Remarks:** Accepts advertising. **Circ:** Mon.-Sat. ★**22455**, Sun. ★**23246**.

271 ■ WAAX-AM - 570
6510 Whorton Bend Rd.
Gadsden, AL 35901
Phone: (256)546-6397
Fax: (256)543-8777

Format: Talk; News. **Owner:** iHeartMedia Inc., 200 E Basse Rd., San Antonio, TX 78209, Ph: (210)832-3314. **Operating Hours:** Continuous. **ADI**: Birmingham (Gadsden), AL. **Key Personnel:** Jason Mack, Prog. Dir., jasonmack@iheartmedia.com. **Wattage**: 5,000. **Ad Rates:** Advertising accepted; rates available upon request. **URL:** http://www.waax570.com/main.html.

272 ■ WJBY-AM - 930
301 N 12th St.
Gadsden, AL 35901

Format: Classic Rock; Oldies; Information. **Owner:** Hinton Mitchem, Hwy.431 Albertsville, Albertville, AL 35950, Fax: (205)878-1631. **Founded:** 1926. **Operating Hours**: 5:30 a.m.-10 p.m. **Key Personnel:** Mike Hooks, Music Dir., Program Mgr.; Hinton Mitchem, President, hm@wjby.com. **Wattage**: 5,000 KW. **Ad Rates:** $4 for 10 seconds; $8-14 for 30 seconds; $10-16 for 60 seconds. **URL:** http://www.jeffbeckmedia.com/radio-stations/wgad-930-am.

273 ■ WJXS-TV - 24
2111 Hwy 78 E Ste. 1
Anniston, AL 36207
Phone: (256)831-4624

Owner: Alabama Heritage Communications L.L.C., 92 Edgewater Ct., Anniston, AL 36207. **Key Personnel:** Mickey Shadrix, Sports Dir., Prog. Dir., mshadix@tv24.tv. **Mailing address:** PO Box 3248, Oxford, AL 36203. **URL:** http://www.tv24.tv.

274 ■ WMGJ-AM - 1240
815 Tuscaloosa Ave.
Gadsden, AL 35901
Phone: (256)546-4434
Fax: (256)546-9645

Format: Urban Contemporary. **Operating Hours**: Continuous. **Key Personnel:** David Lawson, Operations Mgr. **Ad Rates:** Advertising accepted; rates available upon request. **URL:** http://wmgjam.com.

275 ■ WSGN-FM
1001 George Wallace Dr.
Gadsden, AL 35902-0227
Phone: (205)549-8439
Fax: (205)549-8404

Format: Educational; Classical; Information. **Networks:** National Public Radio (NPR); Public Radio International (PRI). **Owner:** Gadsden State Community College, 1801 Coleman Rd., Anniston, AL 36207. **Founded:** 1975. **Formerly**: WEXP. **Key Personnel:** Neil D. Mullin, Gen. Mgr., nmullin@gadsdenst.ate.edu. **Ad Rates:** Accepts Advertising.

276 ■ WTJP-TV - 60
313 Rosedale Ave.
Gadsden, AL 35901-5361
Email: cr@tbn.org

Format: Religious; Public Radio. **Owner:** Trinity Broadcasting Network Inc., PO Box A, Santa Ana, CA 92711, Ph: (714)832-2950, Free: 888-731-1000. **Operating Hours**: Continuous; 97% network, 3% local. **ADI**: Birmingham (Gadsden), AL. **Key Personnel:** Gary Hodges, Contact. **Ad Rates:** Noncommercial. **URL:** http://www.tbn.org.

GARDENDALE

C. AL. Jefferson Co. 10 mi. NE of Birmingham.

277 ■ The North Jefferson News
Community Newspaper Holdings Inc.
1110 Main St.
Gardendale, AL 35071
Phone: (205)631-8716
Fax: (205)631-9902
Publication E-mail: newsroom@njeffersonnews.com

Community newspaper. **Freq:** Weekly (Thurs.). **Print Method:** Offset. Accepts mats. **Cols./Page:** 6. **Col. Width:** 22 nonpareils. **Col. Depth:** 301 agate lines. **Key Personnel:** Melanie Patterson, Editor, phone: (205)631-8716; Becky Johnson, Director, Advertising. **Subscription Rates:** $25 By mail; $22.50 By mail seniors; $39 Out of country. **URL:** http://www.njeffersonnews.com. **Mailing address:** PO Box 849, Gardendale, AL 35071. **Remarks:** Accepts advertising. **Circ:** (Not Reported).

GENEVA

SE AL. Geneva Co. On Choctawhatchee River, 33 mi. SW of Dothan. Manufactures textiles, aluminum registers, cotton goods, veneer. Timber. Agriculture. Soybeans, peanuts, corn, cattle, hogs, cotton.

278 ■ WGEA-AM - 1150
605 W Camellia Ave.
Geneva, AL 36340
Phone: (334)684-7079
Fax: (334)684-7079
Format: Country; Talk; Southern Gospel. **Networks:** USA Radio; Precision Racing. **Founded:** 1953. **Operating Hours:** 6 a.m.-5 p.m. **Key Personnel:** Doc Parker, Gen. Mgr. **Wattage:** 1,000. **Ad Rates:** $3 for 30 seconds; $4 for 60 seconds. **URL:** http://www.wgea.us/component/content/article/default/geneva-church-of-christ-banner.

GILBERTOWN

279 ■ Choctaw Sun-Advocate
The Choctaw Sun-Advocate
PO Box 269
Gilbertown, AL 36908
Phone: (251)843-6397
Fax: (251)843-3233
Publisher's E-mail: choctawsun@millry.net
Community newspaper. **Freq:** Weekly (Thurs.). **Print Method:** Offset. **Trim Size:** 13 x 21. **Cols./Page:** 6. **Col. Width:** 25 nonpareils. **Col. Depth:** 301 agate lines. **Key Personnel:** Dee Ann Campbell, Publisher, Managing Editor. **USPS:** 106-200. **Subscription Rates:** $30 Individuals print only; $40 Individuals print and e-edition; $20 Individuals senior citizen (print only); $50 Out of state print; $35 Out of state online. **URL:** http://choctawsun.com. **Formed by the merger of:** Choctaw Sun; Choctaw Advocate. **Ad Rates:** BW $441; PCI $4. **Remarks:** Accepts advertising. **Circ:** ‡5100.

GREENVILLE

S. AL. Butler Co. 44 mi. SW of Montgomery. Manufactures textiles, fertilizer, automobile seat belts, gloves, store fixtures, generators, air conditioners, electrical connectors, heavy logging equipments, plywood. Lumber, feed mills; cotton gins. Pecan shelling. Timber. Agriculture. Cotton, strawberries.

280 ■ WGYV-AM - 1380
PO Box 585
Greenville, AL 36037
Phone: (334)382-5444
Operating Hours: Sunrise to sunset. **Wattage:** 1,000 ERP.

281 ■ WKXK-FM
Manningham Rd., At I-65
Greenville, AL 36037
Phone: (334)382-6555
Fax: (334)382-7770
Format: Country. **Networks:** American Urban Radio; Mutual Broadcasting System. **Founded:** 1989. **Formerly:** WXKO-FM. **Wattage:** 41,000 ERP.

282 ■ WKXN-FM - 95.9
PO Box 369
Greenville, AL 36037
Phone: (334)382-6555
Fax: (334)382-7770
Format: Urban Contemporary. **Networks:** Alabama Radio (ALANET); American Urban Radio. **Owner:** Autaugaville Radio, Inc., at above address. **Founded:** 1977. **Operating Hours:** Continuous. **Key Personnel:** Chelli Merrett, Traffic Mgr., Office Mgr., chelli@wkxn.com; Roscoe Miller, Dir. of Programs. **Wattage:** 4,000. **Ad Rates:** Noncommercial. $10-25 for 30 seconds; $12-30 for 60 seconds.

283 ■ WQZX-FM - 94.3
205 W Commerce St.
Greenville, AL 36037-2217
Phone: (334)382-6633
Format: Country; Sports; News. **Networks:** ABC; AP. **Owner:** Haynes Broadcasting Inc. **Founded:** 1985. **Operating Hours:** Continuous; 60% network, 40% local. **Key Personnel:** Kyle Haynes, Sales Mgr., kyle@q94.net; Kim Herman, Bus. Mgr., Mgr. of Admin., kim@q94.net; Mark Ritchie, Program Mgr., programmingmark@q94.net. **Wattage:** 6,000. **Ad Rates:** $6.60-9.60 for 30 seconds; $8.95-12.15 for 60 seconds. **URL:** http://www.q94.net.

GROVE HILL

SW AL. Clarke Co. 50 mi. N. of Mobile.

284 ■ Clarke County Democrat
Clarke County Democrat
PO Box 39
Grove Hill, AL 36451
Phone: (251)275-3375
Fax: (251)275-3060
Publisher's E-mail: clarkecountydem@tds.net
Community newspaper. **Freq:** Weekly. **Subscription Rates:** $52 Individuals online. **URL:** http://www.clarkecountydemocrat.com. **Ad Rates:** BW $645; PCI $3.80. **Remarks:** Accepts advertising. **Circ:** ‡5000.

GULF SHORES

SW AL. Baldwin Co. 7 mi. SW of Orange Beach. Residential.

285 ■ ConventionSouth
Convention South Magazine
2001 W 1st St.
Gulf Shores, AL 36542-4447
Phone: (251)968-5300
Fax: (251)968-2033
Free: 800-968-0712
Publisher's E-mail: info@conventionsouth.com
Trade magazine for planners of meetings, conferences, seminars, and related events in the southern U.S. **Freq:** Monthly. **Print Method:** Web offset. **Trim Size:** 10 3/8 x 12 3/4. **Cols./Page:** 4. **Col. Width:** 2 3/8 inches. **Key Personnel:** J. Talty O'Connor, President, Publisher; Marlane A. Bundock, Associate Publisher; Ashley Brokowsky, Manager, Circulation, phone: (251)968-6716. **ISSN:** 1074--0627 (print). **URL:** http://www.conventionsouth.com. **Mailing address:** PO Box 2267, Gulf Shores, AL 36547. **Ad Rates:** BW $2,915; 4C $3,900. **Remarks:** Accepts advertising. **Circ:** (Not Reported).

286 ■ Crossties
Covey Communications Corp.
2001 W First St.
Gulf Shores, AL 36542
Phone: (251)968-5300
Free: 800-968-0712
Publisher's E-mail: info@sportseventsmagazine.com
Trade magazine for users and producers of treated wood crossties. **Freq:** Bimonthly. **Print Method:** Sheetfed offset. **Trim Size:** 8 1/2 x 11. **Cols./Page:** 3. **Col. Width:** 2 3/8 inches. **Key Personnel:** Kristen S. McIntosh, Editor. **ISSN:** 0097--4536 (print). **URL:** http://www.rta.org/crossties-magazine. **Formerly:** Crosstie Bulletin. **Mailing address:** PO Box 2267, Gulf Shores, AL 36547. **Ad Rates:** BW $3,580; 4C $4,650. **Remarks:** Accepts advertising. **Circ:** Controlled ‡3600.

287 ■ Islander
Gulf Coast Newspaper
128 Cove Ave.
Gulf Shores, AL 36547
Phone: (251)968-6414
Fax: (251)968-5233
Publisher's E-mail: islander@gulfcoastnewspapers.com
Community newspaper. **Founded:** 1977. **Freq:** Biweekly. **Key Personnel:** John Mullen, Editor; Dale Jones, Writer. **Subscription Rates:** $37.25 Individuals. **URL:** http://www.gulfcoastnewstoday.com/the_islander/. **Mailing address:** PO Box 1128, Gulf Shores, AL 36547. **Ad Rates:** GLR $3.02; PCI $13.95. **Remarks:** Accepts advertising. **Circ:** 4,000.

288 ■ WCSN-FM
PO Box 1919
Gulf Shores, AL 36547
Phone: (251)967-1057
Fax: (251)967-1050
Email: sunny105@gulftel.com
Format: News; Talk. **Owner:** Gulf Coast Broadcasting Co., Inc., 26946 Martinique Dr., Orange Beach, AL 36561, Ph: (251)981-7671, Fax: (251)981-7680. **Founded:** Sept. 15, 2006. **Wattage:** 5,000 ERP. **Ad Rates:** $10 for 30 seconds; $12 for 60 seconds. **URL:** http://sunny1057.com.

GUNTERSVILLE

N. AL. Marshall Co. On southern point of Tennesse River, 35 mi. SE of Huntsville. Recreation and tourist center. Manufactures high tech components, disposable clothing.

289 ■ The Advertiser-Gleam
The Advertiser-Gleam
2218 Taylor St.
Guntersville, AL 35976
Publisher's E-mail: news@advertisergleam.com
Community newspaper. **Freq:** Semiweekly (Wed. and Sat.). **Print Method:** Offset. **Trim Size:** 13 x 21 1/2. **Cols./Page:** 6. **Col. Width:** 2 1/16 inches. **Col. Depth:** 21 1/2 inches. **Subscription Rates:** $30 Individuals 1 year subscription of print + digital edition; $38 Individuals 1 year subscription of digital edition; $55 Out of area 1 year subscription of print + digital; $64 Out of state 1 year subscription of print + digital. **Mailing address:** PO Box 190, Guntersville, AL 35976. **Ad Rates:** 4C $320; SAU $6.15; PCI $6.30. **Remarks:** Accepts advertising. **Circ:** Paid ★**10954**.

290 ■ WGSV-AM
PO Box 220
Guntersville, AL 35976-0221
Phone: (256)582-8131
Format: Adult Contemporary. **Networks:** ABC. **Owner:** Guntersville Broadcasting Co., at above address. **Founded:** 1950. **Key Personnel:** Kerry Jackson, Operations Mgr. **Wattage:** 1,000 Day; 124 Night.

291 ■ WJIA-FM - 88.5
5025 Spring Creek Dr.
Guntersville, AL 35976
Phone: (256)505-0885
Format: Country; Contemporary Christian; Gospel. **Owner:** Lake City Educational Broadcasting Inc., 5025 Spring Creek Dr., Guntersville, AL 35976, Ph: (256)505-0885. **Key Personnel:** Mary Cody, Contact; Kelly Beason, Contact. **Wattage:** 2,200 ERP V. **Ad Rates:** Accepts Advertising. **URL:** http://www.wjia885.com.

292 ■ WTWX-FM
PO Box 220
Guntersville, AL 35976-0221
Phone: (256)582-4946
Fax: (256)582-4347
Format: Country. **Networks:** ABC. **Owner:** Guntersville Broadcasting Co., at above address. **Founded:** 1969. **Wattage:** 10,500 ERP.

HALEYVILLE

N. AL. Winston Co. 40 mi. S. of Florence. Cotton, lumber and grist mills. Manufactures textiles, furniture, mobile homes, truck trailers. Timber. Hatcheries. Agriculture. Cotton, cattle.

293 ■ Northwest Alabamian
Northwest Alabamian
PO Box 430
Haleyville, AL 35565
Phone: (205)486-9461
Community newspaper. **Freq:** Semiweekly (Wed. and Sat.). **Print Method:** Offset. **Trim Size:** 13 3/4 x 22 1/2. **Cols./Page:** 6. **Col. Width:** 25 nonpareils. **Col. Depth:** 301 agate lines. **Key Personnel:** Roger Carden, Director, Advertising; Horace Moore, Publisher; Melica Allen, Managing Editor. **Subscription Rates:** $34.50 Individuals Winston County only; $38.50 Individuals adjoining counties; $30 Individuals senior; $50.50 Out of area; $26 Individuals 6 months subscription, Winston County only; $28 Individuals 6 months subscription, adjoining counties; $22 Individuals 6 months subscription, senior; $32 Out of area 6 months subscription. **Remarks:** Adver-

Circulation: ★ = AAM; △ or • = BPA; ♦ = CAC; ❑ = VAC; ⊕ = PO Statement; ‡ = Publisher's Report; Boldface figures = sworn; Light figures = estimated.

tising accepted; rates available upon request. **Circ:** ‡7200.

294 ■ The Times-Record
Northwest Alabamian
PO Box 430
Haleyville, AL 35565
Phone: (205)486-9461
Local newspaper. **Founded:** Aug. 24, 1977. **Freq:** Weekly (Wed.). **Print Method:** Offset. **Trim Size:** 13 x 21. **Cols./Page:** 6. **Col. Width:** 2 1/16 inches. **Col. Depth:** 21 inches. **Key Personnel:** Robert Long, Managing Editor, phone: (207)504-8233; James McCarthy, Editor, phone: (207)504-8231; Chris P. Miles, Publisher, phone: (207)504-8202. **USPS:** 390-130. **Subscription Rates:** $130.05 Individuals 1 year home subscription; $115.50 By mail 1 year mail subscription, Armed Forces; $129.10 By mail 1 year mail subscription, Maine & U.S.; $89.99 Individuals 1 year online subscription. **URL:** http://www.timesrecord.com/; http://www.mytrpaper.com. **Ad Rates:** GLR $.32; BW $504; PCI $4.50. **Remarks:** Accepts advertising. **Circ:** Mon.-Thurs. ★**9800**, Fri. ★**11573**.

295 ■ WJBB-AM - 1230
PO Box 370
Haleyville, AL 35565
Phone: (205)486-2277
Fax: (205)486-3905
Email: info@wjbb.cjb.net
Format: News; Southern Gospel. **Networks:** Mutual Broadcasting System. **Owner:** Haleyville Broadcasting Co., Inc., 807 Highway 13, Haleyville, AL 35565, Ph: (205)486-2277. **Founded:** 1949. **Operating Hours**: 5 a.m.-midnight; 10% network, 90% local. **ADI**: Birmingham (Gadsden), AL. **Key Personnel:** Brian Walker, Operations Mgr., bwalker@wjbb.cjb.net; Aubrey Haynes, Sales Mgr., ahaynes@wjbb.cjb.net; Robert Wakefield, Dir. of Programs, rwakefield@wjbb.cjb.net. **Wattage**: 1,000. **Ad Rates:** $5-6.30 for 30 seconds; $8-9 for 60 seconds. WJBB-FM.

296 ■ WJBB-FM - 92.7
PO Box 370
Haleyville, AL 35565
Phone: (205)486-2277
Fax: (205)486-3905
Email: info@wjbb.cjb.net
Format: Country. **Networks:** Mutual Broadcasting System. **Owner:** Haleyville Broadcasting Co., Inc., 807 Highway 13, Haleyville, AL 35565, Ph: (205)486-2277. **Founded:** 1979. **Operating Hours**: 5 a.m.-midnight; 5% network, 95% local. **Key Personnel:** Aubrey Haynes, Sales Mgr., ahaynes@wjbb.cjb.net. **Wattage**: 4,000. **Ad Rates:** $6.50-7.20 for 30 seconds; $9.25-10.25 for 60 seconds. WJBB-AM. **URL:** http://www.angelfire.com/al4/wjbb/index1.html.

HAMILTON

NW AL. Marion Co. 4 mi. S. of Weston. Residential.

297 ■ WERH-AM - 970
PO Box 1119
Hamilton, AL 35570
Phone: (205)921-3481
Fax: (205)921-7187
Format: Eclectic. **Owner:** Kate F. Fite. **Founded:** 1950. **Operating Hours**: Sunrise-sunset. **Wattage**: 5,000. **Ad Rates:** Advertising accepted; rates available upon request. Combined advertising rates available with WERH-FM.

HARTSELLE

N. AL. Morgan Co. 12 mi. S. of Decatur. Manufactures air conditioner compressors, insulated electrical wire, electronics components, wood products, textiles, doors, metal cable reels, seat cushions. Timber. Agriculture. Cotton, soybeans, cattle, poultry.

298 ■ Hartselle Enquirer
Hartselle Newspapers L.L.C.
PO Box 929
Hartselle, AL 35640-0929
Community newspaper. **Freq:** Weekly (Thurs.). **Print Method:** Offset. **Trim Size:** 13 1/2 x 21 1/2. **Cols./Page:** 6. **Col. Width:** 12 picas. **Col. Depth:** 21.5 picas. **Key Personnel:** Randy Garrison, President, Publisher; Brent Maze, Managing Editor. **USPS:** 236-380. **Subscription Rates:** $39 Individuals /year (in county); $78 Individuals 2 years (in county); $78 Out of state /year. **URL:** http://www.hartselleenquirer.com. **Remarks:** Accepts advertising. **Circ:** (Not Reported).

299 ■ Hartselle Shopping Guide
Hartselle Newspapers L.L.C.
407 W Chestnut St.
Hartselle, AL 35640
Phone: (256)773-6566
Fax: (256)773-1953
Shopper. **Freq:** Weekly. **Print Method:** Offset. **Cols./Page:** 6. **Col. Width:** 12 picas. **Col. Depth:** 21 1/2 inches. **Key Personnel:** Leada DeVaney, Publisher. **Ad Rates:** GLR $6; BW $716; 4C $853; SAU $6.50; PCI $7.40. **Remarks:** Accepts advertising. **Circ:** Combined ‡5000.

WQAH-AM - See Priceville, AL

300 ■ WYAM-AM - 890
3002 Riley Rd.
Huntsville, AL 35801
Phone: (256)355-4567
Fax: (256)351-1234
Format: Hispanic. **Founded:** 1956. **Operating Hours**: Daytime. **ADI**: Huntsville-Decatur-Florence, AL. **Wattage**: 2,500. **Ad Rates:** $5 for 60 seconds. $5 for 60 seconds. Combined advertising rates available with WYAM TV56. **URL:** http://www.fccinfo.com.

301 ■ WYAM-FM - 106.1
809 N Sparkman St.
Hartselle, AL 35640
Phone: (205)351-2345
Format: Adult Contemporary. **Networks:** Satellite Music Network. **Owner:** Gene Newman, at above address. **Founded:** 1992. **Operating Hours**: Continuous. **Key Personnel:** Gene Newman, Gen. Mgr. **Wattage**: 6,000. **Ad Rates:** $60 for 60 seconds. WAJF-AM, WHRT-AM, and WJRA-FM.

HEFLIN

NE AL. Cleburne Co. 15 mi. E. of Anniston. Manufactures business forms, chenille, mica products, textiles. Saw and planning mills. Cotton gins. Yellow pine timber. Agriculture. Poultry, cotton, corn, hay.

302 ■ WPIL-FM - 91.7
256 Brockford Rd.
Heflin, AL 36264
Phone: (256)463-4226
Fax: (256)463-4232
Email: wpil@wpilfm.com
Format: Gospel; Country; Bluegrass. **URL:** http://www.wpilfm.com.

HIGDON

303 ■ WGNQ-AM - 1480
1237 County Road 295
Higdon, AL 35979
Fax: (914)730-9820
Free: 877-237-6259
Email: manager@wgnq.net
Format: Contemporary Christian. **Formerly**: WYMR-AM.

HOMEWOOD

304 ■ WBPT-FM - 106.9
301 Beacon Pkwy. W, Ste. 200
Homewood, AL 35209
Phone: (205)916-1100
Fax: (205)290-1061
Format: Classic Rock. **Owner:** Cox Radio Inc., 6205 Peachtree Dunwood Rd., Atlanta, GA 30328-4524, Ph: (678)645-0000, Fax: (678)645-5002. **Operating Hours**: Continuous. **Key Personnel:** Justin Ragland, Div. Mgr., justin.ragland@coxradio.com; Natalie Smith, Sales Mgr., natalie.smith@summitmediacorp.com. **Ad Rates:** Advertising accepted; rates available upon request. **URL:** http://www.birminghamseagle.com.

305 ■ WNCB-FM - 97.3
301 Beacon Pky. W, Ste. 200
Homewood, AL 35209
Phone: (205)916-1100
Fax: (205)916-1150
Format: Country. **Owner:** Cox Radio Inc., 6205 Peachtree Dunwood Rd., Atlanta, GA 30328-4524, Ph: (678)645-0000, Fax: (678)645-5002. **Founded:** 1971. **Operating Hours**: Continuous; 100% local. **ADI**: Duluth, MN-Superior, WI. **Key Personnel:** Justin Ragland, Dir. of Mktg., Promotions Dir., justin.ragland@coxradio.com; Justin Case, Dir. of Programs, justin.case@coxradio.com; David Walls, Gen. Sales Mgr., david.walls@coxradio.com. **Wattage**: 2,400. **Ad Rates:** Advertising accepted; rates available upon request.

306 ■ WUHT-FM - 107.7
244 Goodwin Crest Dr., No. 300
Homewood, AL 35209
Phone: (205)945-4646
Email: hertisene.riley@cumulus.com
Format: Blues. **Owner:** Citadel Broadcasting Corp., 7201 W Lake Mead Blvd., Ste. 400, Las Vegas, NV 89128-8366, Ph: (702)804-5200, Fax: (702)804-8250. **Operating Hours**: Continuous. **Ad Rates:** Advertising accepted; rates available upon request. **URL:** http://www.hot1077radio.com.

307 ■ WZZK-FM - 104.7
301 Beacon Pky. W, Ste. 200
Homewood, AL 35209
Phone: (205)916-1100
Fax: (205)290-1061
Free: 866-998-1047
Format: Contemporary Country. **Simulcasts:** WZZK-AM. **Owner:** Cox Radio Inc., 6205 Peachtree Dunwood Rd., Atlanta, GA 30328-4524, Ph: (678)645-0000, Fax: (678)645-5002. **Founded:** 1948. **Operating Hours**: Continuous. **ADI**: Birmingham (Gadsden), AL. **Key Personnel:** Justin Case, Dir. of Programs, justin.case@coxradio.com; David Walls, Sales Mgr., david.walls@coxradio.com; Dave Dunaway, Prog. Dir., Dave@wzzk.com; Justin Ragland, Promotions Mgr., Justin.Ragland@summitmediacorp.com. **Wattage**: 100,000. **Ad Rates:** Noncommercial. **URL:** http://www.wzzk.com.

HOOVER

308 ■ Journal of School Safety
National Association of School Resource Officers
2020 Valleydale Rd., Ste. 207A
Hoover, AL 35244-4803
Phone: (205)739-6060
Fax: (205)536-9255
Free: 888-316-2776
Journal promoting a proper relationship between law enforcement officers and America's youth and providing safe and secure learning environments. **Freq:** Quarterly. **Subscription Rates:** Included in membership. **Remarks:** Advertising not accepted. **Circ:** (Not Reported).

HUNTSVILLE

N. AL. Madison Co. 85 mi. N. of Birmingham. Madison Co. (N). 85 m N of Birmingham. Manufactures cotton goods, compact audio discs, sheet metal products, flags, missiles, polyvinyl chloride film, ballistic missile fuel, electronic components, cottonseed oil, veneer, stoves, electric heaters, wire staples, farm implements, abrasives, toys, telephone instruments, auto tires, airplane glass, air handling equipment, modular buildings, hardware, space metals, aircraft instruments, perfumes, machine tools & parts, plastics, fiberglass bathroom fixtures, refrigeration equipment, electric generating units. Timber. Agriculture.

309 ■ The Exponent
University of Alabama in Huntsville
301 Sparkman Dr.
Huntsville, AL 35899
Phone: (256)824-2773
Free: 800-UAH-CALL
Publication E-mail: editor@exponent.uah.edu
Collegiate magazine. **Founded:** 1966. **Freq:** Weekly (Thurs.) during the school year. **Print Method:** Offset. **Cols./Page:** 4. **Col. Width:** 2 1/4 inches. **Col. Depth:** 15 inches. **Key Personnel:** Joseph Terrell, Editor-in-Chief; Heather Evans, Editor; Johnson Clay, Distribution Manager, Editor; Madison Young, Managing Editor; Patrick Collins, Editor; Tammy Smith, Editor. **URL:** http://uah.edu. **Formerly**: Slaton Press. **Ad Rates:** BW $750; 4C $1,300. **Remarks:** Accepts advertising. **Circ:** Non-paid 3500.

310 ■ The Huntsville Times
Alabama Media Group
200 Westside Sq., Ste. 100
Huntsville, AL 35801

Phone: (256)532-4000
Free: 800-239-5271

General newspaper. **Freq:** 3/week. **Print Method:** Offset. **Trim Size:** 13 1/2 x 21 1/4. **Cols./Page:** 6. **Col. Width:** 12 picas. **Col. Depth:** 21 inches. **USPS:** 254-640. **Online:** Alabama Media Group Alabama Media Group. **Alt. Formats:** Handheld. **URL:** http://member.al.com/index.aspx?sitecode=HT; http://www.alabamamediagroup.com/about/brands. **Ad Rates:** BW $4207; 4C $4682.14; SAU $33.39. **Remarks:** Accepts advertising. **Circ:** Mon.-Fri. ★**53194**, Sun. ★**71786**, Sat. 50981.

311 ■ Journal of Cave and Karst Studies
National Speleological Society
6001 Pulaski Pke.
Huntsville, AL 35810-1122
Phone: (256)852-1300
Publication E-mail: nss@caves.org

Freq: 3/year. **Key Personnel:** Malcolm S. Field, Editor. **ISSN:** 1090--6924 (print). **Subscription Rates:** $45 Individuals /year; $90 Individuals two years; $135 Individuals three years. **URL:** http://caves.org/pub/journal. **Remarks:** Accepts advertising. **Circ:** (Not Reported).

312 ■ Poem
Huntsville Literary Association
PO Box 919
Huntsville, AL 35804
Phone: (256)534-9964

Scholarly magazine of poetry. **Freq:** Semiannual spring and fall. **Key Personnel:** Rebecca Harbou Jones, Editor; Nancy Williams, Advisor, Board Member. **ISSN:** 0032--1885 (print). **Subscription Rates:** $20 Out of area /year; $10 Single issue /issue; $7 Single issue sample copy of back issue. **URL:** http://hlahsv.org/POEM. **Remarks:** Advertising not accepted. **Circ:** 400.

313 ■ Predator & Prey
JNE Publishing Inc.
PO Box 5647
Huntsville, AL 35814

Magazine for hunters. **Key Personnel:** Bill Bynum, Editor-in-Chief; Paula Buccellato, Office Manager. **Circ:** (Not Reported).

314 ■ Southwest Philosophy Review: The Journal of the Southwestern Philosophical Society
Southwestern Philosophical Society
c/o Deborah K. Heikes, Secretary-Treasurer
University of Alabama in Huntsville
332 Morton Hall
Huntsville, AL 35899
Phone: (256)824-2335

Professional journal covering philosophy. **Freq:** Semiannual. **Trim Size:** 6 x 9. **Cols./Page:** 1. **Col. Width:** 6 inches. **Col. Depth:** 9 inches. **Key Personnel:** Todd M. Stewart, Jr., Editor. **ISSN:** 0897--2346 (print); **EISSN:** 2154--1116 (electronic). **Subscription Rates:** $100 Institutions online. **URL:** http://www.southwesternphilosophical.org/publications. **Formerly:** Southwestcan Journal of Philosophy. **Remarks:** Advertising not accepted. **Circ:** Paid 250.

315 ■ UAH Magazine
University of Alabama in Huntsville
301 Sparkman Dr.
Huntsville, AL 35899
Phone: (256)824-2773
Free: 800-UAH-CALL
Publication E-mail: omc@uah.edu

Alumni and university interest magazine. **Freq:** Semiannual. **Print Method:** Offset. **Trim Size:** 81/2 x 11. **Cols./Page:** 3. **URL:** http://www.uah.edu/magazine. **Also known as:** The University of Alabama in Huntsville Magazine. **Remarks:** Advertising not accepted. **Circ:** ‡19000.

316 ■ Mediacom Communications Corp.
123 Ware Dr.
Huntsville, AL 35811
Free: 800-239-8411

Key Personnel: Rocco B. Commisso, CEO, Chairman; Mark E. Stephan, CFO. **Cities Served:** 80 channels. **URL:** http://www.mediacomcable.com.

317 ■ WAAY-TV - 31
1000 Monte Sano Blvd.
Huntsville, AL 35801
Phone: (256)533-3131

Format: News; Sports. **Networks:** ABC. **Operating Hours:** Continuous. **ADI:** Huntsville-Decatur-Florence, AL. **Wattage:** 468,000 ERP H. **Ad Rates:** Advertising accepted; rates available upon request. **URL:** http://www.waaytv.com.

318 ■ WAFF-TV - 48
1414 N Memorial Pky.
Huntsville, AL 35801
Phone: (256)533-4848
Fax: (256)533-1337
Email: pix@waff.com

Format: Commercial TV. **Networks:** NBC. **Owner:** Raycom Media Inc., 201 Monroe St., RSA Twr., 20th Fl., Montgomery, AL 36104-3731, Ph: (334)206-1400. **Founded:** 1954. **Formerly:** WYUR-TV. **Operating Hours:** Continuous. **ADI:** Huntsville-Decatur-Florence, AL. **Key Personnel:** Vanessa Oubre, Gen. Mgr., voubre@waff.com. **Ad Rates:** Advertising accepted; rates available upon request. **URL:** http://www.waff.com.

319 ■ WAHR-FM - 99.1
1555 The Boardwalk, Ste. 1
Huntsville, AL 35816
Phone: (256)534-9900

Format: Adult Contemporary. **Networks:** NBC. **Founded:** 1959. **Operating Hours:** Continuous. **ADI:** Huntsville-Decatur-Florence, AL. **Key Personnel:** Jimbo Wood. **Wattage:** 100,000. **Ad Rates:** $35-125 for 30 seconds; for 60 seconds. **URL:** http://www.star99.fm.

320 ■ WAMY-TV - 8
1309 N Memorial Pky.
Huntsville, AL 35801
Phone: (256)533-5454
URL: http://www.fox54.com.

321 ■ WAYH-FM - 88.1
9582 Madison Blvd., No. 8
Madison, AL 35758
Phone: (256)837-9293
Free: 888-239-2936

Format: Contemporary Christian. **Owner:** WAY-FM Media Group Inc., 5540 Tech Center Dr., Ste. 200, Colorado Springs, CO 80919, Ph: (719)533-0300. **Founded:** 1987. **Key Personnel:** Thom Ewing, Gen. Mgr.; Lisa Shelton, Dir. of Dev.; Dusty Rhodes, Sr. VP. **URL:** http://www.wayfm.com.

322 ■ WDJL-AM - 1000
603 Governors Dr.
Huntsville, AL 35801
Phone: (256)852-1223
Fax: (256)852-1900

Format: Urban Contemporary; Gospel. **Networks:** Independent. **Founded:** 1968. **Formerly:** WTAK-AM; WVOV-AM. **Operating Hours:** Sunrise-sunset; 100% local. **ADI:** Huntsville-Decatur-Florence, AL. **Wattage:** 10,000. **Ad Rates:** $10 for 30 seconds. **URL:** http://www.ontheradio.net/radiostations/wdjlam.aspx.

323 ■ WEUP-AM - 1600
2609 Jordan Ln. NW
Huntsville, AL 35816
Phone: (205)837-9387
Fax: (205)837-9404

Format: Urban Contemporary. **Networks:** American Urban Radio. **Founded:** 1958. **Operating Hours:** Continuous. **ADI:** Huntsville-Decatur-Florence, AL. **Key Personnel:** Dee Handley, Station Mgr.; Virginia Caples, Contact; Virginia Caples, Contact; Hundley Batts, Contact; Steve Murry, Contact. **Wattage:** 5,000 day; 500 night. **Ad Rates:** $18-56 for 30 seconds; $22-70 for 60 seconds. **URL:** http://www.weupam.com/page.php?page_id=71.

324 ■ WEUP-FM - 103.1
2609 Jordan Ln. NW
Huntsville, AL 35816
Phone: (256)837-9387
Fax: (256)837-9404

Format: Hip Hop; Blues. **ADI:** Huntsville-Decatur-Florence, AL. **Wattage:** 25,000. **URL:** http://www.103weup.com.

325 ■ WEUV-AM - 1700
2609 Jordan Ln. NW
Huntsville, AL 35816
Phone: (256)837-9387
Fax: (256)837-9404

Format: Gospel. **Owner:** WEUP Radio, 2609 Jordan Ln. NW, Huntsville, AL 35816, Ph: (256)837-9387, Fax: (256)837-9404. **ADI:** Huntsville-Decatur-Florence, AL. **Wattage:** 10,000. **URL:** http://www.weupam.com/upload/EEOPUBLICFILEREPORT2014.pdf.

326 ■ WEUZ-FM - 92.1
2609 Jordan Ln. NW
Huntsville, AL 35816
Phone: (256)837-9387
Fax: (256)837-9404

Format: Urban Contemporary. **Owner:** WEUP Radio, 2609 Jordan Ln. NW, Huntsville, AL 35816, Ph: (256)837-9387, Fax: (256)837-9404. **ADI:** Huntsville-Decatur-Florence, AL. **Wattage:** 6,000. **URL:** http://www.103weup.com.

327 ■ WHDF-TV - 15
200 Andrew Jackson Way
Huntsville, AL 35801
Phone: (256)536-1550

Owner: Lockwood Broadcast Group, 3914 Wistar Rd., Richmond, VA 23228, Ph: (804)672-6565, Fax: (804)672-6571. **Founded:** 1957. **Key Personnel:** Dale Stafford, Gen. Mgr., dstafford@thevalleyscw.tv. **URL:** http://www.lbgtelevision.com.

WHIQ-Digital Channel 24 - See Huntsville

328 ■ WHIQ-Digital Channel 24 - 25
c/o Alabama Public Television
2112 11th Ave. S, Ste. 400
Huntsville, AL 35801
Phone: (205)328-8756
Fax: (205)251-2192
Free: 800-239-5233
Email: wwood@aptv.org

Format: Public TV. **Simulcasts:** WBIQ-TV. **Networks:** Public Broadcasting Service (PBS). **Owner:** Alabama Public Television, 2112 11th Ave. S, Birmingham, AL 35205, Ph: (205)328-8756, Fax: (205)251-2192, Free: 800-239-5233. **Founded:** 1967. **Operating Hours:** Continuous. **ADI:** Huntsville-Decatur-Florence, AL. **Key Personnel:** Rhonda Colvin, Producer, rcolvin@aptv.org. **Local Programs:** *For the Record.* **Wattage:** 1,225,000 ERP. **Ad Rates:** Noncommercial. **URL:** http://www.aptv.org.

329 ■ WHIY-AM - 1600
2609 Jordan Ln. NW
Huntsville, AL 35816
Phone: (256)837-9387
Fax: (256)837-9404

Format: News; Gospel; Information. **Owner:** Broadcast One, 1501 Dahlia St., Denver, CO 80220, Ph: (303)331-1730, Fax: (303)331-1729. **Founded:** 1963. **ADI:** Huntsville-Decatur-Florence, AL. **Key Personnel:** Virginia Caples, Owner. **Wattage:** 5,000 Day; 500 Night. **Ad Rates:** Accepts Advertising. **URL:** http://www.whiyam.com.

330 ■ WHNT-TV - 19
200 Holmes Ave.
Huntsville, AL 35801
Phone: (256)533-1919
Fax: (256)536-9468
Free: 800-533-8819
Email: hancock@whnt.com

Format: News. **Networks:** CBS. **Founded:** 1963. **Operating Hours:** Continuous. **Key Personnel:** Denise Vickers, VP, denise.vicker@whnt.com. **Ad Rates:** Advertising accepted; rates available upon request. **URL:** http://www.whnt.com.

331 ■ WJOU-FM - 90.1
7000 Adventist Blvd.
Huntsville, AL 35896
Phone: (256)722-9990
Fax: (256)837-7918
Email: wjou@oakwood.edu

Format: Religious. **Networks:** USA Radio. **Owner:** Oakwood University, 7000 Adventist Blvd. NW, Huntsville, AL 35896, Ph: (256)726-7000, Fax: (256)726-7154. **Founded:** 1979. **Formerly:** WOCG-FM. **Operating Hours:** Continuous; 10% network, 90% local. **ADI:**

Circulation: ★ = AAM; △ or • = BPA; ♦ = CAC; ❑ = VAC; ⊕ = PO Statement; ‡ = Publisher's Report; Boldface figures = sworn; Light figures = estimated.

Huntsville-Decatur-Florence, AL. **Key Personnel:** Victoria Miller, Gen. Mgr. **Wattage:** 25,000. **Ad Rates:** Noncommercial. **URL:** http://www.wjou.org.

332 ■ WLOR-AM
1555 The Boardwalk, Ste. 1
Huntsville, AL 35816
Phone: (256)536-1568
Fax: (256)536-4416
Format: Oldies. **Wattage**: 50,000 Day; 044 Night. **URL:** http://www.jammin1550.am.

333 ■ WLRH-FM - 89.3
UAH Campus
John Wright Dr.
Huntsville, AL 35899
Phone: (256)895-9574
Free: 800-239-9574
Format: Public Radio. **Networks:** National Public Radio (NPR). **Owner:** Alabama ETV Commission, at above address. **Founded:** 1976. **Operating Hours:** Continuous. **ADI**: Huntsville-Decatur-Florence, AL. **Wattage:** 100,000. **Ad Rates:** Noncommercial. **URL:** http://www.wlrh.org.

334 ■ WOWL-TV - 15
200 Andrew Jackson Way
Huntsville, AL 35801
Phone: (919)839-0300
Format: Commercial TV. **Networks:** NBC. **Founded:** 1957. **Operating Hours**: 6 a.m.-1 a.m.; 80% network, 20% local. **Key Personnel:** Thomas Shannon, Gen. Mgr., Contact; Verbon Jones, Gen. Sales Mgr.; Carol Strength, Bus. Mgr.; Debbie Summers, Traffic Mgr.; Tim Rovere, Chief Engineer; David Yancey, Operations Mgr.; David Hale, Comm. Aff. Dir., Promotions Mgr; Thomas Shannon, Contact. **Ad Rates:** $50-175 for 30 seconds. **URL:** http://www.lbgtelevision.com.

335 ■ WRSA-FM - 96.9
8402 Memorial Pky. S
Huntsville, AL 35802
Phone: (256)885-9797
Fax: (256)885-9796
Free: 888-503-4969
Email: studio@lite969.com
Owner: NCA, Inc., 287 Tel. Tower Rd., Laceys Spring, AL 35754, Ph: (205)498-5259. **Founded:** 1965. **ADI**: Huntsville-Decatur-Florence, AL. **Key Personnel:** Bonny O'Brien, News Dir., bonny@lite969.com. **Wattage**: 100,000 ERP. **Ad Rates:** $75-110 for 30 seconds; $95-140 for 60 seconds. **URL:** http://www.lite969.com/.

336 ■ WRTT-FM - 95.1
1555 The Boardwalk, Ste. 1
Huntsville, AL 35816
Phone: (256)536-1568
Fax: (256)536-4416
Format: Album-Oriented Rock (AOR). **Owner:** BCA Radio, LLC, at above address. **Operating Hours:** Continuous. **Key Personnel**: Tom Panucci, Gen. Mgr., t.panucci@radiohuntsville.com. **Ad Rates:** Advertising accepted; rates available upon request. **URL:** http://www.therocket951.com.

337 ■ W67CO - 67
PO Box A
Santa Ana, CA 92711
Phone: (714)832-2950
Free: 888-731-1000
Email: comments@tbn.org
Owner: Trinity Broadcasting Network Inc., PO Box A, Santa Ana, CA 92711, Ph: (714)832-2950, Free: 888-731-1000. **URL:** http://www.tbn.org.

338 ■ WTKI-AM - 1450
2305 Holmes Ave. NW
Huntsville, AL 35816
Phone: (256)533-1450
Fax: (256)551-9865
Email: info@wtkiradio.com
Format: Sports. **Networks:** Jones Satellite; ESPN Radio. **Founded:** 1946. **Formerly**: WFIX-AM. **Operating Hours**: Continuous. **Wattage:** 1,000. **Ad Rates:** Advertising accepted; rates available upon request. **URL:** http://wtkiradio.com.

339 ■ W209BL-FM - 89.7
PO Box 391
Twin Falls, ID 83303
Fax: (208)736-1958
Free: 800-357-4226
Format: Religious; Contemporary Christian. **Owner:** CSN International, PO Box 391, Twin Falls, ID 83303, Ph: (208)736-1958, Fax: (208)736-1958, Free: 800-357-4226. **URL:** http://www.csnradio.com.

340 ■ WWFF-FM - 93.3
1717 US Hwy. 72 E
Huntsville, AL 35811
Phone: (256)830-8300
Fax: (256)232-6842
Format: Country. **Owner:** Cumulus Broadcasting Inc., 3280 Peachtree Rd. NW, Ste. 2300, Atlanta, GA 30305-2447, Ph: (404)949-0700, Fax: (404)949-0740. **Key Personnel:** John Wolfe, Prog. Dir., john.wolfe@cumulus.com. **Ad Rates:** Advertising accepted; rates available upon request. **URL:** http://www.933nashicon.com.

WYAM-AM - See Hartselle, AL

341 ■ WZDX-TV - 54
1309 N Memorial Pkwy.
Huntsville, AL 35801
Phone: (256)533-5454
Fax: (256)533-5315
Format: Commercial TV. **Networks:** Fox. **Founded:** 1985. **ADI:** Huntsville-Decatur-Florence, AL. **Key Personnel:** Milton Grant, Founder; Everett Lawrence, Sales Mgr. **Ad Rates:** Noncommercial. **Mailing address:** PO Box 3889, Huntsville, AL 35801. **URL:** http://www.fox54.com.

IRONDALE

WSPP-FM - See Hopkinsville, KY

JACKSON

SW AL. Clarke Co. On Tombigbee River, 63 mi. N. of Mobile. Manufactures tricot cloth, textiles, fine printing papers. Lumber, oil, pulpwood, grist mills; cotton gin. Pine timber. Agriculture. Cotton, corn, sweet potatoes.

342 ■ North Jackson Progress
North Jackson Progress
128 Oak Hill Cir.
Stevenson, AL 35772-0625
Phone: (256)437-2395
Community newspaper. **Freq:** Semiweekly (Mon. and Thurs.). **Cols./Page:** 6. **Col. Width:** 2 inches. **Col. Depth:** 21 1/2 inches. **Key Personnel:** Larry O. Glass, Publisher. **Subscription Rates:** $17 Individuals local; $14 Individuals Senior citizens; $23 Out of area. **Ad Rates:** PCI $5.90. **Remarks:** Accepts advertising. **Circ:** 4500.

343 ■ The South Alabamian
The South Alabamian
1064 Coffeeville Rd.
Jackson, AL 36545
Phone: (251)246-4494
Publisher's E-mail: news@thesouthalabamian.com
Community newspaper. **Freq:** Weekly (Thurs.). **Print Method:** Offset. **Cols./Page:** 6. **Col. Width:** 12 INS. **Col. Depth:** 21 inches. **USPS:** 501-840. **Subscription Rates:** $52 Individuals /year (online); $22 Individuals 3 month (online); $12 Individuals 1 month (online). **URL:** http://www.southalabamian.com. **Mailing address:** PO Box 68, Jackson, AL 36545. **Ad Rates:** GLR $5; BW $441; SAU $4; PCI $4.75. **Remarks:** Advertising accepted; rates available upon request. **Circ:** ‡4900.

344 ■ WHOD-FM - 94.5
4428 Hwy. 43 N
Jackson, AL 36545-0518
Phone: (251)246-4431
Format: Classic Rock. **Owner:** Capital Assets, Inc., 8002 S 101st East Ave., Tulsa, OK 74133. **Founded:** 1967. **ADI:** Mobile, AL-Pensacola, FL. **Wattage**: 30,000 ERP. **Ad Rates:** Advertising accepted; rates available upon request. $7 for 30 seconds; $9 for 60 seconds. **Mailing address:** PO Box 518, Jackson, AL 36545-0518. **URL:** http://www.bamadixie.com.

JACKSONVILLE

NE AL. Calhoun Co. 11 mi. N. of Anniston. Jacksonville State University. Residential.

345 ■ Journal of the Alabama Academy of Science
Journal of the Alabama Academy of Science
c/o Safaa Al-Hamdani, Ph.D., Editor
Jacksonville State University
Dept. of Biology
700 Pelham Rd. N
Jacksonville, AL 36265-1623
Phone: (205)782-5801
Publisher's E-mail: info@alabamaacademyofscience.org
Science journal. **Freq:** Quarterly. **Print Method:** Offset. Accepts mats. **Trim Size:** 6 x 9. **Cols./Page:** 1. **Col. Width:** 54 nonpareils. **Col. Depth:** 105 agate lines. **Key Personnel:** Prof. Safaa Al-Hamdani, PhD, Editor. **ISSN:** 0002--4112 (print). **Alt. Formats:** PDF. **URL:** http://www.alabamaacademyofscience.org/jcurrent.php. **Circ:** ‡1200.

346 ■ WJXL-AM - 1010
188 John Turner Broadcast Blvd.
Jacksonville, AL 36265
Phone: (904)641-1011
Fax: (904)641-1022
Format: Sports. **Simulcasts:** WJXL-FM. **Networks:** ESPN Radio. **Owner:** Bussey-Hayes Communications Inc., at above address. **Founded:** 1987. **ADI**: Jacksonville (Brunswick), FL. **Key Personnel:** Stewart Young, Contact. **Wattage**: 50,000 Daytime; 300. **Ad Rates:** Advertising accepted; rates available upon request. **URL:** http://www.1010xl.com/.

347 ■ WLJS-FM - 91.9
700 Pelham Rd. N
Jacksonville, AL 36265
Phone: (256)782-5572
Fax: (256)782-8204
Format: Talk; Full Service; Information; Folk. **Networks:** National Public Radio (NPR). **Owner:** Board of Trustees of Jacksonville State University, 700 Pelham Rd. N, Jacksonville, AL 36265. **Founded:** 1975. **Operating Hours**: 7:00 a.m. - 3:00 a.m. **Local Programs**: *Brutal Reality*. **Wattage**: 610 ERP. **Ad Rates:** Accepts Advertising. **URL:** http://919wljs.webs.com.

JASPER

N. AL. Walker Co. 35 mi. NW of Birmingham. Manufactures lumber, textiles, golf bags. Poultry, poultry processing. Coal mines; timber. Agriculture. Cattle.

348 ■ Alabama Weddings
PRO-Motion Marketing
1065 Whittemore Rd.
Jasper, AL 35503
Phone: (205)387-5571
Fax: (205)387-5572
Publisher's E-mail: info@alabamaweddingsmagazine.com
Magazine covering weddings in Alabama. Provides information on clothing, event planning, and more. **Freq:** Annual. **Key Personnel:** Michelle Van Every Tubbs, Publisher, Owner; Tracy Jennison Cotter, Managing Editor. **URL:** http://alabamaweddingsmagazine.com. **Remarks:** Accepts advertising. **Circ:** 150000.

349 ■ Jasper Daily Mountain Eagle
Daily Mountain Eagle
1301 Viking Dr.
Jasper, AL 35501
Phone: (205)221-2840
Fax: (205)221-6203
Publisher's E-mail: jasper@mountaineagle.com
Newspaper with a Democratic orientation. **Freq:** Daily and Sun. (eve.). **Print Method:** Offset. **Cols./Page:** 6. **Col. Width:** 25 nonpareils. **Col. Depth:** 308 agate lines. **Key Personnel:** Ron Harris, Managing Editor; J.H. Boshell, Manager, Circulation. **Subscription Rates:** $126 Individuals by carrier; $114 Individuals by mail; $138 Out of area by mail; $166 Out of state by mail. **URL:** http://mountaineagle.com. **Mailing address:** PO Box 1469, Jasper, AL 35502. **Ad Rates:** SAU $6.30; PCI $12.91. **Remarks:** Accepts advertising. **Circ:** Mon.-Sat. ★**10883**, Sun. ★**10668**.

350 ■ WJBE-FM - 88.5
310 Hwy. 195, Ste. 4
Jasper, AL 35503
Phone: (205)221-2222
Fax: (205)221-2222
Email: info@countrylegends885.com
Format: Country. **Key Personnel:** Brett Elmore, Gen. Mgr., brett@countrylegends885.com; Barry Patilla, Dir. of Programs, barry@countrylegends885.com; Terry Madison, News Dir., terrell@countrylegends885.com.

URL: http://www.countrylegends885.com/.

351 ■ WJLX-AM - 1240
310 Hwy. 195, Ste. 4
Jasper, AL 35503
Phone: (205)221-2222
Fax: (205)221-2222
Email: whatshappening@oldies1015fm.com
Format: Oldies; Religious. **Owner:** Wal Win L.L.C., 310 Highway 195 , Jasper, AL 35503, Ph: (205)221-2222. **Formerly:** WLYJ-AM. **Key Personnel:** Brett Elmore, Gen. Mgr., brett@oldies1015fm.com. **Ad Rates:** Noncommercial; underwriting available. **URL:** http://oldies1015fm.com.

352 ■ WQJJ-FM - 97.7
830 Hillsdale Rd.
Jasper, AL 35504
Phone: (205)265-1369
Email: wqjj@monsterfm.com
Format: Information; Classical. **Owner:** North Alabama Public Service Broadcasters, 5332 North Walston Bridge Road, Jasper, AL 35504, Ph: (225)384-6498. **Founded:** 2000. **URL:** http://www.monsterfm.com/977.

353 ■ W25DR - 25
PO Box A
Santa Ana, CA 92711
Phone: (714)832-2950
Free: 888-731-1000
Owner: Trinity Broadcasting Network Inc., PO Box A, Santa Ana, CA 92711, Ph: (714)832-2950, Free: 888-731-1000. **URL:** http://www.tbn.org.

KENNEDY

354 ■ Christian Voice Magazine
Christian Voice Magazine
PO Box 147
Kennedy, AL 35574
Phone: (205)596-4371
Fax: (205)596-4375
Publication E-mail: editor@christianvoicemagazine.com
Religious magazine. **Freq:** Monthly. **Key Personnel:** John Lanier, Executive Editor; Kim Vail, Manager, Circulation. **Subscription Rates:** $20 Individuals U.S. only, 1 year; $40 Individuals U.S only. 2 years; $10 Individuals U.S only, 1 year digital; $20 Individuals U.S only, 2 years digital. **URL:** http://www.christianvoicemagazine.com. **Formerly:** Mid-South Gospel News; U.S. Gospel News. **Ad Rates:** 4C $800. **Remarks:** Accepts advertising. **Circ:** Paid 60000, Non-paid 25000.

LAFAYETTE

355 ■ Lafayette Sun
The Lafayette Sun
PO Box 378
Lafayette, AL 36862
Phone: (334)864-8885
Fax: (334)864-8310
Community newspaper. **Freq:** Weekly (Wed.). **Print Method:** Offset. **Cols./Page:** 6. **Col. Width:** 1.833 inches. **Col. Depth:** 21 1/2 inches. **Subscription Rates:** $18 Individuals /year; $20 Other countries /year. **Ad Rates:** BW $638.55; 4C $788.55; SAU $9.50; PCI $4.95. **Remarks:** Accepts advertising. **Circ:** 3000.

LANETT

E. AL. Chambers Co. 75 mi. NE of Montgomery. Manufactures textiles, textile machinery, cleaning and polishing preparations. Agriculture. Corn, grain, peaches.

356 ■ The Valley Times-News
Valley Newspapers Inc.
220 N 12th St.
Lanett, AL 36863
Phone: (334)644-8100
Fax: (334)644-5587
Publisher's E-mail: advertising@valleytimes-news.com
General newspaper. **Freq:** Daily. **Key Personnel:** Cy Wood, Editor, Publisher; Martha Milner, Manager, Advertising. **Subscription Rates:** $88 Individuals print, home delivery; $50 Individuals online. **URL:** http://www.valleytimes-news.com. **Mailing address:** PO Box 850, Lanett, AL 36863. **Remarks:** Advertising accepted; rates available upon request. **Circ:** (Not Reported).

WBRQ-FM - See Cidra

LINEVILLE

E. AL. Clay Co. 25 mi. SE of Anniston. Lumber, saw and grist mills. Cotton gins. Bottling works. Timber. Agriculture. Cotton, corn, hay.

357 ■ The Clay Times Journal
The Clay Times Journal
60132 Hwy. 49
Lineville, AL 36266
Phone: (205)396-5760
Publisher's E-mail: timesjournal@centurytel.net
Community newspaper. **Freq:** Weekly (Thurs.). **Print Method:** Web. **Cols./Page:** 6. **Col. Width:** 24 nonpareils. **Col. Depth:** 297 agate lines. **Key Personnel:** C. David Proctor, Editor; Linda D. McDonald, Contact. **ISSN:** 1053--9123 (print). **USPS:** 314-240. **Subscription Rates:** $27 Individuals; $33 Out of area. **URL:** http://www.theclay-timesjournal.com. **Formed by the merger of:** The Ashland Progress. **Formerly:** The Lineville Tribune. **Mailing address:** PO Box 97, Lineville, AL 36266. **Ad Rates:** GLR $6; BW $645; 4C $985; PCI $6.25. **Remarks:** Accepts advertising. **Circ:** 3600.

358 ■ SIFAT Journal
Servants in Faith and Technology
2944 County Road 113
Lineville, AL 36266
Phone: (256)396-2015
Fax: (256)396-2501
Publisher's E-mail: info@sifat.org
Freq: Monthly. **Subscription Rates:** Free for contributors. **Alt. Formats:** PDF. **URL:** http://sifat.org/category/journal. **Remarks:** Advertising not accepted. **Circ:** 2200.

LIVINGSTON

359 ■ Alabama Counseling Association Journal
Alabama Counseling Association
217 Darryl St.
Livingston, AL 35470
Phone: (205)652-1712
Fax: (205)652-1576
Free: 888-655-5460
Publisher's E-mail: alca@alabamacounseling.org
Professional journal covering mental health and counseling issues. **Freq:** Quarterly. **Key Personnel:** Ervin L. Wood, Executive Director; Florence Hemphill, Executive Assistant. **ISSN:** 1546-2781 (print). **Alt. Formats:** PDF. **URL:** http://www.alabamacounseling.org/journals.html. **Remarks:** Advertising not accepted. **Circ:** Non-paid 2000.

360 ■ The Alabama Review: A Quarterly Journal of Alabama History
Alabama Historical Association
The Alabama Review
University of West Alabama
UWA Station 3
Livingston, AL 35470
Phone: (205)652-5562
Publication E-mail: alabamareview@uwa.edu
Journal covering historical analysis of the Alabama region. **Freq:** Quarterly. **Print Method:** Offset. **Trim Size:** 11 x 15. **Cols./Page:** 5. **Col. Width:** 22 nonpareils. **Col. Depth:** 196 agate lines. **Key Personnel:** R. Volney Riser, Editor. **ISSN:** 0009--7810 (print). **Subscription Rates:** Included in membership. **URL:** http://www.uwa.edu/alabamareview. **Remarks:** Advertising not accepted. **Circ:** (Not Reported).

361 ■ Sumter County Record-Journal
Sumter County Record-Journal
PO Box B
Livingston, AL 35470
Phone: (205)652-6100
Fax: (205)652-4466
Community newspaper. **Freq:** Weekly (Thurs.). **Print Method:** Offset. **Cols./Page:** 6. **Col. Width:** 2 inches. **Col. Depth:** 21 1/2 inches. **Key Personnel:** Tommy McGraw, Owner, Publisher; Herman Ward, Associate Editor. **USPS:** 579-740. **Subscription Rates:** $37 By mail in Sumter county (print or online); $39 By mail out of county (print); $44 By mail out of state (print). **URL:** http://www.therecordjournal.net. **Formed by the merger of:** Sumter County Record. **Formerly:** Home Record; Sumter County Journal. **Ad Rates:** BW $722.40; 4C $1012.70; PCI $7.30. **Remarks:** Accepts advertising. **Circ:** 5225.

LOUISVILLE

SE AL. Barbour Co. 50 mi. SE of Montgomery.

362 ■ WGIQ-TV - 43
c/o Alabama Public Television, 2112 11th Ave. S, Ste. 400
2112 11th Ave. S, Ste. 400
Birmingham, AL 35205
Phone: (205)328-8756
Fax: (205)251-2192
Free: 800-239-5233
Format: Public TV. **Simulcasts:** WBIQ-TV. **Networks:** Public Broadcasting Service (PBS). **Owner:** Alabama Public Television, 2112 11th Ave. S, Birmingham, AL 35205, Ph: (205)328-8756, Fax: (205)251-2192, Free: 800-239-5233. **Founded:** Sept. 09, 1968. **Operating Hours:** 12 a.m.-11.30 p.m. **ADI:** Birmingham (Gadsden), AL. **Key Personnel:** Sandy Boyd, Asst. Dir. **Wattage:** 5,000,000 ERP. **Ad Rates:** Noncommercial. **URL:** http://www.aptv.org.

LUVERNE

S. AL. Crenshaw Co. 45 mi. S. of Montgomery. Cotton gins and warehouses; bottling works; lumber, grist mills. Timber. Agriculture. Cotton, peanuts, corn.

363 ■ Crenshaw Cable
90 S Forest Ave.
Luverne, AL 36049
Phone: (334)335-3435
Free: 800-735-9546
Founded: Sept. 05, 2006. **URL:** http://www.troycable.net.

364 ■ WAOQ 100.3 FM - 100.3
PO Box 699
Luverne, AL 36049
Phone: (334)335-2877
Free: 866-421-1003
Email: office@waoq.com
Format: Country. **Founded:** Sept. 14, 2006. **Ad Rates:** Noncommercial. **URL:** http://www.waoq.com.

MADISON

N. AL. Madison Co. 5 mi. W. of Huntsville. Residential.

365 ■ Journal of the Rossica Society of Russian Philately
Rossica Society of Russian Philately
c/o Ray Pietruszka, President
211 Evalyn St.
Madison, AL 35758-2203
Freq: Semiannual. **ISSN:** 0035- 8363 (print). **Subscription Rates:** Included in membership; $7.50 Members single issues; $9 Nonmembers single issues; $5 Members Additionally single issues as a download for a reduced price; 8 Nonmembers Additionally single issues as a download for a reduced price. **Alt. Formats:** CD-ROM; PDF. **URL:** http://www.rossica.org/journal.php. **Remarks:** Accepts advertising. **Circ:** 500.

366 ■ Madison County Record
Madison County Record
151-C Hughes Rd.
Madison, AL 35758
Phone: (256)772-6677
Fax: (256)772-6655
Publisher's E-mail: news@madisoncountyrecord.com
Community newspaper. **Founded:** 1968. **Freq:** Weekly (Wed.). **Print Method:** Offset. Accepts mats. **Cols./Page:** 6. **Col. Width:** 25 nonpareils. **Col. Depth:** 301 agate lines. **Key Personnel:** Alan Brown, President, Publisher; Wendy Graf, Office Manager. **ISSN:** 0889-4205 (print). **Subscription Rates:** $28.08 Individuals; $112.32 Out of country. **URL:** http://www.madisoncountyrecord.com/. **Ad Rates:** BW $967.50; 4C $1,099.15; SAU $7.50. **Remarks:** Accepts advertising. **Circ:** Paid 4000.

WAYH-FM - See Huntsville

367 ■ WBHP-AM - 1230
26869 Peoples Rd.
Madison, AL 35756
Phone: (256)534-3521

Circulation: ★ = AAM; △ or • = BPA; ♦ = CAC; ❑ = VAC; ⊕ = PO Statement; ‡ = Publisher's Report; Boldface figures = sworn; Light figures = estimated.

Fax: (256)350-2653
Format: Talk; News. **Owner:** iHeartMedia Inc., 200 E Basse Rd., San Antonio, TX 78209, Ph: (210)832-3314. **Operating Hours:** Continuous. **ADI:** Huntsville-Decatur-Florence, AL. **Key Personnel:** Carmelita Palmer, Contact, sales@wdrm.com; Stuart Langston, Contact, stuartlangston@clearchannel.com. **Wattage:** 1,000. **Ad Rates:** Noncommercial; Advertising accepted; rates available upon request. **URL:** http://www.wbhpam.com.

368 ■ WDRM-FM - 102.1
26869 Peoples Rd.
Madison, AL 35756
Phone: (256)309-2400
Fax: (256)350-2653
Free: 866-302-0102
Format: Contemporary Country. **Networks:** Independent. **Founded:** 1948. **Operating Hours:** Continuous. **Key Personnel:** Jim Tice, Programmer, Computer, jimtice@clearchannel.com; David Turner, Promotions Mgr., davidturner@clearchannel.com; Stuart Langston, Production Mgr., stuart@wdrm.com. **Wattage:** 100,000. **Ad Rates:** Advertising accepted; rates available upon request. **URL:** http://www.wdrm.com.

369 ■ WHOS-AM - 800
26869 Peoples Rd.
Madison, AL 35756
Phone: (256)309-2400
Fax: (256)350-2653
Format: News; Talk. **Owner:** iHeartMedia Inc., 200 E Basse Rd., San Antonio, TX 78209, Ph: (210)832-3314. **Operating Hours:** Continuous. **ADI:** Huntsville-Decatur-Florence, AL. **Key Personnel:** Carmelita Palmer, Dir. of Sales, carmelitapalmer@iheartmedia.com. **Wattage:** 1,000 ERP. **Ad Rates:** Noncommercial. **URL:** http://www.wbhpam.com.

370 ■ WQRV-FM - 100.3
26869 Peoples Rd.
Madison, AL 35756
Phone: (256)309-2400
Free: 877-628-0100
Format: Contemporary Hit Radio (CHR). **Operating Hours:** Continuous. **Key Personnel:** Carmelita Palmer, Contact, sales@wtak.com; Erich West, Contact, erich@wtak.com; Carmelita Palmer, Contact, sales@wtak.com. **Ad Rates:** Advertising accepted; rates available upon request. **URL:** http://www.1003theriver.com.

371 ■ WTAK-FM - 106.1
26869 Peoples Rd.
Madison, AL 35756
Phone: (256)309-2400
Fax: (256)350-2653
Format: Classic Rock. **Owner:** iHeartMedia Inc., 200 E Basse Rd., San Antonio, TX 78209, Ph: (210)832-3314. **Key Personnel:** Rick Brown, Contact, RickBrown@Clearchannel.com. **Wattage:** 5,400. **Ad Rates:** Noncommercial. **URL:** http://www.wtak.com.

MARION

C. AL. Perry Co. 28 mi. NW of Selma. Judson College (women). Marion Military Institute (men). Cotton gins, lumber, grist mills. Pine timber. Agriculture. Cotton, corn, cattle, poultry.

372 ■ The Triangle
Judson College
PO Box 120
Marion, AL 36756
Phone: (205)683-6161
Fax: (205)683-6675
Collegiate magazine. **Founded:** 1924. **Freq:** 5/year (during the academic year). **Print Method:** Offset. **Cols./Page:** 6. **Col. Width:** 18 nonpareils. **Col. Depth:** 186 agate lines. **Key Personnel:** Paula Webb, Editor. **URL:** http://thetriangleonline.com/. **Ad Rates:** BW $100. **Remarks:** Accepts advertising. **Circ:** Non-paid 700.

373 ■ WJUS-AM - 1310
5053 NW Hwy. 225A
5053 NW Hwy., 225A
Ocala, FL 34482
Phone: (352)671-1909
Format: Urban Contemporary. **Founded:** 1984. **Formerly:** WJAM-AM. **Operating Hours:** Sunrise-sunset. **Key Personnel:** Gary Cooper, Founder, President. **Wattage:** 5,000. **Ad Rates:** Noncommercial. **URL:** http://www.southeastagnet.com.

MAXWELL AFB

374 ■ Air and Space Power Journal
Air and Space Power Journal
Cadre/ARJ
401 Chennault Cir.
Maxwell AFB, AL 36112-6428
Phone: (334)953-5322
Fax: (334)953-5811
Publisher's E-mail: aspj@maxwell.af.mil
Professional military journal covering the development, fielding, and application of air combat power. **Founded:** 1947. **Freq:** Bimonthly. **Print Method:** Offset. **Trim Size:** 7 5/8 x 9 3/4. **Cols./Page:** 2. **Col. Width:** 17 picas. **Col. Depth:** 48 picas. **Key Personnel:** Tawanda Eaves, Managing Editor. **ISSN:** 1554-2505 (print). **Subscription Rates:** $32 Individuals; $44.80 Other countries. **URL:** http://www.airpower.au.af.mil/. **Formerly:** Air University Review; Airpower Journal; Aerospace Power Journal. **Remarks:** Advertising not accepted. **Circ:** Paid ‡1200, Controlled ‡20000.

MENTONE

375 ■ Telemedicine and E-Health
Mary Ann Liebert Inc., Publishers
c/o Ronald C. Merrell, MD, Ed.-in-Ch.
Virginia Commonwealth University
Mentone, AL 35984
Phone: (256)634-0206
Publisher's E-mail: info@liebertpub.com
International peer-reviewed journal covering medicine and telecommunications. **Freq:** Monthly. **Print Method:** Offset. **Trim Size:** 8 1/2 x 11. **Cols./Page:** 2. **Col. Width:** 3 1/4 inches. **Col. Depth:** 9 1/2 inches. **Key Personnel:** Charles R. Doarn, Editor-in-Chief; Ronald C. Merrell, MD, Editor-in-Chief. **ISSN:** 1530--5627 (print); **EISSN:** 1556--3669 (electronic). **Subscription Rates:** $275 Individuals print and online, USA ; $343 Other countries print and online, outside USA ; $267 Individuals online only; $2778 Institutions print and online, USA ; $3194 Institutions, other countries print and online, outside USA ; $2645 Institutions online only ; $2513 Institutions, other countries print only, USA ; $2890 Institutions print only, outside USA. **URL:** http://www.liebertpub.com/overview/telemedicine-and-e-health/54/. **Formerly:** Telemedicine Journal. **Mailing address:** PO Box 165, Mentone, AL 35984. **Ad Rates:** BW $1,010; 4C $1,760. **Remarks:** Advertising accepted; rates available upon request. **Circ:** (Not Reported).

MOBILE

SW AL. Mobile Co. On Mobile River, 157 mi. NE of New Orleans, LA. Important seaport. Shipbuilding and repair center. Commerce in cotton, lumber, coal, aluminum, tobacco, naval stores, citrus fruit, pitch pine, pecans, vegetables, cattle, hog raising. Principal manufacturing: chemicals, lumber, paper, textiles, ships, barges, roofing materials, petroleum products, natural gas, drugs, dyewood extracts, heating and plumbing materials, oxygen and acetylene, soft drinks, rayon. Seafood canning. Fish, shrimp, oyster fisheries. Resort.

376 ■ Business Alabama
PMT Publishing Company Inc.
PO Box 66200
Mobile, AL 36660-1200
Phone: (205)802-6363
Fax: (205)802-9396
Publisher's E-mail: wsorrell@pmtpublishing.com
Magazine for owners, managers, and presidents of companies covering issues and people in business in Alabama. **Freq:** Monthly. **Print Method:** Offset. **Trim Size:** 8 1/8 x 11. **Cols./Page:** 3. **Col. Width:** 25 1/2 nonpareils. **Col. Depth:** 140 agate lines. **Key Personnel:** Walker Sorrell, Associate Publisher; Anita Miller, Manager, Circulation, phone: (251)473-6269, fax: (251)479-8822; Erica West, Editor. **ISSN:** 0886--3024 (print). **Subscription Rates:** $22.95 Individuals 12 issues; $32.95 Two years 24 issues; $42.95 Individuals three years and 36 issues. **URL:** http://www.businessalabama.com; http://www.pmtpublishing.com. **Ad Rates:** BW $1662; 4C $2349. **Remarks:** Accepts advertising. **Circ:** Controlled 15000.

377 ■ The Catholic Week: Official Weekly Publication of the Archdiocese of Mobile
Archdiocese of Mobile
356 Government St.
Mobile, AL 36601
Phone: (351)432-3529
Fax: (351)434-1547
Roman Catholic (tabloid) publication. **Freq:** Weekly (Fri.). **Print Method:** Offset. **Trim Size:** 11 1/2 x 15. **Cols./Page:** 5. **Col. Width:** 26 nonpareils. **Col. Depth:** 196 agate lines. **Key Personnel:** Mary Ann Stevens, Director, Advertising, phone: (251)434-1543; Larry Wahl, Editor, phone: (251)432-3529; Pamela C. Wheeler, Manager, Production, phone: (251)434-1545. **URL:** http://www.mobilearchdiocese.org/catholicweek. **Ad Rates:** BW $718; PCI $10.75. **Remarks:** Accepts advertising. **Circ:** Paid 16797, Non-paid 400.

378 ■ College Student Journal
Project Innovation Inc.
PO Box 8508
Spring Hill Station
Mobile, AL 36608
Phone: (251)343-1878
Fax: (251)343-1878
Education periodical. **Freq:** Quarterly. **Print Method:** Offset. **Trim Size:** 5 x 8. **Cols./Page:** 2. **Col. Width:** 30 nonpareils. **Col. Depth:** 110 agate lines. **Key Personnel:** George Uhlig, Editor. **ISSN:** 0146--3934 (print). **Subscription Rates:** $80 Institutions; $120 Institutions 2 years; $70 Individuals; $110 Two years; $15 Canada; $25 Other countries. **URL:** http://www.projectinnovation.biz/csj_2006.html. **Remarks:** Advertising not accepted. **Circ:** ‡800.

379 ■ Education
Project Innovation Inc.
PO Box 8508
Spring Hill Station
Mobile, AL 36608
Phone: (251)343-1878
Fax: (251)343-1878
Education magazine. **Founded:** 1880. **Freq:** Quarterly. **Print Method:** Letterpress. **Trim Size:** 7 x 10. **Cols./Page:** 2. **Col. Width:** 30 nonpareils. **Col. Depth:** 110 agate lines. **Key Personnel:** Phil Feldman, Editor, fax: (251)639-7360. **ISSN:** 0013-1172 (print). **Subscription Rates:** $80 Institutions; $120 Institutions 2 years; $155 Institutions 3 years; $70 Individuals; $110 Two years; $145 Individuals 3 years; $15 Canada /year; $25 Other countries /year. **URL:** http://www.projectinnovation.biz/education_2006.html. **Remarks:** Advertising not accepted. **Circ:** ‡2900.

380 ■ Elevator World
Elevator World Inc.
356 Morgan Ave.
Mobile, AL 36606-1737
Phone: (251)479-4514
Fax: (251)479-7043
Free: 800-730-5093
Publisher's E-mail: sales@elevator-world.com
Magazine for the elevator industry. **Founded:** 1953. **Freq:** Monthly. **Print Method:** Offset. **Trim Size:** 8 1/2 x 11. **Cols./Page:** 3. **Col. Width:** 35 nonpareils. **Col. Depth:** 136 agate lines. **Key Personnel:** Bruce T. MacKinnon, Executive Vice President; Ricia Sturgeon-Hendrick, President, Publisher; Patricia Cartee, Director; Robert S. Caporale, Editor. **ISSN:** 0013-6158 (print). **Subscription Rates:** $75 Individuals; $125 Two years; $175 Individuals 3 years. **URL:** http://www.elevatorworld.com/. **Mailing address:** PO Box 6507, Mobile, AL 36606-0507. **Ad Rates:** BW $3,300. **Remarks:** Accepts advertising. **Circ:** Paid ‡7000.

381 ■ The Mobile Press
The Mobile Press
PO Box 2488
Mobile, AL 36652
Phone: (251)219-5374
General newspaper. Combined weekend edition with the Mobile Register as The Mobile Press Register. **Freq:** Daily (eve.), Sat. and Sun. (morn.). **Print Method:** Letterpress. **Cols./Page:** 6. **Col. Width:** 2 1/16 inches. **Col. Depth:** 20 1/4 inches. **Key Personnel:** Thomas A. Taylor, Editor; William J. Hearin, Publisher; John W. Winter, Manager, Advertising. **Circ:** Mon.-Fri. 9471.

382 ■ Negative Capability
Negative Capability Press
62 Ridgelawn Dr. E
Mobile, AL 36608-6116
Phone: (251)591-2922

Publication E-mail: negcap@negativecapabilitypress.org Literary review. **Freq:** 1/yr. **Trim Size:** 5 1/2 x 8 1/2. **Key Personnel:** Sue B. Walker, Editor; Reighter North, Managing Editor. **ISSN:** 0227-5166 (print). **Subscription Rates:** $15; $20 Other countries; $5 Single issue. **URL:** http://negativecapabilitypress.org. **Ad Rates:** BW $50; 4C $150. **Remarks:** Accepts advertising. **Circ:** ‡1000.

383 ■ Reading Improvement
Project Innovation Inc.
PO Box 8508
Spring Hill Station
Mobile, AL 36608
Phone: (251)343-1878
Fax: (251)343-1878
Publication E-mail: philfeldman@projectinnovation.biz
Magazine for teachers of reading and language arts. **Freq:** Quarterly. **Print Method:** Offset. **Trim Size:** 8 1/2 x 11. **Cols./Page:** 2. **Col. Width:** 30 nonpareils. **Col. Depth:** 112 agate lines. **Key Personnel:** Phil Feldman, Editor, fax: (251)639-7360. **ISSN:** 0034--0510 (print). **Subscription Rates:** $145 Individuals online only; $200 Institutions print and online. **URL:** http://www.projectinnovation.com/reading-improvement.html. **Remarks:** Advertising not accepted. **Circ:** ‡2500.

384 ■ The Springhillian
Spring Hill College
4000 Dauphin St.
Mobile, AL 36608
Phone: (251)380-3030
Free: 800-742-6704
Collegiate newspaper. **Freq:** Biweekly. **Print Method:** Offset. **Cols./Page:** 5. **Col. Width:** 2 inches. **Col. Depth:** 14.5 inches. **URL:** http://www.shc.edu; http://issuu.com/thespringhillian. **Circ:** Free ‡2000.

385 ■ The Vanguard
University of South Alabama
Office of Admissions
2500 Meisler Hall
390 Alumni Cir.
Mobile, AL 36688
Phone: (251)460-6101
Fax: (251)460-7876
Free: 800-USA-JAGS
Collegiate weekly newspaper. **Founded:** 1964. **Freq:** Weekly. **Print Method:** Offset. **Trim Size:** 13 x 21. **Cols./Page:** 6. **Col. Width:** 2 1/16 inches. **Col. Depth:** 21 inches. **Key Personnel:** Alyssa Newton, Editor-in-Chief. **URL:** http://www.thevanguardonline.com/. **Ad Rates:** BW $1,008; 4C $1,328; SAU $8; PCI $8. **Remarks:** Accepts advertising. **Circ:** Combined ‡8000.

386 ■ WABB-AM - 1480
1551 Springhill Ave.
Mobile, AL 36604
Phone: (251)432-5572
Fax: (251)438-4044
Format: Talk; News. **Networks:** ABC; NBC; CBS. **Owner:** The Dittman Corp. **Founded:** 1948. **Operating Hours**: Continuous; 75% network, 25% local. **ADI**: Mobile, AL-Pensacola, FL. **Wattage:** 5,000. **Ad Rates:** $6-20 for 30 seconds; $8-25 for 60 seconds. $6-$20 for 30 seconds; $8-$25 for 60 seconds. Combined advertising rates available with WABB-FM.

387 ■ WABB-FM - 97.5
1551 Springhill Ave.
Mobile, AL 36604
Phone: (251)432-5572
Fax: (251)438-4044
Format: Contemporary Hit Radio (CHR). **Networks:** ABC. **Owner:** The Dittman Corp. **Founded:** 1973. **Operating Hours**: Continuous; 10% network, 90% local. **ADI**: Mobile, AL-Pensacola, FL. **Key Personnel:** Cathy Kaufman, Dir. of Sales, ckaufman@wabb.com. **Wattage:** 100,000. **Ad Rates:** $24-70 for 30 seconds; $29-88 for 60 seconds. Combined advertising rates available with WABB-AM.

388 ■ WALA-TV - 10
1501 Satchel Paige Dr.
Mobile, AL 36606
Phone: (251)434-1110
Format: Commercial TV. **Networks:** Fox. **Founded:** 1953. **Operating Hours**: Continuous; 25% network, 75% local. **ADI**: Mobile, AL-Pensacola, FL. **Key Personnel:** Roland Fields, Chief Engineer, rfields@fox10tv.com. **Ad Rates:** Noncommercial. **URL:** http://www.fox10tv.com.

389 ■ WBHY-AM - 840
PO Box 1328
Mobile, AL 36633-1328
Phone: (251)473-8488
Free: 888-473-8488
Format: Talk; Contemporary Christian. **Owner:** Goforth Media Inc., 6530 Spanish Fort Blvd., Spanish Fort, AL 36527, Ph: (251)473-8488. **Founded:** 1943. **Operating Hours**: Sunrise-sunset. **ADI**: Mobile, AL-Pensacola, FL. **Key Personnel:** Wilbur Goforth, Gen. Mgr., Dir. of Mktg., wilbur@goforth.org; Charlie Smith, VP, charlie@goforth.org; Robert Barber, Mgr., VP, robert@goforth.org; Kenny Fowler, Music Dir., kenny@goforth.org. **Wattage:** 10,000. **Ad Rates:** Noncommercial. **URL:** http://www.goforth.org.

390 ■ WBHY-FM - 88.5
PO Box 1328
Mobile, AL 36633
Phone: (251)473-8488
Free: 888-473-8488
Format: Contemporary Christian. **Networks:** Sun Radio. **Owner:** Goforth Media Inc., 6530 Spanish Fort Blvd., Spanish Fort, AL 36527, Ph: (251)473-8488. **Founded:** 1991. **Operating Hours**: Continuous. **ADI**: Mobile, AL-Pensacola, FL. **Key Personnel:** Wilbur Goforth, Gen. Mgr., President, wilbur@goforth.org; Robert Barber, Station Mgr., VP, robert@goforth.org; Kenny Fowler, Music Dir., kenny@goforth.org. **Wattage**: 33,000. **Ad Rates:** Noncommercial. **URL:** http://www.goforth.org.

391 ■ WBLX-FM - 92.9
2800 Dauphin St., Ste. 104
Mobile, AL 36606
Phone: (251)471-9393
Fax: (251)652-2001
Format: Urban Contemporary. **Networks:** ABC. **Owner:** Cumulus Broadcasting Inc., 3280 Peachtree Rd. NW, Ste. 2300, Atlanta, GA 30305-2447, Ph: (404)949-0700, Fax: (404)949-0740. **Founded:** 1973. **Operating Hours**: Continuous. **ADI**: Mobile, AL-Pensacola, FL. **Key Personnel:** James Alexander, CPBE, CBNT, Operations Mgr., Prog. Dir., james.alexander@cumulus.com. **Wattage:** 100,000. **Ad Rates:** $80-110 per unit. **URL:** http://www.thebigstation93blx.com.

392 ■ WDLT-AM - 98.3
1204 Dauphin St.
Mobile, AL 36604
Phone: (334)432-7609
Fax: (334)432-2054
Format: News. **Networks:** CNN Radio. **Owner:** Cumulus Broadcasting, One Office Park St., Ste. 416, Mobile, AL 36607, Ph: (334)652-2000, Fax: (334)652-2001. **Founded:** 1965. **Formerly**: WHOZ-AM; WBLX-AM. **Operating Hours**: Continuous. **Key Personnel:** Bernie Barker, Gen. Mgr.; Joe Vincent, Gen. Sales Mgr.; Rick James, Dir. of Programs. **Wattage**: 10,000 day; 850 night. **Ad Rates:** $25 for 30 seconds; $50 for 60 seconds.

393 ■ WDLT-FM - 104.1
2800 Dauphin St., Ste. 104
Mobile, AL 36606
Phone: (251)652-2007
Fax: (251)652-2001
Free: 866-468-1041
Format: Full Service. **Networks:** CNN Radio. **Owner:** Cumulus Broadcasting Inc., 3280 Peachtree Rd. NW, Ste. 2300, Atlanta, GA 30305-2447, Ph: (404)949-0700, Fax: (404)949-0740. **Founded:** 1992. **ADI**: Mobile, AL-Pensacola, FL. **Key Personnel:** James Alexander, CPBE, CBNT, Operations Mgr., Prog. Dir., james.alexander@cumulus.com. **Wattage:** 98,000 ERP. **Ad Rates:** Advertising accepted; rates available upon request. **URL:** http://www.1041wdlt.com.

WEIQ-Digital Channel 42 - See Mobile

394 ■ WEIQ-Digital Channel 42 - 42
c/o Alabama Public Television
2112 11th Ave. S, Ste. 400
Mobile, AL 36601
Phone: (205)328-8756
Fax: (205)251-2192
Free: 800-239-5233
Format: Public TV. **Simulcasts:** WBIQ-TV Birmingham, AL. **Networks:** Public Broadcasting Service (PBS). **Owner:** Alabama Educational Television Commission, 2112 11th Ave. S, Ste. 400, Birmingham, AL 35205. **Founded:** 1963. **Operating Hours**: Continuous (sign off for maintenance Sunday 11 p.m.-Monday 4 a.m.). **ADI**: Mobile, AL-Pensacola, FL. **Key Personnel:** Sandy Boyd, Asst. Dir., sboyd@aptv.org. **Wattage:** 1,170,000 ERP. **Ad Rates:** Noncommercial. **URL:** http://www.aptv.org.

395 ■ WGOK-AM - 900
2800 Dauphin St., Ste. 104
Mobile, AL 36606
Phone: (251)432-9900
Fax: (251)652-2007
Format: Religious. **Networks:** Southern Broadcasting. **Founded:** 1958. **Operating Hours**: Continuous. **ADI**: Mobile, AL-Pensacola, FL. **Key Personnel:** James Alexander, CPBE, CBNT, Operations Mgr., james.alexander@cumulus.com; Vinny Duncan, Dir. of Mktg., Promotions Dir., vinny.d@cumulus.com. **Wattage:** 1,000. **Ad Rates:** Noncommercial. **URL:** http://www.gospel900.com.

396 ■ WHIL-FM - 91.3
4000 Dauphin St.
Mobile, AL 36608
Phone: (205)348-6644
Free: 800-654-4262
Email: whil@whil.org
Format: Classical; News; Educational. **Networks:** BBC World Service. **Owner:** Spring Hill College and Gulf Coast Public Broadcasting, Inc., at above address. **Founded:** Sept. 05, 1979. **Operating Hours**: Continuous. **ADI**: Mobile, AL-Pensacola, FL. **Wattage**: 100,000 ERP. **Ad Rates:** Noncommercial. **URL:** http://apr.org.

397 ■ WIJD-AM - 1270
273 Azalea Rd., Two Office Pk., Ste. 403
Mobile, AL 36609
Phone: (251)340-0442
Format: Religious. **Owner:** Wilkins Communications Network Inc., 292 S Pine St., Spartanburg, SC 29302, Ph: (864)585-1885, Fax: (864)597-0687, Free: 888-989-2299. **Key Personnel:** Tom Alexander, Station Mgr. **Wattage:** 5,000. **URL:** http://www.wilkinsradio.com.

398 ■ WKRG-TV - 5
555 Broadcast Dr.
Mobile, AL 36606
Phone: (251)479-5555
Fax: (251)473-8130
Format: Commercial TV. **Networks:** CBS. **Owner:** Media General Communications Holdings L.L.C., 333 E Franklin St., Richmond, VA 23219, Ph: (804)649-6000. **Founded:** 1955. **Operating Hours**: Continuous. **ADI**: Mobile, AL-Pensacola, FL. **Ad Rates:** Noncommercial. **URL:** http://www.wkrg.com.

399 ■ WKSJ-FM - 94.9
555 Broadcast Dr., 3rd Fl.
Mobile, AL 36606
Phone: (251)770-9536
Format: Contemporary Country. **Networks:** ABC. **Founded:** 1970. **Operating Hours**: Continuous; 1% network, 99% local. **ADI**: Mobile, AL-Pensacola, FL. **Key Personnel:** Andrea Farrell, Sales Mgr.; Bill Black, Dir. of Programs. **Wattage**: 100,000. **Ad Rates:** Noncommercial. **URL:** http://www.95ksj.com.

400 ■ WMPV-TV - 21
1668 S Beltline Hwy.
Mobile, AL 36693-5102
Format: Religious. **Owner:** Sonlight Broadcasting Systems, Inc., at above address. **Founded:** 1989. **Wattage**: 700,000 ERP. **Ad Rates:** $55 for 30 seconds; $77 for 60 seconds.

401 ■ WMXC-FM - 99.9
555 Broadcast Dr., 3rd Fl.
Mobile, AL 36606
Phone: (251)450-0100
Free: 800-527-8643
Format: Adult Contemporary. **Networks:** Independent. **Owner:** iHeartMedia Inc., 200 E Basse Rd., San Antonio, TX 78209, Ph: (210)832-3314. **Founded:** 1947. **Formerly**: WKRG-FM; WKRD-FM. **Operating Hours**: Continuous; 100% local. **ADI**: Mobile, AL-Pensacola,

Circulation: ★ = AAM; △ or • = BPA; ♦ = CAC; ❑ = VAC; ⊕ = PO Statement; ‡ = Publisher's Report; Boldface figures = sworn; Light figures = estimated.

FL. **Key Personnel:** Dan Mason, Contact, mason@litemix.com; Ronnie Bloodworth, Gen. Mgr. **Wattage:** 100,000. **Ad Rates:** Advertising accepted; rates available upon request. **URL:** http://www.litemix.com.

402 ■ WNSP-FM - 105.5
1100 Dauphin St., Ste. E
Mobile, AL 36604
Phone: (251)438-5460
Fax: (251)438-5462
Format: Sports. **Networks:** ESPN Radio. **Founded:** Sept. 1993. **Operating Hours:** Continuous. **Key Personnel:** Kenny Johnson, VP of Sales, kj@wnsp.com. **Wattage:** 5,300. **Ad Rates:** Advertising accepted; rates available upon request. Combined advertising rates available with WZEW-FM. **URL:** http://wnsp.com/wordpress.

403 ■ WNTM-AM - 710
555 Broadcast Dr., 3rd Fl.
Mobile, AL 36606
Phone: (251)450-0100
Free: 800-527-8643
Format: News; Talk; Sports. **Networks:** CBS; Mutual Broadcasting System. **Owner:** Clear Channel Radio, 555 Broadcast Dr., Mobile, AL 36606, Ph: (334)450-0100, Fax: (334)450-9307. **Founded:** 1946. **Formerly:** WPMI-AM; WKRG-AM. **Operating Hours:** Continuous. **Key Personnel:** Scott O'Brien, Contact, tom@comobile.com; Jessica Hall, Contact, jessica@ccmobile.com; Dan Mason, Dir. of Programs, danmason@clearchannel.com; Scott O'Brien, Contact, tom@comobile.com; Uncle Henry, Contact, michaelp@comobile.com; Jessica Hall, Contact, jessica@ccmobile.com; Jim Bohannon, Contact. **Local Programs:** *Ask the Expert*, Monday Tuesday Wednesday Thursday Friday 10:00 a.m.; *Handel on the Law*, Sunday Saturday 3:00 p.m. - 6:00 p.m.; 6:00 p.m. - 9:00 p.m. 8:00 a.m. - 9:00 a.m.; *Tee Time on the Gulf Coast*, Sunday 11:00 a.m. - 1:00 p.m. **Wattage:** 1,000. **Ad Rates:** Advertising accepted; rates available upon request. **URL:** http://www.newsradio710.com.

404 ■ WPAS-FM - 89.1
PO Box 2440
Tupelo, MS 38803
Phone: (662)844-8888
Format: Religious. **Owner:** American Family Radio, at above address. **Key Personnel:** Ron Meyers, Station Mgr., ron@waoy.com. **URL:** http://www.afa.net.

405 ■ WPMI-TV - 15
661 Azalea Rd.
Mobile, AL 36609
Phone: (251)602-1500
Fax: (251)602-1547
Email: local15@local15tv.com
Format: News. **Networks:** NBC. **Owner:** Newport Television, LLC, 460 Nichols Rd., Ste. 250, Kansas City, MO 64112, Ph: (816)751-0200, Fax: (816)751-0250. **Founded:** 1982. **Operating Hours:** Continuous Mon.-Sat.; 5 a.m.-midnight Sun. **ADI:** Mobile, AL-Pensacola, FL. **Ad Rates:** Advertising accepted; rates available upon request. **URL:** http://www.local15tv.com.

406 ■ WRKH-FM - 96.1
555 Broadcast Dr., 3rd Fl.
Mobile, AL 36606
Phone: (251)450-0100
Fax: (251)479-3418
Free: 800-666-9696
Format: Classic Rock. **Operating Hours:** Continuous. **Key Personnel:** Ronnie Bloodworth, Gen. Sales Mgr., ronniebloodworth@iheartmedia.com; Ronnie Bloodworth, Contact, ronniebloodworth@clearchannel.com. **Wattage:** 73,000. **Ad Rates:** Advertising accepted; rates available upon request. **URL:** http://www.961therocket.com.

407 ■ WYOK-FM
2800 Dauphin St., Ste. 104
Mobile, AL 36606
Phone: (251)652-2000
Fax: (251)652-2001
Key Personnel: James Alexander, CPBE, CBNT, Operations Mgr., Prog. Dir., james.alexander@cumulus.com. **Ad Rates:** Accepts Advertising.

408 ■ WZEW-FM - 92.1
1100-E Dauphin St.
Mobile, AL 36604
Phone: (251)438-5460
Fax: (251)438-5462
Email: 92zew@92zew.net
Format: Album-Oriented Rock (AOR); Jazz. **Networks:** Independent. **Owner:** WZEW Inc., 1100 Dauphin St., Suite E , Mobile, AL 36604, Ph: (251)438-5460, Fax: (251)438-5462. **Founded:** 1982. **Operating Hours:** Continuous. **ADI:** Mobile, AL-Pensacola, FL. **Key Personnel:** Tim Camp, Operations Mgr., timc@wnsp.com; Gene Murrell, Dir. of Programs, gene@92zew.net. **Wattage:** 6,000. **URL:** http://92zew.net.

MONROEVILLE

S. AL. Monroe Co. 65 mi. SW of Selma. Manufactures pulp, plywood, furniture, precast cement panels, textiles, aluminum doors and windows. Cotton gins. Timber. Agriculture. Cotton, corn, potatoes. Beef cattle.

409 ■ The Monroe Journal
Bolton Newspapers Inc.
PO Box 826
Monroeville, AL 36461
Phone: (251)575-3282
Publisher's E-mail: news@monroejournal.com
Newspaper. **Freq:** Weekly. **Print Method:** Offset. **Trim Size:** 13 3/4 x 22 3/4. **Cols./Page:** 6. **Col. Width:** 24 nonpareils. **Col. Depth:** 294 agate lines. **Key Personnel:** Bo Bolton, Publisher; Jodie Bolton, Art Director, Associate Publisher; Mike Qualls, Managing Editor. **ISSN:** 0884--8750 (print). **Subscription Rates:** $31 Individuals in county (print); $37 Individuals out of county, in state (print); $42 Out of state print; $25 Individuals online; $41 Individuals in county (print and online); $47 Individuals out of county, in state (print and online); $52 Out of state print and online. **URL:** http://www.monroejournal.com/32701/2083/1/this-weeks-issuepdf. **Remarks:** Accepts advertising. **Circ:** Combined ‡19000.

MONTEVALLO

C. AL. Shelby Co. 30 mi. S. of Birmingham. Residential.

410 ■ The Alabamian
The Alabamian
University of Montevallo
Sta. 6222
Montevallo, AL 35115
Phone: (205)665-6000
Publisher's E-mail: music@montevallo.edu
Collegiate newspaper. **Freq:** Bimonthly. **Print Method:** Offset. **Trim Size:** 11 1/2 x 12 1/2. **Cols./Page:** 5. **Col. Width:** 24 nonpareils. **Col. Depth:** 294 agate lines. **Key Personnel:** Hannah Stein, Managing Editor. **URL:** http://www.thealabamian.com; http://www.montevallo.edu/campus-life/um-life/organizations/publications. **Ad Rates:** BW $300; 4C $375; SAU $2.80. **Remarks:** Accepts advertising. **Circ:** Paid 40, Non-paid 2500.

MONTGOMERY

S. AL. Montgomery Co. On Alabama River, 90 mi. SE of Birmingham. The State Capital. Maxwell Air Force Base. Alabama State University, Faulkner University, Huntingdon College, U.S.A.F Air University. Auburn University at Montgomery, Troy State University. Large livestock and meat packing market; regional distribution center. Manufactures lumber, glass products, furniture, canned foods, fertilizer, textiles, syrup, chemicals, plumbing, heating and air conditioning supplies, cottonseed oil, soft drinks, plastic products, electronics, automotive products.

411 ■ Alabama Arts
Alabama State Council on the Arts Georgine Clarke Alabama Artists Gallery
201 Monroe St.
Montgomery, AL 36130-1800
Phone: (334)242-4076
Fax: (334)240-3269
Publisher's E-mail: staff@arts.albama.gov
Magazine covering the arts and artists in Alabama. **Freq:** Quarterly. **Trim Size:** 8 1/2 x 11. **Key Personnel:** Barbara Reed, Officer; Albert Head, Executive Director. **URL:** http://arts.state.al.us/resources.aspx#alabamaarts. **Remarks:** Advertising not accepted. **Circ:** (Not Reported).

412 ■ The Alabama Cattleman
Alabama Cattlemen's Association
201 S Bainbridge St.
Montgomery, AL 36104-4332
Phone: (334)265-1867
Fax: (334)834-5326
Freq: Monthly. **Print Method:** Offset. **Trim Size:** 7 1/4 X 9 1/2. **Cols./Page:** 3. **Col. Width:** 28 nonpareils. **Col. Depth:** 133 agate lines. **Key Personnel:** William E. Powell, III, Editor. **URL:** http://www.bamabeef.org/al_cattleman_receive_magazine.html. **Ad Rates:** BW $545; 4C $880. **Remarks:** Accepts advertising. **Circ:** 17000.

413 ■ Alabama Forests
Alabama Forestry Association
555 Alabama St.
Montgomery, AL 36104-4309
Phone: (334)265-8733
Fax: (334)262-1258
Magazine devoted to forest management and wood products. **Freq:** 5/year. **Print Method:** Offset. **Trim Size:** 8 1/2 x 11. **Cols./Page:** 3. **Col. Width:** 26 nonpareils. **Col. Depth:** 126 agate lines. **ISSN:** 0275--6625 (print). **URL:** http://www.alaforestry.org/?page=128. **Remarks:** Accepts advertising. **Circ:** ‡3500.

414 ■ Alabama Living: Alabama's Largest Consumer Publication
Alabama Rural Electric Association of Cooperatives
340 Technacenter Dr.
Montgomery, AL 36117
Phone: (334)215-2732
Free: 800-410-2732
Magazine featuring stories of interest to suburban and rural residents of Alabama. **Freq:** Monthly. **Print Method:** Offset. **Trim Size:** 8 1/8 x 10 7/8. **Cols./Page:** 3. **Col. Width:** 2 1/4 inches. **Col. Depth:** 10 inches. **Key Personnel:** Melissa Henninger, Managing Editor. **ISSN:** 1047--031X (print). **USPS:** 029-920. **Subscription Rates:** $3 Members; $6 Nonmembers. **URL:** http://alabamaliving.coop; http://areapower.coop/news/alabama-living-magazine. **Formerly:** Area Magazine. **Mailing address:** PO Box 244014, Montgomery, AL 36124. **Ad Rates:** GLR $14; BW $4491; 4C $5446. **Remarks:** Accepts advertising. **Circ:** 400000.

415 ■ Alabama Municipal Journal
Alabama League of Municipalities
535 Adams Ave.
Montgomery, AL 36104
Phone: (334)262-2566
Fax: (334)263-0200
Magazine covering municipal government activities. **Freq:** 6/year. **Print Method:** Offset. **Trim Size:** 8.5 x 11. **Cols./Page:** 3. **Col. Width:** 14 picas. **Col. Depth:** 57 picas. **Key Personnel:** Perrie C. Roquemore, Jr., Executive Director; Ken Smith, Executive Director; Stephen S. Martin, Director, Finance. **ISSN:** 0002--4309 (print). **Subscription Rates:** $24 Individuals. **URL:** http://www.alalm.org/alabama-municipal-journal.html. **Mailing address:** PO Box 1270, Montgomery, AL 36104. **Ad Rates:** BW $500; 4C $500. **Remarks:** Accepts advertising. **Circ:** Controlled ‡4500.

416 ■ Alabama Sheriffs' Star
Alabama Sheriffs Association
514 Washington Ave.
Montgomery, AL 36104-4385
Phone: (334)264-7827
Fax: (334)269-5588
Free: 800-622-7827
Publisher's E-mail: info@alabamasheriffs.com
Journal containing general information for sherriffs, also featuring a sheriff each issue from the Alabama Sheriffs Association. **Freq:** Quarterly. **ISSN:** 0199- 0509 (print). **Subscription Rates:** included in membership dues. **Alt. Formats:** CD-ROM; Magnetic tape. **URL:** http://www.alabamasheriffs.com/sponsorship_program.php. **Remarks:** Accepts advertising. **Circ:** 2,200.

417 ■ Aumnibus
Auburn University at Montgomery
PO Box 244023
Montgomery, AL 36124-4023
Phone: (334)244-3000
Free: 800-227-2694
Publisher's E-mail: askaum@aum.edu
Collegiate newspaper. **Freq:** Weekly. **Print Method:** Offset. **Cols./Page:** 4. **Col. Width:** 2.5 nonpareils. **Subscription Rates:** Free. **URL:** http://theaumnibus.com/aumnibus. **Ad Rates:** SAU $5; PCI $5. **Remarks:** Advertising accepted; rates available upon request. **Circ:** ‡1600.

418 ■ Bassmaster Magazine: Published for B.A.S.S. Members
ESPN
5845 Carmichael Rd.
Montgomery, AL 36117-2329
Phone: (334)272-9530
Fax: (334)270-8549
Publisher's E-mail: customerservice@bassmaster.com
Magazine covering boating and freshwater bass fishing. **Freq:** 9/year. **Print Method:** Offset. Uses mats. **Trim Size:** 7 7/8 x 10 1/2. **Cols./Page:** 3. **Col. Width:** 28 nonpareils. **Col. Depth:** 138 agate lines. **Key Personnel:** Dean Kessel, General Manager; James Hall, Editor; Dave Precht, Editor-in-Chief. **ISSN:** 0199--3291 (print). **URL:** http://espn.go.com/outdoors/bassmaster/news/story?page=b_news_102406_Bassmaster_magazine. **Ad Rates:** BW $29840; 4C $43650. **Remarks:** Accepts advertising. **Circ:** Paid ‡511794.

419 ■ Buckmasters Whitetail Magazine
Buckmasters
PO Box 244022
Montgomery, AL 36124-4022
Phone: (334)215-3337
Consumer magazine covering hunting. **Freq:** Bimonthly. **Print Method:** Web. **Trim Size:** 7 3/4 x 10 1/2. **Key Personnel:** Margaret Ann Huggins, Vice President, Advertising, Vice President, Sales; Scott Maloch, Director, Advertising. **URL:** http://buckmasters.com/Magazines; http://www.buckmasters.com. **Ad Rates:** BW $7194; 4C $8956. **Remarks:** Accepts advertising. **Circ:** (Not Reported).

420 ■ Civil Air Patrol News
Civil Air Patrol Inc.
105 S Hansell St., Bldg. 714
Maxwell AFB
Montgomery, AL 36112
Fax: (334)953-4262
Free: 877-227-9142
Publication E-mail: capnews@cap.gov
Newspaper covering aerospace education. **Founded:** Nov. 1968. **Freq:** Monthly. **Print Method:** Offset. **Trim Size:** 11 x 15. **Cols./Page:** 5. **Col. Width:** 22 nonpareils. **Col. Depth:** 196 agate lines. **Key Personnel:** James F. Tynan, Editor-in-Chief, phone: (334)953-5700; Donna Sparks, Assistant Editor, phone: (334)953-2599. **ISSN:** 0009-7810 (print). **URL:** http://www.gocivilairpatrol.com/html/index.htm. **Circ:** ‡60000.

421 ■ The Danville News
Community Newspaper Holdings Inc.
445 Dexter Ave., Ste. 7000
Montgomery, AL 36104-3742
Phone: (334)293-5800
Fax: (334)293-5910
General newspaper. **Freq:** Daily (eve.) and Sat. (morn.). **Print Method:** Offset. **Cols./Page:** 6. **Col. Width:** 26 nonpareils. **Col. Depth:** 301 agate lines. **Key Personnel:** Ed Christine, Business Manager; Brian Weaver, Manager, Circulation; Larry Kauffman, Manager, Production; Holly Brandon, Managing Editor; Pam Christine, Editor, General Manager; Scott Jeffrey, Director, Marketing; Donna Keefer, Manager, Advertising. **Subscription Rates:** $20.99 Individuals /year; total access; $16.99 Individuals /year; digital access. **URL:** http://www.dailyitem.com/news. **Ad Rates:** GLR $6.35; BW $748.20; SAU $6.35; PCI $6.35. **Remarks:** Accepts advertising. **Circ:** ‡3839.

422 ■ First Draft
Alabama Writers' Forum
PO Box 4777
Montgomery, AL 36103-4777
Phone: (334)265-7728
Fax: (334)262-2150
Free: 866-901-1117
Publisher's E-mail: writersforum@writersforum.org
Journal containing information about writers from the Alabama Writers' Forum and literary activities in Alabama. **Founded:** 1992. **Freq:** Semiannual. **Key Personnel:** Danny Gamble, Director, Communications. **URL:** http://www.writersforum.org/news_and_reviews/. **Remarks:** Accepts advertising. **Circ:** (Not Reported).

423 ■ Fishing Tackle Retailer
ESPN
5845 Carmichael Rd.
Montgomery, AL 36117-2329
Phone: (334)272-9530
Fax: (334)270-8549
Publisher's E-mail: customerservice@bassmaster.com
Magazine for the fishing tackle industry. **Freq:** 11/year. **Print Method:** Offset. **Trim Size:** 8 1/8 x 10 7/8. **Cols./Page:** 3. **Col. Width:** 13 picas. **Col. Depth:** 10 inches. **Key Personnel:** Dave Ellison, Editor; Deborah Johnson, Managing Editor. **ISSN:** 8750--1287 (print). **URL:** http://fishingtackleretailer.com; http://espn.go.com/outdoors/bassmaster/about/news/story?page=bass_media_fishing_tackle_retailer. **Ad Rates:** BW $2728; 4C $4330; PCI $139. **Remarks:** Accepts advertising. **Circ:** (Not Reported).

424 ■ Free Press
Community Newspaper Holdings Inc.
445 Dexter Ave., Ste. 7000
Montgomery, AL 36104-3742
Phone: (334)293-5800
Fax: (334)293-5910
Publisher's E-mail: editor@mankatofreepress.com
General newspaper. **Founded:** 1887. **Freq:** Mon.-Sat. (morn.). **Print Method:** Offset. **Cols./Page:** 6. **Col. Width:** 26 nonpareils. **Col. Depth:** 301 agate lines. **Key Personnel:** David Habrat, Director, Advertising, phone: (507)344-6351; Glen Asleson, Director, Production, phone: (507)344-6370; Joe Spear, Managing Editor, phone: (507)344-6382; Brooke High, Business Manager, phone: (507)344-6313; Roxanne Deegan, Manager, Advertising, phone: (507)344-6359; Barb Wass, Assistant, phone: (507)344-6364. **Subscription Rates:** $180.45 Individuals carrier delivery; $190.25 Individuals motor route; $218.90 Individuals postal delivery. **URL:** http://www.mankatofreepress.com/. **Mailing address:** PO Box 3287, Mankato, MN 56002-3287. **Ad Rates:** BW $2,193; 4C $2,443; SAU $14. **Remarks:** Accepts classified advertising. **Circ:** Mon.-Sat. ★**22072**, Sun. ★**21734**.

425 ■ Friends & Family
Alabama Farmers Federation
2108 E South Blvd.
Montgomery, AL 36116-2410
Phone: (334)288-3900
Publisher's E-mail: info@alfafarmers.org
Fitness magazine with articles on diet and exercise. **Freq:** Quarterly March, June, September and December. **Trim Size:** 8 1/4 x 10 3/4. **Cols./Page:** 3. **Col. Width:** 33 nonpareils. **Col. Depth:** 154 agate lines. **Key Personnel:** Paula Culver, Contact. **URL:** http://alfafarmers.org/stories/publications/magazines/publications_friends_family/summer-friends-family. **Formerly:** Alfa News. **Mailing address:** PO Box 11000, Montgomery, AL 36111-1113. **Ad Rates:** GLR $6; BW $4110; 4C $4485; PCI $205. **Remarks:** Accepts advertising. **Circ:** ‡330000.

426 ■ Intelligence Report, SPLC
Intelligence Project
Southern Poverty Law Ctr.
400 Washington Ave.
Montgomery, AL 36104
Phone: (334)956-8200
Free: 888-414-7752
Freq: Quarterly spring, summer, winter and fall. **Subscription Rates:** Free to law enforcement, journalists, scholars and community activists. **URL:** http://www.splcenter.org/intelligence-report. **Remarks:** Advertising not accepted. **Circ:** (Not Reported).

427 ■ Intelligence Report, SPLC
Southern Poverty Law Center
400 Washington Ave.
Montgomery, AL 36104-4344
Phone: (334)956-8200
Fax: (334)956-8481
Freq: Quarterly spring, summer, winter and fall. **Subscription Rates:** Free to law enforcement, journalists, scholars and community activists. **URL:** http://www.splcenter.org/intelligence-report. **Remarks:** Advertising not accepted. **Circ:** (Not Reported).

428 ■ International Journal of Applied Mathematical Analysis and Applications
Serials Publications Private Ltd.
Prof. Wendong Chang, Editorial Board Member
Department of Mathematics & Computer Science
Alabama State University
915 S Jackaon St.
Montgomery, AL 36104
Publisher's E-mail: serials@mail.com
Journal covering applied mathematical analysis and applications. **Freq:** Semiannual. **Key Personnel:** P.S. Rama Chandra Rao, Editor-in-Chief; Prof. Ilijas Farah, Board Member; Prof. Ke Chen, Board Member; Prof. Wendong Chang, Board Member. **ISSN:** 0973--3868 (print). **URL:** http://serialsjournals.com/journal-detail.php?journals_id=230. **Circ:** (Not Reported).

429 ■ The Land
Community Newspaper Holdings Inc.
445 Dexter Ave., Ste. 7000
Montgomery, AL 36104-3742
Phone: (334)293-5800
Fax: (334)293-5910
Publication E-mail: theland@thelandonline.com
Farm magazine. **Founded:** 1976. **Freq:** Weekly. **Print Method:** Offset. **Cols./Page:** 6. **Col. Width:** 10 picas. **Col. Depth:** 11.625 inches. **Key Personnel:** Kevin Schulz, Editor, phone: (507)344-6342; Kim Henrickson, Advertising Representative; Vail Belgard, General Manager; Tom Royer, Managing Editor. **ISSN:** 0279-1633 (print). **Subscription Rates:** $15 Individuals voluntary; $24 Individuals. **URL:** http://www.thelandonline.com. **Mailing address:** PO Box 3287, Mankato, MN 56002-3287. **Ad Rates:** GLR $14; BW $1,700.16; 4C $2,100.16; PCI $27.72. **Remarks:** Advertising accepted; rates available upon request. **Circ:** Non-paid ★**30813**.

430 ■ Mayo Free Press
Community Newspaper Holdings Inc.
445 Dexter Ave., Ste. 7000
Montgomery, AL 36104-3742
Phone: (334)293-5800
Fax: (334)293-5910
Publication E-mail: mayofreepress@windstream.net
Newspaper serving Mayo, Florida. **Key Personnel:** Linda Smith, Manager; Myra Regan, Publisher; Monja Slater, Director, Advertising. **Subscription Rates:** $26 Individuals out of county delivery; $18 Individuals in county delivery. **URL:** http://www.suwanneedemocrat.com/mayo. **Remarks:** Accepts advertising. **Circ:** (Not Reported).

431 ■ The Montgomery Advertiser
Gannett Company Inc.
425 Molton St.
Montgomery, AL 36104
Phone: (334)262-1611
General newspaper. **Freq:** Mon.-Sun. (morn.). **Print Method:** Offset. **Cols./Page:** 6. **Col. Width:** 2 1/16 inches. **Col. Depth:** 21 inches. **Key Personnel:** Pat Daugherty, Manager, Circulation, phone: (334)240-0136; Wanda S. Lloyd, Executive Editor, phone: (334)261-1509; Samuel Martin, President, Publisher, phone: (334)261-1582. **Subscription Rates:** $12 Individuals /month, Sunday and Wednesday; $18 Individuals /month, Wednesday to Sunday; $20 Individuals /month, Monday to Sunday. **URL:** http://www.montgomeryadvertiser.com. **Remarks:** Accepts advertising. **Circ:** Mon.-Sat. ★**35827**, Sun. ★**44120**.

432 ■ Neighbors
Alabama Farmers Federation
2108 E South Blvd.
Montgomery, AL 36116-2410
Phone: (334)288-3900
Publication E-mail: jhelms@alfafarmers.org
Magazine covering agriculture, gardening, and rural lifestyles. **Founded:** 1975. **Freq:** Monthly. **Print Method:** Offset. **Trim Size:** 8 1/4 x 10 3/4. **Cols./Page:** 3. **Col. Width:** 27 nonpareils. **Col. Depth:** 140 agate lines. **Key Personnel:** Jerry Newby, President. **ISSN:** 0162-2274 (print). **URL:** http://www.alfafarmers.org/neighbors/. **Mailing address:** PO Box 11000, Montgomery, AL 36111-1113. **Ad Rates:** BW $2,520; 4C $2,150; PCI $130. **Remarks:** Accepts advertising. **Circ:** 105000.

433 ■ The Orange Leader
Community Newspaper Holdings Inc.
445 Dexter Ave., Ste. 7000
Montgomery, AL 36104-3742
Phone: (334)293-5800
Fax: (334)293-5910
General newspaper. **Founded:** July 24, 1875. **Freq:** Daily Tue., Thu., and Sat. **Print Method:** Offset. **Cols./**

Circulation: ★ = AAM; △ or • = BPA; ♦ = CAC; ❑ = VAC; ⊕ = PO Statement; ‡ = Publisher's Report; Boldface figures = sworn; Light figures = estimated.

Page: 6. **Col. Width:** 1.833 inches. **Col. Depth:** 294 agate lines. **Key Personnel:** Van Wade, Editor, phone: (409)721-2817; Dawn Burleigh, Editor. **Subscription Rates:** $66 Individuals 1 year; print; mail home delivery. **URL:** http://orangeleader.com. **Remarks:** Accepts advertising. **Circ:** Mon.-Sat. ★**3936**, Sun. ★**4460**.

434 ■ Panel World
Hatton-Brown Publishers Inc.
225 Hanrick St.
Montgomery, AL 36102
Phone: (334)834-1170
Fax: (334)834-4525
Free: 800-699-5613
Publisher's E-mail: mail@hattonbrown.com
Business magazine serving the worldwide veneer, plywood, and panel board industry. **Freq:** Bimonthly. **Print Method:** Offset. **Trim Size:** 8 1/8 x 10 7/8. **Cols./Page:** 3. **Col. Width:** 2 1/4 inches. **Col. Depth:** 10 inches. **Key Personnel:** Jennifer McCary, Associate Editor; Rich Donnell, Editor-in-Chief; Dan Shell, Managing Editor; David Abbott, Associate Editor. **ISSN:** 0889--731X (print). **URL:** http://www.panelworldmag.com. **Formerly:** Plywood & Panel World. **Mailing address:** PO Box 2268, Montgomery, AL 36102. **Ad Rates:** BW $2525; 4C $945. **Remarks:** Accepts advertising. **Circ:** ‡7832.

435 ■ Paper Industry: North America's New Product News Leader
Paper Industry
PO Box 5675
Montgomery, AL 36103-5675
Fax: (604)264-1397
Free: 888-224-6611
Publication E-mail: info@paperindustrymag.com
Tabloid magazine describing new products, machinery processes and services and their application in the North America pulp and paper industries. **Freq:** Bimonthly. **Print Method:** Offset. **Trim Size:** 11 x 14 1/2. **Cols./Page:** 4 and 3. **Col. Width:** 36 and 28 nonpareils. **Col. Depth:** 210 agate lines. **Key Personnel:** Tim Shaddick, Publisher; Peter N. Williamson, Editor, phone: (450)458-4571. **URL:** http://www.paperindustrymag.com. **Formerly:** Paper Industry Equipment. **Ad Rates:** BW $2655; 4C $695; PCI $85. **Remarks:** Accepts advertising. **Circ:** 15400.

436 ■ Power Equipment Trade: First Choice of Power Equipment Professionals
Hatton-Brown Publishers Inc.
225 Hanrick St.
Montgomery, AL 36102
Phone: (334)834-1170
Fax: (334)834-4525
Free: 800-699-5613
Publisher's E-mail: mail@hattonbrown.com
Magazine covering outdoor power equipment trade for servicing power equipment and power sports dealers. **Freq:** 6/year. **Print Method:** Offset. **Trim Size:** 8 1/8 x 10 7/8. **Cols./Page:** 3. **Col. Width:** 2 1/4 inches. **Col. Depth:** 10 inches. **Key Personnel:** Rich Donnell, Editor-in-Chief; Jennifer McCary, Associate Editor; Dan Shell, Managing Editor; David Abbott, Associate Editor. **ISSN:** 0009-093X (print). **Subscription Rates:** Free. **Alt. Formats:** PDF. **URL:** http://www.powerequipmenttrade.com. **Mailing address:** PO Box 2268, Montgomery, AL 36102. **Remarks:** Accepts advertising. **Circ:** ■ **21896**.

437 ■ Southern Business & Economic Journal
Auburn University at Montgomery College of Business
PO Box 244023
Montgomery, AL 36124-4023
Phone: (334)244-3000
Free: 800-227-2649
Trade journal covering business and busines research. **Freq:** Semiannual. **Key Personnel:** Evan Moore, Editor; Joe Newman, Editor. **ISSN:** 0743--779X (print). **Subscription Rates:** $50 Individuals; $50 Libraries; $50 Individuals goverment; $50 Individuals submission. **URL:** http://www.business.aum.edu/about/southern-business-economic-journal. **Remarks:** Advertising not accepted. **Circ:** Combined 950.

438 ■ Southern Loggin' Times: The Southern Logger's Best Friend
Hatton-Brown Publishers Inc.
225 Hanrick St.
Montgomery, AL 36102
Phone: (334)834-1170
Fax: (334)834-4525
Free: 800-699-5613
Publisher's E-mail: mail@hattonbrown.com
Magazine serving the Southern U.S. logging industry. **Freq:** Monthly. **Print Method:** Offset. **Trim Size:** 10 1/4 x 13 3/4. **Cols./Page:** 4. **Col. Width:** 2 1/4 inches. **Col. Depth:** 13 inches. **Key Personnel:** Dan Shell, Editor; Rich Donnell, Editor-in-Chief; David Abbott, Associate Editor; Jennifer McCary, Associate Editor. **ISSN:** 0744--2106 (print). **Subscription Rates:** Free to qualified subscribers. **URL:** http://www.southernloggintimesmagazine.com. **Mailing address:** PO Box 2268, Montgomery, AL 36102. **Ad Rates:** BW $2305. **Remarks:** Accepts advertising. **Circ:** (Not Reported).

439 ■ Teaching Tolerance
Southern Poverty Law Center
400 Washington Ave.
Montgomery, AL 36104-4344
Phone: (334)956-8200
Fax: (334)956-8481
Magazine focusing on reducing prejudice, improving intergroup relations and supporting equitable school experiences for children. **Freq:** Semiannual. **Subscription Rates:** Free for teachers. **URL:** http://www.tolerance.org. **Mailing address:** PO Box 548, Montgomery, AL 36101-0548. **Remarks:** Advertising not accepted. **Circ:** (Not Reported).

440 ■ Timber Harvesting & Wood Fiber Operations™
Hatton-Brown Publishers Inc.
225 Hanrick St.
Montgomery, AL 36102
Phone: (334)834-1170
Fax: (334)834-4525
Free: 800-699-5613
Publisher's E-mail: mail@hattonbrown.com
National magazine for the U.S. logging industry. **Freq:** 6/year. **Print Method:** Offset. **Trim Size:** 8 1/8 x 10 7/8. **Cols./Page:** 3. **Col. Width:** 2 1/4 inches. **Col. Depth:** 10 inches. **Key Personnel:** Jennifer McCary, Associate Editor; David Abbott, Associate Editor; Rich Donnell, Editor-in-Chief; Dan Shell, Editor. **ISSN:** 0160--6433 (print). **Subscription Rates:** Free to qualified subscribers. **URL:** http://www.timberharvesting.com. **Formerly:** Timber Harvesting: America's Only National Logging & Forestry Magazine. **Mailing address:** PO Box 2268, Montgomery, AL 36102. **Ad Rates:** BW $3825; 4C $945. **Remarks:** Advertising accepted; rates available upon request. **Circ:** ■ **19375**.

441 ■ Timber Processing: Lumber, Composites, Engineered Products
Hatton-Brown Publishers Inc.
225 Hanrick St.
Montgomery, AL 36102
Phone: (334)834-1170
Fax: (334)834-4525
Free: 800-699-5613
Publisher's E-mail: mail@hattonbrown.com
North American lumber and wood products industries magazine. **Freq:** 10/year. **Print Method:** Offset. **Trim Size:** 8 1/8 x 10 7/8. **Cols./Page:** 3. **Col. Width:** 2 1/4 inches. **Col. Depth:** 10 inches. **Key Personnel:** Rich Donnell, Editor-in-Chief; Jennifer McCary, Associate Editor; Dan Shell, Managing Editor; David Abbott, Associate Editor. **ISSN:** 0885--906X (print). **Subscription Rates:** Free to qualified subscribers. **URL:** http://www.timberprocessing.com. **Formerly:** Timber Processing Industry. **Mailing address:** PO Box 2268, Montgomery, AL 36102. **Ad Rates:** BW $2390. **Remarks:** Accepts advertising. **Circ:** ■ **14065**.

442 ■ Tribune-Star
Community Newspaper Holdings Inc.
445 Dexter Ave., Ste. 7000
Montgomery, AL 36104-3742
Phone: (334)293-5800
Fax: (334)293-5910
Newspaper serving Terre Haute and the Wabash Valley with news coverage of Terre Haute and the Wabash Valley. **Freq:** Mon.-Sun. (morn.). **Print Method:** Offset. **Trim Size:** 22 3/4 x 27 1/4. **Cols./Page:** 6. **Col. Width:** 24 nonpareils. **Col. Depth:** 301 agate lines. **Key Personnel:** Max Jones, Editor, phone: (812)231-4336. **Remarks:** Accepts advertising. **Circ:** Mon.-Fri. ★**25920**, Sat. ★**26364**, Sun. ★**31643**.

443 ■ Young Bucks Outdoors
Buckmasters
PO Box 244022
Montgomery, AL 36124-4022
Phone: (334)215-3337
Publication E-mail: ybo@buckmasters.com
Consumer magazine covering youth interests. **Freq:** Monthly. **Print Method:** Web. **Subscription Rates:** $19.95 Individuals. **URL:** http://buckmasters.com/Resources/YBO. **Remarks:** Accepts advertising. **Circ:** Paid 50000.

444 ■ Bright House Networks
150 S Perry St.
Montgomery, AL 36104

445 ■ KTXC-FM - 104.7
RSA Twr., 20th Fl., 201 Monroe St.
Montgomery, AL 36104
Phone: (915)362-0401
Free: 800-683-0878
Format: Country. **Networks:** Jones Satellite. **Formerly:** KCOT-FM; KIOL-K-LITE. **ADI:** Odessa-Midland, TX. **Wattage:** 100,000. **Ad Rates:** $10-17 for 30 seconds; $17-27 for 60 seconds.

446 ■ WACV-AM - 1170
4101 A Wall St.
Montgomery, AL 36106
Phone: (334)352-9104
Format: Talk; Sports; News. **Networks:** CBS; Sun Radio; Mutual Broadcasting System. **Owner:** Bluewater Broadcasting Inc., 4101-A Wall St., Montgomery, AL 36106, Ph: (334)244-0961, Fax: (334)279-9563. **Founded:** 1986. **Formerly:** WCOV-AM. **Operating Hours:** Continuous; 50% network, 50% local. **Key Personnel:** Rick Peters, Gen. Mgr., President; Jay Scott, Dir. of Production; John Rodriguez, Sales Mgr.; Mary Brazell, Div. Dir., mbrazell@bluewaterbroadcasting.com. **Wattage:** 10,000 Day; 1,000 Night. **Ad Rates:** $8-25 for 30 seconds; $10-35 for 60 seconds. **URL:** http://www.1049thegump.com.

447 ■ WAIQ-TV - 26
2112 11th Ave. S, Ste. 400
Birmingham, AL 35205
Phone: (205)328-8756
Fax: (205)251-2192
Free: 800-239-5233
Format: Public TV. **Simulcasts:** WBIQ-TV. **Networks:** Public Broadcasting Service (PBS). **Owner:** Alabama Public Television, 2112 11th Ave. S, Birmingham, AL 35205, Ph: (205)328-8756, Fax: (205)251-2192, Free: 800-239-5233. **Founded:** 1955. **Operating Hours:** 7 a.m.-11 p.m. weekdays; 7 a.m-11 p.m. Sat.; 7 a.m.-11 p.m. Sun. **ADI:** Montgomery-Selma, AL. **Key Personnel:** Harvey Wilson, Asst. Dir., hwilson@aptv.org. **Ad Rates:** Noncommercial. **URL:** http://www.aptv.org.

448 ■ WAKA-TV - 8
3251 Harrison Rd.
Montgomery, AL 36109
Phone: (334)271-8888
Fax: (334)272-6444
Free: 800-467-0424
Format: News; Sports. **Networks:** CBS. **Founded:** 1960. **Operating Hours:** Continuous. **Key Personnel:** Dee Jackson, Sports Dir. **Wattage:** 316 KW ERP. **Ad Rates:** Noncommercial. **URL:** http://www.waka.com.

449 ■ WBAM-FM - 98.9
4101 A Wall St.
Montgomery, AL 36106
Phone: (334)244-0961
Fax: (334)279-9563
Format: Country. **Networks:** Unistar. **Owner:** Bluewater Broadcasting Inc., 4101-A Wall St., Montgomery, AL 36106, Ph: (334)244-0961, Fax: (334)279-9563. **Founded:** 1978. **Formerly:** WFMI-FM. **Operating Hours:** Continuous; 100% local. **Key Personnel:** Mary Brazell, Dir. of Traffic; Jay Scott, Dir. of Production; John Rodriguez, Sales Mgr.; Rick Peters, President, Gen. Mgr., rpeters@bluewaterbroadcasting.com; Mike Alan, Operations Mgr., malan@bluewaterbroadcasting.com; Terry Barber, Gen. Mgr., tbarber@bluewaterbroadcasting.com. **Wattage:** 100,000. **Ad Rates:** $45-75 for 30 seconds. WJWZ, WQKS, WACV. **URL:** http://www.bamacountry.com.

450 ■ WBMM-TV - 22
3251 Harrison Rd.
Montgomery, AL 36109
Phone: (334)270-3200
Fax: (334)271-2972

Key Personnel: Jesse Grear, Station Mgr., jgrear@wncftv.com. **URL:** http://www.cwmontgomery.com.

451 ■ WCOV-TV - 20
1 Wcov Ave.
Montgomery, AL 36111-2099
Phone: (334)288-7020
Fax: (334)288-5414
Email: mail@wcov.com

Format: Commercial TV. **Networks:** Fox. **Owner:** David Woods, at above address. **Founded:** 1953. **Operating Hours:** Continuous. **ADI:** Montgomery-Selma, AL. **Key Personnel:** Matt Johnson, Creative Dir., matt@wcov.com; Jennifer L. Weaver, Contact. **Wattage:** 460,000. **Ad Rates:** Advertising accepted; rates available upon request. $15-2000 per unit. **URL:** http://www.wcov.com.

WDYF-FM - See Dothan

452 ■ WHLW-FM - 104.3
203 Gunn Rd.
Montgomery, AL 36117
Phone: (334)274-6464
Fax: (334)274-6467

Format: Religious; Gospel; Contemporary Christian. **Operating Hours:** Continuous. **ADI:** Montgomery-Selma, AL. **Key Personnel:** Kimberly Parker, Bus. Mgr.; Becky Sweeney, Gen. Mgr., beckysweeney@clearchannel.com. **Wattage:** 13,500 ERP. **Ad Rates:** Advertising accepted; rates available upon request. **URL:** http://www.1043hallelujahfm.com.

453 ■ WIYC-TV - 48
4266 Lomac Dr.
Montgomery, AL 36106

Formerly: WRJM-TV. **URL:** http://www.eclectic-wiyc.net.

454 ■ WJWZ-FM - 97.9
4101-A Wall St.
Montgomery, AL 36106
Phone: (334)244-0961
Fax: (334)279-9563

Format: Hip Hop. **Operating Hours:** Continuous. **Key Personnel:** Terry Barber, Gen. Mgr., tbarber@bluewaterbroadcasting.com; Rick Peters, President, Gen. Mgr., rpeters@bluewaterbroadcasting.com. **Ad Rates:** Advertising accepted; rates available upon request. **URL:** http://www.979jamz.com.

455 ■ WLBF-FM - 89.1
381 Mendel Pkwy. E
Montgomery, AL 36117
Phone: (334)271-8900
Fax: (334)260-8962
Free: 800-239-8900
Email: mail@faithradio.org

Format: Religious. **Simulcasts:** WSTF-FM and WDYF-FM. **Networks:** Moody Broadcasting. **Owner:** Faith Broadcasting Inc., 381 Mendel Pky. E, Montgomery, AL 36117, Ph: (334)271-8900, Fax: (334)260-8962, Free: 800-239-8900. **Founded:** 1984. **Operating Hours:** Continuous; 90% network. **Key Personnel:** Bob Crittenden, Div. Dir.; Russell Dean, Gen. Mgr.; Jeremy Smith, Operations Mgr. **Wattage:** 100,000. **Ad Rates:** Noncommercial. **URL:** http://www.faithradio.org.

456 ■ WLWI-AM - 1440
One Commerce St., Ste. 300
Montgomery, AL 36104
Phone: (334)240-9274
Fax: (334)240-9219
Free: 800-239-9544

Format: News; Talk; Sports. **Networks:** NBC; ESPN Radio; Westwood One Radio. **Owner:** Cumulus Broadcasting Inc., 3280 Peachtree Rd. NW, Ste. 2300, Atlanta, GA 30305-2447, Ph: (404)949-0700, Fax: (404)949-0740. **Founded:** 1953. **Formerly:** WBAM-AM. **Operating Hours:** Continuous. **ADI:** Montgomery-Selma, AL. **Wattage:** 50,000 Day; 183 Night. **Ad Rates:** Advertising accepted; rates available upon request. $10-30 for 30 seconds; $15-35 for 60 seconds. **URL:** http://www.newsradio1440.com.

457 ■ WLWI-FM - 92.3
Colonial Financial Ctr., 1 Commerce St.
1 Commerce St., Ste. 300
Montgomery, AL 36104
Phone: (334)240-9274
Fax: (334)240-9219
Free: 800-757-9594

Format: News. **Networks:** ABC. **Owner:** Cumulus Broadcasting Inc., 3280 Peachtree Rd. NW, Ste. 2300, Atlanta, GA 30305-2447, Ph: (404)949-0700, Fax: (404)949-0740. **Founded:** 1978. **ADI:** Montgomery-Selma, AL. **Key Personnel:** Marvin Kopman, Mktg. Mgr., marvin.kopman@cumulus.com. **Wattage:** 100,000 ERP. **Ad Rates:** Advertising accepted; rates available upon request. **URL:** http://www.wlwi.com.

458 ■ WMCF-TV - 46
300 Mendel Pky. W
Montgomery, AL 36117-5406
Phone: (334)272-0045
Email: cr@tbn.org

Format: Religious. **Networks:** Independent. **Owner:** Trinity Broadcasting Network Inc., PO Box A, Santa Ana, CA 92711, Ph: (714)832-2950, Free: 888-731-1000. **Formerly:** WMPV-TV. **Operating Hours:** Continuous. **Key Personnel:** Aaron Motley, Station Mgr. **Ad Rates:** $40 for 30 seconds; $56 for 60 seconds. **URL:** http://www.tbn.org.

459 ■ WMGY-AM - 800
2305 Upper Wetumpka Rd.
Montgomery, AL 36107
Phone: (334)834-3710
Email: info@wmgyradio.com

Format: Southern Gospel. **Networks:** USA Radio; Satellite Radio. **Founded:** July 26, 1946. **Operating Hours:** Continuous; 50% local, 50% network. **ADI:** Montgomery-Selma, AL. **Key Personnel:** Dane Harris, Gen. Mgr., Music Dir.; Blaine Harris, Traffic Mgr., Office Mgr. **Wattage:** 1,000. **Ad Rates:** Noncommercial. **URL:** http://www.wmgyradio.com.

460 ■ WNCF-TV - 32
3251 Harrison Rd.
Montgomery, AL 36109
Phone: (334)270-3200
Fax: (334)271-6348

Format: Commercial TV. **Networks:** ABC. **Owner:** Channel 32 Montgomery L.L.C., at above address. **Founded:** 1964. **Formerly:** WHOA; WKAB-TV. **Operating Hours:** Continuous. **ADI:** Montgomery-Selma, AL. **Key Personnel:** Jesse Grear, Gen. Mgr. **Wattage:** 004 MW. **Ad Rates:** Noncommercial. $15-450 for 30 seconds. **URL:** http://www.wncftv.com.

461 ■ WNZZ-AM - 950
1 Commerce St., Ste. 300
Montgomery, AL 36101
Phone: (334)240-9274

Format: Adult Contemporary. **Owner:** Cumulus Media Inc., 3280 Peachtree Rd. NW, Ste. 2300, Atlanta, GA 30305-2455, Ph: (404)949-0700, Fax: (404)949-0740. **Key Personnel:** Lewis W. Dickey, Jr., Chairman, CEO, President. **URL:** http://www.wnzz950.com.

462 ■ WQKS-FM - 96.1
4101-A Wall St.
Montgomery, AL 36106
Phone: (334)244-0961
Fax: (334)279-9563

Format: Classic Rock. **Owner:** Bluewater Broadcasting Inc., 4101-A Wall St., Montgomery, AL 36106, Ph: (334)244-0961, Fax: (334)279-9563. **Operating Hours:** Continuous. **Key Personnel:** Terry Barber, Gen. Mgr., tbarber@bluewaterbroadcasting.com; Mike Alan, Operations Mgr., malan@bluewaterbroadcasting.com; Vivian Mills, Bus. Mgr., vmills@bluewaterbroadcasting.com; Tom Jones, Chief Engineer, tjones@bluewaterbroadcasting.com. **Ad Rates:** Advertising accepted; rates available upon request. **URL:** http://www.q961fm.com.

463 ■ WSFA-TV - 12
12 E Delano Ave.
Montgomery, AL 36105
Phone: (334)288-1212
Email: my12@wsfa.com

Format: Commercial TV. **Networks:** NBC. **Owner:** Raycom Media Inc., 201 Monroe St., RSA Twr., 20th Fl., Montgomery, AL 36104-3731, Ph: (334)206-1400. **Founded:** 1954. **Operating Hours:** Continuous. **ADI:** Montgomery-Selma, AL. **Key Personnel:** Ken Selvaggi, Gen. Mgr., VP, kselvaggi@wsfa.com; Scott Duff, News Dir., sduff@wsfa.com. **Wattage:** 316,000. **Ad Rates:** Advertising accepted; rates available upon request. **URL:** http://www.wsfa.com.

464 ■ WSTF-FM - 91.5
381 Mendel Pkwy.
Montgomery, AL 36117
Phone: (334)271-8900
Fax: (334)260-8962
Free: 800-239-8900
Email: mail@faithradio.org

Format: Religious; Contemporary Christian. **Owner:** Faith Radio, 381 Mendel Pky. E, Montgomery, AL 36117, Ph: (334)271-8900, Fax: (334)260-8962, Free: 800-239-8900. **Founded:** 1996. **Operating Hours:** Continuous. **Key Personnel:** Russell Dean, Gen. Mgr.; Bob Crittenden, Director; Mark Williams, President. **Ad Rates:** Noncommercial; underwriting available. **Mailing address:** PO Box 210789, Montgomery, AL 36117. **URL:** http://www.faithradio.org.

465 ■ WTXK-AM - 1210
1359 Carmichael Way
Montgomery, AL 36106
Phone: (334)517-1210
Fax: (334)356-9776

Format: Sports. **Networks:** ESPN Radio. **Owner:** Frontdoor Broadcasting, LLC, 1359 Carmichael Way, Montgomery, AL 36116. **Operating Hours:** Continuous. **Key Personnel:** Rad Dodson, Contact, rad@wtxktheticket.com. **Wattage:** 10,000 ERP; 003 ERP. **Ad Rates:** Advertising accepted; rates available upon request. **URL:** http://www.wtxktheticket.com.

466 ■ WVAS-FM - 90.7
915 S Jackson St.
Montgomery, AL 36101-0271
Phone: (334)229-4708
Fax: (334)269-4995
Free: 800-631-2893

Format: Jazz. **Networks:** National Public Radio (NPR). **Owner:** Alabama State University, 915 S Jackson St., Montgomery, AL 36101, Ph: (334)293-4100, Free: 800-253-5037. **Founded:** 1984. **Operating Hours:** Continuous; 10% network, 90% local. **ADI:** Montgomery-Selma, AL. **Key Personnel:** Mel Marshall, Dir. of Programs, mmarshall@wvasfm.org; Candy Capel, Station Mgr., ccapel@alasu.edu. **Wattage:** 80,000. **Ad Rates:** Noncommercial. **Mailing address:** PO Box 271, Montgomery, AL 36101-0271. **URL:** http://www.wvasfm.org.

467 ■ WWMG-FM - 97.1
203 Gunn Rd.
Montgomery, AL 36117
Phone: (334)274-9197
Fax: (334)274-6467

Format: Urban Contemporary. **Owner:** iHeartMedia Inc., 200 E Basse Rd., San Antonio, TX 78209, Ph: (210)832-3314. **Founded:** 1948. **Operating Hours:** Continuous. **Key Personnel:** James Belton, Gen. Mgr., jbelton@clearchannel.com; Alberta Jackson, Sales Mgr., albertajackson@clearchannel.com; Michael Long, Operations Mgr., michaellong@clearchannel.com. **Wattage:** 100,000. **Ad Rates:** WEND-FM. **URL:** http://www.mymagic97.com.

468 ■ WXFX-FM - 95.1
1 Commerce St., Ste. 300
Montgomery, AL 36104
Phone: (334)240-9274
Fax: (334)240-9219

Format: Classic Rock. **Owner:** Cumulus Broadcasting Inc., 3280 Peachtree Rd. NW, Ste. 2300, Atlanta, GA 30305-2447, Ph: (404)949-0700, Fax: (404)949-0740. **Founded:** 1982. **Operating Hours:** Continuous. **ADI:** Montgomery-Selma, AL. **Key Personnel:** Marvin Kopman, Gen. Mgr., marvin.kopman@cumulus.com. **Wattage:** 50,000. **Ad Rates:** Advertising accepted; rates available upon request. **URL:** http://www.wxfx.com.

469 ■ WXVI-AM
422 South Ct.
Montgomery, AL 36104
Phone: (205)263-3459
Fax: (205)263-3483

Circulation: ★ = AAM; △ or • = BPA; ♦ = CAC; ❑ = VAC; ⊕ = PO Statement; ‡ = Publisher's Report; Boldface figures = sworn; Light figures = estimated.

Format: Blues. **Networks:** Southern Broadcasting. **Owner:** Sunshine 16 Radio Network Inc., at above address. **Founded:** 1947. **Wattage:** 5,000 Day; 1,000 Nig.

470 ■ WZHT-FM - 105.7
203 Gunn Rd.
Montgomery, AL 36117
Phone: (334)274-6464
Fax: (334)274-6467
Format: Urban Contemporary. **Founded:** Sept. 07, 2006. **Key Personnel:** James Belton, Gen. Mgr., jbelton@clearchannel.com; Alberta Jackson, Gen. Sales Mgr., albertajackson@clearchannel.com; Michael Long, Operations Mgr., michaellong@clearchannel.com. **Ad Rates:** Advertising accepted; rates available upon request. **URL:** http://www.myhot105.com.

MOODY

471 ■ WURL-AM - 760
2999 Radio Park Dr.
Moody, AL 35004
Phone: (205)699-9875
Fax: (205)640-4379
Free: 800-262-9875
Format: Gospel. **Networks:** Independent. **Founded:** 1984. **Operating Hours:** Sunrise-sunset. **Key Personnel:** Bill Davison, Gen. Mgr. **Wattage:** 1,000. **Ad Rates:** $3.50-5.90 for 30 seconds; $4.70-7.10 for 60 seconds. **URL:** http://www.wurlradio.com.

MOULTON

N. AL. Lawrence Co. 20 mi. SW of Decatur. Manufactures textiles, paper. Cotton gins, metal fabrication, sawmill. Timber. Agriculture. Cotton, corn, hay.

472 ■ WALW-FM - 98.3
531 Walnut St.
Moulton, AL 35650
Phone: (256)905-4400
Email: walwfm@bellsouth.net
Format: Eclectic. **URL:** http://www.walw.org.

MOUNT CHEAHA

473 ■ WCIQ-TV - 7
c/o Alabama Public Television
2112 11th Ave. S, Ste. 400
Birmingham, AL 35205-2884
Phone: (205)328-8756
Fax: (205)251-2192
Free: 800-239-5233
Format: Public TV. **Simulcasts:** WBIQ-TV. **Networks:** Public Broadcasting Service (PBS). **Owner:** Alabama Public Television, 2112 11th Ave. S, Birmingham, AL 35205, Ph: (205)328-8756, Fax: (205)251-2192, Free: 800-239-5233. **Founded:** 1955. **Operating Hours:** Continuous. **ADI:** Birmingham (Gadsden), AL. **Key Personnel:** Jon Beans, Dir. Pub. Aff., jbeans@aptv.org; Jim Hyatt, Asst. Dir., jhyatt@aptv.org. **Wattage:** 316,000 ERP. **Ad Rates:** Noncommercial. **URL:** http://www.aptv.org.

NEW HOPE

NC AL. Madison Co. 20 mi. SE of Huntsville.

474 ■ New Hope Telephone Cooperative Inc.
5415 Main Dr.
New Hope, AL 35760-9758
Phone: (256)723-4211
Fax: (256)723-2800
Free: 877-474-4211
Email: support@nehp.net
Founded: 1952. **Key Personnel:** David Ayers, VP; Robert Patterson, Engineer, robertp@nehp.net. **Cities Served:** Grant, Owens Cross Road, Alabama; United States; 57 channels. **Mailing address:** PO Box 452, New Hope, AL 35760. **URL:** http://www.nhtc.coop.

NORMAL

475 ■ WJAB-FM - 90.9
Telecommunications Ctr.
Normal, AL 35762
Phone: (256)372-5793
Email: info@aamu.edu
Format: Jazz. **Networks:** National Public Radio (NPR). **Founded:** 1991. **Operating Hours:** Continuous. **Key Personnel:** Erica Fox Coleman, Director; Lois Watkins, Production Mgr.; Michael Morris, Chief Engineer. **Wattage:** 100,000. **Ad Rates:** Noncommercial. **Mailing address:** PO Box 1687, Normal, AL 35762. **URL:** http://www.aamu.edu/wjab.

NORTHPORT

476 ■ WMFT-FM - 88.9
5710 Watermelon Rd., Ste. 316
Northport, AL 35473
Phone: (205)758-7900
Fax: (205)758-0059
Email: wmft@moody.edu
Format: Religious; Gospel. **Owner:** Moody Bible Institute, 820 N LaSalle Blvd., Chicago, IL 60610, Free: 800-356-6639. **Key Personnel:** Rob Moore, Station Mgr.; John Rogers, Dir. of Programs. **URL:** http://www.moodyradiosouth.fm.

ONEONTA

N. AL. Blount Co. 36 mi. NE of Birmingham. Manufactures aluminum utensils, plastic tubing, textiles, lime, cement. Lumber, coal. Agriculture. Cotton, hay, truck crops, soybeans, beef, cattle, dairying.

477 ■ Oneonta Telephone Co.
PO Box 1500
Oneonta, AL 35121-0017
Key Personnel: Brian Corr, Gen. Mgr. **Cities Served:** subscribing households 2,200.

478 ■ WCRL-AM
111 1ST Ave. E
Oneonta, AL 35121
Phone: (205)625-3333
Fax: (205)625-5433
Format: Oldies. **Networks:** Jones Satellite; Alabama Radio (ALANET). **Founded:** 1952. **Key Personnel:** Danny Bentley, Contact. **Wattage:** 2,500 Day; 064 Night. **Ad Rates:** $3-7 for 30 seconds; $4-8 for 60 seconds.

OPELIKA

E. AL. Lee Co. 26 mi. NW of Columbus, GA. Manufactures cotton goods, magnetic tape, auto tires, plastics, lumber, fertilizer, athletic equipment, bakery and dairy products. Pine timber. Agriculture. Dairying.

479 ■ Bovine Practitioner
American Association of Bovine Practitioners
3320 Skyway Dr., Ste. 802
Opelika, AL 36801
Phone: (334)821-0442
Fax: (334)821-9532
Publisher's E-mail: aabphq@aabp.org
Freq: Annual. **Subscription Rates:** Included in membership; $20 Nonmembers /year. **URL:** http://www.aabp.org/members/publications/practitioner.asp. **Mailing address:** PO Box 3610, Auburn, AL 36831-3610. **Remarks:** Accepts advertising. **Circ:** (Not Reported).

480 ■ Opelika-Auburn News
Opelika-Auburn News
2901 Society Hill Rd.
Opelika, AL 36803
Phone: (334)749-6271
Fax: (334)749-1228
General newspaper. **Freq:** Daily and Sun. (morn.). **Print Method:** Offset. **Cols./Page:** 6. **Col. Width:** 25 nonpareils. **Col. Depth:** 303 agate lines. **ISSN:** 1044--7539 (print). **Subscription Rates:** $13.95 Individuals Monday to Sunday (home delivery); $14.95 Individuals digital only; $8.40 Individuals Monday to Friday (home delivery); $8.80 Individuals Friday to Sunday (home delivery). **URL:** http://www.oanow.com. **Mailing address:** PO Box 2208, Opelika, AL 36803. **Remarks:** Accepts advertising. **Circ:** (Not Reported).

WCJM-FM - See West Point, GA

481 ■ WKKR-FM - 97.7
915 Veterans Pky.
Opelika, AL 36801
Phone: (334)274-6424
Format: Contemporary Country. **Networks:** ABC. **Owner:** Fuller Broadcasting, at above address. **Founded:** 1968. **Formerly:** WFRI-FM. **Operating Hours:** Continuous; 100% local. **ADI:** Columbus, GA (Opelika, AL). **Key Personnel:** Russell Bath, Sports Dir., News Dir. **Wattage:** 3,000. **Ad Rates:** $13.65-18.15 for 30 seconds; $17-22.70 for 60 seconds. **URL:** http://kickerfm.iheart.com.

482 ■ WMXA-FM - 96.7
915 Veterans Pky.
Opelika, AL 36801
Phone: (334)274-6424
Format: Top 40. **Key Personnel:** John Bodiford, Station Mgr.; Jay Jeffcoat, Dir. of Programs; Glenn Buxton, Gen. Mgr., glennbuxton@mindspring.com; Don Brown, Mktg. Mgr.; Sandra Smith, Bus. Mgr. **URL:** http://mix967online.iheart.com.

483 ■ WTLM-AM - 1520
915 Veterans Pky.
Opelika, AL 36801
Phone: (334)745-4656
Fax: (334)749-1520
Format: Oldies. **Owner:** Qantum of Auburn L.L.C., 915 Veterans Pkwy., Opelika, AL 36801. **Key Personnel:** John Bodiford, Dir. of Mktg., Mktg. Mgr., john.bodiford@qantumofauburn.com; Ben Taylor, Dir. of Sales, ben.taylor@qantumofauburn.com. **URL:** http://www.qantumofauburn.com.

484 ■ WZMG-AM - 910
915 Veterans Pkwy.
Opelika, AL 36801
Phone: (334)745-4656
Fax: (334)749-1520
Format: Urban Contemporary; Oldies. **Networks:** ABC. **Owner:** Qantum of Auburn L.L.C., 915 Veterans Pkwy., Opelika, AL 36801. **Founded:** 1968. **Formerly:** WAOA-AM. **Operating Hours:** Continuous. **ADI:** Columbus, GA (Opelika, AL). **Key Personnel:** Ben Taylor, Dir. of Sales, ben.taylor@qantumofauburn.com; John Bodiford, Dir. of Mktg., Mktg. Mgr., john.bodiford@qantumofauburn.com. **Wattage:** 1,000. **Ad Rates:** $9.20-10.90 for 30 seconds; $11.45-13.65 for 60 seconds.

OPP

S. AL. Covington Co. 75 mi. S. of Montgomery. Manufactures textiles, lumber. Agriculture. Hogs, cotton, peanuts.

485 ■ Opp Cablevision
108 N Main St.
Opp, AL 36467
Phone: (334)493-4571
Email: support@oppcatv.com
Owner: Opp Utilities. **Founded:** Sept. 01, 2006. **Cities Served:** Kinston, Alabama.

486 ■ WAMI-AM - 860
PO Box 40
Opp, AL 36467
Phone: (334)493-3588
Email: wami@oppcatv.com
Format: Country. **Simulcasts:** WAMI-FM. **Owner:** Opp Broadcasting Co., Inc., 1807 North Main St, Opp, AL 36467, Ph: (334)493-3588. **Founded:** 1952. **Operating Hours:** 5 a.m.-midnight; 100% local. **Wattage:** 1,000. **Ad Rates:** Noncommercial. **URL:** http://wami1023.webs.com/aboutus.htm.

487 ■ WAMI-FM - 102.3
1807 N Main St.
Opp, AL 36467
Phone: (334)493-3588
Fax: (334)493-4182
Format: Country. **Simulcasts:** WAMI-AM. **Networks:** ABC. **Owner:** Opp Broadcasting Co., Inc., 1807 North Main St, Opp, AL 36467, Ph: (334)493-3588. **Founded:** 1974. **Operating Hours:** Continuous; 100% local. **Wattage:** 3,400. **Ad Rates:** $5-7 for 30 seconds; $8-10 for 60 seconds.

488 ■ WOPP-AM - 1290
1101 Cameron Rd.
Opp, AL 36467
Phone: (334)493-4545
Fax: (334)493-4546
Email: wopp@wopp.com
Format: Country; Oldies; Southern Gospel. **Networks:** Sun Radio. **Founded:** 1980. **Operating Hours:** Continuous. **Key Personnel:** Robert H. Boothe, Jr., Gen. Mgr., rbt@wopp.com; Frank Shuford, Contact. **Wattage:** 2,500. **Ad Rates:** $5 for 30 seconds; $9 for 60 seconds. **URL:** http://www.wopp.com.

OXFORD

NE AL. Talladega Co. 5 mi. S. of Anniston. Manufactures machinery, prefabricated buildings, cordage, feed, cleaning preparations. Hatcheries. Agriculture. Cotton, dairying, poultry.

489 ■ WTBJ-FM - 91.3
1500 Airport Rd.
Oxford, AL 36203
Phone: (256)831-3333
Fax: (256)831-5895
Email: office@trinityoxford.org
Format: Religious. **Simulcasts:** WTBB. **Owner:** Trinity Christian Academy, at above address, Addison, TX. **Founded:** May 1994. **Operating Hours:** Continuous. **Local Programs:** *The Front Porch Fellowship*, Monday Tuesday Wednesday Thursday Friday Saturday 12:05 a.m.; 12:05 p.m. 12:05 a.m.; *A New Song for A New Day*, Monday Tuesday Wednesday Thursday Friday Saturday 1:05 a.m.; 7:07 a.m. 1:05 a.m. **Wattage:** 170. **Ad Rates:** Noncommercial. **URL:** http://www.trinityoxford.org.

490 ■ WVOK-FM - 97.9
1215 Church St.
Oxford, AL 36203
Phone: (256)835-1580
Fax: (256)831-1500
Format: Music of Your Life. **Owner:** Woodward Broadcasting Co., Inc., at above address. **Founded:** Feb. 19, 1990. **Key Personnel:** Chuck Woodard, Gen. Mgr. **Wattage:** 510 ERP. **Ad Rates:** Advertising accepted; rates available upon request. Combined advertising rates available with WVOK-AM. **URL:** http://www.979wvok.com.

OZARK

SE AL. Dale Co. 30 mi. N. of Florida.

491 ■ Bullwhip Squadron News
Bullwhip Squadron Association
c/o Joe Bowen, President
5566 County Road 18
Ozark, AL 36360-5927
Magazine containing history, accomplishments and other relevant ideas regarding Combat Veterans. **Alt. Formats:** PDF. **Remarks:** Advertising not accepted. **Circ:** (Not Reported).

492 ■ WOAB-FM - 104.9
PO Box 911
Ozark, AL 36361-1109
Phone: (334)774-5600
Email: woab@charter.net
Format: Oldies. **Networks:** Independent. **Owner:** Ozark Broadcasting Corp. **Founded:** 1967. **Operating Hours:** Continuous; 100% local. **Wattage:** 6,000. **Ad Rates:** $5 for 30 seconds; $7 for 60 seconds.

493 ■ WOZK-AM - 900
PO Box 911
Ozark, AL 36361-1109
Phone: (334)774-5600
Email: wozk@alaweb.com
Format: Middle-of-the-Road (MOR); Easy Listening; Oldies. **Networks:** Independent. **Owner:** Ozark Broadcasting Corp. **Founded:** 1953. **Operating Hours:** Daytime; 100% local. **Wattage:** 1,000. **Ad Rates:** $4.90 for 30 seconds; $6.90 for 60 seconds.

494 ■ WRJM-FM - 93.7
285 E Broad St.
Ozark, AL 36360
Phone: (334)774-7673
Fax: (334)774-6450
Format: News; Talk. **Founded:** 1969. **Operating Hours:** Continuous. **Wattage:** 100,000. **Ad Rates:** Advertising accepted; rates available upon request. **URL:** http://www.wrjmfm.com.

PELHAM

495 ■ Fabricating & Metalworking
Cygnus Business Media
262 Yeager Pkwy., Ste. C
Pelham, AL 35124
Fax: (205)987-3237
Free: 800-366-0676
Publisher's E-mail: info@cygnus.com
Magazine providing technical information, new products and technology, new literature and industry news to corporate managers, engineers and others across the U.S. and Canada. Technical features cover diverse processes within the metalforming, welding and metalcutting industries. Business and editorial reports analyze the critical issues shared across each industry. **Freq:** 10/year. **Trim Size:** 7.812 x 10.5. **Key Personnel:** Tony Morrison, Publisher, phone: (866)832-8473; Mike Riley, Editor, phone: (205)681-3393. **URL:** http://www.fabricatingandmetalworking.com. **Remarks:** Advertising accepted; rates available upon request. **Circ:** Controlled ‡38800.

496 ■ WAYE-AM
100 Yeager Pky.
Pelham, AL 35124
Phone: (205)786-9293
Fax: (205)786-9296
Format: Gospel. **Networks:** Independent. **Owner:** Willis Broadcasting, 645 Church St., Ste. 400, Norfolk, VA 23510, Ph: (804)888-7180. **Founded:** 1972. **Wattage:** 1,000 Day; 075 Night. **Ad Rates:** $35 for 60 seconds.

PELL CITY

N. AL. St. Clair Co. On Coosa River, 32 mi. NE of Birmingham. Manufactures cotton goods, lumber, barrel heads, plastic pipe. Timber. Agriculture. Cotton, corn.

497 ■ St. Clair Times
Consolidated Publishing
1911 Martin St. S, Ste. 7
Pell City, AL 35128
Fax: (205)814-9194
Free: 888-653-8229
Publisher's E-mail: news@cleburnenews.com
Newspaper covering the St. Clair County. **Freq:** Weekly (Thurs.). **Key Personnel:** Ed Fowler, Publisher, phone: (256)299-2101; Will Heath, Editor, phone: (205)884-3400; Gary Hanner, Associate Editor, phone: (205)884-3400. **Subscription Rates:** Free. **URL:** http://www.thestclairtimes.com. **Remarks:** Accepts advertising. **Circ:** (Not Reported).

498 ■ WFHK-AM - 1430
22 Cogswell Ave.
Pell City, AL 35125-2438
Phone: (205)338-1430
Fax: (205)338-2238
Format: Country. **Networks:** ABC; Alabama Radio (ALANET). **Founded:** 1956. **Operating Hours:** 6 a.m.-6 p.m.; 5% network, 95% local. **Key Personnel:** Doug Williamson, Contact. **Wattage:** 5,000. **Ad Rates:** $4.70 for 30 seconds; $7.35 for 60 seconds. Combined advertising rates available with WSSY-FM.

PIEDMONT

NE AL. Cherokee Co. 75 mi. NE of Birmingham. Cotton yarn, lumber mills; cotton gins. Iron mines; mineral springs. Dairy, poultry, fruit, grain farms.

499 ■ WJCK-FM - 88.3
9423 Hwy. 21 N
Piedmont, AL 36272
Phone: (256)447-6008
Format: Gospel. **Owner:** Immanuel Broadcasting Network, 779 S Erwin St., Cartersville, GA 30120, Ph: (770)387-0917, Fax: (770)387-2856. **URL:** http://www.ibn.org.

PLEASANT GROVE

500 ■ WQOH-AM - 1480
40 Park Rd., Ste. B
Pleasant Grove, AL 35127
Phone: (205)744-4456
Format: Religious. **Owner:** EWTN Global Catholic Network, 5817 Old Leeds Rd., Irondale, AL 35210, Ph: (205)271-2900. **Formerly:** WRLM-AM. **Operating Hours:** Continuous. **Key Personnel:** Michael Deering, VP; John Martignoni, President, john@queenofheavenradio.com. **Wattage:** 5,000. **Ad Rates:** Advertising accepted; rates available upon request. **URL:** http://www.queenofheavenradio.com.

PRATTVILLE

C. AL. Elmore Co. 12 mi. NW of Montgomery. Manufactures cotton gin machinery, textiles, cotton, paper, rope, boxes, brake shoes, webbing. Timber. Agriculture.

501 ■ WIQR-AM - 1410
921 E Main St.
Prattville, AL 36066
Phone: (334)358-0410
Format: Sports. **Ad Rates:** Advertising accepted; rates available upon request.

PRICEVILLE

502 ■ WQAH-AM - 1310
1431 Hwy. 31 N
Hartselle, AL 35640
Phone: (256)353-4060
Format: Gospel; Religious. **Networks:** Independent. **Owner:** Abercrombie Broadcasting Co., 219 Chestnut St. NE, Hartselle, AL 35640, Ph: (256)502-9896. **Founded:** 1986. **Formerly:** WJRA-AM. **Operating Hours:** 6 a.m.-6 p.m.; 100% local. **ADI:** Huntsville-Decatur-Florence, AL. **Key Personnel:** Ray Mosley, Contact; Rob Lawler, Contact. **Wattage:** 1,000. **Ad Rates:** Noncommercial. $10 for 60 seconds. Combined advertising rates available with WAJF-AM, WHRT-AM, and WYAM-FM. **URL:** http://wqah.com.

RAGLAND

503 ■ Ragland Telephone Company Inc.
630 Main St.
Ragland, AL 35131-0577
Phone: (205)472-2141
Fax: (205)472-2145
Email: support@ragland.net
Cities Served: United States; 21 channels. **Mailing address:** PO Box 577, Ragland, AL 35131-0577. **URL:** http://www.ragland.net.

RAINSVILLE

NE AL. DeKalb Co. 30 mi. N. of Gadsden. State College at Rainsville. Manufactures textiles, furniture, feed. Agriculture. Cotton, poultry.

504 ■ WVSM-AM - 1500
PO Box 339
Rainsville, AL 35986
Phone: (205)638-2137
Format: Religious. **Networks:** Interstate Radio. **Owner:** Sand Mountain Advertising Company Inc., 368 McCurdy Ave. N, Rainsville, AL 35986, Ph: (256)638-4237. **Founded:** 1967. **Operating Hours:** Sunrise-sunset; 100% local. **Wattage:** 1,000. **Ad Rates:** for 15 seconds; $8-9 for 30 seconds; $8-9 for 60 seconds; $10-11 for 60 seconds. **URL:** http://wvsmam.com.

RED BAY

NW AL. Franklin Co. 38 mi. SW of Florence. Recreation areas. Feed mills. Manufactures mobile and motor homes, textiles. Lumber. Agriculture. Cotton, grain, soybeans, livestock, poultry.

505 ■ WRMG-AM - 1430
PO Box 656
Red Bay, AL 35582-0656
Format: Contemporary Christian; Sports. **Networks:** Alabama News. **Owner:** Redmont Broadcasting Corp., at above address. **Founded:** 1968. **Wattage:** 1,000. **Ad Rates:** $4 for 30 seconds; $5.50 for 60 seconds. **URL:** http://www.wrmgradio.com/.

ROANOKE

E. AL. Randolph Co. 25 mi. NW of La Grange, GA. Manufactures art supplies, doors, industrial fabrics, textile yarns, metal furniture, textiles, lumber. Pine, hardwood timber. Agriculture. Apples, corn, poultry, cattle.

506 ■ CommuniComm Services
3164 Hwy. 431
Roanoke, AL 36274
Phone: (334)863-8112
Free: 800-239-5367
Cities Served: Roanoke, Alabama; 71 channels. **URL:** http://www.netcommander.com.

507 ■ WELR-AM - 1360
6855 Hwy. 431
Roanoke, AL 36274

Circulation: ★ = AAM; △ or • = BPA; ♦ = CAC; ❑ = VAC; ⊕ = PO Statement; ‡ = Publisher's Report; Boldface figures = sworn; Light figures = estimated.

Phone: (334)863-2540
Fax: (334)863-2540
Email: welr@eagle1023.com
Format: News; Sports. **Simulcasts:** WLAG-AM. **Networks:** ABC; ESPN Radio; Precision Racing; Meadows Racing. **Owner:** Eagle's Nest Inc., 112 E 9th Ave., Winfield, KS 67156, Ph: (620)229-8282, Fax: (620)229-8236. **Founded:** 1950. **Operating Hours:** 5 a.m.-6 p.m.; 98% network, 2% local. **Wattage:** 1,000. **Ad Rates:** $6 for 30 seconds; $11 for 60 seconds. **URL:** http://www.eagle1023.com.

508 ■ WELR-FM - 102.3
6855 Hwy. 431
Roanoke, AL 36274
Phone: (334)863-4139
Fax: (334)863-2540
Email: welr@eagle1023.com
Format: Contemporary Country. **Simulcasts:** no. **Networks:** ABC. **Owner:** Eagle's Nest Inc., 112 E 9th Ave., Winfield, KS 67156, Ph: (620)229-8282, Fax: (620)229-8236. **Founded:** 1964. **Operating Hours:** Continuous. **Key Personnel:** Jim Vice, Contact. **Wattage:** 25,000. **Ad Rates:** $12 for 30 seconds; $18 for 60 seconds. yes - WELR-AM - WLAG-AM. **URL:** http://www.eagle1023.com.

ROBERTSDALE

SW AL. Baldwin Co. 20 mi. SE of Mobile. Residential.

509 ■ Flint Hills Independent
Gulf Coast Newspapers
PO Box 509
Robertsdale, AL 36567
Publication E-mail: indy96@gulftel.com
Community newspaper. **Founded:** 1900. **Freq:** Weekly (Thurs.). **Print Method:** Web offset. **Trim Size:** 13 x 20. **Cols./Page:** 5 and 6. **Col. Width:** 11 picas and 26 nonpareils. **Col. Depth:** 15 and 294 21 1/2 inches. **Subscription Rates:** $21.50; $25 Out of state; $18 Individuals county; $22 Out of area state of WA; $24 Out of state; $23 Individuals; $13.50 senior citizens. **Formerly**: The Independent. **Mailing address:** PO Box 27, Eskridge, KS 66423. **Ad Rates:** GLR $8; BW $375; 4C $575; BW $529.20; PCI $4.20; GLR $1,064.25; BW $741.75; 4C $1,121.75; SAU $8.25; CNU $7.25; PCI $1,444.25. **Remarks:** Color advertising not accepted. **Circ:** 3100, ‡2350, 4500.

510 ■ WNSI-FM - 105.9
PO Box 578
Robertsdale, AL 36567
Phone: (251)209-5828
Email: wnsi@gulftel.com
Format: News; Talk; Information; Sports. **Owner:** Southern Media Communication, Inc., at above address. **Operating Hours:** Continuous. **Key Personnel:** Walter Bowen, President, walter@wnsiradio.com. **Ad Rates:** Noncommercial; underwriting available. **URL:** http://www.wnsiradio.com.

RUSSELLVILLE

NW AL. Franklin Co. 20 mi. S. of Florence. Manufactures textiles, artificial flowers. Aluminum reduction plants. Stone quarries. Agriculture. Cotton, corn, hay.

511 ■ Franklin County Times
Franklin County Times Inc.
14131 Hwy. 43
Russellville, AL 35653
Phone: (256)332-1881
Fax: (256)332-1883
Newspaper. **Freq:** Weekly (Wed.). **Print Method:** Offset. **Cols./Page:** 6. **Col. Width:** 26 nonpareils. **Col. Depth:** 301 agate lines. **Key Personnel:** Jonathan Willis, Publisher. **Subscription Rates:** $42.51 Individuals /year in-county; $85.02 Out of area /year. **Mailing address:** PO Box 1088, Russellville, AL 35653. **Remarks:** Accepts advertising. **Circ:** (Not Reported).

512 ■ WKAX-AM - 1500
113 Washington Ave.
Russellville, AL 35653
Phone: (256)777-3181
Format: Religious; Music of Your Life. **Founded:** 1974. **Wattage:** 1,000 ERP. **Ad Rates:** $6 for 60 seconds. **URL:** http://www.wkaxam.com/.

SCOTTSBORO

NE AL. Jackson Co. 40 mi. E. of Huntsville. Manufactures textiles, lumber, aluminum, store fixtures, air conditioner components, plastic liter bottles, polyester tire cord, lace goods, hardwood flooring. Vending operations. Timber. Agriculture.

513 ■ The Daily Sentinel
Ohio Valley Publishing
701 Veterans Dr.
Scottsboro, AL 35768
Phone: (256)259-1020
General newspaper. **Founded:** 1872. **Freq:** Daily (eve.). **Print Method:** Offset. **Cols./Page:** 6. **Col. Width:** 1 13/16 inches. **Col. Depth:** 294 agate lines. **Key Personnel:** Junior Lewis, Manager, Production; Greg Gardner, Manager, Circulation; Sara Graves, Business Manager; Ken Bonner, Managing Editor. **Subscription Rates:** $83 Individuals carrier; $75 Individuals senior, carrier; $84 By mail in County; $91 Out of area. **URL:** http://thedailysentinel.com. **Mailing address:** PO Box 220, Scottsboro, AL 35768. **Ad Rates:** SAU $7.25. **Remarks:** Accepts advertising. **Circ:** Paid ♦**3270**.

514 ■ Jackson County Chronicle
Jackson County, Alabama Historical Association
435 Barbee Ln.
Scottsboro, AL 35769-3745
Phone: (256)574-3556
Publication E-mail: rabc123@scottsboro.org
Journal covering local history. **Freq:** Quarterly. **Trim Size:** 8 1/2 x 11. **Key Personnel:** Matthew Perenchio, Executive Editor; Chris Hardie, Publisher. **URL:** http://lacrossetribune.com/jacksoncochronicle. **Remarks:** Advertising not accepted. **Circ:** Paid 400.

515 ■ Scottsboro Electric Power Board
PO Box 550
Scottsboro, AL 35768
Phone: (256)574-2682
Fax: (256)574-5085
Founded: Sept. 05, 2006. **Cities Served:** 83 channels. **URL:** http://www.scottsboropower.com.

516 ■ WKEA-FM - 98.3
19784 John T. Reid Pkwy.
Scottsboro, AL 35768
Phone: (256)259-2341
Fax: (256)574-2156
Format: Contemporary Country. **Networks:** Fox. **Owner:** Kea Radio Inc., 19784 John T. Reid Pky., Scottsboro, AL 34768, Ph: (256)259-2341, Fax: (256)574-2156. **Founded:** 1966. **Formerly**: WCNA-FM. **Operating Hours**: Continuous; 5% network, 95% local. **ADI**: Huntsville-Decatur-Florence, AL. **Key Personnel:** Ronald H. Livengood, Gen. Mgr., President, ron@wkeafm.com; Gene Sisk, VP. **Wattage:** 6,000 ERP. **Ad Rates:** $8 for 30 seconds; $13.70 for 60 seconds. **URL:** http://www.wkeafm.com.

517 ■ WMXN-FM - 101.7
19784 John T. Reid Pky.
Scottsboro, AL 35768
Phone: (256)259-2341
Format: Classic Rock. **Networks:** Westwood One Radio. **Owner:** Kea Radio Inc., 19784 John T. Reid Pky., Scottsboro, AL 34768, Ph: (256)259-2341, Fax: (256)574-2156. **Founded:** 1941. **Formerly**: WFPA-AM. **Operating Hours**: Continuous; 95% network, 5% local. **ADI**: Huntsville-Decatur-Florence, AL. **Key Personnel:** Ronald H. Livengood, Gen. Mgr., President. **Wattage:** 1,000. **Ad Rates:** $5.95 for 30 seconds; $8 for 60 seconds. Combined advertising rates available with WKEA-FM. **Mailing address:** PO Box 966, Scottsboro, AL 35768. **URL:** http://www.wkeafm.com.

518 ■ W27CV - 27
PO Box A
Santa Ana, CA 92711
Phone: (714)832-2950
Free: 888-731-1000
Owner: Trinity Broadcasting Network Inc., PO Box A, Santa Ana, CA 92711, Ph: (714)832-2950, Free: 888-731-1000.

519 ■ WWIC-AM - 1050
815 W Willow St.
Scottsboro, AL 35768
Phone: (256)259-1050
Fax: (256)575-2411
Email: wwic@scottsboro.org
Format: Country. **Networks:** Mutual Broadcasting System. **Owner:** Scottsboro Broadcasting Co., Inc., 815 W Willow Street, Scottsboro, AL 35768, Ph: (256)259-1050. **Founded:** 1950. **Operating Hours**: Continuous; 5% network, 95% local. **ADI**: Chattanooga (Cleveland), TN. **Key Personnel:** Greg Bell, Contact; Greg Bell, Contact. **Wattage:** 1,000. **Ad Rates:** $2.40-2.95 for 15 seconds; $4.60-5.97 for 30 seconds; $6.24-7.62 for 60 seconds. **URL:** http://www.wwicradio.com.

520 ■ WZCT-AM - 1330
1111 E Willow St.
Scottsboro, AL 35768
Phone: (256)574-1330
Format: Full Service; Southern Gospel. **Networks:** Alabama Radio (ALANET). **Owner:** Bonner-Carlisle Enterprises, Inc., 2002 East Willow St., Scottsboro, AL 35768. **Founded:** 1952. **Formerly**: WROS-AM. **Operating Hours**: Continuous. **ADI**: Huntsville-Decatur-Florence, AL. **Key Personnel:** Rob Carlile, Contact. **Wattage**: 5,000. **Ad Rates:** $6.15 for 30 seconds; $8.25 for 60 seconds. **URL:** http://southerngospelam1330.com.

SELMA

S. AL. Dallas Co. On Alabama River, 50 mi. W. of Montgomery. Manufactures lumber, cottonseed oil and meal, furniture, farm machinery, lawn mowers, cigars, glazed tile blocks, bricks, architectural gravel. Cotton warehouses; cotton gins; aircraft repair; bottling works; meat packing and magnesium plants, paper and textile mills, stockyards; slaughter house. Grain elevators. Timber. Agriculture. Hay, livestock, cotton.

521 ■ The Selma Times-Journal
Selma Newspapers Inc.
1018 Water Ave.
Selma, AL 36701
Phone: (334)875-2110
General newspaper. **Freq:** Daily and Sun. (morn.). **Print Method:** Offset. **Cols./Page:** 6. **Col. Width:** 25 nonpareils. **Col. Depth:** 301 agate lines. **Key Personnel:** Jay Davis, Business Manager, Vice President; Dennis Palmer, President, Publisher; Stephanie Reeves, Account Manager. **Subscription Rates:** $15.50 Individuals 1 month; $62 Individuals 4 months; $124 Individuals 8 months; $186 Individuals 12 months. **URL:** http://www.selmatimesjournal.com. **Remarks:** Accepts advertising. **Circ:** (Not Reported).

522 ■ WAQU-FM - 91.1
PO Box 2440
Tupelo, MS 38803
Free: 800-326-4543
Format: Religious. **Owner:** American Family Radio, at above address. **URL:** http://www.afa.net.

523 ■ WDXX-FM - 100.1
505 Lauderdale St.
Selma, AL 36702-1055
Phone: (334)875-3350
Fax: (334)874-6959
Format: Religious; Full Service. **Networks:** Independent. **Owner:** BroadSouth Communications Inc., 4141 Wall St , Montgomery, AL 36106, Ph: (334)593-9500. **Founded:** 1970. **Formerly**: WTUN-FM. **Operating Hours**: Continuous; 100% local. **ADI**: Montgomery-Selma, AL. **Key Personnel:** George Henry, Dir. of Programs. **Wattage:** 50,000. **Ad Rates:** Noncommercial. **URL:** http://www.dixiecountry.net/home.

524 ■ WHBB-AM - 1490
505 Lauderdale St.
Selma, AL 36702-1055
Phone: (334)875-3350
Fax: (334)874-6959
Format: News; Religious; Talk. **Networks:** ABC. **Owner:** BroadSouth Communications Inc., 4141 Wall St , Montgomery, AL 36106, Ph: (334)593-9500. **Founded:** 1935. **Operating Hours**: 5:00 a.m.-12:00 a.m. **ADI**: Montgomery-Selma, AL. **Key Personnel:** George Henry, Dir. of Programs; Marlene Lynn, Contact. **Wattage**: 1,000. **Ad Rates:** $10-40 for 30 seconds; $12-48 for 60 seconds. $8-$20 for 30 seconds; $10-$30 for 60 seconds. Combined advertising rates available with WDXX-FM. **Mailing address:** PO Box 1055, Selma, AL 36702-1055.

525 ■ WMRK-AM - 1340
PO Box 1150
Selma, AL 36702-1150
Phone: (334)875-7101
Fax: (334)875-1340
Email: walx@bellsouth.net

Format: Urban Contemporary. **Founded:** 1946. **Key Personnel:** Scott Alexander, Gen. Mgr. **Wattage:** 1,000 ERP. **Ad Rates:** Advertising accepted; rates available upon request. **URL:** http://walxradio.com.

526 ■ WRNF-FM - 89.5
PO Box 10
Selma, AL 36702
Free: 888-624-7234

Format: Religious. **Owner:** Moody Radio, 820 N La Salle Blvd., Chicago, IL 60610, Ph: (312)329-4000, Free: 800-356-6639.

527 ■ W24CK - 24
PO Box A
Santa Ana, CA 92711
Phone: (714)832-2950
Free: 888-731-1000

Owner: Trinity Broadcasting Network Inc., PO Box A, Santa Ana, CA 92711, Ph: (714)832-2950, Free: 888-731-1000.

SHEFFIELD

NW AL. Colbert Co. 5 mi. SE of Florence.

528 ■ WAKD-FM - 89.9
PO Box 2440
Tupelo, MS 38803
Phone: (662)844-8888

Format: Religious. **Owner:** American Family Association, at above address. **Ad Rates:** Noncommercial. **URL:** http://www.afa.net.

529 ■ WBTG-AM
1605 Gospel Rd.
Sheffield, AL 35660-0518
Phone: (205)381-6800
Fax: (205)381-6801

Format: Talk. **Owner:** Slatton & Associates Broadcasters Inc., at above address. **Founded:** 1962. **Formerly:** WSHF-AM; WHCM-AM. **Key Personnel:** Paul Slatton, Contact. **Wattage:** 1,000 Day; 079 Night. **Ad Rates:** $7-9 for 30 seconds. **Mailing address:** PO Box 518, Sheffield, AL 35660-0518. **URL:** http://www.wbtgradio.com/.

530 ■ WBTG-FM - 106.3
1605 Gospel Rd.
Sheffield, AL 35660-0518
Phone: (256)381-6800
Fax: (256)381-6801

Format: Gospel; Contemporary Christian. **Owner:** Slatton & Associates Broadcasters Inc., at above address. **Founded:** 1977. **Formerly:** WRCK-FM. **Operating Hours:** Continuous. **Wattage:** 6,000 ERP. **Ad Rates:** $12-28 for 30 seconds; $14-34 for 60 seconds. $12-$28 for 30 seconds; $14-$34 for 60 seconds. Combined advertising rates available with WBTG-AM. **Mailing address:** PO Box 518, Sheffield, AL 35660-0518. **URL:** http://www.wbtgradio.com/.

SPANISH FORT

531 ■ WLPR-AM - 960
6530-B Spanish Fort Blvd.
Spanish Fort, AL 36527
Phone: (251)473-8080
Email: wbhy@goforth.org

Format: Southern Gospel. **Owner:** Goforth Media Inc., 6530 Spanish Fort Blvd., Spanish Fort, AL 36527, Ph: (251)473-8488. **Founded:** 1964. **Operating Hours:** Continuous; 98% network, 2% local. **ADI:** Mobile, AL-Pensacola, FL. **Key Personnel:** Wilbur Goforth, Gen. Mgr., President, wilbur@goforth.org; Charlie Smith, Dir. of Mktg., charlie@goforth.org; Robert Barber, Station Mgr., robert@goforth.org; Kenny Fowler, Music Dir., kenny@goforth.org. **Wattage:** 5,000. **Ad Rates:** Noncommercial. **URL:** http://www.goforth.org.

STEVENSON

North Jackson Progress - See Jackson

SULLIGENT

NW AL. Lamar Co. 82 mi. NW of Birmingham. Timber, metal working industry. Textile plants. Oil, natural gas.

532 ■ Lamar Leader
Lamar Leader
PO Box 925
Sulligent, AL 35586
Phone: (205)698-8148
Fax: (205)698-8146
Publisher's E-mail: news@lamarleader.com

Community newspaper. **Freq:** Weekly (Wed.). **Print Method:** Offset. **Trim Size:** 13 x 21 1/2. **Cols./Page:** 6. **Col. Width:** 12.5 picas. **Col. Depth:** 129 picas. **Key Personnel:** Stephanie Wilson, Office Manager. **USPS:** 002-510. **Subscription Rates:** $40 Individuals 1 year print and online; $25 Individuals 1 year print - in county; $27.50 Individuals 1 year print - neighboring counties; $30 Individuals 1 year print - other counties in Alabama; $35 Individuals 1 year print - out of state; $30 Individuals 1 year - online only. **Remarks:** Accepts advertising. **Circ:** (Not Reported).

SYLACAUGA

EC AL. Talladega Co. 40 mi. SE of Birmingham.

533 ■ Sylacauga
Sylacauga Chamber of Commerce
17 W Ft. Williams St.
Sylacauga, AL 35150-2427
Phone: (256)249-0308
Fax: (256)249-0315

Magazine covering local information, local attractions, and listings of other civic, social, and professional organizations. **Freq:** Annual. **Key Personnel:** Carol Pappas, Editor; Pam Adamson, Director, Advertising. **Subscription Rates:** Included in membership. **URL:** http://sylacaugachamber.com/magazine.as. **Mailing address:** PO Box 185, Sylacauga, AL 35150-0185. **Circ:** (Not Reported).

534 ■ WAWV-FM - 98.3
PO Box 629
Sylacauga, AL 35150
Phone: (205)245-3281
Fax: (256)245-4355
Email: thev983@mindspring.com

Format: Adult Contemporary. **Networks:** ABC. **Owner:** Coosa Valley Broadcasting, Inc., at above address, Ph: (256)249-4263. **Founded:** 1959. **Formerly:** WMLS-FM; Alabama Broacasting Co., Inc. **Operating Hours:** 24 hours. **Key Personnel:** Brad Isbell, Contact; Brad Isbell, Contact, bradisbell@webtv.net; Brad Isbell, Contact, bradisbell@webtv.net. **Wattage:** 5,000. **Ad Rates:** $6.50-13.25 for 30 seconds; $8.50-15 for 60 seconds.

535 ■ WFEB-AM - 1340
1209 Millerville Hwy.
Sylacauga, AL 35150
Phone: (256)245-3144
Fax: (256)245-3148

Format: News; Talk; Oldies; Contemporary Christian. **Networks:** Mutual Broadcasting System. **Founded:** 1945. **Operating Hours:** Continuous. **Key Personnel:** Bruce C. Carr, Gen. Mgr. **Wattage:** 1,000. **Ad Rates:** $8.65 for 30 seconds; $10.45 for 60 seconds. **Mailing address:** PO Box 358, Sylacauga, AL 35150. **URL:** http://wfebsylacauga.com/.

536 ■ WYEA-AM - 1290
1 Motes Rd
Sylacauga, AL 35150-0629
Phone: (256)249-4263
Fax: (256)245-4355
Email: info@wyea.net

Format: Gospel. **Networks:** Alabama Radio (ALANET); Arkansas Radio; Interstate Radio. **Founded:** 1948. **Formerly:** WMLS-AM. **Operating Hours:** 6:00 a.m. - 8:00 p.m. **Key Personnel:** John Vogel, Owner. **Wattage:** 1,000 per Day; 050 Watts per Night. **Ad Rates:** $3.95-4.75 for 30 seconds; $4.30-5.75 for 60 seconds. **Mailing address:** PO Box 629, Sylacauga, AL 35150-1731. **URL:** http://www.wyea.net.

TALLADEGA

Talladega Co. 24 mi. SW of Anniston. Talladega College (Black); State Schools for the Deaf and Blind. Federal Correctional Institute. Manufactures cotton yarn, textiles, bags, soil pipe fittings, plywood, textile machine parts, sawmill machinery, insecticides, lumber. Timber. Agriculture. Cotton, corn, soybeans, hay, cattle.

537 ■ The Daily Home
Consolidated Publishing Company Inc.
6 Sylacauga Hwy
Talladega, AL 35160-0977
Phone: (205)362-1000

General newspaper. **Freq:** Tuesday - Sunday(morning). **Print Method:** Offset. **Trim Size:** 13 3/4 x 22 3/4. **Cols./Page:** 6. **Col. Width:** 25 nonpareils. **Col. Depth:** 21 1/2 inches. **Key Personnel:** Ed Fowler, Publisher; Pam Adamson, Director, Advertising; Kandi Macy, Manager, Circulation. **USPS:** 143-180. **Subscription Rates:** $110 Individuals /year (online). **URL:** http://www.annistonstar.com/the_daily_home. **Remarks:** Advertising accepted; rates available upon request. **Circ:** (Not Reported).

TALLASSEE

EC AL. Tallapoosa Co. 25 mi. NE of Montgomery.

538 ■ The Tallassee Tribune
The Tallassee Tribune
301 Gilmer
Tallassee, AL 36078-1211
Phone: (334)283-6568
Publisher's E-mail: editor@tallasseetribune.com

Community newspaper. **Freq:** Weekly (Thurs.). **Print Method:** Offset. **Cols./Page:** 6. **Col. Width:** 12 1/5 picas. **Col. Depth:** 21 1/2 inches. **Key Personnel:** Griffin Pritchard, Managing Editor. **Mailing address:** PO Box 780730, Tallassee, AL 36078-1211. **Ad Rates:** PCI $5. **Remarks:** Accepts classified advertising. **Circ:** 3736.

539 ■ WACQ-AM - 1130
320 Barnett Blvd.
Tallassee, AL 36078
Phone: (334)283-6888
Free: 800-923-4699

Owner: Progressive United Comm. Inc., at above address. **Founded:** 1979. **Key Personnel:** Fred Randall Hughey, Contact; Debra Hughey, Contact. **Ad Rates:** $5 for 30 seconds; $7.50 for 60 seconds. **URL:** http://www.wacqradio.com/contact-us/.

540 ■ WACQ-FM - 99.9
320 Barnett Blvd.
Tallassee, AL 36078

Format: Adult Contemporary. **Networks:** Alabama Radio (ALANET); USA Radio. **Owner:** Tuskegee Communication Co. Inc., at above address. **Operating Hours:** Continuous. **ADI:** Montgomery-Selma, AL. **Key Personnel:** Fred Randall Hughey, Contact; Debra Hughey, Contact. **Wattage:** 6,000. **Ad Rates:** $10 for 30 seconds; $15 for 60 seconds. **URL:** http://www.wacqradio.com/about-us/.

541 ■ WTLS-AM - 1300
2045 Alabama Hwy. 229
Tallassee, AL 36078
Phone: (334)283-8200
Fax: (334)283-8622
Free: 877-329-0197

Format: Talk; Sports. **Owner:** Michael Butler. **Founded:** 1954. **Operating Hours:** Sunrise-Sunset. **Key Personnel:** Miles Hathcook, Contact; Shane Yankey, Contact; Rick Dorley, Contact. **Local Programs:** *Wake-Up Call*, Monday Tuesday Wednesday Thursday Friday 6:00 a.m. - 9:00 a.m. **Wattage:** 1,200. **Ad Rates:** Noncommercial; Advertising accepted; rates available upon request. **Mailing address:** PO Box 780146, Tallassee, AL 36078. **URL:** http://www.1300wtls.com.

THOMASVILLE

SW AL. Clarke Co. 55 mi. SW of Selma. Saw, planing, stave, and paper mills.; Cotton gins; machine shop. Textile factory. Pine and hardwood timber. Agriculture. Cotton, corn, peanuts.

542 ■ The Thomasville Times
The Thomasville Times
24 W Front St. S
Thomasville, AL 36784

Circulation: ★ = AAM; △ or • = BPA; ♦ = CAC; ❑ = VAC; ⊕ = PO Statement; ‡ = Publisher's Report; Boldface figures = sworn; Light figures = estimated.

Phone: (334)636-2214
Fax: (334)636-9822
Publisher's E-mail: newsroom@thethomasvilletimes.com
Newspaper. **Freq:** Weekly (Thurs.). **Print Method:** Offset. **Trim Size:** 13 x 21 1/2. **Cols./Page:** 6. **Col. Width:** 12.5 picas. **Key Personnel:** Arthur Mclean, Contact. **USPS:** 628-060. **Subscription Rates:** $30 Individuals print; $29 Individuals senior citizen (print); $40 Elsewhere print; $39 Elsewhere senior citizen (print); $52 Individuals online. **Alt. Formats:** PDF. **Mailing address:** PO Box 367, Thomasville, AL 36784. **Remarks:** Advertising accepted; rates available upon request. **Circ:** (Not Reported).

543 ■ Mediacom
32761 Hwy. 43
Thomasville, AL 36784
Free: 800-239-8411
Cities Served: 80 channels. **URL:** http://www.mediacomcable.com.

544 ■ WJDB-AM
PO Box 219
Thomasville, AL 36784
Phone: (334)636-4438
Fax: (334)636-4439
Free: 800-245-9532
Format: Southern Gospel. **Networks:** CBS. **Owner:** Griffin Broadcasting Corp., at above address, Ph: (334)636-4438. **Founded:** 1956. **Wattage:** 1,000 Day; 049 Night. **Ad Rates:** $5.00 for 30 seconds; $7.00 for 60 seconds.

545 ■ WJDB-FM - 95.5
PO Box 219
Thomasville, AL 36784
Format: Country. **Networks:** CBS. **Owner:** Griffin Broadcasting Corp., at above address, Ph: (334)636-4438. **Founded:** 1972. **Operating Hours:** Continuous. **Wattage:** 25,000. **Ad Rates:** $5-7 for 30 seconds; for 60 seconds. **URL:** http://www.wjdb955.com.

TROY

SE AL. Pike Co. 43 mi. SE of Montgomery. Troy State University. Manufactures truck bodies, latex products, plastic containers, textiles, wood products, circuit boards. Pecan shelling plants. Timber. Agriculture. Cotton, peanuts, pecans.

546 ■ Carmina Philosophiae
International Boethius Society
c/o Noel Harold Kaylor Jr., Executive Director
Smith Hall 274
Dept. of English
Troy University
Troy, AL 36082
Phone: (334)670-3519
Journal covering the study of Boethius, his age, and his influence, and soliciting full-length articles, review essays, and book reviews for upcoming issues. **Freq:** Annual. **Subscription Rates:** Included in membership. **URL:** http://boethius.blogspot.com/p/carmina-philosophiae.html. **Remarks:** Advertising not accepted. **Circ:** (Not Reported).

547 ■ Tropolitan
Troy University
Troy, AL 36082
Phone: (334)670-3289
Free: 800-414-5756
Publisher's E-mail: ask@troy.edu
Collegiate newspaper (broadsheet). **Freq:** Weekly (Thurs.) during the academic year. **Print Method:** Offset. **Trim Size:** 10 x 12 3/4. **Cols./Page:** 6. **Col. Width:** 28 nonpareils. **Col. Depth:** 181 agate lines. **Key Personnel:** Virginia Spears, Editor; Thomas King, Managing Editor; Edward Bailey, Editor. **Alt. Formats:** PDF. **URL:** http://tropnews.com. **Remarks:** Advertising accepted; rates available upon request. **Circ:** (Not Reported).

548 ■ Troy Messenger
Boone Newspapers Inc.
918 S Brundidge St.
Troy, AL 36081
Phone: (334)566-4270
Independent newspaper. **Freq:** Tues.-Fri. (morn.), Sun. (morn.). **Print Method:** Offset. **Cols./Page:** 6. **Col. Width:** 25 nonpareils. **Col. Depth:** 21 1/2 inches. **Key Personnel:** Wendy Ward, Office Manager, phone: (334)670-6301; Stacy G. Graning, Editor; Deedie Carter, Director, Advertising, phone: (334)670-6305. **URL:** http://www.troymessenger.com. **Feature Editors:** Jaine Treadwell, *Features*, phone: (334)670-6302, jaine.treadwell@troymessenger.com. **Mailing address:** PO Box 727, Troy, AL 36081. **Ad Rates:** SAU $5.88. **Remarks:** Accepts advertising. **Circ:** Combined 3000, Non-paid 14000.

549 ■ Troy Cablevision & Entertainment
1006 S Brundidge St.
Troy, AL 36081
Phone: (334)566-3310
Free: 800-735-9546
Cities Served: 69 channels. **URL:** http://www.troycable.net.

550 ■ WRWA-FM - 88.7
Troy University
Wallace Hall
Troy, AL 36082
Fax: (334)670-3934
Free: 800-800-6616
Email: publicradiocomments@troy.edu
Format: Public Radio. **Simulcasts:** WTSU and WTJB. **Networks:** National Public Radio (NPR); Public Radio International (PRI). **Owner:** Troy University, Troy, AL 36082, Ph: (334)670-3289, Free: 800-414-5756. **Founded:** 1985. **Operating Hours:** Continuous. **Key Personnel:** Fred Azbell, Program Mgr.; John Brunson, Chief Engineer, jbrunson@troy.edu. **Wattage:** 50,000. **Ad Rates:** Noncommercial. **URL:** http://www.troypublicradio.org.

551 ■ WTBF-AM - 970
67 Court Sq.
Troy, AL 36081
Phone: (334)566-0300
Fax: (334)566-5689
Email: wtbfjennifer@troycable.net
Format: Sports; Talk. **Simulcasts:** WTBF-FM. **Networks:** ABC. **Owner:** Troy Broadcasting Corp., 67 W Court Sq., Troy, AL 36081, Ph: (334)566-0300. **Founded:** 1947. **Operating Hours:** Continuous. **ADI:** Dothan, AL. **Key Personnel:** Dave Kirby, Contact; Jennifer Smith, Traffic Mgr; Jim Roling, Contact; Ralph Black, Contact; Dave Kirby, Contact. **Local Programs:** *Dennis Miller*, Monday Tuesday Wednesday Thursday Friday 6:00 p.m. - 9:00 p.m.; *Morning Show*, Saturday Monday Tuesday Wednesday Thursday Friday 8:00 a.m. - 9:00 a.m. 5:30 a.m. - 9:00 a.m.; *On the Bookshelf*, Sunday 9:00 a.m. - 10:00 a.m.; 3:30 p.m. - 4:00 p.m. **Wattage:** 5,000. **Ad Rates:** $6.50 for 15 seconds; $11 for 30 seconds; $15 for 30 seconds; $18 for 60 seconds; $22.50 for 60 seconds. Combined advertising rates available with WTBF-FM. **URL:** http://www.wtbf.com.

552 ■ WTBF-FM - 94.7
67 Court Sq.
Troy, AL 36081
Phone: (334)566-0300
Fax: (334)566-5689
Format: News; Sports. **Simulcasts:** WTBF-AM. **Owner:** Troy Broadcasting Corp., 67 W Court Sq., Troy, AL 36081, Ph: (334)566-0300. **Founded:** Nov. 1997. **Operating Hours:** Continuous. **ADI:** Albany-Schenectady-Troy, NY. **Key Personnel:** Jennifer Smith, Traffic Mgr. **Local Programs:** *Morning Show*, Monday Tuesday Wednesday Thursday Friday 5:30 a.m. - 9:00 a.m.; *Best of Rick & Bubba*, Monday Tuesday Wednesday Thursday Friday 6:00 a.m. - 10:00 a.m.; *Twilight Zone*, Saturday 3:00 a.m. - 4:00 a.m.; 6:00 a.m. - 7:00 a.m.; 10:00 p.m. - 12:00 a.m.; *Driving Home With Doc*; *Roger Hedgecock Weekend*, Saturday 11:00 a.m. - 2:00 p.m.; *Saturday Night America*, Saturday 7:00 p.m. - 10:00 p.m; *The Dirt Doctor*, Sunday 8:00 a.m. - 9:00 a.m.; *Chronicles of the Old West*, Saturday Sunday 4:00 a.m. - 5:00 a.m. 11:00 p.m. - 12:00 a.m. **Wattage:** 16,500 ERP. **Ad Rates:** Combined advertising rates available with WTBF-AM. **URL:** http://www.wtbf.com.

553 ■ WTJB-FM - 91.7
Wallace Hall
Troy, AL 36082
Phone: (334)670-3000
Free: 800-800-6616
Email: publicradio@troy.edu
Format: Public Radio; Full Service; Jazz; Talk. **Simulcasts:** WTSU and WRWA. **Networks:** National Public Radio (NPR); Public Radio International (PRI); BBC World Service; WFMT Fine Arts. **Owner:** Troy State University, at above address. **Founded:** 1984. **Operating Hours:** Continuous. **Key Personnel:** John Brunson, Chief Engineer, jbrunson@troy.edu; Fred Azbell, Program Mgr., fazbell@troy.edu. **Wattage:** 5,000 ERP Horizontal. **Ad Rates:** Accepts Advertising. **URL:** http://troypublicradio.org.

554 ■ WTSU-FM - 89.9
Troy University
Wallace Hall
Troy, AL 36082
Phone: (334)670-3268
Fax: (334)670-3934
Free: 800-800-6616
Email: publicradio@troy.edu
Format: Public Radio. **Simulcasts:** WRWA-FM, WTJB-FM. **Networks:** National Public Radio (NPR); Public Radio International (PRI). **Owner:** Troy University, Troy, AL 36082, Ph: (334)670-3289, Free: 800-414-5756. **Founded:** 1977. **Operating Hours:** Continuous. **Key Personnel:** John Brunson, Chief Engineer. **Wattage:** 100,000. **Ad Rates:** Noncommercial. **URL:** http://www.troy.edu.

TUSCALOOSA

W. AL. Tuscaloosa Co. On Black Warrior River, 56 mi. SW of Birmingham. Manufactures chemicals, paper, lumber, cast iron pipe, veneer, fertilizer, feeds, cottonseed products, auto and truck tires and tubes. Meat packing plants, oil refinery.

555 ■ Aggregates Manager
Randall-Reilly Publishing Company L.L.C.
3200 Rice Mine Rd. NE
Tuscaloosa, AL 35406
Free: 800-633-5953
Publisher's E-mail: an@randallreilly.com
Magazine covering the full range of information needs for aggregates professionals. **Freq:** Monthly. **Key Personnel:** Amanda Bayhi, Managing Editor; Joe Donald, Board Member; Therese Dunphy, Editor-in-Chief, phone: (330)920-9737. **URL:** http://www.aggman.com/; http://www.randallreilly.com/solutions/media-services/our-brands/aggregates-manager. **Circ:** (Not Reported).

556 ■ Alabama Alumni Magazine
National Alumni Association University of Alabama Chapter
Box 861928
224 Paul W. Bryant Dr.
Tuscaloosa, AL 35401
Phone: (205)348-5963
Fax: (205)348-5958
Publisher's E-mail: alumni@alumni.ua.edu
University alumni magazine. **Freq:** Quarterly. **Print Method:** Offset. **Trim Size:** 8 1/4 x 10 3/4. **Cols./Page:** 3. **Col. Width:** 28 nonpareils. **Col. Depth:** 134 agate lines. **Key Personnel:** Lydia Avant, Editor; Janice M. Fink, Associate Editor; Calvin Brown, Director, phone: (205)348-5966. **USPS:** 011-040. **URL:** http://alumni.ua.edu/publications/alumni-magazine. **Ad Rates:** BW $2100. **Remarks:** Accepts advertising. **Circ:** 38000.

557 ■ Alabama Economic Outlook
University of Alabama Culverhouse College of Commerce and Business Administration Center for Business and Economic Research
Box 870221
Tuscaloosa, AL 35487
Phone: (205)348-6191
Fax: (205)348-2951
Publisher's E-mail: uacber@cba.ua.edu
Trade magazine covering economic conditions in the nation and Alabama. **Founded:** 1980. **Freq:** Annual. **Subscription Rates:** $30 Individuals. **URL:** http://cber.cba.ua.edu/publications.html#outlook. **Mailing address:** PO Box 870221, Tuscaloosa, AL 35487-0221. **Remarks:** Advertising not accepted. **Circ:** (Not Reported).

558 ■ Alabama Heritage
University of Alabama
PO Box 870342
Tuscaloosa, AL 35487-0342
Phone: (205)348-7467
Fax: (205)348-7473
Free: 877-925-2323
Publication E-mail: alabama.heritage@ua.edu

Historical magazine for the general public. Covers cultural heritage of Alabama and the South. **Freq:** Quarterly. **Print Method:** Offset. **Trim Size:** 8 1/2 x 11. **Cols./Page:** 3. **Key Personnel:** Donna L. Cox, Editor-in-Chief; Sara Martin, Director, Marketing. **ISSN:** 0887--493X (print). **Subscription Rates:** $18.95 Individuals; $32.95 Two years. **URL:** http://www.alabamaheritage.com. **Remarks:** Accepts advertising. **Circ:** (Not Reported).

559 ■ Black Warrior Review
University of Alabama
PO Box 2389
Tuscaloosa, AL 35403
Phone: (205)348-7257
Publication E-mail: bwr@ua.edu
Literary a journal. **Freq:** Semiannual. **Print Method:** Offset. **Trim Size:** 6 x 9. **Key Personnel:** Bronwyn Valentine, Editor. **ISSN:** 0193--6301 (print). **Subscription Rates:** $20 Individuals 1 year; $40 Individuals 2 years; $12 Individuals single issue. **URL:** http://bwr.ua.edu. **Ad Rates:** BW $150. **Remarks:** Accepts advertising. **Circ:** Paid 2000.

560 ■ Christian Higher Education
Routledge
c/o Barry D. Lumsden, Editor-in-Chief
University of Alabama
Education Policy Center
Tuscaloosa, AL 35487-0231
Phone: (940)597-7923
Publisher's E-mail: book.orders@tandf.co.uk
Peer-reviewed journal focusing on issues in finance, enrollment management, innovative teaching methods, higher education administration, program assessment, faculty development, curriculum development, and student services. **Freq:** 5/year. **Key Personnel:** Karen A. Longman, Editor-in-Chief; Laurie A. Schreiner, Editor-in-Chief; Barry D. Lumsden, Editor-in-Chief; Perry Glanzer, Editor; Todd C. Ream, Editor. **ISSN:** 1536--3759 (print); **EISSN:** 1539--4107 (electronic). **Subscription Rates:** $215 Individuals print only; $379 Institutions online only; $433 Institutions print and online. **URL:** http://www.tandfonline.com/toc/uche20/current#.UvWuF9lW2qY. **Mailing address:** PO Box 870231, Tuscaloosa, AL 35487-0231. **Circ:** (Not Reported).

561 ■ Commercial Carrier Journal
Randall-Reilly Publishing Company L.L.C.
3200 Rice Mine Rd. NE
Tuscaloosa, AL 35406
Free: 800-633-5953
Publisher's E-mail: an@randallreilly.com
Magazine containing management, maintenance, and operations information for truck and bus fleets. **Founded:** 1911. **Freq:** Monthly. **Print Method:** Offset. **Key Personnel:** Stacy McCants, Publisher; Dean Smallwood, Managing Editor; Avery Vise, Director, Editorial. **ISSN:** 0734-1423 (print). **Subscription Rates:** Free. **URL:** http://www.randallreilly.com/portfolio-item/commercial-carrier-journal/. **Ad Rates:** 4C $15,140. **Remarks:** Accepts advertising. **Circ:** Combined 96500.

562 ■ Dreams and Nightmares
Dreams and Nightmares
1300 Kicker Rd.
Tuscaloosa, AL 35404
Journal covering science fiction, fantasy, and horror. **Freq:** Irregular. **Print Method:** Photocopy. **Trim Size:** 8 1/2 x 5 1/2. **Key Personnel:** David Kopaska-Merkel, Editor. **ISSN:** 0897--0238 (print). **Subscription Rates:** $25 Individuals six-issue subscription within North America; $30 Other countries six-issue subscription outside North America; $90 U.S. and other countries lifetime subscription. **URL:** http://dreamsandnightmaresmagazine.com. **Ad Rates:** BW $25. **Remarks:** Accepts advertising. **Circ:** Combined 200.

563 ■ Equipment World
Randall-Reilly Publishing Company L.L.C.
3200 Rice Mine Rd. NE
Tuscaloosa, AL 35406
Free: 800-633-5953
Publisher's E-mail: an@randallreilly.com
Magazine featuring construction contractors, equipment manufacturers, and dealers and providers of services and supplies to the construction industry. **Freq:** Monthly. **Key Personnel:** Gregg Terry, Publisher; Amy Materson, Managing Editor; Tom Jackson, Executive Editor. **URL:** http://www.equipmentworld.com. **Circ:** ‡78000.

564 ■ International Journal of Security & Networks
Inderscience Publishers
c/o Prof. Yang Xiao, Ed.-in-Ch.
University of Alabama, Department of Computer Science
101 Houser Hall
Box 870290
Tuscaloosa, AL 35487-0290
Publisher's E-mail: editor@inderscience.com
Journal covering on dissemination of network security related issues. **Founded:** 2006. **Freq:** Quarterly. **Key Personnel:** Prof. Yang Xiao, Editor-in-Chief. **ISSN:** 1747-8405 (print); **EISSN:** 1747-8413 (electronic). **Subscription Rates:** €520 Individuals print or online only for 1 user; €882 Individuals online only for 2-3 users; €520 Individuals print & online; €1292 Individuals online only for 4-5 users; €1680 Individuals online only for 6-7 users; €2048 Individuals online only for 8-9 users; €2390 Individuals online only for 10-14 users; €2709 Individuals online only for 15-19 users; €3171 Individuals online only for 20 users. **URL:** http://www.inderscience.com/info/inprice.php?jcode=ijsn. **Circ:** (Not Reported).

565 ■ International Journal of Sensor Networks
Inderscience Publishers
c/o Prof. Yang Xiao, Ed.-in-Ch.
University of Alabama
101 Houser Hall
Tuscaloosa, AL 35487-0290
Publisher's E-mail: editor@inderscience.com
Journal focused on knowledge systems and advanced information systems. **Freq:** 12/yr. **Key Personnel:** Prof. Yang Xiao, Editor-in-Chief; Dr. Xiuzhen Cheng, Board Member; Dr. Sghaier Guizani, Board Member; Dr. Maggie Cheng, Board Member; Prof. Mohsen Guizani, Board Member; Prof. Hsiao-Hwa Chen, Board Member; Prof. Christos Douligeris, Board Member. **ISSN:** 1748--1279 (print); **EISSN:** 1748--1287 (electronic). **Subscription Rates:** $1415 Individuals print or online; $1981 Individuals print and online. **URL:** http://www.inderscience.com/jhome.php?jcode=ijsnet. **Mailing address:** PO Box 870290, Tuscaloosa, AL 35487-0290. **Circ:** (Not Reported).

566 ■ Journal of Creative Behavior
Creative Education Foundation
c/o Thomas B. Ward, Ed.
Department of Psychology
University of Alabama
Tuscaloosa, AL 35487-0348
Phone: (205)348-3178
Fax: (205)348-8648
Journal covering creative education. **Freq:** Quarterly. **Key Personnel:** Ronald Beghetto, Editor. **ISSN:** 0022-0175 (print). **Subscription Rates:** $107 Individuals print or online; $135 Individuals print and online; $339 Institutions print or online; $390 Institutions print and online. **URL:** http://www.creativeeducationfoundation.org/what-we-do/journal-of-creative-behavior. **Mailing address:** PO Box 870348, Tuscaloosa, AL 35487-0348. **Remarks:** Advertising not accepted. **Circ:** 2000.

567 ■ Journal of Interactive Online Learning
National Center for Online Learning Research
PO Box 870232
Tuscaloosa, AL 35487-0232
Phone: (205)348-1401
Fax: (205)348-9863
Online academic journal that provides a venue for manuscripts, critical essays, and reviews. **Freq:** Quarterly. **Key Personnel:** Dr. Cynthia S. Sunal, Board Member, Editor; Jason T. Abbitt, PhD, Board Member, Managing Editor. **ISSN:** 1541--4914 (print). **Subscription Rates:** Free online. **URL:** http://www.ncolr.org. **Circ:** (Not Reported).

568 ■ Journal of the Legal Profession
University of Alabama School of Law
101 Paul W. Bryant Dr. E
Tuscaloosa, AL 35487-0382
Phone: (205)348-5440
Publisher's E-mail: admissions@law.ua.edu
Journal covering topics related to legal ethics and professional responsibility. **Freq:** Semiannual. **Key Personnel:** Robby Marcum, Editor-in-Chief. **Subscription Rates:** $24 Individuals. **URL:** http://www.law.ua.edu/jlp. **Mailing address:** PO Box 870382, Tuscaloosa, AL 35487-0382. **Circ:** (Not Reported).

569 ■ NANO Fiction
NANO Fiction
904 Anna Ave.
Tuscaloosa, AL 35401
Publisher's E-mail: managingeditor@nanofiction.org
Magazine featuring short stories, prose, experimental works, and comics. **Freq:** Semiannual spring and fall. **Key Personnel:** Andrew Bales, Associate Editor; Kirby Johnson, Editor; Glenn Shaheen, Editor. **ISSN:** 1935--844X (print). **Subscription Rates:** $14 Individuals; $8 Single issue; $24 Other countries. **URL:** http://www.nanofiction.org. **Circ:** (Not Reported).

570 ■ Overdrive: The Magazine for the American Trucker
Overdrive Magazine Inc.
3200 Rice Mine Rd. NE
Tuscaloosa, AL 35406
Phone: (205)349-2990
Free: 855-288-3783
Publication E-mail: editors@overdriveonline.com
Business/lifestyle publication for owner-operators in the trucking industry. **Freq:** Monthly. **Key Personnel:** Brad Holthaus, Publisher; Jeff Mason, Vice President; Linda Longton, Editor. **ISSN:** 0030--7394 (print). **URL:** http://www.overdriveonline.com. **Ad Rates:** 4C $19,739. **Remarks:** Accepts advertising. **Circ:** ‡103310.

571 ■ Roanoke-Chowan News-Herald
Boone Newspapers Inc.
1060 Fairfax Pk., Ste. B
Tuscaloosa, AL 35406-2837
Phone: (205)330-4100
Newspaper covering the local news, sports, business, and entertainment in Roanoke-Chowan region. **Freq:** Weekly (Thurs.). **Key Personnel:** Cal Bryant, Editor. **URL:** http://www.roanoke-chowannewsherald.com. **Mailing address:** PO Box 2370, Northport, AL 35475. **Remarks:** Accepts advertising. **Circ:** (Not Reported).

572 ■ Theatre History Studies
The University of Alabama Press
200 Hackberry Ln., 2 Flr.
Tuscaloosa, AL 35847-0380
Phone: (205)348-5180
Fax: (800)621-8476
Free: 800-621-2736
Publication E-mail: aharper@uapress.ua.edu
Scholarly journal covering theatre history. **Freq:** Annual. **Key Personnel:** Robert A. Schanke, Editor. **ISSN:** 0733-2033 (print). **Subscription Rates:** $15 Individuals; $30 Institutions; $29.95 Single issue. **URL:** http://www.uapress.ua.edu/pages/THS.aspx. **Mailing address:** PO Box 870380, Tuscaloosa, AL 35847-0380. **Ad Rates:** BW $150. **Remarks:** Accepts advertising. **Circ:** Paid 1000.

573 ■ Total Landscape Care
Randall-Reilly Publishing Company L.L.C.
3200 Rice Mine Rd. NE
Tuscaloosa, AL 35406
Free: 800-633-5953
Publisher's E-mail: an@randallreilly.com
Magazine focusing on landscaping. **Key Personnel:** Dan Tidwell, Publisher, Vice President; Jeff Cull, Associate Publisher. **URL:** http://www.randallreilly.com/portfolio-item/total-landscape-care. **Circ:** ‡72000.

574 ■ Truck Parts & Service
Randall-Reilly Publishing Company L.L.C.
3200 Rice Mine Rd. NE
Tuscaloosa, AL 35406
Free: 800-633-5953
Publication E-mail: truckparts&service@halldata.com
Trade magazine for truck parts and service market. **Freq:** Monthly. **Print Method:** Offset. **Trim Size:** 8 1/4 x 11. **Cols./Page:** 3. **Col. Width:** 13 picas. **Col. Depth:** 59 picas. **Key Personnel:** Denise L. Rondini, Executive Editor; Derek Smith, Editor. **ISSN:** 0895--3856 (print). **URL:** http://www.truckpartsandservice.com. **Formerly:** Heavy Duty Distribution. **Remarks:** Accepts advertising. **Circ:** 30000.

Circulation: ★ = AAM; △ or • = BPA; ♦ = CAC; ❑ = VAC; ⊕ = PO Statement; ‡ = Publisher's Report; Boldface figures = sworn; Light figures = estimated.

575 ■ Truckers News
Randall-Reilly Publishing Company L.L.C.
3200 Rice Mine Rd. NE
Tuscaloosa, AL 35406
Free: 800-633-5953
Publisher's E-mail: an@randallreilly.com
Magazine containing trucking news, the coolest rigs, timely health tips, and a list of top jobs from the extensive Randall-Reilly recruiting networks. **Freq:** Monthly. **ISSN:** 1040--2284 (print). **URL:** http://www.truckersnews.com; http://www.randallreilly.com/solutions/media-services/our-brands/truckers-news. **Remarks:** Accepts advertising. **Circ:** 225000.

576 ■ The Tuscaloosa News
The Tuscaloosa News
315 28th Ave.
Tuscaloosa, AL 35401
Phone: (205)345-0505
General newspaper. **Freq:** Daily (eve.), Sat. and Sun. (morn.). **Print Method:** Offset. **Cols./Page:** 6. **Col. Width:** 25 nonpareils. **Col. Depth:** 301 agate lines. **Key Personnel:** Tim Thompson, Publisher, phone: (205)722-0115; Doug Ray, Executive Editor, phone: (205)722-0190. **USPS:** 644-320. **Subscription Rates:** $26.07 Individuals /month - 7-day (print and digital); $21.73 Individuals /month - weekend (print and digital); $14.30 Individuals /month (digital). **Remarks:** Accepts advertising. **Circ:** (Not Reported).

577 ■ Waxahachie Daily Light
Boone Newspapers Inc.
1060 Fairfax Pk., Ste. B
Tuscaloosa, AL 35406-2837
Phone: (205)330-4100
Newspaper. **Freq:** Daily and Sun. (eve.). **Print Method:** Offset. **Trim Size:** 13 3/4 x 22 1/2. **Cols./Page:** 6. **Col. Width:** 12.5 picas. **Col. Depth:** 301 agate lines. **Key Personnel:** Neal White, Editor; Joe Constancio, Manager, Production; Aaron Schwaderer, Managing Editor. **Subscription Rates:** $71.99 Individuals online. **URL:** http://www.waxahachiedailylight.com. **Mailing address:** PO Box 2370, Northport, AL 35475. **Ad Rates:** GLR $.375; BW $677.25; 4C $867.25; SAU $6. **Remarks:** Accepts advertising. **Circ:** Combined ‡33000.

578 ■ WACT-AM
3900 11th Ave.
Tuscaloosa, AL 35402-0126
Phone: (205)349-3200
Fax: (205)752-9269
Format: Gospel; Southern Gospel. **Networks:** USA Radio. **Founded:** 1958. **ADI**: Tuscaloosa, AL. **Wattage**: 5,000 Day; 108 Night. **Ad Rates:** $8-18 for 30 seconds; $10-24 for 60 seconds. **Mailing address:** PO Box 020126, Tuscaloosa, AL 35402-0126.

579 ■ WAPR-FM - 88.3
920 Paul W Bryant Dr.
Tuscaloosa, AL 35487
Phone: (205)348-6644
Format: Public Radio. **Networks:** National Public Radio (NPR). **Founded:** May 1996. **Operating Hours**: Continuous. **Key Personnel:** Brian Poellnitz, Operations Mgr.; Kathy Henslee, Dir. of Dev.; Pat Duggins, News Dir. **Wattage**: 53,000. **Ad Rates:** Advertising accepted; rates available upon request. **URL:** http://www.apr.org/index.html.

580 ■ WBEI-FM - 101.7
142 Skyland Blvd. E
Tuscaloosa, AL 35405
Phone: (205)345-7200
Fax: (205)349-1715
Format: Alternative/New Music/Progressive. **Owner:** Citadel Broadcasting Corp., 7201 W Lake Mead Blvd., Ste. 400, Las Vegas, NV 89128-8366, Ph: (702)804-5200, Fax: (702)804-8250. **ADI**: Tuscaloosa, AL. **Key Personnel:** David Dubose, Gen. Mgr., david.dubose@townsquaremedia.com; Greg Thomas, Div. Mgr., greg.thomas@townsquaremedia.com; Todd Livingston, Contact, todd.livingston@citcomm.com. **URL:** http://www.b1017online.com.

581 ■ WDGM-FM - 99.1
142 Skyland Blvd.
Tuscaloosa, AL 35405
Phone: (205)345-7200
Format: Oldies. **Owner:** Citadel Broadcasting Corp., 7201 W Lake Mead Blvd., Ste. 400, Las Vegas, NV 89128-8366, Ph: (702)804-5200, Fax: (702)804-8250. **ADI**: Tuscaloosa, AL.

582 ■ WFFN-FM - 95.3
142 Skyland Blvd. E
Tuscaloosa, AL 35405
Phone: (205)339-4953
Format: Contemporary Country. **Owner:** Cumulus Media Inc., 3280 Peachtree Rd. NW, Ste. 2300, Atlanta, GA 30305-2455, Ph: (404)949-0700, Fax: (404)949-0740. **Founded:** 1987. **Operating Hours**: Continuous. **ADI**: Tuscaloosa, AL. **Key Personnel:** Greg Thomas, Operations Mgr. **Wattage**: 3,000. **Ad Rates:** Noncommercial. **URL:** http://www.953thebear.com.

583 ■ W46BU - 46
PO Box A
Santa Ana, CA 92711
Phone: (714)832-2950
Free: 888-731-1000
Email: comments@tbn.org
Owner: Trinity Broadcasting Network Inc., PO Box A, Santa Ana, CA 92711, Ph: (714)832-2950, Free: 888-731-1000. **URL:** http://www.tbn.org.

584 ■ WJRD-AM - 1150
142 Skyland Blvd.
Tuscaloosa, AL 35405
Phone: (205)345-7200
Format: News; Talk. **Owner:** Citadel Broadcasting Corp., 7201 W Lake Mead Blvd., Ste. 400, Las Vegas, NV 89128-8366, Ph: (702)804-5200, Fax: (702)804-8250. **ADI**: Tuscaloosa, AL.

585 ■ WQPR-FM - 88.7
PO Box 870370
Tuscaloosa, AL 35487-0370
Phone: (205)348-6644
Free: 800-654-4262
Format: Public Radio; Jazz; Classical. **Networks:** National Public Radio (NPR); American Public Radio (APR). **Owner:** University of Alabama, Tuscaloosa, AL 35487, Ph: (205)348-6010. **Founded:** 1987. **Operating Hours**: Continuous. **Key Personnel:** Elizabeth Brock, Exec. Dir.; Brian Poellnitz, Operations Mgr.; Kathy Henslee, Dir. of Dev., khenslee@apr.org; Pat Duggins, News Dir.; Jackie Howell, Contact. **Wattage**: 20,000. **Ad Rates:** Noncommercial. **URL:** http://www.apr.org.

586 ■ WRTR-FM - 105.9
3900 11th Ave. S
Tuscaloosa, AL 35401
Phone: (205)349-3200
Fax: (205)752-9269
Format: Full Service; Classic Rock. **Owner:** iHeartMedia Inc., 200 E Basse Rd., San Antonio, TX 78209, Ph: (210)832-3314. **Founded:** 1966. **Operating Hours**: Continuous. **ADI**: Tuscaloosa, AL. **Key Personnel:** Bill Seckbach, Operations Mgr. **Wattage**: 6,000. **Ad Rates:** $16-28 for 30 seconds; $18-30 for 60 seconds. **URL:** http://www.iheart.com.

587 ■ WTBC-AM - 1230
2110 McFarland Blvd.
Tuscaloosa, AL 35404
Phone: (205)752-9822
Fax: (205)752-9696
Free: 800-518-1977
Format: News; Talk. **Networks:** ABC; ESPN Radio. **Owner:** Sisty Enterprises. **Founded:** 1946. **Operating Hours**: Continuous. **ADI**: Tuscaloosa, AL. **Key Personnel:** Ronnie Quarles, Gen. Mgr. **Local Programs**: *The Morning Show*, Monday Tuesday Wednesday Thursday Friday 6:00 a.m. - 9:00 a.m. **Wattage**: 1,000. **Ad Rates:** $14 for 30 seconds; $18 for 60 seconds. **Mailing address:** PO Box 2000, Tuscaloosa, AL 35404. **URL:** http://www.wtbc1230.com.

588 ■ WTSK-AM - 790
142 Skyland Blvd.
Tuscaloosa, AL 35405-4015
Phone: (205)345-7200
Fax: (205)349-1715
Format: Music of Your Life. **Founded:** 1958. **Operating Hours**: Continuous. **ADI**: Tuscaloosa, AL. **Wattage**: 5,000 ERP. **Ad Rates:** Advertising accepted; rates available upon request. **URL:** http://790wtsk.com/.

589 ■ WTUG-FM - 92.9
142 Skyland Blvd. E
Tuscaloosa, AL 35405
Phone: (205)391-0093
Format: Urban Contemporary. **Networks:** American Urban Radio. **Owner:** Citadel Broadcasting Corp., 7201 W Lake Mead Blvd., Ste. 400, Las Vegas, NV 89128-8366, Ph: (702)804-5200, Fax: (702)804-8250. **Founded:** 1979. **Operating Hours**: Continuous. **Key Personnel:** Charles Anthony, Dir. of Programs; Jade Nicole, Dir. Pub. Aff., News Dir.; Greg Thomas, Operations Mgr. **Wattage**: 100,000. **Ad Rates:** Noncommercial. **URL:** http://www.wtug.com.

590 ■ WTXT-FM - 98.1
3900 11th Ave. S
Tuscaloosa, AL 35401
Phone: (205)344-4589
Fax: (205)366-9774
Format: Country. **Owner:** Clear Channel Radio, 2601 Nicholasville Rd., Lexington, KY 40503, Ph: (859)422-1000. **Key Personnel:** Jackie Toye, Promotions Dir., jackietoye@iheartmedia.com; Gigi South, Gen. Mgr., gigisouth@clearchannel.com. **Ad Rates:** Advertising accepted; rates available upon request. **URL:** http://www.98txt.com.

591 ■ WUAL-FM - 91.5
920 Paul W Bryant Dr.
166 Reese Phifer Hall
Tuscaloosa, AL 35487
Phone: (205)348-6644
Free: 800-654-4262
Email: aprnews@apr.org
Format: Public Radio; News; Educational. **Networks:** National Public Radio (NPR); American Public Radio (APR). **Owner:** University of Alabama, Tuscaloosa, AL 35487, Ph: (205)348-6010. **Founded:** 1982. **Operating Hours**: Continuous. **Key Personnel:** Pat Duggins, News Dir.; Elizabeth Brock, Director. **Wattage**: 100,000. **Ad Rates:** Noncommercial. **Mailing address:** PO Box 870370, Tuscaloosa, AL 35487. **URL:** http://www.apr.org.

592 ■ WVUA-FM - 90.7
414 Campus Dr. E
Tuscaloosa, AL 35487
Phone: (205)348-6061
Email: wvua@sa.ua.edu
Format: Full Service; Alternative/New Music/Progressive. **Networks:** Independent. **Owner:** Board of Trustees-Communication School, at above address. **Founded:** 1972. **Operating Hours**: Continuous. **ADI**: Tuscaloosa, AL. **Key Personnel:** Chris Dodson, Station Mgr. **Wattage**: 150. **Ad Rates:** Advertising accepted; rates available upon request. **Mailing address:** PO Box 870170, Tuscaloosa, AL 35487-0170. **URL:** http://www.wvuafm.ua.edu.

593 ■ WVUA-TV - 7
901 University Blvd.
Tuscaloosa, AL 35401
Phone: (205)348-7000
Fax: (205)348-7002
Email: news@wvuatv.com
Key Personnel: Lynn Brooks, Contact, lbrooks@wvuatv.com. **URL:** http://www.wvuatv.com.

594 ■ WWPG-AM - 1280
601 Greensboro Ave., Ste. 507
Tuscaloosa, AL 35407
Phone: (205)345-4787
Format: Talk; Gospel. **Simulcasts:** WSLY-FM. **Owner:** Lawson of Tuscaloosa Inc. **Founded:** 1951. **Formerly**: WNPT-AM. **Operating Hours**: Continuous; 10% network, 90% local. **Wattage**: 5,000. **Ad Rates:** $10 for 30 seconds; $15 for 60 seconds. WQZZ-FM. **Mailing address:** PO Box 70427, Tuscaloosa, AL 35407.

595 ■ WZBQ-FM - 94.1
3900 11th Ave. S
Tuscaloosa, AL 35401
Phone: (205)344-4589
Fax: (205)366-9774
Format: Top 40; Contemporary Hit Radio (CHR). **Founded:** 1962. **Formerly**: WWWB-FM; WCKO-FM. **Operating Hours**: Continuous. **ADI**: Tuscaloosa, AL. **Key Personnel:** Rick L. Jones, Contact; Gigi South, Gen. Mgr., gigisouth@clearchannel.com; Jackie Toye, Sr. VP of Sales; Rick L. Jones, Contact. **Wattage**: 100,000. **Ad Rates:** Noncommercial. **URL:** http://www.941zbq.com.

TUSCUMBIA

NW AL. Colbert Co. 10 mi. NE of Montgomery.

596 ■ WLAY-AM - 1450
509 N Main St.
Tuscumbia, AL 35674
Phone: (256)383-2525
Owner: iHeartMedia Inc., 200 E Basse Rd., San Antonio, TX 78209, Ph: (210)832-3314. **Founded:** Sept. 15, 2006. **Wattage:** 1,000. **Ad Rates:** Accepts Advertising. **URL:** http://www.wlay1035.com.

597 ■ WLAY-FM - 103.5
509 N Main St.
Tuscumbia, AL 35674
Phone: (256)383-2525
Format: Country. **Networks:** Jones Satellite; ABC. **Owner:** Urban Radio Broadcasting, LLC, 134 S Dixie Hwy., Ste. 206, Hallandale Beach, FL 33009, Ph: (786)787-0404, Fax: (786)787-0405. **Founded:** 1964. **Operating Hours:** Continuous. **ADI:** Tuscaloosa, AL. **Wattage:** 100,000 W. **Ad Rates:** Noncommercial. **URL:** http://www.wlay1035.com.

598 ■ WMSR-FM - 94.9
509 N Main St.
Tuscumbia, AL 35674
Format: News. **Wattage:** 7,700.

599 ■ WVNA-AM - 1590
509 N Main St.
Tuscumbia, AL 35674
Phone: (256)383-2525
Fax: (256)383-4450
Format: News; Talk. **Owner:** Urban Radio Broadcasting, LLC, 134 S Dixie Hwy., Ste. 206, Hallandale Beach, FL 33009, Ph: (786)787-0404, Fax: (786)787-0405. **Key Personnel:** Brian Landrum, Dir. of Programs, brianlandrum@urbanradio.fm.

600 ■ WZZA-AM - 1410
1570 Woodmont Dr.
Tuscumbia, AL 35674
Phone: (256)381-1862
Fax: (256)381-6006
Email: promotions@wzzaradio.com
Format: Gospel; Hip Hop; Blues; Jazz; News; Information. **Owner:** Muscle Shoals Broadcasting, at above address. **Founded:** 1972. **Key Personnel:** Tori Bailey, Gen. Mgr., toribailey@wzzaradio.com. **Local Programs:** *A Look at the Shoals.* **Wattage:** 500 Day; 051 Night. **Ad Rates:** Advertising accepted; rates available upon request. **URL:** http://www.wzzaradio.com.

TUSKEGEE

E. AL. Macon Co. 40 mi. E. of Montgomery. Tuskegee University.

601 ■ The Tuskegee News: Macon County's Newspaper Since 1895
Tuskegee Newspapers Inc.
103 S Main St.
Tuskegee, AL 36083
Phone: (334)727-3020
Fax: (334)727-7700
Publication E-mail: tuskegeenews@bellsouth.net
Local newspaper serving the communities of Macon county. **Freq:** Weekly. **Print Method:** Offset. **Cols./Page:** 6. **Col. Width:** 2 inches. **Col. Depth:** 21 1/2 inches. **Key Personnel:** Paul Davis, Publisher; Scott Richardson, Manager, Advertising. **Subscription Rates:** $33 Individuals /year in Macon County; $57 Two years in Macon County; $39 Out of area /year; $66 Out of area two years; $44 Out of state; $78 Out of state two years. **URL:** http://www.thetuskegeenews.com. **Remarks:** Accepts advertising. **Circ:** 4200.

602 ■ Charter Communications
204C S Elm St.
Tuskegee, AL 36083
Owner: Charter Communications Inc., 400 Atlantic St., Stamford, CT 06901, Ph: (203)905-7801. **Founded:** Sept. 1972. **Formerly:** Tuskegee Cablevision; Bece Cable Inc. **Key Personnel:** Peggy Tuck, Bus. Mgr. **Cities Served:** Tuskegee, Alabama: subscribing households 3000; 35 channels; 1 community access channel; 24 hours per week community access programming. **URL:** http://www.charter.com.

UNION SPRINGS

603 ■ Union Springs Herald
Union Springs Herald
324 Ellis St.
Union Springs, AL 36089
Phone: (334)738-2360
Free: 800-738-6860
Community newspaper. Mailed all over the United States. **Freq:** Weekly (Wed.). **Cols./Page:** 6. **Col. Width:** 12 1/5 picas. **Col. Depth:** 21 1/2 inches. **Key Personnel:** Kim Graham, Publisher. **Subscription Rates:** $35 Individuals in county (print and online); $40 Individuals out of county (print and online). **URL:** http://www.unionspringsherald.com. **Ad Rates:** PCI $6. **Remarks:** Accepts advertising. **Circ:** 2400.

604 ■ Union Springs Telephone Co.
206 Hardaway Ave. E
Union Springs, AL 36089
Phone: (334)738-4400
Fax: (334)738-5555
Free: 800-352-8156
Founded: 1955. **Cities Served:** 60 channels. **Mailing address:** PO Box 272, Union Springs, AL 36089. **URL:** http://www.ustconline.net.

VERNON

NW AL. Lamar Co. 27 mi. NE of Columbus, MS. Cotton gins. Textile factories, timber products. Agriculture. Cotton, corn, potatoes.

605 ■ WJEC-FM - 106.5
PO Box 630
Vernon, AL 35592
Phone: (205)695-9191
Fax: (205)695-9131
Email: info@wjec1065.com
Format: Southern Gospel. **Owner:** Lamar County Broadcasting Co., Inc., at above address. **Founded:** 1991. **Operating Hours:** Continuous. **Key Personnel:** Glenn Crawford, Gen. Mgr., President, VP; Curt Smith, Div. Mgr. **Wattage:** 6,000. **Ad Rates:** Noncommercial. Combined advertising rates available with WVSA. **URL:** http://www.wjec1065.com.

606 ■ WVSA-AM - 1380
PO Box 630
Vernon, AL 35592
Phone: (205)695-9191
Fax: (205)695-9131
Format: Sports; Talk. **Networks:** ESPN Radio. **Owner:** Lamar City Broadcasting Company Inc., at above address. **Founded:** 1966. **Operating Hours:** 12 HRS Daily. **Key Personnel:** Brandon Crawford, President, Gen. Mgr.; Glenn Crawford, VP; Curt Smith, Station Mgr. **Wattage:** 5,000. **Ad Rates:** Advertising accepted; rates available upon request. **URL:** http://www.wvsa1380.com.

VESTAVIA HILLS

607 ■ Charter Communications
2100 S Columbiana Rd.
Vestavia Hills, AL 35216
Phone: (205)733-8778
Fax: (205)823-0353
Founded: 1967. **Formerly:** TCI Cablevision of Alabama, Inc. **Cities Served:** Jefferson and Shelby Counties. **URL:** http://www.charter.com/browse/content/store-locations-adp#/search.

WETUMPKA

C. AL. Elmore Co. On Coosa River, 13 mi. NE of Montgomery. Recreation, tourism. Textile, lumber and grist mills; cotton gins. Agriculture. Cotton, corn, oats. Beef and dairy products.

608 ■ The Wetumpka Herald
The Wetumpka Herald Inc.
PO Box 99
Wetumpka, AL 36092
Phone: (334)567-7811
Publication E-mail: news@thewetumpkaherald.com
Local newspaper. **Freq:** Semiweekly (Wed. and Sat.). **Print Method:** Offset. **Trim Size:** 12 1/2 x 22 3/4. **Cols./Page:** 6. **Col. Width:** 1.833 nonpareils. **Col. Depth:** 295 agate lines. **Key Personnel:** Peggy Blackburn, Managing Editor. **ISSN:** 1536--688X (print). **USPS:** 681-260. **Subscription Rates:** $44 Individuals; $49 Out of area; $54 Out of state; $25 Individuals senior citizen; $30 Out of area senior citizen; $35 Out of state senior citizen. **URL:** http://www.thewetumpkaherald.com. **Ad Rates:** BW $715.95; 4C $250; SAU $6; PCI $5.55. **Remarks:** Color advertising accepted; rates available upon request. **Circ:** ‡5300.

609 ■ Bright House Networks
3996 US Hwy. 231
Wetumpka, AL 36093
Free: 866-876-1872
Founded: Sept. 05, 2006. **Key Personnel:** Joe Schoenstein, Div. Pres. **URL:** http://www.brighthouse.com.

610 ■ WAPZ-AM - 1250
2821 US Hwy. 231
Wetumpka, AL 36093-1222
Phone: (334)567-9279
Fax: (334)567-7971
Format: Gospel. **Networks:** American Urban Radio. **Owner:** J and W Promotion Inc., at above address. **Founded:** 1954. **Operating Hours:** Continuous. **Key Personnel:** Pat Sullivan, Operations Mgr. **Wattage:** 5,000. **Ad Rates:** $20 for 30 seconds; $25 for 60 seconds.

YORK

W. AL. Sumter Co. 28 mi. NE of Meridian, MS. Lumber mills; cotton ginning. Pine, hickory timber. Agriculture. Cotton, beans, potatoes.

611 ■ WSLY-FM - 104.9
11474 US Hwy. 11
York, AL 36925
Phone: (205)392-5234
Free: 877-396-5536
Format: Gospel. **Owner:** Grantell Broadcasting Co., at above address. **Founded:** 1976. **Operating Hours:** Continuous. **ADI:** Meridian, MS. **Key Personnel:** Dr. Ken Michaels, Sr., Director, ken@y104radio.com; Clifford E. Holloway, III, Producer; Wayne B. Grant, Sr., Gen. Mgr.; Sarah P. Grant, President. **Wattage:** 50,000. **Ad Rates:** $6 for 30 seconds; $10 for 60 seconds. **URL:** http://www.espn1049.com.

612 ■ WYLS-AM - 670
11474 Hwy. 11 N
York, AL 36925
Phone: (205)392-5234
Fax: (205)392-5536
Format: Middle-of-the-Road (MOR); Big Band/Nostalgia; Gospel. **Networks:** CBS; Alabama Radio (ALANET); Mississippi. **Founded:** 1970. **Operating Hours:** Sunrise-sunset. **ADI:** Tuscaloosa, AL. **Wattage:** 4,800. **Ad Rates:** $6 for 30 seconds; $10 for 60 seconds.

Circulation: ★ = AAM; △ or • = BPA; ♦ = CAC; ❑ = VAC; ⊕ = PO Statement; ‡ = Publisher's Report; Boldface figures = sworn; Light figures = estimated.

ANCHORAGE

Anchorage Borough. Anchorage Census Div. (S). Situated on a broad plain at the head of Cook Inlet in Southcentral Alaska. Tourism. Wholesale retail trade. Oil.

613 ■ Alaska Business Monthly
Alaska Business Publishing Company Inc.
501 W Northern Lights Blvd., Ste. 100
Anchorage, AK 99503
Phone: (907)276-4373
Fax: (907)279-2900
Free: 800-770-4373
Publisher's E-mail: editor@akbizmag.com
Magazine featuring news, analysis, and profiles related to business in Alaska. **Founded:** 1985. **Freq:** Monthly. **Print Method:** Offset. **Trim Size:** 8 1/4 x 10 5/8. **Cols./Page:** 3. **Col. Width:** 27 nonpareils. **Col. Depth:** 140 agate lines. **Key Personnel:** Susan Harrington, Managing Editor; Bill Morris, Account Manager. **ISSN:** 8756-4092 (print). **Subscription Rates:** $39.95 Individuals; $59.95 Two years. **URL:** http://www.akbizmag.com/. **Ad Rates:** BW $1,560; 4C $3,179. **Remarks:** Accepts advertising. **Circ:** Paid 3500, Non-paid 7500.

614 ■ Alaska History
Alaska Historical Society
PO Box 100299
Anchorage, AK 99510-0299
Phone: (907)276-1596
Publisher's E-mail: members@alaskahistoricalsociety.org
Journal covering original research on Alaskan and northern U.S. history. **Freq:** Semiannual. **Trim Size:** 6 x 9. **Key Personnel:** James D. Ducker, Editor. **ISSN:** 0890--6149 (print). **Subscription Rates:** $4 Members; $6 Nonmembers. **URL:** http://alaskahistoricalsociety.org/publications/alaska-history. **Circ:** Paid 500.

615 ■ Alaska Journal of Commerce
Morris Communications Company L.L.C.
725 Broad St.
Augusta, GA 30901
Phone: (706)724-0851
Free: 800-622-6358
Publisher's E-mail: allaccessprogram@morris.com
Newspaper (tabloid) featuring business and legal news. **Freq:** Weekly. **Print Method:** Offset. **Trim Size:** 11 x 17. **Cols./Page:** 4. **Col. Width:** 14 picas. **Col. Depth:** 15 1/2 inches. **Key Personnel:** Andrew Jensen, Managing Editor; Tim Bradner, Reporter. **ISSN:** 0271--3276 (print). **Subscription Rates:** $45 Individuals Anchorage; $52 Individuals rest of Alaska; $70 Individuals outside Alaska. **URL:** http://www.morris.com/divisions/magazine-publishing/alaska-journal-commerce. **Ad Rates:** GLR $.33; BW $1,064; 4C $1,525; PCI $23. **Remarks:** Accepts advertising. **Circ:** Paid ‡4865, Free ‡1662.

616 ■ Alaska Quarterly Review: A Literary Magazine of Consequence
University of Alaska Anchorage
3211 Providence Dr.
Anchorage, AK 99508-4614
Phone: (907)786-1800
Publication E-mail: aaqr@uaa.alaska.edu
Student literary magazine. **Freq:** Semiannual. **Key Personnel:** Ronald Spatz, Editor-in-Chief; Billy Collins, Editor; Stuart Dischell, Editor. **Subscription Rates:** $20 Individuals; $40 Two years; $60 Individuals three years. **URL:** http://www.uaa.alaska.edu/aqr. **Circ:** (Not Reported).

617 ■ The Arctic Sounder
Alaska Media LLC
Community Newspaper serving the Arctic Alaska communities of Kotzebue, Barrow and the North Slope Borough. **Freq:** Weekly (Thurs.). **Print Method:** Web press. **USPS:** 002-382. **URL:** http://www.thearcticsounder.com. **Remarks:** Accepts advertising. **Circ:** (Not Reported).

618 ■ The Bristol BayTimes
Alaska Newspapers Inc.
301 Calista Ct., Ste. B
Anchorage, AK 99518
Phone: (907)272-9830
Fax: (907)272-9512
Free: 800-770-9830
Publication E-mail: jevans@reportalaska.com
Community newspaper. **Freq:** Weekly. **Print Method:** Web offset. **Cols./Page:** 5. **Col. Width:** 2 1/2 inches. **Col. Depth:** 15 1/2 inches. **Key Personnel:** Jason Evans, President, Publisher. **USPS:** 010-399. **Available online. URL:** http://www.thebristolbaytimes.com. **Ad Rates:** PCI $15. **Remarks:** Accepts advertising. **Circ:** Controlled ⊕**2076**.

619 ■ The Dutch Harbor Fisherman
Alaska Newspapers Inc.
301 Calista Ct., Ste. B
Anchorage, AK 99518
Phone: (907)272-9830
Fax: (907)272-9512
Free: 800-770-9830
Publication E-mail: fisherman@alaskanewspapers.com
Community newspaper. **Freq:** Weekly. **Print Method:** Web offset. **Cols./Page:** 5. **Col. Width:** 2 1/2 inches. **Col. Depth:** 15 1/2 inches. **Key Personnel:** Margaret Nelson, President, Publisher; Tony Hall, Managing Editor; Rose Cox, Editor. **USPS:** 015-185. **URL:** http://www.thedutchharborfisherman.com. **Ad Rates:** GLR $1.50; BW $150; 4C $400; PCI $26.25. **Remarks:** Accepts advertising. **Circ:** Paid ⊕**1002**, Controlled 1046.

620 ■ First Alaskans: A Statewide Magazine of Business and Culture
Alaska Newspapers Inc.
301 Calista Ct., Ste. B
Anchorage, AK 99518
Phone: (907)272-9830
Fax: (907)272-9512
Free: 800-770-9830
Consumer magazine covering business and culture in Alaska. **Freq:** Quarterly. **Key Personnel:** Tony Hall, Editor. **Subscription Rates:** $16 Individuals. **Ad Rates:** BW $190; 4C $425. **Remarks:** Accepts advertising. **Circ:** (Not Reported).

621 ■ Fish Alaska Magazine
Fish Alaska Publications L.L.C.
PO Box 113403
Anchorage, AK 99511
Phone: (907)345-4337
Fax: (907)345-2087
Publisher's E-mail: info@fishalaskamagazine.com
Magazine covering how-to fish articles, gear reviews, and other stories of interest to Alaskan anglers. **Freq:** 10/year. **Key Personnel:** Melissa Norris, Publisher; Marcus Weiner, Publisher. **Subscription Rates:** $30 Individuals; $55 Two years; $50 Canada; $80 Other countries. **URL:** http://www.fishalaskamagazine.com/. **Remarks:** Advertising accepted; rates available upon request. **Circ:** (Not Reported).

622 ■ GreatLander Bush Mailer
GreatLander Bush Mailer
3110 Spenard Rd.
Anchorage, AK 99503
Phone: (907)274-0611
Fax: (907)272-2105
Free: 888-746-7452
Publication E-mail: marketingak@greatlander.com
Shopper. **Freq:** Monthly. **Print Method:** Offset. **Trim Size:** 11 1/2 x 14. **Cols./Page:** 4. **Col. Width:** 24 nonpareils. **Col. Depth:** 171 agate lines. **Key Personnel:** Linda Bedal, Contact, phone: (907)274-0611; Dennis Ford, Director, Marketing, phone: (907)274-0611. **URL:** http://greatlander.com/great-lander-bushmailer. **Ad Rates:** BW $700; 4C $1,200; SAU $10; PCI $32. **Remarks:** Accepts advertising. **Circ:** Free 36300.

623 ■ NORTHVIEW
Identity
336 E 5th Ave.
Anchorage, AK 99501
Phone: (907)929-4528
Fax: (907)334-1992
Publisher's E-mail: info@identityinc.org
Magazine featuring gays and lesbians. **Freq:** Quarterly. **URL:** http://www.identityinc.org. **Ad Rates:** BW $140. **Remarks:** Accepts advertising. **Circ:** (Not Reported).

624 ■ Petroleum News
Petroleum Newspapers of Alaska L.L.C.
PO Box 231647
Anchorage, AK 99523-1651
Phone: (907)522-9469
Fax: (907)522-9583
Free: 877-411-1484
Publisher's E-mail: publisher@petroleumnews.com
Newspaper covering Alaska and Canada petroleum industry. **Freq:** Weekly (Sun.). **Key Personnel:** Kay Cashman, Editor, Publisher, phone: (907)245-2297, fax: (907)522-9583; Clint Lasley, General Manager; Kristen Nelson, Editor-in-Chief, phone: (907)522-9469, fax: (907)248-3437; Susan Crane, Director, Advertising, phone: (907)770-5592, fax: (907)522-9583. **ISSN:** 1093--6297 (print). **Subscription Rates:** $118 U.S.; $206 Canada and Mexico; $240 Other countries; $89 Individuals online only. **URL:** http://www.petroleumnews.com. **Formerly:** Petroleum News Alaska. **Ad Rates:** BW $1945, full page; BW $1340, half page. **Remarks:** Accepts advertising. **Circ:** Paid ‡1600, Non-paid ‡800.

625 ■ Senior Voice: Official Publication of Older Persons Action Group
Older Persons Action Group Inc.

Circulation: ★ = AAM; △ or • = BPA; ♦ = CAC; ❑ = VAC; ⊕ = PO Statement; ‡ = Publisher's Report; Boldface figures = sworn; Light figures = estimated.

3340 Arctic Blvd., Ste. 106
Anchorage, AK 99503
Phone: (907)276-1059
Free: 800-478-1059
News/features for Alaska's seniors. **Freq:** Monthly. **Print Method:** Offset. **Trim Size:** Tab 16. **Cols./Page:** 5. **Col. Width:** 22 nonpareils. **Col. Depth:** 224 agate lines. **ISSN:** 0741--2894 (print). **URL:** http://www.seniorvoicealaska.com. **Ad Rates:** BW $1,097; 4C $1,476.50. **Remarks:** Accepts advertising. **Circ:** Mon.-Fri. 14000.

626 ■ Alaska Communications Systems Group Inc.
600 Telephone Ave.
Anchorage, AK 99503-6091
Phone: (907)564-7556
Free: 888-234-9383
Formerly: ATU Telecommunications (1999); Alec Holdings Inc. (1999). **Key Personnel:** Michael Todd, Sr. VP of Engg., Sr. VP of Operations; Anand Vadapalli, CEO, President. **Cities Served:** United States. **URL:** http://www.alsk.com.

627 ■ Eyecom Cable-Galena
201 E 56th Ave.
Anchorage, AK 99518
Phone: (907)563-2003
Email: customerservice@telalaska.com
Founded: Sept. 05, 2006. **Key Personnel:** Brenda Shepard, CEO; David J. Goggins, VP of Operations. **Cities Served:** 32 channels. **URL:** http://www.telalaska.com.

628 ■ Eyecom Cable - Girdwood
201 E 56th Ave.
Anchorage, AK 99518
Phone: (907)563-2003
Email: customerservice@telalaska.com
Key Personnel: David J. Goggins, President, Gen. Mgr. **Cities Served:** 46 channels. **URL:** http://www.telalaska.com.

629 ■ GCI Inc.
2550 Denali St., Ste. 1000
Anchorage, AK 99503
Phone: (907)265-5600
Free: 800-770-7886
Email: noreply@gci.com
Owner: Kevin Sheridan. **Founded:** 1979. **Key Personnel:** Ronald Duncan, CEO, President; Wilson G. Hughes, Exec. VP; Dana L. Tindall, Sr. VP; William C. Behnke, Sr. VP. **Cities Served:** Palmer, Wasilla, Alaska; 248 channels. **Mailing address:** PO Box 99016, Anchorage, AK 99509-9016. **URL:** http://www.gci.com.

630 ■ KADX-FM - 94.7
2509 Eide St., Ste. 6
Anchorage, AK 99503
Phone: (907)277-5652
Fax: (907)344-5728
Email: x-fm@chugach.net
Format: Jazz. **Networks:** Westwood One Radio; CBS. **Owner:** American Radio Brokers Inc., 1255 Post St., Ste. 1011, San Francisco, CA 94109. **Founded:** May 24, 1999. **Operating Hours**: Continuous. **ADI**: Anchorage, AK. **Key Personnel:** Chester Coleman, Gen. Mgr., Prog. Dir.; Matt Sherman, Dir. of Programs; John Speeney, Sales Mgr. **Wattage**: 50,000. **Ad Rates:** $30 for 15 seconds; $35 for 30 seconds; $45 for 60 seconds. Combined advertising rates available with KAXX-AM.

631 ■ KAFC-FM - 93.7
PO Box 201839
Anchorage, AK 99521
Phone: (907)333-5282
Fax: (907)337-0003
Format: Contemporary Christian. **Owner:** Christian Broadcasting Inc., PO Box 201839, Anchorage, AK 99521. **Operating Hours**: Continuous. **Key Personnel:** Tom Steigleman, Contact. **Wattage:** 27,000. **Ad Rates:** Advertising accepted; rates available upon request. **URL:** http://www.katb.org.

632 ■ KAKL-FM - 88.5
PO Box 2098
Omaha, NE '68103-2098
Free: 800-525-5683
Format: Contemporary Christian. **Owner:** Educational Media Foundation, 5700 W Oaks Blvd., CA 95765, Free: 800-800434-8400. **ADI**: Anchorage, AK. **Key Personnel:** Mike Novak, President, CEO; Alan Mason, COO. **Wattage**: 11,000. **URL:** http://www.klove.com.

633 ■ KAKM-TV - 7
3877 University Dr.
Anchorage, AK 99508-4676
Phone: (907)550-8400
Fax: (907)550-8401
Email: web@alaskapublic.org
Founded: May 07, 1975. **Key Personnel:** Constance Huff, Contact; Pat Yack, Contact; Bede Trantina, Prog. Dir.; Bob Wyatt, Chief Tech. Ofc. **Ad Rates:** Noncommercial. **URL:** http://www.alaskapublic.org.

634 ■ KASH-FM - 107.5
800 E Dimond Blvd., Ste. 3-370
Anchorage, AK 99515
Phone: (907)522-1515
Fax: (907)743-5186
Format: Contemporary Country. **Founded:** 1985. **Operating Hours**: Continuous; 100% local. **Key Personnel:** Steve Chapma, Program Mgr.; Steve Hood, Sales Mgr. **Wattage**: 100,000. **URL:** http://kashcountry1075.iheart.com/.

635 ■ KATB-FM - 89.3
PO Box 210389
Anchorage, AK 99521
Phone: (907)333-5282
Fax: (907)337-0003
Format: Religious. **Networks:** Moody Broadcasting; International Broadcasting. **Owner:** Christian Broadcasting Inc., PO Box 201839, Anchorage, AK 99521. **Founded:** 1985. **Operating Hours**: Continuous. **ADI**: Anchorage, AK. **Wattage**: 4,900. **Ad Rates:** Advertising accepted; rates available upon request. **URL:** http://www.katb.org.

636 ■ KATN-TV - 2
2700 E Tudor Rd.
Anchorage, AK 99507
Phone: (907)561-1313
Fax: (907)561-8934
Email: info@youralaskalink.com
Format: Commercial TV. **Networks:** ABC. **Owner:** Smith Broadcast Group, Inc., at above address. **Founded:** 1955. **Operating Hours**: Continuous; 90% network, 10% local. **ADI**: Fairbanks (North Pole), AK. **Key Personnel:** John Thompson, Div. Dir. **Wattage**: 10,000. **Ad Rates:** Advertising accepted; rates available upon request. **URL:** http://www.youralaskalink.com.

637 ■ KBBO-FM - 92.1
833 Gambell St.
Anchorage, AK 99501
Phone: (907)344-4045
Fax: (907)522-6053
Format: Adult Contemporary. **Owner:** New Northwest Broadcasters, 315 Fifth Ave. S, Ste. 700, Seattle, WA 98104, Ph: (206)204-0213, Fax: (206)204-0214. **URL:** http://www.921bob.fm.

638 ■ KBFX-FM - 100.5
800 E Dimond Blvd Ste. 3-370
Anchorage, AK 99515
Phone: (907)522-1515
Format: Classic Rock. **Networks:** Independent. **Founded:** 1981. **Formerly**: KHVN-FM. **Operating Hours**: Continuous. **Key Personnel:** Andy Lohman, Gen. Mgr., andylohman@clearchannel.com. **Wattage**: 25,000. **Ad Rates:** Noncommercial. **URL:** http://www.1005thefox.com.

639 ■ KBRJ-FM - 104.1
301 Arctic Slope Ave., Ste. 200
Anchorage, AK 99518
Fax: (907)344-9622
Format: Hot Country. **Networks:** AP. **Owner:** Morris Communications Company L.L.C., 725 Broad St., Augusta, GA 30901, Ph: (706)724-0851, Free: 800-622-6358. **Founded:** 1976. **Formerly**: KKLV-FM. **Operating Hours**: Continuous. **ADI**: Anchorage, AK. **Wattage**: 55,000. **Ad Rates:** $15-37 for 30 seconds; $18-41 for 60 seconds. **URL:** http://www.kbrj.com.

640 ■ KBYR-AM - 700
833 Gambell St.
Anchorage, AK 99503
Phone: (907)344-4045
Fax: (907)522-6053
Format: Talk. **Networks:** ABC. **Owner:** KMBQ-FM, 851 E Westpoint Dr., Ste. 301, Wasilla 99654-7355, Ph: (907)373-0222, Fax: (907)376-1575. **Operating Hours**: Continuous. **ADI**: Anchorage, AK. **Wattage**: 10,000. **Ad Rates:** Advertising accepted; rates available upon request. **URL:** http://www.kbyr.com.

KCUK-FM - See Chevak

641 ■ KDBZ-FM
833 Gambell St.
Anchorage, AK 99501
Phone: (907)344-4045
Fax: (907)522-6053
Owner: New Northwest Broadcasters, LLC, at above address.

642 ■ KDMD-TV - 33
1310 E 66th Ave.
Anchorage, AK 99518-1915
Phone: (907)562-5363
Email: info@kdmd.tv
Format: Commercial TV. **Networks:** Home Shopping Club. **Founded:** 1989. **Operating Hours**: Continuous. **ADI**: Anchorage, AK. **Ad Rates:** Advertising accepted; rates available upon request. **URL:** http://www.kdmd.tv.

643 ■ KEAG-FM - 97.3
725 Broad St.
Augusta, GA 30903
Phone: (706)724-0851
Format: Oldies. **Networks:** Independent. **Owner:** Morris Communications Company L.L.C., 725 Broad St., Augusta, GA 30901, Ph: (706)724-0851, Free: 800-622-6358. **Founded:** 1987. **Operating Hours**: Continuous. **ADI**: Anchorage, AK. **Key Personnel:** Dave Stroh, Dir. of Programs; Ed Riley, Contact, ed.riley@anchoragemediagroup.com. **Wattage**: 100,000. **Ad Rates:** $24-45 per unit. Combined advertising rates available with KPXR-FM. **URL:** http://www.kool973.com.

644 ■ KENI-AM - 650
800 E Dimond Blvd., Ste. 3-370
Anchorage, AK 99515
Phone: (907)522-1515
Format: Talk; News. **Networks:** ABC; NBC; Mutual Broadcasting System. **Operating Hours**: Continuous; 75% network, 25% local. **ADI**: Anchorage, AK. **Key Personnel:** Mark Murphy, Prog. Dir., markmurphy@iheartmedia.com; Andy Lohman, Gen. Mgr., andylohman@iheartmedia.com. **Wattage**: 5,000. **Ad Rates:** $21-51 per unit. **URL:** http://www.650keni.com.

645 ■ KFAT-FM - 92.9
833 Gambell St.
Anchorage, AK 99501
Phone: (907)344-4045
Fax: (907)522-6053
Format: Contemporary Hit Radio (CHR). **Owner:** New Northwest Broadcasters, 315 Fifth Ave. S, Ste. 700, Seattle, WA 98104, Ph: (206)204-0213, Fax: (206)204-0214. **Key Personnel:** Bill Sigmar, Dir. of Sales, Gen. Mgr. **URL:** http://www.kfat929.com.

646 ■ KHAR-AM
301 Arctic Slope
Anchorage, AK 99518
Phone: (907)344-9622
Fax: (907)349-3299
Format: Big Band/Nostalgia. **Networks:** NBC. **Owner:** Alaska Broadcast Communications, at above address. **Founded:** 1961. **ADI**: Anchorage, AK. **Key Personnel:** John Ruby, Gen. Mgr.; Ron Clements, Sales Mgr., ron.clement@anchoragemediagroup.com. **Wattage**: 5,000. **Ad Rates:** $10-25 for 30 seconds; $13-28 for 60 seconds.

647 ■ KIMO-TV - 13
2700 E Tudor Rd.
Anchorage, AK 99507
Phone: (907)561-1313
Fax: (907)561-8934
Email: news@youralaskalink.com
Format: Commercial TV. **Simulcasts:** KATN, KJUD. **Networks:** ABC. **Founded:** 1967. **Operating Hours**: Continuous. **Ad Rates:** Noncommercial. **URL:** http://www.youralaskalink.com/about/fcc.

KJLP-FM - See Palmer

648 ■ KJUD-TV - 8
2700 E Tudor Rd.
Anchorage, AK 99507
Phone: (907)561-1313
Fax: (907)561-8934

Format: Commercial TV. **Networks:** ABC. **Operating Hours:** 4 a.m.-4 a.m.; 90% network, 10% local. **ADI:** Juneau, AK. **Key Personnel:** Kip Jarmon, Contact. **Ad Rates:** Advertising accepted; rates available upon request. **URL:** http://www.youralaskalink.com.

649 ■ KKRO-FM - 102.1
3700 Woodland Dr., Ste. 800
Anchorage, AK 99517
Phone: (907)243-3141
Fax: (907)243-3291
Format: Contemporary Hit Radio (CHR). **Networks:** Independent. **Owner:** Tom Ingstad Broadcast Group, 8500 Normandale Lake Blvd., No. 1740, Bloomington, MN 55437, Ph: (612)921-2434. **Founded:** 1986. **Formerly:** KRKN-FM; KPXR-FM. **Operating Hours:** Continuous. **Key Personnel:** Don Nordin, Contact; Jay Perry, Sales Mgr.; Jason Palmer, Dir. of Programs; Don Nordin, Contact. **Wattage:** 25,000. **Ad Rates:** $10-28 per unit.

650 ■ KLEF-FM - 98.1
3601 C St.
Anchorage, AK 99503
Phone: (907)522-1018
Format: Classical. **Networks:** Concert Music Network (CMN). **Owner:** Chinook Concert Broadcasters Inc., at above address. **Founded:** 1988. **Operating Hours:** 5 a.m.-midnight. **ADI:** Alaska. **Key Personnel:** Rick Goodfellow, Gen. Mgr., President. **Local Programs:** *Sacred Concert*; *Saturday Night at the Opera*. **Wattage:** 25,000. **Ad Rates:** Noncommercial. **URL:** http://www.wfffradio.com.

651 ■ KMXS-FM - 103.1
301 Artic Slope, Ste. 200
Anchorage, AK 99518
Phone: (907)344-9622
Email: winner@kmxs.com
Format: Adult Contemporary. **Owner:** Morris Communications Company L.L.C., 725 Broad St., Augusta, GA 30901, Ph: (706)724-0851, Free: 800-622-6358. **Operating Hours:** Continuous. **ADI:** Anchorage, AK. **Wattage:** 100,000. **Ad Rates:** Noncommercial. **URL:** http://www.kmxs.com.

652 ■ KNBA-FM - 90.3
3600 San Jeronimo Dr., Ste. 480
Anchorage, AK 99508
Phone: (907)793-3500
Fax: (907)793-3536
Free: 888-278-5622
Email: feedback@knba.org
Format: Country; News. **Networks:** National Public Radio (NPR); Public Radio International (PRI); Corporation for Public Broadcasting. **Operating Hours:** Continuous. **ADI:** Anchorage, AK. **Key Personnel:** Jaclyn Sallee, Producer, asallee@koahnic.org; Charles Sather, Chief Engineer; Loren Dixon, Dir. of Operations, Dir. of Programs. **Wattage:** 100,000 ERP. **Ad Rates:** Noncommercial. Underwriting available. **URL:** http://www.knba.org.

653 ■ KNLT-FM - 95.5
4700 Business Pk. Blvd.,Bldg. E, Ste. 44
4700 Business Park Blvd.
Anchorage, AK 99503
Format: Adult Contemporary. **Formerly:** KNIK-FM. **Operating Hours:** Continuous; 100% local. **Wattage:** 1,500. **Ad Rates:** $14-21 for 60 seconds. **URL:** http://www.knlt.com.

654 ■ KRUA-FM - 88.1
3211 Providence Dr.
Anchorage, AK 99508
Fax: (907)786-6805
Format: Educational; News; Sports. **Networks:** NBC. **Owner:** UAA Board of Regents, at above address. **Founded:** 1987. **Operating Hours:** Continuous. **ADI:** Anchorage, AK. **Wattage:** 155 ERP. **Ad Rates:** Noncommercial. Underwriting available. **URL:** http://www.kruaradio.org.

655 ■ KSKA-FM - 91.1
3877 University Dr.
Anchorage, AK 99508-4676
Phone: (907)550-8400
Fax: (907)550-8401
Format: Public Radio; News. **Networks:** National Public Radio (NPR); Alaska Public Radio; Public Radio International (PRI). **Owner:** Alaska Public Media, 3877 University Dr., Anchorage, AK 99508-4676, Ph: (907)550-8400, Fax: (907)550-8401. **Founded:** 1975. **Operating Hours:** Continuous; 57% network, 43% local. **Key Personnel:** Bede Trantina, Dir. of Programs; Constance Huff, Prog. Dir., chuff@kska.org. **Wattage:** 100,000. **Ad Rates:** Noncommercial. **URL:** http://www.alaskapublic.org.

656 ■ KTBY-TV - 4
2700 E Tudor Rd.
Suite 1
Anchorage, AK 99507
Phone: (907)561-1313
Fax: (907)561-8934
Format: News; Sports; Information. **Networks:** Fox; ABC. **Founded:** 1983. **ADI:** Anchorage, AK. **Key Personnel:** Laurie Taylor, Contact, itaylor@fox4ktby.com. **Wattage:** 234,400 ERP H. **Ad Rates:** $15-425. **URL:** http://www.youralaskalink.com.

657 ■ KTUU-TV - 2
701 E Tudor Rd., Ste. 220
Anchorage, AK 99503-7488
Phone: (907)762-9202
Fax: (907)561-0874
Email: web@ktuu.com
Format: Commercial TV. **Networks:** NBC. **Founded:** 1953. **ADI:** Anchorage, AK. **Key Personnel:** Nancy Johnson, Dir. of Sales; Andrew MacLeod, Gen. Mgr., President, amacleod@ktuu.com; Steve MacDonald, News Dir.; Maria Downey, Asst. Dir. **Ad Rates:** Noncommercial. **URL:** http://www.ktuu.com.

658 ■ KTVA-TV - 11
1007 W 32nd Ave.
Anchorage, AK 99503
Phone: (907)273-3192
Email: 11news@ktva.com
Format: Commercial TV. **Networks:** CBS. **Owner:** Alaska Broadcasting Company Inc., 700 W 41st Ave., Ste. 102, Anchorage, AK 99503, Fax: (907)258-2414. **Operating Hours:** Continuous. **ADI:** Anchorage, AK. **Wattage:** 28,900 ERP. **Ad Rates:** Advertising accepted; rates available upon request. $20-550 for 30 seconds; $40-110 for 60 seconds. **URL:** http://www.ktva.com.

659 ■ KTZN-AM - 550
800 E Dimond Blvd., Ste. 3-370
Anchorage, AK 99515
Phone: (907)522-1515
Format: Sports. **ADI:** Anchorage, AK. **Key Personnel:** Andy Lohman, Gen. Mgr.; Mark Murphy, Prog. Dir. **Wattage:** 5,000. **Ad Rates:** Noncommercial. **URL:** http://www.550thezone.com//main.html.

660 ■ KUDO-AM - 1080
4700 Business Park Blvd., Bldg. E, Ste. 44-A
Anchorage, AK 99503
Phone: (907)947-7344
Fax: (907)522-1027
Format: Talk. **Wattage:** 10,000. **Ad Rates:** Advertising accepted; rates available upon request. **URL:** http://www.1080koan.com.

661 ■ KWHL-FM - 106.5
301 Artic Slope Ave., Ste. 200
Anchorage, AK 99518
Phone: (907)344-9622
Email: studio@kwhl.com
Format: Album-Oriented Rock (AOR). **Owner:** MCC Radio L.L.C., 725 Broad St., Augusta, GA 30901, Ph: (706)724-0851. **Founded:** 1982. **Operating Hours:** Continuous. **ADI:** Anchorage, AK. **Key Personnel:** Brad Stennett, Contact. **Wattage:** 100,000. **Ad Rates:** Noncommercial. Combined advertising rates available with KFQD-AM. **URL:** http://www.kwhl.com.

662 ■ KXDZ-FM - 103.1
301 Arctic Slope Ave., Ste. 200
Anchorage, AK 99518
Phone: (907)344-9622
Format: Adult Contemporary. **Founded:** 1987. **Key Personnel:** Bill Lawrence, Gen. Mgr.; Larry Yarow, Dir. of Programs. **Wattage:** 3,000. **URL:** http://www.kmxs.com.

663 ■ KXLW-FM - 96.3
833 Gambell St.
Anchorage, AK 99501
Phone: (907)344-4045
Fax: (907)522-6053
Format: Classic Rock. **Founded:** Nov. 01, 2006. **Operating Hours:** Continuous. **ADI:** Anchorage, AK. **Key Personnel:** Bill Sigmar, Dir. of Sales, Gen. Mgr., bill.sigmar@nnbradio.com; Tom Oakes, Dir. of Programs, tom.oakes@nnbradio.com. **URL:** http://www.963thewolf.com.

664 ■ KYES-TV - 5
3700 Woodland Dr.
Anchorage, AK 99517
Phone: (907)248-5937
Format: Commercial TV. **Networks:** United Paramount Network. **Owner:** Fireweed Communications Corp., 3700 Woodland Dr., Anchorage, AK 99517, Ph: (907)248-5937. **Founded:** 1990. **Operating Hours:** Continuous. **ADI:** Anchorage, AK. **Key Personnel:** Jim Hill, Dir. of Programs; Jeremy Lansman, Chief Engineer; Monica Marcott, Sales Mgr. **Wattage:** 100,000. **Ad Rates:** Advertising accepted; rates available upon request. **URL:** http://www.kyes.com.

665 ■ KYMG-FM - 98.9
800 E Diamond Blvd., Ste. 3-370
Anchorage, AK 99515
Phone: (907)743-0989
Fax: (907)743-5183
Format: Adult Contemporary. **Networks:** Independent. **Founded:** 1989. **Operating Hours:** Continuous; 100% local. **ADI:** Anchorage, AK. **Key Personnel:** Dave Flavin, Dir. of Programs, daveflavin@clearchannel.com. **Wattage:** 100,000. **Ad Rates:** Noncommercial. **URL:** http://www.magic989fm.com.

666 ■ KZND-FM - 94.7
4700 Business Park Blvd., Bldg. E, Ste. 44-a
Anchorage, AK 99503
Phone: (907)522-1018
Format: News; Talk; Classic Rock. **Owner:** Tati Broadcasting, LLC, at above address. **Operating Hours:** 12:00 a.m. - 7:00 p.m. Monday - Friday 2:00 p.m. - 10:00 p.m. Midnight Saturday 01:00 a.m. - 10:00 p.m. Midnight Sunday. **ADI:** Houston, TX. **Wattage:** 15,000 ERP. **Ad Rates:** Accepts Advertising. **URL:** http://www.947kznd.com/.

KZPA-AM - See Fort Yukon

667 ■ 101.3 KGOT - 101.3
800 E Dimond Blvd., Ste. 3-370
Anchorage, AK 99515
Phone: (907)522-1515
Fax: (907)743-5186
Email: kgot@alaskanet.com
Format: Top 40; Contemporary Hit Radio (CHR). **Owner:** iHeartMedia Inc., 200 E Basse Rd., San Antonio, TX 78209, Ph: (210)832-3314. **Founded:** 1967. **Operating Hours:** Continuous. **ADI:** Anchorage, AK. **Key Personnel:** Bill Stewart, Dir. of Programs, stewart@clearchannel.com; Andy Lohman, Sales Mgr., andylohman@clearchannel.com. **Wattage:** 26,000. **Ad Rates:** Noncommercial. $43-48 per unit. **URL:** http://www.kgot.com.

BARROW

North Slope Borough. North Slope Borough. (C). 60 m NE of Wainwright.

668 ■ KBRW-AM - 680
PO Box 109
Barrow, AK 99723
Format: Public Radio; Eclectic; Educational. **Networks:** Public Radio International (PRI); National Public Radio (NPR); Alaska Public Radio. **Owner:** Silakkuagvik Communications Inc., at above address. **Founded:** 1974. **Operating Hours:** Continuous; 33% network 67% local. **Key Personnel:** Isaac Tuckfield, Prog. Dir. **Wattage:** 10,000. **Ad Rates:** Noncommercial. **URL:** http://www.kbrw.org/.

669 ■ KBRW-FM - 91.9
PO Box 109
Barrow, AK 99723
Format: Public Radio; Educational. **Networks:** National Public Radio (NPR); Alaska Radio Network; Public Radio International (PRI). **Owner:** Silakkuagvik Communications Inc., at above address. **Operating Hours:** Continuous, 88% network, 12% local. **Wattage:** 890. **Ad Rates:** Noncommercial. **URL:** http://www.kbrw.org.

Circulation: ★ = AAM; △ or • = BPA; ♦ = CAC; ❑ = VAC; ⊕ = PO Statement; ‡ = Publisher's Report; Boldface figures = sworn; Light figures = estimated.

BETHEL

Bethel Census Area. Bethel Census Div. (SW). 5 m W of Kwenthluk. Residential.

670 ■ KYKD-FM - 100.1
406 Ptarmigan Rd.
Bethel, AK 99559
Phone: (907)543-5953
Email: kykd@vfcm.org
Format: Easy Listening; Religious. **Networks:** USA Radio. **Owner:** Voice For Christ Ministries, PO Box 474, Nenana, AK 99760, Ph: (907)832-5426. **Founded:** 1983. **Operating Hours**: Continuous. **ADI**: Bethel, AK. **Wattage**: 7,900. **Ad Rates:** Advertising accepted; rates available upon request. **Mailing address:** PO Box 2428, Bethel, AK 99559. **URL:** http://www.vfcm.org.

671 ■ KYUK-AM - 640
PO Box 468
Bethel, AK 99559
Phone: (907)543-5985
Format: Public Radio. **Networks:** National Public Radio (NPR); Alaska Public Radio; Public Radio International (PRI). **Founded:** 1971. **Operating Hours**: 6 a.m.-midnight. **ADI**: Bethel, AK. **Key Personnel:** Mike Martz, Gen. Mgr., mike@kyuk.org; Joseph Seibert, Chief Engineer, joe@kyuk.org; Angela Denning-Barnes, News Dir., angela@kyuk.org. **Wattage**: 10,000. **Ad Rates:** Underwriting available. **URL:** http://www.kyuk.org.

672 ■ KYUK-TV - 4
PO Box 468
Bethel, AK 99559
Phone: (907)543-3131
Format: Public TV. **Networks:** Public Broadcasting Service (PBS). **Owner:** Bethel Broadcasting, Inc., PO Box 468, Bethel, AK 99559, Ph: (907)543-0222. **Founded:** 1973. **Operating Hours**: 9 a.m.-midnight. **ADI**: Bethel, AK. **Key Personnel:** Mike Martz, Gen. Mgr., mike@kyuk.org; Joseph Seibert, Chief Engineer, joe@kyuk.org. **Wattage**: 5,000. **Ad Rates:** Noncommercial. **URL:** http://www.kyuk.org.

CHEVAK

673 ■ KCUK-FM - 88.1
3877 University Dr.
Anchorage, AK 99508
Phone: (907)550-8400
Fax: (907)550-8401
Free: 800-478-5256
Email: web@alaskapublic.org
Format: Public Radio. **Owner:** Alaska Public Radio Network, 3877 University Dr., Anchorage, AK 99508-4676, Ph: (907)550-8401, Fax: (907)550-8401, Free: 800-478-5256. **URL:** http://www.alaskapublic.org.

CORDOVA

Valdez-Cordova Census Area. Valdez-Cordova Census Div. (S). On Gulf of Alaska, 140 m SE of Anchorage. Ferry connections. Crab, clam, herring, black cod, halibut, salmon canneries. Fisheries. Coal mining. Oil drilling in vicinity. Cold storage plants. Spruce, hemlock, timber.

674 ■ KCDV-FM - 100.9
112 Forestry Way
Cordova, AK 99574-0060
Phone: (907)242-3796
Fax: (907)242-3737
Email: email@cordovaradio.com
Format: Adult Contemporary. **Owner:** Bayview Communications, at above address. **Wattage**: 970. **Mailing address:** PO Box 60, Cordova, AK 99574-0060. **URL:** http://www.cordovaradio.com.

675 ■ KLAM-AM - 1450
112 Forestry Way
Cordova, AK 99574
Phone: (907)424-3796
Fax: (907)424-3737
Email: email@cordovaradio.com
Format: Country; Classic Rock; Talk. **Networks:** ABC. **Owner:** Bay View Communications, at above address. **Founded:** May 02, 1954. **Operating Hours**: Continuous. **Wattage**: 250. **Ad Rates:** $6.50-12 for 30 seconds; $7.50-15 for 60 seconds. **Mailing address:** PO Box 60, Cordova, AK 99574. **URL:** http://www.cordovaradio.com.

DELTA JUNCTION

Southeast Fairbanks Census Area. Fairbanks Census Div. (C). 100 m SE of Fairbanks. Residential.

676 ■ Delta Wind
TriDelta Inc.
2887 Alaska Hwy.
Delta Junction, AK 99737-0609
Community newspaper. **Freq:** Weekly (Thurs.). **Print Method:** Offset. **Trim Size:** 11 1/4 x 17 1/2. **Cols./Page:** 4. **Col. Width:** 14 picas. **Col. Depth:** 16 1/4 inches. **Subscription Rates:** $26 Individuals print; $33.80 Out of area print; $39 Out of state print. **URL:** http://www.deltawindonline.com. **Formerly**: The Delta Paper. **Mailing address:** PO Box 986, Delta Junction, AK 99737-0609. **Ad Rates:** BW $552.50; 4C $1,252.50; PCI $8.50. **Remarks:** Accepts advertising. **Circ:** Paid ‡1150, Free ‡75.

DILLINGHAM

Dillingham Census Area. On the Alaskan Peninsula.

677 ■ KDLG-AM - 670
PO Box 670
Dillingham, AK 99576
Phone: (907)842-5281
Fax: (907)842-5281
Format: Public Radio; Full Service. **Networks:** BBC World Service; National Public Radio (NPR). **Owner:** Dillingham City Schools, PO Box 170, Dillingham, AK 99576. **Founded:** 1975. **ADI**: Dillingham, AK. **Key Personnel:** Jody Seitz, News Dir. **Wattage**: 10,000. **Ad Rates:** Accepts Advertising. **URL:** http://kdlg.org/.

678 ■ Nushagak Cooperative Inc.
557 Kenny Wren Rd.
Dillingham, AK 99576
Phone: (907)842-5251
Fax: (907)842-2799
Founded: 1973. **Formerly**: Nushagak Telephone Cooperative Inc. **Key Personnel:** Henry Strub, VP; Pete Andrew, President. **Cities Served:** United States. **Mailing address:** PO Box 350, Dillingham, AK 99576. **URL:** http://www.nushtel.com.

EAGLE RIVER

Anchorage Census Div. (S). 20 m S of Palmer. Gateway to Chugach State Park. Service businesses, construction and land development.

679 ■ Alaska Star
Morris Communications Company L.L.C.
725 Broad St.
Augusta, GA 30901
Phone: (706)724-0851
Free: 800-622-6358
Publisher's E-mail: allaccessprogram@morris.com
Community newspaper. **Freq:** Weekly (Thurs.). **Print Method:** Offset. **Trim Size:** 11 x 17. **Cols./Page:** 5. **Col. Width:** 23 nonpareils. **Col. Depth:** 224 agate lines. **Key Personnel:** Cinthia Ritchie, Editor. **USPS:** 939-280. **Subscription Rates:** $25 Individuals home delivery; $13 Individuals 6 months, home delivery; $15 Individuals 6 months, mail; $30 Individuals mail; $16.50 Individuals 6 months, mail, rest of state; $32 Individuals mail, rest of state; $18 Out of state 6 months; $34 Out of state. **URL:** http://www.alaskastar.com. **Formerly**: Chugiak-Eagle River Alaska Star. **Ad Rates:** BW $1170; 4C $1,620; PCI $14.80. **Remarks:** Accepts advertising. **Circ:** Paid ‡7380, Free ‡1200.

ESTER

680 ■ The Ester Republic: National Rag of the Independent People's republic of Ester
Ester Republic Press
2922 Parks Hwy.
Ester, AK 99725
Phone: (907)451-0636
Publisher's E-mail: info@esterrepublic.com
Community newspaper. **Freq:** Monthly. **Key Personnel:** Deirdre Helfferich, Publisher, Editor; Amy Cameron, Manager, Advertising. **Subscription Rates:** $24 Individuals /year; $69 Other countries /year; $20 Individuals PDF. **URL:** http://esterrepublic.com/Republicwelcome.html. **Mailing address:** PO Box 24, Ester, AK 99725. **Ad Rates:** PCI $18.75; BW $360. **Remarks:** Accepts advertising. **Circ:** (Not Reported).

FAIRBANKS

Fairbanks North Star Borough. Fairbanks North Star Census Div. 300 m NE OF Anchorage. University of Alaska. Terminus Alaska Highway and Alaska Railroad. Distribution and Supply Center for Interior and Northern Alaska, including North Slope, petroleum development and pipeline distribution system. Diversified mining.

681 ■ Agroborealis
University of Alaska Fairbanks School of Natural Resources and Agricultural Sciences
505 S Chandalar Dr.
Fairbanks, AK 99775
Phone: (907)474-7034
Publication E-mail: fndlf2@uaf.edu
Trade magazine covering agriculture, forestry research, and natural resources management and education. **Founded:** 1969. **Freq:** Semiannual. **ISSN:** 0002-1822 (print). **Alt. Formats:** PDF. **URL:** http://www.uaf.edu/snras/research/publications/agroborealis. **Mailing address:** PO Box 757500, Fairbanks, AK 99775. **Remarks:** Advertising not accepted. **Circ:** Non-paid 2500.

682 ■ Fairbanks Daily News-Miner
Fairbanks Daily News-Miner
200 N Cushman St.
Fairbanks, AK 99707
Phone: (907)456-6661
Publication E-mail: circulation@newsminer.com
General newspaper. **Freq:** Mon.-Sun. **Print Method:** Offset. **Trim Size:** 12 1/2 x 22 3/4. **Cols./Page:** 6. **Col. Width:** 11.2 nonpareils. **Col. Depth:** 294 agate lines. **Key Personnel:** Tom Gilligan, Manager, Circulation, phone: (907)459-7528; Rod Boyce, Managing Editor, phone: (907)459-7585. **ISSN:** 8750-5495 (print). **Subscription Rates:** $15.23 Individuals daily/Sunday 1 month; $49.50 Individuals daily/Sunday 13 weeks; $94 Individuals daily/Sunday 26 weeks; $188 Individuals daily/Sunday; $9.55 Individuals daily only 1 month; $31.08 Individuals daily only 13 weeks; $62.10 Individuals daily only 26 weeks; $124.20 Individuals daily only; $7.94 Individuals Friday, Saturday & Sunday 1 month; $103.20 Individuals Friday, Saturday & Sunday. **URL:** http://www.newsminer.com/. **Mailing address:** PO Box 70710, Fairbanks, AK 99707-0710. **Remarks:** Accepts advertising. **Circ:** (Not Reported).

683 ■ Sun Star: University of Alaska Fairbanks
University of Alaska Fairbanks School of Natural Resources and Agricultural Sciences
PO Box 756640
Fairbanks, AK 99775-6640
Phone: (907)474-6039
Publication E-mail: fystar@uaf.edu
Collegiate newspaper. **Freq:** Weekly (Tues.). **Print Method:** Offset. **Trim Size:** 11 x 17. **Cols./Page:** 4. **Col. Width:** 2 7/16 inches. **Col. Depth:** 204 agate lines. **Key Personnel:** Andrew Sheeler, Editor-in-Chief; Alex Kinn, Manager, Advertising. **URL:** http://www.uafsunstar.com. **Formerly**: Polar Star. **Ad Rates:** BW $435; 4C $935; PCI $7.85. **Remarks:** Accepts advertising. **Circ:** Free ‡4000.

684 ■ Western Historical Quarterly
Western History Association
University of Alaska Fairbanks
Dept. of History
605 Gruening Bldg.
Fairbanks, AK 99775-6460
Phone: (907)474-6509
Fax: (435)797-3899
Publication E-mail: whq@usu.edu
Journal covering history of the Western U.S. **Freq:** Quarterly Spring (Feb), Summer (May), Autumn (Aug), and Winter (Nov). **Key Personnel:** Colleen O'Neill, Associate Editor; David Rich Lewis, Editor. **ISSN:** 0043--3810 (print); **EISSN:** 1939--8603 (electronic). **Subscription Rates:** $130 Institutions print; $140 Institutions print and online; $140 Institutions online; Included in membership. **URL:** http://www.usu.edu/whq. **Ad Rates:** BW $250. **Remarks:** Accepts advertising. **Circ:** Paid ⊕**2500**.

685 ■ GCI
3637 Airport Way, Spc. 110
Fairbanks, AK 99701
Phone: (907)452-7191
Owner: GCI Cable, at above address. **Founded:** 1979. **Formerly**: ACN; Alaskan Cable Network. **Key Personnel:** Mike Baker, Regional Mgr.; William C. Behnke, Sr.

VP. **Cities Served:** Eielson, Fairbanks, Fort Greely, Fort Wainwright, North Pole, North Star Borough, Alaska: subscribing households 10,000; 51 channels; 1 community access channel. **URL:** http://www.gci.com/store-locations.

686 ■ KCBF-AM - 820
819 First Ave., Ste. A
Fairbanks, AK 99701
Phone: (907)451-5910
Fax: (907)451-5999
Format: Sports. **Networks:** ESPN Radio. **Owner:** New Northwest Broadcasters, LLC, at above address. **Founded:** 1948. **Operating Hours:** Continuous. **Wattage:** 10,000. **Ad Rates:** Noncommercial. $14-21 for 30 seconds; $20-35 for 60 seconds. Combined advertising rates available with KLXR-FM, KUWL-FM, KWLF-FM, KFAR-AM. **URL:** http://www.820sports.com.

687 ■ KFAR-AM - 660
819 1st Ave., Ste. A
Fairbanks, AK 99701
Phone: (907)451-5910
Fax: (907)451-5999
Format: Talk; News; Public Radio. **Networks:** CBS; NBC; Westwood One Radio. **Owner:** New Northwest Broadcasters, LLC, at above address. **Founded:** 1939. **Operating Hours:** Continuous; 63% network, 37% local. **ADI:** Fairbanks (North Pole), AK. **Local Programs:** *Problem Corner*, Monday Tuesday Wednesday Thursday Friday 11:00 a.m. - 1:00 p.m.; *Better Breakfast Show*, Monday Tuesday Wednesday Thursday Friday 6:00 a.m. - 8:00 a.m. **Wattage:** 10,000. **Ad Rates:** Noncommercial. Combined advertising rates available with KWLF-FM, KUWL-FM, KXLR-FM, KCBF-AM. **URL:** http://www.kfar660.com.

688 ■ KFBX-AM - 970
546 9th Ave.
Fairbanks, AK 99701
Phone: (907)450-1000
Fax: (907)450-1092
Email: kfbx@clearchannel.com
Format: News; Talk. **Operating Hours:** Continuous. **ADI:** Alaska. **Key Personnel:** Charlie O'Toole, Prog. Dir. **Wattage:** 10,000. **Ad Rates:** Advertising accepted; rates available upon request. **URL:** http://970kfbx.iheart.com.

689 ■ KFXF-TV - 7
3650 Bradock St.
Fairbanks, AK 99701
Wattage: 6,100 ERP. **Ad Rates:** Advertising accepted; rates available upon request.

690 ■ KIAK-AM - 970
546 9th Ave.
Fairbanks, AK 99701-4902
Phone: (907)457-1921
Fax: (907)457-2128
Format: Contemporary Country. **ADI:** Fairbanks (North Pole), AK. **Wattage:** 5,000. **URL:** http://970kfbx.iheart.com/.

691 ■ KKED-FM - 104.7
546 Ninth Ave.
Fairbanks, AK 99701
Phone: (907)450-1000
Fax: (907)450-1092
Format: Album-Oriented Rock (AOR). **ADI:** Alaska. **Key Personnel:** Denise Omstead, Account Exec. **Wattage:** 46,000. **Ad Rates:** Noncommercial. **URL:** http://www.1047theedge.com.

692 ■ KSUA-FM - 91.5
PO Box 750113
Fairbanks, AK 99775
Format: Educational; Alternative/New Music/Progressive. **Networks:** Pacifica; Independent. **Owner:** University of Alaska, Butrovich Bldg., Ste. 206 910 Yukon Drive, Fairbanks, AK 99775-5340, Ph: (907)450-8100, Fax: (907)450-8101. **Founded:** 1984. **Operating Hours:** 6 a.m.-4 a.m. **ADI:** Fairbanks (North Pole), AK. **Key Personnel:** Matt Schroder, Gen. Mgr.; Shayna Hawkins, Dir. of Programs; John Bolds, Program Mgr., fytv21@uaf.edu; Ephy Wheeler, Music Dir. **Wattage:** 3,000. **Ad Rates:** Underwriting available. $3-10 per unit. **URL:** http://www.ksuaradio.com.

693 ■ KTDZ-FM - 103.9
819 1st Ave., Ste. A
Fairbanks, AK 99701
Format: Oldies. **Owner:** New Northwest Broadcasters, 315 Fifth Ave. S, Ste. 700, Seattle, WA 98104, Ph: (206)204-0213, Fax: (206)204-0214. **Ad Rates:** Advertising accepted; rates available upon request. **URL:** http://www.mytedfm.com.

694 ■ KTVF-TV - 11
3528 International St.
Fairbanks, AK 99701
Phone: (907)458-1800
Fax: (907)458-1820
Email: comments@ktvf11.com
Format: Commercial TV. **Networks:** NBC. **Founded:** 1955. **Operating Hours:** 6 a.m.-2:45 a.m. **ADI:** Fairbanks (North Pole), AK. **Key Personnel:** Dee Dee Caciari, Div. Dir., deedeecaciari@ktvf11.com; Larry Rhody, CFO, larryrhody@ktvf11.com; Celia Vissers, Contact, celiavissers@ktvf11.com. **Ad Rates:** $20-400 per unit. **URL:** http://www.webcenter11.com.

695 ■ KUAC-FM - 89.9
312 Tanana Dr.
Fairbanks, AK 99775-5620
Phone: (907)474-7491
Fax: (907)474-5064
Free: 800-393-8539
Format: Public Radio; Classical. **Networks:** National Public Radio (NPR); Public Radio International (PRI); Alaska Public Radio; BBC World Service. **Founded:** Oct. 01, 1962. **Operating Hours:** 1.00 a.m.-11.00 p.m. **ADI:** Fairbanks (North Pole), AK. **Wattage:** 38,000 ERP. **Mailing address:** PO Box 775620, Fairbanks, AK 99775-5620. **URL:** http://www.kuac.org.

696 ■ KUAC-TV - 9
University of Alaska at Fairbanks
312 Tanana Dr., Ste. 202
Fairbanks, AK 99775-5620
Phone: (907)474-7491
Fax: (907)474-5064
Format: Public TV. **Networks:** Public Broadcasting Service (PBS). **Founded:** 1971. **Operating Hours:** Continuous. **ADI:** Fairbanks (North Pole), AK. **Key Personnel:** Keith Martin, Dir. of Engg., Gen. Mgr. **Wattage:** 47,000 ERP. **Ad Rates:** Noncommercial. **Mailing address:** PO Box 755620, Fairbanks, AK 99775-5620. **URL:** http://www.kuac.org.

697 ■ KUWL-FM - 91.5
202 Butrovich Bldg.
Fairbanks, AK 99775
Format: Religious. **Owner:** Fairbanks Educational Broadcasting Foundation, Inc., at above address. **Founded:** 1985. **Operating Hours:** Continuous. **Key Personnel:** Gary Wells, Gen. Mgr.; Keith Andree, Chief Engineer; Karina E. Hogan, Contact; Alan Corrick, Contact; Mike Nafpliotis, Contact. **Wattage:** 374.

698 ■ KWLF-FM - 98.1
819 1st St. Ave., Ste. A
Fairbanks, AK 99701
Phone: (907)451-5910
Fax: (907)451-5999
Format: Contemporary Hit Radio (CHR); Adult Contemporary. **Owner:** New Northwest Brodcasters L.L.C., at above address. **Founded:** 1987. **Operating Hours:** Continuous; 67% network, 33% local. **ADI:** Fairbanks (North Pole), AK. **Wattage:** 10,000 (25,000 ERP). **Ad Rates:** $14-24 for 30 seconds. Combined advertising rates available with KXLR-FM, KCBF-AM, KFAR-AM, KUWL-FM. **URL:** http://www.kwolf981.com.

699 ■ KXLR-FM - 95.9
819 1st Ave., Ste. A
Fairbanks, AK 99701
Phone: (907)452-5121
Fax: (907)452-5120
Format: Classic Rock. **Networks:** Satellite Music Network. **Owner:** Northern Television Inc., at above address. **Founded:** 1990. **Formerly:** KINQ-FM. **Operating Hours:** Continuous. **ADI:** Fairbanks (North Pole), AK. **Key Personnel:** Tim Palmer, Operations Mgr; Bill Holzheimer, Contact. **Wattage:** 25,000. **Ad Rates:** Combined advertising rates available with KCBF-AM. **URL:** http://xrock959.com.

FORT RICHARDSON

700 ■ Alaska Post
U.S. Army Alaska
Public Affairs Office
724 Postal Service Loop, No. 5900
Fort Richardson, AK 99505-5900
Phone: (907)353-1110
Army newspaper. **Freq:** Weekly. **Print Method:** Offset. **Key Personnel:** Kamryn Jaroszewski, Editor. **Subscription Rates:** Free. **URL:** http://www.dvidshub.net/publication/561/alaska-post#.Veo2ztKeDGc. **Formerly:** Arctic Star. **Ad Rates:** GLR $8.50; BW $658.75; 4C $883.75; SAU $8.50; PCI $8.50. **Remarks:** Accepts advertising. **Circ:** Controlled 10000.

FORT YUKON

701 ■ KZPA-AM - 900
3877 University Dr.
Anchorage, AK 99508
Phone: (907)550-8400
Fax: (907)550-8401
Format: Public Radio. **Owner:** Alaska Public Radio Network, 3877 University Dr., Anchorage, AK 99508-4676, Ph: (907)550-8401, Fax: (907)550-8401, Free: 800-478-5256. **URL:** http://www.alaskapublic.org.

GALENA

702 ■ KIYU-AM - 910
PO Box 165
Galena, AK 99741
Phone: (907)656-1488
Fax: (907)656-1734
Email: raven@kiyu.com
Format: Public Radio; Eclectic; News. **Simulcasts:** KSKO, KZPA. **Networks:** Alaska Public Radio; National Public Radio (NPR). **Owner:** Big River Public Broadcasting Corp., at above address, Galena, AK 99741. **Founded:** 1986. **Operating Hours:** Continuous; 40% network, 60% local. **ADI:** Alaska. **Key Personnel:** Russ Sweetsir, President. **Wattage:** 5,000. **Ad Rates:** Noncommercial. Combined advertising rates available with KSKO, KUAC, KZPA, KTNA. **URL:** http://www.kiyu.com.

GIRDWOOD

703 ■ KEUL-FM - 88.9
PO Box 29
Girdwood, AK 99587-0029
Phone: (907)754-2489
Email: radio@glaciercity.us
Format: Information; News. **Founded:** 1997. **Key Personnel:** Lewis Leonard, COO. **Ad Rates:** Noncommercial. **URL:** http://www.glaciercity.us.

GLENNALLEN

704 ■ KCAM-AM - 790
Mile 187 Glenn Hwy.
Glennallen, AK 99588
Phone: (907)822-5226
Email: kcam@kcam.org
Format: Religious. **Networks:** SkyLight Satellite; Ambassador Inspirational Radio; Moody Broadcasting; USA Radio. **Owner:** Northern Lights Library Network, 1104 7th Ave. S, Moorhead, MN 56563, Ph: (218)477-2934. **Founded:** 1964. **Operating Hours:** Continuous; 80% network, 20% local. **Key Personnel:** Scott Yahr, Station Mgr.; Michelle Eastty, Dir. of Programs. **Wattage:** 5,000. **Ad Rates:** $6-14 for 30 seconds; $14-20.50 for 60 seconds. **Mailing address:** PO Box 249, Glennallen, AK 99588. **URL:** http://www.kcam.org.

HAINES

Haines Borough. Haines Census Div. (SE). 75 m NW of Juneau. Tourism center. Outdoor recreation, state park camping facilities. Chilkat Indian dancers. State preserve for world's largest gathering of bald eagles. Sport and commercial fishing.

705 ■ Haines Cable TV
PO Box 1229
Haines, AK 99827
Phone: (907)766-2337
Fax: (907)766-2345
Owner: Patty Campbell, 810 N Union, Ste. 601, Whitesboro, TX. **Founded:** 1964. **Key Personnel:** Patty Campbell, Owner. **Cities Served:** Skagway, Alaska: subscribing households 123; 30 channels; 1 community

Circulation: ★ = AAM; △ or • = BPA; ♦ = CAC; ❑ = VAC; ⊕ = PO Statement; ‡ = Publisher's Report; Boldface figures = sworn; Light figures = estimated.

access channel; 168 hours per week community access programming. **URL:** http://www.hainescable.com.

706 ■ KHNS-FM - 102.3
PO Box 1109
Haines, AK 99827
Phone: (907)766-2020
Fax: (907)766-2022
Email: khns@khns.org
Format: Public Radio; Eclectic. **Networks:** National Public Radio (NPR); Public Radio International (PRI). **Owner:** Lynn Canal Broadcasting, 1 Theatre Dr., Haines, AK 99827, Ph: (907)766-2020, Fax: (907)766-2022. **Founded:** 1980. **Operating Hours:** Continuous. **Key Personnel:** Kay Clements, Gen. Mgr., gm@khns.org. **Local Programs:** *With Strings Attached*, Wednesday 8:00 p.m. - 10:00 p.m. **Wattage:** 3,000. **Ad Rates:** Noncommercial. **URL:** http://www.khns.org.

707 ■ Skagway Cable TV
715 Main St.
Haines, AK 99827
Phone: (907)766-2337
Fax: (907)766-2345
Owner: Educated Design & Development Inc., 901 Sheldon Dr., Cary, NC 27513, Ph: (919)469-9434, Fax: (919)469-5743, Free: 800-806-6236. **Founded:** Apr. 1979. **Key Personnel:** Patty Campbell, Owner. **Cities Served:** Skagway, Alaska: subscribing households 40; 30 channels; 1 community access channel; 168 hours per week community access programming. **Mailing address:** PO Box 1229, Haines, AK 99827. **URL:** http://www.hainescable.com.

HOMER

Kenai Peninsula Borough. Kenai Peninsula Census Div. (SC) 115 m SW of Anchorage. Recreational area. Sport fishing. Manufactures boats. Canning.

708 ■ Homer News
Homer News
3482 Landings St.
Homer, AK 99603
Phone: (907)235-7767
Fax: (907)235-6571
Publication E-mail: news@homernews.com
Community newspaper. **Freq:** Weekly (Thurs.). **Print Method:** Offset. **Trim Size:** 10 x 16. **Cols./Page:** 6. **Col. Width:** 19 nonpareils. **Col. Depth:** 210 agate lines. **Key Personnel:** Lori Evans, Editor, Publisher. **Subscription Rates:** $40 Individuals in Homer distribution area; $50 Out of area out of county; $60 Out of state Lower 48 & Hawai; $110 Individuals first class. **URL:** http://homernews.com. **Ad Rates:** GLR $.40; BW $840; 4C $1,140; PCI $9.80. **Remarks:** Accepts advertising. **Circ:** (Not Reported).

709 ■ Homer Tribune
The Homer Tribune
435 E Pioneer Ave.
Homer, AK 99603-7142
Phone: (907)235-3714
Fax: (907)235-3716
Community newspaper. **Freq:** Weekly. **Key Personnel:** Jane M. Pascall, Publisher. **Subscription Rates:** $39 Individuals; $48 Out of area; $58 Out of state. **URL:** http://homertribune.com. **Remarks:** Accepts advertising. **Circ:** (Not Reported).

710 ■ KBBI-AM - 890
3913 Kachemak Way
Homer, AK 99603
Phone: (907)235-7721
Fax: (907)235-2357
Email: info@kbbi.org
Format: Public Radio. **Simulcasts:** partial @ KDLL-FM in Kenai. **Networks:** National Public Radio (NPR); Alaska Public Radio; American Public Radio (APR); Public Radio International (PRI). **Owner:** Kachemak Bay Broadcasting Inc., at above address, Homer, AK 99603. **Founded:** 1979. **Operating Hours:** Continuous; 60% network, 40% local. **Key Personnel:** Dave Anderson, Gen. Mgr., dave@kbbi.org; Dorle Harness, Bus. Mgr., dorle@kbbi.org; Terry Rensel, Dir. of Programs, terry@kbbi.org. **Local Programs:** *Coffee Table*, Wednesday 9:00 a.m. - 10:00 a.m.; *Classical 24*, Monday Tuesday Wednesday Thursday 11:00 a.m. - 12:00 p.m. **Wattage:** 10,000. **Ad Rates:** Noncommercial. **URL:** http://www.kbbi.org.

711 ■ KGTL-AM - 620
PO Box 109
Homer, AK 99603
Phone: (907)235-6000
Fax: (907)235-6683
Email: kwavefm@xyz.net
Format: Country. **Networks:** Independent. **Owner:** Peninsula Communication Inc., 6 Rossi Cir., Salinas, CA 93907. **Founded:** 1981. **Formerly:** KCNL-AM. **Operating Hours:** 5 a.m.-midnight; 100% local. **Key Personnel:** David F. Becker, Contact. **Wattage:** 5,000. **Ad Rates:** $6-13 for 30 seconds; $9-18 for 60 seconds. Combined advertising rates available with KWVV-FM, KPEN-FM, KXBA-FM.

KPEN-FM - See Soldotna, AK

712 ■ KWVV-FM - 103.5
PO Box 109
Homer, AK 99603-0109
Phone: (907)235-6000
Fax: (907)235-6683
Email: kwavefm@atxyz.net
Format: Adult Contemporary. **Owner:** Peninsula Communications, Inc., at above address. **Founded:** Sept. 1979. **Operating Hours:** Continuous. **Wattage:** 100,000. **Ad Rates:** $12-18 per unit.

HOUSTON

713 ■ KAGV-AM - 1110
4723 King David St.
Houston, AK 99694
Phone: (907)892-8820
Email: kagv@vfcm.org
Format: Gospel. **Owner:** Voice For Christ Ministries, PO Box 474, Nenana, AK 99760, Ph: (907)832-5426. **Operating Hours:** Continuous. **Ad Rates:** Noncommercial. **Mailing address:** PO Box 940096, Houston, AK 99694. **URL:** http://www.vfcm.org.

JUNEAU

Juneau Borough. Juneau Census Div. (SE) 175 m N of Wrangell. State Capital. Residential.

714 ■ Juneau Empire
Morris Communications Company L.L.C.
3100 Channel Dr.
Juneau, AK 99801-7814
Phone: (907)586-3740
Fax: (907)586-3028
Publisher's E-mail: allaccessprogram@morris.com
General newspaper. **Freq:** Daily (eve.). **Print Method:** Offset. **Cols./Page:** 6. **Col. Width:** 2 1/32 inches. **Col. Depth:** 294 agate lines. **Key Personnel:** Rustan Burton, Publisher. **Subscription Rates:** $15.50 Individuals all access per month; $13.95 Individuals digital only, per month. **URL:** http://juneauempire.com. **Ad Rates:** BW $1,586; 4C $2,141; PCI $12.59. **Remarks:** Advertising accepted; rates available upon request. **Circ:** Paid 7066, Free 190.

715 ■ Southeast Alaska Catholic
Diocese of Juneau
415 6th St., Ste. 300
Juneau, AK 99801-1074
Phone: (907)586-2237
Fax: (907)463-3237
Publication E-mail: juneaudiocese@gci.net
Official newspaper of the Catholic Diocese of Juneau. **Freq:** Biweekly except for the months of June, July and August. **Print Method:** Offset. **Trim Size:** 11 1/2 x 14. **Cols./Page:** 5. **Col. Width:** 1 15/16 inches. **Col. Depth:** 12 inches. **Key Personnel:** Karla Donaghey, Editor; Rev. Edward J. Burns, Publisher. **USPS:** 877-080. **Subscription Rates:** $30 Individuals donation. **Alt. Formats:** PDF. **URL:** http://akseac.com. **Formerly:** Inside Passage: Serving the Church of Southeast Alaska. **Remarks:** Advertising not accepted. **Circ:** Paid 2267.

716 ■ UAS Explorations
UAS Explorations
11120 Glacier Hwy.
Juneau, AK 99801-8671
Phone: (907)796-6000
Free: 877-465-4827
Publisher's E-mail: uas.info@uas.alaska.edu
Literary journal covering poetry and fiction. **Freq:** Annual. **Print Method:** Offset. **Trim Size:** 5 1/2 x 8 1/2. **Key Personnel:** Art Petersen, Editor. **ISSN:** 1081--325X (print). **URL:** http://www.uas.alaska.edu. **Remarks:** Advertising not accepted. **Circ:** 650.

717 ■ GCI
8390 Airport Blvd., Ste. 101
Juneau, AK 99801
Phone: (907)586-3320
Free: 800-800-4800
Email: noreply@gci.com
Owner: GCI Cable/Juneau, 2550 Denali St., Ste. 1000, Anchorage, AK 99503, Free: 800-770-7886. **Founded:** 1970. **Key Personnel:** William C. Behnke, Sr. VP; G. Wilson Hughes, Exec. VP; Dean Bardenheuer, Contact; Dean D. Bardenheuer, Contact, dbardenheur@gci.com; Terry Dunlap, Contact, tdunlap@gci.com; Lea J. Ike, Contact, like@gci.com. **Cities Served:** Douglas, Juneau County, Alaska; United States; 251 channels. **URL:** http://www.gci.com.

718 ■ KINY-AM - 800
3161 Channel Dr.
Juneau, AK 99801
Phone: (907)586-1800
Fax: (907)463-3685
Format: Adult Contemporary; Talk. **Networks:** ABC. **Owner:** Juneau Alaska Communications L.L.C., 3161 Channel Dr., Juneau, AK 99801, Ph: (907)586-3630, Fax: (907)463-3685. **Founded:** 1935. **Operating Hours:** Continuous. **Key Personnel:** Pete Carran, News Dir. **Wattage:** 10,000 Day; 7,500 Night. **Ad Rates:** $16-33 for 30 seconds; $29-50 for 60 seconds. **URL:** http://www.kinyradio.com.

719 ■ KJNO-AM - 630
3161 Channel Dr., Ste. 202
Juneau, AK 99801
Phone: (907)586-3630
Fax: (907)463-3685
Format: Talk; Sports. **Networks:** CBS. **Owner:** Alaska Broadcast Communications, at above address. **Founded:** 1952. **Operating Hours:** 5 a.m.-midnight Sun.-Thurs.; Continuous Fri.-Sat. **ADI:** Juneau, AK. **Wattage:** 5,000 Day; 1,000 Night. **Ad Rates:** $20-30 for 30 seconds; $24-35 for 60 seconds. Combined advertising rates available with KTKU-FM.

720 ■ KSBZ-FM - 103.1
3161 Channel Dr., Ste. 2
Juneau, AK 99801
Fax: (907)747-8455
Format: Classic Rock. **Networks:** Jones Satellite. **Owner:** Alaska Broadcasting Co. Inc., 3161 Channel Dr., Juneau, AK 99801, Ph: (907)586-3630, Fax: (907)463-3685. **Founded:** 1990. **Operating Hours:** Continuous. **ADI:** Sitka, AK. **Wattage:** 3,000. **Ad Rates:** Noncommercial. KIFW-AM.

KSCT-TV - See Sitka

721 ■ KSUP-FM - 106.3
3161 Channel Dr., Ste. 2
Juneau, AK 99801
Phone: (907)586-3630
Format: Adult Contemporary. **Networks:** ABC; Westwood One Radio. **Owner:** Juneau Alaska Communications L.L.C., 3161 Channel Dr., Juneau, AK 99801, Ph: (907)586-3630, Fax: (907)463-3685. **Founded:** 1984. **ADI:** Juneau, AK. **Wattage:** 10,000. **Ad Rates:** Combined advertising rates available with KINY-AM. **URL:** http://www.ptialaska.net.

722 ■ KTKU-FM - 105.1
3161 Channel Dr.
Juneau, AK 99801
Phone: (907)586-3630
Format: Hot Country. **Owner:** Alaska Broadcast Communications, at above address. **Operating Hours:** Continuous. **ADI:** Juneau, AK. **Wattage:** 3,800. **Ad Rates:** Advertising accepted; rates available upon request. Combined advertising rates available with KUNO-AM. **URL:** http://www.taku105.com.

723 ■ KTOO-FM - 104.3
360 Egan Dr.
Juneau, AK 99801
Phone: (907)586-1670
Format: Public Radio; News; Classical; Jazz; Alternative/New Music/Progressive. **Simulcasts:** KRNN,KXLL. **Networks:** National Public Radio (NPR); Public Radio International (PRI). **Owner:** Capital Community Broadcasting Inc., 360 Egan Dr., Juneau, AK 99801-1748. **Founded:** 1974. **ADI:** Juneau, AK. **Key**

Personnel: Jeff Brown, Dir. of Programs; Rosemarie Alexander, Contact. **Wattage:** 1,400 ERP. **Ad Rates:** Advertising accepted; rates available upon request. **URL:** http://www.ktoo.org.

724 ■ KTOO-TV - 3
360 Egan Dr.
Juneau, AK 99801-1748
Phone: (907)586-1670
Fax: (907)586-5692
Email: questions@ktoo.org
Format: Public TV. **Networks:** Public Broadcasting Service (PBS). **Owner:** Capital Community Broadcasting Inc., 360 Egan Dr., Juneau, AK 99801-1748. **Founded:** 1978. **Operating Hours:** Continuous. **ADI:** Juneau, AK. **Key Personnel:** Barbara Sheinberg, Contact; Bill Legere, Gen. Mgr., President; Beth Weigel, Contact. **Ad Rates:** Noncommercial. **URL:** http://www.ktoo.org.

725 ■ KXLJ-TV - 24
1105 W Ninth St.
Juneau, AK 99801
Phone: (907)586-2455
Fax: (907)586-2495
Networks: CBS. **ADI:** Juneau, AK.

726 ■ KXLL-FM - 100.7
360 Egan Dr.
Juneau, AK 99801-1748
Phone: (907)586-1670
Fax: (907)586-3612
Free: 800-478-3636
Format: Adult Album Alternative; Album-Oriented Rock (AOR). **Operating Hours:** Continuous. **Key Personnel:** Cheryl Levitt, Mgr.; Andy Kline, Mgr., Comm.; Rosemarie Alexander, Contact. **Ad Rates:** Noncommercial; underwriting available. **URL:** http://www.ktoo.org/kxll.

KENAI

Kenai Peninsula Borough. Kenai Peninsula Census Div. (SC). 53 m SW of Anchorage. Residential.

727 ■ Peninsula Clarion
Morris Communications Company L.L.C.
725 Broad St.
Augusta, GA 30901
Phone: (706)724-0851
Free: 800-622-6358
Publisher's E-mail: allaccessprogram@morris.com
General newspaper. **Freq:** Daily (morn.) except Sat. and federal holidays. **Print Method:** Offset. **Trim Size:** 13 x 21 1/2. **Cols./Page:** 6. **Col. Width:** 1.833 inches. **Col. Depth:** 210 agate lines. **Key Personnel:** Will Morrow, Editor, phone: (907)335-1251. **USPS:** 438-410. **Subscription Rates:** $130 Individuals home delivery; $200 Individuals mail, in Borough; $250 Individuals mail, in state; $300 Individuals mail, out of state. **URL:** http://peninsulaclarion.com. **Ad Rates:** 4C $600; PCI $18. **Remarks:** Accepts advertising. **Circ:** Mon.-Thurs. ⊕**6140**, Fri. ⊕**6574**, Sun. ⊕**6358**.

728 ■ Peninsula Clarion
Southeastern Newspapers Inc.
PO Box 3009
Kenai, AK 99611
Phone: (907)283-7551
Fax: (907)283-3299
Publisher's E-mail: allaccessprogram@morris.com
General newspaper. **Freq:** Daily (morn.) except Sat. and federal holidays. **Print Method:** Offset. **Trim Size:** 13 x 21 1/2. **Cols./Page:** 6. **Col. Width:** 1.833 inches. **Col. Depth:** 210 agate lines. **Key Personnel:** Will Morrow, Editor, phone: (907)335-1251. **USPS:** 438-410. **Subscription Rates:** $130 Individuals home delivery; $200 Individuals mail, in Borough; $250 Individuals mail, in state; $300 Individuals mail, out of state. **URL:** http://peninsulaclarion.com. **Ad Rates:** 4C $600; PCI $18. **Remarks:** Accepts advertising. **Circ:** Mon.-Thurs. ⊕**6140**, Fri. ⊕**6574**, Sun. ⊕**6358**.

729 ■ KDLL-FM - 91.9
14896 Kenai Spur Hwy., Ste. 103
Kenai, AK 99611
Phone: (907)283-8433
Format: Public Radio. **Networks:** National Public Radio (NPR); Public Radio International (PRI); American Public Radio (APR). **Owner:** Pickle Hill Broadcasting Inc., at above address, Kenai, AK. **Operating Hours:** Continuous. **Key Personnel:** Terry Rensel, Prog. Dir., terry@kbbi.org; Dave Anderson, Gen. Mgr., dave@kbbi.org. **Local Programs**: *Coffee Table*, Wednesday 9:00 a.m. - 10:00 a.m. **Wattage**: 4,900. **Ad Rates:** Noncommercial. KBBI Homer, AK. **Mailing address:** PO Box 2111, Kenai, AK 99611. **URL:** http://www.kdllradio.org.

730 ■ KKIS-FM - 96.5
40960 Kalifornsky Beach Rd.
Kenai, AK 99611
Phone: (907)283-5821
Fax: (907)283-9177
Free: 800-247-4487
Format: Contemporary Hit Radio (CHR). **Owner:** KSRM Inc., 40960 Kalifornsky Beach Rd., Kenai, AK 99611. **Key Personnel:** Jake Thompson, Contact. **URL:** http://www.radiokenai.net/kkis/contact.

731 ■ KSLD-AM - 1140
40960 Kalifornsky Beach Rd.
Kenai, AK 99611
Phone: (907)283-8700
Fax: (907)283-9177
Free: 855-631-3995
Format: Classic Rock; Information. **Owner:** KSRM Inc., 40960 Kalifornsky Beach Rd., Kenai, AK 99611. **URL:** http://www.radiokenai.net.

732 ■ KSRM-AM - 920
40960 Kalifornsky Beach Rd.
Kenai, AK 99611
Phone: (907)283-5811
Fax: (907)283-9177
Free: 888-872-5776
Email: rken18@radiokenai.com
Format: Talk; News; Sports. **Owner:** KSRM Inc., 40960 Kalifornsky Beach Rd., Kenai, AK 99611. **Founded:** 1967. **Operating Hours**: 8:00 a.m. - 5:00 p.m. Monday - Friday. **Key Personnel:** Dan Gensel, Sports Dir., dangensel@radiokenai.com; John C. Davis, CEO, President, johndavis@radiokenai.com; Mark Gage, Consultant, mgage@radiokenai.com. **Wattage**: 5,000 ERP. **Ad Rates:** Noncommercial. **URL:** http://www.radiokenai.net.

733 ■ K206DG-FM - 89.1
PO Box 391
Twin Falls, ID 83303
Free: 800-357-4226
Format: Religious; Contemporary Christian. **Owner:** CSN International, PO Box 391, Twin Falls, ID 83303, Ph: (208)736-1958, Fax: (208)736-1958, Free: 800-357-4226. **Key Personnel:** Don Mills, Prog. Dir., Music Dir.; Kelly Carlson, Dir. of Engg.; Ray Gorney, Asst. Dir. **URL:** http://www.csnradio.com.

734 ■ KWHQ-FM - 100.1
40960 Kalifornsky Beach Rd.
Kenai, AK 99611
Phone: (907)283-8700
Fax: (907)283-9177
Free: 888-872-5776
Email: info@radiokenai.com
Format: Contemporary Country. **Networks:** ABC. **Owner:** KSRM Inc., 40960 Kalifornsky Beach Rd., Kenai, AK 99611. **Founded:** 1976. **Formerly:** KQOK-FM. **Operating Hours:** Continuous. **Key Personnel:** John C. Davis, CEO, Gen. Mgr., President, johndavis@radiokenai.com; Jake Thompson, Production Mgr., jakethompson@radiokenai.com; Joe Nicks, News Dir., news@radiokenai.com. **Wattage:** 3,000. **Ad Rates:** $14-30 for 30 seconds; $26-60 for 60 seconds. Combined advertising rates available with KSRM-AM, KSLD-AM, KKIS-FM. **URL:** http://www.radiokenai.net.

KETCHIKAN

Ketchikan Gateway Borough. Ketchikan Census Div. (SE). 237 m SE of Juneau. Ferry connections. Soft drink factory; pulp and saw mills; salmon canning and freezing and packing plants. Important shipping center. Commercial fisheries. Uranium, molybdenum mine. Logging camps.

735 ■ Ketchikan Daily News
Pioneer Printing Company Inc.
501 Dock St.
Ketchikan, AK 99901
Phone: (907)225-3157
Fax: (907)225-1096
Publisher's E-mail: news@ketchikandandailynews.net
General newspaper. **Freq:** Daily. **Print Method:** Offset. **Cols./Page:** 6. **Col. Width:** 27 nonpareils. **Col. Depth:** 294 agate lines. **USPS:** 293-940. **Alt. Formats:** PDF. **URL:** http://www.ketchikandailynews.com. **Mailing address:** PO Box 7900, Ketchikan, AK 99901. **Ad Rates:** BW $1,827; 4C $2,027; PCI $14.50. **Remarks:** Accepts advertising. **Circ:** ‡5823.

736 ■ KFMJ-FM - 99.9
516 Stedman St.
Ketchikan, AK 99901
Phone: (907)247-3699
Fax: (907)247-5365
Email: kfmj@alaska.fm
Format: Oldies. **Owner:** TLP Communications Inc., at above address. **URL:** http://www.alaska.fm/kfmj.

737 ■ KGTW-FM - 106.7
526 Stedman St.
Ketchikan, AK 99901
Phone: (907)225-2193
Format: Country. **Networks:** ABC. **Founded:** 1987. **Operating Hours**: Continuous. **ADI**: Ketchikan, AK. **Wattage**: 5,000. **Ad Rates:** Advertising accepted; rates available upon request. $21-$32 for 30 seconds; $24-$36 for 60 seconds. Combined advertising rates available with KTKN-AM.

738 ■ KRBD-FM - 105.3
1101 Copper Ridge Rd.
Ketchikan, AK 99901
Phone: (907)225-9655
Fax: (907)247-0808
Free: 800-557-5723
Email: news@krbd.org
Format: Eclectic; Public Radio. **Networks:** National Public Radio (NPR); Alaska Public Radio; Public Radio International (PRI). **Owner:** Rainbird Community Broadcasting Corp., 1101 Copper Ridge Ln., Ketchikan, AK 99901-6250, Ph: (907)225-9655, Fax: (907)247-0808, Free: 800-557-5723. **Founded:** 1976. **Operating Hours**: Continuous. **ADI**: Ketchikan, AK. **Key Personnel:** Sheila Miller, VP; Nathan Grambau, Gen. Mgr.; Deanna Garrison, News Dir. **Wattage**: 15,000. **Ad Rates:** Noncommercial. **URL:** http://www.krbd.org.

739 ■ KTKN-AM - 930
526 Stedman St.
Ketchikan, AK 99901
Phone: (907)225-2193
Fax: (907)255-0444
Format: Talk; Adult Contemporary. **Networks:** ABC. **Owner:** Alaska Broadcasters Association, c/o Cathy Hiebert, Executive Director 700 W 41st St., Ste. 102, Anchorage, AK 99503, Ph: (907)258-2424, Fax: (907)258-2414. **Founded:** 1942. **Operating Hours:** Continuous. **ADI:** Ketchikan, AK. **Key Personnel:** Mary Biggerstaff, Station Mgr., mary@abcstations.com. **Ad Rates:** $21-32 for 30 seconds; $24-36 for 60 seconds. $21-$32 for 30 seconds; $24-$36 for 60 seconds. Combined advertising rates available with KGTW-FM. **URL:** http://ketchikanradio.com/station.php.

740 ■ K216DG-FM - 91.1
PO Box 391
Twin Falls, ID 83303
Fax: (208)736-1958
Free: 800-357-4226
Format: Religious; Contemporary Christian. **Owner:** CSN International, PO Box 391, Twin Falls, ID 83303, Ph: (208)736-1958, Fax: (208)736-1958, Free: 800-357-4226. **ADI**: Ketchikan, AK. **Key Personnel:** Don Mills, Prog. Dir., Music Dir.; Ray Gorney, Asst. Dir.; Kelly Carlson, Dir. of Engg. **Wattage**: 075. **URL:** http://www.csnradio.com.

741 ■ KUBD-TV - 4
2417 Tongass Ave.
Ketchikan, AK 99901
Phone: (907)225-4613
Fax: (907)225-4613
Networks: CBS. **ADI:** Ketchikan, AK. **URL:** http://www.cbssoutheastak.com.

Circulation: ★ = AAM; △ or • = BPA; ♦ = CAC; ❑ = VAC; ⊕ = PO Statement; ‡ = Publisher's Report; Boldface figures = sworn; Light figures = estimated.

KING SALMON

742 ■ Bay Cablevision Inc.
One Main St.
King Salmon, AK 99613
Phone: (907)246-3403
Fax: (907)246-1115
Free: 800-478-9100
Email: bbtccsr@bristolbay.com
Cities Served: 39 channels. **Mailing address:** PO Box 297, King Salmon, AK 99613. **URL:** http://www.bristolbay.com.

KODIAK

Kodiak Island Borough. Kodiak Island Census Div. (S). On Gulf of Alaska, 250 m SW of Anchorage. Boat connections. U.S. Coast Guard Base. Salmon, herring, tanner crab & shrimp canneries. Fisheries. Spruce timber. Stock farms.

743 ■ Kodiak Daily Mirror
Kodiak Daily Mirror
1419 Selig St.
Kodiak, AK 99615
Phone: (907)486-3227
Fax: (907)486-3088
General newspaper. **Freq:** Daily. **Print Method:** Offset. **Trim Size:** 11 x 21. **Cols./Page:** 6. **Col. Width:** 11 3/4 picas. **Key Personnel:** Janet Baker, Specialist, Circulation; Drew Herman, Editor, Reporter. **URL:** http://www.kodiakdailymirror.com. **Ad Rates:** 4C $800; PCI $12.75. **Remarks:** Advertising accepted; rates available upon request. **Circ:** Paid 3313.

744 ■ KMXT-FM - 100.1
620 Egan Way
Kodiak, AK 99615
Phone: (907)486-3181
Format: Public Radio; News; Eclectic. **Networks:** Alaska Public Radio; National Public Radio (NPR); Public Radio International (PRI); Corporation for Public Broadcasting. **Owner:** Kodiak Public Broadcasting Corp., 620 Egan Way, Kodiak, AK 99615. **Founded:** 1976. **Operating Hours:** Continuous. **Key Personnel:** Pam Foreman, Dir. of Dev., pam.foreman@kmxt.org; Mike Wall, Gen. Mgr., Prog. Dir. **Local Programs:** *Alaska Fisheries Report,* Thursday 9:00 a.m.; *Swinging Down the Lane.* **Wattage:** 3,000 ERP. **Ad Rates:** Noncommercial. **URL:** http://www.kmxt.org.

745 ■ KMXT-TV - 9
620 Egan Way
Kodiak, AK 99615
Phone: (907)486-3181
Key Personnel: Mike Wall, Gen. Mgr., Music Dir., Prog. Dir., gm@kmxt.org. **URL:** http://www.kmxt.org.

746 ■ Kodiak Cablevision
170 Von Sheele Way
Kodiak, AK 99615
Phone: (907)486-3334
Owner: GCI Cable Inc., 2550 Denali St., Ste. 1000, Anchorage, AK 99503-2751, Ph: (907)265-5600, Free: 800-770-7886. **Founded:** 1982. **Key Personnel:** Ronald Duncan, President, CEO, Founder. **Cities Served:** subscribing households 2,900. **URL:** http://www.gci.com.

747 ■ KRXX-FM - 101.1
1315 Mill Bay Rd.
Kodiak, AK 99615
Phone: (907)486-5159
Fax: (907)486-3044
Format: Adult Contemporary. **Simulcasts:** KVOK-AM. **Networks:** ABC. **Owner:** Kodiak Island Broadcasting Company Inc., at above address, Kodiak, AK 99615. **Founded:** 1985. **Formerly:** KJJZ-FM. **Operating Hours:** Continuous; 90% network, 10% local. **Key Personnel:** Clifford Kay, Operations Mgr., clifford@kvok.com. **Wattage:** 3,100. **Ad Rates:** $12-35 for 30 seconds; $15-40 for 60 seconds. Combined advertising rates available with KVOK-AM.

748 ■ K216DF-FM - 91.1
PO Box 391
Twin Falls, ID 83303
Fax: (208)736-1958
Free: 800-357-4226
Format: Religious; Contemporary Christian. **Owner:** CSN International, PO Box 391, Twin Falls, ID 83303, Ph: (208)736-1958, Fax: (208)736-1958, Free: 800-357-4226. **Key Personnel:** Don Mills, Prog. Dir., Music Dir.; Kelly Carlson, Dir. of Engg.; Ray Gorney, Asst. Dir. **Wattage:** 015.005. **URL:** http://www.csnradio.com.

749 ■ KVOK-AM - 560
1315 Mill Bay Rd.
Kodiak, AK 99615
Phone: (907)486-5159
Fax: (907)486-3044
Email: kvok@ak.net
Format: Country; News. **Networks:** ABC. **Owner:** Kodiak Island Broadcasting Company Inc., at above address, Kodiak, AK 99615. **Founded:** 1974. **Operating Hours:** Continuous; 20% network, 80% local. **Key Personnel:** Chuck Wright, Operations Mgr., chuck@kvok.com. **Wattage:** 1,000. **Ad Rates:** $12-35 for 30 seconds; $15-40 for 60 seconds. KRXX-FM. **Mailing address:** PO Box 708, Kodiak, AK 99615. **URL:** http://www.kvok.com.

KOTZEBUE

Northwest Arctic Borough. Northwest Artic Borough Co. (NW). 200 m NE of Nome.

750 ■ KOTZ-AM - 89.9
PO Box 78
Kotzebue, AK 99752
Phone: (907)442-3434
Fax: (907)442-2292
Format: Public Radio; News; Eclectic; Talk. **Networks:** American Public Radio (APR); Alaska Radio Network; AP. **Owner:** Kotzebue Broadcasting Inc., 396 Lagoon St., Kotzebue, AK 99752, Ph: (907)442-3434, Fax: (907)442-2292. **Founded:** 1973. **Operating Hours:** 6 p.m.-midnight; 20% network, 80% local. **Key Personnel:** Pierre Lonewolf, Chief Engineer, plonewolf@kotz.org; Rosie Hensley, Gen. Mgr., rhensley@kotz.org; Johnson Greene, Dir. of Programs, jgreene@kotz.org. **Wattage:** 10,000. **Ad Rates:** Underwriting available. **URL:** http://www.kotz.org.

MCGRATH

751 ■ KSKO-AM - 870
PO Box 70
McGrath, AK 99627
Phone: (907)524-3001
Fax: (907)524-3436
Format: Eclectic. **Networks:** Public Radio International (PRI). **Owner:** Kuskokwim Public Broadcasting Corp., at above address. **Founded:** 1981. **Operating Hours:** Continuous. **Wattage:** 10,000. **Ad Rates:** Noncommercial.

NAKNEK

752 ■ KAKN-FM - 100.9
PO Box 214
Naknek, AK 99633
Format: Religious. **Networks:** AP. **Owner:** Bay Broadcasting, Mile 2 Alaska Peninsula Hwy., Naknek, AK 99633. **Operating Hours:** 6 a.m.-midnight; Continuous June and July. **Wattage:** 3,000. **Ad Rates:** Noncommercial. **Mailing address:** PO Box 214, Naknek, AK 99633. **URL:** http://www.kaknradio.org.

NENANA

753 ■ KIAM-AM - 630
409 1st St.
Nenana, AK 99760
Phone: (907)832-5426
Email: alaskaradio@vfcm.org
Format: Religious; Gospel. **Owner:** Voice for Christ Ministries Inc., at above address. **Founded:** 1985. **Operating Hours:** Continuous. **Key Personnel:** Brian Blair, Station Mgr; Ron Heagy, Contact. **Wattage:** 10,000 Day 3,100 Night. **Ad Rates:** $12 for 30 seconds; $18 for 60 seconds. Combined advertising rates available with KYKD. **Mailing address:** PO Box 474, Nenana, AK 99760. **URL:** http://www.vfcm.org.

NOME

Nome Census Area. Nome Census Div. (NW) On Norton Sound, 500 m W of Fairbanks. Tourism. Winter sports. Recreation center. Boat and air connections. Gold mines. Commercial fisheries.

754 ■ KICY-AM - 850
408 W D St.
Nome, AK 99762
Phone: (907)443-2213
Fax: (907)443-2344
Free: 800-478-5429
Email: office@kicy.org
Format: Southern Gospel; Religious. **Networks:** ABC; Moody Broadcasting. **Owner:** Arctic Broadcasting Association Inc., PO Box 820, Nome, AK 99762. **Founded:** 1960. **Operating Hours:** Continuous. **Key Personnel:** Dennis Weidler, Gen. Mgr., dennisw@kicy.org; Candace Weidler, Div. Dir; Luda Kinok, Contact. **Wattage:** 50,000. **Ad Rates:** $7-13 for 30 seconds; $10-17 for 60 seconds. $7-$13 for 30 seconds; $10-$17 for 60 seconds. Combined advertising rates available with KICY-FM. **Mailing address:** PO Box 820, Nome, AK 99762. **URL:** http://www.kicy.org.

755 ■ KICY-FM - 100.3
408 W D St.
Nome, AK 99762
Phone: (907)443-2213
Fax: (907)443-2344
Free: 800-478-5429
Email: office@kicy.org
Format: Contemporary Christian. **Networks:** Independent. **Owner:** Arctic Broadcasting Association Inc., PO Box 820, Nome, AK 99762. **Founded:** 1977. **Operating Hours:** Continuous; 100% local. **Key Personnel:** Dennis Weidler, Gen. Mgr., dennisw@kicy.org. **Wattage:** 084. **Ad Rates:** $7-13 for 30 seconds; $10-17 for 60 seconds. $7-$13 for 30 seconds; $10-$17 for 60 seconds. Combined advertising rates available with KICY-AM. **Mailing address:** PO Box 820, Nome, AK 99762. **URL:** http://www.kicy.org.

756 ■ KNOM-AM - 780
PO Box 988
Nome, AK 99762
Phone: (907)443-5221
Fax: (907)443-5757
Free: 855-445-7131
Email: story49@knom.org
Format: News; World Beat. **Simulcasts:** KNOM-FM. **Networks:** AP. **Founded:** 1971. **Operating Hours:** Continuous. **Key Personnel:** Ric Schmidt, Gen. Mgr.; Laureli Kinneen, Contact; Kelly Brabec, Dir. of Programs; Lynette Schmidt, Bus. Mgr. **Wattage:** 25,000 Day; 14,000 N. **Ad Rates:** Accepts Advertising. **URL:** http://www.knom.org.

757 ■ KNOM-FM - 96.1
PO Box 988
Nome, AK 99762
Phone: (907)443-5221
Fax: (907)443-5757
Free: 800-478-5666
Email: business@knom.org
Format: Educational; Religious; News; Oldies; Jazz. **Networks:** CNN Radio. **Owner:** Catholic Bishop of Northern Alaska, at above address. **Founded:** May 17, 1993. **Operating Hours:** Continuous. **Key Personnel:** Kelly Brabec, Dir. of Programs, programdirector@knom.org; Laureli Kinneen, News Dir., newsdirector@knom.org; Lynette Schmidt, Bus. Mgr., business@knom.org; Ric Schmidt, Gen. Mgr., generalmanager@knom.org. **Wattage:** 1,000 ERP. **Ad Rates:** Noncommercial. **URL:** http://www.knom.org.

NORTH POLE

Fairbanks North Star Borough. Fairbanks North Star Borough Co. (NE). 20 m S of Fairbanks.

758 ■ KJNP-AM - 1170
PO Box 56359
North Pole, AK 99705
Phone: (907)488-2216
Fax: (907)488-5246
Email: kjnp@mosquitonet.com
Format: Religious. **Networks:** AP. **Owner:** Evangelistic Alaska Missionary Fellowship, at above address. **Founded:** 1967. **Operating Hours:** 5:30 a.m.-midnight summer; 5:30 a.m.-1:15 a.m. winter. **Wattage:** 50,000. **Ad Rates:** $4-5 for 15 seconds; $6-9 for 30 seconds; $10.80-16.20 for 60 seconds. **URL:** http://www.mosquitonet.com/~kjnp/am.html.

759 ■ KJNP-FM - 100.3
PO Box 56359
North Pole, AK 99705-1359
Email: kjnp@mosquitonet.com
Format: Religious. **Networks:** Moody Broadcasting. **Owner:** Evangelistic Alaska Missionary Fellowship, at above address. **Founded:** 1977. **Operating Hours:** Continuous; 75% network, 25% local. **ADI:** Fairbanks (North Pole), AK. **Wattage:** 25,000. **Ad Rates:** $10 for 30 seconds. **URL:** http://www.mosquitonet.com/~kjnp/volunteer.html.

760 ■ KJNP-TV - 4
PO Box 56359
North Pole, AK 99705-1359
Phone: (907)488-2216
Fax: (907)488-5246
Email: kjnp@mosquitonet.com
Format: Commercial TV; Religious. **Founded:** 1981. **Operating Hours:** Continuous. **ADI:** Fairbanks (North Pole), AK. **Local Programs:** *Closing Comments*, Tuesday Thursday 9:00 p.m. - 10:00 p.m. **Wattage:** 18,000. **Ad Rates:** $32-60 for 30 seconds; $57.60-108 for 60 seconds. **URL:** http://www.mosquitonet.com/~kjnp.

PALMER

Matanuska-Susitna Borough. Matanuska-Susitna Borough Co. (SC). 20 m NE of Anchorage.

761 ■ KJLP-FM - 88.9
PO Box 210389
Anchorage, AK 99521
Phone: (907)333-5282
Free: 800-478-4483
Format: Religious. **Owner:** Christian Broadcasting Inc., PO Box 201839, Anchorage, AK 99521. **Wattage:** 250. **URL:** http://www.katb.org.

PETERSBURG

Wrangell-Petersburg Census Area. Wrangell-Petersburg Census Div. (SE). 140 m S of Juneau. Boat connections. Fish packing plants; seafood canneries; saw, pulp mills. Commercial fisheries. Spruce timber.

762 ■ Petersburg Pilot
Pilot Publishing Inc.
PO Box 930
Petersburg, AK 99833
Publication E-mail: pilotpub@gmail.com
Local newspaper serving Mitkof Island and surrounding area. **Freq:** Weekly. **Print Method:** Offset. **Trim Size:** 11 3/8 x 16. **Cols./Page:** 5. **Col. Width:** 22 nonpareils. **Col. Depth:** 196 agate lines. **ISSN:** 0535--7000 (print). **Subscription Rates:** $47 Individuals; $94 Two years. **URL:** http://www.petersburgpilot.com. **Remarks:** Accepts classified advertising. **Circ:** ‡1800.

763 ■ Wrangell Sentinel
Pilot Publishing Inc.
PO Box 930
Petersburg, AK 99833
Publisher's E-mail: info@petersburgpilot.com
Community newspaper. **Freq:** Weekly (Thurs.). **Print Method:** Offset. **Cols./Page:** 5. **Col. Width:** 11 picas. **Col. Depth:** 14.5 inches. **USPS:** 626-480. **Subscription Rates:** $42 Individuals; $84 Individuals 2 years; $126 Individuals 3 years. **URL:** http://www.wrangellsentinel.com. **Ad Rates:** GLR $6.50; BW $471.25; 4C $971.25; SAU $8.09; CNU $8.40; PCI $6.50. **Remarks:** Advertising accepted; rates available upon request. **Circ:** Paid ‡1475, Free ‡25.

764 ■ GCI
1270 Howkan Space 3
Petersburg, AK 99833
Phone: (907)772-3292
Free: 800-770-7886
Email: support@gci.net
Founded: 1979. **Key Personnel:** Ronald Duncan, CEO; G. Wilson Hughes, Exec. VP; William C. Behnke, Sr. VP of Strategic Bus. Operations. **Cities Served:** 53 channels. **URL:** http://www.gci.com.

765 ■ KFSK-FM - 100.9
404 N 2nd St.
Petersburg, AK 99833
Phone: (907)772-3808
Fax: (907)772-9296
Free: 888-772-3808
Format: News; Eclectic. **Owner:** Narrows Broadcasting Corp., 404 N Second St., Petersburg, AK 99833. **Founded:** 1977. **Operating Hours:** Continuous. **Key Personnel:** Tom Abbott, Gen. Mgr. **Wattage:** 2,000. **Ad Rates:** Noncommercial. **Mailing address:** PO Box 149, Petersburg, AK 99833. **URL:** http://www.kfsk.org.

766 ■ KRSA-AM - 580
PO Box 650
Petersburg, AK 99833
Phone: (907)772-3891
Fax: (907)772-4538
Free: 800-478-5772
Format: Religious. **Networks:** Sun Radio; SkyLight Satellite. **Owner:** Northern Lights Library Network, 1104 7th Ave. S, Moorhead, MN 56563, Ph: (218)477-2934. **Founded:** 1982. **Operating Hours:** Continuous; 50% network, 50% local. **ADI:** Alaska. **Key Personnel:** Amy Long-Drew, Office Mgr. **Wattage:** 5,000. **Ad Rates:** $10-16 for 30 seconds; $16-18 for 60 seconds.

SAINT PAUL ISLAND

767 ■ KUHB-FM - 91.9
PO Box 905
Saint Paul Island, AK 99660
Phone: (907)546-2254
Format: Country; Album-Oriented Rock (AOR). **Founded:** 1985. **Wattage:** 3,000. **URL:** http://www.kuhbradio.org.

SAND POINT

768 ■ KSDP-AM - 830
100 Main St.
Sand Point, AK 99661
Email: cw@apradio.org
Format: Full Service. **Networks:** Alaska Public Radio; National Public Radio (NPR); Public Radio International (PRI). **Owner:** Aleutian Peninsula Broadcasting, Inc., at above address. **Founded:** 1983. **Operating Hours:** Continuous. **Key Personnel:** Kells Hetherington, Contact. **Wattage:** 1,000. **Ad Rates:** Noncommercial. **Mailing address:** PO Box 328, Sand Point, AK 99661. **URL:** http://www.apradio.org.

SELDOVIA

769 ■ K220FW-FM - 91.9
PO Box 391
Twin Falls, ID 83303
Fax: (208)736-1958
Free: 800-357-4226
Format: Religious; Contemporary Christian. **Owner:** CSN International, PO Box 391, Twin Falls, ID 83303, Ph: (208)736-1958, Fax: (208)736-1958, Free: 800-357-4226. **URL:** http://www.csnradio.com.

SITKA

Sitka Borough. Sitka Census Div. (SE). 100 m S of Juneau. Daily jet connections to Seattle & points north; regular Alaska ferry connections. Mt. Edgecunbe Boarding School; Sheldon Jackson College; Coast Guard Air station. Rich historical, area, former capital of Russian America. Pulp manufacture for export; logging; commercial fishing and processing center.

770 ■ The Daily Sitka Sentinel: A Home-owned Newspaper Serving Sitka Since 1940
The Daily Sitka Sentinel
112 Barracks St.
Sitka, AK 99835
Phone: (907)747-3219
Fax: (907)747-8898
Publisher's E-mail: sitkanews@hotmail.com
General newspaper. **Freq:** Daily (eve.). **Print Method:** Offset. **Cols./Page:** 6. **Col. Width:** 2 3/16 inches. **Col. Depth:** 294 agate lines. **Key Personnel:** Thad Poulson, Editor; Sandy Poulson, Publisher. **USPS:** 146-160. **Subscription Rates:** $50 Individuals online only. **URL:** http://sitkasentinel.com. **Ad Rates:** GLR $8.80; BW $1,155; 4C $1,875; PCI $10.20. **Remarks:** Advertising accepted; rates available upon request. **Circ:** 3020.

771 ■ GCI
208-A Lake St.
Sitka, AK 99835
Phone: (907)747-3535
Free: 800-770-7886
Email: support@gci.net
Founded: 1979. **Key Personnel:** Ronald Duncan, CEO, Founder, President; William C. Behnke, Sr. VP. **Cities Served:** 91 channels. **URL:** http://www.gci.com.

772 ■ KCAW-FM - 104.7
2B Lincoln St.
Sitka, AK 99835
Phone: (907)747-5877
Fax: (907)747-5977
Free: 800-478-5877
Format: Public Radio. **Networks:** National Public Radio (NPR); Public Radio International (PRI); Alaska Public Radio. **Owner:** Raven Radio Foundation Inc., 2B Lincoln St., Sitka, AK 99835, Ph: (907)747-5877, Fax: (907)747-5977, Free: 800-478-5877. **Founded:** 1982. **Operating Hours:** Continuous. **ADI:** Sitka, AK. **Wattage:** 5,000. **Ad Rates:** Noncommercial. **URL:** http://www.kcaw.org.

773 ■ KIFW-AM - 1230
611 Lake St.
Sitka, AK 99835
Phone: (907)747-6626
Email: kifw@abcstations.com
Format: Information; News. **Owner:** Alaska Broadcasting Co. Inc., 3161 Channel Dr., Juneau, AK 99801, Ph: (907)586-3630, Fax: (907)463-3685. **Founded:** 1949. **Operating Hours:** Continuous. **ADI:** Sitka, AK. **Wattage:** 1,000. **Ad Rates:** $12-25 for 30 seconds; $19-40 for 60 seconds. $7-$19 for 30 seconds; $13-$30 for 60 seconds. Combined advertising rates available with KSBZ-FM. **URL:** http://www.kifw.com/.

774 ■ KRAW-FM - 90.1
2 Lincoln St., Ste. B
Sitka, AK 99835
Phone: (907)747-5877
Fax: (907)747-5977
Free: 800-478-5877
Format: Talk; Jazz; Alternative/New Music/Progressive. **Owner:** Raven Radio Foundation Inc., 2B Lincoln St., Sitka, AK 99835, Ph: (907)747-5877, Fax: (907)747-5977, Free: 800-478-5877. **Operating Hours:** Continuous. **Ad Rates:** Noncommercial; underwriting available.

775 ■ KSCT-TV - 5
1107 W Eight St., Ste. 1
Juneau, AK 99801
Phone: (907)586-8384
Fax: (907)586-8394
Format: News; Sports; Information. **Networks:** NBC. **Founded:** 1993. **ADI:** Sitka, AK. **Key Personnel:** Charlie Ellis, Station Mgr., charlie@kath.tv; Rik Pruett, Production Mgr., rik@kath.tv; Mikko Wilson, Contact, mikko@kath.tv. **Wattage:** 049 ERP. **Ad Rates:** Accepts Advertising. **URL:** http://www.kath.tv.

776 ■ KTNL-TV - 13
208 Lake St.
Sitka, AK 99835
Format: Commercial TV. **Networks:** CBS. **Owner:** Ketchikan Television, 2208 Tongass Ave , Ketchikan, AK 99901, Ph: (907)225-4613. **Formerly:** KIFW-TV. **Operating Hours:** 2 a.m.-12:35 a.m. **ADI:** Sitka, AK. **Wattage:** 1,000. **Ad Rates:** $25 for 30 seconds; $50 for 60 seconds. **URL:** http://www.cbssoutheastak.com/.

777 ■ K220FY-FM - 91.9
PO Box 391
Twin Falls, ID 83303
Fax: (208)736-1958
Free: 800-357-4226
Format: Religious; Contemporary Christian. **Owner:** CSN International, PO Box 391, Twin Falls, ID 83303, Ph: (208)736-1958, Fax: (208)736-1958, Free: 800-357-4226. **ADI:** Sitka, AK. **Key Personnel:** Don Mills, Prog. Dir., Music Dir.; Kelly Carlson, Dir. of Engg.; Ray Gorney, Asst. Dir. **Wattage:** 085. **URL:** http://www.csnradio.com.

SKAGWAY

Skagway-Yakutat-Angoon Census Area. Skagway Census Div. (SE) 100 m NW of Juneau. Residential.

778 ■ The Skagway News
The Skagway News

Circulation: ★ = AAM; △ or • = BPA; ♦ = CAC; ❑ = VAC; ⊕ = PO Statement; ‡ = Publisher's Report; Boldface figures = sworn; Light figures = estimated.

264 Broadway St.
Skagway, AK 99840-0498
Phone: (907)983-2354
Publisher's E-mail: skagnews@aptalaska.net
Community newspaper. **Freq:** Semimonthly. **Print Method:** Offset. **Trim Size:** 10 1/8 x 13 1/2. **Cols./Page:** 5. **Col. Width:** 28 nonpareils. **Col. Depth:** 196 agate lines. **Key Personnel:** William J. Brady, Editor, Publisher. **ISSN:** 0745--872X (print). **Subscription Rates:** $45 Individuals second class; $55 Individuals first class anywhere in North America; $65 Elsewhere first class international; $30 Individuals local; $39.95 Individuals online. **URL:** http://www.skagwaynews.com. **Mailing address:** PO Box 498, Skagway, AK 99840-0498. **Ad Rates:** BW $573.75; 4C $500; PCI $11. **Remarks:** Accepts advertising. **Circ:** ‡1000.

SOLDOTNA

Kenai Peninsula Borough. Kenai Peninsula Census Div. (SC). On Sterling Highway, 145 m SW of Anchorage. Residential.

779 ■ GCI
44661 Sterling Hwy.
Soldotna, AK 99669
Phone: (907)262-3266
Free: 800-770-7886
Founded: 1979. **Key Personnel:** Ronald Duncan, Founder, President; William C. Behnke, Sr. VP of Strategic Bus. Operations. **Cities Served:** 48 channels. **URL:** http://www.gci.com.

780 ■ KPEN-FM - 101.7
PO Box 109
Homer, AK 99603
Phone: (907)235-6000
Fax: (907)235-6683
Format: Country. **Networks:** Independent. **Owner:** Peninsula Communications, Inc., at above address. **Founded:** 1984. **Formerly:** KENY-FM. **Operating Hours:** Continuous; 100% local. **Wattage:** 25,000. **Ad Rates:** $9-13 for 30 seconds; $13-18 for 60 seconds. Combined advertising rates available with KWVV-FM, KXBA-FM, KGTL-AM.

TOK

781 ■ KUDU-FM - 91.9
PO Box 719
Tok, AK 99780
Phone: (907)883-5838
Fax: (907)883-5845
Format: Religious. **Owner:** LifeTalk Radio Network, 11291 Pierce St., Riverside, CA 92505, Ph: (615)469-5122, Free: 800-775-4673. **URL:** http://www.lifetalk.net.

UNALASKA

782 ■ KUCB-FM - 89.7
PO Box 181
Unalaska, AK 99685
Phone: (907)581-1888
Fax: (907)581-1634
Free: 855-257-3377
Email: info@kucb.org
Format: Public Radio; Educational. **Networks:** National Public Radio (NPR); Alaska Public Radio. **Owner:** Unalaska Community Broadcasting, at above address, Unalaska, AK 99685. **Founded:** 1983. **Operating Hours:** 24/7; 87% network, 13% local. **Key Personnel:** Lauren Adams, Gen. Mgr., lauren@kial.org. **Wattage:** 100. **Ad Rates:** Noncommercial. **URL:** http://www.kucb.org.

VALDEZ

Valdez-Cordova Census Area. Valdez-Cordova Census Div. (SC). 150 m S of Seward. Tourism. Main economy of the community is oil industry. Fisheries. Foreign Trade Zone.

783 ■ GCI
104 Harbor Dr.
Valdez, AK 99686
Phone: (907)835-4930
Free: 800-770-7886
Founded: 1979. **Key Personnel:** Ronald Duncan, President, CEO, Founder. **Cities Served:** 48 channels. **URL:** http://www.gci.com.

784 ■ KCHU-AM - 770
128 Pioneer Dr.
Valdez, AK 99686
Phone: (907)835-5880
Fax: (907)835-2847
Free: 800-478-5080
Format: Full Service. **Networks:** National Public Radio (NPR); Public Radio International (PRI); American Public Radio (APR). **Founded:** 1986. **Operating Hours:** Continuous; 75% network, 25% local. **Key Personnel:** Mr. John Anderson, Operations Mgr., johnnyops@kchu.org. **Wattage:** 10,000. **Ad Rates:** Noncommercial. **Mailing address:** PO Box 467, Valdez, AK 99686. **URL:** http://www.kchu.org.

785 ■ KVAK-AM - 1230
501 E Bremner St.
Valdez, AK 99686
Phone: (907)835-5825
Fax: (907)835-5158
Format: Country; News. **Simulcasts:** KVAK-FM. **Networks:** ABC. **Founded:** 1981. **Operating Hours:** Continuous; 90% network. **Wattage:** 1,000. **Ad Rates:** Advertising accepted; rates available upon request. Combined advertising rates available with 93.3 FM. **Mailing address:** PO Box 367, Valdez, AK 99686. **URL:** http://www.kvakradio.com.

786 ■ KVAK-FM - 93.3
501 E Bremner, No. 2
Valdez, AK 99686
Phone: (907)835-5825
Fax: (907)835-5158
Format: Sports; Information. **Founded:** 1981. **Wattage:** 1,200. **Ad Rates:** Advertising accepted; rates available upon request. **Mailing address:** PO Box 367, Valdez, AK 99686. **URL:** http://www.kvakradio.com.

WASILLA

Matanuska-Susitna Borough. Matanuska - Susitna Census Div. (CS). 5 m W of Palmer. Residential

787 ■ Alaska Horse Journal
Alaska Horse Journal
4311 E Crane Rd.
Wasilla, AK 99654
Phone: (907)376-4470
Fax: (907)373-3276
Publication E-mail: office@alaskahorsejournal.com
Magazine for horse enthusiasts. **Freq:** Monthly. **Trim Size:** 7 x 9 1/2. **Key Personnel:** Sandy Shacklett, Editor. **Subscription Rates:** $22.50 Individuals; $37.50 Individuals first class; $3 Single issue. **URL:** http://alaskahorsejournal.printroom.com/. **Ad Rates:** BW $300. **Remarks:** Accepts advertising. **Circ:** 5000.

788 ■ KAYO-FM - 100.9
501 E Bogard Rd.
Wasilla, AK 99654
Phone: (907)631-0493
Email: eddie@countrylegends1009.com
Format: Hot Country. **Networks:** Independent. **Founded:** 1981. **Formerly:** KJDM-FM. **Operating Hours:** Continuous. **Wattage:** 50,000. **Ad Rates:** Advertising accepted; rates available upon request. KFMY. **URL:** http://www.countrylegends1009.com.

789 ■ KMBQ-FM - 99.7
2200 E Parks Hwy.
Wasilla, AK 99654
Phone: (907)373-0222
Fax: (907)376-1575
Format: Adult Contemporary. **Networks:** NBC; CNN Radio. **Founded:** 1985. **Operating Hours:** Continuous. **ADI:** Anchorage, AK. **Key Personnel:** Ray Knight, Dir. of Corp. Operations. **Wattage:** 51,000. **Ad Rates:** $20-35 for 30 seconds; $25-40 for 60 seconds. Combined advertising rates available with KBYR-AM. **URL:** http://www.kmbq.com.

WILLOW

790 ■ Mushing: The Magazine of Dog Powered Adventure
Mushing Magazine
PO Box 1195
Willow, AK 99688
Phone: (907)495-2468
Publisher's E-mail: info@mushing.com
Magazine dealing with all aspects of dog-powered sports. **Freq:** Bimonthly. **Key Personnel:** Jacob Witkop, Editor, Owner. **Subscription Rates:** $26 Individuals; $48 Two years; $35 Canada; $63 Canada two years; $47 Other countries; $84 Other countries two years. **Remarks:** Advertising accepted; rates available upon request. **Circ:** (Not Reported).

WRANGELL

Wrangell-Petersburg Census Area. Wrangell-Petersburg Census Div. (SE). Seaport on Wrangell Island, at mouth of Stikine River, 175 m S of Juneau. Boat connections. Saw mills; fish canneries. Commercial fisheries. Logging. Mineral exploration. Tourism.

791 ■ GCI
325 Front St.
Wrangell, AK 99929
Phone: (907)874-2392
Founded: 1979. **Key Personnel:** Ronald Duncan, CEO; G. Wilson Hughes, Exec. VP; Richard P. Dowling, Sr. VP; William C. Behnke, Sr. VP. **Cities Served:** 80 channels. **URL:** http://www.gci.com.

792 ■ KSTK-FM - 101.7
PO Box 1141
Wrangell, AK 99929
Phone: (907)874-2345
Fax: (907)874-3293
Free: 800-874-KSTK
Format: Public Radio; News. **Networks:** Alaska Public Radio; AP; Public Radio International (PRI); National Public Radio (NPR). **Founded:** 1977. **Operating Hours:** Continuous; 15% network, 85% local. **Local Programs:** *Mountain Stage*, Sunday Saturday 2:00 a.m. - 4:00 a.m. 10:00 a.m. 12:00 p.m.; *The Midnight Special*, Saturday 2:00 a.m. - 4:00 a.m. **Wattage:** 3,000. **Ad Rates:** Noncommercial. **URL:** http://www.kstk.org.

PAGO PAGO

793 ■ KKHJ-FM - 93.1
PO Box 6758
Pago Pago, American Samoa 96799
Phone: (684)633-7793
Fax: (684)633-4493
Format: Top 40. **Operating Hours**: Continuous. **Key Personnel:** Larry Fuss, President, larry@khjradio.com; Joey Cummings, Gen. Mgr., joey@khjradio.com; Monica Miller, News Dir., monica@khjradio.com. **Wattage**: 1,100. **URL:** http://www.khjradio.com.

Circulation: ★ = AAM; △ or • = BPA; ♦ = CAC; ❑ = VAC; ⊕ = PO Statement; ‡ = Publisher's Report; Boldface figures = sworn; Light figures = estimated.

AJO

Pima Co. (S). 110 m SW of Phoenix. Winter resort. Copper, gold, silver, lead mines.

794 ■ Ajo Copper News
Ajo Copper News
PO Box 39
Ajo, AZ 85321
Phone: (520)387-7688
Fax: (520)387-7505
Publisher's E-mail: cunews@cunews.info
Community newspaper. **Freq:** Weekly. **Print Method:** Offset. **Cols./Page:** 5. **Col. Width:** 24 nonpareils. **Key Personnel:** Mike Mekelburg, Contact; Gabrielle David, Editor; H.J. David, Publisher. **ISSN:** 1546--2846 (print). **USPS:** 010-660. **Subscription Rates:** $43 By mail 1 year print edition; $25 Individuals 1 year digital download. **URL:** http://www.cunews.info. **Ad Rates:** BW $300; PCI $3.75. **Remarks:** Accepts advertising. **Circ:** ‡1700.

APACHE JUNCTION

Pinal Co. Pinal Co. (S). 30 m SE of Phoenix. Residential.

795 ■ Apache Junction Independent
Independent Newspapers Inc.
2066 W Apache Trl., Ste. 110
Apache Junction, AZ 85120
Phone: (480)982-7799
Publication E-mail: ajeditor@newszap.com
Community newspaper. **Freq:** Weekly (Wed.). **Print Method:** Offset. **Trim Size:** 13 x 21. **Cols./Page:** 6. **Col. Width:** 2 1/16 inches. **Col. Depth:** 21 1/2 inches. **URL:** http://apachejunctionindependent.com. **Remarks:** Accepts advertising. **Circ:** Non-paid ♦**20000**.

796 ■ Mesa Independent
Independent Newspapers Inc.
2066 W Apache Trl., Ste. 110
Apache Junction, AZ 85120
Publication E-mail: eastmesa@newszap.com
Community newspaper. **Freq:** Weekly (Wed.). **Print Method:** Offset. **Trim Size:** 13 x 21. **Cols./Page:** 6. **Col. Width:** 2 1/16 inches. **Col. Depth:** 21 1/2 inches. **Subscription Rates:** $26 Individuals e-edition; Free print subscription. **URL:** http://mesaindependent.com. **Formerly**: East Mesa Independent. **Ad Rates:** PCI $25.96. **Remarks:** Accepts advertising. **Circ:** Non-paid ♦**25978**.

797 ■ Queen Creek/San Tan Valley Independent
Independent Newsmedia Inc.
2066 W. Apache Trail, Ste. 110
Apache Junction, AZ 85220
Phone: (480)982-7799
Publisher's E-mail: help@newszap.com
Community newspaper. **Freq:** Weekly (Wed.). **Key Personnel:** Richard Dyer, Managing Editor; Terrance Thornton, Editor, phone: (623)445-2774. **Subscription Rates:** $26 Individuals e-edition. **URL:** http://queencreekindependent.com. **Remarks:** Accepts advertising. **Circ:** Combined ♦**15945**.

798 ■ RV Times
RVing Women
PO Box 1940
Apache Junction, AZ 85117-4074
Phone: (480)671-6226
Fax: (480)671-6230
Publisher's E-mail: rvwoffice@rvingwomen.org
Freq: Bimonthly. **Subscription Rates:** C$55 U.S. print only; C$62 Canada print only; C$70 Other countries print only. **URL:** http://www.rvtimes.com; http://www.rvingwomen.org/default.asp?resource_publication. **Remarks:** Accepts advertising. **Circ:** 4000.

799 ■ RVing Women Magazine
RVing Women
PO Box 1940
Apache Junction, AZ 85117-4074
Phone: (480)671-6226
Fax: (480)671-6230
Publisher's E-mail: rvwoffice@rvingwomen.org
Freq: Bimonthly. **URL:** http://www.rvingwomen.org; http://www.rvingwomen.org/default.asp?resource_publication. **Remarks:** Advertising not accepted. **Circ:** (Not Reported).

AVONDALE

Maricopa Co. Maricopa Co. (C). 15 m W of Phoenix. Industrial. Agriculture. Cattle, grain, cotton.

800 ■ West Valley View
West Valley View
1050 E Riley Dr.
Avondale, AZ 85323
Phone: (623)535-8439
Fax: (623)935-2103
Community newspaper. **Founded:** Apr. 1986. **Freq:** Weekly. **Key Personnel:** Elliott Freireich, Publisher. **Subscription Rates:** $150 Individuals within county; $175 Out of area; $90 Out of country 6 months; $80 Individuals 6 months. **URL:** http://www.westvalleyview.com. **Ad Rates:** BW $2,084.88; 4C $2,597.88. **Remarks:** Accepts advertising. **Circ:** Controlled 67461.

BENSON

Cochise Co. Cochise Co. (SE). 40 m SE of Tucson. Tourism. Manufactures explosives. Mining. Stock, poultry, dairy farms.

801 ■ San Pedro Valley News-Sun
Wick Communications
200 S Ocotillo Ave.
Benson, AZ 85602
Phone: (520)586-3382
Fax: (520)586-2382
Publication E-mail: newssun@bensonnews-sun.com
Community newspaper. **Freq:** Weekly (Wed.). **Print Method:** Offset. **Trim Size:** 13 x 21 1/2. **Cols./Page:** 6. **Key Personnel:** Jane Amari, Editor; Chris Dabovich, Managing Editor; Joan Hancoc, Business Manager. **USPS:** 480-680. **Subscription Rates:** $31 Individuals Cochise County; $35 Elsewhere in Arizona; $38 Out of state; $30 Individuals online only. **URL:** http://www.bensonnews-sun.com. **Mailing address:** PO Box Drawer 1000, Benson, AZ 85602. **Ad Rates:** BW $65; 4C $190. **Remarks:** Accepts advertising. **Circ:** 3600.

BISBEE

Cochise Co. Cochise Co. (SE). 85 m SE of Tucson. Retirement community. Historic old mining camp. Tourism. Live theater and concerts. Agriculture. Cattle.

802 ■ The Bisbee Observer
The Bisbee Observer
7 Bisbee Rd., Ste. L
Bisbee, AZ 85603
Phone: (520)432-7254
Fax: (520)432-4192
Community newspaper. **Freq:** Weekly (Thurs.). **Print Method:** Offset. **Cols./Page:** 5. **Col. Width:** 1 19/20 inches. **Col. Depth:** 15 3/4 inches. **Key Personnel:** Laura Swan, Publisher. **ISSN:** 0895--2450 (print). **Subscription Rates:** $24 Individuals in Cochise County (6 months); $27 Elsewhere in Arizona (6 months); $40 Individuals online (one year); $40 Individuals in Cochise County (one year); $45 Elsewhere in Arizona (one year); $50 Out of state one year. **URL:** http://thebisbeeobserver.com. **Formerly**: The Ketchum Co./Bisbee Observer. **Ad Rates:** PCI $4.35. **Remarks:** Accepts advertising. **Circ:** Controlled ‡2300.

803 ■ KBRP-FM - 96.1
43 Howell Ave.
Bisbee, AZ 85603
Phone: (520)432-1400
Email: kbrp@kbrp.org
Format: Information. **Key Personnel:** Jim Mahoney, President. **Ad Rates:** Noncommercial. **Mailing address:** PO Box 1501, Bisbee, AZ 85603. **URL:** http://www.kbrpradio.com.

804 ■ KRMB-FM - 90.1
PO Box 2520
Douglas, AZ 85608-2520
Email: krmc@lwrn.org
Format: Hispanic. **Owner:** World Radio Network, Inc., PO Box 3765, McAllen, TX 78502, Ph: (956)787-9788. **URL:** http://www.worldradionetwork.org/.

BLYTHE

805 ■ Parker/Blythe White Sheet
Associated Desert Shoppers Inc.
2099 W Acoma
Lake Havasu City, AZ 86403
Phone: (928)855-7871
Fax: (928)855-8183
Shopper. **Freq:** Weekly (Tues.). **Print Method:** Web. **Trim Size:** 11 x 12 1/2. **Cols./Page:** 6. **Col. Width:** 9.5 picas. **Col. Depth:** 11 3/4 inches. **Alt. Formats:** Download; PDF. **URL:** http://www.greenandwhitesheet.com/white_sheet_home.php. **Formed by the merger of**: The Blythe Advertiser. **Formerly**: White Sheet--The Blythe Advertiser. **Remarks:** Advertising accepted; rates available upon request. **Circ:** Free ‡25000.

BULLHEAD CITY

Mohave Co. (W). Fishing, boating, recreation area.

Circulation: ★ = AAM; △ or • = BPA; ♦ = CAC; ❑ = VAC; ⊕ = PO Statement; ‡ = Publisher's Report; Boldface figures = sworn; Light figures = estimated.

806 ■ Booster Advertiser
News West Publishing Co.
PO Box 21209
Bullhead City, AZ 86439
Phone: (928)763-2505
Free: 800-571-3835
Publisher's E-mail: publisher@nwppub.com
Shopping guide. **Freq:** Semiweekly. **Print Method:** Offset. **Remarks:** Accepts classified advertising. **Circ:** Combined 14751.

807 ■ Colorado River Weekender
News West Publishing Co.
PO Box 21209
Bullhead City, AZ 86439
Phone: (928)763-2505
Free: 800-571-3835
Publisher's E-mail: publisher@nwppub.com
Community newspaper. **Freq:** Weekly (Fri.). **Print Method:** Offset. **Subscription Rates:** Free. **URL:** http://www.mohavedailynews.com/site/about.html. **Remarks:** Accepts classified advertising. **Circ:** (Not Reported).

808 ■ Laughlin Nevada Entertainer
News West Publishing Co.
PO Box 21209
Bullhead City, AZ 86439
Phone: (928)763-2505
Free: 800-571-3835
Publisher's E-mail: publisher@nwppub.com
Entertainment. **Freq:** Weekly (Wed.). **Print Method:** Offset. **Key Personnel:** Chuck Rathbun, Publisher; Alan Marciocchi, Editor. **Ad Rates:** 4C $575. **Remarks:** Accepts classified advertising. **Circ:** Combined 50000.

809 ■ Mohave Valley Daily News
Mohave Valley Daily News
2435 Miracle Mile
Bullhead City, AZ 86442-7311
Phone: (928)763-2505
Fax: (928)763-2369
Newspaper covering Mohave County. **Freq:** Weekly. **Print Method:** Offset. **Cols./Page:** 6. **Col. Width:** 12 picas. **Col. Depth:** 21 inches. **Key Personnel:** Paul Stubler, General Manager. **ISSN:** 1061--8569 (print). **Subscription Rates:** $240 By mail 52 weeks, home delivery; $129.84 Individuals 52 weeks, home delivery and online; $124.35 Individuals 52 weeks, home delivery. **URL:** http://www.mohavedailynews.com. **Formerly:** Mohave Valley News. **Mailing address:** PO Box 21209, Bullhead City, AZ 86439. **Ad Rates:** BW $2,449.44; 4C $2,809.44; PCI $19.44. **Remarks:** Accepts advertising. **Circ:** Non-paid ★**9016**, Paid ★**10259**.

810 ■ KFLG-AM - 1000
2350 Miracle Mile Rd., Ste. 300.
Bullhead City, AZ 86442
Phone: (928)763-5586
Format: Contemporary Country. **Simulcasts:** KFLG-FM. **Networks:** ABC. **Owner:** Continental Bradcasting Inc., at above address. **Founded:** 1976. **Formerly:** KRHS-AM. **Operating Hours:** Sunrise-sunset. **Key Personnel:** Cal Hall, Gen. Mgr; Julie Songster, Contact. **Wattage:** 1,000. **Ad Rates:** $12-14 for 15 seconds; $14-20 for 30 seconds; $16-22 for 60 seconds. **URL:** http://www.kflg947.com/contact_us.html.

811 ■ KFLG-FM - 94.7
1531 Jill Way, Ste. 7
Bullhead City, AZ 86426
Phone: (928)704-5354
Fax: (602)763-3957
Format: Country; Contemporary Country. **Owner:** Cameron Broadcasting Inc., 2350 Miracle Mile Rd., Ste. 300, Bullhead City, AZ 86442, Ph: (928)763-5586; Guyann Corp., at above address. **Founded:** 1974. **Formerly:** KZZZ-FM; The Park Lane Group; H&R Green River Broadcasting; KCRR-FM. **Key Personnel:** Tamie Phillips, Contact. **Wattage:** 19,500 ERP. **Ad Rates:** $12-14 for 15 seconds; $14-20 for 30 seconds; $16-22 for 60 seconds. **URL:** http://www.kflg947.com.

812 ■ KLUK-FM
2350 Miracle Mile Rd.
Bullhead City, AZ 86442
Format: Classic Rock. **Wattage:** 29,500 ERP.

813 ■ KMOH-TV - 6
2160 S Hwy 95, Ste.8
Bullhead City, AZ 86442-7100
Phone: (520)758-7333
Fax: (520)758-8139
Format: Commercial TV. **Networks:** Independent. **Owner:** Grand Canyon Television Co., Inc., 2525 W Camelback Rd., No. 800, Phoenix, AZ 85016. **Operating Hours:** Continuous. **ADI:** Phoenix (Kingman, Prescott), AZ. **Key Personnel:** Dan Robbins, Sales Mgr., VP; Joel Gable, Sales Mgr.

814 ■ KNKK-FM - 107.1
2350 Miracle Mile Rd., Ste. 300
Bullhead City, AZ 86442
Phone: (928)704-8800
Email: info@theknack107.com
Format: Top 40. **URL:** http://www.theknack107.com.

815 ■ KZZZ-AM - 1490
2350 Miracle Mile Rd., Ste. 300
Bullhead City, AZ 86442
Format: Talk. **Owner:** Cameron Broadcasting Inc., 2350 Miracle Mile Rd., Ste. 300, Bullhead City, AZ 86442, Ph: (928)763-5586. **Operating Hours:** Continuous. **Key Personnel:** Mike Fletcher, Gen. Sales Mgr. **Ad Rates:** Advertising accepted; rates available upon request. **URL:** http://www.talkatoz.com.

CAMP VERDE

Yavapai Co. Yavapai Co. (NE). 35 m E of Prescott on Verde River. Cattle raising and farming.

816 ■ The Camp Verde Journal: Voice of Camp Verde and the Lower Verde Valley
The Camp Verde Journal
PO Box 2048
Camp Verde, AZ 86322
Phone: (928)567-3341
Fax: (928)567-2373
Publisher's E-mail: cveditor@larsonnewspapers.com
Local newspaper. **Freq:** Weekly. **Print Method:** Offset. **Cols./Page:** 6. **Col. Width:** 12.60 picas. **Col. Depth:** 21 inches. **USPS:** 664-770. **Subscription Rates:** $16 Individuals local; $22 Out of area. **URL:** http://www.journalaz.com. **Mailing address:** PO Box 2048, Camp Verde, AZ 86322. **Ad Rates:** GLR $8.90; BW $1,121.40; 4C $1,411.40; SAU $8.90; PCI $8.90. **Circ:** Controlled ‡40000.

817 ■ K220GI-FM - 91.9
PO Box 391
Twin Falls, ID 83303
Fax: (208)736-1958
Free: 800-357-4226
Format: Religious; Contemporary Christian. **Owner:** CSN International, PO Box 391, Twin Falls, ID 83303, Ph: (208)736-1958, Fax: (208)736-1958, Free: 800-357-4226. **Key Personnel:** Ray Gorney, Asst. Dir.; Don Mills, Prog. Dir., Music Dir.; Kelly Carlson, Dir. of Engg. **Wattage:** 010. **URL:** http://www.csnradio.com.

CASA GRANDE

Pinal Co. Pinal Co. (S). 45 m SE of Phoenix. Manufactures textiles, furniture, mobile homes, shotgun shell components. Copper mines. Health resort. Agriculture. Cotton, alfalfa, grain, cattle.

818 ■ Casa Grande Dispatch
Casa Grande Valley Newspapers
200 W Second St.
Casa Grande, AZ 85130-5002
Phone: (520)836-7461
Publisher's E-mail: ads@trivalleycentral.com
General newspaper. **Freq:** Daily and Sun. (morn.). **Print Method:** Offset. **Cols./Page:** 6. **Col. Width:** 26 nonpareils. **Col. Depth:** 301 agate lines. **Key Personnel:** Kramer M. Donovan, Jr., Managing Editor, Publisher. **Subscription Rates:** $63 Individuals 6 months, home delivery; $126 Individuals home delivery; $156 By mail in Pinal County; $218.75 By mail outside Pinal County; $243.75 Out of state; $500 Other countries. **URL:** http://www.trivalleycentral.com/casa_grande_dispatch. **Ad Rates:** BW $1,052; 4C $1,352; SAU $18.58; PCI $8.20. **Circ:** Paid ★**9830**.

819 ■ KCAB-LP - 28
318 E Cottonwood Ln., Ste. D
Casa Grande, AZ 85222
Phone: (520)876-4080
Format: Commercial TV. **Networks:** Independent. **Owner:** Central Arizona Broadcasting, L.L.C., at above address, Casa Grande, AZ. **Founded:** Apr. 01, 1999. **Formerly:** K47FW-TV. **Operating Hours:** Continuous. **Key Personnel:** Bea Lueck, Contact. **Local Programs:** *Local News.* **Ad Rates:** $50 for 30 seconds. **URL:** http://www.tvnewscheck.com.

CAVE CREEK

Maricopa Co. Maricopa Co (C). 3 m N of Carefree. Residential.

820 ■ Sonoran News: The Conservative Voice of Arizona
Sonoran News
6702 E Cave Creek Rd., Ste. 3
Cave Creek, AZ 85331
Phone: (480)488-2021
Fax: (480)488-6216
Publication E-mail: editor@sonorannews.com
Community newspaper. **Freq:** Bimonthly. **Key Personnel:** Don Sorchych, Editor, Publisher; Rachel Karls-Gomes, Manager, Production. **Subscription Rates:** $25.50 Individuals 12 issues; $49.30 Individuals 24 weeks; $98.55 Individuals 45 weeks; Free to all customers within zip codes 85327, 85331, 85377, 85255, 85266 and 85262. **URL:** http://www.sonorannews.com. **Ad Rates:** PCI $28. **Remarks:** Accepts advertising. **Circ:** Combined 43000.

821 ■ True West
True West Magazine
6702 E Cave Creek Rd., Ste. 5
Cave Creek, AZ 85331
Phone: (480)575-1881
Fax: (480)575-1903
Free: 888-687-1881
Magazine covering the American West. Topics covered include history, travel and entertainment. **Freq:** Monthly. **Print Method:** Offset. **Trim Size:** 8 x 10 7/8. **Cols./Page:** 3. **Col. Width:** 27 nonpareils. **Col. Depth:** 140 agate lines. **Key Personnel:** Meghan Saar, Editor-in-Chief; Carole Compton Glenn, General Manager; Trish Brink, Publisher. **ISSN:** 0041--3615 (print). **Subscription Rates:** $29.95 Individuals 1 year; $49.95 Individuals 2 years. **Remarks:** Advertising accepted; rates available upon request. **Circ:** (Not Reported).

CHANDLER

Maricopa Co. Maricopa Co. (SC). 22 m SE of Phoenix. Winter resort. Manufactures fertilizer, electronics. Cotton gins. Agriculture. Citrus fruits.

822 ■ Comparative Economic Studies
Association for Comparative Economic Studies
c/o Josef C. Brada, Executive Secretary
333 N Pennington Dr., No. 57
Chandler, AZ 85224-8269
Publisher's E-mail: univinn@rci.rutgers.edu
Scholarly journal concerning comparative studies of economic systems, planning, and development. **Freq:** Quarterly. **Key Personnel:** Josef C. Brada, Editor; Paul Wachtel, Editor. **ISSN:** 0888--7233 (print); **EISSN:** 1478--3320 (electronic). **Subscription Rates:** £362 Institutions print only; $614 Institutions print only; $503 Institutions online only. **URL:** http://www.springer.com/economics/journal/41294. **Formerly:** ACES Bulletin. **Remarks:** Accepts advertising. **Circ:** (Not Reported).

CHINO VALLEY

823 ■ Chino Valley Review
Western News & Info Inc.
1260 S Hwy. 89, Ste. D
Chino Valley, AZ 86323
Phone: (928)636-2653
Newspaper. **Freq:** Weekly (Wed.). **Key Personnel:** Kelly Soldwedel, Publisher. **Subscription Rates:** $130 Individuals 1 year; $65 Individuals 26 weeks; $30 Individuals 12 weeks; $20 Individuals 8 weeks. **URL:** http://cvrnews.com/index.asp. **Mailing address:** PO Box 428, Chino Valley, AZ 86323. **Circ:** (Not Reported).

824 ■ Creation Research Society Quarterly
Creation Research Society
6801 N Highway 89
Chino Valley, AZ 86323
Phone: (928)636-1153
Fax: (928)636-8444
Free: 877-277-2665
Publication E-mail: contact@creationresearch.org
Freq: Quarterly. **Print Method:** Offset. **Trim Size:** 8 1/2 x 11. **Cols./Page:** 2. **Col. Width:** 39 nonpareils. **Col.**

Depth: 126 agate lines. **ISSN:** 0092--9166 (print). **Subscription Rates:** $34 Nonmembers online only; $68 Nonmembers online only, 2 years; $41 Nonmembers print only; $82 Nonmembers print only, 2 years. **URL:** http://www.creationresearch.org/index.php/extensions/crs-quarterly. **Remarks:** Advertising not accepted. **Circ:** 2000, 1800.

825 ■ Creation Research Society Quarterly
CRS Van Andel Creation Research Center
6801 N Highway 89
Chino Valley, AZ 86323-9186
Phone: (928)636-1153
Publication E-mail: contact@creationresearch.org
Freq: Quarterly. **Print Method:** Offset. **Trim Size:** 8 1/2 x 11. **Cols./Page:** 2. **Col. Width:** 39 nonpareils. **Col. Depth:** 126 agate lines. **ISSN:** 0092--9166 (print). **Subscription Rates:** $34 Nonmembers online only; $68 Nonmembers online only, 2 years; $41 Nonmembers print only; $82 Nonmembers print only, 2 years. **URL:** http://www.creationresearch.org/index.php/extensions/crs-quarterly. **Remarks:** Advertising not accepted. **Circ:** 2000, 1800.

CLIFTON

Greenlee Co. Greenlee Co. (SE) 169 m NE of Tucson. Residential.

826 ■ The Copper Era
Wick Communications
1 Wards Canyon
Clifton, AZ 85533
Phone: (520)865-3162
Fax: (928)428-3110
Community newspaper. **Freq:** Weekly (Wed.). **Print Method:** Offset. **Cols./Page:** 6. **Col. Width:** 2 inches. **Col. Depth:** 21 1/2 inches. **Key Personnel:** Richard Schneider, Publisher; John M. Mathew, Chief Executive Officer, President; Robert Wick, Chairman, Secretary, Treasurer; Walt Wick, Chairman, Vice President. **Subscription Rates:** $25 Individuals Grenlee, 6 months; $35 Individuals Grenlee; $45 Elsewhere in Arizona; $50 Out of state. **URL:** http://www.eacourier.com. **Mailing address:** PO Box 1357, Clifton, AZ 85533. **Remarks:** Accepts advertising. **Circ:** Paid ‡1557.

827 ■ KJJJ-FM - 95.3
2919 E Broadway
Tucson, AZ 85716
Phone: (928)505-6917
Fax: (928)505-6980
Format: Country. **Founded:** 1986. **Wattage:** 250. **URL:** http://kjjjfm.com/.

828 ■ K220IO-FM - 91.9
PO Box 391
Twin Falls, ID 83303
Fax: (208)736-1958
Free: 800-357-4226
Format: Religious; Contemporary Christian. **Owner:** CSN International, PO Box 391, Twin Falls, ID 83303, Ph: (208)736-1958, Fax: (208)736-1958, Free: 800-357-4226. **URL:** http://www.csnradio.com.

COOLIDGE

Pinal Co. Pinal Co. (S). 65 m SE of Phoenix. Tourism. Casa Grande Ruins National Monument. Cotton gin. Diversified farming. Cotton, alfalfa, vegetables.

829 ■ Coolidge Examiner
Casa Grande Valley Newspapers
353 W Central Ave.
Coolidge, AZ 85128
Phone: (520)723-5441
Fax: (520)723-7899
Publication E-mail: coolidgeexaminer@yahoo.com
Newspaper. **Freq:** Weekly (Wed.). **Print Method:** Offset. **Cols./Page:** 6. **Col. Width:** 26 nonpareils. **Col. Depth:** 301 agate lines. **Key Personnel:** Sean Higgins, Editor; Donavan Kramer, Jr., Managing Editor, Publisher. **Subscription Rates:** $29 By mail in Pinal County; $45 Out of area by mail; $56 Out of state; $125 Other countries. **URL:** http://www.trivalleycentral.com/coolidge_examiner. **Remarks:** Accepts advertising. **Circ:** ‡2364.

830 ■ Cable America Corp.
775 N Arizona Blvd.
Coolidge, AZ 85228-3900
Phone: (520)723-7874
Key Personnel: William H. Lewis, VP; William G. Jackson, President; Christopher A. Dyrek, Exec. VP; Alan C. Jackson, VP; Eric W. Jackson, VP; John A. Mori, Dir. of Mktg. **URL:** http://www.cableamerica.com/.

COTTONWOOD

Yavapai Co. Yavapai Co. (C). 30 m NE of Prescott. Cement plant. Electronic assembly. Construction materials. Mining.

831 ■ Cottonwood Journal Extra
Cottonwood Journal Extra
830 S Main St., Ste. 1E
Cottonwood, AZ 86326
Phone: (928)634-8551
Fax: (928)634-0823
Community newspaper. **Freq:** Weekly. **Key Personnel:** Todd Etshman, Editor. **Mailing address:** PO Box 2266, Cottonwood, AZ 86326. **Remarks:** Accepts advertising. **Circ:** (Not Reported).

832 ■ Verde Independent
Western News & Info Inc.
116 S Main St.
Cottonwood, AZ 86326
Phone: (928)634-2241
Community newspaper (printed in 2 zoned editions). **Freq:** Triweekly Wed., Fri., Sun. **Print Method:** Offset. **Cols./Page:** 6. **Col. Width:** 2 1/8 inches. **Col. Depth:** 21 1/2 inches. **Key Personnel:** Pam Miller, Chief Executive Officer, Publisher; Dan Engler, Editor. **Subscription Rates:** $108 Individuals home delivery; 2 year; $57 Individuals home delivery; 1 year; $32 Individuals home delivery; 6 months; $17 Individuals home delivery; 3 months; $49 Individuals 6 months mail delivered; $27 Individuals 3 months mail delivered. **URL:** http://verdenews.com. **Ad Rates:** PCI $13.92. **Remarks:** Accepts advertising. **Circ:** Paid ‡3650.

833 ■ Cable One
235 s 6th S
Cottonwood, AZ 86326
Owner: Post-Newsweek Cable, at above address. **Founded:** 1959. **Formerly:** Cablecom; Post-Newsweek Cable. **Cities Served:** subscribing households 4,700. **URL:** http://www.cableone.net/li/pages/cottonwood-az.aspx.

834 ■ KKLD-FM
PO Box 187
Cottonwood, AZ 86326-0187
Format: Oldies. **Wattage:** 21,000 ERP. **Ad Rates:** Noncommercial.

835 ■ KQST-FM
PO Box 187
Cottonwood, AZ 86326-0187
Phone: (602)282-1111
Fax: (602)282-7031
Format: Easy Listening; Jazz; New Age; Big Band/Nostalgia. **Owner:** American Aircasting Corp., PO Box 182, Scottsdale, AZ 85252. **Founded:** 1984. **Key Personnel:** Gary R. Gilbert, Dir. of Programs. **Wattage:** 90,000 ERP.

836 ■ KVRD-FM - 105.7
3405 E State Route 89A
Cottonwood, AZ 86326
Phone: (928)634-2286
Email: kvrd@myradioplace.com
Format: Country. **Owner:** Yavapai Broadcasting Corp., at above address. **Operating Hours:** Continuous. **Wattage:** 300. **Ad Rates:** Advertising accepted; rates available upon request. Combined advertising rates available with KVRD-AM, KKCD-FM, KZGL-FM. **URL:** http://www.kvrdfm.com.

837 ■ KYBC-AM - 1600
PO Box 187
Cottonwood, AZ 86326
Phone: (928)634-2286
Fax: (928)634-2295
Email: news@myradioplace.com
Format: Adult Contemporary. **Networks:** Westwood One Radio. **Owner:** Yavapai Broadcasting Corp., at above address. **Founded:** 1964. **Formerly:** KVRD-AM; KVIO-AM. **Operating Hours:** Continuous. **Key Personnel:** Chit Watkins, Dir. of Programs. **Wattage:** 1,000. **Ad Rates:** $8-27 for 30 seconds. $8-$27 for 30 seconds. Combined advertising rates available with KVRD-FM; KKLD-FM; KZGL-FM. **URL:** http://www.myradioplace.com.

838 ■ KZGL-FM - 95.9
PO Box 187
Box 10
Cottonwood, AZ 86326
Phone: (602)634-3693
Fax: (602)634-8481
Format: Album-Oriented Rock (AOR). **Owner:** The Parklane Group, 750 Menlo Ave Suite 340, Menlo Park, CA 94025. **Founded:** 1983. **Formerly:** KSMK-FM. **Key Personnel:** Gary Hershey, Gen. Mgr. **Wattage:** 21,000 ERP. **Ad Rates:** $7-16 for 30 seconds. **URL:** http://myradioplace.com.

DOUGLAS

Cochise Co. Cochise Co. (SE). 105 m SE of Tucson. Tourism. Art gallery. Parks. Recreation center. Industrial park. Garment, electronic manufactures. Food processing firms. Food packing industry. Copper smelter. Agriculture and ranching.

839 ■ The Cochise County Historical Journal
Cochise County Historical Society
PO Box 818
Douglas, AZ 85608-0818
Phone: (520)364-7370
Publisher's E-mail: cchs@cochisecountyhistory.org
Journal featuring historical articles of Cochise County, AZ. **Freq:** Semiannual. **Subscription Rates:** $10 Individuals including postage and handling; Free for members. **URL:** http://www.mycochise.com/journal.php. **Formerly:** Cochise Journal. **Remarks:** Advertising not accepted. **Circ:** (Not Reported).

840 ■ The Mirage
Cochise College
4190 W Highway 80
Douglas, AZ 85607-6190
Free: 800-966-7943
Publication E-mail: mirage@cochise.edu
Literary arts magazine. **Freq:** Annual. **Trim Size:** 6 x 9. **Cols./Page:** 1. **Col. Width:** 5 1/2 inches. **Col. Depth:** 8 1/2 inches. **Key Personnel:** Jeff Sturges, Faculty Advisor, phone: (520)515-5435; Jay Treiber, Faculty Advisor, phone: (520)417-4765. **Subscription Rates:** Free. **URL:** http://www.cochise.edu/mirage. **Remarks:** Accepts advertising. **Circ:** (Not Reported).

841 ■ KDAP-AM
901 E 13TH St.
Douglas, AZ 85607
Format: Ethnic; Hispanic. **Owner:** KDAP, Inc., at above address. **Founded:** 1946. **Key Personnel:** Howard Henderson, Gen. Mgr.; Luis Aguilar, Dir. of Programs. **Wattage:** 1,000. **Ad Rates:** $5.85-8.90 for 30 seconds; $8.15-12.45 for 60 seconds.

842 ■ KDAP-FM
PO Box 1179
Douglas, AZ 85608
Phone: (602)364-3484
Format: Contemporary Country. **Networks:** Satellite Music Network. **Owner:** KDAP, Inc., at above address. **Founded:** 1990. **Key Personnel:** Howard Henderson, Gen. Mgr. **Wattage:** 3,000 ERP. **Ad Rates:** Advertising accepted; rates available upon request.

KRMB-FM - See Bisbee

843 ■ KRMC-FM - 91.7
PO Box 2520
Douglas, AZ 85608-2520
Phone: (520)364-5392
Fax: (520)364-5392
Email: krmc@lwrn.org
Format: Hispanic. **Owner:** World Radio Network, Inc., PO Box 3765, McAllen, TX 78502, Ph: (956)787-9788. **URL:** http://www.worldradionetwork.org/.

ELOY

Pinal Co. Pinal Co. (S). 50 m NW of Tucson. Light industrial. Agri-business. Agriculture. Wheat, alfalfa, cotton.

844 ■ Eloy Enterprise
Casa Grande Valley Newspapers
710 N Main St.
Eloy, AZ 85131

Circulation: ★ = AAM; △ or • = BPA; ♦ = CAC; ❑ = VAC; ⊕ = PO Statement; ‡ = Publisher's Report; Boldface figures = sworn; Light figures = estimated.

Phone: (520)466-7333
Fax: (520)466-7334
Publication E-mail: editor@eloyenterprise.com
Newspaper. **Freq:** Weekly (Thurs.). **Print Method:** Offset. **Cols./Page:** 6. **Col. Width:** 26 nonpareils. **Col. Depth:** 301 agate lines. **Key Personnel:** Donovan M. Kramer, Editor, Publisher. **Subscription Rates:** $29 By mail in Pinal County; $45 Out of area by mail; $56 Out of state; $125 Other countries; $32 Out of state 6 months. **URL:** http://www.trivalleycentral.com/eloy_enterprise. **Ad Rates:** PCI $4.40. **Remarks:** Accepts advertising. **Circ:** ‡1154.

FLAGSTAFF

Coconino Co. Coconino Co. (N). 90 m SE OF Grand Canyon. Northern Arizona University. Resort. National parks and monuments. Lumber mill.

845 ■ Arizona Daily Sun
Lee Enterprises Inc.
1751 S Thomson
Flagstaff, AZ 86001
Phone: (928)774-4545
Fax: (928)773-1934
General newspaper. **Freq:** Daily (eve.), Sat. and Sun. (morn.). **Print Method:** Offset. **Cols./Page:** 6. **Col. Width:** 24 nonpareils. **Col. Depth:** 301 agate lines. **Key Personnel:** Don Rowley, Publisher, phone: (928)556-2240; Randy Wilson, Editor, phone: (928)556-2254. **ISSN:** 1054--9536 (print). **Subscription Rates:** $219.02 Individuals 52 weeks, home delivery 6 days a week (Tue-Sun); $156.16 Individuals 52 weeks, weekend home delivery (Fri, Sat, Sun). **Remarks:** Accepts advertising. **Circ:** Mon.-Sat. ★**10464**, Sun. ★**10287**.

846 ■ Plateau: Land and People of the Colorado Plateau
Museum of Northern Arizona
3101 N Fort Valley Rd.
Flagstaff, AZ 86001-8348
Phone: (928)774-5213
Publisher's E-mail: info@musnaz.org
Magazine covering the biology, geology, anthropology, arts, and crafts of the Colorado Plateau. **Freq:** Semiannual. **Print Method:** Offset. **Trim Size:** 8 1/2 x 11. **Cols./Page:** 2. **Col. Width:** 26 nonpareils. **Col. Depth:** 120 agate lines. **Key Personnel:** Diana Lubick, Editor; Donna A. Boyd, Assistant Editor; Robin Smith, Manager, Circulation, phone: (602)774-5213, fax: (602)774-1527. **ISSN:** 0032--1346 (print). **Subscription Rates:** $17 Members; $30 Two years members. **Formerly:** Plateau: Plateau. **Remarks:** Advertising not accepted. **Circ:** ‡6000.

847 ■ Social Science Journal
Western Social Science Association
2307 Chof Trl.
Flagstaff, AZ 86005
Freq: Quarterly. **ISSN:** 0362-3319 (print). **Subscription Rates:** included in membership dues. **URL:** http://www.wssaweb.com/journal.html. **Remarks:** Advertising not accepted. **Circ:** (Not Reported).

848 ■ Studies in American Indian Literatures
Association for the Study of American Indian Literatures
c/o Jeff Berglund, Treasurer
PO Box 6032
Flagstaff, AZ 86011-6032
Publisher's E-mail: pressmail@unl.edu
Journal presenting literature created by Native Americans. **Freq:** Quarterly. **Key Personnel:** Chadwick Allen, Editor. **ISSN:** 0730--3238 (print). **Subscription Rates:** $50 Individuals 1 year - U.S; $74 Individuals 1 year - foreign; $38 Individuals 1 year - online; $141 Institutions 1 year - U.S; $165 Institutions, other countries 1 year - online; $38 /year for individuals; $95 /year for institutions. **Alt. Formats:** PDF. **URL:** http://www.nebraskapress.unl.edu/product/Studies-in-American-Indian-Literat%20ures,673235.aspx. **Ad Rates:** BW $265. **Remarks:** Accepts advertising. **Circ:** (Not Reported).

849 ■ Thin Air
Northern Arizona University College of Arts & Letters
Building 15/Room 304
Flagstaff, AZ 86011
Phone: (928)523-8632
Fax: (928)523-7074
Magazine featuring original poetry, fiction, creative nonfiction and visual art. **Freq:** Annual. **Key Personnel:** Chelsea Burk, Editor-in-Chief; Jeff Huizinga, Managing Editor. **Subscription Rates:** $14 Individuals. **URL:** http://thinairmagazine.org; http://nau.edu/CAL/English/Sponsored-Programs. **Mailing address:** PO Box 5064, Flagstaff, AZ 86011. **Circ:** (Not Reported).

850 ■ KAFF-AM - 930
1117 W Route 66
Flagstaff, AZ 86001
Phone: (928)774-5231
Format: Country; Talk. **Simulcasts:** KAFF-FM. **Networks:** ABC. **Owner:** Guyann Corp., at above address. **Founded:** 1963. **Operating Hours:** Continuous. **Wattage:** 5,000. **Ad Rates:** $20-23.50 for 15 seconds; $22.50-47 for 30 seconds; $27-50.50 for 60 seconds. **URL:** http://www.kaff.com.

851 ■ KAFF-FM - 92.9
1117 W Rte. 66
Flagstaff, AZ 86001
Format: Country. **Owner:** Guyann Corp., at above address. **Founded:** 1963. **Ad Rates:** $20-23.50 for 15 seconds; $22.50-47 for 30 seconds; $27-50.50 for 60 seconds.

852 ■ KBXZ-AM - 1650
1016 W University Ave., Ste. 205
Flagstaff, AZ 86001
Phone: (928)774-5250
Fax: (928)774-5247
Format: Sports. **Owner:** Fox Sports Radio, 407 N Maple Dr., Beverly Hills, CA 90210, Ph: (310)969-7192. **Ad Rates:** Advertising accepted; rates available upon request. **URL:** http://www.reachoutthewindow.com.

853 ■ KFLX-FM - 105.1; 97.1
2409 N 4th St., Ste. 101
Flagstaff, AZ 86004
Phone: (928)779-1177
Fax: (928)774-5179
Format: Adult Album Alternative. **Networks:** NBC. **Owner:** Red Rock Communications, Ltd., at above address. **Founded:** Feb. 1995. **Operating Hours:** 8 a.m.-5 p.m. **Wattage:** 50,000. **Ad Rates:** Advertising accepted; rates available upon request. **URL:** http://www.bigtalkerradio.com/common/page.php?pt=eeo&id=72.

854 ■ KJTA-FM - 89.9
PO Box 35300
Tucson, AZ 85740
Free: 800-776-1070
Format: Religious. **Owner:** Family Life Communication Inc., 7355 N Oracle Rd., Tucson, AZ 85740, Free: 800-776-1070. **Founded:** Mar. 13, 2001. **ADI:** Flagstaff, AZ. **Wattage:** 1,000. **Ad Rates:** Noncommercial. **URL:** http://www.myflr.org.

855 ■ KMGN-FM - 93.9
1117 W Rte. 66
Flagstaff, AZ 86001
Phone: (928)774-5231
Fax: (928)779-2988
Format: Adult Contemporary. **Networks:** AP. **Owner:** Guyann Corp., at above address. **Founded:** 1975. **Formerly:** KSOJ-FM. **Operating Hours:** Continuous; 100% local. **Wattage:** 100,000. **Ad Rates:** $23-53 for 60 seconds. **URL:** http://www.939themountain.gcmaz.com.

856 ■ KNAU-FM - 88.7
PO Box 5764
Flagstaff, AZ 86011
Phone: (928)523-5628
Fax: (928)523-7647
Free: 800-523-5628
Email: knau@nau.edu
Format: News; Talk; Information; Classical. **Simulcasts:** KPUB, KNAA, KNAD, KNAQ, KNAG. **Networks:** National Public Radio (NPR); AP; Public Radio International (PRI). **Owner:** Northern Arizona University, South San Francisco St., Flagstaff, AZ 86001, Ph: (928)523-9011, Fax: (928)523-1848. **Founded:** 1983. **Formerly:** KAXR-FM. **Operating Hours:** Continuous. **ADI:** Flagstaff, AZ. **Key Personnel:** John Stark, Gen. Mgr., john.stark@nau.edu; Brian Sanders, Operations Mgr. **Wattage:** 100,000. **Ad Rates:** Noncommercial; underwriting available. $20-30 per unit. **URL:** http://www.knau.org.

857 ■ KVNA-AM - 600
1800 S Milton Rd., Ste. 105
Flagstaff, AZ 86001
Phone: (928)526-2700
Email: news@myradioplace.com
Format: Talk; Sports; News. **Networks:** ABC. **Owner:** Yavapai Broadcasting Corp., at above address. **Founded:** 1958. **Formerly:** KZKZ; KEOS. **Operating Hours:** Continuous; 90% network, 10% local. **ADI:** Flagstaff, AZ. **Key Personnel:** David Kessel, Contact, dave@myradioplace.com. **Wattage:** 1,000 Day; 048 Night. **Ad Rates:** $25 for 30 seconds. Combined advertising rates available with KVNA-FM. **URL:** http://www.myradioplace.com/am600/am600.htm.

858 ■ KVNA-FM - 100.1
1800 S Milton Rd., Ste. 105
Flagstaff, AZ 86001
Phone: (928)526-2700
Fax: (928)774-5852
Email: news@myradioplace.com
Format: Adult Contemporary. **Owner:** Yavapai Broadcasting Corp., PO Box 187, Cottonwood, AZ 86326. **Founded:** 1958. **Operating Hours:** Continuous; 100% Local. **ADI:** Flagstaff, AZ. **Key Personnel:** David J. Kessel, Contact, dave@myradioplace.com; Rich Malone, Contact, malone@myradioplace.com. **Wattage:** 100,000. **Ad Rates:** $15 for 30 seconds. $22 for 30 seconds; Combined advertising rates available with KVNA-AM. **URL:** http://www.myradioplace.com/am600/am600.htm.

859 ■ KWMX-FM - 96.7
112 E Rte. 66, Ste. 105
Flagstaff, AZ 86001
Phone: (928)779-1177
Format: Classic Rock. **Owner:** Grenax Broadcasting II L.L.C., 131 W Navajo Dr., Prescott, AZ 86301. **Wattage:** 10,500 ERP. **Ad Rates:** Noncommercial.

FLORENCE

Pinal Co. Pinal Co. (S). On Gila River, 68 m N of Tucson. Health resort. Copper mines. Agriculture. Cotton, wheat, alfalfa.

860 ■ Florence Reminder & Blade-Tribune
Casa Grande Valley Newspapers
244 N Main St.
Florence, AZ 85132
Phone: (520)868-5897
Fax: (520)868-5898
Publisher's E-mail: ads@trivalleycentral.com
Newspaper. **Freq:** Weekly (Thurs.). **Print Method:** Offset. **Cols./Page:** 6. **Col. Width:** 26 nonpareils. **Col. Depth:** 301 agate lines. **Key Personnel:** Donovan M. Kramer, Jr., Managing Editor, Publisher; Mark Cowling, Editor; Kara K. Cooper, Contact. **Subscription Rates:** $29 By mail in Pinal County; $45 Out of area by mail; $56 Out of state; $125 Other countries. **URL:** http://www.trivalleycentral.com/florence_reminder_blade_tribune. **Ad Rates:** SAU $5.35. **Remarks:** Accepts advertising. **Circ:** ‡1700.

FOUNTAIN HILLS

Maricopa Co. Maricopa Co. (C). 12 m E of Scottsdale. Residential.

861 ■ The Fountain Hills Times
Western States Publishers Inc.
16508 E Laser Dr., Ste. 101
Fountain Hills, AZ 85268
Phone: (480)837-1925
Fax: (480)837-1951
Local newspaper. **Freq:** Weekly. **Print Method:** Offset. **Cols./Page:** 6. **Col. Width:** 26 nonpareils. **Col. Depth:** 294 agate lines. **Key Personnel:** Kip Kirkendoll, Business Manager; Michael G. Scharnow, Editor; Alan L. Cruikshank, Publisher. **ISSN:** 0607--5000 (print). **Subscription Rates:** $42 Individuals Maricopa County; $48 Individuals part time resident; $53 Individuals out of county including all states within US. **URL:** http://www.fhtimes.com. **Ad Rates:** BW $125; SAU $12; PCI $10.35. **Remarks:** Accepts advertising. **Circ:** (Not Reported).

862 ■ The Shekel
American-Israel Numismatic Association
PO Box 20255
Fountain Hills, AZ 85269-0255
Phone: (818)225-1348

Publisher's E-mail: ainapresident@lycos.com
Freq: Bimonthly. **Col. Depth:** 8 inches. **ISSN:** 0087--3486 (print). **Subscription Rates:** $25 Individuals 1 year (U.S. and Israel); $48 Individuals 2 years (U.S. and Israel); $35 Other countries 1 year; $67 Other countries 2 years; $500 Individuals lifetime; Included in membership. **URL:** http://www.amerisrael.com/shekel.html. **Remarks:** Advertising not accepted. **Circ:** (Not Reported).

863 ■ VITA Technologies
OpenSystems Media
16872 E Ave. of the Fountains, Ste. 203
Fountain Hills, AZ 85268
Phone: (480)967-5581
Fax: (480)837-6466
Publisher's E-mail: lab@opensystemsmedia.com
Magazine covering VMEbus computer technology. **Freq:** Bimonthly. **Print Method:** Web Press. **Trim Size:** 8 x 10 7/8. **Cols./Page:** 2 and 3. **Col. Width:** 3 5/16 INS2 1/8 INS. **Col. Depth:** 20 INS20 INS. **Key Personnel:** Patrick Hopper, Publisher; Jerry Gipper, Director, Editorial. **ISSN:** 0884-1357 (print). **Subscription Rates:** Free. **URL:** http://vita.mil-embedded.com. **Formerly**: VMEbus Systems; VME and Critical Systems: The Magazine for Engineers by Engineers. **Ad Rates:** BW $3,680; 4C $4,555. **Remarks:** Accepts advertising. **Circ:** Combined ‡22490.

GILBERT

864 ■ BMXer
USA BMX
1645 W Sunrise Blvd.
Gilbert, AZ 85233
Phone: (480)961-1903
Fax: (480)961-1842
Membership magazine covering national BMX racing, product evaluation, member point standings, future events, and buyers' guide. **Freq:** Monthly. **Key Personnel:** Dan Mooney, Editor; Cheryl Bustamante, Art Director. **Subscription Rates:** $2.50 /issue; $16 Single issue. **Mailing address:** PO Box 718, Chandler, AZ 85244. **Remarks:** Advertising accepted; rates available upon request. **Circ:** 49000, 49000.

GLENDALE

Maricopa Co. Maricopa Co. (SC). 9 m NW of Phoenix. Manufactures avionics, instrumentations, cable connections, precision machined parts, building materials, packaging materials. Food processing. Plastic extrusions.

865 ■ Das Tor
Thunderbird School of Global Management
1 Global Pl.
Glendale, AZ 85306
Publisher's E-mail: tlcc@t-bird.edu
Newspaper (tabloid) covering international and business affairs. **Freq:** Weekly (Thurs.). **Print Method:** Offset. **Trim Size:** 11 x 17. **Cols./Page:** 5. **Col. Width:** 1 7/8 inches. **Col. Depth:** 16 inches. **Key Personnel:** Bala Rajendran, Editor-in-Chief. **URL:** http://dastornews.com/about. **Ad Rates:** BW $460; PCI $5.75. **Remarks:** Accepts advertising. **Circ:** Free ‡1600.

866 ■ For Formulation Chemists Only
CITA International
5331 W Montebello Ave.
Glendale, AZ 85301
Phone: (602)447-0480
Fax: (623)847-4454
Publisher's E-mail: esam@citainternational.com
Online journal covering chemical industrial technology for technicians in the chemical specialty and consumer product industries. **Freq:** Monthly. **Key Personnel:** E.M. Mosby, Editor-in-Chief, Founder. **ISSN:** 1930-1723 (print). **Subscription Rates:** $95 Individuals; $110 Other countries. **URL:** http://www.citainternational.com/f2co.htm. **Remarks:** Advertising accepted; rates available upon request. **Circ:** (Not Reported).

867 ■ The Glendale Star
Pueblo Publishers Inc.
7122 N 59th Ave.
Glendale, AZ 85301-2436
Phone: (623)842-6000
Publisher's E-mail: subscribe@star-times.com
Community newspaper. **Freq:** Weekly (Thurs.). **Print Method:** Offset. **Trim Size:** 11 x 17. **Cols./Page:** 6. **Col. Width:** 9.5 picas. **Col. Depth:** 16 picas. **Key Personnel:** Carolyn Castillo; Mike Kenny, Manager, Circulation, phone: (623)847-4606; Carolyn Dryer, Editor, phone: (623)847-4604; Connie Williams, Manager, Advertising, phone: (623)847-4601; Roger W. Toops, Business Manager, phone: (623)847-4603; William E. Toops, Publisher, phone: (623)847-4602. **USPS:** 998-340. **Subscription Rates:** $25 Individuals in Maricopa County; $30 Out of area; $40 Two years in Maricopa County; $45 Out of area 2 years. **URL:** http://www.glendalestar.com. **Ad Rates:** BW $692; 4C $1,067; SAU $8.65; PCI $6. **Circ:** Mon.-Sun. ‡20000.

868 ■ Peoria Times: Peoria's Hometown Newspaper
Pueblo Publishers Inc.
7122 N 59th Ave.
Glendale, AZ 85301-2436
Phone: (623)842-6000
Publisher's E-mail: subscribe@star-times.com
Community newspaper. **Freq:** Weekly (Fri.). **Print Method:** Offset. **Trim Size:** 11x17. **Cols./Page:** 6. **Col. Width:** 9 1/2 inches. **Col. Depth:** 16 inches. **Key Personnel:** Connie Williams, Manager, Advertising, phone: (623)847-4601; Roger W. Toops, Business Manager, phone: (623)847-4603; William E. Toops, Publisher, phone: (623)847-4602; Carolyn Dryer, Editor, phone: (623)847-4604. **USPS:** 427-760. **Subscription Rates:** $25 Individuals in Maricopa County; $40 Two years in Maricopa County; $55 Individuals 3 years (in Maricopa County); $30 Out of area; $45 Out of area 2 years; $60 Out of area 3 years. **URL:** http://www.peoriatimes.com. **Ad Rates:** BW $576; 4C $951; SAU $7.20; PCI $5. **Remarks:** Accepts advertising. **Circ:** Mon.-Sun. ‡20000.

869 ■ UIM Magazine
United Indian Missions International
6419 W Maryland Ave.
Glendale, AZ 85301-3718
Phone: (623)847-9227
Fax: (623)934-5996
Magazine containing articles regarding United Indian Mission Association and other related ideas. **Freq:** Annual. **Subscription Rates:** Free. **Alt. Formats:** Download; PDF. **URL:** http://www.uiminternational.org/resources/publications/uim-magazine-archive. **Mailing address:** PO Box 6429, Glendale, AZ 85312-6429. **Remarks:** Advertising not accepted. **Circ:** (Not Reported).

GLOBE

Gila Co. Gilla Co. (C). 94 m E of Phoenix. Copper. Cattle raising.

870 ■ Arizona Silver Belt
Arizona Silver Belt
298 N Pine St.
Globe, AZ 85501
Phone: (928)425-7121
Fax: (928)425-7001
Community newspaper. **Freq:** Weekly. **Print Method:** Offset. **Cols./Page:** 6. **Col. Width:** 21 nonpareils. **Col. Depth:** 294 agate lines. **Key Personnel:** Bethel Baker, Manager, Production. **Subscription Rates:** $11.64 Individuals 10 weeks manual pay (in Area); $10.94 Individuals 10 weeks auto pay (in Area); $42.25 Individuals 1 year auto pay (in Area); $44.25 Individuals 1 year manual pay (in Area); $13.38 Out of area 10 weeks manual pay; $12.57 Out of area 10 weeks auto pay; $48.55 Out of area 1 year auto pay; $50.85 Out of area 1 year manual pay. **URL:** http://silverbelt.com/v2_main_page.php. **Ad Rates:** BW $722.40; 4C $992.40; SAU $5.60. **Remarks:** Accepts advertising. **Circ:** ‡7336.

871 ■ KJAA-AM - 1240
5734 S McKinney Ave.
Globe, AZ 85501
Fax: (928)425-6397
Format: News; Sports; Hispanic; Oldies; Talk. **Owner:** Gila Co. Broadcasting Co., Inc., at above address. **Founded:** 1971. **Formerly**: KSML-AM. **Key Personnel:** John Rau, News Dir. **Wattage:** 1,000. **Ad Rates:** $10 for 30 seconds; $12 for 60 seconds. **Mailing address:** PO Box 292, Miami, AZ 85539. **URL:** http://www.jukebox1240.com.

872 ■ KLKA-FM - 88.5
PO Box 2098
Omaha, NE 68103-2098
Format: Contemporary Christian. **Owner:** Educational Media Foundation, 5700 W Oaks Blvd., CA 95765, Free: 800-800434-8400. **Key Personnel:** Mike Novak, President, CEO; Alan Mason, COO. **Wattage:** 1,500. **URL:** http://www.klove.com.

873 ■ KRDE-FM - 94.1
800 N Main St.
Globe, AZ 85501
Phone: (928)402-9222
Fax: (928)425-5063
Email: krde@cableone.net
Format: Country. **Wattage**: 4,700. **Ad Rates:** Advertising accepted; rates available upon request. **URL:** http://www.krde.com.

GOODYEAR

Maricopa Co.

874 ■ Key Magazine Phoenix/Scottsdale
Key Magazines Inc.
c/o Thomas Ruberto, Owner/Publisher
18346 W Sweet Acacia Dr.
Goodyear, AZ 85338
Phone: (623)217-6574
Fax: (623)218-6574
Publisher's E-mail: info@keymilwaukee.com
Visitor's guide publication featuring coverage of events, dining, shopping, and more. **Freq:** Monthly. **Trim Size:** 51/2 x 81/2. **Key Personnel:** Brian Malthaner, Owner; Thomas Ruberto, Owner, Publisher; Sue Malthaner, Editor, Owner. **URL:** http://keymagazine.com/arizona/attractions.html. **Remarks:** Accepts advertising. **Circ:** Combined **40000**.

GREEN VALLEY

Pima Co. (S). 23 m S of Tucson. Residential.

875 ■ Green Valley News
Green Valley News & Sun
18705 S I-19 Frontage Rd., Ste. 125
Green Valley, AZ 85614
Phone: (520)625-5511
Fax: (520)625-8046
Publication E-mail: editorial@gvnews.com
Community newspaper serving the Santa Cruz Valley and Green Valley area. **Freq:** Weekly (Wed.). **Print Method:** Offset. **Cols./Page:** 6. **Col. Width:** 25 nonpareils. **Col. Depth:** 294 agate lines. **Key Personnel:** Dan Shearer, Editor, phone: (520)547-9770; Irene Redondo, Business Manager, phone: (520)547-9734. **USPS:** 228-440. **Subscription Rates:** $133 By mail; $118.50 Individuals carrier/mail; $30 Individuals web only. **URL:** http://www.gvnews.com. **Formerly**: Green Valley News & Sun. **Feature Editors:** Karen Walenga, kwalenga@gvnews.com. **Mailing address:** PO Box 567, Green Valley, AZ 85614. **Ad Rates:** PCI $15.85. **Remarks:** Accepts advertising. **Circ:** Free ‡566, Paid ‡7946, Combined ‡8512.

876 ■ Santa Cruz Valley Sun
Green Valley News & Sun
18705 S I-19 Frontage Rd., Ste. 125
Green Valley, AZ 85614
Phone: (520)625-5511
Fax: (520)625-8046
Publisher's E-mail: dshearer@gvnews.com
Community newspaper. **Freq:** Weekly. **Key Personnel:** Pamela K. Mox, Publisher, phone: (520)547-9722; Dan Shearer, Editor, phone: (520)547-9770. **Subscription Rates:** Free. **URL:** http://www.nogalesinternational.com/santa_cruz_valley_sun/. **Mailing address:** PO Box 567, Green Valley, AZ 85614. **Remarks:** Accepts advertising. **Circ:** Free ■ **11161**.

GROOM CREEK

877 ■ K258AL-FM - 99.5
PO Box 391
Twin Falls, ID 83303
Free: 800-357-4226
Format: Religious; Contemporary Christian. **Owner:** CSN International, PO Box 391, Twin Falls, ID 83303, Ph: (208)736-1958, Fax: (208)736-1958, Free: 800-357-4226.

Circulation: ★ = AAM; △ or • = BPA; ♦ = CAC; ❑ = VAC; ⊕ = PO Statement; ‡ = Publisher's Report; Boldface figures = sworn; Light figures = estimated.

HIGLEY

878 ■ Sport Horse Guide
American Warmblood Society
PO Box 1561
Higley, AZ 85236
Phone: (480)251-0348
Fax: (520)568-3318
Publisher's E-mail: awsdir2013@gmail.com
Journal publishing information for American Warmblood Society members. **Freq:** Annual. **Remarks:** Accepts advertising. **Circ:** (Not Reported).

HOLBROOK

Navajo Co. Navajo Co. (NE). 90 m SE of Flagstaff. Trading and tourist center. Petrified Forest. National Park and Painted Desert. Lakes. Navajo Hopi, and Apache Reservations. Ponderosa pine timber. Coal fired electric generating. Agriculture. Cattle, sheep, pigs, poultry, dairying.

879 ■ KBMH-FM - 90.3
PO Box 3206
Tupelo, MS 38803
Format: Religious. **Owner:** American Family Radio, at above address. **Wattage:** 250. **URL:** http://Afa.Net.

880 ■ KDJI-AM - 1270
250 N Broadcast Ln.
Holbrook, AZ 86025
Phone: (928)368-8100
Fax: (928)368-8108
Free: 800-581-9292
Email: production@whitemountainradio.com
Format: Talk; News; Sports. **Simulcasts:** KVWM-AM. **Owner:** Petracom of Holbrook L.L.C., at above address. **Founded:** 1959. **Key Personnel:** Roy Roberts, Contact; Roy Roberts, Contact. **Wattage:** 5,000 Daytime; 130 N. **Ad Rates:** $6.80-8.40 for 30 seconds; $8-9.90 for 60 seconds. Combined advertising rates available with KZUA-FM. **URL:** http://www.whitemountainradio.com.

881 ■ K217CN-FM - 91.3
PO Box 391
Twin Falls, ID 83303
Fax: (208)736-1958
Free: 800-357-4226
Format: Religious; Contemporary Christian. **Owner:** CSN International, PO Box 391, Twin Falls, ID 83303, Ph: (208)736-1958, Fax: (208)736-1958, Free: 800-357-4226. **URL:** http://www.csnradio.com.

KEAMS CANYON

882 ■ KUYI-FM - 88.1
PO Box 1500
Keams Canyon, AZ 86034
Phone: (928)738-5530
Email: info@kuyi.net
Format: Public Radio; Educational; Ethnic. **Founded:** Sept. 13, 2000. **Key Personnel:** Monica Nuvamsa, Gen. Mgr.; Richard Alun Davis, Mgr., richard.davis@kuyi.net. **Ad Rates:** Noncommercial. **URL:** http://www.kuyi.net.

KEARNY

Pinal Co. Pinal Co. (S). 80 m SE of Phoenix. Retirement community. Copper. Cattle.

883 ■ Copper Basin News
Copper Area Publishing
PO Box 579
Kearny, AZ 85137
Community newspaper. **Freq:** Weekly (Wed.). **Print Method:** Offset. **Cols./Page:** 6. **Col. Width:** 12 nonpareils. **Col. Depth:** 290 agate lines. **URL:** http://www.copperarea.com/pages/category/kearny. **Ad Rates:** GLR $0.28; SAU $4.75. **Remarks:** Accepts advertising. **Circ:** ‡2600.

884 ■ Superior Sun
Superior Sun
PO Box 579
Kearny, AZ 85237-0579
Phone: (520)363-5554
Fax: (520)363-9663
Community newspaper. **Freq:** Weekly (Wed.). **Print Method:** Offset. **Cols./Page:** 6. **Col. Width:** 12 nonpareils. **Col. Depth:** 294 agate lines. **Subscription Rates:** $35.50 Individuals; $31.50 Individuals six months in Pinal County in Arizona; $40.50 Out of area; $36.50 Out of area six months. **URL:** http://www.copperarea.com/pages/category/publications/superior-sun. **Ad Rates:** PCI $5.50. **Remarks:** Advertising accepted; rates available upon request. **Circ:** ‡1300.

KINGMAN

Mohave Co. Mohave Co. (NW). 100 m NW of Prescott. Industrial park. Gold, silver, lead, zinc, copper, feldspar mines. Cattle raising.

885 ■ Kingman Daily Miner
Western News & Info Inc.
3015 Stockton Hill Rd.
Kingman, AZ 86401
Phone: (928)753-6397
Publication E-mail: opinion@kdminer.com
General newspaper. **Founded:** Aug. 1882. **Freq:** Daily and Sun. (eve.). **Print Method:** Offset. **Cols./Page:** 6. **Col. Width:** 25 nonpareils. **Col. Depth:** 294 agate lines. **Key Personnel:** Robin Mauser, Chief Executive Officer, Publisher; Storm Chamberlain, Director, Personnel; Rich Thurlow, Editor; Nirali Dave, Business Manager. **Subscription Rates:** $93.60 Individuals home delivery; $72.45 Individuals 9 months home delivery; $49.80 Individuals 6 months home delivery; $26.40 Individuals 3 months home delivery; $8.80 Individuals 1 month home delivery. **URL:** http://kdminer.com. **Formerly:** Mohave Daily Miner. **Remarks:** Accepts advertising. **Circ:** Combined 8200, Paid 7419.

886 ■ KAAA-AM - 1230
2535 Hualapai Mountain Rd., Ste. D
Kingman, AZ 86401
Phone: (928)753-2537
Format: News; Talk. **Networks:** ABC. **Owner:** Cameron Broadcasting Inc., 2350 Miracle Mile Rd., Ste. 300, Bullhead City, AZ 86442, Ph: (928)763-5586. **Founded:** 1949. **Operating Hours:** Continuous; 10% network, 10% local, 80% satellite. **ADI:** Phoenix (Kingman, Prescott), AZ. **Key Personnel:** Mike Fletcher, Gen. Sales Mgr. **Wattage:** 1,000. **Ad Rates:** Advertising accepted; rates available upon request. KZZZ/KFLG Radio. **URL:** http://www.talkatoz.com.

887 ■ KGMN-FM - 100.1
812 E Beale St.
Kingman, AZ 86401
Fax: (928)753-1978
Format: Country. **Networks:** USA Radio. **Owner:** New West Broadcasting Systems Inc., 812 E Beale St., Kingman, AZ 86401, Ph: (928)753-9100, Fax: (928)753-1978. **Founded:** 1984. **Operating Hours:** Continuous. **ADI:** Phoenix (Kingman, Prescott), AZ. **Key Personnel:** Joe Hart, President, joe@kgmn.net; Rhonda Hart, Gen. Mgr., VP, rhonda@kgmn.net; Deana Campbell, Dir. of Traffic, Operations Mgr., kgmntraffic@citlink.net; Dave Hawkins, News Dir., newshawk22@hotmail.com. **Wattage:** 5,000. **Ad Rates:** $13 for 30 seconds; $15 for 60 seconds. **URL:** http://www.kgmn.net.

888 ■ KGPS-FM - 98.7
500 Stowell
500 Stowell Ave.
Kingman, AZ 86401
Phone: (928)753-3730
Email: calvarykingman@gmail.com
Format: Religious. **ADI:** Phoenix (Kingman, Prescott), AZ. **Wattage:** 100. **URL:** http://www.calvarychapelkingman.com.

889 ■ KZKE-FM - 104.9
812 E Beale St.
Kingman, AZ 86401
Phone: (928)753-9100
Fax: (928)753-1978
Free: 800-996-5466
Format: Oldies. **Key Personnel:** Joe Hart, President, joe@kgmn.net; Rhonda Hart, Gen. Mgr., VP, rhonda@kgmn.net; Deana Campbell, Dir. of Traffic, Operations Mgr., kgmntraffic@citlink.net. **Ad Rates:** Advertising accepted; rates available upon request. **URL:** http://www.kgmn.net.

LAKE HAVASU CITY

Mohave Co. Mohave Valley Co. (NW). 185 m E of Phoenix. London bridge. Chain saw & boat plants.

Parker/Blythe White Sheet - See Blythe

890 ■ River Extra
River City Newspapers L.L.C.
2225 W Acoma Blvd. W
Lake Havasu City, AZ 86403
Phone: (928)453-4237
Publisher's E-mail: service@havasunews.com
Newspaper. **Freq:** Weekly (Sun.). **Print Method:** Offset. **Cols./Page:** 6. **Col. Width:** 2 1/16 inches. **Col. Depth:** 21 inches. **Key Personnel:** Mike Quinn, President. **Subscription Rates:** $97.92 Out of country; $286.05 Out of country; $230.43; $3.99 Individuals 1 week online; $8.99 Individuals 1 month online; $71.40 Individuals 1 year online. **Ad Rates:** PCI $4.25. **Circ:** Paid ■ **10364**, Paid ■ **10920**.

891 ■ Smart Buyer
River City Newspapers L.L.C.
2225 W Acoma Blvd. W
Lake Havasu City, AZ 86403
Phone: (928)453-4237
Publisher's E-mail: service@havasunews.com
Shopper. **Freq:** Weekly (Tues.). **Key Personnel:** Michael Quinn, President. **Subscription Rates:** Free. **URL:** http://www.havasunews.com/app/pdfs/advrates_tnh.pdf. **Remarks:** Accepts advertising. **Circ:** Free ■ **25419**.

892 ■ Today's News-Herald
River City Newspapers L.L.C.
2225 W Acoma Blvd. W
Lake Havasu City, AZ 86403
Phone: (928)453-4237
Publisher's E-mail: service@havasunews.com
Daily newspaper. **Freq:** Daily except Saturday. **Print Method:** Offset. **Cols./Page:** 6. **Col. Width:** 2 1/16 inches. **Col. Depth:** 21 inches. **Key Personnel:** Mike Quinn, President, Publisher. **ISSN:** 1084--9009 (print). **Subscription Rates:** $126.43 Individuals home delivery; $286.05 Out of area mail delivery. **URL:** http://www.havasunews.com. **Ad Rates:** GLR $2.96; BW $2,332; 4C $215; PCI $23.42. **Circ:** Mon.-Fri. 11239, Sun. 13484.

893 ■ White Sheet--The Lake Havasu
Associated Desert Shoppers Inc.
2099 W Acoma
Lake Havasu City, AZ 86403
Phone: (928)855-7871
Fax: (928)855-8183
Free: 800-298-8162
Shopper. **Freq:** Weekly (Tues.). **Print Method:** Web. **Trim Size:** 11 x 12 1/2. **Cols./Page:** 6. **Col. Width:** 9.5 picas. **Col. Depth:** 11 1/2 inches. **Alt. Formats:** Download; PDF. **URL:** http://www.greenandwhitesheet.com/white_sheet_home.php. **Remarks:** Advertising accepted; rates available upon request. **Circ:** Free ‡30000.

894 ■ White Sheet-The Tri-State Advertiser
Associated Desert Shoppers Inc.
2099 W Acoma
Lake Havasu City, AZ 86403
Phone: (928)855-7871
Fax: (928)855-8183
Free: 800-298-8162
Shopper. **Freq:** Weekly (Tues.). **Print Method:** Web. **Trim Size:** 11 x 12 1/2. **Cols./Page:** 6. **Col. Width:** 9.5 picas. **Col. Depth:** 11 1/2 inches. **Key Personnel:** John Schneider, Manager, Sales. **Alt. Formats:** PDF. **URL:** http://www.greenandwhitesheet.com/white_sheet_home.php. **Ad Rates:** BW $365; 4C $650. **Remarks:** Accepts advertising. **Circ:** Non-paid ‡10500.

895 ■ KADD-FM - 93.5
PO Box 1866
Lake Havasu City, AZ 86403
Phone: (928)855-1051
Format: Adult Contemporary. **Key Personnel:** Rick L. Murphy, CEO. **Ad Rates:** Advertising accepted; rates available upon request.

896 ■ KBBC-FM - 101.1
1642 McCulloch Blvd. N, No. 193
Lake Havasu City, AZ 86403-0961
Fax: (602)855-5395
Format: Top 40; Contemporary Hit Radio (CHR). **Owner:** London Bridge Broadcasting, Inc., at above address. **Operating Hours:** Continuous. **Key Personnel:** Lee Shoblom, Gen. Mgr.; Terry Watt, VP; Doreen Ridenour, Office Mgr. **Wattage:** 100,000. **Ad Rates:**

$9.50 for 30 seconds; $11.25 for 60 seconds.

897 ■ KJJJ-FM - 102.3
1845 McCulloch Blvd., Ste. A-14
Lake Havasu City, AZ 86403
Phone: (928)855-9336
Fax: (928)855-9333
Format: Country. **Ad Rates:** Noncommercial. **URL:** http://www.kjjjfm.com.

898 ■ KLHU-TV - 45
1600 W Acoma Blvd., Ste. 34
Lake Havasu City, AZ 86403
Phone: (928)453-8888
Email: info@klhu.tv
URL: http://klhu.tv.

899 ■ KMDX-FM - 99.3
1930 Mesquite Ave., Ste. 3-A
Lake Havasu City, AZ 86403
Phone: (602)669-6176
Fax: (602)669-8090
Format: Contemporary Hit Radio (CHR). **Networks:** Westwood One Radio. **Owner:** Gilbert Leivas, at above address. **Founded:** 1977. **Operating Hours:** Continuous; 17% network, 83% local. **Key Personnel:** Chris Pappas, Gen. Mgr.; Chuck Harold, Sales Mgr; Rick W. Kurtis, Contact; Gilbert Leivas, Contact. **Wattage:** 3,000 ERP. **Ad Rates:** $8-17 for 30 seconds; $10-20 for 60 seconds.

900 ■ KNLB-FM - 91.1
510 N Acoma Blvd.
Lake Havasu City, AZ 86404
Phone: (928)855-9110
Fax: (928)453-2588
Free: 800-721-9313
Email: info@knlb.com
Format: Religious. **Networks:** USA Radio; International Broadcasting. **Owner:** Advance Ministries, 12391 Lyra Dr., Willis, TX 77318, Ph: (936)856-3419, Fax: (936)856-3419. **Founded:** 1983. **Operating Hours:** Continuous; 40% network, 60% local. **Key Personnel:** Faron Eckelbarger, Station Mgr., faron@knlb.com. **Wattage:** 1,000. **Ad Rates:** Noncommercial. **URL:** http://www.knlb.com.

901 ■ KNTR-AM - 980
1845 McCulloch Blvd., Ste. A-14
Lake Havasu City, AZ 86403
Phone: (928)855-9336
Email: office@myradiocentral.com
Format: Talk; News; Sports. **Founded:** Sept. 14, 2006. **Operating Hours:** Continuous. **Wattage:** 1,000 Day; 049 Night. **Ad Rates:** Accepts Advertising. **URL:** http://www.kntrtalk.com.

902 ■ KRCY-FM
PO Box 1866
Lake Havasu City, AZ 86405
Phone: (602)855-1051
Fax: (602)855-7966
Free: 800-582-ROCK
Format: Oldies. **Networks:** Satellite Music Network. **Owner:** Mad Dog Wireless, Inc., at above address. **Founded:** 1990. **Key Personnel:** Steven Reno, Dir. of Programs. **Wattage:** 260 ERP. **Ad Rates:** $11-16 for 30 seconds; $16.50-24 for 60 seconds.

903 ■ KRRK-FM
PO Box 1866
Lake Havasu City, AZ 86405
Format: Classic Rock. **Wattage:** 275 ERP.

904 ■ KWFH-FM - 90.1
510 Acoma Blvd. N
Lake Havasu City, AZ 86403-4838
Phone: (928)855-9110
Free: 866-999-5934
Email: comment@alivefm.org
Format: Contemporary Christian. **Networks:** Moody Broadcasting. **Owner:** Advance Ministries, 12391 Lyra Dr., Willis, TX 77318, Ph: (936)856-3419, Fax: (936)856-3419. **Founded:** 1984. **Operating Hours:** Continuous. **Wattage:** 460. **Ad Rates:** Noncommercial. **URL:** http://www.kwfh.org.

905 ■ KZUL-FM - 104.5
Ten Media Center Dr.
Lake Havasu City, AZ 86403
Phone: (928)855-1051
Free: 800-582-7625
Format: Adult Contemporary. **Networks:** Unistar. **Owner:** Murphy Broadcasting, at above address, Lake Havasu City, AZ 86403. **Founded:** 1986. **Operating Hours:** Continuous; 70% network, 30% local. **Key Personnel:** Julie Cummings, VP of Sales; Melissa Hughes, Operations Mgr., mediacenter@maddog.net; Mike Anthony, Gen. Sales Mgr., manthony@maddog.net. **Wattage:** 286. **Ad Rates:** $11-16 for 30 seconds; $16.50-24 for 60 seconds. **URL:** http://www.murphybroadcasting.com.

LAKESIDE

Navajo Co. (SE). Part of Pinetop-Lakeside.

906 ■ KVWM-AM - 970
1838 W Commerce Dr., Ste. A
Lakeside, AZ 85929
Format: Talk. **Operating Hours:** 6 a.m. to 10 p.m. **Wattage:** 5,000. **Ad Rates:** Advertising accepted; rates available upon request. **URL:** http://970kvwm.com.

MESA

Maricopa Co. Maricopa Co. (SC). 16 m SE of Phoenix. Culture and art centers. Museums. Fishing and hunting. Manufactures integrated circuits, heavy equipment, propellant, rocket motors, electronic interconnectors, helicopters, steel doors & frames, metal corrals and horse trailer, plastic counter tops; frozen food. Agriculture.

907 ■ Mesa Legend
Mesa Legend
1833 W. Southern Ave.
Mesa, AZ 85202
Phone: (480)461-7333
Collegiate newspaper. **Freq:** Biweekly. **Print Method:** Offset. **Trim Size:** 21.5 x 13. **Cols./Page:** 6. **Col. Width:** 2.125 inches. **Col. Depth:** 20 5/8 inches. **Key Personnel:** Ryan Scott, Editor-in-Chief. **Ad Rates:** BW $808. **Remarks:** Accepts advertising. **Circ:** Free ‡24000.

908 ■ New Thought
International New Thought Alliance
5003 E Broadway Rd.
Mesa, AZ 85206
Phone: (480)830-2461
Publisher's E-mail: info@newthoughtalliance.org
Freq: Quarterly. **Print Method:** Offset. **Trim Size:** 8 1/2 x 11. **Cols./Page:** 3. **Col. Width:** 28 nonpareils. **Col. Depth:** 130 agate lines. **Key Personnel:** Dr. Mimi Ronnie, Chief Operating Officer, Managing Editor. **ISSN:** 0146--7832 (print). **USPS:** 382--380. **Subscription Rates:** $25 Individuals; Included in membership; $45 Other countries. **URL:** http://www.newthoughtalliance.org/new-thought-magazine.html. **Ad Rates:** BW $608.50; PCI $26. **Remarks:** Accepts advertising. **Circ:** ‡3000.

909 ■ Psychotherapy: Theory, Research, Practice, Training
APA Division 29: The Society for the Advancement of Psychology
c/o Tracey Martin
6557 E Riverdale St.
Mesa, AZ 85215
Phone: (602)363-9211
Fax: (480)854-8966
Publisher's E-mail: assnmgmt1@cox.net
Journal containing articles on theory, research, practice, and training in psychotherapy. **Freq:** Quarterly. **Print Method:** Offset. **Trim Size:** 6 3/4 x 10. **Cols./Page:** 2. **Col. Width:** 2 3/4 inches. **Col. Depth:** 8 inches. **Key Personnel:** Mark Hilsenroth, Editor; Jesse J. Owens, Associate Editor; Lisa Wallner Samstag, Associate Editor. **ISSN:** 0033-3204 (print). **Subscription Rates:** $64 Members domestic; $84 Other countries member, surface; $310 Institutions; $352 Institutions, other countries surface; $115 Nonmembers domestic. **URL:** http://societyforpsychotherapy.org/publications/journal/; http://www.apa.org/pubs/journals/pst/index.aspx. **Formerly:** Psychotherapy: Theory, Research, and Practice. **Ad Rates:** BW $425; 4C $1,400. **Remarks:** Accepts advertising. **Circ:** ‡3000.

910 ■ KDKB-FM - 93.3
1167 W Javelina Ave.
Mesa, AZ 85210
Phone: (480)897-9300
Format: Album-Oriented Rock (AOR). **Networks:** Independent. **Owner:** Sandusky Radio. **Founded:** 1968. **Operating Hours:** Continuous. **Wattage:** 100,000. **Ad Rates:** Advertising accepted; rates available upon request. **URL:** http://www.altaz933.com.

911 ■ KFXY-FM
550 W Baseline Rd.
Mesa, AZ 85210
Fax: (504)384-2351
Format: Contemporary Hit Radio (CHR). **Founded:** 1967. **Wattage:** 002 ERP.

MIAMI

912 ■ KIKO-FM
4501 Broadway
Miami, AZ 85539
Phone: (928)425-7500
Fax: (928)425-9393
Format: Easy Listening. **Networks:** Westwood One Radio. **Owner:** Shoecraft Broadcasting, Inc., at above address. **Founded:** 1991. **Wattage:** 40,000 ERP. **Ad Rates:** Noncommercial.

913 ■ KQSS-FM - 101.9
PO Box 292
Miami, AZ 85539
Phone: (928)425-7186
Fax: (928)425-7982
Email: news4susank@yahoo.com
Format: Contemporary Country. **Owner:** Bill Taylor, at above address. **Founded:** 1987. **Operating Hours:** Continuous; 100% local. **Key Personnel:** Bill Taylor, Gen. Mgr., Owner. **Wattage:** 3,000. **Ad Rates:** $9-15.50 for 60 seconds. **URL:** http://www.gila1019.com.

NOGALES

Santa Cruz Co. Santa Cruz Co. (S). 65 m S of Tucson. Port of entry on Mexican border with important export and import trade. Ships winter vegetables. Copper, silver, lead mines. Cattle farms.

914 ■ Nogales International
Nogales International
268 W View Point Dr.
Nogales, AZ 85621
Phone: (520)375-5760
Publisher's E-mail: publisher@nogalesinternational.com
Community newspaper. **Freq:** Biweekly Tuesday and Friday. **Print Method:** Offset. **Cols./Page:** 6. **Col. Width:** 12.3 picas. **Col. Depth:** 21.5 inches. **Key Personnel:** Manuel C. Coppola, Editor, phone: (520)375-5766; Jonathan Clark, Editor, phone: (520)375-5767. **Subscription Rates:** $52 Individuals in county mail delivery; $62 Individuals out of county mail delivery. **URL:** http://www.nogalesinternational.com. **Ad Rates:** GLR $0.30; BW $1,136.33; 4C $1,436.33; SAU $8.70; PCI $8.70. **Remarks:** Accepts advertising. **Circ:** Paid ■ **2220**.

915 ■ KOFH-FM - 99.1
934 Bejarano St., Ste. 2
Nogales, AZ 85621
Phone: (520)287-6885
Fax: (520)287-8290
Wattage: 6,000 ERP. **Ad Rates:** Accepts Advertising.

916 ■ Mediacom Communications Corp.
181 N Arroyo Blvd.
Nogales, AZ 85621
Free: 800-239-8411
Owner: Mediacom Communications Corp., 100 Crystal Run Rd., Middletown, NY 10941, Ph: (845)695-2600, Fax: (845)698-4570, Free: 888-847-6228. **Founded:** 1996. **Key Personnel:** Rocco B. Commisso, CEO, Chairman; Mark E. Stephan, CFO, Exec. VP. **Cities Served:** Ajo, Amado, Arivaca Junction, Rio Rico, Arizona: subscribing households 8,500; 62 channels; 1 community access channel; 24 hours per week community access programming. **URL:** http://mediacomcable.com.

ORO VALLEY

917 ■ KVOI-AM - 1030
3222 S Richey Ave.
Tucson, AZ 85713
Phone: (520)790-2440

Circulation: ★ = AAM; △ or • = BPA; ♦ = CAC; ❑ = VAC; ⊕ = PO Statement; ‡ = Publisher's Report; Boldface figures = sworn; Light figures = estimated.

Email: info@kvoi.com
Format: Talk. **Owner:** Good News Radio Broadcasting. **Founded:** 1953. **Operating Hours:** Continuous. **ADI:** Tucson, AZ. **Key Personnel:** Doug Martin, President, doug@kvoi.com; Mary Martin, Mgr., Ad./Sales, marymartin@kvoi.com. **Wattage:** 10,000 Day; 1,000 Ni. **Ad Rates:** Advertising accepted; rates available upon request. Combined advertising rates available with KGMS-AM. **URL:** http://www.kvoi.com.

PAGE

Coconino Co. Coconino Co. (N). On Lake Powell, 139 m N of Flagstaff. National recreation area. Glen Canyon, Lake Powell, Rainbow Bridge. Navajo generating station.

918 ■ KPGE-AM - 1340
91 E 7th Ave.
Page, AZ 86040
Phone: (928)645-8181
Free: 800-498-7741
Format: Country. **Networks:** ABC. **Owner:** Lake Powell Communications Inc., at above address. **Founded:** 1962. **Operating Hours:** Continuous. **Wattage:** 1,000. **Ad Rates:** Advertising accepted; rates available upon request. KXAZ-FM. **Mailing address:** PO Box 1030, Page, AZ 86040. **URL:** http://www.kpge.com.

PARADISE VALLEY

919 ■ Town of Paradise Valley Independent
Independent Newspapers Inc.
23043 N 16th Ln.
Phoenix, AZ 85027
Community newspaper. **Freq:** Weekly (Wed.). **Print Method:** Offset. **Trim Size:** 13 x 21. **Cols./Page:** 6. **Col. Width:** 2 1/16 inches. **Col. Depth:** 21 1/2 inches. **Ad Rates:** PCI $21.16. **Remarks:** Accepts advertising. **Circ:** Non-paid ♦**7862**.

PARKER

La Paz Co. Yumba Co. (SW). 135 m W of Phoenix. Residential.

920 ■ Parker Pioneer
Wick Communications
1001 12th St.
Parker, AZ 85344
Phone: (928)669-2275
Fax: (928)669-9624
Community newspaper. **Freq:** Weekly (Wed.). **Print Method:** Offset. **Cols./Page:** 6. **Col. Width:** 26 nonpareils. **Col. Depth:** 294 agate lines. **Key Personnel:** Brandon Bowers, Editor. **USPS:** 422-120. **Subscription Rates:** $126.43 Individuals print; $71.40 Individuals online; $230.43 Individuals in county. **URL:** http://www.havasunews.com. **Mailing address:** PO Box 3365, Parker, AZ 85344. **Ad Rates:** BW $750; 4C $210; SAU $6.30; PCI $5.25. **Remarks:** Accepts advertising. **Circ:** Paid ■ **3296**.

921 ■ KLPZ-AM - 1380
816 W 6th St.
Parker, AZ 85344
Phone: (928)669-9274
Fax: (928)669-9300
Email: info@klpz1380.com
Format: Contemporary Country; News; Talk. **Networks:** ABC; Satellite Network News; Jones Satellite. **Owner:** Learn Broadcasting. **Founded:** 1974. **Formerly:** KZUL-AM. **Operating Hours:** Continuous. **Local Programs:** *Mornings with Keith and Juanita*, Monday Tuesday Wednesday Thursday Friday Saturday Sunday 6:00 a.m. - 10:00 a.m. **Wattage:** 2,500. **Ad Rates:** for 30 seconds; for 60 seconds. **URL:** http://www.klpz1380.com.

PAYSON

Gila Co. Gila Co. (NC). 70 m NE of Phoenix. Tourism, cattle, and lumber.

922 ■ Payson Roundup and Advisor
WorldWest L.L.C.
PO Box 2520
Payson, AZ 85547
Phone: (928)474-5251
Fax: (928)474-1893
Community newspaper. **Freq:** Semiweekly Tues. and Fri. **Print Method:** Offset. **Trim Size:** 13 1/2 x 23. **Cols./Page:** 6. **Col. Width:** 12.5 picas. **Col. Depth:** 301 agate lines. **Key Personnel:** John Naughton, Publisher, phone: (928)474-5251; Bobby Davis, Director, Advertising, phone: (928)474-5251. **URL:** http://www.paysonroundup.com. **Remarks:** Accepts advertising. **Circ:** 7000.

923 ■ KMOG-AM - 1420
500 E Tyler Pkwy.
Payson, AZ 85541
Phone: (928)474-5214
Fax: (928)474-0236
Email: kmog@1420kmog.com
Format: Country. **Networks:** ABC. **Owner:** Farrell Enterprises LLC, at above address. **Founded:** 1983. **Operating Hours:** Continuous; 15% network, 85% local. **Wattage:** 2,500. **Ad Rates:** $11-14 for 30 seconds; $14-16 for 60 seconds. **URL:** http://www.rimcountryradio.com.

924 ■ KRIM-FM - 96.3
500 E Parkway Plz.
Payson, AZ 85541
Format: Eclectic; Oldies. **Simulcasts:** KBZR-FM. **Owner:** Payson Council for the Musical Arts, 963 E Highline Dr., Payson, AZ 85541. **Formerly:** KKJJ-FM. **Operating Hours:** Continuous. **Key Personnel:** Tom Vorce, Contact. **Wattage:** 004. **Ad Rates:** Noncommercial; underwriting available; Advertising accepted; rates available upon request. **Mailing address:** PO Box 2579, Payson, AZ 85547-2579. **URL:** http://www.krim-fm.com.

925 ■ K219KQ-FM - 91.7
PO Box 391
Twin Falls, ID 83303
Fax: (208)736-1958
Free: 800-357-4226
Format: Religious; Contemporary Christian. **Owner:** CSN International, PO Box 391, Twin Falls, ID 83303, Ph: (208)736-1958, Fax: (208)736-1958, Free: 800-357-4226. **Key Personnel:** Don Mills, Prog. Dir., Music Dir.; Kelly Carlson, Dir. of Engg.; Ray Gorney, Asst. Dir. **Wattage:** 010. **URL:** http://www.csnradio.com.

PEORIA

Maricopa Co.

926 ■ Thai Philately
Society for Thai Philately
9379 W Escuda Dr.
Peoria, AZ 85382
Journals including specialized research, articles of general interest and related news. **Freq:** 3/year. **ISSN:** 0198--7992 (print). **Subscription Rates:** Included in membership. **Alt. Formats:** CD-ROM; Download; PDF. **URL:** http://www.thaiphilately.org/journals. **Remarks:** Accepts advertising. **Circ:** (Not Reported).

PHOENIX

Maricopa Co. Maricopa Co. (C). The State Capital, 107 m NW of Tucson. Arizona State University. Trade and Business center of the State. Winter resort. Private and ranch schools. American Graduate School for International Management is located in NW Phoenix. Manufactures aircraft and aircraft parts, electronic equipment, steel castings, flour, boxes and crates, agricultural chemicals, aluminum products, radios, mobile homes, air conditioning machinery, steel fabrications, creamery products, beer, liquor, saddles and leather goods, men's and women's apparel, Indian and Mexican novelties, textile goods. Meat packing plants; citrus juices, pickle and olive canneries; sugar refinery; lettuce, cantaloupe, vegetable packing and shipping; cotton products.

927 ■ Ahwatukee Foothills News
Ahwautkee Foothills News
10631 S 51st St., Ste. 1
Phoenix, AZ 85044
Phone: (480)898-7900
Fax: (480)893-1684
Community newspaper. **Freq:** Triweekly Wednesdays, Fridays and Sundays. **Key Personnel:** Holli Roach, Manager, Advertising, Manager, Production; Jason Joseph, Publisher; Brian Johnson, Photographer. **URL:** http://www.ahwatukee.com. **Formerly:** Ahwatakee Weekly News. **Remarks:** Advertising accepted; rates available upon request. **Circ:** Combined ‡28000.

928 ■ Arizona Archaeologist
Arizona Archaeological Society
PO Box 9665
Phoenix, AZ 85068
Phone: (928)684-3251
Publisher's E-mail: aas@azarchsoc.org
Professional magazine covering Southwest US archaeology. **Freq:** Annual. **Trim Size:** 8 x 11. **Key Personnel:** Bill Burkett, Editor. **Subscription Rates:** Included in membership. **Alt. Formats:** PDF. **URL:** http://www.azarchsoc.org/page-807608. **Remarks:** Advertising not accepted. **Circ:** Controlled 780.

929 ■ Arizona Business Gazette
Phoenix Newspapers Inc.
200 E Van Buren St.
Phoenix, AZ 85004
Phone: (602)444-8000
Free: 800-331-9303
Publisher's E-mail: fullaccess@republicmedia.com
Business and legal newspaper. **Freq:** Daily. **Print Method:** Offset. **Trim Size:** 14 x 22 1/2. **Cols./Page:** 5. **Col. Width:** 2 1/8 inches. **Col. Depth:** 182 agate lines. **Key Personnel:** David Proffitt, Editor, phone: (602)444-7346. **ISSN:** 0273--6950 (print). **Subscription Rates:** $25.99 Individuals monthly (monday-sunday); $16.99 Individuals monthly (wednesday and sunday). **URL:** http://www.azcentral.com/topic/98835572-F5D3-4661-8274-EFE190D9D69A. **Remarks:** Accepts advertising. **Circ:** (Not Reported).

930 ■ Arizona Food Industry Journal
Arizona Food Marketing Alliance
120 E Pierce St.
Phoenix, AZ 85004
Phone: (602)252-9761
Fax: (602)252-9021
Magazine containing information regarding the food market, features trade information. **Freq:** Monthly. **Subscription Rates:** $60 Individuals. **URL:** http://www.afmaaz.org/journal.asp. **Ad Rates:** BW $1,650, full page - member; BW $940, half page - member; BW $2,145, full page - non member; BW $1,185, half page - non member. **Remarks:** Accepts advertising. **Circ:** 3000.

931 ■ Arizona Highways
Arizona Highways
2039 W Lewis Ave.
Phoenix, AZ 85009-2819
Phone: (602)712-2200
Fax: (602)254-4505
Free: 800-543-5432
Publisher's E-mail: arizonahighways@emailcustomerservice.com
Travel magazine covering regional history, natural science, folklore, and natural history. **Freq:** Monthly. **Print Method:** Offset. **Trim Size:** 9 x 12. **Cols./Page:** 2. **Col. Width:** 42 nonpareils. **Col. Depth:** 140 agate lines. **Key Personnel:** Win Holden, Publisher; Peter Aleshire, Editor. **ISSN:** 0004--1521 (print). **Subscription Rates:** $24 Individuals; $44 Other countries; $43 Individuals 2 years; $83 Other countries 2 years; $59 Individuals 3 years; $119 Other countries 3 years. **URL:** http://www.arizonahighways.com. **Remarks:** Advertising not accepted. **Circ:** ‡300000000.

932 ■ Arizona Informant
Arizona Informant
1301 E Washington St.
Phoenix, AZ 85034
Phone: (602)257-9300
Fax: (602)257-0547
Black community newspaper. **Founded:** 1958. **Freq:** Weekly (Wed.). **Print Method:** Web offset. **Trim Size:** 9 3/4 x 16. **Cols./Page:** 6. **Col. Width:** 1.625 inches. **Col. Depth:** 116 agate lines. **Key Personnel:** Roland Campbell, Chief Executive Officer, Publisher; Cloves C. Campbell, Jr., Chairman, Publisher. **USPS:** 051-770. **Subscription Rates:** $30 Individuals; $35 Out of state. **URL:** http://www.azinformant.com. **Ad Rates:** GLR $4.57; BW $1,300; 4C $1,702; PCI $32. **Remarks:** Accepts advertising. **Circ:** ‡1800.

933 ■ Arizona Jazz Magazine
Targeted Media Communications Inc.
1241 E Washington St., Ste. 206
Phoenix, AZ 85034
Phone: (602)230-8161
Fax: (602)230-8162
Publisher's E-mail: sales@azjazz.com

Consumer magazine covering local jazz music. **Freq:** Quarterly. **Key Personnel:** D.A. Peartree, Publisher. **URL:** http://www.azjazz.com. **Remarks:** Advertising accepted; rates available upon request. **Circ:** (Not Reported).

934 ■ Arizona Parks and Recreation
Arizona Parks and Recreation Association
12950 N 7th St.
Phoenix, AZ 85022-5500
Phone: (602)335-1962
Publisher's E-mail: info@azpra.org
Freq: Quarterly latest issue: Fall 2011. **Key Personnel:** Teresa Jackson, Managing Editor. **Subscription Rates:** $25 Members; free for members. **URL:** http://www.azpra.org/news?mode=PostView&bmi=1129861; http://www.azpra.org/magazine. **Remarks:** Accepts advertising. **Circ:** 1200.

935 ■ The Arizona Republic
Phoenix Newspapers Inc.
PO Box 1950
Phoenix, AZ 85001-9943
Phone: (602)444-8000
Publication E-mail: AZRepublicCustomerService@gannett.com
General newspaper. **Freq:** Mon.-Sun. (morn.). **Print Method:** Letterpress and Offset. **Cols./Page:** 6. **Col. Width:** 25 nonpareils. **Col. Depth:** 301 agate lines. **Subscription Rates:** $32 Individuals /month (Monday-Sunday); $16 Individuals /month (Wednesday and Sunday); $9.99 Individuals /month (digital only). **URL:** http://www.azcentral.com/topic/e85b7e4c-ae59-4084-9af1-020df1406d1d/the-arizona-republic-online. **Remarks:** Accepts classified advertising. **Circ:** (Not Reported).

936 ■ Asian SUNews
Asian Chamber of Commerce
Bldg. A, Ste. C
1402 S Central Ave.
Phoenix, AZ 85004
Phone: (602)371-8452
Fax: (602)314-5974
Newspaper including national and local news pertinent to the Asian community in Arizona. **Freq:** Semiannual. **Key Personnel:** Madeline Ong-Sakata, Editor, Publisher. **Subscription Rates:** Free. **Alt. Formats:** PDF. **URL:** http://www.asianchamber.org/news.php. **Remarks:** Accepts advertising. **Circ:** (Not Reported).

937 ■ AZMedicine
Arizona Medical Association
810 W Bethany Home Rd.
Phoenix, AZ 85013
Phone: (602)246-8901
Fax: (602)242-6283
Free: 800-482-3480
Publisher's E-mail: armacommunications@azmed.org
Freq: Quarterly. **Key Personnel:** Jeffrey Singer, MD, Editor. **URL:** http://www.azmed.org/publications; http://azmed.org/?page_id=433. **Formerly:** Arizona Medicine. **Remarks:** Accepts advertising. **Circ:** Controlled 5,000.

938 ■ Baseball Research Journal
Society for American Baseball Research
4455 E Camelback Rd., Ste. D140
Phoenix, AZ 85018-2847
Phone: (602)343-6455
Fax: (602)595-5690
Free: 800-969-7227
Magazine about the game of baseball. **Freq:** Semiannual. **Trim Size:** 8 1/2 x 11. **Key Personnel:** Nicholas Frankovich, Director, Publications. **Subscription Rates:** Included in membership. **URL:** http://sabr.org/content/baseball-research-journal-archives. **Remarks:** Advertising not accepted. **Circ:** (Not Reported).

939 ■ Billing & OSS World
Virgo Publishing L.L.C.
3300 N Central Ave., Ste. 300
Phoenix, AZ 85012-2501
Phone: (480)990-1101
Fax: (480)990-0819
Publisher's E-mail: cp.contracts@vpico.com
Magazine featuring coverage and analysis of the telecommunications billing and operations support services. **Freq:** Bimonthly. **Key Personnel:** Tim McElligott, Editor-in-Chief, phone: (480)990-1101; Buffy Naylor, Managing Editor, fax: (480)990-1101. **URL:** http://www.channelpartnersonline.com. **Mailing address:** PO Box 40079, Phoenix, AZ 85067-0079. **Remarks:** Accepts advertising. **Circ:** (Not Reported).

940 ■ BUSRide
Power Trade Media L.L.C.
4742 N 24th St., Ste. 340
Phoenix, AZ 85016
Phone: (602)265-7600
Fax: (602)227-7588
Free: 800-541-2670
Magazine covering all aspects of transit and motorcoach industry. **Freq:** Monthly. **Print Method:** Offset. **Trim Size:** 8 1/4 x 11. **Cols./Page:** 2 and 3. **Col. Width:** 2 1/4 and 0 inches. **Col. Depth:** 133 agate lines. **Key Personnel:** Valerie Valtierra, Director, Production; Steve Kane, Editor-in-Chief, Publisher; David Hubbard, Executive Editor, Editor. **ISSN:** 0192--8902 (print). **URL:** http://busride.com. **Ad Rates:** BW $2800; 4C $3275. **Remarks:** Accepts advertising. **Circ:** Combined 16000.

941 ■ Caloosa Belle
Independent Newspapers Inc.
23043 N 16th Ln.
Phoenix, AZ 85027
Publication E-mail: readerservices@newszap.com
Community newspaper. **Freq:** Weekly (Thurs.). **Print Method:** Offset. **Cols./Page:** 6. **URL:** http://caloosabelle.com. **Ad Rates:** PCI $12.24. **Remarks:** Accepts advertising. **Circ:** Free 5000.

942 ■ The Catholic Sun
Roman Catholic Diocese of Phoenix
400 E Monroe St.
Phoenix, AZ 85004-2336
Phone: (602)354-2000
Fax: (602)354-2427
Publication E-mail: info@catholicsun.org
Religious newspaper providing news, information, and commentary about the Catholic church and the Catholic Diocese of Phoenix, Arizona. **Founded:** Apr. 04, 1985. **Freq:** Semimonthly. **Print Method:** Offset. **Trim Size:** 11 x 13 3/4. **Cols./Page:** 5. **Col. Width:** 11 picas. **Col. Depth:** 180 agate lines. **Key Personnel:** Alana Kearns, Contact, phone: (602)354-2138; Jennifer Ellis, Representative, Advertising and Sales, phone: (602)354-2136; Bishop Thomas J. Olmsted, Publisher; J.D. Long-Garcia, Editor, phone: (602)354-2131. **ISSN:** 1533-0230 (print). **USPS:** 741-630. **URL:** http://www.catholicsun.org. **Ad Rates:** PCI $42; BW $2,625, full page; BW $1,575, half page - vertical; BW $1,312.50, half page - horizontal. **Remarks:** Accepts advertising. **Circ:** 117000.

943 ■ Church Executive: The First Source of Information for Business Administrators of America's Largest Churches
Power Trade Media L.L.C.
4742 N 24th St., Ste. 340
Phoenix, AZ 85016
Phone: (602)265-7600
Fax: (602)227-7588
Free: 800-541-2670
Magazine for church leaders. **Freq:** Monthly. **Key Personnel:** Steve Kane, Editor-in-Chief, Publisher. **Subscription Rates:** $39 Individuals; $64 Two years; $89 Individuals 3 years. **Ad Rates:** 4C $6,270. **Remarks:** Accepts advertising. **Circ:** 40000.

944 ■ Dental Town
Dental Town
9633 S 48th St., Ste. 200
Phoenix, AZ 85044
Phone: (480)598-0001
Fax: (480)598-3450
Publisher's E-mail: promotions@dentaltown.com
Magazine that offers information on the dental industry and latest dental equipment. **Freq:** Monthly. **Key Personnel:** Howard Farran, Founder; Thomas J. Giacobbi, Director, Editorial; Lorie Xelowski, President. **ISSN:** 1555--404X (print). **Subscription Rates:** Free print for U.S. and Canada; Free digital (worldwide). **URL:** http://www.dentaltown.com/Dentaltown/SiteDefault.aspx. **Ad Rates:** BW $8900, full page. **Remarks:** Accepts advertising. **Circ:** ‡90995.

945 ■ Destination I Do: Passport to Paradise
Destination Media L.L.C.
1220 E Osborn Rd., Ste. 102
Phoenix, AZ 85014
Publisher's E-mail: info@destinationidomag.com
Magazine offering information on destinations to get married and information to plan the wedding and how to make it legally binding. **Freq:** Semiannual. **Print Method:** Web Offset. **Trim Size:** 8.375 x 10.875. **Key Personnel:** Jennifer Stein, Editor; Mike Walker, Director, Advertising; Carolyn Steere, Chief Executive Officer, Owner. **Subscription Rates:** $9.90 Individuals; $13.90 Canada; $29.90 Other countries. **URL:** http://destinationido.com. **Ad Rates:** 4C $11058. **Remarks:** Advertising accepted; rates available upon request. **Circ:** (Not Reported).

946 ■ Edible Phoenix
Edible Communities Inc.
PO Box 9519
Phoenix, AZ 85068
Phone: (602)361-7363
Fax: (602)374-4217
Publication E-mail: info@ediblephoenix.com
Magazine focusing on the local food of Phoenix. **Freq:** Quarterly. **Trim Size:** 7.5 x 9.5. **Key Personnel:** Pamela Hamilton, Founder, Publisher, Editor. **Subscription Rates:** $28 Individuals one year; $56 Two years; 48 one year plus thirty back issues. **URL:** http://ediblephoenix.ediblefeast.com. **Ad Rates:** BW $1650; 4C $2375. **Remarks:** Accepts advertising. **Circ:** (Not Reported).

947 ■ ENR Southwest
McGraw-Hill Inc.
4747 E Elliot Rd., Ste. 29-339
Phoenix, AZ 85044
Fax: (480)656-7984
Regional trade magazine for the contracting industries including highway, municipal, utility, heavy construction, and mining. Serving Arizona, New Mexico and Nevada. **Freq:** Monthly. **Print Method:** Offset. **Trim Size:** 8 1/8 x 10 7/8. **Cols./Page:** 2 and 3. **Col. Width:** 21 and 14 picas. **Col. Depth:** 10 inches. **Key Personnel:** Scott Blair, Senior Editor, phone: (480)656-7615, fax: (480)656-7984. **ISSN:** 1064--6914 (print). **URL:** http://www.enr.com/southwest. **Formerly:** Contractor Engineer; Southwest Contractor. **Ad Rates:** BW $1630; 4C $2180. **Remarks:** Accepts advertising. **Circ:** Paid ***5715**.

948 ■ EquiShopper
Active Interest Media
22601 N 19th Ave., Ste.131
Phoenix, AZ 85027
Publisher's E-mail: admin@aimmedia.com
Magazine publishing articles about shopping for horses. **URL:** http://www.aimmedia.com/es.html. **Remarks:** Accepts advertising. **Circ:** (Not Reported).

949 ■ Gilbert Independent
Independent Newspapers Inc.
23043 N 16th Ln.
Phoenix, AZ 85027
Publication E-mail: gilbertnews@newszap.com
Community newspaper. **Freq:** Weekly (Wed.). **Print Method:** Offset. **Trim Size:** 13 x 21. **Cols./Page:** 6. **Col. Width:** 2 1/16 inches. **Col. Depth:** 21 1/2 inches. **Subscription Rates:** $26 Individuals e-edition. **URL:** http://arizona.newszap.com/gilbertindependent. **Ad Rates:** PCI $21.92. **Remarks:** Accepts advertising. **Circ:** Non-paid ♦**15015**.

950 ■ HQ: Good Design is Good Business
McGraw-Hill Inc.
4747 E Elliot Rd., Ste. 29-339
Phoenix, AZ 85044
Fax: (480)656-7984
Design magazine for C-level executives, building owners and developers, and design and construction professionals. **Freq:** Quarterly. **Key Personnel:** Norbert W. Young, Jr., President; Laura Viscusi, Publisher; Stephen R. Weiss, Manager, Production. **Subscription Rates:** Free. **Remarks:** Advertising accepted; rates available upon request. **Circ:** (Not Reported).

951 ■ Immokalee Bulletin
Independent Newspapers Inc.
23043 N 16th Ln.
Phoenix, AZ 85027
Publication E-mail: readerservices@newszap.com
Serves the northeastern Collier County area. **Freq:** Weekly (Thurs.). **Cols./Page:** 6. **Col. Width:** 1.833 inches. **Col. Depth:** 21.5 picas. **Key Personnel:** Patty

Circulation: ★ = AAM; △ or • = BPA; ♦ = CAC; ❑ = VAC; ⊕ = PO Statement; ‡ = Publisher's Report; Boldface figures = sworn; Light figures = estimated.

Brant, Managing Editor. **URL:** http://immokaleebulletin.com. **Ad Rates:** PCI $10.56. **Remarks:** Accepts advertising. **Circ:** Free ‡3500.

952 ■ Inside Self-Storage
Informa Exhibitions L.L.C.
3300 N Central Ave. Ste. 300
Phoenix, AZ 85012
Phone: (480)990-1101
Magazine reporting about products to self-storage professionals in Australia, Canada, Europe, the United Kingdom and other countries. **Freq:** Monthly. **Key Personnel:** Amy Campbell, Editor. **URL:** http://www.insideselfstorage.com. **Ad Rates:** BW $6655; 4C $1199. **Remarks:** Accepts advertising. **Circ:** 1800.

953 ■ Java Magazine
Java Magazine
PO Box 45448
Phoenix, AZ 85064
Phone: (480)966-6352
Publication E-mail: javamag@cox.net
Consumer magazine covering alternative arts and culture. **Freq:** Monthly. **Print Method:** Web offset. **Trim Size:** 10 x 10 3/4. **URL:** http://www.javamagaz.com. **Ad Rates:** BW $745; 4C $1,675. **Remarks:** Accepts advertising. **Circ:** Controlled 27,000.

954 ■ Jewish News of Greater Phoenix
Phoenix Jewish News Inc.
1625 E Northern Ave., Ste. 106
Phoenix, AZ 85020
Phone: (602)870-9470
Fax: (602)870-0426
Jewish community newspaper (tabloid). **Freq:** Weekly (Fri.). **Print Method:** Offset. **Trim Size:** 11 x 13 3/4. **Cols./Page:** 5. **Col. Width:** 22 nonpareils. **Col. Depth:** 175 agate lines. **Key Personnel:** Leisah Woldoff, Managing Editor; Becky Globokar, Manager, Production; Jaime Stern, Publisher. **ISSN:** 0747--444X (print). **Subscription Rates:** $99 Individuals three years; $79 Two years; $48 Individuals 1 year subscription. **URL:** http://www.jewishaz.com. **Formerly**: Greater Phoenix Jewish News. **Remarks:** Advertising accepted; rates available upon request. **Circ:** ‡7200.

955 ■ Journal of Medical Toxicology
American College of Medical Toxicology
10645 N Tatum Blvd., Ste. 200-111
Phoenix, AZ 85028
Phone: (623)533-6340
Fax: (623)533-6520
Publisher's E-mail: info@acmt.net
Journal advancing the science and practice of medical toxicology, a medical subspecialty focusing on the diagnosis, management, and prevention of poisoning/toxicity and other adverse health effects resulting from medications, chemicals, occupational and environmental substances, and biological hazards. **Freq:** Quarterly. **ISSN:** 1556--9039 (print); **EISSN:** 1937--6995 (electronic). **Subscription Rates:** $335 Institutions. **URL:** http://www.acmt.net/cgi/page.cgi/journals.html; http://www.springer.com/biomed/pharmacology+%26+toxicology/journal/13181. **Remarks:** Accepts advertising. **Circ:** (Not Reported).

956 ■ LOOKING FIT
Virgo Publishing L.L.C.
3300 N Central Ave., Ste. 300
Phoenix, AZ 85012-2501
Phone: (480)990-1101
Fax: (480)990-0819
Publisher's E-mail: cp.contracts@vpico.com
Magazine featuring news and information in the indoor tanning industry. **Key Personnel:** Karen Butler, Editor, Publisher, phone: (480)990-1101. **URL:** http://www.vpico.com/tanning.html. **Mailing address:** PO Box 40079, Phoenix, AZ 85067-0079. **Remarks:** Accepts advertising. **Circ:** (Not Reported).

957 ■ MAGAZine Newsletter
Maricopa Association of Governments
302 N 1st Ave., Ste. 300
Phoenix, AZ 85003
Phone: (602)254-6300
Fax: (602)254-6490
Magazine featuring updates on Maricopa Association of Governments issues. **Freq:** Quarterly. **Key Personnel:** Kelly Taft, Editor; Dennis Smith, Executive Director. **Subscription Rates:** Free. **URL:** http://www.azmag.gov/Projects/Project.asp?CMSID=1009&CMSID2=1111. **Formerly**: MAG Newsletter. **Remarks:** Advertising not accepted. **Circ:** (Not Reported).

958 ■ The Mini-Storage Messenger
Mini-Storage Messenger
2531 W Dunlap Ave.
Phoenix, AZ 85021
Free: 800-528-1056
Publisher's E-mail: info@minico.com
Magazine for the mini-storage trade. **Freq:** Monthly. **Print Method:** Offset. **Trim Size:** 8 1/2 x 11. **Cols./Page:** 3. **Col. Width:** 14 picas. **Col. Depth:** 59 picas. **Key Personnel:** Poppy Behrens, Publisher. **ISSN:** 0273--5822 (print). **Subscription Rates:** $21.95 Individuals online only; $59.95 Individuals print only; $69.95 Individuals print and online; $79 Canada and Mexico print only; $145 Other countries print only; $155.95 Other countries print and online. **Remarks:** Advertising accepted; rates available upon request. **Circ:** Paid 18000.

959 ■ National Pastime
Society for American Baseball Research
4455 E Camelback Rd., Ste. D140
Phoenix, AZ 85018-2847
Phone: (602)343-6455
Fax: (602)595-5690
Free: 800-969-7227
Publication covering sports and history. **Freq:** Annual. **Key Personnel:** Jim Charlton, Editor. **ISSN:** 0734--6905 (print). **Subscription Rates:** $14.95 Individuals. **Alt. Formats:** PDF. **URL:** http://sabr.org/about/publications; http://research.sabr.org/journals/archive/np. **Circ:** (Not Reported).

960 ■ PC AI Online: Where Intelligent Technology Meets the Real World
Knowledge Technology Inc.
PO Box 30130
Phoenix, AZ 85046-0130
Phone: (602)971-1869
Fax: (602)971-2321
Publisher's E-mail: info@pcai.com
Geared toward practical application of intelligent technology, covers developments in robotics, expert systems, neural networks, fuzzy logic, object-oriented development, languages and all other areas of artificial intelligence. **Freq:** Bimonthly. **Key Personnel:** Robin Okun, Managing Editor; Terry Hengl, Publisher. **ISSN:** 0894--0711 (print). **Subscription Rates:** $400 Individuals entire set. **Alt. Formats:** PDF. **URL:** http://www.pcai.com. **Remarks:** 0. **Circ:** Combined 10,000.

961 ■ PetSmart News
Media American Corporation for PetSmart Inc.
5555 N 7th Ave., Ste. B-200
Phoenix, AZ 85013-1755
Phone: (602)207-3750
Fax: (602)207-3777
Magazine about caring and raising companion animals. **Freq:** Monthly. **Print Method:** Offset. **Trim Size:** 8 x 10 3/4. **Cols./Page:** 3. **Col. Width:** 2 3/16 inches. **Col. Depth:** 9 9/16 inches. **Key Personnel:** Nancy Case, Editor; Burt Kennedy, Director; Michel le Powers, Manager, Advertising; Kay Morrow, Director; Winfield L. Holden, General Manager. **Ad Rates:** BW $24,310; 4C $29,170. **Remarks:** Accepts advertising. **Circ:** Controlled 1100000.

962 ■ Phoenix Clipper Marketplace
Echo Media
900 Circle 75 Pky., Ste. 1600
Atlanta, GA 30339
Phone: (770)955-3535
Fax: (770)955-3599
Publisher's E-mail: salesinfo@echo-media.com
Glossy coupon magazine. **Freq:** Monthly. **URL:** http://echomedia.com/medias/details/824. **Formerly**: Phoenix Value Clipper. **Remarks:** Accepts advertising. **Circ:** 750000.

963 ■ Phoenix Magazine
MAC America Communications Inc.
5555 N. 7th Ave.
Phoenix, AZ 85013
Phone: (602)207-3333
Fax: (602)207-3777
Magazine with local interest news, features, and style. **Founded:** 1966. **Freq:** Monthly. **Print Method:** Web Offset. **Trim Size:** 8 3/8 x 10 7/8. **Cols./Page:** 3. **Col. Width:** 13 picas. **Col. Depth:** 58 picas. **Subscription Rates:** $14.95 Individuals; $24 Two years. **URL:** http://www.phoenixmag.com/. **Formerly**: Phoenix Metro Magazine. **Ad Rates:** GLR $35; BW $3,725; 4C $5,495; PCI $145. **Remarks:** Accepts advertising. **Circ:** Paid 55097.

964 ■ Phoenix New Times
New Times Inc.
1201 E Jefferson
Phoenix, AZ 85034
Phone: (602)271-0040
Fax: (602)340-8806
Weekly newspaper serving as a comprehensive news, arts, entertainment, and restaurant guide for Phoenix. **Freq:** Weekly (Thurs.). **Print Method:** Offset. **Trim Size:** 10 x 12 7/8. **Cols./Page:** 8. **Col. Width:** 6.5 picas. **Col. Depth:** 77 picas. **Key Personnel:** Nate Richey, Manager, Production; Jennifer Meister, Director, Advertising; Rick Barrs, Editor; Amy Silverman, Managing Editor. **ISSN:** 0279--3962 (print). **Mailing address:** PO Box 2510, Phoenix, AZ 85034. **Remarks:** Advertising accepted; rates available upon request. **Circ:** (Not Reported).

965 ■ Phoenix Saguaro Gold
Echo Media
900 Circle 75 Pky., Ste. 1600
Atlanta, GA 30339
Phone: (770)955-3535
Fax: (770)955-3599
Publisher's E-mail: salesinfo@echo-media.com
Glossy coupon magazine. **Freq:** 7/year. **URL:** http://echomedia.com/medias/details/833. **Remarks:** Accepts advertising. **Circ:** (Not Reported).

966 ■ Phoenix TV y Mas
Echo Media
900 Circle 75 Pky., Ste. 1600
Atlanta, GA 30339
Phone: (770)955-3535
Fax: (770)955-3599
Publisher's E-mail: salesinfo@echo-media.com
Magazine covering advertising and distribution. **Freq:** Weekly (Fri.). **URL:** http://echomedia.com/medias/details/6031. **Remarks:** Accepts advertising. **Circ:** 90000.

967 ■ Professional Case Management
Wolters Kluwer Health Inc.
c/o Suzanne K. Powell, Ed.-in-Ch.
237 W Ridgecrest Rd.
Phoenix, AZ 85086
Phone: (623)465-0684
Fax: (623)465-0642
Publication E-mail: pcmjournal@aol.com
Peer-reviewed journal featuring best practices and industry benchmarks for the professional case manager. **Founded:** 1996. **Freq:** Bimonthly. **Trim Size:** 7 3/4 x 10 3/4. **Key Personnel:** Suzanne K. Powell, Editor-in-Chief. **ISSN:** 1932-8087 (print); **EISSN:** 1932-8095 (electronic). **Subscription Rates:** $124 Individuals print; $225 Other countries print; $410 Institutions print; $607 Institutions, other countries print; $72 Individuals in-training. **URL:** http://journals.lww.com/professionalcasemanagementjournal. **Formerly**: Lippincott's Case Management. **Ad Rates:** BW $1,830; 4C $945. **Remarks:** Accepts classified advertising. **Circ:** 10762.

968 ■ Scottsdale Independent
Independent Newspapers Inc.
23043 N 16th Ln.
Phoenix, AZ 85027
Community newspaper. **Freq:** Weekly (Wed.). **Print Method:** Offset. **Trim Size:** 13 x 21. **Cols./Page:** 6. **Col. Width:** 2 1/16 inches. **Col. Depth:** 21 1/2 inches. **Key Personnel:** Bret McKeand, Publisher. **Subscription Rates:** Free. **URL:** http://www.newszap.com/delmarvamediakit. **Formerly**: North Scottsdale Independent. **Ad Rates:** PCI $16.92. **Remarks:** Accepts advertising. **Circ:** Non-paid ♦**16679**.

969 ■ Sonoran Quarterly
Desert Botanical Garden
1201 N Galvin Pkwy.
Phoenix, AZ 85008
Phone: (480)941-1225
Fax: (480)481-8124

Free: 888-314-9480
Publisher's E-mail: administration@dbg.org
Freq: Quarterly. **ISSN:** 0735--8652 (print). **Subscription Rates:** Included in membership. **URL:** http://www.dbg.org/sonoran-quarterly. **Remarks:** Advertising not accepted. **Circ:** (Not Reported).

970 ■ Sports 'n Spokes
Paralyzed Veterans of America
2111 E Highland Ave., Ste. 180
Phoenix, AZ 85016-4732
Phone: (602)224-0500
Fax: (602)224-0507
Free: 888-888-2201
Publication E-mail: snsmagaz@aol.com
Magazine covering wheelchair sports and recreation news. **Founded:** May 1975. **Freq:** Bimonthly 8/year Jan, Mar, May, June, July, Sept, Nov and Dec. **Print Method:** Web. **Trim Size:** 8 1/8 x 10 7/8. **Cols./Page:** 3. **Col. Width:** 14 picas. **Col. Depth:** 9 5/8 inches. **Key Personnel:** Cliff Crase, Editor; Sherri Shea, Manager, Advertising. **ISSN:** 0161-6706 (print). **Subscription Rates:** $21 Individuals; $27 Other countries; $43 Canada and Mexico; $63 By mail. **URL:** http://www.pva.org. **Ad Rates:** BW $1072; 4C $1,795; PCI $45. **Remarks:** Accepts advertising. **Circ:** ‡14000.

971 ■ Swimming World Magazine: The World's Leading Independent Resource For Swimming
Sports Publications International Inc.
2744 E Glenrosa
Phoenix, AZ 85016
Phone: (602)522-0778
Fax: (602)522-0744
Free: 800-511-3029
Magazine that publishes swimming news, tips, and product reviews for competitive and fitness swimmers as well as their families and coaches. **Freq:** Monthly. **Trim Size:** 8 x 10-3/4. **Key Personnel:** Richard Deal, Chairman; Brent Rutemiller, Publisher; Jason Marsteller, Managing Editor. **Subscription Rates:** $39.95 Individuals print & premium; $59.95 Two years; $74.95 Individuals three years; $3.95 Individuals online; $29.95 Individuals print. **URL:** http://www.swimmingworldmagazine.com. **Ad Rates:** BW $1395; 4C $2235. **Remarks:** Accepts advertising. **Circ:** (Not Reported).

972 ■ TechConnect
Arizona Technology Council
2800 N Central Ave., Ste. 1920
Phoenix, AZ 85004
Phone: (602)343-8324
Publisher's E-mail: info@aztechcouncil.org
Magazine that covers issues and trends in the high technology industry in Arizona. **Freq:** Quarterly. **Key Personnel:** Don Rodriguez, Editor. **URL:** http://www.aztechcouncil.org/techconnect. **Ad Rates:** 4C $3,930. **Remarks:** Accepts advertising. **Circ:** ‡25000.

Town of Paradise Valley Independent - See Paradise Valley

973 ■ Wing World Magazine
Gold Wing Road Riders Association
21423 N 11th Ave.
Phoenix, AZ 85027-2813
Phone: (623)581-2500
Fax: (877)348-9416
Free: 800-843-9460
Publisher's E-mail: customerservice@gwrra.org
Freq: Monthly. **ISSN:** 0745--273X (print). **Subscription Rates:** $40 Individuals. **URL:** http://gwrra.org/magazine_subscribe.html. **Remarks:** Accepts advertising. **Circ:** (Not Reported).

974 ■ AZ-TV - 7
4343 E Camelback Rd., Ste. 130
Phoenix, AZ 85018
Phone: (602)977-7700
Fax: (602)224-2214
Email: programming@aztv.com
Format: Classical; Commercial TV. **Networks:** Fox; ABC. **Operating Hours:** Continuous. **Ad Rates:** Advertising accepted; rates available upon request. **URL:** http://www.aztv.com.

975 ■ Cable One Inc.
210 E Earll Dr.
Phoenix, AZ 85012
Fax: (602)364-6010
Email: user@cableone.net
Owner: Graham Holdings Co., 1300 N 17th St., 17th Fl., Arlington, VA 22209, Ph: (703)345-6300; Cable One Inc., 210 E Earll Dr., Phoenix, AZ 85012, Fax: (602)364-6010. **Founded:** Sept. 07, 2006. **Formerly:** Post-Newsweek Cable; Cablecom General; Capital Cities. **Key Personnel:** Thomas O. Might, CEO. **Cities Served:** Bisbee, Central Heights, Clifton, Miami, Morenci, Naco, Wheatfield, Arizona; Salmon, Idaho; Gulfport, Long Beach, Pass Christian, Mississippi: subscribing households 700,000; **Postal Areas Served:** 39507; 39560; 39571. **URL:** http://www.cableone.net.

976 ■ Cox Communication Inc.
PO Box 78071
Phoenix, AZ 85062-8071
Phone: (860)432-6000
Founded: 1982. **Formerly:** Dimension Cable. **Key Personnel:** F. William Farina, Sr. VP of Sales; Patrick J. Esser, President; Joseph J. Rooney, Sr. VP of Advertising, Sr. VP of Mktg.; William J. Fitzsimmons, Chief Acct. Ofc., Sr. VP of Fin.; Mark Greatrex, Sr. VP, Chief Mktg. Ofc.; Marilyn Burrows, Sr. VP; Jill Campbell, Exec. VP, COO. **Cities Served:** subscribing households 86,000. **URL:** http://cox.com.

977 ■ Indevideo Co. Inc.
PO Box 56339
Phoenix, AZ 85079
Phone: (602)248-8333
Fax: (602)248-0690
Free: 800-234-8333
Owner: Indevideo Co., Inc., at above address. **Founded:** 1972. **Cities Served:** Gisela, Grand Canyon, Leupp, Spring Valley, Tuba City, Tusayan, Arizona: subscribing households 2000; 51 channels; 1 community access channel; 28 hours per week community access programming.

978 ■ KAET-TV - 8
Arizona State University
555 N Central Ave., Ste. 500
Phoenix, AZ 85004-1252
Phone: (602)496-8888
Email: eight@asu.edu
Format: Public TV. **Networks:** Public Broadcasting Service (PBS). **Owner:** Arizona State University Board of Regents, 2020 N Central Ave., Ste. 230, Phoenix, AZ 85004-4593, Ph: (602)229-2500, Fax: (602)229-2555. **Founded:** 1961. **Operating Hours:** Continuous. **ADI:** Phoenix (Kingman, Prescott), AZ. **Wattage:** 316 KW E001RP. **Ad Rates:** Noncommercial. **URL:** http://www.asu.edu.

979 ■ KASA-AM
1445 W Baseline Rd.
Phoenix, AZ 85041
Phone: (602)276-5272
Fax: (602)276-8119
Format: Religious. **Networks:** Independent. **Owner:** Kasa Radio Hogar, Inc., Seattle, WA, Ph: (206)324-2000. **Founded:** 1966. **Key Personnel:** Donna R. Phelps, Contact; Tom Bogner, Contact. **Wattage:** 10,000 Day; 019 Night. **Ad Rates:** $6-8 for 30 seconds; $8-12 for 60 seconds.

980 ■ KASC-AM - 1260
555 N Central Ave., Ste. 302
Phoenix, AZ 85004
Phone: (602)496-5156
Format: Alternative/New Music/Progressive. **Owner:** Arizona State University, 1151 S Forest Ave. , Tempe, AZ 85287, Ph: (480)965-2100, Fax: (480)965-0076. **Founded:** Oct. 18, 1982. **Formerly:** KASR-AM. **Operating Hours:** Continuous. **Wattage:** 010. **Ad Rates:** Noncommercial. **URL:** http://www.blazeradioonline.com.

981 ■ KCKY-AM - 1150
1445 W Baseline Rd.
Phoenix, AZ 85041
Phone: (520)723-5448
Fax: (520)723-5961
Format: Sports; News; Talk. **Networks:** Mutual Broadcasting System. **Founded:** 1948. **Operating Hours:** 5:45 a.m.-midnight; 80% network, 20% local. **ADI:** Phoenix (Kingman, Prescott), AZ. **Key Personnel:** Bill Oostenburg, Contact. **Wattage:** 5,000 day; 1,000 night. **Ad Rates:** $10-16 for 30 seconds; $17-25 for 60 seconds.

982 ■ KDVA-FM - 106.9
501 N 44th St., Ste. 425
Phoenix, AZ 85008
Phone: (602)776-1400
Fax: (602)279-2921
Format: Hispanic. **Owner:** Entravision Communications Corporation, 2425 Olympic Blvd., Ste. 6000 W, Santa Monica, CA 90404-4030, Ph: (310)447-3870, Fax: (310)447-3899. **ADI:** Phoenix (Kingman, Prescott), AZ. **Key Personnel:** Walter F. Ulloa, Exec. Chmn. of the Bd., CEO; Karl Meyer, Exec. VP of Mktg.; Chris Moncayo, Exec. VP of Mktg. **URL:** http://www.entravision.com.

983 ■ KEDJ-FM
4745 N 7th St. No. 410
Phoenix, AZ 85014
Phone: (602)266-1360
Owner: Big City Radio, Inc., at above address, Fax: (602)263-4844. **Founded:** 1975. **Formerly:** KWAO-FM; KMZK-FM; KONC-FM. **Key Personnel:** Michael Mallace, Gen. Mgr., VP; Nancy Stevens, Dir. of Programs; Derk Chamberlin, Gen. Sales Mgr. **Ad Rates:** Accepts Advertising. **URL:** http://www.univision.com/.

984 ■ KESZ-FM - 99.9
4686 E Van Buren St., Ste. 300
Phoenix, AZ 85008
Phone: (602)374-6000
Format: Adult Contemporary. **Founded:** 1982. **Formerly:** KTWC-FM. **Operating Hours:** Continuous. **Key Personnel:** Jerry Ryan, Gen. Mgr.; Jeff England, Gen. Mgr; Beth McDonald, Contact, bethmcdonald@clearchannel.com. **Wattage:** 100,000. **Ad Rates:** Noncommercial. **URL:** http://www.kez999.com.

985 ■ KFLR-FM - 90.3
PO Box 35300
Tucson, AZ 85740
Free: 800-776-1070
Format: Religious. **Networks:** Moody Broadcasting. **Owner:** Family Life Communications, Inc., 7355 N Oracle Rd., Tucson, AZ 85704, Ph: (520)544-5950, Fax: (520)742-6979, Free: 800-776-1070. **Founded:** 1985. **Operating Hours:** Continuous; 25% network, 75% local. **ADI:** Phoenix (Kingman, Prescott), AZ. **Key Personnel:** Dr. Randy L. Carlson, President. **Wattage:** 3,900. **Ad Rates:** Noncommercial. **URL:** http://www.myflr.org.

986 ■ KFNN-AM - 1510
4800 N Central Ave.
Phoenix, AZ 85012
Phone: (602)241-1510
Fax: (602)241-1540
Free: 800-293-5366
Format: News. **Networks:** ABC; CNN Radio. **Owner:** CRC Broadcasting, at above address. **Founded:** 1988. **Formerly:** KJAA-AM. **Operating Hours:** Continuous. **ADI:** Phoenix (Kingman, Prescott), AZ. **Wattage:** 23,000. **Ad Rates:** $85-195 for 60 seconds. **URL:** http://www.moneyradio1510.com.

987 ■ KFNX-AM - 1100
2001 N 3rd St., Ste. 102
Phoenix, AZ 85004
Phone: (602)277-1100
Fax: (602)248-1478
Format: Talk; News. **Founded:** 2003. **Key Personnel:** Francis Battaglia, President, fbattaglia@1100kfnx.com; Matthew Battaglia, Bus. Mgr., mbattaglia@1100kfnx.com; Michael O'Connor, Dept. Head. **Ad Rates:** Noncommercial. **URL:** http://www.1100kfnx.com.

988 ■ KFYI-AM - 550
4686 E Van Burden St., Ste. 300
Phoenix, AZ 85008
Phone: (602)374-6000
Format: News; Talk. **Networks:** CBS. **Owner:** iHeartMedia Inc., 200 E Basse Rd., San Antonio, TX 78209, Ph: (210)832-3314. **Founded:** 1940. **Formerly:** KJJJ-AM. **Operating Hours:** Continuous. **ADI:** Phoenix (Kingman, Prescott), AZ. **Wattage:** 5,000. **Ad Rates:** Noncommercial. **URL:** http://www.kfyi.com.

989 ■ KGME-AM - 910
4686 E Van Buren St., Ste. 300
Phoenix, AZ 85008
Phone: (602)374-6000

Circulation: ★ = AAM; △ or • = BPA; ♦ = CAC; ❑ = VAC; ⊕ = PO Statement; ‡ = Publisher's Report; Boldface figures = sworn; Light figures = estimated.

Format: Sports. **Founded:** 1946. **Formerly**: KNNS-AM; KLFF-AM; KRUX-AM. **Operating Hours**: Continuous. **ADI**: Phoenix (Kingman, Prescott), AZ. **Wattage**: 50,000 Day; 1,000 Night. **Ad Rates:** Advertising accepted; rates available upon request. **URL:** http://www.foxsports910.com//main.html.

990 ■ KHOT-FM - 105.9
4745 N 7th St., Ste. 140
Phoenix, AZ 85014
Phone: (602)308-7900
Fax: (602)308-7979
Format: Hispanic. **Owner:** Univision Radio Inc., 3102 Oak Lawn Ave., Ste. 215, Dallas, TX 75219-4259, Ph: (214)525-7700, Fax: (214)525-7750. **ADI**: Phoenix (Kingman, Prescott), AZ. **Key Personnel:** Mary McEvilly Hernandez, Gen. Mgr.; Nelson Oseida, Dir. of Programs; Edgar Zambrano, Dir. of Production. **URL:** http://www.univision.com.

991 ■ KHOV-FM - 105.3
4745 N 7th St., Ste. 140
Phoenix, AZ 85014
Phone: (602)308-7900
Fax: (602)308-7979
Format: Hispanic. **Owner:** Univision Radio Inc., 3102 Oak Lawn Ave., Ste. 215, Dallas, TX 75219-4259, Ph: (214)525-7700, Fax: (214)525-7750. **Key Personnel:** Aide G. Gonzalez, Promotions Dir. **URL:** http://1059phoenix.univision.com.

992 ■ KIDR-AM - 740
3030 N Central Ave.
Phoenix, AZ 85012
Format: Hispanic; News; Talk. **Owner:** Multicultural Radio Broadcasting Inc., 27 William St., 11th Fl., New York, NY 10005, Ph: (212)966-1059, Fax: (212)966-9580. **Formerly**: KMEO-AM. **Operating Hours**: Continuous. **Key Personnel:** Dave Sweeney, Contact, daves@mrbi.net; Dave Sweeney, Contact, daves@mrbi.net. **Wattage**: 1,000. **Ad Rates:** $45 for 30 seconds. Combined advertising rates available with KQTL-AM. **URL:** http://enfamilia.org.

993 ■ KIHP-AM - 1310
3256 Penryn Rd., Ste. 100
Loomis, CA 95650-8052
Phone: (916)535-0500
Fax: (916)535-0504
Free: 888-887-7120
Format: Religious. **Networks:** ABC; Westwood One Radio. **Owner:** Immaculate Heart Radio, 3256 Penryn Rd., Ste. 100, Loomis, CA 95650-8052. **Founded:** 1946. **Formerly**: KXAM-AM. **Operating Hours**: Continuous. **ADI**: Phoenix (Kingman, Prescott), AZ. **Key Personnel:** Dick Jenkins, Gen. Mgr. **Wattage**: 5,000. **Ad Rates:** Noncommercial. **URL:** http://www.ihradio.com.

994 ■ KJAG-AM - 1640
5401 S 7th St.
Phoenix, AZ 85040
Phone: (602)764-5000
Format: Educational. **Key Personnel:** Ann Miles, Gen. Mgr. **URL:** http://www.phxhs.k12.az.us/education/staff/staff.php?sectionid=715.

995 ■ KKFR-FM - 98.3
4745 N 7th St., Ste. 410
Phoenix, AZ 85014
Phone: (602)648-9800
Fax: (602)283-0923
Format: Hip Hop; Urban Contemporary. **Networks:** CBS. **Owner:** Riviera Broadcast Group, at above address. **Founded:** 1979. **Operating Hours**: Continuous. **ADI**: Phoenix (Kingman, Prescott), AZ. **Key Personnel:** Deonne McBean, Contact, dmcbean@power983fm.com. **Wattage**: 100,000. **Ad Rates:** Advertising accepted; rates available upon request. **URL:** http://www.power983fm.com.

996 ■ KKNT-AM - 960
2425 E Camelback Rd., Ste. 570
Phoenix, AZ 85016
Phone: (602)955-9600
Fax: (602)955-7860
Format: News; Talk. **Founded:** 1947. **ADI**: Phoenix (Kingman, Prescott), AZ. **Key Personnel:** Heath Garlutzo, Dir. of Sales; Diane Johnson, Bus. Mgr. **URL:** http://www.kknt960.com.

997 ■ KLNZ-FM - 103.5
501 N 44th St., Ste. 425
Phoenix, AZ 85008
Phone: (602)776-1400
Fax: (602)279-2921
Free: 866-560-5673
Format: Hispanic. **Owner:** Entravision Communications Corporation, 2425 Olympic Blvd., Ste. 6000 W, Santa Monica, CA 90404-4030, Ph: (310)447-3870, Fax: (310)447-3899. **ADI**: Phoenix (Kingman, Prescott), AZ. **Key Personnel:** Chris Moncayo, Gen. Mgr., Gen. Sales Mgr. **URL:** http://www.entravision.com.

998 ■ KLVA-FM - 105.5
PO Box 2098
Omaha, NE 68103
Free: 800-434-8400
Email: info@klove.com
Format: Contemporary Christian. **Networks:** Independent. **Owner:** Educational Media Foundation, 5700 W Oaks Blvd., CA 95765, Free: 800-800434-8400. **Operating Hours**: Continuous. **Wattage**: 50,000. **Ad Rates:** Noncommercial. **URL:** http://www.klove.com.

999 ■ KMIK-AM - 1580
4020 N 20th St.
Phoenix, AZ 85016
Phone: (917)612-5693
Format: Contemporary Hit Radio (CHR). **Ad Rates:** Noncommercial.

1000 ■ KMLE-FM - 107.9
840 N Central Ave.
Phoenix, AZ 85004
Phone: (602)452-1000
Fax: (602)440-6530
Format: Contemporary Country. **Owner:** CBS Radio Inc., 1271 Avenue of the Americas, 44th Fl., New York, NY 10020-1401, Ph: (212)649-9600. **Founded:** 1980. **Operating Hours**: Continuous; 100% local. **Wattage**: 96,000. **Ad Rates:** Advertising accepted; rates available upon request. **URL:** http://kmle1079.cbslocal.com.

1001 ■ KMVA-FM - 97.5
4747 N Seventh St., Ste. 424
Phoenix, AZ 85014
Phone: (602)222-9750
Fax: (602)222-2297
Format: Urban Contemporary. **ADI**: Phoenix (Kingman, Prescott), AZ.

1002 ■ KMVP-AM - 860
5300 N Central Ave.
Phoenix, AZ 85012-1410
Phone: (602)274-6200
Format: Sports. **Owner:** Bonneville International Corp., 55 North 300 West, Salt Lake City, UT 84101-3502, Ph: (801)575-7500. **Key Personnel:** Paul Ihander, Div. Dir.; Ryan Hatch, VP of Operations; Jessica Webb, VP of Sales; Scott Sutherland, VP, Mktg. Mgr. **URL:** http://arizonasports.com.

1003 ■ KMXP-FM - 96.9
4686 E Van Buren St., Ste. 300
Phoenix, AZ 85008
Phone: (602)374-6000
Format: Adult Contemporary. **Formerly**: KMEO-FM; KPSN-FM. **ADI**: Phoenix (Kingman, Prescott), AZ. **Wattage**: 98,000. **Ad Rates:** Advertising accepted; rates available upon request. **URL:** http://www.mix969.com.

1004 ■ KNAI-FM - 88.3
3602 W Thomas Rd., Ste. 6
Phoenix, AZ 85019
Format: Educational. **Simulcasts:** KCEC 104.5, KRCW 96.3, KMYX 92.5, KSEA 107.9, KUFW 90.5. **Owner:** Radio Campesina Network, at above address, Ph: (602)269-3121, Fax: (602)269-3020. **Founded:** 1996. **Operating Hours**: 8a.m.-5p.m. . **ADI**: Phoenix (Kingman, Prescott), AZ. **Wattage**: 22,500. **Ad Rates:** Advertising accepted; rates available upon request.

1005 ■ KNIX-FM - 102.5
4686 E Van Buren St., Ste. 300
Phoenix, AZ 85008
Phone: (602)374-6000
Format: Full Service; Country. **ADI**: Phoenix (Kingman, Prescott), AZ. **Wattage**: 98,000. **Ad Rates:** Advertising accepted; rates available upon request. **URL:** http://www.knixcountry.com.

1006 ■ KNUV-AM - 1190
1601 N 7th St., Ste. 310
Phoenix, AZ 85006
Phone: (602)433-6244
Fax: (602)759-1776
Format: Hispanic. **Networks:** Westwood One Radio. **Owner:** New Radio Venture, at above address. **Founded:** 1979. **Formerly**: KMYL-AM. **Operating Hours**: Continuous; 50% network, 50% local. **Key Personnel:** Ulises Ortez, Contact. **Wattage**: 5,000 Day; 250 Night. **Ad Rates:** $25-40 for 30 seconds; $45-65 for 60 seconds. **URL:** http://www.1190-am.com.

1007 ■ KNXV-TV - 15
515 N 44th St.
Phoenix, AZ 85008
Phone: (602)685-6397
Fax: (602)685-6363
Format: Commercial TV. **Networks:** ABC. **Owner:** The E. W. Scripps Co., 312 Walnut St., Cincinnati, OH 45202, Ph: (513)977-3000. **Founded:** 1979. **Operating Hours**: Continuous. **ADI**: Phoenix (Kingman, Prescott), AZ. **Ad Rates:** Noncommercial. **URL:** http://www.abc15.com.

1008 ■ KOMR-FM - 106.3
4745 N 7th St., Ste. 140
Phoenix, AZ 85014
Phone: (602)308-7900
Fax: (602)308-7979
Owner: Univision Communication Inc., 3102 Oak Lawn Ave., Ste. 215, Dallas, TX 75219, Fax: (214)525-7750. **Wattage**: 23,000 ERP.

1009 ■ KOOL-FM - 94.5
840 N Central
Phoenix, AZ 85004
Phone: (602)260-9494
Fax: (602)440-6530
Format: Oldies. **Owner:** CBS Radio Inc., 40 W 57th St., New York, NY 10019, Ph: (212)846-3939, Fax: (212)315-2162. **Founded:** 1956. **Operating Hours**: Continuous. **ADI**: Phoenix (Kingman, Prescott), AZ. **Key Personnel:** Jeff Garrison, Contact, jeff.garrison@cbsradio.com; Karla Kruz, Contact, sunday@cbsradiophoenix.com; Jeff Garrison, Contact, jeff.garrison@cbsradio.com; Chris Crawford, Contact, chris.crawford@cbsradio.com. **Wattage**: 95,600. **Ad Rates:** KMLE KZON. **URL:** http://www.kool.cbslocal.com.

1010 ■ KOY-AM - 1230
4686 E Van Buren St., Ste. 300
Phoenix, AZ 85008
Phone: (602)374-6000
Format: Big Band/Nostalgia. **Networks:** CNN Radio; Unistar. **Owner:** iHeartMedia Inc., 200 E Basse Rd., San Antonio, TX 78209, Ph: (210)832-3314. **Founded:** 1921. **Operating Hours**: Continuous. **ADI**: Phoenix (Kingman, Prescott), AZ. **Wattage**: 5,000 Day; 1,000 Night. **Ad Rates:** Advertising accepted; rates available upon request. **URL:** http://www.kfyi2.com//main.html.

1011 ■ KPAZ-TV - 21
3551 E McDowell Rd.
Phoenix, AZ 85008
Phone: (602)273-1477
Format: Commercial TV. **Operating Hours**: Continuous. **ADI**: Phoenix (Kingman, Prescott), AZ. **Key Personnel:** Oralena Valero, Contact. **Ad Rates:** Noncommercial. **URL:** http://www.tbn.org.

1012 ■ KPHE-TV - 44
2412 E University Dr.
Phoenix, AZ 85034
Phone: (602)220-9944
Email: info@kphetv.com
Owner: Lotus Communications Corp., 3301 Barham Blvd., Ste. 200, Los Angeles, CA 90068, Ph: (323)512-2225, Fax: (323)512-2224. **URL:** http://www.kphetv.com.

1013 ■ KPHF-FM - 88.3
290 Hegenberger Rd.
Oakland, CA 94621
Free: 800-543-1495
Email: familyradio@familyradio.org
Format: Religious. **Owner:** Family Stations Inc., 290 Hegenberger Rd., Oakland, CA 94621, Free: 800-543-1495. **URL:** http://www.familyradio.org.

1014 ■ KPHO-TV - 5
4016 N Black Canyon Hwy.
Phoenix, AZ 85017

Phone: (602)264-1000
Format: Commercial TV. **Networks:** Independent; CBS. **Owner:** Meredith Corp., 1716 Locust St., Des Moines, IA 50309-3038, Ph: (515)284-3000. **Founded:** 1949. **Operating Hours**: Continuous. **ADI**: Phoenix (Kingman, Prescott), AZ. **Key Personnel:** Steve Hammel, Contact. **Ad Rates:** Noncommercial. **URL:** http://www.kpho.com.

1015 ■ KPHX-AM - 1480
824 E Washington St.
Phoenix, AZ 85034
Phone: (602)257-1351
Format: Talk; News. **Networks:** UPI. **Owner:** All Comedy Networks. **Founded:** 1958. **Operating Hours**: Continuous. **ADI**: Phoenix (Kingman, Prescott), AZ. **Wattage**: 5,000. **Ad Rates:** Advertising accepted; rates available upon request. **URL:** http://www.1480kphx.com.

1016 ■ KPKX-FM - 98.7
5300 N Central Ave.
Phoenix, AZ 85012
Format: Adult Contemporary. **Networks:** Independent. **Owner:** Bonneville International Corp., 55 North 300 West, Salt Lake City, UT 84101-3502, Ph: (801)575-7500. **Founded:** 1960. **Formerly**: KKLT-FM. **Operating Hours**: Continuous. **ADI**: Phoenix (Kingman, Prescott), AZ. **Wattage**: 115,000 ERP. **Ad Rates:** Advertising accepted; rates available upon request. **URL:** http://www.bonneville.com.

1017 ■ KPNX-TV - 12
200 E Van Buren
Phoenix, AZ 85004
Phone: (602)257-1212
Free: 800-331-9303
Email: sales@12news.com
Format: Commercial TV. **Networks:** NBC. **Owner:** Gannett Company Inc., 7950 Jones Branch Dr., McLean, VA 22107-0150, Ph: (703)854-6089. **Founded:** 1953. **Formerly**: KTYL-TV. **Operating Hours**: Continuous; 60% network, 40% local. **ADI**: Phoenix (Kingman, Prescott), AZ. **Key Personnel:** Chip Hale, Mgr. **Ad Rates:** Advertising accepted; rates available upon request. **URL:** http://www.azcentral.com/?from=global&sessionKey=&autologin=.

1018 ■ KPXQ-AM - 1360
2425 E Camelback Rd.
Phoenix, AZ 85016
Format: Contemporary Christian. **Owner:** Salem Media Group Inc., 4880 Santa Rosa Rd., Camarillo, CA 93012, Ph: (805)987-0400, Fax: (805)384-4520. **Formerly**: KOOL-AM; KARL-AM. **Operating Hours**: Continuous. **ADI**: Phoenix (Kingman, Prescott), AZ. **Wattage**: 50,000 Day; 1,000 Night. **Ad Rates:** $49-105 for 60 seconds. **URL:** http://kpxq1360.com.

1019 ■ KQEZ-FM - 103.9
4745 N 7th St., Ste. 410
Phoenix, AZ 85014
Phone: (602)898-8881
Format: Country; Hot Country; News. **Networks:** Independent. **Owner:** Scott Chistenson, PO Box 1437, Coolidge, AZ 85228, Ph: (602)391-9859. **Founded:** 1981. **Operating Hours**: Continuous. **ADI**: Phoenix (Kingman, Prescott), AZ. **Key Personnel:** Tim Rapp, Contact; Tim Rapp, Contact; Cindy Farris, Contact; Hank Calhane, Contact. **Wattage**: 99,590 ERP. **Ad Rates:** $4-24 for 30 seconds; $6-26 for 60 seconds. **URL:** http://hot975phoenix.com.

1020 ■ KQMR-FM - 100.3
4745 N 7th St., Ste. 140
Phoenix, AZ 85014
Phone: (602)308-7900
Fax: (602)308-7979
Format: Hispanic. **ADI**: Phoenix (Kingman, Prescott), AZ. **Key Personnel:** Robbie Ramirez, Dir. of Programs; Edgar Zambrano, Dir. of Production. **URL:** http://1063masvariedad.univision.com.

1021 ■ KSAZ-TV - 10
511 W Adams St.
Phoenix, AZ 85003-1608
Phone: (602)257-1234
Format: Commercial TV. **Networks:** Fox. **Owner:** Fox Television Stations Inc., 1211 Ave. of the Americas, 21st Fl., New York, NY 10036, Ph: (212)301-5400. **Founded:** 1953. **Formerly**: KTSP-TV; KOOL-TV. **Operating Hours**: Continuous. **ADI**: Phoenix (Kingman, Prescott), AZ. **Key Personnel:** Michael Miller, Contact. **Ad Rates:** Advertising accepted; rates available upon request. **URL:** http://www.fox10phoenix.com.

1022 ■ KSUN-AM - 1400
714 N Third St.
Phoenix, AZ 85004
Phone: (602)252-0030
Fax: (602)252-4211
Format: Adult Contemporary; Hispanic. **Networks:** Independent. **Owner:** Radio Fiesta Inc., 714 3rd St., Phoenix, AZ 85004, Ph: (602)252.0030. **Founded:** 1986. **Operating Hours**: Continuous. **ADI**: Phoenix (Kingman, Prescott), AZ. **Wattage**: 1,000. **Ad Rates:** $15-45 for 30 seconds; $25-60 for 60 seconds. **URL:** http://www.lamejor1400.wix.com.

1023 ■ KTAR-AM - 620
7740 N 16th St., Ste. 200
Phoenix, AZ 85020
Phone: (602)274-6200
Format: News; Talk; Sports. **Networks:** ABC; AP. **Owner:** Bonneville International Corp., 55 North 300 West, Salt Lake City, UT 84101-3502, Ph: (801)575-7500. **Founded:** 1922. **Operating Hours**: Continuous. **ADI**: Phoenix (Kingman, Prescott), AZ. **Key Personnel:** Jessica Webb, Gen. Sales Mgr., jwebb@ktar.com. **Local Programs**: *Arizona's Morning News*, Monday Tuesday Wednesday Thursday Friday 5:00 a.m. - 9:00 a.m.; *Rosie on the House*, Saturday 7:00 a.m. - 11:00 a.m. **Wattage**: 5,000 Day; 1,000 Night. **Ad Rates:** Advertising accepted; rates available upon request. **URL:** http://ktar.com.

1024 ■ KTAR-FM - 92.3
7740 N 16th St., Ste. 200
Phoenix, AZ 85020
Phone: (602)274-6200
Fax: (602)266-3858
Format: Talk; News. **Operating Hours**: Continuous. **Key Personnel:** Ryan Hatch, VP, rhatch@ktar.com; Scott Sutherland, VP, Mktg. Mgr.; Paul Ihander, News Dir.; Jessica Webb, VP of Sales. **Ad Rates:** Advertising accepted; rates available upon request. **URL:** http://www.ktar.com.

1025 ■ KTVK-TV - 3
5555 N 7th Ave.
Phoenix, AZ 85013
Phone: (602)207-3333
Fax: (602)207-3477
Email: feedback@azfamily.com
Format: News. **Owner:** KTVK Inc., 5555 N 7th Ave., Phoenix, AZ 85013, Ph: (602)207-3333, Fax: (602)207-3308. **Founded:** 1955. **Operating Hours**: Continuous. **Key Personnel:** Lea-Ann Clement, Dir. of HR. **Ad Rates:** Advertising accepted; rates available upon request. Combined advertising rates available with KASW-TV. **URL:** http://www.azfamily.com.

1026 ■ KTVW-TV - 33
6006 30th St.
Phoenix, AZ 85042
Phone: (310)348-3600
Format: Commercial TV; Ethnic. **Networks:** Univision. **Founded:** Sept. 1979. **Operating Hours**: Continuous;. **ADI**: Phoenix (Kingman, Prescott), AZ. **Key Personnel:** Tom Kioski, Production Mgr.; Virginia Luna, Dir. of Programs. **URL:** http://www.univision.com.

1027 ■ KUTP-TV - 45
511 W Adams St.
Phoenix, AZ 85003
Phone: (602)257-1234
Format: Commercial TV. **Networks:** United Paramount Network. **Owner:** Fox/UTV Holdings Inc., 11358 Viking Dr, Eden Prairie, MN 55344, Ph: (952)946-5767. **Founded:** 1985. **Operating Hours**: Continuous; 100% local. **ADI**: Phoenix (Kingman, Prescott), AZ. **Ad Rates:** Advertising accepted; rates available upon request. **URL:** http://www.my45.com.

1028 ■ KVJC-FM - 91.1
PO Box 391
Twin Falls, ID 83303
Fax: (208)736-1958
Free: 800-357-4226
Format: Religious; Contemporary Christian. **Owner:** CSN International, PO Box 391, Twin Falls, ID 83303, Ph: (208)736-1958, Fax: (208)736-1958, Free: 800-357-4226. **Key Personnel:** Mike Kestler, Contact. **URL:** http://www.csnradio.com.

1029 ■ KVVA-FM - 107.1
501 N 44th St., Ste. 125
Phoenix, AZ 85008
Phone: (602)776-1400
Fax: (602)279-2921
Format: Hispanic; Adult Contemporary. **Owner:** Z-Spanish Radio Network, 1436 Auburn Blvd., Sacramento, CA 95815, Ph: (916)646-4000. **Founded:** 1983. **Formerly**: KSTM-FM. **Operating Hours**: Continuous; 100% local. **ADI**: Phoenix (Kingman, Prescott), AZ. **Key Personnel:** Ricardo Torres, Gen. Mgr; Veronica Ortiz, Contact. **Wattage**: 25,000. **Ad Rates:** Advertising accepted; rates available upon request. **URL:** http://www.josephoenix.com.

1030 ■ KXEG-AM - 1280
4020 N 20th St.
Phoenix, AZ 85008
Phone: (602)296-3600
Fax: (602)296-3624
Format: Contemporary Christian; Gospel; Religious. **Networks:** Mid-America Gospel. **Founded:** 1962. **Operating Hours**: Continuous. **Key Personnel:** Richard Dugan, Contact; Jess Spurgin, Dir. of Sales, jspurgin@communicon.com; Richard Dugan, Contact. **URL:** http://www.1280kxeg.com.

1031 ■ KXXT-AM - 1010
2425 E Camelback Rd., Ste. 570
Phoenix, AZ 85016
Phone: (602)296-3600
Fax: (602)955-7860
Format: Contemporary Christian. **Owner:** Communicom Broadcasting. **Key Personnel:** Ramon Bonilla, Contact, rbonilla@communicom.com. **Ad Rates:** Noncommercial. **URL:** http://www.1280kxeg.com.

1032 ■ KYOT-FM - 95.5
4686 E Van Buren St., Ste. 300
Phoenix, AZ 85008
Phone: (602)374-6000
Format: Jazz. **Networks:** Independent. **Founded:** 1963. **Formerly**: KOY-FM. **Operating Hours**: Continuous. **ADI**: Phoenix (Kingman, Prescott), AZ. **Key Personnel:** Tom Duran, Sales Mgr., tomduran@clearchannel.com. **Wattage**: 96,000. **Ad Rates:** Advertising accepted; rates available upon request. **URL:** http://www.955themountain.com.

1033 ■ KZON-FM - 101.5
840 N Central Ave.
Phoenix, AZ 85004
Phone: (602)452-1000
Fax: (602)440-6530
Format: Contemporary Hit Radio (CHR); Top 40. **Networks:** Radio-Radio. **Owner:** CBS Radio Inc., 40 W 57th St., New York, NY 10019, Ph: (212)846-3939, Fax: (212)315-2162. **Founded:** 1964. **Formerly**: KAMJ-FM; KMXX-FM. **Operating Hours**: Continuous. **ADI**: Phoenix (Kingman, Prescott), AZ. **Wattage**: 100,000. **Ad Rates:** $200-500 for 60 seconds. KKFR-AM. **URL:** http://www.live1015phoenix.cbslocal.com.

1034 ■ KZZP-FM - 104.7
4686 E Van Buren St., Ste. 300
Phoenix, AZ 85008
Phone: (602)374-6000
Format: Contemporary Hit Radio (CHR). **Networks:** American Public Radio (APR). **Founded:** 1976. **Formerly**: KZZP-AM; KVRY-FM. **Operating Hours**: Continuous. **ADI**: Phoenix (Kingman, Prescott), AZ. **Wattage**: 100,000. **Ad Rates:** Advertising accepted; rates available upon request. **URL:** http://www.1047kissfm.com.

1035 ■ Qwest Choice TV
20 E Thomas Rd., 11th Fl.
Phoenix, AZ 85012
Founded: Sept. 07, 2006. **Cities Served:** 25 channels. **URL:** http://www.qwest.com/vdsl/phoenix.

PINETOP

Navajo Co. (SE). Part of Pinetop-Lakeside.

1036 ■ K219CG-FM - 102.1
PO Box 391
Twin Falls, ID 83303

Circulation: ★ = AAM; △ or • = BPA; ◆ = CAC; ❑ = VAC; ⊕ = PO Statement; ‡ = Publisher's Report; Boldface figures = sworn; Light figures = estimated.

Phone: (208)733-3133
Format: Religious; Contemporary Christian; News. **Owner:** CSN International, PO Box 391, Twin Falls, ID 83303, Ph: (208)736-1958, Fax: (208)736-1958, Free: 800-357-4226. **URL:** http://www.csnradio.com.

PRESCOTT

Yavapai Co. Yavapai Co. (C). 90 m NW of Phoenix. Tourism. Prescott National Forest.

1037 ■ The Daily Courier
Prescott Newspapers Inc.
PO Box 312
Prescott, AZ 86302
Phone: (928)445-3333
Publisher's E-mail: jgrimaldi@prescottaz.com
General newspaper. **Founded:** 1882. **Freq:** Daily and Sun. (eve.). **Print Method:** Offset. **Trim Size:** 13 3/4 x 22 5/8. **Cols./Page:** 6. **Col. Width:** 26 nonpareils. **Col. Depth:** 21 1/2 inches. **Key Personnel:** Kelly Soldwedel, Chief Executive Officer, Publisher; Tim Wiederaenders, Editor. **Subscription Rates:** $14 Individuals 4 weeks; $28 Individuals 8 weeks; $40.47 Individuals 12 weeks; $86.45 Individuals 26 weeks; $167.44 Individuals 52 weeks. **URL:** http://www.dcourier.com/index.asp. **Ad Rates:** BW $1,184.22; 4C $1,544.22; SAU $9.18. **Remarks:** Accepts advertising. **Circ:** Mon.-Sat. 17000.

1038 ■ Handloader: Ammunition Reloading Journal
Wolfe Publishing Co.
2180 Gulfstream, Ste. A
Prescott, AZ 86301
Phone: (928)445-7810
Fax: (928)778-5124
Free: 800-899-7810
Publisher's E-mail: circ@riflemag.com
Magazine covering ammunition handloading. **Freq:** Bimonthly. **Print Method:** Web. **Trim Size:** 8 1/8 x 10 7/8. **Cols./Page:** 3. **Col. Width:** 27 nonpareils. **Col. Depth:** 140 agate lines. **ISSN:** 0017--7393 (print). **Subscription Rates:** $22.97 Individuals. **Alt. Formats:** DVD; PDF. **URL:** http://www.riflemagazine.com/magazine/index.cfm?magid=701. **Ad Rates:** BW $2926; 4C $3745; PCI $91. **Remarks:** Accepts advertising. **Circ:** ‡150000.

1039 ■ Reader's Digest
Trusted Media Brands, Inc.
PO Box 50005
Prescott, AZ 86301-5005
General interest non-fiction magazine. **Founded:** 1922. **Freq:** Monthly. **Print Method:** Offset. **Trim Size:** 5 3/8 x 7 7/16. **Cols./Page:** 2. **Col. Width:** 12.5 picas. **Col. Depth:** 42 agate lines. **Key Personnel:** Peggy Northrop, Editor. **Subscription Rates:** $10 Individuals; $15 Two years. **URL:** http://www.rd.com. **Ad Rates:** BW $216,400; 4C $185,300. **Remarks:** Accepts advertising. **Circ:** Paid ‡5500000.

1040 ■ Rifle: The Sporting Firearms Journal
Wolfe Publishing Co.
2180 Gulfstream, Ste. A
Prescott, AZ 86301
Phone: (928)445-7810
Fax: (928)778-5124
Free: 800-899-7810
Publisher's E-mail: circ@riflemag.com
Covers all types of rifles-centerfires, rimfires, air rifles and muzzle loaders. **Freq:** Bimonthly. **Print Method:** Offset. **Trim Size:** 8 1/8 x 10 7/8. **Cols./Page:** 3. **Col. Width:** 27 nonpareils. **Col. Depth:** 140 agate lines. **Key Personnel:** Mark Harris, Associate Publisher; Don Polacek, Publisher; Dave Scovill, Editor-in-Chief. **ISSN:** 0162--3583 (print). **Subscription Rates:** $19.97 Individuals. **URL:** http://www.riflemagazine.com/magazine/index.cfm?magid=702. **Ad Rates:** BW $3150, full page; BW $1901, half page; 4C $3839, full page; 4C $2679, half page. **Remarks:** Accepts advertising. **Circ:** ‡95000.

1041 ■ Successful Hunter
Wolfe Publishing Co.
2180 Gulfstream, Ste. A
Prescott, AZ 86301
Phone: (928)445-7810
Fax: (928)778-5124
Free: 800-899-7810
Publication E-mail: editor@riflemag.com
Magazine featuring hunting tips and techniques, product reviews, and interviews. **Freq:** Bimonthly. **Key Personnel:** Dave Scovill, Editor-in-Chief; Lee J. Hoots, Editor; Roberta Scovill, Managing Editor. **ISSN:** 1541--6249 (print). **Subscription Rates:** $19.97 Individuals. **URL:** http://www.riflemagazine.com. **Ad Rates:** BW $3342; 4C $4074. **Remarks:** Accepts advertising. **Circ:** (Not Reported).

1042 ■ KDDL-FM - 94.3
3755 Karicio Ln., Ste. 2C
Prescott, AZ 86303
Phone: (928)445-8289
Free: 800-264-5449
Format: Country. **Founded:** 1985. **Ad Rates:** Advertising accepted; rates available upon request. **Mailing address:** PO Box 26523, Prescott Valley, AZ 86312. **URL:** http://www.cattlecountryradio.com.

1043 ■ KGCB-FM - 90.9
3741 Karicio Ln.
Prescott, AZ 86303
Phone: (928)776-0909
Fax: (928)776-1736
Free: 800-720-0909
Email: info@arizonashine.org
Format: Contemporary Christian. **Founded:** 1994. **Operating Hours:** Continuous. **Key Personnel:** Steve White, Gen. Mgr., VP. **Wattage:** 58,000. **Ad Rates:** Noncommercial. **URL:** http://www.kgcb.org.

1044 ■ KJZA-FM
923 E Gurley St.
Prescott, AZ 86301
Phone: (928)541-1008
Format: Public Radio. **Wattage:** 250 ERP. **URL:** http://www.kjza.com.

1045 ■ KNOT-AM - 1450
116 S Alto
Prescott, AZ 86301
Phone: (928)445-6880
Fax: (928)445-6852
Format: Oldies. **Networks:** ABC. **Owner:** Guyann Corp., at above address. **Operating Hours:** Continuous. **ADI:** Phoenix (Kingman, Prescott), AZ. **Wattage:** 1,000. **Ad Rates:** Advertising accepted; rates available upon request. Combined advertising rates available with KTMG-FM. **URL:** http://www.funoldies.gcmaz.com.

1046 ■ KPPV-FM - 106.7
3755 Karicio Ln., Ste. 2C
Prescott, AZ 86303
Phone: (928)445-8289
Free: 800-374-5888
Email: contact@kppv.com
Format: Adult Contemporary. **Networks:** Fox. **Founded:** Sept. 01, 1985. **Formerly:** KIHX. **Operating Hours:** Continuous; 10% network; 90% local. **ADI:** Phoenix (Kingman, Prescott), AZ. **Key Personnel:** Sanford Cohen, President. **Wattage:** 50,000 ERP. **Ad Rates:** $20-26 per unit. Combined advertising rates available with KQNA-AM. **URL:** http://www.kppv.com.

1047 ■ KTMG-FM - 99.1
116 S Alto
Prescott, AZ 86301
Phone: (928)445-6880
Fax: (928)445-6852
Format: Adult Contemporary. **Networks:** ABC. **Owner:** Guyann Corp., at above address. **Founded:** 1977. **Operating Hours:** 10% network; 90% local. **ADI:** Phoenix (Kingman, Prescott), AZ. **Wattage:** 6,000. **Ad Rates:** Advertising accepted; rates available upon request. Combined advertising rates available with KNOT-AM.

1048 ■ KUSK-TV - 7
3211 Tower Rd.
Prescott, AZ 86305
Phone: (928)778-6770
Fax: (928)445-5210
Email: team@kusk.com
Format: Commercial TV. **Networks:** Independent. **Owner:** KUSK, Inc, at above address. **Founded:** 1982. **Operating Hours:** Continuous. **Key Personnel:** Arnold Corella, Production Mgr; Richard C. Howe, Contact, rich@kusk.com; Patricia Gray, Contact, pat@kusk.com. **Wattage:** 8,700. **Ad Rates:** $20-250 per unit. **URL:** http://www.aztv.com.

1049 ■ KYCA-AM
PO Box 1631
Prescott, AZ 86302
Phone: (602)445-1700
Format: News; Sports; Talk. **Networks:** CBS; Mutual Broadcasting System; Wall Street Journal Radio. **Founded:** 1940. **Wattage:** 1,000.

PRESCOTT VALLEY

Yavapai Co. Yavapai Co.

1050 ■ The Journal of Educational Technology Development and Exchange
Society of International Chinese in Educational Technology
c/o Dr. Hong Zhan, Treasurer
7200 E Pioneer Ln.
Prescott Valley, AZ 86314
Phone: (928)523-0408
Fax: (928)523-1929
Journal providing a multidisciplinary forum and focal points for SICET members with the aim of aiding the needs of Chinese scholars and experts in education technology. **Freq:** Quarterly. **ISSN:** 1941--8027 (print). **URL:** http://sicet.org/web/journals/jetde/jetde.html; http://tnet1.ioe.tsinghua.edu.cn/evaluate/index.do?groupId=3. **Remarks:** Advertising not accepted. **Circ:** (Not Reported).

1051 ■ Prescott Valley Tribune
Western News & Info Inc.
8307 State Rte. 69
Prescott Valley, AZ 86314
Newspaper. **Freq:** Weekly (Wed.). **Key Personnel:** Kelly Soldwedel, Publisher. **Subscription Rates:** $260 Individuals; $130 Individuals 26 weeks; $60 Individuals 12 weeks; $40 Individuals 8 weeks. **URL:** http://pvtrib.com. **Remarks:** Accepts advertising. **Circ:** (Not Reported).

1052 ■ KQNA-AM - 1130
PO Box 26523
Prescott Valley, AZ 86312
Phone: (928)445-8289
Email: talkofthetown@kqna.com
Format: Talk; News; Sports. **Owner:** Prescott Valley Broadcasting Company Inc., at above address. **Founded:** June 26, 1986. **Operating Hours:** Sunrise-sunset. **Wattage:** 1,000. **Ad Rates:** Noncommercial. **URL:** http://www.kqna.com.

QUARTZSITE

La Paz Co. LaPaz Co. (SW). 60 m NE of Yuma.

1053 ■ KBUX-FM - 94.3
101 W Camel St.
Quartzsite, AZ 85346
Phone: (928)927-5111
Format: Oldies; Music of Your Life; News. **Founded:** 1988. **Operating Hours:** Continuous. **Wattage:** 3,000 ERP. **Ad Rates:** Advertising accepted; rates available upon request. $3-7.50 for 30 seconds; $5-10 for 60 seconds. **Mailing address:** PO Box 1, Quartzsite, AZ 85346. **URL:** http://www.kbuxradio.com.

SAFFORD

Graham Co. Graham Co. (SE). 85 m NE of Tucson. Copper.Stock, poultry, grain farms. Cotton, cattle.

1054 ■ KCUZ-AM - 1490
301B E Hwy. 70
Safford, AZ 85546
Phone: (928)428-0916
Fax: (928)428-7797
Format: Classic Rock. **Simulcasts:** KFMM-FM. **Networks:** ABC; Mutual Broadcasting System. **Owner:** Marketron Broadcast Solutions L.L.C., at above address. **Founded:** 1969. **Operating Hours:** Continuous; 95% network, 5% local. **Wattage:** 1,000. **Ad Rates:** $6-12 for 30 seconds; $8-16 for 60 seconds.

1055 ■ KFMM-FM - 99.1
301B E Hwy. 70
Safford, AZ 85546
Phone: (928)428-0916
Fax: (928)428-7797
Email: k-rock@kfmmradio.com
Owner: Marketron Broadcast Solutions L.L.C., at above address. **Founded:** 1977. **Wattage:** 6,200 ERP. **Ad Rates:** $5.25-10.50 for 30 seconds; $7-15.50 for 60

seconds. **URL:** http://www.classicrockexperience.com/home.asp?callsign=KFMM-FM.

1056 ■ KJIK-FM - 100.7
1850 W Thatcher Blvd.
Safford, AZ 85546
Phone: (928)428-4100
Email: traffic@kjik.fm
Format: Contemporary Hit Radio (CHR); Easy Listening; Eighties; Adult Contemporary; Soft Rock. **Owner:** Country Mountain Airwaves L.L.C., 1850 W Thatcher Boulevard, Safford, AZ 85546, Ph: (928)428-4100. **Key Personnel:** Dan Curtis, Gen. Mgr., dan@kjik.fm. **Wattage:** 9,730 ERP. **URL:** http://www.kjik.fm.

SAHUARITA

1057 ■ KGVY-AM - 1080
1510 W Camino Antigua
Sahuarita, AZ 85629
Phone: (520)399-1000
Email: news@kgvy1080.com
Format: Music of Your Life; Full Service. **Networks:** Independent. **Owner:** KGVY L.L.C., at above address. **Founded:** 1981. **Operating Hours:** 6 a.m.-sunset; 5% network, 95% local. **ADI:** Tucson, AZ. **Key Personnel:** DeAnna Stenman, Operations Mgr., deannas@kgvy1080.com; Joey Lessa, Contact, joeyl@kgvy1080.com. **Wattage:** 1,000. **Ad Rates:** $28 per unit. for 30 seconds 25 times per week-$32 for 60 seconds one time. **URL:** http://www.kgvy1080.com.

SAN MANUEL

Pinal Co. (SE).

1058 ■ San Manuel Miner
San Manuel Miner
PO Box 60
San Manuel, AZ 85631
Phone: (520)385-2266
Fax: (520)385-4666
Publisher's E-mail: miner@minersunbasin.com
Community newspaper. **Freq:** Weekly. **Print Method:** Offset. **Trim Size:** 14 x 22. **Cols./Page:** 6. **Col. Width:** 12 picas. **Col. Depth:** 290.5 picas. **Key Personnel:** James Carnes, Manager, Advertising, Publisher; Jennifer Carnes, Managing Editor. **Subscription Rates:** $35.50 Individuals mail; $40.50 Out of area mail; $24 Individuals home delivery. **URL:** http://www.copperarea.com/pages/category/publications/san-manuel-miner. **Ad Rates:** GLR $.29; BW $504; 4C $500; SAU $5.50. **Remarks:** Accepts advertising. **Circ:** Mon.-Sat. 3400.

SCOTTSDALE

Maricopa Co. Maricopa Co. (C). 13 m NE of Phoenix. Tourism. Electronic and ceramic plants. Regional trade. Stock.

1059 ■ Arizona Foothills
Arizona Foothills Magazine
8132 N 87th Pl.
Scottsdale, AZ 85258
Phone: (480)460-5203
Fax: (480)460-2345
Luxury and lifestyle magazine. **Freq:** Monthly. **Key Personnel:** Michael Dee, President, Publisher. **Subscription Rates:** S$12 Individuals; S$4.99 Single issue. **URL:** http://www.arizonafoothillsmagazine.com. **Circ:** (Not Reported).

1060 ■ Construction Superintendent: The Commercial Builder's Source for Current News, technology & Methods
Inform Publishing Group L.L.C.
8040 E Morgan Trl., Ste. 23
Scottsdale, AZ 85258
Phone: (480)361-6300
Fax: (480)361-6394
Magazine featuring current news, technology, and methods in the construction field. **Freq:** Quarterly. **Key Personnel:** Gary Amsinger, Vice President; Stuart Mann, Director, Publications, phone: (480)361-6300; Evan Mann, Publisher. **ISSN:** 2155--9473 (print). **Subscription Rates:** $25 U.S.; $45 Canada and Mexico; $60 Other countries. **URL:** http://www.consupt.com. **Circ:** (Not Reported).

1061 ■ Cryonics
Alcor Life Extension Foundation
7895 E Acoma Dr., Ste. 110
Scottsdale, AZ 85260-6916
Phone: (480)905-1906
Fax: (480)922-9027
Free: 877-462-5267
Freq: 12/year. **Subscription Rates:** Included in membership. **Alt. Formats:** PDF. **URL:** http://www.alcor.org/CryonicsMagazine/index.html. **Remarks:** Accepts advertising. **Circ:** (Not Reported).

1062 ■ Distance Learning
Information Age Publishing Inc.
7500 E McCormick Pkwy.
Scottsdale, AZ 85258
Phone: (704)752-9125
Fax: (704)752-9113
Publisher's E-mail: infoage@infoagepub.com
Magazine information for those who provide instruction to all types of learners, of all ages, using telecommunications technologies of all types. **Freq:** Quarterly. **Key Personnel:** Michael Simonson, Editor; Charles Schlosser, Managing Editor; John Flores, Associate Editor; George Johnson, Founder, Publisher. **Subscription Rates:** $60 Individuals; $175 Institutions; $35 Students; $205 Other countries institutional; $90 Other countries; $65 Other countries student. **URL:** http://www.infoagepub.com/distance-learning.html. **Mailing address:** PO Box 79049, Charlotte, NC 28271-7047. **Circ:** (Not Reported).

1063 ■ The Educational Facility Planner
Association for Learning Environments
11445 E Via Linda, Ste. 2-440
Scottsdale, AZ 85259
Phone: (480)391-0840
Magazine publishing articles concerning the latest in school building research and hot topics. **Freq:** 3/year. **Subscription Rates:** Included in membership. **URL:** http://events.cefpi.org/i4a/pages/index.cfm?pageid=3372. **Remarks:** Advertising not accepted. **Circ:** (Not Reported).

1064 ■ Emerging
Teleos Institute
7439 E Beryl Ave.
Scottsdale, AZ 85258
Phone: (480)948-1800
Fax: (480)948-1870
Publisher's E-mail: teleosinst@aol.com
Freq: Semiannual. **ISSN:** 0890- 538X (print). **Subscription Rates:** Included in membership. **URL:** http://www.consciousnesswork.com/emergingindex.htm. **Remarks:** Advertising not accepted. **Circ:** 300.

1065 ■ Frank Lloyd Wright Quarterly
Frank Lloyd Wright Foundation
12621 N Frank Lloyd Wright Blvd.
Scottsdale, AZ 85259
Phone: (480)860-2700
Publisher's E-mail: info@franklloydwright.org
Scholarly magazine covering the life and work of architect Frank Lloyd Wright. **Freq:** Quarterly. **Print Method:** Offset. **Trim Size:** 8 1/2 x 11. **Cols./Page:** 3. **Subscription Rates:** $20 Nonmembers approximately 20-25 issues; $5 Individuals back issue; included in membership dues. **URL:** http://www.franklloydwright.org/about/quarterly.html. **Remarks:** Advertising not accepted. **Circ:** Controlled 10000, 10000.

1066 ■ Kono
Kono Magazine Corp.
7329 E Sixth Ave.
Scottsdale, AZ 85251
Phone: (480)421-2065
Fax: (480)421-2068
Free: 877-411-5666
Magazine covering martial arts for children. **Freq:** 10/yr. **Key Personnel:** Cory Michael Skaaren, Creative Director, Publisher; HK Kim, Editor-in-Chief. **Subscription Rates:** $14.99 Individuals; $19.99 Two years; $44 Canada; $4.99 Single issue. **URL:** http://www.konomag.com/. **Circ:** (Not Reported).

1067 ■ Lovin' Life News
Nevada Senior World
3200 Hayden, Ste. 330
Scottsdale, AZ 85251
Newspaper for senior citizens. **Founded:** 1976. **Freq:** Monthly. **Print Method:** Offset. Uses mats. **Trim Size:** 10.5 x 11.5. **Cols./Page:** 4. **Col. Depth:** 85 INS. **Key Personnel:** Steve Fish, Publisher; Zac Reynolds, Director, Advertising and Sales. **Subscription Rates:** $18 Individuals; $35 Two years. **URL:** http://lovinlife.com. **Formerly:** Senior Times; Arizona/Nevada Senior World Newspaper. **Ad Rates:** BW $1500; 4C $1750. **Remarks:** Advertising accepted; rates available upon request. **Circ:** ‡125,000.

1068 ■ Medical Construction & Design
Inform Publishing Group L.L.C.
8040 E Morgan Trl., Ste. 23
Scottsdale, AZ 85258
Phone: (480)361-6300
Fax: (480)361-6394
Magazine covering healthcare construction and design process. **Freq:** Bimonthly. **Key Personnel:** Stuart Mann, Publisher, Publisher, phone: (480)361-6300; Michelle Tennis, Editor, phone: (480)361-6300; Evan Mann, Publisher. **URL:** http://mcdmag.com. **Circ:** (Not Reported).

1069 ■ National Horseman
The National Horseman
16101 N 82nd St., Ste. 10
Scottsdale, AZ 85260-1830
Phone: (480)922-5202
Fax: (480)922-5212
Publication E-mail: info@tnh1865.com
Magazine featuring horse breeding, training, and showing. **Freq:** 17/yr. **Print Method:** Offset. **Trim Size:** 8 1/2 x 11. **Cols./Page:** 2. **Col. Width:** 22 picas. **Col. Depth:** 60 picas. **Key Personnel:** Allison Lambert, Publisher. **ISSN:** 0027--9455 (print). **USPS:** 373-380. **Subscription Rates:** $199 Individuals print, 3 years (51 issues); $159 Individuals print, 2 years (34 issues); $99 Individuals print, 1 year (17 issues); $49 Individuals online. **URL:** http://www.nationalhorseman.com. **Ad Rates:** BW $565; 4C $1025. **Remarks:** Advertising accepted; rates available upon request. **Circ:** Paid 3800, Non-paid 1000.

1070 ■ New Homes Today
Mino Media, LLC
Magazine featuring home builders and communities in the Greater Phoenix Area. **URL:** http://www.newhomestoday.com. **Formerly:** New Homes & Lifestyles. **Remarks:** Accepts advertising. **Circ:** (Not Reported).

1071 ■ Phoenix Home & Garden: The Magazine of Southwest Living
Phoenix Home and Garden
8501 E Princess Dr., Ste. 190
Scottsdale, AZ 85255
Phone: (480)664-3960
Fax: (480)664-3963
Free: 866-481-6971
Home and garden magazine. **Freq:** Monthly. **Print Method:** Offset. **Trim Size:** 8 1/4 x 10 3/4. **Cols./Page:** 3. **Col. Width:** 13 3/5 picas. **Col. Depth:** 136 agate lines. **ISSN:** 0270--9341 (print). **Subscription Rates:** $19.95 Individuals 12 issues; $29.95 Two years 24 issues. **Ad Rates:** BW $4105; 4C $6300. **Remarks:** Accepts advertising. **Circ:** Paid ★**83373**.

1072 ■ Phoenix Woman
LPI Multimedia Inc.
15170 N Hayden Rd., Ste. 5
Scottsdale, AZ 85260
Phone: (480)443-7750
Magazine for women in Phoenix. **Freq:** Bimonthly. **Trim Size:** 9 x 10.875. **Key Personnel:** Trif Kupanoff, President; Jessica Parsons, Editor; Hillary Cerchia, Manager, Production. **Subscription Rates:** $12 Individuals; $18 Two years individual. **Remarks:** Accepts advertising. **Circ:** 60000.

1073 ■ Runway
Runway Beauty Inc.
4413 N SaddleBag Trail Ste. 1
Scottsdale, AZ 85251
Phone: (562)802-3344
Free: 800-417-1387
Magazine featuring fashion and beauty. **Freq:** Quarterly. **Key Personnel:** Vincent Mazzotta, Editor-in-Chief; Lauren Wise, Managing Editor. **Subscription Rates:** $17.99 Individuals; $31.99 Canada and Mexico; $37.99 Other countries Europe. **URL:** http://www.runwaybeauty.

Circulation: ★ = AAM; △ or • = BPA; ♦ = CAC; ❑ = VAC; ⊕ = PO Statement; ‡ = Publisher's Report; Boldface figures = sworn; Light figures = estimated.

com. **Ad Rates:** 4C $8700. **Remarks:** Accepts display advertising. **Circ:** ★**100000**.

1074 ■ Scottsdale Health
Richman Media Group
8300 N Hayden Rd., Ste. 207
Scottsdale, AZ 85258
Magazine featuring the latest in health and wellness. **Freq:** Monthly. **Trim Size:** 8.375 x 10.875. **Key Personnel:** Bill Richman, Publisher; Michelle Glicksman, Editor-in-Chief; Anthony Cox, Creative Director. **Subscription Rates:** $36 Individuals. **URL:** http://www.allyouneedforhappiness.com. **Ad Rates:** 4C $2,650. **Remarks:** Accepts advertising. **Circ:** ‡30000.

1075 ■ Skin Inc.
American Association of Cosmetology Schools
9927 E Bell Rd., Ste. 110
Scottsdale, AZ 85260
Phone: (480)281-0431
Fax: (480)905-0993
Free: 800-831-1086
Publication E-mail: skininc@allured.com
Freq: Monthly. **URL:** http://www.skininc.com/magazine. **Remarks:** Advertising accepted; rates available upon request. **Circ:** (Not Reported).

1076 ■ So Scottsdale!: A Fashion and Beauty Magazine for Women
Richman Media Group
8300 N Hayden Rd., Ste. 207
Scottsdale, AZ 85258
Magazine featuring the latest fashion and beauty trends for women. **Freq:** Monthly. **Trim Size:** 8.375 x 10.875. **Key Personnel:** Bill Richman, Publisher; Michelle Glicksman, Editor-in-Chief; Anthony Cox, Creative Director. **Subscription Rates:** $36 Individuals. **URL:** http://www.soscottsdale.com. **Ad Rates:** 4C $2,650. **Remarks:** Accepts advertising. **Circ:** Combined ‡25000.

1077 ■ WorldatWork Journal
WorldatWork
14040 N Northsight Blvd.
Scottsdale, AZ 85260
Phone: (480)922-2020
Fax: (480)483-8352
Free: 866-816-2962
Publisher's E-mail: customerrelations@worldatwork.org
Freq: Quarterly. **ISSN:** 1068--0918 (print). **Subscription Rates:** $130 U.S. Annual; $165 Other countries Annual. **URL:** http://www.worldatwork.org/waw/worldatworkjournal/html/journal-home.html. **Remarks:** Advertising not accepted. **Circ:** 25000.

1078 ■ KAJM-FM - 104.3
7434 E Stetson Dr., Ste. 255
Scottsdale, AZ 85251
Phone: (480)994-9100
Fax: (480)423-8770
Format: Oldies. **Key Personnel:** Michael Mallace, Gen. Mgr.; Matt Kirkpatrick, Promotions Dir. **Ad Rates:** Advertising accepted; rates available upon request. **URL:** http://www.mega1043.com.

1079 ■ KBSZ-AM - 1260
4301 N 75th St., No. 105
Scottsdale, AZ 85251
Phone: (480)423-1260
Email: press@tunein.com
Format: Talk. **Founded:** 1968. **Formerly:** KTIM-AM; KCIW-AM. **Operating Hours:** Continuous. **Wattage:** 1,000 Day; 202 Night. **Ad Rates:** $2 for 15 seconds; $3 for 30 seconds; $5 for 60 seconds. **URL:** http://www.tunein.com.

1080 ■ KNRJ-FM - 101.1
7434 E Stetson Dr., Ste. 255
Scottsdale, AZ 85251
Phone: (602)260-4927
Fax: (480)423-8770
Key Personnel: Michael Mallace, Gen. Mgr. **Wattage:** 4,000 ERP. **Ad Rates:** Accepts Advertising.

1081 ■ KVIB-FM - 95.1
4343 N Scottsdale Rd., No. 200
Scottsdale, AZ 85251
Phone: (480)222-3300
Fax: (480)970-1759
Format: Hispanic. **Key Personnel:** Jose Rodiles, Gen. Mgr.; Jackie Bosque Diaz, Gen. Sales Mgr.

SEDONA

Yavapai Co. Coconino Co. (C) 102 m N. of Phoenix. Residential.

1082 ■ Sedona Excentric: Sedona's Finest Restaurant & Arts Guide
Sedona Excentric
PO Box 843
Sedona, AZ 86339
Phone: (928)639-4224
Alternative, local newspaper covering travel, entertainment and events. **Freq:** Monthly. **URL:** http://www.sedonausa.com; http://www.sedonaexcentric.com. **Ad Rates:** 4C $580. **Remarks:** Accepts advertising. **Circ:** Non-paid ‡10000.

1083 ■ Sedona Red Rock News: The Voice of Sedona and Oak Creek Canyon for 42 years
Sedona Red Rock News
PO Box 619
Sedona, AZ 86339
Phone: (928)282-7795
Fax: (928)282-6011
Local newspaper. **Freq:** Semiweekly (Wed. and Fri.). **Print Method:** Offset. **Cols./Page:** 6. **Col. Width:** 2 1/10 inches. **Col. Depth:** 21 inches. **Key Personnel:** Christopher Fox Graham, Managing Editor. **USPS:** 458-460. **Subscription Rates:** $43 Individuals; $64 Out of area. **URL:** http://www.redrocknews.com. **Formerly:** Red Rock News. **Remarks:** Accepts classified advertising. **Circ:** (Not Reported).

1084 ■ Swimming World and Junior Swimmer
Sports Publications Inc.
PO Box 20337
Sedona, AZ 86341
Phone: (520)284-4005
Fax: (520)284-2477
Publication E-mail: swimworld@aol.com
Magazine on competitive swimming, diving and water polo. **Freq:** Monthly. **Print Method:** Offset. **Trim Size:** 8 1/4 x 10 3/4. **Cols./Page:** 2 and 3. **Col. Width:** 42 and 26 nonpareils. **Col. Depth:** 140 agate lines. **Key Personnel:** Bob Ingram, Senior Editor; Richard Deal, Chairman; Jason Marsteller, Managing Editor. **ISSN:** 0039--7431 (print). **Subscription Rates:** $39.95 Individuals print & total access (one year); $74.95 Individuals print & total access (three years); $59.95 Two years print & total access; $3.95 Individuals 30 day online. **URL:** http://www.swimmingworldmagazine.com. **Ad Rates:** BW $2155; 4C $3150. **Remarks:** Accepts advertising. **Circ:** ‡33000.

1085 ■ KAZM-AM - 780
PO Box 1525
Sedona, AZ 86336
Phone: (928)282-4154
Fax: (928)282-2230
Email: info@kazmradio.com
Format: Talk; News; Sports; Contemporary Hit Radio (CHR). **Networks:** Independent. **Owner:** Tabback Broadcasting Company Inc., PO Box 4259, Sedona, AZ 86340, Ph: (928)282-4154, Fax: (928)282-2230. **Founded:** 2000. **Operating Hours:** Continuous; 100% local. **ADI:** Flagstaff, AZ. **Key Personnel:** Tom Tayback, Gen. Mgr., President, tom@kazmradio.com; Mike Tabback, Sales Mgr., mike@kazmradio.com. **Local Programs:** *The Duo*, Monday Tuesday Wednesday Thursday Friday 7:15 a.m. - 8:00 a.m.; *Tech Talk*, Wednesday 9:15 a.m. - 10:00 a.m. **Wattage:** 5,000 Day; 250 Night. **Ad Rates:** $26-33 for 30 seconds; $35-41 for 60 seconds. **URL:** http://www.kazmradio.com.

KDKT-AM - See Beulah, ND

SHOW LOW

Navajo Co. Navajo Co. (NE). 45 m S of Holbrook. Lumber mill. Timber. Agriculture. Cattle.

1086 ■ White Mountain Independent: Navajo Edition/Apache Edition
White Mountain Publishing Co.
3191 S White Mountain Rd., Ste. 4
Show Low, AZ 85901-7409
Phone: (928)537-5721
Fax: (928)537-1780
Publisher's E-mail: postmaster@wmicentral.com
Community newspaper. **Freq:** Semiweekly Tues. & Fri. **Print Method:** Offset. **Cols./Page:** 6. **Col. Width:** 2 1/16 inches. **Col. Depth:** 21 1/2 inches. **Key Personnel:** Brian D. Kramer, Publisher; Wiley Acheson, Director, Advertising. **ISSN:** 0002--7520 (print). **Subscription Rates:** $50 Individuals Apache & Navajo county print & digital; $70 Individuals in AZ out of county print & digital; $82 Out of state print & digital. **URL:** http://www.wmicentral.com. **Mailing address:** PO Box 1570, Show Low, AZ 85902-1570. **Ad Rates:** 4C $2169.24. **Remarks:** Accepts advertising. **Circ:** (Not Reported).

1087 ■ KQAZ-FM - 101.7
PO Box 2020
Show Low, AZ 85902
Phone: (928)532-1010
Fax: (928)532-0101
Format: Adult Contemporary. **Networks:** Jones Satellite; CNN Radio. **Founded:** 1984. **Operating Hours:** Continuous. **Wattage:** 55,000 ERP. **Ad Rates:** $12 for 30 seconds; $15 for 60 seconds. **URL:** http://www.majik101.com/.

1088 ■ KRFM-FM
700 E Savage
Show Low, AZ 85901-3714
Phone: (602)537-2921
Format: Adult Contemporary. **Networks:** ABC. **Founded:** 1983. **Wattage:** 100,000 ERP. **Ad Rates:** $8.80-12 for 30 seconds; $10-14 for 60 seconds.

1089 ■ KVSL-AM - 1470
PO Box 2770
Show Low, AZ 85902
Phone: (928)251-4351
Format: Information; News; Contemporary Hit Radio (CHR). **Founded:** 1968. **Operating Hours:** Continuous. **Wattage:** 1,000. **Ad Rates:** $5.50-7 for 30 seconds; $6.50-8.25 for 60 seconds. $5.50-$7 for 30 seconds; $6.50-$8.25 for 60 seconds. Combined advertising rates available with KRFM-FM. **URL:** http://www.rewind108.com/contact.asp.

1090 ■ KWKM-FM - 95.7
1520 B Commerce Dr.
Show Low, AZ 85901
Phone: (928)532-2949
Fax: (928)532-3176
Format: Classic Rock. **URL:** http://www.kwkm.com.

SIERRA VISTA

Cochise Co. Cochise Co. (SE). 70 m SE of Tucson. Tourism. Electronic devices manufactured. Ranching.

1091 ■ Bisbee Daily Review
Sierra Vista Herald
102 Fab Ave.
Sierra Vista, AZ 85635
Phone: (520)458-9440
Fax: (520)459-0120
Publisher's E-mail: dana.cole@svherald.com
Daily newspaper. **Freq:** Daily and Sun. **Print Method:** Web offset. **Key Personnel:** Eric Petermann, Editor. **URL:** http://www.svherald.com. **Remarks:** Accepts advertising. **Circ:** (Not Reported).

1092 ■ Daily Herald
Wick Communications
333 W Wilcox Dr., Ste. 302
Sierra Vista, AZ 85635-1756
Phone: (520)458-0200
Fax: (520)458-6166
General newspaper serving the Roanoke Valley, Lake Gaston, and Southside Virginia. **Founded:** 1914. **Freq:** Daily and Sun. (eve.) Tuesday-Friday & Sunday. **Print Method:** Offset. **Cols./Page:** 6. **Col. Width:** 25 nonpareils. **Col. Depth:** 301 agate lines. **Key Personnel:** Titus Workman, Publisher; Stephen Hemelt, Managing Editor; Carol Moseley, Manager, Circulation. **Subscription Rates:** $174.72 By mail. **URL:** http://www.rrdailyherald.com. **Remarks:** Accepts advertising. **Circ:** Tues.-Fri. ■ **9,296**, Sun. ■ **9,815**.

1093 ■ Douglas Dispatch
Wick Communications
333 W Wilcox Dr., Ste. 302
Sierra Vista, AZ 85635-1756
Phone: (520)458-0200
Fax: (520)458-6166
Newspaper featuring arts and entertainment, restaurant reviews, horoscope, classifieds and more. **Freq:** Weekly (Wed.). **Key Personnel:** Francis Wick, Publisher. **URL:** http://www.douglasdispatch.com. **Remarks:** Accepts advertising. **Circ:** (Not Reported).

1094 ■ Eastern Arizona Courier
Wick Communications
333 W Wilcox Dr., Ste. 302
Sierra Vista, AZ 85635-1756
Phone: (520)458-0200
Fax: (520)458-6166
Local newspaper. **Freq:** Weekly (Wed.). **Print Method:** Offset. **Cols./Page:** 6. **Col. Width:** 26 nonpareils. **Col. Depth:** 294 agate lines. **Key Personnel:** Monica Watson, Publisher. **Subscription Rates:** $52 Individuals; $67 Elsewhere; $72.80 Out of state. **URL:** http://www.eacourier.com. **Ad Rates:** GLR $.56; BW $1058; 4C $1303; SAU $8.20. **Remarks:** Accepts advertising. **Circ:** Free ‡30, Paid ‡5805, Combined ‡5835.

1095 ■ Half Moon Bay Review and Pescadero Pebble
Wick Communications
333 W Wilcox Dr., Ste. 302
Sierra Vista, AZ 85635-1756
Phone: (520)458-0200
Fax: (520)458-6166
Publication E-mail: letters@hmbreview.com
Newspaper with Republican orientation. **Freq:** Weekly (Wed.). **Print Method:** Offset. **Cols./Page:** 6. **Col. Width:** 24 nonpareils. **Col. Depth:** 301 agate lines. **Key Personnel:** Clay Lambert, Editor. **Subscription Rates:** $46.80 Individuals in San Mateo County; $88.40 Two years in San Mateo County; $57.20 Out of country; $104 Out of country two years. **URL:** http://hmbreview.com. **Remarks:** Advertising accepted; rates available upon request. **Circ:** ‡7500.

1096 ■ Sahuarita Sun
Wick Communications
333 W Wilcox Dr., Ste. 302
Sierra Vista, AZ 85635-1756
Phone: (520)458-0200
Fax: (520)458-6166
Newspaper providing information and serving Sahuarita and surrounding areas. **Freq:** Weekly (Wed.). **Key Personnel:** Rebecca Bradner, Publisher. **URL:** http://www.sahuaritasun.com. **Remarks:** Accepts advertising. **Circ:** (Not Reported).

1097 ■ Sierra Vista Herald
Sierra Vista Herald
102 Fab Ave.
Sierra Vista, AZ 85635
Phone: (520)458-9440
Fax: (520)459-0120
Publisher's E-mail: dana.cole@svherald.com
General newspaper. **Freq:** Mon.-Sun. (morn.). **Print Method:** Offset. **Cols./Page:** 6. **Col. Width:** 1.833 inches. **Col. Depth:** 21.25 inches. **Key Personnel:** Matt Hickman, Editor; Sam Aselstine, Editor; Scott Green, Director, Production; Philip Vega, Publisher; Steven Byerly, Managing Editor. **Ad Rates:** 4C $290; SAU $10.20. **Remarks:** Advertising accepted; rates available upon request. **Circ:** Mon.-Sat. ‡8505, Sun. ‡9167.

1098 ■ Wahpeton Daily News
Wick Communications
333 W Wilcox Dr., Ste. 302
Sierra Vista, AZ 85635-1756
Phone: (520)458-0200
Fax: (520)458-6166
Newspaper featuring news section, classifieds and more. **Key Personnel:** Ken Harty, Publisher. **URL:** http://www.wahpetondailynews.com. **Remarks:** Accepts advertising. **Circ:** (Not Reported).

1099 ■ KTAN-AM - 1420
2300 Busby Dr.
Sierra Vista, AZ 85636
Phone: (520)458-4313
Fax: (520)458-4317
Format: News; Talk. **Owner:** Cherry Creek Radio LLC, 501 S Cherry St., Ste. 480, Denver, CO 80246, Ph: (303)468-6500, Fax: (303)468-6555. **Founded:** 1958. **Formerly:** KLTW-AM. **Operating Hours:** Continuous; 90% network, 10% local. **ADI:** Tucson, AZ. **Key Personnel:** Joe Schwartz, CEO, President; Travis L. Cronen, Dir. of Operations, VP; Kelley Cheatwood, Exec. VP, Regional Mgr. **Wattage:** 1,500. **Ad Rates:** Advertising accepted; rates available upon request. Combined advertising rates available with KZMK, KWCD. **Mailing address:** PO Box 2770, Sierra Vista, AZ 85636. **URL:** http://www.cherrycreekradio.com.

1100 ■ KWCD-FM - 92.3
2300 Busby Dr.
Sierra Vista, AZ 85636
Phone: (520)458-4313
Fax: (520)458-4317
Format: Country; Adult Contemporary. **Networks:** Westwood One Radio. **Owner:** Cherry Creek Radio LLC, 501 S Cherry St., Ste. 480, Denver, CO 80246, Ph: (303)468-6500, Fax: (303)468-6555. **Founded:** 1983. **Formerly:** KZMK-FM; KFFN-FM; KTAZ-FM. **Operating Hours:** Continuous. **ADI:** Tucson, AZ. **Key Personnel:** Paul Orlando, Gen. Mgr., porlando@cherrycreekradio.com. **Wattage:** 3,000. **Ad Rates:** Noncommercial; Advertising accepted; rates available upon request. Combined advertising rates available with KZMK, KTAN. **Mailing address:** PO Box 2770, Sierra Vista, AZ 85636. **URL:** http://www.cherrycreekradio.com.

1101 ■ KWRB-FM - 90.9
3320 E Fry Blvd.
Sierra Vista, AZ 85635
Phone: (520)452-8022
Fax: (520)452-0927
Free: 877-909-5972
Format: Educational. **Networks:** Moody Broadcasting. **Owner:** World Radio Network, Inc., PO Box 3765, McAllen, TX 78502, Ph: (956)787-9788. **Founded:** Dec. 10, 1996. **Operating Hours:** Continuous. **Key Personnel:** Arron Daniels, Station Mgr. **Local Programs:** *Paws & Tales*, Saturday 8:00 a.m - 8:30 a.m.; *Weekend 20 Countdown*, Saturday 8:00 p.m. - 10:00 p.m.; *Truth for Life Weekend*, Sunday 6:00 a.m. - 6:30 a.m.; *Sunday In The Country*, Sunday 7:30 a.m. - 8:00 a.m.; *Adventures in Odyssey*, Saturday 8:30 a.m. - 9:00 a.m.; *The Alternative - Dr. Tony Evans*, Monday Tuesday Wednesday Thursday Friday 11:20 a.m. - 12:20 p.m. **Wattage:** 088. **Ad Rates:** Noncommercial. **URL:** http://www.kwrb.org.

SPRINGERVILLE

1102 ■ KRVZ-AM - 1400
PO Box 1069
Springerville, AZ 85938
Simulcasts: KQAZ 101.7 FM/KTHQ 92.5 FM. **Owner:** Country Mountain Airwaves L.L.C., 1850 W Thatcher Boulevard, Safford, AZ 85546, Ph: (928)428-4100. **Founded:** 1982. **Ad Rates:** $4 for 30 seconds; $5 for 60 seconds.

SUN CITY

Maricopa Co. (C). 3 m W of Peoria. Retirement Community.

1103 ■ Daily News-Sun
Northwest Valley Newspapers
10102 Santa Fe Dr.
Sun City, AZ 85351
Phone: (623)977-8351
General newspaper. **Freq:** six days a week. **Print Method:** Offset. **Cols./Page:** 6. **Col. Width:** 12 picas. **Col. Depth:** 21.5 inches. **Key Personnel:** Kristy Kollman, Publisher. **Subscription Rates:** $8.16 Individuals Tuesday thru Saturday/4 Weeks - 5 Day Delivery; $25.74 Individuals Tuesday thru Saturday/13 Weeks - 5 Day Delivery. **URL:** http://www.yourwestvalley.com. **Remarks:** Advertising accepted; rates available upon request. **Circ:** Mon.-Sat. ★**11000**.

1104 ■ Peoria Independent
Independent Newsmedia Inc.
17220 N Boswell Blvd., Ste. 101
Sun City, AZ 85373
Phone: (623)972-6101
Publication E-mail: wvnews@newszap.com
Community newspaper. **Freq:** Weekly (Wed.). **Key Personnel:** Rusty Bradshaw, Editor. **Subscription Rates:** $26 Individuals e-subscription. **URL:** http://arizona.newszap.com/peoriaindependent; http://peoriaindependent.com. **Remarks:** Accepts advertising. **Circ:** Non-paid ♦**15536**.

1105 ■ Sun Cities Independent
Independent Newspapers Inc.
17220 N Boswell Blvd., Ste. 101
Sun City, AZ 85373
Community newspaper. **Freq:** Weekly (Wed.). **Print Method:** Offset. **Trim Size:** 13 x 21. **Cols./Page:** 6. **Col. Width:** 2 1/16 inches. **Col. Depth:** 21 1/2 inches. **Subscription Rates:** Free; $26 Individuals e-edition. **URL:** http://arizona.newszap.com/suncitiesindependent. **Remarks:** Advertising accepted; rates available upon request. **Circ:** Combined ♦**21175**.

TEMPE

Maricopa Co. Maricopa Co. (SC). 10 m SE of Phoenix. Arizona State University. Electronic plants; semi conductor plants; garment factories. Diversified farming. Alfalfa, wheat, cotton, citrus fruit.

1106 ■ Arizona Journal of Pharmacy
Arizona Pharmacy Association
1845 E Southern Ave.
Tempe, AZ 85282-5831
Phone: (480)838-3385
Fax: (480)838-3557
Publisher's E-mail: admin@azpharmacy.org
Educational journal containing social and industry information for pharmacists. **Freq:** Quarterly. **Print Method:** Offset. **Trim Size:** 8 1/2 x 11. **Cols./Page:** 2. **Col. Width:** 3 3/8 INS. **Key Personnel:** Leslie Rodriguez, Board Member; Julie Hernandez, Board Member; Jonathan Merchen, Board Member; Whitney Rice, Board Member. **ISSN:** 0004--1602 (print). **Subscription Rates:** $40 Nonmembers; Included in membership. **Alt. Formats:** PDF. **URL:** http://www.azpharmacy.org/?page=AJP. **Formerly:** Arizona Pharmacist. **Remarks:** Accepts advertising. **Circ:** 1000.

1107 ■ Arizona State Law Journal
Arizona State University Sandra Day O'Connor College of Law
Armstrong Hall
1100 S McAllister Ave.
Tempe, AZ 85287-7906
Phone: (480)965-6181
Fax: (480)965-2427
Publisher's E-mail: asulaw.admissions@asu.edu
Journal covering law and law-related topics. **Freq:** Quarterly. **Key Personnel:** Julie Hedberg, Editor-in-Chief. **URL:** http://arizonastatelawjournal.org. **Mailing address:** PO Box 877906, Tempe, AZ 85287-7906. **Circ:** (Not Reported).

1108 ■ Bilingual Review/Revista Bilingue
Bilingual Review Press
Arizona State University
Tempe, AZ 85287-5303
Phone: (480)965-3867
Fax: (480)965-0315
Free: 866-965-3867
Publication E-mail: brp@asu.edu
Scholarly journal covering literature, poetry and reviews in Spanish and English. **Freq:** Triennial. **Trim Size:** 7 1/2 x 10. **Key Personnel:** Gary D. Keller, Editor-in-Chief. **ISSN:** 0094--5366 (print). **Subscription Rates:** $32 Individuals 1 volume - 3 issues; $60 Individuals 2 volumes - 6 issues; $84 Individuals 3 volumes - 9 issues; $55 Institutions 1 volume - 3 issues; $110 Institutions 2 volumes - 6 issues; $165 Institutions 3 volumes - 9 issues. **URL:** http://www.asu.edu/brp/bilin/bilin.html. **Mailing address:** PO Box 875303, Tempe, AZ 85287-5303. **Remarks:** Accepts advertising. **Circ:** (Not Reported).

1109 ■ Computer Aided Geometric Design
Elsevier
c/o G.E. Farin, Ed.-in-Ch.
Department of Computer Science & Engineering
Arizona State University
Brickyard Eng 414
Tempe, AZ 85287-8809
Publisher's E-mail: t.reller@elsevier.com
Journal devoted to developers dealing with mathematical and computational methods. **Freq:** 9/year. **Key Personnel:** G.E. Farin, Editor-in-Chief; R. Farouki, Associate Editor; M.S. Floater, Associate Editor; R.N. Goldman, Associate Editor; H. Prautzsch, Editor-in-Chief; O. Davydov, Associate Editor. **ISSN:** 0167--8396 (print). **Subscription Rates:** $131 Individuals print; $1416 Institutions online or print. **URL:** http://www.journals.elsevier.com/computer-aided-geometric-design. **Circ:** (Not Reported).

1110 ■ East Valley Tribune
Freedom Communications Inc.
1620 W Fountainhead Prkwy

Circulation: ★ = AAM; △ or • = BPA; ♦ = CAC; ❑ = VAC; ⊕ = PO Statement; ‡ = Publisher's Report; Boldface figures = sworn; Light figures = estimated.

Ste. 219
Tempe, AZ 85282
Publisher's E-mail: info@freedom.com
General newspaper. **Freq:** Daily. **Print Method:** Offset. **Trim Size:** 13 3/4 x 22. **Cols./Page:** 6. **Col. Width:** 21 nonpareils. **Col. Depth:** 294 agate lines. **Key Personnel:** Steve Pope, Publisher, General Manager. **ISSN:** 0888--0271 (print). **URL:** http://www.eastvalleytribune.com. **Formerly**: Tempe Daily News Tribune. **Remarks:** Accepts classified advertising. **Circ:** (Not Reported).

1111 ■ Education and Training in Autism and Developmental Disabilities
Council for Exceptional Children
Arizona State University
Special Education Program
Tempe, AZ 85287-2011
Phone: (480)965-1449
Fax: (480)965-4942
Publication E-mail: etdd@asu.edu
Journal covering theory and research in education of individuals with mental retardation and/or developmental disabilities. **Freq:** Quarterly. **Trim Size:** 10 x 7. **Cols./Page:** 2. **Col. Width:** 15 INS. **Key Personnel:** Stanley H. Zucker, PhD, Editor. **ISSN:** 1547-0350 (print). **Subscription Rates:** $60 Individuals; $64 Other countries; $195 Institutions; $199.50 Institutions, other countries; $30 Single issue. **URL:** http://daddcec.org/Publications/ETADDJournal.aspx. **Formerly**: Education and Training of the Mentally Retarded; Education and Training in Mental Retardation and Development Disabilities; Education and Training in Developmental Disabilities. **Ad Rates:** BW $500. **Remarks:** Accepts advertising. **Circ:** (Not Reported).

1112 ■ French Historical Studies
Duke University Press
Arizona State University
School of Historical, Philosophical & Religious Studies
Tempe, AZ 85287-4302
Phone: (480)965-2429
Fax: (480)965-0310
Publication E-mail: fhs@asu.edu
Scholarly journal covering French history. **Freq:** Quarterly. **Key Personnel:** Kathryn A. Edwards, Editor. **ISSN:** 0016-1071 (print). **Subscription Rates:** $50 Individuals; $208 Institutions print and electronic; $177 Institutions electronic version; $1201 Institutions print only; $25 Students. **URL:** http://www.dukeupress.edu/Catalog/ViewProduct.php?productid=45611. **Mailing address:** PO Box 874302, Tempe, AZ 85287-4302. **Ad Rates:** BW $400. **Remarks:** Accepts advertising. **Circ:** Paid 1277.

1113 ■ Hayden's Ferry Review
Arizona State University Virginia G. Piper Center for Creative Writing
PO Box 875002
Tempe, AZ 85287-5002
Phone: (480)965-6018
Fax: (480)727-0820
Publication E-mail: hfr@asu.edu
Journal featuring poetry, fiction and art. **Freq:** Semiannual. **Key Personnel:** Chelsea Hickok, Editor-in-Chief. **URL:** http://haydensferryreview.com. **Circ:** (Not Reported).

1114 ■ The Indexer
American Society for Indexing
1628 E Southern Ave., No. 9-223
Tempe, AZ 85282
Phone: (480)245-6750
Publication E-mail: info@theindexer.org
Professional journal for indexers. **Freq:** Quarterly March, June, September and December. **Key Personnel:** Maureen MacGlashan, Editor. **ISSN:** 0019--4131 (print); **EISSN:** 1756--0632 (electronic). **Subscription Rates:** £60 Nonmembers royal mail 2nd class/overseas priority mail; £38.50 Members; £160 Institutions print or online; £200 Institutions print and online. **URL:** http://www.theindexer.org; http://www.indexers.org.uk. **Ad Rates:** 4C $210, full page; 4C £120, half page; BW £210. **Remarks:** Accepts advertising. **Circ:** 2200.

1115 ■ Inside Supply Management: Resources to Create Your Future
Institute for Supply Management
2055 E Centennial Cir.
Tempe, AZ 85284
Phone: (480)752-6276
Fax: (480)752-7890
Free: 800-888-6276
Publisher's E-mail: custsvc@ism.ws
Trade magazine for purchasing and supply managers. **Freq:** Monthly. **Print Method:** Web offset. **Trim Size:** 8 1/8 x 10 7/8. **Cols./Page:** 3. **Col. Width:** 13.5 picas. **Col. Depth:** 57 picas. **Key Personnel:** Debbie Webber, CAE, Senior Vice President, Treasurer; Cindy Urbaytis, Vice President, Sales and Marketing; Terri Tracey, Editor-in-Chief. **ISSN:** 1538--733X (print). **Subscription Rates:** Included in membership. **URL:** http://www.instituteforsupplymanagement.org/Pubs/ISMMag/index.cfm. **Formerly**: NAPM Insights; Purchasing Today. **Remarks:** Accepts advertising. **Circ:** (Not Reported).

1116 ■ International Journal of Paleopathology
Elsevier
c/o Jane Buikstra, Editor-in-Chief
900 S Cady Mall, Rm. 233
School of Human Evolution & Social Change
Arizona State University
Tempe, AZ 85287-2402
Publisher's E-mail: t.reller@elsevier.com
Journal publishing research studies on paleopathology. **Freq:** Quarterly 4/yr. **Key Personnel:** Jane Buikstra, Editor-in-Chief. **ISSN:** 1879--9817 (print). **Subscription Rates:** $100 Individuals print; $365 Institutions print; $118.93 Institutions; Included in membership. **Alt. Formats:** Electronic publishing. **URL:** http://www.journals.elsevier.com/international-journal-of-paleopathology; http://paleopathology-association.wildapricot.org/IJPP; http://www.sciencedirect.com/science/journal/18799817. **Remarks:** Advertising not accepted. **Circ:** (Not Reported).

1117 ■ Journal of American Indian Education
Arizona State University College of Liberal Arts and Sciences School of Social Transformation Center for Indian Education
Payne Hall, Ste. 302
Tempe, AZ 85287-4902
Phone: (480)965-6292
Fax: (480)965-8115
Publisher's E-mail: bryan.brayboy@asu.edu
Journal focusing on research covering the education of American, Indians and Alaska Natives. **Founded:** 1961. **Freq:** 3/year. **Key Personnel:** Bryan Brayboy, PhD, Editor; Jeston Morris, Managing Editor. **ISSN:** 0021-8731 (print). **Subscription Rates:** $35 Individuals; $75 Institutions; $38.50 Other countries; $78.50 Institutions, other countries; $8 Single issue. **URL:** http://jaie.asu.edu. **Mailing address:** PO Box 876403, Tempe, AZ 85287-6403. **Circ:** (Not Reported).

1118 ■ Journal of Policy History
Pennsylvania State University Press
Arizona State University
975 S Myrtle Ave.
Tempe, AZ 85287-4302
Phone: (480)727-7280
Publication E-mail: jpolhist@asu.edu
Peer-reviewed journal focusing on application of historical perspectives to public policy studies. **Freq:** Quarterly. **Key Personnel:** Prof. Donald T. Critchlow, PhD, Editor; Prof. David B. Robertson, PhD, Associate Editor. **ISSN:** 0898--0306 (print). **Subscription Rates:** $42 Individuals; $103 Institutions print only; $115 Institutions print & online; $92 Institutions online only. **URL:** http://jph.asu.edu. **Mailing address:** PO Box 874302, Tempe, AZ 85287-4302. **Remarks:** Accepts advertising. **Circ:** (Not Reported).

1119 ■ The Journal of Supply Chain Management
Institute for Supply Management
2055 E Centennial Cir.
Tempe, AZ 85284
Phone: (480)752-6276
Fax: (480)752-7890
Free: 800-888-6276
Publisher's E-mail: custsvc@ism.ws
Journal covering high-quality, high-impact behavioral research focusing on theory-building and empirical methodologies. **Freq:** Quarterly. **ISSN:** 1523- 2409 (print); **EISSN:** 1745- 493X (electronic). **Subscription Rates:** $113 Individuals America; Print and Online.; $356 Institutions America; Print Only.; $428 Institutions America; Print and Online.; $356 Institutions America; Online Only. **URL:** http://www.ism.ws/pubs/JournalSCM/Index.cfm; http://www.ism.ws/pubs/journalscm/index.cfm?navItemNumber=22792. **Remarks:** Advertising not accepted. **Circ:** 3500.

1120 ■ The Journal of Supply Chain Management: A Global Review of Purchasing and Supply
Institute for Supply Management
2055 E Centennial Cir.
Tempe, AZ 85284
Phone: (480)752-6276
Fax: (480)752-7890
Free: 800-888-6276
Publisher's E-mail: custsvc@ism.ws
Academic journal covering purchasing and supply management. **Founded:** 1965. **Freq:** Quarterly. **Print Method:** Offset. **Trim Size:** 8 1/2 x 11. **Cols./Page:** 2. **Col. Width:** 41 nonpareils. **Col. Depth:** 115 agate lines. **Key Personnel:** Craig R. Carter, PhD, Editor-in-Chief; Lisa M. Ellram, PhD, Editor-in-Chief. **ISSN:** 1523-2409 (print). **Subscription Rates:** $113 Individuals Americas print + online; €107 Individuals print + online; £71 Individuals rest of world print + online; $428 Institutions print + online; €341 Institutions print + online; £268 Institutions, other countries print + online. **URL:** http://www.ism.ws/pubs/journalscm/index.cfm?navItemNumber=5474. **Formerly**: Journal of Purchasing & Materials Management; International Journal of Purchasing & Materials Management. **Remarks:** Accepts advertising. **Circ:** ‡1800.

1121 ■ Jurimetrics: The Journal of Law, Science and Technology
Arizona State University Sandra Day O'Connor College of Law
c/o Deborah J. Pogson, Mng. Ed.
Sandra Day O'Connor College of Law
Arizona State University
Tempe, AZ 85287-7906
Phone: (480)965-6181
Publication E-mail: jurimetrics@asu.edu
Legal journal. **Freq:** Quarterly. **Print Method:** Offset. **Trim Size:** 6 x 9. **Cols./Page:** 1. **Col. Width:** 26 picas. **Col. Depth:** 43.5 picas. **Key Personnel:** Racheal White Hawk, Editor-in-Chief; Deborah J. Pogson, Managing Editor. **ISSN:** 0897--1277 (print); **EISSN:** 2154- 4344 (electronic). **Subscription Rates:** $55 Members; $85 Nonmembers per year. **URL:** http://www.law.asu.edu/student-life/organizations/jj; http://www.americanbar.org/publications/jurimetrics/2011/spring/publishing_policystatements.html. **Formerly**: Jurimetrics Journal. **Mailing address:** PO Box 877906, Tempe, AZ 85287-7906. **Remarks:** Advertising not accepted. **Circ:** 12200.

1122 ■ Mathematical Biosciences and Engineering
American Institute of Mathematical Sciences
Dept. of Math & Statistics
College of Liberal Arts & Sciences
Arizona State University
Tempe, AZ 85287
Publisher's E-mail: general@aimsciences.org
Journal that publishes papers on subjects of general mathematical methods and their applications in biology, medical sciences and engineering. **Freq:** Bimonthly. **Key Personnel:** Dr. Yang Kuang, Editor-in-Chief; Zhiming Zheng, Editor-in-Chief; David M. Bortz, Associate Editor. **ISSN:** 1547--1063 (print); **EISSN:** 1551--0018 (electronic). **Subscription Rates:** $955 Individuals online only. **URL:** http://www.aimsciences.org/journals/home.jsp?journalID=8. **Remarks:** Advertising not accepted. **Circ:** (Not Reported).

1123 ■ MDA/ALS NewsMagazine
Muscular Dystrophy Association - Arizona
4500 S Lakeshore Dr., No. 440
Tempe, AZ 85282
Phone: (480)496-4530
Publisher's E-mail: phoenixeast@mdausa.org
Freq: Bimonthly. **Subscription Rates:** Free. **URL:** http://www.mda.org/alsn. **Remarks:** Accepts advertising. **Circ:** (Not Reported).

1124 ■ MDA Quest
Muscular Dystrophy Association - Arizona
4500 S Lakeshore Dr., No. 440
Tempe, AZ 85282
Phone: (480)496-4530
Publisher's E-mail: phoenixeast@mdausa.org
Freq: Quarterly. **Subscription Rates:** free to individuals

served by MDA; $15 Individuals /year in U.S.; $24 Individuals /year outside U.S.; $24 Two years /year in U.S.; $37 Two years /year outside U.S. **Alt. Formats:** PDF. **URL:** http://www.mda.org/quest. **Remarks:** Accepts advertising. **Circ:** (Not Reported).

1125 ■ Pool Dust
Pool Dust
PO Box 419
Tempe, AZ 85280-0419
Publication E-mail: wez@pooldust.com
Magazine covering skateboarding and music. **Freq:** Irregular. **Key Personnel:** Chris Lundry, Editor. **Subscription Rates:** $2.50 U.S. and Canada; $4.50 Elsewhere. **URL:** http://www.pooldust.com/. **Ad Rates:** BW $100. **Remarks:** Accepts advertising. **Circ:** Non-paid ‡5000.

1126 ■ Quest
Muscular Dystrophy Association - Arizona
4500 S Lakeshore Dr., No. 440
Tempe, AZ 85282
Phone: (480)496-4530
Publication E-mail: publications@mdausa.org
Magazine focusing on issues important to people who have muscular dystrophy and other neuromuscular diseases. **Founded:** 1994. **Freq:** Bimonthly. **Print Method:** Offset. **Trim Size:** 8 3/8 x 10 7/8. **Key Personnel:** Carol Sowell, Editor, phone: (520)529-5355, fax: (520)529-5383; Maureen Tuncer, Manager, Advertising. **ISSN:** 1087-1578 (print). **Subscription Rates:** $15 Individuals; $24 Other countries; $24 Two years; $37 Two years other countries; $32 Individuals 3 years; $50 Other countries 3 years. **URL:** http://quest.mda.org. **Ad Rates:** BW $3,185; 4C $3,770. **Remarks:** Advertising accepted; rates available upon request. **Circ:** Non-paid 130000.

1127 ■ Sports and Entertainment Law Journal
Arizona State University Sandra Day O'Connor College of Law
Armstrong Hall
1100 S McAllister Ave.
Tempe, AZ 85287-7906
Phone: (480)965-6181
Fax: (480)965-2427
Publisher's E-mail: asulaw.admissions@asu.edu
Journal covering scholarly articles on local, national, and international sports business and entertainment law issues that enlighten academic legal debate and advance the understanding, proper interpretation, and application of the law. **Freq:** Semiannual. **Key Personnel:** Tyler Brown, Editor-in-Chief. **URL:** http://www.law.du.edu/index.php/sports-and-entertainment-law-journal. **Mailing address:** PO Box 877906, Tempe, AZ 85287-7906. **Circ:** (Not Reported).

1128 ■ State Press
Arizona State University
c/o Arizona State University
Student Media
950 S Cady Mall
Tempe, AZ 85287-1502
Phone: (480)965-2292
Fax: (480)965-0689
Publication E-mail: state.press@asu.edu
Collegiate newspaper (tabloid) published by the students of Arizona State University. **Freq:** Mon.-Fri. in Fall and Spring, Weekly in Summer. **Print Method:** Offset. **Trim Size:** 10 5/16 x 16. **Cols./Page:** 6. **Col. Width:** 19 nonpareils. **Col. Depth:** 224 agate lines. **Key Personnel:** Shelby Slade, Editor-in-Chief. **Subscription Rates:** $125 Individuals fall, spring & summer; $75 Individuals fall semester only; $75 Individuals spring semester only; $15 Individuals summer semester only. **URL:** http://www.statepress.com. **Remarks:** Accepts advertising. **Circ:** Free ‡18000.

1129 ■ Today's Astrologer
American Federation of Astrologers
6535 S Rural Rd.
Tempe, AZ 85283-3746
Phone: (480)838-1751
Fax: (480)838-8293
Free: 888-301-7630
Publisher's E-mail: info@astrologers.com
Journal publishing astrological information and education and general membership news. **Freq:** Monthly. **ISSN:** 0735-4797 (print). **Subscription Rates:** Included in membership. **URL:** http://www.astrologers.com/get-involved/. **Remarks:** Advertising not accepted. **Circ:** 3000.

1130 ■ Wicazo Sa Review: A Journal of Native American Studies
Wicazo Sa Review
Arizona State University
Tempe, AZ 85287-4603
Publisher's E-mail: ump@umn.edu
Scholarly journal covering Native American studies. **Freq:** Semiannual. **Key Personnel:** James Riding In, Editor. **ISSN:** 0749--6427 (print); **EISSN:** 1533--7901 (electronic). **Subscription Rates:** $20 Individuals; $25 Other countries; $50 Institutions; $55 Institutions, other countries. **URL:** http://www.upress.umn.edu/journals/wsr/default.html. **Formerly**: Red Pencil Review; Wicazo Sa Review/Red Pencil Review. **Mailing address:** PO Box 874603, Tempe, AZ 85287-4603. **Remarks:** Accepts advertising. **Circ:** (Not Reported).

1131 ■ Women's Community Connection
Women's Community Connection
2544 N Champlain Ave.
Tempe, AZ 85281
Phone: (480)946-5570
Publication E-mail: publisher@womenscommunityconnection.com
Magazine for the lesbian community in Phoenix. **Key Personnel:** Sherrie Nist, Publisher. **URL:** http://www.womenscommunityconnection.com. **Ad Rates:** BW $1800. **Remarks:** Accepts advertising. **Circ:** (Not Reported).

1132 ■ Insight Communications
6820 S Harl Ave.
Tempe, AZ 85283
Free: 800-467-4448
Owner: Insight Communications Company L.P. **Formerly**: Sammons Communications. **Cities Served:** subscribing households 2,500. **URL:** http://www.insight.com.

1133 ■ KBAQ-FM - 89.5
2323 W 14th St.
Tempe, AZ 85281
Phone: (480)833-1122
Fax: (480)774-8475
Format: Classical. **Networks:** National Public Radio (NPR). **Owner:** Maricopa County Community College District, 2411 W 14th St., Tempe, AZ 85281, Ph: (480)731-8000. **Founded:** Apr. 1993. **Operating Hours**: Continuous. **ADI:** Phoenix (Kingman, Prescott), AZ. **Key Personnel:** Sterling Beeaff, Music Dir; Katrina Becker, Contact. **Wattage**: 12,500. **Ad Rates:** Noncommercial. **URL:** http://www.kbaq.org.

1134 ■ KDUS-AM - 1060
1900 W Carmen St.
Tempe, AZ 85283
Format: Sports. **Operating Hours**: Monday – Friday; 8:30 AM – 5:30 PM. **Key Personnel:** Kevin McCabe, Contact. **Wattage:** 5,000 Day Time/500 Ni. **Ad Rates:** Accepts Advertising.

1135 ■ KJZZ-FM - 91.5
2323 W 14th St.
Tempe, AZ 85281
Phone: (480)834-5627
Fax: (480)774-8475
Email: mail@kjzz.org
Format: Public Radio. **Networks:** National Public Radio (NPR). **Owner:** Maricopa Community Colleges District, 2411 W 14th St., Tempe, AZ 85281, Ph: (480)731-8000. **Founded:** 1951. **Formerly**: KMCR-FM. **Operating Hours**: Continuous; 60% network, 40% local. **Key Personnel:** Blaise Lantana, Music Dir. **Wattage**: 96,000. **Ad Rates:** Noncommercial. KBAQ. **URL:** http://www.kjzz.org.

1136 ■ KNIX-FM - 102.5
600 Gilbert Dr.
Tempe, AZ 85280
Phone: (602)966-6236
Fax: (602)966-7435
Format: Country. **Networks:** Independent. **Owner:** Owens Broadcasting, LLC., 3223 Sillect, Bakersfield, CA 93308, Ph: (805)326-1011, Fax: (805)328-7503. **Founded:** 1968. **Operating Hours**: Continuous. **Key Personnel:** Michael Owens, Gen. Mgr. **Wattage**: 100,000. **Mailing address:** PO Box 3174, Tempe, AZ 85280.

1137 ■ KTRX-FM - 93.5
2334 E Southern Ave.
Tempe, AZ 85282
Format: Country. **Networks:** ABC. **Founded:** 1977. **Operating Hours**: Continuous. **Key Personnel:** Mike L. Carter, President; Roger Houts, Operations Mgr.; Wayne Combs, News Dir.; Jay Truitt, Director. **Wattage**: 6,000. **Ad Rates:** $56-72 for 30 seconds; $70-90 for 60 seconds. **URL:** http://krss.me.

1138 ■ KUPD-FM - 97.9
1900 W Carmen St.
Tempe, AZ 85283
Phone: (480)838-0400
Format: Album-Oriented Rock (AOR). **Networks:** Independent. **Founded:** 1960. **Operating Hours**: Continuous. **Key Personnel:** Mark Randall, Promotions Dir. **Wattage:** 100,000. **Ad Rates:** Advertising accepted; rates available upon request. **URL:** http://www.98kupd.com.

THATCHER

Graham Co. Graham Co. (SE). 120 m NE of Tucson. Eastern Arizona College. Agriculture. Stock, poultry, grain farm, cotton & cattle.

1139 ■ KATO-AM - 1230
3335 W Eighth St.
Thatcher, AZ 85552
Phone: (928)428-4994
Fax: (928)428-6818
Email: traffic@mcmurrayradio.com
Format: News; Talk; Sports. **Networks:** ABC. **Owner:** McMurray Communications, Inc., 3335 W 8th St, Thatcher, AZ 85552, Ph: (928)428-1230, Fax: (928)428-1311. **Founded:** 1961. **Operating Hours:** 5 a.m.-midnight; 75% network, 25% local. **Key Personnel:** William Perry, News Dir., bperry@mcmurrayradio.com; Reed Richins, Operations Mgr., reed@mcmurrayradio.com. **Wattage:** 1,000. **Ad Rates:** $10 for 30 seconds; $15 for 60 seconds. Combined advertising rates available with KXKQ/KWRQ. **URL:** http://www.mysouthernaz.com.

1140 ■ KXKQ-FM - 94.3
3335 W Eighth St.
Thatcher, AZ 85552
Phone: (928)428-9494
Fax: (928)428-1311
Email: kat@mcmurrayradio.com
Format: Contemporary Country. **Networks:** Jones Satellite. **Owner:** McMurray Communications, Inc., 3335 W 8th St, Thatcher, AZ 85552, Ph: (928)428-1230, Fax: (928)428-1311. **Founded:** 1979. **Operating Hours**: Continuous. **ADI:** Tucson, AZ. **Wattage:** 100,000. **Ad Rates:** $10-15 per unit. Combined advertising rates available with KATO-AM/KWRQ. **URL:** http://www.mysouthernaz.com.

TUBA CITY

1141 ■ KGHR-FM - 91.3
PO Box 160
Tuba City, AZ 86045
Format: Ethnic; News; Adult Album Alternative. **Owner:** Tuba City High School Board Inc., at above address. **Operating Hours**: Continuous. **Wattage:** 100,000. **Ad Rates:** $0 per unit. **URL:** http://kghr.org.

TUCSON

Pima Co. Pima Co. (S). 125 m SE of Phoenix. University of Arizona, State School for Deaf and Blind, Pima Community College, private schools. Health and winter resort. Manufactures aerospace weapons, air conditioners, airplane instruments, electronics, ammunition, bricks, clay, cement, dairy products, dental tools, filters, optics, paint, plastics, women's wear. Poultry processing, meat packing plants. Copper, silver, gold mines. Agriculture. Cotton, cattle, grain, pecans.

1142 ■ American Journal of Medicine
Excerpta Medica Inc.
c/o Joseph S. Alpert, MD, Ed.-in-Ch.
University of Arizona College of Medicine
Tucson, AZ 85724

Circulation: ★ = AAM; △ or • = BPA; ♦ = CAC; ❑ = VAC; ⊕ = PO Statement; ‡ = Publisher's Report; Boldface figures = sworn; Light figures = estimated.

Phone: (520)207-9418
Publisher's E-mail: info@excerptamedica.com
Medical journal. **Freq:** Monthly. **Print Method:** Offset. **Cols./Page:** 2. **Col. Width:** 41 nonpareils. **Col. Depth:** 140 agate lines. **Key Personnel:** Pamela J. Powers, Managing Editor; Joseph S. Alpert, MD, Editor-in-Chief; David B. Hellmann, MD, Associate Editor; Thomas D. Boyer, MD, Associate Editor; Richard M. Mandel, MD, Associate Editor; James E. Dalen, MD, Associate Editor. **ISSN:** 0002--9343 (print); **EISSN:** 1552--4833 (electronic). **Subscription Rates:** $210 U.S. and Canada print and online; $509 Other countries print and online; $122 Students print and online US; $131 Students print and online - Canada/International. **URL:** http://www.amjmed.com/. **Ad Rates:** BW $4,850. **Remarks:** Accepts advertising. **Circ:** (Not Reported).

1143 ■ Animal Keepers' Forum
American Association of Zoo Keepers
8476 E Speedway Blvd., Ste. 204
Tucson, AZ 85710-1728
Phone: (520)298-9688
Publisher's E-mail: visitor@aazk.org
Professional journal of the American Association of Zoo Keepers, Inc. **Freq:** Monthly. **Print Method:** Offset. **Trim Size:** 6 x 9. **Cols./Page:** 1. **Key Personnel:** Susan D. Chan, Managing Editor; Barbara Manspeaker, Secretary, Administration. **ISSN:** 0164--9531 (print). **Subscription Rates:** $15 Individuals; $17.50 Other countries. **URL:** http://www.aazk.org/animal-keepers-forum. **Ad Rates:** BW $215. **Remarks:** Accepts advertising. **Circ:** Controlled 2850.

1144 ■ Arizona Gourmet Living
Oser Communications Group Inc.
1877 N Kolb
Tucson, AZ 85715
Phone: (520)721-1300
Fax: (520)721-6300
Publication E-mail: info@azgourmet.com
Consumer magazine covering food and beverages. **Freq:** Quarterly. **Key Personnel:** Lee M. Oser, Jr., Editor-in-Chief; Jenna Crisostomo, Managing Editor; Tara Neal, Manager, Circulation. **Subscription Rates:** $21.95 Individuals; $33.95 Two years. **Alt. Formats:** PDF. **URL:** http://www.osercomm.com/arizona-gourmet-living; http://www.arizonagourmetliving.com. **Formerly:** Arizona Gourmet. **Remarks:** Accepts advertising. **Circ:** Free ■ **24519**, Paid ■ **4**, Combined ■ **24523**.

1145 ■ Arizona Jewish Post
Jewish Federation of Southern Arizona
5546 E 4th St., Ste. 101
Tucson, AZ 85711
Phone: (520)319-1112
Jewish interest newspaper. **Freq:** Biweekly. **Print Method:** Offset. **Cols./Page:** 6. **Col. Depth:** 13 inches. **Key Personnel:** Phyllis Braun, Executive Editor. **URL:** http://azjewishpost.com. **Formerly:** Arizona Post. **Remarks:** Advertising accepted; rates available upon request. **Circ:** 6300.

1146 ■ Arizona Journal of International and Comparative Law
University of Arizona James E. Rogers College of Law
1201 E Speedway
Tucson, AZ 85721-0176
Phone: (520)621-1373
Fax: (520)626-9140
Journal containing articles on a wide variety of international and comparative law topics. **Freq:** Semiannual. **Key Personnel:** Derek Graffious, Editor-in-Chief. **Subscription Rates:** $29 Individuals; $33 Other countries; $10 Single issue domestic shipping; $12 Single issue foreign shipping. **URL:** http://arizonajournal.org. **Circ:** (Not Reported).

1147 ■ Arizona Quarterly: A Journal of American Literature, Culture and Theory
Arizona Quarterly
University of Arizona
1731 E 2nd St.
Tucson, AZ 85721
Fax: (520)621-7397
Publication E-mail: azq@u.arizona.edu
Scholarly journal on American literature, culture, and theory. **Freq:** Quarterly. **Print Method:** Offset. **Trim Size:** 6 x 9. **Cols./Page:** 1. **Col. Width:** 54 nonpareils. **Col. Depth:** 81 agate lines. **Key Personnel:** Tenney Nathanson, Associate Editor; Lynda Zwinger, Associate Editor; Edgar A. Dryden, Editor. **ISSN:** 0004--1610 (print). **Subscription Rates:** $40 Individuals; $80 Individuals three years; $55 Institutions; $110 Institutions three years; $15 Single issue; $20 Single issue special issues. **URL:** http://azq.arizona.edu. **Ad Rates:** BW $150. **Remarks:** Accepts advertising. **Circ:** Paid ‡350, Non-paid ‡300.

1148 ■ AzGS Journal
Arizona Geriatrics Society
c/o Mindy Fain, MD, Journal Editor
University of Arizona College of Medicine
1821 East Elma St.
Tucson, AZ 85719
Publisher's E-mail: AskUs@ArizonaGeriatrics.org
Freq: Annual. **Key Personnel:** Carol L. Howe, MD, Editor; Dr. Mindy Fain, Editor. **Alt. Formats:** PDF. **URL:** http://www.arizonageriatrics.org/journal. **Ad Rates:** $525-600. BW $. **Remarks:** Accepts advertising. **Circ:** ★**1000**, 1200.

1149 ■ Aztec Press
Pima County Community College
4905 E Broadway Blvd.
Tucson, AZ 85709-1000
Phone: (520)206-4500
Free: 800-860-PIMA
Publication E-mail: aztecpress@pima.edu
Collegiate newspaper. **Founded:** 1973. **Freq:** Weekly (Thurs.). **Print Method:** Web Offset. **Trim Size:** 11 x 16. **Cols./Page:** 5. **Col. Width:** 24 nonpareils. **Col. Depth:** 224 agate lines. **Key Personnel:** Debbie Hadley, Editor-in-Chief; Astrid Verdugo, Editor; Anthony French, Manager, Advertising. **Subscription Rates:** Free. **Alt. Formats:** PDF. **URL:** http://aztecpressonline.com. **Formerly:** Aztec News; Campus News. **Ad Rates:** PCI $11. **Remarks:** Advertising accepted; rates available upon request. **Circ:** ‡5000.

1150 ■ Collegiate Baseball Newspaper
Collegiate Baseball Newspaper Inc.
2515 N Stone Ave.
Tucson, AZ 85705
Phone: (520)623-4530
Fax: (520)624-5501
Publication E-mail: cbn@azstarnet.com
Amateur baseball magazine. **Freq:** 14/yr. **Print Method:** Offset. **Cols./Page:** 5. **Col. Width:** 23 nonpareils. **Col. Depth:** 194 agate lines. **Key Personnel:** Dianne Pavlovich, Manager, Advertising. **ISSN:** 0530--9751 (print). **Subscription Rates:** $28 Individuals one year; $48 Two years; $45 Individuals first class one year; $50 Other countries airmail one year; $32 Canada one year; $4 Single issue past issue. **URL:** http://www.baseballnews.com. **Mailing address:** PO Box 50566, Tucson, AZ 85703. **Ad Rates:** BW $1530; 4C $2070; PCI $25. **Circ:** ‡7500.

1151 ■ The Daily Territorial
Territorial Newspapers
3280 E Hemisphere Loop, Ste. 180
Tucson, AZ 85706
Phone: (520)294-1200
Fax: (520)294-4040
Newspaper featuring business and legal news. **Freq:** Daily Monday through Friday. **Print Method:** Offset. **Cols./Page:** 4. **Col. Width:** 2 3/8 inches. **Col. Depth:** 14 inches. **Key Personnel:** Thomas P. Lee, Publisher. **ISSN:** 0743--8397 (print). **Subscription Rates:** $45 Individuals 3 months; $70 Individuals 6 months; $110 Individuals 1 year; $190 Two years. **URL:** http://www.insidetucsonbusiness.com/daily_territorial; http://www.insidetucsonbusiness.com/subscribe-to-the-daily-territorial/article_4cbba691-ac64-572f-ada6-4256fae3a7d4.html. **Mailing address:** PO Box 872, Tucson, AZ 85726. **Ad Rates:** GLR $.39; BW $390; 4C $840; PCI $7.50. **Remarks:** Accepts advertising. **Circ:** Paid 892, Free 100.

1152 ■ Desert Plants
University of Arizona College of Agriculture and Life Sciences
2120 E Allen Rd.
Tucson, AZ 85719
Phone: (520)305-3586
Professional journal covering plants in arid and semi-arid environments. **Founded:** 1979. **Freq:** Semiannual. **Cols./Page:** 2. **Key Personnel:** Margaret Norem, Editor. **ISSN:** 0734-3434 (print). **Subscription Rates:** $20 Individuals; $3 Individuals single back issue; $30 Other countries; $50 Institutions. **URL:** http://cals.arizona.edu/desertplants/. **Remarks:** Advertising not accepted. **Circ:** Combined 1000.

1153 ■ The Ecofeminist Journal
Feminists for Animal Rights
PO Box 41355
Tucson, AZ 85717
Phone: (520)825-6852
Publisher's E-mail: far@farinc.org
Remarks: Advertising not accepted. **Circ:** (Not Reported).

1154 ■ Fibromyalgia Network Journal
Fibromyalgia Network
7371 E Tanque Verde Rd.
Tucson, AZ 85715
Phone: (520)290-5508
Fax: (520)290-5550
Free: 800-853-2929
Contains articles, new treatments, and the latest advancements in research about the fibromyalgia syndrome. **Freq:** Quarterly. **Subscription Rates:** $28. **URL:** http://fmnetnews.iraherman.com/publications/quarterly-journal. **Remarks:** Advertising not accepted. **Circ:** (Not Reported).

1155 ■ First Days
American First Day Cover Society
PO Box 16277
Tucson, AZ 85732-6277
Phone: (520)321-0880
Publisher's E-mail: afdcs@afdcs.org
Freq: 6/year. **ISSN:** 0428- 4836 (print). **Subscription Rates:** Included in membership. **Alt. Formats:** PDF. **URL:** http://www.afdcs.org/firstdays.html. **Remarks:** Accepts advertising. **Circ:** 5000.

1156 ■ General Music Today
SAGE Publications Inc.
c/o Shelly Cooper, Ed.
9684 N Deimos Dr.
Tucson, AZ 85743-7461
Publisher's E-mail: sales@pfp.sagepub.com
Professional journal covering general music from early childhood through high school for teachers. **Freq:** 3/year January, April and October. **Key Personnel:** Shelly Cooper, Editor, phone: (520)744-9091, fax: (520)621-8118. **ISSN:** 1048-3713 (print); **EISSN:** 1931-3756 (electronic). **Subscription Rates:** $88 Institutions e-access; $97 Institutions e-acces +back file; Members free; $61 Institutions backfile lease, E-access plus backfile (All online content); $55 Institutions backfile purchase, E-access (content through 1998). **URL:** http://www.sagepub.com/journalsProdDesc.nav?ct_p=subscribe&prodId=Journal201902. **Remarks:** Advertising not accepted. **Circ:** (Not Reported).

1157 ■ Geoarchaeology: An International Journal
John Wiley & Sons Inc.
c/o Gary Huckleberry, Co-Ed.
Department of Geoscience, The University of Arizona
Gould-Simpson Bldg., No. 77
1040 E 4th St.
Tucson, AZ 85721
Publisher's E-mail: info@wiley.com
Publication dedicated to the exploration of the relationships between the various disciplines of anthropologists, archaeologists, geologists, geographers and geomorphologists. Focuses primarily on the application of the geological sciences in furthering the interpretation of archaeological materials. **Freq:** Bimonthly. **Print Method:** Offset. **Trim Size:** 7 1/4 x 10 1/4. **Cols./Page:** 2. **Col. Width:** 13 picas. **Col. Depth:** 45 picas. **Key Personnel:** Rolfe D. Mandel, Associate Editor; Gary Huckleberry, Editor; Paul Goldberg, Associate Editor; Richard MacPhail, Associate Editor; Jamie C. Woodward, Editor; Barry Taylor, Assistant Editor. **ISSN:** 0883--6353 (print); **EISSN:** 1520--6548 (electronic). **Subscription Rates:** $2567 Institutions online only - Canada & Mexico/ROW print or online - USA; $3081 Institutions print + online; $322 Individuals print only - USA/Canada & Mexico; $3215 Institutions, Canada and Mexico print + online; $2679 Institutions, Canada and Mexico print only; £1312 Institutions online only UK; £1678 Institutions print + online UK; £1398 Institutions print only UK; $378 Other countries print only; €1656 Institutions online only; €2117 Institutions print + online; €1764 Institutions print only; $3282 Institutions, other countries

print + online; $2735 Institutions, other countries print only. **URL:** http://onlinelibrary.wiley.com/journal/10.1002/(ISSN)1520-6548. **Ad Rates:** BW $757; 4C $1,009. **Remarks:** Accepts advertising. **Circ:** 3850.

1158 ■ Handball
United States Handball Association
2333 N Tucson Blvd.
Tucson, AZ 85716
Phone: (520)795-0434
Fax: (520)795-0465
Free: 800-289-8742
Publication E-mail: handball@ushandball.org
Magazine featuring handball game. **Print Method:** Offset. **Trim Size:** 8 1/8 x 10 3/8. **Cols./Page:** 3. **Col. Width:** 27 nonpareils. **Col. Depth:** 140 agate lines. **Key Personnel:** Vern Roberts, Executive Editor. **ISSN:** 0046--6778 (print). **Subscription Rates:** Included in membership. **URL:** http://www.ushandball.org. **Remarks:** Accepts advertising. **Circ:** ‡10000.

1159 ■ IEEE Antennas & Propagation
IEEE - Antennas and Propagation Society
c/o J. Scott Tyo, Secretary/Treasurer
University of Arizona
Meinel Bldg., Rm. 623
Tucson, AZ 85745
Phone: (520)626-8183
Fax: (520)621-4358
Membership magazine covering antennas, propogation, telecommunications, electromagnetics, and computational methods. Non-member subscriptions are available. **Freq:** Bimonthly. **Key Personnel:** W. Ross Stone, Editor-in-Chief, phone: (619)222-1915, fax: (619)222-1606. **ISSN:** 1045--9243 (print). **Alt. Formats:** PDF. **URL:** http://ieeexplore.ieee.org/xpl/RecentIssue.jsp?punumber=74. **Ad Rates:** BW $630; 4C $1,375. **Remarks:** Accepts advertising. **Circ:** Controlled 10400.

1160 ■ IEEE Antennas and Propagation Magazine
IEEE - Antennas and Propagation Society
c/o J. Scott Tyo, Secretary/Treasurer
University of Arizona
Meinel Bldg., Rm. 623
Tucson, AZ 85745
Phone: (520)626-8183
Fax: (520)621-4358
Magazine featuring articles that describe engineering activities taking place in industry, government, and universities. **Freq:** Bimonthly. **Key Personnel:** W. Ross Stone, Editor-in-Chief, phone: (619)222-1915, fax: (619)222-1606. **URL:** http://www.ieeeaps.org/publications/ieee-antennas-and-propagation-magazine. **Remarks:** Advertising not accepted. **Circ:** (Not Reported).

1161 ■ Inside Tucson Business
Territorial Newspapers
7225 N Mona Lisa Rd., Ste. 125
Tucson, AZ 85741
Phone: (520)797-4384
Fax: (520)575-8891
Newspaper featuring business news. **Freq:** Weekly. **Print Method:** Offset. **Cols./Page:** 4. **Col. Width:** 2 1/2 inches. **Col. Depth:** 12 1/2 inches. **Key Personnel:** Greg Day, Manager, Production; Jill A'Hearn, Director, Advertising; David Hatfield, Editor; Thomas Lee, Publisher. **ISSN:** 1069--5184 (print). **Subscription Rates:** $50 Individuals; $85 Two years; $35 Individuals new subscriber; $105 Individuals 3 years. **URL:** http://www.insidetucsonbusiness.com. **Ad Rates:** BW $1,552; 4C $2,002; PCI $29.85. **Remarks:** Accepts advertising. **Circ:** Paid ■ **3919**, Non-paid ■ **1687**.

1162 ■ International Journal of Computational Cognition
Yang's Scientific Research Institute
1303 E University Blvd., No. 20882
Tucson, AZ 85719-0521
Fax: (760)418-8415
Publication E-mail: ijcc@yangsky.com
Journal that aims to provide a forum for interdisciplinary discourse about computational cognition among scientists, educators, students, and engineers. **Freq:** Quarterly. **Key Personnel:** Tao Yang, Editor-in-Chief; Goong Chen, Editor; Yoshiyuki Suzuki, Editor. **ISSN:** 1542--8060 (print); **EISSN:** 1542--5908 (electronic). **Remarks:** Accepts advertising. **Circ:** (Not Reported).

1163 ■ Journal of Aging Life Care
Aging Life Care Association
3275 W Ina Rd., Ste. 130
Tucson, AZ 85741-2198
Phone: (520)881-8008
Fax: (520)325-7925
Journal containing topics that is relevant to care managers' clinical and business interests. **Freq:** Semiannual. **Key Personnel:** Jennifer E. Voorlas, MSG, CMC, Editor-in-Chief. **URL:** http://www.aginglifecarejournal.org. **Formerly:** Journal of Geriatric Care Management. **Remarks:** Accepts advertising. **Circ:** (Not Reported).

1164 ■ Journal of American Physicians and Surgeons
Association of American Physicians and Surgeons
1601 N Tucson Blvd., No. 9
Tucson, AZ 85716
Phone: (520)323-3110
Fax: (520)326-3529
Free: 800-635-1196
Publisher's E-mail: aaps@aapsonline.org
Freq: Quarterly. **Subscription Rates:** $75 Individuals; $125 Institutions. **URL:** http://www.jpands.org. **Remarks:** Advertising not accepted. **Circ:** (Not Reported).

1165 ■ Journal of Applied Business and Economics
National Business and Economics Society
PO Box 65657
Tucson, AZ 85728
Phone: (520)395-2622
Fax: (520)395-2622
Publisher's E-mail: info@nbesonline.com
Refereed journal that is dedicated to the advancement and dissemination of business and economic knowledge by ongoing results of research. **Key Personnel:** Dr. Andy Bertsch, Board Member. **ISSN:** 1499--691X (print). **Subscription Rates:** $360 Individuals. **URL:** http://www.na-businesspress.com/jabeopen.html. **Circ:** (Not Reported).

1166 ■ Journal of Arizona History
Arizona Historical Society
949 E 2nd St.
Tucson, AZ 85719
Phone: (520)617-1165
Fax: (520)628-5695
Journal covering the history of the Southwestern U.S., northern Mexico, and Arizona, particularly. **Freq:** Quarterly. **Key Personnel:** Bruce J. Dinges, Editor. **ISSN:** 0021--9053 (print). **Subscription Rates:** $7 Single issue back issue; $12.50 Single issue current issues. **URL:** http://www.arizonahistoricalsociety.org/publications. **Remarks:** Advertising not accepted. **Circ:** Controlled 2300.

1167 ■ Journal of Biological Dynamics
Taylor & Francis Group Journals
c/o J.M. Cushing, Ed.-in-Ch.
University of Arizona
617 N Santa Rita
Tucson, AZ 85721-0089
Publisher's E-mail: customerservice@taylorandfrancis.com
Journal providing information on dynamic phenomena, ecology and ecosystems. **Freq:** Continuous. **Key Personnel:** J.M. Cushing, Editor-in-Chief; Saber Elaydi, Editor-in-Chief. **ISSN:** 1751--3758 (print); **EISSN:** 1751--3766 (electronic). **URL:** http://www.tandfonline.com/toc/tjbd20/current; http://www.tandfonline.com/loi/tjbd20#.VzVmaTWrQdU. **Circ:** (Not Reported).

1168 ■ Journal of Non-Crystalline Solids
RELX Group P.L.C.
c/o B.G. Potter, Ed.
University of Arizona
Arizona Materials Laboratory
4715 E Ft. Lowell Rd.
Tucson, AZ 85712-1201
Publisher's E-mail: amsterdam@relx.com
Journal dealing with topics on oxide and non- oxide glasses, amorphous semiconductors, and non-crystalline films. **Freq:** Semimonthly. **Key Personnel:** B.G. Potter, Editor. **ISSN:** 0022--3093 (print). **Subscription Rates:** $10155 Institutions print; $7996 Institutions ejournal. **URL:** http://www.journals.elsevier.com/journal-of-non-crystalline-solids. **Circ:** (Not Reported).

1169 ■ Journal of the Southwest
University of Arizona Southwest Center
1052 N Highland Ave.
Tucson, AZ 85721-0185
Phone: (520)621-2484
Fax: (520)621-9922
Publisher's E-mail: jwilder@email.arizona.edu
Scholarly journal covering natural and human history, literature, folklore, politics, and anthropology of the Southwest U.S. **Freq:** Quarterly. **Trim Size:** 6 x 9. **Key Personnel:** Joseph C. Wilder, Editor. **ISSN:** 0894--8410 (print); **EISSN:** 2158--1371 (electronic). **Subscription Rates:** $25 Individuals /year; $65 Institutions /year; $50 Other countries individual per year; $75 Institutions, other countries. **URL:** http://muse.jhu.edu/journal/530. **Formerly:** Arizona and the West. **Ad Rates:** BW $100. **Remarks:** Accepts advertising. **Circ:** Paid 1000.

1170 ■ The Journal for Specialists in Group Work
Routledge
c/o Sheri Bauman, Ed.
Dept. of Educational Psychology
University of Arizona
Tucson, AZ 85721-0069
Publisher's E-mail: book.orders@tandf.co.uk
Journal reviewing theory, empirical research related to group work, counseling, and therapy. **Founded:** 1976. **Freq:** Quarterly (March, June, September, and December). **Print Method:** Web Offset. **Trim Size:** 6 x 9. **Key Personnel:** Christopher J. McCarthy, Ph.D., Editor. **ISSN:** 0193-3922 (print). **Subscription Rates:** $115 Individuals print only; $401 Institutions print and online; $351 Institutions online only. **URL:** http://www.tandf.co.uk/journals/titles/01933922.asp. **Mailing address:** PO Box 210069, Tucson, AZ 85721-0069. **Remarks:** Accepts advertising. **Circ:** ‡2300.

1171 ■ Light of Consciousness: A Journal of Spiritual Awakening
Truth Consciousness at Desert Ashram
3403 W Sweetwater Dr.
Tucson, AZ 85745-9301
Phone: (520)743-8821
Publisher's E-mail: info@truthconsciousness.org
Consumer magazine on spirituality. **Freq:** Quarterly. **Print Method:** Offset. **Trim Size:** 8 1/2 x 10 7/8. **Cols./Page:** 2. **ISSN:** 1040--7448 (print). **Subscription Rates:** $23.99 Individuals print and online; $34.99 Canada print and online; $35.99 Other countries print and online; $19.99 Individuals print; $30.99 Canada print; $35.99 Other countries print. **URL:** http://light-of-consciousness.org. **Ad Rates:** BW $750; 4C $850. **Remarks:** Advertising accepted; rates available upon request. **Circ:** Paid 22500.

1172 ■ Lymphology
International Society of Lymphology
PO Box 245200
Tucson, AZ 85724
Phone: (520)626-6118
Fax: (520)626-0822
Freq: Quarterly. **ISSN:** 0024--7766 (print). **Subscription Rates:** $75 with 10% discount for vendors. **URL:** http://journals.uair.arizona.edu/index.php/lymph/index. **Remarks:** Advertising not accepted. **Circ:** (Not Reported).

1173 ■ Meteoritics and Planetary Science
The Meteoritical Society
University of Arizona
Department of Geosciences
4717 E Fort Lowell Rd., Rm. 104
Tucson, AZ 85712-1201
Phone: (520)881-0857
Fax: (520)881-0554
Publication E-mail: office@meteoritics.org
Journal covering research on meteorites, lunar samples, interplanetary dust, impact processes, asteroids and meteors. **Freq:** Monthly. **Key Personnel:** Prof. A.J. Timothy Jull, Editor; Agnieszka P. Baier, Managing Editor. **ISSN:** 1086--9379 (print); **EISSN:** 1945--5100 (electronic). **Subscription Rates:** $2055 Institutions print + online; £1257 Institutions print + online; €1473 Institutions print + online; $1712 Institutions online only; £1047 Institutions online only; €1227 Institutions online only. **URL:** http://onlinelibrary.wiley.com/journal/10.1111/

Circulation: ★ = AAM; △ or • = BPA; ♦ = CAC; ❑ = VAC; ⊕ = PO Statement; ‡ = Publisher's Report; Boldface figures = sworn; Light figures = estimated.

%28ISSN%291945-5100. **Remarks:** Advertising not accepted. **Circ:** 1200.

1174 ■ New Tucson Shopper
The Tucson Shopper
1861 W Grant Rd.
Tucson, AZ 85745
Phone: (520)622-0101
Publication E-mail: sgallagher@newtucsonshopper.com
Shopping guide zoned in 26 community editions. **Freq:** Weekly (Wed.). **Formerly**: Tucson Shopper. **Circ:** 260000.

1175 ■ Newspapers & Technology
Conley Magazines L.L.C.
7000 E Tanque Verde, Ste. 11
Tucson, AZ 85715-5318
Phone: (520)721-2929
Trade journal for newspaper publishers. **Freq:** Monthly. **Print Method:** Web Offset. **Trim Size:** 10.75 x 14.5. **Key Personnel:** Mary Van Meter, Publisher; Tara McMeekin, Editor. **ISSN:** 1052--5572 (print). **URL:** http://www.newsandtech.com. **Remarks:** Accepts advertising. **Circ:** (Not Reported).

1176 ■ Physica D: Nonlinear Phenomena
RELX Group P.L.C.
c/o Joceline Lega, Editor-in-Chief
Dept. of Mathematics
University of Arizona
Tucson, AZ 85721
Publisher's E-mail: amsterdam@relx.com
Journal reporting on advances in the nonlinear phenomena including wave motion in physical, chemical and biological systems; chaotic motion in models relevant to turbulence, physical and biological phenomena governed by nonlinear field equations; instability, bifurcation, pattern formation and cooperative phenomena. **Freq:** 24/yr. **Key Personnel:** S. Coombes, Editor; T. Sauer, Editor-in-Chief. **ISSN:** 0167--2789 (print). **Subscription Rates:** $2716.67 Institutions online; $4412 Institutions print. **URL:** http://www.journals.elsevier.com/physica-d-nonlinear-phenomena. **Circ:** (Not Reported).

1177 ■ Roadhouse Music Magazine
Southwest Alternatives Institute Inc.
PO Box 3355
Tucson, AZ 85722
Phone: (520)623-3733
Publisher's E-mail: sai@emol.org
Newspaper of the Southwest Alternatives Institute. **URL:** http://emol.org/sai. **Circ:** (Not Reported).

1178 ■ Safari Magazine
Safari Club International
4800 W Gates Pass Rd.
Tucson, AZ 85745-9490
Phone: (520)620-1220
Fax: (520)622-1205
Free: 888-486-8724
Freq: 7/year. **Print Method:** Web offset. **Trim Size:** 7 3/4 x 10 3/4. **Cols./Page:** 3. **Col. Width:** 26 nonpareils. **Col. Depth:** 140 agate lines. **Key Personnel:** Angelia Sagi, Manager, Sales, phone: (910)875-8781, fax: (520)618-3555. **ISSN:** 0199--5316 (print). **Subscription Rates:** Included in membership. **URL:** http://www.scifirstforhunters.org/coverage/pubs. **Ad Rates:** BW $2590; 4C $3750. **Remarks:** Accepts advertising. **Circ:** Controlled ‡39000.

1179 ■ Spirit & Life: Inspiration for Christian Living
Benedictine Sisters of Perpetual Adoration
800 N Country Club Rd.
Tucson, AZ 85716-4583
Phone: (520)325-6401
Spiritual growth magazine for Christians. **Freq:** Bimonthly. **Key Personnel:** Lenora Black, Editor; Mary DeSales, Editor. **ISSN:** 0038-7592 (print). **Subscription Rates:** $2.50 Single issue. **URL:** http://www.benedictinesisters.org/spirit-and-life-magazine-home.php. **Formerly**: Tabernacle & Purgatory. **Remarks:** Advertising not accepted. **Circ:** 10000.

1180 ■ Terrain.org: A Journal of the Built & Natural Environments
Terrain Publishing
PO Box 19161
Tucson, AZ 85731-9161
Publication E-mail: info@terrain.org
Journal dealing with all aspects of built and natural environments. **Freq:** Semiannual. **Key Personnel:** Todd Ziebarth, Board Member; Simmons B. Buntin, Editor-in-Chief. **ISSN:** 1932--9474 (print). **Circ:** (Not Reported).

1181 ■ Tree-Ring Research
University of Arizona Laboratory of Tree-Ring Research
1215 E Lowell St., Box 210045
Tucson, AZ 85721
Phone: (520)621-1608
Fax: (520)621-8229
Publisher's E-mail: trslori@gmail.com
Peer-reviewed journal publishing articles and research on growth rings of trees and the applications of tree-ring in a wide variety of fields. **Freq:** Semiannual. **Key Personnel:** Steven Leavitt, Editor. **ISSN:** 1536--1098 (print); **EISSN:** 2162--4585 (electronic). **URL:** http://www.treeringsociety.org/journal.html. **Formerly**: Tree-Ring Bulletin. **Remarks:** Advertising not accepted. **Circ:** 333.

1182 ■ Tucson Lifestyle Magazine
Conley Magazines L.L.C.
7000 E Tanque Verde, Ste. 11
Tucson, AZ 85715-5318
Phone: (520)721-2929
Publication E-mail: tlm@tucsonlifestyle.com
Tucson lifestyle magazine. **Freq:** Monthly. **Print Method:** Offset. **Trim Size:** 8 1/8 x 10 3/4. **Cols./Page:** 3. **Col. Width:** 120 picas. **Col. Depth:** 58.5 picas. **Key Personnel:** Sue Giles, Editor-in-Chief; Anne Kellogg, Associate Editor; Scott Barker, Executive Editor. **ISSN:** 1062--2861 (print). **Subscription Rates:** $18 Individuals 1 year; $25 Out of state 1 year; $32 Two years; $39 Out of state 2 years; $42 Individuals 3 years; $49 Out of state 3 years. **URL:** http://www.tucsonlifestyle.com; http://www.tucsonlifestyle.com/magazine/current-issue/. **Ad Rates:** BW $2746; 4C $4130. **Remarks:** Accepts advertising. **Circ:** 29000.

1183 ■ Tucson Weekly
Tucson Weekly
7225 N Mona Lisa Rd., Ste. 125
Tucson, AZ 85741
Phone: (520)797-4384
Fax: (520)575-8891
Publisher's E-mail: mailbag@tucsonweekly.com
Tucson metropolitan newspaper (tabloid) covering news and arts. **Freq:** Weekly (Thurs.). **Key Personnel:** Mari Herreras, Editor; Steve Pope, Publisher. **ISSN:** 0742--0692 (print). **URL:** http://www.tucsonweekly.com; http://issuu.com/tucsonweekly/docs. **Remarks:** Accepts advertising. **Circ:** Free ‡41509.

1184 ■ University of Arizona Journal of Medicine
University of Arizona College of Medicine
1501 N Campbell Ave.
Tucson, AZ 85724
Phone: (520)626-4555
Publisher's E-mail: sgoldsch@email.arizona.edu
Contains articles by medical students on basic science, clinical and translational research, and humanities essays. **Freq:** Semiannual. **URL:** http://journals.uair.arizona.edu/index.php/UAJOM/index. **Mailing address:** PO Box 245017, Tucson, AZ 85724. **Circ:** (Not Reported).

1185 ■ Water Conditioning & Purification
Publicom Inc.
2800 E Fort Lowell Rd.
Tucson, AZ 85716
Phone: (520)323-6144
Fax: (520)323-7412
Publication E-mail: info@wcponline.com
Magazine on residential and commercial water conditioning and purification. **Freq:** Monthly. **Print Method:** Web offset. **Trim Size:** 8 1/4 x 10 7/8. **Cols./Page:** 3. **Col. Width:** 26 nonpareils. **Col. Depth:** 140 agate lines. **Key Personnel:** Kurt C. Peterson, Publisher, Director, Advertising; Denise M. Roberts, Executive Editor; Sharon M. Peterson, Founder. **ISSN:** 0746--4029 (print). **Subscription Rates:** Free. **URL:** http://www.wcponline.com. **Ad Rates:** 4C $3000, full page; 4C $2000, 1/2 page island; 4C $1850, 1/2 page. **Remarks:** Accepts advertising. **Circ:** (Not Reported).

1186 ■ The Weekly Observer
The Weekly Observer
PO Box 50733
Tucson, AZ 85703
Phone: (520)622-7176
Publication E-mail: info@tucsonobserver.com
Community newspaper primarily for a gay and lesbian audience. **Founded:** Sept. 29, 1976. **Freq:** Weekly (Wed.). **Print Method:** Offset. **Key Personnel:** Bob Ellis, Editor-in-Chief; Mark Kerr, Managing Editor. **Alt. Formats:** PDF. **URL:** http://www.tucsonobserver.com. **Remarks:** Accepts advertising. **Circ:** (Not Reported).

1187 ■ KAMP-AM - 1570
615 N Park Ave., No. 101
Tucson, AZ 85721
Phone: (520)621-8173
Fax: (520)626-5986
Format: Contemporary Hit Radio (CHR). **Founded:** 1988. **Key Personnel:** Michael Lemons, Dir. of Engg. **Ad Rates:** Noncommercial. **URL:** http://www.kamp.arizona.edu.

1188 ■ KAMY-FM - 90.1
PO Box 35300
Tucson, AZ 85740
Free: 800-776-1070
Format: Religious. **Owner:** Family Life Communications, Inc., 7355 N Oracle Rd., Tucson, AZ 85704, Ph: (520)544-5950, Fax: (520)742-6979, Free: 800-776-1070. **Founded:** Sept. 15, 2006. **ADI:** Lubbock, TX. **Wattage**: 63,000. **Ad Rates:** Noncommercial. **URL:** http://www.myflr.org.

1189 ■ KAVV-FM - 97.7
PO Box 18899
Tucson, AZ 85731
Phone: (520)586-9797
Format: Country. **Key Personnel:** Paul Lotsof, Mgr.

1190 ■ KCEE-AM - 690
3222 S Richey Ave.
Tucson, AZ 85713
Phone: (520)790-2440
Fax: (520)790-2937
Email: info@690kcee.com
Format: Big Band/Nostalgia. **Owner:** Good News Radio Broadcasting. **Key Personnel:** Doug Martin, Gen. Mgr., President. **URL:** http://www.690kcee.com.

1191 ■ KCMT-FM - 92.1
3871 N Commerce Dr.
Tucson, AZ 85705
Phone: (520)407-4500
Format: Hispanic. **Founded:** Sept. 07, 2006. **Wattage**: 50,000. **URL:** http://www.kcmt.com.

1192 ■ KCUB-AM - 1290
575 W Roger Rd.
Tucson, AZ 85705
Phone: (520)887-1000
Format: Country. **Networks:** Independent. **Owner:** Slone Broadcasting Co., 3222 S Richey Avenue, Tucson, AZ 85713-5498, Ph: (520)790-2440. **Founded:** 1929. **Operating Hours**: Continuous; 100% local. **ADI:** Tucson, AZ. **Key Personnel:** Keith Rosenblatt, Sales Mgr., keith.rosenblatt@citcomm.com. **Wattage**: 1,000. **Ad Rates:** Noncommercial. **URL:** http://www.sportsradio1290am.com.

1193 ■ KEYU-FM - 98.5
7355 N Oracle Rd.
Tucson, AZ 85704
Free: 800-776-1070
Format: Contemporary Christian. **Owner:** Family Life Broadcasting Inc., PO Box 35300, Tucson, AZ 85740. **Founded:** 1966. **Formerly**: KRGN-FM. **Operating Hours**: Continuous. **Wattage**: 079. **Ad Rates:** Noncommercial. **URL:** http://www.myflr.org.

1194 ■ KFFN-AM - 1490
7280 E Rosewood St.
Tucson, AZ 85710
Phone: (520)722-5486
Format: Sports; Talk. **Networks:** ABC; ESPN Radio. **Owner:** Journal Broadcast Group Inc., 333 W State St., Milwaukee, WI 53203-1305, Ph: (414)332-9611, Fax: (414)967-5400. **Founded:** 1957. **Formerly**: KJYK-AM; KKND-AM. **Operating Hours**: Continuous. **ADI:** Tucson, AZ. **Wattage**: 1,000. **Ad Rates:** Noncommercial. KMXZ-FM, KZPT-FM, KGMG-FM. **URL:** http://www.espntucson.com.

1195 ■ KFLB-AM - 920
PO Box 35300
Tucson, AZ 85740
Free: 800-776-1070
Format: Religious. **Ad Rates:** Noncommercial. **URL:** http://www.myflr.org.

KFLQ-FM - See Albuquerque, NM

KFLR-FM - See Phoenix, AZ

1196 ■ KFLT-AM - 830
PO Box 35300
Tucson, AZ 85740
Free: 800-776-1070
Format: Religious. **Networks:** USA Radio; Moody Broadcasting. **Owner:** Family Life Communications, Inc., 7355 N Oracle Rd., Tucson, AZ 85704, Ph: (520)544-5950, Fax: (520)742-6979, Free: 800-776-1070. **Founded:** 1977. **Formerly:** KOPO-AM. **Operating Hours:** Continuous; 10% network, 90% local. **ADI:** Tucson, AZ. **Wattage:** 50,000 Day; 1,000 Night. **Ad Rates:** Noncommercial. **URL:** http://www.myflr.org.

1197 ■ KFMA-FM - 102.1
3871 N Commerce Dr.
Tucson, AZ 85705
Phone: (520)407-4500
Email: only@kfma.com
Format: Country. **ADI:** Tucson, AZ. **Key Personnel:** Ken Kwilosz, Gen. Mgr., kkwilosz@azlotus.com; Larry Mac, Operations Mgr., lmac@azlotus.com. **Wattage:** 100,000 ERP. **Ad Rates:** Advertising accepted; rates available upon request. **URL:** http://www.kfma.com.

1198 ■ KGMG-FM - 106.3
7280 E Rosewood St.
Tucson, AZ 85710
Phone: (520)722-5486
Email: feedback@1063thegroove.com
Format: Oldies; Blues. **Owner:** Journal Broadcast Corp., 333 W State St., Milwaukee, WI 53203, Ph: (414)332-9611, Fax: (414)967-5400. **Key Personnel:** Ken Carr, Dir. of Programs, kcarr@journalbroadcastgroup.com. **URL:** http://www.1063thegroove.com.

1199 ■ KGMS-AM - 940
3222 S Richey Ave.
Tucson, AZ 85713
Phone: (520)790-2440
Format: Sports. **Owner:** Good News Communication, 2510 N Las Posas Rd., Camarillo, CA 93010, Ph: (520)790-2440. **Operating Hours:** Continuous. **ADI:** Tucson, AZ. **Key Personnel:** Christina Willits, Operations Mgr.; Mary Martin, Sales Mgr., Advertising Mgr.; Doug Martin, President. **Wattage:** 1,000 Day; 250 Night. **Ad Rates:** Advertising accepted; rates available upon request. **URL:** http://www.kgms.com.

1200 ■ KGUN-TV - 9
7280 E Rosewood St.
Tucson, AZ 85710
Phone: (520)722-5486
Fax: (520)733-7050
Format: Commercial TV. **Networks:** ABC. **Owner:** Journal Broadcast Group, 5257 Fairview Ave., No. 260, Boise, ID 83706. **Founded:** 1956. **Operating Hours:** Continuous. **ADI:** Tucson, AZ. **Key Personnel:** Jay Clifford, Contact, jclifford@kgun9.com. **Ad Rates:** Advertising accepted; rates available upon request. **URL:** http://www.jrn.com.

1201 ■ KHRR-TV - 40
2919 E Broadway
Tucson, AZ 85716
Phone: (602)322-6888
Fax: (602)881-7926
Format: Hispanic. **Networks:** Telemundo. **Founded:** 1989. **Formerly:** KHR-TV. **ADI:** Tucson, AZ. **Key Personnel:** Jay S. Zucker, Contact. **Wattage:** 396,000 ERP. **Ad Rates:** Advertising accepted; rates available upon request.

1202 ■ KHYT-FM - 107.5
575 W Roger Rd.
Tucson, AZ 85705
Phone: (520)880-1075
Fax: (520)887-1000
Format: Classic Rock. **Owner:** Citadel Broadcasting Corp., 7201 W Lake Mead Blvd., Ste. 400, Las Vegas, NV 89128-8366, Ph: (702)804-5200, Fax: (702)804-8250. **Operating Hours:** Monday – Friday ; 8:00 AM – 5:00 PM. **Wattage:** 82,000. **Ad Rates:** Advertising accepted; rates available upon request. **URL:** http://www.khit1075.com.

1203 ■ KIIM-FM - 99.5
575 W Roger Rd.
Tucson, AZ 85705
Phone: (520)887-1000
Fax: (520)887-6397
Format: Contemporary Country. **Owner:** Citadel Broadcasting Corp., 7201 W Lake Mead Blvd., Ste. 400, Las Vegas, NV 89128-8366, Ph: (702)804-5200, Fax: (702)804-8250. **Founded:** 1983. **Operating Hours:** Continuous. **ADI:** Tucson, AZ. **Key Personnel:** Keith Rosenblatt, Dir. of Sales, keith.rosenblatt@cumulus.com; Chuck Meyer, Contact, chuck.meyer@citcomm.com. **Wattage:** 90,000 ERP. **Ad Rates:** Advertising accepted; rates available upon request. **URL:** http://www.kiimfm.com.

KJJJ-FM - See Clifton

1204 ■ KJLL-AM - 1330
4433 E Broadway, Ste. 210
Tucson, AZ 85711
Phone: (520)529-5865
Fax: (520)529-9324
Format: Talk; News. **Founded:** Sept. 13, 2006. **Key Personnel:** Dawn Avalon, Gen. Mgr., dawn.avalon@ymail.com; Randal Howard, Chief Engineer, rwilliamhoward@aol.com. **Ad Rates:** Advertising accepted; rates available upon request.

KJTA-FM - See Flagstaff

KJTY-FM - See Topeka, KS

1205 ■ KLPX-FM - 96.1
3871 N Commerce Dr.
Tucson, AZ 85705
Phone: (520)407-4500
Email: online@klpx.com
Format: Classic Rock. **Owner:** Arizona Lotus Broadcasting, at above address. **Founded:** 1979. **Operating Hours:** Continuous. **ADI:** Tucson, AZ. **Key Personnel:** Ken Kwilosz, Gen. Mgr., kkwilosz@azlotus.com; Larry Mac, Operations Mgr., lmac@klpx.com. **Wattage:** 82,000 ERP. **Ad Rates:** Advertising accepted; rates available upon request. Combined advertising rates available with KFMA-FM, KTKT-AM. **URL:** http://www.klpx.com.

1206 ■ KLTU-FM - 88.1
PO Box 779002
Rocklin, CA 95677-9972
Free: 800-525-5683
Format: Contemporary Christian. **Owner:** Educational Media Foundation, PO Box 2098, Omaha, NE 68103-2098, Free: 800-434-8400. **URL:** http://www.klove.com.

1207 ■ KMSB-TV - 11
1855 N 6th Ave.
Tucson, AZ 85705
Phone: (520)770-1123
Format: Commercial TV. **Networks:** Fox. **Owner:** A.H. Belo Corp., 508 Young St. , Dallas, TX 75202-4808, Ph: (214)977-8200, Fax: (214)977-8201. **Founded:** 1967. **Formerly:** KZAZ-TV. **Operating Hours:** Continuous. **ADI:** Tucson, AZ. **Ad Rates:** Noncommercial. **URL:** http://www.tucsonnewsnow.com.

1208 ■ KMXZ-FM - 94.9
7280 E Rosewood St.
Tucson, AZ 85710
Phone: (520)722-5486
Format: Adult Contemporary. **Owner:** Journal Broadcast Group Inc., 1533 Amherst Rd., Knoxville, TN 37909. **Founded:** 1973. **Formerly:** KKLD-FM. **Operating Hours:** Continuous; 100% local. **ADI:** Tucson, AZ. **Key Personnel:** Bobby Rich, Contact; Bobby Rich, Contact. **Local Programs:** *The Morning Mix*, Monday Tuesday Wednesday Thursday Friday 5:00 a.m. - 9:00 a.m. **Wattage:** 97,000. **Ad Rates:** Advertising accepted; rates available upon request. Combined advertising rates available with KZPT-FM, KGMG-FM, KFFN-AM. **URL:** http://www.mixfm.com.

1209 ■ KNST-AM - 790
3202 N Oracle Rd.
Tucson, AZ 85705
Phone: (520)618-2100
Format: Talk; News. **Networks:** ABC; Westwood One Radio; ESPN Radio. **Owner:** iHeartMedia Inc., 200 E Basse Rd., San Antonio, TX 78209, Ph: (210)832-3314. **Founded:** 1981. **Formerly:** KMGX-AM; KHOS-AM. **Operating Hours:** Continuous. **ADI:** Tucson, AZ. **Key Personnel:** Paul Birmingham, News Dir., paul@790knst.com. **Local Programs:** *Week in Review*, Monday Tuesday Wednesday Thursday Friday. **Wattage:** 5,000 Day; 500 Night. **Ad Rates:** Advertising accepted; rates available upon request. **URL:** http://www.knst.com.

1210 ■ KNXN-AM
3222 S Richey Ave.
Tucson, AZ 85713
Phone: (602)459-1470
Fax: (602)459-5418
Email: mix1470@theriver.com
Format: Full Service; News; Talk. **Networks:** NBC; Sun Radio; Southern Farm. **Owner:** Blue Horizon Broadcasting, at above address. **Founded:** 1980. **Formerly:** KSVA-AM; KMFI-AM. **Wattage:** 2,500 Day; 039 Night. **Ad Rates:** $5-7 for 30 seconds; $8-11 for 60 seconds.

1211 ■ KOAZ-FM - 97.5
575 W Roger Rd.
Tucson, AZ 85705
Phone: (520)887-1000
Format: Jazz; Soft Rock; Hip Hop. **Owner:** Citadel Broadcasting Corp., 7201 W Lake Mead Blvd., Ste. 400, Las Vegas, NV 89128-8366, Ph: (702)804-5200, Fax: (702)804-8250. **Operating Hours:** 6:00 a.m. - 12:00 a.m. Monday – Friday, 6:00 p.m. - 12:00 a.m. Sunday. **Wattage:** 6,000. **URL:** http://www.975thevibe.com/station-information.

1212 ■ KOHT-FM - 98.3
3202 N Oracle Rd.
Tucson, AZ 85705
Phone: (520)618-2100
Fax: (520)618-2165
Format: Hip Hop. **Founded:** 1985. **Formerly:** KXMG-FM; KOPO-FM. **Operating Hours:** Continuous; 100% local. **ADI:** Tucson, AZ. **Wattage:** 6,000. **Ad Rates:** $45-50 for 30 seconds; $50-65 for 60 seconds. **URL:** http://www.hot983.com.

1213 ■ KOLD-TV - 13
7831 N Business Park Dr.
Tucson, AZ 85743
Phone: (520)744-1313
Fax: (520)744-5233
Format: News. **Networks:** CBS. **Owner:** Raycom Media Inc., 201 Monroe St., RSA Twr., 20th Fl., Montgomery, AL 36104-3731, Ph: (334)206-1400. **Founded:** Jan. 13, 1953. **Operating Hours:** 12 a.m. - 11 p.m. **Key Personnel:** Debbie Bush, Gen. Mgr.; Bob McCaughey, Gen. Sales Mgr.; List Tuft, Traffic Mgr.; Michelle Germano, News Dir.; Lorne Earle, Chief Engineer. **Ad Rates:** Noncommercial. **URL:** http://www.TucsonNewsNow.com.

1214 ■ KPYT-FM - 100.3
7474 S Camino De Oeste
Tucson, AZ 85757
Phone: (520)883-5000
Fax: (520)883-5014
Format: Ethnic. **Owner:** Pascua Yaqui Tribe, 7474 S Camino De Oeste, Tucson, AZ 85746, Ph: (520)883-5000. **Key Personnel:** Hector Youtsey, Gen. Mgr., hector.youtsey@pascuayaqui-nsn.gov. **Ad Rates:** Noncommercial.

1215 ■ KQTH-FM - 104.1
7280 E Rosewood St.
Tucson, AZ 85710
Phone: (520)722-5486
Format: News; Talk. **ADI:** Tucson, AZ. **Key Personnel:** Ryan McCredden, Dir. of Programs. **URL:** http://www.1041kqth.com.

1216 ■ KQTL-AM - 1210
11850 S Old Nogales Hwy.
Tucson, AZ 85756-9560
Phone: (602)628-1200
Fax: (602)326-4927
Format: Ethnic; Hispanic. **Networks:** Independent. **Owner:** Cima Broadcasting, L.L.C., at above address. **Founded:** 1985. **Operating Hours:** Continuous. **ADI:** Tucson, AZ. **Key Personnel:** Bertha Gallego, Opera-

Circulation: ★ = AAM; △ or • = BPA; ♦ = CAC; ❑ = VAC; ⊕ = PO Statement; ‡ = Publisher's Report; Boldface figures = sworn; Light figures = estimated.

tions Mgr.; Frank Fregoso, Chief Engineer; Amparo Maldonado, News Dir. **Wattage**: 10,000 day; 1,000 night.

1217 ■ KRQ-FM - 93.7
3202 N Oracle Rd.
Tucson, AZ 85705
Phone: (520)618-2100
Format: Big Band/Nostalgia. **Networks:** NBC. **Owner:** iHeartMedia and Entertainment Inc. , 200 E Basse Rd., San Antonio, TX 78209, Ph: (210)822-2828. **Operating Hours**: Continuous. **ADI**: Tucson, AZ. **Wattage**: 93,000 ERP. **Ad Rates:** Advertising accepted; rates available upon request. $50-160 per unit. **URL:** http://krq.iheart.com.

1218 ■ KRQQ-FM - 93.7
3202 N Oracle Rd.
Tucson, AZ 85705
Phone: (520)618-2100
Fax: (520)618-2165
Format: Top 40. **Networks:** Independent. **Founded:** 1971. **Operating Hours**: Continuous; 100% local. **Wattage:** 91,000. **Ad Rates:** Advertising accepted; rates available upon request. **URL:** http://www.krq.com.

1219 ■ KSZR-FM - 97.5
575 W Roger Rd.
Tucson, AZ 85705
Phone: (520)887-1000
Format: Adult Contemporary. **Owner:** Citadel Broadcasting Corp., 7201 W Lake Mead Blvd., Ste. 400, Las Vegas, NV 89128-8366, Ph: (702)804-5200, Fax: (702)804-8250. **Wattage**: 6,000. **Ad Rates:** Advertising accepted; rates available upon request. **URL:** http://www.i975tucson.com.

1220 ■ KTTU-TV - 18
1855 N Sixth Ave.
Tucson, AZ 85705
Phone: (520)744-1313
Format: Commercial TV. **Networks:** United Paramount Network. **Owner:** Belo Corp., 400 S Record St., Dallas, TX 75202-4841, Ph: (214)977-6606, Fax: (214)977-6603. **Founded:** Dec. 1984. **Operating Hours**: Continuous. **ADI**: Tucson, AZ. **Ad Rates:** Advertising accepted; rates available upon request. **URL:** http://www.tucsonnewsnow.com.

1221 ■ KTUC-AM - 1400
2761 N Country Club Rd., Ste. 201
Tucson, AZ 85716-2271
Phone: (602)326-8788
Fax: (602)326-9655
Format: News; Talk; Sports. **Networks:** CBS; NBC. **Owner:** KTUC, Inc., at above address. **Founded:** 1926. **Operating Hours**: Continuous. **ADI**: Tucson, AZ. **Wattage**: 1,000. **Ad Rates:** $35.

1222 ■ KTZR-AM
2475 N Jack Rabbitt Dr.
Tucson, AZ 85745
Phone: (602)670-1450
Fax: (602)670-1601
Format: Hispanic. **Networks:** Independent. **Founded:** 1947. **ADI**: Tucson, AZ. **Wattage**: 1,000. **Ad Rates:** $10-20 for 30 seconds.

1223 ■ KTZR-FM - 97.1
3202 N Oracle Rd.
Tucson, AZ 85705
Phone: (520)618-2100
Format: Hispanic. **ADI**: Tucson, AZ. **Key Personnel:** Shanna McCoy, Gen. Mgr. **Wattage**: 330. **Ad Rates:** Advertising accepted; rates available upon request.

1224 ■ KUAS-TV - 27
c/o KUAT-TV
University of Arizona
Tucson, AZ 85721
Fax: (602)621-3360
Email: serres@kuat.pbs.org
Simulcasts: KUAT. **Networks:** Public Broadcasting Service (PBS). **ADI**: Tucson, AZ. **Wattage**: 50,000 Horizontal. E. **Ad Rates:** Accepts Advertising. **URL:** http://www.azpm.org.

1225 ■ KUAT-FM - 90.5
University of Arizona
Tucson, AZ 85721
Phone: (520)621-5828
Fax: (520)621-3360
Email: kuatpab@wechv.com
Format: Public Radio; News; Jazz. **Owner:** University of Arizona Board of Regents, The University of Arizona, Tucson, AZ 85721. **Founded:** 1975. **Operating Hours**: 6:09 a.m. - 8:00 p.m. Monday - Friday; 6:00 a.m. - 3:30 p.m. Saturday; 6:00 a.m. - 8:00 p.m. Sunday. **ADI**: Tucson, AZ. **Wattage**: 12,000 ERP. **Ad Rates:** Accepts Advertising. **Mailing address:** PO Box 210067, Tucson, AZ 85721. **URL:** http://radio.azpm.org/classical/.

1226 ■ KUAT-TV - 6
PO Box 210067
Tucson, AZ 85721
Phone: (520)621-5828
Format: Public TV. **Networks:** Public Broadcasting Service (PBS). **Owner:** Arizona Board of Regents, 2020 N Central Ave., Ste. 230, Phoenix, AZ 85004, Ph: (602)229-2500, Fax: (602)229-2555. **Founded:** 1959. **Operating Hours**: 17 hours Daily; 97.5% network, 2.5% local. **ADI**: Tucson, AZ. **Ad Rates:** Noncommercial. **URL:** http://www.azpm.org.

1227 ■ KUAZ-AM
PO Box 5764
Tucson, AZ 85703-0764
Phone: (520)621-5828
Format: Public Radio; News. **Networks:** National Public Radio (NPR); Public Radio International (PRI). **Owner:** University of Arizona Board of Regents, The University of Arizona, Tucson, AZ 85721. **Founded:** 1968. **Formerly**: KUAT-AM. **ADI**: Tucson, AZ. **Key Personnel:** John Kelley, Station Mgr.; Peter Michaels, News Dir. **Wattage**: 50,000 Day. **Ad Rates:** Noncommercial.

1228 ■ KUAZ-FM - 89.1
University of Arizona
Tucson, AZ 85721
Phone: (520)621-5805
Format: Public Radio. **Simulcasts:** KUAZ-AM. **Networks:** National Public Radio (NPR); AP; Public Radio International (PRI). **Owner:** Board of Regents, at above address. **Founded:** 1992. **Operating Hours:** Continuous. **Wattage**: 3,000. **Ad Rates:** Noncommercial. **Mailing address:** PO Box 210067, Tucson, AZ 85721. **URL:** http://www.about.azpm.org.

1229 ■ KVOA-TV - 4
PO Box 5188
Tucson, AZ 85703
Phone: (520)792-2270
Format: Commercial TV. **Networks:** NBC. **Owner:** Evening Post Industries Inc., 134 Columbus St., Charleston, SC 29403, Ph: (843)577-7111. **Operating Hours:** Continuous Sun.-Fri.; 5:30 a.m.-12:30 a.m. Sat. **ADI**: Tucson, AZ. **Key Personnel:** Bill Shaw, Gen. Mgr., President; Dave Kerrigan, Operations Mgr., dkerrigan@kvoa.com; Jeff Green, Sales Mgr., jgreen@kvoa.com. **Ad Rates:** Noncommercial. **URL:** http://www.kvoa.com.

KVOI-AM - See Oro Valley

1230 ■ KWFM-AM - 1450
3202 N Oracle Rd.
Tucson, AZ 85705
Phone: (520)618-2100
Format: Oldies. **ADI**: Tucson, AZ. **Key Personnel:** Shanna McCoy, Gen. Mgr. **Wattage**: 1,000. **Ad Rates:** Noncommercial.

1231 ■ KWMT-FM - 92.9
3202 N Oracle Rd.
Tucson, AZ 85705
Format: Adult Album Alternative; Alternative/New Music/Progressive. **Operating Hours**: Continuous. **ADI**: Tucson, AZ. **Wattage**: 90,000. **Ad Rates:** Noncommercial; Advertising accepted; rates available upon request. **URL:** http://my929.iheart.com.

1232 ■ KWXL-FM - 98.7
3500 S 12th Ave.
Tucson, AZ 85713-5913
Phone: (520)225-4383
Format: Oldies. **Operating Hours**: Continuous. **ADI**: Tucson, AZ. **Key Personnel:** Tara Bulleigh, Contact, tara.bulleigh@tusd1.org. **Wattage**: 050. **URL:** http://edweb.tusd.k12.az.us/tbulleigh/index.html.

1233 ■ KXCI-FM - 91.3
220 S 4th Ave.
Tucson, AZ 85701
Phone: (520)623-1000
Email: lonelyheartsclub@kxci.org
Format: Full Service. **Networks:** CBS. **Founded:** 1983. **ADI**: Tucson, AZ. **Key Personnel:** Randy Peterson, Dir. of Dev., Gen. Mgr., randy@kxci.org; Duncan Hudson, Music Dir., duncan@kxci.org. **Wattage**: 340 ERP. **Ad Rates:** Noncommercial. **URL:** http://www.kxci.org.

1234 ■ KXEW-AM - 1600
3202 N Oracle Rd.
Tucson, AZ 85705
Phone: (520)880-1600
Fax: (520)618-2165
Format: Tejano. **Founded:** 1962. **Operating Hours**: Continuous. **ADI**: Tucson, AZ. **Key Personnel:** Melissa Santa Cruz, Dir. of Programs, Promotions Dir., melissa@tejano1600.com. **Wattage**: 1,000. **Ad Rates:** Advertising accepted; rates available upon request. **URL:** http://www.tejano1600.com.

1235 ■ KZPT-FM - 104.1
7280 E Rosewood St.
Tucson, AZ 85710
Phone: (520)880-1041
Format: Adult Contemporary. **Owner:** Journal Broadcast Group Inc., 1533 Amherst Rd., Knoxville, TN 37909. **Key Personnel:** Ryan McCredden, Dir. of Programs. **Wattage**: 3,000. **Ad Rates:** Noncommercial. **URL:** http://www.1041kqth.com.

1236 ■ WBFN-AM
7355 N Oracle Rd.
Tucson, AZ 85704
Phone: (520)742-6976
Format: Urban Contemporary. **Key Personnel:** Terry Bonner, Contact; Micheal Fairchild, Contact. **Wattage**: 1,000. **Ad Rates:** $6 for 30 seconds; $7.50 for 60 seconds.

WJBP-FM - See Chattanooga, TN

1237 ■ WJTG-FM - 91.3
7355 N Oracle Rd.
Tucson, AZ 85704
Free: 800-776-1070
Email: wjtg@wjtg.org
Format: Religious. **Mailing address:** PO Box 35300, Tucson, AZ 85740. **URL:** http://www.myflr.org.

WJTY-FM - See Lancaster, WI

WUFL-AM - See Detroit, MI

1238 ■ WUFN-FM - 96.7
7335 N Oracle, Ste. 200
Tucson, AZ 85704
Free: 800-776-1070
Format: Religious; Gospel. **Owner:** Family Life Communications, Inc., 7355 N Oracle Rd., Tucson, AZ 85704, Ph: (520)544-5950, Fax: (520)742-6979, Free: 800-776-1070. **Founded:** 1971. **Operating Hours**: Continuous. **Key Personnel:** Randy Carlson, President. **Wattage**: 3,000 ERP. **Ad Rates:** Noncommercial. **URL:** http://www.myflr.org.

1239 ■ WUGN-FM - 99.7
PO Box 35300
Tucson, AZ 85740
Free: 800-776-1070
Format: Religious. **Owner:** Family Life Communications, Inc., 7355 N Oracle Rd., Tucson, AZ 85704, Ph: (520)544-5950, Fax: (520)742-6979, Free: 800-776-1070. **Key Personnel:** Dr. Randy L. Carlson, President. **Wattage**: 100,000. **Ad Rates:** Noncommercial. **URL:** http://www.myflr.org.

WUNN-AM - See Mason, MI

WHITERIVER

1240 ■ KNNB-FM
PO Box 310
Box 310
Whiteriver, AZ 85941
Phone: (520)338-5211
Fax: (520)338-1744
Format: Eclectic; Ethnic. **Owner:** White Mountain Apache Tribe, 501 E Fatco Rd., Whiteriver, AZ 85941, Ph: (928)338-4346, Fax: (928)338-4150. **Founded:** 1982. **Wattage**: 630 ERP. **Ad Rates:** Underwriting available.

WICKENBURG

Maricopa Co. Maricopa Co. (SC). 52 m NW of Phoenix. Winter resort. Gold, silver, lead mines. Cattle.

1241 ■ Wickenburg Shopper News
Brehm Communications Inc.
180 N Washington St.
Wickenburg, AZ 85390
Shopper. **Freq:** Weekly (Tues.). **Print Method:** Offset. **Trim Size:** 10 1/4 x 16. **Cols./Page:** 5. **Col. Width:** 12 picas. **Col. Depth:** 16 inches. **Key Personnel:** Kevin Cloe, Publisher. **Subscription Rates:** Free. **URL:** http://www.brehmcommunications.com/publications. **Ad Rates:** BW $480; SAU $6. **Remarks:** Accepts advertising. **Circ:** Free ‡7000.

1242 ■ KSWG-FM - 96.3
801 W Wickenburg Way
Wickenburg, AZ 85390
Phone: (602)254-6644
Format: Country. **Operating Hours**: Continuous. **Wattage**: 6,400. **Ad Rates:** Noncommercial. $50-70 per unit. **URL:** http://www.kswgradio.com.

WILLCOX

Cochise Co. Cochise Co. (SE). 65 m E of Tucson. Agriculture. Cattle and apples.

1243 ■ Arizona Range News
Wick Communications
122 S Haskell Ave.
Willcox, AZ 85644
Phone: (520)384-3571
Fax: (520)384-3572
Publication E-mail: rangenews@willcoxrangenews.com
Community newspaper. **Freq:** Weekly (Wed.). **Print Method:** Offset. **Trim Size:** 13 x 21 1/2. **Cols./Page:** 6. **Col. Width:** 19 nonpareils. **Col. Depth:** 294 agate lines. **Key Personnel:** Ainslee S. Wittig, Managing Editor. **USPS:** 030-860. **Subscription Rates:** $21 Individuals in Cochise County 6 months; $31 Individuals in Cochise County 1 year; $23 Individuals elsewhere in Arizona 6 months; $35 Individuals elsewhere in Arizona 1 year; $24 Other countries 6 months; $38 Other countries 1 year; $30 online; annual. **URL:** http://www.willcoxrangenews.com. **Mailing address:** PO Box 1155, Willcox, AZ 85644. **Ad Rates:** BW $65; 4C $190. **Remarks:** Accepts advertising. **Circ:** Paid 3100.

WINDOW ROCK

Apache Co. (NE). 100 m NE of Winslow. Agriculture. Cattle, sheep, grains.

1244 ■ The Navajo Times: The Newspaper of the Navajo People
The Navajo Times
Hwy. 264 & Rte. 12
Window Rock, AZ 86515-0310
Phone: (928)871-1130
Fax: (928)871-1159
Publisher's E-mail: editor@navajotimes.com
Weekly newspaper for the Navajo people and Native Americans. **Freq:** Weekly (Thurs.). **Print Method:** Offset. **Trim Size:** 13 x 21. **Cols./Page:** 6. **Col. Width:** 12.5 picas. **Col. Depth:** 21 inches. **Key Personnel:** Duane A. Beyal, Editor, phone: (928)871-1136; Bobby Martin, Manager, Production, phone: (928)871-1152; Rhonda Joe, Manager, Circulation, phone: (928)871-1149. **USPS:** 375-040. **Subscription Rates:** $35 U.S. 3 months; $70 U.S. 6 months; $120 U.S. 1 year; $6.25 Individuals per month, 1 year e-edition; $7.50 Individuals per month, 6 months e-edition; $8.50 Individuals per month, 3 months e-edition; $2 Single issue one week access for e-edition; $60 Canada and Mexico 3 months; $125 Canada and Mexico 6 months; $200 Canada and Mexico 1 year; $125 Other countries 3 months; $225 Other countries 6 months; $400 Other countries 1 year. **URL:** http://www.navajotimes.com. **Formerly:** Navajo Times Today. **Mailing address:** PO Box 310, Window Rock, AZ 86515-0310. **Remarks:** alcohol & tobacco. **Circ:** Paid ‡22800.

1245 ■ KHAC-AM - 880
PO Box 9090
Window Rock, AZ 86515
Phone: (505)371-5587
Fax: (505)371-5588
Email: kwim@westernindian.org
Format: Religious. **Networks:** Moody Broadcasting. **Owner:** Western Indian Ministries Inc., PO Box 9090, Window Rock, AZ 86515, Ph: (505)371-5749, Fax: (505)371-5588. **Founded:** 1967. **Operating Hours:** Sunrise-sunset; 20% network, 80% local. **Key Personnel:** Greg Lewis, Director. **Wattage:** 10,000 Day; 430 Night. **Ad Rates:** $4.75-10 for 30 seconds; $5-11.50 for 60 seconds. **URL:** http://www.khac.westernindian.net.

1246 ■ KTBA-AM - 1050
PO Box 9090
Window Rock, AZ 86515-9090
Phone: (505)371-5749
Fax: (505)371-5588
Email: wim@westernindian.org
Format: Religious. **Networks:** Moody Broadcasting. **Owner:** Western Indian Ministries Inc., PO Box 9090, Window Rock, AZ 86515, Ph: (505)371-5749, Fax: (505)371-5588. **Founded:** 1964. **Operating Hours**: Continuous. **Wattage**: 5,000. **Ad Rates:** $8-11 for 30 seconds; $6-9 for 60 seconds. **URL:** http://www.westernindian.org/history.

1247 ■ KTNN-AM - 660
Window Rock Shopping Ctr.
Window Rock, AZ 86515
Phone: (928)871-3553
Fax: (928)871-3479
Format: Sports; News. **Owner:** KTNN Radio Station, at above address, Window Rock, AZ 86515. **Founded:** 1986. **Operating Hours**: Continuous; 8% network, 92% local. **Wattage**: 50,000 Day; 50,000 N. **Ad Rates:** Advertising accepted; rates available upon request. **Mailing address:** PO Box 2569, Window Rock, AZ 86515. **URL:** http://www.ktnnonline.com.

1248 ■ KWIM-FM - 102.7
PO Box 9090
Window Rock, AZ 86515
Phone: (505)371-5749
Fax: (505)371-5588
Email: wim@westernindian.org
Format: Religious. **Owner:** Western Indian Ministries, at above address. **Wattage**: 30,000. **URL:** http://www.westernindian.org.

WINSLOW

Navajo Co. Navajo Co. (NE). 55 m SE of Flagstaff. Indian Reservation. Sawmills. Manufactures women's and children's garments. Sheep, cattle.

1249 ■ KINO-AM - 1230
Drawer K
Winslow, AZ 86047
Phone: (928)289-3364
Owner: Sunflower Communications, Inc., at above address. **Founded:** 1962. **Key Personnel:** Loy Engelhardt, Contact. **Wattage**: 1,000. **Ad Rates:** $4-5.50 for 30 seconds; $5.25-7.75 for 60 seconds. **URL:** http://www.kinoampool.ch/.

1250 ■ K206DH-FM - 89.1
PO Box 391
Twin Falls, ID 83303
Fax: (208)736-1958
Free: 800-357-4226
Format: Religious; Contemporary Christian. **Owner:** CSN International, PO Box 391, Twin Falls, ID 83303, Ph: (208)736-1958, Fax: (208)736-1958, Free: 800-357-4226. **URL:** http://www.csnradio.com.

YUMA

Yuma Co. Yuma Co. (SW). On Colorado River 180 m SW of Phoenix on Calif./Mexico border. Tourism. Resort. Modest manufacturing complex. Predominately agricultural.

1251 ■ Bajo El Sol
The Yuma Daily Sun
2055 S Arizona Ave.
Yuma, AZ 85364
Phone: (928)783-3333
Publisher's E-mail: newsroom@yumasun.com
Shopping guide for the local Hispanic market. **Freq:** Daily. **Print Method:** Photo Offset. **Key Personnel:** Rodriguez Duvi, Editor; John Vuaughn, Editor. **Subscription Rates:** $168 Individuals 1 year, 7 days delivery; $84 Individuals 6 months, 7 days delivery; $42 Individuals 3 months, 7 days delivery; $14 Individuals 1 months, 7 days delivery. **URL:** http://www.bajoelsol.com; http://www.yumasun.com/bajo_el_sol. **Remarks:** Accepts advertising. **Circ:** Non-paid ♦14261.

1252 ■ Imperial Valley White Sheet
Associated Desert Shoppers Inc.
1355 W 16th St., Ste. 10
Yuma, AZ 85364
Phone: (928)782-3663
Fax: (928)782-3403
Shoppers' publication serving the Imperial Valley, California area. **Freq:** Weekly. **URL:** http://www.greenandwhitesheet.com/white_sheet_home.php. **Ad Rates:** BW $500. **Remarks:** Accepts advertising. **Circ:** Non-paid 30000.

1253 ■ The Prospector
Western News & Info Inc.
1748 S Arizona Ave.
Yuma, AZ 85364
Newspaper. **Founded:** 1882. **Freq:** Weekly (Sun.). **Print Method:** Offset. **Trim Size:** 11 3/8 x 13 3/4. **Key Personnel:** Robin Mauser, Publisher; Rich Thurlow, Editor. **ISSN:** 0746-9764 (print). **URL:** http://www.kingmandailyminer.com. **Formerly**: Mohave Daily Miner. **Ad Rates:** GLR $3; BW $1,377.72; 4C $1,807.32; PCI $7.40. **Remarks:** 3. **Circ:** Sun. ■ **10938**.

1254 ■ Williams-Grand Canyon News
Williams-Grand Canyon News
1748 S Arizona Ave.
Yuma, AZ 85364
Phone: (928)635-4426
Fax: (928)635-4887
Free: 800-408-4726
Publication E-mail: editorial@williamsnews.com
Community newspaper. **Freq:** Weekly (Wed.). **Print Method:** Offset. **Cols./Page:** 6. **Col. Width:** 27 nonpareils. **Col. Depth:** 21 1/2 inches. **Key Personnel:** Debbie White-Hoel, Publisher; Connie Hiemenz, Manager, Advertising. **USPS:** 684-640. **Subscription Rates:** $16.50 Individuals 3 months, In-county; $21.50 Individuals 6 months, In-county; $32.50 Individuals 12 months, In-county; $55 Two years In-county; $18.50 Individuals 3 months, Out of county; $26.50 Individuals 6 months, Out of county; $42.50 Individuals 12 months, Out of county; $75 Two years Out of county; $20.50 Out of state 3 months; $28.50 Out of state 6 months; $46.50 Out of state 12 months; $80 Out of state 24 months. **URL:** http://www.grandcanyonnews.com. **Ad Rates:** GLR $.81; BW $1180.59; 4C $1430.54; SAU $11.30; PCI $11.30. **Remarks:** Accepts advertising. **Circ:** ‡5000.

1255 ■ Yuma Sun
The Yuma Daily Sun
2055 S Arizona Ave.
Yuma, AZ 85364
Phone: (928)783-3333
Publisher's E-mail: newsroom@yumasun.com
General newspaper. **Freq:** Daily. **Print Method:** Offset. **Cols./Page:** 6. **Col. Width:** 24 nonpareils. **Col. Depth:** 126 agate lines. **Key Personnel:** Randy Hoeft, Editor, phone: (928)539-6869. **Subscription Rates:** $186 Individuals 1 year (7 days a week; print and online); $96 Individuals 6 months (7 days a week; print and online); $46.50 Individuals 3 months (7 days a week; print and online); $15.50 Individuals 1 month (7 days a week; print and online). **Alt. Formats:** PDF. **URL:** http://www.yumasun.com. **Formerly**: The Yuma Daily Sun. **Remarks:** Accepts advertising. **Circ:** Mon.-Sat. ♦**12261**, Sun. ♦**14315**.

1256 ■ Yuma White Sheet
Associated Desert Shoppers Inc.
1355 W 16th St., Ste. 10
Yuma, AZ 85364
Phone: (928)782-3663
Fax: (928)782-3403
Shoppers' publication serving Yuma, Arizona area. **Freq:** Weekly. **URL:** http://www.greenandwhitesheet.com/white_sheet_home.php. **Remarks:** Accepts advertising. **Circ:** (Not Reported).

1257 ■ Beamspeed LLC
2481 E Palo Verde St.
Yuma, AZ 85365
Phone: (928)343-0300
Email: support@beamspeed.net
URL: http://www.beamspeed.net.

1258 ■ KAWC-FM - 88.9
PO Box 929
Yuma, AZ 85366

Circulation: ★ = AAM; △ or • = BPA; ♦ = CAC; ❑ = VAC; ⊕ = PO Statement; ‡ = Publisher's Report; Boldface figures = sworn; Light figures = estimated.

Phone: (928)344-7690
Fax: (928)344-7740
Free: 877-838-5292
Email: info@kawc.org
Format: Classical; Jazz; News. **Networks:** National Public Radio (NPR). **Owner:** Arizona Western College, 2020 S Ave. 8E, Yuma, AZ 85365, Ph: (928)317-6000, Free: 888-293-0392. **Founded:** 1992. **Operating Hours:** Continuous. **ADI**: El Centro, CA-Yuma, AZ. **Key Personnel:** Jim Anderson, Div. Mgr., jim.anderson@kawc.org; Dave Riek, Gen. Mgr., dave.riek@kawc.org; Mark Reynolds, Prog. Dir., mark.reynolds@kawc.org. **Wattage:** 3,000. **Ad Rates:** Noncommercial. **URL:** http://www.kawc.org.

1259 ■ KBLU-AM - 560
755 W 28th St.
Yuma, AZ 85364
Phone: (928)344-4980
Fax: (928)344-4983
Format: News; Talk. **Networks:** CNN Radio; Westwood One Radio. **Founded:** 1940. **Formerly**: KYUM-AM. **Operating Hours**: Continuous. **ADI**: El Centro, CA-Yuma, AZ. **Key Personnel:** Jeff Harris, Gen. Mgr., jeffharris@edbroadcasters.com. **Wattage**: 1,000. **Ad Rates:** Noncommercial. $4-$22 for 30 seconds; $7-$28 for 60 seconds. Combined advertising rates available with KTTI-FM. **URL:** http://www.kbluam.com.

1260 ■ KCEC-FM - 104.5
670 E 32nd St., Ste. 12A
Yuma, AZ 85365
Phone: (928)782-5995
Fax: (928)782-3874
Format: Hispanic. **ADI**: El Centro, CA-Yuma, AZ. **Key Personnel:** Rosella Lopez, Gen. Mgr., rosella.lopez@campesina.com. **URL:** http://www.campesina.com.

1261 ■ KCFY-FM - 88.1
1921 S Rail Ave.
Yuma, AZ 85365
Phone: (928)341-9730
Fax: (928)341-9099
Email: kcfy@kcfyfm.com
Format: Contemporary Christian. **Owner:** Relevant Media, Inc., at above address. **Founded:** 1992. **Operating Hours**: Continuous. **ADI**: El Centro, CA-Yuma, AZ. **Key Personnel:** Greg S. Myers, Gen. Mgr. **Local Programs:** *My Money Life.* **Wattage**: 3,000 ERP. **Ad Rates:** Noncommercial. **URL:** http://www.kcfyfm.com.

1262 ■ KCYK-AM - 1400
949 S Ave. B
Yuma, AZ 85364
Phone: (928)782-4321
Free: 888-534-7664
Format: Country. **Networks:** AP; Jones Satellite. **Owner:** MonsterMedia, LLC, at above address, Orlando, FL; Monster Media L.L.C., 555 S Lake Destiny, Orlando, FL 32810, Ph: (407)478-8163. **Founded:** 1950. **Formerly**: KEZC-AM; KVOY-AM; KJOK-AM. **Operating Hours**: Continuous. **ADI**: El Centro, CA-Yuma, AZ. **Key Personnel:** Keith Lewis, Gen. Mgr., Gen. Sales Mgr., Owner; Christina Collom, Bus. Mgr. **Wattage**: 1,000. **Ad Rates:** $6-24 per unit. Combined advertising rates available with KLJZ-FM: $18-$48. **URL:** http://outlawcountry1400.com.

1263 ■ KLJZ-FM - 93.1
949 S Ave. B
Yuma, AZ 85364
Phone: (928)782-4321
Format: Adult Contemporary. **Networks:** Jones Satellite. **Owner:** MonsterMedia, LLC, at above address, Orlando, FL. **Founded:** 1970. **Formerly**: KJOK-FM. **Operating Hours**: Continuous. **ADI**: El Centro, CA-Yuma, AZ. **Key Personnel:** Keith Lewis, CEO, Gen. Mgr., klewis@z93yuma.com. **Wattage**: 100,000. **Ad Rates:** $12-42 per unit. Combined advertising rates available with KJOK: $18-$48. **URL:** http://www.z93yuma.com.

1264 ■ KSWT-TV - 13
1965 S 4th Ave.
Yuma, AZ 85364
Phone: (928)782-5113
Email: news@kswt.com
Format: Commercial TV. **Networks:** CBS. **Owner:** Pappas Telecasting of AZ, LLC. **Founded:** 1963. **Operating Hours**: Continuous. **ADI**: El Centro, CA-Yuma, AZ. **Key Personnel:** Julie Muhe, Sales Mgr. **Ad Rates:** Noncommercial. **URL:** http://www.kswt.com.

1265 ■ KTTI-FM - 95.1
755 W 28th St.
Yuma, AZ 85364
Phone: (928)344-4980
Fax: (928)344-4983
Format: Country. **Networks:** Independent. **Founded:** 1972. **Formerly:** KALJ-FM. **Operating Hours**: Continuous; 100% local. **Key Personnel:** Starr Favreau, Contact, starrfavreau@edbroadcasters.com. **Wattage**: 25,000. **Ad Rates:** $4-22 for 30 seconds; $7-28 for 60 seconds. $4-22 for 30 seconds; $7-28 for 60 seconds. Combined advertising rates available with KBLU-AM: $7-$36 for 30 seconds; $11-$46. **URL:** http://www.kttifm.com.

1266 ■ KYMA-TV - 11
1385 S Pacific Ave.
Yuma, AZ 85365
Phone: (928)782-1111
Email: kyma1@kyma.com
Format: News. **Networks:** NBC. **Owner:** SunBelt Broadcasting, 1500 Foremaster Ln., Las Vegas, NV 89101, Ph: (702)642-3333. **Founded:** 1988. **Operating Hours**: Continuous; 65% network, 35% local. **Local Programs**: *First News 11*, Monday Tuesday Wednesday Thursday Friday 6:00 a.m. - 7:00 a.m. **Ad Rates:** Advertising accepted; rates available upon request. **URL:** http://www.kyma.com.

1267 ■ KYRM-FM - 91.9
PO Box 5965
Yuma, AZ 85366
Format: Hispanic. **ADI**: El Centro, CA-Yuma, AZ. **Wattage:** 6,300. **URL:** http://www.manantialyuma.org.

ARKADELPHIA

SW AR. Clark Co. On Ouachita River, 36 mi. S. of Hot Springs. Henderson State University. Ouachita Baptist University. Manufactures lumber, bearings, boats, roofing materials, rebuilt brake shoes, hotel-motel furniture. Saw mills. Timber. Diversified farming.

1268 ■ Daily Siftings Herald
GateHouse Media Inc.
205 S 26th St.
Arkadelphia, AR 71923
Phone: (870)246-5525
Publication E-mail: advertising@siftingsherald.com
General newspaper. **Freq:** Daily (eve.). **Print Method:** Offset. **Key Personnel:** Shane Allen, Publisher; James Leigh, Editor. **URL:** http://www.siftingsherald.com. **Remarks:** Accepts classified advertising. **Circ:** Paid ‡3100, Non-paid ‡125.

1269 ■ KDEL-FM
PO Box 40
Arkadelphia, AR 71923
Phone: (870)246-9272
Fax: (870)246-5878
Format: Adult Contemporary. **Networks:** Arkansas Radio. **Owner:** Clark County Broadcasting, Inc., at above address. **Founded:** 1974. **Wattage:** 3,000 ERP. **Ad Rates:** $5.50 for 30 seconds; $7.50 for 60 seconds.

1270 ■ KETG-TV - 9
350 S Donaghey Ave.
Conway, AR 72034
Phone: (501)682-2386
Free: 800-662-2386
Email: info@aetn.org
Format: Public TV. **Networks:** Public Broadcasting Service (PBS). **Owner:** Arkansas Educational Television Commission, at above address. **Founded:** 1976. **Operating Hours:** 6 a.m.-11:30 p.m. weekdays; 7 a.m.-11:30 p.m. Saturday and Sunday. **Key Personnel:** Allen Weatherly, Exec. Dir., aweatherly@aetn.org; Tony Brooks, Dep. Dir., tbrooks@aetn.org. **Ad Rates:** Advertising accepted; rates available upon request. **URL:** http://www.aetn.org.

1271 ■ KSWH 102.5 FM – Pulse 102 - 99.9
PO Box 7872
Arkadelphia, AR 71999
Phone: (870)230-5185
Email: kswh@hsu.edu
Format: Alternative/New Music/Progressive. **Owner:** Henderson State College Board of Trustees, Not Available. **Founded:** 1968. **Operating Hours:** 7 a.m.-12 a.m. **Wattage:** 010. **Ad Rates:** Noncommercial. **URL:** http://pulse102.net.

1272 ■ KVRC-AM
PO Box 40
Arkadelphia, AR 71923
Phone: (501)246-4561
Fax: (501)246-4562
Owner: Noalmark Broadcasting, at above address.

ASHDOWN

SW AR. Little River Co. 20 mi. NW of Texarkana, near Lake Millwood. Manufactures lumber, trailers, lingerie, paper. Sawmills. Timber. Agriculture. Cotton, corn, oats, soybeans. Cattle.

1273 ■ Little River News: The Oldest Business Institution in Little River County
Little River News
45 E Commerce St.
Ashdown, AR 71822
Phone: (870)898-3462
Fax: (870)898-6213
Newspaper with Democratic orientation. **Freq:** Weekly (Thurs.). **Print Method:** Offset. **Cols./Page:** 7. **Col. Width:** 26 nonpareils. **Col. Depth:** 294 agate lines. **Key Personnel:** Carolyn Myers, Editor. **Subscription Rates:** $35 Individuals in Ashdown, Foreman, Wilton, Ogden, Horatio, Ben, Lomond, De Queen and Lockesburg; $40 Individuals in Mineral Springs, Nashville, Saratoga, Columbus and Washington; $52 Out of state. **URL:** http://www.littlerivernews.net. **Ad Rates:** BW $882; SAU $7.25; PCI $6.50. **Remarks:** Accepts advertising. **Circ:** 3700.

ATKINS

NWC AR. Pope Co. 50 mi. NW of Little Rock. Lumber mill. Manufactures aluminum containers. Pickle plant. Oak, gum, cypress timber. Diversified farming. Cucumbers, peppers, spinach, tomatoes, cotton, rice, wheat & soybeans.

1274 ■ The Atkins Chronicle: The Heart of Arkansas River Valley
The Atkins Chronicle
204 Ave. 1 NE
Atkins, AR 72823
Phone: (479)641-7161
Fax: (479)641-1604
Publisher's E-mail: news@atkinschronicle.com
Newspaper with Democratic orientation. **Freq:** Weekly (Wed.). **Print Method:** Offset. **Trim Size:** 12 5/8' x 22'. **Cols./Page:** 6. **Col. Width:** 12 picas. **Col. Depth:** 294 agate lines. **Key Personnel:** Van A. Tyson, Editor; Ginnie Tyson, Business Manager; Beckie Tyson, Managing Editor. **USPS:** 035-740. **Subscription Rates:** $30 Individuals in-town; $35 Individuals in-state; $40 Out of state. **URL:** http://www.atkinschronicle.com. **Formerly:** Chronicle: The Heart of Arkansas River valley. **Mailing address:** PO Box 188, Atkins, AR 72823. **Ad Rates:** PCI $4.50. **Remarks:** Accepts advertising. **Circ:** 2400.

BARLING

1275 ■ KERX-FM - 95.3
1912 Church St.
Barling, AR 72923
Phone: (479)484-7285
Fax: (479)484-7290
Format: Adult Album Alternative. **Owner:** Pearson Broadcasting Group, 9530 Midlothian Pike, Richmond, VA 23235, Ph: (804)276-0300. **Formerly:** KCCL-FM. **Operating Hours:** Continuous. **Wattage:** 50,000. **Ad Rates:** Advertising accepted; rates available upon request. Combined advertising rates available with KTTG-FM; KBCN-FM. **URL:** http://www.pearsonbroadcasting.com.

BATESVILLE

N. AR. Independence Co. On White River, 80 mi. NE of Little Rock. Arkansas College. Manufactures white lime, marble and silica, rubber, lumber, staves, shoes, dairy products. Cotton ginning and compressing; saw mills; bottling works. Manganese, white and black marble, limestone, silica quarries; hardwood, pine timber. Diversified farming. Corn, hay, livestock, poultry.

1276 ■ Batesville Daily Guard
Batesville Guard-Record Company Inc.
258 W Main St.
Batesville, AR 72503
Phone: (870)793-2383
General newspaper. **Freq:** Daily (eve.). **Print Method:** Offset. **Cols./Page:** 6. **Col. Width:** 12 picas. **Col. Depth:** 21 inches. **Key Personnel:** Angelia Roberts, Executive Director. **USPS:** 045-220. **Subscription Rates:** $7.50 Individuals per month, online edition. **Alt. Formats:** Download; PDF. **URL:** http://www.guardonline.com. **Mailing address:** PO Box 2036, Batesville, AR 72503. **Remarks:** Advertising accepted; rates available upon request. **Circ:** Paid 8786.

1277 ■ KAAB-AM
PO Box 2077
Batesville, AR 72503-2077
Phone: (501)793-4196
Fax: (501)793-5222
Format: Religious. **Owner:** W.R.D. Entertainment, Inc., at above address. **Founded:** 1980. **Key Personnel:** Bob Connell, Contact. **Wattage:** 1,000 Day; 020 Night. **Ad Rates:** $4.50-5 for 30 seconds; $5.50-6 for 60 seconds.

1278 ■ KBTA-AM
PO Box 2077
Batesville, AR 72503-2077
Phone: (870)793-4196
Fax: (870)793-5222
Format: Oldies. **Networks:** AP. **Owner:** W.R.D. Entertainment, Inc., at above address. **Founded:** 1950. **Key Personnel:** Rob Grace, President. **Wattage:** 1,000. **Ad Rates:** $4-7 for 30 seconds; $5-8 for 60 seconds.

1279 ■ K15FW - 15
PO Box A
Santa Ana, CA 92711
Phone: (714)832-2950
Free: 888-731-1000
Owner: Trinity Broadcasting Network Inc., PO Box A, Santa Ana, CA 92711, Ph: (714)832-2950, Free: 888-731-1000. **URL:** http://www.tbn.org.

1280 ■ KFXV-FM - 105.7
555 St. Louis St.
Batesville, AR 72501
Phone: (501)542-5000
Format: Eighties; Alternative/New Music/Progressive. **Key Personnel:** Doug Holt, Dir. of Operations, Promotions Dir., creative@searcyradiogroup.com; Daren James, News Dir., news@searcyradiogroup.com. **URL:** http://mybullcountry.com.

Circulation: ★ = AAM; △ or • = BPA; ♦ = CAC; ❑ = VAC; ⊕ = PO Statement; ‡ = Publisher's Report; Boldface figures = sworn; Light figures = estimated.

1281 ■ KWOZ-FM - 103.3
920 Harrison St., Ste. C
Batesville, AR 72501-6949
Phone: (870)793-4196
Fax: (870)793-5222
Format: Country. **Key Personnel:** Rob Stanley, Contact. **Wattage:** 100,000. **Ad Rates:** Noncommercial. **URL:** http://www.ar1033.com.

1282 ■ KZLE-FM - 93.1
920 Harrison St., Ste. C
Batesville, AR 72501
Phone: (870)793-4196
Fax: (870)793-5222
Format: Classic Rock. **Networks:** AP. **Owner:** W.R.D. Entertainment, Inc., at above address. **Founded:** 1982. **Operating Hours:** Continuous; 100% local. **ADI:** Little Rock, AR. **Key Personnel:** Rob Grace, Music Dir., President, rob@cr93.com. **Local Programs:** *Rockin Ride Home*, Monday Tuesday Wednesday Thursday Friday 3:00 p.m. - 7:00 p.m. **Wattage:** 100,000. **Ad Rates:** $8.50-12.50 for 30 seconds; $11.50-15 for 60 seconds. **URL:** http://www.cr93.com.

BEEBE

SW AR. White Co. 27 mi. NE of Little Rock. Agriculture and sawmills.

1283 ■ Beebe News
Beebe News
107 E Center St.
Beebe, AR 72012
Phone: (501)882-5414
Fax: (501)882-3576
Community newspaper. **Freq:** Weekly (Thurs.). **Print Method:** Offset. **Cols./Page:** 6. **Col. Width:** 2 1/16 inches. **Col. Depth:** 21 1/2 inches. **Key Personnel:** Christian McLane, Contact; Lee McLane, Editor, Publisher; Charlotte Paquette, Secretary. **USPS:** 047-880. **Subscription Rates:** $10 Individuals for six months. **URL:** http://www.beebenews.com. **Mailing address:** PO Box 910, Beebe, AR 72012. **Ad Rates:** SAU $8. **Remarks:** Accepts advertising. **Circ:** ‡2500.

BELLA VISTA

NC AR. Benton Co. 4 mi. N. of Bentonville in the Ozarks. Mineral springs.

1284 ■ The Weekly Vista
Community Publishers
313 Town Center W
Bella Vista, AR 72714
Phone: (479)855-3724
Fax: (479)855-6992
Publication E-mail: weeklyvista@nwanews.com
Community newspaper. **Freq:** Weekly. **Print Method:** Offset. **Cols./Page:** 5. **Col. Width:** 2 inches. **Col. Depth:** 15 3/4 inches. **Key Personnel:** Rusty Turner, Editor. **USPS:** 067-130. **Subscription Rates:** $3.99 Individuals per month, online only; $49 Individuals per year, home delivery & online. **URL:** http://bvwv.nwaonline.com/. **Remarks:** Accepts advertising. **Circ:** Paid ‡5000.

BENTON

C. AR. Saline Co. 23 mi. SW of Little Rock. Aluminum ore mines. Manufactures furniture, pulpwood, lumber. Agriculture. Poultry, beef. Dairy farming.

1285 ■ Saline Courier
Benton Publishing Company Inc.
321 N Market St.
Benton, AR 72015
Phone: (501)315-8228
Fax: (501)315-1920
Publication E-mail: news@bentoncourier.com
Community newspaper. **Freq:** Daily. **Print Method:** Offset. **Trim Size:** 14 x 22 3/4. **Cols./Page:** 6. **Col. Width:** 26 nonpareils. **Col. Depth:** 301 agate lines. **Key Personnel:** Megan Reynolds, Editor. **Subscription Rates:** $95 Individuals carrier delivery print 12 months; $150 By mail 12 months/print; $159 Out of area 12 months print ; $55 Individuals Saturdays & Sundays only /print 12 months. **URL:** http://www.bentoncourier.com. **Formerly:** The Benton Courier. **Mailing address:** PO Box 207, Benton, AR 72018. **Remarks:** Accepts advertising. **Circ:** Paid 1000.

1286 ■ KEWI-AM - 690
115 S Main St.
Benton, AR 72015
Phone: (501)778-6677
Format: Classical. **Owner:** Landers Broadcasting Company Inc., at above address. **Ad Rates:** Noncommercial.

BENTONVILLE

NW AR. Benton Co. 79 mi. N. of Fort Smith. Resort. Manufactures plastics, lumber, injection molds, electronic controls, textile items, canned fruits and vegetables, cabinets, cheese, butter, evaporated fruits, clothing. Monument plants. Ships poultry. Hardwood timber. Agriculture. Poultry, apples, grapes.

1287 ■ Backtracker
Northwest Arkansas Genealogical Society
405 S Main St.
Bentonville, AR 72712
Phone: (479)271-6820
Fax: (479)271-6775
Publisher's E-mail: genealogy@bentonvillear.com
Genealogical journal of Northwest Arkansas. **Freq:** Quarterly. **ISSN:** 0094--6915 (print). **URL:** http://www.rootsweb.ancestry.com/~arnwags/indexBacktracker.html. **Remarks:** Advertising not accepted. **Circ:** Combined 200.

1288 ■ Republic Monitor
Community Publishers
125 W Central Ave., Ste. 318
Bentonville, AR 72712
Community newspaper. **Freq:** Weekly (Thurs.). **Cols./Page:** 6. **Col. Width:** 2 inches. **Col. Depth:** 21 1/2 inches. **Key Personnel:** Ryan Squibb, Editor; Greg White, General Manager; Rodger Wheeler, Editor; Karen Keaton, Office Manager. **Subscription Rates:** $38.50 Individuals print or digital Greene and adjoining countries - 52 issues; $23.83 Individuals Greene and adjoining countries, 26 issues; $52.09 Elsewhere in Missouri - 52 issues; $33.97 Elsewhere in Missouri - 26 issues; $56.70 Out of state 52 issues; $35.70 Out of state 26 issues. **URL:** http://republicmonews.com. **Mailing address:** PO Box 1049, Bentonville, AR 72712. **Ad Rates:** BW $1246, full page; BW $958, 3/4 page; BW $660, 1/2 page; BW $450, 1/3 page; BW $340, 1/4 page; BW $276, 1/5 page; BW $234, 1/6 page; BW $176, 1/8 page; BW $138, 1/10; BW $92, 1/16 page; BW $48, 1/32 page. **Remarks:** Accepts advertising. **Circ:** 3,500.

1289 ■ KAPG-FM - 88.1
PO Box 3206
Tupelo, MS 38803
Format: Religious. **Owner:** American Family Radio, at above address. **Wattage:** 750. **URL:** http://Afa.Net.

1290 ■ K268AQ-FM - 101.5
PO Box 391
Twin Falls, ID 83303
Fax: (208)736-1958
Free: 800-357-4226
Format: Religious; Contemporary Christian. **Owner:** CSN International, PO Box 391, Twin Falls, ID 83303, Ph: (208)736-1958, Fax: (208)736-1958, Free: 800-357-4226. **URL:** http://www.csnradio.com.

BERRYVILLE

NW AR. Carroll Co. 80 mi. SE of Joplin, MO. Lumber mill; corrugated box factory; electronic components plant. Timber. Dairy, fruit, truck farms. Poultry processing.

1291 ■ Carroll County News
Carroll County Newspapers
PO Box 232
Berryville, AR 72616
Phone: (870)423-6636
Fax: (870)423-6640
Free: 800-524-2087
Publisher's E-mail: ccnnews@cox-internet.com
Local newspaper. **Founded:** 1872. **Freq:** Weekly (Tues.). **Print Method:** Offset. **Cols./Page:** 6. **Col. Width:** 26 nonpareils. **Col. Depth:** 301 agate lines. **Key Personnel:** Bob Moore, Publisher; Scott Loftis, Managing Editor. **USPS:** 519-220. **Subscription Rates:** $36 Individuals in Carroll county; $49 Individuals in Arkansas; $52 Out of state; $27 Individuals online. **URL:** http://www.carrollconews.com/. **Formed by the merger of:** Berryville Star Progress; Green Forest Tribune; Times-Echo; Star-Tribune. **Remarks:** Accepts advertising. **Circ:** ‡4007.

1292 ■ KTHS-AM - 1480
PO Box 191
Berryville, AR 72616
Phone: (870)423-2147
Email: frontdesk@kthsradio.com
Format: Country; Sports; News. **Networks:** ABC. **Founded:** 1958. **Operating Hours:** 6 am-8:30 pm; network five-minute newscasts; remainder local. **ADI:** Springfield, MO. **Key Personnel:** Jim Earls, Gen. Mgr.; Linda Boyer, News Dir; Jamie Hussey, Contact, jamieh@kthsradio.com; Tim Poynter, Contact, timpoynter@hotmail.com; Bree Adams, Contact, breeadams@kthsradio.com. **Wattage:** 5,000. **Ad Rates:** $9.42 for 30 seconds; $13.57 for 60 seconds. **URL:** http://www.kthsradio.com.

1293 ■ KTHS-FM - 107.1
PO Box 191
Berryville, AR 72616
Phone: (870)423-2147
Fax: (870)423-2146
Format: Country; Sports. **Networks:** ABC. **Founded:** 1974. **Formerly:** KSCC-FM. **Operating Hours:** Continuous; five minute network newscasts, remainder local. **ADI:** Springfield, MO. **Key Personnel:** Linda Boyer, News Dir., lindaboyer12@hotmail.com; Carroll Autry, Sales Mgr. **Wattage:** 18,000. **Ad Rates:** $9.42-11.18 for 30 seconds; $13.53-16.47 for 60 seconds. **URL:** http://www.kthsradio.com/.

BLYTHEVILLE

NE AR. Mississippi Co. 70 mi. N. of Memphis, TN. Mississippi County Community College.Manufactures industrial valves, electric tools, automotive emission controls, flexible duct systems, metal work, cable assemblies, canned goods, agri-chemicals and fertilizers, battery chargers Agriculture. Soybeans, cotton, milo, wheat rice.

1294 ■ Blytheville Courier News
Blytheville Courier News
PO Box 1108
Blytheville, AR 72316
Phone: (870)763-4461
Fax: (870)763-6874
Publisher's E-mail: aweld@couriernews.net
Newspaper. **Freq:** Tues.-Sat. **Cols./Page:** 9. **Key Personnel:** Andy Weld, Editor; Bess Ann Pease, Representative, Advertising and Sales; Mark Brasfield, Managing Editor. **Subscription Rates:** $21 Individuals print and All Digital the first three months, then $10.50 per month; $10.50 Individuals /month, online access. **URL:** http://www.couriernews.net. **Ad Rates:** BW $125; 4C $325; PCI $7.25. **Remarks:** Accepts advertising. **Circ:** Paid ‡2438, Combined ‡9954.

1295 ■ KBCM-FM - 88.3
PO Box 2440
Tupelo, MS 38803
Phone: (622)844-8888
Owner: American Family Association, at above address. **Wattage:** 1,200.

1296 ■ KHLS-FM - 96.3
PO Box 989
Blytheville, AR 72316
Phone: (870)762-2093
Fax: (870)763-8459
Free: 800-737-0096
Format: Country. **Networks:** ABC; Progressive Farmer. **Owner:** Sudbury Broadcasting Group, 125 S 2nd St., Blytheville, AR 72315, Ph: (870)762-2093, Free: 800-737-0096. **Founded:** 1948. **Operating Hours:** Continuous. **Key Personnel:** Jean Anderson, Gen. Mgr., jwhite@sudburybroadcastinggroup.com; Keith Michaels, Dir. of Operations, keith@thundercountry963.com. **Wattage:** 100,000. **Ad Rates:** $6.20-7.15 for 15 seconds; $7.60-14.30 for 30 seconds; $9.85-19 for 60 seconds. **URL:** http://www.thundercountry963.com.

1297 ■ KLCN-AM
PO Box 989
Blytheville, AR 72316
Phone: (870)762-2093
Fax: (870)763-8459
Free: 800-737-0096

Format: News. **Founded:** 1922. **Key Personnel:** Harold Sudbury, President; Ed White, Sales Mgr., Station Mgr. **Wattage:** 5,000 Day; 085 Night. **Ad Rates:** Advertising accepted; rates available upon request.

BOONEVILLE

SW AR. Logan Co. 34 mi. SE of Fort Smith. Sawmills, natural gas; tuberculosis sanatorium.

1298 ■ Booneville Democrat
Stephens Media L.L.C.
72 W 2nd St.
Booneville, AR 72927
Phone: (479)675-4455
Fax: (479)675-5457
Publisher's E-mail: sfrederick@stephensmedia.com
Community newspaper. **Freq:** Monthly. **Key Personnel:** Glenn Parrish, Editor; Vickey Wiggins, Publisher; Manuel Mann, Manager, Advertising. **Subscription Rates:** $29 Individuals print home delivery & online access. **URL:** http://www.boonevilledemocrat.com. **Mailing address:** PO Box 208, Booneville, AR 72927. **Remarks:** Advertising accepted; rates available upon request. **Circ:** (Not Reported).

CABOT

C. AR. Lonoke Co. 20 mi. NE of Little Rock. Manufactures furniture, net hoops, wearing apparel, military caps, satellite antenna dishes, mobile homes. Agriculture. Dairying. Soybeans, Corn, potatoes, strawberries. Poultry.

1299 ■ Cabot Star-Herald
Magie Enterprises Inc.
903 S Pine
Cabot, AR 72023
Phone: (501)843-3534
Fax: (501)843-6447
Community newspaper. **Freq:** Weekly (Wed.). **Print Method:** Offset. **Cols./Page:** 6. **Col. Width:** 2 1/8 inches. **Col. Depth:** 21 inches. **Key Personnel:** Byron Tate, Publisher; Jeremy Peppas, Editor. **USPS:** 082-320. **Subscription Rates:** $36 Individuals home delivery & online access one year. **URL:** http://lonokenews.net/cabot-star-herald. **Mailing address:** PO Box 1058, Cabot, AR 72023. **Ad Rates:** BW $1449; 4C $1724; SAU $11.50; PCI $11.50. **Remarks:** Advertising accepted; rates available upon request. **Circ:** (Not Reported).

CAMDEN

S. AR. Ouachita Co. On Ouachita River at head of navigation, 30 mi. N. of El Dorado. Manufactures paper, paper bags, disposable diapers, roofing materials, industrials ceramics, rubber adhesives, defense systems. lumber, monuments, fertilizer. Pine, hardwood timber. Hatcheries. Agriculture. Poultry, cotton, corn.

1300 ■ Cam-Tel Co.
113 Madison Ave. NE
Camden, AR 71701
Free: 800-903-0508
Owner: WEHCO Video, Inc., 115 E Capitol Ave., Little Rock, AR 72201, Ph: (501)378-3400, Fax: (501)376-8594. **Founded:** 1963. **Formerly**: Cam-Telco. **Cities Served:** subscribing households 5,577. **URL:** http://www.camdencabletv.com/cable-tv.html.

1301 ■ KAMD-FM - 97.1
612 Fairview Rd.
Camden, AR 71701
Phone: (870)836-9567
Fax: (870)836-9500
Format: Oldies. **Owner:** Radio Works L.L.C., 3207 Dogwood Dr., Portsmouth, VA 23703, Ph: (757)484-0140. **Founded:** 1968. **Operating Hours**: Continuous; 5% network, 95% local. **ADI**: Little Rock, AR. **Wattage**: 50,000. **Ad Rates:** $14-19 for 30 seconds; $19-26 for 60 seconds.

1302 ■ KCXY-FM - 95.3
612 Fairview Rd.
Camden, AR 71701
Phone: (870)836-9567
Format: Contemporary Country. **Networks:** ABC. **Owner:** Radio Works L.L.C., 3207 Dogwood Dr., Portsmouth, VA 23703, Ph: (757)484-0140. **Founded:** 1987. **Operating Hours**: Sunrise-sunset. **Key Personnel:** Donna Bradshaw, Gen. Mgr.; Jay Phillips, Dir. of Programs. **Wattage:** 100,000. **Ad Rates:** $14.11-18.23 for 30 seconds; $19.41-25.88 for 60 seconds.

1303 ■ KMGC-FM - 104.5
612 Fairview Rd.
Camden, AR 71701
Phone: (870)836-9567
Fax: (870)836-9500
Email: radioworks@camdenfm.net
Format: Urban Contemporary. **Founded:** Sept. 13, 2006. **Ad Rates:** Advertising accepted; rates available upon request. **URL:** http://www.yesradioworks.com/contact.

CARLISLE

C. AR. Lonoke Co. 35 mi. E. of Little Rock. Rice and sawmills; cotton ginning; cheese factory. Hardwood timber. Agriculture. Rice, oats, cotton.

1304 ■ Carlisle Independent
Stephens Media L.L.C.
220 W Main St.
Carlisle, AR 72024
Phone: (870)552-3111
Fax: (870)552-3111
Publication E-mail: cgoodman@carlisleindependent.com
Community newspaper. **Freq:** Weekly (Wed.). **Print Method:** Offset. **Cols./Page:** 6. **Col. Width:** 21 nonpareils. **Col. Depth:** 294 agate lines. **Key Personnel:** Byron Tate, Publisher; Jeremy Peppas, Editor. **USPS:** 090-800. **Subscription Rates:** $32 Individuals print home delivery & online access one year. **URL:** http://lonokenews.net/carlisle-independent. **Mailing address:** 220 W Main St., Carlisle, AR 72024. **Ad Rates:** GLR $.21; BW $441; SAU $3. **Remarks:** Accepts advertising. **Circ:** Paid 1515, Free 109.

CHARLESTON

SW AR. Franklin Co.

1305 ■ Charleston Express
Stephens Media L.L.C.
511 E Main
Charleston, AR 72933
Phone: (479)965-7368
Fax: (479)965-7206
Publisher's E-mail: sfrederick@stephensmedia.com
Community newspaper. **Freq:** Weekly (Wed.). **Print Method:** Offset. **Cols./Page:** 6. **Col. Width:** 13 inches. **Col. Depth:** 21 1/2 inches. **Key Personnel:** Paul Gramlich, Editor; Kristyn Sims, General Manager. **Subscription Rates:** $29 Individuals print home delivery and online. **URL:** http://www.charlestonexpress.com. **Ad Rates:** BW $416.67; 4C $666.67; SAU $3.53. **Remarks:** Accepts advertising. **Circ:** Paid 2250, Free 25.

CHEROKEE VILLAGE

1306 ■ KFCM-FM - 98.3
PO Box 909
Cherokee Village, AR 72525
Phone: (870)856-3630
Fax: (870)856-4408
Format: Oldies. **Owner:** KFCM, Inc., at above address. **Operating Hours:** Continuous. **Wattage:** 25,000. **Ad Rates:** Noncommercial. **URL:** http://www.myhometownradiostations.com.

CLARKSVILLE

NW AR. Johnson Co. 60 mi. E. of Fort Smith. College of the Ozarks. Lumber and stave mills. Brick, shoes, power tools, stainless steel tubing plants. Gas wells; coal mines; pine, oak timber. Poultry and sweet potato processing. Dairy, poultry, stock farms. Peaches.

1307 ■ Johnson County Graphic
Johnson County Graphic Inc.
203 E Cherry St.
Clarksville, AR 72830-0289
Phone: (479)754-2005
Fax: (479)754-2098
Community newspaper. **Freq:** Weekly (Wed.). **Print Method:** Offset. **Trim Size:** 13 1/8 x 21 1/2. **Cols./Page:** 6. **Col. Width:** 25 nonpareils. **Col. Depth:** 301 agate lines. **Key Personnel:** Ron Wylie, Publisher; Margaret Wylie, Manager, Advertising, Managing Editor; Debra Gray, Manager, Circulation. **USPS:** 276-380. **Subscription Rates:** $45 Individuals print and online in Johnson, Franklin, Pope, Newton or Logan counties; $35 Individuals online; $55 Elsewhere print and online; $3.50 Individuals online per month. **URL:** http://www.thegraphic.org. **Mailing address:** PO Box 289, Clarksville, AR 72830-0289. **Remarks:** Accepts advertising. **Circ:** ‡8200.

1308 ■ KLYR-AM - 1360
PO Box 188
Clarksville, AR 72830-0188
Phone: (479)754-3092
Fax: (479)667-5214
Free: 800-905-8020
Format: Country. **Networks:** Independent. **Founded:** 1957. **Operating Hours**: 6 a.m.-10 p.m. **Key Personnel:** Randall Forrester, Contact. **Wattage**: 500 day; 098 nights. **Ad Rates:** $3.53-8.09 for 30 seconds; $5.31-12.14 for 60 seconds. **URL:** http://kdyn.com/-station-info--links.html.

1309 ■ KUOZ-FM - 100.5
415 N College Ave.
Clarksville, AR 72830
Free: 800-264-8636
Format: Information; Eclectic. **Owner:** University of the Ozarks, 415 N College Ave., Clarksville, AR 72830-2880, Free: 800-264-8636. **Wattage**: 100. **URL:** http://www.ozarks.edu/visitors/comm/kuoz/default.asp.

1310 ■ KUOZ-TV - 6
415 N College Ave.
Clarksville, AR 72830-2880
Free: 800-264-8636
Owner: University of the Ozarks, 415 N College Ave., Clarksville, AR 72830-2880, Free: 800-264-8636. **Founded:** 1956. **URL:** http://www.ozarks.edu/visitors/comm.

1311 ■ KWXT-AM - 1490
PO Box 215
Clarksville, AR 72830
Phone: (479)754-3399
Email: kwxt1490am@yahoo.com
Format: Public Radio. **Key Personnel:** George Domerese, Contact. **URL:** http://www.kwxt1490am.com/.

1312 ■ KXIO-FM - 106.9
901 S Rogers St.
Clarksville, AR 72830
Format: Country. **Wattage:** 5,900. **URL:** http://www.kxio.nu/.

CLEVELAND COUNTY

1313 ■ Cleveland County Herald
Talent Publishing L.L.C.
215 Main St.
Rison, AR 71665
Phone: (870)325-6412
Fax: (870)325-6127
Publisher's E-mail: ccherald@tds.net
Community newspaper. **Freq:** Weekly (Wed.). **Print Method:** Offset. **Trim Size:** Quarter. **Cols./Page:** 6. **Col. Width:** 12 picas. **Col. Depth:** 21 inches. **Key Personnel:** Britt K. Talent, Editor; Shannon Ingram, Manager, Circulation. **USPS:** 117-660. **Subscription Rates:** $22 By mail digital; $24 Individuals print, Cleveland County and surrounding counties; $30 Out of area print; $33 Out of state print. **Mailing address:** PO Box 657, Rison, AR 71665. **Ad Rates:** SAU $4; SAU $4; PCI $4. **Remarks:** Accepts advertising. **Circ:** 2700.

CLINTON

NWC AR. Van Buren Co. 70 mi. N. of Little Rock. Manufactures electrical cord. Diversified farming. Poultry processing; beef and dairy cattle, hay.

1314 ■ Van Buren County Democrat
Stephens Media L.L.C.
197 Court St.
Clinton, AR 72031
Phone: (501)745-5175
Fax: (501)745-8865
Publisher's E-mail: sfrederick@stephensmedia.com
Community newspaper. **Freq:** Weekly (Wed.). **Print Method:** Offset. **Cols./Page:** 6. **Col. Width:** 2.4 inches. **Col. Depth:** 21 inches. **Key Personnel:** Byron Tate,

Circulation: ★ = AAM; △ or • = BPA; ♦ = CAC; ❑ = VAC; ⊕ = PO Statement; ‡ = Publisher's Report; Boldface figures = sworn; Light figures = estimated.

Publisher; Joe Lamb, Editor. **USPS:** 656-540. **Subscription Rates:** $34 Individuals print home delivery/online access. **URL:** http://www.vanburencountydem.com. **Mailing address:** PO Box 119, Clinton, AR 72031. **Ad Rates:** SAU $5.90; PCI $5. **Remarks:** Accepts advertising. **Circ:** Paid ‡4700.

1315 ■ KGFL-AM
PO Box 1349
Clinton, AR 72031-1349
Phone: (501)745-4474
Format: News; Talk; Oldies. **Wattage:** 5,000 Day; 1,000 CH. **Ad Rates:** Noncommercial.

1316 ■ KHPQ-FM - 92.1
PO Box 33
Clinton, AR 72031
Format: Country. **Wattage:** 10,000. **Ad Rates:** Noncommercial. **URL:** http://www.khpq.com.

CONWAY

C. AR. Faulkner Co. 32 mi. NW of Little Rock. Hendrix College; University of Central Arkansas. Manufactures shoes, school & office furniture, bus bodies, refrigerated cabinets, folding boxes, automotive testing equipment, dance floors, machine tools, vending machines. Dairy, stock, poultry farms.

1317 ■ Log Cabin Democrat
Log Cabin Democrat
1058 Front St.
Conway, AR 72032
Phone: (501)327-6621
Fax: (501)327-6787
Free: 800-678-4523
Publisher's E-mail: mail@thecabin.net
General newspaper. **Freq:** Daily and Sun. (eve.). **Key Personnel:** Waylon Harris, Editor, phone: (501)505-1212; Rick Fahr, Publisher; Rhonda Overbey, Director, Advertising, phone: (501)505-1273. **USPS:** 142-780. **Subscription Rates:** $150 Individuals /year daily; $119.40 Individuals /year (fri-sun); $83.40 Individuals /year Sunday only; $230 Other countries /year daily; $116 Other countries /year Sunday only; $6.95 Individuals monthly, online. **Mailing address:** PO Box 969, Conway, AR 72032. **Ad Rates:** GLR $.72; BW $1077.15; PCI $8.35. **Remarks:** Accepts advertising. **Circ:** (Not Reported).

1318 ■ The Oxford American
The Oxford American
PO Box 3235
Conway, AR 72035
Phone: (501)450-5376
Fax: (501)450-3490
Publication E-mail: oamag@oxfordamericanmag.com
General-interest literary magazine. **Freq:** Quarterly. **Key Personnel:** Roger Hodge, Editor. **ISSN:** 1074--4525 (print). **Subscription Rates:** $24.98 U.S.; $34.98 Canada; $44.98 Other countries. **URL:** http://www.oxfordamericanmag.com. **Ad Rates:** BW $2,925; 4C $3,650. **Remarks:** Accepts advertising. **Circ:** (Not Reported).

1319 ■ Conway Corp.
1307 Prairie St.
Box 99
Conway, AR 72034
Phone: (501)450-6000
Fax: (501)450-6099
Email: comments@conwaycorp.net
Founded: 1980. **Key Personnel:** Richie Arnold, CEO, richiea@conwaycorp.net; Bret Carroll, CFO, bretc@conwaycorp.net; Linda Johnson, Mgr., ljohnson@conwaycorp.net; Mike Bailey, Mgr., mikeb@conwaycorp.net; Roger Mills, Contact, rogerm@conwaycorp.net. **Cities Served:** Conway, Arkansas: subscribing households 14,917; 79 channels; 1 community access channel; 168 hours per week community access programming. **URL:** http://www.conwaycorp.com.

KAFT-TV - See Fayetteville

1320 ■ KASR-FM - 92.7
1072 Markham St.
Conway, AR 72032
Phone: (501)327-6611
Fax: (501)327-6614
Email: kasr@sbcglobal.net
Format: Sports. **Owner:** Creative Media, Inc., at above address. **Key Personnel:** Mike Harrison, Sales Mgr.; Josh Harrison, Prog. Dir., Traffic Mgr., josh@kasrfm.com; Elaine Harrison, Traffic Mgr. **Ad Rates:** Noncommercial. **URL:** http://www.kasrfm.com.

1321 ■ KCON-AM - 1230
201 Donaghey Ave.
Conway, AR 72035
Phone: (501)450-3326
Fax: (501)450-5874
Format: Adult Contemporary; News; Sports. **Networks:** Arkansas Radio. **Owner:** University of Central Arkansas, 201 Donaghey Ave., Conway, AR 72035, Ph: (501)450-5000. **Founded:** 1950. **Operating Hours:** Continuous. **Key Personnel:** Mike Reynolds, Contact; Steve Owens, Contact; Gary Roberts, Dean; Monty Rowell, Contact; Steve Owens, Contact. **Wattage:** 1,000. **Ad Rates:** $2.50 for 30 seconds; $3 for 60 seconds. **URL:** http://www.uca.edu/ubulletin/02/211.php.

KEMV-TV - See Mountain View

KETG-TV - See Arkadelphia

1322 ■ KETS-TV - 2
350 S Donaghey
Conway, AR 72032
Phone: (501)682-2386
Fax: (501)682-4122
Free: 800-662-2386
Format: Public TV. **Networks:** Public Broadcasting Service (PBS). **Owner:** Arkansas Educational Television Commission, at above address. **Founded:** 1966. **Operating Hours:** Continuous. **Key Personnel:** Kathy Atkinson, Dir. of Programs; Kathleen Stafford, Dir. Ed.; Allen Weatherly, Exec. Dir.; Carole Adornetto, Dir. of Production; Ron Johnson, Dir. of Comm.; Tony Brooks, Dep. Dir. **Local Programs:** *Arkansas Week*, Friday Sunday 7:30 p.m. 11:00 a.m. **Wattage:** 26,730 ERP horizontal. **Ad Rates:** Accepts Advertising. **URL:** http://www.aetn.com.

1323 ■ KETZ-TV - 12
350 S Donaghey Ave.
Conway, AR 72034
Phone: (501)450-1727
Free: 800-662-2386
Owner: Arkansas Educational Television Network, 350 S Donaghey Ave., Conway, AR 72034, Ph: (501)682-2386, Fax: (501)537-9815, Free: 800-662-2386. **Key Personnel:** Allen Weatherly, Exec. Dir. **URL:** http://www.aetn.org.

1324 ■ KHDX-FM - 93.1
1600 Washington Ave.
Conway, AR 72032
Format: Alternative/New Music/Progressive. **Owner:** Hendrix College, 1600 Washington Ave., Conway, AR 72032, Ph: (501)329-6811, Free: 800-277-9017. **Founded:** 1971. **Operating Hours:** midnight. **Wattage:** 008. **Ad Rates:** Noncommercial. **URL:** http://www.khdx.fm.

KTEJ-TV - See Jonesboro

CORNING

1325 ■ Clay County Courier
810 N Missouri Ave.
Corning, AR 72422-0085
Phone: (870)857-3531
Community newspaper. **Freq:** Weekly (Wed.). **Cols./Page:** 8. **Col. Width:** 12.5 picas. **Col. Depth:** 21 1/2 inches. **Key Personnel:** Jan Rockwell, Publisher. **URL:** http://www.claycountyliving.com/; http://www.corningpublishing.com. **Mailing address:** PO Box 85, Corning, AR 72422-0085. **Circ:** 3400.

1326 ■ KCCB-AM
PO Box 398
Corning, AR 72422
Format: Country. **Networks:** Arkansas Radio. **Owner:** Clay County Broadcasting Co., at above address, Fax: (501)857-6795. **Founded:** 1959. **Wattage:** 1,000 Day; 031 Night.

CROSSETT

SE AR. Ashley Co. 15 mi. S. of Hamburg. Residential

1327 ■ Ashley News Observer
Ashley County Publishing Inc.
102 Pine St.
Crossett, AR 71635
Phone: (870)364-5186
Fax: (870)364-2216
Publisher's E-mail: news@ashleynewsobserver.com
General newspaper. **Freq:** Weekly. **Print Method:** Offset. **Cols./Page:** 6. **Col. Width:** 2 1/16 inches. **Col. Depth:** 21 1/2 inches. **URL:** http://www.ashleynewsobserver.com. **Ad Rates:** GLR $0.45; BW $823.02; 4C $1,223.02; SAU $6.82; PCI $6.82. **Remarks:** Advertising accepted; rates available upon request. **Circ:** 4950.

1328 ■ KAGH-AM - 800
PO Box 697
Crossett, AR 71635
Phone: (870)364-2181
Fax: (870)364-2183
Email: kagh@alltel.net
Format: Oldies. **Networks:** Arkansas Radio; Westwood One Radio; CNN Radio. **Owner:** Ashley County Broadcasters Inc., at above address. **Founded:** 1951. **Operating Hours:** Continuous. **Key Personnel:** Barry Medlin, Contact. **Wattage:** 240. **Ad Rates:** $2.15-7.15 for 15 seconds; $3.20-8 for 30 seconds; $4.70-10.85 for 60 seconds. Combined advertising rates available with KWLT-FM, KAGH-FM. **URL:** http://www.crossettradio.com.

1329 ■ KAGH-FM - 104.9
PO Box 697
Crossett, AR 71635
Phone: (870)364-2182
Fax: (870)364-2183
Email: kagh@alltel.net
Format: Country. **Networks:** Arkansas Radio; Mutual Broadcasting System; Westwood One Radio. **Owner:** Ashley County Broadcasters Inc., at above address. **Founded:** 1967. **Operating Hours:** Continuous. **Wattage:** 6,000 ERP. **Ad Rates:** $2.15-7.15 for 15 seconds; $3.20-8 for 30 seconds; $4.70-10.85 for 60 seconds. Combined advertising rates available with KWLT-FM, KAGH-AM. **URL:** http://www.crossettradio.com.

1330 ■ KHMB-FM - 99.5
203 Fairview Rd.
Crossett, AR 71635
Phone: (870)364-4700
Fax: (870)364-4770
Free: 888-276-7047
Email: qlite@arkansas.net
Format: Adult Contemporary. **Wattage:** 3,200. **URL:** http://www.qliteradio.com.

1331 ■ KWLT-FM - 102.7
PO Box 697
Crossett, AR 71635
Phone: (870)364-2181
Fax: (870)364-2183
Email: comments@crossettradio.com
Format: Classic Rock. **Networks:** ABC. **Owner:** South Ark Broadcasting Inc., at above address. **Founded:** May 1995. **Operating Hours:** Continuous. **Wattage:** 25,000. **Ad Rates:** Advertising accepted; rates available upon request. Combined advertising rates available with KAGH-AM, KAGH-FM. **URL:** http://www.crossettradio.com.

DE QUEEN

SW AR. Sevier Co. 45 mi. NW of Texarkana. Timber and pole treating plant. Poultry processing, broiler chickens, beef cattle. Pine, oak, gum, timber.

1332 ■ De Queen Bee
De Queen Bee Co.
404 De Queen Ave.
De Queen, AR 71832
Phone: (870)642-2111
Fax: (870)642-3138
Newspaper with a Democratic orientation. **Freq:** Weekly (Fri.). **Print Method:** Offset. **Cols./Page:** 7. **Col. Width:** 25 nonpareils. **Col. Depth:** 294 agate lines. **Key Personnel:** Patrick Massey, Managing Editor. **URL:** http://www.dequeenbee.com. **Mailing address:** PO Box 1000, De Queen, AR 71832. **Remarks:** Accepts advertising. **Circ:** ‡1677.

1333 ■ KDQN-AM - 1390
921 W Collin Raye Dr.
De Queen, AR 71832
Phone: (870)642-2446
Email: numberonecountry@yahoo.com

Format: Hispanic. **Founded:** 1956. **Operating Hours:** Daytime. **Wattage:** 500. **Ad Rates:** $6 for 30 seconds; $12 for 60 seconds. KDQN-FM; KMJI-FM. **Mailing address:** PO Box 311, De Queen, AR 71832. **URL:** http://www.kdqn.net.

1334 ■ KDQN-FM - 92.1
921 W Collin Raye Dr.
De Queen, AR 71832
Phone: (870)642-2446
Fax: (870)642-2442
Email: numberonecountry@yahoo.com
Format: Country. **Founded:** 1978. **Operating Hours:** Continuous. **Wattage:** 50,000. **Ad Rates:** $8 for 30 seconds; $16 for 60 seconds. **Mailing address:** PO Box 311, De Queen, AR 71832. **URL:** http://www.kdqn.net.

1335 ■ KENA-FM - 102.1
PO Box 311
De Queen, AR 71832
Phone: (479)394-1450
Fax: (479)394-1459
Free: 877-394-5459
Format: Contemporary Country. **Networks:** ABC. **Owner:** Ouachita Broadcasting, Inc., at above address. **Founded:** 1969. **Operating Hours:** Continuous; 90% network, 10% local. **Wattage:** 25,000. **Ad Rates:** $12 for 30 seconds; $18 for 60 seconds. KQOR-FM; KILX-FM;##.

KMTB-FM - See Murfreesboro, AR

DE WITT

C. AR. Arkansas Co. 40 mi. E. of Pine Bluff. Rice mills, cotton gins, shipping.

1336 ■ De Witt Era-Enterprise
De Witt Publishing Co.
140 Court Sq.
De Witt, AR 72042-2049
Phone: (870)946-3933
Community newspaper. **Freq:** Weekly (Wed.). **Key Personnel:** Valenya Franks, Editor. **URL:** http://dewittee.com. **Mailing address:** PO Box 678, De Witt, AR 72042-0678. **Remarks:** Accepts advertising. **Circ:** 3300.

DES ARC

EC AR. Prairie Co. On White River, 48 mi. NE of Little Rock. Manufactures cables for auto industry. Soft and hardwood timber. Diversified farming. Rice, soybeans, wheat, corn, milo.

1337 ■ KBDO-FM - 91.7
PO Box 2440
Tupelo, MS 38803
Phone: (662)844-8888
Free: 800-326-4543
Format: Religious. **Owner:** American Family Association, at above address. **Ad Rates:** Noncommercial. **URL:** http://www.afa.net.

DEWITT

1338 ■ Front Porch
Arkansas Farm Bureau
1710 S Whitehead Dr.
Dewitt, AR 72042-2911
Phone: (870)946-3501
Association magazine of interest to general membership. **Freq:** Quarterly. **Print Method:** Offset. **Trim Size:** 8 3/8 x 10 7/8. **Cols./Page:** 4. **Col. Width:** 2 1/4 inches. **Col. Depth:** 10 1/2 inches. **Key Personnel:** Gregg Patterson, Editor. **URL:** http://www.arfb.com/media-communications/front-porch. **Formerly:** Farm Bureau Press. **Ad Rates:** BW $3,010; 4C $3,635; PCI $98. **Remarks:** Accepts advertising. **Circ:** Combined ■ **190000.**

DEWITT

1339 ■ KDEW-FM - 96.7
Hwy. 152-A
DeWitt, AR 72042
Phone: (501)946-1470
Format: Contemporary Country. **Owner:** Quadras Broadcasting Co., Inc., at above address. **Founded:** 1970. **Operating Hours:** 6 a.m.-10 p.m. **Key Personnel:** Ben Allen, Gen. Mgr. **Wattage:** 3,000 ERP. **Mailing address:** PO Box 566, DeWitt, AR 72042.

EL DORADO

S. AR. Union Co. 85 mi. E. of Texarkana. Manufactures refined petroleum, petro-chemical products, asphalt and foundry products, lighting fixtures, wood fabricators, oil well equipment, lumber, fertilizer, tool and diecasting, industrial rubber products. Saw mill; nursery. Gas and oil wells; pine and hardwood timber. Livestock, poultry.

1340 ■ El Dorado News-Times
El Dorado News Times
111 N Madison Ave.
El Dorado, AR 71730
Phone: (870)862-6611
Fax: (870)862-9482
General newspaper. **Freq:** Mon.-Sun. (morn.). **Print Method:** Offset. **Trim Size:** 13 3/4 x 22 1/2. **Cols./Page:** 6. **Col. Width:** 13 inches. **Col. Depth:** 21 1/2 inches. **Key Personnel:** Nicole Patterson, Manager, Advertising; Wayne Warren, Manager, Circulation; Betty Chatham, General Manager; Chris Qualls, Managing Editor; IvaGail Riser, Manager, Production. **Subscription Rates:** $12.95 Individuals /monthly online; $155.40 Individuals /year online; $.99 Individuals /day online. **URL:** http://www.eldoradonews.com. **Ad Rates:** GLR $0.86; BW $1,560.90; 4C $1,810.90; PCI $12. **Remarks:** Accepts advertising. **Circ:** Mon.-Sat. ★**9357.**

1341 ■ KAGL-FM - 93.3
2525 NW Ave.
El Dorado, AR 71730
Phone: (870)863-6126
Fax: (870)863-4555
Format: Classic Rock. **Owner:** Noalmark Broadcasting, at above address. **Ad Rates:** Noncommercial. **URL:** http://www.totalradio.com.

1342 ■ KAKV-FM - 88.9
PO Box 779002
Rocklin, CA 95677-9972
Fax: (916)251-1901
Free: 800-525-5683
Format: Contemporary Christian. **Owner:** Educational Media Foundation, PO Box 2098, Omaha, NE 68103-2098, Free: 800-434-8400. **ADI:** Monroe, LA-El Dorado, AR. **Key Personnel:** Mike Novak, President, CEO; Alan Mason, COO. **Wattage:** 26,000. **URL:** http://www.klove.com.

1343 ■ KELD-AM - 1400
2525 N West Ave.
El Dorado, AR 71730
Phone: (870)863-6126
Fax: (870)863-4555
Format: Sports. **Networks:** USA Radio; Independent Broadcasting. **Owner:** Noalmark Broadcasting, at above address. **Founded:** 1935. **Operating Hours:** Continuous. **ADI:** Monroe, LA-El Dorado, AR. **Key Personnel:** Orlando Garza, Gen. Sales Mgr. **Wattage:** 1,000. **Ad Rates:** $10 for 30 seconds; $14 for 60 seconds. Combined advertising rates available with KIXB, KXZX, KAGL, KMLK. **URL:** http://www.totalradio.com/fcc.htm.

1344 ■ KLBQ-FM - 98.7
1904 W Hillsboro St.
El Dorado, AR 71730
Phone: (870)863-5121
Fax: (870)863-6221
Email: klbq@infogo.com
Format: Adult Contemporary; Top 40. **Networks:** ABC. **Owner:** El Dorado Communications Inc., at above address. **Founded:** 1963. **Operating Hours:** Continuous. **ADI:** Monroe, LA-El Dorado, AR. **Wattage:** 25,000. **Ad Rates:** Noncommercial.

1345 ■ KMLK-FM - 101.5
2525 Northwest Ave.
El Dorado, AR 71730
Phone: (870)863-6126
Fax: (870)863-4555
Format: Oldies; Urban Contemporary. **Owner:** Noalmark Broadcasting, at above address. **ADI:** Monroe, LA-El Dorado, AR. **URL:** http://www.totalradio.com/kmlk.htm.

1346 ■ KMRX-FM - 96.1
2525 NW Ave.
El Dorado, AR 71730
Phone: (870)863-6126
Free: 800-247-4487
Email: requests@todaysbesthits.com
Format: Adult Contemporary. **Owner:** Noalmark Broadcasting, at above address. **ADI:** Monroe, LA-El Dorado, AR. **URL:** http://www.totalradio.com.

1347 ■ KVMA-AM - 630
202 W 19th St.
El Dorado, AR 71730
Phone: (870)234-9901
Format: Country. **Networks:** ABC; Arkansas Radio. **Owner:** Noalmark Broadcasting @COR, 2525 N West Ave., El Dorado, AR 71730. **Founded:** 1948. **Operating Hours:** 6 a.m.-sunset; 5% network, 95% local. **Wattage:** 1,000. **Ad Rates:** Noncommercial. **URL:** http://pro.knro-am.tritonflex.com.

1348 ■ KVMZ-FM - 99.1
202 W 19TH St.
El Dorado, AR 71730-3115
Phone: (870)234-9901
Free: 888-822-5862
Format: Country. **Owner:** Noalmark Broadcasting, at above address. **Key Personnel:** Amanda Smith, Contact, amanda.smith@suddenlinkmail.com; Ken Sibley, Contact, ken.sibley@suddenlinkmail.com; Dan Gregory, Contact, dan.gregory@suddenlinkmail.com; Amanda Smith, Contact, amanda.smith@suddenlinkmail.com. **Wattage:** 4,100. **URL:** http://www.magnoliaradio.com.

EUREKA SPRINGS

NW AR. Carroll Co. 80 mi. NE of Fort Smith. Manufactures lumber. Saw mills. Tourism, health resort; mineral springs. Oak, pine timber. Agriculture. Corn, wheat, poultry, livestock.

1349 ■ The Anglican Digest
Society for Promoting and Encouraging Arts and Knowledge of the Church
805 County Road 102
Eureka Springs, AR 72632-9705
Phone: (479)253-9701
Fax: (479)253-1277
Free: 800-572-7929
Publisher's E-mail: anglicandigest@att.net
Religious magazine. **Freq:** Quarterly. **Print Method:** Offset. **Trim Size:** 5 1/8 x 7 1/2. **Cols./Page:** 2. **Col. Width:** 24 nonpareils. **Col. Depth:** 88 agate lines. **Key Personnel:** Rev. Kendall Harmon, Editor; Rev. John Dryden Burton, Managing Editor; Tom Walker, General Manager. **ISSN:** 0003--3278 (print). **Subscription Rates:** $25 Individuals; free, contribution requested. **URL:** http://www.anglicandigest.org. **Ad Rates:** BW $800. **Remarks:** Accepts advertising. **Circ:** Non-paid 145000, 115000.

1350 ■ The Anglican Digest
SPEAK Inc.
805 County Rd. 102
Eureka Springs, AR 72632-9705
Phone: (501)253-9701
Fax: (479)253-1277
Publisher's E-mail: anglicandigest@att.net
Religious magazine. **Freq:** Quarterly. **Print Method:** Offset. **Trim Size:** 5 1/8 x 7 1/2. **Cols./Page:** 2. **Col. Width:** 24 nonpareils. **Col. Depth:** 88 agate lines. **Key Personnel:** Rev. Kendall Harmon, Editor; Rev. John Dryden Burton, Managing Editor; Tom Walker, General Manager. **ISSN:** 0003--3278 (print). **Subscription Rates:** $25 Individuals; free, contribution requested. **URL:** http://www.anglicandigest.org. **Ad Rates:** BW $800. **Remarks:** Accepts advertising. **Circ:** Non-paid 145000, 115000.

1351 ■ The Lovely County Citizen
PO Box 679
Eureka Springs, AR 72632
Phone: (479)253-0070
Fax: (479)253-0080
Community newspaper. **Freq:** Weekly (Thurs.). **Key Personnel:** Bob Moore, Publisher. **Subscription Rates:** $50 Individuals. **URL:** http://www.lovelycitizen.com/. **Remarks:** Accepts advertising. **Circ:** Non-paid ♦**5784.**

FAIRFIELD BAY

Van Buren Co.

Circulation: ★ = AAM; △ or • = BPA; ♦ = CAC; ❑ = VAC; ⊕ = PO Statement; ‡ = Publisher's Report; Boldface figures = sworn; Light figures = estimated.

1352 ■ KFFB-FM - 106.1
PO Box 1050
Fairfield Bay, AR 72088
Phone: (800)356-5106
Fax: (501)723-4861
Email: calendar@kffb.com
Format: News; Talk; Oldies. **Networks:** ABC; Arkansas Radio. **Owner:** Freedom Broadcasting., Inc., at above address, Irvine, CA. **Founded:** 1985. **Operating Hours:** Continuous. **ADI:** Little Rock, AR. **Key Personnel:** Bob Connell, Gen. Mgr., bob@kffb.com; Pamela Connell, Contact, pam@kffb.com; Weldon Smith, Contact, weldon@kffb.com. **Wattage:** 50,000. **Ad Rates:** Advertising accepted; rates available upon request. **URL:** http://www.kffb.com.

FAYETTEVILLE

NW AR. Washington Co. 60 mi. NE of Fort Smith. University of Arkansas. Manufactures tools, clothing, business forms, steel towers, electronic organs, wheels, pipe fittings, electrical components. Poultry processing; bottling works; hatchery. Resort. Hardwood timber. Poultry, fruit, dairy, stock farms.

1353 ■ Arkansas Historical Quarterly
Arkansas Historical Association
c/o University of Arkansas
416 Old Main
Fayetteville, AR 72701
Phone: (479)575-5884
Fax: (479)575-2775
Historical magazine. **Freq:** Quarterly. **Print Method:** Offset. **Trim Size:** 6 x 9. **Cols./Page:** 1. **Col. Width:** 48 nonpareils. **Col. Depth:** 91 agate lines. **Key Personnel:** Michael Pierce, Associate Editor; Patrick Williams, Editor; Charles S. Bolton, Board Member; Michael B. Dougan, Board Member; Kenneth C. Barnes, Board Member; Carl Moneyhon, Board Member. **ISSN:** 0004--1823 (print). **URL:** http://arkansashistoricalassociation.org/?page_id=10. **Ad Rates:** BW $100. **Remarks:** Accepts advertising. **Circ:** ‡1600.

1354 ■ Arkansas Law Review
William S. Hein and Company Inc.
University of Arkansas
School of Law
Waterman Hall 107
Fayetteville, AR 72701-1201
Phone: (479)575-5610
Publication E-mail: lawrev@uark.edu
Law journal. **Freq:** Quarterly. **Key Personnel:** Haley Heath, Editor-in-Chief. **ISSN:** 0004--1831 (print). **Subscription Rates:** $25 Individuals /year; $30 Other countries /year; $9 Single issue. **URL:** http://lawreview.law.uark.edu; http://www.wshein.com/catalog/863. **Remarks:** Advertising not accepted. **Circ:** (Not Reported).

1355 ■ The Arkansas Traveler
The Arkansas Traveler
119 Kimpel Hall,University of Arkansas
Fayetteville, AR 72701
Publication E-mail: traveler@uark.edu
Student newspaper of the University of Arkansas. **Freq:** Triweekly Mon., Wed., and Friday. **Print Method:** Web offset. **Trim Size:** 11.625 x 11.833. **Cols./Page:** 6. **Col. Width:** 2.065 inches. **Col. Depth:** 21 inches. **Key Personnel:** Isabel Dobrin, Editor-in-Chief. **URL:** http://www.uatrav.com. **Ad Rates:** BW $1,042; 4C $1,292; SAU $8.27; PCI $8.42. **Remarks:** Accepts advertising. **Circ:** Non-paid ‡5000.

1356 ■ Central States Archaeological Journal
Central States Archaeological Societies
c/o Kevin Farmer, President
3515 E Redwood Dr.
Fayetteville, AR 72703
Archaeological journal. **Freq:** Quarterly January, April, July, and October. **Print Method:** Offset. **Trim Size:** 6 1/2 x 10. **Cols./Page:** 2. **Col. Width:** 30 nonpareils. **Col. Depth:** 98 agate lines. **Key Personnel:** Steven R. Cooper, Editor-in-Chief. **ISSN:** 0008--9559 (print). **Subscription Rates:** Included in membership. **URL:** http://csasi.org/journal_articles.htm. **Remarks:** Advertising not accepted. **Circ:** (Not Reported).

1357 ■ Countdown
JDRF Northwest Arkansas Chapter
4241 Gabel Dr., Ste. 2B
Fayetteville, AR 72703
Phone: (479)443-9190
Fax: (479)443-2692
Publisher's E-mail: orangecounty@jdrf.org
Magazine containing information about juvenile diabetes research progress. **Freq:** Quarterly. **URL:** http://countdown.jdrf.org. **Remarks:** Accepts advertising. **Circ:** (Not Reported).

1358 ■ Flashback
Washington County Historical Society
118 E Dickson St.
Fayetteville, AR 72701-4207
Phone: (479)521-2970
Publisher's E-mail: info@washcohistoricalsociety.org
Magazine covering local history. **Freq:** Quarterly. **ISSN:** 0428--5573 (print). **Subscription Rates:** $6 Individuals. **URL:** http://www.washcohistoricalsociety.org/flashback. **Remarks:** Advertising not accepted. **Circ:** (Not Reported).

1359 ■ IEEE Transactions on Engineering Management
IEEE - Engineering Management Society
c/o Rajiv Sabherwal, Ed.-in-Ch.
Sam M. Walton College of Business
University of Arkansas
Fayetteville, AR 72701
Phone: (479)575-4500
Publication E-mail: ieee-tem@umsl.edu
Journal covering research regarding the theory and practice of engineering management. **Freq:** Quarterly. **Key Personnel:** Rajiv Sabherwal, Editor-in-Chief. **ISSN:** 0018-9391 (print). **URL:** http://ieeexplore.ieee.org/xpl/RecentIssue.jsp?punumber=17. **Remarks:** Accepts advertising. **Circ:** (Not Reported).

1360 ■ Journal of Food Law and Policy
University of Arkansas School of Law
Robert A. Leflar Law Ctr.
Waterman Hall
1045 W Maple St.
Fayetteville, AR 72701
Phone: (479)575-5601
Fax: (479)575-3937
Publisher's E-mail: lawadmit@uark.edu
Journal covering topics on food safety and labeling, consumer interest in food policy, international food safety laws and regulations, the legal effects of food technology, traceability issues, and a wide variety of other dynamic issues affecting food law and policy. **Freq:** Semiannual. **Key Personnel:** Jordan Broyles, Editor-in-Chief. **URL:** http://law.uark.edu/academics/journals/journal-food-law-policy.php. **Circ:** (Not Reported).

1361 ■ Northwest Arkansas Times
Northwest Arkansas Times
PO Box 1607
Fayetteville, AR 72702
Fax: (479)571-6418
Publication E-mail: email@nwarktimes.com
General newspaper. **Freq:** Mon.-Sun. (morn.). **Print Method:** Letterpress and offset. **Cols./Page:** 6. **Col. Width:** 25 nonpareils. **Col. Depth:** 301 agate lines. **Key Personnel:** Greg Harton, Editor. **Subscription Rates:** $28 Individuals /month. **URL:** http://www.nwaonline.com. **Remarks:** Accepts advertising. **Circ:** (Not Reported).

1362 ■ The Times of Northeast Benton County
The Times of Northeast Benton County
212 N East Ave.
Fayetteville, AR 72701
Phone: (479)442-1700
Community newspaper. **Freq:** Weekly (Wed.). **Print Method:** Offset. **Cols./Page:** 6. **Col. Width:** 24 nonpareils. **Col. Depth:** 297 agate lines. **Key Personnel:** Annette Beard, Managing Editor, phone: (479)451-1196, fax: (479)451-9456. **Subscription Rates:** $39 Individuals /year, home delivery and online; $3.99 Individuals /year, online. **URL:** http://tnebc.nwaonline.com. **Ad Rates:** GLR $.19; BW $318.75; SAU $4; PCI $3.25. **Remarks:** Accepts advertising. **Circ:** ‡1690.

1363 ■ Cox Communications
637 E Joyce Blvd.
Fayetteville, AR 72703
Founded: 1953. **Formerly:** TCA Cable-TV; TCA Cable TV. **Key Personnel:** Dennis Yocum, Gen. Mgr., dryyool@tca-cable.com. **Cities Served:** subscribing households 20,500. **URL:** http://www.cox.com.

1364 ■ KAFT-TV - 13
350 S Donaghey Ave.
Conway, AR 72034
Phone: (501)682-2386
Free: 800-662-2386
Email: info@aetn.org
Format: Public TV. **Networks:** Public Broadcasting Service (PBS). **Owner:** Arkansas Educational Television Commission, at above address. **Founded:** 1976. **Operating Hours:** 6 a.m.-11:30 p.m. weekdays; 7 a.m.-11:30 p.m. Saturday and Sunday. **Key Personnel:** Tony Brooks, Dep. Dir., tbrooks@aetn.org; Allen Weatherly, Exec. Dir. **Ad Rates:** Noncommercial. **URL:** http://www.aetn.org.

1365 ■ KAMO-FM - 94.3
4209 Frontage Rd.
Fayetteville, AR 72703
Phone: (479)521-5566
Fax: (479)521-0751
Format: Country. **Simulcasts:** KAMO-AM. **Networks:** ABC. **Owner:** Cumulus Broadcasting Inc., 3280 Peachtree Rd. NW, Ste. 2300, Atlanta, GA 30305-2447, Ph: (404)949-0700, Fax: (404)949-0740. **Founded:** 1971. **Operating Hours:** Continuous. **Key Personnel:** Anita Cowan, Contact, anita.cowan@cumulus.com; Dan Hentschel, Dir. of Programs, dan.hentschel@cumulus.com; Anita Cowan, Contact, anita.cowan@cumulus.com. **Wattage:** 28,000. **Ad Rates:** Noncommercial. **URL:** http://www.nashfm943.com.

1366 ■ KBNV-FM - 90.1
PO Box 2440
Tupelo, MS 38803
Phone: (662)844-8888
Format: Religious. **Owner:** American Family Association, at above address. **URL:** http://www.afa.net.

1367 ■ KEZA-FM - 107.9
2049 E Joyce Blvd., Ste. 101
Fayetteville, AR 72703
Format: Adult Contemporary. **Networks:** Independent. **Founded:** 1983. **Operating Hours:** Continuous; 100% local. **Key Personnel:** Tony Beringer, Gen. Mgr; Duce Foreman, Contact, duceforeman@clearchannel.com. **Wattage:** 100,000. **Ad Rates:** $28-42 for 30 seconds; $40-75 for 60 seconds. **URL:** http://www.magic1079.com.

1368 ■ KFAY-AM - 1030
4209 Frontage Rd.
Fayetteville, AR 72703
Phone: (479)521-5566
Fax: (479)521-0751
Format: News; Talk. **Networks:** ABC; Westwood One Radio. **Owner:** Cumulus Broadcasting Inc., 3280 Peachtree Rd. NW, Ste. 2300, Atlanta, GA 30305-2447, Ph: (404)949-0700, Fax: (404)949-0740. **Operating Hours:** Continuous; 50% network, 50% local. **Wattage:** 10,000 Day : 1,000 Night. **Ad Rates:** Advertising accepted; rates available upon request. **URL:** http://newstalk1030.com.

1369 ■ KFTA-TV - 24
15 S Block Ave., Ste. 101
Fayetteville, AR 72701
Phone: (479)571-5100
Free: 866-946-5692
Format: Commercial TV. **Networks:** NBC. **Founded:** 1978. **Formerly:** KLMN-TV. **Operating Hours:** 6 a.m. **ADI:** Fort Smith, AR. **Ad Rates:** Advertising accepted; rates available upon request. **URL:** http://nwahomepage.com.

1370 ■ KIGL-FM - 93.3
2049 E Joyce Blvd., Ste. 101
Fayetteville, AR 72703
Phone: (479)521-0104
Fax: (479)587-TALK
Format: Classic Rock. **Key Personnel:** Judy Hudson, Bus. Mgr., judyhudson@clearchannel.com. **Wattage:** 100,000. **Ad Rates:** Advertising accepted; rates available upon request. **URL:** http://www.933theeagle.com.

1371 ■ KIX-FM - 104
2049 E Joyce Blvd., Ste. 101
Fayetteville, AR 72703
Phone: (479)521-0104
Format: Country. **Founded:** 1993. **Key Personnel:** Judy Hudson, Bus. Mgr. **Ad Rates:** Advertising ac-

cepted; rates available upon request. **URL:** http://www.kix104.com.

1372 ■ KJEM-FM - 93.3
2049 E Joyce Blvd., Ste. 101
Fayetteville, AR 72703
Format: Classic Rock. **Networks:** ABC. **Owner:** iHeartMedia and Entertainment Inc. , 200 E Basse Rd., San Antonio, TX 78209, Ph: (210)822-2828. **Founded:** 1986. **Formerly**: KHHC-FM. **Operating Hours**: Monday - Sunday : 12:00 am - 7.00 pm. **Wattage**: 100,000. **Ad Rates:** Accepts Advertising. **URL:** http://933theeagle.iheart.com.

1373 ■ KKEG-FM - 98.3
4209 Frontage Rd.
Fayetteville, AR 72701
Phone: (479)521-5566
Format: Album-Oriented Rock (AOR). **Networks:** AP. **Owner:** Cumulus Media Inc., 3280 Peachtree Rd. NW, Ste. 2300, Atlanta, GA 30305-2455, Ph: (404)949-0700, Fax: (404)949-0740. **Operating Hours**: Continuous; 1% network, 99% local. **ADI**: Fort Smith, AR. **Key Personnel:** Sheila Lewis, Dir. of Sales, sheila.lewis@cumulus.com. **Wattage:** 3,000. **Ad Rates:** $10-25 per unit. **URL:** http://www.983thekeg.com.

1374 ■ KKIX-FM - 103.9
2049 E Joyce Blvd., Ste. 101
Fayetteville, AR 72703
Phone: (479)521-0104
Format: Country. **Networks:** Independent. **Owner:** iHeartMedia Inc., 200 E Basse Rd., San Antonio, TX 78209, Ph: (210)832-3314. **Founded:** 1983. **Formerly**: KNWA-FM. **Operating Hours**: Continuous; 100% local. **ADI**: Fort Smith, AR. **Key Personnel:** Dave Ashcraft, Dir. of Programs, davetyler@kix104.com; Tony Beringer, Gen. Mgr., VP, tonyberinger@clearchannel.com. **Wattage:** 100,000. **Ad Rates:** $125 for 60 seconds. **URL:** http://www.kix104.com.

1375 ■ KMXF-FM - 101.9
2049 E Joyce Blvd., Ste. 101
Fayetteville, AR 72703
Format: Contemporary Hit Radio (CHR). **Wattage:** 24,000. **Ad Rates:** Advertising accepted; rates available upon request. **URL:** http://www.hotmix1019.com.

1376 ■ KNWA-TV - 51
609 W Dickson St. 3rd Fl.
Fayetteville, AR 72701
Phone: (479)571-5100
Owner: Nexstar Broadcasting Group Inc., 545 E John Carpenter Fwy., Ste. 700, Irving, TX 75062, Ph: (972)373-8800. **URL:** http://nwahomepage.com.

1377 ■ KOFC-AM
2553 N College
Fayetteville, AR 72703-3311
Phone: (501)443-2900
Fax: (501)443-2978
Email: kofc@ipa.net
Format: Talk; Southern Gospel; Contemporary Christian. **Networks:** USA Radio; Ambassador Inspirational Radio; Voice of Christian Youth America. **Founded:** 1987. **Key Personnel:** Terry Evans, Sales Mgr.; Robert Johnson, Gen. Mgr., Contact; Robert Johnson, Contact. **Wattage**: 920 Day; 045 Night. **Ad Rates:** $3-9 for 30 seconds; $5-11 for 60 seconds.

1378 ■ KREB-AM - 1190
1780 W Holly St.
Fayetteville, AR 72703-1307
Format: Eclectic; News; Talk. **Networks:** ABC. **Founded:** 1954. **Formerly**: KAMO-AM. **Operating Hours**: Continuous. **Key Personnel:** Dave Clark, Dir. of Programs; Stephen Butler, President. **Wattage**: 5,000 KW. **Ad Rates:** $8 for 30 seconds; $10 for 60 seconds. **URL:** http://1190thefan.com.

1379 ■ K215EE-FM - 90.9
PO Box 391
Twin Falls, ID 83303
Fax: (208)736-1958
Free: 800-357-4226
Format: Religious; Contemporary Christian. **Owner:** CSN International, PO Box 391, Twin Falls, ID 83303, Ph: (208)736-1958, Fax: (208)736-1958, Free: 800-357-4226. **URL:** http://www.csnradio.com.

1380 ■ KUAF-FM - 91.3
Nine S School Ave.
Fayetteville, AR 72701
Phone: (479)575-2556
Fax: (479)575-8440
Free: 800-522-5823
Format: Public Radio; Talk; News; Educational; Classical. **Networks:** National Public Radio (NPR). **Owner:** University of Arkansas System Board of Trustees, 2404 North University Ave., Little Rock, AR 72207, Ph: (501)686-2500. **Founded:** 1973. **Operating Hours**: Continuous; 45% network, 55% local. **Key Personnel:** Rick Stockdell, Station Mgr.; Kyle Kellams, News Dir.; Pete Hartman, Operations Mgr. **Wattage**: 60,000. **Ad Rates:** Noncommercial; underwriting available. $22-27 per unit. **URL:** http://www.kuaf.com.

1381 ■ KXNA-FM - 104.9
1780 Holly St.
Fayetteville, AR 72703
Phone: (479)582-3776
Fax: (479)571-0995
Format: Album-Oriented Rock (AOR). **Owner:** Butler Broadcasting Corp., at above address. **Operating Hours**: Continuous. **Wattage**: 2,750. **Ad Rates:** Advertising accepted; rates available upon request. **URL:** http://www.newrock1049x.com.

1382 ■ KXUA-FM - 88.3
A665 Arkansas Union
Fayetteville, AR 72701
Phone: (479)575-4273
Email: kxua@uark.edu
Format: Eclectic. **Founded:** 1973. **Key Personnel:** David Martin, Station Mgr. **Ad Rates:** Noncommercial. **URL:** http://kxua.uark.edu.

1383 ■ KYNF-FM - 94.9
4209 Frontage Rd.
Fayetteville, AR 72703
Phone: (479)521-5566
Format: Adult Contemporary. **Owner:** Cumulus Broadcasting Inc., 3280 Peachtree Rd. NW, Ste. 2300, Atlanta, GA 30305-2447, Ph: (404)949-0700, Fax: (404)949-0740. **Key Personnel:** Sarah Leftwich, Dir. of Mktg., Mktg. Mgr., sarah.leftwich@cumulus.com. **URL:** http://www.949nashicon.com.

FORDYCE

S. AR. Dallas Co. 48 mi. SW of Pine Bluff. Manufactures picture frames, garments, folders & filing systems, telephone, electrical cable, wire, plywood, lumber, caskets, furniture, cross ties. Hardwood, pine timber & pulpwood. Poultry, livestock, truck crops, fruit.

1384 ■ KBJT-AM - 1590
303 Spring St.
Fordyce, AR 71742
Phone: (870)352-7137
Fax: (870)352-7139
Email: kbjt@windstream.net
Format: News; Information. **Owner:** KBJT/KQEW Radio, 303 Spring St., Fordyce, AR 71742. **Founded:** 1977. **Operating Hours**: Continuous; 90% network, 10% local. **Key Personnel:** Carna Coates, Contact. **Wattage**: 810. **Ad Rates:** $3.77-6 for 30 seconds; $6.19-8 for 60 seconds. **URL:** http://www.kbjtkq.com.

1385 ■ KQEW-FM - 102.3
303 Spring St.
Fordyce, AR 71742
Phone: (870)352-7137
Fax: (870)352-7139
Email: kbjt@alltel.net
Format: Country. **Networks:** Independent. **Owner:** Dallas Properties, Inc., 303 N Spring St , Fordyce, AR 71742-3317, Ph: (870)352-7137. **Founded:** 1982. **Operating Hours**: Continuous. 100% local. **Key Personnel:** Carna Coates, Contact. **Wattage**: 25,000. **Ad Rates:** Noncommercial. Combined advertising rates available with KBJT-AM. **URL:** http://www.kbjtkq.com.

FORREST CITY

E. AR. St. Francis Co. 9 mi. SW of Palestine. Residential.

1386 ■ Times Herald
Times Herald
PO Box 1699
Forrest City, AR 72336-1699
Phone: (870)633-3130
Fax: (870)633-0599
Publisher's E-mail: addept@thnews.com
General newspaper. **Founded:** 1871. **Freq:** Daily. **Print Method:** Offset. **Cols./Page:** 6. **Col. Width:** 2 1/16 inches. **Col. Depth:** 21 inches. **Key Personnel:** Bonner McCollum, Publisher; Weston McCollum Lewey, Publisher. **Subscription Rates:** $8.50 Individuals per month; carrier; $139 By mail 1 year in county; $169 Out of area 1 year by mail; $100 Students 9 months college subscription. **URL:** http://www.thnews.com. **Ad Rates:** PCI $11.64. **Remarks:** Accepts advertising. **Circ:** Mon.-Fri. 4500.

1387 ■ East Arkansas Cable TV
4804 N Washington St.
Forrest City, AR 72335
Free: 800-903-0508
URL: http://eastarkansasvideo.com.

1388 ■ KARH-FM - 88.1
PO Box 3206
Tupelo, MS 38803
Format: Gospel. **Owner:** American Family Radio, at above address. **Wattage:** 4,200. **URL:** http://Afa.Net.

1389 ■ KBFC-FM - 93.5
501 E Broadway St.
Forrest City, AR 72335
Phone: (870)633-1252
Fax: (870)633-1259
Free: 800-246-5955
Email: radio@arkansas.net
Format: Country. **Owner:** Forrest City Broadcasting Co., PO Box 707, Forrest City, AR, Ph: (870)633-1252, Fax: (870)633-1259, Free: 800-246-5955. **Operating Hours**: 6 a.m.-10 p.m. **Wattage**: 25,000. **Ad Rates:** $5.25-10 for 30 seconds; $8.50-13 for 60 seconds. **Mailing address:** PO Box 707, Forrest City, AR 72336-0707. **URL:** http://www.kbfc.com.

1390 ■ KXJK-AM - 950
PO Box 707
Forrest City, AR 72336-0707
Phone: (870)633-1252
Fax: (870)633-1259
Free: 800-246-5955
Email: radio@arkansas.net
Format: News; Sports. **Founded:** Sept. 13, 2006. **Key Personnel:** Jeff Fogg, Gen. Mgr., jeff@arkradio.com; Rob Johnson, Sales Mgr., rob@arkradio.com; Rick Holt, News Dir., rick@arkradio.com. **Ad Rates:** Noncommercial. **URL:** http://www.kxjk.com.

FORT SMITH

W. AR. Sebastian Co. On Arkansas River, 134 mi. SE of Tulsa, Okla. Livestock, feed and food processors. Furniture, glass, bottles, bricks, chimneys, mattresses, cottonseed oil, lumber, kitchen cabinets, handles, tents, caskets, auto bodies, refrigerators, air conditioners, paper cups, concrete pipe and concrete blocks, iron and sheet metal, optical goods, paper boxes, scissors, coal briquettes, heavy trailers, rubber products, clothing, electrical appliances manufactured. Coal mines; hardwood timber.

1391 ■ The Journal
Fort Smith Historical Society Inc.
PO Box 3676
Fort Smith, AR 72913
Phone: (479)452-2415
Publisher's E-mail: info@fortsmithhistory.org
Journal of the Fort Smith Historical Society. **Freq:** Semiannual. **ISSN:** 0736-4261 (print). **URL:** http://www.fortsmithhistory.org/. **Remarks:** Advertising not accepted. **Circ:** (Not Reported).

1392 ■ The Lions' Chronicle
University of Arkansas, Fort Smith
5210 Grand Ave.
Fort Smith, AR 72913
Phone: (479)788-7000
Publication E-mail: lionschronicle@uafs.edu
Student newspaper for the University of Arkansas, Fort Smith. **Freq:** Monthly. **Key Personnel:** Dr. Monica Lubeke, Faculty Advisor, phone: (479)788-7966. **URL:** http://lionschronicle.uafs.edu. **Mailing address:** PO Box 3649, Fort Smith, AR 72913-3649. **Circ:** (Not Reported).

Circulation: ⋆ = AAM; △ or • = BPA; ♦ = CAC; ❑ = VAC; ⊕ = PO Statement; ‡ = Publisher's Report; Boldface figures = sworn; Light figures = estimated.

1393 ■ Southwest Times Record
Stephens Media L.L.C.
3600 Wheeler Ave.
Fort Smith, AR 72901
Phone: (479)785-7700
Publisher's E-mail: sfrederick@stephensmedia.com
General newspaper. **Freq:** Daily. **Print Method:** Offset. **Cols./Page:** 6. **Col. Width:** 10.4 picas. **Col. Depth:** 21 inches. **Key Personnel:** Judith Hansen, Editor; Glen Hogue, Manager, Circulation; Carla Gardner, Business Manager. **Subscription Rates:** $115.20 Individuals daily home delivery - carrier; $228.00 By mail. **URL:** http://www.swtimes.com. **Ad Rates:** PCI $37.6. **Remarks:** Accepts advertising. **Circ:** Paid ♦**29258**, Paid ♦**33204**.

1394 ■ KAOW-FM - 88.9
PO Box 2440
Tupelo, MS 38803
Phone: (662)844-8888
Format: Contemporary Christian. **Owner:** American Family Association, at above address. **URL:** http://www.afa.net.

1395 ■ KFPW-AM - 1230
321 N Greenwood Ave.
Fort Smith, AR 72901
Phone: (479)288-1047
Fax: (479)785-2638
Format: Talk. **Networks:** ABC; Arkansas Radio. **Owner:** Fort Smith Radio Group, 321 N Greenwood Ave., Fort Smith, AR 72901-3453, Ph: (479)288-1047, Fax: (479)785-2638. **Founded:** 1930. **Operating Hours**: Continuous; 90% network, 10% local. **ADI**: Fort Smith, AR. **Key Personnel:** Jeff Clunn, Sales Mgr. **Wattage**: 1,000. **Ad Rates:** Noncommercial. Combined advertising rates available with KRBK/KHGG/KOLX. **URL:** http://www.sportshog1031.com/page.php?page_id=28031.

1396 ■ KFPW-FM - 94.5
PO Box 908
Fort Smith, AR 72902
Phone: (479)783-5379
Fax: (501)785-2638
Format: Classic Rock; Oldies. **Networks:** ABC; Arkansas Radio. **Owner:** Fort Smith Radio Group, 321 N Greenwood Ave., Fort Smith, AR 72901-3453, Ph: (479)288-1047, Fax: (479)785-2638; Gordon Brown, at above address. **Founded:** 1978. **Operating Hours**: Continuous. **ADI**: Fort Smith, AR. **Key Personnel:** Gordon Brown, Contact; Margie Cole, Contact; Jack Riley, Contact. **Wattage**: 50,000. **Ad Rates:** Advertising accepted; rates available upon request. $4-6 for 15 seconds; $9-14 for 30 seconds; $16-20 for 60 seconds. $4-$6 for 15 seconds; $9-$11 for 30 seconds; $12-$14 for 60 seconds. Combined advertising rates available with KFPW-AM. **URL:** http://www.thefort945fm.com.

1397 ■ KFSA-AM - 950
Four Glen Haven Dr.
Fort Smith, AR 72901
Phone: (479)785-2526
Fax: (479)646-1373
Email: kzkzfm@kzkzfm.com
Format: News; Southern Gospel; Talk. **Networks:** ABC. **Owner:** The Fred Rogers Co., 6420 Zero St, Fort Smith, AR 72903, Ph: (479)646-6700. **Founded:** 1947. **Operating Hours**: Continuous. **ADI**: Fort Smith, AR. **Key Personnel:** David Burdue, Dir. of Programs. **Wattage**: 1,000 Day; 500 Night. **Ad Rates:** $5-10 for 30 seconds; $8-15 for 60 seconds.

1398 ■ KFSM-TV - 5
PO Box 369
Fort Smith, AR 72902
Phone: (479)783-3131
Fax: (479)783-3295
Format: News; Sports. **Networks:** CBS. **Owner:** The New York Times Co., 620 8th Ave., New York, NY 10018, Ph: (212)204-4000, Fax: (212)204-1727, Free: 888-698-6397. **Operating Hours**: 12:00 a.m.-6:00 p.m. **ADI**: Fort Smith, AR. **Key Personnel:** Gene Graham, VP; Mark Howell, Controller, VP. **Wattage**: 550,000 ERP Horizon. **URL:** http://5newsonline.com/.

1399 ■ KHBS-TV - 40
2415 N Albert Pke.
Fort Smith, AR 72904
Phone: (479)783-4040
Fax: (479)785-5375
Format: News. **Networks:** ABC. **Owner:** Arkansas Argyle Television Inc., 300 W 57th St., New York, NY 10019-3789, Ph: (212)887-6800, Fax: (212)887-6855. **Operating Hours**: Continuous Sun.-Thurs.; 6:30 a.m.-1:40 a.m. Sat. **ADI**: Fort Smith, AR. **Key Personnel:** Mike Burgess, Sales Mgr. **Wattage**: 310. **Ad Rates:** Advertising accepted; rates available upon request. **URL:** http://www.4029tv.com.

1400 ■ KHGG-FM - 103.1
321 N Greenwood Ave.
Fort Smith, AR 72901-3453
Phone: (479)288-1047
Fax: (479)785-2638
Format: Sports. **Owner:** Pharis Broadcasting Inc., at above address. **Operating Hours**: Continuous. **Key Personnel:** Bill Pharis, President, CEO, billpharis40@yahoo.com; Dennis McCaslin, Mktg. Coord., dmc0796@msn.com. **Ad Rates:** Advertising accepted; rates available upon request. **URL:** http://www.sportshog1031.com/index.php.

1401 ■ KISR-FM
117 Belle Ave.
Fort Smith, AR 72901
Phone: (501)785-2526
Format: Hip Hop. **ADI**: Fort Smith, AR. **Wattage**: 100,000 ERP. **Ad Rates:** Noncommercial.

1402 ■ KKBD-FM - 95.9
311 Lexington Ave.
Fort Smith, AR 72901
Phone: (479)782-8888
Fax: (479)782-0366
Free: 866-503-1398
Format: Classic Rock. **Operating Hours**: Continuous. **ADI**: Fort Smith, AR. **Wattage**: 50,000. **Ad Rates:** Noncommercial. Combined advertising rates available with KZBB-FM, KWHN-AM, KMAG-FM. **URL:** http://www.bigdog959.com.

1403 ■ KLFS-FM - 90.3
PO Box 779002
Rocklin, CA 95677-9972
Fax: (916)251-1901
Free: 800-525-5683
Format: Contemporary Christian. **Owner:** Educational Media Foundation, PO Box 2098, Omaha, NE 68103-2098, Free: 800-434-8400. **Key Personnel:** Mike Novak, President, CEO; Alan Mason, COO. **Wattage**: 2,400. **URL:** http://www.klove.com.

1404 ■ KLSZ-FM - 100.7
3101 Free Ferry Rd., Ste. E
Fort Smith, AR 72903
Phone: (501)452-0681
Format: Classic Rock. **Owner:** Cumulus Broadcasting Inc., 3280 Peachtree Rd. NW, Ste. 2300, Atlanta, GA 30305-2447, Ph: (404)949-0700, Fax: (404)949-0740. **Founded:** 1983. **Formerly**: KXXI-FM. **Operating Hours**: Continuous. **ADI**: Fort Smith, AR. **Key Personnel:** Matt Miller, Dir. of Programs, matt.miller2@cumulus.com. **Wattage**: 25,000. **Ad Rates:** $25-50 per unit. Combined advertising rates available with KAYR-FM, KOMS-FM, KBBQ-FM. **URL:** http://www.1007nashicon.com.

1405 ■ KMAG-FM - 99.1
311 Lexington Ave.
Fort Smith, AR 72901
Phone: (479)782-8888
Fax: (479)782-0366
Format: Country. **Operating Hours**: Continuous. **ADI**: Fort Smith, AR. **Key Personnel:** Steve Knoll, Dir. of Programs, steveknoll@clearchannel.com; Dave Ashcraft, Operations Mgr., daveashcraft@cleachannel.com; Judy Hudson, Bus. Mgr.; Mike Burgess, Dir. of Sales. **Wattage**: 100,000. **Ad Rates:** Noncommercial. Combined advertising rates available with KZBB-FM, KWHN-AM, KKBD-FM, KYHN-AM. **URL:** http://www.kmag991.com.

1406 ■ KRBK-FM
PO Box 908
Fort Smith, AR 72902
Phone: (479)783-5379
Owner: Fort Smith Radio Group, 321 N Greenwood Ave., Fort Smith, AR 72901-3453, Ph: (479)288-1047, Fax: (479)785-2638.

1407 ■ KRWA-FM - 103.1
321 N Greenwood Ave.
Fort Smith, AR 72901-3453
Phone: (479)288-0940
Fax: (479)785-2638
Format: News; Religious; Sports. **Networks:** ABC. **Founded:** 1984. **Operating Hours**: Continuous. **Key Personnel:** Neil Raines, Dir. of Programs; Bob Sachs, Music Dir.; Janet Carnahan, Dir. of Traffic. **Wattage**: 6,100 ERP. **Ad Rates:** $2.50 for 30 seconds; for 60 seconds. **URL:** http://www.sportshog1031.com.

1408 ■ K16ER - 16
PO Box A
Santa Ana, CA 92711
Phone: (714)832-2950
Free: 888-731-1000
Owner: Trinity Broadcasting Network Inc., PO Box A, Santa Ana, CA 92711, Ph: (714)832-2950, Free: 888-731-1000. **URL:** http://www.tbn.org.

1409 ■ KTCS-AM - 1410
PO Box 180188
Fort Smith, AR 72918
Phone: (479)646-6151
Format: Contemporary Country. **Simulcasts:** KTCS-FM. **Networks:** Independent. **Owner:** Big Chief Broadcasting Co., at above address. **Operating Hours**: Continuous. **ADI**: Fort Smith, AR. **Wattage**: 1,000. **Ad Rates:** $10 for 30 seconds; $15 for 60 seconds. Combined advertising rates available with KTCS-FM: $25-$48 for 30 seconds; $34-$65 for 60 seconds. **URL:** http://www.ktcs.com.

1410 ■ KTCS-FM - 99.9
5304 Hwy. 45 E
Fort Smith, AR 72916
Email: ktcs@ktcs.com
Format: Country; News. **Owner:** Big Chief Broadcasting Co., at above address. **ADI**: Fort Smith, AR. **Wattage**: 100,000 ERP. **Ad Rates:** Advertising accepted; rates available upon request. **URL:** http://www.ktcs.com.

1411 ■ KWHN-AM - 1320
311 Lexington Ave.
Fort Smith, AR 72901
Format: News; Talk. **Simulcasts:** KYHN. **Networks:** ABC. **Founded:** 2000. **Operating Hours**: Continuous; 25% network, 75% other. **ADI**: Fort Smith, AR. **Key Personnel:** Kelley Ray, Dir. of Public Rel., Prog. Dir.; Tony Montgomery, Dir. of Sales, tonymontgomery@clearchannel.com. **Wattage**: 10,000. **Ad Rates:** Noncommercial. KMAG-FM, KZBB-FM, KKBD-FM, KYHN-AM. **URL:** http://www.kwhn.com.

1412 ■ KYHN-AM - 1320
311 Lexington Ave.
Fort Smith, AR 72901
Phone: (479)782-8888
Fax: (479)785-5946
Format: News; Talk. **Networks:** ABC. **Owner:** Clear Channel Communication, Inc., 200 E Basse Rd., San Antonio, TX 78209, Ph: (210)822-2828, Fax: (210)822-2828. **Operating Hours**: Continuous; 25% network, 75% other. **ADI**: Fort Smith, AR. **Wattage**: 1,320. **Ad Rates:** Combined advertising rates available with KMAG-FM, KZBB-FM, KKBD-FM, KWHN-AM. **URL:** http://www.kwhn.com.

1413 ■ KZBB-FM - 97.9
311 Lexington Ave.
Fort Smith, AR 72901
Phone: (479)782-8888
Fax: (479)782-0366
Format: Contemporary Hit Radio (CHR). **Owner:** iHeartMedia Inc., 200 E Basse Rd., San Antonio, TX 78209, Ph: (210)832-3314. **Founded:** 1947. **Operating Hours**: Continuous. **ADI**: Fort Smith, AR. **Key Personnel:** Tony Montgomery, Dir. of Sales; Bobby Baldwin, Dir. of Programs. **Wattage**: 100,000. **Ad Rates:** $36-85 for 30 seconds; $56-120 for 60 seconds. KMAG-FM, KKBD-FM, KWHN-AM, KYHN-AM. **URL:** http://www.kzbb.com.

1414 ■ KZKZ-FM - 106.3
6420 S Zero St.
Fort Smith, AR 72903
Phone: (479)646-6700
Fax: (479)646-1373
Format: Contemporary Christian. **Networks:** USA Radio. **Owner:** The Fred Rogers Co., 6420 Zero St, Fort Smith, AR 72903, Ph: (479)646-6700. **Founded:**

1993. **Operating Hours**: Continuous; 100% local. **ADI**: Fort Smith, AR. **Key Personnel:** Bertha James, Sales Rep., bertha@kzkzfm.com; Dave Burdue, Contact, dave@kzkzfm.com. **Local Programs**: *Exciting E.T.*, Monday Tuesday Wednesday Thursday Friday Sunday 7:51 a.m. 8:00 a.m. - 8:30 a.m.; *Overnight Show*, Monday Tuesday Wednesday Thursday Friday 12:00 a.m. - 5:30 a.m. **Wattage**: 6,000. **Ad Rates:** Noncommercial. **URL:** http://www.kzkzfm.com.

GLENWOOD

SW AR. Pike Co. 81 mi. SW of Little Rock. Residential.

1415 ■ KWXI-AM - 670
PO Box 740
Glenwood, AR 71943
Phone: (870)356-2151
Fax: (870)356-4684
Email: info@kwxi.net
Format: News; Sports; Contemporary Christian. **Simulcasts:** KWXE. **Networks:** CBS. **Founded:** 1980. **Operating Hours**: Continuous. **ADI**: Little Rock, AR. **Wattage**: 5,000. **Ad Rates:** $5.88 for 30 seconds; $8.82 for 60 seconds. KWXE-FM.

GRAVETTE

NW AR. Benton Co. 15 mi. W. of Bentonville. Black walnut plant. Precision machine shop. Manufactures pharmaceuticals, plastics insulation, garments. Timber. Agriculture. Poultry; dairy products.

1416 ■ KBVA-FM - 106.5
1512 W Hwy. 72
Gravette, AR 72736
Phone: (479)787-6411
Format: Music of Your Life. **Wattage**: 37,000. **URL:** http://variety1065.com.

GREEN FOREST

NW AR. Carroll Co. 80 mi. NE of Fort Smith. Many tomato canneries. Agriculture. Corn, oats, hay.

1417 ■ KGSF-FM - 88.7
PO Box 391
Twin Falls, ID 83303
Fax: (208)736-1958
Free: 800-357-4226
Format: Religious; Contemporary Christian. **Owner:** CSN International, PO Box 391, Twin Falls, ID 83303, Ph: (208)736-1958, Fax: (208)736-1958, Free: 800-357-4226. **Key Personnel:** Kelly Carlson, Dir. of Engg.; Ray Gorney, Asst. Dir.; Don Mills, Music Dir., Director. **URL:** http://www.csnradio.com.

GREENWOOD

W. AR. Sebastian Co. 15 mi. S. of Fort Smith. Residential

1418 ■ Greenwood Democrat
Stephens Media L.L.C.
PO Box 398
Greenwood, AR 72936
Phone: (479)996-4494
Fax: (479)996-4122
Publication E-mail: info@greenwooddemocrat.com
Community newspaper. **Freq:** Weekly (Wed.). **Print Method:** Offset. **Cols./Page:** 6. **Col. Width:** 1.833 inches. **Col. Depth:** 21 inches. **Key Personnel:** Dustin Graham, Editor. **Subscription Rates:** $30 Individuals print home delivery and online access; $30 Individuals digital only. **URL:** http://greenwooddemocrat.stephensmedia.com. **Ad Rates:** GLR $6.50; BW $819; 4C $826.70; PCI $6.50. **Remarks:** Advertising accepted; rates available upon request. **Circ:** (Not Reported).

GURDON

SW AR. Clark Co. 65 mi. NE of Texarkana. Lumber mills. Plywood plant. Pine timber. Agriculture. Cattle, poultry.

1419 ■ Hoo-Hoo Log and Tally Magazine
Hoo-Hoo International
207 Main St.
Gurdon, AR 71743
Phone: (870)353-4997
Fax: (870)353-4151
Publisher's E-mail: info@hoo-hoo.org
Magazine containing reports from International Board of Directors and Officers, local club reports from around the world and other stories and reprints of interest to those in the forest products industry. **Freq:** 3/year. **Subscription Rates:** Included in membership. **Alt. Formats:** Download; PDF. **URL:** http://www.hoo-hoo.org/log-tally.php. **Mailing address:** PO Box 118, Gurdon, AR 71743. **Ad Rates:** BW $425. **Remarks:** Accepts advertising. **Circ:** (Not Reported).

HAMBURG

SE AR. Ashley Co. 15 mi. NE of Crossett. Lakes. Manufactures die & moulding, apparel, shirts.

1420 ■ Ashley County Ledger
Ashley Publishing Company Inc.
PO Box 471
Hamburg, AR 71646
Phone: (870)853-2424
Fax: (870)853-8203
Publisher's E-mail: editor@ashleycountyledger.com
Newspaper. **Freq:** Daily. **Print Method:** Offset. **Cols./Page:** 6. **Col. Width:** 2 1/16 inches. **Col. Depth:** 21 1/2 inches. **Subscription Rates:** $30 Individuals in Ashley County; $35 Out of area. **URL:** http://www.ashleycountyledger.com. **Remarks:** Accepts advertising. **Circ:** ‡3000.

HAMPTON

SE AR. Calhoun Co. 8 mi. NW of Harrell. Residential.

1421 ■ KBPW-FM - 88.1
PO Box 3206
Tupelo, MS 38803
Format: Religious; Contemporary Christian. **Owner:** American Family Radio, at above address. **Operating Hours**: Continuous. **Wattage**: 60,000 ERP. **URL:** http://www.afr.net/newafr/default.asp.

HARDY

NE AR. Sharp Co. 50 mi. NW of Paragould. Residential.

1422 ■ KOOU-FM - 104.7
PO Box 480
Hardy, AR 72542
Phone: (870)856-2179
Fax: (870)856-4001
Format: Oldies. **Wattage**: 6,000.

HARRISON

NW AR. Boone Co. 30 mi. SE of Berryville. Residential.

1423 ■ Newton County Times
Newton County Times
PO Box 40
Harrison, AR 72602-0040
Phone: (870)741-2625
Local newspaper. **Freq:** Weekly (Wed.). **Print Method:** Offset. **Cols./Page:** 6. **Col. Width:** 24 nonpareils. **Col. Depth:** 301 agate lines. **Key Personnel:** Jeff Dezort, Editor; Ronnie Bell, Publisher; Jason Overman, Director, Advertising. **Subscription Rates:** $25.20 Individuals. **URL:** http://newtoncountytimes.com. **Ad Rates:** BW $670; 4C $735; PCI $5.20. **Remarks:** Advertising accepted; rates available upon request. **Circ:** ‡3000.

1424 ■ Harrison Radio Station Inc.
600 S Pine St.
Harrison, AR 72601
Email: info@kcwdradio.com
Format: Oldies; Eighties; Sports. **Operating Hours**: Continuous. **Ad Rates:** , Rate for 30 spots between 3:00 a.m. - 7:00 a.m.; , Rate for 30 spots for best time available (6am – 7pm); , Rate for 60 spots for best time available (6am – 7pm); , Rate for 60 spots for Run of Station (6am – 12 midnight); , Rate for 60 spots between 10:00 a.m. - 3:00 a.m.; , Rate for 60 spots between 6:00 a.m. - 10:00 a.m.; , Rate for 30 spots between 10:00 a.m. - 3:00 a.m.; , Rate for 30 spots between 6:00 a.m. - 10:00 a.m.; , Rate for 30 spots for Run of Station (6am – 12 midnight); , Rate for 60 spots between 3:00 a.m. - 7:00 a.m. Combined advertising rates available for KOOL 96.1 FM KCWD. **URL:** http://www.kcwdradio.com.

1425 ■ KCWD-FM - 96.1
600 S Pine St.
Harrison, AR 72601
Phone: (870)741-1402
Free: 866-853-5293
Email: info@kcwdradio.com
Format: Classic Rock. **Networks:** ABC. **Owner:** Harrison Radio Station Inc., 600 S Pine St., Harrison, AR 72601. **Founded:** 1982. **Operating Hours**: Continuous. **ADI**: Springfield, MO. **Key Personnel:** Roger Lowery, Mgr.; Barbara Dean, Office Mgr. **Wattage**: 50,000. **Ad Rates:** $8.50-15 for 30 seconds; $14-17 for 60 seconds. **URL:** http://www.kcwdradio.com.

1426 ■ KHOZ-AM - 900
1111 Radio Ave.
Harrison, AR 72601
Phone: (870)741-2301
Fax: (870)741-3299
Format: Talk; Sports. **Networks:** CBS. **Founded:** 1946. **Operating Hours**: Continuous. **Key Personnel:** Scottie Earls, Gen. Mgr.; Marilyn Wallis, Station Mgr., marilynwallis@khoz.com; Rob McBee, Production Mgr., robmcbee@khoz.com. **Local Programs**: *Party Line*, Monday Tuesday Wednesday Thursday Friday 9:00 a.m. - 11:00 a.m. **Wattage**: 1,000. **Ad Rates:** Noncommercial. Combined advertising rates available with KHOZ-FM. **URL:** http://www.1029thez.com.

1427 ■ KHOZ-FM - 102.9
1111 Radio Ave.
Harrison, AR 72601
Phone: (870)741-2301
Fax: (870)741-3299
Email: khozradio@khoz.com
Format: Adult Contemporary. **Owner:** Harrison Broadcasting Corp., at above address. **Founded:** 1963. **Formerly**: KWNQ-FM. **Operating Hours**: Continuous. **Key Personnel:** Marilyn Wallis, Station Mgr., marilynwallis@khoz.com; Scottie Earls, Gen. Mgr., scottieearls@krzk.com. **Wattage**: 100,000. **Ad Rates:** $12-28 for 30 seconds; $17-36 for 60 seconds. Combined advertising rates available with KHOZ-AM. **URL:** http://www.1029thez.com.

1428 ■ Ritter Communications
9444 Hwy. 65 S
Harrison, AR 72601
Phone: (870)429-5211
Free: 800-758-5790
Email: customerservice@rittercommunications.com
Cities Served: 327 community access channels. **URL:** http://www.rittercommunications.com.

HATFIELD

1429 ■ HeartBeat
Christian Motorcyclists Association
4278 Highway 71 S
Hatfield, AR 71945-7119
Phone: (870)389-6196
Freq: Monthly. **Subscription Rates:** free, for members only. **URL:** http://www.cmausa.org/cma_national/heartbeat.asp. **Mailing address:** PO Box 9, Hatfield, AR 71945-0009. **Remarks:** Accepts advertising. **Circ:** 50000.

HAZEN

EC AR. Prairie Co. 40 mi. E. of Little Rock. Manufactures men's shirts. Agriculture. Rice, soybeans, cotton.

1430 ■ The DeValls Bluff Times
Herald Publishing Company Inc.
111 Hwy. 70 East
Hazen, AR 72064
Phone: (870)255-4538
Fax: (870)255-4539
Publisher's E-mail: editor@herald-publishing.com
Local newspaper. **Freq:** Weekly (Wed.). **Print Method:** Offset. **Cols./Page:** 6. **Col. Depth:** 294 agate lines. **Key Personnel:** Martha Shinley, Editor; Nathaniel Bradow, Managing Editor. **USPS:** 150-380. **Subscription Rates:** $17.50 Individuals in Prairie County; $22.50 Individuals in Arkansas; $27.50 Out of state. **URL:** http://www.herald-publishing.com. **Mailing address:** PO Box 370, Hazen, AR 72064. **Ad Rates:** GLR $.25; PCI $2.75. **Remarks:** Accepts advertising. **Circ:** Paid 486, Free 14.

1431 ■ Grand Prairie Herald
Herald Publishing Company Inc.
111 Hwy. 70 East
Hazen, AR 72064
Phone: (870)255-4538
Fax: (870)255-4539
Publisher's E-mail: editor@herald-publishing.com

Circulation: ⋆ = AAM; △ or • = BPA; ♦ = CAC; ❑ = VAC; ⊕ = PO Statement; ‡ = Publisher's Report; Boldface figures = sworn; Light figures = estimated.

Newspaper community. **Freq:** Weekly (Wed.). **Print Method:** Offset. **Cols./Page:** 6. **Col. Depth:** 21 inches. **Key Personnel:** Martha Shinley, Editor, Manager, Circulation; Nathaniel Bradow, Managing Editor. **USPS:** 225-680. **Subscription Rates:** $25 Individuals 1 year print and online subscription; $30 Out of area 1 year print and online subscription; $35 Out of state 1 year print and online subscription; $17.50 Individuals 1 year print subscription; $22.50 Out of area 1 year print subscription; $27.50 Out of state 1 year print subscription; $15 Individuals 1 year online subscription. **URL:** http://www.herald-publishing.com. **Mailing address:** PO Box 370, Hazen, AR 72064. **Ad Rates:** GLR $.25; BW $370.44; PCI $3.75. **Remarks:** Accepts advertising. **Circ:** Paid 1650, Free 50.

HEBER SPRINGS

NC AR. Cleburne Co. 62 mi. N. of Little Rock. Resort, mineral springs. Manufactures lumber, gloves, circular saws, weed eaters, bendable hose, concrete handling products, men's shirts. Stone quarries. Dairy, stock, poultry and cattle.

1432 ■ KAWW-AM
422 W Main St.
Heber Springs, AR 72543
Phone: (501)362-5863
Fax: (501)362-5864
Format: Southern Gospel. **Networks:** Arkansas Radio. **Founded:** 1967. **Key Personnel:** Clay Marshall, Dir. of Pub. Prog. & Svcs.; Connie Owens, Dir. of Traffic; Karol Berry, Contact. **Wattage:** 1,000 Day. **Ad Rates:** $5 for 30 seconds; $9 for 60 seconds. **Mailing address:** PO Box 324, Heber Springs, AR 72543.

1433 ■ KBMJ-FM - 89.5
PO Box 3206
Tupelo, MS 38803
Format: Religious. **Owner:** American Family Radio, at above address. **Wattage:** 70,000. **URL:** http://www.afa.net.

HELENA

E. AR. Phillips Co. On Mississippi River, 90 mi. SW of Memphis, TN. Port of entry. Manufactures cottonseed oil, bean oil, chemicals, lumber, swim pools, soybean products, luggage, men's clothing, farm implements, barges; fertilizer. Cotton ginning and compressing; cannery; sawmills. Ships cotton, lumber. Crude oils. Timber. Agriculture. Rice, wheat, soybeans.

1434 ■ KFFA-AM - 1360
1360 Radio Dr.
Helena, AR 72342
Phone: (870)338-8361
Fax: (870)338-8332
Email: kffa@arkansas.net
Format: Country. **Networks:** Agrinet Farm Radio; AP; St. Louis Cardinals; UPI. **Owner:** Delta Broadcasting, Inc., at above address. **Founded:** 1941. **Operating Hours:** Continuous. **Key Personnel:** Nancy Howe, VP. **Local Programs:** *King Biscuit Time*, Monday Tuesday Wednesday Thursday Friday 12:15 p.m. - 12:45 p.m. **Wattage:** 1,000. **Ad Rates:** Noncommercial. Combined advertising rates available with KFFA-FM. **URL:** http://www.kffa.com.

1435 ■ KFFA-FM - 103.1
1360 Radio Dr.
Helena, AR 72342
Phone: (870)338-8361
Fax: (870)338-8332
Email: kffa@arkansas.net
Format: Adult Contemporary. **Owner:** BP Internet Solutions, Inc, at above address. **Formerly:** KCRI-FM. **Operating Hours:** Continuous. **Key Personnel:** Nancy Howe, VP. **Wattage:** 13,000. **Ad Rates:** Noncommercial. Combined advertising rates available with KFFA-AM. **URL:** http://www.kffa.com.

1436 ■ KJIW-FM - 94.5
204 Moore St.
Helena, AR 72342-3438
Phone: (870)338-2700
Fax: (870)338-3166
Format: Gospel; Contemporary Christian. **Key Personnel:** Elijah Mondy, Owner, em@lordradio.com; April Monday, Dir. of Operations, april@lordradio.com; Zipporah Monday, Dir. of Sales, Music Dir., zm@lordradio.com. **URL:** http://www.kjiwfm.com.

HOPE

SW AR. Hempstead Co. 34 mi. NE of Texarkana. Lumber; insecticide, floor sweep, electronic speaker factories; brickworks; hatcheries, egg processing plants. Hard and softwood timber. Diversified farming. Poultry, livestock.

1437 ■ KHPA-FM - 104.9
PO Box 424
Hope, AR 71802
Phone: (870)777-8868
Fax: (870)777-8888
Format: Contemporary Country. **Networks:** Independent. **Owner:** Sudbury Broadcasting Group, 125 S 2nd St., Blytheville, AR 72315, Ph: (870)762-2093, Free: 800-737-0096. **Founded:** 1976. **Operating Hours:** midnight. **Key Personnel:** Amanda Smith, Contact; Amanda Smith, Contact. **Wattage:** 6,000. **Ad Rates:** Advertising accepted; rates available upon request. **URL:** http://www.supercountry105.com.

1438 ■ KTPA-AM
PO Box 424
Hope, AR 71801
Phone: (501)887-2638
Fax: (501)778-8888
Format: Country. **Networks:** Arkansas Radio. **Owner:** Newport Broadcasting Co., PO Box 989, Blytheville, AR 72315, Ph: (501)762-2093. **Founded:** 1959. **Key Personnel:** David Paul, Contact. **Wattage:** 1,000 Day. **Ad Rates:** $2.50-4.30 for 15 seconds; $3.30-5.50 for 30 seconds; $4.30-6.50 for 60 seconds.

1439 ■ KTSS-TV - 50
206 S Main St.
Hope, AR 71801
Phone: (870)722-5588
Fax: (870)722-5555
Owner: ArTex TV L.L.C., 206 S Main, Hope, AR 71801, Ph: (870)722-5588, Fax: (870)722-5555. **URL:** http://www.ktss.tv.

1440 ■ KXAR-AM - 1490
PO Box 424
Hope, AR 71802
Phone: (870)777-8868
Fax: (870)777-8888
Format: Talk. **Networks:** ABC; Arkansas Radio. **Owner:** Sudbury Broadcasting Group, 125 S 2nd St., Blytheville, AR 72315, Ph: (870)762-2093, Free: 800-737-0096. **Founded:** 1988. **Operating Hours:** Continuous; 30% network, 70% local. **Key Personnel:** Amanda Smith, Contact; Amanda Smith, Contact. **Wattage:** 3,000. **Ad Rates:** Advertising accepted; rates available upon request. **URL:** http://www.supercountry105.com.

HOT SPRINGS

WC AR. Garland Co. 47 mi. SW of Little Rock. Manufactures lumber, aluminum, bottled mineral water, ladies' shoes, rubber bands, mail handling equipment, hydraulic cylinders auto fabricast parts; cables. Vanadium oxide mill. Aluminum storm doors and windows. Pine timber.

1441 ■ The Record
Garland County Historical Society
PO Box 21335
Hot Springs, AR 71903-1335
Phone: (501)321-2159
Publisher's E-mail: gchsweb@gmail.com
Journal containing the historical and genealogical articles pertaining to Hot Springs and Garland County, AR. **Freq:** Annual. **Key Personnel:** Liz Robbins, Editor, Executive Director. **ISSN:** 0163-6820 (print). **Subscription Rates:** $25 Nonmembers. **URL:** http://www.garlandcountyhistoricalsociety.com/html/therecord.php. **Remarks:** Advertising not accepted. **Circ:** (Not Reported).

1442 ■ The Sentinel-Record
The Sentinel-Record
300 Spring St.
Hot Springs, AR 71901
Phone: (501)623-7711
Publication E-mail: questions@hotsr.com
General newspaper. **Freq:** Mon.-Sun. (morn.). **Print Method:** Offset. **Cols./Page:** 6. **Col. Width:** 26 nonpareils. **Col. Depth:** 301 agate lines. **USPS:** 490-720. **Subscription Rates:** $24.50 Individuals /month; $294 Individuals /year. **URL:** http://www.hotsr.com. **Ad Rates:** GLR $1.73; BW $2,193.30; 4C $2,543; PCI $31.67. **Remarks:** Accepts advertising. **Circ:** Mon.-Sat. ★**17943**, Sun. ★**18998**.

1443 ■ KBHS-AM
Attn: Greg Shinn
Hot Springs, AR 71913
Phone: (501)623-6661
Format: Adult Contemporary. **Networks:** Satellite Music Network. **Wattage:** 5,000 Day; 087 Night.

1444 ■ KLAZ-FM - 105.9
208 Buena Vista Rd.
Hot Springs, AR 71913
Phone: (501)525-4600
Email: sales@klaz.com
Format: Contemporary Hit Radio (CHR). **Owner:** Noalmark Broadcasting, 202 W 19th St., El Dorado, AR 71730, Ph: (501)862-7777. **Founded:** 1971. **ADI:** Little Rock, AR. **Wattage:** 95,000 ERP. **Ad Rates:** Advertising accepted; rates available upon request. $8.50 for 30 seconds; $19.75 for 60 seconds. **URL:** http://www.klaz.com.

1445 ■ KLXQ-FM - 101.9
125 Corporate Ter.
Hot Springs, AR 71913
Phone: (501)525-9700
Fax: (501)525-9739
Free: 866-425-9600
Format: Classic Rock; Adult Contemporary. **Founded:** Feb. 1992. **Operating Hours:** Continuous. **Key Personnel:** Gary Terrell, Gen. Mgr., gterrell@usstations.com. **Wattage:** 6,000. **Ad Rates:** Noncommercial. $8 for 30 seconds; $12 for 60 seconds.

1446 ■ KQUS-FM - 97.5
125 Corporate Ter.
Hot Springs, AR 71913
Phone: (501)525-8797
Free: 888-507-9538
Format: Country. **Networks:** ABC. **Owner:** U.S. Stations LLC, at above address, Hot Springs, AR 71913. **Founded:** 1969. **Operating Hours:** Continuous. **ADI:** Little Rock, AR. **Key Personnel:** Dick Antoine, Contact, dck_antoine@yahoo.com; Dick Antoine, Contact, dck_antoine@yahoo.com. **Wattage:** 100,000. **Ad Rates:** $15-28 for 30 seconds; $18-40 for 60 seconds. **URL:** http://www.myhotsprings.com.

1447 ■ KTTG-FM - 96.3
1411 Central Ave.
Hot Springs, AR 71901
Phone: (479)484-7285
Fax: (479)484-7290
Format: Sports. **Networks:** ESPN Radio. **Owner:** Pearson Broadcasting Group, 9530 Midlothian Pike, Richmond, VA 23235, Ph: (804)276-0300. **Operating Hours:** Continuous. **Wattage:** 100,000. **Ad Rates:** Advertising accepted; rates available upon request. **URL:** http://www.espnarkansas.net.

1448 ■ K23GT - 23
PO Box A
Santa Ana, CA 92711
Phone: (714)832-2950
Free: 888-731-1000
Owner: Trinity Broadcasting Network Inc., PO Box A, Santa Ana, CA 92711, Ph: (714)832-2950, Free: 888-731-1000. **URL:** http://www.tbn.org.

1449 ■ KZNG-AM - 1340
125 Corporate Ter.
Hot Springs, AR 71913
Phone: (501)525-9700
Format: Talk; News. **Networks:** ABC. **Owner:** U.S. Stations LLC, at above address, Hot Springs, AR 71913. **Founded:** 1953. **Operating Hours:** Continuous. **ADI:** Hartford-New Haven (New London), CT. **Wattage:** 1,000. **Ad Rates:** $5-18 for 30 seconds; $8-25 for 60 seconds. **URL:** http://www.myhotsprings.com.

1450 ■ Resort TV Cable Company Inc.
410 Airport Rd., Ste. H
Hot Springs, AR 71913
Email: resort@cablelynx.com
Owner: WEHCO Video, Inc., 115 E Capitol Ave., Little Rock, AR 72201, Ph: (501)378-3400, Fax: (501)376-8594. **Key Personnel:** Chuck Launius, VP, Gen. Mgr. **Cities Served:** Mount Pine, Arkansas; 280 channels. **URL:** http://www.resorttvcable.com/services.html.

HUNTSVILLE

SC AR. Madison Co.

1451 ■ The Madison County Musings
Madison County Genealogical & Historical Society
PO Box 427
Huntsville, AR 72740
Phone: (479)738-6408
Magazine containing the history of Madison County and its residents. **Freq:** Quarterly. **ISSN:** 1071--1937 (print). **Subscription Rates:** $18 Individuals. **URL:** http://www.mcghs.info/Publications/musingsintro.html. **Remarks:** Advertising not accepted. **Circ:** (Not Reported).

1452 ■ Madison County Record
Madison County Record
201 Church St.
Huntsville, AR 72740
Phone: (479)738-2141
Fax: (479)738-1250
Publication E-mail: mcrecord@madisoncounty.net
Community newspaper. **Founded:** May 29, 1879. **Freq:** Weekly (Thurs.). **Print Method:** Offset. **Cols./Page:** 6. **Col. Width:** 2 1/4 inches. **Key Personnel:** Matt Shelnutt, Editor, General Manager. **Subscription Rates:** $31 Individuals Madison County; $34 Individuals out of county; $37 Out of state; $27 Individuals e-edition. **URL:** http://www.mcrecordonline.com/. **Ad Rates:** BW $4.50; 4C $6.50; PCI $5. **Remarks:** Accepts advertising. **Circ:** 5200.

1453 ■ KAKS-FM - 99.5
230 Park Ave.
New York, NY 10169
Phone: (646)435-5781
Format: Hispanic. **Owner:** Davidson Media Group, at above address. **Operating Hours:** Continuous. **URL:** http://www.davidsonmediagroup.com/Stations/PAGES/KAKS.htm.

1454 ■ Madison County Cable
113 Court St.
PO Drawer D
Huntsville, AR 72740
Phone: (479)738-2121
Email: info@madisoncounty.net
URL: http://www.madisoncounty.net.

JACKSONVILLE

C. AR. Pulaski Co. 9 mi. N of Galloway. Residential.

1455 ■ Jacksonville Patriot
Stephens Media L.L.C.
PO Box 5329
Jacksonville, AR 72078
Publisher's E-mail: sfrederick@stephensmedia.com
Community newspaper. **Founded:** 1958. **Freq:** Biweekly. **Print Method:** Offset. **Cols./Page:** 6. **Col. Width:** 12 picas. **Col. Depth:** 294 agate lines. **Key Personnel:** Byron Tate. **ISSN:** 0891-5601 (print). **USPS:** 582-500. **Subscription Rates:** $36 Individuals 1 year online access; $28 Individuals 1 year print home delivery and online access (carrier). **URL:** http://pulaskinews.net/jacksonville-patriot. **Formerly**: Jacksonville News. **Ad Rates:** BW $944; 4C $1,219; SAU $7.49; PCI $7.49. **Remarks:** Accepts advertising. **Circ:** Paid ‡2762, Non-paid ‡504.

1456 ■ The Leader
Worrall Community Newspapers Inc.
404 Graham Rd.
Jacksonville, AR 72076
Phone: (501)982-9421
Publication E-mail: leadernews@arkansasleader.com
Local newspaper serving Kenilworth and Roselle Park, NJ. **Founded:** Mar. 04, 1987. **Freq:** Weekly (Thurs.). **Print Method:** Offset. **Cols./Page:** 6. **Col. Width:** 25 nonpareils. **Col. Depth:** 294 agate lines. **Key Personnel:** Christy Hendricks, Editor; John Henderson, General Manager; Eileen Feldman, Executive Editor; John Hofheimer, Writer; Matt Robinson, Director, Publications; Garrick Feldman, Editor; Clay Knupp, Contact. **URL:** http://www.arkansasleader.com. **Formerly**: Kenilworth Leader. **Ad Rates:** SAU $18; PCI $15.75. **Remarks:** Accepts advertising. **Circ:** ‡4,237.

1457 ■ KVDW-AM - 1530
204 Bucky Beaver St.
Jacksonville, AR 72076
Format: Gospel; Contemporary Christian. **URL:** http://www.victory1530.com/.

JONESBORO

NE AR. Craighead Co. 70 mi. NW of Memphis. Arkansas State University. Manufactures lift equipment, tool boxes, agriculture machinery, aluminum castings, drapery hardware, medical testing equipment, truck transmissions, tennis balls, conveyor equipment, electric motors, shoes, lumber products, brakes; rice milling; beverage bottling. Agriculture. Rice, wheat, cotton, soybeans.

1458 ■ The Jonesboro Sun
Jonesboro Sun
518 Carson
Jonesboro, AR 72401-3128
Phone: (870)935-5525
Fax: (870)935-1674
Free: 800-237-5341
Publisher's E-mail: support@jonesborosun.com
Newspaper with a Democratic orientation. **Founded:** 1903. **Freq:** Mon.-Sun. (morn.). **Print Method:** Offset. **Cols./Page:** 6. **Col. Width:** 24 nonpareils. **Col. Depth:** 294 agate lines. **Key Personnel:** David Mosesso, Publisher, fax: (870)935-5823; Lisa Lynn, Director, Advertising, fax: (870)935-1674. **Subscription Rates:** $1.25 Individuals 1 day online edition; $9 Individuals 4 weeks online edition; $27 Individuals 12 weeks online edition; $54 Individuals 24 weeks online edition; $117 Individuals 52 weeks online edition. **URL:** http://www.jonesborosun.com/. **Mailing address:** PO Box 1249, Jonesboro, AR 72403-1249. **Ad Rates:** GLR $1.20; BW $2,160.75; 4C $2,635.75; PCI $27.25. **Remarks:** Accepts advertising. **Circ:** Mon.-Sat. ★**19830**, Sun. ★**22564**.

1459 ■ KAIT-TV - 8
472 County Rd. 766
Jonesboro, AR 72401
Phone: (870)931-8888
Fax: (870)931-1371
Email: news@kait8.com
Format: Commercial TV. **Networks:** ABC. **Owner:** Raycom Media Inc., 201 Monroe St., RSA Twr., 20th Fl., Montgomery, AL 36104-3731, Ph: (334)206-1400. **Founded:** 1963. **Operating Hours**: Continuous. **ADI**: Jonesboro, AR. **Key Personnel:** Tim Ingram, Gen. Mgr., VP, tingram@kait8.com; Hatton Weeks, News Dir., hweeks@kait8.com; Ralph Caudill, Sales Mgr., rcaudill@kait8.com; Joe Sciortino, Gen. Sales Mgr., sduckworth@kait8.com; Debi Gann, Dir. of Programs, Dir. of Traffic, dgann@kait8.com. **Ad Rates:** $25-850 per unit. **Mailing address:** PO Box 790, Jonesboro, AR 72401. **URL:** http://www.kait8.com.

1460 ■ KAOG-FM - 90.5
PO Box 2440
Tupelo, MS 38803
Phone: (662)844-5036
Email: faq@afa.net
Format: Contemporary Christian. **Owner:** American Family Association, at above address. **ADI:** Jonesboro, AR. **Wattage:** 40,000. **Ad Rates:** Noncommercial. **URL:** http://afa.net.

1461 ■ KBTM-AM - 1230
PO Box 1737
Jonesboro, AR 72403
Phone: (870)935-5597
Fax: (870)932-0892
Format: News; Talk. **Owner:** East Arkansas Broadcasters Of Jonesboro, LLC, PO Box 789, Wynne, AR 72396, Ph: (870)238-8141. **Operating Hours**: Continuous. **ADI**: Jonesboro, AR. **Wattage**: 1,000. **Ad Rates:** Noncommercial.

1462 ■ KDXY-FM - 104.9
314 Union Ave.
Jonesboro, AR 72401
Phone: (870)933-8800
Fax: (870)933-0403
Format: Country. **Networks:** ABC. **Owner:** Saga Communications of Arkansas L.L.C., 73 Kercheval Ave., Grosse Pointe Farms, MI 48236. **Founded:** 1971. **Operating Hours**: Continuous; 5% network, 95% local. **Key Personnel:** Trey Stafford, Gen. Mgr., President, trey@jonesbororadiogroup.com. **Wattage:** 3,000. **Ad Rates:** Noncommercial. **URL:** http://www.thefox1049.com.

1463 ■ KEGI-FM - 100.5
314 Union
Jonesboro, AR 72401
Phone: (870)933-8800
Fax: (870)933-0403
Format: Oldies. **ADI**: Jonesboro, AR. **Key Personnel:** Trey Stafford, Gen. Mgr., trey@triplefm.com; Rick Christian, Dir. of Programs, rick@triplefm.com. **URL:** http://eagle1005.com.

1464 ■ KFIN-FM - 107.9
403 West Parker Rd.
Drawer 1737
Jonesboro, AR 72403
Phone: (870)932-1079
Fax: (870)932-3814
Format: Contemporary Country. **Networks:** CNN Radio. **Founded:** 1974. **ADI**: Memphis, TN. **Key Personnel:** Pam Statler, Director. **Wattage**: 98,000 ERP. **Ad Rates:** Advertising accepted; rates available upon request. $30-45 for 30 seconds; $38-57 for 60 seconds. **URL:** http://www.kfin.com.

1465 ■ K42GX - 42
PO Box A
Santa Ana, CA 92711
Phone: (714)832-2950
Free: 888-731-1000
Owner: Trinity Broadcasting Network Inc., PO Box A, Santa Ana, CA 92711, Ph: (714)832-2950, Free: 888-731-1000. **URL:** http://www.tbn.org.

1466 ■ KJBX-FM - 106.7
314 Union
Jonesboro, AR 72401
Phone: (870)933-8800
Fax: (870)933-0403
Format: Eclectic. **Owner:** Saga Communications of Arkansas L.L.C., 73 Kercheval Ave., Grosse Pointe Farms, MI 48236. **Key Personnel:** Trey Stafford, Gen. Mgr., trey@thefox1049.com; Kevin Neathery, Sales Mgr., kevin@triplefm.com; Ben Blankenship, Dir. of Production, ben@thefox1049.com. **Ad Rates:** Noncommercial. **URL:** http://themix1063.com.

1467 ■ KJLV-FM - 105.3
PO Box 779002
Rocklin, CA 95677-9972
Fax: (916)251-1901
Free: 800-525-5683
Format: Contemporary Christian. **Owner:** Educational Media Foundation, PO Box 2098, Omaha, NE 68103-2098, Free: 800-434-8400. **Key Personnel:** Mike Novak, President, CEO; Alan Mason, COO. **Wattage**: 25,000. **URL:** http://www.klove.com.

1468 ■ KNEA-AM - 970
PO Box 789
Wynne, AR 72396
Phone: (870)238-8141
Format: Talk; Sports. **Networks:** Arkansas Radio. **Owner:** East Arkansas Broadcasters of Jonesboro, LLC, at above address. **Founded:** 1950. **Operating Hours**: 7 a.m.-6 p.m.;. **ADI**: Jonesboro, AR. **Wattage**: 1,000. **Ad Rates:** Advertising accepted; rates available upon request. $6-8 for 30 seconds; $12 for 60 seconds. **URL:** http://www.953theticket.com.

1469 ■ KTEJ-TV - 19
350 S Donaghey
Conway, AR 72032
Phone: (501)682-2386
Free: 800-682-2386
Format: News; Educational; Talk; Contemporary Christian. **Networks:** Public Broadcasting Service (PBS). **Owner:** Arkansas Educational Television Commission, at above address. **Founded:** 1976. **ADI**: Jonesboro, AR. **Key Personnel:** Gary Schultz, Dir. of Engg.; Ron Johnson, Dir. of Comm.; Allen Weatherly, Exec. Dir.; Tony Brooks, Dep. Dir.; Kathy Atkinson, Dir. of Programs; Carole Adornetto, Dir. of Production; Kathleen Stafford, Dir. of Operations. **Local Programs**: *Cooking on the Wild Side*, Tuesday 6:30 p.m.; *Arkansas Week*, Friday Sunday 7:30 p.m. 11:00 a.m.; *A New Island.* **Wattage**: 322,900 ERP. **Ad Rates:** Advertising accepted; rates available upon request. **URL:** http://www.aetn.org.

Circulation: ★ = AAM; △ or • = BPA; ♦ = CAC; ❑ = VAC; ⊕ = PO Statement; ‡ = Publisher's Report; Boldface figures = sworn; Light figures = estimated.

1470 ■ K218DE-FM - 91.5
PO Box 391
Twin Falls, ID 83303
Fax: (208)736-1958
Free: 800-357-4226
Format: Religious; Contemporary Christian. **Owner:** CSN International, PO Box 391, Twin Falls, ID 83303, Ph: (208)736-1958, Fax: (208)736-1958, Free: 800-357-4226. **ADI:** Jonesboro, AR. **Key Personnel:** Don Mills, Prog. Dir., Music Dir.; Kelly Carlson, Dir. of Engg.; Ray Gorney, Asst. Dir. **Wattage:** 250. **URL:** http://www.csnradio.com.

1471 ■ Ritter Communications
2400 Ritter Dr.
Jonesboro, AR 72401
Phone: (870)336-3434
Free: 888-336-4249
Email: customerservice@rittercommunications.com
Founded: 1906. **URL:** http://www.ritterbusiness.com.

LITTLE ROCK

C. AR. Pulaski Co. In the center of the state on the Arkansas River. The State Capital. University of Arkansas School of Medicine, Nursing, Pharmacy; University of Arkansas Graduate School of Technology; University of Arkansas at Little Rock; several colleges; many state institutions. Retail and wholesale trading center. Manufactures chemicals, furniture, cottonseed products, clothing, building and plumbing supplies, lumber, paper boxes, paint, pumps, valves, plastic piping, fertilizer, light bulbs, watches, radio and television cabinets, electrical equipment, cameras, teletypes, innertubes and related rubber products. Steel foundry; packing houses. Crushed stone, bauxite mines.

1472 ■ Arkansas Banker
Arkansas Bankers Association
1220 W 3rd St.
Little Rock, AR 72201
Phone: (501)376-3741
Fax: (501)376-9243
The official publication of The Arkansas Bankers Association. **Freq:** Monthly. **Print Method:** Offset. **Trim Size:** 9 3/8 x 12 1/2. **Cols./Page:** 4. **Col. Width:** 27 nonpareils. **Col. Depth:** 156 agate lines. **Key Personnel:** Mary Beth Brooks, Board Member. **ISSN:** 0004--1726 (print). **Subscription Rates:** $40 Members; $60 Nonmembers. **Ad Rates:** BW $1,177. **Remarks:** Accepts advertising. **Circ:** ‡10000.

1473 ■ Arkansas Bride
Arkansas Business Publishing Group
114 Scott St.
Little Rock, AR 72201
Phone: (501)372-1443
Fax: (501)375-7933
Free: 888-322-6397
Publisher's E-mail: abnews@abnews.com
Magazine containing wedding stories, fashion shoots and guide to Arkansas wedding professionals. **Freq:** Semiannual. **Key Personnel:** Rachel Bradbury, Publisher. **URL:** http://www.arkansasbride.com. **Mailing address:** PO Box 3686, Little Rock, AR 72203. **Remarks:** Accepts advertising. **Circ:** (Not Reported).

1474 ■ Arkansas Business
Arkansas Business Publishing Group
114 Scott St.
Little Rock, AR 72201
Phone: (501)372-1443
Fax: (501)375-7933
Free: 888-322-6397
Publisher's E-mail: abnews@abnews.com
Business magazine on the Arkansas business community, covering people and recent news events statewide. **Freq:** Weekly. **Print Method:** Offset. **Trim Size:** 11 x 13 3/4. **Cols./Page:** 4. **Col. Width:** 14 picas. **Col. Depth:** 74 picas. **Key Personnel:** Jeff Hankins, Editor. **USPS:** 730-650. **Subscription Rates:** $64.95 Individuals in state; $194.95 Other countries; $94.95 Individuals out of state; $119.95 Two years in state; $179.95 Two years out of state. **URL:** http://store.arkansasbusiness.com/collections/publications/products/arkansas-business. **Mailing address:** PO Box 3686, Little Rock, AR 72203. **Remarks:** Accepts advertising. **Circ:** Paid 6500, Controlled 2000.

1475 ■ Arkansas Catholic
Arkansas Catholic
PO Box 7417
Little Rock, AR 72217
Phone: (501)664-0125
Fax: (501)664-6572
Catholic newspaper of the Diocese of Little Rock. **Founded:** 1911. **Freq:** Weekly (Sat.). **Print Method:** Offset. **Trim Size:** 10.25 x 14. **Cols./Page:** 4. **Col. Width:** 28 nonpareils. **Col. Depth:** 182 agate lines. **USPS:** 006-793. **Subscription Rates:** $22 Individuals print; $42 Two years print. **URL:** http://www.arkansas-catholic.org/. **Formerly**: The Guardian. **Ad Rates:** GLR $1; BW $616; PCI $14. **Circ:** ‡7000.

1476 ■ Arkansas Cattle Business
Arkansas Cattlemen's Association
310 Executive Ct.
Little Rock, AR 72205
Phone: (501)224-2114
Fax: (501)224-5377
Publisher's E-mail: info@arbeef.org
Freq: Monthly. **Print Method:** Offset/Web. **Trim Size:** 8 1/2 x 11. **Cols./Page:** 3. **Col. Width:** 27 nonpareils. **Col. Depth:** 140 agate lines. **Subscription Rates:** $40 Individuals; Included in membership. **URL:** http://www.arbeef.org/cattlebusiness.aspx. **Ad Rates:** BW $600; 4C $910; PCI $27. **Remarks:** Accepts advertising. **Circ:** Paid 10000, Controlled 1000, 15000.

1477 ■ Arkansas Democrat-Gazette
Arkansas Democrat-Gazette Inc.
121 E Capitol Ave.
Little Rock, AR 72201
Phone: (501)378-3400
Fax: (501)399-3663
Free: 800-482-1121
General newspaper. **Founded:** Nov. 20, 1819. **Freq:** Mon.-Sun. (morn.). **Print Method:** Offset. **Trim Size:** 12 1/2 x 22. **Cols./Page:** 6. **Col. Width:** 11 nonpareils. **Col. Depth:** 301 agate lines. **Key Personnel:** Celia Storey; David Bailey, Managing Editor, phone: (501)378-3594; Walter E. Hussman, Jr., Publisher; Griffin Smith, Jr., Executive Editor; John Mobbs, Director, Advertising; Paul Greenberg, Editor, phone: (501)378-3482. **ISSN:** 1060-4332 (print). **Subscription Rates:** $28 Individuals per month, 7 days home delivery and online; $28 Individuals per month, online only; $30 Individuals per month, outside Central Arkansas. **URL:** http://www.arkansasonline.com. **Formerly**: Arkansas Democrat. **Feature Editors:** Bill Simmons, *Political*, phone: (501)399-3657, bsimmons@arkansasonline.com. **Mailing address:** PO Box 2221, Little Rock, AR 72203. **Ad Rates:** GLR $208; BW $26,832; 4C $28,482; SAU $195; PCI $208; GLR $315; BW $40,635; 4C $42,285; SAU $295; PCI $315. **Remarks:** Advertising accepted; rates available upon request. **Circ:** (Not Reported).

1478 ■ Arkansas Educator
Arkansas Education Association
1500 W 4th St.
Little Rock, AR 72201
Phone: (501)375-4611
Fax: (501)375-4620
Free: 800-632-0624
Educational magazine. **Freq:** Monthly. **Print Method:** Offset. **Cols./Page:** 4. **Col. Width:** 28 nonpareils. **Col. Depth:** 224 agate lines. **Alt. Formats:** PDF. **Ad Rates:** BW $800. **Remarks:** Accepts advertising. **Circ:** ‡18268.

1479 ■ Arkansas Family Historian
Arkansas Genealogical Society
PO Box 26374
Little Rock, AR 72221-6374
Publisher's E-mail: AskAGS@agsgenealogy.org
Journal covering genealogy and history in Arkansas. **Freq:** Quarterly. **Trim Size:** 8 1/2 x 11. **ISSN:** 0571--0472 (print). **Subscription Rates:** $15 Individuals 1962-2011 - CD. **Alt. Formats:** CD-ROM; PDF. **URL:** http://agsgenealogy.org/publications/default.html; http://www.agsgenealogy.org/databases/AFHissues.html. **Remarks:** Advertising not accepted. **Circ:** Paid 1,000.

1480 ■ Arkansas Green Guide
Arkansas Business Publishing Group
114 Scott St.
Little Rock, AR 72201
Phone: (501)372-1443
Fax: (501)375-7933
Free: 888-322-6397
Publisher's E-mail: abnews@abnews.com
Magazine covering tips and trends and comprehensive resource guide of eco-friendly products and services in Arkansas. **Freq:** Annual. **Key Personnel:** Lindsay Irvin, Editor. **URL:** http://www.arkansasgreenguide.com. **Mailing address:** PO Box 3686, Little Rock, AR 72203. **Remarks:** Accepts advertising. **Circ:** (Not Reported).

1481 ■ Arkansas Journal of Social Change and Public Service
University of Arkansas William H. Bowen School of Law
1201 McMath Ave.
Little Rock, AR 72202-5142
Phone: (501)324-9903
Fax: (501)324-9909
Publisher's E-mail: law@ualr.edu
Journal covering issues lying at the intersection of policy, public interest, academia, and the law, raising awareness of topics insufficiently examined in traditional scholarly publications. **Freq:** Semiannual. **Key Personnel:** Kendall Lewellen, Editor-in-Chief. **URL:** http://ualr.edu/socialchange. **Circ:** (Not Reported).

1482 ■ Arkansas Living
Arkansas Times
PO Box 34010
Little Rock, AR 72203-4010
Phone: (501)375-2985
Fax: (501)375-3623
Publisher's E-mail: arktimes@arktimes.com
Consumer newspaper covering lifestyle in Arkansas. **Freq:** Monthly. **Print Method:** Web offset. **Trim Size:** 10 1/16 x 12 5/16. **Cols./Page:** 4. **Col. Width:** 2 1/3 inches. **Col. Depth:** 12 5/16 inches. **Key Personnel:** Sheila Yount, Editor. **Subscription Rates:** $7 Individuals. **URL:** http://arkansaslivingmagazine.com. **Formerly**: Arkansas Homes. **Ad Rates:** BW $4554. **Remarks:** Accepts advertising. **Circ:** Controlled 383000.

1483 ■ Arkansas Next: A Guide to Life After High School
Arkansas Business Publishing Group
114 Scott St.
Little Rock, AR 72201
Phone: (501)372-1443
Fax: (501)375-7933
Free: 888-322-6397
Publisher's E-mail: abnews@abnews.com
Magazine with articles on helping students choose a college, pick a major and find financial aid. **Freq:** Annual Latest edition 2016. **URL:** http://www.arkansasnext.com. **Mailing address:** PO Box 3686, Little Rock, AR 72203. **Remarks:** Accepts advertising. **Circ:** (Not Reported).

1484 ■ Arkansas Pharmacist
Arkansas Pharmacists Association
417 S Victory St.
Little Rock, AR 72201
Phone: (501)372-5250
Fax: (501)372-0546
Publisher's E-mail: support@arrx.org
Professional journal for pharmacists. **Freq:** Quarterly Published at the end of January, April, July and October each year. **Key Personnel:** Barbara McMillan, Director. **Subscription Rates:** Included in membership. **Alt. Formats:** PDF. **URL:** http://www.arpharmacists.org/arrx-the-arkansas-pharmacist. **Remarks:** Advertising accepted; rates available upon request. **Circ:** (Not Reported).

1485 ■ Arkansas Register
Arkansas Secretary of State
State Capitol
500 Woodlane Ave., Ste. 256
Little Rock, AR 72201
Phone: (501)682-1010
Fax: (501)682-3510
Publisher's E-mail: corporations@sos.arkansas.gov
Professional magazine. **Freq:** Monthly. **Cols./Page:** 2. **Key Personnel:** Jon Davidson, Editor, phone: (501)682-3527; Charlie Daniels, Publisher. **Subscription Rates:** $40 Individuals; $3.50 Single issue. **Alt. Formats:** PDF. **URL:** http://www.sos.arkansas.gov/rulesRegs/Pages/ArkansasRegister.aspx. **Remarks:** Advertising not accepted. **Circ:** Combined 206.

1486 ■ Arkansas Times: Arkansas Weekly Newspaper of Politics & Culture
Arkansas Times

PO Box 34010
Little Rock, AR 72203-4010
Phone: (501)375-2985
Fax: (501)375-3623
Publisher's E-mail: arktimes@arktimes.com
Newspaper aimed at informing and educating readers about life in Arkansas; including articles on people, places, history, environment, politics, and current events. **Freq:** Weekly (Thurs.). **Print Method:** Cold press. **Trim Size:** 11 x 13 3/4. **Cols./Page:** 4. **Col. Width:** 14 picas. **Col. Depth:** 74 picas. **Key Personnel:** Alan Leveritt, Publisher. **Subscription Rates:** $42 Individuals In State; $49 Out of state; $168 Other countries. **URL:** http://www.arktimes.com. **Ad Rates:** BW $2,250; 4C $2,700. **Remarks:** Advertising accepted; rates available upon request. **Circ:** Free ‡24252, Paid ‡1584, Combined ‡25836.

1487 ■ Arkansas Trucking Report: Regional Publication of the Arkansas Trucking Association
Arkansas Trucking Association
1401 W Capitol Ave.
Little Rock, AR 72201
Phone: (501)372-3462
Fax: (501)376-1810
Publisher's E-mail: getinfo@arkansastrucking.com
Trade magazine containing articles for executives and management personnel of the trucking industry. **Freq:** Bimonthly. **Print Method:** Offset. **Trim Size:** 8 1/2 x 11. **Cols./Page:** 3. **Key Personnel:** Jennifer Matthews Kidd, Publisher. **URL:** http://www.arkansastrucking.com/publications/arkansastruckingreport. **Formerly**: TAB; The Arkansas Motor Carrier; AMCA Trucking Report. **Mailing address:** PO Box 3476, Little Rock, AR 72203. **Ad Rates:** BW $1,395; 4C $1,530. **Remarks:** Accepts advertising. **Circ:** 9000.

1488 ■ The Armiger's News
American College of Heraldry
1818 N Taylor St., Ste. B, No. 312
Little Rock, AR 72207
Publisher's E-mail: info@americancollegeofheraldry.org
Freq: Quarterly. **Subscription Rates:** Included in membership. **URL:** http://www.americancollegeofheraldry.org/achpubs.html. **Remarks:** Advertising not accepted. **Circ:** (Not Reported).

1489 ■ At Home in Arkansas
At Home in Arkansas Magazine
2207 Cottondale Ln.
Little Rock, AR 72202
Phone: (501)666-5510
Lifestyle magazine for the Arkansas region. **Freq:** 11/year. **Trim Size:** 8.625 x 11.125. **Key Personnel:** Kelly Fraiser, Publisher; Chip Jones, Editor-in-Chief; Tiffany Burgess, Managing Editor. **Subscription Rates:** $12.95 Individuals 1 year (print); $21.95 Two years (print). **URL:** http://www.athomearkansas.com. **Remarks:** Advertising accepted; rates available upon request. **Circ:** (Not Reported).

1490 ■ ATLA Docket
Arkansas Trial Lawyers Association
1400 W Markham St., Ste. 307
Little Rock, AR 72201
Phone: (501)376-2852
Free: 800-442-2852
Publisher's E-mail: arktla@arktla.org
Journal featuring the latest trends in the law, law office management, and legal research technology. **Freq:** Quarterly. **Key Personnel:** Karen Smith, Contact, phone: (501)376-2852. **URL:** http://www.arktla.org/index.cfm?pg=ATLADocket. **Remarks:** Accepts advertising. **Circ:** 1000.

1491 ■ Baptist Trumpet
Baptist Missionary Association of Arkansas
PO Box 192208
Little Rock, AR 72219-2208
Phone: (501)565-4601
Fax: (501)565-6397
Baptist tabloid. **Freq:** Weekly. **Print Method:** Offset. **Trim Size:** 11 1/2 x 14. **Cols./Page:** 5. **Col. Width:** 11 picas. **Key Personnel:** Diane Spriggs, Business Manager, Editor; Joyce Lowe, Specialist, Circulation. **ISSN:** 0888--9074 (print). **Subscription Rates:** $23.50 Individuals both mailed and e-mailed version; $18.50 Individuals mailed version only; $12 Individuals e-mailed version only; $23.50 Individuals mailed and e-mailed. **URL:** http://www.baptisttrumpet.com. **Ad Rates:** GLR $.28; BW $180; PCI $5. **Circ:** 11600.

1492 ■ Collaborative Case Management Magazine
National Institute for Case Management
11701 W 36th St.
Little Rock, AR 72211
Phone: (501)227-2262
Fax: (501)227-4247
Freq: Quarterly. **Subscription Rates:** Included in membership. **URL:** http://www.acmaweb.org/section.aspx?sID=52. **Remarks:** Advertising accepted; rates available upon request. **Circ:** (Not Reported).

1493 ■ Dimensions of Early Childhood
Southern Early Childhood Association
1123 S University Ave., Ste. 255
Little Rock, AR 72204-1618
Free: 800-305-7322
Publisher's E-mail: info@southernearlychildhood.org
Freq: 3/year. **ISSN:** 1068--6177 (print). **Subscription Rates:** $50 Individuals; $10 Single issue. **URL:** http://www.southernearlychildhood.org/product-category/dimension-of-early-childhood. **Remarks:** Accepts advertising. **Circ:** (Not Reported).

1494 ■ Drug Metabolism Reviews
Informa Healthcare
c/o Jack A. Hinson, Exec. Ed.
Division of Toxicology-Slot 638
University of Arkansas for Medical Sciences
4301 W Markham St.
Little Rock, AR 72205
Publisher's E-mail: healthcare.enquiries@informa.com
Journal covering drug metabolism Research. **Freq:** Quarterly. **Print Method:** Offset. **Trim Size:** 8 1/4 x 10 7/8. **Key Personnel:** Anna Radominska-Pandya; Jack A. Hinson, Executive Editor; B. Clement, Associate Editor; Frederick J. Di Carlo, Editor, Founder. **ISSN:** 0360--2532 (print); **EISSN:** 1097--9883 (electronic). **Subscription Rates:** £2225 Institutions; €2939 Institutions; $3667 Institutions. **URL:** http://informahealthcare.com/dmr. **Ad Rates:** BW $890; 4C $1,935. **Remarks:** Accepts advertising. **Circ:** 275.

1495 ■ Executive Golfer
Arkansas Business Publishing Group
114 Scott St.
Little Rock, AR 72201
Phone: (501)372-1443
Fax: (501)375-7933
Free: 888-322-6397
Publisher's E-mail: abnews@abnews.com
Magazine featuring informative topics for golf enthusiasts. **Subscription Rates:** $5 Single issue. **URL:** http://store.arkansasbusiness.com/publications/view/publication_id/30. **Mailing address:** PO Box 3686, Little Rock, AR 72203. **Circ:** (Not Reported).

1496 ■ The Fulton Sun
WEHCO Media Inc.
115 E Capitol Ave.
Little Rock, AR 72201-3819
Phone: (501)378-3400
Fax: (501)376-8594
General newspaper. **Freq:** Daily except Saturdays and Mondays. **Print Method:** Offset. **Trim Size:** 13 3/4 x 22 1/2. **Cols./Page:** 6. **Col. Width:** 28 nonpareils. **Col. Depth:** 294 agate lines. **Key Personnel:** Rick Kennedy, Editor; Ryan Boland, Reporter, phone: (573)826-2422. **ISSN:** 1084--5275 (print). **Subscription Rates:** $89 Individuals 1 year (carrier delivery); $94 By mail 1 year (in county); $114 By mail 1 year (out of area). **URL:** http://www.fultonsun.com. **Formerly**: The Kingdom Daily Sun-Gazette. **Mailing address:** PO Box 2221, Little Rock, AR 72203-2221. **Remarks:** Accepts advertising. **Circ:** Paid ‡4300.

1497 ■ Geriatric Nursing
Mosby Inc.
10801 Executive Center Dr., Ste. 509
Little Rock, AR 72211
Magazine for nurses in geriatric and gerontologic nursing practice, the primary professional providers of care for the aging. Provides news on issues affecting elders and clinical information on techniques and procedures. **Freq:** Bimonthly. **Print Method:** Offset. **Trim Size:** 8 1/8 x 10 7/8. **Cols./Page:** 3. **Col. Width:** 26 nonpareils. **Col. Depth:** 140 agate lines. **Key Personnel:** S. Magee, Publisher; A. O'Meara, Managing Editor; Barbara Resnick, PhD, Editor, fax: (410)828-0494; J. Milton, Designer. **ISSN:** 0197--4572 (print). **Subscription Rates:** $107 U.S., Canada, and Mexico online only, other countries; $119 U.S. online and print, individuals; $202 Other countries online and print. **URL:** http://www.gnjournal.com. **Ad Rates:** BW $1,925. **Remarks:** Accepts advertising. **Circ:** Paid ‡6050.

1498 ■ Greenhead
Arkansas Business Publishing Group
114 Scott St.
Little Rock, AR 72201
Phone: (501)372-1443
Fax: (501)375-7933
Free: 888-322-6397
Publisher's E-mail: abnews@abnews.com
Magazine featuring articles and photos showcasing Arkansas' rich duck hunting tradition. **Freq:** Annual. **Key Personnel:** Brent Birch, Editor. **URL:** http://www.greenhead.net. **Mailing address:** PO Box 3686, Little Rock, AR 72203. **Remarks:** Accepts advertising. **Circ:** (Not Reported).

1499 ■ The Journal of Appellate Practice and Process
University of Arkansas William H. Bowen School of Law
1201 McMath Ave.
Little Rock, AR 72202-5142
Phone: (501)324-9903
Fax: (501)324-9909
Publisher's E-mail: law@ualr.edu
Journal covering exclusively on issues, practices, and procedures of appellate court systems, both federal and state, both American and international. **Freq:** Semiannual. **Key Personnel:** Nancy Bellhouse May, Editor-in-Chief. **Subscription Rates:** $25 U.S.; $30 Other countries. **URL:** http://ualr.edu/law/publications/the-journal-of-appellate-practice-and-process. **Circ:** (Not Reported).

1500 ■ The Journal of the Arkansas Medical Society
Arkansas Medical Society
10 Corporate Hill Dr., Ste. 300
Little Rock, AR 72205
Phone: (501)224-8967
Fax: (501)224-6489
Free: 800-542-1058
Publication E-mail: journal@arkmed.org
Medical journal. **Freq:** Monthly. **Print Method:** Offset. **Trim Size:** 8 1/4 x 10 7/8. **Cols./Page:** 2. **Col. Width:** 34 nonpareils. **Col. Depth:** 126 agate lines. **ISSN:** 0004--1858 (print). **Subscription Rates:** $30 Individuals mail. **URL:** http://www.arkmed.org/resources/publications/jams. **Mailing address:** PO Box 55088, Little Rock, AR 72215. **Ad Rates:** BW $1,070; 4C $1,420. **Remarks:** Accepts advertising. **Circ:** Combined ‡4500.

1501 ■ Little Rock Family
Arkansas Business Publishing Group
114 Scott St.
Little Rock, AR 72201
Phone: (501)372-1443
Fax: (501)375-7933
Free: 888-322-6397
Publisher's E-mail: abnews@abnews.com
Magazine featuring parenting-related topics. **Freq:** Monthly. **Key Personnel:** Heather Bennett, Editor. **Subscription Rates:** $15 Individuals; $2.50 Single issue. **URL:** http://www.littlerockfamily.com. **Mailing address:** PO Box 3686, Little Rock, AR 72203. **Remarks:** Accepts advertising. **Circ:** (Not Reported).

1502 ■ NeuroToxicology
RELX Group P.L.C.
c/o Joan Marie Cranmer, Ed.-in-Ch.
Department of Pediatrics
Univ. of Arkansas for Medical Science & Arkansas Children's Hospital
1 Children's Way, Mail No. 512-19C
Little Rock, AR 72202-3591
Phone: (501)320-2986
Fax: (501)320-4978
Publisher's E-mail: amsterdam@relx.com
Peer-reviewed journal dealing with the effects of toxic substances on the nervous system of humans and

Circulation: ★ = AAM; △ or • = BPA; ♦ = CAC; ❑ = VAC; ⊕ = PO Statement; ‡ = Publisher's Report; Boldface figures = sworn; Light figures = estimated.

experimental animals. **Freq:** 6/year. **Key Personnel:** Joan Marie Cranmer, Editor-in-Chief; Michael Aschner, Associate Editor; Lucio G. Costa, Associate Editor. **ISSN:** 0161--813X (print). **Subscription Rates:** $363 Individuals print; $702 Institutions online; $841 Institutions print. **URL:** http://www.journals.elsevier.com/neurotoxicology. **Circ:** (Not Reported).

1503 ■ SCA Journal
Society for Commercial Archeology
PO Box 2500
Little Rock, AR 72203
Publisher's E-mail: office@sca-roadside.org
Freq: Semiannual Summer and Winter. **Subscription Rates:** $1 back issues - 1978 to 1983; $3 back issue - 1990; $6 year 1991 up to present. **Circ:** (Not Reported).

1504 ■ Small Ruminant Research
International Goat Association
c/o Christian De Vries
12709 Grassy Dr.
Little Rock, AR 72210-2708
Phone: (501)454-1641
Fax: (501)251-9391
Journal publishing original, basic and applied research articles, technical notes, and review articles on research relating to goats, sheep, deer and the New World camelids llama, alpaca and vicuna. **Freq:** Monthly. **Trim Size:** 8 1/4 X 11. **Key Personnel:** J. Boyazoglu, Editor-in-Chief; A.L. Goetsch, Associate Editor; M.S.A. Kumar, Associate Editor; G.F.W. Haenlein, Editor-in-Chief. **ISSN:** 0921--4488 (print). **Subscription Rates:** $3512 Institutions print or online. **URL:** http://www.journals.elsevier.com/small-ruminant-research; http://www.iga-goatworld.com/srr-journal.html. **Ad Rates:** BW $1610; 4C $2875. **Remarks:** Accepts advertising. **Circ:** (Not Reported).

1505 ■ The Times
Stephens Media L.L.C.
119 Main St.
Little Rock, AR 72201
Phone: (501)370-8300
Fax: (501)370-8391
Publisher's E-mail: sfrederick@stephensmedia.com
Suburban newspaper serving North Pulaski County. **Founded:** 1898. **Freq:** Weekly (Thurs.). **Print Method:** Offset. **Trim Size:** 11.58 x 21 1/2. **Cols./Page:** 6. **Col. Width:** 1.799 inches. **Col. Depth:** 126 inches. **USPS:** 617-620. **Subscription Rates:** $27 Individuals in county; $31 Individuals in state; $39 Out of state. **URL:** http://www.nlrtimes.com. **Remarks:** Accepts advertising. **Circ:** ‡8091.

1506 ■ Comcast Cablevision
1020 W Fourth St.
Little Rock, AR 72201
Phone: (501)376-5700
Email: we_can_help@comcast.com
Key Personnel: Brian L. Roberts, Chairman, CEO; Stephen B. Burke, Exec. VP. **Cities Served:** Pulaski and Saline Counties. **URL:** http://www.comcast.com.

1507 ■ KAAY-AM - 1090
700 Wellington Hills Rd.
Little Rock, AR 72212
Phone: (501)401-0288
Format: Gospel. **Networks:** USA Radio. **Owner:** Cumulus Media Inc., 3280 Peachtree Rd. NW, Ste. 2300, Atlanta, GA 30305-2455, Ph: (404)949-0700, Fax: (404)949-0740. **Founded:** 1953. **Formerly:** Beasley Broadcast. **Operating Hours:** Continuous. **ADI:** Little Rock, AR. **Wattage:** 50,000. **Ad Rates:** $4.50-8 for 30 seconds; $9-14 for 60 seconds. **URL:** http://www.1090kaay.com.

1508 ■ KABF-FM - 88.3
2101 S Main St.
Little Rock, AR 72206
Phone: (501)433-0088
Format: Bluegrass; Gospel; Jazz; Full Service; Eclectic. **Networks:** ESPN Radio. **Owner:** Arkansas Broadcasting Foundation/KABF, at above address. **Founded:** 1983. **Operating Hours:** Continuous. **ADI:** Little Rock, AR. **Key Personnel:** John Cain, Program Mgr. **Wattage:** 91,000 ERP. **Ad Rates:** Noncommercial. Underwriting available. **URL:** http://www.kabf.org.

1509 ■ KABZ-FM - 103.7
2400 Cottondale Ln.
Little Rock, AR 72202
Phone: (501)661-1037
Fax: (501)664-5871
Format: Talk. **Owner:** Signal Media of Arkansas, 2400 Cottondale Ln., Little Rock, AR 72202. **Key Personnel:** Tommy Smith, Contact; David Bazzel, Contact. **Ad Rates:** Noncommercial. **URL:** http://www.1037thebuzz.com.

1510 ■ KAKI-FM - 106.7
2400 Cottondale Ln.
Little Rock, AR 72202
Phone: (501)778-8257
Format: Country. **Networks:** Unistar; CNN Radio. **Owner:** Bridges Broadcasting Service, at above address. **Founded:** 1979. **Operating Hours:** 6 am- 7 pm. **Wattage:** 13,000 ERP. **Ad Rates:** $12 for 30 seconds; $15 for 60 seconds. **URL:** http://1067theride.com.

1511 ■ KARK-TV - 4
1401 W Capitol Ave., Ste. 104
Little Rock, AR 72201-2940
Phone: (501)340-4444
Email: news4@kark.com
Format: Commercial TV. **Networks:** NBC. **Owner:** Nexstar Broadcasting Group Inc., 545 E John Carpenter Fwy., Ste. 700, Irving, TX 75062, Ph: (972)373-8800. **Founded:** 1954. **Operating Hours:** Continuous. **ADI:** Little Rock, AR. **Key Personnel:** Austin Kellerman, News Dir., akellerman@kark.com; Mike Vaughn, Gen. Mgr.; Greg Yarbrough, Managing Ed., gyarbrough@kark.com; Brandon Scott, Div. Mgr., bscott@kark.com. **URL:** http://www.arkansasmatters.com.

1512 ■ KARN-AM - 920
700 Wellington Hills Rd.
Little Rock, AR 72211
Format: Talk; News; Sports. **Simulcasts:** KARN-FM; KKRN-FM. **Networks:** CBS. **Owner:** Citadel Broadcasting Corp., 7201 W Lake Mead Blvd., Ste. 400, Las Vegas, NV 89128-8366, Ph: (702)804-5200, Fax: (702)804-8250. **Founded:** 1928. **Formerly:** KGJF-AM. **Operating Hours:** Continuous; 40% network, 60% local. **ADI:** Little Rock, AR. **Key Personnel:** Bob Steel, Contact. **Wattage:** 50,000. **Ad Rates:** Advertising accepted; rates available upon request. **URL:** http://www.sportsanimal920.com.

1513 ■ KARN-FM - 102.9
700 Wellington Hills Rd.
Little Rock, AR 72211-2026
Format: News; Talk. **Wattage:** 50,000. **Ad Rates:** Advertising accepted; rates available upon request. **URL:** http://www.karnnewsradio.com.

1514 ■ KATV-TV - 7
PO Box 77
Little Rock, AR 72203
Phone: (501)324-7777
Email: rhoffmeyer@katv.com
Format: Commercial TV. **Networks:** ABC. **Owner:** Allbritton Communications Co., 808 17th St. NW, Washington, DC 20006-3910. **Founded:** 1953. **Operating Hours:** 4:30 a.m.-1:30 a.m. **ADI:** Little Rock, AR. **Ad Rates:** Advertising accepted; rates available upon request. **URL:** http://www.katv.com.

1515 ■ KCDI-FM - 93.3
415 N McKinley St., Ste. 700
Little Rock, AR 72205
Phone: (501)332-6981
Fax: (501)332-6984
Email: listeners@kcdifm.com
Format: Hot Country. **Networks:** Jones Satellite. **Owner:** Malvern Entertainment Corporation, at above address. **Founded:** 1989. **Operating Hours:** Continuous. **Key Personnel:** Scott Gray, Contact; Scott A. Gray, Gen. Mgr., President, sgray@kcdifm.com; Melanie Rock, Sales Mgr; Scott Gray, Contact. **Wattage:** 6,000 ERP. **Ad Rates:** $18-36 for 30 seconds. **URL:** http://www.933fmthefish.com.

1516 ■ KDIS-FM - 99.5
415 N McKinley St., Ste. 610
Little Rock, AR 72205
Phone: (501)404-6560
Fax: (501)404-6560
Email: info@faithtalk995.com
Format: Educational. **Owner:** Radio Disney, 500 S Buena Vista St. MC 7663, Burbank, CA 91521-7716. **ADI:** Little Rock, AR. **Wattage:** 6,000. **URL:** http://www.faithtalk995.com.

1517 ■ KDJE-FM - 100.3
10800 Colonel Glenn Rd.
Little Rock, AR 72204
Phone: (501)217-5000
Fax: (501)374-0808
Email: jeffcage@clearchannel.com
Format: Alternative/New Music/Progressive. **ADI:** Little Rock, AR. **Key Personnel:** Ron Collar, Gen. Mgr. **Wattage:** 85,000. **Ad Rates:** Noncommercial. **URL:** http://www.edgelittlerock.com.

1518 ■ KHKN-FM - 106.7
10800 Colonel Glenn Rd.
Little Rock, AR 72204
Phone: (501)217-5000
Format: Country. **ADI:** Little Rock, AR. **Key Personnel:** Kevin Waltman, Dir. of Sales, kevinwaltman@clearchannel.com; Keli Williams, Sales Mgr., keliwilliams@clearchannel.com. **Wattage:** 16,000.

1519 ■ KHLR-FM - 106.7
10800 Colonel Glenn Rd.
Little Rock, AR 72204
Phone: (501)217-5000
Format: Gospel; Religious; Contemporary Christian. **Owner:** Clear Channel Communications Inc., at above address, Ph: (210)822-2828, Fax: (210)822-2299. **Operating Hours:** 6 a.m. - 12 a.m. **Ad Rates:** Advertising accepted; rates available upon request. **URL:** http://www.heartbeat1067.com.

1520 ■ KHTE-FM - 96.5
400 Hardin Rd., Ste. 150
Little Rock, AR 72211
Format: Contemporary Hit Radio (CHR). **Wattage:** 10,500. **Ad Rates:** Advertising accepted; rates available upon request. **URL:** http://www.965thevoice.com.

1521 ■ KIPR-FM - 92.3
700 Wellington Hills Rd.
Little Rock, AR 72211
Phone: (501)401-0200
Fax: (501)401-0374
Format: Urban Contemporary. **Networks:** ABC. **Owner:** Citadel Broadcasting Corp., 7201 W Lake Mead Blvd., Ste. 400, Las Vegas, NV 89128-8366, Ph: (702)804-5200, Fax: (702)804-8250. **Operating Hours:** Continuous. **Wattage:** 100,000. **Ad Rates:** Noncommercial. **URL:** http://www.power923.com.

1522 ■ KKPT-FM - 94.1
2400 Cottondale Ln.
Little Rock, AR 72202
Phone: (501)664-9410
Free: 800-844-0094
Format: Classic Rock. **Networks:** Independent. **Owner:** Signal Media of Arkansas, 2400 Cottondale Ln., Little Rock, AR 72202. **Founded:** 1960. **Formerly:** KLPQ-FM; KHLT-FM. **Operating Hours:** Sunrise-sunset. **ADI:** Little Rock, AR. **Key Personnel:** Mike Kennedy, Prog. Dir., mikek@kkpt.com; Chuck Gatlin, Contact, chuck@kkpt.com. **Wattage:** 100,000. **Ad Rates:** Noncommercial. **URL:** http://www.point941.com/contact.

1523 ■ KKRN-FM - 102.9
700 Wellington Hills Rd.
Little Rock, AR 72211
Phone: (501)401-0200
Free: 800-264-0092
Format: News; Talk. **Simulcasts:** KARN-FM. **Owner:** Cumulus Media Inc., 3280 Peachtree Rd. NW, Ste. 2300, Atlanta, GA 30305-2455, Ph: (404)949-0700, Fax: (404)949-0740. **Wattage:** 50,000. **Ad Rates:** Noncommercial. **URL:** http://kkrn.org.

1524 ■ KKYK-FM - 103.7
2400 Cottondale Ln.
Little Rock, AR 72202
Phone: (501)378-0104
Fax: (501)375-4887
Format: Talk; Sports. **Owner:** Shepard Communications of Arkansas, Inc., 209A Waters Bldg., Grand Rapids, MI 49503, Ph: (616)456-8002. **Founded:** 1967. **Formerly:** KARK-FM. **Operating Hours:** Continuous; 100% local. **ADI:** Little Rock, AR. **Key Personnel:** Michael Rosen, Contact; Laurie Allen, News Dir.; Bill Pressly, Dir. of Programs; Madison Taylor, Music Dir; Michael Rosen, Contact. **Wattage:** 100,000 ERP. **Ad Rates:** $27-102 for 30 seconds; $37-117 for 60 seconds. **URL:** http://1037thebuzz.com.

1525 ■ KLAL-FM - 107.7
700 Wellington Hills Rd.
Little Rock, AR 72211
Phone: (501)433-1077
Format: Top 40. **Wattage**: 100,000. **Ad Rates:** Noncommercial. **URL:** http://www.alice1077.com.

1526 ■ KLRA-FM - 96.5
415 N McKinley St., Ste. 700
Little Rock, AR 72205
Phone: (501)842-2581
Format: Contemporary Country; Agricultural. **Networks:** CBS; CNN Radio. **Owner:** Diamond State Broadcasting Inc., at above address. **Founded:** 1988. **Operating Hours:** Continuous. **Key Personnel:** Keith B. Dodd, Contact. **Wattage:** 10,500 ERP. **Ad Rates:** $15-25 for 30 seconds; $20-30 for 60 seconds. **URL:** http://965fmtheanswer.com.

1527 ■ KLRE-FM - 90.5
2801 S University Ave.
Little Rock, AR 72204-1099
Phone: (501)569-8485
Free: 800-952-2528
Email: comments@ualrpublicradio.org
Format: Classical. **Networks:** National Public Radio (NPR). **Owner:** Little Rock School District, 810 W Markham St., Little Rock, AR 72201, Ph: (501)477-1002, Fax: (501)447-2061. **Founded:** 1973. **Operating Hours**: Continuous. **Key Personnel:** Ben Fry, Gen. Mgr.; Ron Breeding, News Dir., Prog. Dir.; Kevin Delaney, Director. **Wattage:** 40,000. **Ad Rates:** Noncommercial. **URL:** http://www.ualrpublicradio.org.

1528 ■ KLRT-TV - 16
10800 Colonel Glenn Rd.
Little Rock, AR 72204-8017
Phone: (501)340-4444
Fax: (501)375-1961
Email: info@fox16.com
Format: News. **Networks:** Fox. **Owner:** iHeartMedia Inc., 200 E Basse Rd., San Antonio, TX 78209, Ph: (210)832-3314. **Founded:** 1983. **Operating Hours**: Continuous. **ADI**: Little Rock, AR. **Key Personnel:** Brandon Scott, Contact; Austin Kellerman, News Dir.; Chuck Stanley, Dir. of Engg.; Ed Trauschke, News Dir., etrauschke@fox16.com; Shane Deitert, Managing Ed., shane@fox16.com; Vicki McRae, Sales Mgr., vmcrae@fox16.com; Chuck Spohn, Gen. Mgr., cspohn@fox16.com; Dean Wetherbee, Asst. Dir., dwetherbee@fox16.com; Mike Vaughn, Gen. Mgr. **Wattage:** 5,000,000. **Ad Rates:** $20-950 per unit. **URL:** http://www.fox16.com.

1529 ■ KMJX-FM - 105.1
10800 Colonel Glenn Rd.
Little Rock, AR 72204
Phone: (501)217-5000
Fax: (501)217-5080
Email: request@1051thewolf.com
Format: Country. **Networks:** ABC. **Founded:** 1979. **Operating Hours:** Continuous; 3% network, 97% local. **Key Personnel:** Kelli Williams, Sales Mgr., keliwilliams@clearchannel.com. **Wattage**: 79,000. **Ad Rates:** Noncommercial. **URL:** http://kmud.org.

1530 ■ KMSX-FM - 94.9
10800 Colonel Glenn Rd.
Little Rock, AR 72204
Phone: (501)217-5000
Format: Adult Contemporary. **ADI**: Little Rock, AR. **Wattage**: 100,000. **Ad Rates:** Noncommercial.

1531 ■ KOKY-FM - 102.1
700 Wellington Hills Rd.
Little Rock, AR 72211
Phone: (501)401-0200
Fax: (501)401-0374
Format: Urban Contemporary. **Owner:** Citadel Broadcasting Corp., 7201 W Lake Mead Blvd., Ste. 400, Las Vegas, NV 89128-8366, Ph: (702)804-5200, Fax: (702)804-8250. **Key Personnel:** Rich Nickols, Sales Mgr. **Wattage**: 4,100. **Ad Rates:** Noncommercial. **URL:** http://www.koky.com.

1532 ■ KOLL-FM - 106.3
400 Hardin Rd., Ste. 150
Little Rock, AR 72211-3507
Phone: (501)219-1919
Format: Adult Contemporary. **Networks:** ABC. **Founded:** 1985. **Operating Hours**: Continuous. **ADI**: Little Rock, AR. **Key Personnel:** Neal Gladner, Gen. Mgr., VP, nealgladner@crainmedia.com; Sonny Victory, Dir. of Operations, sonnyvictory@crainmedia.com. **Wattage**: 100,000. **Ad Rates:** $60 for 60 seconds.

1533 ■ KPZK-FM - 102.5
700 Wellington Hills Rd.
Little Rock, AR 72211
Phone: (501)401-0200
Fax: (501)401-0366
Wattage: 3,000 ERP.

1534 ■ KQAR-FM - 100.3
10800 Colonel Glenn Rd.
Little Rock, AR 72204
Phone: (918)664-4581
Format: Contemporary Hit Radio (CHR); Country; Hot Country. **Founded:** 1969. **Formerly**: KDDK-FM; KEZQ-FM. **Operating Hours**: Continuous. **ADI**: Little Rock, AR. **Key Personnel:** Joe Rook, Sales Mgr., joerook@clearchannel.com; Wally Tucker, Gen. Mgr.; Ted Jones, Station Mgr.; Nancy Murray, VP of Admin.; Stephanie Sherwin, Gen. Sales Mgr. **Wattage:** 85,000. **Ad Rates:** Noncommercial. $50 for 60 seconds. Combined advertising rates available with KOLL-FM. **URL:** http://edgelittlerock.iheart.com.

1535 ■ KSSN-FM - 95.7
10800 Colonel Glenn Rd.
Little Rock, AR 72204
Phone: (501)217-5000
Fax: (501)374-0808
Format: Country. **Owner:** iHeartMedia Inc., 200 E Basse Rd., San Antonio, TX 78209, Ph: (210)832-3314. **Founded:** 1965. **Operating Hours**: Continuous; 100% local. **ADI**: Little Rock, AR. **Key Personnel:** Keli Williams, Sr. VP of Sales, keliwilliams@clearchannel.com. **Wattage:** 92,000. **Ad Rates:** $50-250 for 60 seconds. Combined advertising rates available with KDDK-FM. **URL:** http://www.kssn.com.

1536 ■ K34FH - 34
PO Box A
Santa Ana, CA 92711
Phone: (714)832-2950
Free: 888-731-1000
Owner: Trinity Broadcasting Network Inc., PO Box A, Santa Ana, CA 92711, Ph: (714)832-2950, Free: 888-731-1000.

1537 ■ KTHV-TV - 11
PO Box 269
Little Rock, AR 72203
Phone: (501)376-1111
Fax: (501)376-3324
Email: sales@thv11.com
Format: Commercial TV. **Networks:** CBS. **Owner:** Arkansas Television Co., 720 S Izard St., Little Rock, AR 72201, Ph: (501)376-9935. **Founded:** 1955. **Operating Hours**: Sunday-Thurs Continuous; Friday & Saturday 4:30 a.m.-1:30 a.m. **ADI**: Little Rock, AR. **Wattage**: 316 KW. **Ad Rates:** Noncommercial. **Mailing address:** PO Box 269, Little Rock, AR 72203. **URL:** http://www.static.thv11.com.

1538 ■ KTUV-AM - 1440
21700 Northwestern Hwy., Twr. 14, Ste. 1190
Southfield, MI 48075
Phone: (248)557-3500
Fax: (248)557-2950
Email: sima@birach.com
Format: Hispanic. **Owner:** Birach Broadcasting Corp., at above address. **Key Personnel:** Sima Birach, CEO, President. **URL:** http://www.birach.com/ktuv.htm.

1539 ■ KUAR-FM - 89.1
2801 S University Ave.
Little Rock, AR 72204-1099
Phone: (501)569-8485
Free: 800-952-2528
Email: comments@ualrpublicradio.org
Format: News; Information. **Networks:** National Public Radio (NPR). **Owner:** Board of Trustees of the University of Arkansas, at above address, Little Rock, AR. **Founded:** 1986. **Operating Hours**: Continuous. **ADI**: Little Rock, AR. **Key Personnel:** Ben Fry, Gen. Mgr. **Wattage**: 100,000. **Ad Rates:** Noncommercial. **URL:** http://www.kuar.org.

1540 ■ KURB-FM - 98.5
700 Wellington Hills Rd.
Little Rock, AR 72211
Phone: (501)401-0200
Fax: (501)401-0349
Format: Adult Contemporary. **Simulcasts:** KURB-AM. **Owner:** Cumulus Media Inc., 3280 Peachtree Rd. NW, Ste. 2300, Atlanta, GA 30305-2455, Ph: (404)949-0700, Fax: (404)949-0740. **Founded:** 1972. **Formerly**: KZOU-FM. **Operating Hours**: Continuous. **Key Personnel:** Becky Rogers, Contact. **Wattage:** 100,000. **Ad Rates:** Advertising accepted; rates available upon request. **URL:** http://www.b98.com.

1541 ■ KVLO-FM - 102.9
700 Wellington Hills Rd.
244 Jackson St., 4th Fl.
Little Rock, AR 72211
Free: 800-264-0092
Email: karn@karnnewsradio.com
Format: Country. **Wattage**: 50,000. **Ad Rates:** Advertising accepted; rates available upon request. **URL:** http://www.newsradio1029.com.

1542 ■ KVTH-TV - 26
PO Box 22007
Little Rock, AR 72221
Phone: (501)223-2525
Owner: Victory Television Network, 701 Napa Valley Dr., Little Rock, AR 72211, Fax: (888)317-1427, Free: 888-317-1427. **URL:** http://www.vtntv.com.

1543 ■ KVTJ-TV - 48
PO Box 22007
Little Rock, AR 72221
Phone: (501)223-2525
Owner: Victory Television Network, 701 Napa Valley Dr., Little Rock, AR 72211, Fax: (888)317-1427, Free: 888-317-1427. **URL:** http://www.vtntv.com.

1544 ■ KVTN-TV - 25
PO Box 22007
Little Rock, AR 72221
Phone: (501)223-2525
Format: Religious. **Owner:** Agape Church Inc., 701 Napa Valley Dr., Little Rock, AR 72211, Ph: (501)225-0612. **Founded:** 1988. **Operating Hours**: Continuous. **ADI**: Little Rock, AR. **Local Programs**: *Live from Studio B*; *Acquire the Fire*; *Way of the Master*; *Ever Increasing Faith*, Sunday 8:30 a.m. - 9:30 a.m.; *Lester Sumrall Teaching*; *Burnnie the Bunny*, Saturday 11:30 a.m.; *Make Your Day Count*; *Gaither Homecoming Hour*; *John Hagee Today*, Monday Tuesday Wednesday Thursday Friday 9:30 p.m.; *YouthBytes*; *VTN Drive-In*; *In His Presence*, Monday Tuesday Thursday Friday 1:00 p.m. 7:00 p.m. 10:30 p.m. 12:00 p.m.; *Where Life Begins*; *Destined to Win*; *Ministry of Compassion*; *Victory in Jesus*, Saturday Sunday Wednesday 5:00 p.m. 9:00 a.m.; 11:00 a.m.; 6:00 p.m. 7:00 p.m.; *Inspiration Time*; *Arkansas Alive*, Monday Tuesday Wednesday Thursday Friday 7:00 a.m.; 5:00 p.m.; 10:00 p.m.; *The Harvest Show*; *The Place for Miracles with Richard Roberts*, Monday Tuesday Wednesday Thursday Friday 1:00 a.m.; 5:00 p.m.; *Believer's Voice of Victory with Kenneth Copeland*; *The Gospel Truth with Andrew Wommack*; *Faith Life Church with Keith Moore*, Sunday Friday 9:00 a.m. 6:30 p.m. **Ad Rates:** $40 for 30 seconds; $60 for 60 seconds. Combined advertising rates available with KVTH-TV. **URL:** http://www.vtntv.com.

LONOKE

C. AR. Lonoke Co. 23 mi. E. of Little Rock. Manufactures wood products, women's apparel, ammunition. Cottonginning. Agriculture. Rice, wheat, soybeans; cotton. Fish farming.

1545 ■ Lonoke Democrat
Stephens Media L.L.C.
402 N Center St.
Lonoke, AR 72086
Phone: (501)676-2463
Fax: (501)676-6231
Publisher's E-mail: sfrederick@stephensmedia.com
Community newspaper. **Freq:** Weekly (Thurs.). **Print Method:** Offset. **Cols./Page:** 6. **Col. Width:** 26 nonpareils. **Col. Depth:** 294 agate lines. **Key Personnel:** Dennis Byrd, Publisher; Tania Johnston, Business Manager. **USPS:** 153-040. **Subscription Rates:** $32

Circulation: ★ = AAM; △ or • = BPA; ♦ = CAC; ❑ = VAC; ⊕ = PO Statement; ‡ = Publisher's Report; Boldface figures = sworn; Light figures = estimated.

Individuals print home delivery; $36 Individuals online access. **URL:** http://stephensmedia.com/lonoke-democrat. **Mailing address:** PO Box 747, Lonoke, AR 72086. **Remarks:** Accepts advertising. **Circ:** (Not Reported).

MAGNOLIA

SW AR. Columbia Co. 50 mi. SE of Texarkana. Southern Arkansas University. Manufactures fabric dams, bromine, aluminum extrusion, steel, plastic pipe, rubber coated fabric. Oil and natural gas. Pine, oak, gum timber. Agriculture. Cotton, corn, hogs.

1546 ■ Banner-News
Banner-News Publishing Co.
130 S Washington
Magnolia, AR 71753
Phone: (870)234-5130
Fax: (870)234-2551
Publisher's E-mail: news@bannernews.net
General newspaper. **Freq:** Daily (eve.). **Print Method:** Offset. **Cols./Page:** 6. **Col. Width:** 24 nonpareils. **Col. Depth:** 303 agate lines. **Key Personnel:** Susan Gill, General Manager; Jamie Davis, Managing Editor; Chris Gilliam, Editor. **Subscription Rates:** $123 Individuals 1 year (internet only). **URL:** http://www.magnoliabannernews.com. **Mailing address:** PO Box 100, Magnolia, AR 71753. **Ad Rates:** BW $2,109.54; 4C $2,384.54; SAU $16.53; PCI $16.35. **Remarks:** Accepts advertising. **Circ:** (Not Reported).

1547 ■ KZHE-FM - 100.5
406 W Union St.
Magnolia, AR 71753
Phone: (870)234-7790
Fax: (870)234-7791
Format: Country. **Founded:** 1981. **Formerly**: KQIT-FM. **Operating Hours**: Continuous. **Key Personnel:** Troy Alphin, Contact; Dave Sehon, Contact. **Wattage**: 50,000. **Ad Rates:** $1.75-3.40 for 15 seconds; $.75-6 for 30 seconds; $1.15-7 for 60 seconds. **URL:** http://www.kzhe.com.

MALVERN

SWC AR. Hot Spring Co. 20 mi. SE of Hot Spring. Manufactures brick, aluminum, telephone and electrical cable, lumber, building board, plastic utility pipe, brass fittings, aluminum and fiberglass boats, window frames, portable buildings, camper trailers, egg cartons. Mining barite. Poultry, livestock, timber.

1548 ■ Malvern Daily Record
Horizon Publishing Company L.L.C.
PO Box 70
Malvern, AR 72104
Phone: (501)337-7523
Fax: (501)337-1226
Publisher's E-mail: custserv@horizonpublishing.com
Newspaper. **Freq:** Daily (eve.). **Print Method:** Offset. **Trim Size:** 13 x 21 1/2. **Cols./Page:** 6. **Col. Width:** 2 1/16 inches. **Col. Depth:** 21 1/2 inches. **Key Personnel:** Richard Folds, Publisher; Kim Taber, Business Manager. **USPS:** 326-860. **Subscription Rates:** $96 Individuals carrier delivery; $123 By mail. **URL:** http://www.malvern-online.com. **Ad Rates:** 4C $260; SAU $7.80; PCI $8.48. **Remarks:** Accepts advertising. **Circ:** Paid ‡5300, Free ‡4000.

MANILA

NE AR. Mississippi Co. 20 mi. W. of Blytheville. Residential.

1549 ■ The Town Crier
The Town Crier
100 W Lake St.
Manila, AR 72442-1326
Phone: (870)561-4634
Fax: (870)561-3602
Publisher's E-mail: towncrier@centurytel.net
Local newspaper. **Founded:** 1971. **Freq:** Weekly (Tues.). **Print Method:** Offset. **Cols./Page:** 6. **Col. Width:** 24 nonpareils. **Col. Depth:** 294 agate lines. **Key Personnel:** Kaye Farrow, Contact; Ron Kemp, Publisher. **Subscription Rates:** $30 Individuals in County; $38 Individuals in Arkansas; $44 Out of state. **URL:** http://www.thetown-crier.com/. **Mailing address:** PO Box 1326, Manila, AR 72442-1326. **Ad Rates:** BW $409.50; 4C $609.50; SAU $5; PCI $5.25. **Remarks:** Accepts advertising. **Circ:** Paid 3000, Free 4400.

MARSHALL

N. AR. Searcy Co. 90 mi. N. of Little Rock. Recreation area in Ozark Mountains. Buffalo National River. Hardwood timber. Agriculture. Vegetables. Dairy products.

1550 ■ KCGS-AM - 960
208 Battle St.
Marshall, AR 72650
Phone: (870)448-5566
Fax: (870)448-5384
Format: Gospel. **Networks:** Independent; USA Radio. **Founded:** 1975. **Operating Hours**: Continuous; 100% local. **Key Personnel:** Peggy Ragland, Station Mgr. **Local Programs:** *Swap Shop*, Tuesday Wednesday Thursday 9:30 a.m. - 10:50 a.m. **Wattage**: 5,000. **Ad Rates:** $5-7 for 30 seconds; $7-8 for 60 seconds. **URL:** http://www.kcgsam.com.

MARVELL

E. AR. Phillips Co. 80 mi. NE of Little Rock. Cotton ginning, saw, hosiery mills. Agriculture. Cotton, rice.

1551 ■ KLMK-FM - 90.7
PO Box 2098
Omaha, NE 68103-2098
Free: 800-525-5683
Email: klove@klove.com
Format comprises contemporary Christian music programming. **Format:** Contemporary Christian. **Owner:** Educational Media Foundation, 2351 Sunset Blvd., Ste. 170-218, Rocklin, CA 95677, Ph: (800)434-8400; Educational Media Foundation, 5700 W Oaks Blvd., CA 95765, Free: 800-800434-8400. **Formerly**: WKFP-FM. **Operating Hours**: Continuous. **Key Personnel:** Mike Novak, President, CEO; Alan Mason, COO. **Wattage**: 25,000. **Ad Rates:** Advertising accepted; rates available upon request. **URL:** http://www.klove.com.

MAUMELLE

1552 ■ KWLR-FM - 96.9
6080 Mt. Moriah
Memphis, TN 38115
Phone: (901)375-9324
Fax: (901)375-5889
Email: mail@flinn.com
Format: Contemporary Christian. **Owner:** Flinn Broadcasting Corporation, at above address. **Key Personnel:** Mike Novak, President, CEO; Alan Mason, COO. **Wattage**: 4,600. **Ad Rates:** Noncommercial. **URL:** http://www.flinn.com.

MCCRORY

C. AR. Woodruff Co. Shoes, cotton gin.

1553 ■ McCrory Monitor-Leader-Advocate: The Monitor
Gladys Price Press
PO Box 898
McCrory, AR 72101
Phone: (870)731-2263
Fax: (870)731-5899
Publication E-mail: wcm@ipa.net
Local newspaper. **Freq:** Weekly. **Print Method:** Offset. **Cols./Page:** 6. **Col. Width:** 2 1/4 inches. **Col. Depth:** 21 1/2 inches. **Key Personnel:** Bill Riddle, Editor; Maryln Moody, Manager, Advertising; Paula Davis, Publisher. **USPS:** 006-506. **Subscription Rates:** $18 Individuals; $22 Out of area; $25 Out of state. **Formerly**: McCrory Leader; McCrory Monitor; Augusta Advocate. **Ad Rates:** GLR $.10; SAU $5; CNU $6; PCI $4. **Remarks:** Accepts advertising. **Circ:** ‡1800.

MCGEHEE

SE AR. Desha Co. 45 mi. NW of Greenville, MS. Cotton ginning; logging; paper & rice mills; glove factory. Agriculture. Cotton, corn, rice, hay.

1554 ■ KVSA-AM
PO Box 110
McGehee, AR 71654-0110
Fax: (501)538-3389
Format: Full Service. **Owner:** Southeast Arkansas Broadcasters, Inc., at above address, Ph: (501)538-5200. **Founded:** 1953. **Key Personnel:** Abbott F. Kinney, Contact. **Wattage**: 1,000 Day; 040 Night. **Ad Rates:** $3.35-4.20 for 30 seconds; $4.25-5.25 for 60 seconds.

MENA

W. AR. Polk Co. 65 mi S. of Fort Smith. Manufactures jeans, furniture rubber and plastic products, electric motors. Sawmills. Timber. Agriculture. Corn, potatoes, berries, poultry, dairy products. Cattle.

1555 ■ The Mena Star
Mena Star Company Inc.
PO Box 1307
Mena, AR 71953
Phone: (479)394-1900
Fax: (479)394-1908
General newspaper. **Freq:** Weekly (Thurs.). **Print Method:** Offset. **Cols./Page:** 6. **Col. Width:** 2 1/16 inches. **Col. Depth:** 21 1/2 inches. **Key Personnel:** Joe Ben Oller, Editor; Andy Philpot, Managing Editor. **ISSN:** 0747--1513 (print). **URL:** http://www.menastar.com. **Ad Rates:** BW $722.40; SAU $5.60; PCI $5.60. **Remarks:** Accepts advertising. **Circ:** 4750.

1556 ■ KENA-AM
PO Box 1450
Mena, AR 71953
Phone: (501)394-1450
Fax: (501)394-1459
Format: Southern Gospel. **Owner:** Ouachita Broadcasting, Inc., at above address. **Founded:** 1950. **Formerly**: Quachita Communications, Inc. **Key Personnel:** Dwight Douglas, Mgr. **Wattage**: 1,000. **Ad Rates:** $8 for 30 seconds; $12 for 60 seconds.

1557 ■ KRMN-FM - 88.9
1100 College Dr.
Mena, AR 71953
Phone: (479)394-7622
Format: Eclectic. **Owner:** Rich Mountain Community College, at above address. **Key Personnel:** Rudi Timmermann, Contact. **Wattage**: 500. **URL:** http://www.rmcc.edu/index.php?option=com_content&view=article&id=87.

1558 ■ RMCC-TV - 19
1100 College Dr.
Mena, AR 71953
Phone: (479)394-7622
Owner: Rich Mountain Community College, at above address. **Key Personnel:** Rudi Timmermann, Contact. **URL:** http://www.rmcc.edu/index.php?option=com_content&view=article&id=87.

MONTICELLO

SE AR. Drew Co. 50 mi. SE of Pine Bluff. University of Arkansas. Manufactures boats, paper and plastic bags, Rugs, yarn mills. Bottling works. Timber. Tomatoes, soybeans.

1559 ■ Community Communications Co.
1920 Hwy. 425 N
Monticello, AR 71655-4463
Phone: (870)367-7300
Fax: (870)367-9770
Free: 800-272-2191
Email: cccaccounts@ccc-cable.net
Founded: Sept. 06, 2006. **Key Personnel:** Paul Gardner, Gen. Mgr. **Cities Served:** Amity, Arkansas City, Bismarck, Bismarck, Carpenter Dam, Clark County, Diamondhead, Donaldson, East Camden, Eudora, Friendship, Garland County, Gillet, Glenwood, Gould, Gum Springs, Hooker, Jones Mill, Kilbourne, Kingsland, Ladd, Magic Springs, Magic Springs, Monticello, Norman, Ouachita County, Reed, Rison, Rosedale, Royal, Royal, Saline County, Star City, Tillar, Warren, Watson, Yorktown, Arkansas; 35 channels. **URL:** http://www.ccc-cable.net/.

1560 ■ KHBM-FM - 93.7
539 W Gaines
Monticello, AR 71655
Phone: (870)367-6854
Fax: (870)367-9564
Format: Adult Contemporary. **Networks:** AP; Arkansas Radio; ABC. **Owner:** Pines Broadcasting, Inc., 279 Midway Rte, Monticello, AR 71655, Ph: (870)367-6854. **Founded:** 1955. **Operating Hours:** Continuous; 1% network, 99% local. **Wattage:** 50,000. **Ad Rates:** Advertising accepted; rates available upon request.

1561 ■ KXSA-FM - 103.1
539 W Gaines
Monticello, AR 71655
Phone: (870)367-8528
Fax: (870)367-9564
Email: crn@ccc-cable.net
Format: Country. **Owner:** Pines Broadcasting, Inc., 279 Midway Rte, Monticello, AR 71655, Ph: (870)367-6854. **Founded:** 1983. **Operating Hours**: Continuous. **Wattage**: 6,000. **Ad Rates:** Noncommercial.

MORRILTON

C. AR. Conway Co. 40 mi. NW of Little Rock. Petit Jean State Park. Manufactures lumber, clothing, auto-parts, cottonseed oil, saw, pulp, and paper mills; meat packing plant, bottling works. Pine and hardwood timber. Agriculture. Cotton, soybeans, poultry, Livestock. rice.

1562 ■ KVLD-FM - 99.3
PO Box 541
Morrilton, AR 72110
Email: lagrand@rivervalleyradio.com
Format: Hispanic; Tejano. **Ad Rates:** Advertising accepted; rates available upon request. **URL:** http://993theeagle.com.

1563 ■ KVOM-AM - 800
PO Box 541
Morrilton, AR 72110
Phone: (501)354-2484
Fax: (501)354-5629
Email: kvom@kvom.com
Format: News. **Owner:** Max Media of Arkansas L.L.C., 1360 Hwy. 22, Dardanelle, AR 72834, Ph: (479)968-6816, Fax: (479)968-2946. **Key Personnel:** Rich Moellers, Mktg. Mgr., rich@rivervalleyradio.com. **Ad Rates:** Advertising accepted; rates available upon request. **URL:** http://www.kvom.com.

1564 ■ KVOM-FM - 101.7
PO Box 541
Morrilton, AR 72110
Phone: (501)354-2484
Fax: (501)354-5629
Email: kvom@kvom.com
Format: Country. **Owner:** Max Media of Arkansas L.L. C., 1360 Hwy. 22, Dardanelle, AR 72834, Ph: (479)968-6816, Fax: (479)968-2946. **Key Personnel:** Rich Moellers, Mktg. Mgr., rich@rivervalleyradio.com. **Wattage**: 6,000. **Ad Rates:** Advertising accepted; rates available upon request. **URL:** http://www.kvom.com.

MOUNTAIN HOME

N. AR. Baxter Co. 18 mi. N. of Buffalo City. Residential

1565 ■ The Baxter Bulletin
The Baxter Bulletin
16 W Sixth St.
Mountain Home, AR 72653
Phone: (870)508-8000
Fax: (870)508-8020
General newspaper. **Freq:** Mon.-Sat. (morn.). **Print Method:** Offset. **Trim Size:** 13 3/4 x 22 3/4. **Cols./Page:** 6. **Col. Width:** 24 nonpareils. **Col. Depth:** 294 agate lines. **Key Personnel:** Bob Heist, Managing Editor. **ISSN:** 0745--7707 (print). **Subscription Rates:** $.99 Individuals monthly (digital only); $4.30 Individuals monthly (print home delivery). **URL:** http://www.baxterbulletin.com. **Ad Rates:** BW $976.50; 4C $1,171.50; SAU $7.75; PCI $7.75. **Remarks:** Accepts advertising. **Circ:** Paid 10229.

1566 ■ KCMH-FM - 91.5
126 S Church St.
Mountain Home, AR 72653
Phone: (870)425-2525
Fax: (870)424-2626
Free: 888-577-5264
Format: Religious. **Networks:** Moody Broadcasting. **Owner:** Christian Broadcasting Group of Mountain Home Inc., 126 S Church St., Mountain Home, AZ 72653. **Founded:** 1988. **Operating Hours**: Continuous. **Wattage**: 26,000 ERP. **Ad Rates:** Accepts Advertising. **URL:** http://www.kcmhradio.com.

1567 ■ KCTT-FM - 101.7
620 Hwy. 5 N
Mountain Home, AR 72654-2010
Phone: (870)425-3101
Fax: (870)424-4314
Format: Oldies; Classical. **Owner:** KTLO L.L.C., at above address. **Founded:** 1983. **Operating Hours**: Continuous. **Key Personnel:** Danny Ward, Station Mgr., danny@ktlo.com; Bob Knight, Gen. Mgr., bob@ktlo.com; Robin Hawkins, Sales Mgr. **Wattage**: 3,000. **Ad Rates:** $4-6 for 30 seconds; $7-10 for 60 seconds. **Mailing address:** PO Box 2010, Mountain Home, AR 72654-2010. **URL:** http://www.ktlo.com.

1568 ■ K41HC - 41
PO Box A
Santa Ana, CA 92711
Phone: (714)832-2950
Free: 888-731-1000
Owner: Trinity Broadcasting Network Inc., PO Box A, Santa Ana, CA 92711, Ph: (714)832-2950, Free: 888-731-1000. **URL:** http://www.tbn.org.

1569 ■ KKTZ-FM - 93.5
2352 Hwy. 62 B
Mountain Home, AR 72653
Phone: (870)492-6022
Fax: (870)492-2137
Format: Adult Contemporary. **Networks:** ABC. **Founded:** 1985. **Operating Hours**: Continuous. **ADI**: Springfield, MO. **Key Personnel:** Stewart Brunner, Gen. Mgr., VP, stewartbrunner@twinlakesradio.com; Kim Garrett, Office Mgr., kimgarrett@twinlakesradio.com. **Wattage**: 25,000. **Ad Rates:** Advertising accepted; rates available upon request. **URL:** http://www.twinlakesradio.com.

1570 ■ KLRM-FM - 90.7
PO Box 2098
Omaha, NE 68103-2098
Free: 800-525-5683
Format: Contemporary Christian. **Owner:** Education Media Foundation, 2351 Sunset Blvd., Ste. 170-218, Rocklin, CA 95765, Ph: (916)251-1600, Free: 800-434-8400. **Key Personnel:** Mike Novak, President, CEO; Alan Mason, COO. **Wattage**: 7,000. **URL:** http://www.klove.com.

1571 ■ KOMT-FM - 107.5
2352 Highway 62 B
Mountain Home, AR 72653
Phone: (870)492-6022
Fax: (870)492-2137
Format: Adult Contemporary. **Operating Hours**: Continuous. **Key Personnel:** Stewart Brunner, Gen. Mgr., VP, stewartbrunner@twinlakesradio.com; Kim Garrett, Office Mgr., kimgarrett@twinlakesradio.com. **Wattage**: 100,000. **Ad Rates:** Advertising accepted; rates available upon request. **URL:** http://www.twinlakesradio.com.

1572 ■ KPFM-FM - 105.5
2352 Hwy. 62 B
Mountain Home, AR 72653
Phone: (870)492-6022
Fax: (870)492-2137
Format: Country. **Networks:** ABC. **Founded:** 1985. **Formerly:** KGHI-FM. **Operating Hours**: Continuous. **Key Personnel:** Stewart Brunner, Gen. Mgr., VP; Kim Garrett, Office Mgr. **Wattage**: 50,000. **Ad Rates:** Advertising accepted; rates available upon request. **URL:** http://www.twinlakesradio.com.

1573 ■ KTLO-AM - 1240
620 Hwy. 5 N
Mountain Home, AR 72653
Phone: (870)425-3101
Fax: (870)424-4314
Free: 800-884-0364
Email: news@ktlo.com
Format: Country. **Networks:** ABC. **Founded:** 1953. **Operating Hours**: Continuous; 75% network, 25% local. **ADI**: Springfield, MO. **Key Personnel:** Matt Sharp, Contact; Linda Knight, Contact; Robin Hawkins, Asst. Mgr., robin@ktlo.com; Bob Knight, Gen. Mgr., bob@ktlo.com; Danny Ward, Station Mgr., danny@ktlo.com; Sue Knight, Contact, sue@ktlo.com. **Wattage**: 1,000. **Ad Rates:** Noncommercial. $5.50-$8 for 30 seconds; $10.50-$11 for 60 seconds. Combined advertising rates available with KTLO-FM, KCTT-FM. **URL:** http://www.ktlo.com.

1574 ■ KTLO-FM - 97.9
620 Hwy. 5 N
Mountain Home, AR 72653
Phone: (870)425-3101
Fax: (870)424-4314
Email: news@ktlo.com
Format: Contemporary Hit Radio (CHR). **Networks:** ABC. **Founded:** 1970. **Operating Hours**: Continuous; 60% network, 40% local. **ADI**: Springfield, MO. **Key Personnel:** Patty Sindlinger, Producer; Bob Knight, Station Mgr., bob@ktlo.com; Danny Ward, Dir. of Traffic, danny@ktlo.com; Robin Hawkins, Asst. Mgr., robin@ktlo.com; Brad Haworth, Contact, brad@ktlo.com; Sue Knight, Contact, sue@ktlo.com. **Wattage**: 50,000. **Ad Rates:** $8-11 for 30 seconds; $13-17 for 60 seconds. $7-$10 for 30 seconds; $12-$17 for 60 seconds. Combined advertising rates available with KTLO-AM, KCTT-FM. **URL:** http://www.ktlo.com.

MOUNTAIN VIEW

NC AR. Stone Co. 30 mi. NW of Independence.

1575 ■ Stone County Leader
Stone County Publishing Co.
104 W Main St.
Mountain View, AR 72560
Phone: (870)269-3841
Fax: (870)269-2171
Local newspaper. **Freq:** Weekly (Wed.). **Key Personnel:** Lori Freeze, Editor; James R. Fraser, Owner, Publisher; Karen Younger, Manager, Circulation. **USPS:** 009-255. **Subscription Rates:** $25 Individuals in Stone and surrounding counties; $50 Out of area out of area; $12.50 Individuals in Stone and surrounding counties - 6 months; $25 Out of area 6 months; $25 Individuals online only; $3 Individuals trial access. **URL:** http://www.stonecountyleader.com/. **Mailing address:** PO Box 509, Mountain View, AR 72560. **Ad Rates:** PCI $7.60. **Remarks:** Accepts advertising. **Circ:** Paid ‡5000.

1576 ■ KEMV-TV - 6
350 S Donaghey Ave.
Conway, AR 72034
Phone: (501)682-2386
Free: 800-662-2386
Email: info@aetn.org
Format: Public TV. **Networks:** Public Broadcasting Service (PBS). **Owner:** Arkansas Educational Television Commission, at above address. **Founded:** 1980. **Operating Hours**: 6 a.m.-11:30 p.m. weekdays; 7 a.m.-11:30 p.m. Saturday and Sunday. **Key Personnel:** Allen Weatherly, Exec. Dir., aweatherly@aetn.org; Tony Brooks, Dep. Dir., tbrooks@aetn.org. **Ad Rates:** Noncommercial. **URL:** http://www.aetn.org.

MURFREESBORO

1577 ■ KMTB-FM - 99.5
PO Box 311
De Queen, AR 71832-0311
Phone: (870)845-3601
Fax: (870)845-3680
Email: pag@iosa.com
Format: Country. **Networks:** Arkansas Radio. **Owner:** Arklatex Radio, Inc., at above address. **Operating Hours**: Continuous. **Key Personnel:** Brent Pinkerton, Gen. Mgr. **Wattage**: 20,500. **Ad Rates:** Advertising accepted; rates available upon request. Combined advertising rates available with KBH and KNAS.

NASHVILLE

SW AR. Howard Co. 39 mi. NE of Texarkana. Manufactures cement products, gypsum wallboard, chainsaws, baskets, garments, Sawmills; cutlery plants. Major poultry area. Cattle. peaches.

1578 ■ Montgomery County News
Graves Publishing Co.
PO Box 297
Nashville, AR 71852
Local newspaper. **Founded:** 1951. **Freq:** Weekly (Thurs.). **Print Method:** Offset. **Cols./Page:** 5. **Col. Width:** 11 picas. **Col. Depth:** 180 agate lines. **Subscription Rates:** $20 Individuals 1 year digital edition; $1 Single issue; $10 Individuals 6 months digital edition. **URL:** http://swarkansasnews.com/. **Ad Rates:** GLR

Circulation: ★ = AAM; △ or • = BPA; ♦ = CAC; ❑ = VAC; ⊕ = PO Statement; ‡ = Publisher's Report; Boldface figures = sworn; Light figures = estimated.

$.23; PCI $3.21. **Remarks:** Accepts advertising. **Circ:** ‡1950.

1579 ■ Murfreesboro Diamond
Graves Publishing Co.
PO Box 297
Nashville, AR 71852
Community newspaper (tabloid). **Freq:** Weekly (Wed.). **Print Method:** Offset. **Cols./Page:** 5. **Col. Width:** 2 inches. **Col. Depth:** 13 inches. **Key Personnel:** Heather Grabin, Editor. **URL:** http://swarkansasnews.com/newspaper-archives/murfreesboro-diamond. **Ad Rates:** PCI $2.92. **Remarks:** Accepts advertising. **Circ:** ‡1800.

1580 ■ The Nashville News
The Nashville News
418 N Main St.
Nashville, AR 71852
Phone: (870)845-2010
Fax: (870)845-5091
Publisher's E-mail: contact@swarkansasnews.com
Community newspaper. **Founded:** Jan. 1878. **Key Personnel:** Ellen Ward, Manager, Circulation; Mike Graves, Publisher; Jim Pinson, Editor. **Subscription Rates:** $30 Individuals 104 issues; $50 Elsewhere; $20 Individuals digital edition; $10 Individuals 6 months, digital edition; $1 Individuals digital edition. **URL:** http://www.nashvillenews.org. **Formerly:** The News. **Mailing address:** PO Box 297, Nashville, AR 71852. **Remarks:** Accepts classified advertising. **Circ:** (Not Reported).

1581 ■ KBHC-AM - 1260
1513 S 4th St.
Nashville, AR 71852
Phone: (870)845-3601
Fax: (870)845-3680
Format: Country; Religious. **Networks:** Arkansas Radio. **Owner:** Arklatex Radio, Inc., at above address. **Founded:** 1959. **Operating Hours:** Sunrise-sunset. **Key Personnel:** Pete Gathright, Contact; Ann Gathright, Contact; Rick Castleberry, Contact. **Wattage:** 500. **Ad Rates:** $3-4.12 for 30 seconds; $3.50-5 for 60 seconds. **URL:** http://southwestarkansasradio.com/.

1582 ■ KNAS-FM
1513 S 4th St.
Nashville, AR 71852
Phone: (501)845-3601
Fax: (501)845-3680
Format: Oldies. **Networks:** Arkansas Radio. **Owner:** Arklatex Radio, Inc., at above address. **Founded:** 1977. **Key Personnel:** Pete Gathright, Contact; Ann Gathright, Contact; Rick Castleberry, Contact. **Wattage:** 6,000 ERP. **Ad Rates:** $3-4.12 for 30 seconds; $4.12-5.88 for 60 seconds.

1583 ■ KNLL-FM - 90.5
PO Box 3206
Tupelo, MS 38803
Format: Religious. **Owner:** American Family Radio, at above address. **Wattage:** 100,000. **URL:** http://www.afa.net.

NEWARK

1584 ■ KLLN-FM
1502 N Hill St.
Newark, AR 72562
Phone: (870)799-8969
Fax: (870)799-8647
Format: Southern Gospel. **Wattage:** 4,000 ERP. **Ad Rates:** Noncommercial.

NEWPORT

NE AR. Jackson Co. On White River, 91 mi. NW of Memphis, TN. Lumber mills; furniture, lighting fixtures, mobile homes, electrical wires, metal tube factories; soybean cotton compressing. Agriculture. Cotton, rice, livestock.

1585 ■ Newport Independent
GateHouse Media Inc.
2408 Hwy. 367 N
Newport, AR 72112
Phone: (870)523-5855
Fax: (870)523-6540
Community newspaper. **Freq:** Semiweekly (Wed. and Fri.). **Key Personnel:** Gina Slagley, Editor, Publisher. **URL:** http://www.newportindependent.com; http://www.gatehousemedia.com. **Formerly:** Newport Daily Independent. **Remarks:** Accepts advertising. **Circ:** (Not Reported).

1586 ■ KNBY-AM - 1280
2025 McLarty Dr.
Newport, AR 72112
Phone: (870)523-5891
Fax: (870)523-2967
Email: legends@rivercountry967.com
Format: Talk. **URL:** http://www.rivercountry967.com.

NORTH LITTLE ROCK

C. AR. Pulaski Co. On Arkansas River, opposite Little Rock. Manufactures chemicals, coke, fertilizer, excelsior, furniture, baking powder, concrete products. Soybeans, cottonseed. Pulp mill; stock yards; poultry processing plant.

1587 ■ The Baptist Challenge: A Voice of Independent Baptists
The Central Baptist Church of Little Rock
5200 Fairway Ave.
North Little Rock, AR 72116-7071
Phone: (501)771-1125
Religious magazine. **Freq:** Monthly. **Print Method:** Offset. **Trim Size:** 8 1/2 x 11. **Cols./Page:** 4. **Col. Width:** 28 nonpareils. **Col. Depth:** 140 agate lines. **Key Personnel:** M.L. Moser, Editor. **USPS:** 547-400. **Subscription Rates:** Free. **Ad Rates:** BW $250; PCI $8. **Remarks:** Accepts advertising. **Circ:** Free ‡6000.

1588 ■ City & Town: official publication of the Arkansas Municipal League
Arkansas Municipal League
301 W 2nd
North Little Rock, AR 72114
Phone: (501)374-3484
Fax: (501)374-0541
Publication E-mail: citytown@arml.org
Municipal government. **Freq:** Monthly. **Print Method:** Offset. **Trim Size:** 8.5 x 11. **Cols./Page:** 2 and 3. **Col. Width:** 26 and 40 nonpareils. **Col. Depth:** 140 agate lines. **Key Personnel:** Andrew Morgan, Editor; Don Zimmerman, Publisher. **ISSN:** 0193--8371 (print). **Subscription Rates:** $20 Individuals; $1.67 Single issue. **Alt. Formats:** PDF. **URL:** http://www.arml.org/services/publications/city-town. **Mailing address:** PO Box 38, North Little Rock, AR 72115. **Ad Rates:** BW $375; 4C $555. **Remarks:** Accepts advertising. **Circ:** ‡6800.

OSCEOLA

NE AR EC AR. Mississippi Co Mississippi Co. 25 mi. S. of Blytheville On Mississippi River, 16 mi. S. of Blytheville. Feed, cottonseed, oil and alphafa.

1589 ■ KOSE-AM - 860
509 S Walnut St.
Osceola, AR 72370
Phone: (501)563-2641
Format: Oldies. **Networks:** ABC; Arkansas Radio. **Owner:** Pollack Broadcasting, at above address, Memphis, TN. **Founded:** 1949. **Operating Hours:** 17 hours daily; 100% local. **Key Personnel:** Jamie Williams, Dir. of Traffic; Bob Abel, News Dir., Contact; Chris Webster, Dir. of Operations; Ed White, Sales Mgr., Prog. Dir; Bob Abel, Contact; Craig Koon, Contact. **Wattage:** 1,000. **Ad Rates:** $8-10.50 for 30 seconds; $10-13 for 60 seconds. **Mailing address:** PO Box 249, Osceola, AR 72370.

OZARK

1590 ■ KDYN-AM - 1540
PO Box 1086
Ozark, AR 72949
Phone: (501)667-4567
Fax: (501)667-5214
Free: 888-325-5396
Email: kdyn@centurytel.net
Format: Contemporary Country. **Networks:** ABC; Arkansas Radio. **Owner:** Ozark Communications Inc., 1591 1st Commercial Bldg., Little Rock, AR 72204. **Operating Hours:** Continuous. **Wattage:** 500. **Ad Rates:** Advertising accepted; rates available upon request. KDYN-FM. **URL:** http://www.kdyn.com.

PARAGOULD

NE AR. Greene Co. 69 mi. NW of Memphis, TN. Manufactures electric motors. shock absorbers, sprockets and gears, gas grills, shirts, burial vaults, trailers. Cotton ginning; bottling works. Soybeans, cotton, corn, hay. Cattle, hogs. Milk, dairy products.

1591 ■ Paragould Daily Press
Paragould Daily Press
1401 W Hunt St.
Paragould, AR 72450
Phone: (870)239-8562
Fax: (870)239-3636
Publisher's E-mail: newsinfo@paragoulddailypress.com
Community newspaper. **Freq:** Tuesday through Friday and Sunday morning. **Key Personnel:** Steve Gillespie, Editor; Tammy Thompson, Consultant; Scott Perkins, Publisher. **URL:** http://www.paragoulddailypress.com. **Mailing address:** PO Box 38, Paragould, AR 72450. **Remarks:** Accepts advertising. **Circ:** ‡5539, ‡6291.

1592 ■ KDRS-AM - 1490
400 Tower Dr.
Paragould, AR 72450
Phone: (870)236-7627
Fax: (870)239-4583
Format: Talk. **Networks:** Arkansas Radio. **Owner:** MOR Media, Inc., at above address, Paragould, AR. **Operating Hours:** Continuous. **Key Personnel:** Dina Mason, Contact, dina@kdrs.com; Dina Mason, Contact, dina@kdrs.com; Brian Osborn, Contact, brian@kdrs.com. **Wattage:** 1,000. **Ad Rates:** Advertising accepted; rates available upon request. KDRS AM/FM. **URL:** http://www.neajackfm.com.

1593 ■ KDRS-FM - 107.1
400 Tower Dr.
Paragould, AR 72450
Phone: (870)236-7627
Fax: (870)239-4583
Format: Adult Contemporary. **Networks:** Fox; Arkansas Radio. **Owner:** MOR Media, Inc., at above address, Paragould, AR. **Operating Hours:** Continuous. **Key Personnel:** Dina Mason, Contact, dina@kdrs.com; Dina Mason, Contact, dina@kdrs.com; Brian Osborn, Contact, brian@kdrs.com; Peggy Richardson, Contact, peggy@kdrs.com. **Wattage:** 3,000. **Ad Rates:** Advertising accepted; rates available upon request. KDRS AM/FM. **URL:** http://www.neajackfm.com.

1594 ■ K27FC - 27
PO Box A
Santa Ana, CA 92711
Phone: (714)832-2950
Free: 888-731-1000
Owner: Trinity Broadcasting Network Inc., PO Box A, Santa Ana, CA 92711, Ph: (714)832-2950, Free: 888-731-1000. **URL:** http://www.tbn.org.

1595 ■ K204DN-FM - 88.7
PO Box 391
Twin Falls, ID 83303
Fax: (208)736-1958
Free: 800-357-4226
Format: Religious; Contemporary Christian. **Owner:** CSN International, PO Box 391, Twin Falls, ID 83303, Ph: (208)736-1958, Fax: (208)736-1958, Free: 800-357-4226. **URL:** http://www.csnradio.com.

PARIS

1596 ■ Paris Express
Stephens Media L.L.C.
PO Box 551
Paris, AR 72855
Phone: (479)963-2901
Publication E-mail: news@paris-express.com
Community newspaper. **Freq:** Weekly (Wed.). **Print Method:** Offset. **Cols./Page:** 6. **Col. Width:** 12 picas. **Col. Depth:** 21 1/2 inches. **Key Personnel:** Vickey Wiggins, Publisher; Pat McHughes, Editor; Mary Harrison, Manager, Advertising. **Subscription Rates:** $34 Individuals print or online. **URL:** http://paris-express.com. **Mailing address:** PO Box 551, Paris, AR 72855. **Remarks:** Advertising accepted; rates available upon request. **Circ:** 3600.

1597 ■ KCCL-FM - 95.3
24 S Express St.
Paris, AR 72855
Format: Country; Agricultural. **Owner:** Diamond State Broadcasting Inc., at above address. **Founded:** 1981. **Operating Hours:** Sunrise-sunset. **Key Personnel:** Willie Harris, M.D., President; Keith Dodd, Gen. Mgr.;

Rhonda Price, Station Mgr. **Wattage:** 4,500 ERP.

1598 ■ K207CW-FM - 89.3
PO Box 391
Twin Falls, ID 83303
Fax: (208)736-1958
Free: 800-357-4226
Format: Religious; Contemporary Christian. **Owner:** CSN International, PO Box 391, Twin Falls, ID 83303, Ph: (208)736-1958, Fax: (208)736-1958, Free: 800-357-4226. **URL:** http://www.csnradio.com.

PINE BLUFF

SEC AR. Jefferson Co. 45 mi. SE of Little Rock, on Arkansas River. University of Arkansas at Pine Bluff. Pine Bluff Convention Center. Manufactures lumber, agricultural machinery, wood products, cotton pickers, electric transformers, pillow cases, bed sheets, furniture, paper bags, & cartons, chemicals, aluminum & steel casting, archery equipment, newsprint, jumbo barges, towboats. Cotton market and livestock; cotton oil mills; cotton compresses and warehouses; stockyards. Pine, gum, oak timber. Agriculture. Cattle, hogs, cotton, rice, soybeans.

1599 ■ Pine Bluff Commercial
Stephens Media L.L.C.
PO Box 6469
Pine Bluff, AR 71611
Phone: (870)534-3400
Fax: (870)534-0113
Publisher's E-mail: sfrederick@stephensmedia.com
General newspaper. **Freq:** Daily (morn.). **Print Method:** Letterpress. **Cols./Page:** 6. **Col. Depth:** 293 agate lines. **Key Personnel:** Byron Tate, Editor, Publisher. **Subscription Rates:** $155.40 Individuals home deliver (daily and Sunday); $93 Individuals home delivery (Sunday only); $207.92 By mail In Jefferson County (daily and Sunday); $112.60 By mail In Jefferson County (Sunday only); $234.92 By mail Outside Jefferson County (daily and Sunday); $130.60 By mail Outside Jeffersn County (Sunday only). **URL:** http://stephensmedia.com/pine-bluff-commercial; http://www.pbcommercial.com. **Ad Rates:** GLR $.49; BW $1,542.24; 4C $1,842.24; SAU $12.24. **Remarks:** Accepts advertising. **Circ:** Mon.-Sat. ♦**10889**, Sun. ♦**11347**.

1600 ■ KCAT-AM - 1340
1207 W 6th St.
Pine Bluff, AR 71601-3927
Phone: (870)534-5001
Fax: (870)534-7985
Format: Gospel; Contemporary Christian. **Networks:** American Urban Radio. **Founded:** 1963. **Operating Hours:** Continuous; 10% network, 90% local. **Key Personnel:** Elijah Mondy, Jr., Owner, em@lordradio.com. **Wattage:** 1,000. **Ad Rates:** $12-16 for 30 seconds; $15-20 for 60 seconds. **URL:** http://www.kcatam.com.

1601 ■ K204DO-FM - 88.7
PO Box 391
Twin Falls, ID 83303
Fax: (208)736-1958
Free: 800-357-4226
Format: Religious; Contemporary Christian. **Owner:** CSN International, PO Box 391, Twin Falls, ID 83303, Ph: (208)736-1958, Fax: (208)736-1958, Free: 800-357-4226. **URL:** http://www.csnradio.com.

1602 ■ KUAP-FM - 89.7
1200 N University Dr.
Pine Bluff, AR 71601
Phone: (870)575-8000
Format: Jazz. **Owner:** University of Arkansas at Pine Bluff, 1200 N University Dr., Pine Bluff, AR 71601, Ph: (870)575-8000. **Founded:** 1873. **Operating Hours:** Continuous. **Key Personnel:** Robert Wall, Director. **Ad Rates:** Noncommercial. **URL:** http://www.uapb.edu.

1603 ■ Pine Bluff Cable TV Co., Inc.
715 S Poplar Ave.
Pine Bluff, AR 71601
Free: 800-903-0508
Email: pinebluffcabletvcs@cablelynx.com
Cities Served: 63 channels. **URL:** http://www.pinebluffcabletv.com/customer-service.html.

POCAHONTAS

NE AR. Randolph Co. On Black River, 35 mi. NW of Jonesboro. Manufactures handles, tool chests, shoes, electronic component parts, heavy trailers, pickup campers. Timber. Dairy, poultry, grain and hog farms.

1604 ■ KPOC-FM - 104.1
PO Box 508
Pocahontas, AR 72455
Phone: (870)892-5234
Fax: (870)892-5235
Email: kpoc-krlw@centurytel.net
Owner: Combined Media Group Inc., at above address. **Wattage:** 6,000 ERP.

PRESCOTT

SW AR. Nevada Co. 48 mi. NE of Texarkana. Lumber, cottonseed oil mills. Pine timber. Agriculture. Cotton, corn.

1605 ■ The Gurdon Times
GateHouse Media Inc.
100 E Elm
Prescott, AR 71857
Phone: (870)353-4482
Community newspaper. **Freq:** Weekly (Thurs.). **Print Method:** Offset. **Trim Size:** 13 3/4 x 22 3/4. **Cols./Page:** 6. **Col. Width:** 2 1/16 inches. **Col. Depth:** 21 1/2 inches. **Key Personnel:** Clark Smith, Publisher; Wendy Ledbetter, Editor; Mandie Shelton, Reporter. **USPS:** 232-180. **URL:** http://www.thegurdontimes.com/section/?template=onlinesubscription. **Mailing address:** PO Box 60, Prescott, AR 71857. **Ad Rates:** BW $409.50; SAU $3.25. **Remarks:** Advertising accepted; rates available upon request. **Circ:** ‡1200.

RECTOR

1606 ■ Clay County Democrat
Delta Publishing Co.
PO Box 366
Rector, AR 72461
Phone: (870)598-2201
Community newspaper. **Freq:** Weekly (Wed.). **Print Method:** Offset. **Trim Size:** 6 x 21. **Cols./Page:** 6. **Col. Width:** 12.5 picas. **Col. Depth:** 21 inches. **Key Personnel:** Nancy Kemp, Editor; Ron Kemp, Publisher. **USPS:** 116-620. **Remarks:** Accepts advertising. **Circ:** 2000.

RISON

SC AR. Cleveland Co. 20 mi. S. of Pine Bluff.

Cleveland County Herald - See Cleveland County

ROGERS

NW AR. Benton Co. 75 mi. N. of Fort Smith. Lake and mountain resort. Manufactures electric motors, air guns, vinegar, brooder equipment, corrugated paper products, plastic bags. Hatchery, poultry processing, meat packing, and rabbit processing. Beef, dairy, cattle; turkey, chicken raising. Grape, apple growing.

1607 ■ KHOG-TV - 29
2809 Ajax Ave., Ste. 200
Rogers, AR 72758
Phone: (479)631-4029
Fax: (479)878-6077
Format: Commercial TV. **Networks:** ABC. **Owner:** Hearst Television Inc., 300 W 57th St., New York, NY 10019-3741, Ph: (212)887-6800, Fax: (212)887-6855. **Founded:** 1977. **Formerly:** KTVP-TV. **Operating Hours:** 6 a.m.-1 a.m.; 90% network, 10% local. **ADI:** Fort Smith, AR. **Key Personnel:** Mark Lericos, Sports Dir. **URL:** http://www.4029tv.com.

1608 ■ KURM-AM - 790
113 E New Hope Rd.
Rogers, AR 72758
Phone: (479)636-7979
Fax: (479)631-9711
Free: 800-767-7979
Format: News; Talk. **Networks:** CBS. **Owner:** Kern Inc., 3940 Gantz Rd., Ste. A, Grove City, OH 43123-4845, Ph: (614)317-2600, Fax: (614)491-9529. **Founded:** 1979. **Operating Hours:** 5 a.m.-midnight. **Wattage:** 5,000. **Ad Rates:** $8 for 30 seconds; $12 for 60 seconds. **URL:** http://www.kurm.net.

1609 ■ Southern Cablecom
221 N 3rd St.
Rogers, AR 72756
Phone: (501)631-1650
Fax: (501)631-7831
Founded: 1981. **Cities Served:** subscribing households 2,600. **Mailing address:** PO Box 474, Rogers, AR 72756.

RUSSELLVILLE

NW AR. Pope Co. 75 mi. NW of Little Rock. Arkansas Tech University. Manufactures furniture, shoes, frozen foods, inner tubes, corrugated boxes, concrete forms, chlorine extraction cells, metal products; rendering plant. Timber. Diversified farming. Feed producers hatcheries.

1610 ■ The Arka Tech
Arkansas Tech University
1605 N Coliseum Dr.
Russellville, AR 72801
Phone: (479)968-0238
Publisher's E-mail: snicholson@atu.edu
Collegiate newspaper. **Freq:** Weekly (Tues.). **Print Method:** Offset. **Cols./Page:** 6. **Col. Width:** 11 picas. **Col. Depth:** 21.5 inches. **Key Personnel:** Laura Bean, Editor. **URL:** http://arkatechnews.wordpress.com/category/news. **Ad Rates:** PCI $3. **Remarks:** Advertising accepted; rates available upon request. **Circ:** Free ‡2500.

1611 ■ The Courier
Russellville Newspaper
201 E 2nd St.
Russellville, AR 72801-5102
General newspaper. **Freq:** Daily (morn.) (except Mon.). **Subscription Rates:** $146.27 Individuals Tues. thru Sunday; $154.70 By mail Tues. thru Sunday; $178.75 Elsewhere Tues. thru Sunday; $96.85 Individuals Saturday & Sunday Only. **URL:** http://www.couriernews.com. **Remarks:** Accepts advertising. **Circ:** Paid ‡20000.

1612 ■ Nebo: A Literary Journal
Arkansas Tech University Department of English
1605 Coliseum Dr., Ste. 141
Russellville, AR 72801
Free: 800-582-6953
Student publication covering poetry and prose. **Freq:** Semiannual. **Key Personnel:** Ryan Smith, Editor. **Subscription Rates:** $10 Individuals. **URL:** http://www.atu.edu/worldlanguages/Nebo.php. **Remarks:** Advertising not accepted. **Circ:** (Not Reported).

1613 ■ KCAB-AM - 980
2705 East Pkwy.
Russellville, AR 72802
Phone: (479)968-6816
Fax: (479)968-2946
Format: News; Talk; Sports. **Owner:** Max Media of Arkansas, LLC, 900 Laskin Rd., Virginia Beach, VA 23451, Ph: (757)437-9800. **Founded:** 1998. **Key Personnel:** Rich Moellers, Gen. Mgr., rich@rivervalleyradio.com; Rhonda Dilbeck, Dir. of Sales, rhonda@rivervalleyradio.com; Aaron Thomas, Operations Mgr., aaron@rivervalleyradio.com. **Wattage:** 5,000. **Ad Rates:** Noncommercial. **URL:** http://www.rivertalk980.com.

1614 ■ KCJC-FM - 102.3
2705 East Pkwy.
Russellville, AR 72802
Phone: (479)968-6816
Fax: (479)968-2946
Format: Country. **Networks:** ABC. **Owner:** Max Media of Arkansas L.L.C., 1360 Hwy. 22, Dardanelle, AR 72834, Ph: (479)968-6816, Fax: (479)968-2946. **Formerly:** KAIO-FM. **Operating Hours:** Continuous. **Key Personnel:** Aaron Thomas, Operations Mgr.; Rhonda Dilbeck, Dir. of Sales. **Wattage:** 1,450. **Ad Rates:** Noncommercial. **URL:** http://rivercountrykcjc.com.

1615 ■ KMTC-FM - 91.1
305 Lake Front Dr.
Russellville, AR 72811
Phone: (479)968-7965
Email: rcc@rccenter.org
Format: Contemporary Christian. **Networks:** USA Radio. **Owner:** Russellville Educational Broadcast Foundation, at above address. **Founded:** 1987. **Operating Hours:** Continuous. **Key Personnel:** Melissa Krueger, Station Mgr., kmtc@rccenter.org. **Wattage:** 360. **Ad Rates:** $6-8 for 30 seconds; $8-10 for 60 seconds. **URL:** http://www.rccenter.org.

Circulation: ★ = AAM; △ or • = BPA; ♦ = CAC; ❑ = VAC; ⊕ = PO Statement; ‡ = Publisher's Report; Boldface figures = sworn; Light figures = estimated.

1616 ■ KWKK-FM - 100.9
PO Box 10310
Russellville, AR 72812
Phone: (479)890-4796
Format: Adult Contemporary. **Ad Rates:** Advertising accepted; rates available upon request.

1617 ■ KXRJ-FM - 91.9
Crabaugh 106
Russellville, AR 72801-2222
Phone: (479)964-0806
Fax: (479)498-6024
Email: kxrj.news@atu.edu
Format: Educational; Jazz; News. **Owner:** Arkansas Tech University, at above address. **Founded:** 1985. **Operating Hours**: Sunrise-sunset. **Key Personnel:** George Cotton, Chief Engineer, gcotton@atu.edu. **Wattage**: 100. **Ad Rates:** Noncommercial. **URL:** http://www.atu.edu.

1618 ■ KYXK-FM - 92.7
805 Wood Duck Ln.
Russellville, AR 72801
Phone: (501)353-2927
Fax: (501)353-2928
Format: Country; Eclectic; Religious; Soft Rock. **Networks:** ABC. **Owner:** Two Rivers Broadcasting Inc., PO Box 129, Gurdon, AR 71743, Ph: (501)353-2584. **Founded:** 1984. **Formerly**: KGAP. **Operating Hours**: 24 hours. **Wattage**: 3,000. **Ad Rates:** $3-5 per unit.

SALEM

NC AR. Fulton Co. 30 mi. NW of Ash Flat.

1619 ■ The News
Delta Publishing Co.
PO Box 248
Salem, AR 72576
Phone: (870)895-3207
Fax: (870)895-4277
Free: 800-995-3209
Publication E-mail: news@areawidenews.com
Community newspaper. **Freq:** Weekly (Thurs.). **Cols./Page:** 6. **Col. Width:** 12 picas. **Col. Depth:** 21 inches. **Key Personnel:** Janie Flynn, Publisher; Erma Harris, Managing Editor; Debra Perryman, Manager, Circulation. **USPS:** 477-627. **Subscription Rates:** $17.50 Individuals print and online, 6 months; $24 Out of area online, 6 months. **URL:** http://www.areawidenews.com. **Formerly**: Salem News; Salem Headlight. **Ad Rates:** BW $756; SAU $7; PCI $5. **Remarks:** Advertising accepted; rates available upon request. **Circ:** (Not Reported).

1620 ■ The South Missourian News
Areawide Media Inc.
PO Box 248
Salem, AR 72576
Phone: (870)895-3207
Fax: (870)895-4277
Free: 800-995-3209
Publisher's E-mail: news@areawidenews.com
Rural county newspaper. **Freq:** Weekly (Thurs.). **Print Method:** Offset. Accepts mats. **Cols./Page:** 6. **Col. Width:** 2 inches. **Col. Depth:** 21 inches. **Key Personnel:** Debra Perryman, Manager, Circulation; Dennis Moss, Manager, Production; Janie Flynn, Publisher; Tammy Curtis, Managing Editor. **URL:** http://www.areawidenews.com. **Formed by the merger of**: Thayer News; South Missourian Democrat. **Ad Rates:** BW $630; SAU $7; PCI $5. **Remarks:** Accepts advertising. **Circ:** (Not Reported).

1621 ■ Villager Journal
Villager Journal
PO Box 248
Salem, AR 72576
Phone: (870)895-3207
Fax: (870)895-4277
Free: 800-995-3209
Publisher's E-mail: news@areawidenews.com
Local newspaper. **Freq:** Weekly. **Print Method:** Offset. **Trim Size:** 11 5/16 x 17 7/16. **Cols./Page:** 5. **Col. Width:** 2 1/16 inches. **Col. Depth:** 16 inches. **Key Personnel:** Janie Flynn, Publisher; Debra Perryman, Manager, Circulation; Tammy Curtis, Managing Editor. **ISSN:** 0899--7780 (print). **Subscription Rates:** $25 Individuals online; $33 Individuals; $40 Out of area; $17.50 Individuals six months. **URL:** http://www.areawidenews.com. **Remarks:** Accepts advertising. **Circ:** (Not Reported).

1622 ■ KSAR-FM - 92.3
Hillside Plz., Hwy. 62
Salem, AR 72576
Phone: (870)895-2665
Fax: (870)856-4408
Format: Country; News. **Networks:** ABC. **Owner:** Bragg Broadcasting Corp., at above address. **Operating Hours**: Continuous. **ADI**: Springfield, MO. **Key Personnel:** James Bragg, Gen. Mgr. **Wattage**: 50,000. **Ad Rates:** $6.50-8 for 30 seconds; $13-16 for 60 seconds. **URL:** http://www.myhometownradiostations.com.

SEARCY

NEC AR. White Co. 50 mi. NE of Little Rock. Harding University. Manufactures refrigeration and aircraft components, printer's and industrial rollers, hydraulic valves, washing machines, leather goods. Food and egg processing. Pine, oak timber. Cattle, livestock.

1623 ■ The Daily Citizen
Paxton Media Group
3000 E Race Ave.
Searcy, AR 72143
Phone: (501)268-8621
Fax: (501)268-6277
Free: 800-400-3142
Publication E-mail: editor@thedailycitizen.com
General newspaper. **Founded:** 1854. **Freq:** Daily (morn.) except Monday and Saturday. **Print Method:** Offset. **Cols./Page:** 6. **Col. Width:** 25 nonpareils. **Col. Depth:** 258 agate lines. **Key Personnel:** Mike Murphy, Publisher; Warren Watkins, Managing Editor; Wendy Jones, Editor. **Subscription Rates:** $136 Individuals home delivery; $72 Individuals home delivery; for 6 months; $39 Individuals home delivery; for 3 months; $12 Individuals home delivery; monthly; $42.25 Out of area 3 months; $80 Out of area 6 months; $156 Out of area; $6 Individuals 1 month online subscription; $18 Individuals 3 months online subscription; $32.50 Individuals 6 months online subscription; $65 Individuals 1 year online subscription. **URL:** http://www.thedailycitizen.com. **Formerly**: The Searcy Citizen. **Ad Rates:** GLR $.65; BW $1,174; 4C $1,444; SAU $9.10; PCI $9.52. **Circ:** ‡7251, Sun. ‡7833.

1624 ■ KAWW-FM - 100.7
111 N Spring
Searcy, AR 72143
Phone: (501)268-7123
Fax: (501)279-2900
Format: Adult Contemporary; Country. **Networks:** Arkansas Radio. **Founded:** 1972. **Operating Hours**: Continuous. **Wattage**: 50,000. **Ad Rates:** $8 for 30 seconds; $12 for 60 seconds.

1625 ■ KOKR-FM - 96.7
401 S Spring St.
Searcy, AR 72143
Phone: (501)268-9700
Format: Country. **Owner:** Sudbury Broadcasting Group, 125 S 2nd St., Blytheville, AR 72315, Ph: (870)762-2093, Free: 800-737-0096. **Key Personnel:** Kevin Pearce, Contact, Gen. Mgr; Rhonda Pounders, Contact. **URL:** http://www.rivercountry967.com.

1626 ■ KVHU-FM - 95.3
915 E Market
Searcy, AR 72149
Email: druginfo@harding.edu
Format: Eclectic. **Operating Hours**: Continuous. **URL:** http://www.harding.edu/academics/colleges-departments/arts-humanities/communication/streaming.

1627 ■ White County Cable TV
1927 W Beebe Capps Exp.
Searcy, AR 72143
Phone: (501)903-0508
Cities Served: 61 channels. **URL:** http://www.whitecountycabletv.com/.

SHERIDAN

1628 ■ Sheridan Headlight
Sheridan Headlights
PO Box 539
Sheridan, AR 72150
Phone: (870)942-2142
Fax: (870)942-8823
Publisher's E-mail: info@thesheridanheadlight.com
Community newspaper. **Freq:** Weekly. **Ad Rates:** BW $490.20; 4C $565.20; SAU $5.20; PCI $4.26. **Remarks:** Accepts advertising. **Circ:** ‡4050.

1629 ■ KANX-FM - 91.1
PO Box 3206
Tupelo, MS 38803
Phone: (662)844-8888
Format: Contemporary Christian. **Owner:** American Family Association, at above address. **URL:** http://www.afr.net.

SHERWOOD

NE AR. Pulaski Co. 5 mi NE of Little Rock.

1630 ■ KMTL-AM - 760
301 Brookswood Rd., Ste. 208
Sherwood, AR 72120
Phone: (479)754-3399
Format: Gospel. **Founded:** 1983. **Operating Hours**: Sunrise-sunset. **Wattage**: 10,000 Day. **URL:** http://www.kmtl760am.com.

SILOAM SPRINGS

NW AR. Benton Co. 60 mi. N. of Fort Smith. John Brown University. Manufactures gates, rubber, telephone cables, cutting tools, motors, plastic pipes. Diversified farming. Fruit, poultry, livestock.

1631 ■ KLRC-FM - 90.9
110 N Broadway
Siloam Springs, AR 72761
Phone: (479)238-8600
Fax: (479)238-8601
Email: klrc@klrc.com
Format: Contemporary Christian. **Owner:** John Brown University, 2000 W University St., Siloam Springs, AR 72761, Ph: (479)524-9500. **Founded:** 1984. **Operating Hours**: Continuous. **Key Personnel:** Mark Michaels, Prog. Dir.; Jeremy Louis, Asst. Dir; Jane Clayberg, Contact. **Wattage**: 100,000 ERP. **Ad Rates:** Noncommercial. **URL:** http://www.klrc.com.

SPRINGDALE

NW AR. Washington Co. 10 mi. N. of Fayetteville. Manufactures paper bags, nails, wood office furniture, forging tools, aluminum extrusions. Poultry hatcheries; processing plants; vegetable canning, feed mills. Agriculture; grapes.

1632 ■ KSEC-FM - 95.7
2323-D S Old Missouri Rd.
Springdale, AR 72764
Phone: (479)756-8686
Fax: (479)756-8687
Email: info@ezspanishmedia.com
Format: Hispanic. **Operating Hours**: Continuous. **Wattage**: 6,000. **URL:** http://www.ezspanishmedia.com.

1633 ■ KUOA-AM - 1290
2250 W Sunset, Ste. 3
Springdale, AR 72762
Phone: (479)303-2034
Fax: (479)303-2037
Free: 866-265-4005
Format: Talk; Sports. **Networks:** CNN Radio; Jones Satellite. **Founded:** 1923. **Operating Hours**: Continuous. **ADI**: Fort Smith, AR. **Wattage**: 5,000. **Ad Rates:** $7-9 for 15 seconds; $9-11 for 30 seconds; $12-14 for 60 seconds. **URL:** http://www.hogsportsradio.com.

STATE UNIVERSITY

1634 ■ Arkansas Review: A Journal of Delta Studies
Arkansas Review
Arkansas State University
Dept. of English & Philosophy
State University, AR 72467
Phone: (870)972-3043
Fax: (870)972-3045
Regional studies review. **Freq:** 3/year spring, summer, winter. **Print Method:** Offset. **Trim Size:** 8 1/2 x 11. **Cols./Page:** 2. **Col. Width:** 3 INS. **Col. Depth:** 9 INS. **Key Personnel:** Janelle Collins, Editor. **ISSN:** 0022--8745 (print). **Subscription Rates:** $20 U.S.; $7.50

Single issue; C$25 Canada; $26 Elsewhere. **URL:** http://altweb.astate.edu/arkreview. **Formerly:** Kansas Quarterly; Kansas Quarterly/Arkansas Review. **Mailing address:** PO Box 1890, State University, AR 72467. **Remarks:** Accepts advertising. **Circ:** (Not Reported).

1635 ■ Explorations in Renaissance Culture
Arkansas State University Department of English and Philosophy
c/o Frances Malpezzi, Ed.
Department of English & Philosophy
Arkansas State University
State University, AR 72467
Phone: (870)972-2545
Publication E-mail: fmalpezz@astate.edu
Scholarly journal covering Renaissance and Early Modern European studies. **Freq:** Biennial. **Print Method:** Offset. **Trim Size:** 6 x 9. **Cols./Page:** 1. **Col. Width:** 4 1/4 inches. **Col. Depth:** 7 1/4 inches. **Key Personnel:** Pat Garcia, Contact; Frances Malpezzi, Editor. **Subscription Rates:** $20 Institutions; $20 Individuals; $10 Students; $10 back issue plus S&H on large and international orders. **URL:** http://www.astate.edu/college/humanities-and-social-sciences/departments/english-and-philosophy/journals/. **Mailing address:** PO Box 1890, State University, AR 72467. **Remarks:** Advertising not accepted. **Circ:** Combined 314.

1636 ■ The Herald of Arkansas State University
Arkansas State University
PO Box 600
State University, AR 72467
Phone: (870)972-2100
Fax: (870)972-3545
Publication E-mail: herald@astate.edu
Collegiate newspaper. **Freq:** Sat. and Sun. **Print Method:** Offset. **Key Personnel:** Samuel G. Smith, Editor-in-Chief; Raven Hearton, Editor. **URL:** http://www.asuherald.com. **Mailing address:** PO Box 600, State University, AR 72467. **Ad Rates:** GLR $.218; BW $567; PCI $7.25. **Remarks:** Advertising accepted; rates available upon request. **Circ:** ‡8000.

1637 ■ KASU-FM - 91.9
PO Box 2160
State University, AR 72467
Phone: (870)972-2200
Fax: (870)972-2997
Format: Blues; Folk; Bluegrass; New Age. **Networks:** National Public Radio (NPR); AP; Public Radio International (PRI). **Owner:** Arkansas State University, State University, AR 72467, Ph: (870)972-2100, Fax: (870)972-3545. **Founded:** 1957. **Operating Hours:** Continuous; 30% network, 70% local. **Key Personnel:** Marty Scarbrough, Dir. of Programs; Mark Smith, Dir. of Dev. **Wattage:** 100,000. **Ad Rates:** Noncommercial. **URL:** http://www.kasu.org.

STUTTGART

E. AR. Arkansas Co. 50 mi. SE of Little Rock. Rice mills. Soybean plant. Hardwood lumber mill. Oak, Gum timber. Agriculture; rice, soybeans, and oats.

1638 ■ The Stuttgart Daily Leader
GateHouse Media Inc.
111 W 6th St.
Stuttgart, AR 72160
Phone: (870)673-8533
Fax: (870)673-3671
General newspaper. **Freq:** Daily. **Print Method:** Offset. **Cols./Page:** 6. **Col. Width:** 25 nonpareils. **Col. Depth:** 301 agate lines. **Key Personnel:** Willene Boehn, Manager, Circulation; Stephanie Fischer, Managing Editor. **USPS:** 143-170. **URL:** http://www.stuttgartdailyleader.com. **Remarks:** Accepts classified advertising. **Circ:** Paid 3600, Non-paid 6000.

1639 ■ KWAK-AM
PO Box 907
Stuttgart, AR 72160-0907
Phone: (870)673-1595
Fax: (870)673-8445
Format: News; Contemporary Country. **Networks:** ABC. **Founded:** May 01, 1948. **Key Personnel:** Jay Toddy, Contact. **Wattage:** 960. **Ad Rates:** $12 for 30 seconds; $17 for 60 seconds.

TEXARKANA

SW AR. Miller Co. 157 mi. S. of Little Rock. Lumber. Cotton seed oil. Cotton ginning and Compressing. Creosoted Poles. Clay, sulphur. Sheet metal products, ammunition, crossarms, medicine, caskets, lead manufactured. Timber, Agriculture. Cattle.

1640 ■ KFYX-FM - 107.1
3161 Channel Dr., Ste. 2
Texarkana, AR 71854
Phone: (907)586-3630
Format: Contemporary Hit Radio (CHR). **Owner:** Ark-La-Tex, LLC, at above address. **Founded:** 1961. **Formerly:** KTWN; KQIX. **Operating Hours:** Continuous. **ADI:** Shreveport, LA-Texarkana, TX. **Wattage:** 6,000. **Ad Rates:** $16-28 for 30 seconds; $22-40 for 60 seconds.

1641 ■ KKLT-FM - 89.3
PO Box 779002
Rocklin, CA 95677-9972
Fax: (916)251-1901
Free: 800-525-5683
Format: Contemporary Christian. **Owner:** Educational Media Foundation, PO Box 2098, Omaha, NE 68103-2098, Free: 800-434-8400. **Key Personnel:** Mike Novak, President, CEO; Alan Mason, COO. **Wattage:** 001 H;23,000 V. **URL:** http://www.klove.com.

1642 ■ KKYR-FM - 102.5
2324 Arkansas Blvd.
Texarkana, AR 71854
Phone: (870)772-3771
Format: Country. **Owner:** Townsquare Media Inc., 240 Greenwich Ave., Greenwich, CT 06830-6507, Ph: (203)861-0900. **Founded:** 1989. **Formerly:** KOSY-FM. **Operating Hours:** Continuous; 100% local. **Key Personnel:** Mario Garcia, Dir. of Programs, mariogarcia@gapbroadcasting.com; Jackie Zimmerman, Contact, jackiezimmerman@gapbroadcasting.com. **Wattage:** 100,000. **Ad Rates:** Advertising accepted; rates available upon request. **URL:** http://www.kkyr.com.

1643 ■ KLLI-FM - 95.9
2324 Arkansas Blvd.
Texarkana, AR 71854
Fax: (870)772-0364
Email: chip@kpanradio.com
Format: Country. **Owner:** John T. Mitchell, at above address. **Founded:** 1985. **Operating Hours:** Continuous. **ADI:** Shreveport, LA-Texarkana, TX. **Key Personnel:** Bob Gipson, Gen. Mgr.; Rob Ryan, Dir. of Programs; Chuck Zach, News Dir.; Jay James, Operations Mgr.; Phil O'Brian, Dir. of Production. **Wattage:** 11,500 ERP. **Ad Rates:** $18 for 30 seconds; $23 for 60 seconds. **URL:** http://power959.com.

1644 ■ KMJI-FM - 93.3
2324 Arkansas Blvd.
Texarkana, AR 71854
Phone: (870)772-3771
Format: Adult Contemporary. **ADI:** Shreveport, LA-Texarkana, TX. **Key Personnel:** Brian Purdy, Gen. Mgr. **Wattage:** 7,400. **URL:** http://mix933fm.com/help.

1645 ■ KOSY-AM - 790
2324 Arkansas Blvd.
Texarkana, AR 71854
Phone: (870)772-2753
Format: Oldies; Contemporary Country. **Owner:** GAP Broadcasting, LLC, 12900 Preston Rd., Ste. 525, Dallas, TX 75230, Ph: (214)295-3530, Fax: (972)386-4445; Broadcasters Unlimited Inc., Tyler, TX, Ph: (214)581-0606. **Founded:** 1989. **Operating Hours:** Continuous; 100% local. **ADI:** Shreveport, LA-Texarkana, TX. **Key Personnel:** Mitzi Dowd, Contact, mitzidowd@townsquaremedia.com; Melvin C. Jones, Contact. **Wattage:** 1,000. **Ad Rates:** Noncommercial. **URL:** http://www.kosy790am.com.

1646 ■ KPWW-FM - 95.9
2324 Arkansas Blvd.
Texarkana, AR 71854
Phone: (870)772-3771
Format: Contemporary Hit Radio (CHR). **Owner:** Townsquare Media Inc., 240 Greenwich Ave., Greenwich, CT 06830-6507, Ph: (203)861-0900. **Wattage:** 11,500. **Ad Rates:** Noncommercial. **URL:** http://www.power959.com.

1647 ■ KXAR-FM - 101.7
615-618 Olive St.
Texarkana, AR 71854
Phone: (903)793-4671
Fax: (501)777-3535
Format: Country. **Networks:** American Urban Radio. **Owner:** KdB, Inc., 2806 Country Club Ln., Hope, AR 71801, Ph: (870)722-2299, Fax: (870)722-5927. **Founded:** 1988. **Operating Hours:** Continuous; 5% network, 95% local. **Key Personnel:** Bill Hoglund, President; Scott Neal, Sales Mgr., Operations Mgr.; Patti Bryant, Office Mgr.; Jodi Neal, Sales Mgr. **Wattage:** 50,000 ERP. **Ad Rates:** Advertising accepted; rates available upon request. **URL:** http://www.texarkanaradio.com.

1648 ■ KYGL-FM - 106.3
2324 Arkansas Blvd.
Texarkana, AR 71854
Phone: (870)772-3771
Format: Classic Rock. **Owner:** Townsquare Media Inc., 240 Greenwich Ave., Greenwich, CT 06830-6507, Ph: (203)861-0900. **ADI:** Shreveport, LA-Texarkana, TX. **Wattage:** 50,000. **Ad Rates:** Noncommercial. **URL:** http://kygl.com.

TRUMANN

NE AR. Poinsett Co. 16 mi. S. of Jonesboro. Lumber. Cotton gin. Manufacturing plant. Warehouse. Oak, gum timber. Agriculture. Cotton, corn, hay.

1649 ■ Ritter Communications
106 E Main
106 E Main St.
Trumann, AR 72472
Free: 888-336-4466
Email: customerservice@rittercommunications.com
Founded: Sept. 06, 1906. **Cities Served:** 317 community access channels. **URL:** http://rittercommunications.com.

VAN BUREN

NW AR. Crawford Co. On Arkansas River, 5 mi. NE of Fort Smith. Steel and concrete plants. Furniture factories. Canneries. Natural gas wells. River navigation port. Timber; oak, gum, hickory. Agriculture. Spinach, peaches, strawberries.

1650 ■ Press Argus-Courier
Stephens Media L.L.C.
100 N 11th St.
Van Buren, AR 72956
Phone: (479)474-5215
Publication E-mail: jmcclure@pressargus.com
Local newspaper. **Freq:** Semiweekly Sunday & Thursday. **Print Method:** Offset. **Cols./Page:** 6. **Col. Width:** 25 nonpareils. **Col. Depth:** 294 agate lines. **Key Personnel:** Kenneth Fry, Editor; Kim Hattaway, Office Manager; Judy Weese, Manager, Advertising. **Subscription Rates:** $49 Individuals print & online. **URL:** http://www.pressargus.com. **Mailing address:** PO Box 369, Van Buren, AR 72956. **Remarks:** Advertising accepted; rates available upon request. **Circ:** ‡9400.

WALDRON

WC AR. Scott Co. 40 mi. NW of Montgomery. Scott Co. (WC). 40 m NW of Montgomery.

1651 ■ Waldron News
Waldron News
200 Main St.
Waldron, AR 72958
Phone: (479)637-4161
Fax: (479)637-4162
Community newspaper. **Freq:** Weekly (Wed.). **USPS:** 049-045. **Subscription Rates:** $22 Individuals in County. **Mailing address:** PO Box 745, Waldron, AR 72958. **Ad Rates:** BW $315; SAU $5.20; PCI $4.15. **Remarks:** Accepts advertising. **Circ:** 2250.

WALNUT RIDGE

NE AR. Lawrence Co. 20 mi W. of Jonesboro. Southern Baptist College. Vacuum cleaner, auto parts, power tools, striking tool, shoe, dress and shoe-last factories. Timber. Agriculture. Rice, wheat, milo, soybeans.

Circulation: ★ = AAM; △ or • = BPA; ♦ = CAC; ❑ = VAC; ⊕ = PO Statement; ‡ = Publisher's Report; Boldface figures = sworn; Light figures = estimated.

1652 ■ Herpetological Review
Society for the Study of Amphibians and Reptiles
c/o Ann Paterson, Treasurer
60 W Fulbright Ave.
Walnut Ridge, AR 72476
Journal comprising of articles and notes concerning the study of amphibians and reptiles, book reviews, commentaries, regional and international herpetological society news, and letters from readers directed to the field of herpetology. **Freq:** Quarterly. **URL:** http://ssarherps.org/publications/journals/herpetological-review. **Mailing address:** Po Box 3692, Walnut Ridge, AR 72476. **Ad Rates:** 4C $675. **Remarks:** Accepts advertising. **Circ:** (Not Reported).

1653 ■ The Times Dispatch
The Times Dispatch
225 W Main St.
Walnut Ridge, AR 72476
Phone: (870)886-2464
Fax: (870)886-9369
Publication E-mail: help@thetd.com
Newspaper with a democratic orientation. **Freq:** Weekly (Wed.). **Print Method:** Offset. **Cols./Page:** 6. **Col. Width:** 26 nonpareils. **Col. Depth:** 294 agate lines. **Key Personnel:** John A. Bland, Publisher; Janice Hibbard, Manager, Advertising; Gretchen Hunt, Editor. **Subscription Rates:** $36 Individuals print + online (elsewhere in Arkansas); $28 Out of state print + online; $22 Individuals online full edition; $30 By mail print & online (mailed in Lawrence, Greene, Jackson, Craighead, Sharp, Independence, and Randolph counties). **URL:** http://www.thetd.com. **Mailing address:** PO Box 389, Walnut Ridge, AR 72476. **Remarks:** Advertising accepted; rates available upon request. **Circ:** Paid ‡6000.

WARREN

1654 ■ KHBM-AM - 1430
1255 N Myrtle St.
Warren, AR 71671
Phone: (870)226-2653
Format: Big Band/Nostalgia. **Owner:** Pines Broadcasting, Inc., 279 Midway Rte, Monticello, AR 71655, Ph: (870)367-6854. **Founded:** 1955. **Wattage:** 1,000. **Ad Rates:** Advertising accepted; rates available upon request.

1655 ■ KWRF-AM - 860
1255 N Myrtle
Warren, AR 71671
Phone: (870)226-2653
Fax: (870)226-3039
Email: squirt@ipa.net
Format: Oldies. **Networks:** Arkansas Radio. **Owner:** Pines Broadcasting, Inc., 279 Midway Rte, Monticello, AR 71655, Ph: (870)367-6854. **Founded:** 1953. **Operating Hours:** Continuous. **Key Personnel:** Jimmy Sledge, Operator, Owner. **Wattage:** 250. **Ad Rates:** $7.25 for 30 seconds; $9 for 60 seconds.

1656 ■ KWRF-FM - 105.5
1255 N Myrtle
Warren, AR 71671
Phone: (870)226-2653
Fax: (870)226-3039
Email: kwrf@ipa.net
Format: Country. **Networks:** Arkansas Radio; Satellite Music Network. **Owner:** Pines Broadcasting, Inc., 279 Midway Rte, Monticello, AR 71655, Ph: (870)367-6854. **Founded:** 1953. **Operating Hours:** Continuous. **Key Personnel:** Jimmy Sledge, Gen. Mgr. **Wattage:** 3,000. **Ad Rates:** $7.25 for 30 seconds; $9 for 60 seconds.

WEINER

1657 ■ Ritter Communications
123 W 2nd St.
123 W 2nd St.
Weiner, AR 72479
Free: 888-336-4466
Cities Served: 311 community access channels. **URL:** http://www.getritter.info.

WEST HELENA

1658 ■ KCLT-FM - 104.9
PO Box 2870
West Helena, AR 72390
Phone: (870)572-9506
Fax: (870)572-1845
Email: force2@sbcglobal.net
Format: Urban Contemporary. **Networks:** ABC. **Founded:** 1984. **Operating Hours:** Continuous. **Wattage:** 3,000 ERP.

WEST MEMPHIS

E. AR. Crittenden Co. Two bridges to Memphis, TN. Manufactures flakeboard, box, bleach, gypsum, and concrete slab. Oil refinery and terminal. Cotton seed oil compressing. Agricultural equipment. Agriculture. Cotton, soybeans, rice.

1659 ■ KKLV-FM - 94.7
102 N 5th St.
West Memphis, AR 72301
Format: Religious. **Owner:** Pollack Broadcasting Co., 1303 Southwest Dr., Kennett, MO 63857. **Formerly:** KSUD-FM. **Operating Hours:** Continuous. **ADI:** Memphis, TN. **Key Personnel:** Frank Hammond, Contact. **Wattage:** 6,000. **URL:** http://www.klove.com/contact/.

WYNNE

E. AR. Cross Co. 45 mi. W. of Memphis, TN. Manufactures copper tubing and air conditioning components, men's slacks, shoes, horse trailers, building equipment. Cotton ginning; farm machinery, rice drier. Fruit shipped. Agriculture. Peaches, cotton, cucumbers, rice, soybeans.

1660 ■ East Arkansas News Leader
Wynne Progress Inc.
702 N Falls Blvd.
Wynne, AR 72396
Phone: (870)238-2375
Free Newspaper. **Founded:** 1971. **Freq:** Weekly (Wed.). **Print Method:** Offset. **Cols./Page:** 6. **Col. Width:** 26 nonpareils. **Col. Depth:** 294 agate lines. **URL:** http://www.mediatico.com/en/goto.asp?url=5093. **Formerly:** Shoppers News. **Mailing address:** PO Box 308, Wynne, AR 72396. **Ad Rates:** GLR $9; BW $1,260; 4C $1,660; PCI $10. **Circ:** 21340.

KNEA-AM - See Jonesboro, AR

1661 ■ KPOC-AM - 1420
PO Box 789
Wynne, AR 72396
Phone: (870)238-8141
Email: kpoc-krlw@centurytel.net
Format: Adult Contemporary. **Networks:** ABC; ESPN Radio. **Owner:** Combined Media Group Inc., at above address. **Founded:** 1950. **Operating Hours:** network, 90% local fulltime. **ADI:** Jonesboro, AR. **Wattage:** 1,000. **Ad Rates:** $24-28 per unit.

1662 ■ KRLW-AM - 1320
PO Box 789
Wynne, AR 72396
Phone: (501)238-8141
Fax: (501)886-5719
Email: kpoc-krlw@centurytel.net
Format: Oldies. **Networks:** ABC; Arkansas Radio. **Owner:** Combined Media Group Inc., at above address. **Founded:** 1951. **Operating Hours:** Continuous. **ADI:** Jonesboro, AR. **Wattage:** 1,000. **Ad Rates:** $24 for 30 seconds; $28 for 60 seconds. Combined advertising rates available with KRLW-FM.

1663 ■ KWHF-FM - 95.9
Hwy. 64 W
Wynne, AR 72396
Phone: (870)238-8141
Fax: (870)932-3814
Format: Country. **ADI:** Jonesboro, AR. **Key Personnel:** Larry James, Gen. Mgr. **Wattage:** 34,000. **Ad Rates:** Noncommercial. **Mailing address:** PO Box 789, Wynne, AR 72396.

1664 ■ KWYN-AM - 1400
Hwy. 64 W
Wynne, AR 72396
Phone: (870)238-8141
Fax: (870)238-5997
Format: Country; Talk. **Owner:** East Arkansas Broadcasters, Inc., PO Box 789, Wynne, AR 72396. **Founded:** 1956. **Key Personnel:** Steve Chapman, Contact; Bobby Caldwell, Contact; Steve Chapman, Contact; Lindell Staggs, Contact. **Wattage:** 1,000 Daytime;1,000 Ni. **Ad Rates:** $16 for 30 seconds; $20 for 60 seconds. **URL:** http://kwyn.com/.

1665 ■ KWYN-FM - 92.5
PO Box 789
Wynne, AR 72396
Phone: (870)238-8141
Fax: (870)238-5997
Format: Country. **Owner:** East Arkansas Broadcasters, Inc., at above address. **Founded:** 1969. **Operating Hours:** Continuous. **ADI:** Memphis, TN. **Key Personnel:** Bobby Caldwell, Contact; Steve Chapman, Contact; Lindell Staggs, Contact. **Wattage:** 35,000. **Ad Rates:** $16 for 30 seconds; $20 for 60 seconds. **URL:** http://www.kwyn.com/common/more.php?m=33&r=11.

ACTON

1666 ■ Acton/Agua Dulce News
Joyce Media Inc.
3413 Soledad Cyn Rd.
Acton, CA 93510-0057
Phone: (661)269-1169
Fax: (661)269-2139
Publication E-mail: aadnews@joycemediainc.com
Community newspaper. **Freq:** Weekly (Mon.). **Print Method:** Web Offset. **Trim Size:** 11 x 17. **Subscription Rates:** $33 By mail 1 year - electronic only. **URL:** http://joycemediainc.com/papers/aadmall.html. **Formerly:** Acton News. **Mailing address:** PO Box 57, Acton, CA 93510-0057. **Remarks:** Accepts advertising. **Circ:** Controlled 4700.

AGOURA HILLS

Los Angeles Co. Los Angeles Co.

1667 ■ The Acorn
J. Bee NP Publishing Ltd.
30423 Canwood St., Ste. 108
Agoura Hills, CA 91301
Publication E-mail: moreinfo@theacorn.com
Local newspaper. **Founded:** 1983. **Freq:** Weekly (Wed.). **Print Method:** Offset. **Cols./Page:** 6. **Col. Width:** 18 nonpareils. **Col. Depth:** 224 agate lines. **Key Personnel:** John Loesing, Editor, phone: (818)706-0266; Jim Rule, Publisher. **Alt. Formats:** PDF. **URL:** http://www.theacorn.com/Current/Front_page/. **Ad Rates:** GLR $1.97; BW $1,354.56; PCI $14.11. **Remarks:** Accepts advertising. **Circ:** Free ■ **30815**.

1668 ■ Biker
Paisano Publications L.L.C.
28210 Dorothy Dr.
Agoura Hills, CA 91301
Free: 800-323-3484
Publisher's E-mail: bulkmagazines@paisanopub.com
Motorcycle lifestyle magazine. **Founded:** Mar. 12, 1987. **Freq:** 9/yr. **Print Method:** Offset. **Trim Size:** 8 x 10 7/8. **Cols./Page:** 3. **Col. Width:** 2 1/4 inches. **Col. Depth:** 10 inches. **ISSN:** 1058-7926 (print). **Subscription Rates:** $19.95 Individuals. **URL:** http://www.easyriders.com. **Formerly:** Biker Lifestyle. **Ad Rates:** BW $2,525; 4C $2,910; PCI $64. **Remarks:** Accepts advertising. **Circ:** (Not Reported).

1669 ■ Easyriders: World's Largest Selling Motorcycle Magazine
Paisano Publications L.L.C.
28210 Dorothy Dr.
Agoura Hills, CA 91301
Free: 800-323-3484
Publisher's E-mail: bulkmagazines@paisanopub.com
Motorcycle magazine. **Freq:** Monthly. **Print Method:** Web Offset. **Trim Size:** 7 3/4 x 10 1/2. **Cols./Page:** 3. **Col. Depth:** 133 agate lines. **Key Personnel:** Dave Nichols, Editor. **ISSN:** 0046--0990 (print). **Subscription Rates:** $19.99 Individuals. **URL:** http://www.paisanopub.com/index.cfm?id=www.easyriders.com; http://www.paisanopub.com/easyriders/index-main.php. **Remarks:** Advertising accepted; rates available upon request. **Circ:** Paid ★**109390**.

1670 ■ In the Wind: If It's out There, It's in Here
Paisano Publications L.L.C.
28210 Dorothy Dr.
Agoura Hills, CA 91301
Free: 800-323-3484
Publisher's E-mail: bulkmagazines@paisanopub.com
Motorcycle lifestyle magazine. **Freq:** Quarterly. **Print Method:** Offset. **Trim Size:** 8 x 10 7/8. **Cols./Page:** 3. **Col. Depth:** 10 inches. **ISSN:** 1059--759X (print). **Subscription Rates:** $29.99 Individuals; $49.99 Two years. **URL:** http://www.easyriders.com. **Remarks:** Accepts advertising. **Circ:** (Not Reported).

1671 ■ Mainsheet Magazine
Coronado 15 National Association
30025 Torrepines Pl.
Agoura Hills, CA 91301-4070
Phone: (916)832-8015
Publisher's E-mail: info@coronado15.org
Magazine featuring information about boats, stories, news, programs, activities, events and accomplishments of Coronado 15 National Association and its members. **Freq:** Quarterly. **Subscription Rates:** Included in membership. **URL:** http://www.mainsheet.net. **Remarks:** Advertising not accepted. **Circ:** (Not Reported).

1672 ■ Moorpark Acorn
J. Bee NP Publishing Ltd.
30423 Canwood St., Ste. 108
Agoura Hills, CA 91301
Community newspaper. **Freq:** Weekly (Fri.). **Key Personnel:** Daniel Wolowicz, Editor; Jim Rule, Publisher; John Loesing, Managing Editor. **Subscription Rates:** Free. **URL:** http://www.mpacorn.com/current/front_page. **Remarks:** Advertising accepted; rates available upon request. **Circ:** Free ■ **11230**.

1673 ■ Savage
Paisano Publications L.L.C.
28210 Dorothy Dr.
Agoura Hills, CA 91301
Free: 800-323-3484
Publisher's E-mail: bulkmagazines@paisanopub.com
Consumer magazine covering body modification, including piercing, branding, tatooing, and related issues. **Freq:** Monthly. **Subscription Rates:** $19.99 Individuals. **URL:** http://www.paisanopub.com/savage. **Remarks:** Advertising accepted; rates available upon request. **Circ:** (Not Reported).

1674 ■ Simi Valley Acorn
J. Bee NP Publishing Ltd.
30423 Canwood St., Ste. 108
Agoura Hills, CA 91301
Community newspaper. **Freq:** Weekly (Fri.). **Key Personnel:** Darleen Principe, Editor; Jim Rule, Publisher; John Loesing, Managing Editor. **Subscription Rates:** Free. **URL:** http://www.simivalleyacorn.com/current/front_page. **Remarks:** Advertising accepted; rates available upon request. **Circ:** Free ■ **24162**.

1675 ■ Tattoo: The Magazine of Dermagraphics
Paisano Publications L.L.C.
28210 Dorothy Dr.
Agoura Hills, CA 91301
Free: 800-323-3484
Publisher's E-mail: bulkmagazines@paisanopub.com
Magazine for tattoo enthusiasts. **Freq:** Monthly. **Print Method:** Offset. **Trim Size:** 8 x 10 7/8. **Cols./Page:** 3. **Col. Width:** 2 1/4 inches. **Col. Depth:** 10 inches. **ISSN:** 1041--3146 (print). **Subscription Rates:** $29.99 Individuals; $9.99 Individuals digital (10 issues). **URL:** http://www.paisanopub.com/tattoo/. **Ad Rates:** BW $5,180; 4C $7,508; CNU $1,630; PCI $64. **Remarks:** Accepts advertising. **Circ:** (Not Reported).

1676 ■ Thousand Oaks Acorn
J. Bee NP Publishing Ltd.
30423 Canwood St., Ste. 108
Agoura Hills, CA 91301
Community newspaper. **Freq:** Weekly (Thurs.). **Key Personnel:** Kyle Jorrey, Editor, phone: (805)367-8232, fax: (805)367-8237; Jim Rule, Publisher; John Loesing, Managing Editor. **Subscription Rates:** Free. **URL:** http://www.toacorn.com/current/front_page. **Remarks:** Advertising accepted; rates available upon request. **Circ:** Free ■ **40212**.

1677 ■ V-Twin: Motorcycles
Paisano Publications L.L.C.
28210 Dorothy Dr.
Agoura Hills, CA 91301
Free: 800-323-3484
Publisher's E-mail: bulkmagazines@paisanopub.com
Consumer magazine covering new motorcycles, products, apparel and news for riders. **Freq:** Monthly. **Subscription Rates:** $19.99 Individuals print and online. **URL:** http://www.paisanopub.com/vtwin. **Remarks:** Advertising accepted; rates available upon request. **Circ:** (Not Reported).

ALAMEDA

W. CA. Alameda Co. An island in San Francisco Bay, 12 mi. E. of San Francisco. U.S. Navel Air Base. Recreation. Manufactures pumps, diesel engines, boxes. Military aircraft engine repair. Marine related products. High tech hardware and software products, biogenetics.

1678 ■ The Latham Letter
Latham Foundation
1320 Harbor Bay Pky., Ste. 200
Alameda, CA 94502
Phone: (510)521-0920
Fax: (510)521-9861
Freq: Quarterly. **Subscription Rates:** $15 U.S.; $20 Canada and Mexico; $27 Other countries. **Alt. Formats:** PDF. **URL:** http://www.latham.org/research-and-resources/latham-letter-articles. **Remarks:** Advertising not accepted. **Circ:** (Not Reported).

1679 ■ Overheard Cams
Alfa Romeo Association
PO Box 1458
Alameda, CA 94501
Freq: Monthly. **Subscription Rates:** included in membership dues. **URL:** http://www.alfaromeoassociation.org/Overheard. **Remarks:** Accepts advertising. **Circ:** 600.

Circulation: ★ = AAM; △ or • = BPA; ♦ = CAC; ❑ = VAC; ⊕ = PO Statement; ‡ = Publisher's Report; Boldface figures = sworn; Light figures = estimated.

1680 ■ Parents' Press: The Monthly Newspaper for Bay Area Parents
Parents' Press
1416 Park Ave.
Alameda, CA 94501
Phone: (510)747-1060
Fax: (510)747-1067
Publisher's E-mail: editor@parentspress.com
Local consumer magazine covering parenting. **Freq:** Monthly. **Key Personnel:** Debbi Murzyn, Art Director; Robert McKean, Publisher; Judith M. Gallman, Editor. **ISSN:** 0889-8863 (print). **Subscription Rates:** $15 By mail. **URL:** http://www.parentspress.com. **Ad Rates:** BW $2,860; 4C $3,360. **Remarks:** Accepts advertising. **Circ:** Combined 40000.

1681 ■ Alameda Municipal Power
2000 Grand St.
Alameda, CA 94501
Phone: (510)748-3900
Email: media@alamedamp.com
Founded: 1887. **Formerly**: Alameda Power & Telecom. **Cities Served:** 100 channels. **URL:** http://www.alamedamp.com.

KDFR-FM - See Des Moines, IA

1682 ■ KEDR-FM - 88.1
1350 S Loop Rd., Ste. 130
Alameda, CA 94502
Format: Gospel. **URL:** http://www.familyradio.org.

KPOR-FM - See Emporia, KS

1683 ■ KTXB-FM - 89.7
1350 S Loop Rd., Ste. 130
Alameda, CA 94502
Phone: (409)745-1737
Format: Religious; Gospel. **ADI**: Beaumont-Port Arthur, TX. **URL:** http://www.familyradio.org.

1684 ■ WCTF-AM - 1170
1350 S Loop Rd., Ste. 130
Alameda, CA 94502
Format: Religious. **Owner:** Family Stations Inc., 290 Hegenberger Rd., Oakland, CA 94621, Free: 800-543-1495. **Founded:** 1986. **Formerly**: WRTT-AM. **Operating Hours**: Sunrise-sunset; 98% network, 2% local. **Key Personnel:** DJ White, Station Mgr. **Wattage**: 1,000 KW. **URL:** http://www.familyradio.org.

1685 ■ WFBF-FM - 89.9
1350 S Loop Rd., Ste. 130
910 Union Rd.
Alameda, CA 94502
Phone: (712)246-5151
Free: 800-543-1495
Format: Contemporary Christian; Middle-of-the-Road (MOR). **Networks:** Family Stations Radio. **Owner:** Family Stations Inc., 290 Hegenberger Rd., Oakland, CA 94621, Free: 800-543-1495. **Founded:** 1989. **Operating Hours**: Continuous. **Key Personnel:** Mike Zeiman, Contact. **Wattage**: 16,000 KW. **Ad Rates:** Noncommercial. **URL:** http://www.familyradio.org.

WFRS-FM - See Smithtown, NY

ALBANY

NW CA. Alameda Co. N. of Oakland on San Francisco Bay. Residential.

1686 ■ Bulletin of the Seismological Society of America
Seismological Society of America
400 Evelyn Ave., Ste. 201
Albany, CA 94706-1375
Phone: (510)525-5474
Fax: (510)525-7204
Publisher's E-mail: info@seismosoc.org
Journal publishing research in seismology, earthquake engineering and related fields. **Freq:** Bimonthly February, April, June, August, October, and December. **ISSN:** 0037--1106 (print); **EISSN:** 1943--3573 (electronic). **Subscription Rates:** $555 Individuals online only; $620 U.S. print and online; $670 Other countries print and online; $710 Individuals India; print and online. **URL:** http://www.seismosoc.org/publications/bssa. **Remarks:** Advertising not accepted. **Circ:** 2800.

1687 ■ Seismological Research Letters
Seismological Society of America
400 Evelyn Ave., Ste. 201
Albany, CA 94706-1375
Phone: (510)525-5474
Fax: (510)525-7204
Publisher's E-mail: info@seismosoc.org
Scholarly journal covering seismology and earthquake engineering. **Freq:** Bimonthly. **Print Method:** Offset. **Trim Size:** 8 1/2 x 11. **Cols./Page:** 2. **Col. Width:** 3 2/5 inches. **Col. Depth:** 9 3/10 inches. **Key Personnel:** Zhigang Peng, Editor. **ISSN:** 0895--0695 (print). **Subscription Rates:** $170 U.S. print and online; $190 Individuals print and online (out of state); $225 Individuals print and online (shipping to India); $160 Individuals online; $165 Institutions; $185 Institutions, other countries. **URL:** http://srl.geoscienceworld.org; http://www.seismosoc.org/publications/srl. **Formerly**: Earthquake Notes. **Remarks:** Advertising not accepted. **Circ:** (Not Reported).

ALISO VIEJO

1688 ■ American Journal of Critical Care
American Association of Critical-Care Nurses
101 Columbia
Aliso Viejo, CA 92656-4109
Phone: (949)362-2000
Fax: (949)362-2020
Publisher's E-mail: info@aacn.org
Freq: Bimonthly. **Trim Size:** 8 1/8 x 10 7/8. **Key Personnel:** Peter E. Morris, MD, Board Member; Cindy L. Munro, Editor. **ISSN:** 1062--3264 (print); **EISSN:** 1937--710X (electronic). **Subscription Rates:** Included in membership; $59 Individuals 1 year; $98 Individuals 2 years; $599 Institutions 1 year, print and online (U.S.); $957 Institutions 2 years, print and online (U.S.); $434 Institutions 1 year, print only (U.S.); $694 Institutions 2 years, print only (U.S.); $414 Institutions 1 year, online only; $663 Institutions 2 years, online only. **URL:** http://ajcc.aacnjournals.org. **Ad Rates:** BW $7315; 4C $1840. **Remarks:** Accepts advertising. **Circ:** Combined 66500.

1689 ■ Critical Care Nurse
American Association of Critical-Care Nurses
101 Columbia
Aliso Viejo, CA 92656-4109
Phone: (949)362-2000
Fax: (949)362-2020
Publisher's E-mail: info@aacn.org
Nursing journal. **Freq:** Bimonthly. **Print Method:** Web offset. **Trim Size:** 8 1/8 x 10 7/8. **Cols./Page:** 3. **Col. Width:** 12.5 picas. **Col. Depth:** 140 agate lines. **Key Personnel:** Rebecka Wulf, Managing Editor; Thomas Ahrens, Board Member; Susan D. Bell, Board Member; LeRoy Hinton, Art Director; JoAnn Grif Alspach, Editor. **ISSN:** 0279-5442 (print); **EISSN:** 1940-8250 (electronic). **Subscription Rates:** $39 Individuals; $66 Other countries; $322 Institutions print only; $442 Institutions, other countries print only; $451 Institutions print and online; $577 Institutions, other countries print and online; Included in membership; $65 Two years; $110 Other countries 2 years; $720 Institutions print and online; $302 Institutions online only. **URL:** http://ccn.aacnjournals.org. **Ad Rates:** GLR $32; BW $4,985; 4C $6,530. **Remarks:** Accepts advertising. **Circ:** ‡96000, 100,000.

ALPINE

S. CA. San Diego Co. 30 mi. E. of San Diego. Established as a stage stop in 1760. Light industry. Small ranches.

1690 ■ Alpine Sun
Alpine Sun
2144 Alpine Blvd.
Alpine, CA 91901
Phone: (619)445-3288
Fax: (619)445-6776
Publisher's E-mail: editor@thealpinesun.com
Community newspaper. **Freq:** Weekly. **Print Method:** Offset. Uses mats. **Trim Size:** 10 x 13. **Cols./Page:** 5. **Col. Width:** 11.5 picas. **Col. Depth:** 65 picas. **Key Personnel:** Vonnie Sanchez, Associate Publisher; Christy Scott, Editor, Web Administrator. **ISSN:** 8750--8257 (print). **Subscription Rates:** Included in membership. **URL:** http://www.thealpinesun.com. **Remarks:** Advertising accepted; rates available upon request. **Circ:** Paid ‡4400.

1691 ■ KRLY-FM - 107.9
2065 Arnold Way, Ste. 104
Alpine, CA 91901
Format: Adult Contemporary. **Operating Hours**: Continuous. **Wattage**: 004. **Ad Rates:** Advertising accepted; rates available upon request. **URL:** http://www.my1079.com/.

ALTADENA

S. CA. Los Angeles Co. 4 mi. N. of Pasadena. Space age research center. Residential.

1692 ■ Coast Defense Journal
Coast Defense Study Group
1577 Braeburn Rd.
Altadena, CA 91001-2603
Freq: Quarterly. **ISSN:** 1085--9675 (print). **Subscription Rates:** Included in membership. **Alt. Formats:** PDF. **URL:** http://cdsg.org/cdsg-journal-index. **Remarks:** Advertising not accepted. **Circ:** (Not Reported).

1693 ■ Mythic Circle
Mythopoeic Society
PO Box 6707
Altadena, CA 91003-6707
Publisher's E-mail: webmaster@mythsoc.org
Freq: Annual. **Subscription Rates:** $8 Individuals /year in US. **URL:** http://www.mythsoc.org/mythic-circle.htm. **Remarks:** Advertising not accepted. **Circ:** (Not Reported).

1694 ■ Skeptic
The Skeptics Society
PO Box 338
Altadena, CA 91001
Phone: (626)794-3119
Fax: (626)794-1301
Publisher's E-mail: skepticsociety@skeptic.com
Freq: Quarterly. **ISSN:** 1063- 9330 (print). **Subscription Rates:** Included in membership; $30 U.S. for nonmembers; $40 Canada and Mexico for nonmembers; $50 Other countries for nonmembers; $50 U.S. 2 years for nonmembers; $70 Canada and Mexico 2 years for nonmembers; $90 Other countries 2 years for nonmembers. **URL:** http://www.skeptic.com/magazine. **Remarks:** Accepts advertising. **Circ:** (Not Reported).

1695 ■ Skeptic: Extraordinary Claims, Revolutionary Ideas, and the Promotion of Science
Skeptic Magazine
PO Box 338
Altadena, CA 91001
Phone: (626)794-3119
Fax: (626)794-1301
Publisher's E-mail: skepticssociety@skeptic.com
Magazine promoting scientific method, critical thinking and the skepticism of the paranormal and superstition. **Freq:** Quarterly. **Key Personnel:** Michael Shermer, Editor-in-Chief; Pat Linse, Art Director. **ISSN:** 1063--9330 (print). **Subscription Rates:** $30 Individuals U.S.; $50 Two years U.S.; $40 Canada and Mexico; $70 Two years Canada & Mexico; $50 Other countries; $90 Two years other countries. **Alt. Formats:** Download. **URL:** http://www.skeptic.com/magazine/about_the_magazine. **Remarks:** Accepts advertising. **Circ:** (Not Reported).

ALTURAS

NE CA. Modoc Co. 3 mi. E. of Cederville. Residential.

1696 ■ Modoc County Record
Modoc County Record
201 W Carlos St.
Alturas, CA 96101
Phone: (530)233-2632
Fax: (530)233-5113
Publication E-mail: record1@modocrecord.com
Newspaper. **Freq:** Weekly (Thurs.). **Print Method:** Offset. **Cols./Page:** 6. **Col. Width:** 26 nonpareils. **Col. Depth:** 294 agate lines. **Key Personnel:** Jane S. Holloway, Publisher. **Subscription Rates:** $25 Individuals Modoc, Lassen & Siskiyou Counties; $30 Elsewhere; $15 Individuals electronic version; $20 Students. **URL:** http://www.modocrecord.com/news.html. **Mailing address:** PO Box 531, Alturas, CA 96101. **Ad Rates:** GLR $4; BW $504; 4C $400; SAU $3.35; PCI $4. **Remarks:** Accepts advertising. **Circ:** 4125.

ANAHEIM

S. CA. Orange Co. 26 mi. SE of Los Angeles. Home of Disneyland. Seaside and mountain resort. Manufactures aircraft parts, surface to air missile launchers. Mobile homes. Electronic computer components, electric motors, auto batteries, citrus fruit packing plants. Agriculture. Strawberries.

1697 ■ The Automotive Booster of California
KAL Publications Inc.
559 S Harbor Blvd., Ste. A
Anaheim, CA 92805-4525
Phone: (714)563-9300
Fax: (714)563-9310
Publisher's E-mail: sales@kalpub.com
Trade magazine for members of Automotive Booster Clubs, automotive distributors, automotive parts jobbers, and others. **Freq:** 7/year. **Print Method:** Web offset. **Trim Size:** 8 1/2 x 11. **Cols./Page:** 3. **Col. Width:** 14 picas. **Col. Depth:** 10 inches. **USPS:** 908-240. **Subscription Rates:** $25 Individuals 1 year; $40 Individuals 2 years. **URL:** http://www.kalpub.com/Booster/booster.html. **Ad Rates:** BW $2,425; 4C $700; PCI $35. **Remarks:** Accepts advertising. **Circ:** Non-paid ‡4700.

1698 ■ DRIVE!
DRIVE! Magazine
2400 E Katella Ave., Ste. 300
Anaheim, CA 92806
Phone: (714)939-9991
Consumer magazine covering automobiles for enthusiasts. **Founded:** 1986. **Freq:** Monthly. **Key Personnel:** Matt Emery, Editor; Brent Diamond, Chief Executive Officer, President. **Subscription Rates:** $19.95 Individuals 3rd class; $35 Individuals 1st class; $50 Canada and Mexico airmail; $86 Out of country airmail. **URL:** http://www.motortopia.com/driveonline/. **Ad Rates:** BW $2,912; 4C $3,392; PCI $35. **Remarks:** Accepts advertising. **Circ:** (Not Reported).

1699 ■ MiniTruckin'
McMullen Argus Publishing Inc.
2400 E Katella Ave., 11th Fl.
Anaheim, CA 92806
Phone: (714)939-2400
Fax: (714)978-6390
Magazine for mini-truck enthusiasts. **Freq:** Monthly. **Print Method:** Web Offset. **Trim Size:** 8 x 10 7/8. **Key Personnel:** Brad Christopher, Publisher, phone: (714)769-7419; Mike Alexander, Editor; Steve Von Seggern, Publisher, phone: (714)939-2581. **Subscription Rates:** $25 Individuals 13 issues; $40 Individuals 26 issues; $38 Canada; $51 Other countries. **URL:** http://www.minitruckinweb.com. **Ad Rates:** BW $4,805; 4C $5,585. **Remarks:** Accepts advertising. **Circ:** ‡30107.

1700 ■ O & A Marketing News
KAL Publications Inc.
559 S Harbor Blvd., Ste. A
Anaheim, CA 92805-4525
Phone: (714)563-9300
Fax: (714)563-9310
Publisher's E-mail: sales@kalpub.com
News magazine (tabloid) targeting people engaged in the marketing, distribution, merchandising, installation, and servicing of gasoline, fuels, oil, tires, batteries, accessories, and automotive aftermarket products for service stations, convenience stores and carwashes in the thirteen Pacific Western states. **Freq:** 7/year. **Print Method:** Web. **Trim Size:** 11 1/2 x 17. **Cols./Page:** 4. **Col. Width:** 14 picas. **Col. Depth:** 16 inches. **Key Personnel:** Kathy Laderman, Editor; Doreen Philbin, Representative, Advertising and Sales. **ISSN:** 0192--009X (print). **Subscription Rates:** $25 Individuals; $40 Two years. **URL:** http://www.kalpub.com/OANews/oa.html. **Ad Rates:** BW $2,425; 4C $4,000; SAU $50; PCI $55. **Remarks:** Accepts advertising. **Circ:** Paid ‡4522, Free ‡2732.

1701 ■ Off-Road
McMullen Argus Publishing Inc.
2400 E Katella Ave., 11th Fl.
Anaheim, CA 92806
Phone: (714)939-2400
Fax: (714)978-6390
Illustrated magazine focusing on the sport of off-roading. Features four-wheel drive vehicles, pick-ups, vans, and trail bikes. Includes trip information, race reports, photos, technical tips, equipment and accessories, and road tests. **Freq:** Monthly. **Print Method:** Offset. **Cols./Page:** 3. **Col. Width:** 27 nonpareils. **Col. Depth:** 140 agate lines. **ISSN:** 0363--1745 (print). **Subscription Rates:** $11.97 Individuals 1 year ; $19.97 Two years 24 issues. **URL:** http://www.off-roadweb.com; http://www.fourwheeler.com/off-road-magazine. **Ad Rates:** BW $5855; 4C $8275. **Remarks:** Accepts advertising. **Circ:** 47353.

1702 ■ Pakistan Link
JAZ LLC
PO Box 1238
Anaheim, CA 92815
Phone: (714)400-3400
Fax: (714)400-3404
Publication E-mail: editor@pakistanlink.com
Newspaper. **Freq:** Weekly. **Key Personnel:** Akhtar M. Faruqui, Editor; Arif Mansuri, Managing Editor, President. **ISSN:** 1074--0406 (print). **Subscription Rates:** $49.95 Individuals; $89.95 Two years; $129.95 Individuals three years. **URL:** http://pakistanlink.org. **Remarks:** Accepts advertising. **Circ:** (Not Reported).

1703 ■ Travel Guide
Anaheim/Orange County Visitor and Convention Bureau
800 W Katella Ave.
Anaheim, CA 92802
Phone: (714)740-4440
Fax: (714)867-5669
Free: 855-405-5020
Magazine containing guide to facilities and services of Anaheim/Orange County Area. **Freq:** Annual. **URL:** http://anaheimoc.org/plan-your-trip/travel-guide. **Circ:** (Not Reported).

1704 ■ Turbo & High-Tech Performance
Illustrated Graphic Communications
2400 E Katella Ave., 11th Fl.
Anaheim, CA 92806
Phone: (714)939-2400
Fax: (714)978-6390
Magazine covering automotive performance and engineering. **Founded:** 1984. **Freq:** Monthly. **Print Method:** Offset. Uses mats. **Trim Size:** 8 x 10 7/8. **Cols./Page:** 3. **Col. Width:** 27 nonpareils. **Col. Depth:** 140 agate lines. **Key Personnel:** Maria Jamison, Contact, phone: (714)939-2455. **ISSN:** 0894-5039 (print). **Subscription Rates:** $19.95 Individuals; $29.95 Two years. **URL:** http://www.turbomagazine.com. **Ad Rates:** BW $5,160; 4C $6,305. **Remarks:** Accepts advertising. **Circ:** ‡27587.

1705 ■ World of Pageantry: Band & Drill Team News
Harvey Berish
150 S Magnolia Ave.
Anaheim, CA 92804
Phone: (714)952-2263
Publication E-mail: admin@worldofpageantry.com
Newspaper for marching bands, drill teams, cheerleaders and related groups. **Freq:** Monthly. **Print Method:** Offset. **URL:** http://www.worldofpageantry.com. **Formerly**: Pageantry Press. **Remarks:** Advertising accepted; rates available upon request. **Circ:** Paid ⊕**12000**.

1706 ■ KIKF-FM - 94.3
1045 South East St.
Anaheim, CA 92805
Phone: (714)977-1943
Fax: (714)502-9400
Email: tract@pacbell.net
Format: Country. **Networks:** AP. **Owner:** N. Art Astor., at above address. **Founded:** 1961. **Formerly:** KGGK-FM. **Operating Hours**: Continuous; 1% network, 99% local. **Key Personnel:** Frank Cisco, Contact. **Wattage**: 3,000. **Ad Rates:** $50-100 for 30 seconds; $80-150 for 60 seconds. **URL:** http://www.kikf.com.

1707 ■ KLAA-AM - 830
2000 Gene Autry Way
Anaheim, CA 92806
Phone: (910)293-4209
Fax: (910)293-3600
Email: comments@am830klaa.com
Format: Sports. **Formerly:** KSRT. **Key Personnel:** Michael Means, Sales Mgr., mmeans@am830klaa.com; Jorge Sevilla, Promotions Dir., jsevilla@am830klaa.com. **Wattage**: 50,000 day; 20,000 night. **Ad Rates:** Advertising accepted; rates available upon request. **URL:** http://www.am830klaa.com.

1708 ■ KSPA-AM - 1510
1045 S East St.
Anaheim, CA 92805
Format: Adult Contemporary; News; Information; Sports. **Owner:** Astor Broadcast Group, at above address. **Ad Rates:** Noncommercial. **URL:** http://www.financialnewsandtalk.com.

ANGWIN

Napa Co.

1709 ■ KDFC-FM - 89.9
95 LaJota Dr.
Angwin, CA 94508
Phone: (707)965-4155
Fax: (707)965-4161
Free: 877-207-1063
Owner: Howell Mtn. Broadcasting, at above address. **Wattage**: 800 ERP. **Ad Rates:** Accepts Advertising.

APTOS

W. CA. Santa Cruz Co. 20 mi. E. of Santa Cruz. Residential.

1710 ■ International California Mining Journal
International California Mining Journal
PO Box 2260
Aptos, CA 95001-2260
Phone: (831)479-1500
Fax: (831)479-4385
Mining trade magazine covering prospecting and mining throughout the world. **Freq:** Monthly. **Print Method:** Offset. Uses mats. **Trim Size:** 8 1/2 x 11. **Cols./Page:** 3. **Col. Width:** 28 nonpareils. **Col. Depth:** 133 agate lines. **Key Personnel:** Scott Harn, Editor, Publisher. **ISSN:** 0008--1299 (print). **Subscription Rates:** $27.95 U.S. print or online; $31.95 U.S. print and online; $41.95 Canada print only; $45.95 Canada print and online; $27.95 Canada online only; $44.95 Other countries print only; $48.95 Other countries print and online; $27.95 Other countries online only. **URL:** http://www.icmj.com/the-magazine.php. **Formerly**: California Mining Journal. **Ad Rates:** BW $711; 4C $689.50; PCI $25. **Remarks:** Accepts advertising. **Circ:** ‡10000.

ARCADIA

S. CA. Los Angeles Co. 15 mi. NE of Los Angeles. Manufactures sash and doors, plastics, boats, airplane tools. Nurseries. Hatcheries. Ranches. Orange and walnut groves.

1711 ■ Butane-Propane News
Butane-Propane News Inc.
338 E Foothill Blvd.
Arcadia, CA 91066
Phone: (626)357-2168
Fax: (626)303-2854
Free: 800-214-4386
Publisher's E-mail: npeal@bpnews.com
Magazine for the liquefied petroleum gas industry. **Freq:** Monthly. **Print Method:** Offset. **Trim Size:** 8 1/8 x 10 7/8. **Cols./Page:** 3. **Col. Width:** 27 nonpareils. **Col. Depth:** 140 agate lines. **Key Personnel:** Natalie Peal, Publisher; Kurt Ruhl, Manager, Sales. **ISSN:** 0007-7259 (print). **Subscription Rates:** $34 Individuals; $50 Two years. **URL:** http://www.bpnews.com/. **Mailing address:** PO Box 660698, Arcadia, CA 91066. **Ad Rates:** 4C $3,950. **Remarks:** Advertising accepted; rates available upon request. **Circ:** (Not Reported).

1712 ■ California Thoroughbred
California Thoroughbred Breeders Association
201 Colorado Pl.
Arcadia, CA 91007
Phone: (626)445-7800
Fax: (626)574-0852
Free: 800-573-2822
Publisher's E-mail: ctbainfo@ctba.com
Magazine about horse breeding and racing. **Freq:** Monthly. **Print Method:** Offset. **Trim Size:** 8 1/2 x 11. **Cols./Page:** 3. **Col. Width:** 2 1/8 inches. **Col. Depth:** 12 3/4 inches. **Key Personnel:** Doug Burge, Editor, Executive Vice President, General Manager; Loretta Veiga, Manager, Advertising. **ISSN:** 0049--3821 (print). **Subscription Rates:** $55 Individuals; $85 Other countries; $100 Two years; $170 Other countries two years. **URL:** http://ctba.com/california-thoroughbred-magazine.

Circulation: ★ = AAM; △ or • = BPA; ♦ = CAC; ❑ = VAC; ⊕ = PO Statement; ‡ = Publisher's Report; Boldface figures = sworn; Light figures = estimated.

Formerly: The Thoroughbred of California. **Mailing address:** PO Box 60018, Arcadia, CA 91066. **Ad Rates:** BW $490; 4C $980; PCI $41. **Remarks:** Accepts advertising. **Circ:** 5500.

1713 ■ Electrical News: The industry's choice for news in the West
Electrical News
135 E La Porte St.
Arcadia, CA 91006
Publication E-mail: editor@electricalnews.com
Trade magazine serving the electrical building and maintenance industry in the western states. Audience includes wholesale distributors, contractors, and plant engineers. **Freq:** Monthly. **Print Method:** Offset. **Trim Size:** 10 x 16. **Cols./Page:** 5. **Col. Width:** 1 13/16 inches. **Col. Depth:** 16 inches. **Subscription Rates:** $36 Individuals. **Alt. Formats:** PDF. **URL:** http://www.electricalnews.com. **Ad Rates:** BW $3,953; 4C $5,453. **Remarks:** Accepts advertising. **Circ:** Paid 31000.

1714 ■ Psychology for Living
Narramore Christian Foundation
250 W Colorado Blvd., Ste. 100
Arcadia, CA 91007
Phone: (626)821-8400
Fax: (626)821-8409
Freq: Annual. **URL:** http://ncfliving.org/psychology-for-living-literature/psychology-for-living-magazine.html. **Remarks:** Advertising not accepted. **Circ:** (Not Reported).

1715 ■ KSSE-FM - 107.1
5700 Wilshire Blvd., Ste. 250
Los Angeles, CA 90036
Phone: (323)900-6100
Fax: (323)900-6127
Format: Hispanic. **Owner:** Entravision Radio, Los Angeles, at above address. **Key Personnel:** Karl Meyer, Gen. Mgr. **Ad Rates:** Advertising accepted; rates available upon request. **URL:** http://www.entravision.com.

ARCATA

NW CA. Humboldt Co. On Humboldt Bay and Pacific Ocean, 8 mi. NE of Eureka. Humboldt State University. Tourism. Lumbering. Light industry. Mobile homes. Trucking. Construction, machine shops. Timber. Agriculture.

1716 ■ The Arcata Eye
Arcata Eye
PO Box 451
Arcata, CA 95518
Phone: (707)826-7000
Newspaper serving Arcata and nearby Blue Lake in California. **Freq:** Weekly (Tues.). **Key Personnel:** Kevin L. Hoover, Editor, Publisher. **ISSN:** 1091-1510 (print). **Subscription Rates:** $35 Individuals in Humboldt County; $37 Elsewhere in California; $40 Out of state. **URL:** http://www.arcataeye.com/. **Remarks:** Accepts advertising. **Circ:** (Not Reported).

1717 ■ The Lumberjack Newspaper
Humboldt State University Schatz Energy Research Center
1 Harpst St.
Arcata, CA 95521
Phone: (707)826-4345
Fax: (707)826-4347
Publication E-mail: thejack@humboldt.edu
Collegiate newspaper (tabloid). **Freq:** Weekly (Wed.). **Print Method:** Offset. **Trim Size:** 5 x 12 1/2. **Cols./Page:** 5. **Col. Width:** 11.5 picas. **Col. Depth:** 12.5 inches. **Key Personnel:** Yelena Kisler, Editor-in-Chief; Adrian Emery, Managing Editor. **Subscription Rates:** Free; $14 By mail. **URL:** http://thelumberjack.org. **Ad Rates:** GLR $5; BW $491.25; 4C $340; PCI $7.86. **Remarks:** Accepts advertising. **Circ:** Free ‡6500.

1718 ■ KCHP-FM - 97.1
1575 L St.
Arcata, CA 95521
Format: Religious. **Owner:** Calvary Chapel Of Arcata. **Operating Hours**: Continuous. **Wattage**: 093. **Ad Rates:** Noncommercial; underwriting available. **URL:** http://www.telioschurch.com.

1719 ■ KHSR-FM - 91.9
1 Harpst St.
Arcata, CA 95521
Format: Eclectic. **Founded:** July 26, 1999. **Ad Rates:** Noncommercial. **URL:** http://www.khsu.org/.

1720 ■ KHSU-FM - 90.5
1 Harpst St.
Arcata, CA 95521
Phone: (707)826-4805
Fax: (707)826-6082
Email: calendar@khsu.org
Format: Classical. **Networks:** Public Radio International (PRI); National Public Radio (NPR); Fox; ABC. **Owner:** Humboldt State University, at above address. **Founded:** 1960. **Operating Hours**: Continuous. **Key Personnel:** David Reed, Dir. of Dev., david@khsu.org; Kevin Sanders, Chief Engineer, ksanders@khsu.org; Ed Subkis, Gen. Mgr., esubkis@khsu.org. **Local Programs**: *KHSU Homepage*, Monday Tuesday Wednesday Thursday Friday 1:00 p.m. - 1:30 p.m.; *Thursday Night Talk*, Thursday 7:00 p.m. - 8:00 p.m. **Wattage**: 8,500 ERP. **Ad Rates:** Noncommercial. KHSR-FM. **URL:** http://www.khsu.org.

ATASCADERO

SW CA. San Luis Obispo Co. 19 mi. N. of San Luis Obispo. Residential. Meat plant. Agriculture. Grain.

1721 ■ Atascadero News
Atascadero News
5660 El Camino Real
Atascadero, CA 93422
Phone: (805)466-2585
Fax: (805)466-2714
Publisher's E-mail: editor@atascaderonews.com
Community newspaper. **Freq:** Weekly. **Key Personnel:** Jason Cross, Publisher; Jennifer Porter, Office Manager. **Subscription Rates:** $10 Individuals in area, print home delivery 10 weeks manual pay; $34.75 Individuals in area, 1 year auto pay; $39.95 Individuals in area, 1 year manual pay; $13 Out of area print home delivery, 10 weeks manual pay; $45.25 Out of area 1 year auto pay; $50.95 Out of area 1 year manual pay. **URL:** http://www.atascaderonews.com/v2_main_page.php. **Ad Rates:** BW $642.60; PCI $6.50. **Remarks:** Accepts advertising. **Circ:** ‡6450.

ATHERTON

1722 ■ KCEA-FM - 89.1
555 Middlefield Rd.
Atherton, CA 94027
Phone: (650)306-8823
Format: Oldies. **Founded:** 1979. **Key Personnel:** Michael Isaacs, Gen. Mgr.; Trish Millet, Office Mgr.; John Mylod, Sports Dir., sports@kcea.org. **Ad Rates:** Noncommercial.

AUBURN

NE CA. Placer Co. 35 mi. NE of Sacramento. Mountain resort. Gold mines. Fruits, poultry products shipped. Saw, planing mills; nursery. Fruit, stock, poultry farms.

1723 ■ Auburn Journal
Gold Country Media
1030 High St.
Auburn, CA 95604
Phone: (530)888-2471
Fax: (530)885-4902
Publication E-mail: ajournal@goldcountrymedia.com
General newspaper. **Founded:** 1872. **Freq:** Daily and Sun. (morn.). **Print Method:** Offset. **Cols./Page:** 6. **Col. Width:** 12 picas. **Col. Depth:** 294 agate lines. **Key Personnel:** Deric Rothe, Contact. **USPS:** 036-860. **Subscription Rates:** $96.53 Individuals. **URL:** http://www.auburnjournal.com/. **Ad Rates:** BW $1,828; 4C $2,128; SAU $14.51. **Remarks:** Accepts advertising. **Circ:** Mon.-Fri. ★**10164**, Sun. ★**10135**.

1724 ■ Colfax Record
Gold Country Media
1030 High St.
Auburn, CA 95604
Phone: (530)888-2471
Fax: (530)885-4902
Community newspaper. **Freq:** Weekly (Tues.). **Print Method:** Offset. **Cols./Page:** 6. **Col. Width:** 2 1/16 inches. **Col. Depth:** 21 1/2 inches. **Key Personnel:** Martha Garcia, Editor, phone: (530)346-2232. **URL:** http://www.colfaxrecord.com. **Ad Rates:** GLR $.63; SAU $5. **Remarks:** Accepts advertising. **Circ:** Paid ■ **1090.**

1725 ■ FPC/Fire Protection Contractor
Haden B. Brumbeloe and Associates Inc.
550 High St., Ste. 220
Auburn, CA 95603
Phone: (530)823-0706
Fax: (530)823-6937
Publication E-mail: info@fpcmag.com
Trade magazine for fire sprinkler industry professionals. **Freq:** Monthly. **Print Method:** Offset. **Trim Size:** 8 1/2 x 11. **Key Personnel:** Brant Brumbeloe, Editor. **ISSN:** 1043--2485 (print). **Subscription Rates:** $68 U.S. 1 year; $124 U.S. 2 years; $171 U.S. 3 years; $102 Canada 1 year; $192 Canada 2 years; $272 Canada 3 years; $145 Other countries 1 year; $275 Other countries 2 years; $399 Other countries 3 years; $10 Single issue first classmail; $15 Single issue priority mail; $30 Single issue FedEx overnight. **URL:** http://www.fpcmag.com. **Ad Rates:** BW $1372; 4C $1837. **Remarks:** Accepts advertising. **Circ:** Controlled 2,300.

1726 ■ Shotgun Sports: America's Leading Shotgun Magazine
Shotgun Sports Inc.
PO Box 6810
Auburn, CA 95604
Phone: (530)889-2220
Fax: (530)889-9106
Free: 800-676-8920
Magazine for clay target shooting and hunting. **Freq:** Monthly. **Print Method:** Offset. **Trim Size:** 7 1/2 x 10 1/2. **Cols./Page:** 3. **Col. Width:** 27 nonpareils. **Col. Depth:** 140 agate lines. **ISSN:** 0774--3773 (print). **Subscription Rates:** $30 Individuals; $45 Canada; $79.95 Other countries. **URL:** http://www.shotgunsportsmagazine.com. **Ad Rates:** BW $4,010; 4C $5,000. **Remarks:** Accepts advertising. **Circ:** ‡108000.

1727 ■ KAHI-AM - 950
985 Lincoln Way, Ste. 103
Auburn, CA 95603
Phone: (530)885-5636
Fax: (530)885-0166
Email: info@kahi.com
Format: Sports. **Owner:** IHR Educational Broadcasting, 605 W Lake Blvd., Ste. 5, Tahoe City, CA 96145. **Founded:** 1957. **Key Personnel:** Jerry Henry, Gen. Mgr., jerry@kahi.com; Eva Thomas, Bus. Mgr., eva@kahi.com. **Wattage**: 5,000. **Ad Rates:** Advertising accepted; rates available upon request. $18 for 30 seconds; $24 for 60 seconds. **URL:** http://www.kahi.com.

1728 ■ WaveDivision Holdings L.L.C.
1225 Lincoln Way
Auburn, CA 95603
Email: customerservice@wavebroadband.com
Founded: Sept. 05, 2006. **Cities Served:** 95 channels. **URL:** http://www.wavebroadband.com.

1729 ■ WSER-AM - 1550
PO Box 99
Auburn, CA 95604
Format: News; Talk. **Networks:** ABC. **Owner:** First Philadelphia Properties, 311 French Rd., Newtown Square, PA 19073, Ph: (610)356-3946. **Founded:** 1963. **Operating Hours**: 6 a.m.-6p.m. **ADI**: Baltimore, MD. **Wattage**: 1,000. **Ad Rates:** $12-20 for 30 seconds; for 60 seconds. **URL:** http://www.wser.org/contact-us/.

AVALON

S. CA. Los Angeles Co. 50 mi. S. of Los Angeles. Resort.

1730 ■ Catalina Cable TV Co.
PO Box 2143
Avalon, CA 90704
Phone: (310)510-0255
Cities Served: Avalon, California: subscribing households 1,380; 110 channels; 3 community access channels; 50 hours per week community access programming. **Postal Areas Served:** 90704. **URL:** http://catalinabb.com/contact-catalina.

1731 ■ KISL-FM - 88.7
PO Box 1980
Avalon, CA 90704
Phone: (310)510-7469
Email: cshel@kislavalon.com
Format: Public Radio. **Key Personnel:** David Markowitz, Station Mgr. **Ad Rates:** Noncommercial. **URL:** http://kislavalon.com.

AZUSA

S. CA. Los Angeles Co. 3 mi. E. of Duarte. Residential.

1732 ■ Clause
Azusa Pacific University
Unit 5165
Azusa, CA 91702-9521
Phone: (626)815-6000
Fax: (626)815-2045
Publication E-mail: clause@apu.edu
College newspaper. **Freq:** Weekly. **Col. Depth:** 16 inches. **Key Personnel:** Kelyn Struiksma, Editor-in-Chief. **URL:** http://www.theclause.org. **Mailing address:** BP 83, 26802 Portes les Valence, France. **Ad Rates:** BW $480; PCI $1.50; 4C $576. **Remarks:** Accepts advertising. **Circ:** 7900.

BAKERSFIELD

S. CA. Kern Co. 109 mi. N. of Los Angeles. Oil wells and refineries. Borax, tungsten mines. Manufactures oil well tools, pumps, steel castings & riveted pipe, cottonseed oil, furniture, textile bags, Meat packing plant; bottling works. Ships citrus fruits, grapes, melons, cotton, cottonseed, potatoes, alfalfa, wheat.

1733 ■ The Bakersfield Californian: family-owned newspaper
The Bakersfield Californian
PO Box BIN 440
Bakersfield, CA 93302-0440
Phone: (661)395-7500
Free: 800-953-5353
Publisher's E-mail: onlinesales@bakersfield.com
General newspaper. **Freq:** Mon.-Sun. (morn.). **Print Method:** Offset. **Cols./Page:** 6. **Col. Width:** 25 nonpareils. **Col. Depth:** 294 agate lines. **Key Personnel:** Richard Beene, Chief Executive Officer, President; John Wells, Senior Vice President, Marketing; Logan Molen, Chief Operating Officer, Senior Vice President; Ginger Moorhouse, Chairman, Publisher. **Subscription Rates:** $7.99 Individuals monthly access to digital edition; $79.99 Individuals yearly access to digital edition; $15.50 Individuals 7 day per week print delivery; $11.99 Individuals 4 day per print delivery. **URL:** http://www.bakersfield.com. **Remarks:** Advertising accepted; rates available upon request. **Circ:** Mon.-Fri. ★**59433**, Sun. ★**68825**, Sat. ★**60719**.

1734 ■ Cicada
Cricket Media, Inc.
13625A Dulles Technology Dr.
Herndon, VA 20171
Phone: (703)885-3400
Publisher's E-mail: donations@cricketmedia.com
Literary magazine featuring haiku and Japanese-oriented fiction. **Freq:** Quarterly. **Print Method:** Offset. **Trim Size:** 5 1/2 x 8 1/2. **Cols./Page:** 1. **Col. Width:** 4 1/2 inches. **Col. Depth:** 7 1/2 inches. **Key Personnel:** Frederick A. Raborg, Jr., Editor, Contact. **ISSN:** 0891-2386 (print). **Subscription Rates:** $18 Individuals; $6 Single issue; $25 Individuals out of country; $8.50 Single issue out of country. **Ad Rates:** BW $100; PCI $10. **Remarks:** Accepts advertising. **Circ:** Paid 800, Non-paid 100.

1735 ■ El Popular
El Popular
208 Truxtun Ave.
Bakersfield, CA 93301
Phone: (661)325-7725
Fax: (661)325-1351
Publication E-mail: news@elpopularnews.com
Community newspaper (Hispanic) with one edition, serving Bakersfield, and Fresno. **Founded:** 1983. **Freq:** Weekly. **Print Method:** Offset. **Cols./Page:** 6. **Col. Width:** 2 inches. **Col. Depth:** 21 inches. **Key Personnel:** Raul R. Camacho, Sr., Editor. **Subscription Rates:** $30 Individuals. **URL:** http://elpopularnews.com. **Ad Rates:** GLR $15; BW $1,890; 4C $500; SAU $36; PCI $17.50. **Remarks:** Advertising accepted; rates available upon request. **Circ:** ‡23100.

1736 ■ Strategy & Tactics
Decision Games
PO Box 21598
Bakersfield, CA 93390
Phone: (661)587-9633
Fax: (661)587-5031
Publisher's E-mail: tbomba@strategyandtacticspress.com
Consumer magazine covering military history including board game of featured battle. **Freq:** Bimonthly. **Key Personnel:** Joseph Miranda, Editor-in-Chief; Christopher Cummins, Publisher. **ISSN:** 1040-886X (print). **Subscription Rates:** $29.97 U.S.; $36 Canada; $42 Other countries; $49.97 Two years U.S.; $62 Two years Canada; $74 Two years overseas. **URL:** http://strategyandtacticsmagazine.com. **Remarks:** Advertising accepted; rates available upon request. **Circ:** Paid ⊕**5200**.

1737 ■ Bright House Networks
3701 N Sillect Ave.
Bakersfield, CA 93308
Founded: 1966. **Formerly:** Warner Cable; Time Warner Cable. **Key Personnel:** Joe Schoenstein, Gen. Mgr., VP, joe.schoenstein@twcbak.com; Don Stone, Rep., Ad./Sales, don.stone@twcbak.com. **Cities Served:** subscribing households 90,022. **URL:** http://brighthouse.com/static/documents/BAKWinbackCreditForm.pdf.

1738 ■ KAFY-AM - 970
1100 Mohawk St., Ste. 280
Bakersfield, CA 93309
Fax: (805)327-9459
Format: Hispanic. **Networks:** UPI; CBS. **Owner:** Barro Broadcasting Corp., at above address. **Founded:** 1946. **Operating Hours:** Continuous. **Wattage:** 1,000 day; 5,000 night. **Ad Rates:** $18-25 for 30 seconds; $24-29 for 60 seconds. **URL:** http://foxsports970am.iheart.com.

1739 ■ KAXL-FM - 88.3
110 S Montclair, Ste. 205
Bakersfield, CA 93309
Phone: (661)832-2800
Fax: (661)832-3164
Email: kaxl@kaxl.com
Format: Gospel. **Networks:** Fox; CBS. **Owner:** Skyride Unlimited, at above address. **Founded:** May 1994. **Operating Hours:** Continuous. **Key Personnel:** Sheryl Giesbrecht, Contact. **Wattage:** 21,000 ERP. **Ad Rates:** Combined advertising rates available with KERI. **URL:** http://www.kaxl.com.

1740 ■ KBAK-TV - 29
1901 Westwind Dr.
Bakersfield, CA 93301
Phone: (661)327-7955
Format: Commercial TV. **Networks:** CBS. **Owner:** Fisher Communications Inc., 140 4th Ave. N, Ste. 500, Seattle, WA 98109-4940, Ph: (206)404-7000, Fax: (206)404-6037. **Founded:** 1953. **Operating Hours:** Continuous weekdays; 6 a.m.-2 a.m. Saturday and Sunday. **ADI:** Bakersfield, CA. **Key Personnel:** Cristi Jessee, News Dir., cjessee@bakersfieldnow.com; Teresa Burgess, Gen. Mgr., tburgess@bakersfieldnow.com; Pete Capra, Contact, pcapra@bakersfieldnow.com. **Wattage:** 1,700,000. **Ad Rates:** Noncommercial. **URL:** http://www.bakersfieldnow.com.

1741 ■ KBFP-AM - 800
1100 Mohawk St., Ste. 280
Bakersfield, CA 93309
Phone: (661)322-9929
Fax: (661)322-7239
Format: Hispanic. **Key Personnel:** Jim A. Bell, Gen. Mgr. **URL:** http://www.iheartmedia.com.

1742 ■ KBFP-FM - 105.3
1100 Mohawk St., Ste. 280
Bakersfield, CA 93309
Phone: (661)322-9929
Format: Hispanic. **Founded:** 1972. **Key Personnel:** Gary Larkin, Exec. VP; Chris Williams, Sr. VP; Bob Pittman, Chairman, CEO; Jim A. Bell, Gen. Mgr. **URL:** http://www.iheartmedia.com.

1743 ■ KBFX-TV - 58
1901 Westwind Dr.
Bakersfield, CA 93301
Phone: (661)327-7955
Fax: (661)327-5603
Networks: Fox. **ADI:** Bakersfield, CA. **Key Personnel:** Tom Murphy, Reporter; Teresa Burgess, Gen. Mgr., VP, tburgess@bakersfieldnow.com; Cristi Jessee, News Dir., cjessee@bakersfieldnow.com. **URL:** http://www.bakersfieldnow.com.

1744 ■ KBKO-FM - 96.5
5100 Commerce Dr.
Bakersfield, CA 93309-0864
Phone: (661)327-9711
Fax: (661)327-0797
Format: Country. **ADI:** Bakersfield, CA. **Key Personnel:** Kenn McCloud, Dir. of Programs; Vikki Peterson, Sales Mgr. **Wattage:** 50,000. **Ad Rates:** Noncommercial. **URL:** http://www.concierto965.com/contacto-concierto.

1745 ■ KERI-AM - 1180
1400 Easton Dr., Ste. 144
Bakersfield, CA 93309
Phone: (661)328-1410
Fax: (661)328-0873
Format: Contemporary Christian. **Networks:** USA Radio; International Broadcasting; Moody Broadcasting. **Owner:** American General Media, PO Box 2700, Bakersfield, CA 93303, Ph: (661)328-0118, Fax: (661)328-1648. **Founded:** 1950. **Formerly:** KWSO-AM. **Operating Hours:** Continuous; 75% network, 25% local. **ADI:** Bakersfield, CA. **Key Personnel:** Toni Snyder, Gen. Mgr., tsnyder@americangeneralmedia.com. **Wattage:** 50,000 Day; 10,000 Night. **Ad Rates:** $7.50-15 for 30 seconds; $9.50-18.75 for 60 seconds. Combined advertising rates available with KAXL. **URL:** http://www.keri.com.

1746 ■ KERN-AM - 1180
1400 Easton Dr., Ste. 144
Bakersfield, CA 93309
Phone: (661)328-1410
Fax: (661)328-0873
Email: kindnesscrew@kernradio.com
Format: Talk; News. **Owner:** American General Media, PO Box 2700, Bakersfield, CA 93303, Ph: (661)328-0118, Fax: (661)328-1648. **Founded:** 1932. **Operating Hours:** Continuous. **Wattage:** 50,000 Day; 10,000 N. **Ad Rates:** Advertising accepted; rates available upon request. **URL:** http://www.kernradio.com.

1747 ■ KERO-TV - 23
321 21st St.
Bakersfield, CA 93301
Phone: (661)637-2320
Fax: (661)323-5538
Format: Commercial TV. **Networks:** ABC. **Owner:** S&P Global Inc., 55 Water St., New York, NY 10041, Ph: (212)438-1000, Free: 888-806-5541. **Founded:** 1953. **Operating Hours:** 20 hours Daily; 62% network, 38% local. **ADI:** Bakersfield, CA. **Key Personnel:** Steven McEvoy, Contact. **Wattage:** 1,750,000. **Ad Rates:** Advertising accepted; rates available upon request. **URL:** http://www.turnto23.com.

1748 ■ KGEO-AM
PO Box 2700
Bakersfield, CA 93303
Phone: (661)328-1410
Fax: (661)328-0873
Owner: American General Media, 1400 Easton Dr., Ste. 144, Bakersfield, CA 93309, Ph: (661)328-1410, Fax: (661)328-0873. **URL:** http://www.americangeneralmedia.com/station.html?id=9.

1749 ■ KGET-TV - 17
2120 L St.
Bakersfield, CA 93301
Phone: (661)283-1700
Fax: (661)283-1843
Format: Commercial TV. **Networks:** NBC. **Operating Hours:** Continuous. **ADI:** Bakersfield, CA. **Key Personnel:** Shirley Sanford, Program Mgr., shirleysanford@kget.com; John Pilios, News Dir., johnpilios@kget.com; Derek Jeffery, Dir. of Sales, derekjeffery@kget.com; Jim Tripeny, Div. Mgr., jimtripeny@kget.com. **Ad Rates:** Advertising accepted; rates available upon request. **URL:** http://www.kerngoldenempire.com.

1750 ■ KGFM-FM - 101.5
1400 Easton Dr., Ste.144
Bakersfield, CA 93303-2700
Phone: (661)328-1410
Fax: (661)328-0873
Founded: 1964. **Formerly:** KGEE-FM. **Operating Hours:** Continuous. **ADI:** Bakersfield, CA. **Key Personnel:** Roger Fessler, Gen. Mgr.; Chris Edwards, Operations Mgr., chris@kgfm.com. **Wattage:** 6,700 ERP. **Ad Rates:** Advertising accepted; rates available upon

Circulation: ★ = AAM; △ or • = BPA; ♦ = CAC; ❑ = VAC; ⊕ = PO Statement; ‡ = Publisher's Report; Boldface figures = sworn; Light figures = estimated.

request. **Mailing address:** PO Box 2700, Bakersfield, CA 93303-2700. **URL:** http://www.kgfm.com/.

1751 ■ KIQO-FM - 104.5
1400 Easton Dr., Ste. 144
Bakersfield, CA 93309
Phone: (805)466-6511
Fax: (805)466-5362
Email: oldies@fix.net
Format: Adult Contemporary. **Owner:** Garry & Virginia Brill, at above address. **Founded:** 1979. **ADI**: Bakersfield, CA. **Key Personnel:** Garry Brill, Mgr.; Dell McCulley, Sales Mgr.; Seth Blackburn, Operations Mgr. **Wattage**: 4,700 ERP. **Ad Rates:** Combined advertising rates available with KWEZ-FM. **URL:** http://www.americangeneralmedia.com.

1752 ■ KISV-FM - 94.1
1400 Easton Dr., Ste. 144B
Bakersfield, CA 93309
Phone: (661)328-1410
Fax: (661)328-0873
Email: listeners@hot941.com
Format: Contemporary Hit Radio (CHR); Hip Hop; Blues. **Owner:** American General Media, 1400 Easton Dr., Ste. 144, Bakersfield, CA 93309, Ph: (661)328-1410, Fax: (661)328-0873. **Ad Rates:** Advertising accepted; rates available upon request. **URL:** http://www.hot941.com.

1753 ■ KIWI-FM - 102.9
5100 Commerce Dr.
Bakersfield, CA 93309
Phone: (661)327-9711
Fax: (661)327-0797
Format: Hispanic. **Networks:** Independent. **Owner:** Lotus Bakersfield Corp., 5100 Commerce Dr., Bakersfield, CA 93309. **Founded:** 1986. **Operating Hours**: Continuous; 100% local. **Wattage**: 25,000. **Ad Rates:** Noncommercial. **URL:** http://www.radiolobo.com.

1754 ■ KKBB-FM - 99.3
3651 Pegasus Dr., Ste. 107
Bakersfield, CA 93308
Phone: (661)393-1900
Owner: Buckley RADIO, 166 W Putnam Ave., Greenwich, CT 06830, Ph: (203)661-4307. **ADI**: Bakersfield, CA. **Wattage**: 1,000 ERP. **Ad Rates:** Accepts Advertising.

1755 ■ KLLY-FM - 95.3
3651 Pegasus Dr., Ste. 107
Bakersfield, CA 93308
Phone: (661)393-1900
Fax: (661)393-1915
Owner: Buckley Broadcasting Corp. Inc., 166 W Putnam Ave., Greenwich, CT 06830-5241, Ph: (203)661-4309. **Key Personnel:** Otis Warren, Contact. **Wattage**: 12,500 ERP.

1756 ■ KMYX-FM - 92.5
6313 Schirra Ct.
Bakersfield, CA 93313
Phone: (661)837-0745
Fax: (661)837-1612
Format: Hispanic; Adult Contemporary. **Founded:** 1994. **Operating Hours**: Continuous. **Key Personnel:** Cesar Chavez, Gen. Mgr. **Wattage**: 6,000. **Ad Rates:** $15-50 per unit.

1757 ■ KNZR-AM - 1560
3651 Pegasus Dr., Ste. 107
Bakersfield, CA 93308
Phone: (661)393-1900
Fax: (661)393-1915
Format: Talk; News. **Networks:** CNN Radio. **Owner:** Buckley RADIO, 166 W Putnam Ave., Greenwich, CT 06830, Ph: (203)661-4307. **Formerly**: KPMC-AM. **Operating Hours**: Continuous. **ADI**: Bakersfield, CA. **Wattage**: 25,000. **Ad Rates:** Noncommercial. **URL:** http://www.knzr.com.

1758 ■ KRAB-FM - 106.1
1100 Mohawk St., Ste. 280
Bakersfield, CA 93309
Phone: (661)322-9929
Fax: (661)322-7239
Format: Alternative/New Music/Progressive; Album-Oriented Rock (AOR). **Owner:** iHeartMedia Inc., 200 E Basse Rd., San Antonio, TX 78209, Ph: (210)832-3314. **Founded:** Sept. 15, 2006. **ADI**: Bakersfield, CA. **Key Personnel:** Danny Spanks, Contact, dannyspanks@clearchannel.com. **Wattage**: 25,000. **Ad Rates:** Noncommercial. **URL:** http://www.krab.com.

1759 ■ KSMJ-FM - 97.7
3651 Pegasus Dr., Ste. 107
Bakersfield, CA 93308
Phone: (661)393-1900
Fax: (661)393-1915
Format: Soft Rock. **Owner:** Buckley Broadcasting Corp. Inc., 166 W Putnam Ave., Greenwich, CT 06830-5241, Ph: (203)661-4309. **Key Personnel:** E.J. Tyler, Dir. of Programs; Steve Darnell, Gen. Mgr., VP; Otis Warren, Sales Mgr. **Ad Rates:** Advertising accepted; rates available upon request.

1760 ■ K21FP - 21
PO Box A
Santa Ana, CA 92711
Phone: (714)832-2950
Free: 888-731-1000
Owner: Trinity Broadcasting Network Inc., PO Box A, Santa Ana, CA 92711, Ph: (714)832-2950, Free: 888-731-1000. **URL:** http://www.tbn.org.

1761 ■ K289AN-FM - 105.7
PO Box 391
Twin Falls, ID 83303
Free: 800-357-4226
Format: Religious; Contemporary Christian. **Owner:** CSN International, PO Box 391, Twin Falls, ID 83303, Ph: (208)736-1958, Fax: (208)736-1958, Free: 800-357-4226.

1762 ■ K214ED-FM - 90.7
PO Box 391
Twin Falls, ID 83303
Fax: (208)736-1958
Free: 800-357-4226
Format: Religious; Contemporary Christian. **Owner:** CSN International, PO Box 391, Twin Falls, ID 83303, Ph: (208)736-1958, Fax: (208)736-1958, Free: 800-357-4226. **Key Personnel:** Don Mills, Prog. Dir., Music Dir.; Kelly Carlson, Dir. of Engg.; Ray Gorney, Asst. Dir. **Wattage**: 010. **URL:** http://www.csnradio.com.

1763 ■ KUVI-TV - 45
5801 Truxtun Ave.
Bakersfield, CA 93309-0609
Phone: (661)324-0045
Fax: (661)334-2693
Email: dtvinfo@kuvi45.com
Format: Commercial TV. **Networks:** United Paramount Network. **Owner:** Buck Owens Prod. Inc., 3223 Sillect Ave, Bakersfield, CA 93308-6332, Ph: (661)326-1011. **Founded:** 1988. **Formerly**: KDOB-TV, KUZZ-TV. **Operating Hours**: Continuous; 100% local. **ADI**: Bakersfield, CA. **Wattage**: 5,000,000. **Ad Rates:** Advertising accepted; rates available upon request. **URL:** http://www.kuvi45.com.

1764 ■ KUZZ-AM - 550
3223 Sillect Ave.
Bakersfield, CA 93308
Phone: (661)326-1011
Fax: (661)328-7503
Format: Country. **Simulcasts:** KUZZ-FM. **Owner:** Buck Owens Production Company Inc., at above address. **Founded:** 1958. **Formerly**: KCWR-AM. **Operating Hours**: Continuous. **ADI**: Bakersfield, CA. **Wattage**: 5,000. **Ad Rates:** Noncommercial. **URL:** http://www.kuzzradio.com.

1765 ■ KUZZ-FM - 107.1
3223 Sillect Ave.
Bakersfield, CA 93308
Phone: (661)326-1011
Fax: (661)328-7503
Format: Country; Urban Contemporary. **Simulcasts:** KUZZ-AM. **Networks:** ABC; Independent. **Owner:** Buck Owens Production Company Inc., at above address. **Founded:** 1993. **Operating Hours**: Continuous. **ADI**: Bakersfield, CA. **Key Personnel:** Harvey Campbell, Gen. Sales Mgr.; Jerry Hufford, Promotions Dir. **Wattage**: 6,000. **Ad Rates:** Noncommercial. Combined advertising rates available with KUZZ-AM. **URL:** http://www.kuzz.com.

1766 ■ KYLU-FM - 88.7
PO Box 2098
Omaha, NE 68103-2098
Free: 800-525-5683
Format: Contemporary Christian. **Owner:** Educational Media Foundation, 2351 Sunset Blvd., Ste. 170-218, Rocklin, CA 95677, Ph: (800)434-8400. **URL:** http://www.klove.com.

1767 ■ Lotus Bakersfield Corp.
5100 Commerce Dr.
Bakersfield, CA 93309
Key Personnel: Howard A. Kalmenson, President, CEO; John Paley, VP of Corp. Affairs. **URL:** http://www.lotuscorp.com.

BALDWIN PARK

Los Angeles Co.

1768 ■ Charter Communications
4781 Irwindale Ave.
Baldwin Park, CA 91706-2175
Owner: Charter Communications Inc., 400 Atlantic St., Stamford, CT 06901, Ph: (203)905-7801. **Founded:** 1981. **Formerly**: Cencom Cable Television; Falcon. **Key Personnel:** Kevin Maguire, Mgr. **Cities Served:** subscribing households 116,804. **URL:** http://www.charter.com.

BANNING

SE CA. Riverside Co. 22 mi. NW of Palm Springs. Resort. Industrial park. Electronic components, shirts, cabinets and trailers manufactured. Fruit farms. Apricots, peaches. Livestock.

1769 ■ The Record-Gazette
Record Inc.
218 N Murray St.
Banning, CA 92220
Phone: (951)849-4586
Fax: (951)849-2437
Newspaper. **Founded:** 1908. **Freq:** Weekly (Fri.). **Print Method:** Offset. **Cols./Page:** 6. **Col. Width:** 25 nonpareils. **Col. Depth:** 294 agate lines. **Key Personnel:** Virginia Bradford, Office Manager; David Berkowitz, Publisher. **Subscription Rates:** $15.95 Individuals 6 months, local delivery; $24.95 Individuals 1 year, local delivery. **URL:** http://www.recordgazette.net. **Ad Rates:** GLR $10.55; BW $10.08; SAU $8.50; PCI $10.08. **Remarks:** Accepts advertising. **Circ:** Free ■ **18171**, Paid ■ **1670**, Combined ■ **19721**.

BARSTOW

SE CA. San Bernardino Co. 55 mi. NE of San Bernardino. Silver, borax, salt, barium mines. Agriculture. Alfalfa, cotton, melons, poultry.

1770 ■ Desert Dispatch
Freedom Communications Inc.
130 Coolwater Ln.
Barstow, CA 92311
Phone: (760)256-8589
Publication E-mail: jackie_parsons@link.freedom.com
General newspaper. **Founded:** 1917. **Freq:** Mon.-Sat. (eve.). **Print Method:** Offset. **Cols./Page:** 8. **Col. Width:** 21 nonpareils. **Col. Depth:** 301 agate lines. **Key Personnel:** Stephan Wingert, Publisher, phone: (760)955-5345; Scott Shackford, Editor-in-Chief, phone: (760)256-4104. **Subscription Rates:** $42 Individuals e-edition; $98 Individuals print and e-edition. **URL:** http://www.desertdispatch.com/; http://www.highdesert.com. **Ad Rates:** PCI $7.56. **Remarks:** Accepts advertising. **Circ:** Mon.-Sat. ♦**2612**.

1771 ■ KBTW-FM - 104.5
125 E Fredericks St.
Barstow, CA 92311-2809
Phone: (760)255-1316
Format: Hispanic. **Owner:** Lazer Broadcasting Corp., 200 S A St., Ste. 400, Oxnard, CA 93030, Ph: (805)240-2070, Fax: (805)240-5960. **Key Personnel:** Dino Mercado, Mgr. **Ad Rates:** Noncommercial.

1772 ■ KDUC-FM - 94.3
PO Box 250
Barstow, CA 92311
Free: 800-944-5382
Email: kduc943@aol.com
Format: News; Sports. **Networks:** Westwood One Radio; Satellite Music Network; ABC; EFM. **Owner:** Tele-Media Broadcasting, 4414 Lafayette Blvd., Ste. 100, Fredericksburg, VA 22408, Ph: (540)891-9959, Free: 888-760-1045. **Founded:** 1986. **Formerly**: KPRD-

FM; First American Communications Corp.; KWTC-AM. **Wattage:** 4,600 ERP. **Ad Rates:** $11; $8-12 for 30 seconds; $15-20 for 60 seconds; $12-15 for 60 seconds. Combined advertising rates available with KSZL-AM. **URL:** http://theduckradio.net.

1773 ■ KHDR-FM - 96.9
1611 E Main St.
Barstow, CA 92312
Phone: (760)256-0326
Fax: (760)256-9507
Format: Heavy Metal; Alternative/New Music/ Progressive. **Owner:** Highway Radio Corp., 101 Convention Center Dr., P119, Las Vegas, NV 89109, Ph: (702)737-9899. **Ad Rates:** Advertising accepted; rates available upon request.

1774 ■ KHRQ-FM - 94.9
1611 E Main St.
Barstow, CA 92311
Phone: (760)256-0326
Fax: (760)256-9507
Format: Heavy Metal; Classic Rock. **Owner:** Highway Radio Corp., 101 Convention Center Dr., P119, Las Vegas, NV 89109, Ph: (702)737-9899. **Key Personnel:** Matt Phillips, Mgr. **Ad Rates:** Advertising accepted; rates available upon request. **Mailing address:** PO Box 1668, Barstow, CA 92312. **URL:** http://www.highwayradio.com.

1775 ■ KHWY-FM - 98.9
1611 E Main St.
Barstow, CA 92311
Format: Adult Contemporary. **Ad Rates:** Noncommercial. **URL:** http://www.highwayradio.com.

1776 ■ KHWZ-FM - 100.1
1611 E Main St.
Barstow, CA 92312
Phone: (760)256-0326
Fax: (760)256-9507
Format: Contemporary Country. **Founded:** 1970. **Ad Rates:** Advertising accepted; rates available upon request.

1777 ■ KHYZ-FM
1611 E Main St.
Barstow, CA 92311
Format: Adult Contemporary. **Wattage**: 8,400 ERP.

1778 ■ KIXF-FM - 101.5
1611 E Main St.
Barstow, CA 92312
Phone: (760)256-0326
Fax: (760)256-9507
Email: info@highwayradio.com
Format: Country. **Mailing address:** PO Box 1668, Barstow, CA 92312. **URL:** http://www.highwayradio.com.

1779 ■ KIXW-FM - 107.3
1611 E Main St.
Barstow, CA 92312
Phone: (760)256-0326
Fax: (760)256-9507
Email: info@highwayradio.com
Format: Country. **Wattage**: 1,000. **URL:** http://www.highwayradio.com.

1780 ■ K212BD-FM - 90.3
PO Box 391
Twin Falls, ID 83303
Fax: (208)736-1958
Free: 800-357-4226
Format: Religious; Contemporary Christian. **Owner:** CSN International, PO Box 391, Twin Falls, ID 83303, Ph: (208)736-1958, Fax: (208)736-1958, Free: 800-357-4226. **Key Personnel:** Ray Gorney, Asst. Dir.; Don Mills, Prog. Dir., Music Dir.; Kelly Carlson, Dir. of Engg. **Wattage**: 006. **URL:** http://www.csnradio.com.

1781 ■ KXIF-FM - 101.5
1611 E Main St.
Barstow, CA 92312
Free: 800-231-9899
Format: Contemporary Country; Country. **Founded:** 1970. **Ad Rates:** Advertising accepted; rates available upon request.

BELMONT

W. CA. San Mateo Co. 21 mi. SE of San Francisco. Residential. Electronic equipment manufactured.

1782 ■ Terrae Incognitae: The Journal for the History of Discoveries
Society for the History of Discoveries
c/o William Brandenburg, Treasurer
631 Masonic Way, Apt. 1
Belmont, CA 94002
Phone: (650)591-1601
Peer-reviewed journal covering the history of geographic exploration and cross-cultural interaction around the world and its effects. **Freq:** Semiannual. **Key Personnel:** Lauren Beck, Editor; Marguerite Ragnow, Board Member; David Buisseret, Editor. **ISSN:** 0082--2884 (print); **EISSN:** 2040--8706 (electronic). **Subscription Rates:** $300 Institutions print and online or online only; $30 /year for members and institutions, in U.S. and Canada; $35 /year for members and institutions, outside U.S. and Canada. **URL:** http://www.tandfonline.com/loi/ytin20; http://www.sochistdisc.org/terrae_incognitae/terrae-incognitae.htm?PHPSESSID=fe99dc71e1632fa90f3d47a44f4094fe. **Remarks:** Accepts advertising. **Circ:** (Not Reported).

BENICIA

W. CA. Solano Co. 30 mi. NE of San Francisco, on Strait of Carquinez. Boat connections. Dredges manufactured. Agriculture.

1783 ■ Wine Country International Magazine
Wine Country International Magazine
PO Box 515
Benicia, CA 94510-0515
Phone: (707)746-0741
Fax: (707)746-1579
Magazine about wine, food, travel, and other aspects of fine living. **Freq:** Quarterly. **Print Method:** Offset. **Trim Size:** 8 1/8 x 10 7/8. **Cols./Page:** 3. **Col. Width:** 28 nonpareils. **Col. Depth:** 140 agate lines. **Key Personnel:** Christopher J. Davies, Publisher. **Subscription Rates:** $16 Individuals annual. **URL:** http://www.winecountrynetwork.com/mag.html. **Ad Rates:** BW $2,541; 4C $3,569. **Remarks:** Accepts advertising. **Circ:** ‡50000.

BERKELEY

W. CA. Alameda Co. On San Francisco Bay, adjoining Oakland. Boat connections. University of California at Berkeley and several religious colleges, private schools. Manufactures gasoline engines, castings, steel tanks, structural aluminum, computer software, pumps, carbon dioxide, dry ice, silicate of soda.

1784 ■ Algebraic & Geometric Topology
Mathematical Sciences Publishers
University of California
University of California, Berkeley
Berkeley, CA 94720-3840
Phone: (510)643-8638
Fax: (510)295-2608
Publication E-mail: agt@msp.warwick.ac.uk
Peer-reviewed journal covering topology and advancement of mathematics. **Freq:** Bimonthly. **Key Personnel:** John Etnyre, Editor; Kathryn Hesser, Editor. **ISSN:** 1472--2747 (print); **EISSN:** 1472--2739 (electronic). **Subscription Rates:** $410 Individuals electronic only; $650 Individuals print and electronic. **URL:** http://msp.org/agt/2014/14-2; http://msp.org/publications/journals/#agt. **Circ:** (Not Reported).

1785 ■ Anarchy: A Journal of Desire Armed
CAL Press
Berkeley, CA
Anti-authoritarian publication addressing worldwide anarchist and libertarian issues. **Freq:** Quarterly. **ISSN:** 1044--1387 (print). **Subscription Rates:** $25 U.S. 1 year; $48 U.S. 2 years, with free book or t-shirt; $48 Out of state 1 year; $50 Libraries in the U.S; $64 Libraries outside U.S; $10 Individuals PDF, 1 year; $20 Individuals PDF, 4 years. **URL:** http://anarchymag.org. **Remarks:** Advertising not accepted. **Circ:** (Not Reported).

1786 ■ Asian American Law Journal
University of California, Berkeley Safe Transportation Research & Education Center
2614 Dwight Way
Berkeley, CA 94720-7374
Fax: (510)643-9922
Publisher's E-mail: admissions@law.berkeley.edu
Journal focusing on legal issues of concern to Asian Americans. **Freq:** Annual. **Cols./Page:** 2. **Key Personnel:** Joseph Bui, Editor-in-Chief. **ISSN:** 1939--8417 (print). **Subscription Rates:** $45 Canada and Mexico institutional; $60 Other countries; $45 Single issue back issue. **URL:** http://scholarship.law.berkeley.edu/aalj. **Formerly**: Asian Law Journal. **Remarks:** Advertising not accepted. **Circ:** (Not Reported).

1787 ■ Asian American Law Journal
University of California School of Law
Boalt Hall No. 7200
Berkeley, CA 94720-7200
Phone: (510)642-1741
Publisher's E-mail: admissions@law.berkeley.edu
Journal focusing on legal issues of concern to Asian Americans. **Freq:** Annual. **Cols./Page:** 2. **Key Personnel:** Joseph Bui, Editor-in-Chief. **ISSN:** 1939--8417 (print). **Subscription Rates:** $45 Canada and Mexico institutional; $60 Other countries; $45 Single issue back issue. **URL:** http://scholarship.law.berkeley.edu/aalj. **Formerly**: Asian Law Journal. **Remarks:** Advertising not accepted. **Circ:** (Not Reported).

1788 ■ Bay Nature: Exploring Nature in the San Francisco Bay Area
Clapperstick Institute
1328 6th St., Ste. 2
Berkeley, CA 94710
Magazine that publishes articles about local creatures, wild places, and natural history of the California Bay area. **Freq:** Quarterly. **Trim Size:** 8 1/2 x 11. **Key Personnel:** David Loeb, Executive Director, Publisher. **ISSN:** 1531--5193 (print). **Subscription Rates:** $21.95 Individuals; $39.95 Two years; $53.95 Individuals 3 years. **URL:** http://baynature.org. **Ad Rates:** BW $1175; 4C $1780. **Remarks:** Accepts advertising. **Circ:** 8000.

1789 ■ Berkeley Business Law Journal
University of California School of Law
University of California
Boalt Hall School of Law
158 Boalt Hall
Berkeley, CA 94720-7200
Phone: (510)642-5268
Fax: (775)593-5187
Publication E-mail: bblj@law.berkeley.edu
Journal that aims to create innovative business law-oriented commentary created by professors, professionals, and students. **Freq:** Semiannual. **Key Personnel:** Katie Glynn, Editor-in-Chief; Joe Santiesteban, Editor-in-Chief. **ISSN:** 1548--7067 (print). **Subscription Rates:** $45 Individuals; $60 Other countries; $24 Single issue. **URL:** http://businesslawjournal.org; http://www.law.berkeley.edu/newsroom/student-journals. **Remarks:** Accepts advertising. **Circ:** (Not Reported).

1790 ■ Berkeley Journal of African American Law and Policy
University of California School of Law
Boalt Hall No. 7200
Berkeley, CA 94720-7200
Phone: (510)642-1741
Publisher's E-mail: admissions@law.berkeley.edu
Journal serving as an alternative forum to address legal and policy issues of concern to African Americans. **Freq:** Annual. **ISSN:** 1943--4278 (print). **Subscription Rates:** $58 Individuals. **URL:** http://scholarship.law.berkeley.edu/bjalp. **Circ:** (Not Reported).

1791 ■ Berkeley Journal of Criminal Law
University of California School of Law
Boalt Hall No. 7200
Berkeley, CA 94720-7200
Phone: (510)642-1741
Publisher's E-mail: admissions@law.berkeley.edu
Journal containing discussions on regional, national, and international criminal law issues. **URL:** http://www.bjcl.org. **Circ:** (Not Reported).

1792 ■ Berkeley Journal of Employment and Labor Law
University of California School of Law
Boalt Hall No. 7200
Berkeley, CA 94720-7200
Phone: (510)642-1741
Publication E-mail: journalpublications@law.berkeley.edu
Professional journal covering employment and labor law. **Freq:** Semiannual. **Print Method:** offset. **Trim Size:**

Circulation: ★ = AAM; △ or • = BPA; ♦ = CAC; ❑ = VAC; ⊕ = PO Statement; ‡ = Publisher's Report; Boldface figures = sworn; Light figures = estimated.

7 x 10. **Key Personnel:** Jonathan Helfgott, Editor-in-Chief; Caleb Webster, Editor. **ISSN:** 1067--7666 (print). **Alt. Formats:** PDF. **URL:** http://scholarship.law.berkeley.edu/bjell. **Remarks:** Accepts advertising. **Circ:** (Not Reported).

1793 ■ Berkeley Journal of Entertainment and Sports Law
University of California School of Law
Boalt Hall No. 7200
Berkeley, CA 94720-7200
Phone: (510)642-1741
Publisher's E-mail: admissions@law.berkeley.edu
Journal containing current legal issues that impact the sports and entertainment industries, domestically and internationally. **Freq:** Annual. **URL:** http://www.bjesl.net. **Circ:** (Not Reported).

1794 ■ Berkeley Journal of Gender, Law & Justice, a continuation of the Berkeley Women's Law Journal
Joe Christensen Inc.
University of California
38 W Wing
Berkeley, CA 94720
Phone: (510)642-6263
Publication E-mail: bwlj@socrates.berkeley.edu
journalpublications@law.berkeley.edu
Journal covering women and law. **Freq:** Semiannual. **Key Personnel:** Aditi Fruitwala, Editor-in-Chief; Louisa Irving, Editor-in-Chief. **Subscription Rates:** $32 Single issue; $75 Institutions, other countries; $60 Institutions domestic; $15 Students. **URL:** http://genderlawjustice.berkeley.edu; http://scholarship.law.berkeley.edu/bglj/. **Formerly**: Berkeley Women's Law Journal. **Ad Rates:** BW $275. **Remarks:** Accepts advertising. **Circ:** (Not Reported).

1795 ■ Berkeley Journal of International Law
University of California School of Law
Boalt Hall No. 7200
Berkeley, CA 94720-7200
Phone: (510)642-1741
Publisher's E-mail: admissions@law.berkeley.edu
Journal containing a broad range of scholarship that spans public international, private international, and comparative law disciplines. **Freq:** Semiannual. **URL:** http://scholarship.law.berkeley.edu/bjil. **Circ:** (Not Reported).

1796 ■ Berkeley Journal of Middle Eastern and Islamic Law
University of California School of Law
Boalt Hall No. 7200
Berkeley, CA 94720-7200
Phone: (510)642-1741
Publisher's E-mail: admissions@law.berkeley.edu
Journal serving as a forum for the discussion of legal and philosophical issues relating to the Middle East and Islamic world. **Freq:** Annual. **URL:** http://scholarship.law.berkeley.edu/jmeil. **Circ:** (Not Reported).

1797 ■ Berkeley La Raza Law Journal
University of California School of Law
Boalt Hall No. 7200
Berkeley, CA 94720-7200
Phone: (510)642-1741
Publisher's E-mail: admissions@law.berkeley.edu
Journal containing legal issues affecting the Latina/o community. **Freq:** Annual. **URL:** http://www.boalt.org/LRLJ. **Circ:** (Not Reported).

1798 ■ Berkeley Technology Law Journal
University of California, Berkeley Safe Transportation Research & Education Center
University of California, Berkeley
587 Simon Hall
Berkeley, CA 94720
Fax: (510)643-6816
Publication E-mail: btlj@law.berkeley.edu
Journal covering technology and law. **Freq:** Quarterly 4/yr (Spring, Summer, Fall, and Annual Review). **Key Personnel:** Emily Chen, Editor-in-Chief; Wyatt Glynn, Editor. **ISSN:** 1086--3818 (print). **Subscription Rates:** $65 Individuals; $85 Institutions; $27 Single issue back issue. **URL:** http://btlj.org. **Formerly**: High Technology Law Journal. **Remarks:** Accepts advertising. **Circ:** (Not Reported).

1799 ■ Biotechnology & Bioengineering
John Wiley & Sons Inc.
c/o Douglas S. Clark, Ed.-in-Ch.
Department of Chemical Engineering
University of California
Berkeley, CA 94720-1462
Publisher's E-mail: info@wiley.com
Journal providing an international forum for original research on all aspects of biochemical and microbial technology, including products, process development and design, and equipment. **Founded:** 1958. **Freq:** 18/yr. **Print Method:** Offset. **Trim Size:** 8 1/2 x 11 1/4. **Cols./Page:** 2. **Col. Width:** 20 picas. **Col. Depth:** 60 picas. **Key Personnel:** Lee R. Lynd, Advisor, Board Member; Douglas S. Clark, Editor-in-Chief; James D. Bryers, Board Member; Elmer L. Gaden, Jr., Editor, Founder; Vassily Hatzimanikatis, Associate Editor; Pauline M. Doran, Associate Editor; Michael J. Betenbaugh, Board Member; Jens Nielsen, Associate Editor; Tadashi Matsunaga, Associate Editor. **ISSN:** 0006-3592 (print); **EISSN:** 1097-0290 (electronic). **Subscription Rates:** $11417 U.S., Canada, and Mexico online only; institutions; £5826 Institutions online only; €7367 Institutions online only; $13701 U.S. print and online; $14003 Canada and Mexico print and online; £7223 Institutions print and online; €9134 Institutions print and online; $11417 U.S. print only; $11669 Canada and Mexico print only; £6019 Institutions print only; €7611 Institutions print only. **URL:** http://onlinelibrary.wiley.com/journal/10.1002/(ISSN)1097-0290; http://www.wiley.com/WileyCDA/WileyTitle/productCd-BIT.html. **Ad Rates:** BW $1,217; 4C $1,545. **Remarks:** Accepts advertising. **Circ:** Paid 11900.

1800 ■ California Engineer
California Engineer Publishing Co.
University of California, Berkeley
221 Bechtel Engineering Ctr.
Berkeley, CA 94720-0001
Collegiate engineering journal serving the students, faculty, and staff of the University of California Engineering Colleges at Berkeley, Los Angeles, Davis, Irvine, San Diego, and Santa Barbara. **Freq:** Quarterly during academic year. **Print Method:** Offset. **Trim Size:** 8 1/2 x 11. **Cols./Page:** 3. **Col. Width:** 15 picas. **Col. Depth:** 9 inches. **Key Personnel:** Pavan Yedavalli, Editor-in-Chief. **ISSN:** 0008--1027 (print). **Subscription Rates:** $5 Individuals. **Ad Rates:** BW $2,100; 4C $2,800. **Remarks:** Accepts advertising. **Circ:** Controlled ‡10000.

1801 ■ California Law Review
Joe Christensen Inc.
University of California, School of Law
40 Boalt Hall
Berkeley, CA 94720
Phone: (510)642-7562
Fax: (510)642-3476
Legal journal. **Freq:** Bimonthly February, April, June, August, October, and December. **Print Method:** Offset. **Trim Size:** 5 1/2 x 8. **Cols./Page:** 1. **Col. Width:** 57 nonpareils. **Col. Depth:** 105 agate lines. **Key Personnel:** Jonas Lerman, Editor-in-Chief; Sarah Chilim Ihm, Managing Editor. **ISSN:** 0088--1221 (print). **Subscription Rates:** $85 Individuals; $100 Institutions. **URL:** http://www.californialawreview.org. **Remarks:** Advertising not accepted. **Circ:** ‡1500.

1802 ■ California Management Review
University of California, Berkeley Safe Transportation Research & Education Center
2614 Dwight Way
Berkeley, CA 94720-7374
Fax: (510)643-9922
Publication E-mail: cmr@haas.berkeley.edu
Magazine covering research and creative thought in business and public policy, corporate strategy and organization, and the international economy. **Founded:** 1958. **Freq:** Quarterly. **Key Personnel:** David Vogel, Editor-in-Chief; Gundars Strads, Senior Editor, phone: (510)642-7321; Kora Cypress, Managing Editor. **ISSN:** 0008-1256 (print); **EISSN:** 2162--8564 (electronic). **Subscription Rates:** $75 Individuals; $120 Two years; $115 Other countries; $200 Other countries two years; $40 Students; $40 Individuals Haas Alumni. **URL:** http://cmr.berkeley.edu/. **Also known as:** CMR. **Mailing address:** PO Box 1737, Santiago, Chile. **Ad Rates:** BW $350. **Remarks:** Color advertising not accepted. **Circ:** ‡5500.

1803 ■ California Monthly
California Alumni Association
1 Alumni House
Berkeley, CA 94720
Phone: (510)900-8225
Fax: (510)642-6252
Free: 888-225-2586
Publication E-mail: californiamag@alumni.berkeley.edu
University alumni magazine. **Freq:** Bimonthly. **Print Method:** Web offset. **Trim Size:** 9 x 10.875. **Cols./Page:** 4. **Col. Width:** 32 nonpareils. **Col. Depth:** 194 agate lines. **Key Personnel:** Pat Joseph, Executive Editor; Wendy Miller, Editor. **ISSN:** 0008--1302 (print). **URL:** http://alumni.berkeley.edu/california-magazine. **Ad Rates:** BW $4,710; 4C $6,000. **Remarks:** Accepts advertising. **Circ:** Combined ‡95000.

1804 ■ Cambridge Quarterly of Healthcare Ethics
Cambridge University Press
c/o Dr. Thomasine Kushner, Editor
Health & Medical Sciences Program
University of California, Berkeley
Berkeley, CA 94720
Publication E-mail: ad_sales@cambridge.org
Journal focusing on ethics as applied to medicine. **Freq:** Quarterly. **Key Personnel:** Dr. Doris Thomasma, Managing Editor; Steve Heilig, Editor; Dr. Thomasine Kushner, Editor. **ISSN:** 0963-1801 (print). **Subscription Rates:** $360 Institutions online & print; $300 Institutions online; $45 Single issue article; £225 Institutions online & print; £188 Institutions online. **URL:** http://journals.cambridge.org/action/displayJournal?jid=CQH. **Ad Rates:** BW $895. **Remarks:** Accepts advertising. **Circ:** 950.

1805 ■ Catalysis Letters
Springer Netherlands
c/o Gabor A. Somorjai, Ed.-in-Ch.
D58 Hildebrand Hall
Dept. of Chemistry
University of California, Berkeley
Berkeley, CA 94720-1460
Phone: (510)642-4053
Journal covering the science of catalysis and functions as a vehicle of communication and exchange of seminal ideas and advances among practitioners. **Freq:** Monthly. **Key Personnel:** Hajo Freund, Editor-in-Chief; E.A. Lombardo, Board Member; Sir John Meurig Thomas, Editor, Founder; Gabor A. Somorjai, Editor-in-Chief; Sir John Meurig Thomas, Editor, Founder. **ISSN:** 1011--372X (print); **EISSN:** 1572--879X (electronic). **Subscription Rates:** €4778 Institutions print or online only; €5734 Institutions print and enhanced access; $4894 Institutions print or online only; $5873 Institutions print and enhanced access. **URL:** http://link.springer.com/journal/10562; http://www.springer.com/chemistry/catalysis/journal/10562. **Remarks:** Accepts advertising. **Circ:** (Not Reported).

1806 ■ Cellular Microbiology
Wiley-Blackwell
c/o Richard S. Stephens, Co-Founding Editor
Division of Infectious Diseases
University of California
16 Warren Hall
Berkeley, CA 94720-7360
Fax: (510)643-1537
Journal focusing on microbial and host-cell biology. **Freq:** Monthly. **Key Personnel:** Richard S. Stephens, Founder, Editor; Philippe Sansonetti, Founder, Editor. **ISSN:** 1462--5814 (print); **EISSN:** 1462--5822 (electronic). **Subscription Rates:** £1290 Institutions online only; $2384 Institutions online only; €1638 Institutions online only; $2779 Institutions, other countries online only. **URL:** http://onlinelibrary.wiley.com/journal/10.1111/(ISSN)1462-5822. **Remarks:** Accepts advertising. **Circ:** (Not Reported).

1807 ■ Chicana/Latina Studies: The Journal of MALCS
Mujeres Activas en Letras Y Cambio Social
1404 66th St.
Berkeley, CA 94702
Publisher's E-mail: chicanas@malcs.org
Journal containing peer-reviewed research articles, literary criticism, creative writing, review essays, occasional commentaries, and book reviews about Chicana/Latina experiences and conditions. **Freq:** Annual. **Alt. Formats:** PDF. **URL:** http://malcs.org/chicanalatina-studies-the-journal-of-malcs. **Formerly**: Trabajos Monograficos: Studies in Chicana/Latina Research. **Remarks:** Advertising not accepted. **Circ:** (Not Reported).

1808 ■ The Coffee Review
The Coffee Review
2625 Alcatraz Ave., No. 263
Berkeley, CA 94705
Fax: (510)653-8131
Trade magazine focused on educating and entertaining coffee enthusiasts. **Freq:** Monthly. **Key Personnel:** Kenneth Davids, Editor. **URL:** http://www.coffeereview.com. **Remarks:** Accepts advertising. **Circ:** (Not Reported).

1809 ■ Communications in Applied Mathematics and Computational Science
Mathematical Sciences Publishers
c/o John B. Bell, Managing Editor
Center for Computational Sciences & Engineering
Lawrence Berkeley National Laboratory
One Cyclotron Rd., MS 50A-1148
Berkeley, CA 94720-8142
Publisher's E-mail: contact@mathscipub.org
Peer-reviewed journal covering applied mathematics and computational science. **Freq:** 2/yr. **Key Personnel:** John B. Bell, Managing Editor. **ISSN:** 1559--3940 (print); **EISSN:** 2157--5452 (electronic). **Subscription Rates:** $100 Individuals electronic; $150 Individuals print and electronic. **URL:** http://msp.org/publications/journals/#camcos; http://msp.org/camcos/about/cover/cover.html. **Circ:** (Not Reported).

1810 ■ Cultural Analysis: An Interdisciplinary Forum on Folklore and Popular Culture
University of California, Berkeley Institute of International Studies
215 Moses Hall
Berkeley, CA 94720-2309
Phone: (510)642-2474
Fax: (510)642-9493
Publisher's E-mail: iis@berkeley.edu
Peer-reviewed journal dedicated to folklore and investigating expressive and everyday culture. **Key Personnel:** Pertti J. Anttonen, Board Member; Hande Birkalan, Board Member; Regina Bendix, Board Member; Charles Briggs, Board Member; Veronique Campion-Vincent, Board Member; Galit Hasan-Rokem, Board Member; Kimberly Lau, Board Member. **ISSN:** 1537--7873 (print). **URL:** http://socrates.berkeley.edu/~caforum/. **Circ:** (Not Reported).

1811 ■ The Daily Californian: Berkeley's Independent Daily: Established 1871
Independent Berkeley Student Publishing Company Inc.
600 Eshleman Hall
University of California Berkeley
Berkeley, CA 94701-0949
Phone: (510)548-8300
Fax: (510)849-2803
Publication E-mail: dailycal@dailycal.org
Tabloid newspaper covering both the University of California and the city of Berkeley. **Freq:** Weekly. **Print Method:** Offset. **Trim Size:** 10 1/4 x 16. **Cols./Page:** 5. **Col. Width:** 1 7/8 inches. **Col. Depth:** 96 picas. **Key Personnel:** Chloe Hunt, Editor-in-Chief, President. **ISSN:** 1050--2300 (print). **URL:** http://www.dailycal.org. **Mailing address:** PO Box 1949, Berkeley, CA 94701-0949. **Ad Rates:** GLR $7; PCI $25. **Remarks:** Accepts advertising. **Circ:** ‡10000.

1812 ■ Early China
University of California, Berkeley Center for Chinese Studies
2223 Fulton St., Rm. 505
Berkeley, CA 94720-2328
Phone: (510)643-6321
Fax: (510)643-7062
Publisher's E-mail: ccs@berkeley.edu
Scholarly journal covering prehistoric China history. **Freq:** Annual. **Trim Size:** 6 x 9. **Cols./Page:** 1. **Col. Width:** 26 picas. **Key Personnel:** Katherine Lawn Chouta, Managing Editor, phone: (510)643-3378. **ISSN:** 0362--5028 (print); **EISSN:** 2325--2324 (electronic). **Subscription Rates:** $50 Individuals volume 35-36 (2012-2013) - current; $40 Individuals volume 33-34 or 32; $30 Individuals volume 30 or 31. **URL:** http://ieas.berkeley.edu/publications/early_china.html; http://www.dartmouth.edu/~earlychina/publications/early_china_journal/index.html; http://journals.cambridge.org/action/displayJournal?jid=EAC. **Remarks:** Advertising not accepted. **Circ:** Controlled 350, 400.

1813 ■ Earth Island Journal: An International Environmental News Magazine
Earth Island Institute
2150 Allston Way, Ste. 460
Berkeley, CA 94704-1375
Phone: (510)859-9100
Fax: (510)859-9091
Magazine publishing environmental alerts and success stories from around the world. **Freq:** Quarterly Winter, Autumn, Summer, Spring. **Print Method:** Web Offset. **Trim Size:** 8.375 x 10.875. **Cols./Page:** 3. **Col. Width:** 2 1/4 inches. **Key Personnel:** John A. Knox, Executive Director; Jason Mark, Editor; Erin Palmerston, Office Manager. **ISSN:** 1041-0406 (print). **Subscription Rates:** $10 Individuals; $20 Other countries. **URL:** http://www.earthisland.org/journal. **Ad Rates:** BW $875; 4C $1,090. **Remarks:** Accepts advertising. **Circ:** Combined 18000.

1814 ■ Earthquake Engineering and Structural Dynamics: The Journal of the International Association for Earthquake Engineering
John Wiley & Sons Inc.
c/o Prof. Anil K. Chopra, Exec. Ed.
Department of Civil & Environmental Engineering
University of California
721 Davis Hall
Berkeley, CA 94720-1710
Publisher's E-mail: info@wiley.com
Journal focusing on earthquake engineering, including such topics as seismicity, ground motion characteristics, and soil amplification and failure. **Freq:** 15/yr. **Key Personnel:** Prof. Anil K. Chopra, Executive Editor; Prof. Peter Fajfar, Editor; Prof. Ray W. Clough, Editor; Prof. Masayoshi Nakashima, Editor. **ISSN:** 0098--8847 (print); **EISSN:** 1096--9845 (electronic). **Subscription Rates:** $8108 Institutions print or online - USA/Canada & Mexico/ROW; $9730 Institutions print & online - USA/Canada & Mexico/ROW; £4141 Institutions print or online - UK; £4970 Institutions print & online - UK; €5235 Institutions print or online - Europe; €6282 Institutions print & online - Europe. **URL:** http://onlinelibrary.wiley.com/journal/10.1002/(ISSN)1096-9845. **Remarks:** Accepts advertising. **Circ:** (Not Reported).

1815 ■ Ecology Law Quarterly
University of California Boalt Hall School of Law
396 Simon Hall
Berkeley, CA 94720-7200
Phone: (510)642-6483
Fax: (510)642-9893
Publication E-mail: JournalPublications@law.berkeley.edu
Journal covering ecology and law. **Freq:** Quarterly (Feb., May, Aug., Nov.). **Key Personnel:** Sheri Hani, Managing Editor; Danny Kramer, Editor-in-Chief. **ISSN:** 0046--1121 (print). **Subscription Rates:** $35 Individuals; $60 Institutions. **URL:** http://www.ecologylawquarterly.org; http://ecologylawquarterly.org. **Remarks:** Accepts advertising. **Circ:** (Not Reported).

1816 ■ Experimental Heat Transfer
Taylor & Francis Group Journals
c/o Per F. Peterson, Editorial Advisory Board
Department of Nuclear Engineering
University of California
4155 Etcheverry Hall
Berkeley, CA 94720-1730
Publisher's E-mail: customerservice@taylorandfrancis.com
Forum for original research on heat and mass transfer and in related fluid flows. **Freq:** Bimonthly. **Print Method:** Offset. **Trim Size:** 7 x 10. **Key Personnel:** Melany L. Hunt, Advisor; Ishwar K. Puri, Editor; Prof. J.P. Meyer, Editor; J.W. Rose, Editor; J.H. Lienhard, Editor; Suresh V. Garimella, Editor; Ping Cheng, Advisor; Prof. Dimos Poulikakos, Editor-in-Chief. **ISSN:** 0891--6152 (print); **EISSN:** 1521--0480 (electronic). **Subscription Rates:** $1217 Institutions print & online; $1065 Institutions online only; $549 Individuals. **URL:** http://www.tandfonline.com/toc/ueht20/current. **Remarks:** Accepts advertising. **Circ:** Paid ‡267.

1817 ■ The Four Seasons: Journal of the Regional Parks Botanic Garden
Regional Parks Botanic Garden
Tilden Regional Pk.
Berkeley, CA 94708-2396
Phone: (510)544-3169
Publisher's E-mail: bgarden@ebparks.org
Professional journal covering natural history, biology, ecology, conservation, botany, and horticulture, with an emphasis on California's native plants. **Freq:** Annual. **Print Method:** Offset. **Trim Size:** 6 1/2 x 9 1/2. **Cols./Page:** 1. **Col. Width:** 4 1/2 inches. **Col. Depth:** 7 1/10 inches. **Subscription Rates:** $10 Single issue back issues from 2004 to present; $4 Single issue back issue before 2004; $50 Individuals; $30 Included in membership Student; $75 Included in membership Family. **URL:** http://www.nativeplants.org/fourseasons.html. **Remarks:** Advertising not accepted. **Circ:** Combined 500.

1818 ■ Greater Good
University of California, Berkeley - Greater Good Science Center
2425 Atherton St., Ste. 6070
Berkeley, CA 94720-6070
Phone: (510)642-2451
Magazine highlighting ground breaking scientific research into the roots of happiness, compassion, and altruism. **Freq:** Quarterly. **Key Personnel:** Dacher Keltner, Executive Editor; Ann Shulman, Executive Director; Jason Marsh, Editor-in-Chief. **URL:** http://greatergood.berkeley.edu. **Circ:** (Not Reported).

1819 ■ Here Comes the Guide
Hopscotch Press Inc.
930 Carlton St.
Berkeley, CA 94710-9727
Phone: (510)548-0400
Fax: (510)548-0144
Publisher's E-mail: info@herecomestheguide.com
Magazine that aims to the wedding resource for California event locations and services. **Freq:** Annual. **Key Personnel:** Jan Brenner, Editor-in-Chief; Meredith Monday Schwartz, Chief Executive Officer; Lisa Edd, Managing Editor, phone: (877)826-2646. **Subscription Rates:** Free online. **URL:** http://www.herecomestheguide.com. **Remarks:** Accepts advertising. **Circ:** (Not Reported).

1820 ■ Home Energy
Energy Auditor & Retrofitter, Inc.
1250 Addison St. Ste. 211 B
Berkeley, CA 94702
Phone: (510)524-5405
Fax: (510)981-1406
Publisher's E-mail: contact@homeenergy.org
Trade magazine covering residential energy conservation issues. **Freq:** Bimonthly. **Print Method:** Web offset. **Trim Size:** 8.75 x 11.125. **Key Personnel:** Tom White, Publisher; Jim Gunshinan, Editor; Carol Markell, Manager, Advertising, Manager, Marketing; Maggie Forti, Office Manager; Alana Shindler, Manager. **ISSN:** 0896--9442 (print). **Subscription Rates:** $85 Individuals print and online; $55 Individuals online; $150 Two years print & online; $90 Two years online. **URL:** http://www.homeenergy.org. **Formerly:** Energy Auditor and Retro Filter; Energy auditor and retrofitter. **Ad Rates:** BW $1,100; 4C $1,715. **Remarks:** Accepts advertising. **Circ:** Combined ‡5500.

1821 ■ Human Development
S. Karger Publishers Inc.
Institute of Human Development
University of California
1121 Tolman Hall
Berkeley, CA 94720
Phone: (510)642-7969
Publication E-mail: humandev@uic.edu
Scientific medical journal. **Founded:** 1958. **Freq:** Bimonthly. **Print Method:** Offset. **Trim Size:** 177 x 252 mm. **Cols./Page:** 1. **Col. Width:** 84 nonpareils. **Col. Depth:** 141 agate lines. **Key Personnel:** Dr. Geoffrey B. Saxe, Editor; L. Nucci, Editor; Terezinha Nunes, Associate Editor. **ISSN:** 0018-716X (print). **Subscription Rates:** 917 FR Institutions online or print, combined; 229 FR Individuals online or print, combined. **URL:** http://www.karger.com/Journal/Home/224249. **Formerly:** Vita Humana. **Ad Rates:** BW $1,950. **Remarks:** Accepts advertising. **Circ:** 1850.

1822 ■ Industrial and Corporate Change
Oxford University Press
c/o David Teece, Ed.
Institute for Business Innovation, F402
Haas School of Business, No. 1930

Circulation: ★ = AAM; △ or • = BPA; ♦ = CAC; ❑ = VAC; ⊕ = PO Statement; ‡ = Publisher's Report; Boldface figures = sworn; Light figures = estimated.

University of California
Berkeley, CA 94720-1930
Phone: (510)642-1075
Fax: (510)642-2826
Publisher's E-mail: webenquiry.uk@oup.com
Journal discussing the structure of industries and the causes of change in a variety of disciplines. **Freq:** 6/yr. **Key Personnel:** J. Chytry, Managing Editor, phone: (510)642-1075, fax: (510)642-2826; David Teece, Editor; Giovanni Dosi, Editor; Nick Von Tunzelmann, Member; Glenn R. Carroll, Editor. **ISSN:** 0960--6491 (print); **EISSN:** 1464--3650 (electronic). **Subscription Rates:** £100 Individuals print only; $197 Individuals print only; €150 Individuals print only; £635 Institutions print only; $1249 Institutions print only; €952 Institutions print only; £862 Institutions corporate, print and online; $1697 Institutions corporate, print and online; €1293 Institutions corporate, print and online. **URL:** http://icc.oxfordjournals.org/. **Remarks:** Advertising accepted; rates available upon request. **Circ:** (Not Reported).

1823 ■ International Journal of Nanotechnology
Inderscience Publishers
c/o Dr. Lionel Vayssieres, Ed.-in-Ch.
Chemical Sciences Division
Lawrence Berkeley National Laboratory
MS 70A-1150, One Cyclotron Rd.
Berkeley, CA 94720
Publication E-mail: info@inderscience.com
Journal offering a multidisciplinary source of information in all subjects and topics related to nanotechnology, with fundamental, technological, as well as societal and educational perspectives. **Freq:** Monthly. **Key Personnel:** Dr. Lionel Vayssieres, Editor-in-Chief; Samuel S. Mao, Associate Editor. **ISSN:** 1475--7435 (print); **EISSN:** 1741--8151 (electronic). **Subscription Rates:** $1415 Individuals print or online only for 1 user; $2405 Individuals online only for 2-3 users; $1981 Individuals print and online; $3537.50 Individuals online only for 4-5 users; $4598.75 Individuals online only for 6-7 users; $5589.25 Individuals online only for 8-9 users; $6509 Individuals online only for 10-14 users; $7428.75 Individuals online only for 15-19 users; $8773 Individuals online only for 20+ users. **URL:** http://www.inderscience.com/jhome.php?jcode=ijnt. **Circ:** (Not Reported).

1824 ■ International Journal of Transitional Justice
Oxford University Press
Human Rights Center & School of Public Health
University of California
Berkeley, CA 94720
Journal focusing on the study of those strategies employed by states and international institutions to deal with a legacy of human rights abuses and to effect social reconstruction in the wake of widespread violence. Covering truth commissions, universal jurisdiction, post-conflict social reconciliation, victim and perpetrator studies, international and domestic prosecutions, institutional transformation, vetting, memorialization, reparations and ex-combatant reintegration. **Freq:** 3/year. **Print Method:** Offset. **Trim Size:** 11 3/8 x 14 1/2. **Cols./Page:** 5. **Col. Width:** 11 picas. **Col. Depth:** 13 1/2 inches. **Key Personnel:** Hugo van der Merwe, Editor-in-Chief; Harvey M. Weinstein, Editor; Nahla Valji, Board Member. **ISSN:** 1752--7716 (print); **EISSN:** 1752--7724 (electronic). **USPS:** 094-480. **Subscription Rates:** $451 Institutions print and online; $564 print and online (corporate); $143 Students print. **URL:** http://ijtj.oxfordjournals.org. **Remarks:** Accepts advertising. **Circ:** (Not Reported).

1825 ■ Involve: A Journal of Mathematics
Mathematical Sciences Publishers
University of California
University of California, Berkeley
Berkeley, CA 94720-3840
Phone: (510)643-8638
Fax: (510)295-2608
Publisher's E-mail: contact@mathscipub.org
Peer-reviewed journal covering mathematics. **Freq:** 5/year. **Key Personnel:** Kenneth S. Berenhaut, Managing Editor. **ISSN:** 1944--4176 (print); **EISSN:** 1944--4184 (electronic). **Subscription Rates:** $175 Individuals electronic; $235 Individuals print and electronic; $270 Other countries electronic + print , international shipping. **URL:** http://msp.org/involve/about/cover/cover.html; http://msp.org/publications/journals/#involve. **Remarks:** Accepts advertising. **Circ:** (Not Reported).

1826 ■ Journal of Cognitive Neuroscience
The MIT Press
University of California
Helen Wills Neuroscience Institute
132 Baker Hall
Berkeley, CA 94720-3190
Publication E-mail: jocn@jocn.berkeley.edu
Forum for research of interaction between brain and behavior. **Freq:** Monthly. **Print Method:** Offset. **Trim Size:** 8 1/2 x 11. **Cols./Page:** 2. **Col. Width:** 20 picas. **Col. Depth:** 57 picas. **Key Personnel:** Mark E'Esposito, Editor-in-Chief; Amy F. Arnsten, Board Member; Anjan Chatterjee, Board Member; Marlene Behrman, Board Member; Richard B. Ivry, Associate Editor. **ISSN:** 0898-929X (print); **EISSN:** 1530-8898 (electronic). **Subscription Rates:** $195 Individuals online only; $102 Students retired, online only; $1063 Institutions online. **URL:** http://www.mitpressjournals.org/loi/jocn. **Remarks:** Accepts advertising. **Circ:** (Not Reported).

1827 ■ Journal of Irreproducible Results
JIR Publishers
2625 Alcatraz Ave., Ste. 235
Berkeley, CA 94705
Phone: (650)573-7125
Journal of humor and satire. **Founded:** 1955. **Freq:** Bimonthly. **Print Method:** Offset. Uses mats. **Trim Size:** 8 1/2 x 11. **Cols./Page:** 2. **Col. Width:** 37 nonpareils. **Col. Depth:** 125 agate lines. **Key Personnel:** Norman Sperling, Editor. **ISSN:** 0022-2038 (print). **Subscription Rates:** $26.95 Individuals; $38.95 Canada and Mexico; $49.95 Other countries. **URL:** http://www.jir.com/index.html. **Ad Rates:** BW $850; 4C $1,750; PCI $7. **Remarks:** Accepts advertising. **Circ:** ‡5000.

1828 ■ Journal of Law, Economics, and Organization
Oxford University Press
c/o Pablo T. Spiller, Ed.
Haas School of Business
University of California, Berkeley
Berkeley, CA 94720
Phone: (203)432-1670
Fax: (203)432-8260
Publication E-mail: jleo@pantheon.yale.edu
Journal covering the study of organization within firms and political institutions. **Freq:** 6/year. **Trim Size:** 6 x 9. **Key Personnel:** Al Klevorick, Editor; Cathy Orcutt, Assistant Editor; Henry Hansmann, Board Member; Francine Lafontaine, Board Member; Robert Kagan, Board Member; Aaron Edlin, Board Member; Lee Epstein, Editor; Guido Calabresi, Board Member; Morris Fiorina, Board Member; Gary Cox, Board Member; Pablo T. Spiller, Editor. **ISSN:** 8756--6222 (print); **EISSN:** 1465--7341 (electronic). **Subscription Rates:** £133 Institutions online; £153 Institutions print; £166 Institutions print and online; $253 Institutions online; $291 Institutions print; $316 Institutions print and online; €199 Institutions online; €229 Institutions print; €249 Institutions print and online; £65 Individuals print; $125 Individuals print; €98 Individuals print. **URL:** http://jleo.oxfordjournals.org. **Remarks:** Accepts advertising. **Circ:** (Not Reported).

1829 ■ Journal of Mathematical Logic
World Scientific Publishing Company Private Ltd.
c/o W. Hugh Woodin, Mng. Ed.
University of California, Berkeley
Department of Mathematics
Berkeley, CA 94720
Fax: (510)642-8204
Publisher's E-mail: wspc@wspc.com.sg
Peer-reviewed journal in mathematics. **Freq:** Semiannual. **Key Personnel:** W. Hugh Woodin, Managing Editor; Theodore A. Slaman, Managing Editor; Chitat Chong, Managing Editor. **ISSN:** 0219--0613 (print); **EISSN:** 1793--6691 (electronic). **Subscription Rates:** $242 Institutions and libraries; print & electronic; $216 Institutions and libraries; electronic only; £168 Institutions and libraries; print & electronic; £149 Institutions and libraries; electronic only; S$384 Institutions and libraries; print & electronic; S$342 Institutions and libraries; electronic only. **URL:** http://www.worldscientific.com/worldscinet/jml. **Circ:** (Not Reported).

1830 ■ Journal of Mechanics of Materials and Structures
Mathematical Sciences Publishers
University of California
University of California, Berkeley
Berkeley, CA 94720-3840
Phone: (510)643-8638
Fax: (510)295-2608
Publisher's E-mail: contact@mathscipub.org
Peer-reviewed journal covering areas of engineering, materials, and biology, the mechanics of solids, materials, and structures. **Freq:** 5/year. **Key Personnel:** Charles R. Steele, Founder; Davide Bigoni, Editor; Iwona Jasiuk, Editor. **ISSN:** 1559--3959 (print); **EISSN:** 1559--3959 (electronic). **Subscription Rates:** $615 Individuals electronic; $775 Individuals print and electronic; $835 Individuals electronic + print, international shipping. **URL:** http://msp.org/publications/journals/#jomms; http://msp.org/jomms. **Circ:** (Not Reported).

1831 ■ Journal of Occupational and Environmental Hygiene
American Conference of Governmental Industrial Hygienists
c/o Mark Nicas, PhD, Ed.-in-Ch.
University of California
School of Public Health
University Hall, Rm. 50
Berkeley, CA 94720-7360
Publisher's E-mail: mail@acgih.org
Freq: Monthly. **Key Personnel:** Michael S. Morgan, Editor-in-Chief; Mark Nicas, PhD, Editor-in-Chief; Joseph Bowman, PhD, Board Member; Kevin Ashley, PhD, Board Member; Farhang Akbar-Khanzadeh, PhD, Board Member; Jonathan Borak, MD, Board Member; Stephen Bowes, PhD, Board Member; Lisa M. Brosseau, PhD, Board Member; Howard Cohen, Board Member; Elliott Berger, Board Member. **ISSN:** 1545--9624 (print); **EISSN:** 1545--9632 (electronic). **Subscription Rates:** $352 Individuals print only; $1109 Institutions print & online; $970 Institutions online only; Included in membership. **URL:** http://tandfonline.com/toc/uoeh20/current; http://acgih.org/publications/journal/journal-of-occupational-and-environmental-hygiene; http://aiha.org/publications-and-resources/JOEH/Pages/default.aspx. **Formerly:** AIHA Journal; Applied Occupational and Environmental Hygiene. **Remarks:** Advertising accepted; rates available upon request. **Circ:** 6100.

1832 ■ Journal of Public Deliberation
bepress
2809 Telegraph Ave., Ste. 202
Berkeley, CA 94705
Phone: (510)665-1200
Fax: (510)665-1201
Publisher's E-mail: info@bepress.com
Journal covering research, projects, opinion, experiments and experiences of practitioners and academics in the rising multi-disciplinary field and political movement. **Key Personnel:** Lyn Carson, Board Member; Laura W. Black, Editor. **ISSN:** 1937--2841 (print). **URL:** http://www.publicdeliberation.net/jpd. **Circ:** (Not Reported).

1833 ■ Jump Cut: A Review of Contemporary Media
Jump Cut Associates
PO Box 865
Berkeley, CA 94701
Journal covering film, video, and media criticism. **Freq:** Annual. **Print Method:** Web offset. **Trim Size:** 8 1/4 x 10 3/4. **Key Personnel:** Julia Lesage, Editor; John Hess, Editor. **ISSN:** 0146--5546 (print). **URL:** http://www.ejumpcut.org/home.html. **Remarks:** Accepts advertising. **Circ:** (Not Reported).

1834 ■ Login
USENIX Association
2560 9th St., Ste. 215
Berkeley, CA 94710
Phone: (510)528-8649
Fax: (510)548-5738
Publisher's E-mail: office@usenix.org
Magazine covering all aspects of computing systems. **Freq:** 6/year. **Key Personnel:** Rik Farrow, Editor. **Subscription Rates:** $90 Individuals print and online; $65 Individuals online only. **URL:** http://www.usenix.org/publications/login. **Remarks:** Advertising not accepted. **Circ:** 5,000, 15000.

1835 ■ Madrono: A West American Journal of Botany
California Botanical Society
c/o Jepson Herbarium
1001 Valley Life Sciences Bldg.
Berkeley, CA 94720-2466
Phone: (510)643-7008
Botanical journal. **Freq:** Quarterly (Jan., April, July, Oct.). **Print Method:** Letterpress. Uses mats. **Cols./Page:** 1. **Col. Width:** 50 nonpareils. **Col. Depth:** 98 agate lines. **Key Personnel:** Matt Ritter, Editor. **ISSN:** 0024--9637 (print); **EISSN:** 1943--6297 (electronic). **Subscription Rates:** $10 Single issue. **URL:** http://calbotsoc.org/madrono. **Remarks:** Advertising not accepted. **Circ:** ‡1200.

1836 ■ Mystery Readers Journal
Mystery Readers International
PO Box 8116
Berkeley, CA 94707-8116
Freq: Quarterly. **Key Personnel:** Janet A. Rudolph, Editor. **ISSN:** 1043--3473 (print). **Subscription Rates:** $6.50 Single issue /issue - PDF download; $11 Single issue back issue; $15 Single issue back issue - other countries; included in membership; $39 U.S. and Canada /year; $50 U.S. /year, for overseas airmail; $15 Individuals online. **Alt. Formats:** PDF. **URL:** http://www.mysteryreaders.org/journal.html. **Remarks:** Advertising not accepted. **Circ:** Controlled 2000, 2000.

1837 ■ New Oxford Review
New Oxford Review Inc.
1069 Kains Ave.
Berkeley, CA 94706
Phone: (510)526-5734
Fax: (510)526-3492
Religious magazine. **Freq:** 10/year. **Print Method:** Offset. **Trim Size:** 8 1/2 x 11. **Cols./Page:** 2 and 3. **Col. Width:** 26 and 41 nonpareils. **Col. Depth:** 133 agate lines. **Key Personnel:** Elena M. Vree, Managing Editor; Pieter Vree, Editor, phone: (510)526-5374. **ISSN:** 0149--4244 (print). **Subscription Rates:** $24 Individuals 1 year print edition; $43 Two years; $59 Individuals 3 years print edition; $29 Individuals 1 year online access; $52 Two years online access; $64 Individuals 3 years online access; $38 Individuals 1 year, print and online; $69 Individuals 2 years, print and online; $97 Individuals 3 years, print and online. **URL:** http://www.newoxfordreview.org. **Ad Rates:** BW $640. **Remarks:** Accepts advertising. **Circ:** ‡12000.

1838 ■ News from Native California: An Inside View of the California Indian World
Heyday Books
PO Box 9145
Berkeley, CA 94709
Phone: (510)549-3564
Fax: (510)549-1889
Publication E-mail: nnc@heydaybooks.com
Magazine featuring material relating to California Indians, past and present. **Freq:** Quarterly. **Print Method:** Offset. **Trim Size:** 7 1/2 x 10. **Cols./Page:** 3. **Col. Width:** 14 picas. **Col. Depth:** 57 picas. **Key Personnel:** Margaret Dubin, Managing Editor; Malcolm Margolin, Publisher. **ISSN:** 1040-5437 (print). **Subscription Rates:** $21 Individuals; $5.95 Single issue; $40 Two years; $57 Individuals 3 years. **URL:** http://heydaybooks.com/news-from-native-california; http://newsfromnativecalifornia.com. **Ad Rates:** BW $750. **Remarks:** Accepts advertising. **Circ:** Paid 5000, Controlled 500.

1839 ■ Poetry Flash: A Poetry Review & Literary Calendar for the West
Poetry Flash Inc.
1450 4th St., Ste. 4
Berkeley, CA 94710
Literary magazine (tabloid) containing reviews, interviews and essays on poetry and literary topics. **Freq:** Quarterly. **Print Method:** Web offset. **Trim Size:** 11 1/2 x 15. **Cols./Page:** 3. **Col. Width:** 3 1/8 inches. **Col. Depth:** 13 3/4 inches. **Key Personnel:** Joyce Jenkins, Editor; Richard Silberg, Associate Editor. **ISSN:** 0737--4747 (print). **URL:** http://www.poetryflash.org. **Ad Rates:** BW $715; PCI $17.30. **Remarks:** Accepts advertising. **Circ:** ‡22000.

1840 ■ Post-Soviet Affairs
Bellwether Publishing, Ltd.
c/o George W. Breslauer, Ed.
210 Barrows Hall
Department of Political Science
University of California, Berkeley
Berkeley, CA 94720-1950
Phone: (510)642-4655
Fax: (510)642-9515
Journal featuring the work of prominent Western scholars in Russia. **Freq:** 6/year. **Key Personnel:** George W. Breslauer, Editor. **ISSN:** 1060--586X (print); **EISSN:** 1938--2855 (electronic). **Subscription Rates:** $527 Institutions online; $602 Institutions online and print; $112 Individuals print. **URL:** http://tandfonline.com/toc/rpsa20/current; http://www.bellpub.com/psa. **Circ:** (Not Reported).

1841 ■ San Diego International Law Journal
Law of the Sea Institute
University of California, Berkeley
381 Boalt Hall
Berkeley, CA 94720-7200
Phone: (510)643-5699
Publisher's E-mail: losi@law.berkeley.edu
Freq: Semiannual. **Subscription Rates:** $27 Individuals. **URL:** http://sandiego.edu/law/academics/journals/ilj. **Remarks:** Advertising not accepted. **Circ:** (Not Reported).

1842 ■ ScienceWriters
National Association of Science Writers
PO Box 7905
Berkeley, CA 94707
Phone: (510)647-9500
Publisher's E-mail: director@nasw.org
Magazine featuring analytical reporting and commentary on issues in science journalism and public information. **Freq:** Quarterly. **Key Personnel:** Lynne Friedmann, Editor. **Subscription Rates:** accessible only to members. **URL:** http://www.nasw.org/sciencewriters. **Remarks:** Accepts advertising. **Circ:** (Not Reported).

1843 ■ SCP Journal
Spiritual Counterfeits Project, Inc.
PO Box 4308
Berkeley, CA 94704
Phone: (510)540-0300
Fax: (510)540-1107
Publisher's E-mail: scp@scp-inc.org
Magazine covering spiritual phenomena and cultural trends such as near-death experiences, deep ecology, Gaia, witchcraft, and UFOs. Analyzes spiritual trends from a Christian perspective. **Founded:** 1973. **Freq:** Quarterly. **Key Personnel:** Tal Brooke, Editor, President; John Moore, Associate Editor. **Subscription Rates:** $25 Individuals; $35 Out of country. **URL:** http://www.scp-inc.org. **Remarks:** Advertising not accepted. **Circ:** Paid 15000.

1844 ■ Share International
Transmission Meditation Group
c/o Share International USA
PO Box 5537
Berkeley, CA 94705
Phone: (818)785-6300
Publication E-mail: share@shareintl.org
Magazine reporting on world events and emergence of Maitreya, the World Teacher. **Freq:** Monthly. **Print Method:** Offset. **Trim Size:** 8 1/2 x 11. **Cols./Page:** 3. **Col. Width:** 2 3/8 inches. **Col. Depth:** 9 3/8 inches. **Key Personnel:** Benjamin Creme, Editor, phone: 44-207-482-1113. **ISSN:** 0169--1341 (print). **Subscription Rates:** $38 Individuals USA and Philippines; $42 Individuals Canada, Central & South America, Australia and New Zealand. **Alt. Formats:** PDF. **URL:** http://share-international.org/magazine/SI_main.htm. **Remarks:** Advertising not accepted. **Circ:** Paid 5000, Non-paid 1000.

1845 ■ Share International
Share International
PO Box 5537
Berkeley, CA 94705
Phone: (818)785-6300
Publication E-mail: share@shareintl.org
Magazine reporting on world events and emergence of Maitreya, the World Teacher. **Freq:** Monthly. **Print Method:** Offset. **Trim Size:** 8 1/2 x 11. **Cols./Page:** 3. **Col. Width:** 2 3/8 inches. **Col. Depth:** 9 3/8 inches. **Key Personnel:** Benjamin Creme, Editor, phone: 44-207-482-1113. **ISSN:** 0169--1341 (print). **Subscription Rates:** $38 Individuals USA and Philippines; $42 Individuals Canada, Central & South America, Australia and New Zealand. **Alt. Formats:** PDF. **URL:** http://share-international.org/magazine/SI_main.htm. **Remarks:** Advertising not accepted. **Circ:** Paid 5000, Non-paid 1000.

1846 ■ Sinister Wisdom: A Journal for the Lesbian Imagination in the Arts and Politics
Sinister Wisdom Inc.
PO Box 3252
Berkeley, CA 94703
Publisher's E-mail: sue_lenaerts@hotmail.com
Lesbian literary journal. **Freq:** Quarterly. **Print Method:** Offset. **Trim Size:** 5 1/2 x 8 1/2. **Cols./Page:** 1. **Col. Width:** 24 picas. **Col. Depth:** 100 agate lines. **Key Personnel:** Susan Levinkind, Office Manager. **ISSN:** 0196--1853 (print). **Subscription Rates:** $14.75 Individuals 1 year. **URL:** http://www.sinisterwisdom.org. **Ad Rates:** BW $200. **Remarks:** Color advertising not accepted. **Circ:** Paid ‡3000, Non-paid ‡500.

1847 ■ Teaching English as a Second or Foreign Language: An Electronic Journal
University of California College Writing Programs
112 Wheeler Hall, No. 2500
Berkeley, CA 94720-2500
Phone: (510)642-5570
Fax: (510)642-6963
Publisher's E-mail: collegewriting@berkeley.edu
Journal publishing wide array of articles and reviews relating to teaching English as a Second or foreign language. **Freq:** Quarterly. **Key Personnel:** Vance Stevens, Contact; Spencer Salas, Reviewer; Thomas Delaney, Media Specialist; Maggie Sokolik, Editor; Thomas Robb, Editor. **ISSN:** 1072--4303 (print). **Subscription Rates:** Free. **URL:** http://www.tesl-ej.org/wordpress. **Remarks:** Accepts advertising. **Circ:** (Not Reported).

1848 ■ The Threepenny Review
The Threepenny Review
PO Box 9131
Berkeley, CA 94709
Phone: (510)849-4545
Publisher's E-mail: wlesser@threepennyreview.com
Liberal left-wing literary arts magazine. **Freq:** Quarterly. **Print Method:** Offset. **Trim Size:** 10 x 15. **Cols./Page:** 4. **Col. Width:** 27 nonpareils. **Col. Depth:** 203 agate lines. **Key Personnel:** Wendy Lesser, Editor. **ISSN:** 0275--1410 (print). **Subscription Rates:** $25 Individuals; $45 Two years; $50 Other countries; $7 Single issue. **URL:** http://www.threepennyreview.com. **Ad Rates:** BW $1800; PCI $60. **Remarks:** Accepts advertising. **Circ:** ‡6000.

1849 ■ Tikkun Magazine: A Bimonthly Jewish Critique of Politics, Culture and Society
Tikkun Magazine
2342 Shattuck Ave., Ste. 1200
Berkeley, CA 94704
Phone: (510)644-1200
Fax: (510)644-1255
Magazine featuring world politics and social issues. **Freq:** Quarterly. **Print Method:** Web offset. **Cols./Page:** 3. **Col. Width:** 2 nonpareils. **Col. Depth:** 9 1/8 agate lines. **Key Personnel:** Michael Lerner, Editor-in-Chief; Pete Cattrell, Manager, Operations; Alana Yu-lan Price, Managing Editor. **ISSN:** 0887--9982 (print). **Subscription Rates:** $29 Individuals. **URL:** http://www.tikkun.org. **Ad Rates:** BW $2250; 4C $2500. **Remarks:** Accepts advertising. **Circ:** Combined 24000.

1850 ■ Transactions on Circuits and Systems II: Express Briefs
IEEE - Circuits and Systems Society
c/o Vojin Oklobdzija, President
1285 Grizzly Peak Blvd.
Berkeley, CA 94708-2127
Phone: (510)230-3267
Journal focusing on video systems architecture, video quality assessment, and other video-technology related topics. **Freq:** Monthly. **Key Personnel:** Yong Lian, Editor-in-Chief; Albert Wang, Associate Editor; Antonio Liscidini, Associate Editor. **ISSN:** 1549--7747 (print). **Subscription Rates:** $20 Nonmembers; $10 Members. **URL:** http://tcas2.polito.it; http://ieee-cas.org/publications/transactions-on-circuits-and-systems-part-ii-

Circulation: ★ = AAM; △ or • = BPA; ♦ = CAC; ❑ = VAC; ⊕ = PO Statement; ‡ = Publisher's Report; Boldface figures = sworn; Light figures = estimated.

express-briefs. **Circ:** (Not Reported).

1851 ■ Transit
University of California Department of German
5319 Dwinelle Hall
Berkeley, CA 94720-3243
Phone: (510)643-2004
Fax: (510)642-3243
Publication E-mail: transitjournal@berkeley.edu
Journal publishing in the field of German studies and shed new light on debates about transnational connections. **ISSN:** 1551-9627 (print). **URL:** http://german.berkeley.edu/transit. **Circ:** (Not Reported).

1852 ■ Turning Wheel
Buddhist Peace Fellowship
PO Box 3470
Berkeley, CA 94703
Phone: (510)239-3764
Publisher's E-mail: info@bpf.org
Freq: Semiannual. **ISSN:** 1065- 058X (print). **Subscription Rates:** Included in membership. **URL:** http://www.buddhistpeacefellowship.org/our-work/turning-wheel-media. **Remarks:** Accepts advertising. **Circ:** 10000.

1853 ■ Yoga Journal: For Health and Conscious Living
California Yoga Teachers Association
2054 University Ave.
Berkeley, CA 94704
Phone: (510)841-9200
Fax: (510)644-3101
Free: 800-IDO-YOGA
Magazine devoted to holistic living and yoga. **Freq:** Bimonthly. **Print Method:** Web Offset. **Trim Size:** 8 x 10 1/2. **Cols./Page:** 3. **Col. Width:** 2 1/4 inches. **Col. Depth:** 9 3/8 inches. **Key Personnel:** Claudia Smukler, Director, Production; Kathryn Arnold, Editor; Bill Harper, Publisher; Kaitlin Quistgaard, Editor-in-Chief; Diane Anderson, Senior Editor; Kelle Walsh, Managing Editor. **ISSN:** 0191-0965 (print). **Subscription Rates:** $27.95 Individuals in Canada; $51.95 Two years in Canada; $16.95 Individuals in U.S.; $37.95 Other countries includes postage for one-year.; $71.95 Two years elsewhere. **Remarks:** Advertising accepted; rates available upon request. **Circ:** Paid ★334026.

1854 ■ KALX-FM - 90.7
26 Barrows Hall, No. 5650
Berkeley, CA 94720-5650
Phone: (510)642-1111
Email: mail@kalx.berkeley.edu
Format: Educational. **Owner:** University of California, at above address. **Founded:** 1967. **Operating Hours:** Sunrise-sunset. **Key Personnel:** Sandra Wasson, Gen. Mgr., mail@kalx.berkeley.edu. **Local Programs:** *Film Close-Ups*, Saturday 5:30 p.m. - 6:30 p.m.; *The Next Big Thing*, Monday 6:00 p.m. - 7:00 p.m.; *Women Hold Up Half The Sky*, Saturday 11:00 a.m. - 12:00 p.m. **Wattage:** 500. **Ad Rates:** Noncommercial. **URL:** http://www.kalx.berkeley.edu.

1855 ■ KPFA-FM - 94.1
1929 Martin Luther King Jr. Way
Berkeley, CA 94704
Phone: (510)848-6767
Fax: (510)848-3812
Format: Full Service; Eclectic. **Networks:** Pacifica. **Owner:** Pacifica Foundation, 120 Wall St., New York, NY 10005. **Founded:** 1949. **Operating Hours:** Continuous; 2% network, 98% local. **Key Personnel:** Michael Yoshida, Chief Engineer; Maria Negret, Bus. Mgr., mariabiz@kpfa.org; Andrew Leslie Phillips, Gen. Mgr., andrew@kpfa.org. **Local Programs:** *Morning Show*, Monday Tuesday Wednesday Thursday Friday 8:00 a.m.; *The Bonnie Simmons Show*, Thursday 8:00 p.m. - 10:00 p.m.; *Flashpoints*, Monday Tuesday Wednesday Thursday Friday 5:00 p.m. - 6:00 p.m. **Wattage:** 59,000. **Ad Rates:** Noncommercial. **URL:** http://www.kpfa.org.

BEVERLY HILLS

S. CA. Los Angeles Co. Surrounded by city of Los Angeles. Manufactures cameras, aircraft parts, recording instruments, building materials, tools, food, clothing, plastics, heating equipment, petroleum products. Residential.

1856 ■ AFCI Newsletter
Association of Film Commissioners International
9595 Wilshire Blvd., Ste. 900
Beverly Hills, CA 90211
Phone: (323)461-2324
Fax: (413)375-2903
Magazine featuring stories, news, programs, activities, events and accomplishments of the Association of Film Commissioners International (AFCI) and its members. **Freq:** Monthly. **Subscription Rates:** Included in membership. **Remarks:** Advertising not accepted. **Circ:** (Not Reported).

1857 ■ Aromatherapy Thymes
Aromatherapy Thymes Magazine
8950 W Olympic Blvd., Ste. 282
Beverly Hills, CA 90211
Phone: (323)272-3637
Publisher's E-mail: info@aromatherapythymes.com
Magazine focusing on the use of aromatic plant oils for health and well being. **Freq:** Quarterly. **Key Personnel:** Patricia Carol Brooks, Editor-in-Chief, Founder. **URL:** http://www.aromatherapythymes.com. **Remarks:** Advertising accepted; rates available upon request. **Circ:** (Not Reported).

1858 ■ Art and Living
Art and Living
8306 Wilshire Blvd., Ste. 2029
Beverly Hills, CA 90211
Phone: (310)313-3171
Fax: (310)313-2125
Publisher's E-mail: sales@artandliving.com
Magazine covering art and art topics. **Freq:** 3/year. **Key Personnel:** Jeff Marinelli, Publisher. **URL:** http://www.artandliving.com. **Remarks:** Accepts advertising. **Circ:** (Not Reported).

1859 ■ The Beverly Hills Courier
The Beverly Hills Courier
9100 Wilshire Blvd., Ste. 360 E
Beverly Hills, CA 90212
Phone: (310)278-1322
Fax: (310)271-5118
Local Community newspaper (tabloid). **Freq:** Weekly (Fri.). **Print Method:** Offset. **Trim Size:** 11 x 14. **Cols./Page:** 5. **Col. Width:** 12 picas. **Col. Depth:** 14 inches. **Key Personnel:** Marcia W. Hobbs, Publisher. **Subscription Rates:** Free. **URL:** http://bhcourier.com; http://bhcourier.com/archives. **Ad Rates:** GLR $40; BW $2800; 4C $490; PCI $40. **Remarks:** Accepts advertising. **Circ:** ‡40000.

1860 ■ Beverly Hills Weekly
Beverly Hills Weekly Inc.
140 S Beverly Dr., Ste. 201
Beverly Hills, CA 90210
Community newspaper serving Los Angeles County. **Freq:** Weekly (Thurs.). **Key Personnel:** Josh E. Gross, Chief Executive Officer, Publisher; Melanie Anderson, Editor. **ISSN:** 1528-851X (print). **Subscription Rates:** $75 By mail. **URL:** http://www.bhweekly.com/. **Remarks:** Accepts advertising. **Circ:** (Not Reported).

1861 ■ Beyond Cinema
Association of Film Commissioners International
9595 Wilshire Blvd., Ste. 900
Beverly Hills, CA 90211
Phone: (323)461-2324
Fax: (413)375-2903
Magazine containing articles on the field of film, television, and digital and interactive media industry of producers, directors, writers, executives, location managers, talents and fans of cinematic arts and beyond. **Freq:** 3/year. **Alt. Formats:** Handheld. **URL:** http://www.afci.org/beyond-cinema. **Formerly:** AFI Locations. **Remarks:** Accepts advertising. **Circ:** 30000.

1862 ■ Canyon News
Canyon News
9465 Wilshire Blvd., Ste. 300
Beverly Hills, CA 90210
Fax: (310)807-4394
Publisher's E-mail: staff@canyon-news.com
Newspaper serving Beverly Hills, Bel Air, Malibu and nearby areas. **Founded:** Aug. 2001. **Freq:** Weekly (Sun.). **Key Personnel:** Glenn Kelly, Publisher; Irma Ramos, Editor-in-Chief. **URL:** http://canyon-news.com/artman/publish/index.php. **Ad Rates:** BW $1,680. **Remarks:** Accepts advertising. **Circ:** (Not Reported).

1863 ■ Computer Technology Review
WestWorldWide L.L.C.
420 N Camden Dr.
Beverly Hills, CA 90210-4507
Phone: (310)276-9500
Fax: (310)432-7130
Publisher's E-mail: editorial@wwpi.com
Computer tabloid. **Freq:** Monthly. **Print Method:** Web offset. **Trim Size:** 10 x 14 3/8. **Cols./Page:** 5 and 3. **Col. Width:** 11 and 15 nonpareils. **Col. Depth:** 80 and 60 agate lines. **Key Personnel:** Yuri R. Spiro, Publisher. **Subscription Rates:** Free. **URL:** http://www.wwpi.com. **Ad Rates:** BW $11047; 4C $12997. **Remarks:** Accepts advertising. **Circ:** Controlled 50000.

1864 ■ The Ethiopian Mirror
The Ethiopian Mirror
PO Box 6881
Beverly Hills, CA 90212
Phone: (323)939-3059
Fax: (323)419-1118
Publication E-mail: mirrormedia@aol.com
A Monthly Publication Featuring News, Interviews, Arts & Entertainment. **Freq:** Monthly. **Trim Size:** 11 x 15. **Cols./Page:** 4. **Key Personnel:** Tesfaye Davino, Publisher. **Subscription Rates:** $24 Individuals; $2 Single issue. **Alt. Formats:** Large print. **Ad Rates:** BW $400; 4C $450. **Remarks:** Accepts advertising. **Circ:** Paid 11000, Non-paid 15000.

1865 ■ Hustler Busty Beauties: North America's Breast Magazine
Larry Flynt Publications Inc.
8484 Wilshire Blvd., Ste. 900
Beverly Hills, CA 90211-3218
Phone: (323)651-5400
Adult magazine. **Freq:** Monthly. **Print Method:** Offset. **Trim Size:** 8 1/4 x 10 7/8. **Cols./Page:** 3. **Col. Width:** 14 picas. **Col. Depth:** 58.5 picas. **Key Personnel:** Morgen N. Hagen, Editor; Larry Flynt, Publisher. **ISSN:** 1058-6798 (print). **Subscription Rates:** Included in membership. **URL:** http://BustyBeauties.com/mansion; http://www.bustybeauties.com. **Ad Rates:** BW $1,250; 4C $1,750. **Remarks:** Accepts advertising. **Circ:** ‡160000.

1866 ■ Hustler Magazine
Larry Flynt Publications Inc.
8484 Wilshire Blvd., Ste. 900
Beverly Hills, CA 90211-3218
Phone: (323)651-5400
Men's entertainment magazine. **Freq:** Monthly. **Print Method:** Offset. **Trim Size:** 8 1/2 x 11. **Cols./Page:** 3. **Col. Width:** 28 nonpareils. **Col. Depth:** 140 agate lines. **Key Personnel:** Allan MacDonell, Editor; Larry Flynt, Publisher. **ISSN:** 0149--4635 (print). **URL:** http://www.hustler.com/magazines. **Remarks:** Advertising accepted; rates available upon request. **Circ:** 1066537.

1867 ■ Inside Film Magazine
Inside Film Magazine
8306 Wilshire Blvd., Ste 1826
Beverly Hills, CA 90211
Fax: (323)653-6554
Publisher's E-mail: editor@insidefilm.com
Magazine covering the film industry. **Freq:** Bimonthly. **Key Personnel:** Susan Royal, Editor-in-Chief. **Formerly:** American Premiere. **Remarks:** Advertising not accepted. **Circ:** (Not Reported).

1868 ■ Los Angeles Confidential
Niche Media L.L.C.
8530 Wilshire Blvd., Ste. 500
Beverly Hills, CA 90211
Phone: (310)289-7300
Fax: (310)289-0444
Publication E-mail: advertising@la-confidential-magazine.com
Luxury lifestyle and entertainment magazine covering Los Angeles and the vicinity. **Freq:** 8/year. **Print Method:** Web offset. **Trim Size:** 10 x 12. **Key Personnel:** Alison Miller, Publisher; Spencer Beck, Editor-in-Chief. **Subscription Rates:** $42 U.S. **URL:** http://www.la-confidential-magazine.com. **Remarks:** Accepts advertising. **Circ:** ★65000.

1869 ■ PC Portables Magazine
Larry Flynt Publications Inc.
8484 Wilshire Blvd., Ste. 900
Beverly Hills, CA 90211-3218
Phone: (323)651-5400
Consumer magazine focusing on portable computers,

their software, and applications. **Freq:** Monthly. **Print Method:** Web offset. **Trim Size:** 8 x 10 7/8. **Cols./Page:** 3. **Key Personnel:** Mark A. Kellner, Editor-in-Chief, Contact; Michelle Anderson, Director, Advertising. **ISSN:** 1043--1314 (print). **Formerly**: PC Laptop Computers Magazine. **Ad Rates:** BW $2,500; 4C $3,150. **Remarks:** Accepts advertising. **Circ:** Paid 70000.

1870 ■ Produced By
Producers Guild of America
8530 Wilshire Blvd., Ste. 400
Beverly Hills, CA 90211
Phone: (310)358-9020
Fax: (310)358-9520
Publisher's E-mail: info@producersguild.org
Magazine featuring stories on producers in film, television and new media. **Freq:** 5/year. **Subscription Rates:** Included in membership; $30 Nonmembers. **Alt. Formats:** PDF. **URL:** http://www.producersguild.org/?page=produced_by. **Remarks:** Accepts advertising. **Circ:** 3500.

1871 ■ Splash Magazine
Splash Magazine
311 N Robertson Blvd., 372
Beverly Hills, CA 90211
Phone: (323)362-6282
Publication E-mail: contact@lasplash.com
Online trade magazine covering the water leisure industry. Targets owners, managers, suppliers, and developers of private and community owned water leisure facilities, in addition to hotels and resorts with these facilities. **Founded:** July 1981. **Freq:** Monthly. **Key Personnel:** Barbara Keer, Editor; Lawrence Davis, Founder. **Subscription Rates:** Free. **URL:** http://www.lasplash.com. **Remarks:** Advertising accepted; rates available upon request. **Circ:** (Not Reported).

1872 ■ Under the Radar: The Solution to Music Pollution
Under the Radar
238 S Tower Dr. Ste. 204
Beverly Hills, CA 90211
Publisher's E-mail: subscriptions@undertheradarmag.com
Magazine featuring indie music. **Freq:** Quarterly. **Key Personnel:** Mark Redfern, Senior Editor. **Subscription Rates:** $16.99 U.S.; $24.99 Canada and Mexico; $51.99 Other countries. **URL:** http://www.undertheradarmag.com. **Remarks:** Advertising accepted; rates available upon request. **Circ:** Paid ‡65000.

1873 ■ URB
URB
8484 Wilshire Blvd., Ste. 560
Beverly Hills, CA 90211-3234
Consumer magazine covering hip-hop and dance music. **Freq:** 10/yr. **Key Personnel:** Raymond L. Roker, Publisher; Clarissa Butler, Office Manager; Joshua Glazer, Editor-in-Chief; Amy Grabisch, Manager, Advertising, Manager, Marketing, phone: (323)315-1728; Michael Vasquez, Editor. **ISSN:** 1081-9924 (print). **Subscription Rates:** $14.95 Individuals. **URL:** http://urb.com; http://www.urb.ro. **Ad Rates:** 4C $4200. **Remarks:** Accepts advertising. **Circ:** Non-paid 70,000.

BIG BEAR LAKE

SE CA. San Bernardino Co. 25 mi. NE of San Bernardino. Mountain resort. Fishing, skiing center.

1874 ■ Big Bear Grizzly
Big Bear Grizzly
42007 Fox Farm Rd., Ste. 3B
Big Bear Lake, CA 92315
Phone: (909)866-3456
Fax: (909)866-2302
Publisher's E-mail: jwright@bigbeargrizzly.net
General newspaper. **Freq:** Weekly (Wed.). **Print Method:** Offset. **Cols./Page:** 6. **Col. Width:** 26 nonpareils. **Col. Depth:** 301 agate lines. **Key Personnel:** Judi Bowers, Publisher; Karen Osuna-Sharamitaro, Business Manager. **ISSN:** 1073--6867 (print). **Subscription Rates:** $27 Individuals within San Bernardino County 6 months; $34 Individuals within San Bernardino County 1 year; $57 Individuals within San Bernardino County 2 years; $35 Individuals outside San Bernardino County 6 months; $45 Individuals outside San Bernardino County 1 year; $42 Individuals outside of California 6 months; $57 Individuals outside of California 1 year; $24 Individuals e-edition 1 year; $5 Individuals e-edition 1 month. **URL:** http://www.bigbeargrizzly.net. **Formerly:** Big Bear Life & the Grizzly. **Mailing address:** PO Box 1789, Big Bear Lake, CA 92315. **Remarks:** Accepts advertising. **Circ:** ‡9000.

1875 ■ Charter Communications
41490 Big Bear Blvd.
Box 1771
Big Bear Lake, CA 92315
Email: jlichti@chartercom.com
Owner: Charter Communications Inc., 400 Atlantic St., Stamford, CT 06901, Ph: (203)905-7801. **Founded:** 1952. **Key Personnel:** Marti Kinson, Mktg. Mgr., mkinson@chartercom.com. **Cities Served:** subscribing households 13,000. **URL:** http://www.charter.com.

1876 ■ KWBB-FM - 105.5
713 Stocker Rd.
Big Bear Lake, CA 92315
Format: Religious. **Wattage:** 008. **Ad Rates:** Noncommercial. **Mailing address:** PO Box 1965, Big Bear Lake, CA 92315. **URL:** http://kwbb.org.

BISHOP

SE CA. Inyo Co. 265 mi. N. of Los Angeles. Gateway high sierra ski, mountain resort. Ancient bristlecone pines. Old west museums. Dairy, livestock grazing, poultry, grain farms.

1877 ■ Inyo Register
Horizon California Publications Inc.
1180 N Main St. Ste. 108
Bishop, CA 93514
Phone: (760)873-3535
Fax: (760)873-3591
Free: 800-293-3535
Newspaper. **Freq:** 3/week Tuesday, Thursday and Saturday. **Print Method:** Offset. **Cols./Page:** 8. **Col. Width:** 18 nonpareils. **Col. Depth:** 294 agate lines. **Key Personnel:** Terrance Vestal, Editor. **Subscription Rates:** $65 Individuals home delivery 12 months; $82 By mail 12 months; $92 Out of area 12 months; $60 Individuals e-edition 12 months. **URL:** http://www.inyoregister.com. **Ad Rates:** GLR $.675; BW $1194; 4C $1494; PCI $9.71. **Remarks:** Accepts advertising. **Circ:** 7590.

1878 ■ KBOV-AM - 1230
S Hwy. 395
Bishop, CA 93515
Phone: (760)873-6324
Email: kibskbov@yahoo.com
Format: Oldies. **Networks:** ABC. **Owner:** Great Country Broadcasting, Inc., at above address. **Founded:** 1953. **Formerly**: KIBS-AM. **Operating Hours**: Continuous; 90% network, 10% local. **Local Programs**: *Dodger Baseball*. **Wattage**: 1,000. **Ad Rates:** $9-10.40 for 30 seconds; $13-15 for 60 seconds. Combined advertising rates available with KIBS-FM. **Mailing address:** PO Box 757, Bishop, CA 93515. **URL:** http://www.kibskbov.com.

1879 ■ KIBS-FM - 100.7
S Hwy. 395
Bishop, CA 93515
Phone: (760)873-6324
Email: kibskbov@kibskbov.com
Format: Country. **Networks:** Jones Satellite; ABC. **Owner:** Great Country Broadcasting, Inc., at above address. **Founded:** 1974. **Formerly:** KIOQ-FM. **Operating Hours:** Continuous; 67% network, 33% local. **Wattage:** 50,000 ERP. **Ad Rates:** $10 for 30 seconds; $12 for 60 seconds. $13 for 30 seconds; $16 for 60 seconds. Combined advertising rates available with KBOV-AM. **URL:** http://www.kibskbov.com.

1880 ■ KWTD-FM - 91.9
PO Box 637
Bishop, CA 93515-0637
Free: 866-466-5989
Format: Religious. **Owner:** Living Proof Broadcasting, PO Box 637, Bishop, CA 93515, Free: 866-466-5989. **Wattage:** 7,000. **URL:** http://www.kwtw.org/kwtd.html.

1881 ■ KWTH-FM - 91.3
PO Box 637
Bishop, CA 93515
Free: 866-466-5989
Email: friar@schat.com
Format: Religious. **Owner:** Living Proof Inc., 12131 Malcomson Rd., Houston, TX 77070, Ph: (281)257-3344, Fax: (888)700-1999, Free: 888-700-1999. **Wattage:** 1,550. **URL:** http://www.kwtw.org/kwth.html.

1882 ■ KWTM-FM - 90.9
PO Box 637
Bishop, CA 93515
Free: 866-466-5989
Email: recep@kwtw.org
Format: Religious. **Owner:** Living Proof Broadcasting, PO Box 637, Bishop, CA 93515, Free: 866-466-5989. **Wattage:** 910. **URL:** http://www.kwtw.org/kwtm.html.

1883 ■ KWTW-FM - 88.5
PO Box 637
Bishop, CA 93515
Free: 866-466-5989
Email: friar@schat.com
Format: Religious. **Wattage:** 900. **Ad Rates:** Advertising accepted; rates available upon request. **URL:** http://www.kwtw.org.

BLYTHE

SE CA. Riverside Co. 169 mi. W. of Phoenix, AZ. Hunting and fishing. cotton gins; feed mills; seed plants. Stock, truck farms. Cotton, alfalfa, lettuce, cantaloupes. Citrus fruits.

1884 ■ Palo Verde Valley Times
Palo Verde Valley Times
153 S Broadway
Blythe, CA 92225
Phone: (760)922-3181
Newspaper. **Freq:** Semiweekly (Wed. and Fri.). **Print Method:** Offset. **Trim Size:** 6 x 21 1/2. **Cols./Page:** 6. **Col. Width:** 25 nonpareils. **Col. Depth:** 294 agate lines. **Key Personnel:** Debbie White-Hoel, Publisher. **USPS:** 419-240. **Subscription Rates:** $26 Individuals carrier rates 6 months; $48 Individuals carrier rates 12 months; $31 Individuals in-county mail rates 6 months; $49.50 Individuals in-county mail rates 12 months; $38.50 Individuals out of county mail rates 6 months; $66 Individuals out of county mail rates 12 months. **URL:** http://www.paloverdevalleytimes.com. **Ad Rates:** GLR $.43; 4C $1494.54; SAU $8.04; PCI $9.84. **Remarks:** Accepts advertising. **Circ:** Paid ‡4076.

1885 ■ Blythe Radio Inc.
681 N Fourth St.
Blythe, CA 92225
Phone: (760)922-7143
Fax: (760)922-2844
URL: http://www.kjmbfm.com.

1886 ■ KERU-FM
PO Box 910
Blythe, CA 92226-0910
Phone: (760)899-4565
Email: keru88.5@yahoo.com
Format: Hispanic. **Wattage:** 1,000 ERP. **Ad Rates:** Noncommercial.

1887 ■ KJMB-FM - 100.3
681 N Fourth St.
Blythe, CA 92225
Phone: (760)922-7143
Fax: (760)922-2844
Email: kjmbfm@hotmail.com
Format: Adult Contemporary. **Owner:** Blythe Radio Inc., 681 N Fourth St., Blythe, CA 92225, Ph: (760)922-7143, Fax: (760)922-2844. **Founded:** 1975. **Operating Hours:** Continuous. **Key Personnel:** Jim Morris, Station Mgr. **Wattage:** 36,400. **Ad Rates:** Noncommercial. **URL:** http://www.kjmbfm.com.

1888 ■ K209CY-FM - 89.7
PO Box 391
Twin Falls, ID 83303
Fax: (208)736-1958
Free: 800-357-4226
Format: Religious; Contemporary Christian. **Owner:** CSN International, PO Box 391, Twin Falls, ID 83303, Ph: (208)736-1958, Fax: (208)736-1958, Free: 800-357-4226. **URL:** http://www.csnradio.com.

Circulation: ★ = AAM; △ or • = BPA; ♦ = CAC; □ = VAC; ⊕ = PO Statement; ‡ = Publisher's Report; Boldface figures = sworn; Light figures = estimated.

BOLINAS

1889 ■ Coastal Post
Marin County's News Monthly-Free Press
PO Box 31
Bolinas, CA 94924
Phone: (415)868-1600
Fax: (415)868-0502
Publication E-mail: editor@coastalpost.com
Environmental and political newspaper. **Freq:** Monthly. **Key Personnel:** Pam Carey, Office Manager; Don Deane, Editor. **Subscription Rates:** $30 Individuals one year subscription; $60 Two years. **URL:** http://www.coastalpost.com. **Ad Rates:** PCI $12. **Remarks:** Advertising accepted; rates available upon request. **Circ:** Combined 9000.

BONSALL

1890 ■ Journal of Dredging Engineering
Western Dredging Association
c/o Thomas P. Cappellino, Executive Director
PO Box 1393
Bonsall, CA 92003
Phone: (949)422-8231
Publisher's E-mail: weda@comcast.net
Freq: Quarterly. **Key Personnel:** Dr. Ram Mohan, Editor. **Alt. Formats:** PDF. **URL:** http://www.westerndredging.org/index.php/information/weda-journal. **Circ:** (Not Reported).

BOONVILLE

NW CA. Mendocino Co. On Pacific Ocean, 50 mi. NW of Santa Rosa. Sawmill. Wineries. Orchards, vineyards, sheep, cattle.

1891 ■ The Anderson Valley Advertiser
The Anderson Valley Advertiser
PO Box 459
Boonville, CA 95415
Phone: (707)895-3016
Fax: (707)895-3355
Publisher's E-mail: ava@pacific.net
Socialist rural newspaper. **Freq:** Weekly (Wed.). **Print Method:** Offset. **Cols./Page:** 8. **Col. Width:** 19 nonpareils. **Col. Depth:** 308 agate lines. **Key Personnel:** Bruce Anderson, Publisher, Editor. **Subscription Rates:** $50 Individuals per year in California print; $100 Out of state per year print. **Alt. Formats:** E-book. **URL:** http://theava.com. **Ad Rates:** GLR $.95; SAU $1.25; PCI $2.95. **Remarks:** Accepts advertising. **Circ:** 4000.

BORREGO SPRINGS

S. CA. San Diego Co. 90 mi. NE of San Diego. Resort. State Park.

1892 ■ Borrego Sun
Copley Press Inc.
707 Christmas Cir.
Borrego Springs, CA 92004-0249
Phone: (760)767-5338
Fax: (760)767-4971
Publication E-mail: generalmail@borregosun.com
Community newspaper (tabloid). **Freq:** Semimonthly every other Thursday. **Print Method:** Offset. **Trim Size:** 10 1/4 x 11 1/4. **Cols./Page:** 4. **Col. Width:** 14.5 picas. **Col. Depth:** 11 1/4 inches. **Key Personnel:** Judy Winter Meier, Editor, General Manager; Patrick Meehan, Publisher. **USPS:** 061-260. **Subscription Rates:** $4 By mail single copy; $36 By mail per year; $65 U.S. domestic; first class; $78 Canada first class; $135 Individuals Europe; first class; $1 Single issue newsstand copy. **URL:** http://www.borregospringschamber.com/borregonews.html; http://www.borregosun.com/. **Mailing address:** PO Box 249, Borrego Springs, CA 92004-0249. **Ad Rates:** BW $520; 4C $780; PCI $11.35. **Remarks:** Accepts advertising. **Circ:** ‡4200.

1893 ■ K217EL-FM - 91.3
PO Box 391
Twin Falls, ID 83303
Fax: (208)736-1958
Free: 800-357-4226
Format: Religious; Contemporary Christian. **Owner:** CSN International, PO Box 391, Twin Falls, ID 83303, Ph: (208)736-1958, Fax: (208)736-1958, Free: 800-357-4226. **URL:** http://www.csnradio.com.

BRAWLEY

SE CA. Imperial Co Imperial Co. SE corner of California in Imperial Valley, south of Salton Sea. Fruit.

1894 ■ KMXX-FM - 99.3
1603 N Imperial Dr.
El Centro, CA 92243-1333
Phone: (760)482-7777
Format: Hispanic. **Founded:** 1980. **Operating Hours:** Continuous. **ADI:** El Centro, CA-Yuma, AZ. **Key Personnel:** Cal Mandel, Gen. Mgr. **Wattage:** 6,000. **URL:** http://www.tricolor993.com/.

1895 ■ KROP-AM - 1300
120 S Plz.
Brawley, CA 92227
Phone: (760)344-1300
Fax: (760)344-1763
Format: Country; Eclectic. **Networks:** ESPN Radio; CBS. **Owner:** LarDog Communications LLC, 120 S Plaza St., Brawley, CA 92227, Ph: (760)344-2172. **Founded:** 1946. **Formerly:** KKSC-AM. **Operating Hours:** Continuous. **Wattage:** 500 ERP. **Ad Rates:** $14-18 for 30 seconds; $17-24 for 60 seconds. Combined advertising rates available with KSIQ-FM. **Mailing address:** PO Box 238, Brawley, CA 92227. **URL:** http://www.krop.info/.

BREA

S. CA. Orange Co. 12 mi. S. of Anaheim. Residential.

1896 ■ The California Parent Educator
Christian Home Educators Association of California
595 W Lambert Rd., Ste. 101
Brea, CA 92821
Phone: (562)864-2432
Fax: (562)864-3747
Publisher's E-mail: cheainfo@cheaofca.org
Magazine featuring home education news and articles for CHEA members. **Freq:** Bimonthly. **URL:** http://www.cheaofca.org/index.cfm?fuseaction=Page.viewPage&pageId=564&parentID=527. **Remarks:** Accepts advertising. **Circ:** 5500.

1897 ■ Singing Wires
Telephone Collectors International
3805 Spurr Cir.
Brea, CA 92823
Phone: (714)528-3561
Publisher's E-mail: info@telephonecollectors.org
Freq: Monthly. **Subscription Rates:** $35 /year; Included in membership. **URL:** http://www.telephonecollectors.org/JournalsSamples/singwire.htm. **Remarks:** Accepts advertising. **Circ:** 600.

1898 ■ Switchers' Quarterly
Telephone Collectors International
3805 Spurr Cir.
Brea, CA 92823
Phone: (714)528-3561
Publisher's E-mail: info@telephonecollectors.org
Journal containing articles about Central Office and PBX switching technology and other relevant topics providing the interests of telephone collectors. **Freq:** Quarterly. **Subscription Rates:** $15 Members print; $8 Members online. **URL:** http://www.telephonecollectors.org/JournalsSamples/SwitchersQuartely.htm. **Remarks:** Accepts advertising. **Circ:** (Not Reported).

BRISBANE

San Mateo Co.

1899 ■ KTSF-TV - 26
100 Valley Dr.
Brisbane, CA 94005
Phone: (415)468-2626
Fax: (415)467-7559
Format: Commercial TV. **Networks:** Independent. **Owner:** Lincoln Broadcasting Co., at above address, Brisbane, CA 94005. **Founded:** 1976. **Operating Hours:** Continuous; 100% local. **ADI:** San Francisco-Oakland-San Jose. **Local Programs:** *Cantonese News*, Saturday Sunday; *TV Patrol World*, Monday Tuesday Wednesday Thursday Friday 6:00 p.m. - 6:45 p.m.; *Balitang America*, Monday Tuesday Wednesday Thursday Friday 6:45 p.m. - 7:00 p.m.; *Filipino-American Journal*, Saturday 5:30 a.m. - 6:00 a.m.; *Talk Tonight*, Friday Sunday 11:00 p.m. 7:30 p.m. - 8:00 p.m.; *Vietnamese Journal*, Saturday 5:30 a.m. - 6:00 a.m.; *KBS News*, Monday Tuesday Wednesday Thursday Friday 7:30 a.m. - 8:00 a.m.; *Korean Journal*, Saturday 5:30 a.m. - 6:00 a.m.; *Namaste America*, Saturday 9:00 a.m. - 10:00 a.m.; *Showbiz India*, Saturday 10:00 a.m. - 11:00 a.m.; *CMC Beat Lounge*, Monday Tuesday Wednesday Thursday Friday 4:30 p.m. - 5:00 p.m.; *CMC Late Night*, Saturday 12:30 a.m. - 1:00 a.m.; *China News*, Monday Tuesday Wednesday Thursday Friday 8:30 a.m. - 9:00 a.m.; *Divine Plan*, Tuesday 6:00 a.m. - 6:30 a.m.; *Nima TV*, Sunday 12:00 p.m. - 1:00 p.m.; *Greek TV*, Saturday 3:00 p.m. - 4:00 p.m.; *Business & Lifestyle*, Sunday 6:30 p.m. - 7:00 p.m.; *California Music Channel [CMC]*, Monday Tuesday Wednesday Thursday Friday 4:30 p.m. - 5:00 p.m. **Wattage:** 2,500,000 ERP. **Ad Rates:** Noncommercial. **URL:** http://www.ktsf.com.

BROWNSVILLE

1900 ■ K217EA-FM - 91.3
PO Box 391
Twin Falls, ID 83303
Free: 800-357-4226
Format: Religious; Contemporary Christian. **Owner:** CSN International, PO Box 391, Twin Falls, ID 83303, Ph: (208)736-1958, Fax: (208)736-1958, Free: 800-357-4226. **Key Personnel:** Don Mills, Prog. Dir., Music Dir.; Kelly Carlson, Dir. of Engg.; Ray Gorney, Asst. Dir. **URL:** http://www.csnradio.com.

BURBANK

S. CA. Los Angeles Co. 10 mi. N. of Los Angeles. Manufactures airplanes, aircraft equipment and instruments, motion picture films and sound equipment, electronics equipment, plastics.

1901 ■ Burbank Business Journal
Burbank Chamber of Commerce
200 W Magnolia Blvd.
Burbank, CA 91502-1724
Phone: (818)846-3111
Fax: (818)846-0109
Publisher's E-mail: info@burbankchamber.org
Newspaper containing a variety of articles about Burbank, CA businesses, chamber members and the community at large. **Freq:** Monthly. **Key Personnel:** Sheri Rang, Contact. **Subscription Rates:** Free to members. **Alt. Formats:** PDF. **URL:** http://www.burbankchamber.org/html/advertising.asp. **Remarks:** Accepts advertising. **Circ:** 7500, 8000.

1902 ■ California Broker
McGee Publishers
217 E Alameda Ave., Ste. 207
Burbank, CA 91502-2622
Phone: (818)848-2957
Fax: (818)843-3489
Free: 800-675-7563
Magazine providing financial planning information for life and health insurance brokers. **Freq:** Monthly. **Print Method:** Offset. **Trim Size:** 8 3/8 x 10 7/8. **Cols./Page:** 3. **Col. Width:** 28 nonpareils. **Col. Depth:** 140 agate lines. **Key Personnel:** Richard Madden, Publisher; Leila Morris, Editor; Kate Kinkade, Editor-in-Chief. **ISSN:** 0883--6159 (print). **Subscription Rates:** $21 Individuals 1 year; $31.50 Two years; $4 Single issue plus shipping fee. **URL:** http://www.calbrokermag.com. **Ad Rates:** GLR $10; BW $4990, full page; 4C $5875, full page; PCI $80. **Remarks:** Accepts advertising. **Circ:** ‡25000.

1903 ■ The Caucus Journal
Caucus for Producers, Writers & Directors
PO Box 11236
Burbank, CA 91510-1236
Phone: (818)843-7572
Fax: (818)221-0347
Publisher's E-mail: info@caucus.org
Freq: Quarterly. **Subscription Rates:** $5. **URL:** http://caucus.org/caucusjournal/index.html. **Remarks:** Advertising not accepted. **Circ:** 2000.

1904 ■ German-American Genealogy
Immigrant Genealogical Society
1310-B W Magnolia Blvd.
Burbank, CA 91506
Phone: (818)848-3122
Fax: (818)716-6300
Freq: Semiannual. **Subscription Rates:** Included in membership. **Mailing address:** PO Box 7369, Burbank,

CA 91510. **Remarks:** Advertising not accepted. **Circ:** 700.

1905 ■ Insider Magazine
Association of Correctional Food Service Affiliates
PO Box 10065
Burbank, CA 91510
Phone: (818)843-6608
Fax: (818)843-7423
Freq: Quarterly. **Subscription Rates:** Included in membership. **Alt. Formats:** PDF. **URL:** http://www.acfsa.org/insider.php. **Ad Rates:** BW $600; 4C $1200. **Remarks:** Accepts advertising. **Circ:** (Not Reported).

1906 ■ KBIG-FM - 104.3
3400 W Olive Ave., Ste. 550
Burbank, CA 91505
Phone: (818)559-2252
Fax: (818)955-8303
Email: lahr@clearchannel.com
Format: Adult Contemporary. **Networks:** Independent. **Founded:** 1959. **Operating Hours:** Continuous. **ADI:** Los Angeles (Corona & San Bernardino), CA. **Wattage:** 105,000. **Ad Rates:** Advertising accepted; rates available upon request. **URL:** http://www.1043myfm.com.

1907 ■ KBUA-FM
1845 Empire Ave.
Burbank, CA 91504
Phone: (818)729-5300
Email: advertising@aquisuena.com
Format: Ethnic. **Owner:** Liberman Broadcasting, Inc., 3000 Bering Dr., Houston, TX 77057. **Wattage:** 6,000 ERP. **Ad Rates:** Noncommercial.

1908 ■ KBUE-FM
1845 Empire Ave.
Burbank, CA 91504
Phone: (818)729-5300
Email: advertising@aquisuena.com
Format: Hispanic. **Wattage:** 3,000 ERP. **Ad Rates:** Noncommercial.

1909 ■ KEBN-FM - 94.3
1845 W Empire Ave.
Burbank, CA 91504
Phone: (818)563-5722
Format: Hispanic. **Ad Rates:** Advertising accepted; rates available upon request.

KFAC-FM - See Santa Barbara, CA

1910 ■ KIIS-AM - 102.7
3400 W Olive Ave., Ste. 550
Burbank, CA 91505
Phone: (818)559-2252
Free: 800-520-1027
Format: Top 40. **Simulcasts:** KIIS-FM. **Networks:** Independent. **Founded:** 1927. **Operating Hours:** Continuous. **Wattage:** 5,000. **Ad Rates:** Advertising accepted; rates available upon request. **URL:** http://www.kiisfm.com.

1911 ■ KIIS-FM - 102.7
3400 W Olive Ave., Ste. 550
Burbank, CA 91505
Phone: (818)559-2252
Free: 800-520-1027
Format: Top 40. **Simulcasts:** KXTA-AM, XTRA-AM. **Networks:** Independent. **Founded:** 1948. **Operating Hours:** Continuous. **Wattage:** 8,000. **Ad Rates:** Advertising accepted; rates available upon request. **URL:** http://www.kiisfm.com.

1912 ■ KLAC-AM - 570
3400 W Olive Ave., Ste. 550
Burbank, CA 91505
Phone: (818)559-2252
Format: Sports. **Networks:** AP; Unistar; Westwood One Radio. **Founded:** 1970. **Operating Hours:** Continuous. **ADI:** Los Angeles (Corona & San Bernardino), CA. **Key Personnel:** Greg Ashlock, President. **Wattage:** 5,000. **Ad Rates:** Advertising accepted; rates available upon request. **URL:** http://www.am570radio.com.

1913 ■ KNBC-TV - 4
3000 W Alameda Ave.
Burbank, CA 91523
Format: Commercial TV. **Networks:** NBC. **Founded:** 1949. **Operating Hours:** Continuous. **ADI:** Los Angeles (Corona & San Bernardino), CA. **Key Personnel:** Patrick Healy, Reporter; Chuck Henry, Reporter. **Ad Rates:** Advertising accepted; rates available upon request. **URL:** http://www.nbclosangeles.com.

1914 ■ KOST-FM - 103.5
3400 W Olive Ave., Ste. 550
Burbank, CA 91505
Phone: (818)559-2252
Fax: (818)729-2600
Free: 800-929-5678
Format: Adult Contemporary. **Owner:** iHeartMedia Inc., 200 E Basse Rd., San Antonio, TX 78209, Ph: (210)832-3314. **Founded:** 1957. **Operating Hours:** Continuous. **ADI:** Los Angeles (Corona & San Bernardino), CA. **Key Personnel:** Greg Ashlock, Station Mgr.; Melissa Carbone, Gen. Sales Mgr. **Wattage:** 12,500. **Ad Rates:** Advertising accepted; rates available upon request. **URL:** http://www.kost1035.com.

1915 ■ KPNZ-TV - 24
1845 Empire Ave.
Burbank, CA 91504
Phone: (818)729-5300
Email: info@utahs24tv.com
Wattage: 450,000 ERP.

1916 ■ KPWR-FM - 106
2600 W Olive Ave., 8th Fl.
Burbank, CA 91505
Phone: (818)953-4200
Fax: (818)848-0961
Format: Contemporary Hit Radio (CHR); Hip Hop. **Networks:** Independent. **Owner:** Emmis Communications Corp., One Emmis Plz., 40 Monument Cir., Ste. 700, Indianapolis, IN 46204-3011, Ph: (317)266-0100. **Founded:** 1986. **Operating Hours:** Continuous. **Key Personnel:** Jimmy Steal, Dir. of Programs. **Wattage:** 25,000. **Ad Rates:** Noncommercial. **URL:** http://www.emmis.com.

KPXN-TV - See Los Angeles

1917 ■ KRRL-FM - 98.9
3400 W Olive Ave., Ste. 550
Burbank, CA 91505
Phone: (818)559-2252
Fax: (818)955-8439
Free: 866-246-8923
Format: Urban Contemporary. **Owner:** iHeartMedia Inc., 200 E Basse Rd., San Antonio, TX 78209, Ph: (210)832-3314. **Formerly:** KHHT-FM. **Key Personnel:** David Howard, Contact, davidhoward2@clearchannel.com; David Howard, Contact, davidhoward2@clearchannel.com. **Wattage:** 1,400. **Ad Rates:** Advertising accepted; rates available upon request. **URL:** http://www.hot923.com/main.html.

1918 ■ KSDX-TV - 29
1845 Empire Ave.
Burbank, CA 91504
Phone: (818)563-5722
Email: ksdxinfo@lbimedia.com
Owner: Liberman Broadcasting, Inc., 3000 Bering Dr., Houston, TX 77057. **Founded:** 1987. **URL:** http://www.lbimedia.com.

1919 ■ KTLK-AM - 1150
3400 W Olive Ave., Ste. 550
Burbank, CA 91505-5544
Phone: (818)559-2252
Format: Talk. **Owner:** iHeartMedia Inc., 200 E Basse Rd., San Antonio, TX 78209, Ph: (210)832-3314. **Founded:** 1946. **Formerly:** KIST-AM. **Operating Hours:** Continuous. **ADI:** Santa Barbara-Santa Maria-San Luis Obispo,CA. **Wattage:** 1,000. **Ad Rates:** Noncommercial. $10.40-$40 for 30 seconds; $13-$50 for 60 seconds. Combined advertising rates available with KMGQ-FM. **URL:** http://www.patriot.la//main.html.

KVNR-AM - See Los Angeles

1920 ■ KXOS-FM - 93.9
2600 W Olive Ave., 8th Fl.
Burbank, CA 91505
Phone: (818)525-5000
Email: ir@emmis.com
Format: Top 40. **Owner:** Emmis Communication, 1 EMMIS Plz., 40 Monument Cir., Ste. 700 40 Monument Cir., Ste. 700, Indianapolis, IN 46204, Ph: (317)266-0100. **Formerly:** KMVN-FM. **Key Personnel:** Jimmy Steal, Dir. of Programs; Ricci Filiar, Asst. Dir., Music Dir.; Dennis Martin, Chief Engineer. **Ad Rates:** Advertising accepted; rates available upon request.

1921 ■ KXTA-AM - 1150
3400 W Olive Ave., Ste. 550
Burbank, CA 91505
Phone: (210)832-3149
Format: Sports. **ADI:** Los Angeles (Corona & San Bernardino), CA. **Wattage:** 5,000 Watts. **Ad Rates:** Noncommercial. **URL:** http://patriotla.iheart.com/articles/contact-us-120972/employment-opportunities-7777116.

1922 ■ KYSR-FM - 98.7
3400 W Olive Ave., Ste. 550
Burbank, CA 91505
Phone: (818)559-2252
Format: Classic Rock. **Founded:** 1954. **Operating Hours:** Continuous. **Key Personnel:** Lisa Foxx, Contact. **Wattage:** 75,000. **Ad Rates:** Advertising accepted; rates available upon request. **URL:** http://www.alt987fm.com.

1923 ■ KZLA-FM - 93.9
2600 W Olive Ave., Ste. 850
Burbank, CA 91505
Phone: (818)525-5000
Email: kzlamail@kzla.com
Format: Country; News; Talk. **Owner:** Emmis Interactive, One Emmis Plz. 40 Monument Cir., Ste. 700, Indianapolis, IN 46204, Ph: (317)266-0100. **Founded:** 1978. **Formerly:** KPOL-FM. **Operating Hours:** Continuous. **ADI:** Los Angeles (Corona & San Bernardino), CA. **Key Personnel:** Brian Bartolo, Sales Mgr., bbartolo@power106.com. **Wattage:** 18,500 ERP H; 16,000. **Ad Rates:** Advertising accepted; rates available upon request. **URL:** http://radiocentro939.com/rc939.

1924 ■ XETRA-AM - 690
3500 W Olive Ave., Ste. 250
Burbank, CA 91505
Phone: (619)291-9191
Fax: (619)291-5622
Key Personnel: Bob Bollinger, Gen. Mgr. **URL:** http://www.wradio690.com/.

BURLINGAME

W. CA. San Mateo Co. 15 mi. S. of San Francisco. Residential. Independent retail. Light industry.

1925 ■ California Educator
California Teachers Association
1705 Murchison Dr.
Burlingame, CA 94010-4504
Phone: (650)697-1400
Fax: (650)552-5023
Freq: Monthly. **Print Method:** web press. **Trim Size:** 8 3/8 x 10 7/8. **Cols./Page:** 4. **Key Personnel:** Katharine Fong, Editor-in-Chief. **ISSN:** 1091--6148 (print). **Subscription Rates:** Included in membership. **URL:** http://www.cta.org/en/Professional-Development/Publications.aspx. **Formerly:** CTA/NEA Action; CTA Action. **Mailing address:** PO Box 921, Burlingame, CA 94010-0921. **Ad Rates:** BW $5235; 4C $6855. **Remarks:** Color advertising accepted; rates available upon request. **Circ:** ‡330000.

1926 ■ Journal of Libertarian Studies
Center for Libertarian Studies
PO Box 4091
Burlingame, CA 94011
Phone: (650)020-0358
Journal covering Libertarianism. **Freq:** Semiannual. **Key Personnel:** Hans-Hermann Hoppe, Editor; Judith Thommesen, Managing Editor. **URL:** http://mises.org/library/journal-libertarian-studies. **Circ:** (Not Reported).

1927 ■ Junior Statement
Junior State of America
111 Anza Blvd., Ste. 109
Burlingame, CA 94010
Phone: (650)347-1600
Fax: (650)347-7200
Free: 800-334-5353
Publisher's E-mail: jsa@jsa.org
Membership magazine of the Junior State of America covering youth activities in politics and government. **Freq:** Quarterly. **Print Method:** Offset. **Trim Size:** 11 X 17. **Cols./Page:** 5. **Key Personnel:** Jack Cahn, Editor-in-Chief. **URL:** http://jsa.org/?s=Junior+Statement+&x=0&y=0. **Remarks:** Advertising not accepted. **Circ:** Paid 10000.

1928 ■ Los Angeles Philippine News
Los Angeles Philippine News

Circulation: ★ = AAM; △ or • = BPA; ♦ = CAC; ❑ = VAC; ⊕ = PO Statement; ‡ = Publisher's Report; Boldface figures = sworn; Light figures = estimated.

1415 Rollins Rd., Ste. 202
Burlingame, CA 94010
Phone: (562)513-1831
Fax: (562)892-1406
Newspaper for Filipino communities. **Freq:** Weekly. **Remarks:** Accepts advertising. **Circ:** (Not Reported).

BURNEY

N. CA. Shasta Co. 51 mi. NE of Redding. Tourism. Resort. Saw pulp, veneer mills. Agriculture. Cattle, grain.

1929 ■ Intermountain News
Intermountain News
37095 Main St.
Burney, CA 96013-1030
Phone: (530)335-4533
Fax: (530)335-5335
Publication E-mail: editor@im-news.com
Local newspaper. **Freq:** Weekly (Wed.). **Print Method:** Offset. **Cols./Page:** 6. **Col. Width:** 2 1/8 inches. **Col. Depth:** 21 inches. **Key Personnel:** Craig Harrington, Publisher; Katie Harrington, Manager; Debbie Crone, Manager, Circulation. **Subscription Rates:** $59 Individuals one year. **URL:** http://www.theimnews.com. **Mailing address:** PO Box 1030, Burney, CA 96013-1030. **Ad Rates:** BW $693; 4C $879; PCI $7.23. **Remarks:** Accepts advertising. **Circ:** ‡3254.

1930 ■ KIBC-FM - 90.5
PO Box 1717
Burney, CA 96013
Phone: (530)335-5422
Format: Religious; Educational. **Founded:** 1984. **Operating Hours:** Continuous. **Key Personnel:** Pastor Hennessey, Gen. Mgr., pastorbud@kibcfm.org. **Wattage:** 3,000. **Ad Rates:** Noncommercial. **URL:** http://www.kibcfm.org.

1931 ■ K203CU-FM - 88.5
PO Box 391
Twin Falls, ID 83303
Fax: (208)736-1958
Free: 800-357-4226
Format: Religious; Contemporary Christian. **Owner:** CSN International, PO Box 391, Twin Falls, ID 83303, Ph: (208)736-1958, Fax: (208)736-1958, Free: 800-357-4226. **URL:** http://www.csnradio.com.

BYRON

1932 ■ K207DN-FM - 89.3
PO Box 391
Twin Falls, ID 83303
Free: 800-357-4226
Format: Religious; Contemporary Christian. **Owner:** CSN International, PO Box 391, Twin Falls, ID 83303, Ph: (208)736-1958, Fax: (208)736-1958, Free: 800-357-4226. **Key Personnel:** Don Mills, Prog. Dir., Music Dir.; Kelly Carlson, Dir. of Engg.; Ray Gorney, Asst. Dir. **URL:** http://www.csnradio.com.

CALABASAS

S. CA. Los Angeles Co. 5 mi. W. of Los Angeles. Residential. Aerospace.

1933 ■ CRM Buyer
NewsFactor Network
23679 Calabasas Rd., Ste. 805
Calabasas, CA 91302
Phone: (818)713-2500
Magazine covering customer relationship management solutions. **Freq:** Monthly. **URL:** http://www.crmbuyer.com/. **Remarks:** Advertising accepted; rates available upon request. **Circ:** (Not Reported).

1934 ■ NewsFactor Magazine
NewsFactor Network
23679 Calabasas Rd., Ste. 805
Calabasas, CA 91302
Phone: (818)713-2500
Magazine covering technology news. **Freq:** Monthly. **ISSN:** 1557--2323 (print). **URL:** http://www.newsfactor.com/whitepapers/category.xhtml?category_id=14. **Remarks:** Advertising accepted; rates available upon request. **Circ:** (Not Reported).

CALEXICO

S. CA. Imperial Co. 95 mi. SE of San Diego. Ships fruit and vegetables for eastern markets. Cotton gins; cottonseed oil mill; sheet metal works. Diversified farming. Lettuce, cantaloupes, alfalfa, flax.

1935 ■ KQVO-FM - 97.7
5200 Campanile Dr.
San Diego, CA 92182
Phone: (619)594-1515
Format: Adult Contemporary; Hispanic. **Founded:** 1984. **Operating Hours:** Continuous. **Key Personnel:** Tom Karlo, Gen. Mgr.; David Bull, Director; John Decker, Director. **Wattage:** 6,000. **Ad Rates:** $16-23 for 30 seconds; $20-28 for 60 seconds. Combined advertising rates available with KICO-AM. **URL:** http://www.kpbs.org.

CALIFORNIA CITY

S. CA. Kern Co. 12 mi. SE of Boron. Residential.

1936 ■ The Mojave Desert News
MOCAL News Corp.
8148 California City Blvd.
California City, CA 93505
Phone: (760)373-4812
Local newspaper. **Founded:** 1938. **Freq:** Weekly (Thurs.). **Print Method:** Offset. **Cols./Page:** 6. **Col. Width:** 12 picas. **Col. Depth:** 21.5 inches. **Key Personnel:** James H. Quiggle, Editor; Linda Love-Quiggle, Publisher. **Subscription Rates:** $22.50 Individuals Kern County; $45 Out of area; $60 Out of state. **URL:** http://www.desertnews.com/. **Formerly:** The Enterprise. **Mailing address:** PO Box 2698, California City, CA 93504. **Ad Rates:** GLR $1.20; BW $945; SAU $8. **Remarks:** Accepts advertising. **Circ:** Paid ‡6000, Free ‡200.

CAMARILLO

SW CA. Ventura Co. 15 mi. E. of Ventura. Fruit and nuts shipped. Nurseries. Agriculture. Beans, oranges, lemons, walnuts.

1937 ■ Camarillo Acorn
J. Bee NP Publishing Ltd.
1203 Flynn Rd., Ste. 140
Camarillo, CA 93012
Phone: (805)484-2403
Fax: (805)484-2313
Community newspaper. **Freq:** Weekly (Thurs.). **Key Personnel:** Daniel Wolowicz, Editor; Jim Rule, Publisher; John Loesing, Managing Editor. **Subscription Rates:** Free. **URL:** http://www.thecamarilloacorn.com/Current/Front_page. **Remarks:** Advertising accepted; rates available upon request. **Circ:** Free ■ **26904**.

1938 ■ CCM: Contemporary Christian Music
Salem Media Group Inc.
4880 Santa Rosa Rd.
Camarillo, CA 93012
Phone: (805)987-0400
Fax: (805)384-4520
Publisher's E-mail: privacy@salempublishing.com
Magazine on Christian music and entertainment. **Freq:** Monthly. **Print Method:** Offset. **Trim Size:** 8 1/4 x 10 7/8. **Cols./Page:** 3. **Col. Width:** 29 nonpareils. **Col. Depth:** 130 agate lines. **Key Personnel:** Michael Miller, Publisher. **ISSN:** 0746--0066 (print). **Subscription Rates:** $11.99 Individuals. **URL:** http://salemmedia.com/stationcat/contemporary-christian-music. **Formerly:** Contemporary Christian Magazine. **Ad Rates:** BW $3,168; 4C $3,918. **Remarks:** Advertising accepted; rates available upon request. **Circ:** (Not Reported).

1939 ■ Conejo Valley
Ventura County Star
PO Box 6006
Camarillo, CA 93011
Phone: (805)437-0000
Free: 800-221-7827
General newspaper. **Freq:** Daily (morn.). **Print Method:** Offset. **Cols./Page:** 6. **Col. Width:** 25 nonpareils. **Col. Depth:** 301 agate lines. **Key Personnel:** John Moore, Editor. **Subscription Rates:** $5.99 Individuals /month - print and digital; $4.99 Individuals /month - digital only. **URL:** http://www.vcstar.com/news/local/conejo-valley. **Formerly:** News Chronicles; Thousand Oaks Star. **Ad Rates:** SAU $13.50; PCI $12.50. **Remarks:** Accepts advertising. **Circ:** (Not Reported).

1940 ■ Import Automotive Parts & Accessories
Meyers Publishing
799 Camarillo Springs Rd.
Camarillo, CA 93012-8111
Phone: (805)445-8881
Fax: (805)445-8882
Trade magazine for the automotive aftermarket. **Freq:** Monthly. **Print Method:** Offset. **Trim Size:** 8 x 10 7/8. **Cols./Page:** 3. **Col. Width:** 27 nonpareils. **Col. Depth:** 142 agate lines. **Key Personnel:** Harriet Kaplan, Assistant Editor; Lana Meyers, Director, Advertising; Steve Relyea, Editor; Andrew Meyers, Publisher. **ISSN:** 0199--4468 (print). **Subscription Rates:** $105 Canada and Mexico; $50 Individuals domestic; $125 Other countries; $10 Single issue; $25 Individuals import industry sourcebook; $35 Individuals import industry sourcebook outside the U.S.; $20 Single issue outside the U.S. **URL:** http://meyerspublishing.com/iapa-magazine. **Remarks:** Advertising accepted; rates available upon request. **Circ:** ‡30000.

1941 ■ Journal of the Holy Roman Empire
Society for the Study of the Holy Roman Empire
California State University, Channel Islands
History Dept.
One University Dr.
Camarillo, CA 93012
Publication E-mail: jhreditors@gmail.com
Journal covering the research works on the history and culture of the Roman Empire. **Freq:** Semiannual. **Key Personnel:** Dr. Tryntje Helfferich, Editor. **Subscription Rates:** Free. **URL:** http://www.jrhe.org/welcome-to-journal-of-the-holy-roman-empire/. **Remarks:** Advertising not accepted. **Circ:** (Not Reported).

1942 ■ Preaching
Salem Media Group Inc.
4880 Santa Rosa Rd.
Camarillo, CA 93012
Phone: (805)987-0400
Fax: (805)384-4520
Interdenominational professional magazine for ministers. **Freq:** Bimonthly. **Key Personnel:** Michael Duduit, Executive Editor. **ISSN:** 0862--7036 (print). **Subscription Rates:** $24 Individuals print only; $32 Other countries print and online; $14.99 Individuals online only. **URL:** http://www.preaching.com. **Ad Rates:** BW $500; 4C $700. **Remarks:** Accepts advertising. **Circ:** ‡8000.

1943 ■ Specialty Automotive Magazine
Meyers Publishing
799 Camarillo Springs Rd.
Camarillo, CA 93012-8111
Phone: (805)445-8881
Fax: (805)445-8882
Trade magazine for the automotive aftermarket. **Freq:** Bimonthly January, March, May, July, September and November. **Print Method:** Offset. **Trim Size:** 8 x 10 7/8. **Cols./Page:** 3. **Col. Width:** 27 nonpareils. **Col. Depth:** 142 agate lines. **Key Personnel:** Steve Relyea, Editor; Andrew Meyers, Publisher; Harriet Kaplan, Assistant Editor; Lana Meyers, Director, Advertising; Bill Meyers, Art Director. **ISSN:** 0894--7414 (print). **Subscription Rates:** $40 Individuals domestic; $25 Individuals specialty and performance industry sourcebook; $80 Canada and Mexico; $95 Other countries; $35 Other countries Import Industry Sourcebook; $10 Single issue in the U.S; $20 Single issue outside the U.S. **URL:** http://meyerspublishing.com/sam-magazine. **Remarks:** Advertising accepted; rates available upon request. **Circ:** ‡25000.

1944 ■ Ventura County Star
The E. W. Scripps Co.
550 Camarillo Center Dr.
Camarillo, CA 93010
Phone: (805)437-0000
Fax: (805)482-6167
Publisher's E-mail: corpcomm@scripps.com
General newspaper. **Freq:** Mon.-Sun. **Cols./Page:** 6. **Col. Width:** 25 nonpareils. **Col. Depth:** 301 agate lines. **Key Personnel:** John Moore, Editor, phone: (805)437-0200. **URL:** http://www.vcstar.com. **Formerly:** Ventura County Star Free Press. **Remarks:** Accepts advertising. **Circ:** Mon.-Fri. 86276, Sun. 94708, Sat. ★**85642**.

1945 ■ KBBX-AM - 1420
4880 Santa Rosa Rd.
Camarillo, CA 93012
Phone: (805)987-0400

Format: Urban Contemporary. **Networks:** ABC; Satellite Music Network. **Owner:** Oma, Inc., at above address. **Founded:** 1957. **Formerly**: KESY-AM; KOOO-AM. **Operating Hours**: Continuous. **Key Personnel:** Dana Webb, Gen. Mgr; Gus Rodino, Contact. **Wattage**: 1,000.

KEYQ-AM - See Fresno

1946 ■ KGZO-FM - 90.9
PO Box 500
Camarillo, CA 93011
Free: 800-260-5676
Owner: Association for Community Education, 2310 E Ponderosa Dr Ste 28, Camarillo, CA 93010, Ph: (805)482-4797. **Wattage**: 19,000 ERP. **Ad Rates:** Accepts Advertising.

KHCM-AM - See Honolulu, HI

1947 ■ KMRO-FM - 90.3
2310 E Ponderosa Dr., Ste. 28
Camarillo, CA 93010-4747
Owner: Association for Community Education, 2310 E Ponderosa Dr Ste 28, Camarillo, CA 93010, Ph: (805)482-4797. **Founded:** 1987. **Operating Hours**: Continuous. **Wattage**: 10,500. **Ad Rates:** Noncommercial.

KRLA-AM - See Los Angeles

1948 ■ KTNO-AM
4880 Santa Rosa Rd.
Camarillo, CA 93012
Phone: (817)469-1540
Fax: (817)261-2137
Format: Hispanic; Religious. **Networks:** Independent. **Formerly**: KMIA-AM; KSGB-AM. **Wattage**: 50,000 Day; 350 Nigh.

1949 ■ KXTZ-FM - 94.1
149 Estaban Dr.
2300 Paseo del Prado
Bldg. B, Ste. 112
Camarillo, CA 93010
Phone: (702)367-4563
Fax: (702)367-4846
Founded: 1971. **Wattage**: 100,000. **Ad Rates:** $55-95 per unit.

1950 ■ WLTA-AM
4880 Santa Rosa Rd.
Camarillo, CA 93012
Phone: (805)987-0400
Format: Album-Oriented Rock (AOR). **Founded:** May 17, 1988. **Key Personnel:** Jeff Carter, Operations Mgr., jeff@wniv.com. **Wattage**: 1,000. **Ad Rates:** Noncommercial.

1951 ■ WROL-AM - 950
4880 Santa Rosa Rd.
Camarillo, CA 93012
Phone: (617)423-0210
Fax: (617)482-9305
Format: Gospel; Ethnic. **Founded:** 1950. **Operating Hours**: Continuous. **ADI**: Boston-Worcester,MA-Derry-Manchester,NH. **Key Personnel:** Pat Ryan, Gen. Mgr., patr@salemradioboston.com; Pauline Rockwell, Bus. Mgr., prockwell@wezeradio.com; Ken Carter, Contact. **Wattage:** 5,000 Day; 090 Night. **Ad Rates:** Accepts Advertising. **URL:** http://www.wrolradio.com.

CAMBRIA

SW CA. San Luis Obispo Co. On Pacific Ocean, halfway between Los Angeles and San Francisco. Resort. Hearst-San Simeon State Park.

1952 ■ Arabian Horse World
Arabian Horse World
1316 Tamson Dr., Ste. 101
Cambria, CA 93428
Phone: (805)771-2300
Fax: (805)927-6522
Free: 800-955-9423
Publication E-mail: info@ahwmagazine.com
Magazine covering Arabian horse-breeding news and information for owners, breeders, and admirers. **Freq:** Monthly. **Print Method:** Offset. **Trim Size:** 8 3/8 x 10 7/8. **Key Personnel:** Denise Hearst, Publisher; Mary Jane Parkinson, Editor. **ISSN:** 0003--7494 (print). **Subscription Rates:** $36 U.S. print and online; $25 Individuals online only. **URL:** http://www.arabianhorseworld.com/home.asp. **Ad Rates:** BW $450; 4C $950. **Remarks:** Accepts advertising. **Circ:** 10000.

1953 ■ KTEA-FM - 103.5
2976 Burton Dr.
Cambria, CA 93428
Phone: (805)924-0103
Format: Oldies. **Owner:** James R. Kampschroer. **Founded:** 2003. **Operating Hours**: Continuous. **Wattage:** 6,000. **Ad Rates:** Advertising accepted; rates available upon request. **URL:** http://www.ktea-fm.com.

CAMPBELL

W. CA. Santa Clara Co. 5 mi. SW of San Jose. Residential.

1954 ■ Campbell Express
Hanchett Publishing
334 E Campbell Ave.
Campbell, CA 95008
Phone: (408)374-9700
Fax: (408)374-0813
Independent newspaper (tabloid). **Freq:** Weekly (Wed.). **Print Method:** Offset. **Trim Size:** 11 x 17. **Cols./Page:** 6. **Col. Width:** 1 3/4 inches. **Col. Depth:** 16 inches. **Key Personnel:** Roberta C. Howe, Editor; Matthew C. Howe, Editor. **USPS:** 086-440. **Subscription Rates:** $20 By mail per year. **URL:** http://www.campbellexpress.com. **Formerly**: Cambrian News. **Ad Rates:** GLR $.20; BW $268; PCI $2.80. **Remarks:** Accepts advertising. **Circ:** ‡1562.

1955 ■ Journal of the Society for Information Display
Society for Information Display
1475 S Bascom Ave., Ste. 114
Campbell, CA 95008-0628
Phone: (408)879-3901
Fax: (408)879-3833
Publisher's E-mail: office@sid.org
Journal featuring original technical papers regarding information display. **Freq:** Quarterly. **ISSN:** 0734- 1768 (print). **Subscription Rates:** $340 Institutions America's, USA, Canada and Mexico, ROW (online); £215 Institutions UK, (online); €256 Institutions Europe, (online); $408 Institutions America's, USA, Canada and Mexico, ROW (print and online); £258 Institutions UK, (print and online); €308 Institutions Europe, (print and online); $340 Institutions America's, USA, Canada and Mexico, ROW (print); £215 Institutions UK, (print) ; €256 Institutions Europe, (print). **URL:** http://www.sid.org/Publications/JournaloftheSID.aspx. **Remarks:** Advertising not accepted. **Circ:** 4,000.

CANOGA PARK

S. CA. Los Angeles Co. Suburb of Los Angeles. Aerospace, rocket engines for space shuttle. Residential.

1956 ■ Na'amat Woman
Na'amat U.S.A.
21515 Vanowen St., Ste. 102
Canoga Park, CA 91303
Phone: (818)431-2200
Fax: (818)937-6883
Free: 844-777-5222
Publisher's E-mail: naamat@naamat.org
Magazine of NA'AMAT USA, the Women's Labor Zionist Organization of America. **Freq:** Quarterly. **Print Method:** Sheetfed Offset. **Trim Size:** 8 1/2 x 11. **Cols./Page:** 3. **Col. Width:** 2 3/8 inches. **Col. Depth:** 9-3/4 inches. **Key Personnel:** Judith A. Sokoloff, Editor. **ISSN:** 0888--191X (print). **URL:** http://naamat.org/magazine. **Formerly**: Pioneer Woman. **Ad Rates:** BW $750; PCI $30. **Remarks:** Accepts advertising. **Circ:** ‡15000.

CAPISTRANO BEACH

S. CA. Orange Co. 30 mi. S. of Santa Ana. Residential.

1957 ■ San Clemente Times
San Clemente Times
34932 Calle del Sol, Ste. B
Capistrano Beach, CA 92624
Phone: (949)388-7700
Fax: (949)388-9977
Newspaper focusing on the human-interest stories, small business, and personalities issues of San Clemente residents. **Freq:** Weekly (Thurs.). **Key Personnel:** Andrea Swayne, Senior Editor; Norb Garrett, Chief Executive Officer; Lauralyn Loynes, Associate Publisher. **Subscription Rates:** $90 Individuals. **URL:** http://www.sanclementetimes.com. **Remarks:** Accepts advertising. **Circ:** 20000.

CARLSBAD

S. CA. San Diego Co. 35 mi. N. of San Diego. Resort. Tourism. Industrial parks. Electronics, computers, silicon chips. Agriculture. Fruit, vegetables, flowers.

1958 ■ American Journal of Forensic Psychiatry
American College of Forensic Psychiatry
PO Box 130458
Carlsbad, CA 92013-0458
Phone: (760)929-9777
Fax: (760)929-9803
Publisher's E-mail: psychlaw@sover.net
Freq: Quarterly. **ISSN:** 0163--1942 (print). **Subscription Rates:** $80 Individuals; $110 Institutions; $29 Individuals single issue. **URL:** http://www.forensicpsychonline.com/journal.htm. **Remarks:** Accepts advertising. **Circ:** (Not Reported).

1959 ■ American Journal of Forensic Psychiatry: Interfacing Issues of Psychiatry and Law
American College of Forensic Psychiatry
PO Box 130458
Carlsbad, CA 92013-0458
Phone: (760)929-9777
Fax: (760)929-9803
Publisher's E-mail: psychlaw@sover.net
Professional journal covering interfacing issues of psychiatry and law. **Freq:** Quarterly. **Print Method:** Offset. **Trim Size:** 7 x 10. **Cols./Page:** 1. **Col. Width:** 63 nonpareils. **Col. Depth:** 124 agate lines. **Key Personnel:** Ronald Shlensky, Contact. **ISSN:** 0163--1942 (print). **Subscription Rates:** $80 Individuals domestic; $115 Other countries; $45 Students; $150 Two years domestic; $210 Other countries 2 years; $110 Institutions domestic; $145 Institutions, other countries; $200 Two years; $29 Single issue; $270 Institutions, other countries 2 years. **URL:** http://www.forensicpsychonline.com/journal.htm. **Ad Rates:** BW $250. **Remarks:** Accepts advertising. **Circ:** ‡1000.

1960 ■ American Journal of Forensic Psychology: Interfacing Issues of Psychology and Law
American College of Forensic Psychiatry
PO Box 130458
Carlsbad, CA 92013-0458
Phone: (760)929-9777
Fax: (760)929-9803
Publisher's E-mail: psychlaw@sover.net
Professional journal covering psychology as it relates to law. **Freq:** Quarterly. **Print Method:** Offset. **Trim Size:** 7 x 10. **Cols./Page:** 1. **Col. Width:** 63 nonpareils. **Col. Depth:** 116 agate lines. **ISSN:** 0733--1290 (print). **Subscription Rates:** $85 Individuals domestic; $120 Other countries; $45 Students; $80 Students, other countries; $160 Two years; $230 Other countries 2 years; $125 Institutions; $160 Institutions, other countries; $230 Institutions 2 years; $35 Single issue; $300 Other countries 2 years. **URL:** http://www.forensicpsychology.org/journal.htm. **Remarks:** Accepts advertising. **Circ:** ‡800.

1961 ■ Business Opportunities Journal
Business Service Corp.
5365 Avenida Encinas, Ste. E
Carlsbad, CA 92008
Fax: (619)263-1763
Publisher's E-mail: boj@boj.com
Newspaper covering businesses for sale. **Freq:** Monthly. **Print Method:** Offset. **Cols./Page:** 6. **Col. Width:** 19 nonpareils. **Col. Depth:** 196 agate lines. **URL:** http://www.franchiseopportunitiesjournal.com. **Remarks:** Accepts advertising. **Circ:** ‡132000.

1962 ■ Ride BMX
TransWorld Business
2052 Corte del Nogal, Ste. B
Carlsbad, CA 92011
Phone: (760)722-7777
Magazine covering freestyle and dirt-biking. **Freq:** 9/year. **Print Method:** Offset. **Trim Size:** 9 x 10 1/2. **Cols./Page:** 3. **Col. Width:** 27 nonpareils. **Col. Depth:** 138 agate lines. **Key Personnel:** Keith Mulligan, Editor-in-Chief. **ISSN:** 0362--8841 (print). **Subscription Rates:**

Circulation: ★ = AAM; △ or • = BPA; ♦ = CAC; ❑ = VAC; ⊕ = PO Statement; ‡ = Publisher's Report; Boldface figures = sworn; Light figures = estimated.

$18.97 Individuals 6 issues; $23.97 Individuals 12 issues. **URL:** http://bmx.transworld.net. **Remarks:** Accepts advertising. **Circ:** (Not Reported).

1963 ■ TransWorld Business
TEN: The Enthusiast Network
2052 Corte Del Nogal
Carlsbad, CA 92011
Phone: (760)722-7777
Publication E-mail: business@transworld.net
Magazine featuring board-sports news and information. **Key Personnel:** Adam Cozens, Publisher; Michael Lewis, Editor-in-Chief. **URL:** http://business.transworld.net/magazine. **Remarks:** Accepts advertising. **Circ:** 17700.

1964 ■ Transworld Motocross Magazine
TransWorld Media
2052 Corte del Nogal Ste. 100
Carlsbad, CA 92011
Phone: (760)722-7777
Publisher's E-mail: business@transworld.net
Magazine about motocross. **Freq:** Monthly. **Subscription Rates:** $26.97 Two years; $16.97 Individuals; $11.99 Individuals digital; $17.99 Two years digital. **URL:** http://motocross.transworld.net. **Remarks:** Accepts advertising. **Circ:** (Not Reported).

1965 ■ TransWorld Ride BMX
TEN: The Enthusiast Network
2052 Corte Del Nogal
Carlsbad, CA 92011
Phone: (760)722-7777
Magazine featuring information for BMX bike owners. **Freq:** Bimonthly. **Key Personnel:** Jeff Zielinski, Managing Editor. **Subscription Rates:** $18.97 Individuals print. **URL:** http://bmx.transworld.net. **Remarks:** Accepts advertising. **Circ:** (Not Reported).

1966 ■ Adelphia
5720 El Camino Real
Carlsbad, CA 92008
Free: 800-340-4308
Owner: Time Warner Inc., 1 Time Warner Ctr., New York, NY 10019-8016, Ph: (212)484-8000. **Founded:** 1977. **Key Personnel:** Robert D. Marcus, CFO, Sr. Exec. VP. **Cities Served:** subscribing households 65,000.

1967 ■ KCEO-AM - 1000; 900
2888 Loker Ave. E, Ste. 211
Carlsbad, CA 92010
Phone: (760)729-1000
Fax: (760)931-8201
Owner: Astor Broadcast Group, at above address. **Wattage:** 1,000. **Ad Rates:** Combined advertising rates available with KFSD, KSPA.

1968 ■ KFSD-AM - 1450
1835 Aston Ave.
Carlsbad, CA 92008
Phone: (760)729-1000
Fax: (760)931-8201
Email: contact@am1510kspa.com
Format: Classical. **Owner:** Astor Broadcast Group, at above address. **Founded:** 1958. **Formerly:** KOWN-AM; KSPA-AM. **Operating Hours:** Continuous; 100% local. **ADI:** San Diego, CA. **Local Programs:** *SPA Music Weekend*, Saturday Sunday 12:00 a.m. - 8:00 a.m.; 8:30 a.m. - 10:00 a.m.; 10:30 a.m. - 11:00 a.m. 12:00 a.m. - 6:00 a.m.; 7:00 a.m. - 10:00 a.m.; 3:00 p.m. - 4:00 p.m.; 5:00 p.m. - 6:00 p.m.; 8:00 p.m. - 12:00 a.m. **Wattage:** 1,000. **Ad Rates:** Advertising accepted; rates available upon request. Combined advertising rates available with KECD-FM, KCED-AM. **URL:** http://www.am1510kspa.com/.

CARMEL

W. CA. Monterey Co. On Pacific Ocean, 4 mi. SW of Monterey. Exclusive residential community.

1969 ■ Key Magazine, Carmel and Monterey Peninsula
Key Magazines Inc.
PO Box 223859
Carmel, CA 93922
Phone: (831)392-1311
Fax: (831)899-1305
Publication E-mail: keymonterey@sbcglobal.net
Tourist magazine for the peninsula area. **Freq:** Monthly. **Print Method:** Offset. **Trim Size:** 5 1/2 x 8 1/2. **Cols./Page:** 2. **Col. Width:** 14 picas. **Col. Depth:** 7 3/4 inches. **Key Personnel:** Dane Riggenbach, Publisher. **URL:** http://www.keymagazine.com/carmel/index.html. **Ad Rates:** BW $670; 4C $810. **Remarks:** Accepts advertising. **Circ:** 38000.

1970 ■ Shivas Irons Society Journal
Shivas Irons Society
PO Box 222339
Carmel, CA 93922-2339
Phone: (831)216-6252
Publisher's E-mail: connect@shivas.org
Publishes literature and essays about the mystical and metaphysical aspects of golf. Inspired by the fictional character Shivas Irons, a mystical and talented golf professional from Michael Murphy's novel, Golf in the Kingdom. **Freq:** 3/yr. **URL:** http://shivas.org/the-journal-of-the-shivas-irons-society-issue-4. **Circ:** (Not Reported).

1971 ■ KRML Radio - 1410
27300 RANCHO SAN CARLOS RD.
Carmel, CA 93923
Phone: (831)244-0102
Format: Jazz. **Networks:** Independent. **Founded:** 1957. **Operating Hours:** Continuous. **ADI:** Salinas-Monterey, CA. **Key Personnel:** David C. Kimball, Contact. **Wattage:** 2,500. **Ad Rates:** $20-30 for 30 seconds; $50 for 60 seconds. **URL:** http://www.krml.com.

CARMICHAEL

NC CA. Sacramento Co. 80 mi. NE of San Francisco.

1972 ■ Carmichael Times
Carmichael Times
PO Box 14
Carmichael, CA 95609-0014
Phone: (916)773-1111
Fax: (916)773-2999
Publisher's E-mail: publisher@carmichaeltimes.com
Community newspaper. **Freq:** Weekly. **Print Method:** Web Offset. **Key Personnel:** Paul V. Scholl, Publisher. **ISSN:** 1948--1918 (print). **Subscription Rates:** $42 Individuals /year - within Carmichael. **Alt. Formats:** PDF. **URL:** http://www.carmichaeltimes.com. **Ad Rates:** GLR $1; BW $830.40; PCI $17. **Remarks:** Accepts advertising. **Circ:** (Not Reported).

1973 ■ Edible Sacramento
Edible Communities Inc.
1681 Del Dayo Dr.
Carmichael, CA 95608
Phone: (916)335-7262
Publication E-mail: ediblesacramento@gmail.com
Magazine covering Sacramento County's local food. **Freq:** Quarterly. **Key Personnel:** Jennifer Cliff, Founder. **Subscription Rates:** $36 Individuals; $60 Two years. **URL:** http://ediblesacramento.ediblefeast.com. **Remarks:** Advertising accepted; rates available upon request. **Circ:** (Not Reported).

1974 ■ KYDS-FM - 91.5
3738 Walnut Ave.
Carmichael, CA 95609-0477
Phone: (916)971-7453
Format: Eclectic. **Owner:** San Juan Unified School District, 5641 Mariposa Ave., Citrus Heights, CA 95610, Ph: (916)867-2098, Fax: (916)867-2083. **Founded:** 1979. **Operating Hours:** 7 a.m.-5 p.m. **ADI:** Sacramento-Stockton, CA. **Wattage:** 414. **Ad Rates:** Noncommercial.

CARNELIAN BAY

1975 ■ KODS-FM - 103.7
961 Matley Ln., Ste. 120
Reno, NV 89502
Phone: (775)829-1964
Fax: (775)825-3183
Format: Oldies. **Networks:** Independent. **Owner:** Americom Broadcasting, 6225 Sunset Blvd., Ste. 1900, Los Angeles, CA 90028. **Founded:** 1974. **Formerly:** KHTZ-FM. **Operating Hours:** Continuous. **ADI:** Reno, NV. **Wattage:** 6,300. **Ad Rates:** $17-72 per unit. **URL:** http://www.river1037.com.

CARPINTERIA

SW CA. Santa Barbara Co. On Pacific Ocean, 12 mi. S. of Santa Barbara. Tourism. Light manufacturing. Agriculture.

1976 ■ Coastal View News
Coastal View
4856 Carpinteria Ave.
Carpinteria, CA 93013
Phone: (805)684-4428
Publisher's E-mail: news@coastalview.com
Community newspaper. **Freq:** Weekly. **Print Method:** Web offset. **Trim Size:** 11 x 17. **Cols./Page:** 4. **Col. Width:** 2 1/2 inches. **Col. Depth:** 16 inches. **Key Personnel:** Lea Boyd, Managing Editor. **Subscription Rates:** Free. **URL:** http://coastalview.com. **Remarks:** Accepts advertising. **Circ:** (Not Reported).

CARSON

1977 ■ Lakeshore Flashes Shopping Guide: Lakeshore Flashes
Flashes Publishers Inc.
2695 E Dominguez St.
Carson, CA 90895
Shopper/weekly newspaper. **Freq:** Weekly (Mon.). **Print Method:** Offset. **Trim Size:** 11 3/8 x 13 3/4. **Cols./Page:** 4. **Col. Width:** 2 7/16 inches. **Col. Depth:** 12 inches. **Key Personnel:** Peter Esser, Publisher, phone: (616)546-4259; Debbie Sloan, Manager, phone: (269)673-1720. **Alt. Formats:** Download. **Ad Rates:** GLR $6; BW $545; PCI $7.90. **Remarks:** Color advertising accepted; rates available upon request. **Circ:** (Not Reported).

CASTRO VALLEY

1978 ■ Radiance: The Magazine for Large Women
Radiance
4788 Heyer Ave., Ste. B
Castro Valley, CA 94546
Phone: (510)885-1505
Publication E-mail: info@radiancemagazine.com
Online magazine encouraging women to feel good about their bodies, whatever their size. Featuring articles on health, media, fashion and politics. **Freq:** Quarterly. **Key Personnel:** Alice Ansfield, Editor, Founder, Publisher. **Subscription Rates:** Free. **URL:** http://www.radiancemagazine.com. **Mailing address:** PO Box 2352, Carlsbad, CA 92018. **Remarks:** Advertising accepted; rates available upon request. **Circ:** (Not Reported).

CATHEDRAL CITY

Riverside Co.

1979 ■ KRTM-FM - 88.1
PO Box 2260
Cathedral City, CA 92235
Phone: (760)770-6545
Format: Religious; Contemporary Christian. **Operating Hours:** 18 hours Daily. **Key Personnel:** Lee Alan, Engineer, Station Mgr., lee.alan@krtmradio.com; Bradley Smith, Dir. of Programs. **Ad Rates:** Noncommercial; underwriting available. **URL:** http://www.krtmradio.com.

1980 ■ KTWD-FM
35200 Cathedral Canyon Dr.
Cathedral City, CA 92234
Format: Religious. **Wattage:** 1,600 ERP.

1981 ■ KWXY-AM - 1340
68700 Dinah Shore Dr.
Cathedral City, CA 92234
Phone: (619)328-1104
Fax: (619)328-7814
Format: News. **Founded:** 1964. **Operating Hours:** Continuous. **Wattage:** 1,000. **Ad Rates:** $18 for 30 seconds; $25 for 60 seconds. Combined advertising rates available with KWXY-AM. **URL:** http://www.kwxy.com/.

CEDAR RIDGE

1982 ■ The Mountain Astrologer
The Mountain Astrologer
PO Box 970
Cedar Ridge, CA 95924
Free: 800-287-4828
Publisher's E-mail: subs@mountainastrologer.com
Astrology magazine. **Freq:** Bimonthly. **Trim Size:** 8.5 x 11. **Key Personnel:** Tem Tarriktar, Publisher; Nan Geary, Senior Editor; Janette deProsse, Managing Editor. **Subscription Rates:** $42 By mail; $48 Canada;

$64 Individuals Mexico. **URL:** http://mountainastrologer.com/tma. **Ad Rates:** BW $825; 4C $1,025. **Remarks:** Accepts advertising. **Circ:** 19000.

CERES

C. CA. Stanislaus Co. 4 mi. S. of Modesto. Residential. Industrial. Diversified farming.

1983 ■ The Ceres Courier
The Ceres Courier
2940 4th St.
Ceres, CA 95307
Phone: (209)537-5032
Fax: (209)537-0543
Publication E-mail: circulation@cerescourier.com
Community newspaper. **Freq:** Weekly (Wed.). **Print Method:** Offset. **Cols./Page:** 6. **Col. Width:** 11.2 picas. **Col. Depth:** 294 agate lines. **Key Personnel:** Jeff Benziger, Editor. **Subscription Rates:** $24 Individuals. **URL:** http://www.cerescourier.com. **Mailing address:** PO Box 7, Ceres, CA 95307. **Ad Rates:** GLR $.42; BW $185; PCI $5.88. **Remarks:** Advertising accepted; rates available upon request. **Circ:** Free 19500.

1984 ■ KADV-FM - 90.5
2020 Academy Pl.
Ceres, CA 95307
Format: Religious. **Networks:** Moody Broadcasting; Ambassador Inspirational Radio; SkyLight Satellite; USA Radio. **Operating Hours:** 4 a.m.-11:30 p.m.; 100% local. **Wattage:** 1,500. **Ad Rates:** Noncommercial; underwriting available. **URL:** http://mypromisefm.com.

CHATSWORTH

1985 ■ Adult Video News
AVN Media Network Inc.
9400 Penfield Ave.
Chatsworth, CA 91311
Phone: (818)718-5788
Fax: (818)718-5799
Trade magazine for the adult entertainment industry. **Freq:** Monthly. **Print Method:** Web Offset. **Trim Size:** 8 3/8 x 10 7/8. **Cols./Page:** 3. **Col. Width:** 2 1/2 inches. **Col. Depth:** 10 1/4 inches. **Key Personnel:** Mark Kernes, Senior Editor; Dan Miller, Editor-in-Chief; Paul Fishbein, Chairman. **ISSN:** 0883-7090 (print). **Ad Rates:** BW $2,405; 4C $4,185. **Remarks:** Accepts advertising. **Circ:** (Not Reported).

1986 ■ Air Classics
Challenge Publications Inc.
9509 Vassar Ave., Unit A
Chatsworth, CA 91311-0883
Phone: (818)700-6868
Fax: (818)700-6282
Publisher's E-mail: customerservice@challengeweb.com
Consumer magazine covering aviation for pilots and others. **Freq:** Monthly. **Subscription Rates:** $41.95 U.S. 12 issues; $69.95 U.S. 24 issues; $65.95 Other countries 12 issues; $117.95 Other countries 24 issues. **URL:** http://www.challengeweb.com/air-classics.html. **Remarks:** Accepts advertising. **Circ:** (Not Reported).

1987 ■ Campus Technology
Syllabus Press
9121 Oakdale Ave., Ste. 101
Chatsworth, CA 91311-6526
Phone: (818)814-5277
Fax: (818)734-1522
Publisher's E-mail: wladuke@1105media.com
Trade magazine covering issues for educators worldwide. **Freq:** Monthly. **Key Personnel:** Geoffrey H. Fletcher, Editor, phone: (206)463-1750; Rhea Kelly, Executive Editor; Wendy LaDuke, Chief Revenue Officer. **Subscription Rates:** Free. **Alt. Formats:** PDF. **URL:** http://campustechnology.com/Research/List/Digital-Edition.aspx. **Formerly:** Syllabus Magazine. **Remarks:** Advertising accepted; rates available upon request. **Circ:** (Not Reported).

1988 ■ College Planning and Management
1105 Media Inc.
9200 Oakdale Ave. Rm 101
Chatsworth, CA 91311-6526
Phone: (818)734-1520
Fax: (818)734-1522
Publisher's E-mail: info@1105media.com
Periodical covering education and business. **Freq:** Monthly. **Key Personnel:** Laurie Layman, Art Director, phone: (937)550-9874; Shannon O'Cannor, Managing Editor; Deborah P. Moore, Executive Editor, Publisher. **ISSN:** 1523-0910 (print). **Subscription Rates:** $28.95 Other countries; $57.90 Other countries 2 years. **URL:** http://webcpm.com/Home.aspx. **Ad Rates:** BW $5,910; 4C $1,000. **Remarks:** Accepts advertising. **Circ:** △**30061**.

1989 ■ Enterprise Linux
101communications LLC
9121 Oakdale Ave., Ste. 101
Chatsworth, CA 91311
Phone: (818)814-5200
Fax: (818)734-1522
Technical magazine covering Linux for computing professionals. **Freq:** Monthly. **Key Personnel:** Charlie Simpson, Editor-in-Chief; Eric Derby, Associate Publisher. **Available online. URL:** http://www.enterpriselinuxmag.com/. **Ad Rates:** BW $9,875; 4C $11,875. **Remarks:** Accepts advertising. **Circ:** (Not Reported).

1990 ■ Federal Computer Week: The Newspaper for Federal IT Decision Makers
101communications LLC
9121 Oakdale Ave., Ste. 101
Chatsworth, CA 91311
Phone: (818)814-5200
Fax: (818)734-1522
Computer newsweekly for government systems decision-makers. **Freq:** 40/yr. **Print Method:** Web Offset. **Trim Size:** 8 3/4 x 10 7/8. **Cols./Page:** 3. **Col. Width:** 14 picas. **Col. Depth:** 57 picas. **Key Personnel:** Christopher Dorobek, Editor-in-Chief, fax: (703)876-5143; Florence Olsen, Managing Editor, phone: (703)876-5118; Sean Gallagher, Editor, phone: (410)504-6616. **ISSN:** 0893--052X (print). **Subscription Rates:** Free U.S.; $165 Other countries. **URL:** http://www.fcw.com. **Ad Rates:** 4C $25,937. **Remarks:** Accepts advertising. **Circ:** (Not Reported).

1991 ■ The National Notary
National Notary Association
9350 De Soto Ave.
Chatsworth, CA 91313-2402
Free: 800-876-6827
Publication E-mail: publications@nationalnotary.org
Legal trade magazine. **Freq:** Bimonthly. **Print Method:** Offset. **Cols./Page:** 3 and 2. **Col. Width:** 28 and 42 nonpareils. **Col. Depth:** 138 agate lines. **Key Personnel:** Armando Aguirre, Senior Editor, phone: (818)739-4055. **ISSN:** 0894--7872 (print). **Subscription Rates:** $45 Members includes magazine & bulletin. **URL:** http://www.nationalnotary.org/knowledge-center/news/the-national-notary. **Ad Rates:** BW $1,400; 4C $1,700. **Remarks:** Accepts advertising. **Circ:** ‡200000.

1992 ■ Networking Times
Gabriel Media Group Inc.
11418 Kokopeli Pl.
Chatsworth, CA 91311
Phone: (818)727-2000
Fax: (818)727-9110
Free: 866-343-4005
Magazine that contains articles and features on network marketing and communication. **Freq:** 6/year. **Key Personnel:** Bob Proctor, Publisher; Josephine M. Gross, PhD, Editor-in-Chief. **ISSN:** 1539--3151 (print). **Subscription Rates:** $47.77 U.S. print + online; $33.77 Individuals online. **URL:** http://www.networkingtimes.com. **Remarks:** Accepts advertising. **Circ:** (Not Reported).

1993 ■ School Planning and Management
1105 Media Inc.
9200 Oakdale Ave. Rm 101
Chatsworth, CA 91311-6526
Phone: (818)734-1520
Fax: (818)734-1522
Publisher's E-mail: info@1105media.com
Professional publication covering education. **Freq:** Monthly. **Key Personnel:** Patty James, Director, Publications; Jerry Enderle, Editor-in-Chief, phone: (937)550-9874; Deborah P. Moore, Executive Editor, Publisher, phone: (602)867-2085. **ISSN:** 1086--4628 (print). **Subscription Rates:** Free. **URL:** http://webspm.com/Home.aspx; http://1105media.com/pages/shs.aspx. **Remarks:** Accepts advertising. **Circ:** (Not Reported).

1994 ■ Sea Classics
Challenge Publications Inc.
9509 Vassar Ave., Unit A
Chatsworth, CA 91311-0883
Phone: (818)700-6868
Fax: (818)700-6282
Publisher's E-mail: customerservice@challengeweb.com
Consumer magazine covering current and historical maritime and naval events. **Freq:** Monthly. **ISSN:** 0048--9867 (print). **Subscription Rates:** $41.95 Individuals 1 year; $69.95 Two years; $65.95 Individuals 1 year; other countries; $117.95 Two years other countries. **URL:** http://www.challengeweb.com/sea-classics.html. **Remarks:** Accepts advertising. **Circ:** Paid ⊕**57346**.

1995 ■ T.H.E. Journal
T.H.E. Journal
9201 Oakdale Ave., Ste. 101
Chatsworth, CA 91311
Phone: (818)734-1520
Fax: (818)734-1522
Publisher's E-mail: wladuke@1105media.com
Application of technology journal for educators and administrators in higher education, K-12 and industry training. **Founded:** 1973. **Freq:** 11/year. **Print Method:** Offset. **Trim Size:** 7 7/8 x 10 1/2. **Cols./Page:** 3. **Col. Width:** 26 nonpareils. **Col. Depth:** 138 agate lines. **Key Personnel:** Wendy LaDuke, Publisher, phone: (949)265-1520. **ISSN:** 0192-592X (print). **URL:** http://thejournal.com/Home.aspx. **Also known as:** Technological Horizons in Education. **Ad Rates:** BW $9,950; 4C $1,700. **Remarks:** Advertising accepted; rates available upon request. **Circ:** 100000.

1996 ■ UFO Journal
National Investigations Committee on Unidentified Flying Objects
PO Box 3847
Chatsworth, CA 91313-9998
Phone: (818)882-0039
Fax: (818)998-6712
Publisher's E-mail: nicufo@gmail.com
Provides accounts of sightings of UFOs worldwide; includes book reviews and articles on miscellaneous space/science phenomena. **Freq:** Quarterly. **Subscription Rates:** Included in membership. **URL:** http://www.nicufo.org/others.htm. **Remarks:** Accepts advertising. **Circ:** (Not Reported).

1997 ■ Warbirds International
Challenge Publications Inc.
9509 Vassar Ave., Unit A
Chatsworth, CA 91311-0883
Phone: (818)700-6868
Fax: (818)700-6282
Publisher's E-mail: customerservice@challengeweb.com
Consumer magazine covering vintage and veteran military aircraft. **Freq:** Monthly. **Subscription Rates:** $41.95 U.S. 12 issues; $69.95 U.S. 24 issues; $65.95 Other countries 12 issues; $117.95 Other countries 24 issues. **URL:** http://www.challengeweb.com/warbirds-international.html. **Remarks:** Accepts advertising. **Circ:** (Not Reported).

CHESTER

NE CA. Plumas Co. 70 mi. E. of Red Bluff. Residential. Tourism. Forest products.

1998 ■ Chester Progressive
Feather Publishing Company Inc.
135 Main St.
Chester, CA 96020
Phone: (530)258-3115
Fax: (530)258-2365
Publication E-mail: chesterprogressive@frontiernet.net
Community newspaper serving Plumas and Lassen counties. **Freq:** Weekly (Wed.). **Print Method:** Offset. **Cols./Page:** 6. **Col. Width:** 11 picas. **Col. Depth:** 301 agate lines. **Key Personnel:** Michael C. Taborski, Publisher. **ISSN:** 0010--2880 (print). **Subscription Rates:** $26 Individuals in County; $37 Individuals in California; $44 Out of state. **URL:** http://www.plumasnews.com. **Remarks:** Accepts advertising. **Circ:** (Not Reported).

Circulation: ★ = AAM; △ or • = BPA; ♦ = CAC; ❑ = VAC; ⊕ = PO Statement; ‡ = Publisher's Report; Boldface figures = sworn; Light figures = estimated.

1999 ■ KWLU-FM - 98.9
PO Box 779002
Rocklin, CA 95677-9972
Fax: (916)251-1901
Free: 800-525-5683
Email: klove@klove.com
Format: Contemporary Christian. **Owner:** Educational Media Foundation, PO Box 2098, Omaha, NE 68103-2098, Free: 800-434-8400. **Key Personnel:** Mike Novak, President, CEO; Alan Mason, COO. **Wattage:** 1,000. **URL:** http://www.klove.com.

CHICO

N. CA. Butte Co. 90 mi. N. of Sacramento. California State University At Chico. Manufactures aluminum, lumber, canned goods, pruning saws, foundry, concrete products, beverages. Fruit drying and packing, almond & walnut hulling and processing plants; Agriculture.

2000 ■ Animals Voice Magazine
The Animals Voice
1692 Mangrove Ave., No. 276
Chico, CA 95926
Publisher's E-mail: 4rights@animalsvoice.com
Freq: Quarterly. **URL:** http://animalsvoice.com/the-animals-voice/the-magazine. **Remarks:** Accepts advertising. **Circ:** (Not Reported).

2001 ■ Chico Enterprise-Record
Digital First Media
400 E Park Ave.
Chico, CA 95928
Phone: (530)891-1234
Fax: (530)891-9204
General newspaper. **Freq:** Daily. **Print Method:** Offset. **Cols./Page:** 6. **Col. Width:** 25 nonpareils. **Col. Depth:** 294 agate lines. **Key Personnel:** Sean Johnson, Manager, Production, phone: (530)896-7794; David Little, Editor, phone: (530)896-7793. **URL:** http://www.chicoer.com. **Ad Rates:** BW $3653; 4C $4013; SAU $18.16; PCI $28.99. **Remarks:** Accepts advertising. **Circ:** Mon.-Fri. ★27229, Sat. ★25180, Sun. ★31339.

2002 ■ Chico News & Review
Chico Community Publishing Inc.
353 E 2nd St.
Chico, CA 95928
Phone: (530)894-2300
Fax: (530)894-0143
Publication E-mail: chicosubs@newsreview.com
Community newspaper (tabloid). **Freq:** Weekly (Thurs.). **Print Method:** Offset. Uses mats. **Cols./Page:** 5. **Col. Width:** 2 1/16 inches. **Col. Depth:** 13 1/8 inches. **Key Personnel:** Jeff von Kaenel, Chief Executive Officer, President; Melissa Daugherty, Editor. **URL:** http://www.newsreview.com/chico/Home. **Remarks:** Advertising accepted; rates available upon request. **Circ:** Free ‡34716, Paid ‡5, Combined ‡34721.

2003 ■ Edible Shasta-Butte
Edible Communities Inc.
7 Hidden Brooke Way
Chico, CA 95928
Phone: (530)345-9509
Publication E-mail: info@edibleshastabutte.com
Magazine featuring the local food of Shasta and Butte Counties. **Freq:** Quarterly. **Key Personnel:** Candace Byrne, Contact; Earl Bloor, Contact. **Subscription Rates:** $28 Individuals /year. **URL:** http://edibleshastabutte.com. **Ad Rates:** 4C $1200. **Remarks:** Accepts advertising. **Circ:** (Not Reported).

2004 ■ Macrobiotics Today
George Ohsawa Macrobiotic Foundation
1277 Marian Ave.
Chico, CA 95928-6914
Phone: (530)566-9765
Fax: (530)566-9768
Free: 800-232-2372
Publisher's E-mail: gomf@earthlink.net
Magazine covering macrobiotics, health, and nutrition. **Freq:** Quarterly. **Print Method:** Web press. **Trim Size:** 8 1/8 x 10 3/4. **Cols./Page:** 3. **Col. Width:** 2 1/4 inches. **Col. Depth:** 9 inches. **Key Personnel:** Carl Ferre, Publisher; Bob Ligon, Contact. **Subscription Rates:** $25 Individuals /year; print; $40 Elsewhere /year; print; $15 Individuals /year; PDF download. **Alt. Formats:** PDF. **URL:** http://www.ohsawamacrobiotics.com/macrobiotics-today?id=18. **Mailing address:** PO Box 3998, Chico, CA 95927-3998. **Remarks:** Advertising accepted; rates available upon request. **Circ:** Paid 2000, Controlled 5000.

2005 ■ Synthesis
Synthesis Network Inc.
210 W Sixth St.
Chico, CA 95928
Phone: (530)899-7708
Online entertainment magazine featuring music and movie reviews, interviews, and audio downloads. **Founded:** 1995. **Freq:** Weekly. **Key Personnel:** Bill Fishkin, Chief Executive Officer; Karen Potter, Editor; Ryan Prado, Managing Editor. **Subscription Rates:** Free online. **URL:** http://synthesisweekly.com/. **Remarks:** Accepts advertising. **Circ:** (Not Reported).

2006 ■ Videomaker Magazine
Videomaker Inc.
1350 E 9th St.
Chico, CA 95928
Phone: (530)891-8410
Fax: (530)891-8443
Free: 800-284-3226
Publisher's E-mail: customerservice@videomaker.com
Videomaker covers camcorders, video editing, desktop video and audio production for video. Includes a buyer's guide to a relevant product type in every issue. **Freq:** Monthly. **Print Method:** Offset. **Trim Size:** 7 7/8 x 10 1/12. **Key Personnel:** Scott Memmott, Contact. **ISSN:** 0889--4973 (print). **Subscription Rates:** $19.97 Individuals; $71.88 newsstand price. **URL:** http://www.videomaker.com; http://www.videomaker.com/magazine. **Mailing address:** PO Box 4591, Chico, CA 95927. **Remarks:** Advertising accepted; rates available upon request. **Circ:** Paid ★65396.

2007 ■ KBQB-FM - 92.7
856 Manzanita Ct.
Chico, CA 95926
Phone: (530)342-2200
Fax: (530)342-2260
Format: Contemporary Hit Radio (CHR). **Owner:** Results Radio L.L.C., 970 Tripoli St., Johnstown, PA 15902. **Operating Hours:** Continuous. **ADI:** Chico-Redding, CA. **Wattage:** 1,500. **Ad Rates:** Advertising accepted; rates available upon request. **URL:** http://www.927bobfm.com.

2008 ■ KCEZ-FM - 102.1
856 Manzanita Ct.
Chico, CA 95926
Phone: (530)342-2200
Fax: (530)342-2260
Format: Oldies. **Key Personnel:** Jon Graham, Mktg. Mgr. **Ad Rates:** Advertising accepted; rates available upon request. **URL:** http://power102radio.com/contact-2.

2009 ■ KCHO-FM - 91.7
California State University
35 Main St.
Chico, CA 95929-0500
Phone: (530)898-5896
Fax: (530)898-4348
Email: info@kcho.org
Format: Information; Educational. **Key Personnel:** Mike Birdsill, Chief Engineer, mbirdsill@csuchico.edu. **Ad Rates:** Noncommercial. **URL:** http://mynspr.org.

2010 ■ KFMF-FM - 93.9
1459 Humboldt Rd., No. D
Chico, CA 95928
Phone: (530)899-3600
Format: Classic Rock. **Networks:** Independent. **Owner:** Mapleton Communication L.L.C., 10900 Wilshire Blvd., No. 1500, Los Angeles, CA 90024, Ph: (310)209-7221, Fax: (310)209-7239. **Founded:** 1974. **Operating Hours:** Continuous; 100% local. **ADI:** Chico-Redding, CA. **Wattage:** 25,000. **Ad Rates:** $65 for 60 seconds. Combined advertising rates available with KALF-FM; KPPL-FM. **URL:** http://939thehippo.com.

2011 ■ KFPR-FM - 88.9
400 W 1st St.
Chico, CA 95929-0999
Phone: (530)898-5896
Email: info@kcho.org
Format: Jazz. **Key Personnel:** Mike Birdsill, Chief Engineer, mbirdsill@csuchico.edu. **Ad Rates:** Noncommercial. **Mailing address:** PO Box 990061, Redding, CA 96099-0061. **URL:** http://www.kcho.org.

2012 ■ KHAP-FM - 89.1
290 Hegenberger Rd.
Oakland, CA 94621
Free: 800-543-1495
Email: info@familyradio.org
Format: Religious. **Networks:** Family Stations Radio. **Owner:** Family Stations Inc., 290 Hegenberger Rd., Oakland, CA 94621, Free: 800-543-1495. **Wattage:** 12,000. **URL:** http://www.familyradio.org.

2013 ■ KHHZ-FM - 97.7
2654 Cramer Ln.
Chico, CA 95928
Format: Hispanic. **Owner:** Deer Creek Broadcasting, at above address. **Key Personnel:** Dino Corbin, Gen. Mgr., dcorbin@dcbchico.com. **Ad Rates:** Advertising accepted; rates available upon request. **URL:** http://www.khhz.com.

2014 ■ KHSL-FM - 103.5
2654 Cramer Ln.
Chico, CA 95928-8838
Phone: (530)345-0021
Fax: (530)893-2121
Format: Country. **Owner:** Deer Creek Broadcasting, at above address. **Founded:** 1983. **Formerly:** KRIJ-FM; KCHH-FM. **Operating Hours:** Continuous. **ADI:** Chico-Redding, CA. **Key Personnel:** Jaime Perry, Sales Mgr., jperry@dcbchico.com. **Wattage:** 1,600. **URL:** http://www.khsl.com.

2015 ■ KHSL-TV - 12
3460 Silverbell Rd.
Chico, CA 95973
Phone: (530)342-0141
Format: News. **Networks:** CBS. **Founded:** 1953. **Operating Hours:** Continuous; 50% network, 50% local. **ADI:** Chico-Redding, CA. **Key Personnel:** John Stall, Gen. Mgr., jstall@khsltv.com. **Wattage:** 316. **Ad Rates:** $45-650 per unit. **URL:** http://www.actionnewsnow.com/home.

2016 ■ KKXX-AM - 930
1363 Longfellow Ave.
Chico, CA 95926
Phone: (530)894-7325
Fax: (530)894-5372
Format: Contemporary Christian. **Networks:** USA Radio; International Broadcasting; American Ag Net. **Owner:** Butte Broadcasting Inc., 660 Dewey Blvd., Butte, MT 59701, Ph: (406)494-7777. **Founded:** 1965. **Operating Hours:** Continuous; 20% network, 80% local. **ADI:** Chico-Redding, CA. **Key Personnel:** Andrew Palmquist, Gen. Mgr., andrew@kkxx.net. **Local Programs:** *Hope for Today*, Monday Tuesday Wednesday Thursday Friday 5:00 a.m. - 5:30 a.m.; 8:00 a.m. - 8:30 a.m.; *The Hugh Hewitt Show*, Monday Tuesday Wednesday Thursday Friday 3:00 p.m. - 6:00 p.m. **Wattage:** 1,000. **Ad Rates:** Advertising accepted; rates available upon request. **URL:** http://www.chicochristianradio.com.

2017 ■ KLRS-FM - 92.7
856 Manzanita Ct.
Chico, CA 95926
Phone: (530)342-2200
Email: info@colorsradio.com
Format: Top 40. **Ad Rates:** Noncommercial. **URL:** http://www.927bobfm.com/.

2018 ■ KMJE-FM - 101.5
PO Box 7568
Chico, CA 95927
Phone: (530)342-2200
Fax: (530)342-2260
Format: Adult Contemporary. **Key Personnel:** Gordon Rowntree, Dir. of Mktg., Mktg. Mgr., growntree@resultsradiomail.com; Matthew Reisz, Web Adm., mreisz@resultsradiomail.com; Christopher Rey, Dir. of Operations, chrisrey@gosunny.com. **Ad Rates:** Advertising accepted; rates available upon request.

2019 ■ KMXI-FM - 95.1
2654 Cramer Ln.
Chico, CA 95928-8838
Phone: (530)345-0021
Fax: (530)893-2121
Format: Adult Contemporary. **Owner:** Deer Creek Broadcasting, at above address. **Founded:** 1972. **Formerly:** KPAY-FM. **Operating Hours:** Continuous. **ADI:** Chico-Redding, CA. **Key Personnel:** Dino Corbin, Contact; Jaime Perry, Sales Mgr. **Wattage:** 8,700. **Ad**

Rates: Advertising accepted; rates available upon request. **URL:** http://www.kmxi.com.

2020 ■ KNSN-AM - 1290
2654 Cramer Ln.
Chico, CA 95928
Phone: (916)893-8926
Fax: (916)893-8937
Format: Country; Talk; News; Sports. **Networks:** CBS. **Founded:** 1935. **Operating Hours:** Continuous. **ADI:** Chico-Redding, CA. **Key Personnel:** Gus Smith, Gen. Mgr.; Phil Papeman, Gen. Sales Mgr.; Ron Woodward, Operations Mgr., Prog. Dir.; Ken Carpenter, Chief Engineer. **Wattage:** 5,000 KW. **Ad Rates:** $10-20 per unit. **URL:** http://kpay.com.

2021 ■ KNVN-TV - 24
3460 Silverbell Rd.
Chico, CA 95973
Phone: (530)342-0141
Founded: Sept. 06, 2006. **Key Personnel:** John Stall, Contact, jstall@khsltv.com. **Ad Rates:** Advertising accepted; rates available upon request. **URL:** http://www.actionnewsnow.com/home.

2022 ■ KPAY-AM - 1290
2654 Cramer Ln.
Chico, CA 95928-8838
Phone: (530)345-0021
Fax: (530)893-2121
Format: Talk; News. **Owner:** Deer Creek Broadcasting, at above address. **Founded:** 1949. **Operating Hours:** Continuous. **ADI:** Chico-Redding, CA. **Key Personnel:** Mike Baca, Sports Dir., mbaca@dcbchico.com. **Local Programs:** *KPAY Morning News*, Monday Tuesday Wednesday Thursday Friday 6:00 a.m. - 9:00 a.m.; *Hidden Treasures*, Saturday 7:00 a.m. - 8:00 a.m. **Wattage:** 5,000. **Ad Rates:** Advertising accepted; rates available upon request. **URL:** http://www.kpay.com.

2023 ■ KPPL-FM - 107.5
1459 Humboldt Rd., Ste. A
Chico, CA 95928
Phone: (530)342-5775
Fax: (530)343-0243
Format: Hip Hop; News; Talk. **Owner:** KPPL-FM, Menlo Park, CA, Ph: (415)324-8464. **Founded:** 1987. **Formerly:** KTMX-FM. **Operating Hours:** Continuous. **Key Personnel:** Dick Stein, VP. **Wattage:** 28,000 ERP. **Ad Rates:** $50 for 60 seconds. **URL:** http://www.1075nowfm.com.

2024 ■ KQPT-FM - 107.5
1459 Humboldt Rd., Ste. D
Chico, CA 95928
Phone: (530)899-3600
Format: Adult Contemporary; Top 40. **Owner:** Mapleton Communication L.L.C., 10900 Wilshire Blvd., No. 1500, Los Angeles, CA 90024, Ph: (310)209-7221, Fax: (310)209-7239. **Operating Hours:** Continuous. **Wattage:** 28,000. **Ad Rates:** Advertising accepted; rates available upon request. **URL:** http://www.nowfmonline.com.

2025 ■ KRQR-FM - 106.7
856 Manzanita Ct.
Chico, CA 95926
Phone: (530)342-2200
Fax: (530)342-2260
Format: Heavy Metal; Album-Oriented Rock (AOR). **Key Personnel:** Jon Graham, Contact; Jon Graham, Contact. **Wattage:** 50,000. **Ad Rates:** Advertising accepted; rates available upon request. **URL:** http://www.zrockfm.com.

2026 ■ KTHU-FM - 100.7
856 Manzanita Ct.
Chico, CA 95926
Phone: (530)342-2200
Fax: (530)342-2260
Format: Classic Rock. **Wattage:** 50,000. **Ad Rates:** Noncommercial. **URL:** http://chicothunderheads.com.

2027 ■ K213EH-FM - 90.5
PO Box 391
Twin Falls, ID 83303
Fax: (208)736-1958
Free: 800-357-4226
Format: Religious; Contemporary Christian. **Owner:** CSN International, PO Box 391, Twin Falls, ID 83303, Ph: (208)736-1958, Fax: (208)736-1958, Free: 800-357-4226. **ADI:** Chico-Redding, CA. **Key Personnel:** Don Mills, Prog. Dir., Music Dir.; Kelly Carlson, Dir. of Engg.; Ray Gorney, Asst. Dir. **Wattage:** 010. **URL:** http://www.csnradio.com.

2028 ■ KYIX-FM - 104.9
PO Box 2118
Omaha, NE 68103-2118
Free: 888-937-2471
Email: info@air1.com
Format: Contemporary Christian. **Founded:** Sept. 12, 2006. **Key Personnel:** Mike Novak, CEO, President. **Ad Rates:** Noncommercial. **URL:** http://www.air1.com.

2029 ■ KZFR-FM - 90.1
341 Broadway, Ste. 411
Chico, CA 95928
Phone: (530)895-0706
Fax: (530)895-0775
Email: info@kzfr.org
Format: Contemporary Hit Radio (CHR). **Owner:** Golden Valley Community Broadcasters, 341 Broadway, Ste. 411, Chico, CA 95928-5321. **Founded:** July 08, 1990. **Operating Hours:** 6 a.m.-12 a.m. **Key Personnel:** Rick Anderson, Gen. Mgr.; John Dubois, Operations Mgr. **Wattage:** 6,300. **Ad Rates:** Noncommercial. **URL:** http://www.kzfr.org.

2030 ■ KZZP-FM - 96.7
PO Box 7590
Chico, CA 95927-7568
Phone: (916)343-5253
Fax: (916)343-5491
Format: Album-Oriented Rock (AOR). **Networks:** Independent. **Owner:** Phoenix Broadcasting, 407 W 9th St., Chico, CA 95928, Ph: (916)895-1197. **Founded:** 1977. **Formerly:** KNVR-FM. **Operating Hours:** Continuous. **Key Personnel:** Bruce O'Brien, Dir. of Programs; Keith Cross, Station Mgr.; Bruce Sessions, News Dir; Dave Kindig, Contact; Steve Shea, Contact. **Wattage:** 3,000. **Ad Rates:** $5-26 for 30 seconds; $7-28 for 60 seconds.

CHINO

SW CA. San Bernardino Co. 37 mi. E. of Los Angeles. Manufactures computer components, lumber, bricks. Diversified farming. Poultry, and horses, Dairying.

2031 ■ Chino Champion: Chino Valley News
Champion Newspapers
13179 9th St.
Chino, CA 91710
Phone: (909)628-5501
Fax: (909)590-1217
Publisher's E-mail: forum08@championnewspapers.com
Community newspaper. **Freq:** Weekly (Sat.). **Print Method:** Offset. **Trim Size:** 12 1/2 x 21 1/2. **Cols./Page:** 6. **Col. Width:** 1.81 inches. **Col. Depth:** 21 inches. **Key Personnel:** Bruce Wood, Publisher. **USPS:** 106-000. **Subscription Rates:** $10 Individuals by carrier 26 weeks; $15 Individuals by carrier 52 weeks; $25 Individuals by carrier 104 weeks; $35 By mail by carrier 156 weeks; $20 Individuals VIP 26 weeks; $25 Individuals VIP 52 weeks; $45 Individuals VIP 104 weeks; $65 Individuals VIP 156 weeks; $80 U.S. US mail 26 weeks; $110 U.S. US mail 52 weeks; $220 U.S. US mail 104 weeks; $330 U.S. US mail 156 weeks. **URL:** http://www.championnewspapers.com; http://championnewspapers-dot-com.bloxcms.com/site/forms/subscription_services/subscribe/. **Ad Rates:** GLR $2.44; BW $3301; 4C $3641; SAU $34.05; PCI $34.05. **Remarks:** Accepts advertising. **Circ:** Combined ‡42800.

2032 ■ Chino Hills Champion: Chino Hills News
Champion Newspapers
13179 9th St.
Chino, CA 91710
Phone: (909)628-5501
Fax: (909)590-1217
Publisher's E-mail: forum08@championnewspapers.com
Community newspaper. **Freq:** Weekly (Sat.). **Print Method:** Offset. **Trim Size:** 12 1/2 x 21 1/2. **Cols./Page:** 6. **Col. Width:** 1.81 inches. **Col. Depth:** 21 inches. **Key Personnel:** Allen P. McCombs, Owner, Publisher. **USPS:** 106-000. **Subscription Rates:** $10 Individuals by carrier (26 weeks); $15 By mail by carrier (52 weeks); $25 Individuals by carrier (104 weeks); $35 By mail by carrier (156 weeks). **Ad Rates:** GLR $2.44; BW $3301; 4C $3641; SAU $34.05; PCI $34.05. **Remarks:** Accepts advertising. **Circ:** Combined ‡42800.

CHOWCHILLA

SC CA. Madera Co. 38 mi. N. of Fresno. Manufactures cottonseed oil, steel buildings, Compressed wood, chemicals, fertilizer, alfalfa pellets, creamery products. Agriculture. Cotton, almonds, seed crops, dairying, grain.

2033 ■ KFVR-AM - 1310
24626 Rd. 19
Chowchilla, CA 93610-9686
Format: Oldies. **Key Personnel:** Silvia Meza, Bus. Mgr. **Ad Rates:** Noncommercial.

CHUBBUCK

2034 ■ KRCD-FM
5999 Center Dr.
Los Angeles, CA 90045
Phone: (208)232-0010
Format: Talk. **Networks:** People's Network. **Founded:** 1981. **Formerly:** KKLB-FM. **Wattage:** 4,100 ERP.

CHULA VISTA

S. CA. San Diego Co. 6 mi. SE of San Diego. Manufactures cabinets, aircraft and motor vehicle parts, chemicals, electric motors, machinery, metal, concrete products.

2035 ■ Berwick Gazette
Star News
296 3rd Ave.
Chula Vista, CA 91910
Phone: (619)427-3000
Fax: (619)426-6346
Publisher's E-mail: info@thestarnews.com
General newspaper. **URL:** http://berwick.starcommunity.com.au. **Remarks:** Accepts advertising. **Circ:** (Not Reported).

2036 ■ Ferntree Gully, Belgrave Mail
Star News
296 3rd Ave.
Chula Vista, CA 91910
Phone: (619)427-3000
Fax: (619)426-6346
Publisher's E-mail: info@thestarnews.com
Newspaper covering community issues and business news for the people of Melbourne and Geelong. **Freq:** Weekly (Tues.). **URL:** http://ferntreegully.starcommunity.com.au. **Remarks:** Accepts advertising. **Circ:** (Not Reported).

2037 ■ La Prensa San Diego
La Prensa Munoz Inc.
651 3rd Ave., Ste. C
Chula Vista, CA 91910
Phone: (619)425-7400
Publication E-mail: laprensa@ix.netcom.com
Community newspaper (Spanish and English). **Freq:** Weekly (Fri.). **Cols./Page:** 8. **Col. Width:** 1 1/2 inches. **Col. Depth:** 21.5 inches. **Key Personnel:** Daniel L. Munoz, Editor. **ISSN:** 0738--9183 (print). **Subscription Rates:** $130 Individuals. **URL:** http://laprensa-sandiego.org. **Remarks:** Advertising accepted; rates available upon request. **Circ:** ‡30000.

2038 ■ Star-News
Star News
296 3rd Ave.
Chula Vista, CA 91910
Phone: (619)427-3000
Fax: (619)426-6346
Publisher's E-mail: info@thestarnews.com
Community newspaper (tabloid). **Founded:** 1881. **Freq:** Weekly (Fri.). **Print Method:** Offset. **Cols./Page:** 6. **Col. Width:** 9 picas. **Col. Depth:** 16 inches. **Key Personnel:** Carlos R. Davalos, Editor; John Moreno, Publisher. **URL:** http://www.thestarnews.com/. **Ad Rates:** GLR $5.40; BW $1,320; 4C $1,590; SAU $19.95; PCI $17.60. **Remarks:** Accepts advertising. **Circ:** Fri. 33,500.

Circulation: ★ = AAM; △ or • = BPA; ♦ = CAC; ❑ = VAC; ⊕ = PO Statement; ‡ = Publisher's Report; Boldface figures = sworn; Light figures = estimated.

2039 ■ KSDO-AM - 1130
344 F St., Ste. 200
Chula Vista, CA 91910
Format: Music of Your Life. **Owner:** Hi-Favor Broadcasting, LLC, 344 F St., Ste. 200, Chula Vista, CA 91910, Ph: (619)985-8432. **Founded:** 1946. **Operating Hours:** Continuous. **ADI:** San Diego, CA. **Wattage:** 10,000. **Ad Rates:** Accepts Advertising. **URL:** http://nuevavida.com.

2040 ■ XEWT-TV - 12
637 3d Ave., Ste. B
Chula Vista, CA 91910
Phone: (619)585-9398
Fax: (619)585-9463
Email: moreinfo@xewt12.tv
Format: Commercial TV; Hispanic. **Owner:** Televisa, SA News, Avenida Vasco de Quiroga 2000 Colonia Santa Fe, 01210 Mexico, DF, Mexico, Ph: 52-55-5261-2000, Fax: 52-55-5261-2494. **Founded:** 1960. **Operating Hours:** Continuous. **ADI:** San Diego, CA. **Wattage:** 325,000. **Ad Rates:** Noncommercial. Combined advertising rates available with XHVAA Ch. 57.

2041 ■ XLNC-FM - 90.7
1690 Frontage Rd.
Chula Vista, CA 91911
Phone: (619)575-9090
Fax: (619)423-1818
Email: membership@xlnc1.org
Format: Classical. **Operating Hours:** Continuous. **Key Personnel:** Daniel Rumley, Production Mgr., Traffic Mgr., drumley@xlnc1.org. **Ad Rates:** Advertising accepted; rates available upon request. **URL:** http://www.xlnc1.org.

CLAREMONT

S. CA. Los Angeles Co. 35 mi. E. of Los Angeles. Pomona College. Claremont College. Retirement Center. Rancho Santa Ana Botanical Gardens. Air cleaners, scientific instruments.

2042 ■ Bulletin of Mathematical Biology
Society for Mathematical Biology
c/o Lisette de Pillis, Treasurer
Department of Mathematics
Harvey Mudd College
Claremont, CA 91711
Journal publishing research on junction of computational, theoretical and experimental biology. **Freq:** Monthly Bimonthly. **Print Method:** Offset. **Trim Size:** 6 1/2 x 9 7/8. **Cols./Page:** 1. **Col. Width:** 66 nonpareils. **Col. Depth:** 124 agate lines. **Key Personnel:** Philip Maini, Editor. **ISSN:** 0092-8240 (print); **EISSN:** 1522- 9602 (electronic). **Subscription Rates:** Included in membership; $1218 Institutions print incl free access; $1462 Institutions print plus enhanced access. **URL:** http://link.springer.com/journal/11538; http://smb.org/publications/index.shtml. **Ad Rates:** BW $750; 4C $1,750. **Remarks:** Advertising not accepted. **Circ:** ‡2500.

2043 ■ Cactus and Succulent Journal
Cactus and Succulent Society of America
PO Box 1000
Claremont, CA 91711-1000
Journal covering cactus and succulents. **Freq:** Bimonthly. **Trim Size:** 6 3/4 x 10. **Key Personnel:** Myron Kimnach, Editor. **ISSN:** 0007--9367 (print). **Ad Rates:** GLR $11; BW $433. **Remarks:** Accepts advertising. **Circ:** Paid ‡3500.

2044 ■ Claremont Courier
Claremont Courier
1420 N Claremont Blvd.
Claremont, CA 91711
Phone: (909)621-4761
Fax: (909)621-4072
Newspaper. **Freq:** Weekly (Fri.). **Print Method:** Offset. **Trim Size:** 11 x 15. **Cols./Page:** 6. **Col. Width:** 19 nonpareils. **Col. Depth:** 196 agate lines. **Key Personnel:** Peter Weinberger, Editor, Owner, Publisher; Kathryn Dunn, Editor. **USPS:** 115-180. **Subscription Rates:** $56 Individuals print and online; $51 Individuals seniors (print and online); $93 Two years seniors (print and online); $49 Individuals online; $91 Two years online; $15 Individuals online one month; $47 Students one year online. **URL:** http://www.claremont-courier.com. **Ad Rates:** GLR $.52; BW $638.40; 4C $838.40; PCI $7.60. **Remarks:** Accepts advertising. **Circ:** Paid 4520.

2045 ■ Pomona College Magazine
Pomona College
550 N College Ave.
Claremont, CA 91711
Publisher's E-mail: webmaster@pomona.edu
Magazine featuring articles and opinions about Pomona College. **Freq:** 3/year. **Key Personnel:** Mark Wood, Editor. **URL:** http://magazine.pomona.edu; http://www.pomona.edu/administration/communications/publications. **Circ:** (Not Reported).

2046 ■ KSPC-FM - 88.7
Thatcher Music Bldg.
340 N College Ave.
Claremont, CA 91711
Phone: (909)621-8157
Format: Alternative/New Music/Progressive. **Networks:** Independent. **Owner:** Pomona College Board of Trustees, at above address. **Founded:** 1956. **Operating Hours:** Continuous; 100% local. **Local Programs:** *Public Affairs Show*, Monday 10:00 p.m. - 11:00 p.m. **Wattage:** 3,000 ERP. **Ad Rates:** Noncommercial. **URL:** http://www.kspc.org.

2047 ■ KWEB-FM - 91.1
1175 W Baseline Rd.
Claremont, CA 91711
Phone: (909)626-3587
Fax: (909)621-4582
Format: Full Service; Classical. **Founded:** 1957. **Operating Hours:** 6:15 pm - 7:45 pm and 8:45 pm - 10:30 pm Sun.-Fri. **Key Personnel:** Peter Bartlett, Div. Dir., pbartlett@webb.org; Leo Marshall, Dir. of Fin. **URL:** http://www.webb.org/kweb/index.aspx.

CLIPPER MILLS

N. CA. Butte Co. 17 mi SW of Downieville. Residential. Tourism. Timber.

2048 ■ Rabbit Creek Journal
Rabbit Creek Journal
PO Box 309
Clipper Mills, CA 95930
Phone: (530)675-2270
Publisher's E-mail: daysnews@rcj.net
Community newspaper. **Freq:** Weekly. **Print Method:** Offset. **Cols./Page:** 5. **Col. Width:** 26 nonpareils. **Col. Depth:** 301 agate lines. **Subscription Rates:** $30 By mail. **URL:** http://www.rcj.net. **Ad Rates:** BW $393.25; PCI $6.50. **Remarks:** Accepts advertising. **Circ:** ‡2000.

CLOVERDALE

NW CA. Sonoma Co. 35 mi. NW of Santa Rosa. Residential.

2049 ■ Cloverdale Reveille
Cloverdale Reveille
207 N Cloverdale Blvd.
Cloverdale, CA 95425-3318
Phone: (707)894-3339
Publication E-mail: reveille@thegrid.net
Local newspaper. **Freq:** Weekly (Wed.). **Print Method:** Offset. **Cols./Page:** 6. **Col. Width:** 24 nonpareils. **Col. Depth:** 294 agate lines. **Subscription Rates:** $50 Individuals in county residents 1 year; $75 Individuals out of county residents 1 year; $80 Two years in county residents; $125 Two years out of county residents. **URL:** http://www.sonomawest.com/cloverdale_reveille. **Mailing address:** PO Box 157, Cloverdale, CA 95425-3318. **Ad Rates:** BW $126; SAU $5.50; PCI $5. **Remarks:** Accepts advertising. **Circ:** Paid ‡2300.

CLOVIS

C. CA. Fresno Co. 4 mi. NE of Fresno. Fruit packing and concrete plants. Granite quarries; timber. Diversified farming. Dairy products, grapes.

2050 ■ The Clovis Independent
The Clovis Independent
PO Box 2355
Clovis, CA 93613
Phone: (559)298-8081
Fax: (559)441-6740
Community newspaper. **Freq:** Weekly (Fri.). **Print Method:** Offset. **Trim Size:** 14 x 22 3/4. **Cols./Page:** 6. **Col. Width:** 21 inches. **Col. Depth:** 301 agate lines. **Key Personnel:** Tom Cullinan, Publisher, President. **USPS:** 119-060. **URL:** http://www.fresnobee.com/news/local/community/clovis-news. **Ad Rates:** BW $1983.24; 4C $2243.24; PCI $14.28. **Remarks:** Accepts advertising. **Circ:** Free ‡28000.

2051 ■ KAIL-TV - 53
1590 Alluvial Ave.
Clovis, CA 93611
Phone: (559)299-9753
Fax: (559)299-1523
Format: Commercial TV. **Networks:** United Paramount Network. **Founded:** 1965. **Operating Hours:** Continuous. **ADI:** Fresno-Visalia (Hanford), CA. **Wattage:** 2,548,000. **Ad Rates:** $15-250 for 30 seconds. **URL:** http://www.kail.tv.

2052 ■ KPRX-FM - 89.1
2589 Alluvial Ave.
Clovis, CA 93611
Phone: (559)275-0764
Format: Public Radio. **Ad Rates:** Noncommercial. **URL:** http://www.kvpr.org/.

COALINGA

C. CA. Fresno Co. 67 mi. SW of Fresno. Oil well supplies; machinery, iron works, creamery products, asbestos fibre, concrete pipes manufactured. Oil wells; quicksilver mines. Agriculture. Livestock, grain, melons, dairying.

2053 ■ K217EQ-FM - 91.3
PO Box 391
Twin Falls, ID 83303
Fax: (208)736-1958
Free: 800-357-4226
Format: Religious; Contemporary Christian. **Owner:** CSN International, PO Box 391, Twin Falls, ID 83303, Ph: (208)736-1958, Fax: (208)736-1958, Free: 800-357-4226. **Key Personnel:** Don Mills, Prog. Dir., Music Dir.; Kelly Carlson, Dir. of Engg.; Ray Gorney, Asst. Dir. **Wattage:** 010. **URL:** http://www.csnradio.com.

COARSEGOLD

2054 ■ Turning Wheels
Studebaker Driver's Club
43306 Running Deer Dr.
Coarsegold, CA 93614-9662
Phone: (763)420-7829
Freq: Monthly. **ISSN:** 1052- 3251 (print). **Subscription Rates:** Included in membership. **Alt. Formats:** PDF. **URL:** http://www.studebakerdriversclub.com/turningwheels.asp. **Remarks:** Accepts advertising. **Circ:** 13000.

COLTON

SE CA. San Bernardino Co. 3 mi. SW of San Bernardino. Manufactures cement, lime, animal feeds, concrete pipe, evaporative air coolers, china & porcelain bathroom fixtures, meat packing plant.

2055 ■ Colton City News
City Newspaper Group
PO Box 1604
Colton, CA 92324
Phone: (909)370-2774
Fax: (909)370-1193
Publisher's E-mail: citynews@local.net
Community newspaper. **Freq:** Weekly (Thurs.). **Subscription Rates:** $10 Individuals /year; $15 Two years; $20 Individuals 3 years. **URL:** http://colton.citynewsgroup.com/index.php. **Remarks:** Advertising accepted; rates available upon request. **Circ:** (Not Reported).

2056 ■ Colton Courier
Inland Empire Community Newspapers
PO Box 6247
San Bernardino, CA 92412-6247
Phone: (909)381-9898
Fax: (909)384-0406
Publisher's E-mail: iecn1@mac.com
Newspaper. **Freq:** Weekly (Thurs.). **Print Method:** Offset. **Cols./Page:** 5. **Col. Width:** 1 7/8 inches. **Col. Depth:** 14.5 inches. **Key Personnel:** Maryjoy Duncan, Managing Editor; Diana Macias Harrison, Director, Advertising, General Manager, Publisher. **URL:** http://www.ieweekly.biz/page5/page5.html. **Ad Rates:** GLR $1; BW $1512; 4C $2162; PCI $17. **Remarks:** Accepts advertising. **Circ:** Free ‡16000, Paid ‡1000.

2057 ■ Loma Linda City News
City Newspaper Group
PO Box 1604
Colton, CA 92324
Phone: (909)370-2774
Fax: (909)370-1193
Publisher's E-mail: citynews@local.net
Community newspaper. **Freq:** Weekly (Thurs.). **Key Personnel:** Margie Miller, Publisher. **Subscription Rates:** $10 Individuals; $15 Two years; $20 Individuals 3 years; $25 Individuals 4 years; $30 Individuals 5 years. **URL:** http://lomalinda.citynewsgroup.com/index.php. **Remarks:** Accepts advertising. **Circ:** (Not Reported).

2058 ■ KFRG-FM - 95.1
900 E Washington St., Ste. 315
Colton, CA 92324
Phone: (909)825-9525
Format: Country. **Owner:** CBS Radio Inc., at above address. **Founded:** 1959. **Operating Hours:** Continuous. **ADI:** Los Angeles (Corona & San Bernardino), CA. **Key Personnel:** Scott Ward, Music Dir.; Tom Hoyt, Gen. Mgr.; Lee Douglas, Dir. of Programs. **Wattage:** 6,000. **Ad Rates:** Advertising accepted; rates available upon request. **URL:** http://kfrog.cbslocal.com.

2059 ■ KXFG-FM - 92.9
900 E Washington St., Ste. 315
Colton, CA 92324
Phone: (909)825-9525
Free: 888-431-3764
Format: Country. **Owner:** CBS Radio Inc., 1271 Avenue of the Americas, 44th Fl., New York, NY 10020-1401, Ph: (212)649-9600. **Key Personnel:** Jeff Davis, News Dir; Heather Froglear, Contact, heather@kfrog.net; Christy McLeap, Contact, christy@kfrog.net. **URL:** http://www.kfrog.cbslocal.com.

COLUSA

N. CA. Colusa Co. On Sacramento River, 65 mi. NW of Sacramento. Manufactures Cables. Agriculture. Barley, sugar beets, rice, almonds. Prunes, safflower.

2060 ■ Colusa Sun-Herald
Appeal-Democrat Inc.
249 5th St.
Colusa, CA 95932
Phone: (530)458-2121
Fax: (530)458-5711
Publisher's E-mail: info@appealdemocrat.com
General newspaper. **Freq:** Weekly. **Print Method:** Offset. **Cols./Page:** 6. **Col. Width:** 25 nonpareils. **Col. Depth:** 294 agate lines. **Key Personnel:** Paula Patton, Publisher. **URL:** http://www.appeal-democrat.com/colusa_sun_herald. **Ad Rates:** SAU $4.25. **Remarks:** Accepts advertising. **Circ:** 1281.

COMPTON

S. CA. Los Angeles Co. 6 mi. S. of Los Angeles. Manufactures aircraft parts, oil well supplies, steel castings, furniture. Mobile homes. Nurseries. Oil Wells. Truck, dairy, poultry farms.

2061 ■ Compton Bulletin
American Print Media
800 E Compton Blvd.
Compton, CA 90221
Phone: (310)635-6776
Fax: (310)635-4045
Publisher's E-mail: news@thecomptonbulletin.com
Black community newspaper. **Freq:** Weekly (Wed.). **Cols./Page:** 6. **Col. Width:** 12 1/2 picas. **Col. Depth:** 21 1/2 inches. **Key Personnel:** O. Ray Watkins, Publisher. **Subscription Rates:** $75 Individuals /year (print); $15 Individuals /year (online); $100 Individuals /year (print and online). **URL:** http://www.thebulletinweekly.com/node/5837. **Ad Rates:** BW $3225; 4C $6470; PCI $25. **Remarks:** Accepts advertising. **Circ:** Paid 12000, Free 10000.

CONCORD

W. CA. Contra Costa Co. 25 mi. E. of Oakland. Oil refineries; cement plant; winery; electronic parts manufactured. Fruit, grain.

2062 ■ Contra Costa Lawyer
Contra Costa County Bar Association
2300 Clayton Rd., Ste. 520
Concord, CA 94520
Phone: (925)686-6900
Fax: (925)686-9867
Professional magazine covering law for members. **Freq:** Monthly 6/yr. **Print Method:** Litho. **Trim Size:** 8 1/2 x 11. **Key Personnel:** Nicole Mills, Editor, phone: (925)351-3171; Candice Stoddard, Editor, phone: (925)942-5100. **ISSN:** 1063--4444 (print). **Subscription Rates:** $25 Individuals. **URL:** http://cclawyer.cccba.org; http://www.cccba.org/attorney/cclawyer/index.php. **Ad Rates:** BW $400; 4C $700. **Remarks:** Accepts advertising. **Circ:** Combined 1500, 1,500.

2063 ■ ETC: A Review of General Semantics
International Society for General Semantics
Box 728
Concord, CA 94522
Phone: (925)798-0311
Fax: (925)798-0312
Publisher's E-mail: isgs@generalsemantics.org
Scholarly journal covering language, behavior, and education. **Founded:** 1943. **Freq:** Quarterly. **Trim Size:** 6 x 9. **Subscription Rates:** $55 Individuals; $25 Single issue. **URL:** http://www.generalsemantics.org/store/69-recent-issues. **Remarks:** Advertising accepted; rates available upon request. **Circ:** 1500.

2064 ■ Healthcare Design
Center for Health Design
1850 Gateway Blvd., Ste. 1083
Concord, CA 94520
Phone: (925)521-9404
Fax: (925)521-9405
Publisher's E-mail: info@healthdesign.org
Freq: Monthly. **Subscription Rates:** Free. **URL:** http://www.healthcaredesignmagazine.com. **Remarks:** Advertising accepted; rates available upon request. **Circ:** 40000.

2065 ■ Herd
Center for Health Design
1850 Gateway Blvd., Ste. 1083
Concord, CA 94520
Phone: (925)521-9404
Fax: (925)521-9405
Publisher's E-mail: info@healthdesign.org
Freq: Quarterly. **ISSN:** 1937--5867 (print); **EISSN:** 2167--5112 (electronic). **Alt. Formats:** PDF. **URL:** http://her.sagepub.com. **Remarks:** Advertising not accepted. **Circ:** 450.

2066 ■ Journal of Magnetic Resonance Imaging
International Society for Magnetic Resonance in Medicine
2300 Clayton Rd., Ste. 620
Concord, CA 94520
Phone: (510)841-1899
Fax: (510)841-2340
Publisher's E-mail: info@ismrm.org
International journal covering basic and clinical research, educational and review articles, and other information related to the diagnostic applications of magnetic resonance. **Freq:** Monthly. **Trim Size:** 8 1/4 x 11. **Key Personnel:** Leon C. Partain, MD, Editor. **ISSN:** 1053--1807 (print); **EISSN:** 1522--2586 (electronic). **Subscription Rates:** $3560 Institutions print and online (U.S, Canada and Mexico); $2966 Institutions, other countries online only; $3249 Institutions, other countries print only; $3899 Institutions, other countries print and online; $806 Individuals print or online; $896 Individuals print only (U.K, Europe and other Countries); £1515 Institutions online only; £1660 Institutions print only; £1992 Institutions print and online; €1916 Institutions online only; €2099 Institutions print only; €2519 Institutions print and online. **URL:** http://onlinelibrary.wiley.com/journal/10.1002/(ISSN)1522-2586; http://www.ismrm.org/membership-journals/journals. **Ad Rates:** BW $1205; 4C $1545. **Remarks:** Accepts advertising. **Circ:** Paid 1010.

2067 ■ Magnetic Resonance in Medicine
International Society for Magnetic Resonance in Medicine
2300 Clayton Rd., Ste. 620
Concord, CA 94520
Phone: (510)841-1899
Fax: (510)841-2340
Publisher's E-mail: info@ismrm.org
Journal covering radiology imaging worldwide. **Freq:** Monthly. **Trim Size:** 6 7/8 x 10. **Key Personnel:** Prof. Felix W. Wehrli, Editor; Matt A. Bernstein, Editor-in-Chief. **ISSN:** 0740--3194 (print); **EISSN:** 1522--2594 (electronic). **Subscription Rates:** $3434 U.S. and other countries print or online; £1754 Institutions online; €2218 Institutions online; $4121 U.S. and Canada print and online; $4442 Institutions print and online - rest of the world; £2268 Institutions print and online; €2870 Institutions print and online; £1890 Institutions print; €2391 Institutions print; $3701 Institutions print - rest of the world; $1018 U.S. and other countries print or online. **URL:** http://www.ismrm.org/journals.htm; http://onlinelibrary.wiley.com/journal/10.1002/(ISSN)1522-2594. **Ad Rates:** 4C $1,365; BW $760; 4C $1,650. **Remarks:** Accepts advertising. **Circ:** 766.

2068 ■ Astound Broadband
215 Mason Cir.
Concord, CA 94520
Free: 800-427-8686
Cities Served: Walnut Creek, California; 83 channels. **URL:** http://www.astound.net.

KEGR Radio - See Fort Dodge, IA

2069 ■ KTNC-TV - 42
5101 Port Chicago Hwy.
Concord, CA 94520
Phone: (925)686-4242
Fax: (925)825-4242
Format: Commercial TV. **Networks:** Independent. **Owner:** Pappas Telecasting, at above address. **Founded:** 1983. **Key Personnel:** Gary Johnson, Production Mgr. **Local Programs:** *A Que No Puedes*, Monday Tuesday Wednesday Thursday Friday 8:00 p.m.; *Estrellas Hoy*, Saturday Monday Tuesday Wednesday Thursday Friday 12:00 p.m. 4:00 p.m.; 5:30 p.m.; *Jose Luis Sin Censura*, Monday Tuesday Wednesday Thursday Friday Saturday 11:00 a.m.; 6:00 p.m. 9:00 p.m. **Wattage:** 40,000 ERP.

2070 ■ KVHS-FM - 90.5
1101 Alberta Way, Rm. S-2
Concord, CA 94521
Phone: (925)682-5847
Fax: (925)609-5847
Format: Alternative/New Music/Progressive. **Networks:** Independent. **Founded:** 1969. **Operating Hours:** 6 a.m.-10 p.m.; 100% local. **Key Personnel:** Melissa Foster-Wilson, Gen. Mgr. **Wattage:** 410. **Ad Rates:** Noncommercial. **URL:** http://www.kvhs.com.

CORCORAN

SC CA. Kings Co. 45 mi. S. of Fresno. Flour, feed, cottonseed oil mills; cotton gins. Agriculture. Dairying. Cotton, grain, beef cattle.

2071 ■ The Corcoran Journal
The Corcoran Journal
1012 Hale
Corcoran, CA 93212
Phone: (559)992-3115
Fax: (559)992-5543
Community newspaper. **Freq:** Weekly (Thurs.). **Print Method:** Offset. **Trim Size:** 13 x 21 1/2. **Cols./Page:** 6. **Col. Width:** 19 nonpareils. **Col. Depth:** 301 agate lines. **Key Personnel:** Jeanette Todd, Managing Editor, Publisher, phone: (559)992-3115. **Subscription Rates:** $48 Individuals. **URL:** http://www.thecorcoranjournal.net. **Mailing address:** PO Box 487, Corcoran, CA 93212. **Ad Rates:** GLR $1; BW $548; SAU $4. **Remarks:** Accepts advertising. **Circ:** Paid 2,100.

CORONA

SE CA. Riverside Co. 15 mi. SE of Riverside. Citrus fruit packed. Fiberglass insulation, plywood paneling, furniture, mattresses, die castings manufactured. Fruit, dairy farms.

2072 ■ Autograph
Autograph Magazine
PO Box 25559
Santa Ana, CA 92799
Magazine for museums, manuscript libraries, and worldwide collectors of autographs, signed photos, first day covers, and documents of historical significance. **Freq:** Monthly. **Print Method:** Offset. **Trim Size:** 8 3/8 x

Circulation: ★ = AAM; △ or • = BPA; ♦ = CAC; ❑ = VAC; ⊕ = PO Statement; ‡ = Publisher's Report; Boldface figures = sworn; Light figures = estimated.

10 7/8. **Cols./Page:** 3. **Col. Width:** 2 1/4 inches. **Col. Depth:** 10 inches. **Key Personnel:** Steve Cyrkin, Publisher; Nicole LeMaster, Advertising Representative. **URL:** http://autographmagazine.com. **Formerly:** Autograph Collector. **Circ:** (Not Reported).

2073 ■ Elearning!: Building Smarter Companies
B2B Media Co.
PO Box 77694
Corona, CA 92877
Fax: (888)201-2841
Free: 888-201-2841
Publisher's E-mail: cupton@b2bmediaco.com
Magazine that covers new and emerging computer technology in business. **Freq:** Bimonthly. **Key Personnel:** Jerry Roche, Executive Editor. **URL:** http://www.2elearning.com. **Remarks:** Accepts advertising. **Circ:** (Not Reported).

2074 ■ KGIC-FM - 105.5
Iglesia La Senda
1717 Via Del Rio
Corona, CA 92882
Phone: (951)737-1717
Email: andres@radioimpacto.org
Format: Hispanic. **Operating Hours:** 6 a.m. - 7 p.m. **Wattage:** 059. **Ad Rates:** Noncommercial. **URL:** http://www.radioimpacto.org.

CORTE MADERA

W. CA. Marin Co. 12 mi. NW of San Francisco. Residential.

2075 ■ ELDR Magazine
ELDR Media L.L.C.
Nine Hickory Ave.
Corte Madera, CA 94925
Phone: (415)425-9205
Publisher's E-mail: eldr@pubservice.com
Magazine focusing on aging. **Freq:** 6/yr. **Key Personnel:** Chad Lewis, Chief Executive Officer, Founder, Publisher; David Bunnell, Editor-in-Chief, Founder; Ed Williams, Associate Publisher. **Subscription Rates:** $14.97 Individuals. **URL:** http://www.eldr.com. **Circ:** (Not Reported).

COSTA MESA

S. CA. Orange Co. 8 mi. S. of Santa Ana. Orange Coast College. Southern California College. University of California. Manufactures boats, electronic and airplane parts, plastics, fiberglass fabrications.

2076 ■ Ability Magazine: An Informative Resource on Disability Issues
Ability Magazine
PO Box 10878
Costa Mesa, CA 92627
Phone: (949)854-8700
Fax: (949)548-5966
Publication E-mail: editorial@abilitymagazine.com
Lifestyle magazine featuring celebrity interviews about health and diabetes, new technologies, and general human interest. **Freq:** Bimonthly. **Print Method:** Web heatset. **Trim Size:** 8 x 10 7/8. **Cols./Page:** 3. **Key Personnel:** Gillian Friedman, MD, Contact. **ISSN:** 1062--5321 (print). **Subscription Rates:** $29.70 Individuals print; $49.70 Canada print; $9.95 Single issue print; $19.70 Individuals digital. **URL:** http://www.abilitymagazine.com. **Remarks:** Accepts advertising. **Circ:** (Not Reported).

2077 ■ Cycle News
CN Publishing
PO Box 5084
Costa Mesa, CA 92628-5084
Publication E-mail: editor@cyclenews.com
Newspaper (tabloid) for motorcycle enthusiasts. **Freq:** Weekly. **Print Method:** Offset. **Trim Size:** 11 x 14 1/2. **Cols./Page:** 4. **Col. Width:** 27 nonpareils. **Col. Depth:** 193 agate lines. **Key Personnel:** Henny Ray Abrams, Editor; Robert NorVelle, Publisher; Paul Carruthers, Editor. **Subscription Rates:** Free to qualified subscribers. **URL:** http://cyclenews.com. **Remarks:** Accepts advertising. **Circ:** (Not Reported).

2078 ■ Dune Buggies & Hot VWs
Dune Buggies and Hot VWs
3176 Pullman, Ste. 107
Costa Mesa, CA 92626-6019
Phone: (714)979-2560
Fax: (714)979-3998
Publisher's E-mail: info@hotvws.com
Magazine offering VW automotive news for the consumer. **Freq:** Monthly. **Print Method:** Offset. **Trim Size:** 8 x 10 7/8. **Cols./Page:** 3. **Col. Width:** 27 nonpareils. **Col. Depth:** 140 agate lines. **Key Personnel:** Bruce Simurda, Editor. **ISSN:** 0012--7132 (print). **Subscription Rates:** $22.97 Individuals. **URL:** http://www.hotvws.com. **Ad Rates:** BW $2150; 4C $2990. **Remarks:** Accepts advertising. **Circ:** (Not Reported).

2079 ■ Environmental Forensics
Taylor & Francis Group Journals
c/o Ioana G. Petrisor, PhD, Editor-in-Chief
3187 Red Hill Ave., Ste. 155
Costa Mesa, CA 92626-3453
Publisher's E-mail: customerservice@taylorandfrancis.com
Journal focusing on contamination within the environmental media of air, water, soil, and biota. **Freq:** Quarterly. **Key Personnel:** Ioana G. Petrisor, PhD, Editor-in-Chief; Robert Morrison, PhD, Board Member; Mohamad A. Ghazi, Associate Editor; Robert Kalin, PhD, Board Member; Zhendi Wang, PhD, Board Member; Amvrossios C. Bagtzoglou, PhD, Board Member; Andy Davis, PhD, Board Member; Bill Burnett, Board Member; Jean Christophe Balouet, PhD, Associate Editor. **ISSN:** 1527--5922 (print); **EISSN:** 1527--5930 (electronic). **Subscription Rates:** $191 Individuals print only; $691 Institutions online only; $790 Institutions print and online. **URL:** http://www.tandf.co.uk/journals/journal.asp?issn=1527-5922&linktype=1. **Remarks:** Advertising not accepted. **Circ:** (Not Reported).

2080 ■ O.C. Weekly
O.C. Weekly Media Inc.
2975 Red Hill Ave., Ste. 150
Costa Mesa, CA 92626
Phone: (714)550-5900
Fax: (714)550-5908
Community newspaper. Alternative News Weekly. **Freq:** Weekly. **Key Personnel:** Pat Connell, Director, Circulation; Matt Coker, Writer; Nick Schou, Managing Editor. **URL:** http://www.ocweekly.com. **Remarks:** Accepts advertising. **Circ:** Paid ‡78000.

2081 ■ Paralegal Today
James Publishing
3505 Cadillac Ave., Ste. H
Costa Mesa, CA 92626
Phone: (714)755-5450
Fax: (714)751-2709
Free: 800-400-4780
Publisher's E-mail: customer-service@jamespublishing.com
Magazine for paralegals. Covers career development and ethics; products, services, and technology. **Freq:** Quarterly. **Print Method:** Web offset. **Trim Size:** 8 x 10 7/8. **Cols./Page:** 3. **Col. Width:** 14 picas. **Col. Depth:** 136 agate lines. **Key Personnel:** Charles Buckwalter, Publisher. **ISSN:** 1051--3663 (print). **Subscription Rates:** $32 Individuals U.S.A.; $26 Students U.S.A.; $19.50 Individuals online only. **URL:** http://paralegaltoday.com. **Formerly:** Legal Assistant Today. **Ad Rates:** BW $2,099; 4C $2,621. **Remarks:** Accepts advertising. **Circ:** Paid 8000.

2082 ■ Riviera Interiors
Modern Luxury Media
3200 Bristol St., Ste. 150
Costa Mesa, CA 92626
Phone: (714)557-2700
Fax: (714)371-9988
Magazine featuring the latest styles and trends in interior design. **Freq:** Semiannual. **Key Personnel:** Alan Klein, President, Publisher; Alexandria Abramian-Mott, Editor-in-Chief. **Subscription Rates:** $20 Individuals; $40 Two years. **URL:** http://www.modernluxury.com/Riviera-interiors. **Remarks:** Accepts advertising. **Circ:** (Not Reported).

2083 ■ Riviera Orange County
Modern Luxury Media
3200 Bristol St., Ste. 150
Costa Mesa, CA 92626
Phone: (714)557-2700
Fax: (714)371-9988
Magazine covering affluent lifestyle in the Orange County. **Freq:** Monthly. **Key Personnel:** Chris Gialanella, Publisher; Kedric Francis, Editor-in-Chief. **Subscription Rates:** $40 Individuals; $60 Two years. **URL:** http://modernluxury.com/riviera-orange-county. **Remarks:** Accepts advertising. **Circ:** (Not Reported).

2084 ■ Whittier Journal of Child and Family Advocacy
Whittier Law School
3333 Harbor Blvd.
Costa Mesa, CA 92626
Phone: (714)444-4141
Fax: (714)444-0855
Publisher's E-mail: info@law.whittier.edu
Journal containing articles on child and family issues. **Freq:** Annual summer. **Subscription Rates:** $15 Single issue. **URL:** http://www.law.whittier.edu/index/student-organizations/whittier-journal-of-child-family-advocacy1. **Circ:** (Not Reported).

2085 ■ KBRT-AM - 740
3183 Airway Ave., Ste. D
Costa Mesa, CA 92626
Phone: (714)754-4450
Fax: (714)754-0735
Free: 800-227-5278
Format: Religious; Talk. **Networks:** Independent. **Owner:** Crawford Broadcasting Co., 2821 S Parker Rd., Ste. 1205, Denver, CO 80014, Ph: (303)433-5500, Fax: (303)433-1555. **Founded:** 1952. **Operating Hours:** Sunrise-sunset. **Key Personnel:** Sarah Davis, Contact. **Local Programs:** *Living Word*, Monday Tuesday Wednesday Thursday Friday 2:30 p.m. - 3:00 p.m.; *Talk from the Heart*, Saturday 5:00 p.m. - 6:00 p.m. **Wattage:** 10,000. **Ad Rates:** Noncommercial. **URL:** http://kbrt740.com.

2086 ■ KSON-AM - 1240
3183 Airway Ave., Ste. D
Costa Mesa, CA 92626
Format: Contemporary Hit Radio (CHR); Hip Hop; Gospel; Blues. **Key Personnel:** Darnell Forde, Gen. Mgr., darnell.forde@thesoulofsandiego.com. **Ad Rates:** Advertising accepted; rates available upon request. **URL:** http://crawfordbroadcasting.com.

COTTONWOOD

2087 ■ K207CE-FM - 89.3
PO Box 391
Twin Falls, ID 83303
Fax: (208)736-1958
Free: 800-357-4226
Format: Religious; Contemporary Christian. **Owner:** CSN International, PO Box 391, Twin Falls, ID 83303, Ph: (208)736-1958, Fax: (208)736-1958, Free: 800-357-4226. **Key Personnel:** Don Mills, Prog. Dir., Music Dir.; Kelly Carlson, Dir. of Engg.; Ray Gorney, Asst. Dir. **Wattage:** 001. **URL:** http://www.csnradio.com.

COVINA

S. CA. Los Angeles Co. 9 mi. W. of Pomona. Citrus fruit packing and cold storage plants; steel fabricating. Spray products, ladders manufactured. Agriculture. Oranges, lemons, walnuts.

2088 ■ SAMPE Journal
Society for the Advancement of Material and Process Engineering
1161 Park View Dr., Ste. 200
Covina, CA 91724-3759
Phone: (626)331-0616
Fax: (626)332-8929
Free: 800-562-7360
Magazine covering materials and process engineering. **Freq:** 6/year. **Print Method:** Offset. **Trim Size:** 8 1/8 x 10 7/8. **Cols./Page:** 3. **Col. Width:** 27 nonpareils. **Col. Depth:** 140 agate lines. **ISSN:** 0091--1062 (print). **USPS:** 518-510. **Subscription Rates:** $125 Individuals print only; $122 Individuals online only. **URL:** http://www.sampe.org/sampe-journal.html. **Ad Rates:** BW $1,590; 4C $2,655. **Remarks:** Accepts advertising. **Circ:** Paid ‡5000, 5000.

2089 ■ SAMPE Journal of Advanced Materials
Society for the Advancement of Material and Process Engineering
1161 Park View Dr., Ste. 200
Covina, CA 91724-3759
Phone: (626)331-0616
Fax: (626)332-8929

Free: 800-562-7360
Freq: Quarterly. **ISSN:** 1070- 9789 (print). **Subscription Rates:** $70 /year for nonmembers; $30 /year for members. **Remarks:** Advertising not accepted. **Circ:** 4500.

CRESCENT CITY

NW CA. Del Norte Co. On Pacific Ocean, 70 mi. N. of Eureka. Redwood National Park. Resort. Light Industry. Lumber, wooden novelties manufactured. Creamery. Redwood timber; fisheries. Dairy farms.

2090 ■ Charter Communications Inc.
1286 Northcrest Dr.
Crescent City, CA 95531-2321
Free: 888-438-2427
Founded: 1993. **Key Personnel:** Eric L. Zinterhofer, Chairman; Christopher L. Winfrey, CFO, Exec. VP; Michael J. Lovett, CEO, President. **Cities Served:** 77 channels. **URL:** http://www.charter.com.

2091 ■ KCRE-FM - 94.3
1345 Northcrest Dr.
Crescent City, CA 95531
Phone: (707)464-9561
Fax: (707)464-4303
Email: kcre@bicoastalmedia.com
Format: Adult Contemporary. **Owner:** Bicostal Media L.L.C., 1 Blackfield Dr., Ste. 333, Tiburon, CA 94920, Ph: (415)789-5035, Fax: (415)789-5036. **Operating Hours:** 3:00 a.m. - 3:00 p.m. Sunday - Saturday. **Wattage:** 25,000 ERP. **Ad Rates:** Advertising accepted; rates available upon request. **URL:** http://www.kcrefm.com.

2092 ■ KPOD-AM - 1240
1345 Northcrest Dr.
Crescent City, CA 95531
Phone: (707)464-4303
Format: Talk; News; Sports. **Networks:** Fox. **Owner:** Bicoastal Media L.L.C., at above address, Ph: (707)263-6113, Fax: (707)263-0939. **Founded:** 1958. **Operating Hours:** Continuous. **Key Personnel:** Rene Shanle-Hutzell, Contact. **Wattage:** 1,000,000. **Ad Rates:** for 30 seconds; for 60 seconds. Combined advertising rates available with KPOD-FM, KCRE-FM. **URL:** http://www.kpod.com.

2093 ■ KPOD-FM - 97.9
1345 Northcrest Dr.
Crescent City, CA 95531
Phone: (707)464-3183
Fax: (707)464-4303
Format: Country. **Networks:** ABC. **Owner:** Bicoastal Media L.L.C., at above address, Ph: (707)263-6113, Fax: (707)263-0939. **Founded:** 1989. **Wattage:** 6,000 ERP. **Ad Rates:** Accepts Advertising. **URL:** http://www.kpodfm.com.

CULVER CITY

S. CA. Los Angeles Co. 7 mi. SE of Santa Monica. Motion picture studios. Aircraft, textiles, plastics, machine tools, electronics, draperies, auto batteries, rubber products, industrial alcohol, shoes manufactured. Truck farms.

2094 ■ Culver City Chronicle
Los Angeles Independent Newspaper Group
1730 W Olympic Blvd., No. 500
Los Angeles, CA 90015
Phone: (323)556-5720
Community newspaper. **Freq:** Weekly. **Print Method:** Offset. **Trim Size:** 13 x 22. **Cols./Page:** 6. **Col. Width:** 1.8 inches. **Col. Depth:** 21 inches. **Key Personnel:** Andre Herndon, Executive Editor; Marisela Santana, Writer; John A. Moreno, Editor. **Remarks:** Accepts advertising. **Circ:** Paid 7, Non-paid 10770.

2095 ■ Culver City News
Coast Media Newspaper
4043 Irving Pl.
Culver City, CA 90232-2809
Phone: (310)839-5271
Fax: (310)839-9372
Publication E-mail: info@culvercitynews.org
Community newspaper. **Freq:** Weekly. **Print Method:** Offset. **Cols./Page:** 6. **Col. Width:** 18 nonpareils. **Col. Depth:** 301 agate lines. **URL:** http://www.culvercitynews.org. **Ad Rates:** BW $1,382.88; 4C $2,082.88. **Remarks:** Accepts advertising. **Circ:** 16500.

2096 ■ The Culver City Observer
California Community Newspapers
4346 Sepulveda Blvd.
Culver City, CA 90230
Phone: (310)398-6397
Publisher's E-mail: info@culvercityobserver.com
Community newspaper. **Freq:** Weekly (Thurs.). **Subscription Rates:** $100 Individuals; $200 Individuals 2 years; $300 Individuals 3 years. **URL:** http://www.culvercityobserver.com. **Remarks:** Accepts classified advertising. **Circ:** (Not Reported).

2097 ■ L.A. Weekly
L.A. Weekly
3861 Sepulveda Blvd.
Culver City, CA 90230
Phone: (310)478-6677
Publisher's E-mail: editor@laweekly.com
Newspaper (tabloid) featuring news, people, entertainment, and the arts. **Freq:** Weekly. **Print Method:** Offset. **Trim Size:** 10 3/4 x 14 1/2. **Cols./Page:** 4. **Col. Width:** 14 picas. **Col. Depth:** 13 inches. **Key Personnel:** Jill Stewart, Editor; Drex Heikes, Editor. **USPS:** 461-370. **Subscription Rates:** Free. **URL:** http://www.laweekly.com. **Remarks:** Accepts advertising. **Circ:** (Not Reported).

2098 ■ The Rangefinder
The Rangefinder Publishing Company Inc.
6059 Bristol Pky., Ste. 100
Culver City, CA 90230
Phone: (310)846-4770
Fax: (310)846-5995
Trade publication for portrait, commercial and wedding photographers. **Founded:** July 1952. **Freq:** Monthly. **Print Method:** Offset. **Trim Size:** 8 3/8 x 10 13/16. **Cols./Page:** 3. **Col. Width:** 27 nonpareils. **Col. Depth:** 140 agate lines. **Key Personnel:** Jacqueline Tobin, Editor-in-Chief; Lauren Wendle, Vice President, Publisher. **ISSN:** 0033-9202 (print). **Subscription Rates:** $18 Individuals. **URL:** http://www.rangefinderonline.com/index.shtml. **Ad Rates:** BW $8,663; 4C $7,470; PCI $224. **Remarks:** Accepts advertising. **Circ:** (Not Reported).

2099 ■ Turning the Tide: A Journal of Intercommunal Solidarity
Anti-Racist Action-Los Angeles/People Against Racist Terror
PO Box 1055
Culver City, CA 90232
Phone: (323)636-7388
Magazine detailing antiracist, antisexist, and anti-imperialist beliefs and information. **Freq:** Quarterly. **Print Method:** Web press. **Trim Size:** 11 x 17. **Cols./Page:** 4. **Col. Width:** 2 1/4 inches. **Col. Depth:** 16 inches. **Key Personnel:** Michael Novick, Editor. **ISSN:** 1082--6491 (print). **Subscription Rates:** $16 Individuals; $26 Institutions. **Online:** Lexis-Nexis; Softline Ethnic Newswatch. **URL:** http://antiracist.org. **Ad Rates:** BW $200. **Remarks:** Accepts display advertising. **Circ:** Non-paid 7250.

2100 ■ Comcast Cable
6695 Green Valley Cir.
Culver City, CA 90230
Free: 888-255-5789
Founded: June 1999. **Cities Served:** 70 channels. **URL:** http://www.comcast.com.

CUPERTINO

W. CA. Santa Clara Co. 10 mi. W. of San Jose. Residential. Winery. Electronic products manufactured.

2101 ■ Annals of Genealogical Research
Annals of Genealogical Research
PO Box 2201
Cupertino, CA 95015
Publisher's E-mail: techsupport@genlit.org
Journal that offers research papers on genealogy and family history. **Freq:** Quarterly. **Key Personnel:** Robert S. Shaw, Editor. **ISSN:** 1555--9904 (print). **Subscription Rates:** Free. **URL:** http://www.genlit.org/agr. **Remarks:** Advertising not accepted. **Circ:** (Not Reported).

2102 ■ Red Wheelbarrow
De Anza College
21250 Stevens Creek Blvd.
Cupertino, CA 95014
Phone: (408)864-8948
Literary journal. **Freq:** Semiannual. **Print Method:** Offset. **Trim Size:** 6 x 9. **Key Personnel:** Randolph Splitter, Contact. **ISSN:** 1543--1983 (print). **URL:** http://www.deanza.edu/redwheelbarrow; http://faculty.deanza.fhda.edu/splitterrandolph/stories/storyReader$147. **Formerly:** Bottomfish. **Remarks:** Accepts advertising. **Circ:** (Not Reported).

2103 ■ La Voz: The Voice of De Anza
De Anza College
21250 Stevens Creek Blvd.
Cupertino, CA 95014
Phone: (408)864-8948
Collegiate newspaper broadsheet. **Freq:** Weekly. **Print Method:** Offset. **Trim Size:** 11 1/2 x 17 1/2. **Cols./Page:** 5. **Col. Width:** 11.5 picas. **Col. Depth:** 16 inches. **Key Personnel:** April Seo, Managing Editor; Michael Mannina, Editor-in-Chief. **URL:** http://lavozdeanza.com. **Ad Rates:** BW $630; 4C $450; PCI $8.25. **Remarks:** Accepts advertising. **Circ:** Free ‡3500.

CUTTEN

2104 ■ Human Power
International Human Powered Vehicle Association
PO Box 357
Cutten, CA 95534-0357
Phone: (707)443-8261
Fax: (707)444-2579
Free: 877-333-1029
Freq: Periodic. **ISSN:** 0898- 6908 (print). **Subscription Rates:** Included in membership; $5 for nonmembers. **Alt. Formats:** PDF. **URL:** http://www.ihpva.org/hparchive.htm. **Remarks:** Advertising not accepted. **Circ:** 800.

CYPRESS

Orange Co.

2105 ■ Journal of Minimally Invasive Gynecology
American Association of Gynecologic Laparoscopists
6757 Katella Ave.
Cypress, CA 90630-5105
Phone: (714)503-6200
Free: 800-554-2245
Publisher's E-mail: generalmail@aagl.com
Professional journal covering endoscopic procedures. **Freq:** Quarterly February, May, August, November. **Key Personnel:** Tommaso Falcone, Editor-in-Chief. **ISSN:** 1074--3804 (print). **Subscription Rates:** $329 U.S. and other countries online and print ; $280 U.S. and other countries online; $130 Students online and print - U.S, Canada and other countries; $110 Students online - U.S, Canada and other countries. **URL:** http://www.jmig.org; http://www.aagl.org/jmig2014. **Formerly:** Journal of the American Association of Gynecologic Laparoscopists. **Ad Rates:** BW $3195; 4C $1570. **Remarks:** Accepts advertising. **Circ:** 5200.

DALY CITY

W. CA. San Mateo Co. 5 mi. N. of San Francisco. Residential.

2106 ■ Manila Mail
Manila Mail Newspaper
12 Avalon Dr.
Daly City, CA 94015
Phone: (650)992-5474
Fax: (650)997-0673
Community newspaper for Filipino-Americans. **Freq:** Weekly (Tues.). **Trim Size:** 19 1/2 x 12. **URL:** http://emanilamail.com. **Ad Rates:** BW $1548; 4C $500; PCI $12. **Remarks:** Accepts advertising. **Circ:** Combined ‡25806.

DANA POINT

S. CA. Orange Co. 40 mi. SE of Long Beach. Residential. Tourism. Boat harbor. Manufactures surf boards. Nurseries.

2107 ■ Bike
TEN: The Enthusiast Network
PO Box 1028
Dana Point, CA 92629
Phone: (949)325-6200

Circulation: ★ = AAM; △ or • = BPA; ♦ = CAC; ❑ = VAC; ⊕ = PO Statement; ‡ = Publisher's Report; Boldface figures = sworn; Light figures = estimated.

Fax: (949)325-6196
Publication E-mail: bikemag@sorc.com
Magazine focusing on trends and issues that define the sport of mountain biking. Staff tests bikes and equipment in every issue. **Freq:** 8/yr. **Key Personnel:** Joe Parkin, Editor; Brice Minnigh, Editor. **Subscription Rates:** $11.97 Individuals; $19.97 Two years; $19.97 Canada; $35.97 Canada 2 years; $27.97 Other countries; $51.97 Other countries 2 years. **URL:** http://www.bikemag.com/. **Ad Rates:** BW $5540; 4C $8265. **Remarks:** Accepts advertising. **Circ:** Paid ★**56371**.

DAVIS

C. CA. Yolo Co. 14 mi. W. of Sacramento. University of California at Davis. Manufactures almond hullers, farm equipment, Agriculture. Sugar beets, grain, tomatoes.

2108 ■ Acta Materialia
RELX Group P.L.C.
c/o Prof. S. Mahajan, Coord. Ed.
University of California at Davis
Dept. of Chemical Engineering & Materials Science
1 Shields Ave.
Davis, CA 95616
Phone: (530)752-5132
Fax: (530)752-1031
Publisher's E-mail: amsterdam@relx.com
International journal for the science and engineering of materials. Focused on structural and functional properties of materials, such as metals and alloys, ceramics, high polymers and glasses. **Freq:** 20/yr. **Key Personnel:** Prof. S. Mahajan, Coordinator, Education Resources; Prof. G. Gottstein, Editor; Prof. M. Harmer, Editor; Prof. R. Wagner, Editor; Prof. R. Kirchheim, Editor. **ISSN:** 1359--6454 (print). **URL:** http://www.journals.elsevier.com/acta-materialia. **Circ:** (Not Reported).

2109 ■ American Journal of Enology and Viticulture
American Society for Enology and Viticulture
PO Box 1855
Davis, CA 95617-1855
Phone: (530)753-3142
Fax: (530)753-3318
Publisher's E-mail: society@asev.org
Professional journal covering abstracts, technical briefs, and reviews for the viticulture and enology industry in the U.S. **Freq:** Quarterly. **Key Personnel:** Linda F. Bisson, Editor; Veronique Cheynier, Associate Editor; Judith McKibben, Managing Editor. **ISSN:** 0002--9254 (print). **Subscription Rates:** $265 Institutions print only (USA); $285 Institutions, other countries print only. **URL:** http://www.ajevonline.org; http://www.asev.org/american-journal-enology-and-viticulture-ajev. **Ad Rates:** BW $570. **Remarks:** Advertising accepted; rates available upon request. **Circ:** (Not Reported).

2110 ■ Animal Feed Science and Technology
Mosby Inc.
Dairy & Nutrition
Department of Animal Science
University of California
Davis, CA 95616-8521
Journal publishing research on animal nutrition, feeding, and technology. **Freq:** Monthly. **Key Personnel:** G.G. Mateos, Board Member; C. De Blas, Editor-in-Chief. **ISSN:** 0377--8401 (print). **Subscription Rates:** $5128 Institutions online; $5163 Institutions print. **URL:** http://www.journals.elsevier.com/animal-feed-science-and-technology. **Remarks:** Accepts advertising. **Circ:** (Not Reported).

2111 ■ Aquatic Toxicology
Elsevier
c/o Ronald Tjeerdema, Editor-in-Chief
University of California at Davis
Department of Environmental Toxicology
4138 Meyer Hall
Davis, CA 95616-8501
Phone: (530)754-5192
Fax: (530)752-3394
Publisher's E-mail: t.reller@elsevier.com
Journal covering information on the mechanisms of toxicity in aquatic environments. **Freq:** Monthly. **Print Method:** Web offset. **Trim Size:** 10 x 14 3/8. **Cols./Page:** 5 and 3. **Col. Width:** 11 and 15 nonpareils. **Col. Depth:** 80 and 60 agate lines. **Key Personnel:** G.A. LeBlanc, Board Member; R.J. Van Beneden, Board Member; M. Celander, Editor; J.K. Chipman, Board Member; K.R. Cooper, Board Member; R.S. Tjeerdema, Editor-in-Chief. **ISSN:** 0166--445X (print). **Subscription Rates:** $1518.13 Institutions online; $4554 Institutions print. **URL:** http://www.journals.elsevier.com/aquatic-toxicology. **Circ:** (Not Reported).

2112 ■ ARA Journal
American Romanian Academy of Arts and Sciences
University of California Davis
1 Shields Ave.
Davis, CA 95616
Publisher's E-mail: info@americanromanianacademy.org
Freq: Annual. **ISSN:** 0896- 1018 (print). **Subscription Rates:** included in membership dues. **URL:** http://www.americanromanianacademy.org/#!ara-journal/c7np. **Remarks:** Accepts advertising. **Circ:** 500.

2113 ■ Bamboo: The Magazine of the American Bamboo Society
American Bamboo Society
1607 5th St.
Davis, CA 95616
Publication E-mail: magazine@americanbamboo.org
Magazine covering bamboo. **Freq:** Bimonthly. **Key Personnel:** Betty Shor, Editor; Don Shor, Editor. **Subscription Rates:** Included in membership. **Alt. Formats:** PDF. **URL:** http://www.americanbamboo.org/About.html#Publications. **Remarks:** Advertising not accepted. **Circ:** (Not Reported).

2114 ■ Business Law Journal
University of California School of Law
400 Mrak Hall Dr.
Davis, CA 95616-5201
Phone: (530)752-6477
Publisher's E-mail: admissions@law.ucdavis.edu
Journal containing articles on legal and business analysis. **Freq:** Semiannual. **Subscription Rates:** $44.50 Individuals. **URL:** http://blj.ucdavis.edu. **Circ:** (Not Reported).

2115 ■ Journal of International Law & Policy
University of California School of Law
400 Mrak Hall Dr.
Davis, CA 95616-5201
Phone: (530)752-6477
Publisher's E-mail: admissions@law.ucdavis.edu
Journal containing articles in the field of international law. **Freq:** Semiannual. **ISSN:** 1080--6687 (print). **Subscription Rates:** $44.50 U.S. **URL:** http://jilp.law.ucdavis.edu. **Circ:** (Not Reported).

2116 ■ Journal of Juvenile Law & Policy
University of California School of Law
400 Mrak Hall Dr.
Davis, CA 95616-5201
Phone: (530)752-6477
Publisher's E-mail: admissions@law.ucdavis.edu
Journal containing information about current juvenile, family and educational law issues. **Freq:** Semiannual. **Subscription Rates:** $40 Institutions; $20 Students; $40 Individuals. **URL:** http://jjlp.law.ucdavis.edu. **Circ:** (Not Reported).

2117 ■ Journal of Mathematical Physics
American Institute of Physics
Journal of Mathematical Physics Editorial Office
Dept. of Mathematics
University of California
3125 MSB
Davis, CA 95616
Phone: (530)752-0268
Publication E-mail: jmp@aip.org
Journal presenting original work of interest to theoretical and mathematical physicists. **Freq:** Monthly. **Print Method:** Offset. **Trim Size:** 8 1/4 x 11. **Cols./Page:** 2. **Col. Width:** 41 nonpareils. **Col. Depth:** 138 agate lines. **Key Personnel:** Bruno L.Z. Nachtergaele, Editor. **ISSN:** 0022-2488 (print). **Subscription Rates:** $5025 Institutions tier 1, print & online; $2955 Institutions tier 1, online. **URL:** http://scitation.aip.org/content/aip/journal/jmp. **Remarks:** Advertising not accepted. **Circ:** (Not Reported).

2118 ■ Mechanics Based Design of Structures and Machines: An International Journal
Informa Healthcare
c/o S.A. Velinsky, Editor-in-Chief
University of California
Dept. of Mechanical Engineering
Davis, CA 95616
Publisher's E-mail: healthcare.enquiries@informa.com
Journal covering Research of application to aerospace, automotive, civil and mechanical engineering, marine and related structures. **Freq:** Quarterly. **Print Method:** Offset. **Trim Size:** 8 1/4 x 10 7/8. **Cols./Page:** 1. **Key Personnel:** S. Azarm, Board Member; S.A. Velinsky, Editor-in-Chief; N. Banichuk, Board Member; D. Bestle, Board Member; J. Cuadrado, Board Member. **ISSN:** 1539--7734 (print); **EISSN:** 1539--7742 (electronic). **Subscription Rates:** $681 Individuals print; $2325 Institutions online; $2657 Institutions print & online. **URL:** http://www.tandfonline.com/toc/lmbd20/current#.Uvh7KmJLXlc. **Formerly:** Mechanics of Structures and Machines. **Ad Rates:** BW $890; 4C $1,935. **Remarks:** Accepts advertising. **Circ:** (Not Reported).

2119 ■ Veterinary Surgery
American College of Veterinary Surgeons
c/o John R. Pascoe, Ed.-in-Ch.
Dean's Office
University of California
School of Veterinary Medicine
Davis, CA 95616-8734
Publisher's E-mail: acvs@acvs.org
Print Method: Sheetfed Offset. **Trim Size:** 8 1/8 x 11. **Cols./Page:** 2. **Col. Width:** 39 nonpareils. **Col. Depth:** 140 agate lines. **Key Personnel:** John R. Pascoe, Editor-in-Chief. **ISSN:** 0161-3499 (print); **EISSN:** 1532-950X (electronic). **Subscription Rates:** $279 Individuals print & online; $115 Students print & online; $786 Institutions print & online; $655 Institutions print or online; £235 Individuals print & online; £97 Students print & online; £603 Institutions print + online; £502 Institutions print or online; €350 Individuals print & online; €147 Students print & online; €638 Institutions print or online; €766 Institutions print and online; $982 Institutions, other countries print or online; $1179 Institutions, other countries print and online. **URL:** http://www.wiley.com/WileyCDA/WileyTitle/productCd-VSU.html; http://www.acvs.org/veterinary-surgery-journal; http://onlinelibrary.wiley.com/journal/10.1111/(ISSN)1532-950X. **Ad Rates:** BW $1180; BW $1,239, full page; BW $809, half page. **Remarks:** Accepts advertising. **Circ:** ‡2,454, 2,445.

2120 ■ Women and Health: A Multi Disciplinary Journal of Women's Health Issues
Routledge Journals Taylor & Francis Group
c/o Ellen B. Gold, PhD, Ed.-in-Ch.
Division of Epidemiology
Dept. of Public Health Sciences
University of California
Davis, CA 95616-8638
Multidisciplinary journal on health for women. **Freq:** 8/year. **Trim Size:** 6 x 8 3/8. **Key Personnel:** Ellen B. Gold, PhD, Editor-in-Chief; Janis Barry, Board Member. **ISSN:** 0363-0242 (print); **EISSN:** 1541-0331 (electronic). **Subscription Rates:** $297 Individuals online only; $330 Individuals print + online; $1739 Institutions online only; $1987 Institutions print + online. **URL:** http://www.tandfonline.com/loi/wwah20#.Ve7bg9Kqqko; http://www.tandfonline.com/toc/wwah20/current#.Ve7cUNKqqko. **Ad Rates:** BW $315; 4C $550. **Remarks:** Accepts advertising. **Circ:** Controlled ‡1010.

2121 ■ KQBR-FM - 104.3
1260 Lake Blvd., No. 210
Davis, CA 95616-2617
Phone: (916)756-6800
Format: Country. **Networks:** Independent. **Founded:** 1979. **Formerly:** KLCO-FM. **Operating Hours:** Continuous. **Key Personnel:** Mik Benedek, Gen. Mgr.; Sheila Hatfield, Office Mgr. **Wattage:** 6,000.

DEL MAR

W. CA. San Diego Co. 20 mi. N. of San Diego. Residential.

2122 ■ Chronicle of Holistic Health
Mandala Society
c/o David J. Harris
PO Box 1233
Del Mar, CA 92014
Phone: (858)481-7751
Publisher's E-mail: info@year2020vision.net
Journal consisting of articles, stories and information from people who have healed, and maintaining a lifestyle inspired by the different contemporary health care approach, including interpersonal relationships and the

relationship to nature and physical environment. **Freq:** Annual. **Subscription Rates:** $150 Individuals. **URL:** http://www.year2020vision.net/journals.htm. **Remarks:** Advertising not accepted. **Circ:** (Not Reported).

2123 ■ Del Mar Times
MainStreet Media Group L.L.C.
3702 Via de la Valle, No. 202W
Del Mar, CA 92014
Phone: (858)756-1403
Community newspaper. **Freq:** Weekly. **Key Personnel:** Phyllis Pfeiffer, Publisher, phone: (858)875-5940; Lorine Wright, Executive Editor, phone: (858)756-1451; Ann Marie Gabaldon, Director, Advertising, phone: (858)876-1403. **Subscription Rates:** $125 Out of area by first class mail. **URL:** http://www.delmartimes.net. **Remarks:** Accepts advertising. **Circ:** Combined ■ **7460.**

2124 ■ Rancho Santa Fe Review
MainStreet Media Group L.L.C.
3702 Via de la Valle, No. 202W
Del Mar, CA 92014
Phone: (858)756-1403
Community newspaper. **Freq:** Weekly. **Key Personnel:** Phyllis Pfeiffer, Publisher, phone: (858)875-5940; Lorine Wright, Executive Editor, phone: (858)756-1451. **Subscription Rates:** $150 Out of area by first class mail. **URL:** http://www.ranchosantafereview.com. **Remarks:** Accepts advertising. **Circ:** Combined ■ **7350.**

2125 ■ Solana Beach Sun
MainStreet Media Group L.L.C.
3702 Via de la Valle, No. 202W
Del Mar, CA 92014
Phone: (858)756-1403
Community newspaper. **Freq:** Weekly. **Key Personnel:** Phyllis Pfeiffer, Publisher, phone: (858)875-5940; Lorine Wright, Executive Editor, phone: (858)756-1451; Ann Marie Gabaldon, Director, Advertising, phone: (858)876-1403. **Subscription Rates:** $125 Out of area by first class mail. **URL:** http://www.delmartimes.net/news/local-news/solana-beach. **Remarks:** Accepts advertising. **Circ:** Combined ■ **4725.**

DELANO

S. CA. Kern Co. 32 mi. NW of Bakersfield. Vegetables, fruit shipped. Wineries; cotton gin; concrete pipe factory. Diversified farming. Grapes, potatoes, cotton.

2126 ■ KCHJ-AM - 1010
3301 Brham Blvd., Ste. 200
Los Angeles, CA 90068
Phone: (323)512-2225
Fax: (323)512-2224
Format: Hispanic. **Networks:** Independent. **Owner:** Lotus Communications, at above address. **Founded:** 1949. **Operating Hours**: Continuous. **ADI**: Bakersfield, CA. **Key Personnel:** Howard A. Kalmenson, President. **Wattage**: 5,000 Day; 1,000 Night. **Ad Rates:** Advertising accepted; rates available upon request. **URL:** http://www.lotuscorp.com.

DESERT HOT SPRINGS

SE CA. Riverside Co. 10 mi. N. of Palm Springs. Health resort. Retirement Community.

2127 ■ K288DR-FM - 105.5
PO Box 391
Twin Falls, ID 83303
Fax: (208)736-1958
Free: 800-357-4226
Format: Religious; Contemporary Christian. **Owner:** CSN International, PO Box 391, Twin Falls, ID 83303, Ph: (208)736-1958, Fax: (208)736-1958, Free: 800-357-4226. **URL:** http://www.csnradio.com.

DIAMOND BAR

2128 ■ SEMA News
Specialty Equipment Market Association
1575 S Valley Vista Dr.
Diamond Bar, CA 91765-0910
Phone: (909)610-2030
Fax: (909)860-0184
Publisher's E-mail: sema@sema.org
Freq: Monthly. **Subscription Rates:** free access for members. **URL:** http://www.sema.org/sema-news. **Remarks:** Accepts advertising. **Circ:** 30,000.

DINUBA

NW CA. Tulare Co. 25 mi. SE of Fresno. Irrigated region.

2129 ■ KRDU-AM - 1130
597 N Alta Ave.
Dinuba, CA 93618
Fax: (559)591-4822
Format: Religious. **Networks:** Independent. **Founded:** 1946. **Operating Hours**: Continuous. **ADI**: Fresno-Visalia (Hanford), CA. **Key Personnel:** Jeff Negrete, Gen. Mgr. **Wattage**: 5,000. **Ad Rates:** $15 for 60 seconds. KSOT-FM, KEZL-FM, KFSO-AM, KCBL-AM, KVBL-AM. **URL:** http://www.krdu1130.com.

DIXON

NWC CA. Solano Co. 25 mi. SW of Sacramento. Meat packing, alfalfa dehydrators, wool processing plants; feed mill. Diversified farming. Sheep.

2130 ■ Dixon's Independent Voice: The Dixon Newspaper
Dixon's Independent Voice
PO Box 1106
Dixon, CA 95620
Phone: (707)678-8917
Publication E-mail: staff@independentvoice.com
Community newspaper. **Freq:** Weekly (Wed.). **Print Method:** Off standard. **Key Personnel:** Dave Scholl, Publisher; John Dawson, Author. **URL:** http://independentvoice.com. **Remarks:** Accepts advertising. **Circ:** (Not Reported).

DORRIS

N. CA. Siskiyou Co. 22 mi. S. of Klamath Falls, OR. Lumber mills. Fir, cedar, pine timber. Agriculture. Potatoes, alfalfa. Grain.

2131 ■ K235AG-FM - 94.9
PO Box 391
Twin Falls, ID 83303
Fax: (208)736-1958
Free: 800-357-4226
Format: Religious; Contemporary Christian. **Owner:** CSN International, PO Box 391, Twin Falls, ID 83303, Ph: (208)736-1958, Fax: (208)736-1958, Free: 800-357-4226. **Key Personnel:** Don Mills, Prog. Dir., Music Dir.; Kelly Carlson, Dir. of Engg.; Ray Gorney, Asst. Dir. **Wattage**: 010. **URL:** http://www.csnradio.com.

DOS PALOS

C. CA. Merced Co. 55 mi. NW of Fresno. Agriculture. Vegetables, alfalfa, cotton.

2132 ■ KDPT-FM - 102.9
1742 Almond St.
Dos Palos, CA 93620
Phone: (209)392-8622
Format: Educational; Public Radio. **Owner:** Dos Palos Radio, 42198 Valeria Ave., Dos Palos, CA 93620-9418. **Operating Hours**: Continuous. **Ad Rates:** Advertising accepted; rates available upon request.

DOWNEY

S. CA. Los Angeles Co. 12 mi. SE of Los Angeles. Manufactures asbestos, textiles, aerospace products, farm machinery, cement pipe, soap, chemicals, carpeting, plastics, food, wire, rubber products, furniture, industrial castings and blowers, brass fittings, mobile homes. Nurseries.

2133 ■ Downey Herald American
Wave Newspaper Group
3731 Wilshire Blvd., Ste. 840
Los Angeles, CA 90010
Phone: (323)556-5720
Fax: (213)835-0584
Newspaper. **Freq:** Semiweekly Thurs. and Sat. **Print Method:** Offset. Uses mats. **Cols./Page:** 6. **Col. Width:** 26 nonpareils. **Col. Depth:** 301 agate lines. **Key Personnel:** Jarrette Fellows, Executive Editor. **Subscription Rates:** $125 Individuals. **URL:** http://wavenewspapers.com/category/news/local/herald_american. **Remarks:** Accepts advertising. **Circ:** Paid 291.

2134 ■ Continental Cablevision
10839 La Reina Ave.
Downey, CA 90241
Phone: (310)869-5301
Fax: (310)861-4522
Owner: Continental Cablevision Inc., The Pilot House, Lewis Wharf, Boston, MA 02110, Ph: (617)742-9500. **Founded:** 1982.

DUARTE

SW CA. Los Angeles Co. 40 mi. N. of West Covina.

2135 ■ Duarte View
Duarte Chamber of Commerce
1634 3rd St.
Duarte, CA 91009-4438
Phone: (626)357-3333
Fax: (626)357-3645
Newspaper containing information about the general interests, columns and local business oriented news features of Duarte, CA. **Freq:** Bimonthly. **Alt. Formats:** PDF. **URL:** http://www.duartechamber.com/duarte-view-archive.htm. **Mailing address:** PO Box 1438, Duarte, CA 91009. **Remarks:** Accepts advertising. **Circ:** (Not Reported).

2136 ■ Journal of Hospice and Palliative Nursing: The Official Journal of the Hospice and Palliative Nursing Association
Wolters Kluwer Health Inc.
City of Hope
1500 E Duarte Rd.
Duarte, CA 91010-3000
Phone: (626)256-4673
Peer-reviewed journal for nurses in hospice and palliative care settings, which focuses on the clinical, educational and research aspects of care. **Freq:** 6/year. **Print Method:** Offset, Sheetfed. **Trim Size:** 7 7/8 x 10 7/8. **Key Personnel:** Betty Rolling Ferrell, PhD, Editor-in-Chief; Andrea Garcia, Associate Editor. **ISSN:** 1522--2179 (print); **EISSN:** 1539--0705 (electronic). **Subscription Rates:** $110 Individuals print; $386 Institutions print; $118 Canada and Mexico print; $421 Institutions, Canada and Mexico print; $206 Individuals print - UK/Australia; $564 Institutions, other countries print; $203 Other countries print; $104 Elsewhere online. **URL:** http://journals.lww.com/jhpn/pages/default.aspx. **Ad Rates:** BW $1,585; 4C $1,445. **Remarks:** Accepts advertising. **Circ:** 9875.

DUBLIN

2137 ■ The Luso-American
Luso-American Fraternal Federation
c/o Luso-American Life Insurance Society
7080 Donlon Way, Ste. 200
Dublin, CA 94568
Phone: (925)828-4884
Fax: (925)828-4554
Free: 877-525-5876
Freq: Semiannual. **Subscription Rates:** Included in membership. **Alt. Formats:** PDF. **URL:** http://www.luso-american.org/media.php. **Remarks:** Advertising not accepted. **Circ:** (Not Reported).

2138 ■ The Luso-American
Luso-American Life Insurance Society
7080 Donlon Way, Ste. 200
Dublin, CA 94568-2787
Phone: (925)828-4884
Fax: (925)828-4554
Free: 877-525-5876
Freq: Semiannual. **Subscription Rates:** Included in membership. **Alt. Formats:** PDF. **URL:** http://www.luso-american.org/media.php. **Remarks:** Advertising not accepted. **Circ:** (Not Reported).

EDWARDS

2139 ■ Desert Wings
Aerotech
AFFTC/PAI
1 S Rosamond Blvd.
Edwards, CA 93524-0001
Phone: (661)277-2345
Fax: (661)277-2732
Publication E-mail: afftc.pa.desertwings@edwards.af.mil
Military and family interest newspaper distributed to Air Force families, government employees and contractor personnel. **Freq:** Weekly (Fri.). **Print Method:** Offset. **Trim Size:** 11 1/2 x 13 3/4. **Cols./Page:** 5. **Col. Width:**

Circulation: ★ = AAM; △ or • = BPA; ♦ = CAC; ❑ = VAC; ⊕ = PO Statement; ‡ = Publisher's Report; Boldface figures = sworn; Light figures = estimated.

1 7/8 inches. **Col. Depth:** 13 inches. **Key Personnel:** Paul Kinison, Publisher; 2d Lt. Tony Wickman, Editor. **Subscription Rates:** Free. **Alt. Formats:** PDF. **URL:** http://www.aerotechnews.com/edwardsafb. **Ad Rates:** BW $1189.50. **Remarks:** Advertising accepted; rates available upon request. **Circ:** Non-paid 10000.

EL CAJON

S. CA. San Diego Co. 15 mi. NE of San Diego. Light industry. Citrus truck, poultry farms. Recreation.

2140 ■ Sun Newspapers
Pacific Sierra Publishing Company Inc.
150 Chambers St., Ste. 9
El Cajon, CA 92020-3366
Publisher's E-mail: news@turlockjournal.com
Community newspaper. **Freq:** Weekly (Thurs.). **Print Method:** Offset. **Cols./Page:** 5. **Col. Width:** 26 nonpareils. **Col. Depth:** 224 agate lines. **URL:** http://www.sunnews.org/local-news. **Formerly**: Seal Beach Journal; Seal Beach Sun. **Remarks:** Advertising accepted; rates available upon request. **Circ:** Paid 300, Free 13700.

2141 ■ Youthworker Journal
Salem Publishing
c/o Youth Specialties
300 South Pierce St.
El Cajon, CA 92020
Phone: (619)440-2333
Fax: (619)440-8542
Free: 800-346-4179
Publisher's E-mail: privacy@salempublishing.com
Trade magazine covering professional and personal issues for serious youth workers in church and parachurch settings. **Freq:** 6/year. **Key Personnel:** Jay Howver, Publisher; Roni Meek, Managing Editor. **ISSN:** 0747-3486 (print). **Subscription Rates:** $24 Individuals print, 1 year; $45 Individuals print, 2 years; $60 Individuals print, 3 years; $31 Other countries print; $14.99 Individuals PDF download, 1 year; $29.98 Individuals PDF download, 2 years; $44.97 Individuals PDF download, 3 years. **Alt. Formats:** PDF. **URL:** http://www.youthworker.com; http://salem.cc/prints/youth-worker-journal. **Formerly**: Youthworker. **Circ:** 20000.

2142 ■ KECR-AM
312 W Douglas Ave.
El Cajon, CA 92020
Phone: (619)442-4414
Format: Religious. **Networks:** Family Stations Radio. **Founded:** 1955. **Formerly**: KMJC. **Key Personnel:** Michael Wood, Contact. **Wattage**: 5,000. **Ad Rates:** Noncommercial.

EL CENTRO

S. CA. Imperial Co. 120 mi. E. of San Diego. Mines. Agriculture.

2143 ■ Adelante Valle
Imperial Valley Press
205 N Eighth St.
El Centro, CA 92243-2301
Phone: (760)337-3400
Fax: (760)353-3003
Newspaper in Spanish language featuring local and national news, family, and entertainment stories. **Freq:** Weekly (Thurs.). **Key Personnel:** Arturo Bojorquez, Editor, phone: (760)335-4646. **Subscription Rates:** $124 Individuals /year; by carrier; $163 By mail /year; within Imperial County; $216 Out of area /year; by mail. **URL:** http://www.ivpressonline.com/adelantevalle. **Remarks:** Accepts advertising. **Circ:** Paid ♦9530.

2144 ■ Imperial Valley Press
Imperial Valley Press
205 N Eighth St.
El Centro, CA 92243-2301
Phone: (760)337-3400
Fax: (760)353-3003
General newspaper. **Freq:** Daily and Sun. (eve.). **Print Method:** Offset. **Trim Size:** 13 3/4 x 27 1/2. **Cols./Page:** 6. **Col. Width:** 21.5 nonpareils. **Col. Depth:** 301 agate lines. **Key Personnel:** Peggy Dale, Editor. **USPS:** 260-060. **Subscription Rates:** $163 By mail within Imperial County; $216 By mail outside Imperial County; $124 Individuals Carrier Delivery; $132 Individuals Rural Delivery. **URL:** http://www.ivpressonline.com. **Remarks:** Accepts advertising. **Circ:** Mon.-Sat. ♦**8835**, Sun. ♦**9105**.

2145 ■ KAJB-TV - 54
1803 N Imperial Ave.
El Centro, CA 92243
Phone: (760)482-7777
Fax: (760)482-0099
Owner: Entravision Communications Corporation, 2425 Olympic Blvd., Ste. 6000 W, Santa Monica, CA 90404-4030, Ph: (310)447-3870, Fax: (310)447-3899. **Key Personnel:** Veronica Avila, Station Mgr., vavila@entravision.com. **URL:** http://www.entravision.com.

2146 ■ KECY-TV - 9
646 Main St.
El Centro, CA 92243
Phone: (619)353-9990
Fax: (619)352-5471
Format: Commercial TV. **Networks:** CBS. **Owner:** Pacific Media Corp., at above address. **Founded:** 1968. **Key Personnel:** Pete Sieler, Gen. Mgr; Gloria Flores, Contact. **Wattage**: 50,000 ERP.

2147 ■ KGBA-FM - 100.1
605 State St.
El Centro, CA 92243
Phone: (760)352-9860
Fax: (760)352-1883
Email: kgba@kgba.org
Format: Religious; Talk. **Owner:** The Voice of International Christian Evangelism Inc., 100 N Main St., Ste. 308, Corsicana, TX 75110, Ph: (903)872-0180, Fax: (903)872-5886. **Founded:** 1983. **Operating Hours**: Continuous. **ADI**: El Centro, CA-Yuma, AZ. **Wattage**: 6,000. **Ad Rates:** Accepts Advertising. **URL:** http://www.kgba.org/.

KMXX-FM - See Brawley

2148 ■ KSEH-FM - 94.5
1803 N Imperial Ave.
El Centro, CA 92243
Phone: (760)482-7777
Format: Hispanic. **Owner:** Entravision Communications Corporation, 2425 Olympic Blvd., Ste. 6000 W, Santa Monica, CA 90404-4030, Ph: (310)447-3870, Fax: (310)447-3899. **Key Personnel:** Veronica Avila, Station Mgr., vavila@entravision.com. **URL:** http://www.entravision.com.

2149 ■ KUBO-FM - 88.7
531 Main St., Ste. 2
El Centro, CA 92243
Phone: (760)337-8051
Email: info@radiobilingue.org
Format: Hispanic. **Owner:** Radio Bilingue, Inc., at above address. **Operating Hours**: Continuous. **Key Personnel:** Carol Dowell, Dir. of Dev. **Wattage**: 3,000. **URL:** http://www.radiobilingue.org.

2150 ■ KVYE-TV - 7
1803 N Imperial Ave.
El Centro, CA 92243
Phone: (760)482-7777
Fax: (760)482-0099
Owner: Entravision Communications Corporation, 2425 Olympic Blvd., Ste. 6000 W, Santa Monica, CA 90404-4030, Ph: (310)447-3870, Fax: (310)447-3899. **Key Personnel:** Ray Nieves, Gen. Mgr., VP. **URL:** http://www.kvyetv.com.

2151 ■ KWST-AM - 1430
1803 N Imperial Ave
El Centro, CA 92243
Phone: (760)482-7777
Free: 866-560-5673
Founded: 1958. **Operating Hours**: 24 hrs. **ADI**: El Centro, CA-Yuma, AZ. **Wattage**: 1,000. **URL:** http://www.jose945.com.

2152 ■ KXO-AM - 1230
420 Main St.
El Centro, CA 92243
Phone: (760)352-1230
Format: Oldies; News; Sports; Agricultural. **Networks:** CBS. **Owner:** Gene P. Brister and Carroll Buckley, at above address. **Founded:** 1927. **Operating Hours**: Continuous. **ADI**: El Centro, CA-Yuma, AZ. **Key Personnel:** Gene P. Brister, Gen. Mgr., President. **Wattage**: 1,000. **Ad Rates:** $18-22 for 30 seconds; $20-25 for 60 seconds. $16-19 for 30 seconds; $17-21 for 60 seconds. Combined advertising rates available with KXO-FM. **URL:** http://kxoradio.com.

2153 ■ KXO-FM - 107.5
420 Main St.
El Centro, CA 92243
Phone: (760)352-1230
Email: gbrister@kxoradio.com
Format: Adult Contemporary. **Owner:** Gene Brister/Carroll Buckley, at above address, El Centro, CA. **Founded:** 1976. **Operating Hours**: Continuous. **ADI**: El Centro, CA-Yuma, AZ. **Key Personnel:** Gene Brister, Gen. Mgr., President. **Wattage**: 25,500. **Ad Rates:** $20-25 for 30 seconds; $22-30 for 60 seconds. $16.00-$19.00 for 30 seconds; $17.00-$21.00 for 60 seconds. Combined advertising rates available with KXO-AM. **Mailing address:** PO Box 140, El Centro, CA 92243. **URL:** http://www.kxoradio.com.

2154 ■ XHMIX-FM - 98.3
350 W Ross Ave., Ste. H
El Centro, CA 92243
Phone: (760)352-9833
Fax: (760)352-9444
Format: Classic Rock. **Operating Hours**: 19 hours Daily. **Key Personnel:** Javier Fimbres, Administrator, jfimbres@zona98.com; Francisco Padilla, Contact, fpadilla@zona98.com. **Ad Rates:** Advertising accepted; rates available upon request. **URL:** http://power98jams.com/power.

EL CERRITO

2155 ■ Journal of International Wildlife Law and Policy
Taylor & Francis Group Journals
c/o William C. G. Burns, Editor-in-Chief
Journal of International Wildlife Law & Policy
1702 Arlington Blvd.
El Cerrito, CA 94530
Phone: (650)281-9126
Fax: (801)838-4710
Publication E-mail: jiwlp@internationalwildlifelaw.org
Journal covering legal and political issues concerning the ways in which humans beings relate to and manage wildlife species, their habitats, and the biosphere. **Freq:** Quarterly. **Key Personnel:** William C.G. Burns, Editor-in-Chief; Geoffrey Wandesfore-Smith, Associate Editor; Paul Boudreaux, Board Member; Stephen De Vincent, Editor; Dr. Michael Bowman, Editor. **ISSN:** 1388--0292 (print); **EISSN:** 1548--1476 (electronic). **Subscription Rates:** $185 Individuals print only; $324 Institutions online only; $370 Institutions online and print. **Online:** Kluwer Online. **URL:** http://www.tandfonline.com/toc/uwlp20/current. **Circ:** (Not Reported).

2156 ■ KECG-FM - 88.1
540 Ashbury Ave.
El Cerrito, CA 94530
Phone: (510)525-0234
Format: Eclectic. **Networks:** USA Radio. **Owner:** El Cerrito High School, 540 Ashbury Ave., El Cerrito, CA 94530, Ph: (510)231-1437, Fax: (510)525-1810. **Founded:** 1978. **Operating Hours**: Continuous. **Wattage**: 100. **Ad Rates:** Noncommercial.

EL MONTE

S. CA. Los Angeles Co. 12 mi. E. of Los Angeles. Manufactures dairy, cement, chemical, pressed steel and wood products, electric appliances, electronic products, steam generators, airplane accessories. Walnut packing.

2157 ■ Chinese L.A. Daily News
Chinese L.A. Daily News
9639 Telstar Ave.
El Monte, CA 91731
Phone: (626)453-8800
Chinese language general newspaper. **Freq:** Daily. **URL:** http://www.chinesedaily.com. **Formerly**: Chinese Free Daily News. **Ad Rates:** BW $680; 4C $1220. **Remarks:** Accepts advertising. **Circ:** Combined 103000.

EL SEGUNDO

S. CA. Los Angeles Co. 13 mi. NW of Los Angeles. Residential.

2158 ■ Amazing Wellness
Active Interest Media

300 Continental Blvd., Ste. 650
El Segundo, CA 90245-5067
Phone: (310)356-4100
Fax: (310)356-4110
Publisher's E-mail: admin@aimmedia.com
Magazine publishing articles and information on nutritional supplements, personal care, beauty products, fitness and natural foods and beverages. **Key Personnel:** Joanna Shaw, Publisher. **URL:** http://amazingwellnessmag.com. **Remarks:** Accepts advertising. **Circ:** 240000.

2159 ■ Better Nutrition Magazine
Active Interest Media
300 Continental Blvd., Ste. 650
El Segundo, CA 90245-5067
Phone: (310)356-4100
Fax: (310)356-4110
Publisher's E-mail: admin@aimmedia.com
Magazine focusing on 'all-natural dietary and lifestyle approaches to optimal nutrition and health. **Freq:** Monthly. **Print Method:** Offset. **Trim Size:** 8 1/8 x 10 7/8. **Cols./Page:** 3. **Col. Width:** 27 nonpareils. **Col. Depth:** 140 agate lines. **Key Personnel:** Nicole Brechka, Editor-in-Chief, phone: (707)604-7531; Joanna Shaw, Publisher. **ISSN:** 0405--568X (print). **URL:** http://www.betternutrition.com. **Formerly:** Better Nutrition for Today's Living. **Remarks:** Accepts advertising. **Circ:** (Not Reported).

2160 ■ Black Belt Magazine: World's Leading Magazine of Martial Arts
Active Interest Media
300 Continental Blvd., Ste. 650
El Segundo, CA 90245-5067
Phone: (310)356-4100
Fax: (310)356-4110
Self-defense magazine featuring various martial arts, including how-to's, historical and current events in the martial arts. Audience ranges from pre-teens to 50's. **Freq:** Monthly. **Print Method:** Offset. **Trim Size:** 8 x 10 7/8. **Cols./Page:** 3. **Col. Width:** 13.5 picas. **Col. Depth:** 10 inches. **Key Personnel:** Robert W. Young, Executive Editor. **ISSN:** 0277--3066 (print). **Subscription Rates:** $24 Individuals; $45 Two years; $36 Canada; $69 Canada two years; $48 Other countries; $93 Other countries two years. **URL:** http://www.blackbeltmag.com. **Mailing address:** PO Box 918, Santa Clarita, CA 91355. **Ad Rates:** BW $1521; 4C $2121. **Remarks:** Accepts advertising. **Circ:** ‡105000.

2161 ■ Journal of Artificial Intelligence Research
AI Access Foundation
Fetch Technologies
326 Loma Vista St.
El Segundo, CA 90245
Publication E-mail: jair-ed@isi.edu
Scholarly, scientific journal covering artificial intelligence. **Freq:** Semiannual Volume 50. **Key Personnel:** Shlomo Zilberstein, Editor-in-Chief; Craig Boutilier, Associate Editor; Steven Minton, Managing Editor. **ISSN:** 1076-9757 (print). **Subscription Rates:** $90 for nonmembers; $425 Individuals current issue; $85 Individuals back issues. **URL:** http://www.jair.org. **Remarks:** Advertising not accepted. **Circ:** (Not Reported).

2162 ■ Old-House Journal
Active Interest Media
300 Continental Blvd., Ste. 650
El Segundo, CA 90245-5067
Phone: (310)356-4100
Fax: (310)356-4110
Publisher's E-mail: admin@aimmedia.com
Magazine containing practical articles about the restoration, decoration, and maintenance of houses built before 1940. **Freq:** Bimonthly. **Cols./Page:** 3. **ISSN:** 0094--0178 (print). **Subscription Rates:** $24.95 Individuals /year; $44.95 Two years. **URL:** http://www.oldhousejournal.com. **Remarks:** Advertising accepted; rates available upon request. **Circ:** (Not Reported).

2163 ■ Super Street
TEN: The Enthusiast Network
831 S Douglas St.
El Segundo, CA 90245
Publication E-mail: superstreet@emailcustomerservice.com inquiries@automotive.com
Magazine dedicated to the personalization and performance enhancement of compact street cars. Combines extensive technical information with feature coverage of the rapidly-growing performance compact car aftermarket. Defines the trends in this constantly evolving market with features and event coverage from across the globe. **Freq:** Monthly. **Key Personnel:** Michael Febbo, Editor. **Subscription Rates:** $14.97 Individuals; $24.97 Two years; $26.97 Canada; $48.97 Canada two years; $38.97 Other countries; $72.97 Other countries two years. **URL:** http://www.superstreetonline.com. **Remarks:** Accepts advertising. **Circ:** Paid ★**145205**.

ELK GROVE

NC CA. Sacramento Co. 6 mi. SE of Sacramento. Wineries. Light industry. Chemicals. Feed mill. Fruit, dairy, grain farms. Grapes, hops, Ladino clover.

2164 ■ The California Veteran: Official Publication of the Veterans of Foreign Wars Department of California
Veterans of Foreign Wars of the U.S.
9136 Elk Grove Blvd.,
Elk Grove, CA 95624
Phone: (916)509-8712
Fax: (916)509-8720
Publication E-mail: martin@vfwca.org
Newspaper (tabloid) for veterans and their families. **Freq:** Bimonthly. **Print Method:** Web Offset. **Cols./Page:** 4. **Col. Width:** 2 inches. **Col. Depth:** 16 inches. **Key Personnel:** Steve Milano, Editor, Business Manager. **Subscription Rates:** $1 Members for life; $1.75 Members for continuous or annual members; $5 Nonmembers. **Alt. Formats:** PDF. **URL:** http://www.vfwca.org/in-the-news/publications. **Ad Rates:** BW $1500. **Remarks:** Accepts advertising. **Circ:** 120000.

2165 ■ Elk Grove Citizen
Herburger Publications Inc.
8970 Elk Grove Blvd.
Elk Grove, CA 95624
Phone: (916)685-3945
Community newspaper. **Freq:** Weekly (Wed.). **Print Method:** Offset. **Trim Size:** 12 1/2 x 22 1/2. **Cols./Page:** 6. **Col. Depth:** 21 inches. **Key Personnel:** Keith Gebers, Editor; Jim O'Donnell, Director, Advertising; David Herburger, Publisher. **Subscription Rates:** $22 Individuals 6 months; $38 Individuals; $68 Two years. **URL:** http://www.egcitizen.com. **Ad Rates:** GLR $800; BW $1,008; 4C $1,303; SAU $8. **Remarks:** Accepts advertising. **Circ:** Paid ■ **9211**, Free ■ **250**, Combined ■ **9461**.

2166 ■ The Fish Sniffer
Northern California Angler Publications
10535-H E Stockton Blvd.
Elk Grove, CA 95759
Phone: (916)685-2245
Free: 800-748-6599
Publication E-mail: info@fishsniffer.com
Tabloid covering recreational fishing in northern California and Nevada. **Freq:** Biweekly Fri. **Print Method:** Web offset. **Trim Size:** 10 x 14 1/2. **Cols./Page:** 4. **Col. Width:** 14 picas. **Key Personnel:** Paul Kneeland, Publisher, phone: (530)346-8696; Dan Bacher, Editor. **ISSN:** 0747--3397 (print). **Subscription Rates:** $39.99 Individuals; $69.99 Two years; $89.99 Individuals 3 years; $1.50 Single issue. **URL:** http://www.fishsniffer.com. **Ad Rates:** BW $1,779; 4C $2,668; PCI $19.55. **Remarks:** Accepts advertising. **Circ:** 23770.

2167 ■ Theatre Organ
American Theatre Organ Society, Inc.
7800 Laguna Vega Dr.
Elk Grove, CA 95758
Phone: (503)372-6987
Publisher's E-mail: info@atos.org
Journal covering organizational events and conventions, articles on significant people, including the preservation, restoration and presentation of the theatre pipe organ and its music. **Freq:** Bimonthly. **URL:** http://www.atos.org/tojournal/archives. **Ad Rates:** 4C $1000, full page; BW $425, full page; 4C $500, half page; BW $280, half page. **Remarks:** Accepts advertising. **Circ:** (Not Reported).

EMERYVILLE

W. CA. Alameda Co. 4 mi. N. of Oakland. Residential.

2168 ■ The East Bay Monthly
Klaber Publishing Corp.
1301 59th St.
Emeryville, CA 94608
Phone: (510)658-9811
Fax: (510)658-9902
Publication E-mail: letters@themonthly.com
General interest magazine emphasizing food, health, science, the environment, entertainment, personal essays, interviews, investigative features, and local history. **Freq:** Monthly. **Print Method:** Offset. **Trim Size:** 10 7/8 x 14 5/8. **Cols./Page:** 5. **Col. Width:** 11 picas. **Col. Depth:** 13 3/4 picas. **Key Personnel:** Karen Klaber, Founder, Publisher. **Subscription Rates:** $25 Individuals annual. **URL:** http://www.themonthly.com. **Formerly:** The Berkeley Monthly; The Monthly. **Ad Rates:** GLR $6; BW $3,920; 4C $5,600. **Remarks:** Accepts advertising. **Circ:** ‡62000.

2169 ■ Molecules
Molecular Diversity Preservation International
c/o Dr. Derek J. McPhee, Ed.-in-Ch.
Director of Chemistry
Amyris Biotechnologies, Inc.
5885 Hollis St., Ste. 100
Emeryville, CA 94608
Phone: (510)450-0761
Fax: (510)225-2645
Publisher's E-mail: samples@mdpi.org
Journal focusing on synthetic chemistry and natural product chemistry. **Freq:** Monthly. **Key Personnel:** Dr. Derek J. McPhee, Editor-in-Chief. **ISSN:** 1420--3049 (print). **Subscription Rates:** Free online. **URL:** http://www.mdpi.com/journal/molecules. **Remarks:** Accepts advertising. **Circ:** (Not Reported).

2170 ■ Pact's Point of View
Pact, An Adoption Alliance
5515 Doyle St., Ste. 1
Emeryville, CA 94608-2510
Phone: (510)243-9460
Fax: (510)243-9970
Free: 800-750-7590
Publisher's E-mail: info@pactadopt.org
Freq: Quarterly. **Subscription Rates:** Members free. **URL:** http://www.pactadopt.org/adoptive/services/education/point_of_view.html. **Remarks:** Advertising not accepted. **Circ:** (Not Reported).

ENCINITAS

S. CA. San Diego Co. On Pacific Ocean, 25mi. N. of San Diego. Quail. Botanical garden, rare plants. Floriculture. Ships bulbs, poinsettia roots, carnations. Diversified farming.

2171 ■ Bamboo Science and Culture
American Bamboo Society
315 S Coast Highway 101, Ste. U
Encinitas, CA 92024-3555
Publisher's E-mail: help@bamboo.org
Peer-reviewed journal publishing scientific and cultural articles on all aspects of bamboo. **Freq:** Annual. **ISSN:** 0197--3789 (print); **EISSN:** 2162--7967 (electronic). **URL:** http://www.bamboo.org/About.html#Publications. **Remarks:** Advertising not accepted. **Circ:** 1400.

ENCINO

S. CA. Los Angeles Co. 20 mi. NW of Los Angeles. Nursery. Residential.

2172 ■ E-Commerce Times
ECT News Network, Inc.
17555 Ventura Blvd., Ste. 200
Encino, CA 91316
Phone: (818)461-9700
Fax: (818)461-9710
Free: 877-328-5500
Newspaper pertaining to e-business and technology trends. **Founded:** 1985. **Freq:** Daily. **URL:** http://www.ectnews.com/about; http://www.ecommercetimes.com. **Remarks:** Accepts advertising. **Circ:** (Not Reported).

ESCONDIDO

S. CA. San Diego Co. 30 mi. N. of San Diego. Manufactures clothing, aircraft tools, chemicals, electronic components. Wineries, fruit, meat, egg packing plants. Diversified farming. Avocados, citrus fruit, poultry.

Circulation: ★ = AAM; △ or • = BPA; ♦ = CAC; ❑ = VAC; ⊕ = PO Statement; ‡ = Publisher's Report; Boldface figures = sworn; Light figures = estimated.

2173 ■ DesertUSA.com
Digital West Media Inc.
15011 Highland Valley Rd.
Escondido, CA 92025
Phone: (760)740-1787
Fax: (760)546-0321
Publication E-mail: dusa_feedback@desertusa.com
Magazine providing information on life and culture of the North American deserts. Covers topics such as plants, animals, geology, cultural and natural history, recreation, parks, cities, travel and people. **Freq:** Monthly. **Key Personnel:** Lynn Bremner, Director, Sales and Marketing; Jay W. Sharp, Editor. **URL:** http://www.desertusa.com. **Remarks:** Accepts advertising. **Circ:** (Not Reported).

2174 ■ Interweave Crochet
Interweave Press L.L.C.
PO Box 469076
Escondido, CA 92046-9076
Phone: (760)291-1531
Fax: (760)291-1567
Free: 888-403-5986
Publication E-mail: interweavecrochet@pcspublink.com
Magazine featuring ideas and articles about crochet. **Freq:** Quarterly. **Key Personnel:** Kim Werker, Editor. **Subscription Rates:** $21.95 Individuals; $38.95 Two years; $25.95 Canada; $26.95 Other countries; $46.95 Canada 2 years; $52.95 Other countries 2 years. **URL:** http://www.crochetme.com/blogs/interweavecrochet/default.aspx. **Remarks:** Accepts advertising. **Circ:** (Not Reported).

2175 ■ Interweave Knits
Interweave Press L.L.C.
Escondido, CA 92046-9117
Publication E-mail: interweaveknits@pcspublink.com
Magazine featuring step-by-step instructions and illustrations for knitting. **Freq:** Quarterly. **Key Personnel:** Laura Rintala, Managing Editor. **Subscription Rates:** $17.99 Individuals CD. **Alt. Formats:** CD-ROM. **URL:** http://www.interweavestore.com/knitting-magazines-interweave-knits-cd-collections. **Remarks:** Accepts advertising. **Circ:** (Not Reported).

2176 ■ Jewelry Stringing
Interweave Press L.L.C.
PO Box 469126
Escondido, CA 92046-9126
Phone: (760)291-1531
Fax: (760)291-1567
Free: 800-782-1054
Publisher's E-mail: customerservice@interweave.com
Magazine featuring jewelry design. **Freq:** 4/yr. **Key Personnel:** Leigh Trotter, Manager, Circulation; Danielle Fox, Editor; Marlene Blessing, Managing Editor. **Subscription Rates:** $21.95 Individuals; $39.95 Two years. **URL:** http://www.beadingdaily.com/blogs/stringing/default.aspx. **Formerly**: Stringing. **Remarks:** Accepts advertising. **Circ:** (Not Reported).

2177 ■ Quilting Arts Magazine
Interweave Press L.L.C.
PO Box 469087
Escondido, CA 92046
Phone: (760)291-1519
Free: 800-406-5283
Publisher's E-mail: customerservice@interweave.com
Magazine for quilting enthusiasts. **Freq:** 6/year. **Key Personnel:** Pokey Bolton, Editor-in-Chief; Helen Gregory, Managing Editor. **Subscription Rates:** $29.95 Individuals; $59.95 Two years. **URL:** http://www.quiltingdaily.com/blogs/quiltingarts/default.aspx; http://www.interweave.com/advertising/quilting.html. **Remarks:** Accepts advertising. **Circ:** (Not Reported).

EUREKA

NW CA. Humboldt Co. On Humboldt Bay, 2 mi. from Pacific Ocean, 285 mi. N. of San Francisco. Boat Connections. Manufactures lumber, plywood, paper pulp, woolen goods, wine. Halibut, salmon, crab, cod fisheries. Redwood timber. Dairy, truck, stock farms.

2178 ■ The Journal of Borderland Research
Borderland Sciences Research Foundation
PO Box 6250
Eureka, CA 95502
Phone: (707)497-6911
Publication E-mail: cqc@borderlandsciences.org
Journal for scholars and researchers on the frontiers of science and awareness. **Freq:** Annual. **Print Method:** Web offset. **Trim Size:** 8 1/2 x 11. **Cols./Page:** 2. **Key Personnel:** Michael Theroux, Contact. **ISSN:** 0897--0394 (print). **Subscription Rates:** $7.95 Single issue. **URL:** http://borderlandsciences.org/journal/index.html. **Remarks:** Accepts advertising. **Circ:** Paid ‡1100, Non-paid ‡100, 2000.

2179 ■ North Coast Journal
North Coast Journal Inc.
310 F St.
Eureka, CA 95501
Phone: (707)442-1400
Fax: (707)442-1401
Publisher's E-mail: ncjournal@northcoastjournal.com
Community publication serving the Humboldt county area. **Freq:** Weekly (Thurs.). **ISSN:** 1099--7571 (print). **Subscription Rates:** $39 Individuals domestic bulk mail. **URL:** http://www.northcoastjournal.com. **Remarks:** Accepts advertising. **Circ:** Free ■ **22000**.

2180 ■ Times-Standard: A Division of Garden State Newspapers
Times-Standard
930 Sixth St.
Eureka, CA 95501
Phone: (707)441-0500
Fax: (707)441-0501
Free: 800-564-5630
Publisher's E-mail: business@times-standard.com
General newspaper. **Freq:** Daily (eve.), Sat. and Sun. (morn.). **Print Method:** Offset. **Cols./Page:** 6. **Col. Width:** 12.25 picas. **Col. Depth:** 301 agate lines. **Key Personnel:** Kimberly Wear, Managing Editor, phone: (770)441-0520. **Subscription Rates:** $11.66 Individuals only home delivery - 4 weeks; $31.09 Individuals only home delivery - 12 weeks; $61.62 Individuals only home delivery - 26 weeks; $116.64 Individuals only home delivery - 52 weeks. **URL:** http://www.times-standard.com. **Ad Rates:** GLR $1.42; BW $1,568.70; 4C $240; SAU $19.94; PCI $19.94. **Remarks:** Accepts advertising. **Circ:** Mon.-Sat. ★**19425**, Sun. ★**20963**, Sat. ★**17980**.

2181 ■ KATA-AM - 1340
5640 S Broadway
Eureka, CA 95502
Phone: (707)442-2000
Format: Sports. **Networks:** ESPN Radio. **Owner:** Bicoastal Media L.L.C., at above address, Ph: (707)263-6113, Fax: (707)263-0939. **Founded:** 1956. **Operating Hours**: 3:00 a.m. - 5:30 p.m. Monday - Thursday, 3:00 a.m. - 4:00 p.m. Friday. **Wattage**: 1,000. **Ad Rates:** Combined advertising rates available with KKHB, KGOE, KRED, and KFMI. **URL:** http://www.kata1340.com.

2182 ■ KBVU-TV - 28
730 7th St., Ste. 201
Eureka, CA 95501
Owner: Eureka Television Group, 730 7th St., Ste.100, Eureka, CA.

2183 ■ KEET-TV - 13
PO Box 13
Eureka, CA 95502
Phone: (707)445-0813
Email: letters@keet-tv.org
Format: Public TV. **Networks:** Public Broadcasting Service (PBS). **Owner:** Redwood Empire Public Television Inc., PO Box 13, Eureka, CA 95502, Ph: (707)445-0813. **Founded:** 1962. **Operating Hours**: Continuous; 75% network, 25% local. **Key Personnel:** Carol Johnson, President; Monta Genter, Contact. **Wattage**: 5,000. **Ad Rates:** Noncommercial. **URL:** http://www.keet.org.

2184 ■ KEKA-FM - 101.5
1101 Marsh Rd.
Eureka, CA 95501
Phone: (707)442-5744
Format: Country. **Networks:** ABC. **Owner:** Eureka Broadcasting Comapny Inc., at above address. **Operating Hours**: Continuous. **ADI**: Eureka, CA. **Wattage**: 89,000. **Ad Rates:** Advertising accepted; rates available upon request. **URL:** http://www.eurekaradio.com.

2185 ■ KFMI-FM - 96.3
5640 S Broadway St.
Eureka, CA 95503
Phone: (707)442-2000
Format: Adult Contemporary. **Networks:** Jones Satellite. **Owner:** Bicoastal Media L.L.C., at above address, Ph: (707)263-6113, Fax: (707)263-0939. **Founded:** 1968. **Operating Hours**: Continuous. **ADI**: Eureka, CA. **Key Personnel:** Laurie Tate, Traffic Mgr., Office Mgr.; Tom Sebourn, Dir. of Operations, Program Mgr., tsebourn@nccradio.com. **Wattage**: 30,000. **Ad Rates:** Noncommercial. Combined advertising rates available with KATA-AM, KBOE-AM, KRED-FM, KKHB-FM. **URL:** http://www.power963.com.

2186 ■ K47EH - 47
PO Box A
Santa Ana, CA 92711
Phone: (714)832-2950
Free: 888-731-1000
Owner: Trinity Broadcasting Network Inc., PO Box A, Santa Ana, CA 92711, Ph: (714)832-2950, Free: 888-731-1000. **URL:** http://www.tbn.org.

2187 ■ KGOE-AM - 1480
5640 S Broadway
Eureka, CA 95503
Phone: (707)442-2000
Format: News; Talk; Sports. **Owner:** Bicoastal Media L.L.C., at above address, Ph: (707)263-6113, Fax: (707)263-0939. **Formerly**: KRED-AM; KTMA-AM. **Operating Hours**: Continuous. **ADI**: Eureka, CA. **Local Programs**: *Childhood Matters.* **Wattage**: 5,000 Day; 1,000 Night. **Ad Rates:** Noncommercial. Combined advertising rates available with KFMI, KRED, KKHB, and KATA. **URL:** http://www.kgoe.com.

2188 ■ KIEM-TV - 3
5650 S Broadway
Eureka, CA 95503
Phone: (707)443-3123
Fax: (707)268-8109
Format: Commercial TV. **Networks:** NBC. **Founded:** 1953. **Operating Hours**: Continuous; 60% network, 40% local. **ADI**: Eureka, CA. **Key Personnel:** Philip Wright, Div. Dir. **Wattage**: 100,000. **Ad Rates:** Noncommercial. **URL:** http://www.kiem-tv.com.

2189 ■ KINS-AM - 980
1101 Marsh Rd.
Eureka, CA 95501
Phone: (707)442-5744
Founded: 1958. **Operating Hours**: Continuous. **ADI**: El Centro, CA-Yuma, AZ. **Key Personnel:** Brian Papstein, Mgr.; Barbara Papstein, Office Mgr.; Hugo Papstein, Contact; Mark Householder, Contact. **Wattage**: 5,000. **URL:** http://www.kins1063.com.

2190 ■ KKDS-FM - 97.7
One X St.
Eureka, CA 95501
Phone: (707)444-3437
Format: Eclectic. **Owner:** Blue Ox Community School, One "X" St., Eureka, CA 95501-0847, Ph: (707)444-3437, Fax: (800)248-4259, Free: 800-248-4259. **Founded:** 2000. **Operating Hours**: Continuous. **ADI**: Eureka, CA. **Wattage**: 100. **Ad Rates:** Noncommercial. **URL:** http://blueoxradio.org.

2191 ■ KKHB-FM - 105.5
Eureka, CA
Phone: (707)442-2000
Format: Oldies. **URL:** http://www.cool1055.com/page.php?page_id=60.

2192 ■ KLVG-FM - 103.7
PO Box2098
Omaha, NE 68103
Free: 800-525-5683
Format: Contemporary Christian. **Networks:** Independent. **Owner:** Educational Media Foundation, 2351 Sunset Blvd., Ste. 170-218, Rocklin, CA 95677, Ph: (800)434-8400. **Founded:** 1995. **Formerly**: KWEO-FM. **Operating Hours**: Continuous. **Key Personnel:** Alan Mason, COO; Mike Novak, President, CEO. **Wattage**: 10,000. **Ad Rates:** Noncommercial. **URL:** http://www.klove.com.

2193 ■ KMUE-FM - 88.3
PO Box 135
Redway, CA 95560-0135
Phone: (707)923-2513
Fax: (707)923-2501
Free: 800-568-3723

Format: Public Radio; News. **Owner:** Redwood Community Radio Inc., 1144 Redway Dr., Redway, CA 95560, Ph: (707)923-2605. **Founded:** May 28, 1987. **Key Personnel:** Simon Frech, Tech. Dir., simon@kmud.org; Cynthia Click, Music Dir.; Marianne Knorzer, Dir. of Programs; Terri Klemetson, Contact, terri@kmud.org. **Wattage:** 1,250 ERP. **Ad Rates:** Noncommercial. **URL:** http://kmud.org.

2194 ■ KRED-FM - 92.3
5640 S Broadway
Eureka, CA 95503
Phone: (707)442-2000
Format: Country. **Networks:** Jones Satellite. **Owner:** Bicoastal Media L.L.C., at above address, Ph: (707)263-6113, Fax: (707)263-0939. **Operating Hours:** Continuous. **ADI:** Eureka, CA. **Local Programs:** *The Big Red Weekend Crew.* **Wattage:** 25,000. **Ad Rates:** Advertising accepted; rates available upon request. **URL:** http://www.kred923.com.

2195 ■ K229AF-FM - 93.7
PO Box 391
Twin Falls, ID 83303
Fax: (208)736-1958
Free: 800-357-4226
Format: Religious; Contemporary Christian. **Owner:** CSN International, PO Box 391, Twin Falls, ID 83303, Ph: (208)736-1958, Fax: (208)736-1958, Free: 800-357-4226. **URL:** http://www.csnradio.com.

KURY-AM - See Brookings, OR

2196 ■ KVIQ-TV - 6
1800 Broadway
Eureka, CA 95501
Phone: (707)443-3061
Fax: (707)443-4435
Free: 800-310-4246
Format: Commercial TV; News; Sports. **Networks:** CBS. **Owner:** Ackerley Group, 1301 Fifth Ave. , Seattle, WA 98101, Ph: (206)624-2888, Fax: (206)623-7853. **Founded:** 1958. **ADI:** Eureka, CA. **Key Personnel:** John Burgess, Gen. Mgr., VP, Gen. Mgr., johnburgess@clearchannel.com; Dave Silverbrand, News Dir., davesilverbrand@clearchannel.com; Eric Casella, Program Mgr., ericcasella@clearchannel.com. **Wattage:** 30,000 ERP Horizonta. **Ad Rates:** Advertising accepted; rates available upon request. **URL:** http://www.kviq.com.

2197 ■ KXGO-FM - 93.1
603 F St.
Eureka, CA 95501
Phone: (707)445-3699
Fax: (707)445-3906
Format: Classic Rock. **Networks:** ABC. **Owner:** Redwood Broadcasting Co., at above address. **Founded:** 1970. **Operating Hours:** Continuous; 20% network, 80% local. **ADI:** Eureka, CA. **Wattage:** 100,000. **Ad Rates:** Noncommercial. **URL:** http://www.kxgo.com.

2198 ■ Redwood Community Radio Inc.
1144 Redway Dr.
Redway, CA 95560
Phone: (707)923-2605
Format: News; Information. **Key Personnel:** Jeanette Todd, Station Mgr., jeanette@kmud.org; Cynthia Click, Music Dir.; Simon Frech, Tech. Dir., simon@kmud.org. **Ad Rates:** Underwriting available. **Mailing address:** PO Box 135, Redway, CA 95560. **URL:** http://www.kmud.org.

FAIRFIELD

NWC CA. Solano Co. 45 mi. SW of San Francisco. Residential. Wineries. Explosives, Canvas products, can manufacturing. Ranching.

2199 ■ Daily Republic
Daily Republic
PO Box 47
Fairfield, CA 94533
Phone: (707)427-6989
General newspaper. **Founded:** 1855. **Freq:** Mon.-Sun. (morn.). **Print Method:** Offset. **Cols./Page:** 6. **Col. Width:** 2 1/16 inches. **Col. Depth:** 21 1/2 inches. **Key Personnel:** Foy S. McNaughton, Owner, Publisher, phone: (707)427-6962. **ISSN:** 0746-5858 (print). **Subscription Rates:** $182.56 Individuals 48 weeks; $95.76 By mail 24 weeks; $47.88 Individuals 12 weeks. **URL:** http://www.dailyrepublic.com. **Ad Rates:** GLR $23.47; BW $3,027.63; 4C $3,521.75; PCI $23.47. **Remarks:** Accepts advertising. **Circ:** Paid ♦**13311**, Paid ♦**16847**.

FALL RIVER MILLS

N. CA. Shasta Co. 10 mi. N. of Burmey. Residential.

2200 ■ Mountain Echo
Mountain Echo Inc.
PO Box 224
Fall River Mills, CA 96028
Phone: (530)336-6262
Fax: (530)336-5814
Free: 800-327-6471
Publication E-mail: mtecho@shasta.com
Community newspaper. **Founded:** Oct. 03, 1977. **Freq:** Weekly (Tues.). **Print Method:** Offset. **Cols./Page:** 6. **Col. Width:** 24 nonpareils. **Col. Depth:** 298 agate lines. **Key Personnel:** Walt Caldwell, Editor; Katie Clift, Advertising Representative; Donna Caldwell, Business Manager. **USPS:** 052-610. **Subscription Rates:** $35 Individuals local; $40 Individuals other California counties; $45 Individuals other states; $50 Individuals print & online; $15 Individuals online access. **URL:** http://www.mountainecho.com. **Remarks:** Accepts advertising. **Circ:** (Not Reported).

FERNDALE

NW CA. Humboldt Co. 20 mi. S. of Eureka. Residential. Art galleries. Dairy products manufactured. Dairy, stock, mushroom farms. Potatoes.

2201 ■ The Ferndale Enterprise
Ferndale Enterprise Inc.
PO Box 1066
Ferndale, CA 95536
Phone: (707)786-3068
Fax: (707)786-4311
Publisher's E-mail: editor@ferndaleenterprise.us
Newspaper. **Freq:** Weekly (Thurs.). **Print Method:** Offset. **Cols./Page:** 6. **Col. Width:** 2 inches. **Col. Depth:** 280 agate lines. **Key Personnel:** Caroline Titus, Editor. **Subscription Rates:** $55 Individuals; $110 Two years; $77 Other countries; $154.14 Other countries 2 years. **URL:** http://www.ferndaleenterprise.us. **Ad Rates:** SAU $10.50; PCI $5.95. **Remarks:** Color advertising not accepted. **Circ:** Paid 1400.

2202 ■ KHUM-FM - 104.7
PO Box 25
Ferndale, CA 95536
Phone: (707)786-5104
Fax: (707)786-5100
Email: info@khum.com
Format: Adult Album Alternative. **Wattage:** 24,500. **Ad Rates:** Noncommercial. **URL:** http://www.khum.com.

2203 ■ KSLG-FM - 93.1
PO Box 25
Ferndale, CA 95536
Phone: (707)786-5104
Fax: (707)786-5104
Format: Alternative/New Music/Progressive; Album-Oriented Rock (AOR). **Owner:** Lost Coast Communications Inc., at above address. **Key Personnel:** John Matthews, Contact, jmatthews@kslg.com; Jen Savage, Contact, jen@kslg.com. **Wattage:** 50,000. **Ad Rates:** Advertising accepted; rates available upon request. **URL:** http://www.kslg.com.

2204 ■ KWPT-FM - 100.3
PO Box 25
Ferndale, CA 95536
Phone: (707)786-5104
Fax: (707)786-5100
Format: Classic Rock. **Owner:** Lost Coast Communications Inc., at above address. **Founded:** 2006. **Wattage:** 12,000. **URL:** http://www.kwpt.com.

FIREBAUGH

2205 ■ K211DG-FM - 90.1
PO Box 391
Twin Falls, ID 83303
Free: 800-357-4226
Format: Religious; Contemporary Christian. **Owner:** CSN International, PO Box 391, Twin Falls, ID 83303, Ph: (208)736-1958, Fax: (208)736-1958, Free: 800-357-4226.

2206 ■ KYAF-FM - 94.7
1572 10th St.
Firebaugh, CA 93622
Format: Oldies. **Wattage:** 900. **URL:** http://www.kyafm.com.

FOLSOM

NC CA. Sacramento Co. 22 mi. NE of Sacramento. Recreation. Stock farms.

2207 ■ Converge
e.Republic Inc.
100 Blue Ravine Rd.
Folsom, CA 95630
Fax: (916)932-1470
Publisher's E-mail: info@erepublic.com
Online monthly magazine featuring timely reports and articles on K-12 and higher education technology policies. **Freq:** Monthly. **Print Method:** Online. **Trim Size:** 9 x 10 3/4. **Key Personnel:** Jessica Mulholland, Editor, phone: (916)932-1349; Tanya Roscorla, Managing Editor, phone: (916)932-1343; Marina Leight, Editor-in-Chief, phone: (916)932-1374. **URL:** http://www.centerdigitaled.com. **Remarks:** Accepts advertising. **Circ:** (Not Reported).

2208 ■ El Dorado Hills Telegraph
Brehm Communication
921 Sutter St., Ste. 100
Folsom, CA 95630
Phone: (916)985-2581
Fax: (916)985-0720
Publisher's E-mail: debbiel@brehmmail.com
Newsletter covering news and local happenings in El Dorado, California. **Freq:** Weekly (Wed.). **Key Personnel:** Ryan Schuyler, Publisher. **URL:** http://www.edhtelegraph.com. **Remarks:** Accepts advertising. **Circ:** Free ■ **7959**, Paid ■ **48**, Combined ■ **8007**.

2209 ■ Folsom Telegraph
Gold Country Media
921 Sutter St., Ste. 100
Folsom, CA 95630
Phone: (916)985-2581
Fax: (916)985-0720
Community newspaper. **Freq:** Weekly (Wed.). **Print Method:** Offset. **Cols./Page:** 6. **Col. Width:** 2 1/16 inches. **Col. Depth:** 21 1/2 inches. **Key Personnel:** Don Chaddock, Managing Editor. **URL:** http://www.folsomtelegraph.com. **Remarks:** Accepts advertising. **Circ:** Free ■ **12105**, Paid ■ **2950**, Combined ■ **15055**.

2210 ■ Government Technology: Solutions for State and Local Government
e.Republic Inc.
100 Blue Ravine Rd.
Folsom, CA 95630
Fax: (916)932-1470
Publisher's E-mail: info@erepublic.com
Magazine covering various aspects of information technology such as case studies, applications, news and best practices by and for all levels of government. Provides information on information technology events and other resources for managers, elected officials, chief information officers and technology staff at all levels of government. **Freq:** Monthly. **Trim Size:** 9 x 10.75. **Key Personnel:** Elaine Pittman, Managing Editor. **Subscription Rates:** Free. **URL:** http://www.govtech.com. **Ad Rates:** BW $16950; 4C $2840. **Remarks:** Accepts advertising. **Circ:** (Not Reported).

2211 ■ National Masters News: The Official World and U.S. Publication for Masters Track & Field Long Distance Running and Racewalking
National Masters News
PO Box 1601
Folsom, CA 95763-1601
Phone: (916)989-6667
Publisher's E-mail: nminfo@nationalmastersnews.com
Newspaper (tabloid) on long distance running, racewalking and track and field in the U.S., Canada, and internationally for masters athletes 30+. **Freq:** Monthly. **Print Method:** Offset. **Trim Size:** 10 x 13. **Cols./Page:** 4. **Col. Width:** 2.25 picas. **Key Personnel:** Tish Ceccarelli, Manager, Circulation. **ISSN:** 0744--2416 (print). **Subscription Rates:** $39 Individuals second class; $59 Canada and Mexico; $84 Other countries airmail; $25 Individuals online only; $5 U.S.; $10 Institutions, Canada; $15 Other countries. **URL:** http://www.

Circulation: ★ = AAM; △ or • = BPA; ♦ = CAC; ❑ = VAC; ⊕ = PO Statement; ‡ = Publisher's Report; Boldface figures = sworn; Light figures = estimated.

nationalmastersnews.com. **Ad Rates:** BW $350; 4C $400. **Remarks:** Accepts advertising. **Circ:** Paid ‡6775, Free ‡1000.

2212 ■ Public CIO: Technology Leadership in the Public Sector
e.Republic Inc.
100 Blue Ravine Rd.
Folsom, CA 95630
Fax: (916)932-1470
Publisher's E-mail: info@erepublic.com
Magazine that publishes information of interest to Chief Information Officers. **Freq:** Quarterly. **Trim Size:** 18 x 10 3/4. **Key Personnel:** Steve Towns, Editor; Matt Williams, Associate Editor; Chad Vander Veen, Associate Editor. **Subscription Rates:** Free. **URL:** http://www.govtech.com/magazines/pcio. **Ad Rates:** BW $13220; 4C $1770. **Remarks:** Accepts advertising. **Circ:** ‡25833.

FONTANA

SE CA. San Bernardino Co. 10 mi. W. of San Bernardino. Manufacturing steel, ceramics, clothing, electronic products, explosives. Poultry.

2213 ■ Fontana Herald-News
Fontana Herald Publishing
16981 Foothill Blvd., Ste. N
Fontana, CA 92335
Phone: (909)822-2231
Fax: (909)355-9358
Publisher's E-mail: news@fontanaheraldnews.com
General newspaper. **Freq:** Weekly. **Print Method:** Offset. **Cols./Page:** 6. **Col. Width:** 25 nonpareils. **Col. Depth:** 301 agate lines. **Key Personnel:** Russell Ingold, Editor; Grace Barnett, Publisher. **Subscription Rates:** $15.95 Individuals 6 months home delivery; $14.95 Individuals senior local delivery. **URL:** http://fontanaheraldnews.com. **Remarks:** Accepts advertising. **Circ:** Combined 9511.

FORT BRAGG

NW CA. Mendocino Co. On Pacific Ocean, 165 mi. N. of San Francisco. Year round resort. Manufactures lumber. Nurseries. Fisheries. Redwood, pine, fir timber.

2214 ■ Fort Bragg Advocate-News
Digital First Media
450 N Franklin St.
Fort Bragg, CA 95437
Phone: (707)964-5642
Fax: (707)964-0424
Publication E-mail: advocatenews@mcn.org
Community newspaper. **Founded:** 1889. **Freq:** Weekly (Thurs.). **Key Personnel:** Sharon DiMauro, Publisher. **Subscription Rates:** $37 Individuals in county; $34 Individuals senior citizen, in county; $21 Individuals 6 months in county; $50 Out of area. **URL:** http://www.advocate-news.com. **Mailing address:** PO Box 1188, Fort Bragg, CA 95437. **Remarks:** Accepts advertising. **Circ:** Thurs. 5400.

2215 ■ Mendocino Beacon
Mendocino Beacon
450 N Franklin St.
Fort Bragg, CA 95437
Phone: (707)964-5642
Fax: (707)964-0424
Publisher's E-mail: beacon@mcn.org
Community newspaper. **Founded:** 1877. **Freq:** Weekly (Thurs.). **Print Method:** Offset. **Cols./Page:** 6. **Col. Width:** 72.6 picas. **Col. Depth:** 129 picas. **Key Personnel:** Sharon DiMauro, Publisher; Terri Parks, Office Manager. **Subscription Rates:** $37 Individuals in County; $34 Out of area senior, in County; $21 Individuals 6 months in County; $47 Out of area; $33 Out of area 6 months; $21 Out of area 3 months. **URL:** http://www.mendocinobeacon.com. **Ad Rates:** GLR $5.85; BW $754.65; 4C $1,029.65. **Remarks:** Accepts advertising. **Circ:** (Not Reported).

2216 ■ KMFB-FM - 92.7
101 Boatyard, Ste. E
Fort Bragg, CA 95437
Phone: (707)964-5307
Email: general_mail@kmfb-fm.com
Format: Sports; Eclectic. **Owner:** Four Rivers Broadcasting Corp., PO Box 1557, Gualala, CA 95445. **Founded:** 1966. **Key Personnel:** Bob Woelfel, Gen. Mgr.; Lindy Peters, Sports Dir. **Wattage**: 3,000 ERP. **Ad Rates:** $8-12 for 30 seconds; $12-15 for 60 seconds. Combined advertising rates available with KPMO-AM. **URL:** http://theskunkfm.com.

2217 ■ KOZT-FM - 95.3
110 S Franklin St.
Fort Bragg, CA 95437
Phone: (707)964-7277
Email: thecoast@kozt.com
Format: Album-Oriented Rock (AOR). **Owner:** California Radio Partners, at above address. **Founded:** 1981. **Operating Hours**: 9:00 p.m. - 11:00 p.m. Monday - Friday; 9:00 p.m. - 10:00 p.m. Saturday; 8:00 a.m. - 11:00 p.m. Sunday. **Key Personnel:** Tom Yates, Owner; Joe Regelski, News Dir; Vicky Watts, Contact. **Local Programs:** *Breakfast with the Beatles*, Sunday 8:00 a.m. - 10:00 a.m.; *Local Licks*, Wednesday 9:00 p.m. - 10:00 p.m. **Wattage**: 35,000 ERP. **URL:** http://www.kozt.com.

2218 ■ KSAY-FM - 98.5
PO Box 2269
Fort Bragg, CA 95437
Phone: (707)964-5729
Fax: (707)964-2722
Format: Adult Contemporary. **Networks:** Jones Satellite. **Owner:** Axell Broadcasting, at above address. **Founded:** 1988. **Operating Hours**: Continuous. **ADI**: San Francisco-Oakland-San Jose. **Wattage**: 3,500. **Ad Rates:** $12 per unit.

FOSTER CITY

San Mateo Co San Mateo Co. 20 mi. S. of San Francisco. San Mateo County. 20 miles S. of San Francisco. Residential.

2219 ■ National Motorist
National Automobile Club
373 Vintage Park Dr., Ste. E
Foster City, CA 94404
Phone: (650)294-7000
Fax: (650)294-7040
Free: 800-622-2136
Motor and travel magazine covering western U.S. **Freq:** Quarterly. **Print Method:** Offset. **Trim Size:** 8 x 10 3/4. **Cols./Page:** 3. **Col. Width:** 26 nonpareils. **Col. Depth:** 140 agate lines. **ISSN:** 0279--3083 (print). **Ad Rates:** BW $2225; 4C $2,825. **Remarks:** Accepts advertising. **Circ:** ‡64313.

FOUNTAIN VALLEY

S. CA. Orange Co. 10 mi. NE of Santa Ana. Residential.

2220 ■ Boating World: The Leader in Recreational Trailer Boating
Duncan McIntosh Company Inc.
18475 Bandilier
Fountain Valley, CA 92708
Phone: (949)660-6150
Magazine covering topics like fishing, camping & caravanning, walking, golfing, hunting, and boating. Also offering information on the outdoors in Ireland. **Freq:** Bimonthly. **Print Method:** Offset. **Trim Size:** 8.5 x 10.5. **Cols./Page:** 6. **Col. Width:** 26 nonpareils. **Col. Depth:** 294 agate lines. **Subscription Rates:** $10 Individuals print + online. **URL:** http://www.boatingworld.com. **Formerly:** Go Boating. **Remarks:** Accepts advertising. **Circ:** (Not Reported).

2221 ■ Contemporary Economic Policy: A Journal of the Western Economic Association International
Western Economic Association International
18837 Brookhurst St., Ste. 304
Fountain Valley, CA 92708-7302
Phone: (714)965-8800
Fax: (714)965-8829
Journal exploring ways in which economic policy shapes the world of politics, commerce, and industry. **Freq:** Quarterly. **Print Method:** Offset. **Trim Size:** 6 7/8 x 10. **Cols./Page:** 2. **Col. Width:** 2 2/3 inches. **Col. Depth:** 8 1/2 inches. **Key Personnel:** Brad R. Humphreys, Editor. **ISSN:** 1074--3529 (print); **EISSN:** 1465--7287 (electronic). **Subscription Rates:** $312 Institutions online; $375 Institutions print & online; £194 Institutions online ; £233 Institutions print & online ; €246 Institutions online; €296 Institutions print & online ; $379 Institutions, other countries online; $455 Institutions, other countries print & online. **URL:** http://www.weai.org/CEP; http://onlinelibrary.wiley.com/journal/10.1111/(ISSN)1465-7287. **Formerly:** Contemporary Policy Issues. **Remarks:** Advertising accepted; rates available upon request. **Circ:** Paid ‡3200, Non-paid ‡75.

2222 ■ Economic Inquiry
Western Economic Association International
18837 Brookhurst St., Ste. 304
Fountain Valley, CA 92708-7302
Phone: (714)965-8800
Fax: (714)965-8829
Publication E-mail: journals@weai.org
Journal covering research in all areas of economics. **Freq:** Quarterly. **Print Method:** Offset. **Trim Size:** 6 7/8 x 10. **Cols./Page:** 2. **Key Personnel:** R. Preston McAfee, Editor; Wesley W. Wilson, Editor; Prof. R. Preston McAfee, Editor. **ISSN:** 0095-2583 (print); **EISSN:** 1465-7295 (electronic). **Subscription Rates:** $491 Institutions print and online; €378 Institutions print and online; £298 Institutions print and online; $409 Institutions online only; €315 Institutions online only; £248 Institutions online only; $450 Institutions print and online; $534 Institutions, other countries print and online; €346 Institutions print and online; £248 Institutions, other countries online; $485 Institutions, other countries online only; £273 Institutions UK (print and online). **URL:** http://www.weai.org/EI; http://onlinelibrary.wiley.com/journal/10.1111/(ISSN)1465-7295; http://onlinelibrary.wiley.com/journal/10.1111/%28ISSN%291465-7295. **Formerly**: Western Economic Journal. **Ad Rates:** BW $350. **Remarks:** Accepts advertising. **Circ:** Paid 3500, 3400.

2223 ■ Sea Magazine: America's Western Boating Magazine
Duncan McIntosh Company Inc.
18475 Bandilier
Fountain Valley, CA 92708
Phone: (949)660-6150
Publication E-mail: mike@goboating.com
Recreational boating magazine printing news and features for power boat enthusiasts in 13 western states. **Freq:** Monthly. **Print Method:** Offset. **Trim Size:** 8 x 10 7/8. **Cols./Page:** 3 and 4. **Col. Width:** 13 and 9.5 picas. **Col. Depth:** 9.5 inches. **Key Personnel:** Duncan McIntosh, Jr., Editor. **ISSN:** 0746--8601 (print). **Subscription Rates:** $10 Individuals. **URL:** http://www.seamagazine.com. **Remarks:** Advertising accepted; rates available upon request. **Circ:** (Not Reported).

2224 ■ ST Quarterly Magazine
National Spasmodic Torticollis Association
9920 Talbert Ave.
Fountain Valley, CA 92708
Phone: (714)378-9837
Free: 800-487-8385
Publisher's E-mail: nstamail@aol.com
Freq: Quarterly. **Subscription Rates:** Included in membership. **URL:** http://www.torticollis.org/patient-support. **Remarks:** Advertising not accepted. **Circ:** (Not Reported).

2225 ■ Venues Today
Venues Today
18350 Mt. Langley, Ste. 201
Fountain Valley, CA 92708
Phone: (714)378-5400
Fax: (714)378-0040
Publisher's E-mail: subscribe@venuestoday.com
Magazine covering the venue management industry, including convention centers, sports arenas, concert halls, and others. **Freq:** Monthly. **Trim Size:** 8 1/2 x 11. **Key Personnel:** Linda Deckard, Publisher, Editor-in-Chief, phone: (714)378-5400. **ISSN:** 1547--4135 (print). **Subscription Rates:** $200 Individuals. **URL:** http://www.venuestoday.com. **Ad Rates:** BW $2727; 4C $3227. **Remarks:** Accepts advertising. **Circ:** (Not Reported).

FREMONT

W. CA. Alameda Co. 17 mi. SE of Oakland. Manufactures automobiles, building materials, fabricated metal, electronics.

2226 ■ Kung Fu/Qigong
Pacific Rim Publishing Inc.
40748 Encyclopedia Cr.
Fremont, CA 94538
Publication E-mail: gigi@tcmedia.com
Magazine featuring ancient Chinese holistic exercise for the body, mind, and breath. **Freq:** Bimonthly. **Trim Size:**

8 x 10 7/8. **Key Personnel:** Gigi Oh, Publisher; Patrick Lugo, Designer; Gene Ching, Associate Publisher; Gary Shockley, Editor; Thomas J. Oh, Founder. **ISSN:** 1050--2173 (print). **Subscription Rates:** $15 Individuals; $24 Two years. **URL:** http://www.kungfumagazine.com. **Formerly**: World of Martial Arts. **Ad Rates:** BW $1200. **Remarks:** Accepts advertising. **Circ:** (Not Reported).

2227 ■ KDOW-AM - 1220
39138 Fremont Blvd., 3rd Fl.
Fremont, CA 94538
Phone: (510)713-1100
Format: News; Talk. **Owner:** Salem Media Group Inc., 4880 Santa Rosa Rd., Camarillo, CA 93012, Ph: (805)987-0400, Fax: (805)384-4520. **Key Personnel:** Brian J. Rechten, Dir. of Sales; Mike Shields, Gen. Mgr.; Margo Wiggins, Bus. Mgr.; Greg Edwards, Operations Mgr. **URL:** http://www.kdow.biz.

2228 ■ KFAX-AM - 1100
39138 Fremont Blvd., 3rd Fl.
Fremont, CA 94538
Phone: (510)713-1100
Email: comments@kfax.com
Format: Religious. **Owner:** Salem Media Group Inc., 4880 Santa Rosa Rd., Camarillo, CA 93012, Ph: (805)987-0400, Fax: (805)384-4520. **Key Personnel:** Greg Edwards, Operations Mgr., grege@salemsf.com; Mike Shields, Gen. Mgr., mikes@salemsf.com; Margo Wiggins, Bus. Mgr., margow@salemsf.com. **Ad Rates:** Noncommercial. **URL:** http://www.kfax.com.

2229 ■ KOHL-FM - 89.3
43600 Mission Blvd.
Fremont, CA 94539
Phone: (510)659-6221
Fax: (510)659-6001
Format: Top 40. **Networks:** Independent. **Operating Hours**: Continuous. **Wattage**: 145 Horizontal ERP; 115 Vertical ERP. **Ad Rates:** Noncommercial. **URL:** http://www.kohlradio.com.

FRESNO

C. CA. Fresno Co. 189 mi. SE of San Francisco. California State University at Fresno. Center of cotton, grapes, dried fruit and sweet wine industry; fresh and dried fruit packing and processing; vegetable oil mills; stock and poultry feed, plastics, olive oil, metal fabrication, machinery, vending machines manufactured.

2230 ■ American Tanka
American Tanka Inc.
9230 N Stoneridge Ln.
Fresno, CA 93720
Publisher's E-mail: editor@americantanka.com
Literary journal. **Freq:** Semiannual. **Trim Size:** 8 x 5 1/2. **Key Personnel:** Laura Maffei, Editor, Founder; Michael McClintock, Editor. **URL:** http://www.americantanka.com. **Circ:** (Not Reported).

2231 ■ California Advocate
California Advocate
1555 E St.
Fresno, CA 93706
Phone: (559)268-0941
Black community newspaper. **Freq:** Weekly. **Cols./Page:** 6. **Col. Width:** 2 inches. **Col. Depth:** 21 inches. **Key Personnel:** Pauline Kimber, Editor. **URL:** http://www.caladvocate.com/thismonth/default.asp. **Ad Rates:** PCI $39.50. **Remarks:** Accepts advertising. **Circ:** Paid 33013.

2232 ■ The California-Hawaii Elk
California-Hawaii Elks Association
5450 E Lamona Ave.
Fresno, CA 93727
Phone: (559)255-4531
Fax: (559)456-2659
Publisher's E-mail: chea@chea-elks.org
Freq: 5/year. **Key Personnel:** Ian Lanouette, Editor. **Alt. Formats:** PDF. **URL:** http://chea-elks.org/chea-magazine-2. **Remarks:** Advertising not accepted. **Circ:** 98588.

2233 ■ The California Southern Baptist
California Southern Baptist Convention
678 E Shaw Ave.
Fresno, CA 93710-7704
Phone: (559)229-9533
Fax: (559)229-2824
Publication E-mail: thecsb@csbc.com
Southern Baptist magazine. **Freq:** Monthly. **Print Method:** Offset. **Trim Size:** 11 x 14. **Cols./Page:** 4. **Col. Width:** 12 picas. **Col. Depth:** 57 picas. **Key Personnel:** Terry Barone, Editor; Holly Smith, Managing Editor. **ISSN:** 0008--1558 (print). **Subscription Rates:** $9.50 Individuals print; $5 Individuals digital edition. **URL:** http://www.csbc.com/ministry-resources/the-california-southern-baptist-newsjournal. **Ad Rates:** BW $900; 4C $1050; PCI $30. **Circ:** ‡8000.

2234 ■ The Central California Catholic Life
The Central California Catholic Life
1550 N Fresno St.
Fresno, CA 93703-3711
Phone: (559)488-7464
Fax: (559)488-7464
Publication E-mail: srrosalie@dioceseoffresno.org
Newspaper of the Catholic Diocese of Fresno, CA. **Founded:** 1929. **Freq:** 6/year. **Print Method:** Offset. **Cols./Page:** 5. **Col. Width:** 2 inches. **Col. Depth:** 17 inches. **Key Personnel:** Rev. Jim Rude Rude, S.J., Editor. **Subscription Rates:** Free. **URL:** http://dioceseoffresno.org/index.cfm?load=page&page=258. **Formerly**: The Register. **Ad Rates:** PCI $6. **Remarks:** Accepts advertising. **Circ:** Non-paid 20000.

2235 ■ The Collegian
California State University--Fresno
MS 42
Fresno, CA 93740-0042
Phone: (559)278-5735
Fax: (559)278-2679
Publication E-mail: collegian@csufresno.edu
Collegiate newspaper. **Founded:** 1921. **Freq:** Monday, Wednesday and Friday. **Print Method:** Offset. **Cols./Page:** 5. **Col. Width:** 11 1/2 inches. **Col. Depth:** 17 1/2 inches. **Subscription Rates:** $25 Individuals. **Alt. Formats:** PDF. **URL:** http://collegian.csufresno.edu. **Formerly**: The Daily Collegian. **Ad Rates:** BW $460; PCI $6.40. **Remarks:** Color advertising not accepted. **Circ:** Free ‡3500.

2236 ■ Global Finance Journal
RELX Group P.L.C.
c/o Manuchehr Shahrokhi, Ed.
Craig School of Business
California State University
Fresno, CA 93740-0007
Fax: (559)278-4058
Publisher's E-mail: amsterdam@relx.com
Journal presenting issues relevant to the international financial scene. **Freq:** 3/year. **Key Personnel:** Philippe Jorion, Board Member; Yong Kim, Board Member; Arvind Mahajan, Board Member; Jack D. Glen, Board Member; Michael Frenkel, Board Member; Jeff Madura, Board Member; Giovanni Barone-Adesi, Board Member; R. Aggarwal, Board Member; Manuchehr Shahrokhi, Editor. **ISSN:** 1044--0283 (print). **Subscription Rates:** $137 Individuals print; $637.27 Institutions online; $697 Institutions print. **URL:** http://www.journals.elsevier.com/global-finance-journal. **Circ:** (Not Reported).

2237 ■ Journal of the Society for Armenian Studies
Society for Armenian Studies
c/o Armenian Studies Program
California State University
5245 N Backer Ave., PB4
Fresno, CA 93740-8001
Phone: (559)278-2669
Fax: (559)278-2129
Journal promoting the study of Armenia and related geographic areas, as well as contains issues related to the history and culture of Armenia. **Freq:** Annual. **ISSN:** 0747--9301 (print). **Subscription Rates:** $9.99 Individuals online. **URL:** http://societyforarmenianstudies.com/journal-of-the-society-for-armenian-studies-jsas; http://www.fresnostate.edu/artshum/armenianstudies/sas/sas-journal.html. **Remarks:** Accepts advertising. **Circ:** (Not Reported).

2238 ■ The Normal School
California State University, Fresno
California State University Fresno
5254 N Backer Ave.
M/S PB 98
Fresno, CA 93740-8001
Publication E-mail: editors@thenormalschool.com
Journal featuring nonfiction, fiction, poetry, criticism, and culinary adventure journalism. **Freq:** Semiannual spring and fall. **Key Personnel:** Steven Church, Editor; Sophie Beck, Editor, Managing Editor; Matt Roberts, Editor. **ISSN:** 1943--0760 (print). **Subscription Rates:** $12 Individuals 1 year; $24 Individuals 2 years. **URL:** http://thenormalschool.com. **Remarks:** Advertising not accepted. **Circ:** (Not Reported).

2239 ■ Philosophy in the Contemporary World
Philosophy Documentation Center
c/o Andrew Fiala, Ed.
California State University
2380 E Keats Ave.
MB 105
Fresno, CA 93740
Publisher's E-mail: order@pdcnet.org
Journal publishing peer-reviewed articles on the application of philosophy in contemporary ethical and conceptual problems. **Freq:** Biennial. **Key Personnel:** Joseph Orosco, Editor. **ISSN:** 1077-1999 (print). **Subscription Rates:** $55 Institutions; $165 Institutions online only. **URL:** http://secure.pdcnet.org/pdc/bvdb.nsf/journal?openform&journal=pdc_pcw. **Circ:** (Not Reported).

2240 ■ Pollstar
Pollstar USA
4697 W Jacquelyn Ave.
Fresno, CA 93722
Phone: (559)271-7900
Fax: (559)271-7979
Free: 800-344-7383
Publisher's E-mail: customerservice@pollstar.com
Trade magazine covering the international concert business. **Founded:** 1984. **Freq:** Weekly. **Print Method:** Offset. **Trim Size:** 8 1/2 x 11. **Key Personnel:** Gary Bongiovanni, Editor-in-Chief; Gary Smith, Chief Operating Officer; Brian Bradley, Representative, Advertising and Sales. **Subscription Rates:** $399 Individuals. **URL:** http://www.pollstarpro.com. **Ad Rates:** BW $1399. **Remarks:** Accepts advertising. **Circ:** (Not Reported).

2241 ■ Central Valley Cable
2441 N Grove Industrial Dr.
Fresno, CA 93727-1535
Free: 800-726-3212
Owner: Comcast Cable Communication, 1500 Market St., Philadelphia, PA 19102, Ph: (215)665-1700. **Founded:** 1982. **Formerly:** Northland Cable. **Key Personnel:** Andrew Baer, CIO. **Cities Served:** Chowchilla, Le Grand, Planada, Riverdale, California: subscribing households 1,800; 50 channels; 1 community access channel. **URL:** http://www.cvcca.com.

2242 ■ KALZ-FM - 96.7
83 E Shaw Ave., Ste. 150
Fresno, CA 93710
Phone: (559)230-4300
Fax: (559)243-4301
Format: Alternative/New Music/Progressive. **Key Personnel:** Jeff Negrete, Gen. Mgr., jeffnegrete@clearchannel.com; Paul Wilson, Dir. of Programs, pd@krzr.com. **Wattage**: 50,000. **Ad Rates:** Advertising accepted; rates available upon request. **URL:** http://www.alice967.com/main.html.

2243 ■ KAVT-AM - 1680
139 W Olive St.
Fresno, CA 93728
Phone: (559)499-1680
Format: Educational. **Owner:** Radio Disney, 500 S Buena Vista St. MC 7663, Burbank, CA 91521-7716. **ADI**: Fresno-Visalia (Hanford), CA.

2244 ■ KBFK-TV - 36
706 W Herndon Ave.
Fresno, CA 93650-1033
Phone: (559)435-7000
Fax: (559)435-3201
Email: info@cocolatv.com
Owner: Cocola Broadcasting Companies L.L.C., 706 W Herndon Ave., Fresno, CA 93650-1033, Ph: (559)435-7000, Fax: (559)435-3201. **Founded:** 1980. **URL:** http://www.cocolatv.com.

2245 ■ KBIF-AM - 900
2811 N Wishon Ave.
Fresno, CA 93704-5572
Phone: (559)222-0900
Fax: (559)222-1573

Circulation: ★ = AAM; △ or • = BPA; ♦ = CAC; ❑ = VAC; ⊕ = PO Statement; ‡ = Publisher's Report; Boldface figures = sworn; Light figures = estimated.

Format: Religious. **Operating Hours:** 6 a.m.-midnight. **Wattage:** 1,000. **Ad Rates:** Advertising accepted; rates available upon request. **URL:** http://900kbif.com/.

2246 ■ KBOS-FM - 94.9
83 E Shaw Ave., Ste. 150
Fresno, CA 93710
Phone: (559)230-4300
Format: Top 40; Hip Hop; Blues; Urban Contemporary. **Networks:** ABC. **Owner:** iHeartMedia Inc., 200 E Basse Rd., San Antonio, TX 78209, Ph: (210)832-3314. **Operating Hours:** Continuous. **ADI:** Fresno-Visalia (Hanford), CA. **Key Personnel:** Tony Rainaldi, Contact, tonyrainaldi@iheartmedia.com; David Abenojar, Promotions Dir. **Wattage:** 16,500. **Ad Rates:** $50-100 per unit. **URL:** http://www.b95forlife.com//main.html.

2247 ■ KBTI-TV - 41
706 W Herndon Ave.
Fresno, CA 93650
Phone: (559)435-7000
Fax: (559)435-3201
Email: info@cocolatv.com
Owner: Cocola Broadcasting Companies L.L.C., 706 W Herndon Ave., Fresno, CA 93650-1033, Ph: (559)435-7000, Fax: (559)435-3201. **URL:** http://www.cocolatv.com.

2248 ■ KCBL-AM - 1340
83 E Shaw Ave., Ste. 150
Fresno, CA 93710
Phone: (559)230-4300
Fax: (559)243-4301
Format: Sports. **ADI:** Fresno-Visalia (Hanford), CA. **Key Personnel:** Jeff Negrete, Gen. Mgr. **Wattage:** 1,000. **Ad Rates:** Noncommercial. **URL:** http://www.foxsportsradio1340.com//main.html.

2249 ■ KCWB-TV - 13
706 W Herndon Ave.
Fresno, CA 93650
Phone: (559)435-7000
Fax: (559)435-3201
Email: info@cocolatv.com
Owner: Cocola Broadcasting Companies L.L.C., 706 W Herndon Ave., Fresno, CA 93650-1033, Ph: (559)435-7000, Fax: (559)435-3201. **URL:** http://www.cocolatv.com.

2250 ■ KEYQ-AM - 980
PO Box 500
Camarillo, CA 93011
Phone: (805)482-4797
Fax: (805)388-5202
Free: 800-260-5676
Email: info@nuevavida.com
Format: Hispanic; Religious. **Simulcasts:** KMRO. **Networks:** Independent. **Owner:** Association for Communication Education. **Founded:** 1957. **Formerly:** KEAP-AM. **Operating Hours:** Continuous. **ADI:** Fresno-Visalia (Hanford), CA. **Key Personnel:** Mary Guthrie, Gen. Mgr. **Wattage:** 500. **Ad Rates:** Noncommercial. **URL:** http://www.nuevavida.com.

2251 ■ KEZL-FM - 96.7
83 E Shaw Ave., Ste. 150
Fresno, CA 93710
Phone: (918)664-4581
Format: News; Sports; Talk. **Networks:** Independent. **Owner:** Clear Channel Communications Inc., at above address, Ph: (210)822-2828, Fax: (210)822-2299. **Formerly:** KTED-FM. **Operating Hours:** 12:00 a.m. - 10:00 p.m. Monday - Sunday. **Key Personnel:** Jeff Negrete, Gen. Mgr.; JAY Weidenheimer, Dir. of Programs. **Wattage:** 25,000. **Ad Rates:** Advertising accepted; rates available upon request. **URL:** http://powertalk967.iheart.com.

2252 ■ KFAZ-TV - 8
706 W Herndon Ave.
Fresno, CA 93650
Phone: (559)255-0039
Fax: (559)435-3201
Owner: Cocola Broadcasting Companies L.L.C., 706 W Herndon Ave., Fresno, CA 93650-1033, Ph: (559)435-7000, Fax: (559)435-3201. **URL:** http://www.kmsgtv.com.

2253 ■ KFCF-FM - 88.1
1449 N Wishon
Fresno, CA 93728
Phone: (559)233-2221
Fax: (559)233-5776
Format: Eclectic. **Networks:** Pacifica. **Owner:** Fresno Free College Foundation, at above address. **Founded:** 1975. **Operating Hours:** Continuous; 85% network, 15% local. **ADI:** Fresno-Visalia (Hanford), CA. **Key Personnel:** Rychard Withers, Contact, rwithers@kfcf.org; Rebecca Caraveo, Contact, becky@kfcf.org; Frank Delgado, Contact, frankd@kfcf.org. **Wattage:** 2,400. **Ad Rates:** Noncommercial. **Mailing address:** PO Box 4364, Fresno, CA 93728. **URL:** http://www.kfcf.org.

2254 ■ K56DZ - 56
PO Box A
Santa Ana, CA 92711
Phone: (714)832-2950
Free: 888-731-1000
Owner: Trinity Broadcasting Network Inc., PO Box A, Santa Ana, CA 92711, Ph: (714)832-2950, Free: 888-731-1000.

2255 ■ KFIG-AM - 1430
1415 Fulton St.
Fresno, CA 93721
Phone: (559)447-3570
Fax: (559)447-3579
Email: 1430news@1430espn.com
Format: Sports. **Founded:** 1938. **Operating Hours:** Continuous. **ADI:** Fresno-Visalia (Hanford), CA. **Key Personnel:** Kathy Simonia, Sales Mgr., kathy@1430espn.com; Drew Vertiz, Dir. of Mktg., Dir. of Operations; Paul Swearengin, Contact, paul@1430espn.com. **Wattage:** 5,000. **Ad Rates:** $38-45 for 60 seconds. **URL:** http://www.1430espn.com.

2256 ■ KFPT-AM
1415 Fulton St.
Fresno, CA 93721-1609
Phone: (559)497-5118
Format: Talk. **Owner:** CBS Radio, New York, NY, Ph: (614)249-7676, Fax: (614)249-6995. **Wattage:** 5,000 Day; 2,500 Nig. **Ad Rates:** Underwriting available.

2257 ■ KFRR-FM - 104.1
1415 Fulton St.
Fresno, CA 93721
Phone: (559)228-1041
Format: Alternative/New Music/Progressive; Album-Oriented Rock (AOR); Heavy Metal. **Wattage:** 17,000. **Ad Rates:** Advertising accepted; rates available upon request. **URL:** http://www.newrock1041.fm.

2258 ■ KFSN-TV - 30
1777 G St.
Fresno, CA 93706
Phone: (559)442-1170
Fax: (559)233-5844
Free: 800-423-3030
Format: News. **Networks:** ABC. **Owner:** ABC Inc., 77 W 66th St., New York, NY 10023, Ph: (212)456-7777, Fax: (212)456-4297. **Operating Hours:** Continuous. **ADI:** Fresno-Visalia (Hanford), CA. **Key Personnel:** Mike Carr, News Dir.; Susan Blaze, Gen. Sales Mgr., susan.blaze@abc.com. **Ad Rates:** Noncommercial. **URL:** http://www.abc30.com.

2259 ■ KFSO-FM - 92.9
83 E Shaw Ave., Ste. 150
Fresno, CA 93710
Phone: (559)230-4300
Fax: (559)243-4301
Free: 888-820-6120
Format: Hispanic; Adult Contemporary. **Founded:** 1974. **Formerly:** KONG-FM. **Operating Hours:** Continuous; 100% local. **ADI:** Fresno-Visalia (Hanford), CA. **Key Personnel:** Javier Solis, Dir. of Production. **Wattage:** 50,000. **Ad Rates:** $45-110 per unit. KBOS-FM/KRZA-FM/KCEL-AM/KROLL-AM/KALZ-FM/KEZL-FM. **URL:** http://www.lapreciosa929.com.

2260 ■ KFTV-TV - 21
3239 W Ashlan Ave.
Fresno, CA 93722
Phone: (559)222-2121
Format: Commercial TV. **Networks:** Univision. **Owner:** Univision Communications Inc., 24 Meadowland Pky., Secaucus, NJ 07094. **Founded:** 1972. **Operating Hours:** Continuous. **ADI:** Fresno-Visalia (Hanford), CA. **Ad Rates:** Advertising accepted; rates available upon request. **URL:** http://univisionfresno.univision.com.

2261 ■ KGMC-TV - 43
706 W Herndon Ave.
Fresno, CA 93650-1033
Phone: (559)435-7000
Fax: (559)435-3201
Email: info@cocolatv.com
Format: Commercial TV. **Networks:** Independent. **Owner:** Cocola Broadcasting Companies L.L.C., 706 W Herndon Ave., Fresno, CA 93650-1033, Ph: (559)435-7000, Fax: (559)435-3201. **Founded:** Sept. 1992. **Operating Hours:** Continuous. **ADI:** Fresno-Visalia (Hanford), CA. **Key Personnel:** Gary M. Cocola, CEO, President, garyc@cocolatv.com; Nick Giotto, Dir. of Sales, nickg@cocolatv.com; Federico Galindo, Gen. Mgr., fgalindo@kmsgtv.com. **Wattage:** 1,400,000. **Ad Rates:** Noncommercial. **URL:** http://www.cocolatv.com.

2262 ■ KGST-AM - 1600
3301 Barham Blvd., Ste. 200
Los Angeles, CA 90068
Phone: (323)512-2225
Fax: (323)512-2224
Format: Hispanic; Sports. **Networks:** Independent. **Owner:** Lotus Communication Corp., 3301 Barham Blvd., Ste. 200, CA 90068. **Founded:** 1949. **Operating Hours:** Continuous. **ADI:** Fresno-Visalia (Hanford), CA. **Key Personnel:** Howard A. Kalmenson, CEO, President. **Wattage:** 5,000. **Ad Rates:** $31-43 for 30 seconds; $40-54 for 60 seconds. **URL:** http://www.lotuscorp.com.

2263 ■ KHGE-FM - 102.7
83 E Shaw Ave., Ste. 150
Fresno, CA 93710
Phone: (559)230-4300
Fax: (559)243-4301
Format: Country. **ADI:** Fresno-Visalia (Hanford), CA. **Wattage:** 50,000. **URL:** http://www.1027thewolf.com.

2264 ■ KHOT-AM - 1250
3256 Penryn Rd., Ste. 100
Loomis, CA 95650-8052
Phone: (916)535-0500
Fax: (916)535-0504
Free: 888-887-7120
Format: Religious. **Owner:** Immaculate Heart Radio, 3256 Penryn Rd., Ste. 100, Loomis, CA 95650-8052. **Founded:** 2001. **Formerly:** KQMD-AM. **Operating Hours:** Continuous. **ADI:** Fresno-Visalia (Hanford), CA. **Wattage:** 500. **Ad Rates:** Advertising accepted; rates available upon request. **URL:** http://www.ihradio.com.

2265 ■ KIWB-TV - 43
706 W Herndon Ave.
Fresno, CA 93650
Phone: (559)435-7000
Fax: (559)435-3201
Email: info@cocolatv.com
Owner: Cocola Broadcasting Companies L.L.C., 706 W Herndon Ave., Fresno, CA 93650-1033, Ph: (559)435-7000, Fax: (559)435-3201. **URL:** http://www.cocolatv.com.

2266 ■ KJEO-TV - 32
706 W Herndon Ave.
Fresno, CA 93650
Phone: (559)435-7000
Fax: (559)435-3201
Email: info@cocolatv.com
Format: Commercial TV. **Networks:** CBS. **Owner:** Cocola Broadcasting Companies L.L.C., 706 W Herndon Ave., Fresno, CA 93650-1033, Ph: (559)435-7000, Fax: (559)435-3201. **Founded:** 1953. **Operating Hours:** Continuous; 68% network, 32% local. **ADI:** Fresno-Visalia (Hanford), CA. **Key Personnel:** George Takata, Contact, gtakata@cbsfresno.com. **Local Programs:** *47 On Your Side*, Monday Tuesday Wednesday Thursday Friday 9:00 p.m. **Ad Rates:** Noncommercial. **URL:** http://www.cocolatv.com.

2267 ■ KJFX-FM - 95.7
1066 E Shaw Ave.
Fresno, CA 93710
Phone: (559)230-0104
Format: Classic Rock. **Networks:** Independent. **Owner:** Wilks Broadcast Group L.L.C., 6470 E Johns Crossing, Ste. 450, Duluth, GA 30097, Ph: (678)240-8976, Fax: (678)240-8989. **Founded:** 1970. **Formerly:** KYNO-FM. **Operating Hours:** Continuous. **ADI:** Fresno-Visalia (Hanford), CA. **Wattage:** 17,500. **Ad Rates:** Advertising

accepted; rates available upon request. **URL:** http://www.957thefox.com.

2268 ■ KJKZ-TV - 27
706 W Herndon Ave.
Fresno, CA 93650
Phone: (559)435-7000
Fax: (559)435-3201
Email: info@cocolatv.com
Owner: Cocola Broadcasting Companies L.L.C., 706 W Herndon Ave., Fresno, CA 93650-1033, Ph: (559)435-7000, Fax: (559)435-3201. **Key Personnel:** Gary M. Cocola, President, CEO. **URL:** http://www.cocolatv.com.

2269 ■ KJWL-FM - 99.3
1415 Fulton Ave.
Fresno, CA 93721
Phone: (559)497-5118
Fax: (559)497-9760
Format: Big Band/Nostalgia. **Key Personnel:** John Ostlund, Owner, jostlund@kjwl.com; Layne Ryan, VP, Gen. Mgr., layne@940espnfresno.com. **Ad Rates:** Advertising accepted; rates available upon request. **URL:** http://www.kjwl.com.

2270 ■ KKBZ-FM - 105.1
1110 E Olive Ave.
Fresno, CA 93728
Phone: (559)497-1100
Fax: (559)497-1125
Format: Classic Rock. **Founded:** 1990. **Key Personnel:** John Sterling, Sales Mgr.; Kevin O'Rorke, Gen. Mgr., kororke@lotusfresno.com. **Wattage**: 600. **Ad Rates:** Advertising accepted; rates available upon request. **URL:** http://www.1051theblaze.com.

2271 ■ KKJB-TV - 39
706 W Herndon Ave.
Fresno, CA 93650
Phone: (559)435-7000
Fax: (559)435-3201
Email: info@cocolatv.com
Owner: Cocola Broadcasting Companies L.L.C., 706 W Herndon Ave., Fresno, CA 93650-1033, Ph: (559)435-7000, Fax: (559)435-3201. **URL:** http://www.cocolatv.com.

2272 ■ KLBN-FM - 101.9
1110 E Olive Ave.
Fresno, CA 93728
Phone: (559)497-1100
Fax: (559)497-1125
Format: Hispanic. **Owner:** Lotus Communications Corp., 3301 Barham Blvd., Ste. 200, Los Angeles, CA 90068, Ph: (323)512-2225, Fax: (323)512-2224. **Key Personnel:** Kevin O'Rorke, Gen. Mgr., kororke@lotusfresno.com. **Ad Rates:** Advertising accepted; rates available upon request. **URL:** http://www.1019labuena.com/pages/4150945.php?.

2273 ■ KLLE-FM - 107.9
601 W Univision Plz.
Fresno, CA 93727
Phone: (559)430-8500
Fax: (559)430-8545
Format: Hispanic. **Owner:** Univision Radio Inc., 3102 Oak Lawn Ave., Ste. 215, Dallas, TX 75219-4259, Ph: (214)525-7700, Fax: (214)525-7750. **ADI**: Fresno-Visalia (Hanford), CA. **Key Personnel:** Al Sanchez, Dir. of Programs. **URL:** http://1079fresno.univision.com.

2274 ■ KMCF-TV - 35
706 W Herndon Ave.
Fresno, CA 93650
Phone: (559)435-7000
Fax: (559)435-3201
Email: info@cocolatv.com
Owner: Cocola Broadcasting Companies L.L.C., 706 W Herndon Ave., Fresno, CA 93650-1033, Ph: (559)435-7000, Fax: (559)435-3201. **URL:** http://www.cocolatv.com.

2275 ■ KMGV-FM - 97.9
1071 W Shaw Ave.
Fresno, CA 93711
Phone: (559)490-9800
Free: 800-265-6342
Format: Oldies. **ADI**: Fresno-Visalia (Hanford), CA. **Key Personnel:** Jeff Davis, Contact; Jeff Davis, Contact. **Wattage:** 2,100. **Ad Rates:** Advertising accepted; rates available upon request. **URL:** http://www.mega979.com.

2276 ■ KMJ-AM - 580
1071 W Shaw Ave.
Fresno, CA 93711
Phone: (559)490-5800
Fax: (559)490-5878
Email: patty.hixson@cumulus.com
Format: Talk. **Networks:** CBS. **Owner:** Peak Broadcasting, at above address. **Founded:** 1925. **Operating Hours**: Continuous; 50% network, 50% local. **ADI**: Fresno-Visalia (Hanford), CA. **Key Personnel:** Patty Hixson, Gen. Mgr., patty.hixson@cumulus.com. **Wattage**: 50,000. **Ad Rates:** Advertising accepted; rates available upon request. **URL:** http://www.kmjnow.com.

2277 ■ KMPH-FM - 107.5
601 W Univision Plz.
Fresno, CA 93704
Fax: (209)255-1060
Format: News. **Networks:** CBS. **Formerly**: KCLQ-FM; KCML-FM. **Operating Hours**: Continuous. **ADI**: Fresno-Visalia (Hanford), CA. **Key Personnel:** John F. Carpenter, Exec. VP, Gen. Mgr. **Wattage**: 50,000. **Ad Rates:** Advertising accepted; rates available upon request. **URL:** http://www.univision.com/fresno/kond.

2278 ■ KMPH-TV - 26
5111 E McKinley Ave.
Fresno, CA 93727
Phone: (559)255-2600
Fax: (559)255-9626
Format: Commercial TV. **Networks:** Fox. **Owner:** Pappas Telecasting, at above address. **Founded:** 1971. **Operating Hours**: Continuous. **ADI**: Fresno-Visalia (Hanford), CA. **Ad Rates:** Advertising accepted; rates available upon request. **URL:** http://www.kmph.com.

KMPO-FM - See Modesto

2279 ■ KMSG-TV - 39
706 W Herndon Ave.
Fresno, CA 93650
Phone: (559)255-0039
Fax: (559)435-3201
Email: info@kmsgtv.com
Format: Commercial TV. **Owner:** Cocola Broadcasting Companies L.L.C., 706 W Herndon Ave., Fresno, CA 93650-1033, Ph: (559)435-7000, Fax: (559)435-3201. **Founded:** 2002. **Operating Hours**: Continuous; 85% network, 15% local. **ADI**: Fresno-Visalia (Hanford), CA. **Local Programs**: *Zona Azteca*, Friday 6:00 p.m. - 6:30 p.m. **Ad Rates:** $30-300 per unit. **URL:** http://www.kmsgtv.com.

2280 ■ KNXT-TV - 49
1550 N Fresno St.
Fresno, CA 93703
Phone: (559)488-7440
Email: knxt@pacbell.net
Format: News; Classical; Talk; Religious; Contemporary Christian; Information. **Networks:** Eternal Word TV. **Owner:** Education Corp.-Diocese of Fresno, at above address. **Founded:** 1986. **Operating Hours**: Continuous. **ADI**: Fresno-Visalia (Hanford), CA. **Wattage**: 185,000 ERP. **Ad Rates:** Noncommercial. **URL:** http://www.knxt.tv.

2281 ■ KOND-FM - 92.1
601 W Univision Plz.
Fresno, CA 93704
Phone: (559)430-8500
Format: Hispanic. **Owner:** Univision Communication Inc., 3102 Oak Lawn Ave., Ste. 215, Dallas, TX 75219, Fax: (214)525-7750. **ADI**: Fresno-Visalia (Hanford), CA. **Key Personnel:** Angela Navarrete, Gen. Mgr., VP; Jose Luis Sanchez, Promotions Dir.; Dennis Rosales, Bus. Mgr.

2282 ■ KPMC-TV - 43
2144 N Fine Ave.
Fresno, CA 93727
Phone: (559)455-5511
Owner: Cocola Broadcasting Companies L.L.C., 706 W Herndon Ave., Fresno, CA 93650-1033, Ph: (559)435-7000, Fax: (559)435-3201. **URL:** http://www.cocolatv.com.

2283 ■ KRDA-FM - 107.5
1981 N Gateway, Ste. 101
Fresno, CA 93727
Phone: (559)456-4000
Fax: (559)251-9555
Format: Hispanic; Adult Contemporary. **Owner:** Univision Communications, Inc., at above address.

2284 ■ KRZR-FM - 103.7
83 E Shaw Ave., Ste. 150
Fresno, CA 93711
Phone: (559)243-4300
Fax: (559)243-4301
Founded: 1976. **Formerly**: KMGX-FM. **Operating Hours**: Midnight - 7:00 p.m. Monday - Friday; Midnight - 6:00 p.m. Saturday; Midnight - 4:00 p.m. Sunday. **Key Personnel:** David Abenojar, Promotions Mgr.; Jeff Negrete, Gen. Mgr.; Bob Berger, Dir. of Sales; Rita Walls, Regional Mgr. **Wattage**: 9,000 ERP. **Ad Rates:** Advertising accepted; rates available upon request. **URL:** http://thebeat1037.iheart.com.

2285 ■ KSAO-TV - 49
706 W Herndon Ave.
Fresno, CA 93650
Phone: (559)435-7000
Fax: (559)435-3201
Owner: Cocola Broadcasting Companies L.L.C., 706 W Herndon Ave., Fresno, CA 93650-1033, Ph: (559)435-7000, Fax: (559)435-3201. **Key Personnel:** Jose Diaz, Production Mgr., josed@cocolatv.com; Gary M. Cocola, President, CEO, garyc@cocolatv.com. **URL:** http://www.cocolatv.com.

2286 ■ KSDI-TV - 33
706 W Herndon Ave.
Fresno, CA 93650
Phone: (559)435-7000
Fax: (559)435-3201
Format: Sports. **Owner:** Cocola Broadcasting Companies L.L.C., 706 W Herndon Ave., Fresno, CA 93650-1033, Ph: (559)435-7000, Fax: (559)435-3201. **Key Personnel:** Jose Diaz, Production Mgr., josed@cocolatv.com; Gary M. Cocola, President, CEO, garyc@cocolatv.com. **URL:** http://www.cocolatv.com.

2287 ■ KSEE-TV - 24
5035 E McKinley Ave.
Fresno, CA 93727-1964
Phone: (559)454-2424
Format: Commercial TV. **Networks:** NBC. **Owner:** Granite Broadcasting Corp., 767 3rd Ave., 34th Fl., New York, NY 10017-2083, Ph: (212)826-2530, Fax: (212)826-2858. **Founded:** 1953. **Formerly**: KMJ-TV. **Operating Hours**: Continuous; 75% network, 25% local. **ADI**: Fresno-Visalia (Hanford), CA. **Local Programs**: *KSEE 24 Hour News*, Monday Tuesday Wednesday Thursday Friday Saturday Sunday 11:00 p.m. **Ad Rates:** Advertising accepted; rates available upon request. **URL:** http://www.yourcentralvalley.com.

2288 ■ KSJV-FM - 91.5
5005 E Belmont Ave.
Fresno, CA 93727
Phone: (559)455-5777
Free: 800-509-4772
Email: info@radiobilingue.org
Format: Eclectic; Hispanic; Talk; News. **Networks:** Independent. **Owner:** Radio Bilingue, Inc., at above address. **Founded:** 1980. **Operating Hours**: 6 a.m.-1 a.m.; 90% local. **Key Personnel:** Hugo Morales, Exec. Dir. **Wattage**: 16,000. **Ad Rates:** $20 per unit. **URL:** http://radiobilingue.org.

2289 ■ KSKS-FM - 93.7
1071 W Shaw Ave.
Fresno, CA 93711
Phone: (559)490-5800
Fax: (559)490-5878
Free: 800-767-5477
Format: Country. **Networks:** CBS. **Owner:** Peak Broadcasting, at above address. **Founded:** 1946. **Operating Hours**: Continuous; 100% local. **ADI**: Fresno-Visalia (Hanford), CA. **Key Personnel:** Karen Franz, Gen. Mgr.; Lori Garcia, Dir. of Mktg. **Wattage**: 68,000. **Ad Rates:** Advertising accepted; rates available upon request. **URL:** http://www.ksks.com.

2290 ■ KSOF-FM - 98.9
83 E Shaw Ave., Ste. 150
Fresno, CA 93710
Phone: (559)230-4300
Fax: (559)243-4301
Format: Soft Rock. **Networks:** Independent. **Founded:** 1975. **Formerly**: KOJY-FM; KJOI-FM. **Operating Hours**:

Circulation: ★ = AAM; △ or • = BPA; ♦ = CAC; ❑ = VAC; ⊕ = PO Statement; ‡ = Publisher's Report; Boldface figures = sworn; Light figures = estimated.

Continuous. **ADI**: Fresno-Visalia (Hanford), CA. **Key Personnel**: Mike Brady, Dir. of Programs, michaelbrady@clearchannel.com. **Wattage**: 19,000. **Ad Rates**: Noncommercial. KEZL-FM, KFSO-FM, KROLL-AM, KCBL-AM/KBOS-FM/KRZR-FM/KALZ-FM. **URL**: http://www.softrock989.com.

2291 ■ KSXY-FM - 101.1
1071 W Shaw Ave.
Fresno, CA 93711
Phone: (209)247-5867
Fax: (209)268-1289
Free: 800-345-9101
Format: Music of Your Life; News. **Simulcasts**: KFIG-AM. **Networks**: Independent. **Founded**: 1963. **Formerly**: KFIG-FM. **Operating Hours**: Continuous. **ADI**: Fresno-Visalia (Hanford), CA. **Key Personnel**: Ron Ostlund, Gen. Mgr.; Diane Maze-Ostlund, Station Mgr.; Steve Randall, Operations Mgr. **Wattage**: 10,000 ERP. **Ad Rates**: Accepts Advertising. **URL**: http://www.y101hits.com.

2292 ■ KTHT-FM - 102.7
83 E Shaw Ave., Ste. 150
Fresno, CA 93711
Phone: (209)294-1234
Fax: (209)294-7931
Format: Country. **Networks**: Independent. **Owner**: WP Radio Corp., 427 Bedford Rd. #330, Pleasantville, NY 10570, Ph: (914)741-1133. **Formerly**: KKNU-FM. **Operating Hours**: Continuous Monday - Friday, Sunday; 12:00 a.m. - 9:00 p.m. Saturday. **ADI**: Fresno-Visalia (Hanford), CA. **Key Personnel**: Chris Pachelo, Gen. Mgr.; Jeff Negrete, Sales Mgr; Leah Shapiro, Contact. **Wattage**: 50,000. **Ad Rates**: Accepts Advertising. **URL**: http://1027thewolf.iheart.com.

2293 ■ KTRB-AM - 860
5111 E Mckinley Ave.
Fresno, CA 93727
Phone: (510)713-1100
Fax: (510)897-1451
Format: News. **Owner**: Pappas Radio of Fresno, LLC, 500 S Chinawth, Visalia, CA 93277, Ph: (559)733-7800, Fax: (559)733-7878. **Founded**: 1933. **Operating Hours**: Continuous. **ADI**: San Francisco-Oakland-San Jose. **Wattage**: 50,000 ERP. **Ad Rates**: $25-100 per unit. **URL**: http://860amtheanswer.com/.

2294 ■ KVBL-AM - 1400
83 E Shaw Ave., Ste. 150
Fresno, CA 93710
Phone: (918)664-4581
Format: Sports. **ADI**: Fresno-Visalia (Hanford), CA. **Wattage**: 1,000. **Ad Rates**: Noncommercial. **URL**: http://www.powertalk967.com.

2295 ■ KVHF-TV - 4
706 W Herndon Ave.
Fresno, CA 93650
Phone: (559)435-7000
Fax: (559)435-3201
Owner: Cocola Broadcasting Companies L.L.C., 706 W Herndon Ave., Fresno, CA 93650-1033, Ph: (559)435-7000, Fax: (559)435-3201. **Key Personnel**: Gary M. Cocola, President, CEO, garyc@cocolatv.com; Jose Diaz, Production Mgr., josed@cocolatv.com. **URL**: http://www.cocolatv.com.

2296 ■ KVPR-FM - 89.3
3437 W Shaw Ave Ste. 101
Fresno, CA 93711
Phone: (559)275-0764
Fax: (559)275-2202
Free: 800-275-0764
Email: kvpr@kvpr.org
Format: Public Radio. **Key Personnel**: Joe Garcia, Div. Dir., jgarcia@kvpr.org; John English, Div. Mgr., jenglish@kvpr.org; Mariam Stepanian, Gen. Mgr., President, mariam@kvpr.org; Don Weaver, Production Mgr., dweaver@kvpr.org; Joe Moore, Dir. of Programs, jmoore@kvpr.org. **Ad Rates**: Noncommercial. **URL**: http://www.kvpr.org.

2297 ■ KVPT-TV - 18
1544 Van Ness Ave.
Fresno, CA 93721
Phone: (559)266-1800
Fax: (559)650-1880
Free: 800-801-6500
Format: Public TV. **Networks**: Public Broadcasting Service (PBS). **Owner**: Valley Public Television Inc., 1544 Van Ness Ave., Fresno, CA 93721, Ph: (559)266-1800, Fax: (800)801-6500. **Founded**: 1977. **Formerly**: KMTF-TV. **Operating Hours**: Continuous. **ADI**: Fresno-Visalia (Hanford), CA. **Key Personnel**: Douglas Noll, Chairman; Russell Smith, V. Chmn. of the Bd. **Local Programs**: *Art of Gardening*, Tuesday 7:30 p.m.; *Los Ninos En Su Casa*, Monday Tuesday Wednesday Thursday Friday 5:00 a.m.; *A Place of Our Own*, Monday Tuesday Wednesday Thursday Friday 5:30 a.m.; *Between the Lions*, Monday Tuesday Wednesday Thursday Friday 6:00 a.m.; *Super Why!*, Monday Tuesday Wednesday Thursday Friday 8:30 a.m.; *Best of Joy of Painting*, Saturday 9:30 a.m. - 10:00 a.m.; *Rick Steves' Europe*, Saturday Tuesday 2:00 p.m. - 3:00 p.m. 7:00 p.m.; *O to 5 in 30 Minutes!*, Sunday 10:00 a.m. - 10:30 a.m.; *California's Gold*, Saturday 12:00 p.m.; 12:30 p.m.; *Victory Garden*, Saturday 10:00 a.m. - 10:30 a.m.; *Austin City Limits*, Sunday 1:30 a.m.; *In the Life*, Friday 11:30 p.m. - 12:00 a.m.; *Lawrence Welk Show*, Saturday 7:00 p.m. - 8:00 p.m.; *Keeping Up Appearances*, Saturday 8:00 p.m. - 9:00 p.m.; *As Time Goes By*, Saturday 9:00 p.m. - 10:00 p.m.; *The National Parks: America's Best Idea*, Sunday 11:30 a.m.; 1:30 p.m. **Wattage**: 1,410. **Ad Rates**: Noncommercial. Combined advertising rates available with KVIE, KIXE. **URL**: http://www.valleypbs.org.

2298 ■ KVVG-TV - 54
706 W Herndon Ave.
Fresno, CA 93650
Phone: (559)435-7000
Fax: (559)435-3201
Owner: Cocola Broadcasting Companies L.L.C., 706 W Herndon Ave., Fresno, CA 93650-1033, Ph: (559)435-7000, Fax: (559)435-3201. **Key Personnel**: Gary M. Cocola, President, CEO, garyc@cocolatv.com; Jose Diaz, Production Mgr., josed@cocolatv.com. **URL**: http://www.cocolatv.com.

2299 ■ KWRU-AM - 940
1415 Fulton St.
Fresno, CA 93721
Phone: (559)452-0940
Fax: (559)452-0948
Simulcasts: AG Show. **Founded**: 1937. **Formerly**: KFRE. **Operating Hours**: Continuous. **ADI**: Chico-Redding, CA. **Key Personnel**: Alberto Martinez, Gen. Mgr., amartinez@radioonica.com; Alberto Felix, Operations Mgr. **Wattage**: 50,000. **Ad Rates**: Advertising accepted; rates available upon request. Community events. **URL**: http://www.940espnfresno.com.

2300 ■ KWSM-TV - 40
706 W Herndon Ave.
Fresno, CA 93650
Phone: (559)435-7000
Fax: (559)435-3201
Owner: Cocola Broadcasting Companies L.L.C., 706 W Herndon Ave., Fresno, CA 93650-1033, Ph: (559)435-7000, Fax: (559)435-3201. **Key Personnel**: Gary M. Cocola, President, CEO, garyc@cocolatv.com; Jose Diaz, Production Mgr., josed@cocolatv.com. **URL**: http://www.cocolatv.com.

2301 ■ KWYE-FM - 101.1
1071 W Shaw Ave.
Fresno, CA 93711
Phone: (559)490-5800
Format: Adult Contemporary; Alternative/New Music/Progressive; Classical. **Owner**: Peak Broadcasting Radio, at above address. **Key Personnel**: Patty Hixson, Gen. Mgr., patty.hixson@cumulus.com; Lori Garcia, Sales Mgr., lori.garcia@cumulus.com; Chris Miller, Promotions Dir., chris.miller@peakbroadcasting.com. **Ad Rates**: Advertising accepted; rates available upon request. **URL**: http://www.y101hits.com.

2302 ■ KYMB-TV - 27
706 W Herndon Ave.
Fresno, CA 93650
Phone: (559)435-7000
Fax: (559)435-3201
Email: info@cocolatv.com
Owner: Cocola Broadcasting Companies L.L.C., 706 W Herndon Ave., Fresno, CA 93650-1033, Ph: (559)435-7000, Fax: (559)435-3201. **URL**: http://www.cocolatv.com.

2303 ■ KYNO-AM - 940
1415 Fulton St.
Fresno, CA 93721
Phone: (559)497-5118
Email: jostlund@kjwl.com
Format: Talk; Religious. **Operating Hours**: Continuous. **ADI**: Fresno-Visalia (Hanford), CA. **Key Personnel**: Layne Ryan, VP, Gen. Mgr.; John Ostlund, Owner. **Wattage**: 5,000. **Ad Rates**: $15-35 per unit. **URL**: http://www.kjwl.com.

2304 ■ KZAK-TV - 49
706 W Herndon Ave.
Fresno, CA 93650
Phone: (559)435-7000
Fax: (559)435-3201
Owner: Cocola Broadcasting Companies L.L.C., 706 W Herndon Ave., Fresno, CA 93650-1033, Ph: (559)435-7000, Fax: (559)435-3201. **URL**: http://www.cocolatv.com.

2305 ■ KZOL-FM - 107.9
601 W Univision Plz.
Fresno, CA 93704
Phone: (310)348-3600
Format: Hispanic. **Ad Rates**: Noncommercial. **URL**: http://www.univision.com/fresno/klle.

FULLERTON

S. CA. Orange Co. 25 mi. SE of Los Angeles. Manufactures canned fruit juices, vegetables, preserves; musical instruments, aircraft parts, missile electronics, fabricated metal, transportation equipment, textiles. Citrus fruits, walnuts packed. Oil wells. Fruit, truck farms, Oranges, lemons.

2306 ■ Autism File
Autism File
1816 W Houston Ave.
Fullerton, CA 92833
Publisher's E-mail: info@autismfile.com
Journal covering all aspects of autism. **Freq**: Quarterly. **Key Personnel**: Polly Tommey, Editor-in-Chief. **Subscription Rates**: $24 Individuals; $34 Canada. **URL**: http://www.autismfile.com. **Circ**: (Not Reported).

2307 ■ Inside Hope
Hope International University Alumni Association
2500 Nutwood Ave.
Fullerton, CA 92831
Phone: (714)879-3901
Fax: (714)681-7450
Free: 888-352-HOPE
Magazine containing topics regarding spiritual aspect of the students, alumni, faculty, staff and friends of the University. **Subscription Rates**: Free. **Alt. Formats**: PDF. **URL**: http://www.hiu.edu/news/publications/. **Remarks**: Advertising not accepted. **Circ**: (Not Reported).

2308 ■ Red Hat Society LifeStyle
The Red Hat Society Inc.
431 S Acacia Ave.
Fullerton, CA 92831
Phone: (714)738-0001
Fax: (714)738-0005
Free: 866-386-2850
Publisher's E-mail: info@redhatsociety.com
Freq: Bimonthly. **Remarks**: Advertising not accepted. **Circ**: (Not Reported).

2309 ■ TTOS Order Board
Toy Train Operating Society
PO Box 6710
Fullerton, CA 92834-6710
Phone: (714)449-9391
Fax: (714)449-9631
Publisher's E-mail: ttos@ttos.org
Magazine that contains articles on operating and repairing trains or on special collections or pieces acquired. **Freq**: Bimonthly. **Subscription Rates**: Included in membership. **URL**: http://www.ttos.org/publications. **Remarks**: Accepts display advertising. **Circ**: (Not Reported).

2310 ■ KBPK-FM - 90.1
321 E Chapman Ave.
Fullerton, CA 92832
Phone: (714)992-7419
Fax: (714)447-4097
Format: Adult Contemporary. **Owner**: Buena Park School District, 6885 Orangethorpe Ave., Buena Park,

CA 90620, Ph: (714)522-8412. **Founded:** 1970. **Operating Hours:** Continuous. **Key Personnel:** Peg Stewart Donahoe, Dir. of Programs; Edward Ford, Operations Mgr.; Steve Hassler, Sports Dir. **Wattage:** 019. **Ad Rates:** Noncommercial. **URL:** http://kbpk-fm.com.

2311 ■ VNFM-FM - 96.1
PO Box 2468
Fullerton, CA 92837
Phone: (714)533-2278
Email: radio@tinlanh.org
Format: Religious; Gospel. **Founded:** 1988. **Ad Rates:** Advertising accepted; rates available upon request. **URL:** http://www.tinlanh.org.

GALT

NC CA. Sacramento Co. 26 mi. S. of Sacramento. Condensed milk factory. Winery. Seed mill. Dairying. Stock, poultry farms. Grain. Ladino clover.

2312 ■ The Galt Herald
Herburger Publications Inc.
604 N Lincoln Way
Galt, CA 95632
Phone: (209)745-1551
Fax: (209)745-4402
Community newspaper. **Freq:** Weekly (Wed.). **Print Method:** Offset. **Trim Size:** 12 1/2 x 22 1/2. **Cols./Page:** 6. **Col. Depth:** 21 inches. **Key Personnel:** David Herburger, Publisher; Roy Herburger, President; Rachael Ackerman, Editor. **Subscription Rates:** $14 Individuals 6 months; $20 Individuals one year; $36 Two years. **URL:** http://www.galtheraldonline.com. **Ad Rates:** BW $1008; 4C $1303; SAU $8. **Remarks:** Accepts advertising. **Circ:** Paid ■ **3499**.

2313 ■ Laguna Citizen
Herburger Publications Inc.
604 N Lincoln Way
Galt, CA 95632
Phone: (209)745-1551
Fax: (209)745-4402
Community newspaper. **Freq:** Weekly (Thurs.). **Trim Size:** 12 1/2 x 22 1/2. **Cols./Page:** 6. **Col. Depth:** 294 agate lines. **Key Personnel:** Roy Herburger, President; David Herburger, Publisher; Jim O'Donnell, Director, Advertising. **Subscription Rates:** Free. **Remarks:** Accepts advertising. **Circ:** (Not Reported).

2314 ■ River Valley Times
Herburger Publications Inc.
604 N Lincoln Way
Galt, CA 95632
Phone: (209)745-1551
Fax: (209)745-4402
Newspaper featuring news section, classifieds and more. **URL:** http://www.herburger.net. **Remarks:** Accepts advertising. **Circ:** (Not Reported).

GARBERVILLE

NW CA. Humboldt Co. 22 mi. N. of Bridgeville. Residential.

2315 ■ K201HL-FM - 88.1
PO Box 391
Twin Falls, ID 83303
Fax: (208)736-1958
Free: 800-357-4226
Format: Religious; Contemporary Christian. **Owner:** CSN International, PO Box 391, Twin Falls, ID 83303, Ph: (208)736-1958, Fax: (208)736-1958, Free: 800-357-4226. **URL:** http://www.csnradio.com.

2316 ■ Wave Broadband
615 Bear Creek Rd.
Garberville, CA 95542
Free: 866-928-3123
Email: customerservice@wavebroadband.com
Owner: Wave Broadband, 401 Kirkland Parkplace, Suite 500, Kirkland, WA 98033, Ph: (425)576-8200, Fax: (425)576-8221. **Cities Served:** Auburn, Benbow, Colfax, Lincoln, Rocklin, California: subscribing households 900; Hickman Air Force Base, HI.; 75 channels; 1 community access channel. **Postal Areas Served:** 95677; 95648; 95713; 95603; 95542. **URL:** http://www.wavebroadband.com.

GARDEN GROVE

S. CA. Orange Co. 4 mi. E. of Long Beach. Residential. Citrus fruit, beans packed. Chili and rubber products manufactured. Agriculture. Oranges, walnuts, chili peppers, beans.

2317 ■ RFVN-FM
12755 Brookhurst St., Ste. 104
Garden Grove, CA 92840
Phone: (714)636-9514
Fax: (714)639-9997
URL: http://rfvn.tk.

2318 ■ Time Warner Cable - Orange County
11935 Valley View St.
Garden Grove, CA 92845
Free: 888-892-2253
Founded: 1973. **Key Personnel:** Glenn A. Brit, CEO, Chairman. **Cities Served:** 200 channels. **URL:** http://www.timewarnercable.com.

GARDENA

S. CA. Los Angeles Co. 15 mi. S. of Los Angeles. Plastics, trailers, fishing tackle, poultrymen's equipment, drugs, feed, furniture, bricks, soap, glass, aircraft parts, chemicals, oil tools, electronics.

2319 ■ Audrey: The Asian American Women's Lifestyle Magazine
Audrey Magazine
17000 S Vermont Ave., Ste. A
Gardena, CA 90247
Phone: (310)769-4913
Fax: (310)769-4903
Publisher's E-mail: marketing@audreymagazine.com
Magazine offers lifestyle, entertainment and fashion articles geared toward Asian-American women. **Freq:** Quarterly. **Key Personnel:** James Y. Ryu, Publisher, Chief Executive Officer; Anna M. Park, Editor-in-Chief. **Subscription Rates:** $9.95 Individuals. **URL:** http://audreymagazine.com. **Remarks:** Accepts advertising. **Circ:** (Not Reported).

2320 ■ Gardena Valley News
Gardena Valley News
16417 S W Ave.
Gardena, CA 90247-4635
Phone: (310)329-6351
Fax: (310)329-7501
Free: 800-329-6351
Community newspaper. **Freq:** Weekly (Thurs.). **Print Method:** Offset. **Trim Size:** 14 x 22 3/4. **Cols./Page:** 6. **Col. Width:** 26 nonpareils. **Col. Depth:** 294 agate lines. **Key Personnel:** Gary Kohatsu, Editor. **URL:** http://www.gardenavalleynews.org. **Remarks:** Advertising accepted; rates available upon request. **Circ:** Paid ‡5700.

2321 ■ GMC Directions: An Official General Motors Magazine
GP Sandy
7777 Center Ave., Ste. 550
Gardena, CA 90248
Fax: (248)729-4701
Free: 800-733-4739
Publisher's E-mail: info@sandycorp.com
Consumer magazine covering news for owners of General Motors GMC automobiles. **Freq:** Triennial. **Print Method:** Web offset. **Trim Size:** 8 1/8 x 10 3/4. **Key Personnel:** Jim Bigley, Editor. **Ad Rates:** 4C $22800. **Remarks:** Accepts advertising. **Circ:** Non-paid 850000.

2322 ■ Latin Beat Magazine: Latin Beat
Latin Beat Magazine
2722 W 146th St.
Gardena, CA 90249
Phone: (310)404-3353
Fax: (310)532-6784
Publication E-mail: info@latinbeatmagazine.com
Consumer magazine covering Latin and world music. **Freq:** 10/yr. **Trim Size:** 8 1/2 x 11. **Cols./Page:** 2. **Key Personnel:** Rudolph Mangual, Editor-in-Chief, Publisher; Yvette Mangual, Art Director, Publisher. **URL:** http://www.latinbeatmagazine.com. **Remarks:** Accepts advertising. **Circ:** Combined 50,000.

2323 ■ Right of Way
International Right of Way Association
19210 S Vermont Ave.
Bldg. A, Ste. 100
Gardena, CA 90248
Phone: (310)538-0233
Fax: (310)538-1471
Free: 888-340-4792
Publisher's E-mail: info@irwaonline.org
Trade magazine offering technical articles on right of way management and acquisition, real estate appraisal, and property management. **Freq:** Bimonthly. **Print Method:** Offset. **Trim Size:** 8 1/2 x 11. **Cols./Page:** 3. **Col. Width:** 28 nonpareils. **Col. Depth:** 133 agate lines. **ISSN:** 0035--5275 (print). **USPS:** 466-080. **Subscription Rates:** $30 U.S.; $40 Canada; $48 Individuals outside North America. **URL:** http://www.irwaonline.org/eweb/DynamicPage.aspx?WebCode=Magazine. **Ad Rates:** BW $1000. **Remarks:** Accepts advertising. **Circ:** ‡9000, 7000.

GEORGETOWN

EC CA. El Dorado Co. 40 mi. NE of Sacramento. Tourism. Forestry. Vinyards. Agriculture.

2324 ■ The Anvil's Ring
Artist-Blacksmith's Association of North America
Sebastian Publishing
6690 Wentworth Spring Rd.
Georgetown, CA 95634
Phone: (530)333-2687
Fax: (530)333-2689
Publication E-mail: rob@sebastianpublishing.com
Trade magazine for blacksmiths. **Freq:** Quarterly. **Key Personnel:** Valerie Ostenak, Editor. **ISSN:** 0889--177X (print). **Subscription Rates:** Included in membership. **URL:** http://www.abana.org/publications/ar/index.shtml. **Mailing address:** PO Box 1849, Georgetown, CA 95634. **Ad Rates:** BW $815; 4C $1400. **Remarks:** Accepts advertising. **Circ:** Paid 4574.

2325 ■ KFOK-FM - 95.1
PO Box 4238
Georgetown, CA 95634
Phone: (530)333-4335
Fax: (732)364-3253
Free: 800-526-2163
Email: events@kfok.org
Format: Full Service; Eclectic; Reggae; Jazz; Blues; Oldies; Album-Oriented Rock (AOR). **Founded:** Dec. 04, 2000. **Operating Hours:** Continuous. **Ad Rates:** Advertising accepted; rates available upon request. **URL:** http://www.kfok.org.

GILROY

W. CA. Santa Clara Co. 29 mi. S. of San Jose. Fruit drying, fruit and vegetable canning; wineries, nurseries. Agriculture.

2326 ■ Amador Ledger-Dispatch
MainStreet Media Group L.L.C.
6400 Monterey Rd.
Gilroy, CA 95020
Phone: (408)842-6400
Community newspaper. **Freq:** Weekly (Fri.). **Print Method:** Offset. **Cols./Page:** 6. **Col. Width:** 18 nonpareils. **Col. Depth:** 301 agate lines. **Key Personnel:** Jack Mitchell, Publisher. **Subscription Rates:** $125 Individuals by mail. **Remarks:** Accepts advertising. **Circ:** Free ■ **29**, Paid ■ **5191**, Combined ■ **5220**.

2327 ■ Clout Magazine
Clout Magazine
PO Box 659
Gilroy, CA 95021-0659
Phone: (408)762-8624
Publication E-mail: info@cloutonline.com
Lifestyle magazine specializing in graffiti art in the United States. **Trim Size:** 8.375 x 10.875. **Key Personnel:** Roger Gastman, Editor. **URL:** http://www.cloutonline.com. **Circ:** (Not Reported).

2328 ■ The Dispatch
The Gilroy Dispatch
6400 Monterey Rd.
Gilroy, CA 95020
Phone: (408)842-6400
Fax: (408)842-7105
Local newspaper. **Founded:** 1868. **Freq:** Daily (morn.). **Print Method:** Offset. **Trim Size:** 22 1/2 x 13 1/2. **Cols./Page:** 6. **Col. Width:** 26 nonpareils. **Col. Depth:** 301 agate lines. **Key Personnel:** Jeff Mitchell, Publisher. **Subscription Rates:** $45 Individuals. **URL:** http://www.gilroydispatch.com. **Mailing address:** PO Box 516, Gilroy, CA 95021. **Ad Rates:** GLR $1.27; BW $1,238.47;

Circulation: ★ = AAM; △ or • = BPA; ♦ = CAC; ❑ = VAC; ⊕ = PO Statement; ‡ = Publisher's Report; Boldface figures = sworn; Light figures = estimated.

PCI $9.60. **Remarks:** Accepts advertising. **Circ:** Mon.-Fri. ★**4233**.

2329 ■ The Free Lance
MainStreet Media Group L.L.C.
6400 Monterey Rd.
Gilroy, CA 95020
Phone: (408)842-6400
General newspaper. **Freq:** Daily (eve.). **Print Method:** Offset. **Cols./Page:** 6. **Col. Width:** 25 nonpareils. **Col. Depth:** 302 agate lines. **Key Personnel:** Kollin Kosmicki, Editor, phone: (831)637-5566. **Subscription Rates:** $17.55 Individuals three months (newspaper carrier); $35 Individuals six months (newspaper carrier); $65 Individuals one year (newspaper carrier); $55 Individuals six months (US postal carrier); $100 Individuals one year (US postal carrier). **URL:** http://www.sanbenitocountytoday.com. **Remarks:** Advertising accepted; rates available upon request. **Circ:** (Not Reported).

2330 ■ La Jolla Light
MainStreet Media Group L.L.C.
6400 Monterey Rd.
Gilroy, CA 95020
Phone: (408)842-6400
Local newspaper. **Freq:** Weekly (Thurs.). **Print Method:** Offset. **Trim Size:** 13 x 21 1/2. **Cols./Page:** 6. **Col. Width:** 2 1/16 inches. **Col. Depth:** 21 1/2 inches. **Key Personnel:** Phyllis Pfeiffer, Vice President, General Manager, phone: (858)875-5940; Douglas F. Manchester, Publisher. **URL:** http://www.lajollalight.com. **Remarks:** Advertising accepted; rates available upon request. **Circ:** Combined ■ **18080**.

GLENDALE

S. CA. Los Angeles Co. 7 mi. N. of Los Angeles. Manufactures airplanes, aircraft engines, parachutes, lubricating oils, cameras, glass, clay and plastic products, pharmaceuticals, display signs, cleaning compounds, beverages, optical instruments. Dairying.

2331 ■ Computer Graphics World
PennWell Corp., Advanced Technology Div.
c/o Karen Moltenbrey, Ed.-in-Ch.
620 W Elk Ave.
Glendale, CA 91204
Publication reporting on the use of modeling, animation, and multimedia in the areas of science and engineering, art and entertainment, and presentation and training. **Founded:** Jan. 1978. **Freq:** Monthly. **Print Method:** Offset. Uses mats. **Trim Size:** 8 x 10 3.4. **Cols./Page:** 3 and 2. **Col. Width:** 26 and 39 nonpareils. **Col. Depth:** 140 agate lines. **Key Personnel:** Karen Moltenbrey, Editor-in-Chief. **Subscription Rates:** $68 Individuals; $90 Canada; $105 Other countries; $126 Two years; $178 Canada 2 years; $205 Other countries 2 years; $12 Single issue. **URL:** http://www.cgw.com. **Ad Rates:** BW $7,905; 4C $9,565. **Remarks:** Accepts advertising. **Circ:** (Not Reported).

2332 ■ Cumulative Index to Nursing & Allied Health Literature Print Index: The CINAHL Database
CINAHL Information Systems
1509 Wilson Ter.
Glendale, CA 91206
Phone: (818)409-8005
Fax: (818)546-5679
Free: 800-959-7167
Publisher's E-mail: cinahl@cinahl.com
Index to nursing and allied health literature. **Freq:** 3/year. **Print Method:** Offset. **Cols./Page:** 3. **Col. Width:** 27 nonpareils. **Col. Depth:** 130 agate lines. **ISSN:** 0146--5554 (print). **URL:** http://www.ebscohost.com/nursing/products/cinahl-databases. **Mailing address:** PO Box 871, Glendale, CA 91206-0871. **Remarks:** Advertising accepted; rates available upon request. **Circ:** ‡1800.

2333 ■ El Vaquero
Glendale College
1500 North Verdugo Rd.
Glendale, CA 91208
Phone: (818)240-1000
Collegiate newspaper. **Freq:** seven to eight times during the fall and spring semesters. **Print Method:** Offset. **Cols./Page:** 5. **Col. Width:** 22 nonpareils. **Col. Depth:** 217 agate lines. **Key Personnel:** Mike Eberts, Advisor. **URL:** http://www.elvaq.com; http://issuu.com/el_vaquero. **Ad Rates:** PCI $5.35. **Remarks:** Accepts advertising. **Circ:** Free ‡3500.

2334 ■ Pilot Getaways: The Magazine for Backcountry Aviation Enthusiasts
Airventure Publishing L.L.C.
PO Box 550
Glendale, CA 91209-0550
Phone: (818)241-1890
Fax: (818)241-1895
Free: 877-745-6849
Publication E-mail: info@pilotgetaways.com
Magazine for back country, bush, and mountain flying. **Freq:** Bimonthly. **Key Personnel:** John T. Kounis, Editor; Rick Vachon, Director, Advertising; George A. Kounis, Publisher. **ISSN:** 1523-6412 (print). **Subscription Rates:** $19.95 Individuals; $33.95 Individuals two years; $44.95 Individuals three years. **URL:** http://www.pilotgetaways.com/; http://www.northernpilot.com. **Formed by the merger of:** Northern Pilot Magazine. **Remarks:** Accepts advertising. **Circ:** Paid 15000.

2335 ■ The REACTer
REACT International
PO Box 21064
Glendale, CA 91221
Phone: (301)316-2900
Fax: (800)608-9755
Publisher's E-mail: info@goreact.org
ISSN: 1055--9167 (print). **Subscription Rates:** accessible only to members. **URL:** http://reactintl.org/forums/viewforum.php?f=12. **Remarks:** Accepts advertising. **Circ:** (Not Reported).

2336 ■ Weekend Balita
Balita Media Inc.
520 E Wilson Ave., Ste. 210
Glendale, CA 91206
Phone: (818)552-4503
Fax: (818)550-7635
Publication E-mail: editor@balita.com
Community newspaper for a Filipino audience. **Freq:** Weekly (Sat.). **Key Personnel:** Rhony Laigo, Editor; Gary Escarilla, Manager, Sales; Luchie Mendoza Allen, Publisher. **URL:** http://www.balita.com/weekend-balita-digital-edition. **Remarks:** Accepts advertising. **Circ:** 80000.

2337 ■ KFSH-FM - 95.9
PO Box 29023
Glendale, CA 91209
Phone: (714)796-4458
Free: 866-347-4959
Format: Contemporary Christian. **Owner:** Salem Media Group Inc., 4880 Santa Rosa Rd., Camarillo, CA 93012, Ph: (805)987-0400, Fax: (805)384-4520. **Ad Rates:** Advertising accepted; rates available upon request. **URL:** http://www.thefishla.com.

2338 ■ KKLA-AM - 99.5
PO Box 29023
Glendale, CA 91209
Phone: (818)956-5552
Format: Religious. **Networks:** Independent. **Owner:** Salem Media Group Inc., 4880 Santa Rosa Rd., Camarillo, CA 93012, Ph: (805)987-0400, Fax: (805)384-4520. **Founded:** 1947. **Operating Hours:** Continuous. **Wattage:** 1,000. **Ad Rates:** Advertising accepted; rates available upon request. **URL:** http://www.kkla.com.

2339 ■ KKLA-FM - 99.5
PO Box 29023
Glendale, CA 91209
Phone: (818)956-5552
Format: Religious. **Networks:** Independent. **Owner:** Salem Media Group Inc., 4880 Santa Rosa Rd., Camarillo, CA 93012, Ph: (805)987-0400, Fax: (805)384-4520. **Founded:** 1985. **Operating Hours:** Continuous. **Key Personnel:** Katherine Worthington, Contact, katherine@kkla.com; Jim Governale, Contact, jim@jimgovernale.com. **Local Programs:** *The Frank Sontag Show*, Monday Tuesday Wednesday Thursday Friday 4:00 p.m. - 6:00 p.m. **Wattage:** 30,000. **Ad Rates:** Advertising accepted; rates available upon request. **URL:** http://www.kkla.com.

2340 ■ KSCA-FM - 101.9
655 N Central Ave., Ste. 2500
Glendale, CA 91203-1447
Phone: (818)500-4500
Fax: (818)500-4580
Format: Hispanic. **Networks:** Univision. **Owner:** Univision Radio Inc., 3102 Oak Lawn Ave., Ste. 215, Dallas, TX 75219-4259, Ph: (214)525-7700, Fax: (214)525-7750. **Founded:** 1951. **Operating Hours:** Continuous. **Wattage:** 4,800 ERP. **Ad Rates:** Accepts Advertising.

GLENDORA

S. CA. Los Angeles Co. 12 mi. NW of Pomona. Residential. Light industry.

2341 ■ National Dragster
National Hot Rod Association
2035 Financial Way
Glendora, CA 91741
Phone: (626)914-4761
Fax: (626)963-5360
Publisher's E-mail: nhra@nhra.com
Freq: Weekly (Fri.) Weekly. **Print Method:** Offset. **Trim Size:** 10 x 12. **Cols./Page:** 4. **Col. Width:** 13 picas. **Col. Depth:** 12.5 inches. **Key Personnel:** Lorraine Vestal, Managing Editor; Juan Torres, Managing Editor; Steve Waldron, Senior Editor; Kevin McKenna, Senior Editor; Jeff Morton, Director, Advertising; Phil Burgess, Editor; Adriane Ridder, Vice President. **ISSN:** 0466--2199 (print). **Subscription Rates:** Included in membership. **URL:** http://www.nhra.com/nhra101/join.aspx; http://www.nationaldragster.net. **Ad Rates:** BW $3472; 4C $4663. **Remarks:** Accepts advertising. **Circ:** Paid ‡82666, Non-paid ‡2627, 80000.

2342 ■ OCB Tracker: California's Native news
OCB Tracker
657 E Arrow Hwy., Ste. M
Glendora, CA 91740
Phone: (626)914-0306
Publisher's E-mail: pixelpicks@ocbtracker.com
Community newspaper. **Remarks:** Accepts advertising. **Circ:** Combined 10000.

GOLETA

SW CA. Santa Barbara Co. 7 mi. W. of Santa Barbara. Research development. Manufactures electric measuring instruments, test equipment, electronic components accessories. Avocados, Lemons. Grapes and pickles.

2343 ■ CSA Journal
Cymbidium Society of America
c/o Stanley Fuelscher, Secretary
5710 Hollister Ave., No. 270
Goleta, CA 93117-3421
Journal featuring information related to the growth or advanced growth of Cymbidiums, Paphiopedilums and other cool-growing orchids. **Freq:** Bimonthly. **ISSN:** 1541--5341 (print). **Subscription Rates:** Included in membership. **URL:** http://www.cymbidium.org/csa-journals. **Remarks:** Accepts advertising. **Circ:** (Not Reported).

2344 ■ Origin and Design
Access Research Network
7668 Dartmoor Ave.
Goleta, CA 93117
Phone: (805)448-9505
Journal containing articles that examine theories of origins, their philosophical foundations, and their bearing on culture and all aspects of the idea of design. **Freq:** Periodic. **ISSN:** 0748--9919 (print). **Subscription Rates:** $5 Individuals per back issue (add $1.50 shipping and handling). **URL:** http://www.arn.org/odesign/odesign.htm. **Remarks:** Advertising not accepted. **Circ:** (Not Reported).

2345 ■ KPMR-TV - 38
7000 Hollister Ave.
Goleta, CA 93117
Phone: (805)685-3800
Fax: (805)685-6892
Owner: Entravision Communications Corporation, 2425 Olympic Blvd., Ste. 6000 W, Santa Monica, CA 90404-4030, Ph: (310)447-3870, Fax: (310)447-3899. **Key Personnel:** Gabriel Quiroz, Gen. Mgr.; Philip C. Wilkinson, COO, President; Walter F. Ulloa, Chairman, CEO. **URL:** http://www.entravision.com.

GRANADA HILLS

2346 ■ Instinct
Instinct Publishing Inc.

11856 Balboa Blvd, Ste. 312
Granada Hills, CA 91344
Phone: (818)843-1536
Magazine featuring lifestyle information for gay men. **Freq:** Monthly. **Key Personnel:** J.R. Pratts, Publisher, phone: (818)843-1536, fax: (866)653-9823; Mike Wood, Editor-in-Chief, fax: (818)845-5490. **URL:** http://instinctmagazine.com. **Remarks:** Accepts advertising. **Circ:** (Not Reported).

2347 ■ Pilota
Ferrari Owners Club
PO Box 3671
Granada Hills, CA 91394-0671
Phone: (714)213-4775
Fax: (714)960-4262
Publisher's E-mail: info@ferrariownersclub.org
Freq: Monthly. **Key Personnel:** Tex K. Otto, Editor. **Circ:** (Not Reported).

GRANITE BAY

2348 ■ KIID-AM - 1470
8842 Quail Ln.
Granite Bay, CA 95746
Phone: (916)780-1470
Free: 877-870-5678
Format: Educational. **Owner:** Radio Disney, 500 S Buena Vista St. MC 7663, Burbank, CA 91521-7716.

GRASS VALLEY

NE CA. Nevada Co. 50 mi. NE of Sacramento. Tourism. Electronic plants, saw, planing mills, sheet metal works. Fruit shipped. Timber. Agriculture. Pears, apples, plums, dairying.

2349 ■ The Union
The Union
464 Sutton Way
Grass Valley, CA 95945
Phone: (530)273-9561
General newspaper. **Founded:** 1864. **Freq:** Mon.-Sat. (eve.). **Print Method:** Offset. **Trim Size:** 13 1/8 x 27 3/4. **Cols./Page:** 6. **Col. Width:** 24 nonpareils. **Col. Depth:** 301 agate lines. **Key Personnel:** Brian Hamilton, Editor. **Subscription Rates:** $11.95 Individuals all access, monthly (online and print); $10.50 Individuals unlimited web pass, monthly (online); $2.00 Individuals single day pass (online). **Alt. Formats:** Electronic publishing. **URL:** http://www.theunion.com. **Ad Rates:** PCI $19.50. **Remarks:** Accepts advertising. **Circ:** Mon.-Sat. ♦**13553**.

2350 ■ KNCO-AM - 830
1255 E Main St., Ste. A
Grass Valley, CA 95945
Phone: (530)272-3424
Format: News; Talk; Sports. **Networks:** ABC; CNN Radio. **Owner:** Nevada County Broadcasters, Inc., at above address, Grass Valley, CA. **Founded:** 1978. **Operating Hours**: Continuous; 50% network, 50% local. **ADI**: Sacramento-Stockton, CA. **Key Personnel:** Dave Anderson, Chmn. of the Bd; Tom Fitzsimmons, Contact, tom@knco.com. **Wattage**: 5,000. **Ad Rates:** $25-35 for 30 seconds; $30-40 for 60 seconds. KNCO-FM. **URL:** http://www.knco.com.

2351 ■ KNCO-FM - 94.1
1255 E Main St., Ste. A
Grass Valley, CA 95945
Phone: (530)272-3424
Fax: (530)272-2872
Email: psa@mystarradio.com
Format: Country. **Owner:** Nevada County Broadcasters, Inc., at above address, Grass Valley, CA. **Founded:** 1983. **Operating Hours**: Continuous. **ADI**: Sacramento-Stockton, CA. **Wattage**: 6,000. **Ad Rates:** $11-26 per unit. Combined advertising rates available with KNCO-AM. **URL:** http://www.mystarradio.com.

2352 ■ K272DX-FM - 102.3
PO Box 391
Twin Falls, ID 83303
Fax: (208)736-1958
Free: 800-357-4226
Format: Religious; Contemporary Christian. **Owner:** CSN International, PO Box 391, Twin Falls, ID 83303, Ph: (208)736-1958, Fax: (208)736-1958, Free: 800-357-4226. **Key Personnel:** Don Mills, Prog. Dir., Music Dir.; Kelly Carlson, Dir. of Engg.; Ray Gorney, Asst. Dir. **Wattage**: 010. **URL:** http://www.csnradio.com.

GREENVILLE

NE CA. Plumas Co. 150 mi. NE of Sacramento. Lumber mills. Gold mines. Summer resort. Timber. Agriculture. Hay, grain, cattle.

2353 ■ Indian Valley Record
Feather Publishing Company Inc.
PO Box 469
Greenville, CA 95947
Phone: (530)284-7800
Publication E-mail: aknadler@plumasnews.com
Newspaper serving Plumas and Lassen counties. **Freq:** Weekly (Wed.). **Print Method:** Offset. **Cols./Page:** 6. **Col. Width:** 11.0 picas. **Col. Depth:** 301 agate lines. **Key Personnel:** Alicia Knadler, Editor; Delaine Fragnoli, Managing Editor; Michael C. Taborski, Publisher. **USPS:** 775-460. **URL:** http://www.plumasnews.com. **Remarks:** Advertising accepted; rates available upon request. **Circ:** (Not Reported).

2354 ■ KPJP-FM - 89.3
3256 Penryn Rd., Ste. 100
Loomis, CA 95650-8052
Phone: (916)535-0500
Fax: (916)535-0504
Free: 888-887-7120
Format: Religious; Contemporary Christian. **Owner:** Immaculate Heart Radio, 3256 Penryn Rd., Ste. 100, Loomis, CA 95650-8052. **Founded:** 2004. **Operating Hours**: Continuous. **Ad Rates:** Noncommercial; underwriting available. **URL:** http://www.ihradio.org/stations/california-stations/kpjp-89-3-fm-greenville-ca.

GRIDLEY

N. CA. Butte Co. 70 mi. N. of Sacramento. Cannery, fruit dryer, feed mill. Diversified farming. Poultry, seeds, livestock.

2355 ■ The Gridley Herald
Gridley Area Chamber of Commerce
890 Hazel St., Ste. 14
Gridley, CA 95948
Phone: (530)846-3142
Publisher's E-mail: publisher@gridleyherald.com
Newspaper (tabloid) with Republican orientation. **Freq:** Semiweekly (Wed. and Fri.). **Print Method:** Offset. **Trim Size:** 15 x 23. **Cols./Page:** 6. **Col. Width:** 20 nonpareils. **Col. Depth:** 301 agate lines. **Key Personnel:** Lisa Van De Hey, Publisher; Rachel Marubashi, Manager, Circulation. **USPS:** 859-420. **URL:** http://www.gridleyherald.com; http://gridleyareachamber.com/?page_id=66. **Ad Rates:** GLR $.45; BW $761.10; SAU $6.75. **Remarks:** Advertising accepted; rates available upon request. **Circ:** ‡3400.

2356 ■ The Gridley Herald
The Gridley Herald
680 Washington St.
Gridley, CA 95948
Phone: (530)846-3661
Fax: (530)846-4519
Publisher's E-mail: publisher@gridleyherald.com
Newspaper (tabloid) with Republican orientation. **Freq:** Semiweekly (Wed. and Fri.). **Print Method:** Offset. **Trim Size:** 15 x 23. **Cols./Page:** 6. **Col. Width:** 20 nonpareils. **Col. Depth:** 301 agate lines. **Key Personnel:** Lisa Van De Hey, Publisher; Rachel Marubashi, Manager, Circulation. **USPS:** 859-420. **URL:** http://www.gridleyherald.com; http://gridleyareachamber.com/?page_id=66. **Ad Rates:** GLR $.45; BW $761.10; SAU $6.75. **Remarks:** Advertising accepted; rates available upon request. **Circ:** ‡3400.

GUALALA

C. CA. Mendocino Co. 130 mi. N. of San Francisco. Fort Ross Historical Park. State and county beach parks. Fishing and Lumbering.

2357 ■ Independent Coast Observer
Independent Coast Observer Inc.
PO Box 1200
Gualala, CA 95445-1200
Phone: (707)884-3501
Fax: (707)884-1710
Community newspaper (tabloid). **Freq:** Weekly (Fri.). **Print Method:** Offset. **Cols./Page:** 6. **Col. Width:** 9.5 picas. **Col. Depth:** 15 inches. **Key Personnel:** David Torres, Editor. **USPS:** 881-280. **Subscription Rates:** $55 Individuals mailed paper, online; $345 Other countries airmail. **URL:** http://www.mendonoma.com. **Ad Rates:** BW $12.00, open rate. **Remarks:** Accepts advertising. **Circ:** ‡3100.

2358 ■ Central Valley Cable TV
38958 Cypress Way
Gualala, CA 95445
Phone: (707)884-4111
Fax: (707)884-4117
Email: cvccable@mcn.org
Owner: Central Valley Cable TV L.L.C., PO Box 3200, Clovis, CA 93613, Ph: (559)298-1464, Fax: (559)325-6095. **Founded:** Mar. 01, 2000. **Formerly**: Coast Cable TV; Wander Cable. **Key Personnel:** Nancy Harrison, Office Mgr. **Cities Served:** subscribing households 1,350. **URL:** http://www.cvcca.com/files/2010/06/customer-letter-052010.pdf.

2359 ■ KTDE-FM - 100.5
PO Box 1557
Gualala, CA 95445
Phone: (707)884-1000
Format: Classical. **Operating Hours**: Continuous. **Wattage**: 6,000. **Ad Rates:** Advertising accepted; rates available upon request. **URL:** http://www.ktde.com.

HALF MOON BAY

W. CA. San Mateo Co. 24 mi. SW of San Francisco. Commercial and sport fishing. Floriculture. Fruit, vegetables packed. Nurseries. Resort. Agriculture. Cattle.

2360 ■ Half Moon Bay Review and Pescadero Pebble
Half Bay Review
PO Box 68
Half Moon Bay, CA 94019
Phone: (415)726-4424
Fax: (415)726-7054
Publication E-mail: letters@hmbreview.com
Newspaper with Republican orientation. **Freq:** Weekly (Wed.). **Print Method:** Offset. **Cols./Page:** 6. **Col. Width:** 24 nonpareils. **Col. Depth:** 301 agate lines. **Key Personnel:** Clay Lambert, Editor. **Subscription Rates:** $46.80 Individuals in San Mateo County; $88.40 Two years in San Mateo County; $57.20 Out of country; $104 Out of country two years. **URL:** http://hmbreview.com. **Remarks:** Advertising accepted; rates available upon request. **Circ:** ‡7500.

HANFORD

SC CA. Kings Co. 33 mi. S. of Fresno. Milk condensery, oil refinery, flour, planing mills, canned and dried fruit, meat, poultry, cold storage packing plants; granite works; concrete pipe, tire factories. Oil wells. Agriculture. Dairying, cotton, grain.

2361 ■ KIGS-AM - 620
10238 6th Ave.
Hanford, CA 93230
Phone: (559)582-0361
Format: Hispanic; Top 40; News; Talk. **Networks:** Independent. **Owner:** Joan Parair, at above address. **Formerly**: KNGS-AM; KCLQ-AM. **Operating Hours**: Continuous; 100% local. **ADI**: Fresno-Visalia (Hanford), CA. **Key Personnel:** Tony Vieira, Contact; Herminio Quadros, Contact. **Wattage**: 1,000. **URL:** http://www.kigs.com.

2362 ■ KQKL-FM - 88.5
PO Box 779002
Rocklin, CA 95677
Free: 800-525-5683
Email: info@klove.com
Format: Contemporary Christian. **Owner:** Educational Media Foundation, 2351 Sunset Blvd., Ste. 170-218, Rocklin, CA 95677, Ph: (800)434-8400. **URL:** http://www.klove.com.

Circulation: ★ = AAM; △ or • = BPA; ♦ = CAC; ❑ = VAC; ⊕ = PO Statement; ‡ = Publisher's Report; Boldface figures = sworn; Light figures = estimated.

HAPPY CAMP

2363 ■ K216EC-FM - 91.1
PO Box 391
Twin Falls, ID 83303
Fax: (208)736-1958
Free: 800-357-4226
Format: Religious; Contemporary Christian. **Owner:** CSN International, PO Box 391, Twin Falls, ID 83303, Ph: (208)736-1958, Fax: (208)736-1958, Free: 800-357-4226. **URL:** http://www.csnradio.com.

HAVILAH

2364 ■ K260BI-FM - 99.9
PO Box 391
Twin Falls, ID 83303
Fax: (208)736-1958
Free: 800-357-4226
Format: Religious; Contemporary Christian. **Owner:** CSN International, PO Box 391, Twin Falls, ID 83303, Ph: (208)736-1958, Fax: (208)736-1958, Free: 800-357-4226. **URL:** http://www.csnradio.com.

HAYWARD

W. CA. Alameda Co. 22 mi. SE of San Francisco. California State University at Hayward. Manufactures truck assembly steel, fabrication, construction equipment machine shops, chemicals and electronics.

2365 ■ KCRH-FM - 89.9
25555 Hesperian Blvd.
Hayward, CA 94545
Phone: (510)723-6954
Email: promotions@kcrhradio.com
Format: Educational; Full Service. **Owner:** South County Community College District, at above address, Mission Viejo, CA. **Founded:** 1980. **Operating Hours:** 6:00 a.m. - Midnight. **Wattage:** 018 ERP. **Ad Rates:** Noncommercial. Underwriting available. **URL:** http://kcrhradio.com.

HEALDSBURG

NW CA. Sonoma Co. On Russian River, 65 mi. N. of San Francisco. Wineries. Wood products, machine shops, electronics, ceramics. Agriculture. Prunes, grapes.

2366 ■ Cloverdale Reveille
Sonoma West Publishers Inc.
PO Box 518
Healdsburg, CA 95448
Phone: (707)823-7845
Publication E-mail: reveille@thegrid.net
Local newspaper. **Freq:** Weekly (Wed.). **Print Method:** Offset. **Cols./Page:** 6. **Col. Width:** 24 nonpareils. **Col. Depth:** 294 agate lines. **Subscription Rates:** $50 Individuals in county residents 1 year; $75 Individuals out of county residents 1 year; $80 Two years in county residents; $125 Two years out of county residents. **URL:** http://www.sonomawest.com/cloverdale_reveille. **Mailing address:** PO Box 157, Cloverdale, CA 95425-3318. **Ad Rates:** BW $126; SAU $5.50; PCI $5. **Remarks:** Accepts advertising. **Circ:** Paid ‡2300.

2367 ■ The Healdsburg Tribune
Sonoma West Publishers Inc.
PO Box 518
Healdsburg, CA 95448
Phone: (707)823-7845
Publisher's E-mail: news@sonomawest.com
Community newspaper. **Freq:** Weekly (Wed.). **Print Method:** Offset. **Trim Size:** 13 3/4 x 22 3/4. **Cols./Page:** 6. **Col. Width:** 24 nonpareils. **Col. Depth:** 294 agate lines. **Key Personnel:** Cherie Kelsay, Director, Advertising; Rollie Atkinson, Publisher; Grace Garner, Manager, Circulation; Kerrie Lindecker, Editor; Greg Clementi, Editor; Jeanne Ellis, Contact. **Subscription Rates:** $50 Individuals in county; $75 Out of country; $80 Two years in county; $125 Out of country 2 years. **Alt. Formats:** Electronic publishing. **URL:** http://www.sonomawest.com/the_healdsburg_tribune. **Formerly**: The Healdsburg Tribune and The Windsor Times. **Ad Rates:** BW $1669; 4C $1969; SAU $12.94. **Remarks:** Advertising accepted; rates available upon request. **Circ:** ‡4100, Free 3000.

2368 ■ Sonoma West Times & News
Sonoma West Publishers Inc.
PO Box 518
Healdsburg, CA 95448
Phone: (707)823-7845
Publication E-mail: news@sonomawest.com
Community newspaper. **Freq:** Weekly (Wed.). **Print Method:** Offset. **Cols./Page:** 6. **Col. Width:** 25 nonpareils. **Col. Depth:** 294 agate lines. **Key Personnel:** Rollie Atkinson, Publisher. **Subscription Rates:** $50 Individuals; $75 Out of country; $80 Two years in county residents; $125 Two years out of county residents. **URL:** http://www.sonomawest.com. **Formerly**: Sebastopol Times & News. **Ad Rates:** BW $2,200; 4C $2,630; SAU $10.95; PCI $17.50. **Remarks:** Accepts advertising. **Circ:** 6000.

2369 ■ UltraRunning
UltraRunning
5825 W Dry Creek Rd.
Healdsburg, CA 95448
Phone: (707)431-9898
Publisher's E-mail: help@ultrarunning.com
Magazine featuring comprehensive and informative articles about all aspects of ultrarunning. **Freq:** 10/year. **Trim Size:** 8 1/4 x 10 7/8. **Key Personnel:** Karl Hoagland, Publisher. **Subscription Rates:** $39 Individuals; $74 Canada and Mexico; $20 Individuals online. **URL:** http://www.ultrarunning.com. **Remarks:** Advertising accepted; rates available upon request. **Circ:** Paid ‡6100.

HERMOSA BEACH

S. CA. Los Angeles Co. 20 mi. SW of Los Angeles. Manufactures dye and print textiles, clay products, aircraft parts. Summer resort. Oil wells. Residential.

2370 ■ The Beach Reporter: The Newspaper of the Beach Cities
Equal Access Media Inc.
2615 Pacific Coast Hwy., Ste. 329
Hermosa Beach, CA 90256
Phone: (310)372-0388
Fax: (310)372-6113
Community newspaper. **Freq:** Weekly (Thurs.). **Print Method:** Offset. **Key Personnel:** Simon Grieve, Editor-in-Chief. **URL:** http://tbrnews.com/. **Ad Rates:** BW $1,447. **Remarks:** Accepts advertising. **Circ:** ‡55500.

2371 ■ Easy Reader: The South Bay's Hometown News
Easy Reader/Redondo Beach Hometown News
2200 Pacific Coast Hwy., Ste. 101
Hermosa Beach, CA 90254
Phone: (310)372-4611
Publisher's E-mail: contest@easyreadernews.com
Community newspaper. **Freq:** Weekly (Thurs.). **Print Method:** Offset. **Cols./Page:** 5. **Col. Width:** 24 nonpareils. **Col. Depth:** 175 agate lines. **Key Personnel:** Kevin Cody, Publisher; Lee Craft, Director, Advertising; Tom Fitt, Editor. **URL:** http://www.easyreadernews.com. **Mailing address:** PO Box 427, Hermosa Beach, CA 90254. **Ad Rates:** GLR $1.35; BW $1250; 4C $1850. **Remarks:** Accepts advertising. **Circ:** Combined 57000.

HESPERIA

SE CA. San Bernardino Co. 20 mi. N. of San Bernardino. Cement, wooden crates manufactured. Diversified farming.

2372 ■ Hesperia Resorter
Valley Wide Newspaper
16925 Main St.
Hesperia, CA 92345
Phone: (760)244-0021
Fax: (760)244-6609
Publisher's E-mail: questions@valleywidenewspaper.com
Newspaper. **Freq:** Weekly (Thurs.). **Print Method:** Offset. **Trim Size:** 27 x 1/2. **Cols./Page:** 8. **Col. Width:** 18 nonpareils. **Col. Depth:** 308 agate lines. **Key Personnel:** Linda Martinez Garber, Publisher; Raymond Pryke, Editor. **Subscription Rates:** $19 Individuals per year. **Alt. Formats:** PDF. **URL:** http://www.valleywidenewspaper.com; http://valleywidenewspaper.com/selectapaper.html. **Mailing address:** PO Box 400937, Hesperia, CA 92345. **Ad Rates:** GLR $6; BW $1383.75; 4C $1500; SAU $10.25. **Remarks:** Accepts advertising. **Circ:** Paid ‡2200, Free ‡12000.

2373 ■ Hesperia Star
Freedom Communications Inc.
15550 Main, Ste. C-11
Hesperia, CA 92345
Phone: (760)956-STAR
Publisher's E-mail: info@freedom.com
Newspaper serving the area of Hesperia, California. **Freq:** Weekly. **URL:** http://www.hesperiastar.com. **Remarks:** Accepts advertising. **Circ:** (Not Reported).

2374 ■ KIQQ-AM
11920 Hesperia Rd.
Hesperia, CA 92345
Phone: (619)244-2000
Fax: (619)244-1198
Format: Adult Contemporary; News; Talk. **Owner:** Eneida Orchard, at above address. **Founded:** 1960. **Key Personnel:** Eneida Orchard, Contact. **Wattage:** 5,000 Day; 118 Night. **Ad Rates:** $15 for 60 seconds.

KVFG-FM - See Riverside, CA

HOLLISTER

W. CA. San Benito Co. 90 mi. S. of San Francisco. Aero space aircraft. Fruit, tomatoes, canneries and packing houses. Wineries. Beef slaughtering. Fruit, truck, stock farms.

2375 ■ KMPG-AM - 1520
PO Box 2245
Hollister, CA 95023
Phone: (408)637-7476
Fax: (408)637-4031
Format: Hispanic. **Networks:** Spanish Information Service; Notiuno. **Operating Hours:** Day time. **ADI:** Salinas-Monterey, CA. **Key Personnel:** Adeia Martinez, President. **Wattage:** 5,000. **Ad Rates:** $20 for 60 seconds.

HOLLYWOOD

S. CA. Los Angeles Co. A residential suburb, NW of and part of Los Angeles. Center of motion picture industry. Pacific coast headquarters of four national radio broadcasting networks. Busy retail commercial center, second only to downtown Los Angeles business district.

2376 ■ Americana
Institute for the Study of American Popular Culture
7095-1240 Hollywood Blvd.
Hollywood, CA 90028-8903
Peer-reviewed journal that publishes information on American culture and history in the twentieth and twenty-first centuries. **Freq:** Semiannual. **Key Personnel:** Leslie Kreiner Wilson, PhD, Editor. **ISSN:** 1553--8923 (print). **URL:** http://www.americanpopularculture.com/journal/index.htm. **Remarks:** Advertising not accepted. **Circ:** (Not Reported).

2377 ■ Ben is Dead
Ben is Dead
PO Box 3166
Hollywood, CA 90028
Phone: (213)960-7674
Fax: (310)479-2336
Alternative consumer magazine covering social and cultural issues. **Freq:** Monthly. **Print Method:** Web. **Trim Size:** 8 1/8 x 10 6/8. **Key Personnel:** Darby Romeo, Contact. **Subscription Rates:** $15 Individuals; $5 Single issue. **URL:** http://www.benisdead.com. **Ad Rates:** BW $550; 4C $900. **Remarks:** Accepts advertising. **Circ:** Controlled 12000.

2378 ■ Hollywood Business
Hollywood Chamber of Commerce
7018 Hollywood Blvd.
Hollywood, CA 90028
Phone: (323)469-8311
Fax: (323)469-2805
Publisher's E-mail: info@hollywoodchamber.net
Freq: Monthly. **Subscription Rates:** Free to members; Included in membership. **URL:** http://www.hollywoodchamber.net. **Remarks:** Accepts advertising. **Circ:** 2000.

2379 ■ Update Magazine: The Magazine of film, video, and digital production
Production Update Magazine
5419 Hollywood Blvd., Ste. C227
Hollywood, CA 90027
Phone: (323)786-0340

Fax: (323)395-5954
Publisher's E-mail: contact_p3@p3update.com
Magazine focusing on film, digital, and video production. **Freq:** Monthly. **Trim Size:** 8 3/8 x 10 7/8. **Key Personnel:** James Thompson, Editor; Diane Lesko Thompson, Vice President, Finance; Sally Kemper, Editor. **ISSN:** 1058-3238 (print). **Subscription Rates:** $23.50 Individuals; $61.50 Other countries. **Formerly:** Location Update. **Ad Rates:** BW $2,800; 4C $3,800. **Remarks:** Accepts advertising. **Circ:** 24000.

HOOPA

2380 ■ KIDE-FM - 91.3
PO Box 1220
Hoopa, CA 95546
Phone: (530)625-4245
Email: kide@hoopa-nsn.gov
Format: Eclectic. **Networks:** National Public Radio (NPR). **Owner:** The Hoopa Valley Tribal Council, PO Box 1220, Hoopa, CA 95546, Ph: (530)625-4245. **Founded:** 1980. **Operating Hours:** Continuous. **Key Personnel:** Joseph R. Orozco, Station Mgr.; Floriene McCovey, Announcer, Traffic Mgr., Producer; Jay Renzulli, Announcer, Music Dir. **Wattage**: 195. **Ad Rates:** Noncommercial. **URL:** http://www.kidefm.org.

HUGHSON

2381 ■ KBYN-FM - 95.9
4043 Greer Rd.
Hughson, CA 95326
Phone: (209)883-8760
Format: Hispanic. **Operating Hours**: Continuous.

2382 ■ KNTO-FM - 93.3
4043 Geer Rd.
Hughson, CA 95326
Phone: (209)883-8760
Fax: (209)883-8769
Email: lafavorita@lafavorita.net
Owner: La Favorita Radio Network, Inc., at above address. **Wattage**: 3,000. **Ad Rates:** $16-22 for 30 seconds; $19-25 for 60 seconds.

HUNTINGTON BEACH

S. CA. Orange Co. 12 mi. SW of Santa Ana. Manufactures oil well equipment. Astronautics space missles, brooms, tile. Oil refineries. Oil wells. Agriculture.

2383 ■ Apartment Management Magazine
Apartment News Publications Inc.
15502 Graham St.
Huntington Beach, CA 92649
Phone: (714)893-3971
Fax: (714)893-6484
Free: 800-931-6666
Publisher's E-mail: editor@aptmags.com
Trade magazine serving owners, builders, and managers of apartment buildings. **Freq:** Monthly. **Print Method:** Offset. **Trim Size:** 8 1/8 x 10 1/4. **Cols./Page:** 3. **Col. Width:** 14 picas. **Col. Depth:** 9 7/8 inches. **Key Personnel:** Donn R. Smeallie, Jr., President, Publisher; David Gale, Art Director, Editor; Jordan Smith, Director, Marketing. **Subscription Rates:** $20 Individuals California only; $69 Out of area. **URL:** http://www.aptmags.com. **Formerly**: Apartment Owner/Builder. **Remarks:** Accepts advertising. **Circ:** Combined 80000.

2384 ■ Dynamic Chiropractic: Chiropractic News Source
Dynamic Chiropractic
PO Box 4109
Huntington Beach, CA 92605
Phone: (714)230-3150
Fax: (714)899-4273
Free: 800-324-7758
Magazine for chiropractic professionals. **Freq:** Biweekly. **Print Method:** Web offset. **Trim Size:** 10 7/8 x 16 1/8. **Cols./Page:** 4. **Key Personnel:** Peter Crownfield, Executive Editor; Ramon McLeod, Editor-in-Chief. **ISSN:** 1076--9684 (print). **Subscription Rates:** $104 Individuals; $156 Canada; $308 Other countries. **URL:** http://www.chiroweb.com. **Ad Rates:** BW $5,250; 4C $3,236. **Remarks:** Accepts advertising. **Circ:** Controlled 55184.

2385 ■ Home Business
United Marketing and Research Company Inc.
9582 Hamilton Ave.
Huntington Beach, CA 92646
Phone: (714)968-0331
Fax: (714)962-7722
Free: 800-734-7042
Magazine covering the home-based business market, including sales and marketing, business start-ups, business operations, raising money, productivity, and related issues. **Freq:** Bimonthly. **Print Method:** Web. **Trim Size:** 8 1/8 x 10-7/8. **Cols./Page:** 3. **Key Personnel:** Shannon Needham, Director, Advertising, phone: (949)218-8729, fax: (714)388-3883; Dennis Porti, Manager, Circulation. **ISSN:** 1092--4779 (print). **Subscription Rates:** $19 Individuals; $29 Two years; $39 Canada; $59 Other countries; $8 Single issue. **URL:** http://www.homebusinessmag.com. **Mailing address:** PO Box 368, Huntington Beach, CA 92646. **Ad Rates:** BW $3,275, full page; BW $2,620, 2/3 page; BW $2,160, 1/2 page; BW $1,540, 1/3 page; BW $1,180, 1/4 page; 4C $3,930, full page; 4C $3,145, 2/3 page; 4C $2,595, 1/2 page; 4C $1,845, 1/3 page; 4C $1,415, 1/4 page. **Remarks:** Accepts advertising. **Circ:** Paid 120000.

2386 ■ Huntington Beach News
Huntington Beach News Inc.
18582 Beach Blvd., No. 204
Huntington Beach, CA 92648
Phone: (714)378-1243
Fax: (714)378-1244
Publication E-mail: hbnews@hb.quik.com
Local newspaper (tabloid). **Freq:** Weekly (Fri.). **Print Method:** Web offset. **Cols./Page:** 6. **Col. Width:** 2 inches. **Col. Depth:** 21.5 inches. **Key Personnel:** Jerry Person, Editor. **Subscription Rates:** Free. **URL:** http://www.hbnews.us. **Mailing address:** PO Box 228, Huntington Beach, CA 92648. **Ad Rates:** GLR $15; BW $1150; PCI $7.50. **Remarks:** Color advertising not accepted. **Circ:** Paid ‡200, Free ‡20000.

2387 ■ Skinned Knuckles: A Journal of Car Restoration
SK Publications
PO Box 6983
Huntington Beach, CA 92615
Phone: (714)963-1558
Publisher's E-mail: sk_publishing@yahoo.com
Consumer magazine covering automobile restoration. **Freq:** Monthly. **Print Method:** Newsprint. **ISSN:** 0164--3509 (print). **Subscription Rates:** $28 U.S.; $53 U.S. 2 years; $43 Canada; $83 Canada 2 years; $46 Other countries; $89 Other countries 2 years. **Ad Rates:** BW $152. **Remarks:** Accepts advertising. **Circ:** Paid 7500.

2388 ■ The Western Sun
Golden West College
15744 Goldenwest St.
Huntington Beach, CA 92647
Phone: (714)892-7711
Publisher's E-mail: outreach@gwc.com
Collegiate newspaper. **Founded:** Oct. 06, 1966. **Freq:** Biweekly every wednesday. **Print Method:** Offset. **Trim Size:** 13 x 21 1/2. **Cols./Page:** 6. **Col. Width:** 24 nonpareils. **Col. Depth:** 301 agate lines. **Key Personnel:** Lance Tonelli, Managing Editor; Brooklyn Paxson, Executive Editor. **Subscription Rates:** Free. **URL:** http://www.westernsun.us/category/contact-us/. **Formerly**: Branding Iron. **Ad Rates:** GLR $.71; BW $756; 4C $1,170; PCI $6. **Remarks:** Color advertising accepted; rates available upon request. **Circ:** Free ‡4500.

2389 ■ KVLA-AM - 1400
7291 Heil Ave.
Huntington Beach, CA 92647
Fax: (714)988-4288
Email: dcupit@iamerica.net
Format: Country; Talk. **Networks:** CBS. **Owner:** Bob Cupit, at above address. **Founded:** 1984. **Operating Hours:** 5 a.m.-11 p.m. **Wattage:** 1,000. **Ad Rates:** $7-9 for 30 seconds; $8.50-10.50 for 60 seconds. **URL:** http://kvla.tv/.

IDYLLWILD

SE CA. Riverside Co. 40 mi. SE of Riverside. Resort Area.

2390 ■ Idyllwild Town Crier
Idyllwild Town Crier
54295 Village Center Dr.
Idyllwild, CA 92549-0157
Phone: (951)659-2145
Fax: (951)659-2071
Free: 888-535-6663
Publisher's E-mail: idyllwildtowncrier@towncrier.com
News tabloid. **Freq:** Weekly (Thurs.). **Print Method:** Offset. **Cols./Page:** 6. **Col. Width:** 9.5 picas. **Col. Depth:** 182 agate lines. **Key Personnel:** J.P. Crumrine, Editor. **USPS:** 635-260. **Subscription Rates:** $29 Individuals online ; $34 Individuals print and online; $38 Out of area print and online. **URL:** http://idyllwildtowncrier.com. **Mailing address:** PO Box 157, Idyllwild, CA 92549-0157. **Ad Rates:** PCI $12. **Remarks:** Accepts advertising. **Circ:** 3800.

IMPERIAL

2391 ■ White Sheet-The Imperial Valley Advertiser
Associated Desert Shoppers Inc.
73400 Hwy. 111
Palm Desert, CA 92260
Shopper. **Freq:** Weekly (Tues.). **Print Method:** Offset. **Trim Size:** 11 1/2 x 14. **Cols./Page:** 6. **Col. Width:** 9 1/2 picas. **Col. Depth:** 13 inches. **Key Personnel:** Glen Feigum, Publisher; Roy Morton, Editor. **Alt. Formats:** PDF. **URL:** http://www.greenandwhitesheet.com/white_sheet_home.php. **Ad Rates:** BW $334; 4C $684; PCI $4.28. **Remarks:** Accepts advertising. **Circ:** Non-paid 10000.

INDIO

SW CA. Riverside Co. 125 mi. E. of Los Angeles. Dates, grapefruit, vegetable packing. Truck, fruit farms. grapes, cotton, cattle.

2392 ■ K205DT-FM - 88.9
PO Box 391
Twin Falls, ID 83303
Fax: (208)736-1958
Free: 800-357-4226
Format: Religious; Contemporary Christian. **Owner:** CSN International, PO Box 391, Twin Falls, ID 83303, Ph: (208)736-1958, Fax: (208)736-1958, Free: 800-357-4226. **URL:** http://www.csnradio.com.

INGLEWOOD

S. CA. Los Angeles Co. 10 mi. S. of Los Angeles. Manufactures airplanes. Electronics. Import export, air ground freight.

2393 ■ Poker Player
Gambling Times Inc.
3883 W Century Blvd.
Inglewood, CA 90303
Phone: (310)674-3365
Fax: (310)674-3205
Publisher's E-mail: advertising@gamblingtimes.com
Magazine featuring gambling, horseracing, lotteries and casino games. **Founded:** Nov. 1962. **Freq:** 26/yr. **Print Method:** Offset. **Trim Size:** 14 1/2 x 10 1/4. **Cols./Page:** 5. **Col. Width:** 13.2 nonpareils. **Col. Depth:** 140 agate lines. **Key Personnel:** Stanley R. Sludikoff, Editor. **Alt. Formats:** PDF. **URL:** http://www.pokerplayernewspaper.com. **Formerly**: Win Magazine; Gambling Times. **Ad Rates:** 4C $3,690. **Remarks:** Accepts advertising. **Circ:** 125000.

2394 ■ KJLH-FM - 102.3
161 N La Brea Ave.
Inglewood, CA 90301
Phone: (310)330-2200
Fax: (310)330-5555
Format: Urban Contemporary. **Networks:** ABC; American Urban Radio. **Founded:** 1965. **Operating Hours**: Continuous. **ADI**: Los Angeles (Corona & San Bernardino), CA. **Key Personnel:** Al Ward, Sales Mgr., VP. **Wattage**: 3,000. **Ad Rates:** Noncommercial. **URL:** http://www.kjlhradio.com.

2395 ■ KTYM-AM - 1460
6803 West Blvd.
Inglewood, CA 90302
Phone: (310)672-3700
Fax: (310)673-2259
Format: Religious. **Owner:** Trans America Broadcasting Corp., at above address. **Founded:** 1958. **Key Personnel:** Gerardo Borrego, Gen. Mgr., President, mrb@ktym.com; Bobby Howe, Dir. Pub. Aff., ktympublicaffairs@

Circulation: ★ = AAM; △ or • = BPA; ♦ = CAC; ❑ = VAC; ⊕ = PO Statement; ‡ = Publisher's Report; Boldface figures = sworn; Light figures = estimated.

sbcglobal.net. **Ad Rates:** Advertising accepted; rates available upon request. $15-22 for 30 seconds; $25-35 for 60 seconds. **URL:** http://www.ktym.com/.

IRVINE

S. CA. Orange Co. 9 mi. SE of Santa Ana. Manufacturers machinery, electric instruments, test equipment, tools and dies, aircraft parts, industrial chemicals. Truck, fruit farms.

2396 ■ Advances in Aerospace Science and Technology
Scientific Research Publishing Inc.
PO Box 54821
Irvine, CA 92619-4821
Publisher's E-mail: service@scirp.org
Journal containing various issues and developments in all areas of aerospace science and technology. **Key Personnel:** Prof. Dieter Scholz, Editor-in-Chief. **URL:** http://www.scirp.org/journal/aast. **Circ:** (Not Reported).

2397 ■ Advances in Aging Research
Scientific Research Publishing Inc.
PO Box 54821
Irvine, CA 92619-4821
Publisher's E-mail: service@scirp.org
Journal covering issues and developments in different areas of aging research. **Freq:** Quarterly Latest edition: 2015. **ISSN:** 2169--0499 (print); **EISSN:** 2169--0502 (electronic). **Subscription Rates:** $298 Individuals Volume 3. **URL:** http://www.scirp.org/journal/aar. **Circ:** (Not Reported).

2398 ■ Advances in Alzheimer's Disease
Scientific Research Publishing Inc.
PO Box 54821
Irvine, CA 92619-4821
Publisher's E-mail: service@scirp.org
Journal promoting, sharing and discussing new issues and developments in different areas of Alzheimer's Disease. **Freq:** Quarterly Latest edition: 2015. **Key Personnel:** Lei Xue, Editor-in-Chief. **ISSN:** 2169--2459 (print); **EISSN:** 2169--2467 (electronic). **Subscription Rates:** $298 Individuals Volume 4. **URL:** http://www.scirp.org/journal/aad. **Circ:** (Not Reported).

2399 ■ Advances in Anthropology
Scientific Research Publishing Inc.
PO Box 54821
Irvine, CA 92619-4821
Publisher's E-mail: service@scirp.org
Peer-reviewed journal publishing articles on the latest advancement in anthropology. **Freq:** Quarterly Latest edition 2015. **Key Personnel:** Anatole Klyosov, Editor-in-Chief. **ISSN:** 2163--9353 (print); **EISSN:** 2163--9361 (electronic). **Subscription Rates:** $398 Individuals Volume 5. **URL:** http://www.scirp.org/journal/aa. **Circ:** (Not Reported).

2400 ■ Advances in Applied Sociology
Scientific Research Publishing Inc.
PO Box 54821
Irvine, CA 92619-4821
Publisher's E-mail: service@scirp.org
Journal covering the latest advancements in applied sociology. **Freq:** Monthly. **Key Personnel:** Prof. Wing Hong Chui, Editor-in-Chief. **ISSN:** 2165--4328 (print); **EISSN:** 2165--4336 (electronic). **Subscription Rates:** $998 Individuals. **URL:** http://www.scirp.org/journal/aasoci. **Circ:** (Not Reported).

2401 ■ Advances in Biological Chemistry
Scientific Research Publishing Inc.
PO Box 54821
Irvine, CA 92619-4821
Publisher's E-mail: service@scirp.org
Journal discussing latest advancements and issues in biological chemistry. **Freq:** Bimonthly. **Key Personnel:** Gary W. Black, Editor-in-Chief. **ISSN:** 2162--2183 (print); **EISSN:** 2162--2191 (electronic). **Subscription Rates:** $599 Individuals article processing charge; Free open access. **URL:** http://www.scirp.org/journal/abc. **Circ:** (Not Reported).

2402 ■ Advances in Bioscience and Biotechnology
Scientific Research Publishing Inc.
PO Box 54821
Irvine, CA 92619-4821
Publisher's E-mail: service@scirp.org
Peer-reviewed journal publishing the latest advancements in biosciences. **Freq:** Monthly. **Key Personnel:** Prof. Abass Alavi, Editor-in-Chief. **ISSN:** 2156--8456 (print); **EISSN:** 2156--8502 (electronic). **Subscription Rates:** $1298 Individuals. **URL:** http://www.scirp.org/journal/abb. **Circ:** (Not Reported).

2403 ■ Advances in Chemical Engineering and Science
Scientific Research Publishing Inc.
PO Box 54821
Irvine, CA 92619-4821
Publisher's E-mail: service@scirp.org
Peer-reviewed journal covering advances in chemical engineering and sciences. **Freq:** Quarterly. **Key Personnel:** Prof. SungCheal Moon, Editor-in-Chief. **ISSN:** 2160--0392 (print); **EISSN:** 2160--0406 (electronic). **Subscription Rates:** $398 Individuals. **URL:** http://www.scirp.org/journal/aces. **Circ:** (Not Reported).

2404 ■ Advances in Computed Tomography
Scientific Research Publishing Inc.
PO Box 54821
Irvine, CA 92619-4821
Publisher's E-mail: service@scirp.org
Journal covering various new issues and developments in all areas of computed tomography. **Freq:** Quarterly. **Key Personnel:** Prof. Jun Ni, Editor-in-Chief. **ISSN:** 2169--2475 (print); **EISSN:** 2169--2483 (electronic). **URL:** http://www.scirp.org/journal/act. **Circ:** (Not Reported).

2405 ■ Advances in Entomology
Scientific Research Publishing Inc.
PO Box 54821
Irvine, CA 92619-4821
Publisher's E-mail: service@scirp.org
Journal covering issues and developments in entomology research. **Freq:** Quarterly Latest edition: 2015. **ISSN:** 2331--1991 (print); **EISSN:** 2331--2017 (electronic). **Subscription Rates:** $198 Individuals Volume 3. **URL:** http://www.scirp.org/journal/ae. **Circ:** (Not Reported).

2406 ■ Advances in Enzyme Research
Scientific Research Publishing Inc.
PO Box 54821
Irvine, CA 92619-4821
Publisher's E-mail: service@scirp.org
Journal discussing new issues and developments in different areas of enzyme research. **Freq:** Latest edition 2014. **Key Personnel:** Prof. Bechan Sharma, Editor-in-Chief. **ISSN:** 2328--4846 (print); **EISSN:** 2328--4854 (electronic). **Subscription Rates:** $156 Individuals Volume 2. **URL:** http://www.scirp.org/journal/aer. **Circ:** (Not Reported).

2407 ■ Advances in Historical Studies
Scientific Research Publishing Inc.
PO Box 54821
Irvine, CA 92619-4821
Publisher's E-mail: service@scirp.org
Journal covering the latest advancements in the study of history. **Freq:** Quarterly. **Key Personnel:** Raffaele Pisano, PhD, Editor-in-Chief. **ISSN:** 2327--0438 (print); **EISSN:** 2327--0446 (electronic). **Subscription Rates:** $298 Individuals. **URL:** http://www.scirp.org/journal/ahs. **Circ:** (Not Reported).

2408 ■ Advances in Infectious Diseases
Scientific Research Publishing Inc.
PO Box 54821
Irvine, CA 92619-4821
Publisher's E-mail: service@scirp.org
Journal promoting, sharing and discussing various topics related to infectious diseases. **Freq:** Quarterly. **Key Personnel:** Yung-Fu Chang, Editor-in-Chief. **ISSN:** 2164--2648 (print); **EISSN:** 2164--2656 (electronic). **Subscription Rates:** $398 Individuals. **URL:** http://www.scirp.org/journal/AID. **Circ:** (Not Reported).

2409 ■ Advances in Internet of Things
Scientific Research Publishing Inc.
PO Box 54821
Irvine, CA 92619-4821
Publisher's E-mail: service@scirp.org
Peer-reviewed journal discussing issues on the impact of Internet to society. **Freq:** Quarterly. **Key Personnel:** Prof. Ammar Rayes, Editor-in-Chief. **ISSN:** 2161--6817 (print); **EISSN:** 2161--6825 (electronic). **Subscription Rates:** $398 Individuals. **URL:** http://www.scirp.org/journal/ait. **Circ:** (Not Reported).

2410 ■ Advances in Journalism and Communication
Scientific Research Publishing Inc.
PO Box 54821
Irvine, CA 92619-4821
Publisher's E-mail: service@scirp.org
Journal discussing various practices, developments and theories in journalism and communication. **Freq:** Quarterly. **ISSN:** 2328--4927 (print); **EISSN:** 2328--4935 (electronic). **Subscription Rates:** $198 Individuals. **URL:** http://www.scirp.org/journal/ajc. **Circ:** (Not Reported).

2411 ■ Advances in Linear Algebra & Matrix Theory
Scientific Research Publishing Inc.
PO Box 54821
Irvine, CA 92619-4821
Publisher's E-mail: service@scirp.org
Journal covering the latest advancements in linear algebra. **Freq:** Quarterly. **Key Personnel:** Prof. Mubariz Garayev, Editor-in-Chief. **ISSN:** 2165--333X (print); **EISSN:** 2165--3348 (electronic). **URL:** http://www.scirp.org/journal/alamt. **Circ:** (Not Reported).

2412 ■ Advances in Literary Study
Scientific Research Publishing Inc.
PO Box 54821
Irvine, CA 92619-4821
Publisher's E-mail: service@scirp.org
Journal promoting various new issues and developments in all areas of literary study. **Freq:** Quarterly. **ISSN:** 2327--4034 (print); **EISSN:** 2327--4050 (electronic). **Subscription Rates:** $298 Individuals. **URL:** http://www.scirp.org/journal/als. **Circ:** (Not Reported).

2413 ■ Advances in Lung Cancer
Scientific Research Publishing Inc.
PO Box 54821
Irvine, CA 92619-4821
Publisher's E-mail: service@scirp.org
Peer-reviewed journal featuring new issues and developments in all aspects of basic and clinical lung cancer research. **Freq:** Quarterly Latest edition 2015. **Key Personnel:** Prof. William N. Rom, Editor-in-Chief. **ISSN:** 2169--2718 (print); **EISSN:** 2169--2726 (electronic). **Subscription Rates:** $398 Individuals Volume 4. **URL:** http://www.scirp.org/journal/ALC. **Circ:** (Not Reported).

2414 ■ Advances in Materials Physics and Chemistry
Scientific Research Publishing Inc.
PO Box 54821
Irvine, CA 92619-4821
Publisher's E-mail: service@scirp.org
Journal containing articles relating to physics and chemistry. **Freq:** Monthly. **Key Personnel:** Prof. Zhiwen Chen, Editor-in-Chief. **ISSN:** 2162--531X (print); **EISSN:** 2162--5328 (electronic). **Subscription Rates:** $1098 Individuals volume 5. **URL:** http://www.scirp.org/journal/ampc. **Circ:** (Not Reported).

2415 ■ Advances in Microbiology
Scientific Research Publishing Inc.
PO Box 54821
Irvine, CA 92619-4821
Publisher's E-mail: service@scirp.org
Journal dedicated to the latest advancements in microbiology. **Freq:** Quarterly. **Key Personnel:** Prof. Alan W. Decho, Editor-in-Chief. **ISSN:** 2165--3402 (print); **EISSN:** 2165--3410 (electronic). **Subscription Rates:** $1098 Individuals Volume 5. **URL:** http://www.scirp.org/journal/aim. **Circ:** (Not Reported).

2416 ■ Advances in Molecular Imaging
Scientific Research Publishing Inc.
PO Box 54821
Irvine, CA 92619-4821
Publication E-mail: ami@scirp.org
Peer-reviewed journal publishing clinical studies in all areas of molecular imaging. **Freq:** Quarterly. **Key Personnel:** Prof. Orhan Nalcioglu, Editor-in-Chief. **ISSN:** 2161--6728 (print); **EISSN:** 2161--6752 (electronic). **Subscription Rates:** $298 Individuals. **URL:** http://www.scirp.org/journal/ami. **Circ:** (Not Reported).

2417 ■ Advances in Nanoparticles
Scientific Research Publishing Inc.
PO Box 54821
Irvine, CA 92619-4821

Publisher's E-mail: service@scirp.org
Journal discussing issues and developments in all aspects of nanoparticle science and their applications. **Freq:** Quarterly Latest edition 2015. **Key Personnel:** Dr. Virginia Yong, Editor-in-Chief. **ISSN:** 2169--0510 (print); **EISSN:** 2169--0529 (electronic). **Subscription Rates:** $298 Individuals Volume 4. **URL:** http://www.scirp.org/journal/anp. **Circ:** (Not Reported).

2418 ■ Advances in Parkinson's Disease
Scientific Research Publishing Inc.
PO Box 54821
Irvine, CA 92619-4821
Publisher's E-mail: service@scirp.org
Journal promoting, sharing and discussing new issues and developments in all aspects of Parkinson's disease. **Freq:** Quarterly. **Key Personnel:** Dr. Marie-Helene Saint-Hilaire, Editor-in-Chief. **ISSN:** 2169--9712 (print); **EISSN:** 2169--9720 (electronic). **Subscription Rates:** $398 Individuals Volume 4. **URL:** http://www.scirp.org/journal/apd. **Circ:** (Not Reported).

2419 ■ Advances in Physical Education
Scientific Research Publishing Inc.
PO Box 54821
Irvine, CA 92619-4821
Publisher's E-mail: service@scirp.org
Journal covering the latest advancements in physical education. **Freq:** Quarterly. **Key Personnel:** Prof. Marilyn Mitchell, Editor-in-Chief. **ISSN:** 2164--0386 (print); **EISSN:** 2164--0408 (electronic). **Subscription Rates:** $398 Individuals. **URL:** http://www.scirp.org/journal/ape. **Circ:** (Not Reported).

2420 ■ Advances in Pure Mathematics
Scientific Research Publishing Inc.
PO Box 54821
Irvine, CA 92619-4821
Publisher's E-mail: service@scirp.org
Peer-reviewed journal publishing articles on the advancement of algebraic structures. **Freq:** Monthly. **Key Personnel:** Prof. De-Xing Kong, Editor-in-Chief. **ISSN:** 2160--0368 (print); **EISSN:** 2060--0384 (electronic). **Subscription Rates:** $1098 Individuals print + online. **URL:** http://www.scirp.org/journal/apm. **Circ:** (Not Reported).

2421 ■ Advances in Remote Sensing
Scientific Research Publishing Inc.
PO Box 54821
Irvine, CA 92619-4821
Publisher's E-mail: service@scirp.org
Journal promoting, sharing and discussing various new issues and developments in all areas of remote sensing. **Freq:** Quarterly. **Key Personnel:** Prof. Gunter Menz, Editor-in-Chief. **ISSN:** 2169--267X (print); **EISSN:** 2169--2688 (electronic). **Subscription Rates:** $398 Individuals. **URL:** http://www.scirp.org/journal/ars. **Remarks:** Advertising not accepted. **Circ:** (Not Reported).

2422 ■ Advances in Reproductive Sciences
Scientific Research Publishing Inc.
PO Box 54821
Irvine, CA 92619-4821
Publisher's E-mail: service@scirp.org
Journal promoting new issues and developments in different areas of reproductive research. **Freq:** Quarterly. **Key Personnel:** Abdel Halim Harrath, Editor-in-Chief. **ISSN:** 2330--0744 (print); **EISSN:** 2330--0752 (electronic). **Subscription Rates:** $198 Individuals. **URL:** http://www.scirp.org/journal/arsci. **Circ:** (Not Reported).

2423 ■ Advances in Sexual Medicine
Scientific Research Publishing Inc.
PO Box 54821
Irvine, CA 92619-4821
Publisher's E-mail: service@scirp.org
Journal covering the latest advancements in sexual medicine. **Freq:** Quarterly. **ISSN:** 2164--5191 (print); **EISSN:** 2164--5205 (electronic). **Subscription Rates:** $398 Individuals. **URL:** http://www.scirp.org/journal/ASM. **Circ:** (Not Reported).

2424 ■ Agricultural Sciences
Scientific Research Publishing Inc.
PO Box 54821
Irvine, CA 92619-4821
Publication E-mail: as@scirp.org
Peer-reviewed journal publishing articles on agricultural science. **Freq:** Monthly. **Key Personnel:** Prof. De Wrachien Daniele, Editor-in-Chief; Prof. M.B. Goli, Editor-in-Chief. **ISSN:** 2156--8553 (print); **EISSN:** 2156--8561 (electronic). **Subscription Rates:** $1098 Individuals. **URL:** http://www.scirp.org/journal/as. **Circ:** (Not Reported).

2425 ■ American Journal of Analytical Chemistry
Scientific Research Publishing Inc.
PO Box 54821
Irvine, CA 92619-4821
Publication E-mail: ajac@scirp.org
Peer-reviewed journal featuring the latest advancements in analytical chemistry. **Freq:** Monthly. **Key Personnel:** Prof. Raman Venkataramanan, Editor-in-Chief. **ISSN:** 2156--8251 (print); **EISSN:** 2156--8278 (electronic). **Subscription Rates:** $1198 Individuals. **URL:** http://www.scirp.org/journal/ajac. **Circ:** (Not Reported).

2426 ■ American Journal of Climate Change
Scientific Research Publishing Inc.
PO Box 54821
Irvine, CA 92619-4821
Publisher's E-mail: service@scirp.org
Journal featuring research articles and review papers on all aspects of climate change. **Freq:** Quarterly. **Key Personnel:** John C. Moore, Editor-in-Chief. **ISSN:** 2167--9495 (print); **EISSN:** 2167--9509 (electronic). **Subscription Rates:** $298 Individuals. **URL:** http://www.scirp.org/journal/ajcc. **Circ:** (Not Reported).

2427 ■ American Journal of Computational Mathematics
Scientific Research Publishing Inc.
PO Box 54821
Irvine, CA 92619-4821
Publisher's E-mail: service@scirp.org
Peer-reviewed journal publishing articles about mathematical research in areas of science. **Freq:** Quarterly. **Key Personnel:** Hari M. Srivastava, Prof., Editor-in-Chief. **ISSN:** 2161--1203 (print); **EISSN:** 2161--1211 (electronic). **Subscription Rates:** $398 Individuals. **URL:** http://www.scirp.org/journal/ajcm. **Circ:** (Not Reported).

2428 ■ American Journal of Industrial and Business Management
Scientific Research Publishing Inc.
PO Box 54821
Irvine, CA 92619-4821
Publisher's E-mail: service@scirp.org
Journal publishing high quality, original papers and research developments in all areas of industrial and business management. **Freq:** Monthly Latest edition 2015. **Key Personnel:** Prof. Yuan-Shyi Peter Chiu, Editor-in-Chief. **ISSN:** 2164--5167 (print); **EISSN:** 2164--5175 (electronic). **Subscription Rates:** $1098 Individuals Volume 5. **URL:** http://www.scirp.org/journal/ajibm. **Circ:** (Not Reported).

2429 ■ American Journal of Molecular Biology
Scientific Research Publishing Inc.
PO Box 54821
Irvine, CA 92619-4821
Publisher's E-mail: service@scirp.org
Peer-reviewed journal featuring the latest advancements in molecular biology. **Freq:** Quarterly. **Key Personnel:** Prof. Wei Du, Editor-in-Chief. **ISSN:** 2161--6620 (print); **EISSN:** 2161--6663 (electronic). **Subscription Rates:** $398 Individuals. **URL:** http://www.scirp.org/Journal/ajmb. **Circ:** (Not Reported).

2430 ■ American Journal of Operations Research
Scientific Research Publishing Inc.
PO Box 54821
Irvine, CA 92619-4821
Publication E-mail: ajor@scirp.org
Peer-reviewed journal covering all aspects of operational research methodology and decision making practice. **Freq:** Bimonthly. **Key Personnel:** Jinfeng Yue, Editor-in-Chief. **ISSN:** 2160--8830 (print); **EISSN:** 2160--8849 (electronic). **Subscription Rates:** $498 Individuals. **URL:** http://www.scirp.org/journal/ajor. **Circ:** (Not Reported).

2431 ■ American Journal of Plant Sciences
Scientific Research Publishing Inc.
PO Box 54821
Irvine, CA 92619-4821
Publication E-mail: ajps@scirp.org
Peer-reviewed journal publishing articles on the latest advancements in plant science. **Freq:** Monthly. **Key Personnel:** Dr. Sukumar Saha, Editor-in-Chief. **ISSN:** 2158--2742 (print); **EISSN:** 2158--2750 (electronic). **Subscription Rates:** $1498 Individuals. **URL:** http://www.scirp.org/journal/ajps. **Circ:** (Not Reported).

2432 ■ Applied Mathematics
Scientific Research Publishing Inc.
PO Box 54821
Irvine, CA 92619-4821
Publisher's E-mail: service@scirp.org
Peer-reviewed journal publishing articles on the latest advancements in applied mathematics. **Freq:** Monthly. **Key Personnel:** Prof. Chris Cannings, Editor-in-Chief. **ISSN:** 2152--7385 (print); **EISSN:** 2152--7393 (electronic). **Subscription Rates:** $1298 Individuals. **URL:** http://www.scirp.org/journal/am. **Circ:** (Not Reported).

2433 ■ Archaeological Discovery
Scientific Research Publishing Inc.
PO Box 54821
Irvine, CA 92619-4821
Publisher's E-mail: service@scirp.org
Journal covering latest advancement of the study of archaeology. **Freq:** Quarterly. **ISSN:** 2331--1959 (print); **EISSN:** 2331--1967 (electronic). **Subscription Rates:** $198 Individuals. **URL:** http://www.scirp.org/journal/ad. **Circ:** (Not Reported).

2434 ■ Art and Design Review
Scientific Research Publishing Inc.
PO Box 54821
Irvine, CA 92619-4821
Publisher's E-mail: service@scirp.org
Journal promoting new issues and developments in all areas of art and design. **Freq:** Quarterly. **Key Personnel:** Prof. Vladimir J. Konecni, Editor-in-Chief. **ISSN:** 2332--1997 (print); **EISSN:** 2332--2004 (electronic). **Subscription Rates:** $198 Individuals. **URL:** http://www.scirp.org/journal/adr. **Circ:** (Not Reported).

2435 ■ Atmospheric and Climate Sciences
Scientific Research Publishing Inc.
PO Box 54821
Irvine, CA 92619-4821
Publication E-mail: acs@scirp.org
Journal publishing articles on climate atmospheric science. **Freq:** Quarterly. **Key Personnel:** Dr. Shaocai Yu, Editor-in-Chief. **ISSN:** 2160--0414 (print); **EISSN:** 2160--0422 (electronic). **Subscription Rates:** $398 Individuals. **URL:** http://www.scirp.org/journal/acs. **Circ:** (Not Reported).

2436 ■ Beijing Law Review
Scientific Research Publishing Inc.
PO Box 54821
Irvine, CA 92619-4821
Publication E-mail: blr@scirp.org
Peer-reviewed journal publishing latest advancements in law review. **Freq:** Quarterly. **Key Personnel:** Prof. Jin Huang, Editor-in-Chief. **ISSN:** 2159--4627 (print); **EISSN:** 2159--4635 (electronic). **Subscription Rates:** $498 Individuals. **URL:** http://www.scirp.org/Journal/blr. **Circ:** (Not Reported).

2437 ■ Case Reports in Clinical Medicine
Scientific Research Publishing Inc.
PO Box 54821
Irvine, CA 92619-4821
Publisher's E-mail: service@scirp.org
Journal featuring case reports on new issues and developments in the field of clinical medicine. **Freq:** Monthly. **Key Personnel:** Prof. Shang I Brian Jiang, Editor-in-Chief. **ISSN:** 2325--7075 (print); **EISSN:** 2325--7083 (electronic). **Subscription Rates:** $998 Individuals. **URL:** http://www.scirp.org/journal/crcm. **Circ:** (Not Reported).

2438 ■ CellBio
Scientific Research Publishing Inc.
PO Box 54821
Irvine, CA 92619-4821
Publisher's E-mail: service@scirp.org
Journal promoting the advancement of the study of Cell Biology. **Freq:** Quarterly Latest edition 2015. **Key**

Circulation: ★ = AAM; △ or • = BPA; ♦ = CAC; ❑ = VAC; ⊕ = PO Statement; ‡ = Publisher's Report; Boldface figures = sworn; Light figures = estimated.

Personnel: Dr. Bor Luen Tang, Editor-in-Chief. **ISSN:** 2325--7776 (print); **EISSN:** 2325--7792 (electronic). **Subscription Rates:** $398 Individuals Volume 4. **URL:** http://www.scirp.org/journal/CellBio. **Circ:** (Not Reported).

2439 ■ CFMA Building Profits
Orange County Chapter of the Construction Financial Management Association
PO Box 17081
Irvine, CA 92623-7081
Phone: (714)632-2600
Trade magazine covering the financial side of the construction industry. Features employment opportunities for financial professionals in the construction industry. **Freq:** Bimonthly. **Print Method:** Sheetfed offset. **Trim Size:** 8 3/8 x 10 7/8. **Cols./Page:** 3. **Key Personnel:** Kristi L. Domboski, Managing Editor; Kirby E. Baldwin, Assistant Editor; Ron Kress, Manager, Advertising and Sales; Paula Wristen, Director, Editorial. **ISSN:** 1078-2435 (print). **Subscription Rates:** Included in membership; free for members. **Alt. Formats:** Print. **URL:** http://www.cfma.org/; http://www.cfma.org/resources/content.cfm?ItemNumber=847&navItemNumber=581. **Ad Rates:** GLR $10; BW $1,650; 4C $2,625. **Remarks:** Accepts advertising. **Circ:** Combined 7,000, 7000, Controlled .

2440 ■ Chevrolet High Performance
RentPath Inc.
1733 Alton Pkwy.
Irvine, CA 92606
Magazine covering the performance and restoration spectrum involving mid-1950's Chevys, Shoeboxes, Camaros, Corvettes, and muscle cars. **Freq:** Monthly. **Print Method:** Web Offset. **Trim Size:** 7 7/8 x 10 1/2. **Cols./Page:** 3. **Key Personnel:** Tim Foss, Contact, phone: (949)705-3325. **ISSN:** 1062-192X (print). **Subscription Rates:** $15 Individuals 1 year (12 issues) print; $25 Two years print (24 issues); $49 Canada 2 years print; $27 Canada 1 year print; $39 Other countries print 1 year; $73 Other countries print 2 years; $11.99 Individuals digital. **URL:** http://www.superchevy.com/chevy-high-performance-magazine. **Circ:** (Not Reported).

2441 ■ Chinese Medicine
Scientific Research Publishing Inc.
PO Box 54821
Irvine, CA 92619-4821
Publication E-mail: cm@scirp.org
Peer-reviewed journal publishing articles on the latest advancements in Chinese medicine. **Freq:** Quarterly. **Key Personnel:** Prof. Maythem Saeed, Editor-in-Chief. **ISSN:** 2151-1918 (print); **EISSN:** 2151-1926 (electronic). **Subscription Rates:** $316 Individuals. **URL:** http://www.scirp.org/journal/cm/. **Circ:** (Not Reported).

2442 ■ Chinese Studies
Scientific Research Publishing Inc.
PO Box 54821
Irvine, CA 92619-4821
Publisher's E-mail: service@scirp.org
Journal promoting topics related to China and its civilization. **Freq:** Quarterly Latest edition 2015. **Key Personnel:** Dr. Shaodan Luo, Editor-in-Chief. **ISSN:** 2168--5428 (print); **EISSN:** 2168--541X (electronic). **Subscription Rates:** $398 Individuals volume 4. **URL:** http://www.scirp.org/journal/CHNSTD. **Circ:** (Not Reported).

2443 ■ Circuits and Systems
Scientific Research Publishing Inc.
PO Box 54821
Irvine, CA 92619-4821
Publisher's E-mail: service@scirp.org
Peer-reviewed journal publishing articles on the latest advancement of theories, methods and applications in electronics, circuits and systems. **Freq:** Monthly. **Key Personnel:** Prof. Gyungho Lee, Editor-in-Chief; Prof. Jichai Jeong, Associate Editor; Mehdi Anwar, Editor-in-Chief. **ISSN:** 2153--1285 (print); **EISSN:** 2153--1293 (electronic). **Subscription Rates:** $998 Individuals. **URL:** http://www.scirp.org/journal/cs. **Circ:** (Not Reported).

2444 ■ Classic Auto Restorer
Bowtie Inc.
3 Burroughs
Irvine, CA 92618
Phone: (949)855-8822
Fax: (949)855-3045
Publisher's E-mail: ppneditor@fancypubs.com
Magazine focusing on how to restore and enjoy collector cars. **Freq:** Monthly. **Print Method:** Offset. **Trim Size:** 8 x 10 3/4. **Cols./Page:** 3. **Col. Width:** 2 1/8 inches. **Col. Depth:** 10 inches. **Key Personnel:** Ted Kade, Editor. **ISSN:** 1042-5683 (print). **Subscription Rates:** $20 Individuals; $32 Other countries. **URL:** http://www.autorestorermagazine.com/ar. **Remarks:** Accepts advertising. **Circ:** (Not Reported).

2445 ■ Communications and Network
Scientific Research Publishing Inc.
PO Box 54821
Irvine, CA 92619-4821
Publisher's E-mail: service@scirp.org
Journal publishing articles on the latest advancements in communications and network technologies. **Freq:** Quarterly. **Key Personnel:** Prof. Hamed Al-Raweshidy, Editor-in-Chief. **ISSN:** 1949--2421 (print); **EISSN:** 1947--3826 (electronic). **Subscription Rates:** $598 Individuals. **URL:** http://www.scirp.org/journal/cn. **Circ:** (Not Reported).

2446 ■ Computational Chemistry
Scientific Research Publishing Inc.
PO Box 54821
Irvine, CA 92619-4821
Publisher's E-mail: service@scirp.org
Journal featuring fundamental advances in all aspects of computational chemistry. **Freq:** Quarterly. **ISSN:** 2332--5968 (print); **EISSN:** 2332--5984 (electronic). **Subscription Rates:** $198 Individuals volume 3. **URL:** http://www.scirp.org/journal/cc. **Circ:** (Not Reported).

2447 ■ Computational Molecular Bioscience
Scientific Research Publishing Inc.
PO Box 54821
Irvine, CA 92619-4821
Publisher's E-mail: service@scirp.org
Journal containing the latest advancements in Computational Molecular Bioscience. **Freq:** Quarterly Latest edition 2015. **Key Personnel:** Dr. Christo Z. Christov, Editor-in-Chief. **ISSN:** 2165--3445 (print); **EISSN:** 2165--3453 (electronic). **Subscription Rates:** $398 Individuals Volume 5. **URL:** http://www.scirp.org/journal/cmb. **Circ:** (Not Reported).

2448 ■ Computational Water, Energy, and Environmental Engineering
Scientific Research Publishing Inc.
PO Box 54821
Irvine, CA 92619-4821
Publisher's E-mail: service@scirp.org
Peer-reviewed journal discussing problems and solutions governing the atmosphere, hydrosphere, lithosphere and biosphere ecosystems. **Freq:** Quarterly. **Key Personnel:** Prof. Ahmad Qasaimeh, Editor-in-Chief. **ISSN:** 2168--1562 (print); **EISSN:** 2168--1570 (electronic). **Subscription Rates:** $298 Individuals. **URL:** http://www.scirp.org/journal/cweee. **Circ:** (Not Reported).

2449 ■ Countdown
JDRF Orange County Chapter
2 Corporate Park, Ste. 106
Irvine, CA 92606
Phone: (949)553-0363
Fax: (949)553-8813
Publisher's E-mail: orangecounty@jdrf.org
Magazine containing information about juvenile diabetes research progress. **Freq:** Quarterly. **URL:** http://countdown.jdrf.org. **Remarks:** Accepts advertising. **Circ:** (Not Reported).

2450 ■ Creative Education
Scientific Research Publishing Inc.
PO Box 54821
Irvine, CA 92619-4821
Publication E-mail: ce@scirp.org
Peer-reviewed journal publishing articles on the latest advancements in creative education. **Freq:** Monthly. **Key Personnel:** Dr. Stephen Rushton, Editor-in-Chief. **ISSN:** 2151--4755 (print); **EISSN:** 2151--4771 (electronic). **Subscription Rates:** $1098 Individuals. **URL:** http://www.scirp.org/journal/ce. **Circ:** (Not Reported).

2451 ■ Crystal Structure Theory and Applications
Scientific Research Publishing Inc.
PO Box 54821
Irvine, CA 92619-4821
Publisher's E-mail: service@scirp.org
Journal featuring new issues and developments in crystal structure theory and applications. **Freq:** Quarterly. **Key Personnel:** Prof. Jorge M. Seminario, Editor-in-Chief. **ISSN:** 2169--2491 (print); **EISSN:** 2169--2505 (electronic). **Subscription Rates:** $499 Individuals article processing charge; Free open access. **Alt. Formats:** PDF. **URL:** http://www.scirp.org/journal/csta. **Circ:** (Not Reported).

2452 ■ Current Urban Studies
Scientific Research Publishing Inc.
PO Box 54821
Irvine, CA 92619-4821
Publisher's E-mail: service@scirp.org
Journal covering the latest advancement in the study of urban studies. **Freq:** Quarterly. **ISSN:** 2328--4900 (print); **EISSN:** 2328--4919 (electronic). **Subscription Rates:** $499 Individuals article Processing Charges; Free access on internet. **URL:** http://www.scirp.org/journal/CUS. **Circ:** (Not Reported).

2453 ■ Cycle World
Bonnier Corp.
15215 Alton Pkwy., Ste. 100
Irvine, CA 92618
Phone: (760)707-0100
Publication E-mail: cycleworld@neodata.com
Magazine on street, dirt, dual-purpose, and all-terrain motorcylces. Covering tests, aftermarket products, parts and accessories, competition, personalities, travel, and nostalgia. **Freq:** Monthly. **Print Method:** Offset. **Trim Size:** 7 7/8 x 10 1/2. **Cols./Page:** 3. **Col. Width:** 27 nonpareils. **Col. Depth:** 140 agate lines. **Key Personnel:** Andrew Leisner, Publisher. **ISSN:** 0011--4286 (print). **Subscription Rates:** $12 Individuals /year; $22 Canada; $31.93 Other countries. **URL:** http://www.cycleworld.com. **Ad Rates:** BW $22435; 4C $36180. **Remarks:** Advertising accepted; rates available upon request. **Circ:** Paid ★**227950**.

2454 ■ Dealernews: The Voice Of The Powersports Industry
Advanstar Holdings Inc.
2525 Main St., Ste. 400
Irvine, CA 92614
Phone: (949)954-8400
Fax: (949)954-8414
Publisher's E-mail: info@advanstar.com
Magazine covering dealers of motorcycles, ATV/off-road vehicles, watercraft, other powersport vehicles, and related aftermarket and apparel products. **Freq:** Monthly. **Trim Size:** 8 x 10.75. **Key Personnel:** Mary Slepicka; Arlo Redwine, Senior Editor; Dennis Johnson, Senior Editor. **ISSN:** 0893--2522 (print). **Subscription Rates:** $50 Individuals; $66.50 Canada and Mexico; $103.25 Other countries. **URL:** http://www.dealernews.com. **Formerly**: Motorcycle Dealernews. **Ad Rates:** BW $3,771; 4C $8,153. **Remarks:** Accepts advertising. **Circ:** Paid 18700.

2455 ■ E-Health Telecommunication Systems and Networks
Scientific Research Publishing Inc.
PO Box 54821
Irvine, CA 92619-4821
Publisher's E-mail: service@scirp.org
Refereed journal promoting the state-of-the-art research in the field of e-health applications in telecommunication systems and networks. **Freq:** Quarterly Latest edition 2015. **Key Personnel:** Prof. Mohamad Abou El-Nasr, Editor-in-Chief. **ISSN:** 2167--9517 (print); **EISSN:** 2167--9525 (electronic). **Subscription Rates:** $398 Individuals Volume 4. **URL:** http://www.scirp.org/journal/etsn. **Circ:** (Not Reported).

2456 ■ Editor & Publisher
Editor & Publisher Magazine
17782 Cowan, Ste. C
Irvine, CA 92614
Phone: (949)660-6150
Fax: (949)660-6172
Magazine focusing on newspaper journalism, advertising, printing equipment and interactive services. **Freq:** Weekly (Mon.). **Print Method:** Offset. **Trim Size:** 8 x 10 7/8. **Cols./Page:** 3. **Col. Width:** 2 1/4 inches. **Col. Depth:** 10 inches. **Key Personnel:** Charles McKeown, Publisher, phone: (646)654-5120; Mark Fitzgerald, Edi-

tor, phone: (949)660-6150; Shawn Moynihan, Managing Editor. **ISSN:** 0013--094X (print). **Subscription Rates:** $49 Individuals print and digital 12 issues; $75 Two years print and digital 24 issues; $49 Individuals 12 Issues Digital. **URL:** http://www.editorandpublisher.com. **Ad Rates:** BW $5,207; 4C $6,719. **Remarks:** Accepts advertising. **Circ:** (Not Reported).

2457 ■ Energy and Materials for Aerospace Engineering
Scientific Research Publishing Inc.
PO Box 54821
Irvine, CA 92619-4821
Publisher's E-mail: service@scirp.org
Journal featuring the latest advancements of energy and materials in the area of aerospace engineering. **Freq:** Bimonthly. **Key Personnel:** Prof. Jianglong Yu, Editor-in-Chief. **Subscription Rates:** $299 Individuals. **URL:** http://www.scirp.org/journal/EMAE. **Circ:** (Not Reported).

2458 ■ Energy and Power Engineering
Scientific Research Publishing Inc.
PO Box 54821
Irvine, CA 92619-4821
Publisher's E-mail: service@scirp.org
Journal publishing information on all important aspects of electric power engineering. **Freq:** Monthly. **Key Personnel:** Fermin Mallor, PhD, Editor-in-Chief. **ISSN:** 1949--243X (print); **EISSN:** 1947-3818 (electronic). **Subscription Rates:** $1298 Individuals. **URL:** http://www.scirp.org/journal/epe. **Circ:** (Not Reported).

2459 ■ Engineering
Scientific Research Publishing Inc.
PO Box 54821
Irvine, CA 92619-4821
Publication E-mail: eng@scirp.org
Peer-reviewed journal publishing articles on the latest advancements in engineering. **Freq:** Monthly. **Key Personnel:** Prof. David L. Carroll, Editor-in-Chief. **ISSN:** 1947-3931 (print); **EISSN:** 1947-3818 (electronic). **Subscription Rates:** $1068 Individuals. **URL:** http://www.scirp.org/journal/eng/. **Circ:** (Not Reported).

2460 ■ Entrepreneur Magazine
Entrepreneur Press
18061 Fitch
Irvine, CA 92614-6244
Phone: (949)261-2325
Fax: (949)261-7729
Free: 800-421-2300
Publication E-mail: entmag@entrepreneur.com
Freq: Monthly. **Print Method:** Offset. **Trim Size:** 8 x 10 3/4. **Cols./Page:** 3. **Col. Width:** 28 nonpareils. **Col. Depth:** 140 agate lines. **Key Personnel:** Rieva Lesonsky, Director, Editorial; Ryan Shea, President, Publisher, Chief Executive Officer. **ISSN:** 0163--3341 (print). **Subscription Rates:** $9.99 Individuals print or online. **URL:** http://www.entrepreneur.com/magazine/entrepreneur/index.html. **Ad Rates:** BW $62625; 4C $83480. **Remarks:** Accepts advertising. **Circ:** Paid ★**606770**, 200000.

2461 ■ Entrepreneur's Bizstartups.com
Entrepreneur Press
18061 Fitch
Irvine, CA 92614-6244
Phone: (949)261-2325
Fax: (949)261-7729
Free: 800-421-2300
Magazine for Generation X entrepreneurs (age 35 and under). Articles cover hot businesses to start; ideas for running and growing a business; cutting-edge technology; management; motivation and more. **Freq:** Monthly. **Col. Width:** 28 nonpareils. **Col. Depth:** 140 agate lines. **Key Personnel:** Jim Kahn, Publisher, phone: (212)563-8080, fax: (212)563-3852; Karen Axelton, Executive Editor, Publisher, phone: (212)563-8080, fax: (212)563-3852; Maria Anton, Executive Editor; Mike Hogan, Editor; Teresa Ciulla, Executive Editor. **ISSN:** 1522--1814 (print). **Subscription Rates:** $11.97 Individuals. **URL:** http://www.entrepreneur.com/startingabusiness/index.html. **Formerly:** Entrepreneur's Start-Ups; New Business Opportunities; Business Start-Ups. **Remarks:** Accepts classified advertising. **Circ:** (Not Reported).

2462 ■ Executive Golfer
Pazdur Publishing Inc.
2171 Campus Dr., Ste. 330
Irvine, CA 92612
Phone: (949)752-6474
Fax: (949)752-0398
Publisher's E-mail: june@executivegolfermagazine.com
Magazine providing private country club golfers with information on resorts for meetings, guest policies at private clubs, and golf communities for investment and retirement. Contains instructive articles for executives over 40. **Founded:** May 1972. **Freq:** Bimonthly. **Print Method:** Offset. **Trim Size:** 8 3/8 x 10 7/8. **Cols./Page:** 3. **Col. Width:** 27 nonpareils. **Col. Depth:** 98 agate lines. **Key Personnel:** Mark Pazdur, Publisher; Joyce Stevens, Managing Editor. **Subscription Rates:** $15 Two years. **URL:** http://www.executivegolfermagazine.com/. **Ad Rates:** BW $8,680; 4C $9,980. **Remarks:** Accepts advertising. **Circ:** Controlled 75000.

2463 ■ FJ Cruiser
Haymarket Worldwide L.L.C.
16842 Von Karman Ave., Ste. 125
Irvine, CA 92606
Phone: (949)417-6700
Publisher's E-mail: hello@haymarket.com
Magazine highlighting the vehicle's off-road capabilities. **Key Personnel:** Laurence Foster, Editor-in-Chief, phone: (44)20 82678887; Ian Havard, President, Publisher, phone: (949)417-6749. **URL:** http://www.fjc-mag.com/fj-cruiser. **Circ:** (Not Reported).

2464 ■ Food and Nutrition Sciences
Scientific Research Publishing Inc.
PO Box 54821
Irvine, CA 92619-4821
Publisher's E-mail: service@scirp.org
Peer-reviewed journal publishing articles on the latest advancements in food and nutrition science and technology. **Freq:** Monthly. **Key Personnel:** Prof. Alessandra Bordoni, Editor-in-Chief. **ISSN:** 2157--944X (print); **EISSN:** 2157--9458 (electronic). **Subscription Rates:** $1298 Individuals. **URL:** http://www.scirp.org/journal/fns. **Circ:** (Not Reported).

2465 ■ Forensic Medicine and Anatomy Research
Scientific Research Publishing Inc.
PO Box 54821
Irvine, CA 92619-4821
Publisher's E-mail: service@scirp.org
Peer-reviewed journal covering reviews and developments in the various branches of the anatomy sciences and forensic sciences. **Freq:** Quarterly. **Key Personnel:** Prof. Bofeng Zhu, Editor-in-Chief. **ISSN:** 2327--4115 (print); **EISSN:** 2327--4107 (electronic). **Subscription Rates:** $398 Individuals. **URL:** http://www.scirp.org/journal/fmar. **Circ:** (Not Reported).

2466 ■ Geomaterials
Scientific Research Publishing Inc.
PO Box 54821
Irvine, CA 92619-4821
Publication E-mail: gm@scirp.org
Journal publishing articles on rock and soil as materials. **Freq:** Quarterly. **Key Personnel:** Prof. Zhijian Peng, PhD, Editor-in-Chief. **ISSN:** 2161--7538 (print); **EISSN:** 2161--7546 (electronic). **Subscription Rates:** $498 Individuals. **URL:** http://www.scirp.org/journal/gm. **Circ:** (Not Reported).

2467 ■ Global Societies Journal
University of California, Irvine Center for Learning in the Arts, Sciences and Sustainability
2656 Biological Sciences III
Irvine, CA 92697-4540
Phone: (949)824-2418
Fax: (949)824-9103
Publication E-mail: Globalsocietiesucsb@gmail.com
Peer-reviewed journal containing articles on global issues. **Key Personnel:** John Soboslai, Editor-in-Chief. **EISSN:** 2373--7611 (electronic). **URL:** http://www.global.ucsb.edu/globalsocieties. **Circ:** (Not Reported).

2468 ■ Graphene
Scientific Research Publishing Inc.
PO Box 54821
Irvine, CA 92619-4821
Publisher's E-mail: service@scirp.org
Journal promoting, sharing and discussing new issues and developments in all aspects of graphene. **Freq:** Quarterly Latest edition 2015. **Key Personnel:** Prof. Michael Keidar, Editor-in-Chief. **ISSN:** 2169--3439 (print); **EISSN:** 2169--3471 (electronic). **Subscription Rates:** $398 Individuals volume 4. **URL:** http://www.scirp.org/journal/graphene. **Circ:** (Not Reported).

2469 ■ Green and Sustainable Chemistry
Scientific Research Publishing Inc.
PO Box 54821
Irvine, CA 92619-4821
Publication E-mail: gsc@scirp.org
Peer-reviewed journal publishing articles related to reducing the environmental impact of chemicals and fuels. **Freq:** Quarterly. **Key Personnel:** Prof. Nour-Eddine Es-Safi, Editor-in-Chief; Prof. Liang-Nian He, Editor-in-Chief. **ISSN:** 2160--6951 (print); **EISSN:** 2160--696X (electronic). **Subscription Rates:** $498 Individuals. **URL:** http://www.scirp.org/journal/gsc. **Circ:** (Not Reported).

2470 ■ Health
Scientific Research Publishing Inc.
PO Box 54821
Irvine, CA 92619-4821
Publication E-mail: health@scirp.org
Peer-reviewed journal publishing articles on the latest advancements in human health. **Freq:** Monthly. **Key Personnel:** Prof. Leonid P. Titov, Editor-in-Chief. **ISSN:** 1949-4998 (print). **Subscription Rates:** $948 Individuals. **URL:** http://www.scirp.org/journal/health/. **Circ:** (Not Reported).

2471 ■ Honda Tuning
TEN: The Enthusiast Network
1733 Alton Pkwy.
Irvine, CA 92606
Publication E-mail: hondatuning@emailcustomerservice.com
Magazine catering to the 18-34 year old Honda & Acura enthusiast, recognizing that Honda & Acura owners make up over forty-five percent of the sport compact market. Staff conducts road tests of the newest cars, testing of performance parts, accessories and covers the best performance tuner Hondas & Acuras in the market. Features tech tips by the country's leading tuners, dyno testing, new product evaluations and comprehensive how-to articles. **Freq:** 9/year. **Key Personnel:** Michael Febbo, Editor. **URL:** http://www.superstreetonline.com/honda-tuning-magazine/. **Remarks:** Accepts advertising. **Circ:** (Not Reported).

2472 ■ iBusiness
Scientific Research Publishing Inc.
PO Box 54821
Irvine, CA 92619-4821
Publisher's E-mail: service@scirp.org
Peer-reviewed journal publishing articles on the latest advancements in internet and business, and the intersection of economics with business applications. **Freq:** Quarterly. **Key Personnel:** Prof. Hengjin Cai, Editor-in-Chief. **ISSN:** 2150--4075 (print); **EISSN:** 2150--4083 (electronic). **Subscription Rates:** $498 Individuals. **URL:** http://www.scirp.org/journal/ib. **Circ:** (Not Reported).

2473 ■ InfraMatics
Scientific Research Publishing Inc.
PO Box 54821
Irvine, CA 92619-4821
Publisher's E-mail: service@scirp.org
Peer-reviewed journal presenting observational and theoretical studies of atmospheric infrasound generation, propagation and reception. **Freq:** Quarterly. **Key Personnel:** Dr. Michael A. H. Hedlin, Editor-in-Chief. **ISSN:** 2169--270X (print); **EISSN:** 2169--2696 (electronic). **Subscription Rates:** $298 Individuals. **URL:** http://www.scirp.org/journal/inframatics. **Circ:** (Not Reported).

2474 ■ Intelligent Control and Automation
Scientific Research Publishing Inc.
PO Box 54821
Irvine, CA 92619-4821
Publisher's E-mail: service@scirp.org
Peer-reviewed journal publishing articles on theories, methods and applications in intelligent control and automation. **Freq:** Quarterly. **Key Personnel:** Prof. Theodore B. Trafalis, Editor-in-Chief. **ISSN:** 2153--0653 (print); **EISSN:** 2153--0661 (electronic). **Subscription Rates:** $398 Individuals. **URL:** http://www.scirp.org/

Circulation: ★ = AAM; △ or • = BPA; ♦ = CAC; ❑ = VAC; ⊕ = PO Statement; ‡ = Publisher's Report; Boldface figures = sworn; Light figures = estimated.

journal/ica. **Circ:** (Not Reported).

2475 ■ Intelligent Information Management
Scientific Research Publishing Inc.
PO Box 54821
Irvine, CA 92619-4821
Publisher's E-mail: service@scirp.org
Peer-reviewed journal publishing articles on the latest advancements in intelligent information management. **Freq:** Bimonthly. **Key Personnel:** Prof. Damon Shing-Min Liu, Editor-in-Chief. **ISSN:** 2160--5912 (print); **EISSN:** 2160--5920 (electronic). **Subscription Rates:** $698 Individuals. **URL:** http://www.scirp.org/journal/iim. **Circ:** (Not Reported).

2476 ■ International Journal of Analytical Mass Spectrometry and Chromatography
Scientific Research Publishing Inc.
PO Box 54821
Irvine, CA 92619-4821
Publisher's E-mail: service@scirp.org
Journal presenting the latest developments and issues in all areas of mass spectrometry and chromatography. **Freq:** Quarterly. **Key Personnel:** Dr. Ilia Brondz, Editor-in-Chief. **ISSN:** 2332--1768 (print); **EISSN:** 2332--1776 (electronic). **URL:** http://www.scirp.org/journal/ijamsc. **Circ:** (Not Reported).

2477 ■ International Journal of Astronomy and Astrophysics
Scientific Research Publishing Inc.
PO Box 54821
Irvine, CA 92619-4821
Publication E-mail: ijaa@scirp.org
Peer-reviewed journal publishing research on fields of astrophysics and space sciences. **Freq:** Quarterly. **Key Personnel:** Prof. Michael D. Smith, Editor-in-Chief. **ISSN:** 2161--4717 (print); **EISSN:** 2161--4725 (electronic). **Subscription Rates:** $498 Individuals. **URL:** http://www.scirp.org/journal/ijaa. **Circ:** (Not Reported).

2478 ■ International Journal of Clean Coal and Energy
Scientific Research Publishing Inc.
PO Box 54821
Irvine, CA 92619-4821
Publisher's E-mail: service@scirp.org
Journal discussing new issues and developments in clean coal and energy. **Freq:** Quarterly. **Key Personnel:** Dr. Ke Liu, Editor-in-Chief. **ISSN:** 2168--152X (print); **EISSN:** 2168--1538 (electronic). **Subscription Rates:** $398 Individuals. **URL:** http://www.scirp.org/journal/ijcce. **Circ:** (Not Reported).

2479 ■ International Journal of Clinical Medicine
Scientific Research Publishing Inc.
PO Box 54821
Irvine, CA 92619-4821
Publisher's E-mail: service@scirp.org
Peer-reviewed journal publishing articles on the latest advancements in clinical medicine. **Freq:** Monthly. **Key Personnel:** Dr. Michael L. Moritz, Editor-in-Chief. **ISSN:** 2158--284X (print); **EISSN:** 2158--2882 (electronic). **Subscription Rates:** $1098 Individuals. **URL:** http://www.scirp.org/journal/ijcm. **Circ:** (Not Reported).

2480 ■ International Journal of Communications, Network and System Sciences
Scientific Research Publishing Inc.
PO Box 54821
Irvine, CA 92619-4821
Publisher's E-mail: service@scirp.org
Peer-reviewed journal publishing articles on the latest advancements in communications and network technologies. **Freq:** Monthly. **Key Personnel:** Prof. Boris S. Verkhovsky, Editor-in-Chief. **ISSN:** 1913--3715 (print); **EISSN:** 1913--3723 (electronic). **Subscription Rates:** $1298 Individuals. **URL:** http://www.scirp.org/journal/ijcns. **Circ:** (Not Reported).

2481 ■ International Journal of Geosciences
Scientific Research Publishing Inc.
PO Box 54821
Irvine, CA 92619-4821
Publisher's E-mail: service@scirp.org
Peer-reviewed journal publishing articles on the latest advancements in geosciences. **Freq:** Monthly. **Key Personnel:** Prof. Shuanggen Jin, Editor-in-Chief; Dr. Jacques Bourgois, Editor-in-Chief. **ISSN:** 2156--8359 (print); **EISSN:** 2156--8367 (electronic). **Subscription Rates:** $1198 Individuals. **URL:** http://www.scirp.org/journal/ijg. **Circ:** (Not Reported).

2482 ■ International Journal of Intelligence Science
Scientific Research Publishing Inc.
PO Box 54821
Irvine, CA 92619-4821
Publisher's E-mail: service@scirp.org
Journal featuring refereed papers on intelligence science. **Freq:** Quarterly. **Key Personnel:** Prof. Zhong-zhi Shi, Editor-in-Chief. **ISSN:** 2163--0283 (print); **EISSN:** 2163--0356 (electronic). **Subscription Rates:** $498 Individuals. **URL:** http://www.scirp.org/journal/ijis/. **Remarks:** Advertising not accepted. **Circ:** (Not Reported).

2483 ■ International Journal of Internet and Distributed Systems
Scientific Research Publishing Inc.
PO Box 54821
Irvine, CA 92619-4821
Publisher's E-mail: service@scirp.org
Journal featuring topics in all aspects of Internet and distributed systems. **Freq:** Quarterly. **ISSN:** 2327--7157 (print); **EISSN:** 2327--7165 (electronic). **URL:** http://www.scirp.org/journal/ijids. **Circ:** (Not Reported).

2484 ■ International Journal of Medical Physics, Clinical Engineering and Radiation Oncology
Scientific Research Publishing Inc.
PO Box 54821
Irvine, CA 92619-4821
Publisher's E-mail: service@scirp.org
Journal featuring research and clinical articles relevant to medical physics, biomedical engineering and radiation. **Freq:** Quarterly. **Key Personnel:** Huan Bosco Giap, Editor-in-Chief. **ISSN:** 2168--5436 (print); **EISSN:** 2168--5444 (electronic). **Subscription Rates:** $398 Individuals. **URL:** http://www.scirp.org/journal/IJMPCERO. **Circ:** (Not Reported).

2485 ■ International Journal of Modern Nonlinear Theory and Application
Scientific Research Publishing Inc.
PO Box 54821
Irvine, CA 92619-4821
Publisher's E-mail: service@scirp.org
Journal discussing all topics related to nonlinear dynamics and its applications. **Freq:** Quarterly. **Key Personnel:** Prof. Ahmad M. Harb, Editor-in-Chief. **ISSN:** 2167--9479 (print); **EISSN:** 2167--9487 (electronic). **Subscription Rates:** $398 Individuals. **URL:** http://www.scirp.org/journal/ijmnta. **Circ:** (Not Reported).

2486 ■ International Journal of Nonferrous Metallurgy
Scientific Research Publishing Inc.
PO Box 54821
Irvine, CA 92619-4821
Publisher's E-mail: service@scirp.org
Peer-reviewed journal discussing latest developments and issues in nonferrous metallurgy research. **Freq:** Quarterly. **Key Personnel:** Prof. Francesco Veglio, Editor-in-Chief. **ISSN:** 2168--2054 (print); **EISSN:** 2168--2062 (electronic). **Subscription Rates:** $499 Individuals article processing charges; Free open access. **URL:** http://www.scirp.org/journal/ijnm. **Circ:** (Not Reported).

2487 ■ International Journal of Organic Chemistry
Scientific Research Publishing Inc.
PO Box 54821
Irvine, CA 92619-4821
Publisher's E-mail: service@scirp.org
Peer-reviewed journal publishing articles in the field of organic chemistry. **Freq:** Quarterly. **Key Personnel:** Prof. Bouzid Menna, Editor-in-Chief. **ISSN:** 2161--4687 (print); **EISSN:** 2161--4695 (electronic). **Subscription Rates:** $398 Individuals. **URL:** http://www.scirp.org/journal/ijoc. **Circ:** (Not Reported).

2488 ■ International Journal of Otolaryngology and Head & Neck Surgery
Scientific Research Publishing Inc.
PO Box 54821
Irvine, CA 92619-4821
Publisher's E-mail: service@scirp.org
Peer-reviewed journal containing the latest advancements in otorhinolaryngology, head, and neck surgery. **Freq:** Bimonthly. **ISSN:** 2168--5452 (print); **EISSN:** 2168--5460 (electronic). **Subscription Rates:** $498 Individuals. **URL:** http://www.scirp.org/journal/ijohns. **Circ:** (Not Reported).

2489 ■ Journal of Agricultural Chemistry and Environment
Scientific Research Publishing Inc.
PO Box 54821
Irvine, CA 92619-4821
Publisher's E-mail: service@scirp.org
Journal covering topics dealing with chemical, biological and physical processes affecting the environmental changes in agriculture. **Freq:** Quarterly February, May, August and November. **Key Personnel:** Sun Chul Kang, Editor-in-Chief. **ISSN:** 2325--7458 (print); **EISSN:** 2325--744X (electronic). **Subscription Rates:** $498 Individuals. **URL:** http://www.scirp.org/journal/jacen. **Circ:** (Not Reported).

2490 ■ Journal of Analytical Sciences, Methods and Instrumentation
Scientific Research Publishing Inc.
PO Box 54821
Irvine, CA 92619-4821
Publisher's E-mail: service@scirp.org
Journal featuring scientific and technological advances in analytical sciences, experimental protocols, methods and characterization techniques. **Freq:** Quarterly. **Key Personnel:** Dr. Bouzid Menaa, Editor-in-Chief. **ISSN:** 2164--2745 (print); **EISSN:** 2164--2753 (electronic). **URL:** http://www.scirp.org/journal/jasmi. **Circ:** (Not Reported).

2491 ■ Journal of Behavioral and Brain Science
Scientific Research Publishing Inc.
PO Box 54821
Irvine, CA 92619-4821
Publisher's E-mail: service@scirp.org
Peer-reviewed journal publishing original research articles and reviews in the field of behavioral and brain function. **Freq:** Monthly. **Key Personnel:** Dr. Juan J. Canales, Editor-in-Chief. **ISSN:** 2160--5866 (print); **EISSN:** 2160--5874 (electronic). **Subscription Rates:** $1098 Individuals. **URL:** http://www.scirp.org/journal/jbbs. **Circ:** (Not Reported).

2492 ■ Journal of Biomaterials and Nanobiotechnology
Scientific Research Publishing Inc.
PO Box 54821
Irvine, CA 92619-4821
Publisher's E-mail: service@scirp.org
Peer-reviewed journal covering the basic science and engineering aspects of biomaterials and nanotechnology. **Freq:** Quarterly. **Key Personnel:** Dr. Bouzid Menaa, Editor-in-Chief. **ISSN:** 2158--7027 (print); **EISSN:** 2158--7043 (electronic). **Subscription Rates:** $598 Individuals. **URL:** http://www.scirp.org/journal/jbnb. **Circ:** (Not Reported).

2493 ■ Journal of Biomedical Science and Engineering
Scientific Research Publishing Inc.
PO Box 54821
Irvine, CA 92619-4821
Publisher's E-mail: service@scirp.org
Peer-reviewed journal covering all aspects of biomedical science and engineering. **Freq:** Monthly. **Key Personnel:** Prof. Kuo-Chen Chou, Editor-in-Chief. **ISSN:** 1937--6871 (print); **EISSN:** 1937--688X (electronic). **Subscription Rates:** $1298 Individuals. **URL:** http://www.scirp.org/journal/jbise. **Circ:** (Not Reported).

2494 ■ Journal of Biophysical Chemistry
Scientific Research Publishing Inc.
PO Box 54821
Irvine, CA 92619-4821
Publisher's E-mail: service@scirp.org
Peer-reviewed journal publishing the latest advancements in biophysical chemistry. **Freq:** Quarterly. **Key Personnel:** Prof. Cornelis J. Van der Schyf, Editor-in-Chief. **ISSN:** 2153--036X (print); **EISSN:** 2153--0378 (electronic). **Subscription Rates:** $498 Individuals. **URL:** http://www.scirp.org/journal/jbpc. **Circ:** (Not Reported).

2495 ■ Journal of Biosciences and Medicines
Scientific Research Publishing Inc.
PO Box 54821
Irvine, CA 92619-4821
Publisher's E-mail: service@scirp.org
Journal featuring the latest advancement in biosciences and medicines. **Freq:** Monthly Latest edition 2014. **ISSN:** 2327--5081 (print); **EISSN:** 2327--509X (electronic). **Subscription Rates:** $468 Individuals volume 2. **URL:** http://www.scirp.org/journal/jbm. **Circ:** (Not Reported).

2496 ■ Journal of Building Construction and Planning Research
Scientific Research Publishing Inc.
PO Box 54821
Irvine, CA 92619-4821
Publisher's E-mail: service@scirp.org
Peer-reviewed journal covering technical and scientific advances in building construction and planning. **Freq:** Quarterly. **Key Personnel:** Dr. Gwang-Hee Kim, Editor-in-Chief. **ISSN:** 2328--4889 (print). **Subscription Rates:** $298 Individuals. **URL:** http://www.scirp.org/journal/jbcpr. **Circ:** (Not Reported).

2497 ■ Journal of Cancer Therapy
Scientific Research Publishing Inc.
PO Box 54821
Irvine, CA 92619-4821
Publisher's E-mail: service@scirp.org
Peer-reviewed journal publishing the latest advancements in cancer therapy. **Freq:** Monthly. **Key Personnel:** Prof. Sibu P. Saha, Editor-in-Chief. **ISSN:** 2151--1934 (print); **EISSN:** 2151--1942 (electronic). **Subscription Rates:** $1298 Individuals. **URL:** http://www.scirp.org/journal/jct. **Circ:** (Not Reported).

2498 ■ Journal of Computer and Communications
Scientific Research Publishing Inc.
PO Box 54821
Irvine, CA 92619-4821
Publisher's E-mail: service@scirp.org
Journal containing topics regarding the latest advancements in communications and computers. **Freq:** Quarterly. **Key Personnel:** Prof. Vicente Milanes, Editor-in-Chief. **ISSN:** 2327--5219 (print); **EISSN:** 2327--5227 (electronic). **URL:** http://www.scirp.org/journal/JCC. **Circ:** (Not Reported).

2499 ■ Journal of Cosmetics, Dermatological Sciences and Applications
Scientific Research Publishing Inc.
PO Box 54821
Irvine, CA 92619-4821
Publisher's E-mail: service@scirp.org
Peer-reviewed journal covering the basic sciences, engineering aspects and applied technology of cosmetics, toiletries, perfumery and related fields. **Freq:** Quarterly. **Key Personnel:** Dr. Bouzid Menaa, Editor-in-Chief. **ISSN:** 2161--4105 (print); **EISSN:** 2161--4512 (electronic). **Subscription Rates:** $498 Individuals. **URL:** http://www.scirp.org/journal/jcdsa. **Circ:** (Not Reported).

2500 ■ Journal of Crystallization Process and Technology
Scientific Research Publishing Inc.
PO Box 54821
Irvine, CA 92619-4821
Publication E-mail: jcpt@scirp.org
Peer-reviewed journal covering all aspects of the crystallization process, studies and properties of crystalline materials. **Freq:** Quarterly. **Key Personnel:** Prof. Bouzid Menna, Editor-in-Chief. **ISSN:** 2161--7678 (print); **EISSN:** 2161--7686 (electronic). **Subscription Rates:** $398 Individuals. **URL:** http://www.scirp.org/journal/jcpt. **Circ:** (Not Reported).

2501 ■ Journal of Data Analysis and Information Processing
Scientific Research Publishing Inc.
PO Box 54821
Irvine, CA 92619-4821
Publisher's E-mail: service@scirp.org
Journal covering topics in different areas of data analysis and information processing. **Freq:** Quarterly. **Key Personnel:** Prof. Feng Shi, Editor-in-Chief. **ISSN:** 2327--7211 (print); **EISSN:** 2327--7203 (electronic). **Subscription Rates:** $298 Individuals. **URL:** http://www.scirp.org/journal/jdaip/. **Circ:** (Not Reported).

2502 ■ Journal of Diabetes Mellitus
Scientific Research Publishing Inc.
PO Box 54821
Irvine, CA 92619-4821
Publisher's E-mail: service@scirp.org
Peer-reviewed journal publishing research on diabetes mellitus. **Freq:** Quarterly. **Key Personnel:** Prof. Sharma S. Prabhakar, Editor-in-Chief. **ISSN:** 2160--5831 (print); **EISSN:** 2160--5858 (electronic). **Subscription Rates:** $498 Individuals. **URL:** http://www.scirp.org/journal/jdm. **Circ:** (Not Reported).

2503 ■ Journal of Electromagnetic Analysis and Applications
Scientific Research Publishing Inc.
PO Box 54821
Irvine, CA 92619-4821
Publisher's E-mail: service@scirp.org
Peer-reviewed journal covering the field of electromagnetic analysis testing and application. **Freq:** Monthly. **Key Personnel:** Prof. James L. Drewniak, Editor-in-Chief; Prof. Yuanzhang Sun, Editor-in-Chief. **ISSN:** 1942--0730 (print); **EISSN:** 1942--0749 (electronic). **Subscription Rates:** $1198 Individuals. **URL:** http://www.scirp.org/journal/jemaa. **Circ:** (Not Reported).

2504 ■ Journal of Electronics Cooling and Thermal Control
Scientific Research Publishing Inc.
PO Box 54821
Irvine, CA 92619-4821
Publisher's E-mail: service@scirp.org
Peer-reviewed journal providing reviews pertaining to the electronic cooling and thermal system control technology in the computer and electronics industries. **Freq:** Quarterly volume 5. **Key Personnel:** Prof. Dayong Gao, Editor-in-Chief. **ISSN:** 2162--6162 (print); **EISSN:** 2162--6170 (electronic). **Subscription Rates:** $398 Individuals. **URL:** http://www.scirp.org/journal/jectc. **Circ:** (Not Reported).

2505 ■ Journal of Encapsulation and Adsorption Sciences
Scientific Research Publishing Inc.
PO Box 54821
Irvine, CA 92619-4821
Publisher's E-mail: service@scirp.org
Peer-reviewed journal covering all aspects of encapsulation and adsorption sciences. **Freq:** Quarterly. **Key Personnel:** Dr. Bouzid Menaa, Editor-in-Chief. **ISSN:** 2161--4865 (print); **EISSN:** 2161--4873 (electronic). **Subscription Rates:** $398 Individuals. **URL:** http://www.scirp.org/journal/jeas. **Circ:** (Not Reported).

2506 ■ Journal of Environmental Protection
Scientific Research Publishing Inc.
PO Box 54821
Irvine, CA 92619-4821
Publisher's E-mail: service@scirp.org
Peer-reviewed journal publishing articles on the latest advancements in environmental protection. **Freq:** Monthly. **Key Personnel:** Prof. Thangarasu Pandiyan, Editor-in-Chief; Dr. Qingren Wang, Editor-in-Chief. **ISSN:** 2152--2197 (print); **EISSN:** 2152--2219 (electronic). **Subscription Rates:** $1298 Individuals. **URL:** http://www.scirp.org/journal/jep. **Circ:** (Not Reported).

2507 ■ Journal of Financial Risk Management
Scientific Research Publishing Inc.
PO Box 54821
Irvine, CA 92619-4821
Publisher's E-mail: service@scirp.org
Journal promoting to advance the knowledge and understanding of the practice of financial risk management. **Freq:** Quarterly Latest edition 2015. **Key Personnel:** Prof. Robin H. Luo, Editor-in-Chief. **ISSN:** 2167--9533 (print); **EISSN:** 2167--9541 (electronic). **Subscription Rates:** $398 Individuals Volume 4. **URL:** http://www.scirp.org/journal/jfrm. **Circ:** (Not Reported).

2508 ■ Journal of Flow Control, Measurement & Visualization
Scientific Research Publishing Inc.
PO Box 54821
Irvine, CA 92619-4821
Publisher's E-mail: service@scirp.org
Journal covering experimental and computational articles in the fields of flow control, measurement and visualization. **Freq:** Quarterly latest edition 2015. **Key Personnel:** Nobuyuki Fujisawa, Editor-in-Chief. **ISSN:** 2329--3322 (print); **EISSN:** 2329--3330 (electronic). **Subscription Rates:** $498 Individuals volume 3. **URL:** http://www.scirp.org/journal/JFCMV. **Circ:** (Not Reported).

2509 ■ Journal of Geographic Information System
Scientific Research Publishing Inc.
PO Box 54821
Irvine, CA 92619-4821
Publisher's E-mail: service@scirp.org
Peer-reviewed journal featuring the latest advancements in geographic information system. **Freq:** Bimonthly. **Key Personnel:** Prof. Jordi Marti Henneberg, Editor-in-Chief. **ISSN:** 2151--1950 (print); **EISSN:** 2151--1969 (electronic). **Subscription Rates:** $698 Individuals. **URL:** http://www.scirp.org/journal/jgis. **Circ:** (Not Reported).

2510 ■ Journal of Geoscience and Environment Protection
Scientific Research Publishing Inc.
PO Box 54821
Irvine, CA 92619-4821
Publisher's E-mail: service@scirp.org
Journal covering the latest advancement of natural sciences. **ISSN:** 2327--4336 (print); **EISSN:** 2327--4344 (electronic). **URL:** http://www.scirp.org/journal/gep. **Circ:** (Not Reported).

2511 ■ Journal of Human Resource and Sustainability Studies
Scientific Research Publishing Inc.
PO Box 54821
Irvine, CA 92619-4821
Publisher's E-mail: service@scirp.org
Journal featuring the latest advancements related to topics of human resource, work, and ecological sustainability. **Freq:** Quarterly Latest edition 2015. **Key Personnel:** Prof. Pascal Paille, Editor-in-Chief. **ISSN:** 2328--4862 (print); **EISSN:** 2328--4870 (electronic). **Subscription Rates:** $198 Individuals Volume 3. **URL:** http://www.scirp.org/journal/jhrss. **Circ:** (Not Reported).

2512 ■ Journal of Immune Based Therapies, Vaccines and Antimicrobials
Scientific Research Publishing Inc.
PO Box 54821
Irvine, CA 92619-4821
Publisher's E-mail: service@scirp.org
Journal discussing all aspects of therapeutic and prophylactic applications of immunology and microbiology. **Freq:** Quarterly Latest edition 2015. **Key Personnel:** Prof. Ronald B. Moss, Editor-in-Chief. **ISSN:** 2168--1546 (print); **EISSN:** 2168--1554 (electronic). **Subscription Rates:** $298 Individuals volume 4. **URL:** http://www.scirp.org/journal/jibtva. **Circ:** (Not Reported).

2513 ■ Journal of Information Security
Scientific Research Publishing Inc.
PO Box 54821
Irvine, CA 92619-4821
Publication E-mail: jis@scirp.org
Peer-reviewed journal publishing articles on different areas of information security. **Freq:** Quarterly. **Key Personnel:** Prof. Gyungho Lee, Editor-in-Chief; Prof. Lina Wang, Board Member. **ISSN:** 2153--1234 (print); **EISSN:** 2153--1242 (electronic). **Subscription Rates:** $398 Individuals. **URL:** http://www.scirp.org/journal/jis. **Circ:** (Not Reported).

2514 ■ Journal of Intelligent Learning Systems and Applications
Scientific Research Publishing Inc.
PO Box 54821
Irvine, CA 92619-4821
Publisher's E-mail: service@scirp.org
Peer-reviewed journal covering all aspects of intelligent learning systems and applications. **Freq:** Quarterly. **Key Personnel:** Prof. Xin Xu, Editor-in-Chief; Steve S.H. Ling, Editor-in-Chief. **ISSN:** 2150--8402 (print); **EISSN:** 2150--8410 (electronic). **Subscription Rates:** $498 Individuals. **URL:** http://www.scirp.org/journal/jilsa. **Circ:** (Not Reported).

2515 ■ Journal of Materials Science and Chemical Engineering
Scientific Research Publishing Inc.
PO Box 54821
Irvine, CA 92619-4821

Circulation: ★ = AAM; △ or • = BPA; ♦ = CAC; ❑ = VAC; ⊕ = PO Statement; ‡ = Publisher's Report; Boldface figures = sworn; Light figures = estimated.

Publisher's E-mail: service@scirp.org
Journal featuring latest advancement in materials science and chemical engineering. **Freq:** Monthly. **Key Personnel:** Dr. Jiyu Fang, Editor-in-Chief. **ISSN:** 2327--6045 (print); **EISSN:** 2327--6053 (electronic). **Subscription Rates:** $598 Individuals. **URL:** http://www.scirp.org/journal/msce. **Circ:** (Not Reported).

2516 ■ Journal of Mathematical Finance
Scientific Research Publishing Inc.
PO Box 54821
Irvine, CA 92619-4821
Publisher's E-mail: service@scirp.org
Journal presenting the latest developments in pure and applied financial mathematics. **Freq:** Quarterly Latest edition 2015. **Key Personnel:** Prof. Moawia Alghalith, Editor-in-Chief. **ISSN:** 2162--2434 (print); **EISSN:** 2162--2442 (electronic). **Subscription Rates:** $498 Individuals volume 5. **URL:** http://www.scirp.org/journal/jmf. **Circ:** (Not Reported).

2517 ■ Journal of Modern Physics
Scientific Research Publishing Inc.
PO Box 54821
Irvine, CA 92619-4821
Publisher's E-mail: service@scirp.org
Peer-reviewed journal publishing articles on the latest advancements in modern physics. **Freq:** Monthly. **Key Personnel:** Prof. Moshe Gai, Editor-in-Chief; Prof. Yang-Hui He, Editor-in-Chief; Prof. Marko Markov, Editor-in-Chief; Prof. Chang Liu, Managing Editor. **ISSN:** 2153--1196 (print); **EISSN:** 2153--120X (electronic). **Subscription Rates:** $1298 Individuals. **URL:** http://www.scirp.org/journal/jmp. **Circ:** (Not Reported).

2518 ■ Journal of Power and Energy Engineering
Scientific Research Publishing Inc.
PO Box 54821
Irvine, CA 92619-4821
Publisher's E-mail: service@scirp.org
Journal covering the latest advancements in power and energy engineering. **Freq:** Monthly. **Key Personnel:** Prof. Elias K. Stefanakos, PhD, Editor-in-Chief. **ISSN:** 2327--588X (print); **EISSN:** 2327--5901 (electronic). **Subscription Rates:** $598 Individuals. **URL:** http://www.scirp.org/journal/jpee. **Circ:** (Not Reported).

2519 ■ Journal of Quantum Information Science
Scientific Research Publishing Inc.
PO Box 54821
Irvine, CA 92619-4821
Publisher's E-mail: service@scirp.org
Journal containing research articles in the field of quantum information science. **Freq:** Quarterly. **Key Personnel:** Prof. Arun Kumar Pati, Editor-in-Chief. **ISSN:** 2162--5751 (print); **EISSN:** 2162--576X (electronic). **URL:** http://www.scirp.org/journal/jqis. **Circ:** (Not Reported).

2520 ■ Journal of Sensor Technology
Scientific Research Publishing Inc.
PO Box 54821
Irvine, CA 92619-4821
Publisher's E-mail: service@scirp.org
Journal providing topics on sensor technologies and related studies. **Freq:** Quarterly. **Key Personnel:** Prof. Ashok Srvastava, Editor-in-Chief. **ISSN:** 2161--122X (print); **EISSN:** 2161--1238 (electronic). **Subscription Rates:** $398 Individuals. **URL:** http://www.scirp.org/journal/jst. **Circ:** (Not Reported).

2521 ■ Journal of Service Science and Management
Scientific Research Publishing Inc.
PO Box 54821
Irvine, CA 92619-4821
Publisher's E-mail: service@scirp.org
Peer-reviewed journal covering all aspects of service science and management. **Freq:** Bimonthly. **Key Personnel:** Prof. Samuel Mendlinger, Editor-in-Chief. **ISSN:** 1940--9893 (print); **EISSN:** 1940--9907 (electronic). **Subscription Rates:** $598 Individuals. **URL:** http://www.scirp.org/journal/jssm. **Circ:** (Not Reported).

2522 ■ Journal of Signal and Information Processing
Scientific Research Publishing Inc.
PO Box 54821
Irvine, CA 92619-4821
Publisher's E-mail: service@scirp.org
Peer-reviewed journal publishing articles on the latest advancements in signal and information processing. **Freq:** Quarterly. **Key Personnel:** Prof. Baozong Yuan, Editor-in-Chief; Prof. Qiuqi Ruan, Editor-in-Chief. **ISSN:** 2159--4465 (print); **EISSN:** 2159--4481 (electronic). **Subscription Rates:** $398 Individuals. **URL:** http://www.scirp.org/journal/jsip. **Circ:** (Not Reported).

2523 ■ Journal of Software Engineering and Applications
Scientific Research Publishing Inc.
PO Box 54821
Irvine, CA 92619-4821
Publisher's E-mail: service@scirp.org
Peer-reviewed journal covering software engineering and applications. **Freq:** Monthly. **Key Personnel:** Prof. Yashwant K. Malaiya, Editor-in-Chief. **ISSN:** 1945--3116 (print); **EISSN:** 1945--3124 (electronic). **Subscription Rates:** $1198 Individuals. **URL:** http://www.scirp.org/journal/jsea. **Circ:** (Not Reported).

2524 ■ Journal of Surface Engineered Materials and Advanced Technology
Scientific Research Publishing Inc.
PO Box 54821
Irvine, CA 92619-4821
Publisher's E-mail: service@scirp.org
Peer-reviewed journal publishing articles on surface sciences, surface properties, techniques of characterization and generated applications. **Freq:** Quarterly. **Key Personnel:** Prof. Bouzid Menaa, Editor-in-Chief. **ISSN:** 2161--4881 (print); **EISSN:** 2161--489X (electronic). **Subscription Rates:** $398 Individuals. **URL:** http://www.scirp.org/journal/jsemat. **Circ:** (Not Reported).

2525 ■ Journal of Sustainable Bioenergy Systems
Scientific Research Publishing Inc.
PO Box 54821
Irvine, CA 92619-4821
Publisher's E-mail: service@scirp.org
Journal promoting and sharing the advancements of Sustainable Bioenergy Systems. **Freq:** Quarterly latest edition 2015. **Key Personnel:** Dr. Lijun Wang, Editor-in-Chief. **ISSN:** 2165--400X (print); **EISSN:** 2165--4018 (electronic). **Subscription Rates:** $1592 Individuals volume 5. **URL:** http://www.scirp.org/journal/jsbs. **Circ:** (Not Reported).

2526 ■ Journal of Transportation Technologies
Scientific Research Publishing Inc.
PO Box 54821
Irvine, CA 92619-4821
Publication E-mail: jtts@scirp.org
Peer-reviewed journal publishing articles on the latest advancement of transportation technologies. **Freq:** Quarterly. **Key Personnel:** Prof. Tschangho Kim, Editor-in-Chief. **ISSN:** 2160--0473 (print); **EISSN:** 2160--0481 (electronic). **Subscription Rates:** $498 Individuals. **URL:** http://www.scirp.org/journal/jtts. **Circ:** (Not Reported).

2527 ■ Journal of Tuberculosis Research
Scientific Research Publishing Inc.
PO Box 54821
Irvine, CA 92619-4821
Publisher's E-mail: service@scirp.org
Journal promoting, sharing and discussing new issues and developments in different areas of tuberculosis research. **Freq:** Quarterly Latest edition 2015. **Key Personnel:** Dr. Wing Cheong Yam, Editor-in-Chief. **ISSN:** 2329--843X (print); **EISSN:** 2329--8448 (electronic). **Subscription Rates:** $398 Individuals Volume 3. **URL:** http://www.scirp.org/journal/jtr. **Circ:** (Not Reported).

2528 ■ Journal of Water Resource and Protection
Scientific Research Publishing Inc.
PO Box 54821
Irvine, CA 92619-4821
Publisher's E-mail: service@scirp.org
Peer-reviewed journal publishing articles on the latest advancements in water resources and protection. **Freq:** Monthly. **Key Personnel:** Prof. Jian Shen, Editor-in-Chief; Prof. Ni-Bin Chang, Editor-in-Chief. **ISSN:** 1945--3094 (print); **EISSN:** 1945--3108 (electronic). **Subscription Rates:** $1298 Individuals. **URL:** http://www.scirp.org/Journal/jwarp. **Circ:** (Not Reported).

2529 ■ The Log
The Log Newspapers
17782 Cowan, Ste. C
Irvine, CA 92614
Phone: (949)660-6150
Fax: (949)660-6172
Newspaper for the southern California boating communities. **Founded:** Nov. 1971. **Freq:** Semimonthly 26/yr. **Print Method:** Offset. **Trim Size:** 11 5/8 x 17 1/8. **Cols./Page:** 4. **Col. Width:** 2 3/8 inches. **Col. Depth:** 224 agate lines. **Key Personnel:** Eston Ellis, Managing Editor; Taylor Hill, Associate Editor. **Subscription Rates:** $39.90 Individuals (one year) via third class mail; $125 Individuals (one year) via first class mail. **URL:** http://www.thelog.com/. **Formerly:** San Diego Log. **Ad Rates:** BW $1,706; 4C $1,961. **Remarks:** Accepts advertising. **Circ:** Paid 1600, Free 80000.

2530 ■ Low Carbon Economy
Scientific Research Publishing Inc.
PO Box 54821
Irvine, CA 92619-4821
Publisher's E-mail: service@scirp.org
Peer-reviewed journal publishing articles on the latest advancements of applied research toward a more efficient and equitable carbon neutral economic society. **Freq:** Quarterly. **Key Personnel:** Prof. Hans Schnitzer, Editor-in-Chief. **ISSN:** 2158--7000 (print); **EISSN:** 2158--7019 (electronic). **Subscription Rates:** $498 Individuals. **URL:** http://www.scirp.org/journal/lce. **Circ:** (Not Reported).

2531 ■ Lowrider
TEN: The Enthusiast Network
1733 Alton Pky.
Irvine, CA 92606
Publication E-mail: lowrider@emailcustomerservice.com
Magazine focusing on the Lowrider industry and its enthusiasts and promoting lowriding as a positive automotive lifestyle. **Freq:** Monthly. **Key Personnel:** Rudy Rivas, Publisher, phone: (949)705-3169. **Subscription Rates:** $20 Individuals; $35 Two years; $32 Canada; $59 Canada 2 years; $44 Other countries; $83 Other countries 2 years. **URL:** http://www.lowridermagazine.com/. **Remarks:** Accepts advertising. **Circ:** Paid ★**154147**.

2532 ■ Lowrider Arte
TEN: The Enthusiast Network
1733 Alton Pky.
Irvine, CA 92606
Publication E-mail: inquiries@automotive.com
Magazine celebrating America's foremost amateur and underground artists. Features highlight creative talent; submissions are received from readers and artists around the world. Each issue features the popular "Artist Profile" series, which explores the legendary talents of the Masters as well as the innovations of new, emerging artists. **Freq:** Quarterly. **Key Personnel:** Rudy Rivas, Publisher, phone: (949)705-3169. **URL:** http://www.lowrider.com/brand/lowrider-arte-magazine. **Remarks:** Accepts advertising. **Circ:** (Not Reported).

2533 ■ Materials Sciences and Applications
Scientific Research Publishing Inc.
PO Box 54821
Irvine, CA 92619-4821
Publication E-mail: msa@scirp.org
Peer-reviewed journal publishing articles on different areas of materials sciences and applications. **Freq:** Monthly. **Key Personnel:** Prof. Young W. Kwon, Editor-in-Chief. **ISSN:** 2153--117X (print); **EISSN:** 2153--1188 (electronic). **Subscription Rates:** $1198 Individuals. **URL:** http://www.scirp.org/journal/msa. **Circ:** (Not Reported).

2534 ■ Mexican Studies-Estudios Mexicanos
University of California Press - Journals and Digital Publishing Division
c/o Jacobo Sefami, Ed.
University of California
300 Krieger Hall
Irvine, CA 92697-3275
Publication E-mail: estumex@uci.edu
Publication covering Mexican studies. **Freq:** Semiannual February, August. **Trim Size:** 6 x 9. **Key Personnel:** Jaime E. Rodriguez O, Editor. **ISSN:** 0742--9797 (print); **EISSN:** 1533--8320 (electronic). **Subscription Rates:** $52 Individuals print & online; $235 Institutions print & online; $29 Individuals single issue; $125 Institu-

tions single issue. **URL:** http://msem.ucpress.edu. **Ad Rates:** BW $325. **Remarks:** Accepts advertising. **Circ:** Paid 400.

2535 ■ Microscopy Research
Scientific Research Publishing Inc.
PO Box 54821
Irvine, CA 92619-4821
Publisher's E-mail: service@scirp.org
Journal promoting, sharing and discussing new issues and developments in all areas of Microscopy Research. **Freq:** Quarterly latest edition 2015. **ISSN:** 2329--3306 (print); **EISSN:** 2329--3314 (electronic). **Subscription Rates:** $198 Individuals volume 3. **URL:** http://www.scirp.org/journal/MR. **Circ:** (Not Reported).

2536 ■ Microsoft Certified Professional Magazine
101communications LLC
16271 Laguna Canyon Rd.
Irvine, CA 92618
Phone: (949)265-1520
Fax: (949)265-1528
Professional magazine for Windows NT/200 experts. **Freq:** Daily. **Key Personnel:** Doug Barney, Editor-in-Chief; Lafe Low, Executive Editor; Michael Domingo, Editor; Wendy Gonchar, Managing Editor; Keith Ward, Editor. **Subscription Rates:** Free. **URL:** http://www.mcpmag.com. **Remarks:** Advertising accepted; rates available upon request. **Circ:** (Not Reported).

2537 ■ Modeling and Numerical Simulation of Material Science
Scientific Research Publishing Inc.
PO Box 54821
Irvine, CA 92619-4821
Publisher's E-mail: service@scirp.org
Journal featuring latest advancement in modeling and numerical simulation of material science. **Freq:** Quarterly. **Key Personnel:** Prof. Hai-Liang Yu, Editor-in-Chief. **ISSN:** 2164--5345 (print); **EISSN:** 2164--5353 (electronic). **Subscription Rates:** $298 Individuals. **URL:** http://www.scirp.org/journal/mnsms. **Circ:** (Not Reported).

2538 ■ Modern Chemotherapy
Scientific Research Publishing Inc.
PO Box 54821
Irvine, CA 92619-4821
Publisher's E-mail: service@scirp.org
Journal featuring latest issues and developments in all aspects of anti-infective and anti-tumor chemotherapy. **Freq:** Quarterly. **Key Personnel:** Prof. Stephen L. Chan, Editor-in-Chief. **ISSN:** 2169--348X (print); **EISSN:** 2169--3498 (electronic). **Subscription Rates:** $398 Individuals. **URL:** http://www.scirp.org/journal/mc. **Circ:** (Not Reported).

2539 ■ Modern Economy
Scientific Research Publishing Inc.
PO Box 54821
Irvine, CA 92619-4821
Publication E-mail: me@scirp.org
Peer-reviewed journal publishing articles on all areas of international economics. **Freq:** Monthly. **Key Personnel:** Prof. Cuihong Yong, Editor-in-Chief. **ISSN:** 2152--7245 (print); **EISSN:** 2152--7261 (electronic). **Subscription Rates:** $898 Individuals. **URL:** http://www.scirp.org/journal/me. **Circ:** (Not Reported).

2540 ■ Modern Instrumentation
Scientific Research Publishing Inc.
PO Box 54821
Irvine, CA 92619-4821
Publisher's E-mail: service@scirp.org
Journal featuring the latest advancements in instrumentation. **Freq:** Quarterly. **Key Personnel:** Prof. P. Balasubramaniam, Editor-in-Chief. **ISSN:** 2165--9257 (print); **EISSN:** 2165--9273 (electronic). **Subscription Rates:** $298 Individuals. **URL:** http://www.scirp.org/journal/mi. **Circ:** (Not Reported).

2541 ■ Modern Mechanical Engineering
Scientific Research Publishing Inc.
PO Box 54821
Irvine, CA 92619-4821
Publisher's E-mail: service@scirp.org
Journal covering the latest advancements in mechanical engineering. **Freq:** Quarterly. **Key Personnel:** Prof. C.W. Lim, Editor-in-Chief. **ISSN:** 2164--0165 (print); **EISSN:** 2164--0181 (electronic). **Subscription Rates:** $298 Individuals. **URL:** http://www.scirp.org/Journal/mme. **Circ:** (Not Reported).

2542 ■ Modern Plastic Surgery
Scientific Research Publishing Inc.
PO Box 54821
Irvine, CA 92619-4821
Publisher's E-mail: service@scirp.org
Journal discussing various new issues and developments in plastic surgery. **Freq:** Quarterly. **Key Personnel:** Randal Tanh Hoang Pham, Editor-in-Chief; Prof. Salvatore Carlucci, Board Member. **ISSN:** 2164--5213 (print); **EISSN:** 2164--5280 (electronic). **Subscription Rates:** $398 Individuals. **URL:** http://www.scirp.org/journal/mps. **Circ:** (Not Reported).

2543 ■ Modern Research in Catalysis
Scientific Research Publishing Inc.
PO Box 54821
Irvine, CA 92619-4821
Publisher's E-mail: service@scirp.org
Journal promoting, sharing and discussing various new issues and developments in all aspects of catalyst. **Freq:** Quarterly. **Key Personnel:** Dr. Ismail Ibrahem, Editor-in-Chief. **ISSN:** 2168--4480 (print); **EISSN:** 2168--4499 (electronic). **URL:** http://www.scirp.org/journal/mrc. **Circ:** (Not Reported).

2544 ■ Modern Research in Inflammation
Scientific Research Publishing Inc.
PO Box 54821
Irvine, CA 92619-4821
Publisher's E-mail: service@scirp.org
Journal promoting, sharing and discussing new issues and developments in different areas of Inflammation. **Freq:** Quarterly Latest edition 2015. **Key Personnel:** Prof. Alpana Ray, Editor-in-Chief. **ISSN:** 2169--9682 (print); **EISSN:** 2169--9690 (electronic). **Subscription Rates:** $398 Individuals Volume 4. **URL:** http://www.scirp.org/journal/mri. **Circ:** (Not Reported).

2545 ■ Natural Resources
Scientific Research Publishing Inc.
PO Box 54821
Irvine, CA 92619-4821
Publication E-mail: nr@scirp.org
Peer-reviewed journal publishing articles on the latest advancements in natural resources. **Freq:** Monthly. **Key Personnel:** Prof. Alevtina Smirnova, Editor-in-Chief. **ISSN:** 2158--706X (print); **EISSN:** 2158--7086 (electronic). **Subscription Rates:** $1098 Individuals. **URL:** http://www.scirp.org/journal/nr. **Circ:** (Not Reported).

2546 ■ Natural Science
Scientific Research Publishing Inc.
PO Box 54821
Irvine, CA 92619-4821
Publication E-mail: ns@scirp.org
Peer-reviewed journal publishing articles on the latest advancements in natural sciences. **Freq:** Monthly. **Key Personnel:** Prof. Kuo-Chen Chou, Editor-in-Chief. **ISSN:** 2150--4091 (print); **EISSN:** 2150--4105 (electronic). **Subscription Rates:** $1298 Individuals. **URL:** http://www.scirp.org/journal/ns. **Circ:** (Not Reported).

2547 ■ Neuroscience and Medicine
Scientific Research Publishing Inc.
PO Box 54821
Irvine, CA 92619-4821
Publisher's E-mail: service@scirp.org
Peer-reviewed journal publishing the latest advancements in neuroscience. **Freq:** Quarterly. **Key Personnel:** Prof. Thomas Muller, Editor-in-Chief. **ISSN:** 2158--2912 (print); **EISSN:** 2158--2947 (electronic). **Subscription Rates:** $498 Individuals. **URL:** http://www.scirp.org/journal/nm. **Circ:** (Not Reported).

2548 ■ New Journal of Glass and Ceramics
Scientific Research Publishing Inc.
PO Box 54821
Irvine, CA 92619-4821
Publisher's E-mail: service@scirp.org
Peer-reviewed journal publishing articles on all branches of glass and ceramics. **Freq:** Quarterly. **Key Personnel:** Prof. Bouzid Menaa, Editor-in-Chief. **ISSN:** 2161--7554 (print); **EISSN:** 2161--7562 (electronic). **Subscription Rates:** $498 Individuals. **URL:** http://www.scirp.org/journal/njgc. **Circ:** (Not Reported).

2549 ■ New University
University of California, Irvine
260 Aldrich Hall
Irvine, CA 92697-1075
Phone: (949)824-6703
Fax: (949)824-2951
Collegiate newspaper featuring campus/community news. **Freq:** Weekly (Mon.). **Print Method:** Offset. **Trim Size:** 11 x 17. **Cols./Page:** 5. **Col. Width:** 23 nonpareils. **Col. Depth:** 224 agate lines. **Key Personnel:** Natasha Monnereau, Manager, Advertising, phone: (949)824-4284. **Subscription Rates:** Free. **URL:** http://www.newuniversity.org. **Ad Rates:** BW $812; 4C $1298.22. **Remarks:** Accepts advertising. **Circ:** Combined ‡41859.

2550 ■ Occupational Diseases and Environmental Medicine
Scientific Research Publishing Inc.
PO Box 54821
Irvine, CA 92619-4821
Publisher's E-mail: service@scirp.org
Journal discussing new issues and developments in all areas of occupational diseases and environmental medicine. **Freq:** Quarterly. **Key Personnel:** Hesham M. Korashy, Editor-in-Chief. **ISSN:** 2333--3561 (print); **EISSN:** 2333--357X (electronic). **URL:** http://www.scirp.org/journal/odem. **Circ:** (Not Reported).

2551 ■ Open Journal of Accounting
Scientific Research Publishing Inc.
PO Box 54821
Irvine, CA 92619-4821
Publisher's E-mail: service@scirp.org
Journal promoting and discussing various new issues and developments in different areas of accounting. **Freq:** Quarterly Latest edition 2015. **ISSN:** 2169--3404 (print); **EISSN:** 2169--3412 (electronic). **Subscription Rates:** $298 Individuals Volume 4. **URL:** http://www.scirp.org/journal/ojacct. **Circ:** (Not Reported).

2552 ■ Open Journal of Acoustics
Scientific Research Publishing Inc.
PO Box 54821
Irvine, CA 92619-4821
Publisher's E-mail: service@scirp.org
Journal covering the advancements of the study of acoustics. **Freq:** Quarterly. **Key Personnel:** Dr. Wen L. Li, Editor-in-Chief. **ISSN:** 2162--5786 (print); **EISSN:** 2162--5794 (electronic). **Subscription Rates:** $498 Individuals. **URL:** http://www.scirp.org/journal/oja/. **Circ:** (Not Reported).

2553 ■ Open Journal of Air Pollution
Scientific Research Publishing Inc.
PO Box 54821
Irvine, CA 92619-4821
Publisher's E-mail: service@scirp.org
Journal promoting various issues and developments in different areas of air pollution. **Freq:** Quarterly. **Key Personnel:** Prof. Kalliat T. Valsaraj, Editor-in-Chief. **ISSN:** 2169--2653 (print); **EISSN:** 2169--2661 (electronic). **Subscription Rates:** $398 Individuals. **URL:** http://www.scirp.org/journal/ojap. **Circ:** (Not Reported).

2554 ■ Open Journal of Anesthesiology
Scientific Research Publishing Inc.
PO Box 54821
Irvine, CA 92619-4821
Publisher's E-mail: service@scirp.org
Journal covering the latest advancements in anesthesiology. **Freq:** Monthly. **Key Personnel:** Prof. Praveen Kumar Neema, Editor-in-Chief. **ISSN:** 2164--5531 (print); **EISSN:** 2164--5558 (electronic). **Subscription Rates:** $1198 Individuals. **URL:** http://www.scirp.org/journal/ojanes. **Circ:** (Not Reported).

2555 ■ Open Journal of Animal Sciences
Scientific Research Publishing Inc.
PO Box 54821
Irvine, CA 92619-4821
Publisher's E-mail: service@scirp.org
Journal containing the latest advancements in animal sciences. **Freq:** Quarterly Latest edition: 2015. **Key Personnel:** Prof. Young W. Park, Editor-in-Chief. **ISSN:** 2161--7597 (print); **EISSN:** 2161--7627 (electronic). **Subscription Rates:** $498 Individuals Volume 5. **URL:** http://www.scirp.org/journal/ojas. **Circ:** (Not Reported).

Circulation: ★ = AAM; △ or • = BPA; ♦ = CAC; ❑ = VAC; ⊕ = PO Statement; ‡ = Publisher's Report; Boldface figures = sworn; Light figures = estimated.

2556 ■ Open Journal of Antennas and Propagation
Scientific Research Publishing Inc.
PO Box 54821
Irvine, CA 92619-4821
Publisher's E-mail: service@scirp.org
Journal featuring new issues and developments in the research of antennas and propagation. **Freq:** Quarterly. **Key Personnel:** Prof. Ahmed M. Attiya, Editor-in-Chief. **ISSN:** 2329--8421 (print); **EISSN:** 2329--8413 (electronic). **Subscription Rates:** $298 Individuals. **URL:** http://www.scirp.org/journal/ojapr. **Circ:** (Not Reported).

2557 ■ Open Journal of Apoptosis
Scientific Research Publishing Inc.
PO Box 54821
Irvine, CA 92619-4821
Publisher's E-mail: service@scirp.org
Journal promoting, sharing and discussing new issues and developments in different areas of apoptosis. **Freq:** Quarterly Latest edition: 2015. **ISSN:** 2168--3832 (print); **EISSN:** 2168--3840 (electronic). **Subscription Rates:** $298 Individuals Volume 4. **URL:** http://www.scirp.org/journal/OJApo. **Circ:** (Not Reported).

2558 ■ Open Journal of Applied Biosensor
Scientific Research Publishing Inc.
PO Box 54821
Irvine, CA 92619-4821
Publisher's E-mail: service@scirp.org
Journal covering new issues and developments in different areas of Biosensor. **Freq:** Quarterly latest edition 2015. **Key Personnel:** Prof. Arun K. Bhunia, Editor-in-Chief. **ISSN:** 2168--5401 (print); **EISSN:** 2168--5398 (electronic). **Subscription Rates:** $298 Individuals volume 4. **URL:** http://www.scirp.org/journal/ojab. **Circ:** (Not Reported).

2559 ■ Open Journal of Applied Sciences
Scientific Research Publishing Inc.
PO Box 54821
Irvine, CA 92619-4821
Publisher's E-mail: service@scirp.org
Peer-reviewed journal promoting interdisciplinary studies in applied sciences. **Freq:** Monthly latest edition 2015. **Key Personnel:** Prof. Harry E. Ruda, Editor. **ISSN:** 2165--3917 (print); **EISSN:** 2165--3925 (electronic). **Subscription Rates:** $1098 Individuals volume 5. **URL:** http://www.scirp.org/journal/ojapps. **Circ:** (Not Reported).

2560 ■ Open Journal of Biophysics
Scientific Research Publishing Inc.
PO Box 54821
Irvine, CA 92619-4821
Publisher's E-mail: service@scirp.org
Journal covering new issues and developments in different areas of biophysics. **Freq:** Quarterly. **Key Personnel:** Prof. Tatyana Karabencheva, Editor-in-Chief. **ISSN:** 2164--5388 (print); **EISSN:** 2164--5396 (electronic). **Subscription Rates:** $316 Individuals. **URL:** http://www.scirp.org/journal/ojbiphy. **Circ:** (Not Reported).

2561 ■ Open Journal of Blood Diseases
Scientific Research Publishing Inc.
PO Box 54821
Irvine, CA 92619-4821
Publisher's E-mail: service@scirp.org
Peer-reviewed journal covering the advancement of the study of blood diseases. **Freq:** Quarterly. **Key Personnel:** Prof. Ricardo Forastiero, Editor-in-Chief. **ISSN:** 2164--3180 (print); **EISSN:** 2164--3199 (electronic). **Subscription Rates:** $498 Individuals. **URL:** http://www.scirp.org/journal/ojbd. **Circ:** (Not Reported).

2562 ■ Open Journal of Business and Management
Scientific Research Publishing Inc.
PO Box 54821
Irvine, CA 92619-4821
Publisher's E-mail: service@scirp.org
Journal presenting the latest advancement in the study of business and management. **Freq:** Quarterly Latest edition 2015. **ISSN:** 2329--3284 (print); **EISSN:** 2329--3292 (electronic). **Subscription Rates:** $398 Individuals volume 3. **URL:** http://www.scirp.org/journal/ojbm. **Circ:** (Not Reported).

2563 ■ Open Journal of Civil Engineering
Scientific Research Publishing Inc.
PO Box 54821
Irvine, CA 92619-4821
Publisher's E-mail: service@scirp.org
Journal covering the latest advancements in civil engineering. **Freq:** Quarterly. **Key Personnel:** Dr. Hwai-Chung Wu, Editor-in-Chief. **ISSN:** 2164--3164 (print); **EISSN:** 2164--3172 (electronic). **Subscription Rates:** $398 Individuals. **URL:** http://www.scirp.org/journal/ojce. **Circ:** (Not Reported).

2564 ■ Open Journal of Clinical Diagnostics
Scientific Research Publishing Inc.
PO Box 54821
Irvine, CA 92619-4821
Publisher's E-mail: service@scirp.org
Journal featuring the latest advancements in clinical diagnostics. **Freq:** Quarterly. **Key Personnel:** Dr. Natalia Bizunok, Editor-in-Chief. **ISSN:** 2162--5816 (print); **EISSN:** 2162--5824 (electronic). **Subscription Rates:** $398 Individuals. **URL:** http://www.scirp.org/journal/ojcd. **Circ:** (Not Reported).

2565 ■ Open Journal of Composite Materials
Scientific Research Publishing Inc.
PO Box 54821
Irvine, CA 92619-4821
Publisher's E-mail: service@scirp.org
Journal presenting the latest advancements in composite materials. **Freq:** Quarterly. **Key Personnel:** Dr. Chengye Fan, Editor-in-Chief. **ISSN:** 2164--5612 (print); **EISSN:** 2164--5655 (electronic). **Subscription Rates:** $398 Individuals. **URL:** http://www.scirp.org/journal/ojcm. **Circ:** (Not Reported).

2566 ■ Open Journal of Depression
Scientific Research Publishing Inc.
PO Box 54821
Irvine, CA 92619-4821
Publisher's E-mail: service@scirp.org
Journal discussing depression-related topics. **Freq:** Quarterly latest edition 2015. **ISSN:** 2169--9658 (print); **EISSN:** 2169--9674 (electronic). **Subscription Rates:** $498 Individuals volume 4. **URL:** http://www.scirp.org/journal/ojd. **Circ:** (Not Reported).

2567 ■ Open Journal of Discrete Mathematics
Scientific Research Publishing Inc.
PO Box 54821
Irvine, CA 92619-4821
Publisher's E-mail: service@scirp.org
Journal covering the latest advances in discrete mathematics. **Freq:** Quarterly. **Key Personnel:** Prof. Hosam M. Mahmoud, Editor-in-Chief. **ISSN:** 2161--7635 (print); **EISSN:** 2161--7643 (electronic). **Subscription Rates:** $498 Individuals. **URL:** http://www.scirp.org/journal/ojdm. **Circ:** (Not Reported).

2568 ■ Open Journal of Earthquake Research
Scientific Research Publishing Inc.
PO Box 54821
Irvine, CA 92619-4821
Publisher's E-mail: service@scirp.org
Journal covering various issues and developments in all aspects of earthquake research. **Freq:** Quarterly. **Key Personnel:** Dr. Hing-Ho Tsang, Editor-in-Chief. **ISSN:** 2169--9623 (print); **EISSN:** 2169--9631 (electronic). **Subscription Rates:** $398 Individuals. **URL:** http://www.scirp.org/journal/ojer. **Circ:** (Not Reported).

2569 ■ Open Journal of Emergency Medicine
Scientific Research Publishing Inc.
PO Box 54821
Irvine, CA 92619-4821
Publisher's E-mail: service@scirp.org
Journal promoting various new issues and developments in all areas of emergency medicine. **Freq:** Quarterly. **Key Personnel:** Prof. Boyd D. Burns, Editor. **ISSN:** 2332--1806 (print); **EISSN:** 2332--1814 (electronic). **Subscription Rates:** $398 Individuals. **URL:** http://www.scirp.org/journal/ojem. **Circ:** (Not Reported).

2570 ■ Open Journal of Endocrine and Metabolic Diseases
Scientific Research Publishing Inc.
PO Box 54821
Irvine, CA 92619-4821
Publisher's E-mail: service@scirp.org
Journal covering the latest advancements in endocrine and metabolic diseases. **Freq:** Monthly. **Key Personnel:** Prof. Yuh-Min Song, Editor-in-Chief. **ISSN:** 2165--7424 (print); **EISSN:** 2165--7432 (electronic). **Subscription Rates:** $998 Individuals. **URL:** http://www.scirp.org/Journal/ojemd. **Circ:** (Not Reported).

2571 ■ Open Journal of Energy Efficiency
Scientific Research Publishing Inc.
PO Box 54821
Irvine, CA 92619-4821
Publisher's E-mail: service@scirp.org
Journal promoting new issues and developments in all areas of energy efficiency. **Freq:** Quarterly. **Key Personnel:** Prof. Qianchuan Zhao, Editor-in-Chief. **ISSN:** 2169--2637 (print); **EISSN:** 2169--2645 (electronic). **Subscription Rates:** $1192 Individuals. **URL:** http://www.scirp.org/journal/ojee. **Circ:** (Not Reported).

2572 ■ Open Journal of Epidemiology
Scientific Research Publishing Inc.
PO Box 54821
Irvine, CA 92619-4821
Publisher's E-mail: service@scirp.org
Journal featuring topics related to the latest advancements in epidemiology. **Freq:** Quarterly. **Key Personnel:** Prof. Inmaculada Failde, Editor-in-Chief. **ISSN:** 2165--7459 (print); **EISSN:** 2165--7467 (electronic). **Subscription Rates:** $498 Individuals. **URL:** http://www.scirp.org/journal/ojepi. **Circ:** (Not Reported).

2573 ■ Open Journal of Fluid Dynamics
Scientific Research Publishing Inc.
PO Box 54821
Irvine, CA 92619-4821
Publisher's E-mail: service@scirp.org
Journal covering the latest advancements in fluid dynamics. **Freq:** Quarterly. **Key Personnel:** Prof. Heuy-Dong Kim, Editor-in-Chief. **ISSN:** 2165--3852 (print); **EISSN:** 2165--3860 (electronic). **Subscription Rates:** $498 Individuals. **URL:** http://www.scirp.org/journal/ojfd. **Circ:** (Not Reported).

2574 ■ Open Journal of Forestry
Scientific Research Publishing Inc.
PO Box 54821
Irvine, CA 92619-4821
Publisher's E-mail: service@scirp.org
Journal containing articles on latest issues and developments in different areas of forestry. **Freq:** Quarterly. **Key Personnel:** Prof. Valeriy Perminov, Editor-in-Chief. **ISSN:** 2163--0429 (print); **EISSN:** 2163--0437 (electronic). **Subscription Rates:** $498 Individuals. **URL:** http://www.scirp.org/journal/ojf. **Circ:** (Not Reported).

2575 ■ Open Journal of Gastroenterology
Scientific Research Publishing Inc.
PO Box 54821
Irvine, CA 92619-4821
Publisher's E-mail: service@scirp.org
Journal covering the latest advancement in gastroenterology. **Freq:** Monthly. **Key Personnel:** Prof. Weizhen Zhang, Editor-in-Chief. **ISSN:** 2163--9450 (print); **EISSN:** 2163--9469 (electronic). **Subscription Rates:** $1098 Individuals. **URL:** http://www.scirp.org/journal/ojgas. **Circ:** (Not Reported).

2576 ■ Open Journal of Genetics
Scientific Research Publishing Inc.
PO Box 54821
Irvine, CA 92619-4821
Publisher's E-mail: service@scirp.org
Journal featuring new issues and developments in different areas of Genetics. **Freq:** Quarterly latest edition 2015. **ISSN:** 2162--4453 (print); **EISSN:** 2162--4461 (electronic). **Subscription Rates:** $1992 Individuals volume 5. **URL:** http://www.scirp.org/journal/ojgen. **Circ:** (Not Reported).

2577 ■ Open Journal of Immunology
Scientific Research Publishing Inc.
PO Box 54821
Irvine, CA 92619-4821
Publisher's E-mail: service@scirp.org
Journal featuring the latest advancements in immunology. **Freq:** Quarterly Latest edition: 2015. **Key Personnel:** Dr. Zhiwei Hu, Editor-in-Chief. **ISSN:** 2162--450X (print); **EISSN:** 2162--4526 (electronic). **Subscription Rates:** $498 Individuals Volume 5. **URL:** http://www.scirp.org/journal/oji. **Circ:** (Not Reported).

2578 ■ Open Journal of Inorganic Chemistry
Scientific Research Publishing Inc.

PO Box 54821
Irvine, CA 92619-4821
Publisher's E-mail: service@scirp.org
Journal promoting and discussing new issues and developments in different areas of inorganic chemistry. **Freq:** Quarterly. **Key Personnel:** Prof. Rajni Kant, Editor-in-Chief. **ISSN:** 2161--7406 (print); **EISSN:** 2161--7414 (electronic). **Subscription Rates:** $298 Individuals. **URL:** http://www.scirp.org/journal/ojic. **Circ:** (Not Reported).

2579 ■ Open Journal of Inorganic Non-metallic Materials
Scientific Research Publishing Inc.
PO Box 54821
Irvine, CA 92619-4821
Publisher's E-mail: service@scirp.org
Journal featuring latest developments in different areas of inorganic non-metallic material. **Freq:** Quarterly. **Key Personnel:** Prof. Ahmed Arafat Khamis, Editor-in-Chief. **ISSN:** 2164--6791 (print); **EISSN:** 2164--6805 (electronic). **Subscription Rates:** $298 Individuals. **URL:** http://www.scirp.org/journal/ojinm. **Circ:** (Not Reported).

2580 ■ Open Journal of Internal Medicine
Scientific Research Publishing Inc.
PO Box 54821
Irvine, CA 92619-4821
Publisher's E-mail: service@scirp.org
Journal covering the advancement of the study of internal medicine. **Freq:** Quarterly. **Key Personnel:** Dr. Jorge-Shmuel Delgado, Editor-in-Chief. **ISSN:** 2162--5972 (print); **EISSN:** 2162--5980 (electronic). **Subscription Rates:** $498 Individuals. **URL:** http://www.scirp.org/journal/ojim. **Circ:** (Not Reported).

2581 ■ Open Journal of Leadership
Scientific Research Publishing Inc.
PO Box 54821
Irvine, CA 92619-4821
Publisher's E-mail: service@scirp.org
Journal featuring articles on various practices, development and theories of leadership. **Freq:** Quarterly. **Key Personnel:** Prof. Michael G. Brizek, Editor-in-Chief. **ISSN:** 2167--7743 (print); **EISSN:** 2167--7751 (electronic). **Subscription Rates:** $298 Individuals. **URL:** http://www.scirp.org/journal/ojl. **Circ:** (Not Reported).

2582 ■ Open Journal of Marine Science
Scientific Research Publishing Inc.
PO Box 54821
Irvine, CA 92619-4821
Publisher's E-mail: service@scirp.org
Journal presenting the latest advancements in marine science. **Freq:** Quarterly. **Key Personnel:** David Alberto Salas-de-Leon, Editor-in-Chief. **ISSN:** 2161--7384 (print); **EISSN:** 2161--7392 (electronic). **Subscription Rates:** $899 Individuals. **URL:** http://www.scirp.org/journal/ojms. **Circ:** (Not Reported).

2583 ■ Open Journal of Medical Imaging
Scientific Research Publishing Inc.
PO Box 54821
Irvine, CA 92619-4821
Publisher's E-mail: service@scirp.org
Journal featuring the advancement in the study of medical imaging. **Freq:** Quarterly. **Key Personnel:** Prof. Michael L. Goris, Editor-in-Chief. **ISSN:** 2164--2788 (print); **EISSN:** 2164--2796 (electronic). **Subscription Rates:** $498 Individuals. **URL:** http://www.scirp.org/journal/ojmi. **Circ:** (Not Reported).

2584 ■ Open Journal of Medical Microbiology
Scientific Research Publishing Inc.
PO Box 54821
Irvine, CA 92619-4821
Publisher's E-mail: service@scirp.org
Journal promoting, sharing and discussing the latest advancements in Medical Microbiology. **Freq:** Quarterly Latest edition 2015. **Key Personnel:** Prof. Arun K. Bhunia, Editor-in-Chief. **ISSN:** 2165--3372 (print); **EISSN:** 2165--3380 (electronic). **Subscription Rates:** $398 Individuals Volume 5. **URL:** http://www.scirp.org/journal/ojmm. **Circ:** (Not Reported).

2585 ■ Open Journal of Medical Psychology
Scientific Research Publishing Inc.
PO Box 54821
Irvine, CA 92619-4821
Publisher's E-mail: service@scirp.org
Journal promoting the latest advancements in medical psychology. **Freq:** Quarterly. **ISSN:** 2165--9370 (print); **EISSN:** 2165--9389 (electronic). **Subscription Rates:** $398 Individuals. **URL:** http://www.scirp.org/journal/ojmp. **Circ:** (Not Reported).

2586 ■ Open Journal of Medicinal Chemistry
Scientific Research Publishing Inc.
PO Box 54821
Irvine, CA 92619-4821
Publisher's E-mail: service@scirp.org
Peer-reviewed journal presenting the latest advancements in medicinal chemistry. **Freq:** Quarterly. **Key Personnel:** Prof. James A. Radosevich, Editor-in-Chief. **ISSN:** 2164--3121 (print); **EISSN:** 2164--313X (electronic). **Subscription Rates:** $398 Individuals. **URL:** http://www.scirp.org/journal/ojmc. **Circ:** (Not Reported).

2587 ■ Open Journal of Metal
Scientific Research Publishing Inc.
PO Box 54821
Irvine, CA 92619-4821
Publisher's E-mail: service@scirp.org
Journal discussing topics regarding the latest advancements in metals and related disciplines. **Freq:** Quarterly. **Key Personnel:** Dr. M. Jayachandran, Editor-in-Chief. **ISSN:** 2164--2761 (print); **EISSN:** 2164--277X (electronic). **Subscription Rates:** $398 Individuals volume 5. **URL:** http://www.scirp.org/journal/ojmetal. **Circ:** (Not Reported).

2588 ■ Open Journal of Microphysics
Scientific Research Publishing Inc.
PO Box 54821
Irvine, CA 92619-4821
Publisher's E-mail: service@scirp.org
Journal containing articles on the advancement of the study of microphysics. **Freq:** Monthly. **Key Personnel:** Prof. Stefano Moretti, Editor-in-Chief. **ISSN:** 2162--2450 (print); **EISSN:** 2162--2469 (electronic). **Subscription Rates:** $1298 Individuals. **URL:** http://www.scirp.org/journal/ojm. **Circ:** (Not Reported).

2589 ■ Open Journal of Modelling and Simulation
Scientific Research Publishing Inc.
PO Box 54821
Irvine, CA 92619-4821
Publisher's E-mail: service@scirp.org
Journal discussing various new issues and developments in all aspects of modelling and simulation. **Freq:** Quarterly. **Key Personnel:** Prof. Bilal Chanane, Editor-in-Chief. **ISSN:** 2327--4018 (print); **EISSN:** 2327--4026 (electronic). **Subscription Rates:** $298 Individuals. **URL:** http://www.scirp.org/journal/ojmsi. **Circ:** (Not Reported).

2590 ■ Open Journal of Modern Hydrology
Scientific Research Publishing Inc.
PO Box 54821
Irvine, CA 92619-4821
Publisher's E-mail: service@scirp.org
Journal covering the latest advances in various areas of hydrology. **Freq:** Quarterly. **Key Personnel:** Prof. Andrea Vacca, Editor-in-Chief. **ISSN:** 2163--0461 (print); **EISSN:** 2163--0496 (electronic). **Subscription Rates:** $398 Individuals. **URL:** http://www.scirp.org/journal/ojmh. **Circ:** (Not Reported).

2591 ■ Open Journal of Modern Linguistics
Scientific Research Publishing Inc.
PO Box 54821
Irvine, CA 92619-4821
Publisher's E-mail: service@scirp.org
Journal covering the latest advancements in modern linguistics. **Freq:** Quarterly. **Key Personnel:** Maria Jose de la Fuente, Editor-in-Chief. **ISSN:** 2164--2818 (print); **EISSN:** 2164--2834 (electronic). **Subscription Rates:** $398 Individuals; Free access on internet; $599 Individuals article processing charge. **URL:** http://www.scirp.org/journal/ojml. **Circ:** (Not Reported).

2592 ■ Open Journal of Modern Neurosurgery
Scientific Research Publishing Inc.
PO Box 54821
Irvine, CA 92619-4821
Publisher's E-mail: service@scirp.org
Journal discussing various advancements in all aspects of neurosurgery. **Freq:** Quarterly. **Key Personnel:** Prof. Vincenzo Cuomo, Editor-in-Chief. **ISSN:** 2163--0569 (print); **EISSN:** 2163--0585 (electronic). **Subscription Rates:** $398 Individuals. **URL:** http://www.scirp.org/journal/ojmn. **Circ:** (Not Reported).

2593 ■ Open Journal of Molecular and Integrative Physiology
Scientific Research Publishing Inc.
PO Box 54821
Irvine, CA 92619-4821
Publisher's E-mail: service@scirp.org
Journal promoting, sharing and discussing developments in different areas of Physiology. **Freq:** Quarterly. **Key Personnel:** Prof. Weizhen Zhang, Editor-in-Chief. **ISSN:** 2162--2159 (print); **EISSN:** 2162--2167 (electronic). **Subscription Rates:** $398 Individuals Volume 5. **URL:** http://www.scirp.org/journal/OJMIP. **Circ:** (Not Reported).

2594 ■ Open Journal of Nephrology
Scientific Research Publishing Inc.
PO Box 54821
Irvine, CA 92619-4821
Publisher's E-mail: service@scirp.org
Journal containing articles discussing various new issues and developments in different areas of nephrology. **Freq:** Quarterly. **Key Personnel:** Prof. Zheng Dong, Editor-in-Chief. **ISSN:** 2164--2842 (print); **EISSN:** 2164--2869 (electronic). **Subscription Rates:** $398 Individuals. **URL:** http://www.scirp.org/journal/ojneph. **Circ:** (Not Reported).

2595 ■ Open Journal of Nursing
Scientific Research Publishing Inc.
PO Box 54821
Irvine, CA 92619-4821
Publisher's E-mail: service@scirp.org
Journal covering latest advancements in nursing. **Freq:** Monthly. **Key Personnel:** Prof. Geraldine MacDonald, Editor-in-Chief. **ISSN:** 2162--5336 (print); **EISSN:** 2162--5344 (electronic). **Subscription Rates:** $1098 Individuals. **URL:** http://www.scirp.org/journal/ojn. **Circ:** (Not Reported).

2596 ■ Open Journal of Obstetrics and Gynecology
Scientific Research Publishing Inc.
PO Box 54821
Irvine, CA 92619-4821
Publisher's E-mail: service@scirp.org
Journal promoting the latest advancements in obstetrics and gynecology. **Freq:** Monthly. **Key Personnel:** Prof. Chris Constantinou, Editor-in-Chief. **ISSN:** 2160--8792 (print); **EISSN:** 2160--8806 (electronic). **Subscription Rates:** $1198 Individuals. **URL:** http://www.scirp.org/Journal/ojog. **Circ:** (Not Reported).

2597 ■ Open Journal of Ophthalmology
Scientific Research Publishing Inc.
PO Box 54821
Irvine, CA 92619-4821
Publisher's E-mail: service@scirp.org
Peer-reviewed journal covering the latest advancements in ophthalmology. **Freq:** Quarterly. **Key Personnel:** Pinakin Gunvant Davey, Editor-in-Chief. **ISSN:** 2165--7408 (print); **EISSN:** 2165--7416 (electronic). **Subscription Rates:** $398 Individuals. **URL:** http://www.scirp.org/journal/ojoph. **Circ:** (Not Reported).

2598 ■ Open Journal of Optimization
Scientific Research Publishing Inc.
PO Box 54821
Irvine, CA 92619-4821
Publisher's E-mail: service@scirp.org
Journal covering latest issues and developments in all aspects of optimization. **Freq:** Quarterly. **Key Personnel:** Prof. Moran Wang, Editor-in-Chief. **ISSN:** 2325--7105 (print); **EISSN:** 2325--7091 (electronic). **URL:** http://www.scirp.org/journal/ojop. **Circ:** (Not Reported).

2599 ■ Open Journal of Organ Transplant Surgery
Scientific Research Publishing Inc.
PO Box 54821
Irvine, CA 92619-4821
Publisher's E-mail: service@scirp.org

Circulation: ★ = AAM; △ or • = BPA; ♦ = CAC; ❑ = VAC; ⊕ = PO Statement; ‡ = Publisher's Report; Boldface figures = sworn; Light figures = estimated.

Journal discussing the latest advancements in organ transplant surgery. **Freq:** Quarterly. **Key Personnel:** Prof. Rubin Zhang, Editor-in-Chief. **ISSN:** 2163--9485 (print); **EISSN:** 2163--9493 (electronic). **Subscription Rates:** $398 Individuals. **URL:** http://www.scirp.org/journal/ojots. **Circ:** (Not Reported).

2600 ■ Open Journal of Organic Polymer Materials
Scientific Research Publishing Inc.
PO Box 54821
Irvine, CA 92619-4821
Publisher's E-mail: service@scirp.org
Journal covering the developments in different areas of organic polymer materials. **Freq:** Quarterly. **Key Personnel:** Prof. Richard J. Spontak, Editor-in-Chief. **ISSN:** 2164--5736 (print); **EISSN:** 2164--5752 (electronic). **Subscription Rates:** $298 Individuals. **URL:** http://www.scirp.org/journal/ojopm. **Circ:** (Not Reported).

2601 ■ Open Journal of Orthopedics
Scientific Research Publishing Inc.
PO Box 54821
Irvine, CA 92619-4821
Publisher's E-mail: service@scirp.org
Journal covering the latest advancements in orthopedics. **Freq:** Monthly. **ISSN:** 2164--3008 (print); **EISSN:** 2164--3016 (electronic). **Subscription Rates:** $1098 Individuals. **URL:** http://www.scirp.org/journal/ojo. **Circ:** (Not Reported).

2602 ■ Open Journal of Pathology
Scientific Research Publishing Inc.
PO Box 54821
Irvine, CA 92619-4821
Publisher's E-mail: service@scirp.org
Journal covering the latest advancements in pathology. **Freq:** Quarterly. **Key Personnel:** Prof. Takuji Tanaka, Editor-in-Chief. **ISSN:** 2164--6775 (print); **EISSN:** 2164--6783 (electronic). **Subscription Rates:** $498 Individuals. **URL:** http://www.scirp.org/journal/ojpathology/. **Circ:** (Not Reported).

2603 ■ Open Journal of Pediatrics
Scientific Research Publishing Inc.
PO Box 54821
Irvine, CA 92619-4821
Publisher's E-mail: service@scirp.org
Journal promoting, sharing and discussing new issues and developments in different areas of Pediatrics. **Freq:** Quarterly Latest edition 2015. **Key Personnel:** Prof. Carl E. Hunt, Editor-in-Chief. **ISSN:** 2160--8741 (print); **EISSN:** 2160--8776 (electronic). **Subscription Rates:** $498 Individuals volume 5. **URL:** http://www.scirp.org/journal/OJPED. **Circ:** (Not Reported).

2604 ■ Open Journal of Philosophy
Scientific Research Publishing Inc.
PO Box 54821
Irvine, CA 92619-4821
Publisher's E-mail: service@scirp.org
Journal covering the latest advancements in philosophy. **Freq:** Quarterly. **Key Personnel:** Prof. Kuang-Ming Wu, Editor-in-Chief. **ISSN:** 2163--9434 (print); **EISSN:** 2163--9442 (electronic). **URL:** http://www.scirp.org/journal/ojpp. **Circ:** (Not Reported).

2605 ■ Open Journal of Physical Chemistry
Scientific Research Publishing Inc.
PO Box 54821
Irvine, CA 92619-4821
Publisher's E-mail: service@scirp.org
Journal publishing the latest advancements in physical chemistry. **Freq:** Quarterly. **Key Personnel:** Prof. Kalliat T. Valsaraj, Editor-in-Chief. **ISSN:** 2162--1969 (print); **EISSN:** 2162--1977 (electronic). **Subscription Rates:** $398 Individuals volume 5. **URL:** http://www.scirp.org/journal/ojpc. **Circ:** (Not Reported).

2606 ■ Open Journal of Political Science
Scientific Research Publishing Inc.
PO Box 54821
Irvine, CA 92619-4821
Publisher's E-mail: service@scirp.org
Journal covering the latest advancements in political science. **Freq:** Quarterly. **ISSN:** 2164--0505 (print); **EISSN:** 2164--0513 (electronic). **Subscription Rates:** $398 Individuals. **URL:** http://www.scirp.org/journal/ojps. **Circ:** (Not Reported).

2607 ■ Open Journal of Polymer Chemistry
Scientific Research Publishing Inc.
PO Box 54821
Irvine, CA 92619-4821
Publisher's E-mail: service@scirp.org
Peer-reviewed journal featuring the latest advancements in polymer chemistry and related disciplines. **Freq:** Quarterly. **Key Personnel:** Prof. Emilio Bucio, Editor-in-Chief. **ISSN:** 2165--6681 (print); **EISSN:** 2165--6711 (electronic). **Subscription Rates:** $398 Individuals. **URL:** http://www.scirp.org/journal/ojpchem. **Circ:** (Not Reported).

2608 ■ Open Journal of Preventive Medicine
Scientific Research Publishing Inc.
PO Box 54821
Irvine, CA 92619-4821
Publisher's E-mail: service@scirp.org
Journal promoting and sharing the latest advancements in Preventive Medicine. **Freq:** Monthly Latest edition 2015. **Key Personnel:** Prof. Maciej Buchowski, Editor-in-Chief. **ISSN:** 2162--2477 (print); **EISSN:** 2162--2485 (electronic). **Subscription Rates:** $1098 Individuals Volume 5. **URL:** http://www.scirp.org/journal/ojpm. **Circ:** (Not Reported).

2609 ■ Open Journal of Psychiatry
Scientific Research Publishing Inc.
PO Box 54821
Irvine, CA 92619-4821
Publisher's E-mail: service@scirp.org
Journal containing the latest advancements in psychiatry. **Freq:** Quarterly Latest edition 2014. **Key Personnel:** Gjumrakch Aliev, Editor-in-Chief. **ISSN:** 2161--7325 (print); **EISSN:** 2161--7333 (electronic). **Subscription Rates:** $316 Individuals Volume 4; $498 Individuals Volume 5. **URL:** http://www.scirp.org/journal/ojpsych. **Circ:** (Not Reported).

2610 ■ Open Journal of Radiology
Scientific Research Publishing Inc.
PO Box 54821
Irvine, CA 92619-4821
Publisher's E-mail: service@scirp.org
Peer-reviewed journal presenting the latest advancements in medical imaging. **Freq:** Quarterly Latest edition 2015. **Key Personnel:** Prof. Joseph Sekiguchi Yu, Editor-in-Chief. **ISSN:** 2164--3024 (print); **EISSN:** 2164--3032 (electronic). **Subscription Rates:** $398 Individuals Volume 5. **URL:** http://www.scirp.org/journal/ojrad. **Circ:** (Not Reported).

2611 ■ Open Journal of Regenerative Medicine
Scientific Research Publishing Inc.
PO Box 54821
Irvine, CA 92619-4821
Publisher's E-mail: service@scirp.org
Peer-reviewed journal containing original research studies, reviews and case reports in all aspects of Regenerative Medicine. **Freq:** Quarterly Latest edition 2015. **Key Personnel:** Prof. Peter K. Law, Editor-in-Chief. **ISSN:** 2169--2513 (print); **EISSN:** 2169--2521 (electronic). **Subscription Rates:** $498 Individuals Volume 4. **URL:** http://www.scirp.org/journal/ojrm. **Circ:** (Not Reported).

2612 ■ Open Journal of Respiratory Diseases
Scientific Research Publishing Inc.
PO Box 54821
Irvine, CA 92619-4821
Publisher's E-mail: service@scirp.org
Journal covering the latest advancements in respiratory diseases. **Freq:** Quarterly. **ISSN:** 2163--940X (print); **EISSN:** 2163--9418 (electronic). **Subscription Rates:** $498 Individuals. **URL:** http://www.scirp.org/journal/ojrd. **Circ:** (Not Reported).

2613 ■ Open Journal of Rheumatology and Autoimmune Diseases
Scientific Research Publishing Inc.
PO Box 54821
Irvine, CA 92619-4821
Publisher's E-mail: service@scirp.org
Peer-reviewed journal discussing the latest advancements in rheumatology and autoimmune diseases. **Freq:** Quarterly. **Key Personnel:** Prof. Remzi Cevik, Editor-in-Chief. **ISSN:** 2163--9914 (print); **EISSN:** 2164--005X (electronic). **Subscription Rates:** $398 Individuals. **URL:** http://www.scirp.org/journal/ojra. **Circ:** (Not Reported).

2614 ■ Open Journal of Safety Science and Technology
Scientific Research Publishing Inc.
PO Box 54821
Irvine, CA 92619-4821
Publisher's E-mail: service@scirp.org
Journal promoting and discussing new issues and developments in different areas of safety science and technology. **Freq:** Quarterly Latest edition 2015. **Key Personnel:** Prof. Singiresu S. Rao, Editor-in-Chief. **ISSN:** 2162--5999 (print); **EISSN:** 2162--6006 (electronic). **Subscription Rates:** $398 Individuals volume 5. **URL:** http://www.scirp.org/journal/ojsst. **Circ:** (Not Reported).

2615 ■ Open Journal of Social Sciences
Scientific Research Publishing Inc.
PO Box 54821
Irvine, CA 92619-4821
Publisher's E-mail: service@scirp.org
Journal promoting interdisciplinary studies in social science. **Freq:** Monthly Latest edition 2015. **Key Personnel:** Prof. Aqueil Ahmad, Editor-in-Chief. **ISSN:** 2327--5952 (print); **EISSN:** 2327--5960 (electronic). **Subscription Rates:** $598 Individuals Volume 3. **URL:** http://www.scirp.org/journal/jss. **Circ:** (Not Reported).

2616 ■ Open Journal of Soil Science
Scientific Research Publishing Inc.
PO Box 54821
Irvine, CA 92619-4821
Publisher's E-mail: service@scirp.org
Journal covering the latest advancements and issues in soil science. **Freq:** Monthly. **Key Personnel:** Prof. Haiyan Chu, Editor-in-Chief. **ISSN:** 2162--5360 (print); **EISSN:** 2162--5379 (electronic). **Subscription Rates:** $998 Individuals. **URL:** http://www.scirp.org/journal/ojss. **Circ:** (Not Reported).

2617 ■ Open Journal of Statistics
Scientific Research Publishing Inc.
PO Box 54821
Irvine, CA 92619-4821
Publisher's E-mail: service@scirp.org
Journal covering the latest advancements in statistics. **Freq:** Bimonthly. **Key Personnel:** Prof. Qihua Wang, Editor-in-Chief. **ISSN:** 2161--718X (print); **EISSN:** 2161--7198 (electronic). **Subscription Rates:** $498 Individuals. **URL:** http://www.scirp.org/journal/ojs/. **Circ:** (Not Reported).

2618 ■ Open Journal of Stomatology
Scientific Research Publishing Inc.
PO Box 54821
Irvine, CA 92619-4821
Publisher's E-mail: service@scirp.org
Journal covering the latest advancements in stomatology. **Freq:** Monthly. **Key Personnel:** Prof. Junichi Asaumi, Editor-in-Chief. **ISSN:** 2160--8709 (print); **EISSN:** 2160--8717 (electronic). **Subscription Rates:** $1098 Individuals. **URL:** http://www.scirp.org/journal/ojst. **Circ:** (Not Reported).

2619 ■ Open Journal of Synthesis Theory and Applications
Scientific Research Publishing Inc.
PO Box 54821
Irvine, CA 92619-4821
Publisher's E-mail: service@scirp.org
Journal providing new issues and developments in different areas of synthesis. **Freq:** Quarterly. **Key Personnel:** Prof. Changle Chen, Editor-in-Chief. **ISSN:** 2168--1244 (print); **EISSN:** 2168--1252 (electronic). **Subscription Rates:** $398 Individuals. **URL:** http://www.scirp.org/journal/ojsta. **Circ:** (Not Reported).

2620 ■ Open Journal of Therapy and Rehabilitation
Scientific Research Publishing Inc.
PO Box 54821
Irvine, CA 92619-4821
Publisher's E-mail: service@scirp.org
Journal promoting various new issues and developments in all aspects of therapy and rehabilitation. **Freq:** Quarterly. **Key Personnel:** Prof. Masahiro Kohzuki, Editor-in-Chief. **ISSN:** 2332--1822 (print); **EISSN:** 2332--1830 (electronic). **Subscription Rates:** $398 Individuals. **URL:** http://www.scirp.org/journal/ojtr. **Circ:** (Not Reported).

2621 ■ Open Journal of Thoracic Surgery
Scientific Research Publishing Inc.
PO Box 54821
Irvine, CA 92619-4821

Publisher's E-mail: service@scirp.org
Journal covering the latest advancements in thoracic surgery. **Freq:** Quarterly. **Key Personnel:** Prof. Filipe Moreira de Andrade, Editor-in-Chief. **ISSN:** 2164--3059 (print); **EISSN:** 2164--3067 (electronic). **Subscription Rates:** $498 Individuals. **URL:** http://www.scirp.org/journal/ojts. **Circ:** (Not Reported).

2622 ■ Open Journal of Urology
Scientific Research Publishing Inc.
PO Box 54821
Irvine, CA 92619-4821
Publisher's E-mail: service@scirp.org
Journal featuring articles that promote, share, and discuss various issues and developments in urology. **Freq:** Monthly. **Key Personnel:** Dr. Phillip Mucksavage, Editor-in-Chief. **ISSN:** 2160--5440 (print); **EISSN:** 2160--5629 (electronic). **Subscription Rates:** $998 Individuals. **URL:** http://www.scirp.org/journal/oju. **Circ:** (Not Reported).

2623 ■ Open Journal of Veterinary Medicine
Scientific Research Publishing Inc.
PO Box 54821
Irvine, CA 92619-4821
Publisher's E-mail: service@scirp.org
Journal featuring the latest advancements in Veterinary Medicine. **Freq:** Monthly Latest edition 2015. **Key Personnel:** Prof. Hung-Jen Liu, Editor-in-Chief. **ISSN:** 2165--3356 (print); **EISSN:** 2165--3364 (electronic). **Subscription Rates:** $1098 Individuals Volume 5. **URL:** http://www.scirp.org/journal/ojvm. **Circ:** (Not Reported).

2624 ■ Optics and Photonics Journal
Scientific Research Publishing Inc.
PO Box 54821
Irvine, CA 92619-4821
Publisher's E-mail: service@scirp.org
Peer-reviewed journal publishing articles on all areas of optics and photonics. **Freq:** Monthly. **Key Personnel:** Dr. Bouzid Menaa, Editor-in-Chief. **ISSN:** 2160--8881 (print); **EISSN:** 2160--889X (electronic). **Subscription Rates:** $1098 Individuals. **URL:** http://www.scirp.org/journal/opj. **Circ:** (Not Reported).

2625 ■ Orange County Business Journal
Orange County Business Journal
18500 Von Karman Ave., Ste. 150
Irvine, CA 92612
Phone: (949)833-8373
Regional business news journal. **Founded:** 1978. **Freq:** Weekly. **Print Method:** Digital direct to plate. **Cols./Page:** 4. **Col. Width:** 29 nonpareils. **Col. Depth:** 195 agate lines. **Key Personnel:** Jerry Sullivan, Editor. **ISSN:** 1051-7480 (print). **Subscription Rates:** $89 Individuals; $158 Two years. **URL:** http://www.ocbj.com. **Remarks:** Accepts advertising. **Circ:** Paid 23052.

2626 ■ Pain Studies and Treatment
Scientific Research Publishing Inc.
PO Box 54821
Irvine, CA 92619-4821
Publisher's E-mail: service@scirp.org
Journal discussing various issues and developments in all aspects of pain studies and treatment. **Freq:** Quarterly. **ISSN:** 2329--3268 (print); **EISSN:** 2329--3276 (electronic). **Subscription Rates:** $298 Individuals. **URL:** http://www.scirp.org/journal/pst. **Circ:** (Not Reported).

2627 ■ Pharmacology and Pharmacy
Scientific Research Publishing Inc.
PO Box 54821
Irvine, CA 92619-4821
Publisher's E-mail: service@scirp.org
Peer-reviewed journal publishing articles on pharmacology and pharmacy. **Freq:** Monthly. **Key Personnel:** Prof. George Perry, Editor-in-Chief. **ISSN:** 2157--9423 (print); **EISSN:** 2157--9431 (electronic). **Subscription Rates:** $1098 Individuals. **URL:** http://www.scirp.org/journal/pp. **Circ:** (Not Reported).

2628 ■ Philosophy of Science
Philosophy of Science Association
Dept. of Logic & Philosophy of Science
University of California, Irvine
Irvine, CA 92697
Publication E-mail: journal@philsci.org
Journal devoted to the philosophy of science. **Freq:** 5/year Jan., Apr., Jul., Oct., Dec. **Print Method:** Offset. **Trim Size:** 5-7/8 x 9. **Cols./Page:** 1. **Col. Width:** 51 nonpareils. **Col. Depth:** 105 agate lines. **Key Personnel:** Jeffrey Barrett, Editor-in-Chief; Laura Ruetsche, Board Member; Jim Weatherall, Associate Editor. **ISSN:** 0031--8248 (print); **EISSN:** 1539--767X (electronic). **Subscription Rates:** $289 Institutions; included in membership dues. **URL:** http://journal.philsci.org; http://www.jstor.org/journal/philscie; http://www.journals.uchicago.edu/toc/phos/current. **Ad Rates:** BW $578. **Remarks:** Accepts advertising. **Circ:** 1949, 2200.

2629 ■ Physiological and Biochemical Zoology
The University of Chicago Press
Dept. of Ecology & Evolutionary Biology
University of California
321 Steinhaus Hall
Irvine, CA 92697-2525
Phone: (949)824-9626
Fax: (949)824-9628
Publication E-mail: pbz@uci.edu
Professional publication covering biological issues in zoology. **Freq:** Bimonthly. **Trim Size:** 8 1/2 x 11. **Key Personnel:** Michael Castellini, Board Member; Theodore Garland, Jr., Associate Editor; Kathleen M. Gilmour, Editor; Perry Barboza, Board Member; Barbara Block, Board Member; Andrea L. Canfield, Managing Editor; Patricia M. Schulte, Editor; Jon Harrison, Associate Editor. **ISSN:** 1522--2152 (print); **EISSN:** 1537--5293 (electronic). **Subscription Rates:** $102 Individuals print and electronic; $91 Individuals electronic; $93 Individuals print only; $80 Members print & electronic; $51 Students print and electronic. **URL:** http://www.jstor.org/action/showPublication?journalCode=physbioczool; http://www.press.uchicago.edu/ucp/journals/journal/pbz.html. **Ad Rates:** BW $551. **Remarks:** Accepts advertising. **Circ:** 671.

2630 ■ Positioning
Scientific Research Publishing Inc.
PO Box 54821
Irvine, CA 92619-4821
Publication E-mail: pos@scirp.org
Peer-reviewed journal publishing articles on different areas of navigation and positioning. **Freq:** Quarterly. **Key Personnel:** Dr. Chuang Shi, Editor-in-Chief. **ISSN:** 2150--850X (print); **EISSN:** 2150--8526 (electronic). **Subscription Rates:** $598 Individuals. **URL:** http://www.scirp.org/journal/pos. **Circ:** (Not Reported).

2631 ■ Psychology
Scientific Research Publishing Inc.
PO Box 54821
Irvine, CA 92619-4821
Publisher's E-mail: service@scirp.org
Journal featuring the latest advancements in psychology. **Freq:** Monthly. **Key Personnel:** Prof. Peter Walla, Editor-in-Chief. **ISSN:** 2152--7180 (print); **EISSN:** 2152--7199 (electronic). **Subscription Rates:** $1198 Individuals. **URL:** http://www.scirp.org/journal/psych. **Circ:** (Not Reported).

2632 ■ Racer
Racer Communications Inc.
16842 Von Karman Ave., Ste. 125
Irvine, CA 92606
Phone: (949)417-6700
Fax: (949)417-6750
Publisher's E-mail: sportscar@racer.com
Motorsports magazine covering all aspects of local and international racing. **Founded:** May 1992. **Freq:** 8/year. **Print Method:** Web offset. **Trim Size:** 8 1/2 x 10 7/8. **Key Personnel:** Mark Carballo, Sales Executive, phone: (949)417-6713. **Subscription Rates:** $39 Individuals; $69 Two years; $59 Canada; $99 Two years Canada; $79 Other countries; $139 Two years international. **URL:** http://www.racer.com/. **Ad Rates:** 4C $4694. **Remarks:** Accepts advertising. **Circ:** (Not Reported).

2633 ■ The Review of Financial Studies
Oxford University Press
c/o David Hirshleifer, Executive Editor
The Paul Merage School of Business
The Review of Financial Studies
University of California
Irvine, CA 92679
Phone: (949)824-2022
Fax: (949)824-8469
Publisher's E-mail: uk@oup.com
Journal focusing on financial economics. **Freq:** Monthly. **Trim Size:** 6 x 9. **Cols./Page:** 1. **Col. Width:** 4 5/8 inches. **Col. Depth:** 7 1/8 inches. **Key Personnel:** Bruce Carlin, Associate Editor; David Hirshleifer, Executive Editor. **ISSN:** 0893--9454 (print); **EISSN:** 1465--7368 (electronic). **Subscription Rates:** $778 Institutions print and online; $623 Institutions online only; $716 Institutions print only; $2096 corporate (print and online) ; $1676 corporate (online only); $1928 corporate (print only). **URL:** http://rfs.oxfordjournals.org. **Ad Rates:** BW $225. **Remarks:** Advertising accepted; rates available upon request. **Circ:** Paid ‡2025.

2634 ■ Smart Grid and Renewable Energy
Scientific Research Publishing Inc.
PO Box 54821
Irvine, CA 92619-4821
Publication E-mail: sgre@scirp.org
Peer-reviewed journal publishing articles on the latest advancements in all aspects of smart grid and renewable energy. **Freq:** Monthly. **Key Personnel:** Prof. Victor Sreeram, Editor-in-Chief; Prof. Yuanzhang Sun, Editor-in-Chief. **ISSN:** 2151--481X (print); **EISSN:** 2151--4844 (electronic). **Subscription Rates:** $1098 Individuals. **URL:** http://www.scirp.org/journal/sgre. **Circ:** (Not Reported).

2635 ■ Social Networking
Scientific Research Publishing Inc.
PO Box 54821
Irvine, CA 92619-4821
Publisher's E-mail: service@scirp.org
Journal covering new issues and developments in all areas of social networking. **Freq:** Quarterly. **Key Personnel:** Prof. Li Weigang, Editor-in-Chief. **ISSN:** 2169--3285 (print); **EISSN:** 2169--3323 (electronic). **Subscription Rates:** $398 Individuals. **URL:** http://www.scirp.org/journal/sn. **Circ:** (Not Reported).

2636 ■ Sociology Mind
Scientific Research Publishing Inc.
PO Box 54821
Irvine, CA 92619-4821
Publication E-mail: sm@scirp.org
Peer-reviewed journal covering sociological inquiry and research. **Freq:** Quarterly. **Key Personnel:** Prof. Asafa Jalata, Editor-in-Chief. **ISSN:** 2160--083X (print); **EISSN:** 2160--0848 (electronic). **Subscription Rates:** $398 Individuals. **URL:** http://www.scirp.org/journal/sm. **Circ:** (Not Reported).

2637 ■ Soft
Scientific Research Publishing Inc.
PO Box 54821
Irvine, CA 92619-4821
Publisher's E-mail: service@scirp.org
Journal containing topics on soft condensed matter systems. **Freq:** Quarterly Latest edition 2015. **Key Personnel:** Dr. Anderson Ho Cheung Shum, Editor-in-Chief. **ISSN:** 2327--0799 (print); **EISSN:** 2327--0802 (electronic). **Subscription Rates:** $398 Individuals volume 4. **URL:** http://www.scirp.org/journal/soft. **Circ:** (Not Reported).

2638 ■ Soft Nanoscience Letters
Scientific Research Publishing Inc.
PO Box 54821
Irvine, CA 92619-4821
Publisher's E-mail: service@scirp.org
Peer-reviewed journal publishing articles in the field of soft nanoscience. **Freq:** Quarterly. **Key Personnel:** Prof. Richard J. Spontak, Editor-in-Chief. **ISSN:** 2160--0600 (print); **EISSN:** 2160--0740 (electronic). **Subscription Rates:** $498 Individuals. **URL:** http://www.scirp.org/journal/snl. **Circ:** (Not Reported).

2639 ■ Spectral Analysis Review
Scientific Research Publishing Inc.
PO Box 54821
Irvine, CA 92619-4821
Publisher's E-mail: service@scirp.org
Journal promoting, sharing and discussing various issues and developments in all aspects of Spectroscopy. **Freq:** Quarterly Latest edition 2015. **ISSN:** 2331--2092 (print); **EISSN:** 2331--2106 (electronic). **Subscription Rates:** $298 Individuals volume 3. **URL:** http://www.scirp.org/journal/sar. **Circ:** (Not Reported).

2640 ■ Stem Cell Discovery
Scientific Research Publishing Inc.

Circulation: ★ = AAM; △ or • = BPA; ♦ = CAC; ❑ = VAC; ⊕ = PO Statement; ‡ = Publisher's Report; Boldface figures = sworn; Light figures = estimated.

PO Box 54821
Irvine, CA 92619-4821
Publisher's E-mail: service@scirp.org
Peer reviewed journal discussing primary discoveries from stem cell basic and translational research. **Freq:** Quarterly Latest edition 2015. **Key Personnel:** Prof. Ming Zhan, Editor-in-Chief. **ISSN:** 2161--6760 (print); **EISSN:** 2161--6787 (electronic). **Subscription Rates:** $398 Individuals Volume 5. **URL:** http://www.scirp.org/journal/scd. **Circ:** (Not Reported).

2641 ■ Street Chopper
Bonnier Corp.
1733 Alton Pky.
Irvine, CA 92606
Publication E-mail: inquiries@automotive.com
Magazine featuring custom long choppers, bobbers, and more. Includes comprehensive tech articles to help readers build their own chopper, as well as the newest parts and accessories. **Freq:** Monthly. **Key Personnel:** Dave Roe, Associate Publisher, phone: (310)265-1876. **Subscription Rates:** $29.97 U.S. 6 issues; $41.97 Canada 6 issues; $53.97 Other countries 6 issues. **URL:** http://www.streetchopperweb.com. **Remarks:** Accepts advertising. **Circ:** (Not Reported).

2642 ■ Surgical Science
Scientific Research Publishing Inc.
PO Box 54821
Irvine, CA 92619-4821
Publication E-mail: ss@scirp.org
Peer-reviewed journal publishing articles on the latest developments in surgery. **Freq:** Monthly. **Key Personnel:** Prof. Vahit Ozmen, Editor-in-Chief. **ISSN:** 2157--9407 (print); **EISSN:** 2157--9415 (electronic). **Subscription Rates:** $1198 Individuals. **URL:** http://www.scirp.org/journal/ss. **Circ:** (Not Reported).

2643 ■ Technology and Investment
Scientific Research Publishing Inc.
PO Box 54821
Irvine, CA 92619-4821
Publisher's E-mail: service@scirp.org
Peer-reviewed journal publishing articles on technology and investment. **Freq:** Quarterly. **Key Personnel:** Dr. Lucas M. Bernard, Editor-in-Chief; Prof. Willi Semmler, Editor-in-Chief. **ISSN:** 2150--4059 (print); **EISSN:** 2150--4067 (electronic). **Subscription Rates:** $498 Individuals. **URL:** http://www.scirp.org/journal/ti. **Circ:** (Not Reported).

2644 ■ Theoretical Economics Letters
Scientific Research Publishing Inc.
PO Box 54821
Irvine, CA 92619-4821
Publisher's E-mail: service@scirp.org
Journal containing papers on economic theory and mathematical economics. **Freq:** Bimonthly Latest edition 2015. **Key Personnel:** Prof. Moawia Alghalith, Editor-in-Chief. **ISSN:** 2162--2078 (print); **EISSN:** 2162--2086 (electronic). **URL:** http://www.scirp.org/journal/tel. **Circ:** (Not Reported).

2645 ■ Truckin' Magazine
McMullen Argus Publishing Inc.
1733 Alton Pky.
Irvine, CA 92606
Magazine about custom vans, mini trucks, and pickups. **Freq:** 13/yr. **Print Method:** Web Offset. **Trim Size:** 8 x 10 7/8. **Cols./Page:** 3. **Col. Width:** 27 nonpareils. **Col. Depth:** 140 agate lines. **ISSN:** 0277--5743 (print). **Subscription Rates:** $24.95 Individuals 13 issues; $39.95 Individuals 26 issues. **URL:** http://www.truckinweb.com. **Ad Rates:** BW $15,370; 4C $20,280. **Remarks:** Accepts advertising. **Circ:** ★114110.

2646 ■ UCLA Entertainment Law Review
University of California, Irvine Center for Learning in the Arts, Sciences and Sustainability
2656 Biological Sciences III
Irvine, CA 92697-4540
Phone: (949)824-2418
Fax: (949)824-9103
Publisher's E-mail: lbrouill@uci.edu
Journal containing topics on entertainment law community. **Freq:** Semiannual. **ISSN:** 1073--2896 (print); **EISSN:** 1939--5523 (electronic). **URL:** http://escholarship.org/uc/uclalaw_elr. **Circ:** (Not Reported).

2647 ■ UCLA Historical Journal
University of California, Irvine Center for Learning in the Arts, Sciences and Sustainability
2656 Biological Sciences III
Irvine, CA 92697-4540
Phone: (949)824-2418
Fax: (949)824-9103
Publisher's E-mail: lbrouill@uci.edu
Journal containing student research and writing. **ISSN:** 0276--864X (print). **URL:** http://escholarship.org/uc/ucla_history_historyjournal. **Circ:** (Not Reported).

2648 ■ Wireless Engineering and Technology
Scientific Research Publishing Inc.
PO Box 54821
Irvine, CA 92619-4821
Publication E-mail: wet@scirp.org
Peer-reviewed journal publishing articles on wireless engineering and technology. **Freq:** Quarterly. **Key Personnel:** Dr. Yi Huang, Editor-in-Chief. **ISSN:** 2152--2294 (print); **EISSN:** 2152--2308 (electronic). **Subscription Rates:** $498 Individuals. **URL:** http://www.scirp.org/journal/wet. **Circ:** (Not Reported).

2649 ■ Wireless Sensor Network
Scientific Research Publishing Inc.
PO Box 54821
Irvine, CA 92619-4821
Publisher's E-mail: service@scirp.org
Peer-reviewed journal publishing the latest advancement in the study of wireless sensor network and applications. **Freq:** Monthly. **Key Personnel:** Prof. Kosai Raoof, Editor-in-Chief. **ISSN:** 1945--3078 (print); **EISSN:** 1945--3086 (electronic). **Subscription Rates:** $1198 Individuals. **URL:** http://www.scirp.org/journal/wsn. **Circ:** (Not Reported).

2650 ■ World Dredging, Mining & Construction
World Dredging Magazine
PO Box 17479
Irvine, CA 92623-7479
Phone: (949)553-0836
Fax: (949)863-9261
Publication E-mail: info@worlddreging.com
Trade magazine discussing current issues and technological developments relating to the worldwide dredging and dredge mining industries. **Freq:** Bimonthly. **Print Method:** Offset. **Trim Size:** 8 1/2 x 11. **Cols./Page:** 3. **Col. Width:** 26 nonpareils. **Col. Depth:** 140 agate lines. **Key Personnel:** Steve Richardson, Editor, phone: (949)553-0836. **ISSN:** 1045--0343 (print). **Subscription Rates:** $100 Individuals 1 year; $180 Individuals 2 years; $270 Individuals 3 years; $200 Individuals 1 year airmail. **URL:** http://www.worlddredging.com. **Ad Rates:** BW $1,100; 4C $1,385. **Remarks:** Accepts advertising. **Circ:** ‡2400.

2651 ■ World Journal of AIDS
Scientific Research Publishing Inc.
PO Box 54821
Irvine, CA 92619-4821
Publication E-mail: wja@scirp.org
Peer-reviewed journal publishing articles on research data and education in all aspects of HIV and AIDS. **Freq:** Quarterly. **Key Personnel:** Dr. Jayashree Seema Nandi, Editor-in-Chief. **ISSN:** 2160--8814 (print); **EISSN:** 2160--8822 (electronic). **Subscription Rates:** $398 Individuals. **URL:** http://www.scirp.org/journal/wja. **Circ:** (Not Reported).

2652 ■ World Journal of Cardiovascular Diseases
Scientific Research Publishing Inc.
PO Box 54821
Irvine, CA 92619-4821
Publisher's E-mail: service@scirp.org
Journal featuring the latest advancement in cardiovascular diseases. **Freq:** Monthly. **Key Personnel:** Prof. Luca Masotti, Editor-in-Chief. **ISSN:** 2164--5329 (print); **EISSN:** 2164--5337 (electronic). **Subscription Rates:** $998 Individuals. **URL:** http://www.scirp.org/journal/wjcd. **Circ:** (Not Reported).

2653 ■ World Journal of Cardiovascular Surgery
Scientific Research Publishing Inc.
PO Box 54821
Irvine, CA 92619-4821
Publisher's E-mail: service@scirp.org
Journal covering the latest advancements in cardiovascular surgery. **Freq:** Monthly. **Key Personnel:** Prof. Tomas A. Salerno, Editor-in-Chief. **ISSN:** 2164--3202 (print); **EISSN:** 2164--3210 (electronic). **Subscription Rates:** $1098 Individuals. **URL:** http://www.scirp.org/journal/wjcs. **Circ:** (Not Reported).

2654 ■ World Journal of Condensed Matter Physics
Scientific Research Publishing Inc.
PO Box 54821
Irvine, CA 92619-4821
Publication E-mail: wjcmp@scirp.org
Peer-reviewed journal publishing information on condensed matter physics. **Freq:** Quarterly. **Key Personnel:** Prof. Wen-Jeng Hsueh, Editor-in-Chief. **ISSN:** 2160--6919 (print); **EISSN:** 2160--6927 (electronic). **Subscription Rates:** $498 Individuals. **URL:** http://www.scirp.org/journal/wjcmp. **Circ:** (Not Reported).

2655 ■ World Journal of Engineering and Technology
Scientific Research Publishing Inc.
PO Box 54821
Irvine, CA 92619-4821
Publisher's E-mail: service@scirp.org
Journal covering latest developments and issues in all aspects of engineering and technology. **Freq:** Quarterly. **Key Personnel:** Dr. Gwang-Hee Kim, Editor-in-Chief. **ISSN:** 2331--4222 (print); **EISSN:** 2331--4249 (electronic). **URL:** http://www.scirp.org/journal/WJET. **Circ:** (Not Reported).

2656 ■ World Journal of Mechanics
Scientific Research Publishing Inc.
PO Box 54821
Irvine, CA 92619-4821
Publisher's E-mail: service@scirp.org
Peer-reviewed journal publishing articles in the general field of mechanics. **Freq:** Monthly. **Key Personnel:** Prof. Dan Mateescu, Editor-in-Chief; Prof. Kumar K. Tamma, Editor-in-Chief. **ISSN:** 2160--049X (print); **EISSN:** 2160--0503 (electronic). **Subscription Rates:** $998 Individuals. **URL:** http://www.scirp.org/journal/wjm. **Circ:** (Not Reported).

2657 ■ World Journal of Nano Science and Engineering
Scientific Research Publishing Inc.
PO Box 54821
Irvine, CA 92619-4821
Publisher's E-mail: service@scirp.org
Peer-reviewed journal publishing articles on applications of physical, chemical and biological sciences to engineering. **Freq:** Quarterly. **ISSN:** 2161--4954 (print); **EISSN:** 2161--4962 (electronic). **Subscription Rates:** $398 Individuals. **URL:** http://www.scirp.org/journal/wjnse. **Circ:** (Not Reported).

2658 ■ World Journal of Neuroscience
Scientific Research Publishing Inc.
PO Box 54821
Irvine, CA 92619-4821
Publisher's E-mail: service@scirp.org
Journal featuring the latest issues and developments in Neuroscience. **Freq:** Quarterly Latest edition 2015. **Key Personnel:** Gjumrakch Aliev, Editor-in-Chief. **ISSN:** 2162--2000 (print); **EISSN:** 2162--2019 (electronic). **Subscription Rates:** $1992 Individuals Volume 5. **URL:** http://www.scirp.org/journal/wjns. **Circ:** (Not Reported).

2659 ■ World Journal of Nuclear Science and Technology
Scientific Research Publishing Inc.
PO Box 54821
Irvine, CA 92619-4821
Publisher's E-mail: service@scirp.org
Peer-reviewed journal publishing articles on nuclear science and technology. **Freq:** Quarterly. **Key Personnel:** Prof. Andrzej Grzegorz Chmielewski, Editor-in-Chief. **ISSN:** 2161--6795 (print); **EISSN:** 2161--6809 (electronic). **Subscription Rates:** $498 Individuals. **URL:** http://www.scirp.org/journal/wjnst. **Circ:** (Not Reported).

2660 ■ World Journal of Vaccines
Scientific Research Publishing Inc.
PO Box 54821
Irvine, CA 92619-4821
Publication E-mail: wjv@scirp.org
Peer-reviewed journal publishing articles on the latest advancements in vaccine. **Freq:** Quarterly. **Key Personnel:** Prof. Andrew W. Heath, Editor-in-Chief. **ISSN:**

2160--5815 (print); **EISSN:** 2160--5823 (electronic). **Subscription Rates:** $498 Individuals for year 2015. **URL:** http://www.scirp.org/journal/wjv. **Circ:** (Not Reported).

2661 ■ Young Rider
Lumina Media L.L.C.
3 Burroughs
Irvine, CA 92618
Phone: (949)855-8822
Fax: (949)855-3045
Consumer magazine covering horse riding. **Freq:** Bimonthly. **Subscription Rates:** $14.99 U.S.; $20.99 Other countries surface delivery. **URL:** http://www.youngrider.com. **Circ:** Paid ***85411**.

2662 ■ KUCI-FM - 88.9
PO Box 4362
Irvine, CA 92616
Phone: (949)824-6868
Format: Eclectic. **Networks:** Independent. **Owner:** Regents of the University of California, 1111 Franklin St., 12th Fl., Oakland, CA 94607. **Founded:** 1969. **Operating Hours:** Continuous. **Key Personnel:** Elizabeth Wood, Dir. of Mktg.; Kevin Stockdale, Engineer, Contact; Kevin Stockdale, Contact. **Wattage:** 200. **Ad Rates:** Noncommercial. **URL:** http://www.kuci.org.

JOSHUA TREE

2663 ■ KCDZ-FM - 107.7
6448 Hallee Rd., Ste. 5
Joshua Tree, CA 92252
Phone: (760)366-8471
Fax: (760)366-2976
Format: Adult Contemporary. **Networks:** ABC. **Founded:** July 15, 1989. **Operating Hours:** Continuous. **ADI:** Palm Springs, CA. **Key Personnel:** Gary Daigneault, Owner, Prog. Dir; Cindy Daigneault, Contact, kcdzfmgm@gmail.com. **Wattage:** 7,200. **Ad Rates:** Advertising accepted; rates available upon request. **URL:** http://www.kcdzfm.com.

2664 ■ KQCM-FM - 92.1
PO Box 1437
Joshua Tree, CA 92252
Phone: (760)362-4264
Format: Hip Hop; News; Information; Top 40. **Owner:** Copper Mountain Broadcasting, at above address, Joshua Tree, CA. **URL:** http://www.copperxrocks.com.

2665 ■ KXCM-FM - 96.3
PO Box 1437
Joshua Tree, CA 92252
Phone: (760)362-4264
Format: Country. **Owner:** Copper Mountain Broadcasting, at above address, Joshua Tree, CA. **Wattage:** 6,000. **URL:** http://www.kxcmradio.com//home/main.

JULIAN

SW CA. San Diego Co. 30 mi. SE of Escondido.

2666 ■ Julian News
Julian News
PO Box 639
Julian, CA 92036
Phone: (760)765-2231
Fax: (760)765-2231
Publisher's E-mail: publisher@juliannews.com
Community newspaper. **Freq:** Weekly (Wed.). **Key Personnel:** Michael Hart, Publisher; Michele Harway, Publisher. **Subscription Rates:** $40 By mail standard mail - 1 year; $120 By mail first class mail - 1 year. **URL:** http://www.juliannews.com. **Ad Rates:** GLR $12; SAU $12; PCI $15. **Remarks:** Accepts advertising. **Circ:** Controlled 2500.

KEENE

2667 ■ KBDS-FM - 103.9
PO Box 62
Keene, CA 93531
Phone: (661)837-0745
Fax: (661)837-1612
Format: Hip Hop.

KENSINGTON

2668 ■ Blue Unicorn: A Tri-Quarterly of Poetry
Blue Unicorn Inc.
22 Avon Rd.
Kensington, CA 94707
Phone: (510)526-8439
Publication E-mail: staff@blueunicorn.com
Poetry journal. **Freq:** 3/year Feb, June, & Oct. **Trim Size:** 8 1/2 x 11. **Key Personnel:** James Schevill, Editor; Darlene Mathis-Eddy, Editor; X.J. Kennedy, Editor; Daniel J. Langton, Editor; John Hart, Editor; Joan LaBombard, Editor; Fred Ostrander, Editor; Ruth G. Iodice, Editor. **ISSN:** 0960--8574 (print). **Subscription Rates:** $20 Individuals add $8 (mailing cost) for outside the USA; $15 Single issue add $5 (mailing cost) for outside the USA. **URL:** http://www.blueunicorn.org. **Remarks:** Advertising not accepted. **Circ:** Combined 475.

KERMAN

C. CA. Fresno Co. 15 mi. W. of Fresno. Sugar factory. Alfalfa mill, cotton gins. Agriculture. Sugar beets, grapes, cotton, rice, alfalfa, cattle.

2669 ■ The Kerman News
Kerwest
PO Box 336
Kerman, CA 93630
Phone: (559)846-6689
Fax: (209)846-8045
Publisher's E-mail: kerwest@msn.com
Community newspaper. **Freq:** Weekly (Wed.). **Print Method:** Offset. **Cols./Page:** 6. **Col. Width:** 2 1/16 inches. **Col. Depth:** 21 inches. **Key Personnel:** Mark Kilen, Contact. **URL:** http://www.kerwestnewspapers.com/news.htm. **Ad Rates:** GLR $.59; BW $1,036.98; SAU $8.23. **Remarks:** Accepts advertising. **Circ:** ‡6500.

KERNVILLE

SC CA. Kern Co. 50 mi. NE of Bakersfield.

2670 ■ KCNQ-FM - 102.5
14 Sierra Dr.
Kernville, CA 93238-2008
Phone: (760)376-4500
Format: Country. **Networks:** ABC. **Operating Hours:** Continuous. **Wattage:** 130. **Ad Rates:** $5.60-24 per unit. Combined advertising rates available with KVLI-FM and KQAB-AM. **Mailing address:** PO Box 1184, Kernville, CA 93238. **URL:** http://www.kernriverradio.com.

2671 ■ K216EW-FM - 91.1
PO Box 391
Twin Falls, ID 83303
Free: 800-357-4226
Format: Religious; Contemporary Christian. **Owner:** CSN International, PO Box 391, Twin Falls, ID 83303, Ph: (208)736-1958, Fax: (208)736-1958, Free: 800-357-4226. **Key Personnel:** Don Mills, Prog. Dir., Music Dir.; Kelly Carlson, Dir. of Engg.; Ray Gorney, Asst. Dir. **URL:** http://www.csnradio.com.

2672 ■ KVLI-FM - 104.5
14 Sierra Dr., Ste. A
Kernville, CA 93238
Format: Oldies. **Owner:** QAB Media, LLC, at above address. **Founded:** Oct. 28, 1992. **Operating Hours:** Continuous. **Key Personnel:** Scott Allen, Gen. Mgr., Contact; Scott Allen, Contact. **Wattage:** 200. **Ad Rates:** $11-15 for 30 seconds; $13-18 for 60 seconds. Combined advertising rates available with KCNQ-FM and KQAB-AM. **Mailing address:** PO Box 3434, Lake Isabella, CA 93240. **URL:** http://www.kernriverradio.com.

KING CITY

W. CA. Monterey Co. 48 mi. SE of Salinas. Wax, asbestos products. Garlic onion dehydration. Carrots and tomatoes packed. Agriculture. Cattle, grain, potatoes.

2673 ■ Greenfield News
South County Newspapers
522-A Broadway
King City, CA 93930
Phone: (831)385-4880
Fax: (831)385-4799
Community newspaper. **Freq:** Weekly (Wed.). **Print Method:** Offset. **Cols./Page:** 6. **Col. Width:** 26 nonpareils. **Col. Depth:** 294 agate lines. **Key Personnel:** Tricia Bergeron, General Manager, phone: (831)385-4880. **Subscription Rates:** $49.70 Individuals in area; $52.95 Out of area. **URL:** http://greenfieldnews.com/v2_main_page.php. **Ad Rates:** SAU $9.50. **Remarks:** Accepts advertising. **Circ:** ‡1475.

2674 ■ King City Rustler
South County Newspapers
522-A Broadway
King City, CA 93930
Phone: (831)385-4880
Fax: (831)385-4799
Newspaper. **Freq:** Weekly (Wed.). **Print Method:** Offset. **Cols./Page:** 6. **Col. Width:** 26 nonpareils. **Col. Depth:** 294 agate lines. **Key Personnel:** Tricia Bergeron, General Manager. **Subscription Rates:** $49.70 Individuals in county; $52.95 Out of area. **URL:** http://www.kingcityrustler.com/v2_main_page.php. **Ad Rates:** SAU $9.50. **Remarks:** Accepts advertising. **Circ:** (Not Reported).

2675 ■ Soledad Bee
Soledad Bee
522-A Broadway
King City, CA 93930
Phone: (831)385-4880
Fax: (831)385-4799
Publisher's E-mail: publisher@southcountynewspapers.com
Community newspaper. **Freq:** Weekly (Wed.). **Print Method:** Offset. **Trim Size:** 14 x 22 3/4. **Cols./Page:** 6. **Col. Width:** 26 nonpareils. **Col. Depth:** 294 agate lines. **Key Personnel:** John Bartlett, Publisher. **USPS:** 500-740. **Subscription Rates:** $12.75 Individuals 10 weeks (manual pay); $12 Individuals 10 weeks (auto pay); $47.50 Individuals 1 year (auto pay); $49.70 Individuals 1 year (manual pay); $13.85 Out of area 10 weeks (manual pay); $13 Out of area 10 weeks (auto pay); $50.55 Out of area 1 year (auto pay); $52.95 Out of area 1 year (manual pay). **URL:** http://www.soledadbee.com/v2_main_page.php. **Ad Rates:** PCI $8.45. **Remarks:** Advertising accepted; rates available upon request. **Circ:** 1125.

2676 ■ KDKL-FM - 88.3
PO Box 2098
Omaha, NE 68103
Free: 800-525-5683
Format: Contemporary Christian. **Owner:** Educational Media Foundation, 5700 W Oaks Blvd., CA 95765, Free: 800-800434-8400. **Key Personnel:** Mike Novak, President, CEO; Alan Mason, COO. **Wattage:** 1,400. **URL:** http://www.klove.com.

2677 ■ KRKC-AM - 1490
1134 San Antonio Dr.
King City, CA 93930
Phone: (831)385-5421
Email: krkc@dedot.com
Format: News; Agricultural; Sports. **Key Personnel:** Bill Gittler, Contact, bill@krkc.com; Jim Barker, Contact. **Wattage:** 1,000. **Ad Rates:** Accepts Advertising. **URL:** http://www.krkc.com.

2678 ■ KRKC-FM - 102.1
1134 San Antonio Dr.
King City, CA 93930-3317
Phone: (831)385-5421
Email: krkc@dedot.com
Format: Country. **Owner:** Radio del Rey Inc., at above address. **Founded:** 1989. **Key Personnel:** Bill Gittler, Contact, bill@krkc.com; Michael Davis, Contact. **Wattage:** 2,850 ERP. **Ad Rates:** Combined advertising rates available with KRKC-AM. **URL:** http://www.krkc.com.

LA CANADA

S. CA. Los Angeles Co. 5 mi. NW of Pasadena. Residential.

2679 ■ La Canada Valley Sun
La Canada Valley Sun
727 Foothill Blvd.
La Canada, CA 91011
Publication E-mail: lcnews@valleysun.com
Local newspaper. **Freq:** Weekly (Thurs.). **Print Method:** Offset. **Cols./Page:** 6. **Col. Width:** 19 nonpareils. **Col. Depth:** 224 agate lines. **Key Personnel:** Carol Cormaci, Managing Editor; Dan Evans, Editor, phone: (818)637-3234. **URL:** http://www.latimes.com/socal/la-canada-valley-sun. **Remarks:** Accepts advertising. **Circ:** 6763.

Circulation: ⋆ = AAM; △ or • = BPA; ♦ = CAC; ❑ = VAC; ⊕ = PO Statement; ‡ = Publisher's Report; Boldface figures = sworn; Light figures = estimated.

LA HABRA

S. CA. Orange Co. 25 mi. E. of Los Angeles. Citrus fruit packing, electronic products manufactured. Agriculture.

2680 ■ The Restorer
Model A Ford Club of America
250 S Cypress St.
La Habra, CA 90631-5515
Phone: (562)697-2712
Fax: (562)690-7452
Publisher's E-mail: info@mafca.com
Freq: Bimonthly. **Subscription Rates:** Included in membership. **URL:** http://www.mafca.com/pub_restorer.html. **Remarks:** Accepts classified advertising. **Circ:** (Not Reported).

LA HONDA

2681 ■ Terrier Type
Dan Kiedrowski Co.
PO Box A
La Honda, CA 94020
Phone: (650)747-0549
Publication E-mail: editor@terriertype.com
Trade magazine covering show dogs for breeders, handlers, and owners. **Freq:** Monthly. **Print Method:** Offset. **Trim Size:** 6 x 9. **Cols./Page:** 1. **Col. Width:** 4 3/4 inches. **Col. Depth:** 7 3/4 inches. **Key Personnel:** Shawn Nichols, Editor, phone: (403)264-9559; Cherie Virden, Creative Director. **ISSN:** 0199--6495 (print). **Subscription Rates:** $55 U.S. regular/surface; $75 U.S. first class; $65 Canada first/class airmail; $95 Other countries first/class airmail; $85 Individuals first/class airmail - Mexico. **URL:** http://www.terriertype.com. **Remarks:** Advertising not accepted. **Circ:** Combined ‡1900.

LA JOLLA

San Diego Co. On Pacific Ocean, 15 mi. NW of San Diego. University of California at San Diego. Winter and summer resort. Residential.

2682 ■ Biology of the Cell
Biochemical Society
c/o Dr.Sharon Schendel, Admin Ed.
BoC USA
The Burnham Institute
10901 N Torrey Pines Rd.
La Jolla, CA 92037
Phone: (858)795-5283
Fax: (858)795-5284
Publication E-mail: editorial@biolcellusa.org
Journal covering all issues related to cellular and molecular biology and cell physiology, in connection with the Societe Francaise desMicroscopies and the Societe de Biologie Cellulairede. **Freq:** Monthly. **Key Personnel:** Thierry Galli, Editor-in-Chief. **ISSN:** 0248--4900 (print); **EISSN:** 1768--322X (electronic). **Subscription Rates:** $1716 Institutions online only; €1367 Institutions online only; £945 Institutions online only; $1716 Institutions rest of world. **URL:** http://onlinelibrary.wiley.com/journal/10.1111/(ISSN)1768-322X. **Remarks:** Advertising accepted; rates available upon request. **Circ:** (Not Reported).

2683 ■ Bioorganic & Medicinal Chemistry Letters
Elsevier
c/o Prof. D.L. Boger, Advisory Board
The Scripps Institute
Dept. of Chemistry
La Jolla, CA 92037
Publisher's E-mail: t.reller@elsevier.com
Journal focused on chemistry and biology and on major advances in drug design and development. **Freq:** 24/yr. **Print Method:** Offset. **Trim Size:** 13 3/4 x 22. **Cols./Page:** 6. **Col. Width:** 13 picas. **Col. Depth:** 21 1/8 inches. **Key Personnel:** Prof. D.L. Boger, Board Member. **ISSN:** 0960--894X (print). **Subscription Rates:** $529 Individuals print; $2127.73 Institutions ejournal; $6382 Individuals print. **URL:** http://www.journals.elsevier.com/bioorganic-and-medicinal-chemistry-letters. **Circ:** (Not Reported).

2684 ■ Clinical Science
Portland Press Ltd.
c/o Dr. Sharon Schendel, Admin. Ed.
The Burnham Institute
10901 N Torrey Pines Rd.
La Jolla, CA 92037
Phone: (858)713-5283
Fax: (858)713-5284
Publisher's E-mail: sales@portland-services.com
Journal covering research related to health and disease. **Founded:** 1906. **Freq:** Monthly. **Key Personnel:** Rhian M. Touyz. **ISSN:** 0143-5221 (print). **Subscription Rates:** $1125 Institutions online only; $1251 Institutions online and print. **URL:** http://www.clinsci.org/; http://www.portlandpress.com/pcs/journals/journal.cfm?product=CLI. **Remarks:** Advertising accepted; rates available upon request. **Circ:** (Not Reported).

2685 ■ Communications in Algebra
Taylor & Francis Group Journals
c/o Lance W. Small, Ed.
University of California
La Jolla, CA 92093-0112
Publisher's E-mail: customerservice@taylorandfrancis.com
Journal covering areas of algebraic interest. **Freq:** 12/yr. **Print Method:** Offset. **Trim Size:** 8 1/4 X 10 7/8. **Cols./Page:** 1. **Col. Width:** 71 nonpareils. **Col. Depth:** 126 agate lines. **Key Personnel:** Lance W. Small, Editor; Earl J. Taft, Editor, Founder. **ISSN:** 0092--7872 (print); **EISSN:** 1532-4125 (electronic). **Subscription Rates:** $1776 Individuals print only; $6378 Institutions online only; $7289 Institutions print and online. **URL:** http://www.tandfonline.com/toc/lagb20/current#.VGs6rTQwrld. **Ad Rates:** BW $890; 4C $1,935. **Remarks:** Accepts advertising. **Circ:** 725.

2686 ■ Dream Home Magazine
Dream Homes Magazine
PO Box 2988
La Jolla, CA 92038
Phone: (619)275-9104
Publisher's E-mail: admin@dreamhomesmagazine.com
Magazine for Cincinnati area builders, remodelers, and home buyers. **Freq:** Monthly. **Key Personnel:** Andrew Dremak, Contact. **Subscription Rates:** $45 Individuals. **URL:** http://www.dreamhomesmagazine.com. **Ad Rates:** BW $335. **Remarks:** Advertising accepted; rates available upon request. **Circ:** Controlled 13000.

2687 ■ High Altitude Medicine & Biology
Mary Ann Liebert Inc., Publishers
c/o John B. West, MD, Ed.-in-Ch.
UCSD Dept. of Medicine 0623A
9500 Gilman Dr.
La Jolla, CA 92093-0623
Phone: (858)534-4192
Fax: (858)534-4812
Publisher's E-mail: info@liebertpub.com
Peer-reviewed journal covering the latest advances in high altitude life sciences. **Freq:** Quarterly. **Trim Size:** 8 1/2 x 11. **Cols./Page:** 2. **Col. Width:** 19 nonpareils. **Col. Depth:** 57.5 agate lines. **Key Personnel:** Andrew M. Luks, MD, Associate Editor; Peter H. Hackett, Board Member; Cynthia Beall, PhD, Board Member; Buddha Basnyat, MD, Board Member; Inder S. Anand, MD, Board Member; Peter Bartsch, MD, Board Member; John B. West, MD, Editor-in-Chief; Hermann Brugger, MD, Associate Editor; Franz Berghold, MD, Board Member; Tom Brutsaert, PhD, Board Member. **ISSN:** 1527-0297 (print); **EISSN:** 1557--8682 (electronic). **Subscription Rates:** $696 Individuals online only; $1215 Institutions online only; $717 Individuals online. **URL:** http://www.liebertpub.com/overview/high-altitude-medicine-and-biology/65; http://ismm.org/index.php/journal.html. **Ad Rates:** BW $1,800; 4C $2,550. **Remarks:** Advertising accepted; rates available upon request. **Circ:** (Not Reported).

2688 ■ The Journal of Film Music
Equinox Publishing Ltd.
c/o William H. Rosar, Ed.
Department of Psychology
University of California, San Diego
Mandler Hall, Rm. 2541
La Jolla, CA 92093-0109
Publisher's E-mail: info@equinoxpub.com
Journal focusing on original articles and reviews that address any aspect of film music. **Freq:** Semiannual April & September. **Key Personnel:** William H. Rosar, Editor; Michael Beckerman, Board Member; David Cooper, Board Member. **ISSN:** 1087-7142 (print); **EISSN:** 1758-860X (electronic). **Subscription Rates:** $84 Individuals print only; $47 Other countries online only; $68 Individuals print only; $35 Other countries online only; $315 Institutions print and online; $195 Other countries print and online; $240 Institutions online only; $158 Other countries online only. **URL:** http://www.equinoxpub.com/index.php/JFM. **Circ:** (Not Reported).

2689 ■ Journal of Financial Markets
RELX Group P.L.C.
c/o B. Lehman, Co-Ed.
Graduate School of International Relations & Pacific Studies
University of California at San Diego
La Jolla, CA 92093
Phone: (858)534-0945
Fax: (858)534-3939
Publisher's E-mail: amsterdam@relx.com
Journal covering applied issues related to securities trading and pricing. **Freq:** 5/yr. **Key Personnel:** B. Lehmann, Editor; A. Subrahmanyam, Editor. **ISSN:** 1386--4181 (print). **Subscription Rates:** $84 Individuals print; $671 Institutions print. **URL:** http://www.journals.elsevier.com/journal-of-financial-markets. **Circ:** (Not Reported).

2690 ■ Leading Companies
University of California - San Diego Rady School of Management Beyster Institute
Otterson Hall S, 4th Fl.
9500 Gilman Dr.
La Jolla, CA 92093-0553
Phone: (858)246-0654
Publisher's E-mail: beysterinfo@rady.ucsd.edu
Freq: Monthly. **Subscription Rates:** free. **Remarks:** Advertising not accepted. **Circ:** (Not Reported).

2691 ■ Marine Mammal Science
Society for Marine Mammalogy
c/o Jay Barlow, President
8901 La Jolla Shores Dr.
La Jolla, CA 92037-1508
Phone: (858)546-7178
Fax: (910)962-4066
Journal covering the research on marine mammals. **Freq:** Quarterly. **Key Personnel:** Daryl J. Boness, Editor. **ISSN:** 0824--0469 (print); **EISSN:** 1748--7692 (electronic). **Subscription Rates:** $359 Institutions online only; £223 Institutions online only, UK; €280 Institutions online only, Europe; $429 Institutions, other countries online only. **URL:** http://onlinelibrary.wiley.com/journal/10.1111/(ISSN)1748-7692; http://www.marinemammalscience.org/journal. **Remarks:** Accepts advertising. **Circ:** (Not Reported).

2692 ■ Neural Computation
The MIT Press
c/o Dr. Terrence Sejnowski, Ed.-in-Ch.
The Salk Institute-CNL
10010 N Torrey Pines Rd.
La Jolla, CA 92037
Phone: (858)453-4100
Fax: (858)587-0417
Publisher's E-mail: sales@mitpress.mit.edu
Disseminating research results in the neural computation field. **Freq:** Monthly. **Print Method:** Offset. **Trim Size:** 6 x 9. **Cols./Page:** 1. **Col. Width:** 26 picas. **Col. Depth:** 43 picas. **Key Personnel:** Terrence J. Sejnowski, Editor-in-Chief; Mary Ellen Perryri, Managing Editor; Laurence Abbott, Associate Editor. **ISSN:** 0899-7667 (print); **EISSN:** 1530-888X (electronic). **Subscription Rates:** $134 Individuals electronic access; $1075 Institutions electronic access; $75 Students print & electronic access. **URL:** http://www.mitpressjournals.org/loi/neco. **Ad Rates:** BW $450. **Remarks:** Accepts advertising. **Circ:** Controlled ‡600.

2693 ■ PLOS Computational Biology
International Society for Computational Biology
9500 Gilman Dr.
MC 0505
La Jolla, CA 92093-0505
Phone: (858)534-0852
Fax: (619)374-2894
Publication E-mail: ploscompbiol@plos.org
Open access, peer-reviewed journal that publishes works that further understanding of living systems at all scales through the application of computational methods. Publication fees are charged to authors, institutions, or funders for each article published. **Freq:** Monthly. **Key Personnel:** Philip E. Bourne, Editor-in-Chief; Ruth Nussinov, Editor-in-Chief. **ISSN:** 1553--7358 (print);

EISSN: 1553--734X (electronic). **Subscription Rates:** $2250 Individuals. **Alt. Formats:** Database. **URL:** http://journals.plos.org/ploscompbiol. **Remarks:** Accepts advertising. **Circ:** (Not Reported).

2694 ■ Progress in Oceanography
RELX Group P.L.C.
c/o Cisco Werner, Editor
PO Box 271
La Jolla, CA 92038
Phone: (858)546-7081
Fax: (858)546-7003
Publisher's E-mail: amsterdam@relx.com
Journal for oceanographers. Covers the whole range of fields in oceanography. **Founded:** 1963. **Freq:** 10/year. **Key Personnel:** Cisco Werner, Editor-in-Chief. **ISSN:** 0079-6611 (print). **Subscription Rates:** $4237 Institutions print; $4237.60 online; $255 Individuals print. **URL:** http://www.journals.elsevier.com/progress-in-oceanography. **Circ:** (Not Reported).

2695 ■ Think Spanish! Audio Magazine
Second Language Publishing
PO Box 2732
La Jolla, CA 92038-2732
Fax: (858)777-5551
Free: 800-741-0773
Magazine devoted to teaching Spanish language. **Freq:** Monthly. **Print Method:** Offset. **Trim Size:** 7 7/8 x 10 3/4. **Cols./Page:** 3 and 2. **Col. Width:** 26 and 40 nonpareils. **Col. Depth:** 140 agate lines. **ISSN:** 0017--9434 (print). **Subscription Rates:** $99 Individuals. **URL:** http://www.thinklanguage.com/spanish. **Remarks:** Accepts advertising. **Circ:** (Not Reported).

2696 ■ UCSD Guardian
University of California at San Diego
9500 Gilman Dr.
La Jolla, CA 92093
Phone: (858)534-2230
Publication E-mail: editor@ucsdguardian.org
College newspaper. **Founded:** 1964. **Freq:** Semiweekly (Mon. & Thurs.). **Print Method:** Offset. **Trim Size:** 10 x 16. **Cols./Page:** 5. **Col. Width:** 1 7/8 inches. **Col. Depth:** 16 inches. **Key Personnel:** Angela Chen, Editor-in-Chief; Arielle Sallai, Managing Editor; Monica Bachmeier, General Manager; Nicole Chan, Associate Editor. **Subscription Rates:** $38 Individuals per quarter; $100 Individuals academic year. **URL:** http://library.ucsd.edu/dc/object/bb5496181f. **Formerly:** Triton Times. **Ad Rates:** GLR $4; BW $880; 4C $1,270; PCI $11. **Remarks:** Accepts advertising. **Circ:** Combined 10000.

2697 ■ KSDT-FM - 95.5
9500 Gilman Dr., Ste. 0077
La Jolla, CA 92093-0315
Phone: (858)534-3673
Fax: (858)534-0480
Format: Educational. **Simulcasts:** KSDT-AM 1320. **Owner:** University of California, San Diego, 9500 Gilman Dr., CA 92093-0021. **Founded:** 1967. **URL:** http://ksdt.ucsd.edu/contact-us.

LA MESA

S. CA. San Diego Co. 10 mi. E. of San Diego. Residential. Retirement community.

2698 ■ San Diego Jewish Times
Schwarz Publishing Inc.
4731 Palm Ave.
La Mesa, CA 91941
Phone: (619)463-5515
Fax: (619)463-1309
Publication E-mail: sdjt@sdjewishtimes.com
Newspaper containing information of interest to the Jewish community. **Freq:** Biweekly. **Key Personnel:** Mike Schwarz, Publisher; Mike Sirota, Editor. **Subscription Rates:** $36 Individuals one year; $65 Individuals two years. **URL:** http://sdjewishtimes.com. **Ad Rates:** 4C $2,460; PCI $60. **Remarks:** Accepts advertising. **Circ:** (Not Reported).

LA MIRADA

S. CA. Los Angeles Co. 12 mi. SE of Los Angeles. Biola University. Manufactures plastics, tools, steel, paper products, chemicals, furniture.

2699 ■ The Chimes
Biola University
13800 Biola Ave.
La Mirada, CA 90639-0001
Phone: (562)903-6000
Publisher's E-mail: ucm@biola.edu
Collegiate newspaper. **Founded:** 1935. **Freq:** Weekly (Thurs.). **Print Method:** Offset. **Cols./Page:** 5. **Col. Width:** 22 nonpareils. **Col. Depth:** 210 agate lines. **URL:** http://chimes.biola.edu/. **Remarks:** Accepts advertising. **Circ:** Free 2000.

2700 ■ Great Commission Research Journal: to communicate recent thinking and research related to American Church Growth
Great Commission Research Network
13800 Biola Ave.
La Mirada, CA 90639
Publication covering churches in the U.S. **Freq:** 3/year. **Key Personnel:** Gary L. McIntosh, Editor, Founder; Alan McMahan, Editor. **ISSN:** 1091--2711 (print). **Subscription Rates:** $30 Individuals regular; $20 Students; $38 Other countries; $60 Individuals two years; $76 Other countries two years. **URL:** http://journals.biola.edu/gcr/about. **Formerly:** Journal of the American Society of Church Growth. **Remarks:** Advertising accepted; rates available upon request. **Circ:** 400.

2701 ■ Journal of Psychology and Christianity: An Official Publication of the Christian Association for Psychological Studies
Christian Association for Psychological Studies
c/o Peter C. Hill, PhD, Ed.
Rosemead School of Psychology
Biola University
13800 Biola Ave.
La Mirada, CA 90639
Publication E-mail: jpc@caps.net
Journal on topics relating Christianity with psychological and pastoral professions. **Freq:** Quarterly. **Print Method:** Offset. **Trim Size:** 6 x 9. **Cols./Page:** 1. **Col. Width:** 54 nonpareils. **Col. Depth:** 100 agate lines. **ISSN:** 0733--4273 (print). **Subscription Rates:** Included in membership; $103 Libraries member; $103 Nonmembers Individual per year. **URL:** http://caps.net/membership/publications/jpc. **Remarks:** Advertising accepted; rates available upon request. **Circ:** Paid ‡2300, Non-paid ‡200.

2702 ■ Journal of Psychology and Theology: An Evangelical Forum for the Integration of Psychology & Theology
Rosemead School of Psychology
Biola University
13800 Biola Ave.
La Mirada, CA 90639
Phone: (562)903-4867
Free: 800-652-4652
Publisher's E-mail: graduate.admissions@biola.edu
Theoretical, research, and applied articles on the interrelationships of psychological and theological concepts. Also includes reviews of relevant books. **Freq:** Quarterly. **Print Method:** Offset. **Trim Size:** 6 3/4 x 10. **Cols./Page:** 2. **Col. Width:** 32 nonpareils. **Col. Depth:** 109 agate lines. **ISSN:** 0091--6471 (print). **Subscription Rates:** $46 Individuals; $66 Individuals print + CD; $35 Students; $60 Individuals other countries; $105 Individuals other countries, print + CD. **Alt. Formats:** CD-ROM. **URL:** http://www.rosemead.edu/faculty/journal-psychology-and-theology. **Remarks:** Advertising accepted; rates available upon request. **Circ:** ‡1350.

LA VERNE

S. CA. Los Angeles Co. 30 mi. E. of Los Angeles. Residential.

2703 ■ Campus Times
University of La Verne
1950 3rd St.
La Verne, CA 91750
Phone: (909)593-3511
Fax: (909)392-0364
Publication E-mail: ctimes@ulv.edu
College newspaper. **Founded:** 1919. **Freq:** Weekly. **Print Method:** Offset. **Trim Size:** 11 x 17. **Cols./Page:** 5. **Col. Width:** 10.8 nonpareils. **Col. Depth:** 96 agate lines. **Key Personnel:** Eric Borer, Assistant. **URL:** http://www.ulv.edu/ctimes. **Ad Rates:** BW $650; 4C $1,000; PCI $8. **Remarks:** Advertising accepted; rates available upon request. **Circ:** Free 2000.

2704 ■ KULV-AM - 107.9
1950 3rd St.
La Verne, CA 91750
Phone: (909)593-3511
Fax: (909)392-2706
Email: kulv@ulv.edu
Format: Alternative/New Music/Progressive. **Owner:** University of La Verne, at above address. **Founded:** 1976. **Operating Hours:** Continuous. **Key Personnel:** Shane Rodrigues, Operations Mgr., srodrigu@ulv.edu; Mike Laponis, Gen. Mgr., laponism@ulv.edu. **Wattage:** 130. **Ad Rates:** Advertising accepted; rates available upon request. **URL:** http://laverne.edu.

2705 ■ KULV-FM - 107.9
1950 3rd St.
La Verne, CA 91750
Phone: (909)593-3511
Fax: (909)392-2706
Format: Alternative/New Music/Progressive. **Simulcasts:** KULV-AM. **Owner:** University of La Verne, at above address. **Founded:** 1976. **Operating Hours:** 7 a.m.-11 p.m. Mon.-Fri.,Continuous Sat.-Sun. **Key Personnel:** Mike Laponis, Gen. Mgr.; Shane Rodrigues, Operations Mgr. **Wattage:** 001. **Ad Rates:** $2-8 for 30 seconds; $3-10 for 60 seconds. **URL:** http://laverne.edu.

LADERA RANCH

2706 ■ Vows: The Bridal and Wedding Business Journal
Grimes and Associates
24 Daisy St.
Ladera Ranch, CA 92694
Phone: (949)388-4848
Fax: (949)388-8448
Publisher's E-mail: info@vowsmagazine.com
Trade journal for bridal and wedding professionals. **Freq:** Bimonthly. **Key Personnel:** Kori Grimes; Peter Grimes, Publisher, phone: (949)388-4848; Karl Nazarro, Creative Director. **Subscription Rates:** $30 Individuals; $52 Two years; $55 Canada; $89 Other countries surface; $129 Other countries air. **URL:** http://vowsmagazine.com. **Ad Rates:** BW $1,775; 4C $2,570. **Remarks:** Accepts advertising. **Circ:** 11000.

LAFAYETTE

W. CA. Contra Costa Co. 10 mi. NE of Berkeley. Residential.

2707 ■ Allcarcentral.com
All Car Central Publishing
3622B Mount Diablo Blvd.
Lafayette, CA 94549-3737
Phone: (925)951-7100
Fax: (925)609-9481
Publisher's E-mail: info@allcarcentral.com
Automotive news and archival web-based publication. **Freq:** Daily. **Key Personnel:** Frank Cunnigham, Manager. **Subscription Rates:** Free. **URL:** http://www.allcarcentral.com. **Remarks:** Advertising accepted; rates available upon request. **Circ:** Free 900000.

2708 ■ Journal of Investment Management: Serving the Profession and Academia
Journal of Investment Management
3658 Mt. Diablo Blvd., Ste. 200
Lafayette, CA 94549
Phone: (925)299-7800
Fax: (925)299-7815
Publisher's E-mail: editor@joim.com
Refereed journal that seeks to bridge the gap between investment management theory and practice. **Freq:** Quarterly. **Key Personnel:** Gifford H. Fong, Editor; Keith Brown, Associate Editor; Elroy Dimson, Associate Editor. **ISSN:** 1545--9144 (print); **EISSN:** 1545--9152 (electronic). **Subscription Rates:** $310 Individuals; $340 Individuals other countries; $575 Libraries premium; $640 Libraries premium, international; $1100 Elsewhere corporate library, per site. **URL:** http://www.joim.com/library.asp. **Remarks:** Advertising accepted; rates available upon request. **Circ:** (Not Reported).

LAGUNA BEACH

S. CA. Orange Co. On Pacific Ocean, 18 mi. SW of Santa Ana. Summer and winter resort.

Circulation: ★ = AAM; △ or • = BPA; ♦ = CAC; ❑ = VAC; ⊕ = PO Statement; ‡ = Publisher's Report; Boldface figures = sworn; Light figures = estimated.

2709 ■ American Bankruptcy Law Journal
National Conference of Bankruptcy Judges
c/o Jeanne Sleeper, Executive Director
954 La Mirada St.
Laguna Beach, CA 92651-3751
Phone: (949)497-3673
Fax: (949)497-2523
Publisher's E-mail: NCBJadmin@NCBJmeeting.org
Peer-reviewed journal focusing on bankruptcy law and related subjects. **Freq:** Quarterly. **Key Personnel:** Judge J. Rich Leonard, Editor-in-Chief; Judge Mary F. Walrath, Business Manager. **ISSN:** 0027--9048 (print). **Subscription Rates:** $45 Individuals /year for new lawyers (less than two years in practice); $75 Individuals /year for new and renewals; $85 Other countries. **URL:** http://www.ncbj.org/?page=AmerBankLawJour. **Remarks:** Advertising not accepted. **Circ:** (Not Reported).

2710 ■ The Laguna Journal
Laguna Journal
301 Forest Ave.
Laguna Beach, CA 92651
Phone: (949)494-7121
Publisher's E-mail: mvwsr@aol.com
General newspaper. **Freq:** Daily. **Key Personnel:** Michael Webster, Publisher, phone: (949)494-7121. **URL:** http://paper.li/e-1424380550. **Remarks:** Accepts advertising. **Circ:** (Not Reported).

2711 ■ Left Side Lines
Sidelines National High-Risk Pregnancy Support Network
PO Box 1808
Laguna Beach, CA 92652
Free: 888-447-4754
Publisher's E-mail: sidelines@sidelines.org
Freq: Annual. **Subscription Rates:** $3 /copy. **URL:** http://www.sidelines.org/index.php/about-our-volunteers. **Remarks:** Advertising not accepted. **Circ:** (Not Reported).

2712 ■ Los Cabos Magazine
Promociones Tyson S.A. de C.V.
303 Magnolia Dr.
Laguna Beach, CA 92651-1720
Phone: (858)569-0172
Fax: (858)333-7000
Publication E-mail: info@loscabosguide.com
Magazine covering hotel, resort, restaurant and shopping information on the Mexican resort area of Los Cabos. **Freq:** Quarterly. **Print Method:** Web offset. **Trim Size:** 8 1/8 x 10 7/8. **Cols./Page:** 3. **Col. Width:** 2 1/4 inches. **Col. Depth:** 10 inches. **Key Personnel:** Joseph A. Tyson, Publisher. **Subscription Rates:** $8 Individuals 1 year; $14 Individuals 2 years; $24 Individuals 4 years. **URL:** http://www.loscabosmagazine.com. **Ad Rates:** 4C $5,650. **Remarks:** Accepts advertising. **Circ:** 240000.

KYHO-FM - See Poplar Bluff, MO

WVXR-FM - See Richmond, IN

LAGUNA HILLS

S. CA. Orange Co. 2 mi. S. of El Toro.

2713 ■ Altered Couture
Stampington & Co.
22992 Mill Creek, Ste. B
Laguna Hills, CA 92653
Phone: (949)380-7318
Fax: (949)380-9355
Free: 877-782-6737
Publisher's E-mail: wholesale@stampington.com
Fashion magazine. **Freq:** Quarterly. **Key Personnel:** Darcy Fowkes, Contact. **Subscription Rates:** $59.99 Individuals. **URL:** http://www.alteredcouture.com; http://stampington.com/altered-couture. **Circ:** (Not Reported).

2714 ■ Art Doll Quarterly
Stampington & Co.
22992 Mill Creek, Ste. B
Laguna Hills, CA 92653
Phone: (949)380-7318
Fax: (949)380-9355
Free: 877-782-6737
Publisher's E-mail: wholesale@stampington.com
Magazine featuring art dolls and sculptural figures made from cloth, polymer clay, creative paperclay, wire armatures, and mixed media. **Freq:** Quarterly. **Key Personnel:** Laura Burns, Manager, Advertising and Sales. **Subscription Rates:** $34.99 Individuals; $44.99 Canada; $59.99 Other countries. **URL:** http://www.artdollquarterly.com; http://stampington.com/art-doll-quarterly. **Circ:** (Not Reported).

2715 ■ Artful Blogging
Stampington & Co.
22992 Mill Creek, Ste. B
Laguna Hills, CA 92653
Phone: (949)380-7318
Fax: (949)380-9355
Free: 877-782-6737
Publisher's E-mail: wholesale@stampington.com
Magazine featuring artful blogging. **Freq:** Quarterly. **Trim Size:** 8.375 x 10.875. **Key Personnel:** Laura Burns, Manager, Advertising and Sales; Melissa Mercer, Account Executive. **Subscription Rates:** $59.99 Individuals; $67.99 Canada; $75.99 Other countries. **URL:** http://artfulblogging.com; http://stampington.com/artful-blogging. **Circ:** (Not Reported).

2716 ■ Bell Armoire
Stampington & Co.
22992 Mill Creek, Ste. B
Laguna Hills, CA 92653
Phone: (949)380-7318
Fax: (949)380-9355
Free: 877-782-6737
Publisher's E-mail: wholesale@stampington.com
Magazine featuring fabric arts, handmade garments, creative jewelry, and accessories. **Freq:** Bimonthly. **Trim Size:** 8.375 x 10.875. **Key Personnel:** Laura Burns, Manager, Advertising and Sales; Melissa Mercer, Account Executive. **Subscription Rates:** $64.95 Individuals; $84.95 Canada; $104.95 Other countries. **URL:** http://www.bellearmoire.com; http://stampington.com/belle-armoire. **Ad Rates:** 4C $1722. **Remarks:** Accepts advertising. **Circ:** (Not Reported).

2717 ■ Life Images
Stampington & Co.
22992 Mill Creek, Ste. B
Laguna Hills, CA 92653
Phone: (949)380-7318
Fax: (949)380-9355
Free: 877-782-6737
Publisher's E-mail: wholesale@stampington.com
Magazine featuring original and full-page photographs. **Freq:** Quarterly. **Key Personnel:** Melissa Mercer, Account Executive; Laura Burns, Manager, Advertising and Sales. **Subscription Rates:** $14.99 Individuals print - plus shipping and handling; $9.99 Individuals online. **URL:** http://stampington.com/life-images. **Circ:** (Not Reported).

2718 ■ Somerset Life
Stampington & Co.
22992 Mill Creek, Ste. B
Laguna Hills, CA 92653
Phone: (949)380-7318
Fax: (949)380-9355
Free: 877-782-6737
Publication E-mail: somersetlife@stampington.com
Magazine featuring tips and guides to an inspired and artful way of living. **Freq:** Annual. **Subscription Rates:** $14.99 Individuals. **URL:** http://www.stampington.com/somersetlife. **Circ:** (Not Reported).

2719 ■ Somerset Studio
Stampington & Co.
22992 Mill Creek, Ste. B
Laguna Hills, CA 92653
Phone: (949)380-7318
Fax: (949)380-9355
Free: 877-782-6737
Publisher's E-mail: wholesale@stampington.com
Magazine featuring papercrafting, art stamping, and lettering arts. **Freq:** Bimonthly. **Trim Size:** 8.375 x 10.875. **Key Personnel:** Laura Burns, Manager, Advertising and Sales; Melissa Mercer, Account Executive. **Subscription Rates:** $32.99 Individuals. **URL:** http://stampington.com/somerset-studio. **Ad Rates:** BW $1855; 4C $2195. **Remarks:** Accepts advertising. **Circ:** (Not Reported).

2720 ■ Stampers' Sampler
Stampington & Co.
22992 Mill Creek, Ste. B
Laguna Hills, CA 92653
Phone: (949)380-7318
Fax: (949)380-9355
Free: 877-782-6737
Publisher's E-mail: wholesale@stampington.com
Magazine featuring hand-stamped artworks. **Freq:** Bimonthly. **Key Personnel:** Laura Burns, Manager, Advertising and Sales; Melissa Mercer, Account Executive. **Subscription Rates:** $32.99 Individuals. **URL:** http://stampington.com/the-stampers-sampler. **Circ:** (Not Reported).

2721 ■ Where Women Create
Stampington & Co.
22992 Mill Creek, Ste. B
Laguna Hills, CA 92653
Phone: (949)380-7318
Fax: (949)380-9355
Free: 877-782-6737
Publisher's E-mail: wholesale@stampington.com
Magazine covering inspiring work spaces of extraordinary women. **Freq:** Quarterly. **Key Personnel:** Jo Packham, Editor-in-Chief; Janet Southwick, Office Manager; Kellene Giloff, Publisher. **Subscription Rates:** $59.99 Individuals. **URL:** http://www.wherewomencreate.com/where-women-create. **Circ:** (Not Reported).

LAKE ARROWHEAD

SE CA. San Bernardino Co. 10 mi. NE of San Bernardino. Residential. Year-round resort.

2722 ■ Crestline Courier-News
Mountain News
PO Box 2410
Lake Arrowhead, CA 92352
Phone: (909)337-6145
Community newspaper. **Freq:** Weekly (Thurs.). **Print Method:** Offset. **Trim Size:** 13 3/4 x 21 1/2. **Cols./Page:** 6. **Col. Width:** 12 1/3 picas. **Col. Depth:** 20.5 inches. **Key Personnel:** Harry Bradley, Publisher, phone: (909)337-6145; Mary-Justine Lanyon, Editor; Angela Yap, Director, Marketing. **USPS:** 137-780. **Subscription Rates:** $29.95 Individuals 1 year subscription in San Bernardino County; $49.95 Two years in San Bernardino County; $39.95 Individuals 1 year subscription out of the County; $75.90 Two years out of the County; $60 Out of state 1 year subscription; $99 Out of state 2 years subscription. **URL:** http://www.mountain-news.com. **Remarks:** Accepts advertising. **Circ:** ‡2850.

2723 ■ Mountain News
Brehm Communications Inc.
PO Box 2410
Lake Arrowhead, CA 92352
Phone: (909)336-3555
Fax: (909)337-5275
Community newspaper. **Founded:** 1920. **Freq:** Weekly (Thurs.). **Print Method:** Offset. **Cols./Page:** 6. **Col. Width:** 26 nonpareils. **Col. Depth:** 280 agate lines. **Key Personnel:** Harry Bradley, Publisher, phone: (909)337-6145. **Subscription Rates:** $29.95 Individuals; $39.95 Individuals out of county; $60 Individuals outside state. **URL:** http://www.mountain-news.com; http://www.brehmcommunications.com/publications/. **Ad Rates:** SAU $7.65. **Remarks:** Accepts advertising. **Circ:** ‡7500.

2724 ■ Mountain Shopper
Brehm Communications Inc.
28200 Hwy. 189, Ste. 200
Lake Arrowhead, CA 92352
Phone: (909)336-3555
Fax: (909)337-5275
Shopping guide. **Freq:** Weekly (Tues.). **Print Method:** Offset. **Cols./Page:** 6. **Col. Width:** 26 nonpareils. **Col. Depth:** 280 agate lines. **Key Personnel:** Harry Bradley, Publisher. **URL:** http://www.brehmcommunications.com/publications. **Remarks:** Advertising accepted; rates available upon request. **Circ:** (Not Reported).

LAKE ELSINORE

2725 ■ Roadracing World & Motorcycle Technology
Roadracing World and Motorcycle Technology
PO Box 1428
Lake Elsinore, CA 92531
Phone: (951)245-6411
Fax: (951)245-6417
Publisher's E-mail: customerservice@roadracingworld.com
Consumer magazine covering motorcycle racing and and high performance motorcycles. **Freq:** Monthly. **Key Personnel:** John D. Ulrich, Editor; Chris Ulrich, Editor;

Sam Fleming, Editor. **ISSN:** 1056--4845 (print). **Subscription Rates:** $19.95 Individuals print - 13 issues; $24.95 Individuals print + digital - 13 issues; $34.95 Individuals print - 2 years 26 issues; $44.95 Individuals print & online - 2 years 26 issues; $47.95 Individuals print & online - 3 years 39 issues; $49.95 Canada and Mexico print - 1 year 13 issues; $54.95 Canada and Mexico print & online - 1 year 13 issues; $74.95 Other countries print - 1 year 13 issues; $79.95 Other countries print - 1 year 13 issues; $12 Individuals digital only; $22 Individuals digital only; $30 Individuals digital only. **Alt. Formats:** PDF. **URL:** http://roadracingworld.com; http://www.roadracingworld.com/magazine. **Remarks:** Accepts advertising. **Circ:** Paid ‡20000.

LAKE FOREST

Capistrano Valley News - See San Juan Capistrano

2726 ■ Dana Point News
Freedom Communications Inc.
22481 Aspan St.
Lake Forest, CA 92630
Fax: (949)454-7354
Publisher's E-mail: info@freedom.com
Community newspaper. **Founded:** 1965. **Freq:** Weekly (Thurs.). **Print Method:** Offset. **Cols./Page:** 5. **Col. Width:** 12 1/16 inches. **Col. Depth:** 13 inches. **Key Personnel:** Michael Colorado, Team Leader, phone: (949)454-7351; Rob Vardon, Editor. **URL:** http://www.ocregister.com/sections/city-pages/danapoint/. **Formerly**: Dana Point/Laguna Niguel News. **Ad Rates:** PCI $32.17. **Remarks:** Accepts advertising. **Circ:** Free ■ **9642**.

2727 ■ Information Technology and Disabilities
Equal Access to Software and Information
PO Box 818
Lake Forest, CA 92609
Phone: (949)916-2837
Publisher's E-mail: info@easi.cc
Journal covering issues related to the development of new technologies by computer users with disabilities. **Freq:** Annual. **Key Personnel:** Tom McNulty, Editor, phone: (212)998-2519; Steve Noble, Editor. **ISSN:** 1073--5127 (print). **Remarks:** Advertising not accepted. **Circ:** Non-paid 1900.

2728 ■ Laguna Niguel News
Freedom Communications Inc.
22481 Aspan St.
Lake Forest, CA 92630
Fax: (949)454-7300
Publisher's E-mail: info@freedom.com
Community newspaper. **Founded:** 1965. **Freq:** Weekly (Thurs.). **Print Method:** Offset. **Cols./Page:** 5. **Col. Width:** 12 1/16 inches. **Col. Depth:** 13 inches. **Key Personnel:** Freda Freeman, Editor; Chris Boucly, Team Leader. **Subscription Rates:** Free; $12 By mail. **URL:** http://www.ocregister.com. **Formerly**: Dana Point/Laguna Niguel News. **Ad Rates:** PCI $32.17. **Remarks:** Accepts advertising. **Circ:** Free ‡17515.

LAKE ISABELLA

SC CA. Kern Co. 40 mi. NE of Bakersfield. Kern Co. (SC). 40 m NE of Bakersfield.

2729 ■ Kern Valley Sun
Kern Valley Sun
PO Box 3074
Lake Isabella, CA 93240-3074
Phone: (619)379-3667
Fax: (619)379-4343
Community newspaper. **Freq:** Weekly (Wed.). **Print Method:** Offset. **Cols./Page:** 6. **Col. Width:** 2 inches. **Col. Depth:** 21 inches. **USPS:** 293-740. **Subscription Rates:** $44 Individuals. **URL:** http://www.kernvalleysun.com. **Ad Rates:** PCI $6.80. **Remarks:** Accepts advertising. **Circ:** 6800.

LAKE LOS ANGELES

2730 ■ The Lake Los Angeles News
Joyce Media Inc.
4030 N 170th St. E
Lake Los Angeles, CA 93591-0109
Phone: (661)269-1169
Fax: (661)269-2139
Publisher's E-mail: help@joycemediainc.com
Community newspaper. **Freq:** Weekly. **URL:** http://joycemediainc.com/papers/llamall.html. **Mailing address:** PO Box 500109, Lake Los Angeles, CA 93591-0109. **Remarks:** Advertising accepted; rates available upon request. **Circ:** (Not Reported).

LAKEHEAD

2731 ■ K207CT-FM - 89.3
PO Box 391
Twin Falls, ID 83303
Fax: (208)736-1958
Free: 800-357-4226
Format: Religious; Contemporary Christian. **Owner:** CSN International, PO Box 391, Twin Falls, ID 83303, Ph: (208)736-1958, Fax: (208)736-1958, Free: 800-357-4226. **Key Personnel:** Ray Gorney, Asst. Dir.; Don Mills, Prog. Dir., Music Dir.; Kelly Carlson, Dir. of Engg. **Wattage**: 010. **URL:** http://www.csnradio.com.

LAKEPORT

N. CA. Lake Co. On Clear Lake, 45 mi. N. of Santa Rosa. Summer resort. Diversified farming. Livestock.

2732 ■ Cancer Victors Journal: Voice of IACVF
The International Association of Cancer Victors and Friends
PO Box 745
Lakeport, CA 95453
Phone: (480)636-6611
Free: 877-558-4286
Publisher's E-mail: contact@cancervictors.net
Association magazine. **Freq:** Quarterly. **Print Method:** Offset or Desk. **Trim Size:** 8 1/2 x 11. **Cols./Page:** 3. **Key Personnel:** Ann Cinquina, Contact. **ISSN:** 0891--0766 (print). **URL:** http://www.cancervictors.net. **Formerly**: Cancer News Journal. **Ad Rates:** BW $300; 4C $500. **Remarks:** Accepts advertising. **Circ:** Paid ‡20000.

2733 ■ Lake County Record-Bee
Lake County Publishing
PO Box 849
Lakeport, CA 95453
Phone: (707)263-5636
Fax: (707)263-0600
Publisher's E-mail: letters@record-bee.com
Newspaper with a Republican orientation. **Founded:** 1873. **Freq:** Tues.-Sat. (morn.). **Print Method:** Offset. **Cols./Page:** 6. **Col. Width:** 25 nonpareils. **Col. Depth:** 287 agate lines. **Key Personnel:** Kevin McConnell, Publisher. **ISSN:** 0746-4304 (print). **Subscription Rates:** $2.30 Individuals online; $2.91 Individuals print. **URL:** http://www.record-bee.com/. **Ad Rates:** SAU $6.05. **Remarks:** Accepts advertising. **Circ:** Tues.-Fri. ★**6825**, Sat. ★**7739**.

2734 ■ KNTI-FM - 99.5
140 N Main St.
Lakeport, CA 95453
Phone: (707)263-6113
Fax: (707)263-0939
Format: Classical. **Networks:** Mutual Broadcasting System. **Owner:** Bicoastal Media L.L.C., at above address, Ph: (707)263-6113, Fax: (707)263-0939. **Founded:** 1984. **Operating Hours**: Continuous; 25% network, 75% local. **ADI**: San Francisco-Oakland-San Jose. **Key Personnel:** Alan Mathews, Contact. **Wattage**: 50,000. **Ad Rates:** $10-15 for 30 seconds; $14-20 for 60 seconds. **URL:** http://www.knti.com.

2735 ■ KUKI-FM - 103.3
140 N Main St.
Lakeport, CA 95453
Phone: (707)466-5868
Fax: (707)466-5852
Format: Country. **Networks:** ABC; CBS. **Owner:** Bicoastal Media L.L.C., at above address, Ph: (707)263-6113, Fax: (707)263-0939. **Founded:** 1974. **Formerly**: KKTU-FM; KIAH-FM; KAFF-FM. **Operating Hours**: Continuous. **Key Personnel:** Allan Mathews, Contact. **Wattage**: 2,900. **Ad Rates:** Noncommercial. **URL:** http://www.kukifm.com.

2736 ■ KXBX-AM - 1270
140 N Main St.
Lakeport, CA 95453
Phone: (707)263-6113
Fax: (707)263-0939
Format: Middle-of-the-Road (MOR). **Networks:** Satellite Music Network. **Owner:** Bi-Coastal Media L.L.C., 1 Blackfield Dr., Ste. 333, Tiburon, CA 94920, Ph: (415)789-5035, Fax: (415)789-5036. **Formerly**: KWTR-AM. **Operating Hours**: Continuous. **Wattage**: 500. **Ad Rates:** $8.75 per unit. **URL:** http://www.kxbx.com.

2737 ■ KXBX-FM - 98.3
445 N Main St.
Lakeport, CA 95453
Phone: (707)263-6113
Format: Adult Contemporary. **Networks:** Satellite Music Network; NBC. **Owner:** Bicoastal Media L.L.C., at above address, Ph: (707)263-6113, Fax: (707)263-0939. **Formerly**: KBLC-FM. **Operating Hours**: Continuous; 90% network, 10% local. **Wattage**: 4,800. **Ad Rates:** Noncommercial. **URL:** http://www.kxbxfm.com.

LAKEWOOD

S. CA. Los Angeles Co. 5 mi. E. of Cerritos. Residential.

2738 ■ Journal of the American Society of Questioned Document Examiners
American Society of Questioned Document Examiners
PO Box 6140
Lakewood, CA 90714
Professional journal covering forensic sciences. **Freq:** Semiannual. **Key Personnel:** Tobin Tanaka, Editor; Susan E. Morton, Editor. **Subscription Rates:** $80 Individuals USA/Canada; $95 Individuals other countries; $120 Institutions USA/Canada; $135 Institutions, other countries. **Alt. Formats:** CD-ROM; DVD. **URL:** http://www.asqde.org/journal/journal.html. **Remarks:** Advertising not accepted. **Circ:** (Not Reported).

LAMONT

S. CA. Kern Co. 10 mi. S. of Bakersfield. Truck, fruit, poultry farms.

2739 ■ KTQX-FM - 90.1
8787 Hall Rd.
Lamont, CA 93241-1953
Phone: (760)331-8874
Format: Hispanic. **Owner:** Radio Bilingue Inc., 5005 Belmont Ave., Fresno, CA 93727, Ph: (559)264-9191, Free: 800-200-5758. **Operating Hours**: Continuous. **Key Personnel:** Hugo Morales, Exec. Dir. **Wattage**: 570. **Ad Rates:** Noncommercial. **URL:** http://www.radiobilingue.org.

LANCASTER

SW CA. Los Angeles Co. 70 mi. NE of Los Angeles.

2740 ■ Aerotech News & Review: Journal of Aerospace and Defense Industry News
Aerotech
456 East Ave. K-4, Ste. 8
Lancaster, CA 93535
Fax: (877)247-9188
Publisher's E-mail: printing@aerotechnews.com
Professional journal for the aerospace industry. **Freq:** Weekly (Fri.). **Print Method:** Offset. **Trim Size:** 11 1/2 x 13 3/4. **Cols./Page:** 5. **Col. Width:** 1.875 inches. **Col. Depth:** 13 inches. **Key Personnel:** Lisa Kinison, Business Manager; Paul Kinison, Publisher; Stuart Ibberson, Editor. **Subscription Rates:** $89 Individuals. **URL:** http://www.aerotechnews.com/about-us. **Ad Rates:** PCI $11.55. **Remarks:** Accepts advertising. **Circ:** Non-paid 15000.

2741 ■ KAVL-AM - 610
352 E Ave. K-4
Lancaster, CA 93535
Phone: (661)942-1121
Format: Sports. **Networks:** USA Radio. **Founded:** 1950. **Operating Hours:** Continuous. **ADI:** Los Angeles (Corona & San Bernardino), CA. **Key Personnel:** Linda Foster, Contact, lindafoster@clearchannel.com. **Local Programs:** *Petros & Money Show*, Monday Tuesday Wednesday Thursday Friday 3:00 p.m. - 7:00 p.m.; *Gametime React*, Saturday Sunday 8:00 p.m. - 11:00 p.m. **Wattage**: 5,000 Daytime; 4,000 Nighttime. **Ad Rates:** Noncommercial.

2742 ■ KAVS-FM - 97.7
352 E Avenue K4
Lancaster, CA 93535

Circulation: ★ = AAM; △ or • = BPA; ♦ = CAC; ❑ = VAC; ⊕ = PO Statement; ‡ = Publisher's Report; Boldface figures = sworn; Light figures = estimated.

Phone: (805)942-1121
Fax: (805)723-5512
Free: 866-790-1031
Email: lvn@avcn.com
Format: Country; Contemporary Hit Radio (CHR). **Owner:** Antelope Broadcasting Co., at above address. **Founded:** 1966. **Operating Hours:** Continuous. **Key Personnel:** Ivan Ladizinsky, Gen. Mgr.; Rob Deshay, Dir. of Programs; Debi Strickland, Bus. Mgr. **Wattage:** 003.000 ERP. **Ad Rates:** $34-50 for 30 seconds; $37-57 for 60 seconds. **URL:** http://www.ktpifm.com.

2743 ■ KBET-AM - 1220
348 East Ave. K4
Lancaster, CA 93535-4505
Fax: (805)252-2679
Format: Adult Contemporary. **Networks:** CNN Radio; Westwood One Radio. **Founded:** 1989. **Operating Hours:** Continuous. **ADI:** Los Angeles (Corona & San Bernardino), CA. **Key Personnel:** A.J. Morgan, News Dir.; Carl Goldman, Gen. Mgr.; Chip Ehrhardt, Sales Mgr. **Wattage:** 1,000.

2744 ■ KFXM-FM - 96.7
PO Box 5478
Lancaster, CA 93539
Phone: (661)729-0202
Email: kfxmfm@kfxm.com
Format: Oldies. **Wattage:** 100. **URL:** http://www.kfxm.com.

2745 ■ KTLW-FM - 88.9
PO Box 2227
Lancaster, CA 93539
Fax: (818)779-8411
Free: 888-779-5859
Format: Religious. **Networks:** Ambassador Inspirational Radio; Moody Broadcasting; Family Stations Radio. **Operating Hours:** Continuous. **Key Personnel:** Gary Curtis, Gen. Mgr., VP. **Wattage:** 5,800. **Ad Rates:** Noncommercial. **URL:** http://ktlw.net.

2746 ■ KTPI-AM - 1340
348 E Ave. K-4
Lancaster, CA 93535
Phone: (661)942-1121
Fax: (661)723-5512
Format: Adult Contemporary. **Key Personnel:** Jim Bell, Gen. Mgr. **Wattage:** 1,000. **Ad Rates:** Noncommercial.

2747 ■ KTPI-FM - 97.7
352 E Ave. K-4
Lancaster, CA 93535
Fax: (661)942-1121
Free: 866-790-1031
Format: Country. **Operating Hours:** Continuous. **Key Personnel:** Linda Foster, Contact. **Wattage:** 3,000 ERP. **Ad Rates:** Combined advertising rates available with KAVC-AM, and KOSS-FM. **URL:** http://www.ktpifm.com.

KYHT-FM - See Los Angeles

LANDERS

2748 ■ K212EP-FM - 90.3
PO Box 391
Twin Falls, ID 83303
Free: 800-357-4226
Format: Religious; Contemporary Christian. **Owner:** CSN International, PO Box 391, Twin Falls, ID 83303, Ph: (208)736-1958, Fax: (208)736-1958, Free: 800-357-4226. **Key Personnel:** Don Mills, Prog. Dir., Music Dir.; Kelly Carlson, Dir. of Engg.; Ray Gorney, Asst. Dir. **URL:** http://www.csnradio.com.

LAUREL

2749 ■ K216AX-FM - 91.1
PO Box 391
Twin Falls, ID 83303
Fax: (208)736-1958
Free: 800-357-4226
Format: Religious; Contemporary Christian. **Owner:** CSN International, PO Box 391, Twin Falls, ID 83303, Ph: (208)736-1958, Fax: (208)736-1958, Free: 800-357-4226. **Key Personnel:** Don Mills, Prog. Dir., Music Dir.; Kelly Carlson, Dir. of Engg.; Ray Gorney, Asst. Dir. **Wattage:** 010. **URL:** http://www.csnradio.com.

LAYTONVILLE

2750 ■ KHKL-FM - 91.9
PO Box 779002
Rocklin, CA 95677-9972
Fax: (916)251-1901
Free: 800-525-5683
Format: Contemporary Christian. **Owner:** Educational Media Foundation, PO Box 2098, Omaha, NE 68103-2098, Free: 800-434-8400. **Key Personnel:** Mike Novak, President, CEO; Alan Mason, COO. **Wattage:** 100. **URL:** http://www.klove.com.

2751 ■ KLAI-FM - 90.3
PO Box 135
Redway, CA 95560
Phone: (707)923-3911
Fax: (707)923-2501
Free: 800-568-3723
Format: Public Radio. **Owner:** Redwood Community Radio Inc., 1144 Redway Dr., Redway, CA 95560, Ph: (707)923-2605. **Key Personnel:** Cynthia Click, Music Dir.; Jeanette Todd, Tech. Dir., Station Mgr. **URL:** http://www.kmud.org.

LEMON GROVE

S. CA. San Diego Co. 8 mi. E. of San Diego. Residential.

2752 ■ PPNF Health Journal: Health and Healing Wisdom
Price-Pottenger Nutrition Foundation
7890 Broadway
Lemon Grove, CA 91945
Phone: (619)462-7600
Fax: (619)433-3136
Free: 800-366-3748
Publisher's E-mail: info@ppnf.org
Freq: Quarterly. **Subscription Rates:** $40 Individuals. **URL:** http://ppnf.org/resources/ppnf-journals-digital. **Remarks:** Accepts advertising. **Circ:** 2000.

LEMOORE

SC CA. Kings Co. 32 mi. S. of Fresno. Carpet. Dairy products manufactured, cotton, fruit, grain, poultry, truck farms. Dairying.

2753 ■ KGAR-FM - 93.3
101 E Bush St.
Lemoore, CA 93245-3601
Phone: (559)924-6600
Format: Educational. **Owner:** Lemoore Union High School District, 5 Powell Ave., Lemoore, CA 93245, Ph: (559)924-6610. **Wattage:** 091. **URL:** http://www.luhsd.k12.ca.us/Departments_and_Courses/KGAR_Radio.

2754 ■ KJOP-AM - 1240
PO Box 327
Lemoore, CA 93245-0327
Phone: (559)924-2562
Format: Contemporary Country; Hispanic. **Founded:** 1981. **Operating Hours:** 6 a.m.-6 p.m. **Key Personnel:** Bob Jones, Gen. Mgr., Contact; Jesus Gonzalez, News Dir., Prog. Dir; Bob Jones, Contact. **Wattage:** 250 day; 1,000 night. **Ad Rates:** $12-32 for 30 seconds; $16-36 for 60 seconds. **URL:** http://ihradio.com/listen/stations/california-stations/kjop-1240-am-lemoore-ca/.

LINCOLN

NE CA. Placer Co. 28 mi. NE of Sacramento. Manufactures formica. Pottery, electronics. Cold storage, grain warehouses. Clay pits. Fruit, grain, dairy & beef farms.

2755 ■ Lincoln News-Messenger
Gold Country Media
553 F St.
Lincoln, CA 95648
Phone: (916)645-7733
Fax: (916)645-2776
Publication E-mail: messenger@goldcountrymedia.com
Community newspaper. **Freq:** Weekly (Thurs.). **Print Method:** Offset. **Trim Size:** 14 x 22. **Cols./Page:** 6. **Col. Width:** 12.5 picas. **Col. Depth:** 21 inches. **Key Personnel:** Carol Feineman, Editor, phone: (916)774-7972. **USPS:** 386-980. **URL:** http://www.lincolnnewsmessenger.com. **Remarks:** Accepts advertising. **Circ:** Free ■ **116**, Paid ■ **5274**, Combined ■ **5390**.

LINDEN

C. CA. San Joaquin Co. 10 mi. NE of Stockton. Walnut harvesters, church fruniture manufactured. Agriculture. Walnuts, cherries, peaches, livestock.

2756 ■ California Odd Fellow and Rebekah
Linden Publications
19033 E Main St.
Linden, CA 95236-0129
Phone: (209)887-3829
Official magazine of Odd Fellows and Rebekahs of California. **Freq:** Quarterly. **Print Method:** Offset. **Trim Size:** 8 1/2 x 11. **Cols./Page:** 3. **Col. Width:** 21 INS. **Col. Depth:** 60 INS. **Key Personnel:** Carol A. Fraher, Editor. **USPS:** 084-600. **Alt. Formats:** PDF. **URL:** http://caioof.org/odd-fellow-and-rebekah-publication. **Mailing address:** PO Box 129, Linden, CA 95236-0129. **Remarks:** Advertising not accepted. **Circ:** ‡8125.

2757 ■ The Linden Herald
The Linden Herald
18974 E Main St.
Linden, CA 95236
Phone: (209)887-3112
Community newspaper. **Freq:** Weekly (Thurs.). **Print Method:** Offset. **Cols./Page:** 8. **Col. Width:** 22 inches. **Col. Depth:** 13 & 22 inches. **Key Personnel:** Brian Reilly, Editor, Contact. **USPS:** 587-180. **Subscription Rates:** $35 Individuals; $40 Out of area. **URL:** http://www.lindenherald.com. **Mailing address:** PO Box 929, Linden, CA 95236. **Ad Rates:** GLR $5; BW $784; SAU $8; PCI $5.50. **Remarks:** Color advertising accepted; rates available upon request. **Circ:** Paid ‡1200.

LITTLE RIVER

2758 ■ Marine Ornithology
Pacific Seabird Group
c/o Ron LeValley, Treas.
Little River, CA 95456
Publication E-mail: marine.ornithology@ec.gc.ca
Peer-reviewed international journal on marine seabirds. **Freq:** Semiannual. **Key Personnel:** John Cooper, Founder, Editor; Scott Hatch, Editor; Rob Barrett, Editor. **ISSN:** 1018--3337 (print); **EISSN:** 2074--1235 (electronic). **Subscription Rates:** $100 Institutions; $45 Individuals; $25 Individuals low/mid income country. **URL:** http://www.marineornithology.org. **Formerly:** Cormorant. **Mailing address:** PO Box 324, Little River, CA 95456. **Circ:** (Not Reported).

LIVERMORE

W. CA. Alameda Co. 33 mi. SE of Oakland. Nuclear weapons, energy research. Wineries. Agriculture.

2759 ■ High Energy Density Physics
Elsevier
c/o Richard W. Lee, Ed.-in-Ch.
University of California at Berkeley
Livermore, CA 94550
Publisher's E-mail: t.reller@elsevier.com
Journal covering original experimental and related theoretical work studying the physics of matter and radiation under extreme conditions. **Freq:** Quarterly. **Print Method:** Web. **Trim Size:** 8 3/8 x 10 7/8. **Cols./Page:** 3. **Col. Width:** 2 1/4 INS. **Col. Depth:** 9 3/4 INS. **Key Personnel:** Steven J. Rose, Board Member; Richard W. Lee, Editor-in-Chief. **ISSN:** 1574--1818 (print). **Subscription Rates:** $193 Individuals print; $629.87 Institutions online; $944 Institutions print. **URL:** http://www.journals.elsevier.com/high-energy-density-physics. **Circ:** (Not Reported).

2760 ■ Numerical Linear Algebra with Applications
John Wiley & Sons Inc.
c/o Dr. Panayot S. Vassilevski, Ed.-in-Ch.
Centre for Applied Scientific Computing
Lawrence Livermore National Lab
7000 E Ave., Mail Stop L-560
Livermore, CA 94550
Publication E-mail: panayot@llnl.gov
Journal emphasizing new methods in numerical linear algebra, including their analysis and applications. **Freq:** 12/yr. **Key Personnel:** Prof. Owe Axelsson, Editor; Dr. Panayot S. Vassilevski, Editor-in-Chief; Z.Z. Bai, Board Member; Maya Neytcheva, Associate Editor. **ISSN:** 1070--5325 (print); **EISSN:** 1099--1506 (electronic). **Subscription Rates:** $2420 Institutions online only -

USA/Canada & Mexico/ROW; £1236 Institutions online only - UK; €1563 Institutions online only - Europe. **URL:** http://onlinelibrary.wiley.com/journal/10.1002/(ISSN)1099-1506. **Remarks:** Accepts advertising. **Circ:** (Not Reported).

2761 ■ Science & Technology Review
U.S. Department of Energy Lawrence Livermore National Laboratory
7000 East Ave.
Livermore, CA 94550-9234
Phone: (925)422-1100
Fax: (925)422-1370
Journal focusing on the accomplishments of Lawrence Livermore National Laboratory. **Freq:** 8/year. **Key Personnel:** Ray Marazzi, Managing Editor. **URL:** http://str.llnl.gov. **Mailing address:** PO Box 808, Livermore, CA 94551-0808. **Circ:** (Not Reported).

LODI

C. CA. San Joaquin Co. 14 mi. N. of Stockton. Extensive fruit packing and shipping. Manufactures canned fruit and vegetables, cereals, cake mixes, wine, olive oil, pumps, concrete pipes, brace aluminum, iron foundries, trailer hitches, juicers. Agriculture. Fruit, poultry, grain.

2762 ■ Lodi News-Sentinel
Lodi News-Sentinel
125 N Church St.
Lodi, CA 95240-2102
Phone: (209)369-2761
Fax: (209)369-1084
Publication E-mail: news@lodinews.com
General newspaper. **Print Method:** Offset. **Trim Size:** 13 3/4 x 22 3/4. **Cols./Page:** 6. **Col. Width:** 33 picas. **Col. Depth:** 21.5 inches. **Key Personnel:** Tracy Kelly, Director, Advertising; Richard Hanner, Editor; Marty Weybret, Publisher. **Subscription Rates:** $8.25 Individuals /month, online; $10 Individuals /month, print. **URL:** http://www.lodinews.com. **Mailing address:** PO Box 1360, Lodi, CA 95241-1360. **Ad Rates:** GLR $1.32; BW $2,380.05; 4C $2,755.05; SAU $8.05; PCI $19.18. **Circ:** Paid ♦**12116**.

LOMA LINDA

SE CA. San Bernardino Co. Residential.

2763 ■ Scope
Loma Linda University
Office of University Relations
24941 Stewart St.
Loma Linda, CA 92350
Phone: (909)558-4526
Publication E-mail: scope@llu.edu
University alumni magazine. **Founded:** 1933. **Freq:** Quarterly. **Print Method:** Offset. **Trim Size:** 8 1/2 x 11. **Cols./Page:** 3. **Col. Width:** 26 nonpareils. **Col. Depth:** 126 agate lines. **URL:** http://www.llu.edu/news/scope/index.page. **Remarks:** Accepts advertising. **Circ:** Free ‡40000.

2764 ■ Today
Loma Linda University
Office of University Relations
24941 Stewart St.
Loma Linda, CA 92350
Phone: (909)558-4526
Collegiate newspaper. **Founded:** 1969. **Freq:** 2/month on Wed. during academic school and 1/month during summer. **Print Method:** Web. **Trim Size:** 11 x 15. **Cols./Page:** 5. **Col. Width:** 22 nonpareils. **Col. Depth:** 224 agate lines. **Subscription Rates:** Free. **URL:** http://www.llu.edu/news/today/adinfo.page. **Formerly**: Observer. **Ad Rates:** PCI $10. **Remarks:** Accepts advertising. **Circ:** Non-paid 4000.

LOMPOC

SW CA. Santa Barbara Co. 55 mi. NW of Santa Barbara. Insulation, filtration products manufactured. Oil wells. Truck farms. Flower seeds, sugar beets.

2765 ■ HopeDance: Celebrating Transition, Opportunity & Resilience
HopeDance
PO Box 1741
Lompoc, CA 93438
Phone: (805)762-4848
Publisher's E-mail: info@hopedance.org
Magazine featuring the outrageous, pioneering and inspiring activities of outstanding individuals and organizations that are creating a new world regardless of their spiritual tradition or political agenda. **Freq:** Bimonthly. **Key Personnel:** Bob Banner, Editor. **Subscription Rates:** $10 Students; $20 Individuals regular; $50 Individuals family. **URL:** http://www.hopedance.org. **Remarks:** Accepts advertising. **Circ:** 30000.

2766 ■ Lompoc Record
Tower Media Inc.
Lompoc Record
115 N H St.
Lompoc, CA 93436
Phone: (805)736-2313
General newspaper. **Freq:** Daily (eve.). **Print Method:** Offset. **Trim Size:** 14 x 22. **Cols./Page:** 6. **Col. Width:** 12.3 picas. **Col. Depth:** 301 agate lines. **Key Personnel:** Cynthia Schur, Publisher, phone: (805)739-2154; Rich Pulsifer, Manager, Circulation, phone: (805)739-2147; George Fischer, Manager, Production, phone: (805)739-2234. **Subscription Rates:** $25 Individuals six months. **URL:** http://www.lompocrecord.com/. **Ad Rates:** BW $1,766; 4C $2,216; PCI $13.69. **Circ:** Mon.-Fri. ★**6529**, Sun. ★**6775**.

2767 ■ KRQZ-FM - 91.5
500 E North Ave.
Lompoc, CA 93436
Phone: (805)736-6415
Fax: (805)736-2642
Format: Contemporary Christian. **Ad Rates:** Advertising accepted; rates available upon request.

2768 ■ KTME-AM - 1410
PO Box 606
Lompoc, CA 93438
Phone: (805)736-5656
Fax: (805)735-6000
Format: Eclectic. **Owner:** Jaime Bonilla Valdez, 269 H Street 3rd Floor, Chula Vista, CA 91910, Ph: (619)429-5877. **Founded:** 1979. **Formerly**: KLLB-AM. **Operating Hours**: Continuous. **Wattage**: 500 Day; 077 Night. **Ad Rates:** Accepts Advertising. **URL:** http://www.radioktnk.com.

LONE PINE

NE CA. Inyo Co. 5 mi. S. of Independence.

2769 ■ Lone Pine Television
223 Jackson St.
Lone Pine, CA 93545
Phone: (760)876-5461
Free: 855-827-0815
Owner: Bruce James Branson, at above address. **Founded:** 1956. **Cities Served:** Lone Pine, California: subscribing households 625; 36 channels; 1 community access channel; 24 hours per week community access programming. **Postal Areas Served:** 93545. **URL:** http://www.lonepinetv.com/?page_id=34.

LONG BEACH

S. CA. Los Angeles Co. On Pacific Ocean, 22 mi. S. of Los Angeles. Long Beach City College; California State University at Long Beach. Summer and winter resort. America's most modern port. U. S. Naval Base and shipyard. Oil and gas wells. Oil production and refining, oil drilling equipment; fisheries, sardines, tuna, mackerel, meat packing plants; soft drink bottlers; shipbuilding and repair; aircraft and aircraft parts; chemicals, technical instruments, machinery, clothing, furnaces and heaters, building and insulation products, glass paper products, plastics manufactured.

2770 ■ The Cuddly News
Incest Survivors Anonymous
PO Box 17245
Long Beach, CA 90807
Phone: (562)428-5599
Freq: Semiannual. **Remarks:** Advertising not accepted. **Circ:** (Not Reported).

2771 ■ Daily 49er: The Student Publication of California State University Long Beach
Forty-Niner Publications
California State University, Long Beach
1250 Bellflower Blvd.
SSPA 010B
Long Beach, CA 90840-4601
Fax: (562)985-1740
Daily newspaper. **Freq:** Periodic 4/wk, Mon.-Thurs. **Print Method:** Offset. **Trim Size:** 10 1/4 x 16. **Cols./Page:** 6. **Col. Width:** 1 1/2 inches. **Key Personnel:** Paige Pelonis, Editor-in-Chief. **URL:** http://www.daily49er.com. **Formerly**: Daily 49er. **Remarks:** Accepts advertising. **Circ:** Free ‡42125.

2772 ■ International Journal of Instructional Technology and Distance Learning
The Reading Matrix
Meena Singhal, Ph.D., Ed.
Long Beach City College
Dept. of English as a Second Language
Long Beach, CA 90806
Phone: (562)938-4311
Fax: (562)938-4628
Publisher's E-mail: msinghal@lbcc.edu
Online journal covering topics in the field of second and foreign language teaching and research. **Freq:** Monthly. **Print Method:** Offset. **Trim Size:** 7 7/8 x 10 5/8. **Cols./Page:** 1. **Col. Width:** 84 nonpareils. **Col. Depth:** 133 agate lines. **Key Personnel:** Brent Muirhead, PhD, Senior Editor; Muhammad Betz, Editor; Donald G. Perrin, PhD, Executive Editor; Elizabeth Perrin, PhD, Editor-in-Chief. **ISSN:** 1550--6908 (print). **Alt. Formats:** E-book; PDF. **URL:** http://www.itdl.org. **Circ:** (Not Reported).

2773 ■ The International Review of Research in Open and Distance Learning
The Reading Matrix
Meena Singhal, Ph.D., Ed.
Long Beach City College
Dept. of English as a Second Language
Long Beach, CA 90806
Phone: (562)938-4311
Fax: (562)938-4628
Publisher's E-mail: msinghal@lbcc.edu
Peer-reviewed e-journal for advanced research. **Key Personnel:** Insung Jung, Board Member; Terry Anderson, Editor; Patrick J. Fahy, Board Member; Heather Kanuka, Board Member. **ISSN:** 1492--3831 (print). **URL:** http://www.irrodl.org/index.php/irrodl/index. **Remarks:** Advertising not accepted. **Circ:** (Not Reported).

2774 ■ Invertebrate Biology
American Microscopical Society
Dept. of Biological Sciences
CSU, Long Beach
1250 Bellflower Blvd.
Long Beach, CA 90840
Phone: (562)985-5378
Fax: (562)985-8878
Scientific journal covering the biology of invertebrate animals and research in the fields of cell and molecular biology, ecology, physiology, systematics, genetics, biogeography and behavior. **Freq:** Quarterly. **Trim Size:** 8 1/2 x 11. **Key Personnel:** Bruno Pernet, Editor-in-Chief; Maria Byrne, Board Member. **ISSN:** 1077--8306 (print); **EISSN:** 1744--7410 (electronic). **Subscription Rates:** $364 Institutions; £221 Institutions UK; €280 Institutions Europe; $430 Institutions, other countries; $437 Institutions print and online; £266 Institutions print and online, UK; €336 Institutions print and online, Europe; $516 Institutions, other countries print and online. **URL:** http://amicros.org/?page_id=2; http://onlinelibrary.wiley.com/journal/10.1111/(ISSN)1744-7410. **Formerly**: Transactions of the American Microscopial Society. **Remarks:** Advertising not accepted. **Circ:** (Not Reported).

2775 ■ The Journal of Educators Online
The Reading Matrix
Meena Singhal, Ph.D., Ed.
Long Beach City College
Dept. of English as a Second Language
Long Beach, CA 90806
Phone: (562)938-4311
Fax: (562)938-4628
Publisher's E-mail: msinghal@lbcc.edu
Journal covering online courses in arts, business, education, engineering, medicine, and sciences. **Key Personnel:** Kirsti A. Dyer, MD, Advisor, Board Member; Jean B. Mandernach, PhD, Advisor, Board Member; Sharmila Basu Conger, PhD, Advisor, Board Member; Kathryn Ley, PhD, Associate Editor. **URL:** http://www.thejeo.com. **Remarks:** Advertising not accepted. **Circ:** (Not Reported).

Circulation: ★ = AAM; △ or • = BPA; ♦ = CAC; ❑ = VAC; ⊕ = PO Statement; ‡ = Publisher's Report; Boldface figures = sworn; Light figures = estimated.

2776 ■ Journal of Electronic Commerce Research
California State University
401 Golden Shore
Long Beach, CA 90802-4210
Phone: (562)951-4000
Publisher's E-mail: webmaster@calstate.edu
Journal dealing with topics relating to electronic commerce theories and applications. **Freq:** Quarterly. **Key Personnel:** Melody Kiang, Editor-in-Chief; Robert Chi, Editor-in-Chief. **ISSN:** 1938--9027 (print); **EISSN:** 1526--6133 (electronic). **Subscription Rates:** $100 Individuals. **URL:** http://www.csulb.edu/journals/jecr/a_j.htm. **Circ:** (Not Reported).

2777 ■ The Journal of Human Performance in Extreme Environments
The Society for Human Performance in Extreme Environments
790 E Willow St.
Long Beach, CA 90806
Publisher's E-mail: Contact@hpee.org
Freq: Semiannual. **Key Personnel:** Jason Kring, Ph.D., President; Kelley Krokos, Ph.D., Vice President. **ISSN:** 1529--5168 (print). **Subscription Rates:** Included in membership. **URL:** http://www.hpee.org/journal. **Remarks:** Accepts advertising. **Circ:** Paid 200.

2778 ■ The Orion
California State University
401 Golden Shore
Long Beach, CA 90802-4210
Phone: (562)951-4000
Publication E-mail: orion@csuchico.edu
College newspaper. **Freq:** Weekly (Wed.). **Print Method:** Offset. **Trim Size:** 13 1/3 x 21. **Cols./Page:** 6. **Col. Width:** 12.5 picas. **Col. Depth:** 126 picas. **Key Personnel:** Stephanie Schmieding, Editor-in-Chief. **URL:** http://theorion.com. **Ad Rates:** BW $958. **Remarks:** Accepts advertising. **Circ:** 9000.

2779 ■ Press-Telegram
Digital First Media
727 Pine Ave.
Long Beach, CA 90844
Phone: (562)435-1161
General newspaper. **Founded:** 1888. **Freq:** Daily. **Print Method:** Letterpress. **Cols./Page:** 6. **Col. Width:** 25 nonpareils. **Col. Depth:** 301 agate lines. **Key Personnel:** Rich Archbold, Editor, phone: (562)499-1285; Tim Grobaty, Columnist. **Subscription Rates:** $20 Individuals 1 month; $10 Individuals /per, online. **URL:** http://www.presstelegram.com. **Remarks:** Accepts advertising. **Circ:** Mon.-Fri. ★**69761**, Sat. ★**69263**, Sun. ★**68477**.

2780 ■ The Reading Matrix
The Reading Matrix
Meena Singhal, Ph.D., Ed.
Long Beach City College
Dept. of English as a Second Language
Long Beach, CA 90806
Phone: (562)938-4311
Fax: (562)938-4628
Publisher's E-mail: msinghal@lbcc.edu
Peer-reviewed journal that exists to disseminate knowledge in the fields of second language acquisition and applied linguistics. **Freq:** Semiannual. **Key Personnel:** Meena Singhal, Editor-in-Chief; John Liontas, Managing Editor; Adrian Wurr, Editor. **ISSN:** 1533--242X (print). **Subscription Rates:** Free. **URL:** http://www.readingmatrix.com/journal.html; http://readingmatrix.com. **Circ:** (Not Reported).

2781 ■ Reporter
Pfanstiel Publishers and Printers Inc.
PO Box 4278
Long Beach, CA 90804
Phone: (562)438-5641
Publisher's E-mail: reporter.lb@verison.net
Legal newspaper. **Founded:** 1933. **Freq:** Semiweekly (Tues. and Fri.). **Print Method:** Offset. **Trim Size:** 17 1/2 x 22 1/2. **Cols./Page:** 5. **Col. Width:** 11.5 picas. **Col. Depth:** 280 agate lines. **Subscription Rates:** $51.89 Individuals 12 weeks; $100.51 Individuals 24 weeks; $180.38 Individuals 48 weeks. **URL:** http://www.thereporter.com/. **Ad Rates:** PCI $5.75. **Remarks:** Accepts advertising. **Circ:** ‡650.

2782 ■ Sexuality & Culture: An Interdisciplinary Quarterly
Springer Science + Business Media LLC
Dept. of Sociology
California State University
Long Beach, CA 90840-0906
Publisher's E-mail: service-ny@springer.com
Analysis of ethical, cultural, social, and political issues related to sexual relationships and sexual behavior. **Freq:** Quarterly. **Trim Size:** 4 3/4 x 7 3/4. **Key Personnel:** Barry M. Dank, Editor, Founder; Roberto Refinetti, Editor-in-Chief; Jakob Pastoetter, Editor. **ISSN:** 1095--5143 (print); **EISSN:** 1936--4822 (electronic). **Subscription Rates:** $637 Institutions print incl. free access or e-only; $764 Institutions print plus enhanced access; €463 Institutions print incl. free access or e-only; €556 Institutions print plus enhanced access. **URL:** http://www.springer.com/social+sciences/journal/12119. **Remarks:** Accepts advertising. **Circ:** 1000.

2783 ■ Troy Gazette
Gazette Newspapers Inc.
5225 E 2nd St.
Long Beach, CA 90803-5326
Phone: (562)433-2000
Fax: (562)434-8826
Publisher's E-mail: editor@gazettes.com
Community newspaper (tabloid). **Freq:** Weekly. **Print Method:** Offset. **Trim Size:** 11 1/2 x 30. **Cols./Page:** 5. **Col. Width:** 11.06 picas. **Col. Depth:** 13 1/2 inches. **Key Personnel:** Cynthia Kmett, Editor; Claire M. Weber, Editor. **URL:** http://rrhgazette.com. **Ad Rates:** BW $1,050; 4C $1,050; SAU $14.60; PCI $14.70. **Remarks:** Advertising accepted; rates available upon request. **Circ:** Free ‡20000.

2784 ■ Turkish Journal: The First Published Turkish Newspaper in California
California Turkish Times
PO Box 50018
Long Beach, CA 90815
Phone: (562)491-1223
Fax: (562)491-1227
Newspaper covering American news and current events in Turkish language and relating to the Turkish community. **Freq:** Weekly. **Subscription Rates:** Free to qualified subscribers. **URL:** http://www.turkishjournal.com. **Formerly:** California Turkish Times. **Remarks:** Accepts advertising. **Circ:** (Not Reported).

2785 ■ Viking
Long Beach City College
4901 E Carson St.
Long Beach, CA 90808
Phone: (562)938-4111
Publisher's E-mail: geninfo@lbcc.edu
Collegiate newspaper. **Founded:** 1927. **Freq:** Biweekly. **Print Method:** Offset. **Cols./Page:** 5. **Col. Width:** 24 nonpareils. **Col. Depth:** 196 agate lines. **Subscription Rates:** Free. **URL:** http://www.lbccvikingnews.com/. **Ad Rates:** GLR $.70; BW $480; SAU $1.78; PCI $6. **Circ:** Free 6500.

2786 ■ Weight Engineering
Society of Allied Weight Engineers
5734 E Lucia Walk
Long Beach, CA 90803-4015
Phone: (562)596-2873
Fax: (562)596-2874
Freq: Periodic. **Subscription Rates:** Included in membership; $60 Nonmembers /year. **URL:** http://www.sawe.org/technical/publications/journal. **Mailing address:** PO Box 60024, Los Angeles, CA 90060. **Remarks:** Accepts advertising. **Circ:** 1000.

2787 ■ Charter Communications
2310 Bellflower Blvd., Unit 102
Long Beach, CA 90815-2019
Founded: 1965. **Formerly:** Simmons Cable TV. **Key Personnel:** John Craig, Contact; John Craig, Contact. **Cities Served:** subscribing households 75,000. **URL:** http://www.charter.com.

2788 ■ KKJZ-FM
6300 E State University Dr.
Long Beach, CA 90815
Phone: (562)985-2999
Fax: (562)985-2982
Format: Jazz. **Networks:** AP. **Owner:** California State University, Long Beach, 1250 Bellflower Blvd., CA 90840. **Founded:** 1974. **Formerly:** KMXI-FM; KMJK-FM. **Wattage:** 30,000 ERP. **Ad Rates:** Noncommercial.

LOOMIS

NE CA. Placer Co. 20 mi. NE of Sacramento. Nurseries. Ships fruit. Agriculture. Pears, plums, peaches.

2789 ■ Loomis News
Loomis News
3550 Taylor Rd.
Loomis, CA 95650
Phone: (916)652-7939
Fax: (916)652-7879
Community newspaper. **Freq:** Weekly (Thurs.). **Print Method:** Offset. **Cols./Page:** 6. **Col. Width:** 2 inches. **Col. Depth:** 21 inches. **Key Personnel:** Andrew DiLuccia, Editor. **Subscription Rates:** $125 Individuals; $0.50 Single issue. **URL:** http://www.theloomisnews.com. **Ad Rates:** GLR $1.50; BW $515.34; 4C $700; SAU $4.09. **Remarks:** Accepts advertising. **Circ:** Free ■ **2927**, Paid ■ **1233**, Combined ■ **4160**.

KHOT-AM - See Fresno
KIHM-AM - See Reno, NV
KIHP-AM - See Phoenix, AZ
KPJP-FM - See Greenville
KSFB-AM - See San Francisco
K237EQ-FM - See Farmington, NM
KWG-AM - See Stockton
KXXQ-FM - See Gallup, NM

2790 ■ KYAA-AM - 1200
3256 Penryn Rd., Ste. 100
Loomis, CA 95650-8052
Phone: (916)535-0500
Fax: (916)535-0504
Free: 888-887-7120
Format: Oldies. **Networks:** Westwood One Radio. **Owner:** People's Radio, Inc. **Founded:** 2002. **Operating Hours:** Continuous. **Key Personnel:** Dick Jenkins, Gen. Mgr. **Wattage:** 25,000. **Ad Rates:** $28 for 30 seconds; $44 for 60 seconds. **URL:** http://ihradio.com.

LOS ALTOS

W. CA. Santa Clara Co. 6 mi. SE of Palo Alto. Nurseries. Fruit packed. Residential. Fruit, truck farms.

2791 ■ The Future of Children
David and Lucile Packard Foundation
343 2nd St.
Los Altos, CA 94022-3632
Phone: (650)948-7658
Publisher's E-mail: communications@packard.org
Journal covering issues related to children's well-being. **Freq:** Semiannual. **Key Personnel:** Sara McLanahan, Editor-in-Chief. **ISSN:** 1054--8289 (print). **URL:** http://www.futureofchildren.org; http://blogs.princeton.edu/futureofchildren. **Remarks:** Advertising not accepted. **Circ:** (Not Reported).

2792 ■ Los Altos Town Crier
The Town Crier Company Inc.
138 Main St.
Los Altos, CA 94022
Phone: (650)948-9000
Fax: (650)948-9213
Publisher's E-mail: info@latc.com
Community newspaper. **Freq:** Weekly. **Key Personnel:** Bruce Barton, Editor-in-Chief; Paul Nyberg, Publisher; Howard Bischoff, Specialist, Circulation. **Subscription Rates:** $30 Individuals /year in Santa Clara County; $20 Individuals /year senior; $50 Out of state /year; $30.50 Individuals /year (digital only). **URL:** http://www.losaltosonline.com. **Remarks:** Advertising accepted; rates available upon request. **Circ:** Combined 16500.

2793 ■ Narrow Gauge and Short Line Gazette
Benchmark Publications Ltd.
PO Box 26
Los Altos, CA 94023
Phone: (650)941-3823
Fax: (650)941-3845
Free: 800-545-4102
Magazine for narrow gauge and short line scale model railroad enthusiasts. **Freq:** Bimonthly. **Print Method:** Offset. **Trim Size:** 8 3/8 x 10 15/16. **Cols./Page:** 2 and 3. **Col. Width:** 2 1/4 and 2 1/4 inches. **Col. Depth:** 10 and 10 inches. **ISSN:** 0148--2122 (print). **Subscription Rates:** $40 Individuals; $45 Canada; $55 Other coun-

tries; $80 U.S. 2 years; $90 Canada 2 years; $110 Other countries 3 years. **URL:** http://www.ngslgazette.com/issue.htm. **Ad Rates:** BW $642; 4C $814. **Remarks:** Advertising accepted; rates available upon request. **Circ:** Paid ‡16300, Non-paid ‡219.

LOS ALTOS HILLS

W. CA. Santa Clara Co.

2794 ■ KFJC-FM - 89.7
12345 El Monte Rd.
Los Altos Hills, CA 94022
Phone: (650)949-7260
Fax: (650)948-1085
Format: Country. **Owner:** Foothill College Board of Trustees, at above address. **Founded:** 1959. **Operating Hours:** Continuous; 100% local. **Key Personnel:** Eric Johnson, Gen. Mgr.; Doc Pelzel, Station Mgr., doc@kfjc.org. **Wattage:** 110. **Ad Rates:** Noncommercial. **URL:** http://www.kfjc.org.

LOS ANGELES

S. CA. Los Angeles Co. A city of 450 square miles on the southern Pacific Coast. Largest city in area in United States, second largest retail center in the nation, largest industrial center west of Chicago and a leading agricultural center. University of Southern California; University of California at Los Angeles, and many other colleges and schools. A diversified economy with a variety of enterprises in agriculture. Manufacturing. Trade fishing, mining, entertaining, constructions, transportation services. Leads in value and added by manufactures of aircraft and aircraft parts, furniture fixtures, ordnance missiles. Other major manufacturing sectors include, electrical equipment, stone, clay, glass, apparel, fabricated metals, rubber, plastics, motion pictures, petroleum, coal, transportation equipment, printing and publishing. Lumber and wood products.

2795 ■ ACM Transactions on Design Automation of Electronic Systems
Association for Computing Machinery
c/o Massoud Pedram, Ed.-in-Ch.
Dept. of Electrical Engineering
University of Southern California
EEB 344, 3740 McClintock Ave.
Los Angeles, CA 90089-2562
Phone: (213)740-4458
Fax: (213)740-9803
Publisher's E-mail: acmhelp@acm.org
Journal of the Association for Computing Machinery. Intends to provide a comprehensive coverage of innovative works concerning the specification, design, analysis, simulation, testing, and evaluation of very large scale integrated electronic systems, emphasizing a computer science/engineering orientation. Editorial board invites submission of technical papers describing recent results of research and development efforts in the area of design automation of electronic systems. **Freq:** Quarterly. **Key Personnel:** Davide Bertozzi, Associate Editor, phone: (053)297-4832, fax: (053)297-4870; Shaahin Hessabi, Associate Editor; Naehyuck Chang, Editor-in-Chief; Bill Lin, Associate Editor, phone: (858)822-1383. **ISSN:** 1084-4309 (print); **EISSN:** 1557-7309 (electronic). **Subscription Rates:** $245 Nonmembers print only; $192 Nonmembers online only; $288 Nonmembers print & online; $46 Members print only; $37 Members online only; $55 Members print & online. **URL:** http://todaes.acm.org. **Circ:** (Not Reported).

2796 ■ Advances in Anatomic Pathology
Lippincott Williams & Wilkins
c/o Mahul B. Amin, Ed.-in-Ch.
Cedars-Sinai Medical Ctr.
Dept. of Pathology & Laboratory Medicine
8700 Beverly Blvd., Ste. 8728
Los Angeles, CA 90048
Phone: (310)423-6631
Fax: (310)423-0170
Peer-reviewed journal covering the key developments in anatomic and surgical pathology, and focuses on significant changes in knowledge, techniques, and equipment. **Freq:** 6/year. **Print Method:** Sheetfed Offset. **Trim Size:** 8 1/4 x 11. **Key Personnel:** Mahul B. Amin, MD, Editor-in-Chief; Thomas Pacific, Publisher. **ISSN:** 1072--4109 (print); **EISSN:** 1533--4031 (electronic). **URL:** http://journals.lww.com/anatomicpathology/pages/default.aspx. **Ad Rates:** BW $830; 4C $1,180. **Remarks:** Accepts advertising. **Circ:** 830.

2797 ■ The Advocate
Here Media Inc.
PO Box 4371
Los Angeles, CA 90078
Phone: (310)943-5858
Fax: (310)806-6350
Publication E-mail: newsroom@advocate.com
National gay and lesbian news and lifestyle magazine. **Founded:** Sept. 1967. **Freq:** Bimonthly. **Print Method:** Offset. Uses mats. **Trim Size:** 7 7/8 x 10 7/8. **Cols./Page:** 3. **Col. Width:** 2 1/8 inches. **Col. Depth:** 10 1/8 inches. **Key Personnel:** Matthew Breen, Editor-in-Chief. **ISSN:** 0001-8996 (print). **Subscription Rates:** $29.95 Individuals print; $44 Two years print; $14.95 Individuals online; $24 Two years online. **URL:** http://www.advocate.com. **Ad Rates:** GLR $58.50; BW $6,940; 4C $9,690. **Remarks:** Accepts advertising. **Circ:** (Not Reported).

2798 ■ African Arts
African Studies Center
10244 Bunche Hall
405 Hilgard Ave.
Los Angeles, CA 90095-1310
Phone: (310)825-3686
Fax: (310)206-2250
Publisher's E-mail: africa@international.ucla.edu
Journal featuring contemporary and traditional arts of Africa. **Founded:** Nov. 1967. **Freq:** Quarterly. **Print Method:** Offset. **Trim Size:** 8 1/2 x 11. **Cols./Page:** 3. **Col. Width:** 27 nonpareils. **Col. Depth:** 140 agate lines. **Key Personnel:** Eva P. Howard, Manager, Operations; Marla C. Berns, Editor; Leslie Ellen Jones, Executive Editor. **ISSN:** 0001-9933 (print); **EISSN:** 1937-2108 (electronic). **Subscription Rates:** $205. **URL:** http://www.international.ucla.edu/africa/africanarts. **Ad Rates:** BW $1,900; 4C $1,825. **Remarks:** Accepts advertising. **Circ:** 1000.

2799 ■ AI EDAM: Artificial Intelligence for Engineering Design, Analysis and Manufacturing
Cambridge University Press
c/o Yan Jin, Editor
Dept. of Aerospace & Mechanical Engineering
University of Southern California
3650 McClintock Ave., OHE-430
Los Angeles, CA 90089-1453
Publication E-mail: aiedam@cs.wpi.edu
Peer-reviewed journal on artificial intelligence technologies. **Freq:** Quarterly. **Key Personnel:** Yan Jin, Editor; Jonathan Cagan, Board Member. **ISSN:** 0890--0604 (print); **EISSN:** 1469--1760 (electronic). **Subscription Rates:** $983 Institutions online only; £597 Institutions online only. **URL:** http://journals.cambridge.org/action/displayJournal?jid=AIE. **Remarks:** Accepts advertising. **Circ:** (Not Reported).

2800 ■ Al Talib: The Muslim Magazine at UCLA
Student Media UCLA
118 Kerckhoff Hall
308 Westwood Plz.
Los Angeles, CA 90024-1641
Phone: (310)825-2787
Fax: (210)206-0906
Publication E-mail: altalib@media.ucla.edu
Community magazine for Muslims. **Freq:** Quarterly. **Print Method:** Offset. **Trim Size:** 10 x 16. **Cols./Page:** 5. **Col. Width:** 2 inches. **Col. Depth:** 16 inches. **Key Personnel:** Mustafa Siddique, Editor; Jeremy Wildman, Manager, Advertising; Marissa Vogt, Chairperson; Mussarat Bata, Vice Chairperson. **URL:** http://www.ucla.edu; http://al-talib.org. **Remarks:** Advertising accepted; rates available upon request. **Circ:** (Not Reported).

2801 ■ Amerasia Journal: Asian American Studies
University of California, Los Angeles Asian American Studies Center AASC Press
3230 Campbell Hall
Box 951546
Los Angeles, CA 90095-1546
Phone: (310)825-2968
Fax: (310)206-9844
Publication E-mail: ytu@aasc.ucla.edu aascpress@aasc.ucla.edu
Journal addressing intercultural interests. **Freq:** 3/year Spring, Summer/Fall, Winter. **Trim Size:** 6 x 9. **Cols./Page:** 1. **Col. Width:** 4 1/2 INS. **Col. Depth:** 7 1/2 INS. **Key Personnel:** Russell C. Leong, Editor, phone: (310)206-2892, fax: (310)206-9844. **ISSN:** 0044--7471 (print). **Subscription Rates:** $445 Institutions print plus online; $99 Individuals print plus online; $25 Other countries; $35 Individuals print only; $15 Single issue print. **URL:** http://www.aasc.ucla.edu/aascpress/aj.aspx. **Ad Rates:** BW $300. **Remarks:** Accepts advertising. **Circ:** Paid 2000, Non-paid 45.

2802 ■ American Cinematographer
American Society of Cinematographers
1782 N Orange Dr.
Los Angeles, CA 90078
Phone: (323)969-4333
Free: 800-448-0145
Publisher's E-mail: office@theasc.com
Magazine featuring on the art and craft of cinematography, covering domestic and foreign feature productions, television productions, short films, music videos and commercials. **Freq:** Monthly. **Subscription Rates:** $29.95 Individuals print or online. **URL:** http://www.theasc.com/ac_magazine/October2014/current.php. **Mailing address:** PO Box 2230, Hollywood, CA 90078. **Remarks:** Accepts advertising. **Circ:** 26582.

2803 ■ American Indian Culture and Research Journal
American Indian Studies Center Press
3220 Campbell Hall
Los Angeles, CA 90095-1548
Phone: (310)206-7508
Fax: (310)206-7060
Publisher's E-mail: sales@aisc.ucla.edu
Scholarly journal covering Native American studies. **Freq:** Quarterly. **Trim Size:** 6 x 9. **ISSN:** 0161--6463 (print). **Subscription Rates:** $15 Individuals. **URL:** http://www.books.aisc.ucla.edu/books/aicrjv35n4.aspx. **Mailing address:** PO Box 951548, Los Angeles, CA 90095-1548. **Ad Rates:** BW $150. **Remarks:** Accepts advertising. **Circ:** Combined ‡1000.

2804 ■ American Sailing
American Sailing Association
5301 Beethoven St., Ste. No. 265
Los Angeles, CA 90066-7052
Phone: (310)822-7171
Fax: (310)822-4741
Publisher's E-mail: info@asa.com
Journal containing feature stories, facilities, schools, programs, travel guides, news, and events about boat sailing. **Freq:** Quarterly. **Subscription Rates:** Included in membership. **Online:** Google Inc.; Apple Inc. **Alt. Formats:** PDF. **URL:** http://www.asa.com/asj.html; http://asa.com/american-sailing-journal/. **Remarks:** Advertising not accepted. **Circ:** (Not Reported).

2805 ■ American Sailing
American Sailing Association Foundation
5301 Beethoven St., Ste. 265
Los Angeles, CA 90066-7052
Phone: (310)822-7171
Fax: (310)822-4741
Publisher's E-mail: info@asa.com
Journal containing feature stories, facilities, schools, programs, travel guides, news, and events about boat sailing. **Freq:** Quarterly. **Subscription Rates:** Included in membership. **Online:** Google Inc.; Apple Inc. **Alt. Formats:** PDF. **URL:** http://www.asa.com/asj.html; http://asa.com/american-sailing-journal/. **Remarks:** Advertising not accepted. **Circ:** (Not Reported).

2806 ■ Anaerobe
Anaerobe Society of the Americas
PO Box 452058
Los Angeles, CA 90045
Phone: (310)216-9265
Fax: (310)216-9274
Publisher's E-mail: asa@anaerobe.org
Journal publishing the study and application of knowledge of anaerobic bacteriology. **Freq:** Periodic. **Subscription Rates:** $342 Individuals print ; $529.07 Individuals online; $792 Institutions print. **URL:** http://www.journals.elsevier.com/anaerobe/#description. **Remarks:** Advertising not accepted. **Circ:** (Not Reported).

Circulation: ★ = AAM; △ or • = BPA; ♦ = CAC; ❑ = VAC; ⊕ = PO Statement; ‡ = Publisher's Report; Boldface figures = sworn; Light figures = estimated.

2807 ■ Angeleno
Modern Luxury Media
5455 Wilshire Blvd., Ste. 1412
Los Angeles, CA 90036
Magazine covering affluent lifestyle in Los Angeles. **Freq:** Monthly. **Trim Size:** 10 x 12. **Key Personnel:** Spencer Beck, Director, Editorial; Lisa Sweetingham, Editor-in-Chief; Alan Klein, President, Publisher. **Subscription Rates:** $40 Individuals; $60 Two years. **URL:** http://media.modernluxury.com/magazines/city-magazines.php. **Remarks:** Advertising accepted; rates available upon request. **Circ:** 75000.

2808 ■ Angeleno Interiors
Modern Luxury Media
5455 Wilshire Blvd., Ste. 1412
Los Angeles, CA 90036
Magazine featuring the latest styles in interior design. **Freq:** Semiannual. **Key Personnel:** Alan Klein, President, Publisher; Alexandria Abramian-Mott, Editor-in-Chief. **Subscription Rates:** $20 Individuals; $40 Two years. **URL:** http://www.modernluxury.com/angeleno/digital-edition. **Remarks:** Accepts advertising. **Circ:** (Not Reported).

2809 ■ Animal Defender
Animal Defenders International U.S.A.
6100 Wilshire Blvd., No. 1150
Los Angeles, CA 90048
Phone: (323)935-2234
Publisher's E-mail: usa@ad-international.org
Magazine containing articles that create awareness and promote the interest of humanity in the cause of justice and the suppression of all forms of cruelty to animals, and topics that helps to conserve and protect animals and their environment. **Freq:** Semiannual. **ISSN:** 2158-5032 (print). **Subscription Rates:** $ Posted: 12 January 2015. Updated: 12 January 2015 - UK; Posted: 12 January 2015 - USA. **URL:** http://ad-international.org/publications. **Circ:** (Not Reported).

2810 ■ Anthem Magazine
Anthem Magazine
1250 Elysian Park Ave.
Los Angeles, CA 90026
Magazine featuring emerging talents in music, film and fashion, along with media icons. **Freq:** Quarterly. **Key Personnel:** Dustin Beatty, Editor-in-Chief. **Subscription Rates:** $35 Individuals; $55 Canada. **URL:** http://anthemmagazine.com. **Circ:** (Not Reported).

2811 ■ Apartment Age Magazine
Apartment Age Magazine
621 S Westmoreland Ave.
Los Angeles, CA 90005-3995
Phone: (213)384-4131
Fax: (213)382-3970
Publisher's E-mail: info@aagla.org
Magazine for residential rental property owners. **Freq:** Monthly. **Print Method:** Offset. **Trim Size:** 8 3/8 x 10 5/8. **Cols./Page:** 3. **Col. Width:** 27 nonpareils. **Col. Depth:** 140 agate lines. **Key Personnel:** Kevin B. Postema, Editor. **ISSN:** 0192--0030 (print). **Subscription Rates:** Free to qualified subscribers; $48 Nonmembers; $4 Single issue. **URL:** http://aagla.org/magazine. **Ad Rates:** BW $749; 4C $1,049. **Remarks:** Accepts advertising. **Circ:** ‡12000.

2812 ■ Apparel News South
Apparel News Group
110 E 9th St., Ste. A-777
Los Angeles, CA 90079-1777
Phone: (213)627-3737
Fax: (213)623-5707
Publisher's E-mail: info@apparelnews.net
Clothing industry magazine containing textile information on garments for women and children. **Freq:** Weekly. **Print Method:** Offset. **Trim Size:** 7 1/8 x 10. **Cols./Page:** 5. **Col. Width:** 22 nonpareils. **Col. Depth:** 210 agate lines. **Key Personnel:** Martin Wernicke, Chief Executive Officer, Publisher; Alison A. Nieder, Executive Editor. **ISSN:** 0744--6403 (print). **Subscription Rates:** $69.95 Individuals print and online; $135 Canada print and online; $180 Other countries print and online. **URL:** http://www.apparelnews.net. **Ad Rates:** BW $426; 4C $869; PCI $40. **Remarks:** Accepts advertising. **Circ:** 19248.

2813 ■ Applied Immunohistochemistry & Molecular Morphology
Lippincott Williams & Wilkins
c/o Clive R. Taylor, MD, Ed.-in-Ch.
University of Southern California
Keck School of Medicine, Dept. of Pathology
2011 Zonal Ave., HMR 204
Los Angeles, CA 90089
Phone: (323)442-1180
Fax: (626)799-1643
Peer-reviewed journal focusing on diagnostic and prognostic applications of immunohistochemistry to human disease. **Freq:** 10/year. **Print Method:** Sheetfed Offset. **Trim Size:** 8 1/4 x 11. **Key Personnel:** Clive R. Taylor, MD, Editor-in-Chief; Jiang Gu, MD, Editor-in-Chief; Thomas Pacific, Publisher. **ISSN:** 1062--3345 (print); **EISSN:** 153-3-4058 (electronic). **URL:** http://journals.lww.com/appliedimmunohist/Pages/default.aspx. **Ad Rates:** BW $1,340; 4C $2,815; SAU $670. **Remarks:** Accepts advertising. **Circ:** 315.

2814 ■ Aquatics International
Hanley Wood Media Inc.
6222 Wilshire Blvd., Ste. 600
Los Angeles, CA 90048
Phone: (323)801-4900
Magazine providing in-depth information about designing, building, maintaining, promoting, managing and outfitting commercial and public pool facilities. **Founded:** 1989. **Freq:** Monthly. **Key Personnel:** Gary Thill, Editor; Dick Coleman, Publisher, phone: (323)801-4903. **ISSN:** 1058-7039 (print). **Subscription Rates:** $30 Individuals; $45 Canada and Mexico; $95 Other countries; $58 Two years; $88 Canada and Mexico two years. **URL:** http://hanleywood.omeda.com/aqi/main.do. **Formerly:** Aquatics. **Ad Rates:** BW $4,185. **Remarks:** Accepts classified advertising. **Circ:** Non-paid ‡22500.

2815 ■ Architectural Digest
Conde Nast Publications
6300 Wilshire Blvd.
Los Angeles, CA 90048
Phone: (323)965-3700
Fax: (323)965-4975
Magazine on interior design, art, and antiques. **Freq:** Monthly. **Print Method:** Offset. **Cols./Page:** 3. **Col. Width:** 34 nonpareils. **Col. Depth:** 154 agate lines. **Key Personnel:** Guilio Capua, Publisher, Vice President; Margaret Russell, Editor-in-Chief. **Subscription Rates:** $29.99 Individuals online; $70 Canada print. **URL:** http://www.architecturaldigest.com. **Ad Rates:** BW $73,060; 4C $130,502. **Remarks:** Accepts advertising. **Circ:** Paid ***823280.**

2816 ■ Asian Journal: Los Angeles Edition
Asian Journal Publications Inc.
1150 Wilshire Blvd.
Los Angeles, CA 90017
Phone: (213)250-9797
Fax: (213)481-0854
Community newspaper for Filipinos. **Freq:** Biweekly Wednesday and Saturday. **Alt. Formats:** PDF. **URL:** http://asianjournal.com/interactive/digital-editions/los-angeles-weekend-edition. **Remarks:** Accepts advertising. **Circ:** (Not Reported).

2817 ■ Asian Pacific American Law Journal
University of California School of Law
1242 Law Bldg.
385 Charles E. Young Dr. E
Los Angeles, CA 90095
Phone: (310)825-4841
Publisher's E-mail: admissions@law.ucla.edu
Journal containing articles on legal, social and political issues affecting Asian Pacific American communities. **EISSN:** 2169--7809 (electronic). **URL:** http://escholarship.org/uc/uclalaw_apalj; http://www.law.ucla.edu/student-life/law-reviews-and-journals/asian-pacific-american-law-journal. **Circ:** (Not Reported).

2818 ■ Association News: America's Most-Read Magazine for State and Regional Associations
Schneider Publishing Company Inc.
11835 W Olympic Blvd., 12th Fl.
Los Angeles, CA 90064
Phone: (310)577-3700
Fax: (310)577-3715
Free: 877-577-3700
Publisher's E-mail: info@schneiderpublishing.com
Magazine containing management and meeting plan information for association executives and meeting planners. **Founded:** 1976. **Freq:** Monthly. **Print Method:** Sheet fed Offset. **Trim Size:** 8 1/2 x 11. **Cols./Page:** 3. **Col. Width:** 13.5 picas. **Col. Depth:** 10 inches. **Key Personnel:** Ann Shepphird, Editor; Timothy Schneider, Publisher. **ISSN:** 1062-5771 (print). **Subscription Rates:** Free. **URL:** http://www.associationnews.com/. **Formerly:** Western Association News. **Ad Rates:** BW $2,600; 4C $3,710. **Remarks:** Accepts advertising. **Circ:** Controlled ‡42000.

2819 ■ Automundo Magazine
AutoMundo Productions Inc.
880 W First St., Ste. 310
Los Angeles, CA 90012
Automotive magazine in Spanish language. **Freq:** Monthly. **Print Method:** Offset. **Trim Size:** 8 1/2 x 11. **Cols./Page:** 3. **Col. Width:** 26 nonpareils. **Col. Depth:** 140 agate lines. **URL:** http://www.automundomagazinetv.com. **Remarks:** Accepts advertising. **Circ:** △**75000.**

2820 ■ Aztlan: A Journal of Chicano Studies
UCLA Chicano Studies Research Center
193 Haines Hall
Los Angeles, CA 90095-1544
Phone: (310)825-2363
Fax: (310)206-1784
Publisher's E-mail: csrcinfo@chicano.ucla.edu
Peer-reviewed journal covering Chicano studies. **Founded:** 1970. **Freq:** Semiannual. **Print Method:** Offset. **Trim Size:** 6 x 9. **Cols./Page:** 1. **Col. Width:** 4 inches. **Col. Depth:** 7 inches. **Key Personnel:** Chon A. Noriega, Editor. **ISSN:** 0005-2604 (print). **Subscription Rates:** $30 Individuals; $50 Two years; $40 U.S., Canada, and Mexico; $210 Institutions; $15 Single issue. **URL:** http://www.chicano.ucla.edu/press/journals/default.asp. **Ad Rates:** BW $225. **Remarks:** Accepts advertising. **Circ:** Paid ‡700.

2821 ■ Back Stage West
Screen Actors Guild - American Federation of Television and Radio Artists
5757 Wilshire Blvd., 7th Fl.
Los Angeles, CA 90036
Phone: (323)954-1600
Free: 855-724-2387
Trade publication covering the entertainment industry. **Freq:** Weekly 51/yr (plus 2 free issues). **Key Personnel:** Mark Peikert, Editor-in-Chief. **ISSN:** 1076-5379 (print). **Subscription Rates:** $144 Individuals; $95.70 Individuals 6 months; $12 Individuals monthly. **URL:** http://www.backstage.com. **Ad Rates:** BW $2,300; 4C $3,200. **Remarks:** Accepts advertising. **Circ:** 24000.

2822 ■ Bell Gardens Sun
Eastern Group Publications Inc.
111 South Ave. 59
Los Angeles, CA 90042
Phone: (323)341-7970
Fax: (323)341-7976
Publisher's E-mail: service@egpnews.com
Community newspaper. **Freq:** Weekly (Thurs.). **Key Personnel:** Dolores Sanchez, Editor-in-Chief, Publisher; Gloria Alvarez, Managing Editor. **URL:** http://egpnews.com/category/editions/bell-gardens-sun. **Remarks:** Advertising accepted; rates available upon request. **Circ:** Paid ♦**7000.**

2823 ■ Belvedere Citizen
Wave Newspaper Group
3731 Wilshire Blvd., Ste. 840
Los Angeles, CA 90010
Phone: (323)556-5720
Fax: (213)835-0584
Community newspaper. **Freq:** Weekly. **Trim Size:** 6 x 21 1/2. **Cols./Page:** 6. **Col. Depth:** 21 INS. **Key Personnel:** Arthur J. Aguilar, Executive Editor, Publisher. **Subscription Rates:** Free; $15. **Circ:** (Not Reported).

2824 ■ Black Lace
Blk Publishing Company Inc.
6709 La Tijera Blvd., Ste. 402
Los Angeles, CA 90045-2017
Publication E-mail: newsroom@blk.com
Magazine published by and for African-American lesbians. Includes erotica and politically focused articles and analysis. **Freq:** Quarterly. **Trim Size:** 8 1/8 x 10 7/8. **ISSN:** 1049-3298 (print). **Subscription Rates:** $20

Individuals; $36 Two years; $36 Other countries; $5.95 Single issue; $6.95 Other countries single copy. **URL:** http://www.blacklace.org. **Mailing address:** PO Box 83912, Los Angeles, CA 90083-0912. **Ad Rates:** BW $300; 4C $429. **Remarks:** Advertising accepted; rates available upon request. **Circ:** Paid 9000, Non-paid 200.

2825 ■ Blackfire
Blk Publishing Company Inc.
6709 La Tijera Blvd., Ste. 402
Los Angeles, CA 90045-2017
Consumer magazine covering black erotica for a gay audience. **Freq:** Bimonthly. **Trim Size:** 8 1/8 x 10 3/4. **Key Personnel:** Alan Bell, Editor. **ISSN:** 1049--3271 (print). **Subscription Rates:** $30 Individuals; $54 Two years; $24 Other countries; $6.95 Single issue. **URL:** http://www.blackfire.com. **Mailing address:** PO Box 83912, Los Angeles, CA 90083-0912. **Ad Rates:** BW $1,800; 4C $2,574. **Remarks:** Accepts advertising. **Circ:** (Not Reported).

2826 ■ The Braille Mirror
Braille Institute Press
741 N Vermont Ave.
Los Angeles, CA 90029-3514
Phone: (323)663-1111
Fax: (323)663-0867
Free: 800-272-4553
Publisher's E-mail: la@brailleinstitute.org
General interest magazine (Braille). **Freq:** Bimonthly. **Print Method:** Heidelberg Cylinder Press adapted for zinc braille plates. **Trim Size:** 11 x 11 1/2. **Cols./Page:** 1. **Col. Width:** 9 inches. **Col. Depth:** 10 inches. **Key Personnel:** Douglas Menville, Editor; Peter Gray Mansinne, ´Director. **Subscription Rates:** $15 Individuals. **Alt. Formats:** Braille. **Remarks:** Advertising not accepted. **Circ:** Controlled 3000.

2827 ■ California Apparel News
Apparel News Group
110 E 9th St., Ste. A-777
Los Angeles, CA 90079-1777
Phone: (213)627-3737
Fax: (213)623-5707
Publisher's E-mail: info@apparelnews.net
Weekly newspaper covering the apparel industry and providing information about textiles, trimmings, fashion trends, retailing and business. **Freq:** Monthly. **Print Method:** Web Press. **Trim Size:** 10 3/4 x 14 5/8. **Cols./Page:** 5. **Col. Width:** 24 nonpareils. **Col. Depth:** 196 agate lines. **Key Personnel:** Deborah Belgum, Senior Editor; Alison A. Nieder, Executive Editor; Kendall In, Manager, Production. **ISSN:** 0008--0896 (print). **Subscription Rates:** $69.95 Individuals; $135 Canada; $180 Other countries. **URL:** http://www.apparelnews.net. **Ad Rates:** BW $5,855; 4C $6,870. **Remarks:** Accepts advertising. **Circ:** 15872.

2828 ■ California Real Estate Magazine
California Association of Realtors
525 S Virgil Ave.
Los Angeles, CA 90020-1403
Phone: (213)739-8200
Fax: (213)480-7724
Magazine promoting professionalism and skills of real estate brokers and agents. 'Offers in depth news and information focusing on California's residential real estate issues and trends'. **Freq:** Monthly. **Print Method:** Web Offset (SWOP). **Trim Size:** 8 1/4 x 10 3/4. **Cols./Page:** 3. **Col. Width:** 27 nonpareils. **Col. Depth:** 128 agate lines. **Key Personnel:** Anna Framroze, Publisher, Vice President. **ISSN:** 0008--1450 (print). **Subscription Rates:** $24 Nonmembers one year; $40 Nonmembers two years; $3 Single issue. **URL:** http://www.car.org/newsstand/crem. **Ad Rates:** BW $6100; 4C $7900. **Remarks:** Accepts advertising. **Circ:** △**151882**.

2829 ■ The Calligraph
Society for Calligraphy
PO Box 64174
Los Angeles, CA 90064-0174
Publisher's E-mail: president@societyforcalligraphy.org
Freq: 3/year. **Remarks:** Advertising not accepted. **Circ:** (Not Reported).

2830 ■ Cancer Control Journal
Cancer Control Society
2043 N Berendo St.
Los Angeles, CA 90027-1906
Phone: (323)663-7801
Fax: (323)663-7757
Publisher's E-mail: cancercontrolsociety@outlook.com
Freq: Periodic. **Subscription Rates:** Included in membership. **Remarks:** Advertising not accepted. **Circ:** 13,000.

2831 ■ Children and Youth Services Review
RELX Group P.L.C.
c/o Duncan Lindsey, Ed.
3815 McLaughlin Ave. No.101
Los Angeles, CA 90066
Publisher's E-mail: amsterdam@relx.com
Journal providing a platform for scholarly discussion on service programs for children and youth. **Freq:** Monthly. **Key Personnel:** Duncan Lindsey, Editor; A. Shlonsky, Editor; N. Trocme, Editor. **ISSN:** 0190--7409 (print). **Subscription Rates:** $309 Individuals print; $1936.67 Institutions eJournal; $2325 Institutions print. **URL:** http://www.journals.elsevier.com/children-and-youth-services-review. **Circ:** (Not Reported).

2832 ■ City Terrace Comet
Eastern Group Publications Inc.
111 South Ave. 59
Los Angeles, CA 90042
Phone: (323)341-7970
Fax: (323)341-7976
Publisher's E-mail: service@egpnews.com
Community newspaper (English and Spanish). **Freq:** Weekly (Thurs.). **Print Method:** Offset. **Trim Size:** 13 x 21 1/2. **Cols./Page:** 6. **Col. Width:** 2 1/16 inches. **Col. Depth:** 294 agate lines. **Key Personnel:** Dolores Sanchez, Editor-in-Chief, Publisher; Gloria Alvarez, Managing Editor; Bianca Sanchez, Manager, Operations. **URL:** http://egpnews.com/category/editions/city-terrace-comet. **Ad Rates:** GLR $2.50; BW $4788; 4C $5238; SAU $38; PCI $38. **Remarks:** Accepts advertising. **Circ:** 3000.

2833 ■ Clinical Lab Products: The Product News Magazine for the Clinical Laboratory
Clinical Lab Products
6100 Center Dr., Ste. 1020
Los Angeles, CA 90045
Phone: (310)642-4400
Fax: (310)641-4444
Magazine (tabloid) for medical labs. **Freq:** Monthly. **Print Method:** Offset. **Trim Size:** 10 x 13. **Cols./Page:** 4. **Col. Width:** 13 picas. **Col. Depth:** 224 agate lines. **Key Personnel:** Steve Halasey, Editor, phone: (626)219-0199; Drew Thornley, Publisher. **ISSN:** 0192--1282 (print). **Subscription Rates:** Free. **URL:** http://www.clpmag.com. **Ad Rates:** 4C $7400. **Remarks:** Accepts advertising. **Circ:** (Not Reported).

2834 ■ Colleague Alumni Magazine
Pepperdine University
c/o Editor, Pepperdine Colleague
Pepperdine University
Graduate School of Education and Psychology
6100 Center Dr.
Los Angeles, CA 90045
Phone: (310)568-5773
Publisher's E-mail: graphic@pepperdine.edu
Magazine covering the latest faculty, alumni and student news. **Freq:** Semiannual. **Key Personnel:** Keith Lungwitz, Contact; Jennifer Scharnikow, Director, Marketing; Ron Hall, Photographer; Marie Lindgren, Editor; Vincent Way, Editor. **URL:** http://colleague.pepperdine.edu. **Remarks:** Advertising not accepted. **Circ:** (Not Reported).

2835 ■ Compassionate Living
Mercy For Animals
8033 Sunset Blvd., Ste. 864
Los Angeles, CA 90046
Free: 866-632-6446
Publisher's E-mail: info@mercyforanimals.org
Freq: Semiannual. **Subscription Rates:** Included in membership. **Alt. Formats:** PDF. **URL:** http://www.mercyforanimals.org/magazine. **Remarks:** Advertising not accepted. **Circ:** (Not Reported).

2836 ■ Contraception: Official Journal of the Association of Reproductive Health Professionals and the Society of Family Planning
Mosby Inc.
University of Southern California School of Medicine
Dept. of Obstetrics & Gynecology
Women's & Children's Hospital
1240 N Mission Rd., RL-1009
Los Angeles, CA 90033
Journal for researchers and clinicians about advances in contraception. **Freq:** Monthly. **Print Method:** Sheetfed. **Trim Size:** 8 1/4 x 11. **Key Personnel:** D.R. Mishell, Jr., Editor; Carolyn Westhoff, MD, Editor-in-Chief. **ISSN:** 0010--7824 (print). **Subscription Rates:** $523 U.S. print and online; $575 Other countries print and online; $427 Individuals online. **URL:** http://www.contraceptionjournal.org. **Ad Rates:** BW $2260; 4C $1695. **Remarks:** Accepts advertising. **Circ:** Combined ‡1150.

2837 ■ Cosmic Voice
Aetherius Society
6202 Afton Pl.
Los Angeles, CA 90028-8205
Phone: (323)465-9652
Free: 800-800-1354
Publisher's E-mail: info@aetherius.org
Publication covering mysticism. **Freq:** Quarterly Bimonthly. **Key Personnel:** Brian Keneipp, Editor. **ISSN:** 1058- 4196 (print). **Subscription Rates:** £20 in UK; $20 in America and Canada; $16 /year for nonmembers; included in membership dues. **Remarks:** Advertising not accepted. **Circ:** (Not Reported).

2838 ■ The Cue Sheet
Film Music Society
1516 S Bundy Dr., Ste. 305
Los Angeles, CA 90025
Phone: (310)820-1909
Fax: (310)820-1301
Publisher's E-mail: info@filmmusicsociety.org
Freq: Quarterly January, April, July and October. **ISSN:** 0888--9015 (print). **Subscription Rates:** Included in membership. **URL:** http://www.filmmusicsociety.org/merchandise/merchandise.html; http://www.filmmusicsociety.org/special/cuesheet/cuesheet.html. **Remarks:** Advertising not accepted. **Circ:** 700.

Culver City Chronicle - See Culver City

2839 ■ Current Rheumatology Reviews
Bentham Science Publishers Ltd.
David Geffen School of Medicine at UCLA
UCLA
Los Angeles, CA 90095
Publisher's E-mail: subscriptions@benthamscience.org
Journal publishing frontier reviews on all the latest advances on rheumatology and its related areas, e.g. pharmacology, pathogenesis, epidemiology, clinical care, and therapy. **Freq:** Semiannual. **Key Personnel:** Serena Guiducci, Editor-in-Chief. **ISSN:** 1573--3971 (print); **EISSN:** 1875--6360 (electronic). **Subscription Rates:** $180 Individuals print; $450 print and online - academic; $410 print or online - academic; $1030 print and online - corporate; $860 print or online - corporate. **URL:** http://benthamscience.com/journals/current-rheumatology-reviews. **Ad Rates:** BW $600; 4C $800. **Remarks:** Accepts advertising. **Circ:** ‡400.

2840 ■ Daily Bruin
University of California, Los Angeles
118 Kerckhoff Hall
308 Westwood Plz.
Los Angeles, CA 90024
Phone: (310)825-9898
Fax: (310)206-0906
Collegiate newspaper (tabloid). **Freq:** Daily (morn.) (during the academic year). **Print Method:** Offset. Uses mats. **Cols./Page:** 5. **Col. Width:** 11.5 picas. **Col. Depth:** 16 inches. **Key Personnel:** Jeremy Wildman, Manager, Advertising. **ISSN:** 1080--5060 (print). **Subscription Rates:** Free to the students of partner schools. **URL:** http://dailybruin.com. **Remarks:** Accepts advertising. **Circ:** Free 22000.

2841 ■ Daily Trojan
University of Southern California
University Park Campus
Los Angeles, CA 90089
Phone: (213)740-2311
Collegiate newspaper. **Freq:** Daily (morn.) except Saturday, Sunday, examination week and university holidays. **Print Method:** Offset. **Trim Size:** 11 x 17. **Cols./Page:** 5. **Col. Width:** 22 nonpareils. **Col. Depth:** 224 agate lines. **Key Personnel:** Sheridan Watson, Editor-in-Chief. **Subscription Rates:** Free. **URL:** http://dailytrojan.com. **Remarks:** tobacco, liquor, beer, wine,

Circulation: ★ = AAM; △ or • = BPA; ♦ = CAC; ❑ = VAC; ⊕ = PO Statement; ‡ = Publisher's Report; Boldface figures = sworn; Light figures = estimated.

gambling, term paper sales,. **Circ:** ‡10000.

2842 ■ Diesel Power
National Hot Rod Diesel Association
6420 Wilshire Blvd.
Los Angeles, CA 90048-5515
Free: 800-381-1288
Publisher's E-mail: info@nhrda.com
Automotive magazine. **Freq:** Monthly. **Key Personnel:** Steve VonSeggern, Contact, phone: (714)769-7499. **Subscription Rates:** $19.95 Individuals print; $14.99 Individuals online. **URL:** http://www.trucktrend.com/diesel-power-magazine; http://www.nhrda.com/Membership2.php. **Remarks:** Advertising not accepted. **Circ:** (Not Reported).

2843 ■ Digital Photo
Werner Publishing Corp.
12121 Wilshire Blvd., 12th Fl.
Los Angeles, CA 90025
Phone: (310)820-1500
Fax: (310)826-5008
Publication E-mail: editor@dpmag.com
Magazine covering the desktop darkroom or home photo lab technologies, trends and methods for modern photo and computer enthusiasts. **Freq:** 7/year. **Print Method:** Offset. **Cols./Page:** 6. **Col. Width:** 2 1/4 inches. **Col. Depth:** 21 1/2 inches. **Subscription Rates:** $11.97 Individuals; $21.97 Two years; $26.97 Other countries /year. **URL:** http://www.dpmag.com. **Formerly**: PCPhoto. **Remarks:** Accepts advertising. **Circ:** (Not Reported).

2844 ■ Digital Photo Pro
Werner Publishing Corp.
12121 Wilshire Blvd., 12th Fl.
Los Angeles, CA 90025
Phone: (310)820-1500
Fax: (310)826-5008
Magazine covering digital photography. **Freq:** 7/year. **Subscription Rates:** $9 Individuals. **URL:** http://store.madavor.com/digital-photo-pro.html. **Remarks:** Accepts advertising. **Circ:** (Not Reported).

2845 ■ Documentary
International Documentary Association
3470 Wilshire Blvd., Ste. 980
Los Angeles, CA 90010
Phone: (213)232-1660
Fax: (213)232-1669
Publisher's E-mail: info@documentary.org
Journal promoting non-fiction film and video. **Freq:** Quarterly. **Print Method:** sheet-fed. **Trim Size:** 8 1/2 x 11. **Cols./Page:** 3. **Col. Width:** 2 1/4 INS. **Col. Depth:** 9 1/4 INS. **Key Personnel:** Jana Green, Editor; Thomas White, Editor; Tamara Krinsky, Associate Editor. **ISSN:** 0742-533X (print). **Subscription Rates:** Included in membership. **URL:** http://www.documentary.org/magazine. **Formerly**: International Documentary. **Ad Rates:** GLR $.75; BW $630; 4C $1,950. **Remarks:** Accepts advertising. **Circ:** 3,000.

Downey Herald American - See Downey

2846 ■ Dukeminier Awards Journal of Sexual Orientation & Gender Identity Law
University of California School of Law
1242 Law Bldg.
385 Charles E. Young Dr. E
Los Angeles, CA 90095
Phone: (310)825-4841
Publisher's E-mail: admissions@law.ucla.edu
Journal containing topics about sexual orientation and gender identity law and public policy. **Freq:** Annual. **URL:** http://law.ucla.edu/student-life/law-reviews-and-journals/dukeminier-awards-journal. **Circ:** (Not Reported).

2847 ■ Earth and Planetary Science Letters
Elsevier
c/o T.M. Harrison, Ed.
Dept. of Earth and Space Science, 2810 Geology B1
University of California at Los Angeles
595 Charles E. Young Dr. E.
Los Angeles, CA 90095-1567
Phone: (310)206-3051
Publisher's E-mail: t.reller@elsevier.com
Journal presenting high-quality research articles on earth and planetary science letters. **Founded:** 1966. **Freq:** 24/yr. **Print Method:** Offset. **Trim Size:** 13 x 21. **Cols./Page:** 6. **Col. Width:** 2 1/2 inches. **Col. Depth:** 294 agate lines. **Key Personnel:** T. Elliott, Editor. **ISSN:** 0012-821X (print). **Subscription Rates:** $6516 Institutions print; $6516.80 Institutions ejournal; $337 Individuals print. **URL:** http://www.journals.elsevier.com/earth-and-planetary-science-letters. **Circ:** (Not Reported).

2848 ■ Eastside Journal
Wave Newspaper Group
3731 Wilshire Blvd., Ste. 840
Los Angeles, CA 90010
Phone: (323)556-5720
Fax: (213)835-0584
Community newspaper. **Freq:** Weekly. **Trim Size:** 6 x 21 1/2. **Cols./Page:** 6. **Col. Depth:** 21 INS. **Remarks:** Advertising accepted; rates available upon request. **Circ:** (Not Reported).

2849 ■ Eastside Sun
Eastern Group Publications Inc.
111 South Ave. 59
Los Angeles, CA 90042
Phone: (323)341-7970
Fax: (323)341-7976
Publisher's E-mail: service@egpnews.com
Hispanic community newspaper (English and Spanish). **Freq:** Weekly (Thurs.). **Print Method:** Offset. **Trim Size:** 13 x 21. **Cols./Page:** 6. **Col. Width:** 2 1/16 inches. **Col. Depth:** 294 agate lines. **Key Personnel:** Gloria Alvarez, Managing Editor; Dolores Sanchez, Editor-in-Chief, Publisher; Bianca Sanchez, Manager, Operations. **URL:** http://egpnews.com/category/editions/eastside-sun. **Ad Rates:** GLR $3.80; BW $4788; 4C $5238; SAU $38; PCI $38. **Remarks:** Accepts advertising. **Circ:** 24000.

2850 ■ Economic Development and Cultural Change
The University of Chicago Press
University of Southern California
837 Downey Way
Stonier Hall 100
Los Angeles, CA 90089-0377
Phone: (213)740-2091
Fax: (213)740-2773
Publication E-mail: edcc@press.uchicago.edu
Journal focusing on economic development. **Founded:** 1952. **Freq:** Quarterly. **Print Method:** Offset. **Trim Size:** 6 x 9. **Cols./Page:** 1. **Col. Width:** 52 nonpareils. **Col. Depth:** 90 agate lines. **Key Personnel:** John Strauss, Associate Editor; Marcel Fafchamps, Editor-in-Chief; Lisa McKamy, Managing Editor. **ISSN:** 0013-0079 (print). **Subscription Rates:** $77 Individuals print and electronic; $68 Individuals electronic only; $70 Individuals print only; $39 Students electronic only; $139 Two years print and electronic; $70 Two years student, electronic only; $302 Institutions print and electronic; $282 Institutions print only; $270 Institutions electronic only. **URL:** http://www.jstor.org/action/showPublication?journalCode=econdevecultchan. **Ad Rates:** BW $690. **Remarks:** Accepts advertising. **Circ:** 708.

2851 ■ E.L.A. Brooklyn-Belvedere Comet
Eastern Group Publications Inc.
111 South Ave. 59
Los Angeles, CA 90042
Phone: (323)341-7970
Fax: (323)341-7976
Publisher's E-mail: service@egpnews.com
Hispanic community newspaper (English and Spanish). **Freq:** Weekly (Thurs.). **Print Method:** Offset. **Trim Size:** 13 x 21 1/2. **Cols./Page:** 6. **Col. Width:** 2 1/16 inches. **Col. Depth:** 294 agate lines. **Key Personnel:** Gloria Alvarez, Managing Editor; Bianca Sanchez, Manager, Operations; Dolores Sanchez, Editor-in-Chief, Publisher. **URL:** http://egpnews.com/category/editions/ela-brooklyn-belvedere-comet. **Ad Rates:** GLR $38; BW $4,788; 4C $5,238; SAU $38; PCI $38. **Remarks:** Accepts advertising. **Circ:** Mon.-Fri. 3000.

2852 ■ The Episcopal News
The Episcopal Diocese of Los Angeles
840 Echo Pk. Ave.
Los Angeles, CA 90026
Phone: (213)482-2040
Fax: (213)482-5304
Publisher's E-mail: news@ladiocese.org
Newspaper covering the Episcopal Diocese of Los Angeles, the Episcopal Church in the U.S., the Anglican Communion, and the wider Christian fellowship. **Freq:** Bimonthly except August and November. **ISSN:** 0195--0681 (print). **URL:** http://www.episcopalnews.ladiocese.net/. **Mailing address:** PO Box 512164, Los Angeles, CA 90026. **Ad Rates:** BW $1,204.50; PCI $24.25. **Remarks:** Color advertising not accepted. **Circ:** ‡30000.

2853 ■ Fem: UCLA's Feminist Newsmagazine
University of California, Los Angeles
405 Hilgard Ave.
Los Angeles, CA 90095
Phone: (310)825-4321
Publication E-mail: fem@media.ucla.edu
News magazine for women and feminist students at the University and the surrounding community. **Freq:** Weekly (Fri.). **Print Method:** Offset. **Trim Size:** 11 1/2 x 17 5/8. **Cols./Page:** 5. **Col. Width:** 1 7/8 inches. **Key Personnel:** Jennifer Wang, Editor. **URL:** http://femmagazine.com. **Formerly**: ASCULA Together; Together - The Feminist Newsletter at UCLA. **Ad Rates:** BW $350; 4C $1,450; PCI $7.10. **Remarks:** Accepts advertising. **Circ:** ‡5000.

2854 ■ Film Score Magazine: Your Soundtrack Source since 1990
Film Score Monthly
4470 W Sunset Blvd., No. 705
Los Angeles, CA 90027
Phone: (323)461-2240
Consumer magazine covering music in movies and television. **Freq:** Bimonthly. **Print Method:** Offset. **Key Personnel:** Lukas Kendall, President. **ISSN:** 1077-4289 (print). **Subscription Rates:** Accessible only to members. **URL:** http://www.filmscoremonthly.com/fsmonline/faq.cfm. **Formerly**: Film Score Monthly. **Ad Rates:** BW $450; 4C $625; PCI $55. **Remarks:** Accepts advertising. **Circ:** Combined 7000.

2855 ■ Film Threat
Film Threat
5042 Wilshire Blvd.
Los Angeles, CA 90036
Phone: (818)248-4549
Fax: (818)248-4533
Magazine covering alternative/underground films and the film industry; online only. **Key Personnel:** Chris Gore, Writer; Mark Bell, Editor-in-Chief, Founder, Publisher. **Mailing address:** PO Box 1500, Los Angeles, CA 90036. **Remarks:** Accepts advertising. **Circ:** (Not Reported).

2856 ■ Filter: Good Music Will Prevail
Filter Magazine & Filtermmm L.L.C.
5908 Barton Ave.
Los Angeles, CA 90038
Phone: (323)464-4217
Publisher's E-mail: info@filtermmm.com
Music magazine. **Freq:** 5/year. **Key Personnel:** Pat McGuire, Editor-in-Chief; Christopher Saltzman, Art Director. **Subscription Rates:** $24.95 Individuals. **URL:** http://filtermagazine.com; http://filtermagazine.com/index.php/magazine. **Circ:** (Not Reported).

2857 ■ Flowers&
Teleflora
11444 W Olympic Blvd.
Los Angeles, CA 90064
Publisher's E-mail: customerservice@teleflora.com
Trade magazine for retail florists. **Freq:** Monthly. **Print Method:** Offset. **Trim Size:** 8 1/8 x 10 3/4. **Cols./Page:** 2. **Col. Width:** 38 nonpareils. **Key Personnel:** Richard Salvaggio, Publisher. **ISSN:** 0199--4751 (print). **Subscription Rates:** $66 U.S.; $102 Other countries; $19.95 Individuals digital only - yearly; $90 Canada. **URL:** http://www.myteleflora.com/flowers-and-magazine.aspx. **Ad Rates:** 4C $2430, full page; 4C $1510, half page; BW $1475, full page; BW $835, half page. **Remarks:** Accepts advertising. **Circ:** (Not Reported).

2858 ■ FREEDOM Magazine: Investigative Reporting in the Public Interest
Church of Scientology International
6331 Hollywood Blvd., Ste. 1200
Los Angeles, CA 90028
Phone: (323)960-3500
Magazine emphasizing social reform, national news and human rights. **Freq:** Bimonthly. **Print Method:** Offset. **Trim Size:** 9 x 11. **Cols./Page:** 3. **Col. Width:** 2 1/2 inches. **Col. Depth:** 10 inches. **Key Personnel:** Thomas G. Whittle, Editor. **URL:** http://www.freedommag.org. **Remarks:** Advertising not accepted. **Circ:** ‡150000.

2859 ■ F2 eZine
Women in Photography International
569 N Rossmore Ave., No. 604
Los Angeles, CA 90004

Phone: (323)462-1444
Publisher's E-mail: info@womeninphotography.org
Magazine featuring member profiles and portfolios, interviews, book reviews, product information and gallery listings. **Freq:** Quarterly. **URL:** http://www.womeninphotography.org/wipihome.html. **Remarks:** Advertising not accepted. **Circ:** (Not Reported).

2860 ■ Giant Robot: Asian American Pop Culture and Beyond
Giant Robot
PO Box 642053
Los Angeles, CA 90064
Phone: (310)479-7311
Publisher's E-mail: info@giantrobot.com
Consumer magazine covering Asian and Asian-American pop culture. **Freq:** 6/year. **Key Personnel:** Martin Wong, Editor; Eric Nakamura, Editor, Publisher; Kiyoshi Nakazawa, Contact, phone: (323)668-9330. **Subscription Rates:** $4.95 Individuals. **URL:** http://www.giantrobot.com/collections/giant-robot-magazine. **Remarks:** Accepts advertising. **Circ:** (Not Reported).

2861 ■ Glendale News Press
Times Community News
202 W 1st St., 2nd Fl.
Los Angeles, CA 90012
Phone: (818)637-3200
Fax: (818)241-1975
Free: 800-234-4444
Publisher's E-mail: gnp@latimes.com
General newspaper. **Freq:** Mon.-Sat. (morn.). **Print Method:** Offset. **Cols./Page:** 6. **Col. Width:** 12.25 picas. **Col. Depth:** 301 agate lines. **Subscription Rates:** $1.99 Individuals /week (online); $2.49 Individuals /week (print and online). **URL:** http://www.glendalenewspress.com. **Ad Rates:** $7.50-26. BW $. **Remarks:** Accepts advertising. **Circ:** Mon.-Fri. ■ **21766**, Wed. ■ **20966**, Sat. ■ **36176**.

2862 ■ Golf Tips
Werner Publishing Corp.
12121 Wilshire Blvd., 12th Fl.
Los Angeles, CA 90025
Phone: (310)820-1500
Fax: (310)826-5008
Consumer magazine covering golf. **Trim Size:** 8 1/4 x 10 3/4. **Subscription Rates:** $7 Individuals single issue. **URL:** http://store.wernerpublishing.com/golf-tips.html. **Ad Rates:** BW $23,825; 4C $21,425. **Remarks:** Accepts advertising. **Circ:** Paid ★**226749**.

2863 ■ GOOD
GOOD Worldwide, Inc.
6380 Wilshire Boulevard, 15th Floor
Los Angeles, CA 90048
Phone: (323)556-6780
Publisher's E-mail: info@goodinc.com
Magazine focusing on businesses, NGOs, and communities. **Key Personnel:** Brent Sanet, Manager, Advertising; Christopher Butterick, Manager, Operations. **Subscription Rates:** $40 U.S. and Canada; $60 Other countries. **URL:** http://magazine.good.is. **Remarks:** Accepts advertising. **Circ:** (Not Reported).

2864 ■ The Griffith Observer
Griffith Observatory
2800 E Observatory Rd.
Los Angeles, CA 90027
Phone: (213)473-0800
Magazine covering astronomy and related sciences for the general reader, including monthly sky calendar and monthly star charts. **Freq:** Monthly. **Print Method:** Offset. **Trim Size:** 6 x 8 1/2. **Cols./Page:** 2. **Col. Width:** 15 picas. **Col. Depth:** 46 picas. **Key Personnel:** Dr. E.C. Krupp, Editor-in-Chief. **ISSN:** 0195--3982 (print). **Subscription Rates:** $23 U.S. third class; $30 U.S. and Canada first class; $35 Other countries surface mail; $40 Other countries airmail; $2.50 Single issue back issues for current year; $8 Single issue for photocopies of old issues that are no longer in print. **URL:** http://www.griffithobs.org/programs/observer.html. **Remarks:** Advertising not accepted. **Circ:** Paid 2400, Controlled 80.

2865 ■ Ha'Am
Student Media UCLA
118 Kerckhoff Hall
308 Westwood Plz.
Los Angeles, CA 90024-1641
Phone: (310)825-2787
Fax: (210)206-0906
Publisher's E-mail: studentmedia@media.ucla.edu
Journal devoted to the Jewish community. **Freq:** Quarterly. **Print Method:** Offset. **Trim Size:** 8 3/8 x 10 7/8. **Cols./Page:** 3. **Key Personnel:** Tessa Nath, Editor-in-Chief; Alexa Lucas, Editor, Writer. **ISSN:** 0026--914X (print). **URL:** http://haam.org. **Remarks:** Accepts advertising. **Circ:** (Not Reported).

2866 ■ Harte-Hanks Pennysaver
Echo Media
900 Circle 75 Pky., Ste. 1600
Atlanta, GA 30339
Phone: (770)955-3535
Fax: (770)955-3599
Publisher's E-mail: salesinfo@echo-media.com
Advertising shopper. **Freq:** 52/yr. **Subscription Rates:** By mail. **URL:** http://echomedia.com/medias/details/6618/harte+hanks+pennysaver+hispanicel+pennysaver. **Remarks:** Accepts advertising. **Circ:** 1200000.

2867 ■ House Calls
House Research Institute
2100 W 3rd St.
Los Angeles, CA 90057
Phone: (213)483-4431
Fax: (213)483-8789
Free: 800-388-8612
Publisher's E-mail: info@hei.org
Freq: Semiannual. **Remarks:** Advertising not accepted. **Circ:** (Not Reported).

2868 ■ Hoy, Los Angeles
The Tribune Media Co.
202 W 1st St., 2nd Fl.
Los Angeles, CA 90012
Phone: (213)237-3001
Publisher's E-mail: sales@atlanticsyndication.com
Newspaper for the Hispanic households in Los Angeles. **Key Personnel:** Reynaldo Mena, Editor, phone: (213)237-4395. **URL:** http://www.tribpub.com/topic/hoy-los-angeles; http://hoylosangeles.com. **Remarks:** Accepts advertising. **Circ:** (Not Reported).

2869 ■ ICG Magazine
International Cinematographers Guild
7755 Sunset Blvd.
Los Angeles, CA 90046-3911
Phone: (323)876-0160
Fax: (323)876-6383
Trade magazine covering cinematography lighting techniques in film and video. **Freq:** Monthly. **Print Method:** Sheetfed offset. **Trim Size:** 8.5 x 11. **Key Personnel:** David Geffner, Executive Editor, phone: (323)969-2715. **ISSN:** 0020--8299 (print). **Subscription Rates:** $48 U.S. 1 year print + digital; $24 Other countries 1 year print + digital; $82 Other countries 1 year print + digital (surface mail); $117 Other countries 1 year print + digital (air mail); $36 Students 1 year print + digital. **URL:** http://www.icgmagazine.com/web. **Formerly:** International Photographer. **Remarks:** Accepts advertising. **Circ:** (Not Reported).

2870 ■ Information Technologies and International Development
The MIT Press
c/o Ernest J. Wilson, III, Founding Ed.-in.-Ch.
University of Southern California
3503 Watt Way, Ste. 304
Los Angeles, CA 90089
Publisher's E-mail: sales@mitpress.mit.edu
Journal focusing on the intersection of information and communication technologies (ICT) with international development. Aims to create a networked community of leading thinkers and strategists to discuss the critical issues of ICT and development, an epistemic community that crosses disciplines (especially technologists and social scientists), national boundaries, and the North and South hemispheres. Audience comes from academia, the private sector, NGOs, and government. **Freq:** Quarterly fall, winter, spring, summer. **Key Personnel:** Ernest J. Wilson, III, Editor-in-Chief, Founder; Arlene Luck, Managing Editor; Michael L. Best, Editor, Founder; K.Y. Amoako, Advisor, Board Member; Francois Bar, Editor-in-Chief; Kentaro Toyama, Editor-in-Chief. **ISSN:** 1544--7529 (print). **Subscription Rates:** $27 Individuals back issue; $54 Institutions back issue. **URL:** http://itidjournal.org/itid. **Remarks:** Accepts advertising. **Circ:** (Not Reported).

2871 ■ Inside Weddings
Inside Weddings
9229 Sunset Blvd., Ste. 950
Los Angeles, CA 90069
Phone: (310)281-6400
Fax: (310)281-6406
Magazine that offers information for brides on wedding spots, dresses, and accessories. **Freq:** Quarterly. **Key Personnel:** Walt Shepard, Editor-in-Chief, Publisher; Art Scangas, Creative Director. **ISSN:** 1552--4647 (print). **Subscription Rates:** $16 Individuals print + digital. **URL:** http://insideweddings.com. **Remarks:** Accepts advertising. **Circ:** (Not Reported).

2872 ■ Integration: Mathematical Theory and Applications
Nova Science Publishers Inc.
c/o Mark Burgin, Editor-in-Chief
Dept. of Mathematics
University of California, Los Angeles
520 Portola Pl., Box 951555
Los Angeles, CA 90095
Publisher's E-mail: nova.main@novapublishers.com
Journal that publishes research that contribute new results in all areas related to mathematical problems of integration. **Freq:** Quarterly. **Key Personnel:** Mark Burgin, Editor-in-Chief; Marcia Federson, Board Member; Louis H. Kauffman, Board Member; Gerald W. Johnson, Board Member; Peter A. Loeb, Board Member; Pat Muldowney, Board Member; Tepper L. Gill, Board Member; Michel L. Lapidus, Board Member. **ISSN:** 1948--5972 (print). **Subscription Rates:** $400 Individuals. **URL:** http://www.novapublishers.com/catalog/product_info.php?products_id=1674. **Circ:** (Not Reported).

2873 ■ The Inter-City Express
Daily Journal Corp.
915 E First St.
Los Angeles, CA 90012
Phone: (213)229-5300
Fax: (213)229-5481
Legal and real estate newspaper. **Founded:** 1909. **Freq:** Monday-Friday. **Print Method:** Offset. **Cols./Page:** 4. **Col. Width:** 2 1/2 inches. **Col. Depth:** 13 1/2 inches. **USPS:** 265-620. **Subscription Rates:** $150 Individuals. **URL:** http://www.dailyjournal.com. **Ad Rates:** BW $347; PCI $6.20. **Remarks:** Accepts advertising. **Circ:** Paid ‡1023, Non-paid ‡14.

2874 ■ Internet Journal of Pulmonary Medicine
Internet Scientific Publications L.L.C.
c/o Dr. Armando J. Huaringa, MD, Ed.-in-Ch.
Loma Linda University School of Medicine
1720 Cesar E. Chavez Ave.
Los Angeles, CA 90033
Publisher's E-mail: support@ispub.com
Online journal covering pulmonary medicine for medical professionals. **Freq:** Semiannual. **Key Personnel:** Dr. Armando J. Huaringa, MD, Editor-in-Chief. **ISSN:** 1531--2984 (print). **Subscription Rates:** Free. **URL:** http://ispub.com/IJPM. **Remarks:** Advertising accepted; rates available upon request. **Circ:** (Not Reported).

2875 ■ Issues in Applied Linguistics
UCLA Applied Linguistics/TESL
3300 Rolfe Hall
Los Angeles, CA 90095-1531
Phone: (310)825-4631
Fax: (310)206-4118
Publication E-mail: ial@humnet.ucla.edu
Journal concerning issues in applied linguistics. **Freq:** Semiannual. **Key Personnel:** Bahiyyih Hardacre, Editor-in-Chief; Jinhee Lee, Managing Editor. **ISSN:** 1050--4273 (print). **URL:** http://ial.humanities.ucla.edu; http://appling.ucla.edu/issuesinappliedlinguistics. **Remarks:** Advertising accepted; rates available upon request. **Circ:** (Not Reported).

2876 ■ Jonathan
Jonathan Club
545 S Figueroa St.
Los Angeles, CA 90071
Phone: (213)624-0881
Club magazine featuring California art, member news, and social activities. **Freq:** Monthly. **Print Method:** Offset. **Trim Size:** 9 x 12. **Cols./Page:** 3. **Col. Width:**

Circulation: ★ = AAM; △ or • = BPA; ♦ = CAC; ❏ = VAC; ⊕ = PO Statement; ‡ = Publisher's Report; Boldface figures = sworn; Light figures = estimated.

28 nonpareils. **Col. Depth:** 144 agate lines. **USPS:** 276-720. **Subscription Rates:** $24 Other countries. **URL:** http://www.jc.org. **Ad Rates:** BW $691; 4C $1091. **Remarks:** Advertising accepted; rates available upon request. **Circ:** Controlled ‡3800.

2877 ■ Journal of the American Academy of Religion
Oxford University Press
c/o Amir Hussain, Ed.
Department of Theological Studies
Loyola Marymount University
1 LMU Dr., Ste. 3700
Los Angeles, CA 90045
Publisher's E-mail: uk@oup.com
Journal containing articles on world religious traditions and research methodology studies. **Freq:** Quarterly. **Print Method:** Offset. **Trim Size:** 6 x 9. **Cols./Page:** 1. **Col. Width:** 54 nonpareils. **Col. Depth:** 96 agate lines. **Key Personnel:** Amir Hussain, Editor; David A. Sanchez, Editor; Francis X. Clooney, SJ, Associate Editor; Charles Mathewes, Board Member; Anna M. Gade, Associate Editor; Kimberly Connor, Associate Editor; Jack Miles, Associate Editor; Ebrahim Moosa, Associate Editor; Jonathan Schofer, Board Member. **ISSN:** 0002--7189 (print); **EISSN:** 1477--4585 (electronic). **Subscription Rates:** $276 Institutions print & online; £185 Institutions Print & online; €264 Institutions print & online; £170 Institutions print only; $254 Institutions print only; €243 Institutions print only. **URL:** http://jaar.oxfordjournals.org. **Ad Rates:** BW $650. **Remarks:** Accepts advertising. **Circ:** 11000.

2878 ■ Journal of Atmospheric and Solar-Terrestrial Physics
RELX Group P.L.C.
c/o R.J. Strangeway, Editor-in-Chief
Earth and Space Sciences Dept.
University of California at Los Angeles
405 Hilgard Ave.
Los Angeles, CA 90095-1567
Publisher's E-mail: amsterdam@relx.com
Journal devoted to the physics of the Earth's atmospheric and space environment. Publishes articles and research papers on the physical processes operating in the troposphere, stratosphere, mesosphere, thermosphere, ionosphere, magnetosphere, the Sun, interplanetary medium, and heliosphere. **Freq:** 15/yr. **Key Personnel:** R.J. Strangeway, Editor-in-Chief; M. Rapp, Board Member. **ISSN:** 1364--6826 (print). **Subscription Rates:** $280 Individuals print; $2660.40 Institutions online; $5321 Institutions print. **URL:** http://www.journals.elsevier.com/journal-of-atmospheric-and-solar-terrestrial-physics. **Circ:** (Not Reported).

2879 ■ Journal of Cellular Biochemistry
John Wiley & Sons Inc.
c/o C. Fred Fox, Exec. Ed.
Department of Microbiology & Molecular Genetics
609 CE Young Dr. E, 1602 MSB
University of California
Los Angeles, CA 90095-1489
Publisher's E-mail: info@wiley.com
Research journal. **Freq:** 18/yr. **Print Method:** Offset. **Trim Size:** 8 1/2 x 11 1/4. **Cols./Page:** 1. **Col. Width:** 56 nonpareils. **Col. Depth:** 126 agate lines. **Key Personnel:** C. Fred Fox, Executive Editor; Priscilla Vasquez, Managing Editor; Gary S. Stein, Executive Editor. **ISSN:** 0730--2312 (print); **EISSN:** 1097--4644 (electronic). **Subscription Rates:** $14129 Institutions, Canada and Mexico online only; £7212 Institutions UK; online only; €9118 Institutions Europe; online only; $14129 Institutions, other countries online only. **URL:** http://onlinelibrary.wiley.com/journal/10.1002/(ISSN)1097-4644. **Ad Rates:** BW $795; 4C $1040. **Remarks:** Accepts advertising. **Circ:** Paid 5950.

2880 ■ Journal of Early Intervention
Division for Early Childhood of the Council for Exceptional Children
3415 S Sepulveda Blvd., Ste. 1100
Los Angeles, CA 90034
Phone: (310)428-7209
Fax: (855)678-1989
Publisher's E-mail: sales@pfp.sagepub.com
Journal related to research and practice in early intervention for infants and young children with special needs and their families. **Freq:** Quarterly. **Trim Size:** 7 x 9 1/4. **Cols./Page:** 2. **Key Personnel:** William H. Brown, PhD, Board Member; Mary Hemmeter, Editor. **ISSN:** 0885- 3460 (print). **Subscription Rates:** Included in membership; $77 Individuals print only; $286 Institutions print only; $263 Institutions e-access; $292 Institutions print and e-access; $79 Institutions single issue; $25 Individuals single issue. **URL:** http://www.dec-sped.org/journal; http://jei.sagepub.com. **Formerly**: Journal of the Division for Early Childhood. **Remarks:** Accepts advertising. **Circ:** (Not Reported).

2881 ■ Journal of Environmental Law and Policy
University of California School of Law
405 Hilgard Ave.
Los Angeles, CA 90095-9000
Publication E-mail: jelp@lawnet.ucla.edu
Journal containing topics regarding environmental legal and policy matters. **Freq:** Semiannual. **Key Personnel:** Lucas Grunbaum, Editor-in-Chief. **EISSN:** 1942--8553 (electronic). **URL:** http://escholarship.org/uc/uclalaw_jelp; http://law.ucla.edu/student-life/law-reviews-and-journals/journal-of-environmental-law-and-policy. **Mailing address:** PO Box 951476, Los Angeles, CA 90095-1476. **Circ:** (Not Reported).

2882 ■ Journal of Film and Video
University of Illinois Press
c/o Stephen Tropiano, Editor
Ithaca College Los Angeles Program
3800 Barham Blvd., Ste. 305
Los Angeles, CA 90068
Fax: (323)851-6748
Free: 800-280-7709
Publication E-mail: ufvajournal@aol.com
Film and video journal. **Freq:** Quarterly. **Print Method:** Letterpress. **Trim Size:** 6 x 9. **Cols./Page:** 2. **Col. Width:** 28 nonpareils. **Col. Depth:** 102 agate lines. **Key Personnel:** Stephen Tropiano, Editor. **ISSN:** 0742--4671 (print); **EISSN:** 1934--6018 (electronic). **Subscription Rates:** $75 Institutions print or online (1 year); $95 Institutions print & online (1year); $20 Single issue; $10 Canada and Mexico non-U.S. postage; $35 Other countries non-U.S. postage. **URL:** http://www.press.uillinois.edu/journals/jfv.html. **Formerly:** Journal of the University Film & Video Association. **Ad Rates:** BW $250, full page; BW $185, half page. **Remarks:** Accepts advertising. **Circ:** 1100.

2883 ■ Journal of International Law and Foreign Affairs
University of California School of Law
1242 Law Bldg.
385 Charles E. Young Dr. E
Los Angeles, CA 90095
Phone: (310)825-4841
Publisher's E-mail: admissions@law.ucla.edu
Journal containing articles on immigration or international gender and race discrimination, and other various topics. **Key Personnel:** Laura Shi, Editor-in-Chief; Jessica Temple, Editor-in-Chief. **URL:** http://law.ucla.edu/student-life/law-reviews-and-journals/journal-of-international-law-and-foreign-affairs. **Circ:** (Not Reported).

2884 ■ Journal of Intravenous Therapy
Journal of Intravenous Therapy
PO Box 67159
Los Angeles, CA 90067-7159
Phone: (310)475-5339
Fax: (310)475-5339
Journal covering nursing, pharmacology, and I.V. Therapy. **Freq:** Biennial. **Print Method:** Letterpress and offset. **Cols./Page:** 3. **Col. Width:** 36 nonpareils. **Col. Depth:** 98 agate lines. **ISSN:** 0194--1658 (print). **Subscription Rates:** $24 Individuals; $34 Canada; $44 Other countries. **Remarks:** Advertising accepted; rates available upon request. **Circ:** ‡1000.

2885 ■ Journal of Islamic and Near Eastern Law
University of California School of Law
385 Charles E Young Dr. E
Los Angeles, CA 90095-1476
Publication E-mail: jinel@lawnet.ucla.edu
Journal featuring articles dealing with the complex and multifaceted issues of Islamic and Near Eastern law and its applications and effects within and outside of the Near East. **Freq:** Annual. **Key Personnel:** Seelai Ludin, Editor-in-Chief. **EISSN:** 2169--7884 (electronic). **URL:** http://escholarship.org/uc/uclalaw_jinel; http://law.ucla.edu/student-life/law-reviews-and-journals/journal-of-islamic-and-near-eastern-law. **Mailing address:** PO Box 951476, Los Angeles, CA 90095-1476. **Circ:** (Not Reported).

2886 ■ Journal of Law and Technology
University of California School of Law
1242 Law Bldg.
385 Charles E. Young Dr. E
Los Angeles, CA 90095
Phone: (310)825-4841
Publisher's E-mail: admissions@law.ucla.edu
Journal discussing relevant materials on the law's attempt to keep pace with technological innovation. **Freq:** Semiannual. **Key Personnel:** Stacy Yae, Editor-in-Chief. **URL:** http://journals.law.ucla.edu/jolt/Pages/default.aspx. **Circ:** (Not Reported).

2887 ■ Journal of Materials Engineering and Performance
ASM International
Loyola Marymount University
1 LMU Dr.
Los Angeles, CA 90045-2659
Phone: (310)338-2700
Fax: (310)338-5896
Publisher's E-mail: memberservicecenter@asminternational.org
Metal/materials engineering technical journal. **Freq:** Bimonthly. **Print Method:** Offset. **Trim Size:** 8 1/2 x 11. **Cols./Page:** 2. **Key Personnel:** David E. Alman, Chairperson; Rajiv Asthana, Associate Editor; Jeffrey A. Hawk, Editor. **ISSN:** 1059--9495 (print); **EISSN:** 1544--1024 (electronic). **Subscription Rates:** $224.91 Members; $3096 Nonmembers; $1801 Nonmembers online ; $2128 Nonmembers online and print ; $746 Members online; $808 Members print and online. **URL:** http://www.asminternational.org/materials-resources/journals/journal-of-materials-engineering-performance. **Formerly**: Journal of Materials Technology and Performance. **Remarks:** Accepts advertising. **Circ:** Paid ⊕**541**, Non-paid ⊕**141**.

2888 ■ Journal of Pediatric Nursing
Elsevier Inc.
c/o Cecily Lynn Betz, PhD, Ed.-in-Ch.
University of South California
Dept. of Nursing
University Affiliated Program at Children's Hospital Los Angeles
Los Angeles, CA 90027
Publication E-mail: elspcs@elsevier.com
Professional journal covering current information in pediatric nursing. **Founded:** Feb. 1986. **Freq:** 6/yr. **Print Method:** Sheetfed. **Trim Size:** 8 1/4 x 11. **Key Personnel:** Angela Green, PhD, Board Member; Cecily Lynn Betz, PhD, Editor-in-Chief. **ISSN:** 0882-5963 (print). **Subscription Rates:** $476 Institutions, other countries; $122 Individuals; $343 Institutions; $283 Other countries. **URL:** http://www.journals.elsevier.com/journal-of-pediatric-nursing. **Ad Rates:** BW $1,185; 4C $1,360. **Remarks:** Accepts advertising. **Circ:** Paid ‡4410.

2889 ■ Journal of Pure and Applied Algebra
RELX Group P.L.C.
c/o E.M. Friedlander, Mng. Ed.
Department of Mathematics
University of Southern California
3620 S Vermont Ave.
Los Angeles, CA 90089
Publisher's E-mail: amsterdam@relx.com
Journal dealing with topics relating to pure and applied algebra. **Freq:** 12/yr. **Key Personnel:** Chuck Weibel, Managing Editor; J. Adamek, Editor; Eric Friedlander, Managing Editor. **ISSN:** 0022--4049 (print). **Subscription Rates:** $2905 Institutions print; $2264 Institutions ejournal. **URL:** http://www.journals.elsevier.com/journal-of-pure-and-applied-algebra. **Circ:** (Not Reported).

2890 ■ LA Hollywood Independent: Los Angeles Independent Newspaper Group
Los Angeles Independent Newspaper Group
1730 W Olympic Blvd., No. 500
Los Angeles, CA 90015
Phone: (323)556-5720
Community newspaper. **Freq:** Weekly. **Print Method:** Offset. **Trim Size:** 13 1/2 x 22 1/2. **Cols./Page:** 6. **Col. Width:** 2 1/16 inches. **Col. Depth:** 21 inches. **Key Personnel:** Andre Herndon, Executive Editor; John A. Moreno, Managing Editor. **URL:** http://laindependent.com. **Formerly**: Wilshire Independent. **Remarks:** Ac-

cepts advertising. **Circ:** Combined 33000.

2891 ■ LACMA Physician: Magazine of the Los Angeles County Medical Association
Los Angeles County Medical Association
801 S Grand Ave., Ste. 425
Los Angeles, CA 90017
Phone: (213)683-9900
Fax: (213)226-0350
Free: 800-786-4262
Publisher's E-mail: info@lacmanet.org
Professional magazine for the Los Angeles County medical community. **Freq:** Monthly. **Print Method:** Offset. **Trim Size:** 8 3/8 x 10 7/8. **Cols./Page:** 4 and 3. **Col. Width:** 1.7 and 2.25 inches. **Col. Depth:** 140 agate lines. **Key Personnel:** Cheryl England, Editor, Publisher, phone: (213)226-0335, fax: (213)226-0350. **ISSN:** 0162--7163 (print). **Subscription Rates:** $39 Individuals 1 year. **URL:** http://www.lacmanet.org/NewsandPublications/Magazine.aspx; http://www.lacmanet.org. **Remarks:** Advertising accepted; rates available upon request. **Circ:** Paid ‡10154, Non-paid ‡651.

2892 ■ Lambda Literary Review
Lambda Literary Foundation
5482 Wilshire Blvd., No. 1595
Los Angeles, CA 90036
Phone: (323)643-4281
Publisher's E-mail: admin@lambdaliterary.org
Magazine covering gay and lesbian literature. **Freq:** 4/yr (January, April, July, & October). **Key Personnel:** William Johnson, Managing Editor. **ISSN:** 1048--9487 (print). **URL:** http://www.lambdaliterary.org. **Formerly:** Lambda Rising Book Report; Lambda Book Report. **Remarks:** Accepts advertising. **Circ:** (Not Reported).

2893 ■ Lithuanian Days
Lithuanian Days
4364 Sunset Blvd.
Los Angeles, CA 90029
Phone: (213)664-2919
Lithuanian interest magazine (Lithuanian and English). **Freq:** Monthly. **Print Method:** Offset. **Trim Size:** 9 1/2 x 12. **Cols./Page:** 2 and 4. **Col. Width:** 24 and 40 nonpareils. **Col. Depth:** 154 agate lines. **Key Personnel:** A.F. Skirius, Publisher. **ISSN:** 0024--2950 (print). **Subscription Rates:** $20 Individuals. **Also known as:** Lietuviu Dienos. **Ad Rates:** BW $200; PCI $20. **Remarks:** Color advertising not accepted. **Circ:** Paid ‡3000, Non-paid ‡2000.

2894 ■ Los Angeles Bulletin
Metropolitan News Co.
210 S Spring St.
Los Angeles, CA 90012
Phone: (213)346-0033
Fax: (213)687-3886
Publisher's E-mail: info@mnc.net
Daily newspaper. **Freq:** Daily except Saturdays, Sundays and postal holidays. **Print Method:** Offset. **Cols./Page:** 4. **Col. Width:** 15 picas. **Col. Depth:** 15 1/2 inches. **Key Personnel:** Don E. Parret, Editor; Jo-Ann W. Grace, Publisher; Roger M. Grace, Publisher. **Subscription Rates:** $69 Individuals plus tax. **URL:** http://www.mnc.net/bulletin.htm. **Ad Rates:** PCI $6. **Remarks:** Accepts advertising. **Circ:** Paid 200, Non-paid 4000.

2895 ■ The Los Angeles Business Journal
The Los Angeles Business Journal
5700 Wilshire, No. 170
Los Angeles, CA 90036
Phone: (213)549-5225
Fax: (213)549-5255
Newspaper (tabloid) covering local business news, business trends, executive profiles, and information for the Los Angeles area executive. **Founded:** 1979. **Freq:** Weekly (Mon.). **Print Method:** Offset. **Trim Size:** 11 3/8 x 15. **Cols./Page:** 4. **Col. Width:** 2 1/4 inches. **Col. Depth:** 13 1/2 inches. **Key Personnel:** Charles Crumpley, Editor. **Subscription Rates:** $129.95 Individuals; $219.95 Two years. **URL:** http://www.labusinessjournal.com. **Ad Rates:** BW $4,011; 4C $4,611. **Remarks:** Accepts advertising. **Circ:** Paid 20956.

2896 ■ Los Angeles Daily Journal
Daily Journal Corp.
915 E First St.
Los Angeles, CA 90012
Phone: (213)229-5300
Fax: (213)229-5481
Newspaper for the legal community. **Freq:** Mon.-Fri. **Print Method:** Offset. **Cols./Page:** 6. **Col. Width:** 2 1/4 inches. **Col. Depth:** 20 1/2 inches. **Key Personnel:** David Houston, Editor; Sharon Liang, Editor. **ISSN:** 0362--5575 (print). **Subscription Rates:** $804 Individuals 1 year; $477 Individuals 6 months; $318 Individuals 3 months. **URL:** http://www.dailyjournal.com. **Ad Rates:** BW $5320. **Remarks:** Accepts advertising. **Circ:** Paid 12433.

2897 ■ Los Angeles Downtown News
Los Angeles Downtown News
1264 W 1st St.
Los Angeles, CA 90026
Phone: (213)481-1448
Fax: (213)250-4617
Publisher's E-mail: realpeople@downtownnews.com
Community newspaper. **Freq:** Weekly. **Key Personnel:** Sue Laris, Publisher; Dawn Eastin, General Manager. **Subscription Rates:** $150 By mail /year; $75 By mail 6 months. **URL:** http://www.ladowntownnews.com. **Formerly:** Civic Center News, Inc. **Ad Rates:** 4C $575; PCI $45. **Remarks:** Accepts advertising. **Circ:** Combined ‡46468.

2898 ■ Los Angeles Independent: Los Angeles Independent Newspaper Group
Equal Access Media Inc.
4201 Wilshire Blvd., Ste. 600
Los Angeles, CA 90010
Community newspaper. **Founded:** 1927. **Freq:** Weekly. **Print Method:** Offset. **Trim Size:** 13 x 22 1/2. **Cols./Page:** 6. **Col. Width:** 1.8 inches. **Col. Depth:** 21 inches. **Key Personnel:** Sharia Hamilton, Manager, Sales; John A. Moreno, Managing Editor; Pluria Marshall, Jr., Publisher. **URL:** http://laindependent.com. **Formerly:** Sunday Independent. **Remarks:** Accepts advertising. **Circ:** (Not Reported).

2899 ■ Los Angeles Lawyer: The Magazine of the Los Angeles County Bar Assn
Los Angeles County Bar Association
1055 W 7th St., Ste. 2700
Los Angeles, CA 90017-2533
Phone: (213)627-2727
Fax: (213)833-6717
Publisher's E-mail: msd@lacba.org
Magazine featuring scholarly legal articles. **Freq:** Monthly July/August issues combined. **Print Method:** Offset. **Trim Size:** 8 3/8 x 10 7/8. **Cols./Page:** 3. **Col. Width:** 2 1/4 inches. **Col. Depth:** 10 inches. **Key Personnel:** Sam Lipsman, Editor. **ISSN:** 0162--2900 (print). **Subscription Rates:** $28 Nonmembers; $4 Single issue plus handling. **Alt. Formats:** PDF. **URL:** http://www.lacba.org/news-and-publications/los-angeles-lawyer. **Mailing address:** PO Box 55020, Los Angeles, CA 90055. **Remarks:** Advertising accepted; rates available upon request. **Circ:** △**22150**.

2900 ■ Los Angeles Loyolan
Loyola Marymount University
One LMU Dr.
Los Angeles, CA 90045-2659
Phone: (310)338-2700
Free: 800-568-4636
Publication E-mail: editor@theloyolan.com
Collegiate newspaper. **Freq:** Semiweekly. **Print Method:** Web offset. **Cols./Page:** 5. **Col. Width:** 11 picas. **Col. Depth:** 16 picas. **Key Personnel:** Jose Martinez, Senior Editor; Kenzie O'Keefe, Editor-in-Chief; Laura Riparbelli, Editor. **URL:** http://www.laloyolan.com. **Ad Rates:** 4C $440, Half page; 4C $880, Full page. **Remarks:** Accepts advertising. **Circ:** Free ‡10000.

2901 ■ Los Angeles Sentinel
Los Angeles Sentinel
3800 Crenshaw Blvd.
Los Angeles, CA 90008
Phone: (323)299-3800
Publisher's E-mail: generalinfo@lasentinel.net
Black community newspaper. **Freq:** Weekly (Thurs.). **Print Method:** Offset. **Trim Size:** 13 x 22 1/2. **Cols./Page:** 6. **Col. Width:** 26 nonpareils. **Col. Depth:** 294 agate lines. **Key Personnel:** Danny Bakewell, Jr., Editor, President. **Subscription Rates:** $48 Individuals. **URL:** http://www.lasentinel.net. **Ad Rates:** BW $2,835; 4C $3,335; SAU $22.50; PCI $22.50. **Remarks:** Accepts advertising. **Circ:** (Not Reported).

2902 ■ Los Angeles Times
Los Angeles Times latimes.com
202 W. 1st St.
Los Angeles, CA 90012
Phone: (213)237-5000
Publisher's E-mail: letters@latimes.com
General newspaper. **Freq:** Daily. **Print Method:** Offset. **Cols./Page:** 6. **Col. Width:** 24 nonpareils. **Col. Depth:** 301 agate lines. **Key Personnel:** Davan Maharaj, Editor. **URL:** http://www.latimes.com. **Remarks:** Accepts advertising. **Circ:** Mon.-Fri. ★**641369**, Sun. ★**962193**.

2903 ■ Los Angeles Watts Times
Echo Media
900 Circle 75 Pky., Ste. 1600
Atlanta, GA 30339
Phone: (770)955-3535
Fax: (770)955-3599
Publisher's E-mail: salesinfo@echo-media.com
Local newspaper. **Freq:** Mon.-Sun. **Subscription Rates:** Free. **URL:** http://echomedia.com/medias/details/9617. **Remarks:** Accepts advertising. **Circ:** Free 25000.

2904 ■ Los Angeles Wave
Wave Newspaper Group
3731 Wilshire Blvd., Ste. 840
Los Angeles, CA 90010
Phone: (323)556-5720
Fax: (213)835-0584
Community newspaper. **Freq:** Weekly. **Trim Size:** 6 x 20.5. **URL:** http://wavenewspapers.com. **Ad Rates:** BW $43,050; 4C $5000. **Remarks:** Accepts advertising. **Circ:** Paid ★**240000**.

2905 ■ Los Angeles Wave: East Edition
Wave Newspaper Group
3731 Wilshire Blvd., Ste. 840
Los Angeles, CA 90010
Phone: (323)556-5720
Fax: (213)835-0584
Community newspaper. **Freq:** Weekly. **Trim Size:** 6 x 20.5. **URL:** http://wavenewspapers.com/category/news/local/east_edition. **Ad Rates:** BW $43,050; 4C $5000. **Remarks:** Accepts advertising. **Circ:** Paid ★**240000**.

2906 ■ Los Angeles Wave: Lynwood Press Edition
Wave Newspaper Group
3731 Wilshire Blvd., Ste. 840
Los Angeles, CA 90010
Phone: (323)556-5720
Fax: (213)835-0584
Community newspaper. **Freq:** Weekly. **Trim Size:** 6 x 20.5. **URL:** http://wavenewspapers.com/category/news/local/lynwood_press. **Ad Rates:** BW $43,050; 4C $5000. **Remarks:** Accepts advertising. **Circ:** Paid ★**240000**.

2907 ■ Los Angeles Wave: Northeast Edition
Wave Newspaper Group
3731 Wilshire Blvd., Ste. 840
Los Angeles, CA 90010
Phone: (323)556-5720
Fax: (213)835-0584
Community newspaper. **Freq:** Weekly. **Trim Size:** 6 x 20.5. **URL:** http://wavenewspapers.com/category/news/local/northeast_edition. **Ad Rates:** BW $43,050; 4C $5000. **Remarks:** Accepts advertising. **Circ:** Paid ★**240000**.

2908 ■ Los Angeles Wave: West Edition
Wave Newspaper Group
3731 Wilshire Blvd., Ste. 840
Los Angeles, CA 90010
Phone: (323)556-5720
Fax: (213)835-0584
Community newspaper. **Freq:** Weekly. **Trim Size:** 6 x 20.5. **URL:** http://wavenewspapers.com/category/news/local/west_edition. **Ad Rates:** BW $43,050; 4C $5000. **Remarks:** Accepts advertising. **Circ:** Paid ★**240000**.

2909 ■ Lynwood Press
Wave Newspaper Group
3731 Wilshire Blvd., Ste. 840
Los Angeles, CA 90010
Phone: (323)556-5720
Fax: (213)835-0584
Black community newspaper. **Freq:** Semiweekly. **Print Method:** Offset. **Trim Size:** 13 3/4 x 21 1/2. **Cols./Page:**

Circulation: ★ = AAM; △ or • = BPA; ♦ = CAC; ❑ = VAC; ⊕ = PO Statement; ‡ = Publisher's Report; Boldface figures = sworn; Light figures = estimated.

6. **Col. Width:** 5 nonpareils. **Col. Depth:** 21 1/2 inches. **Subscription Rates:** $106 Individuals; $53 Individuals 6 months. **URL:** http://wavenewspapers.com/category/news/local/lynwood_press. **Remarks:** Accepts advertising. **Circ:** 12500.

2910 ■ Memoirs of the American Mathematical Society
American Mathematical Society
c/o Robert Guralnick, Managing Editor
Dept. of Mathematics
University of S California
Los Angeles, CA 90089-2532
Publisher's E-mail: cust-serv@ams.org
Peer-reviewed journal of research in pure and applied mathematics. **Freq:** 6/year. **Key Personnel:** Robert Guralnick, Managing Editor. **ISSN:** 0065--9266 (print); **EISSN:** 1947--6221 (electronic). **Subscription Rates:** $757 Individuals list; $605.60 Members institutional - domestic or foreign. **URL:** http://www.ams.org/cgi-bin/mstrack/accepted_papers/memo. **Remarks:** Advertising not accepted. **Circ:** Paid 522.

2911 ■ MEN
S.L. Inc.
PO Box 4356
Los Angeles, CA 90078-4356
Phone: (323)960-5400
Fax: (323)960-1163
Publisher's E-mail: illoinfo@freshmen.com
Magazine featuring gay, male erotica. **Founded:** 1984. **Freq:** Monthly. **Trim Size:** 8 x 10 7/8. **Key Personnel:** Austin Foxxe, Editor-in-Chief. **ISSN:** 0742-4701 (print). **Subscription Rates:** $39.96 Individuals; $70 Two years; $54.98 Other countries. **URL:** http://www.men20.com/. **Formerly**: AdvocateMEN. **Ad Rates:** BW $3,502; 4C $5,306. **Remarks:** Accepts advertising. **Circ:** (Not Reported).

2912 ■ Mercury
Los Angeles Athletic Club
431 W Seventh St.
Los Angeles, CA 90014
Phone: (213)625-2211
Fax: (213)689-1194
Publisher's E-mail: laac@laac.net
Private club magazine. **Founded:** June 01, 1912. **Freq:** Monthly. **Print Method:** Offset. **Trim Size:** 8 1/2 x 11. **Cols./Page:** 3. **Col. Width:** 17 nonpareils. **Col. Depth:** 154 agate lines. **ISSN:** 0025-9969 (print). **URL:** http://www.laac.com/Default.aspx?p=DynamicModule&pageid=243734&ssid=99204&v nf=1. **Ad Rates:** BW $650; 4C $814. **Remarks:** Accepts advertising. **Circ:** ‡6000.

2913 ■ Metropolitan News
Metropolitan News Co.
210 S Spring St.
Los Angeles, CA 90012
Phone: (213)346-0033
Fax: (213)687-3886
Publisher's E-mail: info@mnc.net
Community newspaper. **Freq:** Daily Monday through Friday. **Print Method:** Offset. **Cols./Page:** 6. **Col. Width:** 18 nonpareils. **Col. Depth:** 200 agate lines. **Key Personnel:** Roger M. Grace, Editor, Publisher; Jo-Ann W. Grace, Publisher; Vahn Babigian, General Manager. **URL:** http://www.metnews.com/metnews.htm; http://mnc.net/papers.htm. **Ad Rates:** PCI $7.35, Classified rate; PCI $9, Display rate; BW $375, Display rate. **Remarks:** Accepts advertising. **Circ:** 142600.

2914 ■ Mission Magazine
Society for the Propagation of the Faith
3424 Wilshire Blvd.
Los Angeles, CA 90010-2241
Phone: (213)637-7223
Fax: (213)637-6223
Publisher's E-mail: missionoffice@la-archdiocese.org
Magazine seeking to foster a missionary spirit among Catholics. **Founded:** 1951. **Freq:** Quarterly. **Key Personnel:** Rev. John Kozar, Director, phone: (212)563-8726; Monica Yehle, Editor, phone: (212)563-8706. **URL:** http://www.onefamilyinmission.org/society-propfaith/read-mission-magazine.html. **Remarks:** Advertising not accepted. **Circ:** Non-paid 1000000.

2915 ■ Montebello Comet
Eastern Group Publications Inc.
111 South Ave. 59
Los Angeles, CA 90042
Phone: (323)341-7970
Fax: (323)341-7976
Publisher's E-mail: service@egpnews.com
Hispanic community newspaper (English and Spanish). **Freq:** Weekly (Thurs.). **Print Method:** Offset. Uses mats. **Trim Size:** 13 x 21 1/2. **Cols./Page:** 6. **Col. Width:** 2 1/16 inches. **Col. Depth:** 294 agate lines. **Key Personnel:** Dolores Sanchez, Editor-in-Chief, Publisher; Gloria Alvarez, Managing Editor. **URL:** http://egpnews.com/category/editions/montebello-comet. **Ad Rates:** GLR $3.80; BW $4788; 4C $5238; SAU $38; PCI $38. **Remarks:** Accepts advertising. **Circ:** Combined 17000.

2916 ■ Monterey Park Comet
Eastern Group Publications Inc.
111 South Ave. 59
Los Angeles, CA 90042
Phone: (323)341-7970
Fax: (323)341-7976
Publisher's E-mail: service@egpnews.com
Newspaper with a Democratic orientation (English and Spanish). **Freq:** Weekly (Thurs.). **Print Method:** Offset. Uses mats. **Trim Size:** 13 x 21. **Cols./Page:** 6. **Col. Width:** 2 1/16 inches. **Col. Depth:** 294 agate lines. **Key Personnel:** Jonathan Sanchez, Associate Publisher, Chief Operating Officer; Bianca Sanchez, Manager, Operations; Dolores Sanchez, Editor-in-Chief, Publisher; Gloria Alvarez, Managing Editor. **URL:** http://egpnews.com/category/editions/monterey-park-comet. **Ad Rates:** GLR $3.80; BW $4788; 4C $5238; SAU $38. **Remarks:** Accepts advertising. **Circ:** 7000.

2917 ■ Monterey Park Progress
Wave Newspaper Group
3731 Wilshire Blvd., Ste. 840
Los Angeles, CA 90010
Phone: (323)556-5720
Fax: (213)835-0584
Newspaper. **Freq:** Biweekly Thurs. and Sat. **Print Method:** Offset. **Cols./Page:** 6. **Col. Width:** 26 nonpareils. **Col. Depth:** 301 agate lines. **Key Personnel:** Pluria Marshall, Jr., Publisher. **Subscription Rates:** $125 By mail /year; Free local. **URL:** http://wavenewspapers.com. **Remarks:** Advertising accepted; rates available upon request. **Circ:** (Not Reported).

2918 ■ Mutineer Magazine
Wine Mutineer L.L.C.
7510 Sunset Blvd.
Los Angeles, CA 90046
Fax: (888)837-7072
Publisher's E-mail: general@mutineermagazine.com
Magazine featuring fine beverages with an emphasis on wine, beer, and spirits. **Freq:** Bimonthly. **Key Personnel:** Alan Kropf, Editor-in-Chief. **Subscription Rates:** $14.99 Individuals; $25 Two years. **URL:** http://mutineermagazine.com. **Remarks:** Accepts advertising. **Circ:** (Not Reported).

2919 ■ New Resources
MnM Publishing Corp.
110 E Ninth St., Ste. A777
Los Angeles, CA 90079
Phone: (213)627-3737
Publisher's E-mail: info@apparelnews.net
Digest magazine. **Freq:** Semiannual in March and October. **Trim Size:** 5 1/2 X 8 1/2. **Key Personnel:** John Irwin, Manager; Alison A. Nieder, Executive Editor; Deborah Belgum, Senior Editor. **URL:** http://www.apparelnews.net/categories/news/new-resources. **Remarks:** Advertising accepted; rates available upon request. **Circ:** (Not Reported).

2920 ■ News-Herald and Journal
Wave Newspaper Group
3731 Wilshire Blvd., Ste. 840
Los Angeles, CA 90010
Phone: (323)556-5720
Fax: (213)835-0584
Community newspaper. **Freq:** Semiweekly (Wed. and Sat.). **Print Method:** Letterpress. **Cols./Page:** 6. **Col. Width:** 21 1/2 nonpareils. **Key Personnel:** Pluria Marshall, Jr., Publisher. **Subscription Rates:** $106 By mail. **Remarks:** Advertising accepted; rates available upon request. **Circ:** (Not Reported).

2921 ■ NOMMO
University of California, Los Angeles
405 Hilgard Ave.
Los Angeles, CA 90095
Phone: (310)825-4321
Publication E-mail: nommo@media.ucla.edu
A UCLA magazine focusing on African Americans. **Founded:** 1968. **Freq:** Quarterly. **Print Method:** Offset. **Trim Size:** 11 1/2 x 17 5/8. **Col. Width:** 1 7/8 INS. **Col. Depth:** 5 INS. **URL:** http://apply.uclastudentmedia.com/applications/nommo/. **Remarks:** Advertising accepted; rates available upon request. **Circ:** Non-paid 5000.

Norwalk Herald American - See Norwalk

2922 ■ Nutrition Bytes
University of California, Los Angeles
405 Hilgard Ave.
Los Angeles, CA 90095
Phone: (310)825-4321
Journal publishing outstanding contributions by the first year medical students of David Geffen School of Medicine at UCLA on various topics relating to nutrition. **Key Personnel:** John Edmond, PhD, Board Member; Felice Kurtzman, Editor; Leonard Rome, Board Member; Eryn Ujita Lee, Editor. **ISSN:** 1548--4327 (print). **URL:** http://escholarship.org/uc/uclabiolchem_nutritionbytes. **Circ:** (Not Reported).

2923 ■ Nutrition Noteworthy
University of California, Los Angeles
405 Hilgard Ave.
Los Angeles, CA 90095
Phone: (310)825-4321
Journal publishing contributions by David Geffen School of Medicine at UCLA medical students on topics relating to diet and nutrition. **Key Personnel:** Felice Kurtzman, Editor; John Edmond, Board Member; Eryn Ujita Lee, Editor; Leonard Rome, Board Member; Arash Shahangian, Editor; Leo Treyzon, Editor; Christie V. Papagiannis, Editor; Erin Sanders, Editor; Nima Gharavi, Editor; Steve Chen, Editor. **ISSN:** 1556--1895 (print). **Circ:** (Not Reported).

2924 ■ The Occidental Weekly
Occidental College
1600 Campus Rd.
Los Angeles, CA 90041
Phone: (323)259-2500
Fax: (323)259-2958
Publication E-mail: weeklyads@oxy.edu
Collegiate newspaper. **Freq:** Weekly (Wed.). **Print Method:** Offset. **Trim Size:** 12 x 16. **Cols./Page:** 5. **Col. Width:** 23 nonpareils. **Col. Depth:** 224 agate lines. **Key Personnel:** Juliet Suess, Editor-in-Chief. **Subscription Rates:** $55 Individuals per year ; $2.30 Single issue. **URL:** http://occidentalweekly.com. **Ad Rates:** BW $424.80; SAU $6.75; PCI $6.50. **Remarks:** Color advertising not accepted. **Circ:** Combined 2000.

2925 ■ OrthoKinetic Review
Novicom Inc.
6100 Center Dr., Ste. 1000
Los Angeles, CA 90045
Magazine featuring new products and services available in the podiatric field. **Freq:** Bimonthly. **Print Method:** Web Offset. **Trim Size:** 8 1/8 x 10 7/8. **Cols./Page:** 3. **ISSN:** 0890-3972 (print). **URL:** http://www.laspineinstitute.com/OrthoKineticReview.htm. **Formerly**: Podiatric Products. **Ad Rates:** BW $2,245; 4C $2,970. **Remarks:** Accepts advertising. **Circ:** Controlled 20000.

2926 ■ Our Weekly: Our Truth, Our Voice, Our Weekly
Our Weekly
8732 S Western Ave.
Los Angeles, CA 90047
Phone: (323)905-1300
Fax: (323)753-0456
Publisher's E-mail: editor@ourweekly.com
Community newspaper for African-American citizens of Los Angeles. **Freq:** Weekly (Thurs.). **Key Personnel:** Natalie Cole, Chief Executive Officer, Publisher. **Subscription Rates:** Free. **URL:** http://ourweekly.com. **Remarks:** Accepts advertising. **Circ:** 50000.

2927 ■ Out Magazine: America's Best-Selling, Gay and Lesbian Magazine
Out Magazine
10960 Wilshire Blvd., Ste. 1050
Los Angeles, CA 90024

Phone: (310)943-5858
Fax: (310)806-6351
Publisher's E-mail: letters@out.com
Consumer magazine for gay men and lesbians. Features articles on culture, people, and current issues of concern to the gay community. **Freq:** 11/year. **Key Personnel:** Aaron Hicklin, Editor-in-Chief. **ISSN:** 1062-7928 (print). **Subscription Rates:** $19.95 Individuals; $34 Two years. **URL:** http://www.out.com. **Ad Rates:** BW $9,865; 4C $14275; PCI $225. **Remarks:** Advertising accepted; rates available upon request. **Circ:** Paid ★**125,755**.

2928 ■ Outdoor Photographer
Werner Publishing Corp.
12121 Wilshire Blvd., 12th Fl.
Los Angeles, CA 90025
Phone: (310)820-1500
Fax: (310)826-5008
Magazine for amateur and professional photographers interested in nature, sports, travel, and wildlife. **Freq:** 11/year. **Print Method:** Web Offset. **Trim Size:** 7 7/8 x 10 3/4. **Cols./Page:** 3. **Col. Width:** 13 picas. **Col. Depth:** 10 inches. **ISSN:** 0890--5304 (print). **Subscription Rates:** $14.97 Individuals /year; $25.97 Two years. **Alt. Formats:** Handheld. **URL:** http://www.outdoorphotographer.com. **Ad Rates:** BW $7,780; 4C $10,795. **Remarks:** Accepts advertising. **Circ:** Paid ★**193676**.

2929 ■ OutWrite: UCLA's Lesbian, Gay and Bisexual Magazine
University of California, Los Angeles
405 Hilgard Ave.
Los Angeles, CA 90095
Phone: (310)825-4321
Publication E-mail: outwritebruins@gmail.com
Lesbian, gay, and bisexual community magazine. **Freq:** Quarterly. **Print Method:** Offset. **Trim Size:** 10 x 16. **Cols./Page:** 5. **Col. Width:** 2 inches. **Col. Depth:** 16 inches. **Key Personnel:** Bryan Platz, Editor-in-Chief. **URL:** http://outwritenewsmag.org. **Formerly:** TenPercent. **Remarks:** Accepts advertising. **Circ:** 5000.

2930 ■ Overture
Professional Musicians Local 47
817 Vine St.
Los Angeles, CA 90038
Phone: (323)462-2161
Fax: (323)461-3090
Publication E-mail: overture@promusic47.org
Union newspaper (tabloid). **Founded:** 1921. **Freq:** Monthly. **Print Method:** Offset. Uses mats. **Cols./Page:** 4. **Col. Width:** 27 nonpareils. **Col. Depth:** 189 agate lines. **Key Personnel:** Linda Rapka, Manager, Advertising, Managing Editor. **ISSN:** 0030-7556 (print). **URL:** http://www.promusic47.org/overture.html. **Ad Rates:** BW $855; PCI $25. **Remarks:** Accepts advertising. **Circ:** Paid ‡8000.

2931 ■ Pacific Basin Law Journal
University of California School of Law
1242 Law Bldg.
385 Charles E. Young Dr. E
Los Angeles, CA 90095
Phone: (310)825-4841
Publisher's E-mail: admissions@law.ucla.edu
Journal containing legal issues that directly affect trade flows and international transactions in the Pacific Basin. **Freq:** Semiannual. **Key Personnel:** Zachary Simmons, Editor-in-Chief. **EISSN:** 2169--7728 (electronic). **URL:** http://escholarship.org/uc/uclalaw_pblj; http://law.ucla.edu/student-life/law-reviews-and-journals/pacific-basin-law-journal. **Circ:** (Not Reported).

2932 ■ Pacific Journal of Mathematics
University of California at Los Angeles
PO Box 951555
Los Angeles, CA 90095-1555
Phone: (310)825-4321
Research journal in mathematics. **Freq:** Monthly (except July and August). **Key Personnel:** Paul Balmer, Editor. **ISSN:** 0030-8730 (print). **Subscription Rates:** $600 Individuals print and electronic; $440 Individuals electronic only. **URL:** http://msp.berkeley.edu/pjm/2011/251-2/index.xhtml. **Remarks:** Advertising not accepted. **Circ:** (Not Reported).

2933 ■ Pacific Ties: UCLA's Asian Pacific Islander Newsmagazine
Student Media UCLA
118 Kerckhoff Hall
308 Westwood Plz.
Los Angeles, CA 90024-1641
Phone: (310)825-2787
Fax: (210)206-0906
Publisher's E-mail: studentmedia@media.ucla.edu
Student magazine. **Freq:** Quarterly. **Cols./Page:** 4. **Col. Width:** 2 inches. **Col. Depth:** 15.5 inches. **Key Personnel:** Karin Chan, Editor-in-Chief. **URL:** http://pacificties.org. **Remarks:** Accepts advertising. **Circ:** (Not Reported).

2934 ■ Palaeogeography, Palaeoclimatology, Palaeoecology
RELX Group P.L.C.
c/o D.J. Bottjer, Editor
Dept. of Earth Sciences
University of Southern California
University Park
Los Angeles, CA 90089-0740
Phone: (213)740-6100
Fax: (213)740-8801
Publisher's E-mail: amsterdam@relx.com
Journal publishing multidisciplinary, original studies and comprehensive reviews in the field of palaeo-environmental geology. **Freq:** 24/yr. **Key Personnel:** Prof. D.J. Bottjer, Editor; Prof. T. Correge, Editor; Prof. A.P. Kershaw, Editor. **ISSN:** 0031--0182 (print). **Subscription Rates:** $454 Individuals print; $5852 Institutions online; $7022 Institutions print. **URL:** http://www.journals.elsevier.com/palaeogeography-palaeoclimatology-palaeoecology. **Circ:** (Not Reported).

2935 ■ Pancreas: Journal of Neuroendocrine Tumors and Pancreatic Diseases and Sciences
Lippincott Williams & Wilkins
c/o Vay Liang W. Go, MD, Editor-in-Chief
Warren Hall 13-146
900 Veteran Ave.
Los Angeles, CA 90095-1786
Phone: (310)208-2530
Fax: (310)824-5990
Publication E-mail: pancreasofc@ucla.edu
Peer-reviewed journal providing a central forum for communication of original works involving both basic and clinical research on the exocrine and endocrine pancreas and their interrelationship and consequences in disease states. **Freq:** 8/year. **Print Method:** Sheetfed Offset. **Trim Size:** 8 1/8 x 10 7/8. **Key Personnel:** Vay Liang W. Go, MD, Editor-in-Chief; Nina J. Chang, Publisher. **ISSN:** 0885--3177 (print); **EISSN:** 1536--4828 (electronic). **Subscription Rates:** $1507 Individuals; $4099 Institutions; $713 Individuals in-training; $1672 Other countries individual; $4247 Institutions, other countries; $732 Other countries in-training. **URL:** http://journals.lww.com/pancreasjournal/pages/default.aspx; http://www.lww.com/Product/0885-3177. **Ad Rates:** BW $1100; 4C $1580. **Remarks:** Accepts advertising. **Circ:** 226.

2936 ■ Park Labrea News and Beverly Press
Park Labrea News and Beverly Press
5150 Wilshire Blvd. Ste. 330
Los Angeles, CA 90036
Phone: (323)933-5518
Community newspaper. **Freq:** Weekly (Thurs.). **Print Method:** Offset. **Cols./Page:** 5. **Col. Width:** 12 picas. **Col. Depth:** 16 inches. **Key Personnel:** Karen Villalpando, Publisher; Edwin Folven, Editor; Michael Villalpando, Publisher. **URL:** http://parklabreanewsbeverlypress.com/news. **Mailing address:** PO Box 36036, Los Angeles, CA 90036. **Remarks:** Advertising accepted; rates available upon request. **Circ:** Free ‡13000.

2937 ■ Performances Magazine
Echo Media
900 Circle 75 Pky., Ste. 1600
Atlanta, GA 30339
Phone: (770)955-3535
Fax: (770)955-3599
Publisher's E-mail: salesinfo@echo-media.com
For upscale art patrons, distributed in theatres, concert halls and amphitheaters in Southern California. **Freq:** Monthly. **URL:** http://echomedia.com/medias/details/10030. **Remarks:** Accepts advertising. **Circ:** 265000.

2938 ■ Physical Therapy Products
Novicom Inc.
6100 Center Dr., Ste. 1000
Los Angeles, CA 90045
Magazine featuring new products and services available in the physical therapy field. **Freq:** Monthly. **Print Method:** Web Offset. **Trim Size:** 8 1/8 x 10 7/8. **Cols./Page:** 3. **Key Personnel:** Jody Rich, Publisher; Frank Long, Editor. **ISSN:** 1059-096X (print). **Subscription Rates:** Free to qualified subscribers. **URL:** http://www.ptproductsonline.com. **Ad Rates:** BW $3,325; 4C $850. **Remarks:** Accepts advertising. **Circ:** Controlled 30000.

2939 ■ Pomona Civil Citizen's Journal
Echo Media
900 Circle 75 Pky., Ste. 1600
Atlanta, GA 30339
Phone: (770)955-3535
Fax: (770)955-3599
Publisher's E-mail: salesinfo@echo-media.com
African-American oriented community journal. **Freq:** Monthly delivered on the 2nd Thursday of every month. **Remarks:** Accepts advertising. **Circ:** 10000.

2940 ■ Pool & Spa News
Leisure Publications Inc.
4160 Wilshire Blvd.
Los Angeles, CA 90010-3500
Phone: (323)964-4800
Fax: (323)417-4840
Free: 800-222-7209
Publication E-mail: poolspanews@hanleywood.com
Magazine focusing on the swimming pool and spa industries. **Freq:** Semimonthly. **Print Method:** Web Offset. **Trim Size:** 8 1/4 x 10 7/8. **Cols./Page:** 3. **Col. Width:** 27 nonpareils. **Col. Depth:** 140 agate lines. **Key Personnel:** Joanne McClain, Managing Editor, phone: (323)801-4979; Dick Coleman, Publisher, phone: (323)801-4903; Erika Taylor, Editor, phone: (972)536-6439; Steve Honum, Account Executive, phone: (323)801-4926; Gary Carr, Manager, Sales, phone: (323)801-4922. **Subscription Rates:** $19.97 Individuals pool & spa news; $45 Other countries; $29.97 Two years; $68 Other countries two years. **URL:** http://www.poolspanews.com. **Ad Rates:** BW $2730; 4C $915. **Remarks:** Accepts advertising. **Circ:** (Not Reported).

2941 ■ Psychological Perspectives
C. G. Jung Institute of Los Angeles
10349 W Pico Blvd.
Los Angeles, CA 90064-2608
Phone: (310)556-1193
Fax: (310)556-2290
Publication E-mail: psych_perspectives@junginla.org
Journal of Jungian thought featuring articles, interviews, poetry, fiction, and book and film reviews. **Freq:** Quarterly. **Trim Size:** 6 x 9. **Cols./Page:** 1. **Col. Width:** 4 1/2 inches. **Key Personnel:** Caroline Green, Assistant Editor; Gilda Frantz, Editor-in-Chief; Margaret P. Johnson, PhD, Managing Editor. **ISSN:** 0033--2925 (print). **Subscription Rates:** $94 Individuals; $267 Institutions online only; $305 Institutions print and online. **URL:** http://www.junginla.org/words&images/psychological_perspectives. **Remarks:** Accepts advertising. **Circ:** (Not Reported).

2942 ■ The Rafu Shimpo
The Rafu Shimpo
138 Onizuka St.
Los Angeles, CA 90012
Phone: (213)629-2231
Fax: (213)687-0737
Publisher's E-mail: online@rafu.com
Community newspaper (English and Japanese). **Freq:** Daily Tuesday, Wednesday, Thursday and Saturday. **Key Personnel:** Gwen Muranaka, Editor; Mario G. Reyes, Editor; Michael Komai, Publisher; Michael Hirano Culross, Contact. **Subscription Rates:** $149 Individuals standard; $119 Individuals senior; $75 Students for 9 months. **Remarks:** Accepts advertising. **Circ:** (Not Reported).

2943 ■ Razorcake
Razorcake/Gorsky Press, Inc.
PO Box 42129
Los Angeles, CA 90042
Publisher's E-mail: customerservice@razorcake.org
Magazine covering punk and hardcore music. **Freq:** 6/year. **Subscription Rates:** $15 Individuals bulk; $21

Circulation: ★ = AAM; △ or • = BPA; ♦ = CAC; ❑ = VAC; ⊕ = PO Statement; ‡ = Publisher's Report; Boldface figures = sworn; Light figures = estimated.

Individuals 1st Class; $25 Canada Sent air mail; 50 Other countries sent air mail; $33 By mail Mexican; $21 U.S. prisoner. **Circ:** (Not Reported).

2944 ■ Reason
The Reason Foundation
5737 Mesmer Ave.
Los Angeles, CA 90230
Phone: (310)391-2245
Fax: (310)391-4395
Magazine covering politics, culture, and ideas through a provocative mix of news, analysis, commentary, and reviews. **Founded:** 1968. **Freq:** Monthly. **Print Method:** Web offset. **Trim Size:** 7.33 x 9.33. **Cols./Page:** 10. **Col. Width:** 6.6 picas. **Col. Depth:** 301 agate lines. **Key Personnel:** Ronald Bailey, Correspondent; Brian Doherty, Senior Editor; Nick Gillespie, Editor-in-Chief; Jacob Sullum, Senior Editor; Radley Balko, Senior Editor; Jesse Walker, Managing Editor. **ISSN:** 0048-6906 (print). **Subscription Rates:** $25.97 Two years; $14.97 Individuals; $37.97 Individuals three years. **URL:** http://reason.com. **Ad Rates:** BW $1,915; 4C $2,525. **Remarks:** Print and Online. **Circ:** Paid ■ **55000.**

2945 ■ RT: For Decision Makers in Respiratory Care
CurAnt Communications Inc.
6701 Ctr. Dr. W, Ste. 450
Los Angeles, CA 90045
Phone: (310)642-4400
Fax: (310)641-4444
Publication E-mail: rtmag@aol.com
Trade magazine serving as a buyer's guide for the respiratory care practitioner. **Freq:** Semiannual. **Print Method:** Web offset. **Trim Size:** 8 3/8 x 10 7/8. **Key Personnel:** Roy Felts, Director, Advertising; Anne Welsbacher, Editor. **ISSN:** 1068--963X (print). **Subscription Rates:** Free. **URL:** http://www.rtmagazine.com. **Formerly:** Respiratory Therapy Products. **Ad Rates:** 4C $5,320. **Remarks:** Accepts advertising. **Circ:** Combined ‡28136.

2946 ■ Self-Realization: A Magazine Devoted to Healing of Body, Mind, and Soul
Self-Realization Fellowship Publishers
3880 San Rafael Ave.
Los Angeles, CA 90031-1835
Phone: (323)276-6002
Fax: (323)927-1624
Free: 888-773-8680
Publisher's E-mail: sales@srfpublishers.org
Magazine promoting the practical application of spiritual principles for healing of body, removing mental harmonies by concentration and positive thinking, and freeing the soul from ignorance by yoga meditation. **Freq:** Quarterly. **Print Method:** Offset. **Trim Size:** 5 1/4 x 7 3/4. **Cols./Page:** 1. **Col. Width:** 49 nonpareils. **Col. Depth:** 87 agate lines. **ISSN:** 0037--1564 (print). **Subscription Rates:** $19 Individuals; $23 Other countries; $54 Individuals 3 years; $66 Other countries 3 years. **Alt. Formats:** CD-ROM. **URL:** http://www.yogananda-srf.org/self-realization_magazine/self-realization_magazine.aspx#.VrgFhxh94dU. **Remarks:** Advertising not accepted. **Circ:** 25000.

2947 ■ Self-Realization Magazine
Self-Realization Fellowship
3880 San Rafael Ave.
Los Angeles, CA 90065-3219
Phone: (818)549-5151
Fax: (818)549-5100
Magazine containing fascinating and informative articles providing insight and information on a wide range of subjects: finding balance in today's complex world; the nature of life, death and reincarnation; a spiritual perspective on world events; developing mind power; creating a personal relationship with God; and much more. Magazine with a unique blend of ancient wisdom and modern thought. **Freq:** Quarterly. **Subscription Rates:** $19 U.S. /year; $23 Other countries /year; $54 U.S. 3 years; $66 Other countries 3 years. **Alt. Formats:** CD-ROM. **URL:** http://www.yogananda-srf.org/Self-Realization_Magazine/Self-Realization_Magazine.aspx#.VUIxS9KUeqa. **Remarks:** Advertising not accepted. **Circ:** (Not Reported).

2948 ■ Seminars in Respiratory and Critical Care Medicine
Thieme Medical Publishers, Inc.
c/o Joseph P. Lynch, III, Editor-in-Chief
Div. of Pulmonary, Critical Care, & Hospitals
David Geffen School of Medicine at UCLA
10833 Le Conte Ave., Rm. 37-131 CHS
Los Angeles, CA 90095-1690
Phone: (310)825-5988
Fax: (310)206-8622
Publisher's E-mail: customerservice@thieme.com
Medical journal covering respiratory and pulmonary disorders. **Freq:** Bimonthly February, April, June, August, October, December. **Print Method:** Web Offset. **Trim Size:** 8 1/8 x 10 7/8. **Cols./Page:** 2. **Col. Width:** 38 nonpareils. **Col. Depth:** 133 agate lines. **Key Personnel:** Ulrich Costabel, MD, Board Member; Joseph P. Lynch, III, Editor-in-Chief; Nicholas S. Hill, MD, Board Member; Robert P. Baughman, MD, Board Member; Steve Nelson, MD, Board Member; Victor F. Tapson, MD, Board Member; Wesley E. Ely, MD, Board Member; Steven A. Sahn, MD, Board Member. **ISSN:** 1069--3424 (print). **Subscription Rates:** $330 Individuals print and online; $1235 Institutions print and online; $128 Individuals resident rate. **URL:** http://www.thieme.com/books-main/internal-medicine/product/2166-seminars-in-respiratory-and-critical-care-medicine. **Formerly:** Seminars in Respiratory Medicine. **Ad Rates:** BW $1420; 4C $1500. **Remarks:** Accepts advertising. **Circ:** Paid ‡2312.

2949 ■ Slavic and East European Journal
American Association of Teachers of Slavic and East European Languages
c/o Elizabeth Durst, PhD, Executive Director
University of Southern California
3501 Trousdale Pky., THH 255L
Los Angeles, CA 90089
Phone: (213)740-2734
Fax: (213)740-8550
Publisher's E-mail: aatseel@usc.edu
Journal publishing research in the areas of Slavic and East European languages, literatures, cultures, linguistics, and methodology. **Freq:** Quarterly. **Key Personnel:** Prof. Irene Delic, Editor. **Subscription Rates:** Included in membership. **URL:** http://www.aatseel.org/publications/see_journal. **Remarks:** Accepts advertising. **Circ:** (Not Reported).

2950 ■ South Gate Press
Wave Newspaper Group
3731 Wilshire Blvd., Ste. 840
Los Angeles, CA 90010
Phone: (323)556-5720
Fax: (213)835-0584
Community Newspaper. **Freq:** Semiweekly Thurs. and Sat. **Print Method:** Uses mats. Offset. **Trim Size:** 6 x 21 1/2. **Cols./Page:** 6. **Col. Width:** 37 nonpareils. **Col. Depth:** 301 agate lines. **Subscription Rates:** Free; $125 yr/mailed. **URL:** http://wavenewspapers.com/?s=South+Gate+Press. **Remarks:** Accepts advertising. **Circ:** (Not Reported).

2951 ■ Southern California Interdisciplinary Law Journal
University of Southern California Gould School of Law
699 Exposition Blvd.
Los Angeles, CA 90089-0040
Phone: (213)740-9244
Publisher's E-mail: admissions@law.usc.edu
Journal containing articles on interdisciplinary law. **Freq:** 3/year. **Subscription Rates:** $36 Individuals domestic; $45 Individuals international; $10.50 Single issue plus $6 shipping. **URL:** http://lawreview.usc.edu; http://gould.usc.edu/why/students/orgs/ilj. **Circ:** (Not Reported).

2952 ■ Southern California Law Review
University of Southern California
University Park Campus
Los Angeles, CA 90089
Phone: (213)740-2311
College law Journal. **Freq:** Bimonthly 6/year. **Print Method:** Offset. **Trim Size:** 17 x 25 cm. **Cols./Page:** 1. **Col. Width:** 55 nonpareils. **Col. Depth:** 105 agate lines. **Key Personnel:** Ravi Mahesh, Editor-in-Chief. **ISSN:** 0038--3910 (print). **USPS:** 856-100. **Subscription Rates:** $36 Individuals domestic; $45 Individuals foreign. **URL:** http://lawreview.usc.edu. **Circ:** Paid ‡1033, Non-paid ‡100.

2953 ■ Southern California Law Review
University of Southern California Gould School of Law
699 Exposition Blvd.
Los Angeles, CA 90089-0074
Phone: (213)740-7331
College law Journal. **Freq:** Bimonthly 6/year. **Print Method:** Offset. **Trim Size:** 17 x 25 cm. **Cols./Page:** 1. **Col. Width:** 55 nonpareils. **Col. Depth:** 105 agate lines. **Key Personnel:** Ravi Mahesh, Editor-in-Chief. **ISSN:** 0038--3910 (print). **USPS:** 856-100. **Subscription Rates:** $36 Individuals domestic; $45 Individuals foreign. **URL:** http://lawreview.usc.edu. **Circ:** Paid ‡1033, Non-paid ‡100.

2954 ■ Southern California Review
University of Southern California
c/o Master of Professional Writing
University of Southern California
Mark Taper Hall, THH 355J
3501 Trousdale Pky.
Los Angeles, CA 90089-0355
Publication E-mail: scr@dornsife.usc.edu
Magazine featuring fiction and poetry. **Freq:** Annual. **Key Personnel:** Mellinda Hensley, Editor-in-Chief. **Subscription Rates:** $15 Single issue. **URL:** http://dornsife.usc.edu/mpw/literary-journal. **Circ:** (Not Reported).

2955 ■ Southwestern Journal of International Law
Southwestern Law School
3050 Wilshire Blvd.
Los Angeles, CA 90010
Phone: (213)738-6700
Publisher's E-mail: admissions@swlaw.edu
Journal containing topics on international insolvency, environmental law, international trade issues, NAFTA, international arbitration, privatization in Central and South American countries, immigration, human rights, international crime, and other comparative issues. **Freq:** Semiannual. **Subscription Rates:** $30 Individuals domestic; $35 Individuals foreign; $17 Single issue. **URL:** http://www.swlaw.edu/academics/cocurricular/journaloflaw. **Circ:** (Not Reported).

2956 ■ Spiritus: A Journal of Christian Spirituality
Johns Hopkins University Press
c/o Douglas Burton-Christie, Ed.
Loyola Marymount University
Dept. of Theological Studies
1 LMU Dr.
Los Angeles, CA 90045
Publisher's E-mail: webmaster@jhupress.jhu.edu
Peer-reviewed journal exploring the connections between spirituality and cultural analysis including literary and artistic expression, social activism, and spiritual practice. Promotes research in the field of Christian spirituality while fostering creative dialogue with other nonChristian traditions. Sponsored by the Society for the Study of Christian Spirituality. **Freq:** Semiannual. **Key Personnel:** Nadia Pandolfo, Managing Editor. **ISSN:** 1533--1709 (print); **EISSN:** 1535--3117 (electronic). **Subscription Rates:** $130 Institutions print; $260 Institutions print, 2 years. **URL:** http://www.press.jhu.edu/journals/spiritus/index.html; http://sscs.press.jhu.edu/publications/order_spiritus.html. **Ad Rates:** BW $325. **Remarks:** Accepts advertising. **Circ:** 664.

2957 ■ Studies in American Political Development
Cambridge University Press
c/o Scott James
Dept. of Political Science
University of California, Los Angeles
Los Angeles, CA 90024-1472
Publication E-mail: ad_sales@cambridge.org
Journal covering American political changes and institutional developments. **Freq:** Semiannual. **Key Personnel:** Daniel Carpenter, Board Member; Stephen Skowronek, Editor, Founder; Prof. Elisabeth Clemens, Board Member; Scott James, Board Member. **ISSN:** 0898--588X (print); **EISSN:** 1469--8692 (electronic). **Subscription Rates:** $265 Institutions online only; £159 Institutions online only; $331 Institutions print & online; £198 Institutions print & online; $305 Institutions print only; £183 Institutions print only. **URL:** http://journals.cambridge.org/action/displayJournal?jid=SAP. **Ad Rates:** BW $845. **Remarks:** Accepts advertising. **Circ:** 400.

2958 ■ T'ai Chi: International Magazine of T'ai Chi Ch'uan
Wayfarer Publications
2601 Silver Ridge Ave.
Los Angeles, CA 90039
Phone: (323)665-7773
Fax: (323)665-1627
Free: 800-888-9119
Publication E-mail: taichi@tai-chi.com
A magazine for practitioners of T'ai Chi and related martial arts, health and fitness disciplines. **Freq:** Quarterly. **Print Method:** Offset. **Trim Size:** 8 3/8 x 10 7/8. **Cols./Page:** 3. **Col. Width:** 2 1/4 inches. **Col. Depth:** 9 3/4 inches. **Key Personnel:** Marvin Smalheiser, Editor. **ISSN:** 0730--1049 (print). **Subscription Rates:** $20 U.S. one year; $30 U.S. two years; $30 Other countries one year; $50 Other countries two years; $5.99 Single issue U.S.; $6.25 Single issue international. **URL:** http://www.tai-chi.com. **Mailing address:** PO Box 39938, Los Angeles, CA 90039. **Ad Rates:** BW $825; 4C $1,030; PCI $25. **Remarks:** Advertising accepted; rates available upon request. **Circ:** (Not Reported).

2959 ■ TDmonthly: A Trade Magazine For The Toy, Hobby, Game and Gift Industry
ToyDirectory.com Inc.
12340 Santa Monica Blvd., Ste. 226
Los Angeles, CA 90025
Phone: (310)979-4330
Fax: (310)979-4350
Free: 888-732-2378
Publisher's E-mail: contact2@toydirectory.com
Trade magazine covering the toy, hobby and game industry. **Freq:** Monthly. **Key Personnel:** Bob Naimi, Publisher, Editor. **Subscription Rates:** $9.99 Individuals e-newsletter. **URL:** http://www.toydirectory.com/monthly/. **Remarks:** Advertising accepted; rates available upon request. **Circ:** (Not Reported).

2960 ■ TelevisionWeek
Crain Communications Inc.
6500 Wilshire Blvd., Ste. 2300
Los Angeles, CA 90048
Phone: (323)370-2417
Publisher's E-mail: info@crain.com
Newspaper covering management, programming, cable and trends in the television and the media industry. **Founded:** Aug. 1982. **Freq:** Weekly. **Print Method:** Heat-set Web Offset. **Trim Size:** 10 7/8 x 14 1/2. **Cols./Page:** 5. **Col. Width:** 1 7/8 inches. **Col. Depth:** 14 inches. **Key Personnel:** Rance Crain, Editor-in-Chief, President; Chuck Ross, Managing Director, phone: (323)370-2417; Dennis Liff, Executive Editor. **Subscription Rates:** $119 Individuals; $171 Canada incl. GST; $309 Other countries airmail. **URL:** http://www.tvweek.com/. **Formerly**: Electronic Media. **Ad Rates:** BW $12670; 4C $17210. **Remarks:** Accepts advertising. **Circ:** (Not Reported).

2961 ■ Theosophy: The Synthesis of Science, Religion and Philosophy
The Theosophy Co.
245 W 33rd St.
Los Angeles, CA 90007
Phone: (213)748-7244
Publisher's E-mail: theosco@sbcglobal.net
Magazine devoted to philosophy and science. **Freq:** Quarterly. **Print Method:** Offset. **Trim Size:** 5 1/2 x 8 1/2. **Cols./Page:** 1. **Col. Width:** 48 nonpareils. **Col. Depth:** 100 agate lines. **ISSN:** 0040--5906 (print). **Subscription Rates:** $15 Individuals; $25 Two years; $4.50 Single issue. **Alt. Formats:** PDF. **URL:** http://www.theosophycompany.org/pubs.html. **Remarks:** Advertising not accepted. **Circ:** Paid 800.

2962 ■ The Tidings
The Tidings Corp.
3424 Wilshire Blvd.
Los Angeles, CA 90010
Phone: (213)637-7360
Fax: (213)637-6360
Publisher's E-mail: info@the-tidings.com
Catholic newspaper. **Founded:** 1895. **Freq:** Weekly. **Print Method:** Offset. **Cols./Page:** 8. **Col. Width:** 18 nonpareils. **Col. Depth:** 294 agate lines. **Key Personnel:** Mike Nelson, Editor, phone: (213)637-7543. **ISSN:** 0040-6791 (print). **Subscription Rates:** $23 Individuals 51 issues; $42 Two years individuals. **URL:** http://www.angelusnews.com/. **Ad Rates:** GLR $1.56; BW $2,757; 4C $3,407; SAU $21.88; PCI $21.88. **Remarks:** Accepts advertising. **Circ:** ‡100000.

2963 ■ Transactions on Design Automation of Electronic Systems
Association for Computing Machinery
c/o Massoud Pedram, Editorial Assistant
Dept. of Electrical Engineering
University of Southern California
3740 McClintock Ave.
Los Angeles, CA 90089-2562
Phone: (213)740-4465
Publisher's E-mail: acmhelp@acm.org
Professional journal covering system design, high level synthesis, physical layout, and related topics. **Freq:** Quarterly. **Print Method:** Offset. **Trim Size:** 6 1/2 X 10. **Key Personnel:** Naehyuck Chang, Editor-in-Chief; Yuan Xie, Associate Editor. **ISSN:** 1084--4309 (print). **URL:** http://todaes.acm.org. **Remarks:** Advertising not accepted. **Circ:** (Not Reported).

2964 ■ Transactions in GIS
Wiley-Blackwell
c/o Dr. John P. Wilson, Editor
University of Southern California
Los Angeles, CA 90089
Phone: (213)740-1908
Fax: (213)740-9687
Publisher's E-mail: info@wiley.com
Journal publishing original research papers, review papers, short notes and book reviews on GIS. **Freq:** Bimonthly. **Key Personnel:** Alex Singleton, Editor; Dr. John P. Wilson, Editor. **ISSN:** 1361--1682 (print); **EISSN:** 1467--9671 (electronic). **Subscription Rates:** $2077 Institutions online; $45 Members online; $2565 Institutions, other countries online; £30 Institutions, other countries online. **URL:** http://www.wiley.com/bw/journal.asp?ref=1361-1682. **Remarks:** Advertising accepted; rates available upon request. **Circ:** (Not Reported).

2965 ■ TravelAge West
Northstar Travel Media L.L.C.
11400 W Olympic Blvd., Ste. 325
Los Angeles, CA 90064
Fax: (310)954-2510
Publication E-mail: letters@travelagewest.com
Magazine for retail travel agents in western U.S. and western Canada. **Freq:** Biweekly. **Print Method:** Offset. **Trim Size:** 8 1/2 x 11. **Cols./Page:** 4. **Col. Width:** 20 nonpareils. **Col. Depth:** 140 agate lines. **Key Personnel:** Bruce Shulman, Publisher. **ISSN:** 0041--1973 (print). **Subscription Rates:** $79 Individuals. **URL:** http://www.travelagewest.com; http://www.northstartravelgroup.com/audiences/retail-travel/travelage-west. **Ad Rates:** 4C $22375. **Remarks:** Accepts advertising. **Circ:** △**22144**.

2966 ■ U. The National College Magazine
American Collegiate Network
1800 Century Pk. E, Ste. 820
Los Angeles, CA 90067-1501
Phone: (310)551-1381
Fax: (310)551-1659
National collegiate magazine. **Freq:** 3/year. **Print Method:** Rotogravure. **Trim Size:** 9 1/2 x 11 1/2. **Cols./Page:** 4. **Col. Width:** 2.25 picas. **Col. Depth:** 14 inches. **Key Personnel:** John Carrieri, Editor-in-Chief, Publisher; Nancy Kennedy, Managing Editor; Gabriel Jacobs, Manager, Circulation. **Subscription Rates:** $18 Individuals; $2 Single issue. **URL:** http://www.colleges.com/Umagazine/index.html#. **Formerly**: U. The National College Newspaper. **Ad Rates:** BW $50300; 4C $55800; PCI $295. **Remarks:** Accepts advertising. **Circ:** Paid 3233, Non-paid 1509925.

2967 ■ UCLA Magazine
University of California, Los Angeles
405 Hilgard Ave.
Los Angeles, CA 90095
Phone: (310)825-4321
General interest magazine reporting on the university and its impact of the world around it. Covers research, people, the arts, sports and critical issues while also serving as a guide to UCLA's cultural and recreational offerings. **Freq:** Quarterly. **Print Method:** Web Offset. **Trim Size:** 8 3/4 x 10 3/4. **Key Personnel:** Jack Feuer, Editor, phone: (310)794-0281, fax: (310)794-6883. **ISSN:** 1075--2749 (print). **USPS:** 011-191. **Subscription Rates:** $8 Individuals; $2 Single issue. **URL:** magazine.ucla.edu/v2/?utm_expid=669409-4.e5lBhzzNQu2z3hVlnKKAgQ.1&utm_referrer=https%3A%2F%2Fwww.google.com.ph%2F. **Formerly**: The UCLA Monthly. **Ad Rates:** BW $4,450; 4C $8,100. **Remarks:** Accepts advertising. **Circ:** 135000.

2968 ■ Ufahamu: Journal of African Studies
University of California at Los Angeles - James S. Coleman African Studies Center
10244 Bunche Hall
405 Hilgard Ave.
Los Angeles, CA 90095-1310
Phone: (310)825-3686
Fax: (310)206-2250
Publication E-mail: ufahamu@gmail.com
Journal covering multidisciplinary African studies. **Freq:** Biennial. **Key Personnel:** Jeremy Jacob Peretz, Editor-in-Chief. **ISSN:** 0041--5715 (print); **EISSN:** 2150--5802 (electronic). **URL:** http://escholarship.org/uc/international_asc_ufahamu. **Remarks:** Accepts advertising. **Circ:** Combined 250.

2969 ■ Urban History
Cambridge University Press
c/o Philip J. Ethington, Multimedia Ed.
University of Southern California
Dept. of History
3520 Trousdale Pky., SOS 254
Los Angeles, CA 90089-0034
Publisher's E-mail: newyork@cambridge.org
Journal focusing on urban historical research. **Freq:** 3/year. **Key Personnel:** Prof. Philip J. Ethington, Editor; Prof. Rosemary Sweet, Editor; Prof. Simon Gunn, Editor. **ISSN:** 0963--9268 (print); **EISSN:** 1469--8706 (electronic). **Subscription Rates:** $104 Individuals online & print; £59 Individuals online & print; $418 Institutions online only; £239 Institutions online only; $502 Institutions online & print; £286 Institutions online & print; $473 Institutions print only; £274 Institutions print only. **URL:** http://journals.cambridge.org/action/displayJournal?jid=UHY. **Ad Rates:** BW $825. **Remarks:** Accepts advertising. **Circ:** 750.

2970 ■ USC Trojan Family Magazine
University of Southern California
3434 S Grand Ave., CAL 140 1st Flr.
Los Angeles, CA 90089-2818
Alumni magazine. Includes reviews of faculty publications. **Freq:** Quarterly. **Print Method:** Offset. **Trim Size:** 10 1/4 x 13 3/8. **Cols./Page:** 3 and 5. **Col. Width:** 16.5 and 10 picas. **Col. Depth:** 70 picas. **Key Personnel:** Alicia Di Rado, Editor-in-Chief. **ISSN:** 8750--7927 (print). **URL:** http://tfm.usc.edu. **Formerly**: Trojan Family; University of Southern California Alumni Review. **Remarks:** Advertising accepted; rates available upon request. **Circ:** Controlled ‡200000.

2971 ■ USC Viterbi
USC Viterbi School of Engineering
Olin Hall of Engineering
3650 McClintock Ave.
Los Angeles, CA 90089-1450
Phone: (213)740-9677
Publisher's E-mail: viterbi.careers@usc.edu
Engineering magazine. **Freq:** Semiannual spring and fall. **Print Method:** Offset. **Key Personnel:** Nancy Mack, Editor. **URL:** http://viterbi.usc.edu/viterbiengineer. **Formerly**: USC Engineer. **Ad Rates:** BW $540; 4C $870. **Remarks:** Accepts advertising. **Circ:** Non-paid ‡5000.

2972 ■ Viator
Brepols Publishers
c/o Ctr. for Medieval & Renaissance Studies
University of California, Los Angeles
302 Royce Hall, Box 951485
Los Angeles, CA 90095-1485
Phone: (310)825-1880
Publisher's E-mail: info@brepols.net
Journal of the Center for Medieval and Renaissance Studies, featuring articles on the middle ages and renaissance period. **Freq:** 3/year. **Key Personnel:** Henry Ansgar Kelly, Editor; Blair Sullivan, Associate Editor. **ISSN:** 0083--5897 (print). **URL:** http://cmrs.ucla.edu/publications/journals/viator. **Circ:** (Not Reported).

2973 ■ Vida Nueva
The Tidings Corp.
3424 Wilshire Blvd.
Los Angeles, CA 90010

Circulation: ★ = AAM; △ or • = BPA; ♦ = CAC; ❑ = VAC; ⊕ = PO Statement; ‡ = Publisher's Report; Boldface figures = sworn; Light figures = estimated.

Phone: (213)637-7360
Fax: (213)637-6360
Publisher's E-mail: info@the-tidings.com
Newspaper. **Freq:** Weekly. **Cols./Page:** 5. **Key Personnel:** Victor Aleman, Editor, phone: (213)637-7327. **Subscription Rates:** $20 Individuals. **URL:** http://www.vidanueva.com. **Remarks:** Advertising accepted; rates available upon request. **Circ:** Free ‡215000.

2974 ■ Waterwear
MnM Publishing Corp.
110 E Ninth St., Ste. A777
Los Angeles, CA 90079
Phone: (213)627-3737
Publisher's E-mail: info@apparelnews.net
Magazine featuring swimwear design. **Freq:** 3/week January, July and September. **Trim Size:** 8.125 X 10.875. **Key Personnel:** Alison A. Nieder, Executive Editor; Rhea Cortado, Associate Editor; Terry Martinez, Director, Sales and Marketing. **URL:** http://www.apparelnews.net/documents/sets/waterwear. **Remarks:** Advertising accepted; rates available upon request. **Circ:** (Not Reported).

2975 ■ West Hollywood Independent
Los Angeles Independent Newspaper Group
1730 W Olympic Blvd., No. 500
Los Angeles, CA 90015
Phone: (323)556-5720
Community newspaper. **Freq:** Weekly. **Print Method:** Offset. **Trim Size:** 13 x 22. **Cols./Page:** 6. **Col. Width:** 1.8 inches. **Col. Depth:** 21 inches. **URL:** http://laindependent.com. **Remarks:** Accepts advertising. **Circ:** Paid 9, Non-paid 31680.

2976 ■ Women's Law Journal
University of California School of Law
PO Box 951476
Los Angeles, CA 90095-1476
Publisher's E-mail: admissions@law.ucla.edu
Journal containing articles on issues of gender, race and sexual orientation. **Freq:** Semiannual. **Key Personnel:** Jessica Backer, Editor-in-Chief; Sabrina Lu, Editor-in-Chief. **EISSN:** 1943--1708 (electronic). **URL:** http://escholarship.org/uc/uclalaw_wlj; http://law.ucla.edu/student-life/law-reviews-and-journals/womens-law-journal. **Circ:** (Not Reported).

2977 ■ Woodworkers West
Woodworkers West
PO Box 452058
Los Angeles, CA 90045
Phone: (310)216-9265
Publication E-mail: editor@woodwest.com
Magazine covering woodworking in the Western U.S. **Freq:** Bimonthly January, March, May, July, September & November. **Print Method:** Web offset. **Trim Size:** 8 1/2 x 11. **Cols./Page:** 2. **Col. Width:** 3 1/2 inches. **Col. Depth:** 9 3/4 inches. **ISSN:** 1080--0042 (print). **Subscription Rates:** $4 Single issue Single Current Copy Price; $12 Individuals 1 year(6 issues); $20 Two years 12 issues; $27 Individuals 3 years(18 issues); $5 Canada and Mexico Current issue; $9 Other countries Current issue; $12 U.S. 1 year(6 issues); $22 Canada and Mexico 1 year(6 issues); $40 Other countries 1 year(6 issues); $20 Two years U.S. Delivery 12 issues; 27 U.S. 3 years(18 issues). **Formerly**: Southern California Woodworker. **Remarks:** Accepts advertising. **Circ:** (Not Reported).

2978 ■ World Neurosurgery: An International Journal of Neurosurgery and Neuroscience
Mosby Inc.
1420 San Pablo St.
PMB A-106
Los Angeles, CA 90033
Journal publishing peer-reviewed articles about the latest developments in the field of neurosurgery for neurosurgeons and residents. **Freq:** Monthly. **Print Method:** Web offset. **Trim Size:** 8 X 10 3/4. **Key Personnel:** Edward Benzel, Editor-in-Chief. **ISSN:** 1878--8750 (print). **Subscription Rates:** $777 Individuals print and online; $889 Other countries print and online; $288 Students; $336 Students, other countries. **URL:** http://www.journals.elsevier.com/world-neurosurgery; http://www.worldneurosurgery.org. **Formerly**: Surgical Neurology. **Ad Rates:** BW $1270; 4C $1410. **Remarks:** Accepts advertising. **Circ:** ‡750.

2979 ■ Written By
Writers Guild of America West
7000 W 3rd St.
Los Angeles, CA 90048
Phone: (323)951-4000
Fax: (323)782-4800
Free: 800-548-4532
Freq: Quarterly. **ISSN:** 1092--468X (print). **Subscription Rates:** $40 Individuals domestic fulfillment ; $10 Single issue limited availability on back issues. **URL:** http://www.wga.org/writtenby/writtenby.aspx. **Remarks:** Accepts advertising. **Circ:** (Not Reported).

2980 ■ Wyvernwood Chronicle
Eastern Group Publications Inc.
111 South Ave. 59
Los Angeles, CA 90042
Phone: (323)341-7970
Fax: (323)341-7976
Publisher's E-mail: service@egpnews.com
Hispanic community newspaper (English and Spanish). **Freq:** Weekly (Thurs.). **Print Method:** Offset. **Trim Size:** 13 x 21. **Cols./Page:** 6. **Col. Width:** 2 1/2 inches. **Col. Depth:** 294 agate lines. **Key Personnel:** Dolores Sanchez, Editor-in-Chief, Publisher; Gloria Alvarez, Managing Editor; Bianca Sanchez, Manager, Operations. **URL:** http://egpnews.com/category/editions/wyvernwood-chronicle. **Ad Rates:** GLR $2.50; BW $3,150; 4C $3,570; SAU $25; PCI $25. **Remarks:** 2.50. **Circ:** 2000.

2981 ■ Young Exceptional Children
Division for Early Childhood of the Council for Exceptional Children
3415 S Sepulveda Blvd., Ste. 1100
Los Angeles, CA 90034
Phone: (310)428-7209
Fax: (855)678-1989
Publisher's E-mail: dec@dec-sped.org
Freq: Quarterly. **ISSN:** 1096- 2506 (print). **Subscription Rates:** Included in membership; $33 Individuals print only; $132 Institutions print only; $122 Institutions e-access; $135 Institutions print & e-access; $36 Institutions single issue; $11 Individuals single issue. **URL:** http://www.dec-sped.org/yec; http://yec.sagepub.com. **Remarks:** Advertising not accepted. **Circ:** (Not Reported).

2982 ■ Zoo View
Greater Los Angeles Zoo Association
5333 Zoo Dr.
Los Angeles, CA 90027
Phone: (323)644-4200
Fax: (323)644-4720
Publisher's E-mail: webmaster@lazoo.org
L.A. Zoo Magazine. **Freq:** Quarterly. **Print Method:** Web offset. **Trim Size:** 8 1/2 x 11. **Key Personnel:** Brenda Posada, Editor, phone: (323)644-4783. **ISSN:** 0276--3303 (print). **Subscription Rates:** $11 Individuals. **URL:** http://www.lazoo.org/membership/publications; http://www.lazoo.org/zooview. **Remarks:** Advertising not accepted. **Circ:** Paid 65000, Non-paid 1000.

2983 ■ KABC-AM - 790
3321 S La Cienega Blvd.
Los Angeles, CA 90016-3114
Phone: (310)840-4900
Free: 800-222-5222
Format: Talk; News. **Founded:** 1929. **Operating Hours**: Continuous. **ADI**: Los Angeles (Corona & San Bernardino), CA. **Key Personnel:** Bill Sommers, Gen. Mgr; Lindsay Trumbull, Contact. **Wattage**: 5,000. **Ad Rates:** Advertising accepted; rates available upon request. **URL:** http://www.kabc.com/.

2984 ■ KACE-FM - 103.9
5999 Center Dr.
Los Angeles, CA 90045
Phone: (310)846-2800
Fax: (213)380-4214
Free: 800-540-1039
Networks: Fox; CBS; NBC. **Owner:** Cox Broadcasting, 322 N Glenwood Blvd., Tyler, TX 75702, Ph: (903)595-4321. **Founded:** 1959. **Operating Hours**: Continuous. **ADI**: Los Angeles (Corona & San Bernardino), CA. **Key Personnel:** Howard Neal, Gen. Mgr.; Kevin Fleming, Dir. of Programs; Chuck Rios, Mktg. Mgr., Promotions Mgr., Contact; Chuck Rios, Contact. **Wattage:** 4,100 ERP. **Ad Rates:** Accepts Advertising. **URL:** http://www.univision.com.

2985 ■ KALF-FM - 95.7
10900 Wilshire Blvd.
Los Angeles, CA 90024
Phone: (310)209-7333
Format: Country. **Owner:** Mapleton Communication, 513 Main St., Mapleton, IA 51034, Ph: (712)881-4000. **Founded:** 1978. **Operating Hours**: Continuous; 100% local. **ADI**: Chico-Redding, CA. **Key Personnel:** Chad Gammage, Dir. of Mktg., Mktg. Mgr. **Wattage**: 50,000. **Ad Rates:** $20-45 per unit. **URL:** http://www.957thewolfonline.com.

2986 ■ KAMP-FM - 97.1
5670 Wilshire Blvd., Ste. 200
Los Angeles, CA 90036
Phone: (323)930-5500
Owner: CBS Radio Inc., 1271 Avenue of the Americas, 44th Fl., New York, NY 10020-1401, Ph: (212)649-9600. **ADI**: Los Angeles (Corona & San Bernardino), CA. **Wattage**: 21,000 ERP. **Ad Rates:** Accepts Advertising.

2987 ■ KBJZ-FM - 103.1
5700 Wilshire Blvd
Los Angeles, CA 90036
Phone: (310)447-3870
Format: Adult Contemporary. **Networks:** CBS. **Founded:** 1992. **Formerly**: KSFR-FM; KOCM-FM. **Operating Hours**: Continuous. **Key Personnel:** Susan Wallace, Gen. Sales Mgr.; Manon Hennessey, Dir. of Programs. **Wattage:** 3,000. **Ad Rates:** $100 for 60 seconds. **URL:** http://www.joseradio.com/contacto.

2988 ■ KBRG-FM - 104.9
1149 S Hill St., Ste. H-100
Los Angeles, CA 90015
Phone: (408)274-1170
Fax: (408)274-1818
Format: Classical; Educational. **Simulcasts:** KDFC-FM. **Networks:** Independent. **Owner:** EXCL Communications, Inc., at above address. **Founded:** 1961. **Operating Hours**: Continuous; 100% local. **Key Personnel:** Jeffrey Liberman, Contact; Guillermo Prince, Contact; Athena Marks, Gen. Mgr; Jeffrey Liberman, Contact; Guillermo Prince, Contact. **Wattage:** 6,000 ERP. **Ad Rates:** Underwriting available. **URL:** http://www.usc.edu.

2989 ■ KCBS-FM - 93.1
5901 Venice Blvd.
Los Angeles, CA 90034
Phone: (323)937-9331
Free: 866-931-5225
Email: jack@931jackfm.com
Format: Adult Contemporary. **Networks:** Westwood One Radio. **Founded:** 1950. **Formerly:** KNX-FM; KODJ-FM; KKHR-FM. **Operating Hours:** Continuous. **Wattage**: 29,000. **Ad Rates:** Advertising accepted; rates available upon request. **URL:** http://www.931jackfm.cbslocal.com.

2990 ■ KCET-TV - 13
4401 Sunset Blvd.
Los Angeles, CA 90027
Phone: (323)666-6500
Email: viewerservices@kcet.org
Format: Public TV. **Networks:** Public Broadcasting Service (PBS). **Owner:** Community Television of Southern California, at above address. **Founded:** 1964. **Operating Hours**: Continuous. **ADI**: Los Angeles (Corona & San Bernardino), CA. **Key Personnel:** Al Jerome, CEO, President; Camille Gonzalez, CFO, VP; Lourdes Nunez-Burgess, VP of HR; Val Zavala, VP of Public Affairs. **Local Programs**: *Generations of Violence*; *Hungary: Pushing the Limits*; *Diet for a New America*. **Wattage**: 5,000. **Ad Rates:** Noncommercial. **URL:** http://www.kcet.org.

KCHJ-AM - See Delano

2991 ■ KCOP-TV - 13
1999 S Bundy Dr.
Los Angeles, CA 90025
Phone: (310)584-2000
Format: Commercial TV. **Networks:** Independent; United Paramount Network. **Owner:** Fox Television Stations Inc., 1211 Ave. of the Americas, 21st Fl., New York, NY 10036, Ph: (212)301-5400. **Founded:** 1948. **Operating Hours**: Continuous. **ADI**: Los Angeles (Corona & San Bernardino), CA. **Key Personnel:** Pat Jones, VP, pat.jones@foxtv.com. **Ad Rates:** Noncommercial. **URL:** http://www.myfoxla.com.

2992 ■ KCOR-AM
5999 Center Dr.
Los Angeles, CA 90045
Format: Hispanic. **Founded:** 1946. **Key Personnel:** Dan Wilson, Gen. Mgr. **Wattage:** 5,000. **Ad Rates:** Advertising accepted; rates available upon request.

2993 ■ KDAY-FM - 93.5
5055 Wilshire Blvd., Ste. 720
Los Angeles, CA 90036
Email: kday@members.kday.com
Operating Hours: Continuous. **Wattage:** 4,200 ERP. **Ad Rates:** Advertising accepted; rates available upon request. **URL:** http://www.935kday.com.

2994 ■ KDLD-FM - 103.1
5700 Wilshire Blvd., No. 250
Los Angeles, CA 90036
Phone: (323)900-6100
Format: Album-Oriented Rock (AOR); Hispanic. **Owner:** Entravision Communication Corp., 2425 Olympic Blvd. W, Ste. 6000, Santa Monica, CA 90404; Entravision Communications Corporation, 2425 Olympic Blvd., Ste. 6000 W, Santa Monica, CA 90404-4030, Ph: (310)447-3870, Fax: (310)447-3899. **Operating Hours:** Continuous. **Key Personnel:** Karl Meyer, Contact. **Ad Rates:** Advertising accepted; rates available upon request. **URL:** http://www.joseradio.com.

2995 ■ KDLE-FM - 103.1
5700 Wilshire Blvd., No. 250
Los Angeles, CA 90036
Phone: (323)560-5673
Format: Alternative/New Music/Progressive. **Ad Rates:** Advertising accepted; rates available upon request. **URL:** http://www.joseradio.com/.

KDSC-FM - See Thousand Oaks, CA

2996 ■ KENO-AM - 1460
3301 Barham Blvd., Ste. 200
Los Angeles, CA 90068
Phone: (702)876-1460
Email: info@wearelv.com.com
Format: News; Sports. **Networks:** Unistar. **Owner:** Lotus Communications Corp., 3301 Barham Blvd., Ste. 200, Los Angeles, CA 90068, Ph: (323)512-2225, Fax: (323)512-2224. **Founded:** 1940. **ADI:** Las Vegas, NV. **Wattage:** 10,000 KW. **Ad Rates:** $120-175 per unit. **URL:** http://www.lvsportsnetwork.com.

2997 ■ KFTR-TV - 11
5999 Center Dr.
Los Angeles, CA 90045
Phone: (219)665-6427
Format: Commercial TV. **Networks:** Independent. **Owner:** Marina D. Leathers, at above address. **Wattage:** 370,000 ERP.

2998 ■ KFWB-AM - 980
5670 Wilshire Blvd., Ste. 200
Los Angeles, CA 90036
Phone: (323)569-1070
Format: News; Talk. **Networks:** CNN Radio; AP. **Founded:** 1925. **Operating Hours:** Continuous; 30% network, 70% local. **ADI:** Los Angeles (Corona & San Bernardino), CA. **Wattage:** 5,000. **Ad Rates:** Advertising accepted; rates available upon request. **URL:** http://kfwbam.com/2014/10/02/hilary-knight-to-join-ducks-in-practice.

2999 ■ KGBT-AM
5999 Center Dr.
Los Angeles, CA 90045
Phone: (512)423-3910
Fax: (512)425-4930
Format: Hispanic. **Networks:** Independent. **Founded:** 1941. **Wattage:** 50,000 Day; 10,000 N. **Ad Rates:** $18-60 for 30 seconds; $22-75 for 60 seconds.

KGST-AM - See Fresno

KHIT-AM - See Reno

KHIT-FM - See Madera

3000 ■ KHSC-TV - 46
5999 Center Dr.
Los Angeles, CA 90045
Phone: (310)348-3600
Format: Commercial TV. **Networks:** Home Shopping Network. **Owner:** Silver King Communications, 2425 Olympic Blvd., Santa Monica, CA 90404, Ph: (310)247-7930. **Founded:** 1986. **Formerly:** KIHS-TV. **Operating Hours:** Continuous. **ADI:** Los Angeles (Corona & San Bernardino), CA. **Key Personnel:** Bart Pearce, Station Mgr.; Julio Brito, Chief Engineer; Brian Walek, Operations Mgr., Traffic Mgr. **Ad Rates:** Advertising accepted; rates available upon request. **URL:** http://www.univision.com.

3001 ■ KIDD-AM - 630
1500 Conter Ave.
Los Angeles, CA 90001
Phone: (831)649-0969
Fax: (831)649-3335
Free: 800-550-3663
Email: kkhal@magic63.com
Format: Adult Contemporary. **Simulcasts:** KXDC-FM. **Networks:** Independent. **Owner:** Buckley Communications, Inc., 166 W Putnam Ave., Greenwich, CT 06830, Ph: (203)661-4307, Fax: (203)622-7341. **Founded:** 1963. **Formerly:** KXDC-AM; KWST-AM. **Operating Hours:** Continuous. **ADI:** Salinas-Monterey, CA. **Key Personnel:** Kevin Kahl, Contact. **Wattage:** 1,000. **Ad Rates:** $30-55 per unit.

KIOT-FM - See Los Lunas, NM

3002 ■ KJLA-TV - 57
2323 Corinth Ave.
Los Angeles, CA 90064
Phone: (310)943-5288
Fax: (310)943-5299
Free: 800-588-5788
Format: Commercial TV. **Operating Hours:** Continuous. **Key Personnel:** Francis X. Wilkinson, Gen. Mgr., fwilkinson@kjla.com. **Wattage:** 1,000,000 ERP H. **URL:** http://www.kjla.com.

3003 ■ KKGO-FM - 105.1
1500 Cotner Ave.
Los Angeles, CA 90025
Phone: (310)478-5540
Fax: (310)445-1439
Free: 866-479-1051
Email: mail@gocountry105.com
Format: Country. **Networks:** Independent. **Owner:** Mount Wilson FM Broadcasters Inc., at above address, Los Angeles, CA 90025. **Founded:** 1959. **Formerly:** KMZT-FM. **Operating Hours:** Continuous. **ADI:** Los Angeles (Corona & San Bernardino), CA. **Key Personnel:** Kane Biscaya, Gen. Sales Mgr.; Michael Levine, Dir. of Mktg. **Wattage:** 18,000. **Ad Rates:** Advertising accepted; rates available upon request. **URL:** http://www.gocountry105.com.

3004 ■ KKPN-FM - 102.9
5999 Centre Dr.
Los Angeles, CA 90045
Phone: (713)830-8000
Fax: (713)780-0036
Format: Full Service. **Owner:** WMXB-FM, 812 Moorefield Park Dr., Ste. 300, Richmond, VA 23236, Ph: (804)330-5700. **Founded:** 1960. **Formerly:** KQUE-FM. **ADI:** Houston, TX. **Key Personnel:** John Cook, Contact; Michael Nasser, Gen. Mgr.; Russell Lindley, Sales Mgr; John Cook, Contact; Mary Smith, Contact. **Wattage:** 99,500 ERP. **Ad Rates:** Accepts Advertising. **URL:** http://www.univision.com/houston/kltn.

3005 ■ KLAX-AM - 97.9
10281 W Pico Bl.
Los Angeles, CA 90064
Phone: (310)203-0900
Fax: (310)843-4969
Email: promociones@979laraza.com
Format: Hispanic. **Ad Rates:** Noncommercial. **URL:** http://www.979laraza.lamusica.com.

3006 ■ KLAX-FM - 97.9
10281 W Pico Blvd.
Los Angeles, CA 90064
Phone: (310)203-0900
Fax: (310)843-4969
Format: Hispanic. **Networks:** Spanish Broadcasting System. **Owner:** Spanish Broadcasting System Inc., Pablo Raul Alarcon Media Ctr., 7007 NW 77th Ave., Miami, FL 33166, Ph: (305)441-6901, Fax: (305)883-3375. **Founded:** 1987. **Formerly:** KSKQ-FM. **Operating Hours:** Continuous. **Wattage:** 50,000. **Ad Rates:** Noncommercial. **URL:** http://www.979laraza.lamusica.com.

3007 ■ KLCS-TV - 58
1061 W Temple St.
Los Angeles, CA 90012
Phone: (213)241-4000
Fax: (213)481-1019
Email: info@klcs.pbs.org
Format: Public TV. **Networks:** Public Broadcasting Service (PBS). **Owner:** Los Angeles Unified School District, 333 S Beaudry Ave., Los Angeles, CA 90017, Ph: (213)241-1000, Fax: (213)241-8442. **Founded:** 1973. **Operating Hours:** Continuous. **ADI:** Los Angeles (Corona & San Bernardino), CA. **Local Programs:** *Homework Hotline*, Tuesday Wednesday Thursday Friday Saturday Sunday Monday 10:30 a.m.; 10:30 p.m. 6:30 a.m.; 6:30 p.m.; 10:30 a.m.; 10:30 p.m. **Wattage:** 90,000 H ERP. **Ad Rates:** Noncommercial. Underwriting available. **URL:** http://www.klcs.org.

3008 ■ KLOS-FM - 95.5
3321 S La Cienega Blvd.
Los Angeles, CA 90016
Phone: (310)676-1149
Free: 800-955-5567
Format: Album-Oriented Rock (AOR). **Networks:** ABC. **Owner:** ABC Entertainment Group, 500 S Buena Vista St., Burbank, CA 91521-4588. **Founded:** 1957. **Formerly:** KABC-FM. **Operating Hours:** Continuous. **ADI:** Los Angeles (Corona & San Bernardino), CA. **Key Personnel:** Bill Sommers, Gen. Mgr., President; Leonard Madrid, Gen. Sales Mgr.; CW West, Promotions Mgr. **Wattage:** 63,100. **Ad Rates:** Advertising accepted; rates available upon request. **URL:** http://www.955klos.com/station-information.

3009 ■ KLYY-FM - 97.5
5700 Wilshire Blvd., Ste. 250
Los Angeles, CA 90036
Phone: (323)900-6100
Fax: (323)900-6127
Format: Hispanic. **Owner:** Entravision Communications Corporation, 2425 Olympic Blvd., Ste. 6000 W, Santa Monica, CA 90404-4030, Ph: (310)447-3870, Fax: (310)447-3899. **ADI:** Los Angeles (Corona & San Bernardino), CA. **Key Personnel:** Karl Meyer, Gen. Mgr. **URL:** http://www.entravision.com.

3010 ■ KMAX-FM - 107.1
5700 Wilshire Blvd., Ste. 250
Los Angeles, CA 90036
Phone: (323)900-6100
Fax: (818)351-6218
Format: Ethnic. **Networks:** Independent. **Founded:** 1960. **Operating Hours:** Continuous. **Key Personnel:** Glenn Vaagen, Dir. of Programs; Randy Byers, Promotions Dir.; Steve Grubbs, Sports Dir. **Wattage:** 6,000 ERP. **Ad Rates:** $15-70 for 30 seconds; $25-95 for 60 seconds. **URL:** http://www.superestrella.com.

3011 ■ KMEX-TV - 34
5999 Center Dr. W
Los Angeles, CA 90045
Phone: (310)348-3447
Fax: (310)348-3459
Format: Classic Rock. **Networks:** Univision. **Owner:** Univision Communications, Inc., at above address. **Founded:** 1962. **ADI:** Los Angeles (Corona & San Bernardino), CA. **Key Personnel:** Joe Uva, CEO. **Wattage:** 40,000 ERP Horizonta. **Ad Rates:** Accepts Advertising. **URL:** http://www.univision.com.

3012 ■ KNAC-FM
1700 N Alvarado St.
Los Angeles, CA 90026-1726
Founded: 1961. **Key Personnel:** Gary Price, Gen. Mgr. **Ad Rates:** $135-180 per unit. **URL:** http://www.knac.com.

3013 ■ KNX-AM - 1070
5670 Wilshire Blvd., Ste. 200
Los Angeles, CA 90036
Phone: (323)900-2070
Format: News. **Networks:** CBS. **Owner:** Infinity Broadcasting Corp., 1515 Broadway, 46th Fl., New York, NY 10036-8901, Ph: (212)846-3939. **Founded:** 1920. **Operating Hours:** Continuous. **ADI:** Los Angeles (Corona & San Bernardino), CA. **Local Programs:** *The Gabe Wisdom Show*, Tuesday Wednesday Thursday; *Food News*, Saturday Monday Tuesday Wednesday Thursday Friday 10:00 a.m. - 12:00 p.m. 12:57 p.m. **Wattage:**

Circulation: ★ = AAM; △ or • = BPA; ♦ = CAC; ❑ = VAC; ⊕ = PO Statement; ‡ = Publisher's Report; Boldface figures = sworn; Light figures = estimated.

50,000. **Ad Rates:** Advertising accepted; rates available upon request. **URL:** http://www.losangeles.cbslocal.com.

3014 ■ KPFK-FM - 90.7
3729 Cahuenga Blvd. W
North Hollywood, CA 91604
Phone: (818)985-2711
Fax: (818)763-7526
Format: Public Radio; News. **Networks:** Pacifica. **Owner:** Pacifica Foundation, 1925 Martin Luther King Jr. Way, Berkeley, CA 94704-1037, Ph: (510)849-2590. **Founded:** 1959. **Operating Hours**: Continuous. **Key Personnel:** Alan Minsky, Producer, aminsky@kpfk.org; Christine Blosdale, Producer, cblosdale@kpfk.org; Roy Tuckman, Producer, rtuckman@kpfk.org; Terry Guy, Dir. of Member Svcs., tguy@kpfk.org. **Local Programs**: *Background Briefing*, Sunday Monday Tuesday Wednesday Thursday 11:00 a.m. - 12:00 p.m. 5:00 p.m. - 6:00 p.m.; *Restless Soul*, Monday 10:30 p.m. - 12:00 a.m.; *Pocho Hour of Power*, Friday 4:00 p.m. - 5:00 p.m. **Wattage**: 110,000. **Ad Rates:** Noncommercial. **URL:** http://www.kpfk.org.

KPLY-AM - See Reno, NV

KPSC-FM - See Palm Springs, CA

3015 ■ KPXN-TV - 30
2600 Olive Ave., Ste. 900
Burbank, CA 91505
Phone: (818)563-1005
Fax: (818)524-1999
Key Personnel: Brandon Burgess, Chairman, CEO. **Ad Rates:** Noncommercial. **URL:** http://www.ionmedia.tv.

3016 ■ KQSR-FM
4311 Wilshire Blvd.
Los Angeles, CA 90010
Phone: (928)344-4980
Fax: (928)344-4983
Format: Classical; Soft Rock. **Founded:** Sept. 15, 2006. **Wattage**: 3,000 ERP. **Ad Rates:** Noncommercial.

KRCD-FM - See Chubbuck

3017 ■ KRCD-FM
5999 Center Dr.
Los Angeles, CA 90045
Phone: (818)500-4500
Format: Hispanic. **Owner:** Univision Communications Inc., 5999 Center Dr., Los Angeles, CA 90045, Ph: (310)556-7676, Fax: (310)556-3568. **Founded:** 1998. **Wattage**: 4,100 ERP.

3018 ■ KRCV-FM
5999 Center Dr.
Los Angeles, CA 90045
Phone: (818)500-4500
Format: Hispanic. **Owner:** Univision Communications Inc., 5999 Center Dr., Los Angeles, CA 90045, Ph: (310)556-7676, Fax: (310)556-3568. **Wattage**: 6,000 ERP.

3019 ■ KRLA-AM - 870
4880 Santa Rosa Rd., Ste. 300
Camarillo, CA 93012
Phone: (805)987-0400
Free: 800-499-5552
Format: Talk; News; Information. **Owner:** Salem Media Group Inc., 4880 Santa Rosa Rd., Camarillo, CA 93012, Ph: (805)987-0400, Fax: (805)384-4520. **Founded:** 1928. **Formerly**: KIEV-AM. **Operating Hours**: Continuous. **Local Programs:** *A Touch of Grey*, Sunday 12:00 p.m. - 1:00 p.m. **Wattage**: 20,000 Day; 3,000 Night. **Ad Rates:** Advertising accepted; rates available upon request. **URL:** http://salemmedia.com.

3020 ■ KRLV-AM - 1340
3301 Barham Blvd., Ste., 200
Los Angeles, CA 90068
Phone: (702)739-9600
Fax: (702)739-0083
Free: 800-227-7685
Format: News; Educational; Sports. **Networks:** Fox; NBC; ESPN Radio; ABC. **Founded:** 1962. **Formerly**: KRAM-AM; KMTW-AM. **Operating Hours**: Continuous; 100% network. **ADI:** Las Vegas, NV. **Local Programs**: *Nutricion Al Dia*, Monday Tuesday Wednesday Thursday Friday Saturday 10:00 a.m. - 12:00 p.m. **Wattage**: 1,000. **Ad Rates:** $5-15 per unit. **URL:** http://www.lvsportsnetwork.com/fox-sports.

3021 ■ KROQ-FM - 106.7
5901 Venice Blvd.
Los Angeles, CA 90034
Phone: (323)930-1067
Format: Album-Oriented Rock (AOR); Alternative/New Music/Progressive. **Networks:** Independent. **Owner:** CBS Radio Inc., 1271 Avenue of the Americas, 44th Fl., New York, NY 10020-1401, Ph: (212)649-9600. **Founded:** 1974. **Operating Hours**: Continuous. **ADI**: Los Angeles (Corona & San Bernardino), CA. **Wattage**: 5,600. **Ad Rates:** Noncommercial. **URL:** http://www.kroq.cbslocal.com.

3022 ■ KRTH-FM - 101.1
5670 Wilshire Blvd., Ste. 200
Los Angeles, CA 90036
Phone: (323)936-5784
Fax: (323)933-6072
Free: 800-232-5784
Format: Oldies. **Networks:** Westwood One Radio. **Owner:** CBS Radio Inc., 1271 Avenue of the Americas, 44th Fl., New York, NY 10020-1401, Ph: (212)649-9600. **Founded:** 1941. **Operating Hours**: Continuous. **ADI**: Los Angeles (Corona & San Bernardino), CA. **Wattage**: 51,000. **Ad Rates:** Noncommercial. **URL:** http://www.kearth101.cbslocal.com.

3023 ■ KSPN-AM
800 W Olympic Blvd.
Los Angeles, CA 90015
Phone: (213)284-7100
Free: 877-710-3776
Format: Sports. **Key Personnel:** Chris Berry, Gen. Mgr.; Larry Gifford, Dir. of Programs; Bill Lennert, Dir. of Mktg. **Wattage**: 50,000 Day; 10,000 N. **Ad Rates:** Advertising accepted; rates available upon request. **URL:** http://sports.espn.go.com/stations/710espn/.

3024 ■ KSSC-FM - 107.1
5700 Wilshire Blvd., Ste. 250
Los Angeles, CA 90036
Phone: (323)900-6100
Fax: (323)900-6119
Format: Hispanic. **Owner:** Entravision Radio, Los Angeles, at above address. **Key Personnel:** Walter F. Ulloa, Chairman, CEO. **Ad Rates:** Advertising accepted; rates available upon request. **URL:** http://www.entravision.com.

KSSE-FM - See Arcadia

3025 ■ KTFF-TV - 61
5999 Center Dr.
Los Angeles, CA 90045

3026 ■ KTKT-AM - 990
3301 Barham Blvd., Ste. 200
Los Angeles, CA 90068
Phone: (323)461-8225
Format: News; Oldies; Eighties. **Networks:** CNN Radio. **Owner:** Lotus Communications, at above address. **Founded:** 1949. **Operating Hours**: Continuous. **ADI**: Tucson, AZ. **Key Personnel:** Jim Cooley, Gen. Mgr. **Wattage**: 10,000 KW. **Ad Rates:** $20-25 for 60 seconds. **URL:** http://www.ktkt99.com.

3027 ■ KTLA-TV - 5
5800 Sunset Blvd.
Los Angeles, CA 90028
Phone: (323)460-5500
Fax: (323)460-5333
Format: Commercial TV. **Owner:** Tribune Broadcasting, 7700 Westpark Dr., Houston, TX 77063. **Founded:** Jan. 22, 1947. **Operating Hours**: Continuous. **ADI**: Los Angeles (Corona & San Bernardino), CA. **Local Programs:** *KTLA Morning News*, Monday Tuesday Wednesday Thursday Friday Saturday Sunday 4:00 a.m. - 10:00 a.m.; 1:00 p.m. - 2:00 p.m.; 6:00 p.m. - 7:00 p.m.; 10:00 p.m. - 11:00 p.m. 5:00 a.m. - 7:00 a.m.; 6:00 p.m. - 7:00 p.m.; 10:00 p.m. - 11:00 p.m. 6:00 a.m. - 9:00 a.m.; 6:00 p.m. - 7:00 p.m.; 8:00 p.m. - 11:00 p.m.; *KTLA 5 Morning News at 9am*, Monday Tuesday Wednesday Thursday Friday 9:00 a.m. - 10:00 a.m.; *KTLA 5 News at 6*, Monday Tuesday Wednesday Thursday Friday 6:00 p.m. - 6:30 p.m.; *KTLA 5 News at 1*, Monday Tuesday Wednesday Thursday Friday 1:00 p.m. - 2:00 p.m.; *KTLA 5 News at 10*, Monday Tuesday Wednesday Thursday Friday 10:00 p.m. - 11:00 p.m. **Ad Rates:** Advertising accepted; rates available upon request. **URL:** http://www.ktla.com.

3028 ■ KTTV-TV - 11
1999 S Bundy Dr.
Los Angeles, CA 90025
Phone: (310)584-2000
Format: Commercial TV. **Networks:** Fox. **Owner:** Fox Television Stations Inc., 1211 Ave. of the Americas, 21st Fl., New York, NY 10036, Ph: (212)301-5400. **Founded:** 1949. **Operating Hours**: Continuous. **Key Personnel:** Pat Jones, VP, pat.jones@foxtv.com. **Local Programs**: *Good Day LA*, Monday Tuesday Wednesday Thursday Friday 7:00 a.m. - 10:00 a.m. **Ad Rates:** Advertising accepted; rates available upon request. **URL:** http://www.myfoxla.com.

3029 ■ KTWV-FM - 94.7
5670 Wilshire Blvd., Ste. 200
Los Angeles, CA 90036
Phone: (323)937-9283
Fax: (323)634-0947
Free: 800-520-9283
Format: Urban Contemporary; Adult Contemporary; Jazz. **Networks:** Independent. **Owner:** CBS Radio Inc., 1271 Avenue of the Americas, 44th Fl., New York, NY 10020-1401, Ph: (212)649-9600; CBS Radio Inc., 40 W 57th St., New York, NY 10019, Ph: (212)846-3939, Fax: (212)315-2162. **Founded:** Feb. 14, 1987. **Formerly**: KMET-FM. **Operating Hours**: Continuous. **Key Personnel:** Steve carver, Gen. Mgr.; Jhani Kaye, Dir. of Programs; John Bassanelli, Gen. Sales Mgr.; Ed Krampf, Gen. Mgr. of Mktg. & Sales; Lisa Hornick, Sales Mgr.; Jamie Kanai, Dir. of Mktg., Promotions Dir; Anita Dominguez, Contact. **Local Programs**: *The WAVE's Sunday Brunch*, Sunday; *Smooth Jazz Top 20 Countdown*. **Wattage**: 58,000. **Ad Rates:** Advertising accepted; rates available upon request. **URL:** http://947thewave.cbslocal.com.

3030 ■ KUSC-FM - 91.5
1149 S Hill St., Ste. H100
Los Angeles, CA 90015
Phone: (213)225-7400
Email: kusc@kusc.org
Format: Classical. **Networks:** National Public Radio (NPR). **Owner:** University of Southern California, University Park Campus, Los Angeles, CA 90089, Ph: (213)740-2311. **Founded:** 1946. **Operating Hours**: Continuous. **ADI**: Los Angeles (Corona & San Bernardino), CA. **Key Personnel:** Brenda Barnes, President, bbarnes@kusc.org. **Wattage**: 39,000 ERP. **Ad Rates:** Noncommercial. **URL:** http://www.kusc.org.

3031 ■ KVNR-AM - 1480
1845 Empire Ave.
Burbank, CA 91504
Phone: (818)729-5300
Email: lbiinfo@lbimedia.com
Format: News; Information. **Owner:** Liberman Broadcasting, Inc., 3000 Bering Dr., Houston, TX 77057. **URL:** http://www.lbimedia.com.

3032 ■ KWAC-AM - 1490
3301 Barham Blvd., Ste. 200
Los Angeles, CA 90068
Phone: (323)512-2225
Fax: (323)512-2224
Format: Hispanic. **Owner:** Lotus Bakersfield Corp., 5100 Commerce Dr., Bakersfield, CA 93309. **Founded:** 1963. **Operating Hours**: Continuous; 2% network, 98% local. **ADI**: Bakersfield, CA. **Wattage**: 1,000. **Ad Rates:** Advertising accepted; rates available upon request. **URL:** http://www.lotuscorp.com.

3033 ■ KWKW-AM - 1330
3301 Barham Blvd., Ste. 200
Los Angeles, CA 90068
Phone: (323)512-2225
Fax: (323)512-2224
Format: Talk; Hispanic; Sports. **Simulcasts:** KWKU-AM. **Networks:** Lotus. **Owner:** Lotus Communications, at above address. **Founded:** 1942. **Operating Hours**: Continuous. **Key Personnel:** John Paley, VP of Corp. Rel. **Local Programs**: *Nutricion Al Dia*, Monday Tuesday Wednesday Thursday Friday Saturday 10:00 a.m. - 12:00 p.m.; *Balon Latino Americano*; *La Maquina Deportiva*. **Ad Rates:** $51-196 for 30 seconds; $80-245 for 60 seconds. **URL:** http://www.lotuscorp.com.

3034 ■ KXLA-AM - 990
2323 Corinth Ave
Box 990
Los Angeles, CA 90064
Phone: (310)478-0055
Fax: (310)478-8070
Format: Gospel. **Networks:** American Urban Radio. **Owner:** Red Bear Management, 1990 N 18th Suite 330, Monroe, LA 71201, Ph: (318)361-0347, Fax: (318)361-9885. **Founded:** 1957. **Formerly**: KRIH-AM. **Operating Hours**: 6 a.m.-12 a.m.; 10% network, 90% local. **Wattage**: 1,000. **Ad Rates:** $8 for 30 seconds; $12 for 60 seconds. **URL:** http://www.kxlatv.com/contact.asp.

3035 ■ KXLA-TV - 44
2323 Corinth Ave.
Los Angeles, CA 90064
Phone: (310)478-0055
Fax: (310)478-8070
Key Personnel: Carolina Gonzalez, Traffic Mgr., cgonzalez@kxlatv.com. **URL:** http://www.kxlatv.com/index.asp.

3036 ■ KXLU-FM - 88.9
One LMU Dr.
Malone 402
Los Angeles, CA 90045
Phone: (310)338-2866
Format: Eclectic. **Owner:** Loyola Marymount University, One LMU Dr., Los Angeles, CA 90045-2659, Ph: (310)338-2700, Free: 800-568-4636. **Founded:** 1973. **Operating Hours**: Continuous. **ADI**: Los Angeles (Corona & San Bernardino), CA. **Key Personnel:** Maki Tamura, Chief Engineer, kxlumaki@gmail.com; Daniel Lees, Gen. Mgr., dankxlu@gmail.com; Alyssa Bailey, Dir. of Programs, alyssakxlu@gmail.com; Erin Walsh, Dir. of Programs, erinkxlu@gmail.com; Stefan Richter, Chief Engineer, stefankxlu@gmail.com. **Local Programs**: *Demolisten*, Friday 6:00 p.m. - 8:00 p.m.; *Neuz Pollution*, Wednesday 10:00 p.m. - 11:00 a.m.; *Psychotechnics*, Wednesday 12:00 a.m. - 2:00 a.m. **Wattage**: 3,000. **Ad Rates:** Noncommercial. **URL:** http://www.kxlu.com.

3037 ■ KXOL-FM - 96.3
10281 W Pico Blvd.
Los Angeles, CA 90064
Phone: (310)229-3200
Format: Hispanic; Contemporary Hit Radio (CHR). **ADI**: Los Angeles (Corona & San Bernardino), CA. **Wattage**: 6,600. **Ad Rates:** Advertising accepted; rates available upon request. **URL:** http://mega963fm.lamusica.com.

3038 ■ KXTF-TV - 35
4311 Wilshire Blvd.
Los Angeles, CA 90010
Phone: (208)733-0035
Fax: (208)733-0160
Format: Commercial TV. **Networks:** Fox; United Paramount Network. **Owner:** Sunbelt Communications Co., 1500 Foremaster Ln., Las Vegas, NV 89101, Ph: (702)642-3333, Fax: (702)657-3423. **Founded:** Oct. 23, 1995. **Operating Hours**: 6 a.m.-2 a.m. **Key Personnel:** Ted Meairs, Station Mgr., tmeairs@kxtf.com; Tom Nelson, Sales Mgr., tnelson@magiclink.com. **Ad Rates:** Advertising accepted; rates available upon request.

3039 ■ KYHT-FM
2501 West Ave.
Lancaster, CA 93536
Format: Adult Album Alternative; Alternative/New Music/Progressive. **Simulcasts:** KAVS-FM. **Owner:** Antelope Broadcasting Co., at above address. **Founded:** Nov. 1996. **Operating Hours**: Continuous. **ADI**: Los Angeles (Corona & San Bernardino), CA. **Key Personnel:** Ron Carter, President; Ivan Ladizinsky, Gen. Mgr.; Clay Roe, Dir. of Programs; Henry Schindel, Sales Mgr.; Larry Thornhill, Operations Mgr. **Wattage**: 25,000. **Ad Rates:** Advertising accepted; rates available upon request.

KYNS-AM - See San Luis Obispo

3040 ■ KZAP-FM - 96.7
10900 Wilshire Blvd.
Los Angeles, CA 90024
Phone: (530)899-3600
Fax: (530)895-3740
Email: info@club967.com
Format: Urban Contemporary. **Owner:** Mappleton License of Chico, LLC, at above address. **Founded:** 1977. **Operating Hours**: Continuous. **Key Personnel:** Robb Cheal, Gen. Mgr., VP. **Wattage**: 1,500. **Ad Rates:** Noncommercial. $10-14 per unit. **URL:** http://www.club967.com.

3041 ■ Radio Fiesta Network L.L.C. - 720
4887 Melrose Ave.
Los Angeles, CA 90029
Phone: (323)462-0903
Format: News; Talk. **Networks:** ABC. **Operating Hours**: Continuous. **ADI**: Los Angeles (Corona & San Bernardino), CA. **Wattage**: 10,000 Day; 184 Nigh. **Ad Rates:** Advertising accepted; rates available upon request. **URL:** http://www.radiofiestanetwork.com.

3042 ■ Time Warner Communications
900 N Cahuenga Blvd.
Los Angeles, CA 90038
Free: 888-892-2253
Owner: Time Warner Inc., 1 Time Warner Ctr., New York, NY 10019-8016, Ph: (212)484-8000. **Founded:** 1989. **Formerly**: Paragon Cable. **Key Personnel:** Robert D. Marcus, COO, President. **Cities Served**: subscribing households 130,000. **URL:** http://www.timewarnercable.com.

3043 ■ WLII-TV - 11
5999 Center Dr.
Los Angeles, CA 90045
Fax: (809)721-0777
Format: Commercial TV. **Networks:** Independent. **Founded:** 1960. **Key Personnel:** David E. Murphy, Contact. **Wattage**: 48,000 ERP.

3044 ■ WQBA-AM
5999 Center Dr.
Los Angeles, CA 90045
Phone: (305)441-2073
Fax: (305)445-8908
Format: Full Service; Talk; Hispanic. **Founded:** 1967. **Formerly**: WMIE-AM. **Key Personnel:** Claudia Puig, Gen. Mgr; Augustin Acosta, Contact. **Wattage**: 50,000 Day; 10,000 N. **Ad Rates:** $100 for 30 seconds; $150 for 60 seconds.

3045 ■ WQHS-TV - 61
5999 Center Dr.
Los Angeles, CA 90045
Phone: (440)888-0061
Fax: (440)888-7023
Format: Commercial TV. **Networks:** Home Shopping Network. **Founded:** Dec. 23, 1986. **Formerly**: WCLQ-TV. **Key Personnel:** Sharon Roman, Dir. of Operations, sharon.roman@prodigy.net. **Wattage**: 525,000 ERP.

3046 ■ WSUR-TV - 9 & 11
5999 Center Dr.
Los Angeles, CA 90045
Phone: (809)843-0910
Fax: (809)841-7358
Format: Commercial TV. **Networks:** Independent. **Owner:** TeleOnce Corp., Box S-4189, San Juan, Puerto Rico 00915. **Founded:** 1958. **Key Personnel:** Anne P. Jones, Contact. **Wattage**: 21,600 ERP.

WTAM-TV - See Tampa, FL

3047 ■ WUVC-TV - 40
1999 Avenue of the Stars, Ste. 3050
Los Angeles, CA 90067
Phone: (310)556-7676
Format: Commercial TV. **Networks:** Independent. **Owner:** Univision Communications, Inc., at above address. **Founded:** June 01, 1981. **Operating Hours**: Continuous. **ADI**: Raleigh-Durham, NC. **Key Personnel:** Jerrold A. Perenchio, CEO; Ray Rodriguez, COO; Douglas C. Kranwinkle, Gen. Counsel, Exec. VP. **Wattage**: 5,000,000. **Ad Rates:** Advertising accepted; rates available upon request. **URL:** http://www.corporate.univision.com.

LOS BANOS

C. CA. Merced Co. 60 mi. NW of Fresno. Creamery. Diversified farming. Dairying, alfalfa, vegetables, cotton, melons.

3048 ■ KLBS-AM - 1330
401 Pacheco Blvd.
Los Banos, CA 93635
Phone: (209)826-0578
Fax: (209)826-1906
Email: pr@klbs.com
Format: Ethnic. **Owner:** Coyote Communications Inc., PO Box 5015, Lakeland, FL 33807, Ph: (863)660-6825. **Founded:** 1961. **Operating Hours**: Continuous; 100% local. **Key Personnel:** Cidalia Sequeira Aguiar, Office Mgr., cidalia@klbs.com. **Wattage**: 5,000. **Ad Rates:** Noncommercial. **URL:** http://www.klbs.com.

3049 ■ KQLB-FM - 106.9
401-A Pacheco Blvd.
Los Banos, CA 93635
Phone: (209)827-0123
Fax: (209)826-1906
Format: Hispanic. **Owner:** VLB Broadcasting Inc., 401-A Pacheco Blvd., Los Banos, CA 93635-4227. **Wattage**: 6,000. **URL:** http://www.kqlb.com.

3050 ■ VLB Broadcasting Inc.
401-A Pacheco Blvd.
Los Banos, CA 93635-4227
URL: http://www.kqlb.com.

LOS GATOS

W. CA. Santa Clara Co. 50 mi. S. of San Francisco. Residential. Wineries. Nurseries. Prunes, appricots, peaches.

3051 ■ Los Gatos Weekly Times
Silicon Valley Community Newspapers
634 N Sta. Cruz Ave.
Los Gatos, CA 95030
Phone: (408)354-3110
Fax: (408)354-3917
Local newspaper. **Freq:** Weekly (Wed.). **Print Method:** Offset. **Cols./Page:** 5. **Col. Width:** 2 1/6 inches. **Col. Depth:** 13 1/4 inches. **Key Personnel:** Jeannette Close, Manager, Advertising, phone: (408)200-1069; Dale Bryant, Executive Editor, phone: (408)200-1021; David Cohen, Publisher; Tomasz Mackowiak, Manager, Circulation, phone: (408)200-1063; Dick Sparrer, Editor. **URL:** http://www.mercurynews.com/los-gatos. **Formerly**: Los Gatos Weekly; Los Gatos Times Observer. **Remarks:** Accepts advertising. **Circ:** Combined ♦**20912**.

3052 ■ K201FW-FM - 88.1
PO Box 391
Twin Falls, ID 83303
Fax: (208)736-1958
Free: 800-357-4226
Format: Religious; Contemporary Christian. **Owner:** CSN International, PO Box 391, Twin Falls, ID 83303, Ph: (208)736-1958, Fax: (208)736-1958, Free: 800-357-4226. **URL:** http://www.csnradio.com.

LOS OSOS

3053 ■ Rapa Nui Journal: The Journal of the Easter Island Foundation
Easter Island Foundation
PO Box 6774
Los Osos, CA 93412-6774
Phone: (805)528-8558
Publisher's E-mail: books@islandheritage.org
Professional journal covering Easter Island and East Polynesia history, archaeology, and anthropology. **Freq:** Semiannual. **Print Method:** Offset. **Trim Size:** 8 1/2 x 11. **Cols./Page:** 2. **Col. Width:** 3 1/2 inches. **Col. Depth:** 10 inches. **Key Personnel:** Georgia Lee, Advisor. **ISSN:** 1040-1385 (print). **Subscription Rates:** Included in membership. **Alt. Formats:** PDF. **URL:** http://islandheritage.org/wordpress/?page_id=295. **Remarks:** Accepts advertising. **Circ:** 400.

LOTUS

3054 ■ Journal of Rational Recovery
Rational Recovery Systems, Inc.
PO Box 800
Lotus, CA 95651
Phone: (530)621-2667
Freq: Quarterly. **ISSN:** 1065--2019 (print). **Remarks:** Accepts advertising. **Circ:** (Not Reported).

LOYALTON

NE CA. Sierra Co. 42 mi. NW of Reno, NV. Recreation. Sawmills. Gold mining. Cattle.

3055 ■ Sierra Booster
Plumas-Sierra Rural Electric Cooperative

Circulation: ★ = AAM; △ or • = BPA; ♦ = CAC; ❑ = VAC; ⊕ = PO Statement; ‡ = Publisher's Report; Boldface figures = sworn; Light figures = estimated.

PO Box 8
Loyalton, CA 96118
Phone: (530)933-4379
Local newspaper (tabloid). **Freq:** every other Friday. **Print Method:** Offset. **Trim Size:** 11 1/2 x 13. **Cols./Page:** 6. **Col. Width:** 1 5/8 inches. **Col. Depth:** 12 inches. **Key Personnel:** Janice W. Buck, Editor. **USPS:** 495-900. **Subscription Rates:** $20 Individuals; $32 Two years. **URL:** http://www.sierrabooster.com. **Ad Rates:** BW $345; PCI $4. **Remarks:** Accepts advertising. **Circ:** Paid ‡226, Free ‡930.

MADERA

SC CA. Madera Co. 22 mi. NW of Fresno. Manufactures air conditioners, wrought iron, fiber glass insulation, electronics, oil, lumber mills, wineries, sheet metal works, nursery, hatcheries. Granite quarry. Sugar pine timber. Chinchilla farms.

3056 ■ KHIT-FM - 107.1
3301 Barham Blvd., Ste. 200
Los Angeles, CA 90068
Phone: (323)512-2225
Fax: (323)512-2224
Format: Adult Contemporary; Hispanic. **Owner:** Lotus Communications, at above address. **Formerly:** KXOB-FM. **Key Personnel:** Howard A. Kalmenson, President, CEO; John Paley, VP of Corp. Rel.; William H. Shriftman, Sr. VP. **Wattage:** 9,900. **URL:** http://www.lotuscorp.com.

MALIBU

S. CA. Los Angeles Co. Adjacent to Santa Monica. Residential.

3057 ■ Dispute Resolution Law Journal
Pepperdine University School of Law
24255 Pacific Coast Hwy.
Malibu, CA 90263
Phone: (310)506-4611
Publisher's E-mail: lawadmis@pepperdine.edu
Journal containing intellectual discourse in the field of alternative dispute resolution. **Freq:** 3/year. **URL:** http://law.pepperdine.edu/dispute-resolution-law-journal. **Circ:** (Not Reported).

3058 ■ European Tool & Mould Making: The Trade Magazine for Tool, Mould & Die Making
Access Communications Inc.
30765 Pacific Coast Hwy., PMB 351
Malibu, CA 90265-3643
Magazine focusing on sourcing solutions and the tool and mold making industry. **Freq:** 9/year. **Key Personnel:** Britta Solloway, Manager, Sales. **Subscription Rates:** $150 Individuals; $275 Two years. **URL:** http://www.etmm-online.com. **Ad Rates:** BW €4,110; 4C €1,090. **Remarks:** Accepts advertising. **Circ:** (Not Reported).

3059 ■ Graphic
Pepperdine University
24255 Pacific Coast Hwy.
Malibu, CA 90263
Phone: (213)456-4000
Fax: (310)506-4411
Publication E-mail: graphic@pepperdine.edu
Collegiate newspaper. **Founded:** 1937. **Freq:** Weekly. **Print Method:** Offset. **Trim Size:** 13 x 21. **Cols./Page:** 6. **Col. Width:** 2 1/16 inches. **Col. Depth:** 21 inches. **Key Personnel:** Shannon Urtnowski, Editor-in-Chief. **URL:** http://pepperdine-graphic.com/. **Formerly:** The Graphic Weekly. **Ad Rates:** BW $900; 4C $1,400. **Remarks:** Accepts advertising. **Circ:** Free ‡3750.

3060 ■ Journal of Business, Entrepreneurship, and the Law
Pepperdine University School of Law
24255 Pacific Coast Hwy.
Malibu, CA 90263
Phone: (310)506-4611
Publisher's E-mail: lawadmis@pepperdine.edu
Journal containing articles from students, academics, practitioners, lawmakers, regulators, and entrepreneurs in the fields of business law and entrepreneurship. **Freq:** Semiannual. **Subscription Rates:** $28 Individuals; $15 Single issue. **URL:** http://law.pepperdine.edu/jbel. **Circ:** (Not Reported).

3061 ■ Journal of the National Association of Administrative Law Judiciary
Pepperdine University School of Law
24255 Pacific Coast Hwy.
Malibu, CA 90263
Phone: (310)506-4611
Publisher's E-mail: lawadmis@pepperdine.edu
Journal covering articles on developments affecting the administrative judiciary. **Freq:** Semiannual. **Key Personnel:** Samantha Koopman, Editor-in-Chief. **URL:** http://law.pepperdine.edu/naalj. **Circ:** (Not Reported).

3062 ■ Malibu
Malibu Monthly Inc.
23410 Civic Center Way, Ste. C-1
Malibu, CA 90265
Publication E-mail: subscriptions@malibumag.com
Magazine covering Malibu lifestyle. **Founded:** 2002. **Subscription Rates:** $29.95 Individuals; $4.95 Single issue. **URL:** http://www.malibumag.com/site. **Ad Rates:** BW $3,740; 4C $5,195. **Remarks:** Accepts advertising. **Circ:** Controlled 35000.

3063 ■ The Malibu Surfside News: Malibu News and Entertainment Voice
The Malibu Surfside News
28990 Pacific Coast Hwy., Ste. 108
Malibu, CA 90265
Phone: (310)457-2112
Publication E-mail: editor@malibusurfsidenews.com
Regional newspaper. **Freq:** Weekly (Wed.). **Print Method:** Offset. **Trim Size:** 10 1/2 x 14. **Cols./Page:** 6. **Col. Width:** 18 nonpareils. **Col. Depth:** 224 agate lines. **ISSN:** 0191--7307 (print). **Subscription Rates:** $95 Out of area; $150 Out of country; $25 Individuals online. **URL:** http://www.malibusurfsidenews.com. **Ad Rates:** BW $1,600; 4C $325; SAU $10; PCI $9. **Remarks:** Accepts advertising. **Circ:** Paid 13500.

3064 ■ Robb Report Collection: The Global Luxury Source
CurtCo Media Labs L.L.C.
29160 Heathercliff Rd., Ste. 200
Malibu, CA 90265
Phone: (310)589-7700
Fax: (310)589-7701
Free: 800-777-1851
Publication E-mail: editorial@robbreport.com
Magazine that covers the benefits of a luxury lifestyle. **Freq:** Monthly. **Subscription Rates:** $65 Individuals; C$75 Individuals; $100 Two years; C$120 Two years; $135 Individuals 3 years. **URL:** http://robbreport.com. **Remarks:** Accepts advertising. **Circ:** (Not Reported).

3065 ■ Robb Report: For the Luxury Lifestyle
CurtCo Media Labs L.L.C.
29160 Heathercliff Rd., Ste. 200
Malibu, CA 90265
Phone: (310)589-7700
Fax: (310)589-7701
Free: 800-777-1851
Publication E-mail: webfeedback@curtco.com
Lifestyle magazine focusing on vintage and exotic automobiles, lifestyle and interiors, upscale travel, boating, investment opportunities, technology, profiles, and recreation. **Freq:** Monthly. **Print Method:** Offset. **Trim Size:** 8.125" x 10.8125". **Cols./Page:** 3. **Col. Width:** 2 1/4 inches. **Col. Depth:** 9 3/4 inches. **Key Personnel:** Dan Phillips, Publisher, fax: (978)263-3812. **ISSN:** 0279--1447 (print). **Subscription Rates:** $65 Individuals 1 year, 12 issues, print; $100 Individuals 2 years, 24 issues, print; $135 Individuals 3 years, 36 issues, print; $120 Canada 2 years; $105 Other countries; $180 Other countries 2 years. **URL:** http://www.robbreport.com. **Remarks:** Advertising accepted; rates available upon request. **Circ:** Paid ‡104206.

3066 ■ Robb Report Home Entertainment: The Finest in Audio/Video Technology & Design
CurtCo Media Labs L.L.C.
29160 Heathercliff Rd., Ste. 200
Malibu, CA 90265
Phone: (310)589-7700
Fax: (310)589-7701
Free: 800-777-1851
Publication E-mail: theed@homeentertainmentmag.com
Magazine that covers home theaters, home automation systems, architecture and interior design. **Subscription Rates:** $15 Individuals. **URL:** http://www.hedmag.com. **Circ:** (Not Reported).

3067 ■ KWVS-FM - 101.5
24255 Pacific Coast Hwy.
Malibu, CA 90263-4211
Phone: (310)506-4000
Email: info@mysite.com
Format: Contemporary Christian. **Key Personnel:** Brittany Pearce, Dir. of Programs, brittany.pearce@pepperdine.edu; Karen Yang, Station Mgr., karen.yang@pepperdine.edu; Lida Manukyan, News Dir., lida.manukyan@pepperdine.edu; Amanda Kopang, Contact, amanda.kopang@pepperdine.edu. **Wattage:** 100. **Ad Rates:** Noncommercial. **URL:** http://radiopepperdine.wix.com/pepperdinekwvsradio.

MAMMOTH LAKES

E. CA. Mono Co. 120 mi. S. of Carson City, NV. Mountain and winter sports resort. Manufactures air pumps, cement and archery products.

3068 ■ Mammoth Times: Eastern Sierra Times
New Times Publishing Inc.
452 Old Mammoth Rd., 2nd Fl.
Mammoth Lakes, CA 93546
Phone: (760)934-3929
Fax: (760)934-3951
Weekly community newspaper. **Freq:** Weekly (Thurs.). **Print Method:** Web offset. **Trim Size:** 10 3/4 x 14 1/2. **Cols./Page:** 4. **Col. Width:** 2 1/4 inches. **Col. Depth:** 13 1/4 inches. **Key Personnel:** Aleksandra Gajewski, Publisher, Editor. **Subscription Rates:** $38 Individuals print; $64 Out of area print; $24 Individuals online. **URL:** http://www.mammothtimes.com. **Mailing address:** PO Box 3929, Mammoth Lakes, CA 93546. **Ad Rates:** BW $710. **Remarks:** Advertising accepted; rates available upon request. **Circ:** ‡7500.

3069 ■ KMMT-FM - 106.5
94 Laurel Mountain Rd.
Mammoth Lakes, CA 93546
Phone: (760)934-8888
Email: info@kmmtradio.com
Format: Top 40. **Networks:** Mutual Broadcasting System. **Owner:** Mammoth Mountain FM Associates Inc., at above address. **Founded:** 1973. **Operating Hours:** Continuous. **Key Personnel:** Dave Digerness, Owner; Paul Payne, Div. Mgr.; Lisa Meuret, Dir. of Programs. **Wattage:** 75,000. **Ad Rates:** $12 for 30 seconds; $14 for 60 seconds. **Mailing address:** PO Box 1284, Mammoth Lakes, CA 93546. **URL:** http://www.kmmtradio.com.

3070 ■ KRHV-FM - 93.3
94 Laurel Mountain Rd.
Mammoth Lakes, CA 93546
Phone: (760)934-8888
Format: Classic Rock. **Owner:** Dave and Maryann Digerness. **Operating Hours:** Continuous. **Key Personnel:** Paul Payne, Sales Mgr., Station Mgr.; Lisa Meuret, Dir. of Programs. **Ad Rates:** Advertising accepted; rates available upon request. **Mailing address:** PO Box 1284, Mammoth Lakes, CA 93546. **URL:** http://www.kmmtradio.com.

MANTECA

C. CA. San Joaquin Co. 12 mi. S. of Stockton. Manufactures electronic components. Wineries. Diversified farming.

3071 ■ Manteca Bulletin
Manteca Bulletin Daily Newspaper
531 E Yosemite Ave.
Manteca, CA 95336
Phone: (209)249-3500
Fax: (209)249-3551
Publisher's E-mail: news@mantecabulletin.com
Newspaper with a local orientation. **Freq:** Daily. **Print Method:** Offset. **Trim Size:** 12 1/2 x 22 3/4. **Cols./Page:** 6. **Col. Width:** 11.2 picas. **Col. Depth:** 294 agate lines. **Key Personnel:** Jennifer Marek, Publisher; Dennis Wyatt, Managing Editor, phone: (209)249-3532. **Subscription Rates:** $84 Individuals online; $104 Individuals print and online. **URL:** http://mantecabulletin.com. **Remarks:** Accepts advertising. **Circ:** Paid ■ **5660**.

MARINA DEL REY

S. CA. Los Angeles Co. 13 mi. SW of Los Angeles. Residential. Recreation and tourist areas. Small craft harbor.

3072 ■ The Structural Design of Tall and Special Buildings
John Wiley & Sons Inc.
c/o Gary C. Hart, Ed.
Department of Civil & Environmental Engineering, University of California
Principal of Weidlinger Associates, Inc.
4551 Glencoe Ave., Ste. 350
Marina del Rey, CA 90292
Publisher's E-mail: info@wiley.com
Journal containing information on the structural design and construction of tall buildings. **Freq:** 18/year. **Trim Size:** 7 7/8 x 10 1/4. **Key Personnel:** Nabih Youssef, Associate Editor; Gregg E. Brandow, Board Member; Gary C. Hart, Editor; Jefferson Asher, Board Member; Lauren D. Carpenter, Board Member; John A. Martin, Jr., Board Member. **ISSN:** 1541--7794 (print); **EISSN:** 1541--7808 (electronic). **Subscription Rates:** $1653 Institutions online only - USA/Canada & Mexico/ROW; £846 Institutions online only - UK; €1068 Institutions online only - Europe. **URL:** http://onlinelibrary.wiley.com/journal/10.1002/(ISSN)1541-7808. **Formerly:** The Structural Design of Tall Buildings. **Remarks:** Advertising accepted; rates available upon request. **Circ:** (Not Reported).

MARIPOSA

C. CA. Mariposa Co. 6 mi. N. of Fresno. Tourist. Lumber. Mining. Cattle.

3073 ■ Mariposa Gazette and Miner
Mariposa Gazette and Miner
5108 Hwy. 140
Mariposa, CA 95338
Phone: (209)966-2500
Fax: (209)966-3384
Publisher's E-mail: editor@mariposagazette.com
Community newspaper. **Freq:** Weekly (Thurs.). **Print Method:** Offset. **Cols./Page:** 6. **Col. Width:** 12.5 picas. **Col. Depth:** 21.5 inches. **Key Personnel:** Tracy Guenthart, Office Manager; Erik Skindrud, Editor; R.D. Tucker, Publisher. **Subscription Rates:** $36.50 Individuals; $21 Individuals 6 months; $52 Out of area; $29 Out of area 6 months. **URL:** http://www.mariposagazette.com. **Mailing address:** PO Box 38, Mariposa, CA 95338. **Ad Rates:** BW $1,000; 4C $1,340; PCI $12.75. **Remarks:** Accepts advertising. **Circ:** Paid ‡5300.

3074 ■ K214CT-FM - 90.7
PO Box 391
Twin Falls, ID 83303
Fax: (208)736-1958
Free: 800-357-4226
Format: Religious; Contemporary Christian. **Owner:** CSN International, PO Box 391, Twin Falls, ID 83303, Ph: (208)736-1958, Fax: (208)736-1958, Free: 800-357-4226. **Key Personnel:** Don Mills, Prog. Dir., Music Dir.; Kelly Carlson, Dir. of Engg.; Ray Gorney, Asst. Dir. **Wattage:** 010. **URL:** http://www.csnradio.com.

MARTINEZ

W. CA. Contra Costa Co. On Strait of Carquinez, 20 mi. by water NE of San Francisco. Boat connections. Oil refineries. Copper smelter. Wineries. Chemicals, valves.

3075 ■ Contra Costa News Register
Contra Costa News Register
617 Main St.
Martinez, CA 94553-1226
Phone: (925)229-2910
Fax: (925)934-2532
Legal and business newspaper. **Freq:** Semiweekly Tuesday and Friday. **Cols./Page:** 3. **Col. Width:** 28 nonpareils. **Col. Depth:** 182 agate lines. **Subscription Rates:** Free. **URL:** http://www.ccnewsregister.com. **Remarks:** Advertising not accepted. **Circ:** ‡500.

3076 ■ Martinez News-Gazette
Gibson Publications Inc.
615 Estudillo St.
Martinez, CA 94553
Phone: (925)228-6400
Fax: (925)228-1536
Community newspaper covering local news. **Freq:** 3/week Tues, Thursday, and Sun. (morn.). **Print Method:** Web. **Cols./Page:** 6. **Col. Width:** 12 picas. **Col. Depth:** 21 inches. **Key Personnel:** David L. Payne, President, Publisher; Jenny Croghan, General Manager, Managing Editor. **USPS:** 363-220. **Subscription Rates:** $54 Individuals; $16 Out of area monthly (mailed). **Ad Rates:** GLR $.20; PCI $6.95. **Remarks:** Accepts advertising. **Circ:** Free ■ **6791**, Paid ■ **2201**, Combined ■ **8992**.

MARYSVILLE

NC CA. Yuba Co. On Feather River, 50 mi. N. of Sacramento. Yuba College. Fruit canning and drying; quick freezing plant, logging, welding, boat works. Manufactures fishing tackle, trailers, gunstocks; Fruit, dairying, cattle raising.

3077 ■ Appeal Democrat
Vista California News Media
PO Box 431
Marysville, CA 95901
Phone: (530)741-2345
Free: 800-831-2345
Publication E-mail: info@appealdemocrat.com
General newspaper. **Freq:** Daily (eve.) and Sat. (morn.). **Print Method:** Offset. **Cols./Page:** 6. **Col. Width:** 26 nonpareils. **Col. Depth:** 294 agate lines. **Key Personnel:** Glenn Stifflemire, Publisher; Ursula Myers, Accountant, phone: (530)749-4774; Donna Blair, Director, Human Resources, phone: (530)749-4781. **Subscription Rates:** $144 Individuals 1 year online; $72 Individuals 6 months online; $36 Individuals 3 months online; $12 Individuals 1 month online; $162 Individuals 1 year online+print; $81 Individuals 6 months online+print; $40.50 Individuals 3 months online+print; $13.50 Individuals 1 month online+print. **URL:** http://www.appeal-democrat.com. **Remarks:** Accepts classified advertising. **Circ:** Mon.-Sat. ♦**15048**, Sun. ♦**15684**.

3078 ■ Arts
Yuba-Sutter Regional Arts Council
624 and 630 E St.
Marysville, CA 95901
Phone: (530)742-2787
Publisher's E-mail: email@yubasutterarts.org
Magazine featuring arts information and community calendars for the Yuba-Sutter Regional Arts Council. **Freq:** Bimonthly. **URL:** http://yubasutterarts.org/?section=about&page=newsletter.php. **Circ:** (Not Reported).

3079 ■ Corning Observer
Freedom Communications Inc.
1530 Ellis Lake Drive
Marysville, CA 95901
Phone: (530)749-4700
Publisher's E-mail: info@freedom.com
General newspaper. **Freq:** Triweekly. **Print Method:** Offset. **Cols./Page:** 6. **Col. Width:** 26 nonpareils. **Col. Depth:** 301 agate lines. **Key Personnel:** Paula Patton, Publisher; Julie Johnson, Reporter. **USPS:** 132-940. **URL:** http://www.appeal-democrat.com/corning_observer. **Ad Rates:** SAU $4.76; PCI $3.61. **Remarks:** Accepts advertising. **Circ:** 648.

MENDOCINO

3080 ■ KAKX-FM - 89.3
PO Box 769
Mendocino, CA 95460
Owner: Mendocino High School, 10700 Ford St., Mendocino, CA 95460. **Operating Hours:** Continuous. **Key Personnel:** Marshall Brown, Mgr., marshall@kakx.org. **Wattage:** 250 Vertical. ERP. **Ad Rates:** Accepts Advertising. **URL:** http://www.kakx.org/news/.

3081 ■ KPMO-AM - 1300
14200 Prairie Way
Mendocino, CA 95460
Phone: (541)552-6301
Free: 800-782-6191
Format: Talk; Information; Folk; Full Service; Jazz; Religious. **Owner:** Jefferson Public Radio, 1250 Siskiyou Blvd., Ashland, OR 97520, Ph: (541)552-6301, Free: 800-782-6191. **Founded:** 1966. **Operating Hours:** Continuous. **Wattage:** 5,000. **Ad Rates:** $8.25-9.50 for 30 seconds; $10.25-11.50 for 60 seconds. $8.25-$9.50 for 30 seconds; $10.25-$11.50 for 60 seconds. Combined advertising rates available with KMFB-FM. **URL:** http://ijpr.org.

MENIFEE

3082 ■ Bayou Talk
Jo Val Inc.
27101 Yorba Linda Ct.
Menifee, CA 92584
Publisher's E-mail: submissions@bayoutalk.com
Cajun Creole community newspaper. **Freq:** Monthly. **Key Personnel:** Louis H. Metoyer, Editor. **URL:** http://bayoutalk.com. **Ad Rates:** PCI $15. **Remarks:** Accepts advertising. **Circ:** Paid 3000, Non-paid 3000.

MENLO PARK

W. CA. San Mateo Co. 1 mi. NW of Palo Alto. St. Patrick's Seminary (men). Stanford Research Institute. Residential. Electronics manufactured.

3083 ■ Communication Arts Magazine
Communication Arts
110 Constitution Dr.
Menlo Park, CA 94025
Phone: (650)326-6040
Fax: (650)326-1648
Magazine covering design, advertising, photography, illustration, and multimedia. **Freq:** 6/year. **Print Method:** Web offset. **Trim Size:** 8 5/8 x 10 7/8. **Cols./Page:** 2. **Col. Width:** 41 nonpareils. **Col. Depth:** 140 agate lines. **ISSN:** 0010--3519 (print). **Subscription Rates:** $53 U.S. print and digital; $70 Canada print and digital; $110 Other countries print and digital; $199 Other countries 2 years, print and digital; $30 Individuals digital. **URL:** http://www.commarts.com. **Ad Rates:** BW $8280; 4C $11330. **Remarks:** Accepts advertising. **Circ:** Paid ⋆**62504**.

3084 ■ Gentry Magazine
18 Media Inc.
1162 El Camino Real
Menlo Park, CA 94025
Phone: (650)324-1818
Publication E-mail: edit@18media.com
Consumer magazine covering Northern California people, community, and homes. **Freq:** Monthly. **Print Method:** Web. **Key Personnel:** Mike Kanemura, Manager, Production. **Alt. Formats:** PDF. **URL:** http://www.18media.com. **Ad Rates:** 4C $3,395. **Remarks:** Accepts advertising. **Circ:** Combined ‡36150.

3085 ■ Palo Alto Daily News
The Daily News
255 Constitution Dr.
Menlo Park, CA 94025-1108
Publication E-mail: letters@dailynewsgroup.com
General newspaper. **Freq:** Tue.-Sat. **Print Method:** Offset. **Key Personnel:** Tomasz Mackowiak, Manager, Circulation, phone: (408)200-1063; Mario Dianda, Editor, phone: (650)391-1342. **URL:** http://www.mercurynews.com/peninsula. **Remarks:** Advertising accepted; rates available upon request. **Circ:** Paid 18500.

3086 ■ The Pharos
Alpha Omega Alpha Honor Medical Society
525 Middlefield Rd., Ste. 130
Menlo Park, CA 94025
Phone: (650)329-0291
Fax: (650)329-1618
Publisher's E-mail: info@alphaomegaalpha.org
Scholarly journal featuring non-technical articles on broad aspects of medicine, including history, ethics, medical care, and education. **Freq:** Quarterly. **Trim Size:** 8 1/2 x 11. **Cols./Page:** 3. **Col. Width:** 2 1/4 inches. **Col. Depth:** 8 1/4 inches. **Key Personnel:** Dr. Robert Glaser, Editor; Debbie Lancaster, Managing Editor. **ISSN:** 0031--7179 (print). **URL:** http://www.alphaomegaalpha.org/the_pharos.html. **Remarks:** Advertising not accepted. **Circ:** Controlled 70000, 72000.

3087 ■ Reviews of Accelerator Science and Technology
World Scientific Publishing Company Inc.
c/o Alexander W. Chao, Editor
National Accelerator Laboratory
2575 Sand Hill Rd.
Menlo Park, CA 94025
Publisher's E-mail: wspc@wspc.com
Peer-reviewed journal covering the field of accelerator science and technology. **Freq:** Annual. **Key Personnel:** Alexander W. Chao, Editor; Weiren Chou, Editor. **ISSN:** 1793--6268 (print); **EISSN:** 1793--8058 (electronic).

Circulation: ⋆ = AAM; △ or • = BPA; ♦ = CAC; ❑ = VAC; ⊕ = PO Statement; ‡ = Publisher's Report; Boldface figures = sworn; Light figures = estimated.

Subscription Rates: $229 Institutions print + electronic; $204 Institutions electronic only; £145 Institutions print + electronic; £129 Institutions electronic only; S$346 Institutions print + electronic; S$308 Institutions electronic only. **URL:** http://www.worldscientific.com/worldscinet/rast. **Circ:** (Not Reported).

3088 ■ Sunset Magazine: The Magazine of Western Living
Sunset Publishing Corp.
80 Willow Rd.
Menlo Park, CA 94025-3661
Phone: (650)321-3600
Free: 800-777-0117
Publisher's E-mail: readerletters@sunset.com
Magazine covering western homes, gardens, food and travel (5 regional editions). **Freq:** Monthly. **Print Method:** Letterpress and offset. **Trim Size:** 8 x 10 3/4. **Cols./Page:** 3. **Col. Width:** 27 nonpareils. **Col. Depth:** 140 agate lines. **Key Personnel:** Brian Gruseke, Publisher, phone: (212)526-5386. **ISSN:** 0039--5404 (print). **Subscription Rates:** $16 Individuals print and online. **URL:** http://www.sunset.com/magazine. **Ad Rates:** BW $132,800. **Remarks:** Accepts advertising. **Circ:** Paid 1265934.

3089 ■ KPPL-FM
Menlo Park, CA
Phone: (415)324-8464
Owner: KPPL-FM, Menlo Park, CA, Ph: (415)324-8464. **Wattage:** 25,000 ERP.

MERCED

C. CA. Merced Co. 55 mi. N. of Fresno. Manufactures pharmaceuticals. Dairy products cannery. Nurseries. Pine timber, diversified farming, alfalfa, peaches sweet potatoes, tomatoes, walnuts, almonds, rice. Cattle.

3090 ■ Current Anthropology
The University of Chicago Press
c/o Mark Aldenderfer, Ed.
University of California, Merced
The University of Arizona
School of Social Science, Humanities & Arts
Merced, CA 95343
Phone: (209)228-4418
Fax: (209)228-4007
Publication E-mail: curranth@ucdavis.edu
Journal presenting research, theory, and critical analysis in anthropology and related subdisciplines. **Freq:** 6/year. **Print Method:** Offset. **Trim Size:** 8 1/2 x 11. **Cols./Page:** 2. **Col. Width:** 40 nonpareils. **Col. Depth:** 116 agate lines. **Key Personnel:** Mark Aldenderfer, Editor; Jose Luis Lanata, Editor; Lisa McKamy, Managing Editor, phone: (773)753-2294, fax: (773)753-4247. **ISSN:** 0011--3204 (print); **EISSN:** 1537--5382 (electronic). **Subscription Rates:** $79 Individuals print and electronic; $46 Individuals electronic only; $47 Individuals print only; $158 Two years print and electronic; $92 Two years electronic only; $94 Two years print only. **URL:** http://www.press.uchicago.edu/ucp/journals/journal/ca.html; http://www.jstor.org/journal/curranth. **Ad Rates:** BW $730. **Remarks:** Accepts advertising. **Circ:** ‡1246.

3091 ■ E-Z Shopper
E-Z Shopper
PO Box 9210
Merced, CA 95344
Phone: (209)935-5313
Shopping guide (tabloid). **Freq:** Weekly. **Print Method:** Offset. **Trim Size:** 10 1/2 x 11. **Cols./Page:** 6. **Col. Width:** 1 1/2 inches. **Col. Depth:** 10 inches. **Subscription Rates:** Free. **Ad Rates:** BW $25.90. **Remarks:** Accepts advertising. **Circ:** Free ‡131000.

3092 ■ Merced Sun-Star
McClatchy Newspapers Inc.
3033 North G St.
Merced, CA 95340
Phone: (209)722-1511
Publisher's E-mail: pensions@mcclatchy.com
Local newspaper. **Founded:** Nov. 04, 1910. **Freq:** Daily. **Print Method:** Offset. **Cols./Page:** 6. **Col. Width:** 2 inches. **Col. Depth:** 21 inches. **Key Personnel:** Dave Hill, Editor. **USPS:** 432-340. **Subscription Rates:** $.22 Individuals /day, print and digital; $.99 Individuals /month, digital only. **URL:** http://www.mercedsunstar.com; http://www.mcclatchy.com/2006/06/15/426/merced-sun-star.html. **Formerly:** The Gustine Standard. **Ad Rates:** PCI $6.16. **Remarks:** Accepts advertising. **Circ:** Mon.-Fri. 14219, Sat. 18569.

3093 ■ Training and Development in Human Services
National Staff Development and Training Association
2115 Wardrobe Ave.
Merced, CA 95341
Phone: (209)385-3000
Fax: (209)354-2501
Journal providing a venue for both human services training scholars and practitioners to contribute to the knowledge base and advance the field of human services training and development. **ISSN:** 1941-2193 (print). **Subscription Rates:** $25. **Alt. Formats:** PDF. **Mailing address:** PO Box 112, Merced, CA 95341. **Remarks:** Advertising not accepted. **Circ:** (Not Reported).

3094 ■ KAMB-FM - 101.5
90 E 16th St.
Merced, CA 95340
Phone: (209)723-1015
Fax: (209)723-1945
Free: 800-692-5777
Email: kamb@celebrationradio.com
Format: Religious. **Networks:** Moody Broadcasting; SkyLight Satellite; Ambassador Inspirational Radio. **Owner:** Central Valley Broadcasting, at above address. **Founded:** 1967. **Formerly:** Good News Radio. **Operating Hours:** Continuous. **Key Personnel:** Tim Land, Gen. Mgr; Dave Benton, Contact, dave@celebrationradio.com. **Wattage:** 1,850. **Ad Rates:** Noncommercial. **URL:** http://www.celebrationradio.com.

3095 ■ KBKY-FM - 94.1
450 Grogan Ave., Ste. A
Merced, CA 95340-6402
Phone: (209)726-1351
Format: Music of Your Life. **Operating Hours:** Continuous. **Wattage:** 6,000 ERP. **Ad Rates:** Advertising accepted; rates available upon request. **URL:** http://radioalfayomega941fm.com.

3096 ■ KBRE-FM - 92.5
1020 W Main St.
Merced, CA 95340
Phone: (209)723-2191
Format: Album-Oriented Rock (AOR). **Owner:** Mapleton Communications, 10900 Wilshire Blvd., No. 1500, Los Angeles, CA 90024, Ph: (310)209-7229, Fax: (310)209-7239. **Founded:** Nov. 16, 1995. **Formerly:** KVRQ-FM; KJMQ-FM. **Operating Hours:** Continuous. **Wattage:** 6,000. **Ad Rates:** $12-21 for 30 seconds; $15-25 for 60 seconds. KLOQ; KABX; KYOS; KNAH. **URL:** http://www.radiomerced.com.

3097 ■ KHTN-FM - 104.7
510 W 19th St.
Merced, CA 95340
Phone: (209)383-7900
Fax: (209)723-8461
Email: hot1047email@aol.com
Format: Adult Contemporary; Contemporary Hit Radio (CHR). **Networks:** Satellite Music Network. **Owner:** Buckley Communications, Inc., 166 W Putnam Ave., Greenwich, CT 06830, Ph: (203)661-4307, Fax: (203)622-7341. **Founded:** 1982. **Formerly:** KSNN-FM. **Operating Hours:** Continuous; 25% network, 75% local. **Key Personnel:** John Sterling, Gen. Sales Mgr., sterling@kubb.com. **Wattage:** 50,000. **Ad Rates:** for 30 seconds; $25 for 60 seconds. **URL:** http://www.hot1047fm.com.

3098 ■ KLOQ-FM - 98.7
1020 W Main St.
Merced, CA 95340-4521
Phone: (209)723-2191
Format: Hispanic. **Owner:** Mapleton Communications, 10900 Wilshire Blvd., No. 1500, Los Angeles, CA 90024, Ph: (310)209-7229, Fax: (310)209-7239. **Operating Hours:** Continuous. **Wattage:** 6,000. **Ad Rates:** $11-27 for 30 seconds; $14-32 for 60 seconds. Combined advertising rates available with KTIQ; KVVY; KABX; KYOS; KIBG; KBRE. **URL:** http://www.radiolobo987.com.

3099 ■ KUBB-FM - 96.3
510 W 19th St.
Merced, CA 95340
Phone: (209)383-7900
Fax: (209)723-8461
Format: Country. **Networks:** Westwood One Radio. **Owner:** Buckley Broadcasting Corp. Inc., 166 W Putnam Ave., Greenwich, CT 06830-5241, Ph: (203)661-4309. **Founded:** 1977. **Operating Hours:** Continuous; 25% network, 75% local. **Wattage:** 1,900. **Ad Rates:** $8-38 for 60 seconds. **URL:** http://www.kubb.com.

3100 ■ KYOS-AM - 1480
1020 West Main St.,
Merced, CA 95340
Phone: (209)723-2191
Format: News; Talk. **Networks:** ABC. **Owner:** Mapleton Communications, 10900 Wilshire Blvd., No. 1500, Los Angeles, CA 90024, Ph: (310)209-7229, Fax: (310)209-7239. **Founded:** 1936. **Operating Hours:** Continuous. **Local Programs:** *The Savage Nation*, Monday Tuesday Wednesday Thursday Friday 6:00 p.m. - 8:00 p.m.; *The Jerry Doyle Show*, Monday Tuesday Wednesday Thursday Friday 7:00 p.m. - 10:00 p.m. **Wattage:** 5,000 Day; 5,000 Nig. **URL:** http://www.1480kyos.com.

MI WUK VILLAGE

3101 ■ Meyerhoff Cable Systems Inc.
PO Box 340
Mi Wuk Village, CA 95346
Cities Served: County of Tolumne, CA. **URL:** http://kepler.sos.ca.gov/.

MIDWAY CITY

3102 ■ The Royal Spaniels
Premiere Publications
14531 Jefferson St.
Midway City, CA 92655
Phone: (714)893-0053
Fax: (714)893-5085
Publication E-mail: royalspaniels@frontiernet.net
Consumer magazine covering the breeding and exhibiting of show dogs of the breeds, Cavalier King Charles Spaniels and King Charles Spaniels. **Freq:** Quarterly March, June, September, and December. **Key Personnel:** Holly Cornwell, Editor; John Garrison, Contact. **ISSN:** 1096--0759 (print). **Subscription Rates:** $50 U.S.; $60 Canada; $85 Other countries. **URL:** http://www.the-royal-spaniels.com. **Remarks:** Accepts advertising. **Circ:** (Not Reported).

MILL VALLEY

W. CA. Marin Co. On Richardson Bay, 14 mi. N. of San Francisco. Nurseries. Creamery, hardware manufactured. Residential. Dairy, grain farms.

3103 ■ Edible Marin & Wine Country
Edible Communities Inc.
160 Summit Ave.
Mill Valley, CA 94941
Phone: (415)515-4456
Fax: (415)384-0635
Publication E-mail: info@ediblemarinandwinecountry.com
Magazine focusing on the local food and wine of Marin, Napa, and Sonoma Counties. **Freq:** Quarterly. **Key Personnel:** Gibson Thomas, Publisher. **Subscription Rates:** $28 Individuals. **URL:** http://ediblemarinandwinecountry.ediblefeast.com. **Ad Rates:** 4C $3145. **Remarks:** Accepts advertising. **Circ:** (Not Reported).

3104 ■ Latitude 38
Latitude 38
15 Locust Ave.
Mill Valley, CA 94941
Phone: (415)383-8200
Fax: (415)383-5816
Consumer magazine covering sailing. **Freq:** Monthly. **Print Method:** Newsprint. **Trim Size:** 8 1/16 x 10 1/4. **Key Personnel:** Andy Turpin, Managing Editor; John Arndt, Associate Publisher, Specialist, Advertising and Sales; Colleen Levine, General Manager; Richard Spindler, Executive Editor, Publisher; LaDonna Bubak, Editor; Christine Weaver, Contact. **Subscription Rates:** $36 Individuals 3rd class; $55 U.S. and Canada 1st class; $6 Single issue. **URL:** http://www.latitude38.com/index.lasso. **Remarks:** Accepts advertising. **Circ:** (Not Reported).

3105 ■ Shamanism
Foundation for Shamanic Studies
PO Box 1939
Mill Valley, CA 94942
Phone: (415)897-6416
Fax: (415)897-4583
Publisher's E-mail: info@shamanism.org
Freq: Annual. **ISSN:** 1042--1513 (print). **Subscription Rates:** Included in membership. **URL:** http://shamanism.org/news/2011/07/23/the-shamanism-annual-fss-scholarly-journal. **Remarks:** Advertising not accepted. **Circ:** (Not Reported).

MILPITAS

W. CA. Santa Clara Co. 5 mi. N. of San Jose. Manufactures electric transformers, batteries, industrial water. Auto assembly plant. Agriculture. truck crops.

3106 ■ Jain Digest
Federation of Jain Associations in North America
722 S Main St.
Milpitas, CA 95035
Phone: (510)730-0204
Publisher's E-mail: info@jaina.org
Freq: Quarterly. **URL:** http://www.jaina.org/?page=JD_Publication. **Remarks:** Advertising not accepted. **Circ:** (Not Reported).

3107 ■ Milpitas Post
Milpitas Post
59 Marylinn Dr.
Milpitas, CA 95035
Phone: (408)262-2454
Fax: (408)763-9710
Publication E-mail: news@themilpitaspost.com
Local newspaper. **Founded:** 1955. **Freq:** Weekly (Wed.). **Print Method:** Offset. **Cols./Page:** 5. **Col. Width:** 2 1/16 inches. **Col. Depth:** 13 1/4 inches. **Key Personnel:** Robert J. Devincenzi, Editor; Gloria Guillen, Business Manager; Paul E. Baca, Director, Production. **URL:** http://www.mercurynews.com/milpitas. **Ad Rates:** GLR $1.65; BW $718.15; 4C $1,000; PCI $23.10. **Remarks:** Accepts advertising. **Circ:** (Not Reported).

MISSION VIEJO

S. CA. Orange Co. 4 mi. NE of San Juan Capistrano. Residential.

3108 ■ Barter News: The Official Journal of the Reciprocal Trade Industry
Barter News
PO Box 3024
Mission Viejo, CA 92690
Phone: (949)831-0607
Trade magazine covering bartering information. **Freq:** Quarterly. **Key Personnel:** Robert Meyer, Editor, Owner, Publisher; Marcia Meyer, Manager, Operations. **ISSN:** 1092--3608 (print). **Subscription Rates:** $350 U.S. back issues; $395 Other countries back issues; $298 Individuals FastStart programs I or II; $496 Individuals FastStart programs I and II. **URL:** http://barternews.com/issues.htm. **Ad Rates:** BW $3,000; 4C $4,000. **Remarks:** Accepts advertising. **Circ:** Controlled 30000.

3109 ■ Toastmaster
Gavel Clubs
PO Box 9052
Mission Viejo, CA 92690-9052
Phone: (949)858-8255
Fax: (949)858-1207
Publisher's E-mail: newclubs@toastmasters.org
Freq: Monthly. **Print Method:** Offset. **Trim Size:** 8 1/4 x 10 7/8. **Cols./Page:** 3. **Col. Width:** 27 nonpareils. **Col. Depth:** 133 agate lines. **Key Personnel:** Paul Sterman, Senior Editor; Suzanne Frey, Managing Editor, Contact. **ISSN:** 0040--8263 (print). **Subscription Rates:** Included in membership. **Alt. Formats:** PDF. **URL:** http://www.toastmasters.org/Magazine. **Remarks:** Advertising accepted; rates available upon request. **Circ:** ‡250000.

3110 ■ Veterinary Practice News
Bowtie Inc.
PO Box 6050
Mission Viejo, CA 92690-6050
Phone: (949)855-8822
Fax: (949)855-3045
Magazine covering veterinary practice in the United States featuring developments and trends affecting companion animals and livestock. **Freq:** Monthly. **Print Method:** Offset. **Trim Size:** 13 x 21. **Cols./Page:** 6. **Col. Width:** 2 1/16 inches. **Col. Depth:** 21 1/2 inches. **Key Personnel:** Marilyn Iturri, Editor. **Subscription Rates:** $42 U.S. and Canada digital; $48 Individuals print. **URL:** http://www.veterinarypracticenews.com. **Remarks:** Accepts classified advertising. **Circ:** (Not Reported).

3111 ■ KSBR-FM - 88.5
28000 Marguerite Pkwy.
Mission Viejo, CA 92692
Phone: (949)582-5727
Fax: (949)347-9693
Format: Jazz; Blues. **Networks:** AP. **Owner:** South Orange County Community College District, 28000 Marguerite Pkwy., Mission Viejo, CA 92692. **Founded:** 1975. **Operating Hours:** Continuous; 5% network, 95% local. **Key Personnel:** Terry Wedel, Contact, twedel@saddleback.cc.ca.us; Dawn Kamber, Contact, dkamber@saddleback.edu. **Wattage:** 600. **Ad Rates:** Noncommercial. **URL:** http://www.ksbr.org.

MODESTO

C. CA. Stanislaus Co. 94 mi. SE of San Francisco. Frozen foods, canning and packing plants. Meat, poultry, dairy products, olive oil, crates, dehydrators, chemicals, wine manufactured. Diversified farming. Peaches, walnuts, almonds.

3112 ■ Carnets de Geologie: Notebooks on Geology
Carnets de Geologie
1916 Temescal Dr.
Modesto, CA 95355-9171
Publisher's E-mail: carnets@univ-brest.fr
Journal presenting papers in the field of sedimentology, stratigraphy, and paleontology. **Key Personnel:** Bruno Granier, Editor; Christian C. Emig, Associate Editor. **ISSN:** 2108--5196 (print); **EISSN:** 1634--0744 (electronic). **Alt. Formats:** Electronic publishing. **URL:** http://paleopolis.rediris.es/cg. **Circ:** (Not Reported).

3113 ■ The Modesto Bee
McClatchy Newspapers Inc.
1325 H St.
Modesto, CA 95352
Phone: (209)578-2000
Free: 800-776-4237
Publisher's E-mail: pensions@mcclatchy.com
General newspaper. **Freq:** Daily. **Print Method:** Flexography. **Cols./Page:** 6. **Col. Width:** 26 nonpareils. **Col. Depth:** 297 agate lines. **Key Personnel:** Ken Riddick, President, Publisher, phone: (209)578-2090. **Subscription Rates:** $79.95 Individuals online only. **URL:** http://www.modbee.com. **Ad Rates:** GLR $3.36; BW $6,447; 4C $7,047; PCI $51.17. **Remarks:** Accepts advertising. **Circ:** 60595, 72680.

3114 ■ KATM-FM - 103.3
1581 Cummins Dr., No. 135
Modesto, CA 95358
Phone: (209)766-5103
Fax: (209)571-1033
Free: 800-499-5103
Format: Country. **Owner:** Citadel Broadcasting Corp., 7201 W Lake Mead Blvd., Ste. 400, Las Vegas, NV 89128-8366, Ph: (702)804-5200, Fax: (702)804-8250. **Founded:** 1958. **Formerly:** KBEE-AM. **Operating Hours:** Continuous. **ADI:** Sacramento-Stockton, CA. **Wattage:** 50,000. **Ad Rates:** Advertising accepted; rates available upon request. **URL:** http://www.katm.com.

3115 ■ KAZV-TV - 14
1064 Woodland Ave., Ste. P
Modesto, CA 95351
Phone: (209)566-9135
Key Personnel: George Baker, Contact; George Baker, Contact; Warda Designs, Contact.

3116 ■ KBES-FM - 89.5
PO Box 4116
Modesto, CA 95352
Phone: (209)538-4130
Fax: (209)538-2795
Format: Ethnic. **Owner:** Bet-Nahrain, 3119 S Central Ave., Ceres, CA 95307-3632, Ph: (209)538-4130. **Founded:** 1977. **Key Personnel:** Dr. Sargon Dadesho, President. **Ad Rates:** Noncommercial. **URL:** http://www.wordpress.betnahrain.org.

3117 ■ KBSV-TV - 23
PO Box 4116
Modesto, CA 95352
Phone: (209)538-4130
Fax: (209)538-2795
Email: kbsv@aol.com
Owner: Bet-Nahrain, 3119 S Central Ave., Ceres, CA 95307-3632, Ph: (209)538-4130. **Key Personnel:** Dr. Sargon Dadisho, President; Jannet Shamon, Director. **URL:** http://wordpress.betnahrain.org/htdocs.

3118 ■ KCIV-FM - 99.9
1031 15th St., Ste. 1
Modesto, CA 95354-1102
Format: Religious. **Owner:** Bott Radio Network, 10550 Barkley, Overland Park, KS 66212, Ph: (913)642-7770, Fax: (913)642-1319, Free: 800-345-2621. **Founded:** 1989. **Operating Hours:** Continuous. **Key Personnel:** Rich Bott, Exec. VP. **Wattage:** 1,900. **Ad Rates:** Noncommercial.

3119 ■ KDJK-FM - 104.1
1581 Cummins Dr., Ste. 135
Modesto, CA 95358
Phone: (209)766-5000
Format: Classic Rock. **Owner:** Citadel Broadcasting Corp., 7201 W Lake Mead Blvd., Ste. 400, Las Vegas, NV 89128-8366, Ph: (702)804-5200, Fax: (702)804-8250. **Founded:** 1985. **ADI:** Sacramento-Stockton, CA. **Wattage:** 071. **Ad Rates:** Advertising accepted; rates available upon request.

3120 ■ KEQP-FM - 106.9
4300 America Ave.
Modesto, CA 95356
Phone: (209)545-5530
Owner: Calvary Chapel of Modesto, 4300 American Ave., Modesto, CA 95356, Ph: (209)545-5530.

3121 ■ KFIV-AM
2121 Lancey Dr.
Modesto, CA 95351
Phone: (209)551-1306
Fax: (209)551-1359
Format: Talk; News. **Networks:** ABC. **Owner:** Clear Channel Inc., 200 E Basse Rd., San Antonio, TX 78209, Ph: (612)336-9700, Fax: (612)336-9701. **Founded:** 1950. **Key Personnel:** Gary L. Halladay, Contact. **Wattage:** 4,000 Day; 950 Night. **Ad Rates:** $35 per unit.

3122 ■ K49EO - 49
PO Box A
Santa Ana, CA 92711
Phone: (714)832-2950
Free: 888-731-1000
Owner: Trinity Broadcasting Network Inc., PO Box A, Santa Ana, CA 92711, Ph: (714)832-2950, Free: 888-731-1000. **URL:** http://www.tbn.org.

3123 ■ KJSN-FM - 102.3
2121 Lancey Dr.
Modesto, CA 95355
Phone: (209)551-1306
Fax: (209)551-1359
Format: Adult Contemporary. **Networks:** Independent. **Owner:** Clear Channel Communication, Inc., 200 E Basse Rd., San Antonio, TX 78209, Ph: (210)822-2828, Fax: (210)822-2828. **Founded:** 1977. **Formerly:** KFIV-FM. **Operating Hours:** Continuous. **ADI:** Sacramento-Stockton, CA. **Wattage:** 6,000. **Ad Rates:** Noncommercial. Combined advertising rates available with KFIV-AM, KUYL-AM, KOSO-FM, KMR0-FM, KQOD-FM. **URL:** http://www.sunny102fm.com.

3124 ■ KLVN-FM - 88.3
PO Box 2098
Omaha, NE 68103
Free: 800-525-5683
Format: Contemporary Christian. **Networks:** Independent. **Owner:** Educational Media Foundation, 2351 Sunset Blvd., Ste. 170-218, Rocklin, CA 95677, Ph: (800)434-8400. **Founded:** 1991. **Operating Hours:** Continuous. **Key Personnel:** Mike Novak, President, CEO; Alan Mason, COO. **Wattage:** 7,500. **Ad Rates:** Noncommercial. **URL:** http://www.klove.com.

Circulation: ★ = AAM; △ or • = BPA; ♦ = CAC; ❑ = VAC; ⊕ = PO Statement; ‡ = Publisher's Report; Boldface figures = sworn; Light figures = estimated.

3125 ■ KMPO-FM - 88.7
5005 E Belmont Ave.
Fresno, CA 93727
Phone: (559)455-5777
Free: 800-200-5758
Email: info@radiobilingue.org
Format: Hispanic. **Networks:** Independent. **Owner:** Radio Bilingue, Inc., at above address. **Founded:** 1980. **Operating Hours:** Continuous; 90% local. **Key Personnel:** Hugo Morales, Exec. Dir. **Wattage:** 2,000. **Ad Rates:** Noncommercial. **URL:** http://www.radiobilingue.org.

3126 ■ KMRQ-FM - 96.7
2121 Lancey Dr., No. 1
Modesto, CA 95355
Format: Alternative/New Music/Progressive. **ADI:** Sacramento-Stockton, CA. **Wattage:** 1,500. **URL:** http://rock967.iheart.com/features/contact-rock-967-1537/.

3127 ■ KOSO-FM - 93.1
2121 Lancey Dr.
Modesto, CA 95355
Phone: (209)551-1306
Fax: (209)551-3791
Format: Contemporary Hit Radio (CHR). **Networks:** AP. **Owner:** Clear Channel Inc., 200 E Basse Rd., San Antonio, TX 78209, Ph: (612)336-9700, Fax: (612)336-9701. **Founded:** 1966. **Operating Hours:** Continuous. **Wattage:** 50,000 ERP. **Ad Rates:** $250 for 60 seconds. Combined advertising rates available with KFIV-AM, KUYL-AM, KJJN-FM. **URL:** http://929thebigdog.iheart.com.

3128 ■ KQOD-FM - 100.1
2121 Lancey Dr.
Modesto, CA 95355
Phone: (209)551-1306
Fax: (209)551-3791
Free: 888-868-7707
Format: Oldies. **Networks:** ABC. **Owner:** iHeartMedia Inc., 200 E Basse Rd., San Antonio, TX 78209, Ph: (210)832-3314. **Founded:** 1980. **Operating Hours:** Continuous. **ADI:** Sacramento-Stockton, CA. **Wattage:** 6,000 ERP. **Ad Rates:** Advertising accepted; rates available upon request. **URL:** http://www.mega100fm.com/main.html.

3129 ■ KRVR-FM - 105.5
961 N Emerald Ave., Ste. A
Modesto, CA 95351-1556
Phone: (209)544-1055
Email: theriver@krvr.com
Format: Jazz. **Owner:** Threshold Communications, 16541 Redmond Way, Redmond, WA 98052, Ph: (206)812-6200, Fax: (206)686-7800, Free: 844-844-1382. **Operating Hours:** Continuous. **Wattage:** 1,000. **Ad Rates:** Noncommercial. KVIN-AM. **URL:** http://www.krvr.com.

3130 ■ KUYL-AM - 1280
2121 Lancey Dr.
Modesto, CA 95355
Phone: (918)664-4581
Format: Religious. **Founded:** 1947. **Formerly:** KJAX-AM. **Operating Hours:** Continuous. **ADI:** Sacramento-Stockton, CA. **Key Personnel:** Gary Granger, Contact, garygranger@clearchannel.com; Gary Granger, Contact, garygranger@clearchannel.com. **Wattage:** 1,000. **Ad Rates:** Advertising accepted; rates available upon request. **URL:** http://powertalk1280.iheart.com.

3131 ■ KWNN-FM - 98.3
1581 Cummins Dr.
Modesto, CA 95358
Phone: (209)766-5000
Fax: (209)523-4018
Format: Top 40. **Founded:** Sept. 13, 2006. **Ad Rates:** Advertising accepted; rates available upon request. **URL:** http://www.kwin.com/.

3132 ■ KWSX-AM - 1280
2121 Lancey Dr., Ste. 1
Modesto, CA 95355
Phone: (209)551-1306
Fax: (209)551-1359
ADI: Sacramento-Stockton, CA. **Wattage:** 1,000.

MOJAVE

S. CA. Kern Co. 58 mi. SE of Bakersfield. Residential. Industry. Mining. Aviation.

3133 ■ Charter Communications
15713 K St.
Mojave, CA 93501
Free: 888-438-2427
Owner: Charter Communications Inc., 400 Atlantic St., Stamford, CT 06901, Ph: (203)905-7801. **Formerly:** Falcon Cable TV. **Key Personnel:** Tom Rutledge, President, CEO. **Cities Served:** Boron, California; 70 channels. **URL:** http://www.charter.com.

MONROVIA

S. CA. Los Angeles Co. 17 mi. NE of Los Angeles. Tourism. Manufactures chemicals, electronics, furniture, hardware. Dairy products.

3134 ■ Health Freedom News
National Health Federation
PO Box 688
Monrovia, CA 91017
Phone: (626)357-2181
Publisher's E-mail: contact-us@thenhf.com
Consumer magazine. **Freq:** Quarterly. **Trim Size:** 8 3/8 x 10 7/8. **Cols./Page:** 2. **Key Personnel:** Scott Tips, Editor. **ISSN:** 0749--4742 (print). **Subscription Rates:** $36 Members; $5 Single issue plus shipping and handling. **URL:** http://www.thenhf.com/health-freedom-news. **Ad Rates:** $640-795, full page; $480-595, 2/3 page; $360-450, 1/2 page; $260-325, 1/3 page; $195-250, 1/4 page; $140-175, 1/6 page; $50-75, business card; $1800-2000, covers. BW $800; 4C $1,000. **Remarks:** Accepts advertising. **Circ:** Non-paid 20000.

3135 ■ Champion Broadband
911 S Primrose Ave., Ste. E
Monrovia, CA 91016
Free: 877-899-8898
Cities Served: Arcadia, Monrovia, Monrovia, Pasadena, California; Denver, Lakewood, Limon, Lyons, Colorado; Guernsey, Pine Bluffs, Wyoming; 23 channels. **URL:** http://www.championbroadband.com.

MONTEREY

W. CA. Monterey Co. On Monterey Bay, 125 mi. S. of San Francisco. Resort. Military. Light industry.

3136 ■ Applied Language Learning
Defense Language Institute Foreign Language Center
Presidio of Monterey
1759 Lewis Rd., Bldg. 614, Ste. 251
Monterey, CA 93944
Phone: (831)242-5119
Fax: (831)242-5850
Professional journal covering information on foreign language instruction and acquisition. **Freq:** Semiannual. **Trim Size:** 6 x 9. **Cols./Page:** 1. **Col. Width:** 4 3/4 inches. **Col. Depth:** 7 3/4 inches. **Key Personnel:** Dr. Lidia Woytak, Editor, phone: (831)242-5638, fax: (831)242-5850. **ISSN:** 1041--679X (print); **EISSN:** 1041--6791 (electronic). **Subscription Rates:** Free. **Alt. Formats:** PDF. **URL:** http://www.dliflc.edu/#homepage-tabl3. **Remarks:** Advertising not accepted. **Circ:** Non-paid 4500.

3137 ■ The Monterey County Herald
Monterey Peninsula Herald Co.
Eight Upper Ragsdale
Monterey, CA 93940
Phone: (831)372-3311
Publisher's E-mail: newsroom@montereyherald.com
General newspaper. **Founded:** 1922. **Freq:** Mon.-Sun. (morn.). **Print Method:** Flexography. **Cols./Page:** 6. **Col. Width:** 25 nonpareils. **Col. Depth:** 294 agate lines. **Subscription Rates:** $74.40 Individuals daily service, 12 weeks; $148.81 Individuals daily service, 24 weeks; $322.41 Individuals daily service, 52 weeks; $50.40 Individuals weekend service (Friday, Saturday and Sunday), 12 weeks; $100.80 Individuals weekend service (Friday, Saturday and Sunday), 24 weeks; $218.41 Individuals weekend service (Friday, Saturday and Sunday), 52 weeks; $33.96 Individuals Sunday only, 12 weeks; $67.92 Individuals Sunday only, 24 weeks; $147.16 Individuals Sunday only, 52 weeks. **URL:** http://www.montereyherald.com/. **Formerly:** The Herald. **Ad Rates:** GLR $4.56; BW $2,961; 4C $3,411; SAU $23.50. **Remarks:** Accepts advertising. **Circ:** Mon.-Sat. *31813, Sun. *34699.

3138 ■ The Observer
Diocese of Monterey
580 Fremont St.
Monterey, CA 93940
Phone: (831)373-4345
Publication E-mail: observer@dioceseofmonterey.org
Official newspaper of the Catholic Diocese of Monterey. **Founded:** 1969. **Freq:** Monthly. **Print Method:** Offset. **Trim Size:** 11 x 14. **Cols./Page:** 5. **Col. Width:** 1 15/16 inches. **Col. Depth:** 13 inches. **Subscription Rates:** $20 Individuals. **URL:** http://www.dioceseofmonterey.org/ministries/ministry.php?id=21235. **Mailing address:** PO Box 2048, Monterey, CA 93940-3216. **Ad Rates:** BW $600; 4C $800; PCI $12. **Remarks:** Accepts advertising. **Circ:** (Not Reported).

3139 ■ KBOQ-FM - 103.9
60 Garden Ct., Ste. 300
Monterey, CA 93940
Format: Classical. **Owner:** Mapleton Communications, 10900 Wilshire Blvd., No. 1500, Los Angeles, CA 90024, Ph: (310)209-7229, Fax: (310)209-7239. **Founded:** 1993. **Ad Rates:** $25-40 per unit.

3140 ■ KCDU-FM - 101.7
60 Garden Ct., Ste. 300
Monterey, CA 93940
Phone: (831)658-5200
Free: 888-636-1017
Email: 1017thebeach@radiomontereybay.com
Format: Eighties. **Owner:** Mapleton Communication L.L.C., 10900 Wilshire Blvd., No. 1500, Los Angeles, CA 90024, Ph: (310)209-7221, Fax: (310)209-7239. **Ad Rates:** Noncommercial. **URL:** http://www.1017thebeach.com.

3141 ■ KHIP-FM - 104.3
60 Garden Ct., Ste. 300
Monterey, CA 93940
Phone: (831)658-5200
Free: 877-762-5104
Format: Classic Rock. **Owner:** Mapleton Communications, 10900 Wilshire Blvd., No. 1500, Los Angeles, CA 90024, Ph: (310)209-7229, Fax: (310)209-7239. **Operating Hours:** Continuous. **Wattage:** 2,600. **Ad Rates:** Advertising accepted; rates available upon request. **URL:** http://www.thehippo.com.

3142 ■ KMBX-AM - 700
67 Garden Ct.
Monterey, CA 93940
Phone: (831)333-9735
Fax: (831)333-9750
Format: Hispanic. **Owner:** Entravision Communications Corporation, 2425 Olympic Blvd., Ste. 6000 W, Santa Monica, CA 90404-4030, Ph: (310)447-3870, Fax: (310)447-3899. **ADI:** Salinas-Monterey, CA. **Key Personnel:** Aaron Scoby, Gen. Mgr. **URL:** http://www.entravision.com.

3143 ■ KOTR-TV - 11
2511 Garden Rd., Ste. C150
Monterey, CA 93940
Phone: (831)655-5687
Fax: (831)649-5687
Key Personnel: Randy Rogers, Gen. Mgr., Gen. Sales Mgr.; Christine Jaege, Dir. of Mktg. **URL:** http://www.mytvmonterey.com.

3144 ■ KSES-FM - 107.1
67 Garden Ct.
Monterey, CA 93940
Phone: (831)373-6767
Free: 877-354-3646
Format: World Beat; Ethnic. **Owner:** Entravision Communication Corp., 2425 Olympic Blvd. W, Ste. 6000, Santa Monica, CA 90404. **Operating Hours:** Continuous. **Key Personnel:** Aaron Scoby, Gen. Mgr. **Ad Rates:** Advertising accepted; rates available upon request. **URL:** http://www.jose1071.com.

3145 ■ KSFN-AM
60 Garden Ct.
Monterey, CA 93940
Phone: (831)658-5281
Format: Talk. **Wattage:** 8,000 Day; 2,400 Nig. **Ad Rates:** Advertising accepted; rates available upon request.

3146 ■ KSMS-TV - 67
67 Garden Ct.
Monterey, CA 93940
Phone: (831)757-6711

Fax: (831)373-6700
Format: Commercial TV. **Networks:** Univision. **Founded:** 1986. **Key Personnel:** Carlos Romos, Contact. **Wattage:** 1,000,000 ERP.

3147 ■ KWAV-FM - 96.9
60 Garden Ct., Ste. 300
Monterey, CA 93940
Phone: (831)658-5200
Free: 800-304-5928
Format: Adult Contemporary. **Owner:** Buckley Broadcasting Corporation of Monterey, at above address. **Operating Hours:** Continuous. **ADI:** Salinas-Monterey, CA. **Wattage:** 18,000 ERP. **Ad Rates:** Advertising accepted; rates available upon request. **URL:** http://www.kwav.com.

3148 ■ KYZZ-FM - 97.9
Five Harris Ct., Bldg. C
Monterey, CA 93940
Phone: (831)649-0969
Fax: (831)649-3335
Format: Hip Hop. **Owner:** Buckley Radio, at above address, Stratford, CT. **ADI:** Salinas-Monterey, CA. **Key Personnel:** Kathy Baker, Exec. VP, Gen. Mgr. **Wattage:** 2,900.

MONTEREY PARK

S. CA. Los Angeles Co. 2 mi. S. of Alhambra. Residential. Illuminating signs, shoes, electronics, chemicals, hardware, diesel replacement parts manufactured.

3149 ■ Campus News
East Los Angeles College
1301 Avenida Cesar Chavez
Monterey Park, CA 91754-6099
Phone: (323)265-8650
Community college newspaper. **Founded:** 1945. **Freq:** Weekly (Wed.). **Print Method:** Offset. **Cols./Page:** 6. **Col. Width:** 26 nonpareils. **Col. Depth:** 294 agate lines. **Key Personnel:** Lindsey Maeda, Editor-in-Chief; Jean Stapleton, Advisor. **URL:** http://elaccampusnews.com/. **Ad Rates:** GLR $.44; SAU $4.50; PCI $5. **Remarks:** Accepts advertising. **Circ:** Free ‡500.

3150 ■ Global Business Education
International Society for Business Education
c/o Ruth DiPieri, President
1301 Avenida Cesar Chavez
Monterey Park, CA 91754
Phone: (619)469-5067
Remarks: Advertising not accepted. **Circ:** (Not Reported).

MOORPARK

3151 ■ Ultimate Motorcycling
Coram Publishing L.L.C.
887 Patriot Dr., Unit B
Moorpark, CA 93021
Phone: (805)367-4432
Fax: (805)715-3718
Journal covering motorcycling. **Freq:** 5/year. **Key Personnel:** Arthur C. Coldwells, President, Publisher; Mary Buch, Vice President, Associate Publisher. **Subscription Rates:** $18.97 U.S. 1 year; $32.87 Two years; $41.97 U.S. 3 years; $49.97 Other countries. **URL:** http://ultimatemotorcycling.com. **Formerly:** Robb Report MotorCycling. **Remarks:** Advertising accepted; rates available upon request. **Circ:** 40000.

MORAGA

W. CA. Contra Costa Co. 8 mi. SE of Berkeley. Residential.

3152 ■ The Collegian: Oldest Fortnightly in the East Bay
St. Mary's College
1928 Saint Mary's Rd.
Moraga, CA 94575-2715
Phone: (925)631-4000
Publication E-mail: collegia@stmarys-ca.edu
Collegiate newspaper. **Freq:** Weekly (Tues.). **Print Method:** Offset. **Trim Size:** 11 x 17. **Cols./Page:** 5. **Col. Width:** 24 nonpareils. **Col. Depth:** 203 agate lines. **Key Personnel:** Alex Choy, Business Manager; Ashley Hagin, Editor-in-Chief. **URL:** http://www.stmarys-ca.edu/the-collegian; http://www.stmaryscollegian.com. **Formerly:** St. Mary's Collegian. **Ad Rates:** GLR $2.50; BW $627; PCI $8.25. **Remarks:** Accepts advertising. **Circ:** 4500.

3153 ■ The Cryptogram
American Cryptogram Association
56 Sanders Ranch Rd.
Moraga, CA 94556-2806
Freq: Bimonthly. **ISSN:** 0045- 9151 (print). **Subscription Rates:** Included in membership. **Alt. Formats:** CD-ROM. **Remarks:** Advertising not accepted. **Circ:** (Not Reported).

3154 ■ KSMC-FM - 89.5
St. Mary's College
Moraga, CA 94575
Phone: (925)631-4000
Format: Educational. **Owner:** St. Mary's College, at above address. **Founded:** 1973. **Key Personnel:** Alex Green, Contact. **Wattage:** 800 ERP Horizontal. **Ad Rates:** for 30 seconds; for 60 seconds. **Mailing address:** PO Box 3223, Moraga, CA 94575. **URL:** http://www.stmarys-ca.edu/ksmc.

MORENO VALLEY

SE CA. Riverside Co. 8 mi. E. of Riverside. Recreation. Agriculture. Commercial.

3155 ■ Marantha Christian Journal
Maranatha Christian Journal
12240 Perris Blvd., No. 112
Moreno Valley, CA 92557
Phone: (909)247-0958
Consumer magazine covering news and information for Christians. **Remarks:** Advertising accepted; rates available upon request. **Circ:** (Not Reported).

MOUNT SHASTA

N. CA. Siskiyou Co. 90 mi. S. of Medford, OR. Sawmill. Pine, fir, cedar timber. Mountain resort. Agriculture.

3156 ■ Journal of the Order of Buddhist Contemplatives
Order of Buddhist Contemplatives
3724 Summit Dr.
Mount Shasta, CA 96067-9102
Phone: (530)926-4208
Journal contains articles on Buddhist meditation and practice written by priests of the Order and lay members of the congregation. **Freq:** Quarterly. **Print Method:** Offset. **Trim Size:** 5 1/2 x 8 1/2. **Key Personnel:** Rev. Eko Little, Contact. **ISSN:** 0891--1177 (print). **URL:** http://journal.obcon.org; http://obcon.org. **Formerly:** Journal of Shasta Abbey. **Remarks:** Advertising not accepted. **Circ:** (Not Reported).

3157 ■ KLDD-FM - 91.9
1250 Siskiyou Blvd.
Ashland, OR 97520
Phone: (541)552-6301
Free: 800-782-6191
Format: Public Radio. **Owner:** Jefferson Public Radio, 1721 Market St., Redding, CA 96001. **Key Personnel:** Dave Jackson, Host. **URL:** http://www.ijpr.org/Page.

3158 ■ K267AJ-FM - 101.3
PO Box 391
Twin Falls, ID 83303
Fax: (208)736-1958
Free: 800-357-4226
Format: Religious; Contemporary Christian. **Owner:** CSN International, PO Box 391, Twin Falls, ID 83303, Ph: (208)736-1958, Fax: (208)736-1958, Free: 800-357-4226. **Key Personnel:** Don Mills, Prog. Dir., Music Dir.; Kelly Carlson, Dir. of Engg.; Ray Gorney, Asst. Dir. **Wattage:** 013. **URL:** http://www.csnradio.com.

3159 ■ KZRO-FM - 100.1
PO Box 1234
Mount Shasta, CA 96067
Phone: (530)926-1332
Fax: (530)926-0737
Email: zmail@zchannelradio.com
Format: Classic Rock. **Key Personnel:** Dennis Michaels, Gen. Mgr., Sales Mgr. **URL:** http://www.zchannelradio.com.

MOUNTAIN VIEW

W. CA. Santa Clara Co. 34 mi. S. of San Francisco. Residential. Electronics.

3160 ■ International Journal of Multisensor Information Fusion
International Society of Information Fusion
PO Box 4631
Mountain View, CA 94040
Publisher's E-mail: membership@isif.org
Journal containing information on all aspects of research and development in the field of information fusion. **Freq:** Bimonthly. **ISSN:** 1566--2535 (print). **Subscription Rates:** $179 Individuals print only; $514.27 Individuals eJournal; $881 Institutions print only. **URL:** http://www.journals.elsevier.com/information-fusion. **Remarks:** Advertising not accepted. **Circ:** (Not Reported).

3161 ■ International Journal of Offshore and Polar Engineering
International Society of Offshore and Polar Engineers
495 N Whisman Rd., Ste. 300
Mountain View, CA 94043-5711
Phone: (650)254-1871
Fax: (650)254-2038
Publisher's E-mail: info@isope.org
Scholarly journal covering mechanics, materials, energy/resources, engineering, ocean/offshore, hydrodynamics, marine, polar, ice technology, geotechnical, and environmental issues. **Freq:** Quarterly Mar., June, Sept., Dec. **Print Method:** Perfectbound. **Trim Size:** 8 3/8 x 10 7/8. **Cols./Page:** 2. **Key Personnel:** W. Koterayama, Editor; Prof. Jin S. Chung, Editor. **ISSN:** 1053--5381 (print). **Subscription Rates:** $170 Individuals per year; $100 Individuals set of back issues, nonmembers; $60 Single issue; $20 Individuals per pdf file. **Alt. Formats:** PDF. **URL:** http://www.isope.org/publications/publications.htm. **Mailing address:** PO Box 189, Cupertino, CA 95015-0189. **Circ:** Combined 1400.

3162 ■ International Journal of Offshore and Polar Engineers
International Society of Offshore and Polar Engineers
495 N Whisman Rd., Ste. 300
Mountain View, CA 94043-5711
Phone: (650)254-1871
Fax: (650)254-2038
Publisher's E-mail: info@isope.org
Freq: Quarterly. **ISSN:** 1053- 5381 (print). **Subscription Rates:** $150 for nonmembers. **Alt. Formats:** CD-ROM. **URL:** http://www.isope.org/publications/publicationsjournal.htm. **Mailing address:** PO Box 189, Cupertino, CA 95015-0189. **Remarks:** Accepts advertising. **Circ:** 1050.

3163 ■ Journal of Advances in Information Fusion
International Society of Information Fusion
PO Box 4631
Mountain View, CA 94040
Publisher's E-mail: membership@isif.org
Journal discussing latest development related to information integration. **Freq:** Semiannual. **Key Personnel:** Uwe D. Hanebeck, Editor-in-Chief. **ISSN:** 1557--6418 (print). **URL:** http://isif.org/journals/all. **Remarks:** Advertising not accepted. **Circ:** (Not Reported).

3164 ■ The National Fantasy Fan
National Fantasy Fan Federation
PO Box 1925
Mountain View, CA 94042
Freq: Quarterly. **Key Personnel:** David Speakman, Editor. **ISSN:** 2169-3595 (print). **Subscription Rates:** Included in membership. **Alt. Formats:** Download; PDF. **URL:** http://n3f.org/zines/tnff. **Remarks:** Advertising not accepted. **Circ:** (Not Reported).

3165 ■ The People
Socialist Labor Party of America
PO Box 218
Mountain View, CA 94042-0218
Phone: (650)938-8359
Fax: (650)938-8392
Publisher's E-mail: socialists@slp.org
News journal with a socialist orientation. **Freq:** Bimonthly Monthly. **Print Method:** Offset. **Trim Size:** 11 3/8 x 17 1/2. **Cols./Page:** 4. **Col. Width:** 14 3/4 nonpareils. **Col. Depth:** 230 agate lines. **ISSN:** 0199--350X (print). **Subscription Rates:** $5 /year. **Alt. Formats:** Download; PDF. **URL:** http://www.slp.org/tp.htm. **Remarks:** Advertising not accepted. **Circ:** (Not Reported).

Circulation: ★ = AAM; △ or • = BPA; ♦ = CAC; ❑ = VAC; ⊕ = PO Statement; ‡ = Publisher's Report; Boldface figures = sworn; Light figures = estimated.

3166 ■ La Red--The Net: The Hispanic Journal of Education Commentary and Reviews
Floricanto Press Inc.
650 Castro St., Ste. 120-331
Mountain View, CA 94041-2055
Phone: (415)552-1879
Fax: (702)995-1410
Publisher's E-mail: sales@floricantopress.com
Hispanic book review journal. **Freq:** Quarterly. **Print Method:** Web. **Trim Size:** 8 1/2 x 11. **Cols./Page:** 2. **Col. Width:** 3 1/4 inches. **Col. Depth:** 7 1/2 inches. **ISSN:** 1043--3321 (print). **Remarks:** Accepts advertising. **Circ:** (Not Reported).

3167 ■ Track & Field News
Track and Field News
2570 W El Camino Real, Ste. 220
Mountain View, CA 94040
Phone: (650)948-8188
Fax: (650)948-9445
Free: 800-438-8725
Publisher's E-mail: business@trackandfieldnews.com
Track and field magazine. **Freq:** Monthly. **Print Method:** Offset. **Trim Size:** 8 1/2 x 11. **Cols./Page:** 3. **Col. Width:** 28 nonpareils. **Col. Depth:** 152 agate lines. **Key Personnel:** E. Garry Hill, Editor; Sieg Lindstrom, Managing Editor; Ed Fox, Publisher; Janet Vitu, Publisher. **ISSN:** 0041--0284 (print). **Subscription Rates:** $48.95 Individuals print and online; $63.95 Individuals first class;print and online; $55 Canada standard delivery-;print and online; $69 Other countries air mail;print and online. **URL:** http://www.trackandfieldnews.com. **Remarks:** Accepts advertising. **Circ:** Paid 24000.

MURRIETA

3168 ■ Global Writes
International Food, Wine and Travel Writers Association
39252 Winchester Rd., Ste. 107, No. 418
Murrieta, CA 92563
Fax: (877)439-8929
Free: 877-439-8929
Publisher's E-mail: admin@ifwtwa.org
Magazine featuring journalists who cover the hospitality and lifestyle fields, and the people who promote them. **Freq:** Weekly. **URL:** http://global-writes.com. **Remarks:** Accepts advertising. **Circ:** (Not Reported).

3169 ■ Murrieta Chamber of Commerce Business Directory and Community Resource Guide
Murrieta Chamber of Commerce
25125 Madison Ave., Ste. 108
Murrieta, CA 92562
Phone: (951)677-7916
Fax: (951)677-9976
Publisher's E-mail: pellis@murrietachamber.org
Magazine contains a 70 page bound business directory and community resource guide. **Freq:** Annual. **Key Personnel:** Patrick Ellis, President, Chief Executive Officer; Rhonda Warner, Contact. **Subscription Rates:** Included in membership. **URL:** http://www.murrietachamber.org/. **Remarks:** Accepts advertising. **Circ:** (Not Reported).

MUSCOY

3170 ■ K276EF-FM - 103.1
PO Box 391
Twin Falls, ID 83303
Fax: (208)736-1958
Free: 800-357-4226
Format: Religious; Contemporary Christian. **Owner:** CSN International, PO Box 391, Twin Falls, ID 83303, Ph: (208)736-1958, Fax: (208)736-1958, Free: 800-357-4226. **Key Personnel:** Don Mills, Prog. Dir., Music Dir.; Kelly Carlson, Dir. of Engg.; Ray Gorney, Asst. Dir. **Wattage:** 010. **URL:** http://www.csnradio.com.

NAPA

W. CA. Napa Co. On Napa River, 15 mi. E. of Vallejo. Fruit canning and drying. Premier grape growing regions. Manufactures wine. Clothing, dairy products. Quicksilver gold mines. Diversified farming. Grapes, fruits, poultry.

3171 ■ The Napa Valley Register
The Napa Valley Register
1615 Second St.
Napa, CA 94559
Phone: (707)226-3711
Publisher's E-mail: bkisliuk@napanews.com
General newspaper. **Freq:** Mon.-Sun. (eve.). **Print Method:** Offset. **Trim Size:** 14 x 22 3/4. **Cols./Page:** 6. **Col. Width:** 25 nonpareils. **Col. Depth:** 301 agate lines. **Key Personnel:** Brenda Speth, Publisher, phone: (707)256-2234; Norma Kostecka, Director, Advertising. **URL:** http://napavalleyregister.com. **Formerly:** The Napa Register. **Remarks:** Accepts advertising. **Circ:** (Not Reported).

3172 ■ The Weekly Calistogan
The Weekly Calistogan
1615 2nd St.
Napa, CA 94559-2818
Phone: (707)226-5582
Publication E-mail: circulation@napanews.com
Newspaper with a liberal orientation. **Freq:** Weekly (Thurs.). **Print Method:** Offset. **Cols./Page:** 6. **Col. Width:** 25 nonpareils. **Col. Depth:** 301 agate lines. **Key Personnel:** Sean Scully, Editor. **USPS:** 672-180. **URL:** http://napavalleyregister.com./calistogan. **Formerly:** Independent Calistogan; Calistoga Calistogian. **Remarks:** Accepts advertising. **Circ:** ‡3000.

3173 ■ KEWE-AM - 1340
198 Monte Vista Dr.
Napa, CA 94559
Phone: (530)345-0021
Format: Sports. **Owner:** Deer Creek Broadcasting, at above address. **Key Personnel:** Dino Corbin, Contact; Dino Corbin, Contact. **URL:** http://newstalk1290.wordpress.com.

3174 ■ KVON-AM - 1440
1124 Foster Rd.
Napa, CA 94558
Phone: (707)258-1111
Format: Talk; News. **Networks:** ABC; Westwood One Radio. **Owner:** Wine Country Broadcasting, 1124 Foster Rd., Napa, CA 94558. **Founded:** 1947. **Operating Hours:** Continuous. **Key Personnel:** Ira C. Smith, Sports Dir., ira@kvon.com; Tracy Green, Bus. Mgr., Dir. of Traffic, tracy@kvon.com; Carmen Shantz, Dir. of Sales. **Wattage:** 5,000. **Ad Rates:** Noncommercial. Combined advertising rates available with KVYN-FM. **URL:** http://www.kvon.com.

3175 ■ KVYN-FM - 99.3
1124 Foster Rd.
Napa, CA 94558
Fax: (707)252-1440
Email: lsharp@winecountrybroadcasting.com
Format: Adult Contemporary; Oldies. **Networks:** ABC. **Owner:** Wine Country Broadcasting, 1124 Foster Rd., Napa, CA 94558. **Founded:** 1976. **Operating Hours:** Continuous. **Wattage:** 6,000. **Ad Rates:** $34-48 for 30 seconds; $42-60 for 60 seconds. Combined advertising rates available with KVON-AM. **URL:** http://www.993thevine.com.

3176 ■ VINE-FM - 99.3
1124 Foster Rd.
Napa, CA 94558
Phone: (707)258-1111
Format: Ethnic; World Beat. **Operating Hours:** Continuous. **Ad Rates:** Advertising accepted; rates available upon request. **URL:** http://www.kvon.com.

NEEDLES

SE CA. San Bernardino Co. On Colorado River, 160 mi. NE of San Bernardino. Mojave indian reservation. Tourism. Power & food packing plants. Agriculture.

3177 ■ Needles Desert Star
Needles Desert Star
800 W Broadway, Ste. E
Needles, CA 92363
Phone: (760)326-2222
Community newspaper. **Founded:** Sept. 01, 1888. **Freq:** Weekly (Wed.). **Print Method:** Offset. **Cols./Page:** 6. **Col. Width:** 24 nonpareils. **Col. Depth:** 294 agate lines. **Key Personnel:** Robin Richards, Editor; Gary L. Milks, President, Publisher. **Subscription Rates:** $18 Individuals. **URL:** http://www.mohavedailynews.com/needles_desert_star. **Formerly:** Booth's Bazoo; Needles Eye; Needles Nugget. **Ad Rates:** GLR $.15; SAU $7.50. **Remarks:** Accepts advertising. **Circ:** 4000.

3178 ■ KTOX-AM - 1340
100 Balboa Pl.
Needles, CA 92363
Phone: (760)326-4500
Format: Talk; News. **Networks:** CBS; Mutual Broadcasting System; People's Network. **Owner:** Coburn Communications Corp., 130 W 42nd St., Ste. 950, New York, NY 10036. **Founded:** 1948. **Formerly:** KSFE-AM. **Operating Hours:** Continuous. **Key Personnel:** Andy Ward, Contact. **Wattage:** 1,000. **Ad Rates:** Advertising accepted; rates available upon request. $3-9 for 30 seconds; $4.10-12 for 60 seconds. **URL:** http://www.ktox1340.com.

NEVADA CITY

NE CA. Nevada Co. 2 mi. SW of Grass Valley. Residential.

3179 ■ International Research Journal Online
Flower Essence Society
PO Box 459
Nevada City, CA 95959
Phone: (530)265-9163
Fax: (530)265-0584
Free: 800-736-9222
Publisher's E-mail: info@flowersociety.org
Journal containing current clinical research, plant study, humanitarian outreach efforts utilizing flower essences and educational opportunities. **Subscription Rates:** Included in membership. **URL:** http://www.flowersociety.org/ejournals-links.htm. **Formerly:** Calix. **Remarks:** Advertising not accepted. **Circ:** (Not Reported).

3180 ■ KVMR-FM - 89.5
401 Spring St.
Nevada City, CA 95959
Phone: (530)265-9073
Fax: (530)265-9077
Free: 800-355-5867
Email: news@kvmr.org
Format: Eclectic. **Networks:** Independent. **Owner:** Nevada City Community Broadcast Group, at above address. **Founded:** 1978. **Operating Hours:** Continuous; 100% local. **Key Personnel:** Erica Randall, Bus. Mgr., businessmgr@kvmr.org; Steve Baker, Dir. of Programs, program@kvmr.org; Alice MacAllister, Music Dir., music@kvmr.org; Paul Paterson, Chief Engineer, engineer@kvmr.org; David Levin, Gen. Mgr., gm@kvmr.org. **Wattage:** 2,000. **Ad Rates:** Noncommercial. **URL:** http://www.kvmr.org.

NEWMAN

C. CA. Stanislaus Co. 25 mi. SW of Modesto. Manufactures dairy products. Poultry. Dairy, grain farms. Alfalfa, green peppers, cauliflower, tomatoes Spinach.

3181 ■ The West Side Index
Mattos Newspapers Inc.
1021 Fresno St.
Newman, CA 95360
Phone: (209)862-2222
Publisher's E-mail: advertising@mattosnews.com
Community newspaper. **Freq:** Weekly (Thurs.). **Print Method:** Offset. **Cols./Page:** 6. **Col. Width:** 21 nonpareils. **Col. Depth:** 287 agate lines. **Key Personnel:** Susan Mattos, Publisher. **Subscription Rates:** $30 Individuals in county; $40 Out of area; $30 Individuals senior; $38 Out of area senior. **URL:** http://www.westsideconnect.com. **Ad Rates:** PCI $8. **Remarks:** Accepts advertising. **Circ:** 1850.

NEWPORT BEACH

S. CA. Orange Co. On Pacific Ocean, 12 mi. SW of Santa Ana. Beach resort. Finanical center. Electronics research and development, guidance control systems, boats.

3182 ■ Builder and Developer
Peninsula Publishing Inc.
1602 Monrovia Ave.
Newport Beach, CA 92663-2808
Phone: (949)631-0308
Fax: (949)631-2475
Publisher's E-mail: nslevin@penpubinc.com
Magazine for homebuilders. **Freq:** 11/year. **Trim Size:** 9 x 10.875. **Key Personnel:** Nick Slevin, Editor-in-Chief, Publisher; Kristen Eichenmuller, Contact. **URL:** http://bdmag.com. **Ad Rates:** BW $5,967; 4C $7,227. **Re-**

marks: Accepts advertising. **Circ:** △**40000**.

3183 ■ Building Products Digest
Cutler Publishing Inc.
4500 Campus Dr., Ste. 480
Newport Beach, CA 92660-1872
Magazine covering lumber yards, home centers, retailers, and wholesalers. **Freq:** Monthly. **Print Method:** Offset. **Trim Size:** 8 1/4 x 10 7/8. **Cols./Page:** 3. **Col. Width:** 26 nonpareils. **Col. Depth:** 140 agate lines. **Key Personnel:** Heather Kelly, Contact; Alan Oakes, Publisher; Chuck Casey, Manager, Advertising and Sales. **ISSN:** 0742--5691 (print). **Subscription Rates:** $22 Individuals; $36 Two years; $50 Individuals 3 years. **URL:** http://www.building-products.com. **Remarks:** Accepts advertising. **Circ:** Controlled 17161.

3184 ■ Civilitas
Newport Institute for Ethics, Law and Public Policy
PO Box 9044
Newport Beach, CA 92658
Free: 800-811-4770
Publisher's E-mail: info@newportinstitute.org
Freq: Quarterly. **Remarks:** Advertising not accepted. **Circ:** (Not Reported).

3185 ■ Fibromyalgia AWARE
National Fibromyalgia Association
1000 Bristol St. N, Ste. 17-247
Newport Beach, CA 92660
Publisher's E-mail: nfa@fmaware.org
Freq: Quarterly. **Subscription Rates:** $34.95 U.S. three issues; $44.95 Canada three issues; $69.95 Other countries three issues. **Remarks:** Accepts advertising. **Circ:** (Not Reported).

3186 ■ 50 Plus Builder
Peninsula Publishing Inc.
1602 Monrovia Ave.
Newport Beach, CA 92663-2808
Phone: (949)631-0308
Fax: (949)631-2475
Publisher's E-mail: nslevin@penpubinc.com
Magazine for homebuilders, architects, interior designers and allied residential building professionals who market their products and services to the 50-plus demographic. **Freq:** Monthly. **Key Personnel:** Nick Slevin, Editor-in-Chief, Publisher; Kristen Eichenmuller, Contact. **Subscription Rates:** Free. **URL:** http://www.50plusbuilder.com. **Remarks:** Accepts advertising. **Circ:** (Not Reported).

3187 ■ Green Home Builder: America's Premier Green Homebuilding Resource
Peninsula Publishing Inc.
1602 Monrovia Ave.
Newport Beach, CA 92663-2808
Phone: (949)631-0308
Fax: (949)631-2475
Publisher's E-mail: nslevin@penpubinc.com
Magazine for home builders and home building industry. **Freq:** Quarterly. **Trim Size:** 9 x 10.875. **Key Personnel:** Nick Slevin, Editor-in-Chief, Publisher. **URL:** http://greenhomebuildermag.com; http://www.penpubinc.com. **Remarks:** Accepts advertising. **Circ:** 19000.

3188 ■ The Journal of Historical Review
Institute for Historical Review
PO Box 2739
Newport Beach, CA 92659-1339
Phone: (714)593-9725
Fax: (714)465-3176
Publisher's E-mail: ihr@ihr.org
Journal containing articles and reviews in the tradition of Historical Revisionism. **Freq:** Bimonthly. **Print Method:** Web. **Trim Size:** 8 1/2 x 11. **Cols./Page:** 2. **Key Personnel:** Mark Weber, Editor. **ISSN:** 0195-6752 (print). **Alt. Formats:** DVD; PDF. **URL:** http://ihr.org/main/journal.shtml. **Ad Rates:** BW $500. **Remarks:** Accepts advertising. **Circ:** 1500.

3189 ■ The Merchant Magazine
Cutler Publishing Inc.
4500 Campus Dr., Ste. 480
Newport Beach, CA 92660-1872
Lumber and building materials magazine for the retailer and wholesaler of lumber & building materials. **Freq:** Monthly. **Print Method:** Offset. **Trim Size:** 8 1/4 x 10 7/8. **Cols./Page:** 3 and 2. **Col. Width:** 30 and 39 nonpareils. **Col. Depth:** 140 agate lines. **Key Personnel:** Chuck Casey, Manager, Advertising; Alan Oakes, Publisher. **ISSN:** 0739--9723 (print). **Subscription Rates:** $22 Individuals; $36 Two years; $50 Individuals 3 years. **URL:** http://www.building-products.com/Merchant-Magazine-Current-Issue. **Remarks:** Accepts advertising. **Circ:** Controlled ‡4000.

3190 ■ MUFON UFO Journal
Mutual UFO Network
3822 Campus Dr., Ste. 201
Newport Beach, CA 92660
Phone: (949)476-8366
Publisher's E-mail: hq@mufon.com
Contains statistics, research reports, book reviews and information on UFO sightings. **Freq:** Monthly. **Key Personnel:** Roger Marsh, Editor. **ISSN:** 0270--6822 (print). **Subscription Rates:** Included in membership. **URL:** http://www.mufon.com/e-journal.html. **Ad Rates:** BW $350. **Remarks:** Accepts advertising. **Circ:** 3000.

3191 ■ OC Register Metro: The Business Lifestyle Magazine
Churm Media Inc.
1451 Quail St., Ste. 201
Newport Beach, CA 92660
Professional magazine covering finance, politics and technology for executives. **Freq:** Semimonthly. **Key Personnel:** Kimberly A. Porrazzo, Editor; Craig Reem, Executive Editor; Steve Churm, Publisher; Guida Quon, Vice President, Human Resources, Vice President, Sales; Brian D. O'Neill, Chief Financial Officer. **URL:** http://www.ocregister.com. **Remarks:** Accepts advertising. **Circ:** ‡130,000.

3192 ■ Orange Coast: The Magazine of Orange County
Orange Coast
3701 Birch St., Ste. 100
Newport Beach, CA 92660
Phone: (949)862-1133
Fax: (949)862-0133
Publisher's E-mail: editorial@orangecoast.com
Consumer magazine for residents and visitors of Orange County, CA. **Freq:** Monthly. **Print Method:** Offset. **Trim Size:** 8 3/8 x 10 7/8. **Cols./Page:** 3. **Col. Width:** 13.5 picas. **Col. Depth:** 44 picas. **Key Personnel:** Martin J. Smith, Editor-in-Chief; Linda Goldstein, Executive Vice President. **ISSN:** 0279-0483 (print). **Subscription Rates:** $19.99 Individuals print and digital; $14.99 Individuals print; $9.99 Individuals digital. **Alt. Formats:** Download. **Remarks:** Accepts advertising. **Circ:** Paid ★**54220**.

3193 ■ Residential Contractor
Peninsula Publishing Inc.
1602 Monrovia Ave.
Newport Beach, CA 92663-2808
Phone: (949)631-0308
Fax: (949)631-2475
Publisher's E-mail: nslevin@penpubinc.com
Magazine for small volume residential builders, contractors, and specialty trades. **Freq:** Quarterly. **Trim Size:** 9 x 10.875. **Key Personnel:** Nick Slevin, Editor-in-Chief, Publisher; Carina Calhoun, Editor. **URL:** http://residentialcontractormag.com. **Remarks:** Accepts advertising. **Circ:** (Not Reported).

NORTH HOLLYWOOD

S. CA. Los Angeles Co. 15 mi. NW of Los Angeles. Manufactures aircraft, motion pictures and equipment, missiles, electronics, television, plastics. Residential.

3194 ■ Emmy
Academy of Television Arts and Sciences
5220 Lankershim Blvd.
North Hollywood, CA 91601
Phone: (818)754-2800
Freq: Bimonthly. **Print Method:** Offset. **Trim Size:** 8.375" x 10.875". **Key Personnel:** Juan Morales, Editor-in-Chief; Gail Polevoi, Editor. **ISSN:** 0164--3495 (print). **Subscription Rates:** $28 Individuals /year in U.S.; $7.95 Single issue print; $42 Individuals /year, Canada; $65 Individuals /year, international (non-U.S. and Canada); $5 Single issue digital; $19.95 Individuals One year digital subscription.; Included in membership. **URL:** http://www.emmys.com/emmy-magazine. **Ad Rates:** BW $2475; 4C $5000. **Remarks:** Accepts advertising. **Circ:** 14000.

3195 ■ Set Decor
Set Decorators Society of America
7100 Tujunga Ave., Ste. A
North Hollywood, CA 91605-6216
Phone: (818)255-2425
Fax: (818)982-8597
Publisher's E-mail: sdsa@setdecorators.org
Magazine covering art, craft and profession of set decoration. **Freq:** Quarterly. **Subscription Rates:** $24 Individuals /year; $10 Single issue. **Alt. Formats:** PDF. **URL:** http://www.setdecorators.org/?name=Set-Decor&art=setdecor; http://www.setdecorators.org/?art=setdecor_magazine_archives. **Remarks:** Accepts advertising. **Circ:** (Not Reported).

KAEH-FM - See Tooele, UT

KPFK-FM - See Los Angeles

NORTHRIDGE

S. CA. Los Angeles Co. 25 mi. N. of Los Angeles. California State University, Northridge. Citrus juices, electronic parts, boats, carbon paper manufactured.

3196 ■ Archeological Papers of the American Anthropological Association
Blackwell Publishing Inc.
Dept. of Anthropology
California State University, Northridge
18111 Nordhoff St.
Northridge, CA 91330
Publisher's E-mail: journaladsusa@bos.blackwellpublishing.com
Journal presenting manuscripts related to anthropological archeology for The American Anthropological Association. **Freq:** Annual. **Key Personnel:** Lynne Goldstein, Editor. **ISSN:** 1551--823X (print); **EISSN:** 1551--8248 (electronic). **Subscription Rates:** $40 Institutions online; £22 Institutions; €28 Institutions; $40 Institutions, other countries. **URL:** http://onlinelibrary.wiley.com/journal/10.1111/(ISSN)1551-8248. **Remarks:** Accepts advertising. **Circ:** (Not Reported).

3197 ■ The Daily Sundial
Santa Susana Press
University Library
18111 Nordhoff St.
Northridge, CA 91330-8326
Phone: (818)667-2638
Fax: (818)677-2676
Publisher's E-mail: santa.susana@csun.edu
Key Personnel: Manuel D. Araujo, Editor-in-Chief. **URL:** http://sundial.csun.edu. **Remarks:** Accepts advertising. **Circ:** (Not Reported).

3198 ■ Northridge
California State University Northridge Alumni Association
18111 Nordhoff St.
Northridge, CA 91330-8385
Phone: (818)677-2786
Fax: (818)677-4823
Publisher's E-mail: alumni@csun.edu
Freq: 3/year. **Subscription Rates:** free for members. **URL:** http://www.csun.edu/magazine. **Remarks:** Advertising not accepted. **Circ:** (Not Reported).

3199 ■ Perfume Bottle Quarterly
International Perfume Bottle Association
PO Box 7644
Northridge, CA 91327
Publisher's E-mail: membership@perfumebottles.org
Freq: Quarterly. **Subscription Rates:** Included in membership; $12 Nonmembers back issues. **Alt. Formats:** CD-ROM. **URL:** http://www.perfumebottles.org/pbq_archive.html. **Remarks:** Accepts advertising. **Circ:** 1300.

3200 ■ KCSN-FM - 88.5
18111 Nordhoff St.
Northridge, CA 91330
Phone: (818)677-3090
Email: feedback@kcsn.org
Format: Adult Album Alternative. **Networks:** National Public Radio (NPR). **Owner:** California State University, Northridge, 18111 Nordhoff St., Northridge, CA 91330, Ph: (818)677-1200. **Founded:** 1963. **Operating Hours:** Continuous. **Key Personnel:** Yvonne Wolfe, Bus. Mgr., yvonne.wolfe@csun.edu. **Wattage:** 370 ERP. **Ad Rates:** Noncommercial. **URL:** http://www.kcsn.org.

Circulation: ★ = AAM; △ or • = BPA; ♦ = CAC; ❑ = VAC; ⊕ = PO Statement; ‡ = Publisher's Report; Boldface figures = sworn; Light figures = estimated.

NORWALK

S. CA. Los Angeles Co. 10 mi. SE of Anaheim. Residential.

3201 ■ Norwalk Herald American
Wave Newspaper Group
3731 Wilshire Blvd., Ste. 840
Los Angeles, CA 90010
Phone: (323)556-5720
Fax: (213)835-0584
Newspaper. **Freq:** Weekly (Thurs.). **Cols./Page:** 6. **Col. Width:** 26 nonpareils. **Col. Depth:** 301 agate lines. **Key Personnel:** Arnold Adler. **Subscription Rates:** $125 By mail; Free local. **URL:** http://wavenewspapers.com. **Remarks:** Accepts advertising. **Circ:** (Not Reported).

3202 ■ Talon Marks
Cerritos College
11110 Alondra Blvd.
Norwalk, CA 90650-6298
Phone: (562)860-2451
Collegiate newspaper. **Freq:** Weekly during school year. **Print Method:** Offset. **Cols./Page:** 6. **Col. Width:** 25 nonpareils. **Col. Depth:** 294 agate lines. **Key Personnel:** Karla Enriquez, Editor-in-Chief. **URL:** http://www.talonmarks.com. **Ad Rates:** GLR $6; PCI $7. **Remarks:** Accepts advertising. **Circ:** Free 4000.

NOVATO

W. CA. Marin Co. 28 mi. N. of San Francisco. Suburban residential.

3203 ■ Diabetes Health: Investigate, Inform, Inspire
Diabetes Health
365 Bel Marin Keys Blvd., Ste. 100
Novato, CA 94949
Magazine focusing on diabetes health. **Trim Size:** 8 1/4 x 10 3/4. **Key Personnel:** Nadia Al-Samarrie, Editor-in-Chief, Publisher, Editor; Dick Young, Director, Operations. **Subscription Rates:** $19.95 Individuals print; $29.95 Two years print. **URL:** http://diabeteshealth.com. **Remarks:** Accepts advertising. **Circ:** 150000.

3204 ■ Ross Valley Reporter
Marin Scope Community Newspapers Inc.
1301 B Grant Ave.
Novato, CA 94948
Phone: (415)892-1516
Local community newspaper. **Freq:** Weekly (Thurs.). **Print Method:** Offset. **Trim Size:** 13 x 21. **Cols./Page:** 8. **Col. Width:** 8.5 picas. **Col. Depth:** 21 INS. **Key Personnel:** Soren Hemmila, Editor. **Subscription Rates:** $49 Individuals. **URL:** http://www.marinscope.com/ross_valley_reporter. **Ad Rates:** 4C $400; PCI $12.75. **Remarks:** Advertising accepted; rates available upon request. **Circ:** ‡10000.

3205 ■ San Rafael Newspointer
Marin Scope Community Newspapers Inc.
1301 B Grant Ave.
Novato, CA 94948
Phone: (415)892-1516
Community newspaper serving San Rafael, Terra Linda, and Lucas Valley. **Freq:** Weekly (Wed.). **Print Method:** Offset. **Trim Size:** 13 x 21. **Cols./Page:** 8. **Col. Width:** 8.5 INS. **Col. Depth:** 2 INS. **Key Personnel:** Joe Wolfcale, Managing Editor. **URL:** http://www.marinscope.com/news_pointer. **Ad Rates:** 4C $4; PCI $12.75. **Remarks:** Advertising accepted; rates available upon request. **Circ:** Combined ‡11500.

3206 ■ Sausalito Marin Scope
Marin Scope Community Newspapers Inc.
1301 B Grant Ave.
Novato, CA 94948
Phone: (415)892-1516
Community newspaper serving Sausalito, CA. **Freq:** Weekly (Tues.). **Print Method:** Web offset. **Trim Size:** 13 x 21. **Key Personnel:** Soren Hemmila, Editor; Linda Mallin, Manager, Circulation. **URL:** http://www.marinscope.com/sausalito_marin_scope. **Ad Rates:** PCI $7.60; SAU $16.10. **Remarks:** Accepts advertising. **Circ:** Combined ‡1487.

3207 ■ Somatics
Somatics Society
1516 Grant Ave., Ste. 212
Novato, CA 94945
Phone: (415)892-0617
Fax: (415)892-4388
Publisher's E-mail: info@somaticsed.com
Freq: Semiannual. **Subscription Rates:** Included in membership. **Remarks:** Advertising not accepted. **Circ:** (Not Reported).

3208 ■ Somatics: Magazine-Journal of the Mind/Body Arts and Sciences
Somatics Society
1516 Grant Ave., Ste. 212
Novato, CA 94945
Phone: (415)892-0617
Fax: (415)892-4388
Publisher's E-mail: info@somaticsed.com
Magazine covering health and fitness, movement, dance, yoga, and philosophy for professionals and a general audience. **Freq:** Semiannual. **Key Personnel:** Eleanor Criswell Hanna, Director, Editor, phone: (415)892-0617, fax: (415)382-4388; Thomas Hanna, Founder. **ISSN:** 0147--5231 (print). **Subscription Rates:** $20 Individuals /year; $25 Institutions /year. **URL:** http://www.somaticsed.com/magJournal.html. **Remarks:** Accepts advertising. **Circ:** (Not Reported).

3209 ■ Twin Cities Times
Marin Scope Community Newspapers Inc.
1301 B Grant Ave.
Novato, CA 94948
Phone: (415)892-1516
Community newspaper serving Corte Madera, Larkspur, and Greenbrae. **Freq:** Weekly (Wed.). **Print Method:** Web offset. **Trim Size:** 13 x 21. **Cols./Page:** 8. **Col. Width:** 8.5 picas. **Col. Depth:** 21 INS. **Key Personnel:** Greg Andersen, Editor. **URL:** http://www.marinscope.com/twin_cities_times. **Ad Rates:** 4C $400; PCI $12. **Remarks:** Advertising accepted; rates available upon request. **Circ:** Combined ‡7706.

OAKDALE

C. CA. Stanislaus Co. 16 mi. N. of Modesto. Manufactures chocolate, fire trucks. Poultry and egg processing; fruit, vegetable cannery; winery, Diversified farming. Sheep, poultry, dairy, cattle, almonds, peaches.

3210 ■ Escalon Times
Morris Newspaper of California
122 S 3rd Ave.
Oakdale, CA 95361
Phone: (209)847-3021
Newspaper. **Freq:** Weekly (Wed.). **Print Method:** Offset. **Col. Width:** 2 1/16 inches. **Col. Depth:** 294 agate lines. **Key Personnel:** Marg Jackson, Editor. **Subscription Rates:** $15 Individuals 3 months online only; $25 Individuals 6 months online only; $35 Individuals 6 months print and online; $35 Individuals 1 year online only; $52 Individuals 1 year print and online. **URL:** http://www.escalontimes.com. **Ad Rates:** BW $1,260; PCI $10. **Remarks:** Accepts advertising. **Circ:** 11000.

3211 ■ Oakdale Leader
Oakdale Leader
122 S 3rd Ave.
Oakdale, CA 95361
Phone: (209)847-3021
Publisher's E-mail: report@oakdaleleader.com
Community newspaper. **Freq:** Weekly (Wed.). **Print Method:** Offset. **Trim Size:** 13 1/4 x 21. **Cols./Page:** 8. **Col. Width:** 1 1/2 inches. **Col. Depth:** 21 inches. **Key Personnel:** Marg Jackson, Editor. **Subscription Rates:** $35 Individuals online only; $52 Individuals print + online. **URL:** http://www.oakdaleleader.com. **Ad Rates:** BW $1,278.48; 4C $1,618.48; SAU $12.45; PCI $9.35. **Remarks:** Accepts advertising. **Circ:** Paid ‡4899, Free ‡5911.

3212 ■ Top Gun
World Fast-Draw Association
6000 Wilkins Ave.
Oakdale, CA 95361-9797
Phone: (209)847-0483
Publisher's E-mail: wfda@fastdraw.org
Freq: Bimonthly. **Subscription Rates:** Included in membership. **URL:** http://www.fastdraw.org/wfda/wfd_topgun.html. **Remarks:** Accepts advertising. **Circ:** 500.

3213 ■ KCBC-AM - 770
10948 Cleveland Ave.
Oakdale, CA 95361-0077
Phone: (209)847-7700
Fax: (209)847-1769
Free: 800-593-5222
Owner: Crawford Broadcasting Co., 2821 S Parker Rd., Ste. 1205, Denver, CO 80014, Ph: (303)433-5500, Fax: (303)433-1555. **Founded:** 1987. **Formerly:** KPLA-AM. **Operating Hours:** 5 a.m.-10:00 p.m.; 80% network. **ADI:** San Francisco-Oakland-San Jose. **Key Personnel:** Don Crawford, Jr., Gen. Mgr.; Virginia Marsau, Operations Mgr.; Debbie Sill, Office Mgr. **Wattage:** 50,000 day; 1,000 night. **Ad Rates:** $15 for 30 seconds; $30 for 60 seconds. **URL:** http://770kcbc.com.

OAKHURST

SC CA. Madena Co. 45 mi. NW of Fresno. Residential. Mountain resort.

3214 ■ Sierra Home Advertiser
Pacific-Sierra Publishing
49165 Crane Valley Rd.
Oakhurst, CA 93644-8621
Phone: (559)683-4464
Fax: (559)683-8102
Shopper. **Freq:** Semiweekly (Wed. and Fri.). **Print Method:** Offset. **Cols./Page:** 6. **Col. Width:** 12.5 picas. **Col. Depth:** 21.5 inches. **Subscription Rates:** $46 Individuals includes Sunday Fresno Bee home delivery. **URL:** http://www.sierrastar.com. **Mailing address:** PO Box 305, Oakhurst, CA 93644-8621. **Ad Rates:** BW $1,251.30; 4C $1,491.30; SAU $9.95; PCI $9.70. **Remarks:** Accepts advertising. **Circ:** Free ‡12500.

3215 ■ KAAT-FM - 103.1
40356 Oak Pkwy.
Oakhurst, CA 93644
Phone: (559)683-1031
Fax: (559)683-5488
Format: Adult Contemporary; Soft Rock; Big Band/Nostalgia. **Networks:** Jones Satellite. **Owner:** California Sierra Corp., 4965 Joule St., Reno, NV 89502, Ph: (775)856-8008, Fax: (775)856-8009. **Founded:** 1982. **Operating Hours:** Continuous; 75% network, 25% local. **ADI:** Fresno-Visalia (Hanford), CA. **Key Personnel:** Larry W. Gamble, Gen. Mgr. **Wattage:** 25,000. **Ad Rates:** Noncommercial.

3216 ■ KTNS-AM - 1060
40356 Oak Pky.
Oakhurst, CA 93644
Phone: (559)683-1090
Fax: (559)683-5488
Email: mtkaat@sierratel.com
Format: Easy Listening. **Networks:** Jones Satellite. **Owner:** California Sierra Corp., 4965 Joule St., Reno, NV 89502, Ph: (775)856-8008, Fax: (775)856-8009. **Founded:** 1988. **Operating Hours:** Continuous. **Wattage:** 5,000. **Ad Rates:** Noncommercial.

3217 ■ Northland Communications
40092 Hwy. 49, Ste. A
Oakhurst, CA 93644
Phone: (559)683-7388
Fax: (559)642-2432
Free: 800-736-1414
Founded: Sept. 05, 2006. **Formerly:** Northland Cable Television. **Cities Served:** 120 channels. **Mailing address:** PO Box 2110, Oakhurst, CA 93644. **URL:** http://www.yournorthland.com.

OAKLAND

W. CA. Alameda Co. On east side of San Francisco Bay, connected by a bridge with San Francisco. Mills College (women). California College of Arts and Crafts. College of Holy Name (women). Coliseum Arena. World's 2nd largest container cargo port. Important seaport. Principally manufactures steel. Iron Paper, tin, building materials, food processing, engines.

3218 ■ Alameda County Bar Association Bulletin
Alameda County Bar Association
1000 Broadway, Ste. 480
Oakland, CA 94607
Phone: (510)302-2222
Fax: (510)452-2224
Professional magazine covering law. **Freq:** 5/year. **Print Method:** Offset. **Key Personnel:** Wayne S. Nishioka, President; Shannon Goecke, Editor-in-Chief, phone: (510)302-2215. **URL:** http://www.acbanet.org. **Remarks:** Accepts advertising. **Circ:** Controlled 2000.

3219 ■ Asian Survey: A Bimonthly Review of Contemporary Asian Affairs
University of California Press - Journals and Digital Publishing Division
Journals Fulfillment Dept., Ste. 400
155 Grand Ave.
Oakland, CA 94612-3758
Phone: (510)883-8232
Fax: (510)836-8910
Publication E-mail: asiasrvy@uclink.berkeley.edu
Political science journal covering Asia. **Freq:** Bimonthly. **Trim Size:** 6 x 9. **Key Personnel:** Tun-Jen Cheng, Board Member; Martin K. Whyte, Board Member; David Fraser, Managing Editor; Lowell Dittmer, Editor. **ISSN:** 0004--4687 (print); **EISSN:** 1533--838X (electronic). **Subscription Rates:** $99 Individuals online; $130 Individuals print and online; $49 Students; $35 Single issue. **URL:** http://as.ucpress.edu. **Remarks:** Accepts advertising. **Circ:** (Not Reported).

3220 ■ Bad Subjects: Political Education for Everyday Life
University of California
1111 Franklin St.
Oakland, CA 94607
Publication E-mail: bad@uclink.berkeley.edu
Journal that focuses on broadening the views on leftist and progressive work. **Freq:** 6/year. **Key Personnel:** Charlie Bertsch, Editor, Writer; Kim Nicolini, Editor. **URL:** http://bad.eserver.org. **Remarks:** Advertising not accepted. **Circ:** (Not Reported).

3221 ■ Beeswax: A Journal of Literature & Art
Valley Business Front L.L.C.
248 Third St., No. 733
Oakland, CA 94607
Phone: (510)282-5971
Publication E-mail: editors@beeswaxmagazine.com
Journal featuring literature and art. **Freq:** Bimonthly. **Trim Size:** 8 x 8. **Key Personnel:** Laureen Mahler, Editor; John Peck, Editor. **Subscription Rates:** $35 Individuals. **URL:** http://www.voltapress.com/Beeswax-Magazine. **Circ:** (Not Reported).

3222 ■ Berkeley Journal of Employment and Labor Law
University of California Press - Journals and Digital Publishing Division
Journals Fulfillment Dept., Ste. 400
155 Grand Ave.
Oakland, CA 94612-3758
Phone: (510)883-8232
Fax: (510)836-8910
Publication E-mail: journalpublications@law.berkeley.edu
Professional journal covering employment and labor law. **Freq:** Semiannual. **Print Method:** offset. **Trim Size:** 7 x 10. **Key Personnel:** Jonathan Helfgott, Editor-in-Chief; Caleb Webster, Editor. **ISSN:** 1067--7666 (print). **Alt. Formats:** PDF. **URL:** http://scholarship.law.berkeley.edu/bjell. **Remarks:** Accepts advertising. **Circ:** (Not Reported).

3223 ■ Boom: A Journal of California
University of California Press - Journals and Digital Publishing Division
Journals Fulfillment Dept., Ste. 400
155 Grand Ave.
Oakland, CA 94612-3758
Phone: (510)883-8232
Fax: (510)836-8910
Publisher's E-mail: library@ucpressjournals.com
Journal containing articles on vital social, cultural, and political issues in California. **Freq:** Quarterly March, June, September, December. **ISSN:** 2153--8018 (print); **EISSN:** 2153--764X (electronic). **URL:** http://boom.ucpress.edu. **Circ:** (Not Reported).

3224 ■ California Business Law Reporter
Continuing Education of the Bar
2100 Franklin St., Ste. 500
Oakland, CA 94612-3098
Phone: (510)302-2000
Fax: (800)640-6994
Free: 800-232-3444
Publisher's E-mail: customer_service@ceb.ucop.edu
Legal recent developments in business law. **Freq:** Bimonthly. **Print Method:** Offset. **Cols./Page:** 2. **Col. Width:** 21 picas. **Col. Depth:** 55 picas. **ISSN:** 0199--669X (print). **Subscription Rates:** $385 Individuals. **URL:** http://www.ceb.com/CEBSite/product.asp?catalog%5Fname=CEB&menu%5Fcategory=Bookstore&main%5Fcategory=Reporters&product%5Fid=BU90040&Page=1. **Circ:** (Not Reported).

3225 ■ California Journal of Politics and Policy
University of California California Digital Library
415 20th St., 4th Fl.
Oakland, CA 94612-2901
Phone: (510)987-0425
Fax: (510)893-5212
Publisher's E-mail: cdl@www.cdlib.org
Peer-reviewed journal covering the policy and politics in California. **Freq:** Quarterly. **Key Personnel:** Jack Citrin, Editor; Bruce E. Cain, Editor. **ISSN:** 1944--4370 (print). **URL:** http://escholarship.org/uc/cjpp. **Circ:** (Not Reported).

3226 ■ The Catholic Voice: A Publication of the Roman Catholic Diocese of Oakland
Roman Catholic Diocese of Oakland
2121 Harrison St., Ste. 100
Oakland, CA 94612
Phone: (510)893-5339
Fax: (510)893-4734
Publication E-mail: cathvoice@aol.com
Catholic newspaper. **Freq:** Bimonthly. **Print Method:** Offset. **Cols./Page:** 6. **Col. Width:** 21 nonpareils. **Col. Depth:** 231 agate lines. **Key Personnel:** Albert C. Pacciorini, Editor, phone: (510)419-1073; Sandi Gearhart, Manager, Circulation, phone: (510)893-5339. **URL:** http://www.catholicvoiceoakland.org. **Ad Rates:** BW $2697; PCI $27. **Remarks:** Accepts advertising. **Circ:** (Not Reported).

3227 ■ Classical Antiquity
University of California Press - Journals and Digital Publishing Division
Journals Fulfillment Dept., Ste. 400
155 Grand Ave.
Oakland, CA 94612-3758
Phone: (510)883-8232
Fax: (510)836-8910
Publisher's E-mail: library@ucpressjournals.com
Peer-reviewed scholarly journal covering interdisciplinary research and issues in Classics-Greek and Roman literature, history, art, philosophy, archaeology, and philology. **Freq:** Semiannual April and October. **Trim Size:** 7 x 10. **Key Personnel:** Steven Johnstone, Board Member; Ellen Finkelpearl, Board Member; Alain Gowing, Board Member; Mark Griffith, Editor. **ISSN:** 0278--6656 (print); **EISSN:** 1067--8344 (electronic). **Subscription Rates:** $217 Institutions online only; $49 Individuals online only; $24 Individuals online only, student/retired. **URL:** http://ca.ucpress.edu. **Ad Rates:** BW $325. **Remarks:** Accepts advertising. **Circ:** 600.

3228 ■ ColorLines
Race Forward: The Center for Racial Justice Innovation
900 Alice St., Ste. 400
Oakland, CA 94607
Phone: (510)653-3415
Fax: (510)986-1062
Publisher's E-mail: media@raceforward.org
Freq: Quarterly. **Key Personnel:** Akiba Solomon, Director, Editorial; Rinku Sen, Publisher. **URL:** http://www.colorlines.com. **Remarks:** Accepts advertising. **Circ:** (Not Reported).

3229 ■ Continuing Education of the Bar
California Continuing Education of the Bar
2100 Franklin St., Ste. 500
Oakland, CA 94612-3098
Phone: (510)302-2000
Free: 800-232-3444
Publisher's E-mail: customer_service@ceb.ucop.edu
Trade magazine concentrating on recent legislation and court decisions affecting estates, trusts, and related taxation in California. **Freq:** Bimonthly. **Print Method:** Offset/Electronic. **Trim Size:** 8 1/2 x 11. **Cols./Page:** 2. **Col. Width:** 21 picas. **Col. Depth:** 55 picas. **Key Personnel:** Jeffrey A. Dennis-Strathmeyer, Editor. **ISSN:** 0273--7027 (print). **Formerly:** Estate Planning and California Probate Reporter. **Remarks:** Advertising not accepted. **Circ:** (Not Reported).

3230 ■ Diseased Pariah News
Men's Support Center
PO Box 30564
Oakland, CA 94604
Publication E-mail: dpnmail@netcom.com
Publication focusing on HIV infected gay men. **Freq:** Quarterly. **Subscription Rates:** $10. **URL:** http://www.stim.com/Stim-x/6.1/readthis/readthis-06.1.html. **Circ:** (Not Reported).

3231 ■ EarthLight Magazine: Magazine of Spirituality and Ecology
EarthLight Magazine
111 Fairmount Ave.
Oakland, CA 94611
Phone: (510)451-4926
Publication E-mail: admin@earthlight.org
Publication on sacred ecology. **Freq:** Quarterly. **Print Method:** Web offset. **Trim Size:** 8 1/2 x 11. **Cols./Page:** 3. **Col. Width:** 14 picas. **Col. Depth:** 49 picas. **Key Personnel:** Lauren K. De Boer, Editor. **ISSN:** 1050-0413 (print). **URL:** http://www.earthlight.org. **Ad Rates:** GLR $3; BW $400; 4C $600; PCI $15. **Remarks:** Accepts advertising. **Circ:** Paid 6,500, Non-paid 500.

3232 ■ Edible East Bay
Edible Communities Inc.
4200 Park Blvd., No. 267
Oakland, CA 94602
Phone: (510)225-5776
Publisher's E-mail: info@ediblecommunities.com
Magazine covering the local food in the East Bay region. **Freq:** Quarterly. **Key Personnel:** Cheryl Koehler, Editor, Publisher, phone: (520)225-5776. **Subscription Rates:** $28 Individuals; $46 Two years. **URL:** http://ediblee astbay.com. **Remarks:** Accepts advertising. **Circ:** (Not Reported).

3233 ■ The Employee Advocate
National Employment Lawyers Association
2201 Broadway, Ste. 402
Oakland, CA 94612
Phone: (415)296-7629
Free: 866-593-7521
Publisher's E-mail: nelahq@nelahq.org
Freq: Quarterly. **Subscription Rates:** Included in membership. **URL:** http://www.nela.org/index.cfm?pg=join. **Remarks:** Accepts advertising. **Circ:** 3,000.

3234 ■ Federal Sentencing Reporter
University of California Press - Journals and Digital Publishing Division
Journals Fulfillment Dept., Ste. 400
155 Grand Ave.
Oakland, CA 94612-3758
Phone: (510)883-8232
Fax: (510)836-8910
Publisher's E-mail: library@ucpressjournals.com
Journal featuring information about the law of sentencing as it has evolved under the United States Sentencing Commission guidelines. **Freq:** 5/yr October, December, February, April, June. **Trim Size:** 8 1/2 x 11. **Key Personnel:** Douglas A. Berman, Managing Editor; Frank O. Bowman, III, Editor; Mark D. Harris, Editor; Aaron Rappaport, Editor; Daniel J. Freed, Editor; Nora V. Demleitner, Managing Editor; Steven L. Chanenson, Editor. **ISSN:** 1053-9867 (print). **Subscription Rates:** $176 Individuals print only; $97 Students print only; $97 Individuals retired, print only. **URL:** http://www.ucpressjournals.com/journal.asp?j=fsr. **Remarks:** Advertising not accepted. **Circ:** (Not Reported).

3235 ■ Film Quarterly
University of California Press - Journals and Digital Publishing Division
Journals Fulfillment Dept., Ste. 400
155 Grand Ave.
Oakland, CA 94612-3758
Phone: (510)883-8232
Fax: (510)836-8910
Publisher's E-mail: library@ucpressjournals.com
Peer-reviewed journal covering the art of cinema. **Freq:** Quarterly. **Print Method:** Offset. **Trim Size:** 8 1/2 x 11. **Cols./Page:** 2. **Col. Width:** 39 nonpareils. **Col. Depth:** 125 agate lines. **Key Personnel:** Christine Acham, Board Member; Marsha Kinder, Board Member; Leo Braudy, Board Member; Ann Martin, Editor. **ISSN:** 0015--1386 (print); **EISSN:** 1533--8630 (electronic). **Subscription Rates:** $45 Individuals online only; $59 Individuals print and online; $20 Single issue; $25 Students individual; $225 Institutions online only; $303 Institutions print and online; $66 Single issue institutional. **URL:** http://fq.ucpress.edu. **Ad Rates:** GLR $540; BW $615.

Circulation: ★ = AAM; △ or • = BPA; ♦ = CAC; ❑ = VAC; ⊕ = PO Statement; ‡ = Publisher's Report; Boldface figures = sworn; Light figures = estimated.

Remarks: Accepts advertising. **Circ:** 3591.

3236 ■ Global Pesticide Campaigner
Pesticide Action Network North America
1611 Telegraph Ave., Ste. 1200
Oakland, CA 94612-2130
Phone: (510)788-9020
Publisher's E-mail: panna@panna.org
Freq: Quarterly. **ISSN:** 1055--548X (print). **Remarks:** Advertising not accepted. **Circ:** (Not Reported).

3237 ■ Global Pesticide Campaigner
Pesticide Action Network North America Regional Center
1611 Telegraph Ave., Ste. 1200
Oakland, CA 94612-2130
Phone: (510)788-9020
Publisher's E-mail: panna@panna.org
Freq: Quarterly. **ISSN:** 1055--548X (print). **Remarks:** Advertising not accepted. **Circ:** (Not Reported).

3238 ■ Historical Studies in the Natural Sciences
University of California Press - Journals and Digital Publishing Division
Journals Fulfillment Dept., Ste. 400
155 Grand Ave.
Oakland, CA 94612-3758
Phone: (510)883-8232
Fax: (510)836-8910
Publisher's E-mail: library@ucpressjournals.com
Scholarly journal covering intellectual and social history of the physical sciences and experimental biology from the 17th century to the present. **Freq:** 5/year February, April, June, September and November. **Trim Size:** 6 x 9. **Key Personnel:** Cathryn Carson, Editor; Diana Wear, Managing Editor. **ISSN:** 1939--1811 (print); **EISSN:** 1939--182X (electronic). **Subscription Rates:** $237 Institutions online only; $60 Individuals online only; $30 Individuals online only, single/retired. **URL:** http://hsns.ucpress.edu. **Formerly**: Historical Studies in the Physical and Biological Sciences. **Ad Rates:** BW $325. **Remarks:** Accepts advertising. **Circ:** 400.

3239 ■ The Independent Review
The Independent Institute
100 Swan Way
Oakland, CA 94621-1428
Phone: (510)632-1366
Fax: (510)568-6040
Journal ranging across the fields of economics, political science, law, history, philosophy and sociology. **Freq:** Quarterly. **Subscription Rates:** $28.95 /year; $7.50 Individuals single copy; $25 Institutions single copy. **URL:** http://www.independent.org/publications/tir/. **Ad Rates:** BW $775. **Remarks:** Accepts advertising. **Circ:** (Not Reported).

3240 ■ International Review of Qualitative Research
University of California Press - Journals and Digital Publishing Division
Journals Fulfillment Dept., Ste. 400
155 Grand Ave.
Oakland, CA 94612-3758
Phone: (510)883-8232
Fax: (510)836-8910
Publisher's E-mail: library@ucpressjournals.com
Peer-reviewed journal advancing the use of critical, experimental, and traditional forms of qualitative inquiry towards the pursuit of social justice. **Freq:** Quarterly May, August, November, February. **ISSN:** 1940--8447 (print); **EISSN:** 1940--8455 (electronic). **Subscription Rates:** $47 Individuals /year (online); $26 Individuals single issue; $63 Individuals /year (print and online); $341 Institutions /year (online); $53 Institutions single issue; $387 Institutions /year (print and online). **URL:** http://irqr.ucpress.edu. **Circ:** (Not Reported).

3241 ■ Journal of Musicology
University of California Press - Journals and Digital Publishing Division
Journals Fulfillment Dept., Ste. 400
155 Grand Ave.
Oakland, CA 94612-3758
Phone: (510)883-8232
Fax: (510)836-8910
Publisher's E-mail: library@ucpressjournals.com
Peer-reviewed journal dealing with field and methodology of musicological scholarship. **Freq:** Quarterly latest volume: 3 Summer 2016. **Trim Size:** 6 x 9. **Key Personnel:** Klara Moricz, Editor; Christopher Hailey, Editor; Karol Berger, Board Member. **ISSN:** 0277--9269 (print); **EISSN:** 1533--8347 (electronic). **Subscription Rates:** $55 Individuals online (1 year); $69 Individuals online & print (1 year); $20 Individuals single issue; $80 Institutions single issue. **URL:** http://jm.ucpress.edu. **Remarks:** Accepts advertising. **Circ:** 875.

3242 ■ Journal of Vietnamese Studies
University of California Press - Journals and Digital Publishing Division
Journals Fulfillment Dept., Ste. 400
155 Grand Ave.
Oakland, CA 94612-3758
Phone: (510)883-8232
Fax: (510)836-8910
Publisher's E-mail: library@ucpressjournals.com
Journal containing Vietnamese history, culture and society. **Freq:** Quarterly Published: February, May, August, November. **Key Personnel:** Liam C. Kelley, Editor. **ISSN:** 1559--372X (print); **EISSN:** 1559--3738 (electronic). **URL:** http://vs.ucpress.edu. **Circ:** (Not Reported).

3243 ■ Left Curve
Left Curve Publications
PO Box 472
Oakland, CA 94604-0472
Phone: (510)763-7193
Publisher's E-mail: editor@leftcurve.org
Artist-produced journal that addresses the problems of cultural forms emerging from one crises of modernity that strive to be independent from the control of dominant institutions. **Freq:** Irregular. **Print Method:** Offset. **Trim Size:** 8 1/2 x 11. **Cols./Page:** 2. **Col. Width:** 3 1/2 inches. **Col. Depth:** 9 inches. **Key Personnel:** Richard Olsen, Associate Editor; John Hutnyk, Associate Editor; Jack Hirschman, Associate Editor; Agneta Falk, Associate Editor; Csaba Polony, Editor; Des McGuinness, Associate Editor; Peter Laska, Associate Editor. **ISSN:** 0160--1857 (print). **Subscription Rates:** $35 Individuals; $50 Institutions; $12 Single issue. **URL:** http://www.leftcurve.org. **Ad Rates:** GLR $1.50; BW $200; PCI $15. **Remarks:** Accepts advertising. **Circ:** Paid 2000, 2000.

3244 ■ Locus: News, Reviews, Resources, and Perspectives of Science Fiction, Fantasy, and Horror
Locus Publications
PO Box 13305
Oakland, CA 94661
Fax: (510)339-9198
Trade magazine on science fiction publishing. **Freq:** Monthly. **Print Method:** Offset. **Trim Size:** 8 3/8 x 10 7/8. **Cols./Page:** 3. **Col. Width:** 30 nonpareils. **Col. Depth:** 140 agate lines. **Key Personnel:** Charles N. Brown, Editor-in-Chief, Publisher; Liza Groen Trombi, Editor-in-Chief; Kirsten Gong-Wong, Managing Editor. **ISSN:** 0047--4959 (print). **Subscription Rates:** $63 U.S. print - periodical, 12 issues; $76 U.S. print - first class, 12 issues; $75 U.S. print and digital - periodical, 12 issues; $88 U.S. print and online - first class, 12 issues; $77 Canada and Mexico International Surface Airlift - 12 issues; $89 Canada and Mexico print and digital - 12 issues; $100 Other countries International Surface Airlift - 12 issues; $5.50 Individuals electronic publishing/ PDF - single current issue; $48 Individuals electronic publishing/ PDF - 12 issues. **Alt. Formats:** Electronic publishing; PDF. **URL:** http://www.locusmag.com. **Ad Rates:** GLR $2; BW $600, full page; 4C $1225; PCI $20. **Remarks:** Accepts advertising. **Circ:** ‡10000, 6000.

3245 ■ MEDICC Review
Medical Education Cooperation with Cuba
1814 Franklin St., Ste. 820
Oakland, CA 94612
Phone: (678)904-8092
EISSN: 1527--3172 (electronic). **URL:** http://medicc.org/mediccreview. **Remarks:** Advertising not accepted. **Circ:** (Not Reported).

3246 ■ Music Perception: An Interdisciplinary journal
University of California Press - Journals and Digital Publishing Division
Journals Fulfillment Dept., Ste. 400
155 Grand Ave.
Oakland, CA 94612-3758
Phone: (510)883-8232
Fax: (510)836-8910
Publisher's E-mail: library@ucpressjournals.com
Journal on music. **Freq:** 5/year. **Print Method:** Offset. **Trim Size:** 7 x 10. **Cols./Page:** 1. **Col. Width:** 56 nonpareils. **Col. Depth:** 105 agate lines. **Key Personnel:** Lola L. Cuddy, Editor; Jay W. Dowling, Associate Editor; Christine K. Koh, Managing Editor; Eric Clarke, Associate Editor. **ISSN:** 0730--7829 (print); **EISSN:** 1533--8312 (electronic). **Subscription Rates:** $89 Individuals online only; $115 Individuals print and online; $25 Single issue individuals; $441 Institutions online only; $594 Institutions print and online; $128 Single issue institution. **URL:** http://mp.ucpress.edu. **Ad Rates:** BW $325. **Remarks:** Advertising accepted; rates available upon request. **Circ:** ‡685.

3247 ■ The Negro Spiritual
Friends of Negro Spirituals
PO Box 71956
Oakland, CA 94612-8156
Phone: (510)869-4359
Journal containing educational articles and news about Negro Spirituals. **Freq:** 3/year. **Subscription Rates:** Included in membership. **URL:** http://www.dogonvillage.com/negrospirituals. **Circ:** (Not Reported).

3248 ■ New Criminal Law Review
University of California Press - Journals and Digital Publishing Division
Journals Fulfillment Dept., Ste. 400
155 Grand Ave.
Oakland, CA 94612-3758
Phone: (510)883-8232
Fax: (510)836-8910
Publisher's E-mail: library@ucpressjournals.com
Journal focusing on examinations of crime and punishment in domestic, transnational, and international context. **Freq:** Quarterly January, April, July, October. **ISSN:** 1933--4192 (print); **EISSN:** 1933--4206 (electronic). **URL:** http://nclr.ucpress.edu. **Circ:** (Not Reported).

3249 ■ Nineteenth-Century Literature
University of California Press - Journals and Digital Publishing Division
Journals Fulfillment Dept., Ste. 400
155 Grand Ave.
Oakland, CA 94612-3758
Phone: (510)883-8232
Fax: (510)836-8910
Publication E-mail: ncl@humnet.ucla.edu
Journal on literature. **Freq:** Quarterly. **Print Method:** Offset. **Trim Size:** 6 x 9. **Cols./Page:** 1. **Col. Width:** 52 nonpareils. **Col. Depth:** 100 agate lines. **Key Personnel:** Jonathan H. Grossman, Advisor, Board Member; Ronald Lear, Assistant Editor; Evan Carton, Advisor, Board Member; Elizabeth K. Helsinger, Advisor, Board Member; Regenia Gagnier, Advisor, Board Member; Nancy Bentley, Advisor, Board Member; Claudia L. Johnson, Advisor, Board Member; Rosemarie Bodenheimer, Advisor, Board Member; Saree Makdisi, Editor; Thomas Wortham, Advisor, Board Member. **ISSN:** 0891--9356 (print); **EISSN:** 1067--8352 (electronic). **Subscription Rates:** $49 Individuals online only; $65 Individuals print and online; $20 Single issue individual; $200 Institutions online only; $268 Institutions print and online; $73 Single issue institution. **URL:** http://ncl.ucpress.edu. **Remarks:** Advertising accepted; rates available upon request. **Circ:** 1614.

3250 ■ 19th-Century Music
University of California Press - Journals and Digital Publishing Division
Journals Fulfillment Dept., Ste. 400
155 Grand Ave.
Oakland, CA 94612-3758
Phone: (510)883-8232
Fax: (510)836-8910
Publisher's E-mail: library@ucpressjournals.com
Scholarly journal covering music. **Freq:** 3/year July, November and March. **Print Method:** Offset. **Trim Size:** 8.5 x 10. **Key Personnel:** Lawrence Kramer, Editor; Christina Acosta, Managing Editor. **ISSN:** 0148--2076 (print); **EISSN:** 1533--8606 (electronic). **Subscription Rates:** $49 Individuals /year (online); $65 Individuals /year (print and online); $25 Individuals single issue; $29 Students /retired, /year (online); $239 Institutions /year (online; $306 Institutions /year (print and online);

$110 Institutions single issue. **URL:** http://ncm.ucpress.edu. **Remarks:** Accepts advertising. **Circ:** (Not Reported).

3251 ■ Nova Religio: The Journal of Alternative and Emergent Religions
University of California Press - Journals and Digital Publishing Division
Journals Fulfillment Dept., Ste. 400
155 Grand Ave.
Oakland, CA 94612-3758
Phone: (510)883-8232
Fax: (510)836-8910
Publisher's E-mail: library@ucpressjournals.com
Peer-reviewed journal presenting a comprehensive interpretation and examination of alternative religious movements. **Freq:** Quarterly. **Key Personnel:** Joel E. Tishken, Editor; Catherine Wessinger, Editor; Eugene V. Gallagher, Editor. **ISSN:** 1092--6690 (print); **EISSN:** 1541--8480 (electronic). **Subscription Rates:** $80 Institutions /issue; $65 Individuals /yr. online; $85 Individuals /yr. print & online; $25 Individuals /issue; $35 Individuals /yr. **URL:** http://nr.ucpress.edu. **Remarks:** Accepts advertising. **Circ:** (Not Reported).

3252 ■ Our Truths
Exhale
1714 Franklin St., No. 100-141
Oakland, CA 94612
Phone: (510)446-7900
Fax: (309)410-1127
Publisher's E-mail: info@exhaleprovoice.org
Freq: Semiannual. **Alt. Formats:** PDF. **URL:** http://exhaleprovoice.org/our-truths-nuestras-verdades-zine. **Remarks:** Advertising not accepted. **Circ:** (Not Reported).

3253 ■ The Public Historian
University of California Press - Journals and Digital Publishing Division
Journals Fulfillment Dept., Ste. 400
155 Grand Ave.
Oakland, CA 94612-3758
Phone: (510)883-8232
Fax: (510)836-8910
Publisher's E-mail: ncph@iupui.edu
Journal covering public history and policy. **Freq:** Quarterly February, May, August, November. **Print Method:** Offset. **Trim Size:** 6 x 9. **Key Personnel:** Randolph Bergstrom, Editor; Shelley Bookspan, Senior Editor; Lindsey Reed, Senior Editor. **ISSN:** 0272-3433 (print); **EISSN:** 1533-8576 (electronic). **Subscription Rates:** $218 Institutions 1 year - online only; $76 Single issue institution; $20 Single issue; $273 Institutions 1 year - print and online. **URL:** http://tph.ucpress.edu. **Ad Rates:** BW $325. **Remarks:** Advertising accepted; rates available upon request. **Circ:** 1600, 1500.

3254 ■ Real Property Law Reporter
Continuing Education of the Bar
2100 Franklin St., Ste. 500
Oakland, CA 94612-3098
Phone: (510)302-2000
Fax: (800)640-6994
Free: 800-232-3444
Publisher's E-mail: customer_service@ceb.ucop.edu
Legal publication on real property law developments in California. **Freq:** 6/year. **Print Method:** Offset/Electronic. **Trim Size:** 8 1/2 x 11. **Cols./Page:** 3. **Col. Width:** 21 picas. **Col. Depth:** 55 picas. **ISSN:** 0898--1698 (print). **Subscription Rates:** $385 Individuals. **URL:** http://www.ceb.com/CEBSite/product.asp?catalog_name=CEB&menu_category=Bookstore&main_category=Reporters&product_id=RE73000&Page=1. **Remarks:** Advertising not accepted. **Circ:** (Not Reported).

3255 ■ Reports of the National Center for Science Education
National Center for Science Education
1904 Franklin St., Ste. 600
Oakland, CA 94612-2922
Phone: (510)601-7203
Fax: (510)788-7971
Publisher's E-mail: info@ncse.com
Journal covering all aspects of the creationism/evolution controversy, and controversies over instruction in global warming and other climate change issues. **Freq:** Bimonthly. **ISSN:** 2159- 9270 (print). **Subscription Rates:** Included in membership. **URL:** http://reports.ncse.com/index.php/rncse; http://ncse.com/media. **Remarks:** Advertising not accepted. **Circ:** (Not Reported).

3256 ■ Representations
University of California Press - Journals and Digital Publishing Division
Journals Fulfillment Dept., Ste. 400
155 Grand Ave.
Oakland, CA 94612-3758
Phone: (510)883-8232
Fax: (510)836-8910
Publisher's E-mail: library@ucpressjournals.com
Journal featuring literary and art criticisms and cultural studies. **Freq:** Quarterly February, May, August and November. **Print Method:** Offset. **Trim Size:** 7 x 10. **Cols./Page:** 1. **Col. Width:** 56 nonpareils. **Col. Depth:** 105 agate lines. **Key Personnel:** Catherine Gallagher, Board Member; Thomas Laqueur, Board Member; Ian Duncan, Editor; Stephen Best, Board Member; David Henkin, Editor; Whitney Davis, Board Member; T.J. Clark, Board Member; Carol J. Clover, Board Member; Jean Day, Associate Editor. **ISSN:** 0734--6018 (print); **EISSN:** 1533--855X (electronic). **Subscription Rates:** $55 Individuals online only; $69 Included in membership print and online; $20 Single issue individual; $292 Institutions online only; $376 Institutions print and online; $102 Single issue institution. **URL:** http://rep.ucpress.edu. **Ad Rates:** BW $360. **Remarks:** Advertising accepted; rates available upon request. **Circ:** 1097.

3257 ■ Revolution Magazine: The Journal for RNs and Patient Advocacy
National Nurses Organizing Committee California Nurses Association
2000 Franklin St.
Oakland, CA 94612
Phone: (510)273-2200
Fax: (510)663-1625
Publisher's E-mail: press@calnurses.org
Professional magazine covering news and issues for registered nurses. **Freq:** Bimonthly. **Key Personnel:** Kay McVay, RN, President; Charles Idelson, Editor, phone: (510)273-2246. **ISSN:** 1059-0927 (print). **Subscription Rates:** $30 Individuals; $100 Institutions. **URL:** http://www.calnurses.org/publications/revolution/. **Ad Rates:** GLR $20; BW $2,600; 4C $2,600; PCI $180. **Remarks:** Accepts advertising. **Circ:** (Not Reported).

3258 ■ Rhetorica: A Journal of the History of Rhetoric
University of California Press - Journals and Digital Publishing Division
Journals Fulfillment Dept., Ste. 400
155 Grand Ave.
Oakland, CA 94612-3758
Phone: (510)883-8232
Fax: (510)836-8910
Publisher's E-mail: library@ucpressjournals.com
Journal covering the theory and practice of rhetoric in all aspects. **Freq:** Quarterly February, May, August, November. **Print Method:** Offset. **Trim Size:** 6 x 9. **Key Personnel:** Marc van der Poel, Editor; Mike Edwards, Board Member; Laurent Pernot, Board Member. **ISSN:** 0734-8584 (print). **Subscription Rates:** $16 Single issue; $64 Single issue intitutions; $16 Single issue student/retired. **URL:** http://www.jstor.org/page/journal/rhetorica/about.html. **Ad Rates:** BW $325. **Remarks:** Advertising accepted; rates available upon request. **Circ:** 725.

3259 ■ Sierra: The Magazine of the Sierra Club
Sierra Club
2101 Webster St., Ste. 1300
Oakland, CA 94612
Phone: (415)977-5500
Fax: (510)208-3140
Publication E-mail: sierra.mail@sierraclub.org
Magazine on conservation and the environment. **Freq:** Bimonthly. **Print Method:** Offset. **Trim Size:** 8 x 10 1/2. **Cols./Page:** 3. **Col. Width:** 27 nonpareils. **Col. Depth:** 128 agate lines. **Key Personnel:** Jason Marks, Editor-in-Chief. **USPS:** 495-920. **Subscription Rates:** Included in membership. **URL:** http://www.sierraclub.org/sierra. **Circ:** Paid ★**742083**.

3260 ■ Social Problems
University of California Press - Journals and Digital Publishing Division
Journals Fulfillment Dept., Ste. 400
155 Grand Ave.
Oakland, CA 94612-3758
Phone: (510)883-8232
Fax: (510)836-8910
Publication E-mail: socialproblems@fsu.edu
Journal addressing social issues. **Founded:** 1952. **Freq:** Quarterly February, May, August, November. **Print Method:** Offset. **Trim Size:** 7 x 10. **Key Personnel:** Kristin Lavin, Managing Editor; Ted Chiricos, Editor. **ISSN:** 0037-7791 (print). **Subscription Rates:** $83 Institutions single issue; $293 Nonmembers individual; $80 Nonmembers individual, single issue. **URL:** http://www.ucpressjournals.com/journal.asp?j=sp. **Ad Rates:** 4C $350. **Remarks:** Advertising accepted; rates available upon request. **Circ:** 3050.

3261 ■ TEST Engineering & Management
The Mattingley Publishing Company Inc.
3756 Grand Ave., Ste. 205
Oakland, CA 94610-1545
Phone: (510)839-0909
Fax: (510)839-2950
Publication E-mail: testmag@testmagazine.biz
Trade publication that covers physical and mechanical testing and environmental simulation; edited for test engineering professionals. **Freq:** 6/year. **Print Method:** Offset. **Trim Size:** 8 x 10 7/8. **Cols./Page:** 3. **Col. Width:** 26 nonpareils. **Col. Depth:** 140 agate lines. **Key Personnel:** Eve Mattingley-Hannigan, Editor. **ISSN:** 0193--4120 (print). **Subscription Rates:** $65 U.S. individual, 1 year; $55 U.S. agency, 1 year; $75 Other countries individual, 1 year; $64 Other countries agency, 1 year. **URL:** http://www.mattingley-publ.com. **Ad Rates:** BW $2950; 4C $3850; PCI $90. **Remarks:** Accepts advertising. **Circ:** (Not Reported).

3262 ■ Ultra Cycling
Ultra Marathon Cycling Association
c/o Paul Carpenter, President
7982 Hillmont Dr., Apt. B
Oakland, CA 94605
Phone: (303)545-9566
Fax: (303)545-9619
Publisher's E-mail: executivedirector@ultracycling.com
Freq: Quarterly. **Subscription Rates:** Included in membership. **Alt. Formats:** PDF. **URL:** http://www.ultracycling.com/sections/magazine/samples.php. **Mailing address:** PO Box 18028, Boulder, CO 80308-1028. **Remarks:** Accepts advertising. **Circ:** (Not Reported).

3263 ■ VIA: AAA Traveler's Companion
AAA Northern California, Nevada and Utah
PO Box 24502
Oakland, CA 94623
Magazine covering worldwide and regional travel and recreation, restaurants, cars and car care, motorists issues, and traffic safety. **Freq:** Bimonthly. **Print Method:** Offset. **Trim Size:** 8 x 10 7/8. **Cols./Page:** 3. **Col. Width:** 27 nonpareils. **Col. Depth:** 140 agate lines. **Key Personnel:** Anne McSilver, Editor-in-Chief; Karen Zuercher, Executive Editor; Leslie Endicott, Editor. **URL:** http://www.viamagazine.com. **Formerly:** Motorland. **Remarks:** Advertising accepted; rates available upon request. **Circ:** (Not Reported).

3264 ■ Youth Law News
National Center for Youth Law
405 14th St., 15th Fl.
Oakland, CA 94612
Phone: (510)835-8098
Fax: (510)835-8099
Publisher's E-mail: info@youthlaw.org
Journal publishing articles on children's issue, policies and new developments in law. **Freq:** Quarterly. **ISSN:** 0882-8520 (print). **Subscription Rates:** $60 Individuals; $125 Institutions. **URL:** http://www.youthlaw.org/publications/yln/. **Remarks:** Advertising not accepted. **Circ:** 4,500.

KARR-AM - See Kirkland, WA

KBFR-FM - See Bismarck, ND

3265 ■ KDVS-FM - 90.3
1111 Franklin St.
Oakland, CA 94607-5201
Phone: (530)752-0728
Fax: (530)752-8548
Owner: Regents of the University of California, 1111 Franklin St., 12th Fl., Oakland, CA 94607. **Founded:**

Circulation: ★ = AAM; △ or • = BPA; ♦ = CAC; ❑ = VAC; ⊕ = PO Statement; ‡ = Publisher's Report; Boldface figures = sworn; Light figures = estimated.

1964. **Formerly**: KCD-FM; 9XM. **Key Personnel:** Ben Johnson, Gen. Mgr., gm@kdvs.org; Roxanne Ahmadpour, Music Dir., musicdept@kdvs.org; Julia Litman Cleper, Dir. of Production, psa@kdvs.org; Rich Luscher, Chief Engineer, engineering@kdvs.org. **Wattage**: 13,000 ERP. **Ad Rates:** Accepts Advertising. **URL:** http://www.kdvs.org.

KEAR-AM - See San Francisco, CA

KEAR-FM - See Sacramento, CA

KEBR-AM - See Rocklin

3266 ■ KEFR-FM - 89.9
290 Hegenberger Rd.
Oakland, CA 94621
Free: 800-543-1495
Email: info@familyradio.org
Owner: Family Radio, Inc., at above address. **Founded:** 1985. **Operating Hours**: Continuous. **Wattage**: 1,800 ERP. **Ad Rates:** Noncommercial. **URL:** http://www.familyradio.com.

KFRD-FM - See Butte, MT

3267 ■ KFRN-AM - 1280
290 Hegenberg Rd.
Oakland, CA 94621
Free: 800-543-1495
Email: info@familyradio.org
Format: Religious. **Networks:** Family Stations Radio. **Owner:** Family Stations Inc., 290 Hegenberger Rd., Oakland, CA 94621, Free: 800-543-1495. **Founded:** 1977. **Formerly:** KFOX-AM. **Operating Hours**: Continuous. **Key Personnel:** Harold Camping, President. **Wattage:** 1,000. **Ad Rates:** Noncommercial. **URL:** http://www.familyradio.org.

KFRS-FM - See Soledad, CA

KFRW-FM - See Black Eagle, MT

KHAP-FM - See Chico

KHFR-FM - See Santa Maria, CA

3268 ■ KICU-TV - 36
Two Jack London Sq.
Oakland, CA 94607
Format: Commercial TV. **Networks:** Independent. **Owner:** Cox Enterprises Inc., 6205 Peachtree Dunwoody Rd., Atlanta, GA 30328, Ph: (678)645-0000, Fax: (678)645-1079. **Founded:** 1967. **Formerly**: KGSC-TV. **Operating Hours**: Continuous. **ADI:** San Francisco-Oakland-San Jose. **Wattage:** 4,070 KW GRP. **URL:** http://www.ktvu.com.

KKAA-AM - See Aberdeen, SD

KPHF-FM - See Phoenix, AZ

KPRA-FM - See Ukiah

KQFE-FM - See Springfield, OR

KQFR-FM - See Rapid City, SD

3269 ■ KTVU-TV - 2
PO Box 22222
Oakland, CA 94623
Format: Commercial TV. **Networks:** Fox; Independent. **Owner:** Cox Enterprises Inc., 6205 Peachtree Dunwoody Rd., Atlanta, GA 30328, Ph: (678)645-0000, Fax: (678)645-1079. **Founded:** 1958. **Operating Hours**: Continuous; 3% network, 97% local. **ADI**: San Francisco-Oakland-San Jose. **Ad Rates:** Advertising accepted; rates available upon request. **URL:** http://www.ktvu.com.

KUFR-FM - See Salt Lake City, UT

KYFR-AM - See Shenandoah, IA

WBFR-FM - See Birmingham, AL

WBMD-AM - See Baltimore, MD

3270 ■ WCUE-AM - 1150
290 Hegenberger Rd.
Oakland, CA 94621
Free: 800-543-1495
Email: info@familyradio.org
Format: Religious. **Networks:** Family Stations Radio. **Owner:** Family Stations Inc., 290 Hegenberger Rd., Oakland, CA 94621, Free: 800-543-1495. **Founded:** 1949. **Operating Hours**: Continuous; 100% network, 15% local. **ADI:** Cleveland (Akron, Canton, & Sandusky), OH. **Wattage:** 5,400 Day; 500 Night. **Ad Rates:** Noncommercial. **URL:** http://www.familyradio.org.

WEFR-FM - See Erie, PA

WFME-FM - See Newark, NJ

WFRC-FM - See Columbus, GA

WFRH-FM - See Kingston, NY

WFRJ-FM - See Johnstown, PA

WFRP-FM - See Americus, GA

WFRW-FM - See Webster, NY

WFSI-FM - See Annapolis, MD

WFTI-FM - See Saint Petersburg, FL

3271 ■ WJCH-FM - 91.9
290 Hegenberger Rd.
Oakland, CA 94621
Free: 800-543-1495
Format: Religious. **Networks:** Family Stations Radio. **Owner:** Family Stations Inc., 290 Hegenberger Rd., Oakland, CA 94621, Free: 800-543-1495. **Founded:** 1986. **Operating Hours**: Continuous; 90% network, 10% local. **Wattage:** 50,000. **Ad Rates:** Noncommercial. **URL:** http://www.familyradio.com.

WKDN-FM - See Camden, NJ

WOFR-FM - See Schoolcraft, MI

3272 ■ WOTL-FM - 90.3
290 Hegenberger Rd.
Oakland, CA 94621
Free: 800-543-1495
Email: info@familyradio.org
Format: Religious. **Networks:** Family Stations Radio. **Owner:** Family Stations Inc., 290 Hegenberger Rd., Oakland, CA 94621, Free: 800-543-1495. **Founded:** 1987. **Operating Hours**: Continuous; 96% network, 4% local. **ADI:** Toledo, OH. **Wattage:** 700. **Ad Rates:** Noncommercial. **URL:** http://www.familyradio.org.

WWFR-FM - See Stuart, FL

WYTN-FM - See Youngstown, OH

OCEANSIDE

S. CA. San Diego Co. On Pacific Ocean, 38 mi. N. of San Diego. Resort. Manufactures Electrical connectors, electronic components, military hardware.

3273 ■ Reunion Journal
1st Marine Division Association
PO Box 9000
Oceanside, CA 92051
Phone: (760)763-3268
Journal featuring news, events, activities, advertisements, travel guides and other military-interest materials of the Southern California Chapter of the 1st Marine Division Association. **Remarks:** Advertising not accepted. **Circ:** (Not Reported).

3274 ■ Snowboard Life
TransWorld Media
353 Airport Rd.
Oceanside, CA 92054
Phone: (760)722-7777
Fax: (760)722-7530
Publisher's E-mail: business@transworld.net
Consumer magazine covering snowboarding for enthusiasts. **Freq:** 9/year. **URL:** http://www.snowboard-life.com; http://snowboarding.transworld.net/tag/snowboard-life. **Remarks:** Accepts advertising. **Circ:** (Not Reported).

3275 ■ TransWorld Skateboarding Magazine
TransWorld Media
353 Airport Rd.
Oceanside, CA 92054
Phone: (760)722-7777
Fax: (760)722-7530
Publisher's E-mail: business@transworld.net
Magazine for skateboarders. **Freq:** Monthly. **Print Method:** Web offset. **Trim Size:** 8 x 10 7/8. **Key Personnel:** Lauren N. Machen, Contact; Carleton Curtis, Managing Editor; Jayme Stone, Associate Publisher, phone: (760)722-7777. **ISSN:** 0748-7401 (print). **Subscription Rates:** $16.97 Individuals; $23.97 Two years; $47.97 Two years Canada; $28.97 Canada; $71.97 Other countries 2 years; $40.97 Other countries. **URL:** http://skateboarding.transworld.net. **Ad Rates:** 4C $21,417. **Remarks:** Accepts advertising. **Circ:** 100000.

3276 ■ TransWorld Snowboarding Magazine
TransWorld Media
353 Airport Rd.
Oceanside, CA 92054
Phone: (760)722-7777
Fax: (760)722-7530
Publisher's E-mail: business@transworld.net
Magazine for the snowboarding community. **Freq:** 10/year. **Print Method:** Web Offset. **Trim Size:** 8 1/8 x 10 7/8. **Key Personnel:** Annie Fast, Senior Editor; Liam Gallagher, Associate Editor; Adam Cozens, Associate Publisher. **Subscription Rates:** $16.97 Individuals print. **URL:** http://snowboarding.transworld.net. **Remarks:** Advertising accepted; rates available upon request. **Circ:** (Not Reported).

3277 ■ Transworld Surf Magazine
TransWorld Media
353 Airport Rd.
Oceanside, CA 92054
Phone: (760)722-7777
Fax: (760)722-7530
Publisher's E-mail: business@transworld.net
Magazine on water surfing. **Freq:** Monthly. **Subscription Rates:** $12 Individuals print; $20 Two years print; $8.99 Individuals digital; $14.99 Two years digital. **URL:** http://www.grindtv.com/topic/transworld-surf-magazine/#yGtq5ku2rTpMkD07.97. **Ad Rates:** 4C $7,416. **Remarks:** Accepts advertising. **Circ:** (Not Reported).

OJAI

SW CA. Ventura Co. 14 mi. NE of Ventura. Ventura Co. (SW). 14 m NE of Ventura. Mountain resort. Private schools. Fruit packed. Diversified farming.

3278 ■ AeroSpaceNews.com
AeroSpaceNews.com
PO Box 1748
Ojai, CA 93024-1748
Phone: (805)985-2320
Journal reporting on the insights, impressions and images of tomorrow's technological wonders in the field of aerospace. **Freq:** Monthly. **Key Personnel:** Craig Schmitman, Editor-in-Chief, Publisher. **URL:** http://aerospacenews.com. **Remarks:** Accepts advertising. **Circ:** (Not Reported).

3279 ■ Edible Ojai & Ventura County
Edible Communities Inc.
PO Box 184
Ojai, CA 93024
Phone: (805)646-6678
Publication E-mail: info@edibleojai.com
Magazine featuring Ojai City's local food. **Freq:** Quarterly. **Trim Size:** 7.5 x 9.5. **Key Personnel:** Ron Wallace, Publisher. **Subscription Rates:** $28 Individuals. **URL:** http://edibleventuracounty.ediblefeast.com. **Formerly**: Edible Ojai. **Remarks:** Accepts advertising. **Circ:** (Not Reported).

3280 ■ Imaging News: Guide
Diamond Research Corp.
530 W Ojai Ave., Ste. 108
Ojai, CA 93023-2471
Phone: (805)640-7177
Fax: (805)640-7178
Trade magazine covering imaging materials, technologies, and markets. Available online only. **Freq:** Monthly. **Key Personnel:** Arthur S. Diamond, Editor. **Subscription Rates:** $175 Individuals. **URL:** http://www.imagingnews.com/imagingnews.html. **Formerly:** Imaging News Online; R & R News. **Remarks:** Banner advertising. **Circ:** (Not Reported).

3281 ■ Ojai Valley News
Ojai Valley Newspapers L.L.C.
408 Bryant Cir., Ste. A
Ojai, CA 93023
Phone: (805)646-1476
Fax: (805)646-4281
Local newspaper. **Freq:** Semiweekly (Wed. and Fri.). **Print Method:** Offset. **Cols./Page:** 6. **Col. Width:** 18 nonpareils. **Col. Depth:** 294 agate lines. **Key Personnel:** Misty Volaski, Managing Editor; Bill Buchanan, Editor; Jodie Miller, Business Manager. **ISSN:** 4059--8000 (print). **Subscription Rates:** $52 Individuals print; $25 Individuals online only. **URL:** http://www.ojaivalleynews.com. **Mailing address:** PO Box 277, Ojai, CA 93024-0277. **Remarks:** Accepts advertising. **Circ:** ‡5000.

ONTARIO

SE CA. San Bernardino Co. 30 mi. E. of Los Angeles. Manufactures aircraft and aircraft parts, electrical equipment, tile, steel products, aluminum roofing, missile components. Wineries. Nurseries. Ships citrus fruit. Agriculture. Oranges, lemons, olives, grapes.

3282 ■ Daily Bulletin
Tower Media Inc.
2041 E 4th St.
Ontario, CA 91764
Phone: (909)987-6397
Publication E-mail: citydesk@inlandnewspapers.com
Daily newspaper. **Freq:** Daily. **Key Personnel:** Ron Hasse, President, Publisher; Frank Pine, Managing Editor. **URL:** http://www.dailybulletin.com/. **Remarks:** Accepts advertising. **Circ:** (Not Reported).

3283 ■ Inland Valley Daily Bulletin
California Newspaper Partnership
2041 E 4th St.
Ontario, CA 91764
Phone: (909)987-6397
Publication E-mail: webmaster@dailybulletin.com
General newspaper serving Chino, Chino Hills, Claremont, Diamond Bar, Fontana, La Verne, Montclair, Ontario, Pomona, Rancho Cucamonga, Rialto, San Dimas, and Upland, CA. **Founded:** 1882. **Freq:** Daily. **Print Method:** Offset. **Cols./Page:** 6. **Col. Width:** 26 nonpareils. **Col. Depth:** 301 agate lines. **Key Personnel:** Frank Pine, Editor, General Manager. **Subscription Rates:** $20 Individuals 7-day home delivery; 4 weeks; $10 Individuals Sunday only home delivery; 4 weeks. **URL:** http://www.dailybulletin.com. **Remarks:** Accepts advertising. **Circ:** Mon.-Fri. ★**60505**, Sat. ★**58566**, Sun. ★**68656**.

3284 ■ Karter News
International Kart Federation
1609 S Grove Ave., Ste. 105
Ontario, CA 91761
Phone: (909)923-4999
Fax: (909)923-6940
Publisher's E-mail: results@ikfkarting.com
Freq: Monthly. **ISSN:** 0096- 3216 (print). **Subscription Rates:** Included in membership. **Alt. Formats:** PDF. **URL:** http://www.ikfkarting.com/OfficePages/News/KarterNewsArchives.html. **Remarks:** Accepts advertising. **Circ:** 5000.

3285 ■ Official Magazine
International Association of Plumbing and Mechanical Officials
4755 E Philadelphia St.
Ontario, CA 91761
Phone: (909)472-4100
Fax: (909)472-4150
Publisher's E-mail: iapmo@iapmo.org
Trade publication containing articles of interest to anyone involved in the plumbing, heating, cooling, building codes and standards. **Freq:** Quarterly. **Print Method:** Offset. **Trim Size:** 8.5 x 11. **Cols./Page:** 2. **Col. Width:** 3 1/2 inches. **Col. Depth:** 10 inches. **Key Personnel:** Jeff Ortiz, Editor, phone: (909)472-4119. **ISSN:** 0192--5784 (print). **Subscription Rates:** Included in membership. **URL:** http://www.iapmo.org/Pages/OFFICIALMagazine.aspx. **Ad Rates:** 4C $2100. **Remarks:** Accepts advertising. **Circ:** ‡29000.

ORANGE

S. CA. Orange Co. 35 mi. SE of Los Angeles. Chapman College. Manufactures copper wire, rope, twine, electronic equipment, concrete pipe, steel tanks, plastic hose and bags. Nurseries.

3286 ■ Cottages and Bungalows
Action Pursuit Group
265 S Anita Dr., Ste. 120
Orange, CA 92868-3343
Publication E-mail: editorial@cottagesandbungalowsmag.com
Magazine featuring cottages and bungalow. **Freq:** Bimonthly. **Key Personnel:** Jickie Torres, Editor; Meryl Schoenbaum, Managing Editor. **Subscription Rates:** $19.95 Individuals. **URL:** http://www.cottagesandbungalowsmag.com. **Remarks:** Accepts advertising. **Circ:** (Not Reported).

3287 ■ Nexus Journal
Chapman University Dale E. Fowler School of Law
Donald P. Kennedy Hall
1 University Dr.
Orange, CA 92866
Phone: (714)628-2500
Fax: (714)628-2501
Publisher's E-mail: lawadm@chapman.edu
Journal containing topics where law, politics, economics, and media converge. **Key Personnel:** Allison Scott, Editor-in-Chief. **URL:** http://www.chapman.edu/law/publications/nexus-journal. **Circ:** (Not Reported).

3288 ■ The Panther
Chapman University
1 University Dr.
Orange, CA 92866
Phone: (714)997-6815
Publication E-mail: thepanthernewspaper@gmail.com
Collegiate newspaper. **Freq:** Weekly (Mon.). **Print Method:** Offset. **Trim Size:** 11 x 17. **Cols./Page:** 5. **Col. Width:** 2 inches. **Col. Depth:** 13 inches. **Key Personnel:** Mark Pampanin, Editor-in-Chief; Stefani Peterson, Contact. **Alt. Formats:** Download. **URL:** http://www.thepantheronline.com. **Ad Rates:** GLR $5; BW $596.75; 4C $1193.50; PCI $12. **Remarks:** Accepts advertising. **Circ:** Mon. ‡2500.

3289 ■ Romantic Homes
Action Pursuit Group
265 S Anita Dr., Ste. 120
Orange, CA 92868-3343
Lifestyle magazine featuring home products, ideas, decorating style and latest trends. **Freq:** Monthly. **Key Personnel:** Jacqueline deMontravel, Editor; Meryl Schoenbaum, Executive Editor. **ISSN:** 1086--4083 (print). **Subscription Rates:** $21.95 Individuals print; $14.99 Individuals online; $30 Individuals print and online. **URL:** http://www.romantichomes.com. **Remarks:** Accepts advertising. **Circ:** (Not Reported).

3290 ■ Ultimate MMA: Mixed Martial Arts
Action Pursuit Group
265 S Anita Dr., Ste. 120
Orange, CA 92868-3343
Magazine featuring the grappling sport for fans and grapplers. **Freq:** Bimonthly. **Key Personnel:** Doug Jeffrey, Editor. **Subscription Rates:** $17.95 Individuals. **URL:** http://www.ultimatemmamag.com. **Formerly:** Ultimate Grappling. **Remarks:** Accepts advertising. **Circ:** (Not Reported).

ORANGEVALE

3291 ■ Sacramento Bride and Groom
Pre-Nup Publishing
9073 Pecor Way
Orangevale, CA 95662
Phone: (916)987-3058
Fax: (916)987-3058
Magazine featuring information for couples planning their wedding in the Sacramento and Lake Tahoe area. **Freq:** Semiannual. **Key Personnel:** Tami Miller, Publisher; Lisa Duncan, Manager, Sales, phone: (916)532-3563. **URL:** http://www.sacbride.com. **Circ:** (Not Reported).

ORCUTT

3292 ■ KGDP-AM - 660
2225 Skyway Dr., Ste. B
Santa Maria, CA 93455
Phone: (805)928-7707
Fax: (805)922-8582
Email: kgdp660@yahoo.com
Format: Religious. **Networks:** USA Radio. **Owner:** Radio Representatives Inc., 1416 Hollister Ln., Los Osos, CA 93402. **Founded:** 1987. **Operating Hours:** 5 a.m.-11 p.m., Mon.-Fri.; 6 a.m.-11 p.m., Sat.-Sun. **ADI:** Santa Barbara-Santa Maria-San Luis Obispo,CA. **Wattage:** 10,000 Day; 1,000 Night. **Ad Rates:** $12-20 for 30 seconds; $15-25 for 60 seconds.

ORINDA

W. CA. Contra Costa Co. 7 mi. NE of Oakland. Residential.

3293 ■ Exclusive Reports Online
Tradeline Inc.
115 Orinda Way
Orinda, CA 94563
Phone: (925)254-1744
Fax: (925)254-1093
Publication E-mail: pr@tradelineinc.com
Online trade journal covering facilities planning, architecture, engineering, and management of universities, research laboratories, high-tech corporations, manufacturers, financial institutions, and general government agencies. **Freq:** Weekly. **Key Personnel:** Steven L. Westfall, Executive Editor; Bill Nothofer, Contact. **ISSN:** 1096--4894 (print). **URL:** http://www.tradelineinc.com. **Formerly:** Facilities Planning News; FM Data Monthly; Tradeline's Exclusive Reports Online. **Remarks:** Advertising accepted; rates available upon request. **Circ:** 7000.

OROVILLE

N. CA. Butte Co. On Feather River, 75 mi. N. of Sacramento. Olive, fruit, vegetable canning and packing. Olive oil, lumber manufactured. Pine timber. Farming.

3294 ■ The Digger Shopper & News
Great Ad-ventures Publishing Inc.
2057 Mitchell Ave.
Oroville, CA 95966
Phone: (530)533-2170
Fax: (530)533-2181
Publication E-mail: digger@cncnet.com
Shopping guide with community news. **Founded:** Aug. 21, 1977. **Freq:** Weekly (Tues.). **Print Method:** Offset. **Trim Size:** 11 1/2 x 12 3/4. **Cols./Page:** 4. **Col. Width:** 2 3/8 picas. **Col. Depth:** 11 3/8 inches. **Key Personnel:** Pat Miller, Editor. **Subscription Rates:** Free; $75 By mail. **URL:** http://diggernews.com. **Formerly:** The Digger. **Mailing address:** PO Box 5006, Oroville, CA 95966. **Ad Rates:** GLR $0.77; BW $544.80; 4C $614.80; PCI $9.65. **Remarks:** Accepts advertising. **Circ:** Free ‡13620.

3295 ■ KRBS-FM - 107.1
2360 Oro Quincy Hwy.
Oroville, CA 95965
Phone: (530)534-1200
Format: Public Radio. **Key Personnel:** Lee Edwards, President; Por Yang, VP; Erv Knorzer, Treasurer. **Ad Rates:** Noncommercial; underwriting available.

OXNARD

SW CA. Ventura Co. 10 mi. SE of Ventura. Manufactures aircraft components, lumber. Seafood, fruit, vegetable canneries, frozen food plants; oil refineries. Nurseries. Agriculture. Citrus fruit, celery, strawberries, tomatoes.

3296 ■ Automated Builder: The No. 1 Engineered Housing Technology Transfer Magazine for Manufacturing and Marketing
CMN Associates Inc.
2401 Grapevine Dr.
Oxnard, CA 93036
Phone: (805)351-5931
Fax: (805)351-5755
Publication E-mail: info@automatedbuilder.com
cms03@pacbell.net
Covers factory-built housing industry. **Freq:** Monthly. **Print Method:** Offset. **Trim Size:** 8 x 10 3/4. **Cols./Page:** 3. **Col. Width:** 2 3/16 INS. **Col. Depth:** 9 5/8 inches. **Key Personnel:** Don O. Carlson, Editor; Lance Carlson, Manager, Advertising. **ISSN:** 0899--5540 (print). **USPS:** 000-869. **URL:** http://www.componentadvertiser.com. **Formed by the merger of:** Automation in Housing; Manufactured Home Dealer. **Ad Rates:** BW $5,730; 4C $1,945. **Remarks:** Accepts advertising. **Circ:** 25000.

3297 ■ Iron Man: Real Bodybuilding Training, Nutrition and Supplementation
Ironman Publishing
1701 Ives Ave.
Oxnard, CA 93033
Phone: (805)385-3500
Fax: (805)385-3515
Free: 800-447-0008
Publisher's E-mail: info@ironmanmagazine.com
Magazine on bodybuilding and fitness. **Freq:** Monthly. **ISSN:** 0047--1496 (print). **Subscription Rates:** $79 U.S. 1 year; $158 U.S. 2 years; $99 Other countries 1 year. **URL:** http://www.ironmanmagazine.com. **Remarks:** Accepts advertising. **Circ:** Paid 225000.

Circulation: ★ = AAM; △ or • = BPA; ♦ = CAC; ❑ = VAC; ⊕ = PO Statement; ‡ = Publisher's Report; Boldface figures = sworn; Light figures = estimated.

3298 ■ KDAR-FM - 98.3
500 Esplanade Dr.
Oxnard, CA 93036
Phone: (805)485-8881
Email: radiomail@kdar.com
Format: Contemporary Christian. **Networks:** Christian Broadcasting (CBN). **Owner:** Salem Media Group Inc., 4880 Santa Rosa Rd., Camarillo, CA 93012, Ph: (805)987-0400, Fax: (805)384-4520. **Founded:** 1974. **Operating Hours:** Continuous; 80% network, 20% local. **Key Personnel:** Kim Pummill-Talon, Bus. Mgr., Traffic Mgr., kim@kdar.com. **Wattage:** 1,500 ERP. **Ad Rates:** $27-40 per unit. **URL:** http://www.kdar.com.

OXNARD

3299 ■ KLUN-FM - 103.1
200 S A St., Ste. 400
oxnard, CA 93030
Phone: (805)928-9796
Format: Hispanic. **Wattage:** 1,100. **URL:** http://www.radiolazer.com.

OXNARD

SW CA. Ventura Co. 10 mi. SE of Ventura. Manufactures aircraft components, lumber. Seafood, fruit, vegetable canneries, frozen food plants; oil refineries. Nurseries. Agriculture. Citrus fruit, celery, strawberries, tomatoes.

3300 ■ KMLA-FM - 103.7
355 S A St., No. 103
Oxnard, CA 93030
Phone: (805)385-5656
Fax: (805)385-5690
Email: willy@lam1037.com
Format: Hispanic. **Owner:** Gold Coast Radio L.L.C., at above address. **Operating Hours:** Continuous. **Key Personnel:** Guillermo Gonzalez, Contact. **Wattage:** 3,000. **Ad Rates:** Noncommercial. **URL:** http://www.lam1037.com.

3301 ■ KOXR-AM
200 S A St.
Oxnard, CA 93030
Phone: (805)487-0444
Fax: (805)487-2117
Free: 800-852-0444
Format: Hispanic. **Owner:** Lazer Broadcasting Corp., 200 S A St., Ste. 400, Oxnard, CA 93030, Ph: (805)240-2070, Fax: (805)240-5960. **Founded:** 1955. **Wattage:** 5,000 Day; 1,000 Nig. **Ad Rates:** $35 for 30 seconds; $40 for 60 seconds.

3302 ■ KSBQ-AM - 1480
200 S A St., Ste. 400
Oxnard, CA 93030
Phone: (805)922-3312
Format: Hispanic. **Owner:** Jaime Bonilla Valdez, 269 H Street 3rd Floor, Chula Vista, CA 91910, Ph: (619)429-5877. **Founded:** 1961. **Operating Hours:** 24 hrs. **ADI:** Santa Barbara-Santa Maria-San Luis Obispo,CA. **Wattage:** 1,000 day; 061 night. **Ad Rates:** $17-22 for 30 seconds; $19-24 for 60 seconds.

3303 ■ KSMY-FM - 106.7
200 S A St., Ste. 400
Oxnard, CA 93030
Phone: (323)931-1745
Fax: (805)541-5303
Format: Adult Contemporary. **ADI:** Santa Barbara-Santa Maria-San Luis Obispo,CA. **Wattage:** 3,500. **Ad Rates:** Noncommercial.

3304 ■ KXLM-FM - 102.9
200 S A St., Ste. 400
Oxnard, CA 93035
Phone: (805)240-2070
Fax: (805)240-5960
Format: Hispanic. **Owner:** Lazer Broadcasting Corp., 200 S A St., Ste. 400, Oxnard, CA 93030, Ph: (805)240-2070, Fax: (805)240-5960. **Key Personnel:** Terry Janisch, Mgr. **Ad Rates:** Advertising accepted; rates available upon request. **URL:** http://www.radiolazer.com.

PACIFIC GROVE

W. CA. Monterey Co. 20 mi. S. of Santa Cruz. Residential.

3305 ■ Carmel Pine Cone
Carmel Communications
734 Lighthouse Ave.
Pacific Grove, CA 93950
Phone: (831)624-0162
Fax: (831)375-5018
Publisher's E-mail: mail@carmelpinecone.com
Community newspaper. **Freq:** Weekly (Fri.). **Print Method:** Offset. **Cols./Page:** 6. **Col. Width:** 21 nonpareils. **Col. Depth:** 224 agate lines. **Key Personnel:** Paul Miller, Publisher, phone: (831)274-8653; Jackie Edwards, Manager, Production, phone: (831)274-8634; Irma Garcia, Office Manager, phone: (831)274-8645. **Subscription Rates:** Free. **URL:** http://www.pineconearchive.com. **Ad Rates:** GLR $19.10; PCI $17.20. **Remarks:** Accepts advertising. **Circ:** 20000.

3306 ■ Surfing Medicine
Surfer's Medical Association
PO Box 51881
Pacific Grove, CA 93950
Publisher's E-mail: sma_website@yahoo.com
URL: http://surfingmedicine.com/. **Remarks:** Advertising not accepted. **Circ:** (Not Reported).

PACIFIC PALISADES

S. CA. Los Angeles Co. 4 mi. N. of Santa Monica. Residential suburb.

3307 ■ Palisadian-Post
Palisadian-Post
881 Alma Real Dr., Ste. 213
Pacific Palisades, CA 90272-0725
Publisher's E-mail: sports@palipost.com
Local newspaper. **Freq:** Weekly (Thurs.). **Print Method:** Offset. **Cols./Page:** 6. **Col. Width:** 24 nonpareils. **Col. Depth:** 294 agate lines. **Key Personnel:** Roberta Donohue, Publisher; Bill Bruns, Managing Editor; Libby Motika, Senior Editor. **Subscription Rates:** $69 Individuals one year. **URL:** http://palipost.com. **Ad Rates:** GLR $28; PCI $33. **Remarks:** Accepts advertising. **Circ:** Free ‡121, Paid ‡4741, Combined ‡4862.

3308 ■ Post Shopper
Post Shopper
839 Via De La Paz
Pacific Palisades, CA 90272-0725
Free shopper. **Freq:** Weekly (Thurs.). **Print Method:** Offset. **Trim Size:** 12 3/4 x 21 1/2. **Cols./Page:** 6. **Col. Width:** 17 nonpareils. **Col. Depth:** 294 agate lines. **Key Personnel:** Roberta Donohue, Publisher; Tom Small, President; Bill Bruns, Managing Editor. **Subscription Rates:** $47 Individuals; $65 Two years; $70 Out of country. **Ad Rates:** GLR $.85; PCI $33. **Remarks:** Accepts advertising. **Circ:** (Not Reported).

3309 ■ Rental Equipment Register: Serving the Rental Profession
Penton Business Media, Inc.
c/o Michael Roth, Ed.
17383 Sunset Blvd., Ste. A220
Pacific Palisades, CA 90272
Phone: (310)230-7177
Fax: (310)230-7169
Magazine for the rental equipment industry. **Freq:** Monthly. **Print Method:** Offset. **Trim Size:** 7 7/8 x 10 3/4. **Cols./Page:** 3. **Col. Width:** 27 nonpareils. **Col. Depth:** 140 agate lines. **Key Personnel:** Michael Roth, Editor; David Miller, Publisher; Brandey Chewning Smith, Managing Editor. **ISSN:** 0034--4524 (print). **URL:** http://rermag.com. **Ad Rates:** BW $4,280; 4C $1,220. **Remarks:** Accepts advertising. **Circ:** 21204.

3310 ■ Rev Magazine
Rev Magazine
PO Box 1052
Pacific Palisades, CA 90272
Publication E-mail: sysop2@rev-mag.com
Online auto magazine featuring pin-up style model photographs, car and racing tips, and product reviews. **Freq:** Weekly. **Subscription Rates:** $5.95 Individuals monthly. **URL:** http://www.rev-mag.com. **Remarks:** Accepts advertising. **Circ:** (Not Reported).

PACIFICA

W. CA. San Mateo Co. On Pacific Ocean, 10 mi. S. of San Francisco. Residential. Beach oriented. Recreation.

3311 ■ Pacifica Tribune
Pacifica Tribune
59 Bill Drake Way
Pacifica, CA 94044
Phone: (650)359-6666
Fax: (650)359-3821
Newspaper. **Founded:** 1947. **Freq:** Weekly (Wed.). **Print Method:** Offset. **Trim Size:** 6 x 20 1/2. **Cols./Page:** 6. **Col. Depth:** 287 agate lines. **Key Personnel:** Elaine Larsen, Editor, phone: (650)738-4542. **Subscription Rates:** $2.50 Individuals home delivery; per week; $2.38 Individuals Friday-Sunday edition; per week; $1.50 Individuals Sunday only; per week. **URL:** http://www.mercurynews.com/pacifica. **Mailing address:** PO Box 1189, Pacifica, CA 94044. **Ad Rates:** BW $1,734.30; SAU $14.10. **Remarks:** Accepts advertising. **Circ:** 3500.

3312 ■ Western Birds
Western Field Ornithologists
1359 Solano Dr.
Pacifica, CA 94044-4258
Publication E-mail: birds@sdnhm.org
Peer-reviewed journal focusing on field oriented descriptive ornithology. **Freq:** Quarterly. **Key Personnel:** Philip Unitt, Editor; Kathy Molina, Assistant Editor; Doug Faulkner, Associate Editor. **ISSN:** 0160--1121 (print). **Subscription Rates:** $35 Individuals; $60 Two years; $85 Individuals three years; $40 U.S. Family - 1 year; $70 U.S. Family - 2 years; $100 U.S. Family - 3 years; $10 Students 1 year; $40 Canada 1 year; $70 Canada 2 years; $100 Canada 3 years; $20 Members Mexico - 1 year; $40 Mexico - 2 years; $60 Mexico - 3 years. **URL:** http://www.westernfieldornithologists.org/publications.php; http://www.westernfieldornithologists.org/journal.php. **Formerly:** California Birds. **Remarks:** Accepts advertising. **Circ:** Paid 1100.

PALM DESERT

SE CA. Riverside Co. 75 mi. SE of Redland. Winter resort.

3313 ■ Business to Business
Palm Desert Area Chamber of Commerce
72559 Highway 111
Palm Desert, CA 92260
Phone: (760)346-6111
Fax: (760)346-3263
Newspaper containing articles that offer several ways to enhance your business. **Freq:** Monthly. **URL:** http://www.pdcc.org/links.html#publications. **Remarks:** Accepts advertising. **Circ:** 1500.

3314 ■ Coachella Valley White Sheet
Associated Desert Shoppers Inc.
73400 Hwy. 111
Palm Desert, CA 92260
Shoppers' publication serving Coachella Valley, California area. **Freq:** Weekly. **URL:** http://www.greenandwhitesheet.com/white_sheet_home.php. **Remarks:** Accepts advertising. **Circ:** (Not Reported).

3315 ■ Saludos Hispanos
Saludos Hispanos
73-121 Fred Waring Dr., Ste. 100
Palm Desert, CA 92260
Phone: (760)776-1206
Fax: (760)776-1214
Free: 800-371-4456
Publisher's E-mail: info@saludos.com
Magazine showcasing successful Hispanic Americans and promoting higher education (English and Spanish). **Freq:** Bimonthly. **Trim Size:** 10 1/4 x 13. **Key Personnel:** Rosemarie Garcia-Solomon, Managing Editor. **URL:** http://www.saludos.com/newslette/index.html. **Remarks:** Accepts advertising. **Circ:** 300,000.

White Sheet-The Imperial Valley Advertiser - See Imperial

3316 ■ White Sheet-The Palm Springs Advertiser
Associated Desert Shoppers Inc.
73400 Hwy. 111
Palm Desert, CA 92260
Shopper. **Freq:** Weekly (Tues.). **Print Method:** Web. **Trim Size:** 11 x 12 1/2. **Cols./Page:** 6. **Col. Width:** 9 1/2 picas. **Col. Depth:** 11 3/4 inches. **Alt. Formats:** PDF. **URL:** http://www.greenandwhitesheet.com. **Ad Rates:** BW $365; 4C $650. **Remarks:** Advertising accepted; rates available upon request. **Circ:** Free ‡10000.

3317 ■ KESQ-TV - 3
42-650 Melanie Pl.
Palm Desert, CA 92211

Phone: (760)773-3333
Fax: (760)773-5128
Email: newsline3@kesq.com
Format: News. **Networks:** Fox. **Owner:** News Press & Gazette Co., 825 Edmond St., Saint Joseph, MO. **Founded:** 1968. **Operating Hours**: Continuous. **ADI**: Palm Springs, CA. **Key Personnel:** John White, Contact; John White, Contact. **Ad Rates:** Noncommercial. **URL:** http://www.kesq.com.

3318 ■ KEZN-FM - 103.1
72-915 Parkview Dr.
Palm Desert, CA 92260
Phone: (760)340-9383
Fax: (760)340-5756
Format: Adult Contemporary. **Owner:** CBS Radio, New York, NY, Ph: (614)249-7676, Fax: (614)249-6995. **Founded:** 1977. **Operating Hours**: Continuous. **Key Personnel:** Rob Zavitka, Sales Mgr., rob.zavitka@cbsradio.com; Vicki Steele, Dir. of Production, production@ez103.com. **Local Programs**: *Saturday Night Disco Fever*, Saturday 8:00 p.m. **Wattage**: 001. **Ad Rates:** Advertising accepted; rates available upon request. **URL:** http://sunny1031fm.cbslocal.com.

3319 ■ KLOB-FM - 94.7
41601 Corporate Way
Palm Desert, CA 92260
Phone: (760)341-5837
Fax: (760)341-0951
Format: Hispanic. **Owner:** Entravision Communications Corporation, 2425 Olympic Blvd., Ste. 6000 W, Santa Monica, CA 90404-4030, Ph: (310)447-3870, Fax: (310)447-3899. **Key Personnel:** Victor Tocco, Gen. Mgr. **Mailing address:** PO Box 13750, Palm Desert, CA 92260. **URL:** http://www.entravision.com.

3320 ■ KMIR-TV - 6
72920 Park View Dr.
Palm Desert, CA 92260
Phone: (760)568-3636
Fax: (760)568-1176
Format: Commercial TV. **Networks:** NBC. **Founded:** 1968. **Operating Hours**: Continuous; 67% network, 33% local. **ADI**: Palm Springs, CA. **Wattage**: 10,000. **Ad Rates:** Advertising accepted; rates available upon request. **URL:** http://www.kmir6.com.

3321 ■ KPLM-FM - 106.1
75153 Merle Dr., Ste. G
Palm Desert, CA 92211
Phone: (760)568-4550
Fax: (760)341-7600
Format: Country. **Networks:** AP. **Owner:** RM Broadcasting LLC, at above address. **Founded:** 1983. **Operating Hours:** Continuous; 1% network, 99% local. **ADI**: Palm Springs, CA. **Key Personnel:** Todd Marker, Gen. Sales Mgr.; Al Gordon, Dir. of Programs. **Wattage**: 50,000. **Ad Rates:** $18-40 for 30 seconds; $28-60 for 60 seconds. **URL:** http://thebig106.com.

3322 ■ KPSE-TV - 13
72920 Parkview Dr.
Palm Desert, CA 92260
Phone: (760)568-3636
Fax: (760)568-1176
Owner: Journal Broadcast Corp., 333 W State St., Milwaukee, WI 53203, Ph: (414)332-9611, Fax: (414)967-5400. **Founded:** 2007. **Key Personnel:** Alison Shaw, Contact. **URL:** http://www.kmir.com.

3323 ■ KRCK-FM - 97.7
73-733 Fred Waring Dr., Ste. 201
Palm Desert, CA 92260
Phone: (760)341-0123
Fax: (760)341-7455
Format: Classic Rock. **Ad Rates:** Noncommercial. **URL:** http://www.krck.com.

3324 ■ KUNA-FM - 96.7
42-650 Melanie Pl.
Palm Desert, CA 92211
Phone: (760)568-6830
Fax: (619)568-3984
Format: Ethnic; Hispanic; Religious. **Owner:** Gulf California Broadcasting, at above address, palm springs, CA 92276. **Founded:** 1987. **Formerly**: KBZT-FM; KUNA-AM. **Operating Hours**: Continuous. **ADI**: Palm Springs, CA. **Key Personnel:** Martin Serna, Station Mgr. **Wattage**: 650. **Ad Rates:** $25-35 for 30 seconds; $35-80 for 60 seconds.

3325 ■ KVER-TV - 4
41601 Corporate Way
Palm Desert, CA 92260
Phone: (760)341-5837
Fax: (760)837-3711
Owner: Entravision Communications Corporation, 2425 Olympic Blvd., Ste. 6000 W, Santa Monica, CA 90404-4030, Ph: (310)447-3870, Fax: (310)447-3899. **Founded:** 2012. **Key Personnel:** Victor Tocco, Sr. VP. **Mailing address:** PO Box 13750, Palm Desert, CA 92260. **URL:** http://www.kvertv.com.

3326 ■ KXPS-AM - 1010
75-153 Merle Dr.
Palm Desert, CA 92211
Phone: (760)621-0100
Format: Sports. **Key Personnel:** Norman Feuer, Gen. Mgr., norman.feuer@morris.com; Virginia Nelson, Dir. of Sales, virginia.nelson@desertfun.com; Sean Flannigan, Promotions Dir., sean.flannigan@morris.com. **Ad Rates:** Advertising accepted; rates available upon request. **URL:** http://www.team1010.com.

PALM SPRINGS

SE CA. Riverside Co. 56 mi. E. of Riverside. Desert resort.

3327 ■ Coachella Valley Sun
Desert Sun Publishing Co.
750 N Gene Autry Terr.
Palm Springs, CA 92262
Phone: (760)322-8889
Fax: (760)778-4504
Free: 800-834-6052
Newspaper. **Freq:** Daily. **Print Method:** Offset. **Cols./Page:** 6. **Col. Width:** 24 nonpareils. **Col. Depth:** 295 agate lines. **URL:** http://www.thedesertsun.com. **Mailing address:** PO Box 2734, Palm Springs, CA 92263. **Remarks:** Accepts advertising. **Circ:** 174000.

3328 ■ The Desert Sun
Gannett Company Inc.
PO Box 2734
Palm Springs, CA 92263
Phone: (760)322-8889
Local newspaper of Coachella Valley. **Freq:** Mon.-Sun. (morn.). **Print Method:** Offset. **Trim Size:** 13 x 21. **Cols./Page:** 6. **Col. Width:** 27 nonpareils. **Col. Depth:** 301 agate lines. **Key Personnel:** Dominique Shwe, Director, Advertising; Mark Kurtich, Director, Production. **Subscription Rates:** $19.99 Individuals online. **URL:** http://www.mydesert.com. **Ad Rates:** BW $4017; 4C $4899; PCI $31.88. **Remarks:** Accepts advertising. **Circ:** Mon.-Fri. ★**46063**, Sun. ★**51569**, Sat. ★**48844**.

3329 ■ Guest Life Monterey Bay
Desert Publications Inc.
303 N Indian Canyon Dr.
Palm Springs, CA 92262
Phone: (760)325-2333
Fax: (760)325-7008
Publisher's E-mail: editorial@palmspringslife.com
General interest magazine serving local areas. **Freq:** Annual. **Trim Size:** 8 3/8 x 10 7/8. **Key Personnel:** Franklin W. Jones, Associate Publisher; Milton W. Jones, Publisher; Joseph Hinman, Chief Financial Officer. **ISSN:** 1047--3610 (print). **URL:** http://www.guestlife.com/media/GuestLife/Monterey-Bay. **Formerly**: Pacific, The Monterey Bay; Monterey Bay. **Mailing address:** PO Box 2724, Palm Springs, CA 92263. **Remarks:** Advertising accepted; rates available upon request. **Circ:** (Not Reported).

3330 ■ Palm Springs Life: California's Prestige Magazine
Desert Publications Inc.
303 N Indian Canyon Dr.
Palm Springs, CA 92262
Phone: (760)325-2333
Fax: (760)325-7008
Publication E-mail: desertpubs@aol.com
Lifestyle magazine containing upscale local and social news. **Freq:** Monthly. **Print Method:** Offset. **Trim Size:** 8 3/8 x 10 7/8. **Cols./Page:** 3. **Col. Width:** 28 nonpareils. **Col. Depth:** 147 agate lines. **Key Personnel:** Joseph Hinman, Chief Financial Officer; Stuart Funk, Creative Director; Franklin W. Jones, Associate Publisher; Olga Reyes, Managing Editor. **ISSN:** 0331--0425 (print). **Subscription Rates:** $19.99 Individuals annual digital only. **URL:** http://www.palmspringslife.com. **Mailing address:** PO Box 2724, Palm Springs, CA 92263. **Remarks:** Accepts advertising. **Circ:** Paid ‡17142.

3331 ■ Palm Springs Life's Desert Guide
Desert Publications Inc.
303 N Indian Canyon Dr.
Palm Springs, CA 92262
Phone: (760)325-2333
Fax: (760)325-7008
Publisher's E-mail: editorial@palmspringslife.com
Visitor's guide for the Coachella Valley. **Freq:** 15/yr. **Trim Size:** 8 1/2 x 10 7/8. **Cols./Page:** 3. **Col. Width:** 2 1/4 inches. **Col. Depth:** 9 3/4 inches. **Key Personnel:** Franklin W. Jones, Associate Publisher; Joseph Hinman, Chief Financial Officer; Stuart Funk, Creative Director; Olga Reyes, Managing Editor; Susan Stein, Editor; Todd May, Director; Milton W. Jones, Publisher; Janice Kleinschmidt, Editor; Julie Sinclair, Editor-in-Chief. **Subscription Rates:** $42 Individuals print and online; $66 Two years print and online; $1.99 Single issue online; $19.95 Individuals online. **URL:** http://www.palmspringslife.com/palm-springs-lifes-desert-guide. **Mailing address:** PO Box 2724, Palm Springs, CA 92263. **Remarks:** Advertising accepted; rates available upon request. **Circ:** Paid 18011.

3332 ■ Professional Candy Buyer
Adams Business Media
420 S Palm Canyon Dr., 2nd Fl.
Palm Springs, CA 92262
Phone: (760)318-7000
Fax: (760)323-4310
Trade publication covering the candy industry. **Freq:** Bimonthly. **Key Personnel:** Charles Forman, Publisher, Executive Vice President; Paula Trapalis, Editor; Karen Kalinyak, Manager, Production. **ISSN:** 1090--1914 (print). **Subscription Rates:** $39 Individuals; $50 Canada and Mexico; $130 Other countries; $8 Single issue print only. **URL:** http://www.professionalcandybuyer.com. **Ad Rates:** BW $5,070; 4C $6,630; PCI $85. **Remarks:** Accepts advertising. **Circ:** (Not Reported).

3333 ■ The Public Record
ThePublicRecord
303 N Indian Canyon Dr.
Palm Springs, CA 92263-2724
Phone: (760)771-1155
Fax: (760)322-2533
Journal. **Freq:** Weekly (Fri.). **Print Method:** Offset. **Trim Size:** 11 1/2 x 13 1/2. **Cols./Page:** 4. **Col. Width:** 2 3/8 inches. **Col. Depth:** 12 1/2 inches. **Key Personnel:** Bob Marra, Publisher. **USPS:** 662-010. **Subscription Rates:** $59.95 Individuals 52 weeks. **URL:** http://www.desertpublicrecord.com. **Mailing address:** PO Box 2724, PalmSprings, CA 92263-2724. **Ad Rates:** BW $800. **Remarks:** Accepts advertising. **Circ:** Paid ‡500, Free ‡500.

3334 ■ KCLB-AM - 970
1321 N Gene Autry Trl.
Palm Springs, CA 92262
Phone: (503)517-6200
Format: Sports; Adult Contemporary; Country; Classic Rock; Top 40. **Networks:** CBS. **Owner:** Coachella Valley Broadcasting, at above address. **Founded:** 1954. **Formerly**: KVIM-AM. **Operating Hours**: Continuous. **Key Personnel:** Gene Abraham, Station Mgr.; Alfonso Garfias, News Dir.; Susan Gorges, Gen. Mgr; Ramiro Islas, Contact. **Wattage**: 5,000 Day;360 Night. **Ad Rates:** Advertising accepted; rates available upon request. **URL:** http://www.943knews.com.

3335 ■ KCLB-FM - 93.7
1321 N Gene Autry Trl.
Palm Springs, CA 92262-7944
Phone: (760)322-7890
Format: Album-Oriented Rock (AOR). **Owner:** Coachella Valley Broadcasting, at above address. **Founded:** 1960. **Formerly**: KCHV-FM; KELB-FM. **Operating Hours**: Continuous. **Key Personnel:** Gene Abraham, Contact. **Wattage**: 26,500 ERP. **Ad Rates:** Advertising accepted; rates available upon request. **URL:** http://www.937kclb.com.

Circulation: ★ = AAM; △ or • = BPA; ♦ = CAC; ❑ = VAC; ⊕ = PO Statement; ‡ = Publisher's Report; Boldface figures = sworn; Light figures = estimated.

3336 ■ KCMJ-FM - 92.7
PO Box 1626
Palm Springs, CA 92263
Fax: (619)320-1493
Email: kcmjamfm@worldnet.att.net
Format: Classic Rock; Oldies. **Owner:** Claridge Broadcasting, Inc., at above address. **Founded:** 1942. **Operating Hours:** Continuous. **ADI:** Palm Springs, CA. **Key Personnel:** Barry Gorfine, Gen. Sales Mgr., Contact; Gary DeMaroney, Dir. of Programs; Bruce Johnson, Gen. Mgr; Barry Gorfine, Contact. **Wattage:** 3,000. **Ad Rates:** $25 per unit.

3337 ■ KDES-FM - 98.5
2100 Tahquitz Canyon Way
Palm Springs, CA 92262
Phone: (760)325-2582
Fax: (760)322-3562
Format: Oldies. **Owner:** RR Broadcasting, 2100 Tahquitz Canyon Wy., Palm Springs, CA 92262, Ph: (760)325-2582, Fax: (760)322-3562. **Founded:** 1954. **Operating Hours:** Continuous; 100% local. **ADI:** Palm Springs, CA. **Key Personnel:** Gene Nichols, News Dir., gene@rrbroadcasting.com; Gregg Aratin, VP of Sales, gregg@rrbroadcasting.com; Mel Hill, Sales Mgr., mel@rrbroadcasting.com; Jack Broady, Dir. of Production; Kacy Consiglio, Traffic Mgr. **Wattage:** 42,000. **Ad Rates:** $50 for 30 seconds; $75 for 60 seconds. Combined advertising rates available with KGAM-AM; $7-$50 for 30 seconds; $10-$60 for 60 seconds. **URL:** http://www.kdes.com.

3338 ■ KDGL-FM - 106.9
1321 N Gene Autry Trl.
Palm Springs, CA 92262
Phone: (760)866-1069
Fax: (760)322-7890
Free: 800-955-5567
Format: Classical. **Owner:** Morris Radio, 725 Broad St., Augusta, GA 30901, Ph: (706)724-0851, Fax: (800)622-6358. **ADI:** Palm Springs, CA. **Key Personnel:** Jennifer Shevlin, Operations Mgr., Prog. Dir., jennifer.shevlin@morris.com. **URL:** http://www.theeagle1069.com.

3339 ■ K40ID - 40
PO Box A
Santa Ana, CA 92711
Phone: (714)832-2950
Free: 888-731-1000
Owner: Trinity Broadcasting Network Inc., PO Box A, Santa Ana, CA 92711, Ph: (714)832-2950, Free: 888-731-1000. **URL:** http://www.tbn.org.

3340 ■ KFUT-AM - 1270
1321 N Gene Autry Trl.
Palm Springs, CA 92262
Phone: (760)322-7890
Owner: Morris Communications Company L.L.C., 725 Broad St., Augusta, GA 30901, Ph: (706)724-0851, Free: 800-622-6358.

3341 ■ KHCS-FM - 91.7
PO Box 2507
Palm Springs, CA 92263
Phone: (760)864-9620
Fax: (760)864-9633
Format: Religious. **Founded:** 1993. **Wattage:** 960. **Ad Rates:** Noncommercial. **URL:** http://www.khcs.us.

3342 ■ KKUU-FM - 92.7
1321 N Gene Autry Trl.
Palm Springs, CA 92262
Fax: (760)322-5493
Format: Top 40; Alternative/New Music/Progressive. **Wattage:** 4,200. **Ad Rates:** Noncommercial. **URL:** http://www.927kkuu.com.

3343 ■ KMRJ-FM - 99.5
PO Box 1825
Palm Springs, CA 92263
Phone: (760)320-4550
Fax: (760)320-3037
Email: info@995theheat.com
Format: Alternative/New Music/Progressive. **Networks:** Westwood One Radio. **Owner:** Mitchell Media, Inc., at above address, Arlington, VA 22201-3391. **Founded:** July 17, 1998. **Operating Hours:** Continuous. **ADI:** Palm Springs, CA. **Key Personnel:** Todd Marker, Gen. Mgr., toddmarker@dc.rr.com. **Local Programs:** *The Bob & Tom Show*, Monday Tuesday Wednesday Thursday Friday 6:00 a.m. - 10:00 a.m.; *Theatre of the Mind with Lord Tim*. **Wattage:** 3,000. **Ad Rates:** Noncommercial. Combined advertising rates available with KPLM, KJJZ, KPSI, KDES, KDSI-AM, KGAM.

3344 ■ KNWQ-AM - 1140
1321 N Gene Autry Trl.
Palm Springs, CA 92262
Phone: (760)322-7890
Fax: (760)322-5493
Free: 888-589-6397
Format: News; Talk. **Key Personnel:** Sean Flannigan, Promotions Dir., sean.flannigan@morris.com; Virginia Nelson, Dir. of Sales, virginia.nelson@morris.com. **URL:** http://www.943knews.com.

3345 ■ KPDC-TV - 25
630 S Sunrise Way
Palm Springs, CA 92264
URL: http://kpdctv.com.

3346 ■ KPSC-FM - 88.5
PO Box 77913
Los Angeles, CA 90007
Phone: (213)225-7400
Email: info@thegrandtour.com
Format: Classical. **Networks:** National Public Radio (NPR); Public Radio International (PRI). **Owner:** University of Southern California, University Park Campus, Los Angeles, CA 90089, Ph: (213)740-2311. **Founded:** 1985. **Operating Hours:** Continuous. **Key Personnel:** Brenda Barnes, President, bbarnes@kusc.org; Eric DeWeese, Gen. Mgr.; Ron Thompson, Dir. of Engg. **Wattage:** 39,000. **Ad Rates:** Noncommercial. **URL:** http://www.kusc.org.

3347 ■ KPSI-AM - 920
2100 Tahquitz Canyon Way
Palm Springs, CA 92262
Phone: (760)325-2582
Fax: (760)322-3562
Format: News; Talk. **Networks:** ABC. **Owner:** R & R Radio Corporation, at above address. **Founded:** 1954. **Operating Hours:** Continuous; 75% network, 25% local. **ADI:** Palm Springs, CA. **Key Personnel:** Mel Hill, Sales Mgr., mel@rrbroadcasting.com; Gregg Aratin, Gen. Sales Mgr., gregg@rrbroadcasting.com; Scott Crisman, CFO, scott@rrbroadcasting.com. **Wattage:** 1,000. **Ad Rates:** $9-13 for 15 seconds; $12-16 for 30 seconds; $15-21 for 60 seconds. **URL:** http://www.rrbroadcasting.com.

3348 ■ KPSI-FM - 100.5
2100 Tahquitz Canyon Way
Palm Springs, CA 92262
Phone: (760)325-2582
Fax: (760)322-3562
Format: Adult Contemporary. **Owner:** RR Broadcasting, 2100 Tahquitz Canyon Wy., Palm Springs, CA 92262, Ph: (760)325-2582, Fax: (760)322-3562. **Founded:** 1980. **Operating Hours:** Continuous. **ADI:** Palm Springs, CA. **Key Personnel:** Gene Nichols, News Dir., gene@rrbroadcasting.com; Gregg Aratin, Gen. Sales Mgr., gregg@rrbroadcasting.com. **Wattage:** 25,000. **Ad Rates:** Advertising accepted; rates available upon request. **URL:** http://www.rrbroadcasting.com.

PALMDALE

S. CA. Los Angeles Co. 40 mi. NE of Los Angeles. Air craft manufacturing. Air force flight test center. Rocket lab.

3349 ■ Antelope Valley Lifestyle
Antelope Valley Newspapers Inc.
37404 Sierra Hwy.
Palmdale, CA 93550-9343
Phone: (661)273-2700
Fax: (661)947-4870
Publisher's E-mail: letters@avpress.com
Magazine featuring places, individuals and community events in Antelope Valley. **Freq:** Monthly. **Key Personnel:** Karen Maeshiro, Editor. **URL:** http://avpress.com/avlifestyle/index.html. **Mailing address:** PO Box 4050, Palmdale, CA 93590-4050. **Ad Rates:** BW $1478, full page; BW $813, half page. **Remarks:** Accepts advertising. **Circ:** (Not Reported).

3350 ■ Antelope Valley Press
Antelope Valley Newspapers Inc.
37404 Sierra Hwy.
Palmdale, CA 93550-9343
Phone: (661)273-2700
Fax: (661)947-4870
Publisher's E-mail: letters@avpress.com
General newspaper. **Freq:** Daily. **Print Method:** Offset. **Cols./Page:** 6. **Col. Width:** 25 nonpareils. **Col. Depth:** 301 agate lines. **URL:** http://www.avpress.com. **Mailing address:** PO Box 4050, Palmdale, CA 93590-4050. **Remarks:** Accepts advertising. **Circ:** Mon.-Sat. ■ **21237**, Sun. ■ **24943**.

3351 ■ High Desert Broadcasting
570 E Ave. Q-9
Palmdale, CA 93550
Phone: (661)947-3107
Format: News; Talk; Classic Rock; Top 40. **URL:** http://www.highdesertbroadcasting.com.

3352 ■ KCEL-FM - 96.1
570 E Ave. Q-9
Palmdale, CA 93550
Phone: (661)947-3107
Format: Hispanic. **Networks:** ABC. **Owner:** High Desert Broadcasting, 570 E Ave. Q-9, Palmdale, CA 93550, Ph: (661)947-3107. **Operating Hours:** Continuous. **Wattage:** 630. **Ad Rates:** Noncommercial. **URL:** http://www.laquebuena961.com.

3353 ■ KGMX-FM - 106.3
570 East Ave., Q-9
Palmdale, CA 93550
Phone: (661)947-3107
Fax: (661)272-5688
Email: psa@highdesertbroadcasting.com
Format: Adult Contemporary. **Networks:** Westwood One Radio; NBC. **Owner:** High Desert Broadcasting, 570 E Ave. Q-9, Palmdale, CA 93550, Ph: (661)947-3107. **Founded:** 1956. **Operating Hours:** Continuous. **Key Personnel:** Nelson Rasse, Gen. Sales Mgr. **Wattage:** 3,000. **Ad Rates:** $21 for 30 seconds; $24 for 60 seconds. **URL:** http://www.kmix1063.com.

3354 ■ KKZQ-FM - 100.1
570 E Ave., Ste. Q-9
Palmdale, CA 93550
Phone: (661)947-3107
Format: Alternative/New Music/Progressive. **Owner:** High Desert Broadcasting, 570 E Ave. Q-9, Palmdale, CA 93550, Ph: (661)947-3107. **Wattage:** 340. **Ad Rates:** Advertising accepted; rates available upon request. **URL:** http://www.edge100.com.

3355 ■ KLKX-FM - 93.5
570 E Ave., Q-9
Palmdale, CA 93550
Phone: (661)947-3107
Format: Classic Rock. **Ad Rates:** Noncommercial. **URL:** http://www.935thequake.com.

3356 ■ KOSS-AM 1380 - 1380
570 E Ave. Q-9
Palmdale, CA 93550
Phone: (661)947-3107
Format: News; Talk. **Networks:** NBC; Westwood One Radio. **Owner:** High Desert Broadcasting, 570 E Ave. Q-9, Palmdale, CA 93550, Ph: (661)947-3107. **Operating Hours:** Sunrise-sunset. **Wattage:** 1,000. **Ad Rates:** $15 for 30 seconds; $20 for 60 seconds. **URL:** http://newstalk1380.com.

3357 ■ KUTY-AM - 1470
570 E Ave., Q-9
Palmdale, CA 93550
Phone: (661)947-3107
Format: Hispanic. **Owner:** High Desert Broadcasting, 570 E Ave. Q-9, Palmdale, CA 93550, Ph: (661)947-3107. **Founded:** 1981. **Operating Hours:** Continuous. **Wattage:** 5,000. **Ad Rates:** $15 for 30 seconds; $20 for 60 seconds. **URL:** http://www.highdesertbroadcasting.com.

PALO ALTO

W. CA. Santa Clara Co. 30 mi. S. of San Francisco. Residential. Stanford University and several private schools. Electronic missile research. Pharmaceuticals. Film processing.

3358 ■ AI Magazine
Association for the Advancement of Artificial Intelligence
2275 E Bayshore Rd., Ste. 160
Palo Alto, CA 94303
Phone: (650)328-3123

Fax: (650)321-4457
Publisher's E-mail: info@aaai.org
Magazine about artificial intelligence. **Freq:** Quarterly. **Print Method:** Offset. **Trim Size:** 8 3/8 x 10 7/8. **Cols./Page:** 3. **Col. Width:** 13.5 picas. **Col. Depth:** 54 picas. **Key Personnel:** David B. Leake, Editor-in-Chief; David M. Hamilton, Managing Editor; Carol M. Hamilton, Publisher. **ISSN:** 0738- 4602 (print). **Subscription Rates:** $145 Individuals print and online; $75 Individuals online ; $290 Institutions online; $580 Institutions 2 IPs (online); $870 Institutions 3 IPs (online); $1020 Institutions 4 IPs (online). **Alt. Formats:** PDF. **URL:** http://www.aaai.org/Magazine/magazine.php. **Ad Rates:** BW $1375. **Remarks:** Accepts advertising. **Circ:** 7,000.

3359 ■ The Almanac: Menlo Park's Country Almanac
Embarcadero Publishing Co.
450 Cambridge Ave.
Palo Alto, CA 94306
Phone: (650)326-8210
Publisher's E-mail: info@embarcaderomediagroup.com
Newspaper. **Freq:** Weekly (Wed.). **Print Method:** Offset. **Cols./Page:** 5. **Col. Width:** 11.5 picas. **Col. Depth:** 197 agate lines. **Key Personnel:** Richard Hine, Managing Editor; Tom Gibboney, Editor, Publisher; Neal Fine, Manager. **ISSN:** 0192--0111 (print). **Subscription Rates:** $30 Individuals; $50 Out of area 2 years. **URL:** http://www.almanacnews.com. **Ad Rates:** GLR $0.56; BW $1,287; 4C $1,617; PCI $15.85. **Remarks:** Accepts advertising. **Circ:** Free ‡17500.

3360 ■ Annual Review of Biochemistry
Annual Reviews
4139 El Camino Way
Palo Alto, CA 94306
Phone: (650)493-4400
Fax: (650)855-9815
Free: 800-523-8635
Publisher's E-mail: service@annualreviews.org
Journal covering analytic reviews in 32 disciplines within the biomedical, physical, and social sciences. **Freq:** Annual. **Key Personnel:** Roger D. Kornberg, Editor; Christian Raetz, Associate Editor. **ISSN:** 0066--4154 (print). **Subscription Rates:** $105 Individuals print and online; $269 Institutions print or online; $417 Institutions print and online. **URL:** http://www.annualreviews.org/journal/biochem. **Mailing address:** PO Box 10139, Palo Alto, CA 94303-0139. **Remarks:** Advertising not accepted. **Circ:** (Not Reported).

3361 ■ Annual Review of Earth and Planetary Sciences
Annual Reviews
4139 El Camino Way
Palo Alto, CA 94306
Phone: (650)493-4400
Fax: (650)855-9815
Free: 800-523-8635
Publisher's E-mail: service@annualreviews.org
Scholarly journal covering earth sciences, geology, and astronomy. **Freq:** Annual. **Print Method:** Offset. **Trim Size:** 6 x 8 1/2. **Cols./Page:** 1. **Col. Width:** 26 picas. **Col. Depth:** 42 picas. **Key Personnel:** Katherine H. Freeman, Editor, phone: (814)863-8177, fax: (814)863-7823; Raymond Jeanloz, Editor, phone: (510)642-2639, fax: (510)643-9980. **ISSN:** 0084--6597 (print). **URL:** http://www.annualreviews.org/journal/earth. **Mailing address:** PO Box 10139, Palo Alto, CA 94303-0139. **Remarks:** Advertising not accepted. **Circ:** (Not Reported).

3362 ■ Annual Review of Genetics
Annual Reviews
4139 El Camino Way
Palo Alto, CA 94306
Phone: (650)493-4400
Fax: (650)855-9815
Free: 800-523-8635
Publisher's E-mail: service@annualreviews.org
Periodical covering issues in genetics and the biological sciences. **Freq:** Annual November. **Key Personnel:** Bonnie L. Bassler, Editor; Michael Lichten, Associate Editor; Absolom J. Hagg, Editor, phone: (650)843-6673. **ISSN:** 0066-4197 (print). **Subscription Rates:** $99 Individuals print only; $255 Institutions print or online; $383 Institutions print and online. **URL:** http://www.annualreviews.org/journal/genet. **Mailing address:** PO Box 10139, Palo Alto, CA 94303-0139. **Circ:** (Not Reported).

3363 ■ Annual Review of Immunology
Annual Reviews
4139 El Camino Way
Palo Alto, CA 94306
Phone: (650)493-4400
Fax: (650)855-9815
Free: 800-523-8635
Publisher's E-mail: service@annualreviews.org
Journal covering active research in immunobiology. Topics include cytokines, cell surface receptors, transcription factors, immune response to disease, signal transduction and interactions of T cells with antigen presenting cells. **Freq:** Semiweekly Tues-Sat. **Print Method:** Offset. **Cols./Page:** 6. **Col. Width:** 25 nonpareils. **Col. Depth:** 301 agate lines. **Key Personnel:** Daniel Littman, Associate Editor, phone: (212)263-7579, fax: (212)263-5711; Erin Wait, Editor, phone: (650)843-6622. **ISSN:** 0732--0582 (print). **USPS:** 035-640. **Subscription Rates:** $105 Individuals; $278 Institutions print or online; $417 Institutions print & online. **URL:** http://www.annualreviews.org/journal/immunol. **Mailing address:** PO Box 10139, Palo Alto, CA 94303-0139. **Remarks:** Advertising not accepted. **Circ:** (Not Reported).

3364 ■ Annual Review of Law and Social Science
Annual Reviews
4139 El Camino Way
Palo Alto, CA 94306
Phone: (650)493-4400
Fax: (650)855-9815
Free: 800-523-8635
Publisher's E-mail: service@annualreviews.org
Journal covering current issues in law and the social sciences. **Freq:** Annual. **Key Personnel:** John Hagan, Editor; Kim Lane Scheppele, Associate Editor; Tom R. Tyler, Associate Editor. **ISSN:** 1550--3585 (print). **URL:** http://www.annualreviews.org/loi/lawsocsci. **Mailing address:** PO Box 10139, Palo Alto, CA 94303-0139. **Circ:** (Not Reported).

3365 ■ Annual Review of Medicine: Selected Topics in the Clinical Sciences
Annual Reviews
4139 El Camino Way
Palo Alto, CA 94306
Phone: (650)493-4400
Fax: (650)855-9815
Free: 800-523-8635
Publisher's E-mail: service@annualreviews.org
Professional journal covering medicine and clinical science. **Freq:** Periodic. **Key Personnel:** C. Thomas Caskey, Editor, phone: (713)500-2401; Christopher Austin, Associate Editor, phone: (301)402-0955; James Hoxie, Associate Editor, phone: (215)898-0261, fax: (215)573-7356. **ISSN:** 0066-4219 (print). **Subscription Rates:** $99 Individuals. **Alt. Formats:** PDF. **URL:** http://www.annualreviews.org/journal/med. **Mailing address:** PO Box 10139, Palo Alto, CA 94303-0139. **Remarks:** Advertising not accepted. **Circ:** (Not Reported).

3366 ■ Annual Review of Microbiology
Annual Reviews
4139 El Camino Way
Palo Alto, CA 94306
Phone: (650)493-4400
Fax: (650)855-9815
Free: 800-523-8635
Publisher's E-mail: service@annualreviews.org
Periodical covering microbiology and the biological sciences. **Freq:** Annual September. **Key Personnel:** Olaf Schneewind, MD, Associate Editor, phone: (773)834-9060, fax: (773)834-8150; Caroline Harwood, Associate Editor; Susan Gottesman, Editor, phone: (301)496-3524, fax: (301)496-3875. **ISSN:** 0066--4227 (print). **Subscription Rates:** $99 Individuals; $255 Institutions print or online; $383 Institutions print and online. **URL:** http://www.annualreviews.org/journal/micro. **Mailing address:** PO Box 10139, Palo Alto, CA 94303-0139. **Circ:** (Not Reported).

3367 ■ Annual Review of Psychology
Annual Reviews
4139 El Camino Way
Palo Alto, CA 94306
Phone: (650)493-4400
Fax: (650)855-9815
Free: 800-523-8635
Publisher's E-mail: service@annualreviews.org
Publication covering psychology and mental health issues. **Freq:** Annual January. **Key Personnel:** Daniel L. Schacter, Associate Editor, phone: (617)495-3855, fax: (617)496-3122; Susan T. Fiske, Editor, phone: (609)258-0655, fax: (609)258-1113. **ISSN:** 0066--4308 (print). **Subscription Rates:** $93 Individuals; $234 Institutions print or online; $351 Institutions print and online. **URL:** http://www.annualreviews.org/journal/psych. **Mailing address:** PO Box 10139, Palo Alto, CA 94303-0139. **Circ:** (Not Reported).

3368 ■ Annual Review of Sociology
Annual Reviews
4139 El Camino Way
Palo Alto, CA 94306
Phone: (650)493-4400
Fax: (650)855-9815
Free: 800-523-8635
Publisher's E-mail: service@annualreviews.org
Publication covering the field of sociology and the social sciences. **Freq:** Annual July. **Key Personnel:** Karen S. Cook, Editor; Douglas S. Massey, Editor. **ISSN:** 0360--0572 (print). **Subscription Rates:** $93 Individuals; $234 Institutions print or online; $351 Institutions print and online. **URL:** http://www.annualreviews.org/journal/soc. **Mailing address:** PO Box 10139, Palo Alto, CA 94303-0139. **Circ:** (Not Reported).

3369 ■ ARTWEEK
ARTWEEK
PO Box 52100
Palo Alto, CA 94303-0751
Publisher's E-mail: laslagunagallery@gmail.com
Magazine containing contemporary West Coast art reviews, commentary, features and interviews. **Freq:** Monthly. **Print Method:** Offset. **Trim Size:** 11 x 14. **Cols./Page:** 5. **ISSN:** 0004--4121 (print). **URL:** http://www.artweek.com. **Ad Rates:** GLR $5; BW $1400; 4C $1815. **Remarks:** Accepts advertising. **Circ:** Paid ‡12000, Non-paid ‡3000.

3370 ■ Astronomy and Astrophysics
Annual Reviews
4139 El Camino Way
Palo Alto, CA 94306
Phone: (650)493-4400
Fax: (650)855-9815
Free: 800-523-8635
Publisher's E-mail: service@annualreviews.org
Professional journal covering astronomy and astrophysics. **Founded:** 1963. **Freq:** Annual. **Key Personnel:** Roselyn Lowe-Webb, Editor, phone: (650)843-6623, fax: (650)855-9815; John Kormendy, Associate Editor, phone: (512)471-8191, fax: (512)471-6016. **ISSN:** 0066-4146 (print). **Subscription Rates:** $96 Individuals print and online; $369 Institutions print and online; $246 Institutions print only; $246 Institutions online only. **URL:** http://www.annualreviews.org/journal/astro. **Formerly:** Annual Review of Astronomy and Astrophysics. **Mailing address:** PO Box 10139, Palo Alto, CA 94303-0139. **Remarks:** Advertising not accepted. **Circ:** (Not Reported).

3371 ■ EPRI Journal
Electric Power Research Institute
3420 Hillview Ave.
Palo Alto, CA 94304
Phone: (650)855-2121
Free: 800-313-3774
Publication E-mail: journal@epri.com
Online publication reporting on global energy technology research and development and related environmental and economic issues. **Key Personnel:** David Dietrich, Managing Editor, phone: (650)855-8519. **Alt. Formats:** Download. **URL:** http://www.epri.com. **Circ:** (Not Reported).

3372 ■ EPRI Online Journal
Electric Power Research Institute
3420 Hillview Ave.
Palo Alto, CA 94304
Phone: (650)855-2121
Free: 800-313-3774
Publisher's E-mail: askepri@epri.com

Circulation: ★ = AAM; △ or • = BPA; ♦ = CAC; ❑ = VAC; ⊕ = PO Statement; ‡ = Publisher's Report; Boldface figures = sworn; Light figures = estimated.

Subscription Rates: free for members. **Remarks:** Advertising not accepted. **Circ:** (Not Reported).

3373 ■ Journal of Artificial Intelligence Research
AAAI Press
2275 E Bayshore Rd., Ste. 160
Palo Alto, CA 94303-3224
Phone: (650)328-3123
Fax: (650)321-4457
Publication E-mail: jair-ed@isi.edu
Scholarly, scientific journal covering artificial intelligence. **Freq:** Semiannual Volume 50. **Key Personnel:** Shlomo Zilberstein, Editor-in-Chief; Craig Boutilier, Associate Editor; Steven Minton, Managing Editor. **ISSN:** 1076-9757 (print). **Subscription Rates:** $90 for nonmembers; $425 Individuals current issue; $85 Individuals back issues. **URL:** http://www.jair.org. **Remarks:** Advertising not accepted. **Circ:** (Not Reported).

3374 ■ Journal of Transpersonal Psychology
Association for Transpersonal Psychology
PO Box 50187
Palo Alto, CA 94303
Phone: (650)424-8764
Publisher's E-mail: info@atpweb.org
Freq: Semiannual summer and winter. **ISSN:** 0022--524X (print). **Subscription Rates:** Included in membership. **URL:** http://atpweb.org/journal.aspx. **Ad Rates:** BW $600. **Remarks:** Accepts advertising. **Circ:** (Not Reported).

3375 ■ Pacific Sun: Alternative Newsweekly
Embarcadero Publishing Co.
450 Cambridge Ave.
Palo Alto, CA 94306
Phone: (650)326-8210
Publication E-mail: letters@pacificsun.com
Community newspaper. **Freq:** Weekly (Fri.). **Print Method:** Offset. **Trim Size:** 11 3/8 x 15. **Cols./Page:** 4. **Col. Width:** 2 1/4 inches. **Col. Depth:** 13 1/2 inches. **Key Personnel:** Gina Allen, Publisher; Linda Black, Director, Advertising. **ISSN:** 0048--2641 (print). **Subscription Rates:** $60 Individuals; $100 Two years. **Ad Rates:** BW $1,920; 4C $100; PCI $25.60. **Remarks:** Accepts advertising. **Circ:** Free 36500.

3376 ■ Palo Alto Weekly
Embarcadero Publishing Co.
450 Cambridge Ave.
Palo Alto, CA 94306
Phone: (650)326-8210
Publication E-mail: pizazz@paloaltoonline.com
Community newspaper. **Freq:** Weekly (Fri.). **Print Method:** Offset. **Cols./Page:** 6. **Col. Width:** 18 nonpareils. **Col. Depth:** 189 agate lines. **Key Personnel:** William S. Johnson, Publisher; Jennifer Lindberg, Manager, Production. **ISSN:** 0199--1159 (print). **Subscription Rates:** $60 Individuals. **Alt. Formats:** Download; PDF. **URL:** http://www.paweekly.com; http://www.embarcaderopublishing.com/paweekly.html. **Remarks:** Accepts advertising. **Circ:** Paid 47000.

3377 ■ Vadeboncoeur Collection of ImageS
JVJ Publishing
3809 Laguna Ave.
Palo Alto, CA 94306-2629
Magazine covering classic illustration. **Freq:** Irregular. **Subscription Rates:** $30 Individuals. **URL:** http://www.bpib.com/imagesmagfolder/imagesmag/index.html. **Remarks:** Accepts advertising. **Circ:** (Not Reported).

PALOS VERDES ESTATES

3378 ■ Moto Retro Illustrated
Moto Retro Illustrated
PO Box 202
Palos Verdes Estates, CA 90274
Publisher's E-mail: info@motoretroillustrated.com
Magazine providing in-depth features and news about bikes and moto-culture. **Freq:** Quarterly. **Key Personnel:** Mitch Boehm, Editor, phone: (310)849-1845. **URL:** http://www.motoretroillustrated.com. **Formerly:** Motorcycle Retro. **Circ:** (Not Reported).

PALOS VERDES PENINSULA

S. CA. Los Angeles Co. 18 mi. SW of Los Angeles. Residential.

3379 ■ The Serendipity Magazine
Serendipity Magazine L.L.C.
PO Box 2171
Palos Verdes Peninsula, CA 90274
Fax: (714)828-2208
Bridal magazine featuring Asian American brides in Southern California. **Freq:** 10/year. **Trim Size:** 8.5 x 11. **Key Personnel:** Caroline Chang, Editor, phone: (714)321-8736; Caroline Wu, Editor, phone: (310)938-6269. **Subscription Rates:** $24.95 Individuals; $30 Two years. **URL:** http://theserendipitymagazine.com. **Remarks:** Advertising accepted; rates available upon request. **Circ:** 10000.

3380 ■ Soundboard Magazine
Guitar Foundation of America
PO Box 2900
Palos Verdes Peninsula, CA 90274
Free: 877-570-1651
Publisher's E-mail: info@guitarfoundation.org
Freq: Quarterly. **ISSN:** 0145- 6237 (print). **Subscription Rates:** $7 /issue; $7.90 for back issues; $12 current issue. **URL:** http://www.guitarfoundation.org/?page=SBFront. **Ad Rates:** BW $695, full page; BW $500, half page vertical or horizontal. **Remarks:** Accepts advertising. **Circ:** 3000.

3381 ■ Soundboard Scholar
Guitar Foundation of America
PO Box 2900
Palos Verdes Peninsula, CA 90274
Free: 877-570-1651
Publisher's E-mail: info@guitarfoundation.org
Freq: Annual. **Subscription Rates:** Included in membership. **URL:** http://www.guitarfoundation.org/?page=SBScholarly. **Remarks:** Advertising not accepted. **Circ:** 3000.

PARADISE

N. CA. Butte Co. 90 mi. NE of Sacramento. Residential. Grape Juice Cannery, machine shop. Agriculture. Apples, grapes.

3382 ■ California Territorial Quarterly
California Territorial Quarterly
6848 U Skyway
Paradise, CA 95969
Phone: (530)872-3363
Free: 877-397-3363
Publication E-mail: info@californiahistory.com
Consumer magazine covering California history. **Freq:** Quarterly. **Key Personnel:** Bill Anderson, Editor. **ISSN:** 1080--7594 (print). **Subscription Rates:** $18 Individuals per year for four quarterly issues - add $3.00 shipping per order; $5.75 Single issue add $3.00 shipping per order; $4.50 Single issue buy four or more copies - add $3.00 shipping per order. **URL:** http://www.californiahistory.com. **Formerly:** Dogtown Territorial Quarterly. **Ad Rates:** BW $459; 4C $499. **Remarks:** Accepts advertising. **Circ:** Controlled ‡3000.

3383 ■ Genealogical Goldmine
Paradise Genealogical Society
PO Box 460
Paradise, CA 95967-0460
Phone: (530)877-2330
Publisher's E-mail: pargenso@att.net
Genealogical journal covering local and general family histories. **Freq:** Annual. **Print Method:** Copy Machine. **Trim Size:** 8 1/2 x 11. **ISSN:** 0738--3770 (print). **Subscription Rates:** $2 Individuals. **URL:** http://www.pargenso.org/publications.html. **Mailing address:** PO Box 460, Paradise, CA 95967-0460. **Remarks:** Advertising not accepted. **Circ:** Combined 200.

3384 ■ The Paradise Post
The Paradise Post
PO Box 70
Paradise, CA 95967
Phone: (530)877-4413
Publication E-mail: newsroom@paradisepost.com
Community newspaper. **Freq:** 3/week Tuesday, Thursday and Saturday. **Print Method:** Offset. **Trim Size:** 14 x 22 3/4. **Cols./Page:** 6. **Col. Width:** 26 nonpareils. **Col. Depth:** 301 agate lines. **Key Personnel:** Gregg McConnell, Publisher, phone: (530)877-4413; Sharon Gingerich, Sales Executive. **URL:** http://www.paradisepost.com. **Mailing address:** PO Box 70, Paradise, CA 95967. **Remarks:** Accepts advertising. **Circ:** (Not Reported).

3385 ■ KRGR-FM - 101.3
1633 Sweetbrier Ln.
Paradise, CA 95969
Phone: (530)872-7839
Format: Religious. **Key Personnel:** Rick Mautz, Station Mgr. **URL:** http://www.lifetalk.net.

PARAMOUNT

S. CA. Los Angeles Co. Adjoins the city of Long Beach. Foundries, machine shops, Oil refinery. Aluminum, aircraft components, hospital equipment, dairy products manufactured.

3386 ■ The Paramount Journal
Community Media Corp.
8007 Somerset Blvd.
Paramount, CA 90723
Phone: (800)540-1870
Publication E-mail: info@paramountjournal.org
Community newspaper. **Freq:** Weekly (Thurs.) every Thursday. **Print Method:** Offset. **Cols./Page:** 5. **Col. Width:** 1 9/10 picas. **Col. Depth:** 15 inches. **Key Personnel:** J. J. Amonette, Publisher; Cheryl Scott. **Subscription Rates:** Free. **URL:** http://www.paramountjournal.org. **Ad Rates:** GLR $8; 4C $275; PCI $8. **Remarks:** Accepts advertising. **Circ:** ‡5000.

PASADENA

S. CA. Los Angeles Co. 12 mi. NE of Los Angeles. California Institute of Technology. Pasadena City College. Art Center and Design. Ambassador College and Foundation. Pacific Oaks College. Residential. Manufactures furniture, aircraft components, aerospace, scientific and precision instruments, chemicals, electronics, pharmaceuticals, plastics, Oil refineries. Nurseries. Citrus fruit packed.

3387 ■ The Argonaut
Southland Publishing
50 S DeLacey Ave., Ste. 200
Pasadena, CA 91105
Phone: (626)584-1500
Community newspaper. **Founded:** Nov. 25, 1971. **Freq:** Weekly (Thurs.). **Print Method:** Offset. **Cols./Page:** 5. **Col. Width:** 25 nonpareils. **Col. Depth:** 224 agate lines. **Key Personnel:** David Comden, Publisher; Joe Piasecki, Editor. **Subscription Rates:** $135 Individuals first class mail; $4 Single issue by mail. **URL:** http://argonautnews.com. **Ad Rates:** GLR $6.50; BW $2,760; 4C $3,310; PCI $34.50. **Remarks:** Accepts advertising. **Circ:** ‡30000.

3388 ■ Arroyo Monthly
Southland Publishing
50 S DeLacey Ave., Ste. 200
Pasadena, CA 91105
Phone: (626)584-1500
Magazine featuring charitable giving. **Freq:** Monthly. **Key Personnel:** Jon Guynn, Publisher; Irene Lacher, Editor. **URL:** http://www.arroyomonthly.com. **Remarks:** Accepts advertising. **Circ:** 27000.

3389 ■ Beirut Times
Beirut Times
PO Box 40277
Pasadena, CA 91114
Phone: (626)844-7777
Fax: (626)795-2222
Publication E-mail: info@beiruttimes.net
Covers events, issues, and social needs unique to Arab Americans. **Freq:** Weekly. **Print Method:** Web. **Trim Size:** 17. **Cols./Page:** 5. **Col. Width:** 1 3/4 inches. **USPS:** 765-440. **Subscription Rates:** $49 Individuals regular mail; $99 Two years regular mail; $99 Individuals first class mail; $190 Two years first class mail; $199 Other countries airmail. **URL:** http://www.beiruttimes.com. **Ad Rates:** GLR $35; BW $1,500; 4C $3,000; PCI $35. **Remarks:** Accepts advertising. **Circ:** Free 20000.

3390 ■ Boxoffice Magazine: The Business Magazine of The Global Motion Picture Industry
Media Enterprises L.P.
155 S El Molino Ave, Ste. 100
Pasadena, CA 91101
Phone: (626)396-0250
Fax: (626)396-0248
Publication E-mail: boxoff@earthlink.net

Trade magazine for the motion picture exhibition industry; including news of film distribution and exhibition, film reviews, and technical articles. **Freq:** Monthly. **Print Method:** Offset. **Trim Size:** 8 1/8 x 10 7/8. **Cols./Page:** 3. **Col. Width:** 27 nonpareils. **Col. Depth:** 140 agate lines. **Key Personnel:** Amy Nicholson, Editor. **ISSN:** 0006--8527 (print). **Subscription Rates:** $59.95 Individuals; $74.95 Canada; $135 Other countries; $89.95 Two years domestic; $109.95 Individuals domestic three years. **URL:** http://pro.boxoffice.com. **Ad Rates:** BW $2680; 4C $3695; PCI $125. **Remarks:** Accepts advertising. **Circ:** Paid 4875.

3391 ■ Global Prayer Digest
Frontier Ventures
1605 Elizabeth St.
Pasadena, CA 91104
Phone: (626)797-1111
Magazine serving as a Christian devotional aid in daily prayer for ethnic groups unreached by the gospel. **Freq:** Monthly. **Trim Size:** 5 3/8 x 8 1/2. **Cols./Page:** 1. **Col. Width:** 3 7/8 inches. **Col. Depth:** 6 1/2 inches. **Key Personnel:** Keith Carey, Managing Editor, phone: (626)398-2241; Marjorie Clark, Contact; Dan Eddy, Contact. **ISSN:** 1045-9731 (print). **Subscription Rates:** $12 Individuals; $18 Other countries surface; $30 Other countries air mail; $18 Canada. **URL:** http://www.globalprayerdigest.org. **Formerly:** Daily Prayer Guide. **Remarks:** Advertising not accepted. **Circ:** (Not Reported).

3392 ■ Journal of the Mechanics and Physics of Solids
Aspen Publishers, Inc.
c/o K. Bhattacharya, Editor
California Institute of Technology
MS 104-44
Pasadena, CA 91125
Phone: (626)395-3389
Fax: (626)583-4963
Publisher's E-mail: order.entry@aspenpublishers.com
Scientific journal for engineers dealing with micro properties. **Freq:** Monthly. **Print Method:** Offset. **Trim Size:** 6 3/4 x 10. **Cols./Page:** 1. **Col. Width:** 66 nonpareils. **Col. Depth:** 124 agate lines. **Key Personnel:** Prof. J.R. Willis, Advisor; L.B. Freund, Advisor; K. Bhattacharya, Editor; H. Gao, Editor, fax: (401)863-9025. **ISSN:** 0022-5096 (print). **Subscription Rates:** $4914.07 Institutions online; $5361 Institutions print; $490 Individuals print. **URL:** http://www.journals.elsevier.com/journal-of-the-mechanics-and-physics-of-solids. **Ad Rates:** BW $600; 4C $1,400. **Remarks:** Accepts advertising. **Circ:** ‡1500.

3393 ■ Life After 50
Southland Publishing
50 S DeLacey Ave., Ste. 200
Pasadena, CA 91105
Phone: (626)584-1500
Magazine for people over fifty years of age in Southern California. **Freq:** Monthly. **Key Personnel:** Ben Malkin, Publisher, phone: (805)444-5016; David Laurell, Editor, phone: (818)563-1007. **URL:** http://lifeafter50.com. **Remarks:** Advertising accepted; rates available upon request. **Circ:** (Not Reported).

3394 ■ Mission Frontiers
Frontier Ventures
1605 Elizabeth St.
Pasadena, CA 91104
Phone: (626)797-1111
Bulletin of the United States Center for World Mission; editorial on evangelical Frontier Christian missions. **Freq:** Bimonthly. **Print Method:** Web offset. **Trim Size:** 10 11/16 x 8 1/4. **Cols./Page:** 2. **Col. Width:** 3 1/2 inches. **Col. Depth:** 9 inches. **Key Personnel:** Rick Wood, Editor. **ISSN:** 0889-9436 (print). **Subscription Rates:** $24 Individuals 6 bi-monthly issues. **Alt. Formats:** PDF. **URL:** http://www.missionfrontiers.org. **Ad Rates:** BW $1,890. **Remarks:** Advertising accepted; rates available upon request. **Circ:** Combined ‡8150.

3395 ■ Pasadena Star-News
San Gabriel Newspaper Group
911 E Colorado Blvd.
Pasadena, CA 91109
Phone: (626)578-6300
Publication E-mail: news.star-news@sgvn.com
General newspaper. **Founded:** Apr. 21, 1886. **Freq:** Weekly. **Print Method:** Offset. **Cols./Page:** 6. **Col. Width:** 26 nonpareils. **Col. Depth:** 301 agate lines. **Key Personnel:** Larry Wilson, Editor; Steve Hunt, Senior Editor. **URL:** http://www.pasadenastarnews.com. **Formerly:** Star-News. **Ad Rates:** GLR $1.80; 4C $3,748; PCI $31.50. **Remarks:** Accepts classified advertising. **Circ:** (Not Reported).

3396 ■ Pasadena Weekly
Southland Publishing
50 S DeLacey Ave., Ste. 200
Pasadena, CA 91105
Phone: (626)584-1500
Community newspaper. **Freq:** Weekly (Thurs.). **Print Method:** Offset. **Trim Size:** 10 13/16 x 15 3/4. **Cols./Page:** 5. **Col. Width:** 12 1/2 nonpareils. **Col. Depth:** 221 agate lines. **Key Personnel:** Kevin Uhrich, Editor; Andre Coleman, Reporter; Jon Guynn, Publisher; Irene Lacher, Editor. **Subscription Rates:** Free Northeast Los Angeles County. **URL:** http://www.pasadenaweekly.com. **Remarks:** Accepts advertising. **Circ:** Free ‡30000.

3397 ■ PCC Courier
Pasadena City College
1570 E Colorado Blvd.
Pasadena, CA 91106
Phone: (626)585-7123
Collegiate newspaper. **Founded:** 1917. **Freq:** Weekly (Thurs.). **Print Method:** Offset. **Cols./Page:** 6. **Col. Width:** 26 nonpareils. **Col. Depth:** 294 agate lines. **URL:** http://pcccourier.com/. **Formerly:** The Courier. **Ad Rates:** PCI $10. **Remarks:** no alcohol or tobacco ads will be accepted. **Circ:** ‡5000.

3398 ■ Planetary Report
The Planetary Society
60 S Los Robles Ave.
Pasadena, CA 91101
Phone: (626)793-5100
Fax: (626)793-5528
Publisher's E-mail: tps@planetary.org
Magazine featuring articles of discoveries on Earth and other planets. **Freq:** Quarterly. **ISSN:** 0736-3680 (print). **Subscription Rates:** Included in membership. **URL:** http://www.planetary.org/explore/the-planetary-report. **Remarks:** Advertising not accepted. **Circ:** (Not Reported).

3399 ■ Ribbons
Tanka Society of America
c/o Kathabela Wilson, Secretary
439 S Catalina Ave., No. 306
Pasadena, CA 91106
Publisher's E-mail: welchm@aol.com
Freq: 3/year. **Subscription Rates:** Included in membership. **URL:** http://sites.google.com/site/tankasocietyofamerica/ribbons. **Remarks:** Advertising not accepted. **Circ:** (Not Reported).

3400 ■ SIAM Journal on Computing
Society for Industrial and Applied Mathematics
c/o Leonard J. Schulman, Editor-in-Chief
California Institute of Technology
Division of Engineering and Applied Science
Pasadena, CA 91125
Publisher's E-mail: service@siam.org
Journal containing research articles dealing with the mathematical and formal aspects of computer science and nonnumerical computing. **Freq:** Bimonthly. **Print Method:** Offset. **Trim Size:** 6 x 9. **Cols./Page:** 1. **Col. Width:** 31 picas. **Col. Depth:** 50 picas. **Key Personnel:** Steven Fortune, Associate Editor; James Aspnes, Associate Editor; Leonard J. Schulman, Editor-in-Chief. **ISSN:** 0097--5397 (print); **EISSN:** 1095--7111 (electronic). **Subscription Rates:** $129 Members domestic; $135 Members foreign; $115 Members electronic only (1997 - present); $811 Individuals list price; $110 Individuals print add on, Volume 44 (six issues). **URL:** http://www.siam.org/journals/sicomp.php. **Remarks:** Advertising accepted; rates available upon request. **Circ:** ‡1324.

3401 ■ Southern California Quarterly
Historical Society of Southern California
PO Box 93487
Pasadena, CA 91109
Phone: (323)222-0546
Fax: (323)645-7466
Publication E-mail: hssc@socalhistory.org
Scholarly journal covering local history. **Freq:** Quarterly February, May, August, November. **Key Personnel:** Merry Ovnick, Editor. **ISSN:** 0038--3930 (print); **EISSN:** 2162- 8637 (electronic). **Subscription Rates:** Free; $62 Individuals; $63 Institutions. **URL:** http://www.socalhistory.org/publications/southern-california-quarterly.html; http://www.socalhistory.org/?page_id=3877; http://ucpressjournals.com/journal.php?j=scq. **Remarks:** Advertising not accepted. **Circ:** Paid 1200.

3402 ■ Theoretical and Computational Fluid Dynamics
Springer-Verlag GmbH & Company KG
c/o T. Colonius, Editor-in-Chief
Division of Engineering and Applied Science
California Institute of Technology
Mail Code 104-44
Pasadena, CA 91125
Publisher's E-mail: customerservice@springer.com
Journal focusing on aeronautical sciences, geophysical and environmental sciences, life sciences and materials sciences that deals with the fundamental aspects of fluid flow. **Key Personnel:** T. Colonius, Editor-in-Chief; M.Y. Hussaini, Founder, Editor-in-Chief. **ISSN:** 0935--4964 (print); **EISSN:** 1432--2250 (electronic). **Subscription Rates:** €125.21 Individuals online. **URL:** http://www.springer.com/materials/mechanics/journal/162. **Remarks:** Advertising accepted; rates available upon request. **Circ:** (Not Reported).

3403 ■ Western Cleaner and Launderer
Wakefield Publishing Co.
800 Canyon Wash Dr.
Pasadena, CA 91107
Phone: (626)793-2911
Fax: (626)793-5540
Free: 800-793-2911
Laundry and dry cleaning trade newspaper. **Freq:** Monthly. **Print Method:** Offset. **Trim Size:** 10 x 13 1/2. **Cols./Page:** 4. **Col. Width:** 2 5/16 inches. **Key Personnel:** Albane F. Wente, Publisher; Randy Wente, Editor. **ISSN:** 0049--741X (print). **USPS:** 414-650. **Subscription Rates:** Free. **URL:** http://www.wcl-online.com/index.html. **Ad Rates:** 4C $720; PCI $65. **Remarks:** Accepts advertising. **Circ:** Non-paid ⊕**16000**.

3404 ■ KALI-AM - 1430
747 E Green St., Ste. 208
Pasadena, CA 91101
Phone: (626)773-1430
Fax: (626)792-8890
Email: gfm75@aol.com
Format: News. **Founded:** 1952. **Operating Hours:** Continuous. **Key Personnel:** Gary Mercer, Station Mgr., Contact; Dave Sweeney, VP; Gary Mercer, Contact. **Wattage:** 50,000 KW. **Ad Rates:** Advertising accepted; rates available upon request. **URL:** http://www.am1430.net.

3405 ■ KAZN-AM - 1300
747 E Green St.
Pasadena, CA 91101
Phone: (626)568-1300
Fax: (626)568-3666
Email: sales@am1300.com
Format: Ethnic. **Owner:** Multicultural Radio Broadcasting Inc., 27 William St., 11th Fl., New York, NY 10005, Ph: (212)966-1059, Fax: (212)966-9580. **URL:** http://www.am1300.com.

KBLA-AM - See Santa Monica, CA

3406 ■ KPPC-AM - 1240
3844 E Foothill Blvd.
Pasadena, CA 91107-2205
Phone: (818)577-1240
Format: Religious. **Networks:** Independent. **Founded:** 1924. **Operating Hours:** Evenings Mon.-Sat.; 6 a.m.-midnight Sun. **Key Personnel:** Mark E. Pompey, Contact. **Wattage:** 250. **Ad Rates:** Advertising accepted; rates available upon request.

3407 ■ KYPA-AM
747 E Green St.
Pasadena, CA 91101
Owner: Multicultural Radio Broadcasting Inc., 27 William St., 11th Fl., New York, NY 10005, Ph: (212)966-1059, Fax: (212)966-9580. **Founded:** 1926. **Ad Rates:** Advertising accepted; rates available upon request.

Circulation: ★ = AAM; △ or • = BPA; ♦ = CAC; ❑ = VAC; ⊕ = PO Statement; ‡ = Publisher's Report; Boldface figures = sworn; Light figures = estimated.

3408 ■ Southern California Public Radio
474 S Raymond Ave.
Pasadena, CA 91105
Free: 866-893-5722
Format: Educational; Talk. **Networks:** BBC World Service; Talknet. **Key Personnel:** Bill Davis, President, CEO. **Ad Rates:** Underwriting available. **URL:** http://www.scpr.org.

PASO ROBLES

SW CA. San Luis Obispo Co. 30 mi. N. of San Luis Obispo. Recreation. Tourism. Light metal fabricating plant, plastic moldings, electronic products manufactured, grain warehouse, nurseries, fruit drying, almonds shipped. Agriculture. Wheat, cattle, almonds, fruits.

3409 ■ Paso Robles Press
Paso Robles Communications Group
PO Box 427
Paso Robles, CA 93447
Phone: (805)237-6060
Fax: (805)237-6066
Publication E-mail: class@pasoroblespress.com
Community newspaper with an agricultural and tourism emphasis. **Founded:** 1886. **Freq:** Semiweekly (Wed. and Fri.). **Print Method:** Offset. **Trim Size:** 13 x 22. **Cols./Page:** 6. **Col. Width:** 2 1/16 inches. **Col. Depth:** 21 1/2 inches. **Key Personnel:** John Bartlett, Publisher. **USPS:** 565-660. **Subscription Rates:** $14 Individuals 10 weeks manual pay; $13.25 Individuals 10 weeks auto pay; $51.80 Individuals 1 year auto pay; $54.25 Individuals 1 year manual pay; $16.50 Out of area 10 weeks manual pay; $15.75 Out of area 10 weeks auto pay; $64.75 Out of area 1 year auto pay; $67.80 Out of area 1 year manual pay. **URL:** http://www.pasoroblespress.com/v2_main_page.php. **Formed by the merger of:** North County Journal; Daily Press; Country News. **Formerly:** Country News-Press. **Ad Rates:** GLR $1.86; BW $1,670.50; 4C $1,920.50; PCI $13.25. **Remarks:** 1.86. **Circ:** Wed. ‡12500, Fri. ‡5000.

3410 ■ KPRL-AM - 1230
531 - 32nd St.
Paso Robles, CA 93446
Phone: (805)238-1230
Fax: (805)238-5332
Email: reception@kprl.com
Format: News; Talk; Sports. **Networks:** ABC; CBS; Mutual Broadcasting System; Sun Radio. **Owner:** North County Communications L.L.C. **Founded:** 1946. **Operating Hours:** Continuous. **Key Personnel:** Kevin Will, Prog. Dir. **Local Programs:** *The Morning Exchange*, Monday Tuesday Wednesday Thursday Friday 6:00 a.m. - 9:00 a.m.; *Sound-off*, Monday Tuesday Wednesday Thursday Friday 12:30 p.m. - 2:00 p.m. **Wattage:** 1,000. **Ad Rates:** $10-16 for 30 seconds; $12-18 for 60 seconds. **Mailing address:** PO Box 7, Paso Robles, CA 93447. **URL:** http://kprl.com.

3411 ■ K288BO-FM - 105.5
PO Box 391
Twin Falls, ID 83303
Fax: (208)736-1958
Free: 800-357-4226
Format: Religious; Contemporary Christian. **Owner:** CSN International, PO Box 391, Twin Falls, ID 83303, Ph: (208)736-1958, Fax: (208)736-1958, Free: 800-357-4226. **Key Personnel:** Ray Gorney, Asst. Dir.; Don Mills, Prog. Dir., Music Dir.; Kelly Carlson, Dir. of Engg. **Wattage:** 010. **URL:** http://www.csnradio.com.

PATTERSON

C. CA. Stanislaus Co. 19 mi. SW of Modesto. Manufactures farm equipment, frozen food; Modular mobile homes. Grain, fruit and vegetable farms.

3412 ■ Patterson Irrigator
Patterson Irrigator
26 N 3rd St.
Patterson, CA 95363
Phone: (209)892-6187
Fax: (209)892-3761
Publication E-mail: news@pattersonirrigator.com
Community newspaper. **Freq:** Semiweekly. **Print Method:** Offset. **Trim Size:** 14 x 22 3/4. **Cols./Page:** 6. **Col. Width:** 24 nonpareils. **Col. Depth:** 294 agate lines. **Key Personnel:** Jonathan Partridge, Managing Editor; Maddy Houk, Reporter. **ISSN:** 4234--6000 (print). **URL:** http://www.goldenstatenewspapers.com/patterson_irrigator. **Ad Rates:** GLR $5.50; BW $693; 4C $948; SAU $6; PCI $5.50. **Remarks:** Accepts advertising. **Circ:** (Not Reported).

PEARBLOSSOM

3413 ■ Medical Veritas: The Journal of Medical Truth
Pearblossom Private School Inc.
Publishing Division
Pearblossom, CA 93553
Fax: (661)944-4483
Free: 800-309-3569
Publisher's E-mail: pearblossominc@aol.com
Academic journal that examines the influence of the medical and pharmaceutical industries on public health policy. **Freq:** Semiannual April & November. **Key Personnel:** Bonnie S. Dunbar, PhD, Editor; Gary Goldman, PhD, Editor-in-Chief. **ISSN:** 1549--1404 (print). **Alt. Formats:** Download. **URL:** http://www.medicalveritas.com. **Mailing address:** PO Box 847, Pearblossom, CA 93553. **Circ:** (Not Reported).

PEBBLE BEACH

NW CA. Monterey Co. 5 mi. W. of Monterey. Monterey Co. (NW). 5 m W of Monterey.

3414 ■ Progress in Aerospace Sciences: An International Review Journal
RELX Group P.L.C.
c/o Prof. M.R. Platzer, Commissioning Editor
Naval Postgraduate School
3070 Hermitage Rd.
Pebble Beach, CA 93953
Publisher's E-mail: amsterdam@relx.com
Journal for those interested in aerospace sciences. **Freq:** 8/year. **Key Personnel:** Prof. M.R. Platzer, Editor; Prof. B.E. Richards, Editor. **ISSN:** 0376--0421 (print). **Subscription Rates:** $988.53 Institutions online; $2965 Institutions print. **URL:** http://www.journals.elsevier.com/progress-in-aerospace-sciences. **Circ:** (Not Reported).

3415 ■ KSPB-FM - 91.9
PO Box 657
Pebble Beach, CA 93953
Phone: (831)625-5078
Owner: Stevenson School, Pebble Beach and Carmel Campus, 24 W 74th St., New York, NY 10024, Ph: (212)787-6400. **Founded:** 1979. **Key Personnel:** Matt Arruda, Gen. Mgr. **Wattage:** 1,000. **Ad Rates:** Noncommercial. **URL:** http://www.stevensonschool.org/arts/pebblebeach/kspb/index.aspx.

PENRYN

3416 ■ Philalethes: The Journal of Masonic Research & Letters
Philalethes Society
PO Box 379
Penryn, CA 95663-0379
Freemasonry magazine. **Freq:** Quarterly. **Print Method:** Offset. **Trim Size:** 8 1/2 x 11. **Cols./Page:** 3. **Col. Width:** 26 nonpareils. **Col. Depth:** 140 agate lines. **Key Personnel:** Kenneth Roberts, Contact; Shawn Eyer, Editor. **Subscription Rates:** Included in membership. **Alt. Formats:** PDF. **URL:** http://www.freemasonry.org/journal.php. **Remarks:** Advertising not accepted. **Circ:** (Not Reported).

PERRIS

SE CA. Riverside Co. 18 mi. S. of Riverside. Manufactures mobile homes. Steel and wire products, heavy foundry machinery. Gold, silver mine area, granite quarry. Agriculture.

3417 ■ The Perris Progress
The Perris Progress
240 W Fourth St.
Perris, CA 92570-2011
Phone: (951)657-1810
Fax: (951)940-1832
Community newspaper. **Freq:** Weekly (Wed.). **Print Method:** Offset. **Cols./Page:** 6. **Col. Width:** 25 nonpareils. **Col. Depth:** 301 agate lines. **USPS:** 428-100. **Subscription Rates:** $14 Individuals In Riverside County; $54 Out of state. **URL:** http://www.theperrisprogress.com. **Ad Rates:** GLR $.26; BW $501.48; 4C $621.48; SAU $6.46; PCI $4.48. **Remarks:** Accepts advertising. **Circ:** Paid ‡4000.

PESCADERO

3418 ■ KPDO-FM - 89.3
PO Box 893
Pescadero, CA 94060
Format: Public Radio. **Wattage:** 100. **URL:** http://www.kpdo.org/.

PETALUMA

NW CA. Sonoma Co. 38 mi. N. of San Francisco. Manufactures oil burners, brooder stoves, poultry and stock foods, egg fillers, milk products, soap, fertilizer. Ships baby chicks. Hatcheries. Dairying. Poultry farms.

3419 ■ Assistive Technology News
Ability Tools
1304 Southpoint Blvd., Ste. 240
Petaluma, CA 94954
Free: 800-900-0706
Newspaper informing employers on the Americans with Disabilities Act and assistance technology products for disabled people. **Freq:** Monthly. **URL:** http://www.atechnews.com/articleindex/atgeneral.html. **Formerly:** Special and Individual Needs Technology Magazine. **Ad Rates:** BW $495; 4C $2,500. **Remarks:** Advertising accepted; rates available upon request. **Circ:** 25000.

3420 ■ Neonatal Network: The Journal of Neonatal Nursing
Neonatal Network
1425 N McDowell Blvd., Ste. 105
Petaluma, CA 94954
Phone: (707)569-1421
Fax: (707)569-0786
Publication E-mail: subscriptions@neonatalnetwork.com
Professional medical journal for neonatal nurses and related health care professionals. **Freq:** Bimonthly. **ISSN:** 0730-0832 (print). **Subscription Rates:** $65 Individuals; $70 Individuals online; $75 Individuals print and online; $100 Individuals; $70 Individuals online; $110 Individuals print and online; $265 Institutions; $250 Institutions online; $275 Institutions print and online; $325 Institutions; $250 Institutions online; $350 Institutions print and online. **URL:** http://neonatalnetwork.com. **Ad Rates:** BW $2,050; 4C $3,550. **Remarks:** Accepts advertising. **Circ:** Controlled 11000.

3421 ■ Petaluma Argus-Courier
Sonoma Media Investments
PO Box 750308
Petaluma, CA 94975
Publication E-mail: argus@arguscourier.com
General newspaper. **Freq:** Weekly. **Print Method:** Offset. **Cols./Page:** 6. **Col. Width:** 12 3/10 picas. **Col. Depth:** 301 agate lines. **Key Personnel:** John Burns, Publisher, phone: (707)776-8450. **Subscription Rates:** $49.50 Individuals print and digital. **URL:** http://www.petaluma360.com. **Ad Rates:** GLR $1.15; BW $2091; 4C $2341; SAU $16.21. **Remarks:** Advertising accepted; rates available upon request. **Circ:** (Not Reported).

3422 ■ Petaluma Business
Petaluma Area Chamber of Commerce
6 Petaluma Blvd. N, Ste. A2
Petaluma, CA 94952
Phone: (707)762-2785
Fax: (707)762-4721
Publisher's E-mail: pacc@petalumachamber.com
Newspaper containing information about business and community information within Petaluma Area, CA. **Freq:** Monthly. **Key Personnel:** Onita Pellegrini, Chief Executive Officer; Kathy Brandal, Contact. **Alt. Formats:** PDF. **URL:** http://Www.petalumachamber.com/PACC_News.asp. **Remarks:** Accepts advertising. **Circ:** 2000.

PHILO

3423 ■ KZYX-FM - 90.7
9300 Hwy. 128
Philo, CA 95466
Phone: (707)895-2324
Fax: (707)895-2451
Free: 800-298-1296
Format: Public Radio. **Simulcasts:** KZYZ-FM. **Networks:** National Public Radio (NPR); Pacifica. **Owner:** Mendocino County Public Broadcasting Inc. **Founded:** 1989. **Operating Hours:** Continuous; 20% network,

80% local. **Key Personnel:** Mary Aigner, Dir. of Programs; John Coate, Exec. Dir., Gen. Mgr.; Rich Culbertson, Dir. of Operations. **Local Programs**: *KZYX Community News*, Monday Tuesday Wednesday Thursday Friday 6:00 p.m. - 7:00 p.m.; 7:45 a.m.; 8:45 a.m.; *The Take Away*, Monday Tuesday Wednesday Thursday Friday 6:00 a.m. - 7:00 a.m.; *Radiogram*, Wednesday 8:00 p.m. - 9:00 p.m; *The Wondrous World of Music*, Friday 10:00 a.m. - 12:00 p.m. **Wattage**: 3,400. **Ad Rates:** Underwriting available. $11-17 per unit. **Mailing address:** PO Box 1, Philo, CA 95466. **URL:** http://www.kzyx.org.

3424 ■ KZYZ-FM - 91.5
PO Box 1
Philo, CA 95466
Phone: (707)895-2324
Fax: (707)895-2451
Email: news@kzyx.org
Format: Eclectic. **Founded:** Oct. 15, 1989. **Key Personnel:** John Coate, Gen. Mgr.; Mary Aigner, Dir. of Programs, mary@kzyx.org; Rich Culbertson, Dir. of Operations, rich@kzyx.org. **URL:** http://www.kzyx.org.

PICO RIVERA

S. CA. Los Angeles Co. 10 mi. SE of Los Angeles. Automobile assembly, electronics, plastics, cement, dairy products, drugs, lumber.

3425 ■ Armenian Numismatic Journal
Armenian Numismatic Society
8511 Beverly Park Pl.
Pico Rivera, CA 90660-1920
Phone: (562)695-0380
Publisher's E-mail: armnumsoc@aol.com
Journal covering Armenian coins, bank notes, and medals. **Freq:** Quarterly. **Trim Size:** 8 1/2 x 11. **Cols./Page:** 1. **ISSN:** 0884-0180 (print). **URL:** http://www.armnumsoc.org/pubs.htm. **Remarks:** Advertising not accepted. **Circ:** Paid 200.

PINE GROVE

Amador Co.

3426 ■ Volcano Vision, Inc.
PO Box 1070
Pine Grove, CA 95665
Phone: (209)296-2288
Email: info@volcanotel.com
Owner: Volcano Communications Group of Cos., 20000 Hwy. 88, Pine Grove, CA 95665, Ph: (209)296-7502, Fax: (209)296-4466. **Founded:** 1982. **Cities Served:** Ione, Kirkwood, Pioneer, West Point, California: subscribing households 8,900; 300 channels; 2 community access channels; 140 hours per week community access programming. **URL:** http://volcanocommunications.com.

PINOLE

W. CA. Contra Costa Co. On San Pablo Bay, 15 mi. N. of Oakland. Manufactures chemicals. Agriculture, livestock.

3427 ■ National Finch and Softbill Society Journal
National Finch and Softbill Society
c/o Sara Roberts, Treasurer
720 Live Oak Ln.
Pinole, CA 94564
Journal comprising of articles, reports, and features on general bird keeping, avian management and husbandry, species specific articles, banding, showing, avian medicine, and legislation affecting aviculture. **Freq:** Bimonthly. **URL:** http://nfss.org/journal/. **Remarks:** Advertising not accepted. **Circ:** (Not Reported).

PITTSBURG

W. CA. Contra Costa Co. 44 mi. NE of Oakland. Boat connections. Manufactures steel, chemicals, rubber goods, building materials. Ship repair yard. Salmon, shad fisheries. Grain, stock farms. Wheat, barley, hay.

3428 ■ Experience
Los Medanos College
2700 E Leland Rd.
Pittsburg, CA 94565
Phone: (925)439-2181
Publisher's E-mail: lmcquestions@losmedanos.edu
Collegiate newspaper. **Founded:** 1974. **Freq:** Weekly (Fri.). **Print Method:** Offset. **Cols./Page:** 6. **Col. Width:** 24 nonpareils. **Col. Depth:** 285 agate lines. **Key Personnel:** Cindy McGrath, Advisor. **URL:** http://www.losmedanos.edu. **Ad Rates:** PCI $4. **Remarks:** Accepts advertising. **Circ:** Free 2000.

PLACENTIA

3429 ■ Street Rodder
McMullen Argus Publishing Inc.
c/o Brian Brennan, Ed.
720 Hundley Way
Placentia, CA 92870
Magazine for automotive enthusiasts interested in building or revamping cars. **Freq:** Monthly. **Print Method:** Offset. **Trim Size:** 8 x 10 7/8. **Cols./Page:** 3. **Col. Width:** 27 nonpareils. **Col. Depth:** 140 agate lines. **Key Personnel:** Craig Reiss, Officer; Kris Hancock, Managing Editor; Eric Geisert, Associate Editor; Ryan Manson, Associate Editor; Alan Alpanian, Creative Director; Sarah Maxwell, Editor; Janeen Web, Manager, Advertising and Sales; Brian Brennan, Editor; Ron Ceridono, Publisher. **Subscription Rates:** $24.95 Individuals; $44.95 Two years. **Ad Rates:** BW $9,535; 4C $13,390. **Remarks:** Accepts advertising. **Circ:** Paid ★**142295**.

PLATINA

N. CA. Shasta Co. 10 mi. S. of Omo. Residential.

3430 ■ The Orthodox Word
St. Herman of Alaska Brotherhood
PO Box 70
Platina, CA 96076
Publisher's E-mail: stherman@stherman.com
Magazine about the Orthodox Christian spirituality and the monastic tradition. Includes lives and teachings of the holy fathers and recent confessors as well as examinations of current topics. **Freq:** Bimonthly. **Print Method:** Offset. **Trim Size:** 6 x 8 1/2. **Cols./Page:** 1. **Col. Width:** 54 nonpareils. **Col. Depth:** 98 agate lines. **ISSN:** 0030--5839 (print). **Subscription Rates:** $19 Individuals; $33 Two years; $46 Students 3 years; $30 Other countries; $54 Other countries two years. **URL:** http://www.sainthermanmonastery.com/category-s/1835.htm. **Remarks:** Advertising not accepted. **Circ:** Paid ‡2790, Controlled ‡400.

PLEASANTON

W. CA. Alameda Co. 42 mi. SE of San Francisco. Residential. Cheese factories, wineries, Research.

3431 ■ The Goodtimes Gazette
Goodguys Rod and Custom Association
PO Box 9132
Pleasanton, CA 94566
Phone: (925)838-9876
Freq: Monthly. **Subscription Rates:** Included in membership. **URL:** http://www.good-guys.com/info/about-the-gazette. **Remarks:** Accepts advertising. **Circ:** (Not Reported).

3432 ■ Transactional Analysis Journal
International Transactional Analysis Association
2843 Hopyard Rd., Ste. 155
Pleasanton, CA 94588
Phone: (925)600-8110
Fax: (925)600-8112
Publisher's E-mail: info@itaaworld.org
Journal containing topics focusing on transactional analysis theory, principles, and application in various fields, including psychotherapy, counseling, education, and organizational development. **Freq:** Quarterly January, April, July, October. **Key Personnel:** Robin Fryer, Managing Editor. **ISSN:** 0362--1537 (print); **EISSN:** 2329--5244 (electronic). **Subscription Rates:** £234 Included in membership print & e-access; £211 Institutions e-access ; £229 Institutions print only; £78 Individuals print only; £63 Institutions single print issue; £25 Individuals single print issue. **URL:** http://www.itaaworld.org/transactional-analysis-journal; http://tax.sagepub.com. **Remarks:** Accepts advertising. **Circ:** (Not Reported).

3433 ■ Valley Times
Hills Publications Inc.
127 Spring St.
Pleasanton, CA 94566
Phone: (510)847-2111
Fax: (510)847-2189
Daily newspaper. **Founded:** 1971. **Freq:** Daily and Sun. **Print Method:** Offset. **Trim Size:** 13 3/4 x 23. **Cols./Page:** 6. **Col. Width:** 25 nonpareils. **Col. Depth:** 301 agate lines. **Subscription Rates:** $53.50 Individuals; $102 Out of area. **URL:** http://www.contracostatimes.com. **Mailing address:** PO Box 607, Pleasanton, CA 94566. **Ad Rates:** GLR $5.80; BW $2,089.80; 4C $2,474.80; SAU $16.20. **Remarks:** Accepts advertising. **Circ:** (Not Reported).

3434 ■ KKDV-FM - 92.1
7901 Stoneridge Dr., Ste. 525
Pleasanton, CA 94588
Fax: (925)416-1211
Email: programming@kkdv.com
Format: Adult Contemporary. **URL:** http://www.kkdv.com.

3435 ■ KKIQ-FM - 101.7
7901 Stoneridge Dr., Ste. 525
Pleasanton, CA 94588
Phone: (925)455-4500
Fax: (925)416-1211
Free: 800-398-1017
Format: News. **Owner:** Coast Radio Co., Inc., 600 Main St., Vacaville, CA 95688. **Founded:** 1969. **Operating Hours**: Continuous. **Key Personnel:** Jim Hampton, Contact, jhampton@kkiq.com. **Wattage:** 4,500 ERP. **Ad Rates:** Advertising accepted; rates available upon request. $80 per unit. Combined advertising rates available with KUIC Vacaville CA. **URL:** http://kkiq.com.

POINT REYES STATION

W. CA. Marin Co. On Pacific Ocean, 35 mi. NW of San Francisco. Resort. Commercial fisheries. Dairying.

3436 ■ Point Reyes Light
Point Reyes Light
PO Box 210
Point Reyes Station, CA 94956
Phone: (415)669-1200
Fax: (415)669-1216
Community newspaper. **Freq:** Weekly (Thurs.). **Print Method:** Offset. **Cols./Page:** 6. **Col. Width:** 19 nonpareils. **Col. Depth:** 200 agate lines. **Key Personnel:** Tess Elliott, Editor. **Subscription Rates:** $70 Individuals; $119 Individuals two years; $76 Out of state; $130 Out of state two years. **URL:** http://www.ptreyeslight.com. **Remarks:** Accepts advertising. **Circ:** Paid ‡2250.

3437 ■ Horizon Cable T.V. Inc.
520 Mesa Rd.
Point Reyes Station, CA 94956
Phone: (415)663-9610
Fax: (415)663-9608
Free: 888-663-9610
Cities Served: subscribing households 2,300. **Mailing address:** PO Box 1240, Point Reyes Station, CA 94956-1240. **URL:** http://www.horizoncable.com.

POMONA

S. CA. Los Angeles Co. 30 mi. E. of Los Angeles. Mount San Antonio College. California State Polytechnic University, Pomona. Manufactures tile bricks, fruit processing and citrus packing equipment. Guided missile plant. Fruit packing, oil refinery, paper reclaiming. Fruit, dairy, stock farms. Oranges, lemons, grapefruit.

3438 ■ Biology of Sex Differences
Organization for the Study of Sex Differences
c/o Dr. Arbi Nazarian, Treasurer
College of Pharmacy
Western University of Health Sciences
309 E 2nd St.
Pomona, CA 91766-1854
ISSN: 204-2-6410 (print). **URL:** http://bsd.biomedcentral.com; http://www.ossd.wildapricot.org/Journal. **Remarks:** Advertising not accepted. **Circ:** (Not Reported).

3439 ■ The Poly Post
California State Polytechnic University
3801 W Temple Ave.
Pomona, CA 91768-2557
Phone: (909)869-7659

Circulation: ★ = AAM; △ or • = BPA; ♦ = CAC; ❑ = VAC; ⊕ = PO Statement; ‡ = Publisher's Report; Boldface figures = sworn; Light figures = estimated.

Collegiate newspaper. **Founded:** 1945. **Freq:** Weekly Tues. during academic year. **Print Method:** Offset. **Trim Size:** 14 x 22. **Cols./Page:** 6. **Col. Width:** 2 inches. **Col. Depth:** 21 inches. **Key Personnel:** Adrian Danganan, Editor-in-Chief. **Subscription Rates:** Free to the campus. **URL:** http://www.thepolypost.com. **Formerly:** The Post. **Ad Rates:** GLR $1; BW $720; PCI $8.50; 4C $300. **Remarks:** Accepts advertising. **Circ:** Free ‡7000.

3440 ■ Teaching Philosophy: A Journal for Philosophy Teachers at all Levels
Philosophy Documentation Center
c/o Michael Cholbi, Editor
California State Polytechnic University at Pomona
3801 W Temple Ave.
Pomona, CA 91768
Publisher's E-mail: order@pdcnet.org
Philosophy education journal covering the practical and the theoretical aspects of teaching and learning philosophy. **Freq:** Quarterly. **Key Personnel:** Michael Cholbi, Editor; David Boersema, Editor. **ISSN:** 0145-5788 (print); **EISSN:** 215-3-6619 (electronic). **Subscription Rates:** $33 Individuals print; $40 Individuals 0nline; $53 Individuals print & online; $86 Institutions print; $234 Institutions 0nline; $281 Institutions print & online. **URL:** http://www.pdcnet.org/teachphil/Teaching-Philosophy. **Remarks:** Accepts advertising. **Circ:** Paid ‡1110, Non-paid ‡47.

PORTERVILLE

SC CA. Tulare Co. 56 mi. N. of Bakersfield. Recreation. Extensive orange and deciduous fruit packing. Electronics, medical instruments, sportswear, paper products. Carpet yarn manufactured. Diversified farming.

3441 ■ Porterville Recorder
Glacier Media Inc.
115 E Oak
Porterville, CA 93257
Publisher's E-mail: info@glaciermedia.ca
General newspaper. **Freq:** Mon.-Sat. (eve.). **Print Method:** Offset. **Cols./Page:** 6. **Col. Width:** 24 nonpareils. **Col. Depth:** 21 inches. **Key Personnel:** Rick Elkins, Publisher, Editor, phone: (559)784-5000. **Subscription Rates:** $135 Individuals. **URL:** http://www.recorderonline.com. **Remarks:** Advertising accepted; rates available upon request. **Circ:** Mon.-Sat. ★**8904**.

3442 ■ KTIP-AM - 1450
1660 Newcomb St.
Porterville, CA 93257
Format: Talk; News. **Simulcasts:** KTIP.COM. **Networks:** CBS; Westwood One Radio. **Owner:** Mayberry Broadcasting Co. **Operating Hours**: Continuous; 75% network, 25% local. **Local Programs**: *Trader's Market*, Saturday 9:00 a.m. - 12:00 p.m.; *Hopper In The Morning with PK the Redhead*, Monday Tuesday Wednesday Thursday Friday 6:00 a.m. - 9:00 a.m. **Wattage:** 1,000. **Ad Rates:** $9-30 for 30 seconds. **URL:** http://www.ktip.com/mysgmediatesting.info/wsdindex.html.

PORTOLA

NE CA. Plumas Co. 40 mi. W. of Reno, NV. Resort. Tourism, recreation. Lumbering. Pine, cedar timber. Dairy, stock farms.

3443 ■ Portola Reporter
Feather Publishing Company Inc.
96 E Sierra Ave.
Portola, CA 96122
Phone: (530)832-4646
Fax: (530)832-5319
Publication E-mail: mail@plumasnews.com
Newspaper serving Plumas and Lassen counties. **Freq:** Weekly (Wed.). **Print Method:** Offset. **Cols./Page:** 6. **Col. Width:** 26 nonpareils. **Col. Depth:** 301 agate lines. **Key Personnel:** Michael C. Taborski, Publisher. **Subscription Rates:** $26 Individuals in County; $37 Individuals in California; $44 Out of state. **URL:** http://www.plumasnews.com. **Remarks:** Accepts advertising. **Circ:** ‡1950.

POWAY

S. CA. San Diego Co. 10 mi. N. of San Diego. San Diego Co. (S). 10 m N of San Diego. Residential.

3444 ■ Poway News Chieftain: Serving Poway, Rancho Bernardo and 4S Ranch
Pomerado Publishing
13475 Danielson St., Ste. 110
Poway, CA 92064
Phone: (858)748-2311
Fax: (858)748-2418
Publisher's E-mail: news@pomeradonews.com
Community newspaper. **Freq:** Weekly (Thurs.). **Print Method:** Offset. **Cols./Page:** 6. **Col. Width:** 25 nonpareils. **Col. Depth:** 294 agate lines. **Key Personnel:** Steve Dreyer, Executive Editor. **USPS:** 440-760. **URL:** http://www.pomeradonews.com. **Remarks:** Accepts advertising. **Circ:** Paid 14434.

3445 ■ Rancho Bernardo News Journal
Pomerado Publishing
13475 Danielson St., Ste. 110
Poway, CA 92064
Phone: (858)748-2311
Fax: (858)748-2418
Publisher's E-mail: news@pomeradonews.com
Local newspaper. **Freq:** Weekly (Thurs.). **Print Method:** Offset. **Cols./Page:** 6. **Col. Width:** 25 nonpareils. **Col. Depth:** 294 agate lines. **Key Personnel:** Steve Dreyer, Editor, phone: (858)218-7207. **URL:** http://www.pomeradonews.com/news/local-news/rancho-bernardo. **Ad Rates:** 4C $1995. **Remarks:** Accepts advertising. **Circ:** 17076.

QUARTZ HILL

3446 ■ Quartz Hill Journal of Theology
Quartz Hill Journal of Theology
43543 51st St. W
Quartz Hill, CA 93536
Phone: (661)722-0891
Fax: (661)943-3484
Publication E-mail: info@theology.edu
Religious magazine containing reviews, poetry, and articles. A journal of Bible and Contemporary Theological Thought. **Freq:** Quarterly. **Trim Size:** 8.5 x 11. **Key Personnel:** Dandi Moyers, Assistant Editor; R.P. Nettlehost, Editor. **ISSN:** 1075--0126 (print). **URL:** http://www.theology.edu/more.htm. **Remarks:** Advertising accepted; rates available upon request. **Circ:** (Not Reported).

3447 ■ KGBB-FM - 103.9
42010 50th St. W
Quartz Hill, CA 93536
Phone: (661)718-1552
Fax: (661)552-1553
Format: Eclectic. **Owner:** Adelman Broadcasting, 731 N Balsam St., Ridgecrest, CA 93555, Ph: (760)371-1700. **Wattage:** 6,000. **URL:** http://www.bobfm1039.com.

QUINCY

NE CA. Plumas Co. 25 mi. NW of Portola. Resort. Sawmills, bottling works, lumber mills, machine shop. Fir, pine timber. Dairying. Stock farms.

3448 ■ Feather River Bulletin
Feather Publishing Company Inc.
287 Lawrence St.
Quincy, CA 95971-9477
Phone: (530)283-0800
Fax: (530)283-3952
Publication E-mail: mail@plumasnews.com
Community newspaper serving Plumas and Lassen counties. **Freq:** Weekly (Wed.). **Print Method:** Offset. **Cols./Page:** 6. **Col. Width:** 11 picas. **Col. Depth:** 301 agate lines. **Key Personnel:** Michael C. Taborski, Publisher; Delaine Fragnoli, Managing Editor; Mary Newhouse, Manager, Circulation; Sherri McConnell, Manager, Advertising. **USPS:** 118-550. **URL:** http://www.plumasnews.com. **Mailing address:** PO Box B, Quincy, CA 95971-3586. **Ad Rates:** BW $774; 4C $1,074; SAU $6. **Remarks:** Accepts advertising. **Circ:** ‡3380.

3449 ■ KNLF-FM - 95.9
440 Lawrence St.
Quincy, CA 95971
Phone: (530)283-4144
Fax: (530)283-5135
Email: Listener@KNLFRadio.Com
Format: Talk; Sports; Religious; Gospel. **Owner:** New Life Broadcasting, at above address. **Founded:** 1984. **Operating Hours**: Continuous. **Key Personnel:** Ron Trumbo, Owner. **Wattage:** 500. **Ad Rates:** Advertising accepted; rates available upon request. **Mailing address:** PO Box 117, Quincy, CA 95971. **URL:** http://www.knlfradio.com.

RAMONA

3450 ■ Wildlife Art: The Art Journal of the Natural World
Pothole Publications Inc.
PO Box 219
Ramona, CA 92065
Phone: (760)788-9453
Fax: (760)788-9454
Free: 800-221-6547
Magazine for wildlife art collectors. **Freq:** Semiannual. **Print Method:** Web offset. **Trim Size:** 8 1/4 x 10 13/16. **Cols./Page:** 3. **Key Personnel:** Keith Hansen, Publisher; Patricia Hansen, Publisher; Rose Marie Scott-Blair, Editor. **ISSN:** 0746-9640 (print). **Subscription Rates:** $24.95 Individuals; $4.95 Single issue; $38.95 Two years. **URL:** http://www.wildlifeartmag.com. **Formerly:** Wildlife Art News. **Ad Rates:** 4C $2,195. **Remarks:** Accepts advertising. **Circ:** 22000.

RANCHO CORDOVA

NC CA. Sacramento Co. 5 mi. NE of Mather A.F.B.

3451 ■ KSPX-TV - 29
3352 Mather Field Rd.
Rancho Cordova, CA 95670
Phone: (212)757-3100
Fax: (646)597-5903
Free: 888-467-2988
Format: Commercial TV. **Networks:** Independent. **Founded:** 1984. **Formerly:** KCMY-TV. **Operating Hours**: Continuous. **ADI:** Sacramento-Stockton, CA. **Key Personnel:** Daniel Briggs, Gen. Mgr., briggsd@calweb.com. **Wattage:** 1,000,000 H. **Ad Rates:** Accepts Advertising. **URL:** http://www.ionmedianetworks.com.

RANCHO SANTA FE

WC CA. San Diego Co. 21 mi. N. of San Diego. Citrus fruit, avocado groves; residential.

3452 ■ Carmel Valley News
MainStreet Media Group L.L.C.
16236 San Dieguito Rd., Ste. 5-25
Rancho Santa Fe, CA 92067
Community newspaper. **Freq:** Weekly. **Key Personnel:** Phyllis Pfeiffer, Publisher, phone: (858)756-1403; Lorine Wright, Executive Editor, phone: (858)756-1451; Ann Marie Gabaldon, Director, Advertising, phone: (858)876-1403. **URL:** http://www.delmartimes.net/news/local-news/carmel-valley/. **Mailing address:** PO Box 9077, Rancho Santa Fe, CA 92067. **Remarks:** Accepts advertising. **Circ:** Combined ■ **19805**.

RANCHO SANTA MARGARITA

3453 ■ Reeves Journal: Plumbing, Heating, Cooling
BNP Media
30211 Avenida de las Banderas, Ste. 200
Rancho Santa Margarita, CA 92688
Publisher's E-mail: asm@halldata.com
Regional plumbing, heating, and cooling magazine. **Freq:** Monthly. **Print Method:** Offset. **Trim Size:** 8 1/4 x 11. **Cols./Page:** 3. **Col. Width:** 13.5 picas. **Col. Depth:** 140 agate lines. **Key Personnel:** Souzan Azar, Manager, Production; Jack Sweet, Editor, phone: (949)716-2053; Ellyn Fishman, Publisher, phone: (949)766-6779. **ISSN:** 0048--7066 (print). **Subscription Rates:** Free. **URL:** http://www.reevesjournal.com. **Ad Rates:** BW $4,400; 4C $1,680. **Remarks:** Accepts advertising. **Circ:** Controlled ‡13001.

3454 ■ Toastmaster
Toastmasters International
23182 Arroyo Vista
Rancho Santa Margarita, CA 92688-2620
Phone: (949)858-8255
Fax: (949)858-1207
Publisher's E-mail: newclubs@toastmasters.org
Freq: Monthly. **Print Method:** Offset. **Trim Size:** 8 1/4 x 10 7/8. **Cols./Page:** 3. **Col. Width:** 27 nonpareils. **Col. Depth:** 133 agate lines. **Key Personnel:** Paul Sterman, Senior Editor; Suzanne Frey, Managing Editor, Contact. **ISSN:** 0040--8263 (print). **Subscription Rates:** Included in membership. **Alt. Formats:** PDF. **URL:** http://www.toastmasters.org/Magazine. **Remarks:** Advertising ac-

cepted; rates available upon request. **Circ:** ‡250000.

RED BLUFF

N. CA. Tehama Co. On Sacramento River, 115 mi. N. of Sacramento. Residential. Lumber mills, box factories, pulp plant. Diversified farming. Livestock, fruit, grain.

3455 ■ Daily News
Digital First Media
545 Diamond Ave.
Red Bluff, CA 96080
Phone: (530)527-2151
Fax: (530)527-9251
General newspaper. **Founded:** Nov. 1885. **Freq:** Mon.-Sat. (eve.). **Print Method:** Offset. **Cols./Page:** 6. **Col. Width:** 24 nonpareils. **Col. Depth:** 301 agate lines. **Key Personnel:** Chip Thompson, Editor; Sandy Valdivia, Manager, Production; Greg Stevens, Publisher; Rich Greene, Reporter; Kathy Hogan, Manager, Circulation. **USPS:** 458-200. **Subscription Rates:** $66 Individuals. **URL:** http://www.redbluffdailynews.com/. **Mailing address:** PO Box 220, Red Bluff, CA 96080. **Ad Rates:** BW $1,193.25; 4C $1,378.25; SAU $9.25. **Remarks:** Accepts advertising. **Circ:** Mon.-Sat. ★**6760**.

3456 ■ KBLF-AM - 1490
20639 W Walnut St.
Box 1490
Red Bluff, CA 96080-1490
Phone: (530)727-5253
Fax: (530)527-3525
Format: News. **Networks:** CBS. **Owner:** KBLF Inc., at above address. **Founded:** 1946. **Ad Rates:** Advertising accepted; rates available upon request. $4-10 for 30 seconds; $6-12 for 60 seconds. **URL:** http://kblfam.com/.

3457 ■ K212DF-FM - 90.3
PO Box 391
Twin Falls, ID 83303
Fax: (208)736-1958
Free: 800-357-4226
Format: Religious; Contemporary Christian. **Owner:** CSN International, PO Box 391, Twin Falls, ID 83303, Ph: (208)736-1958, Fax: (208)736-1958, Free: 800-357-4226. **Key Personnel:** Don Mills, Prog. Dir., Music Dir.; Kelly Carlson, Dir. of Engg.; Ray Gorney, Asst. Dir. **Wattage:** 015.005. **URL:** http://www.csnradio.com.

REDDING

N. CA. Shasta Co. On Sacramento River, 70 mi. N. of Chico. Mountain resort. Pine timber. Saw, planing mills, box and veneer, machine shops, bottling works, creameries. Diversified farming.

3458 ■ After Five Magazine: The North State Magazine
After Five Magazine
PO Box 492905
Redding, CA 96049
Phone: (530)402-7440
Fax: (530)335-5335
Publisher's E-mail: editorial@after5online.com
Lifestyle magazine covering northern California, and southern Oregon. **Freq:** Monthly. **Alt. Formats:** PDF. **URL:** http://northstate.news. **Remarks:** Advertising accepted; rates available upon request. **Circ:** (Not Reported).

3459 ■ The Lance
Shasta Community College
11555 Old Oregon Trail
Redding, CA 96049-6006
Phone: (530)242-7500
Collegiate newspaper (tabloid). **Founded:** 1950. **Freq:** 15/yr (September to May). **Print Method:** Offset. **Cols./Page:** 5. **Col. Width:** 22 nonpareils. **Col. Depth:** 196 agate lines. **Subscription Rates:** Free. **URL:** http://www.thelanceonline.com/. **Mailing address:** PO Box 496006, Redding, CA 96049. **Ad Rates:** BW $435; 4C $90; PCI $5. **Remarks:** Accepts advertising. **Circ:** (Not Reported).

3460 ■ The Record Searchlight Newspaper
The E. W. Scripps Co.
1101 Twin View Blvd.
Redding, CA 96003
Phone: (530)243-2424
Publisher's E-mail: corpcomm@scripps.com
General newspaper. **Freq:** Daily. **Print Method:** Offset. **Cols./Page:** 6. **Col. Width:** 11.5 inches. **Col. Depth:** 21 1/4 inches. **Key Personnel:** Carole Ferguson, Managing Editor, phone: (530)225-8232; Silas Lyons, Editor, phone: (530)225-8210. **USPS:** 458-520. **Subscription Rates:** $19.99 Individuals 13 weeks/7 day home delivery; $13.99 Individuals 13 weeks/weekend delivery; $12.99 Individuals 13 weeks/Sunday only delivery. **URL:** http://www.redding.com. **Formerly:** Record Searchlight. **Ad Rates:** GLR $4.68; BW $4,553.03; 4C $5,416.20; SAU $46.78; PCI $42.48. **Remarks:** Accepts advertising. **Circ:** Mon.-Fri. ★**32147**, Sat. ★**32101**, Sun. ★**35004**.

3461 ■ Redding Directions
Greater Redding Chamber of Commerce
747 Auditorium Dr.
Redding, CA 96001
Phone: (530)225-4433
Fax: (530)225-4398
Publisher's E-mail: info@reddingchamber.com
Magazine containing information regarding Greater Redding, CA. **Freq:** Monthly. **Subscription Rates:** Included in membership. **URL:** http://reddingchamber.com/about-the-chamber. **Remarks:** Accepts advertising. **Circ:** 1100.

3462 ■ KESR-FM - 107.1
1588 Charles Dr.
Redding, CA 96003
Phone: (530)244-9700
Fax: (530)244-9707
Format: Eclectic. **Owner:** Results Radio L.L.C., 1355 N Dutton Ave., Ste. 225, Santa Rosa, CA 95401, Ph: (707)546-9185. **Wattage:** 1,400. **Ad Rates:** Advertising accepted; rates available upon request. **URL:** http://www.1071bobfm.com.

3463 ■ KGEC-TV - 26
215 Lake Blvd., Ste. 26
Redding, CA 96003
Phone: (530)941-7879
Email: info@kgectv.com
Format: Commercial TV. **Operating Hours:** Continuous. **ADI:** Chico-Redding, CA. **Key Personnel:** George Cooper, Contact; Millie Cooper, Contact. **Wattage:** 7,500 ERP. **Ad Rates:** Advertising accepted; rates available upon request. **URL:** http://www.kgectv.com.

KGRV-AM - See Winston, OR

3464 ■ KHRD-FM - 103.1
1588 Charles Dr.
Redding, CA 96003
Phone: (530)244-9700
Format: Classic Rock; Album-Oriented Rock (AOR). **Owner:** Results Radio Redding, 1588 Charles Dr, Redding, CA 96003. **Operating Hours:** Continuous. **Key Personnel:** Beth Tappan, Mktg. Mgr., btappan@resultsradio.com. **Ad Rates:** Advertising accepted; rates available upon request. **URL:** http://www.red1031.com.

3465 ■ KIXE-TV - 9
603 N Market St.
Redding, CA 96003
Phone: (530)243-5493
Email: captions@kixe.org
Founded: Sept. 07, 2006. **Key Personnel:** Philip Smith, Gen. Mgr; Jack Nehr, Contact. **Wattage:** 115-thousand. **Ad Rates:** Noncommercial. **URL:** http://www.kixe.org.

3466 ■ KLVB-FM - 99.5
PO Box 779002
Rocklin, CA 95677-9972
Fax: (916)251-1901
Free: 800-525-5683
Email: info@klove.com
Format: Contemporary Christian. **Owner:** Educational Media Foundation, 2351 Sunset Blvd., Ste. 170-218, Rocklin, CA 95677, Ph: (800)434-8400. **Key Personnel:** Mike Novak, President, CEO. **URL:** http://www.klove.com.

3467 ■ KLXR-AM
1326 Market St.
Redding, CA 96001
Phone: (916)244-0564
Format: Classic Rock. **Owner:** Redding Broadcasting, at above address. **Founded:** 1956. **Formerly:** KRDG-AM. **Wattage:** 1,000. **Ad Rates:** $10.50 for 30 seconds; $16.50 for 60 seconds.

KMWR-FM - See Brookings, OR

3468 ■ KNCQ-FM - 97.3
1588 Charles Dr.
Redding, CA 96003
Phone: (530)244-9700
Fax: (530)244-9707
Format: Contemporary Country. **Networks:** Independent. **Founded:** 1985. **Operating Hours:** Continuous; 100% local. **ADI:** Chico-Redding, CA. **Wattage:** 100,000. **Ad Rates:** Noncommercial. **URL:** http://www.q97country.com.

3469 ■ KNNN-FM - 99.3
3360 Alta Mesa Dr.
Redding, CA 96002
Phone: (530)226-9500
Fax: (530)221-4940
Format: Country. **Owner:** Mapleton Communicatons, 513 Main St., Mapleton, IA 51034. **Founded:** 1989. **Operating Hours:** Continuous; 100% local. **ADI:** Chico-Redding, CA. **Wattage:** 5,280. **Ad Rates:** Noncommercial. $25-95 for 30 seconds; $30-100 for 60 seconds. Combined advertising rates available with KSHA-FM, KRDG-AM, KQMS-AM, KNRO-AM, KRRX-FM.

3470 ■ KNRO-AM - 1670
3360 Alta Mesa Dr.
Redding, CA 96002
Phone: (530)226-9500
Format: Alternative/New Music/Progressive. **Networks:** ESPN Radio. **Founded:** 1936. **Formerly:** KHTE-AM. **Operating Hours:** Continuous; 100% local. **ADI:** Chico-Redding, CA. **Key Personnel:** Lisa Geraci, Gen. Mgr. **Wattage:** 1,000. **Ad Rates:** Noncommercial. Combined advertising rates available with KSHA-FM, KNNN-FM, KRDG-AM, KQMS-AM, KRRX-FM. **URL:** http://www.bristar.com.

3471 ■ KQMS-AM - 1400
3360 Alta Mesa Dr.
Redding, CA 96002
Phone: (530)226-9500
Fax: (530)221-6653
Format: Talk; News. **Owner:** Mapleton Communications, 10900 Wilshire Blvd., No. 1500, Los Angeles, CA 90024, Ph: (310)209-7229, Fax: (310)209-7239. **Operating Hours:** Continuous. **ADI:** Chico-Redding, CA. **Key Personnel:** Erin Myers, Contact, erin@kqms.com; Steve Gibson, Contact, steve@kqms.com. **Wattage:** 1,000. **URL:** http://www.kqms.com.

3472 ■ KRCR-TV - 7
755 Auditorium Dr.
Redding, CA 96001
Phone: (530)243-7777
Fax: (530)243-0217
Free: 800-222-5727
Email: info@krcrtv.com
Format: Commercial TV. **Networks:** ABC. **Founded:** 1956. **Formerly:** KVIP-TV. **Operating Hours:** 4 a.m.-2 a.m. **ADI:** Chico-Redding, CA. **Key Personnel:** Jennifer Scarborough, News Dir., jscarborough@krcrtv.com; Carlos Casarez, Sales Mgr.; Andrew Stewart, VP, Gen. Mgr., astewart@krcrtv.com; Paula Murphy, Dir. of Programs, pmurphy@bontencalifornia.com. **Local Programs:** *The Insider*, *Entertainment Tonight*, Monday Tuesday Wednesday Thursday Friday Saturday 7:00 p.m. 4:00 p.m.; *KRCR News Channel 7 at 5:30 PM*, Saturday Sunday 5:30 p.m. - 6:00 p.m.; 6:30 p.m. - 7:00 p.m.; 11:00 p.m. - 11:30 p.m. **Wattage:** 115,000 ERP. **Ad Rates:** Noncommercial. **URL:** http://www.krcrtv.com.

3473 ■ KRDG-FM - 105.3
3360 Alta Mesa Dr.
Redding, CA 96002
Phone: (530)226-9500
Fax: (530)221-4940
Owner: Mapleton Communications, 10900 Wilshire Blvd., No. 1500, Los Angeles, CA 90024, Ph: (310)209-7229, Fax: (310)209-7239. **Founded:** 1995. **Wattage:** 28,000. **Ad Rates:** Advertising accepted; rates available upon request.

3474 ■ KRRX-FM - 106.1
3360 Alta Mesa Dr.
Redding, CA 96002
Phone: (530)226-9500

Circulation: ★ = AAM; △ or • = BPA; ♦ = CAC; ❑ = VAC; ⊕ = PO Statement; ‡ = Publisher's Report; Boldface figures = sworn; Light figures = estimated.

Format: Album-Oriented Rock (AOR). **Owner:** Mapleton Communications, 10900 Wilshire Blvd., No. 1500, Los Angeles, CA 90024, Ph: (310)209-7229, Fax: (310)209-7239. **Founded:** 1985. **Formerly:** KARZ-FM. **Operating Hours:** Continuous; 16% network, 84% local. **ADI:** Chico-Redding, CA. **Wattage:** 100,000. **Ad Rates:** Advertising accepted; rates available upon request. Combined advertising rates available with KSHA-FM, KNNN-FM, KRDG-AM, KQMS-AM, KNRO-AM. **URL:** http://www.106x.com.

3475 ■ KSHA-FM - 104.3
3360 Alta Mesa Dr.
Redding, CA 96002
Phone: (530)226-9500
Fax: (530)221-4940
Format: Adult Contemporary. **Networks:** ABC; CBS. **Founded:** 1981. **Operating Hours:** Continuous; 5% network, 95% local. **ADI:** Chico-Redding, CA. **Wattage:** 100,000 ERP. **Ad Rates:** Noncommercial. **URL:** http://www.kshasta.com.

3476 ■ KSYC-AM - 103.9
1721 Market St.
Redding, CA 96001
Phone: (530)552-6301
Format: News; Country; Oldies. **Networks:** Satellite Music Network; CBS. **Owner:** Siskiyou Radio Partners, Inc., at above address. **Founded:** 1945. **Operating Hours:** Continuous. **Key Personnel:** Rick Martin, News Dir. **Wattage:** 10,000 ERP. **Ad Rates:** $12.90-14.50 for 30 seconds; $16-18 for 60 seconds. Combined advertising rates available with KSYC-FM. **URL:** http://ijpr.org/contact-us#stream/0.

3477 ■ K298AF-FM - 107.5
PO Box 391
Twin Falls, ID 83303
Fax: (208)736-1958
Free: 800-357-4226
Format: Religious; Contemporary Christian. **Owner:** CSN International, PO Box 391, Twin Falls, ID 83303, Ph: (208)736-1958, Fax: (208)736-1958, Free: 800-357-4226. **URL:** http://www.csnradio.com.

3478 ■ K225AJ-FM - 92.9
PO Box 391
Twin Falls, ID 83303
Fax: (208)736-1958
Free: 800-357-4226
Format: Religious; Contemporary Christian. **Owner:** CSN International, PO Box 391, Twin Falls, ID 83303, Ph: (208)736-1958, Fax: (208)736-1958, Free: 800-357-4226. **URL:** http://www.csnradio.com.

3479 ■ K220IR-FM - 91.9
PO Box 391
Twin Falls, ID 83303
Fax: (208)736-1958
Free: 800-357-4226
Format: Religious; Contemporary Christian. **Owner:** CSN International, PO Box 391, Twin Falls, ID 83303, Ph: (208)736-1958, Fax: (208)736-1958, Free: 800-357-4226. **Key Personnel:** Mike Kestler, President; Don Mills, Music Dir., Prog. Dir. **URL:** http://www.csnradio.com.

3480 ■ KVIP-AM - 540
1139 Hartnell Ave.
Redding, CA 96002
Phone: (530)222-4455
Fax: (530)222-4484
Email: info@kvip.org
Format: Contemporary Christian. **Networks:** Moody Broadcasting. **Owner:** Pacific Cascade Communications Corp. **Founded:** 1970. **Operating Hours:** Continuous; 35% network, 65% local. **ADI:** Chico-Redding, CA. **Key Personnel:** Steve Hafen, Contact; Ted Hering, Contact. **Local Programs:** *Prayer Time*, Monday Tuesday Wednesday Thursday Friday 11:45 a.m. - 12:00 p.m. **Wattage:** 2,500. **Ad Rates:** Noncommercial. **URL:** http://www.kvip.org.

3481 ■ KVIP-FM - 98.1
1139 Hartnell Ave.
Redding, CA 96002
Phone: (530)222-4455
Fax: (530)222-4484
Free: 800-877-5847
Email: info@kvip.org
Format: Contemporary Christian. **Networks:** Moody Broadcasting. **Owner:** Pacific Cascade Communications Corp. **Founded:** 1975. **Operating Hours:** Continuous; 35% network, 65% local. **ADI:** Chico-Redding, CA. **Key Personnel:** Steve Hafen, Contact; Ted Hering, Contact. **Local Programs:** *Let My People Think*, Sunday 1:00 a.m. - 1:30 a.m.; *Saturday Magazine*, Saturday 11:00 a.m. - 12:00 p.m. **Wattage:** 30,000. **Ad Rates:** Noncommercial. **URL:** http://www.kvip.org.

REDLANDS

SE CA. San Bernardino Co. 9 mi. SE of San Bernardino. University of Redlands. Extensive orange packing and shipping. Storage batteries, display letters, food, dairy products, plastics electric cars, boxes, recapping equipment manufactured. Nurseries; hatcheries. Fruit farms. Citrus, deciduous fruits, truck crops.

3482 ■ ArcNews
ESRI
380 New York St.
Redlands, CA 92373-8100
Phone: (909)793-2853
Fax: (909)793-5953
Free: 800-447-9778
Publisher's E-mail: info@esri.com
Magazine covering geography, maps and mapping, and computers. **Founded:** 1979. **Freq:** Quarterly. **Key Personnel:** Thomas K. Miller, Editor-in-Chief. **ISSN:** 1064-6108 (print). **Subscription Rates:** Free. **URL:** http://www.esri.com/esri-news/arcnews. **Formerly:** ARC News. **Ad Rates:** BW $8,305; 4C $9,520. **Remarks:** Accepts advertising. **Circ:** 390000.

3483 ■ Bulldog Weekly
University of Redlands
1200 E Colton Ave.
Redlands, CA 92373
Phone: (909)793-2121
Fax: (909)793-2029
Collegiate newspaper. **Freq:** Weekly. **Print Method:** Offset. **Trim Size:** 11 x 13 1/2. **Cols./Page:** 4. **Col. Width:** 24 nonpareils. **Col. Depth:** 189 agate lines. **URL:** http://www.redlands.edu/offices-directories/bulldog-weekly-newspaper.aspx. **Mailing address:** PO Box 3080, Redlands, CA 92373. **Remarks:** Accepts advertising. **Circ:** Free ‡2000.

North San Bernardino Green Sheet - See San Bernardino

3484 ■ Redlands Daily Facts
Donrey Media Group
700 Brookside Ave.
Redlands, CA 92373
Phone: (909)793-3221
General interest newspaper. **Founded:** 1891. **Freq:** Daily and Sun. (eve.). **Print Method:** Offset. **Cols./Page:** 6. **Col. Width:** 12.2 picas. **Col. Depth:** 21 1/2 inches. **Key Personnel:** Ron Hasse, President, Publisher; Toni Momberger, Managing Editor. **USPS:** 183-620. **Subscription Rates:** $38 Individuals home delivery. **URL:** http://www.redlandsdailyfacts.com. **Ad Rates:** GLR $1.44; BW $1,575.09; PCI $12.21. **Remarks:** Accepts advertising. **Circ:** Mon.-Fri. ★**7088**, Sun. ★**7154**.

3485 ■ Redlands Green Sheet
Associated Desert Shoppers Inc.
721 Nevada St., Ste. 207
Redlands, CA 92373
Fax: (909)253-0727
Free: 800-678-4237
Publication E-mail: greensheet@desertshoppers.net
Shopper (tabloid). **Freq:** Weekly (Wed.). **Print Method:** Web. **Trim Size:** 11 x 12 1/2. **Cols./Page:** 6. **Col. Width:** 9.5 picas. **Col. Depth:** 11 3/4 inches. **Key Personnel:** Gary Graham, Manager, Circulation. **Alt. Formats:** PDF. **URL:** http://www.greenandwhitesheet.com/green_sheet_home.php. **Remarks:** Accepts advertising. **Circ:** (Not Reported).

Riverside Green Sheet - See Riverside

3486 ■ San Bernardino Green Sheet
Associated Desert Shoppers Inc.
721 Nevada St., Ste. 207
Redlands, CA 92373
Fax: (760)346-3597
Free: 800-678-4237
Shoppers' publication serving Redlands, California area. **Freq:** Weekly. **Key Personnel:** Gary Graham, Manager, Circulation. **URL:** http://www.greenandwhitesheet.com/green_sheet_home.php. **Remarks:** Accepts advertising. **Circ:** (Not Reported).

West San Bernardino Green Sheet - See San Bernardino

3487 ■ KCAL-FM - 96.7
1940 Orange Tree Ln., Ste. 200
Redlands, CA 92374
Phone: (909)793-3554
Fax: (909)793-7225
Email: sales@kcalfm.com
Format: Country. **Networks:** CBS. **Founded:** 1959. **Operating Hours:** Continuous; 100% local. **Key Personnel:** Jeffrey Parke, Contact, jparke@kcalfm.com. **Wattage:** 1,750 ERP. **Ad Rates:** Advertising accepted; rates available upon request. **URL:** http://www.kcalfm.com.

3488 ■ KOLA-FM - 99.9
1940 Orange Tree Ln., Ste. 200
Redlands, CA 92374
Phone: (909)793-3554
Fax: (909)793-7225
Email: sales@kolafm.com
Format: Classical. **Networks:** ABC. **Owner:** Inland Empire Broadcasting Corp., at above address. **Founded:** 1959. **ADI:** Los Angeles (Corona & San Bernardino), CA. **Key Personnel:** Gary Springfield, Dir. of Programs, gary@kolafm.com; Douglas Fleniken, Contact, doug@kolafm.com. **Wattage:** 29,500 ERP. **Ad Rates:** Advertising accepted; rates available upon request. **URL:** http://www.kolafm.com.

3489 ■ KSGN-FM - 89.7
2048 Orange Tree Ln., Ste. 200
Redlands, CA 92374
Phone: (909)583-2150
Fax: (909)583-2170
Free: 800-897-5746
Email: info@ksgn.com
Format: Contemporary Christian. **Networks:** UPI. **Owner:** Good News Radio. **Founded:** 1958. **Formerly:** KSDA-FM; KNFP-FM; KLLU-FM. **Operating Hours:** Continuous; 5% network, 95% local. **ADI:** Los Angeles (Corona & San Bernardino), CA. **Key Personnel:** Melissa Chavez, Producer. **Wattage:** 3,000. **Ad Rates:** Noncommercial. **URL:** http://www.ksgn.com.

3490 ■ KUOR-FM - 89.1
474 S Raymond Ave.
1200 E Colton Ave.
Redlands, CA 92373-0999
Phone: (909)792-0721
Fax: (909)793-2029
Format: Jazz; Adult Contemporary. **Networks:** Independent. **Owner:** University of Redlands, 1200 E Colton Ave., Redlands, CA 92373, Ph: (909)793-2121, Fax: (909)793-2029. **Founded:** 1951. **Operating Hours:** Continuous. **Key Personnel:** Paul Glickman, News Dir. **Wattage:** 035. **Ad Rates:** Noncommercial. **URL:** http://www.scpr.org/about/kuor.

REDONDO BEACH

S. CA. Los Angeles Co. On Pacific Ocean, 19 mi. SW of Los Angeles. Aircraft parts, electronics, missiles, steel, chemicals manufactured; aircraft assembly plant. Residential. Ships cut flowers.

3491 ■ Courts Today
Criminal Justice Media Inc.
116 S Catalina Ave., Ste. 116
Redondo Beach, CA 90277
Phone: (310)374-2700
Fax: (310)347-4174
Publication E-mail: courtstoday@mac.com
Magazine that defines, examines and clarifies the issues, challenges and successes of the court system. **Freq:** Quarterly. **Key Personnel:** Tom Kapinos, Publisher. **Subscription Rates:** Free to qualified subscribers. **URL:** http://www.courtstoday.com. **Ad Rates:** BW $1,900; 4C $3,240. **Remarks:** Accepts advertising. **Circ:** Free 10000.

3492 ■ Lovematters.com
Lovematters.com
1840 S Elena Ave., No. 103
Redondo Beach, CA 90277
Phone: (310)378-0067
Fax: (310)375-4546

Publication E-mail: jtfinn@earthlink.net
Newspaper covering dating, sex, love and life. **Key Personnel:** J.T. Finn, Editor-in-Chief. **Alt. Formats:** PDF. **URL:** http://www.lovematters.com. **Remarks:** Accepts advertising. **Circ:** (Not Reported).

3493 ■ Medical Acupuncture
American Academy of Medical Acupuncture
2512 Artesia Blvd., Ste. 200
Redondo Beach, CA 90278
Phone: (310)379-8261
Fax: (310)379-8283
Publisher's E-mail: info@medicalacupuncture.org
Peer-reviewed journal covering acupuncture. **Freq:** Bimonthly. **Key Personnel:** Richard C. Niemtzow, MD, Editor-in-Chief. **ISSN:** 1933--6586 (print); **EISSN:** 1933--6594 (electronic). **Subscription Rates:** $237 Individuals print and online (U.S.A.); $307 Individuals print and online (outside U.S.A.); $226 Individuals online. **URL:** http://www.medicalacupuncture.org/ForPhysicians/MedicalAcupunctureJournal.aspx. **Ad Rates:** BW $1,075; 4C $1,525. **Remarks:** Advertising accepted; rates available upon request. **Circ:** 4000.

REDWAY

KLAI-FM - See Laytonville

3494 ■ KMUD-FM - 91.1
1144 Redway Dr.
Redway, CA 95560-0135
Phone: (707)923-2513
Fax: (707)923-2501
Free: 800-568-3723
Format: Public Radio. **Simulcasts:** KMUE FM fulltime. **Networks:** Pacifica; Longhorn Radio. **Owner:** Redwood Community Radio Inc., 1144 Redway Dr., Redway, CA 95560, Ph: (707)923-2605. **Founded:** 1986. **Operating Hours**: Continuous; 10% network, 90% local. **Key Personnel:** Marianne Knorzer, Dir. of Programs, pd@kmud.org. **Wattage**: 5,500 KMUD. **Ad Rates:** Noncommercial; underwriting available. **Mailing address:** PO Box 135, Redway, CA 95560-0135. **URL:** http://kmud.org.

KMUE-FM - See Eureka

Redwood Community Radio Inc. - See Eureka

REDWOOD CITY

W. CA. San Mateo Co. 26 mi. SE of San Francisco. Financial center. Computer equipment. Ships food products, lumber and petroleum, recording equipment, electronics-components manufactured. Ships cut flowers. Agriculture.

3495 ■ KKPX-TV - 65
660 Price Ave., Ste. B
Redwood City, CA 94063
Phone: (650)261-1370
Fax: (650)261-1293
Key Personnel: Brandon Burgess, Chairman, CEO. **Ad Rates:** Noncommercial. **URL:** http://www.ionmedia.tv.

REEDLEY

C. CA. Fresno Co. 25 mi. SE of Fresno. Reedley College. Fruit packing, drying plants, olive oil, wine manufactured. Agriculture. peaches, grapes, plums, nectarines.

3496 ■ Reedley Exponent
Reedley Exponent Inc.
1130 G St.
Reedley, CA 93654
Phone: (559)638-2244
Fax: (559)638-5021
Newspaper with a Republican orientation. **Freq:** Weekly (Thurs.). **Print Method:** Offset. **Cols./Page:** 6. **Col. Width:** 25 nonpareils. **Col. Depth:** 291 agate lines. **Key Personnel:** Fred Hall, Publisher. **Subscription Rates:** $25 Individuals for Fresno County; $24.50 Out of area for out of county; $26.50 Out of state for out of state; $23 Individuals age 55 above; $22.50 Out of area age 55 above; $24.50 Out of state age 55 above. **URL:** http://www.reedleyexponent.com. **Mailing address:** PO Box 432, Reedley, CA 93654. **Ad Rates:** BW $938.70; 4C $1238.70; SAU $9.50. **Remarks:** Accepts advertising. **Circ:** Paid ‡3650, Free ‡16400.

RENO

3497 ■ KHIT-AM - 1450
3301 Barham Blvd., Ste. 200
Los Angeles, CA 90068
Phone: (323)512-2225
Fax: (323)512-2224
Format: Sports. **Networks:** ESPN Radio. **Owner:** Lotus Communications, at above address. **Founded:** 1984. **Formerly**: KRCV-AM. **Operating Hours**: Continuous. **ADI**: Reno, NV. **Key Personnel:** John Paley, VP of Rel.; Howard A. Kalmenson, CEO, President. **Wattage**: 1,000. **Ad Rates:** Advertising accepted; rates available upon request. **URL:** http://www.lotuscorp.com.

RESEDA

3498 ■ California Hungarians
California Hungarians
PO Box 370305
Reseda, CA 91337-0305
Phone: (818)996-7685
Fax: (818)996-5306
Publisher's E-mail: calhun@pacificnet.net
Newspaper (tabloid) with an ethnic, political, and cultural orientation (Hungarian). **Freq:** Weekly. **Print Method:** Offset. **Trim Size:** 11 x 17. **Cols./Page:** 5. **Col. Width:** 2 inches. **Col. Depth:** 16 inches. **Key Personnel:** Attila Fenyes, Publisher. **ISSN:** 0744--8600 (print). **Subscription Rates:** $26 Individuals; $19 Individuals senior citizens; $28 Canada; $35 Other countries. **URL:** http://www.magyarsajto.com. **Also known as**: Californiai Magyarsag. **Ad Rates:** GLR $1.50; BW $500; PCI $10. **Remarks:** Accepts advertising. **Circ:** ‡2000.

RIALTO

SE CA. San Bernardino Co. 7 mi. W. of San Bernardino. Residential. Light industry.

3499 ■ Rialto Record
Inland Empire Community Newspapers
PO Box 6247
San Bernardino, CA 92412-6247
Phone: (909)381-9898
Fax: (909)384-0406
Publisher's E-mail: iecn1@mac.com
Newspaper. **Founded:** 1911. **Freq:** Weekly (Thurs.). **Print Method:** Offset. **Cols./Page:** 5. **Col. Width:** 1 7/8 inches. **Col. Depth:** 14.5 inches. **Key Personnel:** Diana Macias Harrison, General Manager. **Subscription Rates:** $75 Out of state. **URL:** http://www.rialtorecord.com/. **Formerly**: The Record. **Ad Rates:** GLR $1; BW $1,512; 4C $2,162; PCI $17. **Remarks:** Accepts advertising. **Circ:** Free ‡16000, Paid ‡1000.

RICHMOND

Contra Costa Co.

3500 ■ California Agriculture
California Agriculture
1301 S 46th St., Blvd. 478
Richmond, CA 94804-4600
Journal reporting agricultural research at the University of California. **Founded:** Dec. 1946. **Freq:** Quarterly. **Print Method:** Offset. **Trim Size:** 8 1/2 x 11. **Cols./Page:** 3. **Col. Width:** 2 1/4 inches. **Col. Depth:** 9 1/2 inches. **Key Personnel:** Will Suckow, Art Director. **ISSN:** 0008-0845 (print). **Subscription Rates:** $24 Individuals outside the U.S.; Free U.S. resident; $40 Two years outside the U.S.; $60 Individuals outside the U.S., 3 years subscription. **URL:** http://californiaagriculture.ucanr.org/. **Remarks:** Accepts advertising. **Circ:** Combined 16700.

3501 ■ House Rabbit Journal
House Rabbit Society
148 Broadway
Richmond, CA 94804
Phone: (510)970-7575
Fax: (510)970-9820
Publisher's E-mail: rabbit-center@rabbit.org
Contains information on rabbit diet, behavior, and environment. Features articles by veterinarians. **Freq:** 2 or 3 times a year. **Subscription Rates:** Included in membership. **URL:** http://rabbit.org/house-rabbit-journal-archive. **Remarks:** Advertising not accepted. **Circ:** 6000, 7000.

3502 ■ Richmond Magazine
Richmond Chamber of Commerce
3925 Macdonald Ave.
Richmond, CA 94805
Phone: (510)234-3512
Fax: (510)234-3540
Freq: Biennial. **Subscription Rates:** Included in membership. **URL:** http://rcoc.com/richmond-magazine-2015-16-is-here. **Remarks:** Advertising not accepted. **Circ:** 5000.

3503 ■ Strings
String Letter Publishing
501 Canal Blvd., Ste. J
Richmond, CA 94804-3505
Phone: (510)215-0010
Fax: (510)231-5824
Publication E-mail: editors.st@stringletter.com subs.st@stringletter.com
Magazine for musicians of bowed instruments. **Freq:** Monthly. **Print Method:** Offset. **Key Personnel:** David A. Lusterman, Publisher. **ISSN:** 0888-3106 (print). **Subscription Rates:** $32 Individuals print or digital. **URL:** http://www.allthingsstrings.com; http://stringletter.com/community/strings. **Remarks:** Accepts advertising. **Circ:** ‡15000.

3504 ■ KDYA-AM - 1190
3260 Blume Dr., Ste. 520
Richmond, CA 94806
Phone: (510)222-4242
Fax: (510)262-9054
Free: 888-467-7754
Format: Gospel. **Key Personnel:** Clifford Brown, Jr., Dir. of Programs, cliffordbrown@gospel1190.net. **Ad Rates:** Advertising accepted; rates available upon request. **URL:** http://www.gospel1190.net.

RIDGECREST

S. CA. Kern Co. 125 mi. E. of Bakersfield. Residential. Naval weapons center. Logging. Lumber mill.

3505 ■ The Daily Independent
GateHouse Media Inc.
224 E Ridgecrest Blvd.
Ridgecrest, CA 93556
Phone: (760)375-4481
Fax: (760)375-4880
General newspaper. **Founded:** 1925. **Freq:** Tues.-Fri. (eve.) Sun. (Mon.). **Print Method:** Offset. **Cols./Page:** 6. **Col. Width:** 2 1/16 inches. **Col. Depth:** 21 1/2 inches. **Key Personnel:** John Watkins, Publisher; Rodney Connors, Manager, Circulation. **Subscription Rates:** $60 Individuals. **URL:** http://www.ridgecrestca.com/. **Ad Rates:** SAU $8.95. **Remarks:** Accepts advertising. **Circ:** Paid 8651.

3506 ■ News-Review
News-Review
109 N Sanders St.
Ridgecrest, CA 93555
Phone: (760)371-4301
Fax: (760)371-4304
Publisher's E-mail: newsreview@iwvisp.com
Newspaper serving the communities of Inyokern and Ridgecrest. **Founded:** 1976. **Freq:** Weekly. **Key Personnel:** Patti Cosner, Managing Editor; Patricia Farris, Publisher. **ISSN:** 0893-9004 (print). **URL:** http://www.news-ridgecrest.com/news/category.pl; http://www.newsreviewiwv.com. **Ad Rates:** GLR $.55; BW $1096.50; 4C $1246.50; PCI $8.50. **Remarks:** Advertising accepted; rates available upon request. **Circ:** (Not Reported).

3507 ■ KFLA-TV - 6
701 Perdew Ave.
Ridgecrest, CA 93555
Format: Commercial TV. **Key Personnel:** Roy Mayhugh, Contact, roy@mayhugh.com. **URL:** http://www.kfla.tv/index.html.

3508 ■ KLOA-AM - 1240
731 N Balsam St.
Ridgecrest, CA 93555
Phone: (760)371-1700
Format: Oldies. **Networks:** CBS; ESPN Radio; ABC. **Owner:** Adelman Broadcasting, 42010 50th St. W, Quartz Hill, CA 93536, Ph: (661)718-1552. **Founded:** 1956. **Operating Hours**: Continuous; 80% network,

Circulation: ★ = AAM; △ or • = BPA; ♦ = CAC; ❑ = VAC; ⊕ = PO Statement; ‡ = Publisher's Report; Boldface figures = sworn; Light figures = estimated.

20% local. **Wattage**: 250. **Ad Rates:** $4.50-13 for 30 seconds; $5.50-14 for 60 seconds. $4.50-$13 for 30 seconds; $5.50-$14 for 60 seconds. Combined advertising rates available with KLOA-FM. **URL:** http://ksfm.cbslocal.com.

3509 ■ KLOA-FM - 104.9
731 N Balsam St.
Ridgecrest, CA 93555
Phone: (760)371-1700
Fax: (760)371-1824
Format: Country. **Networks:** Satellite Music Network. **Owner:** Adelman Communications Inc. **Founded:** 1982. **Formerly**: KFIO-FM. **Operating Hours**: Continuous; 80% network, 20% local. **Wattage:** 25,000. **Ad Rates:** $15-26 for 30 seconds; $20-31 for 60 seconds.

3510 ■ KRAJ-FM - 100.9
731 N Balsam St.
Ridgecrest, CA 93555
Format: Blues; Hip Hop. **Wattage**: 1,500. **Ad Rates:** Noncommercial. **URL:** http://Theheat1009.Com.

3511 ■ KSSI-FM
1621 North Downs St.
Ridgecrest, CA 93555
Email: kssirock@iwvisp.com
Format: Album-Oriented Rock (AOR); Classic Rock. **Owner:** Sound Enterprises, Lawrenceville, GA. **Founded:** Feb. 26, 1996. **Local Programs**: *Christine in the Morning*, Monday Tuesday Wednesday Thursday Friday 6:00 a.m. - 9:00 a.m. **Wattage**: 1,550 ERP. **Ad Rates:** Advertising accepted; rates available upon request.

3512 ■ K218DU-FM - 91.5
PO Box 391
Twin Falls, ID 83303
Fax: (208)736-1958
Free: 800-357-4226
Format: Religious; Contemporary Christian. **Owner:** CSN International, PO Box 391, Twin Falls, ID 83303, Ph: (208)736-1958, Fax: (208)736-1958, Free: 800-357-4226. **URL:** http://www.csnradio.com.

3513 ■ KWDJ-AM - 1360
121 W Ridgecrest Blvd.
Ridgecrest, CA 93555
Phone: (760)384-4937
Fax: (760)384-4978
Format: Talk. **Operating Hours**: Continuous. **Wattage**: 1,000. **Ad Rates:** Advertising accepted; rates available upon request.

3514 ■ KZIQ-FM - 92.7
121 W Ridgecrest Blvd.
Ridgecrest, CA 93555
Phone: (760)384-4937
Fax: (760)384-4978
Format: Contemporary Country; Country. **Owner:** Sunset Media. **Ad Rates:** Advertising accepted; rates available upon request.

RIO VISTA

NWC CA. Solano Co. On Sacramento River, 40 mi. S. of Sacramento. Recreation. Waterways. Fruit packing. Natural gas fields, farm machinery manufactured. Agriculture.

3515 ■ River News Herald & Isleton Journal
River News Herald Co.
PO Box 786
Rio Vista, CA 94571
Phone: (707)374-6431
Fax: (707)374-6322
Publisher's E-mail: rveditor@citlink.net
Community newspaper. **Freq:** Weekly (Wed.). **Print Method:** Offset. **Cols./Page:** 6. **Col. Width:** 20 nonpareils. **Col. Depth:** 301 agate lines. **Key Personnel:** Rich Peters, Editor-in-Chief; Sarah Villec, General Manager; Galen Kusic, Editor. **USPS:** 466-680. **URL:** http://rivernewsherald.org. **Formerly**: Isleton Journal; The River News-Herald. **Remarks:** Accepts advertising. **Circ:** Free ■ **960**, Paid ■ **1560**, Combined ■ **2520**.

RIPON

C. CA. San Joaquin Co. 10 mi. NW of Modesto. Residential. Wineries. Dairy, fruit, poultry farms. Almonds.

3516 ■ The Ripon Record
The Ripon Record
130 W Main St.
Ripon, CA 95366
Phone: (209)599-2194
Publisher's E-mail: editor@riponrecordnews.com
Community newspaper. **Freq:** Weekly (Wed.). **Print Method:** Offset. Uses mats. **Cols./Page:** 6. **Col. Width:** 25 nonpareils. **Col. Depth:** 294 agate lines. **Key Personnel:** Craig Macho, Editor. **URL:** http://www.riponrecordnews.com. **Ad Rates:** GLR $.33; BW $356.58; SAU $3.92. **Remarks:** Accepts advertising. **Circ:** Paid ‡2500.

RIVERSIDE

SE CA. Riverside Co. 53 mi. E. of Los Angeles. University of California at Riverside. Riverside City College. Loma Linda University. California Baptist College. Extensive citrus fruit packing, large food distribution center. Manufactures aircraft components, cement, motors, aircraft precision instruments, plant covers, air conditioning equipment, concrete, asbestos pipe. Seed distribution center. Rock quarry. Tourist center.

3517 ■ Applied Biochemistry and Biotechnology: Enzyme Engineering & Biotechnology
Humana Press Inc.
c/o Ashok Mulchandani, Editor-in-Chief
University of California
Dept. of Chemical & Environmental Engineering
Bourns Hall
Riverside, CA 92521
Phone: (909)787-6419
Fax: (909)787-5696
Publisher's E-mail: orders-ny@springer.com
Scientific journal covering biochemistry and biotechnology. **Freq:** 24/yr. **Print Method:** Sheet Fed. **Trim Size:** 7 x 10. **Key Personnel:** Jonathan Sachs, Editor-in-Chief. **ISSN:** 0273-2289 (print); **EISSN:** 1559-0291 (electronic). **Subscription Rates:** €2548 Institutions print incl. free access; €3058 Institutions print plus enhanced access; €125.21 Individuals. **URL:** http://www.springer.com/humana+press/biotechnology/journal/12010. **Remarks:** Accepts advertising. **Circ:** (Not Reported).

3518 ■ The Banner
California Baptist University
8432 Magnolia Ave.
Riverside, CA 92504-3297
Free: 877-228-3615
Collegiate newspaper. **Founded:** 1955. **Freq:** Biweekly. **Print Method:** Offset. **Trim Size:** 10 3/4 x 13. **Cols./Page:** 5. **Col. Width:** 10 3/4 picas. **Col. Depth:** 13 inches. **Key Personnel:** Maryann Pearson, Contact. **URL:** http://www.cbubanner.com/. **Ad Rates:** BW $200; PCI $5. **Remarks:** Color advertising not accepted. **Circ:** Free ‡1000.

3519 ■ Black Equal Opportunity Employment Journal: The Employment and Entrepreneur Magazine
Black Equal Employment Opportunity Journal
6845 Indiana Ave., Ste. 200
Riverside, CA 92506
Free: 800-487-5099
Publisher's E-mail: info@blackeoejournal.com
Magazine providing information on business and employment opportunities for the African-American community. **Freq:** Quarterly. **Key Personnel:** Sandra Jackson, Director. **Subscription Rates:** $16 Individuals print; $30 Two years print; $11.99 Individuals online. **URL:** http://www.blackeoejournal.com. **Remarks:** Advertising accepted; rates available upon request. **Circ:** (Not Reported).

3520 ■ The Black Voice News
Black Voice News
4290 Brockton Ave.
Riverside, CA 92501
Phone: (951)682-6070
Fax: (951)276-0877
Publisher's E-mail: support@blackvoicenews.com
Newspaper serving African-American communities in what is commonly called the 'Inland Empire': Riverside, Moreno Valley, Perris, Banning, Palm Springs, San Bernardino, Ontario, Redlands, and Fontana. **Freq:** Weekly (Thurs.). **Print Method:** Offset. **Cols./Page:** 6. **Col. Width:** 24 nonpareils. **Col. Depth:** 294 agate lines. **Key Personnel:** Rickerby Hinds, Editor-in-Chief; Lee Ragin, General Manager. **Subscription Rates:** $50 Individuals; $82 Two years; $25 Individuals senior, 65 years old above. **URL:** http://www.blackvoicenews.com. **Mailing address:** PO Box 912, Riverside, CA 92502. **Remarks:** Accepts advertising. **Circ:** ‡7500.

3521 ■ Cinefex
Cinefex
PO Box 20027
Riverside, CA 92516
Phone: (951)781-1917
Fax: (951)788-1793
Free: 800-434-3339
Publisher's E-mail: advertising@cinefex.com
Journal covering motion picture special effects. **Freq:** Quarterly. **Print Method:** Sheetfed offset. **Trim Size:** 9 x 8. **Cols./Page:** 2. **Key Personnel:** Jody Duncan, Contact. **ISSN:** 0198-1056 (print). **Subscription Rates:** $100 Individuals. **URL:** http://www.cinefex.com/next_issue.htm. **Ad Rates:** BW $4,750; 4C $5,975. **Remarks:** Accepts advertising. **Circ:** Paid 36000, Non-paid 1000.

3522 ■ Corona-Norco Independent
Press-Enterprise Co.
1825 Chicago Ave., Ste. 100
Riverside, CA 92507
Phone: (951)684-1200
Free: 800-794-NEWS
Publisher's E-mail: customercare@pe.com
Community newspaper. **Freq:** Daily. **Print Method:** Offset. **Cols./Page:** 5. **Col. Width:** 2 inches. **Col. Depth:** 11.5 inches. **Key Personnel:** Kathy Michalak, Contact. **ISSN:** 0745--3930 (print). **Subscription Rates:** $34.48 Individuals daily delivery; $25.83 Individuals Thursday-Sunday delivery; $17.19 Individuals Sunday only delivery. **Ad Rates:** GLR $.25; BW $520; 4C $150; SAU $5; PCI $8. **Remarks:** Accepts advertising. **Circ:** (Not Reported).

3523 ■ Great Dane Reporter
Tomar Publications
PO Box 150
Riverside, CA 92502-0150
Consumer magazine covering Great Dane breeding, raising and showing. **Freq:** Bimonthly. **Trim Size:** 8 3/8 x 10 7/8. **USPS:** 971-580. **Subscription Rates:** $40 Individuals; $76 Two years individual; $58 Individuals overseas. **URL:** http://cyberpet.com/cyberdog/products/pubmag/gdr.htm. **Ad Rates:** BW $165; 4C $500. **Remarks:** Accepts advertising. **Circ:** Combined 2200.

3524 ■ Healthy Cooking
Inland Empire Magazine
3400 Central Ave., Ste. 160
Riverside, CA 92506
Phone: (951)682-3026
Fax: (951)682-0246
Publisher's E-mail: iemail@iemag.bz
Consumer magazine covering cooking and recipes. **Freq:** Bimonthly. **Subscription Rates:** $12.95 Individuals; $25.98 Other countries; $21.98 Canada. **URL:** http://www.tasteofhome.com/healthy-cooking-magazine/archive. **Remarks:** Accepts advertising. **Circ:** (Not Reported).

3525 ■ Highlander
University of California, Riverside
900 University Ave.
Riverside, CA 92521
Phone: (951)827-1012
Collegiate newspaper. **Founded:** 1954. **Freq:** Weekly (Tues.). **Print Method:** Offset. **Trim Size:** 10 1/4 x 16. **Cols./Page:** 5. **Col. Width:** 1 7/8 inches. **Col. Depth:** 84 agate lines. **Subscription Rates:** Free; $45 By mail. **URL:** http://www.highlandernews.org/. **Ad Rates:** GLR $8; BW $864.80; 4C $1,200; PCI $15. **Remarks:** Accepts advertising. **Circ:** Free ‡10000.

3526 ■ Inland Empire
Inland Empire Magazine
3400 Central Ave., Ste. 160
Riverside, CA 92506
Phone: (951)682-3026
Fax: (951)682-0246
Publisher's E-mail: iemail@iemag.bz
Magazine on business and lifestyles in Southern California. **Freq:** Monthly. **Print Method:** Offset. **Trim Size:** 8 1/4 x 11. **Cols./Page:** 3. **Col. Width:** 27 nonpareils. **Col. Depth:** 140 agate lines. **USPS:** 518-

650. **Subscription Rates:** $12 Individuals 24 issues; $18 Individuals 36 issues. **URL:** http://www.inlandempiremagazine.com. **Ad Rates:** BW $1,295; 4C $1,795. **Remarks:** Accepts advertising. **Circ:** ‡70000.

3527 ■ Insect Biochemistry and Molecular Biology
RELX Group P.L.C.
c/o S. Gill, Editor
Cell Biology and Neuroscience
2103 Biological Sciences
University of California at Riverside
Riverside, CA 92521
Publisher's E-mail: amsterdam@relx.com
Journal publishing original contributions in the areas of insect biochemistry and insect molecular biology. **Founded:** 1971. **Freq:** Monthly. **Key Personnel:** A.S. Raikhel, Board Member; R. Feyereisen, Editor; S. Gill, Editor. **ISSN:** 0965-1748 (print). **Subscription Rates:** $3510 Institutions print. **URL:** http://www.journals.elsevier.com/insect-biochemistry-and-molecular-biology. **Circ:** (Not Reported).

3528 ■ Journal of Economic Entomology
Entomological Society of America
c/o John T. Trumble, Ed.-in-Ch.
Dept. of Entomology
University of California
Riverside, CA 92521-0001
Phone: (951)827-5624
Fax: (951)827-5624
Publisher's E-mail: esa@entsoc.org
Freq: Bimonthly February, April, June, August, October and December. **Trim Size:** 7 x 10. **Key Personnel:** John T. Trumble, Editor-in-Chief; John T. Trumble, Editor-in-Chief; Alan Kahan, Managing Editor, phone: (301)731-4535, fax: (301)731-4538. **ISSN:** 0022--0493 (print); **EISSN:** 1938--291X (electronic). **Subscription Rates:** $298 Individuals print; $239 Individuals online; $625 Institutions print; $543 Institutions online; $680 Institutions print and online; £157 Individuals print; £127 Individuals online; £329 Institutions print; £286 Institutions online; £358 Institutions print and online; €235 Individuals print; €190 Individuals online; €490 Institutions print; €429 Institutions online; €536 Institutions print. **URL:** http://www.entsoc.org/Pubs/Periodicals/JEE. **Ad Rates:** BW $1000. **Remarks:** Accepts advertising. **Circ:** ‡900.

3529 ■ Journal of Nanoelectronics and Optoelectronics
American Scientific Publishers
c/o Prof. Alexander A. Balandin, Ed.-in-Ch.
Department of Electrical Engineering
University of California
Riverside, CA 92521-0425
Phone: (951)827-2351
Fax: (951)827-2425
Publisher's E-mail: order@aspbs.com
Peer-reviewed journal on nanoscale electronic and optoelectronic materials and devices. **Freq:** 4/yr. **Key Personnel:** Dr. Ahmad Umar, Editor-in-Chief. **ISSN:** 1555--130X (print); **EISSN:** 1555--1318 (electronic). **URL:** http://www.aspbs.com/jno/. **Circ:** (Not Reported).

3530 ■ Journal of the Riverside Historical Society
Riverside Historical Society
PO Box 246
Riverside, CA 92502-0246
Phone: (951)688-2854
Publisher's E-mail: info@riversidehistoricalsociety.org
Journal featuring articles on Riverside personalities, events, and institutions of the past. **Freq:** Annual. **Key Personnel:** Steve Lech, Editor. **Alt. Formats:** PDF. **URL:** http://www.riversidehistoricalsociety.org/journal.html. **Circ:** (Not Reported).

3531 ■ Latin American Perspectives: A Journal on Capitalism and Socialism
SAGE Publications Inc.
PO Box 5703
Riverside, CA 92517-5703
Phone: (909)787-5037
Fax: (909)787-5685
Publisher's E-mail: sales@pfp.sagepub.com
Journal on capitalism and socialism in Latin America. **Freq:** Bimonthly. **Print Method:** Offset. **Trim Size:** 5 1/2 x 8 1/2. **Cols./Page:** 1. **Col. Width:** 50 nonpareils. **Col. Depth:** 100 agate lines. **Key Personnel:** Ronald H. Chilcote, Editor. **ISSN:** 0094--582X (print); **EISSN:** 1552--678X (electronic). **Subscription Rates:** $844 Institutions print & e-access; $928 Institutions current volume print & all online content; $760 Institutions e-access; $844 Institutions e-access (all online content); $1669 Institutions e-access (content through 1998); $827 Institutions print only; $74 Individuals print only; $16 Single issue individual; $152 Single issue institution. **URL:** http://lap.sagepub.com. **Ad Rates:** BW $875; 4C $1110. **Remarks:** Accepts advertising. **Circ:** (Not Reported).

3532 ■ The Press-Enterprise
Press-Enterprise Co.
1825 Chicago Ave., Ste. 100
Riverside, CA 92507
Phone: (951)684-1200
Publication E-mail: customercare@pe.com
Local newspaper. **Freq:** Mon.-Sun. (morn.). **Print Method:** Offset. **Trim Size:** 21 1/2 x 13 3/4. **Cols./Page:** 6. **Col. Width:** 26 12 3/10 nonpareils picas. **Col. Depth:** 294 21.5 agate lines inches. **Key Personnel:** Michael Coronado, Editor, phone: (951)368-9413; Tom Bray, Managing Editor, phone: (951)368-9422; Roger Ruvolo, Assistant Managing Editor, phone: (951)368-9419. **Subscription Rates:** $4.99 Individuals /week; print + online; $3.99 Individuals /week; Thurs.-Sun., print; Mon.-Sun., online; $1.99 Individuals /week; Sun., print; Mon.-Sun., online. **Online:** LexisNexis; Press-Enterprise Co. Press-Enterprise Co. **Alt. Formats:** Handheld. **URL:** http://www.pe.com. **Ad Rates:** GLR $.87; BW $1,587; 4C $1,839; SAU $12.30. **Circ:** Mon.-Sat. ★**182682**, Sun. ★**186790**, Paid ♦**18165**, Paid ♦**19395**.

3533 ■ Riverside Green Sheet
Associated Desert Shoppers Inc.
721 Nevada St., Ste. 207
Redlands, CA 92373
Fax: (909)253-0727
Free: 800-678-4237
Shopper (tabloid). **Freq:** Weekly (Wed.). **Print Method:** Web. **Trim Size:** 11 x 12 1/2. **Cols./Page:** 6. **Col. Width:** 9.5 picas. **Col. Depth:** 11 3/4 inches. **Key Personnel:** Gary Graham, Manager, Circulation. **Alt. Formats:** Download; PDF. **URL:** http://www.greenandwhitesheet.com/green_sheet_home.php. **Remarks:** Advertising accepted; rates available upon request. **Circ:** Free 26000.

3534 ■ Southern California Golf
Inland Empire Magazine
3400 Central Ave., Ste. 160
Riverside, CA 92506
Phone: (951)682-3026
Fax: (951)682-0246
Publisher's E-mail: iemail@iemag.bz
Consumer magazine covering golf in Southern California. **Freq:** Annual. **URL:** http://www.inlandempiremagazine.com/products.htm. **Circ:** (Not Reported).

3535 ■ Sun City News
Press-Enterprise Co.
1825 Chicago Ave., Ste. 100
Riverside, CA 92507
Phone: (951)684-1200
Free: 800-794-NEWS
Publisher's E-mail: customercare@pe.com
Retirement community newspaper. **Freq:** Weekly (Thurs.) every second thursday. **Print Method:** Offset. **Trim Size:** 13 x 21 1/2. **Cols./Page:** 5. **Col. Width:** 26 nonpareils. **Col. Depth:** 301 agate lines. **Key Personnel:** Joe Frederickson, Publisher; Maria De Varenne, Editor; John Gryka, Managing Editor. **Subscription Rates:** Free. **URL:** http://www.pe.com; http://www.suncitynews.com.au. **Ad Rates:** GLR $.25; BW $520; 4C $150; PCI $8. **Circ:** (Not Reported).

3536 ■ Valley Times
Press-Enterprise Co.
1825 Chicago Ave., Ste. 100
Riverside, CA 92507
Phone: (951)684-1200
Free: 800-794-NEWS
Publisher's E-mail: customercare@pe.com
General newspaper. **Founded:** 1954. **Freq:** Daily Monday through Friday at noon. **Print Method:** Offset. **Cols./Page:** 5. **Col. Width:** 2 inches. **Col. Depth:** 11.5 inches. **Key Personnel:** Cy Wood, Editor, Publisher. **Subscription Rates:** $24 Individuals delivery - 3 months; $45 Individuals delivery - 6 months; $88 Individuals delivery - 1 year; $15 Individuals digital - 3 months; $27.50 Individuals digital - 6 months; $50 Individuals digital - 1 year. **URL:** http://www.valleytimes-news.com/. **Formerly:** Moreno Valley Butterfield Express. **Ad Rates:** GLR $.25; BW $520; 4C $150; SAU $5; PCI $8. **Remarks:** Accepts advertising. **Circ:** (Not Reported).

3537 ■ KGGI-FM - 99.1
2030 Iowa Ave., Ste. 100
Riverside, CA 92507
Phone: (951)684-1991
Fax: (951)274-4949
Free: 866-991-5444
Format: Top 40. **Networks:** ABC. **Owner:** iHeartMedia Inc., 200 E Basse Rd., San Antonio, TX 78209, Ph: (210)832-3314. **Founded:** Aug. 1979. **Operating Hours:** Continuous; 100% local. **ADI:** Los Angeles (Corona & San Bernardino), CA. **Wattage:** 3,100. **Ad Rates:** $150-200 for 60 seconds. **URL:** http://www.kggiradio.com.

3538 ■ KKDD-AM - 1290
2030 Iowa Ave., Ste. A
Riverside, CA 92507
Phone: (951)684-1991
Format: Eclectic. **Operating Hours:** Continuous. **Wattage:** 5,000. **Ad Rates:** Noncommercial. **URL:** http://www.lapreciosa1290.com.

3539 ■ KPRO-AM - 1570
7351 Lincoln Ave.
Riverside, CA 92504
Phone: (951)688-1570
Fax: (951)688-7009
Email: kproval@aol.com
Format: Religious. **Networks:** CNN Radio. **Founded:** 1957. **Formerly:** KMAY-AM. **Operating Hours:** Continuous. **Key Personnel:** Juan Marcos, Promotions Dir., juanmarcos@clearchannel.com. **Wattage:** 5,000. **Ad Rates:** $18 for 30 seconds; $20 for 60 seconds. **URL:** http://www.bristar.com/kpro/about.htm.

3540 ■ KSVA-AM - 920
PO Box 7150
Riverside, CA 92513
Free: 800-775-4673
Email: ksva@lobo.net
Owner: LifeTalk Radio Network, 11291 Pierce St., Riverside, CA 92505, Ph: (615)469-5122, Free: 800-775-4673.

3541 ■ KTDD-AM - 1350
2030 Iowa Ave., Ste. A
Riverside, CA 92507
Phone: (909)684-1991
Format: Country. **Wattage:** 5,000. **Ad Rates:** Noncommercial. **URL:** http://www.foxsportsradio1350.com.

3542 ■ KUCR-FM - 88.3
University of California
Riverside, CA 92521
Phone: (951)827-5827
Format: Educational; Alternative/New Music/Progressive; Classical; Jazz; Blues; Hip Hop; Talk. **Operating Hours:** Continuous. **Wattage:** 150 ERP. **Ad Rates:** Accepts Advertising. **URL:** http://kucr.org.

3543 ■ KVFG-FM - 103.1
11920 Hesperia Rd.
Hesperia, CA 92345
Phone: (760)244-2000
Format: Sports. **Owner:** CBS Radio Inc., at above address. **Wattage:** 250. **Ad Rates:** Noncommercial. **URL:** http://www.cbsradio.com.

ROCKLIN

NE CA. Placer Co. 20 mi. NE of Sacramento. Sawmill, granite stone quarry. Agriculture. Citrus fruits, poultry, livestock.

3544 ■ Placer Herald
Brehm Inc.
5055 Pacific St.
Rocklin, CA 95677
Phone: (916)774-7981
Fax: (916)783-1183
Publisher's E-mail: circulation@goldcountrymedia.com

Circulation: ★ = AAM; △ or • = BPA; ♦ = CAC; ❑ = VAC; ⊕ = PO Statement; ‡ = Publisher's Report; Boldface figures = sworn; Light figures = estimated.

Community newspaper. **Freq:** Weekly (Wed.). **Print Method:** Offset. **Trim Size:** 13 x 22. **Cols./Page:** 6. **Col. Width:** 2 1/16 inches. **Col. Depth:** 21 inches. **Subscription Rates:** $26 Individuals home delivery; $52 Two years home delivery; $45 Individuals mail in county; $55 Individuals mail out county. **URL:** http://www.placerherald.com. **Ad Rates:** BW $856.80; 4C $156.80; PCI $6.80. **Remarks:** Accepts advertising. **Circ:** Free ■ **13299**, Paid ■ **586**, Combined ■ **13885.**

3545 ■ Reflections of You
American Chronic Pain Association
PO Box 850
Rocklin, CA 95677
Fax: (916)652-8190
Free: 800-533-3231
Publisher's E-mail: acpa@theacpa.org
Subscription Rates: $30. **URL:** http://www.theacpa.org/product.aspx?guid=6e800fba-47cd-4126-8e4c-4d63a97429b2. **Remarks:** Advertising not accepted. **Circ:** (Not Reported).

KAKV-FM - See El Dorado, AR

3546 ■ KALR-FM - 91.5
5700 W Oaks Blvd.
Rocklin, CA 95765
Format: Contemporary Christian. **Key Personnel:** Mike Novak, President, CEO; Alan Mason, COO. **Wattage:** 4,500.

3547 ■ KAPK-FM - 91.1
5700 W Oaks Blvd.
Rocklin, CA 95765
Format: Religious; Music of Your Life; News. **URL:** http://www.klove.com.

3548 ■ KCIL-FM - 107.5
5700 W Oaks Blvd.
Rocklin, CA 95765
Email: info@c1075.com
Format: Contemporary Country. **Networks:** Unistar; Louisiana. **Owner:** Sunburst Media-Louisiana LLC, at above address. **Founded:** 1946. **Operating Hours:** Continuous. **ADI:** New Orleans, LA. **Key Personnel:** Danny Fletcher, Gen. Mgr.; Eric Gill, Promotions Dir. **Wattage:** 100,000. **Ad Rates:** $30-38 for 30 seconds; $34-48 for 60 seconds. Combined advertising rates available with KJIN-AM.

3549 ■ KEBR-AM - 1210
290 Hegenberger Rd.
Oakland, CA 94621
Free: 800-543-1495
Email: info@familyradio.org
Format: Religious. **Simulcasts:** KEBR-FM. **Networks:** Independent. **Owner:** Family Radio Network Inc. **Founded:** 1988. **Operating Hours:** Continuous. **ADI:** Sacramento-Stockton, CA. **Wattage:** 5,000. **Ad Rates:** Noncommercial. **URL:** http://www.familyradio.org.

KEKL-FM - See Las Vegas, NV

3550 ■ KFLB-FM - 90.5
5700 W Oaks Blvd.
Rocklin, CA 95765
Format: Religious; Music of Your Life; News. **URL:** http://www.klove.com.

KGCO-FM - See Fort Collins, CO

KHKL-FM - See Laytonville

KHLV-FM - See Helena, MT

3551 ■ KHRI-FM
5700 W Oaks Blvd.
Rocklin, CA 95765
Format: Contemporary Christian. **Key Personnel:** Dr. David R. Ferry, Director. **Wattage:** 170 ERP. **Ad Rates:** Noncommercial. **URL:** http://www.air1.com/.

KJKL-FM - See Grants Pass, OR

KJLV-FM - See Jonesboro, AR

KKLG-FM - See Newton, IA

KKLJ-FM - See Klamath Falls, OR

KKLM-FM - See Corpus Christi, TX

KKLP-FM - See La Pine, OR

KKLQ-FM - See Fargo, ND

KKLT-FM - See Texarkana, AR

KKLW-FM - See Willmar, MN

KKVO-FM - See Altus, OK

KLBV-FM - See Steamboat Springs, CO

KLDV-FM - See Denver, CO

KLFS-FM - See Fort Smith, AR

KLFV-FM - See Grand Junction, CO

KLGQ-FM - See Grants, NM

KLJV-FM - See Scottsbluff, NE

KLNB-FM - See Grand Island, NE

KLON-FM - See Rockaway Beach, OR

KLOY-FM - See Astoria, OR

KLRH-FM - See Reno, NV

KLRJ-FM - See Aberdeen, SD

KLRQ-FM - See Kansas City, MO

KLRV-FM - See Billings, MT

KLRW-FM - See San Angelo, TX

KLRY-FM - See Gypsum, CO

KLTU-FM - See Tucson, AZ

KLVB-FM - See Redding

3552 ■ KLVC-FM - 88.3
5700 W Oaks Blvd.
Rocklin, CA 95765
Phone: (916)251-1740
Format: Contemporary Christian. **URL:** http://www.klove.com/search/?q=klvc.

3553 ■ KLVH-FM - 88.5
5700 W Oaks Blvd.
Rocklin, CA 95765
Phone: (916)251-1740
Format: Contemporary Christian. **URL:** http://www.klove.com/search/?q=KLVH-FM.

KLVU-FM - See Salem, OR

KLXA-FM - See Alexandria, LA

KLXV-FM - See Glenwood Springs, CO

KLZV-FM - See Sterling, CO

3554 ■ KMKL-FM - 90.3
5700 W Oaks Blvd.
Rocklin, CA 95765
Phone: (916)251-1740
Format: Contemporary Christian. **Key Personnel:** Mike Novak, President, CEO; Alan Mason, COO. **Ad Rates:** Advertising accepted; rates available upon request. **URL:** http://www.klove.com/search/?q=kmkl.

KQKL-FM - See Hanford

KQLR-FM - See Butte, MT

3555 ■ KRKL-FM
5700 W Oaks Blvd.
Rocklin, CA 95765
Format: Contemporary Christian. **Wattage:** 42,000 ERP. **Ad Rates:** Noncommercial. **URL:** http://www.klove.com.

KRLR-FM - See Lake Charles, LA

KRLU-FM - See Roswell, NM

3556 ■ KTCY-FM - 101.7
5700 W Oaks Blvd.
Rocklin, CA 95765
Phone: (916)251-1600
Format: Hispanic. **Owner:** LBI Broadcasting, 1845 Empire Ave., Burbank, CA 91504. **Founded:** 1947. **Formerly:** KMMK-FM; KSSA-FM; KRVA-FM. **Operating Hours:** Continuous. **ADI:** Dallas-Fort Worth, TX. **Key Personnel:** Anthony Gutierrez, Promotions Dir.; Frank Torres, Sales Mgr.; Jabo Casanova, Dir. of Programs. **Wattage:** 92,000. **Ad Rates:** Combined advertising rates available with KZMP-AM, KZMP-FM. **URL:** http://www.air1.com/music/radio-stations/all.aspx.

KTKL-FM - See McAlester, OK

KTLI-FM - See Wichita, KS

KVLK-FM - See Socorro, NM

KWKL-FM - See Lawton, OK

KWLU-FM - See Chester, CA

3557 ■ KWYQ-FM - 90.3
5700 W Oaks Blvd.
Rocklin, CA 95765
Phone: (916)251-1600
Owner: WAY-FM Media Group Inc., 5540 Tech Center Dr., Ste. 200, Colorado Springs, CO 80919, Ph: (719)533-0300. **Key Personnel:** Danny Houle, Gen. Mgr.; Kelli Puzey, Asst. **URL:** http://www.klove.com.

KYKL-FM - See Stockton, CA

KYLA-FM - See Shreveport, LA

KYLR-FM - See Austin, TX

KYLV-FM - See Oklahoma City, OK

3558 ■ KZRI-FM - 90.3
5700 W Oaks Blvd.
Rocklin, CA 95765
Phone: (916)251-1600
Format: Alternative/New Music/Progressive. **Ad Rates:** Noncommercial. **URL:** http://www.kxpc.com.

3559 ■ WAKL-FM - 88.9
5700 W Oaks Blvd.
Rocklin, CA 95765
Format: Contemporary Christian.

WEKV-FM - See Portsmouth, OH

3560 ■ WFZH-FM - 105.3
5700 W Oaks Blvd.
Rocklin, CA 95765
Phone: (916)251-1600
Format: Contemporary Christian. **Key Personnel:** Danny Clayton, Dir. of Programs, dannyc@salemmilwaukee.com; Dave Santrella, Gen. Mgr., VP, dsantrella@salemradiochicago.com; Mark Jaycox, Station Mgr., markj@salemmilwaukee.com. **Ad Rates:** Noncommercial.

WGKV-FM - See Pulaski, NY

WHKV-FM - See Albany, GA

WKIV-FM - See Westerly, RI

WKVE-FM - See Raleigh, NC

3561 ■ WKVF-FM - 94.9
5700 W Oaks Blvd.
Rocklin, CA 95765
Phone: (916)251-1740
Format: Contemporary Christian. **Ad Rates:** Noncommercial. **URL:** http://www.klove.com.

WKVZ-FM - See Ripley, TN

WKYJ-FM - See Rouses Point, NY

WLKA-FM - See Scranton, PA

WMXK-FM - See Morristown, TN

WNLT-FM - See Cincinnati, OH

3562 ■ WNWT-AM - 1520
5700 W Oaks Blvd.
Rocklin, CA 95765
Phone: (916)251-1600
Format: News; Music of Your Life. **Owner:** Matrix Broadcasting Group, LLC, at above address. **URL:** http://urbanfamilytalk.com.

WQRA-FM - See Indianapolis, IN

3563 ■ WSJI-FM - 89.5
5700 W Oaks Blvd.
Rocklin, CA 95765
Phone: (888)937-2471
Email: info@wsji.org
Format: Religious. **Networks:** AP; SkyLight Satellite. **Owner:** Broadcast Learning Center Inc., at above address. **Founded:** 1987. **Formerly:** WEEE-FM. **Operating Hours:** Continuous. **Key Personnel:** Debbie Helbig, Secretary; Ted Boyda, Operations Mgr. **Wattage:** 2,000. **Ad Rates:** Noncommercial. **URL:** http://www.air1.com/terms.aspx.

3564 ■ WTYX-FM - 94.7
5700 W Oaks Blvd.
Rocklin, CA 95765
Phone: (916)251-1600
Email: mail94@arrow94.com
Format: Classic Rock. **Owner:** Proteus Investments, 222 Beasley, Jackson, MS 39206, Fax: (601)956-0370. **Founded:** 1971. **Operating Hours:** Continuous. **Key Personnel:** Sam Blythe, Dir. of Programs, brothersam@arrow94.com; Marshall Magee, President, Gen. Mgr., mmagee@arrow94.com. **Wattage:** 97,000. **Ad Rates:** Advertising accepted; rates available upon request. $30-54 for 30 seconds; $30-54 for 60 seconds.

WYKL-FM - See Mansfield, OH

3565 ■ WYLR-FM
5700 W Oaks Blvd.
Rocklin, CA 95765
Phone: (518)793-4444
Fax: (518)792-3374
Format: Country. **Networks:** ABC. **Owner:** Calvin Carr Via CMA Through Chris Lynch, at above address, Ph:

(518)793-4445. **Founded:** 1968. **Formerly:** WWSC-FM. **Key Personnel:** Paul Vega, Gen. Mgr; P. Vega, Contact. **Wattage:** 3,000 ERP. **Ad Rates:** $11-24 for 30 seconds; $13.50-29 for 60 seconds.

ROHNERT PARK

NW CA. Sonoma Co. 40 mi. N. of San Francisco.

3566 ■ Fort Worth Greensheet
Greensheet Inc.
6145 State Farm Dr.
Rohnert Park, CA 94928-2147
Fax: (707)586-4747
Free: 800-757-4441
Shopper. **Freq:** Semimonthly. **Print Method:** Offset. **Trim Size:** 11 x 14. **Cols./Page:** 6. **Col. Width:** 20 nonpareils. **Col. Depth:** 196 agate lines. **Key Personnel:** Patti Murphy, Senior Editor; Paul Green, Editor-in-Chief. **Ad Rates:** PCI $14.60. **Remarks:** Accepts advertising. **Circ:** 25000.

3567 ■ KRCB-FM - 91.1
5850 Labath Ave.
Rohnert Park, CA 94928
Phone: (707)584-2000
Fax: (707)585-1363
Free: 800-287-2722
Format: Classical. **Key Personnel:** Patrick Campbell, Chairman; Bruce Robinson, News Dir. **Ad Rates:** Noncommercial. **URL:** http://www.krcb.org.

3568 ■ KRCB-TV - 22
5850 Labath Ave.
Rohnert Park, CA 94928
Phone: (707)584-2000
Fax: (707)585-1363
Free: 800-287-2722
Format: Public TV. **Networks:** Public Broadcasting Service (PBS). **Founded:** 1982. **Operating Hours:** Continuous. **ADI:** Sacramento-Stockton, CA. **Key Personnel:** Nancy Dobbs, CEO, President. **Local Programs:** *InnerVIEWS With Ernie*, Friday 8:00 p.m. **Wattage:** 68,000 ERP. **Ad Rates:** Noncommercial. **URL:** http://www.krcb.org.

3569 ■ KSUN-FM - 95
1801 E Cotati Ave.
Rohnert Park, CA 94928
Phone: (707)664-2623
Format: Alternative/New Music/Progressive. **Owner:** Sonoma State University, 1801 E Cotati Ave., Rohnert Park, CA 94928, Ph: (707)664-2880. **Key Personnel:** Eric Ritz, Music Dir., gmksun@yahoo.com; Anthony Marefat, Gen. Mgr., spike65@gmail.com; Nicole Ortega, Dir. of Programs, ortegani@seawolf.sonoma.edu; Ron Pierce, Sports Dir., News Dir., cptmeatman@aol.com. **Ad Rates:** Noncommercial. **URL:** http://www.ksunradio.com.

ROLLING HILLS ESTATES

3570 ■ Palos Verdes Peninsula News
Equal Access Media Inc.
609 Deep Valley Dr., Ste. 200
Rolling Hills Estates, CA 90274
Phone: (310)372-0388
Fax: (310)544-4322
Publication E-mail: mscott@pvnews.com
Community newspaper. **Freq:** Semiweekly Thursday and Saturday. **Print Method:** Offset. **Cols./Page:** 6. **Col. Width:** 2 1/16 nonpareils. **Col. Depth:** 294 agate lines. **Key Personnel:** Chris Boyd, Managing Editor; Mary Scott, Editor-in-Chief. **ISSN:** 0419--0300 (print). **URL:** http://www.pvnews.com. **Formerly:** Rolling Hills Herald. **Remarks:** Accepts advertising. **Circ:** Thurs. ‡13600.

3571 ■ Peninsula Business Journal
Palos Verdes Peninsula Chamber of Commerce
707 Silver Spur Rd., Ste. 100
Rolling Hills Estates, CA 90274-7612
Phone: (310)377-8111
Fax: (310)377-0614
Business journal serving Jefferson and Clallam Counties. **Freq:** Monthly. **Print Method:** Web press. **Trim Size:** 9 3/4 x 14. **Cols./Page:** 5. **Col. Width:** 1 7/8 inches. **Col. Depth:** 16 inches. **Key Personnel:** Sue Ellen Riesau, General Manager; Jim Manders, Editor; Debbi Kanjman, Advertising Representative, Editor; Brown Maloney, Advertising Representative, Publisher. **Available online. Alt. Formats:** PDF. **URL:** http://www.palosverdeschamber.com/april-2016-peninsula-business-journal. **Mailing address:** PO Box 1750, Sequim, WA 98382-1750. **Remarks:** Accepts advertising. **Circ:** (Not Reported).

ROSAMOND

SW CA. Kern Co. 5 mi. N. of Lancaster.

3572 ■ The Rosamond News
Joyce Media Inc.
2969 Sierra Hwy.
Rosamond, CA 93560-0848
Phone: (661)256-0149
Fax: (661)269-2139
Publication E-mail: rosamondnews@joycemediainc.com
Community newspaper. **Freq:** Weekly (Fri.). **Subscription Rates:** $133 By mail; $33 Individuals online only. **URL:** http://joycemediainc.com/papers/rosamondmall.html. **Mailing address:** PO Box 848, Rosamond, CA 93560-0848. **Remarks:** Advertising accepted; rates available upon request. **Circ:** (Not Reported).

ROSEMEAD

S. CA. Los Angeles Co. 8 mi. E. of Los Angeles. Residential.

3573 ■ Rosemead Report
Rosemead Chamber of Commerce
3953 N Muscatel Ave.
Rosemead, CA 91770
Phone: (626)288-0811
Fax: (626)288-2514
Newspaper containing news about Rosemead, CA; includes community news, business developments, membership updates and chamber activities. **Freq:** Monthly. **Key Personnel:** Cathy Brehm, Editor. **Alt. Formats:** PDF. **URL:** http://www.rosemeadchamber.org/latest-news/rosemead-report.html. **Mailing address:** PO Box 425, Rosemead, CA 91770. **Remarks:** Accepts advertising. **Circ:** 18500.

3574 ■ Saigon Times
Saigon Times
9234 E Valley Blvd.
Rosemead, CA 91770
Phone: (626)288-2696
Fax: (626)288-2033
Publisher's E-mail: info@saigontimesusa.com
Vietnamese language community newspaper. **Freq:** Weekly. **Key Personnel:** Ai Cam, Publisher; Thai Tu Hap, Editor-in-Chief; Katherine Le, Managing Editor. **Subscription Rates:** Free. **URL:** http://saigontimesusa.com. **Ad Rates:** BW $500; 4C $800. **Remarks:** Accepts advertising. **Circ:** Combined 20000.

ROSEVILLE

NE CA. Placer Co. 18 mi. NE of Sacramento. High tech industries. Railroad marshaling yards. Tile manufacturing. Sand and gravel pits. Agriculture.

3575 ■ Before & After: How to Design Cool Stuff
Before and After
323 Lincoln St.
Roseville, CA 95678-2229
Phone: (916)784-3880
Fax: (916)784-3995
Trade magazine covering graphic design. **Freq:** Bimonthly. **Print Method:** Offset Lithograph. **Trim Size:** 8 1/2 x 11. **Key Personnel:** John McWade, Creative Director, Founder. **ISSN:** 1049--0035 (print). **Subscription Rates:** $9 Single issue print; $18 Single issue PDF. **Alt. Formats:** PDF. **URL:** http://www.bamagazine.com. **Remarks:** Advertising not accepted. **Circ:** (Not Reported).

3576 ■ Press-Tribune
Brehm Inc.
188 Cirby Way
Roseville, CA 95678
Phone: (916)786-8746
Fax: (916)783-1183
Publisher's E-mail: circulation@goldcountrymedia.com
General newspaper. **Freq:** Semiweekly (Wed. and Sat.). **Print Method:** Web offset. **Cols./Page:** 6. **Col. Width:** 12.2 picas. **Col. Depth:** 21.5 inches. **Key Personnel:** Scott Thomas Anderson, Editor. **Subscription Rates:** $39 Individuals; $70 Two years. **URL:** http://www.thepresstribune.com. **Remarks:** Accepts advertising. **Circ:** Sat. ■ **7253.**

3577 ■ RetailerNOW
Home Furnishings Association
500 Giuseppe Ct., Ste. 6
Roseville, CA 95678
Fax: (916)784-7697
Free: 800-422-3778
Home Furnishings Retail Trade Journal. **Freq:** 10/year. **Print Method:** Web offset. **Trim Size:** 8 x 10 7/8. **Cols./Page:** 3. **Col. Width:** 26 nonpareils. **Col. Depth:** 140 agate lines. **Key Personnel:** Mary Wynn Ryan, Editor. **ISSN:** 1073-5585 (print). **Subscription Rates:** $60 Individuals; $80 Canada; $120 Other countries; $60 /year. **URL:** http://www.retailernowmag.com. **Formerly:** Furniture Retailer Magazine; Home Furnishings Executive; Home Furnishings Retailer. **Ad Rates:** BW $3,355; 4C $4,725. **Remarks:** Accepts advertising. **Circ:** Non-paid 14500, 12000.

3578 ■ TechEvents
Corporate Event Marketing Association
5098 Foothills Blvd., Ste. 3-386
Roseville, CA 95747
Phone: (916)740-3623
Freq: Quarterly. **Remarks:** Advertising not accepted. **Circ:** (Not Reported).

SACRAMENTO

NC CA. Sacramento Co. 88 mi. NE of San Francisco. The State Capital on Sacramento River. California State University at Sacramento. Dairy products, feeds, meat, poultry packing houses, brick and clay products, rocket engines and guided missiles, mining equipment, lumber boxes manufactured.

3579 ■ Ag Alert: The Weekly Newspaper for California Agriculture
California Farm Bureau Federation
2300 River Plaza Dr.
Sacramento, CA 95833
Phone: (916)561-5500
Fax: (916)561-5699
Free: 800-698-FARM
Publication E-mail: agalert@cfbf.com
Agricultural newspaper. **Freq:** Weekly. **Print Method:** Offset. **Cols./Page:** 4. **Col. Width:** 2 1/4 inches. **Col. Depth:** 12 3/4 inches. **Key Personnel:** Dave Kranz, Editor, Manager; Steve Adler, Associate Editor; Margaret Rodriguez, Manager, Operations, Manager, Production. **Subscription Rates:** Included in membership. **URL:** http://agalert.com. **Ad Rates:** BW $5302; 4C $6452; PCI $110. **Circ:** 44000.

3580 ■ Almond Facts
Blue Diamond Growers
1802 C St.
Sacramento, CA 95811
Phone: (916)446-8500
Free: 800-987-2329
Magazine covering almond growing and marketing. **Freq:** Bimonthly. **Print Method:** Offset. **Trim Size:** 8 1/2 x 11. **Cols./Page:** 3. **Col. Width:** 27 nonpareils. **Col. Depth:** 140 agate lines. **URL:** http://bluediamondgrowers.com/news. **Mailing address:** PO Box 1768, Sacramento, CA 95811. **Remarks:** Accepts advertising. **Circ:** Controlled 8000.

3581 ■ Alzheimer Disease and Associated Disorders: An International Journal
Lippincott Williams & Wilkins
c/o Charles DeCarli, MD, Editor-in-Chief
University of California
Dept. of Neurology, Davis Medical Ctr.
4860 Y St., Ste. 3700
Sacramento, CA 95817
Phone: (916)734-8413
Fax: (916)734-6525
Peer-reviewed journal covering groundbreaking advances in basic science and clinical research of Alzheimer's Disease. **Freq:** Quarterly. **Print Method:** Sheetfed Offset. **Trim Size:** 8 1/4 x 11. **Key Personnel:** Charles DeCarli, MD, Editor-in-Chief; Harry Dean, Publisher. **ISSN:** 0893-0341 (print); **EISSN:** 1546-4156 (electronic). **Subscription Rates:** $418 Individuals; $1124 Institutions; $220 Individuals in training; $512 Other countries; $1215 Institutions; $247 Other countries in-training.

Circulation: ★ = AAM; △ or • = BPA; ♦ = CAC; ❑ = VAC; ⊕ = PO Statement; ‡ = Publisher's Report; Boldface figures = sworn; Light figures = estimated.

URL: http://journals.lww.com/alzheimerjournal/pages/default.aspx; http://www.lww.com/product/?0893-0341. **Ad Rates:** BW $1,180; 4C $1,430. **Remarks:** Accepts advertising. **Circ:** Paid 282.

3582 ■ arcCa
American Institute of Architects - California Council
1303 J St., Ste. 200
Sacramento, CA 95814
Phone: (916)448-9082
Fax: (916)442-5346
Publisher's E-mail: mail@aiacc.org
Journal covering architecture, design, urban planning, construction and architectural culture in California. **Freq:** Quarterly. **Print Method:** Offset. **Trim Size:** 7 x 10. **Cols./Page:** 2. **Col. Width:** 45 nonpareils. **Col. Depth:** 126 agate lines. **Key Personnel:** Seth Horowitz, Publisher; Maggie Hartley, Account Manager, phone: (626)932-6174, fax: (626)932-6163. **ISSN:** 0738--1131 (print). **Subscription Rates:** $24 Members; $15 Students; $34 Nonmembers; $38 U.S. and Canada; $42 Other countries. **URL:** http://www.aiacc.org/arcca. **Formerly**: Architecture California. **Ad Rates:** BW $2520; 4C $3070. **Remarks:** Accepts advertising. **Circ:** 10000.

3583 ■ The Business Journal
The Business Journal
1400 X St.
Sacramento, CA 95814-5221
Phone: (916)447-7661
Fax: (916)444-7779
Publisher's E-mail: sacramento@bizjournals.com
Regional business magazine (tabloid). **Founded:** Dec. 13, 1984. **Freq:** Weekly (Fri.). **Print Method:** Offset. **Trim Size:** 11 x 14. **Cols./Page:** 4. **Col. Width:** 28 nonpareils. **Col. Depth:** 196 agate lines. **ISSN:** 8756-5897 (print). **Subscription Rates:** $107 Individuals print and online. **URL:** http://www.bizjournals.com/sacramento/. **Ad Rates:** BW $3,120; 4C $3,720. **Remarks:** Accepts advertising. **Circ:** 10500.

3584 ■ CA Grange News
California State Grange
3830 U St.
Sacramento, CA 95817
Phone: (916)454-5805
Fax: (916)739-8189
Publication E-mail: cgn@californiagrange.org
Newspaper containing published information for members of the California State Grange. **Freq:** Bimonthly. **Key Personnel:** Bob McFarland, Publisher; J.D. Hartz, Editor. **Subscription Rates:** $15 Nonmembers. **Remarks:** Accepts advertising. **Circ:** (Not Reported).

3585 ■ California Builder: The Offcial Publication of the California Building Industry Association and PCBC
California Building Industry Association
1215 K St., Ste. 1200
Sacramento, CA 95814
Phone: (916)443-7933
Fax: (916)443-1960
Publisher's E-mail: mwinn@cbia.org
Official publication of the California Building Industry Association and the Premier Building Show. Covers innovations and developments in the construction industry. **Freq:** Bimonthly. **Key Personnel:** Mike Castillo, Contact; Robert Rivinius, Publisher, phone: (916)443-7933; Greg Robertson, Editor, phone: (916)443-7933. **Subscription Rates:** Free to qualified subscribers. **Remarks:** Accepts advertising. **Circ:** (Not Reported).

3586 ■ California Cattleman
California Cattlemen's Association
1221 H St.
Sacramento, CA 95814
Phone: (916)444-0845
Fax: (916)444-2194
Freq: Monthly except July/August. **Print Method:** Offset. Uses mats. **Trim Size:** 8 1/2 x 11. **Cols./Page:** 3. **Col. Width:** 27 nonpareils. **Col. Depth:** 140 agate lines. **Key Personnel:** Stevie Ipsen, Managing Editor. **ISSN:** 0008--0942 (print). **Subscription Rates:** $20 Individuals per year; Included in membership; $20 Nonmembers. **URL:** http://www.calcattlemen.org/cca_news/california_cattleman_magazine.aspx. **Ad Rates:** BW $625; 4C $1000. **Remarks:** Accepts advertising. **Circ:** Paid ‡3585, Non-paid ‡910.

3587 ■ The California Enrolled Agent
California Society of Enrolled Agents
3200 Ramos Cir.
Sacramento, CA 95827-2513
Phone: (916)366-6646
Fax: (916)366-6674
Free: 800-777-2732
Publisher's E-mail: info@csea.org
Magazine containing technical information regarding tax and tax related issues; also includes California Society of Enrolled Agents news. **Freq:** 9/year. **Key Personnel:** Scarlet D. Vanyi, CAE, Executive Vice President. **ISSN:** 1086--5012 (print). **Subscription Rates:** Included in membership. **URL:** http://www.csea.org/magazine. **Remarks:** Accepts advertising. **Circ:** (Not Reported).

3588 ■ California Fire Service
California State Firefighters' Association
1232 Q St., 2nd Fl.
Sacramento, CA 95811
Fax: (916)446-9889
Free: 800-451-2732
Magazine containing articles on emergency medical services, fire prevention, hazardous materials, disaster response, and legislation of interest to California firefighters. **Freq:** Bimonthly. **Print Method:** Offset. **Trim Size:** 8 1/2 x 11. **Cols./Page:** 3. **Col. Width:** 2.25 picas. **Col. Depth:** 9.5 picas. **Key Personnel:** Gary C. Giacomo, Editor, phone: (916)410-1394. **USPS:** 083-920. **Subscription Rates:** Included in membership. **URL:** http://www.csfa.net/CSFA/CalFF/Membership/Member_Benefits_List/CA_Fire_Service_Magazine.aspx. **Also known as**: CSFA Magazine. **Ad Rates:** GLR $17; BW $1920; 4C $2734. **Remarks:** Accepts advertising. **Circ:** Paid 27442.

3589 ■ California Grocer
California Grocers Association
1215 K St., Ste. 700
Sacramento, CA 95814-3946
Phone: (916)448-3545
Fax: (916)448-2793
Magazine for the California grocery trade. **Founded:** 1986. **Freq:** Bimonthly. **Print Method:** Offset. **Trim Size:** 8 1/2 x 11. **Cols./Page:** 3. **Key Personnel:** Dave Heylen, Editor; Tony Ortega, Associate Editor. **Subscription Rates:** $25. **URL:** http://www.cagrocers.com/news/publications/. **Formerly**: Bulletin. **Ad Rates:** BW $1,900; 4C $2,800. **Remarks:** Accepts advertising. **Circ:** 700.

3590 ■ California Journal of Health-System Pharmacy
California Society of Health-System Pharmacists
1314 H St., Ste. 200
Sacramento, CA 95814
Phone: (916)447-1033
Fax: (916)447-2396
Publisher's E-mail: cshp@cshp.org
Medical journal serving health professionals practicing pharmaceutical care in health-system environments for member of the California Society of Health-System Pharmacists. **Freq:** Bimonthly. **Key Personnel:** Dawn Benton, Chief Executive Officer, Vice President. **ISSN:** 1097--6337 (print). **Subscription Rates:** Included in membership. **URL:** http://www.cshp.org/page/cjhp. **Ad Rates:** 4C $1,600. **Remarks:** Accepts advertising. **Circ:** (Not Reported).

3591 ■ California Manufacturers
California Manufacturers and Technology Association
1115 11th St.
Sacramento, CA 95814
Phone: (916)441-5420
Publisher's E-mail: members@cmta.net
Industrial/political quarterly. **Freq:** Quarterly. **Print Method:** Offset. **Trim Size:** 8 1/2 x 11. **Cols./Page:** 3. **Col. Width:** 28 nonpareils. **Col. Depth:** 133 agate lines. **ISSN:** 1042--2331 (print). **Subscription Rates:** Included in membership. **URL:** http://www.cmta.net. **Formerly**: Sacramento Report. **Ad Rates:** BW $2250; 4C $2900. **Remarks:** Accepts advertising. **Circ:** ‡10000.

3592 ■ California Pharmacist
California Pharmacists Association
4030 Lennane Dr.
Sacramento, CA 95834
Phone: (916)779-1400
Fax: (916)779-1401
Free: 800-444-3851
Publication E-mail: cpha@cpha.com
Peer-reviewed pharmacy journal. **Freq:** Quarterly. **Print Method:** Offset. **Trim Size:** 8 1/2 x 11. **Cols./Page:** 2 and 3. **Col. Width:** 26 and 42 nonpareils. **Col. Depth:** 139 agate lines. **Key Personnel:** Jon R. Roth, Chief Executive Officer, phone: (916)779-4500. **ISSN:** 0739--0483 (print). **Subscription Rates:** Included in membership. **URL:** http://www.cpha.com/Communications/California-Pharmacist-Journal. **Ad Rates:** PCI $125; BW $1569; 4C $2,349.50. **Remarks:** Accepts advertising. **Circ:** ‡5000.

3593 ■ The California Psychologist
California Psychological Association
1231 I St., Ste. 204
Sacramento, CA 95814-2933
Phone: (916)286-7979
Fax: (916)286-7971
Publisher's E-mail: cpa@cpapsych.org
Freq: Bimonthly latest issue 2016. **Trim Size:** 8 3/8 x 10 7/8. **Key Personnel:** Jo Linder-Crow, Chief Executive Officer. **Subscription Rates:** Included in membership. **Alt. Formats:** PDF. **URL:** http://www.cpapsych.org/?page=048. **Ad Rates:** BW $850. **Remarks:** Accepts advertising. **Circ:** 4800.

3594 ■ California Publisher
California Newspaper Publishers Association
2701 K St.
Sacramento, CA 95811
Phone: (916)288-6000
Newspaper (tabloid) reports on newspaper publishers and educators. **Freq:** Quarterly. **Print Method:** Offset. **Trim Size:** 11 1/4 x 16. **Cols./Page:** 4. **Col. Width:** 14 picas. **Col. Depth:** 17.5 inches. **ISSN:** 0008--1434 (print). **Subscription Rates:** Included in membership. **URL:** http://www.cnpa.com/california_publisher/california-publisher/article_72f7b0a2-79c7-11e1-9644-0019bb30f31a.html. **Remarks:** Color advertising accepted; rates available upon request. **Circ:** ‡1300.

3595 ■ The California Surveyor
California Land Surveyors Association
2520 Venture Oaks Way, Ste. 150
Sacramento, CA 95833
Phone: (916)239-4083
Fax: (916)924-7323
Publication E-mail: clsa@californiasurveyors.org
Land surveying magazine. **Freq:** Quarterly. **Print Method:** Offset. **Trim Size:** 8 1/2 x 11. **Cols./Page:** 3. **Col. Width:** 26 nonpareils. **Col. Depth:** 128 agate lines. **Key Personnel:** John P. Wilusz, Editor. **Alt. Formats:** PDF. **URL:** http://www.californiasurveyors.org/calsurv.html. **Ad Rates:** BW $570, full page; 4C $750, full page; BW $340, half page; 4C $520, half page. **Remarks:** Accepts advertising. **Circ:** ‡5000.

3596 ■ California Veterinarian
California Veterinary Medical Association
1400 River Park Dr., Ste. 100
Sacramento, CA 95815-4505
Phone: (916)649-0599
Fax: (916)646-9156
Publisher's E-mail: staff@cvma.net
Magazine containing general association news and scientific material related to veterinary medicine and business management. **Freq:** Bimonthly. **Print Method:** Offset. **Trim Size:** 9 x 10 7/8. **Cols./Page:** 3. **Col. Width:** 27 nonpareils. **Col. Depth:** 133 agate lines. **Key Personnel:** Phil Boerner, Coordinator. **ISSN:** 0008--1612 (print). **Subscription Rates:** Included in membership. **URL:** http://cvma.net/publications/cal-vet. **Ad Rates:** BW $1695. **Remarks:** Accepts advertising. **Circ:** 10000.

3597 ■ California Woman
California Federation of Business and Professional Women
7485 Rush River Dr., Ste. 710
Sacramento, CA 95831
Magazine for business and professional women. **Freq:** 3/year. **Print Method:** Offset. **Trim Size:** 8 1/2 x 11. **Cols./Page:** 3. **Col. Width:** 28 nonpareils. **Col. Depth:** 136 agate lines. **Key Personnel:** Michelle Husby, Editor. **ISSN:** 0008--1663 (print). **URL:** http://bpwcal.org/about-cfbpw/california-woman-magazine. **Mailing address:** Box 370, Sacramento, CA 95831. **Ad Rates:** BW $250; 4C $300. **Remarks:** Accepts advertising. **Circ:** 5500.

3598 ■ Catholic Herald
El Heraldo Catolico

2110 Broadway
Sacramento, CA 95818
Phone: (916)733-0100
Fax: (916)733-0195
Publication E-mail: catholicherald@megapathdsl.net
Catholic newspaper (tabloid). **Founded:** 1908. **Freq:** Bimonthly monthly in July and Dec. **Print Method:** Offset. **Trim Size:** 11 x 16 1/2. **Cols./Page:** 6. **Col. Width:** 10 1/4 inches. **Col. Depth:** 15 1/2 inches. **Key Personnel:** Cathy Joyce, Manager, Advertising, phone: (916)733-0173; Bishop Jaime Soto, Publisher; Julie Sly, Editor, phone: (916)733-0175. **ISSN:** 0746-4185 (print). **Subscription Rates:** $15 Individuals /yr; $2 Single issue. **URL:** http://www.catholicheraldsacramento.org. **Ad Rates:** GLR $1.28; BW $1,953; 4C $824; SAU $6; PCI $21. **Remarks:** Accepts classified advertising. **Circ:** Paid 54500.

3599 ■ CDA Journal
California Dental Association
1201 K St., 14th Fl.
Sacramento, CA 95814
Phone: (916)443-0505
Free: 800-232-7645
Publisher's E-mail: contactcda@cda.org
Freq: Monthly. **Key Personnel:** Kerry K. Carney, DDS, Editor. **Alt. Formats:** PDF. **URL:** http://www.cda.org/member-resources/journal. **Remarks:** Accepts advertising. **Circ:** (Not Reported).

3600 ■ CDA Update
California Dental Association
1201 K St., 14th Fl.
Sacramento, CA 95814
Phone: (916)443-0505
Free: 800-232-7645
Publisher's E-mail: contactcda@cda.org
News publication for California Dental Association members. **Founded:** 1989. **Freq:** Monthly. **Print Method:** Offset. **Trim Size:** 11 x 15 1/2. **Cols./Page:** 4. **Col. Width:** 2 1/4 inches. **Col. Depth:** 14 inches. **Key Personnel:** Corey Gerhard, Manager, Advertising, phone: (916)554-5304. **ISSN:** 1048-3594 (print). **Subscription Rates:** $12 Members ADA; $24 Nonmembers; $36 Other countries; $6 Individuals back issue. **URL:** http://www.cda.org/about-cda/publications. **Ad Rates:** BW $2,050; 4C $825. **Remarks:** Accepts advertising. **Circ:** Paid 21000, Non-paid ‡104.

3601 ■ Cheer Biz News
Inside Publications, LLC
Magazine for owners and coaches of competitive cheer training and gymnastics centers. **Freq:** Bimonthly. **Key Personnel:** Amy Cogan, Publisher, Vice President. **URL:** http://www.cheerbiznews.com. **Ad Rates:** BW $4,500. **Remarks:** Accepts advertising. **Circ:** ‡7500.

3602 ■ Comstock's: Business Insight for California's Capital Region
Comstock Publishing Inc.
1006 4th St., 3rd Fl.
Sacramento, CA 95814
Phone: (916)364-1000
Fax: (916)364-0350
Magazine highlighting business and industry trends, community issues, business leaders and their companies, and regional issues. **Freq:** Monthly. **Key Personnel:** Winnie Comstock-Carlson, President, Publisher. **Subscription Rates:** $20 Individuals; $35 Two years; $50 Individuals 3 years. **URL:** http://www.comstocksmag.com. **Formerly**: Comstock's Business Magazine. **Remarks:** Accepts advertising. **Circ:** (Not Reported).

3603 ■ Contemporary School Psychology Journal
California Association of School Psychologists
1020 12th St., Ste. 200
Sacramento, CA 95814
Phone: (916)444-1595
Fax: (916)444-1597
Journal of the California Association of School Psychologists. **Freq:** Annual. **ISSN:** 2159--2020 (print); **EISSN:** 2161--1505 (electronic). **Subscription Rates:** $20 Individuals; $20 back issues. **Remarks:** Accepts advertising. **Circ:** (Not Reported).

3604 ■ The Current
American River College
4700 College Oak Dr.
Sacramento, CA 95841-4286
Phone: (916)484-8011
Publisher's E-mail: info@arc.losrios.edu
Community college newspaper. **Founded:** 1955. **Freq:** Weekly (Wed.). **Print Method:** Offset. **Cols./Page:** 5. **Col. Width:** 22 nonpareils. **Col. Depth:** 210 agate lines. **Key Personnel:** Ed Gebing, Managing Editor, Manager, Advertising; Barbara Harvey, Editor-in-Chief. **URL:** http://www.arcurrent.com. **Formerly**: The Beaver. **Ad Rates:** GLR $1; PCI $7. **Remarks:** Advertising accepted; rates available upon request. **Circ:** 5000.

3605 ■ The Daily Recorder: Legal/Governmental/R.E.
Daily Journal Corp.
901 H St., Ste. 312
Sacramento, CA 95814-1808
Phone: (916)444-2355
Fax: (916)444-0636
Newspaper (tabloid) on law, real estate, and state government. **Freq:** Daily (morn.). **Print Method:** Offset. **Trim Size:** 10 x 14. **Cols./Page:** 4. **Col. Width:** 2 3/8 inches. **Col. Depth:** 13 1/2 inches. **Key Personnel:** David Houston, Editor. **ISSN:** 0197--8055 (print). **Subscription Rates:** $316 Individuals. **URL:** http://www.dailyjournal.com. **Remarks:** Advertising accepted; rates available upon request. **Circ:** ‡1122.

3606 ■ Education California
Association of California School Administrators
1029 J St., Ste. 500
Sacramento, CA 95814
Phone: (916)444-3216
Fax: (916)444-3739
Free: 800-608-2272
Publisher's E-mail: info@acsa.org
Newspaper on state and national education issues with focus on school administrators. **Freq:** Irregular. **Key Personnel:** London Roberts, Editor. **ISSN:** 0740--0357 (print). **USPS:** 684-390. **Subscription Rates:** Included in membership. **URL:** http://www.acsa.org/publications. **Ad Rates:** BW $2666; PCI $43. **Remarks:** Accepts advertising. **Circ:** (Not Reported).

3607 ■ El Heraldo Catolico
El Heraldo Catolico
2110 Broadway
Sacramento, CA 95818
Phone: (916)733-0100
Fax: (916)733-0195
Catholic newspaper (Spanish). **Freq:** Monthly. **Print Method:** Offset. **Trim Size:** 11 x 17. **Cols./Page:** 6. **Col. Width:** 18 nonpareils. **Col. Depth:** 182 agate lines. **Key Personnel:** Arch. George H. Niederauer, Publisher; Julie Sly, Editor, Administrator; Marina Hinestrosa, Editor. **Subscription Rates:** $15 Individuals; $30 Out of country; $1 Single issue; Free for Spanish & Hispanic business establishments. **URL:** http://www.diocese-sacramento.org/elheraldo. **Ad Rates:** GLR $20.50; 4C $450; PCI $10. **Remarks:** Accepts advertising. **Circ:** 32500.

3608 ■ Fair Dealer
Western Fairs Association
1776 Tribute Rd., Ste. 210
Sacramento, CA 95815
Phone: (916)927-3100
Fax: (916)927-6397
Publisher's E-mail: info@fairsnet.org
Trade magazine covering the fair industry. **Freq:** Quarterly. **Print Method:** Web. **Trim Size:** 8 1/2 x 11. **Cols./Page:** 2 and 3. **Key Personnel:** Stephen Chambers, Executive Director; Carrie Wright, Program Director. **URL:** http://www.westernfairs.org/p/join/211. **Ad Rates:** BW $360; 4C $585,875. **Remarks:** Accepts advertising. **Circ:** Controlled 2000.

3609 ■ Fort Mill Times
McClatchy Newspapers Inc.
2100 Q St.
Sacramento, CA 95816-6899
Phone: (916)321-1855
Publisher's E-mail: pensions@mcclatchy.com
Community newspaper. **Freq:** Weekly (Wed.). **Print Method:** Offset. **Cols./Page:** 6. **Col. Width:** 12 picas. **Col. Depth:** 21 inches. **Key Personnel:** Debbie Abels, Publisher, phone: (803)329-4042; Jennifer Becknell, General Manager, phone: (803)329-4077; Mark Rochester, Editor. **Subscription Rates:** $0.40 Individuals daily (digital and print); $12.99 Individuals monthly (digital only); $99.99 Individuals annual (digital only). **URL:** http://www.fortmilltimes.com; http://www.mcclatchy.com/2012/06/29/2784/the-herald.html. **Ad Rates:** BW $774; 4C $987; PCI $6.55. **Remarks:** Accepts advertising. **Circ:** ‡19000.

3610 ■ Humor Times
Humor Times
PO Box 162429
Sacramento, CA 95816
Phone: (916)455-1217
Publication E-mail: info@humortimes.com
Magazine featuring cartoons and humor. **Freq:** Monthly. **Print Method:** Offset. **Trim Size:** 6 x 9. **Cols./Page:** 1. **Col. Width:** 48 nonpareils. **Col. Depth:** 91 agate lines. **Key Personnel:** James Israel, Editor, Founder, Publisher, Writer. **ISSN:** 0004--1823 (print). **Subscription Rates:** $24.95 Individuals; $9.95 Individuals online. **URL:** http://www.humortimes.com. **Remarks:** Accepts advertising. **Circ:** (Not Reported).

3611 ■ Inside Arden: Get Into the Neighborhood
Inside Publications
3104 O St., Ste. 120
Sacramento, CA 95816
Phone: (916)443-5087
Magazine covering interesting topics on Sacramento's people, places, and events. **Freq:** Monthly. **Key Personnel:** Cecily Hastings, Publisher; Marybeth Bizjak, Editor. **Subscription Rates:** $25 Individuals 3rd class mail. **URL:** http://www.insidepublications.org/. **Remarks:** Accepts advertising. **Circ:** Combined ♦**23000.**

3612 ■ Inside East Sacramento: Get Into the Neighborhood
Inside Publications
3104 O St., Ste. 120
Sacramento, CA 95816
Phone: (916)443-5087
Magazine providing informative news on East Sacramento's lifestyle. **Freq:** Monthly. **Key Personnel:** Cecily Hastings, Publisher; Marybeth Bizjak, Editor. **Subscription Rates:** $25 Individuals 3rd class mail. **URL:** http://www.insidepublications.org/. **Remarks:** Accepts advertising. **Circ:** Combined ♦**18500.**

3613 ■ Inside The City: Get Into the Neighborhood
Inside Publications
3104 O St., Ste. 120
Sacramento, CA 95816
Phone: (916)443-5087
Magazine aiming to provide positive and informative news on Sacramento's interesting people, places, and events. **Freq:** Monthly. **Key Personnel:** Cecily Hastings, Publisher; Marybeth Bizjak, Editor. **Subscription Rates:** $25 Individuals 3rd class mail. **URL:** http://www.insidepublications.org/. **Remarks:** Accepts advertising. **Circ:** Combined ♦**19193.**

3614 ■ International Travel News
Martin Publications Inc.
2120 28th St.
Sacramento, CA 95818
Phone: (916)457-3643
Publisher's E-mail: info@intltravelnews.com
Overseas travel magazine. **Freq:** Monthly. **Print Method:** Offset. **Trim Size:** 8 1/4 x 10 3/4. **Cols./Page:** 3. **Col. Width:** 2.25 inches. **Col. Depth:** 9.5 inches. **Key Personnel:** Armond Noble, Publisher; David Tykol, Editor. **USPS:** 115-550. **Subscription Rates:** $24 Individuals; $40 Two years; $57 Individuals three years; $40 Canada; $50 Individuals Mexico, W. Europe, Japan, New Zealand, Australia; $70 Other countries. **URL:** http://www.intltravelnews.com. **Ad Rates:** BW $1877. **Remarks:** Accepts advertising. **Circ:** 40000.

3615 ■ Journal of Addictions Nursing
Lippincott Williams and Wilkins
c/o Christine Vourakis, Ed.-in-Ch.
Scholarship of Nursing, California State University, Sacramento
Folsom Hall, 2nd Fl., Rm. 2009
7667 Folsom Blvd.
Sacramento, CA 95826
Phone: (916)278-4663
Fax: (916)278-6311

Circulation: ★ = AAM; △ or • = BPA; ♦ = CAC; ❑ = VAC; ⊕ = PO Statement; ‡ = Publisher's Report; Boldface figures = sworn; Light figures = estimated.

Publisher's E-mail: ronna.ekhouse@wolterskluwer.com
Journal for nursing addiction professionals. **Freq:** Quarterly. **Key Personnel:** Tonda Hughes, PhD, Board Member; Carol J. Boyd, PhD, Board Member; Christine Vourakis, Editor-in-Chief; Diane Snow, PhD, Associate Editor; William Lorman, PhD, Associate Editor; Karen Allen, PhD, Associate Editor. **ISSN:** 1088-4602 (print). **Subscription Rates:** £356 Institutions; $578 Institutions; €462 Institutions. **URL:** http://informahealthcare.com/journal/jan. **Circ:** (Not Reported).

3616 ■ Journal of the American Criminal Justice Association
American Criminal Justice Association - Lambda Alpha Epsilon
PO Box 601047
Sacramento, CA 95860-1047
Phone: (916)484-6553
Fax: (916)488-2227
Publisher's E-mail: acjalae@aol.com
Journal covering issues in criminal justice. **Freq:** Semiannual. **Key Personnel:** Fred R. Campbell, Editor. **URL:** http://www.acjalae.org/journal1.html. **Remarks:** Advertising not accepted. **Circ:** (Not Reported).

3617 ■ Journal of the California Dental Association
California Dental Association
1201 K St., 14th Fl.
Sacramento, CA 95814
Phone: (916)443-0505
Free: 800-232-7645
Publisher's E-mail: contactcda@cda.org
Professional magazine for dentists. **Freq:** Monthly. **Print Method:** Half Web Offset. **Trim Size:** 8 3/8 x 10 7/8. **Cols./Page:** 3. **Col. Width:** 13.5 picas. **Col. Depth:** 59.5 picas. **Key Personnel:** Patty Reyes, Coordinator; Kerry K. Carney, DDS, Editor-in-Chief; Corey Gerhard, Manager, Advertising, phone: (916)554-5304. **ISSN:** 1043--2256 (print). **Subscription Rates:** $18 Members; $40 Members domestic; $75 Nonmembers ADA; $80 Other countries; $10 Members back issue. **URL:** http://www.cda.org/member-resources/journal. **Ad Rates:** BW $2965. **Remarks:** Accepts classified advertising. **Circ:** Paid 26000.

3618 ■ Journal of California Law Enforcement
California Peace Officers' Association
555 Capitol Mall, Ste. 1495
Sacramento, CA 95814
Phone: (916)263-0541
Publisher's E-mail: cpoa@cpoa.org
Journal featuring articles on law enforcement, judicial and educational fields. **Freq:** Quarterly. **Subscription Rates:** $40 Members print and online; $55 Nonmembers print and online; $30 Members online only; $40 Nonmembers online only. **URL:** http://cpoa.org/resources/journal-of-ca-law-enforcement. **Remarks:** Advertising not accepted. **Circ:** (Not Reported).

3619 ■ Leadership Magazine
Association of California School Administrators
1029 J St., Ste. 500
Sacramento, CA 95814
Phone: (916)444-3216
Fax: (916)444-3739
Free: 800-608-2272
Publisher's E-mail: info@acsa.org
Practical journal for educators interested in new ways to be effective. **Founded:** 1971. **Freq:** 5/yr. **Print Method:** Offset. **Trim Size:** 8 1/2 x 11. **Cols./Page:** 3. **Col. Width:** 2 1/4 inches. **Col. Depth:** 10 inches. **ISSN:** 1531-3174 (print). **Subscription Rates:** $50 Individuals; $8 Single issue. **URL:** http://www.acsa.org/FunctionalMenuCategories/Media/LeadershipMagazine.aspx. **Formerly**: Thrust for Educational Leadership. **Ad Rates:** BW $1,520; 4C $2,320. **Remarks:** Accepts advertising. **Circ:** Combined 16500.

3620 ■ Leben: A Journal of Reformed Life
City Seminary Press
2150 River Plaza Dr., Ste. 150
Sacramento, CA 95833
Magazine featuring stories of the Protestant Reformers. **Freq:** Quarterly. **Subscription Rates:** $12.95 U.S. /year; $18.95 U.S. two years; $24.95 U.S. three years; $15.95 Other countries /year; $30.95 Other countries two years; $42.95 Other countries three years. **URL:** http://www.leben.us. **Remarks:** Advertising accepted; rates available upon request. **Circ:** (Not Reported).

3621 ■ Management of the California State Water Project
California Department of Water Resources
1416 9th St., Rm. 1620
Sacramento, CA 95814
Phone: (916)653-5791
Fax: (916)653-4684
Trade report covering water delivery in California. **Freq:** Annual. **Alt. Formats:** PDF. **URL:** http://www.water.ca.gov/swpao/bulletin_home.cfm. **Mailing address:** PO Box 942836, Sacramento, CA 94236. **Remarks:** Advertising not accepted. **Circ:** (Not Reported).

3622 ■ McGeorge Law Review: Water Law Symposium
University of the Pacific McGeorge School of Law
3200 5th Ave.
Sacramento, CA 95817
Phone: (916)739-7191
Publisher's E-mail: mcgeorge@pacific.edu
Journal covering legal issues. **Freq:** Quarterly. **Key Personnel:** Danielle Lenth, Editor-in-Chief. **Subscription Rates:** $20 Individuals. **URL:** http://www.mcgeorge.edu/Publications/McGeorge_Law_Review.htm. **Formerly**: Pacific Law Journal. **Remarks:** Advertising not accepted. **Circ:** (Not Reported).

3623 ■ Meeting Planner Guide
Sacramento Convention and Visitors Bureau
1608 St.
Sacramento, CA 95814
Phone: (916)808-7777
Free: 800-292-2334
Magazine containing information regarding the Sacramento Convention and Visitors Bureau, specially including information on convention planning. **Freq:** Periodic. **URL:** http://www.visitsacramento.com. **Circ:** (Not Reported).

3624 ■ The Miami Herald
McClatchy Newspapers Inc.
2100 Q St.
Sacramento, CA 95816-6899
Phone: (916)321-1855
General newspaper. **Freq:** Daily. **Print Method:** Letterpress, Offset, and Flexography. **Cols./Page:** 6. **Col. Width:** 22.5 nonpareils. **Col. Depth:** 315 agate lines. **ISSN:** 0898--865X (print). **Subscription Rates:** $3.99 Individuals /month (Sunday only); $10.99 Individuals /month (Thursday to Sunday). **Online:** ProQuest L.L.C.; McClatchy Newspapers Inc. McClatchy Newspapers Inc. **URL:** http://www.miamiherald.com. **Formerly**: The Miami Evening Record. **Remarks:** Accepts advertising. **Circ:** (Not Reported).

3625 ■ Military: The Press of Freedom
MHR Publishing Corp.
2120 28th St.
Sacramento, CA 95818
Phone: (916)457-8990
Publication E-mail: generalinfo@milmag.com
Magazine for American combat veterans. **Freq:** Monthly. **Key Personnel:** Armond M. Noble, Publisher. **ISSN:** 1046--2511 (print). **Subscription Rates:** $21 Individuals; $40 Canada and Mexico; $64 Other countries; $35 Two years; $49 Individuals 36 issues. **URL:** http://milmag.com. **Formerly**: Military History Review. **Ad Rates:** BW $374; PCI $18. **Remarks:** Accepts advertising. **Circ:** 23000.

3626 ■ Pacific McGeorge Global Business and Development Law Journal
University of the Pacific McGeorge School of Law
3200 5th Ave.
Sacramento, CA 95817
Phone: (916)739-7191
Publisher's E-mail: mcgeorge@pacific.edu
Journal featuring articles on legal and policy issues of local, national, and global concern. **Freq:** Quarterly. **Subscription Rates:** $20 Individuals. **URL:** http://www.mcgeorge.edu/Publications/Global_Business_and_Development_Law_Journal.htm. **Circ:** (Not Reported).

3627 ■ Philadelphia Daily News
McClatchy Newspapers Inc.
2100 Q St.
Sacramento, CA 95816-6899
Phone: (916)321-1855
Publisher's E-mail: pensions@mcclatchy.com
Newspaper (tabloid). **Freq:** Mon.-Sat. (eve.). **Print Method:** Letterpress. **Cols./Page:** 5. **Col. Width:** 2 1/16 inches. **Col. Depth:** 182 agate lines. **Key Personnel:** Terrance C. Z. Egger, Publisher. **Subscription Rates:** $6.60 Individuals /week. **URL:** http://www.phillydailynews.com. **Ad Rates:** PCI $120. **Remarks:** Accepts advertising. **Circ:** (Not Reported).

3628 ■ The Sacramento Bee
The Sacramento Bee
2100 Q St.
Sacramento, CA 95816
Phone: (916)321-1000
Publisher's E-mail: feedback@sacbee.com
General newspaper. **Founded:** Feb. 03, 1857. **Freq:** Daily and Sun. (morn.). **Print Method:** Mon.-Sun. (morn.). **Trim Size:** 13 1/2 x 22 5/16. **Cols./Page:** 6. **Col. Width:** 1.639 inches. **Col. Depth:** 294 agate lines. **Key Personnel:** Melanie Sill, Editor, phone: (916)321-1002; Cheryl Dell, Publisher, President, phone: (916)321-1885. **Subscription Rates:** $156 Individuals; $39 Individuals 13 weeks. **URL:** http://www.sacbee.com. **Remarks:** Accepts classified advertising. **Circ:** Mon.-Sat. 565000, Sun. 707000.

3629 ■ Sacramento Business Journal
Sacramento Business Journal
1400 X St.
Sacramento, CA 95818
Phone: (916)447-7661
Fax: (916)558-7898
Publisher's E-mail: sacramento@bizjournals.com
Local business newspaper. **Freq:** Weekly. **Key Personnel:** Terry Hillman, Publisher, phone: (916)558-7804; Jack Robinson, Editor, phone: (916)558-7862; Gary Chazen, Managing Editor, phone: (916)558-7865. **Subscription Rates:** $115 Individuals print & digital. **Online:** American City Business Journals Inc. **URL:** http://www.bizjournals.com/sacramento. **Remarks:** Advertising accepted; rates available upon request. **Circ:** (Not Reported).

3630 ■ Sacramento City College Express
Sacramento City College Store
3835 Freeport Blvd.
Sacramento, CA 95822-1318
Phone: (916)558-2421
Community college newspaper. **Freq:** Biweekly. **Print Method:** Offset. **Cols./Page:** 5. **Col. Width:** 28 nonpareils. **Col. Depth:** 195 agate lines. **Key Personnel:** Serina Martin, Editor-in-Chief; Zack Schmitz, Manager, Advertising; Nicole Head, Editor. **URL:** http://saccityexpress.com. **Ad Rates:** BW $450. **Remarks:** Accepts advertising. **Circ:** Free 3000.

3631 ■ The Sacramento Gazette: Sacramento's Weekly Newspaper
The Sacramento Gazette
555 University Ave., Ste. 126
Sacramento, CA 95825-6584
Phone: (916)567-9654
Fax: (916)567-9653
Publication E-mail: sacgazette@aol.com
General newspaper. **Freq:** Weekly (Fri.). **Print Method:** Web offset. **Trim Size:** 10 13/16 x 13 15/16. **Cols./Page:** 4. **Col. Width:** 28 nonpareils. **Col. Depth:** 182 agate lines. **Key Personnel:** David A. Fong, Editor. **ISSN:** 1089-9618 (print). **Subscription Rates:** $79.75 Individuals 52 issues; $144.75 Two years; $5 Single issue. **URL:** http://www.sacgazette.com/. **Ad Rates:** GLR $1.65; BW $712.50; PCI $14.25. **Remarks:** Accepts advertising. **Circ:** Paid 1480.

3632 ■ Sacramento Hispanic
Sacramento Hispanic Chamber of Commerce
1491 River Park Dr., Ste. 101
Sacramento, CA 95815-4531
Phone: (916)486-7700
Fax: (916)486-7728
Magazine containing information about businesses in Sacramento, CA. **Freq:** Monthly. **Subscription Rates:** Free. **Alt. Formats:** PDF. **URL:** http://www.sachcc.org/community/SacramentoHispanic/index.html. **Remarks:** Accepts advertising. **Circ:** Combined 2500, 1000.

3633 ■ Sacramento Magazine
Sacramento Magazines Corp.
231 Lathrop Way, Suite A
Sacramento, CA 95815
Phone: (916)426-1720
Publisher's E-mail: wine@sacmag.com
Regional interest magazine serving the five county

Sacramento region. **Freq:** Monthly. **Print Method:** Offset. **Trim Size:** 8 1/8 x 10 7/8. **Cols./Page:** 3. **Col. Width:** 27 nonpareils. **Col. Depth:** 140 agate lines. **Key Personnel:** Krista Minard, Editor; Joe Chiodo, Publisher, Director, Advertising; Darlena Belushin McKay, Managing Editor. **ISSN:** 0191--8796 (print). **Subscription Rates:** $12 Individuals; $20 Two years. **URL:** http://www.sacmag.com. **Remarks:** Advertising accepted; rates available upon request. **Circ:** Combined 42895.

3634 ■ Sacramento News & Review
News & Review
1124 Del Paso Blvd.
Sacramento, CA 95815
Phone: (916)498-1234
Fax: (916)498-7920
Publication E-mail: sactoletters@newsreview.com
Community newspaper. (Tabloid). **Founded:** 1989. **Freq:** Weekly (Thurs.). **Key Personnel:** Jeff von Kaenel, Chief Executive Officer, President; Melinda Welsh, Editor. **Subscription Rates:** $50 By mail; $25 By mail 6 months. **URL:** http://www.newsreview.com/sacramento/home. **Formerly:** News & Review. **Remarks:** Accepts advertising. **Circ:** Free ‡71073, Paid ‡13, Combined ‡71086.

3635 ■ Sacramento Observer
Observer Newspapers
2330 Alhambra Blvd.
Sacramento, CA 95817
Phone: (916)452-4781
Fax: (916)452-7744
Black community newspaper. **Freq:** Weekly (Thurs.). **Print Method:** Offset. **Trim Size:** 10 x 15. **Cols./Page:** 5 and 6. **Key Personnel:** Dr. William H. Lee, Publisher; Joe Stinson, Director, Sales; Larry Lee, Chief Executive Officer, President. **URL:** http://sacobserver.com. **Ad Rates:** 4C $700. **Remarks:** Accepts advertising. **Circ:** ‡49090.

3636 ■ San Francisco Estuary and Watershed Science
State of California Delta Stewardship Council
650 Capitol Mall, Fifth Fl.
Sacramento, CA 95814
Phone: (916)445-5511
Fax: (916)445-7297
Publisher's E-mail: help@solicitation.calwater.ca.gov
Journal focusing on all aspects of San Francisco Bay-Delta estuary, its watershed, and adjacent coastal ocean. **Freq:** Quarterly. **ISSN:** 1546--2366 (print). **Subscription Rates:** Free. **URL:** http://escholarship.org/uc/jmie_sfews. **Circ:** (Not Reported).

3637 ■ Sierra Sacramento Valley Medicine
Media Marketing
5380 Elvas Ave., Ste. 101
Sacramento, CA 95819
Phone: (916)452-2671
Fax: (916)452-2690
Publisher's E-mail: info@ssvms.org
Professional medical journal. **Freq:** Bimonthly. **Print Method:** Offset. **Trim Size:** 8 x 11. **Key Personnel:** Ted Fourkas, Managing Editor; Chris Stincelli, Associate Director; John Loofbourow, MD, Editor; Bill Sandberg, Executive Director. **ISSN:** 0886--2826 (print). **USPS:** 753-570. **Subscription Rates:** $26 Individuals. **URL:** http://www.ssvms.org; http://www.ssvms.org/Publications/SSVMedicine.aspx. **Formerly:** Sacramento Medicine. **Ad Rates:** 4C $1500, inside cover; 4C $1200, full page; 4C $850, 1/2 page; 4C $590, 1/3 page; 4C $400, 1/4 page. **Remarks:** Advertising accepted; rates available upon request. **Circ:** Controlled ‡2500.

3638 ■ The State Hornet
The State Hornet
California State University
6000 J St., University Union
Sacramento, CA 95819-6102
Phone: (916)278-6584
Publisher's E-mail: hornetop@csus.edu
College newspaper. **Freq:** Weekly. **Key Personnel:** Rachel Rosenbaum, Managing Editor. **URL:** http://www.statehornet.com. **Remarks:** Advertising accepted; rates available upon request. **Circ:** ‡12000.

3639 ■ Vida en el Valle
McClatchy Newspapers Inc.
2100 Q St.
Sacramento, CA 95816-6899
Phone: (916)321-1855
Publisher's E-mail: pensions@mcclatchy.com
Community newspaper (Spanish). **Freq:** Weekly. **Key Personnel:** Bill Gutierrez, Manager, Sales, phone: (559)441-6405; Juan Esparza Loera, Editor, phone: (559)441-6781. **Remarks:** Accepts advertising. **Circ:** (Not Reported).

3640 ■ Visitor Guide
Sacramento Convention and Visitors Bureau
1608 St.
Sacramento, CA 95814
Phone: (916)808-7777
Free: 800-292-2334
Magazine containing information regarding convention planning information. **Freq:** 3/year. **URL:** http://www.visitsacramento.com/visit/visitors-guide/. **Remarks:** Accepts advertising. **Circ:** (Not Reported).

3641 ■ The Way of St. Francis
Franciscan Friars Province of Saint Barbara
c/o David Elliott, Ed.
1112 26th St.
Sacramento, CA 95816-5610
Phone: (916)443-5717
Fax: (916)443-2019
Publication E-mail: theway@sbofm.org
Magazine presenting Franciscan vision and spirituality applied to today's issues. **Freq:** Bimonthly. **Print Method:** Offset. **Trim Size:** 5 1/2 x 8 1/2. **Cols./Page:** 1. **Col. Width:** 3 3/4 inches. **Col. Depth:** Varies INS. **Key Personnel:** David Eliott, Editor. **ISSN:** 0273--8295 (print). **Subscription Rates:** $15 Individuals; $30 Two years; $20 Out of country. **URL:** http://www.sbfranciscans.org/franciscan-materials/way-st-francis. **Remarks:** Advertising not accepted. **Circ:** Controlled 5000.

3642 ■ Western City
League of California Cities
1400 K St., Ste. 400
Sacramento, CA 95814
Phone: (916)658-8200
Fax: (916)658-8240
Freq: Monthly. **Print Method:** Offset. **Trim Size:** 8 1/2 x 11. **Cols./Page:** 3. **Col. Width:** 2.25 picas. **Col. Depth:** 60 picas. **Key Personnel:** Eva Spiegel, Managing Editor, phone: (916)658-8228; Jude Hudson, Editor-in-Chief, phone: (916)658-8234; Pam Maxwell-Blodgett, Manager, Advertising, fax: (916)647-0705. **Subscription Rates:** $39 Individuals 1 year; $63 Two years; $52 Other countries 1 year; $26.50 Students 1 year. **URL:** http://www.westerncity.com; http://www.cacities.org/Top/Western-City-Magazine.aspx. **Ad Rates:** BW $2700, full page; 4C $1300; BW $2200, 1/2 page island; BW $1950, 1/2 page horizontal. **Remarks:** Accepts advertising. **Circ:** Combined ‡9358.

3643 ■ WMA Reporter
Western Manufactured Housing Communities Association
455 Capitol Mall, Ste. 800
Sacramento, CA 95814-4420
Phone: (916)448-7002
Fax: (916)448-7085
Magazine featuring articles by industry experts, providing valuable management tips, information on property rights, legislation, utility systems, legal issues and a host of other topics. **Freq:** Monthly. **Key Personnel:** Regina Sanchez, Director. **Subscription Rates:** Included in membership. **URL:** http://www.wma.org/wma-reporter. **Ad Rates:** BW $565, full page - members; BW $330, half page - members; BW $1130, full page - nonmember; BW $660, half page - nonmember. **Remarks:** Accepts advertising. **Circ:** (Not Reported).

3644 ■ KBAA-FM - 103.3
500 Media Pl.
Sacramento, CA 95815
Format: Hispanic. **Owner:** Bustos Media L.L.C., 5110 SE Stark St., Portland, OR 97215. **Wattage:** 530. **URL:** http://www.bustosmedia.com.

3645 ■ KBBU-FM - 93.9
500 Media Pl.
Sacramento, CA 95815
Phone: (209)526-5352
Format: Adult Contemporary; Ethnic; Top 40; Tejano; Classic Rock; Alternative/New Music/Progressive. **Operating Hours:** Continuous. **Ad Rates:** Advertising accepted; rates available upon request. **URL:** http://www.radiolazer.com.

3646 ■ KBEB-FM - 92.5
1440 Ethan Way, Ste. 200
Sacramento, CA 95825
Phone: (916)929-5325
Format: Adult Contemporary. **Owner:** iHeartMedia Inc., 200 E Basse Rd., San Antonio, TX 78209, Ph: (210)832-3314. **Formerly:** KGBY-FM. **Key Personnel:** Paul Boris, Contact, paulboris@my925radio.com. **Wattage:** 50,000. **Ad Rates:** Noncommercial. **URL:** http://www.my925radio.com.

3647 ■ KBMB-FM - 103.5
1436 Auburn Blvd.
Sacramento, CA 95815
Phone: (916)646-4000
Format: Hip Hop. **Operating Hours:** Continuous. **Ad Rates:** Advertising accepted; rates available upon request. **URL:** http://www.hot1035.com.

KBMG-FM - See Evanston, WY

3648 ■ KBZC-FM - 106.5
5345 Madison Ave.
Sacramento, CA 95841
Phone: (916)334-7777
Format: Adult Contemporary. **Networks:** CBS. **Formerly:** KWOD-FM. **Operating Hours:** Continuous. **ADI:** Sacramento-Stockton, CA. **Wattage:** 50,000. **Ad Rates:** $150-275 for 60 seconds. **URL:** http://www.star1065.com.

3649 ■ KCCL-FM - 92.1
298 Commerce Cir.
Sacramento, CA 95815
Phone: (916)576-7333
Fax: (916)929-5330
Format: Adult Contemporary. **Networks:** Independent. **Owner:** Harlan Communications Inc., at above address. **Founded:** 1974. **Formerly:** KXEZ-FM; KHEX-FM; KXCL-FM. **Operating Hours:** Continuous; 100% local. **ADI:** Sacramento-Stockton, CA. **Wattage:** 25,000 ERP. **Ad Rates:** $19-24 per unit. Combined advertising rates available with KUBA-AM. **URL:** http://www.1015khits.com.

3650 ■ KCRA 3 - 3
Three Television Cir.
Sacramento, CA 95814
Phone: (916)446-3333
Format: News. **Networks:** NBC. **Owner:** Hearst Television Inc., 300 W 57th St., New York, NY 10019-3741, Ph: (212)887-6800, Fax: (212)887-6855. **Founded:** 1955. **Operating Hours:** Continuous. **Ad Rates:** Advertising accepted; rates available upon request. **URL:** http://www.kcra.com.

3651 ■ KCSO-TV - 33
500 Media Pl.
Sacramento, CA 95815
Phone: (916)567-3300
Format: Commercial TV. **Networks:** Univision. **Owner:** Univision Communication Inc., 1999 Ave. of the Stars, Ste. 3050, Los Angeles, CA 90067, Ph: (310)556-7665, Fax: (310)556-7615. **Founded:** Sept. 07, 2006. **Operating Hours:** Continuous; 60% network, 40% local. **ADI:** Sacramento-Stockton, CA. **Key Personnel:** Paul Schafer, Gen. Sales Mgr.; Mark Irons, Production Mgr.; Paul Johnson, Chief Engineer; Steve Stuck, Gen. Mgr.; Joe Cruz, Sales Mgr.; Carolina Rojas-Gore, Director. **Ad Rates:** Noncommercial.

3652 ■ KDEE 97.5 FM - 97.7
1600 Sacramento Inn Way, Ste. 232
Sacramento, CA 95815
Phone: (916)921-5333
Fax: (916)463-0190
Email: info@kdeefm.org
Format: Eclectic; Talk. **Owner:** California Black Chamber of Commerce Foundation, 2951 Sunrise Blvd., Rancho Cordova, CA 95742. **Ad Rates:** Advertising accepted; rates available upon request. **URL:** http://www.kdeefm.org.

3653 ■ KDND-FM - 107.9
5345 Madison Ave.
Sacramento, CA 95841

Circulation: ★ = AAM; △ or • = BPA; ♦ = CAC; ❑ = VAC; ⊕ = PO Statement; ‡ = Publisher's Report; Boldface figures = sworn; Light figures = estimated.

Phone: (916)334-7777
Format: Contemporary Hit Radio (CHR). **Networks:** Independent. **Owner:** Entercom Communications Corp., 401 City Ave., Ste. 809, Bala Cynwyd, PA 19004-1130, Ph: (610)660-5610, Fax: (610)660-5620. **Founded:** 1945. **Operating Hours**: Continuous. **ADI**: Sacramento-Stockton, CA. **Wattage**: 50,000. **Ad Rates:** Advertising accepted; rates available upon request. **URL:** http://www.entercom.com.

3654 ■ KEAR-FM - 88.1
290 Hegenberger Rd.
Oakland, CA 94621
Phone: (510)568-6200
Fax: (510)568-6190
Free: 800-543-1495
Format: Religious; Educational. **Networks:** Family Stations Radio. **Owner:** Family Stations Inc., 290 Hegenberger Rd., Oakland, CA 94621, Free: 800-543-1495. **Founded:** 1959. **Operating Hours**: Continuous; 90% network, 10% local. **ADI**: Sacramento-Stockton, CA. **Key Personnel:** Matthew Pearce, Contact, matthew@familyradio.com. **Wattage**: 8,400. **Ad Rates:** Noncommercial. **URL:** http://www.familyradio.org.

3655 ■ KEBR-FM - 88.1
4135 Northgate Blvd., Ste. 1
Sacramento, CA 95834-1226
Format: Religious. **Networks:** Family Stations Radio. **Founded:** 1992. **Operating Hours**: Continuous. **Key Personnel:** Peggy Renschler, Station Mgr. **Wattage**: 3,100. **Ad Rates:** Noncommercial. **URL:** http://www.familyradio.org.

3656 ■ KFBK-AM - 1530
1440 Ethan Way, Ste. 200
Sacramento, CA 95825
Phone: (916)929-5325
Free: 800-282-2882
Email: news@kfbk.com
Format: News; Talk. **Networks:** ABC; CNN Radio. **Founded:** 1922. **Operating Hours**: Continuous. **ADI**: Sacramento-Stockton, CA. **Wattage**: 118,000. **Ad Rates:** Noncommercial. **URL:** http://www.kfbk.com.

3657 ■ KFIA-AM - 710
1425 River Park Dr., Ste. 520
Sacramento, CA 95815
Phone: (916)924-0710
Email: info@kfia.com
Format: News. **Owner:** Salem Media Group Inc., 4880 Santa Rosa Rd., Camarillo, CA 93012, Ph: (805)987-0400, Fax: (805)384-4520. **Founded:** 1979. **Operating Hours**: Continuous. **Local Programs**: *The Eric Hogue Show*, Monday Tuesday Wednesday Thursday Friday 5:00 p.m. **Wattage**: 25,000. **URL:** http://www.kfia.com.

3658 ■ K45HC - 45
PO Box A
Santa Ana, CA 92711
Phone: (714)832-2950
Free: 888-731-1000
Owner: Trinity Broadcasting Network Inc., PO Box A, Santa Ana, CA 92711, Ph: (714)832-2950, Free: 888-731-1000. **URL:** http://www.tbn.org.

3659 ■ KFYE-FM - 106.3
1425 N Market Blvd.
Sacramento, CA 95834
Phone: (707)528-9236
Fax: (707)528-9246
Free: 800-525-5683
Email: klove@klove.com
Format: Contemporary Christian. **Networks:** Independent. **Owner:** Educational Media Foundation, 5700 W Oaks Blvd., CA 95765, Free: 800-800434-8400. **Founded:** 1991. **Formerly**: KJET-FM; KLVS-FM; KLVK-FM. **Operating Hours**: Continuous. **Key Personnel:** Dick Jenkins, President; Mike Novak, Prog. Dir., VP; Lloyd Parker, Gen. Mgr.; Sam Wallington, Dir. of Engg. **Wattage**: 16,000. **Ad Rates:** Noncommercial. **URL:** http://www.klove.com.

3660 ■ KHTK-AM - 1140
5244 Madison Ave.
Sacramento, CA 95841
Phone: (916)338-9200
Free: 800-920-1140
Format: Sports. **Networks:** Independent. **Owner:** CBS Radio Inc., 1271 Avenue of the Americas, 44th Fl., New York, NY 10020-1401, Ph: (212)649-9600. **Founded:** 1926. **Operating Hours**: Continuous. **ADI**: Sacramento-Stockton, CA. **Key Personnel:** Scott Marsh, Sales Mgr., scott.marsh@cbsradio.com; Danny Irwin, Promotions Dir., daniel.irwin@cbsradio.com. **Wattage**: 50,000. **Ad Rates:** Advertising accepted; rates available upon request. **URL:** http://sacramento.cbslocal.com/category/sports.

3661 ■ KHYL-FM - 101.1
1440 Ethan Way, Ste. 200
Sacramento, CA 95825
Phone: (916)929-5325
Fax: (916)925-0118
Format: Hip Hop; Blues. **Networks:** Independent. **Founded:** 1961. **Operating Hours**: Continuous. **ADI**: Sacramento-Stockton, CA. **Wattage**: 36,700. **Ad Rates:** Advertising accepted; rates available upon request. **URL:** http://www.v1011fm.com.

3662 ■ KKFS-FM - 103.9
1425 River Park Dr., Ste. 520
Sacramento, CA 95815
Phone: (916)924-0710
Fax: (916)924-1587
Free: 800-826-3637
Email: info@1039thefish.com
Format: Contemporary Christian. **Wattage**: 6,000. **Ad Rates:** Advertising accepted; rates available upon request. **URL:** http://www.1039thefish.com.

3663 ■ KKTO-FM - 90.5
7055 Folsom Blvd.
Sacramento, CA 95826-2625
Phone: (916)278-8900
Fax: (916)278-8989
Format: Classical. **Key Personnel:** Joe Barr, News Dir. **Ad Rates:** Noncommercial. **URL:** http://www.capradio.org.

3664 ■ KLIB-AM - 1110
3463 Ramona Ave.
Sacramento, CA 95826
Format: Ethnic. **Owner:** Multicultural Radio Broadcasting Inc., 27 William St., 11th Fl., New York, NY 10005, Ph: (212)966-1059, Fax: (212)966-9580. **Key Personnel:** Julie Re, Contact, julier@mrbi.net.

3665 ■ KLMG-FM - 94.3
500 Media Pl.
Sacramento, CA 95815
Phone: (916)368-6300
Fax: (916)441-6480
Free: 888-664-4949
Format: Hispanic. **Owner:** Bustos Media L.L.C., 5110 SE Stark St., Portland, OR 97215. **ADI**: Sacramento-Stockton, CA. **Key Personnel:** John Bustos, Gen. Mgr., jbustos@bustosmedia.com. **URL:** http://radiolazer943.com.

3666 ■ KLVC-FM - 93.7
1425 N Market Blvd.
Sacramento, CA 95834
Free: 800-525-5683
Email: klove@klove.com
Format: Classic Rock. **Networks:** Independent. **Owner:** Educational Media Foundation, 5700 W Oaks Blvd., CA 95765, Free: 800-800434-8400. **Founded:** 1993. **Formerly**: WKXP-FM. **Operating Hours**: Continuous. **Key Personnel:** Mike Novak, Dir. of Programs, mnovak@klove.com; Ed Lenane, News Dir.; Sam Wallington, Engineer, samw@klove.com; Devona Porter, Contact. **Wattage**: 26,500. **Ad Rates:** Noncommercial. **URL:** http://www.klove.com/search/?q=klvc-fm%2093.7.

3667 ■ KNCI-FM - 105.1
5244 Madison Ave.
Sacramento, CA 95841
Phone: (916)338-9200
Free: 800-850-1051
Format: Country. **Networks:** Independent. **Owner:** CBS Radio Inc., 40 W 57th St., New York, NY 10019, Ph: (212)846-3939, Fax: (212)315-2162. **Founded:** 1960. **Operating Hours**: Continuous. **ADI**: Sacramento-Stockton, CA. **Key Personnel:** Mark Evans, Dir. of Programs; Matt Vieira, Promotions Dir. **Wattage**: 50,000. **Ad Rates:** $20-385 per unit. **URL:** http://www.kncifm.com.

3668 ■ KNTY-FM - 101.9
1436 Auburn Blvd.
Sacramento, CA 95815
Phone: (916)646-4000
Fax: (916)646-3237
Format: Country. **Operating Hours**: Continuous. **Key Personnel:** Jim Danzer, Gen. Sales Mgr., jdanzer@entravision.com. **Wattage**: 47,000. **Ad Rates:** Advertising accepted; rates available upon request. **URL:** http://www.1019thewolf.com.

3669 ■ KQCA-TV - 58
3 Television Cir.
Sacramento, CA 95814-0794
Fax: (916)441-4050
Email: web@kcra.com
Format: Commercial TV. **Networks:** United Paramount Network. **Owner:** Hearst Television Inc., 300 W 57th St., New York, NY 10019-3741, Ph: (212)887-6800, Fax: (212)887-6855. **Founded:** 1986. **Operating Hours**: 6 a.m.-5 a.m. **ADI**: Sacramento-Stockton, CA. **Wattage**: 005 Million. **Ad Rates:** Noncommercial. **URL:** http://www.kcra.com/my58-advertise/index.html.

3670 ■ KQJK-FM - 93.7
1545 River Park Dr., Ste. 500
Sacramento, CA 95815
Phone: (916)929-9370
Format: Adult Contemporary. **ADI**: Sacramento-Stockton, CA. **Ad Rates:** Advertising accepted; rates available upon request. **URL:** http://www.937jackfm.com.

3671 ■ KQNC-FM - 88.1
7055 Folsom Blvd.
Sacramento, CA 95826-2625
Phone: (916)278-8900
Fax: (916)278-8989
Free: 877-480-5900
Email: info@capradio.org
Format: Public Radio. **Owner:** Capital Public Radio Inc., at above address. **Founded:** 2003. **Operating Hours**: Continuous. **Key Personnel:** Mark Jones, Production Mgr.; Rick Eytcheson, Gen. Mgr., President. **Ad Rates:** Underwriting available. **URL:** http://www.capradio.org.

3672 ■ KRCX-FM - 99.9
1436 Auburn Blvd.
Sacramento, CA 95815
Phone: (916)646-4000
Fax: (916)646-3237
Format: Hispanic. **Key Personnel:** Walter F. Ulloa, Chairman, CEO; Allyson Maiman, Gen. Mgr. **Ad Rates:** Noncommercial. **URL:** http://www.entravision.com.

3673 ■ KRXQ-FM - 93.7
5345 Madison, Ste. 100
Sacramento, CA 95841-3109
Phone: (916)766-5000
Fax: (916)339-4293
Format: Album-Oriented Rock (AOR). **Networks:** Independent. **Owner:** Jacor Broadcasting Co., Columbus, OH, Ph: (614)249-7676. **Founded:** 1970. **Operating Hours**: Continuous. **ADI**: Sacramento-Stockton, CA. **Key Personnel:** Mike John, Gen. Mgr. **Wattage**: 25,000. **Ad Rates:** Advertising accepted; rates available upon request. **URL:** http://www.krxq.net/.

3674 ■ KSAC-AM
1909 7th St.
Sacramento, CA 95811
Phone: (916)553-3000
Fax: (916)553-3013
Format: Sports; Talk. **Networks:** NBC; CBS. **Owner:** Diamond Broadcasting, at above address. **Founded:** 1937. **Formerly**: KROY-AM. **Operating Hours**: Continuous. **Key Personnel:** Christine Craft, Contact, christine@1240talkcity.com. **Ad Rates:** Advertising accepted; rates available upon request. **URL:** http://radiosantisimosacramento.com.

3675 ■ KSEG-FM - 96.9
5345 Madison Ave.
Sacramento, CA 95841
Phone: (916)334-7777
Email: feedback@eagle969.com
Format: Classic Rock. **Owner:** Entercom Communications Corp., 401 City Ave., Ste. 809, Bala Cynwyd, PA 19004-1130, Ph: (610)660-5610, Fax: (610)660-5620. **Founded:** 1959. **Formerly**: KROY-FM. **Operating Hours**: Continuous. **Key Personnel:** Brian Lopez, Asst. Dir., Music Dir., brian@eagle969.com; Lizann Hunt, Promotions Dir., lhunt@entercom.com; Kat Maudru, Dir. of Pub. Prog. & Svcs., kmaudru@eagle969.com. **Watt-**

age: 50,000. **Ad Rates:** Advertising accepted; rates available upon request. **URL:** http://www.eagle969.com.

3676 ■ KSFM-FM - 102.5
280 Commerce Cir.
Sacramento, CA 95825
Phone: (916)923-6800
Format: Contemporary Hit Radio (CHR). **Networks:** Independent. **Owner:** CBS Radio Inc., 1271 Avenue of the Americas, 44th Fl., New York, NY 10020-1401, Ph: (212)649-9600. **Founded:** 1961. **Operating Hours:** Continuous. **ADI:** Sacramento-Stockton, CA. **Key Personnel:** Byron Kennedy, Prog. Dir., byron.kennedy@cbsradio.com; Kim Piazza, Promotions Dir., kmpiazza@ksfm.com; Christian Salisbury, Gen. Sales Mgr., christian.salisbury@cbsradio.com. **Wattage:** 50,000. **Ad Rates:** Advertising accepted; rates available upon request. **URL:** http://ksfm.cbslocal.com.

3677 ■ KSMH-AM - 1620
2628 El Camino Ave.
Sacramento, CA 95821
Phone: (916)880-4040
Format: Religious. **Ad Rates:** Noncommercial. **URL:** http://ihradio.com.

3678 ■ KSQR-AM - 1240
1909 7th St.
Sacramento, CA 95811
Phone: (916)442-7389
Format: Talk. **ADI:** Sacramento-Stockton, CA. **Ad Rates:** Advertising accepted; rates available upon request. **URL:** http://radiosantisimosacramento.com.

3679 ■ KSSU-AM - 1580
6000 J St.
Sacramento, CA 95819-6011
Phone: (916)278-3343
Format: Alternative/New Music/Progressive. **Owner:** Associated Students Inc., University Student Union, Rm. 316 & 317 Keats Campus Bldg., Fresno, CA 93740-8023, Ph: (559)278-2656, Fax: (559)278-2720. **Founded:** 1991. **Formerly:** KEDG-AM. **Operating Hours:** Continuous. **ADI:** Sacramento-Stockton, CA. **Key Personnel:** Laura Smith, Music Dir., music@kssu.com; Brian Bautista, Station Mgr., manager@kssu.com. **Wattage:** 002. **Ad Rates:** Noncommercial. **URL:** http://www.kssu.com.

3680 ■ KSTE-AM - 650
1545 River Park Dr., Ste. 500
Sacramento, CA 95815
Phone: (916)576-1578
Fax: (916)920-8362
Format: Talk. **Key Personnel:** John Myers, News Dir., johnmyers@clearchannel.com. **Wattage:** 21,500. **Ad Rates:** Advertising accepted; rates available upon request. **URL:** http://kste.iheart.com.

3681 ■ KTKZ-AM - 1380
1425 River Park Dr., Ste. 520
Sacramento, CA 95815
Phone: (916)924-0710
Fax: (916)924-1587
Format: Talk. **Ad Rates:** Advertising accepted; rates available upon request. **URL:** http://am1380theanswer.com.

3682 ■ KTKZ-FM - 105.5
1425 River Park Dr., Ste. 520
Sacramento, CA 95815
Phone: (916)924-0710
Fax: (916)924-1587
Format: News; Talk. **Operating Hours:** Continuous. **Ad Rates:** Advertising accepted; rates available upon request. **URL:** http://www.am1380theanswer.com.

3683 ■ KTTA-FM - 97.9
200 S A St., Ste. 400
Sacramento, CA 95815
Phone: (805)240-2070
Format: World Beat; Ethnic. **Operating Hours:** Continuous. **Ad Rates:** Advertising accepted; rates available upon request. **URL:** http://www.latino979.com/formas-de-contacto.html.

3684 ■ K238AY-FM - 95.5
PO Box 391
Twin Falls, ID 83303
Fax: (208)736-1958
Free: 800-357-4226
Format: Religious; Contemporary Christian. **Owner:** CSN International, PO Box 391, Twin Falls, ID 83303, Ph: (208)736-1958, Fax: (208)736-1958, Free: 800-357-4226. **URL:** http://www.csnradio.com.

3685 ■ KTXL FOX40 - 40
4655 Fruitridge Rd.
Sacramento, CA 95820-5299
Phone: (916)454-4422
Fax: (916)739-1079
Email: news@fox40.com
Format: Commercial TV. **Networks:** Fox; Independent. **Owner:** The Tribune Media Co., 435 N Michigan Ave., Chicago, IL 60611-4066, Ph: (312)222-9100, Fax: (312)222-4206, Free: 800-874-2863. **Founded:** 1968. **Operating Hours:** Continuous. **ADI:** Sacramento-Stockton, CA. **Wattage:** 50,000. **Ad Rates:** Advertising accepted; rates available upon request. **URL:** http://www.fox40.com.

KULE-AM - See Wenatchee, WA

3686 ■ KVIE-TV - 6
2030 W El Camino Ave.
Sacramento, CA 95833
Phone: (916)929-5843
Free: 800-347-5843
Email: member@kvie.org
Format: Public TV. **Networks:** Public Broadcasting Service (PBS). **Founded:** 1959. **Operating Hours:** Continuous. **ADI:** Sacramento-Stockton, CA. **Key Personnel:** David Lowe, President, Gen. Mgr. **Local Programs:** *The Leo Buscaglia Specials.* **Wattage:** 100,000. **Ad Rates:** Noncommercial. **URL:** http://www.kvie.org.

3687 ■ KXJS-FM - 88.7
7055 Folsom Blvd.
Sacramento, CA 95826-2625
Phone: (916)278-8900
Fax: (916)278-8989
Free: 877-480-5900
Email: info@capradio.org
Format: Public Radio. **Owner:** Capital Public Radio Inc., at above address. **Founded:** 2003. **Operating Hours:** Continuous. **Ad Rates:** Underwriting available. **URL:** http://www.capradio.org.

3688 ■ KXJZ-FM - 90.9
7055 Folsom Blvd.
Sacramento, CA 95826-2625
Phone: (916)278-8900
Fax: (916)278-8989
Free: 877-480-5900
Email: info@capradio.org
Format: Jazz; Public Radio; Classical; News. **Founded:** 1991. **Wattage:** 50,000. **Ad Rates:** Noncommercial. **URL:** http://www.capradio.org.

3689 ■ KXPR-FM - 88.9
7055 Folsom Blvd.
Sacramento, CA 95826-2625
Phone: (916)278-8900
Fax: (916)278-8989
Free: 877-480-5900
Email: info@capradio.org
Format: Classical. **Networks:** National Public Radio (NPR). **Owner:** California State University, 6000 J St., Sacramento, CA 95819, Ph: (916)278-6011. **Founded:** 1979. **Operating Hours:** Continuous; 20% network, 80% local. **ADI:** Sacramento-Stockton, CA. **Key Personnel:** Barbara O'Connor, Secretary. **Wattage:** 50,000. **Ad Rates:** Underwriting available. **URL:** http://www.capradio.org.

3690 ■ KXSE-FM - 104.3
1436 Auburn Blvd.
Sacramento, CA 95815
Phone: (916)646-4000
Fax: (916)646-3237
Format: Hispanic. **Owner:** Entravision Communications Corporation, 2425 Olympic Blvd., Ste. 6000 W, Santa Monica, CA 90404-4030, Ph: (310)447-3870, Fax: (310)447-3899. **ADI:** Sacramento-Stockton, CA. **Key Personnel:** Allyson Maiman, Gen. Mgr. **URL:** http://www.entravision.com.

3691 ■ KXSR-FM - 91.7
7055 Folsom Blvd.
Sacramento, CA 95826-2625
Format: Classical. **Founded:** 1306. **URL:** http://www.capradio.org.

3692 ■ KXTV-TV - 10
400 Broadway
Sacramento, CA 95818
Phone: (916)321-3300
Format: News. **Networks:** CBS. **Owner:** Gannett Company Inc., 7950 Jones Branch Dr., McLean, VA 22107-0150, Ph: (703)854-6089. **Operating Hours:** Continuous. **ADI:** Sacramento-Stockton, CA. **Ad Rates:** Noncommercial. **URL:** http://www.news10.net.

3693 ■ KYMX-FM - 96.1
280 Commerce Cir.
Sacramento, CA 95815-4212
Phone: (916)923-6800
Format: Adult Contemporary. **Owner:** CBS Radio Inc., 1271 Avenue of the Americas, 44th Fl., New York, NY 10020-1401, Ph: (212)649-9600. **Founded:** 1947. **Operating Hours:** Continuous. **ADI:** Sacramento-Stockton, CA. **Key Personnel:** Bryan Jackson, Dir. of Programs, bjackson@kymx.com. **Wattage:** 50,000. **URL:** http://kymx.cbslocal.com.

3694 ■ KZZO-FM - 100.5
280 Commerce Cir.
Sacramento, CA 95815
Phone: (916)923-6800
Format: Adult Contemporary. **Founded:** 1945. **Operating Hours:** Continuous. **ADI:** Sacramento-Stockton, CA. **Key Personnel:** Christian Salisbury, Gen. Sales Mgr., christian.salisbury@cbsradio.com. **Wattage:** 5,000 Day; 1,000 Night. **Ad Rates:** Advertising accepted; rates available upon request. **URL:** http://now100fm.cbslocal.com.

SAINT HELENA

W. CA. Napa Co. 50 mi. N. of San Francisco. Residential. Wineries. Agriculture.

3695 ■ St. Helena Star Online
Krsek Publishing L.P.
1200 Main St., Ste. C
Saint Helena, CA 94574-1901
Phone: (707)963-2731
Fax: (707)963-8957
Publication E-mail: dernst@sthelenastar.com
Community newspaper. **Freq:** Weekly (Thurs.). **Print Method:** Offset. **Cols./Page:** 6. **Col. Width:** 11.2 picas. **Col. Depth:** 21.5 inches. **Key Personnel:** David Stoneberg, Editor. **USPS:** 476-020. **Subscription Rates:** $35 Individuals; $52 Out of area daily and Sunday mail. **URL:** http://napavalleyregister.com/star. **Mailing address:** PO Box 346, Saint Helena, CA 94574-1901. **Remarks:** Accepts advertising. **Circ:** ‡12000.

3696 ■ KSHC-FM - 106.5
1777 Main St.
Saint Helena, CA 94574
Phone: (707)963-4461
Fax: (707)963-1159
Email: kshc@sabbathfellowship.org
Format: Religious; Easy Listening; Contemporary Christian. **Wattage:** 002 ERP. **URL:** http://www.shsda.org.

SALIDA

3697 ■ KQRP-FM - 106.1
PO Box 612
Salida, CA 95368
Phone: (209)545-4227
Format: News; Talk; Heavy Metal; Alternative/New Music/Progressive. **Founded:** 2000. **Ad Rates:** Noncommercial. **URL:** http://www.valleymedia.org.

SALINAS

W. CA. Monterey Co. 19 mi. E. of Monterey. Hartnell College. Manufactures canned foods, electrical fixtures. Ships lettuce. Diversified farming. Lettuce, sugar beets, artichokes, beans, peas, strawberries.

3698 ■ The Californian
Salinas Newspapers Inc.
123 W Alisal St.
Salinas, CA 93901
Phone: (831)424-2221
Fax: (831)754-4286

Circulation: ★ = AAM; △ or • = BPA; ♦ = CAC; ❑ = VAC; ⊕ = PO Statement; ‡ = Publisher's Report; Boldface figures = sworn; Light figures = estimated.

Free: 877-424-4917
General newspaper. **Founded:** 1871. **Freq:** Mon.-Sat. (morn.). **Print Method:** Offset. **Cols./Page:** 6 and 7. **Col. Width:** 11 and 9 picas. **Col. Depth:** 301 and 301 agate lines. **Subscription Rates:** $12.23 Individuals. **URL:** http://www.thecalifornian.com/. **Formerly:** The Salinas Californian. **Remarks:** Accepts advertising. **Circ:** Mon.-Fri. *17259, Sat. *19195.

3699 ■ KAXT-FM - 101.7
1 Robar Ctr., Ste. 201
Salinas, CA 93901
Operating Hours: Continuous;100% local. **Wattage:** 6,000. **Ad Rates:** $2-70 for 30 seconds; $2-70 for 60 seconds. **URL:** http://www.radiolazer.com/.

3700 ■ KCBA-TV - 35
1550 Moffett St.
Salinas, CA 93905
Phone: (831)422-3500
Format: News. **Networks:** Fox. **Owner:** iHeartMedia Inc., 200 E Basse Rd., San Antonio, TX 78209, Ph: (210)832-3314. **Founded:** 1981. **Operating Hours:** Continuous. **ADI:** Sacramento-Stockton, CA. **Wattage:** 2,328,000. **Ad Rates:** Advertising accepted; rates available upon request. **URL:** http://www.kcba.com.

3701 ■ KDBV-AM - 980
517 S Main St., Ste. 201
Salinas, CA 93901
Phone: (831)757-5911
Fax: (831)757-8015
Email: radsuprema@aol.com
Owner: Wolfhouse Radio Group, Inc., at above address, Ph: (831)757-1910, Fax: (831)771-1685. **Founded:** 1963. **Formerly:** KCTY-AM. **ADI:** Salinas-Monterey, CA. **Key Personnel:** Rachel Ybarra, Contact. **Ad Rates:** $50-80 for 60 seconds. Combined advertising rates available with KRAY-FM, KLXM-FM. **Mailing address:** PO Box 1939, Salinas, CA 93901. **URL:** http://www.radiovidaabundante.com/.

3702 ■ KDON-FM - 102.5
903 N Main St.
Salinas, CA 93906
Phone: (831)755-8181
Fax: (831)755-8193
Format: Contemporary Hit Radio (CHR). **Networks:** Independent. **Owner:** iHeartMedia Inc., 200 E Basse Rd., San Antonio, TX 78209, Ph: (210)832-3314. **Founded:** 1947. **Operating Hours:** Continuous. **ADI:** Salinas-Monterey, CA. **Key Personnel:** Rhonda McCormack, Gen. Mgr. **Wattage:** 18,500. **Ad Rates:** Advertising accepted; rates available upon request. **URL:** http://www.kdon.com.

3703 ■ KEXA-FM - 93.9
548 E Alisal St.
Salinas, CA 93905
Phone: (831)757-1910
Email: advertising@wolfhouseradio.net
Format: Hispanic. **Owner:** Wolfhouse Radio Group, Inc., at above address, Ph: (831)757-1910, Fax: (831)771-1685. **Key Personnel:** Don Cheto, Contact. **Wattage:** 5,000. **Mailing address:** PO Box 1939, Salinas, CA 93905. **URL:** http://www.wolfhouseradio.net/estaciones.

3704 ■ KHDC-FM - 90.9
161 Main St., Ste. 4
Salinas, CA 93901
Phone: (831)757-8039
Fax: (831)757-9854
Format: Hip Hop. **Owner:** Satellite Radio Bilingue, 5005 E Belmont Ave., Fresno, CA 93727, Ph: (559)455-5777. **Founded:** 1986. **Formerly:** KUBO-FM. **Operating Hours:** 4:00 p.m. - 12:00 a.m. Monday - Friday 5:00 a.m. - Midnight Saturday - Sunday. **ADI:** Salinas-Monterey, CA. **Key Personnel:** Delia Saldivar, Station Mgr., saldivard@radiobilingue.org; Hugo Morales, Exec. Dir., Founder. **Wattage:** 3,000. **Ad Rates:** Accepts Advertising. **URL:** http://www.radiobilingue.org.

3705 ■ KION-TV - 46
1550 Moffett St.
Salinas, CA 93905
Phone: (831)784-6300
Fax: (831)422-9365
Free: 888-678-2871
Format: Commercial TV. **Networks:** CBS. **Founded:** 1965. **Formerly:** KMST-TV; KCCN-TV. **Operating Hours:** Continuous. **Wattage:** 1,350. **Ad Rates:** Advertising accepted; rates available upon request. **URL:** http://www.kionrightnow.com.

3706 ■ KKMC-AM - 880
30 E San Joaquin St., Ste. 105
Salinas, CA 93901
Phone: (831)424-5562
Format: Religious. **Networks:** USA Radio; International Broadcasting; Sun Radio. **Owner:** Monterey County Broadcasters, Inc., at above address. **Operating Hours:** Continuous. **ADI:** Salinas-Monterey, CA. **Local Programs:** *Seeds for Life*, Monday Tuesday Wednesday Thursday Friday Sunday 6:30 a.m.; 5:30 p.m. 8:00 a.m.; 6:00 p.m. **Wattage:** 10,000 KW Day/1,000 Night. **Ad Rates:** Noncommercial. **URL:** http://www.kkmc.com.

3707 ■ KLVM-FM
8145 Prunedale North Rd.
Salinas, CA 93907-8826
Format: Contemporary Christian. **Wattage:** 450 ERP.

3708 ■ KOCN-FM - 105.1
903 N Main St.
Salinas, CA 93906
Phone: (831)755-8181
Free: 888-896-5626
Format: Oldies; Blues. **Networks:** ABC. **Owner:** iHeartMedia Inc., 200 E Basse Rd., San Antonio, TX 78209, Ph: (210)832-3314. **Founded:** 1974. **ADI:** Salinas-Monterey, CA. **Wattage:** 1,800 ERP. **Ad Rates:** Advertising accepted; rates available upon request. **URL:** http://www.1051kocean.com//main.html.

3709 ■ KRAY-FM - 103.5
PO Box 1939
Salinas, CA 93902
Phone: (831)766-1900
Format: Adult Contemporary. **Owner:** Wolfhouse Radio Group Inc., 548 E Alisal St., Ste. A, Salinas, CA 93905-2760, Ph: (831)757-1910, Fax: (831)757-1910. **Founded:** 1976. **Operating Hours:** Continuous. **ADI:** Salinas-Monterey, CA. **Key Personnel:** Ramon Castro, Gen. Mgr. **Wattage:** 10,000. **Ad Rates:** Advertising accepted; rates available upon request. $70 for 60 seconds. **URL:** http://wolfhouseradio.net.

3710 ■ KSBW-TV - 8
PO Box 81651
Salinas, CA 93912
Phone: (831)758-8888
Fax: (831)424-3750
Format: News. **Simulcasts:** KSBY. **Networks:** NBC. **Owner:** STC Broadcasting, 8202 E 21st St N Ste B, Wichita, KS 67206-2906, Ph: (316)652-0093. **Founded:** Sept. 11, 1953. **ADI:** Salinas-Monterey, CA. **Key Personnel:** Wendy Hillan, Gen. Sales Mgr., whillan@hearst.com. **Wattage:** 158,000. **Ad Rates:** Advertising accepted; rates available upon request. **URL:** http://www.KSBW.com.

3711 ■ KSEA-FM - 107.9
229 Pajaro St., Ste. 302D
Salinas, CA 93901
Phone: (831)754-1469
Fax: (831)754-1563
Format: Hispanic. **Owner:** Radio Campesina Network, 3602 W Thomas Rd., Ste. 6, Phoenix, AZ 85019. **Founded:** 1993. **ADI:** Salinas-Monterey, CA. **URL:** http://www.campesina.net.

3712 ■ KTGE-AM
548 E Alisal St.
Salinas, CA 93905
Phone: (408)757-1910
Fax: (408)757-9582
Format: Hispanic. **Networks:** Independent. **Owner:** TGR Broadcasting, at above address. **Founded:** 1987. **Key Personnel:** Hector Villalobos, Gen. Mgr. **Wattage:** 5,000 Day; 500 Night.

3713 ■ KTOM-AM - 1380
903 N Main St.
Salinas, CA 93906
Phone: (831)755-8181
Fax: (831)755-8193
Free: 800-660-5866
Simulcasts: KTOM-FM. **Founded:** 1972. **Operating Hours:** Continuous. **ADI:** Salinas-Monterey, CA. **Key Personnel:** Jess Gibbs, Asst. Dir., jess@ktom.com; Craig Hymovitz, Dir. of Sales; Eric Bishop, Contact, eric@ktom.com. **Wattage:** 5,000. **Ad Rates:** Advertising accepted; rates available upon request. **URL:** http://ktom.iheart.com.

3714 ■ KTOM-FM - 92.7
903 N Main St.
Salinas, CA 93906
Phone: (831)755-8181
Fax: (831)755-8193
Free: 800-660-5866
Format: Country. **Simulcasts:** KTOM-AM. **Networks:** ABC. **Owner:** iHeartMedia Inc., 200 E Basse Rd., San Antonio, TX 78209, Ph: (210)832-3314. **Founded:** 1972. **Operating Hours:** Continuous. **ADI:** Salinas-Monterey, CA. **Key Personnel:** Rhonda McCormack, Gen. Mgr. **Wattage:** 50,000 ERP. **Ad Rates:** Advertising accepted; rates available upon request. **URL:** http://www.ktom.com.

3715 ■ K252CK-FM - 98.3
PO Box 391
Twin Falls, ID 83303
Fax: (208)736-1958
Free: 800-357-4226
Format: Religious; Contemporary Christian. **Owner:** CSN International, PO Box 391, Twin Falls, ID 83303, Ph: (208)736-1958, Fax: (208)736-1958, Free: 800-357-4226. **ADI:** Salinas-Monterey, CA. **Key Personnel:** Don Mills, Prog. Dir., Music Dir.; Kelly Carlson, Dir. of Engg.; Ray Gorney, Asst. Dir. **Wattage:** 010. **URL:** http://www.csnradio.com.

3716 ■ KXSM-FM - 93.5
600 E Market St., Ste. 200
Salinas, CA 93905
Phone: (831)422-5019
Fax: (831)422-5027
Format: Hispanic. **Owner:** Lazer Broadcasting Corp., 200 S A St., Ste. 400, Oxnard, CA 93030, Ph: (805)240-2070, Fax: (805)240-5960. **Key Personnel:** Alfredo Plascencia, CEO, President, alfredop@radiolazer.com. **URL:** http://www.radiolazer.com.

SAN ANDREAS

C. CA. Calaveras Co. 40 mi. NE of Stockton. Residental. Gold mines. Agriculture. Cattle, sheep raising.

3717 ■ The Calaveras Enterprise
Calaveras First Newspapers
15 N Main St.
San Andreas, CA 95249
Phone: (209)754-3861
Fax: (209)754-1805
Free: 888-811-3861
Community newspaper. **Freq:** Semiweekly Tues. and Fri. **Key Personnel:** Stephen Crane, Editor; Ralph Alldredge, Owner, Publisher. **Subscription Rates:** $60 Individuals 1 year home delivery - Calaveras County; $55 Individuals 1 year home delivery senior rate (55+) - Calaveras County ; $45 Individuals 1 year postal delivery - Calaveras County ; $42 Individuals 1 Year (Senior 55+) postal delivery - Calaveras County ; $80 Two years postal delivery - Calaveras County; $72 Two years (Senior 55+) postal delivery - Calaveras County ; $65 Individuals 1 year postal delivery - out of County/State; $115 Two years postal delivery - out of County/State ; $30 online only. **URL:** http://www.calaverasenterprise.com. **Mailing address:** PO Box 1197, San Andreas, CA 95249. **Remarks:** Advertising accepted; rates available upon request. **Circ:** ‡5800.

SAN ANSELMO

W. CA. Marin Co. 20 mi. NW of San Francisco. Manufactures food specialties, automatic weighing machinery, milk products. Nursery.

3718 ■ Acoustic Guitar Magazine
Acoustic Guitar
PO Box 767
San Anselmo, CA 94979
Phone: (415)485-6946
Free: 800-827-6837
Publication E-mail: editors.ag@stringletter.com
Magazine for professional and amateur acoustic guitar enthusiasts offering advice on choosing, maintaining, and playing acoustic guitar. **Freq:** 8/year. **Print Method:** Web Offset. **Trim Size:** 8 3/8 x 10 7/8. **Key Personnel:** David A. Lusterman, Publisher. **ISSN:** 1044-9261 (print). **Subscription Rates:** $40 Individuals print/year; $32 Individuals print or online/month. **URL:** http://www.

acousticguitar.com; http://store.acousticguitar.com/collections/back-issues. **Ad Rates:** BW $3,690; 4C $5,320; PCI $155. **Remarks:** Accepts advertising. **Circ:** Paid ★**54202**.

3719 ■ Western & Eastern Treasures: World's Leading How-To Magazine For Metal Dectorists Since 1966
People's Publishing Co.
PO Box 219
San Anselmo, CA 94979
Phone: (415)454-3936
Publisher's E-mail: treasurenet@prodigy.net
How-to magazine covering metal detecting, gold prospecting, and all forms of treasure hunting. **Freq:** Monthly. **Print Method:** Offset. **Trim Size:** 8 x 10 7/8. **Cols./Page:** 3. **Col. Width:** 27 nonpareils. **Col. Depth:** 142 agate lines. **Key Personnel:** Rosemary Anderson, Editor; Steve Anderson, Manager, Advertising. **ISSN:** 0890--0876 (print). **Subscription Rates:** $37 Individuals print; $65 Two years print; $30 Individuals online. **URL:** http://www.wetreasures.com. **Ad Rates:** BW $900; 4C $1,665; PCI $55. **Remarks:** Accepts advertising. **Circ:** ‡60000.

SAN BERNARDINO

San Bernardino Co. San Bernardino Co. (SE). 60 m E of Los Angeles. San Bernardino Valley College. California State College. Foundry, steel mill, fruit packing. Cement, refrigerator cars, wine, liquor, dairy products, plumbing material, aerospace products manufactured.

3720 ■ Adapted Physical Activity Quarterly
Human Kinetics Inc.
c/o Terry Rizzo, Co-Editor
Dept. of Kinesiology, HP 120
California State University, San Bernardino
5500 University Pky.
San Bernardino, CA 92407-2397
Phone: (909)537-5355
Publisher's E-mail: info@hkusa.com
Journal on the study of physical activity for special populations. **Freq:** Quarterly January, April, July, and October. **Print Method:** Offset. **Trim Size:** 6 x 9. **Cols./Page:** 1. **Col. Width:** 65 nonpareils. **Col. Depth:** 108 agate lines. **Key Personnel:** Terry Rizzo, Advisor, Editor, phone: (909)537-5355; Marcel Bouffard, Advisor, Editor; Yeshayahu Hutzler, Editor. **ISSN:** 0736--5829 (print); **EISSN:** 1543--2777 (electronic). **Subscription Rates:** $96 Individuals online and print; $577 Institutions online and print; $77 Students online and print; $76 Individuals online only; $57 Students online only; $470 Institutions online only. **URL:** http://journals.humankinetics.com/APAQ. **Ad Rates:** BW $399. **Remarks:** Accepts advertising. **Circ:** Paid ‡977, ‡26.

Colton Courier - See Colton

3721 ■ El Chicano: The Voice of the Chicano Community
Inland Empire Community Newspapers
PO Box 6247
San Bernardino, CA 92412-6247
Phone: (909)381-9898
Fax: (909)384-0406
Publisher's E-mail: iecn1@mac.com
Newspaper (Spanish and English). **Freq:** Weekly (Thurs.). **Print Method:** Offset. **Cols./Page:** 5. **Col. Width:** 1 7/8 inches. **Col. Depth:** 14.5 inches. **Key Personnel:** Diana Macias Harrison, General Manager, Publisher, Director, Advertising; Maryjoy Duncan, Managing Editor. **URL:** http://www.ieweekly.biz/page4/page4.html. **Ad Rates:** GLR $1; BW $1512; 4C $2162; PCI $15. **Remarks:** Accepts advertising. **Circ:** Free ‡16000.

3722 ■ Journal of Latinos and Education
Routledge Journals Taylor & Francis Group
c/o Enrique G. Murillo, Jr., Editor
California State University
College of Education
Center for Equity in Education, 5500 University Pky.
San Bernardino, CA 92407-2397
Scholarly, multidisciplinary journal covering educational issues that impact Latinos for researchers, teaching professionals, academics, scholars, institutions, and others. **Freq:** Quarterly. **Key Personnel:** Enrique G. Murillo, Jr., Editor; Corinne Martinez, Associate Editor; Sofia A. Villenas, Associate Editor. **ISSN:** 1534--8431 (print); **EISSN:** 1532--771X (electronic). **Subscription Rates:** $511 Institutions online only; $584 Institutions print and online. **URL:** http://www.tandfonline.com/toc/hjle20/current. **Ad Rates:** BW $400. **Remarks:** Accepts advertising. **Circ:** (Not Reported).

3723 ■ North San Bernardino Green Sheet
Associated Desert Shoppers Inc.
721 Nevada St., Ste. 207
Redlands, CA 92373
Phone: (909)793-3768
Fax: (909)793-8998
Shopper (tabloid). **Freq:** Weekly (Wed.). **Print Method:** Web. **Trim Size:** 11 x 12 1/2. **Cols./Page:** 6. **Col. Width:** 9.5 picas. **Col. Depth:** 11 3/4 inches. **Key Personnel:** Judy Shipley, Contact; Beverly King, Contact; Debra Law, Contact; Jerry Magnant, Contact; Ria Almaraz, Contact; Jamie Kourkos, Contact; Bobbie Demerest, Contact; Gary Graham, Manager, Circulation; Chuck Holcomb, Manager; Shari Dage, Contact. **Alt. Formats:** PDF. **Ad Rates:** BW $564. **Remarks:** Advertising accepted; rates available upon request. **Circ:** Free 19800.

3724 ■ Precinct Reporter
Precinct Reporter
1677 W Baseline St.
San Bernardino, CA 92411
Phone: (909)889-0597
Fax: (909)889-1706
Publisher's E-mail: news@precinctreporter.com
Black community newspaper. **Freq:** Weekly (Thurs.). **Print Method:** Offset. **Cols./Page:** 6. **Col. Width:** 18 nonpareils. **Col. Depth:** 294 agate lines. **URL:** http://online.precinctreporter.com/app.php?bookcode. **Ad Rates:** GLR $1.61; BW $2,902.50; 4C $750; PCI $23.50. **Remarks:** Accepts advertising. **Circ:** ‡55000.

Rialto Record - See Rialto, CA

3725 ■ San Bernardino Bulletin
Metropolitan News Co.
1264 S. Waterman
Suite 41
San Bernardino, CA 92408
Phone: (909)889-6477
Fax: (909)889-3696
Publisher's E-mail: info@mnc.net
Community newspaper. **Freq:** 3/week Monday, Wednesday and Friday. **Print Method:** Offset. **Cols./Page:** 4. **Col. Width:** 15 picas. **Col. Depth:** 15 1/2 inches. **Key Personnel:** Jo-Ann W. Grace, Publisher; Roger M. Grace, Publisher. **Subscription Rates:** $79 Individuals plus tax. **URL:** http://www.mnc.net/sbbulletin.htm; http://www.mnc.net/papers.htm. **Mailing address:** PO Box 13111, San Bernardino, CA 92423-3111. **Ad Rates:** PCI $6. **Remarks:** Accepts advertising. **Circ:** Non-paid 1000.

3726 ■ West San Bernardino Green Sheet
Associated Desert Shoppers Inc.
721 Nevada St., Ste. 207
Redlands, CA 92373
Fax: (760)346-3597
Free: 800-678-4237
Shopper (tabloid). **Freq:** Weekly (Thurs.). **Print Method:** Web. **Trim Size:** 11 x 12 1/2. **Cols./Page:** 6. **Col. Width:** 9.5 picas. **Col. Depth:** 11 3/4 inches. **Key Personnel:** Gary Graham, Manager, Circulation; Chuck Holcomb, Manager. **Subscription Rates:** $164 Free to qualified subscribers. **URL:** http://www.greenandwhitesheet.com/green_sheet_home.php. **Ad Rates:** BW $564. **Circ:** Non-paid 45000.

3727 ■ KCAA-AM - 1050
254 Carousel Mall
San Bernardino, CA 92401
Phone: (909)885-8497
Fax: (909)381-8935
Free: 888-909-1050
Email: info@kcaaradio.com
Format: News; Talk. **Networks:** NBC. **Owner:** Broadcast Management Services Inc., 19939 Gatling Ct., Katy, TX 77449. **Operating Hours:** Continuous. **ADI:** Los Angeles (Corona & San Bernardino), CA. **Key Personnel:** Paul Lane, Bur. Chief; Dennis Baxter, Gen. Mgr., dennis@kcaaradio.com. **Wattage:** 1,400 Day; 350 Night. **Ad Rates:** Advertising accepted; rates available upon request. **URL:** http://www.kcaaradio.com.

3728 ■ KCXX-FM - 103.9
242 E Airport Dr., Ste. 106
San Bernardino, CA 92408
Phone: (909)890-5904
Fax: (909)890-9035
Format: Album-Oriented Rock (AOR). **Networks:** Independent. **Founded:** 1978. **Operating Hours:** Continuous; 100% local. **ADI:** Los Angeles (Corona & San Bernardino), CA. **Key Personnel:** Jim Daniels, Mktg. Mgr., Promotions Mgr., jd@x1039.com; Fred Follmer, Chief Engineer; John DeSantis, Dir. of Programs. **Wattage:** 6,000. **Ad Rates:** $85-110 for 30 seconds; $110-140 for 60 seconds. $45-$65 for 30 seconds; $55-$75 for 60 seconds. **URL:** http://www.x1039.com.

3729 ■ KVCR-FM - 91.9
701 S Mount Vernon Ave.
San Bernardino, CA 92410-2798
Phone: (909)384-4444
Fax: (909)885-2116
Email: info@kvcr.org
Format: Public Radio; Talk; News. **Networks:** National Public Radio (NPR). **Owner:** San Bernardino Community College District, 114 S Del Rosa Dr., San Bernardino, CA 92408, Ph: (909)382-4000, Fax: (909)382-0116. **Founded:** 1953. **Operating Hours:** Continuous; 57% network, 43% local. **ADI:** Los Angeles (Corona & San Bernardino), CA. **Key Personnel:** Ben Holland, Producer; Jim Walker, Prog. Dir. **Wattage:** 003. **Ad Rates:** Noncommercial. **URL:** http://www.kvcr.org.

3730 ■ KVCR-TV - 24
701 S Mt. Vernon Ave.
San Bernardino, CA 92410
Phone: (909)384-4444
Fax: (909)885-2116
Format: Public TV. **Networks:** Public Broadcasting Service (PBS). **Owner:** San Bernardino Community College District, 114 S Del Rosa Dr., San Bernardino, CA 92408, Ph: (909)382-4000, Fax: (909)382-0116. **Founded:** 1962. **Operating Hours:** 8:30 a.m.-12:00 a.m.; 5:30 a.m.-1:30 a.m. Mon.-Fri. **ADI:** Los Angeles (Corona & San Bernardino), CA. **Key Personnel:** Larry Ciecalone, Chmn. of the Bd.; Ben Holland, Prog. Dir.; Kenn Couch, Station Mgr. **Wattage:** 1,300. **Ad Rates:** Noncommercial. **URL:** http://kvcr.org/TV.

3731 ■ KXRS-FM - 105.7
1950 S Sunwest Ln., Ste. 302
San Bernardino, CA 92408
Phone: (909)384-9750
Fax: (909)884-5844
Format: Hispanic. **Owner:** Lazer Broadcasting Corp., 200 S A St., Ste. 400, Oxnard, CA 93030, Ph: (805)240-2070, Fax: (805)240-5960. **Key Personnel:** Armando Gutierrez, Mgr. **Ad Rates:** Advertising accepted; rates available upon request.

3732 ■ KXSB-FM - 101.7
1950 S Sunwest Ln., Ste. 302
San Bernardino, CA 92408
Phone: (951)765-1017
Format: Hispanic. **Owner:** Lazer Broadcasting Corp., 200 S A St., Ste. 400, Oxnard, CA 93030, Ph: (805)240-2070, Fax: (805)240-5960. **Key Personnel:** Alfredo Plascencia, CEO, President, alfredop@radiolazer.com. **URL:** http://www.radiolazer.com.

SAN BRUNO

San Mateo Co. San Mateo Co. (W) 2 m S of South San Francisco. Residential.

3733 ■ Keyboard
Music Player Network
1111 Bayhill Dr., Ste. 125
San Bruno, CA 94066
Phone: (650)238-0300
Fax: (650)238-0261
Magazine dedicated to keyboard technology and techniques. **Founded:** 1875. **Freq:** Monthly. **Print Method:** Offset. **Trim Size:** 14 x 22. **Cols./Page:** 6. **Col. Width:** 12.3 picas. **Col. Depth:** 301 agate lines. **Key Personnel:** Joe Perry, Publisher, phone: (770)343-9978. **Subscription Rates:** $12 Individuals; $25 Two years; $27 Canada and Mexico; $37 Other countries. **URL:** http://www.keyboardmag.com. **Ad Rates:** BW $7925. **Remarks:** Accepts advertising. **Circ:** 16,364.

3734 ■ Philippines Today: Fair News, Fearless Views
Philippines Today

Circulation: ★ = AAM; △ or • = BPA; ♦ = CAC; ❑ = VAC; ⊕ = PO Statement; ‡ = Publisher's Report; Boldface figures = sworn; Light figures = estimated.

883 Sneath Ln., Ste. 222
San Bruno, CA 94066
Phone: (650)872-3200
Newspaper serving the Filipino-American communities in Northern California and Reno, Nevada. **Freq:** Weekly (Thurs.). **Subscription Rates:** Free. **URL:** http://www.philippinestodayus.com. **Remarks:** Accepts advertising. **Circ:** Non-paid ♦**29773**.

3735 ■ Technology & Learning
UBM P.L.C.
1111 Bayhill Dr., Ste. 440
San Bruno, CA 94066
Phone: (650)238-0260
Fax: (650)238-0263
Publication E-mail: techlearning@nbmedia.com
Magazine for educators (K-12) interested in the use of computers and other technology in schools. **Freq:** Monthly. **Print Method:** Offset. **Trim Size:** 7.75 x 10.5. **Cols./Page:** 3. **Col. Width:** 27 nonpareils. **Col. Depth:** 137 agate lines. **Key Personnel:** Allison Knapp, Publisher; Kevin Hogan, Director, Editorial; Christine Weiser, Executive Editor. **ISSN:** 0746--4223 (print). **Subscription Rates:** $20 U.S. and other countries digital; $39.95 Canada print; $69.95 Other countries print; $29.95 U.S. **URL:** http://www.techlearning.com/currentIssue. **Ad Rates:** BW $11150; 4C $14070. **Remarks:** Accepts advertising. **Circ:** ‡94547.

3736 ■ San Bruno Municipal Cable TV
398 El Camino Real
San Bruno, CA 94066
Phone: (650)616-3100
Free: 877-646-6407
Email: info@sanbrunocable.com
Owner: City of San Bruno, 567 El Camino Real, San Bruno, CA 94066. **Founded:** Oct. 18, 1971. **Key Personnel:** Miriam Schalit, Program Mgr. **Cities Served:** San Bruno, California: subscribing households 15,600; 117 channels. **URL:** http://sanbrunocable.com.

SAN CLEMENTE

Orange Co. Orange Co. (S). On Pacific Ocean, 32 m SW of Santa Ana. Resort. Residential.

3737 ■ BodyBoarding Magazine
McMullen Argus Publishing Inc.
950 Calle Amanecer, No. C
San Clemente, CA 92673
Phone: (714)498-6485
Fax: (714)498-6485
Publication E-mail: bbdingmag@aol.com
Action and personality-oriented magazine featuring bodyboarders and their sport. **Freq:** 8/year. **Print Method:** Web offset. **Trim Size:** 10 7/8 x 8. **Cols./Page:** 3. **Col. Width:** 13.6 picas. **Col. Depth:** 61 picas. **Key Personnel:** James Lynch, Manager, Advertising and Sales; Nick Long, Editor; Bob Mignogna, Publisher; Simon Ramsey, Associate Publisher. **ISSN:** 1047-2223 (print). **Subscription Rates:** $3.95 Single issue; $4.95 Single issue Canada; $4.95 Single issue Canada. **URL:** http://www.bodyboardingweb.com. **Ad Rates:** BW $2,389; 4C $3,419. **Remarks:** Accepts advertising. **Circ:** Paid ‡44757, Controlled ‡3727.

3738 ■ Canoe and Kayak Magazine: The 1 Paddlesports Resource
The Enthusiast Network
236 Avenida Fabricante, Ste. 201
San Clemente, CA 92672
Magazine on canoeing, kayaking, camping, and other outdoor recreation activities. **Freq:** Quarterly. **Print Method:** Offset. **Trim Size:** 8 x 10 1/2. **Cols./Page:** 3. **Col. Width:** 28 nonpareils. **Col. Depth:** 140 agate lines. **Key Personnel:** Jeff Moag, Editor-in-Chief; Jim Marsh, Publisher. **Subscription Rates:** $14.95 Individuals 4 issues; $24.95 Two years 8 issues; $19.95 Canada; $24.95 Other countries. **URL:** http://www.canoekayak.com; http://www.canoekayak.com/magazine. **Remarks:** Accepts advertising. **Circ:** (Not Reported).

3739 ■ Outcomes
Christian Leadership Alliance
635 Camino de los Mares, Ste. 216
San Clemente, CA 92673
Phone: (949)487-0900
Fax: (949)487-0927
Publisher's E-mail: info@christianleadershipalliance.org
Magazine featuring inspirational insights about the Christian ministry from the different Christian leaders nationwide. **Freq:** Quarterly. **Subscription Rates:** $29.99 /year. **URL:** http://www.christianleadershipalliance.org/resources/outcomes. **Circ:** (Not Reported).

3740 ■ San Clemente Sun-Post News
Freedom Communications Inc.
95 Avenida Del Mar
San Clemente, CA 92672
Fax: (949)492-5122
Publisher's E-mail: info@freedom.com
Community newspaper. **Freq:** Weekly (Thurs.). **Print Method:** Offset. **Cols./Page:** 5. **Col. Width:** 12.2 inches. **Col. Depth:** 182 agate lines. **URL:** http://www.ocregister.com/tag/insideocr/san-clemente-sun-post-news. **Formerly:** San Clemente News. **Ad Rates:** PCI $32.17. **Remarks:** Accepts advertising. **Circ:** Free ■ **9586**.

3741 ■ Skateboarding
TEN: The Enthusiast Network
236 Avenida Fabricante, Ste. 201
San Clemente, CA 92672
Phone: (949)325-6190
Magazine focusing on skateboarding coverage. Staff comprised of active skaters. **Freq:** Monthly. **Key Personnel:** Jaime Owens, Editor; Jamey Stone, Publisher; Christian Senrud, Associate Editor. **URL:** http://skateboardermag.com. **Ad Rates:** BW $5778; 4C $8256. **Remarks:** Accepts advertising. **Circ:** 92000.

3742 ■ Snowboarder
Source Interlink Media L.L.C.
236 Avenida Fabricante, Ste. 201
San Clemente, CA 92672
Phone: (949)325-6200
Publisher's E-mail: webmastersim@sourceinterlink.com
Consumer magazine covering snowboarding. **Founded:** 1988. **Freq:** 6/year. **Trim Size:** 8 x 10.5. **Key Personnel:** Norb Garrett, Publisher. **Subscription Rates:** $9.97 Individuals; $17.97 Two years. **URL:** http://www.snowboardermag.com; http://www.actionsportsgroup.net/snowboarder/snowboarder-magazine.html. **Ad Rates:** BW $7,353; 4C $10,502. **Remarks:** Accepts advertising. **Circ:** Combined 85000.

SAN DIEGO

San Diego Co. San Diego Co. (S). On San Diego Bay, 125 m SE of Los Angeles. Splendid harbor with extensive commerce. State College, United States International University. University of San Diego. University of California at San Diego, and many other colleges. Private schools. Army, Navy. Marine Corps and Coast Guard installations and schools. Naval hospital. Tourist resort. Sport and commercial fishing. Manufactures acoustical materials, adhesives, airplane parts, bamboo, dairy, electronic transmission and distribution equipment, electronic computing machines and components, plastic, rubber products, awnings, beverages, paper and clothing, dental specialties, detergents, drugs, chemicals, golf carts, wines, wooden boxes, bricks, brooms, building supplies, caskets, citrus by-products, missiles and missile components, farm and garden equipment, furniture, paint, parachute, processing and packing (meat, fish, fruit and food), plumbing supplies, pumps, tools, dies, uniforms, vending machines. Shipyards and marine ways.

3743 ■ ACE ProSource
American Council on Exercise
4851 Paramont Dr.
San Diego, CA 92123-1449
Phone: (858)576-6500
Fax: (858)576-6564
Free: 888-825-3636
Publisher's E-mail: support@acefitness.org
Freq: Monthly. **URL:** http://www.acefitness.org/prosource/115/prosource-january-2016. **Formerly:** ACE Certified News. **Remarks:** Accepts advertising. **Circ:** (Not Reported).

3744 ■ Affluent Living
Affluent Living
1081 Camino Del Rio S, Ste. 224
San Diego, CA 92108
Phone: (619)296-9305
Fax: (619)296-9345
Publisher's E-mail: dave@alpublications.com
Magazine that offers information in fine dining events, health, shopping, trends, travel, lodging, people, nightlife, arts, culture, and style. **Freq:** Bimonthly. **Key Personnel:** Dave Baker, Contact, phone: (619)296-9305, fax: (619)296-9345. **URL:** http://www.alpublications.com. **Remarks:** Accepts advertising. **Circ:** (Not Reported).

3745 ■ AGC Permit Reports
AGC Permit Reports
4355 Ruffin Rd., Ste. 103
San Diego, CA 92123
Phone: (858)874-8560
Fax: (858)874-8569
Publisher's E-mail: permits@agcsd.org
Construction newspaper covering jobs that are out for bid, bid results, building permits, and other information. **Freq:** Daily. **Print Method:** Offset. **Trim Size:** 8 1/2 x 11. **Cols./Page:** 2. **Col. Width:** 42 nonpareils. **Col. Depth:** 140 agate lines. **Subscription Rates:** $225 Individuals. **Formerly:** Daily Construction Reporter. **Ad Rates:** BW $145. **Remarks:** Accepts advertising. **Circ:** 500.

3746 ■ Alaska Contractor Magazine
MARCOA Publishing Inc.
9955 Black Mountain Rd.
San Diego, CA 92126
Phone: (858)695-9600
Free: 800-854-2935
Publisher's E-mail: edit@marcoa.com
Magazine publishing articles in the field of construction industry. **Freq:** Quarterly. **Key Personnel:** Jamie Rogers, Editor; Rachael Fisher, Managing Editor. **URL:** http://www.aqppublishing.com/pub_businessMagazine.html. **Mailing address:** PO Box 509100, San Diego, CA 92150-9100. **Circ:** ‡5000, ‡5000.

3747 ■ Alaska Warriors Magazine
MARCOA Publishing Inc.
9955 Black Mountain Rd.
San Diego, CA 92126
Phone: (858)695-9600
Free: 800-854-2935
Publisher's E-mail: edit@marcoa.com
Magazine for the Alaska Department of Military and Veterans Affairs, covering information for civilian employees, military members, veterans and their families. **Freq:** Quarterly. **Key Personnel:** Kalei Rupp, Managing Editor. **URL:** http://www.aqppublishing.com/pub_nationalGuardMagazine.html. **Mailing address:** PO Box 509100, San Diego, CA 92150-9100. **Circ:** (Not Reported).

3748 ■ American Angler
American Angler
1403 Scott St.
San Diego, CA 92106
Phone: (619)223-5414
Publisher's E-mail: office@americananglersportfishing.com
The American Angler is one of the most beautifully designed and appointed sport fishing boats in the San Diego fleet. **Freq:** Bimonthly. **Print Method:** Offset. **Trim Size:** 8 1/4 x 10 7/8. **Cols./Page:** 3. **Col. Width:** 27 nonpareils. **Col. Depth:** 140 agate lines. **Key Personnel:** Michael Floyd, Director, Advertising, phone: (706)823-3739, fax: (706)724-3873; Steve Walburn, Publisher. **ISSN:** 1055--6737 (print). **USPS:** 451-070. **Subscription Rates:** $19.95 Individuals print; $39.95 Canada print; $59.95 Other countries print; $37.90 Two years. **URL:** http://www.americanangler.com. **Formerly:** American Fly Tyer; American Angler & Fly Tyer. **Ad Rates:** BW $1580; 4C $1995. **Remarks:** Accepts advertising. **Circ:** ‡43,000.

3749 ■ American Cop
Publishers Development Corp.
12345 World Trade Dr.
San Diego, CA 92128
Fax: (858)605-0247
Magazine for police, corrections officers, federal agents, and other security officers. **Freq:** Bimonthly. **Key Personnel:** Suzi Huntington, Editor. **URL:** http://americancopmagazine.com. **Ad Rates:** BW $3,990; 4C $4,940. **Remarks:** Accepts advertising. **Circ:** (Not Reported).

3750 ■ Arts & Activities
Arts & Activities

12345 World Trade Dr.
San Diego, CA 92128
Phone: (858)605-0251
Publisher's E-mail: subs@artsandactivities.com
Elementary and high school art education magazine. **Freq:** 10/year. **Print Method:** Offset. **Trim Size:** 8 x 10 7/8. **Cols./Page:** 3. **Col. Width:** 27 nonpareils. **Col. Depth:** 138 agate lines. **Key Personnel:** Brent Weidemann, Manager, Advertising. **ISSN:** 0004--3931 (print). **Subscription Rates:** $40 U.S.; $80 Two years; $90 Other countries; $180 Other countries 2 years. **URL:** http://www.artsandactivities.com. **Ad Rates:** BW $2324. **Remarks:** Accepts advertising. **Circ:** (Not Reported).

3751 ■ Asia Pacific Journal of Speech, Language and Hearing
Plural Publishing Inc.
5521 Ruffin Rd.
San Diego, CA 92123
Phone: (858)492-1555
Fax: (858)492-1020
Free: 866-758-7251
Publisher's E-mail: information@pluralpublishing.com
Peer-reviewed journal publishing experimental and clinical research papers, reviews, clinical notes, and comments and critiques on any aspect of normal or disordered speech, language or hearing. **Freq:** Quarterly. **Key Personnel:** Michael Robb, Editor-in-Chief. **ISSN:** 1361--3286 (print). **Subscription Rates:** £179 Individuals print & online; £357 Institutions print & online; $570 Institutions print & online. **URL:** http://www.pluralpublishing.com/wp/?p=946. **Remarks:** Accepts advertising. **Circ:** (Not Reported).

3752 ■ Back to Godhead: The Magazine of the Hare Krishna Movement
Back to God Lead
PO Box 90946
San Diego, CA 92169
Phone: (619)272-7384
Fax: (619)272-3673
Publication E-mail: editors@krishna.com
Magazine on Indian philosophy, religion, culture, and literature. English edition; also published in Spanish, Italian, German, Bengali, and Hindi. **Freq:** Bimonthly. **Print Method:** Offset. **Trim Size:** 8 1/2 x 11. **Cols./Page:** 3. **Col. Width:** 27 nonpareils. **Col. Depth:** 138 agate lines. **Key Personnel:** Nagaraja Dasa, Editor. **ISSN:** 0005-3643 (print). **Subscription Rates:** $19.95 Individuals; $37.95 Two years; $23.95 Canada; $44.95 Two years; $29.95 Other countries; $56.95 Two years. **URL:** http://btg.krishna.com. **Circ:** ‡6000.

3753 ■ Battle Born
MARCOA Publishing Inc.
9955 Black Mountain Rd.
San Diego, CA 92126
Phone: (858)695-9600
Free: 800-854-2935
Publisher's E-mail: edit@marcoa.com
Magazine publishing information for employees, retirees and military members of the National Guard of Nevada. **Freq:** Quarterly. **Key Personnel:** April Conway, Managing Editor; Erick Studenicka, Editor. **URL:** http://www.aqppublishing.com/pub_nationalGuardMagazine.html; http://www.nv.ngb.army.mil/nvng/index.cfm/public-affairs/battle-born-magazine/. **Mailing address:** PO Box 509100, San Diego, CA 92150-9100. **Circ:** (Not Reported).

3754 ■ Beach & Bay Press
San Diego Community Newspaper Group
4645 Cass St., 2nd Fl.
San Diego, CA 92109
Phone: (858)270-3103
Fax: (858)713-0095
Publication E-mail: bbp@sdnews.com
Community newspaper. **Freq:** Weekly. **Print Method:** Offset. **Trim Size:** 11 x 17. **Cols./Page:** 5. **Col. Width:** 1 15/16 inches. **Col. Depth:** 15 3/4 inches. **Key Personnel:** Julie Mannis Hoisington, Publisher; Kendra Hartmann, Editor. **ISSN:** 3303--6063 (print). **Subscription Rates:** Free. **URL:** http://www.sdnews.com/pages/home?site=bbp#. **Circ:** (Not Reported).

3755 ■ Big Sky Guardian
MARCOA Publishing Inc.
9955 Black Mountain Rd.
San Diego, CA 92126
Phone: (858)695-9600
Free: 800-854-2935
Publisher's E-mail: edit@marcoa.com
Magazine publishing information for employees, families and military members of the Montana Department of Military and Veterans Affairs. **Freq:** Quarterly. **Key Personnel:** Tim Crowe, Executive Editor; Roger Dey, Managing Editor. **URL:** http://www.aqppublishing.com/pub_nationalGuardMagazine.html. **Mailing address:** PO Box 509100, San Diego, CA 92150-9100. **Circ:** (Not Reported).

3756 ■ Biological Control
Academic Press Inc.
525 B St., Ste. 1900
San Diego, CA 92101-4495
Phone: (619)231-6616
Free: 800-545-2522
Journal containing information on the means of reducing or mitigating pets and pest effects through the use of natural enemies. **Freq:** Monthly. **Key Personnel:** H.K. Kaya, Board Member; J.D. Vandenberg, Board Member; J. Brodeur, Board Member; J.H. Hoffmann, Editor. **ISSN:** 1049--9644 (print). **Subscription Rates:** $368 Individuals print only; $647.60 Institutions eJournal; $1294 Institutions print only. **URL:** http://www.journals.elsevier.com/biological-control/. **Circ:** (Not Reported).

3757 ■ Books
San Diego Union-Tribune L.L.C.
600 B St., Ste. 1201
San Diego, CA 92101
Phone: (619)293-1211
Fax: (619)293-1896
Free: 800-533-8830
Publication E-mail: books@uniontrib.com
Newspaper with books section. **Freq:** Weekly. **Print Method:** Offset. **Cols./Page:** 6. **Col. Width:** 2 1/16 inches. **Col. Depth:** 13 inches. **URL:** http://www.utsandiego.com/news/entertainment/arts-and-culture/books. **Formerly:** Currents in Books. **Mailing address:** PO Box 120191, San Diego, CA 92112-0191. **Remarks:** Advertising accepted; rates available upon request. **Circ:** ‡422000.

3758 ■ California Garden
San Diego Floral Association
1650 El Prado, Rm. 105
San Diego, CA 92101-1684
Phone: (619)232-5762
Publisher's E-mail: presidentsdfloral@gmail.com
Magazine on floriculture and horticulture. **Freq:** Bimonthly. **Print Method:** Offset. **Trim Size:** 8 1/2 x 11. **Cols./Page:** 2. **Col. Width:** 3 1/2 inches. **Col. Depth:** 9 1/4 inches. **ISSN:** 0008--1116 (print). **Subscription Rates:** $4 Individuals. **URL:** http://www.sdfloral.org/magazine.htm. **Ad Rates:** GLR $2; BW $100; PCI $20. **Remarks:** Accepts advertising. **Circ:** 2100.

3759 ■ Capital Guardian
MARCOA Publishing Inc.
9955 Black Mountain Rd.
San Diego, CA 92126
Phone: (858)695-9600
Free: 800-854-2935
Publisher's E-mail: edit@marcoa.com
Magazine publishing information for employees and military members of the District of Columbia National Guard. **Key Personnel:** Bob Ulin, Publisher. **URL:** http://www.aqppublishing.com/pub_nationalGuardMagazine.html. **Mailing address:** PO Box 509100, San Diego, CA 92150-9100. **Circ:** (Not Reported).

3760 ■ Coatings Pro
Four Point Publishing L.L.C.
4501 Mission Bay Dr., Ste. 2G
San Diego, CA 92109
Phone: (858)490-2708
Magazine that features a broad base of articles edited for applicators and specifying engineers of industrial and commercial coatings. **Freq:** Bimonthly. **Key Personnel:** Eliina Lizarraga, Managing Editor; Bill Wageneck, Publisher, phone: (281)228-6441. **Subscription Rates:** Free to qualified subscribers. **URL:** http://www.coatingspromag.com. **Ad Rates:** BW $3390; 4C $4765. **Remarks:** Advertising accepted; rates available upon request. **Circ:** 26300.

3761 ■ Communicative Disorders Review
Plural Publishing Inc.
5521 Ruffin Rd.
San Diego, CA 92123
Phone: (858)492-1555
Fax: (858)492-1020
Free: 866-758-7251
Publication E-mail: cdr@pluralpublishing.com
Journal offering current information in the field of Communicative Disorders. **Freq:** Quarterly. **Key Personnel:** Raymond D. Kent, PhD, Editor-in-Chief. **ISSN:** 1933--2831 (print). **Subscription Rates:** $120 Individuals; $180 Institutions; $170 Other countries; $230 Institutions, other countries. **URL:** http://www.pluralpublishing.com/journals_CDR.htm. **Circ:** (Not Reported).

3762 ■ Continental Newstime
Continental Features/Continental News Service
501 W Broadway, Plz. A
PMB No. 265
San Diego, CA 92101
Publisher's E-mail: continentalnewsservice@yahoo.com
Magazine featuring news and commentary on national and world affairs. **Freq:** Biweekly. **Print Method:** Offset. **Trim Size:** 8 1/2 x 11. **Cols./Page:** 2 and 3. **Col. Width:** 3 1/2 and 2 inches. **Col. Depth:** 7 3/4 and 10 inches. **Key Personnel:** Gary P. Salamone, Editor-in-Chief, President. **ISSN:** 1096--1712 (print). **URL:** http://www.continentalnewsservice.com. **Ad Rates:** BW $12,800; PCI $475. **Remarks:** Accepts advertising. **Circ:** 19700.

3763 ■ Current Immunology Reviews
Bentham Science Publishers Ltd.
La Jolla Institute for Allergy & Immunology
San Diego, CA 92121
Publisher's E-mail: subscriptions@benthamscience.org
Journal publishing frontier reviews on all the latest advances in clinical immunology. **Freq:** Semiannual. **Key Personnel:** Cecil Czerkinsky, Editor-in-Chief. **ISSN:** 1573--3955 (print); **EISSN:** 1875--631X (electronic). **Subscription Rates:** $130 Individuals print; $310 print and online - academic; $280 print or online - academic; $710 print and online - corporate; $590 print or online - corporate. **URL:** http://benthamscience.com/journals/current-immunology-reviews. **Ad Rates:** BW $600; 4C $800. **Remarks:** Accepts advertising. **Circ:** ‡400.

3764 ■ Cyberpsychology, Behavior, and Social Networking
Mary Ann Liebert Inc., Publishers
c/o Brenda K. Wiederhold, PhD, Ed.-in-Ch.
Interactive Media Institute
9565 Waples St., Ste. 200
San Diego, CA 92121
Phone: (858)642-0267
Fax: (858)642-0285
Publication E-mail: cyberpsych@vrphobia.com
Peer-reviewed journal covering the impact of the Internet, multi-media, and virtual reality on behavior and society for psychologists, psychiatrists, sociologists, educators and others. **Freq:** Monthly. **Trim Size:** 8 1/2 x 11. **Key Personnel:** Giuseppe Riva, Editor; Brenda K. Wiederhold, PhD, Editor-in-Chief. **ISSN:** 2152--2715 (print); **EISSN:** 2152--2723 (electronic). **Subscription Rates:** $815 Individuals print and online; $937 Other countries print and online; $759 Individuals online only; $1613 Institutions print and online; $1855 Institutions, other countries print and online; $1536 Institutions online only; $1460 Institutions print only; $1679 Institutions, other countries print only. **URL:** http://www.liebertpub.com/overview/cyberpsychology-behavior-brand-social-networking/10. **Formerly:** CyberPsychology and Behavior. **Ad Rates:** BW $1,095; 4C $1,845. **Remarks:** Accepts advertising. **Circ:** (Not Reported).

3765 ■ The Daily Aztec
San Diego State University
San Diego State University, EBA-2
San Diego, CA 92182-7700
Publication E-mail: letters@thedailyaztec.com
College newspaper. **Freq:** Semiweekly (Mon. and Thurs.). **Print Method:** Offset. **Cols./Page:** 5. **Col. Width:** 24 nonpareils. **Col. Depth:** 224 agate lines. **Key Personnel:** Kelly Hillock, Editor-in-Chief. **URL:** http://www.thedailyaztec.com. **Formerly:** Normal News; Paper Lantern; The Aztec. **Ad Rates:** BW $1050. **Remarks:** Accepts advertising. **Circ:** Free 10000.

3766 ■ Dakota Pack Magazine
MARCOA Publishing Inc.

Circulation: ★ = AAM; △ or • = BPA; ♦ = CAC; ❑ = VAC; ⊕ = PO Statement; ‡ = Publisher's Report; Boldface figures = sworn; Light figures = estimated.

9955 Black Mountain Rd.
San Diego, CA 92126
Phone: (858)695-9600
Free: 800-854-2935
Publisher's E-mail: edit@marcoa.com
Magazine publishing information for service members and the families of South Dakota Army and Air National Guard. **Freq:** Quarterly. **Key Personnel:** Bob Ulin, Publisher. **URL:** http://www.aqppublishing.com/pub_nationalGuardMagazine.html. **Mailing address:** PO Box 509100, San Diego, CA 92150-9100. **Circ:** ‡4500, 5500.

3767 ■ Developmental Neurobiology
John Wiley & Sons Inc.
c/o Eduardo Macagno, Editor
University of California, San Diego
San Diego, CA 92101
Publisher's E-mail: info@wiley.com
Journal publishing original research articles on vertebrate and invertebrate nervous systems. Emphasis is on cellular, genetic, and molecular analyses of neurodevelopment and the ontology of behavior. **Freq:** Monthly. **Print Method:** Offset. **Trim Size:** 11 x 8 1/4. **Cols./Page:** 1. **Col. Width:** 80 nonpareils. **Col. Depth:** 140 agate lines. **Key Personnel:** Darcy B. Kelley, Editor; Eduardo Macagno, Editor; Peter W. Baas, Board Member; Moses V. Chao, Editor; Paola Bovolenta, Editor. **ISSN:** 1932--8451 (print); **EISSN:** 1932--846X (electronic). **Subscription Rates:** $8762 Institutions print only; $8970 Institutions, Canada and Mexico print only; $9074 Institutions, other countries print only; £4633 Institutions print only; €5857 Institutions print only; $10515 Institutions print and online; $10764 Institutions, Canada and Mexico print and online; £5560 Institutions print and online; €7029 Institutions print and online; $10889 Institutions, other countries print and online. **URL:** http://onlinelibrary.wiley.com/journal/10.1002/(ISSN)1932-846X. **Formerly**: Journal of Neurobiology. **Ad Rates:** BW $772; 4C $1009. **Remarks:** Accepts advertising. **Circ:** 5250.

3768 ■ Early Childhood Services: An Interdisciplinary Journal of Effectiveness
Plural Publishing Inc.
5521 Ruffin Rd.
San Diego, CA 92123
Phone: (858)492-1555
Fax: (858)492-1020
Free: 866-758-7251
Publication E-mail: ecs@pluralpublishing.com
Peer-reviewed journal focusing on the interdisciplinary nature of early childhood services. **Freq:** Quarterly. **Key Personnel:** M. Jeanne Wilcox, PhD, Editor; Philippa H. Campbell, PhD, Editor. **ISSN:** 1559--9647 (print). **Subscription Rates:** $79.95 Individuals; $140 Institutions; $130 Other countries; $190 Institutions, other countries. **URL:** http://www.pluralpublishing.com/journals_ECS.htm. **Remarks:** Accepts advertising. **Circ:** (Not Reported).

3769 ■ Edible San Diego
Edible Communities Inc.
PO Box 83549
San Diego, CA 92105
Phone: (619)222-8267
Publication E-mail: info@ediblesandiego.com
Magazine covering the local food of San Diego. **Freq:** Quarterly. **Trim Size:** 7.5 x 10. **Key Personnel:** Riley Davenport, Publisher; John Vawter, Publisher. **Subscription Rates:** $33 Individuals; $54 Two years; $72 Institutions three years. **URL:** http://www.ediblesandiego.com. **Remarks:** Accepts advertising. **Circ:** (Not Reported).

3770 ■ Enlace
San Diego Union-Tribune L.L.C.
600 B St., Ste. 1201
San Diego, CA 92101
Phone: (619)293-1211
Fax: (619)293-1896
Free: 800-533-8830
Newspaper serving the Latino community in the San Diego region. **Founded:** 1998. **Freq:** Weekly (Sat.). **Key Personnel:** Lilia O'Hara, Editor, phone: (619)293-2294. **Subscription Rates:** Free. **URL:** http://www.utsandiego.com. **Mailing address:** PO Box 120191, San Diego, CA 92112-0191. **Circ:** Non-paid ♦**111574**.

3771 ■ Fire-Rescue Magazine: Read it Today, Use it Tomorrow
Jems Communications
525 B St., Ste. 1900
San Diego, CA 92101
Free: 800-266-5367
Publication E-mail: frm.editor@jems.com
Magazine addressing the needs of emergency response personnel, including techniques for extrication, treatment and transport on all terrain. **Founded:** Mar. 1997. **Freq:** Monthly. **Print Method:** Offset. **Trim Size:** 7 7/8 x 10 7/8. **Cols./Page:** 3. **Col. Width:** 13 picas. **Col. Depth:** 9 1/2 inches. **Key Personnel:** Erich Roden, Editor-in-Chief, phone: (414)559-0465. **ISSN:** 1094-0529 (print). **Subscription Rates:** $43 Individuals; $73 Two years; $223 Other countries airmail delivery, 2 years; $118 Other countries airmail delivery; $118 Canada airmail delivery; $220 Canada airmail delivery, 2 years; $78 Canada ground delivery; $143 Canada ground delivery, 2 years. **URL:** http://www.jems.com; http://www.firerescuemagazine.com. **Formed by the merger of:** Firefighter's News; Rescue Magazine. **Ad Rates:** BW $6,010; 4C $7,435. **Remarks:** Accepts advertising. **Circ:** Paid 9709.

3772 ■ Ft. Madison Daily Democrat
Brehm Communication
16644 W Bernardo Dr., Ste. 300
San Diego, CA 92127-1901
Phone: (858)451-6200
Fax: (858)451-3814
Publisher's E-mail: debbiel@brehmmail.com
General newspaper. **Freq:** Daily. **Print Method:** Offset. **Trim Size:** 13 1/2 x 21 3/4. **Cols./Page:** 8. **Col. Width:** 18 nonpareils. **Col. Depth:** 301 agate lines. **Key Personnel:** Robin Delaney, Managing Editor; Tracy Burris, Supervisor; Lee K. Vandenberg, Director, Advertising; Mary Older, Business Manager. **Subscription Rates:** $77 Individuals foot carrier; $86 Individuals motor carrier. **URL:** http://www.dailydem.com. **Remarks:** Accepts advertising. **Circ:** (Not Reported).

3773 ■ Gem State Guardian Magazine
MARCOA Publishing Inc.
9955 Black Mountain Rd.
San Diego, CA 92126
Phone: (858)695-9600
Free: 800-854-2935
Publisher's E-mail: edit@marcoa.com
Magazine publishing information for employees and military members of the State of Idaho Military Division. **Freq:** Quarterly. **Key Personnel:** Tim Marsano, Editor; Tony Vincelli, Assistant Editor. **Alt. Formats:** PDF. **URL:** http://www.aqppublishing.com/pub_nationalGuardMagazine.html. **Mailing address:** PO Box 509100, San Diego, CA 92150-9100. **Circ:** ‡5000, ‡5000.

3774 ■ Guns Magazine: The Finest in the Firearms Field Since 1955
Publishers Development Corp.
12345 World Trade Dr.
San Diego, CA 92128
Fax: (858)605-0247
Magazine on firearms and shooting sports. **Freq:** Monthly. **Print Method:** Offset. **Trim Size:** 8 x 10 7/8. **Cols./Page:** 3. **Col. Width:** 27 nonpareils. **Col. Depth:** 140 agate lines. **ISSN:** 1044--6257 (print). **Subscription Rates:** $24.95 Individuals; $64.95 Other countries; $42.95 Two years; $112.95 Other countries 2 years. **URL:** http://gunsmagazine.com. **Ad Rates:** BW $4,291; 4C $6,887. **Remarks:** Accepts advertising. **Circ:** Paid ★**100011**.

3775 ■ The Hook
Tailhook Association
9696 Businesspark Ave.
San Diego, CA 92131-1643
Phone: (858)689-9223
Free: 800-322-4665
Publication E-mail: thookassn@aol.com
Journal covering U.S. Navy carrier-based aircraft history. Includes book reviews. **Freq:** Quarterly. **Print Method:** Offset. **Trim Size:** 8 1/2 x 11. **Cols./Page:** 3 and 2. **Col. Width:** 27 and 42 nonpareils. **Col. Depth:** 142 agate lines. **Key Personnel:** Dennis Irelan, Editor, phone: (858)689-9227; Jan Jacobs, Managing Editor. **ISSN:** 0736--9220 (print). **Subscription Rates:** Included in membership. **URL:** http://www.tailhook.net/A_Hook_Magazine.html. **Ad Rates:** BW $2525; 4C $3485. **Remarks:** Accepts advertising. **Circ:** Paid ‡12636, Non-paid ‡244.

3776 ■ HPCwire
Tabor Communications Inc.
8445 Camino Santa Fe
San Diego, CA 92121-2649
Phone: (858)625-0070
Fax: (858)625-0088
Journal on High Performance Computing industry covering related topics of hardware, software and integrated systems technology, and also related business, corporate, economic and governmental news among others. **Freq:** Weekly. **Key Personnel:** Tom Tabor, President, Chief Executive Officer. **URL:** http://www.hpcwire.com. **Remarks:** Advertising accepted; rates available upon request. **Circ:** (Not Reported).

3777 ■ Human Antibodies
IOS Press B.V.
c/o Mark C. Glassy, PhD, Ed.-in-Ch.
10246 Parkdale Ave.
San Diego, CA 92126
Phone: (858)566-9490
Publisher's E-mail: info@iospress.nl
International journal covering to bring together all aspects of human hybridomas and antibody technology under a single, cohesive theme, including fundamental research, applied science and clinical applications, emphasizing articles on antisera, monoclonal antibodies, fusion partners, EBV transformation, transfections, in vitro immunization, defined antigens, tissue reactivity, scale-up production, chimeric antibodies, autoimmunity, natural antibodies/immune response, anti-idiotypes, hybridomas secreting interesting growth factors and immunoregulatory molecules, including T cell hybridomas. **Freq:** Quarterly. **Key Personnel:** Mark C. Glassy, PhD, Editor-in-Chief. **ISSN:** 1093--2607 (print); **EISSN:** 1875--869X (electronic). **Subscription Rates:** €575 Institutions print & online; $785 Institutions print & online. **URL:** http://www.iospress.nl/journal/human-antibodies. **Circ:** (Not Reported).

3778 ■ IDEA Fitness Journal
IDEA Health and Fitness Association
10190 Telesis Ct.
San Diego, CA 92121
Phone: (858)535-8979
Fax: (858)535-8234
Free: 800-999-4332
Publisher's E-mail: contact@ideafit.com
Magazine that covers personal training, group exercise, nutrition and mind-body fitness. **Freq:** 10/year. **Key Personnel:** Peter Davies, Chief Executive Officer, Publisher. **ISSN:** 1548--419X (print). **Subscription Rates:** Included in membership. **URL:** http://www.ideafit.com/publications; http://www.ideafit.com/idea-fitness-journal. **Remarks:** Accepts advertising. **Circ:** (Not Reported).

3779 ■ The Insurance Journal of the West
Wells Media Group Inc.
3570 Camino del Rio N, Ste. 200
San Diego, CA 92108
Phone: (619)584-1100
Fax: (619)584-1200
Free: 800-897-9965
Trade journal covering insurance. **Freq:** Semimonthly. **Trim Size:** 8 3/8 x 10 7/8. **Key Personnel:** Dena Kaplan, Associate Publisher; Mark Wells, Chairman, Publisher; Mitch Dunford, Chief Executive Officer. **Subscription Rates:** $195 Individuals print & online; $99 Individuals online only; $195 Individuals print only. **Alt. Formats:** Download. **URL:** http://www.insurancejournal.com; http://www.insurancejournal.com/magazines/west. **Ad Rates:** BW $4,578; 4C $6,473; PCI $82. **Remarks:** Accepts advertising. **Circ:** △**42030**.

3780 ■ JEMS: Journal of Emergency Medical Services
Jems Communications
525 B St., Ste. 1900
San Diego, CA 92101
Free: 800-266-5367
EMS (Emergency Medical Services)professionals journal. **Freq:** Monthly. **Print Method:** Offset. **Trim Size:** 8 3/8 x 10 7/8. **Cols./Page:** 3 and 2. **Col. Width:** 13 and 20 picas. **Col. Depth:** 140 agate lines. **Key Personnel:** A.J. Heightman, Editor-in-Chief, phone: (800)266-5367; Jennifer Berry, Managing Editor. **ISSN:** 0197--2510 (print). **Subscription Rates:** $19.99 U.S. 1 year print and digital; $49 Canada 1 year print and digital; $59

Other countries 1 year print and digital; Free digital only. **URL:** http://www.jems.com/magazine.html. **Ad Rates:** GLR $1.75; BW $4975; 4C $5970; PCI $75. **Remarks:** Accepts advertising. **Circ:** (Not Reported).

3781 ■ Journal of Contemporary Legal Issues
University of San Diego School of Law
Warren Hall, Rm. 201
5998 Alcala Pk.
San Diego, CA 92110-2492
Phone: (619)260-4527
Publisher's E-mail: lawdean@sandiego.edu
Journal containing topics on family law, critical race feminism, law, evolution and biology, the religion clauses of the Constitution, and criminal law. **Freq:** Annual. **Key Personnel:** Paul Horton, Editor. **Subscription Rates:** $37 Individuals domestic or international. **URL:** http://www.sandiego.edu/law/academics/journals/jcli. **Remarks:** Accepts advertising. **Circ:** (Not Reported).

3782 ■ Journal of Infection
Academic Press Inc.
525 B St., Ste. 1900
San Diego, CA 92101-4495
Phone: (619)231-6616
Free: 800-545-2522
Publisher's E-mail: info@elsevier.com
Journal publishing papers on all aspects of infection - clinical, microbiological, epidemiological and molecular. **Freq:** Monthly. **Key Personnel:** R. Read, Editor-in-Chief, phone: (44)114 2724072, fax: (44)114 2739926. **ISSN:** 0163-4453 (print). **Subscription Rates:** $379 Individuals print; $460.53 Institutions e-journal (access for 5 users and to 4 years of archives); $1463 Institutions print. **URL:** http://www.journalofinfection.com; http://www.journals.elsevier.com/journal-of-infection; http://www.britishinfection.org/news/journal-infection. **Mailing address:** PO Box 46908, Saint Louis, MO 63146-3318. **Remarks:** Advertising accepted; rates available upon request. **Circ:** (Not Reported).

3783 ■ The Journal of the Jamestown Rediscovery Center
Preservation Virginia
c/o Seth Mallios, Ed.
San Diego State Univ.
5500 Campanile Dr.
San Diego, CA 92182
Phone: (619)514-4748
Fax: (619)594-1150
Publisher's E-mail: info@preservationvirginia.org
Journal covering the settling of North America by Europeans with an emphasis on life at Jamestown Island during the 16th and 17th century. **Freq:** Annual. **Key Personnel:** Seth Mallios, Editor; Alison Bell, Associate Editor. **ISSN:** 1534--6234 (print). **URL:** http://www.apva.org/resource/jjrc. **Circ:** (Not Reported).

3784 ■ Journal of Mathematical Analysis and Applications
Academic Press Inc.
525 B St., Ste. 1900
San Diego, CA 92101-4495
Phone: (619)231-6616
Free: 800-545-2522
Journal publishing mathematical papers on classical analysis and its applications. **Freq:** 24/yr. **Trim Size:** 6 x 9. **Key Personnel:** Prof. George Leitmann, Editor; Richard M. Aron, Editor-in-Chief. **ISSN:** 0022--247X (print). **Subscription Rates:** $926 Individuals print only; $6577.60 Institutions eJournal; $9867 Institutions print only. **URL:** http://www.journals.elsevier.com/journal-of-mathematical-analysis-and-applications. **Remarks:** Accepts advertising. **Circ:** (Not Reported).

3785 ■ La Jolla Village News
San Diego Community Newspaper Group
4645 Cass St., 2nd Fl.
San Diego, CA 92109
Phone: (858)270-3103
Fax: (858)713-0095
Publisher's E-mail: sales@sdnews.com
Community newspaper. **Freq:** Weekly (Thurs.). **Print Method:** Web offset. **Cols./Page:** 5. **Col. Width:** 1 15/16 inches. **Col. Depth:** 15 3/4 inches. **Key Personnel:** Martin Westlin, Editor; Julie Mannis Hoisington, Publisher; Heather Snyder, Manager, Advertising. **URL:** http://www.sdnews.com/pages/home?site=ljvn#. **Remarks:** Accepts advertising. **Circ:** 20000.

3786 ■ Law Officer
Jems Communications
525 B St., Ste. 1900
San Diego, CA 92101
Free: 800-266-5367
Magazine that covers tactics, training and technology for police officers at all levels in their careers. **Freq:** Bimonthly. **Key Personnel:** Jeff Berend, Publisher; Capt. Dale Stockton, Editor-in-Chief. **Ad Rates:** BW $3,790; 4C $4,785. **Remarks:** Accepts advertising. **Circ:** (Not Reported).

3787 ■ Leaves and Saplings
San Diego Genealogical Society
PO Box 33725
San Diego, CA 92163
Phone: (858)672-2593
Publisher's E-mail: sdgsinfo@yahoo.com
Magazine containing San Diego County genealogical records. **Freq:** Quarterly. **Subscription Rates:** $30 Individuals; $25 Members; $7.50 Single issue back issue. **URL:** http://sdgs.wildapricot.org/page-1075191. **Circ:** (Not Reported).

3788 ■ Legal Theory
Cambridge University Press
c/o Prof. Larry Alexander, Ed.
University of San Diego
School of Law
5998 Alcala Park
San Diego, CA 92110
Publication E-mail: ad_sales@cambridge.org
Peer-reviewed journal focusing on academic law, humanities and social sciences. **Freq:** Quarterly. **Key Personnel:** Brian Leiter, Board Member; Prof. Larry Alexander, Editor; Jules L. Coleman, Board Member. **ISSN:** 1352--3252 (print); **EISSN:** 1469--8048 (electronic). **Subscription Rates:** $337 Institutions online only; £198 Institutions online only; $413 Institutions online and print; £240 Institutions online and print; $396 Institutions print only; £224 Institutions print only. **URL:** http://journals.cambridge.org/action/displayJournal?jid=LEG. **Ad Rates:** BW $845. **Remarks:** Accepts advertising. **Circ:** 600.

3789 ■ Linguistics and Language Behavior Abstracts
Cambridge Scientific Abstracts L.P.
PO Box 22206
San Diego, CA 92192
Phone: (858)571-8979
Fax: (858)571-8694
Publisher's E-mail: sales@proquest.com
Linguistics publication containing abstracts from over 2,000 serials from 30 languages. **Founded:** 1967. **Freq:** Monthly with approximately 14,000 new records added per year. **Print Method:** Offset. **Cols./Page:** 2. **Col. Width:** 36 nonpareils. **Col. Depth:** 122 agate lines. **ISSN:** 0888-8027 (print). **URL:** http://www.csa.com/factsheets/llba-set-c.php; http://www.proquest.com/products-services/llba-set-c.html. **Remarks:** Advertising not accepted. **Circ:** ‡900.

3790 ■ The National Jurist: News and Insights for the Future Lawyer
The National Jurist Crittenden Magazines
7670 Opportunity Rd., Ste. 105
San Diego, CA 92111
Phone: (858)300-3200
Trade magazine covering news, advice, and humor for law students. **Freq:** Bimonthly. **Key Personnel:** Katina Cavagnaro, Publisher, phone: (858)300-3217; Jack Crittenden, Editor-in-Chief, phone: (858)300-3210; Mike Wright, Account Manager. **ISSN:** 1094-866X (print). **Subscription Rates:** $30 Individuals 6 issues; $55 Two years 12 issues; $40 Individuals One Year to National Jurist & preLaw. **URL:** http://www.nationaljurist.com/. **Ad Rates:** BW $4,175; 4C $4,775. **Remarks:** Accepts advertising. **Circ:** Combined 70000.

3791 ■ Network Professional Journal
Network Professional Association
3157 Carmino Del Rio S, Ste. 115
San Diego, CA 92108-4098
Free: 888-NPA-NPA0
Journal publishing articles pertaining to topics of interest to network professionals. **Freq:** Quarterly. **URL:** http://www.npa.org/public/publications_npj.cfm. **Remarks:** Accepts advertising. **Circ:** (Not Reported).

3792 ■ Noesis
Mega Society
c/o Jeff Ward, Administrator
13155 Wimberly Sq., No. 284
San Diego, CA 92128
Freq: Quarterly. **URL:** http://www.megasociety.org. **Remarks:** Advertising not accepted. **Circ:** 50.

3793 ■ Nucleic Acid Therapeutics
Oligonucleotide Therapeutics Society
4377 Newport Ave.
San Diego, CA 92107
Phone: (619)795-9458
Fax: (619)923-3230
Publisher's E-mail: info@oligotherapeutics.org
Peer-reviewed journal focusing on oligonucleotide drug development. **Freq:** Bimonthly. **Print Method:** Offset. **Trim Size:** 8 1/2 x 11. **Cols./Page:** 2. **Col. Width:** 3 1/4 inches. **Col. Depth:** 9 1/2 inches. **Key Personnel:** Bruce A. Sullenger, Editor-in-Chief; C.A. Stein, MD, Editor, phone: (718)920-8980, fax: (718)652-4027. **ISSN:** 2159-3337 (print); **EISSN:** 2159-3345 (electronic). **Subscription Rates:** $440 Individuals print and online; $573 Other countries print and online; $437 Individuals online only; $1993 Institutions print and online; $2292 Institutions, other countries print and online; $1817 Institutions print only; $2090 Institutions, other countries print only; $1954 Institutions online only; $573 Individuals print and online; $2292 Other countries print and online; $2090 Other countries print only. **URL:** http://www.liebertpub.com/NAT. **Formerly:** Antisense Research and Development; Antisense and Nucleic Acid Drug Development; Oligonucleotides. **Ad Rates:** BW $1,095; 4C $1,845. **Remarks:** Advertising accepted; rates available upon request. **Circ:** (Not Reported).

3794 ■ Ocean State Guardian
MARCOA Publishing Inc.
9955 Black Mountain Rd.
San Diego, CA 92126
Phone: (858)695-9600
Free: 800-854-2935
Publisher's E-mail: edit@marcoa.com
Magazine publishing information for employees and military members of the Rhode Island National Guard. **Key Personnel:** Denis Riel, Managing Editor. **Alt. Formats:** PDF. **URL:** http://www.aqppublishing.com/pub_nationalGuardMagazine.html. **Mailing address:** PO Box 509100, San Diego, CA 92150-9100. **Circ:** (Not Reported).

3795 ■ Pelican Dispatch
MARCOA Publishing Inc.
9955 Black Mountain Rd.
San Diego, CA 92126
Phone: (858)695-9600
Free: 800-854-2935
Publisher's E-mail: edit@marcoa.com
Magazine publishing information for employees and military members of Louisiana National Guard. **Freq:** Quarterly. **Key Personnel:** Bob Ulin, Publisher. **Mailing address:** PO Box 509100, San Diego, CA 92150-9100. **Circ:** (Not Reported).

3796 ■ Peninsula Beacon
San Diego Community Newspaper Group
4645 Cass St., 2nd Fl.
San Diego, CA 92109
Phone: (858)270-3103
Fax: (858)713-0095
Publisher's E-mail: sales@sdnews.com
Community newspaper. **Freq:** Weekly. **Print Method:** Offset. **Trim Size:** 11 x 17. **Cols./Page:** 4. **Col. Width:** 2 1/2 inches. **Col. Depth:** 15 3/4 inches. **Key Personnel:** Julie Mannis Hoisington, Publisher; Kevin McKay, Editor. **Subscription Rates:** Free. **URL:** http://www.sdnews.com/pages/home?site=pb#. **Remarks:** Accepts advertising. **Circ:** (Not Reported).

3797 ■ The Point Weekly
Point Loma Nazarene University
3900 Lomaland Dr.
San Diego, CA 92106-2810
Phone: (619)849-2200
Collegiate newspaper (tabloid). **Freq:** Quarterly summer, spring, fall, winter. **Print Method:** Uses mats. Offset. **Trim Size:** 11 x 17. **Cols./Page:** 5. **Col. Width:** 30 nonpareils. **Col. Depth:** 224 agate lines. **Key Personnel:** Kyle Lundberg, Editor-in-Chief. **Remarks:**

Circulation: ★ = AAM; △ or • = BPA; ♦ = CAC; ❑ = VAC; ⊕ = PO Statement; ‡ = Publisher's Report; Boldface figures = sworn; Light figures = estimated.

Advertising accepted; rates available upon request. **Circ:** ‡1500.

3798 ■ Psychiatry Research: Neuroimaging
Elsevier Inc. Health Sciences Division Saunders
Department of Psychiatry & NeuroPET Center
University of California at San Diego
11388 Sorento Valley Rd., Ste. 100
San Diego, CA 92121
Journal publishing manuscripts on positron emission tomography, magnetic resonance imaging, computerized electroencephalographic topography, regional cerebral blood flow, computed tomography, magnetoencephalography, autoradiography, post-mortem regional analyses, and other imaging techniques. **Freq:** 12/yr. **Key Personnel:** T. Dierks, Editor-in-Chief; K. Maurer, Editor-in-Chief; Monte S. Buchsbaum, Editor-in-Chief; H. Anisman, Board Member; S. Buchsbaum, Managing Editor; J.L. Abelson, Board Member. **ISSN:** 0925--4927 (print). **Subscription Rates:** $2143.20 Institutions online; $2143 Institutions print. **URL:** http://www.journals.elsevier.com/psychiatry-research-neuroimaging. **Circ:** (Not Reported).

3799 ■ Riviera San Diego
Modern Luxury Media
1055 F St.
San Diego, CA 92101
Phone: (619)849-6677
Fax: (619)849-6689
Magazine covering affluent lifestyle in San Diego, California. **Freq:** 7/yr. **Key Personnel:** Gillian Flynn, Editor-in-Chief. **Subscription Rates:** $40 Individuals; $60 Two years. **URL:** http://modernluxury.com/riviera-san-diego. **Remarks:** Accepts advertising. **Circ:** (Not Reported).

3800 ■ San Diego Business Journal
San Diego Business Journal
4909 Murphy Canyon Rd., Ste. 200
San Diego, CA 92123
Phone: (858)277-6359
Publisher's E-mail: mdomine@sdbj.com
Metropolitan business newspaper specializing in investigative and enterprise reporting on San Diego County businesses and related issues. **Freq:** Weekly (Mon.). **Print Method:** Offset. **Trim Size:** 10 x 14. **Cols./Page:** 4. **Col. Width:** 27 nonpareils. **Col. Depth:** 196 agate lines. **Key Personnel:** Reo Carr, Executive Editor. **ISSN:** 8750--6890 (print). **Subscription Rates:** $99 Individuals; $180 Two years; $228 Individuals three years. **URL:** http://www.sdbj.com. **Remarks:** Advertising accepted; rates available upon request. **Circ:** (Not Reported).

3801 ■ San Diego City Beat
Southland Publishing
3047 University Ave., Ste. 202
San Diego, CA 92104
Phone: (619)281-7526
Fax: (619)281-5273
Community newspaper. **Freq:** Weekly (Wed.). **Key Personnel:** David Rolland, Editor; Kelly Davis, Associate Editor; Kevin Hellman, Publisher. **URL:** http://www.sdcitybeat.com/sandiego; http://www.southlandpublishing.com/index-2.html. **Remarks:** Accepts classified advertising. **Circ:** Free 50000.

3802 ■ San Diego Commerce
Daily Journal Corp.
2652 4th Ave., 2nd Fl.
San Diego, CA 92103
Phone: (619)232-3486
Fax: (619)232-1159
Publication E-mail: san_diego@dailyjournal.com
Business, real estate, and legal newspaper. **Freq:** Tri-weekly Tuesday, Wednesday, Friday. **Print Method:** Offset. **Trim Size:** 11 1/2 x 15. **Cols./Page:** 4. **Col. Width:** 2 3/8 inches. **Col. Depth:** 13 3/4 inches. **ISSN:** 1063--5513 (print). **URL:** http://www.dailyjournal.com/public/PubMain.cfm?seloption=RenewSub&pubdate=&shNewsType=ContactUs&NewsId=-1&sdivId=&screenHt=430. **Formerly**: Back Country Trader. **Remarks:** Accepts advertising. **Circ:** (Not Reported).

3803 ■ San Diego Earth Times
San Diego Earth Times
PO Box 99179
San Diego, CA 92169
Phone: (858)272-7423
Fax: (858)272-2933
Publisher's E-mail: info@sdearthtimes.com
Magazine covering a wide variety of local, national and international environmental topics. **Key Personnel:** Carolyn Chase, Editor. **URL:** http://www.earthdayweb.org. **Circ:** (Not Reported).

3804 ■ San Diego Family Magazine
San Diego Family Magazine
1475 6th Ave., 5th Fl.
San Diego, CA 92101-3200
Phone: (619)685-6970
Fax: (619)685-6978
Publisher's E-mail: family@sandiegofamily.com
Magazine. **Freq:** Monthly. **Key Personnel:** Giovanni Baldan, Director, Advertising, Director, Marketing, phone: (619)685-6987; Sharon Bay, Editor, Publisher, phone: (619)685-6970; Tony Andrews, Director, Advertising, Director, Marketing, phone: (619)685-6977. **Subscription Rates:** $18 Individuals. **URL:** http://sandiegofamily.com. **Formerly:** San Diego Family Press. **Remarks:** Accepts advertising. **Circ:** ‡120000.

3805 ■ San Diego International Law Journal
University of San Diego School of Law
Warren Hall, Rm. 201
5998 Alcala Pk.
San Diego, CA 92110-2492
Phone: (619)260-4527
Publisher's E-mail: losi@law.berkeley.edu
Freq: Semiannual. **Subscription Rates:** $27 Individuals. **URL:** http://sandiego.edu/law/academics/journals/ilj. **Remarks:** Advertising not accepted. **Circ:** (Not Reported).

3806 ■ San Diego Journal of Climate and Energy Law
University of San Diego School of Law
Warren Hall, Rm. 201
5998 Alcala Pk.
San Diego, CA 92110-2492
Phone: (619)260-4527
Publisher's E-mail: lawdean@sandiego.edu
Journal containing legal issues related to climate change and energy. **Freq:** Annual. **Key Personnel:** Andrew Walters, Editor-in-Chief. **URL:** http://www.sandiego.edu/law/academics/journals/jcel. **Circ:** (Not Reported).

3807 ■ San Diego Law Review
San Diego Law Review Association
c/o University of San Diego, School of Law
5998 Alcala Pk.
San Diego, CA 92110
Phone: (619)260-4531
Fax: (619)260-7497
Publication E-mail: lawreview@sandiego.edu
Law journal. **Freq:** Quarterly. **Cols./Page:** 1. **Col. Width:** 6 1/2 inches. **Col. Depth:** 10 inches. **Key Personnel:** Brandon G. Smith, Editor-in-Chief; Misty Ann Giles, Editor. **ISSN:** 0036-4037 (print). **Subscription Rates:** $30 Individuals; $43 Other countries. **URL:** http://www.sandiego.edu. **Ad Rates:** BW $150. **Remarks:** Accepts advertising. **Circ:** 900.

3808 ■ San Diego Magazine
San Diego Magazine Publishing Co.
707 Broadway Ste. 1100
San Diego, CA 92101-3411
Phone: (619)230-9292
Fax: (619)230-0490
Regional magazine covering San Diego, California. **Freq:** Monthly. **Print Method:** Offset. **Trim Size:** 8 1/4 x 10 3/4. **Cols./Page:** 3. **Col. Width:** 27 nonpareils. **Col. Depth:** 138 agate lines. **ISSN:** 0036--4045 (print). **Subscription Rates:** $18 Individuals print; $12 Individuals online; $98 Other countries print. **Remarks:** Advertising accepted; rates available upon request. **Circ:** Combined 49684.

3809 ■ San Diego Physician
San Diego County Medical Society
5575 Ruffin Rd., Ste. 250
San Diego, CA 92123
Phone: (858)565-8888
Fax: (858)569-1334
Publication E-mail: editor@sdcms.org
Freq: Monthly latest issue: May 2015. **Trim Size:** 8 1/2 x 11. **Key Personnel:** Jennifer Rohr, Contact. **Subscription Rates:** $35 Individuals /year. **Alt. Formats:** Print. **URL:** http://www.sdcms.org/PhysicianQuicklinks/Publications/SanDiegoPhysicianMagazine.aspx. **Ad Rates:** 4C $1,675. **Remarks:** Accepts advertising. **Circ:** Paid 3000, 2100.

3810 ■ San Diego Reader
San Diego Reader
1703 India St. (at Date St.)
Little Italy, downtown San Diego
San Diego, CA 92186
Phone: (619)235-3000
Fax: (619)231-0489
Newspaper covering San Diego lifestyle emphasizing the arts, entertainment, and politics. Features comprehensive listings of movies, events, theater, and pop music; restaurant and film reviews; and free classified advertisements for its readers. **Freq:** Weekly (Thurs.). **Print Method:** Offset. **Trim Size:** 10 1/4 x 13. **Cols./Page:** 6. **Col. Width:** 1 1/2 inches. **Subscription Rates:** $10 Single issue; $125 Individuals third-class mail; $299 Individuals first-class mail. **URL:** http://www.sandiegoreader.com/home. **Mailing address:** PO Box 85803, San Diego, CA 92186-5803. **Remarks:** Advertising accepted; rates available upon request. **Circ:** Free ■ **149687**.

3811 ■ San Diego This Week
Key Magazines Inc.
501 W Broadway, Ste. 800
San Diego, CA 92101
Free: 888-299-1364
Publication E-mail: info@hottengroup.com
Visitor's guide publication featuring coverage of events, dining, shopping, and more. **Freq:** Biweekly. **Circ:** Combined **65000**.

3812 ■ The San Diego Union-Tribune
Union-Tribune Publishing Co.
350 Camino de la Reina
San Diego, CA 92112-0191
Phone: (619)293-1211
Fax: (619)293-1896
Free: 800-533-8830
Publisher's E-mail: customersupport@utsandiego.com
International, national, and local news. **Founded:** Oct. 10, 1868. **Freq:** Daily. **Print Method:** Offset. **Cols./Page:** 6. **Col. Width:** 2 1/16 inches. **Col. Depth:** 21 1/2 inches. **Key Personnel:** Bill Osborne, Director, Editorial; Jeff Light, Editor. **URL:** http://www.utsandiego.com/. **Mailing address:** PO Box 120191, San Diego, CA 92112-0191. **Remarks:** Accepts advertising. **Circ:** Mon.-Fri. ***314279**, Sun. ***416682**, Sat. ***362388**.

3813 ■ The San Diego Voice and Viewpoint
The San Diego Voice & Viewpoint
3619 College Ave.
San Diego, CA 92112
Phone: (619)266-2233
Fax: (619)266-0533
Publisher's E-mail: news@sdvoice.com
Black American newspaper. **Freq:** Weekly (Thurs.). **Print Method:** Offset. Uses mats. **Cols./Page:** 6. **Col. Width:** 23 nonpareils. **Col. Depth:** 224 agate lines. **Key Personnel:** John E. Warren, Dr., Publisher, Chief Executive Officer. **Subscription Rates:** $60 Individuals; $70 Out of state; $90 Two years; $100 Other countries two years. **URL:** http://sdvoice.info. **Remarks:** Advertising accepted; rates available upon request. **Circ:** 13000.

3814 ■ Shooting Industry
Publishers Development Corp.
12345 World Trade Dr.
San Diego, CA 92128
Fax: (858)605-0247
Magazine serving the firearms industry. **Freq:** Monthly. **Print Method:** Offset. **Trim Size:** 8 x 10 7/8. **Cols./Page:** 3. **Col. Width:** 26 nonpareils. **Col. Depth:** 140 agate lines. **Key Personnel:** Russ Thurman, Editor, phone: (858)605-0244; Anita Carson, Director, Advertising and Sales, phone: (866)972-4545. **ISSN:** 0037--4148 (print). **URL:** http://www.shootingindustry.com. **Ad Rates:** BW $4228; 4C $6711; PCI $458. **Remarks:** Accepts advertising. **Circ:** Paid ‡893, Non-paid ‡16462.

3815 ■ Sociological Abstracts
Cambridge Scientific Abstracts L.P.
Sociological Abstracts
San Diego, CA 92192
Phone: (858)571-8979
Fax: (858)571-8694
Publisher's E-mail: sales@proquest.com

Publication containing abstracts of sociology publications worldwide. **Founded:** 1952. **Freq:** Monthly with approximately 30,000 records added per year. **Print Method:** Offset. **Trim Size:** 8 1/2 x 11. **Cols./Page:** 2. **Col. Width:** 49 nonpareils. **Col. Depth:** 135 agate lines. **ISSN:** 0038-0202 (print). **Subscription Rates:** $860 Individuals print + web edition, includes shipping. **URL:** http://www.proquest.com/products-services/socioabsset-c.html. **Mailing address:** PO Box 22206, San Diego, CA 92192. **Remarks:** Advertising not accepted. **Circ:** ‡1900.

3816 ■ The Southern Cross
Roman Catholic Diocese of San Diego
PO Box 81869
San Diego, CA 92138
Phone: (858)490-8279
Roman Catholic newspaper. **Freq:** Monthly the third Wednesday of each month. **Print Method:** Offset. **Trim Size:** 62.5 pica x 96 pica. **Cols./Page:** 4. **Col. Width:** 19 nonpareils. **Col. Depth:** 224 agate lines. **Key Personnel:** Rev. Charles Fuld, Managing Editor, phone: (858)490-8279. **ISSN:** 0745--0257 (print). **Subscription Rates:** $15 Individuals. **URL:** http://www.thesoutherncross.org. **Ad Rates:** 4C $1400; PCI $30. **Remarks:** Advertising accepted; rates available upon request. **Circ:** ‡34000.

3817 ■ SWE Magazine
Society of Women Engineers San Diego County
PO Box 881205
San Diego, CA 92168-1205
Magazine of the Society of Women Engineers, San Diego County Section. **Freq:** Quarterly. **Trim Size:** 8 3/8 X 10 7/8. **Key Personnel:** Alyse Stofer, President. **ISSN:** 1070--6232 (print). **URL:** http://societyofwomenengineers.swe.org/swe-magazine-new. **Ad Rates:** BW $7728; 4C $1295. **Remarks:** Accepts advertising. **Circ:** (Not Reported).

3818 ■ Theoretical Population Biology
Academic Press Inc.
525 B St., Ste. 1900
San Diego, CA 92101-4495
Phone: (619)231-6616
Free: 800-545-2522
Journal presenting articles on the theoretical aspects of the biology of populations, particularly in the areas of ecology, genetics, demography, and epidemiology. **Freq:** Bimonthly. **Trim Size:** 6 x 9. **Key Personnel:** P.L. Chesson, Editor. **ISSN:** 0040--5809 (print). **Subscription Rates:** $333 Individuals print only; $1006.67 Institutions eJournal; $1660 Institutions print only. **URL:** http://www.journals.elsevier.com/theoretical-population-biology. **Circ:** (Not Reported).

3819 ■ Triathlete
Competitor Group Inc.
9401 Waples St., Ste. 150
San Diego, CA 92121
Phone: (858)450-6510
Fax: (858)450-6905
Magazine for multi-sport endurance athletes. **Freq:** Monthly. **Print Method:** Offset. **Trim Size:** 8 1/8 x 10 3/4. **Cols./Page:** 3. **Col. Width:** 27 nonpareils. **Col. Depth:** 140 agate lines. **Key Personnel:** Brad Culp, Editor. **Subscription Rates:** $39.95 Individuals print and online; C$65.95 Canada print and online; $99.95 Other countries print and online. **URL:** http://competitorgroup.com/media/triathlete. **Ad Rates:** BW $4,631; 4C $6,169. **Circ:** Paid ★**65248**.

3820 ■ Uptown San Diego Examiner: Business News
Uptown Examiner Group
3930 Oregon St., Ste. 110
San Diego, CA 92104
Phone: (619)955-8960
Fax: (619)955-8962
Community newspaper. **Freq:** Semiweekly (Wed. and Fri.). **Trim Size:** 8.125 x 10.5. **Cols./Page:** 3. **Col. Depth:** 10 inches. **Key Personnel:** Kevin Specht, Director, Production. **ISSN:** 0898--4581 (print). **Subscription Rates:** $35 Individuals; $40 Out of area. **URL:** http://uptownexaminer.com. **Ad Rates:** BW $183; PCI $5. **Remarks:** Color advertising not accepted. **Circ:** Controlled 40000.

3821 ■ Western Journal of Communication
Routledge Journals Taylor & Francis Group
c/o William Eadie, Ed.
School of Journalism and Media Studies
San Diego State University
5500 Campanile Dr.
San Diego, CA 92182-4561
Publication E-mail: weadie@mail.sdsu.edu
Journal on communication for academicians. **Freq:** Quarterly. **Key Personnel:** William Eadie, Editor. **ISSN:** 1057-0314 (print). **Subscription Rates:** $411 Institutions online only; $15 Institutions print and online. **URL:** http://www.tandfonline.com/toc/rwjc20/current#.VHhF7tIW2qY. **Formerly**: Western Journal of Speech Communications. **Circ:** (Not Reported).

3822 ■ Writers' Monthly
Writers' Monthly
PO Box 4913
San Diego, CA 92164-4913
Literary magazine for local authors. **Freq:** Monthly. **Trim Size:** 8 x 10 1/2. **Key Personnel:** Elizabeth Baldwin, Editor. **ISSN:** 1054--6774 (print). **Subscription Rates:** $38 Individuals; $3 Single issue. **URL:** http://www.writersmonthly.com. **Remarks:** Accepts advertising. **Circ:** (Not Reported).

3823 ■ ZOONOOZ
San Diego Zoo Global
2920 Zoo Dr.
San Diego, CA 92101-1646
Phone: (619)231-1515
Magazine on natural history, animal science, and conservation. **Freq:** Monthly. **Print Method:** Offset. **Trim Size:** 8 1/2 x 11. **Cols./Page:** 4 and 3. **Col. Width:** 20 and 27 nonpareils. **Col. Depth:** 136 agate lines. **ISSN:** 0044--5282 (print). **URL:** http://zoonooz.sandiegozoo.org. **Mailing address:** PO Box 120551, San Diego, CA 92112-0551. **Remarks:** Accepts advertising. **Circ:** ‡250000.

3824 ■ Cox Communications
5159 Federal Blvd.
San Diego, CA 92105
Phone: (619)263-9251
Owner: Cox Communications Inc., 1400 Lake Hearn Dr., Atlanta, GA 30319-1464, Ph: (404)843-5000, Free: 866-456-9944. **Key Personnel:** Patrick J. Esser, President. **Cities Served:** Alpine, Chula Vista, Chula Vista, El Cajon, Imperial Beach, La Mesa, Lemon Grove, National City, Pine Valley, Poway, Santee, California: subscribing households 326,000; San Diego County, CA; 77 channels; 3 community access channels; 380 hours per week community access programming. **URL:** http://ww2.cox.com/aboutus/sandiego/contact-us/residential-local.cox.

3825 ■ KBNT-TV - 17
5770 Ruffin Rd.
San Diego, CA 92123-1013
Phone: (858)715-6424
Fax: (858)435-1505
Networks: Univision. **Owner:** Entravision Communications Corporation, 2425 Olympic Blvd., Ste. 6000 W, Santa Monica, CA 90404-4030, Ph: (310)447-3870, Fax: (310)447-3899. **Founded:** 1990. **Operating Hours:** Continuous. **ADI**: San Diego, CA. **Key Personnel:** Margarita Wilder, Gen. Mgr. **Wattage**: 031. **Ad Rates:** $125-1000 for 30 seconds. **URL:** http://www.entravision.com.

3826 ■ KBZT-FM - 94.9
1615 Murray Canyon Rd., Ste. 710
San Diego, CA 92108
Phone: (619)718-7127
Fax: (619)543-1353
Email: fm949studio@lincolnfinancialmedia.com
Format: Album-Oriented Rock (AOR); Alternative/New Music/Progressive. **Owner:** Lincoln Financial Media Co., 1615 Murray Canyon Rd., San Diego, CA 92108. **Founded:** 1960. **Formerly**: KWLT-FM; KBZS-FM. **Operating Hours**: Continuous. **ADI**: San Diego, CA. **Key Personnel:** Garett Michaels, Dir. of Programs, gmichaels@fm949sd.com. **Wattage:** 22,000. **Ad Rates:** Noncommercial. Combined advertising rates available with KSON-FM &AM; KIPM-FM. **URL:** http://www.fm949sd.com.

3827 ■ KCBQ-AM - 1170
9255 Towne Centre Dr., Ste. 535
San Diego, CA 92121
Phone: (858)535-1210
Fax: (858)535-1212
Format: News; Talk. **Networks:** Westwood One Radio. **Owner:** Salem Media Group Inc., 4880 Santa Rosa Rd., Camarillo, CA 93012, Ph: (805)987-0400, Fax: (805)384-4520. **Operating Hours**: Continuous. **ADI**: San Diego, CA. **Wattage**: 50,000 Day; 1,500 Night. **Ad Rates**: Advertising accepted; rates available upon request. **URL:** http://www.kcbq.com.

3828 ■ KCBQ-FM - 105.3
9660 Granite Ridge Dr., Ste. 100
San Diego, CA 92123
Phone: (858)570-1053
Format: Oldies; Album-Oriented Rock (AOR). **Networks:** AP; Independent. **Owner:** Compass Radio Group, at above address, Fax: (619)449-8548; Clear Channel Communication, Inc., 200 E Basse Rd., San Antonio, TX 78209, Ph: (210)822-2828, Fax: (210)822-2828. **Founded:** 1954. **Formerly**: KGMG-FM. **Operating Hours**: Continuous. **Key Personnel:** Debbie Wagner, Gen. Mgr.; Bob Ferro, Gen. Sales Mgr.; Julian Muschell, Sales Mgr.; Kim Leeds, Promotions Dir.; Jeff Stewart, Coord.; Dan Mitchinson, Director; Mike Aiken, Asst. Dir.; Bill Lipis, Chief Engineer; Bob Hughes, Gen. Mgr. **Wattage**: 26,000 ERP. **Ad Rates:** Noncommercial. **URL:** http://rock1053.iheart.com.

3829 ■ KCR-AM - 98.9
c/o Student Activities & Campus Life
5500 Campanile Dr.
San Diego, CA 92182-7440
Phone: (619)594-7014
Format: Educational. **Owner:** San Diego State University, 5500 Campanile Dr., San Diego, CA 92182, Ph: (619)594-5200. **Founded:** 1969. **Key Personnel:** Johnny White, Promotions Dir., kcrpromotionsdirector@gmail.com. **Ad Rates:** Noncommercial. **URL:** http://www.kcr.sdsu.edu.

3830 ■ KCR-FM - 98.9
5500 Campanile Dr.
San Diego, CA 92182-7440
Phone: (619)594-7014
Email: kcr@mail.sdsu.edu
Format: Educational. **Owner:** San Diego State University, 5500 Campanile Dr., San Diego, CA 92182, Ph: (619)594-5200. **Key Personnel:** Matthew Hoffman, Director; Josh Hoffman, Gen. Mgr., kcrgeneralmanager@gmail.com. **Ad Rates:** Noncommercial. **URL:** http://www.kcr.sdsu.edu.

3831 ■ KEGY-FM. - 99.1
1515 Broadway
New York, NY 10036
Format: Adult Contemporary. **Owner:** Cbs Radio Stations Inc, at above address. **Founded:** 1928. **Formerly**: KSCF-FM. **ADI**: Sacramento-Stockton, CA. **Wattage**: 100. **URL:** http://www.cbsradio.com.

3832 ■ KFMB-AM - 760
7677 Engineer Rd.
San Diego, CA 92111
Phone: (858)292-7600
Free: 800-760-5362
Email: comments@kfmb.com
Format: Talk. **Networks:** CBS. **Owner:** Midwest Television Inc., 509 S Neil St., Champaign, IL 61820, Ph: (217)356-8333, Fax: (217)373-3680. **Founded:** 1941. **Operating Hours**: 5:00 a.m. - 6:00 p.m. Monday - Friday; 7:00 a.m. - 4:00 p.m. Saturday; 9:00 a.m. - 8:00 p.m. Sunday. **ADI**: San Diego, CA. **Local Programs**: *The Lawyer in Blue Jeans*, Saturday 4:00 p.m. - 5:00 p.m. **Wattage**: 5,000 Day; 50,000 Ni. **Ad Rates:** Advertising accepted; rates available upon request. **URL:** http://www.760kfmb.com.

3833 ■ KFMB-FM - 100.7
7677 Engineer Rd.
San Diego, CA 92111
Phone: (858)571-8888
Free: 888-570-1007
Email: radiopromotions@kfmb.com
Format: Adult Contemporary. **Networks:** Independent. **Owner:** Midwest Television Inc., 7677 Engineer Road, San Diego, CA 92111-1582, Ph: (619)495-9308, Fax: (619)279-3519. **Founded:** 1959. **Operating Hours**: Continuous. **ADI**: San Diego, CA. **Key Personnel:** Joyce Bergen, Contact, jbergen@kfmb.com; Mitch Gruber,

Circulation: ★ = AAM; △ or • = BPA; ♦ = CAC; ❑ = VAC; ⊕ = PO Statement; ‡ = Publisher's Report; Boldface figures = sworn; Light figures = estimated.

Contact, websales@kfmb.com. **Wattage**: 36,000. **Ad Rates:** Advertising accepted; rates available upon request. **URL:** http://www.sandiegojack.com.

3834 ■ KFMB-TV - 8
7677 Engineer Rd.
San Diego, CA 92111
Email: news8@kfmb.com
Format: Commercial TV. **Networks:** CBS. **Owner:** Midwest Television Inc., 7677 Engineer Road, San Diego, CA 92111-1582, Ph: (619)495-9308, Fax: (619)279-3519. **Founded:** 1949. **Operating Hours**: Continuous except 2 a.m.-6 a.m. Sat. and Sun. **ADI**: San Diego, CA. **Local Programs**: *CBS Evening News*, Monday Tuesday Wednesday Thursday 6:00 p.m. **Ad Rates:** Noncommercial. **URL:** http://www.cbs8.com.

3835 ■ KGB-FM - 89.7
9660 Granite Ridge Dr., Ste. 100
San Diego, CA 92123
Phone: (858)292-2000
Format: Classic Rock. **Simulcasts:** KGBB, KMYT. **Owner:** iHeartMedia Inc., 200 E Basse Rd., San Antonio, TX 78209, Ph: (210)832-3314. **Formerly**: Nationwide. **Operating Hours**: Continuous. **Key Personnel:** Melissa Forrest, President, Mktg. Mgr.; Terry King, Sales Mgr., marydeary@clearchannel.com; Bill Lennert, Promotions Dir; Mary Deary, Contact, marydeary@clearchannel.com. **Wattage**: 6,800. **Ad Rates:** Advertising accepted; rates available upon request. **URL:** http://www.101kgb.com.

3836 ■ KGTV-TV - 10
4600 Air Way
San Diego, CA 92102
Phone: (619)237-1010
Fax: (619)527-0369
Email: kgtv_marketing@10news.com
Format: Commercial TV. **Networks:** ABC. **Owner:** McGraw-Hill Broadcasting, Inc., PO Box 182604, Columbus, OH 43272, Fax: (614)759-3749, Free: 877-833-5524. **Founded:** 1953. **ADI**: San Diego, CA. **Key Personnel:** Jeff Block, Gen. Mgr., VP. **Ad Rates:** Advertising accepted; rates available upon request. **URL:** http://www.10news.com.

3837 ■ KHTS-FM - 93.3
9660 Granite Ridge Dr., Ste. 100
San Diego, CA 92123
Format: Contemporary Hit Radio (CHR). **Wattage**: 50,000. **Ad Rates:** Noncommercial. **URL:** http://intagme.com.

3838 ■ KIFM-FM - 98.1
1615 Murray Canyon Rd., Ste. 710
San Diego, CA 92108-4321
Phone: (619)297-3698
Fax: (619)543-1353
Format: Jazz. **Networks:** Independent. **Owner:** Lincoln Financial Media Company of California, 1615 Murray Canyon Rd., San Diego, CA 92108, Ph: (619)291-9797. **Founded:** 1960. **Operating Hours**: Continuous. **ADI**: San Diego, CA. **Key Personnel:** Mike Vasquez, Dir. of Programs, mikev@kifm.net; Natasha Collins, Promotions Mgr., natasha.collins@lincolnfinancialmedia.com; John D'Angelo, Promotions Dir., john.dangelo@lincolnfinancialmedia.com. **Wattage**: 28,000. **Ad Rates:** $200-350 for 60 seconds. Combined advertising rates available with KSON, KBZT. **URL:** http://www.easy981.com.

3839 ■ KLNV-FM - 106.5
600 W Broadway, Ste. 2150
San Diego, CA 92101
Phone: (619)235-0600
Fax: (619)744-4300
Free: 866-702-1065
Format: Hispanic. **Key Personnel:** Peter Moore, Gen. Mgr. **Ad Rates:** Noncommercial.

3840 ■ KLQV-FM - 102.9
600 W Broadway, Ste. 2150
San Diego, CA 92101
Phone: (619)235-0600
Fax: (619)744-4300
Format: Hispanic. **Owner:** Univision Radio Inc., 3102 Oak Lawn Ave., Ste. 215, Dallas, TX 75219-4259, Ph: (214)525-7700, Fax: (214)525-7750. **ADI**: San Diego, CA. **Key Personnel:** Peter Moore, Mgr. **URL:** http://www.univision.com.

3841 ■ KLSD-AM - 1360
9660 Granite Ridge Dr., Ste. 100
San Diego, CA 92123
Phone: (858)292-2000
Format: Sports. **ADI**: San Diego, CA. **Wattage**: 5,000. **Ad Rates:** Noncommercial. **URL:** http://www.xtrasports1360.com.

3842 ■ KLVQ-FM - 102.9
600 W Broadway, Ste. 2150
San Diego, CA 92101
Phone: (903)489-1238
Fax: (903)489-2671
Format: Hispanic. **Mailing address:** PO Box 489, Malakoff, TX 92101. **URL:** http://www.kcklfm.com/klvq.

3843 ■ KMYI-FM - 94.1
9660 Granite Ridge Dr., Ste. 100
San Diego, CA 92123
Format: Adult Contemporary. **ADI**: San Diego, CA. **Wattage**: 77,000. **URL:** http://intagme.com.

3844 ■ KNFR-FM - 96.1
750 B. St., Ste. 1920
San Diego, CA 92101
Format: Country. **Owner:** Triathlon Broadcasting, Inc., at above address. **Founded:** Oct. 1992. **Operating Hours**: Continuous. **ADI**: Spokane, WA. **Key Personnel:** Kosta Panidis, Gen. Mgr.; Scott Shannon, Dir. of Programs; Mary Norton, Bus. Mgr.; Brenda Anderson, Dir. of Traffic. **Wattage**: 56,000. **Ad Rates:** Advertising accepted; rates available upon request.

3845 ■ KNSD-TV - 39
225 Broadway, Ste. 100
San Diego, CA 92101
Phone: (619)231-3939
Format: Commercial TV. **Networks:** NBC. **Owner:** NBC Universal Media L.L.C., 30 Rockefeller Plz., New York, NY 10112, Ph: (212)664-4444. **Founded:** 1965. **Formerly**: KAAR-TV. **Operating Hours**: 5:15 a.m.-4:15 a.m.; 57% network, 43% local. **ADI**: San Diego, CA. **Key Personnel:** Michael Bass, Sr. VP. **Ad Rates:** Noncommercial. **URL:** http://www.nbcsandiego.com.

3846 ■ KOGO-AM - 600
9660 Granite Ridge Dr.
San Diego, CA 92123
Phone: (858)292-2000
Free: 800-600-5646
Format: Talk; News. **Simulcasts:** KOGO-FM. **Networks:** CNN Radio; ABC. **Founded:** 1926. **Formerly**: KLZZ-AM; KKLQ-AM. **Operating Hours**: Continuous. **ADI**: San Diego, CA. **Local Programs**: *The Voice of San Diego*, Sunday; *The Movie Guys*; *The Jesus Christ Show*, Sunday 6:00 a.m. - 9:00 a.m. **Wattage**: 5,000. **Ad Rates:** Advertising accepted; rates available upon request. Combined advertising rates available with KSDO-AM. **URL:** http://www.kogo.com.

3847 ■ KPBS-FM - 89.5
5200 Campanile Dr.
San Diego, CA 92182-5400
Phone: (619)594-6983
Free: 888-399-5727
Email: members@kpbs.org
Format: News; Public Radio. **Networks:** National Public Radio (NPR); Public Radio International (PRI). **Founded:** 1960. **Operating Hours**: Continuous; 50% network, 50% local. **ADI**: San Diego, CA. **Key Personnel:** Steve Walsh, Producer; John Decker, Dir. of Programs; Tom Karlo, Gen. Mgr.; Erik Anderson, Dir. of Mktg.; Joe Guerin, Editor. **Local Programs**: *Midday Edition*, Monday Tuesday Wednesday Thursday Friday Monday Tuesday Wednesday Thursday 12:00 p.m. 9:00 p.m. **Wattage**: 1,750. **Ad Rates:** Noncommercial. **URL:** http://www.kpbs.org.

3848 ■ KPBS-TV - 15
5200 Campanile Dr.
San Diego, CA 92182
Phone: (619)594-1515
Free: 888-399-5727
Format: Public TV. **Networks:** Public Broadcasting Service (PBS). **Owner:** Public Broadcasting Service, 2100 Crystal Dr., Arlington, VA 22202, Ph: (703)739-5000. **Founded:** 1967. **Formerly**: KEBS-TV. **Operating Hours**: 6:15 a.m.-2 a.m.; 95% network, 5% local. **ADI**: San Diego, CA. **Key Personnel:** Tom Karlo, Gen. Mgr., tkarlo@kpbs.org; Deanna Mackey, Station Mgr. **Local Programs**: *Teen Issues: Date Rape*; *Teen Issues: Peer Pressure*; *Teen Issues: Teen-Parent Communication*. **Wattage**: 3,020. **Ad Rates:** Advertising accepted; rates available upon request. **URL:** http://www.kpbs.org.

3849 ■ KPRZ-AM - 1210
9255 Towne Centre Dr., Ste. 535
San Diego, CA 92121
Phone: (858)535-1210
Fax: (858)535-1212
Format: Contemporary Christian. **Owner:** Salem Media Group Inc., 4880 Santa Rosa Rd., Camarillo, CA 93012, Ph: (805)987-0400, Fax: (805)384-4520. **Founded:** 1986. **Operating Hours**: Continuous. **ADI**: San Diego, CA. **Key Personnel:** Dave Armstrong, Gen. Mgr. **Local Programs**: *KPRZ Specials*, Monday Tuesday Wednesday Thursday Friday Saturday Sunday 5:00 a.m. - 5:30 a.m. 12:00 a.m. - 12:30 a.m.; 1:00 a.m. - 5:00 a.m.; 6:00 a.m. - 8:00 a.m.; 3:00 p.m. - 4:00 p.m.; 8:00 p.m. - 9:00 p.m. 12:01 a.m. - 5:00 a.m.; 9:30 a.m. - 10:00 a.m.; 11:30 a.m. - 1:00 p.m.; 2:00 p.m. - 4:00 p.m.; 6:30 p.m. - 7:00 p.m.; 8:00 p.m. - 8:30 p.m. **Wattage**: 20,000 Day; 10,000 N. **Ad Rates:** Accepts Advertising. **URL:** http://www.kprz.com.

KQVO-FM - See Calexico

3850 ■ KSDS-FM - 88.3
San Diego City College
1313 Park Blvd.
San Diego, CA 92101
Phone: (619)388-3037
Fax: (619)388-3928
Format: Jazz. **Networks:** Independent. **Owner:** San Diego Community College District, 3375 Camino Del Rio S, San Diego, CA 92108, Ph: (619)388-6500. **Founded:** 1951. **Operating Hours**: Continuous; 100% local. **ADI**: San Diego, CA. **Key Personnel:** Mark Deboskey, Station Mgr.; Joe Kocherhans, Music Dir.; Claudia Russell, Dir. of Programs; Jennifer Weddel, Dir. of Dev.; Leslie Ebner, Office Mgr. **Wattage**: 3,000. **Ad Rates:** Noncommercial. **URL:** http://www.jazz88.org.

3851 ■ KSON-FM - 97.3
1615 Murray Canyon Rd., Ste. 710
San Diego, CA 92108-4321
Phone: (619)291-9797
Fax: (619)543-1353
Format: Country. **Owner:** Lincoln Financial Media Company of California, 1615 Murray Canyon Rd., San Diego, CA 92108, Ph: (619)291-9797. **Founded:** 1946. **Operating Hours**: Continuous Monday - Friday. **ADI**: San Diego, CA. **Wattage**: 50,000 ERP. **Ad Rates:** Combined advertising rates available with KSON-AM. **URL:** http://www.kson.com.

3852 ■ KSWB-TV - 69
7191 Engineer Rd.
San Diego, CA 92111
Phone: (858)492-9269
Format: Commercial TV. **Networks:** Warner Brothers Studios. **Owner:** The Tribune Media Co., 435 N Michigan Ave., Chicago, IL 60611-4066, Ph: (312)222-9100, Fax: (312)222-4206, Free: 800-874-2863. **Founded:** 1984. **Formerly**: KTTY-TV. **Operating Hours**: Continuous. **ADI**: San Diego, CA. **Wattage**: 4,500 KW. **Ad Rates:** Advertising accepted; rates available upon request. **URL:** http://www.fox5sandiego.com.

3853 ■ KUSI-TV - 51
4575 Viewridge Ave.
San Diego, CA 92123
Phone: (858)571-5151
Email: news@kusi.com
Format: News; Talk. **Networks:** United Paramount Network. **Owner:** McKinnon Broadcasting Co., 4575 Viewridge Avenue, San Diego, CA 92123, Ph: (858)505-5100, Fax: (858)571-5711. **Founded:** 1983. **Operating Hours**: Continuous. **ADI**: San Diego, CA. **Ad Rates:** Advertising accepted; rates available upon request. **URL:** http://www.kusi.com.

3854 ■ KUSS-FM - 95.7
9660 Granite Ridge Dr.
San Diego, CA 92123
Phone: (858)292-2000
Free: 888-570-1957
Format: Country. **ADI**: San Diego, CA. **Wattage**: 100,000. **Ad Rates:** Advertising accepted; rates available upon request. **URL:** http://www.957kissfm.com//main.html.

3855 ■ KYDO-FM - 96.1

2550 5th Ave., Ste. 723
San Diego, CA 92102
Phone: (760)344-1300
Fax: (760)344-1763
Founded: 1981. **Ad Rates:** $14-18 for 30 seconds; $17-24 for 60 seconds.

3856 ■ KYXY-FM - 96.5
8033 Linda Vista Rd.
San Diego, CA 92111
Phone: (858)571-7600
Fax: (858)571-0326
Free: 888-560-9650
Format: Soft Rock. **Networks:** Independent. **Owner:** CBS Radio Inc., 1271 Avenue of the Americas, 44th Fl., New York, NY 10020-1401, Ph: (212)649-9600. **Founded:** 1978. **Operating Hours**: Continuous. **ADI**: San Diego, CA. **Wattage**: 26,500. **Ad Rates:** Advertising accepted; rates available upon request. Combined advertising rates available with KPLN-FM. **URL:** http://kyxy.cbslocal.com.

3857 ■ 102.1 KPRI - 102.1
9710 Scranton Rd., Ste. 200
San Diego, CA 92121
Phone: (858)678-0102
Fax: (858)320-7024
Format: Classic Rock; Soft Rock. **Ad Rates:** Noncommercial. **URL:** http://www.kprifm.com.

3858 ■ Time Warner Cable - San Diego
8949 Ware Ct.
San Diego, CA 92121
Fax: (858)566-6248
Email: jim.fellhauer@tvcable.com
Owner: Time Warner Cable Inc., 60 Columbus Cir., New York, NY 10023, Ph: (212)364-8200, Fax: (212)328-0604, Free: 800-892-4357. **Founded:** 1964. **Formerly**: Southwestern Cable TV. **Cities Served:** Clairemont, Del Mar Heights, La Jolla, Linda Vista, Mira Mesa, Mission Beach, North Poway, North Poway, Pacific Beach, San Diego County, Tierrasanta, University City, California: subscribing households 205,000; Bay Park, Carmel Mountain Ranch, Mission Valley, North City West, Poway, Rancho Bernardo, Rancho Penas Quitos, Sabre Springs, Serra Mesa, CA; 78 channels; 1 community access channel; 40 hours per week community access programming. **URL:** http://www.timewarnercable.com/content/dam/Corporate/PDFs/About-Us/Careers/2012-FCC-notices/0561%20EEO%20Public%20File%20Report%202012.pdf.

3859 ■ XDTV-TV - 49
5770 Ruffin Rd.
San Diego, CA 92123
Phone: (858)576-1919
Fax: (858)715-2978
Owner: Entravision Communications Corporation, 2425 Olympic Blvd., Ste. 6000 W, Santa Monica, CA 90404-4030, Ph: (310)447-3870, Fax: (310)447-3899. **Key Personnel:** Robert Moutal, Gen. Mgr., robert@telemundo33.com. **URL:** http://www.mytv13.com.

3860 ■ XEPE-AM - 1700
6160 Cornerstone Ct. E, Ste. 100
San Diego, CA 92121
Phone: (858)535-2500
Format: Talk; Sports. **Wattage**: 10,000. **URL:** http://www.sandiego1700.com/pages/main.

3861 ■ XEPRS-AM - 1090
6160 Cornerstone Ct. E, Ste. 100
San Diego, CA 92121
Phone: (858)535-2500
Free: 877-792-1090
Format: Sports. **Operating Hours**: Continuous. **ADI**: San Diego, CA. **Key Personnel:** Larry Patrick, CEO. **Wattage**: 50,000.

3862 ■ XEPRS-FM - 105.7
3655 Nobel Dr., No. 470
San Diego, CA 92122
Phone: (858)535-2500
Free: 877-792-1090
Format: Sports. **Founded:** 2003. **Operating Hours**: Continuous. **ADI**: San Diego, CA. **Wattage**: 50,000.

3863 ■ XERCN-AM - 1470
5030 Camino de la Siesta, Ste. 403
San Diego, CA 92108
Phone: (619)497-0600
Format: Hispanic; Talk. **Owner:** Uniradio Corp. **ADI**: San Diego, CA. **URL:** http://www.uniradioinforma.com/main.php.

3864 ■ XETV-TV - 6
8253 Ronson Rd.
San Diego, CA 92111
Phone: (858)279-6666
Fax: (858)279-0061
Format: Commercial TV. **Networks:** Fox; United Paramount Network. **Owner:** Grupo Televisa, Av. Vasco de Quiroga No. 2000, Edif. A, Piso 4 Delegación Álvaro Obregón, 01210 Col. Santa Fe, Mexico, Ph: 52 55 5261 2445, Fax: 52 55 5261 2494. **Founded:** 1953. **Operating Hours**: Continuous. **ADI**: San Diego, CA. **Ad Rates:** Advertising accepted; rates available upon request. **URL:** http://www.sandiego6.com.

3865 ■ XHAS-TV - 33
5770 Ruffin Rd.
San Diego, CA 92123
Phone: (858)874-3320
Fax: (858)874-3321
Format: Hispanic. **Networks:** Telemundo. **Owner:** Entravision Communications Corporation, 2425 Olympic Blvd., Ste. 6000 W, Santa Monica, CA 90404-4030, Ph: (310)447-3870, Fax: (310)447-3899. **Founded:** 1990. **Operating Hours**: 6 a.m.-2 a.m. **ADI**: San Diego, CA. **Key Personnel:** Juan Perez, Contact. **Wattage**: 1,000,000 ERP.

3866 ■ XHRM-FM - 92.5
6160 Cornerstone Ct. E
San Diego, CA 92121
Phone: (858)888-7000
Format: Oldies; Adult Contemporary. **Owner:** Finest City Broadcasting, at above address. **Founded:** 1969. **Operating Hours**: Continuous. **Wattage**: 100,000. **Ad Rates:** Noncommercial. **URL:** http://www.magic925.com.

3867 ■ XHTY-FM - 99.7
5030 Camino de la Siesta, Ste. 403
San Diego, CA 92108
Phone: (619)497-0600
Format: Hispanic; Full Service. **Owner:** Uniradio Corp. **Founded:** 1998. **ADI**: San Diego, CA. **Key Personnel:** Jim Smith, Gen. Sales Mgr., jsmith@uniradio.com. **Wattage**: 60,000. **URL:** http://www.uniradio.com.

SAN DIMAS

Los Angeles Co.

3868 ■ ASA Avicultural Bulletin
Avicultural Society of America
PO Box 3161
San Dimas, CA 91773
Publisher's E-mail: info@asabirds.org
Covers the care, feeding, and breeding of birds in captivity. Contains membership roster and listings of bird specialty organizations and new members. **Freq:** Bimonthly. **Key Personnel:** Kelly Tucker, Contact, phone: (505)384-5490. **ISSN:** 0567-2856 (print). **Subscription Rates:** $12 Students; $25 Individuals; $33 Other countries. **URL:** http://asabirds.org/bulletin. **Ad Rates:** 4C $300, full page; 4C $225, half page; BW $120, full page; BW $180, half page. **Remarks:** Accepts advertising. **Circ:** 1000.

3869 ■ The Barbed Wire Collector
Antique Barbed Wire Society
1475 Paseo Maravilla
San Dimas, CA 91773-3908
Freq: Bimonthly. **Subscription Rates:** $6 Individuals single issue; $25 U.S. /year; $35 Other countries /year. **URL:** http://www.antiquebarbedwiresociety.com/magazine.html. **Remarks:** Accepts advertising. **Circ:** (Not Reported).

3870 ■ Recumbent & Tandem Rider
Coyne Publishing
PO Box 337
San Dimas, CA 91773
Publisher's E-mail: rtrmag@earthlink.net
Magazine recumbent and tandem bicycling enthusiasts. Includes product reviews, event coverage, and interviews. **Freq:** Quarterly. **Subscription Rates:** $12 Individuals; $25 Other countries. **URL:** http://www.rtrmag.com. **Remarks:** Accepts advertising. **Circ:** (Not Reported).

3871 ■ Wheel Clicks
Pacific Railroad Society
210 W Bonita Ave.
San Dimas, CA 91773
Phone: (909)394-0616
Publisher's E-mail: info@pacificrailroadsociety.org
Journal of the Pacific Railroad Society. **Freq:** Monthly. **Key Personnel:** Marti Ann Draper, Contact. **ISSN:** 0043--4744 (print). **URL:** http://pacificrailroadsociety.org/PRS_Publications.html. **Remarks:** Advertising not accepted. **Circ:** (Not Reported).

SAN FERNANDO

Los Angeles Co. Los Angeles Co. (S). 20 m NW of Los Angeles. Citrus fruit and vegetable packing. Canning, preserving. Oil refinery. Cement pipe, olive oil, meat products, electronics, shirts, hosiery manufactured. Nurseries. Agriculture. Citrus fruit, vegetables.

3872 ■ The San Fernando Sun Newspaper and Valley View
San Fernando Valley Sun Newspaper
601 S Brand Blvd., Ste. 202
San Fernando, CA 91340
Phone: (818)365-3111
Fax: (818)898-7135
Publisher's E-mail: legals@sanfernandosun.com
Community newspaper covering the San Fernando Valley and surrounding areas. **Freq:** Weekly. **Print Method:** Web Offset. **Cols./Page:** 5. **Subscription Rates:** $85 By mail one year ; $150 By mail two year. **URL:** http://www.sanfernandosun.com. **Ad Rates:** PCI $15.70. **Remarks:** Accepts advertising. **Circ:** (Not Reported).

3873 ■ KURS-AM - 1040
PO Box 471
San Fernando, CA 91341
Phone: (619)426-5645
Format: Gospel. **Owner:** Radio Unica, 8400 N.W. 52nd St., Ste. 101, Miami, FL 33166, Ph: (305)463-5000, Fax: (305)463-5001. **Ad Rates:** Advertising accepted; rates available upon request. **URL:** http://elsembradorministries.com.

SAN FRANCISCO

San Francisco Co. City and County of San Francisco (W). On San Francisco Peninsula bounded by San Francisco Bay, Golden Gate and Pacific Ocean, has one of the finest harbor in the world. University of San Francisco. University of California at San Francisco. San Francisco State College. Other colleges. Law, dental, medical and many private schools. Gateway to the west, ranking in pacific waterborne commerce, financial center, wholesale trade. Printing and publishing houses. Manufactures paper boxes, confectionery, paints, chemicals, glass, leather, lumber, textiles, steel, clothing, bags, furniture, auto parts, electrical machinery, matches, clay, rubber products, tools, beverages. Coffee roasting, meat, fruit, vegetable packing, tea, spice, extract plants, shipyards, foundries, machine shops.

3874 ■ Afar
Afar Media
394 Pacific Ave., 2nd Fl.
San Francisco, CA 94111
Fax: (415)391-1566
Publisher's E-mail: help@afar.com
Magazine covering culture and travel experiences. **Freq:** Bimonthly. **Key Personnel:** Ellen Asmodeo-Giglio, Publisher; Jeremy Saum, Editor. **Subscription Rates:** $20 Individuals print; $32 Two years print. **URL:** http://www.afar.com. **Remarks:** Accepts advertising. **Circ:** (Not Reported).

3875 ■ Aging Today: The Bimonthly Newspaper of the American Society on Aging
American Society on Aging
575 Market St., Ste. 2100
San Francisco, CA 94105-2938
Phone: (415)974-9600
Fax: (415)974-0300
Free: 800-537-9728
Publication E-mail: mktg@asaging.org
Newspaper (tabloid) for health, social service, and other professionals who work with older people. **Freq:**

Circulation: ★ = AAM; △ or • = BPA; ♦ = CAC; ❑ = VAC; ⊕ = PO Statement; ‡ = Publisher's Report; Boldface figures = sworn; Light figures = estimated.

Bimonthly. **Print Method:** Offset. **Trim Size:** 11 x 15. **Cols./Page:** 4. **Col. Width:** 2 3/16 inches. **Col. Depth:** 13 inches. **Subscription Rates:** $60 Individuals; $90 Institutions; $51 Members; $76.50 Institutions member; $114.75 Members package - Aging Today/Generations Subscription; $135 Nonmembers package - Aging Today/Generations Subscription. **URL:** http://www.asaging.org/aging-today. **Formerly:** The ASA Connection; The Aging Connection. **Ad Rates:** BW $1,225. **Remarks:** Advertising accepted; rates available upon request. **Circ:** Paid ‡12,000, 12,000.

3876 ■ Anesthesia and Analgesia
International Anesthesia Research Society
44 Montgomery St., Ste. 1605
San Francisco, CA 94104-4703
Phone: (415)296-6900
Fax: (415)296-6901
Publisher's E-mail: ronna.ekhouse@wolterskluwer.com
Medical journal. **Freq:** Monthly. **Print Method:** Offset. **Trim Size:** 8 1/4 x 11. **Cols./Page:** 2. **Col. Width:** 3 1/4 inches. **Col. Depth:** 10 inches. **Key Personnel:** Steven L. Shafer, MD, Editor-in-Chief; Nancy Lynly, Managing Editor; Steven L. Shafer, Editor-in-Chief. **ISSN:** 0003-2999 (print). **Subscription Rates:** included in membership dues; $1371 Institutions /year for nonmember; $1653 Institutions, other countries; $1607 Institutions, Canada and Mexico. **URL:** http://www.iars.org/publications/about_aa/; http://www.anesthesia-analgesia.org/; http://www.iars.org/publications/; http://www.stahq.org/resources/aanda-magazine/; http://www.lww.com/Product/0003-2999; http://journals.lww.com/anesthesia-analgesia/pages/default.aspx. **Mailing address:** PO Box 908, Philadelphia, PA 19106-3621. **Remarks:** Accepts advertising. **Circ:** 30000, 21000, 16868.

3877 ■ The Argonaut
San Francisco Museum and Historical Society
88 5th St.
San Francisco, CA 94103-1810
Phone: (415)537-1105
Fax: (415)537-1108
Publisher's E-mail: info@sfhistory.org
Journal containing scholarly illustrated articles on San Francisco history. **Freq:** Semiannual. **Subscription Rates:** $12 Individuals back issues; Included in membership. **URL:** http://www.sfhistory.org/publications/the-argonaut. **Mailing address:** PO Box 420470, San Francisco, CA 94142-0470. **Remarks:** Advertising not accepted. **Circ:** (Not Reported).

3878 ■ ASA Generations
American Society on Aging
575 Market St., Ste. 2100
San Francisco, CA 94105-2938
Phone: (415)974-9600
Fax: (415)974-0300
Free: 800-537-9728
Publisher's E-mail: membership@asaging.org
Freq: Quarterly. **ISSN:** 0738- 7806 (print). **Subscription Rates:** included in membership dues; $82.50 Nonmembers individual subscription ; $70.12 Members individual subscription ; $151.80 Nonmembers institutions (print/online subscription); $129.03 Members institutions (print/online subscription) ; $121 Nonmembers institutions (online or print subscription) ; $102.85 Members institutions (online or print subscription). **URL:** http://www.asaging.org/publications. **Ad Rates:** BW $1550. **Remarks:** Accepts advertising. **Circ:** 15,000.

3879 ■ AsianWeek
Pan Asia Venture Capital Corp.
809 Sacramento St.
San Francisco, CA 94108
Phone: (415)373-4002
Fax: (415)397-7258
Publisher's E-mail: asianweek@asianweek.com
Newspaper on Asian-American interests. **Freq:** Weekly. **Print Method:** Offset. **Trim Size:** 10 x 13. **Cols./Page:** 5. **Col. Width:** 24 nonpareils. **Col. Depth:** 196 agate lines. **Key Personnel:** Leila Kang, Editor; Ted Fang, Editor, Publisher; Samson Wong, Consultant; James Fang, President; Jesus Coronel, Manager, Operations; Florence Fang, Chairperson. **ISSN:** 0915--2056 (print). **Alt. Formats:** Download. **URL:** http://asianweek.com. **Ad Rates:** BW $2,465. **Remarks:** Accepts advertising. **Circ:** Combined ■ **58099**.

3880 ■ Bathroom Yearbook
Zinio Systems Inc.
114 Sansome St., 4th Fl.
San Francisco, CA 94107-1922
Phone: (415)494-2700
Fax: (415)494-2701
Magazine featuring bathroom products and designs. **Freq:** Annual. **Trim Size:** 220 x 278 mm. **URL:** http://www.universalmagazines.com.au/magazines/bathroom-yearbook. **Remarks:** Accepts advertising. **Circ:** (Not Reported).

3881 ■ The Baum Bugle
International Wizard of Oz Club
2443 Fillmore St., No. 347
San Francisco, CA 94115
Publisher's E-mail: feedback@ozclub.org
Freq: 3/year spring, autumn and winter. **Key Personnel:** Craig Noble, Editor-in-Chief. **Subscription Rates:** Included in membership; $8 Nonmembers. **URL:** http://ozclub.org/publications/the-baum-bugle. **Remarks:** Accepts advertising. **Circ:** 2500.

3882 ■ Bay Area Reporter
Benro Enterprises Inc.
395 Ninth St.
San Francisco, CA 94103-3831
Phone: (415)861-5019
Publisher's E-mail: baradv@aol.com
Community newspaper. **Freq:** Weekly (Thurs.). **URL:** http://www.ebar.com. **Remarks:** Accepts advertising. **Circ:** (Not Reported).

3883 ■ The Begonian
American Begonia Society
PO Box 471651
San Francisco, CA 94147-1651
Journal containing articles regarding growing techniques and specifics for plants or plant groups. **Freq:** Bimonthly. **Subscription Rates:** Included in membership; $25 Individuals DVD. **Alt. Formats:** DVD. **URL:** http://www.begonias.org/begonian; http://www.begonias.org/shop/shop_front.htm. **Remarks:** Accepts advertising. **Circ:** (Not Reported).

3884 ■ The Believer
McSweeney's
849 Valencia St.
San Francisco, CA 94110
Phone: (415)642-5609
Publisher's E-mail: custservice@mcsweeneys.net
Magazine that features book reviews and interviews without regard to length or timeliness. **Freq:** Monthly. **Key Personnel:** Jordan Bass, Publisher; Heidi Julavits, Editor; Andrew Leland, Managing Editor. **Subscription Rates:** $45 Individuals; $8 Single issue. **URL:** http://www.believermag.com/. **Circ:** (Not Reported).

3885 ■ Bond
Avanti Ragazzi Publishing L.L.C.
2261 Market St., No. 326
San Francisco, CA 94110
Publisher's E-mail: acciones@cmpc.cl
Wedding magazine covering same-sex unions, multi-ethnic couples and offering a non-traditional take on marriage celebrations. **Key Personnel:** Lynn Tsutsumi, Editor-in-Chief, Founder; Dave Carpenter, Executive Editor. **Subscription Rates:** $45 Individuals. **URL:** http://www.bondmag.net/. **Circ:** (Not Reported).

3886 ■ Bulletin of Experimental Treatments for AIDS
San Francisco AIDS Foundation
1035 Market St., Ste. 400
San Francisco, CA 94103
Phone: (415)487-3000
Fax: (415)487-8079
Publication E-mail: beta@sfaf.org
Magazine reporting medical information about treatment for HIV infection. **Freq:** Biennial. **Print Method:** Web press. **Trim Size:** 8 3/8 x 10 7/8. **Cols./Page:** 2. **Col. Depth:** 10 inches. **Key Personnel:** Reilly O'Neal, Editor. **ISSN:** 1058--708X (print). **Subscription Rates:** Free. **URL:** http://www.sfaf.org/hiv-info/hot-topics/beta. **Remarks:** Advertising not accepted. **Circ:** Non-paid 25000.

3887 ■ California Bar Journal
State Bar of California
180 Howard St.
San Francisco, CA 94105
Phone: (415)538-2000
Publisher's E-mail: feedback@calbar.ca.gov
Journal of the State Bar of California covering law. **Freq:** Monthly. **Key Personnel:** David Cunningham, Coordinator; Laura Ernde, Editor, phone: (415)538-2028. **URL:** http://calbarjournal.com/ContactUs.aspx. **Circ:** (Not Reported).

3888 ■ California Family Physician
California Academy of Family Physicians
1520 Pacific Ave.
San Francisco, CA 94109
Phone: (415)345-8667
Fax: (415)345-8668
Publisher's E-mail: cafp@familydocs.org
Medical magazine with a socio-economic and clinical focus. **Freq:** Quarterly. **Print Method:** Offset. **Trim Size:** 8 1/2 x 11. **Cols./Page:** 3. **Col. Width:** 27 nonpareils. **Col. Depth:** 128 agate lines. **Subscription Rates:** Included in membership. **URL:** http://www.familydocs.org/cafp-magazine. **Ad Rates:** 4C $2050. **Remarks:** Accepts advertising. **Circ:** ‡8500.

3889 ■ California History: The Magazine of the California Historical Society
California Historical Society
678 Mission St.
San Francisco, CA 94105
Phone: (415)357-1848
Fax: (415)357-1850
Publisher's E-mail: info@calhist.org
Historical journal about California and the West. **Freq:** Quarterly. **Print Method:** Offset. **Trim Size:** 8 1/2 x 11. **Cols./Page:** 2. **Col. Width:** 20.5 picas. **ISSN:** 0612--2897 (print). **Subscription Rates:** Included in membership. **URL:** http://www.californiahistoricalsociety.org/publications/california_history.html. **Ad Rates:** BW $1200. **Remarks:** Accepts advertising. **Circ:** 5000.

3890 ■ California Home & Design
Hartle Media Ventures L.L.C.
59 Grant Ave., 4th Fl.
San Francisco, CA 94108
Phone: (415)362-7797
Fax: (415)362-9797
Interior design & architecture magazine. **Freq:** Quarterly. **Print Method:** Offset. **Trim Size:** 8.375 x 10.875. **Cols./Page:** 5. **Col. Width:** 23 nonpareils. **Col. Depth:** 194 agate lines. **Key Personnel:** Ali Grosslight, Publisher. **ISSN:** 0530--9751 (print). **URL:** http://www.californiahomedesign.com. **Remarks:** Accepts advertising. **Circ:** 100000.

3891 ■ California Lawyer
Daily Journal Corp.
44 Montgomery St., Ste. 250
San Francisco, CA 94104
Phone: (415)296-2400
Fax: (415)296-2440
Law magazine. **Freq:** Monthly. **Print Method:** Offset. **Trim Size:** 8 1/4 x 10 3/4. **Cols./Page:** 3. **Col. Width:** 25 nonpareils. **Col. Depth:** 140 agate lines. **ISSN:** 0279--4063 (print). **Subscription Rates:** Included in membership. **URL:** http://www.dailyjournal.com; http://www.callawyer.com. **Ad Rates:** BW $8230; 4C $9,957. **Remarks:** Accepts advertising. **Circ:** (Not Reported).

3892 ■ ChinMusic Magazine
Kevin Chanel
PO Box 225029
San Francisco, CA 94122
Consumer magazine covering baseball and punk rock music. **Freq:** Continuous. **Trim Size:** 8 1/2 x 11. **Key Personnel:** Kevin Chanel, Editor. **URL:** http://www.chinmusic.net. **Circ:** (Not Reported).

3893 ■ Chip Design
Extension Media
1786 18th St.
San Francisco, CA 94107
Phone: (415)255-0390
Publisher's E-mail: info@extensionmedia.com
Magazine that aims to fulfill the information needs of the leading-edge, upper-mainstream, and system-level programmable logic IC designers. **Freq:** Quarterly. **Key Personnel:** John Blyler, Director, Editorial, phone: (503)614-1082; Karen Popp, Director, Sales, Publisher, phone: (415)305-5557. **Subscription Rates:** Free to qualified subscribers print (U.S.); Free to qualified subscribers digital (other countries); $150 Individuals print. **Alt. Formats:** PDF. **URL:** http://chipdesignmag.com/index.php. **Ad Rates:** 4C $3500. **Remarks:** Ac-

cepts advertising. **Circ:** 40000.

3894 ■ Cinematograph
San Francisco Cinematheque
145 Ninth St., Ste. 240
San Francisco, CA 94103
Phone: (415)552-1990
Publisher's E-mail: sfc@sfcinematheque.org
Journal covering art film. **Freq:** Occasionally. **Key Personnel:** Steve Polta, Contact; Federico Windhausen, Editor. **ISSN:** 0886--6570 (print). **URL:** http://www.sfcinematheque.org/shop. **Remarks:** Accepts advertising. **Circ:** (Not Reported).

3895 ■ Common Ground: Resources for Personal Transformation
Common Ground
604 Mission St., 10th Fl.
San Francisco, CA 94105
Phone: (415)459-4900
Fax: (415)459-4974
Publication E-mail: info@commongroundmag.com
Magazine (tabloid) listing over700 organizations and individuals offering resources for personal transformation including art, yoga, psychology, psychic arts, spiritual practices, and more in the San Francisco Bay area. **Founded:** 1974. **Freq:** Monthly. **Print Method:** Letterpress and web offset. **Trim Size:** 10 3/4 x 13 1/2. **Cols./Page:** 4. **Col. Width:** 13 picas. **Key Personnel:** Rob Sidon, Director, Advertising, Publisher. **Subscription Rates:** $29 Individuals. **URL:** http://commongroundmag.com/. **Remarks:** Advertising accepted; rates available upon request. **Circ:** Paid ‡2000, Non-paid ‡103000.

3896 ■ Conflict Resolution & Mediation: Journal of the Academy of Family Mediator
Jossey-Bass Publishers
One Montgomery St., Ste. 1200
San Francisco, CA 94104
Phone: (415)433-1740
Fax: (415)433-0499
Free: 888-378-2537
Publisher's E-mail: info@wiley.com
Publication offering information on applications, techniques, and concerns in the family mediation field. **Freq:** Quarterly. **Print Method:** Sheetfed offset. **Trim Size:** 6 x 9. **Cols./Page:** 1. **Col. Width:** 27 picas. **Col. Depth:** 45 picas. **Key Personnel:** Jon Jenkins, Editor; Tricia S. Jones, Editor. **ISSN:** 0739-4098 (print). **Subscription Rates:** $40 Individuals. **URL:** http://www.josseybass.com/WileyCDA/WileyTitle/productCd-0787996092.html. **Circ:** Paid ‡2108, Non-paid ‡98.

3897 ■ Contact Point
University of the Pacific School of Dentistry
155 5th St.
San Francisco, CA 94103
Phone: (415)929-6400
Fax: (415)929-6654
College alumni and dental magazine. **Freq:** Semiannual. **Print Method:** Offset. **Cols./Page:** 3. **Col. Width:** 27 nonpareils. **Col. Depth:** 140 agate lines. **Key Personnel:** Kara Sanchez, Editor, phone: (415)929-6433. **URL:** http://contactpoint.pacific.edu. **Ad Rates:** BW $700; 4C $1400. **Remarks:** Accepts advertising. **Circ:** Non-paid ‡6500.

3898 ■ Culinary Trends
Culinary Trends
211 Sutter St., Ste. 801
San Francisco, CA 94108-4441
Phone: (415)431-1117
Magazine featuring numerous recipes, restaurants, hotels, and chefs. **Freq:** Bimonthly. **Trim Size:** 8 x 10.875. **Key Personnel:** Richard Neubauer, President; Christopher Neubauer, Publisher; Carleigh Connelly, Managing Editor. **URL:** http://www.culinarytrends.net. **Ad Rates:** BW $2,493. **Remarks:** Accepts advertising. **Circ:** Controlled **9521**.

3899 ■ Curve Magazine: Lesbian Magazine
Outspoken Enterprises Inc.
1550 Bryant St., Ste. 510
San Francisco, CA 94103
Phone: (415)863-6538
Fax: (415)863-1609
Free: 800-705-0070
Publisher's E-mail: letters@curvemag.com
National lesbian magazine covering news, politics, sports, arts, entertainment, and trends. **Freq:** 6/year. **Print Method:** Web press. **Trim Size:** 8 3/8 x 10 7/8. **Cols./Page:** 3. **Col. Width:** 2 1/2 inches. **Col. Depth:** 7 1/2 inches. **Key Personnel:** Gretchen Lee, Managing Editor; Frances Stevens, Publisher. **ISSN:** 1062-6247 (print). **Subscription Rates:** $10 Individuals online only; $15 Individuals single issue; $35 Individuals print and online. **URL:** http://www.curvemag.com/Magazine. **Formerly:** Deneuve. **Ad Rates:** GLR $40; BW $3,126; 4C $4,532. **Remarks:** Accepts advertising. **Circ:** ‡68200.

3900 ■ Diagnostic Imaging Asia Pacific
UBM P.L.C.
c/o John Hayes, Editorial Dir.
600 Harrison St.
San Francisco, CA 94107
Phone: (415)874-4572
Fax: (415)947-6099
Publisher's E-mail: communications@ubm.com
Asian-Pacific magazine covering the wide array of modalities that comprise radiology, including ultrasound, magnetic resonance imaging, computer tomography, interventional procedures, digital radiology, socioeconomics, and nuclear medicine. **Freq:** Biennial. **Key Personnel:** Philip Ward, Editor; John Hayes, Director, Editorial. **Subscription Rates:** Free to qualified subscribers. **URL:** http://www.diagnosticimaging.com/journals/diagnostic-imaging-asia-pacific. **Remarks:** Accepts advertising. **Circ:** 10000.

3901 ■ Diagnostic Imaging Europe
UBM P.L.C.
c/o John Hayes, Editorial Dir.
600 Harrison St.
San Francisco, CA 94107
Phone: (415)874-4572
Fax: (415)947-6099
Publisher's E-mail: communications@ubm.com
Pan-European magazine covering the wide array of modalities that comprise radiology, including ultrasound, magnetic resonance imaging, computer tomography, interventional procedures, digital radiology, socioeconomics, and nuclear medicine. **Freq:** Monthly. **Key Personnel:** Philip Ward, Editor; John Hayes, Director, Editorial. **Subscription Rates:** Free to qualified subscribers. **URL:** http://www.diagnosticimaging.com/journals/diagnostic-imaging-europe. **Remarks:** Accepts advertising. **Circ:** 10000.

3902 ■ Diagnostic Imaging: The Newsmagazine of Imaging, Innovation and Economics
UBM Inc.
c/o John Hayes
600 Harrison St.
San Francisco, CA 94107
Phone: (415)874-4572
Fax: (415)947-6099
News and analysis on clinical and economic developments in medical imaging. **Freq:** Monthly. **Print Method:** Web offset. **Trim Size:** 8.125 x 10.875. **Cols./Page:** 3. **Col. Width:** 26 nonpareils. **Col. Depth:** 140 agate lines. **Key Personnel:** Kathy Mischak, Publisher. **URL:** http://www.diagnosticimaging.com. **Remarks:** Accepts advertising. **Circ:** (Not Reported).

3903 ■ Disability Statistics Report
Disability Statistics Center
Institute for Health & Aging
3333 California St., Ste. 340
San Francisco, CA 94118
Magazine containing abstracts, reports, and proceedings that provide statistical data on disability in the U.S. as collected by the Disability Statistics Center. **Freq:** Irregular. **Key Personnel:** Mitch LaPlante, PhD, Director; Steve Kaye, PhD, Director, Research, Director, Research and Development. **Subscription Rates:** Free online. **URL:** http://dsc.ucsf.edu. **Remarks:** Advertising not accepted. **Circ:** (Not Reported).

3904 ■ The Dispatcher: Union Newspaper
International Longshore and Warehouse Union
1188 Franklin St., 4th Fl.
San Francisco, CA 94109-6800
Phone: (415)775-0533
Fax: (415)775-1302
Newspaper containing union and labor news. **Freq:** Monthly. **Print Method:** Offset. **Trim Size:** 11 1/2 x 17 1/2. **Cols./Page:** 4. **Col. Width:** 29 nonpareils. **Col. Depth:** 224 agate lines. **Key Personnel:** Roy San Filippo, Editor; Craig Merrilees, Director, Communications, Senior Editor. **ISSN:** 0012--3765 (print). **URL:** http://www.ilwu.org/the-dispatcher-newspaper. **Remarks:** Advertising not accepted. **Circ:** Non-paid ‡44000.

3905 ■ Edible San Francisco
Edible Communities Inc.
236 W Portal, No. 191
San Francisco, CA 94127
Phone: (415)242-0260
Publication E-mail: ediblesanfrancisco@gmail.com
Magazine featuring San Francisco's local food industry. **Freq:** Quarterly. **Trim Size:** 8.5 x 11. **Key Personnel:** Bruce Cole, Editor, Publisher. **Subscription Rates:** $20 Individuals. **URL:** http://ediblesanfrancisco.ediblefeast.com. **Remarks:** Advertising accepted; rates available upon request. **Circ:** (Not Reported).

3906 ■ Educational Foundations
Caddo Gap Press Inc.
3145 Geary Blvd.
San Francisco, CA 94118
Phone: (415)666-3012
Fax: (415)666-3552
Publisher's E-mail: info@caddogap.com
Professional journal for the educational foundations fields. **Founded:** 1986. **Freq:** Quarterly. **Print Method:** Offset. **Trim Size:** 6 x 9. **Cols./Page:** 1. **Col. Width:** 27 picas. **Col. Depth:** 43 picas. **Key Personnel:** Michael E. Jennings, Editor. **ISSN:** 1047-8248 (print). **Subscription Rates:** $100 Institutions; $50 Individuals. **URL:** http://caddogap.com/periodicals.shtml. **Mailing address:** PO Box 275, San Francisco, CA 94118. **Ad Rates:** BW $200. **Remarks:** Accepts advertising. **Circ:** 800.

3907 ■ El Mensajero
El Mensajero
333 Valencia St., Ste. 410
San Francisco, CA 94103
Hispanic community newspaper. **Freq:** Weekly. **Key Personnel:** Maria Antonieta Mejia, Managing Editor. **URL:** http://www.laopinion.com/categoria/de-la-bahia. **Ad Rates:** PCI $15.26. **Remarks:** Accepts advertising. **Circ:** Non-paid ‡103663.

3908 ■ El Tecolote
El Tecolote
2958 24th St.
San Francisco, CA 94110
Phone: (415)648-1045
Fax: (415)648-1046
Community newspaper (English and Spanish). **Freq:** Monthly. **Print Method:** Offset. **Trim Size:** 10 x 16. **Cols./Page:** 4. **Col. Width:** 2 3/8 inches. **Col. Depth:** 16 inches. **Key Personnel:** Juan Gonzales, Editor, Founder. **Subscription Rates:** $25 Individuals; $25 Institutions non-profit; $35 Institutions corporations. **URL:** http://eltecolote.org/content/en. **Ad Rates:** BW $800. **Remarks:** Accepts advertising. **Circ:** (Not Reported).

3909 ■ EyeNet: The Trusted Source for Clinical Insights
American Academy of Ophthalmology
655 Beach St.
San Francisco, CA 94109
Phone: (415)561-8500
Fax: (415)561-8533
Publisher's E-mail: aaoe@aao.org
Professional magazine of the American Academy of Ophthalmology covering clinical, socioeconomic and political trends affecting their practice for members. **Freq:** Monthly. **Trim Size:** 8 1/8 x 10 7/8. **Key Personnel:** Dr. David W. Parke, MD, Editor-in-Chief; Jane Aguirre, Publisher; Patty Ames, Executive Editor; Chris McDonagh, Senior Editor. **ISSN:** 1097-2986 (print). **Subscription Rates:** $150 Nonmembers within U.S.; $210 Nonmembers outside US; $135 Members international; $75 Individuals inactive member. **URL:** http://www.aao.org/eyenet. **Mailing address:** PO Box 7424, San Francisco, CA 94120-7424. **Ad Rates:** BW $2,135; 4C $4,413. **Remarks:** Accepts advertising. **Circ:** ‡16661.

3910 ■ Film/Tape World: The Film, Video & Computer Media News Magazine

Circulation: ★ = AAM; △ or • = BPA; ♦ = CAC; ❑ = VAC; ⊕ = PO Statement; ‡ = Publisher's Report; Boldface figures = sworn; Light figures = estimated.

Planet Communications
670 5th St., Ste. 401
San Francisco, CA 94107-1517
Trade magazine covering film, video and multimedia in Northern California for professionals. **Freq:** Monthly. **Print Method:** Web offset. **Trim Size:** 11 7/8 x 16 3/4. **Key Personnel:** Wes Dorman, Publisher. **URL:** http://www.filmtapeworld.com. **Remarks:** Accepts advertising. **Circ:** (Not Reported).

3911 ■ Fourteen Hills: The SFSU Review
Fourteen Hills
1600 Holloway Ave.
Dept. of Creative Writing
1600 Holloway Ave.
San Francisco, CA 94132
Phone: (510)524-1668
Publisher's E-mail: orders@spdbooks.org
Magazine containing creative literary work. **Freq:** Semiannual. **Trim Size:** 6 x 9. **Key Personnel:** Esther Patterson, Editor-in-Chief; Monique Mero, Editor-in-Chief. **ISSN:** 1085--4576 (print). **Subscription Rates:** $10 Single issue; $15 one year ; $28 Institutions 2 years ; $30 Institutions one year ; $5 Individuals back issues. **URL:** http://www.14hills.net. **Remarks:** Accepts advertising. **Circ:** Paid 600.

3912 ■ France Today: The Journal of French Travel & Culture
France Press Inc.
944 Market St., Ste. 210
San Francisco, CA 94102
Publication E-mail: info@francetoday.com
Magazine covering contemporary issues, events, trends, and travel in France. **Freq:** 6/year. **Print Method:** Offset. **Trim Size:** 8 x 10 1/4. **Key Personnel:** Louis F. Kyle, Publisher; Vivian Thomas, Associate, Editor; Judy Fayard, Editor-in-Chief; C.C. Glenn, Coordinator, Marketing. **ISSN:** 0895--3651 (print). **Subscription Rates:** $45 U.S. and Canada /year; $85 U.S. and Canada 2 years; £24.95 Individuals /year (United Kingdom); £47.50 Individuals 2 years (United Kingdom); £49.99 Individuals /year (Europe); £84.99 Individuals 2 years (Europe); £49.99 Other countries one year; £84.99 Other countries 2 years. **URL:** http://www.francetoday.com. **Remarks:** Accepts advertising. **Circ:** (Not Reported).

3913 ■ Frogpond
Haiku Society of America
c/o Fay Aoyagi, President
930 Pine St., No. 105
San Francisco, CA 94108
Freq: 3/year. **ISSN:** 8755- 156X (print). **Subscription Rates:** Included in membership; $14 U.S. and Canada single copies of back issues; $15 Other countries for seamail; single copies of back issues; $20 Other countries for airmail; single copies of back issues. **URL:** http://www.hsa-haiku.org/frogpond/index.html. **Remarks:** Advertising not accepted. **Circ:** 600.

3914 ■ Fruit Gardener
California Rare Fruit Growers
66 Farragut Ave.
San Francisco, CA 94112-4050
Magazine featuring articles about fruits and vegetables that are of general interest. **Freq:** Bimonthly. **Subscription Rates:** $7.50 Individuals. **URL:** http://www.crfg.org/fg.html. **Mailing address:** PO Box 6850, Fullerton, CA 92834-6850. **Remarks:** Advertising not accepted. **Circ:** (Not Reported).

3915 ■ Game Developer
Think Services Game Group
600 Harrison St., 6th Fl.
San Francisco, CA 94107
Trade magazine covering video and computer game development. **Freq:** Monthly. **Key Personnel:** Simon Carless, Publisher; Brandon Sheffield, Senior Editor. **URL:** http://www.ubmgamenetwork.com/newsletters/gdmag/GDMag_Update-1102.html. **Ad Rates:** BW $6415; 4C $10665. **Remarks:** Accepts advertising. **Circ:** (Not Reported).

3916 ■ Generations: Journal of the American Society on Aging
American Society on Aging
575 Market St., Ste. 2100
San Francisco, CA 94105-2938
Phone: (415)974-9600
Fax: (415)974-0300
Free: 800-537-9728
Publication E-mail: mktg@asaging.org
Magazine for health, social service, and other professionals who work with older people; presenting in-depth view of a specific topic in aging emphasizing research and practice. **Freq:** Quarterly. **Print Method:** Offset. **Trim Size:** 7.25 x 10. **Cols./Page:** 2. **Col. Width:** 2 3/4 inches. **Col. Depth:** 8 3/4 inches. **ISSN:** 0738--7806 (print). **Subscription Rates:** $82.50 Individuals; $121 Institutions. **URL:** http://asaging.org/generations-journal-american-society-aging. **Ad Rates:** 4C $1500. **Remarks:** Accepts advertising. **Circ:** Combined ‡10500.

3917 ■ GGU Environmental Law Journal
Golden Gate University School of Law
536 Mission St.
San Francisco, CA 94105-2968
Phone: (415)442-6600
Fax: (415)442-6631
Free: 800-GGU-4YOU
Publisher's E-mail: law@ggu.edu
Journal covering all aspects of environmental law, including wildlife, environmental justice, energy, land use and more. **Freq:** Semiannual. **Key Personnel:** Phoebe Moshfegh, Editor-in-Chief. **Subscription Rates:** $25 Individuals; $15 Single issue. **URL:** http://law.ggu.edu/law-library/law-journals. **Circ:** (Not Reported).

3918 ■ Golden Gate University Law Review
Golden Gate University School of Law
536 Mission St.
San Francisco, CA 94105-2968
Phone: (415)442-6600
Fax: (415)442-6631
Free: 800-GGU-4YOU
Publication E-mail: lawreview@ggu.edu
Student-published law review, including Ninth Circuit Survey, Women's Law Forum, and Notes and Comments. **Freq:** 3/year published once a year in three issues. **Key Personnel:** Elizabeth Youngberg, Editor-in-Chief. **ISSN:** 0363--0307 (print). **Subscription Rates:** $35 Individuals international shipping carries an additional 7.00; $15 Single issue. **URL:** http://law.ggu.edu/law-library/law-journals; http://ggulawreview.org. **Remarks:** Advertising not accepted. **Circ:** Paid 375.

3919 ■ The Guardsman
City College of San Francisco
50 Phelan Ave.
San Francisco, CA 94112
Phone: (415)239-3200
Fax: (415)239-3065
Publisher's E-mail: admit@ccsf.edu
Collegiate newspaper. **Freq:** Semiweekly. **Print Method:** Offset. **Cols./Page:** 5. **Col. Width:** 1 7/8 inches. **Col. Depth:** 16 inches. **Key Personnel:** Juan Gonzales, Faculty Advisor; Joe Fitzgerald, Director; Calindra Revier, Editor-in-Chief. **URL:** http://www.theguardsman.com. **Ad Rates:** BW $600. **Remarks:** Accepts advertising. **Circ:** ‡10000.

3920 ■ Hastings Business Law Journal
University of California Hastings College of the Law
200 McAllister St.
San Francisco, CA 94102
Phone: (415)565-4623
Fax: (415)581-8946
Publisher's E-mail: admiss@uchastings.edu
Journal containing issues regarding international and domestic events between law and business. **Freq:** Semiannual. **ISSN:** 1554--849X (print); **EISSN:** 1554--8503 (electronic). **URL:** http://journals.uchastings.edu/journals/websites/business/index.php; http://www.hblj.org. **Circ:** (Not Reported).

3921 ■ Hastings Communications and Entertainment Law Journal
University of California Hastings College of the Law
O'Brien Center for Scholarly Publications
200 McAllister St.
San Francisco, CA 94102
Phone: (415)581-8952
Fax: (415)581-8994
Publisher's E-mail: scholarp@uchastings.edu
Law journal on the legal issues of Communications and entertainment law. **Freq:** 3/yr. **Print Method:** Offset. **Trim Size:** 6 3/4 x 9 3/4. **Key Personnel:** Henna Choi, Editor-in-Chief. **ISSN:** 1061-6578 (print). **Subscription Rates:** $40 Individuals; $50 Out of country; $30 Single issue; $35 Out of country single issue. **URL:** http://journals.uchastings.edu/journals/websites/communications-entertainment/index.php. **Remarks:** Accepts advertising. **Circ:** (Not Reported).

3922 ■ Hastings Law Journal
University of California Hastings College of the Law
200 McAllister St.
San Francisco, CA 94102
Phone: (415)565-4623
Fax: (415)581-8946
Publisher's E-mail: admiss@uchastings.edu
Journal containing scholarly articles on legal thinking. **Freq:** 6/year. **URL:** http://journals.uchastings.edu/journals/websites/law/index.php; http://hastingslawjournal.org. **Circ:** (Not Reported).

3923 ■ Hastings Race and Poverty Law Journal
University of California Hastings College of the Law
200 McAllister St.
San Francisco, CA 94102
Phone: (415)565-4623
Fax: (415)581-8946
Publisher's E-mail: admiss@uchastings.edu
Journal discussing issues on race, poverty, social justice and the law. **Freq:** Semiannual. **URL:** http://journals.uchastings.edu/journals/websites/race-poverty/index.php. **Circ:** (Not Reported).

3924 ■ Hastings Science and Technology Law Journal
University of California Hastings College of the Law
200 McAllister St.
San Francisco, CA 94102
Phone: (415)565-4623
Fax: (415)581-8946
Publisher's E-mail: admiss@uchastings.edu
Journal containing discussion and interpretation of significant developments in science and law. **Freq:** Semiannual. **URL:** http://journals.uchastings.edu/journals/websites/science-technology/index.php. **Circ:** (Not Reported).

3925 ■ Hastings Women's Law Journal
University of California Hastings College of the Law
200 McAllister St.
San Francisco, CA 94102
Phone: (415)565-4623
Fax: (415)581-8946
Publisher's E-mail: admiss@uchastings.edu
Journal containing issues on advancing feminist perspectives and other issues of concern common to all women. **Freq:** Semiannual winter and summer. **Subscription Rates:** $45 Individuals /year (domestic); $55 Individuals /year (foreign); $35 Individuals back issues (domestic); $40 Individuals back issues (foreign). **URL:** http://hastingswomenslj.org; http://journals.uchastings.edu/journals/websites/women/index.php. **Circ:** (Not Reported).

3926 ■ Hastings Women's Law Journal: Not Your Typical Law Journal
University of California Hastings College of the Law
O'Brien Center for Scholarly Publications
200 McAllister St.
San Francisco, CA 94102
Phone: (415)581-8952
Fax: (415)581-8994
Publication E-mail: hwlj@uchastings.edu
Law journal offering beyond the scope of law and influencing legal scholarship with articles on literature, poems, book reviews, personal pieces, among others, and of course, legal analysis. **Freq:** Semiannual winter and summer. **Key Personnel:** Ali Nicollete, Editor-in-Chief. **ISSN:** 1061--0901 (print). **Subscription Rates:** $45 Individuals; $55 Other countries. **URL:** http://hastingswomenslj.org. **Remarks:** Accepts advertising. **Circ:** (Not Reported).

3927 ■ Homeland Protection Professional: Coordinating Domestic Preparedness
Homeland Protection Professional
200 Green St., 2nd Fl.
San Francisco, CA 94111
Phone: (415)962-8340
Publisher's E-mail: customersupport@homeland1.com
Magazine that covers the evolving homeland security marketplace. **Freq:** 10/year. **Key Personnel:** Scott Baltic, Managing Editor. **URL:** http://www.homeland1.com/Homeland-Protection-Professional-Magazine. **Re-**

marks: Accepts advertising. **Circ:** (Not Reported).

3928 ■ Homiletic & Pastoral Review
Homiletic and Pastoral Review
PO Box 591810
San Francisco, CA 94159
Catholic magazine. **Freq:** 11/year. **Print Method:** Offset. **Trim Size:** 6 1/2 x 9 3/4. **Cols./Page:** 2. **Col. Width:** 28 nonpareils. **Col. Depth:** 112 agate lines. **Key Personnel:** Kenneth Baker, Editor. **ISSN:** 0018--4268 (print). **Subscription Rates:** $26 U.S.; $48 Two years. **Alt. Formats:** PDF. **Remarks:** Advertising accepted; rates available upon request. **Circ:** ‡14500.

3929 ■ h2so4: Won't You Join Us We're Drowning in Obscurity but the Water Is Lovely
H2SO4
PO Box 423354
San Francisco, CA 94142
Publication E-mail: h2so4@socrates.berkeley.edu
Literary journal covering philosophy, politics, reviews, humor, and the arts in society. **Freq:** Irregular. **Print Method:** Offset. **Trim Size:** 8 1/2 x 11. **Cols./Page:** 2 and 3. **Key Personnel:** Jill Stauffer, Editor. **ISSN:** 1083--3897 (print). **URL:** http://www.h2so4.net. **Remarks:** Accepts advertising. **Circ:** Combined ‡1000.

3930 ■ Hyphen
Hyphen
17 Walter U Lum Pl.
San Francisco, CA 94108
Publisher's E-mail: hyphen@hyphenmagazine.com
Cultural and political magazine that highlights the Asian American community. **Freq:** 3/year. **Key Personnel:** Abigail Licad, Editor-in-Chief. **Subscription Rates:** $20 Individuals; $28 Canada; $38 Elsewhere; $34 Two years. **URL:** http://www.hyphenmagazine.com. **Remarks:** Accepts advertising. **Circ:** (Not Reported).

3931 ■ IEEE Grid
PC World Communications Inc.
501 Second St.
San Francisco, CA 94107
Phone: (415)243-0500
Fax: (415)442-1891
Publisher's E-mail: copyright@pcworld.com
Electrical engineering. **Freq:** Semimonthly. **Print Method:** Offset. **Cols./Page:** 3. **Col. Width:** 26 nonpareils. **Col. Depth:** 140 agate lines. **Key Personnel:** Paul Wesling, Editor. **Subscription Rates:** Free. **Ad Rates:** BW $870. **Remarks:** Accepts advertising. **Circ:** Paid 30000.

3932 ■ InfoWorld: Defining Technology for Business
InfoWorld Media Group
501 2nd St.
San Francisco, CA 94107
Free: 800-227-8365
Publication E-mail: letters@infoworld.com
Weekly publication. **Freq:** Weekly. **Print Method:** Offset. **Trim Size:** 10 3/8 x 13. **Cols./Page:** 5. **Col. Width:** 1 13/16 inches. **Col. Depth:** 13 inches. **Key Personnel:** Eric Knorr, Editor-in-Chief; Galen Gruman, Executive Editor; Pete Babb, Associate Editor. **ISSN:** 0199--6649 (print). **Subscription Rates:** $180 Individuals. **URL:** http://www.infoworld.com. **Ad Rates:** BW $37,000; 4C $45,500. **Remarks:** Accepts advertising. **Circ:** (Not Reported).

3933 ■ Insight: The Journal of the American Society of Ophthalmic Registered Nurses
American Society of Ophthalmic Registered Nurses
655 Beach St.
San Francisco, CA 94109
Phone: (415)561-8513
Fax: (415)561-8531
Publisher's E-mail: asorn@aao.org
Freq: Quarterly. **ISSN:** 1060--135X (print). **Subscription Rates:** $69 Institutions; $109 Institutions; $79 Other countries; $119 Institutions, other countries; $35 Students; $39 Students, other countries. **URL:** http://www.asorn.org/publications/insight_journal. **Remarks:** Accepts display and classified advertising. **Circ:** (Not Reported).

3934 ■ Intelligent Optimist
The Optimist
22 Montgomery St., Penthouse 2
San Francisco, CA 94104
Free: 888-633-6242
Publication E-mail: ode@odemagazine.com
Magazine featuring positive news, people, and ideas that are changing the world for the better. **Freq:** Monthly except January and July. **Key Personnel:** Jurriaan Kamp, Editor; Marco Visscher, Managing Editor; James Geary, Editor. **ISSN:** 1552--2385 (print). **Subscription Rates:** $29.95 Individuals per month. **URL:** http://theoptimist.com. **Formerly:** Ode: For Intelligent Optimists. **Circ:** 150000.

3935 ■ Issues: A Messianic Jewish Perspective
Jews for Jesus
60 Haight St.
San Francisco, CA 94102-5802
Phone: (415)864-2600
Fax: (415)552-8325
Publisher's E-mail: issuesamjp@aol.com
Freq: Bimonthly. **ISSN:** 0741- 0352 (print). **Alt. Formats:** PDF. **URL:** http://www.jewsforjesus.org/publications/issues. **Remarks:** Advertising not accepted. **Circ:** 27000.

3936 ■ Jewish News Weekly of Northern California
San Francisco Jewish Community Publications Inc.
225 Bush St., Ste. 1480
San Francisco, CA 94104
Phone: (415)263-7200
Fax: (415)263-7222
Free: 800-727-3646
Publisher's E-mail: letters@jweekly.com
Magazine covering news and events that happened during the week. **Founded:** Sept. 19, 2003. **Freq:** 50/yr. **Key Personnel:** Liz Harris, Editor; Sue Fishkoff, Editor. **Subscription Rates:** $46.50 Individuals; $79 Two years; $99 Individuals three years. **URL:** http://www.jweekly.com. **Formerly:** Jewish Bulletin of Northern California. **Remarks:** Accepts advertising. **Circ:** (Not Reported).

3937 ■ Journal of AAPOS
American Association for Pediatric Ophthalmology and Strabismus
655 Beach St.
San Francisco, CA 94109
Phone: (415)561-8505
Fax: (415)561-8531
Publisher's E-mail: aapos@aao.org
Freq: Bimonthly. **ISSN:** 1091--8531 (print). **Subscription Rates:** $319 Individuals in U.S.; $162 Students in U.S.; $383 Individuals in Canada; $198 Students in Canada. **URL:** http://www.jaapos.org. **Remarks:** Advertising not accepted. **Circ:** (Not Reported).

3938 ■ Journal of Pediatric Gastroenterology and Nutrition
Lippincott Williams & Wilkins
c/o Melvin B. Heyman, MD, Ed.
University of California
Dept. of Pediatrics
500 Parnassus Ave., MU-4 E
San Francisco, CA 94143
Peer-reviewed medical journal. **Freq:** Monthly. **Print Method:** Offset, Sheetfed. **Trim Size:** 8 1/4 x 11. **Cols./Page:** 2. **Key Personnel:** Melvin B. Heyman, MD, Editor. **ISSN:** 0277--2116 (print); **EISSN:** 1536--4801 (electronic). **Subscription Rates:** $871 U.S., Canada, and Mexico; $898 Other countries; $1987 Institutions; $2251 Institutions, Canada and Mexico; $2278 Institutions, other countries; $436 U.S., Canada, and Mexico in-training; $463 Other countries in-training. **URL:** http://journals.lww.com/jpgn/pages/default.aspx. **Remarks:** Accepts advertising. **Circ:** (Not Reported).

3939 ■ Journal of Thought
Caddo Gap Press Inc.
3145 Geary Blvd.
San Francisco, CA 94118
Phone: (415)666-3012
Fax: (415)666-3552
Publisher's E-mail: info@caddogap.com
Interdisciplinary journal for scholars, focusing on philosophy of education. **Freq:** Semiannual latest volume:50 Spring-Summer 2016, Numbers 1&2. **Print Method:** Offset. **Trim Size:** 6 x 9. **Cols./Page:** 1. **Col. Width:** 72 nonpareils. **Col. Depth:** 126 agate lines. **Key Personnel:** John Covaleskie, Editor; Sally McMillan, Associate Editor. **ISSN:** 0022--5231 (print). **Subscription Rates:** $50 Individuals; $100 Institutions and libraries; add $60 for subscriptions outside the United States. **URL:** http://journalofthought.com; http://www.caddogap.com/periodicals.shtml. **Mailing address:** PO Box 275, San Francisco, CA 94118. **Ad Rates:** BW $200. **Remarks:** Accepts advertising. **Circ:** ‡400.

3940 ■ Juxtapoz
High Speed Productions Inc.
1303 Underwood Ave.
San Francisco, CA 94124
Free: 888-520-9099
Publisher's E-mail: orders@hsproductions.com
Contains information on underground art and pop culture. **Freq:** Monthly. **Print Method:** Offset. **Trim Size:** 8 1/8 x 10 7/8. **Cols./Page:** 3. **Col. Width:** 15 nonpareils. **Col. Depth:** 60 picas. **Key Personnel:** William Haugh, Director, Advertising; M. Revelli, Editor; Evan Pricco, Managing Editor. **ISSN:** 1077-8411 (print). **Subscription Rates:** $29.99 Individuals; $150 Canada two years; $59.98 Two years; $75 Canada; $80 Other countries; $160 Other countries two years. **URL:** http://www.juxtapoz.com. **Ad Rates:** BW $2,300; 4C $2,950. **Remarks:** Accepts advertising. **Circ:** ‡74000.

3941 ■ Leonardo
The MIT Press
211 Sutter St., Ste. 501
San Francisco, CA 94108
Phone: (415)391-1110
Fax: (415)391-2385
Publication E-mail: isast@leonardo.info
Peer-reviewed journal for readers interested in the application of contemporary science and technology to the arts and music. Features the latest in music, multimedia art, sound science and technology. Subscribers receive a compact disc with subscription, as well as membership to Leonardo/ISAST (the International Society for the Arts, Sciences and Technology) and reduced rates on all Society publications. Subscribers are also granted access to Leonardo Electronic Almanac. **Freq:** 6/year February, April, June, August, October. **Print Method:** Offset. **Trim Size:** 8 1/4 x 11 1/4. **Cols./Page:** 1. **Col. Width:** 86 nonpareils. **Col. Depth:** 147 agate lines. **ISSN:** 0024--094X (print); **EISSN:** 1530--9282 (electronic). **Subscription Rates:** $92 Individuals print and online; $83 Individuals online; $719 Institutions print and online; $644 Institutions online; $59 Students print and online; $53 Students online. **URL:** http://www.mitpressjournals.org/loi/leon. **Ad Rates:** BW $650; 4C $1,450. **Remarks:** Accepts advertising. **Circ:** 2500.

3942 ■ Leonardo Music Journal
The MIT Press
c/o Patricia Bentson, Mng. Ed.
211 Sutter St., Ste. 501
San Francisco, CA 94108
Phone: (415)391-1110
Fax: (415)391-2385
Publisher's E-mail: sales@mitpress.mit.edu
Peer-reviewed journal covering aesthetic and technical issues in contemporary music and sonic arts. **Freq:** Annual December. **Trim Size:** 8 1/2 x 11. **Key Personnel:** Nicolas Collins, Editor-in-Chief; Roger F. Malina, Executive Editor; Pamela Bentson, Managing Editor. **ISSN:** 0961--1215 (print); **EISSN:** 1531--4812 (electronic). **Subscription Rates:** $39 Individuals print only; $36 Individuals online only; $80 Institutions print only; $72 Institutions online only. **URL:** http://www.leonardo.info/lmjinfo.html; http://mitpress.mit.edu/content/leonardo-music-journal. **Ad Rates:** BW $400, full page; BW $300, half page; BW $200, quarter page; BW $650, 2-page spread. **Remarks:** Accepts advertising. **Circ:** ‡1000.

3943 ■ Macworld: The Essential Macintosh Resource
101communications LLC
501 2nd St.
San Francisco, CA 94107-1431
Phone: (415)243-0505
Fax: (415)442-1891
Magazine serving users of the Apple Macintosh personal computer, associated peripheral equipment, and software. **Freq:** Monthly. **Print Method:** Offset. **Trim Size:** 11 x 13. **Cols./Page:** 3. **Col. Width:** 27 nonpareils. **Col. Depth:** 140 agate lines. **Key Personnel:** Jon Phillips, Editor-in-Chief. **USPS:** 749-050. **Subscription Rates:** $19.97 Individuals online. **URL:** http://www.

Circulation: ★ = AAM; △ or • = BPA; ♦ = CAC; ❑ = VAC; ⊕ = PO Statement; ‡ = Publisher's Report; Boldface figures = sworn; Light figures = estimated.

macworld.com. **Remarks:** Accepts advertising. **Circ:** (Not Reported).

3944 ■ Maximumrocknroll
Maximumrocknroll
PO Box 460760
San Francisco, CA 94146-0760
Phone: (415)923-9814
Fax: (415)923-9617
Publication E-mail: mrr@maximumrocknroll.com
Magazine featuring information on punk music, culture and politics. **Freq:** Monthly. **Subscription Rates:** $26 Individuals; $37 Canada; $51 Individuals Mexico; $51 Other countries. **URL:** http://maximumrocknroll.com. **Circ:** (Not Reported).

3945 ■ MediaFile
Media Alliance
2830 20th St., Ste. 102
San Francisco, CA 94110
Phone: (415)746-9475
Fax: (510)238-8557
Publication E-mail: information@media-alliance.org
Newsletter Discussing Progressive Media Issues Including Centralization, Objectivity & Bias, and the Role in Social Justice Movements. **Founded:** 1978. **Freq:** Quarterly. **Trim Size:** 10 x 15 7/8. **Cols./Page:** 3 and 5. **Key Personnel:** Tracy Rosenberg, Executive Director; Ben Clarke, Editor. **URL:** http://www.media-alliance.org; http://www.media-alliance.org/section.php?id=49. **Formerly**: Propaganda Review. **Remarks:** Accepts advertising. **Circ:** 15000.

3946 ■ Mercury: The Magazine of the Astronomical Society of the Pacific
Astronomical Society of the Pacific
390 Ashton Ave.
San Francisco, CA 94112
Phone: (415)337-1100
Fax: (415)337-5205
Free: 800-335-2624
Publication E-mail: editor@astrosociety.org
Magazine outlining new developments in astronomy, astronomy education, and public policy. **Freq:** Quarterly. **Print Method:** Web Offset. **Trim Size:** 8 1/2 x 11. **Cols./Page:** 3. **Col. Width:** 27 nonpareils. **Col. Depth:** 135 agate lines. **Key Personnel:** Paul Deans, Editor, phone: (780)240-4608. **ISSN:** 0047--6773 (print). **USPS:** 184-880. **Subscription Rates:** $15 Individuals within North America; $15 Elsewhere outside North America; $43 U.S. and other countries; $72 Institutions. **URL:** http://www.astrosociety.org/pubs/mercury/mercury.html. **Ad Rates:** 4C $795. **Remarks:** Accepts advertising. **Circ:** (Not Reported).

3947 ■ Mother Jones
Foundation for National Progress
c/o Mother Jones
222 Sutter St., Ste. 600
San Francisco, CA 94108
Phone: (415)321-1700
Fax: (415)321-1701
Freq: Bimonthly. **ISSN:** 0362--8841 (print). **Subscription Rates:** $12 Individuals; $22 Canada; $24 Other countries. **URL:** http://www.motherjones.com. **Remarks:** Accepts advertising. **Circ:** 240000.

3948 ■ Mother Jones: Exposes and Politics
Foundation for National Progress, Mother Jones Magazine
222 Sutter St., 6th Fl.
San Francisco, CA 94108
Phone: (415)321-1700
Fax: (415)321-1701
Free: 800-438-6656
Publisher's E-mail: support@motherjones.com
Magazine covering news, politics, and culture. **Freq:** Bimonthly. **Print Method:** Offset. **Trim Size:** 8 1/4 x 10 1/2. **Cols./Page:** 3. **Col. Width:** 27 nonpareils. **Col. Depth:** 138 agate lines. **Key Personnel:** Steven Katz, Publisher; Clara Jeffery, Editor-in-Chief. **ISSN:** 0362--8841 (print). **Subscription Rates:** $12 U.S.; $24 Other countries. **URL:** http://www.motherjones.com. **Remarks:** Advertising accepted; rates available upon request. **Circ:** Paid ★**259140**.

3949 ■ Multicultural Education
Caddo Gap Press Inc.
3145 Geary Blvd.
San Francisco, CA 94118
Phone: (415)666-3012
Fax: (415)666-3552
Publisher's E-mail: info@caddogap.com
Educational magazine covering the field of multicultural education. **Freq:** Quarterly. **Print Method:** Lithography. **Trim Size:** 8 1/2 x 11. **Cols./Page:** 3. **Col. Width:** 2 inches. **Col. Depth:** 9 inches. **Key Personnel:** Alan H. Jones, Editor; Heather L. Hazuka, Editor. **ISSN:** 1068-3844 (print). **Subscription Rates:** $50 Individuals; $100 Institutions; $40 Students. **URL:** http://www.caddogap.com/periodicals.shtml; http://www.caddogap.com/store/index.html. **Mailing address:** PO Box 275, San Francisco, CA 94118. **Ad Rates:** BW $500. **Remarks:** Accepts advertising. **Circ:** Paid 900.

3950 ■ Musical News
American Federation of Musicians Union - Local 6
116 9th St.
San Francisco, CA 94103-2603
Phone: (415)575-0777
Fax: (415)863-6173
Musicians' union newspaper. **Founded:** 1915. **Freq:** Bimonthly. **Print Method:** Letterpress. **Trim Size:** 7 1/2 x 10. **Cols./Page:** 3. **Key Personnel:** Beth Zare, Editor. **Alt. Formats:** PDF. **URL:** http://afm6.org/our-union/musical-news/. **Ad Rates:** BW $150; PCI $7. **Remarks:** Accepts advertising. **Circ:** Free ‡3200.

3951 ■ New Directions for Community Colleges
Jossey-Bass Publishers
One Montgomery St., Ste. 1200
San Francisco, CA 94104
Phone: (415)433-1740
Fax: (415)433-0499
Free: 888-378-2537
Publisher's E-mail: info@wiley.com
Journal assisting community colleges in their expanding educational mission. **Freq:** Quarterly. **Print Method:** Sheetfed Offset. **Trim Size:** 6 x 9. **Cols./Page:** 1. **Col. Width:** 27 picas. **Col. Depth:** 45 picas. **Key Personnel:** Richard Wagoner, Associate Editor; Arthur M. Cohen, Editor-in-Chief. **ISSN:** 0194-3081 (print). **Subscription Rates:** $98 Individuals print and online; $122 Other countries print and online; $402 Institutions print and online; $476 Institutions, other countries print and online. **URL:** http://as.wiley.com/WileyCDA/WileyTitle/productCd-CC.html; http://onlinelibrary.wiley.com/journal/10.1002/(ISSN)1536-0733. **Remarks:** Accepts advertising. **Circ:** Paid 827, Non-paid 178.

3952 ■ New Directions for Institutional Research
Jossey-Bass Publishers
One Montgomery St., Ste. 1200
San Francisco, CA 94104
Phone: (415)433-1740
Fax: (415)433-0499
Free: 888-378-2537
Publisher's E-mail: info@wiley.com
Journal providing planners and administrators of academic institutions with guidelines for resource coordination, information analysis, program evaluation, and institutional management. **Freq:** Quarterly. **Print Method:** Sheetfed Offset. **Trim Size:** 6 x 9. **Cols./Page:** 1. **Col. Width:** 27 picas. **Col. Depth:** 45 picas. **Key Personnel:** John F. Ryan, Editor. **ISSN:** 0271-0579 (print). **Subscription Rates:** $341 Institutions print or online; $381 Institutions, Canada and Mexico print only; $415 Institutions, other countries; $89 U.S., Canada, and Mexico print or online; $113 Other countries print only. **URL:** http://onlinelibrary.wiley.com/journal/10.1002/(ISSN)1536-075X. **Remarks:** Accepts advertising. **Circ:** Paid 1033, Non-paid 70.

3953 ■ Nikkei Heritage
National Japanese American Historical Society
1684 Post St.
San Francisco, CA 94115-3604
Phone: (415)921-5007
Fax: (415)921-5087
Journal providing timely analysis and insight into the many facets of the Japanese American experience. **Freq:** Quarterly. **Subscription Rates:** Free to qualified subscribers; $5 Individuals published between 1991 - 2003; $7 Individuals published between 2004 - present. **URL:** http://www.njahs.org/nikkei-heritage-archives. **Remarks:** Advertising not accepted. **Circ:** (Not Reported).

3954 ■ Nob Hill Gazette: An Attitude Not An Area
Nob Hill Gazette
950 Mason St., Mezzanine Level
San Francisco, CA 94108
Phone: (415)227-0190
Regional magazine (tabloid) covering the arts, society, and business in the San Francisco Bay area. **Freq:** Monthly. **Print Method:** Offset. **Cols./Page:** 3. **Col. Width:** 36 nonpareils. **Col. Depth:** 224 agate lines. **Key Personnel:** Lois Lehrman, Publisher. **Subscription Rates:** $49 Individuals. **URL:** http://www.nobhillgazette.com. **Ad Rates:** BW $5965; 4C $8155. **Remarks:** Accepts advertising. **Circ:** Controlled ■ **80000**.

3955 ■ Notes and Abstracts in American and International Education
Caddo Gap Press Inc.
3145 Geary Blvd.
San Francisco, CA 94118
Phone: (415)666-3012
Fax: (415)666-3552
Publisher's E-mail: info@caddogap.com
Educational monograph covering the social foundations of education and comparative/international education. **Freq:** Semiannual. **Print Method:** Lithography. **Trim Size:** 5 1/2 x 8 1/2. **Cols./Page:** 1. **Col. Width:** 4 inches. **Col. Depth:** 6 inches. **Key Personnel:** Alan H. Jones, Editor. **ISSN:** 0029-3962 (print). **Subscription Rates:** $30 Individuals; $60 Institutions. **URL:** http://www.caddogap.com/periodicals.shtml; http://www.caddogap.com/store/index.html. **Mailing address:** PO Box 275, San Francisco, CA 94118. **Ad Rates:** BW $200. **Remarks:** Accepts advertising. **Circ:** Paid 125.

3956 ■ Obstetrical & Gynecological Survey
Lippincott Williams and Wilkins
c/o Dr. Robert B. Jaffe, Ed.
University of CA, SF
Dept. of Ob/Gyn & Reproductive Science
505 Parnassuss
San Francisco, CA 94143
Publisher's E-mail: ronna.ekhouse@wolterskluwer.com
Medical journal featuring articles summarizing current topics of clinical interest to obstetricians and gynecologists.Topics includes maternal/fetal medicine, infertility, endocrinology, gynecologic oncology and surgery, infections, contraception and related fields. **Founded:** 1946. **Freq:** Monthly. **Print Method:** Web offset. **Trim Size:** 8 1/8 x 10 7/8. **Cols./Page:** 2. **Col. Width:** 32 nonpareils. **Col. Depth:** 119 agate lines. **Key Personnel:** Dr. Howard W. Jones, Jr., Editor; Dr. Robert B. Jaffe, Editor, phone: (415)476-4303; Matthew Jozwiak, Publisher. **ISSN:** 0029-7828 (print). **Subscription Rates:** $383 Individuals; $968 Institutions; $136 Individuals in-training; $488 Other countries; $1074 Institutions, other countries; $162 Other countries in-training. **URL:** http://journals.lww.com/obgynsurvey/pages/default.aspx; http://www.lww.com/product/?0029-7828. **Ad Rates:** BW $1,055; 4C $2,125. **Remarks:** Accepts advertising. **Circ:** Combined 1349.

3957 ■ Ophthalmology
American Academy of Ophthalmology
655 Beach St.
San Francisco, CA 94109
Phone: (415)561-8500
Fax: (415)561-8533
Publisher's E-mail: t.reller@elsevier.com
Journal publishing original, peer-reviewed reports of research in ophthalmology, including basic science investigations and clinical studies. **Freq:** Monthly. **Print Method:** Web offset. **Trim Size:** 8 1/8 x 10 7/8. **Key Personnel:** George B. Bartley, Editor-in-Chief; May Piotrowski, Managing Editor; Henry Jampel, Deputy. **ISSN:** 0161--6420 (print). **Subscription Rates:** $542 U.S. and Canada online and print; $726 Other countries online and print; 434 Individuals online only. **URL:** http://www.aaojournal.org; http://www.journals.elsevier.com/ophthalmology. **Mailing address:** PO Box 945, New York, NY 10159-0945. **Ad Rates:** BW $2,545; 4C $2,355. **Remarks:** Accepts advertising. **Circ:** ‡27055.

3958 ■ Our Animals: The Magazine of the San Francisco S.P.C.A.
San Francisco SPCA
201 Alabama St.
San Francisco, CA 94103-4213
Phone: (415)554-3000

Publisher's E-mail: ouranimals@sfspca.org
Magazine containing news about cats, dogs, and SPCA programs that help them. **Freq:** Quarterly. **Print Method:** Offset. **Trim Size:** 8 3/8 x 10 7/8. **Cols./Page:** 3. **Col. Width:** 2 3/8 inches. **Col. Depth:** 10 inches. **ISSN:** 0030--6789 (print). **URL:** http://www.sfspca.org/who-we-are/our-mission/videos-publications. **Ad Rates:** BW $770; 4C $1270. **Remarks:** Accepts advertising. **Circ:** Non-paid ‡52000.

3959 ■ Oziana
International Wizard of Oz Club
2443 Fillmore St., No. 347
San Francisco, CA 94115
Publication E-mail: ozianaeic@gmail.com
Freq: Annual. **Key Personnel:** Marcus Mebes, Editor. **Subscription Rates:** Included in membership. **URL:** http://ozclub.org/oziana. **Remarks:** Advertising not accepted. **Circ:** 1000.

3960 ■ Pacific Arts
Pacific Arts Association
c/o Christina Hellmich, Acting Treasurer
Fine Arts Museums of San Francisco
Golden Gate Pk.
Hagiwara Garden Tea Dr.
San Francisco, CA 94118
Publisher's E-mail: paa.treasurer.us@gmail.com
Freq: Semiannual. **ISSN:** 1018--4252 (print). **Subscription Rates:** Included in membership. **URL:** http://www.pacificarts.org/journal. **Remarks:** Advertising not accepted. **Circ:** 300.

3961 ■ Pacific Citizen
Japanese American Citizens League
1765 Sutter St.
San Francisco, CA 94115
Phone: (415)921-5225
Publisher's E-mail: support@southbayjacl.org
Newspaper (tabloid). **Freq:** Bimonthly Biweekly Monthly Semimonthly except once in December and January. **Print Method:** Offset. **Key Personnel:** Allison Haramoto, Executive Editor. **ISSN:** 0030-8579 (print). **USPS:** 308-579. **Subscription Rates:** Included in membership; $40 Nonmembers. **URL:** http://www.southbayjacl.org/membership.html. **Ad Rates:** PCI $20. **Remarks:** Accepts advertising. **Circ:** Paid ‡24000, Free ‡100.

3962 ■ Paul Revere's Horse
Paul Revere's Horse
PO Box 460743
San Francisco, CA 94146
Magazine covering literary and cultural writing. **Founded:** 2008. **Freq:** 2/yr. **Key Personnel:** Christopher Lura, Editor. **Subscription Rates:** $12 Individuals. **URL:** http://www.paulrevereshorse.org. **Also known as:** PRH. **Circ:** (Not Reported).

3963 ■ PC WORLD: The Magazine of Business Computing
101communications LLC
501 2nd St.
San Francisco, CA 94107
Phone: (415)243-0500
Fax: (415)442-1891
Publication E-mail: pcwletters@pcworld.com
Technology or business magazine meeting the informational needs of tech-savvy managers, both at work and at home. **Freq:** Quarterly. **Print Method:** Offset. **Trim Size:** 7 7/8 x 10 1/2. **Cols./Page:** 3. **Col. Width:** 12.5 picas. **Col. Depth:** 55 picas. **Key Personnel:** Jon Phillips, Editor-in-Chief. **ISSN:** 0737--8939 (print). **Subscription Rates:** $19.97 Individuals online. **URL:** http://www.pcworld.com. **Remarks:** Advertising accepted; rates available upon request. **Circ:** Paid ★**880844**.

3964 ■ PI Perspective
Project Inform
273 9th St.
San Francisco, CA 94103
Phone: (415)558-8669
Fax: (415)558-0684
Free: 877-435-7443
Publisher's E-mail: info@help4hep.org
Freq: Monthly. **Subscription Rates:** free. **URL:** http://www.projectinform.org/pi-perspective. **Remarks:** Advertising not accepted. **Circ:** 60000.

3965 ■ Pipelines
Plumbers - Steamfitters, U.A. Local 38
1621 Market St.
San Francisco, CA 94103
Phone: (415)626-2000
Labor union newspaper. **Freq:** Monthly. **Subscription Rates:** Free. **URL:** http://www.ualocal38.org/index.cfm?zone=/unionactive/doc_page.cfm&pageID=12275. **Remarks:** Advertising not accepted. **Circ:** Non-paid 2500.

3966 ■ PLOS Biology
Public Library of Science
Koshland Bldg. E, Ste. 100
1160 Battery St.
San Francisco, CA 94111
Phone: (415)624-1200
Fax: (415)546-4090
Open access, peer-reviewed general biology journal. Publication fees are charged to authors, institutions, or funders for each article published. **Freq:** Monthly. **Trim Size:** 8 3/8 x 10 7/8. **Key Personnel:** Christine Ferguson, Editor-in-Chief; Emma Ganley, Editor-in-Chief; Ines Alvarez-Garcia, Senior Editor; Liza Gross, Senior Editor; Roli Roberts, Senior Editor; Hashi Wijayatilake, Senior Editor. **ISSN:** 1544--9173 (print); **EISSN:** 1545--7885 (electronic). **Subscription Rates:** $2900 Individuals. **URL:** http://journals.plos.org/plosbiology. **Remarks:** Accepts advertising. **Circ:** (Not Reported).

3967 ■ PLOS Computational Biology
Public Library of Science
Koshland Bldg. E, Ste. 100
1160 Battery St.
San Francisco, CA 94111
Phone: (415)624-1200
Fax: (415)546-4090
Publication E-mail: ploscompbiol@plos.org
Open access, peer-reviewed journal that publishes works that further understanding of living systems at all scales through the application of computational methods. Publication fees are charged to authors, institutions, or funders for each article published. **Freq:** Monthly. **Key Personnel:** Philip E. Bourne, Editor-in-Chief; Ruth Nussinov, Editor-in-Chief. **ISSN:** 1553--7358 (print); **EISSN:** 1553--734X (electronic). **Subscription Rates:** $2250 Individuals. **Alt. Formats:** Database. **URL:** http://journals.plos.org/ploscompbiol. **Remarks:** Accepts advertising. **Circ:** (Not Reported).

3968 ■ PLOS Genetics
Public Library of Science
Koshland Bldg. E, Ste. 100
1160 Battery St.
San Francisco, CA 94111
Phone: (415)624-1200
Fax: (415)546-4090
Publication E-mail: plosgenetics@plos.org
Open access, peer-reviewed journal that publishes research and case studies in the field of genetics. Publication fees are charged to authors, institutions, or funders for each article published. **Freq:** Monthly. **Key Personnel:** Gregory P. Copenhaver, Editor-in-Chief; Gregory S. Barsh, Editor-in-Chief. **ISSN:** 1553--7390 (print); **EISSN:** 1553--7404 (electronic). **Subscription Rates:** $2250 Individuals. **URL:** http://journals.plos.org/plosgenetics. **Remarks:** Accepts advertising. **Circ:** (Not Reported).

3969 ■ PLOS Medicine
Public Library of Science
Koshland Bldg. E, Ste. 100
1160 Battery St.
San Francisco, CA 94111
Phone: (415)624-1200
Fax: (415)546-4090
Open-access journal that publishes peer-reviewed advances in all disciplines related to medicine, with the aim of improving human health. Publication fees are charged to authors, institutions, or funders, for each article published. **Freq:** 13/yr. **Key Personnel:** Larry Peiperl, Editor-in-Chief; Amy Ross, Senior Editor; Clare Garvey, Senior Editor. **ISSN:** 1549--1277 (print); **EISSN:** 1549--1676 (electronic). **Subscription Rates:** $2900 Individuals. **URL:** http://journals.plos.org/plosmedicine. **Remarks:** Accepts advertising. **Circ:** (Not Reported).

3970 ■ PLOS ONE
Public Library of Science
Koshland Bldg. E, Ste. 100
1160 Battery St.
San Francisco, CA 94111
Phone: (415)624-1200
Fax: (415)546-4090
Publication E-mail: plosone@plos.org
Print Method: Offset. **Trim Size:** 10 1/8 x 14. **Cols./Page:** 6. **Col. Width:** 19 nonpareils. **Col. Depth:** 196 agate lines. **Key Personnel:** Iratxe Puebla, Editor. **EISSN:** 1932--6203 (electronic). **USPS:** 012-310. **Subscription Rates:** Free online. **URL:** http://www.plosone.org; http://www.plosclinicaltrials.org. **Formerly:** PLoS Clinical Trials. **Remarks:** Accepts advertising. **Circ:** (Not Reported).

3971 ■ PLoS Pathogens
Public Library of Science
Koshland Bldg. E, Ste. 100
1160 Battery St.
San Francisco, CA 94111
Phone: (415)624-1200
Fax: (415)546-4090
Open-access, peer-reviewed journal that publishes new ideas on bacteria, fungi, parasites, prions and viruses that contribute to understanding of the biology of pathogens and pathogen-host interactions. **Freq:** Monthly. **Key Personnel:** Kasturi Haldar, Editor-in-Chief. **ISSN:** 1553--7366 (print); **EISSN:** 1553--7374 (electronic). **Subscription Rates:** $2250 Individuals. **URL:** http://journals.plos.org/plospathogens. **Remarks:** Accepts advertising. **Circ:** (Not Reported).

3972 ■ The Police Marksman
Police Marksman Association
200 Green St., 2nd Fl.
San Francisco, CA 94111
Fax: (415)962-8340
Free: 888-765-4231
Publisher's E-mail: henry@hendonpub.com
Magazine featuring articles on legacy of advancing tactical excellence in law enforcement training. **Freq:** Bimonthly. **Subscription Rates:** $18.95 Individuals; $33.95 Other countries. **URL:** http://www.policeone.com/columnists/marksman. **Remarks:** Accepts advertising. **Circ:** (Not Reported).

3973 ■ Processed World: The Magazine With a Bad Attitude
Processed World
1310 Mission St.
San Francisco, CA 94103
Phone: (415)626-2060
Publisher's E-mail: processedworld@yahoo.com
Publication reviewing the impact of technology on daily life. **Freq:** sporadic. **Print Method:** Web offset. **Trim Size:** 8 3/8 x 10 7/8. **Cols./Page:** 2 and 3. **Col. Width:** 3 1/2 and 2 inches. **Col. Depth:** 9 1/2 inches. **ISSN:** 0735--9381 (print). **Subscription Rates:** $3 Single issue back issues. **Alt. Formats:** PDF. **URL:** http://www.processedworld.com. **Remarks:** Advertising not accepted. **Circ:** Paid 1200, Non-paid 800.

3974 ■ Psychiatric Times
United Business Media
303 2nd St., Ste. 900
San Francisco, CA 94107
Phone: (415)947-6000
Fax: (415)947-6055
Newspaper (tabloid) on psychiatric disorders and issues. **Freq:** 14/yr. **Print Method:** Offset. **Trim Size:** 10 7/16 x 13 3/4. **Cols./Page:** 4. **Key Personnel:** Ronald Pies, MD, Editor-in-Chief; John L. Schwartz, MD, Editor, Founder. **ISSN:** 0893--2905 (print). **Subscription Rates:** Free. **URL:** http://www.psychiatrictimes.com/home. **Remarks:** Accepts advertising. **Circ:** (Not Reported).

3975 ■ Publications of the ASP
Astronomical Society of the Pacific
390 Ashton Ave.
San Francisco, CA 94112
Phone: (415)337-1100
Fax: (415)337-5205
Free: 800-335-2624
Publisher's E-mail: service@astrosociety.org
Journal regarding the Astronomical Society of the Pacific. **Freq:** Monthly. **Key Personnel:** Jeff Mangum, Editor. **ISSN:** 0004--6280 (print); **EISSN:** 1538--3873 (electronic). **URL:** http://www.astrosociety.org/publications/pasp. **Remarks:** Advertising not accepted. **Circ:** (Not Reported).

3976 ■ Pulp and Paper

Circulation: ★ = AAM; △ or • = BPA; ♦ = CAC; ❑ = VAC; ⊕ = PO Statement; ‡ = Publisher's Report; Boldface figures = sworn; Light figures = estimated.

Pulp and Paper
600 Harrison St.
San Francisco, CA 94107
Phone: (415)905-2200
Fax: (415)905-2240
Publisher's E-mail: news@risi.com
Magazine serving the pulp and paper industry. **Freq:** Monthly. **Print Method:** Offset. **Trim Size:** 8 1/8 x 10 7/8. **Cols./Page:** 3. **Col. Width:** 26 nonpareils. **Col. Depth:** 140 agate lines. **Key Personnel:** Mark Rushton, Editor; Graeme Rodden, Executive Editor. **ISSN:** 0033--4081 (print). **Subscription Rates:** Free to qualified subscribers. **URL:** http://www.risiinfo.com/risi-store/do/product/detail/pulp-paper-international.html. **Ad Rates:** BW $7230; 4C $10195. **Remarks:** Accepts advertising. **Circ:** ‡40226.

3977 ■ The Recorder: The Bay Area's Legal Newspaper since 1877
ALM Media Properties L.L.C.
1035 Market St., Ste. 500
San Francisco, CA 94103
Phone: (415)490-9990
Free: 877-256-2472
Publisher's E-mail: customercare@alm.com
Legal newspaper. **Freq:** Daily (morn.). **Print Method:** Offset. **Trim Size:** 11 1/2 x 17 1/2. **Cols./Page:** 10. **Col. Width:** 21 nonpareils. **Col. Depth:** 290 agate lines. **Key Personnel:** Greg Mitchell, Editor-in-Chief. **USPS:** 458-020. **Subscription Rates:** $19.99 Individuals print and online, monthly. **URL:** http://www.therecorder.com; http://www.alm.com/publications/recorder. **Remarks:** Advertising accepted; rates available upon request. **Circ:** ‡6600, Paid 30000.

3978 ■ Research: Ideas for Today's Investment Professional
Research Magazine Inc.
88 Kearny St., Ste. 1800
San Francisco, CA 94108
Fax: (415)956-2401
Publisher's E-mail: jlevaux@researchmag.com
Magazine for stockbrokers including corporate profiles, financial data, articles on investment products, finance selling techniques and tools. **Freq:** Monthly. **Print Method:** Web. **Trim Size:** 7 7/8 X 10 7/8. **Cols./Page:** 3. **Col. Width:** 2 5/16 inches. **Col. Depth:** 9 3/4 inches. **Key Personnel:** Janet Levaux, Editor-in-Chief. **ISSN:** 0192--172X (print). **URL:** http://www.thinkadvisor.com/research-magazine. **Ad Rates:** BW $11900; 4C $14780. **Remarks:** Accepts advertising. **Circ:** Paid 90003.

3979 ■ Revenue Performance
Montgomery Media International
55 New Montgomery St., Ste. 617
San Francisco, CA 94105
Phone: (415)371-8800
Fax: (415)371-0300
Magazine covering internet marketing strategies. **Freq:** Quarterly. **Key Personnel:** Lisa Picarille, Editor-in-Chief, Publisher. **URL:** http://mthink.com/about-revenue-performance. **Formerly**: Revenue. **Remarks:** Accepts advertising. **Circ:** (Not Reported).

3980 ■ The Russian American
Congress of Russian Americans
2460 Sutter St.
San Francisco, CA 94115
Phone: (415)928-5841
Fax: (415)928-5831
Publisher's E-mail: crahq@earthlink.net
Freq: every 1-2 years. **Subscription Rates:** $20 Individuals; $30 Individuals 2 books; $40 Individuals 3 books. **URL:** http://www.russian-americans.org/books-and-publications. **Remarks:** Advertising not accepted. **Circ:** (Not Reported).

3981 ■ The San Francisco Bay Guardian
The San Francisco Bay Guardian
135 Mississippi St.
San Francisco, CA 94107
Fax: (415)487-2506
Alternative news weekly. **Freq:** Weekly. **Print Method:** Offset. **Cols./Page:** 5. **Col. Width:** 25 nonpareils. **Col. Depth:** 196 agate lines. **Key Personnel:** Bruce B. Brugmann, Editor. **URL:** http://www.sfbg.com. **Remarks:** Accepts advertising. **Circ:** Paid ‡95000.

3982 ■ San Francisco Bay View
San Francisco Bay View
4917 Third St.
San Francisco, CA 94124
Phone: (415)671-0789
Fax: (415)671-0789
Publisher's E-mail: editor@sfbayview.com
African American community newspaper. **Freq:** Monthly. **Trim Size:** 12.25 x 20. **Cols./Page:** 6. **Col. Width:** 2 inches. **Col. Depth:** 20 inches. **Key Personnel:** Mary Ratcliff, Editor; Willie Ratcliff, Publisher; Wanda Sabir, Editor. **ISSN:** 1520--7285 (print). **Subscription Rates:** $24 Individuals. **URL:** http://sfbayview.com. **Formerly**: New Bayview. **Ad Rates:** GLR $15.30; BW $1836; 4C $200; PCI $18. **Remarks:** tobacco. **Circ:** (Not Reported).

3983 ■ San Francisco Examiner
San Francisco Examiner
225 Bush, 17th Flr.
San Francisco, CA 94104
General newspaper. **Freq:** Daily. **Print Method:** Letterpress. **Trim Size:** 13 x 21 1/2. **Cols./Page:** 6. **Col. Width:** 24 nonpareils. **Col. Depth:** 301 agate lines. **Key Personnel:** Michael Howerton, Editor-in-Chief. **USPS:** 479-780. **URL:** http://www.sfexaminer.com. **Remarks:** Accepts advertising. **Circ:** ‡155011, ‡255002.

3984 ■ San Francisco Magazine
San Francisco Magazine
55 Francisco St., Ste. 100
San Francisco, CA 94133-2136
Phone: (415)398-2800
Regional interest magazine covering personalities, places, and events in the San Francisco Bay area. **Freq:** Monthly. **Print Method:** Offset. **Trim Size:** 8 1/8 x 10 7/8. **Cols./Page:** 3. **Col. Width:** 2.25 picas. **Col. Depth:** 10 inches. **Key Personnel:** Paul Reulbach, Publisher. **Subscription Rates:** $19.97 Individuals California; $29.97 Out of state; $35 Two years California; $53.97 Canada. **URL:** http://www.modernluxury.com/san-francisco. **Formerly**: San Francisco Focus. **Remarks:** Advertising accepted; rates available upon request. **Circ:** Paid ***115000**.

3985 ■ 7 x 7 Magazine
Hartle Media Ventures L.L.C.
59 Grant Ave., 4th Fl.
San Francisco, CA 94108
Phone: (415)362-7797
Fax: (415)362-9797
Magazine that reflects the lifestyles, attitudes and image of the San Francisco area. **Freq:** 11/year. **Key Personnel:** Tom Hartle, Owner, President, Publisher. **URL:** http://www.7x7mag.com. **Ad Rates:** BW $5,965; 4C $5,965. **Remarks:** Accepts advertising. **Circ:** Combined **■ 35939**.

3986 ■ Sexually Transmitted Diseases: Journal of the American Sexually Transmitted Association
Lippincott Williams and Wilkins
Dept. of Lab Medicine
San Francisco General Hospital
Bldg. 30, Rm. 416
1001 Potrero Ave.
San Francisco, CA 94110
Publisher's E-mail: ronna.ekhouse@wolterskluwer.com
Journal covering all aspects of human sexually transmitted diseases. **Freq:** Monthly. **Print Method:** Sheetfed offset. **Trim Size:** 7 3/4 x 10 3/4. **Cols./Page:** 2. **Col. Width:** 39 nonpareils. **Col. Depth:** 140 agate lines. **Key Personnel:** Jeanne Moncada, Assistant Editor; William C. Miller, PhD, Editor-in-Chief. **ISSN:** 0148--5717 (print); **EISSN:** 1537--4521 (electronic). **Subscription Rates:** $551 Individuals; $1346 Institutions; $587 Other countries; $1372 Institutions, other countries international; $192 U.S. in-training; $218 Other countries in-training. **URL:** http://journals.lww.com/stdjournal/pages/default.aspx. **Remarks:** Accepts advertising. **Circ:** (Not Reported).

3987 ■ Slap
High Speed Productions Inc.
1303 Underwood Ave.
San Francisco, CA 94124
Free: 888-520-9099
Publication E-mail: info@slapmagazine.com
Magazine covering skateboarding, music, art, and youth. **Freq:** Monthly. **Print Method:** Web offset. **Trim Size:** 8 3/8 x 10 1/2. **ISSN:** 1076--9110 (print). **URL:** http://www.slapmagazine.com. **Formerly**: Slap Magazine. **Remarks:** Accepts advertising. **Circ:** (Not Reported).

3988 ■ Social Justice: A Journal of Crime, Conflict, and World Order
Global Options
PO Box 40601
San Francisco, CA 94140-0601
Phone: (415)550-1703
Publication E-mail: socialjust@aol.com
Freq: Quarterly. **Print Method:** Offset. **Trim Size:** 6 x 9. **Cols./Page:** 1. **Col. Width:** 4 3/8 inches. **Col. Depth:** 6 7/8 inches. **Key Personnel:** Stefania De Petris, Managing Editor; Gregory Shank, Managing Editor. **ISSN:** 1043--1578 (print). **Subscription Rates:** $45 Individuals 1 year, U.S.; $47 Individuals 1 year, other countries; $85 Individuals 2 years, U.S.; $89 Individuals 2 years, other countries; $85 Two years US 8 issues; $130.90 Institutions 1 year, U.S.; $136 Institutions 1 year, other countries; $255 Institutions 2 years, U.S.; $263.50 Institutions 2 years, other countries. **URL:** http://www.socialjusticejournal.org/Global_Options.html; http://www.socialjusticejournal.org/. **Formerly**: Crime and Social Justice. **Ad Rates:** BW $250. **Remarks:** Advertising accepted; rates available upon request. **Circ:** Paid ‡3000, Non-paid ‡50.

3989 ■ Social Policy
Organize Training Center
442 Vicksburg St.
San Francisco, CA 94114-3831
Phone: (415)648-6894
Freq: Quarterly. **Subscription Rates:** $45 Individuals; $185 Institutions. **Remarks:** Advertising not accepted. **Circ:** (Not Reported).

3990 ■ Spa Magazine
Islands Publishing Co.
415 Jackson St.
San Francisco, CA 94111
Phone: (415)632-1633
Fax: (415)632-1640
Publisher's E-mail: info@resortsgreathotels.com
Magazine containing articles on travel, well-being, and 'renewal'. **Freq:** 7/yr. **Print Method:** Web Offset. **Trim Size:** 8 3/8 x 10 1/2. **Cols./Page:** 3. **Col. Width:** 2 1/4 inches. **Col. Depth:** 9 1/2 inches. **Key Personnel:** Michelle Gamble, Publisher. **Subscription Rates:** $19.97 U.S.; $28.97 Canada. **Remarks:** Accepts advertising. **Circ:** Paid ‡85,000.

3991 ■ Sports Medicine and Arthroscopy Review
Lippincott Williams & Wilkins
c/o W. Dilworth Cannon, Ed.
University of California, Dept. of Orthopaedic Surgery
San Francisco Medical Ctr.
1701 Divisadero St., No. 240
San Francisco, CA 94115-1351
Phone: (415)353-7566
Fax: (415)353-7593
Peer-reviewed journal covering information and developments in the field of sports medicine and arthroscopy. **Freq:** Quarterly. **Print Method:** Sheetfed Offset. **Trim Size:** 8 1/4 x 11. **Key Personnel:** Gregory C. Fanelli, Associate Editor, phone: (570)271-6541, fax: (570)271-5872; Kenneth E. DeHaven, MD, Editor, phone: (716)275-2970, fax: (716)242-0763; W. Dilworth Cannon, Jr., Editor. **ISSN:** 1062--8592 (print); **EISSN:** 153-8-1951 (electronic). **Subscription Rates:** $416 Individuals paperback; $448 Canada and Mexico paperback; $462 Other countries paperback; $913 Institutions paperback; $975 Institutions, Canada and Mexico paperback; $989 Institutions, other countries paperback. **URL:** http://journals.lww.com/sportsmedarthro/Pages/default.aspx. **Ad Rates:** BW $1,320; 4C $2,805. **Remarks:** Accepts advertising. **Circ:** 202.

3992 ■ Summer Academe: A Journal of Higher Education
Caddo Gap Press Inc.
3145 Geary Blvd.
San Francisco, CA 94118
Phone: (415)666-3012
Fax: (415)666-3552
Publisher's E-mail: info@caddogap.com
Scholarly journal covering the field of higher education summer session administration. **Freq:** Annual. **Print Method:** Lithography. **Trim Size:** 6 x 9. **Cols./Page:** 1. **Col. Width:** 4 1/2 inches. **Col. Depth:** 7 inches. **Key Personnel:** Bill Kops, Editor. **ISSN:** 1091-8515 (print). **Subscription Rates:** $25 Individuals; $50 Institutions.

URL: http://www.caddogap.com/store/index.html. **Mailing address:** PO Box 275, San Francisco, CA 94118. **Ad Rates:** BW $200. **Remarks:** Accepts advertising. **Circ:** Paid 800.

3993 ■ Sun-Reporter - Metro Reporter
Reporter Publications
1791 Bancroft Ave.
San Francisco, CA 94124
Phone: (415)671-1000
Fax: (415)671-1005
Publication E-mail: sunmedia97@aol.com
Black community newspaper (tabloid). **Freq:** Weekly (Thurs.). **Print Method:** Offset. **Cols./Page:** 5. **Col. Width:** 2 1/16 inches. **Col. Depth:** 14 inches. **Key Personnel:** Amelia Ashley-Ward, PhD, Publisher; Gail Berkley, Editor. **Subscription Rates:** $20 Individuals; $35 Two years. **Formerly**: Sun-Reporter. **Ad Rates:** SAU $11.55. **Remarks:** Accepts advertising. **Circ:** (Not Reported).

3994 ■ Super 7
Super7 Media Inc.
1628 Post St.
San Francisco, CA 94115
Phone: (415)409-4701
Fax: (415)409-4703
Publisher's E-mail: info@super7store.com
English-language magazine covering Japanese toy culture. **Freq:** Quarterly. **Key Personnel:** Brian Flynn, Editor. **URL:** http://www.super7store.com. **Remarks:** Accepts advertising. **Circ:** (Not Reported).

3995 ■ Taboo: The Journal of Culture and Education
Caddo Gap Press Inc.
3145 Geary Blvd.
San Francisco, CA 94118
Phone: (415)666-3012
Fax: (415)666-3552
Publisher's E-mail: info@caddogap.com
Scholarly journal covering research, scholarship, and other information about the study of education and culture. **Freq:** Semiannual. **Print Method:** Lithography. **Trim Size:** 6 x 9. **Cols./Page:** 1. **Col. Width:** 4 1/2 inches. **Col. Depth:** 7 inches. **Key Personnel:** Shirley Steinberg, Editor. **ISSN:** 1080-5400 (print). **Subscription Rates:** $50 Individuals; $100 Institutions. **URL:** http://www.caddogap.com/periodicals.shtml; http://www.caddogap.com/store/index.html. **Mailing address:** PO Box 275, San Francisco, CA 94118. **Ad Rates:** BW $200. **Remarks:** Accepts advertising. **Circ:** Paid 125.

3996 ■ Teacher Education Quarterly
Caddo Gap Press Inc.
3145 Geary Blvd.
San Francisco, CA 94118
Phone: (415)666-3012
Fax: (415)666-3552
Publisher's E-mail: info@caddogap.com
Scholarly journal on teacher education. **Freq:** Quarterly. **Print Method:** Offset. **Trim Size:** 6 x 9. **Cols./Page:** 1. **Col. Width:** 27 picas. **Col. Depth:** 43 picas. **Key Personnel:** Christian Faltis, Editor; Alan H. Jones, Publisher. **ISSN:** 0737--5328 (print). **Subscription Rates:** $50 Students outside U.S., add $60 postage (/year); $75 Individuals outside U.S., add $60 postage (/year); $150 Institutions (/year) outside U.S., add $60 postage. **URL:** http://www.caddogap.com; http://www.teqjournal.org; http://www.caddogap.com/periodicals.shtml; http://www.teqjournal.org/ojs/index.php/TEQ. **Mailing address:** PO Box 275, San Francisco, CA 94118. **Ad Rates:** BW $200. **Remarks:** Accepts advertising. **Circ:** 900.

3997 ■ Theatre Bay Area
Theatre Bay Area
1663 Mission St., Ste. 525
San Francisco, CA 94103
Phone: (415)430-1140
Fax: (415)430-1145
Magazine promoting the theatre community in San Francisco Bay Area. **Freq:** Bimonthly. **Key Personnel:** Sam Hurwitt, Editor-in-Chief. **Subscription Rates:** Included in membership. **URL:** http://www.theatrebayarea.org/?page=InPrint. **Remarks:** Accepts advertising. **Circ:** (Not Reported).

3998 ■ THRASHER
High Speed Productions Inc.
1303 Underwood Ave.
San Francisco, CA 94124
Free: 888-520-9099
Publication E-mail: mail@thrashermagazine.com
Skateboard magazine. **Freq:** Monthly. **Print Method:** Offset. **Trim Size:** 8 1/8 x 10.5. **ISSN:** 0889-0692 (print). **Subscription Rates:** $17.95 U.S. one year individual subscription; $48 Canada one year individual subscription; $75 Other countries one year individual subscription. **URL:** http://www.thrashermagazine.com. **Formerly**: THRASHER Skateboard Magazine. **Ad Rates:** BW $4,713; 4C $6,908. **Remarks:** Accepts advertising. **Circ:** ‡250000.

3999 ■ Topics in Antiviral Medicine
International AIDS Society USA
425 California St., Ste. 1450
San Francisco, CA 94104-2120
Phone: (415)544-9400
Fax: (415)544-9401
Publisher's E-mail: info@iasusa.org
Freq: 4-6/year. **Subscription Rates:** Free. **Alt. Formats:** Download. **URL:** http://www.iasusa.org/pub. **Formerly**: Topics in HIV Medicine. **Remarks:** Advertising not accepted. **Circ:** 12000.

4000 ■ Transactions of the American Ophthalmological Society
American Ophthalmological Society
655 Beach St.
San Francisco, CA 94109
Phone: (415)561-8578
Fax: (415)561-8531
Publisher's E-mail: admin@aosonline.org
Freq: Annual in December. **Alt. Formats:** PDF. **Remarks:** Advertising not accepted. **Circ:** (Not Reported).

4001 ■ Translorial
Northern California Translators Association
2261 Market St., No. 160
San Francisco, CA 94114-1600
Phone: (510)845-8712
Publisher's E-mail: administrator@ncta.org
Freq: Quarterly. **Key Personnel:** Sarah Llewellyn, Vice President. **URL:** http://translorial.com. **Remarks:** Accepts advertising. **Circ:** (Not Reported).

4002 ■ Tribal: The Magazine of Tribal Art
Tribarts Inc.
2261 Market St., Ste. 644
San Francisco, CA 94114
Publisher's E-mail: info@tribalartmagazine.com
Magazine covering tribal art worldwide. **Freq:** Quarterly. **Key Personnel:** Stacy Farr, Manager, Circulation; Alex Arthur, Art Director; Jonathan Fogel, Editor-in-Chief; Francoise Barrier, Publisher. **ISSN:** 1354--2990 (print). **Subscription Rates:** $85 Individuals print; €65 Individuals print, Europe; $160 U.S. and Canada 2 years, print; €120 Two years print Europe. **URL:** http://www.tribalartmagazine.com. **Formerly**: The World of Tribal Arts. **Ad Rates:** 4C $1,900. **Remarks:** Accepts advertising. **Circ:** Paid 3000.

4003 ■ Trikon
Trikone
60 29th St., No. 614
San Francisco, CA 94110
Free: 844-903-5663
Publisher's E-mail: contact@trikone.org
Freq: Quarterly. **ISSN:** 1042--735X (print). **Subscription Rates:** $30 Individuals; $40 Other countries; 231.61 &peso; Individuals digital. **URL:** http://www.trikone.org/index.php/magazine/publication; http://www.trikone.org/index.php/magazine/subscription. **Remarks:** Accepts advertising. **Circ:** (Not Reported).

4004 ■ University of San Francisco Magazine
University of San Francisco
2130 Fulton St.
San Francisco, CA 94117-1080
Phone: (415)422-5555
Fax: (415)422-2696
Publication E-mail: usfmagazine@usfca.edu
University magazine. **Freq:** Semiannual. **Key Personnel:** Gary McDonald, Executive Editor. **URL:** http://www.usfca.edu/usfmagazine/. **Remarks:** Advertising not accepted. **Circ:** Controlled 75000.

4005 ■ USF Maritime Law Journal
University of San Francisco School of Law
2130 Fulton St.
San Francisco, CA 94117-1080
Phone: (415)422-6307
Publisher's E-mail: lawcommunications@usfca.edu
Journal containing topics on maritime law, including recent statutory and case law changes. **Freq:** Semiannual. **URL:** http://www.usfca.edu/catalog/course/maritime-law-journal-0. **Circ:** (Not Reported).

4006 ■ VegNews
VegNews
3505 20th St.
San Francisco, CA 94110
Phone: (415)642-6397
Fax: (415)642-6398
Publisher's E-mail: feedback@vegnews.com
Magazine covering vegetarian lifestyle. **Freq:** Bimonthly. **Trim Size:** 8.625 x 10.875. **Key Personnel:** Lyndsay Orwig, Office Manager; Colleen Holland, Publisher. **Subscription Rates:** $20 Individuals; $36 Two years; $50 Individuals three years. **URL:** http://vegnews.com. **Remarks:** Accepts advertising. **Circ:** (Not Reported).

4007 ■ Vitae Scholasticae
Caddo Gap Press Inc.
3145 Geary Blvd.
San Francisco, CA 94118
Phone: (415)666-3012
Fax: (415)666-3552
Publisher's E-mail: info@caddogap.com
Scholarly journal covering research, scholarship, and other information about the study of biography in education. **Freq:** Annual. **Print Method:** Lithography. **Trim Size:** 6 x 9. **Cols./Page:** 1. **Col. Width:** 4 1/2 inches. **Col. Depth:** 7 inches. **Key Personnel:** Patricia Inman, Editor. **ISSN:** 0735-0909 (print). **Subscription Rates:** $50 Individuals; $100 Institutions. **URL:** http://www.caddogap.com/download/CGPorderform.pdf. **Mailing address:** PO Box 275, San Francisco, CA 94118. **Ad Rates:** BW $200. **Remarks:** Accepts advertising. **Circ:** Paid 125.

4008 ■ Weekly Shonen Jump: The World's Most Popular Manga
Viz Media L.L.C.
295 Bay St.
San Francisco, CA 94133
Phone: (415)546-7073
Fax: (415)546-7086
Animation magazine covering the most popular action manga in the world. **Freq:** Weekly. **Trim Size:** 7.125 x 10.125. **Key Personnel:** Yuki Takagaki, Senior Editor, phone: (415)546-7073. **URL:** http://shonenjump.viz.com; http://www.viz.com/anime/streaming/shonen-jump. **Formerly**: Shonen Jump: The World's Most Popular Manga. **Mailing address:** PO Box 77010, San Francisco, CA 94133. **Circ:** Combined 200000.

4009 ■ West-Northwest Journal of Environmental Law and Policy
University of California Hastings College of the Law
200 McAllister St.
San Francisco, CA 94102
Phone: (415)565-4623
Fax: (415)581-8946
Publisher's E-mail: admiss@uchastings.edu
Journal containing issues on environmental law. **Freq:** Semiannual. **URL:** http://www.uchastings.edu/student-life/journals/west-northwest/index.php. **Circ:** (Not Reported).

4010 ■ Wired
Wired News
500 3rd St., Ste. 310
San Francisco, CA 94107
Phone: (415)276-8400
Fax: (415)276-8500
Free: 800-769-4733
Publication E-mail: wirednews@wired.com
Consumer online site focusing on the digital revolution's impact on business, culture, and society. **Freq:** Daily. **Key Personnel:** Evan Hansen, Editor-in-Chief; Kevin Poulsen, Editor. **Alt. Formats:** Handheld. **URL:** http://www.wired.com. **Remarks:** Advertising accepted; rates available upon request. **Circ:** Paid **★611283**.

4011 ■ Words on Plays
American Conservatory Theater

Circulation: ★ = AAM; △ or • = BPA; ♦ = CAC; ❑ = VAC; ⊕ = PO Statement; ‡ = Publisher's Report; Boldface figures = sworn; Light figures = estimated.

30 Grant Ave., 7th Fl.
San Francisco, CA 94108-5834
Phone: (415)834-3200
Publisher's E-mail: tickets@act-sf.org
Freq: 8/year. **Subscription Rates:** $10 Individuals print or online (include postage); $5 Individuals online. **URL:** http://www.act-sf.org/home/education/wop.html. **Remarks:** Advertising not accepted. **Circ:** (Not Reported).

4012 ■ XLR8R: Accelerating Music and Culture
XLR8R
3180 18th St., Ste. 207
San Francisco, CA 94110
Phone: (415)861-7583
Fax: (415)861-7584
Publisher's E-mail: service@xlr8r.com
Magazine covering dance and electronic music, fashion, and politics. **Freq:** Bimonthly. **Print Method:** Web heatset. **Trim Size:** 8.375 x 10.875. **Key Personnel:** Ken Taylor, Editor; Shawn Reynaldo, Managing Editor; Ethan Holben, Manager, Advertising. **ISSN:** 1526--4246 (print). **URL:** http://www.xlr8r.com/magazine. **Remarks:** Accepts advertising. **Circ:** (Not Reported).

4013 ■ ZYZZYVA: The Journal of West Coast Writers and Artists
ZYZZYVA
57 Post St., Ste. 604
San Francisco, CA 94104
Phone: (415)757-0465
Publisher's E-mail: editor@zyzzyva.org
Journal featuring West Coast writers and artists. **Freq:** Quarterly. **Print Method:** Offset. **Trim Size:** 6 x 9. **Cols./Page:** 1. **Col. Width:** 60 nonpareils. **Col. Depth:** 108 agate lines. **Key Personnel:** Oscar Villalon, Managing Editor; Laura Cogan, Editor. **ISSN:** 8756--5633 (print). **Subscription Rates:** $30 Students; $40 Individuals regular; $60 Two years. **URL:** http://www.zyzzyva.org. **Ad Rates:** BW $500. **Remarks:** Color advertising not accepted. **Circ:** Combined ‡2500.

4014 ■ KALW-FM - 91.7
500 Mansell St.
San Francisco, CA 94134
Phone: (415)841-4121
Fax: (415)841-4125
Email: kalw@kalw.org
Format: Talk; News; Eclectic; Public Radio. **Networks:** National Public Radio (NPR); BBC World Service; Canadian Broadcasting Corporation (CBC)/Societe Radio-Canada (SRC). **Owner:** San Francisco Unified School District, 555 Franklin St., San Francisco, CA 94102. **Founded:** 1941. **Operating Hours:** 5 a.m. to 11.30 p.m. **Key Personnel:** Matt Martin, Gen. Mgr., matt@kalw.org; Bill Helgeson, Operations Mgr.; Phil Hartman, Chief Engineer, ph@well.com. **Wattage:** 1,900. **Ad Rates:** Noncommercial. $60-170 for 30 seconds. **URL:** http://www.kalw.org.

4015 ■ KBWF-FM - 95.7
201 3rd St., Ste. 1200
San Francisco, CA 94103
Free: 888-957-9570
Format: Country. **Owner:** Entercom Communications Corp., 401 City Ave., Ste. 809, Bala Cynwyd, PA 19004-1130, Ph: (610)660-5610, Fax: (610)660-5620. **ADI:** San Francisco-Oakland-San Jose. **Key Personnel:** Mike Fadelli, Sales Mgr., mfadelli@entercom.com. **URL:** http://www.957thegame.com.

4016 ■ KCBS-AM - 740
865 Battery St.
San Francisco, CA 94111-1503
Phone: (415)765-4000
Format: News; Information. **Networks:** CBS. **Owner:** CBS Radio Inc., 1271 Avenue of the Americas, 44th Fl., New York, NY 10020-1401, Ph: (212)649-9600. **Founded:** 1909. **Operating Hours:** Continuous. **ADI:** San Francisco-Oakland-San Jose. **Key Personnel:** Justin Erickson, Sales Mgr., erickson@sfradio.cbs.com. **Wattage:** 50,000. **Ad Rates:** Advertising accepted; rates available upon request. **URL:** http://sanfrancisco.cbslocal.com/station/kcbs.

4017 ■ KCNS-TV
449 Broadway
New York, NY 10013
Phone: (212)966-1059
Owner: Multicultural Radio Broadcasting, Inc., at above address. **Founded:** 1986. **Key Personnel:** Julie Re, Contact, julier@mrbi.net. **Ad Rates:** Noncommercial.

4018 ■ KCSF-FM - 90.9
50 Phelan Ave.
San Francisco, CA 94112
Phone: (415)239-3000
Fax: (415)452-5150
Email: kcsf@ccsf.edu
Format: World Beat; News. **Owner:** San Francisco City College, at above address. **Founded:** Sept. 16, 2006. **Ad Rates:** Noncommercial. **URL:** http://www.ccsf.edu.

4019 ■ KDFC-FM - 102.1
201 Third St., Ste. 1200
San Francisco, CA 94103
Phone: (415)546-8710
Email: feedback@kdfc.com
Format: Classical. **Networks:** Independent. **Owner:** Entercom Communications Corp., 401 City Ave., Ste. 809, Bala Cynwyd, PA 19004-1130, Ph: (610)660-5610, Fax: (610)660-5620. **Founded:** 1947. **Operating Hours:** Continuous. **ADI:** San Francisco-Oakland-San Jose. **Key Personnel:** Bill Lueth, President, blueth@entercom.com; Rik Malone, Asst. Dir. **Wattage:** 33,000. **Ad Rates:** Advertising accepted; rates available upon request. **URL:** http://www.kdfc.com.

4020 ■ KDTV-TV - 14
50 Freemont St., 41st Fl.
San Francisco, CA 94105
Phone: (415)538-8000
Fax: (415)538-8053
Format: Commercial TV; Hispanic; News; Sports. **Networks:** Univision. **Founded:** 1975. **Formerly:** KEMO-TV. **Operating Hours:** Continuous. **ADI:** San Francisco-Oakland-San Jose. **Key Personnel:** Zaid F. Alsikafi, Director. **Local Programs:** *Noticiero 14.* **Wattage:** 3,700 ERP. **Ad Rates:** Advertising accepted; rates available upon request. **URL:** http://www.univision.com.

4021 ■ KEAR-AM - 610
290 Hegenberger Rd.
Oakland, CA 94621
Free: 800-543-1495
Email: info@familyradio.org
Format: Religious. **Owner:** Family Stations Inc., 290 Hegenberger Rd., Oakland, CA 94621, Free: 800-543-1495. **URL:** http://www.familyradio.com.

4022 ■ KEST-AM - 1450
44 Gough St., Ste. 301
San Francisco, CA 94103
Phone: (415)978-5378
Fax: (415)865-0738
Email: kest1450@sbcglobal.net
Format: Talk. **Networks:** Independent. **Owner:** Multicultural Radio Broadcasting Inc., 27 William St., 11th Fl., New York, NY 10005, Ph: (212)966-1059, Fax: (212)966-9580. **Founded:** 1926. **Operating Hours:** 5 a.m.-11 a.m. **ADI:** San Francisco-Oakland-San Jose. **Key Personnel:** Julie Re, Contact, julier@mrbi.net. **Wattage:** 1,000. **Ad Rates:** Noncommercial. **URL:** http://www.kestradio.com.

4023 ■ KFOG-FM - 104.5
750 Battery St., 3rd Fl.
San Francisco, CA 94105
Phone: (415)995-6800
Free: 800-300-5364
Email: mindthegap@kfog.com
Format: Classic Rock. **ADI:** San Francisco-Oakland-San Jose. **Key Personnel:** Rosalie Howarth, Contact, sfopsa@cumulus.com. **Wattage:** 7,100 ERP. **Ad Rates:** Advertising accepted; rates available upon request. **URL:** http://www.kfog.com.

4024 ■ KFOX-FM - 98.5
201 3rd St., Ste. 1200
San Francisco, CA 94103
Phone: (408)200-9850
Fax: (408)467-7660
Free: 877-410-5369
Format: News; Sports; Classic Rock. **Operating Hours:** Continuous. **Ad Rates:** Advertising accepted; rates available upon request. **URL:** http://www.kfox.com.

4025 ■ KFRC-FM - 106.9
865 Battery St.
San Francisco, CA 94111
Phone: (415)391-9970
Fax: (415)951-2376
Free: 888-456-KFRC
Format: Oldies. **Networks:** Independent. **Owner:** CBS Radio Inc., 1271 Avenue of the Americas, 44th Fl., New York, NY 10020-1401, Ph: (212)649-9600. **Founded:** 1949. **Formerly:** KXXX-FM. **Operating Hours:** weekdays 5 a.m.-12 a.m.; Saturday and Sunday Continuous. **ADI:** San Francisco-Oakland-San Jose. **Key Personnel:** Liz Saint John, Dir. Pub. Aff., liz@sfradio.cbs.com. **Wattage:** 40,000. **Ad Rates:** $10-650 per unit.

4026 ■ KGO-AM - 810
750 Battery St., 2nd Fl.
San Francisco, CA 94111
Phone: (415)216-1300
Format: News; Talk. **Networks:** ABC. **Owner:** Citadel Broadcasting Corp., 7201 W Lake Mead Blvd., Ste. 400, Las Vegas, NV 89128-8366, Ph: (702)804-5200, Fax: (702)804-8250. **Founded:** 1924. **Operating Hours:** Continuous. **ADI:** San Francisco-Oakland-San Jose. **Wattage:** 50,000. **Ad Rates:** Advertising accepted; rates available upon request. **URL:** http://www.kgoradio.com.

4027 ■ KGO-TV - 7
900 Front St.
San Francisco, CA 94111
Phone: (415)954-7777
Free: 877-222-7777
Networks: ABC. **Founded:** 1949. **Operating Hours:** Continuous. **ADI:** San Francisco-Oakland-San Jose. **Local Programs:** *Perspective 3*; *Interracial Marriage*; *On the Spot—Gangs.* **Ad Rates:** Noncommercial. **URL:** http://www.abc7news.com.

4028 ■ KIOI-FM - 101.3
340 Townsend St., Ste. 5101
San Francisco, CA 94107
Phone: (415)975-5555
Fax: (415)538-5953
Free: 800-800-1013
Format: Adult Contemporary. **Networks:** Independent. **Founded:** 1957. **Operating Hours:** Continuous. **ADI:** San Francisco-Oakland-San Jose. **Key Personnel:** Mark Adams, Dir. of Programs; Val Klein, Promotions Dir., valklein@clearchannel.com. **Local Programs:** *Don Bleu in the Morning*, Monday Tuesday Wednesday Thursday Friday 8:00 a.m. **Wattage:** 125,000. **Ad Rates:** Advertising accepted; rates available upon request. **URL:** http://www.star1013fm.com.

4029 ■ KIQI-AM - 1010
730 Harrison, Ste. 300
San Francisco, CA 94107
Phone: (415)626-1510
Format: Music of Your Life; Talk. **Founded:** 1957. **Operating Hours:** Continuous. **ADI:** San Francisco-Oakland-San Jose. **Key Personnel:** Rene De La Rosa, President. **Wattage:** 10,000. **Ad Rates:** Advertising accepted; rates available upon request. $60-88 for 30 seconds; $75-110 for 60 seconds. **URL:** http://www.kiqi1010am.com.

4030 ■ KISQ-FM - 98.1
340 Townsend St.
San Francisco, CA 94107
Phone: (415)975-5555
Fax: (415)356-5803
Free: 877-547-7329
Format: Adult Contemporary; Talk; News. **Simulcasts:** KABL-AM. **Networks:** Independent. **Founded:** 1959. **Formerly:** KAFE-FM; KABL-FM; KROW-AM; KBGG-FM; KABL-AM. **Operating Hours:** Continuous. **Key Personnel:** J.D. Freeman, Gen. Mgr. **Wattage:** 100,000 ERP. **Ad Rates:** Noncommercial; Advertising accepted; rates available upon request. **URL:** http://www.981kissfm.com.

4031 ■ KITS-FM - 105.3
865 Battery St.
San Francisco, CA 94111
Free: 800-696-1053
Format: Alternative/New Music/Progressive. **Owner:** CBS Radio Inc., 1271 Avenue of the Americas, 44th Fl., New York, NY 10020-1401, Ph: (212)649-9600. **Founded:** 1986. **Operating Hours:** Continuous. **Key Personnel:** Paul Hoffmann, Sales Mgr., phoffmann@live105.com. **Wattage:** 15,000. **Ad Rates:** $200-600 per unit. **URL:** http://live105.cbslocal.com.

4032 ■ KJAZ-FM - 92.7
150 Executive Park Blvd., Ste. 2300
San Francisco, CA 94134
Phone: (415)657-9000
Fax: (415)468-6900

Format: News. **Founded:** 1959. **Operating Hours:** Continuous; 100% local. **Key Personnel:** Jerry Dean, Operations Mgr.; Bob Parlocha, Music Dir; Tim Hodges, Contact; Denise Culver-Nelson, Contact. **Wattage:** 6,000 ERP. **URL:** http://www.927rev.com.

4033 ■ KKHI-FM - 95.7
Hotel St. Francis
335 Powell St.
San Francisco, CA 94102
Phone: (415)986-2151
Fax: (415)398-3770
Format: Classical. **Simulcasts:** KKHI-AM. **Networks:** Independent. **Founded:** 1961. **Operating Hours:** Continuous; 100% local. **Key Personnel:** Victor Ledin, Dir. of Programs; Bruce Beebe, Contact; Leonard Mattson, Contact; Lou Sinclair, Contact; Marita Dorenbecker, Contact. **Wattage:** 8,600. **Ad Rates:** $100-180 for 60 seconds.

4034 ■ KKSF-FM - 103.7
340 Townsend St.
San Francisco, CA 94107
Phone: (415)975-5555
Format: Classic Rock. **Networks:** Independent. **Owner:** iHeartMedia Inc., 200 E Basse Rd., San Antonio, TX 78209, Ph: (210)832-3314. **Founded:** 1987. **Formerly:** KLOK-FM. **Operating Hours:** Continuous. **Wattage:** 7,200. **Ad Rates:** $200-1500 per unit. **URL:** http://www.talk910.com//main.html.

4035 ■ KMBY-FM - 103.9
201 3rd St., Ste. 1200
San Francisco, CA 94103
Phone: (415)546-8710
Free: 888-966-5454
Email: dj@x1039fm.com
Format: Alternative/New Music/Progressive. **Founded:** Sept. 13, 2006. **Key Personnel:** Kenny Allen, Dir. of Programs. **Ad Rates:** Noncommercial. **URL:** http://www.kdfc.com.

4036 ■ KMEL-FM - 106.1
340 Townsend St., Ste. 5101
San Francisco, CA 94107
Phone: (415)975-5555
Fax: (415)538-5953
Email: info@kmel.com
Format: Urban Contemporary. **Networks:** Independent. **Owner:** iHeartMedia Inc., 200 E Basse Rd., San Antonio, TX 78209, Ph: (210)832-3314. **Founded:** 1960. **Operating Hours:** Continuous. **ADI:** San Francisco-Oakland-San Jose. **Wattage:** 69,000. **Ad Rates:** Advertising accepted; rates available upon request. **URL:** http://www.kmel.com.

4037 ■ KMKY-AM - 1310
900 Front St., 3rd Fl.
San Francisco, CA 94111
Phone: (415)788-1310
Fax: (415)788-1312
Format: Eclectic. **Networks:** ABC. **Founded:** 1922. **Formerly:** KDIA-AM; KWBR-AM. **Operating Hours:** Continuous. **ADI:** San Francisco-Oakland-San Jose. **Wattage:** 5,000. **Ad Rates:** $150 for 30 seconds; $200 for 60 seconds. Combined advertising rates available with KGO, KSFO, KIID. **URL:** http://disney.go.com/home/today/index.html.

4038 ■ KMTP-TV - 32
211 Brannan
San Francisco, CA 94107
Phone: (415)777-3232
Format: Public TV. **Networks:** Public Broadcasting Service (PBS). **Formerly:** KQEC-TV. **ADI:** San Francisco-Oakland-San Jose. **Wattage:** 500,000 Horizontal. **Ad Rates:** Noncommercial. **URL:** http://www.kmtp.tv/.

4039 ■ KMVQ-FM - 99.7
865 Battery St.
San Francisco, CA 94111
Phone: (415)391-9970
Free: 888-456-9970
Email: contests@997now.com
Format: Urban Contemporary; Adult Contemporary. **ADI:** San Francisco-Oakland-San Jose. **Key Personnel:** Stephanie Saporita, Sales Mgr., stephanie.saporita@cbsradio.com. **URL:** http://www.997now.cbslocal.com.

4040 ■ KNBR-AM - 680
55 Hawthorne St., Ste. 1100
San Francisco, CA 94105-3914
Phone: (415)995-6800
Fax: (415)995-6867
Format: Sports; Talk. **Owner:** Cumulus Media Inc., 3280 Peachtree Rd. NW, Ste. 2300, Atlanta, GA 30305-2455, Ph: (404)949-0700, Fax: (404)949-0740. **Key Personnel:** Lee Hammer, Dir. of Programs, lee.hammer@cumulus.com. **Ad Rates:** Noncommercial. **URL:** http://www.knbr.com.

4041 ■ KNEW-AM - 910
340 Townsend St.
San Francisco, CA 94107
Phone: (415)975-5555
Fax: (415)356-5803
Format: Talk; News. **Networks:** ABC. **Founded:** 1925. **Formerly:** KEWB-AM. **Operating Hours:** Continuous; 100% local. **ADI:** San Francisco-Oakland-San Jose. **Key Personnel:** Bob Pittman, Chairman, CEO. **Wattage:** 5,000. **Ad Rates:** Advertising accepted; rates available upon request. **URL:** http://www.clearchannel.com/Radio/StationSearch.aspx?RadioSearch=KNEW.

4042 ■ KNGY-FM - 92.7
150 Executive Park Blvd., Ste. 2300
San Francisco, CA 94134
Phone: (415)657-9000
Fax: (415)468-6900
Format: Top 40. **Owner:** Energy 92.7, at above address. **Operating Hours:** Continuous. **Key Personnel:** Don Parker, Dir. of Programs, don@energy927fm.com; Brad Bludau, Gen. Sales Mgr., brad@energy927fm.com; Erik Proctor, Dir. of Mktg., Promotions Dir.; Michelle Bayliss, Dir. of Pub. Prog. & Svcs., mbayliss@energy927fm.com. **Ad Rates:** Advertising accepted; rates available upon request. **URL:** http://www.927rev.com/contact.php.

4043 ■ KOFY-TV - 20
2500 Marin St.
San Francisco, CA 94124-1015
Phone: (415)821-2020
Email: captioning@kofytv.com
Format: Commercial TV. **Networks:** Independent. **Owner:** Granite Broadcasting Corp., 767 3rd Ave., 34th Fl., New York, NY 10017-2083, Ph: (212)826-2530, Fax: (212)826-2858. **Operating Hours:** Continuous. **ADI:** San Francisco-Oakland-San Jose. **Ad Rates:** Noncommercial; Advertising accepted; rates available upon request. **Mailing address:** PO Box 182021, San Francisco, CA 94120-7720. **URL:** http://www.kofytv.com.

4044 ■ KOIT-FM - 96.5
201 Third St., Ste. 1200
San Francisco, CA 94103
Phone: (415)777-0965
Free: 800-564-8965
Email: koit@koit.com
Format: Soft Rock. **Networks:** AP; UPI. **Owner:** Entercom Communications Corp., 401 City Ave., Ste. 809, Bala Cynwyd, PA 19004-1130, Ph: (610)660-5610, Fax: (610)660-5620. **Founded:** 1976. **Operating Hours:** Continuous. **ADI:** San Francisco-Oakland-San Jose. **Key Personnel:** Jude Heller, Dir. of Mktg., jheller@entercom.com. **Wattage:** 33,000. **Ad Rates:** Noncommercial. **URL:** http://www.koit.com.

4045 ■ KPIG-AM - 1510
28 Second St., Ste. 501
San Francisco, CA 94105
Format: Classic Rock. **Owner:** Mapleton Communications, 10900 Wilshire Blvd., No. 1500, Los Angeles, CA 90024, Ph: (310)209-7229, Fax: (310)209-7239. **Operating Hours:** Continuous. **Ad Rates:** Advertising accepted; rates available upon request. **URL:** http://wwwkpigcom.

4046 ■ KPIX-TV - 5
855 Battery St.
San Francisco, CA 94111
Phone: (415)362-5550
Format: Commercial TV. **Networks:** CBS. **Founded:** 1940. **Operating Hours:** 5:30 a.m.-4 a.m. **ADI:** San Francisco-Oakland-San Jose. **Ad Rates:** Advertising accepted; rates available upon request. **URL:** http://sanfrancisco.cbslocal.com.

4047 ■ KPOO-FM - 89.5
1329 Divisadero St.
San Francisco, CA 94115
Phone: (415)346-5373
Fax: (415)346-5173
Email: info@kpoo.com
Format: Full Service. **Networks:** Independent. **Owner:** Poor People's Radio Inc. **Founded:** 1971. **Operating Hours:** Continuous. **ADI:** San Francisco-Oakland-San Jose. **Key Personnel:** Marilyn Fowler, Contact. **Wattage:** 160. **Ad Rates:** Noncommercial. **Mailing address:** PO Box 156650, San Francisco, CA 94115. **URL:** http://www.kpoo.com.

4048 ■ KQED-FM - 88.5
2601 Mariposa St.
San Francisco, CA 94110
Phone: (415)864-2000
Fax: (415)553-2241
Free: 866-733-6786
Email: faq@kqed.org
Format: Public Radio. **Networks:** National Public Radio (NPR). **Owner:** KQED Inc., 2601 Mariposa St., San Francisco, CA 94110, Ph: (415)864-2000; Northern California Public Broadcasting. **Founded:** 1969. **Key Personnel:** Michael Isip, VP; Jo Anne Wallace, VP. **Wattage:** 110,000 ERP. **Ad Rates:** Advertising accepted; rates available upon request. **URL:** http://www.kqed.org.

4049 ■ KQKE-AM - 960
340 Townsend St.
San Francisco, CA 94107
Phone: (415)356-5500
Format: Album-Oriented Rock (AOR). **Founded:** Sept. 15, 2006. **Key Personnel:** Perry Adams, Sales Mgr., perryadams@clearchannel.com; John Scott, Dir. of Programs, john@green960.com. **Wattage:** 5,000. **Ad Rates:** Advertising accepted; rates available upon request. **URL:** http://www.thepatriot960.com.

4050 ■ KRON-TV - 4
1001 Van Ness Ave.
San Francisco, CA 94109
Phone: (415)441-4444
Fax: (415)561-8142
Format: Commercial TV. **Operating Hours:** Continuous. **ADI:** San Francisco-Oakland-San Jose. **Key Personnel:** Mark Sowinski, Contact. **Wattage:** 1,000,000 ERP. **Ad Rates:** Advertising accepted; rates available upon request. **URL:** http://www.kron4.com.

4051 ■ KRZZ-FM - 93.3
455 Market St., Ste. 2300
San Francisco, CA 94105
Owner: Spanish Broadcasting System Inc., Pablo Raul Alarcon Media Ctr., 7007 NW 77th Ave., Miami, FL 33166, Ph: (305)441-6901, Fax: (305)883-3375. **Founded:** 1985. **ADI:** San Francisco-Oakland-San Jose. **Wattage:** 6,000. **Ad Rates:** $60-80 per unit.

4052 ■ KSAN-FM - 107.7
55 Hawthorne St., Ste. 1000
San Francisco, CA 94105-3914
Phone: (415)995-6800
Format: Classic Rock. **Networks:** AP. **Owner:** Cumulus Media Inc., 3280 Peachtree Rd. NW, Ste. 2300, Atlanta, GA 30305-2455, Ph: (404)949-0700, Fax: (404)949-0740. **Founded:** 1954. **Operating Hours:** Continuous. **Wattage:** 8,900. **Ad Rates:** Advertising accepted; rates available upon request. **URL:** http://www.1077thebone.com.

4053 ■ KSFB-AM - 1260
3256 Penryn Rd., Ste. 100
Loomis, CA 95650-8052
Free: 866-774-3278
Format: Religious. **Networks:** AP; UPI. **Owner:** Immaculate Heart Radio, 3256 Penryn Rd., Ste. 100, Loomis, CA 95650-8052. **Operating Hours:** Continuous; 100% local. **ADI:** San Francisco-Oakland-San Jose. **Key Personnel:** Dick Jenkins, Gen. Mgr. **Wattage:** 5,000. **Ad Rates:** Advertising accepted; rates available upon request. **URL:** http://www.ihradio.com.

4054 ■ KSFO-AM - 560
900 Front St.
San Francisco, CA 94111
Format: Talk; Sports; News. **Networks:** Independent. **Owner:** Citadel Broadcasting Corp., 7201 W Lake Mead Blvd., Ste. 400, Las Vegas, NV 89128-8366, Ph: (702)804-5200, Fax: (702)804-8250. **Founded:** 1925. **Operating Hours:** Continuous. **ADI:** San Francisco-

Circulation: ★ = AAM; △ or • = BPA; ♦ = CAC; ❑ = VAC; ⊕ = PO Statement; ‡ = Publisher's Report; Boldface figures = sworn; Light figures = estimated.

Oakland-San Jose. **Wattage**: 5,000. **Ad Rates:** $50-400 per unit. **URL:** http://www.ksfo.com.

4055 ■ KSQL-FM - 99.1
750 Battery St., No. 200
San Francisco, CA 94111
Phone: (415)989-5765
Fax: (415)733-5766
Free: 888-880-5765
Format: Hispanic. **Simulcasts:** KSOL-FM. **Owner:** Univision Radio Inc., 3102 Oak Lawn Ave., Ste. 215, Dallas, TX 75219-4259, Ph: (214)525-7700, Fax: (214)525-7750. **URL:** http://www.univision.com.

4056 ■ KTCT-AM - 1050
55 Hawthorne St., Ste. 1100
San Francisco, CA 94105-3914
Phone: (415)995-6800
Fax: (415)995-6867
Format: Sports; Talk. **Owner:** Cumulus Media Inc., 3280 Peachtree Rd. NW, Ste. 2300, Atlanta, GA 30305-2455, Ph: (404)949-0700, Fax: (404)949-0740. **Operating Hours**: Continuous. **Ad Rates:** Advertising accepted; rates available upon request. **URL:** http://www.knbr.com.

4057 ■ KUSF-FM - 90.3
2130 Fulton St.
San Francisco, CA 94117
Phone: (415)386-5873
Format: News; Classical. **Networks:** Independent. **Owner:** University of San Francisco, 2130 Fulton St., San Francisco, CA 94117-1080, Ph: (415)422-5555, Fax: (415)422-2696. **Founded:** 1962. **Operating Hours**: Continuous; 100% local. **ADI**: San Francisco-Oakland-San Jose. **Key Personnel:** William Ruck, Jr., Chief Engineer. **Wattage**: 3,000. **Ad Rates:** Noncommercial. **URL:** http://www.kusf.org.

4058 ■ KVTO-AM - 1400
256 Laguna Honda Blvd., Ste. B
San Francisco, CA 94116
Phone: (415)566-8808
Fax: (415)566-8901
Email: info@kblx.com
Format: Ethnic; Adult Contemporary. **Networks:** Independent. **Owner:** Inner City Broadcasting Corp., C O Access Comm, 333 7th Ave., 14th Fl., New York, NY 10001-5014. **Founded:** 1994. **Formerly**: KBLX-AM; KRE-AM; KBFN-AM. **Operating Hours**: Continuous. **ADI**: San Francisco-Oakland-San Jose. **Key Personnel:** Kevin Brown, Contact, kbrown@kblx.com; Harvey Stone, Gen. Mgr., President; Barry Rose, Gen. Sales Mgr., VP; Eugene C. Wong, Contact; Kevin Brown, Contact, kbrown@kblx.com; Nikki Thomas, Contact, nthomas@kblx.com. **Wattage**: 1,000. **Ad Rates:** $18-50; $15-40 for 30 seconds; $20-60 for 60 seconds; $70-95 for 60 seconds. **URL:** http://www.kvto.net.

4059 ■ KVVF-FM - 105.7
750 Battery St., Ste. 200
San Francisco, CA 94111
Phone: (415)989-5765
Fax: (415)733-5766
Format: Hispanic. **Wattage**: 50,000. **URL:** http://hot1057fm.univision.com.

4060 ■ KYCY-AM
865 Battery St.
San Francisco, CA 94111
Owner: CBS Radio Inc., 1271 Avenue of the Americas, 44th Fl., New York, NY 10020-1401, Ph: (212)649-9600. **Key Personnel:** Stephen Page, Contact, spage@sfradio.cbs.com.

4061 ■ KYLD-FM - 94.9
340 Townsend St.
San Francisco, CA 94107
Phone: (415)975-5555
Free: 888-333-9490
Format: Contemporary Hit Radio (CHR); Hispanic. **Owner:** Univision Communications, Inc., at above address; iHeartMedia Inc., 200 E Basse Rd., San Antonio, TX 78209, Ph: (210)832-3314. **Formerly**: KSOL-FM. **Operating Hours**: Continuous. **Key Personnel:** Tony Perlongo, Gen. Mgr.; Mark Adams, Sales Mgr.; Anne Hudson, Sales Mgr.; Jose Luis Gonzalez, Contact; Jose Luis Gonzalez, Contact. **Wattage**: 30,000. **Ad Rates:** Noncommercial. **URL:** http://www.wild949.com.

4062 ■ KZCO-FM - 97.7
235 Pine St., Ste. 1675
San Francisco, CA 94104
Phone: (530)533-3700
Fax: (530)648-1688
Email: zspanish@calveb.com
Format: Hispanic; Ethnic. **Owner:** KZCO Broadcasting Inc./Z-Spanish Radio Network, Inc., 4058 Flying C Rd., No. 17, Cameron Park, CA 95682, Ph: (916)676-5996, Fax: (916)677-9799, Free: 800-921-9292. **Founded:** 1996. **Formerly**: KEWE-FM. **Operating Hours**: Continuous; 100% network. **Key Personnel:** Juan Villagrana, Account Exec. **Wattage**: 25,000. **Ad Rates:** $16 for 30 seconds; $23 for 60 seconds.

4063 ■ WOXY-FM - 95.7
201 Third St., Ste. 1200
San Francisco, CA 94103-3143
Format: Contemporary Hit Radio (CHR). **Owner:** iBiquity Digital Corp., 6711 Columbia Gateway Dr., Ste. 500, Columbia, MD 21046-2549, Ph: (410)872-1530, Fax: (443)539-4291. **Operating Hours**: Continuous. **Ad Rates:** Advertising accepted; rates available upon request. **URL:** http://www.957maxfm.com.

SAN JOSE

Santa Clara Co. Santa Clara Co. (W) 38 m SE of Oakland. California State University, at San Jose. West Coast center of research oriented electronic and space industries. Manufactures canning and dried fruit packing machinery; missiles, rocket boosters, computers, atomic electrical equipment, fruit, vegetable and fish cans; foundry, dairy products, chemicals, cement, aluminum, paint, fiberglass, matches, pumps, soaps, motors, cabinets, electronics. Automobile assembly plant. In extensive fruit, wine, nut, berry, grape and row crop growing region.

4064 ■ The Beethoven Journal
American Beethoven Society
San Jose State University
Beethoven Ctr.
1 Washington Sq.
San Jose, CA 95192-0171
Phone: (408)808-2058
Fax: (408)808-2060
Spotlights the life and works of Ludwig van Beethoven (1770-1827). Recurring features include feature articles, news of research, reports of meetings, book reviews, notices of publications available, and columns titled Auction Reports, Studies in Beethoven Bibliography, and Miscellanea. **Freq:** Semiannual summer and winter. **ISSN:** 1087--8262 (print). **Subscription Rates:** $25 Institutions within U.S.; $35 Institutions outside U.S. **URL:** http://americanbeethovensociety.org/journal/beethovenjournal.html; http://www.sjsu.edu/beethoven/research/beethoven_journal. **Formerly**: The Beethoven Newsletter. **Remarks:** Advertising not accepted. **Circ:** 1200, 1000.

4065 ■ Cichlidae Communique
Pacific Coast Cichlid Association
PO Box 28145
San Jose, CA 95159-8145
Phone: (408)243-0434
Journal featuring researches and observational articles about the science and hobby of cichlids. **Freq:** Bimonthly even months. **Subscription Rates:** Included in membership. **URL:** http://cichlidworld.com/membership-info. **Remarks:** Advertising not accepted. **Circ:** (Not Reported).

4066 ■ Cross-Cultural Research
Society for Cross-Cultural Research
c/o Lisa Oliver, Treasurer
Dept. of Counselor Education
San Jose State University
Sweeney Hall 420
San Jose, CA 95192
Publisher's E-mail: societyforcrossculturalresearch@yahoo.com
Journal publishing peer-reviewed articles describing cross-cultural or comparative studies in all the social/behavioral sciences and other sciences dealing with humans, including anthropology, sociology, psychology, political science, economics, human ecology, and evolutionary biology. **Freq:** Quarterly. **Subscription Rates:** Included in membership. **URL:** http://www.sccr.org/JCCR.html. **Remarks:** Advertising not accepted. **Circ:** (Not Reported).

4067 ■ Cupertino Courier
Silicon Valley Community Newspapers
1095 The Alameda
San Jose, CA 95126
Phone: (408)200-1000
Fax: (408)200-1011
Local newspaper. **Freq:** Daily. **Print Method:** Offset. **Trim Size:** 11 1/2 x 14. **Cols./Page:** 5. **Col. Width:** 2 1/16 inches. **Col. Depth:** 13 1/4 inches. **Key Personnel:** Linda Taaffe, Editor, phone: (408)200-1066; Matt Wilson, Writer, phone: (408)200-1065; Dick Sparrer, Editor; Jeannette Close, Manager, Advertising, phone: (408)200-1069. **Subscription Rates:** $2.50 Individuals per week, digital only; $2.50 Individuals per week, all access + sunday print; $5.25 Individuals per week, all access + thrusday, friday and sunday print; $8.95 Individuals per week, all access + 7 days print. **URL:** http://www.mercurynews.com/cupertino. **Remarks:** Accepts advertising. **Circ:** Combined ‡15789.

4068 ■ Discovery Girls
Discovery Girls Inc.
4300 Stevens Creek Blvd., Ste. 190
San Jose, CA 95129
Free: 800-554-8856
Publisher's E-mail: support@discoverygirls.com
Lifestyle magazine for girls ages 8 to 12. **Freq:** Bimonthly. **Key Personnel:** Lisa McKie, Contact. **Subscription Rates:** $19.95 Individuals; $26 Canada; $30 Other countries; $29.95 Two years; $42 Canada two years; $50 Other countries 2 years. **URL:** http://www.discoverygirls.com. **Remarks:** Accepts advertising. **Circ:** (Not Reported).

4069 ■ El Observador
El Observador
99 N 1st St., Ste. 100
San Jose, CA 95113
Phone: (408)938-1700
Bilingual newspaper (Spanish and English). **Freq:** Weekly (Fri.). **Print Method:** Offset. **Trim Size:** 13 x 21. **Cols./Page:** 6. **Col. Width:** 13 inches. **Col. Depth:** 21 inches. **Key Personnel:** Angelica Rossi, Publisher; Hilbert Morales, Publisher; Betty Morales, Publisher. **URL:** http://el-observador.com. **Mailing address:** PO Box 1990, San Jose, CA 95109. **Ad Rates:** GLR $2; BW $3780; SAU $30; PCI $30. **Remarks:** Accepts display advertising. **Circ:** (Not Reported).

4070 ■ Franchise UPDATE
Franchise UPDATE Publications Inc.
PO Box 20547
San Jose, CA 95160
Phone: (408)402-5681
Fax: (408)402-5738
Free: 800-289-4232
Professional magazine covering franchise trade, management and investment activity. **Freq:** Quarterly. **Trim Size:** 8 3/8 X 10 7/8. **Subscription Rates:** $39.95 Individuals; $60 Two years. **URL:** http://www.franchising.com/franchisors; http://subscribe.franchising.com/fum.html. **Ad Rates:** BW $2300; 4C $2800. **Remarks:** Accepts advertising. **Circ:** (Not Reported).

4071 ■ India Currents: The Complete Indian American Magazine.
India Currents
2670 S White Rd., Ste. 165
San Jose, CA 95148
Phone: (408)324-0488
Fax: (408)324-0477
Publication E-mail: editor@indiacurrents.com
Magazine covering articles that are of interest to Indian Americans. **Freq:** Monthly. **Print Method:** Offset. **Trim Size:** 8 1/4 x 10 1/2. **Cols./Page:** 3. **Col. Width:** 2 3/8 inches. **Col. Depth:** 9 3/4 inches. **Key Personnel:** Jaya Padmanabhan, Editor; Vandana Kumar, Publisher. **ISSN:** 0896--095X (print). **Subscription Rates:** Free inside California. **URL:** http://www.indiacurrents.com. **Mailing address:** PO Box 21285, San Jose, CA 95151. **Remarks:** Accepts advertising. **Circ:** Combined 42900.

4072 ■ International Mental Game Coaching Journal
International Mental Game Coaching Association
PO Box 8151
San Jose, CA 95155
Phone: (408)440-2398
Fax: (408)440-2339
Free: 888-445-0291

Contains articles on coaching psychology. **Subscription Rates:** Included in membership. **Remarks:** Advertising not accepted. **Circ:** (Not Reported).

4073 ■ La Oferta Review
La Oferta Review
1376 N 4th St.
San Jose, CA 95112-4713
Phone: (408)436-7850
Fax: (408)436-7861
Free: 800-336-7850
Publisher's E-mail: info@laoferta.com
Community newspaper (English and Spanish). **Freq:** Weekly (Fri.). **Print Method:** Offset. **Trim Size:** 13 x 21. **Cols./Page:** 6. **Col. Width:** 2 1/16 inches. **Col. Depth:** 21 inches. **Key Personnel:** Frank Andrade, Publisher; Mary Andrade, Editor, Publisher; Veronica Andrade, Director, Promotions, Manager, Advertising. **URL:** http://www.laoferta.com. **Remarks:** Accepts advertising. **Circ:** (Not Reported).

4074 ■ Metro
Metro Silicon Valley
550 S First St.
San Jose, CA 95113-2806
Phone: (408)200-1300
Alternative weekly newspaper. **Founded:** Mar. 1985. **Freq:** Weekly. **ISSN:** 0882-4290 (print). **Subscription Rates:** $95 Individuals. **URL:** http://www.metroactive.com/metro/. **Remarks:** Accepts advertising. **Circ:** ‡75000.

4075 ■ Metroactive: Silicon Valley's Weekly Newspaper
Metro Publishing Inc.
380 S First St.
San Jose, CA 95113
Phone: (408)200-1396
Fax: (408)271-3520
Publisher's E-mail: letters@metronews.com
Newspaper (tabloid) covering regional news, arts, and entertainment. **Freq:** Weekly (Thurs.). **Print Method:** Offset. **Trim Size:** 10 3/4 x 13 11/16. **Cols./Page:** 5. **Col. Width:** 26 nonpareils. **Col. Depth:** 196 agate lines. **Key Personnel:** Dan Pulcrano, Executive Editor, Chief Executive Officer. **Subscription Rates:** Free. **URL:** http://www.metroactive.com. **Remarks:** Accepts advertising. **Circ:** Free 85000.

4076 ■ Ministry & Liturgy
Resource Publications Inc.
160 E Virginia St., Ste. 290
San Jose, CA 95112
Phone: (408)286-8505
Fax: (408)287-8748
Free: 888-273-7782
Publication E-mail: editor@rpinet.com
Journal for Roman Catholic church people. **Freq:** Monthly. **Print Method:** Offset. **Trim Size:** 8 3/8 x 10 7/8. **Cols./Page:** 3. **Col. Width:** 13.5 picas. **Col. Depth:** 9.5 inches. **Key Personnel:** Josh Burns, Manager, Advertising and Sales. **ISSN:** 0363--504X (print). **Subscription Rates:** $60 Individuals; $70 Other countries; $145 Individuals premium; $155 Other countries premium. **URL:** http://www.rpinet.com/ml/index15.html. **Formerly:** Modern Liturgy. **Ad Rates:** BW $1326. **Remarks:** Accepts classified advertising. **Circ:** (Not Reported).

4077 ■ Rosicrucian Digest
Ancient Mystical Order Rosae Crucis
1342 Naglee Ave.
San Jose, CA 95191
Phone: (408)947-3600
Fax: (408)947-3677
Free: 800-882-6672
Publisher's E-mail: membership@rosicrucian.org
Magazine covering mysticism, science, and philosophy. **Freq:** Semiannual. **Print Method:** Offset. **Trim Size:** 7 1/2 x 10 1/4. **Cols./Page:** 2. **Col. Width:** 35 nonpareils. **Col. Depth:** 115 agate lines. **ISSN:** 0035--8339 (print). **USPS:** 471-040. **Subscription Rates:** Included in membership. **URL:** http://www.rosicrucian.org/rosicrucian-digest. **Remarks:** Advertising not accepted. **Circ:** (Not Reported).

4078 ■ San Jose Mercury News
Digital First Media
4 N 2nd St., Ste. 800
San Jose, CA 95113
Phone: (408)920-5000
Fax: (408)288-8060
Free: 800-870-NEWS
General newspaper. **Freq:** Daily. **Print Method:** Offset. **Trim Size:** 12 3/4 x 22 1/2. **Cols./Page:** 6. **Col. Width:** 1.81 inches. **Col. Depth:** 21.25 inches. **Key Personnel:** Sharon Ryan, President, Publisher, phone: (408)920-5576; Bert Robinson, Managing Editor, phone: (408)920-5970; Randy Keith, Managing Editor, phone: (408)271-3747; Tiffany Grandstaff, Managing Editor, phone: (925)943-8040. **Online:** Digital First Media Digital First Media. **URL:** http://www.mercurynews.com. **Ad Rates:** BW $2406; 4C $4235; PCI $275; PCI $315. **Remarks:** Advertising accepted; rates available upon request. **Circ:** Mon.-Sat. ***249090**, Sun. ***278420**.

4079 ■ Saratoga News
Silicon Valley Community Newspapers
1095 The Alameda
San Jose, CA 95126
Phone: (408)200-1000
Fax: (408)200-1011
Community newspaper. **Freq:** Weekly (Tues.). **Print Method:** Offset. **Cols./Page:** 5. **Col. Width:** 2 1/16 inches. **Key Personnel:** Dick Sparrer, Editor, phone: (408)200-1035. **ISSN:** 0745--6255 (print). **URL:** http://www.mercurynews.com/saratoga. **Remarks:** Accepts advertising. **Circ:** Combined ♦**13150**.

4080 ■ Song Manh Magazine
Song Sao Cho Manh Inc.
231 O'Connor Dr.
San Jose, CA 95151-1245
Publication E-mail: webmaster@songmanh.org
Magazine promoting Vietnamese awareness of health, health care, and family issues. **Freq:** 3/year. **Subscription Rates:** $12 Individuals; $4 Single issue. **URL:** http://www.songmanh.net/songmanh. **Ad Rates:** BW $600; 4C $975. **Remarks:** Accepts advertising. **Circ:** 10000.

4081 ■ Switch
San Jose State University
1 Washington Sq.
San Jose, CA 95192
Phone: (408)924-1000
Fax: (408)924-4326
Publication E-mail: switch@cadre.sjsu.edu
Scholarly journal covering new media art and technology. **Founded:** 1995. **Key Personnel:** David Spensley, Managing Editor. **URL:** http://switch.sjsu.edu/. **Circ:** (Not Reported).

4082 ■ Thoi Bao
Thoi Bao
447 East Santa Clara St.
San Jose, CA 95113
Phone: (408)292-2276
Fax: (408)292-0346
Vietnamese language community newspaper. **Freq:** Daily (Tues.-Sat.). **Key Personnel:** Ly Vu, Contact. **URL:** http://thoibao.com. **Ad Rates:** BW $380. **Remarks:** Accepts advertising. **Circ:** Combined 12000.

4083 ■ The Valley Catholic Newspaper
Roman Catholic Diocese of San Jose
1150 N First St., Ste. 100
San Jose, CA 95112-4966
Phone: (408)983-0100
Fax: (408)983-0295
Publisher's E-mail: communications@dsj.org
Newspaper for Catholics in Santa Clara County. **Freq:** Monthly. **Print Method:** Offset. **Trim Size:** 10 1/8 x 12 1/4. **Cols./Page:** 5. **Col. Width:** 11 picas. **Col. Depth:** 177 agate lines. **Key Personnel:** Liz Sullivan, Executive Editor, phone: (408)983-0267; Racquel Brown, Contact, phone: (408)983-0262; Yesenia Hall, Contact, phone: (408)983-0174. **ISSN:** 8750--6238 (print). **Subscription Rates:** $17 Individuals; $25 Individuals /year in Santa Clara County.; $35 Individuals /year out of Santa Clara County. **URL:** http://tvc.dsj.org. **Ad Rates:** BW $2321.38; 4C $100; PCI $26. **Remarks:** Accepts advertising. **Circ:** Paid ‡26000.

4084 ■ Vietnam Daily News
Vietnam Daily News
2350 S 10th St.
San Jose, CA 95112
Phone: (408)292-3422
Fax: (408)293-5153
Publication E-mail: vnnb@vietnamdaily.com
Community newspaper serving greater San Francisco area (Vietnamese). **Freq:** Daily. **Print Method:** Offset. **Trim Size:** 15 x 22. **Cols./Page:** 6. **URL:** http://www.vietnamdaily.com. **Remarks:** Accepts advertising. **Circ:** 13000.

4085 ■ Women & Therapy: A Feminist Quarterly
Routledge Journals Taylor & Francis Group
c/o Ellyn Kaschak, PhD, Editor
San Jose State University
San Jose, CA 95192
Focuses on the complex interrelationship between women and the therapeutic experience. **Freq:** Quarterly. **Trim Size:** 6 x 8 3/8. **Cols./Page:** 1. **Col. Width:** 4 3/8 inches. **Col. Depth:** 7 1/8 inches. **Key Personnel:** Ellyn Kaschak, PhD, Editor. **ISSN:** 0270--3149 (print); **EISSN:** 1541--0315 (electronic). **Subscription Rates:** $185 Individuals online only; $1002 Institutions online only; $211 Individuals print and online; $1145 Institutions print and online. **URL:** http://www.tandfonline.com/toc/wwat20/current#.VePybSWqqko. **Ad Rates:** BW $315; 4C $550. **Remarks:** Accepts advertising. **Circ:** (Not Reported).

4086 ■ Comcast Cable
1900 S Tenth St.
San Jose, CA 95112
Email: we_can_help@comcast.com
Founded: 1963. **Key Personnel:** Brian L. Roberts, Chairman, CEO; Stephen B. Burke, COO, President; David L. Cohen, Exec. VP. **Cities Served:** 120 channels. **URL:** http://www.comcast.com.

4087 ■ KAZA-AM - 1290
1982 Senter Rd.
San Jose, CA 95112
Phone: (408)947-7517
Fax: (408)947-0463
Format: Talk. **Networks:** CNN Radio; BBC World Service; ABC. **Founded:** 1967. **ADI:** San Francisco-Oakland-San Jose. **Key Personnel:** Manuel Reyes, Dir. of Programs; Deborah Romero, Promotions Mgr. **Wattage:** 5,000 Day;088 Night. **Ad Rates:** $64-80 for 30 seconds; $70-100 for 60 seconds. **URL:** http://vienthao.com.

4088 ■ KBAY-FM - 94.5
190 Park Center Plz., Ste. 200
San Jose, CA 95113
Phone: (408)287-5775
Free: 800-948-5229
Format: Soft Rock; Music of Your Life; News. **Networks:** Independent. **Operating Hours:** Continuous; 100% local. **Wattage:** 44,000. **Ad Rates:** Advertising accepted; rates available upon request. $75-240 for 60 seconds. **URL:** http://www.kbay.com.

4089 ■ KCNL-FM - 104.9
2905 S King Rd.
San Jose, CA 95122
Phone: (408)440-0851
Format: Hispanic. **Owner:** Principle Broadcasting Network, 726 Exchange St., Ste. 410, Buffalo, NY 14210. **Operating Hours:** Continuous. **ADI:** San Francisco-Oakland-San Jose. **Wattage:** 3,000. **Ad Rates:** Noncommercial.

4090 ■ KEZR-FM - 106.5
190 Park Center Plz., Ste. 200
San Jose, CA 95113
Phone: (408)287-5775
Fax: (408)293-3341
Free: 800-499-1065
Format: Adult Contemporary. **Networks:** Independent. **Operating Hours:** Continuous. **ADI:** San Francisco-Oakland-San Jose. **Wattage:** 42,000. **Ad Rates:** Advertising accepted; rates available upon request. **URL:** http://www.mymix1065.com.

4091 ■ KFFG-FM - 97.7
50 Airport Pky.
San Jose, CA 95134
Phone: (408)817-5364
Fax: (408)437-4926
Format: Contemporary Hit Radio (CHR). **Owner:** Susquehanna Radio Corp., 221 W Philadelphia St.,

Circulation: ★ = AAM; △ or • = BPA; ♦ = CAC; ❑ = VAC; ⊕ = PO Statement; ‡ = Publisher's Report; Boldface figures = sworn; Light figures = estimated.

York, PA 17404, Ph: (717)852-2132, Fax: (717)771-1436. **Founded:** 1987. **Formerly:** KLZE-FM. **Operating Hours:** Continuous; 100% local. **ADI:** San Francisco-Oakland-San Jose. **Key Personnel:** Tony Salvadore, Gen. Mgr., VP; Dwight Walker, VP, Station Mgr.; Julie Kahn, Director, Sales Mgr.; Joe Cunningham, Sales Mgr. **Wattage:** 1,650. **Ad Rates:** per unit.

4092 ■ KHFX-AM - 1460
1982 Senter Rd.
San Jose, CA 95112
Phone: (408)838-4075
Email: info@1460foxsportsradio.com
Format: Country. **Owner:** M&M Broadcasters Ltd., at above address. **Founded:** 1922. **Formerly:** WACO-AM; KKTK-AM; KTFW-AM. **Operating Hours:** Continuous. **Key Personnel:** Mike Crow, Dir. of Programs; Norma Savage, Sales Mgr. **Wattage:** 1,000. **Ad Rates:** Advertising accepted; rates available upon request.

4093 ■ KLIV-AM - 1590
750 Story Rd.
San Jose, CA 95122
Phone: (408)293-8030
Fax: (408)995-0823
Format: News. **Networks:** CNN Radio. **Owner:** Empire Broadcasting Corp., 100 Saratoga Village Blvd., Ste. 21, Ballston Spa, NY 12020, Fax: (518)899-3057. **Operating Hours:** Continuous; 100% local. **ADI:** San Francisco-Oakland-San Jose. **Wattage:** 5,000. **Ad Rates:** Advertising accepted; rates available upon request. **URL:** http://www.kliv.com.

4094 ■ KLOK-AM
2905 S King Rd.
San Jose, CA 95122
Phone: (408)440-0851
Fax: (408)440-0853
Format: Hispanic. **Owner:** EXCL Communications, Inc., at above address. **Founded:** 1946. **Key Personnel:** Martha Garza, Sales Mgr. **Wattage:** 50,000 Day; 5,000 Ni. **Ad Rates:** Advertising accepted; rates available upon request. **URL:** http://www.klok1170am.com/.

4095 ■ KNTV-TV - 11
2450 N 1st St.
San Jose, CA 95131
Phone: (408)432-6221
Free: 888-996-8477
Format: Commercial TV. **Networks:** NBC. **Owner:** Granite Broadcasting Corp., 767 3rd Ave., 34th Fl., New York, NY 10017-2083, Ph: (212)826-2530, Fax: (212)826-2858. **Founded:** 1955. **Operating Hours:** Continuous. **ADI:** San Francisco-Oakland-San Jose. **Local Programs:** *Comunidad del Valle*, Sunday 3:00 p.m.; *In Wine Country*; *Law & Order*, Wednesday; *TechNow*. **Ad Rates:** Noncommercial. **URL:** http://www.nbcbayarea.com.

4096 ■ KRTY-FM - 95.3
750 Story Rd.
San Jose, CA 95122
Phone: (408)293-8030
Fax: (408)293-6124
Email: rudy@rudysabin.com
Format: Country. **Networks:** Independent. **Owner:** Empire Broadcasting Corp., 100 Saratoga Village Blvd., Ste. 21, Ballston Spa, NY 12020, Fax: (518)899-3057. **Founded:** 1966. **Operating Hours:** Continuous. **Key Personnel:** Julie Stevens, Contact. **Wattage:** 870. **URL:** http://www.krty.com.

4097 ■ KSJO-FM - 92.3
2905 S King Rd.
San Jose, CA 95122
Format: Hispanic. **Owner:** Universal Media Access, 2905 S King Rd., San Jose, CA 95122. **Operating Hours:** Continuous. **ADI:** San Francisco-Oakland-San Jose. **Wattage:** 32,000. **Ad Rates:** Noncommercial. **URL:** http://www.u923fm.com.

4098 ■ KSJS-FM - 90.5
Hugh Gillis Hall, Rm. 132
San Jose, CA 95192-0094
Phone: (408)924-4548
Email: ksjs@ksjs.org
Format: Eclectic. **Owner:** San Jose State University, 1 Washington Sq., San Jose, CA 95192, Ph: (408)924-1000, Fax: (408)924-4326. **Founded:** 1963. **Operating Hours:** Continuous. **Key Personnel:** Alexander Scott, Promotions Dir., alexjamesscott91@gmail.com. **Wattage:** 1,500. **Ad Rates:** Noncommercial. $15-40 for 30 seconds. **URL:** http://www.ksjs.org.

4099 ■ KSJX-AM - 1500
545 Parrott St.
San Jose, CA 95112
Phone: (408)947-7517
Fax: (408)947-0463
Email: info@vienthao.com
Format: Ethnic. **Owner:** Vien Thao Media, 1982 Senter Rd., Ste. B, San Jose, CA 95112, Ph: (408)947-7517. **Founded:** 1992. **Operating Hours:** Continuous. **Ad Rates:** Advertising accepted; rates available upon request. **URL:** http://www.vienthao.com.

4100 ■ KSQQ-FM - 96.1
1629 Alum Rock Ave., Ste. 40
San Jose, CA 95116
Phone: (408)258-9699
Fax: (408)258-9770
Format: News; Sports; Information. **Owner:** Coyote Communication, Inc, at above address, Lakeland, FL. **Key Personnel:** Elza Bettencourt, Office Mgr., lucy@ksqq.com; Aida Barbosa, Asst. Mgr., aida@ksqq.com. **Ad Rates:** Noncommercial. **URL:** http://www.ksqq.com.

4101 ■ KUFX-FM - 98.5
1420 Koll Cir., Ste. A
San Jose, CA 95112
Phone: (408)452-7900
Fax: (408)467-7660
Format: Classic Rock. **Networks:** Independent. **Founded:** 1970. **Formerly:** KWSS-FM. **Operating Hours:** Sunrise-sunset. **ADI:** San Francisco-Oakland-San Jose. **Wattage:** 10,000. **Ad Rates:** Advertising accepted; rates available upon request.

4102 ■ KZSF-AM - 1370
2347 Bering Dr.
San Jose, CA 95131
Phone: (408)546-7222
Format: Hispanic. **Key Personnel:** Carlos A. Duharte, Gen. Mgr., President, carlosaduharte@1370am.com; Reyna Santillan, Operations Mgr., reynasantillan@1370am.com. **Ad Rates:** Noncommercial. **URL:** http://www.1370am.com.

SAN JUAN BAUTISTA

4103 ■ K202DU-FM - 88.3
PO Box 391
Twin Falls, ID 83303
Fax: (208)736-1958
Free: 800-357-4226
Format: Religious; Contemporary Christian. **Owner:** CSN International, PO Box 391, Twin Falls, ID 83303, Ph: (208)736-1958, Fax: (208)736-1958, Free: 800-357-4226.

SAN JUAN CAPISTRANO

4104 ■ Capistrano Valley News
Freedom Communications Inc.
22481 Aspan St.
Lake Forest, CA 92630
Fax: (949)454-7354
Publisher's E-mail: info@freedom.com
Community newspaper. **Freq:** Weekly (Thurs.). **Print Method:** Offset. **Cols./Page:** 5. **Col. Width:** 12 1/16 inches. **Col. Depth:** 182 agate lines. **Key Personnel:** Rob Vardon, Editor; Sarah Schurz, Manager, Sales. **Subscription Rates:** $11 Individuals. **Ad Rates:** PCI $32.17. **Remarks:** Accepts advertising. **Circ:** Free ■ **9642.**

4105 ■ Photo District News
Emerald Expositions L.L.C.
31910 Del Obispo St., Ste. 200
San Juan Capistrano, CA 92675
Phone: (949)226-5700
Professional magazine covering photography. **Freq:** Monthly. **Key Personnel:** Holly Stuart Hughes, Editor; David Walker, Executive Editor. **Subscription Rates:** $65 Individuals /year; $105 Canada two years; $45 Individuals /year (online). **URL:** http://www.pdnonline.com/index.shtml. **Ad Rates:** BW $6,460; 4C $9,880. **Remarks:** Accepts advertising. **Circ:** Paid 23264, Non-paid 621.

4106 ■ Worship Leader: Singing to the Lord a New Song
Worship Leader
29122 Rancho Viejo, Ste 110
San Juan Capistrano, CA 92675
Phone: (949)240-9339
Fax: (949)240-0038
Free: 888-881-5861
Magazine featuring articles and commentaries on worship. **Print Method:** Web offset. **Trim Size:** 8.25 x 10.25. **Key Personnel:** Chuck Fromm, PhD, Editor-in-Chief, Publisher; Jeremy Armstrong, Managing Editor. **Subscription Rates:** $24.95 Individuals. **Remarks:** Accepts advertising. **Circ:** (Not Reported).

SAN LEANDRO

Alameda Co. Alameda Co. (W) Adjoins Oakland. Residential. Manufactures tractors, calculating machines, alloy pistons, motor parts, lumber. Nurseries. Rock quarry.

4107 ■ India West
India West Publications
933 MacArthur Blvd.
San Leandro, CA 94577-3062
Phone: (510)383-1140
Fax: (510)383-1155
Publication E-mail: info@indiawest.com
National newspaper specializing in news from India and about the Indian community in the U.S. **Freq:** Weekly (Fri.). **Print Method:** Offset. **Trim Size:** 11 x 17. **Cols./Page:** 5. **Col. Width:** 24 nonpareils. **Col. Depth:** 210 agate lines. **Key Personnel:** Ramesh Murarka, Publisher; Bina Murarka, Editor. **ISSN:** 0883--721X (print). **Subscription Rates:** $30 Individuals; $50 Two years; $120 Individuals 5 years. **URL:** http://www.indiawest.com. **Ad Rates:** BW $1,400; 4C $1,800; PCI $20. **Remarks:** Accepts advertising. **Circ:** 25000.

4108 ■ KFTL-TV - 64
1965 Adams Ave.
San Leandro, CA 94577
Phone: (510)632-5385
Fax: (510)632-8943
Email: kftl64@compuserve.com
Format: Religious; Commercial TV. **Networks:** Family Stations Radio. **Owner:** Family Stations Inc., 290 Hegenberger Rd., Oakland, CA 94621, Free: 800-543-1495. **Founded:** 1988. **Operating Hours:** Continuous, except Sat. -- 18 hrs. **Wattage:** 1,950,000.

SAN LUIS OBISPO

San Luis Obispo Co. San Luis Obispo Co. (SW). 80 m NW of Santa Barbara. California Polytechnic State University. San Luis Obispo. Oil wells. Chromite deposits. Creameries, condensery, bottling, fertilizer works, electronics, motorcycle accessories, hot tub. Wineries. Ships produce. Dairy. Stock, fruit farms. Peas, lettuce, cauliflower. Almonds.

4109 ■ Focus
California Polytechnic State University, City and Regional Planning Department
Dexter Bldg. 34-251
San Luis Obispo, CA 93407
Phone: (805)756-1315
Publisher's E-mail: crp@calpoly.edu
Journal offers information on city and regional planning for the city of San Luis Obispo. **Freq:** Annual. **ISSN:** 1549-3776 (print). **Subscription Rates:** Free. **URL:** http://planning.calpoly.edu/focus/index.html. **Circ:** (Not Reported).

4110 ■ Journal Plus
Plus Magazine
793 Higuera St., Ste. 10
San Luis Obispo, CA 93401-7164
Phone: (805)544-8711
Publisher's E-mail: slojournal@fix.net
Magazine featuring topics of interest for seniors. **Freq:** Monthly. **Print Method:** Offset. **Trim Size:** 8 1/2 x 11. **Cols./Page:** 3. **Key Personnel:** Steve Owens, Publisher. **Subscription Rates:** $20 Individuals. **URL:** http://www.slojournal.com/contactus.html. **Formerly:** Senior Magazine; Plus Magazine: Central Coast Edition. **Ad Rates:** BW $800; 4C $800. **Remarks:** Accepts advertising. **Circ:** Controlled ‡24000.

4111 ■ New Times: News Weekly
New Times

1010 Marsh St.
San Luis Obispo, CA 93401
Phone: (805)546-8208
Fax: (805)546-8641
Free: 800-215-0300
Publisher's E-mail: letters@newtimesslo.com
Newspaper covering local news and entertainment in the San Luis Obispo area. **Freq:** Weekly (Thurs.). **Key Personnel:** Alex Zuniga, Publisher; Bob Rucker, Publisher. **URL:** http://www.newtimesslo.com. **Ad Rates:** BW $2477. **Remarks:** Advertising accepted; rates available upon request. **Circ:** Free ■ **37000.**

4112 ■ The San Luis Obispo County Telegram Tribune: Newspaper of Central Coast
McClatchy Newspapers Inc.
3825 S Higuera St.
San Luis Obispo, CA 93406
Phone: (805)781-7800
Publisher's E-mail: pensions@mcclatchy.com
General newspaper. **Freq:** Daily. **Print Method:** Offset. **Trim Size:** 12 1/2 x 22 3/4. **Cols./Page:** 6. **Col. Width:** 11 picas. **Col. Depth:** 301 agate lines. **Key Personnel:** Sandra Duerr, Vice President, Executive Editor, phone: (805)781-7901. **URL:** http://www.sanluisobispo.com; http://www.mcclatchy.com/2006/06/09/365/the-tribune.html. **Mailing address:** PO Box 112, San Luis Obispo, CA 93406. **Remarks:** Accepts advertising. **Circ:** Mon.-Fri. 35919, Sun. 41511.

4113 ■ SLO County Farmer & Rancher Magazine
San Luis Obispo County Farm Bureau
4875 Morabito Pl.
San Luis Obispo, CA 93401
Phone: (805)543-3654
Fax: (805)543-3697
Publisher's E-mail: info@slofarmbureau.org
Agriculture magazine for members of the San Luis Obispo County Farm Bureau. **Freq:** Monthly. **Key Personnel:** Carlos Castaneda, President; Steve Carter, Director; Jackie Crabb, Executive Director. **Subscription Rates:** Included in membership. **Remarks:** Accepts advertising. **Circ:** (Not Reported).

4114 ■ Charter Communications
PO Box 1205
San Luis Obispo, CA 93406
Phone: (805)238-1397
Fax: (805)541-6042
Owner: Sonic Communications, 235 Montgomery St., Ste. 400, San Francisco, CA 94104, Ph: (415)616-4600. **Founded:** 1977. **Formerly:** Sonic Cable TV of San Luis Obispo. **Key Personnel:** Jeffrey A. Smith, Gen. Mgr. **Cities Served:** Arroyo Grande, Avila Beach, Avila Beach, Cayucos, Grover Beach, Heritage Ranch, Morro Bay, Nipomo, Paso Robles, Pismo Beach, San Luis Obispo, San Miguel, California: subscribing households 47,000; 60 channels; 1 community access channel.

4115 ■ KCBX-FM - 90.1
4100 Vachell Ln.
San Luis Obispo, CA 93401
Phone: (805)549-8855
Free: 800-549-8855
Format: Public Radio; Classical; Jazz; News; Information. **Networks:** National Public Radio (NPR). **Founded:** 1974. **Operating Hours:** Continuous. **ADI:** Santa Barbara-Santa Maria-San Luis Obispo,CA. **Key Personnel:** Hank Hadley, Operations Mgr., hank@kcbx.org; Katherine Johnson, Asst. GM, katherine@kcbx.org; Frank Lanzone, Gen. Mgr., frank@kcbx.org; Neal Losey, Music Dir., neal@kcbx.org; Guy Rathbun, Program Mgr., guy@kcbx.org. **Wattage:** 5,600. **Ad Rates:** Noncommercial. **URL:** http://www.kcbx.org.

4116 ■ KCCE-TV
770 Lawrence Dr., Ste. 130
San Luis Obispo, CA 93401
Phone: (805)545-7770
Email: info@kcce.com
URL: http://www.kcce.com/.

4117 ■ KCPR-FM - 91.3
Graphic Arts Bldg. 26, Rm. 301
San Luis Obispo, CA 93407
Phone: (805)756-5998
Format: Alternative/New Music/Progressive. **Networks:** BBC World Service. **Owner:** California Polytechnic State University, Ph: (805)756-1111. **Founded:** 1968. **Operating Hours:** Continuous; 5% network, 95% local. **Key Personnel:** Alan Fields, Music Dir. **Wattage:** 2,000. **Ad Rates:** Noncommercial. **URL:** http://www.kcpr.org.

4118 ■ KKJG-FM - 98.1
3620 Sacramento Dr., Ste. 204
San Luis Obispo, CA 93401
Phone: (805)781-2750
Format: Country. **Owner:** American General Media, 1400 Easton Dr., Ste. 144, Bakersfield, CA 93309, Ph: (661)328-1410, Fax: (661)328-0873. **Formerly:** KKUS-FM. **Operating Hours:** Continuous. **ADI:** Santa Barbara-Santa Maria-San Luis Obispo,CA. **Wattage:** 4,500. **Ad Rates:** Advertising accepted; rates available upon request. **URL:** http://www.jugcountry.com.

4119 ■ KKJL-AM - 1400
51 Zaca Ln.
San Luis Obispo, CA 93406
Phone: (805)543-9400
Free: 800-896-1669
Format: Big Band/Nostalgia. **Networks:** Westwood One Radio. **Owner:** San Luis Obispo, 51 Zaca Ln., Ste. 100, San Luis Obispo, CA 93401, Ph: (805)543-9400, Fax: (805)541-5303. **Founded:** 1962. **Formerly:** KKCB-AM; KIXT-AM. **Operating Hours:** Continuous; 60% network, 40% local. **ADI:** Santa Barbara-Santa Maria-San Luis Obispo,CA. **Key Personnel:** Guy P. Hackman, Gen. Mgr., Owner; Kyle Ronemus, Owner, VP, kyle@kkjl1400.com. **Wattage:** 1,000. **Ad Rates:** $18 per unit. **Mailing address:** PO Box 1400, San Luis Obispo, CA 93406. **URL:** http://www.kjewel.net.

4120 ■ KLFF-FM - 89.3
560 Higuera St., Ste. G
San Luis Obispo, CA 93406
Phone: (805)541-4343
Fax: (805)541-9101
Free: 888-541-4343
Email: info@klife.org
Format: Contemporary Christian. **Owner:** Logos Broadcasting Corp., 480 Los Osos Valley Rd., Los osos, CA 93402-3122. **Founded:** Sept. 26, 1995. **Operating Hours:** Continuous. **Key Personnel:** Dan Lemburg, Chairman, Founder, President. **Wattage:** 4,400. **Ad Rates:** Noncommercial. **Mailing address:** PO Box 1561, San Luis Obispo, CA 93406. **URL:** http://www.klife.org.

4121 ■ KPYG-FM - 94.9
795 Buckley Rd., Ste. 2
San Luis Obispo, CA 93401
Phone: (805)786-2570
Fax: (805)547-9860
Email: support@kpig.com
Format: Classic Rock. **Owner:** Mapleton Communications, 10900 Wilshire Blvd., No. 1500, Los Angeles, CA 90024, Ph: (310)209-7229, Fax: (310)209-7239. **Operating Hours:** Continuous. **Wattage:** 25,000. **Ad Rates:** Advertising accepted; rates available upon request. **URL:** http://www.kpig.com.

4122 ■ KSBY-TV - 6
1772 Calle Joaquin
San Luis Obispo, CA 93405
Phone: (805)541-6666
Fax: (805)541-5142
Format: News. **Networks:** NBC. **Owner:** Evening Post Industries Inc., 134 Columbus St., Charleston, SC 29403, Ph: (843)577-7111. **Founded:** 1953. **Operating Hours:** Continuous; 85% network, 15% local. **ADI:** Santa Barbara-Santa Maria-San Luis Obispo,CA. **Wattage:** 100,000 ERP. **Ad Rates:** Advertising accepted; rates available upon request. **URL:** http://www.ksby.com.

4123 ■ KSLY-FM - 96.1
51 Zaca Ln., Ste. 110
San Luis Obispo, CA 93401
Phone: (805)545-0101
Fax: (805)541-5303
Format: Country. **Owner:** El Dorado Broadcasters, 12370 Hesperia Rd., Ste. 17, Victorville, CA 92395-5808, Ph: (760)241-1313, Fax: (760)241-0205. **Founded:** 1962. **Operating Hours:** Sunrise-sunset. **ADI:** Santa Barbara-Santa Maria-San Luis Obispo,CA. **Key Personnel:** Mark Mitchell, Dir. of Programs, markmitchell@edbroadcasters.com; Ron Roy, Regional VP, ronroy@edbroadcasters.com. **Wattage:** 5,800. **Ad Rates:** $20-45 per unit. **URL:** http://www.sunnycountry.com.

4124 ■ KSTT-FM - 101.3
51 Zaca Ln., Ste. 110
San Luis Obispo, CA 93401
Phone: (805)545-0101
Fax: (805)541-5303
Format: Adult Contemporary. **Owner:** El Dorado Broadcasters, 12370 Hesperia Rd., Ste. 17, Victorville, CA 92395-5808, Ph: (760)241-1313, Fax: (760)241-0205. **ADI:** Santa Barbara-Santa Maria-San Luis Obispo,CA. **Key Personnel:** Rebecca Crites, Promotions Dir., rebeccacrites@edbroadcasters.com. **Wattage:** 3,400. **Ad Rates:** Noncommercial. **URL:** http://www.kstt.com.

4125 ■ K285EW-FM - 104.9
PO Box 391
Twin Falls, ID 83303
Fax: (208)736-1958
Free: 800-357-4226
Format: Religious; Contemporary Christian. **Owner:** CSN International, PO Box 391, Twin Falls, ID 83303, Ph: (208)736-1958, Fax: (208)736-1958, Free: 800-357-4226. **ADI:** Santa Barbara-Santa Maria-San Luis Obispo,CA. **Key Personnel:** Don Mills, Prog. Dir., Music Dir.; Kelly Carlson, Dir. of Engg.; Ray Gorney, Asst. Dir. **Wattage:** 010. **URL:** http://www.csnradio.com.

4126 ■ K201DF-FM - 88.1
PO Box 391
Twin Falls, ID 83303
Fax: (208)736-1958
Free: 800-357-4226
Format: Religious; Contemporary Christian. **Owner:** CSN International, PO Box 391, Twin Falls, ID 83303, Ph: (208)736-1958, Fax: (208)736-1958, Free: 800-357-4226. **Key Personnel:** Don Mills, Contact. **URL:** http://www.csnradio.com.

4127 ■ KURQ-FM - 107.3
51 Zaca Ln., Ste. 100
San Luis Obispo, CA 93401-7353
Phone: (805)545-0101
Fax: (805)541-5303
Format: Alternative/New Music/Progressive. **Wattage:** 3,500. **Ad Rates:** Noncommercial. **URL:** http://www.newrock1073.com.

4128 ■ KVEC-AM - 920
51 Zaca Ln., Ste. 100
San Luis Obispo, CA 93401
Phone: (805)545-0101
Fax: (805)541-5303
Format: News; Talk. **Networks:** ABC; CNN Radio. **Owner:** El Dorado Broadcasters, 12370 Hesperia Rd., Ste. 17, Victorville, CA 92395-5808, Ph: (760)241-1313, Fax: (760)241-0205. **Founded:** 1937. **Operating Hours:** Continuous; 40% network, 60% local. **ADI:** Santa Barbara-Santa Maria-San Luis Obispo,CA. **Key Personnel:** King Harris, News Dir., king@920kvec.com. **Wattage:** 1,000 Day; 500 Night. **Ad Rates:** Noncommercial. **URL:** http://www.920kvec.com.

4129 ■ KWSP-FM - 106.1
795 Buckley Rd., Ste. 2
San Luis Obispo, CA 93401
Phone: (805)541-1212
Fax: (805)438-3608
Format: Music of Your Life. **Owner:** Hance Communications, Ltd., at above address. **Founded:** 1986. **Operating Hours:** Continuous. **Key Personnel:** Tom Hansen, Gen. Mgr.; Bill Benica, Dir. of Programs. **Wattage:** 1,100 ERP. **Ad Rates:** Accepts Advertising. **URL:** http://www.wild1061.com.

4130 ■ KWWV-FM - 106.1
795 Buckley Rd., No. 2
San Luis Obispo, CA 93401
Format: Hip Hop; Urban Contemporary. **Owner:** Mapleton Communication L.L.C., 10900 Wilshire Blvd., No. 1500, Los Angeles, CA 90024, Ph: (310)209-7221, Fax: (310)209-7239. **Wattage:** 1,100. **Ad Rates:** Advertising accepted; rates available upon request. **URL:** http://www.wild1061.com.

4131 ■ KXTK-AM - 1280
PO Box 14910
San Luis Obispo, CA 93410
Phone: (805)547-1280
Fax: (805)543-1508

Circulation: ★ = AAM; △ or • = BPA; ♦ = CAC; ❑ = VAC; ⊕ = PO Statement; ‡ = Publisher's Report; Boldface figures = sworn; Light figures = estimated.

Email: info@espnradio1280.com
Format: Sports. **Owner:** Pacific Coast Media, LLC, at above address. **Operating Hours**: Continuous. **Key Personnel:** Mike Chellsen, Dir. of Sales, mike@espnradio1280.com; Bill Bordeaux, Exec. Chmn. of the Bd. **Ad Rates:** Advertising accepted; rates available upon request. **URL:** http://www.espnradio1280.com.

4132 ■ KXTZ-FM - 95.3
396 Buckley Rd., Ste. 2
San Luis Obispo, CA 93401
Phone: (805)786-2570
Free: 866-990-4953
Format: Classic Rock. **Owner:** Mapleton Communications, 10900 Wilshire Blvd., No. 1500, Los Angeles, CA 90024, Ph: (310)209-7229, Fax: (310)209-7239. **Founded:** 1974. **Formerly**: KPGA-FM; KWBR-FM. **Wattage**: 4,200 ERP. **Ad Rates:** Advertising accepted; rates available upon request. $15-35 per unit. **URL:** http://953thebeach.com/.

4133 ■ KYNS-AM - 1340
10900 Wilshire Blvd., Ste. 1500
Los Angeles, CA 90024
Format: News; Talk. **Owner:** Mapleton Communications, 10900 Wilshire Blvd., No. 1500, Los Angeles, CA 90024, Ph: (310)209-7229, Fax: (310)209-7239. **Operating Hours**: Continuous. **Ad Rates:** Advertising accepted; rates available upon request. **URL:** http://www.mapletoncomm.com/.

4134 ■ KZOZ-FM - 93.3
3620 Sacramento Dr., Ste. 204
San Luis Obispo, CA 93401
Phone: (805)781-2750
Format: Album-Oriented Rock (AOR). **Owner:** American General Media, PO Box 2700, Bakersfield, CA 93303, Ph: (661)328-0118, Fax: (661)328-1648. **Founded:** 1981. **Operating Hours**: Continuous; 100% local. **ADI**: Santa Barbara-Santa Maria-San Luis Obispo,CA. **Wattage**: 23,000. **Ad Rates:** $26-32 for 30 seconds. **URL:** http://www.kzoz.com.

SAN MARCOS

San Diego Co. San Diego Co. (S) 85 m S of Los Angeles. Palomar Community College. Residential.

4135 ■ KKSM-AM - 1320
c/o Communications Dept.
Palomar College
1140 W Mission Rd.
San Marcos, CA 92069
Phone: (760)744-1150
Format: Alternative/New Music/Progressive; Sports. **Wattage**: 500. **Ad Rates:** Advertising accepted; rates available upon request. **URL:** http://www.palomar.edu.

SAN MARINO

Los Angeles Co. Los Angeles Co. (S). 5 m S of Pasadena. Residential.

4136 ■ Huntington Library Quarterly
University of California Press
c/o Susan Green, Ed.
Huntington Library Press
1151 Oxford Rd.
San Marino, CA 91108
Phone: (626)405-2174
Fax: (626)585-0794
Journal publishing articles on the literature, history and art of the sixteenth to eighteenth centuries in Britain and America. **Freq:** Quarterly March, June, September, December. **Print Method:** Offset. **Trim Size:** 7 x 10. **Cols./Page:** 1. **Col. Width:** 5 inches. **Col. Depth:** 7.5 inches. **Key Personnel:** Susan Green, Editor, phone: (626)405-2174; Jean Patterson, Managing Editor. **ISSN:** 0018--7895 (print); **EISSN:** 1544--399X (electronic). **Subscription Rates:** $54 Individuals print; $79 Individuals print, outside North America. **URL:** http://www.ucpress.edu/blog/15071/from-our-journals-division-some-of-our-faster-growing-journals; http://www.huntington.org/WebAssets/Templates/content.aspx?id=2988. **Ad Rates:** BW $200. **Remarks:** Accepts advertising. **Circ:** 450.

4137 ■ San Marino Tribune
San Marino Tribune
1441 San Marino Ave.
San Marino, CA 91108
Phone: (626)792-6397
Publication E-mail: events@sanmarinotribune.com
Newspaper with a Republican orientation. **Freq:** Weekly. **Print Method:** Offset. **Cols./Page:** 6. **Col. Width:** 2 1/4 inches. **Col. Depth:** 21 1/2 inches. **Key Personnel:** Mitch Lehman, Editor; Andy Salter, Publisher. **Subscription Rates:** $89 Individuals 1 year; $109 Out of state; $178 Two years. **URL:** http://sanmarinotribune.com. **Ad Rates:** BW $812.70; 4C $1,112.70; PCI $6.30. **Remarks:** Accepts advertising. **Circ:** Combined 4400.

SAN MATEO

San Mateo Co. San Mateo Co. (W). On west side of San Francisco Bay, 20 m S of San Francisco. Residential. Tourism. Flower growing and shipping, printing, frozen foods, beverages, feed, precision instruments, rubber, steel products, drugs, paint, wine products, furniture, chemicals, electronics manufactured. Nurseries. Agriculture. Honey, artichokes, peas.

4138 ■ Bay Area Parent--East Bay Edition
United Advertising Publications
1660 S Amphlett Blvd., Ste. 335
San Mateo, CA 94402
Phone: (650)655-7600
Fax: (650)655-7601
Publisher's E-mail: marketing@parenthood.com
Magazine for parents in Central Costra County and the Tri-Valley area of Alameda County, California. **Freq:** Monthly. **Print Method:** Web. **Trim Size:** 10 1/2 x 13 1/2. **Cols./Page:** 4. **Col. Width:** 2 1/4 inches. **Col. Depth:** 11 3/4 inches. **Key Personnel:** Daniel Payomo, Jr., Publisher; Jill Wolfson, Editor; Dawn Hall, Advertising Representative. **URL:** http://bayareaparent.com; http://bap-eastbay.digitalparenthood.com/default.aspx?bhcp=1. **Formerly**: Valley Parent. **Ad Rates:** BW $1,685. **Remarks:** Accepts advertising. **Circ:** 62600.

4139 ■ California CPA
California Society of Certified Public Accountants
1800 Gateway Dr., Ste. 200
San Mateo, CA 94404-4072
Free: 800-922-5272
Professional publication for California CPAs. **Founded:** 1959. **Freq:** 10/yr. **Print Method:** Direct to plate. **Trim Size:** 8 3/8 x 10 7/8. **Cols./Page:** 2. **Col. Width:** 28 nonpareils. **Col. Depth:** 133 agate lines. **Key Personnel:** Bobbi Petrov, Director, Advertising; Aldo Maragoni, Manager, Communications; Clar Rosso, Chief Operating Officer. **ISSN:** 0273-835X (print). **Subscription Rates:** $110 Out of country; $75 Nonmembers; $8.50 Single issue. **URL:** http://www.calcpa.org. **Formerly**: Outlook; Monthly Statement. **Ad Rates:** BW $4,050; 4C $5,375. **Remarks:** Accepts advertising. **Circ:** ‡35000.

4140 ■ The Giant Napkin
Cafepress Inc.
1850 Gateway Dr., Ste. 300
San Mateo, CA 94404-4061
Free: 877-809-1659
Publisher's E-mail: info@cafepress.com
Newspaper featuring funniest satire news. **Key Personnel:** John Curtis, Editor. **URL:** http://thegiantnapkin.com. **Circ:** (Not Reported).

4141 ■ In Flight USA
In Flight USA
PO Box 5402
San Mateo, CA 94402
Phone: (650)358-9908
Fax: (650)358-9254
Publisher's E-mail: staff@inflightusa.com
Magazine on Aviation. **Freq:** Monthly. **Key Personnel:** Victoria Buonocore, Managing Editor, Publisher; Clark Cook, Associate Editor; Ciro Buonocore, Founder. **Subscription Rates:** $24.95 Individuals 1 year; $44.95 Two years. **Remarks:** Accepts advertising. **Circ:** (Not Reported).

4142 ■ The Red Herring
Herring Communications Inc.
1900 Alameda de Las Pulgas, Ste. 112
San Mateo, CA 94403-1295
Phone: (650)215-1520
Fax: (619)923-2792
Trade magazine covering financial and investment news for high-tech companies. **Freq:** Weekly. **Key Personnel:** Joel Dreyfuss, Editor-in-Chief; Alex Vieux, Chairman; Mark Selfe, Art Director. **URL:** http://www.redherring.com. **Remarks:** Accepts advertising. **Circ:** (Not Reported).

4143 ■ KCSM-FM - 91.1
1700 W Hillsdale Blvd.
San Mateo, CA 94402
Phone: (650)574-6586
Format: Jazz. **Networks:** National Public Radio (NPR); American Public Radio (APR). **Owner:** San Mateo County Community College, 3401 CSM Dr., San Mateo, CA 94402, Ph: (650)574-6550. **Founded:** 1964. **Operating Hours**: Continuous; 20% network, 80% local. **ADI**: San Francisco-Oakland-San Jose. **Key Personnel:** Marilyn Lawrence, Gen. Mgr.; Melanie Berzon, Dir. of Programs; Jesse Chuy Varela, Music Dir. **Wattage**: 14,000. **Ad Rates:** Noncommercial. **URL:** http://kcsm.org.

4144 ■ KCSM-TV - 60
1700 W Hillsdale Blvd.
San Mateo, CA 94402
Phone: (650)574-6586
Fax: (650)574-6975
Free: 800-477-5276
Email: tv@kcsm.net
Format: Jazz. **Networks:** Public Broadcasting Service (PBS). **Owner:** San Mateo County Community College District, 3401 CSM Dr., San Mateo, CA 94402. **Founded:** 1964. **Operating Hours**: Continuous; 35% network, 65% local. **Key Personnel:** Jesse Chuy Varela, Music Dir.; Dante Betteo, Station Mgr., dbetteo@kcsm.net; Melanie Berzon, Prog. Dir.; Marilyn Lawrence, Gen. Mgr. **Local Programs**: *Zonya's Health Bites: The Snack Dilemma.* **Wattage**: 1,500,000. **Ad Rates:** Underwriting available. **URL:** http://www.kcsm.org.

SAN PEDRO

Los Angeles Co. (S). On San Pedro Bay, 24 m S of Los Angeles. Port of commerce. Point fermin historic light house. Shipyards and dry docks, fish canneries, oil refineries, lumber mills; paint, fertilizer, roofing material, oil well tool factories. Sardine, tuna, mackerel fisheries.

4145 ■ Whalewatcher
American Cetacean Society
PO Box 1391
San Pedro, CA 90733-1391
Phone: (310)548-6279
Fax: (310)548-6950
Publisher's E-mail: acsoffice@acsonline.org
Journal of the American Cetacean Society (ACS) covering marine science and related world events, conferences, ACS activities, human interest stories, and marine art. **Freq:** Semiannual. **Key Personnel:** Diane Glim, President. **Subscription Rates:** Included in membership. **URL:** http://acsonline.org/publications. **Remarks:** Accepts advertising. **Circ:** (Not Reported).

SAN RAFAEL

Marin Co. Marin Co. (W). On San Pablo Straits, 18 m N of San Francisco. Residential. Dom inican College of San Rafael (Cath.) Manufactures diodes, oil burners, gloves , bricks, beverages, aluminium products, plastics, boats, fish oil, feed, creame ry products. Diversified farming. Artichokes, peas, tomatoes.

4146 ■ Edutopia
The George Lucas Educational Foundation
PO Box 3494
San Rafael, CA 94912
Publisher's E-mail: info@edutopia.org
Magazine focusing on innovative approach in education. **Key Personnel:** Milton Chen, PhD, Executive Director; David Markus, Director, Editorial. **URL:** http://www.edutopia.org. **Ad Rates:** BW $9480; 4C $12000. **Remarks:** Accepts advertising. **Circ:** (Not Reported).

4147 ■ Marin Independent Journal
California Newspapers Inc.
4000 Civic Center Dr.
San Rafael, CA 94903
Publication E-mail: localnews@marinij.com
General newspaper serves Marin County and southern Sonoma County. **Founded:** Mar. 23, 1861. **Freq:** Daily (eve.). **Print Method:** Offset. **Trim Size:** 13 3/4 x 22 7/8. **Cols./Page:** 6. **Col. Width:** 25 nonpareils. **Col. Depth:** 301 agate lines. **Key Personnel:** Robert Sterling, Editor. **Subscription Rates:** $4.09 Individuals 7-days per week home delivery; $1.95 Individuals /week; online.

URL: http://www.marinij.com/marinnews. **Remarks:** Accepts advertising. **Circ:** Mon.-Fri. ★**37322**, Sat. ★**32423**, Sun. ★**36647.**

4148 ■ Wines & Vines
Hiaring Co.
1800 Lincoln Ave.
San Rafael, CA 94901-1298
Phone: (415)453-9700
Fax: (415)453-2517
Free: 866-453-9701
Publication E-mail: info@winesandvines.com
Periodical on wine industry. **Freq:** Monthly. **Print Method:** Offset. **Trim Size:** 8 3/8 x 10 7/8. **Cols./Page:** 3 and 2. **Col. Width:** 27 and 42 nonpareils. **Col. Depth:** 140 agate lines. **Key Personnel:** Jim Gordon, Editor. **ISSN:** 0043--583X (print). **Subscription Rates:** $85 Individuals. **URL:** http://www.winesandvines.com/template.cfm?section=subscribe&product=magazine. **Formerly**: California Grape Grower. **Remarks:** Accepts advertising. **Circ:** ‡10876.

4149 ■ KKHI-FM - 100.7
76 San Pablo Ave., No. 210
San Rafael, CA 94903-4169
Format: Classical. **Networks:** Independent. **Owner:** Mount Wilson FM Broadcasters Inc., at above address, Los Angeles, CA 90025. **Founded:** 1963. **Formerly**: KTIM-FM; KTID-FM. **Operating Hours**: Continuous. **Key Personnel:** Andi Polisky, Gen. Mgr. **Wattage**: 6,000.

4150 ■ KSRH-FM - 88.1
185 Mission St.
San Rafael, CA 94901
Phone: (415)485-2330
Fax: (415)485-2345
Format: Educational. **Networks:** Independent. **Owner:** San Rafael High School, 185 Mission Ave., San Rafael, CA 94901, Ph: (415)485-2330, Fax: (415)485-2345. **Founded:** 1980. **Operating Hours**: MWF: 10 am - 3 pm TTH: 10 am - 5 pm. **Wattage**: 007. **Ad Rates:** Advertising accepted; rates available upon request. **URL:** http://sanrafael.srcs.org.

4151 ■ KTLN-TV - 68
100 Pelican Way, Ste. E & F
San Rafael, CA 94901
Phone: (415)485-5856
Fax: (415)256-9262
Email: ktln@tln.com
Key Personnel: Debra FRaser, Gen. Mgr. **URL:** http://www.ktln.tv.

SAN RAMON

Contra Costa Co. Contra Costa Co. (W) 16 m SE of Berkeley. Residential.

4152 ■ Arthroscopy: The Journal of Arthroscopic and Related Surgery
International Society of Arthroscopy, Knee Surgery and Orthopaedic Sports Medicine
2410 Camino Ramon, Ste. 215
San Ramon, CA 94583
Phone: (925)807-1197
Fax: (925)807-1199
Publisher's E-mail: info@aana.org
Peer-reviewed journal discussing the advantages and disadvantages of arthroscopic techniques. **Freq:** Quarterly. **Key Personnel:** G.G. Poehling, MD, Board Member; Dr. J.H. Lubowitz, Editor-in-Chief. **ISSN:** 0749--8063 (print). **Subscription Rates:** $629 U.S. for personal, online + print; $305 U.S. for student, online + print; $817 Canada for personal, online + print; $597 Canada for student, online + print; $817 Other countries for personal, online + print; $597 Other countries for student, online + print. **URL:** http://www.arthroscopyjournal.org. **Ad Rates:** BW $1745, full page; 4C $1495, full page. **Remarks:** Accepts advertising. **Circ:** ‡9200.

4153 ■ Eugene O'Neill Review
The Eugene O'Neill Society
700 Hawthorn Ct.
San Ramon, CA 94582
Publisher's E-mail: info@seticonsulting.it
Freq: Annual. **Key Personnel:** William Davies King, Editor. **ISSN:** 1040--9483 (print). **Alt. Formats:** Download. **URL:** http://www.eugeneoneillsociety.org/index.php?option=com_content&view=article&id=14&Itemid=24. **Remarks:** Accepts advertising. **Circ:** 400.

4154 ■ The Institutional Real Estate Letter
Institutional Real Estate Inc.
2274 Camino Ramon
San Ramon, CA 94583
Phone: (925)244-0500
Fax: (925)244-0520
Publisher's E-mail: marketing@irei.com
Monthly publication covering the pension, foundation, and endowment investment market. Provides information on investment patterns, trends, and strategies. **Freq:** Monthly. **Key Personnel:** Brigite Thompson, Coordinator, Advertising; Geoffrey Dohrmann, Editor. **ISSN:** 1044--1662 (print). **Subscription Rates:** $2495 Individuals 1 year; $4400 Two years; $5600 Individuals 3 years. **URL:** http://irei.com/publications/institutional-real-estate-americas. **Remarks:** Accepts advertising. **Circ:** (Not Reported).

SAND CITY

4155 ■ KRXA-AM - 540
495 Elder Ave., Ste. 8
Sand City, CA 93955
Phone: (831)899-5792
Fax: (831)480-7897
Format: News; Talk. **Owner:** Carmel Valley, CA, at above address. **Founded:** 1950. **Operating Hours**: Continuous. **Key Personnel:** Hal Ginsberg, Contact, hal@krxa540.com. **Ad Rates:** Advertising accepted; rates available upon request. **URL:** http://radiomonterey.com.

4156 ■ KSRK-AM - 540
495 Elder Ave., Ste. 8
Sand City, CA 93955
Fax: (831)480-7897
Format: Talk; News; Sports. **Networks:** ABC; CNN Radio; ESPN Radio; CBS; Westwood One Radio. **Owner:** People's Radio, Inc. **Operating Hours**: Continuous. **Wattage**: 10,000. **Ad Rates:** Noncommercial. **URL:** http://radiomonterey.com.

SANGER

Fresno Co. Fresno Co. (C). 14 m E of Fresno. Raisins, deciduous and citrus fruit packing houses, frozen food processing plants. Box making machinery, electric cables, cement pipes, overalls, wine manufactured. Agriculture. Grapes, citrus fruit, truck crops.

4157 ■ Bulbs
International Bulb Society
PO Box 336
Sanger, CA 93657-0336
Magazine publishing articles on leading growers, breeders and researchers. **Freq:** Semiannual. **URL:** http://www.bulbsociety.org. **Remarks:** Accepts advertising. **Circ:** (Not Reported).

4158 ■ California Legionnaire: Official Publication of the American Legion Department of California
American Legion Department of California
1601 7th St.
Sanger, CA 93657-2801
Phone: (559)875-8387
Fax: (559)272-5157
Newspaper (tabloid) focusing on the American Legion Family, Legionnaires, Auxiliary, The Sons of the American Leagion and all matters concerning American Veterans. **Freq:** Bimonthly. **Key Personnel:** David L. Eby, Editor; Jenny DeBack, President. **URL:** http://www.calegion.org. **Ad Rates:** BW $2343.75. **Remarks:** Accepts advertising. **Circ:** Paid 153800, Free 1000.

4159 ■ Sanger Herald
Sanger Herald Inc.
740 North St.
Sanger, CA 93657
Phone: (559)875-2511
Community newspaper with a Republican orientation. **Freq:** Weekly (Thurs.). **Print Method:** Offset. **Cols./Page:** 6. **Col. Width:** 24 nonpareils. **Col. Depth:** 294 agate lines. **Key Personnel:** Fred Hall, Publisher; Dick Sheppard, Editor. **USPS:** 481-340. **Subscription Rates:** $25 Individuals Fresno and Tulare County; $23 Individuals Fresno and Tulare County age 55+; $24.50 Out of area; $22.50 Out of area age 55+; 26.50 Dh Out of state; $24.50 Out of state age 55+. **URL:** http://thesangerherald.com. **Ad Rates:** BW $938.70; 4C $1,238.70; SAU $7.45; PCI $9.50. **Circ:** ‡3200.

SANTA ANA

Orange Co. Orange Co. (S). 36 m SE of Los Angeles. Santa Ana College. Manufactures sugar, glass products, plumbing material, foam rubber products, dehydrating, electronic, sport equipment, concentrates, extracts, agricultural machinery, perfumes, feed, cement pipes, soft drinks, rivets, fasteners. Canned and dried fruits and vegetables. Walnuts, oranges packed; hatchery.

4160 ■ Aliso Viejo News
Freedom Communications Inc.
625 N Grand Ave.
Santa Ana, CA 92701
Phone: (714)796-7000
Publisher's E-mail: info@freedom.com
Community newspaper. **Freq:** Daily. **Key Personnel:** Ron Hassen, Publisher. **Subscription Rates:** $4.97 Individuals /week - online and print (7 days delivery); $3.02 Individuals /week - online and print (Thurs-Sunday delivery); $4 Individuals /week - online and print (Sunday delivery). **URL:** http://www.ocregister.com/sections/city-pages/alisoviejo-lagunaniguel. **Remarks:** Accepts advertising. **Circ:** Free ■ **7279.**

4161 ■ Anaheim Bulletin
Freedom Communications Inc.
625 N Grand Ave.
Santa Ana, CA 92701
Phone: (714)796-7000
Publisher's E-mail: info@freedom.com
General newspaper. **Freq:** Weekly (Thurs.). **Print Method:** Offset. **Cols./Page:** 5. **Col. Width:** 11 inches. **Col. Depth:** 13 inches. **Key Personnel:** Terry Horne, President, Publisher, phone: (714)796-7740; Heather McRea, Editor; Sarah Schurz, Manager, Advertising. **URL:** http://www.ocregister.com/tag/insideocr/anaheim-bulletin. **Remarks:** Accepts advertising. **Circ:** Free ■ **32966.**

4162 ■ Azteca News
Azteca News
810 N Broadway
Santa Ana, CA 92701
Phone: (714)972-9912
Fax: (714)973-8117
Publication E-mail: info@aztecanews.com
Community newspaper (Spanish). **Founded:** 1980. **Freq:** Weekly (Wed.). **Print Method:** Offset. **Trim Size:** 12 1/2 x 22. **Cols./Page:** 6. **Col. Width:** 2 inches. **Col. Depth:** 21 1/2 inches. **URL:** http://www.aztecanews.com/. **Formerly**: Semanario Azteca. **Ad Rates:** BW $2,774; 4C $1,948; PCI $21.50. **Remarks:** Accepts advertising. **Circ:** Free ‡33000.

4163 ■ Blood & Thunder Magazine
Black Graves Media
PO Box 11232
Santa Ana, CA 92711
Publication E-mail: editor@bloodandthundermag.com
Magazine featuring all-girl roller. **Trim Size:** 8.5 x 11. **Key Personnel:** Dale Rio, Contact. **URL:** http://bloodandthundermag.com/awesome. **Ad Rates:** $1500-5300. BW $600; 4C $. **Remarks:** Accepts advertising. **Circ:** (Not Reported).

4164 ■ El Mercado
El Mercado
631 S Main St.
Santa Ana, CA 92701
Phone: (714)543-8304
Shopper. **Freq:** Weekly (Wed.). **Remarks:** Advertising accepted; rates available upon request. **Circ:** Free 35000.

4165 ■ Excelsior
The Orange County Register
625 N Grand Ave.
Santa Ana, CA 92701
Free: 877-469-7344
Publisher's E-mail: customerservice@ocregister.com
Spanish-language newspaper. **Freq:** Weekly (Fri.). **Trim Size:** tabloid. **Cols./Page:** 5. **ISSN:** 1077--3916 (print). **Ad Rates:** GLR $33.45; BW $1,973.55; 4C $2,893.55; PCI $27.18. **Remarks:** Accepts advertising. **Circ:** Free ‡51543.

Circulation: ★ = AAM; △ or • = BPA; ♦ = CAC; ❑ = VAC; ⊕ = PO Statement; ‡ = Publisher's Report; Boldface figures = sworn; Light figures = estimated.

4166 ■ Farandula USA
Velazquez Publishing Inc.
2025 S Main St.
Santa Ana, CA 92707
Phone: (714)668-1010
Fax: (714)668-1013
Publisher's E-mail: farandulausa@farandulausa.com
Community publication. **Freq:** Weekly (Wed.). **Key Personnel:** Sergio C. Velasquez, President. **URL:** http://www.farandulausa.com. **Circ:** Free ‡30000.

4167 ■ Fountain Valley View
Freedom Communications Inc.
625 N Grand Ave.
Santa Ana, CA 92701
Phone: (714)796-7000
Publisher's E-mail: info@freedom.com
Community newspaper. **Freq:** Weekly (Thurs.). **Key Personnel:** Greg Lipford, Editor, phone: (714)796-2254; Terry Horne, President, Publisher, phone: (714)796-7740. **Subscription Rates:** Free. **URL:** http://epaper.ocregister.com/Olive/ODE/OCWFountainValleyView. **Remarks:** Accepts advertising. **Circ:** Free ■ **11815.**

4168 ■ GPS World: News and Applications of the Global Positioning System
Questex L.L.C.
201 Sandpointe Ave., Ste. 500
Santa Ana, CA 92707
Publication E-mail: info@gpsworld.com
Magazine for internet engineers. **Freq:** Monthly. **Print Method:** Web Offset. **Trim Size:** 7 3/4 x 10 1/2. **Key Personnel:** Alan Cameron, Editor-in-Chief; Tracy Cozzens, Managing Editor. **ISSN:** 1080-5370 (print). **Subscription Rates:** $80 Individuals; $96 Canada and Mexico; $155 Other countries. **URL:** http://www.gpsworld.com/. **Ad Rates:** BW $8,460; 4C $8,460. **Remarks:** Accepts advertising. **Circ:** Combined ■ **39656.**

4169 ■ Home Media Magazine
Questex L.L.C.
201 E Sandpointe Ave., Ste. 500
Santa Ana, CA 92707
Publication E-mail: homemedia@halldata.com
Business magazine for retailers of prerecorded video software, blank tapes, and accessories. **Freq:** Weekly. **Print Method:** Offset. **Trim Size:** 10 1/2 x 14. **Cols./Page:** 5. **Col. Width:** 11 picas. **Col. Depth:** 13 inches. **Key Personnel:** Thomas K. Arnold, Publisher; Stephanie Prange, Editor-in-Chief. **ISSN:** 0195--1770 (print). **Subscription Rates:** $61 Individuals print; $97 Canada and Mexico print; $121 Elsewhere print. **URL:** http://www.homemediamagazine.com. **Formerly**: Video Store; Home Media Retailing. **Ad Rates:** 4C $8500. **Remarks:** Accepts advertising. **Circ:** ‡18000.

4170 ■ Irvine World News
Freedom Communications Inc.
625 N Grand Ave.
Santa Ana, CA 92701
Phone: (714)796-7000
Publisher's E-mail: info@freedom.com
Community newspaper (tabloid). **Freq:** Weekly (Thurs.). **Print Method:** Offset. Uses mats. **Trim Size:** 11 x 17. **Cols./Page:** 6. **Col. Width:** 19 nonpareils. **Col. Depth:** 224 agate lines. **Key Personnel:** Sarah Schurz, Manager, Advertising. **Subscription Rates:** $155.51 Individuals 52 weeks, (Mon-Sun delivery); $82.56 Individuals 52 weeks, (Thu-Sun delivery); $67.29 Individuals 52 weeks, (Sunday only delivery). **Remarks:** Accepts advertising. **Circ:** Free ■ **54772.**

4171 ■ Laguna Beach News Post
Freedom Communications Inc.
625 N Grand Ave.
Santa Ana, CA 92701
Phone: (714)796-7000
Publisher's E-mail: info@freedom.com
Community newspaper. **Freq:** Weekly (Thurs.). **Print Method:** Offset. **Trim Size:** 10 3/4 x 16 3/4. **Cols./Page:** 5. **Col. Width:** 9 picas. **Col. Depth:** 13 inches. **Key Personnel:** Terry Horne, President, Publisher, phone: (714)796-7740; Freda Freeman, Editor; Chris Boucly, Team Leader. **URL:** http://www.ocregister.com/sections/city-pages/lagunabeach. **Formerly**: Laguna News-Post. **Remarks:** Accepts advertising. **Circ:** Free ■ **9999.**

4172 ■ Miniondas
Velazquez Publishing Inc.
2025 S Main St.
Santa Ana, CA 92707
Phone: (714)668-1010
Fax: (714)668-1013
Publisher's E-mail: farandulausa@farandulausa.com
Community publication. **Freq:** Weekly (Thurs.). **Key Personnel:** Sergio C. Velasquez, President. **URL:** http://www.miniondas.com. **Circ:** Free ‡30000.

4173 ■ Noticiero Semanal
Freedom Communications Inc.
625 N Grand Ave.
Santa Ana, CA 92701
Phone: (714)796-7000
Publisher's E-mail: info@freedom.com
Newspaper serving all of Tulare County and northern Kern County. **Freq:** Weekly. **Key Personnel:** Rick Elkins, Editor, phone: (559)784-5000; Mark Fazzone, Publisher; Brian Williams, Managing Editor. **Subscription Rates:** $135 Individuals 52 weeks, print; $112 Individuals 52 weeks, online; $155 Individuals 52 weeks, print and online. **URL:** http://www.freedom.com. **Remarks:** Accepts advertising. **Circ:** (Not Reported).

4174 ■ Online World of Anime and Manga
Society for the Promotion of Japanese Animation
1522 Brookhollow Dr., No. 1
Santa Ana, CA 92705
Phone: (714)937-2994
Publisher's E-mail: info@spja.org
Remarks: Advertising not accepted. **Circ:** (Not Reported).

4175 ■ Orange City News
Freedom Communications Inc.
625 N Grand Ave.
Santa Ana, CA 92701
Phone: (714)796-7000
Publisher's E-mail: info@freedom.com
Community newspaper. **Freq:** Weekly (Thurs.). **Print Method:** Offset. **Cols./Page:** 5. **Col. Width:** 2 1/16 inches. **Col. Depth:** 13 inches. **Key Personnel:** Theresa Cisneros, Editor; Sarah Schurz, Manager, Advertising; Terry Horne, President, Publisher, phone: (714)796-7740. **Subscription Rates:** $19.99 Individuals for the first four weeks. **Alt. Formats:** Handheld. **URL:** http://www.ocregister.com/sections/city-pages/orange-villapark/; http://www.ocregister.com/sections/login. **Remarks:** Accepts advertising. **Circ:** Free ■ **24592.**

4176 ■ Orange County Register
Freedom Communications Inc.
625 N Grand Ave.
Santa Ana, CA 92701
Free: 877-469-7344
Publication E-mail: customerservice@ocregister.com
General newspaper. **Freq:** Daily (morn.). **Print Method:** Offset. **Trim Size:** 13 x 22 3/4. **Cols./Page:** 6. **Col. Width:** 25 nonpareils. **Col. Depth:** 129 agate lines. **Key Personnel:** Rob Curley, Editor; Rich Mirman, Publisher; Donna Wares, Managing Editor, phone: (714)796-6817. **Subscription Rates:** $39.74 Individuals 8 weeks, (Mon-Sun delivery). **URL:** http://www.ocregister.com. **Formerly**: Santa Ana Daily Register. **Remarks:** Accepts advertising. **Circ:** Mon.-Fri. ★**276881**, Sun. ★**318494.**

4177 ■ Orange County Reporter
Daily Journal Corp.
600 W Santa Ana Blvd., Ste. 205
Santa Ana, CA 92701
Phone: (714)543-2027
Fax: (714)543-6841
Legal and financial newspaper. **Freq:** Triweekly Monday, Wednesday and Friday. **Print Method:** Offset. **Cols./Page:** 4. **Col. Width:** 2 1/2 inches. **Col. Depth:** 12 1/2 inches. **USPS:** 410-200. **Subscription Rates:** $97 Individuals 1 year. **URL:** http://www.dailyjournal.com/public/PubMain.cfm?seloption=RenewSub&pubdate=&shNewsType=SubScribe&NewsId=-1&sdivId=&screenHt=550. **Ad Rates:** BW $108; PCI $6.20. **Remarks:** Accepts advertising. **Circ:** Paid ‡72.

4178 ■ Peacemakers Journal
Peace Officers for Christ International
3000 W MacArthur Blvd., Ste. 426
Santa Ana, CA 92704-6962
Phone: (714)426-7632
Publisher's E-mail: info@pofci.org
Freq: Quarterly. **Remarks:** Advertising not accepted. **Circ:** (Not Reported).

4179 ■ Saddleback Valley News
Freedom Communications Inc.
625 N Grand Ave.
Santa Ana, CA 92701
Phone: (714)835-1234
Publisher's E-mail: info@freedom.com
Community newspaper. **Freq:** Weekly. **Print Method:** Offset. **Cols./Page:** 5. **Col. Width:** 12 1/16 inches. **Col. Depth:** 13 inches. **Key Personnel:** Terry Horne, President, Publisher, phone: (714)796-7740. **URL:** http://www.ocregister.com/tag/insideocr/saddleback-valley-news. **Ad Rates:** PCI $32.17. **Remarks:** Accepts advertising. **Circ:** Free ■ **22963.**

4180 ■ Santa Rosa Press Gazette
Halifax Media Holdings L.L.C.
Daytona Beach, FL 32119
Phone: (386)265-6700
Fax: (386)265-6750
Publication E-mail: news@srpressgazette.com
Community newspaper serving Santa Rosa County. **Freq:** Semiweekly (Wed. and Sat.). **Print Method:** Offset. **Trim Size:** 12 x 21 1/2. **Cols./Page:** 6. **Key Personnel:** Jim Fletcher, Publisher; Bill Gamblin, Editor. **USPS:** 604-360. **Subscription Rates:** $22 Individuals senior citizens; $28 Individuals resident; $40 Out of country. **URL:** http://srpressgazette.com. **Ad Rates:** BW $1,238; 4C $1,503; PCI $9.60. **Remarks:** Accepts advertising. **Circ:** ‡7500.

4181 ■ Tustin News
Freedom Communications Inc.
625 N Grand Ave.
Santa Ana, CA 92701
Phone: (714)796-7000
Publisher's E-mail: info@freedom.com
General interest community newspaper. **Freq:** Weekly (Thurs.). **Print Method:** Offset. **Cols./Page:** 6. **Col. Width:** 12 picas. **Col. Depth:** 21.5 picas. **ISSN:** 0892--6441 (print). **Subscription Rates:** Free. **URL:** http://www.ocregister.com/sections/city-pages/tustin. **Remarks:** Accepts advertising. **Circ:** Free ■ **23338.**

4182 ■ Varsity
Freedom Communications Inc.
625 N Grand Ave.
Santa Ana, CA 92701
Phone: (714)796-7000
Publisher's E-mail: info@freedom.com
High school sports newspaper, available to Orange County Register Subscribers. **Founded:** Sept. 07, 1993. **Freq:** Weekly. **Trim Size:** 5 x 13. **Cols./Page:** 5. **Col. Width:** 12 nonpareils. **Col. Depth:** 13 inches. **Subscription Rates:** $12. **URL:** http://www.ocvarsity.com/. **Ad Rates:** GLR $8.25; BW $455; PCI $8.25. **Remarks:** Accepts advertising. **Circ:** (Not Reported).

4183 ■ Westways: Southern California Lifestyle Magazine
Automobile Club of Southern California
PO Box 25001
Santa Ana, CA 92799-5001
Free: 800-400-4222
Magazine covering regional, domestic and international travel, recreation, and events. **Freq:** Bimonthly. **Print Method:** Web Offset. **Trim Size:** 7 7/8 x 10 1/2. **Cols./Page:** 3. **Col. Width:** 27 nonpareils. **Col. Depth:** 137 agate lines. **URL:** http://www.calif.aaa.com/westways/Pages/index.aspx/. **Formerly**: Avenues. **Ad Rates:** BW $32,070; 4C $40,590. **Remarks:** Accepts advertising. **Circ:** Paid 2652703.

4184 ■ Calvary Radio Network
3000 W MacArthur Blvd., Ste. 500
Santa Ana, CA 92707
Phone: (219)548-5800
Free: 866-303-9457
Email: info@calvaryradionetwork.com
Format: Gospel; Contemporary Christian. **Key Personnel:** Jim Motshagen, Contact, jmots@calvaryradionet.com. **Ad Rates:** Noncommercial. **URL:** http://www.calvaryradionetwork.com.

4185 ■ KDOC-TV - 56
625 N Grand Ave.
Santa Ana, CA 92701
Phone: (949)442-9800
Fax: (949)261-5956
Format: Commercial TV. **Networks:** ABC. **Founded:** 1982. **Operating Hours:** Continuous. **Wattage:**

1,000,000 ERP H. **Ad Rates:** Advertising accepted; rates available upon request. **URL:** http://www.kdoc.tv.

K15CN - See Salina, KS

K15FW - See Batesville, AR

K50JG - See Independence, KS

K51EC - See Lake Charles, LA

K56DZ - See Fresno

K56HW - See Rochester, MN

K40DE - See Williston, ND

K48IT - See Baton Rouge, LA

K45DI - See Mermentau, LA

K45DU - See Ventura

K45HC - See Sacramento

K45IM - See Monroe, LA

K45IY - See Alexandria, LA

K40ID - See Palm Springs

K40JT - See Albert Lea, MN

K49EO - See Modesto

K41HC - See Mountain Home, AR

K47EH - See Eureka

K46DY - See Bismarck, ND

K43HN - See Dodge City, KS

K42AM - See Ottumwa, IA

K42FH - See Bemidji, MN

K42GX - See Jonesboro, AR

K42HI - See Muscatine, IA

K19BG - See Saint Cloud, MN

K19FR - See New Iberia, LA

4186 ■ KOCE-TV Foundation - 50
PO Box 25113
Santa Ana, CA 92799-5113
Phone: (714)241-4100
Fax: (714)668-9689
Free: 800-278-5050
Email: development@pbssocal.org
Format: Public TV. **Networks:** Public Broadcasting Service (PBS). **Founded:** 1972. **Operating Hours:** Continuous. **ADI:** Los Angeles (Corona & San Bernardino), CA. **Local Programs:** *The Friendly Whales*; *Escapeseeker*; *Rocco the Vote*; *Freedom from Despair*; *Bloody Thursday*, Thursday; *Bookmark with Maria Hall-Brown*; *Diocese of Orange: Matters of Faith*; *Greener Buildings/Bluer Skies*; *Inside OC with Rick Reiff*, Monday Tuesday Friday Saturday Sunday 12:30 a.m. 1:00 a.m. 2:30 a.m.; 9:30 a.m.; 5:00 p.m. 4:30 p.m. 11:00 a.m. **Wattage:** 5,000. **URL:** http://www.pbssocal.org.

K17ET - See Cedar Rapids, IA

K16ER - See Fort Smith, AR

4187 ■ KTBN-TV - 40
PO Box A
Santa Ana, CA 92711
Phone: (714)832-2950
Free: 888-731-1000
Format: Religious. **Networks:** Independent. **Wattage:** 1,000,000 ERP. **URL:** http://www.tbn.org/.

K38EE - See Twentynine Palms

K34FH - See Little Rock, AR

K39FW - See Garden City, KS

K39IN - See Opelousas, LA

K31BW - See Manhattan, KS

K31HO - See Shreveport, LA

K33HZ - See Pittsburg, KS

K33IC - See Topeka, KS

K28EP - See Dickinson, ND

K28IL - See New Orleans, LA

K28JB - See Wichita, KS

K25DS - See Junction City, KS

K25IA - See Minneapolis, MN

K29GL - See Lincoln, NE

K21FP - See Bakersfield

K21HS - See Norfolk, NE

K27FC - See Paragould, AR

K26CV - See Ogallala, NE

K23GT - See Hot Springs, AR

4188 ■ KWIZ-FM - 96.7
3101 W 5th St.
Santa Ana, CA 92703
Phone: (714)554-5000
Fax: (714)265-6363
Format: News. **Owner:** Liberman Broadcasting, Inc., 3000 Bering Dr., Houston, TX 77057. **Founded:** 1947. **Operating Hours:** 5:00 a.m. - 12:00 a.m. Monday - Friday, Continuous Saturday - Sunday. **Key Personnel:** Jose Mar, Contact, jmar@lbimedia.com. **Wattage:** 6,000 ERP. **Ad Rates:** Accepts Advertising. **URL:** http://laranchera.estrellatv.com.

4189 ■ KWVE-FM - 107.9
3000 W MacArthur Blvd., Ste. 500
Santa Ana, CA 92704
Free: 866-999-5983
Format: Religious; Contemporary Christian. **Owner:** Calvary Chapel of Costa Mesa Inc., 3800 S Fairview St., Santa Ana, CA 92704, Ph: (714)979-4422. **Operating Hours:** Continuous. **Wattage:** 530. **Ad Rates:** $30 for 30 seconds; $60 per unit. **URL:** http://www.kwve.com.

4190 ■ WDLI-TV - 17
PO Box A
Santa Ana, CA 92711
Phone: (714)832-2950
Free: 888-731-1000
Email: wdli@tbn.org
Format: Religious. **Owner:** Trinity Broadcasting Network Inc., PO Box A, Santa Ana, CA 92711, Ph: (714)832-2950, Free: 888-731-1000. **Founded:** 1967. **Operating Hours:** Continuous. **ADI:** Cleveland (Akron, Canton, & Sandusky), OH. **Wattage:** 900,000 ERP H. **URL:** http://www.tbn.org.

WEID-LP - See Elkhart, IN

W18BT - See Alpena, MI

4191 ■ WFGL-AM - 960
3000 W McArthur Blvd.
Santa Ana, CA 92704
Phone: (714)549-8895
Free: 800-272-9673
Email: wft@primenet.com
Format: Contemporary Christian. **Owner:** CSN International, PO Box 8000, Costa Mesa, CA 92628, Free: 800-272-WORD. **Founded:** 1950. **Formerly:** WXLO-AM. **Operating Hours:** Continuous. **Key Personnel:** George Small, Station Mgr., georgesmall@juno.com; Debbie Doran, Sales Mgr. **Wattage:** 2,500 day 1,000 night. **Ad Rates:** $6-14 per unit.

W50CZ - See Asheville, NC

W58CZ - See Augusta, GA

W59DG - See Elmira, NY

W51CU - See Pascagoula, MS

W51CV - See Utica, NY

W51DY - See Sebring, FL

W57BV - See Florence, AL

W56DY - See Cleveland, MS

W52DF - See Albany, NY

W48BH - See Statesboro, GA

W45CN - See Rocky Mount, NC

W45CO - See Fayetteville, NC

W45CU - See Waycross, GA

W44CN - See Greenville, NC

W47CM - See Glens Falls, NY

W46BU - See Tuscaloosa, AL

W46CY - See Birmingham, AL

W43BV-TV - See Terre Haute, IN

W43CT - See Savannah, GA

W42CY - See Greenville, MS

W14CQ - See Vidalia, GA

WQKO-FM - See Howe, IN

W17CK - See Port Charlotte, FL

W17CS - See Marquette, MI

W16CF - See Charlotte, NC

W16CJ - See Naples, FL

W64CN - See Raleigh, NC

W67CO - See Huntsville, AL

W63CW - See Goldsboro, NC

W10BH - See Jamestown, NY

W30BD - See Eufaula, AL

W30BW - See Olean, NY

W30BY - See Grenada, MS

W38CY - See Syracuse, NY

W35CA - See Lumberton, NC

W34CN - See Medway, ME

W34CZ - See Albany, GA

W34DH - See Panama City, FL

W39CJ - See Elizabethtown, KY

W36AC - See McComb, MS

W36CK - See Bangor, ME

W36CO - See Saint Petersburg, FL

W33AL - See Brunswick, GA

W33BX - See Tifton, GA

W33CM - See Decatur, AL

W32CA - See Portland, ME

W20BA - See Massena, NY

W20BT - See Ithaca, NY

W20BZ - See Escanaba, MI

W25AD - See Columbus, MS

W25DR - See Jasper, AL

W24CK - See Selma, AL

W21CI - See Statesville, NC

W27CQ - See Houghton, MI

W27CV - See Scottsboro, AL

W27CX - See Natchez, MS

W26BS - See Binghamton, NY

W23AQ - See Lake City, FL

W22BP - See Thomasville, GA

W22CH - See Hopkinsville, KY

W22CJ - See Jacksonville, NC

WUDL-LD - See Detroit, MI

SANTA BARBARA

Santa Barbara Co. Santa Barbara Co. (SW). On Pacific Ocean, 97 m NW of Los Angeles. University of California at Santa Barbara. City College. Westmont College. Private schools. research, light industrial, educational, medical, tourist and recreational center. Winter and summer resort. Oil-producing fields. Manufactures electronic products, plastics, aircraft parts, novelties. Oil refineries; meat packing, canning and frozen food processing plants; Nurseries. Ships cattle, lemons, beans, flowers, avocados, tomatoes.

4192 ■ Ancestors West
Santa Barbara County Genealogical Society
316 Castillo St.
Santa Barbara, CA 93101
Phone: (805)884-9909
Publisher's E-mail: info@sbgen.org
Journal covering genealogy and local history. **Freq:** Quarterly. **Key Personnel:** David Petry, Editor. **ISSN:** 0734--4988 (print). **URL:** http://sbgen.org/cpage.php?pt=132. **Remarks:** Advertising not accepted. **Circ:** Combined 640.

4193 ■ Business Energy
Forester Communications Inc.
5638 Hollister No. 301
Santa Barbara, CA 93117
Phone: (805)681-1300
Fax: (805)681-1312
Publication E-mail: adsales@forester.net
Magazine that offers information on minimizing business interruptions by generating power on the business site. **Freq:** 7/year. **Trim Size:** 8 1/8 x 10 7/8. **Key Personnel:** Janice Kaspersen, Editor; Elizabeth Cutright, Editor; John Trotti, Editor. **Subscription Rates:** Free to qualified subscribers. **URL:** http://www.distributedenergy.com/DE/articles.aspx?search=executesearch. **For-**

Circulation: ★ = AAM; △ or • = BPA; ♦ = CAC; ❑ = VAC; ⊕ = PO Statement; ‡ = Publisher's Report; Boldface figures = sworn; Light figures = estimated.

merly: Distributed Energy: The Journal for Onsite Power Solutions. **Ad Rates:** BW $4090; 4C $5375. **Remarks:** Accepts advertising. **Circ:** ‡21000.

4194 ■ Camera Obscura
Duke University Press
Dept. of Film & Media Studies
University of California, Santa Barbara
Santa Barbara, CA 93106-4010
Phone: (805)893-7069
Fax: (805)893-8630
Publication E-mail: cameraobscura@filmandmedia.ucsb.edu
Journal including scholarly essays, reviews and interviews with feminist practitioners in mass or alternative culture industries. **Freq:** 3/year. **Key Personnel:** Lynne Joyrich, Editor; Lalitha Gopalan, Editor; Sharon Willison, Editor. **ISSN:** 0270--5346 (print);. **EISSN:** 1529--1510 (electronic). **Subscription Rates:** $30 Individuals; $20 Students valid student ID required. **URL:** http://www.dukeupress.edu/Camera-Obscura; http://cameraobscura.dukejournals.org. **Ad Rates:** BW $250. **Remarks:** Accepts advertising. **Circ:** 564.

4195 ■ Control Systems
IEEE - Control Systems Society
c/o Francis J. Doyle III, President
Dept. of Chemical Engineering
University of California - Santa Barbara
333 Engineering II
Santa Barbara, CA 93106
Magazine containing articles devoted to all aspects of control systems. **Freq:** Bimonthly. **ISSN:** 0272- 1708 (print). **Subscription Rates:** Included in membership. **URL:** http://www.ieeecss.org/publications/csm. **Remarks:** Accepts advertising. **Circ:** 15000.

4196 ■ DeLorean World
DeLorean Owners Association
879 Randolph Rd.
Santa Barbara, CA 93111
Phone: (805)964-5296
Publisher's E-mail: delorean@impulse.net
Freq: Quarterly. **Subscription Rates:** included in membership dues. **Remarks:** Accepts advertising. **Circ:** (Not Reported).

4197 ■ E-Humanista: Journal of Iberian Studies
University of California, Santa Barbara
Dept. of Spanish & Portuguese
Phelps Hall 4206
Santa Barbara, CA 93106-4150
Phone: (805)893-3161
Fax: (805)893-8341
Open access, peer-reviewed journal publishing original research in the field of Spanish and Portuguese Medieval and Early Modern Literatures and Cultures. **Key Personnel:** Prof. Antonio Cortijo-Ocana, Editor; Erin M. Rebhan, Associate Editor; Prof. Angel Gomez Moreno, Associate Editor. **ISSN:** 1540--5877 (print). **Subscription Rates:** Free online. **URL:** http://www.ehumanista.ucsb.edu. **Remarks:** Advertising not accepted. **Circ:** (Not Reported).

4198 ■ Evolution and Human Behavior
RELX Group P.L.C.
c/o S. Gaulin, Ed.-in-Ch.
Department of Antrhopology
University of California
Santa Barbara, CA 93106
Publisher's E-mail: amsterdam@relx.com
Freq: Bimonthly. **Print Method:** Offset. **Key Personnel:** Ruth Mace, Editor; Robert Kurzban, Editor-in-Chief. **ISSN:** 1090--5138 (print). **Subscription Rates:** $511 Individuals; $1709 Institutions. **URL:** http://www.journals.elsevier.com/evolution-and-human-behavior/#description; http://www.journals.elsevier.com/evolution-and-human-behavior; http://www.ehbonline.org. **Remarks:** Accepts advertising. **Circ:** (Not Reported).

4199 ■ The International Journal for the Psychology of Religion
Routledge Journals Taylor & Francis Group
c/o Dr. Raymond F. Paloutzian, Ed.
Dept. of Psychology
Westmont College
955 La Paz Rd.
Santa Barbara, CA 93108-1099
Phone: (805)565-6233
Fax: (805)565-6116
Journal devoted to psychological studies of religious processes and phenomena in all religious traditions. **Founded:** 1990. **Freq:** Quarterly. **Key Personnel:** Jozef Corveleyn, Associate Editor; Dr. Raymond F. Paloutzian, Editor. **ISSN:** 1050-8619 (print); **EISSN:** 1532-7582 (electronic). **Subscription Rates:** $670 Institutions online only; $83 Individuals print and online; $766 Institutions print and online. **URL:** http://www.tandfonline.com/toc/hjpr20/current. **Ad Rates:** BW $500. **Remarks:** Accepts advertising. **Circ:** (Not Reported).

4200 ■ Journal of IT Financial Management
I.T. Financial Management Association
PO Box 30188
Santa Barbara, CA 93130
Phone: (805)687-7390
Fax: (805)687-7382
Publisher's E-mail: info@itfma.com
Journal covering financial management of information technology organizations. **Founded:** Apr. 1990. **Freq:** 3/year. **ISSN:** 1532-3870 (print). **URL:** http://www.itfma.com/?page=Journal. **Formerly:** Journal of Financial Management for Data Processing.; Journal of IS Financial Management. **Remarks:** Advertising not accepted. **Circ:** (Not Reported).

4201 ■ Journal of School Violence
Routledge Journals Taylor & Francis Group
c/o Michael Furlong, PhD, Editor
Gevirtz Graduate Scholarship of Education
Department of Counseling, Clinical, & Scholarship Psychology
Santa Barbara, CA 93106-9489
Peer-reviewed journal tracking the causes, consequences, and costs of aggressive or violent behavior in children from kindergarten through twelfth grade. **Freq:** Quarterly. **Key Personnel:** Michael Furlong, PhD, Editor; Ilene R. Berson, Board Member; Rami Benbenishty, Board Member; Jeffrey A. Daniels, Board Member; Ron Avi Astor, Board Member. **ISSN:** 1538--8220 (print); **EISSN:** 1538--8239 (electronic). **Subscription Rates:** $176 Individuals online only; $185 Individuals print + online; $548 Institutions online only; $626 Institutions print + online. **URL:** http://tandfonline.com/toc/wjsv20/current#.VIAn59IwpM5. **Ad Rates:** BW $315; 4C $550. **Remarks:** Accepts advertising. **Circ:** (Not Reported).

4202 ■ Pacific Standard
Miller-McCune Inc.
Miller-McCune Ctr.
Santa Barbara, CA 93102
Magazine providing academic research and policy work. **Freq:** Bimonthly. **Trim Size:** 8 1/8 x 10 7/8. **Key Personnel:** Maria Streshinsky, Editor-in-Chief. **ISSN:** 2165--5197 (print). **URL:** http://www.psmag.com. **Formerly:** Miller-McCune. **Mailing address:** PO Box 698, Santa Barbara, CA 93102. **Remarks:** Accepts advertising. **Circ:** (Not Reported).

4203 ■ Qajar Studies
International Qajar Studies Association
PO Box 31107
Santa Barbara, CA 93130
Phone: (805)687-1148
Fax: (805)687-1148
Journal containing topics regarding the Qajar era. **Subscription Rates:** Included in membership. **URL:** http://www.qajarstudies.org/IQSAPubs.html. **Remarks:** Advertising not accepted. **Circ:** (Not Reported).

4204 ■ Santa Barbara Independent
Santa Barbara Independent
1317 State St.
Santa Barbara, CA 93101
Phone: (805)965-5205
Fax: (805)965-5518
Publication E-mail: letters@independent.com
Community newspaper. **Freq:** Weekly (Thurs.). **Print Method:** Offset. **Trim Size:** 11 x 14. **Cols./Page:** 5. **Col. Width:** 11 picas. **Col. Depth:** 13 1/8 inches. **Key Personnel:** Marianne Partridge, Editor-in-Chief; Nick Welsh, Executive Editor; Michelle Drown, Senior Editor. **URL:** http://www.independent.com. **Remarks:** Accepts advertising. **Circ:** ■ **40000**.

4205 ■ Santa Barbara News-Press
Santa Barbara News-Press
715 Anacapa St.
Santa Barbara, CA 93101-2203
Phone: (805)564-5200
Fax: (805)966-6258
Publisher's E-mail: voices@newspress.com
General newspaper. **Freq:** Daily. **Print Method:** Offset. **Cols./Page:** 6. **Col. Width:** 25 nonpareils. **Col. Depth:** 301 agate lines. **Key Personnel:** Arthur von Wiesenberger, Publisher; Wendy McCaw, Publisher. **Subscription Rates:** $60 Individuals online. **URL:** http://www.newspress.com/Top/index.jsp. **Remarks:** Advertising accepted; rates available upon request. **Circ:** Mon.-Fri. ⋆**27189**, Sun. ⋆**24563**, Sat. ⋆**26174**.

4206 ■ School Library Connection
ABC-Clio Inc.
130 Cremona Dr.
Santa Barbara, CA 93117
Phone: (805)968-1911
Fax: (805)685-9685
Free: 800-368-6868
Publisher's E-mail: customerservice@abc-clio.com
Professional magazine school library media and technology specialists. **Freq:** 7/year. **Print Method:** Offset. **Trim Size:** 8 1/2 x 11. **Cols./Page:** 3. **Col. Width:** 14 picas. **Col. Depth:** 60 picas. **Key Personnel:** Marlene Woo-Lun, President, Publisher; Carol Simpson, Director, Editorial; Shelly Glantz, Editor. **ISSN:** 1542--4715 (print). **URL:** http://www.librarymediaconnection.com. **Formerly:** Library Media Connection; Library Talk; The Book Report. **Also known as:** LMC. **Mailing address:** PO Box 1911, Santa Barbara, CA 93117-5516. **Ad Rates:** BW $3130; 4C $4155. **Remarks:** Accepts advertising. **Circ:** ‡18000.

4207 ■ School Library Media Activities Monthly
Libraries Unlimited Inc.
130 Cremona Dr.
Santa Barbara, CA 93116-1911
Fax: (866)270-3856
Free: 800-368-6868
Publisher's E-mail: customerservice@abc-clio.com
School library periodical. **Freq:** Monthly. **Print Method:** Web press. **Trim Size:** 8 3/8 x 11 1/4. **Key Personnel:** Debra Goodrich, Assistant Editor; Deborah D. Levitov, Managing Editor; Paula Jackson, Manager, Advertising. **ISSN:** 0889--9371 (print). **Subscription Rates:** $55 Individuals 7 issues - Canadian and International orders add $13 a year ; $99 Two years 14 issues - Canadian and International orders add $13 a year. **Alt. Formats:** PDF. **URL:** http://www.schoollibrarymedia.com. **Mailing address:** PO Box 1911, Santa Barbara, CA 93116-1911. **Remarks:** Accepts advertising. **Circ:** Paid ⊕**11500**.

4208 ■ Sino-Japanese Studies
Sino-Japanese Studies
History Dept.
University of California
Santa Barbara, CA 93106-9410
Phone: (805)893-2991
Fax: (805)893-8795
Journal covering studies on China and Japan jointly. **Freq:** Semiannual. **Key Personnel:** Joshua A. Fogel, Editor. **ISSN:** 1041-8830 (print). **URL:** http://www.chinajapan.org/. **Circ:** (Not Reported).

4209 ■ The Sunflower
Nuclear Age Peace Foundation
1622 Anacapa St.
Santa Barbara, CA 93101
Phone: (805)965-3443
Magazine for sunflower producers in the U.S. **Freq:** January, February, March/April, August/September, October/November, and December. **Print Method:** Web offset. **Trim Size:** 8 1/2 x 10 7/8. **Cols./Page:** 3. **Col. Width:** 2 1/4 inches. **Col. Depth:** 10 inches. **Key Personnel:** John Sandbakken, Editor. **Subscription Rates:** $15 U.S. and Canada; $40 U.S. and Canada 3 years; $50 Other countries; Free to qualified subscribers. **URL:** http://www.sunflowernsa.com/magazine; http://www.wagingpeace.org/resources/sunflower. **Formerly:** The Sunflower Association. **Ad Rates:** BW $2,016. **Remarks:** Accepts advertising. **Circ:** (Not Reported).

4210 ■ Transactions on Automatic Control
IEEE - Control Systems Society
c/o Francis J. Doyle III, President
Dept. of Chemical Engineering
University of California - Santa Barbara
333 Engineering II
Santa Barbara, CA 93106
Journal publishing papers on the theory, design, and applications of control engineering. **Freq:** Monthly. **Sub-**

scription Rates: Included in membership. **Alt. Formats:** CD-ROM. **URL:** http://www.ieeecss.org/publications/tac; http://www3.nd.edu/~ieeetac. **Remarks:** Advertising not accepted. **Circ:** (Not Reported).

4211 ■ The Veliger
California Malacozoological Society
Santa Barbara Museum Of Natural History
2559 Puesta Del Sol Rd.
Santa Barbara, CA 93105
Phone: (805)682-4711
Publication E-mail: veliger@berkeley.edu
Natural history magazine focusing on the various aspects of malacology (study of mollusks). **Print Method:** Offset. **Trim Size:** 8 1/2 x 11. **Cols./Page:** 2. **Col. Width:** 42 nonpareils. **Col. Depth:** 112 agate lines. **Key Personnel:** David R. Lindberg, Editor-in-Chief. **ISSN:** 0042--3211 (print). **URL:** http://archive.org/details/veliger452002cali. **Remarks:** Advertising not accepted. **Circ:** Paid ‡640, Non-paid ‡10.

4212 ■ Visual Neuroscience
Cambridge University Press
c/o Dr. Benjamin E. Reese, Ed.-in-Ch.
University of California, Santa Barbara
Neuroscience Research Institute
Santa Barbara, CA 93106-5060
Phone: (805)893-2091
Fax: (805)893-2091
Publication E-mail: ad_sales@cambridge.org vns@lifesci.ucsb.edu
Peer-reviewed journal on visual neuroscience. **Freq:** Bimonthly. **Key Personnel:** Dr. Benjamin E. Reese, Editor-in-Chief; Katherine Fite, Editor, Founder. **ISSN:** 0952--5238 (print); **EISSN:** 1469--8714 (electronic). **Subscription Rates:** $1489 Institutions online only; £884 Institutions online only; $45 Individuals /article; £30 Individuals /article. **URL:** http://journals.cambridge.org/action/displayJournal?jid=VNS. **Ad Rates:** BW $885. **Remarks:** Accepts advertising. **Circ:** Combined ‡600.

4213 ■ CKRU-FM - 97.5
403 E Montecito St.
Santa Barbara, CA 93101
Phone: (805)966-1755
Free: 866-965-9797
Format: Album-Oriented Rock (AOR); Contemporary Hit Radio (CHR). **Formerly:** KRUZ-FM. **Operating Hours:** Continuous. **Key Personnel:** Matt Stone, Contact, matt.stone@cumulus.com; Matt Stone, Contact, matt.stone@cumulus.com. **Ad Rates:** Advertising accepted; rates available upon request.

4214 ■ KCSB-FM - 91.9
PO Box 13401
Santa Barbara, CA 93107-3401
Phone: (805)893-3757
Email: info@kcsb.org
Format: Alternative/New Music/Progressive; Eclectic. **Networks:** Pacifica. **Owner:** Regents of the University of California, 1111 Franklin St., 12th Fl., Oakland, CA 94607. **Founded:** 1964. **Operating Hours:** Continuous. **Key Personnel:** Elizabeth Robinson, Contact, elizabeth.robinson@kcsb.org; Alex Smith, Gen. Mgr.; Bryan D. Brown, Chief Engineer, bryan.brown@kcsb.org. **Wattage:** 620. **Ad Rates:** Noncommercial. **URL:** http://www.kcsb.org.

4215 ■ KDB-FM - 93.7
PO Box 91660
Santa Barbara, CA 93190
Phone: (805)966-4131
Fax: (805)966-4788
Email: info@kdb.com
Format: Classical. **Networks:** Independent. **Owner:** Santa Barbara Foundation, 1111 Chapala St., Ste. 200, Santa Barbara, CA 93101, Ph: (805)963-1873. **Founded:** 1926. **Operating Hours:** Continuous. **Wattage:** 12,500. **Ad Rates:** Noncommercial.

4216 ■ KEYT-TV - 3
730 Miramonte Dr.
Santa Barbara, CA 93109
Phone: (805)882-3933
Fax: (805)882-3923
Email: assignmentdesk@keyt.com
Format: Commercial TV. **Networks:** ABC. **Founded:** 1953. **Operating Hours:** Continuous; 60% network, 40% local. **ADI:** Santa Barbara-Santa Maria-San Luis Obispo,CA. **Key Personnel:** Jeff Martin, Dir. of Creative Svcs.; Kim Johnson, Contact, kjohnson@keyt.com; Kim Johnson, Contact, kjohnson@keyt.com. **Ad Rates:** Noncommercial. **URL:** http://www.keyt.com.

4217 ■ KFAC-FM - 92.3
3400 W Olive Ave., Ste. 550
Burbank, CA 91505
Email: kusc@kusc.org
Format: Urban Contemporary; Hip Hop. **Owner:** University of Southern California, at above address. **Founded:** 1985. **Operating Hours:** 12:00 a.m. - 7:00 p.m. Monday - Sunday. **ADI:** Los Angeles (Corona & San Bernardino), CA. **Key Personnel:** Brenda Barnes, President, bpennell@kusc.org; Eric DeWeese, Gen. Mgr. **Wattage:** 47,000 ERP. **Ad Rates:** Advertising accepted; rates available upon request. **URL:** http://real923la.iheart.com.

4218 ■ KIST-FM - 107.7
414 E Cota St.
Santa Barbara, CA 93101
Phone: (805)879-8300
Format: Contemporary Hit Radio (CHR). **Owner:** iHeartMedia Inc., 200 E Basse Rd., San Antonio, TX 78209, Ph: (210)832-3314. **ADI:** Santa Barbara-Santa Maria-San Luis Obispo,CA. **Key Personnel:** Jose Fierros, Contact, jose@radiobronco.com. **Wattage:** 930. **Ad Rates:** Advertising accepted; rates available upon request. **URL:** http://www.radiobronco.com/contactos.

4219 ■ KJEE-FM - 92.9
302 B W Carrillo St.
Santa Barbara, CA 93101
Phone: (805)962-4588
Email: kjee929@aol.com
Format: Album-Oriented Rock (AOR). **Ad Rates:** Noncommercial. **URL:** http://www.kjee.com.

4220 ■ KQSB-AM - 990
414 E Cota St.
Santa Barbara, CA 93101
Phone: (805)879-8300
Email: info@amfm.com
Format: Talk; News. **Networks:** CNN Radio; Westwood One Radio. **Founded:** 1972. **Formerly:** KBBQ-AM; KTVN-AM; KSSM-AM. **Operating Hours:** Continuous. **ADI:** Santa Barbara-Santa Maria-San Luis Obispo,CA. **Key Personnel:** Jennifer VanDonge, Gen. Sales Mgr.; Jim Watkins, Dir. of Programs; Paul Cavanagh, Operations Mgr., pcavanagh@jacor.com; David Hefferman, Dir. of Mktg., Promotions Dir., Operations Mgr., pcavanagh@jacor.com; Paul M. Cavanagh, Contact; Paul M. Cavanagh, Contact. **Wattage:** 5,000 day 500 night.

4221 ■ KSBL-FM - 101.7
414 E Cota St.
Santa Barbara, CA 93101
Phone: (805)879-8300
Format: Adult Contemporary. **Founded:** 1981. **Formerly:** KLIT-FM. **Operating Hours:** Continuous. **ADI:** Santa Barbara-Santa Maria-San Luis Obispo,CA. **Wattage:** 994. **Ad Rates:** Advertising accepted; rates available upon request. **URL:** http://www.ksbl.com.

4222 ■ KSPE-AM
331 N Milpas St., Ste. F
Santa Barbara, CA 93103
Phone: (805)965-1490
Fax: (805)966-7875
Format: Hispanic. **Owner:** Spectacular Broadcasting, Inc., at above address'. **Founded:** 1926. **Formerly:** KDB-AM. **Wattage:** 1,000. **Ad Rates:** Advertising accepted; rates available upon request.

4223 ■ KSPE-FM - 94.5
414 E Cota St.
Santa Barbara, CA 93101
Phone: (805)879-8300
Format: Hispanic. **Owner:** Spectacular Broadcasting, Inc., at above address'. **Founded:** 1989. **Formerly:** KCQR-FM. **Operating Hours:** Continuous. **ADI:** Santa Barbara-Santa Maria-San Luis Obispo,CA. **Key Personnel:** Richard Marsh, Gen. Mgr.; James Farr, Sales Mgr.; Gerardo Lorenz, Dir. of Programs. **URL:** http://www.z945.com.

4224 ■ KTMS-AM - 990
414 E Cota St.
Santa Barbara, CA 93101
Phone: (805)879-8300
Fax: (805)879-8430
Format: News; Talk. **Networks:** ABC; CNN Radio; CBS. **Owner:** Rincon Broadcasting L.L.C., 414 E Cota St., Santa Barbara, CA 93101, Ph: (805)879-8300. **Founded:** 1937. **Operating Hours:** Continuous. **Wattage:** 2,500 Day; 1,000 Night. **Ad Rates:** Advertising accepted; rates available upon request. **URL:** http://www.ktms.com.

4225 ■ K218CP-FM - 91.5
PO Box 391
Twin Falls, ID 83303
Fax: (208)736-1958
Free: 800-357-4226
Format: Religious; Contemporary Christian. **Owner:** CSN International, PO Box 391, Twin Falls, ID 83303, Ph: (208)736-1958, Fax: (208)736-1958, Free: 800-357-4226. **Key Personnel:** Ray Gorney, Asst. Dir.; Don Mills, Prog. Dir., Music Dir.; Kelly Carlson, Dir. of Engg. **Wattage:** 010. **URL:** http://www.csnradio.com.

4226 ■ KTYD-FM - 99.9
414 E Cota St.
Santa Barbara, CA 93101
Phone: (805)879-8300
Fax: (805)879-8430
Format: Classic Rock; Album-Oriented Rock (AOR). **Networks:** Independent. **Owner:** Rincon Broadcasting L.L.C., 414 E Cota St., Santa Barbara, CA 93101, Ph: (805)879-8300. **Founded:** 1972. **Operating Hours:** 6am-12pm-Mon.-Sat.; 6am-10pm-Sun. **Key Personnel:** Keith Royer, Exec. VP, Gen. Mgr. **Wattage:** 34,000. **Ad Rates:** Advertising accepted; rates available upon request. **URL:** http://www.ktyd.com.

4227 ■ KZSB-AM - 1290
715 Anacapa St.
Santa Barbara, CA 93101
Phone: (805)564-5200
Fax: (805)966-6258
Format: News. **Owner:** Santa Barbara Broadcasting, Inc., at above address. **Operating Hours:** Continuous. **Key Personnel:** Wendy McCaw, Publisher; Arthur von Wiesenberger, Publisher. **Ad Rates:** Advertising accepted; rates available upon request. **URL:** http://www.newspress.com/Top.

SANTA CLARA

Santa Clara Co. Santa Clara Co. (W). 3 m NW of San Jose. University of Santa Clara. Fruit packing, canning and drying. Sashes and doors, electronics, fiberglass, pottery, dairy products manufactured. Fruit farms. Apricots, prunes, pears, walnuts.

4228 ■ Always Jukin' Magazine: The Jukebox Supermarket
Always Jukin'
PO Box C
Santa Clara, CA 95051
Phone: (206)652-4005
Publisher's E-mail: alwaysjuke@aol.com
Hobby magazine for jukebox owners and collectors. **Freq:** Monthly. **Print Method:** Web offset. **Trim Size:** 8.5 x 11. **Cols./Page:** 3. **Col. Width:** 2 1/4 inches. **Col. Depth:** 10 inches. **ISSN:** 0896-9345 (print). **Subscription Rates:** $99 Canada 1 year print; $131 Other countries 1 year print; $89 U.S. 1 year digital; $110 U.S. 1 year print. **Alt. Formats:** CD-ROM; PDF. **URL:** http://www.alwaysjukin.com. **Ad Rates:** BW $120, 1 page; 4C $65, 1/2 page horizontal or vertical; BW $40, 1/4 page vertical. **Remarks:** Advertising accepted; rates available upon request. **Circ:** (Not Reported).

4229 ■ Computer and High Technology Law Journal
Santa Clara University School of Law
500 El Camino Real
Santa Clara, CA 95053
Phone: (408)554-4361
Publisher's E-mail: lawadmissions@scu.edu
Journal containing articles on intellectual property (patent, trademark, copyright, and trade secret), technology licensing, contract and tort liability for technology failures, employer/employee relations, unfair competition, venture capital and other financing, computer crime and privacy, biotechnology, and hazardous waste management. **Freq:** Semiannual. **URL:** http://law.scu.

Circulation: ★ = AAM; △ or • = BPA; ♦ = CAC; ❑ = VAC; ⊕ = PO Statement; ‡ = Publisher's Report; Boldface figures = sworn; Light figures = estimated.

edu/courses/computer-and-high-technology-law-journal. **Circ:** (Not Reported).

4230 ■ Connections
Santa Clara County Historical and Genealogical Society
c/o Central Pk. Library
2635 Homestead Rd.
Santa Clara, CA 95051
Phone: (408)615-2986
Journal containing historical articles on local people, events and records of Santa Clara County. **Freq:** Semiannual. **Subscription Rates:** $8 Individuals in addition to membership fee. **URL:** http://www.scchgs.org/main/pubs.html. **Remarks:** Accepts advertising. **Circ:** (Not Reported).

4231 ■ Explorations in Media Ecology
Media Ecology Association
Communication Dept.
Santa Clara University
500 El Camino Real
Santa Clara, CA 95053-0277
Phone: (408)554-4022
Fax: (408)554-4913
Publisher's E-mail: treasurer@media-ecology.org
Journal covering information on understanding of media environments. **Freq:** Quarterly. **Key Personnel:** Brian Cogan, Editor. **Subscription Rates:** Included in membership. **URL:** http://media-ecology.org/publications/Explorations_Media_Ecology/index.html. **Remarks:** Advertising not accepted. **Circ:** (Not Reported).

4232 ■ Journal of International Law
Santa Clara University School of Law
500 El Camino Real
Santa Clara, CA 95053
Phone: (408)554-4361
Publisher's E-mail: lawadmissions@scu.edu
Journal containing articles dealing with issues of international and comparative legal scholarship. **Freq:** Annual. **URL:** http://digitalcommons.law.scu.edu/scujil. **Circ:** (Not Reported).

4233 ■ LonMark Magazine
LonMark International
2901 Patrick Henry Dr.
Santa Clara, CA 95054
Phone: (408)938-5266
Fax: (408)790-3838
Publisher's E-mail: info@lonmark.org
Magazine featuring new technologies, products and applications, industry new, innovative product announcements and industry events. **Freq:** Semiannual. **Subscription Rates:** Included in membership. **URL:** http://www.lmimagazine.com. **Ad Rates:** 4C $1,400, for LMI members in the International Edition. **Remarks:** Accepts advertising. **Circ:** 12,000.

4234 ■ Santa Clara Computer and High Technology Law Journal
Santa Clara University School of Law
500 El Camino Real
Santa Clara, CA 95053
Phone: (408)554-4361
Publisher's E-mail: lawadmissions@scu.edu
Scholarly journal covering legal issues in high technology. **Freq:** 4/yr. **Key Personnel:** Vishal Dave, Editor-in-Chief; Johnathan Elton, Managing Editor. **ISSN:** 0882--3383 (print). **Subscription Rates:** $69.50 Individuals; $79.50 Other countries. **URL:** http://digitalcommons.law.scu.edu/chtlj. **Remarks:** Advertising not accepted. **Circ:** (Not Reported).

4235 ■ Santa Clara Law Review
Santa Clara Law Review
500 El Camino Real
Santa Clara, CA 95053-0426
Phone: (408)554-4074
Fax: (408)554-4018
Professional legal journal. **Freq:** Quarterly. **Key Personnel:** Wesley Dodd, Editor-in-Chief. **ISSN:** 0146--0315 (print). **Subscription Rates:** $54 Individuals /year; $17 Single issue. **Alt. Formats:** PDF. **URL:** http://digitalcommons.law.scu.edu/lawreview. **Remarks:** Advertising not accepted. **Circ:** (Not Reported).

4236 ■ The Santa Clara: SCU's weekly undergraduate newspaper since 1922
Santa Clara University
500 El Camino Real
Santa Clara, CA 95053
Phone: (408)554-4000
Publication E-mail: editor@thesantaclara.com
University and alumni newspaper. **Freq:** Weekly (Thurs.). **Print Method:** Offset. **Trim Size:** 40. **Cols./Page:** 5. **Col. Width:** 18 nonpareils. **Col. Depth:** 224 agate lines. **Key Personnel:** Sophie Mattson, Editor-in-Chief. **Subscription Rates:** Free. **URL:** http://thesantaclara.org. **Formerly:** The Santa Clara: Serving Santa Clara University since 1922. **Mailing address:** PO Box 3190, Santa Clara, CA 95053. **Ad Rates:** BW $600. **Remarks:** Accepts advertising. **Circ:** Free ‡3500.

4237 ■ Techne: Research in Philosophy and Technology
Society for Philosophy and Technology
c/o Shannon Vallor, President
500 El Vamino Real
Santa Clara, CA 95053
Phone: (408)554-5190
Journal covering philosophical analysis of technological systems and to reflections on the art, craft, science and engineering of making things and getting things done in the world. **Freq:** 3/year. **Key Personnel:** Diane P. Michelfelder, Editor. **EISSN:** 1091--8264 (electronic). **Subscription Rates:** $200 Institutions online. **Alt. Formats:** PDF. **URL:** http://www.pdcnet.org/techne. **Remarks:** Advertising not accepted. **Circ:** (Not Reported).

4238 ■ KKUP-FM - 91.5
1275 Franklin Mall
PMB 9150
Santa Clara, CA 95050
Phone: (408)260-2999
Format: Eclectic. **Networks:** Independent. **Owner:** Assurance Science Foundation, at above address, Cupertino, CA. **Founded:** 1972. **Operating Hours:** Continuous; 100% local. **Key Personnel:** Roger Werner, Dept. Head; Michael Berry, Prog. Dir.; Dan Kind, Contact; Jim Thomas, Chairman. **Wattage:** 200. **Ad Rates:** Noncommercial. **URL:** http://www.kkup.com.

4239 ■ KSCU-FM - 103.3
500 El Camino Real, Ste. 3207
Santa Clara, CA 95053-3207
Phone: (408)554-5728
Email: info@kscu.org
Format: Eclectic. **Networks:** Independent. **Owner:** Santa Clara University, 500 El Camino Real, Santa Clara, CA 95053, Ph: (408)554-4000. **Founded:** June 1966. **Operating Hours:** Connecticut. **Key Personnel:** Lauren Duffy, Gen. Mgr., gm@kscu.org. **Wattage:** 030. **Ad Rates:** Noncommercial. **URL:** http://www.kscu.org.

SANTA CLARITA

4240 ■ Hillsboro Sentry-Enterprise
Morris Newspapers Inc.
The Santa Clarita Valley Signal
24000 Creekside Rd.
Santa Clarita, CA 91355
Newspaper. **Freq:** Weekly (Thurs.). **Print Method:** Offset. **Trim Size:** 11 1/2 x 17 1/2. **Cols./Page:** 6. **Col. Width:** 22 nonpareils. **Col. Depth:** 224 agate lines. **Key Personnel:** Harvey Leverenz, Product Manager; Mary Sterba, Office Manager. **Remarks:** Accepts classified advertising. **Circ:** (Not Reported).

4241 ■ Preview Theater Magazine
Hogan Communications
27225 Camp Plenty Rd., Ste. 11
Santa Clarita, CA 91351
Movie, home video, and music magazine for college students. **Freq:** Monthly. **Ad Rates:** BW $7400; 4C $8000. **Remarks:** Accepts advertising. **Circ:** ‡250000.

4242 ■ The Signal
Signal Newspapers Inc.
24000 Creekside Rd.
Santa Clarita, CA 91355
Phone: (661)259-1234
Fax: (661)254-8068
Publication E-mail: atwsignal@cell2000.net
Local newspaper. **Founded:** May 11, 1911. **Freq:** Weekly (Wed.). **Print Method:** Offset. **Trim Size:** 13 x 21 1/2. **Cols./Page:** 6. **Col. Width:** 12 picas. **Col. Depth:** 294 agate lines. **Key Personnel:** David J. Wickenhauser, Editor, phone: (209)722-1511; Tom Schmitt, Publisher, phone: (209)722-1511, fax: (209)384-2221; Sue Devine, Business Manager, phone: (209)722-1511. **Subscription Rates:** $6.25 Individuals a month (7 days delivery); $135.20 Individuals for 52 weeks (7 days delivery); $67.80 Individuals for 26 weeks (7 days delivery); $39 Individuals for 52 weeks (Sunday only delivery). **URL:** http://www.signalscv.com/. **Mailing address:** PO Box 801870, Santa Clarita, CA 91380-1870. **Ad Rates:** PCI $9. **Remarks:** Advertising accepted; rates available upon request. **Circ:** Free ‡1500.

SANTA CRUZ

Santa Cruz Co. Santa Cruz Co. (W). On Pacific Ocean and Monterey Bay, 74 m S of San Francisco. University of California at Santa Cruz. Resort. Manufactures electronics, lime, wire, chewing gum, feed, redwood novelties, lumber. Fruits, vegetables, bulbs, fish packed. Nurseries. hatcheries, wineries. Limestone quarries. redwood timber. Fisheries. Agriculture. Artichokes, blueberries, apples, plums, grapes.

4243 ■ ACM Transactions on Storage
Association for Computing Machinery
c/o Darrell Long, Ed.-in-Ch.
University of California
Jack Baskin School of Engineering
Computer Science Department
Santa Cruz, CA 95064
Phone: (831)459-2616
Fax: (831)459-4829
Publisher's E-mail: acmhelp@acm.org
Archival journal dealing with the field of storage, a broad and multidisciplinary area that comprises of network protocols, resource management, data backup, replication, recovery, devices, security, and theory of data coding, densities, and low-power. **Freq:** Quarterly. **Key Personnel:** Ahmed Amer, Associate Editor, phone: (408)551-6064; Darell Long, Editor-in-Chief; Andre Brinkmann, Associate Editor. **ISSN:** 1553-3077 (print); **EISSN:** 1553-3093 (electronic). **Subscription Rates:** $175 Nonmembers print only; $136 Nonmembers online only; $204 Nonmembers online & print. **URL:** http://tos.acm.org. **Circ:** (Not Reported).

4244 ■ City on a Hill Press
City on a Hill Press
1156 High St.
1156 High St.
Santa Cruz, CA 95064
Phone: (831)459-4350
Fax: (831)459-3818
Publisher's E-mail: business@cityonahillpress.com
Collegiate newspaper. **Freq:** Weekly (Thurs.). **Print Method:** Offset. **Trim Size:** 10 1/4 x 13. **Cols./Page:** 5. **Col. Width:** 18 nonpareils. **Col. Depth:** 182 agate lines. **Subscription Rates:** Free. **URL:** http://www.cityonahillpress.com. **Ad Rates:** 4C $396; PCI $13.13. **Remarks:** Accepts advertising. **Circ:** 24716.

4245 ■ Communication Abstracts
EBSCO Industries Inc.
1651 El Dorado Ave.
Santa Cruz, CA 95062-5703
Phone: (408)475-5020
Fax: (408)475-4544
Publisher's E-mail: sales@pfp.sagepub.com
Journal containing abstracts and references in communications. **Freq:** Bimonthly. **Print Method:** Web Offset. **Trim Size:** 5 1/2 x 8 1/2. **Cols./Page:** 1. **Col. Width:** 50 nonpareils. **Col. Depth:** 100 agate lines. **Key Personnel:** Thomas F. Gordon, Editor, Founder; Karen Cristiano, Editor. **ISSN:** 0162--2811 (print). **URL:** http://www.ebscohost.com/academic/communication-abstracts. **Ad Rates:** BW $445. **Remarks:** Accepts advertising. **Circ:** Paid 600.

4246 ■ GLQ: A Journal of Lesbian and Gay Studies
Duke University Press
Humanities Academic Services
University of California, Santa Cruz
1156 High St.
Santa Cruz, CA 95064
Fax: (831)502-7373
Publisher's E-mail: orders@dukeupress.edu
Scholarly journal covering lesbian and gay studies. **Freq:** Quarterly. **Key Personnel:** Carolyn Dinshaw, Editor, Founder; David M. Halperin, Editor, Founder; Elizabeth Freeman, Editor; Nayan Shah, Editor. **ISSN:** 1064--2684 (print); **EISSN:** 1527--9375 (electronic). **Subscription**

Rates: $40 Individuals; $25 Students a copy of a valid student ID is required. **URL:** http://www.dukeupress.edu/GLQ. **Ad Rates:** BW $300. **Remarks:** Accepts advertising. **Circ:** (Not Reported).

4247 ■ MAPS Bulletin
Multidisciplinary Association for Psychedelic Studies
1115 Mission St.
Santa Cruz, CA 95060-3528
Phone: (831)429-6362
Fax: (831)429-6370
Publisher's E-mail: askmaps@maps.org
Professional magazine covering issues in drugs and pharmacy for association members. **Freq:** 3/year. **Key Personnel:** David Jay Brown, Editor. **ISSN:** 1080--8981 (print). **URL:** http://www.maps.org/maps-media/bulletin. **Remarks:** Advertising not accepted. **Circ:** 4000.

4248 ■ SACNAS News
Society for Advancement of Chicanos/Hispanics and Native Americans in Science
1121 Pacific Ave.
Santa Cruz, CA 95060
Phone: (831)459-0170
Fax: (831)459-0194
Free: 877-722-6271
Publisher's E-mail: info@sacnas.org
Freq: Semiannual. **Subscription Rates:** included in membership dues. **URL:** http://sacnas.org/about/stories/sacnas-news. **Mailing address:** PO Box 8526, Santa Cruz, CA 95061-8526. **Remarks:** Accepts advertising. **Circ:** 19000.

4249 ■ Santa Cruz Weekly
Metro Publishing Inc.
877 Cedar St., Ste. 147
Santa Cruz, CA 95060
Phone: (831)457-9000
Fax: (831)457-5828
Community newspaper. **Freq:** Weekly. **Key Personnel:** Traci Hukill, Editor; Neil Smyth, Manager, Circulation; Debra Whizin, Publisher. **URL:** http://www.santacruzweekly.com; http://www.metronews.com/presssubmiss.html. **Formerly**: Metro Santa Cruz. **Ad Rates:** 4C $2575. **Remarks:** Accepts advertising. **Circ:** Non-paid ■ **28000**.

4250 ■ Traveler's Guide
Santa Cruz County Conference and Visitors Council
303 Water St., Ste. 100
Santa Cruz, CA 95060
Phone: (831)425-1234
Fax: (831)425-1260
Free: 800-833-3494
Magazine featuring business and tourist guides to Santa Cruz County. **Freq:** Annual. **Subscription Rates:** Free; $6 Individuals shipping fee for all international orders. **URL:** http://www.santacruzca.org/partners/publications.php. **Remarks:** Accepts advertising. **Circ:** (Not Reported).

4251 ■ FRSC-FM - 101.1
PO Box 7811
Santa Cruz, CA 95061
Phone: (831)427-3772
Email: frsc@freakradio.org
Format: Information; News; Hip Hop; Alternative/New Music/Progressive; Reggae. **Operating Hours**: Continuous. **Ad Rates:** Advertising accepted; rates available upon request. **URL:** http://www.freakradio.org.

4252 ■ KSCO-AM - 1080
2300 Portola Dr.
Santa Cruz, CA 95062
Phone: (831)475-1080
Format: News; Talk. **Networks:** AP. **Owner:** Zwerling Broadcasting System Ltd., at above address, Santa Cruz, CA. **Founded:** 1947. **Operating Hours**: Continuous. **Key Personnel:** Michael Zwerling, Owner; Rosemary Chalmers, Dir. of Programs; Bill Graff, Dir. of Production, Tech. Dir.; Carol Stafford, Bus. Mgr., Traffic Mgr. **Local Programs**: *Alex Jones*, Monday Thursday Tuesday Wednesday Friday Sunday 8:00 p.m. - 9:30 p.m. 9:00 p.m. - 9:30 p.m.; *Good Morning Monterey Bay*, Monday Tuesday Wednesday Thursday Friday 6:00 a.m. - 9:00 a.m. **Wattage**: 10,000 Day ; 5,000 Night. **Ad Rates:** Noncommercial. **URL:** http://www.ksco.com.

4253 ■ KZSC-FM - 88.1
1156 High St.
Santa Cruz, CA 95064
Phone: (831)459-2811
Format: Eclectic. **Operating Hours**: Continuous. **Wattage**: 1,250. **Ad Rates:** Advertising accepted; rates available upon request. **URL:** http://www.kzsc.org.

SANTA MARIA

Santa Barbara Co. Santa Barbara Co. (SW). 75 m NW of Santa Barbara. Manufactures tire molds, electrical equipment power control cables, flexible cauplings, machine tools, aluminum products, frozen food processing, sugar refinery, Oil refining, & drilling. Cattle ranches. Vegetable farming.

4254 ■ Cessna Pilots Association
Cessna Pilots Association
3409 Corsair Cir.
Santa Maria, CA 93455
Phone: (805)934-0493
Free: 800-343-6416
Freq: Monthly. **Subscription Rates:** Included in membership. **Alt. Formats:** PDF. **URL:** http://www.cessna.org. **Circ:** (Not Reported).

4255 ■ Santa Maria Times
Santa Maria Times
3200 Skyway Dr.
Santa Maria, CA 93455
Phone: (805)739-2200
Free: 888-422-8822
Daily newspaper. **Freq:** Daily. **Print Method:** Offset. **Cols./Page:** 6. **Col. Width:** 21 1/2 nonpareils. **Col. Depth:** 301 agate lines. **Key Personnel:** Cynthia Schur, Publisher, phone: (805)739-2154. **Subscription Rates:** $8 Individuals full access per month. **URL:** http://santamariatimes.com. **Ad Rates:** GLR $1.70; BW $2,160.75; 4C $2,540.75; SAU $18.10; PCI $16.75. **Remarks:** Accepts advertising. **Circ:** Mon.-Sat. ★**16567**, Sun. ★**17895**, Thurs. ★**20729**.

4256 ■ KBID-AM - 1350
121 W Alvin Ave.
Santa Maria, CA 93458
Format: Oldies. **Key Personnel:** Roger Fessler, Gen. Mgr. **Ad Rates:** Noncommercial.

4257 ■ KBOX-FM - 104.1
2325 Skyway Dr., Ste. J
Santa Maria, CA 93455
Phone: (805)922-1041
Fax: (805)928-3069
Owner: American General Media, PO Box 2700, Bakersfield, CA 93303, Ph: (661)328-0118, Fax: (661)328-1648. **Founded:** 1968. **Formerly**: KLPC-FM. **ADI**: Santa Barbara-Santa Maria-San Luis Obispo,CA. **Key Personnel:** Rich Watson, Gen. Mgr., rwatson@americangeneralmedia.com. **Wattage**: 3,300 ERP. **Ad Rates:** Advertising accepted; rates available upon request. $27 for 30 seconds; $30 for 60 seconds. **URL:** http://www.americangeneralmedia.com/station.html?id=20.

4258 ■ KCOY-TV - 12
1211 W McCoy Ln.
Santa Maria, CA 93455
Phone: (805)925-1200
Format: Commercial TV. **Networks:** CBS. **Owner:** iHeartMedia Inc., 200 E Basse Rd., San Antonio, TX 78209, Ph: (210)832-3314. **Operating Hours**: 6 a.m.-2:07 a.m. **ADI**: Santa Barbara-Santa Maria-San Luis Obispo,CA. **Key Personnel:** John Zuchelli, News Dir. **Ad Rates:** Noncommercial. **URL:** http://www.keyt.com.

KGDP-AM - See Orcutt

4259 ■ KHFR-FM - 103.5
290 Hegenberger Rd.
Oakland, CA 94621
Free: 800-543-1495
Email: info@familyradio.org
Format: Religious. **Owner:** Family Stations Inc., 290 Hegenberger Rd., Oakland, CA 94621, Free: 800-543-1495. **Wattage**: 100. **URL:** http://www.familyradio.org.

4260 ■ KLMM-FM - 94.1
312 E Mill St., Ste. 302
Santa Maria, CA 93454-4425
Phone: (805)928-9796
Fax: (805)928-4896
Format: Hispanic. **Wattage**: 340. **URL:** http://www.radiolazer.com/homepage.php.

4261 ■ KPAT-FM - 95.7
2325 Skyway Dr., Ste. J
Santa Maria, CA 93455
Fax: (805)928-3069
Free: 866-957-2328
Format: Hip Hop; Blues; Urban Contemporary. **Owner:** American General Media, PO Box 2700, Bakersfield, CA 93303, Ph: (661)328-0118, Fax: (661)328-1648. **Wattage**: 3,300. **Ad Rates:** Advertising accepted; rates available upon request. **URL:** http://www.957thebeatfm.com.

4262 ■ KRAZ-FM
1101 S Broadway
Santa Maria, CA 93454
Format: Top 40; Country. **Founded:** 1969. **Wattage**: 065 ERP.

4263 ■ KRQK-FM - 100.3
2325 Skyway Dr., Ste. J
Santa Maria, CA 93455
Phone: (805)922-1041
Format: Hispanic; Classic Rock. **Owner:** Jaime Bonilla Valdez, 269 H Street 3rd Floor, Chula Vista, CA 91910, Ph: (619)429-5877. **Formerly**: KRQK FM Radio Aguila. **Operating Hours**: Satellite & local. **Wattage**: 3,700. **Ad Rates:** $17-19 for 30 seconds; $20-27 for 60 seconds. **URL:** http://www.1003laley.com.

4264 ■ KSNI-FM - 102.5
2325 Skyway Dr., Ste. J
Santa Maria, CA 93455
Phone: (805)925-2582
Fax: (805)928-1544
Free: 877-546-JOBS
Format: Country. **Networks:** Westwood One Radio. **Founded:** 1946. **Operating Hours**: Continuous. **Key Personnel:** Ron Roy, Regional VP, ronroy@edbroadcasters.com; Jay Turner, Dir. of Programs, jayturner@sunnycountry.com. **Wattage**: 10,000. **Ad Rates:** Noncommercial. **URL:** http://www.sunnycountry.com.

4265 ■ KTAP-AM
718 E Chapel
Santa Maria, CA 93454
Phone: (805)928-4334
Fax: (805)349-2765
Format: Hispanic. **Networks:** Independent. **Founded:** 1962. **Key Personnel:** Enrique Uribe, Contact. **Wattage**: 470 Day; 026 Night. **Ad Rates:** $25 per unit.

4266 ■ KTAS-TV - 33
330 W Carmen Ln.
Santa Maria, CA 93458
Phone: (805)928-7700
Email: ktastv@fix.net
Format: Commercial TV; Hispanic. **Networks:** Telemundo. **Owner:** R & C Palazuelos, at above address. **Wattage**: 80,400 ERP. **Ad Rates:** Noncommercial.

4267 ■ K216FQ-FM - 91.1
PO Box 391
Twin Falls, ID 83303
Fax: (208)736-1958
Free: 800-357-4226
Format: Religious; Contemporary Christian. **Owner:** CSN International, PO Box 391, Twin Falls, ID 83303, Ph: (208)736-1958, Fax: (208)736-1958, Free: 800-357-4226. **URL:** http://www.csnradio.com.

4268 ■ KUHL-AM - 1440
211 E Fesler
Santa Maria, CA 93456
Phone: (805)922-7727
Fax: (805)349-0265
Format: Talk; News; Information. **Networks:** ABC. **Owner:** El Dorado Broadcasters, 12370 Hesperia Rd., Ste. 17, Victorville, CA 92395-5808, Ph: (760)241-1313, Fax: (760)241-0205; Knight Broadcasting Inc., 1101 S Broadway, Ste. C, Santa Maria, CA 93455, Ph: (805)922-7727, Fax: (805)349-0265; Roger Blaemire, at above address. **Founded:** 1946. **Formerly**: KSMA-AM; KNEZ-AM; Mega Formula Broadcasting; KCLL-AM. **Operating Hours**: Continuous. **ADI**: Santa Barbara-Santa Maria-San Luis Obispo,CA. **Wattage**: 5,000 day; 1,000 night. **Ad Rates:** $15-30 for 30 seconds; $9-22 for 30 seconds;

Circulation: ★ = AAM; △ or • = BPA; ♦ = CAC; ❑ = VAC; ⊕ = PO Statement; ‡ = Publisher's Report; Boldface figures = swom; Light figures = estimated.

$15-35 for 30 seconds; $17-35 for 60 seconds; $20-40 for 60 seconds. **Mailing address:** PO Box 1964, Santa Maria, CA 93456. **URL:** http://www.am1440.com.

4269 ■ KXFM-FM - 99.1
2215 Skyway Dr.
Santa Maria, CA 93455
Phone: (805)925-2582
Fax: (805)928-1554
Format: Classic Rock. **Owner:** El Dorado Broadcasters, 12370 Hesperia Rd., Ste. 17, Victorville, CA 92395-5808, Ph: (760)241-1313, Fax: (760)241-0205. **Founded:** 1946. **Operating Hours**: Continuous. **ADI**: Santa Barbara-Santa Maria-San Luis Obispo,CA. **Key Personnel:** Jennifer Grant, Operations Mgr. **Wattage**: 50,000 ERP. **Ad Rates:** $15-30 for 30 seconds; $17-35 for 60 seconds. **URL:** http://www.991kxfm.com.

SANTA MONICA

Los Angeles Co. Los Angeles Co. (S). On Pacific Ocean, 16 m W of Los Angeles. Santa Monica College. Residential. Beach resort. Manufactures tools, dies, cosmetics, electronics, lubricating equipment.

4270 ■ Bel-Air View
Westside Today L.L.C.
3435 Ocean Park Blvd., Ste. 210
Santa Monica, CA 90405
Phone: (310)310-2637
Fax: (424)744-8821
Community newspaper. **Freq:** Monthly. **URL:** http://www.westsidetoday.com. **Remarks:** Advertising accepted; rates available upon request. **Circ:** (Not Reported).

4271 ■ Beverly Hills 90210
Westside Today L.L.C.
3435 Ocean Park Blvd., Ste. 210
Santa Monica, CA 90405
Phone: (310)310-2637
Fax: (424)744-8821
Community newspaper. **Freq:** Monthly. **URL:** http://westsidetoday.com/2008/09/02/90210-is-back. **Remarks:** Advertising accepted; rates available upon request. **Circ:** (Not Reported).

4272 ■ Brentwood News
Westside Today L.L.C.
3435 Ocean Park Blvd., Ste. 210
Santa Monica, CA 90405
Phone: (310)310-2637
Fax: (424)744-8821
Community newspaper. **Freq:** Semiweekly (Tues. and Fri.). **Print Method:** Offset. **Key Personnel:** Jeffrey Hall, Editor-in-Chief, Publisher. **Subscription Rates:** $36.87 Individuals. **URL:** http://westsidetoday.com/?s=brentwood. **Remarks:** Advertising accepted; rates available upon request. **Circ:** 3728.

4273 ■ Dental Practice Report
Advanstar Holdings Inc.
2450 Colorado Ave., Ste. 300 E
Santa Monica, CA 90404
Phone: (310)857-7500
Fax: (310)857-7510
Free: 800-225-4569
Publisher's E-mail: info@advanstar.com
Periodical covering dental practice and clinical management. **Freq:** Monthly. **Key Personnel:** Daniel Mc Cann, Senior Editor, phone: (847)716-8183, fax: (847)716-8102; Renee Knight, Associate Editor, phone: (847)716-8107, fax: (847)716-8102; Tom Delaney, Publisher, phone: (847)716-8189, fax: (847)716-8195. **URL:** http://www.dentalproductsreport.com; http://practicemanagement.dentalproductsreport.com. **Remarks:** Accepts advertising. **Circ:** (Not Reported).

4274 ■ Ergonomics in Design: The Quarterly of Human Factors Applications
Human Factors and Ergonomics Society
1124 Montana Ave., Ste. B
Santa Monica, CA 90403-1617
Phone: (310)394-1811
Fax: (310)394-2410
Publisher's E-mail: info@hfes.org
Peer-reviewed journal publishing articles in human factors or ergonomics concerned with the usability of products, systems, tools and environments. **Freq:** Quarterly. **Key Personnel:** Carol Stuart-Buttle. **ISSN:** 1064-8046 (print). **Subscription Rates:** $180 Institutions print and E-access; $198 Institutions Backfile Lease, Combined Plus Backfile (Current Volume Print & All Online Content); $137 Institutions E-access; $155 Institutions Backfile Lease, E-access Plus Backfile (All Online Content) ; $136 Institutions E-access (Content through 1998); $153 Institutions print; $115 Individuals print and e-access; $42 Institutions single print issue; $37 Individuals single print issue. **URL:** http://www.hfes.org/Publications/ProductDetail.aspx?ProductID=36. **Mailing address:** PO Box 1369, Santa Monica, CA 90406-1369. **Remarks:** Accepts advertising. **Circ:** 5,400.

4275 ■ Formulary
Advanstar Holdings Inc.
2450 Colorado Ave., Ste. 300 E
Santa Monica, CA 90404
Phone: (310)857-7500
Fax: (310)857-7510
Free: 800-225-4569
Publisher's E-mail: info@advanstar.com
Magazine for physicians, pharmacists and other professionals who are involved with drug therapy decision making in hospitals and other managed care settings. **Freq:** Monthly. **Print Method:** Web Offset. **Trim Size:** 8 x 10.75. **Cols./Page:** 3. **Col. Width:** 26 nonpareils. **Col. Depth:** 140 agate lines. **Key Personnel:** Julie Miller, Editor-in-Chief; James Granato, Publisher; Tracey Walker, Managing Editor, phone: (440)891-2732; David Calabrese, Editor. **URL:** http://formularyjournal.modernmedicine.com. **Remarks:** Accepts advertising. **Circ:** (Not Reported).

4276 ■ Grammy Magazine
National Academy of Recording Arts and Sciences
3030 Olympic Blvd.
Santa Monica, CA 90404
Phone: (310)392-3777
Fax: (310)392-2188
Magazine featuring a series of lists spanning a variety of entertaining GRAMMY and music-related categories. **Freq:** Periodic. **URL:** http://www.grammy.com/news/grammy-magazine-the-list-issue. **Remarks:** Advertising not accepted. **Circ:** (Not Reported).

4277 ■ Human Factors
Human Factors and Ergonomics Society
1124 Montana Ave., Ste. B
Santa Monica, CA 90403-1617
Phone: (310)394-1811
Fax: (310)394-2410
Publisher's E-mail: info@hfes.org
Freq: 8/year. **Subscription Rates:** $849 Institutions print and e-access; $934 Institutions Backfile Lease, Combined Plus Backfile (Current Volume Print & All Online Content); $764 Institutions E-access; $849 Institutions E-access Plus Backfile (All Online Content); 2381 Institutions E-access (Content through 1998); $832 Institutions print ; $508 Individuals print and E-access; $114 Institutions single print issue; $83 Individuals single print issue. **URL:** http://www.hfes.org/Publications/ProductDetail.aspx?ProductID=1. **Mailing address:** PO Box 1369, Santa Monica, CA 90406-1369. **Remarks:** Advertising not accepted. **Circ:** (Not Reported).

4278 ■ Kitten
Kitten Media
1725 Ocean Front Walk, Ste. 614
Santa Monica, CA 90401
Publication E-mail: info@kittenmag.com
Fashion magazine. **Freq:** Monthly. **URL:** http://www.kittenmag.com. **Remarks:** Accepts advertising. **Circ:** (Not Reported).

4279 ■ LCGC Asia Pacific
Advanstar Holdings Inc.
2450 Colorado Ave., Ste. 300 E
Santa Monica, CA 90404
Phone: (310)857-7500
Fax: (310)857-7510
Free: 800-225-4569
Publisher's E-mail: info@advanstar.com
Periodical covering chromatography and the separation sciences throughout Asia. **Freq:** Quarterly. **Key Personnel:** Alasdair Matheson, Editor; Andrew Davies, Publisher. **URL:** http://www.chromatographyonline.com/lcgc-europe-and-lcgc-asia-pacific-editorial-advisory-board. **Remarks:** Accepts advertising. **Circ:** (Not Reported).

4280 ■ LCGC Europe: Solutions for Separation Scientists
Advanstar Holdings Inc.
2450 Colorado Ave., Ste. 300 E
Santa Monica, CA 90404
Phone: (310)857-7500
Fax: (310)857-7510
Free: 800-225-4569
Publisher's E-mail: info@advanstar.com
Publication covering chromatography and the separation sciences in Europe. **Freq:** Monthly. **Key Personnel:** Andrew Davies, Publisher; Alasdair Matheson, Editor. **URL:** http://www.chromatogr aphyonline.com/lcgc/issue/issueList.jsp?id=2555. **Remarks:** Accepts advertising. **Circ:** (Not Reported).

4281 ■ License!
Advanstar Holdings Inc.
2450 Colorado Ave., Ste. 300 E
Santa Monica, CA 90404
Phone: (310)857-7500
Fax: (310)857-7510
Free: 800-225-4569
Publisher's E-mail: info@advanstar.com
Periodical covering for retailers, licensees, manufacturers, wholesalers and distributors. **Freq:** Bimonthly. **Key Personnel:** Carissa Simmerman, Advisor. **URL:** http://www.licensemag.com/license-global. **Circ:** Combined 33,000.

4282 ■ License! Europe
Advanstar Holdings Inc.
2450 Colorado Ave., Ste. 300 E
Santa Monica, CA 90404
Phone: (310)857-7500
Fax: (310)857-7510
Free: 800-225-4569
Publisher's E-mail: info@advanstar.com
Periodical covering for retailers, licensees, manufacturers, wholesalers and distributors in the European market. **Freq:** Monthly. **Key Personnel:** Tony Lisanti, Editor-in-Chief, phone: (212)951-6740; Bernadette Casey, Executive Editor, phone: (212)951-6695; Sam Phillips, Editor. **URL:** http://www.brandlicensing.eu/brand-licensing-europe; http://www.licensemag.com/license-global/category/82. **Remarks:** Accepts advertising. **Circ:** Controlled △**33000**.

4283 ■ Living Buddhism
Soka Gakkai International-United States of America
606 Wilshire Blvd.
Santa Monica, CA 90401
Phone: (310)260-8900
Fax: (310)260-8917
Publisher's E-mail: mail-for-sgi-usa@sgi-usa.org
Freq: Monthly. **URL:** http://www.sgi-usa.org/study-resources/world-tribune/. **Remarks:** Advertising not accepted. **Circ:** 18000.

4284 ■ Motor Age
Advanstar Holdings Inc.
2450 Colorado Ave., Ste. 300 E
Santa Monica, CA 90404
Phone: (310)857-7500
Fax: (310)857-7510
Free: 800-225-4569
Publisher's E-mail: info@advanstar.com
Magazine serving the automotive service industry. **Founded:** 1899. **Freq:** Monthly. **Print Method:** Web offset. **Trim Size:** 8 x 10 3/4. **Cols./Page:** 3. **Key Personnel:** Tschanen Niederkohr, Managing Editor; Larry Silvey, Editor-in-Chief; Chris Miller, Senior Editor. **Subscription Rates:** $70 Individuals; $106 Other countries. **URL:** http://www.searchautoparts.com/motorage. **Ad Rates:** BW $14,480; 4C $16,970. **Remarks:** Accepts advertising. **Circ:** Paid 1111, Non-paid 142036.

4285 ■ Ophthalmology Times: All the Clinical News in Sight
Advanstar Holdings Inc.
2450 Colorado Ave., Ste. 300 E
Santa Monica, CA 90404
Phone: (310)857-7500
Fax: (310)857-7510
Free: 800-225-4569
Publisher's E-mail: info@advanstar.com
Magazine for ophthalmic community. **Freq:** Semimonthly. **Print Method:** Offset. **Trim Size:** 10 3/4 x 14 1/2. **Cols./Page:** 4. **Col. Width:** 27 nonpareils. **Col.**

Depth: 196 agate lines. **Key Personnel:** Peter J. McDonnell, MD, Editor; Lauri Jorgensen, Publisher, phone: (732)346-3013; Erin Schlussel, Account Manager, phone: (732)346-3078; Leo Avila, Associate Publisher, phone: (732)346-3067. **Subscription Rates:** $263 Individuals other countries; $200 Individuals U.S., Canada & Mexico; $20 Single issue U.S., Canada & Mexico. **URL:** http://ophthalmologytimes.modernmedicine.com; http://ubmadvanstar.com. **Remarks:** Accepts advertising. **Circ:** Controlled △**43291**.

4286 ■ Pharmaceutical Executive Europe
Advanstar Holdings Inc.
2450 Colorado Ave., Ste. 300 E
Santa Monica, CA 90404
Phone: (310)857-7500
Fax: (310)857-7510
Free: 800-225-4569
Publisher's E-mail: info@advanstar.com
Periodical covering for Europe's senior pharmaceutical executives. **Freq:** Semiannual. **Key Personnel:** William Looney, Editor-in-Chief; Jeff Schindler, Managing Editor; Walter Armstrong, Senior Editor. **Subscription Rates:** Free to qualified subscribers. **URL:** http://www.pharmexec.com. **Formerly:** European Pharmaceutical Executive. **Circ:** (Not Reported).

4287 ■ Pharmaceutical Technology Europe
Advanstar Holdings Inc.
2450 Colorado Ave., Ste. 300 E
Santa Monica, CA 90404
Phone: (310)857-7500
Fax: (310)857-7510
Free: 800-225-4569
Publisher's E-mail: info@advanstar.com
Periodical serving Europe's pharmaceutical and biopharmaceutical manufacturing industry. **Freq:** Monthly. **Key Personnel:** Bibiana Campos-Seijo, Editor; Corrine Lawrence, Associate Editor; Andy Davies, Publisher. **Subscription Rates:** $185 Individuals; $331 Two years; $263 Canada and Mexico; $458 Canada and Mexico 2 years; $55 Individuals back issue; $85 Individuals Canada/intl back issue. **URL:** http://www.pharmtech.com/pharmtech/About-Us/static/detail/429627. **Remarks:** Accepts advertising. **Circ:** △**18,000**.

4288 ■ RAND Journal of Economics
RAND Corp.
1776 Main St.
Santa Monica, CA 90401-3208
Phone: (310)393-0411
Fax: (310)393-4818
Publication E-mail: rje@rand.org
Journal supports and encourages research in the behavior of regulated industries, the economic analysis of organizations, and, more generally, applied microeconomics. Both empirical and theoretical manuscripts in law and economics are encouraged. **Founded:** 1970. **Freq:** Quarterly. **Print Method:** Offset. **Trim Size:** 6 7/8 x 10. **Cols./Page:** 1. **Col. Width:** 65 nonpareils. **Col. Depth:** 125 1/2 agate lines. **Key Personnel:** James R. Hosek, Editor-in-Chief; Judith Chevalier, Editor; Andrew Daughety, Associate Editor; Mark Armstrong, Editor; Niko Matouschek, Associate Editor. **ISSN:** 0741-6261 (print). **Subscription Rates:** $101 Individuals print + online; $92 Individuals online only; $38 Students print + online; $457 Institutions print + online; $398 Institutions online; €68 Individuals Euro zone, print + online; €62 Individuals Euro zone, online only; €25 Students Euro zone, print + online; €292 Institutions Euro zone, print + online; £53 Individuals non-Euro zone, print + online. **Alt. Formats:** PDF. **URL:** http://www.rje.org; http://onlinelibrary.wiley.com/journal/10.1111/(ISSN)1756-2171. **Formerly:** Bell Journal of Economics. **Mailing address:** PO Box 2138, Santa Monica, CA 90407-2138. **Remarks:** Advertising not accepted. **Circ:** Paid ‡2000, Non-paid ‡80.

4289 ■ Santa Monica College Corsair
Santa Monica Corsair
1900 Pico Blvd.
Santa Monica, CA 90405
Phone: (310)434-4340
Junior college newspaper. **Freq:** Weekly (Wed.). **Print Method:** Offset. **Cols./Page:** 6. **Col. Width:** 18 nonpareils. **Col. Depth:** 295 agate lines. **Key Personnel:** Jacob Hirsohn, Editor-in-Chief. **URL:** http://www.thecorsaironline.com. **Ad Rates:** GLR $11. **Remarks:** Accepts advertising. **Circ:** Free 5000.

4290 ■ Santa Monica Review
Santa Monica College
1900 Pico Blvd.
Santa Monica, CA 90405
Phone: (310)434-4000
Journal featuring literary fiction and non-fiction, including poetry. **Freq:** Semiannual. **Key Personnel:** Andrew Tonkovich, Editor. **Subscription Rates:** $12 Individuals; $7 Single issue. **URL:** http://www2.smc.edu/sm_review/default.htm. **Circ:** (Not Reported).

4291 ■ Spectroscopy
Advanstar Holdings Inc.
2450 Colorado Ave., Ste. 300 E
Santa Monica, CA 90404
Phone: (310)857-7500
Fax: (310)857-7510
Free: 800-225-4569
Publication E-mail: spectroscopyedit@advanstar.com
Periodical covering spectroscopic instrumentation and techniques. **Freq:** Monthly. **Key Personnel:** Edward Fantuzzi, Publisher; Laura Bush, Director, Editorial. **Subscription Rates:** Free to qualified subscribers. **URL:** http://www.spectroscopyonline.com. **Remarks:** Accepts advertising. **Circ:** △**24000**.

4292 ■ Tennis Magazine
Miller Publishing Group L.L.C.
1918 Main St., 3rd Fl.
Santa Monica, CA 90405
Phone: (310)893-5300
Tennis magazine. **Founded:** 1965. **Freq:** 6/year. **Print Method:** Offset. **Trim Size:** 8 x 10 7/8. **Cols./Page:** 3. **Col. Width:** 27 nonpareils. **Col. Depth:** 140 agate lines. **Key Personnel:** Stephen Tignor, Executive Editor; Peter Bodo, Senior Editor. **ISSN:** 0040-3423 (print). **Subscription Rates:** $10 Individuals; $30 Canada. **URL:** http://www.tennis.com/. **Ad Rates:** BW $38,700; 4C $58,050. **Remarks:** Accepts advertising. **Circ:** Paid ★**600000**.

4293 ■ Urology Times: The Leading Newsmagazine for Urologists
Advanstar Holdings Inc.
2450 Colorado Ave., Ste. 300 E
Santa Monica, CA 90404
Phone: (310)857-7500
Fax: (310)857-7510
Free: 800-225-4569
Publication E-mail: ut@advanstar.com
Newsmagazine (tabloid) for patient care urologists. **Freq:** Monthly. **Print Method:** Sheetfed Offset. **Trim Size:** 8 1/2 x 7 1/4. **Cols./Page:** 4. **Key Personnel:** Richard R. Kerr, Editor-in-Chief, phone: (440)891-2758; Patricia M. Fernberg, Managing Editor. **Subscription Rates:** $99 Individuals; $147 Canada and Mexico; $195 Other countries. **URL:** http://urologytimes.modernmedicine.com. **Remarks:** Advertising accepted; rates available upon request. **Circ:** △**11,107**.

4294 ■ Westside Today
Westside Today L.L.C.
3435 Ocean Park Blvd., Ste. 210
Santa Monica, CA 90405
Phone: (310)310-2637
Fax: (424)744-8821
Community newspaper. **Freq:** Monthly. **Key Personnel:** Valerie Westen, Managing Editor. **URL:** http://www.westsidetoday.com. **Remarks:** Advertising accepted; rates available upon request. **Circ:** (Not Reported).

4295 ■ WHERE Boston
Miller Publishing Group L.L.C.
1918 Main St., 3rd Fl.
Santa Monica, CA 90405
Phone: (310)893-5300
Consumer magazine covering local travel and tourism. **Freq:** Monthly. **Key Personnel:** Mark Miller, Publisher, phone: (617)476-2646. **Remarks:** Accepts advertising. **Circ:** (Not Reported).

4296 ■ WHERE Charleston
Miller Publishing Group L.L.C.
1918 Main St., 3rd Fl.
Santa Monica, CA 90405
Phone: (310)893-5300
Travel and tourism magazine focusing on the Charleston, SC area. **Freq:** Quarterly. **Key Personnel:** Michael Andrea, Publisher; Margaret Pilarski, Editor. **Remarks:** Accepts advertising. **Circ:** (Not Reported).

4297 ■ WHERE Chicago
Miller Publishing Group L.L.C.
1918 Main St., 3rd Fl.
Santa Monica, CA 90405
Phone: (310)893-5300
Consumer magazine covering travel and tourism in Chicago. **Freq:** Monthly. **Key Personnel:** Kathy Mitchell, Publisher, phone: (312)566-5221. **Remarks:** Advertising accepted; rates available upon request. **Circ:** (Not Reported).

4298 ■ WHERE Las Vegas
Miller Publishing Group L.L.C.
1918 Main St., 3rd Fl.
Santa Monica, CA 90405
Phone: (310)893-5300
Consumer magazine covering local travel and tourism. **Freq:** Monthly. **Key Personnel:** Courtney Fuhrmann, Publisher, phone: (702)731-4748. **URL:** http://classic.wheretraveler.com/classic/us/nv/las-vegas/where_archive; http://www.wheretraveler.com/las-vegas. **Remarks:** Accepts advertising. **Circ:** (Not Reported).

4299 ■ WHERE Los Angeles
Miller Publishing Group L.L.C.
1918 Main St., 3rd Fl.
Santa Monica, CA 90405
Phone: (310)893-5300
Consumer magazine covering travel and tourism in Los Angeles, CA. **Freq:** Monthly. **Key Personnel:** Jeff Levy, Publisher, phone: (310)280-2880. **URL:** http://wheretraveler.com/los-angeles. **Remarks:** Accepts advertising. **Circ:** (Not Reported).

4300 ■ WHERE Miami
Miller Publishing Group L.L.C.
1918 Main St., 3rd Fl.
Santa Monica, CA 90405
Phone: (310)893-5300
Consumer magazine covering local travel and tourism. **Freq:** Monthly. **Key Personnel:** JaDee Guidice, Associate Publisher, phone: (305)892-4343. **URL:** http://classic.wheretraveler.com/classic/us/fl/miami/where_archive; http://www.wheretraveler.com/miami. **Remarks:** Accepts advertising. **Circ:** (Not Reported).

4301 ■ WHERE New Orleans
Miller Publishing Group L.L.C.
1918 Main St., 3rd Fl.
Santa Monica, CA 90405
Phone: (310)893-5300
Consumer magazine covering local travel and tourism. **Freq:** Monthly. **Key Personnel:** Lois Harris Sutton, Publisher, phone: (504)522-6468. **Remarks:** Accepts advertising. **Circ:** (Not Reported).

4302 ■ WHERE New York
Miller Publishing Group L.L.C.
1918 Main St., 3rd Fl.
Santa Monica, CA 90405
Phone: (310)893-5300
Guide for visitors. **Freq:** Monthly. **Print Method:** Offset. Uses mats. **Cols./Page:** 3. **Col. Width:** 27 nonpareils. **Col. Depth:** 140 agate lines. **Key Personnel:** Merrie L. Davis, Publisher, phone: (212)636-2700; Pat Stacom, Business Manager. **Remarks:** Accepts advertising. **Circ:** (Not Reported).

4303 ■ WHERE Orange County
Miller Publishing Group L.L.C.
1918 Main St., 3rd Fl.
Santa Monica, CA 90405
Phone: (310)893-5300
Consumer magazine covering local travel and tourism. **Key Personnel:** Jeff Levy, Publisher, phone: (310)280-2880. **Remarks:** Accepts advertising. **Circ:** (Not Reported).

4304 ■ WHERE Phoenix/Scottsdale
Miller Publishing Group L.L.C.
1918 Main St., 3rd Fl.
Santa Monica, CA 90405
Phone: (310)893-5300
Consumer magazine covering local travel and tourism. **Freq:** Monthly. **Key Personnel:** Michelle Schneider, Publisher, phone: (480)481-9981. **Remarks:** Accepts advertising. **Circ:** (Not Reported).

4305 ■ WHERE Rome

Circulation: ★ = AAM; △ or • = BPA; ♦ = CAC; ❑ = VAC; ⊕ = PO Statement; ‡ = Publisher's Report; Boldface figures = sworn; Light figures = estimated.

Miller Publishing Group L.L.C.
1918 Main St., 3rd Fl.
Santa Monica, CA 90405
Phone: (310)893-5300
Travel and tourism magazine focusing on Rome, Italy. **URL:** http://www.wherome.it. **Remarks:** Accepts advertising. **Circ:** (Not Reported).

4306 ■ WHERE San Diego
Miller Publishing Group L.L.C.
1918 Main St., 3rd Fl.
Santa Monica, CA 90405
Phone: (310)893-5300
Travel and tourism magazine focusing on the San Diego, CA area. **Freq:** Quarterly. **Key Personnel:** Jeff Levy, Publisher, phone: (310)280-2880; Sarah Daoust, Editor. **Subscription Rates:** $16 Individuals. **Remarks:** Accepts advertising. **Circ:** (Not Reported).

4307 ■ WHERE San Francisco
Miller Publishing Group L.L.C.
1918 Main St., 3rd Fl.
Santa Monica, CA 90405
Phone: (310)893-5300
Consumer magazine covering tourist and travel information on San Francisco, California. **Freq:** Monthly. **Cols./Page:** 3. **Key Personnel:** Nikki Wood, Publisher, phone: (415)901-6260. **URL:** http://wheretraveler.com/classic/us/ca/san-francisco; http://www.wheretraveler.com/san-francisco/tp#. **Remarks:** Accepts advertising. **Circ:** (Not Reported).

4308 ■ WHERE Washington
Miller Publishing Group L.L.C.
1918 Main St., 3rd Fl.
Santa Monica, CA 90405
Phone: (310)893-5300
Consumer magazine covering tourist information for Washington, DC. **Key Personnel:** Courtney Fuhrmann, Vice President, phone: (702)731-4748. **URL:** http://www.wheretraveler.com/washington-dc. **Remarks:** Accepts advertising. **Circ:** Controlled 100000.

4309 ■ KBKO-AM - 1490
715 Broadway, Ste. 320
101 Convention Center Dr., Ste. P119
Santa Monica, CA 90401
Format: Hispanic. **ADI:** Santa Barbara-Santa Maria-San Luis Obispo,CA. **Wattage:** 1,000. **Ad Rates:** Noncommercial. **URL:** http://rinconbroadcasting.com.

4310 ■ KBLA-AM - 1580
747 E Green St.
Pasadena, CA 91101
Phone: (626)844-8882
Fax: (626)844-0156
Format: Urban Contemporary. **Networks:** Unistar. **Owner:** Multicultural Radio Broadcasting Inc., 27 William St., 11th Fl., New York, NY 10005, Ph: (212)966-1059, Fax: (212)966-9580. **Founded:** 1947. **Formerly:** KDAY-AM. **Operating Hours:** Continuous. **ADI:** Los Angeles (Corona & San Bernardino), CA. **Wattage:** 50,000. **Ad Rates:** $110.50-297.50 for 30 seconds; $130-350 for 60 seconds.

4311 ■ KCRI-FM - 89.3
1900 Pico Blvd.
Santa Monica, CA 90405
Phone: (310)450-5183
Format: Public Radio. **Ad Rates:** Noncommercial. **URL:** http://www.kcrw.com.

4312 ■ KCRU-FM - 89.1
1900 Pico Blvd.
Santa Monica, CA 90405
Phone: (310)450-5183
Fax: (310)450-7172
Format: Eclectic. **Ad Rates:** Noncommercial. **URL:** http://www.kcrw.com.

4313 ■ KCRW-FM - 89.9
1900 Pico Blvd.
Santa Monica, CA 90405
Phone: (310)450-5183
Fax: (310)450-7172
Free: 877-600-5279
Email: mail@kcrw.org
Format: Public Radio. **Simulcasts:** KCET. **Networks:** National Public Radio (NPR); Public Radio International (PRI). **Owner:** Santa Monica College, 1900 Pico Blvd., Santa Monica, CA 90405, Ph: (310)434-4000. **Founded:** 1948. **Operating Hours:** Continuous; 35% network, 65% local. **Key Personnel:** Jennifer Ferro, Gen. Mgr.; Steve Herbert, Chief Engineer; Mike Newport, Dir. of Operations, mike.newport@kcrw.org; Bob Carlson, Producer, bob.carlson@kcrw.org. **Local Programs:** *Good Food,* Saturday 11:00 a.m. - 12:00 p.m. **Wattage:** 7,000. **Ad Rates:** Underwriting available. **URL:** http://www.kcrw.com.

4314 ■ KCRY-FM - 88.1
1900 Pico Blvd.
Santa Monica, CA 90405
Phone: (310)450-5183
Fax: (310)450-7172
Format: Eclectic. **URL:** http://www.kcrw.com.

4315 ■ KMPC-AM - 1540
2800 28th St., No. 308
Santa Monica, CA 90405
Phone: (213)487-1300
Fax: (213)487-7455
Email: 1540theticket@1540theticket.com
Format: Sports. **Ad Rates:** Advertising accepted; rates available upon request. **URL:** http://www.radiokorea.com/company/contact.php?t=Address.

4316 ■ KVPA-FM - 101.1
2425 Olympic Blvd. W, Ste. 6000
Santa Monica, CA 90404
Phone: (310)447-3870
Format: Classic Rock. **Networks:** Westwood One Radio. **Founded:** 1992. **Operating Hours:** Continuous. **Key Personnel:** Jim Wilson; Charlie Trub, Gen. Mgr., Owner; Scott Campbell, Dir. of Programs; Teri Murphy, Traffic Mgr., Office Mgr.; John Ross, Chief Engineer. **Wattage:** 3,000. **Ad Rates:** $11-15 for 30 seconds; $13-18 for 60 seconds. **URL:** http://www.jose1011.com/contacto.

SANTA PAULA

Ventura Co. Ventura Co. (SW). 15 m E of Ventura. Manufactures plastics, paper cartons, plastic cups, airplane parts. Fruit packing, canning and drying, walnuts packed, oil refineries. Oil wells. Agriculture. Lemons, oranges. Grapefruit. Avocados.

4317 ■ KKZZ-AM - 1400
2284 S Victoria Ave., Ste. 1-A
Ventura, CA 93003
Phone: (805)656-1400
Fax: (805)644-4257
Format: Adult Contemporary. **Networks:** Westwood One Radio; CNN Radio. **Owner:** Gold Coast Broadcasting, 2284 Victoria Ave., Ste. 2-G, Ventura, CA 93003, Ph: (805)289-1400, Fax: (805)644-7906. **Founded:** 1948. **Operating Hours:** Continuous. **Key Personnel:** Carl Goldman, Gen. Mgr.; Dan Carter, Sales Mgr.; Tom Spence, Operations Mgr. **Wattage:** 1,000.

SANTA ROSA

Sonoma Co. Sonoma Co. (NW). 52 m NW of San Francisco. Fruit canning and drying, wineries, bottling, plating machine works, Shoes, lumber, chemical products, optical coating laboratories, electronics. Agriculture. Apples, grapes. Dairying.

4318 ■ Bike Monkey
Bike Monkey L.L.C.
PO Box 5318
Santa Rosa, CA 95402
Phone: (707)478-9034
Fax: (707)540-6210
Publisher's E-mail: ads@bikemonkey.net
Magazine featuring biking lifestyle. **Freq:** Quarterly. **Trim Size:** 7.5 x 8.75. **Key Personnel:** Carlos Perez, Coordinator, Events, Editor-in-Chief, Publisher; Cheryl Wallace, Manager, Operations; Greg Fisher, Editor. **URL:** http://www.bikemonkey.net. **Remarks:** Accepts advertising. **Circ:** (Not Reported).

4319 ■ Church History: Studies in Christianity and Culture
American Society of Church History
PO Box 2793
Santa Rosa, CA 95405-2793
Phone: (707)538-6005
Fax: (707)538-2166
Publisher's E-mail: asch@churchhistory.org
History of Christianitys and scholarly journal. **Freq:** Quarterly. **Print Method:** Offset. **Trim Size:** 6 x 9. **Cols./Page:** 1. **Col. Width:** 60 nonpareils. **Col. Depth:** 112 agate lines. **Key Personnel:** Tim McDonald, Senior Editor. **ISSN:** 0009-6407 (print). **URL:** http://www.churchhistory.org/church-history-journal. **Ad Rates:** BW $250. **Remarks:** Accepts advertising. **Circ:** ‡3123.

4320 ■ Creag Dhubh
Clan Macpherson Association
c/o Jean Macpherson Duffy, Chairman
6438 Stone Bridge Rd.
Santa Rosa, CA 95409
Publisher's E-mail: cma.vicechairman@clan-macpherson.org
Freq: Annual every spring. **Subscription Rates:** included in membership dues. **Alt. Formats:** DVD. **URL:** http://www.clan-macpherson.org/creagdhubh.html. **Remarks:** Advertising not accepted. **Circ:** (Not Reported).

4321 ■ The Food & Beverage International
Journal Publications Inc.
4343 Sonoma Hwy.
Santa Rosa, CA 95409
Publisher's E-mail: ewalsh@fbworld.com
Trade magazine covering the food and beverage industry. **Freq:** Bimonthly. **Trim Size:** 10 x 13. **Key Personnel:** Rodney Ruppert, Assistant; Ellen Walsh, Vice President; Michael Walsh, President. **URL:** http://www.fbworld.com. **Formerly:** The Food & Beverage Industry. **Ad Rates:** BW $4,932; 4C $5,482. **Remarks:** Accepts advertising. **Circ:** (Not Reported).

4322 ■ The Food & Beverage Journal
Journal Publications Inc.
4343 Sonoma Hwy.
Santa Rosa, CA 95409
Publisher's E-mail: ewalsh@fbworld.com
Trade magazine for the food and beverage industry in the western U.S. **Freq:** Bimonthly. **Trim Size:** 10 x 13. **Key Personnel:** Ellen Walsh, Editor-in-Chief; Michael Walsh, Publisher, Chief Executive Officer; Jason Barlow, Editor. **Subscription Rates:** $30 Individuals; $40 Two years. **Ad Rates:** BW $4,932; 4C $5,482. **Remarks:** Accepts advertising. **Circ:** Combined 27000.

4323 ■ Informing Science
Informing Science Institute
131 Brookhill Ct.
Santa Rosa, CA 95409-2764
Phone: (707)531-4925
Fax: (815)301-6785
Publication E-mail: editor@inform.nu
Peer-reviewed journal providing an understanding of the difficulties in informing clientele. **Key Personnel:** T. Grandon Gill, Associate Editor. **ISSN:** 1547--9684 (print); **EISSN:** 1521--4672 (electronic). **URL:** http://www.informingscience.org/Journals/InformingSciJ/Overview. **Remarks:** Accepts advertising. **Circ:** (Not Reported).

4324 ■ Interdisciplinary Journal of e-Skills and Lifelong Learning
Informing Science Institute
131 Brookhill Ct.
Santa Rosa, CA 95409-2764
Phone: (707)531-4925
Fax: (815)301-6785
Peer-reviewed journal that provides readers with coverage of developments in E-learning and Learning Objects. **Freq:** Annual. **Key Personnel:** Janice Whatley, Editor-in-Chief; Eli Cohen, Managing Editor; Thomas M. Connolly, Editor. **ISSN:** 2375--2084 (print); **EISSN:** 2375--2092 (electronic). **Subscription Rates:** $49.99 Individuals; Free online. **URL:** http://informingscience.org/Journals/IJELL/Overview. **Formerly:** Interdisciplinary Journal of Knowledge and Learning Objects. **Circ:** (Not Reported).

4325 ■ Issues in Informing Science & Information Technology
Informing Science Institute
131 Brookhill Ct.
Santa Rosa, CA 95409-2764
Phone: (707)531-4925
Fax: (815)301-6785
Magazine covering articles on Informing Science and Information Technology. **Freq:** Annual. **Key Personnel:** Eli B. Cohen, Editor-in-Chief. **ISSN:** 1547--5840 (print); **EISSN:** 1547--5867 (electronic). **URL:** http://www.informingscience.us/icarus/journals/iisit. **Remarks:** Advertising not accepted. **Circ:** (Not Reported).

4326 ■ Journal of the Russian Numismatic Society

Russian Numismatic Society
PO Box 3684
Santa Rosa, CA 95402
Phone: (707)527-1007
Fax: (707)527-1204
Publication E-mail: rnsjournals@gmail.com
Journal featuring: original articles; reports on auction results; reports on recent forgeries, with diagnostic details and; reviews of books on Russian numismatic subjects, including original works, translations, and reprints. **Freq:** Quarterly. **Subscription Rates:** $4. **URL:** http://www.russiannumismaticsociety.org. **Remarks:** Advertising not accepted. **Circ:** (Not Reported).

4327 ■ Maledicta: The International Journal of Verbal Aggression
International Maledicta Society
PO Box 14123
Santa Rosa, CA 95402-6123
Phone: (707)795-8178
Journal covering essays and glossaries of insults, curses, slurs, vulgarities and slang in all languages. **Freq:** Periodic. **Print Method:** Offset. **Trim Size:** 5 1/2 x 8 1/2. **Cols./Page:** 1. **Col. Width:** 4 inches. **Col. Depth:** 6 3/4 inches. **Key Personnel:** Dr. Reinhold Aman, Editor. **ISSN:** 0363--3659 (print). **URL:** http://aman.members.sonic.net/journal.html. **Remarks:** Advertising not accepted. **Circ:** Paid 2000.

4328 ■ Maledicta: The International Journal of Verbal Aggression
Maledicta: International Research Center for Verbal Aggression
PO Box 14123
Santa Rosa, CA 95402-6123
Phone: (707)795-8178
Journal covering essays and glossaries of insults, curses, slurs, vulgarities and slang in all languages. **Freq:** Periodic. **Print Method:** Offset. **Trim Size:** 5 1/2 x 8 1/2. **Cols./Page:** 1. **Col. Width:** 4 inches. **Col. Depth:** 6 3/4 inches. **Key Personnel:** Dr. Reinhold Aman, Editor. **ISSN:** 0363--3659 (print). **URL:** http://aman.members.sonic.net/journal.html. **Remarks:** Advertising not accepted. **Circ:** Paid 2000.

4329 ■ North Bay Biz
Gammon L.L.C.
3565 Airway Dr.
Santa Rosa, CA 95403-1605
Phone: (707)575-8282
Fax: (707)546-7368
Business to business magazine emphasizing coverage on the wine, financial, technology, telecommunications, building, and real estate industries in the North Bay Area, Sonoma, Marint Napa Counties. **Freq:** Monthly. **Print Method:** Web. **Trim Size:** 8 1/2 x 11. **Cols./Page:** 3. **Col. Width:** 2 5/16 inches. **Col. Depth:** 9 3/4 inches. **Key Personnel:** Norm Rosinski, Publisher; John P. Dennis, Chief Operating Officer. **USPS:** 097-770. **Subscription Rates:** $35 Individuals; $50 Two years; $65 Individuals 3 years. **URL:** http://www.northbaybiz.com. **Formerly:** Sonoma Business Magazine. **Remarks:** Advertising accepted; rates available upon request. **Circ:** Paid ⊕**8515**, Non-paid ⊕**5485**.

4330 ■ Northwesterner
Northwestern Pacific Railroad Historical Society
PO Box 667
Santa Rosa, CA 95402-0667
Publisher's E-mail: nwprrhs-sec@comcast.net
Historical journal covering railroads. **Freq:** Semiannual. **Key Personnel:** Fred Codoni, Editor. **Subscription Rates:** $5 Individuals print or PDF - back issues. **Alt. Formats:** PDF. **URL:** http://www.nwprrhs.org/publications.html. **Ad Rates:** BW $135; 4C $300. **Remarks:** Accepts advertising. **Circ:** Non-paid 700.

4331 ■ Nuestro Caballo
North American Peruvian Horse Association
PO Box 2187
Santa Rosa, CA 95405
Phone: (707)544-5807
Freq: Periodic. **Subscription Rates:** free for members. **Remarks:** Advertising not accepted. **Circ:** 1200.

4332 ■ The Press Democrat
The Press Democrat
427 Mendocino Ave.
Santa Rosa, CA 95402
Phone: (707)526-8570
Fax: (707)521-5330
Free: 800-675-5056
Publisher's E-mail: assts@pressdemocrat.com
General newspaper. **Freq:** Mon.-Sun. (morn.). **Print Method:** Offset. **Trim Size:** 13 x 21. **Cols./Page:** 6. **Col. Width:** 25 nonpareils. **Col. Depth:** 294 agate lines. **Key Personnel:** Catherine Barnett, Executive Editor, phone: (707)521-5202. **Subscription Rates:** $20 Individuals /month with online access. **URL:** http://www.pressdemocrat.com. **Feature Editors:** Joanne Derbort, *Features*, phone: (707)521-5403, joanne.derbort@pressdemocrat.com. **Mailing address:** PO Box 569, Santa Rosa, CA 95402. **Remarks:** Accepts advertising. **Circ:** Mon.-Fri. ★**78022**, Sat. ★**77887**, Sun. ★**78505**.

4333 ■ Savor Wine Country
The Press Democrat
427 Mendocino Ave.
Santa Rosa, CA 95402
Phone: (707)526-8570
Fax: (707)521-5330
Free: 800-675-5056
Publisher's E-mail: assts@pressdemocrat.com
Magazine covering wine, wineries, and dining. **Freq:** Quarterly. **Mailing address:** PO Box 569, Santa Rosa, CA 95402. **Ad Rates:** 4C $3,080. **Remarks:** Accepts advertising. **Circ:** Combined 42000.

4334 ■ Share Guide
Dennis & Janice Hughes
453 Benicia Dr.
Santa Rosa, CA 95409
Phone: (707)538-0558
Fax: (707)538-2204
Free: 877-488-4938
Publication E-mail: share@shareguide.com
Consumer magazine covering health and general interest information. **Freq:** Bimonthly. **Trim Size:** 8 1/2 x 11. **Key Personnel:** Janice Hughes, Publisher. **Subscription Rates:** Free. **Remarks:** Advertising accepted; rates available upon request. **Circ:** (Not Reported).

4335 ■ Sonoma Medicine
Sonoma County Medical Association
2901 Cleveland Ave., No. 202
Santa Rosa, CA 95403
Phone: (707)525-4375
Fax: (707)525-4328
Publisher's E-mail: info@scma.org
Professional magazine of the Sonoma County Medical Association. **Freq:** Quarterly. **Trim Size:** 8 1/2 x 11. **Cols./Page:** 3. **Key Personnel:** Steve Osborn, Editor, phone: (707)540-0101. **ISSN:** 1534--5386 (print). **Alt. Formats:** PDF. **URL:** http://www.nbcms.org/AboutUs/SonomaCountyMedicalAssociation/Magazine.aspx. **Formerly:** Sonoma County Physician. **Ad Rates:** BW $1,220; 4C $1,220. **Remarks:** Accepts advertising. **Circ:** Combined 1000.

4336 ■ The Urlar
Clan Macpherson Association
c/o Jean Macpherson Duffy, Chairman
6438 Stone Bridge Rd.
Santa Rosa, CA 95409
Publisher's E-mail: cma.vicechairman@clan-macpherson.org
Freq: Quarterly. **Key Personnel:** George McPherson, Editor. **Subscription Rates:** Included in membership. **URL:** http://www.clan-macpherson.org/us/urlar.html. **Remarks:** Advertising not accepted. **Circ:** (Not Reported).

4337 ■ Vineyard & Winery
Vineyard and Winery Management
PO Box 14459
Santa Rosa, CA 95402-6459
Phone: (707)577-7700
Fax: (707)577-7705
Free: 800-535-5670
Publisher's E-mail: feedback@vwm-online.com
Publication focusing on the production and marketing of wine. **Freq:** Bimonthly. **Print Method:** Offset. **Trim Size:** 8 1/4" x 11". **Cols./Page:** 3. **Col. Width:** 13 picas. **Col. Depth:** 10 picas. **Key Personnel:** Robert Merletti, Owner, Chairman, Chief Executive Officer, Publisher. **ISSN:** 1047-4951 (print). **Subscription Rates:** $37 Individuals; $67 Two years; $47 Canada and Mexico; $87 Canada and Mexico two years; $57 Other countries; $107 Other countries two years; $87 Other countries air; $97 Individuals three years; $127 Canada and Mexico three years; $157 Other countries three years; $247 Other countries air; $167 Other countries air; two years. **URL:** http://www.vwmmedia.com. **Ad Rates:** BW $1,859; 4C $2,984. **Remarks:** Accepts advertising. **Circ:** Paid 5385.

4338 ■ KBBF-FM - 89.1
PO Box 7189
Santa Rosa, CA 95407
Phone: (707)545-8833
Email: info@kbbf-fm.org
Format: Hispanic; Educational. **Owner:** Bilingual Broadcasting Foundation Inc. **Founded:** 1973. **Operating Hours:** Continuous. **Wattage:** 420 ERP. **Ad Rates:** Noncommercial. $18 for 30 seconds. **URL:** http://www.kbbf-fm.org.

4339 ■ KFGY-FM - 92.9
1410 Neotomas Ave., Ste. 200
Santa Rosa, CA 95405
Phone: (707)543-0100
Fax: (707)571-1097
Format: Country. **Networks:** Independent. **Owner:** Maverick Media, at above address. **Founded:** 1979. **Formerly:** KVVV-FM; KREO-FM; KLCQ-FM; KHTT-FM. **Operating Hours:** Continuous; 100% local. **Key Personnel:** Jim Murphy, Dir. of Programs, jimmurphy@maverick-media.ws; Stacy Hoblitzell, Music Dir., stacyhoblitzell@maverick-media.ws; Kevin Wodlinger, Sales Mgr. **Wattage:** 2,300. **Ad Rates:** Noncommercial. **URL:** http://www.froggy929.com.

4340 ■ KFTY-TV - 50
50 Twr., 533 Mendocino Ave.
Santa Rosa, CA 95401
Format: News; Sports. **Networks:** Independent. **Founded:** 1981. **Operating Hours:** Continuous. **Key Personnel:** John Burgess, Gen. Mgr., VP, john@metvbayarea.com; Rick Starkey, Operations Mgr., rick@metvbayarea.com. **Wattage:** 360. **Ad Rates:** Advertising accepted; rates available upon request.

4341 ■ KJZY-FM - 93.7
3392 Mendocino Ave.
Santa Rosa, CA 95403
Phone: (707)528-9393
Email: jazzcats@kjzy.com
Format: Jazz. **Key Personnel:** Patrick Stelzner, Dir. of Sales. **Ad Rates:** Advertising accepted; rates available upon request. **Mailing address:** PO Box 100, Santa Rosa, CA 95402. **URL:** http://www.kjzy.com.

4342 ■ KMGG-FM - 97.7
1275 Santa Rosa Ave.
Santa Rosa, CA 95404
Phone: (945)771-9221
Format: Country. **Networks:** Unistar. **Founded:** 1977. **Formerly:** KRJB-FM. **Operating Hours:** Continuous Sunday - Friday, 12:00 a.m. - 7:00 p.m. Saturday. **Key Personnel:** Kent Bjugstad, Gen. Mgr.; Pat Gallagher, Dir. of Pub. Prog. & Svcs.; Kevin Wodlinger, Sales Mgr. **Wattage:** 2,050 ERP. **Ad Rates:** $24-36 per unit. **URL:** http://www.977theriver.com.

4343 ■ KMHX-FM - 104.9
1410 Neotomas Ave., Ste. 200
Santa Rosa, CA 95405
Phone: (707)543-0100
Fax: (707)571-1097
Format: Contemporary Hit Radio (CHR); Oldies. **Operating Hours:** Continuous. **Ad Rates:** Advertising accepted; rates available upon request. **URL:** http://www.mix1049.com.

4344 ■ KNOB-FM - 96.7
3565 Standish Ave.
Santa Rosa, CA 95407
Phone: (707)284-9967
Fax: (707)588-0777
Format: Adult Contemporary. **Operating Hours:** Continuous. **Ad Rates:** Advertising accepted; rates available upon request. **URL:** http://www.96xonline.com.

4345 ■ KRRS-AM
PO Box 2277
Santa Rosa, CA 95405
Phone: (707)545-1460
Fax: (707)545-0112
Email: krrs@sonic.net
Format: Hispanic. **Networks:** UPI. **Owner:** Moon Broadcasting, Corp., 1200 W Venice Blvd., Los Angeles,

Circulation: ★ = AAM; △ or • = BPA; ♦ = CAC; ❑ = VAC; ⊕ = PO Statement; ‡ = Publisher's Report; Boldface figures = sworn; Light figures = estimated.

CA 90006, Ph: (213)745-6224. **Founded:** 1963. **Formerly**: KWFN-AM. **Wattage**: 1,000 Day; 033 Night. **Ad Rates:** Noncommercial.

4346 ■ KRSH-FM - 95.9
3565 Standish Ave.
Santa Rosa, CA 95407
Phone: (707)588-0707
Email: studio@krsh.com
Format: Eclectic. **Key Personnel:** Debbie Morton, Gen. Mgr., debbie@winecountryradio.net; Katie Vrooman, Contact, katie@winecountryradio.net. **Ad Rates:** Advertising accepted; rates available upon request. **URL:** http://www.krsh.com.

4347 ■ KSRO-AM - 1350
1410 Neotomas Ave., Ste. 200
Santa Rosa, CA 95405
Phone: (707)543-0100
Fax: (707)571-1097
Format: Talk; News. **Networks:** CNN Radio; NBC. **Owner:** Maverick Media, at above address. **Founded:** 1937. **Operating Hours**: Continuous. **ADI**: San Francisco-Oakland-San Jose. **Key Personnel:** Kent Bjugstad, Prog. Dir., kentbjugstad@maverick-media.ws. **Local Programs**: *The Danielle Lin Show*, Saturday 1:00 p.m. - 3:00 p.m. **Wattage**: 5,000. **Ad Rates:** Advertising accepted; rates available upon request. **URL:** http://www.ksro.com.

4348 ■ KSRT-FM - 107.1
5510 Skylane Blvd., Ste. 102
Santa Rosa, CA 95403
Phone: (707)284-3069
Fax: (707)284-3174
Format: Hispanic. **Owner:** Lazer Broadcasting Corp., 200 S A St., Ste. 400, Oxnard, CA 93030, Ph: (805)240-2070, Fax: (805)240-5960. **Key Personnel:** Alfredo Plascencia, CEO, alfredop@radiolazer.com. **URL:** http://www.radiolazer.com.

4349 ■ KSXY-FM - 100.9
3565 Standish Ave.
Santa Rosa, CA 95407
Phone: (707)588-0707
Fax: (707)588-0777
Format: Top 40. **Owner:** Sinclair Communications, 999 Waterside Dr., Ste. 500, Norfolk, VA 23510, Ph: (757)640-8500, Fax: (757)640-8552. **Operating Hours**: Continuous. **Wattage**: 2,500. **Ad Rates:** Advertising accepted; rates available upon request. **URL:** http://www.allthehits.fm.

4350 ■ KVRV-FM - 97.7
1410 Neotomas Ave., Ste. 200
Santa Rosa, CA 95405-7533
Phone: (707)636-0977
Fax: (707)571-1097
Format: Classic Rock. **Key Personnel:** Jeff Clark, Gen. Mgr., jeffclark@maverick-media.ws; Jon Snyder, Promotions Dir.; Kevin Wodlinger, Sales Mgr. **URL:** http://www.977theriver.com.

4351 ■ KXFX-FM - 101.7
1410 Neotomas Ave., Ste. 200
Santa Rosa, CA 95405
Phone: (707)543-0100
Fax: (707)571-1097
Format: Adult Contemporary. **Owner:** Maverick Media, at above address. **Founded:** 1988. **Formerly**: KVRE-FM. **Operating Hours**: Continuous. **ADI**: San Francisco-Oakland-San Jose. **Key Personnel:** Jon Snyder, Promotions Dir., jonsnyder@maverick-media.ws; Kent Bjugstad, Dir. of Mktg., Mktg. Mgr., kentbjugstad@maverick-media.ws. **Wattage**: 25,000 ERP. **Ad Rates:** Advertising accepted; rates available upon request.

4352 ■ KXTS-FM - 98.7
3565 Standish Ave.
Santa Rosa, CA 95407
Phone: (707)588-0707
Format: Ethnic; World Beat. **Operating Hours**: Continuous. **Wattage**: 2,650. **Ad Rates:** Advertising accepted; rates available upon request. **URL:** http://www.exitos987.com.

4353 ■ KZST-FM - 100.1
PO Box 100
Santa Rosa, CA 95402
Phone: (707)528-4434
Fax: (707)527-8216
Email: toms@kzst.com
Format: Adult Contemporary. **Networks:** Independent. **Founded:** 1971. **Operating Hours**: Continuous. **ADI**: San Francisco-Oakland-San Jose. **Key Personnel:** Tom Skinner, Gen. Mgr., toms@kzst.com; Brent Farris, Dir. of Programs, brent@kzst.com. **Wattage:** 6,000. **Ad Rates:** $45-90 for 30 seconds; $50-100 for 60 seconds. **URL:** http://www.kzst.com.

SAUSALITO

Marin Co. Marin Co. (W) 8 m NW of San Francisco. Residential.

4354 ■ Marin: Extraordinary Living
Marin Magazine
1 Harbor Dr., Ste. 208
Sausalito, CA 94965
Phone: (415)332-4800
Fax: (415)332-3048
Publisher's E-mail: subscriptions@marinmagazine.com
Magazine offers information about the San Francisco Bay area to affluent peoples. **Freq:** Monthly. **Trim Size:** 8 3/8 x 10 7/8. **Key Personnel:** Nikki Wood, Director, Editorial, President. **Subscription Rates:** $12 Individuals. **URL:** http://marinmagazine.com. **Remarks:** Accepts advertising. **Circ:** Non-paid △**34018**.

4355 ■ Smart Meetings: The Intelligent Way to Plan
Bright Business Media
475 Gate 5 Rd., Ste. 235
Sausalito, CA 94965
Phone: (415)339-9355
Publisher's E-mail: editor@smartmeetings.com
Magazine offering ways to plan professional meetings. **Freq:** Monthly. **Key Personnel:** Marin Bright, Founder, Chief Executive Officer. **Subscription Rates:** Free to qualified subscribers. **URL:** http://www.smartmeetings.com. **Ad Rates:** 4C $8,400. **Remarks:** Accepts advertising. **Circ:** Paid ‡40000.

SCOTIA

4356 ■ K272CH-FM - 102.3
PO Box 391
Twin Falls, ID 83303
Fax: (208)736-1958
Free: 800-357-4226
Format: Religious; Contemporary Christian. **Owner:** CSN International, PO Box 391, Twin Falls, ID 83303, Ph: (208)736-1958, Fax: (208)736-1958, Free: 800-357-4226. **Key Personnel:** Don Mills, Prog. Dir., Music Dir.; Kelly Carlson, Dir. of Engg.; Ray Gorney, Asst. Dir. **Wattage**: 140. **URL:** http://www.csnradio.com.

SCOTTS VALLEY

Santa Cruz Co. Santa Cruz (W) 7 m N of Santa Cruz. Residential.

4357 ■ Family Life Educator
Education, Training and Research Associates
100 Enterprise Way, Ste. G300
Scotts Valley, CA 95066
Phone: (831)438-4284
Free: 800-620-8884
Publisher's E-mail: gsa-info@etr.org
Freq: Quarterly. **ISSN:** 0732--9962 (print). **Subscription Rates:** $45 Individuals /year; $55 Institutions /year. **Remarks:** Advertising not accepted. **Circ:** 5000.

4358 ■ Press-Banner
Johnson Newspapers Inc.
5215 Scotts Valley Dr., Ste. F
Scotts Valley, CA 95066
Phone: (831)438-2500
Fax: (831)438-4114
Publication E-mail: info@pressbanner.com editor@pressbanner.com
Newspaper. **Freq:** Weekly (Wed.). **Print Method:** Offset. **Cols./Page:** 6. **Col. Width:** 26 nonpareils. **Col. Depth:** 294 agate lines. **Subscription Rates:** $52 Individuals /year. **URL:** http://www.pressbanner.com. **Formerly**: Scotts Valley Banner. **Remarks:** Accepts advertising. **Circ:** (Not Reported).

4359 ■ Santa Cruz Sentinel
Digital First Media
1800 Green Hills Rd., Ste. 210
Scotts Valley, CA 95066
Phone: (831)423-4242
Independent newspaper. **Founded:** June 14, 1856. **Freq:** Daily and Sun. (morn.). **Print Method:** Offset. **Cols./Page:** 6. **Col. Width:** 25 nonpareils. **Col. Depth:** 301 agate lines. **Subscription Rates:** $128.27 Individuals. **URL:** http://www.santacruzsentinel.com. **Formerly**: Santa Cruz County Sentinel. **Ad Rates:** GLR $1.44; BW $2,322; 4C $2,723; SAU $18. **Remarks:** Accepts advertising. **Circ:** Mon.-Sat. ★**24954**, Sun. ★**26013**.

SEAL BEACH

Orange Co. Orange Co. (S). On Pacific Ocean, 6 mi. SE of Long Beach. Retirement Community. Marine recreation; surfing.

4360 ■ The Leisure World Golden Rain News
The Leisure World Golden Rain News
PO Box 2338
Seal Beach, CA 90740
Phone: (562)430-0534
Publisher's E-mail: grf@lwsb.com
Official newspaper (tabloid) of the Golden Rain Foundation serving the retirement community of Seal Beach Leisure World. **Freq:** Weekly (Thurs.). **Print Method:** Offset. **Trim Size:** 11 3/8 x 17. **Cols./Page:** 5. **Col. Width:** 1 15/16 INS. **Col. Depth:** 16 inches. **Key Personnel:** David Saunders, Managing Editor. **Ad Rates:** BW $872; 4C $1,322; SAU $11.45; PCI $11.45. **Remarks:** Accepts advertising. **Circ:** Mon.-Sat. 9000.

SEASIDE

Monterey Co. Monterey Co. (W). On Pacific Ocean, 17 m SW of Salinas. Manufactures concrete blocks, molded products, patent medicines, fish canning equipment. Venetian blinds. Agriculture. Pears, apples, apricots.

4361 ■ Monterey County Weekly
Monterey County Weekly
668 Williams Ave.
Seaside, CA 93955
Phone: (831)394-5656
Publication E-mail: erik@mcweekly.com
Local entertainment newspaper. **Freq:** Weekly (Thurs.). **Key Personnel:** Mary Duan, Editor; Erik Cushman, Publisher; Bradley Zeve, Chief Executive Officer, Founder. **URL:** http://www.montereycountyweekly.com/. **Formerly**: Coast Weekly. **Ad Rates:** BW $1,875. **Remarks:** Accepts advertising. **Circ:** Free ■ **38951**, 37054.

4362 ■ KAZU-FM - 90.3
100 Campus Ctr., Bldg. 201, Rm. 317
Box 201
Seaside, CA 93955
Phone: (831)582-5298
Format: Public Radio. **Networks:** National Public Radio (NPR); Public Radio International (PRI); BBC World Service. **Owner:** California State University, Monterey Bay, 100 Campus Ctr., Seaside, CA 93955. **Founded:** 1977. **Operating Hours**: Continuous. **Key Personnel:** Mik Benedek, Gen. Mgr., mbenedek@kazu.org. **Wattage**: 3,100 ERP. **Ad Rates:** Noncommercial. Underwriting available. **URL:** http://www.kazu.org.

SEBASTOPOL

Sonoma Co. Sonoma Co. (NW). 7 m W of Santa Rosa. Fruit packing, canning and drying. Liquor, vinegar, pectin manufactured. Fruit, poultry, dairy farms. Apples, grapes, cherries.

4363 ■ Sonoma West Exchange
Sonoma West Publishers Inc.
135 South Main St.
Sebastopol, CA 95472
Phone: (707)823-7845
Publication E-mail: news@sonomawest.com
Shopper. **Freq:** Weekly (Wed.). **Print Method:** Offset. **Cols./Page:** 6. **Col. Width:** 18 nonpareils. **Col. Depth:** 294 agate lines. **Key Personnel:** Rollie Atkinson, Publisher. **Subscription Rates:** $50 Individuals In County (residents) - 1 year plus 3 months free; $75 Out of country 1 year plus 3 months free; $80 Individuals In County (residents) - 2 years; $125 Out of country 2 years; $50 Individuals online only for 1 year. **URL:** http://www.sonomawest.com. **Formerly**: Sebastopol Times & News Buyers Guide. **Remarks:** Accepts advertising. **Circ:** Free 11300.

4364 ■ Surface Design Journal

Surface Design Association
PO Box 360
Sebastopol, CA 95473-0360
Phone: (707)829-3110
Fax: (707)829-3285
Publisher's E-mail: info@surfacedesign.org
Freq: Quarterly. **Print Method:** Offset. **Trim Size:** 8 1/4 x 10 1/4. **Key Personnel:** Marci Rae Mcdade, Editor; Dale Moyer, Art Director. **ISSN:** 0197-4483 (print). **Subscription Rates:** $15 Single issue; Included in membership. **URL:** http://www.surfacedesign.org/publications.asp; http://www.surfacedesign.org/publications/sda-journal. **Ad Rates:** BW $542; 4C $1,199. **Remarks:** Accepts advertising. **Circ:** Combined 6900.

SELMA

Fresno Co. Fresno Co. (C). 15 m SE of Fresno. Residential. Glass making raisin packing plants, machinery, wineries. Fruit, truck, dairy farms. Grapes, cotton, beef cattle, poultry.

4365 ■ The Selma Enterprise
Lee Enterprises Inc.
2045 Grant St.
Selma, CA 93662
Phone: (559)896-1976
Community newspaper. **Freq:** Weekly (Wed.). **Print Method:** Offset. **Trim Size:** 14 x 21 3/4. **Cols./Page:** 6. **Col. Width:** 24 nonpareils. **Col. Depth:** 294 agate lines. **Key Personnel:** Davis Taylor, Publisher, phone: (559)583-2400. **Subscription Rates:** $7 Individuals per month - digital access only.; $7 Individuals starting price per month - full access (home delivery plus unlimited access). **URL:** http://www.hanfordsentinel.com/selma_enterprise. **Mailing address:** PO Box 100, Selma, CA 93662-0100. **Remarks:** Accepts advertising. **Circ:** ‡4700.

SHAFTER

Kern Co. Kern Co. (S). 18 m NW of Bakersfield. Recreation. Potatoes, onions packed, cotton gins. Cement products, fertilizer manufactured. Truck, fruit, almond vineyards, poultry farms.

4366 ■ Shafter Press
Shafter Press
406 Central Ave.
Shafter, CA 93263
Phone: (661)746-4942
Community newspaper. **Freq:** Weekly (Wed.). **Print Method:** Offset. **Cols./Page:** 6. **Col. Width:** 12 picas. **Col. Depth:** 21 inches. **Key Personnel:** Donald L. Reed, Publisher. **USPS:** 419-700. **Subscription Rates:** $19 Individuals; $21 Out of area; $24 Out of area. **URL:** http://www.shafterpress.net. **Ad Rates:** BW $693; PCI $6.50. **Remarks:** Accepts advertising. **Circ:** Combined 7382.

4367 ■ KKBB-FM - 97.7
5055 California Ave., Ste. 230
Shafter, CA 93263
Phone: (805)326-8000
Fax: (805)326-0937
Format: Album-Oriented Rock (AOR). **Owner:** Kohl Communications Associations Ltd., at above address. **Founded:** 1972. **Key Personnel:** Chuck McKay, Contact; Rick Dames, Gen. Mgr.; Jodie Moser, Gen. Sales Mgr; Chuck McKay, Contact. **Wattage:** 3,000.

SHERMAN OAKS

Los Angeles Co. (SW). Surburban residential section of Los Angeles.

4368 ■ American Fitness
American Fitness
15250 Ventura Blvd., Ste. 200
Sherman Oaks, CA 91403
Free: 877-968-7263
Magazine covering trends in fitness, exercise programs, injury prevention and nutrition. **Freq:** 6/year. **Print Method:** Offset. **Trim Size:** 8 1/8 x 10 7/8. **Cols./Page:** 5. **Key Personnel:** Meg Jordan, Editor. **ISSN:** 0893--5238 (print). **Subscription Rates:** $27 Individuals; $49 Canada and Mexico; $72 Other countries. **URL:** http://www.americanfitness.com. **Formerly:** Aerobics and Fitness. **Ad Rates:** BW $1750; 4C $3500. **Remarks:** Accepts advertising. **Circ:** Combined ‡42000.

4369 ■ Azerbaijan International
Azerbaijan International
PO Box 5217
Sherman Oaks, CA 91413
Phone: (310)440-0800
Fax: (310)440-0801
Publication E-mail: ai@artnet.net
Magazine reporting on Azerbaijani issues worldwide. AZER.com. World's largest website about Azerbaijan. **Freq:** Quarterly. **Trim Size:** 8.5 x 11. **Key Personnel:** Pirouz Khanlou, Publisher; Betty Blair, Editor, Founder. **ISSN:** 1075-086X (print). **URL:** http://www.azer.com/. **Remarks:** Accepts advertising. **Circ:** (Not Reported).

4370 ■ BRE: Black Entertainment's Premiere Magazine Since 1976
BRE Magazine
15030 Ventura Blvd., Ste. 864
Sherman Oaks, CA 91403
Magazine covering the Black entertainment industry. **Freq:** Monthly. **Key Personnel:** Susan Miller, Publisher; Evelyn Miller Randolph, Esq., Chief Executive Officer; Sidney Miller, III, Vice President. **Subscription Rates:** $200 Individuals; $375 Two years; $375 Canada first class; $400 Other countries. **URL:** http://respeconize.com/. **Remarks:** Accepts advertising. **Circ:** 110000.

4371 ■ Classified Flea Market
Classified Flea Market
4954 Van Nuys Blvd.
Sherman Oaks, CA 91403
Publisher's E-mail: service@recycler.com
Shopping guide. **Freq:** Weekly. **Key Personnel:** Josh Siegel, Chief Operating Officer. **URL:** http://www.recycler.com/cfm. **Remarks:** Accepts classified advertising. **Circ:** Combined 100000.

4372 ■ Eligible
Eligible
PO Box 57466
Sherman Oaks, CA 91413
Publisher's E-mail: eligible4@aol.com
Consumer and online magazine exploring issues important to independent women and highlighting some of the most eligible bachelors in the country. **Freq:** Quarterly. **Key Personnel:** Kathy Duliakas, Publisher. **ISSN:** 1073--256X (print). **Formerly:** L.A.'s Eligible. **Ad Rates:** BW $3500; 4C $4500. **Remarks:** Accepts advertising. **Circ:** Paid 95000, Non-paid 5000.

4373 ■ FACT
American Russian Business Council
14044 Ventura Blvd., Ste. 310
Sherman Oaks, CA 91423
Phone: (818)377-2103
Fax: (818)377-9188
Free: 800-428-9308
Publisher's E-mail: contact@russiancouncil.org
Magazine containing interesting and useful information of the American Russian Business Council for California residents of all ages and professions. **Founded:** Jan. 1994. **Freq:** Biweekly. **Subscription Rates:** $20 Individuals; Free throughout California. **URL:** http://www.russiancouncil.org/company/usrussia-business-resources/fact-maga zine-russian-tv-guide/23/. **Remarks:** Accepts advertising. **Circ:** (Not Reported).

SIERRA MADRE

Los Angeles Co. Los Angeles Co. (S). 18 m NE of Los Angeles. Residential. Ceramics, tools, plastic manufactured. Residential.

4374 ■ American Bungalow
American Bungalow Magazine
PO Box 756
Sierra Madre, CA 91025-0756
Fax: (626)355-1220
Free: 800-350-3363
Publisher's E-mail: circulation@ambungalow.com
Consumer magazine covering early American architecture, preservation, and restoration. **Freq:** Quarterly. **URL:** http://www.americanbungalow.com/table-of-contents-inside-past-issues. **Ad Rates:** BW $1707; 4C $2145. **Remarks:** Accepts advertising. **Circ:** (Not Reported).

SIGNAL HILL

4375 ■ The EarlyBird Magazine
Classic Thunderbird Club International
1308 E 29th St.
Signal Hill, CA 90755-1842
Phone: (562)426-2709
Fax: (562)426-7023
Free: 800-488-2709
Publisher's E-mail: ctcioffice@ctci.org
Magazine containing information about restoration, maintenance tips, historical data, parts and cars, plus news from around the world about members, and past and upcoming T-Bird events. **Freq:** 6/year. **Key Personnel:** Lin Somsak, Editor-in-Chief. **URL:** http://www.ctci.org/magazine.php. **Circ:** (Not Reported).

SIMI VALLEY

Ventura Co. Ventura Co. (SW). 30 m NW of Los Angeles. Suburban community.

4376 ■ The Spotter
Dalmatian Club of America
864 Ettin Ave.
Simi Valley, CA 93065-4209
Phone: (805)583-5914
Publisher's E-mail: questions@thedca.org
Magazine covering the Dalmatian and the Dalmatian Club of America club activities. **Freq:** Quarterly. **Subscription Rates:** $56 U.S. /year; $14 U.S. single issue/back issue; $76 Other countries /year in Canada and other countries; $19 Other countries single issue. **URL:** http://www.thespotter.org. **Remarks:** Accepts advertising. **Circ:** (Not Reported).

KSOH-FM - See Yakima, WA

SOLANA BEACH

San Diego Co. San Diego Co. (S). 20 m N of San Diego. Aero-space parts. Commercial flower growing. Nursery. Residential.

4377 ■ KITPLANES Magazine: World's Number One Homebuilt Aircraft Magazine
KITPLANES Magazine
PO Box 1501
Solana Beach, CA 92075
Phone: (760)487-8075
Free: 800-622-1065
Magazine for home-craftsman builders of personal aircraft. **Freq:** 10/year. **Print Method:** Offset. **Trim Size:** 7 7/8 x 10 1/2. **Cols./Page:** 3. **Col. Width:** 26 nonpareils. **Col. Depth:** 140 agate lines. **Key Personnel:** Paul Dye, Editor-in-Chief; Cindy Pedersen, Director, Advertising, Publisher, phone: (760)487-8075. **ISSN:** 0891--1851 (print). **Subscription Rates:** $15.95 Individuals print; $32.95 Other countries. **URL:** http://www.kitplanes.com. **Ad Rates:** BW $4,170. **Remarks:** Accepts advertising. **Circ:** (Not Reported).

4378 ■ Neurobiology of Lipids
The Editorial Group L.L.C.
1051 San Patricio Dr.
Solana Beach, CA 92075
Publisher's E-mail: ask@teg-e.com
Journal publishing original research in neuroscience of lipids. **Key Personnel:** Alexei R. Koudinov, MD, Managing Editor; Joan E. Blanchette-Mackie, Editor; Temirbolat T. Berezov, Editor; Flemming Cornelius, Editor; Luisa Diomede, Editor; Gunter P. Eckert, Editor; Sandra K. Erickson, Editor; Falk Fahrenholz, Editor; Carolyn Harley, Editor; Tobias Hartmann, Editor; Karen J. Horsburgh, Editor. **ISSN:** 1683--5506 (print). **URL:** http://neurobiologyoflipids.org/myjournalindex.html. **Remarks:** Accepts advertising. **Circ:** (Not Reported).

SOLEDAD

Monterey Co. Monterey Co. (W). 26 m SE of Salinas. Residential. Historic Soledad mission. Winery. Agriculture. Dairying, beef cattle, carrots, lettuce.

4379 ■ KFRS-FM - 89.9
290 Hegenberger Rd.
Oakland, CA 94621
Free: 800-543-1495
Email: info@familyradio.org
Format: Religious. **Owner:** Family Stations Inc., 290 Hegenberger Rd., Oakland, CA 94621, Free: 800-543-

Circulation: ★ = AAM; △ or • = BPA; ♦ = CAC; ❑ = VAC; ⊕ = PO Statement; ‡ = Publisher's Report; Boldface figures = sworn; Light figures = estimated.

1495. **Wattage:** 250. **URL:** http://www.familyradio.org.

SOLVANG

Santa Barbara Co. Santa Barbara Co. (SW). 40 m NW of Santa Barbara. Resort area. Cattle, horses, sheep ranching. Wineries, vineyards. Walnuts.

4380 ■ Santa Ynez Valley News
Lee Central Coast Newspapers
423 Second St.
Solvang, CA 93463
Phone: (805)688-5522
Publisher's E-mail: circulation@syvnews.com
Community newspaper. **Freq:** Semiweekly. **Print Method:** Offset. **Cols./Page:** 6. **Col. Width:** 21 nonpareils. **Col. Depth:** 126 agate lines. **Key Personnel:** Cynthia Schur, Publisher; Tom Bolton, Executive Editor; Rich Pulsifer, Manager, Circulation. **Subscription Rates:** $21 Individuals 52 weeks (print); $15 Individuals 52 weeks (online). **URL:** http://syvnews.com. **Mailing address:** PO Box 647, Solvang, CA 93464. **Ad Rates:** GLR $12.85; 4C $180; PCI $12.84. **Remarks:** Accepts advertising. **Circ:** Tues. 13500, Thurs. 7500.

4381 ■ Times Press Recorder
Lee Central Coast Newspapers
423 Second St.
Solvang, CA 93463
Phone: (805)688-5522
Publisher's E-mail: circulation@syvnews.com
Community newspaper. **Freq:** Semiweekly (Wed. and Fri.). **Key Personnel:** Cynthia Schur, Publisher, phone: (805)739-2154; Tom Bolton, Executive Editor, phone: (805)739-2229. **Subscription Rates:** Free. **URL:** http://www.timespressrecorder.com. **Mailing address:** PO Box 647, Solvang, CA 93464. **Remarks:** Accepts advertising. **Circ:** (Not Reported).

4382 ■ KSYV-FM - 96.7
1693 Mission Dr.
Solvang, CA 93463
Phone: (805)922-7727
Fax: (805)349-0265
Email: radio@knightbroadcasting.com
Format: Adult Contemporary. **Owner:** Knight Broadcasting Inc., 1101 S Broadway, Ste. C, Santa Maria, CA 93455, Ph: (805)922-7727, Fax: (805)349-0265. **Founded:** 1982. **ADI**: Santa Barbara-Santa Maria-San Luis Obispo,CA. **Key Personnel:** Shawn Knight, Contact, shawn@knightbroadcasting.com. **Wattage**: 420 ERP. **Ad Rates:** Advertising accepted; rates available upon request. $15-35 for 60 seconds. KRAZ-FM. **URL:** http://www.mix96.com.

SONOMA

Sonoma Co. Sonoma Co. (NW). 21 m S of Santa Rosa. Residential. Wineries. automotive parts, cheese factories. Diversified farming. Grapes, poultry. Dairying. Retirement Community.

4383 ■ The Sonoma Index-Tribune
Sonoma Index-Tribune Inc.
117 W Napa St.
Sonoma, CA 95476
Phone: (707)938-2111
Fax: (707)938-1600
Publisher's E-mail: blynch@sonomanews.com
Community newspaper. **Freq:** Semiweekly (Tues. and Fri.). **Print Method:** Offset. **Trim Size:** 11 3/8 x 13 3/4. **Cols./Page:** 6. **Col. Width:** 11.6 picas. **Col. Depth:** 294 agate lines. **Key Personnel:** Bill Lynch, Editor, phone: (707)933-2721; Bill Hoban, Managing Editor, phone: (707)933-2731. **Subscription Rates:** $80 Individuals annual all access - print and digital; $40 Individuals 6 months all access - print and digital; $5.25 Individuals monthly - digital only. **URL:** http://www.sonomanews.com. **Mailing address:** PO Box C, Sonoma, CA 95476. **Remarks:** Accepts classified advertising. **Circ:** 5300.

4384 ■ Wine Business Monthly: The Industry's Leading Publication for Wineries and Growers
New World Wine Communications Inc.
110 W Napa St.
Sonoma, CA 95476
Phone: (707)939-0822
Fax: (707)939-0833
Publisher's E-mail: services@winebusiness.com
Trade magazine for the wine industry. **Freq:** Monthly. **Print Method:** Web offset. **Key Personnel:** Cyril Penn, Editor; Rachel Nichols, Managing Editor. **Subscription Rates:** $39 U.S.; $49 Canada; $89 Other countries; $58 U.S. two years; $90 Canada two years; $160 Other countries two years; $85 U.S. three years. **URL:** http://www.winebusiness.com/wbm. **Ad Rates:** BW $2658; 4C $3735. **Remarks:** Accepts advertising. **Circ:** △**7060**.

4385 ■ K281BB-FM - 104.1
PO Box 391
Twin Falls, ID 83303
Free: 800-357-4226
Format: Religious; Contemporary Christian. **Owner:** CSN International, PO Box 391, Twin Falls, ID 83303, Ph: (208)736-1958, Fax: (208)736-1958, Free: 800-357-4226.

SONORA

Tuolumne Co. Tuolumne Co. (EC). 50 m E of Stockton. Lumber, lime, foundry products, confectionery manufactured. Mountain resort. Gold mines. limestone quarries. timber. Agriculture. Cattle, apples, pears.

4386 ■ The Pain Practitioner
American Academy of Pain Management
975 Morning Star Dr., Ste. A
Sonora, CA 95370-9249
Phone: (209)533-9744
Fax: (209)533-9750
Publisher's E-mail: info@aapainmanage.org
Magazine covering clinicians who practice pain management about updates in research, diagnosis and treatment. **Freq:** Quarterly. **Key Personnel:** Sheila Miller, Account Manager. **Subscription Rates:** $35 Individuals; Included in membership. **URL:** http://www.aapainmanage.org/category/pain-practitioner. **Ad Rates:** BW $2,590. **Remarks:** Accepts advertising. **Circ:** 10,000.

4387 ■ Union-Democrat
Union Democrat Corp.
84 S Washington St.
Sonora, CA 95370-4711
Phone: (209)532-7151
Fax: (209)532-6451
General newspaper. **Freq:** 5/week. **Print Method:** Offset. **Cols./Page:** 6. **Col. Width:** 24 nonpareils. **Col. Depth:** 294 agate lines. **Key Personnel:** Gary Piech, Publisher; Lynne Fernandez, Business Manager. **Subscription Rates:** subscription required. **Remarks:** Accepts advertising. **Circ:** Mon.-Fri. ★**11626**.

4388 ■ KKBN-FM - 93.5
342 S Washington St.
Sonora, CA 95370-5020
Phone: (209)533-1450
Fax: (209)533-9520
Format: Country. **Owner:** Clarke Broadcasting Corp., 342 S Washington St , Sonora, CA 95370-5020, Ph: (209)533-1450. **Founded:** 1985. **Operating Hours**: Continuous. **Key Personnel:** Larry England, Contact, lenglandcbc@mlode.com. **Wattage:** 400 ERP. **Ad Rates:** $40 for 30 seconds; $60 for 60 seconds. Combined advertising rates available with KVML-AM & KZSQ-FM. **URL:** http://www.kkbn.com.

4389 ■ KVML-AM - 1450
342 S Washington St.
Sonora, CA 95370
Phone: (209)533-1450
Fax: (209)533-9520
Format: News; Sports. **Networks:** ABC. **Owner:** Clarke Broadcasting Corp., 342 S Washington St , Sonora, CA 95370-5020, Ph: (209)533-1450. **Founded:** 1949. **Operating Hours**: Continuous. **Wattage:** 940. **Ad Rates:** for 30 seconds; for 60 seconds. Combined advertising rates available with KZSQ-FM, KKBN-FM. **URL:** http://www.kvml.com.

4390 ■ KZSQ-FM - 92.7
342 S Washington St.
Sonora, CA 95370-5020
Format: Adult Contemporary. **Founded:** 1956. **Operating Hours**: Continuous. **Ad Rates:** Advertising accepted; rates available upon request. **URL:** http://www.kzsq.com.

SOQUEL

4391 ■ Journal of Forensic Vocational Analysis
American Board of Vocational Experts
3121 Park Ave., Ste. C
Soquel, CA 95073
Phone: (831)464-4890
Fax: (831)576-1417
Publisher's E-mail: abve@abve.net
Journal containing source for up-to-date information about rehabilitation, psychology, economics and various aligned disciplines. **Freq:** Annual. **Remarks:** Advertising not accepted. **Circ:** (Not Reported).

SOUTH LAKE TAHOE

El Dorado Co. El Dorado Co. (EC). 100 m NE of Sacramento. Residential. Summer and winter resort area.

4392 ■ Tahoe Daily Tribune
Tahoe Daily Tribune
3079 Harrison Ave.
South Lake Tahoe, CA 96150
Phone: (530)541-3880
Community newspaper. **Freq:** Triweekly Wednesday, Friday and Saturday. **Print Method:** Offset. **Trim Size:** 13 x 21 1/8. **Cols./Page:** 6. **Col. Width:** 24 nonpareils. **Col. Depth:** 301 agate lines. **Key Personnel:** Natasha Schue, Publisher, phone: (530)542-8046. **Subscription Rates:** $9.50 Individuals home-delivery, per 4 weeks; $18.46 By mail per 4 weeks. **URL:** http://www.tahoedailytribune.com. **Remarks:** Accepts classified advertising. **Circ:** Sat. ‡11504.

4393 ■ KTHO-AM - 590
PO Box AM
South Lake Tahoe, CA 96156
Phone: (530)543-0590
Fax: (530)543-1101
Format: Full Service; Talk. **Owner:** Emerald Broadcasting Co., at above address. **Founded:** 1963. **Ad Rates:** Advertising accepted; rates available upon request. **URL:** http://wp.kthoradio.com/.

SOUTH SAN FRANCISCO

San Mateo Co. San Mateo Co. (W). 9 m S of San Francisco. Manufactures auto lifts, metal products, wire, flower pots, air conditioning units, chemicals, pastes, paint, scientific apparatus, airplane parts, radio equipment, magnesium products, plastics, electronics.

4394 ■ Edge
Future Network USA
4000 Shoreline Ct., Ste. 400
South San Francisco, CA 94080
Phone: (650)872-1642
Publisher's E-mail: marketing@futureus.com
Consumer magazine covering computers and games. **Freq:** 13/yr. **Key Personnel:** Frank Mak, Contact, phone: (650)238-2497. **Subscription Rates:** £69.99 U.S.; £147.64 Two years in United States; £34.99 Individuals; £58.49 Individuals 2 years; £74.99 Individuals European and rest of world; £147.64 Two years European and rest of world. **URL:** http://www.futureplc.com/contact/. **Formerly**: Next Generation. **Remarks:** Advertising accepted; rates available upon request. **Circ:** (Not Reported).

4395 ■ Light Metal Age: The International Magazine of the Light Metal Industry
Fellom Publishing Co.
170 S Spruce Ave., Ste. 120
South San Francisco, CA 94080
Phone: (650)588-8832
Fax: (650)588-0901
Publisher's E-mail: lma@lightmetalage.com
Magazine serving primary and semi-fabrication metal plants that produce, semi-fabricate, process or manufacture the light metals: aluminum, magnesium, titanium, beryllium and their alloys, and/or the non-ferrous metals copper and zinc. **Freq:** Bimonthly February, April, June, August, October and December. **Print Method:** Offset. **Trim Size:** 8 1/4 x 11 1/8. **Cols./Page:** 3. **Col. Width:** 27 nonpareils. **Col. Depth:** 140 agate lines. **Key Personnel:** Joseph C. Benedyk, PhD, Editor. **ISSN:** 0024--3345 (print). **Subscription Rates:** $60 Individuals; $100 Other countries; $135 By mail. **URL:** http://www.lightmetalage.com. **Ad Rates:** 4C $3262; PCI $123. **Remarks:** Accepts advertising. **Circ:** Paid 4000.

4396 ■ Maximum PC
Future Network USA
4000 Shoreline Ct., Ste. 400

South San Francisco, CA 94080
Phone: (650)872-1642
Publisher's E-mail: marketing@futureus.com
Consumer magazine covering computing, hardware and software reviews, games and work programs for personal computer users. **Freq:** Monthly. **Trim Size:** 8 x 10 1/2. **Subscription Rates:** $14.95 Individuals; $24.95 Individuals 12 CDs; $29.95 Other countries; $49.95 Other countries two years; $1.95 Single issue. **URL:** http://maximumpc.com. **Ad Rates:** 4C $12,400. **Remarks:** Accepts advertising. **Circ:** Paid ★**274197**.

4397 ■ The Net
Future Network USA
4000 Shoreline Ct., Ste. 400
South San Francisco, CA 94080
Phone: (650)872-1642
Publisher's E-mail: marketing@futureus.com
Trade magazine covering Internet content. **Freq:** Monthly. **Key Personnel:** Dan Oliver, Editor. **Subscription Rates:** $124.99 U.S. 1 year, print; £54.49 Individuals 1 year, UK, print; £82.99 Individuals 1 year, Europe, print; $89.99 Other countries 1 year, print; £44.99 Individuals 1 year, UK, online; €59.99 Individuals 1 year, Europe, online; $64.99 U.S. 1 year, online. **URL:** http://www.creativebloq.com/net-magazine. **Remarks:** Advertising accepted; rates available upon request. **Circ:** (Not Reported).

4398 ■ PC Gamer
Future Network USA
4000 Shoreline Ct., Ste. 400
South San Francisco, CA 94080
Phone: (650)872-1642
Consumer magazine covering computer games. **Freq:** Monthly. **Trim Size:** 10 1/2 x 16. **Key Personnel:** Ashley Kardel, Account Executive, phone: (650)745-9229. **ISSN:** 1080--4471 (print). **Subscription Rates:** $6.99 Single issue; $24 Individuals. **URL:** http://www.futureplc.com/tag/pc-gamer. **Remarks:** Advertising accepted; rates available upon request. **Circ:** ‡158767.

STANFORD

Santa Clara Co. (W). 14 m NW of San Jose. Residential. Stanford University. High tech industrial park.

4399 ■ Communications in Partial Differential Equations
Taylor & Francis Group Journals
c/o R. Mazzeo, Ed.-in-Ch.
Dept. of Mathematics
Stanford University
Stanford, CA 94305
Publisher's E-mail: customerservice@taylorandfrancis.com
Journal exploring mathematical aspects of partial differential equations including the theory of linear and nonlinear equations. **Freq:** 12/yr. **Print Method:** Offset. **Trim Size:** 8 1/4 X 10 7/8. **Cols./Page:** 1. **Col. Width:** 72 nonpareils. **Col. Depth:** 126 agate lines. **Key Personnel:** P.E. Souganidis, Editor-in-Chief, phone: (512)471-1754, fax: (512)232-9484; R. Mazzeo, Editor-in-Chief. **ISSN:** 0360--5302 (print); **EISSN:** 1532--4133 (electronic). **Subscription Rates:** $1138 Individuals print only; $4156 Institutions online only; $4750 Institutions print and online. **URL:** http://www.tandfonline.com/toc/lpde20/current#.VGs7cDQwrld. **Ad Rates:** BW $890; 4C $1,935. **Remarks:** Accepts advertising. **Circ:** 625.

4400 ■ Education Next
Hoover Institution Press
Stanford University
434 Galvez Mall
Stanford, CA 94305-6010
Phone: (650)723-3373
Fax: (650)723-8626
Free: 800-935-2882
Publisher's E-mail: hooverpress@stanford.edu
Journal that aims to publish research, sound ideas, and responsible arguments in the area of K-12 education. **Freq:** Quarterly. **Trim Size:** 8 3/8 x 10 7/8. **Key Personnel:** Paul E. Peterson, Editor-in-Chief; Amanda Olberg, Managing Editor. **ISSN:** 1532--5148 (print). **Subscription Rates:** $20 Individuals print only; $35 Two years print only. **URL:** http://educationnext.org. **Ad Rates:** BW $900; 4C $1,300. **Remarks:** Accepts advertising. **Circ:** (Not Reported).

4401 ■ International Journal of Mathematics
World Scientific Publishing Company Private Ltd.
c/o Yakov Eliashberg, Editor
Department of Mathematics
Stanford University
Stanford, CA 94305
Publisher's E-mail: wspc@wspc.com.sg
Peer-reviewed journal publishing original papers in mathematics. **Freq:** 14/yr. **Key Personnel:** Yakov Eliashberg, Editor. **ISSN:** 0129--167X (print); **EISSN:** 1793--6519 (electronic). **Subscription Rates:** $3005 Institutions and libraries, print & electronic; $2682 Institutions and libraries, electronic only; €2076 Institutions and libraries, print & electronic; €1853 Institutions and libraries, electronic only; S$4662 Institutions and libraries, print & electronic; S$4160 Institutions and libraries, electronic only. **URL:** http://www.worldscientific.com/worldscinet/ijm. **Circ:** (Not Reported).

4402 ■ Jewish Social Studies: History, Culture, and Society
Indiana University Press
c/o Taube Ctr. for Jewish Studies
Stanford University
Bldg. 360, Rm. 362H
Stanford, CA 94305-2190
Publication E-mail: jss@leland.stanford.edu
Journal covering contemporary and historical aspects of Jewish life. **Freq:** 3/year. **Print Method:** Offset. **Trim Size:** 6 x 9. **Cols./Page:** 1. **Col. Width:** 60 nonpareils. **Col. Depth:** 112 agate lines. **Key Personnel:** Steven J. Zipperstein, Board Member; Derek Penslar, Board Member; Tony Michels, Editor. **ISSN:** 0021--6704 (print); **EISSN:** 1527--2028 (electronic). **Subscription Rates:** $49.50 Individuals print and online; $38.25 affiliate, print and online, 1 year; $153 Institutions print and online, 1 year; $45 Individuals print only, 1 year; $34.85 affiliate, print only, 1 year; $115 Institutions print only, 1 year; $40.50 Individuals online only, 1 year; $31.45 affiliate, 1 year, online only; $109.50 Individuals online only, 1 year. **URL:** http://www.jstor.org/action/showPublication?journalCode=jewisocistud. **Ad Rates:** BW $275. **Remarks:** Accepts advertising. **Circ:** (Not Reported).

4403 ■ Lymphatic Research and Biology
Lymphatic Education and Research Network
c/o Stanley G. Rockson, MD, Editor-in-Chief
Division of Cardiovascular Medicine
Falk Cardiovascular Research Center
Stanford University School of Medicine
Stanford, CA 94305
Phone: (650)725-7571
Fax: (650)725-1599
Publisher's E-mail: lern@lymphaticnetwork.org
Peer-reviewed journal providing an interdisciplinary forum for the world's leading biomedical investigators to discuss current and anticipated developments in lymphatic biology and pathology. **Freq:** Quarterly. **Key Personnel:** Francine Blei, MD, Associate Editor; Stanley G. Rockson, MD, Editor-in-Chief. **ISSN:** 1539--6851 (print); **EISSN:** 1557--8585 (electronic). **Subscription Rates:** $646 U.S. print and online; $756 Other countries print and online; $637 Individuals online only. **URL:** http://www.liebertpub.com/overview/lymphatic-research-and-biology/114; http://lymphaticnetwork.org/treating-lymphedema/publications/. **Remarks:** Accepts advertising. **Circ:** (Not Reported).

4404 ■ Stanford Business
Stanford University Stanford Graduate School of Business
655 Knight Way
Stanford, CA 94305-7298
Phone: (650)723-2146
Publisher's E-mail: gsb_info@gsb.stanford.edu
Magazine for business school alumni. **Freq:** Quarterly February, May, August, November. **Print Method:** Offset. **Trim Size:** 8 1/2 x 11. **Key Personnel:** Cathy Castillo, Publisher; Arthur Patterson, Manager, Production; Kathleen O'Toole, Editor. **ISSN:** 1094--5423 (print). **Subscription Rates:** Free. **Alt. Formats:** PDF. **URL:** http://www.gsb.stanford.edu/insights/about/magazine. **Formerly:** Stanford Business School Magazine. **Remarks:** Advertising not accepted. **Circ:** Paid 24000, Controlled 4000.

4405 ■ Stanford Chaparral
Hammer and Coffin Society/Stanford University
PO Box 18916
Stanford, CA 94309
Collegiate magazine. **Freq:** 6/year. **Print Method:** Offset. **Cols./Page:** 3. **Col. Width:** 14 picas. **Col. Depth:** 136 agate lines. **Key Personnel:** Evan Macmillan, Contact. **Subscription Rates:** $19 Individuals. **URL:** http://stanfordchaparral.com. **Ad Rates:** BW $300; 4C $450; PCI $15. **Remarks:** Accepts advertising. **Circ:** Paid 50, Non-paid 6000.

4406 ■ The Stanford Daily: Breaking news from the farm since 1892
The Stanford Daily Publishing Corp.
Storke Publication Bldg.,Ste.101
Stanford, CA 94305-2240
Phone: (650)725-2100
Fax: (650)725-1329
Collegiate newspaper. **Freq:** Daily Monday through Friday. **Print Method:** Offset. **Cols./Page:** 6. **Col. Width:** 25 nonpareils. **Col. Depth:** 294 agate lines. **Key Personnel:** Jana Persky, President, Editor-in-Chief. **USPS:** 518-420. **Subscription Rates:** $21.99 Individuals. **URL:** http://www.stanforddaily.com. **Formerly:** The Daily Palo Alto. **Remarks:** Accepts advertising. **Circ:** Free ‡13500, Mon.-Fri. ‡10000.

4407 ■ Stanford Environmental Law Journal
Stanford Law School
Crown Quadrangle
559 Nathan Abbott Way
Stanford, CA 94305-8610
Phone: (650)723-2465
Fax: (650)725-0253
Publisher's E-mail: deans.office@law.stanford.edu
Journal featuring topics related to law and the environment. **Freq:** 3/year. **Key Personnel:** Adam Bowling, Editor-in-Chief. **ISSN:** 0892-7138 (print). **Subscription Rates:** $40 Individuals; $45 Other countries; $21 Single issue. **URL:** http://journals.law.stanford.edu/stanford-environmental-law-journal-elj. **Circ:** (Not Reported).

4408 ■ Stanford Environmental Law Journal
Stanford Law School
Crown Quadrangle
559 Nathan Abbott Way
Stanford, CA 94305-8610
Phone: (650)723-2465
Fax: (650)725-0253
Publisher's E-mail: deans.office@law.stanford.edu
Journal containing articles on natural resources law, environmental policy, law and economics, international environmental law, and other topics relating to law and the environment. **Freq:** 3/year. **ISSN:** 0892--7138 (print). **Subscription Rates:** $40 Individuals domestic; $45 Individuals international; $21 Single issue; $15 Out of area. **URL:** http://journals.law.stanford.edu/stanford-environmental-law-journal-elj. **Circ:** (Not Reported).

4409 ■ Stanford Journal of Archaeology
Stanford University Department of Sociology
450 Serra Mall Bldg. 120, Rm. 160
Stanford, CA 94305-2047
Phone: (650)723-3956
Fax: (650)725-6471
Publisher's E-mail: sociology@stanford.edu
Online scholarly journal publishing research in archaeology. **Freq:** Irregular. **Key Personnel:** Sebastian De Vivo, Editor; Kathryn Lafrenz, Editor; Darian Totten, Editor. **Subscription Rates:** Free online. **Alt. Formats:** PDF. **URL:** http://web.stanford.edu/dept/archaeology/journal. **Circ:** (Not Reported).

4410 ■ Stanford Journal of Civil Rights and Civil Liberties
Stanford Law School
Crown Quadrangle
559 Nathan Abbott Way
Stanford, CA 94305-8610
Phone: (650)723-2465
Fax: (650)725-0253
Publisher's E-mail: deans.office@law.stanford.edu
Journal covering civil rights and liberties issues. **Freq:** Semiannual. **Key Personnel:** Deepa Kannappan, Editor-in-Chief. **ISSN:** 1553-7226 (print). **Subscription Rates:** $42 Individuals; $47 Other countries; $24 Single issue. **URL:** http://journals.law.stanford.edu/stanford-journal-civil-rights-and-civil-liberties-sjcrcl. **Circ:** (Not Reported).

4411 ■ Stanford Journal of Civil Rights and Civil Liberties

Circulation: ★ = AAM; △ or • = BPA; ♦ = CAC; ❑ = VAC; ⊕ = PO Statement; ‡ = Publisher's Report; Boldface figures = sworn; Light figures = estimated.

Stanford Law School
Crown Quadrangle
559 Nathan Abbott Way
Stanford, CA 94305-8610
Phone: (650)723-2465
Fax: (650)725-0253
Publisher's E-mail: deans.office@law.stanford.edu
Journal containing topics on civil rights and liberties, both domestic and international. **Freq:** Semiannual. **Subscription Rates:** $42 Individuals domestic; $47 Individuals international; $24 Single issue. **URL:** http://journals.law.stanford.edu/stanford-journal-civil-rights-and-civil-liberties-sjcrcl. **Circ:** (Not Reported).

4412 ■ Stanford Journal of Complex Litigation
Stanford Law School
Crown Quadrangle
559 Nathan Abbott Way
Stanford, CA 94305-8610
Phone: (650)723-2465
Fax: (650)725-0253
Publisher's E-mail: deans.office@law.stanford.edu
Journal covering legal topics relating to complex litigation. **Freq:** Semiannual. **Key Personnel:** Demoni Newman, Editor-in-Chief. **ISSN:** 2169-7604 (print). **Subscription Rates:** $45 Individuals; $53 Other countries; $28 Single issue. **URL:** http://journals.law.stanford.edu/stanford-journal-complex-litigation-sjcl/subscriptions. **Circ:** (Not Reported).

4413 ■ Stanford Journal of Complex Litigation
Stanford Law School
Crown Quadrangle
559 Nathan Abbott Way
Stanford, CA 94305-8610
Phone: (650)723-2465
Fax: (650)725-0253
Publisher's E-mail: deans.office@law.stanford.edu
Peer-reviewed journal focusing on complex litigation. **Freq:** Semiannual. **ISSN:** 2169--7604 (print). **Subscription Rates:** $45 Individuals domestic; $53 Individuals international; $28 Single issue; $15 Other countries. **URL:** http://journals.law.stanford.edu/stanford-journal-complex-litigation-sjcl. **Circ:** (Not Reported).

4414 ■ Stanford Journal of Criminal Law and Policy
Stanford Law School
Crown Quadrangle
559 Nathan Abbott Way
Stanford, CA 94305-8610
Phone: (650)723-2465
Fax: (650)725-0253
Publisher's E-mail: deans.office@law.stanford.edu
Journal containing articles exclusively on criminal justice. **Freq:** Semiannual. **URL:** http://journals.law.stanford.edu/stanford-journal-criminal-law-and-policy-sjclp; http://law.stanford.edu/stanford-journal-of-criminal-law-and-policy-sjclp. **Circ:** (Not Reported).

4415 ■ Stanford Journal of International Law
Stanford Law School
Crown Quadrangle
559 Nathan Abbott Way
Stanford, CA 94305-8610
Phone: (650)723-2465
Fax: (650)725-0253
Publisher's E-mail: deans.office@law.stanford.edu
Journal covering analyses of current international legal issues. **Freq:** Semiannual. **Key Personnel:** Enrique Molina, Editor-in-Chief. **ISSN:** 0731-5082 (print). **Subscription Rates:** $46 Individuals; $49 Other countries; $24 Single issue. **URL:** http://journals.law.stanford.edu/sjil. **Circ:** (Not Reported).

4416 ■ Stanford Journal of International Law
Stanford Law School
Crown Quadrangle
559 Nathan Abbott Way
Stanford, CA 94305-8610
Phone: (650)723-2465
Fax: (650)725-0253
Publisher's E-mail: deans.office@law.stanford.edu
Journal covering issues on international and comparative law. **Freq:** Semiannual. **ISSN:** 0731--5082 (print). **Subscription Rates:** $46 Individuals domestic; $56 Individuals international; $24 Single issue; $20 Out of area. **URL:** http://journals.law.stanford.edu/sjil. **Circ:** (Not Reported).

4417 ■ Stanford Journal of Law, Business & Finance
Stanford Law School
Crown Quadrangle
559 Nathan Abbott Way
Stanford, CA 94305-8610
Phone: (650)723-2465
Fax: (650)725-0253
Publisher's E-mail: deans.office@law.stanford.edu
Journal covering legal issues in the fields of business and finance. **Freq:** Semiannual. **Key Personnel:** Michele Cumpston, Editor-in-Chief. **ISSN:** 1078-8794 (print). **Subscription Rates:** $45 Individuals. **URL:** http://www.law.stanford.edu/organizations/student-journals/stanford-journal-of-law-business-finance-sjlbf; http://sjlbf.stanford.edu/. **Circ:** (Not Reported).

4418 ■ Stanford Journal of Law, Business and Finance
Stanford Law School
Crown Quadrangle
559 Nathan Abbott Way
Stanford, CA 94305-8610
Phone: (650)723-2465
Fax: (650)725-0253
Publisher's E-mail: deans.office@law.stanford.edu
Journal containing issues in the fields of business and finance. **Freq:** Semiannual. **ISSN:** 1078--8794 (print). **Subscription Rates:** $45 Individuals domestic; $53 Individuals international; $28 Single issue; $15 Other countries. **URL:** http://journals.law.stanford.edu/stanford-journal-law-business-finance-sjlbf. **Circ:** (Not Reported).

4419 ■ Stanford Journal of Law, Science and Policy
Stanford Law School
Crown Quadrangle
559 Nathan Abbott Way
Stanford, CA 94305-8610
Phone: (650)723-2465
Fax: (650)725-0253
Publisher's E-mail: deans.office@law.stanford.edu
Peer-reviewed journal containing articles on law, science and policy. **Freq:** Semiannual. **Subscription Rates:** Free. **URL:** http://journals.law.stanford.edu/stanford-journal-law-science-policy. **Circ:** (Not Reported).

4420 ■ Stanford Law & Policy Review
Stanford Law School
Crown Quadrangle
559 Nathan Abbott Way
Stanford, CA 94305-8610
Phone: (650)723-2465
Fax: (650)725-0253
Publisher's E-mail: deans.office@law.stanford.edu
Journal containing articles analyzing the intersection of nation's legal system with local, state and federal policy. **Freq:** Semiannual. **Key Personnel:** Kingdar Prussien, Editor-in-Chief. **ISSN:** 1044-4386 (print). **Subscription Rates:** $48 Individuals; $58 Other countries; $27 Single issue. **URL:** http://journals.law.stanford.edu/stanford-law-policy-review. **Circ:** (Not Reported).

4421 ■ Stanford Law Review
Stanford Law School
Crown Quadrangle
559 Nathan Abbott Way
Stanford, CA 94305-8610
Phone: (650)723-2465
Fax: (650)725-0253
Publisher's E-mail: deans.office@law.stanford.edu
Journal on law. **Freq:** Bimonthly Annual. **Key Personnel:** Michael Mestitz, President. **ISSN:** 0038--9765 (print). **URL:** http://www.stanfordlawreview.org; http://stanfordlawreview.org. **Remarks:** Accepts advertising. **Circ:** Combined 2167.

4422 ■ Stanford Lawyer
Stanford Law School
Crown Quadrangle
559 Nathan Abbott Way
Stanford, CA 94305-8610
Phone: (650)723-2465
Fax: (650)725-0253
Publisher's E-mail: deans.office@law.stanford.edu
Law school magazine for alumni, faculty, and students. **Freq:** Semiannual. **Trim Size:** 8 5/16 x 10 7/8. **Key Personnel:** Sharon Driscoll, Editor. **ISSN:** 0585--0576 (print). **URL:** http://law.stanford.edu/stanford-lawyer-magazine. **Remarks:** Advertising not accepted. **Circ:** Controlled 15000.

4423 ■ Stanford Magazine
Stanford Alumni Association Frances C. Arrillaga Alumni Center
326 Galvez St.
Stanford, CA 94305-6105
Phone: (650)725-0672
Fax: (650)725-8676
Publication E-mail: stanford.magazine@stanford.edu
Alumni magazine. **Freq:** Bimonthly. **Print Method:** Offset. **Trim Size:** 8 1/8 x 10 3/4. **Cols./Page:** 3. **Col. Width:** 27 nonpareils. **Col. Depth:** 133 agate lines. **Key Personnel:** Kevin Cool, Editor; Ginny McCormick, Senior Editor; Edie Filice Barry, Publisher. **ISSN:** 1063--2778 (print). **Subscription Rates:** $24 Individuals. **URL:** http://alumni.stanford.edu/get/page/magazine/home. **Ad Rates:** BW $4780; 4C $6830. **Remarks:** Accepts advertising. **Circ:** △**185229**.

4424 ■ Topics in Magnetic Resonance Imaging
Lippincott Williams & Wilkins
c/o Scott W. Atlas, MD, Ed.-in-Ch.
Stanford University Medical Ctr., S-047
300 Pasteur Dr.
Stanford, CA 94305-5105
Peer-reviewed journal covering the latest on magnetic resonance imaging techniques. **Freq:** 6/year. **Print Method:** Sheetfed Offset. **Trim Size:** 8 1/4 x 11. **Key Personnel:** Stella Bebos, Associate Publisher; Scott W. Atlas, MD, Editor-in-Chief. **ISSN:** 0899--3459 (print); **EISSN:** 1536--1004 (electronic). **Subscription Rates:** $564 Individuals paperback; $1087 Institutions paperback; $653 Canada and Mexico paperback; $1273 Institutions, Canada and Mexico paperback; $671 Other countries paperback; $1291 Institutions, other countries paperback. **URL:** http://journals.lww.com/topicsinmri/pages/default.aspx. **Ad Rates:** BW $1,065; 4C $2,520. **Remarks:** Accepts advertising. **Circ:** 108.

4425 ■ KZSU-FM - 90.1
Memorial Hall
540 Memorial Way
Stanford, CA 94305-5010
Phone: (650)725-4868
Email: info@kzsu.stanford.edu
Format: Full Service; Alternative/New Music/Progressive. **Owner:** The Board of Trustees of the Leland Stanford Junior University, 450 Serra Mall, Stanford, CA 94305, Ph: (650)723-2300. **Founded:** 1964. **Operating Hours:** Continuous; 100% local. **Key Personnel:** Mark Lawrence, Chief Engineer, ce@kzsu.stanford.edu; Mark Mollineaux, Dir. of Programs; Francis Dickerson, Dir. Pub. Aff. **Wattage:** 500. **Ad Rates:** Noncommercial. **Mailing address:** PO Box 20190, Stanford, CA 94309-0190. **URL:** http://kzsu.stanford.edu.

STOCKTON

San Joaquin Co. San Joaquin Co. (C). An inland seaport on the San Joaquin River, 78 m E of San Francisco. University of the Pacific. San Joaquin Delta College. Manufactures boxboard, wooden and glass containers, auto windshields, window glass, pencil slats, doors, plows, feeds, fertilizers, bricks, scrapers, farm implement parts, concrete and steel pipes, structural iron and steel, cans, tire camelback, tire repair equipment, electrical equipment, paving machinery, cereal products, canned fruits and vegetables, motor boats, yachts, barges. Shipyards.

4426 ■ AHAF Journal
American Handwriting Analysis Foundation
1011 S Tuxedo Ave.
Stockton, CA 95204-6219
Phone: (209)518-6886
Publisher's E-mail: ahaf@ahafhandwriting.org
Freq: Bimonthly. **Subscription Rates:** Included in membership; $50 U.S. /year; $60 Canada and Mexico /year; $70 Other countries /year. **Remarks:** Accepts advertising. **Circ:** 500.

4427 ■ International Journal of Business Research
International Academy of Business and Economics
IABE, 10940 Trinity Pkwy., Ste. C-185
Stockton, CA 95219
Phone: (702)560-0653

Fax: (702)508-9166
Publisher's E-mail: admin@iabe.eu
Peer-reviewed journal publishing theoretical, conceptual, and applied research on topics related to research, practice and teaching in all areas of business, management, and marketing. **Freq:** 3/year March, June, and October. **Key Personnel:** David Ward, Board Member; Dr. Cheick Wague, Managing Editor; Tahi J. Gnepa, Managing Editor. **ISSN:** 1555--1296 (print); **EISSN:** 2378--8577 (electronic). **URL:** http://www.iabe.eu/domains/iabeX/journalinfo.aspx?JournalID=IJBR. **Circ:** (Not Reported).

4428 ■ Journal of International Business and Economics
International Academy of Business and Economics
IABE, 10940 Trinity Pkwy., Ste. C-185
Stockton, CA 95219
Phone: (702)560-0653
Fax: (702)508-9166
Publisher's E-mail: admin@iabe.eu
Peer-reviewed journal publishing theoretical, conceptual, and applied research on topics related to research, practice and teaching in all areas of business, economics, e-commerce, and related subjects. **Freq:** 3/year March, June, and October. **Key Personnel:** Prof. Tahi J. Gnepa, PhD, Managing Editor; Prof. Zinovy Radovilsky, PhD, Managing Editor; Prof. Phapruke Ussahawanitchakit, PhD, Managing Editor. **ISSN:** 1544--8037 (print); **EISSN:** 2378--9174 (electronic). **URL:** http://www.iabe.eu/domains/iabeX/journal.aspx?journalid=9; http://www.iabe.eu/domains/iabeX/journalinfo.aspx?JournalID=JIBE. **Circ:** (Not Reported).

4429 ■ Journal of International Business Strategy
International Academy of Business and Economics
IABE, 10940 Trinity Pkwy., Ste. C-185
Stockton, CA 95219
Phone: (702)560-0653
Fax: (702)508-9166
Publisher's E-mail: admin@iabe.eu
Peer-reviewed journal publishing theoretical, conceptual, and applied research on topics related to strategy in international business. **Freq:** 3/year March, June, and October. **Key Personnel:** Dr. Wilson Almeida; Prof. Tahi J. Gnepa, PhD, Managing Editor. **ISSN:** 1553--9563 (print); **EISSN:** 2378--8585 (electronic). **URL:** http://www.iabe.eu/domains/iabeX/journal.aspx?journalid=7; http://www.iabe.eu/domains/iabeX/journalinfo.aspx?JournalID=IJBS. **Circ:** (Not Reported).

4430 ■ The Pacifican
University of the Pacific
3601 Pacific Ave.
Stockton, CA 95211
Phone: (209)946-2285
Collegiate newspaper. **Freq:** Weekly. **Print Method:** Photo offset. **Trim Size:** 10 x 15. **Cols./Page:** 5. **Col. Width:** 1.875 inches. **Col. Depth:** 12 inches. **Key Personnel:** Ruben Dominguez, Editor-in-Chief; Jamieson Cox, Publisher; Ruben Moreno, Business Manager. **URL:** http://thepacificanonline.com/wp. **Ad Rates:** BW $360; 4C $400. **Remarks:** Accepts advertising. **Circ:** (Not Reported).

4431 ■ San Joaquin Farm Bureau News
San Joaquin Farm Bureau Federation
3290 N Ad Art Rd.
Stockton, CA 95208
Phone: (209)931-4931
Fax: (209)931-1433
Agricultural newspaper. **Freq:** Monthly. **Print Method:** Offset. **Trim Size:** 11.5 x 15. **Cols./Page:** 4. **Col. Width:** 2 1/4 inches. **Col. Depth:** 13 1/2 inches. **Key Personnel:** Bruce Blodgett, Executive Director. **USPS:** 185-880. **Subscription Rates:** $0.50 Individuals; $5 Nonmembers. **URL:** http://www.sjfb.org. **Ad Rates:** BW $560; 4C $870; PCI $14.20. **Remarks:** Accepts advertising. **Circ:** Paid ‡5000.

4432 ■ Update: Applications of Research in Music Education
National Association for Music Education
c/o Ruth Brittin, Editor
University of the Pacific
104 Buck Hall
3601 Pacific Ave.
Stockton, CA 95211-0110
Phone: (209)946-2408
Publisher's E-mail: memberservices@nafme2.org
Professional journal covering music for music teachers at all levels. **Freq:** Semiannual. **Key Personnel:** Ruth V. Brittin, Editor. **ISSN:** 8755-1233 (print); **EISSN:** 1945-0109 (electronic). **Subscription Rates:** $84 Institutions e-access. **URL:** http://www.sagepub.com/journals/Journal201904. **Remarks:** Advertising not accepted. **Circ:** (Not Reported).

4433 ■ KCVR-AM - 1570
6820 Pacific Ave., Fl. 3A
Stockton, CA 95207
Phone: (209)474-0154
Owner: Stockton Radio Co., at above address. **Founded:** 1946. **Wattage:** 5,000 day. **Ad Rates:** Noncommercial. **Mailing address:** PO Box 7871, Stockton, CA 95207.

4434 ■ KCVR-FM - 98.9
6820 Pacific Ave., 3A Fl.
Stockton, CA 95207
Phone: (209)479-0154
Fax: (209)474-0316
Format: Hispanic. **Owner:** Entravision Communications Corporation, 2425 Olympic Blvd., Ste. 6000 W, Santa Monica, CA 90404-4030, Ph: (310)447-3870, Fax: (310)447-3899. **ADI:** Sacramento-Stockton, CA. **URL:** http://www.entravision.com.

4435 ■ KHKK-FM - 104.1
3127 Transworld Dr., Ste. 270
Stockton, CA 95206
Phone: (209)575-0104
Fax: (209)572-0540
Format: Classic Rock. **Owner:** Citadel Broadcasting Corp., 7201 W Lake Mead Blvd., Ste. 400, Las Vegas, NV 89128-8366, Ph: (702)804-5200, Fax: (702)804-8250. **Operating Hours:** Continuous. **Wattage:** 50,000. **URL:** http://www.104thehawk.com/station-information.

4436 ■ KHOP @ 95-1 - 95.1
3136 Boeing Way, Ste. 125
Stockton, CA 95206
Phone: (209)766-5000
Fax: (209)522-2061
Free: 800-548-0951
Email: khop@khop.com
Format: Top 40. **Owner:** Citadel Communications Corp., San Diego, CA, Ph: (505)767-6700, Fax: (505)767-6767. **Founded:** 1949. **Operating Hours:** Continuous. **Local Programs:** *Ghetto House Radio*, Saturday Sunday 12:00 a.m. - 2:00 a.m.; *Mornings with Madden and Riley*, Monday Tuesday Wednesday Thursday Friday 5:00 a.m. - 10:00 a.m. **Wattage:** 29,500. **Ad Rates:** Advertising accepted; rates available upon request. **URL:** http://www.khop.com.

4437 ■ KJOY-FM - 99.3
3136 Boeing Way, Ste. 25
Stockton, CA 95206
Phone: (209)476-1230
Fax: (209)956-0907
Format: Adult Contemporary. **Owner:** Citadel Broadcasting Corp., 7201 W Lake Mead Blvd., Ste. 400, Las Vegas, NV 89128-8366, Ph: (702)804-5200, Fax: (702)804-8250. **Operating Hours:** Continuous. **ADI:** Sacramento-Stockton, CA. **Wattage:** 4,000 ERP. **Ad Rates:** Advertising accepted; rates available upon request. **URL:** http://www.993kjoy.com.

4438 ■ KLOC-AM - 920
6820 Pacific Ave., Ste. 2
Stockton, CA 95207-2604
Phone: (209)473-7892
Fax: (209)521-4131
Format: Hispanic. **Networks:** Independent. **Founded:** 1963. **Operating Hours:** Continuous; 100% local. **Wattage:** 2,500.

4439 ■ KMIX-FM - 100.9
6820 Pacific Avenue Floor 3A
Stockton, CA 95207
Phone: (209)474-0154
Format: Hispanic. **Networks:** AP. **Owner:** Entravision Communications Corporation, 2425 Olympic Blvd., Ste. 6000 W, Santa Monica, CA 90404-4030, Ph: (310)447-3870, Fax: (310)447-3899. **Founded:** 1921. **Operating Hours:** Continuous. **ADI:** Sacramento-Stockton, CA. **Key Personnel:** Karl Meyer, Exec. VP of Mktg.; David Candelaria, Gen. Mgr.; Walter F. Ulloa, Chairman; Chris Moncayo, Exec. VP; Philip C. Wilkinson, President; Jeff Apodaca, Gen. Mgr. **Wattage:** 6,000. **Ad Rates:** Advertising accepted; rates available upon request. **URL:** http://www.entravision.com.

4440 ■ KSTN-AM - 1420
2171 Ralph Ave.
Stockton, CA 95206
Phone: (209)948-5786
Format: Oldies. **Networks:** NBC. **Founded:** 1949. **Operating Hours:** Continuous. **ADI:** Sacramento-Stockton, CA. **Wattage:** 5,000.

4441 ■ KTSE-FM - 97.1
6820 Pacific Ave., Fl. 3A
Stockton, CA 95207
Phone: (209)474-0154
Fax: (209)474-0316
Format: Hispanic. **Owner:** Entravision Communications Corporation, 2425 Olympic Blvd., Ste. 6000 W, Santa Monica, CA 90404-4030, Ph: (310)447-3870, Fax: (310)447-3899. **ADI:** Sacramento-Stockton, CA. **Key Personnel:** Lisa Sunday, Gen. Mgr. **URL:** http://www.jose971.com.

4442 ■ KWG-AM - 1230
3256 Penryn Rd., Ste. 100
Loomis, CA 95650-8052
Phone: (916)535-0500
Fax: (916)535-0504
Free: 866-774-3278
Format: Religious; Contemporary Christian. **Owner:** Immaculate Heart Radio, 3256 Penryn Rd., Ste. 100, Loomis, CA 95650-8052. **Ad Rates:** Noncommercial; underwriting available. **URL:** http://ihradio.com.

4443 ■ KWIN-FM - 97.7
3136 Boeing Way, Ste. 125
Stockton, CA 95206
Phone: (209)766-5000
Free: 800-585-5946
Email: programming@kwin.com
Format: Urban Contemporary. **Simulcasts:** KWNN-FM. **Networks:** ABC. **Owner:** Citadel Broadcasting Corp., 7201 W Lake Mead Blvd., Ste. 400, Las Vegas, NV 89128-8366, Ph: (702)804-5200, Fax: (702)804-8250. **Founded:** 1959. **Operating Hours:** Continuous. **Key Personnel:** Joe Roberts, Prog. Dir.; Bob Berger, Gen. Mgr., bob.berger@cumulus.com. **Wattage:** 6,000 ERP. **Ad Rates:** Advertising accepted; rates available upon request. **URL:** http://www.kwin.com.

4444 ■ KWNN-FM - 98.3
3136 Boeing Way, Ste. 125
Stockton, CA 95206
Phone: (209)476-1230
Format: Contemporary Hit Radio (CHR). **Simulcasts:** KWIN-FM. **Owner:** Citadel Broadcasting Corp., 7201 W Lake Mead Blvd., Ste. 400, Las Vegas, NV 89128-8366, Ph: (702)804-5200, Fax: (702)804-8250. **Founded:** 1978. **Operating Hours:** Continuous. **ADI:** Sacramento-Stockton, CA. **Key Personnel:** Scott Dwyer, Dir. of Programs. **Wattage:** 3,000. **Ad Rates:** Advertising accepted; rates available upon request. **URL:** http://www.kwin.com.

4445 ■ KXEX-AM - 1550
2171 Ralph Ave.
Stockton, CA 95215
Phone: (559)233-8803
Fax: (559)233-8871
Format: Public Radio. **Simulcasts:** KQEQ-AM. **Owner:** RAK Communications Inc., at above address. **Founded:** 1962. **Operating Hours:** Continuous. **ADI:** Fresno-Visalia (Hanford), CA. **Key Personnel:** Al Perez, Gen. Mgr. **Wattage:** 5,000 day; 2,500 night. **Ad Rates:** $12-15 for 30 seconds; $18-20 for 60 seconds. Combined advertising rates available with KQEQ-AM, KZFO-FM.

4446 ■ KYCC-FM - 89.1
9019 N West Ln.
Stockton, CA 95210-1401
Phone: (209)477-3690
Fax: (209)477-2762
Free: 800-654-5254
Format: Religious; Information. **Simulcasts:** KYCC-FM. **Networks:** USA Radio. **Owner:** Your Christian Companion Network, 9019 W Ln., Stockton, CA 95210-1401, Ph: (209)477-3690, Fax: (209)477-2762, Free: 800-654-

Circulation: ★ = AAM; △ or • = BPA; ♦ = CAC; ❑ = VAC; ⊕ = PO Statement; ‡ = Publisher's Report; Boldface figures = sworn; Light figures = estimated.

5254. **Founded:** 1978. **Formerly:** KCJH-FM. **Operating Hours:** Continuous. **Local Programs:** *Speak Up With Compassion*, Sunday Monday Tuesday Wednesday Thursday Friday 1:20 p.m. 10:20 a.m. **Wattage:** 41,000. **Ad Rates:** Noncommercial. **URL:** http://www.kycc.org.

4447 ■ KYKL-FM
5700 W Oaks Blvd.
Rocklin, CA 95765
Free: 800-525-LOVE
Format: Contemporary Christian. **Owner:** Educational Media Foundation, 2351 Sunset Blvd., Ste. 170-218, Rocklin, CA 95677, Ph: (800)434-8400. **Wattage:** 6,000 ERP.

STUDIO CITY

North Hollywood. South of Burbank.

4448 ■ Fore Magazine
Southern California Golf Association
3740 Cahuenga Blvd.
Studio City, CA 91604-3502
Phone: (818)980-3630
Fax: (818)980-2709
Free: 800-554-7242
Publisher's E-mail: info@scga.org
Freq: Quarterly. **Print Method:** Offset. **Trim Size:** 8 1/4 x 10 1/2. **Cols./Page:** 3. **Col. Width:** 27 nonpareils. **Col. Depth:** 140 agate lines. **ISSN:** 0300--8509 (print). **Subscription Rates:** Included in membership. **URL:** http://www.scga.org/news/fore-magazine. **Ad Rates:** 4C $8,250. **Remarks:** Accepts advertising. **Circ:** Paid 160000, 172000.

4449 ■ Rattle: Poetry for the 21st Century
Rattle Foundation
12411 Ventura Blvd.
Studio City, CA 91604
Phone: (818)505-6777
Fax: (818)505-6778
Magazine featuring poetry, essays and interviews. **Freq:** Quarterly in March, June, September and December. **Key Personnel:** Timothy Green, Editor; Alan Fox, Editor-in-Chief. **ISSN:** 1097--2900 (print); **EISSN:** 2153--8115 (electronic). **Subscription Rates:** $20 Individuals; $35 Two years. **URL:** http://www.rattle.com/poetry. **Circ:** 4700.

4450 ■ KCAL-TV - 9
4200 Radford Ave.
Studio City, CA 91604
Phone: (818)655-2000
Format: Commercial TV. **Networks:** Independent. **Owner:** CBS Corp., 51 W 52nd St., New York, NY 10019-6188, Ph: (212)975-4321, Fax: (212)975-4516, Free: 877-227-0787. **Operating Hours:** Continuous. **ADI:** Los Angeles (Corona & San Bernardino), CA. **URL:** http://www.losangeles.cbslocal.com.

4451 ■ KCBS-TV - 2
4200 Radford Ave.
Studio City, CA 91604
Phone: (818)655-2000
Format: Commercial TV. **Networks:** CBS. **Owner:** CBS Corp., 51 W 52nd St., New York, NY 10019-6188, Ph: (212)975-4321, Fax: (212)975-4516, Free: 877-227-0787. **Founded:** 1931. **Formerly:** Westinghouse/CBS Inc.; KNXT. **Operating Hours:** Continuous. **Key Personnel:** Leslie Moonves, CEO, President. **Ad Rates:** Advertising accepted; rates available upon request. **URL:** http://www.losangeles.cbslocal.com.

SUN VALLEY

4452 ■ The Master's Seminary Journal
The Master's Seminary
13248 Roscoe Blvd.
Sun Valley, CA 91352-3739
Phone: (818)782-6488
Fax: (818)909-5725
Journal containing Biblical text, Theology and Pastoral concerns. **Freq:** Semiannual. **Key Personnel:** Dr. John F. MacArthur, President; Dr. Richard L. Mayhue, Dean, Senior Vice President; Dr. Irvin A. Busenitz, Executive Editor. **ISSN:** 1066--3959 (print). **Subscription Rates:** $40 U.S. print; $35 U.S. alumni discount; $45 Other countries print; $40 Other countries alumni discount. **URL:** http://www.tms.edu/msj. **Circ:** (Not Reported).

SUNNYVALE

Santa Clara Co. Santa Clara Co. (W). 20 m NW of San Jose. Residential. Semi conductors, electronic components, computers, electrical heavy generating and control equipment, missile aerospace systems, paper products, chemicals. Nurseries. Fruit, canneries. Apricots, prunes, cherries.

4453 ■ NATEA Journal
North America Taiwanese Engineers' Association
PO Box 2772
Sunnyvale, CA 94087-0772
URL: http://www.natea.org/hq/journals_index.php. **Remarks:** Accepts advertising. **Circ:** (Not Reported).

SUNSET BEACH

4454 ■ Travel with Spirit
Travel Network Group L.L.C.
PO Box 1318
Sunset Beach, CA 90742
Publication E-mail: press@travelnetworkgroup.com
Magazine featuring Christian travel products and services. **Freq:** Quarterly. **URL:** http://www.travelwithspirit.com. **Remarks:** Accepts advertising. **Circ:** (Not Reported).

SUSANVILLE

Lassen Co. Lassen Co. (NE). 80 m NW of Reno, Nev. Residential. Tourism. Beverages. Pine, fir timber. Dairy, stock, grain farms.

4455 ■ Lassen County Times
Feather Publishing Company Inc.
100 Grand Ave.
Susanville, CA 96130
Phone: (530)257-5321
Fax: (530)257-0408
Publication E-mail: lctimes@lassennews.com
Community newspaper. **Freq:** Weekly (Tues.). **Print Method:** Offset. **Cols./Page:** 6. **Col. Width:** 25 nonpareils. **Col. Depth:** 301 agate lines. **Key Personnel:** Sam Williams, Managing Editor, phone: (530)257-5321; Michael Taborski, Publisher, phone: (530)283-0800; Jill Atkinson, Manager, Advertising. **ISSN:** 5844--9000 (print). **Subscription Rates:** $26 Individuals in County; $37 Individuals in California; $44 Out of state. **URL:** http://www.lassennews.com. **Ad Rates:** GLR $6; BW $720; 4C $1020; SAU $6; PCI $6. **Remarks:** Accepts advertising. **Circ:** Paid 6252, Free 3705.

4456 ■ KJDX-FM - 93.3
3015 Johnstonville Rd.
Susanville, CA 96130-8739
Phone: (530)257-2121
Fax: (530)257-6955
Free: 866-882-1277
Email: radioinfo@theradionetwork.com
Format: Sports; News. **Founded:** 1976. **Formerly:** KSUE-FM. **Operating Hours:** Continuous. **Key Personnel:** Rodney P. Chambers, Contact. **Wattage:** 100,000 ERP. **Ad Rates:** Advertising accepted; rates available upon request. $7-10.50 for 30 seconds; $8.50-12 for 60 seconds. $7-$10.50 for 30 seconds; $8.50-$12 for 60 seconds. Combined advertising rates available with KSUE-AM. **URL:** http://www.sierradailynews.com.

4457 ■ KSUE-AM - 1240
3015 Johnstonville Rd.
Susanville, CA 96130-8739
Phone: (530)257-2121
Fax: (530)257-6955
Format: News; Talk. **Simulcasts:** KJDX-FM. **Networks:** ABC; Westwood One Radio. **Owner:** Sierra Radio Network, 3015 Johnstonville Rd., Susanville, CA 96130, Fax: (530)257-6955, Free: 800-366-9162. **Founded:** 1948. **Operating Hours:** Continuous; 25% network, 75% local. **ADI:** Reno, NV. **Key Personnel:** Suzanne Alliano, Gen. Sales Mgr.; Rod Chambers, Gen. Mgr., rchambers@theradionetwork.com. **Wattage:** 1,000. **Ad Rates:** $7-10.50 for 30 seconds; $8.50-12 for 60 seconds. $7.00-$10.50 for 30 seconds; $8.50-$12.00 for 60 seconds. Combined advertising rates available with KJDE-FM.

SUTTER CREEK

4458 ■ Gold Country Times
Gold Country Times
PO Box 897
Sutter Creek, CA 95685
Phone: (209)267-9886
Fax: (209)267-1601
Community newspaper. **Freq:** Monthly. **Key Personnel:** Martin Johnson, Publisher; Evelina Dunn, Editor-in-Chief. **Subscription Rates:** $20 Individuals first class; $16 Individuals senior/veteran. **URL:** http://www.goldcountrytimes.com/. **Remarks:** Accepts advertising. **Circ:** 6000.

SYLMAR

4459 ■ All Access Magazine
All Access Magazine
15981 Yarnell St., Ste. 122
Sylmar, CA 91342
Phone: (818)833-8852
Magazine covering the best interviews, reviews, CD reviews, columns and photos of celebrities. **Key Personnel:** Debra Stocker, Editor-in-Chief, Publisher; John C. Green, General Manager. **URL:** http://allaccessmagazine.com. **Ad Rates:** BW $550; 4C $650. **Remarks:** Accepts advertising. **Circ:** (Not Reported).

TAHOE CITY

Placer Co. (NE). On Lake Tahoe, 80 m NE of Sacramento. Machine shop. Resort.

4460 ■ North Tahoe/Truckee Week
North Tahoe/Truckee Week
PO Box 87
Tahoe City, CA 96145
Phone: (530)546-5995
Fax: (530)546-8113
Publisher's E-mail: publisher@tahoethisweek.com
Magazine containing current events, entertainment, recreation, and sightseeing information for North Lake Tahoe visitors and residents. Includes classified ads. **Freq:** Weekly (Thurs.). **Print Method:** Offset. **Trim Size:** 11 x 14. **Cols./Page:** 6. **Col. Width:** 9 picas. **Col. Depth:** 14 inches. **Key Personnel:** Katherine E. Hill, Publisher, Editor-in-Chief. **Subscription Rates:** Free. **URL:** http://thetahoeweekly.com. **Formerly:** North Tahoe Week. **Ad Rates:** BW $1,110; 4C $1230; PCI $20. **Remarks:** Accepts advertising. **Circ:** 11250.

TARZANA

Los Angeles Co. (S). 25 m NW of Los Angeles. Residential. Commercial.

4461 ■ Journal of the Fluorescent Mineral Society
Fluorescent Mineral Society
PO Box 572694
Tarzana, CA 91357-2694
Phone: (862)259-2367
Publisher's E-mail: contact@uvminerals.org
Freq: annual or biennial. **URL:** http://uvminerals.org/fms/publications-and-projects. **Remarks:** Advertising not accepted. **Circ:** (Not Reported).

4462 ■ Los Angeles Family Magazine
Family Magazines Group
18801 Ventura Blvd., Ste. 300
Tarzana, CA 91356
Local, consumer magazine covering parenting. **Freq:** Monthly. **Key Personnel:** Laura Diamond, Editor-in-Chief. **Subscription Rates:** Free. **URL:** http://www.lafamily.com. **Formerly:** LA Children Magazine. **Remarks:** Advertising accepted; rates available upon request. **Circ:** (Not Reported).

4463 ■ RePlay Magazine
RePlay Magazine
PO Box 572829
Tarzana, CA 91357
Phone: (818)776-2880
Fax: (818)776-2888
Trade magazine covering the coin-operated amusement game industry. **Freq:** Monthly. **Print Method:** Sheetfed offset. **Trim Size:** 8 1/2 x 11. **Cols./Page:** 3. **Col. Width:** 2 1/4 inches. **Col. Depth:** 10 inches. **Key Personnel:** Steve White, Editor; Barry Zweben, Manager, Advertising. **ISSN:** 1534--2328 (print). **Subscription Rates:** $65 Individuals 1 year; $120 Two years; $160 Individuals 3 years; $90 Canada and Mexico 1 year; $230 Other countries 1 year. **URL:** http://www.replaymag.com. **Formerly:** RePlay. **Ad Rates:** BW

$1380; 4C $1880. **Remarks:** Accepts advertising. **Circ:** 3000.

TEHACHAPI

Kern Co. Kern Co. (S). 46 m SE of Bakersfield. Resort area. Residential. Limestone quarries. Clay pits. Agriculture. wheat, barley, nectarines, peaches.

4464 ■ Tehachapi News
Tehachapi News Publications
411 N Mill St.
Tehachapi, CA 93581
Phone: (661)822-6828
Fax: (661)822-4053
Free: 800-600-2909
Publication E-mail: editorial@tehachapinews.com
Community newspaper. **Freq:** Weekly (Tues.). **Print Method:** Offset. **Cols./Page:** 6. **Col. Width:** 26 nonpareils. **Col. Depth:** 294 agate lines. **Key Personnel:** Claudia Elliott, Editor, General Manager. **USPS:** 536-740. **Subscription Rates:** $26 Individuals in Kern County (home delivery) - one year weekly (every Tuesday); $46 Out of area mail - one year weekly; $56 Out of state mail - one year weekly. **URL:** http://www.tehachapinews.com. **Mailing address:** PO Box 1840, Tehachapi, CA 93561. **Remarks:** Accepts advertising. **Circ:** ‡8500.

TEMECULA

Riverside Co. Riverside Co. (S) 1 m S. of Murrieta. Residential.

4465 ■ Gold Prospector
Gold Prospectors Association of America
43445 Business Park Dr., Ste. 113
Temecula, CA 92590-3671
Phone: (951)699-4749
Fax: (951)699-4062
Free: 800-551-9707
Publisher's E-mail: info@goldprospectors.org
Freq: Bimonthly. **ISSN:** 0745--6344 (print). **Subscription Rates:** Included in membership. **URL:** http://www.goldprospectors.org/Publications. **Remarks:** Accepts advertising. **Circ:** (Not Reported).

4466 ■ Riding: California Riding Magazine
Riding's Publications Inc.
PO Box 893640
Temecula, CA 92589
Phone: (619)445-4020
Fax: (619)566-4100
Publisher's E-mail: info@ridingmagazine.com
Magazine focusing on horses and equestrians. **Freq:** Monthly. **Trim Size:** 8.375 x 10.75. **Key Personnel:** Cheryl Erpelding, Publisher; Kim F. Miller, Managing Editor; Kathy Eble, General Manager. **Subscription Rates:** $20 Individuals; $35 Two years. **URL:** http://www.ridingmagazine.com. **Ad Rates:** BW $495; 4C $1055. **Remarks:** Accepts display advertising. **Circ:** (Not Reported).

4467 ■ Widescreen Review: The Essential Home Theatre Resource
Widescreen Review
PO Box 2587
Temecula, CA 92593-2580
Phone: (951)676-4914
Fax: (951)693-2960
Free: 877-398-3367
Consumer magazine for home theater enthusiasts with widescreen format DVD and covering DVD movie reviews and equipment and technology. **Freq:** Monthly. **Print Method:** Web offset. **Trim Size:** 8 1/8 x 10 1/2. **Key Personnel:** Gary Reber, Editor-in-Chief; Danny Richielieu, Editor. **Subscription Rates:** $30 Canada and Mexico; $50 Other countries; $25 U.S.; $15 By mail. **URL:** http://www.widescreenreview.com. **Ad Rates:** BW $2,975; 4C $3,920. **Remarks:** Accepts advertising. **Circ:** Paid ⊕**50000**.

4468 ■ KATY-FM - 101.3
27431 Enterprise Cir. W, Ste. 101
Temecula, CA 92590
Phone: (951)676-1013
Fax: (951)506-1213
Format: Adult Contemporary. **Networks:** ABC. **Owner:** All Pro Broadcasting, Inc., 242 E Airport Dr., Ste. 106, San Bernardino, CA 92408, Ph: (909)890-5904. **Founded:** Dec. 01, 1989. **Operating Hours:** Continuous. **Wattage:** 1,550 ERP. **Ad Rates:** Noncommercial. **URL:** http://www.1013themix.com.

4469 ■ KMYT-FM - 94.5
27349 Jefferson Ave., No. 116
Temecula, CA 92590
Phone: (909)929-5088
Fax: (909)658-8822
Format: Talk; News. **ADI:** San Diego, CA. **Wattage:** 320. **URL:** http://radio945fm.iheart.com.

4470 ■ KTMQ-FM - 103.3
27349 Jefferson Ave., No. 116
Temecula, CA 92590
Phone: (951)296-9050
Fax: (951)296-9077
Format: Classic Rock. **Owner:** iHeartMedia Inc., 200 E Basse Rd., San Antonio, TX 78209, Ph: (210)832-3314. **ADI:** San Diego, CA. **Key Personnel:** Michael Dellinger, Dir. of Programs; Rich Mena, Chief Engineer. **Wattage:** 1,250. **Ad Rates:** Noncommercial. **URL:** http://www.q1033.com//main.html.

TEMPLE CITY

Los Angeles Co Los Angeles Co. Los Angeles Co. (S) 6 m S of Pasadena. Residential.

4471 ■ 20 de Mayo
20 de Mayo
4509 N Temple City Blvd., Ste. 203
Temple City, CA 91780
Phone: (626)401-0425
Fax: (626)401-9417
Publisher's E-mail: mayo20@aol.com
Newspaper (tabloid, Spanish). **Freq:** Weekly. **Cols./Page:** 6. **Col. Width:** 1 1/2 inches. **Col. Depth:** 16 inches. **Key Personnel:** Abel Perez, Executive Editor. **USPS:** 459-450. **URL:** http://www.20deMayo.org. **Ad Rates:** BW $1,200; PCI $12.50. **Remarks:** Accepts advertising. **Circ:** 25000.

THOUSAND OAKS

Ventura Co. Ventura Co. (SW). 30 m SE of Ventura. Manufactures aircraft parts, electronic parts and parachutes, plastics. Horse breeding. Agriculture. Citrus fruit.

4472 ■ Accounting History
SAGE Publications Inc.
2455 Teller Rd.
Thousand Oaks, CA 91320-2234
Free: 800-818-7243
Publisher's E-mail: sales@pfp.sagepub.com
Journal covering the historical development of accounting. **Freq:** Quarterly February, May, August, and November. **Print Method:** Offset. **Trim Size:** 6 3/4 x 10. **Cols./Page:** 1. **Col. Width:** 50 nonpareils. **Col. Depth:** 100 agate lines. **Key Personnel:** Brian West, Editor; Garry Carnegie, Editor. **ISSN:** 1032--3732 (print); **EISSN:** 1749--3374 (electronic). **Subscription Rates:** $1024 Institutions print & e-access; $922 Institutions e-access; $1004 Institutions print only; $163 Individuals print only; $276 Institutions single print; $53 Individuals single print. **URL:** http://ach.sagepub.com. **Ad Rates:** BW £650. **Remarks:** Accepts advertising. **Circ:** (Not Reported).

4473 ■ Acta Radiologica
SAGE Publications Inc.
2455 Teller Rd.
Thousand Oaks, CA 91320-2234
Free: 800-818-7243
Publisher's E-mail: sales@pfp.sagepub.com
Journal aiming for the prompt publication of original research articles on diagnostic and interventional radiology, clinical radiology, experimental investigations in animals, and all other research related to imaging procedures and providing complete updates on all radiological specialties and technical utilities, as well as physiology and physics related to imaging, including ultrasonography, computed tomography, radionuclide and magnetic resonance imaging. **Freq:** 10/yr. **Key Personnel:** Prof. Arnulf Skjennald, Editor-in-Chief; Andreas Abildgaard, Editor. **ISSN:** 0284--1851 (print); **EISSN:** 1600--0455 (electronic). **Subscription Rates:** £952 Institutions print & e-access; £1047 Institutions combined plus backfile (current volume print & all online content); £857 Institutions e-access; £952 Institutions e-access plus backfile (all online content); £6432 Institutions e-access (content through 1998); £221 Individuals print & e-access; £123 Institutions single print issue; £24 Single issue. **URL:** http://acr.sagepub.com. **Remarks:** Accepts advertising. **Circ:** (Not Reported).

4474 ■ Acta Sociologica
SAGE Publications Inc.
2455 Teller Rd.
Thousand Oaks, CA 91320-2234
Free: 800-818-7243
Publication E-mail: acta@sociology.gu.se
Journal focusing on sociology. **Freq:** Quarterly. **Key Personnel:** Lise Kjolsrod, Editor, Consultant; Arne Mastekaasa, Editor, Consultant. **ISSN:** 0001-6993 (print); **EISSN:** 1502-3869 (electronic). **Subscription Rates:** £340 Institutions combined (print & e-access); £374 Institutions current volume print and all online content; £306 Institutions e-access; £1066 Institutions e-access (content through 1998); £333 Institutions print only; £81 Individuals print only; £92 Institutions single print; £26 Single issue print. **URL:** http://asj.sagepub.com; http://www.uk.sagepub.com/journals/Journal201660. **Remarks:** Accepts advertising. **Circ:** (Not Reported).

4475 ■ Action Research
SAGE Publications Inc.
2455 Teller Rd.
Thousand Oaks, CA 91320-2234
Free: 800-818-7243
Publisher's E-mail: sales@pfp.sagepub.com
Journal focusing on the theory and practice of action research. **Freq:** Quarterly. **Key Personnel:** Peter Reason, Editor; Hilary Bradbury, Editor-in-Chief. **ISSN:** 1476--7503 (print); **EISSN:** 1741--2617 (electronic). **Subscription Rates:** £56 Individuals print only; £484 Institutions e-access; £527 Institutions print only; £538 Institutions print and e-access; £18 Individuals single print issue; £145 Institutions single print issue. **URL:** http://arj.sagepub.com. **Ad Rates:** BW £600. **Remarks:** Accepts advertising. **Circ:** (Not Reported).

4476 ■ Active Learning in Higher Education
SAGE Publications Inc.
2455 Teller Rd.
Thousand Oaks, CA 91320-2234
Free: 800-818-7243
Publisher's E-mail: sales@pfp.sagepub.com
Journal for all those who teach and support learning in Higher Education and those who undertake or use research into effective learning, teaching, and assessment in universities and colleges. **Freq:** 3/year. **Key Personnel:** Lynne P. Baldwin, Editor. **ISSN:** 1469--7874 (print); **EISSN:** 1741--2625 (electronic). **Subscription Rates:** £66 Individuals print only; £441 Institutions e-access; £480 Institutions print only; £490 Institutions print and e-access; £29 Individuals single print issue; £176 Institutions single print issue. **URL:** http://alh.sagepub.com. **Ad Rates:** BW £600. **Remarks:** Accepts advertising. **Circ:** (Not Reported).

4477 ■ Adaptive Behavior
SAGE Publications Inc.
2455 Teller Rd.
Thousand Oaks, CA 91320-2234
Free: 800-818-7243
Publisher's E-mail: sales@pfp.sagepub.com
Peer-reviewed journal focusing on adaptive behavior in animals and autonomous artificial systems. **Freq:** Bimonthly. **Key Personnel:** Ezequiel Di Paolo, Editor; Joanna J. Bryson, Associate Editor; Randall D. Beer, Associate Editor; Peter M. Todd, Associate Editor. **ISSN:** 1059--7123 (print); **EISSN:** 1741--2633 (electronic). **Subscription Rates:** £451 Institutions e-access; £491 Institutions print only; £501 Institutions print and e-access; £90 Institutions single print issue; $767 Institutions content through 1998; $768 Institutions e-access; $836 Institutions print; $853 Institutions print and online; $853 Institutions all online content; $938 Institutions current volume print & all online content; $153 Institutions single issue. **URL:** http://adb.sagepub.com. **Ad Rates:** BW £600. **Remarks:** Accepts advertising. **Circ:** (Not Reported).

4478 ■ Administration & Society
SAGE Publications Inc.
2455 Teller Rd.
Thousand Oaks, CA 91320-2234

Circulation: ★ = AAM; △ or • = BPA; ♦ = CAC; ❑ = VAC; ⊕ = PO Statement; ‡ = Publisher's Report; Boldface figures = sworn; Light figures = estimated.

Free: 800-818-7243
Publisher's E-mail: sales@pfp.sagepub.com
Journal for social scientists and public administrators. **Founded:** 1969. **Freq:** 9/year Jan.-March-April-May-July-Aug-Sept.-Oct.-Nov. **Print Method:** Web Offset. **Trim Size:** 5 1/2 x 8 1/2. **Cols./Page:** 1. **Col. Width:** 50 nonpareils. **Col. Depth:** 100 agate lines. **Key Personnel:** Gary L. Wamsley, Editor; John P. Burns, Associate Editor; Sung Deuk Hahm, Associate Editor. **ISSN:** 0095-3997 (print); **EISSN:** 1552-3039 (electronic). **Subscription Rates:** $1578 Institutions print & e-access; $1736 Institutions current volume print; $1420 Institutions e-access; $1578 Institutions all online content; $3500 Institutions e-access, content through 1998; $1546 Institutions print only; $200 Individuals print only; $189 Institutions single print; $29 Individuals single print. **URL:** http://www.sagepub.com/journalsSubscribe.nav?prodId=Journal200755&. **Ad Rates:** BW $445; 4C $895. **Remarks:** Accepts advertising. **Circ:** Paid ‡700.

4479 ■ Adult Education Quarterly
SAGE Publications Inc.
2455 Teller Rd.
Thousand Oaks, CA 91320-2234
Free: 800-818-7243
Publisher's E-mail: sales@pfp.sagepub.com
Journal focusing on the understanding and practice of adult and continuing education. Published in association with the American Association for Adult and Continuing Education. **Freq:** Quarterly. **Key Personnel:** Leona M. English, Editor; Ashley Gleiman, Assistant Editor; Lisa R. Merriweather, Editor. **ISSN:** 0741--7136 (print); **EISSN:** 1552--3047 (electronic). **Subscription Rates:** $472 Institutions print & e-access; $519 Institutions current volume print & all online content; $472 Institutions backfile lease, e-access plus backfile (online); $1736 Institutions backfile purchase, e-access (content through 1998); $463 Institutions print only; $127 Institutions single print; $35 Individuals single print. **Online:** SAGE Publications Inc. SAGE Publications Inc. **URL:** http://aeq.sagepub.com; http://intl-aeq.sagepub.com online; http://us.sagepub.com/en-us/nam/adult-education-quarterly/journal200765. **Ad Rates:** BW $725. **Remarks:** Accepts advertising. **Circ:** (Not Reported).

4480 ■ Advances in Developing Human Resources
SAGE Publications Inc.
2455 Teller Rd.
Thousand Oaks, CA 91320-2234
Free: 800-818-7243
Publisher's E-mail: sales@pfp.sagepub.com
Journal for professionals working in the field of human resource development. **Freq:** Quarterly. **Key Personnel:** Michael Leimbach, Editor-in-Chief; Kimberly S. McDonald, Editor. **ISSN:** 1523--4223 (print); **EISSN:** 1552--3055 (electronic). **Subscription Rates:** £73 Individuals print only; £421 Institutions e-access; £459 Institutions print only; £468 Institutions print and e-access; £24 Individuals single print issue; £126 Institutions single print issue. **URL:** http://adh.sagepub.com. **Remarks:** Accepts advertising. **Circ:** (Not Reported).

4481 ■ Aesthetic Surgery Journal
Oxford University Press
2455 Teller Rd.
Thousand Oaks, CA 91320
Phone: (805)499-9774
Fax: (805)499-0871
Free: 800-818-7243
Peer-reviewed international journal focusing on scientific developments and clinical techniques in aesthetic surgery. Contains original research and review articles on topics relevant to the safe and effective practice of aesthetic surgery including anatomical studies, outcomes of clinical techniques, and patient safety. **Freq:** 8/year. **Trim Size:** 8 1/4 x 11. **Key Personnel:** Foad Nahai, MD, Editor. **ISSN:** 1090--820X (print); **EISSN:** 1527--330X (electronic). **Subscription Rates:** £248 Individuals print and online; £196 Individuals online only; $390 Individuals print and online; $310 Individuals online only; €294 Individuals print and online; €233 Individuals online only; £251 Institutions print only; £214 Institutions online only; £273 Institutions print and online; $477 Institutions print only; $407 Institutions online only; $519 Institutions print and online; €377 Institutions print only; €321 Institutions online only; €410 Institutions print and online. **URL:** http://asj.oxfordjournals.org; http://www.surgery.org/professionals/aesthetic-surgery-journal. **Formerly:** Aesthetic Surgery Quarterly. **Remarks:** Accepts advertising. **Circ:** Combined ‡5389, 5000.

4482 ■ Alternatives: Global, Local, Political
SAGE Publications Inc.
2455 Teller Rd.
Thousand Oaks, CA 91320-2234
Free: 800-818-7243
Publisher's E-mail: sales@pfp.sagepub.com
Peer-reviewed journal on politics and international relations. **Freq:** Quarterly February, May, August, November. **Key Personnel:** D.L. Sheth, Editor; R.B.J. Walker, Editor. **ISSN:** 0304--3754 (print); **EISSN:** 2163--3150 (electronic). **Subscription Rates:** £14 Individuals single print issue; £42 Individuals print and online; £302 Institutions print only; £83 Institutions single print issue. **URL:** http://uk.sagepub.com/en-gb/asi/alternatives/journal202040. **Ad Rates:** BW $225. **Remarks:** Accepts advertising. **Circ:** 600.

4483 ■ American Behavioral Scientist
SAGE Publications Inc.
2455 Teller Rd.
Thousand Oaks, CA 91320-2234
Free: 800-818-7243
Publication E-mail: journals@sagepub.com
Social and behavioral sciences journal.Offers comprehensive analysis of a single topic, examining such important and diverse arenas as sociology, international and U.S. politics, behavioral sciences, communication and media, economics, education, ethnic and racial studies, terrorism, and public service. **Founded:** 1957. **Freq:** Monthly. **Print Method:** Offset. **Trim Size:** 5 1/2 x 8 1/2. **Cols./Page:** 1. **Col. Width:** 50 nonpareils. **Col. Depth:** 100 agate lines. **Key Personnel:** Laura Lawrie, Editor. **ISSN:** 0002-7642 (print); **EISSN:** 1552-3381 (electronic). **Subscription Rates:** $2556 Institutions print & e-access; $2812 Institutions print & all online; $2300 Institutions e-access; $2556 Institutions backfile lease, e-access plus backfile all online; $7354 Institutions backfile purchase, e-access (content through 1998); $2505 Institutions print only; $261 Individuals print only; $197 Institutions single print; $24 Individuals single print. **URL:** http://www.sagepub.com/journals/Journal200921. **Also known as:** ABS. **Ad Rates:** BW $445. **Remarks:** Accepts advertising. **Circ:** (Not Reported).

4484 ■ American Journal of Cosmetic Surgery
SAGE Publications Inc.
2455 Teller Rd.
Thousand Oaks, CA 91320-2234
Free: 800-818-7243
Journal for professionals in cosmetic surgery. **Freq:** Quarterly. **Trim Size:** 8 1/2 x 11. **Key Personnel:** Jane A. Petro, MD, FACS. **ISSN:** 0748--8068 (print); **EISSN:** 2374--7722 (electronic). **Subscription Rates:** $250 Individuals print only; $255 Individuals print and online; $283 Institutions online only; $308 Institutions print only; $314 Institutions print and online. **URL:** http://acs.sagepub.com. **Ad Rates:** BW $1167.90; 4C $1004.70. **Remarks:** Accepts advertising. **Circ:** ‡3000, ‡2957.

4485 ■ American Journal of Evaluation
SAGE Publications Inc.
2455 Teller Rd.
Thousand Oaks, CA 91320-2234
Free: 800-818-7243
Publisher's E-mail: sales@pfp.sagepub.com
Peer-reviewed journal exploring the challenges related to conducting evaluations, from choosing program theories to implementing an evaluation, to presenting the final report to managing an evaluation's consequences. **Freq:** Quarterly. **Key Personnel:** Sharon F. Rallis, Editor; Thomas A. Schwandt, Editor. **ISSN:** 1098--2140 (print); **EISSN:** 1557--0878 (electronic). **Subscription Rates:** £114 Individuals print; £401 Institutions e-access; £437 Institutions print only; £446 Institutions print and e-access; £37 Individuals single print issue; £120 Institutions single print issue. **URL:** http://aje.sagepub.com. **Remarks:** Accepts advertising. **Circ:** (Not Reported).

4486 ■ American Journal of Hospice and Palliative Medicine
SAGE Publications Inc.
2455 Teller Rd.
Thousand Oaks, CA 91320-2234
Free: 800-818-7243
Publisher's E-mail: sales@pfp.sagepub.com
Journal offering multidisciplinary information on the medical, administrative, and psychosocial aspects of hospice and palliative care. **Freq:** 8/year. **Key Personnel:** Robert E. Enck, Editor-in-Chief; Steven J. Baumrucker, Associate Editor. **ISSN:** 1049-9091 (print). **Subscription Rates:** £555 Institutions print and e-access; £500 Institutions e-access; $544 Institutions print; $149 Individuals print. **URL:** http://ajh.sagepub.com/. **Remarks:** Accepts advertising. **Circ:** (Not Reported).

4487 ■ American Journal of Lifestyle Medicine
SAGE Publications Inc.
2455 Teller Rd.
Thousand Oaks, CA 91320-2234
Free: 800-818-7243
Publisher's E-mail: sales@pfp.sagepub.com
Journal covering professional resource for practitioners seeking to incorporate lifestyle practices into clinical medicine. **Freq:** Bimonthly. **Key Personnel:** James M. Rippe, MD, Editor. **ISSN:** 1559-8276 (print); **EISSN:** 1559-8284 (electronic). **Subscription Rates:** $192 Institutions E-Access; $77 Individuals E-Access. **URL:** http://www.sagepub.com/journalsProdDesc.nav?prodId=Journal201781. **Circ:** (Not Reported).

4488 ■ American Journal of Men's Health
SAGE Publications Inc.
2455 Teller Rd.
Thousand Oaks, CA 91320-2234
Free: 800-818-7243
Publisher's E-mail: sales@pfp.sagepub.com
Journal focusing on men's health, behavioral and social disciplines and illness. **Freq:** Bimonthly. **Print Method:** Web Offset. **Trim Size:** 8 1/8 x 10 7/8. **Key Personnel:** Demetrius James Porche, Editor-in-Chief. **ISSN:** 1557-9883 (print); **EISSN:** 1557-9891 (electronic). **Subscription Rates:** $616 Institutions print and online; $554 Institutions online; $604 Institutions print; $153 Individuals print; $111 Single issue Institutions; $33 Single issue Individuals. **URL:** http://www.sagepub.com/journalsProdDesc.nav?ct_p=boards&prodId=Journal201776. **Ad Rates:** BW $605. **Remarks:** Accepts advertising. **Circ:** (Not Reported).

4489 ■ The American Journal of Sports Medicine
SAGE Publications Inc.
2455 Teller Rd.
Thousand Oaks, CA 91320-2234
Free: 800-818-7243
Publisher's E-mail: info@aossm.org
Medical journal. **Freq:** Monthly. **Print Method:** Web press. **Trim Size:** 8 1/8 x 10 7/8. **Cols./Page:** 2. **Col. Width:** 32 nonpareils. **Col. Depth:** 119 agate lines. **Key Personnel:** Bruce Reider, MD, Editor; Allen Anderson, Associate Editor; Jack Hughston, Founder. **ISSN:** 0363--5465 (print); **EISSN:** 1552--3365 (electronic). **Subscription Rates:** £131 Institutions print and online; £14 Individuals single print issue; £57 Institutions single print issue. **URL:** http://ajs.sagepub.com. **Ad Rates:** BW $1450; 4C $1505. **Remarks:** Accepts advertising. **Circ:** Paid ‡8540, 11000.

4490 ■ American Politics Research
SAGE Publications Inc.
2455 Teller Rd.
Thousand Oaks, CA 91320-2234
Free: 800-818-7243
Publication E-mail: journals@sagepub.com
Political science journal. **Freq:** Bimonthly. **Print Method:** Web Offset. **Trim Size:** 5 1/2 x 8 1/2. **Cols./Page:** 1. **Col. Width:** 50 nonpareils. **Col. Depth:** 100 agate lines. **Key Personnel:** Brady Baybeck, Board Member; Yvette M. Alex-Assensoh, Board Member; Sarah Binder, Board Member; Brian J. Gaines, Editor; John Baughman, Board Member. **ISSN:** 1532--673x (print); **EISSN:** 1552--3373 (electronic). **Subscription Rates:** $160 Individuals print only; $1340 Institutions e-access; $1459 Institutions print only; $1489 Institutions print and e-access; $35 Individuals single issue; $267 Institutions single issue. **URL:** http://apr.sagepub.com. **Formerly:** American Politics Quarterly. **Ad Rates:** BW $875; 4C $1110. **Remarks:** Accepts advertising. **Circ:** (Not Reported).

4491 ■ American Review of Public Administration
SAGE Publications Inc.

2455 Teller Rd.
Thousand Oaks, CA 91320-2234
Free: 800-818-7243
Publisher's E-mail: sales@pfp.sagepub.com
Peer-reviewed journal covering public administration. **Freq:** Quarterly. **Print Method:** Offset. **Trim Size:** 7 x 10. **Cols./Page:** 1. **Col. Width:** 5.5 inches. **Col. Depth:** 8.750 inches. **Key Personnel:** John Clayton Thomas, Editor; Guy Adams, Editor. **ISSN:** 0275--0740 (print); **EISSN:** 1552--3357 (electronic). **Subscription Rates:** $125 Individuals print only; $1100 Institutions e-access; $1198 Institutions print only; $1222 Institutions print & e-access; $1222 Institutions e-access + backfile (all online content); $1344 Institutions combined + backfile (current volume print & all online content); $2616 Institutions e-access (content through 1998); $20 Individuals single print; $165 Institutions single print. **URL:** http://arp.sagepub.com. **Formerly**: Midwest Review of Public Administration. **Ad Rates:** BW $875; 4C $1110. **Remarks:** Accepts advertising. **Circ:** (Not Reported).

4492 ■ Angiology: Journal of Vascular Diseases
SAGE Publications Inc.
2455 Teller Rd.
Thousand Oaks, CA 91320-2234
Free: 800-818-7243
Publisher's E-mail: sales@pfp.sagepub.com
Peer-reviewed journal featuring original papers relating to cerebrovascular, cardiovascular, and peripheral vascular diseases. **Freq:** 10/year. **Print Method:** Offset. **Trim Size:** 8 1/2 x 11. **Cols./Page:** 2. **Key Personnel:** Dimitri P. Mikhailidis, MD, Editor. **ISSN:** 0003--3197 (print); **EISSN:** 1940--1574 (electronic). **Subscription Rates:** £263 Individuals print and e-access; £622 Institutions hospital - print and e-access; £824 Institutions e-access; £897 Institutions print only; £915 Institutions print and e-access; £916 Institutions e-access plus backfile (all online content); £1007 Institutions combined plus backfile (current volume print & all online content); £3145 Institutions e-access (content through 1998); £34 Individuals single print issue; £99 Institutions single print issue. **URL:** http://ang.sagepub.com. **Ad Rates:** BW $1120; 4C $1100, in addition to black & white rate above. **Remarks:** Accepts advertising. **Circ:** (Not Reported).

4493 ■ The Annals of the American Academy of Political and Social Science
SAGE Publications Inc.
2455 Teller Rd.
Thousand Oaks, CA 91320-2234
Free: 800-818-7243
Publisher's E-mail: sales@pfp.sagepub.com
Political and social science journal. **Freq:** Bimonthly. **Print Method:** Letterpress and Offset. **Trim Size:** 6 x 9. **Cols./Page:** 1. **Key Personnel:** Emily Wood, Managing Editor. **ISSN:** 0002--7162 (print); **EISSN:** 1552--3349 (electronic). **Subscription Rates:** $122 Individuals print only; $963 Institutions e-access; $1049 Institutions print ; $1070 Institutions print and e-access; $38 Individuals single print; $192 Individuals single print. **URL:** http://ann.sagepub.com. **Ad Rates:** BW $875; 4C $1110. **Remarks:** Accepts advertising. **Circ:** (Not Reported).

4494 ■ The Annals of Pharmacotherapy
SAGE Publications Inc.
2455 Teller Rd.
Thousand Oaks, CA 91320-2234
Free: 800-818-7243
Publisher's E-mail: sales@pfp.sagepub.com
Peer-reviewed medical journal focusing on the advances of pharmacotherapy throughout the world. **Freq:** Monthly. **Print Method:** Sheetfed. **Trim Size:** 8 1/2 x 11. **Cols./Page:** 2. **Col. Width:** 39 nonpareils. **Col. Depth:** 133 agate lines. **Key Personnel:** Harvey A.K. Whitney, Jr., Publisher; Milap C. Nahata, Editor-in-Chief. **ISSN:** 1060-0280 (print); **EISSN:** 1542-6270 (electronic). **Subscription Rates:** $24 Individuals single print issue; $110 Institutions single print issue; $199 Individuals e-access; $217 Individuals print; $221 Institutions print and e-access; $1102 Institutions e-access; $1200 Institutions print; $1224 Institutions print and e-access; $1346 Institutions print and all online content; $2996 Institutions e-access (content through 1998). **URL:** http://aop.sagepub.com. **Formerly:** Drug Intelligence & Clinical Pharmacy; DICP, The Annals of Pharmacotherapy. **Ad Rates:** BW $2,820; 4C $1,715. **Remarks:** Accepts advertising. **Circ:** ‡5500.

4495 ■ Anthropological Theory
SAGE Publications Inc.
2455 Teller Rd.
Thousand Oaks, CA 91320-2234
Free: 800-818-7243
Publisher's E-mail: sales@pfp.sagepub.com
Journal focusing on a variety of theoretical debates in areas including: Marxism, feminism, political philosophy, historical sociology, hermeneutics, critical theory, anthropology of science, biological anthropology, archaeology, linguistic anthropology, historical anthropology, sociology, and global anthropology. **Freq:** Quarterly. **Key Personnel:** Stephen P. Reyna, Board Member; John Gledhill, Board Member; Julia Eckert, Editor. **ISSN:** 1463--4996 (print); **EISSN:** 1741--2641 (electronic). **Subscription Rates:** $100 Individuals print only; $943 Institutions e-access; $1027 Institutions print only; $1048 Institutions print and e-access; $33 Individuals single print issue; $282 Institutions single print issue. **URL:** http://ant.sagepub.com. **Ad Rates:** BW £600. **Remarks:** Accepts advertising. **Circ:** (Not Reported).

4496 ■ Applied Psychological Measurement
SAGE Publications Inc.
2455 Teller Rd.
Thousand Oaks, CA 91320-2234
Free: 800-818-7243
Publisher's E-mail: sales@pfp.sagepub.com
Journal focusing on ways to use the most current techniques to address measurement problems in the behavioral and social sciences. **Freq:** 8/year. **Key Personnel:** Edison Choe, Managing Editor; Hua-Hua Chang, Editor. **ISSN:** 0146--6216 (print); **EISSN:** 1552--3497 (electronic). **Subscription Rates:** $73 Individuals print only; $645 Institutions online only; $703 Institutions print only; $717 Institutions print and online; $12 Individuals single issue; $97 Institutions single issue. **URL:** http://apm.sagepub.com. **Remarks:** Accepts advertising. **Circ:** (Not Reported).

4497 ■ Armchair General
Armchair General L.L.C.
2060 Avenida De Los Orbes, Ste. 373
Thousand Oaks, CA 91362
Military history magazine featuring analysis of military conflicts and full-color graphics. **Freq:** Bimonthly. **Key Personnel:** Julie Kershenbaum, Director, Advertising. **URL:** http://www.armchairgeneral.com. **Remarks:** Accepts advertising. **Circ:** (Not Reported).

4498 ■ Armed Forces & Society
SAGE Publications Inc.
2455 Teller Rd.
Thousand Oaks, CA 91320-2234
Free: 800-818-7243
Publisher's E-mail: sales@pfp.sagepub.com
Peer-reviewed journal on the military and civil-military relations. Official journal of the Inter-University Seminar on Armed Forces and Society. **Freq:** Quarterly January , April , July , October. **Cols./Page:** 1. **Col. Width:** 4.25 inches. **Col. Depth:** 7.25 inches. **Key Personnel:** Douglas Bland, Associate Editor; Deborah Avant, Associate Editor; Anthony King, Board Member, Editor; Patricia M. Shields, Editor. **ISSN:** 0095-327X (print); **EISSN:** 1556-0848 (electronic). **Subscription Rates:** £27 Single issue print; £84 Individuals print only; £105 Institutions single print issue; £352 Institutions e-access; £383 Institutions print only; £391 Institutions print and e-access; £430 Institutions current volume print and all online content; £720 Institutions e- access (content through 1998); $443 Institutions for print and online; $399 Institutions e-access; $434 Institutions print only; $110 Individuals print only; $119 Institutions single print; $36 Individuals single print; $487 Institutions current volume print and all online content; $814 Institutions online content thru 1999. **URL:** http://afs.sagepub.com; http://www.sagepub.com/journalsProdDesc.nav?prodId=Journal201730; http://uk.sagepub.com/en-gb/asi/armed-forces-society/journal201730; http://www.iusafs.org/about/journal.asp. **Ad Rates:** BW $725. **Remarks:** Accepts advertising. **Circ:** Paid ‡1700, 5000.

4499 ■ Arts and Humanities in Higher Education: An International Journal of Theory, Research & Pratice
SAGE Publications Inc.
2455 Teller Rd.
Thousand Oaks, CA 91320-2234
Free: 800-818-7243
Publisher's E-mail: sales@pfp.sagepub.com
Journal publishing articles, reviews and scholarly comments relating to the arts and humanities in higher education and serving the community of arts and humanities educators internationally. **Freq:** Quarterly. **Key Personnel:** Fred Parker, Senior Editor; Jan Parker, Editor-in-Chief. **ISSN:** 1474--0222 (print); **EISSN:** 1741-2-65X (electronic). **Subscription Rates:** £54 Individuals print only; £383 Institutions e-access; £417 Institutions print only; £425 Institutions print and online; £18 Individuals single print; £115 Institutions single print. **URL:** http://uk.sagepub.com/en-gb/asi/journal/arts-and-humanities-higher-education. **Remarks:** Accepts advertising. **Circ:** (Not Reported).

4500 ■ Asian Journal of Management Cases
SAGE Publications Inc.
2455 Teller Rd.
Thousand Oaks, CA 91320-2234
Free: 800-818-7243
Publisher's E-mail: sales@pfp.sagepub.com
Peer-reviewed journal providing high quality teaching and research cases covering a wide range of management. **Freq:** Semiannual. **Key Personnel:** M. Junaid Ashraf, Editor; Mohan Agarwal, Advisor; Nobuyuki Chikudate, Advisor; Aref Al Ashban, Board Member; Ziguang Chen, Advisor; Robert S. Collins, Advisor. **ISSN:** 0972--8201 (print); **EISSN:** 0973--0621 (electronic). **Subscription Rates:** £48 Individuals print; £176 Institutions e-access; £192 Institutions print only; £196 Institutions print and e-access; £31 Individuals single print; £106 Institutions single print. **URL:** http://ajc.sagepub.com. **Remarks:** Accepts advertising. **Circ:** (Not Reported).

4501 ■ Assessment
SAGE Publications Inc.
2455 Teller Rd.
Thousand Oaks, CA 91320-2234
Free: 800-818-7243
Publisher's E-mail: sales@pfp.sagepub.com
Journal presenting information of direct relevance to the use of assessment measures, including the practical applications of measurement methods, test development and interpretation practices, and advances in the description and prediction of human behavior. **Freq:** Bimonthly. **Key Personnel:** Aaron L. Pincus, Editor. **ISSN:** 1073--1911 (print); **EISSN:** 1552--3489 (electronic). **Subscription Rates:** £76 Individuals print; £428 Institutions e-access; £466 Institutions print only; £475 Institutions print and e-access; £16 Individuals single print; £85 Institutions single print. **URL:** http://asm.sagepub.com. **Remarks:** Accepts advertising. **Circ:** (Not Reported).

4502 ■ Assessment for Effective Intervention
SAGE Publications Inc.
2455 Teller Rd.
Thousand Oaks, CA 91320-2234
Free: 800-818-7243
Publisher's E-mail: sales@pfp.sagepub.com
Journal featuring articles that describe the relationship between assessment and instruction, introduce innovative assessment strategies; outline diagnostic procedures; analyze relationships between existing instruments; and review assessment techniques, strategies, and instrumentation. **Freq:** Quarterly. **Key Personnel:** John L. Hosp, Editor. **ISSN:** 1534--5084 (print); **EISSN:** 1938--7458 (electronic). **Subscription Rates:** £205 Institutions print & e-access; £185 Institutions e-access; £201 Institutions print only; £73 Individuals print & e-access. **URL:** http://aei.sagepub.com. **Ad Rates:** BW $875; 4C $1110. **Remarks:** Accepts advertising. **Circ:** (Not Reported).

4503 ■ Australian & New Zealand Journal of Psychiatry
SAGE Publications Inc.
2455 Teller Rd.
Thousand Oaks, CA 91320-2234
Free: 800-818-7243
Publication E-mail: anzjp@informa.com
Professional journal covering psychiatry. **Founded:** 1965. **Freq:** Monthly. **Print Method:** Offset. **Trim Size:** A4. **Cols./Page:** 2. **Key Personnel:** Sue E. Luty, Board

Circulation: ★ = AAM; △ or • = BPA; ♦ = CAC; ❑ = VAC; ⊕ = PO Statement; ‡ = Publisher's Report; Boldface figures = sworn; Light figures = estimated.

Member; Prof. Gin S. Malhi, Editor; Jan Scott, Board Member; Anthony F. Jorm, Associate Editor; Gavin Andrews, Board Member. **ISSN:** 0004-8674 (print). **Subscription Rates:** £832 Institutions print; £849 Institutions print and e-access; £2240 Institutions e-access. **URL:** http://anp.sagepub.com. **Remarks:** Accepts advertising. **Circ:** Paid 3000.

4504 ■ Autism: The International Journal of Research and Practice
SAGE Publications Inc.
2455 Teller Rd.
Thousand Oaks, CA 91320-2234
Free: 800-818-7243
Publisher's E-mail: sales@pfp.sagepub.com
Journal focusing on autism and other related neurodevelopmental disorders. **Founded:** 1997. **Freq:** 8/year. **Trim Size:** 193 x 118 mm. **Key Personnel:** David Mandell, Editor-in-Chief; Dougal Julian Hare, Editor; Tony Charman, Board Member; Lonnie Zwaigenbaum, Editor; Patrick Bolton, Board Member; Simon Baron-Cohen, Board Member; Dermot M. Bowler, Editor-in-Chief; Prof. Tony Attwood, Board Member; Mohammad Ghaziuddin, Board Member; Rita Jordan, Board Member; Sven Bolte, Editor. **ISSN:** 1362-3613 (print); **EISSN:** 1461-7005 (electronic). **Subscription Rates:** $1510 Institutions combined (print & e-access); $1661 Institutions backfile lease, combined plus backfile; $1359 Institutions e-access; $1510 Institutions backfile lease, e-access plus backfile; $1146 Institutions backfile purchase, e-access (content through 1998); $1480 Institutions print only; $755 Students combined (print & e-access); $137 Individuals print only; $204 Institutions single print; $22 Individuals single print; £781 Institutions electronic & print; £703 Institutions electronic; £765 Institutions print only; £72 Individuals print only; £105 Institutions single print; £12 Individuals single print; £859 Institutions current volume print & all online content; £594 Institutions content through 1998. **URL:** http://www.sagepub.com/journalsProdDesc.nav?prodId=Journal200822; http://www.uk.sagepub.com/journalsProdDesc.nav?prodId=Journal200822; http://aut.sagepub.com/. **Remarks:** Accepts advertising. **Circ:** (Not Reported).

4505 ■ Behavior Modification
SAGE Publications Inc.
2455 Teller Rd.
Thousand Oaks, CA 91320-2234
Free: 800-818-7243
Publication E-mail: journals@sagepub.com
Psychology journal.Offers successful assessment and modification techniques applicable to problems in psychiatric, clinical, educational, and rehabilitative settings, as well as treatment manuals and program descriptions. **Founded:** 1977. **Freq:** Bimonthly January, March, May, July, September, November. **Print Method:** Offset. **Trim Size:** 5 1/2 x 8 1/2. **Cols./Page:** 1. **Col. Width:** 50 nonpareils. **Col. Depth:** 100 agate lines. **Key Personnel:** Alan S. Bellack, PhD, Editor; Robert T. Ammerman, Board Member; Brad Donohue, Board Member; Deborah C. Beidel, Board Member. **ISSN:** 0145-4455 (print); **EISSN:** 1552-4167 (electronic). **Subscription Rates:** $1284 Individuals print & e-access; $1412 Institutions print & all online content; $1156 Institutions e-access; $1284 Institutions all online content, e-access; $2163 Institutions e-access (content through 1998); $1258 Institutions print only; $175 Individuals print only; $231 Institutions single print; $38 Individuals single print. **URL:** http://www.sagepub.com/journals/Journal200900. **Formerly**: Behavior Modification Quarterly. **Ad Rates:** BW $445; 4C $895. **Remarks:** Accepts advertising. **Circ:** Paid 700.

4506 ■ Biological Research for Nursing
SAGE Publications Inc.
2455 Teller Rd.
Thousand Oaks, CA 91320-2234
Free: 800-818-7243
Publisher's E-mail: sales@pfp.sagepub.com
Journal focusing on biological and physiological changes in healthy and unhealthy populations from a nursing perspective. **Freq:** 5/year. **Key Personnel:** Carolyn B. Yucha, PhD, Editor. **ISSN:** 1099--8004 (print); **EISSN:** 1552--4175 (electronic). **Subscription Rates:** £93 Individuals print; £527 Institutions e-access; £572 Institutions print only; £585 Institutions print and e-access; £24 Individuals single print; £126 Individuals single print. **URL:** http://uk.sagepub.com/en-gb/asi/biological-research-for-nursing/journal200861. **Ad Rates:** BW $445. **Remarks:** Accepts advertising. **Circ:** (Not Reported).

4507 ■ Body and Society
SAGE Publications Inc.
2455 Teller Rd.
Thousand Oaks, CA 91320-2234
Free: 800-818-7243
Publisher's E-mail: sales@pfp.sagepub.com
Journal focusing on social and cultural analysis of the human body. **Freq:** 5/year. **Key Personnel:** Mike Featherstone, Editor-in-Chief; Lisa Blackman, Editor. **ISSN:** 1357-034X (print); **EISSN:** 1460-3632 (electronic). **Subscription Rates:** $1120 Institutions print & e-access; $1232 Institutions print & all online; $1008 Institutions e-access; $1120 Institutions backfile lease, e-access plus backfile; $1007 Institutions backfile e-access (content through 1998); $1098 Institutions print only; $111 Individuals print only; $302 Institutions single print; $36 Individuals single print. **URL:** http://www.sagepub.com/journalsProdDesc.nav?ct_p=subscribe&prodId=Journal200799; http://bod.sagepub.com/. **Remarks:** Accepts advertising. **Circ:** (Not Reported).

4508 ■ British Journal of Visual Impairment
SAGE Publications Inc.
2455 Teller Rd.
Thousand Oaks, CA 91320-2234
Free: 800-818-7243
Publisher's E-mail: sales@pfp.sagepub.com
Journal for all professionals concerned with children and adults who have visual impairment. **Freq:** 3/yr. **Key Personnel:** Steve McCall, Board Member; Dr. Stuart Aitken, Board Member; Prof. Gordon Dutton, Board Member; Jill Keeffe, Board Member; Paul J. Pagliano, Board Member; Sue Keil, Board Member; Dr. Graeme Douglas, Board Member; Mike McLinden, Board Member; Dr. Frank Eperjesi, Board Member; Dr. John Ravenscroft, Editor. **ISSN:** 0264-6196 (print); **EISSN:** 1744-5809 (electronic). **Subscription Rates:** $553 Institutions combined (print & e-access); $608 Institutions current volume print and all online content; $498 Institutions e-access; $553 Institutions e-access plus backfile (all online content); $708 Institutions backfile purchase, e-access (content through 1998); $542 Institutions print only; $277 Individuals school, combined (print & e-access); $85 Individuals print only; $199 Single issue institutional, print issue; $37 Single issue individual, print issue. **URL:** http://www.sagepub.com/journals/Journal201712. **Remarks:** Accepts advertising. **Circ:** (Not Reported).

4509 ■ British Journalism Review
SAGE Publications Inc.
2455 Teller Rd.
Thousand Oaks, CA 91320-2234
Free: 800-818-7243
Publisher's E-mail: sales@pfp.sagepub.com
Journal focusing on all aspects of the media, from newspapers and radio to television and online. **Freq:** Quarterly. **Key Personnel:** Julia Langdon, Board Member; Brian Bass, Board Member; Bill Hagerty, Chairman; Kim Fletcher, Editor. **ISSN:** 0956--4748 (print); **EISSN:** 1741--2668 (electronic). **Subscription Rates:** £83 Individuals print; £733 Institutions e-access; £798 Institutions print; £814 Institutions print and e-access; £27 Individuals single print; £219 Institutions single print. **URL:** http://bjr.sagepub.com. **Remarks:** Accepts advertising. **Circ:** (Not Reported).

4510 ■ Bulletin of Science, Technology & Society
SAGE Publications Inc.
2455 Teller Rd.
Thousand Oaks, CA 91320-2234
Free: 800-818-7243
Publisher's E-mail: sales@pfp.sagepub.com
Journal focusing on the role of science and technology in society. **Freq:** Bimonthly. **Key Personnel:** Susan Carol Losh, Editor; Sheila Tobias, Board Member; Braden R. Allenby, Board Member. **ISSN:** 0270-4676 (print); **EISSN:** 1552-4183 (electronic). **Subscription Rates:** $994 Institutions e-access; $1093 Institutions backfile lease, e-access plus backfile (online); $1568 Institutions backfile purchase, e-access (content through 1998); $112 Individuals e-access. **URL:** http://www.sagepub.com/journalsProdDesc.nav?prodId=Journal200908. **Remarks:** Accepts advertising. **Circ:** (Not Reported).

4511 ■ Business Information Review
SAGE Publications Inc.
2455 Teller Rd.
Thousand Oaks, CA 91320-2234
Free: 800-818-7243
Publisher's E-mail: sales@pfp.sagepub.com
Journal for business information professionals. **Freq:** Quarterly. **Key Personnel:** Claire Laybats, Editor; Alan Foster, Board Member; Penny Leach, Board Member. **ISSN:** 0266--3821 (print); **EISSN:** 1741--6450 (electronic). **Subscription Rates:** £64 Individuals print; £866 Institutions e-access; £943 Institutions print; £962 Institutions print and e-access; £21 Individuals single print; £259 Institutions single print. **URL:** http://bir.sagepub.com. **Remarks:** Accepts advertising. **Circ:** (Not Reported).

4512 ■ Business & Society
SAGE Publications Inc.
2455 Teller Rd.
Thousand Oaks, CA 91320-2234
Free: 800-818-7243
Publisher's E-mail: sales@pfp.sagepub.com
Peer-reviewed journal on business and society. Sponsored by the International Association for Business and Society. **Freq:** Bimonthly. **Trim Size:** 5 1/2 x 8 1/2. **Key Personnel:** Duane Windsor, PhD, Editor; Ben Wempe, Associate Editor. **ISSN:** 0007--6503 (print); **EISSN:** 1552--4205 (electronic). **Subscription Rates:** £14 Individuals single print issue; £84 Individuals print; $76 Institutions single print issue; £442 Institutions e-access; £553 Institutions print only; £564 Institutions print and e-access; £620 Institutions current volume print and all online content; £1357 Institutions e-access (content through 1998). **URL:** http://bas.sagepub.com. **Ad Rates:** BW $875; 4C $1110. **Remarks:** Accepts advertising. **Circ:** (Not Reported).

4513 ■ Canadian Journal of School Psychology
SAGE Publications Inc.
2455 Teller Rd.
Thousand Oaks, CA 91320-2234
Free: 800-818-7243
Publisher's E-mail: sales@pfp.sagepub.com
Journal focusing on the interface between psychology and education. **Freq:** Quarterly. **Key Personnel:** Donald H. Saklofske, Editor; Joseph Snyder, Editor. **ISSN:** 0829-5735 (print); **EISSN:** 0829-5735 (electronic). **Subscription Rates:** $329 Institutions print and e-access; $296 Institutions e-access; $322 Institutions print only; $156 Individuals print only; $89 Institutions single print; $51 Individuals single print. **URL:** http://cjs.sagepub.com; http://www.sagepub.com/journalsProdEditBoards.nav?prodId=Journal201846. **Circ:** (Not Reported).

4514 ■ Cardiac Cath Lab Director
SAGE Publications Inc.
2455 Teller Rd.
Thousand Oaks, CA 91320-2234
Free: 800-818-7243
Publisher's E-mail: sales@pfp.sagepub.com
Peer-reviewed journal publishing research on cardiac catheterization procedures. **Freq:** Bimonthly. **Key Personnel:** Linda Paxton, Editor. **ISSN:** 2150--1335 (print); **EISSN:** 2150--1343 (electronic). **URL:** http://ccl.sagepub.com. **Remarks:** Accepts advertising. **Circ:** (Not Reported).

4515 ■ Child Language Teaching and Therapy
National Association of Professionals Concerned with Language Impairment in Children
2455 Teller Rd.
Thousand Oaks, CA 91320
Phone: (805)499-9774
Fax: (805)499-0871
Free: 800-818-7243
Publication E-mail: info@sagepub.com
Peer-reviewed journal covering the field of children's spoken and written language needs. **Freq:** 3/year. **Key Personnel:** Judy Clegg, Editor; Maggie Vance, Editor; John Parrott, Editor. **ISSN:** 0265--6590 (print); **EISSN:** 1477--0865 (electronic). **Subscription Rates:** £74 Individuals e-access; £335 Institutions e-access; £365 Institutions print only; £372 Institutions print & e-access; £32 Individuals single print; £134 Individuals single print; $111 Members print & online; $137 Individuals print &

online; $621 Institutions online; $676 Institutions print; $690 Institutions print & online; $739 Institutions online (content through 1998); $759 Institutions online & print plus backfile (current volume print & all online content); $59 Individuals single issue; $248 Institutions single issue; $58 /issue for individuals; $221 /issue for institutions. **URL:** http://clt.sagepub.com; http://www.sagepub.com/journals/Journal201804; http://www.naplic.org.uk/resources/publications; http://uk.sagepub.com/en-gb/eur/child-language-teaching-and-therapy/journal201804. **Remarks:** Accepts advertising. **Circ:** (Not Reported).

4516 ■ Child Maltreatment
SAGE Publications Inc.
2455 Teller Rd.
Thousand Oaks, CA 91320
Phone: (805)499-9774
Fax: (805)499-0871
Free: 800-818-7243
Publication E-mail: info@sagepub.com
Peer-reviewed journal focusing on original research, information and technical innovations on child abuse and neglect. Published in association with the American Professional Society on the Abuse of Children (APSAC). **Freq:** Quarterly. **Key Personnel:** Candice Feiring, Editor; Ernestine Briggs, Editor; Lucy Berliner, Associate Editor; Judy Donlin, Assistant; Howard Dubowitz, Associate Editor; Steven J. Ondersma, Editor. **ISSN:** 1077--5595 (print); **EISSN:** 1552--6119 (electronic). **Subscription Rates:** $166 Individuals print; $785 Institutions e-access; $855 Institutions print; $872 Institutions print and e-access; $54 Individuals single print; $235 Institutions single print; $235 Single issue Institutions; print; $959 Institutions current volume print and all online content. **URL:** http://cmx.sagepub.com; http://us.sagepub.com/en-us/nam/child-maltreatment/journal200758. **Ad Rates:** BW $725. **Remarks:** Accepts advertising. **Circ:** 45000.

4517 ■ Childhood: A journal of global child research
SAGE Publications Inc.
2455 Teller Rd.
Thousand Oaks, CA 91320-2234
Free: 800-818-7243
Publisher's E-mail: sales@pfp.sagepub.com
Peer-reviewed journal focusing on Research relating to children in global society that spans divisions between geographical regions, disciplines, and social and cultural contexts. **Freq:** Quarterly. **Key Personnel:** Leena Alanen, Editor; Karin Ekberg, Managing Editor; Virginia Morrow, Editor. **ISSN:** 0907--5682 (print); **EISSN:** 1461--7013 (electronic). **Subscription Rates:** £66 Individuals print; £647 Institutions e-access; £705 Institutions print; £719 Institutions print and e-access; £21 Individuals single print; £194 Institutions single print. **URL:** http://uk.sagepub.com/en-gb/eur/journal/childhood. **Remarks:** Accepts advertising. **Circ:** (Not Reported).

4518 ■ China Report: A Journal of East Asian Studies
SAGE Publications Inc.
2455 Teller Rd.
Thousand Oaks, CA 91320-2234
Free: 800-818-7243
Publication E-mail: journals@sagepub.com
Journal promoting the understanding of contemporary China and its East Asian neighbors, including articles on culture, methods of development, and impact on India and other South Asian countries. **Freq:** Quarterly. **Trim Size:** 6 1/4 x 9 1/2. **Key Personnel:** Madhavi Thampi, Editor. **ISSN:** 0009--4455 (print); **EISSN:** 0973--063X (electronic). **Subscription Rates:** $137 Individuals print; $517 Institutions e-access; $563 Institutions print; $574 Institutions print and e-access; $45 Individuals single print; $155 Institutions single print. **URL:** http://chr.sagepub.com. **Remarks:** Accepts advertising. **Circ:** (Not Reported).

4519 ■ Chronic Illness
SAGE Publications Inc.
2455 Teller Rd.
Thousand Oaks, CA 91320-2234
Free: 800-818-7243
Publisher's E-mail: sales@pfp.sagepub.com
Peer-reviewed journal providing a forum in which researchers from a wide range of disciplines, clinicians, policy makers, and people living with chronic illness come together to clarify the common principles underlying the experience and management of chronic illness. **Freq:** Quarterly. **Key Personnel:** James E. Aikens, Editor-in-Chief. **ISSN:** 1742-3953 (print). **Subscription Rates:** £386 Institutions print and e-access; £347 Institutions e-access; £378 Institutions print only; £65 Individuals print and e-access; £104 Institutions single print; £21 Individuals single print. **URL:** http://www.uk.sagepub.com/journalsProdDesc.nav?prodId=Journal201862. **Circ:** (Not Reported).

4520 ■ Clinical and Applied Thrombosis/ Hemostasis: Official Journal of the International Academy of Clincal and Applied Thrombosis/ Hemostasis
SAGE Publications Inc.
2455 Teller Rd.
Thousand Oaks, CA 91320-2234
Free: 800-818-7243
Publisher's E-mail: sales@pfp.sagepub.com
Journal dedicated to reporting original research in all clinical and applied aspects of thrombosis, thrombolysis, and hemorrahagic disorders, including abnormalities of the vasculature. **Freq:** 8/year. **Print Method:** Sheetfed offset. **Trim Size:** 8 1/2 x 11 1/4. **ISSN:** 1076-0296 (print); **EISSN:** 1938-2723 (electronic). **Subscription Rates:** £208 Individuals print and e-access; £824 Institutions e-access; £897 Institutions print; £34 Individuals single print; £123 Institutions single print. **URL:** http://cat.sagepub.com/content/current. **Circ:** 878.

4521 ■ Clinical Case Studies
SAGE Publications Inc.
2455 Teller Rd.
Thousand Oaks, CA 91320-2234
Free: 800-818-7243
Publisher's E-mail: sales@pfp.sagepub.com
Journal focusing on cases involving individual, couples, and family therapy. **Freq:** Bimonthly. **Key Personnel:** Daniel L. Segal, Editor. **ISSN:** 1534--6501 (print); **EISSN:** 1552--3802 (electronic). **Subscription Rates:** $125 Institutions e-access; $706 Individuals e-access. **URL:** http://ccs.sagepub.com. **Remarks:** Accepts advertising. **Circ:** (Not Reported).

4522 ■ Clinical Child Psychology and Psychiatry
SAGE Publications Inc.
2455 Teller Rd.
Thousand Oaks, CA 91320-2234
Free: 800-818-7243
Publisher's E-mail: sales@pfp.sagepub.com
Peer-reviewed journal focusing on clinical and therapeutic aspects of child and adolescent psychology and psychiatry. **Freq:** Quarterly. **Key Personnel:** Rudi Dallos, Associate Editor; Michael Tarren-Sweeney, Editor; Anna Brazier, Editor; Dr. Bernadette Wren, Associate Editor; Arlene Vetere, Associate Editor. **ISSN:** 1359--1045 (print); **EISSN:** 1461--7021 (electronic). **Subscription Rates:** £82 Individuals print; £710 Institutions e-access; £773 Institutions print; £789 Institutions print and e-access; £27 Individuals single print; £213 Institutions single print. **URL:** http://ccp.sagepub.com. **Ad Rates:** BW $300. **Remarks:** Accepts advertising. **Circ:** (Not Reported).

4523 ■ Clinical Ethics
SAGE Publications Inc.
2455 Teller Rd.
Thousand Oaks, CA 91320-2234
Free: 800-818-7243
Publisher's E-mail: sales@pfp.sagepub.com
Journal covering research and policy for clinical ethics. **Freq:** Quarterly. **Key Personnel:** Soren Holm, Editor. **ISSN:** 1477--7509 (print); **EISSN:** 1758--101X (electronic). **Subscription Rates:** $494 Institutions combined (print and e-access); $445 Institutions e-access; $494 Individuals combined (print and e-access). **URL:** http://cet.sagepub.com. **Circ:** (Not Reported).

4524 ■ Clinical Nursing Research: An International Journal
SAGE Publications Inc.
2455 Teller Rd.
Thousand Oaks, CA 91320-2234
Free: 800-818-7243
Publication E-mail: advertising@sagepub.com
Journal on scholarly research focused on clinical practice. **Freq:** Bimonthly. **Trim Size:** 5 1/2 x 8 1/2. **Key Personnel:** Pamela Z. Cacchione, Editor; Norma Metheny, PhD, Associate Editor. **ISSN:** 1054--7738 (print); **EISSN:** 1552--3799 (electronic). **Subscription Rates:** £18 Individuals single print issue; $85 Individuals print only; £101 Institutions single print issue; £465 Institutions e-access (content through 1998); £507 Institutions e-access; £552 Institutions print only; £563 Institutions print and e-access; £619 Institutions current volume print and all online content. **URL:** http://cnr.sagepub.com; http://uk.sagepub.com/en-gb/asi/clinical-nursing-research/journal200890. **Ad Rates:** BW $1120; 4C $1110, in addition to Black & White rate. **Remarks:** Accepts advertising. **Circ:** (Not Reported).

4525 ■ Clinical Pediatrics
SAGE Publications Inc.
2455 Teller Rd.
Thousand Oaks, CA 91320-2234
Free: 800-818-7243
Publisher's E-mail: sales@pfp.sagepub.com
Professional journal for pediatric practitioners. **Freq:** Monthly. **Print Method:** Web Offset. **Trim Size:** 8 1/8 x 10 7/8. **Key Personnel:** Russell W. Steele, MD, Editor. **ISSN:** 0009-9228 (print). **Subscription Rates:** £58 Institutions single issue; £216 Individuals print and online; £678 Institutions online only; £738 Institutions print only; £753 Institutions print and online. **URL:** http://uk.sagepub.com/en-gb/asi/clinical-pediatrics/journal201788; http://cpj.sagepub.com. **Ad Rates:** BW $1,195; 4C $1,180. **Remarks:** Accepts advertising. **Circ:** (Not Reported).

4526 ■ Clinical Rehabilitation
SAGE Publications Inc.
2455 Teller Rd.
Thousand Oaks, CA 91320-2234
Free: 800-818-7243
Publisher's E-mail: sales@pfp.sagepub.com
Peer-reviewed scholarly journal covering the whole field of disability and rehabilitation, publishing research and discussion articles which are scientifically sound and clinically relevant. **Freq:** Monthly. **Key Personnel:** Derick T. Wade, Editor-in-Chief. **ISSN:** 0269-2155 (print); **EISSN:** 1477-0873 (electronic). **Subscription Rates:** $2290 Institutions print and e-access; $2061 Institutions e-access; $2244 Institutions print only; $440 Individuals print and e-access; $206 Institutions single print; $48 Individuals single print. **URL:** http://www.sagepub.com/journalsProdDesc.nav?prodId=Journal201806; http://cre.sagepub.com/. **Ad Rates:** BW $600. **Remarks:** Accepts advertising. **Circ:** (Not Reported).

4527 ■ Clinical Risk
SAGE Publications Inc.
2455 Teller Rd.
Thousand Oaks, CA 91320-2234
Free: 800-818-7243
Publisher's E-mail: sales@pfp.sagepub.com
Journal focusing on patient safety, providing practice guidelines for doctors and managers. **Freq:** Bimonthly. **Key Personnel:** Roger V. Clements, Editor, Founder; Hilary Merrett, Editor-in-Chief. **ISSN:** 1356--2622 (print); **EISSN:** 1758--1028 (electronic). **Subscription Rates:** £433 Institutions combined (print & e-access); £476 Institutions combined plus backfile; £390 Institutions e-access; £433 Institutions e-access plus backfile; £389 Institutions e-access (content hrough 1998); £338 Individuals combined (print & e-access); £65 Institutions single print issue; £73 single print issue. **URL:** http://cri.sagepub.com. **Circ:** (Not Reported).

4528 ■ Communication Disorders Quarterly
SAGE Publications Inc.
2455 Teller Rd.
Thousand Oaks, CA 91320-2234
Free: 800-818-7243
Publisher's E-mail: sales@pfp.sagepub.com
Scholarly journal containing articles on communication disorders in children, including speech, hearing, language, and learning disabilities. **Freq:** Quarterly. **Print Method:** Offset. **Trim Size:** 8 x 10 7/8. **Key Personnel:** Judy Montgomery, Editor; Dolores Battle, PhD, Associate Editor; Karen Hux, PhD, Editor. **ISSN:** 1525-7401 (print). **Subscription Rates:** $67 Individuals print & e-access; $183 Institutions print only; $168 Institutions e-access; $187 Institutions print & e-access; $50 Institu-

Circulation: ★ = AAM; △ or • = BPA; ♦ = CAC; ❑ = VAC; ⊕ = PO Statement; ‡ = Publisher's Report; Boldface figures = sworn; Light figures = estimated.

tions single print; $22 Single issue print. **URL:** http://www.sagepub.com/journalsProdEditBoards.nav?prodId=Journal201874. **Formerly**: Journal of Children's Communication Development. **Ad Rates:** BW $515; 4C $995. **Remarks:** Advertising accepted; rates available upon request. **Circ:** Paid 2300.

4529 ■ Comparative Political Studies
SAGE Publications Inc.
2455 Teller Rd.
Thousand Oaks, CA 91320-2234
Free: 800-818-7243
Publisher's E-mail: sales@pfp.sagepub.com
Political science journal. **Freq:** 14/yr. **Print Method:** Offset. **Trim Size:** 5 1/2 x 8 1/2. **Cols./Page:** 1. **Col. Width:** 50 nonpareils. **Col. Depth:** 100 agate lines. **Key Personnel:** David J. Samuels, Editor. **ISSN:** 0010--4140 (print); **EISSN:** 1552--3829 (electronic). **Subscription Rates:** $193 Individuals print; $1784 Institutions e-access; $1942 Institutions print; $1982 Institutions print and e-access; $18 Individuals single issue; $153 Institutions single issue. **URL:** http://cps.sagepub.com. **Also known as**: CPS. **Ad Rates:** BW $875; 4C $1110. **Remarks:** Accepts advertising. **Circ:** (Not Reported).

4530 ■ Compensation & Benefits Review: The Journal of Total Compensation Strategies
SAGE Publications Inc.
2455 Teller Rd.
Thousand Oaks, CA 91320-2234
Free: 800-818-7243
Publisher's E-mail: sales@pfp.sagepub.com
Journal focusing on issues and trends in the marketplace for senior executives who develop and update compensation and benefits policies. **Freq:** Bimonthly. **Trim Size:** 8 1/8 x 10 7/8. **Key Personnel:** Charles H. Fay, Editor. **ISSN:** 0886-3687 (print); **EISSN:** 1552-3837 (electronic). **Subscription Rates:** $737 Institutions combined (print & e-access); $811 Institutions current volume print & all online content; $663 Institutions e-access; $737 Institutions backfile lease, e-access plus backfile; $722 Institutions print only; $582 Individuals print only; $1694 Institutions backfile online content thru 1998; $132 Institutions single print; $126 Individuals single print. **URL:** http://www.sagepub.com/journalsProdDesc.nav?prodId=Journal200811. **Remarks:** Accepts advertising. **Circ:** (Not Reported).

4531 ■ Concurrent Engineering: Research and Applications
SAGE Publications Inc.
2455 Teller Rd.
Thousand Oaks, CA 91320-2234
Free: 800-818-7243
Publisher's E-mail: sales@pfp.sagepub.com
Peer-reviewed journal publishing the newest and most exciting research arising from parallelism of product life cycle functions. **Freq:** Quarterly. **Trim Size:** 8 1/2 x 11. **Key Personnel:** A.M. Agogino, Associate Editor; Biren Prasad, Editor-in-Chief; M.S. Fox, Associate Editor. **ISSN:** 1063--293X (print); **EISSN:** 1531--2003 (electronic). **Subscription Rates:** $1412 Institutions e-access; $1538 Institutions print; $1569 Institutions print and e-access; $423 Institutions single print. **URL:** http://cer.sagepub.com. **Remarks:** Accepts advertising. **Circ:** 185.

4532 ■ Contexts: Understanding People in their Social Worlds
SAGE Publications Inc.
2455 Teller Rd.
Thousand Oaks, CA 91320-2234
Free: 800-818-7243
Publisher's E-mail: library@ucpressjournals.com
Magazine covering society and social behavior, including developments in social research, social science knowledge, and emerging trends, for sociologists, social and behavioral scientists, and interested others. **Freq:** Quarterly February, May, August, November. **Trim Size:** 8.5 x 11. **Key Personnel:** Carly Chillmon, Managing Editor. **ISSN:** 1536--5042 (print); **EISSN:** 1537--6052 (electronic). **Subscription Rates:** $20 Individuals single print issue; $56 Individuals E-access; $62 Individuals print and E-access; $83 Institutions single print issue; $277 Institutions E-access; $301 Institutions print ; $307 Institutions print and E-access. **URL:** http://ctx.sagepub.com; http://us.sagepub.com/en-us/nam/contexts/journal202013. **Remarks:** Accepts advertising. **Circ:** Paid 3246.

4533 ■ Contributions to Indian Sociology
SAGE Publications Inc.
2455 Teller Rd.
Thousand Oaks, CA 91320-2234
Free: 800-818-7243
Publisher's E-mail: sales@pfp.sagepub.com
Journal focusing on theoretical approaches to the study of society in India. **Freq:** 3/year 3/yr. **Key Personnel:** Janaki Abraham, Editor; Sanjay Srivastava, Editor; Patricia Uberoi, Advisor; Deepak Mehta, Editor. **ISSN:** 0069-9667 (print); **EISSN:** 0973-0648 (electronic). **Subscription Rates:** $460 Institutions print & e-access; $506 Institutions backfile lease, combined plus backfile; $414 Institutions e-access; $460 Institutions all online content; $1127 Institutions backfile purchase, e-access; $451 Institutions print only; $107 Individuals print only; $165 Institutions single print; $46 Individuals single print; $436 Institutions combined (print & e-access); $45 Single issue; $392 Institutions e-access; $436 Institutions backfile lease, e-access; $1068 Institutions backfile purchase, e-access; $427 Institutions print only; $104 Individuals print only; $157 Institutions single print. **URL:** http://www.sagepub.com/journalsProdDesc.nav?prodId=Journal200929. **Remarks:** Accepts advertising. **Circ:** 900.

4534 ■ Convergence: The International Journal of Research into New Media Technologies
SAGE Publications Inc.
2455 Teller Rd.
Thousand Oaks, CA 91320-2234
Free: 800-818-7243
Publication E-mail: convergence@beds.ac.uk
Peer-reviewed journal addressing the creative, social, political and pedagogical issues raised by the advent of new media technologies. **Freq:** Quarterly February, May, August, and November. **Print Method:** Offset. **Trim Size:** 5 1/2 x 8 1/2. **Cols./Page:** 1. **Col. Width:** 50 nonpareils. **Col. Depth:** 100 agate lines. **Key Personnel:** Alexis Weedon, Editor; Julia Knight, Editor; Jeanette Steemers, Associate Editor; Amy Bruckman, Associate Editor; Mark Deuze, Board Member; Jay David Bolter, Board Member; Indrajit Banerjee, Board Member. **ISSN:** 1354--8565 (print); **EISSN:** 1748--7382 (electronic). **Subscription Rates:** $974 Institutions print and e-access; $877 Institutions e-access; $955 Institutions print only; $148 Individuals print only; $175 Institutions single print; $32 Individuals single print. **URL:** http://con.sagepub.com; http://convergence.beds.ac.uk. **Ad Rates:** BW £650. **Remarks:** Accepts advertising. **Circ:** (Not Reported).

4535 ■ Cooperation and Conflict
SAGE Publications Inc.
2455 Teller Rd.
Thousand Oaks, CA 91320-2234
Free: 800-818-7243
Publisher's E-mail: sales@pfp.sagepub.com
Journal promoting research on and understanding of international relations. **Freq:** Quarterly. **Key Personnel:** Martin Hall, Editor; Audie Klotz, Advisor; Eric Einhorn, Advisor; Eiki Berg, Advisor; Iver B. Neumann, Member. **ISSN:** 0010--8367 (print); **EISSN:** 1460--3691 (electronic). **Subscription Rates:** $118 Individuals print; $852 Institutions e-access; $928 Institutions print; $947 Institutions print and e-access; $38 Individuals single print; $255 Institutions single print. **URL:** http://cac.sagepub.com. **Remarks:** Accepts advertising. **Circ:** (Not Reported).

4536 ■ Cornell Hospitality Quarterly
SAGE Publications Inc.
2455 Teller Rd.
Thousand Oaks, CA 91320-2234
Free: 800-818-7243
Publisher's E-mail: sales@pfp.sagepub.com
Journal focusing on critical research, practical applied theories, and useful case studies regarding important industry trends and timely topics in lodging, restaurant, and tourism management. **Freq:** Quarterly. **Key Personnel:** Michael Lynn, Editor; Bruce J. Tracey, Associate Editor. **ISSN:** 0010-8804 (print); **EISSN:** 1938-9663 (electronic). **Subscription Rates:** $609 Institutions print & e-access; $670 Institutions print & all online; $548 Institutions e-access; $609 Institutions e-access & all online; $1820 Institutions e-access (content through 1998); $597 Institutions print only; $162 Individuals e-access; $164 Institutions single; $59 Individuals single. **URL:** http://cqx.sagepub.com/; http://www.sagepub.com/journalsProdDesc.nav?prodId=Journal201681. **Formerly:** Cornell Hotel and Restaurant Administration Quarterly. **Remarks:** Accepts advertising. **Circ:** (Not Reported).

4537 ■ Crime & Delinquency
SAGE Publications Inc.
2455 Teller Rd.
Thousand Oaks, CA 91320-2234
Free: 800-818-7243
Publisher's E-mail: sales@pfp.sagepub.com
Journal on policy studies in criminal justice. **Freq:** Monthly. **Print Method:** Offset. **Trim Size:** 5 1/2 x 8 1/2. **Cols./Page:** 1. **Col. Width:** 50 nonpareils. **Col. Depth:** 100 agate lines. **Key Personnel:** Paul E. Tracy, Editor; Ronald E. Vogel, Board Member; Kimberly Kempf-Leonard, Associate Editor. **ISSN:** 0011--1287 (print); **EISSN:** 1552--387X (electronic). **Subscription Rates:** $2428 Institutions print & e-access; $2671 Institutions current volume print & all online content; $2185 Institutions e-access; $2428 Institutions all online content; $7258 Institutions e-access (content through 1998); $2379 Institutions print only; $211 Individuals print only; $187 Institutions single print; $20 Individuals single print. **URL:** http://cad.sagepub.com. **Ad Rates:** BW $875; 4C $1110. **Remarks:** Accepts advertising. **Circ:** (Not Reported).

4538 ■ Crime, Media, Culture
SAGE Publications Inc.
2455 Teller Rd.
Thousand Oaks, CA 91320-2234
Free: 800-818-7243
Publisher's E-mail: sales@pfp.sagepub.com
Peer-reviewed journal providing the primary vehicle for exchange between scholars who are working at the intersections of criminological and cultural inquiry. **Freq:** 3/year 3/yr. **Key Personnel:** Maggy Lee, Board Member; Jack Katz, Board Member; Michelle Brown, Editor; Roy Coleman, Board Member; Gregg Barak, Board Member; Nachman Ben-Yehuda, Associate Editor; Katja Franko Aas, Associate Editor; Chris Greer, Associate Editor; Jeff Ferrell, Associate Editor. **ISSN:** 1741--6590 (print); **EISSN:** 1741--6604 (electronic). **Subscription Rates:** $91 Individuals print; $715 Institutions e-access; $778 Institutions print; $794 Individuals print and e-access; $39 Individuals single print; $285 Institutions single print. **URL:** http://cmc.sagepub.com. **Remarks:** Accepts advertising. **Circ:** (Not Reported).

4539 ■ Criminal Justice and Behavior: An International Journal
SAGE Publications Inc.
2455 Teller Rd.
Thousand Oaks, CA 91320-2234
Free: 800-818-7243
Publisher's E-mail: sales@pfp.sagepub.com
Journal focusing on the effects of the criminal justice system on human behavior.Promotes scholarly evaluations of assessment, classification, prevention, intervention, and treatment programs to help the correctional professional develop successful programs based on sound and informative theoretical and research foundations. **Freq:** Monthly. **Print Method:** Offset. **Trim Size:** 5 1/2 x 8 1/2. **Cols./Page:** 1. **Col. Width:** 50 nonpareils. **Col. Depth:** 100 agate lines. **Key Personnel:** Emily J. Salisbury, PhD, Editor. **ISSN:** 0093--8548 (print); **EISSN:** 1552--3594 (electronic). **Subscription Rates:** $1280 Institutions print & e-access; $1408 Institutions print & all online content; $1152 Institutions e-access; $1280 Institutions e-access plus backfile (all online content); $2447 Institutions e-access (content through 1998); $1254 Institutions print only; $115 Institutions single print. **URL:** http://cjb.sagepub.com. **Ad Rates:** BW $875; 4C $1110. **Remarks:** Accepts advertising. **Circ:** (Not Reported).

4540 ■ Criminal Justice Policy Review
SAGE Publications Inc.
2455 Teller Rd.
Thousand Oaks, CA 91320-2234
Free: 800-818-7243
Publisher's E-mail: sales@pfp.sagepub.com
Journal publishing articles written by scholars and professionals committed to the study of criminal justice policy through experimental and non-experimental approaches. **Freq:** 8/year. **Key Personnel:** Mitchell Chamlin, Board Member; Leanne F. Alarid, Board

Member; Terry Gingerich, Board Member; David L. Myers, Editor; Kathleen J. Hanrahan, Board Member; Henry Brownstein, Board Member; John K. Cochran, Board Member. **ISSN:** 0887--4034 (print); **EISSN:** 1552--3586 (electronic). **Subscription Rates:** £77 Individuals print; £930 Institutions e-access; £1012 Institutions print; £1033 Institutions print and e-access; £13 Individuals single print; £139 Institutions single print. **URL:** http://cjp.sagepub.com. **Remarks:** Accepts advertising. **Circ:** (Not Reported).

4541 ■ Criminology & Criminal Justice
SAGE Publications Inc.
2455 Teller Rd.
Thousand Oaks, CA 91320-2234
Free: 800-818-7243
Publisher's E-mail: sales@pfp.sagepub.com
Peer-reviewed journal focusing on the general field of criminal justice policy and practice. **Freq:** 5/year. **Key Personnel:** Sarah Armstrong, Editor; Alex Piquero, Advisor, Board Member; Gordon Hughes, Associate Editor; George Mair, Editor, Founder. **ISSN:** 1748--8958 (print); **EISSN:** 1748--8966 (electronic). **Subscription Rates:** $117 Individuals print; $955 Institutions e-access; $1040 Institutions print only; $1061 Institutions print and e-access; $32 Individuals single print; $229 Institutions single print; Included in membership. **URL:** http://crj.sagepub.com; http://www.britsoccrim.org/ccj. **Formerly:** Criminal Justice. **Remarks:** Accepts advertising. **Circ:** 9000.

4542 ■ Critical Social Policy
SAGE Publications Inc.
2455 Teller Rd.
Thousand Oaks, CA 91320-2234
Free: 800-818-7243
Publisher's E-mail: sales@pfp.sagepub.com
Journal aiming to develop an understanding of welfare from socialist, feminist, anti-racist and radical perspectives. **Freq:** Quarterly. **Key Personnel:** Donna Baines, Advisor. **ISSN:** 0261--0183 (print); **EISSN:** 1461--703X (electronic). **Subscription Rates:** £47 Individuals print; £417 Institutions e-access; £454 Institutions print; £463 Institutions print and e-access; £15 Individuals single print; £125 Institutions single print. **URL:** http://csp.sagepub.com. **Remarks:** Accepts advertising. **Circ:** (Not Reported).

4543 ■ Critique of Anthropology
SAGE Publications Inc.
2455 Teller Rd.
Thousand Oaks, CA 91320-2234
Free: 800-818-7243
Publisher's E-mail: sales@pfp.sagepub.com
Journal focusing on the development of anthropology as a discipline that subjects social reality to critical analysis. **Freq:** Quarterly. **Key Personnel:** Patricia Alves de Matos, Editor; Tom Biolsi, Board Member; Keith Hart, Board Member; Nelly Arvelo Jimenez, Board Member; Glenn Bowman, Board Member; Maia Green, Board Member; Michael Blim, Board Member; Stephan Feuchtwang, Board Member; Stephen Nugent, Editor; John Gledhill, Board Member. **ISSN:** 0308--275X (print); **EISSN:** 1460--3721 (electronic). **Subscription Rates:** $115 Individuals print; $1127 Institutions e-access; $1227 Institutions print; $1252 Institutions print and e-access; $37 Individuals single print; $337 Institutions single print. **URL:** http://coa.sagepub.com. **Remarks:** Accepts advertising. **Circ:** (Not Reported).

4544 ■ Cross-Cultural Research: The Journal of Comparative Social Science
SAGE Publications Inc.
2455 Teller Rd.
Thousand Oaks, CA 91320-2234
Free: 800-818-7243
Publication E-mail: advertising@sagepub.com
Journal of cross-cultural research in the social and behavioral sciences. **Freq:** 5/year. **Trim Size:** 5 1/2 x 8 1/2. **Key Personnel:** Lewellyn Hendrix, Editor; Michael Burton, Editor; Garry Chick, Editor; Carol R. Ember, Editor; Herbert Barry, III, Editor; Bobbi Low, Editor; Robert L. Munroe, Editor; Patricia D. Andreucci, Managing Editor. **ISSN:** 1069--3971 (print); **EISSN:** 1552--3578 (electronic). **Subscription Rates:** £22 Individuals single print issue; £84 Individuals print only; £115 Institutions single print issue; £482 Institutions e-access; £524 Institutions print only; £535 Institutions print and e-access; £589 Institutions current volume print and all online content; £1203 Institutions e-access (content through 1998). **URL:** http://ccr.sagepub.com; http://uk.sagepub.com/en-gb/asi/cross-cultural-research/journal200972. **Ad Rates:** BW $875; 4C $1110. **Remarks:** Accepts advertising. **Circ:** (Not Reported).

4545 ■ Cultural Dynamics
SAGE Publications Inc.
2455 Teller Rd.
Thousand Oaks, CA 91320-2234
Free: 800-818-7243
Publisher's E-mail: sales@pfp.sagepub.com
Journal focusing on a relational and dynamic account of socio-cultural phenomena. **Freq:** 3/year 3/yr. **Key Personnel:** Dipesh Chakraborty, Board Member; Rene Devisch, Board Member; Frank van Dun, Board Member; Aant Elzinga, Board Member; Johannes Fabian, Board Member; Barbara Frankel, Board Member; S.N. Balagangadhara, Board Member; Michaeline Crichlow, Editor. **ISSN:** 0921--3740 (print); **EISSN:** 1461--7048 (electronic). **Subscription Rates:** $104 Individuals print; $1242 Institutions e-access; $1352 Institutions print; $1380 Institutions print and e-access; $45 Individuals single print; $496 Institutions single print. **URL:** http://cdy.sagepub.com. **Remarks:** Accepts advertising. **Circ:** (Not Reported).

4546 ■ Cultural Sociology
SAGE Publications Inc.
2455 Teller Rd.
Thousand Oaks, CA 91320-2234
Free: 800-818-7243
Publisher's E-mail: sales@pfp.sagepub.com
Journal covering the sociological comprehension of cultural matters. **Freq:** Quarterly. **Key Personnel:** David Inglis, Editor; Robin Wagner-Pacifici, Editor. **ISSN:** 1749--9755 (print); **EISSN:** 1749--9763 (electronic). **Subscription Rates:** $852 Institutions print & e-access; $767 Institutions e-access; $835 Institutions print only; $107 Individuals print only; $230 Institutions single copy; $35 Single issue. **URL:** http://cus.sagepub.com. **Circ:** (Not Reported).

4547 ■ Cultural Studies - Critical Methodologies
SAGE Publications Inc.
2455 Teller Rd.
Thousand Oaks, CA 91320-2234
Free: 800-818-7243
Publisher's E-mail: sales@pfp.sagepub.com
Journal focusing on the intersections of cultural studies, critical interpretive research methodologies, and cultural critique. **Freq:** Bimonthly. **Key Personnel:** Norman K. Denzin, Editor. **ISSN:** 1532--7086 (print); **EISSN:** 1552--356X (electronic). **Subscription Rates:** $108 Individuals print; $900 Institutions e-access; $980 Institutions print only; $1000 Institutions print and e-access; $23 Individuals single print; $180 Institutions single print. **URL:** http://csc.sagepub.com. **Remarks:** Accepts advertising. **Circ:** (Not Reported).

4548 ■ Culture and Psychology
SAGE Publications Inc.
2455 Teller Rd.
Thousand Oaks, CA 91320-2234
Free: 800-818-7243
Publication E-mail: journals@sagepub.com
Journal addressing the centrality of culture to the understanding of human behavior, identity, intersubjective experiences, emotions, development and language. **Freq:** Quarterly. **Key Personnel:** James V. Wertsch, Associate Editor; Wolfgang Wagner, Associate Editor; Stuart McNaughton, Board Member; Yasuko Minoura, Associate Editor; Michael Cole, Board Member; Jaan Valsiner, Editor. **ISSN:** 1354-067X (print); **EISSN:** 1461-7056 (electronic). **Subscription Rates:** £647 Institutions print & e-access; £712 Institutions current volume print & all online content; £582 Institutions e-access; £647 Institutions backfile lease, e-access plus backfile (online); £582 Institutions e-access (content through 1998); £634 Institutions print only; £64 Individuals print only; £174 Institutions single print; £21 Individuals single print. **URL:** http://cap.sagepub.com/; http://www.uk.sagepub.com/journals/Journal200766?siteId=sage-uk&prodTypes=any&q=Culture+%26+Psychology&fs=1. **Remarks:** Accepts advertising. **Circ:** (Not Reported).

4549 ■ Current Directions in Psychological Science
SAGE Publications Inc.
2455 Teller Rd.
Thousand Oaks, CA 91320
Phone: (805)499-9774
Fax: (805)499-0871
Free: 800-818-7243
Publication E-mail: info@sagepub.com
Journal focusing on trends and controversies in psychology. **Freq:** Bimonthly 6/year February, April, June, August, October, December. **Key Personnel:** Peter Solomon, Executive Director; Randall W. Engle, Editor. **ISSN:** 0963-7214 (print); **EISSN:** 1467-8721 (electronic). **Subscription Rates:** $293 Single issue Institutions; print; Members of the APS receive the journal as part of their annual dues. All others, contact Blackwell Publishers (http://www.blackwellpublishing.com/) for subscription information. **URL:** http://www.psychologicalscience.org/index.php/publications/journals/current_directions; http://cdp.sagepub.com; http://us.sagepub.com/en-us/nam/journal/current-directions-psychological-science. **Ad Rates:** BW $990. **Remarks:** Accepts advertising. **Circ:** 15000.

4550 ■ Current Sociology
SAGE Publications Inc.
2455 Teller Rd.
Thousand Oaks, CA 91320-2234
Free: 800-818-7243
Publisher's E-mail: isa@isa-sociology.org
Freq: 7/year. **Key Personnel:** Eloisa Martin, Editor. **ISSN:** 0011--3921 (print); **EISSN:** 1461--7064 (electronic). **Subscription Rates:** $142 Individuals print only; $1738 Institutions online only; $1892 Institutions print only; $1931 Institutions print and online; $26 Individuals single print issue; $297 Institutions single print issue. **URL:** http://csi.sagepub.com. **Remarks:** Accepts advertising. **Circ:** (Not Reported).

4551 ■ Currents in Biblical Research
SAGE Publications Inc.
2455 Teller Rd.
Thousand Oaks, CA 91320-2234
Free: 800-818-7243
Publisher's E-mail: sales@pfp.sagepub.com
Journal summarizing the spectrum of recent research on particular topics or biblical books. **Freq:** 3/year. **Key Personnel:** Scot McKnight, Editor; Jonathan Klawans, Editor; Alan J. Hauser, Senior Editor. **ISSN:** 1476--993X (print); **EISSN:** 1745--5200 (electronic). **Subscription Rates:** $91 Individuals print; $410 Institutions e-access; $446 Institutions print; $455 Institutions print and e-access; $39 Individuals single print; $164 Institutions single print. **URL:** http://cbi.sagepub.com. **Remarks:** Accepts advertising. **Circ:** (Not Reported).

4552 ■ Dementia: The International Journal of Social Research and Practice
SAGE Publications Inc.
2455 Teller Rd.
Thousand Oaks, CA 91320-2234
Free: 800-818-7243
Publisher's E-mail: sales@pfp.sagepub.com
Journal focusing on social research of direct relevance to improving the quality of life and quality of care for people with dementia and their families. **Founded:** 2002. **Freq:** Bimonthly. **Key Personnel:** John Keady, Editor; Phyllis Braudy Harris, Editor; Jo Moriarty, Editor; Charlotte L. Clarke, Board Member; Heather Wilkinson, Editor. **ISSN:** 1471-3012 (print); **EISSN:** 1741-2684 (electronic). **Subscription Rates:** $1105 Institutions print & e-access; $995 Institutions e-access; $1083 Institutions print; $104 Individuals print; $199 Institutions single print; $23 Individuals single print; $1047 Institutions print & e-access; $942 Institutions e-access; $1026 Institutions print; $100 Individuals print; $188 Institutions single print; $22 Individuals single print. **URL:** http://www.sagepub.com/journalsProdDesc.nav?prodId=Journal201266; http://dem.sagepub.com/. **Ad Rates:** BW $200. **Remarks:** Accepts advertising. **Circ:** (Not Reported).

4553 ■ The Diabetes Educator
American Association of Diabetes Educators
2455 Teller Rd.
Thousand Oaks, CA 91320
Phone: (805)499-9774

Circulation: ★ = AAM; △ or • = BPA; ♦ = CAC; ❑ = VAC; ⊕ = PO Statement; ‡ = Publisher's Report; Boldface figures = sworn; Light figures = estimated.

Fax: (805)499-0871
Free: 800-818-7243
Publication E-mail: info@sagepub.com
Freq: Bimonthly. **ISSN:** 0145-7217 (print); **EISSN:** 1554-6063 (electronic). **Subscription Rates:** Included in membership; $248 Institutions print and online; $223 Institutions online; $243 Institutions print; $118 Individuals print; $45 Single issue Institutions, print; $26 Single issue Individuals, print. **URL:** http://www.sagepub.com/journals/Journal201731; http://www.diabeteseducator.org/ProfessionalResources/Periodicals/Educator/. **Remarks:** Accepts advertising. **Circ:** (Not Reported).

4554 ■ Dialogues in Human Geography
SAGE Publications Inc.
2455 Teller Rd.
Thousand Oaks, CA 91320-2234
Free: 800-818-7243
Publisher's E-mail: sales@pfp.sagepub.com
Peer-reviewed journal covering human geography. **Freq:** 3/year March, July and November. **Key Personnel:** John Paul Jones, III, Editor; Rob Kitchin, Managing Editor. **ISSN:** 2043--8206 (print); **EISSN:** 2043--8214 (electronic). **Subscription Rates:** £316 Institutions print and e-access; £310 Institutions print only; £46 Individuals print only; £114 Institutions single issue; £20 Individuals single issue. **URL:** http://uk.sagepub.com/en-gb/asi/journal/dialogues-human-geography. **Remarks:** Accepts advertising. **Circ:** (Not Reported).

4555 ■ Discourse & Communication
SAGE Publications Inc.
2455 Teller Rd.
Thousand Oaks, CA 91320-2234
Free: 800-818-7243
Publisher's E-mail: sales@pfp.sagepub.com
Journal covering communication research. **Freq:** Quarterly. **Key Personnel:** Teun A. van Dijk, Editor. **ISSN:** 1750--4813 (print); **EISSN:** 1750--4821 (electronic). **Subscription Rates:** $93 Individuals print only; $201 Institutions single print; $30 Individuals single print. **URL:** http://dcm.sagepub.com. **Ad Rates:** BW £650. **Remarks:** Accepts advertising. **Circ:** (Not Reported).

4556 ■ Discourse & Society
SAGE Publications Inc.
2455 Teller Rd.
Thousand Oaks, CA 91320-2234
Free: 800-818-7243
Publisher's E-mail: sales@pfp.sagepub.com
Peer-reviewed journal exploring the relevance of discourse analysis to the social sciences. **Freq:** Bimonthly. **Key Personnel:** Teun A. van Dijk, Editor; Teresa E. Carbo, Editor. **ISSN:** 0957--9265 (print); **EISSN:** 1460--3624 (electronic). **Subscription Rates:** £66 Individuals print only; £977 Institutions Institutional Back file Purchase, E-access (Content through 1998); £14 Individuals single print; £102 Institutions single print. **URL:** http://das.sagepub.com. **Remarks:** Accepts advertising. **Circ:** (Not Reported).

4557 ■ Discourse Studies
SAGE Publications Inc.
2455 Teller Rd.
Thousand Oaks, CA 91320-2234
Free: 800-818-7243
Publisher's E-mail: sales@pfp.sagepub.com
Peer-reviewed journal focusing on cross-disciplinary studies of text and talk in linguistics, anthropology, ethnomethodology, cognitive and social psychology, communication studies and law. **Freq:** Bimonthly. **Key Personnel:** Teun A. van Dijk, Editor. **ISSN:** 1461--4456 (print); **EISSN:** 1461--7080 (electronic). **Subscription Rates:** $115 Individuals print; $1520 Institutions e-access; $1655 Institutions print; $1689 Institutions print and e-access; $25 Individuals single print; $303 Institutions single print. **URL:** http://dis.sagepub.com. **Remarks:** Accepts advertising. **Circ:** (Not Reported).

4558 ■ Drug Information Journal
SAGE Publications Inc.
2455 Teller Rd.
Thousand Oaks, CA 91320-2234
Free: 800-818-7243
Publisher's E-mail: sales@pfp.sagepub.com
Provides latest trends in research and development, distribution, utilization, and regulation of pharmaceuticals, medical devices, and related products. **Freq:** Bimonthly. **ISSN:** 2168--4790 (print); **EISSN:** 2168--4804 (electronic). **Subscription Rates:** Included in membership. **URL:** http://www.diaglobal.org/en/resources/publications; http://dij.sagepub.com/content/by/year. **Remarks:** Accepts advertising. **Circ:** (Not Reported).

4559 ■ East European Politics and Societies
SAGE Publications Inc.
2455 Teller Rd.
Thousand Oaks, CA 91320-2234
Free: 800-818-7243
Publication E-mail: advertising@sagepub.com
Journal covering issues in Eastern Europe from social, political, and economic perspectives. **Freq:** Quarterly. **Trim Size:** 7 x 10. **Key Personnel:** Jan Kubik, Member; Shlomo Avineri, Member; Daniel Chirot, Member; Ilya Prizel, Member; Vladimir Tismaneanu, Committee Chairman; Wendy Bracewell, Editor. **ISSN:** 0888--3254 (print); **EISSN:** 1533--8371 (electronic). **Subscription Rates:** $79 Individuals print or e-access; $454 Institutions e-access; $494 Institutions print only; $504 Institutions print and e-access; $26 Individuals single print issue; $136 Institutions single print issue. **URL:** http://eep.sagepub.com; http://us.sagepub.com/en-us/nam/east-european-politics-and-societies/journal201655. **Ad Rates:** BW $1120; 4C $1100. **Remarks:** Accepts advertising. **Circ:** (Not Reported).

4560 ■ Economic Development Quarterly: The Journal of American Economic Revitalization
SAGE Publications Inc.
2455 Teller Rd.
Thousand Oaks, CA 91320-2234
Free: 800-818-7243
Publisher's E-mail: sales@pfp.sagepub.com
Journal reporting on research programs, policies, and trends in economic development in large cities, small towns, rural areas, and overseas trade and expansion. **Freq:** Quarterly. **Print Method:** Offset. **Trim Size:** 8 1/2 x 11. **Cols./Page:** 1. **Key Personnel:** George A. Erickcek, Editor; Claudette Robey, Managing Editor; Timothy J. Bartik, Editor; Edward W. Hill, Senior Editor; Larry C. Ledebur, Editor. **ISSN:** 0891--2424 (print); **EISSN:** 1552--3543 (electronic). **Subscription Rates:** $1054 Institutions print & e-access; $161 Individuals single print; $949 Institutions e-access; $1054 Institutions e-access (all online content); $967 Institutions e-access (content through 1998); $1033 Institutions print only; $52 Individuals print only; $284 Institutions single print only. **URL:** http://edq.sagepub.com. **Ad Rates:** BW $875; 4C $1110. **Remarks:** Accepts advertising. **Circ:** (Not Reported).

4561 ■ Economic and Industrial Democracy: An International Journal
SAGE Publications Inc.
2455 Teller Rd.
Thousand Oaks, CA 91320-2234
Free: 800-818-7243
Publisher's E-mail: sales@pfp.sagepub.com
Journal for all social scientists concerned with organization of the workplace and economic life. **Freq:** Quarterly. **Key Personnel:** Ann-Britt Hellmark, Associate Editor; Lars Magnusson, Editor; Jan Ottosson, Editor; Elyce Rotella, Board Member; Joan Acker, Board Member; Jacques Freyssinet, Board Member. **ISSN:** 0143--831X (print); **EISSN:** 1461--7099 (electronic). **Subscription Rates:** $144 Individuals print only; $1180 Institutions e-access; $1285 Institutions print only; $1311 Institutions print and e-access; $47 Individuals single print issue; $353 Institutions single print issue. **URL:** http://eid.sagepub.com; http://us.sagepub.com/en-us/nam/economic-and-industrial-democracy/journal200773. **Remarks:** Accepts advertising. **Circ:** (Not Reported).

4562 ■ Education, Citizenship and Social Justice
SAGE Publications Inc.
2455 Teller Rd.
Thousand Oaks, CA 91320-2234
Free: 800-818-7243
Publisher's E-mail: sales@pfp.sagepub.com
Journal focusing on citizenship and social justice. **Freq:** 3/year. **Key Personnel:** Jannette Elwood, Associate Editor; Ruth Leitch, Editor; Bruce Muirhead, Associate Editor; Serdar M. Degirmencioglu, Associate Editor; Peter Evans, Associate Editor; Diana Hess, Associate Editor; Tony Gallagher, Editor; Alan Dyson, Editor; Laurie Johnson, Editor. **ISSN:** 1746--1979 (print); **EISSN:** 1746--1987 (electronic). **Subscription Rates:** $74 Individuals print only; $709 Institutions e-access; $772 Institutions print only; $788 Institutions print and e-access; $32 Individuals single print; $283 Individuals single print. **URL:** http://us.sagepub.com/en-us/nam/education-citizenship-and-social-justice/journal201759; http://esj.sagepub.com. **Remarks:** Accepts advertising. **Circ:** (Not Reported).

4563 ■ Education and Urban Society
SAGE Publications Inc.
2455 Teller Rd.
Thousand Oaks, CA 91320-2234
Free: 800-818-7243
Publisher's E-mail: sales@pfp.sagepub.com
Educational administration journal. **Freq:** 9/year. **Print Method:** Offset. **Trim Size:** 5 1/2 x 8 1/2. **Cols./Page:** 1. **Col. Width:** 50 nonpareils. **Col. Depth:** 100 agate lines. **Key Personnel:** Elizabeth Pearn, Managing Editor; Frank Brown, Board Member; Gerald M. Cattaro, Board Member; Charles J. Russo, Editor. **ISSN:** 0013--1245 (print); **EISSN:** 1552--3535 (electronic). **Subscription Rates:** $1470 Institutions combined print & e-access; $1617 Institutions current volume print & all online content; $1323 Institutions e-access; $1470 Institutions all online content; $2869 Institutions e-access (content through 1998); $1441 Institutions print only; $197 Individuals print only; $176 Institutions single print; $28 Individuals single print. **URL:** http://eus.sagepub.com. **Ad Rates:** BW $785; 4C $1110. **Remarks:** Accepts advertising. **Circ:** (Not Reported).

4564 ■ Educational Administration Quarterly: The Journal of Leadership for Effective & Equitable Organizations
SAGE Publications Inc.
2455 Teller Rd.
Thousand Oaks, CA 91320-2234
Free: 800-818-7243
Publisher's E-mail: sales@pfp.sagepub.com
Educational administration journal. **Freq:** 5/year. **Print Method:** Offset. **Trim Size:** 5 1/2 x 8 1/2. **Cols./Page:** 1. **Col. Width:** 50 nonpareils. **Col. Depth:** 100 agate lines. **Key Personnel:** Casey D. Cobb, Editor. **ISSN:** 0013--161X (print); **EISSN:** 1552--3519 (electronic). **Subscription Rates:** $1069 Institutions print & e-access; $1176 Institutions current volume print & all online content; $962 Institutions e-access; $1069 Institutions e-access plus backfile (all online content); $2779 Institutions e-access (content through 1998); $1048 Institutions print only; $176 Individuals print only; $231 Institutions single print; $46 Individuals single print. **URL:** http://eaq.sagepub.com. **Ad Rates:** BW $875; 4C $1110. **Remarks:** Accepts advertising. **Circ:** (Not Reported).

4565 ■ Educational Management Administration & Leadership
SAGE Publications Inc.
2455 Teller Rd.
Thousand Oaks, CA 91320-2234
Free: 800-818-7243
Publisher's E-mail: sales@pfp.sagepub.com
Peer-reviewed journal focusing on all aspects of leadership, management, administration and policy in education. **Freq:** Bimonthly. **Key Personnel:** Tim Simkins, Associate Editor; Brian Caldwell, Board Member; Jacky Lumby, Associate Editor; Carol Cardno, Board Member; Helen Gunter, Associate Editor; Michael Strain, Associate Editor; Tony Bush, Editor. **ISSN:** 1741-1432 (print); **EISSN:** 1741-1440 (electronic). **Subscription Rates:** $1414 Institutions combined (print & e-access); $1555 Institutions current volume print & all online content; $1273 Institutions e-access; $1414 Institutions e-access plus backfile (all online content); $2812 Institutions backfile purchase, e-access (content through 1998); $1386 Institutions print only; $707 Individuals school, combined (print & e-access); $124 Individuals print only; $254 Single issue institutional; $27 Single issue individual. **URL:** http://ema.sagepub.com; http://www.sagepub.com/journalsProdDesc.nav?prodId=Journal200888. **Remarks:** Accepts advertising. **Circ:** (Not Reported).

4566 ■ Educational Policy
SAGE Publications Inc.
2455 Teller Rd.
Thousand Oaks, CA 91320-2234
Free: 800-818-7243

Publisher's E-mail: sales@pfp.sagepub.com
Peer-reviewed journal for educators, policy makers, administrators, researchers, teachers, and graduate students. **Freq:** Bimonthly. **Key Personnel:** Ana M. Martinez Aleman, Editor; Katya Salkever, Managing Editor. **ISSN:** 0895-9048 (print); **EISSN:** 1552-3896 (electronic). **Subscription Rates:** $1037 Institutions combined (print & e-access); $1141 Institutions backfile lease, combined plus backfile; $933 Institutions e-access; $1037 Institutions backfile lease, e-access plus backfile; $953 Institutions e-access (content through 1998); $1016 Institutions print only; $190 Individuals print only; $186 Institutions single print; $41 Individuals single print. **URL:** http://www.sagepub.com/journalsProdDesc.nav?prodId=Journal200936. **Remarks:** Accepts advertising. **Circ:** (Not Reported).

4567 ■ Educational and Psychological Measurement
SAGE Publications Inc.
2455 Teller Rd.
Thousand Oaks, CA 91320-2234
Free: 800-818-7243
Publication E-mail: advertising@sagepub.com
Journal on problems and research in the areas of education, psychology, industry, and government. **Freq:** Bimonthly. **Print Method:** Offset. **Trim Size:** 5 1/2 x 8 1/2. **Key Personnel:** Xitao Fan, Editor; George A. Marcoulides, Editor. **ISSN:** 0013--1644 (print); **EISSN:** 1552--3888 (electronic). **Subscription Rates:** £27 Individuals single print issue; £123 Individuals print; £139 Institutions single print issue; £698 Institutions e-access; £760 Institutions print only; £775 Institutions print and e-access; £853 Institutions current volume print and all online content; £3443 Institutions e-access (content through 1998). **URL:** http://epm.sagepub.com; http://uk.sagepub.com/en-gb/asi/educational-and-psychological-measurement/journal200914. **Ad Rates:** BW $875; 4C $1110, in addition to Black & White rate. **Remarks:** Accepts advertising. **Circ:** (Not Reported).

4568 ■ Elvis the Magazine
Creative Radio Network
PO Box 7749
Thousand Oaks, CA 91359
Phone: (818)991-3892
Fax: (818)991-3894
Publisher's E-mail: faq@elvisthemagazine.com
Consumer magazine covering entertainment. **Freq:** Quarterly. **Trim Size:** 8 1/2 x 11. **Cols./Page:** 3. **Key Personnel:** Darwin L. Lamm, Publisher. **Subscription Rates:** $39.95 U.S. and other countries plus shipping and handling. **URL:** http://www.elvisthemagazine.com. **Formerly:** Elvis International Forum. **Ad Rates:** 4C $3500. **Remarks:** Accepts advertising. **Circ:** Paid 80000.

4569 ■ Environment and Behavior
SAGE Publications Inc.
2455 Teller Rd.
Thousand Oaks, CA 91320-2234
Free: 800-818-7243
Publisher's E-mail: sales@pfp.sagepub.com
Journal on the effects of environment, geography, and architecture on human behavior.Contains international and interdisciplinary perspectives on the relationships between environment and human behavior. **Founded:** 1969. **Freq:** Bimonthly January , March , May , July , September and November. **Print Method:** Web Offset. **Trim Size:** 5 1/2 x 8 1/2. **Cols./Page:** 1. **Col. Width:** 50 nonpareils. **Col. Depth:** 100 agate lines. **Key Personnel:** Ann Sloan Devlin, Editor. **ISSN:** 0013-9165 (print); **EISSN:** 1552-390X (electronic). **Subscription Rates:** $1569 Individuals print & e-access; $1726 Institutions current volume print & all online content; $1412 Institutions e-access; $1569 Institutions all online content; $3303 Institutions e-access (content through 1998); $1538 Institutions print only; $183 Individuals print only; $169 Institutions single print; $24 Individuals single print. **URL:** http://www.sagepub.com/journalsProdDesc.nav?prodId=Journal200783&. **Ad Rates:** BW $515; 4C $995. **Remarks:** Accepts advertising. **Circ:** Paid ‡1600, Non-paid ‡152.

4570 ■ Environment & Planning A
SAGE Publications Inc.
2455 Teller Rd.
Thousand Oaks, CA 91320-2234
Free: 800-818-7243
Publisher's E-mail: sales@pfp.sagepub.com
Publication focusing on urban and regional research. **Freq:** 7/yr. **Print Method:** Litho. **Trim Size:** 132 x 230 mm. **Key Personnel:** Trevor Barnes, Editor; Henry Yeung, Editor; Nigel Thrift, Editor; Sarah Whatmore, Editor; Jamie Peck, Managing Editor. **ISSN:** 0308--518X (print); **EISSN:** 1472--3409 (electronic). **Subscription Rates:** £166 Individuals print only; £1364 Institutions e-access; £1486 Institutions print only; £1516 Institutions e-access plus backfile (all online content); £1516 Institutions print & e-access; £1668 Institutions combined plus backfile (current volume print & all online content); £3748 Individuals e-access (Content through 1998); £18 Individuals single issue; £136 Institutions single issue. **URL:** http://epn.sagepub.com. **Ad Rates:** BW £650. **Remarks:** Advertising accepted; rates available upon request. **Circ:** (Not Reported).

4571 ■ Environment and Urbanization
SAGE Publications Inc.
2455 Teller Rd.
Thousand Oaks, CA 91320-2234
Free: 800-818-7243
Publication E-mail: subscription@sagepub.co.uk
Journal focusing on the exchange of research findings, ideas and information in the fields of human settlements and environment among researchers, activists and non-governmental organizations (NGOs) in lowland middle-income nations and between these and researchers, international agency staff, students and teachers in high-income nations. **Founded:** 1989. **Freq:** Semiannual April , October. **Print Method:** Offset. **Key Personnel:** David Satterthwaite, Editor; Tade Akin Aina, Board Member; E.J. Anzorena, Board Member; Diana Mitlin, Board Member; Somsook Boonyabancha, Advisor, Board Member; Julio D. Davila, Board Member; Adil M. Ahmad, Advisor, Board Member; Cecilia Tacoli, Advisor, Board Member. **ISSN:** 0956-2478 (print); **EISSN:** 1746-0301 (electronic). **Subscription Rates:** $670 Institutions print & e-access; $603 Institutions e-access; $657 Institutions print only; $80 Individuals print only; $361 Institutions single print issue; $52 Individuals single print issue; $134 Institutions low income, print & e-access; $221 Individuals print & e-access (charity); $737 Institutions Current Volume Print & All Online Content; $221 Institutions Charity - Combined (Print & E-access). **URL:** http://www.sagepub.com/journalsProdDesc.nav?prodId=Journal201733; http://www.environmentandurbanization.org/; http://www.sagepub.com/journals/Journal201733#tabview=subscribe. **Remarks:** Accepts advertising. **Circ:** 3100.

4572 ■ Ethnicities
SAGE Publications Inc.
2455 Teller Rd.
Thousand Oaks, CA 91320-2234
Free: 800-818-7243
Publisher's E-mail: sales@pfp.sagepub.com
Peer-reviewed journal focusing on sociology and politics. **Freq:** Bimonthly. **Key Personnel:** Thomas Hylland Eriksen, Board Member; Stephen May, Editor; Tariq Modood, Editor. **ISSN:** 1468--7968 (print); **EISSN:** 1741--2706 (electronic). **Subscription Rates:** $135 Individuals print only; $1070 Institutions e-access; $1165 Institutions print only; $1189 Institutions print and e-access; $29 Individuals single print; $214 Institutions single print. **URL:** http://us.sagepub.com/en-us/nam/ethnicities/journal200776; http://etn.sagepub.com. **Remarks:** Accepts advertising. **Circ:** (Not Reported).

4573 ■ Ethnography
SAGE Publications Inc.
2455 Teller Rd.
Thousand Oaks, CA 91320-2234
Free: 800-818-7243
Publisher's E-mail: sales@pfp.sagepub.com
Journal focusing on the ethnographic study of social and cultural change. **Freq:** Quarterly. **Key Personnel:** Michel Agier, Board Member; Elijah Anderson, Board Member; Lindsay Hamilton, Editor; Helen Wood, Associate Editor; Peter Geschiere, Editor; Paul Willis, Editor. **ISSN:** 1466--1381 (print); **EISSN:** 1741--2714 (electronic). **Subscription Rates:** $115 Individuals print only; $971 Institutions e-access; $1057 Institutions print only; $1079 Individuals print and e-access; $37 Individuals single print; $291 Institutions single print. **URL:** http://eth.sagepub.com; http://us.sagepub.com/en-us/nam/ethnography/journal200906. **Remarks:** Accepts advertising. **Circ:** (Not Reported).

4574 ■ European History Quarterly
SAGE Publications Inc.
2455 Teller Rd.
Thousand Oaks, CA 91320-2234
Free: 800-818-7243
Publisher's E-mail: sales@pfp.sagepub.com
Peer-reviewed journal focusing on European history from the later Middle Ages to post-1945. **Freq:** Quarterly. **Key Personnel:** Julian Swann, Editor; Laurence Cole, Editor; Lucy Riall, Editor. **ISSN:** 0265--6914 (print); **EISSN:** 1461--7110 (electronic). **Subscription Rates:** $131 Individuals print only; $903 Institutions e-access; $983 Institutions print only; $1003 Institutions print and e-access; $43 Individuals single print; $270 Institutions sinlge print. **URL:** http://ehq.sagepub.com; http://us.sagepub.com/en-us/nam/journal/european-history-quarterly. **Remarks:** Accepts advertising. **Circ:** (Not Reported).

4575 ■ European Journal of Communication
SAGE Publications Inc.
2455 Teller Rd.
Thousand Oaks, CA 91320-2234
Free: 800-818-7243
Publisher's E-mail: sales@pfp.sagepub.com
Peer-reviewed journal focusing on communication research and scholarship. **Freq:** Bimonthly. **Key Personnel:** Helena Sousa, Editor; Peter Golding, Editor; Denis McQuail, Editor. **ISSN:** 0267--3231 (print); **EISSN:** 1460--3705 (electronic). **Subscription Rates:** $131 Individuals print only; $1401 Institutions e-access; $1526 Institutions print only; $1557 Institutions print and e-access; $28 Individuals sinlge print; $280 Institutions single print. **URL:** http://us.sagepub.com/en-us/nam/european-journal-of-communication/journal200857; http://ejc.sagepub.com. **Remarks:** Accepts advertising. **Circ:** (Not Reported).

4576 ■ European Journal of Criminology
SAGE Publications Inc.
2455 Teller Rd.
Thousand Oaks, CA 91320-2234
Free: 800-818-7243
Publisher's E-mail: sales@pfp.sagepub.com
Peer-reviewed journal focusing on crime and criminal justice issues in Europe. **Freq:** Bimonthly. **Key Personnel:** Julian Roberts, Associate Editor; Marzio Barbagli, Board Member; Miklos Levay, Board Member; David J. Smith, Board Member. **ISSN:** 1477--3708 (print); **EISSN:** 1741--2609 (electronic). **Subscription Rates:** $104 Individuals print only; $1172 Institutions e-access; $1276 Institutions print only; $1302 Institutions print and e-access; $23 Individuals single print; $234 Institutions single print. **URL:** http://euc.sagepub.com; http://us.sagepub.com/en-us/nam/european-journal-of-criminology/journal201644. **Remarks:** Accepts advertising. **Circ:** (Not Reported).

4577 ■ European Journal of Cultural Studies
SAGE Publications Inc.
2455 Teller Rd.
Thousand Oaks, CA 91320-2234
Free: 800-818-7243
Publisher's E-mail: sales@pfp.sagepub.com
Peer-reviewed journal promoting a conception of cultural studies rooted in lived experience. **Freq:** Bimonthly February , April , June , August , October , December. **Key Personnel:** Jon Cruz, Editor; Ruth McElroy, Editor; Jaap Kooijman, Associate Editor; Joke Hermes, Editor; Pertti Alasuutari, Editor. **ISSN:** 1367--5494 (print); **EISSN:** 1460--3551 (electronic). **Subscription Rates:** $126 Individuals print only; $1139 Institutions e-access; $1240 Institutions print only; $1265 Institutions print and e-access; $27 Individuals single print; $227 Institutions single print. **URL:** http://ecs.sagepub.com; http://us.sagepub.com/en-us/nam/journal/european-journal-cultural-studies. **Remarks:** Accepts advertising. **Circ:** (Not Reported).

4578 ■ European Journal of Industrial Relations
SAGE Publications Inc.
2455 Teller Rd.
Thousand Oaks, CA 91320-2234
Free: 800-818-7243

Circulation: ★ = AAM; △ or • = BPA; ♦ = CAC; ❑ = VAC; ⊕ = PO Statement; ‡ = Publisher's Report; Boldface figures = sworn; Light figures = estimated.

Publisher's E-mail: sales@pfp.sagepub.com
Journal focusing on European industrial relations and their theoretical and practical implications. **Freq:** Quarterly March , June , September , December. **Key Personnel:** Colin Crouch, Member; Miriam Golden, Member; Sabina Avdagic, Member; Christian Dufour, Member; Richard Hyman, Editor. **ISSN:** 0959--6801 (print); **EISSN:** 1461--7129 (electronic). **Subscription Rates:** $122 Individuals print only; $1202 Institutions e-access; $1309 Institutions print only; $1336 Institutions print and e-access; $40 Individuals single print; $360 Institutions single print. **URL:** http://us.sagepub.com/en-us/nam/european-journal-of-industrial-relations/journal200877; http://ejd.sagepub.com. **Remarks:** Accepts advertising. **Circ:** (Not Reported).

4579 ■ European Journal of International Relations
SAGE Publications Inc.
2455 Teller Rd.
Thousand Oaks, CA 91320-2234
Free: 800-818-7243
Publisher's E-mail: sales@pfp.sagepub.com
Peer-reviewed journal of the Standing Group on International Relations (SGIR) of the European Consortium for Political Research (ECPR). **Freq:** Quarterly March , June , September , December. **Key Personnel:** Tim Dunne, Board Member; Lene Hansen, Board Member; Colin Wight, Board Member; Barry Buzan, Member; Emanuel Adler, Board Member; John Agnew, Board Member; Pierre Allan, Board Member; Esther Barbe, Board Member; Ulrich Beck, Board Member; Kimberley Hutchings, Member; Beate Jahn, Editor-in-Chief. **ISSN:** 1354--0661 (print); **EISSN:** 1460--3713 (electronic). **Subscription Rates:** $122 Individuals print; $1464 Institutions e-access; $1594 Institutions print only; $1627 Institutions print and e-access; $40 Institutions single print; $438 Individuals single print. **URL:** http://ejt.sagepub.com; http://us.sagepub.com/en-us/nam/european-journal-of-international-relations/journal200942. **Remarks:** Accepts advertising. **Circ:** (Not Reported).

4580 ■ European Journal of Political Theory
SAGE Publications Inc.
2455 Teller Rd.
Thousand Oaks, CA 91320-2234
Free: 800-818-7243
Publisher's E-mail: sales@pfp.sagepub.com
Peer-reviewed journal focusing on political thought and theory in a European context. **Freq:** Quarterly. **Key Personnel:** Rob Jubb, Reviewer; Richard North, Board Member; Enzo Rossi, Editor. **ISSN:** 1474--8851 (print); **EISSN:** 1741--2730 (electronic). **Subscription Rates:** $100 Individuals print only; $900 Institutions e-access; $980 Institutions print only; $1000 Institutions print and e-access; $33 Individuals single print; $270 Institutions single print. **URL:** http://us.sagepub.com/en-us/nam/journal/european-journal-political-theory; http://ept.sagepub.com. **Remarks:** Accepts advertising. **Circ:** (Not Reported).

4581 ■ European Journal of Preventive Cardiology
SAGE Publications Inc.
2455 Teller Rd.
Thousand Oaks, CA 91320
Publisher's E-mail: sales@pfp.sagepub.com
Journal publishing articles that address the causes and prevention of cardiovascular disease. **Freq:** 18/yr. **Key Personnel:** Pantaleo Giannuzzi, Senior Editor; Diederick E. Grobbee, Editor-in-Chief; Birna Bjarnason-Wehrens, Board Member; David A. Wood, Senior Editor. **ISSN:** 2047--4873 (print); **EISSN:** 2047--4881 (electronic). **Subscription Rates:** £314 Individuals print and e-access; £1098 Institutions e-access (content through 1998); £1480 Institutions e-access; £1611 Institutions print; £1644 Institutions print and e-access; £1644 Institutions all online content; £1808 Institutions print and all online content; £23 Individuals print - single issue; £98 Institutions print - single issue. **URL:** http://cpr.sagepub.com. **Formerly:** European Journal of Cardiovascular Prevention & Rehabilitation. **Remarks:** Accepts advertising. **Circ:** (Not Reported).

4582 ■ European Physical Education Review
SAGE Publications Inc.
2455 Teller Rd.
Thousand Oaks, CA 91320-2234
Free: 800-818-7243
Publisher's E-mail: sales@pfp.sagepub.com
Journal focusing on the broad field of physical education; including sport and leisure issues and research. **Freq:** Quarterly. **Key Personnel:** Stuart Biddle, Advisor; Jose Campos Granell, Advisor; Ken Green, Editor-in-Chief. **ISSN:** 1356--336X (print); **EISSN:** 1741--2749 (electronic). **Subscription Rates:** $100 Individuals print only; $833 Institutions e-access; $907 Institutions print only; $926 Institutions print and e-access; $33 Individuals single print; $249 Institutions single print. **URL:** http://epe.sagepub.com; http://uk.sagepub.com/en-gb/eur/journal/european-physical-education-review. **Remarks:** Accepts advertising. **Circ:** (Not Reported).

4583 ■ European Urban and Regional Studies
SAGE Publications Inc.
2455 Teller Rd.
Thousand Oaks, CA 91320-2234
Free: 800-818-7243
Publisher's E-mail: sales@pfp.sagepub.com
Journal focusing on urban and regional development issues in Europe. **Freq:** Quarterly. **Key Personnel:** Adrian Smith, Editor-in-Chief; Diane Perrons, Board Member; Neil Coe, Board Member. **ISSN:** 0969--7764 (print); **EISSN:** 1461--7145 (electronic). **Subscription Rates:** $137 Individuals print only; $1048 Institutions e-access; $1141 Institutions print only; $1164 Institutions print and e-access; $45 Individuals single print; $314 Individuals single print. **URL:** http://eur.sagepub.com; http://us.sagepub.com/en-us/nam/journal/european-urban-and-regional-studies. **Remarks:** Accepts advertising. **Circ:** (Not Reported).

4584 ■ Evaluation Review: A Journal of Applied Research
SAGE Publications Inc.
2455 Teller Rd.
Thousand Oaks, CA 91320-2234
Free: 800-818-7243
Publisher's E-mail: sales@pfp.sagepub.com
Journal containing evaluation studies.Contains latest applied evaluation methods used in a wide range of disciplines, including education, public health, criminal justice, child development, mental health, social work, public administration, and environmental studies. **Freq:** Bimonthly. **Print Method:** Offset. **Trim Size:** 5 1/2 x 8 1/2. **Cols./Page:** 1. **Col. Width:** 50 nonpareils. **Col. Depth:** 100 agate lines. **Key Personnel:** Robert F. Boruch, Editor. **ISSN:** 0193--841X (print); **EISSN:** 1552--3926 (electronic). **Subscription Rates:** $1380 Institutions combined (print & e-access); $1518 Institutions current volume print & all online content; $1242 Institutions e-access; $1380 Institutions e-access plus backfile (all online); $2322 Institutions backfile purchase, e-access (content through 1998); $1352 Institutions print only; $186 Individuals print only; $248 Single issue institutions, print only; $40 Single issue individual, print only. **URL:** http://erx.sagepub.com. **Ad Rates:** BW $875; 4C $1110. **Remarks:** Accepts advertising. **Circ:** (Not Reported).

4585 ■ The Expository Times
SAGE Publications Inc.
2455 Teller Rd.
Thousand Oaks, CA 91320-2234
Free: 800-818-7243
Publisher's E-mail: sales@pfp.sagepub.com
Journal focusing on pastoral matters, both practical and theoretical, and the latest international biblical and theological scholarship. **Freq:** Monthly. **Key Personnel:** Duncan Forrester, Board Member; Graeme Auld, Board Member; Larry Hurtado, Board Member; John Riches, Editor; Paul Foster, Editor; Karen Wenell, Editor. **ISSN:** 0014-5246 (print). **Subscription Rates:** $387 Institutions print and online; $348 Institutions online; $379 Institutions print; $63 Individuals print; $35 Institutions single print issue; $7 Individuals single print issue; $426 Institutions current volume print and all online; $387 Institutions e-access plus backfile; $3254 Institutions e-access, backfile through 1998; $271 Individuals print and e-access. **URL:** http://ext.sagepub.com/; http://www.sagepub.com/journalsProdDesc.nav?ct_p=subscribe&prodId=Journal20 1744. **Remarks:** Accepts advertising. **Circ:** (Not Reported).

4586 ■ The Family Journal: Counseling and Therapy for Couples and Families
SAGE Publications Inc.
2455 Teller Rd.
Thousand Oaks, CA 91320-2234
Free: 800-818-7243
Publisher's E-mail: sales@pfp.sagepub.com
Journal focusing on the theory, research, and practice of counseling with couples and families from a family systems perspective. **Freq:** Quarterly. **Key Personnel:** Jill D. Duba, Editor; Stephen Southern, Editor. **ISSN:** 1066--4807 (print); **EISSN:** 1552--3950 (electronic). **Subscription Rates:** $146 Individuals print; $899 Institutions e-access; $979 Institutions print; $999 Institutions print and e-access; $47 Individuals single issue; $269 Institutions single issue. **URL:** http://tfj.sagepub.com; http://www.iamfconline.org/public/department26.cfm. **Remarks:** Accepts advertising. **Circ:** 10000.

4587 ■ Feminism and Psychology
SAGE Publications Inc.
2455 Teller Rd.
Thousand Oaks, CA 91320-2234
Free: 800-818-7243
Publisher's E-mail: sales@pfp.sagepub.com
Journal focusing on feminist research and debate in psychology. **Freq:** Quarterly. **Key Personnel:** Victoria Clarke, Consultant, Editor; Helen Malson, Consultant, Editor; Jeanne Marecek, Editor; Catriona Macleod, Editor-in-Chief. **ISSN:** 0959--3535 (print); **EISSN:** 1461--7161 (electronic). **Subscription Rates:** £66 Individuals print; £590 Institutions e-access; £642 Institutions print; £655 Institutions print and e-access; £21 Individuals single issue; £177 Institutions single print. **URL:** http://fap.sagepub.com. **Remarks:** Accepts advertising. **Circ:** (Not Reported).

4588 ■ Feminist Criminology
SAGE Publications Inc.
2455 Teller Rd.
Thousand Oaks, CA 91320-2234
Free: 800-818-7243
Publisher's E-mail: sales@pfp.sagepub.com
Journal devoted to research pertaining to women, girls and crime within the framework of a feminist critique of criminology, in connection with Division on Women and Crime of the American Society of Criminology. **Freq:** Quarterly. **Trim Size:** 6 x 9. **Key Personnel:** Jana L. Jasinski, Board Member; Joanne Belknap, Editor; Nancy C. Jurik, Editor. **ISSN:** 1557--0851 (print); **EISSN:** 1557--086X (electronic). **Subscription Rates:** £99 Individuals print; £418 Institutions e-access; £455 Institutions print only; £464 Individuals print and e-access; £32 Individuals single print; £125 Institutions single print. **URL:** http://fcx.sagepub.com. **Ad Rates:** BW $875; 4C $1110, in addition to black & white rate above. **Remarks:** Accepts advertising. **Circ:** (Not Reported).

4589 ■ Feminist Theology
SAGE Publications Inc.
2455 Teller Rd.
Thousand Oaks, CA 91320-2234
Free: 800-818-7243
Publisher's E-mail: sales@pfp.sagepub.com
Journal focusing on matters of theology and religion important to the women of Britain and Ireland. **Freq:** 3/year. **Key Personnel:** Lillalou Hughes, Editor; Lisa Isherwood, Editor. **ISSN:** 0966--7350 (print); **EISSN:** 1745--5189 (electronic). **Subscription Rates:** £60 Individuals print; £297 Institutions e-access; £323 Institutions print; £330 Institutions print and e-access; £26 Individuals single print; £118 Institutions single print. **URL:** http://fth.sagepub.com. **Remarks:** Accepts advertising. **Circ:** (Not Reported).

4590 ■ Field Methods
SAGE Publications Inc.
2455 Teller Rd.
Thousand Oaks, CA 91320-2234
Free: 800-818-7243
Publisher's E-mail: sales@pfp.sagepub.com
Journal covering for scholars, students, and professionals who do fieldwork in cultural anthropology. **Freq:** Quarterly. **Key Personnel:** Homero Martinez, Board Member; Gery Ryan, Board Member; Kathleen Carley, Board Member; Jean M. Bartunek, Board Member; Russell H. Bernard, Editor. **ISSN:** 1525--822X (print); **EISSN:** 1552--3969 (electronic). **Subscription Rates:** $171 Individuals e-access; $1043 Institutions e-access. **URL:** http://fmx.sagepub.com. **Formed by the merger of:** Cultural Anthropology Methods. **Remarks:** Accepts

advertising. **Circ:** (Not Reported).

4591 ■ First Language
SAGE Publications Inc.
2455 Teller Rd.
Thousand Oaks, CA 91320-2234
Free: 800-818-7243
Publisher's E-mail: sales@pfp.sagepub.com
Journal focusing on research into how children acquire their first language, and the application of that research into practice. **Freq:** Bimonthly. **Key Personnel:** Kevin Durkin, Editor. **ISSN:** 0142--7237 (print); **EISSN:** 1740--2344 (electronic). **Subscription Rates:** £46 Individuals print ; £549 Institutions e-access; £598 Institutions print; £610 Institutions print and e-access; £10 Individuals single print; £110 Institutions single print. **URL:** http://fla.sagepub.com. **Ad Rates:** BW $250. **Remarks:** Accepts advertising. **Circ:** (Not Reported).

4592 ■ Focus on Autism and Other Developmental Disabilities
SAGE Publications Inc.
2455 Teller Rd.
Thousand Oaks, CA 91320-2234
Free: 800-818-7243
Publisher's E-mail: sales@pfp.sagepub.com
Journal provides practical management, treatment, and planning strategies for professionals working with people with autism and developmental disabilities. **Founded:** 1995. **Freq:** Quarterly. **Print Method:** Offset. **Trim Size:** 8 x 10 7/8. **Cols./Page:** 3. **Col. Width:** 2 1/4 inches. **Col. Depth:** 9 1/4 inches. **Key Personnel:** Richard Simpson, Board Member; Joel Arick, Editor; Diane Adreon, Editor; Kevin Ayres, Editor. **ISSN:** 1088-3576 (print); **EISSN:** 1538-4829 (electronic). **USPS:** 001-259. **Subscription Rates:** $67 Individuals print & e-access; $212 Institutions print & e-access; $191 Institutions e-access; $208 Institutions print only; $57 Institutions Single Print Issue; $22 Individuals Single Print Issue. **URL:** http://www.sagepub.com/journalsProdDesc.nav?ct_p=boards&prodId=Journal201875. **Formerly**: Focus on Autistic Behavior. **Ad Rates:** BW $515; 4C $995. **Remarks:** Accepts advertising. **Circ:** Paid ‡1600.

4593 ■ Food Science and Technology International
SAGE Publications Inc.
2455 Teller Rd.
Thousand Oaks, CA 91320-2234
Free: 800-818-7243
Publisher's E-mail: sales@pfp.sagepub.com
Peer-reviewed journal focusing on research in food science and technology. **Freq:** 8/year. **Cols./Page:** 2. **Col. Width:** 8.5 centimeters. **Key Personnel:** Elvira Costell, Board Member; Franco M. Lajolo, Board Member; Michele Marcotte, Board Member; Antonio Mulet, Board Member; Remedios Melero, Associate Editor; Gustavo V. Barbosa-Canovas, Editor, Board Member; Antonio Martinez Lopez, Editor-in-Chief. **ISSN:** 1082--0132 (print); **EISSN:** 1532--1738 (electronic). **Subscription Rates:** $243 Individuals print; $1724 Institutions e-access; $1878 Institutions print; $1916 Institutions print and e-access; $39 Individuals single print; $258 Institutions single print. **URL:** http://fst.sagepub.com. **Formerly**: Revista Espanola de Ciencia y Tecnologia de Alimentos. **Remarks:** Accepts advertising. **Circ:** (Not Reported).

4594 ■ French Cultural Studies
SAGE Publications Inc.
2455 Teller Rd.
Thousand Oaks, CA 91320-2234
Free: 800-818-7243
Publisher's E-mail: sales@pfp.sagepub.com
Journal focusing on the study of French culture, language, and society. **Freq:** 3/year. **Trim Size:** 243 x 175 mm. **Key Personnel:** Nicholas Hewitt, Editor; Prof. Michael Kelly, Associate Editor; Susan Harris, Associate Editor; Nicola Cooper, Associate Editor. **ISSN:** 0957--1558 (print); **EISSN:** 1740--2352 (electronic). **Subscription Rates:** $87 Individuals print; $857 Institutions e-access; $933 Institutions print; $952 Institutions print and e-access; $28 Individuals single print; $257 Institutions single print. **URL:** http://frc.sagepub.com. **Ad Rates:** BW $200. **Remarks:** Accepts advertising. **Circ:** (Not Reported).

4595 ■ Games and Culture
SAGE Publications Inc.
2455 Teller Rd.
Thousand Oaks, CA 91320-2234
Free: 800-818-7243
Publisher's E-mail: sales@pfp.sagepub.com
Journal focusing on research about games and culture within the context of interactive media. **Freq:** 8/year. **Key Personnel:** Tanya Krzywinska, Editor. **ISSN:** 1555--4120 (print); **EISSN:** 1555--4139 (electronic). **Subscription Rates:** $131 Individuals print and e-access; $830 Institutions e-access; $904 Institutions print only; $922 Individuals print & e-access; $21 Individuals single print; $124 Institutions single print. **URL:** http://gac.sagepub.com. **Remarks:** Accepts advertising. **Circ:** (Not Reported).

4596 ■ Gender, Technology and Development
SAGE Publications Inc.
2455 Teller Rd.
Thousand Oaks, CA 91320-2234
Free: 800-818-7243
Publisher's E-mail: sales@pfp.sagepub.com
Journal exploring the linkages between changing gender relations and technological development. **Freq:** Quarterly. **Key Personnel:** Bernadette Resurreccion, Associate Editor; Joy Clancy, Editor. **ISSN:** 0971-8524 (print); **EISSN:** 0973-0656 (electronic). **Subscription Rates:** $411 Institutions print & e-access; $452 Institutions backfile lease, combined plus backfile; $370 Institutions e-access; $411 Institutions all online content; $370 Institutions backfile purchase, e-access; $403 Institutions print only; $89 Individuals print only; $148 Institutions single print; $38 Individuals single print. **URL:** http://www.sagepub.com/journalsProdDesc.nav?prodId=Journal200816; http://gtd.sagepub.com/. **Remarks:** Accepts advertising. **Circ:** (Not Reported).

4597 ■ Gifted Child Today Magazine
SAGE Publications Inc.
2455 Teller Rd.
Thousand Oaks, CA 91320-2234
Free: 800-818-7243
Publisher's E-mail: sales@pfp.sagepub.com
Magazine for the parents and teachers of gifted, creative, and talented children and youth. **Freq:** Quarterly. **Key Personnel:** Susan Johnsen, PhD, Editor, phone: (254)710-6116; Marjorie Parker, Contact. **ISSN:** 1076--2175 (print); **EISSN:** 2162--951X (electronic). **Subscription Rates:** $18 Individuals single issue; $33 Institutions single issue; $56 Individuals print & online; $120 Institutions print; $122 Institutions print and online; $122 Institutions institutional subscription and back file lease, E-access + back file (all online content); $134 Institutions institutional subscription and back file lease, combined + back file (current volume print and all online content); $196 Institutions institutional back file purchase, E-access (content through 1998). **URL:** http://gct.sagepub.com. **Formerly**: G/C/T. **Remarks:** Accepts advertising. **Circ:** Paid ‡15000.

4598 ■ Global Business Review
SAGE Publications Inc.
2455 Teller Rd.
Thousand Oaks, CA 91320-2234
Free: 800-818-7243
Publisher's E-mail: sales@pfp.sagepub.com
Journal focusing on global management and business practices with an emphasis on Asian and Indian perspectives. **Freq:** Quarterly. **Key Personnel:** Arindam Banik, Editor. **ISSN:** 0972-1509 (print); **EISSN:** 0973-0664 (electronic). **Subscription Rates:** $553 Institutions combined (print & e-access); $498 Institutions e-access; $542 Institutions print only; $111 Individuals print only; $99 Institutions single print; $24 Individuals single print. **URL:** http://www.sagepub.com/journalsProdDesc.nav?prodId=Journal200886. **Remarks:** Accepts advertising. **Circ:** (Not Reported).

4599 ■ Global Media and Communication
SAGE Publications Inc.
2455 Teller Rd.
Thousand Oaks, CA 91320-2234
Free: 800-818-7243
Publisher's E-mail: sales@pfp.sagepub.com
Journal focusing on developments in the global media and communications environment. **Freq:** 3/year 3/yr. **Key Personnel:** Yuezhi Zhao, Editor; Des Freedman, Editor; Daya K. Thussu, Editor; Terhi Rantanen, Editor. **ISSN:** 1742--7665 (print); **EISSN:** 1742--7673 (electronic). **Subscription Rates:** $93 Individuals print; $743 Institutions e-access; $809 Institutions print only; $825 Institutions print and e-access; $40 Individuals single print; $297 Institutions single print. **URL:** http://gmc.sagepub.com. **Remarks:** Accepts advertising. **Circ:** (Not Reported).

4600 ■ Global Social Policy
SAGE Publications Inc.
2455 Teller Rd.
Thousand Oaks, CA 91320-2234
Free: 800-818-7243
Publisher's E-mail: sales@pfp.sagepub.com
Journal aiming to advance the understanding of the impact of globalization upon social policy and social development. **Freq:** 3/year. **Key Personnel:** Rianne Mahon, Editor; Bob Deacon, Editor, Founder. **ISSN:** 1468--0181 (print); **EISSN:** 1741--2803 (electronic). **Subscription Rates:** £52 Individuals print only; £385 Institutions e-access; £419 Institutions print only; £428 Institutions print and e-access; £23 Individuals single print; £157 Institutions single print. **URL:** http://gsp.sagepub.com. **Remarks:** Accepts advertising. **Circ:** (Not Reported).

4601 ■ Group Analysis: The Journal of Group Analytic Psychotherapy
SAGE Publications Inc.
2455 Teller Rd.
Thousand Oaks, CA 91320-2234
Free: 800-818-7243
Publisher's E-mail: sales@pfp.sagepub.com
Journal focusing on the theory, practice, and experience of analytical group psychotherapy; embracing concepts derived from psychoanalytic psychology, social psychology, group dynamics, sociology, and anthropology. **Freq:** Quarterly. **Key Personnel:** Dieter Nitzgen, Editor; Malcolm Pines, Board Member. **ISSN:** 0533--3164 (print); **EISSN:** 1461--717X (electronic). **Subscription Rates:** £79 Individuals print; £473 Institutions e-access; £515 Institutions print; £526 Institutions print and e-access; £26 Individuals single print; £143 Institutions single print. **URL:** http://gaq.sagepub.com. **Remarks:** Accepts advertising. **Circ:** (Not Reported).

4602 ■ Group & Organization Management: An International Journal
SAGE Publications Inc.
2455 Teller Rd.
Thousand Oaks, CA 91320-2234
Free: 800-818-7243
Publisher's E-mail: sales@pfp.sagepub.com
Journal on behavioral studies in human training. Contains international forum for the latest research and analysis in organizational behavior, organization theory, business strategy, and human resources. **Freq:** Bimonthly February , April , June , August , October and December. **Print Method:** Offset. **Trim Size:** 5 1/2 x 8 1/2. **Cols./Page:** 1. **Col. Width:** 50 nonpareils. **Col. Depth:** 100 agate lines. **Key Personnel:** William L. Gardner, Editor; Yehuda Baruch, Board Member. **ISSN:** 1059--6011 (print); **EISSN:** 1552--3993 (electronic). **Subscription Rates:** $1467 Institutions print & e-access; $1614 Institutions current volume print & all online content; $1320 Institutions e-access; $1467 Institutions all online content; $2579 Institutions e-access (content through 1998); $1438 Institutions print only; $220 Individuals print only; $264 Institutions single print; $48 Individuals single print. **URL:** http://gom.sagepub.com. **Formerly**: Group and Organization Studies. **Ad Rates:** BW $875; 4C $1110. **Remarks:** Accepts advertising. **Circ:** (Not Reported).

4603 ■ Group Processes and Intergroup Relations
SAGE Publications Inc.
2455 Teller Rd.
Thousand Oaks, CA 91320-2234
Free: 800-818-7243
Publisher's E-mail: sales@pfp.sagepub.com
Journal focusing on social psychological research into group processes and intergroup relations. **Freq:** Bimonthly. **Key Personnel:** Emanuele Castano, Editor; Bertjan Doosje, Associate Editor; Matthew J. Hornsey, Associate Editor; Norbert L. Kerr, Associate Editor; Craig D. Parks, Associate Editor; Deborah Prentice, Editor; Dominic Abrams, Editor; Michael A. Hogg, Editor. **ISSN:** 1368-4302 (print); **EISSN:** 1461-7188 (electronic). **Sub-**

Circulation: ★ = AAM; △ or • = BPA; ♦ = CAC; ❑ = VAC; ⊕ = PO Statement; ‡ = Publisher's Report; Boldface figures = sworn; Light figures = estimated.

scription Rates: $1322 Institutions combined (print & e-access); $1190 Institutions e-access (content through 1998); $1296 Institutions print only; $117 Individuals print only; $238 Institutions single print; $25 Individuals single print. **URL:** http://www.sagepub.com/journalsProdDesc.nav?prodId=Journal200785; http://gpi.sagepub.com/. **Remarks:** Accepts advertising. **Circ:** (Not Reported).

4604 ■ Handbook of Practice Management
SAGE Publications Inc.
2455 Teller Rd.
Thousand Oaks, CA 91320-2234
Free: 800-818-7243
Publisher's E-mail: sales@pfp.sagepub.com
Journal providing latest information on practice management issues for practice managers. **Freq:** Quarterly. **Key Personnel:** Junaid Bajwa, Contact. **ISSN:** 0962--144X (print); **EISSN:** 2047--718X (electronic). **Subscription Rates:** $256 Institutions combined (print & e-access). **URL:** http://hpm.sagepub.com. **Circ:** (Not Reported).

4605 ■ Health: An Interdisciplinary Journal for the Social Study of Health, Illness and Medicine
SAGE Publications Inc.
2455 Teller Rd.
Thousand Oaks, CA 91320-2234
Free: 800-818-7243
Publisher's E-mail: sales@pfp.sagepub.com
Journal focusing on health and the social sciences. **Founded:** 1997. **Freq:** Bimonthly. **Key Personnel:** Michael Traynor, Editor; Alan Radley, Editor, Founder; Arthur Frank, Editor; Nick Fox, Editor; David Armstrong, Board Member; Susan E. Bell, Board Member. **ISSN:** 1363-4593 (print); **EISSN:** 1461-7196 (electronic). **Subscription Rates:** $1323 Institutions print & e-access; $1455 Institutions print & all online content; $1191 Institutions e-access; $1297 Institutions print only; $111 Individuals print only; $238 Institutions single print; $24 Individuals single print; £60 Individuals print only; £701 Institutions print only; £644 Institutions electronic access only; £715 Institutions print & electronic access; £129 Institutions single print; £13 Individuals single print; £787 Institutions current volume print & all online content; £716 Institutions all online content; £644 Institutions content through 1998. **URL:** http://www.sagepub.com/journalsProdAdv.nav?prodId=Journal200904; http://www.uk.sagepub.com/journalsProdDesc.nav?prodId=Journal200904. **Remarks:** Accepts advertising. **Circ:** (Not Reported).

4606 ■ Health Education & Behavior
SAGE Publications Inc.
2455 Teller Rd.
Thousand Oaks, CA 91320-2234
Free: 800-818-7243
Publisher's E-mail: sales@pfp.sagepub.com
Journal exploring social and behavioral changes as they affect health status and quality of life. **Freq:** Bimonthly. **Key Personnel:** Michael Eriksen, PhD, Board Member; John P. Allegrante, PhD, Editor-in-Chief; Ana F. Abraido-Lanza, PhD, Associate Editor; Marc Zimmerman, PhD, Board Member. **ISSN:** 1090-1981 (print); **EISSN:** 1552-6127 (electronic). **Subscription Rates:** $1380 Institutions combined (print & e-access); $1518 Institutions current volume print & all online content; $193 Individuals print only; $253 Single issue institutional; $42 Single issue individual; $2933 Institutions backfile e-access through 1998. **URL:** http://www.sagepub.com/journalsProdDesc.nav?prodId=Journal200851. **Remarks:** Accepts advertising. **Circ:** (Not Reported).

4607 ■ Health Informatics Journal
SAGE Publications Inc.
2455 Teller Rd.
Thousand Oaks, CA 91320-2234
Free: 800-818-7243
Publisher's E-mail: sales@pfp.sagepub.com
Journal publishing peer-reviewed contributions from the fields of informatics and telematics, the health professions, computer science, engineering and management. **Freq:** Quarterly. **Key Personnel:** Laurence Alpay, Board Member; Matthew Jones, Board Member; Panagiotis D. Bamidis, Board Member; Chris Dowd, Board Member; P.A. Bath, Associate Editor; Rob Procter, Editor. **ISSN:** 1460-4582 (print); **EISSN:** 1741-2811 (electronic). **Subscription Rates:** $705 Institutions print and online; $706 Institutions all online content; $776 Institutions print and all online content; $634 Individuals content through 1998; $635 Institutions e-access; $691 Institutions print only; $163 Individuals print only; $190 Institutions single print; $53 Individuals single print. **URL:** http://www.sagepub.com/journalsProdDesc.nav?prodId=Journal201654. **Remarks:** Accepts advertising. **Circ:** (Not Reported).

4608 ■ Health Promotion Practice
SAGE Publications Inc.
2455 Teller Rd.
Thousand Oaks, CA 91320-2234
Free: 800-818-7243
Publisher's E-mail: sales@pfp.sagepub.com
Peer-reviewed journal focusing on the practical application of health promotion and education. **Freq:** Bimonthly Quarterly. **Key Personnel:** Jesus Ramirez-Valles, PhD, Editor-in-Chief. **ISSN:** 1524--8399 (print); **EISSN:** 1552--6372 (electronic). **Subscription Rates:** $202 Individuals print only; $743 Institutions e-access; $809 Institutions print only; $826 Institutions print and e-access; $44 Individuals single print; $151 Institutions single print; Included in membership. **URL:** http://us.sagepub.com/en-us/nam/health-promotion-practice/journal201271; http://www.sophe.org/Health_Promotion_Practice.cfm. **Ad Rates:** BW $1120; 4C $1100. **Remarks:** Accepts advertising. **Circ:** (Not Reported).

4609 ■ Health Services Management Research
SAGE Publications Inc.
2455 Teller Rd.
Thousand Oaks, CA 91320-2234
Free: 800-818-7243
Publisher's E-mail: sales@pfp.sagepub.com
Journal focusing on practical implementation of research activity in management of health services. **Freq:** Quarterly. **Key Personnel:** Kieran Walshe, Editor. **ISSN:** 0951--4848 (print); **EISSN:** 1758--1044 (electronic). **Subscription Rates:** £283 Institutions combined (print & e-access); £340 Institutions combined plus backfile; £340 Institutions e-access (content through 1998); £378 Institutions e-access plus backfile; £416 Institutions combined (print & e-access); £135 Institutions single print issue ; £92 Individuals single print issue. **URL:** http://hsm.sagepub.com; http://intl-hsm.sagepub.com. **Circ:** (Not Reported).

4610 ■ High Performance Polymers
SAGE Publications Inc.
2455 Teller Rd.
Thousand Oaks, CA 91320-2234
Free: 800-818-7243
Publisher's E-mail: sales@pfp.sagepub.com
Peer-reviewed journal focusing on high performance polymer science and technology. **Freq:** 8/year. **Key Personnel:** M. Bruma, Advisor, Board Member; T.J. Bunning, Advisor, Board Member; B. Banks, Advisor, Board Member; D. Hourston, Advisor, Board Member; H.R. Kricheldorf, Board Member; Benjamin S. Hsiao, Board Member; J.E. McGrath, Advisor, Board Member; John Connell, Editor; M. Kakimoto, Associate Editor. **ISSN:** 0954--0083 (print); **EISSN:** 1361--6412 (electronic). **Subscription Rates:** $1439 Institutions e-access; $1567 Institutions print only; $1599 Institutions print and e-access; $172 Institutions sinlge print. **URL:** http://hip.sagepub.com; http://us.sagepub.com/en-us/nam/journal/high-performance-polymers. **Remarks:** Accepts advertising. **Circ:** (Not Reported).

4611 ■ Hispanic Journal of Behavioral Sciences
SAGE Publications Inc.
2455 Teller Rd.
Thousand Oaks, CA 91320-2234
Free: 800-818-7243
Publication E-mail: advertising@sagepub.com
Journal of research articles, case histories, critical reviews, and scholarly notes that are of theoretical interest or deal with methodological issues related to Hispanic populations. **Founded:** Feb. 1989. **Freq:** Quarterly. **Print Method:** Web Press. **Trim Size:** 5 1/2 x 8 1/2. **Cols./Page:** 1. **Col. Width:** 50 nonpareils. **Col. Depth:** 100 agate lines. **Key Personnel:** Amado M. Padilla, Editor. **ISSN:** 0739-9863 (print); **EISSN:** 1552-6364 (electronic). **Subscription Rates:** $904 Institutions combined (print & e-access); $994 Institutions backfile lease, combined plus backfile; $814 Institutions e-access; $1383 Institutions backfile, e-access (content through 1998); $886 Institutions print only; $138 Individuals print only. **URL:** http://www.sagepub.com/journalsProdDesc.nav?prodId=Journal200809. **Ad Rates:** BW $515; 4C $995. **Remarks:** Accepts advertising. **Circ:** Paid 500.

4612 ■ History of the Human Sciences
SAGE Publications Inc.
2455 Teller Rd.
Thousand Oaks, CA 91320-2234
Free: 800-818-7243
Publisher's E-mail: sales@pfp.sagepub.com
Journal aiming to expand understanding of the human world through a broad interdisciplinary approach, with articles from sociology, psychology, anthropology, and politics. **Freq:** 5/year. **Key Personnel:** Roger Smith, Advisor, Board Member; Thomas Osborne, Advisor, Board Member; Arthur Still, Advisor, Board Member; James Good, Editor; Rhodri Hayward, Editor. **ISSN:** 0952--6951 (print); **EISSN:** 1461--720X (electronic). **Subscription Rates:** $131 Individuals print only; $1564 Institutions e-access; $1703 Institutions print only; $1738 Institutions print and e-access; $34 Individuals single print; $375 Institutions single print. **URL:** http://uk.sagepub.com/en-gb/eur/history-of-the-human-sciences/journal200813. **Remarks:** Accepts advertising. **Circ:** (Not Reported).

4613 ■ History of Psychiatry
SAGE Publications Inc.
2455 Teller Rd.
Thousand Oaks, CA 91320-2234
Free: 800-818-7243
Publisher's E-mail: sales@pfp.sagepub.com
Journal focusing on the history of mental illness and the forms of medicine, psychiatry, cultural response and social policy which have evolved to understand and treat it. **Freq:** Quarterly. **Key Personnel:** G.E. Berrios, Editor. **ISSN:** 0957-154X (print); **EISSN:** 1740-2360 (electronic). **Subscription Rates:** $960 Institutions print & e-access; $1056 Institutions print & all online; $864 Institutions e-access; $941 Institutions print only; $96 Individuals print only; $259 Institutions single print; $31 Individuals single print. **URL:** http://www.sagepub.com/journalsProdDesc.nav?ct_p=&prodId=Journal201666. **Ad Rates:** BW $200. **Remarks:** Accepts advertising. **Circ:** (Not Reported).

4614 ■ Home Health Care Management and Practice
SAGE Publications Inc.
2455 Teller Rd.
Thousand Oaks, CA 91320-2234
Free: 800-818-7243
Publication E-mail: advertising@sagepub.com
Journal covering issues and practical concerns in home health care. **Founded:** 1989. **Freq:** Bimonthly. **Trim Size:** 8 1/2 x 11. **Cols./Page:** 2. **Col. Width:** 16 picas. **Col. Depth:** 45 picas. **Key Personnel:** Robert E. Enck, Editor-in-Chief. **ISSN:** 1084-8223 (print); **EISSN:** 1552-6739 (electronic). **Subscription Rates:** $583 Institutions print & e-access; $641 Institutions current volume print & all online content; $525 Institutions e-access; $583 Institutions all online content; $554 Institutions content through 1998; $571 Institutions print only; $180 Individuals print only; $157 Institutions single print; $59 Individuals single print. **URL:** http://www.sagepub.com/journalsProdDesc.nav?prodId=Journal201504. **Formerly:** Journal of Home Health Care Practice. **Ad Rates:** BW $595; 4C $995. **Remarks:** Accepts advertising. **Circ:** 450.

4615 ■ Homicide Studies
SAGE Publications Inc.
2455 Teller Rd.
Thousand Oaks, CA 91320-2234
Free: 800-818-7243
Publisher's E-mail: sales@pfp.sagepub.com
Journal focusing on research, public policy, and applied knowledge relating to the study of homicide. **Freq:** Quarterly. **Key Personnel:** Gary F. Jensen, Associate Editor; Carolyn Rebecca Block, Associate Editor; Richard Block, Associate Editor; Lynn Addington, Editor. **ISSN:** 1088--7679 (print); **EISSN:** 1552--6720 (electronic). **Subscription Rates:** $153 Individuals print only; $841 Institutions e-access; $915 Institutions print only; $934 Institutions print and e-access; $50 Individuals single print; $252 Institutions sinlge print. **URL:** http://us.sagepub.com/en-us/nam/homicide-studies/journal200817; http://hsx.sagepub.com. **Remarks:**

Accepts advertising. **Circ:** (Not Reported).

4616 ■ Human & Experimental Toxicology
SAGE Publications Inc.
2455 Teller Rd.
Thousand Oaks, CA 91320-2234
Free: 800-818-7243
Publisher's E-mail: sales@pfp.sagepub.com
Peer-reviewed international journal publishes original research and review articles on experimental and clinical studies of functional, biochemical and structural disorders. **Founded:** 1982. **Freq:** Monthly. **Print Method:** Offset. **Trim Size:** 8 1/2 x 11. **Cols./Page:** 2. **Col. Width:** 5 1/4 inches. **Col. Depth:** 9 1/4 inches. **Key Personnel:** Dr. A. Wallace Hayes, Editor; Prof. Kai Savolainen, Editor-in-Chief. **ISSN:** 0960-3271 (print); **EISSN:** 1477-0903 (electronic). **Subscription Rates:** $2619 Institutions print and e-access; $2357 Institutions e-access; $2567 Institutions print; $888 Individuals print and e-access; $235 Institutions single print; $96 Individuals single. **URL:** http://www.sagepub.com/journalsProdDesc.nav?prodId=Journal201813. **Ad Rates:** BW $550; 4C $1,725. **Remarks:** Accepts advertising. **Circ:** Paid 500.

4617 ■ Human Resource Development Review
SAGE Publications Inc.
2455 Teller Rd.
Thousand Oaks, CA 91320-2234
Free: 800-818-7243
Publisher's E-mail: sales@pfp.sagepub.com
Journal for scholars of human resource development and related disciplines. **Freq:** Quarterly. **Trim Size:** 5 1/4 x 8 1/4. **Key Personnel:** Jaime L. Callahan, Editor; Julia Walker, Editor. **ISSN:** 1534--4843 (print); **EISSN:** 1552--6712 (electronic). **Subscription Rates:** $113 Individuals print only; $565 Institutions e-access; $615 Institutions print only; $628 Institutions print and e-access; $37 Individuals single print; $169 Individuals single print. **URL:** http://hrd.sagepub.com; http://us.sagepub.com/en-us/nam/human-resource-development-review/journal201506. **Remarks:** Accepts advertising. **Circ:** (Not Reported).

4618 ■ IFLA Journal
SAGE Publications Inc.
2455 Teller Rd.
Thousand Oaks, CA 91320-2234
Free: 800-818-7243
Publisher's E-mail: sales@pfp.sagepub.com
Peer-reviewed journal of the International Federation of Library Associations and Institutions (IFLA) conference papers & news of current activities. **Freq:** Quarterly. **Key Personnel:** Steve Witt, Editor. **ISSN:** 0340--0352 (print); **EISSN:** 1745--2651 (electronic). **Subscription Rates:** $118 Individuals print only; $479 Institutions e-access; $521 Institutions print only; $532 Institutions print and e-access; $38 Individuals single print; $143 Individuals sinlge print. **URL:** http://www.ifla.org/publications/node/1691; http://us.sagepub.com/en-us/nam/journal/ifla-journal. **Remarks:** Accepts advertising. **Circ:** (Not Reported).

4619 ■ Improving Schools
SAGE Publications Inc.
2455 Teller Rd.
Thousand Oaks, CA 91320-2234
Free: 800-818-7243
Publisher's E-mail: sales@pfp.sagepub.com
Journal focusing on the improvement of schools in difficulty or making successful schools even better. **Freq:** 3/year. **Print Method:** Offset Litho. **Trim Size:** A4. **Col. Width:** 124 millimeters. **Col. Depth:** 202 millimeters. **Key Personnel:** Michael Fielding, Advisor; Jacob Easley, Advisor; Paul Clarke, Advisor. **ISSN:** 1365--4802 (print); **EISSN:** 1475--7583 (electronic). **Subscription Rates:** £56 Individuals print only; £222 Institutions school - print and e-access; £399 Institutions e-access; £434 Institutions print only; £443 Institutions print and e-access; £24 Individuals single print; £159 Institutions single print. **URL:** http://us.sagepub.com/en-us/nam/improving-schools/journal201678; http://imp.sagepub.com. **Remarks:** Advertising accepted; rates available upon request. **Circ:** Paid 1000.

4620 ■ Indian Economic and Social History Review
SAGE Publications Inc.
2455 Teller Rd.
Thousand Oaks, CA 91320-2234
Free: 800-818-7243
Publisher's E-mail: sales@pfp.sagepub.com
Journal encompassing the history, economy, and society of India and South Asia, including comparative studies of world development. **Freq:** Quarterly. **Trim Size:** 6 1/4 x 9 1/2. **Key Personnel:** Sunil Kumar, Board Member; G. Balachandran, Board Member. **ISSN:** 0019--4646 (print); **EISSN:** 0973--0893 (electronic). **Subscription Rates:** $626 Institutions print & e-access; $689 Institutions current volume print & all online; $563 Institutions e-access; $626 Individuals e-access (all online content); $1675 Institutions e-access (content through 1998); $613 Institutions print only; $139 Individuals print only; $169 Institutions single print; $45 Individuals single print. **URL:** http://ier.sagepub.com. **Remarks:** Accepts advertising. **Circ:** (Not Reported).

4621 ■ Indian Journal of Gender Studies
SAGE Publications Inc.
2455 Teller Rd.
Thousand Oaks, CA 91320-2234
Free: 800-818-7243
Publisher's E-mail: sales@pfp.sagepub.com
Journal focusing, among other issues, on violence as a phenomenon, the social organization of the family, the invisibility of women's work, institutional and policy analyses, women and politics, and motherhood and child care. **Freq:** 3/year 3/yr. **Key Personnel:** Bina Agarwal, Advisor; Antoinette Burton, Advisor; Ravinder Pillai, Assistant Editor; Leela Kasturi, Editor; Swapna Guha, Assistant Editor; Aparna Basu, Advisor; Malavika Karlekar, Editor. **ISSN:** 0971-5215 (print); **EISSN:** 0973-0672 (electronic). **Subscription Rates:** $381 Institutions print & e-access; $419 Institutions current volume print & all online content; $343 Institutions e-access; $381 Individuals e-access (all online content); $373 Institutions print only; $91 Individuals print only; $137 Institutions single print; $39 Individuals single print. **URL:** http://www.sagepub.com/journalsProdDesc.nav?prodId=Journal200917. **Remarks:** Accepts advertising. **Circ:** (Not Reported).

4622 ■ Indoor and Built Environment
SAGE Publications Inc.
2455 Teller Rd.
Thousand Oaks, CA 91320-2234
Free: 800-818-7243
Publisher's E-mail: sales@pfp.sagepub.com
Scientific journal. **Freq:** 8/year. **Print Method:** Offset. **Trim Size:** 210 x 280 mm. **Cols./Page:** 1. **Col. Width:** 99 nonpareils. **Key Personnel:** Prof. Chuck Yu, Editor-in-Chief; Prof. Dariush Azimi, Associate Editor. **ISSN:** 1420--326X (print); **EISSN:** 1423--0070 (electronic). **Subscription Rates:** £227 Individuals print only; £1228 Institutions online only; £1337 Institutions print only; £1364 Institutions print and online; £37 Individuals single print issue; £184 Institutions single print issue. **URL:** http://ibe.sagepub.com. **Formerly:** Indoor Environment; Journal of the International Society of the Built Environment. **Ad Rates:** BW $1,195. **Remarks:** Accepts advertising. **Circ:** 1000.

4623 ■ Information Development
SAGE Publications Inc.
2455 Teller Rd.
Thousand Oaks, CA 91320-2234
Free: 800-818-7243
Publisher's E-mail: sales@pfp.sagepub.com
Peer-reviewed journal providing coverage of current developments in the provision, management, and use of information throughout the world, with particular emphasis on the information needs and problems of developing countries. **Freq:** 5/year. **Print Method:** Litho. **Trim Size:** 276 x 210 mm. **Key Personnel:** Kingo McHombu, Advisor; Paul Sturges, Advisor; Stephen J. Parker, Editor; Rashidah Begum Fazal, Advisor. **ISSN:** 0266--6669 (print); **EISSN:** 1741--6469 (electronic). **Subscription Rates:** £64 Individuals print only; £466 Institutions e-access; £508 Institutions print only; £518 Institutions print and e-access; £17 Individuals single print; £112 Institutions single print. **URL:** http://uk.sagepub.com/en-gb/asi/information-development/journal201674; http://idv.sagepub.com. **Remarks:** Advertising accepted; rates available upon request. **Circ:** (Not Reported).

4624 ■ Integrative Cancer Therapies
SAGE Publications Inc.
2455 Teller Rd.
Thousand Oaks, CA 91320-2234
Free: 800-818-7243
Publisher's E-mail: sales@pfp.sagepub.com
Journal emphasizing scientific understanding of alternative medicine and traditional medicine therapies, and their responsible integration with conventional health care. **Freq:** Bimonthly. **Key Personnel:** Daniel Rubin, Assistant Editor; Penny B. Block, Associate Editor; Charlotte Gyllenhaal, PhD, Associate Editor; Keith I. Block, MD, Editor. **ISSN:** 1534--7354 (print); **EISSN:** 1552--695X (electronic). **Subscription Rates:** £112 Individuals print only; £526 Institutions print only; £24 Individuals single print; £96 Institutions single print. **URL:** http://uk.sagepub.com/en-gb/asi/integrative-cancer-therapies/journal201510; http://ict.sagepub.com. **Remarks:** Advertising accepted; rates available upon request. **Circ:** (Not Reported).

4625 ■ International Communication Gazette
SAGE Publications Inc.
2455 Teller Rd.
Thousand Oaks, CA 91320-2234
Free: 800-818-7243
Publication E-mail: journals@sagepub.com
Journal focusing on all aspects of communications including the modern mass media, the traditional media, community and alternative media, telecommunications and information, and communication technologies. **Founded:** 1939. **Freq:** 8/year 8/yr. **Key Personnel:** Cees J. Hamelink, Editor-in-Chief; Ester de Waal, Managing Editor; Jean-Claude Burgelman, Advisor; Richard R. Cole, Advisor; Kwame S.T. Boafo, Advisor; Leen d Heenens, Associate Editor. **ISSN:** 1748-0485 (print); **EISSN:** 1748-0493 (electronic). **Subscription Rates:** $1701 Institutions combined (print & e-access); $1871 Institutions current volume (print & all online content); $1531 Institutions e-access; $1701 Institutions backfile lease, e-access plus backfile; $1667 Institutions print only; $133 Individuals print only; $7806 Institutions backfile online through 1998; $229 Institutions single print; $22 Individuals single print; £870 Institutions Combined (Print & E-access); £957 Institutions Current Volume Print & All Online Content; £783 Institutions E-access; £870 Individuals All Online Content; £3997 Institutions E-access (Content through 1998); £853 Institutions print only; £70 Individuals print only; £117 Institutions single print; £11 Individuals single print. **URL:** http://www.sagepub.com/journalsProdDesc.nav?prodId=Journal200826; http://www.sagepub.co.uk/journalsProdDesc.nav?prodId=Journal200826. **Formerly:** Gazette. **Remarks:** Accepts advertising. **Circ:** (Not Reported).

4626 ■ International Journal of Business Communication
SAGE Publications Inc.
2455 Teller Rd.
Thousand Oaks, CA 91320-2234
Free: 800-818-7243
Publisher's E-mail: sales@pfp.sagepub.com
Journal focusing on professional business communication. **Founded:** 1963. **Freq:** Quarterly. **Print Method:** Offset. **Trim Size:** 6 x 9. **Cols./Page:** 1. **Col. Width:** 51 nonpareils. **Col. Depth:** 102 agate lines. **Key Personnel:** Jim Dubinsky, Managing Editor; Kathryn M. Rybka, Editor, phone: (217)621-2973; Sandra French, Associate Editor; Robyn Walker, Editor; Geert Jacobs, Editor; Daniel Janssen, Associate Editor; John Penrose, Associate Editor; Jason Snyder, Officer; Joel Bowman, Board Member. **ISSN:** 0021-9436 (print); **EISSN:** 2329-489 (electronic). **Subscription Rates:** Included in membership; $497 Institutions online only; $541 Institutions print only; $552 Institutions print and online; $528 Institutions print and e-access; $475 Institutions e-access; $517 Institutions print. **URL:** http://businesscommunication.org; http://job.sagepub.com; http://www.sagepub.com/journalsProdDesc.nav?prodId=Journal201671. **Formerly**: Journal of Business Communication. **Remarks:** Accepts advertising. **Circ:** 2550.

4627 ■ International Journal of Care Coordination
SAGE Publications Inc.
2455 Teller Rd.

Circulation: ★ = AAM; △ or • = BPA; ♦ = CAC; □ = VAC; ⊕ = PO Statement; ‡ = Publisher's Report; Boldface figures = sworn; Light figures = estimated.

Thousand Oaks, CA 91320-2234
Free: 800-818-7243
Publisher's E-mail: sales@pfp.sagepub.com
Peer-reviewed journal focusing on informatics, risk management and quality. **Freq:** Quarterly. **Key Personnel:** H. J. M. Vrijhoef, Editor; Kris Vanhaecht, Board Member. **ISSN:** 2053--4345 (print); **EISSN:** 2053--4353 (electronic). **Subscription Rates:** £397 Institutions combined (print & e-access); £437 Institutions combined plus backfile; £357 Institutions e-access; £397 Institutions e-access plus backfile (all online content); £384 Individuals combined print & e-access (content through 1998); £148 Individuals print and e-access; £152 Institutions single print issue ; £48 Individuals single print issue. **URL:** http://icp.sagepub.com. **Formerly**: Journal of Integrated Care Pathways; International Journal of Care Pathways. **Circ:** (Not Reported).

4628 ■ International Journal of Cross Cultural Management
SAGE Publications Inc.
2455 Teller Rd.
Thousand Oaks, CA 91320-2234
Free: 800-818-7243
Publisher's E-mail: sales@pfp.sagepub.com
Journal serving as a reference for the encouragement and dissemination of research on cross cultural aspects of management, work, and organization. **Freq:** 3/year. **Trim Size:** 190 x 137 mm. **Key Personnel:** Anne-Wil Harzing, Associate Editor; David Thomas, Board Member; Roya Ayman, Board Member; Rabbi S. Bhagat, Board Member; Dharm P.B. Bhawuk, Board Member; Pawan Budhwar, Editor; Nancy J. Adler, Board Member; Allan Bird, Board Member; Terence Jackson, Editor-in-Chief; Zeynep Aycan, Founder, Editor. **ISSN:** 1470--5958 (print); **EISSN:** 1741--2838 (electronic). **Subscription Rates:** £52 Individuals print only; £374 Institutions e-access; £408 Institutions print only; £416 Institutions print and e-access; £23 Individuals single print; £150 Institutions single print. **URL:** http://ccm.sagepub.com; http://uk.sagepub.com/en-gb/asi/international-journal-of-cross-cultural-management/journal201498. **Remarks:** Color advertising accepted; rates available upon request. **Circ:** (Not Reported).

4629 ■ International Journal of Cultural Studies
SAGE Publications Inc.
2455 Teller Rd.
Thousand Oaks, CA 91320-2234
Free: 800-818-7243
Publisher's E-mail: sales@pfp.sagepub.com
Journal providing international perspectives on cultural and media developments across the globe. **Freq:** Bimonthly. **Key Personnel:** William Uricchio, Associate Editor; John Hartley, Editor. **ISSN:** 1367--8779 (print); **EISSN:** 1460--356X (electronic). **Subscription Rates:** £58 Individuals print only; £699 Institutions e-access; £761 Institutions print only; £777 Institutions print and e-access; £13 Individuals single print; £140 Institutions single print. **URL:** http://ics.sagepub.com; http://uk.sagepub.com/en-gb/asi/international-journal-of-cultural-studies/journal200946. **Remarks:** Advertising accepted; rates available upon request. **Circ:** (Not Reported).

4630 ■ International Journal of Damage Mechanics
SAGE Publications Inc.
2455 Teller Rd.
Thousand Oaks, CA 91320-2234
Free: 800-818-7243
Publisher's E-mail: sales@pfp.sagepub.com
Journal focusing on research in the mechanics of fracture and damage assessment. **Freq:** 8/year. **Trim Size:** 6 x 9. **Key Personnel:** Prof. J.W. Ju, Editor-in-Chief; Prof. Vilong Bai, Editor; Prof. Yutaka Toi, Editor; Prof. Chi L. Chow, Editor; Prof. J.L. Chaboche, Editor. **ISSN:** 1056--7895 (print); **EISSN:** 1530--7921 (electronic). **Subscription Rates:** £1013 Institutions e-access; £1103 Institutions print only; £1125 Institutions print and e-access; £152 Institutions single print. **URL:** http://ijd.sagepub.com; http://uk.sagepub.com/en-gb/asi/journal/international-journal-damage-mechanics. **Remarks:** Advertising accepted; rates available upon request. **Circ:** Controlled 160.

4631 ■ International Journal of High Performance Computing Applications
SAGE Publications Inc.
2455 Teller Rd.
Thousand Oaks, CA 91320-2234
Free: 800-818-7243
Publisher's E-mail: sales@pfp.sagepub.com
Journal focusing on the use of supercomputers to solve complex modeling problems in a spectrum of disciplines. **Freq:** Quarterly. **Key Personnel:** Joanne Martin, Editor, Founder; Bronis R. De Supinski, Editor-in-Chief; Jack J. Dongarra, Editor-in-Chief. **ISSN:** 1094--3420 (print); **EISSN:** 1741--2846 (electronic). **Subscription Rates:** £175 Individuals print only; £865 Institutions e-access; £942 Institutions print only; £961 Institutions print and e-access; £57 Individuals single print; £259 Institutions single print. **URL:** http://hpc.sagepub.com; http://uk.sagepub.com/en-gb/asi/journal/international-journal-high-performance-computing-applications. **Remarks:** Advertising accepted; rates available upon request. **Circ:** (Not Reported).

4632 ■ The International Journal of Lower Extremity Wounds
SAGE Publications Inc.
2455 Teller Rd.
Thousand Oaks, CA 91320-2234
Free: 800-818-7243
Publisher's E-mail: sales@pfp.sagepub.com
Journal focusing on the science and practice of lower extremity wound care, from major theoretical advances to tested clinical practice. **Freq:** Quarterly. **Key Personnel:** Mike Edmonds, MD, Board Member; Finn Gottrup, MD, Board Member; Marco Romanelli, MD, Board Member; Xiaobing Fu, MD, Board Member; T.K. Hunt, MD, Editor; Kittipan Rerkasem, MD, Board Member; Raj Mani, PhD, Editor-in-Chief. **ISSN:** 1534-7346 (print); **EISSN:** 1552-6941 (electronic). **Subscription Rates:** $728 Institutions combined (print & e-access); $655 Institutions e-access; $713 Institutions print only; $183 Individuals print only; $196 Institutions single print; $59 Individuals single print. **URL:** http://www.sagepub.com/journalsProdDesc.nav?prodId=Journal201512; http://ijl.sagepub.com. **Remarks:** Accepts advertising. **Circ:** (Not Reported).

4633 ■ International Journal of Music Education
SAGE Publications Inc.
2455 Teller Rd.
Thousand Oaks, CA 91320-2234
Free: 800-818-7243
Publisher's E-mail: sales@pfp.sagepub.com
Journal focusing on music education. **Freq:** Quarterly. **Key Personnel:** Ruth Brittin, Editor. **ISSN:** 0255--7614 (print); **EISSN:** 1744--795X (electronic). **Subscription Rates:** £66 Individuals print only; £434 Institutions e-access; £472 Institutions print only; £482 Institutions print and e-access; £21 Institutions single print; £130 Institutions single print. **URL:** http://ijm.sagepub.com; http://uk.sagepub.com/en-gb/asi/journal/international-journal-music-education. **Formerly**: Music Education International. **Remarks:** Advertising accepted; rates available upon request. **Circ:** Paid ‡1000.

4634 ■ International Journal of Offender Therapy and Comparative Criminology
SAGE Publications Inc.
2455 Teller Rd.
Thousand Oaks, CA 91320-2234
Free: 800-818-7243
Publisher's E-mail: sales@pfp.sagepub.com
Journal focusing on the psychological, genetic/biological, and environmental aspects of offender therapy. **Freq:** 16/yr. **Key Personnel:** George B. Palermo, MD, Editor. **ISSN:** 0306--624X (print); **EISSN:** 1552--6933 (electronic). **Subscription Rates:** £78 Individuals print only; £802 Institutions e-access; £873 Institutions print only; £891 Institutions print and e-access; £6 Individuals single print; £60 Institutions single print. **URL:** http://ijo.sagepub.com; http://uk.sagepub.com/en-gb/asi/international-journal-of-offender-therapy-and-comparative-criminology/journal200930. **Remarks:** Advertising accepted; rates available upon request. **Circ:** (Not Reported).

4635 ■ International Journal of Press/Politics
SAGE Publications Inc.
2455 Teller Rd.
Thousand Oaks, CA 91320-2234
Free: 800-818-7243
Publisher's E-mail: sales@pfp.sagepub.com
Scholarly journal covering the interaction of the press, politics, and public policy-making. **Freq:** Quarterly January , April , July and October. **Trim Size:** 6 x 9. **Key Personnel:** Thomas Patterson, Board Member; Hugo Aguirre, Board Member; James Deane, Board Member; Simon Cottle, Board Member; Catherine M. Conaghan, Board Member; W. Lance Bennett, Board Member; Silvio Waisbord, Editor. **ISSN:** 1081-180X (print); **EISSN:** 1940-1620 (electronic). **Subscription Rates:** $590 Institutions Combined (Print & E-access); $649 Institutions Backfile Lease, Combined Plus Backfile (Current Volume Print & All Online Content); $590 Institutions Backfile Lease, E-access Plus Backfile (All Online Content); $531 Institutions E-access (Content through 1998); $578 Institutions print only; $105 Individuals print only; $159 Institutions single issue; $34 Individuals single issue. **URL:** http://hij.sagepub.com/; http://www.sagepub.com/journalsProdDesc.nav?prodId=Journal201283; http://www.sagepub.com/journals/Journal201283/manuscriptSubmission. **Formerly**: The Harvard International Journal of Press/Politics. **Ad Rates:** BW $605, full page; BW $450, half page; BW $360, quarter page. **Remarks:** Accepts advertising. **Circ:** (Not Reported).

4636 ■ The International Journal of Robotics Research
SAGE Publications Inc.
2455 Teller Rd.
Thousand Oaks, CA 91320-2234
Free: 800-818-7243
Publisher's E-mail: sales@pfp.sagepub.com
Journal for engineers, researchers, and scientist working in the field of robotics. **Freq:** 14/yr. **Key Personnel:** Paul M. Newman, Editor; John M. Hollerbach, Editor; Peter Corke, Editor. **ISSN:** 0278-3649 (print); **EISSN:** 1741-3176 (electronic). **Subscription Rates:** $2364 Institutions print & e-access; $2600 Institutions print & all online; $2128 Institutions e-access; $2364 Institutions e-access & all online; $3075 Institutions e-access (content through 1998); $2317 Institutions print only; $229 Individuals print only; $182 Institutions single print; $21 Individuals single print. **URL:** http://www.sagepub.com/journalsProdDesc.nav?prodId=Journal201324. **Ad Rates:** BW $800. **Remarks:** Accepts advertising. **Circ:** (Not Reported).

4637 ■ International Journal of Rural Management
SAGE Publications Inc.
2455 Teller Rd.
Thousand Oaks, CA 91320-2234
Free: 800-818-7243
Publisher's E-mail: sales@pfp.sagepub.com
Peer-reviewed journal focusing on the practical dimensions of organizing and managing rural enterprises and community based organizations. **Freq:** Semiannual. **Key Personnel:** Tushaar Shah, Editor-in-Chief. **ISSN:** 0973--0052 (print); **EISSN:** 0973--0680 (electronic). **Subscription Rates:** £52 Individuals print only; £193 Institutions e-access; £210 Institutions print only; £214 Institutions print and e-access; £34 Individuals single print; £116 Institutions single print. **URL:** http://irm.sagepub.com; http://uk.sagepub.com/en-gb/asi/international-journal-of-rural-management/journal201713. **Remarks:** Advertising accepted; rates available upon request. **Circ:** (Not Reported).

4638 ■ International Journal of Social Psychiatry
SAGE Publications Inc.
2455 Teller Rd.
Thousand Oaks, CA 91320-2234
Free: 800-818-7243
Publisher's E-mail: sales@pfp.sagepub.com
Journal for psychiatrists and other members of the multidisciplinary team around the world concerned with the impact of social factors on individuals' well being and mental health. **Freq:** 8/year. **Key Personnel:** Peter Jones, Board Member; Kamaldeep Bhui, Board Member; Prof. Dinesh Bhugra, Editor; Inga-Britt Krause, Editor. **ISSN:** 0020-7640 (print); **EISSN:** 1741-2854 (electronic). **Subscription Rates:** $1378 Institutions print and online; $1516 Institutions print & all online content; $1240 Institutions e-access; $1378 Individuals e-access plus backfile (all online content); $1350 Institutions print only; $100 Individuals print only; $186 Institutions single print; $16 Individuals single print. **URL:** http://www.sagepub.

com/journalsProdDesc.nav?prodId=Journal201609. **Remarks:** Accepts advertising. **Circ:** (Not Reported).

4639 ■ International Journal of Surgical Pathology
SAGE Publications Inc.
2455 Teller Rd.
Thousand Oaks, CA 91320-2234
Free: 800-818-7243
Publisher's E-mail: sales@pfp.sagepub.com
Professional publication covering surgical pathology. **Founded:** Jan. 1992. **Freq:** Bimonthly. **Print Method:** Web offset. **Trim Size:** 8 1/8 x 10 7/8. **Key Personnel:** Juan Rosai, MD, Editor-in-Chief; Phillip W. Allen, Board Member; Armanda Locatelli, Managing Editor. **ISSN:** 1066-8969 (print). **Subscription Rates:** £644 Institutions Print & E-access; £708 Institutions Backfile Lease, Combined Plus Backfile (Current Volume Print & All Online Content); £580 Institutions E-access; £644 Institutions Backfile Lease, E-access Plus Backfile (All Online Content); £532 Institutions E-access (Content through 1998); £631 Institutions Print Only; £560 Individuals Hospital - Combined (Print & E-access); £192 Individuals Combined (Print & E-access); £87 Institutions print only; £31 Individuals print only. **URL:** http://ijs.sagepub.com/; http://www.sagepub.com/journals/Journal201789/manuscriptSubmission. **Ad Rates:** BW $1,300; 4C $1,275. **Remarks:** Accepts advertising. **Circ:** Combined 2865.

4640 ■ International Political Science Review
SAGE Publications Inc.
2455 Teller Rd.
Thousand Oaks, CA 91320-2234
Free: 800-818-7243
Publisher's E-mail: sales@pfp.sagepub.com
Peer-reviewed journal of the International Political Science Association (IPSA) that makes a significant contribution to the International Political Science. **Freq:** 5/year. **Key Personnel:** Mark Kesselman, Editor. **ISSN:** 0192--5121 (print); **EISSN:** 1460--373X (electronic). **Subscription Rates:** £74 Individuals print only; £445 Institutions e-access; £484 Institutions print only; £494 Institutions print and e-access; £19 Individuals single print; £106 Institutions single print. **URL:** http://ips.sagepub.com; http://uk.sagepub.com/en-gb/asi/journal/international-political-science-review. **Remarks:** Advertising accepted; rates available upon request. **Circ:** (Not Reported).

4641 ■ International Regional Science Review
SAGE Publications Inc.
2455 Teller Rd.
Thousand Oaks, CA 91320-2234
Free: 800-818-7243
Publisher's E-mail: sales@pfp.sagepub.com
Journal of economists, geographers, planners, and other social scientists. **Freq:** Quarterly. **Key Personnel:** Alan T. Murray, Editor; Carlos R. Azzoni, Board Member; Timothy J. Bartik, Board Member; Bernard Fingleton, Board Member; Luc Anselin, Board Member; Sergio Rey, Board Member. **ISSN:** 0160--0176 (print); **EISSN:** 1552--6925 (electronic). **Subscription Rates:** £75 Individuals print only; £363 Institutions e-access; £395 Institutions print only; £403 Institutions print and e-access; £24 Individuals single print; £109 Institutions single print. **URL:** http://irx.sagepub.com; http://uk.sagepub.com/en-gb/asi/international-regional-science-review/journal200982. **Remarks:** Advertising accepted; rates available upon request. **Circ:** (Not Reported).

4642 ■ International Relations
SAGE Publications Inc.
2455 Teller Rd.
Thousand Oaks, CA 91320-2234
Free: 800-818-7243
Publisher's E-mail: sales@pfp.sagepub.com
Journal focusing on all aspects of international relations including law, economics, ethics, strategy, philosophy, culture, environment, and more. **Freq:** Quarterly. **Key Personnel:** Andrew Linklater, Advisor; Nicholas J. Wheeler, Advisor; Chris Brown, Board Member; Ken Booth, Editor. **ISSN:** 0047--1178 (print); **EISSN:** 1741--2862 (electronic). **Subscription Rates:** $107 Institutions online; $992 Institutions print; $1012 Institutions print and online; $35 Individuals single print issue; $273 Institutions single print issue. **URL:** http://ire.sagepub.com. **Remarks:** Accepts advertising. **Circ:** (Not Reported).

4643 ■ International Review of Administrative Sciences: An International Journal of Comparative Public Administration
SAGE Publications Inc.
2455 Teller Rd.
Thousand Oaks, CA 91320-2234
Free: 800-818-7243
Publisher's E-mail: sales@pfp.sagepub.com
Peer-reviewed journal focusing on academic and professional public Administration. **Freq:** Quarterly. **Key Personnel:** Isabella Proeller, Editor; Anne Marie Berg, Member; Christina W. Andrews, Member; Gavin Drewry, Member; Kenneth Kernaghan, Member. **ISSN:** 0020--8523 (print); **EISSN:** 1461--7226 (electronic). **Subscription Rates:** £78 Individuals print only; £716 Institutions e-access; £779 Institutions print only; £795 Institutions print and e-access; £25 Individuals single print; £214 Institutions single print. **URL:** http://ras.sagepub.com. **Remarks:** Accepts advertising. **Circ:** (Not Reported).

4644 ■ International Review for the Sociology of Sport
SAGE Publications Inc.
2455 Teller Rd.
Thousand Oaks, CA 91320-2234
Free: 800-818-7243
Publisher's E-mail: sales@pfp.sagepub.com
Journal focusing on the research and scholarship of sport throughout the international academic community. **Freq:** 8/year. **Key Personnel:** Lawrence A. Wenner, Editor; David L. Andrews, Board Member; Steven J. Jackson, Editor; Cora Burnett, Editor; Fabien Ohl, Board Member. **ISSN:** 1012--6902 (print); **EISSN:** 1461--7218 (electronic). **Subscription Rates:** £772 Institutions e-access; £841 Institutions print only; £858 Institutions print and e-access; £116 Institutions single print issue. **URL:** http://irs.sagepub.com. **Remarks:** Accepts advertising. **Circ:** (Not Reported).

4645 ■ International Small Business Journal
SAGE Publications Inc.
2455 Teller Rd.
Thousand Oaks, CA 91320-2234
Free: 800-818-7243
Publisher's E-mail: sales@pfp.sagepub.com
Journal focusing on the research on small businesses. **Freq:** 8/year. **Key Personnel:** Robert Blackburn, Editor-in-Chief. **ISSN:** 0266--2426 (print); **EISSN:** 1741--2870 (electronic). **Subscription Rates:** £74 Individuals print only; £1145 Institutions e-access; £1247 Institutions print only; £1272 Institutions print and e-access; £12 Individuals single print; £171 Institutions single print. **Online:** Gale. **URL:** http://isb.sagepub.com. **Remarks:** Accepts advertising. **Circ:** (Not Reported).

4646 ■ International Social Work
SAGE Publications Inc.
2455 Teller Rd.
Thousand Oaks, CA 91320-2234
Free: 800-818-7243
Publisher's E-mail: sales@pfp.sagepub.com
Journal extending knowledge and promoting communication in the fields of social development, social welfare, and human services. **Freq:** Bimonthly Quarterly. **Key Personnel:** Prof. Lena Dominelli, Editor; Prof. Simon Hackett, Board Member. **ISSN:** 0020--8728 (print); **EISSN:** 1461--1234 (electronic). **Subscription Rates:** £73 Individuals print only; £797 Institutions e-access; £868 Institutions print only; £886 Institutions print and e-access; £16 Individuals single print; £159 Institutions single print; Included in membership. **URL:** http://isw.sagepub.com; http://www.iassw-aiets.org/membership. **Remarks:** Accepts advertising. **Circ:** (Not Reported).

4647 ■ International Sociology
Asociación Internacional de Sociologiá
2455 Teller Rd.
Thousand Oaks, CA 91320
Phone: (805)499-9774
Fax: (805)499-0871
Free: 800-818-7243
Publication E-mail: info@sagepub.com
Peer-reviewed journal publishing studies on social organization, societal change, and comparative sociology. **Freq:** Bimonthly. **Key Personnel:** Marta Soler Gallart, Editor. **ISSN:** 0268--5809 (print); **EISSN:** 1461--7242 (electronic). **Subscription Rates:** £68 Individuals print only; £639 Institutions e-access; £696 Institutions print only; £710 Institutions print and e-access; £15 Individuals sinlge print; £128 Institutions, Canada and Mexico single print; $26 /issue for individuals; $213 /issue for institutions. **URL:** http://iss.sagepub.com; http://www.sagepub.com/journals/Journal200944. **Ad Rates:** BW $250. **Remarks:** Accepts advertising. **Circ:** (Not Reported).

4648 ■ International Studies
SAGE Publications Inc.
2455 Teller Rd.
Thousand Oaks, CA 91320-2234
Free: 800-818-7243
Publisher's E-mail: sales@pfp.sagepub.com
Indian research journal in the field of international affairs and area studies. **Founded:** 1959. **Freq:** Quarterly January - April - July - October. **Print Method:** Offset. **Trim Size:** 6 1/4 x 9 1/2. **Cols./Page:** 1. **Col. Width:** 50 nonpareils. **Col. Depth:** 100 agate lines. **Key Personnel:** Varun Sahni, Editor. **ISSN:** 0020- 8817 (print). **Subscription Rates:** $605 Institutions print & e-access; $666 Institutions current volume print & all online content; $545 Institutions e-access; $1619 Institutions e-access, content through 1998; $593 Institutions print only; $131 Individuals print only; $163 Institutions single print; $43 Individuals single print. **URL:** http://www.sagepub.com/journalsProdDesc.nav?prodId=Journal200842&. **Ad Rates:** BW $350. **Remarks:** Accepts advertising. **Circ:** (Not Reported).

4649 ■ Intervention in School and Clinic
SAGE Publications Inc.
2455 Teller Rd.
Thousand Oaks, CA 91320-2234
Free: 800-818-7243
Publisher's E-mail: sales@pfp.sagepub.com
Journal focusing on the daily aspects of special and remedial education. **Founded:** 1965. **Freq:** 5/yr. **Cols./Page:** 3. **Col. Width:** 2 1/8 inches. **Col. Depth:** 9 3/4 inches. **Key Personnel:** Steven P. Chamberlain, Associate Editor; Diane Adreon, Editor; Margaret King-Sears, Editor; Billy T. Ogletree, Editor; Randall Boone, Editor; Kyle Higgins, Editor. **ISSN:** 1053-4512 (print). **Subscription Rates:** $68 Individuals print & e-access; $189 Institutions print only; $174 Institutions e-access; $193 Institutions print & e-access; $42 Institutions single print; $18 Single issue print, individual. **URL:** http://www.sagepub.com/journalsProdEditBoards.nav?prodId=Journal201876. **Ad Rates:** BW $515; 4C $995. **Remarks:** Advertising accepted; rates available upon request. **Circ:** Paid 2500.

4650 ■ Journal of Adolescent Research
SAGE Publications Inc.
2455 Teller Rd.
Thousand Oaks, CA 91320-2234
Free: 800-818-7243
Publication E-mail: advertising@sagepub.com
Journal providing professionals with information on how individuals in the second decade of life (ages 10-20) develop, behave, and are influenced by societal and cultural perspectives. **Founded:** Jan. 1986. **Freq:** Bimonthly. **Print Method:** Offset. **Trim Size:** 5 1/2 x 8 1/2. **Cols./Page:** 1. **Col. Width:** 50 nonpareils. **Col. Depth:** 100 agate lines. **Key Personnel:** Carola Suarez-Orozco, Editor; Ellen E. Thornburg, Editor, Founder. **ISSN:** 0743-5584 (print); **EISSN:** 1552-6895 (electronic). **Subscription Rates:** $879 Institutions e-access; $967 Institutions backfile lease, combined plus backfile; $971 Institutions backfile, e-access (content through 1998); $146 Individuals e-access. **URL:** http://www.sagepub.com/journalsProdDesc.nav?prodId=Journal200883. **Ad Rates:** BW $515; 4C $995. **Remarks:** Accepts advertising. **Circ:** Paid ‡600.

4651 ■ Journal of Advanced Academics: A Journal for Scholars, Administrators, and Policy Makers
SAGE Publications Inc.
2455 Teller Rd.
Thousand Oaks, CA 91320-2234
Free: 800-818-7243
Publisher's E-mail: sales@pfp.sagepub.com
Journal focusing on the advance academic achievements of students of all ages. **Freq:** Quarterly. **Key**

Circulation: ★ = AAM; △ or • = BPA; ♦ = CAC; ❑ = VAC; ⊕ = PO Statement; ‡ = Publisher's Report; Boldface figures = sworn; Light figures = estimated.

Personnel: Matt McBee, Editor; Michael S. Matthews, Editor. **ISSN:** 1932--202X (print); **EISSN:** 2162--9536 (electronic). **Subscription Rates:** $72 Individuals print and online; $203 Institutions online; $221 Institutions print; $225 Institutions print and online; $24 Individuals single print issue; $61 Institutions single print issue. **URL:** http://joa.sagepub.com. **Formerly**: Journal of Secondary Gifted Education. **Remarks:** Accepts advertising. **Circ:** (Not Reported).

4652 ■ Journal of Applied Behavioral Science
SAGE Publications Inc.
2455 Teller Rd.
Thousand Oaks, CA 91320-2234
Free: 800-818-7243
Publication E-mail: advertising@sagepub.com
Journal on research on behavioral science in application to social science. **Founded:** 1965. **Freq:** Quarterly. **Print Method:** Offset. **Trim Size:** 8 x 10 7/8. **Key Personnel:** Mary Pasmore, Managing Editor; Jean M. Bartunek, Associate Editor; William H. Pasmore, Editor. **ISSN:** 0021-8863 (print); **EISSN:** 1552-6879 (electronic). **Subscription Rates:** $943 Institutions combined (print & e-access); $1037 Institutions backfile lease, combined plus backfile; $849 Institutions e-access; $2453 Institutions backfile, e-access (content through 1998); $924 Institutions print only; $146 Individuals print only; $254 Institutions single print; $47 Individuals single print. **URL:** http://www.sagepub.com/journalsProdDesc.nav?prodId=Journal200967. **Ad Rates:** BW $515; 4C $995. **Remarks:** Accepts advertising. **Circ:** Paid 1500.

4653 ■ Journal of Applied Gerontology
SAGE Publications Inc.
2455 Teller Rd.
Thousand Oaks, CA 91320-2234
Free: 800-818-7243
Publisher's E-mail: sales@pfp.sagepub.com
Journal reporting on the subdisciplines of aging and findings applied to the problems encountered by older persons. **Founded:** June 1982. **Freq:** 5/yr. **Print Method:** Offset. **Trim Size:** 5 1/2 x 8 1/2. **Cols./Page:** 1. **Col. Width:** 50 nonpareils. **Col. Depth:** 100 agate lines. **Key Personnel:** Joseph E. Gaugler, Editor. **ISSN:** 0733-4648 (print); **EISSN:** 1552-4523 (electronic). **Subscription Rates:** $1385 Institutions print & e-access; $1524 Institutions current volume print & all online content; $1247 Institutions online; $1386 Individuals e-access & all online; $1801 Institutions e-access (content through 1998); $1357 Institutions print only; $177 Individuals print only; $187 Institutions single print; $29 Individuals single print. **URL:** http://www.sagepub.com/journalsProdDesc.nav?prodId=Journal200744. **Remarks:** Accepts advertising. **Circ:** (Not Reported).

4654 ■ Journal of Attention Disorders
SAGE Publications Inc.
2455 Teller Rd.
Thousand Oaks, CA 91320-2234
Free: 800-818-7243
Publisher's E-mail: sales@pfp.sagepub.com
Journal focusing on research and clinical issues related to attention disorders. **Freq:** Monthly. **Print Method:** Web Offset. **Trim Size:** 8 3/8 x 10 7/8. **Key Personnel:** Sam Goldstein, Editor; Jack Naglieri, Senior Editor. **ISSN:** 1087--0547 (print); **EISSN:** 1557--1246 (electronic). **Subscription Rates:** £64 Individuals print; £410 Institutions e-access; £447 Institutions print; £456 Institutions print and e-access; £7 Individuals single print; £41 Institutions single print. **URL:** http://jad.sagepub.com. **Ad Rates:** BW $570; 4C $1,020. **Remarks:** Accepts advertising. **Circ:** (Not Reported).

4655 ■ Journal of Biological Rhythms
SAGE Publications Inc.
2455 Teller Rd.
Thousand Oaks, CA 91320-2234
Free: 800-818-7243
Publication E-mail: advertising@sagepub.com
Journal focusing on experimental biological research. **Founded:** 1986. **Freq:** Bimonthly February , April , June , August , October , December. **Print Method:** Offset. **Trim Size:** 8 1/2 x 11. **Cols./Page:** 1. **Col. Width:** 72 nonpareils. **Col. Depth:** 126 agate lines. **Key Personnel:** Ueli Schibler, Advisor; Serge Daan, Advisor; Bruce Goldman, Board Member; William J. Schwartz, Editor-in-Chief; Terry Page, Board Member; Martin Zatz, Advisor, phone: (301)656-4655; Michael Hastings, Advisor; Josephine Arendt, Board Member. **ISSN:** 0748-7304 (print); **EISSN:** 1552-4531 (electronic). **Subscription Rates:** $1379 Institutions Combined (Print & E-access); $1517 Institutions Current Volume Print & All Online Content; $1241 Institutions E-access; $1379 Institutions All Online Content; $1372 Institutions E-access (Content through 1998); $1351 Institutions Print Only; $253 Individuals Print Only; $248 Institutions Single Print Issue; $55 Individuals Single Print Issue. **URL:** http://www.sagepub.com/journals/Journal200933/manuscriptSubmission. **Ad Rates:** BW $515; 4C $995. **Remarks:** Accepts advertising. **Circ:** Paid ‡478, Non-paid ‡77.

4656 ■ Journal of Biomolecular Screening
SAGE Publications Inc.
2455 Teller Rd.
Thousand Oaks, CA 91320-2234
Free: 800-818-7243
Publisher's E-mail: sales@pfp.sagepub.com
Peer-reviewed journal focusing on drug discovery sciences, with an emphasis on screening methods and technologies. **Freq:** 10/year. **Key Personnel:** Robert M. Campbell, PhD, Editor-in-Chief; Steven Kahl, Associate Editor; Mark Beggs, Associate Editor. **ISSN:** 1087--0571 (print); **EISSN:** 1552--454X (electronic). **Subscription Rates:** £430 Individuals print; £812 Institutions e-access; £884 Institutions print; £902 Institutions print and e-access; £56 Individuals single print issue; £97 Institutions single print issue; Included in membership; $750 Individuals print only; $1454 Institutions online only. **URL:** http://jbx.sagepub.com; http://www.slas.org/publications/scientific-journals. **Ad Rates:** BW $1,630; 4C $2,165. **Remarks:** Accepts advertising. **Circ:** (Not Reported).

4657 ■ Journal of Black Psychology
SAGE Publications Inc.
2455 Teller Rd.
Thousand Oaks, CA 91320-2234
Free: 800-818-7243
Publication E-mail: advertising@sagepub.com
Journal on psychology with an Afrocentric perspective. Official publication of the Association of Black Psychologists. **Freq:** Bimonthly Quarterly. **Print Method:** Offset. **Trim Size:** 5 1/2 x 8 1/2. **Key Personnel:** Kevin Cokley, Editor-in-Chief. **ISSN:** 0095--7984 (print); **EISSN:** 1552--4558 (electronic). **Subscription Rates:** £17 Single issue print; £80 Institutions print only; £98 Single issue print, Institutions; £492 Institutions e-access; £536 Institutions print only; £547 Institutions print and e-access; £602 Institutions current volume print and all online content; £1004 Institutions e-access (content through 1998); £516 Institutions (Print & E-access); £568 Institutions Backfile Lease, Combined Plus Backfile (Current Volume Print & All Online Content); £464 Institutions E-access; £516 Institutions Backfile Lease, E-access Plus Backfile (All Online Content) ; £947 Institutions E-access (Content through 1998) ; £506 Institutions print only; £78 Individuals print only; £93 Institutions single print ; £17 Individuals single print. **Alt. Formats:** PDF. **URL:** http://jbp.sagepub.com; http://uk.sagepub.com/en-gb/asi/journal-of-black-psychology/journal200978. **Ad Rates:** BW $875; 4C $1110, in addition to Black & White rate. **Remarks:** Accepts advertising. **Circ:** 2500.

4658 ■ Journal of Black Studies
SAGE Publications Inc.
2455 Teller Rd.
Thousand Oaks, CA 91320-2234
Free: 800-818-7243
Publisher's E-mail: sales@pfp.sagepub.com
Journal containing economic, historical, and philosophical research on black people. **Freq:** 8/year. **Print Method:** Offset. **Trim Size:** 5 1/2 x 8 1/2. **Cols./Page:** 1. **Col. Width:** 50 nonpareils. **Col. Depth:** 100 agate lines. **Key Personnel:** Molefi K. Asante, Editor; Ama Mazama, Editor. **ISSN:** 0021--9347 (print); **EISSN:** 1552--4566 (electronic). **Subscription Rates:** $1517 Institutions print & e-access; $1669 Institutions print & all online content; $1365 Institutions e-access; $1517 Institutions e-access (all online content); $1487 Institutions print only; $198 Individuals print only; $204 Institutions single print; $32 Individuals single print. **URL:** http://jbs.sagepub.com. **Ad Rates:** BW $875; 4C $1110. **Remarks:** Accepts advertising. **Circ:** (Not Reported).

4659 ■ Journal of Building Physics
SAGE Publications Inc.
2455 Teller Rd.
Thousand Oaks, CA 91320-2234
Free: 800-818-7243
Journal focusing on the thermal performance of building materials, particularly thermal insulation systems. **Founded:** 1978. **Freq:** Bimonthly. **Print Method:** Offset. **Trim Size:** 6 x 9. **Cols./Page:** 1. **Col. Width:** 54 nonpareils. **Col. Depth:** 100 agate lines. **Key Personnel:** R. Becker, Board Member; Nathan Mendes, Board Member; Hartwig M. Kuenzel, Board Member; Mark Bomberg, Editor. **ISSN:** 1744-2591 (print); **EISSN:** 1744-2583 (electronic). **Subscription Rates:** $1864 Institutions print & e-access; $2050 Institutions current volume print & all online content; $1678 Institutions e-access; $2531 Institutions e-access (content through 1998); $1827 Institutions print only; $335 Institutions single print. **URL:** http://www.sagepub.com/journalsProdDesc.nav?ct_p=societies&prodId=Journal201633; http://www.sagepub.com/journalsProdDesc.nav?prodId=Journal201633. **Formerly**: Journal of Thermal Envelope and Building Science; Journal of Thermal Insulation; Journal of Thermal Envelope and Building Sciences. **Remarks:** Accepts advertising. **Circ:** ‡200.

4660 ■ Journal of Business and Technical Communication
SAGE Publications Inc.
2455 Teller Rd.
Thousand Oaks, CA 91320-2234
Free: 800-818-7243
Publication E-mail: advertising@sagepub.com
Journal focusing on the improvement of communication practices in both industry and academics. **Freq:** Quarterly. **Print Method:** Offset. **Trim Size:** 5 1/2 x 8 1/2. **Cols./Page:** 1. **Col. Width:** 50 nonpareils. **Col. Depth:** 100 agate lines. **Key Personnel:** Lori Peterson, Managing Editor; David R. Russell, Editor. **ISSN:** 1050-6519 (print); **EISSN:** 1552-4574 (electronic). **Subscription Rates:** £465 Institutions e-access; £512 Institutions backfile lease, e-access plus backfile; £474 Institutions backfile, e-access (content through 1998); £84 Individuals e-access. **URL:** http://www.sagepub.com/journalsProdDesc.nav?prodId=Journal200791. **Ad Rates:** BW $515; 4C $995. **Remarks:** Accepts advertising. **Circ:** Paid 500.

4661 ■ Journal of Cardiovascular Pharmacology and Therapeutics
SAGE Publications Inc.
2455 Teller Rd.
Thousand Oaks, CA 91320-2234
Free: 800-818-7243
Publisher's E-mail: sales@pfp.sagepub.com
Scholarly journal covering cardiovascular pharmacology and therapeutics. **Freq:** Bimonthly. **Trim Size:** 8 5/8 x 11 1/8. **Key Personnel:** Jeffrey L. Anderson, MD, Board Member; Inder Anand, MD, Board Member; Charles Antzelevitch, PhD, Board Member; Bramah N. Singh, MD, Editor, Founder. **ISSN:** 1074-2484 (print); **EISSN:** 1940-4034 (electronic). **Subscription Rates:** $1123 Institutions combined (print & e-access); $1011 Institutions e-access; $1101 Institutions print; $1235 Institutions backfile lease, combined + backfile; $741 hospital, combined (print & E-access); $1123 Institutions backfile lease, e-access + backfile; $1011 Institutions backfile purchase, e-access; $332 Individuals combined (print & e-access); $202 Institutions single print; $72 Individuals single print. **URL:** http://www.sagepub.com/journalsProdDesc.nav?prodId=Journal201790&. **Ad Rates:** BW $1,275; 4C $1,250. **Remarks:** Accepts advertising. **Circ:** Paid 430.

4662 ■ Journal of Career Assessment
SAGE Publications Inc.
2455 Teller Rd.
Thousand Oaks, CA 91320-2234
Free: 800-818-7243
Publisher's E-mail: sales@pfp.sagepub.com
Journal covering the various techniques, tests, inventories, rating scales, interview schedules, surveys, and direct observational methods used in scientifically based practice and research to provide an improved understanding of career decision-making. **Freq:** Quarterly. **Key Personnel:** Rosie P. Bingham, Editor; David L. Blustein, Editor; Nancy E. Betz, Editor; Thomas Kriesheok, Editor; Fred H. Borgen, Editor; Bruce W. Walsh, Editor. **ISSN:** 1069--0727 (print); **EISSN:** 1552--4590 (electronic). **URL:** http://jca.sagepub.com. **Remarks:**

Accepts advertising. **Circ:** (Not Reported).

4663 ■ Journal of Career Development
SAGE Publications Inc.
2455 Teller Rd.
Thousand Oaks, CA 91320-2234
Free: 800-818-7243
Publisher's E-mail: sales@pfp.sagepub.com
Journal for professionals in counseling, psychology, education, student personnel, human resources, and business management. **Freq:** Bimonthly. **Key Personnel:** Norman Gysbers, Editor; George V. Gushue, Associate Editor; Lisa Y. Flores, Contact. **ISSN:** 0894--8453 (print); **EISSN:** 1556--0856 (electronic). **Subscription Rates:** $122 Individuals print ; $759 Institutions e-access; $826 Institutions print; $843 Institutions print and e-access; $26 Individuals single print; $151 Institutions single print. **URL:** http://jcd.sagepub.com. **Remarks:** Accepts advertising. **Circ:** (Not Reported).

4664 ■ Journal of Cases in Educational Leadership
SAGE Publications Inc.
2455 Teller Rd.
Thousand Oaks, CA 91320-2234
Free: 800-818-7243
Publisher's E-mail: sales@pfp.sagepub.com
Journal covering cases appropriate for use in programs that prepare educational leaders. **Freq:** Quarterly March, June, September, and December. **Print Method:** Offset. **Trim Size:** 5 1/2 x 8 1/2. **Cols./Page:** 1. **Col. Width:** 50 nonpareils. **Col. Depth:** 100 agate lines. **Key Personnel:** Vonzell Agosto, Editor. **ISSN:** 1555--4589 (print); **EISSN:** 1555--4589 (electronic). **Subscription Rates:** $560 Institutions online; $112 Individuals online. **URL:** http://jel.sagepub.com. **Ad Rates:** BW $875; 4C $1110. **Remarks:** Accepts advertising. **Circ:** (Not Reported).

4665 ■ Journal of Child Health Care
SAGE Publications Inc.
2455 Teller Rd.
Thousand Oaks, CA 91320-2234
Free: 800-818-7243
Publisher's E-mail: sales@pfp.sagepub.com
Peer-reviewed journal focusing on child health issues. **Freq:** Quarterly. **Key Personnel:** Jean B. Ivey, Associate Editor; Helen Langton, Associate Editor; Prof. Bernie Carter, Editor-in-Chief. **ISSN:** 1367-4935 (print); **EISSN:** 1741-2889 (electronic). **Subscription Rates:** $1036 Institutions print & e-access; $1140 Institutions current volume print & all online; $932 Institutions e-access; $905 Institutions backfile purchase, e-access (content through 1998); $1015 Institutions print only; $96 Individuals print only; $279 Institutions single print; $31 Individuals single print. **URL:** http://www.sagepub.com/journalsProdDesc.nav?prodId=Journal201572; http://chc.sagepub.com/. **Remarks:** Accepts advertising. **Circ:** (Not Reported).

4666 ■ Journal of Classical Sociology
SAGE Publications Inc.
2455 Teller Rd.
Thousand Oaks, CA 91320-2234
Free: 800-818-7243
Publisher's E-mail: sales@pfp.sagepub.com
Journal focusing on the origins of sociology and how the classical tradition relates to the sociological imagination in the present. **Freq:** Quarterly. **Key Personnel:** Peter Baehr, Board Member; J.M. Barbalet, Board Member; Kiyomitsu Yui, Board Member; Patrick Baert, Board Member; John O'Neill, Editor; Simon Susen, Editor; Bryan S. Turner, Editor; Roslyn Bologh, Board Member. **ISSN:** 1468--795X (print); **EISSN:** 1741--2897 (electronic). **Subscription Rates:** $104 Individuals print; $1114 Institutions e-access; $1213 Institutions print only; $1238 Institutions print and e-access; $34 Individuals single print issue; $334 Institutions single print issue. **URL:** http://jcs.sagepub.com. **Remarks:** Accepts advertising. **Circ:** (Not Reported).

4667 ■ The Journal of Commonwealth Literature
SAGE Publications Inc.
2455 Teller Rd.
Thousand Oaks, CA 91320-2234
Free: 800-818-7243
Publisher's E-mail: sales@pfp.sagepub.com
Journal focusing on all aspects of Commonwealth and postcolonial literatures. **Freq:** Quarterly. **Print Method:** Litho. **Trim Size:** 148 x 210 mm. **Key Personnel:** Johan Geertsema, Board Member; Laurence Breiner, Board Member; Ralph Crane, Board Member; Elaine Yee-Lin Ho, Board Member; Robert Clark, Board Member; Vassilena Parashkevova, Editor; Elleke Boehmer, Board Member; Claire Chambers, Editor. **ISSN:** 0021--9894 (print); **EISSN:** 1741--6442 (electronic). **Subscription Rates:** £88 Individuals print; £442 Institutions e-access; £481 Institutions print; £491 Institutions print and e-access; £29 Individuals single print issue; £132 Institutions single print issue. **URL:** http://jcl.sagepub.com. **Remarks:** Accepts advertising. **Circ:** (Not Reported).

4668 ■ Journal of Communication Inquiry
SAGE Publications Inc.
2455 Teller Rd.
Thousand Oaks, CA 91320-2234
Free: 800-818-7243
Publication E-mail: advertising@sagepub.com
Academic journal concerning communication. **Freq:** Quarterly Jan., April, July, Oct. **Print Method:** Offset. **Trim Size:** 6 x 9. **Key Personnel:** Meenakshi Gigi Durham, Executive Editor; Shawn Harmsen, Managing Editor. **ISSN:** 0196--8599 (print); **EISSN:** 1552--4612 (electronic). **Subscription Rates:** £21 Single issue print ; £65 Individuals print only; £79 Institutions single print issue; £266 Institutions e-access; £289 Institutions print only; £295 Institutions combined print & e-access; £296 Institutions backfile Lease, E-access Plus Backfile (All Online Content); £325 Institutions backfile Lease, Combined Plus Backfile (Current Volume Print & All Online Content); £196 Institutions backfile Purchase, E-access (Content through 1998). **URL:** http://www.sagepub.com/journalsProdDesc.nav?prodId=Journal200940. **Ad Rates:** BW $515. **Remarks:** Accepts advertising. **Circ:** (Not Reported).

4669 ■ Journal of Conflict Resolution: Journal of the Peace Science Society (International)
SAGE Publications Inc.
2455 Teller Rd.
Thousand Oaks, CA 91320-2234
Free: 800-818-7243
Publisher's E-mail: sales@pfp.sagepub.com
Journal on studies of war, peace, and international relations. **Freq:** 8/year. **Print Method:** Offset. **Trim Size:** 5 1/2 x 8 1/2. **Cols./Page:** 1. **Col. Width:** 50 nonpareils. **Col. Depth:** 100 agate lines. **Key Personnel:** Paul Huth, Editor. **ISSN:** 0022--0027 (print); **EISSN:** 1552--8766 (electronic). **Subscription Rates:** $1821 Institutions print & e-access; $2003 Institutions current volume print & all online content; $1639 Institutions e-access; $1821 Institutions e-access (all online content); $5365 Institutions content through 1998; $1785 Institutions print only; $192 Individuals print only; $196 Institutions single print; $25 Individuals single print. **URL:** http://jcr.sagepub.com. **Ad Rates:** BW $875; 4C $1110. **Remarks:** Accepts advertising. **Circ:** (Not Reported).

4670 ■ Journal of Consumer Culture
SAGE Publications Inc.
2455 Teller Rd.
Thousand Oaks, CA 91320-2234
Free: 800-818-7243
Publisher's E-mail: sales@pfp.sagepub.com
Journal focusing on consumption and consumer culture. **Freq:** 3/year. **Key Personnel:** Prof. George Ritzer, Editor, Founder; Dan Thomas Cook, Advisor, Board Member; Steven Miles, Editor; Don Slater, Board Member; George Ritzer, Editor, Founder; Douglas Kellner, Board Member; Mark Granovetter, Board Member; Zygmunt Bauman, Board Member. **ISSN:** 1469--5405 (print); **EISSN:** 1741--2900 (electronic). **URL:** http://joc.sagepub.com. **Remarks:** Accepts advertising. **Circ:** (Not Reported).

4671 ■ Journal of Contemporary Criminal Justice
SAGE Publications Inc.
2455 Teller Rd.
Thousand Oaks, CA 91320-2234
Free: 800-818-7243
Publisher's E-mail: sales@pfp.sagepub.com
Journal focusing on all aspects of criminal justice. **Freq:** Quarterly. **Key Personnel:** Martin Killias, Board Member; Chris Eskridge, Editor. **ISSN:** 1043--9862 (print); **EISSN:** 1552--5406 (electronic). **Subscription Rates:** $112 Individuals print only; $684 Institutions e-access; $745 Institutions print; $760 Institutions print and e-access; $36 Individuals single print issue; $205 Institutions single print issue. **URL:** http://ccj.sagepub.com. **Remarks:** Accepts advertising. **Circ:** (Not Reported).

4672 ■ Journal of Contemporary Ethnography
SAGE Publications Inc.
2455 Teller Rd.
Thousand Oaks, CA 91320-2234
Free: 800-818-7243
Publisher's E-mail: sales@pfp.sagepub.com
Urban ethnography journal. **Freq:** Bimonthly. **Print Method:** Offset. **Trim Size:** 5 1/2 x 8 1/2. **Cols./Page:** 1. **Col. Width:** 50 nonpareils. **Col. Depth:** 100 agate lines. **Key Personnel:** Robert D. Benford, Associate Editor; Jody Miller, Editor; David Fetterman, Editor; Paul Stoller, Editor; Tamar Katriel, Editor. **ISSN:** 0891--2416 (print); **EISSN:** 1552--5414 (electronic). **Subscription Rates:** $1186 Institutions print & e-access; $1186 Institutions print & all online content; $1067 Institutions e-access; $2450 Institutions e-access (content through 1998); $1186 Institutions print only; $194 Individuals print only; $213 Institutions single print; £42 Individuals single print. **URL:** http://jce.sagepub.com. **Formerly:** Urban Life. **Also known as:** JCE. **Ad Rates:** BW $875; 4C $1110. **Remarks:** Accepts advertising. **Circ:** (Not Reported).

4673 ■ Journal of Contemporary History
SAGE Publications Inc.
2455 Teller Rd.
Thousand Oaks, CA 91320-2234
Free: 800-818-7243
Publisher's E-mail: sales@pfp.sagepub.com
Journal covering a range of historical approaches including social, economic, political, diplomatic, intellectual, and cultural. **Freq:** Quarterly. **Key Personnel:** Walter Laqueur, Editor, Founder; George L. Mosse, Editor, Founder; Stanley Payne, Editor; Richard J. Evans, Editor; Niall Ferguson, Board Member. **ISSN:** 0022--0094 (print); **EISSN:** 1461--7250 (electronic). **Subscription Rates:** £71 Individuals print; £559 Institutions e-access; £609 Institutions print; £621 Institutions print and e-access; £23 Individuals single print; £167 Institutions single print. **URL:** http://jch.sagepub.com. **Remarks:** Accepts advertising. **Circ:** (Not Reported).

4674 ■ Journal of Cross-Cultural Psychology
SAGE Publications Inc.
2455 Teller Rd.
Thousand Oaks, CA 91320-2234
Free: 800-818-7243
Publisher's E-mail: sales@pfp.sagepub.com
Cross-cultural psychology journal. **Freq:** 10/year January , February , April , May , June , July , August , September , October and November. **Print Method:** Offset. **Trim Size:** 7 x 10. **Cols./Page:** 1. **Col. Width:** 50 nonpareils. **Col. Depth:** 100 agate lines. **Key Personnel:** David Matsumoto, Editor; Walter J. Lonner, Editor, Founder; David R. Matsumoto, Editor; Juri Allik, Associate Editor; Deborah L. Best, Editor; Cindy Gallois, Editor; Junko Tanaka-Matsumi, Associate Editor; Walter Lonner, Founder, Senior Editor. **ISSN:** 0022--0221 (print); **EISSN:** 1552--5422 (electronic). **Subscription Rates:** $1648 Institutions print & e-access; $1813 Institutions print & all online content; $1483 Institutions e-access; $3353 Institutions backfile purchase, e-access (1998); $1615 Institutions print only; $191 Individuals print only; $178 Institutions single print; $25 Individuals single print. **URL:** http://jcc.sagepub.com. **Ad Rates:** BW $875; 4C $1110. **Remarks:** Accepts advertising. **Circ:** (Not Reported).

4675 ■ Journal of Dental Research
SAGE Publications Inc.
2455 Teller Rd.
Thousand Oaks, CA 91320-2234
Free: 800-818-7243
Publisher's E-mail: sales@pfp.sagepub.com
Freq: 13/yr. **Print Method:** Offset. **Trim Size:** 8 1/4 x 10 3/4. **Cols./Page:** 2. **Col. Width:** 40 nonpareils. **Col. Depth:** 140 agate lines. **Key Personnel:** Dr. William V. Giannobile, Editor-in-Chief. **ISSN:** 0022--0345 (print); **EISSN:** 1544--0591 (electronic). **Subscription Rates:** £291 Institutions print; £29 Individuals single print issue; £55 Institutions single print issue. **URL:** http://jdr.sagepub.com. **Ad Rates:** BW $945; 4C $1,690; PCI

Circulation: ★ = AAM; △ or • = BPA; ♦ = CAC; ❑ = VAC; ⊕ = PO Statement; ‡ = Publisher's Report; Boldface figures = sworn; Light figures = estimated.

$100. **Remarks:** Accepts advertising. **Circ:** ‡6500, 6,500.

4676 ■ Journal of Developing Societies: A Forum on Issues of Development and Change in All Societies
SAGE Publications Inc.
2455 Teller Rd.
Thousand Oaks, CA 91320-2234
Free: 800-818-7243
Publisher's E-mail: sales@pfp.sagepub.com
Journal focusing on development and social change in all societies. **Freq:** Quarterly. **Key Personnel:** Richard L. Harris, Managing Editor. **ISSN:** 0169--796X (print); **EISSN:** 1745--2546 (electronic). **URL:** http://jds.sagepub.com. **Remarks:** Accepts advertising. **Circ:** (Not Reported).

4677 ■ The Journal of Diagnostic Medical Sonography
Society of Diagnostic Medical Sonography
2455 Teller Rd.
Thousand Oaks, CA 91320
Phone: (805)499-9774
Fax: (805)499-0871
Free: 800-818-7243
Publication E-mail: advertising@sagepub.com info@sagepub.com
Journal publishing peer-reviewed articles for the continuing professional education of diagnostic medical sonographers. **Print Method:** Web Offset. **Trim Size:** 8 x 10 7/8. **Key Personnel:** Jean Lea Spitz, Editor; Julia A. Drose, Editor; Phil Bendick, PhD, Editor-in-Chief. **ISSN:** 8756--4793 (print); **EISSN:** 1552--5430 (electronic). **Subscription Rates:** $41 Individuals single print issue; $152 Institutions single print issue; $191 Individuals print only; $762 Institutions E-access; $830 Institutions print only; $847 Institutions print and online; $908 Institutions back file, e-access (content thru 1998); $932 Institutions Back file Lease, Combined Plus Back file (Current Volume Print & All Online Content). **URL:** http://www.sagepub.com/journalsProdDesc.nav?prodId=Journal201412; http://www.sdms.org/membership/JDMS; http://jdm.sagepub.com. **Ad Rates:** BW $1,915; 4C $1,615; BW $2,815, full page; BW $2,251, half page. **Remarks:** Accepts advertising. **Circ:** Paid 14000, 26500.

4678 ■ Journal of Disability Policy Studies
SAGE Publications Inc.
2455 Teller Rd.
Thousand Oaks, CA 91320-2234
Free: 800-818-7243
Publisher's E-mail: sales@pfp.sagepub.com
Journal addressing a wide range of topics pertaining to disability policy.Addresses timely ethical issues affecting individuals with disabilities. **Freq:** Quarterly March, June, September, December. **Print Method:** Offset. **Trim Size:** 8 x 10 7/8. **Key Personnel:** Mitchell Yell, Editor; Richard L. Allington, Editor; Antonis Katsiyannis, Editor. **ISSN:** 1044--2073 (print); **EISSN:** 1538--4802 (electronic). **Subscription Rates:** £41 Individuals print and online; £113 Institutions online only; £123 Institutions print only; £125 Institutions print and online; £13 Individuals single print issue; £34 Institutions single print issue. **URL:** http://dps.sagepub.com. **Ad Rates:** BW $515; 4C $995. **Remarks:** Advertising accepted; rates available upon request. **Circ:** Paid 400.

4679 ■ The Journal of Early Adolescence
SAGE Publications Inc.
2455 Teller Rd.
Thousand Oaks, CA 91320-2234
Free: 800-818-7243
Publisher's E-mail: sales@pfp.sagepub.com
Journal exploring development in children ages 10 to 14. **Freq:** 8/year. **Print Method:** Offset. **Trim Size:** 5 1/2 x 8 1/2. **Cols./Page:** 1. **Col. Width:** 50 nonpareils. **Col. Depth:** 100 agate lines. **Key Personnel:** Alexander T. Vazsonyi, Editor. **ISSN:** 0272--4316 (print); **EISSN:** 1552--5449 (electronic). **Subscription Rates:** £84 Individuals print only; £707 Institutions e-access; £769 Institutions print only; £785 Institutions print and e-access; £14 Individuals single print issue; £106 Institutions single print issue. **URL:** http://jea.sagepub.com. **Ad Rates:** BW $515; 4C $995. **Remarks:** Accepts advertising. **Circ:** Paid 700.

4680 ■ Journal of Early Childhood Research
SAGE Publications Inc.
2455 Teller Rd.
Thousand Oaks, CA 91320-2234
Free: 800-818-7243
Publisher's E-mail: sales@pfp.sagepub.com
Journal focusing on learning and development in early childhood. **Freq:** 3/year. **Key Personnel:** Rebecca S. New, Editor; Carol Aubrey, Member; Cathy Nutbrown, Editor-in-Chief. **ISSN:** 1476--718X (print); **EISSN:** 1741--2927 (electronic). **Subscription Rates:** $81 Individuals print; $796 Institutions e-access; $866 Institutions print; $884 Institutions print and e-access; $26 Individuals single print issue; $238 Institutions single print issue. **URL:** http://ecr.sagepub.com. **Remarks:** Accepts advertising. **Circ:** (Not Reported).

4681 ■ Journal of Early Intervention
SAGE Publications Inc.
2455 Teller Rd.
Thousand Oaks, CA 91320-2234
Free: 800-818-7243
Publisher's E-mail: sales@pfp.sagepub.com
Journal related to research and practice in early intervention for infants and young children with special needs and their families. **Freq:** Quarterly. **Trim Size:** 7 x 9 1/4. **Cols./Page:** 2. **Key Personnel:** William H. Brown, PhD, Board Member; Mary Hemmeter, Editor. **ISSN:** 0885- 3460 (print). **Subscription Rates:** Included in membership; $77 Individuals print only; $286 Institutions print only; $263 Institutions e-access; $292 Institutions print and e-access; $79 Institutions single issue; $25 Individuals single issue. **URL:** http://www.dec-sped.org/journal; http://jei.sagepub.com. **Formerly:** Journal of the Division for Early Childhood. **Remarks:** Accepts advertising. **Circ:** (Not Reported).

4682 ■ Journal of Elastomers and Plastics
SAGE Publications Inc.
2455 Teller Rd.
Thousand Oaks, CA 91320-2234
Free: 800-818-7243
Publisher's E-mail: sales@pfp.sagepub.com
Peer-reviewed journal focusing on the development and marketing of elastomers and plastics. **Freq:** 8/year. **Print Method:** Offset. **Trim Size:** 6 x 9. **Cols./Page:** 1. **Col. Width:** 54 nonpareils. **Col. Depth:** 100 agate lines. **Key Personnel:** M. El-Halwagi, Board Member; Heshmat A. Aglan, Editor; A.I. Isayev, Board Member. **ISSN:** 0095--2443 (print); **EISSN:** 1530--8006 (electronic). **Subscription Rates:** £1212 Institutions online only; £1320 Institutions print only; £1347 Institutions print and online; £182 Institutions single print issue. **URL:** http://jep.sagepub.com. **Remarks:** Accepts advertising. **Circ:** ‡275.

4683 ■ Journal of Emerging Market Finance
SAGE Publications Inc.
2455 Teller Rd.
Thousand Oaks, CA 91320-2234
Free: 800-818-7243
Publisher's E-mail: sales@pfp.sagepub.com
Peer-reviewed journal focusing on the theory and practice of finance in emerging markets. **Freq:** 3/year. **Key Personnel:** S. Maheshwaran, Editor-in-Chief; Ganesh Balasubramanian, Managing Editor. **ISSN:** 0972--6527 (print); **EISSN:** 0973--0710 (electronic). **Subscription Rates:** £46 Individuals print only; £186 Institutions e-access; £203 Institutions print only; £207 Institutions print and online; £20 Individuals single print issue; £74 Institutions single print issue. **URL:** http://emf.sagepub.com. **Remarks:** Accepts advertising. **Circ:** (Not Reported).

4684 ■ Journal of Emotional and Behavioral Disorders
SAGE Publications Inc.
2455 Teller Rd.
Thousand Oaks, CA 91320-2234
Free: 800-818-7243
Publisher's E-mail: sales@pfp.sagepub.com
Journal of special education. **Founded:** 1993. **Freq:** Quarterly. **Print Method:** Offset. **Trim Size:** 8 x 10 7/8. **Cols./Page:** 3. **Col. Width:** 2 2/8 inches. **Col. Depth:** 9 5/16 inches. **Key Personnel:** Elizabeth Farmer, Editor; Thomas Farmer, Editor. **ISSN:** 1063-4266 (print). **Subscription Rates:** $67 Individuals print & e-access; $212 Institutions print & e-access; $191 Institutions e-access; $208 Institutions print only; $57 Institutions single print. **URL:** http://www.sagepub.com/journalsProdEditBoards.nav?prodId=Journal201878. **Ad Rates:** BW $515; 4C $995. **Remarks:** Accepts advertising. **Circ:** Paid ‡1782, Non-paid ‡94.

4685 ■ Journal of Engineering Manufacture
SAGE Publications Inc.
2455 Teller Rd.
Thousand Oaks, CA 91320-2234
Free: 800-818-7243
Publisher's E-mail: sales@pfp.sagepub.com
Journal covering developments in engineering manufacture. **Freq:** Monthly. **Key Personnel:** Prof. P.G. Maropoulos, Editor. **ISSN:** 0954--4054 (print); **EISSN:** 2041--2975 (electronic). **URL:** http://pib.sagepub.com. **Circ:** (Not Reported).

4686 ■ Journal of English Linguistics
SAGE Publications Inc.
2455 Teller Rd.
Thousand Oaks, CA 91320-2234
Free: 800-818-7243
Publisher's E-mail: sales@pfp.sagepub.com
Journal focusing on all aspects of linguistics in the English language. **Freq:** Quarterly. **Key Personnel:** Mathew Gordon, Editor; Robin Queen, Senior Editor; Anne Curzan, Senior Editor; Peter Grund, Editor. **ISSN:** 0075--4242 (print); **EISSN:** 1552--5457 (electronic). **Subscription Rates:** £74 Individuals print only; £434 Institutions online only; £472 Institutions print only; £482 Institutions print and online; £24 Individuals single print issue; £130 Institutions single print issue. **URL:** http://eng.sagepub.com. **Remarks:** Accepts advertising. **Circ:** (Not Reported).

4687 ■ Journal of Entrepreneurship
SAGE Publications Inc.
2455 Teller Rd.
Thousand Oaks, CA 91320-2234
Free: 800-818-7243
Publisher's E-mail: sales@pfp.sagepub.com
Journal focusing on the changing contours of entrepreneurial research and training, and on trends and directions of explorations in the theory and practice of entrepreneurship. **Freq:** Semiannual March and September. **Key Personnel:** M. Akbar, Board Member; Hrishikes Bhattacharya, Board Member; Dinesh N. Awasthi, Board Member; Sasi Misra, Editor. **ISSN:** 0971--3557 (print); **EISSN:** 0973--0745 (electronic). **Subscription Rates:** £48 Individuals print; £201 Institutions e-access; £219 Institutions print; £223 Institutions print and e-access; £31 Individuals single print issue; £120 Institutions single print issue; Rs 650 Individuals print only; $78 Individuals print only; £42 Individuals print only; Rs 1050 Individuals print and electronic; $296 Individuals print and electronic; £160 Individuals print and electronic. **URL:** http://joe.sagepub.com; http://www.ediindia.org/JOE.asp. **Remarks:** Accepts advertising. **Circ:** (Not Reported).

4688 ■ The Journal of Environment and Development
SAGE Publications Inc.
2455 Teller Rd.
Thousand Oaks, CA 91320-2234
Free: 800-818-7243
Publisher's E-mail: sales@pfp.sagepub.com
Journal covering for anyone concerned with environment and development issues at the local, national, regional and international levels. **Freq:** Quarterly. **Key Personnel:** Steven Charnovitz, Board Member; Raymond Clemencon, Editor-in-Chief; Jessica Marter-Kenyon, Managing Editor. **ISSN:** 1070--4965 (print); **EISSN:** 1552--5465 (electronic). **Subscription Rates:** £80 Individuals online only; £455 Institutions Back file Purchase, Online(Content through 1998); £455 Institutions online only; £501 Institutions Back file Lease, Online Plus Back file (All Online Content). **URL:** http://jed.sagepub.com. **Remarks:** Accepts advertising. **Circ:** (Not Reported).

4689 ■ Journal of European Social Policy
SAGE Publications Inc.
2455 Teller Rd.
Thousand Oaks, CA 91320-2234
Free: 800-818-7243
Publisher's E-mail: sales@pfp.sagepub.com
Journal focusing on European social policy issues and developments. **Freq:** 5/year. **Key Personnel:** Jochen Clasen, Editor; Daniel Clegg, Editor; Traute Meyer, Editor; Karen Anderson, Board Member. **ISSN:** 0958--9287 (print); **EISSN:** 1461--7269 (electronic). **Subscription**

Rates: £76 Individuals print only; £701 Institutions online only; £763 Institutions print only; £779 Institutions print and online; £20 Individuals single print issue; £168 Institutions single print issue. **URL:** http://esp.sagepub.com. **Remarks:** Accepts advertising. **Circ:** (Not Reported).

4690 ■ Journal of European Studies
SAGE Publications Inc.
2455 Teller Rd.
Thousand Oaks, CA 91320-2234
Free: 800-818-7243
Publisher's E-mail: sales@pfp.sagepub.com
Journal focusing on European culture books with European cultural themes. **Founded:** 1970. **Freq:** Quarterly. **Trim Size:** 233 x 153 mm. **Key Personnel:** John Flower, Editor; Philippe Baudoire, Editor; A.G. Cross, Editor. **ISSN:** 0047-2441 (print); **EISSN:** 1740-2379 (electronic). **Subscription Rates:** $1013 Institutions combined (print & e-access); $1114 Institutions current volume print & all online content; $912 Institutions e-access; $1013 Institutions backfile lease, e-access plus backfile; $993 Institutions print only; $89 Individuals print only; $2169 Institutions e-access thru 1998; $273 Institutions single print; $29 Individuals single print; $960 Institutions print & e-access; $1056 Institutions print (all online content); $864 Institutions e-access; $960 Institutions e-access & online; $2056 Institutions e-access (content through 1998); $941 Institutions print only; $87 Individuals print only; $259 Institutions single print; $28 Individuals single print. **URL:** http://www.sagepub.com/journalsProdDesc.nav?prodId=Journal201665. **Ad Rates:** BW $300; BW $200. **Remarks:** Accepts advertising. **Circ:** (Not Reported).

4691 ■ Journal of Evidence Based Complementary & Alternative Medicine
SAGE Publications Inc.
2455 Teller Rd.
Thousand Oaks, CA 91320-2234
Free: 800-818-7243
Publication E-mail: advertising@sagepub.com
Peer-reviewed journal focusing on the cultural, social, demographic, political, economic, and legal implications of the use of alternative and complementary therapies, as well as original basic and applied research from a wide range of health and social science disciplines. **Freq:** Quarterly. **Trim Size:** 7 x 10. **Key Personnel:** Bruce Buehler, Editor. **ISSN:** 1533-2102 (print); **EISSN:** 2156-5899 (electronic). **Subscription Rates:** $586 Institutions print & e-access; $645 Institutions print & all online; $527 Institutions e-access; $574 Institutions print; $88 Individuals print only; $158 Institutions single print; $29 Individuals single print; $528 Institutions online back issue through 1998. **URL:** http://www.sagepub.com/journalsProdDesc.nav?prodId=Journal201646. **Formerly**: Complementary Health Practice Review. **Ad Rates:** BW $625; 4C $995. **Remarks:** Accepts advertising. **Circ:** (Not Reported).

4692 ■ Journal of Family History
SAGE Publications Inc.
2455 Teller Rd.
Thousand Oaks, CA 91320-2234
Free: 800-818-7243
Publisher's E-mail: sales@pfp.sagepub.com
Journal focusing on the history of the family, kinship, and population. Also featuring an expanded editorial focus that encompasses work from a variety of perspectives, including gender, sexuality, race, class, and culture. **Freq:** Quarterly. **Key Personnel:** Roderick Phillips, Editor. **ISSN:** 0363--1990 (print); **EISSN:** 1552--5473 (electronic). **Subscription Rates:** £102 Individuals print only; £560 Institutions online only; £610 Institutions print only; £622 Institutions print and online; £33 Individuals single print issue; £168 Institutions single print issue. **URL:** http://jfh.sagepub.com. **Ad Rates:** BW $445. **Remarks:** Accepts advertising. **Circ:** (Not Reported).

4693 ■ Journal of Family Nursing
SAGE Publications Inc.
2455 Teller Rd.
Thousand Oaks, CA 91320-2234
Free: 800-818-7243
Publication E-mail: advertising@sagepub.com
Scholarly journal on nursing issues pertaining to family health and illness. **Founded:** Feb. 1995. **Freq:** Quarterly. **Print Method:** Offset. **Trim Size:** 5 1/2 x 8 1/2. **Key Personnel:** Janice M. Bell, PhD, Editor. **ISSN:** 1074-8407 (print). **Subscription Rates:** $967 Institutions print & e-access; $1064 Institutions current volume print & all online content; $870 Institutions e-access; $948 Institutions print only; $138 Individuals print only; $261 Institutions single print issue; $45 Individuals single print issue. **URL:** http://www.sagepub.com/journalsProdDesc.nav?prodId=Journal200771; http://jfn.sagepub.com. **Ad Rates:** BW $445. **Remarks:** Accepts advertising. **Circ:** Paid 500.

4694 ■ Journal of Feline Medicine and Surgery
SAGE Publications Inc.
2455 Teller Rd.
Thousand Oaks, CA 91320-2234
Free: 800-818-7243
Publisher's E-mail: sales@pfp.sagepub.com
Journal publishing reviews on all aspects of feline medicine and surgery. **Freq:** Monthly 12/yr. **Key Personnel:** A.H. Sparkes, Editor; M. Scherk, Editor; D. Gunn-Moore, Associate Editor. **ISSN:** 1098--612X (print); **EISSN:** 1532--2750 (electronic). **Subscription Rates:** $385 Individuals print only; $759 Institutions print only; $697 Institutions online only; $774 Institutions print + online; $42 Individuals single print issue; $70 Institutions single print issue; Included in membership. **URL:** http://jfm.sagepub.com; http://www.icatcare.org/vets/jfms; http://icatcare.org/vets/jfms. **Remarks:** Accepts advertising. **Circ:** (Not Reported).

4695 ■ Journal of Geriatric Psychiatry and Neurology
SAGE Publications Inc.
2455 Teller Rd.
Thousand Oaks, CA 91320-2234
Free: 800-818-7243
Publisher's E-mail: sales@pfp.sagepub.com
Journal focusing on all aspects of neuropsychiatric care of aging patients, including age-related biologic, neurological, and psychiatric illnesses; psychosocial problems; forensic issues; and family care. **Freq:** Bimonthly. **Print Method:** Web Offset. **Trim Size:** 8 1/8 x 10 7/8. **Key Personnel:** Sherry P. Becker, Managing Editor; Charles A. Marotta, MD, Associate Editor; George S. Alexopoulos, MD, Board Member; Lee Baer, PhD, Board Member; Marshall Folstein, MD, Board Member; Jeffrey L. Cummings, MD, Associate Editor; Gary D. Miner, PhD, Associate Editor; Cornelia Cremens, MD, Editor; Ned Cassem, MD, Board Member; Alan M. Mellow, MD, Editor. **ISSN:** 0891--9887 (print); **EISSN:** 1552--5708 (electronic). **Subscription Rates:** £138 Individuals print only; £501 Institutions online only; £546 Institutions print only; £557 Institutions print and online; £30 Individuals single print issue; £100 Institutions single print issue. **URL:** http://jgp.sagepub.com. **Ad Rates:** BW $945; 4C $1,200. **Remarks:** Accepts advertising. **Circ:** (Not Reported).

4696 ■ Journal of Health Management
SAGE Publications Inc.
2455 Teller Rd.
Thousand Oaks, CA 91320-2234
Free: 800-818-7243
Publisher's E-mail: sales@pfp.sagepub.com
Journal focusing on health management and policy. **Freq:** Quarterly. **Key Personnel:** Bouchra Assarag, Advisor; S.D. Gupta, Editor; P.R. Sodani, Editor. **ISSN:** 0972-0634 (print); **EISSN:** 0973-0729 (electronic). **Subscription Rates:** $484 Institutions print & e-access; $436 Institutions e-access; $474 Institutions print only; $122 Individuals print only; $130 Institutions single print; $40 Individuals single print. **URL:** http://www.sagepub.com/journalsProdAdv.nav?prodId=Journal200887; http://jhm.sagepub.com/. **Remarks:** Accepts advertising. **Circ:** (Not Reported).

4697 ■ Journal of Health Psychology
SAGE Publications Inc.
2455 Teller Rd.
Thousand Oaks, CA 91320-2234
Free: 800-818-7243
Publisher's E-mail: sales@pfp.sagepub.com
Peer-reviewed journal focusing on research in health psychology. **Freq:** Monthly. **Key Personnel:** Ronan Conroy, Associate Editor; David F. Marks, Editor. **ISSN:** 1359--1053 (print); **EISSN:** 1461--7277 (electronic). **Subscription Rates:** £68 Individuals print only; £1455 Institutions online only; £1585 Institutions print only; £1617 Institutions print and only; £6 Individuals single print issue; £125 Institutions single print issue. **URL:** http://hpq.sagepub.com. **Remarks:** Accepts advertising. **Circ:** (Not Reported).

4698 ■ Journal of Hispanic Higher Education
SAGE Publications Inc.
2455 Teller Rd.
Thousand Oaks, CA 91320-2234
Free: 800-818-7243
Publisher's E-mail: sales@pfp.sagepub.com
Journal focusing on the advancement of knowledge and understanding of issues at Hispanic-serving institutions. **Freq:** Quarterly. **Key Personnel:** Michael William Mulnix, Senior Editor; Esther Elena Lopez-Mulnix, Editor; Noor S. Qasim, Assistant. **ISSN:** 1538--1927 (print); **EISSN:** 1552--5716 (electronic). **Subscription Rates:** £73 Individuals print only; £341 Institutions online only; £371 Institutions print only; £379 Institutions print and only; £24 Individuals single print issue; £102 Institutions single print issue. **URL:** http://jhh.sagepub.com. **Remarks:** Accepts advertising. **Circ:** (Not Reported).

4699 ■ Journal of Holistic Nursing
SAGE Publications Inc.
2455 Teller Rd.
Thousand Oaks, CA 91320-2234
Free: 800-818-7243
Publication E-mail: advertising@sagepub.com
Peer-reviewed journal promoting holism. **Freq:** Quarterly. **Trim Size:** 8 1/8 x 10 7/8. **Key Personnel:** Richard W. Cowling, PhD, Editor. **ISSN:** 0898--0101 (print); **EISSN:** 1552--5724 (electronic). **Subscription Rates:** £26 Individuals single print issue; £384 Institutions print only; £106 Institutions single print issue; £353 Institutions e-access; £384 Institutions print only; £392 Institutions print and e-access; £431 Institutions current volume print and all online content; £481 Institutions e-access (content through 1998); £81 Individuals print only. **URL:** http://jhn.sagepub.com; http://uk.sagepub.com/en-gb/asi/journal-of-holistic-nursing/journal200847. **Ad Rates:** BW $875; 4C $1110, in addition to Black & White rate. **Remarks:** Accepts advertising. **Circ:** (Not Reported).

4700 ■ Journal of Hospitality & Tourism Research
SAGE Publications Inc.
2455 Teller Rd.
Thousand Oaks, CA 91320-2234
Free: 800-818-7243
Publisher's E-mail: publications@chrie.org
Journal focusing on advances in the field of hospitality and tourism. **Freq:** Bimonthly. **Trim Size:** 6 x 9. **Cols./Page:** 1. **Key Personnel:** Chris Roberts, Editor; Linda J. Shea, Editor. **ISSN:** 1096--3480 (print); **EISSN:** 1557--7554 (electronic). **Subscription Rates:** £111 Individuals print only; £392 Institutions online only; £426 Institutions print only; £435 Institutions print and online; £18 Individuals single print issue; £59 Institutions single print issue. **URL:** http://jht.sagepub.com. **Remarks:** Accepts advertising. **Circ:** (Not Reported).

4701 ■ Journal of Human Lactation
SAGE Publications Inc.
2455 Teller Rd.
Thousand Oaks, CA 91320-2234
Free: 800-818-7243
Publisher's E-mail: info@ilca.org
Journal for nurses, lactation consultants, midwives, nutritionists/dieticians, public health and social workers, therapists, and physicians. **Freq:** Quarterly. **Trim Size:** 8 1/2 x 11. **Key Personnel:** Joan E. Dodgson, Editor-in-Chief; Meaghan Kelly, Managing Editor. **ISSN:** 0890--3344 (print); **EISSN:** 1552--5732 (electronic). **Subscription Rates:** £130 Individuals print only; £496 Institutions online only; £540 Institutions print only; £551 Institutions print and online; £42 Individuals single print issue; £149 Institutions single print issue. **URL:** http://jhl.sagepub.com. **Ad Rates:** BW $930; 4C $1030. **Remarks:** Accepts advertising. **Circ:** (Not Reported).

4702 ■ Journal of Human Values
SAGE Publications Inc.
2455 Teller Rd.
Thousand Oaks, CA 91320-2234
Free: 800-818-7243
Publisher's E-mail: info@sagepub.in

Circulation: ★ = AAM; △ or • = BPA; ♦ = CAC; ❑ = VAC; ⊕ = PO Statement; ‡ = Publisher's Report; Boldface figures = sworn; Light figures = estimated.

Journal focusing on the relevance of human values in today's world; human values at the organizational level; and the culture-specificity of human values. **Freq:** 3/week. **Key Personnel:** Kenneth Goodpaster, Advisor; Prof. C. Panduranga Bhatta, Editor; Bhaskar Chakrabarti, Editor; S.K. Chakraborty, Founder, Editor. **ISSN:** 0971--6858 (print); **EISSN:** 0973--0737 (electronic). **Subscription Rates:** £50 Individuals print only; £186 Institutions online only; £203 Institutions print only; £207 Institutions print and only; £22 Individuals single print issue; £74 Institutions single print issue. **URL:** http://jhv.sagepub.com. **Remarks:** Accepts advertising. **Circ:** Paid 600.

4703 ■ Journal of Humanistic Psychology
SAGE Publications Inc.
2455 Teller Rd.
Thousand Oaks, CA 91320-2234
Free: 800-818-7243
Publisher's E-mail: sales@pfp.sagepub.com
Psychology journal.Contains interdisplinary forum for contributions, controversies and diverse statements pertaining to humanistic psychology. **Freq:** Quarterly January , April , July and October. **Print Method:** Offset. **Trim Size:** 5 1/2 x 8 1/2. **Cols./Page:** 1. **Col. Width:** 50 nonpareils. **Col. Depth:** 100 agate lines. **Key Personnel:** Kirk J. Schneider, Editor; Thomas C. Greening, Editor; Shawn Rubin, Editor. **ISSN:** 0022--1678 (print); **EISSN:** 1552--650X (electronic). **Subscription Rates:** $1189 Institutions print & e-access; $33 Individuals single print only; $1070 Institutions e-access; $1189 Institutions e-access (all online content); $3344 Institutions e-access (content through 1998); $1165 Institutions print only; $150 Individuals print only; $214 Institutions single print only; $1308 Institutions combined plus backfile print & all online content. **URL:** http://jhp.sagepub.com. **Ad Rates:** BW $875; 4C $1110. **Remarks:** Accepts advertising. **Circ:** (Not Reported).

4704 ■ Journal of Industrial Relations
SAGE Publications Inc.
2455 Teller Rd.
Thousand Oaks, CA 91320-2234
Free: 800-818-7243
Publisher's E-mail: sales@pfp.sagepub.com
Peer-reviewed journal covering industrial relations including economic, political, and social influences on the power of capital and labor, and the interactions between employers, workers, their collective organizations and the state. **Freq:** 5/year February, April, June, September, and November. **Print Method:** Offset. **Trim Size:** 5 1/2 x 8 1/2. **Cols./Page:** 1. **Col. Width:** 50 nonpareils. **Col. Depth:** 100 agate lines. **Key Personnel:** Marian Baird, Editor; Dr. Bradon Ellem, Editor. **ISSN:** 0022--1856 (print); **EISSN:** 1472--9296 (electronic). **Subscription Rates:** $888 Institutions print and e-access; $799 Institutions e-access; $870 Institutions print only; $96 Individuals print only; $191 Institutions single print; $25 Individuals single print. **URL:** http://jir.sagepub.com. **Ad Rates:** BW £650. **Remarks:** Accepts advertising. **Circ:** (Not Reported).

4705 ■ Journal of Information Science
SAGE Publications Inc.
2455 Teller Rd.
Thousand Oaks, CA 91320-2234
Free: 800-818-7243
Journal for all those researching and working in the sciences of information and knowledge management. **Freq:** Bimonthly. **Print Method:** Litho. **Trim Size:** 276 x 210 mm. **Key Personnel:** Alan Gilchrist, Associate Editor; Eugene Garfield, Board Member; Pia Borlund, Board Member; Ronald N. Kostoff, Associate Editor; Hazel Hall, Board Member; Leo Egghe, Board Member; Adrian Dale, Editor. **ISSN:** 0165--5515 (print); **EISSN:** 1741--6485 (electronic). **Subscription Rates:** £66 Individuals print only; £464 Institutions online only; £505 Institutions print only; £515 Institutions print and online; £14 Individuals single print issue; £93 Institutions single print issue. **URL:** http://jis.sagepub.com. **Remarks:** Accepts advertising. **Circ:** (Not Reported).

4706 ■ Journal of Intensive Care Medicine
SAGE Publications Inc.
2455 Teller Rd.
Thousand Oaks, CA 91320-2234
Free: 800-818-7243
Publication E-mail: journal.icm@hmn.ap.hop-paris.fr
Medical journal for specialists working in intensive care units. **Freq:** 10/year. **Trim Size:** 8 x 10 7/8. **Key Personnel:** Nicholas Smyrnios, MD, Editor; James M. Rippe, MD, Editor; Gordon B. Avery, MD, Advisor; James E. Dalen, MD, Advisor; Ronald Miller, MD, Advisor. **ISSN:** 0885--0666 (print); **EISSN:** 1525--1489 (electronic). **Subscription Rates:** £728 Institutions print & e-access; £801 Institutions current volume print & all online content; £655 Institutions e-access; £728 Institutions all online content; £616 Institutions e-access (Content through 1998); £713 Institutions print only; £78 Institutions single print issue; £26 Individuals single print issue. **URL:** http://jic.sagepub.com. **Ad Rates:** BW $1120; 4C $1110, in addition to Black & White rate. **Remarks:** Advertising accepted; rates available upon request. **Circ:** (Not Reported).

4707 ■ Journal of the International Association of Physicians in AIDS Care
SAGE Publications Inc.
2455 Teller Rd.
Thousand Oaks, CA 91320-2234
Free: 800-818-7243
Publication E-mail: editor@iapac.org
Magazine featuring topics affecting the care of HIV-positive people. **Founded:** Feb. 1995. **Freq:** Bimonthly. **Print Method:** 4-color press. **Trim Size:** 8 1/8 x 11 1/8. **Cols./Page:** 3. **Key Personnel:** John G. Bartlett, MD, Editor; Peter Mugyeni, MD, Editor; Jose Zuniga, Editor-in-Chief; Jose M. Zuniga, Chief Executive Officer, President. **ISSN:** 1545-1097 (print); **EISSN:** 2325-9582 (electronic). **Subscription Rates:** $444 Institutions print & e-access; $400 Institutions e-access; $435 Institutions print; $102 Individuals print; $80 Institutions single print; $22 Individuals single print; $105 Individuals print only; $23 Individuals single print issue. **URL:** http://www.sagepub.com/journalsProdDesc.nav?prodId=Journal201760; http://www.sagepub.com/journalsProdDesc.nav?ct_p=&prodId=Journal201760; http://jia.sagepub.com. **Ad Rates:** BW $3,295; 4C $5,795; 4C $2,550. **Remarks:** Accepts advertising. **Circ:** Paid 5575, Non-paid 2900.

4708 ■ Journal of Interpersonal Violence
SAGE Publications Inc.
2455 Teller Rd.
Thousand Oaks, CA 91320-2234
Free: 800-818-7243
Publisher's E-mail: sales@pfp.sagepub.com
Journal focusing on the study and treatment of victims and perpetrators of violence.Contains information on domestic violence, rape, child sexual abuse and other violent crimes. **Freq:** 20/yr. **Print Method:** Offset. **Trim Size:** 5 1/2 x 8 1/2. **Cols./Page:** 1. **Col. Width:** 50 nonpareils. **Col. Depth:** 100 agate lines. **Key Personnel:** Jon R. Conte, Editor. **ISSN:** 0886--2605 (print); **EISSN:** 1552--6518 (electronic). **Subscription Rates:** $2502 Institutions print & e-access; $2752 Institutions combined & backfile (current volume print & all online content); $2252 Institutions e-access; $2502 Institutions e-access (all online content); $2385 Institutions e-access (content through 1998); $2452 Institutions print only; $358 Individuals print only; $112 Institutions single print; $19 Individuals single print. **URL:** http://jiv.sagepub.com. **Ad Rates:** BW $875; 4C $1110. **Remarks:** Accepts advertising. **Circ:** (Not Reported).

4709 ■ Journal of Laboratory Automation
SAGE Publications Inc.
2455 Teller Rd.
Thousand Oaks, CA 91320-2234
Free: 800-818-7243
Publisher's E-mail: slas@slas.org
Journal publishing current developments in the field of laboratory robotics. **Freq:** Bimonthly. **Key Personnel:** Dean Ho, PhD, Editor-in-Chief. **ISSN:** 2211--0682 (print); **EISSN:** 1540--2452 (electronic). **Subscription Rates:** £185 Individuals print; £284 Institutions online; £310 Institutions print; £316 Institutions combined - print & E-access; £40 Single issue; £57 Institutions single issue. **URL:** http://jla.sagepub.com; http://www.sagepub.com/journals/Journal202089. **Formerly:** Journal of The Association for Laboratory Automation. **Remarks:** Advertising not accepted. **Circ:** (Not Reported).

4710 ■ Journal of Language and Social Psychology
SAGE Publications Inc.
2455 Teller Rd.
Thousand Oaks, CA 91320-2234
Free: 800-818-7243
Publisher's E-mail: sales@pfp.sagepub.com
Journal on the social aspects of language. **Freq:** Quarterly. **Print Method:** Offset. **Trim Size:** 6 x 9. **Key Personnel:** Howard Giles, Editor. **ISSN:** 0261--927X (print); **EISSN:** 1552--6526 (electronic). **Subscription Rates:** PTE21 Individuals single print issue; £99 Individuals print only; £123 Institutions single print issue; £616 Institutions e-access; £670 Institutions print only; £684 Institutions print and e-access; £752 Institutions combined plus backfile (current volume print & all online content); £816 Institutions e-access (content through 1998). **URL:** http://jls.sagepub.com. **Ad Rates:** BW $875; 4C $1110, in addition to Black & White rate. **Remarks:** Accepts advertising. **Circ:** (Not Reported).

4711 ■ Journal of Leadership and Organizational Studies
SAGE Publications Inc.
2455 Teller Rd.
Thousand Oaks, CA 91320-2234
Free: 800-818-7243
Publisher's E-mail: sales@pfp.sagepub.com
Scholarly journal covering leadership studies. **Freq:** Quarterly. **Key Personnel:** Fred Luthans, Editor. **ISSN:** 1548--0518 (print); **EISSN:** 1939--7089 (electronic). **Subscription Rates:** £80 Individuals print only; £271 Institutions print only; £277 Institutions print & e-access; £249 Institutions e-access. **URL:** http://uk.sagepub.com/journals/Journal201858. **Remarks:** Advertising not accepted. **Circ:** (Not Reported).

4712 ■ Journal of Learning Disabilities
SAGE Publications Inc.
2455 Teller Rd.
Thousand Oaks, CA 91320-2234
Free: 800-818-7243
Publisher's E-mail: sales@pfp.sagepub.com
Special education journal. **Freq:** Bimonthly. **Print Method:** Offset. **Trim Size:** 8 x 10 7/8. **Cols./Page:** 3. **Col. Width:** 28 nonpareils. **Col. Depth:** 134 agate lines. **Key Personnel:** Lee H. Swanson, PhD, Editor; Malka Margalit, Associate Editor; Virginia W. Berninger, PhD, Associate Editor. **ISSN:** 0022--2194 (print); **EISSN:** 1538--4780 (electronic). **Subscription Rates:** £49 Individuals print & e-access; £170 Institutions e-access; £185 Institutions print only; £189 Institutions print & e-access; £189 Institutions e-access plus backfile (all online content); £208 Institutions combined plus backfile (current volume print & all online content); £446 Institutions e-access (content through 1998); £11 Individuals single issue; £34 Institutions single issue. **URL:** http://ldx.sagepub.com. **Ad Rates:** BW $875; 4C $1110, in addition to Black & White rate. **Remarks:** Accepts advertising. **Circ:** (Not Reported).

4713 ■ Journal of Librarianship and Information Science
SAGE Publications Inc.
2455 Teller Rd.
Thousand Oaks, CA 91320-2234
Free: 800-818-7243
Publisher's E-mail: sales@pfp.sagepub.com
Peer-reviewed journal for librarians, information scientists, specialists, managers, and educators. **Freq:** Quarterly. **Key Personnel:** Anne Goulding, Editor. **ISSN:** 0961-0006 (print); **EISSN:** 1741-6477 (electronic). **Subscription Rates:** $882 Institutions print & e-access; $970 Institutions print & all online; $794 Institutions e-access; $2023 Institutions e-access (content through 1998); $864 Institutions print only; $118 Individuals print only; $864 Institutions single print; $38 Individuals single print. **URL:** http://www.sagepub.com/journalsProdDesc.nav?prodId=Journal201675. **Ad Rates:** BW £300. **Remarks:** Accepts advertising. **Circ:** (Not Reported).

4714 ■ Journal of Literacy Research
SAGE Publications Inc.
2455 Teller Rd.
Thousand Oaks, CA 91320-2234
Free: 800-818-7243
Publisher's E-mail: sales@pfp.sagepub.com
An interdisciplinary, peer-reviewed journal publishing research related to literacy, language, and literacy and language education from preschool through adulthood. **Freq:** Quarterly. **Key Personnel:** Miriam Martinez, Editor. **ISSN:** 1086--296X (print); **EISSN:** 1554--8430 (electronic). **Subscription Rates:** $47 Individuals print; $250 Institutions e-access; $272 Institutions print only;

$278 Institutions print and online; $15 Individuals single issue; $75 Institutions single issue. **URL:** http://jlr.sagepub.com. **Ad Rates:** BW $550. **Remarks:** Accepts advertising. **Circ:** (Not Reported).

4715 ■ Journal of Macromarketing
Macromarketing Society
Journal examining important social issues, how they are affected by marketing, and how society influences the conduct of marketing. **Freq:** Quarterly. **Key Personnel:** Terence H. Witkowski, Editor. **ISSN:** 0276--1467 (print); **EISSN:** 1552--6534 (electronic). **Subscription Rates:** £363 Institutions print & e-access; £327 Institutions e-access; £498 Institutions e-access (content through 1998); £356 Institutions print only; £73 Individuals print only; £98 Institutions single print; £24 Individuals single print; $127 Individuals print; $594 Institutions online; $647 Institutions print. **URL:** http://us.sagepub.com/en-us/nam/journal-of-macromarketing/journal200954; http://intl-jmk.sagepub.com; http://macromarketing.org/journal-of-macromarketing. **Ad Rates:** BW $725; 4C $1115. **Remarks:** Accepts advertising. **Circ:** (Not Reported).

4716 ■ Journal of Macromarketing
SAGE Publications Inc.
2455 Teller Rd.
Thousand Oaks, CA 91320-2234
Free: 800-818-7243
Journal examining important social issues, how they are affected by marketing, and how society influences the conduct of marketing. **Freq:** Quarterly. **Key Personnel:** Terence H. Witkowski, Editor. **ISSN:** 0276--1467 (print); **EISSN:** 1552--6534 (electronic). **Subscription Rates:** £363 Institutions print & e-access; £327 Institutions e-access; £498 Institutions e-access (content through 1998); £356 Institutions print only; £73 Individuals print only; £98 Institutions single print; £24 Individuals single print; $127 Individuals print; $594 Institutions online; $647 Institutions print. **URL:** http://us.sagepub.com/en-us/nam/journal-of-macromarketing/journal200954; http://intl-jmk.sagepub.com; http://macromarketing.org/journal-of-macromarketing. **Ad Rates:** BW $725; 4C $1115. **Remarks:** Accepts advertising. **Circ:** (Not Reported).

4717 ■ Journal of Management
SAGE Publications Inc.
2455 Teller Rd.
Thousand Oaks, CA 91320-2234
Free: 800-818-7243
Publisher's E-mail: sales@pfp.sagepub.com
Journal publishing research articles focused on the management field as a whole. **Freq:** 7/year. **Key Personnel:** Patrick M. Wright, Editor. **ISSN:** 0149--2063 (print); **EISSN:** 1557--1211 (electronic). **Subscription Rates:** £575 Institutions print & e-access; £576 Institutions current volume print & all online content; £518 Institutions e-access; £1057 Institutions online content through 1998; £564 Institutions print only; £126 Individuals print only; £89 Institutions single print; £23 Individuals single print. **URL:** http://us.sagepub.com/en-us/nam/journal-of-management/journal201724. **Ad Rates:** BW $725; 4C $1115. **Remarks:** Accepts advertising. **Circ:** (Not Reported).

4718 ■ Journal of Management Education
SAGE Publications Inc.
2455 Teller Rd.
Thousand Oaks, CA 91320-2234
Free: 800-818-7243
Publisher's E-mail: sales@pfp.sagepub.com
Journal dedicated to exploring issues of teaching and learning in all areas of management and organizational studies. **Freq:** Bimonthly. **Trim Size:** 5 1/2 x 8 1/2. **Key Personnel:** Jon Billsberry, Board Member; Belinda Allen, Board Member. **ISSN:** 1052--5629 (print); **EISSN:** 1552--6658 (electronic). **Subscription Rates:** £56 Institutions single print issue; £773 Institutions e-access (content through 1998). **URL:** http://jme.sagepub.com. **Formerly:** Organizational Behavior Teaching Review. **Ad Rates:** BW $875; 4C $1110, in addition to Black & White rate. **Remarks:** Accepts advertising. **Circ:** (Not Reported).

4719 ■ Journal of Management Inquiry
SAGE Publications Inc.
2455 Teller Rd.
Thousand Oaks, CA 91320-2234
Free: 800-818-7243
Publisher's E-mail: sales@pfp.sagepub.com
Journal focusing on a wide variety of areas within the management and organization field. **Founded:** 1992. **Freq:** Quarterly. **Print Method:** Offset. **Trim Size:** 8 1/2 x 11. **Key Personnel:** Richard W. Stackman, Editor-in-Chief; Nelson Phillips, Editor-in-Chief. **ISSN:** 1056-4926 (print); **EISSN:** 1552-6542 (electronic). **Subscription Rates:** $807 Institutions combined (print & e-access); $888 Institutions backfile lease, combined plus backfile; $726 Institutions e-access; $791 Institutions print only; $142 Individuals print only; $218 Institutions single print; $46 Individuals single print. **URL:** http://jmi.sagepub.com/; http://www.sagepub.com/journalsProdDesc.nav?prodId=Journal200922. **Remarks:** Accepts advertising. **Circ:** (Not Reported).

4720 ■ Journal of Marketing Education
SAGE Publications Inc.
2455 Teller Rd.
Thousand Oaks, CA 91320-2234
Free: 800-818-7243
Publisher's E-mail: sales@pfp.sagepub.com
Journal publishing articles on new techniques in marketing education. **Freq:** 3/year. **Key Personnel:** Donald R. Bacon, Editor; Denise T. Smart, Board Member; O.C. Ferrell, Board Member. **ISSN:** 0273--4753 (print); **EISSN:** 1552--6550 (electronic). **Subscription Rates:** £422 Institutions print & e-access; £464 Institutions current volume print & all online content; £380 Institutions e-access; £422 Institutions all online content; £414 Institutions print only; £75 Individuals print only; £152 Institutions single print; £33 Individuals single print. **URL:** http://us.sagepub.com/en-us/nam/journal-of-marketing-education/journal200864. **Ad Rates:** BW $725; 4C $1115. **Remarks:** Accepts advertising. **Circ:** (Not Reported).

4721 ■ Journal of Material Culture
SAGE Publications Inc.
2455 Teller Rd.
Thousand Oaks, CA 91320-2234
Free: 800-818-7243
Publisher's E-mail: sales@pfp.sagepub.com
Journal exploring the relationship between artifacts and social relations. **Freq:** Quarterly March , June , September , December. **Key Personnel:** James Clifford, Board Member; Nicholas J. Thomas, Board Member; Paul Basu, Editor; Debbora Battaglia, Board Member; Christopher Pinney, Editor, Board Member; Christopher Tilley, Board Member; Mike Rowlands, Board Member; Victor Buchli, Editor; Danny Miller, Board Member; Russell W. Belk, Board Member. **ISSN:** 1359--1835 (print); **EISSN:** 1460--3586 (electronic). **Subscription Rates:** $1150 Institutions print & e-access; $1265 Institutions backfile lease, combined plus backfile print & all; $1035 Institutions e-access; $1150 Individuals backfile lease, e-access plus backfile all online; $1127 Institutions print only; $100 Individuals print only; $310 Institutions single print; $33 Individuals single print. **URL:** http://us.sagepub.com/en-us/nam/journal/journal-material-culture. **Remarks:** Advertising accepted; rates available upon request. **Circ:** (Not Reported).

4722 ■ Journal of Medical Screening
SAGE Publications Inc.
2455 Teller Rd.
Thousand Oaks, CA 91320-2234
Free: 800-818-7243
Publisher's E-mail: sales@pfp.sagepub.com
Journal concerned with all aspects of medical screening. **Freq:** Quarterly. **Key Personnel:** Prof. Nicholas Wald, Editor. **ISSN:** 0969--1413 (print); **EISSN:** 1475--5793 (electronic). **Subscription Rates:** £399 Institutions combined (print & e-access); £399 Institutions E-access Plus Backfile (All Online Content); £657 Institutions e-access (content through 1998); £174 Individuals combined (print & e-access); £359 Institutions E-access; £154 Institutions single print issue; £57 Individuals single print issue. **URL:** http://msc.sagepub.com. **Circ:** (Not Reported).

4723 ■ Journal of Men's Studies
SAGE Publications Inc.
2455 Teller Rd.
Thousand Oaks, CA 91320-2234
Free: 800-818-7243
Scholarly journal covering men's studies. **Founded:** Aug. 1992. **Freq:** 3/yr. **Trim Size:** 6 x 9. **Cols./Page:** 1. **Key Personnel:** Dr. James Doyle, Editor. **ISSN:** 1060-8265 (print); **EISSN:** 1933-0251 (electronic). **URL:** http://www.mensstudies.com/content/120392/. **Remarks:** Accepts advertising. **Circ:** Paid 400.

4724 ■ Journal of Oncology Pharmacy Practice
International Society of Oncology Pharmacy Practitioners
2455 Teller Rd.
Thousand Oaks, CA 91320
Phone: (805)499-9774
Fax: (805)499-0871
Free: 800-818-7243
Publication E-mail: info@sagepub.com
Journal for pharmacists providing care to cancer patients. Also includes pertinent case reports and consensus guidelines for clinical practice, information on new products, new therapies, and patient management. **Freq:** 6/year Bimonthly February, April, June, August, October, and December. **Print Method:** Offset. **Trim Size:** 5 1/2 x 8 1/2. **Cols./Page:** 1. **Col. Width:** 50 nonpareils. **Col. Depth:** 100 agate lines. **Key Personnel:** Alenxandre Chan, Associate Editor; Barry R. Goldspiel, Editor-in-Chief. **ISSN:** 1078--1552 (print); **EISSN:** 1477--092X (electronic). **Subscription Rates:** $2583 Institutions print and e-access; $2325 Institutions e-access; $2531 Institutions print only; $409 Individuals print and e-access; €348 Institutions single print; €66 Individuals single print. **URL:** http://opp.sagepub.com; http://www.isopp.org/isopp-education-resources/jopp. **Ad Rates:** BW £972; 4C £1136. **Remarks:** Accepts advertising. **Circ:** ‡369.

4725 ■ Journal of Parenteral and Enteral Nutrition
American Society for Parenteral and Enteral Nutrition
2455 Teller Rd.
Thousand Oaks, CA 91320
Phone: (805)499-9774
Fax: (805)499-0871
Free: 800-818-7243
Publisher's E-mail: aspen@nutr.org
Includes current research, book reviews, case reports, and citations from world literature. **Freq:** 8/year. **Key Personnel:** Kelly A. Tappenden, PhD, Editor-in-Chief. **ISSN:** 0148--6071 (print); **EISSN:** 1941--2444 (electronic). **Subscription Rates:** $214 Individuals print and online; $563 Institutions e-access; $613 Institutions print only; $626 Institutions print and e-access; $35 Individuals single issue; $84 Institutions single issue. **URL:** http://pen.sagepub.com. **Remarks:** Accepts advertising. **Circ:** 10500.

4726 ■ Journal of Peace Research
SAGE Publications Inc.
2455 Teller Rd.
Thousand Oaks, CA 91320-2234
Free: 800-818-7243
Publisher's E-mail: sales@pfp.sagepub.com
Peer-reviewed journal focusing on scholary work in peace Research. **Freq:** Bimonthly. **Key Personnel:** Michael Brzoska, Associate Editor; Scott Gates, Associate Editor; Bertrand Lescher-Nuland, Managing Editor; Henrik Urdal, Editor; Han Dorussen, Associate Editor. **ISSN:** 0022-3433 (print); **EISSN:** 1460-3578 (electronic). **Subscription Rates:** $1717 Institutions combined (print & e-access); $1889 Institutions backfile lease, combined plus backfile; $1545 Institutions e-access; $1717 Institutions backfile lease, e-access plus backfile; $4595 Institutions backfile purchase, e-access; $1683 Institutions print only; $148 Individuals print only; $309 Institutions single print; $32 Individuals single print. **URL:** http://jpr.sagepub.com; http://www.sagepub.com/journalsProdDesc.nav?prodId=Journal200751. **Remarks:** Accepts advertising. **Circ:** (Not Reported).

4727 ■ Journal of Pediatric Oncology Nursing: Official Journal of the Association of Pediatric Hematology/Oncology Nurses
SAGE Publications Inc.
2455 Teller Rd.
Thousand Oaks, CA 91320-2234
Free: 800-818-7243
Publisher's E-mail: sales@pfp.sagepub.com
Peer-reviewed journal that provides the latest information regarding childhood cancer, blood disorders, pediatric hematology and oncology nursing. **Freq:** Bimonthly. **Trim Size:** 8 3/8 x 10 7/8. **Key Personnel:**

Circulation: ★ = AAM; △ or • = BPA; ♦ = CAC; ❑ = VAC; ⊕ = PO Statement; ‡ = Publisher's Report; Boldface figures = sworn; Light figures = estimated.

Nancy E. Kline, PhD, Editor-in-Chief. **ISSN:** 1043--4542 (print); **EISSN:** 1532--8457 (electronic). **Subscription Rates:** £296 Institutions print & e-access; £326 Institutions current volume print & all online content; £266 Institutions e-access; £340 Institutions content through 1998; £290 Institutions print only; £84 Individuals print only; £53 Institutions single print issue; £18 Individuals single print issue. **URL:** http://us.sagepub.com/en-us/nam/journal-of-pediatric-oncology-nursing/journal201668. **Ad Rates:** BW $1580; 4C $1235. **Remarks:** Accepts advertising. **Circ:** (Not Reported).

4728 ■ Journal of Planning History
SAGE Publications Inc.
2455 Teller Rd.
Thousand Oaks, CA 91320-2234
Free: 800-818-7243
Publisher's E-mail: sales@pfp.sagepub.com
Peer-reviewed journal focusing on the field of planning history. **Freq:** Quarterly. **Key Personnel:** Sonia Hirt, Editor; David Schuyler, Associate Editor. **ISSN:** 1538--5132 (print); **EISSN:** 1552--6585 (electronic). **Subscription Rates:** £343 Institutions combined (print & e-access); £309 Institutions e-access; £336 Institutions print only; £71 Individuals print only; £92 Institutions single print; £23 Individuals single print. **URL:** http://jph.sagepub.com; http://us.sagepub.com/en-us/nam/journal-of-planning-history/journal201631. **Ad Rates:** BW $725; 4C $1115. **Remarks:** Accepts advertising. **Circ:** (Not Reported).

4729 ■ Journal of Planning Literature: Incorporating the CPL Bibliographies
SAGE Publications Inc.
2455 Teller Rd.
Thousand Oaks, CA 91320-2234
Free: 800-818-7243
Publisher's E-mail: sales@pfp.sagepub.com
Journal on the literature of city and regional planning. Includes reviews of articles on major issues, abstracts of books and articles, and title listings of additional publications. **Freq:** Quarterly. **Print Method:** Offset. **Trim Size:** 8 1/2 x 11. **Cols./Page:** 2. **Col. Width:** 32 nonpareils. **Col. Depth:** 114 agate lines. **Key Personnel:** Bardia Nikrahei, Managing Editor; Tridib Banerjee, Board Member; Jack L. Nasar, Editor. **ISSN:** 0885--4122 (print); **EISSN:** 1552--6593 (electronic). **Subscription Rates:** $1573 Institutions combined (print & e-access); $1730 Institutions backfile lease, combined plus backfile; $1416 Institutions e-access; $1443 Institutions backfile, e-access (content through 1998); $1542 Institutions print only; $171 Individuals print only; $424 Institutions single print; $56 Individuals single print. **URL:** http://jpl.sagepub.com. **Ad Rates:** BW $875; 4C $1110. **Remarks:** Accepts advertising. **Circ:** (Not Reported).

4730 ■ Journal of Plastic Film and Sheeting
SAGE Publications Inc.
2455 Teller Rd.
Thousand Oaks, CA 91320-2234
Free: 800-818-7243
Journal focusing on the science and technology of plastic film and sheeting. **Founded:** 1985. **Freq:** Quarterly. **Print Method:** Offset. **Trim Size:** 6 x 9. **Cols./Page:** 1. **Col. Width:** 54 nonpareils. **Col. Depth:** 100 agate lines. **Key Personnel:** Douglas E. Hirt, Board Member; John R. Wagner, Jr., Editor-in-Chief; A. Ajji, Board Member; James P. Harrington, Editor, Founder; Ananda M. Chatterjee, Associate Editor; Syed S.H. Rizvi, Board Member. **ISSN:** 8756-0879 (print); **EISSN:** 1530-8014 (electronic). **Subscription Rates:** $1435 Institutions combined (print & e-access); $1579 Institutions combined plus backfile current volume print & all; $1292 Institutions e-access; $1436 Institutions e-access plus backfile (all online content); $1494 Institutions backfile purchase, e-access (content through 1998); $1406 Institutions print only; $387 Single issue institutional, print; $1360 Institutions print & e-access; $1496 Institutions print & all online content; $1224 Institutions e-access; $1360 Institutions all online content; $1416 Institutions backfile purchase, e-access; $1333 Institutions print only; $367 Institutions single print. **URL:** http://www.sagepub.com/journalsProdDesc.nav?prodId=Journal201584; http://jpf.sagepub.com. **Remarks:** Accepts advertising. **Circ:** 300.

4731 ■ Journal of Psychoeducational Assessment
SAGE Publications Inc.
2455 Teller Rd.
Thousand Oaks, CA 91320-2234
Free: 800-818-7243
Publisher's E-mail: sales@pfp.sagepub.com
Psychology and educational assessment journal. **Freq:** 8/year. **Print Method:** Offset. **Trim Size:** 7 x 10. **Cols./Page:** 1. **Col. Width:** 5 inches. **Col. Depth:** 8 inches. **Key Personnel:** Donald H. Saklofske, Editor. **ISSN:** 0734--2829 (print); **EISSN:** 1557--5144 (electronic). **Subscription Rates:** $1128 Institutions print only; $146 Individuals print only; $1151 Institutions print and e-access; $1036 Institutions e-access only; $24 Individuals single print; $155 Institutions single print. **URL:** http://jpa.sagepub.com. **Ad Rates:** BW $875; 4C $1110. **Remarks:** Accepts advertising. **Circ:** (Not Reported).

4732 ■ Journal of Psychopharmacology
SAGE Publications Inc.
2455 Teller Rd.
Thousand Oaks, CA 91320-2234
Free: 800-818-7243
Publisher's E-mail: sales@pfp.sagepub.com
Peer-reviewed journal focusing on preclinical and clinical aspects of psychopharmacology. **Freq:** Monthly. **Trim Size:** 215 x 280. **Key Personnel:** Pallab Seth, Manager; Pierre Blier, Editor; David J. Nutt, Editor. **ISSN:** 0269-8811 (print); **EISSN:** 1461-7285 (electronic). **Subscription Rates:** $2221 Institutions print & e-access; $2443 Institutions print & all online; $1999 Institutions e-access; $2039 Institutions e-access (content through 1998); $2177 Institutions print only; $178 Individuals print only; $200 Institutions single print issue; $19 Individuals single print issue. **URL:** http://www.sagepub.com/journalsProdDesc.nav?prodId=Journal200774. **Ad Rates:** BW $650; 4C $1,100. **Remarks:** Accepts advertising. **Circ:** 1400.

4733 ■ Journal of Reinforced Plastics and Composites
SAGE Publications Inc.
2455 Teller Rd.
Thousand Oaks, CA 91320-2234
Free: 800-818-7243
Peer-reviewed journal focusing on achievements in the science, technology, and economics of reinforced plastics and composites. **Freq:** Semimonthly. **Print Method:** Offset. **Trim Size:** 6 x 9. **Cols./Page:** 1. **Col. Width:** 54 nonpareils. **Col. Depth:** 100 agate lines. **Key Personnel:** George S. Springer, Editor-in-Chief. **ISSN:** 0731--6844 (print); **EISSN:** 1530--7964 (electronic). **Subscription Rates:** £5572 Institutions print & e-access; £6129 Institutions current volume print & all online content; £5015 Institutions e-access; £5572 Institutions all online content; £7245 Institutions backfile e-access thru 1998; £5461 Institutions print only; £250 Institutions single print. **URL:** http://jrp.sagepub.com; http://us.sagepub.com/en-us/nam/journal-of-reinforced-plastics-and-composites/journal201585. **Remarks:** Advertising accepted; rates available upon request. **Circ:** 320.

4734 ■ Journal of Research in Crime and Delinquency
SAGE Publications Inc.
2455 Teller Rd.
Thousand Oaks, CA 91320-2234
Free: 800-818-7243
Publisher's E-mail: sales@pfp.sagepub.com
Journal of research in criminology.Offers articles, research notes, review essays and special issues to keep updated on contemporary issues and controversies within the criminal field. **Freq:** Bimonthly February, March, May, July, August and November. **Print Method:** Offset. **Trim Size:** 5 1/2 x 8 1/2. **Cols./Page:** 1. **Col. Width:** 50 nonpareils. **Col. Depth:** 100 agate lines. **Key Personnel:** Michael Maxfield, Editor. **ISSN:** 0022--4278 (print); **EISSN:** 1552--731X (electronic). **Subscription Rates:** $1122 Institutions print & e-access; $1234 Institutions current volume print & all online content; $1010 Institutions e-access; $1122 Institutions all online content; $2758 Institutions e-access (content through 1998); $1100 Institutions print only; $171 Individuals print only; $202 Single issue institutional; $37 Single issue individual. **URL:** http://jrc.sagepub.com. **Ad Rates:** BW $875; 4C $1110. **Remarks:** Accepts advertising. **Circ:** (Not Reported).

4735 ■ Journal of Research in International Education
SAGE Publications Inc.
2455 Teller Rd.
Thousand Oaks, CA 91320-2234
Free: 800-818-7243
Publisher's E-mail: sales@pfp.sagepub.com
Peer-reviewed journal focusing on advancing the understanding and significance of international education. **Freq:** 3/year. **Key Personnel:** Mary Hayden, Editor-in-Chief; Jack Levy, Editor; Jeff Thompson, Editor; George Walker, Board Member; Helen Drennen, Board Member; Samir Chammaa, Board Member; Doug Boughton, Board Member. **ISSN:** 1475--2409 (print); **EISSN:** 1741--2943 (electronic). **Subscription Rates:** £416 Institutions for print and online; £374 Institutions for online; £208 Institutions for print; £52 Individuals print only; £150 Institutions single print; £23 Individuals single print. **URL:** http://jri.sagepub.com; http://us.sagepub.com/en-us/nam/journal-of-research-in-international-education/journal201574. **Remarks:** Advertising accepted; rates available upon request. **Circ:** (Not Reported).

4736 ■ Journal of Research in Nursing
SAGE Publications Inc.
2455 Teller Rd.
Thousand Oaks, CA 91320-2234
Free: 800-818-7243
Publisher's E-mail: sales@pfp.sagepub.com
Journal focusing on nursing topics and themes. **Freq:** 8/year. **Key Personnel:** Ann McMahon, Editor-in-Chief; Andree Le May, Editor-in-Chief; Veronica Bishop, Editor, Founder. **ISSN:** 1744--9871 (print); **EISSN:** 1744--988X (electronic). **Subscription Rates:** £529 Institutions print & e-access; £475 Institutions backfile e-access through 1998; £476 Institutions e-access; £475 Institutions print only; £54 Individuals print only; £71 Institutions single print; £9 Individuals single print. **URL:** http://jrn.sagepub.com; http://us.sagepub.com/en-us/nam/journal-of-research-in-nursing/journal201720. **Ad Rates:** BW $300. **Remarks:** Accepts advertising. **Circ:** (Not Reported).

4737 ■ Journal of Service Research
SAGE Publications Inc.
2455 Teller Rd.
Thousand Oaks, CA 91320-2234
Free: 800-818-7243
Publication E-mail: advertising@sagepub.com
Scholarly journal covering service research in marketing, management, operations, human resources, organizational design and information systems. **Founded:** Aug. 1998. **Freq:** Quarterly. **Key Personnel:** Mary Jo Bitner, Editor; A. Parasuraman, Advisor, Board Member; Katherine Lemon, Associate Editor. **ISSN:** 1094-6705 (print); **EISSN:** 1552-7379 (electronic). **Subscription Rates:** $1019 Institutions print and e-access; $917 Institutions e-access only; $999 Institutions print only; $146 Individuals print only; $47 Individuals single print; $275 Institutions single print. **URL:** http://www.sagepub.com/journalsProdDesc.nav?prodId=Journal200746. **Ad Rates:** BW $605. **Remarks:** Accepts advertising. **Circ:** (Not Reported).

4738 ■ Journal of Social Archaeology
SAGE Publications Inc.
2455 Teller Rd.
Thousand Oaks, CA 91320-2234
Free: 800-818-7243
Publisher's E-mail: sales@pfp.sagepub.com
Journal promoting interdisciplinary research focused on social approaches in archaeology. **Freq:** 3/year. **Key Personnel:** Lynn Meskell, Editor; Joshua Pollard, Editor. **ISSN:** 1469--6053 (print); **EISSN:** 1741--2951 (electronic). **Subscription Rates:** £462 Institutions combined (print & e-access); £416 Institutions e-access; £453 Institutions print only; £52 Individuals print only; £166 Institutions single print; £23 Individuals single print. **URL:** http://jsa.sagepub.com; http://us.sagepub.com/en-us/nam/journal-of-social-archaeology/journal201500. **Remarks:** Advertising accepted; rates available upon request. **Circ:** (Not Reported).

4739 ■ Journal of Social and Personal Relationships
SAGE Publications Inc.
2455 Teller Rd.
Thousand Oaks, CA 91320-2234
Free: 800-818-7243
Publisher's E-mail: sales@pfp.sagepub.com

Peer-reviewed journal focusing on social and personal relationships and on the fields of social psychology, clinical psychology, communication, developmental psychology, and sociology. **Freq:** 8/year. **Key Personnel:** Geoff MacDonald, Editor; John P. Caughlin, Advisor, Board Member; Steve Duck, Editor, Founder; Mario Mikulincer, Board Member; Paul A. Mongeau, Board Member, Advisor. **ISSN:** 0265--4075 (print); **EISSN:** 1460--3608 (electronic). **Subscription Rates:** £1198 Institutions for print and online; £1318 Institutions current volume print and all online content; £1078 Institutions e-access; £85 Individuals for print; £161 Institutions single print; £14 Individuals single print; £1374 Institutions backfile e-access through 1998; £1174 Institutions print only. **URL:** http://spr.sagepub.com; http://us.sagepub.com/en-us/nam/journal-of-social-and-personal-relationships/journal200790. **Remarks:** Advertising accepted; rates available upon request. **Circ:** (Not Reported).

4740 ■ Journal of Social Work
SAGE Publications Inc.
2455 Teller Rd.
Thousand Oaks, CA 91320-2234
Free: 800-818-7243
Publisher's E-mail: sales@pfp.sagepub.com
Journal aiming to advance theoretical understanding, shape policy, and inform practice of social work. **Freq:** Bimonthly. **Key Personnel:** Gayla Rogers, Board Member; Stewart Collins, Editor; Jan Fook, Board Member; David Stanley, Editor; Mel Gray, Board Member; Steven M. Shardlow, Editor-in-Chief. **ISSN:** 1468--0173 (print); **EISSN:** 1741--296X (electronic). **Subscription Rates:** £616 Institutions print & e-access; £554 Institutions e-access; £604 Institutions print only; £56 Individuals print only; £111 Institutions single print; £12 Individuals single print. **URL:** http://jsw.sagepub.com; http://us.sagepub.com/en-us/nam/journal-of-social-work/journal201477. **Ad Rates:** BW $200. **Remarks:** Accepts advertising. **Circ:** (Not Reported).

4741 ■ Journal of Sociology
SAGE Publications Inc.
2455 Teller Rd.
Thousand Oaks, CA 91320-2234
Free: 800-818-7243
Publisher's E-mail: admin@tasa.org.au
Freq: Quarterly. **Key Personnel:** Alphia Possamai-Inesedy, Editor-in-Chief. **ISSN:** 1440--7833 (print); **EISSN:** 1741--2978 (electronic). **Subscription Rates:** £405 Institutions print & e-access; £446 Institutions current volume print & all online content; £365 Institutions e-access; £406 Institutions all online content; £1055 Institutions backfile purchase, e-access (content through 1998); £397 Institutions print only; £52 Individuals print only; £109 Institutions single print; £17 Individuals single print. **URL:** http://us.sagepub.com/en-us/nam/journal/journal-sociology; http://jos.sagepub.com; http://www.tasa.org.au/publications/journal-of-sociology. **Mailing address:** PO Box 218, Hawthorn, VIC 3122, Australia. **Remarks:** Advertising accepted; rates available upon request. **Circ:** (Not Reported).

4742 ■ The Journal of Special Education
SAGE Publications Inc.
2455 Teller Rd.
Thousand Oaks, CA 91320-2234
Free: 800-818-7243
Publisher's E-mail: sales@pfp.sagepub.com
Journal presents research findings in the field of special education. **Freq:** Quarterly. **Print Method:** Offset. **Trim Size:** 8 x 10 7/8. **Cols./Page:** 1. **Col. Width:** 5 inches. **Col. Depth:** 7 1/2 inches. **Key Personnel:** Bob Algozzine, Editor; Fred Spooner, Editor; Ya-yu Lo, Board Member. **ISSN:** 0022--4669 (print); **EISSN:** 1538--4764 (electronic). **USPS:** 005-427. **Subscription Rates:** £41 Individuals print and online; £133 Institutions online only; £145 Institutions print only; £148 Institutions print and online; £13 Individuals single print only; £40 Institutions single print only. **URL:** http://sed.sagepub.com. **Ad Rates:** BW $515; 4C $995. **Remarks:** Advertising accepted; rates available upon request. **Circ:** Paid ‡3268, Non-paid ‡108.

4743 ■ Journal of Sport & Social Issues
SAGE Publications Inc.
2455 Teller Rd.
Thousand Oaks, CA 91320-2234
Free: 800-818-7243
Publication E-mail: advertising@sagepub.com
Journal on contemporary sports issues. The official journal of Northeastern University's Center for the Study of Sport in Society. **Freq:** Bimonthly. **Print Method:** Offset. **Trim Size:** 7 x 10. **Key Personnel:** Adrian Burgos, Jr., Assistant Editor; Monica Casper, Assistant Editor; David L. Andrews, Assistant Editor; C.L. Cole, Editor. **ISSN:** 0193-7235 (print); **EISSN:** 1552-7638 (electronic). **Subscription Rates:** £18 Single issue print; £82 Individuals print only; £83 Single issue print, Institutions; £414 Institutions e-access; £451 Institutions print only; £460 Institutions print and e-access; £560 Institutions current volume print and all online content; £712 Institutions e-access (content through 1998). **URL:** http://jss.sagepub.com; http://uk.sagepub.com/en-gb/asi/journal-of-sport-and-social-issues/journal200897. **Ad Rates:** BW $725. **Remarks:** Accepts advertising. **Circ:** Paid 600.

4744 ■ Journal of Sports Economics
SAGE Publications Inc.
2455 Teller Rd.
Thousand Oaks, CA 91320-2234
Free: 800-818-7243
Publisher's E-mail: sales@pfp.sagepub.com
Journal aiming to further research in the area of sports economics. **Freq:** 8/year. **Key Personnel:** Dennis Coates, Editor; Leo Kahane, Editor, Founder. **ISSN:** 1527--0025 (print); **EISSN:** 1552--7794 (electronic). **Subscription Rates:** £515 Institutions print & e-access; £464 Institutions e-access; £505 Institutions print only; £73 Individuals print only; £69 Institutions single print; £12 Individuals single print. **URL:** http://jse.sagepub.com; http://us.sagepub.com/en-us/nam/journal-of-sports-economics/journal200938. **Ad Rates:** BW $725; 4C $1115. **Remarks:** Accepts advertising. **Circ:** (Not Reported).

4745 ■ Journal of Studies in International Education
SAGE Publications Inc.
2455 Teller Rd.
Thousand Oaks, CA 91320-2234
Free: 800-818-7243
Publisher's E-mail: sales@pfp.sagepub.com
Official journal of the Association for Studies in International Education (ASIE). **Freq:** 5/year. **Key Personnel:** Eric Beerkens, Advisor; Betty Leask, Editor-in-Chief; Jeanine Hermans, Advisor; Philip G. Altbach, Advisor; Hans de Wit, Advisor. **ISSN:** 1028-3153 (print); **EISSN:** 1552-7808 (electronic). **Subscription Rates:** $819 Institutions print & e-access; $901 Institutions current volume print & all online content; $737 Institutions e-access; $819 Institutions all online content; $803 Institutions print only; $108 Individuals print only; $177 Institutions single print; $28 Individuals single print; $738 Institutions backfile e-access through 1998. **URL:** http://jsi.sagepub.com; http://www.sagepub.com/journalsProdDesc.nav?prodId=Journal201378. **Remarks:** Accepts advertising. **Circ:** (Not Reported).

4746 ■ Journal for the Study of the New Testament
SAGE Publications Inc.
2455 Teller Rd.
Thousand Oaks, CA 91320-2234
Free: 800-818-7243
Publisher's E-mail: sales@pfp.sagepub.com
Journal focusing on the study of the New Testament of the Bible. **Freq:** 5/year 5/yr. **Key Personnel:** Dr. Catrin H. Williams, Editor; Daniel K. Falk, Board Member; Peter Oakes, Board Member; Barry Matlock, Board Member; Simon Gathercole, Board Member. **ISSN:** 0142--064X (print); **EISSN:** 1745--5294 (electronic). **Subscription Rates:** £64 Individuals print; £374 Institutions e-access; £408 Institutions print; £416 Institutions print and e-access; £17 Individuals single print issue; £90 Institutions single print issue. **URL:** http://jnt.sagepub.com. **Remarks:** Accepts advertising. **Circ:** (Not Reported).

4747 ■ Journal for the Study of the Old Testament
SAGE Publications Inc.
2455 Teller Rd.
Thousand Oaks, CA 91320-2234
Free: 800-818-7243
Publisher's E-mail: sales@pfp.sagepub.com
Journal focusing on the study of the Old Testament of the Bible. **Freq:** 5/year. **Key Personnel:** Keith Bodner, Board Member; John Day, Board Member; Graeme Auld, Board Member; David Gunn, Board Member; John Jarick, Editor; Yvonne Sherwood, Editor. **ISSN:** 0309--0892 (print); **EISSN:** 1476--6728 (electronic). **Subscription Rates:** £64 Individuals print ; £374 Institutions e-access; £408 Institutions print; £416 Institutions print and e-access; £17 Individuals single print issue; £90 Institutions single print issue. **URL:** http://jot.sagepub.com. **Remarks:** Accepts advertising. **Circ:** (Not Reported).

4748 ■ Journal for the Study of the Pseudepigrapha
SAGE Publications Inc.
2455 Teller Rd.
Thousand Oaks, CA 91320-2234
Free: 800-818-7243
Publisher's E-mail: sales@pfp.sagepub.com
Journal focusing on the study of early Jewish literature. **Freq:** Quarterly. **Key Personnel:** Randall D. Chesnutt, Board Member; Doron Mendels, Board Member; Eileen Schuller, Board Member; Sidnie White Crawford, Board Member; Carol Newsom, Board Member; Phillip R. Davies, Board Member; Lorenzo DiTommaso, Editor; Robert Hayward, Editor; Loren Stuckenbruck, Editor. **ISSN:** 0951--8207 (print); **EISSN:** 1745--5286 (electronic). **Subscription Rates:** $93 Individuals print ; $729 Institutions e-access; $794 Institutions print; $810 Institutions print and e-access; $30 Individuals single print issue; $218 Institutions single print issue. **URL:** http://jsp.sagepub.com. **Remarks:** Accepts advertising. **Circ:** (Not Reported).

4749 ■ Journal of Teacher Education: The Journal of Policy, Practice, and Research in Teacher Education
SAGE Publications Inc.
2455 Teller Rd.
Thousand Oaks, CA 91320-2234
Free: 800-818-7243
Publisher's E-mail: sales@pfp.sagepub.com
Journal focusing on practice, policy, and research in teacher education. **Freq:** 5/year. **Trim Size:** 8 3/8 x 11. **ISSN:** 0022--4871 (print); **EISSN:** 1552--7816 (electronic). **Subscription Rates:** £392 Institutions combined (print & e-access); £392 Institutions current volume print & all content; £353 Institutions e-access; £1470 Institutions e-access (content through 1998); £384 Institutions print only; £76 Individuals print only; £84 Institutions single print; $20 Individuals single print. **URL:** http://jte.sagepub.com; http://uk.sagepub.com/en-gb/asi/journal-of-teacher-education/journal200961. **Ad Rates:** BW $1150; 4C $1475. **Remarks:** Accepts advertising. **Circ:** Paid ‡5800.

4750 ■ Journal of Theoretical Politics
SAGE Publications Inc.
2455 Teller Rd.
Thousand Oaks, CA 91320-2234
Free: 800-818-7243
Journal focusing with the development of theory in the study of political processes. **Freq:** Quarterly January, April, July, and October. **Key Personnel:** Keith Dowding, Board Member; Prof. Torun Dewan, Editor; John Patty, Editor; Gary W. Cox, Board Member; John Dryzek, Board Member; Nicholas R. Miller, Board Member; Kathleen Bawn, Board Member; Burt L. Monroe, Board Member; Jenna Bednar, Board Member; Josep M. Colomer, Board Member. **ISSN:** 0951--6298 (print); **EISSN:** 1460--3667 (electronic). **Subscription Rates:** £773 Institutions print & e-access; £850 Institutions print & all online content; £696 Institutions e-access; £773 Individuals all online content; £758 Institutions print only; £70 Individuals print only; £208 Institutions single print; £23 Individuals single print; £668 Institutions backfile e-access through 1998. **URL:** http://jtp.sagepub.com; http://us.sagepub.com/en-us/nam/journal/journal-theoretical-politics. **Remarks:** Advertising accepted; rates available upon request. **Circ:** (Not Reported).

4751 ■ Journal of Transcultural Nursing
SAGE Publications Inc.
2455 Teller Rd.
Thousand Oaks, CA 91320-2234
Free: 800-818-7243
Publisher's E-mail: staff@tcns.org
Journal focusing on topics that affect nursing and health

Circulation: ★ = AAM; △ or • = BPA; ♦ = CAC; ❑ = VAC; ⊕ = PO Statement; ‡ = Publisher's Report; Boldface figures = sworn; Light figures = estimated.

care clinical practice, research, education, and theory development. **Freq:** Bimonthly. **Key Personnel:** Marilyn Douglas, Editor; Marjory Spraycar, Managing Editor; Norma Cuellar, Editor-in-Chief. **ISSN:** 1043--6596 (print); **EISSN:** 1552--7832 (electronic). **Subscription Rates:** £562 Institutions print & e-access; £618 Institutions current volume print & all online content; £506 Institutions e-access; £562 Institutions all online content; £430 Institutions e-access (content through 1998); £551 Institutions print only; £93 Individuals print only; £101 Institutions single print; £20 Individuals single print. **URL:** http://tcn.sagepub.com; http://uk.sagepub.com/en-gb/asi/journal-of-transcultural-nursing/journal200814. **Remarks:** Advertising accepted; rates available upon request. **Circ:** (Not Reported).

4752 ■ Journal of Transformative Education
SAGE Publications Inc.
2455 Teller Rd.
Thousand Oaks, CA 91320-2234
Free: 800-818-7243
Publisher's E-mail: sales@pfp.sagepub.com
Peer-reviewed journal focusing on advancing the understanding, practice, and experience of transformative education. **Freq:** Quarterly. **Key Personnel:** Laura Markos, Editor, Founder; Ronald M. Cervero, Editor; Patricia Cranton, Editor; John M. Dirkx, Editor; Will McWhinney, Editor, Founder. **ISSN:** 1541--3446 (print); **EISSN:** 1552--7840 (electronic). **Subscription Rates:** £465 Institutions print & e-access; £419 Institutions e-access; £456 Institutions print only; £75 Individuals print only; £125 Institutions single print; £24 Individuals single print. **URL:** http://jtd.sagepub.com; http://uk.sagepub.com/en-gb/asi/journal-of-transformative-education/journal201653. **Remarks:** Advertising accepted; rates available upon request. **Circ:** (Not Reported).

4753 ■ Journal of Travel Research
SAGE Publications Inc.
2455 Teller Rd.
Thousand Oaks, CA 91320-2234
Free: 800-818-7243
Publisher's E-mail: sales@pfp.sagepub.com
Journal focusing on travel and tourism behavior, management and development. **Freq:** Bimonthly. **Key Personnel:** Charles Goeldner, Editor, Founder; Kathleen L. Andereck, Board Member; Richard R. Perdue, Editor. **ISSN:** 0047-2875 (print); **EISSN:** 1552-6763 (electronic). **Subscription Rates:** $804 Institutions for print and e-access; $724 Institutions e-access; $788 Institutions for print; $404 Individuals for print; $144 Institutions single print; $88 Individuals single print; $884 Institutions current volume print & all online content; $2213 Institutions backfile e-access through 1998. **URL:** http://jtr.sagepub.com; http://www.sagepub.com/journalsProdDesc.nav?ct_p=boards&prodId=Journal200788. **Remarks:** Accepts advertising. **Circ:** (Not Reported).

4754 ■ Journal of Urban History
SAGE Publications Inc.
2455 Teller Rd.
Thousand Oaks, CA 91320-2234
Free: 800-818-7243
Publisher's E-mail: sales@pfp.sagepub.com
Urban history journal. **Freq:** Bimonthly. **Print Method:** Offset. **Trim Size:** 7 x 10. **Cols./Page:** 1. **Col. Width:** 50 nonpareils. **Col. Depth:** 100 agate lines. **Key Personnel:** Timothy Gilfoyle, Associate Editor; Blaine A. Brownell, Board Member; Jurgen Buchenau, Board Member; David R. Goldfield, Editor. **ISSN:** 0096--1442 (print); **EISSN:** 1552--6771 (electronic). **Subscription Rates:** $1468 Institutions print & e-access; $1615 Institutions current volume print & all online content; $1321 Institutions e-access; $1468 Institutions e-access (all online content); $2694 Institutions e-access (content through 1998); $1439 Institutions print only; $171 Individuals print only; $264 Institutions single print; $37 Individuals single print. **URL:** http://juh.sagepub.com. **Ad Rates:** BW $875; 4C $1110. **Remarks:** Accepts advertising. **Circ:** (Not Reported).

4755 ■ Journal of Vacation Marketing
SAGE Publications Inc.
2455 Teller Rd.
Thousand Oaks, CA 91320-2234
Free: 800-818-7243
Publisher's E-mail: sales@pfp.sagepub.com
Journal focusing on the latest techniques, thinking and practice in the marketing of hotels, travel, tourism attractions, conventions and destinations. **Freq:** Quarterly. **Key Personnel:** Perry J.S. Hobson, Editor-in-Chief. **ISSN:** 1356--7667 (print); **EISSN:** 1479--1870 (electronic). **Subscription Rates:** £575 Institutions print & e-access; £633 Institutions current volume print & all online content; £518 Institutions e-access; £518 Institutions e-access (content through 1998); £564 Institutions print only; £141 Individuals print only; £155 Institutions single print; £46 Individuals single print. **URL:** http://jvm.sagepub.com; http://uk.sagepub.com/en-gb/asi/journal/journal-vacation-marketing. **Remarks:** Advertising accepted; rates available upon request. **Circ:** (Not Reported).

4756 ■ Journal of Vibration and Control
SAGE Publications Inc.
2455 Teller Rd.
Thousand Oaks, CA 91320-2234
Free: 800-818-7243
Publisher's E-mail: sales@pfp.sagepub.com
Peer-reviewed journal of analytical computational and experimental studies of vibration phenomena. **Freq:** 16/yr. **Key Personnel:** Fabio Casciati, Editor; Thomas Burton, Board Member; Nabil Chalhoub, Associate Editor; Mohamed Abdel Rohman, Board Member; Khaled Asfar, Associate Editor; Balakumar Balachandran, Associate Editor; Mehdi Ahmadian, Editor-in-Chief. **ISSN:** 1077--5463 (print); **EISSN:** 1741--2986 (electronic). **Subscription Rates:** £2150 Institutions print & e-access; £1826 Institutions backfile purchase, e-access (content through 1998); £2107 Institutions print only; £1935 Institutions e-access; £144 Individuals print only; £116 Institutions single print; £9 Individuals single print. **URL:** http://jvc.sagepub.com; http://uk.sagepub.com/en-gb/asi/journal/journal-vibration-and-control. **Remarks:** Advertising accepted; rates available upon request. **Circ:** (Not Reported).

4757 ■ Journal of Visual Culture
SAGE Publications Inc.
2455 Teller Rd.
Thousand Oaks, CA 91320-2234
Free: 800-818-7243
Publisher's E-mail: sales@pfp.sagepub.com
Journal promoting research, scholarship and critical engagement with visual cultures. **Freq:** 3/year. **Key Personnel:** Mark Little, Editor; Dominic Willsdon, Board Member; Raiford Guins, Editor; Joanne Morra, Editor; Susan Pui San Lok, Board Member; Marquard Smith, Editor-in-Chief. **ISSN:** 1470--4129 (print); **EISSN:** 1741--2994 (electronic). **Subscription Rates:** £428 Institutions combined (print & e-access); £385 Institutions e-access; £419 Institutions print only; £50 Individuals print only; £154 Institutions single print; £22 Individuals single print. **URL:** http://vcu.sagepub.com; http://uk.sagepub.com/en-gb/asi/journal/journal-visual-culture. **Remarks:** Advertising accepted; rates available upon request. **Circ:** (Not Reported).

4758 ■ Journalism
SAGE Publications Inc.
2455 Teller Rd.
Thousand Oaks, CA 91320-2234
Free: 800-818-7243
Publisher's E-mail: sales@pfp.sagepub.com
Peer-reviewed journal focusing on the social, economic, political, cultural and practical understanding of journalism. **Freq:** 8/year. **Key Personnel:** Howard Tumber, Editor; Barbie Zelizer, Editor. **ISSN:** 1464-8849 (print); **EISSN:** 1741-3001 (electronic). **Subscription Rates:** $1228 Institutions print & e-access; $1105 Institutions e-access; $1203 Institutions print only; $118 Individuals print only; $165 Institutions single print; $19 Individuals single print. **URL:** http://jou.sagepub.com; http://www.sagepub.com/journalsProdDesc.nav?prodId=Journal200905. **Remarks:** Accepts advertising. **Circ:** (Not Reported).

4759 ■ Labor Studies Journal
SAGE Publications Inc.
2455 Teller Rd.
Thousand Oaks, CA 91320-2234
Free: 800-818-7243
Publisher's E-mail: info@uale.org
Journal exploring the role of the trade union movement in forging American economic and social policy. **Freq:** Quarterly March, June, September, December. **Print Method:** Offset. **Trim Size:** 5 x 9. **Key Personnel:** Bob Bruno; Bruce Nissen, Advisor; Lynn Feekin, Editor; Michelle Kaminski, Editor. **ISSN:** 0160-449X (print); **EISSN:** 1538-9758 (electronic). **Subscription Rates:** $66 Individuals print; $119 Institutions single copy; $432 Institutions print; $397 Institutions electronic; $441 Institutions print and electronic; $21 Individuals Single Print Issue. **URL:** http://us.sagepub.com/en-us/nam/labor-studies-journal/journal201857; http://uale.org/labor-studies-journal; http://www.sagepub.com/journals/Journal201857/subscribe. **Ad Rates:** BW $515; 4C $995. **Remarks:** Accepts advertising. **Circ:** Paid ‡800.

4760 ■ Language and Literature
SAGE Publications Inc.
2455 Teller Rd.
Thousand Oaks, CA 91320-2234
Free: 800-818-7243
Journal of the Poetics and Linguistics Association covering developments in stylistic analysis, the linguistic analysis of literature and related areas. **Freq:** Quarterly. **Key Personnel:** Catherine Emmott, Assistant Editor; Derek Attridge, Board Member; Mick Short, Board Member; David L. Hoover, Board Member; Geoff Hall, Editor. **ISSN:** 0963--9470 (print); **EISSN:** 1461--7293 (electronic). **Subscription Rates:** £610 Institutions combined (print & e-access); £671 Institutions current volume print & all online content; £551 Institutions e-access (content through 1998); £598 Institutions print only; £164 Institutions single print; £21 Individuals single print; £549 Institutions e-access; £66 Individuals e-access (content through 1998). **URL:** http://lal.sagepub.com; http://www.pala.ac.uk/language-and-literature.html; http://uk.sagepub.com/en-gb/asi/language-and-literature/journal200860. **Ad Rates:** BW $250; BW £650. **Remarks:** Accepts advertising. **Circ:** (Not Reported).

4761 ■ Language Testing
SAGE Publications Inc.
2455 Teller Rd.
Thousand Oaks, CA 91320-2234
Free: 800-818-7243
Publisher's E-mail: sales@pfp.sagepub.com
Peer-reviewed journal dedicated to language testing. **Freq:** Quarterly. **Print Method:** Offset. **Trim Size:** 5 1/2 x 8 1/2. **Cols./Page:** 1. **Col. Width:** 50 nonpareils. **Col. Depth:** 100 agate lines. **Key Personnel:** Glenn Fulcher, Editor. **ISSN:** 0265--5322 (print); **EISSN:** 1477--0946 (electronic). **URL:** http://ltj.sagepub.com. **Remarks:** Accepts advertising. **Circ:** (Not Reported).

4762 ■ Leadership
SAGE Publications Inc.
2455 Teller Rd.
Thousand Oaks, CA 91320-2234
Free: 800-818-7243
Publisher's E-mail: sales@pfp.sagepub.com
Peer-reviewed journal focusing on the understanding and significance of leadership in the economic, political, technological and social relations of organization and society. **Freq:** Quarterly. **Key Personnel:** David Collinson, Editor, Reviewer; Richard Badham, Editor, Reviewer; Keith Grint, Editor, Reviewer. **ISSN:** 1742--7150 (print); **EISSN:** 1742--7169 (electronic). **Subscription Rates:** £621 Institutions print & e-access; £559 Institutions e-access; £609 Institutions print only; £73 Individuals print only; £134 Institutions single print; £19 Individuals single print. **URL:** http://lea.sagepub.com; http://uk.sagepub.com/en-gb/asi/journal/leadership. **Remarks:** Advertising accepted; rates available upon request. **Circ:** (Not Reported).

4763 ■ Local Economy
SAGE Publications Inc.
2455 Teller Rd.
Thousand Oaks, CA 91320-2234
Free: 800-818-7243
Publisher's E-mail: sales@pfp.sagepub.com
Journal providing information on local economic policies and social justice. **Freq:** 8/year. **Print Method:** Offset. **Cols./Page:** 6. **Col. Width:** 12 picas. **Col. Depth:** 21 inches. **Key Personnel:** Munir Morad, Editor; Andrew Jones, Executive Editor. **ISSN:** 0269--0942 (print); **EISSN:** 1470--9325 (electronic). **Subscription Rates:** £87 Individuals print; £504 Institutions e-access; £549 Institutions print only; £560 Institutions e-access plus backfile (all online content); £560 Institutions print and e-access; £616 Institutions combined plus backfile (cur-

rent volume print and all online content); £642 Institutions e-access (content through 1998); £14 Individuals single print; £75 Institutions single print. **URL:** http://lec.sagepub.com. **Ad Rates:** BW £650. **Remarks:** Accepts advertising. **Circ:** (Not Reported).

4764 ■ Management Communication Quarterly: An International Journal
SAGE Publications Inc.
2455 Teller Rd.
Thousand Oaks, CA 91320-2234
Free: 800-818-7243
Publisher's E-mail: sales@pfp.sagepub.com
Journal on communication research, with a focus on managerial and organizational effectiveness. **Freq:** Quarterly. **Print Method:** Offset. **Trim Size:** 5 1/2 x 8 1/2. **Cols./Page:** 1. **Col. Width:** 50 nonpareils. **Col. Depth:** 100 agate lines. **Key Personnel:** Patricia M. Sias, Editor; Ling Chen, Board Member; Charles Conrad, Board Member; James Barker, Board Member. **ISSN:** 0893--3189 (print); **EISSN:** 1552--6798 (electronic). **Subscription Rates:** $793 Institutions e-access; $872 Institutions all online content; $810 Institutions e-access (content through 1998); $150 Individuals e-access. **URL:** http://mcq.sagepub.com. **Ad Rates:** BW $875; 4C $1110. **Remarks:** Accepts advertising. **Circ:** (Not Reported).

4765 ■ Management Learning
SAGE Publications Inc.
2455 Teller Rd.
Thousand Oaks, CA 91320-2234
Free: 800-818-7243
Publisher's E-mail: sales@pfp.sagepub.com
Peer-reviewed journal focusing on the understanding of learning in management and organizations. **Freq:** 5/year. **Key Personnel:** Ann Cunliffe, Editor-in-Chief; Russ Vince, Board Member; Craig Prichard, Board Member; Bente Elkjaer, Board Member. **ISSN:** 1350--5076 (print); **EISSN:** 1461--7307 (electronic). **Subscription Rates:** £767 Institutions print & e-access; £844 Institutions print & all online content; £690 Institutions e-access; £767 Institutions e-access (all online content); £1698 Institutions e-access (content through 1998); £752 Institutions print only; £75 Individuals print only; £165 Institutions single print; £20 Individuals single print. **URL:** http://mlq.sagepub.com; http://uk.sagepub.com/en-gb/asi/journal/management-learning. **Remarks:** Advertising accepted; rates available upon request. **Circ:** (Not Reported).

4766 ■ Marketing Theory
SAGE Publications Inc.
2455 Teller Rd.
Thousand Oaks, CA 91320-2234
Free: 800-818-7243
Publisher's E-mail: sales@pfp.sagepub.com
Peer-reviewed journal focusing on the development and dissemination of alternative and critical perspectives on marketing theory. **Freq:** Quarterly March, June, September, and December. **Key Personnel:** Rod Brodie, Associate Editor; Bernard Cova, Board Member; Evert Gummesson, Advisor, Board Member; Jaqueline Pels, Board Member; Gordon R. Foxall, Advisor, Board Member; Michael AJ. Saren, Advisor, Board Member; Les Carlson, Board Member; Pauline Maclaran, Editor-in-Chief. **ISSN:** 1470--5931 (print); **EISSN:** 1741--301X (electronic). **Subscription Rates:** £62 Individuals Print Only; £513 Institutions E-access; £559 Institutions Print Only; £570 Institutions Combined (Print & E-access); £20 Individuals single print issue; £154 Institutions single print issue. **URL:** http://uk.sagepub.com/en-gb/eur/journal/marketing-theory. **Remarks:** Advertising accepted; rates available upon request. **Circ:** (Not Reported).

4767 ■ Mathematics and Mechanics of Solids
SAGE Publications Inc.
2455 Teller Rd.
Thousand Oaks, CA 91320-2234
Free: 800-818-7243
Publisher's E-mail: sales@pfp.sagepub.com
Peer-reviewed journal focusing on research in solid mechanics and materials science. **Freq:** 8/year. **Key Personnel:** R.C. Batra, Editor; L.T. Wheeler, Founder, Editor; David J. Steigmann, Editor-in-Chief; C.O. Horgan, Editor. **ISSN:** 1081--2865 (print); **EISSN:** 1741--3028 (electronic). **Subscription Rates:** £1853 Institutions print & e-access; £2038 Institutions current volume print & all online content; £1668 Institutions e-access; £1816 Institutions print only; £97 Individuals print only; £200 Institutions single print; £13 Individuals single print. **URL:** http://mms.sagepub.com; http://uk.sagepub.com/en-gb/asi/mathematics-and-mechanics-of-solids/journal201478. **Remarks:** Advertising accepted; rates available upon request. **Circ:** (Not Reported).

4768 ■ Measurement and Evaluation in Counseling and Development
SAGE Publications Inc.
2455 Teller Rd.
Thousand Oaks, CA 91320-2234
Free: 800-818-7243
Publisher's E-mail: sales@pfp.sagepub.com
Journal containing professional articles on testing and evaluation. **Founded:** 1968. **Freq:** Quarterly January, April, July, October. **Print Method:** Offset. **Trim Size:** 7 X 10. **Key Personnel:** Paul Peluso, Editor. **ISSN:** 0748-1756 (print). **Subscription Rates:** $24 Individuals print only, single issue; $116 Institutions print only, single issue; $429 Institutions print and e-access. **URL:** http://www.counseling.org/publications/counseling-journals; http://www.sagepub.com/journalsProdDesc.nav?prodId=Journal201951&. **Remarks:** Advertising accepted; rates available upon request. **Circ:** Paid 1500.

4769 ■ Media, Culture and Society
SAGE Publications Inc.
2455 Teller Rd.
Thousand Oaks, CA 91320-2234
Free: 800-818-7243
Publisher's E-mail: sales@pfp.sagepub.com
Journal providing an international forum for the presentation of research and discussion concerning the media, including the newer information and communication technologies, within their political, economic, cultural and historical contexts. **Freq:** 8/year. **Key Personnel:** Lord Asa Briggs, Editor; Jean-Claude Burgelman, Editor; Raymond Boyle, Editor; Anna Reading, Editor; John Corner, Editor; Adigun Agbaje, Editor; Paddy Scannell, Editor; Philip Schlesinger, Editor; Colin Sparks, Editor. **ISSN:** 0163-4437 (print); **EISSN:** 1460-3675 (electronic). **Subscription Rates:** $1979 Institutions combined (print & e-access); $2177 Institutions backfile lease, combined plus backfile; $1781 Institutions e-access; $3028 Institutions backfile purchase, e-access (content through 1998); $1939 Institutions print only; $152 Individuals print only; $267 Institutions single print; $25 Individuals single print. **URL:** http://www.sagepub.com/journalsProdDesc.nav?prodId=Journal200958. **Remarks:** Accepts advertising. **Circ:** (Not Reported).

4770 ■ Medical Care Research and Review
SAGE Publications Inc.
2455 Teller Rd.
Thousand Oaks, CA 91320-2234
Free: 800-818-7243
Publisher's E-mail: sales@pfp.sagepub.com
Journal covering timely aspects of health care. **Freq:** Bimonthly. **Key Personnel:** Gloria Bazzoli, Editor; Laurence Baker, Board Member; Jeffrey A. Alexander, Editor; Thomas A. D'Aunno, Editor. **ISSN:** 1077--5587 (print); **EISSN:** 1552--6801 (electronic). **Subscription Rates:** £741 Institutions for print and online; £815 Institutions current volume print & all online content; £726 Institutions print only; £667 Individuals online only; £133 Institutions single print; £30 Individuals single print; £3120 Institutions backfile e-access through 1998. **URL:** http://mcr.sagepub.com; http://uk.sagepub.com/en-gb/asi/medical-care-research-and-review/journal200970. **Remarks:** Advertising accepted; rates available upon request. **Circ:** (Not Reported).

4771 ■ Medical Decision Making
SAGE Publications Inc.
2455 Teller Rd.
Thousand Oaks, CA 91320-2234
Free: 800-818-7243
Publisher's E-mail: info@smdm.org
Journal focusing on health economics, technology assessment, outcomes research and quality of life research. **Freq:** 8/year. **Key Personnel:** Robert M. Hamm, PhD, Associate Editor; Alan J. Schwartz, PhD, Editor. **ISSN:** 0272--989X (print); **EISSN:** 1552--681X (electronic). **Subscription Rates:** £412 Institutions print & e-access; £453 Institutions print & all online content; £175 Individuals print only; £56 Institutions single print issue; £28 Individuals single print issue. **URL:** http://mdm.sagepub.com; http://uk.sagepub.com/en-gb/asi/medical-decision-making/journal201430. **Ad Rates:** BW $840; 4C $1100. **Remarks:** Accepts advertising. **Circ:** (Not Reported).

4772 ■ The Medieval History Journal
SAGE Publications Inc.
2455 Teller Rd.
Thousand Oaks, CA 91320-2234
Free: 800-818-7243
Publisher's E-mail: sales@pfp.sagepub.com
Journal focusing on all aspects of societies in the medieval universe. **Freq:** Semiannual. **Key Personnel:** Monica Juneja, Editor; Harbans Mukhia, Editor; Rajat Datta, Editor. **ISSN:** 0971--9458 (print); **EISSN:** 0973--0753 (electronic). **Subscription Rates:** £209 Institutions print & e-access; £230 Institutions current volume print & all online content; £188 Institutions e-access; £209 Institutions e-access plus backfile (all online content); £187 Institutions backfile purchase, e-access (content through 1998); £205 Institutions print only; £47 Individuals print only; £113 Single issue institutional; £31 Single issue individual. **URL:** http://mhj.sagepub.com; http://uk.sagepub.com/en-gb/asi/the-medieval-history-journal/journal200760. **Remarks:** Advertising accepted; rates available upon request. **Circ:** (Not Reported).

4773 ■ Men and Masculinities
SAGE Publications Inc.
2455 Teller Rd.
Thousand Oaks, CA 91320-2234
Free: 800-818-7243
Publisher's E-mail: sales@pfp.sagepub.com
Journal exploring the evolving roles and perceptions of men across society. **Freq:** 5/year. **Key Personnel:** Michael Kimmel, Editor; Jeff Hearn, Editor. **ISSN:** 1097--184X (print); **EISSN:** 1552--6828 (electronic). **Subscription Rates:** £438 Institutions e-access; £482 Institutions all online content; £438 Institutions content through 1998; £93 Individuals e-access. **Alt. Formats:** Print. **URL:** http://jmm.sagepub.com; http://uk.sagepub.com/en-gb/asi/men-and-masculinities/journal200971. **Ad Rates:** BW $725; 4C $1115. **Remarks:** Accepts advertising. **Circ:** (Not Reported).

4774 ■ Modern China: An International Quarterly of History and Social Science
SAGE Publications Inc.
2455 Teller Rd.
Thousand Oaks, CA 91320-2234
Free: 800-818-7243
Publisher's E-mail: sales@pfp.sagepub.com
Chinese society and modern history journal. **Freq:** Bimonthly. **Print Method:** Offset. **Trim Size:** 5 1/2 x 8 1/2. **Cols./Page:** 1. **Col. Width:** 50 nonpareils. **Col. Depth:** 100 agate lines. **Key Personnel:** Philip C.C. Huang, Editor. **ISSN:** 0097--7004 (print); **EISSN:** 1552--6836 (electronic). **Subscription Rates:** $1627 Institutions print & e-access; $1790 Institutions current volume print & all online content; $1464 Institutions e-access; $1627 Institutions e-access (all online content); $2989 Institutions e-access (content through 1998); $1594 Institutions print only; $180 Individuals print only; $292 Institutions single print; $39 Individuals single print. **URL:** http://mcx.sagepub.com. **Ad Rates:** BW $875; 4C $1110. **Remarks:** Accepts advertising. **Circ:** (Not Reported).

4775 ■ National Institute Economic Review
SAGE Publications Inc.
2455 Teller Rd.
Thousand Oaks, CA 91320-2234
Free: 800-818-7243
Publisher's E-mail: enquires@niesr.ac.uk
Journal of the National Institute of Economic and Social Research in Britain. **Freq:** Quarterly February, May, August and November. **Key Personnel:** Jonathan Portes, Editor. **ISSN:** 0027--9501 (print); **EISSN:** 1741--3036 (electronic). **Subscription Rates:** £460 Institutions print & e-access; £506 Institutions print & all online; £414 Institutions e-access; £451 Institutions print only; £138 Individuals print only; £124 Institutions single print; £45 Individuals single print; £1395 Institutions backfile e-access through 1998. **URL:** http://ner.sagepub.com; http://www.niesr.ac.uk/national-institute-economic-review; http://us.sagepub.com/en-us/nam/national-institute-economic-review/journal201248. **Remarks:** Ad-

Circulation: ★ = AAM; △ or • = BPA; ♦ = CAC; ❑ = VAC; ⊕ = PO Statement; ‡ = Publisher's Report; Boldface figures = sworn; Light figures = estimated.

vertising accepted; rates available upon request. **Circ:** (Not Reported).

4776 ■ NETWORK Magazine
Pituitary Network Association
PO Box 1958
Thousand Oaks, CA 91358-1958
Phone: (805)499-9973
Fax: (805)480-0633
Publisher's E-mail: info@pituitary.org
Magazine featuring medical and patient articles. **Freq:** Quarterly. **Remarks:** Advertising not accepted. **Circ:** (Not Reported).

4777 ■ Neurohabilitation and Neural Repair
SAGE Publications Inc.
2455 Teller Rd.
Thousand Oaks, CA 91320-2234
Free: 800-818-7243
Publisher's E-mail: sales@pfp.sagepub.com
Journal on functional recovery from neural injury and long term neurologic care.Contains articles designed to appeal to a variety of audiences: clinical practice, research, brief communications, case reports, reviews, and media reviews. **Freq:** 10/year. **Print Method:** Web Offset. **Trim Size:** 8 1/2 x 11. **Cols./Page:** 2. **Col. Width:** 19 picas. **Col. Depth:** 57 picas. **Key Personnel:** Bruce H. Dobkin, Editor; Randolph J. Juno, Editor-in-Chief. **ISSN:** 1545--9683 (print); **EISSN:** 1552--6844 (electronic). **Subscription Rates:** $299 Individuals print only; $1778 Institutions online only; $1936 Institutions print only; $1975 Institutions print and online; $39 Individuals single print; $213 Institutions single print. **URL:** http://nnr.sagepub.com. **Formerly**: Journal of Neurologic Rehabilitation. **Ad Rates:** BW $775; 4C $995. **Remarks:** Accepts advertising. **Circ:** Paid 1850, Non-paid 50.

4778 ■ The Neurohospitalist
SAGE Publications Inc.
2455 Teller Rd.
Thousand Oaks, CA 91320-2234
Free: 800-818-7243
Publisher's E-mail: sales@pfp.sagepub.com
Peer-reviewed journal focusing on practice and performance of neurohospitalist medicine. **Freq:** Quarterly January, April, July, and October. **Key Personnel:** Vanja Douglas, MD, Editor. **ISSN:** 1941--8744 (print); **EISSN:** 1941--8752 (electronic). **Subscription Rates:** $387 Institutions print and e-access; $348 Institutions e-access; $379 Institutions print; $114 Individuals print and e-access; $104 Institutions single issue; $37 Individuals single issue. **URL:** http://us.sagepub.com/en-us/nam/the-neurohospitalist/journal202009. **Remarks:** Accepts advertising. **Circ:** (Not Reported).

4779 ■ The Neuroscientist
SAGE Publications Inc.
2455 Teller Rd.
Thousand Oaks, CA 91320-2234
Free: 800-818-7243
Publisher's E-mail: sales@pfp.sagepub.com
Journal focusing on advances and key trends in molecular, cellular, developmental, behavioral/systems, and cognitive neuroscience. **Freq:** Bimonthly. **Key Personnel:** Cord-Michael Becker, Associate Editor; Thomas N. Byrne, Associate Editor; Eric J. Nestler, Associate Editor; Charles G. Gross, Associate Editor; Benjamin S. Bunney, Jr., Board Member; Eric R. Kandel, Board Member; Albert J. Aguayo, Board Member; Masao Ito, Associate Editor; Stephen Waxman, Editor; Robert L. Barchi, Board Member. **ISSN:** 1073--8584 (print); **EISSN:** 1089--4098 (electronic). **Subscription Rates:** £941 Institutions print & e-access; £941 Institutions current volume print & all online content; £847 Institutions e-access; £922 Institutions print only; £170 Individuals print only; £169 Institutions single print; £37 Individuals single print; £847 Institutions backfile e-access through 1998. **URL:** http://nro.sagepub.com; http://us.sagepub.com/en-us/nam/the-neuroscientist/journal200902. **Remarks:** Advertising accepted; rates available upon request. **Circ:** (Not Reported).

4780 ■ New Media & Society
SAGE Publications Inc.
2455 Teller Rd.
Thousand Oaks, CA 91320-2234
Free: 800-818-7243
Publisher's E-mail: sales@pfp.sagepub.com
Journal focusing on the social dynamics of media and information change. **Freq:** 8/year. **Key Personnel:** Steve Jones, Editor; Dave Park, Editor; Nancy K. Baym, Board Member; Keith Hampton, Editor; Roger Silverstone, Editor. **ISSN:** 1461--4448 (print); **EISSN:** 1461--7315 (electronic). **Subscription Rates:** £58 Individuals for print; PTE140 Institutions single print; £7 Individuals single print. **URL:** http://nms.sagepub.com; http://us.sagepub.com/en-us/nam/journal/new-media-society. **Remarks:** Advertising accepted; rates available upon request. **Circ:** (Not Reported).

4781 ■ Nonprofit and Voluntary Sector Quarterly
SAGE Publications Inc.
2455 Teller Rd.
Thousand Oaks, CA 91320-2234
Free: 800-818-7243
Publication E-mail: advertising@sagepub.com
Journal of research articles on philanthropy, voluntarism, citizen participation, and the nonprofit sector. **Freq:** Quarterly. **Print Method:** Offset. **Trim Size:** 7 x 10 1/2. **Cols./Page:** 1. **Col. Width:** 27 picas. **Col. Depth:** 45 picas. **Key Personnel:** Femida Handy, Editor; Jeffrey Brudney, Editor. **ISSN:** 0899-7640 (print). **Subscription Rates:** $515 Institutions print & e-access; $20 Individuals single print only; $464 Institutions e-access; $516 Institutions all online content; $1063 Institutions content through 1998; $505 Institutions print; $94 Individuals print; $93 Institutions single print. **URL:** http://nvs.sagepub.com; http://www.sagepub.com/journalsProdDesc.nav?prodId=Journal200775. **Formerly**: Journal of Voluntary Action Research. **Ad Rates:** BW $515; 4C $995. **Remarks:** Accepts advertising. **Circ:** 1700.

4782 ■ Nursing Science Quarterly
SAGE Publications Inc.
2455 Teller Rd.
Thousand Oaks, CA 91320-2234
Free: 800-818-7243
Publisher's E-mail: sales@pfp.sagepub.com
Journal focusing on enhancement of nursing knowledge. **Freq:** Quarterly. **Key Personnel:** John R. Phillips, PhD, Board Member; Gail J. Mitchell, PhD, Board Member; Constance L. Milton, PhD, Editor; William K. Cody, PhD, Board Member; Debra A. Bournes, Managing Editor; Sandra Schmidt Bunkers, PhD, Board Member; Rosemarie Rizzo Parse, PhD, Editor. **ISSN:** 0894--3184 (print); **EISSN:** 1552--7409 (electronic). **Subscription Rates:** £454 Institutions combined (print & e-access); £499 Institutions combined plus backfile current volume print & all; £409 Institutions e-access; £454 Institutions e-access plus backfile (all online content); £409 Institutions e-access (content through 1998); £445 Institutions print only; £100 Individuals print only; £122 Institutions single print; £33 Individuals single print. **URL:** http://nsq.sagepub.com; http://us.sagepub.com/en-us/nam/nursing-science-quarterly/journal200789. **Remarks:** Accepts advertising. **Circ:** (Not Reported).

4783 ■ Organization
SAGE Publications Inc.
2455 Teller Rd.
Thousand Oaks, CA 91320-2234
Free: 800-818-7243
Publisher's E-mail: sales@pfp.sagepub.com
Journal focusing on organization studies including current and emergent theoretical and substantive developments in the field. **Freq:** Bimonthly. **Key Personnel:** Martin Parker, Board Member; Robyn Thomas, Editor-in-Chief; Yvonne Benschop, Associate Editor. **ISSN:** 1350--5084 (print); **EISSN:** 1461--7323 (electronic). **Subscription Rates:** £1044 Institutions print & e-access; £1148 Institutions current volume print & all online; £940 Institutions e-access; £1044 Individuals e-access & all online; £1023 Institutions print only; £80 Individuals print only; £188 Institutions single print; £17 Individuals single print; £948 Institutions backfile e-access thru 1998. **URL:** http://org.sagepub.com; http://us.sagepub.com/en-us/nam/journal/organization. **Remarks:** Advertising accepted; rates available upon request. **Circ:** (Not Reported).

4784 ■ Organization & Environment
SAGE Publications Inc.
2455 Teller Rd.
Thousand Oaks, CA 91320-2234
Free: 800-818-7243
Publisher's E-mail: sales@pfp.sagepub.com
Journal focusing on connections between the natural environment and formal and informal patterns of organizing. **Freq:** Quarterly. **Key Personnel:** Carolyn Egri, Board Member; John M. Jermier, Founder, Editor. **ISSN:** 1086--0266 (print); **EISSN:** 1552--7417 (electronic). **Subscription Rates:** £73 Individuals e-access; £498 Institutions e-access content through 1998; £498 Institutions e-access; £548 Institutions e-access plus backfile all online content. **URL:** http://us.sagepub.com/en-us/nam/organization-environment/journal200856; http://oae.sagepub.com. **Ad Rates:** BW $725; 4C $1115. **Remarks:** Accepts advertising. **Circ:** (Not Reported).

4785 ■ Organization Studies
SAGE Publications Inc.
2455 Teller Rd.
Thousand Oaks, CA 91320-2234
Free: 800-818-7243
Publisher's E-mail: sales@pfp.sagepub.com
Journal focusing on the understanding of organizations, organizing, and the organized in and between societies. **Freq:** Monthly. **Key Personnel:** David Courpasson, Editor-in-Chief; Sophia Tzagaraki, Managing Editor. **ISSN:** 0170-8406 (print); **EISSN:** 1741-3044 (electronic). **Subscription Rates:** $2250 Institutions print & e-access; $2475 Institutions print & all online; $2025 Institutions e-access; $3272 Institutions e-access (content through 1998); $2205 Institutions print only; $205 Individuals print only; $202 Institutions single print; $22 Individuals single print. **URL:** http://oss.sagepub.com; http://www.sagepub.com/journalsProdDesc.nav?ct_p=boards&prodId=Journal201657. **Remarks:** Accepts advertising. **Circ:** (Not Reported).

4786 ■ Organizational Psychology Review
SAGE Publications Inc.
2455 Teller Rd.
Thousand Oaks, CA 91320-2234
Free: 800-818-7243
Publisher's E-mail: sales@pfp.sagepub.com
Peer-reviewed journal publishing original conceptual work and meta-analyses in the field of organizational psychology. **Freq:** Quarterly February, May, August, and November. **Key Personnel:** Daan van Knippenberg, Editor. **ISSN:** 2041--3866 (print); **EISSN:** 2041--3874 (electronic). **Subscription Rates:** £522 Institutions print and e-access; £512 Institutions print only; £63 Individuals print only; £141 Institutions single issue; £20 Individuals single issue. **URL:** http://uk.sagepub.com/en-gb/asi/organizational-psychology-review/journal201979. **Remarks:** Accepts advertising. **Circ:** (Not Reported).

4787 ■ Organizational Research Methods
SAGE Publications Inc.
2455 Teller Rd.
Thousand Oaks, CA 91320-2234
Free: 800-818-7243
Publisher's E-mail: sales@pfp.sagepub.com
Peer-reviewed journal focusing on the understanding of current and new methodologies and their application in organizational settings. **Freq:** Quarterly. **Key Personnel:** Jose M. Cortina, Board Member; James M. LeBreton, Editor. **ISSN:** 1094--4281 (print); **EISSN:** 1552--7425 (electronic). **Subscription Rates:** £691 Institutions print & e-access; £760 Institutions current volume print & all online content; £622 Institutions e-access; £622 Institutions content through 1998; £677 Institutions print only; £73 Individuals print only; £186 Institutions single print; £24 Individuals single print. **URL:** http://us.sagepub.com/en-us/nam/organizational-research-methods/journal200894; http://orm.sagepub.com. **Ad Rates:** BW $725; 4C $1115. **Remarks:** Accepts advertising. **Circ:** (Not Reported).

4788 ■ Otolaryngology--Head and Neck Surgery
SAGE Publications Inc.
2455 Teller Rd.
Thousand Oaks, CA 91320-2234
Free: 800-818-7243
Medical journal comprising peer-reviewed papers presented at the annual meeting of the American Academy of Otolarynogolgy-Head and Neck Surgery. Subjects covered include head and neck surgical oncology, otologic surgery and neuro-otology, rhinology, and rhinoplastic surgery. **Freq:** Monthly. **Print Method:**

Offset. **Trim Size:** 8 1/8 x 10 7/8. **Cols./Page:** 2. **Col. Width:** 39 nonpareils. **Col. Depth:** 140 agate lines. **Key Personnel:** John H. Krouse, Ph.D., Editor-in-Chief. **ISSN:** 0194--5998 (print); **EISSN:** 109--76817 (electronic). **Subscription Rates:** £657 Institutions e-access; £738 Institutions print; £753 Institutions print and e-access; £32 Individuals single print issue; £68 Institutions single print issue. **URL:** http://oto.sagepub.com. **Ad Rates:** BW $2005; 4C $1,505; BW $1775, full page; BW $1420, half page. **Remarks:** Accepts advertising. **Circ:** Paid ‡1040.

4789 ■ Outburn: Subversive and Post-Alternative Music
Outburn
PO Box 3187
Thousand Oaks, CA 91359-0187
Publication E-mail: outburn@outburn.com
Online consumer magazine covering music. **Freq:** 5/year. **Trim Size:** 9 x 10 7/8. **Key Personnel:** Rodney Kusano, Editor; Octavia Laird, Editor, Publisher. **ISSN:** 1542--1309 (print). **Subscription Rates:** $10.95 Individuals one year; $16.95 Two years; $16.95 Individuals plus current issue. **URL:** http://www.outburn.com. **Ad Rates:** 4C $2,615. **Remarks:** Accepts advertising. **Circ:** 60000.

4790 ■ Palliative Medicine
SAGE Publications Inc.
2455 Teller Rd.
Thousand Oaks, CA 91320-2234
Free: 800-818-7243
Publisher's E-mail: sales@pfp.sagepub.com
Peer-reviewed journal promoting the palliative care of patients with faradvanced diseases. For medical, nursing, and other patient care professionals. **Freq:** 10/year. **Key Personnel:** Catherine Walshe, Editor-in-Chief; Jim Cleary, Editor. **ISSN:** 0269-2163 (print); **EISSN:** 1477-030X (electronic). **Subscription Rates:** £1342 Institutions print and e-access; £1208 Institutions e-access; £1315 Institutions print; £209 Individuals print and e-access; £145 Institutions single print; £27 Individuals single print. **URL:** http://www.sagepub.co.uk/journalsProdDesc.nav?prodId=Journal201823; http://pmj.sagepub.com/. **Remarks:** Accepts advertising. **Circ:** (Not Reported).

4791 ■ Peace Research Abstracts Journal
SAGE Publications Inc.
2455 Teller Rd.
Thousand Oaks, CA 91320-2234
Free: 800-818-7243
Publisher's E-mail: sales@pfp.sagepub.com
Journal abstracting articles on peace studies from around the world. **Founded:** Feb. 1994. **Freq:** Bimonthly. **Print Method:** Offset. **Trim Size:** 8 1/2 x 11. **Cols./Page:** 2. **Key Personnel:** Henrik Urdal, Editor. **ISSN:** 0031-3599 (print). **Subscription Rates:** $1610 Individuals print only; $144 Individuals print only; $1643 Institutions print + online. **URL:** http://www.sagepub.com/journals/Journal200751?siteId=sage-us&prodTypes=any&q=Peace+Research+Abstracts+Journal&fs=1. **Ad Rates:** BW $445; 4C $895. **Remarks:** Accepts advertising. **Circ:** Paid 200.

4792 ■ Perfusion
SAGE Publications Inc.
2455 Teller Rd.
Thousand Oaks, CA 91320-2234
Free: 800-818-7243
Publisher's E-mail: sales@pfp.sagepub.com
Peer-reviewed journal featuring current information on all aspects of perfusion oxygenation and biocompatibility and their use in modern cardiac surgery. **Freq:** Bimonthly. **Key Personnel:** Prakash Punjabi, Editor-in-Chief; Mark Kurusz, Associate Editor; Peter R. Alston, Advisor. **ISSN:** 0267-6591 (print); **EISSN:** 1477-111X (electronic). **Subscription Rates:** £1325 Institutions print and e-access; £1193 Institutions e-access; £1299 Institutions print only; £190 Individuals print and e-access; £179 Institutions single print; £31 Individuals single print. **URL:** http://www.sagepub.co.uk/journalsProdDesc.nav?prodId=Journal201824; http://prf.sagepub.com/. **Remarks:** Accepts advertising. **Circ:** (Not Reported).

4793 ■ Personality and Social Psychology Review
SAGE Publications Inc.
2455 Teller Rd.
Thousand Oaks, CA 91320-2234
Free: 800-818-7243
Publisher's E-mail: spspinfo@spsp.org
Freq: Quarterly. **Trim Size:** 8 1/2 x 11. **Key Personnel:** Monica Biernat, Editor. **ISSN:** 1088--8683 (print); **EISSN:** 1532--7957 (electronic). **Subscription Rates:** $432 Institutions combined (print & e-access); $475 Institutions combined plus backfile; $389 Institutions e-access; $423 Institutions print only; $78 Individuals combined (print & e-access); $116 Institutions single print; $25 Individuals single print; included in membership dues; $129 /year for individuals, print & online; $677 /year for institutions, print & online; $42 Single issue /issue for individuals; $186 Single issue /issue for institutions. **URL:** http://psr.sagepub.com; http://www.spsp.org/?page=Publications; http://www.spsp.org/?page=pspr; http://www.sagepub.com/journalsProdDesc.nav?ct_p=subscribe&prodId=Journal201783. **Ad Rates:** BW $515; 4C $995. **Remarks:** Accepts advertising. **Circ:** (Not Reported).

4794 ■ Philosophy of the Social Sciences
SAGE Publications Inc.
2455 Teller Rd.
Thousand Oaks, CA 91320-2234
Free: 800-818-7243
Publication E-mail: advertising@sagepub.com
Scholarly journal discussing topics in the social sciences. **Freq:** Bimonthly January , March , June , July , September , December. **Print Method:** Offset. **Trim Size:** 5 1/2 x 8 1/2. **Cols./Page:** 1. **Col. Width:** 54 nonpareils. **Col. Depth:** 101 agate lines. **Key Personnel:** John O'Neill, Editor; Hans Albert, Board Member; Avi J. Cohen, Board Member; Jon Elster, Board Member; Paul A. Roth, Board Member; Joseph Agassi, Board Member; James M. Buchanan, Board Member; Steven Lukes, Board Member; Ian C. Jarvie, Editor; J.N. Hattiangadi, Editor. **ISSN:** 0048--3931 (print); **EISSN:** 1552--7441 (electronic). **Subscription Rates:** £490 Institutions Combined (Print & E-access); £539 Institutions Current Volume Print & All Online Content; £441 Institutions E-access; £490 Institutions All Online Content; £965 Institutions E-access (Content through 1998); £480 Institutions Print Only; £90 Individuals Print Only; £88 Institutions single print; £20 Individuals single print. **URL:** http://us.sagepub.com/en-us/nam/philosophy-of-the-social-sciences/journal200913. **Ad Rates:** BW $515; 4C $995. **Remarks:** Accepts advertising. **Circ:** Paid ‡1350, Non-paid ‡114.

4795 ■ Planning Theory
SAGE Publications Inc.
2455 Teller Rd.
Thousand Oaks, CA 91320-2234
Free: 800-818-7243
Publisher's E-mail: sales@pfp.sagepub.com
Journal focusing on the critical exploration of planning theory. **Freq:** Quarterly. **Key Personnel:** Charles Hoch, Editor; Luigi Mazza, Editor, Founder; Jean Hillier, Editor. **ISSN:** 1473--0952 (print); **EISSN:** 1741--3052 (electronic). **Subscription Rates:** £562 Institutions print and online; £551 Institutions print; £51 Individuals print; £162 Institutions single print; £17 Individuals single print; £506 Institutions e-access. **URL:** http://plt.sagepub.com; http://us.sagepub.com/en-us/nam/journal/planning-theory. **Remarks:** Advertising accepted; rates available upon request. **Circ:** (Not Reported).

4796 ■ Police Quarterly
SAGE Publications Inc.
2455 Teller Rd.
Thousand Oaks, CA 91320-2234
Free: 800-818-7243
Publisher's E-mail: sales@pfp.sagepub.com
Journal emphasizing policy-oriented research of interest to both practitioners and academics. **Freq:** Quarterly. **Trim Size:** 6 x 9. **Key Personnel:** John L. Worrall, PhD, Editor; Ivan Birch, Managing Editor. **ISSN:** 1098--6111 (print); **EISSN:** 1552--745X (electronic). **Subscription Rates:** £466 Institutions print & e-access; £513 Institutions print & all online; £419 Institutions e-access; £457 Institutions print only; £76 Individuals print only; £126 Institutions single print; £25 Individuals single print; £420 Institutions backfile e-access through 1998. **URL:** http://pqx.sagepub.com; http://us.sagepub.com/en-us/nam/police-quarterly/journal201421. **Ad Rates:** BW $725; 4C $1115. **Remarks:** Accepts advertising. **Circ:** (Not Reported).

4797 ■ Policy, Politics, & Nursing Practice
SAGE Publications Inc.
2455 Teller Rd.
Thousand Oaks, CA 91320-2234
Free: 800-818-7243
Publisher's E-mail: sales@pfp.sagepub.com
Journal exploring the multiple relationships between nursing and health policy. **Freq:** Quarterly. **Key Personnel:** Sheila Abood, Associate Editor; Debbie Ward, PhD, Board Member. **ISSN:** 1527--1544 (print); **EISSN:** 1552--7468 (electronic). **Subscription Rates:** £397 Institutions print & e-access; £357 Institutions e-access; £389 Institutions print only; £78 Individuals print only; £107 Institutions single issue; £25 Single issue print. **URL:** http://ppn.sagepub.com; http://us.sagepub.com/en-us/nam/policy-politics-nursing-practice/journal201332. **Ad Rates:** BW $840; 4C $1100. **Remarks:** Accepts advertising. **Circ:** (Not Reported).

4798 ■ Political Theory: An International Journal of Political Philosophy
SAGE Publications Inc.
2455 Teller Rd.
Thousand Oaks, CA 91320-2234
Free: 800-818-7243
Publisher's E-mail: sales@pfp.sagepub.com
Political philosophy journal. **Freq:** Bimonthly. **Print Method:** Offset. **Trim Size:** 5 1/2 x 8 1/2. **Cols./Page:** 1. **Col. Width:** 50 nonpareils. **Col. Depth:** 100 agate lines. **Key Personnel:** Jane Bennett, Editor; J. Peter Euben, Board Member; Stephen K. White, Board Member; Prof. Mary G. Dietz, Board Member. **ISSN:** 0090--5917 (print); **EISSN:** 1552--7476 (electronic). **Subscription Rates:** $1458 Institutions combined (print & e-access); $1604 Institutions current volume print & all online content; $1312 Institutions e-access; $2901 Institutions e-access (content through 1998); $1429 Institutions print only; $181 Individuals print only; $262 Institutions single print; $39 Individuals single print. **URL:** http://ptx.sagepub.com. **Ad Rates:** BW $875; 4C $1110. **Remarks:** Accepts advertising. **Circ:** (Not Reported).

4799 ■ Politics, Philosophy & Economics
SAGE Publications Inc.
2455 Teller Rd.
Thousand Oaks, CA 91320-2234
Free: 800-818-7243
Peer-reviewed journal focusing on the interchange of methods and concepts among political scientists, philosophers and economists interested in the analysis and evaluation of political and economic institutions and practices. **Freq:** Quarterly. **Key Personnel:** Jonathan Riley, Editor; Elizabeth Anderson, Board Member; Ken Binmore, Board Member; David Donaldson, Board Member; Geoff Brennan, Board Member; Paula Casal, Associate Editor; Gillian Brock, Associate Editor; Thomas Christiano, Editor; Norman Daniels, Board Member; Gerald F. Gaus, Editor, Founder; Jack Knight, Associate Editor; Peter Vanderschraaf, Associate Editor; Andrew Williams, Editor; Jeremy Waldron, Board Member. **ISSN:** 1470--594X (print); **EISSN:** 1741--3060 (electronic). **Subscription Rates:** £52 Individuals print only; £497 Institutions e-access; £541 Institutions print only; £552 Institutions print and e-access; £17 Individuals single print; £149 Institutions single print. **URL:** http://uk.sagepub.com/en-gb/asi/journal/politics-philosophy-economics. **Remarks:** Accepts advertising. **Circ:** (Not Reported).

4800 ■ Politics & Society
SAGE Publications Inc.
2455 Teller Rd.
Thousand Oaks, CA 91320-2234
Free: 800-818-7243
Publication E-mail: advertising@sagepub.com
Journal on f politics, sociology, and economics. **Freq:** Quarterly. **Print Method:** Offset. **Trim Size:** 5 1/2 x 8 1/2. **Key Personnel:** Mary-Ann Twist, Editor. **ISSN:** 0032-3292 (print); **EISSN:** 1552-7514 (electronic). **Subscription Rates:** £27 Single issue print; £82 Individuals print only; £163 Single issue print, Institutions; £545 Institutions e-access; £594 Institutions print only; £606 Institutions print and e-access; £667 Institutions current volume print and all online content; £1206 Institutions e-access (content through 1998). **URL:** http://pas.

Circulation: ★ = AAM; △ or • = BPA; ♦ = CAC; ❑ = VAC; ⊕ = PO Statement; ‡ = Publisher's Report; Boldface figures = sworn; Light figures = estimated.

sagepub.com; http://uk.sagepub.com/en-gb/asi/politics-society/journal200925. **Ad Rates:** BW $725. **Remarks:** Accepts advertising. **Circ:** Paid 800.

4801 ■ Politics: Surveys, Debates and Controversies in Politics
SAGE Publications Inc.
2455 Teller Rd.
Thousand Oaks, CA 91320-2234
Free: 800-818-7243
Publisher's E-mail: customerservice@oxon.blackwellpublishing.com
Journal publishing political analysis and providing information on conducting research and teaching politics. **Freq:** Quarterly. **Key Personnel:** Martin Coward, Editor; Kyle Grayson, Editor. **ISSN:** 0263--3957 (print); **EISSN:** 1467--9256 (electronic). **Subscription Rates:** $700 Institutions print and online; $686 Institutions print only; $630 Institutions online only. **URL:** http://us.sagepub.com/en-us/nam/politics/journal202481. **Mailing address:** PO Box 1354, Oxford OX4 2ZG, United Kingdom. **Remarks:** Accepts advertising. **Circ:** (Not Reported).

4802 ■ Post Reproductive Health
SAGE Publications Inc.
2455 Teller Rd.
Thousand Oaks, CA 91320-2234
Free: 800-818-7243
Publisher's E-mail: sales@pfp.sagepub.com
Journal covering news, research and opinion for study and treatment of menopausal conditions. **Freq:** Quarterly. **Key Personnel:** Edward Morris, Editor; Heather Currie, Editor. **ISSN:** 2053-3705 (print); **EISSN:** 2053-3705 (electronic). **Subscription Rates:** £507 Institutions combined (print & e-access); €558 Institutions combined plus backfile; $456 Institutions e-access (content through 1998); $191 Individuals combined (print & e-access). **URL:** http://min.sagepub.com. **Formerly:** Journal of the British Menopause Society; Menopause International. **Circ:** (Not Reported).

4803 ■ The Prison Journal: An International Forum on Incarceration and Alternative Sanctions
SAGE Publications Inc.
2455 Teller Rd.
Thousand Oaks, CA 91320-2234
Free: 800-818-7243
Publication E-mail: journals@sagepub.com
Journal on the field of sentencing, correctional alternatives and penal sanctions. The official publication of the Pennsylvania Prison Society. **Freq:** Bimonthly. **Trim Size:** 5 1/2 x 8 1/2. **Key Personnel:** Rosemary L. Gido, Editor. **ISSN:** 0032--8855 (print); **EISSN:** 1552--7522 (electronic). **Subscription Rates:** £17 Single issue print; £78 Individuals print only; £95 Single issue print, Institutions; £474 Institutions e-access; £516 Institutions print only; £527 Institutions print and e-access; £580 Institutions combined plus backfile (current volume print & all online content); £2688 Institutions e-access (content through 1998). **URL:** http://tpj.sagepub.com. **Ad Rates:** BW $875; 4C $1110, in addition to Black & White rate. **Remarks:** Accepts advertising. **Circ:** (Not Reported).

4804 ■ Probation Journal: The Journal of Community and Criminal Justice
SAGE Publications Inc.
2455 Teller Rd.
Thousand Oaks, CA 91320-2234
Free: 800-818-7243
Publisher's E-mail: sales@pfp.sagepub.com
Journal disseminating criminal justice research and developing debate about the theory and practice of work with offenders. **Freq:** Quarterly. **Key Personnel:** Lol Burke, Editor; Emma Cluley, Managing Editor. **ISSN:** 0264--5505 (print); **EISSN:** 1741--3079 (electronic). **Subscription Rates:** £43 Individuals print only; £1418 Individuals e-access; £14 Individuals single print issue; £68 Institutions single print issue. **URL:** http://uk.sagepub.com/en-gb/asi/journal/probation-journal. **Remarks:** Accepts advertising. **Circ:** (Not Reported).

4805 ■ Progress in Human Geography
SAGE Publications Inc.
2455 Teller Rd.
Thousand Oaks, CA 91320-2234
Free: 800-818-7243
Publisher's E-mail: sales@pfp.sagepub.com
Interdisciplinary journal reporting traditional and new aspects of the study of human geography. **Freq:** Bimonthly. **Key Personnel:** Noel Castree, Managing Editor; Rob Kitchin, Editor. **ISSN:** 0309-1325 (print); **EISSN:** 1477-0288 (electronic). **Subscription Rates:** $54 Individuals single issue; $228 Institutions single issue; $250 Individuals print and online; $1139 Institutions online only; $1241 Institutions print only. **URL:** http://phg.sagepub.com; http://www.uk.sagepub.com/journals/Journal201826. **Remarks:** Accepts advertising. **Circ:** (Not Reported).

4806 ■ Progress in Physical Geography
SAGE Publications Inc.
2455 Teller Rd.
Thousand Oaks, CA 91320-2234
Free: 800-818-7243
Publisher's E-mail: sales@pfp.sagepub.com
Forum for studies on animate and inanimate aspects of earth, ocean, and atmosphere with interest in man-environment interaction. **Freq:** Bimonthly. **Key Personnel:** Nicholas Clifford, Managing Editor. **ISSN:** 0309--1333 (print); **EISSN:** 1477--0296 (electronic). **Subscription Rates:** $52 Individuals single issue; $228 Institutions single issue; $239 Individuals print and online; $1139 Institutions online only; $1241 Institutions print only; $1266 Institutions print and online. **URL:** http://us.sagepub.com/en-us/nam/journal/progress-physical-geography; http://ppg.sagepub.com. **Remarks:** Accepts advertising. **Circ:** (Not Reported).

4807 ■ Psychological Science
SAGE Publications Inc.
2455 Teller Rd.
Thousand Oaks, CA 91320-2234
Free: 800-818-7243
Scientific research journal of the American Psychological Society. **Freq:** Bimonthly. **Key Personnel:** D. Stephen Lindsay, Editor-in-Chief; Michele Nathan, Managing Editor. **ISSN:** 0956--7976 (print); **EISSN:** 1467--9280 (electronic). **Subscription Rates:** $8968 Institutions print and online; $9865 Institutions current volume print & all online content; $8071 Institutions online; $293 Single issue institutions; $8890 Institutions online, content through 1998; $8789 Institutions print only. **URL:** http://pss.sagepub.com; http://www.cpsbeijing.org/en/journals.php; http://www.psychologicalscience.org. **Remarks:** Accepts advertising. **Circ:** 15000.

4808 ■ Psychology & Developing Societies
SAGE Publications Inc.
2455 Teller Rd.
Thousand Oaks, CA 91320-2234
Free: 800-818-7243
Publisher's E-mail: sales@pfp.sagepub.com
Journal aiming to consolidate psychology in developing societies and seeking to further understanding of the problems faced by these societies. **Freq:** Semiannual. **Key Personnel:** Janak Pandey, Board Member; John W. Berry, Board Member; Rashmi Kumar, Associate Editor; Namita Pande, Associate Editor. **ISSN:** 0971-3336 (print); **EISSN:** 0973-0761 (electronic). **Subscription Rates:** $379 Institutions print & e-access; $417 Institutions print & all online; $341 Institutions e-access; $379 Institutions backfile lease, e-access plus backfile (online); $341 Institutions backfile purchase, e-access (content through 1998); $371 Institutions print only; $104 Individuals print only; $204 Institutions single print; $68 Individuals single print. **URL:** http://pds.sagepub.com; http://www.sagepub.com/journalsProdDesc.nav?ct_p=boards&prodId=Journal200945. **Remarks:** Accepts advertising. **Circ:** (Not Reported).

4809 ■ Psychology of Music
SAGE Publications Inc.
2455 Teller Rd.
Thousand Oaks, CA 91320-2234
Free: 800-818-7243
Publisher's E-mail: sales@pfp.sagepub.com
Freq: Bimonthly. **Key Personnel:** Raymond A.R. MacDonald, Associate Editor; Margaret Barrett, Board Member. **ISSN:** 0305--7356 (print); **EISSN:** 1741--3087 (electronic). **Subscription Rates:** $131 Institutions single print. **URL:** http://pom.sagepub.com. **Remarks:** Accepts advertising. **Circ:** (Not Reported).

4810 ■ Public Finance Review
SAGE Publications Inc.
2455 Teller Rd.
Thousand Oaks, CA 91320-2234
Free: 800-818-7243
Publication E-mail: advertising@sagepub.com
Public economy journal. **Freq:** Bimonthly. **Print Method:** Offset. **Trim Size:** 5 1/2 x 8 1/2. **Cols./Page:** 1. **Col. Width:** 50 nonpareils. **Col. Depth:** 100 agate lines. **Key Personnel:** James R. Alm, Editor. **ISSN:** 1091--1421 (print); **EISSN:** 1552--7530 (electronic). **Subscription Rates:** $768 Institutions print & e-access; $845 Institutions current volume print & all online content; $691 Institutions e-access; $768 Institutions e-access (all online content); $1525 Institutions e-access (content through 1998); $753 Institutions print only; $110 Individuals print only; $138 Institutions single print; $24 Individuals single print. **URL:** http://uk.sagepub.com/en-gb/asi/public-finance-review/journal200768. **Ad Rates:** BW $725; 4C $1115. **Remarks:** Accepts advertising. **Circ:** Paid ‡700.

4811 ■ Public Personnel Management
SAGE Publications Inc.
2455 Teller Rd.
Thousand Oaks, CA 91320-2234
Free: 800-818-7243
Publication E-mail: publications@ipma-hr.org
Journal for human resource executives and managers in the public sector. Contains articles on trends, case studies, legislation, and industry research. **Freq:** Quarterly March , June , September , December. **Print Method:** Offset. **Trim Size:** 7 x 10. **Cols./Page:** 1. **Col. Width:** 74 nonpareils. **Col. Depth:** 109 agate lines. **Key Personnel:** Jared J. Llorens, Editor; Leonard Bright, Board Member. **ISSN:** 0091--0260 (print); **EISSN:** 1945--7421 (electronic). **Subscription Rates:** £175 Institutions Combined (Print & E-access); £193 Institutions Current Volume Print & All Online Content; £158 Institutions E-access; £361 Institutions E-access (Content through 1998); £172 Institutions Print Only; £65 Individuals Combined (Print & E-access); $47 Institutions Single Print Issue; £21 Individuals Single Print Issue. **URL:** http://ipma-hr.org/publications/public-personnel-management; http://uk.sagepub.com/en-gb/asi/public-personnel-management/journal202216. **Remarks:** Accepts advertising. **Circ:** (Not Reported).

4812 ■ Public Understanding of Science
SAGE Publications Inc.
2455 Teller Rd.
Thousand Oaks, CA 91320-2234
Free: 800-818-7243
Publisher's E-mail: info@sciencepresidents.org
Peer-reviewed journal covering all aspects of the interrelationships between science (including technology and medicine) and the public. **Freq:** 8/year. **Key Personnel:** Martin Bauer, Editor. **ISSN:** 0963--6625 (print); **EISSN:** 1361--6609 (electronic). **Subscription Rates:** £58 Individuals print; £825 Institutions online; £899 Institutions print; £917 Institutions print and online; £9 Individuals single print; £124 Institutions single print. **URL:** http://pus.sagepub.com. **Remarks:** Accepts advertising. **Circ:** (Not Reported).

4813 ■ Public Works Management & Policy: Research and Practice in Infrastructure, Technology, and the Environment
SAGE Publications Inc.
2455 Teller Rd.
Thousand Oaks, CA 91320-2234
Free: 800-818-7243
Publisher's E-mail: sales@pfp.sagepub.com
Academic journal covering public works and the public infrastructure industry. **Freq:** Quarterly January, April, July, October. **Print Method:** Offset. **Trim Size:** 8 1/2 x 11. **Key Personnel:** Richard G. Little, Editor. **ISSN:** 1087--724X (print); **EISSN:** 1552--7549 (electronic). **Subscription Rates:** $25 Individuals single issue; $78 Individuals print; $150 Institutions single issue; $499 Institutions backfile purchase, E-access (content through 1998); $500 Institutions online only; $545 Institutions print only; $556 Individuals subscription & backfile lease, E-access plus backfile (all online content); $612 Institutions subscription & backfile lease, combined plus backfile (current volume print & all online content). **URL:** http://pwm.sagepub.com. **Ad Rates:** BW $515. **Remarks:** Accepts advertising. **Circ:** Paid 4000.

4814 ■ Punishment & Society: The International Journal of Penology

SAGE Publications Inc.
2455 Teller Rd.
Thousand Oaks, CA 91320-2234
Free: 800-818-7243
Journal focusing on punishment, penal institutions and penal control. **Freq:** 5/year. **Key Personnel:** Prof. Jonathan Simon, Editor; Dario Melossi, Board Member; Pat Carlen, Board Member; Kelly Hannah Moffat, Editor-in-Chief; David Garland, Editor; Anthony Bottoms, Board Member; Shadd Maruna, Editor; Arie Freiberg, Board Member. **ISSN:** 1462--4745 (print); **EISSN:** 1741--3095 (electronic). **Subscription Rates:** £65 Individuals print only; £599 Institutions e-access; £653 Institutions print only; £666 Institutions print and online; £17 Individuals single print; £144 Institutions single print. **URL:** http://pun.sagepub.com. **Ad Rates:** BW £600. **Remarks:** Accepts advertising. **Circ:** (Not Reported).

4815 ■ Qualitative Health Research
SAGE Publications Inc.
2455 Teller Rd.
Thousand Oaks, CA 91320-2234
Free: 800-818-7243
Publication E-mail: advertising@sagepub.com
Journal featuring research, theoretical, and methodological articles on qualitative health issues. **Founded:** 1991. **Freq:** Monthly. **Print Method:** Offset. **Trim Size:** 8 x 10 7/8. **Cols./Page:** 1. **Col. Width:** 50 nonpareils. **Col. Depth:** 100 agate lines. **Key Personnel:** Janice M. Morse, PhD, Editor. **ISSN:** 1049-7323 (print); **EISSN:** 1552-7557 (electronic). **Subscription Rates:** $1542 Institutions combined (print & e-access); $1696 Institutions backfile lease, combined plus backfile; $1388 Institutions e-access; $1542 Institutions backfile lease, e-access plus backfile; $1388 Institutions backfile, e-access (content through 1998); $1511 Institutions print only; $250 Individuals print only; $139 Institutions single print; $27 Individuals single print. **URL:** http://www.sagepub.com/journalsProdDesc.nav?prodId=Journal200926. **Ad Rates:** BW $515; 4C $995. **Remarks:** Accepts advertising. **Circ:** Paid 1100, Non-paid 118.

4816 ■ Qualitative Inquiry
SAGE Publications Inc.
2455 Teller Rd.
Thousand Oaks, CA 91320-2234
Free: 800-818-7243
Publisher's E-mail: sales@pfp.sagepub.com
Journal publishing refereed research articles on qualitative research methodology and related issues in the human sciences. **Freq:** 10/year. **Key Personnel:** Norman K. Denzin, Editor; Yvonna Lincoln, Editor. **ISSN:** 1077--8004 (print); **EISSN:** 1552--7565 (electronic). **Subscription Rates:** £87 Individuals print only; £998 Institutions e-access; £1087 Institutions print only; £1109 Institutions print and e-access; £11 Individuals single print issue; £120 Institutions single print issue. **URL:** http://qix.sagepub.com. **Remarks:** Advertising accepted; rates available upon request. **Circ:** (Not Reported).

4817 ■ Qualitative Social Work
SAGE Publications Inc.
2455 Teller Rd.
Thousand Oaks, CA 91320-2234
Free: 800-818-7243
Publisher's E-mail: sales@pfp.sagepub.com
Journal focusing on qualitative research and evaluation and in qualitative approaches to practice. **Freq:** Bimonthly. **Key Personnel:** Robyn Munford, Associate Editor; Roy Ruckdeschel, Editor, Founder; Ian Shaw, Editor, Founder; Karen M. Staller, Editor. **ISSN:** 1473--3250 (print); **EISSN:** 1741--3117 (electronic). **Subscription Rates:** £56 Individuals print only; £582 Institutions e-access; £634 Institutions print only; £647 Institutions print and e-access; £12 Individuals single print issue; £116 Institutions single print issue. **URL:** http://qsw.sagepub.com. **Remarks:** Advertising accepted; rates available upon request. **Circ:** (Not Reported).

4818 ■ Race and Justice: An International Journal
SAGE Publications Inc.
2455 Teller Rd.
Thousand Oaks, CA 91320-2234
Free: 800-818-7243
Publisher's E-mail: sales@pfp.sagepub.com
Peer-reviewed journal covering the study on race, ethnicity and justice. **Freq:** Quarterly January, April, July and October. **Key Personnel:** Shaun L. Gabbidon, Board Member. **ISSN:** 2153--3687 (print); **EISSN:** 2153--3687 (electronic). **Subscription Rates:** £378 Institutions e-access; £78 Individuals e-access. **URL:** http://www.uk.sagepub.com/journals/Journal201995. **Remarks:** Accepts advertising. **Circ:** (Not Reported).

4819 ■ Reflections on Starting Strong: A New Teachers Journal
Corwin Press Inc.
2455 Teller Rd.
Thousand Oaks, CA 91320
Phone: (805)499-9734
Fax: (800)499-5323
Free: 800-417-2466
Publisher's E-mail: order@corwin.com
Journal providing valuable resource for new teachers. **Trim Size:** 6 x 9. **Subscription Rates:** $9.95 U.S. **URL:** http://www.corwin.com/booksProdDesc.nav?prodId=Book228680&currTree=WebTopic%20s&level1=Web_Topic10. **Remarks:** Advertising not accepted. **Circ:** (Not Reported).

4820 ■ Remedial and Special Education
SAGE Publications Inc.
2455 Teller Rd.
Thousand Oaks, CA 91320-2234
Free: 800-818-7243
Publisher's E-mail: sales@pfp.sagepub.com
Journal interprets research and makes recommendations for practice in the fields of remedial and special education. **Freq:** Bimonthly. **Print Method:** Offset. **Trim Size:** 8 x 10 7/8. **Cols./Page:** 2. **Col. Width:** 3 5/16 inches. **Col. Depth:** 9 5/8 inches. **Key Personnel:** Kathleen Lane, Editor; Chris Schatschneider, Associate Editor; Richard L. Allington, Editor; Susan B. Palmer, Board Member. **ISSN:** 0741--9325 (print); **EISSN:** 1538--4756 (electronic). **Subscription Rates:** $81 Individuals print and online; $265 Institutions online only; £288 Institutions print only; £294 Institutions print and online; £18 Individuals single print issue; £53 Institutions single print issue. **URL:** http://rse.sagepub.com. **Ad Rates:** BW $515; 4C $995. **Remarks:** Accepts advertising. **Circ:** Paid 2587, Non-paid 97.

4821 ■ Research on Aging: An International Bimonthly Journal
SAGE Publications Inc.
2455 Teller Rd.
Thousand Oaks, CA 91320-2234
Free: 800-818-7243
Publisher's E-mail: sales@pfp.sagepub.com
Journal on the problems of the senior citizens.Contains international forum on the aged and the ageing process. Provides with knowledge needed to help improve practices and policies concerning the elderly. **Freq:** 8/year. **Print Method:** Offset. **Trim Size:** 5 1/2 x 8 1/2. **Cols./Page:** 1. **Col. Width:** 50 nonpareils. **Col. Depth:** 100 agate lines. **Key Personnel:** Jeffrey A. Burr, PhD, Editor; William Haley, Board Member. **ISSN:** 0164--0275 (print); **EISSN:** 1552--7573 (electronic). **Subscription Rates:** $766 Institutions combined (print & e-access); $843 Institutions current volume print & all online content; $689 Institutions e-access; $766 Institutions e-access plus backfile (all online content); $1075 Institutions e-access (content through 1998); $751 Institutions print only; $104 Individuals print only; $103 Institutions single print; $17 Individuals single print. **URL:** http://roa.sagepub.com; http://uk.sagepub.com/en-gb/asi/research-on-aging/journal200862. **Formerly:** Research on Aging: A Quarterly of Social Gerontology and Adult Development. **Ad Rates:** BW $725; 4C $1115. **Remarks:** Accepts advertising. **Circ:** Paid ‡1350, Non-paid ‡84.

4822 ■ Research on Social Work Practice
SAGE Publications Inc.
2455 Teller Rd.
Thousand Oaks, CA 91320-2234
Free: 800-818-7243
Publication E-mail: advertising@sagepub.com
Journal covering empirical research on the methods and outcomes of social work practice. **Freq:** 7/year. **Print Method:** Offset. **Trim Size:** 8 x 10 7/8. **Cols./Page:** 1. **Col. Width:** 50 nonpareils. **Col. Depth:** 100 agate lines. **Key Personnel:** Bruce A. Thyer, Editor. **ISSN:** 1049-7315 (print); **EISSN:** 1552-7581 (electronic). **Subscription Rates:** £702 Institutions combined (print & e-access); £772 Institutions backfile lease, combined plus backfile; £632 Institutions e-access; £702 Institutions backfile lease, e-access plus backfile; £688 Institutions print only; £108 Individuals print only; £108 Institutions single print; $33 Individuals single print. **URL:** http://www.sagepub.com/journalsProdDesc.nav?prodId=Journal200896. **Ad Rates:** BW $515; 4C $995. **Remarks:** Accepts advertising. **Circ:** Paid ‡1700.

4823 ■ Review of Public Personnel Administration
SAGE Publications Inc.
2455 Teller Rd.
Thousand Oaks, CA 91320-2234
Free: 800-818-7243
Publisher's E-mail: sales@pfp.sagepub.com
Journal providing research and commentary on personnel and labor relations matters affecting the public sector. **Freq:** Quarterly March, June, September, December. **Print Method:** Offset. **Trim Size:** 6 1/8 x 9 1/4. **Key Personnel:** R. Paul Battaglio, Jr., Editor; Mary Ellen Guy, Board Member; Stephen E. Condrey, Advisor. **ISSN:** 0734--371X (print); **EISSN:** 1552--759X (electronic). **Subscription Rates:** £68 Individuals print only; £556 Institutions e-access; £606 Individuals print only; £618 Institutions e-access plus backfile (all online content); £618 Institutions print & e-access; £680 Institutions print & e-access plus backfile (current volume print & all online content); £851 Institutions e-access (content through 1998); £22 Single issue; £167 Single issue institution. **URL:** http://www.sagepub.com/journalsProdDesc.nav?prodId=Journal201617; http://rop.sagepub.com. **Ad Rates:** BW $875; 4C $1110. **Remarks:** Accepts advertising. **Circ:** (Not Reported).

4824 ■ Review of Radical Political Economics
SAGE Publications Inc.
2455 Teller Rd.
Thousand Oaks, CA 91320-2234
Free: 800-818-7243
Publisher's E-mail: sales@pfp.sagepub.com
Academic journal containing information on radical political economics. **Freq:** Quarterly. **Trim Size:** 7 x 10. **Cols./Page:** 1. **Col. Width:** 30 picas. **Col. Depth:** 42 picas. **Key Personnel:** David Barkin, Editor; Enid Arvidson, Managing Editor. **ISSN:** 0486--6134 (print); **EISSN:** 1552--8502 (electronic). **Subscription Rates:** £348 Institutions e-access; £379 Institutions print only; £387 Institutions print and e-access; £104 Institutions single print issue. **URL:** http://rrp.sagepub.com. **Remarks:** Accepts advertising. **Circ:** 2400.

4825 ■ Science Communication: An Interdisciplinary Social Science Journal
SAGE Publications Inc.
2455 Teller Rd.
Thousand Oaks, CA 91320-2234
Free: 800-818-7243
Publisher's E-mail: sales@pfp.sagepub.com
Social science research journal. **Freq:** Bimonthly. **Print Method:** Offset. **Trim Size:** 5 1/2 x 8 1/2. **Cols./Page:** 1. **Col. Width:** 50 nonpareils. **Col. Depth:** 100 agate lines. **Key Personnel:** Susanna Hornig Priest, Editor; Rick Borchelt, Board Member; JoAnn Myer Valenti, Board Member. **ISSN:** 1075--5470 (print); **EISSN:** 1552--8545 (electronic). **Subscription Rates:** $1335 Institutions combined (print & e-access); $42 Individuals single print only; $1202 Institutions e-access; $1336 Institutions backfile lease, e-access plus backfile (all online content); $1942 Institutions backfile purchase, e-access (content through 1998); $1308 Institutions print only; $194 Individuals print only; $240 Single issue institutional. **URL:** http://scx.sagepub.com. **Formerly:** Knowledge, Creation, Diffusion, Utilization. **Ad Rates:** BW $875; 4C $1110. **Remarks:** Accepts advertising. **Circ:** (Not Reported).

4826 ■ Science, Technology & Human Values
SAGE Publications Inc.
2455 Teller Rd.
Thousand Oaks, CA 91320-2234
Free: 800-818-7243
Publication E-mail: advertising@sagepub.com
Peer-reviewed journal on the ethics of science and technology. **Freq:** Quarterly January, April, July, October. **Print Method:** Offset. **Trim Size:** 5 1/2 x 8 1/2. **Cols./**

Circulation: ★ = AAM; △ or • = BPA; ♦ = CAC; ❑ = VAC; ⊕ = PO Statement; ‡ = Publisher's Report; Boldface figures = sworn; Light figures = estimated.

Page: 1. **Col. Width:** 50 nonpareils. **Col. Depth:** 100 agate lines. **Key Personnel:** Ellsworth R. Fuhrman, Editor; Geoffrey C. Bowker, Editor; Gary Downey, Advisor; Madeleine Akrich, Advisor; Susan Leigh Star, Advisor; Ulrike Felt, Editor. **ISSN:** 0162--2439 (print); **EISSN:** 1552--8251 (electronic). **Subscription Rates:** £17 Single issue print; £78 Individuals print only; £97 Institutions single print issue; £486 Institutions e-access; £529 Institutions print only; £540 Institutions combined print & online; £594 Individuals backfile Lease, Combined Plus Backfile (Current Volume Print & All Online Content); £951 Institutions backfile Purchase, E-access (Content through 1998); £575 Institutions Combined (Print & E-access); £633 Institutions Backfile Lease, Combined Plus Backfile (Current Volume Print & All Online Content); £518 Institutions E-acces; £576 Institutions Backfile Lease, E-access Plus Backfile (All Online Content); £1013 Institutions Backfile Purchase, E-access (Content through 1998); £564 Institutions print; £80 Individuals print; £103 Institutions print, single issue. **URL:** http://sth.sagepub.com; http://www.4sonline.org/sthv; http://uk.sagepub.com/en-gb/asi/science-technology-human-values/journal200858. **Ad Rates:** BW $515; 4C $995; BW $1,120. **Remarks:** Accepts advertising. **Circ:** Paid 1600.

4827 ■ Second Language Research
SAGE Publications Inc.
2455 Teller Rd.
Thousand Oaks, CA 91320-2234
Free: 800-818-7243
Publisher's E-mail: sales@pfp.sagepub.com
Journal covering theoretical and experimental papers concerned with acquisition of a second language. **Freq:** Quarterly January, April, July, and October. **Print Method:** Offset. **Trim Size:** 5 1/2 x 8 1/2. **Cols./Page:** 1. **Col. Width:** 50 nonpareils. **Col. Depth:** 100 agate lines. **Key Personnel:** Michael Sharwood Smith, Founder, Editor. **ISSN:** 0267--6583 (print); **EISSN:** 1477--0326 (electronic). **Subscription Rates:** $961 Institutions print and e-access; $865 Institutions e-access; $942 Institutions print only; $202 Individuals print and e-access; $259 Institutions single print; $66 Individuals single print. **URL:** http://slr.sagepub.com. **Ad Rates:** BW £650. **Remarks:** Accepts advertising. **Circ:** (Not Reported).

4828 ■ Seminars in Cardiothoracic and Vascular Anesthesia
SAGE Publications Inc.
2455 Teller Rd.
Thousand Oaks, CA 91320-2234
Free: 800-818-7243
Publisher's E-mail: sales@pfp.sagepub.com
Scholarly journal covering cardiac, thoracic, and vascular anesthesia and related areas of critical care medicine. **Freq:** Quarterly. **Key Personnel:** Davy C. Cheng, Board Member; Gregory Nuttall, Board Member; John Murkin, Board Member; Nathaen Weitzel, MD, Editor; Eugene A. Hessel, Board Member; Harry van Wezel, Board Member. **ISSN:** 1089-2532 (print). **URL:** http://scv.sagepub.com; http://www.sagepub.com/journalsProdDesc.nav?prodId=Journal201792. **Ad Rates:** BW $1,120; 4C $1,105. **Remarks:** Accepts advertising. **Circ:** (Not Reported).

4829 ■ Simulation & Gaming: An International Journal of Theory, Practice and Research
SAGE Publications Inc.
2455 Teller Rd.
Thousand Oaks, CA 91320-2234
Free: 800-818-7243
Publication E-mail: advertising@sagepub.com
Journal covering theory, practice, and research in simulation and gaming methods used in education, training, consultation, and research. **Freq:** Bimonthly. **Print Method:** Offset. **Trim Size:** 5 1/2 x 8 1/2. **Cols./Page:** 1. **Col. Width:** 50 nonpareils. **Col. Depth:** 100 agate lines. **Key Personnel:** Timothy Clapper, Editor. **ISSN:** 1046--8781 (print); **EISSN:** 1552--826X (electronic). **Subscription Rates:** £822 Institutions e-access; £904 Institutions backfile lease, combined plus backfile; £2023 Institutions e-access (content through 1998); £102 Individuals print issue. **URL:** http://www.unice.fr/sg; http://uk.sagepub.com/en-gb/asi/simulation-gaming/journal200777. **Remarks:** Accepts advertising. **Circ:** Paid ‡600.

4830 ■ Small Group Research: An International Journal of Theory, Investigation, and Application
SAGE Publications Inc.
2455 Teller Rd.
Thousand Oaks, CA 91320-2234
Free: 800-818-7243
Publisher's E-mail: sales@pfp.sagepub.com
Behavioral research and theory journal. **Freq:** Bimonthly. **Print Method:** Offset. **Trim Size:** 5 1/2 x 8 1/2. **Cols./Page:** 1. **Col. Width:** 50 nonpareils. **Col. Depth:** 100 agate lines. **Key Personnel:** Joann Keyton, Editor; Charles Garvin, Board Member; Richard Brian Polley, Board Member. **ISSN:** 1046--4964 (print); **EISSN:** 1552--8278 (electronic). **Subscription Rates:** £113 Individuals print only; £133 Single issue Institutions; £724 Institutions print only; £24 Single issue. **URL:** http://uk.sagepub.com/en-gb/asi/small-group-research/journal200891. **Formerly**: Small Group Behavior. **Ad Rates:** BW $725. **Remarks:** Accepts advertising. **Circ:** Paid ‡1350, Non-paid ‡87.

4831 ■ SMR/Sociological Methods and Research
SAGE Publications Inc.
2455 Teller Rd.
Thousand Oaks, CA 91320-2234
Free: 800-818-7243
Publication E-mail: advertising@sagepub.com smr@wjh.harvard.edu
Sociology journal. **Freq:** Quarterly. **Print Method:** Offset. **Trim Size:** 5 1/2 x 8 1/2. **Cols./Page:** 1. **Col. Width:** 50 nonpareils. **Col. Depth:** 100 agate lines. **Key Personnel:** Prof. Christopher Winship, Editor. **ISSN:** 0049--1241 (print); **EISSN:** 1552--8294 (electronic). **Subscription Rates:** $719 Institutions print & e-access; £791 Institutions current volume print & all online content; £647 Institutions e-access; £719 Institutions e-access (all online content); £1430 Individuals e-access (content through 1998); £705 Institutions print only; £122 Individuals print only; £194 Institutions single print; £40 Individuals single print. **URL:** http://uk.sagepub.com/en-gb/asi/sociological-methods-research/journal200867. **Ad Rates:** BW $725; 4C $1115. **Remarks:** Accepts advertising. **Circ:** Paid ‡700.

4832 ■ Social Science Computer Review
SAGE Publications Inc.
2455 Teller Rd.
Thousand Oaks, CA 91320-2234
Free: 800-818-7243
Publication E-mail: advertising@sagepub.com
Journal covering the social aspects of computers and the application of personal computers to the social sciences. **Freq:** Bimonthly. **Print Method:** Offset. **Trim Size:** 7 x 10. **Cols./Page:** 1. **Col. Width:** 52 nonpareils. **Col. Depth:** 86 agate lines. **Key Personnel:** David G. Garson, Editor. **ISSN:** 0894--4393 (print). **Subscription Rates:** $1009 Institutions combined (print & e-access); $1110 Institutions backfile lease, combined plus backfile; $908 Institutions e-access; $1009 Institutions backfile lease, e-access plus backfile; $1234 Institutions backfile, e-access (content through 1998); $1009 Institutions print and e-access; $146 Individuals print only; $181 Institutions single print; $32 Individuals single print. **URL:** http://www.sagepub.com/journalsProdDesc.nav?prodId=Journal200948&. **Ad Rates:** BW $515; 4C $995. **Remarks:** Accepts advertising. **Circ:** (Not Reported).

4833 ■ Sociological Perspectives: Official Journal of the Pacific Sociological Association
SAGE Publications Inc.
2455 Teller Rd.
Thousand Oaks, CA 91320-2234
Free: 800-818-7243
Sociology journal. **Freq:** Quarterly March, June, September, December. **Print Method:** Offset. **Trim Size:** 7 x 10. **Cols./Page:** 1. **Key Personnel:** James Elliott, Advisor; Matthew Carlson, Editor. **ISSN:** 0731--1214 (print); **EISSN:** 1533--8673 (electronic). **Subscription Rates:** £349 Institutions print & electronic; £314 Institutions electronic only; £342 Institutions print only; £267 Individuals online only; £63 Single issue print only. **URL:** http://uk.sagepub.com/en-gb/asi/sociological-perspectives/journal202165. **Ad Rates:** BW $725. **Remarks:** Accepts advertising. **Circ:** ‡1870.

4834 ■ South Asia Economic Journal
SAGE Publications Inc.
2455 Teller Rd.
Thousand Oaks, CA 91320-2234
Free: 800-818-7243
Publisher's E-mail: sales@pfp.sagepub.com
Journal covering economic analysis and policy options aimed at promoting cooperation among the countries comprising South Asia. **Freq:** Semiannual March and September. **Print Method:** Offset. **Trim Size:** 5 1/2 x 8 1/2. **Cols./Page:** 1. **Col. Width:** 50 nonpareils. **Col. Depth:** 100 agate lines. **Key Personnel:** Saman Kelegama, Editor; Prabir De, Editor. **ISSN:** 1391--5614 (print); **EISSN:** 0973--077X (electronic). **Subscription Rates:** $239 Institutions combined (print & e-access); $215 Institutions e-access; $234 Institutions print only; $85 Individuals print only; $129 Institutions single print; $55 Individuals single print. **URL:** http://sae.sagepub.com. **Remarks:** Advertising not accepted. **Circ:** (Not Reported).

4835 ■ South Asia Research
SAGE Publications Inc.
2455 Teller Rd.
Thousand Oaks, CA 91320-2234
Free: 800-818-7243
Publisher's E-mail: sales@pfp.sagepub.com
Journal covering South Asian studies including the history, politics, law, economics, sociology, visual culture, languages and literatures of the countries of the region. **Freq:** 3/year February, July, and November. **Print Method:** Offset. **Trim Size:** 5 1/2 x 8 1/2. **Cols./Page:** 1. **Col. Width:** 50 nonpareils. **Col. Depth:** 100 agate lines. **Key Personnel:** Werner F. Menski, Editor; Mara Malagodi, Editor. **ISSN:** 0262--7280 (print); **EISSN:** 1741--3141 (electronic). **Subscription Rates:** $621 Institutions print and e-access; $609 Institutions print only; $161 Individuals print only; $559 Institutions e-access; $223 Institutions single issue; $70 Individuals single issue. **URL:** http://sar.sagepub.com. **Remarks:** Advertising not accepted. **Circ:** (Not Reported).

4836 ■ Space and Culture
SAGE Publications Inc.
2455 Teller Rd.
Thousand Oaks, CA 91320-2234
Free: 800-818-7243
Publisher's E-mail: sales@pfp.sagepub.com
Journal covering cultural geography, sociology, cultural studies, architectural theory, ethnography, communications, urban studies, environmental studies and discourse analysis. Focusing on social spaces, such as the home, laboratory, leisure spaces, the city, and virtual spaces. **Freq:** Quarterly February, May, August, and November. **Print Method:** Offset. **Trim Size:** 5 1/2 x 8 1/2. **Cols./Page:** 1. **Col. Width:** 50 nonpareils. **Col. Depth:** 100 agate lines. **Key Personnel:** Justin Lloyd, Editor; Joost van Loon, Editor; Rob Shields, Editor. **ISSN:** 1206--3312 (print); **EISSN:** 1552--8308 (electronic). **Subscription Rates:** $1237 Institutions print and e-access; $1113 Institutions e-access; $1212 Institutions print only; $142 Individuals print only; $333 Institutions single print; $46 Individuals single print. **URL:** http://sac.sagepub.com. **Ad Rates:** BW $875; 4C $1110. **Remarks:** Accepts advertising. **Circ:** (Not Reported).

4837 ■ State Politics & Policy Quarterly
SAGE Publications Inc.
2455 Teller Rd.
Thousand Oaks, CA 91320-2234
Free: 800-818-7243
Publisher's E-mail: sales@pfp.sagepub.com
Official journal of the State Politics and Policy section of the American Political Science Association covering studies that develop general hypotheses of the political behavior and policymaking and test those hypotheses using methodological advantages of the states. **Freq:** Quarterly March , June , September , December. **Trim Size:** 4 3/8 x 7 1/4. **Key Personnel:** Nancy Martorano, Associate Editor; David Lowery, Board Member. **ISSN:** 1532--4400 (print); **EISSN:** 1946--1607 (electronic). **Subscription Rates:** £205 Institutions combined (Print & E-access); £185 Institutions e-access; £201 Institutions print only; £34 Individuals combined (Print & E-access); £31 Individuals e-access; £55 Institutions single print issue; £11 Individuals single print issue. **URL:** http://www.sagepub.com/journals/Journal202001; http://spa.sagepub.com. **Ad Rates:** BW $225. **Remarks:** Accepts advertising. **Circ:** 550.

4838 ■ Statistical Methods in Medical Research
SAGE Publications Inc.
2455 Teller Rd.
Thousand Oaks, CA 91320-2234
Free: 800-818-7243
Publisher's E-mail: sales@pfp.sagepub.com
Peer-reviewed journal covering statistics and medicine. **Freq:** Bimonthly. **Print Method:** Offset. **Trim Size:** 5 1/2 x 8 1/2. **Cols./Page:** 1. **Col. Width:** 50 nonpareils. **Col. Depth:** 100 agate lines. **Key Personnel:** Brian Everitt, Editor-in-Chief. **ISSN:** 0962--2802 (print); **EISSN:** 1477--0334 (electronic). **Subscription Rates:** $1360 Institutions print and e-access; $1224 Institutions e-access; $1333 Institutions print only; $242 Individuals print and e-access; $244 Institutions single print; $52 Individuals single print. **URL:** http://smm.sagepub.com. **Ad Rates:** BW £650. **Remarks:** Accepts advertising. **Circ:** (Not Reported).

4839 ■ Strategic Organization
SAGE Publications Inc.
2455 Teller Rd.
Thousand Oaks, CA 91320-2234
Free: 800-818-7243
Publisher's E-mail: sales@pfp.sagepub.com
Peer-reviewed journal covering research on strategic management and organization. **Freq:** Quarterly February, May, August, and November. **Print Method:** Offset. **Trim Size:** 5 1/2 x 8 1/2. **Cols./Page:** 1. **Col. Width:** 50 nonpareils. **Col. Depth:** 100 agate lines. **Key Personnel:** Robert David, Editor. **ISSN:** 1476--1270 (print); **EISSN:** 1741--315X (electronic). **Subscription Rates:** $1212 Institutions print and e-access; $1188 Institutions print only; $93 Individuals print only; $1091 Institutions e-access; $327 Institutions single print; $30 Individuals single print. **URL:** http://soq.sagepub.com. **Ad Rates:** BW £650. **Remarks:** Accepts advertising. **Circ:** (Not Reported).

4840 ■ Structural Health Monitoring
SAGE Publications Inc.
2455 Teller Rd.
Thousand Oaks, CA 91320-2234
Free: 800-818-7243
Publisher's E-mail: sales@pfp.sagepub.com
Peer-reviewed journal covering experimental or theoretical work on structural health monitoring. **Freq:** Bimonthly. **Print Method:** Offset. **Trim Size:** 5 1/2 x 8 1/2. **Cols./Page:** 1. **Col. Width:** 50 nonpareils. **Col. Depth:** 100 agate lines. **Key Personnel:** Mark J. Schulz, Editor; Fu-Kuo Chang, Editor-in-Chief; William H. Prosser, Editor. **ISSN:** 1475--9217 (print); **EISSN:** 1741--3168 (electronic). **Subscription Rates:** $1435 Institutions print & electronic; $1292 Institutions electronic; $1406 Institutions print; $137 Individuals print; $258 Institutions single issue; $30 Individuals single issue. **URL:** http://shm.sagepub.com. **Ad Rates:** BW £650. **Remarks:** Accepts advertising. **Circ:** (Not Reported).

4841 ■ Studies in Christian Ethics
SAGE Publications Inc.
2455 Teller Rd.
Thousand Oaks, CA 91320-2234
Free: 800-818-7243
Publisher's E-mail: sales@pfp.sagepub.com
Scholarly journal covering Christian ethics and moral theology. **Freq:** Quarterly. **Key Personnel:** Susan Frank Parsons, Editor; David Clough, Editor. **ISSN:** 0953--9468 (print); **EISSN:** 1745--5235 (electronic). **Subscription Rates:** £44 Individuals print only; £342 Institutions e-access; £372 Institutions print only; £380 Institutions print and e-access; £14 Individuals single print issue; £102 Institutions single print issue. **URL:** http://sce.sagepub.com. **Remarks:** Advertising accepted; rates available upon request. **Circ:** (Not Reported).

4842 ■ Surgical Innovation
SAGE Publications Inc.
2455 Teller Rd.
Thousand Oaks, CA 91320-2234
Free: 800-818-7243
Publisher's E-mail: sales@pfp.sagepub.com
Journal covering minimally invasive surgical techniques, instruments such as laparoscopes and endoscopes, and other technologies. Also covers information on clinical practice, research from the basic sciences, surgical education, and insights into the business of surgical practice. **Founded:** 1979. **Freq:** Bimonthly. **Print Method:** Offset. **Trim Size:** 8 1/8 x 10 7/8. **Cols./Page:** 1. **Col. Width:** 50 nonpareils. **Col. Depth:** 100 agate lines. **Key Personnel:** Lee Swanstrom, MD, Editor; Adrian E. Park, MD, Editor. **ISSN:** 1553-3506 (print). **Subscription Rates:** £703 Institutions print and e-access; £187 Individuals print and e-access; £126 Institutions single issue; £41 Individuals single issue; £689 Institutions print; £633 Institutions e-access. **URL:** http://c. **Ad Rates:** BW $1,170; 4C $1,275. **Remarks:** Accepts advertising. **Circ:** (Not Reported).

4843 ■ Teaching of Psychology
SAGE Publications Inc.
2455 Teller Rd.
Thousand Oaks, CA 91320-2234
Free: 800-818-7243
Publisher's E-mail: sales@pfp.sagepub.com
Journal on teaching psychology. **Freq:** Quarterly. **Key Personnel:** Pam Marek, Associate Editor; Bryan K. Saville, Associate Editor; Cynthia S. Koenig, Editor; Andrew N. Christopher, Editor. **ISSN:** 0098--6283 (print); **EISSN:** 1532--8023 (electronic). **Subscription Rates:** £454 Institutions print & e-access; £499 Institutions combined + backfile; £409 Institutions e-access; £454 Institutions e-access + backfile; £869 Institutions e-access (content through 1998); £445 Institutions print only; £38 Individuals print only; £122 Institutions single issue; £12 Individuals single issue. **URL:** http://uk.sagepub.com/en-gb/eur/teaching-of-psychology/journal202003#tabview=title. **Ad Rates:** BW $650. **Remarks:** Accepts advertising. **Circ:** (Not Reported).

4844 ■ Television & New Media
SAGE Publications Inc.
2455 Teller Rd.
Thousand Oaks, CA 91320-2234
Free: 800-818-7243
Publisher's E-mail: sales@pfp.sagepub.com
Journal devoting to the most recent trends in television and new media studies. **Freq:** 8/yr. **Trim Size:** 6 x 9. **Key Personnel:** Toby Miller, Board Member; Vicki Mayer, Editor. **ISSN:** 1527--4764 (print); **EISSN:** 1552--8316 (electronic). **Subscription Rates:** £68 Individuals print; £482 Institutions e-access; £524 Institutions print; £535 Institutions print and e-access; £11 Individuals single print; £72 Institutions single print. **URL:** http://tvn.sagepub.com. **Ad Rates:** BW $875; 4C $1110, in addition to black & white rate above. **Remarks:** Advertising accepted; rates available upon request. **Circ:** (Not Reported).

4845 ■ Textile Research Journal
SAGE Publications Inc.
2455 Teller Rd.
Thousand Oaks, CA 91320-2234
Free: 800-818-7243
Publisher's E-mail: sales@pfp.sagepub.com
Peer-reviewed scientific journal dealing with physical and engineering sciences of fiber and textile materials and processing. **Founded:** 1930. **Freq:** 20/yr. **Print Method:** Offset. **Cols./Page:** 2. **Col. Width:** 37 nonpareils. **Col. Depth:** 122 agate lines. **Key Personnel:** Dong Zhang, Editor-in-Chief. **ISSN:** 0040-5175 (print). **Subscription Rates:** $1862 Institutions print & e-access; $1676 Institutions e-access; $1825 Institutions print only; $494 Individuals print only. **URL:** http://trj.sagepub.com. **Remarks:** Advertising not accepted. **Circ:** ‡2000.

4846 ■ Theory and Research in Education
SAGE Publications Inc.
2455 Teller Rd.
Thousand Oaks, CA 91320-2234
Free: 800-818-7243
Publisher's E-mail: sales@pfp.sagepub.com
Interdisciplinary journal covering normative and theoretical issues concerning education including multi-faceted philosophical analysis of moral, social, political and epistemological problems and issues arising from educational practice. **Freq:** 3/year March, July, and October. **Print Method:** Offset. **Trim Size:** 5 1/2 x 8 1/2. **Cols./Page:** 1. **Col. Width:** 50 nonpareils. **Col. Depth:** 100 agate lines. **Key Personnel:** Marjan Setinc, Editor, Founder; Randall Curren, Editor-in-Chief; Harry Brighouse, Board Member; Mitja Sardoc, Managing Editor. **ISSN:** 1477--8785 (print); **EISSN:** 1741--3192 (electronic). **Subscription Rates:** $743 Institutions print and online; $669 Institutions online; $728 Institutions print; $100 Individuals print; $267 Institutions single print issue; $43 Individuals single print issue. **URL:** http://tre.sagepub.com. **Ad Rates:** BW £650. **Remarks:** Accepts advertising. **Circ:** (Not Reported).

4847 ■ Therapeutic Advances in Drug Safety
SAGE Publications Inc.
2455 Teller Rd.
Thousand Oaks, CA 91320-2234
Free: 800-818-7243
Publisher's E-mail: sales@pfp.sagepub.com
Peer-reviewed journal covering novel and controversial aspects pertaining to the safe use of drugs in different age and ethnic patient groups. **Freq:** Bimonthly. **Key Personnel:** Arduino Mangoni, Editor-in-Chief. **ISSN:** 2042-0986 (print); **EISSN:** 2042-0994 (electronic). **Subscription Rates:** $1181 Institutions print and e-access; $1063 Institutions e-access; $1157 Institutions print; $152 Individuals print. **URL:** http://www.sagepub.com/journalsProdDesc.nav?prodId=Journal201944. **Circ:** (Not Reported).

4848 ■ Topics in Early Childhood Special Education
SAGE Publications Inc.
2455 Teller Rd.
Thousand Oaks, CA 91320-2234
Free: 800-818-7243
Publisher's E-mail: sales@pfp.sagepub.com
Magazine for special education professionals. Provides information on research and teaching practices for young children with disabilities and their families. **Freq:** Quarterly. **Print Method:** Offset. **Trim Size:** 8 x 10 7/8. **Cols./Page:** 2. **Col. Width:** 3 3/8 inches. **Col. Depth:** 9 1/8 inches. **Key Personnel:** Howard Goldstein, Board Member; Judith J. Carta, PhD, Associate Editor; Stephen J. Bagnato, Board Member; Sarah Rule, PhD, Board Member; Glenn Dunlap, Editor. **ISSN:** 0271--1214 (print); **EISSN:** 1538--4845 (electronic). **Subscription Rates:** $71 Individuals print and online; $186 Institutions online only; $203 Institutions online only; $207 Institutions print and online; $23 Individuals single print issue; $56 Institutions single print issue. **URL:** http://tec.sagepub.com. **Ad Rates:** BW $480; 4C $935. **Remarks:** Accepts advertising. **Circ:** Paid 1700.

4849 ■ Toxicologic Pathology
SAGE Publications Inc.
2455 Teller Rd.
Thousand Oaks, CA 91320
Phone: (805)499-9774
Fax: (805)499-0871
Free: 800-818-7243
Publisher's E-mail: sales@pfp.sagepub.com
Journal focusing on the multidisciplinary elements that constitute toxicologic pathology, including spontaneous and experimentally induced morphological and functional changes, environmental exposures, case reports, and risk assessment and investigative techniques. **Freq:** 8/year. **Trim Size:** 8 1/2 x 11. **Key Personnel:** John R. Foster, Advisor; Stephanie Dickinson, BA, Manager, Editor. **ISSN:** 0192--6233 (print); **EISSN:** 1533--1601 (electronic). **Subscription Rates:** £271 Individuals print only; £448 Institutions e-access or print; £498 Institutions print and e-access; £44 Individuals single print issue; £67 Individuals single print issue. **URL:** http://tpx.sagepub.com. **Ad Rates:** BW $850. **Remarks:** Accepts advertising. **Circ:** Paid ‡1350.

4850 ■ Toxicology and Industrial Health
SAGE Publications Inc.
2455 Teller Rd.
Thousand Oaks, CA 91320-2234
Free: 800-818-7243
Publisher's E-mail: sales@pfp.sagepub.com
Peer-reviewed journal covering toxicology and industrial health including biochemical toxicology, genetic and cellular toxicology, pathology, risk assessment associated with hazardous wastes and ground water. **Freq:** 10/year. **Key Personnel:** Ronald W. Hart; Anthony L. Kiorpes, Editor-in-Chief. **ISSN:** 0748-2337 (print); **EISSN:** 1477-0393 (electronic). **Subscription Rates:** $1900 Institutions print and e-access; $1710 Institutions e-access; $1862 Institutions print only; $457 Individuals print and e-access; $205 Institutions single print; $59 Individuals single print. **URL:** http://tih.sagepub.com; http://www.sagepub.com/journalsProdDesc.nav?prodId=

Circulation: ★ = AAM; △ or • = BPA; ♦ = CAC; ❑ = VAC; ⊕ = PO Statement; ‡ = Publisher's Report; Boldface figures = sworn; Light figures = estimated.

Journal201830. **Remarks:** Accepts advertising. **Circ:** (Not Reported).

4851 ■ Trauma, Violence & Abuse
SAGE Publications Inc.
2455 Teller Rd.
Thousand Oaks, CA 91320-2234
Free: 800-818-7243
Publisher's E-mail: sales@pfp.sagepub.com
Journal for expanding knowledge on all force of trauma, abuse, and violence. **Freq:** Quarterly published in January, April, July and October. **Key Personnel:** Jon R. Conte, PhD, Editor; Candace Conte, Managing Editor. **ISSN:** 1524-8380 (print). **Subscription Rates:** $537 Institutions e-access; $129 Individuals e-access. **URL:** http://www.sagepub.com/journalsProdDesc.nav?prodId=Journal200782; http://tva.sagepub.com. **Ad Rates:** BW $515; 4C $995. **Remarks:** Advertising accepted; rates available upon request. **Circ:** (Not Reported).

4852 ■ Trends in Hearing
SAGE Publications Inc.
2455 Teller Rd.
Thousand Oaks, CA 91320-2234
Free: 800-818-7243
Publisher's E-mail: sales@pfp.sagepub.com
Trade publication covering the field of auditory amplification and the care and treatment of hearing disorders. **Freq:** Quarterly March, June, September, December. **Trim Size:** 8 1/2 x 11. **Key Personnel:** Andrew J. Oxenham, PhD, Editor-in-Chief. **ISSN:** 2331-2165 (print); **EISSN:** 2331-2165 (electronic). **Subscription Rates:** $54 Individuals single, print; $166 Individuals print & e-access; $670 Institutions print & e-access; $603 Institutions e-access; $657 Institutions print only. **URL:** http://tia.sagepub.com; http://uk.sagepub.com/en-gb/asi/trends-in-hearing/journal201794. **Formerly:** Trends in Amplification. **Ad Rates:** BW $980; 4C $1,105. **Remarks:** Accepts advertising. **Circ:** Combined 1865.

4853 ■ Urban Affairs Review
SAGE Publications Inc.
2455 Teller Rd.
Thousand Oaks, CA 91320-2234
Free: 800-818-7243
Publisher's E-mail: sales@pfp.sagepub.com
Urban studies journal. **Freq:** Bimonthly. **Print Method:** Offset. **Trim Size:** 5 1/2 x 8 1/2. **Cols./Page:** 1. **Col. Width:** 50 nonpareils. **Col. Depth:** 100 agate lines. **Key Personnel:** Peter Burns, Editor. **ISSN:** 1078--0874 (print); **EISSN:** 1552--8332 (electronic). **Subscription Rates:** £832 Institutions print & e-access; £915 Institutions current volume print & all online content; £749 Institutions e-access; £832 Institutions e-access (all online content); £2099 Institutions e-access (content through 1998); £815 Institutions print only; £107 Individuals print only; £149 Institutions single print; £23 Individuals single print. **URL:** http://uk.sagepub.com/en-gb/asi/urban-affairs-review/journal200784#description. **Formerly:** Urban Affairs Quarterly. **Ad Rates:** BW $725; 4C $1115. **Remarks:** Accepts advertising. **Circ:** Paid ‡1110.

4854 ■ Urban Education
SAGE Publications Inc.
2455 Teller Rd.
Thousand Oaks, CA 91320-2234
Free: 800-818-7243
Publisher's E-mail: sales@pfp.sagepub.com
Journal covering inner city education. **Freq:** 10/year. **Print Method:** Offset. **Trim Size:** 5 1/2 x 8 1/2. **Cols./Page:** 1. **Col. Width:** 50 nonpareils. **Col. Depth:** 100 agate lines. **Key Personnel:** H. Richard Milner, Editor; Lauri Johnson, Board Member. **ISSN:** 0042--0859 (print); **EISSN:** 1552--8340 (electronic). **Subscription Rates:** £912 Institutions combined print and e-access; £821 Institutions e-access; £894 Institutions print only; £129 Individuals print only; £98 Institutions single print; £17 Individuals single print. **URL:** http://uex.sagepub.com; http://uk.sagepub.com/en-gb/asi/urban-education/journal200963. **Ad Rates:** BW $725; 4C $1115. **Remarks:** Accepts advertising. **Circ:** Paid ‡862, Non-paid ‡111.

4855 ■ Vascular and Endovascular Surgery
SAGE Publications Inc.
2455 Teller Rd.
Thousand Oaks, CA 91320-2234
Free: 800-818-7243
Publisher's E-mail: sales@pfp.sagepub.com
Magazine featuring original papers on vascular surgery, including operative procedures, clinical or laboratory research, and case reports. **Founded:** Mar. 1967. **Freq:** Bimonthly. **Print Method:** Offset. **Trim Size:** 8 1/2 x 11. **Cols./Page:** 2. **Key Personnel:** Thomas Maldonado, Editor. **ISSN:** 0042-2835 (print). **Subscription Rates:** $1127 Institutions print & e-access; $1014 Institutions e-access; $1104 Institutions print only; $800 Individuals hospital, print & e-access; $384 Individuals print & e-access; $1240 Institutions current volume (print and online content); $2758 Institutions e-access (content through 1998); $1127 Institutions e-access plus backfile (all online content). **URL:** http://ves.sagepub.com/; http://www.sagepub.com/journals/Journal201795/manuscriptSubmission. **Formerly:** Vascular Surgery. **Ad Rates:** BW $1,445; 4C $1,415. **Remarks:** Accepts advertising. **Circ:** ‡4440.

4856 ■ Vascular Medicine
SAGE Publications Inc.
2455 Teller Rd.
Thousand Oaks, CA 91320-2234
Free: 800-818-7243
Publisher's E-mail: sales@pfp.sagepub.com
Peer-reviewed journal covering vascular biology including the practice of vascular medicine and vascular surgery. **Founded:** June 1982. **Freq:** Bimonthly. **Print Method:** Offset. **Trim Size:** 5 1/2 x 8 1/2. **Cols./Page:** 1. **Col. Width:** 50 nonpareils. **Col. Depth:** 100 agate lines. **Key Personnel:** Mark A. Creager, Editor-in-Chief; Jeffrey W. Olin, Associate Editor; William Hiatt, Associate Editor. **ISSN:** 1358-863X (print); **EISSN:** 1477-0377 (electronic). **Subscription Rates:** $1059 Institutions print & e-access; $953 Institutions e-access; $1038 Institutions print only; $326 Individuals print & e-access; $190 Institutions single print; $71 Individuals single print. **URL:** http://vmj.sagepub.com/; http://www.sagepub.com/journalsProdDesc.nav?prodId=Journal201833. **Circ:** (Not Reported).

4857 ■ Violence Against Women: An International and Interdisciplinary Journal
SAGE Publications Inc.
2455 Teller Rd.
Thousand Oaks, CA 91320-2234
Free: 800-818-7243
Publication E-mail: advertising@sagepub.com
Peer-reviewed journal covering research on violence against women worldwide, including sexual harassment, domestic violence, incest, and sexual assault. **Freq:** Monthly. **Print Method:** Offset. **Trim Size:** 5 1/2 x 8 1/2. **Key Personnel:** Jody Raphael, Associate Editor; Claire M. Renzetti, Editor; Jeffrey Edleson, Associate Editor; Sue Osthoff, Associate Editor. **ISSN:** 1077--8012 (print); **EISSN:** 1552--8448 (electronic). **Subscription Rates:** £18 Individuals single print issue; £75 Institutions single print issue; £199 Individuals print; £872 Institutions e-access; £950 Institutions print; £969 Institutions print and e-access. **URL:** http://vaw.sagepub.com; http://us.sagepub.com/en-us/nam/violence-against-women/journal200837. **Ad Rates:** BW $515. **Remarks:** Accepts advertising. **Circ:** (Not Reported).

4858 ■ War in History
SAGE Publications Inc.
2455 Teller Rd.
Thousand Oaks, CA 91320-2234
Free: 800-818-7243
Publisher's E-mail: sales@pfp.sagepub.com
Peer-reviewed journal covering study of naval forces, maritime power and air forces, as well as military matters. **Freq:** Quarterly January, April, July, and November. **Print Method:** Offset. **Trim Size:** 5 1/2 x 8 1/2. **Cols./Page:** 1. **Col. Width:** 50 nonpareils. **Col. Depth:** 100 agate lines. **Key Personnel:** Dennis Showalter, Board Member; Hew Strachan, Board Member. **ISSN:** 0968--3445 (print); **EISSN:** 1477--0385 (electronic). **Subscription Rates:** $801 Institutions combined print and e-access; $721 Institutions e-access; $785 Institutions print only; $137 Individuals combined print & e-access; $216 Institutions single print issue; $45 Individuals single print issue. **URL:** http://wih.sagepub.com. **Ad Rates:** BW £650. **Remarks:** Accepts advertising. **Circ:** (Not Reported).

4859 ■ Western Journal of Nursing Research: An International Forum for Communicating Nursing Research
SAGE Publications Inc.
2455 Teller Rd.
Thousand Oaks, CA 91320-2234
Free: 800-818-7243
Publisher's E-mail: sales@pfp.sagepub.com
Journal on nursing research.Offers clinical research reports broadened by commentaries and author's responses. **Freq:** 10/year January , February , March , April , May , July , August , September , October and November. **Print Method:** Offset. **Trim Size:** 5 1/2 x 8 1/2. **Cols./Page:** 1. **Col. Width:** 50 nonpareils. **Col. Depth:** 100 agate lines. **Key Personnel:** Vicki Conn, Editor; Susan Rawl, Board Member. **ISSN:** 0193--9459 (print); **EISSN:** 1552--8456 (electronic). **Subscription Rates:** £1283 Institutions print & e-access; £1411 Institutions current volume print & all online content; £1155 Institutions e-access; £1199 Institutions e-access (all online content); £1801 Institutions e-access (content through 1998); £1257 Institutions print only; £119 Individuals print only; £115 Institutions single print; £13 Individuals single print. **URL:** http://uk.sagepub.com/en-gb/asi/western-journal-of-nursing-research/journal200968. **Ad Rates:** BW $725; 4C $1115. **Remarks:** Accepts advertising. **Circ:** Paid ‡1950, Non-paid ‡110.

4860 ■ Work and Occupations: An International Sociological Journal
SAGE Publications Inc.
2455 Teller Rd.
Thousand Oaks, CA 91320-2234
Free: 800-818-7243
Publisher's E-mail: sales@pfp.sagepub.com
Journal covering sociology as related to work, occupations, employment and labor relations. **Freq:** Quarterly. **Print Method:** Offset. **Trim Size:** 5 1/2 x 8 1/2. **Cols./Page:** 1. **Col. Width:** 50 nonpareils. **Col. Depth:** 100 agate lines. **Key Personnel:** Daniel B. Cornfield, Editor. **ISSN:** 0730--8884 (print); **EISSN:** 1552--8464 (electronic). **Subscription Rates:** £690 Institutions print & e-access; £759 Institutions current volume print & all online content; £621 Institutions e-access; £690 Institutions backfile lease, e-access plus backfile -all online; £1319 Institutions e-access (content through 1998); £676 Institutions print only; £93 Individuals print only; £186 Single issue institutional; £30 Single issue individual. **URL:** http://uk.sagepub.com/en-gb/asi/work-and-occupations/journal200911. **Ad Rates:** BW $725; 4C $1115. **Remarks:** Accepts advertising. **Circ:** Paid ‡700.

4861 ■ Workplace Health & Safety: Promoting Environments Conducive to Well-Being and Productivity
SAGE Publications Inc.
2455 Teller Rd.
Thousand Oaks, CA 91320-2234
Free: 800-818-7243
Publication E-mail: aaohn@slackinc.com
Official journal of the American Association of Occupational Health Nurses. **Freq:** Monthly. **Print Method:** Offset. **Trim Size:** 8 1/8 x 10 7/8. **Cols./Page:** 2. **Col. Width:** 19 picas. **Col. Depth:** 58 picas. **Key Personnel:** Joy Wachs, PhD, Editor. **ISSN:** 2165-0799 (print); **EISSN:** 2165-0969 (electronic). **Subscription Rates:** $13 Single issue; $38 Institutions single issue; $117 Individuals print and e-access; $378 Institutions e-access; $412 Institutions print; $420 Institutions print and e-access. **URL:** http://us.sagepub.com/en-us/nam/workplace-health-safety/journal202325. **Formerly:** Occupational Health Nursing; AAOHN Journal. **Ad Rates:** BW $2,520; 4C $4,020. **Remarks:** Accepts advertising. **Circ:** 7100.

4862 ■ Written Communication: An International Quarterly of Research, Theory, and Application
SAGE Publications Inc.
2455 Teller Rd.
Thousand Oaks, CA 91320-2234
Free: 800-818-7243
Publisher's E-mail: sales@pfp.sagepub.com
Journal presenting theory and methodology in the study of the written word. **Freq:** Quarterly. **Print Method:** Offset. **Trim Size:** 5 1/2 x 8 1/2. **Cols./Page:** 1. **Col. Width:** 50 nonpareils. **Col. Depth:** 100 agate lines. **Key Personnel:** Christina Haas, Editor. **ISSN:** 0741--0883 (print); **EISSN:** 1552--8472 (electronic). **Subscription Rates:** £674 Institutions print & e-access; £741 Institu-

tions current volume print & all online content; £607 Institutions e-access only; £674 Institutions e-access & all online; £775 Institutions e-access (content through 1998); £661 Institutions print only; £93 Individuals print only; £182 Single issue institutional; £30 Single issue individual. **URL:** http://uk.sagepub.com/en-gb/asi/written-communication/journal200767. **Ad Rates:** BW $725; 4C $1115. **Remarks:** Accepts advertising. **Circ:** Paid ‡700.

4863 ■ Youth Justice
SAGE Publications Inc.
2455 Teller Rd.
Thousand Oaks, CA 91320-2234
Free: 800-818-7243
Publisher's E-mail: sales@pfp.sagepub.com
Peer-reviewed journal covering analysis of juvenile and youth justice systems, law, policy and practice. **Freq:** 3/year April, August, and December. **Print Method:** Offset. **Trim Size:** 5 1/2 x 8 1/2. **Cols./Page:** 1. **Col. Width:** 50 nonpareils. **Col. Depth:** 100 agate lines. **Key Personnel:** John Muncie, Editor; Chris Cunneen, Board Member; Mark Drakeford, Board Member; Tim Bateman, Board Member; Janet Jamieson, Editor; Barry Goldson, Editor; Jolande Beijerse, Board Member. **ISSN:** 1473--2254 (print); **EISSN:** 1747-0-6283 (electronic). **Subscription Rates:** $881 Institutions print & e-access; $793 Institutions e-access; $863 Institutions print only; $83 Individuals print only; $316 Institutions single issue; $36 Individuals single issue. **URL:** http://yjj.sagepub.com. **Ad Rates:** BW £650. **Remarks:** Accepts advertising. **Circ:** (Not Reported).

4864 ■ Youth & Society
SAGE Publications Inc.
2455 Teller Rd.
Thousand Oaks, CA 91320-2234
Free: 800-818-7243
Publisher's E-mail: sales@pfp.sagepub.com
Journal on the culture and development of youth. **Freq:** Bimonthly. **Print Method:** Offset. **Trim Size:** 5 1/2 x 8 1/2. **Cols./Page:** 1. **Col. Width:** 50 nonpareils. **Col. Depth:** 100 agate lines. **Key Personnel:** Marc Zimmerman, Editor. **ISSN:** 0044--118X (print); **EISSN:** 1552--8499 (electronic). **Subscription Rates:** £722 Institutions print & e-access; £794 Institutions current volume print & all online content; £650 Institutions e-access; £722 Individuals e-access (all online content); £1474 Single issue e-access (content through 1998); $708 Institutions print only; £93 Individuals print only; £97 Single issue institution; £15 Single issue individual. **URL:** http://uk.sagepub.com/en-gb/asi/youth-society/journal200812. **Ad Rates:** BW $725; 4C $1115. **Remarks:** Accepts advertising. **Circ:** Paid ‡700.

4865 ■ Youth Violence and Juvenile Justice
SAGE Publications Inc.
2455 Teller Rd.
Thousand Oaks, CA 91320-2234
Free: 800-818-7243
Publisher's E-mail: sales@pfp.sagepub.com
Journal that provides academics and practitioners with a forum for publishing current empirical research, discussing theoretical issues, and reviewing promising interventions and programs in the areas of youth violence, juvenile justice, and school safety. **Freq:** Quarterly. **Key Personnel:** Eric J. Fritsch, Editor, Founder; Tori J. Caeti, Editor, Founder; Chad R. Trulson, Editor. **ISSN:** 1541--2040 (print); **EISSN:** 1556--9330 (electronic). **Subscription Rates:** $239 Institutions e-access; $75 Individuals e-access. **URL:** http://www.sagepub.com/journalsProdDesc.nav?prodId=Journal201632; http://yvj.sagepub.com; http://www.sagepub.com/journals/Journal201632. **Remarks:** Accepts advertising. **Circ:** (Not Reported).

4866 ■ KAJL-FM - 92.7
99 Long Ct.
Thousand Oaks, CA 91360
Phone: (805)497-8511
Format: Contemporary Hit Radio (CHR); Adult Contemporary; Oldies; Classic Rock; Country. **Key Personnel:** Matthew Rodriguez, Gen. Mgr., matt@playlist927.com; Betsy Zook, Bus. Mgr., betsy@playlist927.com.

4867 ■ KCLU-FM - 88.3
60 W Olsen Rd., No. 4400
Thousand Oaks, CA 91360
Phone: (805)493-3900
Format: Public Radio. **Networks:** National Public Radio (NPR). **Owner:** California Lutheran University, 60 W Olsen Rd., Thousand Oaks, CA 91360. **Founded:** Oct. 20, 1994. **Operating Hours:** Continuous. **Key Personnel:** Mia Karnatz-Shifflett, Dir. of Member Svcs., mkarnatz@callutheran.edu; Lance Orozco, News Dir. **Wattage:** 3,200 ERP. **Ad Rates:** Noncommercial. **URL:** http://www.kclu.org.

4868 ■ KDSC-FM - 91.1
PO Box 77913
Los Angeles, CA 90007
Phone: (213)225-7400
Fax: (213)225-7410
Email: info@thegrandtour.com
Format: Public Radio. **Networks:** National Public Radio (NPR); Public Radio International (PRI). **Owner:** University of Southern California, University Park Campus, Los Angeles, CA 90089, Ph: (213)740-2311. **Founded:** 1982. **Formerly:** KCPB-FM. **Operating Hours:** Continuous. **Key Personnel:** Brenda Barnes, President, bbarnes@kusc.org; Eric DeWeese, Gen. Mgr., edeweese@kusc.org; Ron Thompson, Dir. of Engg., rthompson@kusc.org. **Wattage:** 5,000. **Ad Rates:** Noncommercial. **URL:** http://www.kusc.org.

4869 ■ KHJL-FM - 92.7
99 Long Ct., No. 200
Thousand Oaks, CA 91360
Phone: (805)497-8511
Fax: (805)497-8514
Format: Eclectic. **Key Personnel:** Matthew Rodriguez, Gen. Mgr., matt@playlist927.com; Betsy Zook, Bus. Mgr., betsy@playlist927.com; Pat Duffy, Station Mgr., patduffy@playlist927.com.

4870 ■ KMLT-FM - 92.7
99 Long Ct., No. 200
Thousand Oaks, CA 91360
Phone: (805)497-8511
Format: Adult Contemporary. **Key Personnel:** Matthew Rodriguez, Gen. Mgr., matt@927jillfm.com; Betsy Zook, Bus. Mgr., betsy@playlist927.com; Rick Shaw, Operations Mgr., Prog. Dir., rick@playlist927.com; Jake Hagen, Asst. Dir., Dir. of Traffic, jake@playlilst927.com. **Ad Rates:** Noncommercial.

TIBURON

Marin Co. Marin Co. (W) 5 m N.W. of Sausalito. Residential.

4871 ■ AHP Perspective
Association for Humanistic Psychology
PO Box 1190
Tiburon, CA 94920
Phone: (415)435-1604
Fax: (415)435-1654
Publisher's E-mail: ahpoffice@aol.com
Freq: Bimonthly. **Subscription Rates:** included in membership dues. **Mailing address:** PO Box 1190, Tiburon, CA 94920. **Remarks:** Accepts advertising. **Circ:** 5000.

4872 ■ The Ark
The Ark Publishing Co.
1550 Tiburon Blvd.
Tiburon, CA 94920
Phone: (415)435-2652
Fax: (415)435-0849
Publisher's E-mail: editor@thearknewspaper.com
Newspaper serving Strawberry, Tiburon, and Belvedere. **Freq:** Weekly. **Print Method:** Offset. **Trim Size:** 10 1/8 x 14. **Cols./Page:** 6. **Col. Width:** 19 nonpareils. **Col. Depth:** 196 agate lines. **Key Personnel:** Alison Kern, Publisher; Marilyn Kessler, Editor; Henriette Corn, Director, Advertising. **USPS:** 012-310. **Subscription Rates:** $50 Individuals; $90 Two years; $65 Out of area; $115 Out of area two years; $40 Out of area Students (9 months). **URL:** http://www.thearknewspaper.com/. **Mailing address:** PO Box 1054, Tiburon, CA 94920. **Ad Rates:** BW $642.60; 4C $110; PCI $8.80. **Remarks:** Accepts advertising. **Circ:** Paid ‡3500, Free ‡40.

4873 ■ KEJO-AM - 1240
333 Blackfield Dr., Ste. 333
Tiburon, CA 94920
Phone: (541)754-6633
Fax: (541)754-6725
Email: kfly@proaxis.com
Format: Adult Contemporary. **Networks:** ABC. **Owner:** Madgekal Broadcasting, at above address. **Founded:** 1955. **Formerly:** KFLY-AM. **Operating Hours:** Continuous; 5% network, 95% local. **ADI:** Portland, OR. **Key Personnel:** Pete Young, News Dir; Norm Suiter, Contact. **Wattage:** 1,000. **Ad Rates:** $11 for 30 seconds; $13 for 60 seconds. Combined advertising rates available with KFLY-FM.

TORRANCE

Los Angeles Co. Los Angeles Co. (S). 16 m S of Los Angeles. El Camino College. Manufactures steel, aluminum, oil well machinery, paint, plumbing and heating fixtures, rubber goods, petroleum products, pistons, chemicals, plastics, brick, tile, aircraft, missiles, butter, cheese, insulating material, electronics, steel cable, synthetic rubber. Oil wells.

4874 ■ Automotive Fleet
Bobit Business Media
3520 Challenger St.
Torrance, CA 90503
Phone: (310)533-2400
Fax: (310)533-2500
Automotive magazine covering the car and light truck fleet market. **Freq:** Monthly. **Print Method:** Offset. **Trim Size:** 8 x 10 7/8. **Cols./Page:** 3. **Col. Width:** 26 nonpareils. **Col. Depth:** 140 agate lines. **Key Personnel:** Lauren Fletcher, Managing Editor, phone: (541)213-2097; Sherb Brown, Publisher, Vice President, phone: (310)533-2451; Eric Bearly, Associate Publisher, Manager, Sales, phone: (303)681-2615. **ISSN:** 0005--1519 (print). **Subscription Rates:** Free. **URL:** http://www.automotive-fleet.com. **Ad Rates:** BW $5445; 4C $10850. **Remarks:** Accepts advertising. **Circ:** 23768.

4875 ■ Behold Magazine
Campus Evangelical Fellowship Inc.
1753 Cabrillo Ave.
Torrance, CA 90501
Phone: (310)328-8200
Fax: (310)328-8207
Magazine covering topics on ministry sharing, and spiritual growth. **Freq:** Bimonthly. **Subscription Rates:** $24 Individuals; $36 Other countries. **Circ:** (Not Reported).

4876 ■ Daily Breeze
Daily Breeze
21250 Hawthorne Blvd., Ste. 170
Torrance, CA 90503
Phone: (310)540-5511
Publisher's E-mail: newsroom@dailybreeze.com
General newspaper. **Freq:** Daily. **Key Personnel:** Toni Sciacqua, Editor; Linda Lindus, Publisher. **Subscription Rates:** $20 Individuals /month (print and online) - 7 day home delivery; $15 Individuals /month (print and online) - Thursday to Sunday home delivery; $10 Individuals /month (print and online) - Sunday only home delivery. **URL:** http://www.dailybreeze.com. **Remarks:** Advertising accepted; rates available upon request. **Circ:** Mon.-Fri. ★**68964**, Sun. ★**67782**, Sat. ★**72056**.

4877 ■ Heavy Duty Trucking
Bobit Business Media
3520 Challenger St.
Torrance, CA 90503
Phone: (310)533-2400
Fax: (310)533-2500
Magazine serving large, medium and small fleet managers whose firms operate class 6, 7 and 8 trucks in the U.S. **Freq:** Monthly. **Print Method:** Offset. **Trim Size:** 7 7/8 x 10 3/4. **Cols./Page:** 3 and 2. **Col. Width:** 26 and 40 nonpareils. **Col. Depth:** 140 agate lines. **Key Personnel:** Tom Berg, Senior Editor; Deborah Lockridge, Editor-in-Chief. **ISSN:** 0017--9434 (print). **URL:** http://www.truckinginfo.com. **Remarks:** Advertising accepted; rates available upon request. **Circ:** Paid △**115104**.

4878 ■ The Journal of the Arthur Rackham Society
Arthur Rackham Society
20705 Wood Ave.
Torrance, CA 90503-2755
Publisher's E-mail: the.ar.society@gmail.com
Journal featuring articles of appreciation towards Arthur

Circulation: ★ = AAM; △ or • = BPA; ♦ = CAC; ❑ = VAC; ⊕ = PO Statement; ‡ = Publisher's Report; Boldface figures = sworn; Light figures = estimated.

Rackham and his works. **Freq:** 3/year. **ISSN:** 1076--8912 (print). **Subscription Rates:** Included in membership. **URL:** http://arthur-rackham-society.org/current_issue.html. **Remarks:** Advertising not accepted. **Circ:** (Not Reported).

4879 ■ LCT
Bobit Business Media
3520 Challenger St.
Torrance, CA 90503
Phone: (310)533-2400
Fax: (310)533-2500
Publication E-mail: info@lctmag.com
Magazine for the limousine service industry. #1 Magazine for the limousine service industry. **Freq:** Monthly. **Print Method:** Offset. **Trim Size:** 8 x 10 7/8. **Cols./Page:** 3. **Col. Width:** 26 nonpareils. **Col. Depth:** 130 agate lines. **Key Personnel:** Martin Romjue, Editor, phone: (310)533-2489, fax: (310)533-2514; Heidi Dimaya, Manager, Production, phone: (310)533-2559; Sara Eastwood-McLean, Publisher, phone: (253)983-0515, fax: (253)983-0516. **ISSN:** 8750--7374 (print). **Subscription Rates:** Free to qualified subscribers. **URL:** http://www.lctmag.com. **Also known as:** Limousine & Chauffeured Transportation. **Ad Rates:** BW $2910; 4C $4430. **Remarks:** Accepts advertising. **Circ:** Non-paid △**11756**, Paid △**488**.

4880 ■ The Lesbian News: We've Got You Covered
The Lesbian News
PO Box 55
Torrance, CA 90507
Phone: (310)458-9888
Fax: (310)548-9588
Free: 800-458-9888
Magazine of lesbian and gay-oriented articles, features, and cartoons. **Freq:** Monthly. **Key Personnel:** Ella Matthes, Editor-in-Chief, Publisher. **ISSN:** 0739--1803 (print). **Alt. Formats:** Handheld. **URL:** http://play.google.com/store/apps/details?id=com.lesbiannews.lesbiannews. **Remarks:** Accepts advertising. **Circ:** 40000.

4881 ■ Lighthouse
Lighthouse
2958 Columbia St.
Torrance, CA 90503
Phone: (310)782-6927
Fax: (310)782-6157
Publisher's E-mail: lighthouse@us-lighthouse.com
Japanese language community magazine. **Founded:** 1989. **Freq:** Biweekly. **Key Personnel:** Yoichi Komiyama, Advertising Representative; Hiroko Nishikawa, Contact. **Subscription Rates:** Free; $55 By mail. **URL:** http://www.lce-edu.com/english/profile/index.html. **Ad Rates:** BW $1,800. **Remarks:** Accepts advertising. **Circ:** Combined 65000.

4882 ■ Metro Magazine
Bobit Business Media
3520 Challenger St.
Torrance, CA 90503
Phone: (310)533-2400
Fax: (310)533-2500
Publication E-mail: info@metro-magazine.com
Magazine on public transportation. **Founded:** 1904. **Freq:** 5/yr. **Print Method:** Offset. **Trim Size:** 7 7/8 x 10 3/4. **Cols./Page:** 3. **Col. Width:** 26 nonpareils. **Col. Depth:** 140 agate lines. **Key Personnel:** Frank Di Giacomo, Publisher; Mark Hollenbeck, Associate Publisher; Alex Roman, Managing Editor; Janna Starcic, Executive Editor. **ISSN:** 0162-6221 (print). **Subscription Rates:** Free. **URL:** http://www.metro-magazine.com. **Ad Rates:** BW $5,950; 4C $7,200; PCI $150. **Remarks:** Accepts advertising. **Circ:** Controlled △**24757**.

4883 ■ Minority Business Entrepreneur
Minority Business Entrepreneur
3528 Torrance Blvd., Ste. 101
Torrance, CA 90503-4803
Phone: (310)540-9398
Fax: (310)294-9071
Publication E-mail: boliver@mbemag.com
Business magazine for ethnic minority and women business owners. **Freq:** Bimonthly. **Print Method:** Offset. **Trim Size:** 8 x 10 7/8. **Cols./Page:** 3. **Col. Width:** 13 picas. **Col. Depth:** 10 inches. **Key Personnel:** Ginger Conrad, Managing Editor; Emily Richwine, Managing Editor; Barbara Oliver, Publisher. **ISSN:** 1048--0919 (print). **Subscription Rates:** $25 Individuals print amd digital; $18 Individuals print only; $12 Individuals digital only; $35 Two years print & digital; $30 Two years print only; $20 Two years digital only. **URL:** http://www.mbemag.com. **Ad Rates:** BW $4200; 4C $5200. **Remarks:** Accepts advertising. **Circ:** (Not Reported).

4884 ■ Overseas Campus Magazine
Campus Evangelical Fellowship Inc.
1753 Cabrillo Ave.
Torrance, CA 90501
Phone: (310)328-8200
Fax: (310)328-8207
Magazine focusing on personal testimonies, Christian faith and tracks of life. **Freq:** Bimonthly. **Key Personnel:** Edwin Su, Director. **URL:** http://www.oc.org/eng_txt/about.htm. **Circ:** (Not Reported).

4885 ■ Pacific Citizen
Japanese American Citizens League - South Bay Chapter
PO Box 4135
Torrance, CA 90510
Publisher's E-mail: support@southbayjacl.org
Newspaper (tabloid). **Freq:** Bimonthly Biweekly Monthly Semimonthly except once in December and January. **Print Method:** Offset. **Key Personnel:** Allison Haramoto, Executive Editor. **ISSN:** 0030-8579 (print). **USPS:** 308-579. **Subscription Rates:** Included in membership; $40 Nonmembers. **URL:** http://www.southbayjacl.org/membership.html. **Ad Rates:** PCI $20. **Remarks:** Accepts advertising. **Circ:** Paid ‡24000, Free ‡100.

4886 ■ Police: The Law Enforcement Magazine
Bobit Business Media
3520 Challenger St.
Torrance, CA 90503
Phone: (310)533-2400
Fax: (310)533-2500
Publication E-mail: police@bobit.com
Law enforcement magazine. **Freq:** Monthly. **Print Method:** Offset. **Trim Size:** 7 7/8 x 10 3/4. **Cols./Page:** 3. **Col. Width:** 13 picas. **Col. Depth:** 9 1/4 inches. **Key Personnel:** David Griffith, Editor, phone: (704)527-5182; Melanie Basich, Managing Editor, phone: (310)533-2498; Leslie Pfeiffer, Manager, Sales, Publisher. **ISSN:** 0893--8989 (print). **Subscription Rates:** $25 Individuals 1 year; $40 Canada 1 year; $60 Other countries 1 year. **URL:** http://www.policemag.com. **Formerly:** Police Product News. **Ad Rates:** 4C $4265; PCI $147. **Remarks:** Accepts advertising. **Circ:** △**48120**.

4887 ■ School Bus Fleet
Bobit Business Media
3520 Challenger St.
Torrance, CA 90503
Phone: (310)533-2400
Fax: (310)533-2500
Publication E-mail: sbf@bobit.com
Magazine on pupil transportation. **Freq:** 11/year. **Print Method:** Offset. **Trim Size:** 8 x 10 7/8. **Cols./Page:** 3. **Col. Width:** 26 nonpareils. **Col. Depth:** 140 agate lines. **Key Personnel:** Frank Di Giacomo, Publisher, phone: (856)596-0999, fax: (856)596-0168; Mark Hollenbeck, Associate Publisher, phone: (503)472-8200, fax: (503)472-8228. **ISSN:** 0036--6501 (print). **Subscription Rates:** Free. **URL:** http://www.schoolbusfleet.com. **Remarks:** Advertising accepted; rates available upon request. **Circ:** Controlled △**24741**.

TRACY

San Joaquin Co. San Joaquin Co. (C). 20 m SW of Stockton. Glass containers, milk products, food processing beet sugar factories, construction, sheathing, fruit, vegetable packing plants. Agriculture. Barley, Lima beans, tomatoes, asparagus, alfalfa, apricots, walnuts, almonds.

4888 ■ Tracy Press
Tracy Press
145 W 10th St.
Tracy, CA 95378-0419
Phone: (209)835-3030
Fax: (209)832-5383
General newspaper. **Freq:** Weekly. **Print Method:** Offset. **Cols./Page:** 6. **Col. Width:** 27 nonpareils. **Col. Depth:** 301 agate lines. **Key Personnel:** Robert S. Matthews, President, Publisher. **Subscription Rates:** $34 Individuals; $52 Individuals digital. **URL:** http://www.goldenstatenewspapers.com/tracy_press. **Mailing address:** PO Box 419, Tracy, CA 95378-0419. **Ad Rates:** GLR $.60; BW $1118.43; 4C $1368.43; SAU $8.67; PCI $8.67. **Remarks:** Accepts advertising. **Circ:** (Not Reported).

TRUCKEE

Nevada Co. Nevada Co. (NE). 32 m SW of Reno, Nev. Residential. Summer and winter resort. Lumbering.

4889 ■ The Sierra Sun
Swift Publications
12315 Deerfield Dr.
Truckee, CA 96160
Phone: (530)587-6061
Publication E-mail: editor@sierrasun.com
Local newspaper. **Freq:** Daily. **Print Method:** Offset. **Cols./Page:** 6. **Col. Width:** 24 nonpareils. **Col. Depth:** 301 agate lines. **Key Personnel:** Amy Edgett, Editor, phone: (530)550-2656; Kevin MacMillan, Managing Editor, phone: (530)550-2652. **Subscription Rates:** $150 Individuals. **URL:** http://www.sierrasun.com. **Remarks:** Accepts advertising. **Circ:** Fri. ‡8633, Wed. ‡6655.

4890 ■ KTKE-FM - 101.5
12030 Donner Pass Rd.
Truckee, CA 96161
Phone: (530)587-9999
Email: info@truckeetahoeradio.com
Format: Alternative/New Music/Progressive. **Key Personnel:** Lindsay Romack, Program Mgr., lindsay@truckeetahoeradio.com. **Ad Rates:** Advertising accepted; rates available upon request. **URL:** http://www.truckeetahoeradio.com.

4891 ■ K254AR-FM - 98.7
PO Box 391
Twin Falls, ID 83303
Fax: (208)736-1958
Free: 800-357-4226
Format: Religious; Contemporary Christian. **Owner:** CSN International, PO Box 391, Twin Falls, ID 83303, Ph: (208)736-1958, Fax: (208)736-1958, Free: 800-357-4226. **Key Personnel:** Don Mills, Prog. Dir., Music Dir.; Kelly Carlson, Dir. of Engg.; Ray Gorney, Asst. Dir. **Wattage:** 010. **URL:** http://www.csnradio.com.

TUJUNGA

Los Angeles Co. (S). 12 m NW of Glendale. Residential. Health resort. Manufactures medical instruments, electronic products. Horse country. Light farming.

4892 ■ Comcast Cable
10000 Commerce Ave.
Tujunga, CA 91042
Founded: 1963. **Key Personnel:** Brian L. Roberts, Chairman, CEO; Stephen B. Burke, COO, President; David L. Cohen, Exec. VP. **Cities Served:** 120 channels. **URL:** http://www.comcast.com.

TULARE

Tulare Co. Tulare Co. (SC). 45 m S of Fresno. Creameries. Cotton gins, winery. Diversified farming. Cotton, dairy products, beef cattle, deciduous fruit.

4893 ■ KGEN-AM - 1370
323 E San Joaquin St.
Tulare, CA 93274
Phone: (559)686-1370
Format: Hispanic. **Owner:** Azteca Broadcasting Corp., 323 E San Joaquin St., Tulare, CA 93274-4130. **Founded:** 1986. **Operating Hours:** Continuous. **Wattage:** 1,000. **Ad Rates:** for 30 seconds; for 60 seconds. Combined advertising rates available with KGEN-FM.

4894 ■ KGEN-FM - 94.5
323 E San Joaquin St.
Tulare, CA 93274
Phone: (559)686-1370
Fax: (559)685-1394
Email: kgen@sbcglobal.com
Format: Hispanic; Eclectic. **Owner:** Azteca Broadcasting Corp., 323 E San Joaquin St., Tulare, CA 93274-4130. **Founded:** 1986. **Operating Hours:** Continuous. **Wattage:** 3,300 ERP. **Ad Rates:** Noncommercial. KGEN-AM.

4895 ■ KXEQ-AM - 1340
323 E San Joaquin St.
Tulare, CA 93274

Phone: (775)827-1111
Fax: (775)827-2082
Email: kxeq@sbcglobal.net
Format: Hispanic. **Owner:** Azteca Broadcasting Corp., 323 E San Joaquin St., Tulare, CA 93274-4130. **Founded:** 1991. **Operating Hours**: Continuous. **ADI**: Reno, NV. **Wattage**: 1,000. **Ad Rates:** Noncommercial.

TURLOCK

Stanislaus Co. Stanislaus Co. (C). 40 m SE of Stockton. California State University at Stanislaus. Turkey poultry processing plants, canning, dehydrating fruits and grapes, milk cartons, butter manufactured. Hatcheries. Nurseries. Poultry, fruit, dairy farms. Turkeys, grapes.

4896 ■ International Journal of Business Strategy
International Academy of Business and Economics
983 Woodland Dr.
Turlock, CA 95382
Publisher's E-mail: admin@iabe.org
Peer-reviewed journal that publishes research/conceptual work or applied research/applications on topics related to research, practice, and teaching in all subject areas of Business, Economics, E-Business/E-Commerce. **Freq:** Semiannual. **Key Personnel:** Prof. Tahi J. Gnepa, PhD, Managing Editor; Dr. Sutana Boonlua, Editor-in-Chief. **ISSN:** 1553--9563 (print); **EISSN:** 2378--8585 (electronic). **URL:** http://www.iabe.org/domains/iabeX/journalinfo.aspx?JournalID=IJBS. **Formerly**: International Journal of Business Studies. **Remarks:** Accepts advertising. **Circ:** (Not Reported).

4897 ■ Journal Academy of Business and Economics
International Academy of Business and Economics
983 Woodland Dr.
Turlock, CA 95382
Publisher's E-mail: admin@iabe.org
Peer-reviewed journal that publishes research/conceptual work or applied research/applications on topics related to research, practice, and teaching in all subject areas of Business, Economics, E-Business/E-Commerce. **Freq:** Semiannual. **Key Personnel:** Dr. Cheick Wague, Editor-in-Chief. **ISSN:** 1542--8710 (print); **EISSN:** 2378--8631 (electronic). **URL:** http://www.iabe.org/domains/iabeX/journal.aspx?journalid=4. **Remarks:** Accepts advertising. **Circ:** (Not Reported).

4898 ■ Review of Business Research
International Academy of Business and Economics
983 Woodland Dr.
Turlock, CA 95382
Publisher's E-mail: admin@iabe.org
Peer-reviewed journal that publishes research/conceptual work or applied research/applications on topics related to research, practice, and teaching in all subject areas of Business, Economics, E-Business/E-Commerce. **Freq:** Semiannual. **Key Personnel:** Prof. Dula Borozan, Editor-in-Chief; Dr. Wilson Almeida, Managing Editor. **ISSN:** 1546--2609 (print); **EISSN:** 2378--9670 (electronic). **URL:** http://www.iabe.org/domains/iabeX/journalinfo.aspx?JournalID=RBR. **Remarks:** Accepts advertising. **Circ:** (Not Reported).

4899 ■ The Signal
California State University - Stanislaus
Demergasso-Bava Hall, Rm. 123
California State University, Stanislaus
One University Circle
Turlock, CA 95382
Collegiate newspaper. **Founded:** 1971. **Freq:** Weekly (Thurs.) during the academic year except during vacation breaks. **Print Method:** Offset. **Trim Size:** 10 x 12. **Cols./Page:** 4. **Col. Width:** 2.5 picas. **Col. Depth:** 182 agate lines. **Key Personnel:** Kate Brown, Editor-in-Chief. **URL:** http://www.csusignal.com. **Remarks:** Accepts advertising. **Circ:** Free ‡2200.

4900 ■ Turlock Journal
Merris Multimedia
138 S Center St.
Turlock, CA 95380-4508
Phone: (209)634-9141
Fax: (209)669-1561
General newspaper. **Freq:** Triweekly Wednesdays, Fridays and Saturdays. **Print Method:** Offset. **Cols./Page:** 6. **Col. Width:** 11 picas. **Col. Depth:** 21 1/2 inches. **Key Personnel:** Kristina Hacker, Editor. **Subscription Rates:** $32 Individuals 6 months. **URL:** http://www.turlockjournal.com. **Remarks:** Accepts advertising. **Circ:** (Not Reported).

4901 ■ KCSS-FM - 91.9
1 University Cir.
Turlock, CA 95382
Phone: (209)667-3900
Format: Alternative/New Music/Progressive. **Owner:** California State University, 401 Golden Shore, Long Beach, CA 90802-4210, Ph: (562)951-4000. **Founded:** 1975. **Operating Hours**: Continuous. **Key Personnel:** Frankie Tovar, Tech. Dir., pd@kcss.net; David Rocha, Station Mgr., sm@kcss.net; Eduardo Ruiz, Music Dir., modrock@kcss.net. **Wattage**: 400. **Ad Rates:** Noncommercial. **URL:** http://www.kcss.net.

TUSTIN

Orange Co. Orange Co. (S). 3 m E of Santa Ana. Suburban residential.

4902 ■ Landscape Architect and Specifier News
Landscape Communications Inc.
14771 Plaza Dr., Ste. M
Tustin, CA 92780
Phone: (714)979-5276
Trade magazine covering landscape architecture and planning for professionals. **Freq:** Monthly. **Trim Size:** 8 3/8 x 10 7/8. **Cols./Page:** 4. **Key Personnel:** Stephen Kelly, Editor; Ashley Calabria, Associate Editor; Buck Abbey, Associate Editor; Janet Lennox Moyer, Associate Editor; Larry Shield, Editor; George Schmok, Editor-in-Chief, Publisher. **ISSN:** 1060--9962 (print). **URL:** http://www.landscapeonline.com/contact/contact_mag.php?pub=lasn. **Formerly**: Landscape Construction & Maintenance. **Remarks:** Accepts advertising. **Circ:** Controlled ‡27487.

4903 ■ Landscape Superintendent and Maintenance Professional
Landscape Communications Inc.
14771 Plaza Dr., Ste. M
Tustin, CA 92780
Phone: (714)979-5276
Magazine for landscape professionals. **Key Personnel:** George Schmok, Editor-in-Chief, Publisher; Larry Shield, Editor; Buck Abbey, Associate Editor; Stephen Kelly, Editor; Ashley Calabria, Associate Editor. **URL:** http://www.landscapeonline.com/contact/contact_mag.php?pub=lsmp. **Remarks:** Accepts advertising. **Circ:** (Not Reported).

TWENTYNINE PALMS

San Bernardino Co. San Bernardino Co. (SE). 90 m E of San Bernardino. Health resort.

4904 ■ K38EE - 38
PO Box A
Santa Ana, CA 92711
Phone: (714)832-2950
Free: 888-731-1000
Owner: Trinity Broadcasting Network Inc., PO Box A, Santa Ana, CA 92711, Ph: (714)832-2950, Free: 888-731-1000. **URL:** http://www.tbn.org.

UKIAH

Mendocino Co. Mendocino Co. (NW). 60 m N of Santa Rosa. Residential. Fruit packing houses. Wineries, concrete pipe, sheet metal works, carpet mill lumber mills, masonite plant. Agriculture. Pears, grapes, cattle.

4905 ■ New Dimensions Journal
New Dimensions World Broadcasting Network
PO Box 569
Ukiah, CA 95482
Phone: (707)468-5215
Publisher's E-mail: info@newdimensions.org
Magazine that publishes transcripts from the New Dimensions radio broadcasting network. **Freq:** Irregular. **Key Personnel:** Michael Toms, Co-President, Founder; Justine Toms, Co-President, Founder; Rose Holland, Office Manager. **URL:** http://newdimensions.org. **Circ:** (Not Reported).

4906 ■ Ukiah Daily Journal
Digital First Media
590 S School St.
Ukiah, CA 95482-0749
Phone: (707)468-3500
Fax: (707)468-3544
General newspaper. **Freq:** Daily. **Print Method:** Offset. **Cols./Page:** 6. **Col. Width:** 25 nonpareils. **Col. Depth:** 301 agate lines. **Key Personnel:** K.C. Meadows, Editor; Kevin McConnell, Publisher; Jody Martinez, Editor. **Subscription Rates:** $5 Individuals 1 month (online); $25 Individuals 6 months (online); $45 Individuals 1 year (online). **URL:** http://www.ukiahdailyjournal.com. **Mailing address:** PO Box 749, Ukiah, CA 95482-0749. **Remarks:** Advertising accepted; rates available upon request. **Circ:** Mon.-Sat. ★**6181**, Sun. ★**6477**.

4907 ■ KDAC-AM - 1230
534 S State St.
Ukiah, CA 95482
Phone: (707)468-5578
Fax: (707)468-5361
Format: Tejano. **Simulcasts:** KLLK-AM, KUKI-AM. **Networks:** AP. **Owner:** Bi-Coastal Media L.L.C., 1 Blackfield Dr., Ste. 333, Tiburon, CA 94920, Ph: (415)789-5035, Fax: (415)789-5036. **Operating Hours**: Continuous. **ADI:** San Francisco-Oakland-San Jose. **Key Personnel:** Alan Mathews, Mktg. Mgr.; Mike Wilson, President, COO; Victoria Bennington, Contact. **Wattage**: 1,000. **Ad Rates:** Noncommercial. Combined advertising rates available with KLLK-AM, KUKI-AM. **URL:** http://www.bicoastalmedia.com.

4908 ■ KMEC-FM - 105.1
106 W Standley St.
Ukiah, CA 95482-4812
Phone: (707)468-1660
Format: News; Educational; Information. **Owner:** Mendocino Environmental Center, at above address, Ukiah, CA. **Founded:** 2002. **Operating Hours**: Continuous. **Wattage**: 075. **URL:** http://www.kmecradio.org.

4909 ■ KMKX-FM
1100 'B' Hastings Rd.
Ukiah, CA 95482
Phone: (707)462-0945
Fax: (707)462-4670
Email: info@maxrock.com
Format: Classic Rock. **Networks:** ABC. **Founded:** 1981. **Formerly**: KSIT-FM. **Key Personnel:** Michael Spencer, Contact, capmikey@pacific.net. **Wattage**: 890 ERP. **Ad Rates:** $3.25-4.50 for 15 seconds; $6.50-9 for 30 seconds; $13-18 for 60 seconds.

4910 ■ KPRA-FM - 89.5
290 Hegenberger Rd.
Oakland, CA 94621
Free: 800-543-1495
Format: Religious. **URL:** http://www.familyradio.org.

4911 ■ KUKI-AM - 1400
534 S State St.
Ukiah, CA 95482
Phone: (707)468-5578
Fax: (707)468-5361
Format: News; Talk. **Simulcasts:** KDAC-AM & KLLK-AM. **Networks:** ABC; CBS. **Owner:** Bi-Coastal Media L.L.C., 1 Blackfield Dr., Ste. 333, Tiburon, CA 94920, Ph: (415)789-5035, Fax: (415)789-5036. **Operating Hours**: Continuous. **ADI**: San Francisco-Oakland-San Jose. **Key Personnel:** Mike Wilson, President, COO; Alan Mathews, Mktg. Mgr. **Wattage**: 1,000. **Ad Rates:** $18-25 per unit. Combined advertising rates available with KDAC-AM & KLLK-AM. **URL:** http://www.bicoastalmedia.com.

4912 ■ KWNE-FM - 94.5
PO Box 1056
Ukiah, CA 95482
Phone: (707)462-0945
Fax: (707)462-4670
Format: Adult Contemporary. **Networks:** ABC. **Owner:** Broadcasting Corporation of Mendocino County, 1100 Hastings Rd., Ukiah, CA 95482. **Formerly**: KLIL-FM. **Operating Hours**: Continuous. **Wattage**: 2,200. **Ad Rates:** $4-26 for 30 seconds; $5-31 for 60 seconds. Combined advertising rates available with KMKX-FM. **URL:** http://www.kwine.com.

Circulation: ★ = AAM; △ or • = BPA; ♦ = CAC; ❑ = VAC; ⊕ = PO Statement; ‡ = Publisher's Report; Boldface figures = sworn; Light figures = estimated.

VACAVILLE

Solano Co. Solano Co. (NWC). 27 m SW of Sacramento. Food processing. Mobile homes. Light industry. Diversified farming.

4913 ■ Bingo and Gaming News
Gold Hill Publishing Inc.
349 Flagstone Ct.
Vacaville, CA 95687-4325
Phone: (707)451-4646
Consumer magazine covering bingo and gaming. **Freq:** Monthly. **Subscription Rates:** Free. **URL:** http://www.bingogamingnews.com. **Remarks:** Accepts advertising. **Circ:** (Not Reported).

4914 ■ New Homes Magazine: And Map Guide To New Home Communities
MDM Publications
181 Butcher Rd.
Vacaville, CA 95687
Phone: (707)451-9990
Fax: (707)451-9922
Publication E-mail: info@newhomesmapguide.com
New real estate magazine. **Freq:** Bimonthly. **Print Method:** Offset. **Trim Size:** 8 1/4 x 10 3/4. **Cols./Page:** 3 and 2. **Col. Width:** 27 and 42 nonpareils. **Col. Depth:** 137 agate lines. **URL:** http://www.newhomesca.com. **Ad Rates:** BW $2,600; 4C $2,950. **Remarks:** Accepts advertising. **Circ:** Non-paid ‡100000.

4915 ■ KASK-FM - 91.5
4738 Allendale Rd.
Vacaville, CA 95688
Format: News. **URL:** http://kaskradio.com/.

4916 ■ KFM-FM
PO Box 911
Highfield Rd.
Vacaville, CA 95696
Email: 945webmaster@kfm.co.za
Format: Alternative/New Music/Progressive; Information; News. **Key Personnel:** Ian Bredenkamp, Program Mgr., ianb@primedia.co.za; Colleen Louw, Station Mgr; Yumnah Hendricks, Contact, comments@kfm.co.za; Janine Willemans, Contact, janinew@primedia.co.za. **Wattage:** 3,900 ERP. **Ad Rates:** Advertising accepted; rates available upon request.

4917 ■ KUIC-FM - 95.3
555 Mason St., Ste. 245
Vacaville, CA 95688
Phone: (707)446-0200
Fax: (707)446-0122
Free: 800-698-5842
Email: news@kuic.com
Format: Adult Contemporary. **Simulcasts:** KUIC-2. **Networks:** Independent. **Owner:** 95.3 KUIC Studios, 555 Mason St., Ste. 245, Vacaville, CA 95688, Ph: (707)446-0200, Fax: (707)446-0122. **Operating Hours:** Continuous; 100% local. **Wattage:** 490. **Ad Rates:** $50-150 per unit. **URL:** http://www.kuic.com.

VALENCIA

Los Angeles County. SW of Lake Hughes. Amusement park area.

4918 ■ Advanced Carbon
American Scientific Publishers
26650 The Old Rd., Ste. 208
Valencia, CA 91381-0751
Phone: (661)799-7200
Fax: (661)799-7230
Publisher's E-mail: order@aspbs.com
Peer-reviewed journal featuring articles on manufacturing, synthesis, characterization, physical and chemical properties, and modeling of carbon materials. **Key Personnel:** Dr. Avinash Balakrishnan, Editor-in-Chief. **Subscription Rates:** $750 Institutions domestic and foreign. **URL:** http://www.aspbs.com/ac.htm. **Remarks:** Accepts advertising. **Circ:** (Not Reported).

4919 ■ Advanced Chemistry Letters
American Scientific Publishers
26650 The Old Rd., Ste. 208
Valencia, CA 91381-0751
Phone: (661)799-7200
Fax: (661)799-7230
Publisher's E-mail: order@aspbs.com
Peer-reviewed journal covering all fundamental and applied research areas of chemical sciences. **Freq:** 3/year. **Key Personnel:** Dr. Nikolaos Bouropoulos, Editor-in-Chief. **ISSN:** 2326--747X (print); **EISSN:** 2326--7488 (electronic). **URL:** http://www.aspbs.com/acl. **Remarks:** Accepts advertising. **Circ:** (Not Reported).

4920 ■ Advanced Natural Products
American Scientific Publishers
26650 The Old Rd., Ste. 208
Valencia, CA 91381-0751
Phone: (661)799-7200
Fax: (661)799-7230
Publisher's E-mail: order@aspbs.com
Peer-reviewed journal featuring basic and applied research in all areas of chemical, biological, medical, pharmaceutical and health sciences related to natural products. **Key Personnel:** Dr. Aranya Manosroi, Editor-in-Chief. **URL:** http://www.aspbs.com/anp.htm. **Remarks:** Accepts advertising. **Circ:** (Not Reported).

4921 ■ Advanced Porous Materials
American Scientific Publishers
26650 The Old Rd., Ste. 208
Valencia, CA 91381-0751
Phone: (661)799-7200
Fax: (661)799-7230
Publisher's E-mail: order@aspbs.com
Peer-reviewed journal publishing research activities on the fundamental aspects, synthesis, advanced characterization, structural properties and multiple applications of all kinds of porous materials. **Key Personnel:** Prof. Ajayan Vinu, Editor-in-Chief. **ISSN:** 2327--3941 (print); **EISSN:** 2327--395X (electronic). **URL:** http://www.aspbs.com/apm.htm. **Circ:** (Not Reported).

4922 ■ Advanced Science Letters
American Scientific Publishers
26650 The Old Rd., Ste. 208
Valencia, CA 91381-0751
Phone: (661)799-7200
Fax: (661)799-7230
Publisher's E-mail: order@aspbs.com
Peer-reviewed journal covering physical sciences, biological sciences, mathematical sciences, engineering, computer and information sciences, and geosciences. **Key Personnel:** Hari Singh Nalwa, Editor-in-Chief; Dr. Wolfram Schommers, Editor; Jake Blanchard, Associate Editor. **ISSN:** 1936--6612 (print); **EISSN:** 1936--7317 (electronic). **URL:** http://www.aspbs.com/science. **Remarks:** Accepts advertising. **Circ:** (Not Reported).

4923 ■ Animation Journal
AJ Press
24700 McBean Pkwy.
School of Film/Video, California Institute of the Arts
24700 McBean Pky.
Valencia, CA 91355-2397
Publisher's E-mail: editor@animationjournal.com
Peer-reviewed scholarly journal covering animation history and theory. **Freq:** Annual. **Key Personnel:** Maureen Furniss, Editor. **ISSN:** 1061--0308 (print). **Subscription Rates:** $12 U.S. mail; $17.50 Canada mail; $20 Other countries; $25 Libraries USA; $27.50 Libraries USA and CANADA; $30 Libraries other countries. **URL:** http://www.animationjournal.com. **Remarks:** Advertising not accepted. **Circ:** Paid 200.

4924 ■ BMX Plus!
Hi-Torque Publishing Company Inc.
25233 Anza Dr.
Valencia, CA 91355
Phone: (661)295-1910
Fax: (661)295-1278
Bicycle motocross magazine. **Freq:** Monthly. **Print Method:** Offset. **Trim Size:** 8 x 10 3/4. **Cols./Page:** 3. **Col. Width:** 27 nonpareils. **Col. Depth:** 140 agate lines. **ISSN:** 0195--0320 (print). **Subscription Rates:** $14.99 Individuals U.S, Canada and Other Countries; $27.99 Two years U.S, Canada and Other Countries. **URL:** http://hi-torque.com/product/bmx-plus. **Ad Rates:** BW $2,350; 4C $3,450. **Remarks:** Accepts advertising. **Circ:** ‡47615.

4925 ■ Dirt Bike Magazine
Hi-Torque Publishing Company Inc.
25233 Anza Dr.
Valencia, CA 91355
Phone: (661)295-1910
Fax: (661)295-1278
Cycling magazine. **Freq:** Monthly. **Print Method:** Offset. **Trim Size:** 8 x 10 3/4. **Cols./Page:** 3. **Col. Width:** 26 nonpareils. **Col. Depth:** 140 agate lines. **Key Personnel:** Robert Rex, Manager; Ron Lawson, Editor. **ISSN:** 0364--1546 (print). **Subscription Rates:** $15.99 U.S.; $28.99 Canada; $35.99 Other countries. **URL:** http://dirtbikemagazine.com. **Ad Rates:** BW $4,995; 4C $67,495. **Remarks:** Accepts advertising. **Circ:** Paid 88035.

4926 ■ Dirt Wheels
Hi-Torque Publishing Company Inc.
25233 Anza Dr.
Valencia, CA 91355
Phone: (661)295-1910
Fax: (661)295-1278
ATV magazine. **Freq:** Monthly. **Print Method:** Offset. **Trim Size:** 8 x 10 3/4. **Cols./Page:** 3. **Col. Width:** 27 nonpareils. **Col. Depth:** 140 agate lines. **ISSN:** 0745--0192 (print). **Subscription Rates:** $15.99 U.S. print; $28.99 Canada print; $40.99 Other countries print; $9.99 Individuals online only. **URL:** http://dirtwheelsmag.com. **Ad Rates:** BW $2,995; 4C $5,265. **Remarks:** Accepts advertising. **Circ:** (Not Reported).

4927 ■ 4-Wheel ATV Action
Hi-Torque Publishing Company Inc.
25233 Anza Dr.
Valencia, CA 91355
Phone: (661)295-1910
Fax: (661)295-1278
Publication E-mail: atv@hi-torque.com
Magazine designed for racing and recreational ATV riders. **Freq:** Monthly. **Print Method:** Offset. **Trim Size:** 7 7/8 x 10 1/2. **Cols./Page:** 3. **ISSN:** 0884--7126 (print). **Subscription Rates:** $14.99 U.S. print; $27.99 Canada print; $29.99 Other countries print; $7.99 Individuals online. **URL:** http://utvactionmag.com. **Formerly:** 3 & 4 Wheel Action. **Remarks:** Accepts advertising. **Circ:** Paid 36826.

4928 ■ Genetics and Epigenomics
American Scientific Publishers
26650 The Old Rd., Ste. 208
Valencia, CA 91381-0751
Phone: (661)799-7200
Fax: (661)799-7230
Publisher's E-mail: order@aspbs.com
Peer-reviewed journal featuring topics related to gene regulation or gene modification at the genetic or genomic level. **Key Personnel:** Kai Li, Ph.D., Editor-in-Chief. **URL:** http://www.aspbs.com/geg.htm. **Remarks:** Accepts advertising. **Circ:** (Not Reported).

4929 ■ Journal of Advanced Physics
American Scientific Publishers
26650 The Old Rd., Ste. 208
Valencia, CA 91381-0751
Phone: (661)799-7200
Fax: (661)799-7230
Publisher's E-mail: order@aspbs.com
Peer-reviewed journal containing research activities in all experimental and theoretical aspects of advanced physics. **Freq:** Quarterly. **Key Personnel:** Dr. Sotirios Baskoutas, Editor-in-Chief. **ISSN:** 2168--1996 (print); **EISSN:** 2168--2003 (electronic). **Alt. Formats:** PDF. **URL:** http://www.aspbs.com/jap.htm. **Remarks:** Accepts advertising. **Circ:** (Not Reported).

4930 ■ Journal of Bioinformatics and Intelligent Control
American Scientific Publishers
26650 The Old Rd., Ste. 208
Valencia, CA 91381-0751
Phone: (661)799-7200
Fax: (661)799-7230
Publisher's E-mail: order@aspbs.com
Journal featuring research articles in areas of bioinformatics and intelligent control. **Freq:** Quarterly. **Key Personnel:** Dr. Zhihua Cui, Editor-in-Chief. **ISSN:** 2326--7496 (print); **EISSN:** 2326--750X (electronic). **Alt. Formats:** PDF. **URL:** http://www.aspbs.com/jbic.htm. **Remarks:** Accepts advertising. **Circ:** (Not Reported).

4931 ■ Journal of Biomedical Nanotechnology
American Scientific Publishers
26650 The Old Rd., Ste. 208
Valencia, CA 91381-0751
Phone: (661)799-7200
Fax: (661)799-7230
Publisher's E-mail: order@aspbs.com

Peer-reviewed journal publishing research papers on applications of nanotechnology in biotechnology, medicine, biosciences, and all other related fields of life sciences. **Freq:** 6/year. **Key Personnel:** Dr. Om Perumal, Editor-in-Chief. **ISSN:** 1550--7033 (print); **EISSN:** 1550--7041 (electronic). **URL:** http://www.aspbs.com/jbn.html. **Circ:** (Not Reported).

4932 ■ Journal of Bionanoscience
American Scientific Publishers
26650 The Old Rd., Ste. 208
Valencia, CA 91381-0751
Phone: (661)799-7200
Fax: (661)799-7230
Publisher's E-mail: order@aspbs.com
Journal covering various functions of biological macromolecules. **Freq:** Bimonthly. **Key Personnel:** Dr. Murugan Ramalingam, PhD, Editor-in-Chief. **ISSN:** 1557--7910 (print); **EISSN:** 1557--7929 (electronic). **Subscription Rates:** $300 Individuals; $350 Other countries; $575 Institutions; $595 Institutions, other countries. **URL:** http://www.aspbs.com/jbns. **Remarks:** Accepts advertising. **Circ:** (Not Reported).

4933 ■ Journal of Biopharmaceutics and Biotechnology
American Scientific Publishers
26650 The Old Rd., Ste. 208
Valencia, CA 91381-0751
Phone: (661)799-7200
Fax: (661)799-7230
Publisher's E-mail: order@aspbs.com
Journal covering all aspects of pharmaceutics, biotechnology, and medicine. **Key Personnel:** R. Jayakumar, Prof., Editor-in-Chief. **URL:** http://www.aspbs.com/jbb.htm. **Remarks:** Accepts advertising. **Circ:** (Not Reported).

4934 ■ Journal of Computational and Theoretical Nanoscience
American Scientific Publishers
26650 The Old Rd., Ste. 208
Valencia, CA 91381-0751
Phone: (661)799-7200
Fax: (661)799-7230
Publication E-mail: order@aspbs.com
Peer-reviewed journal that offers articles on computational and theoretical nanoscience. **Freq:** 6/year. **Key Personnel:** Dr. Wolfram Schommers, Editor-in-Chief; Christian Hafner, Associate Editor; Vladimir Basiuk, Board Member. **ISSN:** 1546--1955 (print); **EISSN:** 1546--1963 (electronic). **URL:** http://www.aspbs.com/ctn. **Remarks:** Advertising not accepted. **Circ:** (Not Reported).

4935 ■ Journal of Energy and Environmental Technology
American Scientific Publishers
26650 The Old Rd., Ste. 208
Valencia, CA 91381-0751
Phone: (661)799-7200
Fax: (661)799-7230
Publisher's E-mail: order@aspbs.com
Peer-reviewed journal covering research activities in all areas of energy and environmental technology. **Key Personnel:** Dr. Yuncai Zhou, Editor-in-Chief. **URL:** http://www.aspbs.com/jeet.htm. **Remarks:** Accepts advertising. **Circ:** (Not Reported).

4936 ■ Journal of Genome Science and Technology
American Scientific Publishers
26650 The Old Rd., Ste. 208
Valencia, CA 91381-0751
Phone: (661)799-7200
Fax: (661)799-7230
Publication E-mail: genome@aspbs.com
Peer-reviewed journal that offers information on genome science, genome technology, bioinformatics, biotechnology and medicine. **Freq:** Quarterly. **Key Personnel:** Dr. Burkhard Tummler, Editor-in-Chief, phone: (49)511 5322920, fax: (49)511 5326723; Dan H. Barouch, Board Member. **ISSN:** 1551--7551 (print). **URL:** http://www.aspbs.com/genomelett. **Remarks:** Advertising not accepted. **Circ:** (Not Reported).

4937 ■ Journal of Low Power Electronics
American Scientific Publishers
26650 The Old Rd., Ste. 208
Valencia, CA 91381-0751
Phone: (661)799-7200
Fax: (661)799-7230
Publisher's E-mail: order@aspbs.com
Journal that offers research in the field of low-powered electronics. **Freq:** 3/year. **Key Personnel:** Dr. Patrick Girard, Editor-in-Chief; Mohab H. Anis, Board Member. **ISSN:** 1546--1998 (print). **URL:** http://www.aspbs.com/jolpe. **Remarks:** Advertising not accepted. **Circ:** (Not Reported).

4938 ■ Journal of Nanofluids
American Scientific Publishers
26650 The Old Rd., Ste. 208
Valencia, CA 91381-0751
Phone: (661)799-7200
Fax: (661)799-7230
Publisher's E-mail: order@aspbs.com
Peer-reviewed journal covering a wide range of research topics in the field of nanofluids and fluid science. **Key Personnel:** John Philip, PhD, Editor-in-Chief. **ISSN:** 2169--432X (print); **EISSN:** 2169--4338 (electronic). **Alt. Formats:** PDF. **URL:** http://www.aspbs.com/jon.htm. **Remarks:** Accepts advertising. **Circ:** (Not Reported).

4939 ■ Journal of Nanopharmaceutics and Drug Delivery
American Scientific Publishers
26650 The Old Rd., Ste. 208
Valencia, CA 91381-0751
Phone: (661)799-7200
Fax: (661)799-7230
Publisher's E-mail: order@aspbs.com
Peer-reviewed journal covering nanotechnology and its applications to development, formulation and delivery of pharmaceuticals and diagnostic agents. **Key Personnel:** Dr. Om Perumal, Editor-in-Chief. **ISSN:** 2167--9312 (print); **EISSN:** 2167--9320 (electronic). **Subscription Rates:** $750 Institutions domestic and foreign. **URL:** http://www.aspbs.com/jnd.htm. **Remarks:** Accepts advertising. **Circ:** (Not Reported).

4940 ■ Journal of Nanoscience and Nanotechnology
American Scientific Publishers
26650 The Old Rd., Ste. 208
Valencia, CA 91381-0751
Phone: (661)799-7200
Fax: (661)799-7230
Publication E-mail: jnn@aspbs.com
Peer-reviewed journal covering all aspects of nanoscience and nanotechnology in science, engineering, and medicine. **Freq:** Monthly. **Trim Size:** 8 1/2 X 11. **Key Personnel:** Dr. Hari Singh Nalwa, Editor-in-Chief; Yuehe Lin, PhD, Associate Editor. **ISSN:** 1533-4880 (print); **EISSN:** 1533-4899 (electronic). **Subscription Rates:** $113 Individuals /article. **URL:** http://www.aspbs.com/jnn. **Remarks:** Accepts advertising. **Circ:** Paid 120.

4941 ■ Journal of Neuroscience and Neuroengineering
American Scientific Publishers
26650 The Old Rd., Ste. 208
Valencia, CA 91381-0751
Phone: (661)799-7200
Fax: (661)799-7230
Publisher's E-mail: order@aspbs.com
Peer-reviewed journal that covers all aspects of neuroscience and neuroengineering. **Key Personnel:** Dr. Chin-Teng Lin, Editor-in-Chief. **ISSN:** 2168--2011 (print); **EISSN:** 2168--202X (electronic). **URL:** http://www.aspbs.com/jnsne. **Remarks:** Accepts advertising. **Circ:** (Not Reported).

4942 ■ Journal of Nutritional Ecology and Food Research
American Scientific Publishers
26650 The Old Rd., Ste. 208
Valencia, CA 91381-0751
Phone: (661)799-7200
Fax: (661)799-7230
Publisher's E-mail: order@aspbs.com
Journal covering articles on food production and consumption, with regard to health, environment, society and economy. **Key Personnel:** Prof. Federico Infascelli, Editor-in-Chief. **ISSN:** 2326--4225 (print); **EISSN:** 2326--4233 (electronic). **Alt. Formats:** PDF. **URL:** http://www.aspbs.com/jnef.htm. **Remarks:** Accepts advertising. **Circ:** (Not Reported).

4943 ■ Journal of Surfaces and Interfaces of Materials
American Scientific Publishers
26650 The Old Rd., Ste. 208
Valencia, CA 91381-0751
Phone: (661)799-7200
Fax: (661)799-7230
Publisher's E-mail: order@aspbs.com
Peer-reviewed journal containing topics in the field of surface science and engineering, manufacturing science, processing technology and related applications. **Key Personnel:** Dr. Constantin Politis, Editor-in-Chief. **ISSN:** 2164--7542 (print); **EISSN:** 2164--7550 (electronic). **Alt. Formats:** PDF. **URL:** http://www.aspbs.com/jsim.htm. **Remarks:** Accepts advertising. **Circ:** (Not Reported).

4944 ■ Journal of Ubiquitous Computing and Intelligence
American Scientific Publishers
26650 The Old Rd., Ste. 208
Valencia, CA 91381-0751
Phone: (661)799-7200
Fax: (661)799-7230
Publisher's E-mail: order@aspbs.com
Journal covering all research and application aspects of the ubiquitous computing and ubiquitous intelligence. **Freq:** 3/year. **Key Personnel:** Laurence T. Yang, Editor-in-Chief; Jianhua Ma, Editor-in-Chief. **ISSN:** 1555--1326 (print); **EISSN:** 1555--1334 (electronic). **Subscription Rates:** $200 Individuals; $300 Other countries; $480 Institutions; $495 Institutions, other countries. **URL:** http://www.aspbs.com/juci. **Remarks:** Accepts advertising. **Circ:** (Not Reported).

4945 ■ Materials Focus
American Scientific Publishers
26650 The Old Rd., Ste. 208
Valencia, CA 91381-0751
Phone: (661)799-7200
Fax: (661)799-7230
Publisher's E-mail: order@aspbs.com
Peer-reviewed journal covering fundamental and applied research aspects in all areas of science and engineering of novel advanced materials. **Freq:** 6/year. **Key Personnel:** Prof. Ahmad Umar, PhD, Editor-in-Chief. **ISSN:** 2169--429X (print); **EISSN:** 2169--4303 (electronic). **Alt. Formats:** PDF. **URL:** http://www.aspbs.com/mat.htm. **Remarks:** Accepts advertising. **Circ:** (Not Reported).

4946 ■ Motocross Action
Hi-Torque Publishing Company Inc.
25233 Anza Dr.
Valencia, CA 91355
Phone: (661)295-1910
Fax: (661)295-1278
Motocross racing magazine. **Freq:** Monthly. **Print Method:** Offset. Uses mats. **Trim Size:** 8 x 10 3/4. **Cols./Page:** 3. **Col. Width:** 26 nonpareils. **Col. Depth:** 140 agate lines. **Key Personnel:** Roland S. Hinz, Publisher; Jody Weisel, Editor. **ISSN:** 0146--3292 (print). **Subscription Rates:** $15.99 U.S. print; $31.99 Canada print; $45.99 Other countries print; $9.99 Individuals online. **URL:** http://motocrossactionmag.com. **Ad Rates:** BW $3,670; 4C $5,925. **Remarks:** Accepts advertising. **Circ:** (Not Reported).

4947 ■ Muscle & Performance
Active Interest Media
24900 Anza Dr., Unit E
Valencia, CA 91355
Phone: (661)257-4066
Publisher's E-mail: admin@aimmedia.com
Magazine publishing articles on workouts, diets, supplementation strategies and advice for gaining muscle mass, getting stronger, losing weight and enhancing sports performance. **Freq:** Monthly. **Key Personnel:** Jordana Brown, Editor. **URL:** http://www.muscleandperformance.com. **Remarks:** Accepts advertising. **Circ:** ‡300000.

4948 ■ Nano Communications
American Scientific Publishers
26650 The Old Rd., Ste. 208
Valencia, CA 91381-0751
Phone: (661)799-7200
Fax: (661)799-7230
Publisher's E-mail: order@aspbs.com
Journal publishing peer-reviewed articles on all aspects of nanoscale science, engineering and technology. **Freq:**

Circulation: ★ = AAM; △ or • = BPA; ♦ = CAC; ❑ = VAC; ⊕ = PO Statement; ‡ = Publisher's Report; Boldface figures = sworn; Light figures = estimated.

Latest edition 2015. **Key Personnel:** Prof. Cengiz S. Ozkan, Editor-in-Chief. **ISSN:** 2167--2733 (print); **EISSN:** 2167--2741 (electronic). **Subscription Rates:** $750 Institutions domestic and foreign. **URL:** http://www.aspbs.com/nano.htm. **Circ:** (Not Reported).

4949 ■ Nanomedicine and Nanobiology
American Scientific Publishers
26650 The Old Rd., Ste. 208
Valencia, CA 91381-0751
Phone: (661)799-7200
Fax: (661)799-7230
Publisher's E-mail: order@aspbs.com
Peer-reviewed journal containing topics on nanotechnology for medical applications. **Key Personnel:** Prof. Zhiyong Qian, Editor-in-Chief. **ISSN:** 2167--9290 (print); **EISSN:** 2167--9304 (electronic). **Alt. Formats:** PDF. **URL:** http://www.aspbs.com/nanomed.htm. **Remarks:** Accepts advertising. **Circ:** (Not Reported).

VALLECITO

4950 ■ Faith for All of Life
Chalcedon Foundation
3900 Highway 4
Vallecito, CA 95251
Phone: (209)736-4365
Fax: (209)736-0536
Publisher's E-mail: info@chalcedon.edu
Religious magazine containing articles that explore the relationship of Christian faith to the world. **Freq:** Bimonthly. **Key Personnel:** Mark R. Rushdoony, President; Susan Burns, Managing Editor, phone: (276)963-3696. **Subscription Rates:** $20 U.S. one year print subscription; $35 Canada one year print subscription; $45 Other countries one year print subscription; Free online. **URL:** http://chalcedon.edu/faith-for-all-of-life. **Formerly**: Chalcedon Report. **Mailing address:** PO Box 158, Vallecito, CA 95251. **Ad Rates:** BW $400. **Remarks:** Accepts advertising. **Circ:** Non-paid ‡6000.

VALLEJO

Solano Co. Solano Co. (NWC). On Strait of Carquinez, 27 m NE of San Francisco. Manufactures dairy products, flour, beverages. Offshore oil drilling rigs. Planing mill, sheet metal works. Mare Island Naval Shipyard. Dairy, poultry, fruit farms.

4951 ■ Vallejo Times-Herald
Bay Area News Group
PO Box 3188
Vallejo, CA 94590
Phone: (707)644-1141
General newspaper. **Freq:** Daily. **Print Method:** Uses mats. Offset. **Cols./Page:** 6. **Col. Width:** 26 nonpareils. **Col. Depth:** 301 agate lines. **Key Personnel:** Jack F.K. Bungart, Editor, phone: (707)553-6827; Jim Gleim, Publisher, phone: (707)453-8189. **Subscription Rates:** $7.99 Individuals 1 month (online); $23.97 Individuals 3 month (online); $47.94 Individuals 6 month (online); $95.88 Individuals 1 year (online). **URL:** http://www.timesheraldonline.com. **Remarks:** Accepts classified advertising. **Circ:** Mon.-Fri. ★**14817**, Sat. ★**14707**, Sun. ★**15090**.

VALLEY CENTER

San Diego Co.

4952 ■ Valley Roadrunner
Roadrunner Publications, Inc.
Publication E-mail: editor@valleycenter.com
Community newspaper for Valley Center, Pauma Valley, and Palomar Mountain. **Freq:** Weekly. **Cols./Page:** 6. **Col. Width:** 13 inches. **Col. Depth:** 21 inches. **Key Personnel:** Eric Buskirk, Publisher. **Subscription Rates:** $24 Individuals San Diego county; $42 Two years San Diego county; $35 Elsewhere; $64 Elsewhere 2 years. **URL:** http://www.valleycenter.com. **Ad Rates:** BW $850; 4C $1000. **Remarks:** Advertising accepted; rates available upon request. **Circ:** 2000.

VALLEY GLEN

4953 ■ Valley Star
Los Angeles Valley College Journalism Dept.
Media Arts Dept.
5800 Fulton Ave.
Valley Glen, CA 91401
Phone: (818)947-2600
Publication E-mail: thevalleystar@yahoo.com
Newspaper covering junior college student interests. **Founded:** 1949. **Freq:** Weekly (Wed.). **Print Method:** Web Offset. **Cols./Page:** 6. **Col. Width:** 26 nonpareils. **Col. Depth:** 300 agate lines. **Key Personnel:** Lucas Thompson, Editor-in-Chief. **URL:** http://thevalleystar.com. **Ad Rates:** BW $660; 4C $1,060; PCI $7. **Remarks:** Accepts advertising. **Circ:** Free ‡7000.

VAN NUYS

Los Angeles Co. (S). 18 m NW of Los Angeles. Residential. Aircraft, auto body and trailers, cabinets, chemicals, dairy products, brick and tile, concrete block, pipes, guided missiles, toys, plastics manufactured. Automotive assembly plant. Nurseries.

4954 ■ Beauty Launchpad: What's Taking Off in the World of Beauty
Creative Age Publications Inc.
7628 Densmore Ave.
Van Nuys, CA 91406-2042
Phone: (818)782-7328
Free: 800-634-8500
Publisher's E-mail: subscriptions@creativeage.com
Fashion magazine. **Freq:** Monthly. **Print Method:** Web offset. **Trim Size:** 8 7/8 x 10 3/4. **Key Personnel:** Danielle Timsit, Associate Publisher, Director, Advertising, phone: (818)782-7328; Deborah Carver, Chief Executive Officer, Publisher; Amy Dodds, Executive Editor. **Subscription Rates:** $39.95 Two years print and online; $20.95 Individuals print and online; $23 Two years online only; $13 Individuals online only. **URL:** http://www.creativeage.com/magazine/beauty-launchpad. **Remarks:** Accepts advertising. **Circ:** 61649.

4955 ■ Beauty Store Business
Creative Age Publications Inc.
7628 Densmore Ave.
Van Nuys, CA 91406-2042
Phone: (818)782-7328
Free: 800-634-8500
Publisher's E-mail: subscriptions@creativeage.com
Business magazine for beauty industry professionals and beauty store owners. **Freq:** Monthly. **Print Method:** Web offset. **Trim Size:** 10 7/8 x 13 1/2. **Key Personnel:** Marc Birenbaum, Executive Editor; Jerry Lovell, Associate Publisher, Director, Advertising; Shelley Moench-Kelly, Managing Editor. **URL:** http://beautystorebusiness.com; http://www.creativeage.com/magazine/beauty-store-business. **Remarks:** Accepts advertising. **Circ:** (Not Reported).

4956 ■ Dayspa
Creative Age Publications Inc.
7628 Densmore Ave.
Van Nuys, CA 91406-2042
Phone: (818)782-7328
Free: 800-634-8500
Publisher's E-mail: subscriptions@creativeage.com
Professional magazine covering issues for salon/spa owners. **Freq:** Monthly. **Trim Size:** 8 x 10 3/4. **Cols./Page:** 3. **Key Personnel:** Linda Kossoff, Executive Editor. **ISSN:** 1089--3199 (print). **Subscription Rates:** $9.95 Individuals digital only; $22 Individuals in U.S; $43 Canada; $82 Other countries. **URL:** http://www.dayspamagazine.com. **Ad Rates:** BW $3,000; 4C $4,125. **Remarks:** Accepts advertising. **Circ:** Controlled 32564.

4957 ■ Medesthetics: Business Education for Medical Practitioners
Creative Age Publications Inc.
7628 Densmore Ave.
Van Nuys, CA 91406-2042
Phone: (818)782-7328
Free: 800-634-8500
Publisher's E-mail: subscriptions@creativeage.com
Trade magazine for medical practitioners. **Freq:** Bimonthly. **Print Method:** Web offset. **Trim Size:** 8 x 10 3/4. **Key Personnel:** Deborah Carver, Chief Executive Officer, Publisher; Inga Hansen, Associate Publisher, Editor; Jerry Lovell, Associate Publisher, Director, Advertising. **Subscription Rates:** $48 U.S. print ; $65 Canada print ; $70 Other countries print. **URL:** http://medestheticsmag.com. **Remarks:** Accepts advertising. **Circ:** 17400.

4958 ■ Music Connection Magazine
Music Connection Inc.
14654 Victory Blvd., 1st Fl.
Van Nuys, CA 91411
Phone: (818)995-0101
Fax: (818)995-9235
Publisher's E-mail: contactmc@musicconnection.com
Consumer trade publication covering music. **Freq:** Monthly. **Print Method:** Web. **Trim Size:** 8 3/8 x 11. **Cols./Page:** 4. **Col. Width:** 1 3/14 inches. **Col. Depth:** 10 inches. **Key Personnel:** J. Michael Dolan, Founder; E. Eric Bettelli, Director, Advertising, General Manager, Publisher; Denise Coso, Manager, Operations. **ISSN:** 1091--9791 (print). **USPS:** 447-330. **Subscription Rates:** $35 Individuals one year; $59 Two years. **URL:** http://musicconnection.com. **Ad Rates:** BW $1820; 4C $2580. **Remarks:** Accepts advertising. **Circ:** (Not Reported).

4959 ■ The NA Way Magazine: The International Journal of Narcotics Anonymous
Narcotics Anonymous
PO Box 9999
Van Nuys, CA 91409
Phone: (818)773-9999
Fax: (818)700-0700
Publisher's E-mail: fsmail@na.org
Freq: Quarterly. **ISSN:** 0896--9116 (print). **Alt. Formats:** PDF. **URL:** http://www.na.org/?ID=naway-toc. **Remarks:** Advertising not accepted. **Circ:** (Not Reported).

4960 ■ Nailpro
Creative Age Publications Inc.
7628 Densmore Ave.
Van Nuys, CA 91406-2042
Phone: (818)782-7328
Free: 800-634-8500
Publication E-mail: nailpro@creativeage.com
Salon owners and nail technicians read Nailpro for continuing education in techniques and services, marketing and management tips, product information and industry news. **Freq:** Monthly. **Print Method:** Web Offset. **Trim Size:** 8 x 10 3/4. **Cols./Page:** 3. **Key Personnel:** Nazli Ozen Santana, Associate Publisher, Director, Advertising; Karie L. Frost, Editor; Mindy Rosiejka, Chief Operating Officer, Vice President; Deborah Carver, Chief Executive Officer, Publisher. **ISSN:** 1049-4553 (print). **URL:** http://www.nailpro.com. **Remarks:** Accepts advertising. **Circ:** Paid △**60051**.

4961 ■ Spondylitis Plus Newsletter
Spondylitis Association of America
16360 Roscoe Blvd., Ste. 100
Van Nuys, CA 91406
Phone: (818)892-1616
Fax: (818)892-1611
Free: 800-777-8189
Publisher's E-mail: info@spondylitis.org
Magazine providing a forum for exchange of information about spondylitis. **Freq:** Bimonthly. **Trim Size:** 8 1/2 x 11. **Key Personnel:** Laurie M. Savage, Executive Director; Linda Powell, Administrative Assistant. **Subscription Rates:** Included in membership. **URL:** http://www.spondylitis.org. **Formerly:** Ankylosing Sponylitis News. **Mailing address:** PO Box 5872, Van Nuys, CA 91413. **Remarks:** Advertising not accepted. **Circ:** (Not Reported).

VANDENBERG AFB

4962 ■ Vandenberg Broadband
100 Lake Canyon Rd.
Vandenberg AFB, CA 93437
Cities Served: 61 channels. **URL:** http://www.vandenbergbroadband.com.

VENTURA

Ventura Co. (SW). 70 m N of Los Angeles. Summer and winter resort. Major oil production area. Manufactures gasoline, concrete pipe, electronics, food products, beverages. Ships flowers. Oil, gas wells. Agriculture. Citrus fruit, walnuts, lima beans. poultry, truck farms, cattle. Dairying.

4963 ■ Citations Magazine
Ventura County Bar Association
c/o Erik Feingold
Myers, Widders, Gibson, Jones & Feingold, LLP
PO Box 7209
Ventura, CA 93006

Phone: (805)650-7599
Fax: (805)650-8059
Magazine of the Ventura County Bar Association. **Freq:** Monthly. **Alt. Formats:** PDF. **URL:** http://www.vcba.org/vcbacitations. **Ad Rates:** BW $428. **Remarks:** Accepts advertising. **Circ:** (Not Reported).

4964 ■ MotorHome
Good Sam Enterprises L.L.C.
2575 Vista del Mar Dr.
Ventura, CA 93001
Free: 800-234-3450
Publisher's E-mail: info@goodsamclub.com
Magazine for motorhome enthusiasts. **Freq:** Monthly. **Print Method:** Web Offset. **Trim Size:** 7 7/8 x 10 1/2. **Cols./Page:** 3. **Col. Width:** 28 nonpareils. **Col. Depth:** 140 agate lines. **Key Personnel:** Bruce Hampson, Managing Editor; Barbara Leonard, Director, Editorial; Terry Thompson, Director, Sales. **USPS:** 459-030. **Subscription Rates:** $19.97 Individuals print; $34.97 Two years print. **URL:** http://www.motorhome.com. **Mailing address:** PO Box 6888, Englewood, CO 80155-6888. **Ad Rates:** GLR $46; BW $10,760; 4C $15,485. **Remarks:** Accepts advertising. **Circ:** Paid ★**122031**.

4965 ■ Snow Goer: Canada's Snowmobiling Magazine
Good Sam Enterprises L.L.C.
2575 Vista del Mar Dr.
Ventura, CA 93001
Free: 800-234-3450
Publisher's E-mail: info@goodsamclub.com
Magazine for Canadian snowmobilers. **Freq:** 7/year. **Print Method:** Web offset. **Trim Size:** 8 x 10 7/8. **Key Personnel:** John Prusak, Executive Editor; Andy Swanson, Managing Editor. **ISSN:** 0711-6454 (print). **Subscription Rates:** $16.97 Individuals 1 year; $23.97 Individuals 2 years. **URL:** http://www.snowgoer.com. **Mailing address:** PO Box 6888, Englewood, CO 80155-6888. **Remarks:** Accepts advertising. **Circ:** (Not Reported).

4966 ■ Trailer Life: America's No. 1 RV Magazine
Good Sam Enterprises L.L.C.
2575 Vista del Mar Dr.
Ventura, CA 93001
Free: 800-234-3450
Publisher's E-mail: info@goodsamclub.com
Magazine for recreational vehicle (RV) enthusiasts. **Freq:** Monthly. **Print Method:** Web Offset. **Trim Size:** 7 7/8 x 10 1/2. **Cols./Page:** 3. **Col. Width:** 28 nonpareils. **Col. Depth:** 140 agate lines. **Key Personnel:** Terry Thompson, Vice President, Sales. **ISSN:** 0041--0780 (print). **Subscription Rates:** $17.97 Individuals; $29.97 Two years. **URL:** http://www.trailerlife.com. **Mailing address:** PO Box 6888, Englewood, CO 80155-6888. **Ad Rates:** GLR $62; BW $14,645; 4C $21,220. **Remarks:** Advertising accepted; rates available upon request. **Circ:** Paid ★**196208**.

4967 ■ Ventura County Reporter
Ventura County Reporter
700 E Main St.
Ventura, CA 93001
Phone: (805)648-2244
Fax: (805)648-2245
Publisher's E-mail: editor@vcreporter.com
Weekly newspaper. **Freq:** Weekly (Thurs.). **Print Method:** Offset. **Trim Size:** 10 x 12. **Cols./Page:** 5. **Col. Width:** 1 7/8 inches. **Col. Depth:** 1 inches. **Key Personnel:** Michael Sullivan, Editor; David Comden, Publisher; Diane Newman, Contact. **URL:** http://www.vcreporter.com/cms/index/. **Formerly:** Ventura County & Coast Reporter. **Ad Rates:** 4C $1,635; PCI $19. **Remarks:** Advertising accepted; rates available upon request. **Circ:** Free ‡35000.

4968 ■ Woodall's California RV Traveler
Woodall Publications Corp.
2575 Vista Del Mar Dr.
Ventura, CA 93001
Publisher's E-mail: info@woodallpub.com
Magazine serving RVers in southern and central California. **Freq:** Monthly. **Print Method:** Web. **Cols./Page:** 4. **Col. Width:** 2 3/8 inches. **Col. Depth:** 13 inches. **Subscription Rates:** $12 Individuals; $2.50 Single issue. **URL:** http://www.woodalls.com. **Ad Rates:** BW $1,170; 4C $1,695. **Remarks:** Accepts advertising. **Circ:** Controlled 25000.

4969 ■ Woodall's Carolina RV Traveler
Woodall Publications Corp.
2575 Vista Del Mar Dr.
Ventura, CA 93001-3920
Publisher's E-mail: info@woodallpub.com
Magazine serving RVers in North and South Carolina. **Freq:** Monthly. **Print Method:** Web. **Cols./Page:** 4. **Col. Width:** 2 3/8 inches. **Col. Depth:** 13 inches. **URL:** http://www.woodalls.com. **Ad Rates:** BW $1,325; 4C $1,850. **Remarks:** Accepts advertising. **Circ:** Controlled 22000.

4970 ■ Woodall's Sunny Destinations
Woodall Publications Corp.
2575 Vista Del Mar Dr.
Ventura, CA 93001-3920
Publisher's E-mail: info@woodallpub.com
Guide to camping in the sunbelt region, geared toward the northern population. **Freq:** Annual. **Print Method:** Web. **Cols./Page:** 4. **Col. Width:** 2 3/8 inches. **Col. Depth:** 13 inches. **Subscription Rates:** $2.50 Single issue. **URL:** http://www.woodalls.com. **Ad Rates:** BW $1,048; 4C $1,823. **Remarks:** Accepts advertising. **Circ:** Controlled 55000.

4971 ■ KBBY-FM - 95.1
1376 Walter St.
Ventura, CA 93003
Phone: (805)642-8595
Format: Adult Contemporary. **Networks:** Independent. **Owner:** Cumulus Broadcasting Inc., 3280 Peachtree Rd. NW, Ste. 2300, Atlanta, GA 30305-2447, Ph: (404)949-0700, Fax: (404)949-0740. **Founded:** 1962. **Operating Hours:** Continuous. **Wattage:** 12,500 ERP. **Ad Rates:** Advertising accepted; rates available upon request. **URL:** http://www.951kbby.com.

4972 ■ KCAQ-FM - 104.7
2284 S Victoria Ave., Ste. 2G
Ventura, CA 93003
Phone: (805)289-1400
Format: Contemporary Hit Radio (CHR). **Owner:** Gold Coast Broadcasting, 2284 Victoria Ave., Ste. 2-G, Ventura, CA 93003, Ph: (805)289-1400, Fax: (805)644-7906. **Founded:** 1958. **Formerly:** KACY-FM; KPMJ-FM. **Operating Hours:** Continuous; 100% local. **Key Personnel:** Steve Hess, Sales Mgr., steve.hess@goldcoastbroadcasting.com. **Wattage:** 50,000. **Ad Rates:** $48-110 for 60 seconds. Combined advertising rates available with KKBE, KKZZ, KOLP, KTRO. **URL:** http://www.q1047.com.

4973 ■ K45DU - 45
PO Box A
Santa Ana, CA 92711
Phone: (714)832-2950
Free: 888-731-1000
Owner: Trinity Broadcasting Network Inc., PO Box A, Santa Ana, CA 92711, Ph: (714)832-2950, Free: 888-731-1000. **URL:** http://www.tbn.org.

4974 ■ KFYV-FM - 105.5
2284 S Victoria Ave., Ste. 2G
Ventura, CA 93003
Phone: (805)289-1400
Format: Top 40; Contemporary Hit Radio (CHR). **Owner:** Gold Coast Broadcasting, 2284 Victoria Ave., Ste. 2-G, Ventura, CA 93003, Ph: (805)289-1400, Fax: (805)644-7906. **Operating Hours:** Continuous. **Key Personnel:** Steve Hess, Sales Mgr., steve.hess@goldcoastbroadcasting.com. **Ad Rates:** Advertising accepted; rates available upon request. **URL:** http://www.live1055.fm.

4975 ■ KHAY-FM - 100.7
1376 Walter St.
Ventura, CA 93003
Phone: (805)642-8595
Format: Country. **Owner:** Cumulus Media Inc., 3280 Peachtree Rd. NW, Ste. 2300, Atlanta, GA 30305-2455, Ph: (404)949-0700, Fax: (404)949-0740. **Founded:** 1962. **Operating Hours:** Continuous. **Key Personnel:** Nery Reyes, HR Mgr., nery.reyes@cumulus.com. **Wattage:** 39,000 ERP. **Ad Rates:** Advertising accepted; rates available upon request. **URL:** http://www.khay.com.

KKZZ-AM - See Santa Paula, CA

4976 ■ KOCP-FM - 95.9
2284 S Victoria Ave., Ste. 2G
Ventura, CA 93003
Phone: (805)289-1400
Format: Classic Rock; Oldies. **Ad Rates:** Advertising accepted; rates available upon request. **URL:** http://www.rewind959.com.

4977 ■ KUNX-AM - 1590
2284 Victoria Ave., Ste. 2-G
Ventura, CA 93003
Phone: (805)289-1400
Format: News; Hispanic. **Owner:** Gold Coast Broadcasting, 2284 Victoria Ave., Ste. 2-G, Ventura, CA 93003, Ph: (805)289-1400, Fax: (805)644-7906. **URL:** http://www.goldcoastbroadcasting.com.

4978 ■ KVEN-AM - 1450
1376 Walter St.
Ventura, CA 93003
Phone: (805)642-8595
Format: Sports. **Owner:** Cumulus Broadcasting Inc., 3280 Peachtree Rd. NW, Ste. 2300, Atlanta, GA 30305-2447, Ph: (404)949-0700, Fax: (404)949-0740. **Founded:** 1948. **Wattage:** 1,000 Day. **Ad Rates:** Advertising accepted; rates available upon request. **URL:** http://www.1450kven.com.

4979 ■ KVTA-AM - 1520
2284 S Victoria Ave., Ste. 2G
Ventura, CA 93003
Phone: (805)289-1400
Format: Talk; News. **Key Personnel:** Steve Hess, Contact, steve.hess@goldcoastbroadcasting.com; Jack Clarke, Contact, jack.clarke@goldcoastbroadcasting.com. **Ad Rates:** Noncommercial. **URL:** http://www.kvta.com.

4980 ■ KVYB-FM - 103.3
1376 Walter St.
Ventura, CA 93003
Phone: (805)988-3904
Free: 888-330-1033
Format: Hip Hop. **Operating Hours:** Continuous. **Wattage:** 105,000. **Ad Rates:** Advertising accepted; rates available upon request. **URL:** http://www.1033thevibe.com.

VICTORVILLE

San Bernardino Co. San Bernardino Co. (SE). 42 m N of San Bernardino. Health resort. Dude ranches. Warehousing, electronics. Gold mines. Granite quarries. Agriculture. Alfalfa, cattle, turkeys.

4981 ■ The Daily Press
The Daily Press
13891 Park Ave.
Victorville, CA 92393-1389
Phone: (760)242-7744
Fax: (760)241-7145
Free: 800-553-2006
General newspaper. **Founded:** 1937. **Freq:** Daily. **Key Personnel:** Steven Hunt, Editor; Steve Williams, Editor, phone: (760)955-5332. **Subscription Rates:** $15 Individuals 3 months (online); 30 $U Individuals 6 months (online); $60 Individuals online; $208 Individuals 7 days (online and print); $127.24 Individuals combo; $65.25 Individuals combo, 24 weeks; $39.15 Individuals combo, 12 weeks; $146.25 Individuals 7 day (print); $115.96 Individuals weekender (print); $129.48 Individuals Sunday only (print). **URL:** http://www.vvdailypress.com. **Remarks:** Accepts advertising. **Circ:** Mon.-Sat. ♦**19126**, Sun. ♦**26022**.

4982 ■ Daily Press Preview: Victor Valley Edition
The Daily Press
13891 Park Ave.
Victorville, CA 92393-1389
Phone: (760)242-7744
Fax: (760)241-7145
Free: 800-553-2006
Free Arts & Entertainment weekly. **Freq:** Weekly. **Print Method:** Offset. **Trim Size:** 13 x 21 1/2. **Cols./Page:** 6. **Col. Width:** 2 1/16 inches. **Col. Depth:** 21 1/2 inches. **Key Personnel:** Donnie Welch, Publisher. **Subscription Rates:** $336.18 Individuals California (daily and Sunday); $224.12 Individuals California (Sunday only); $312 Out of state California (daily and Sunday); $208 Out of state California (Sunday only). **URL:** http://www.

Circulation: ★ = AAM; △ or • = BPA; ♦ = CAC; ❑ = VAC; ⊕ = PO Statement; ‡ = Publisher's Report; Boldface figures = sworn; Light figures = estimated.

vvdailypress.com. **Formerly**: Sunday Extra. **Ad Rates:** BW $774; 4C $1,159; SAU $6; PCI $6. **Remarks:** Accepts advertising. **Circ:** Tues. 21012.

4983 ■ El Mojave
Freedom Communications Inc.
13891 Park Ave.
Victorville, CA 92393-1389
Phone: (760)241-7744
Fax: (760)241-1860
Publisher's E-mail: info@freedom.com
Newspaper serving the Latino community in the Mojave area. **Key Personnel:** Al Frattura, Publisher; Fernando Torres, Editor, phone: (760)955-5312. **URL:** http://www.elmojave.com. **Mailing address:** PO Box 1389, Victorville, CA 92393-1389. **Remarks:** Accepts advertising. **Circ:** (Not Reported).

4984 ■ The San Bernardino American News
The American News
PO Box 837
Victorville, CA 92393
Phone: (909)889-7677
Black community newspaper. **Freq:** Weekly (Thurs.). **Print Method:** Offset. **Cols./Page:** 6. **Col. Width:** 26 nonpareils. **Col. Depth:** 294 agate lines. **URL:** http://www.sbnews.us. **Ad Rates:** GLR $.70; BW $787.80; PCI $9.01. **Remarks:** Accepts advertising. **Circ:** 5000.

4985 ■ KATJ-FM - 100.7
12370 Hesperia Rd., Ste. 16
Victorville, CA 92395
Phone: (760)241-1313
Fax: (760)241-0205
Format: Contemporary Country. **Networks:** Independent. **Founded:** 1989. **Operating Hours**: 100% local. **Wattage:** 6,000. **Ad Rates:** Noncommercial. **URL:** http://www.katcountry1007.com.

4986 ■ KHIZ-TV - 64
PO Box 1468
Victorville, CA 92393
Phone: (760)241-6464
Fax: (760)241-0056
Format: News. **Networks:** Independent. **Owner:** Sunbelt Television Inc., 747 E Green St., Ste. 200, Pasadena, CA 91101, Ph: (760)241-6464. **Founded:** 1987. **Formerly**: KVVT-TV. **Operating Hours**: Continuous. **ADI:** Los Angeles (Corona & San Bernardino), CA. **Wattage:** 5,000,000 ERP. **Ad Rates:** $50-200 per unit. **URL:** http://www.khiztv.com.

4987 ■ KIXA-FM - 106.5
12370 Hesperia Rd., Ste. 16
Victorville, CA 92392
Phone: (760)241-1313
Format: Classic Rock. **Key Personnel:** Kim Jennings, Gen. Mgr., kimjennings@edbroadcasters.com. **Wattage:** 560. **Ad Rates:** Noncommercial. **URL:** http://www.thefox1065.com.

4988 ■ KIXW-AM - 960
12370 Hesperia Rd., No. 16
Victorville, CA 92395
Phone: (760)241-1313
Format: Talk. **Founded:** 1988. **Formerly**: KZXY-AM. **Operating Hours**: Continuous; 100% local. **Key Personnel:** Kim Jennings, Sales Mgr., kimjennings@edbroadcasters.com. **Wattage:** 5,000 AM. **Ad Rates:** Advertising accepted; rates available upon request. **URL:** http://www.talk960.com.

4989 ■ K212EK-FM - 90.3
PO Box 391
Twin Falls, ID 83303
Fax: (208)736-1958
Free: 800-357-4226
Format: Religious; Contemporary Christian. **Owner:** CSN International, PO Box 391, Twin Falls, ID 83303, Ph: (208)736-1958, Fax: (208)736-1958, Free: 800-357-4226. **Key Personnel:** Mike Kestler, Contact; Don Mills, Music Dir., Prog. Dir. **URL:** http://www.csnradio.com.

4990 ■ KWRN 1550AM - 1550
15165 7th St., Ste. D
Victorville, CA 92395
Phone: (760)955-8722
Fax: (760)955-5751
Format: Hispanic. **Simulcasts:** 6 p.m.- 6a.m. **Owner:** Major Market Stations Inc., PO Box 10066, glendale, CA 91209. **Founded:** 1991. **Operating Hours**: Continuous. **ADI:** Los Angeles (Corona & San Bernardino), CA. **Wattage:** 5,000 Day; 500 Night. **Ad Rates:** Advertising accepted; rates available upon request. **URL:** http://www.kwrn1550am.com.

4991 ■ KZXY-FM - 102.3
12370 Hesperia Rd., No. 16
Victorville, CA 92395
Phone: (760)241-1313
Fax: (760)241-0205
Format: News. **Owner:** El Dorado Broadcasters, 12370 Hesperia Rd., Ste. 17, Victorville, CA 92395-5808, Ph: (760)241-1313, Fax: (760)241-0205. **Founded:** 1988. **Operating Hours**: Continuous. **Key Personnel:** Coleen Quinn, Prog. Dir., coleenquinn@edbroadcasters.com. **Wattage:** 6,000 ERP. **Ad Rates:** $50 for 60 seconds. **URL:** http://www.y102fm.com.

VISALIA

Tulare Co. Tulare Co. (SC). 42 m SE of Fresno. College of the Sequoias. Fruit canneries. Cheese, butter, transformers, milling products, electronic equipment, beverages manufactured. Walnuts, fruit packed. Diversified farming, Fruit, cattle, eggs.

4992 ■ Advance-Register & Times
Visalia Newspapers Inc.
330 N West St.
Visalia, CA 93279
Phone: (559)735-3200
Fax: (559)735-3399
Free: 888-487-9565
Publisher's E-mail: online@visaliatimesdelta.com
General newspaper. **Freq:** Daily (eve.) and Sat. (morn.). **Print Method:** Offset. **Trim Size:** 14 1/2 x 23. **Cols./Page:** 6. **Col. Width:** 2 1/8 inches. **Col. Depth:** 21 1/2 inches. **Key Personnel:** James Ward, Editor, phone: (559)735-3283; Kessler Vaughn, Director, Advertising, phone: (559)735-3230; Amy Pack, President, Publisher, phone: (559)735-3201. **Subscription Rates:** $12.25 Individuals Monday- Saturday. **URL:** http://www.visaliatimesdelta.com. **Mailing address:** PO Box 31, Visalia, CA 93279-0031. **Ad Rates:** PCI $9.01. **Remarks:** Accepts advertising. **Circ:** Mon.-Sat. 6665, Wed. 6737, Sat. 7238.

4993 ■ Journal of Veterinary Diagnostic Investigation
American Association of Veterinary Laboratory Diagnosticians
PO Box 6396
Visalia, CA 93290-6396
Phone: (559)781-8900
Fax: (559)781-8989
Journal containing informative articles, news, and current events in the field of veterinary science. **Freq:** Bimonthly January, March, May, July, September, November. **ISSN:** 1040- 6387 (print); **EISSN:** 1943-4936 (electronic). **Subscription Rates:** £161 Institutions Combined (Print & E-access); £177 Institutions Combined Plus Backfile (Current Volume Print & All Online Content); £145 Institutions E-access; £161 Institutions E-access Plus Backfile (All Online Content); £145 Institutions E-access (Content through 1998); £158 Institutions Print Only; £111 Individuals Combined (Print & E-access); £100 Individuals E-access; £109 Individuals Print Only; £29 Institutions Single Print Issue; £24 Individuals Single Print Issue. **URL:** http://vdi.sagepub.com/. **Remarks:** Advertising not accepted. **Circ:** 1500.

4994 ■ Visalia Times-Delta
Visalia Daily
330 N West St.
Visalia, CA 93279
Phone: (559)735-3200
Free: 888-487-9565
General newspaper. **Founded:** 1859. **Freq:** Mon.-Sat. (morn.). **Print Method:** Offset. **Cols./Page:** 6. **Col. Width:** 2 1/16 inches. **Key Personnel:** Amy Pack, President, Publisher, phone: (559)735-3201. **Subscription Rates:** $15.50 Individuals 6 days a week (print); $8 Individuals Wednesday and Saturday (print); $8 Individuals online only. **URL:** http://www.visaliatimesdelta.com. **Mailing address:** PO Box 31, Visalia, CA 93279. **Ad Rates:** SAU $16.28. **Remarks:** Accepts advertising. **Circ:** Mon.-Fri. ★**19310**, Sat. ★**22406**.

4995 ■ KARM-FM - 89.7
1300 S Woodland St.
Visalia, CA 93277
Phone: (559)627-5276
Fax: (559)627-5288
Free: 855-427-7664
Format: Religious. **Networks:** USA Radio. **Owner:** Harvest Broadcasting Co., at above address. **Founded:** 1990. **Operating Hours**: Continuous. **ADI:** Fresno-Visalia (Hanford), CA. **Key Personnel:** Loren Olson, Gen. Mgr., loren897@karm.com. **Wattage:** 1,000 ERP. **Ad Rates:** Noncommercial. **URL:** http://www.mypromisefm.com.

4996 ■ KBHH-FM - 95.3
400 W Caldwell Ave.
Visalia, CA 93277
Phone: (559)622-9401
Format: Hispanic. **Operating Hours**: Continuous. **Wattage:** 60,000. **URL:** http://www.campesina.net.

4997 ■ KCRZ-FM - 104.9
1401 W Caldwell
Visalia, CA 93277
Phone: (559)553-1500
Fax: (559)627-1496
Format: Adult Contemporary.

4998 ■ KDUV-FM
130 N Kelsey, Ste. H-123
Visalia, CA 93291
Free: 800-530-5388
Format: Contemporary Christian; Religious. **Key Personnel:** Joe Croft, Contact, joe@kduvfm.com. **Wattage:** 1,000 ERP. **Ad Rates:** Noncommercial.

4999 ■ KIOO-FM - 99.7
166 W Putnam Ave.
Greenwich, CT 06830
Phone: (203)661-4307
Fax: (203)622-7341
Email: info@buckleyradio.com
Format: Classic Rock. **Networks:** NBC. **Founded:** 1976. **Operating Hours**: 6:00 a.m.-midnight; 1% network, 99% local. **ADI:** Fresno-Visalia (Hanford), CA. **Key Personnel:** Bill Lynch, Gen. Mgr., billlynch@q97.com; Genia Taylor, Bus. Mgr.; Clint Showalter, Gen. Sales Mgr., clint@q97.com. **Wattage:** 24,000. **Ad Rates:** Noncommercial.

5000 ■ KJUG-FM - 106.7
1401 W Caldwell Ave.
Visalia, CA 93277
Phone: (559)553-1500
Fax: (559)627-1496
Format: Contemporary Country. **Owner:** Westcoast Broadcasting, Inc., at above address. **Founded:** 1959. **Formerly**: KWSM-FM. **Operating Hours**: Continuous. **Wattage:** 50,000. **Ad Rates:** $10-60 for 30 seconds; $15-70 for 60 seconds. Combined advertising rates available with KJUG-AM; KCRZ-FM. **URL:** http://www.kjug.com.

5001 ■ K100-FM - 99.7
700 E Mineral King Ave.
Visalia, CA 93277
Phone: (559)553-1500
Fax: (559)739-8378
Format: Classic Rock. **Operating Hours**: Continuous. **Key Personnel:** Ray McCarty, Gen. Mgr., raym@q97.com; Clint Showalter, Gen. Sales Mgr., clint@q97.com; Genia Taylor, Bus. Mgr., genia@q97.com. **Ad Rates:** Advertising accepted; rates available upon request. **URL:** http://www.997classicrock.com.

5002 ■ KSEQ-FM - 97.1
617 W Tulare Ave.
Visalia, CA 93277
Phone: (559)627-9710
Format: Top 40. **Networks:** Independent. **Owner:** Buckley Broadcasting Corp. Inc., 166 W Putnam Ave., Greenwich, CT 06830-5241, Ph: (203)661-4309. **Founded:** 1974. **Operating Hours**: Continuous; 100% local. **ADI:** Fresno-Visalia (Hanford), CA. **Wattage:** 17,000. **Ad Rates:** $26 for 30 seconds; $32 for 60 seconds. **URL:** http://www.q97.com.

5003 ■ KUFW-FM - 90.5
400 W Caldwell Ave.
Visalia, CA 93277
Phone: (559)622-9401
Fax: (559)622-9521
Format: Hispanic. **Key Personnel:** Jim Fernandez, Gen. Mgr., jim.fernandez@campesina.com. **URL:** http://campesina.net.

VISTA

San Diego Co. San Diego Co. (SE). 32 m N of San Diego. Light manufacturing. Fruit. truck, poultry farms. Avocados.

5004 ■ Good News Etc.
Good News Publishers Inc.
PO Box 2660
Vista, CA 92085-2660
Phone: (760)724-3075
Fax: (760)724-8311
Publication E-mail: goodnewseditor@cox.net
Community newspaper focusing on the Christian community. **Freq:** Monthly. **Key Personnel:** Colleen Monroe, Publisher; Rick Monroe, Editor. **Subscription Rates:** $30 Individuals first class mail. **URL:** http://www.goodnewsetc.com. **Ad Rates:** BW $1,392; 4C $1,491. **Remarks:** Accepts advertising. **Circ:** Combined 32000.

5005 ■ SIMULATION: Transactions of the Society for Modeling and Simulation International
Society for Modeling & Simulation International
2598 Fortune Way, Ste. I
Vista, CA 92081
Phone: (858)277-3888
Fax: (858)277-3930
Publication E-mail: transactions@scs.org
Freq: Monthly Quarterly. **Print Method:** Offset. **Trim Size:** 8 1/2 x 11. **Cols./Page:** 2. **Key Personnel:** Bernard Zeigler, Editor-in-Chief; Lorrie Mowat, Managing Editor. **ISSN:** 0740--6797 (print); **EISSN:** 1741-3133 (electronic). **Subscription Rates:** £22 Single issue print; £56 Institutions single print issue; £200 Individuals print only; £4715 Institutions backfile Purchase, E-access (Content through 1998); $40 /year for members; $160 /year for nonmembers. **URL:** http://www.scs.org/simulation; http://uk.sagepub.com/en-gb/asi/simulation/journal201571. **Formerly**: Transactions of the Society for Computer Simulation. **Remarks:** Advertising not accepted. **Circ:** 1000.

WALNUT

Los Angeles Co. Los Angeles Co (S) 7 m SW of Pomona. Residential.

5006 ■ Journal of the Los Angeles International Fern Society
Los Angeles International Fern Society
336 Maryville Dr.
Walnut, CA 91789
Phone: (909)598-2494
Publisher's E-mail: laifsfernshow@aol.com
Journal covering ferns worldwide. **Freq:** 6/year. **Trim Size:** 5 1/2 x 8 1/2. **Cols./Page:** 2. **Col. Width:** 2 1/8 inches. **Col. Depth:** 7 1/4 inches. **Key Personnel:** Joan Citron, Editor. **ISSN:** 0416--910X (print). **Subscription Rates:** Included in membership. **URL:** http://www.laifs.org. **Ad Rates:** PCI $10. **Remarks:** Accepts advertising. **Circ:** Combined 400.

5007 ■ SAC Media
Mt. San Antonio College
1100 N Grand Ave.
Walnut, CA 91789
Phone: (909)274-7500
Publisher's E-mail: info@mtsac.edu
Collegiate newspaper (tabloid). **Freq:** Monthly. **Print Method:** Offset. **Trim Size:** 10 x 15. **Cols./Page:** 5. **Col. Width:** 2 inches. **Col. Depth:** 182 agate lines. **Key Personnel:** Albert Serna, Editor-in-Chief. **Subscription Rates:** Free. **URL:** http://www.mtsac.edu/elj/journ/publications.html; http://sac.media. **Formerly**: The Mountaineer: The Student News newspaper of Mt. San Antonio College. **Circ:** (Not Reported).

5008 ■ Skillings Mining Review
Skillings Mining Review
340 S Lemon Ave., No. 7197
Walnut, CA 91789
Phone: (909)962-7321
Fax: (888)261-6014
Publisher's E-mail: subscriptions@skillings.net
Trade magazine for mining business technology, mineral processing, and related fields. **Freq:** Monthly. **Print Method:** Offset. **Trim Size:** 8 1/4 x 11 1/4. **Cols./Page:** 3. **Col. Width:** 2 1/16 inches. **Col. Depth:** 10 inches. **Key Personnel:** Stan Salmi, Contact, phone: (218)525-9555. **USPS:** 376-329. **Subscription Rates:** $72 U.S. hardcopy and online; $140 Two years 2 years; hardcopy and online - U.S; $109 U.S. air mail; $215 Two years 2 years; air mail - U.S; $250 Other countries; $496 Two years other countries; $335 Other countries air mail; $659 Two years 2 years; air mail - other countries. **URL:** http://www.skillings.net. **Ad Rates:** BW $1211; 4C $2265. **Remarks:** Accepts advertising. **Circ:** (Not Reported).

5009 ■ Spotlight La Puente
Armijo Newspapers and Public Relations
20270 E Carrey Rd.
Walnut, CA 91789
Phone: (909)444-0797
Fax: (909)444-1727
Publisher's E-mail: michael@anapr.com
Community newspaper. **Freq:** Quarterly. **Key Personnel:** Michael Armijo, Consultant. **Subscription Rates:** Free. **Alt. Formats:** PDF. **URL:** http://abcpublicrelations.com/Home_Page.html. **Circ:** (Not Reported).

5010 ■ KSAK-FM - 90.1
1100 N Grand Ave.
Walnut, CA 91789
Format: Hip Hop; Contemporary Hit Radio (CHR). **Wattage:** 001.009. **Ad Rates:** Noncommercial. **URL:** http://www.ksak.com.

WALNUT CREEK

Contra Costa Co. Contra Costa Co. (W). 15 m NE of Oakland. Manufactures canned goods, electronic equipment, food processing machinery, hand power tools, plastic coverings, walnut processing plant. Poultry, fruit, dairy farms. Walnuts, apricots, prunes. pears.

5011 ■ American Academy of Gnathologic Orthopedics--Journal
American Academy of Gnathologic Orthopedics
2651 Oak Grove Rd.
Walnut Creek, CA 94598
Fax: (925)934-4531
Free: 800-510-2246
Publisher's E-mail: admin@aago.com
Scientific journal covering orthodontic treatment. **Freq:** Quarterly. **ISSN:** 0886--1064 (print). **Subscription Rates:** Included in membership. **Remarks:** Advertising accepted; rates available upon request. **Circ:** 400.

5012 ■ Design for Living
Diablo Publications
2520 Camino Diablo
Walnut Creek, CA 94597
Phone: (925)943-1111
Fax: (925)943-1045
Magazine focusing on design and inspiration for the affluent homeowner. **Freq:** Semiannual. **Key Personnel:** Steven J. Rivera, Founder, President. **Circ:** (Not Reported).

5013 ■ Diablo Arts
Diablo Publications
2520 Camino Diablo
Walnut Creek, CA 94597
Phone: (925)943-1111
Fax: (925)943-1045
Consumer magazine covering music and the arts. **Freq:** Quarterly. **Print Method:** Web. **Trim Size:** 8 1/4 x 10 3/4. **Key Personnel:** Steven J. Rivera, Founder, President; Barney Fonzi, Publisher; Susan Dowdney Safipour, Editor. **Subscription Rates:** $20 Individuals 12 issues; $40 Two years 24 issues; $60 Individuals 3 years (36 issues). **URL:** http://www.diablomag.com. **Ad Rates:** BW $9089; 4C $9436. **Remarks:** Accepts advertising. **Circ:** 170000.

5014 ■ Diablo: The Magazine of the East Bay
Diablo Publications
2520 Camino Diablo
Walnut Creek, CA 94597
Phone: (925)943-1111
Fax: (925)943-1045
Lifestyle publication for residents of San Francisco's East Bay. **Freq:** Monthly. **Print Method:** Web. **Trim Size:** 8 1/2 x 11. **Cols./Page:** 3. **Col. Width:** 27 nonpareils. **Col. Depth:** 140 agate lines. **Key Personnel:** Susan Safipour, Editor-in-Chief. **Subscription Rates:** $20 Individuals 12 issues; $40 Two years 24 issues; $60 Individuals 3 years (36 issues). **URL:** http://www.diablomag.com. **Remarks:** Advertising accepted; rates available upon request. **Circ:** Combined △**39014**.

5015 ■ Journal of Sandplay Therapy
Sandplay Therapists of America
PO Box 4847
Walnut Creek, CA 94596
Phone: (925)820-2109
Publisher's E-mail: sta@sandplay.org
Freq: Semiannual. **Subscription Rates:** $52 U.S.; $63 Canada; $77 Other countries. **Alt. Formats:** PDF. **URL:** http://www.sandplay.org/journal/about-the-journal. **Remarks:** Advertising not accepted. **Circ:** (Not Reported).

5016 ■ Napa Sonoma
Diablo Publications
2520 Camino Diablo
Walnut Creek, CA 94597
Phone: (925)943-1111
Fax: (925)943-1045
Magazine focusing on luxury living in California Wine country. **Freq:** Semiannual. **Key Personnel:** Susan Dowdney Safipour, Editor-in-Chief. **Subscription Rates:** $13.95 Individuals print; $14.95 Individuals print and tablet; $9.99 Individuals tablet; $4.99 Single issue tablet. **Alt. Formats:** Handheld. **URL:** http://www.napasonomamagazine.com/Napa-Sonoma-Magazine; http://www.diablomag.com/Napa-Sonoma-Magazine. **Remarks:** Accepts advertising. **Circ:** ‡30000.

5017 ■ Rossmoor News: For Seniors
Golden Rain Foundation
1001 Golden Rain Rd.
Walnut Creek, CA 94595-2412
Phone: (510)988-7800
Publication E-mail: news@rossmoor.com
Community newspaper. **Freq:** Weekly (Wed.). **Print Method:** Offset. **Cols./Page:** 5. **Col. Width:** 24 nonpareils. **Col. Depth:** 192 agate lines. **Subscription Rates:** $45 Individuals. **URL:** http://www.rossmoornews.com. **Ad Rates:** PCI $12.50. **Remarks:** Accepts advertising. **Circ:** ‡6700.

WATSONVILLE

Santa Cruz Co. Santa Cruz Co. (W). 20 m N of Salinas. Fruit, Vegetables and lettuce packing houses, evaporating, cold storage, electronics plants, bottling works. Aluminum Extrusions, spray chemicals, vinegar, pectin, boxes, crates, manufactured. Agriculture. Apples, lettuce, berries.

5018 ■ La Ganga
Redgauntlet Publications Ltd.
23 E Beach St., Ste. 205
Plz. Vigil
Watsonville, CA 95076
Phone: (831)724-6564
Fax: (831)724-6399
Newspaper serving the Hispanic communities in the Central Coast area. **Freq:** Weekly (Sat.). **Key Personnel:** Mauricio Urzua, Publisher, Chief Executive Officer. **URL:** http://lagangaonline.com. **Remarks:** Accepts advertising. **Circ:** Non-paid ♦**24522**.

5019 ■ Pacific Citizen
Japanese American Citizens League - Watsonville-Santa Cruz Chapter
PO Box 163
Watsonville, CA 95077
Publisher's E-mail: support@southbayjacl.org
Newspaper (tabloid). **Freq:** Bimonthly Biweekly Monthly Semimonthly except once in December and January. **Print Method:** Offset. **Key Personnel:** Allison Haramoto, Executive Editor. **ISSN:** 0030-8579 (print). **USPS:** 308-579. **Subscription Rates:** Included in membership; $40 Nonmembers. **URL:** http://www.southbayjacl.org/membership.html. **Ad Rates:** PCI $20. **Remarks:** Accepts advertising. **Circ:** Paid ‡24000, Free ‡100.

5020 ■ REG Magazine
REG - The International Roger Waters Fan Club
c/o Michael Simone, President
128 Onyx Dr.
Watsonville, CA 95076
Magazine containing rare and exclusive articles and interviews, as well as news, information and other tidbits. **Freq:** 3-4/year. **Trim Size:** 8 1/2 X 11. **Subscription Rates:** Included in membership; $4 Single issue /back issue, plus shipping and handling. **URL:** http://www.

Circulation: ★ = AAM; △ or • = BPA; ♦ = CAC; ☐ = VAC; ⊕ = PO Statement; ‡ = Publisher's Report; Boldface figures = sworn; Light figures = estimated.

rogerwaters.org/backissues.html. **Remarks:** Advertising not accepted. **Circ:** (Not Reported).

5021 ■ Register-Pajaronian
Watsonville Newspapers Inc.
100 Westridge Dr.
Watsonville, CA 95076
Phone: (831)761-7300
Fax: (831)722-8386
General newspaper. **Freq:** Daily (eve.) and Sat. (morn.). **Print Method:** Offset. **Cols./Page:** 6. **Col. Width:** 12 1/4 picas. **Col. Depth:** 21 inches. **Key Personnel:** John Bartlett, Publisher. **USPS:** 669-540. **Subscription Rates:** $124.65 Individuals in Tri-County area; $132.20 Individuals outside Tri-County area; 12.75 4 weeks manual pay; 11.99 4 weeks auto pay; 124.65 1 year auto pay; 130.50 1 year manual pay. **URL:** http://www.register-pajaronian.com/v2_main_page.php. **Ad Rates:** GLR $.61; BW $1,476.72; 4C $1,744.72; SAU $8.68; PCI $126. **Remarks:** Accepts advertising. **Circ:** (Not Reported).

5022 ■ KAPU-FM - 104.7
250 W Riverside Dr.
Watsonville, CA 95076
Phone: (831)768-7002
Format: Hawaiian; Ethnic. **Operating Hours:** Continuous. **Wattage:** 052. **Ad Rates:** Advertising accepted; rates available upon request. **URL:** http://www.kapu.org.

5023 ■ KOMY-AM - 1340
PO Box 778
Watsonville, CA 95077
Format: News; Talk. **Simulcasts:** KSCO-AM. **Founded:** 1937. **Operating Hours:** Continuous. **Key Personnel:** Rosemary Chalmers, News Dir., mz@ksco.com; Phil Rather, Contact. **Wattage:** 1,000 Daytime; 850 N. **Ad Rates:** Advertising accepted; rates available upon request. **URL:** http://ksco.com/.

5024 ■ KPIG-FM - 107.5
1110 Main St., Ste. 16
Watsonville, CA 95076
Phone: (831)722-9000
Email: sales@kpig.com
Format: Folk; Adult Contemporary. **Owner:** Radio Ranch, at above address, Ph: (408)722-9000. **Founded:** 1976. **Operating Hours:** Continuous. **Wattage:** 5,400 ERP. **Ad Rates:** Advertising accepted; rates available upon request. $30 per unit. **URL:** http://www.kpig.com.

WEAVERVILLE

Trinity Co. (NW). 48 m NW of Redding. Sawmill. Pine, fir, cedar timber.

5025 ■ Trinity Journal
Trinity Journal
218 Main St.
Weaverville, CA 96093
Phone: (530)623-2055
Community newspaper. **Freq:** Weekly (Wed.). **Print Method:** Offset. **Trim Size:** 13 x 21. **Cols./Page:** 6. **Col. Width:** 27 nonpareils. **Col. Depth:** 298 agate lines. **Key Personnel:** Wayne R. Agner, Editor. **USPS:** 673-220. **Subscription Rates:** $33 By mail in-county (includes online); $49 By mail out-of-county (includes online); $25 Individuals online only; $60 Two years by mail in-county (includes online); $92 Two years by mail out-of-county (includes online); $45 Two years online only; $5 Individuals 1 month. **URL:** http://www.trinityjournal.com. **Mailing address:** PO Box 340, Weaverville, CA 96093. **Remarks:** Accepts advertising. **Circ:** (Not Reported).

WEST COVINA

Los Angeles Co Los Angeles Co. Los Angeles County. SW California. West of Los Angeles. Residential community.

5026 ■ The Highlander
San Gabriel Valley Tribune Publishers
1210 N Azusa Canyon Rd.
West Covina, CA 91790
Phone: (818)854-8700
Fax: (818)338-9157
Newspaper. **Founded:** 1948. **Freq:** Weekly. **Print Method:** Letterpress and offset. **Cols./Page:** 6. **Col. Width:** 26 nonpareils. **Col. Depth:** 301 agate lines. **Key Personnel:** William R. Applebee, Publisher. **Subscription Rates:** $10 Individuals all access plus sun print; $15 Individuals all access plus Thursday thru Suday print; $20 Individuals all access plus 7 days print; $10 Individuals all access digital only. **URL:** http://www.sgvtribune.com/highlanders. **Formerly:** Duartean. **Ad Rates:** SAU $13.10. **Remarks:** Accepts advertising. **Circ:** Paid 62, Free 3939.

5027 ■ San Gabriel Valley Tribune
San Gabriel Newspaper Group
1210 N Azusa Canyon Rd.
West Covina, CA 91790
Phone: (626)962-8811
Publication E-mail: news.tribune@sgvn.com
Local newspaper. **Founded:** 1955. **Freq:** Weekly. **Print Method:** Letterpress. **Cols./Page:** 6. **Col. Width:** 12.75 picas. **Col. Depth:** 301 agate lines. **Key Personnel:** Steve Hunt, Senior Editor. **Subscription Rates:** $10 Individuals all access + sun print; $15 Individuals all access + thursday thru sunday print; $20 Individuals all acces + 7 days print; $10 Individuals all access digital only. **URL:** http://www.sgvtribune.com/. **Remarks:** Accepts classified advertising. **Circ:** Mon.-Fri. ⋆**44161**, Sat. ⋆**43021**, Sun. ⋆**44648**.

5028 ■ KCFJ-AM - 570
1773 W San Bernardino Rd., Bldg. C31-34
West Covina, CA 91790
Phone: (626)856-3889
Fax: (626)856-3895
Email: info@edimediainc.com
Format: News. **Owner:** EDI Media Inc., 1773 W San Bernardino Rd., Bldg. C31-34, West Covina, CA 91790, Ph: (626)856-3889, Fax: (626)856-3895. **ADI**: Reno, NV. **Wattage:** 5,000. **Ad Rates:** Advertising accepted; rates available upon request. **URL:** http://edimediainc.com.

KLVP-AM - See Portland, OR

5029 ■ KWRM-AM - 1370
719 N Sunset Ave.
West Covina, CA 91790
Phone: (626)856-3889
Email: mail@am1370-chinese.com
Format: Full Service. **Owner:** Major Market Stations Inc., PO Box 10066, glendale, CA 91209. **Founded:** 1948. **Operating Hours:** Continuous. **Wattage:** 5,000 Daytime; 2,500 N. **Ad Rates:** $40 for 60 seconds. **URL:** http://www.am1370-chinese.com/.

WEST HOLLYWOOD

Los Angeles Co. Los Angeles Co. (SW). NE of Beverly Hills. Urban region.

5030 ■ Cybersocket
Cybersocket Inc.
1017 N La Cienega, Ste. 307
West Hollywood, CA 90069
Phone: (323)650-9906
Fax: (323)650-9926
Magazine featuring gay and lesbian community. **Freq:** Monthly. **Key Personnel:** Tom Terranova, Editor-in-Chief. **Subscription Rates:** $20 Individuals; $40 Two years. **URL:** http://www.cybersocket.com. **Circ:** 70000.

WEST SACRAMENTO

Yolo Co. Yolo Co. (C). Adjacent to Sacramento. Manufactures box shooks. finger joints, moldings furniture, sawdust logs, building materials, boats. Light fixtures, truck trailers bodies, disinfectants, fertilizers, soil conditioning materials, rice millings, envelopes. Geophysical equipment.

5031 ■ Archetype
Woodwork Institute
3188 Industrial Blvd.
West Sacramento, CA 95798-0247
Phone: (916)372-9943
Fax: (916)372-9950
Publisher's E-mail: info@woodinst.com
Journal of the Woodwork Institute. **Freq:** Semiannual. **Key Personnel:** Stanley Gustafson, Chief Executive Officer. **URL:** http://www.wicnet.org/publications/archetype.asp. **Ad Rates:** 4C $750; BW $600. **Remarks:** Accepts advertising. **Circ:** (Not Reported).

5032 ■ California Schools Magazine
California School Boards Association
3251 Beacon Blvd.
West Sacramento, CA 95691
Free: 800-266-3382
School management magazine covering educational issues and policies of vital importance to schools. **Freq:** Quarterly. **Print Method:** Offset. **Trim Size:** 9 x 11. **Cols./Page:** 3. **Col. Width:** 2 1/4 inches. **Col. Depth:** 9 3/4 inches. **Key Personnel:** Susan Swigart, Editor-in-Chief; Brian Taylor, Managing Editor; Cindy Warfe, Advertising Representative. **ISSN:** 1081--8936 (print). **Subscription Rates:** Included in membership; $20 Nonmembers. **URL:** http://www.csba.org/Newsroom/CASchoolsMagazine/2014.aspx. **Ad Rates:** BW $1510; 4C $2160. **Remarks:** Accepts advertising. **Circ:** Combined 7500.

5033 ■ News-Ledger
News-Ledger
1040 W Capitol Ave., Ste. B
West Sacramento, CA 95691-2715
Phone: (916)371-8030
Community newspaper. **Freq:** Weekly (Wed.). **Print Method:** Offset. **Cols./Page:** 6. **Col. Width:** 22 nonpareils. **Col. Depth:** 21 inches. **Key Personnel:** Monica Stark, Editor. **USPS:** 388-320. **Subscription Rates:** $25 Individuals /year in West Sacramento; $30 Out of area /year mailed elsewhere in the U.S. **URL:** http://www.westsac.com/news-ledger. **Ad Rates:** GLR $5.75; BW $724.50; 4C $1,224.50. **Remarks:** Accepts advertising. **Circ:** Free 2100.

5034 ■ KJAY-AM - 1430
5030 S River Rd.
West Sacramento, CA 95691
Phone: (916)371-5101
Format: Gospel; Religious. **Networks:** Independent. **Owner:** Jack L. Powell, at above address. **Founded:** 1963. **Operating Hours:** Sunrise - Sunset Monday-Friday; 6:00 a.m.- 6:30 p.m. Saturday;6:00 a.m.- 4:00 p.m. Sunday. **ADI**: Sacramento-Stockton, CA. **Key Personnel:** Jack L. Powell, Contact. **Wattage:** 500. **Ad Rates:** Accepts Advertising. **URL:** http://www.kjay1430.com.

5035 ■ KMAX-TV - 31
2713 KOVR Dr.
West Sacramento, CA 95605
Phone: (916)374-1313
Fax: (916)374-1304
Free: 800-374-8813
Format: Commercial TV. **Networks:** United Paramount Network. **Founded:** 1981. **Formerly:** KMUV-TV; KRBK-TV; KPWB-TV. **Operating Hours:** Continuous; 100% local. **ADI**: Sacramento-Stockton, CA. **Ad Rates:** Advertising accepted; rates available upon request. **URL:** http://www.gooddaysacramento.cbslocal.com.

5036 ■ KOVR-TV - 13
2713 KOVR Dr.
West Sacramento, CA 95605
Phone: (916)374-1313
Fax: (916)374-1304
Free: 800-374-8813
Format: Commercial TV. **Networks:** CBS. **Founded:** 1954. **Operating Hours:** Continuous. **ADI**: Sacramento-Stockton, CA. **Ad Rates:** Advertising accepted; rates available upon request. **URL:** http://sacramento.cbslocal.com.

WESTLAKE VILLAGE

Los Angeles Co. Los Angeles Co. (SW). 3 m SE of Thousand Oaks.

5037 ■ Gamers' Republic
Millennium Publications
32123 Lindero Canyon Rd. 215
Westlake Village, CA 91361
Phone: (818)889-4372
Fax: (818)889-4606
Consumer magazine covering video and computer games. **Remarks:** Advertising accepted; rates available upon request. **Circ:** (Not Reported).

5038 ■ Pacific Union Recorder
Pacific Union Conference
2686 Townsgate Rd.
Westlake Village, CA 91361-2701
Phone: (805)413-7100
Fax: (805)495-2644
Religious magazine. **Freq:** Monthly. **Print Method:** Web offset. **Trim Size:** 8 x 10 5/8. **Cols./Page:** 4. **Col. Width:**

21 nonpareils. **Col. Depth:** 130 agate lines. **Key Personnel:** Alicia Adams, Contact. **ISSN:** 0744--6381 (print). **Subscription Rates:** Included in membership. **URL:** http://pacificunionrecorder.adventistfaith.org/issue/current. **Mailing address:** PO Box 5005, Westlake Village, CA 91359-5005. **Ad Rates:** BW $3950; 4C $3,650; PCI $55. **Remarks:** Accepts advertising. **Circ:** 80000.

5039 ■ Telemedicine Today
B2BMedia Inc
660 Hampshire Rd., Ste. 200
Westlake Village, CA 91361
Fax: (805)371-7885
Publisher's E-mail: info@telemedtoday.com
Magazine dealing with all aspects of telemedicine industry. **Key Personnel:** Scott Frager, Publisher, phone: (805)371-7877, fax: (805)371-7885. **Subscription Rates:** $125 Individuals; $155 Other countries; $139 Canada and Mexico; $199 Two years; $249 Two years for international order; $229 Two years in Canada and Mexico. **Ad Rates:** 4C $1750. **Remarks:** Accepts advertising. **Circ:** (Not Reported).

WESTMINSTER

Orange Co. Orange Co. (S). 10 m W of Santa Ana. Residential. Light manufacturing. Diversified farming.

5040 ■ Bus Conversions: First and Foremost Bus Converters Magazine
Bus Conversions
7246 Garden Grove Blvd.
Westminster, CA 92683
Phone: (714)799-0062
Fax: (877)783-1667
Publication E-mail: editor@busconversions.com
Magazine about converting buses into motorhomes. **Freq:** Monthly. **Trim Size:** 8 1/4 x 10 3/4. **ISSN:** 1070-6526 (print). **Subscription Rates:** $38 Students print, delivery - 1 year; $70 Students print, delivery - 2 years; $25 Individuals online, 1 year; $45 Individuals online, 2 years; $68 Individuals print, first class U.S delivery; $68 Canada and Mexico print, 1 year; $99 Other countries print, 1 year; $25 Individuals online, 1 year; $45 Individuals online, 2 years. **URL:** http://www.busconversions.com. **Ad Rates:** GLR $10; BW $1,342; 4C $1,610. **Remarks:** Advertising accepted; rates available upon request. **Circ:** Paid 10000.

5041 ■ Nguoi Viet Daily News
Nguoi Viet Daily News
14771 Moran St.
Westminster, CA 92683
Phone: (714)892-9414
Fax: (714)894-1381
Publisher's E-mail: nv2@nguoi-viet.com
General newspaper (Vietnamese). **Freq:** Mon.-Sun. (morn.). **Print Method:** Web. **Trim Size:** 13 x 21. **Cols./Page:** 6. **Col. Width:** 12 picas. **Key Personnel:** Do Ngoc Yen, Publisher. **URL:** http://www.nguoi-viet.com. **Formerly:** Nguoi Vet. **Ad Rates:** BW $659; 4C $1173; PCI $11.75. **Remarks:** Accepts advertising. **Circ:** Paid ■ **16698**.

5042 ■ Viet Bao Kinh Te
Viet Bao Daily News- LA Edition
14841 Moran St.
Westminster, CA 92683
Phone: (714)988-5388
Vietnamese language newspaper for Vietnamese-Americans. **Freq:** Daily. **Print Method:** web. **Trim Size:** Broadsheet. **Ad Rates:** BW $550. **Remarks:** Accepts advertising. **Circ:** (Not Reported).

WESTWOOD

5043 ■ The Informatics Review
Association of Medical Directors of Information Systems
682 Peninsula Dr.
Westwood, CA 96137
Phone: (719)548-9360
Publisher's E-mail: info@amdis.org
Journal covering topics on clinical informatics and computing. **Freq:** Semimonthly. **Key Personnel:** Dean F. Sittig, PhD, Editor-in-Chief. **Circ:** (Not Reported).

WHITTIER

Los Angeles Co. Los Angeles Co. (S). 13 m SE of Los Angeles. Whittier College. Manufacturers oil tools, welding rods, alloy steel products, trailers, automobile polish, auto radiators, gas and oil burners, spray chemicals, tile, paper cartons, bullets, aircraft parts, boxes, cutlery, optical glass, plastics, women's apparel. Citrus fruit, mushrooms packed. Oil, gas wells. Fruit, dairy farms. Oranges, lemons, avocados, walnuts.

5044 ■ Quaker Campus
Whittier College
13406 E Philadelphia St.
Whittier, CA 90608-0634
Phone: (562)907-4200
Fax: (562)907-4870
Publication E-mail: qc@whittier.edu
Collegiate newspaper. **Freq:** Weekly. **Print Method:** Offset. **Cols./Page:** 5. **Col. Width:** 24 nonpareils. **Col. Depth:** 210 agate lines. **URL:** http://thequakercampus.com. **Mailing address:** PO Box 634, Whittier, CA 90608-0634. **Remarks:** Accepts advertising. **Circ:** Free 1800.

5045 ■ Whittier Daily News
San Gabriel Newspaper Group
6737 Brighter Ave., Ste. 109
Whittier, CA 90602
Phone: (562)698-0955
General newspaper. **Founded:** 1900. **Freq:** Daily (morn.). **Print Method:** Offset. **Cols./Page:** 6. **Col. Width:** 12 1/5 picas. **Col. Depth:** 301 agate lines. **Key Personnel:** Ron Hasse, Publisher. **ISSN:** 0746-6188 (print). **Subscription Rates:** $20 Individuals all access plus and print/month. **URL:** http://www.whittierdailynews.com. **Formerly:** Daily News. **Ad Rates:** BW $4,980.45; 4C $5,583.45; SAU $34.93; PCI $15.70. **Remarks:** Accepts classified advertising. **Circ:** Mon.-Fri. ★**16111**, Sat. ★**15723**, Sun. ★**15778**.

WILLITS

Mendocino Co. Mendocino Co. (NW). 110 m N of San Francisco. Manufactures redwood furniture and products, hydraulic cylinders. lumber, sawmills. Ranching.

5046 ■ The Willits News
The Willits News
77 W Commercial St.
Willits, CA 95490
Phone: (707)459-4643
Fax: (707)459-1664
Local newspaper. **Founded:** 1889. **Freq:** Semiweekly (Wed. and Fri.). **Print Method:** Offset. **Trim Size:** 14 x 22 1/4. **Cols./Page:** 6. **Col. Width:** 2 1/8 inches. **Col. Depth:** 21 inches. **Key Personnel:** Debbie Clark, Publisher; Dan McKee, Editor. **USPS:** 685-140. **Subscription Rates:** $53.31 Individuals; $66.34 Out of area. **URL:** http://www.willitsnews.com/. **Ad Rates:** GLR $6.95; SAU $6.95. **Remarks:** Accepts advertising. **Circ:** 3100.

5047 ■ KLLK-AM - 1250
12 W Valley St.
Willits, CA 95490
Format: Alternative/New Music/Progressive. **Simulcasts:** KLLK-FM. **Networks:** Independent. **Owner:** Henry Communications, at above address. **Founded:** 1985. **Operating Hours:** 5 a.m.-midnight; 95% local. **ADI:** San Francisco-Oakland-San Jose. **Key Personnel:** Brian Henry, Gen. Mgr. **Wattage:** 5,400 day; 2,700 night. **Ad Rates:** Advertising accepted; rates available upon request. **URL:** http://www.kuki.com/#.

WILLOWS

Glenn Co. Glenn Co. (NWC). 75 m NW of Sacramento. Manufactures cheese, butter, feed, beverages, roofing material. Rice drying plant. Diversified farming. Rice. sheep, cattle citrus fruit

5048 ■ Glenn Transcript
Vista California News Media
130 N Butte St.
Willows, CA 95988
Phone: (530)934-6800
Fax: (530)934-6815
Newspaper. **Founded:** 1877. **Freq:** 3/week. **Print Method:** Offset. **Cols./Page:** 6. **Col. Width:** 24 nonpareils. **Col. Depth:** 301 agate lines. **Key Personnel:** Glenn Stifflemire, Publisher. **Subscription Rates:** $62 Individuals regular; $44 Individuals senior citizen; $64 Individuals regular; $54 Individuals senior citizen; $65 Individuals regular; $59 Individuals senior citizen; $26 Individuals regular; $24 Individuals senior citizen; $32 Individuals regular; $29 Individuals senior citizen. **URL:** http://www.willows-journal.com/; http://www.freedom.com/newspapers/willows.html. **Formed by the merger of:** The Willows Journal; Orland Press Register. **Remarks:** Advertising not accepted. **Circ:** 1008.

5049 ■ KIQS-AM
118 W Sycamore
Willows, CA 95988
Phone: (916)934-5054
Fax: (916)934-4656
Networks: CNN Radio. **Owner:** Kiqs, Inc, at above address. **Founded:** 1961. **Wattage:** 250 Day. **Ad Rates:** $3.35 for 10 seconds; $3.75-5.95 for 30 seconds; $4.70-7.60 for 60 seconds. **Mailing address:** PO Box 7, Willows, CA 95988.

WINCHESTER

5050 ■ Eye to the Telescope
Science Fiction Poetry Association
PO Box 907
Winchester, CA 92596
Publisher's E-mail: sfpatreasurer@gmail.com
Freq: Quarterly issues on January 15, April 15, July 15, and October 15. **Key Personnel:** Geoffrey A. Landis, Writer; Diane Severson, Editor. **URL:** http://eyetothetelescope.com. **Remarks:** Advertising not accepted. **Circ:** (Not Reported).

WINDSOR

Sonoma Co.

5051 ■ Wine X Magazine: Wine, Food, and an Intelligent Slice of Vice
Wine X Magazine
9903 Old Camp Ln.
Windsor, CA 95492
Phone: (707)545-0992
Free: 866-545-0992
Publisher's E-mail: winexus@winexmagazine.com
Consumer lifestyle magazine covering wine and food, music, video, beer, spirits coffee, fashion, the arts. **Freq:** Bimonthly. **Key Personnel:** Angelina Malhotra-Singh, Editor-in-Chief; Darryl M. Roberts, Director, Sales and Marketing, Publisher. **ISSN:** 1527--3784 (print). **Subscription Rates:** Free only available on-line. **Remarks:** Accepts advertising. **Circ:** (Not Reported).

WINTERS

Yolo Co. Yolo Co. (SC). 28 m W of Sacramento. Fruit drying and packing plants. Agriculture. Apricots, peaches, wheat, almonds.

5052 ■ Winters Express
Winters Express
312 Railroad Ave.
Winters, CA 95694
Phone: (530)795-4551
Publisher's E-mail: news@wintersexpress.com
Newspaper. **Freq:** Weekly (Thurs.). **Print Method:** Offset. **Cols./Page:** 6. **Col. Width:** 25 nonpareils. **Col. Depth:** 280 agate lines. **Key Personnel:** Charles R. Wallace, Publisher; Debra J. DeAngelo, Editor; Elliot Landes, Contact. **Subscription Rates:** $25 Individuals Yolo & Solano counties (home delivery); $30 Individuals Yolo & Solano counties (U.S. mail); $50 Out of area U.S. mail; $25 Individuals online. **URL:** http://wintersexpress.com. **Remarks:** Accepts advertising. **Circ:** ‡2480.

WINTON

Merced Co. (C).

5053 ■ Hilmar Times
Mid-Valley Publications
PO Box 65
Winton, CA 95388
Phone: (209)358-5311
Fax: (209)358-7108
Publication E-mail: info@midvalleypub.com
Local newspaper. **Freq:** Weekly (Wed.). **Print Method:** Offset. **Trim Size:** 14 x 21. **Cols./Page:** 6. **Col. Width:** 2 inches. **Col. Depth:** 294 agate lines. **Key Personnel:** John M. Derby, Contact; Ashley Cahill, Contact. **Subscription Rates:** $30 Individuals out of California, +$1.

Circulation: ★ = AAM; △ or • = BPA; ♦ = CAC; ❑ = VAC; ⊕ = PO Statement; ‡ = Publisher's Report; Boldface figures = sworn; Light figures = estimated.

00. **URL:** http://www.midvalleypublications.com. **Ad Rates:** GLR $9.95; BW $695; 4C $995; SAU $10.95; PCI $7.95. **Remarks:** Accepts advertising. **Circ:** ‡5000.

5054 ■ The Waterford News
Mid-Valley Publications
PO Box 65
Winton, CA 95388
Phone: (209)358-5311
Fax: (209)358-7108
Local newspaper. **Freq:** Weekly (Tues.). **Print Method:** Offset. **Trim Size:** 14 x 21. **Cols./Page:** 6. **Col. Width:** 2 inches. **Col. Depth:** 294 agate lines. **Key Personnel:** Wendy Krier, Editor-in-Chief. **Subscription Rates:** $19.95 Individuals 6 months; $35 Individuals 12 months; $59 Individuals 24 months; $85 Individuals 36 months. **URL:** http://waterfordnews.weebly.com. **Remarks:** Advertising accepted; rates available upon request. **Circ:** ‡6700.

WOODLAND HILLS

Los Angeles Co. (S). Suburb of Los Angeles. Residential. Commerical and industrial.

5055 ■ art ltd.
Lifescape Publishing Inc.
5525 Oakdale Ave., Ste. 430
Woodland Hills, CA 91364
Phone: (818)316-0900
Fax: (818)702-2505
Publication E-mail: editor@artltdmag.com
Art and design magazine. **Freq:** Bimonthly. **Trim Size:** 8.375 x 10.875. **Key Personnel:** George Melrod, Editor; Peter Fehler, Publisher; Kathryn Louyse, Manager, Production. **Subscription Rates:** $23.75 Individuals; $44.75 Two years; $14.99 Individuals digital. **URL:** http://www.artltdmag.com. **Remarks:** Accepts advertising. **Circ:** (Not Reported).

5056 ■ Daily News
Daily News
21860 Burbank Blvd., Ste. 200
Woodland Hills, CA 91367
Phone: (818)713-3000
Fax: (818)713-0058
Publisher's E-mail: feedback@dailynews.com
General newspaper. **Founded:** 1911. **Freq:** Daily. **Print Method:** Offset. **Cols./Page:** 6. **Col. Width:** 24 nonpareils. **Col. Depth:** 294 agate lines. **Key Personnel:** Ron Hasse, Publisher. **Subscription Rates:** $10 Individuals /month; all access digital plus sunday print. **URL:** http://www.dailynews.com/contactus. **Mailing address:** PO Box 4200, Woodland Hills, CA 91365. **Ad Rates:** PCI $91.97. **Remarks:** Accepts classified advertising. **Circ:** Mon.-Fri. ★**169379**, Sat. ★**159561**, Sun. ★**195158**.

5057 ■ Exhibit Builder
Exhibit Builder Magazine
22900 Ventura Blvd., Ste. 245
Woodland Hills, CA 91364
Phone: (818)225-0100
Fax: (818)225-0138
Free: 800-356-4451
Publisher's E-mail: jillb@exhibitbuilder.net
Magazine covering new product information and research related to the exhibit building, including museums and trade shows. **Founded:** 1983. **Freq:** Periodic 7/yr. **Print Method:** Web offset. **Trim Size:** 8 x 10 3/4. **Cols./Page:** 3. **Col. Width:** 27 nonpareils. **Col. Depth:** 138 agate lines. **Key Personnel:** Judy Pomerantz, Managing Editor; Jill Brookman, Publisher; Jollen Ryan, Manager, Circulation. **ISSN:** 0887-6878 (print). **Subscription Rates:** $45 Individuals; $50 Canada; $70 Other countries; $90 Other countries 2 years. **URL:** http://www.exhibitbuilder.net. **Ad Rates:** BW $6,100. **Remarks:** Accepts advertising. **Circ:** ‡15585.

5058 ■ Floor Covering Installer
BNP Media
22801 Ventura Blvd., No. 115
Woodland Hills, CA 91364
Phone: (818)224-8035
Fax: (818)224-8042
Publication E-mail: fci@bnpmedia.com
Trade publication covering issues for floor covering installers. **Freq:** 7/year. **Key Personnel:** Jennifer Allen, Manager, Production; Jeffrey Stouffer, Editor-in-Chief; Michael Chmielecki, Editor, phone: (603)791-0215. **ISSN:** 1099--9647 (print). **Subscription Rates:** Free. **URL:** http://www.fcimag.com; http://www.bnpmedia.com/Articles/Publications/Flooring. **Remarks:** Accepts advertising. **Circ:** (Not Reported).

5059 ■ ICS Cleaning Specialist: Information for Today's Floor Care Professional
Specialist Publications Inc.
22801 Ventura Blvd., Ste. 115
Woodland Hills, CA 91364
Phone: (818)224-8035
Fax: (818)224-8042
Free: 800-835-4398
Publisher's E-mail: ics@bnp.com
Trade magazine for the floor care and service industry. **Freq:** Monthly. **Print Method:** Heat-set Web Offset. **Trim Size:** 8 1/8 x 10 7/8. **Cols./Page:** 2 and 3. **Col. Width:** 40 and 26 nonpareils. **Col. Depth:** 140 agate lines. **Key Personnel:** Evan Kessler, Publisher, phone: (303)255-1263, fax: (248)502-2049; Jeffrey Stouffer, Editor, phone: (818)224-8035, fax: (818)224-8042. **ISSN:** 1522--4708 (print). **URL:** http://www.icsmag.com. **Formerly:** Installation Specialist; Installation & Cleaning Specialist. **Remarks:** Accepts advertising. **Circ:** △**25017**.

5060 ■ L.A. Daily News
Tower Media Inc.
21221 Oxnard St.
Woodland Hills, CA 91367-5015
Phone: (818)713-3000
Fax: (818)713-0058
Daily newspaper. **Freq:** Daily. **Key Personnel:** Ron Hasse, President, Publisher; Carolina Garcia, Managing Editor, phone: (818)713-3639. **URL:** http://www.dailynews.com. **Mailing address:** PO Box 4200, Woodland Hills, CA 91367-4200. **Circ:** (Not Reported).

5061 ■ The Valley Vantage
The Valley Vantage
22025 Ventura Blvd., Ste. 303
Woodland Hills, CA 91364-1107
Phone: (818)223-9545
Publisher's E-mail: wnrcnews@instanet.com
Community newspaper. **Freq:** Weekly (Thurs.). **Print Method:** Offset. **Trim Size:** 10 1/4 x 14. **Cols./Page:** 5. **Col. Width:** 21 nonpareils. **Col. Depth:** 217 agate lines. **URL:** http://www.valleynewsgroup.com/index.html. **Formerly:** Northridger News. **Ad Rates:** BW $1500; PCI $25. **Remarks:** Accepts advertising. **Circ:** Free 20000.

5062 ■ Western States Jewish History
Western States Jewish History Association
22711 Cass Ave.
Woodland Hills, CA 91364
Phone: (818)225-9631
Magazine covering western Jewish history. **Freq:** Quarterly. **Print Method:** Offset. **Trim Size:** 5 1/2 x 8 1/2. **Cols./Page:** 1. **Col. Width:** 51 nonpareils. **Col. Depth:** 93 agate lines. **Key Personnel:** David W. Epstein, Managing Editor, Publisher; Gladys Sturman, Editor-in-Chief, Publisher, phone: (818)222-4694. **ISSN:** 0043--4221 (print). **Subscription Rates:** $36 Individuals per year. **URL:** http://www.jmaw.org/western-states-jewish-history. **Ad Rates:** BW $200. **Remarks:** Accepts advertising. **Circ:** Paid 1200.

WRIGHTWOOD

San Bernardino Co. (SE). 35 m NE of Los Angeles. Suburban. Mt. resort.

5063 ■ Mountaineer Progress
Mountaineer Progress
3407 State Hwy. 2
Wrightwood, CA 92397
Phone: (760)868-3245
Fax: (760)249-4021
Community newspaper. **Freq:** Weekly (Thurs.). **Print Method:** Offset. **Cols./Page:** 6. **Col. Width:** 24 nonpareils. **Col. Depth:** 215 agate lines. **Key Personnel:** Vicky Rinek, Managing Editor; Steven Rinek, Publisher; Eileen Marek, Columnist. **Subscription Rates:** $20 Individuals 12 months; $26 Individuals 24months; $26 Out of state 12 months; $36 Out of state 24 months; $62 Out of state 36 months. **URL:** http://www.mtprogress.net. **Mailing address:** PO Box 248, Wrightwood, CA 92397. **Remarks:** Advertising accepted; rates available upon request. **Circ:** ‡4900.

YANKEE HILL

5064 ■ Feather River Canyon News
Feather River Canyon News
PO Box 4006
Yankee Hill, CA 95965
Publisher's E-mail: frcn@cncnet.com
Community newspaper. **Freq:** Monthly. **Subscription Rates:** Included in membership. **URL:** http://home.surewest.net/frcn. **Circ:** (Not Reported).

YREKA

Siskiyou Co. Siskiyou Co. (N). 50 m S of Medford, Ore. Recreations. Light industry. Historic district. Creamery, bottling, cabinet works, logging, Gold mines. Pine timber. Dairy, stock, grain. Cattle ranching.

5065 ■ Siskiyou Daily News
Siskiyou Daily News
309 S Broadway
Yreka, CA 96097-2905
Phone: (530)842-5777
Fax: (530)842-6787
Publisher's E-mail: publisher@siskiyoudaily.com
General newspaper. **Founded:** 1859. **Freq:** Daily. **Print Method:** Offset. **Cols./Page:** 6. **Col. Width:** 12 4/10 picas. **Col. Depth:** 301 agate lines. **Key Personnel:** Jean Smith, Manager, Circulation; Jolene Foster, Manager, Production; Matt Guthrie, Publisher. **Subscription Rates:** $86.40 Individuals senior; $147 Out of area by mail; $94.50 Individuals regular. **URL:** http://www.siskiyoudaily.com. **Remarks:** Accepts advertising. **Circ:** ‡6000.

5066 ■ KSYC-FM - 103.9
316 Lawrence Ln.
Yreka, CA 96097
Phone: (530)842-4158
Format: Country. **Owner:** Siskiyou Radio Partners, Inc., at above address. **Founded:** 1983. **Operating Hours:** 6:00 a.m. - 9:00 p.m. Monday - Friday. **Key Personnel:** Al Blackmore, Gen. Mgr., Prog. Dir.; Kevin Sponsler, Operations Mgr. **Wattage:** 10,000. **Ad Rates:** Advertising accepted; rates available upon request. $12.90-14.50 for 30 seconds; $16-18 for 60 seconds. Combined advertising rates available with KSYC-AM. **URL:** http://www.ksyc1039.com.

5067 ■ Northland Communications
1836 Fort Jones Rd.
Yreka, CA 96097
Phone: (530)842-4228
Fax: (530)842-2516
Formerly: Northland Cable Television. **Cities Served:** 55 channels. **Mailing address:** PO Box 967, Yreka, CA 96097. **URL:** http://www.northlandcabletv.com/yreka.

YUBA CITY

Sutter Co. Sutter Co. (C). On Feather River, 40 m N of Sacramento. Fruit canning and drying. Fruit and nut packing house. Concrete pipe works. Creamery, feed mill, frozen food, seed cleaning plants. Diversified farming. Peaches, prunes, rice, beans.

5068 ■ The Arrowhead
Jordan Register
2099 Pheasant Dr.
Yuba City, CA 95993
Phone: (530)673-7382
Publisher's E-mail: worledge@succeed.net
Freq: Quarterly. **Subscription Rates:** included in membership dues. **Remarks:** Accepts advertising. **Circ:** 150.

5069 ■ KKCY-FM - 103.1
1479 Sanborn Dr.
Yuba City, CA 95993
Phone: (530)673-2200
Fax: (530)673-3010
Format: Contemporary Country. **Operating Hours:** Continuous. **Key Personnel:** Gordon Rowntree, Mgr; Chris Carothers, Contact, ccarothers@resultsradiomail.com. **Wattage:** 135 ERP. **Ad Rates:** Advertising accepted; rates available upon request. **URL:** http://www.kkcy.com.

5070 ■ KOBO-AM - 1450
350 Del Norte Ave.
Yuba City, CA 95991-4123
Phone: (408)272-5200

Format: Talk; News; Sports. **Networks:** ABC; Sun Radio; AP. **Owner:** Robert M. Peppercorn, MD, 350 Del Norte Ave., Yuba City, CA 95991, Ph: (916)671-4182. **Founded:** 1952. **Operating Hours:** 5 a.m.-midnight; 65% network, 35% local. **Key Personnel:** Robert M. Peppercorn, Contact; Michael Wilson, Contact. **Wattage:** 500. **URL:** http://punjabiradiousa.com/contact-us/.

5071 ■ KUBA-AM - 1600
1479 Sanborn Rd.
Yuba City, CA 95993
Format: News; Oldies. **Networks:** CBS. **Owner:** Nevada County Broadcasters, Inc., at above address, Grass Valley, CA. **Founded:** 1948. **Key Personnel:** Chris Gilbert, News Dir., chris@kubaradio.com. **Wattage:** 5,000 Daytime; 2,500 N. **Ad Rates:** Advertising accepted; rates available upon request. $15-19 per unit. Combined advertising rates available with KNCO-AM, KNCO-FM. **URL:** http://am1600kuba.com/.

YUCAIPA

San Bernardino Co. San Bernardino Co. (SE). 9 m E of Redlands. Retirement living. Mobile home parks. Fruit, poultry, truck farms. Peaches, plums, tomatoes, apples.

5072 ■ News Mirror
News Mirror
35154 Yucaipa Blvd.
Yucaipa, CA 92399
Phone: (909)797-9101
Fax: (909)797-0502
Publication E-mail: newsmir@hcctel.net
Community newspaper. **Founded:** 1891. **Freq:** Weekly. **Print Method:** Offset. **Cols./Page:** 6. **Col. Width:** 14 picas. **Col. Depth:** 21 1/2 inches. **Key Personnel:** Toebe Bush, Publisher; Claire Marie Teeters, Editor. **USPS:** 069-520. **Subscription Rates:** $25 Individuals e-edition. **URL:** http://www.newsmirror.net. **Ad Rates:** BW $630; 4C $850; PCI $6.90. **Remarks:** Accepts advertising. **Circ:** ■ **20000**.

5073 ■ Yucaipa/Calimesa News Mirror
Century Group Newspapers
35154 Yucaipa Blvd.
Yucaipa, CA 92399
Phone: (909)797-9101
Fax: (909)797-0502
Local newspaper. **Freq:** Weekly (Thurs.). **Print Method:** Offset. **Cols./Page:** 8. **Col. Width:** 21 picas. **Col. Depth:** 21 1/2 inches. **Key Personnel:** Toebe Bush, Publisher; Claire Marie Teeters, Editor. **USPS:** 698-640. **Subscription Rates:** $5 Individuals 1 month online; $15 Individuals 3 months online; $20 Individuals 6 months online; $25 Individuals 1 year online. **URL:** http://www.newsmirror.net/news. **Remarks:** Accepts advertising. **Circ:** ■ **69816**.

YUCCA VALLEY

San Bernardino Co. San Bernardino Co. (SE). 31 m N of Palm Springs. Desert and health resort.

5074 ■ Hi-Desert Star
Hi Desert Publishing
56445 29 Palms Hwy.
Yucca Valley, CA 92284
Phone: (760)365-3315
Publisher's E-mail: support@hidesertstar.com
Community newspaper. **Freq:** Semiweekly. **Print Method:** Offset. **Trim Size:** 13 3/4 x 22 3/4. **Cols./Page:** 6 and 9. **Col. Width:** 2 and 1.25 inches. **Col. Depth:** 21.5 and 21.5 inches. **Key Personnel:** Cindy Melland, Publisher; Stacy Moore, Managing Editor. **Subscription Rates:** $30 Individuals 6 months; $45 Individuals 1 year; $73 Individuals 2 years; $106 Individuals 3 years; 53 Elsewhere 6 months; $79 Elsewhere 1 year. **URL:** http://www.hidesertstar.com. **Remarks:** Advertising accepted; rates available upon request. **Circ:** ‡10100.

5075 ■ KJSM-FM - 97.1
57373 Joshua Ln.
Yucca Valley, CA 92284
Phone: (760)365-0769
Format: Gospel; Religious; Contemporary Christian. **Operating Hours:** Continuous. **Key Personnel:** Craig Barnes, Contact. **Ad Rates:** Noncommercial; underwriting available.

5076 ■ K216CX-FM - 91.1
PO Box 391
Twin Falls, ID 83303
Fax: (208)736-1958
Free: 800-357-4226
Format: Religious; Contemporary Christian. **Owner:** CSN International, PO Box 391, Twin Falls, ID 83303, Ph: (208)736-1958, Fax: (208)736-1958, Free: 800-357-4226. **Key Personnel:** Don Mills, Music Dir., Prog. Dir.; Kelly Carlson, Dir. of Engg.; Ray Gorney, Asst. Dir. **URL:** http://www.csnradio.com.

Circulation: ★ = AAM; △ or • = BPA; ♦ = CAC; ❑ = VAC; ⊕ = PO Statement; ‡ = Publisher's Report; Boldface figures = sworn; Light figures = estimated.

AKRON

Washington Co. Washington Co. (NE). 40 m S of Sterling. Residential.

5077 ■ The Akron News-Reporter
The Akron News-Reporter
69 Main Ave.
Akron, CO 80720
Phone: (970)345-2296
Publisher's E-mail: abarry@akronnewsreporter.com
Local newspaper. **Freq:** Weekly (Thurs.). **Print Method:** Offset. **Cols./Page:** 6. **Col. Width:** 23 nonpareils. **Col. Depth:** 297 agate lines. **Key Personnel:** JoAnne Busing, Editor. **USPS:** 010-820. **Subscription Rates:** $39 Individuals in Colorado 1 year; $33 Students 9 months; $43 Other countries 1 year; $38 Students, other countries 9 months. **URL:** http://www.akronnewsreporter.com. **Remarks:** Advertising accepted; rates available upon request. **Circ:** Paid ‡2500, Free ‡30.

ALAMOSA

Alamosa Co. Alamosa Co. (S). 17 m S of Monte Vista.

5078 ■ South Coloradan
Adams State University
208 Edgemont Blvd.
Alamosa, CO 81102
Phone: (719)587-7011
Fax: (719)587-7522
Free: 800-824-6494
Collegiate newspaper (tabloid). **Freq:** Daily. **Print Method:** Offset. **Cols./Page:** 5. **Col. Width:** 34 nonpareils. **Col. Depth:** 206 agate lines. **Key Personnel:** Lance Hostetter, Editor. **URL:** http://southcoloradan.asf.adams.edu. **Feature Editors:** Emma Mueller, muellereg@adams.edu. **Remarks:** Accepts advertising. **Circ:** Free ‡2000.

5079 ■ The Valley Courier
Alamosa Newspapers Inc.
2205 State Ave.
Alamosa, CO 81101
Phone: (719)589-2553
Fax: (719)589-6573
General newspaper. **Founded:** 1925. **Freq:** Daily Tues.-Fri. (Morn.) and Sat. (Morn.). **Print Method:** Offset. **Key Personnel:** Shasta Quintana, Manager, Circulation, phone: (719)589-2553. **ISSN:** 1047-1170 (print). **Subscription Rates:** $90 Individuals e-edition, In Valley; $99 Out of area e-editon; $105 By mail e-edition, In Valley; $105 By mail print and e-edition, In Valley; $142 Out of area print and e-edition. **URL:** http://www.alamosanews.com/v2_main_page.php. **Ad Rates:** GLR $15; BW $1,760.85; 4C $2,010.85; PCI $13.65. **Remarks:** Accepts advertising. **Circ:** (Not Reported).

5080 ■ KALQ-FM - 93.5
PO Box 179
Alamosa, CO 81101-0179
Phone: (719)589-6644
Email: talca@phonefone.net
Format: Adult Contemporary. **Networks:** Unistar. **Owner:** Coummmnity Broadcasting, at above address, Ph: (505)662-4342. **Founded:** 1969. **Formerly:** KGIW-FM. **Operating Hours:** 6 a.m.-11 p.m.; 95% network, 5% local. **Key Personnel:** Mike Tanner, Dir. of Programs. **Wattage:** 3,000. **Ad Rates:** $7.30 for 30 seconds; $12.60 for 60 seconds. **URL:** http://www.kalq935.com/.

5081 ■ KASF-FM - 90.9
208 Edgemont Blvd.
Alamosa, CO 81102
Phone: (719)587-7871
Format: Eclectic. **Owner:** Adams State University, 208 Edgemont Blvd., Alamosa, CO 81102, Ph: (719)587-7011, Fax: (719)587-7522, Free: 800-824-6494. **Founded:** 1967. **Operating Hours:** 7 a.m.-2 a.m. all week. **Key Personnel:** Rita Mays, Gen. Mgr.; Rebekah Colman, Music Dir. **Wattage:** 1,000. **URL:** http://www.blogs.adams.edu.

5082 ■ KGIW-AM - 1450
292 Sanfa Fa Ave.
Alamosa, CO 81101-0179
Phone: (719)589-6644
Email: Palca@fone.net
Format: Full Service. **Networks:** ABC. **Owner:** Community Broadcasting, Inc., at above address, Ph: (505)662-4342. **Founded:** 1929. **Operating Hours:** Continuous. **Wattage:** 1,000. **Ad Rates:** $7.50 for 30 seconds; $13 for 60 seconds. **URL:** http://www.kgiw1450.com/.

5083 ■ KRZA-FM - 88.7
528 Ninth St.
Alamosa, CO 81101
Phone: (719)589-8844
Fax: (719)587-0032
Format: Public Radio; Hispanic. **Owner:** KRZA Radio, at above address. **Founded:** 1985. **Operating Hours:** Continuous. **Key Personnel:** Holly Felmlee, Gen. Mgr., krzamanager@krza.org. **Local Programs:** *The Bioneers*, Wednesday 8:30 a.m. **Wattage:** 9,800 ERP. **Ad Rates:** Noncommercial. **URL:** http://www.krza.org.

ARVADA

5084 ■ Akita World
Hoflin Publishing Inc.
8989 W 51st Ave.
Arvada, CO 80002
Phone: (303)303-2222
Publisher's E-mail: paypal@hoflin.com
Magazine for Akita dog fanciers. **Freq:** Quarterly. **Trim Size:** 8.5 x 11. **Cols./Page:** 4. **Col. Width:** 1.70 inches. **Col. Depth:** 9 1/2 inches. **ISSN:** 0194--6323 (print). **Subscription Rates:** $74 Canada; $54 Individuals; $98 Other countries; $15 Single issue; $105 Two years; $145 Canada two years; $193 Other countries two years. **URL:** http://www.hoflin.com/Magazines/Akita_World. **Ad Rates:** BW $100; 4C $250. **Remarks:** Advertising accepted; rates available upon request. **Circ:** Paid 3000.

5085 ■ The Borzoi Quarterly
Hoflin Publishing Inc.
8989 W 51st Ave.
Arvada, CO 80002
Phone: (303)303-2222
Publisher's E-mail: paypal@hoflin.com
Magazine for lovers of the Borzoi dog breed. **Freq:** Quarterly. **Trim Size:** 8.5x11. **Cols./Page:** 3. **Col. Width:** 2.375 INS. **Col. Depth:** 9.5 INS. **Key Personnel:** Donald R. Hoflin, Editor; Cynthia Kerstiens, Editor. **ISSN:** 0746-2875 (print). **Subscription Rates:** $44 Individuals; $48 Other countries; $13 Single issue. **URL:** http://www.hoflin.com. **Ad Rates:** BW $40; 4C $350. **Remarks:** Advertising accepted; rates available upon request. **Circ:** Paid 393, Non-paid 286.

5086 ■ The Boston Quarterly
Hoflin Publishing Inc.
8989 W 51st Ave.
Arvada, CO 80002
Phone: (303)303-2222
Publisher's E-mail: paypal@hoflin.com
Magazine for fanciers of the Boston Terrier. **Freq:** Quarterly. **Trim Size:** 8.5 x 11. **Cols./Page:** 4. **Col. Width:** 1.7 picas. **Col. Depth:** 9.5 picas. **ISSN:** 0746-4088 (print). **Subscription Rates:** $54 Individuals; $74 Canada; $15 Single issue; $193 Two years; $98 Other countries; $145 Canada 2 years. **URL:** http://www.hoflin.com. **Ad Rates:** BW $100; 4C $400. **Remarks:** Advertising accepted; rates available upon request. **Circ:** Paid 1000.

5087 ■ Cattle Guard: The Official News Publication of the Colorado Cattlemen's Association
Ag Journal
8833 Ralston Rd.
Arvada, CO 80002
Publication E-mail: info@coloradocattle.org
Magazine covering cattle industry news, including legislative updates and management techniques. **Freq:** Quarterly. **Print Method:** Offset. **Trim Size:** 8 1/2 x 11. **Cols./Page:** 3. **Col. Width:** 30 nonpareils. **Col. Depth:** 140 agate lines. **Key Personnel:** Terry Fankhauser, Executive Vice President. **Subscription Rates:** Included in membership. **URL:** http://www.coloradocattle.org/cattleguardmagazine.aspx. **Remarks:** Advertising accepted; rates available upon request. **Circ:** 2500.

5088 ■ The German Shepherd Quarterly
Hoflin Publishing Inc.
8989 W 51st Ave.
Arvada, CO 80002
Phone: (303)303-2222
Publisher's E-mail: paypal@hoflin.com
Magazine for German Shepherd owners and enthusiasts. **Freq:** Quarterly. **Trim Size:** 8.5 x 11. **Cols./Page:** 4. **Col. Width:** 1.7 inches. **Col. Depth:** 9 1/2 inches. **ISSN:** 0745-1849 (print). **Subscription Rates:** $15 Single issue; $54 Individuals; $74 Canada; $98 Other countries; $105 Two years; $145 Canada two years; $193 U.S. and Canada two years. **URL:** http://web.hoflin.com/Magazines/The_German_Shepherd_Qrtly. **Ad Rates:** BW $100; 4C $250. **Remarks:** Advertising accepted; rates available upon request. **Circ:** Paid ‡2000.

5089 ■ Grayson Report
Grayson Associates
c/o Richard C. Leventhal, PhD, Ed.

Circulation: ★ = AAM; △ or • = BPA; ♦ = CAC; ❑ = VAC; ⊕ = PO Statement; ‡ = Publisher's Report; Boldface figures = sworn; Light figures = estimated.

7678 Upham St.
Arvada, CO 80003
Academic journal written for consumer marketing practitioners. **Freq:** Bimonthly. **Print Method:** Offset. **Trim Size:** 8 1/2 x 11. **Cols./Page:** 2. **Col. Width:** 3.5 picas. **Col. Depth:** 10 inches. **Key Personnel:** Susan Grayson, Editor; Robert A. Grayson, Publisher; Geoffrey Lantos, Editor; Richard C. Leventhal, PhD, Editor. **ISSN:** 0736--3761 (print). **Subscription Rates:** $45 U.S. and Canada; $50 Other countries. **Formerly**: Journal of Consumer Marketing. **Circ:** (Not Reported).

5090 ■ The Irish Wolfhound Quarterly
Hoflin Publishing Inc.
8989 W 51st Ave.
Arvada, CO 80002
Phone: (303)303-2222
Publisher's E-mail: paypal@hoflin.com
Magazine for Irish Wolfhound owners and enthusiasts. **Freq:** Quarterly. **Trim Size:** 8.5 x 11. **Cols./Page:** 4. **Col. Width:** 1.7 inches. **Col. Depth:** 9 1/2 inches. **ISSN:** 0746--4087 (print). **Subscription Rates:** $55 Individuals soft cover; $80 Individuals hard cover. **URL:** http://www.hoflin.com/Books/Best_10_IWQ. **Ad Rates:** BW $100; 4C $250. **Remarks:** Advertising accepted; rates available upon request. **Circ:** Paid ‡1000.

5091 ■ The Labrador Quarterly
Hoflin Publishing Inc.
8989 W 51st Ave.
Arvada, CO 80002
Phone: (303)303-2222
Publication E-mail: dogmag@fix.net
Magazine for Labrador retriever owners and enthusiasts. **Freq:** Quarterly. **Trim Size:** 8.5 x 11. **Cols./Page:** 4. **Col. Width:** 1.7 inches. **Col. Depth:** 9 1/2 inches. **ISSN:** 8750-3557 (print). **Subscription Rates:** $58 Individuals; $83 Canada and Mexico airmail only; $135 Other countries airmail only; $113 Two years. **URL:** http://labradorquarterly.com/. **Ad Rates:** BW $100; 4C $250. **Remarks:** Advertising accepted; rates available upon request. **Circ:** Paid ‡7000.

5092 ■ Poodle Review
Hoflin Publishing Inc.
8989 W 51st Ave.
Arvada, CO 80002
Phone: (303)303-2222
Publisher's E-mail: paypal@hoflin.com
Magazine containing poodle breeding and showing information. **Freq:** 5/year. **Print Method:** Offset. **Trim Size:** 6 x 9. **Cols./Page:** 2. **Col. Width:** 14 picas. **Col. Depth:** 112 agate lines. **Subscription Rates:** $55 U.S.; $83 Canada; $111 Other countries; $107 Two years U.S.; $163 Two years Canada; $219 Two years Other countries; $12 Single issue; $35 Single issue special issue - add $8 s&h. **URL:** http://www.hoflin.com/Magazines/Poodle_Review. **Ad Rates:** BW $100; PCI $18. **Remarks:** Accepts advertising. **Circ:** Paid 4000.

5093 ■ The Samoyed Quarterly
Hoflin Publishing Inc.
8989 W 51st Ave.
Arvada, CO 80002
Phone: (303)303-2222
Publisher's E-mail: paypal@hoflin.com
Magazine for Samoyed dog fanciers. **Freq:** Quarterly. **Trim Size:** 8.5 x 11. **Cols./Page:** 4. **Col. Width:** 1.7 inches. **Col. Depth:** 9 1/2 inches. **ISSN:** 8750-3557 (print). **Subscription Rates:** $15 Single issue plus $5 for shipping and handling, $12 outside US; $54 Individuals; $74 Canada; $98 Other countries; $105 Two years; $145 Canada 2 years; $193 Other countries 2 years. **URL:** http://www.hoflin.com/Magazines/The_Samoyed_Quarterly. **Ad Rates:** BW $75; 4C $250. **Remarks:** Advertising accepted; rates available upon request. **Circ:** Paid 1000.

5094 ■ The Siberian Quarterly
Hoflin Publishing Inc.
8989 W 51st Ave.
Arvada, CO 80002
Phone: (303)303-2222
Publisher's E-mail: paypal@hoflin.com
Magazine for Siberian Husky fanciers. **Freq:** Quarterly. **Trim Size:** 8.5 x 11. **Cols./Page:** 4. **Col. Width:** 1.7 inches. **Col. Depth:** 9 1/2 inches. **ISSN:** 0274--7286 (print). **Subscription Rates:** $55 Single issue soft cover; $80 Single issue hard cover, plus $10 shipping and handling, $28 in Canada and $45 outside US/Canada. **URL:** http://www.hoflin.com/Books/Best_10_SHQ. **Ad Rates:** BW $100; 4C $250. **Remarks:** Advertising accepted; rates available upon request. **Circ:** Paid 1000.

5095 ■ KRMT-TV - 41
12014 W 64th Ave.
Arvada, CO 80004
Phone: (817)858-9955
Email: ruben@krmt.com
Format: Educational; Religious; Talk; Contemporary Christian; Gospel. **Owner:** Word of God Fellowship, 4201 Pool Rd., Colleyville, TX 76034, Ph: (817)571-1229, Fax: (817)571-7458. **Founded:** 1987. **Formerly**: KWBI-TV. **Operating Hours:** Continuous. **ADI:** Denver (Steamboat Springs), CO. **Wattage**: 74,800 ERP Horizonta. **Ad Rates:** Noncommercial. **URL:** http://www.daystar.com.

5096 ■ US Cable of Coastal Texas L.P.
14700 W 66th Pl.
Arvada, CO 80004
Cities Served: 40 channels.

ASPEN

Pitkin Co. Pitkin Co. (W). 95 m E of Grand Junction. Winter and summer resort. Timber. Stock, grain, hay.

5097 ■ Aspen Daily News
Ute City Tea Party Ltd.
517 E Hopkins Ave.
Aspen, CO 81611
Phone: (970)925-2220
Fax: (970)925-6397
Publisher's E-mail: letters@aspendailynews.com
General newspaper (tabloid). **Freq:** Daily and Sun. **Key Personnel:** Carolyn Sackariason, Editor; Brent Gardner-Smith, Reporter; Lynn Chaffier, Director, Advertising; Dave Danforth, Owner; Catherine Lutz, Managing Editor; Gail Mason, Business Manager. **Ad Rates:** GLR $8; BW $672; 4C $822; PCI $8. **Remarks:** Accepts advertising. **Circ:** Free 14500.

5098 ■ Aspen Magazine
Ridge Publications
720 E Durant Ave., Ste. E8
Aspen, CO 81611
Phone: (970)920-4040
Fax: (970)920-4044
Publisher's E-mail: aaron@aspenmagazine.com
Regional lifestyle magazine. **Freq:** Bimonthly. **Key Personnel:** Janet O'Grady, Editor-in-Chief, President; Leticia Hanke, Publisher; Jenn Virkus, Manager, Production. **ISSN:** 1043--5085 (print). **Subscription Rates:** $40 Individuals; $60 Individuals two years. **URL:** http://modernluxury.com/aspen. **Remarks:** Advertising accepted; rates available upon request. **Circ:** Paid ‡25,000.

5099 ■ Aspen Peak
Niche Media L.L.C.
300 S Spring St.
Aspen, CO 81611
Phone: (970)429-1215
Fax: (970)429-1280
Publication E-mail: advertising@aspenpeak-magazine.com
Luxury lifestyle and entertainment magazine covering Aspen. **Freq:** Semiannual. **Print Method:** Web offset. **Trim Size:** 10 x 12. **Key Personnel:** Alexandra Halperin, Publisher. **Subscription Rates:** $14 Individuals; $25 Two years. **URL:** http://www.aspenpeak-magazine.com. **Remarks:** Accepts advertising. **Circ:** ★40000.

5100 ■ Aspen Times
Aspen Times
310 E Main St.
Aspen, CO 81611
Phone: (970)925-3414
Fax: (970)925-5647
Publisher's E-mail: classifieds@cmnm.org
Community weekly newspaper (tabloid). **Freq:** Weekly. **Print Method:** Offset. **Trim Size:** 10 1/4 x 16. **Cols./Page:** 5. **Col. Width:** 23 nonpareils. **Col. Depth:** 224 agate lines. **Key Personnel:** Rick Carroll, Managing Editor, phone: (970)429-9141. **Subscription Rates:** Free. **URL:** http://www.aspentimes.com. **Ad Rates:** BW $480; 4C $630; PCI $6. **Remarks:** Accepts advertising. **Circ:** 9000.

5101 ■ Edible Aspen
Edible Communities Inc.
PO Box 11510
Aspen, CO 81611
Phone: (970)925-6000
Publisher's E-mail: info@ediblecommunities.com
Magazine covering the local food in Roaring Fork Valley and neighboring communities. **Freq:** Quarterly. **Key Personnel:** Lisa Houston, Owner, Publisher; Amiee White Beazley, Editor. **Subscription Rates:** $20 Individuals personal; $18 gift. **URL:** http://edibleaspen.ediblefeast.com. **Ad Rates:** 4C $1950. **Remarks:** Accepts advertising. **Circ:** 6000.

5102 ■ KAJX-FM - 91.5
110 E Hallam St., Ste. 134
Aspen, CO 81611
Phone: (970)920-9000
Fax: (970)544-8002
Format: Public Radio. **Networks:** National Public Radio (NPR). **Owner:** Aspen Public Radio, at above address, Aspen, CO 81611. **Founded:** 1987. **Operating Hours:** midnight. **ADI:** Denver (Steamboat Springs), CO. **Key Personnel:** Daniel Shaw, Contact; Andrew Todd, Exec. Dir., andrew@aspenpublicradio.org; Carolyne Heldman, Dir. of Programs, carolyne@aspenpublicradio.org; Carolyn Sackariason, News Dir. **Wattage**: 400. **Ad Rates:** Noncommercial. **URL:** http://aspenpublicradio.org.

5103 ■ KCJX-FM - 91.5
110 E Hallam St., Ste. 134
Aspen, CO 81611-1467
Phone: (970)920-9000
Fax: (970)544-8002
Format: Public Radio. **Owner:** Aspen Public Radio, at above address, Aspen, CO 81611. **Key Personnel:** Mitzi Rapkin, News Dir., mitzi@aspenpublicradio.org; Carolyne Heldman, Exec. Dir., carolyne@aspenpublicradio.org. **Ad Rates:** Noncommercial; underwriting available. **URL:** http://Www.aspenpublicradio.org.

KSPN-FM - See Carbondale

AURORA

Douglas Co. Arapahoe Co. and Adams Co. Adjoins Denver on east. Residential Manufactures fish hooks telephone parts and aircraft ejection seats.

5104 ■ American Indian and Alaska Native Mental Health Research
National Center for American Indian and Alaska Native Mental Health Research
c/o Colorado School of Public Health
13001 E 17th Pl.
Aurora, CO 80045
Phone: (303)724-4585
Freq: Annual. **ISSN:** 1533- 7731 (print). **Subscription Rates:** Free. **Alt. Formats:** PDF. **URL:** http://ucdenver.edu/ACADEMICS/COLLEGES/PUBLICHEALTH/RESEARCH/CENTERS/CAIANH/JOURNAL/Pages/journal.aspx. **Mailing address:** Mail Stop B119, Aurora, CO 80045. **Remarks:** Advertising not accepted. **Circ:** (Not Reported).

5105 ■ Arabian Horse Magazine
Arabian Horse Association
10805 E Bethany Dr.
Aurora, CO 80014
Phone: (303)696-4500
Fax: (303)696-4599
Publisher's E-mail: info@ArabianHorses.org
Magazine providing industry news and features to owners of purebred Arabians, Half-Arabians, and Anglo-Arabians. **Freq:** Bimonthly. **Print Method:** Web offset. **Trim Size:** 8 1/2 x 11. **Key Personnel:** Susan Bavaria, Managing Editor; Eri Hook, Manager, Advertising. **ISSN:** 1082-2984 (print). **Subscription Rates:** $25 Individuals. **URL:** http://www.arabianhorses.org. **Formerly**: Inside International; International Arabian Horse. **Ad Rates:** GLR $.40; BW $500; 4C $775. **Remarks:** Accepts advertising. **Circ:** ‡45000.

5106 ■ Aurora Sentinel
Sentinel Publishing Co.
14305 E Alameda Ave., Second Fl.
Aurora, CO 80012
Phone: (303)750-7555
Fax: (303)750-7699
Publisher's E-mail: advertising@aurorasentinel.com
Community newspaper (tabloid). **Freq:** 3/week. **Print Method:** Offset. **Trim Size:** 11 3/8 x 13 3/4. **Cols./Page:**

5. **Col. Width:** 1 7/8 inches. **Col. Depth:** 13 1/2 inches. **Key Personnel:** H. Harrison Cochran, Publisher, phone: (303)750-7555; Dave Perry, Editor. **Subscription Rates:** $90 Individuals 3 years (weekly issues) ; $70 Two years (weekly issues); $42 Individuals 1 year (weekly issues); $21 Individuals 6 months (weekly issues). **URL:** http://www.aurorasentinel.com. **Ad Rates:** GLR $4.64; BW $4387.50; 4C $5487.50; PCI $65. **Remarks:** Accepts advertising. **Circ:** 7,000, Free 177,422.

5107 ■ Diabetes Technology & Therapeutics
Mary Ann Liebert Inc., Publishers
c/o Satish K. Garg, MD, Ed.-in-Ch.
Barbara Davis Center for Childhood Diabetes
1775 Aurora Ct., A140
Aurora, CO 80045
Phone: (303)724-6770
Fax: (303)724-6784
Publisher's E-mail: info@liebertpub.com
Peer-reviewed journal featuring new devices, drug delivery systems and software for managing diabetes. **Freq:** Monthly. **Trim Size:** 8 1/2 x 11. **Cols./Page:** 2. **Col. Width:** 19 nonpareils. **Col. Depth:** 57.5 agate lines. **Key Personnel:** Jay S. Skyler, MD, Senior Editor; James H. Anderson, MD, Board Member; Mark A. Arnold, PhD, Board Member; Satish K. Garg, MD, Editor-in-Chief. **ISSN:** 1520-9156 (print). **Subscription Rates:** $1013 Individuals print and online; $1210 Other countries print and online; $982 Individuals online only; $2110 Institutions print and online; $2426 Institutions, other countries print and online; $1905 Institutions print only; $2191 Institutions, other countries print only; $2048 Institutions online only. **URL:** http://www.liebertpub.com/publication.aspx?pub_id=11. **Ad Rates:** BW $1,780; 4C $2,630. **Remarks:** Advertising accepted; rates available upon request. **Circ:** (Not Reported).

5108 ■ Energybiz: People, Issues, Strategy, Technology
CyberTech Inc.
2821 S Parker Rd., Ste. 1105
Aurora, CO 80014
Phone: (303)782-5510
Free: 800-459-2233
Publication E-mail: energybiz.editor@energycentral.com
Magazine that covers financial, technological, legal and regulatory of the energy industry. **Freq:** Bimonthly. **Key Personnel:** Martin Rosenberg, Editor-in-Chief, phone: (913)385-9909. **ISSN:** 1554--0073 (print). **Subscription Rates:** $99 Individuals; $129 Other countries print and digital editions; $10 Single issue. **Alt. Formats:** PDF. **URL:** http://www.energycentral.com/centers/energybiz/default_mag.cfm. **Remarks:** Accepts advertising. **Circ:** (Not Reported).

5109 ■ Journal of Electromyography and Kinesiology: Official Journal of the International Society of Electrophysical
Elsevier Inc.
c/o Prof. Moshe Solomonow, Editor-in-Chief
University of Colorado, Health Sciences Center
Mailstop 8343
Aurora, CO 80045
Publisher's E-mail: healthpermissions@elsevier.com
Journal with laboratory and clinical research and specialized reports from scientists worldwide. **Freq:** 6/year. **Print Method:** Sheetfed Offset. **Trim Size:** 8 1/4 x 11. **Key Personnel:** Toshio Moritani, Editor; Prof. Moshe Solomonow, Editor-in-Chief. **ISSN:** 1050-6411 (print). **Subscription Rates:** $1537 Institutions print; $469.60 Institutions online; $290 Individuals print. **URL:** http://www.journals.elsevier.com/journal-of-electromyography-and-kinesiology. **Mailing address:** PO Box 6511, Aurora, CO 80045. **Remarks:** Accepts advertising. **Circ:** 1000.

Northglenn/Thornton Sentinel - See Northglenn, CO, USA

5110 ■ The Retired Enlisted Association--The Voice
The Retired Enlisted Association
1111 S Abilene Ct.
Aurora, CO 80012
Phone: (303)752-0660
Fax: (303)752-0835
Free: 800-338-9337
Publisher's E-mail: treahq@trea.org
Freq: Bimonthly. **Alt. Formats:** PDF. **URL:** http://trea.org/the-voice.html. **Remarks:** Accepts advertising. **Circ:** 85000.

5111 ■ The Voice
Retired Enlisted Association Chapter 87
1111 S Abilene Ct.
Aurora, CO 80012
Phone: (303)752-0660
Fax: (303)752-0835
Free: 888-882-0835
Publisher's E-mail: treahq@trea.org
Magazine containing updates on The Retired Enlisted Association Chapter 87 and progress of the organization with congressional legislation. **Freq:** Monthly. **Subscription Rates:** free to members. **URL:** http://trea.org/the-voice.html. **Remarks:** Accepts advertising. **Circ:** (Not Reported).

5112 ■ KCUV-AM - 1150
3091 S Jamaica Ct., Ste. 230
Aurora, CO 80011
Format: News; Hispanic; Sports; Information. **Owner:** NRC Broadcasting Co., at above address. **Founded:** 1987. **Formerly**: KJIM-AM; KFRR-AM. **Operating Hours**: Continuous. **Key Personnel:** Manuel Fernandez, Gen. Mgr. **Wattage**: 5,000 Day; 1,000 Night. **Ad Rates:** $10-35 for 30 seconds; $15-55 for 60 seconds. $10-$35 for 30 seconds; $15-$55 for 60 seconds. Combined advertising rates available with KXRE-AM and KGRE-AM. **URL:** http://www.onda1150am.com.

5113 ■ KLDC-AM - 1220
2821 S Parker Rd., Ste. 1205
Aurora, CO 80014
Phone: (303)433-5500
Fax: (303)433-1555
Format: Gospel. **Owner:** KLDC AM810 & Crawford Broadcasting Co., at above address. **Operating Hours**: Continuous. **Wattage**: 660. **Ad Rates:** Advertising accepted; rates available upon request. **URL:** http://www.1220kldc.com.

5114 ■ KLTT-AM - 670
2821 S Parker Rd., Ste. 1205
Aurora, CO 80014
Phone: (303)433-5500
Fax: (303)433-1555
Format: Contemporary Christian; Talk. **Networks:** AP. **Owner:** Crawford Broadcasting Co., 725 Skippack St., Ste. 210, Blue Bell, PA 19422. **Founded:** 1956. **Operating Hours**: Continuous. **ADI**: Denver (Steamboat Springs), CO. **Wattage**: 50,000. **Ad Rates:** Advertising accepted; rates available upon request. KLVZ-AM, KLZ-AM. **URL:** http://crawfordbroadcasting.com/kltt.

5115 ■ KLVZ 810AM - 810
2821 S Parker Rd., Ste. 1205
Aurora, CO 80014
Phone: (303)433-5500
Format: Hispanic; Religious. **Owner:** Crawford Broadcasting Network. **Wattage**: 1,200. **Ad Rates:** Advertising accepted; rates available upon request. **URL:** http://810klvz.com.

5116 ■ KNUS-AM - 710
3131 S Vaughn Way, Ste. 601
Aurora, CO 80014
Phone: (303)750-5687
Fax: (303)696-8063
Email: 710knus@710knus.com
Format: Talk; News. **Networks:** CNN Radio. **Owner:** Salem Media of Colorado Inc., 3131 S Vaughn Way, Ste. 601, Aurora, CO 80014, Ph: (303)750-5687. **Founded:** 1941. **Formerly**: KBX-AM; KBXG-AM. **Operating Hours**: Continuous. **Key Personnel:** Brian Taylor, VP, Gen. Mgr.; Cliff Mikkelson, Chief Engineer. **Wattage**: 5,000. **Ad Rates:** $30 for 30 seconds; $50 for 60 seconds. **URL:** http://www.710knus.com.

5117 ■ KPXC-TV - 59
3001 S Jamaica Ct., Ste. 200
Aurora, CO 80014
Phone: (303)751-5959
Fax: (303)751-5993
Format: Commercial TV. **Owner:** ION Media Networks Inc., 601 Clearwater Park Rd., West Palm Beach, FL 33401-6233, Ph: (561)659-4122, Fax: (561)659-4252. **Formerly**: KUBD-TV. **Operating Hours**: Continuous. **ADI**: Denver (Steamboat Springs), CO. **Key Personnel:** Brandon Burgess, Chairman, CEO. **Wattage**: 5,000,000. **Ad Rates:** $125-700 per unit. **URL:** http://www.ionmedia.tv.

5118 ■ KRKS-AM - 990
3131 S Vaughn Way
Aurora, CO 80014
Phone: (303)750-5687
Fax: (303)696-8063
Format: Religious. **Networks:** CNN Radio; Sun Radio. **Owner:** Salem Media of Colorado Inc., 3131 S Vaughn Way, Ste. 601, Aurora, CO 80014, Ph: (303)750-5687. **Founded:** 1953. **Operating Hours**: Continuous. **Key Personnel:** Brian Taylor, Gen. Mgr., VP; Cliff Mikkelson, Dir. of Engg.; Jules Dygert, Sales Mgr. **Ad Rates:** $40 for 30 seconds; $50 for 60 seconds. **URL:** http://www.947krks.com.

AVON

Eagle Co. Eagle Co. (WC). 10 m SW of Vail.

5119 ■ Rocky Mountain Golf Magazine: Celebrating the Lifestyle and the Game
Sagacity Media
PO Box 1397
Avon, CO 81620
Consumer magazine covering golf in the Rocky Mountain region. **Freq:** Semiannual. **Print Method:** Web Offset. **Trim Size:** 8 3/8 x 10 7/8. **Key Personnel:** Don Berger, Editor; Kristin Jennings, Publisher; Heather Trub, Director, Production. **Subscription Rates:** $4.95 Individuals + shipping and handling. **URL:** http://www.rockymountaingolfmag.com. **Formerly**: Vail Valley Golf. **Ad Rates:** 4C $4,137. **Remarks:** Accepts advertising. **Circ:** Combined ‡60000.

5120 ■ Vail-Beaver Creek Magazine
Sagacity Media
PO Box 1397
Avon, CO 81620
Regional consumer magazine. **Freq:** 3/year. **Print Method:** Web offset. **Trim Size:** 10 7/8 x 8 3/8. **Key Personnel:** Kristin Jennings, Publisher; Ted Katauskas, Editor. **URL:** http://www.vailbeavercreekmag.com. **Ad Rates:** 4C $4,059. **Remarks:** Accepts advertising. **Circ:** Combined 62000.

5121 ■ Vail Daily
Vail Daily
40780 US Hwy. 6 & 24
Avon, CO 81620
Phone: (970)949-0555
General tabloid newspaper. **Freq:** Daily. **Print Method:** Offset Web. **Trim Size:** 10 1/2 x 16 1/2. **Cols./Page:** 5. **Col. Width:** 16.5 picas. **Col. Depth:** 16 inches. **Key Personnel:** Claudia Nelson, Editor, phone: (970)748-2988; Don Rogers, Editor, phone: (970)748-2920; Patrick Connolly, Director, Advertising, phone: (970)748-2946; Edward Stoner, Managing Editor, phone: (970)748-2929. **Subscription Rates:** Free. **Mailing address:** PO Box 81, Vail, CO 81658. **Remarks:** Accepts advertising. **Circ:** Free 15000.

5122 ■ KTUN-FM - 94.5
182 Avon Rd., Ste. 240
Avon, CO 81620
Format: Adult Album Alternative; Classic Rock. **Networks:** CNN Radio. **Owner:** NRC Broadcasting Co., at above address. **Formerly**: KWLI-FM; KQMT-FM. **Operating Hours**: Continuous. **Wattage**: 25,000. **Ad Rates:** Advertising accepted; rates available upon request. **Mailing address:** PO Box 7205, Avon, CO 81620. **URL:** http://www.ktunradio.com.

5123 ■ KZYR-FM - 103.1
One Lake St.
Avon, CO 81620
Phone: (970)926-7625
Format: Adult Contemporary; Alternative/New Music/Progressive. **Founded:** 1984. **Operating Hours**: 100% local. **Wattage**: 12,000. **Ad Rates:** $16-24 for 30 seconds; $18-26 for 60 seconds. **URL:** http://kzyr.com/blog.

BAILEY

Park Co. (C). 72 m NE of Aspen. Residential.

5124 ■ UDC Focus
United Doberman Club

Circulation: ★ = AAM; △ or • = BPA; ♦ = CAC; ❑ = VAC; ⊕ = PO Statement; ‡ = Publisher's Report; Boldface figures = sworn; Light figures = estimated.

c/o Bonnie Guzman, Membership Secretary
367 Chickadee Ln.
Bailey, CO 80421
Phone: (303)733-4220
Freq: Quarterly latest: summer 2016. **Subscription Rates:** $4.80 Individuals print & online. **Alt. Formats:** PDF. **URL:** http://uniteddobermanclub.com/udc-focus. **Remarks:** Accepts advertising. **Circ:** (Not Reported).

BASALT

5125 ■ KPVW-FM - 107.1
20 Sunset Dr., Ste. 6-A
Basalt, CO 81621
Phone: (970)927-7600
Fax: (970)927-8001
Format: Hispanic. **Owner:** Entravision Communications Corporation, 2425 Olympic Blvd., Ste. 6000 W, Santa Monica, CA 90404-4030, Ph: (310)447-3870, Fax: (310)447-3899. **Key Personnel:** Mario Carrera, CRO. **URL:** http://www.entravision.com.

BERTHOUD

Larimer Co. Larimer Co. (N). 20 m. S. of Fort Collins. Manufactures store fixtures and displays, modular homes. Agriculture. Sugar beets, wheat, alfalfa. Livestock.

5126 ■ Fjord Herald
Norwegian Fjord Horse Registry
1801 W County Road 4
Berthoud, CO 80513
Phone: (303)684-6466
Fax: (888)646-5613
Freq: Quarterly. **Subscription Rates:** $5 Single issue back issue. **URL:** http://www.nfhr.com/catalog/index.php?cPath=49. **Remarks:** Accepts advertising. **Circ:** 1000.

5127 ■ The Old Berthoud Recorder
The Old Berthoud Recorder
PO Box J
Berthoud, CO 80513
Phone: (970)532-3715
Fax: (970)532-3918
Publisher's E-mail: editor@berthoudrecorder.com
Community newspaper. **Freq:** Weekly (Thurs.). **Print Method:** Offset. **Trim Size:** 11 1/2 x 16. **Cols./Page:** 5. **Col. Width:** 11 1/2 picas. **Col. Depth:** 15 3/4 inches. **Key Personnel:** Gary Wamsley, Editor. **ISSN:** 0896--2812 (print). **Formerly**: The Berthoud Recorder. **Ad Rates:** GLR $1.40; BW $640; 4C $980; SAU $5.50; PCI $8.75. **Remarks:** Accepts advertising. **Circ:** Thurs. ‡1100.

BLACK HAWK

5128 ■ Weekly Register-Call
Weekly Register-Call
PO Box 93
Black Hawk, CO 80422
Phone: (303)582-0133
General newspaper. **Freq:** Weekly (Fri.). **Print Method:** Offset. **Cols./Page:** 6. **Col. Width:** 26 nonpareils. **Col. Depth:** 280 agate lines. **Key Personnel:** Aaron Storms, Publisher, Managing Editor; David Spellman, Publisher. **ISSN:** 0278--5838 (print). **Subscription Rates:** $37 Individuals /year; $32 Individuals /year (seniors rate); $25 Individuals /year (veterans rate). **URL:** http://www.weeklyregistercall.com. **Remarks:** Accepts advertising. **Circ:** (Not Reported).

BOULDER

Boulder Co. Boulder Co. (N). 32 m NW of Denver. Universit of Colorado. Tourism. Manufactures copy machines, chemicals, electronic devices, space hardware, cutlery, recreational equipment. Agriculture. Alfalfa, sugar beets.

5129 ■ American Suzuki Journal
Suzuki Association of the Americas
PO Box 17310
Boulder, CO 80308
Phone: (303)444-0948
Fax: (303)444-0984
Free: 888-378-9854
Publisher's E-mail: info@suzukiassociation.org
Music education journal. **Freq:** Quarterly. **Print Method:** Offset. **Trim Size:** 8 7/8 x 10 7/8. **Key Personnel:** Robert F. Bennett, Editor. **ISSN:** 0193--5372 (print). **Subscription Rates:** Included in membership. **URL:** http://suzukiassociation.org/journal. **Ad Rates:** BW $545; 4C $945. **Remarks:** Accepts advertising. **Circ:** ‡8500, 8200.

5130 ■ Anthropology Now
Paradigm Publishers
2845 Wilderness Pl., Ste. 200
Boulder, CO 80301
Phone: (303)245-9054
Peer-reviewed journal covering issues in anthropology. **Freq:** 3/year. **Key Personnel:** Maria D. Vespari, Editor. **ISSN:** 1942-8200 (print). **Subscription Rates:** $395 Institutions print only; $410 Institutions, other countries print only; $446 Institutions online only; $519 Institutions print and online; $603 Institutions, other countries print and online; $55 Nonmembers print only; $75 Other countries non-member, print only. **URL:** http://paradigm.presswarehouse.com/journals/an/. **Circ:** (Not Reported).

5131 ■ Backpacker Magazine: The Magazine of Wilderness Travel
Backpacker Magazine
2520 55th St., Ste. 210
Boulder, CO 80301
Phone: (610)967-8296
Free: 800-666-3434
Publisher's E-mail: webmaster@backpacker.com
Magazine of self-propelled, low impact, wilderness travel, primarily in North America. **Freq:** 9/year. **ISSN:** 0277--867X (print). **Subscription Rates:** $12 Individuals; $20 Two years; $27 Individuals 3 years. **Alt. Formats:** Handheld. **URL:** http://www.backpacker.com. **Remarks:** Accepts advertising. **Circ:** Paid ★319910.

5132 ■ Boulder County Business Report
Boulder County Business Report
3180 Sterling Cir., Ste. 201
Boulder, CO 80301-2338
Phone: (303)440-4950
Local business newspaper. **Freq:** Biweekly. **Key Personnel:** Chris Wood, Publisher; Dave Thompson, Manager, Production; Kim Oremus, Account Executive; Doug Storum, Editor; Brittany Rauch, Art Director; Rhonda Doyle, Manager, Circulation. **Subscription Rates:** $44.97 Individuals; $79.97 Two years; $114.97 Individuals 3 years. **Ad Rates:** BW $3,440; 4C $4,040; PCI $50. **Remarks:** Accepts advertising. **Circ:** (Not Reported).

5133 ■ Boulder Weekly
Boulder Weekly Inc.
690 S Lashley Ln.
Boulder, CO 80305
Phone: (303)494-5511
Fax: (303)494-2585
Publication E-mail: letters@boulderweekly.com
editorial@boulderweekly.com
Community newspaper. **Freq:** Weekly. **Print Method:** Web offset. **Trim Size:** 11 3/8. **Key Personnel:** Stewart Sallo, Publisher; Pamela White, Editor; Jefferson Dodge, Managing Editor. **URL:** http://www.boulderweekly.com; http://npaper-wehaa.com/boulder-weekly/2009/12/24/s1/?s=issues&output=html. **Ad Rates:** BW $1125. **Remarks:** Accepts advertising. **Circ:** (Not Reported).

5134 ■ Climbing
Active Interest Media
2520 55th St., Ste. 210
Boulder, CO 80301
Phone: (303)625-1600
Fax: (303)440-3618
Free: 800-381-1288
Publication E-mail: climbing@emailcustomerservice.com
Magazine featuring information on alpinism, mountaineering, rock climbing, ice climbing and bouldering. Aims to inspire and inform readers on the latest news on cutting-edge ascents, conservation issues, reviews of the latest gear, features about climbing destinations and tips on how to improve techniques and climb more safely. **Founded:** 1970. **Freq:** 9/yr. **Trim Size:** 8.25 x 10.5. **Key Personnel:** Shannon Davis, Editor. **Subscription Rates:** $29.95 Canada; $55.95 Canada 2 years; $34.95 Other countries; $65.95 Other countries 2 years. **URL:** http://www.climbing.com. **Remarks:** Accepts advertising. **Circ:** (Not Reported).

5135 ■ Colorado Daily: A Publicly Owned Newspaper
Colorado Daily
5450 Western Ave.
Boulder, CO 80301
Phone: (303)473-1111
Publisher's E-mail: letters@coloradodaily.com
Daily newspaper. **Freq:** Daily. **Print Method:** Offset. **Trim Size:** 10 1/4 x 14. **Cols./Page:** 6. **Col. Width:** 19 nonpareils. **Col. Depth:** 196 agate lines. **URL:** http://www.coloradodaily.com/about. **Remarks:** racist and sexist products/services. **Circ:** (Not Reported).

5136 ■ Colorado Engineer
American Association of Teachers of Japanese
366 University of Colorado
1424 Broadway
Boulder, CO 80309-0366
Phone: (303)492-5487
Fax: (303)492-5856
Publisher's E-mail: aatj@aatj.org
Collegiate magazine featuring articles of technical interest. **Freq:** 3/year during the fall, spring and summer sessions. **Print Method:** Offset. **Trim Size:** 8 1/2 x 11. **Cols./Page:** 3. **Col. Width:** 28 nonpareils. **Col. Depth:** 134 agate lines. **Key Personnel:** Hannah Steketee, Editor-in-Chief. **ISSN:** 0010--1583 (print). **Subscription Rates:** $10 Individuals; $20 Two years; $30 Individuals 3 years; $40 Individuals 4 years. **URL:** http://cem.colorado.edu. **Remarks:** Accepts advertising. **Circ:** Non-paid ‡5000, Non-paid ‡5000.

5137 ■ Colorado Research in Linguistics
University of Colorado at Boulder
Boulder, CO 80309
Phone: (303)492-5007
Fax: (303)492-0969
Journal covering research conducted by linguists. **ISSN:** 1937-7029 (print). **URL:** http://www.colorado.edu/ling/CRIL/. **Circ:** (Not Reported).

5138 ■ Colorado Technology Law Journal
University of Colorado School of Law
Office of Admissions
Wolf Law Bldg., UCB 403
Boulder, CO 80309-0403
Phone: (303)492-7203
Fax: (303)492-2542
Publisher's E-mail: lawadmin@colorado.edu
Journal containing articles on national technology and telecommunications law. **Freq:** Semiannual. **ISSN:** 2374--9032 (print). **Subscription Rates:** $50 Individuals domestic; $55 Individuals international. **URL:** http://ctlj.colorado.edu. **Formerly**: Journal on Telecommunications and High Technology Law. **Circ:** (Not Reported).

5139 ■ CU Independent
University of Colorado at Boulder
Boulder, CO 80309
Phone: (303)492-5007
Fax: (303)492-0969
Collegiate newspaper. **Freq:** Monthly. **Print Method:** Offset web. **Cols./Page:** 5. **Col. Width:** 2 1/16 inches. **Col. Depth:** 13 inches. **Key Personnel:** Tommy Wood, Editor-in-Chief. **URL:** http://cuindependent.com. **Formerly**: Campus Press. **Remarks:** Accepts advertising. **Circ:** Controlled 6000.

5140 ■ Culinary Online: A Culinarian's Guide to the Internet
Culinary Software Services Inc.
2930 Center Green Ct.
Boulder, CO 80301
Phone: (303)447-3334
Publication E-mail: questions@culinary-online.com
Journal for culinary professionals, restaurateurs, authors, and famous chefs. **Freq:** 10/year. **Key Personnel:** Alexandra Lynch, Editor. **Subscription Rates:** $29 Individuals. **URL:** http://www.culinary-online.com. **Remarks:** Advertising not accepted. **Circ:** (Not Reported).

5141 ■ Daily Camera
The E. W. Scripps Co.
5450 Western Ave.
Boulder, CO 80301
Phone: (303)442-1202
Fax: (303)449-9358
Publisher's E-mail: corpcomm@scripps.com
General newspaper. **Freq:** Daily (morn.). **Print Method:** Web. **Trim Size:** 11.625 x 21.5. **Cols./Page:** 6. **Col. Width:** 1.533 inches. **Col. Depth:** 21 1/2 inches. **Key**

Personnel: Kevin Kaufman, Executive Editor; Albert J. Manzi, Publisher; Jill Stravolemos, Director, Advertising, Director, Marketing. **Subscription Rates:** $15.18 Individuals daily and Sunday; $8.10 Individuals Friday Monday; $6.26 Individuals Sunday only. **URL:** http://www.scripps.com; http://www.dailycamera.com. **Formerly:** Boulder Camera. **Remarks:** Advertising accepted; rates available upon request. **Circ:** Combined ‡123300.

5142 ■ Delicious Living!: Real Food, natural Health, Green Planet
New Hope Network
1401 Pearl St.
Boulder, CO 80302-5319
Phone: (303)939-8440
Fax: (303)998-9020
Publisher's E-mail: info@newhope.com
Magazine designed to be used as a merchandising and educational tool by natural food stores. **Freq:** Monthly. **Print Method:** Web offset. **Trim Size:** 8 x 10 3/4. **Key Personnel:** Nancy Coulter-Parker, Editor, phone: (303)998-9237; Radha Marcum, Editor-in-Chief, phone: (303)998-9477; Jessica Rubino, Associate Editor, phone: (303)998-9035. **URL:** http://deliciousliving.com. **Formerly:** Delicious! Magazine. **Remarks:** Accepts advertising. **Circ:** (Not Reported).

5143 ■ Delight Gluten Free
Delight Gluten Free Magazine Inc.
PO Box 20428
Boulder, CO 80308
Magazine focusing on gluten intolerance and food allergies. **Freq:** Bimonthly. **Key Personnel:** Julie Ann Luse, Creative Director; Vanessa Maltin Weisbrod, Executive Editor. **Subscription Rates:** $24 Individuals; $35 Canada; $53 Other countries. **URL:** http://www.delightglutenfree.com. **Remarks:** Accepts advertising. **Circ:** (Not Reported).

5144 ■ Edible Frontrange
Edible Communities Inc.
3033 3rd St.
Boulder, CO 80304
Phone: (303)449-4383
Publication E-mail: info@ediblefrontrange.com
Magazine covering the local food of Colorado. **Freq:** Quarterly. **Subscription Rates:** $28 Individuals 4 issues; $40 Individuals 8 issues. **URL:** http://www.ediblefrontrange.com. **Ad Rates:** 4C $2500. **Remarks:** Accepts advertising. **Circ:** (Not Reported).

5145 ■ English Language Notes
University of Colorado at Boulder
Department of English
226 UCB
Boulder, CO 80309-0226
Publication E-mail: eln@colorado.edu
Peer-reviewed journal discussing English language literature. **Freq:** Semiannual. **Print Method:** Offset. **Trim Size:** 6 x 9. **Cols./Page:** 1. **Col. Width:** 51 nonpareils. **Col. Depth:** 102 agate lines. **Key Personnel:** Karen Jacobs, Board Member; Katherine Eggert, Board Member; Jane Garrity, Board Member; Laura Winkiel, Senior Editor. **ISSN:** 0013--8282 (print). **Subscription Rates:** $70 U.S. and Canada institution; $80 Institutions, other countries; $45 U.S. and Canada; $55 Other countries. **URL:** http://english.colorado.edu/eln. **Ad Rates:** BW $350. **Remarks:** Accepts advertising. **Circ:** Paid ‡1100, Non-paid ‡150.

5146 ■ Genders Journal
University of Colorado Dept. of English
University of Colorado
Hellems 101
226 UCB
Boulder, CO 80309-0226
Phone: (303)492-7381
Fax: (303)492-8904
Publisher's E-mail: engldept@colorado.edu
Journal covering gender and sexuality issues. **Key Personnel:** Anna M. Kibbey, Executive Editor; Melissa Mowry, Board Member. **Circ:** (Not Reported).

5147 ■ Geological Society of America Bulletin
Geological Society of America
3300 Penrose Pl.
Boulder, CO 80301
Phone: (303)357-1000
Fax: (303)357-1070
Publisher's E-mail: gsaservice@geosociety.org
Geology journal. **Freq:** Bimonthly. **Print Method:** Offset. **Trim Size:** 8 3/8 x 10 7/8. **Cols./Page:** 3 and 2. **Col. Width:** 28 and 43 nonpareils. **Col. Depth:** 130 agate lines. **Key Personnel:** Nancy Riggs, Editor. **ISSN:** 0016--7606 (print); **EISSN:** 1943--2674 (electronic). **Subscription Rates:** $89 Members print (includes online access); $45 Students members; print (includes online access); $45 Students, other countries members; print (includes online access); $1125 Institutions & nonmembers; print & online; $990 Institutions & nonmembers; online only. **URL:** http://gsabulletin.gsapubs.org; http://www.geosociety.org/pubs/pubdescriptions.htm. **Also known as:** GSA Bulletin. **Mailing address:** PO Box 9140, Boulder, CO 80301. **Ad Rates:** BW $417; 4C $1092. **Remarks:** Accepts advertising. **Circ:** ‡5000.

5148 ■ Geology
Geological Society of America
3300 Penrose Pl.
Boulder, CO 80301
Phone: (303)357-1000
Fax: (303)357-1070
Publisher's E-mail: gsaservice@geosociety.org
Geology journal. **Freq:** Monthly current issue: July 2016. **Print Method:** Offset. **Trim Size:** 8 3/8 x 10 7/8. **Cols./Page:** 3. **Col. Width:** 28 nonpareils. **Key Personnel:** Ronadh Cox, Editor. **ISSN:** 0091--7613 (print); **EISSN:** 1943--2682 (electronic). **Subscription Rates:** $1010 Institutions online; $1185 Institutions print+online; $1320 Institutions Print & Online with Expedited Shipping; $100 Single issue. **URL:** http://geology.gsapubs.org; http://www.geosociety.org/pubs/pubdescriptions.htm. **Mailing address:** PO Box 9140, Boulder, CO 80301. **Ad Rates:** BW $631; 4C $1,231. **Remarks:** Advertising accepted; rates available upon request. **Circ:** Paid ‡6500.

5149 ■ Geosphere
Geological Society of America
3300 Penrose Pl.
Boulder, CO 80301
Phone: (303)357-1000
Fax: (303)357-1070
Publisher's E-mail: gsaservice@geosociety.org
Journal covering all areas of geosciences. **Freq:** Bimonthly. **Key Personnel:** Shan de Silva, Editor, phone: (541)737-1212, fax: (541)737-1200. **ISSN:** 1553--040X (print). **Subscription Rates:** $35 Members online; $119 Members DVD. **Alt. Formats:** DVD. **URL:** http://geosphere.gsapubs.org. **Mailing address:** PO Box 9140, Boulder, CO 80301. **Circ:** (Not Reported).

5150 ■ Global Governance: A Review of Multilateralism and International Organizations
Lynne Rienner Publishers
1800 30th St., Ste. 314
Boulder, CO 80301
Phone: (303)444-6684
Fax: (303)444-0824
Publisher's E-mail: questions@rienner.com
Peer-reviewed journal covering international cooperation and governance. **Freq:** Quarterly. **Key Personnel:** Tom Farer, Board Member; Timothy D. Sisk, Board Member; Roberta Spivak, Managing Editor. **ISSN:** 1075--2846 (print). **Subscription Rates:** $65 Individuals; $155 Institutions. **URL:** http://www.rienner.com/title/Global_Governance_A_Review_of_Multilateralism_ and_International_Organizations. **Ad Rates:** BW $250. **Remarks:** Accepts advertising. **Circ:** 1500.

5151 ■ HerbalGram
Herb Research Foundation
5589 Arapahoe Ave., Ste. 205
Boulder, CO 80303
Phone: (303)449-2265
Fax: (303)449-7849
Publisher's E-mail: info@herbs.org
Consumer magazine covering herbal and botanical products. **Freq:** Quarterly. **Key Personnel:** Lance Lawhon, Manager, Advertising. **ISSN:** 0899--5648 (print). **URL:** http://cms.herbalgram.org/herbalgram. **Ad Rates:** BW $1890, full page bleed; BW B$1720, full page no bleed; 4C $2490, full page bleed; 4C $2320, full page no bleed. **Remarks:** Accepts advertising. **Circ:** 28000, 20000.

5152 ■ Hitch Up
Active Interest Media
2520 55th St., Ste. 210
Boulder, CO 80301
Publisher's E-mail: admin@aimmedia.com
Magazine featuring horse trailer industry news. **Freq:** Quarterly. **Key Personnel:** David Andrick, Publisher. **URL:** http://www.aimmedia.com/hu.html. **Circ:** (Not Reported).

5153 ■ Horse & Rider: With Performance Horseman
Equine Network
2520 55th St., No. 210
Boulder, CO 80301
Phone: (303)625-5450
Publication E-mail: horseandrider@aimmedia.com
Magazine devoted to Western style riding, apparel, products, lifestyle, and general horse care. **Freq:** Monthly. **Print Method:** Offset. **Trim Size:** 8 x 10 3/4. **Cols./Page:** 3. **Col. Width:** 2 1/4 inches. **Col. Depth:** 10 inches. **Key Personnel:** Juli Thorson, Associate Publisher, Editor; Jennifer Paulson, Editor; Adam Purvis, Art Director. **ISSN:** 0018--5159 (print). **Subscription Rates:** $15.95 Individuals; $25.95 Two years. **Alt. Formats:** Download. **URL:** http://horseandrider.com. **Ad Rates:** BW $2670; 4C $8845; PCI $165. **Remarks:** Accepts advertising. **Circ:** Paid ★**157041**.

5154 ■ HorseLink
Active Interest Media
2520 55th St., Ste. 210
Boulder, CO 80301
Publisher's E-mail: admin@aimmedia.com
Magazine publishing articles about shopping for horses. **Freq:** Monthly. **Subscription Rates:** Free. **URL:** http://www.aimmedia.com/hl.html. **Remarks:** Accepts advertising. **Circ:** (Not Reported).

5155 ■ HRF Herb Companion
Herb Research Foundation
5589 Arapahoe Ave., Ste. 205
Boulder, CO 80303
Phone: (303)449-2265
Fax: (303)449-7849
Publisher's E-mail: abc@herbalgram.org
Freq: Bimonthly. **Mailing address:** PO Box 144345, Austin, TX 78714-4345. **Remarks:** Advertising not accepted. **Circ:** (Not Reported).

5156 ■ IMC Journal
1650 38th St., Ste. 205W
Boulder, CO 80301
Phone: (303)440-7085
Fax: (303)440-7234
Magazine publishing application and technical articles for the document-based information systems field. **Freq:** Bimonthly. **Print Method:** Offset. **Cols./Page:** 2. **Col. Width:** 40 nonpareils. **Col. Depth:** 136 agate lines. **Key Personnel:** William McArthur, Editor; Scott Benson, Publisher; Warren A. Cole, Manager, Advertising. **ISSN:** 0019-0012 (print). **Subscription Rates:** $90 Individuals; $115 outside North America. **Ad Rates:** BW $2,925; 4C $3,965. **Remarks:** Accepts advertising. **Circ:** ‡30000.

5157 ■ Inside Triathlon: The Multisport Life
Inside Communications Inc.
1830 55th St.
Boulder, CO 80301-2700
Phone: (303)440-0601
Fax: (303)444-6788
Publisher's E-mail: velnews@aol.com
Consumer magazine covering triathlon events and training. **Freq:** Monthly. **Trim Size:** 18 x 10.875. **Key Personnel:** Brad Culp, Editor. **Subscription Rates:** $39.95 Individuals; $65.95 Canada; $99.95 Other countries. **URL:** http://www.insidetri.com. **Ad Rates:** BW $2,000; 4C $4,118. **Remarks:** Advertising accepted; rates available upon request. **Circ:** Paid ★**22049**.

5158 ■ The Inspector
International Association of Certified Home Inspectors
1750 30th St., Ste. 301
Boulder, CO 80301
Phone: (303)502-6214
Fax: (650)429-2057
Free: 877-346-3467
Magazine publishing articles related to home inspectors. **Freq:** Monthly. **Subscription Rates:** Included in membership. **URL:** http://www.nachi.org/bbsystem/viewtopic.php?t=4242&PHPSESSID=

Circulation: ★ = AAM; △ or • = BPA; ♦ = CAC; ❑ = VAC; ⊕ = PO Statement; ‡ = Publisher's Report; Boldface figures = sworn; Light figures = estimated.

5093079eb32b966f5ed272940ebb8972. **Remarks:** Accepts advertising. **Circ:** Free ‡50000, 200.

5159 ■ Iron Feather Journal
Phun Inc.
PO Box 1905
Boulder, CO 80306
Consumer magazine covering alternative/underground electronic music. **Freq:** Quarterly. **URL:** http://www.ironfeather.com. **Remarks:** Accepts advertising. **Circ:** Combined 3,500.

5160 ■ Journal of Clinical Orthodontics
JCO Inc.
1828 Pearl St.
Boulder, CO 80302
Phone: (303)443-1720
Fax: (303)443-9356
Publisher's E-mail: info@jco-online.com
Dental journal. **Freq:** Monthly. **Print Method:** Offset. **Trim Size:** 8 1/4 x 10 7/8. **Cols./Page:** 2. **Col. Width:** 36 nonpareils. **Col. Depth:** 140 agate lines. **Key Personnel:** Robert G. Keim, DDS, Editor; Eugene L. Gottlieb, DDS, Senior Editor; David S. Vogels, III, Executive Editor; Lynn Bollinger, Business Manager; Carol Varsos, Manager, Circulation. **ISSN:** 0022--3875 (print). **URL:** http://www.jco-online.com. **Remarks:** Accepts advertising. **Circ:** (Not Reported).

5161 ■ Journal of East Asian Studies
Lynne Rienner Publishers
1800 30th St., Ste. 314
Boulder, CO 80301
Phone: (303)444-6684
Fax: (303)444-0824
Publisher's E-mail: questions@rienner.com
International and interdisciplinary journal that publishes social science research on current issues in the East Asian region. **Freq:** 3/year. **Col. Width:** 4.25 inches. **Col. Depth:** 7 inches. **Key Personnel:** Stephan Haggard, Editor; Byung-Kook Kim, Associate Editor; Yun-Han Chu, Associate Editor; Yves Tiberghien, Editor; Steve Chan, Board Member; Andrew MacIntyre, Associate Editor; Young-hwan Shin, Managing Editor; Yoshihide Soeya, Associate Editor; Muthiah Alagappa, Board Member. **ISSN:** 1598--2408 (print). **Subscription Rates:** $57 Individuals; $96 Two years; $32 Students; $135 Institutions; $237 Two years. **URL:** http://www.rienner.com/title/JEAS. **Ad Rates:** BW $200. **Remarks:** Accepts advertising. **Circ:** 500.

5162 ■ Journal of Experiential Education
Association for Experiential Education
1435 Yarmouth Ave., Ste. 104
Boulder, CO 80304
Phone: (303)440-8844
Free: 866-522-8337
Publisher's E-mail: membership@aee.org
Peer-reviewed journal publishing research on experiential education. **Freq:** Quarterly. **Key Personnel:** Patrick Maher, Editor; Philip Mullins, Editor. **Subscription Rates:** $333 Institutions print only; $142 Individuals. **URL:** http://www.sagepub.com/journals/Journal202222?productType=Journals&subject=C00&sortBy=sortTitle+asc&pager.offset=50&fs=1#tabview=title. **Remarks:** Accepts advertising. **Circ:** (Not Reported).

5163 ■ Journal of Sedimentary Research
Rutgers University
446 Pearl St.
Boulder, CO 80301
Phone: (303)447-2020
Fax: (303)357-1071
Publication E-mail: jsedr@colorado.edu
Scientific journal of sedimentary geology. **Founded:** 1931. **Freq:** Bimonthly Feb, Apr, June, Aug, Oct, Dec. **Print Method:** Offset. **Trim Size:** 8 1/2 x 11. **Cols./Page:** 2. **Col. Width:** 3 1/2 inches. **Col. Depth:** 9 inches. **Key Personnel:** Melissa Lester, Managing Editor; Paul McCarthy, Editor; Gene Rankey, Editor. **ISSN:** 0022-4472 (print). **Subscription Rates:** $700 U.S. online with CD; $960 U.S. online with CD and include print option; $700 Other countries online with CD; $1080 Other countries online with CD and include print option. **URL:** http://www.sepm.org/pages.aspx?pageid=117. **Formerly:** Journal of Sedimentary Petrology. **Ad Rates:** BW $500; 4C $1700. **Remarks:** Accepts advertising. **Circ:** 6,000.

5164 ■ Journal on Telecommunications & High Technology Law
University of Colorado at Boulder
Boulder, CO 80309
Phone: (303)492-5007
Fax: (303)492-0969
Publication E-mail: jthtl@colorado.edu
Academic journal that publishes scholarly articles in the developing field of telecommunications law. **Freq:** Semiannual. **Key Personnel:** Dr. Mohamd H. Hamza, Editor-in-Chief. **ISSN:** 1543-8899 (print). **Subscription Rates:** $45 Individuals per-volume; $25 Individuals; $30 Other countries. **URL:** http://www.colorado.edu/law/research/journals/JTHTL; http://www.jthtl.org. **Remarks:** Advertising not accepted. **Circ:** (Not Reported).

5165 ■ Loving More: New Models for Relationships
Pep Publishing
PO Box 4358
Boulder, CO 80306-4358
Phone: (303)543-7540
Publisher's E-mail: lovingmore@lovemore.com
Magazine focusing on polyamory and new models for relationships. **Freq:** Quarterly. **Trim Size:** 8 1/2 x 11. **Key Personnel:** Ryam Nearing, Editor; Mary Wolf, Editor; Robyn Trask, Editor, Executive Director. **ISSN:** 1523-5858 (print). **Formerly:** Pep Talk - Group Marriage News. **Remarks:** Advertising accepted; rates available upon request. **Circ:** ‡12000.

5166 ■ Natural Foods Merchandiser: News, Trends and Ideas for the Business of Natural Products/A Penton Publication
New Hope Network
1401 Pearl St.
Boulder, CO 80302-5319
Phone: (303)939-8440
Fax: (303)998-9020
Publisher's E-mail: info@newhope.com
Natural foods industry trade magazine. **Freq:** Monthly. **Print Method:** Offset. **Trim Size:** 10 3/4 x 14 3/4. **Cols./Page:** 4. **Col. Width:** 27 nonpareils. **Col. Depth:** 140 agate lines. **Key Personnel:** Carlotta Mast, Editor-in-Chief, phone: (303)998-9119; Melaina Juntti, Managing Editor, phone: (303)998-9355. **ISSN:** 0164-338X (print). **Subscription Rates:** Free. **URL:** http://newhope360.com/natural-foods-merchandiser; http://newhope360.com/natural-foods-merchandiser/natural-foods-merchandiser-0. **Ad Rates:** BW $5,680; 4C $9,155. **Remarks:** Accepts advertising. **Circ:** (Not Reported).

5167 ■ Natural Grocery Buyer
New Hope Network
1401 Pearl St.
Boulder, CO 80302-5319
Phone: (303)939-8440
Fax: (303)998-9020
Publisher's E-mail: info@newhope.com
Magazine for retailers of natural and organic groceries. **Freq:** Quarterly. **Print Method:** Web Offset. **Trim Size:** 8 x 10 3/4. **Ad Rates:** BW $3,510; 4C $4,600. **Remarks:** Accepts advertising. **Circ:** 7000.

5168 ■ Natural Solutions: Vibrant Health, Balanced Living
InnoVision Health Media Inc.
2995 Wilderness Pl., Ste. 205
Boulder, CO 80301
Phone: (303)440-7402
Magazine focusing on natural health. **Freq:** 11/year. **Trim Size:** 16 x 10.875. **Key Personnel:** Linda Sparrowe, Editor-in-Chief. **Subscription Rates:** $24.95 Individuals print; $10 Individuals digital edition. **URL:** http://naturalsolutionsmag.com. **Ad Rates:** BW $16454. **Remarks:** Accepts advertising. **Circ:** △225000.

5169 ■ The New Brewer
Brewers Association
1327 Spruce St.
Boulder, CO 80302-5006
Phone: (303)447-0816
Fax: (303)447-2825
Free: 888-822-6273
Publisher's E-mail: info@brewersassociation.org
Magazine containing practical insights and advice for breweries. Featuring topics like brewing technology and problem solving, pub and restaurant management and packaged beer sales and distribution. **Freq:** Bimonthly. **URL:** http://www.brewersassociation.org/resources/the-new-brewer/about. **Mailing address:** PO Box 1679, Boulder, CO 80306-1679. **Remarks:** Accepts advertising. **Circ:** 5000.

5170 ■ Nutrition Business Journal: Strategic Information for Decision Makers in the Nutrition Industry
Penton Business Media, Inc.
1401 Pearl St., Ste. 200
Boulder, CO 80302
Phone: (303)998-9398
Journal catering to nutrition, natural products and alternative health care industries. Publishes information regarding business activities, market size/growth, trends, and opportunities, with a particular emphasis on the nutrition industry. **Freq:** Monthly. **Key Personnel:** Patrick Rea, Director, Editorial, Publisher, phone: (303)998-9229; Carlotta Mast, Editor, phone: (303)998-9249. **Circ:** (Not Reported).

5171 ■ Peaks
Active Interest Media
155 Canon View Rd.
Boulder, CO 80302
Phone: (303)442-7064
Publisher's E-mail: admin@aimmedia.com
Magazine publishing information for skiers and riders. **Freq:** Annual. **Key Personnel:** Andy Bigford, Publisher; Jonathan Dorn, Editor-in-Chief. **URL:** http://www.aimmedia.com/p.html. **Remarks:** Accepts advertising. **Circ:** (Not Reported).

5172 ■ Philosophy and Rhetoric
Pennsylvania State University Press
University of Colorado-Boulder
Comm. Dept., 270 UCB
Boulder, CO 80309-0270
Publication E-mail: pandr@colorado.edu
Journal exploring the relationship between philosophy and rhetoric. **Freq:** Quarterly. **Print Method:** Offset. **Trim Size:** 9 x 6. **Cols./Page:** 1. **Col. Width:** 48 nonpareils. **Col. Depth:** 99 agate lines. **Key Personnel:** Prof. Gerard A. Hauser, Editor. **ISSN:** 0031--8213 (print); **EISSN:** 1527--2079 (electronic). **Subscription Rates:** $50 Individuals print;1 year; $100 Individuals print; 2 years; $50 Individuals online; 1 year; $135 Institutions print; 1 year; $270 Institutions print; 2 years. **URL:** http://www.psupress.org/journals/jnls_pr.html. **Ad Rates:** BW $300. **Remarks:** Advertising accepted; rates available upon request. **Circ:** ‡850.

5173 ■ Recording: The Magazine for the Recording Musician
Music Maker Publications Inc.
5408 Idylwild Trl.
Boulder, CO 80301
Phone: (303)516-9118
Fax: (303)516-9119
Magazine geared toward helping musicians get the most out of their equipment to make the best recording possible. **Freq:** Monthly. **Key Personnel:** Tiffany Sepe, Manager, Circulation; Tom Hawley, President, Publisher; Lorenz Rychner, Editor. **ISSN:** 1078--8352 (print). **Subscription Rates:** $23.97 Individuals; $43.97 Two years; $38.97 Canada; $73.97 Canada 2 years; $16.95 Individuals online only. **URL:** http://www.recordingmag.com. **Formerly:** Home & Studio Recording. **Ad Rates:** BW $1,815; 4C $2,415. **Remarks:** Accepts advertising. **Circ:** Paid ‡24679, Non-paid ‡2857.

5174 ■ Sheet Music Magazine
Piano Today
PO Box 58629
Boulder, CO 80306
Magazine containing sheet music, musical "how to" articles, and information on new keyboard products. **Freq:** Quarterly. **Print Method:** Offset. **Trim Size:** 8 1/4 x 10 3/4. **Cols./Page:** 3. **Col. Width:** 27 nonpareils. **Col. Depth:** 140 agate lines. **ISSN:** 0273--6462 (print). **Ad Rates:** BW $2,750; 4C $4,140. **Remarks:** Accepts advertising. **Circ:** 80000.

5175 ■ Skyscraper
Skyscraper Magazine
PO Box 4432
Boulder, CO 80306
Phone: (303)544-9858
Publisher's E-mail: service@acc.com.tw
Consumer magazine covering music. **Freq:** Quarterly. **Key Personnel:** Andrew Bottomley, Editor-in-Chief, Publisher; Peter Bottomley, Publisher, Director,

Advertising. **Subscription Rates:** $20 Individuals; $30 Canada; $55 Other countries. **URL:** http://www.skyscrapermagazine.com. **Remarks:** Accepts advertising. **Circ:** (Not Reported).

5176 ■ Sociological Focus
Paradigm Publishers
2845 Wilderness Pl., Ste. 200
Boulder, CO 80301
Phone: (303)245-9054
Publisher's E-mail: book.orders@tandf.co.uk
Journal of the North Central Sociological Association. **Freq:** Quarterly. **Key Personnel:** Gustavo Mesch, Editor. **ISSN:** 0038-0237 (print); **EISSN:** 2162-1128 (electronic). **Subscription Rates:** $120 U.S. and Canada non-members; $234 U.S. and Canada libraries; $254 U.S. and Canada libraries; $215 Individuals online only. **URL:** http://www.paradigmpublishers.com/journals/sf/index.htm; http://www.tandfonline.com/toc/usfo20/current. **Circ:** (Not Reported).

5177 ■ Solar Today
American Solar Energy Society
2525 Arapahoe Ave., Ste. E4-253
Boulder, CO 80302
Phone: (303)443-3130
Publisher's E-mail: info@ases.org
Journal covering the business, policy and technology of renewable energy, from wind systems and energy-efficient devices to green building. **Freq:** 8/year. **Print Method:** Web press. **Trim Size:** 8 1/2 x 10 7/8. **Key Personnel:** Brooke Simmons, Manager; Regina Johnson, Associate Publisher, Editor; Brad Collins, Executive Director, Publisher. **ISSN:** 1042-0630 (print). **Subscription Rates:** Included in membership. **URL:** http://solartoday.org. **Ad Rates:** BW $3,485; 4C $2,880. **Remarks:** Accepts advertising. **Circ:** Combined 34764, 4800.

5178 ■ Soldier of Fortune
Soldier of Fortune Magazine
5735 Arapahoe Ave., Ste. A-5
Boulder, CO 80303
Phone: (303)449-3750
Fax: (303)444-5617
Free: 800-377-2789
Monthly publication of military adventure and foreign intrigue. **Freq:** Monthly. **Print Method:** Offset. **Trim Size:** 8 x 10 7/8. **Cols./Page:** 3. **Col. Width:** 26 nonpareils. **Col. Depth:** 142 agate lines. **Key Personnel:** Robert K. Brown, Publisher. **ISSN:** 0145--6784 (print). **Subscription Rates:** $4.95 Single issue online; $4.99 Single issue digital. **URL:** http://www.sofmag.com. **Ad Rates:** PCI $184. **Remarks:** Accepts advertising. **Circ:** (Not Reported).

5179 ■ Timber: A Journal of New Writing
University of Colorado Dept. of English
University of Colorado
Hellems 101
226 UCB
Boulder, CO 80309-0226
Phone: (303)492-7381
Fax: (303)492-8904
Publisher's E-mail: engldept@colorado.edu
Contains original works of prose, poetry, and art. **Freq:** Semiannual. **Subscription Rates:** Free. **URL:** http://www.colorado.edu/timberjournal. **Also known as:** Timber Journal. **Circ:** (Not Reported).

5180 ■ VeloNews: The Journal of Competitive Cycling
Inside Communications Inc.
1830 55th St.
Boulder, CO 80301-2700
Phone: (303)440-0601
Fax: (303)444-6788
Publisher's E-mail: velnews@aol.com
Tabloid magazine for fans of mountain biking and road racing. **Freq:** 14/yr. **Print Method:** Web offset. **Trim Size:** 10 3/4 x 14. **Cols./Page:** 4 and 3. **Col. Width:** 2 1/4 and 3 1/8 inches. **Col. Depth:** 12 5/8 and 12 5/8 inches. **ISSN:** 0161--1798 (print). **USPS:** 017-730. **Subscription Rates:** $29.95 Individuals; $54.95 Two years; $34.95 Individuals print and online; $60.95 Canada print and online; $94.95 Other countries print and online. **URL:** http://velonews.competitor.com. **Remarks:** Advertising accepted; rates available upon request. **Circ:** (Not Reported).

5181 ■ Vibe Magazine: Re-defining Hiphop
Time Ventures
PO Box 59580
Boulder, CO 80322
Publication focusing on popular music and culture. **Freq:** Monthly 12/yr. **Print Method:** Offset. **Trim Size:** 10 x 12. **Key Personnel:** Steve Aaron, Chief Executive Officer; Danyel Smith, Editor-in-Chief; Edgar Hernandez, Associate Publisher. **ISSN:** 1070--4701 (print). **Subscription Rates:** $9.95 Individuals; $14.95 Two years. **URL:** http://www.vibe.com. **Remarks:** Accepts advertising. **Circ:** Paid ★**862933**.

5182 ■ Zymurgy
American Homebrewers Association
1327 Spruce St.
Boulder, CO 80302
Phone: (303)447-0816
Free: 888-822-6273
Publisher's E-mail: info@brewersassociation.org
Magazine featuring articles, recipes, do-it-yourself equipment building, explanations and brewing techniques. **Freq:** Bimonthly. **Key Personnel:** Jill Redding, Editor-in-Chief. **ISSN:** 0196--5921 (print). **Subscription Rates:** $5.50 Single issue; $38 Members Join the AHA to get six issues a year. **URL:** http://www.homebrewersassociation.org/magazine/search-zymurgy-issues. **Mailing address:** PO Box 1679, Boulder, CO 80306. **Remarks:** Advertising not accepted. **Circ:** (Not Reported).

5183 ■ KCFC-AM - 1490
Bridges Broadcast Ctr.
7409 S Alton Ct.
Centennial, CO 80112
Phone: (303)871-9191
Fax: (303)733-3319
Free: 800-722-4449
Format: Public Radio. **Owner:** Colorado Public Radio, at above address. **Key Personnel:** Andrew Shaw, Producer; Doug Clifton, Officer; Mark Coulter, VP of Production, VP of Operations; Mike Flanagan, Prog. Dir.; Jim East, Sr. VP; Max Wycisk, President; Sean Nethery, Sr. VP; Daniel Costello, Operations Mgr.; Jenny Gentry, VP of Fin., VP of Legal Affairs. **URL:** http://www.cpr.org/listen/where.

5184 ■ KGNU-FM - 88.5
4700 Walnut St.
Boulder, CO 80301-2548
Phone: (303)449-4885
Free: 800-737-3030
Format: Educational. **Networks:** Public Radio International (PRI); Pacifica. **Owner:** Boulder Community Broadcasting Assn. Inc., at above address. **Founded:** 1978. **Operating Hours:** 5.30 a.m.- 3 a.m. Wk. Days; 6 a.m. - 3 a.m. Sat. & Sun. **Key Personnel:** Sam Fuqua, Station Mgr.; John Schaefer, Music Dir. **Wattage:** 1,300. **Ad Rates:** Noncommercial. **URL:** http://www.kgnu.org.

5185 ■ KVCU-AM - 1190
University of Colorado
CB 207
Boulder, CO 80309
Phone: (303)492-5031
Fax: (303)492-1369
Email: dj@radio1190.org
Format: Educational. **Owner:** University of Colorado, 1800 Grant St., Suite 800, Denver, CO 80203, Ph: (303)860-5600, Fax: (303)860-5610. **Wattage:** 6,800 Day; 110 Night. **Ad Rates:** Noncommercial. **URL:** http://www.radio1190.org.

5186 ■ KVOD-AM - 1490
7409 S Alton Ct.
Centennial, CO 80112
Phone: (303)871-9191
Fax: (303)733-3319
Free: 800-722-4449
Email: news@cpr.org
Format: Public Radio. **Owner:** Public Broadcasting of Colorado Inc., at above address. **Founded:** Sept. 15, 2006. **Key Personnel:** Dan Murphy, VP; Max Wycisk, President; Jenny Gentry, VP. **Ad Rates:** Noncommercial. **URL:** http://www.cpr.org.

BRECKENRIDGE

Summit Co. Summit Co. (C). 90 m SW of Denver. Summer & winter resort.

5187 ■ KIFT-FM - 106.3
130 Ski Hill Rd., Ste. 240
Breckenridge, CO 80424
Format: Adult Contemporary; Contemporary Hit Radio (CHR). **Owner:** NRC Broadcasting Mountain Group L.L.C., 130 Ski Hill Rd., Breckenridge, CO 80424, Ph: (970)453-2234. **Wattage:** 50,000. **URL:** http://www.alwaysmountaintime.com.

5188 ■ KSMT-FM - 102.3
130 Ski Hill Rd., Ste. 240
Breckenridge, CO 80424
Phone: (970)453-2234
Fax: (303)557-6229
Format: Hip Hop; Album-Oriented Rock (AOR). **Owner:** NRC Broadcasting Co., at above address. **Founded:** 1973. **Formerly:** KLGT-FM. **Operating Hours:** Continuous; 99% local. **Key Personnel:** Pete Benedetti, President, CEO; Kyle McCoy, VP of Operations; John Johnston, Gen. Mgr. **Wattage:** 3,000. **Ad Rates:** $20-35 per unit. Combined advertising rates available with KTUN. **URL:** http://www.alwaysmountaintime.com.

BREEN

5189 ■ KLLV-AM
14780 Hwy. 140
Breen, CO 81326
Phone: (970)259-5558
Format: Religious. **Founded:** 1984. **Wattage:** 1,800 Day.

BRIGHTON

Weld Co. Adams Co. (NEC). 20 m NE of Denver. Canning; beet sugar factories; mobile homes manufactured. Metal fabricating plants. Agriculture. Sugar beets, wheat, corn, cattle feeding; diversified farming.

5190 ■ Ft. Lupton Press
Metro West Publishing
139 N Main St.
Brighton, CO 80601
Community newspaper. **Freq:** Semiweekly (Wed. and Sat.). **Print Method:** Offset. **Cols./Page:** 6. **Col. Width:** 21 nonpareils. **Col. Depth:** 224 agate lines. **Key Personnel:** Steven Smith, Editor. **Subscription Rates:** $32 Individuals print and online - annual; $21 Individuals print and online - semiannual. **URL:** http://www.ftluptonpress.com. **Ad Rates:** SAU $6.75. **Remarks:** Accepts advertising. **Circ:** Paid ‡1100, Non-paid ‡4400.

5191 ■ NAPS Journal
North American Parrot Society
c/o Gary Morgan, Chairman/President
15341 Kingston St.
Brighton, CO 80602-7439
Phone: (303)659-9544
Freq: Quarterly. **Subscription Rates:** included in membership dues. **Remarks:** Advertising not accepted. **Circ:** (Not Reported).

5192 ■ Standard Blade
Metrowest Newspapers
139 N Main St.
Brighton, CO 80601
Community newspaper. **Freq:** Weekly Wednesday & Saturday. **Print Method:** Offset. **Cols./Page:** 6. **Col. Width:** 12 3/10 picas. **Col. Depth:** 12.5 inches. **Key Personnel:** Allen Messick, Publisher. **Subscription Rates:** $32 Individuals in County. **URL:** http://www.thebrightonblade.com. **Ad Rates:** GLR $15; BW $975; 4C $1200; SAU $15; PCI $15. **Remarks:** Accepts advertising. **Circ:** Paid 6593, Non-paid 25227.

BROOMFIELD

Weld Co. Boulder, Adams & Jefferson Co. (NC). 15 m NW of Denver. Residential. Commercial, industrial and high tech centers.

5193 ■ A&E
National Business Media Inc.
2800 West Midway Blvd.
Broomfield, CO 80038
Phone: (303)469-0424
Fax: (303)465-3424
Free: 800-669-0424
Magazine for the awards and engraving industry. **Freq:** Monthly. **Key Personnel:** James Kochevar, Publisher;

Circulation: ★ = AAM; △ or • = BPA; ♦ = CAC; ❏ = VAC; ⊕ = PO Statement; ‡ = Publisher's Report; Boldface figures = sworn; Light figures = estimated.

Steve Wieber, Associate Publisher, Editor; Dave Pomeroy, Vice President. **Subscription Rates:** $45 Individuals print and online. **URL:** http://a-e-mag.com. **Mailing address:** PO Box 1416, Broomfield, CO 80038. **Ad Rates:** 4C $3525. **Remarks:** Accepts advertising. **Circ:** ‡9004.

5194 ■ The Broomfielder
Broomfield Chamber of Commerce
2095 W 6th Ave.
Broomfield, CO 80020
Phone: (303)466-1775
Fax: (303)466-4481
Publisher's E-mail: info@broomfieldchamber.com
Contains information on the Broomfield, CO chamber events, activities and programs. **Freq:** Monthly. **Subscription Rates:** Included in membership. **URL:** http://www.broomfieldchamber.com/memberbenefits.html. **Remarks:** Accepts advertising. **Circ:** (Not Reported).

5195 ■ International Spectrum: The Businessperson's Computer Magazine
IDBMA Inc.
80 Garden Center, Ste. 6
Broomfield, CO 80020
Phone: (720)259-1356
Fax: (603)250-0664
News magazine for the computer industry focusing on the PICK/UNIX/DOS-based computer operating environment. **Freq:** Bimonthly. **Print Method:** Offset. Accepts mats. **Trim Size:** 8 3/8 x 10 7/8. **Cols./Page:** 3. **Col. Width:** 2 1/4 inches. **Col. Depth:** 9 7/8 inches. **Key Personnel:** Clif Oliver, Editor; Gus Giobbi, Publisher; Monica Giobbi, Business Manager. **ISSN:** 1050--9070 (print). **Subscription Rates:** Included in membership. **Alt. Formats:** E-book; PDF. **Ad Rates:** 4C $2475. **Remarks:** Advertising accepted; rates available upon request. **Circ:** Controlled 22500.

5196 ■ Performance and Hotrod Business
National Business Media Inc.
PO Box 1416
Broomfield, CO 80038
Phone: (303)469-0424
Fax: (303)469-5730
Free: 800-669-0424
Magazine for automotive specialists in the street performance and hot rod market segments. **Freq:** Monthly. **Key Personnel:** Jef White, Editor; Kent Bradley, Publisher. **Subscription Rates:** $45 Individuals print and online. **URL:** http://www.nbm.com/what-we-do/publications. **Formerly:** Performance Business. **Ad Rates:** 4C $3,595. **Remarks:** Accepts advertising. **Circ:** 30000.

5197 ■ Printwear
National Business Media Inc.
2800 West Midway Blvd.
Broomfield, CO 80038
Phone: (303)469-0424
Fax: (303)465-3424
Free: 800-669-0424
Trade magazine for garment screen printers and apparel graphics professionals. **Founded:** June 01, 1995. **Freq:** 13/year. **Print Method:** Web. **Trim Size:** 8 1/8 x 10 7/8. **Cols./Page:** 3. **Key Personnel:** Christina Montgomery, Associate Publisher; Emily Kay Thompson, Editor-in-Chief; Dave Pomeroy, Publisher. **Subscription Rates:** $45 Individuals; $76 Canada; $98 Other countries. **URL:** http://printwearmag.com/. **Mailing address:** PO Box 1416, Broomfield, CO 80038. **Ad Rates:** BW $3,470; 4C $1,050. **Remarks:** Accepts advertising. **Circ:** (Not Reported).

5198 ■ RV Pro
National Business Media Inc.
PO Box 1416
Broomfield, CO 80038
Phone: (303)469-0424
Fax: (303)469-5730
Free: 800-669-0424
Magazine for professionals in the recreational vehicle aftermarket industry. **Freq:** Monthly. **Key Personnel:** Dana Nelsen, Publisher; Bradley Worrell, Editor. **Subscription Rates:** Free to qualified subscribers; $45 Individuals print and digital. **URL:** http://rv-pro.com. **Remarks:** Accepts advertising. **Circ:** (Not Reported).

5199 ■ Wraps
National Business Media Inc.
2800 West Midway Blvd.
Broomfield, CO 80038
Phone: (303)469-0424
Fax: (303)465-3424
Free: 800-669-0424
Magazine focusing on digital wraps. **Freq:** Bimonthly. **Key Personnel:** Eddie Wieber, Editor; Mary Tohill, Publisher. **URL:** http://wraps-mag.com; http://www.nbm.com/what-we-do/publications. **Mailing address:** PO Box 1416, Broomfield, CO 80038. **Remarks:** Accepts advertising. **Circ:** (Not Reported).

BRUSH

Morgan Co. Morgan Co. (NE). 61 E of Greeley. Retirement care centers. Manufacturers farm equipment, electronics. Hog processing plant. Livestock markets. Agriculture. Cattle, hogs, daires, horses, alfalfa, grain.

5200 ■ Brush News-Tribune
Brush News-Tribune
109 Clayton St.
Brush, CO 80723
Phone: (970)842-5516
Fax: (970)842-5519
Publisher's E-mail: horner@brushnewstribune.com
Community newspaper. **Founded:** 1894. **Freq:** Weekly (Wed.). **Print Method:** Offset. **Cols./Page:** 5. **Col. Width:** 25 nonpareils. **Col. Depth:** 182 agate lines. **Key Personnel:** Iva Kay Horner, Publisher. **USPS:** 068-240. **Subscription Rates:** $37 Individuals in Morgan County; $47 Out of area. **URL:** http://www.brushnewstribune.com. **Mailing address:** PO Box 8, Brush, CO 80723. **Ad Rates:** BW $312.50; 4C $432.50; SAU $5; PCI $5. **Remarks:** Accepts advertising. **Circ:** ⊕**1832**.

BURLINGTON

Kit Carson Co. Kit Carson Co. (EC). Sugar beets.

5201 ■ Burlington Record & Plains Dealer
Burlington Record
202 South 14th St.
Burlington, CO 80807
Phone: (719)346-5381
Fax: (719)346-5514
Publisher's E-mail: brecord@plainstel.com
Community newspaper with shopper. **Freq:** Weekly (Thurs.). **Print Method:** Web offset. **Cols./Page:** 8. **Col. Width:** 11 inches. **Col. Depth:** 21 inches. **Subscription Rates:** $39 Individuals local; $43 Individuals non-local; $35 Individuals e-edition; $20.50 Individuals e-edition 6 months; $12.50 Individuals e-edition 3 months. **URL:** http://www.burlington-record.com. **Formerly:** Burlington Record. **Remarks:** Accepts advertising. **Circ:** (Not Reported).

5202 ■ KNAB-AM - 1140
17543 County Line Rd. 49
Burlington, CO 80807
Phone: (719)346-8600
Fax: (719)346-8656
Format: Country. **Networks:** ABC; Westwood One Radio. **Owner:** KNAB AM/FM, at above address, Burlington, CO 80807. **Founded:** 1967. **Operating Hours:** 12 hours Daily; 9B network, 2% local. **Wattage:** 1,000. **Ad Rates:** $9.40-14.75 for 30 seconds; $17.40-23 for 60 seconds. Combined advertising rates available with KNAB-FM. **Mailing address:** PO Box 516, Burlington, CO 80807. **URL:** http://www.knabradio.com.

5203 ■ KNAB-FM - 104.1
17543 County Line Rd. 49
Burlington, CO 80807
Phone: (719)346-8600
Fax: (719)346-8656
Email: knab@centurytel.net
Format: Country. **Networks:** ABC. **Owner:** KNAB AM/FM, at above address, Burlington, CO 80807. **Founded:** 1980. **Operating Hours:** Continuous; 98% network, 2% local. **Wattage:** 50,700. **Ad Rates:** $9.40-14.75 for 30 seconds; $17-23 for 60 seconds. Combined advertising rates available with KNAB-AM: $7.20-$10.80 for 20 seconds; $10-$13.80 for 30 seconds. **Mailing address:** PO Box 516, Burlington, CO 80807. **URL:** http://www.knabradio.com.

5204 ■ KPCR-FM - 99.3
1951 28th Ave., Unit 29
Greeley, CO 80634
Phone: (573)324-2283
Fax: (573)324-2670
Email: kpcr@nemonet.com
Owner: Youngers Colorado Broadcasting LLC, at above address. **Founded:** 1975. **Wattage:** 100 ERP. **Ad Rates:** $7.25-11.80 for 30 seconds. **URL:** http://www.joyfmonline.org./.

5205 ■ K201FK-FM - 88.1
PO Box 391
Twin Falls, ID 83303
Fax: (208)736-1958
Free: 800-357-4226
Format: Religious; Contemporary Christian. **Owner:** CSN International, PO Box 391, Twin Falls, ID 83303, Ph: (208)736-1958, Fax: (208)736-1958, Free: 800-357-4226. **Key Personnel:** Don Mills, Prog. Dir., Music Dir.; Kelly Carlson, Dir. of Engg.; Ray Gorney, Asst. Dir. **Wattage:** 250. **URL:** http://www.csnradio.com.

CANON CITY

Fremont Co. Fremont Co. (SC). On Arkansas River, 41 m W of Pueblo. Tourism. Royal Gorge. Light industry.

5206 ■ Daily Record
Royal Gorge Publishing Corp.
701 S 9th St.
Canon City, CO 81212
Phone: (719)275-7565
Fax: (719)275-1353
Newspaper with an Independent orientation. **Founded:** 1875. **Freq:** Daily (eve.). **Print Method:** Offset. **Cols./Page:** 6. **Col. Width:** 2 1/16 inches. **Col. Depth:** 21.5 picas. **USPS:** 088-560. **Subscription Rates:** $18.60 Individuals 3 months; $37.20 Individuals 6 months; $74.40 Individuals; $12 By mail a month. **URL:** http://www.canoncitydailyrecord.com. **Ad Rates:** GLR $.63; BW $1,032; 4C $1,273.95; SAU $8. **Remarks:** Accepts advertising. **Circ:** Mon.-Sat. ★**8265**.

5207 ■ Mining History Journal
Mining History Association
323 Daniels Pl.
Canon City, CO 81212
Phone: (573)290-2453
Freq: Annual. **Subscription Rates:** $10 Single issue; Included in membership. **Alt. Formats:** PDF. **URL:** http://www.mininghistoryassociation.org/journal.htm. **Remarks:** Advertising not accepted. **Circ:** (Not Reported).

5208 ■ KRLN-AM
1615 Central Ave.
Canon City, CO 81212
Phone: (212)688-7908
Owner: Royal Gorge Broadcasting L.L.C., at above address.

CARBONDALE

Garfield Co. (W). 11 m S of Glenwood Springs.

5209 ■ Climbing Magazine
Primedia
326 Hwy. 133, Ste. 190
Carbondale, CO 81623
Publisher's E-mail: climbing@emailcustomerservice.com
Magazine devoted to rock and mountain climbing. **Freq:** 10/year. **Print Method:** Web offset. **Trim Size:** 8 3/8 x 10 7/8. **Cols./Page:** 3. **Col. Width:** 13 picas. **Col. Depth:** 9 5/16 inches. **ISSN:** 0045--7159 (print). **Subscription Rates:** $14.95 Individuals print; $19.55 Individuals digital. **URL:** http://www.climbing.com. **Remarks:** Accepts advertising. **Circ:** Paid ★**37078**.

5210 ■ Home Power
Solar Energy International
520 S 3rd St., Rm. 16
Carbondale, CO 81623
Phone: (970)963-8855
Fax: (970)963-8866
Publisher's E-mail: sei@solarenergy.org
Subscription Rates: included in membership dues (except student/senior membership). **Mailing address:** PO Box 715, Carbondale, CO 81623. **Remarks:** Advertising not accepted. **Circ:** (Not Reported).

5211 ■ KDNK-FM - 88.1
PO Box 1388
Carbondale, CO 81623
Phone: (970)963-0139
Fax: (970)963-0810

Email: news@kdnk.org
Format: Public Radio; Full Service. **Networks:** National Public Radio (NPR). **Owner:** Carbondale Community Access Radio Inc., at above address, Carbondale, CO 81623. **Founded:** 1983. **Operating Hours:** 6 a.m.-1 a.m. weekdays; 7 a.m.-1 a.m. Saturday and Sunday; 20% Network, 80%. **ADI:** Colorado Springs-Pueblo, CO. **Key Personnel:** Steve Skinner, Gen. Mgr. **Wattage:** 215. **Ad Rates:** Noncommercial; underwriting available. **URL:** http://www.kdnk.org.

5212 ■ KSPN-FM - 103.1
402D Aspen Airport Business Ctr., Ste. D
Aspen, CO 81611
Phone: (970)925-5776
Fax: (970)925-1142
Format: Adult Album Alternative. **Networks:** AP; CNN Radio. **Owner:** NRC Broadcasting Co., at above address. **Founded:** 1970. **Formerly:** KTUS-FM; KSNO-FM. **Operating Hours:** Continuous. **Key Personnel:** David Bach, Contact, dbach@nrcbroadcasting.com. **Wattage:** 3,000. **Ad Rates:** Noncommercial. $15-45 for 30 seconds. Combined advertising rates available with KNFO, KKCH, KTUN, KSMT, and KFMU. **URL:** http://www.kspnradio.com.

CASTLE ROCK

Douglas Co. Douglas Co. (C). 20 m S. of Denver.

5213 ■ Lives of Real Estate
REAL Trends Inc.
7501 Village Sq. Dr., Ste. 200
Castle Rock, CO 80108
Phone: (303)741-1000
Fax: (303)741-1070
Publisher's E-mail: tech@realtrends.com
Magazine that profiles personnel in the residential real estate industry. **Freq:** Quarterly. **Trim Size:** 9 x 10.875. **Key Personnel:** Steve Murray, Publisher. **URL:** http://www.realtrends.com/products/LORE-Magazine. **Ad Rates:** 4C $700. **Remarks:** Accepts advertising. **Circ:** ‡40000.

5214 ■ Merry-Go-Roundup
National Carousel Association
c/o Norma Pankratz, Executive Secretary
PO Box 1256
Castle Rock, CO 80104-1256
Freq: Quarterly. **Subscription Rates:** free for members. **URL:** http://carousels.org/MGR.html. **Remarks:** Advertising not accepted. **Circ:** (Not Reported).

5215 ■ The Mining Record
Howell International Enterprises
PO Box 1630
Castle Rock, CO 80104-6130
Phone: (303)663-7820
Fax: (303)663-7823
Free: 800-441-4748
Publisher's E-mail: questions@miningrecord.com
International mining industry newspaper. Features reporting on exploration, discovery, development, production, joint ventures, operating results, legislation, government reports, and metals prices. **Freq:** Monthly. **Print Method:** Offset. **Trim Size:** 11 1/2 x 16 3/4. **Cols./Page:** 5. **Col. Width:** 22 nonpareils. **Col. Depth:** 210 agate lines. **Key Personnel:** Don E. Howell, Editor. **ISSN:** 0026--5241 (print). **Subscription Rates:** $55 U.S. one year - print and online; $90 U.S. two years - print and online; $125 U.S. three years - print and online; $85 U.S. one year, first class mail - print and online; $85 Canada and Mexico one year - print and online; $99 Other countries one year - print and online; $85 U.S. one year - second class mail; $115 U.S. two years - second class mail; $130 U.S. three years - second class mail; $122 U.S. one year - first class mail; $132 Canada and Mexico one year, air mail; $140 Other countries one year, air mail. **URL:** http://www.miningrecord.com. **Remarks:** Accepts advertising. **Circ:** (Not Reported).

CENTENNIAL

5216 ■ Journal of Stroke and Cerebrovascular Diseases
National Stroke Association
9707 E Easter Ln., Ste. B
Centennial, CO 80112
Free: 800-787-6537
Publisher's E-mail: healthpermissions@elsevier.com
Freq: Monthly. **Trim Size:** 8 1/4 x 11. **Cols./Page:** 2. **Key Personnel:** Jose Biller, MD, Editor; Rhonda T. Biller, Managing Editor. **ISSN:** 1052--3057 (print). **Subscription Rates:** $339 U.S. online and print; $441 Canada online and print; $420 Other countries online and print; $3445.33 Institutions e-Journal; $1010 Institutions print. **URL:** http://www.strokejournal.org. **Ad Rates:** BW $1,045; 4C $1,355. **Remarks:** Accepts advertising. **Circ:** Paid ‡5675.

5217 ■ Journal of Stroke and Cerebrovascular Diseases
Elsevier Inc.
1600 John F. Kennedy Blvd., Ste. 1800
Philadelphia, PA 19103-2899
Phone: (215)239-3900
Fax: (215)238-7883
Free: 800-523-1649
Publisher's E-mail: healthpermissions@elsevier.com
Freq: Monthly. **Trim Size:** 8 1/4 x 11. **Cols./Page:** 2. **Key Personnel:** Jose Biller, MD, Editor; Rhonda T. Biller, Managing Editor. **ISSN:** 1052--3057 (print). **Subscription Rates:** $339 U.S. online and print; $441 Canada online and print; $420 Other countries online and print; $3445.33 Institutions e-Journal; $1010 Institutions print. **URL:** http://www.strokejournal.org. **Ad Rates:** BW $1,045; 4C $1,355. **Remarks:** Accepts advertising. **Circ:** Paid ‡5675.

5218 ■ National Cattlemen Magazine
National Cattlemen's Beef Association
9110 E Nichols Ave., No. 300
Centennial, CO 80112
Phone: (303)694-0305
Fax: (303)694-2851
Publisher's E-mail: membership@beef.org
Magazine covering beef-industry business management and issues. **Freq:** Monthly. **Print Method:** Offset. **Trim Size:** 8 1/2 x 11. **Cols./Page:** 3. **ISSN:** 0885--7679 (print). **Subscription Rates:** Included in membership. **URL:** http://www.beefusa.org. **Remarks:** Accepts advertising. **Circ:** (Not Reported).

5219 ■ RadioResource International: Wireless Voice and Data for Mobile and Remote Operations
Pandata Corp.
7108 S Alton Way, Bldg. H
Centennial, CO 80112
Phone: (303)792-2390
Fax: (303)792-2391
Publisher's E-mail: info@rrmediagroup.com
Magazine for mobile mission critical and remote operations. **Freq:** Quarterly. **Print Method:** Web offset. **Trim Size:** 8 1/8 x 10 7/8. **Cols./Page:** 3. **Key Personnel:** Lola Friday, Web Administrator; Mark E. Shira, Vice President; Paulla Nelson-Shira, Director, Editorial, Publisher; Sandra Wendelken, Editor; Lindsay A. Gross, Managing Editor. **ISSN:** 1080--3025 (print). **URL:** http://www.radioresourcemag.com. **Ad Rates:** BW $4,675; 4C $5,550; PCI $104. **Remarks:** Accepts advertising. **Circ:** Non-paid 12443.

5220 ■ Rocky Mountain Baptist
Colorado Baptist General Convention
7393 S Alton Way
Centennial, CO 80112-2302
Phone: (303)771-2480
Fax: (303)771-6272
Free: 888-771-2480
News Journal of Colorado's Southern Baptists. **Freq:** Bimonthly. **Print Method:** Offset. **Trim Size:** 8 1/2 x 11. **Key Personnel:** Mark Edlund, Executive Director. **ISSN:** 0485--294X (print). **Subscription Rates:** $5 Individuals in Colorado; $10 Individuals outside Colorado. **URL:** http://saturatecolorado.com/resources/rocky-mountain-baptists. **Remarks:** Advertising accepted; rates available upon request. **Circ:** ‡6000.

5221 ■ Stroke Smart
National Stroke Association
9707 E Easter Ln., Ste. B
Centennial, CO 80112
Free: 800-787-6537
Publisher's E-mail: info@stroke.org
Magazine containing articles on stroke issues, tips and treatment and other relevant ideas. **Freq:** Bimonthly. **Subscription Rates:** Included in membership. **URL:** http://www.stroke.org/stroke-resources/strokesmart-magazine. **Remarks:** Advertising not accepted. **Circ:** 80000.

5222 ■ Jones Intercable
9697 E Mineral Ave.
No. 7
Centennial, CO 80112
Phone: (303)978-9770
Fax: (303)972-9417
Owner: Jones Intercable Inc., 9697 E Mineral Ave., Englewood, CO 80112-3446, Ph: (303)792-3111, Fax: (303)790-0533. **Key Personnel:** Ann Montague, Bus. Mgr.; Max Romero, Mgr. **Cities Served:** Brighton, Broomfield, Evergreen, Colorado: subscribing households 46,000; Jefferson and Boulder counties; 2 channels; 1 community access channel; 10 hours per week community access programming. **URL:** http://www.jones.com.

KCFC-AM - See Boulder
KCFP-FM - See Pueblo
KCFR-AM - See Denver

5223 ■ KCFR-FM - 90.1
7409 S Alton Ct.
7409 S Alton Ct.
Centennial, CO 80112
Phone: (303)871-9191
Owner: Colorado Public Radio, at above address.

KKPC-AM - See Pueblo

5224 ■ KPRE-FM - 89.9
Bridges Broadcast Ctr.
7409 S Alton Ct.
Centennial, CO 80112
Phone: (303)871-9191
Fax: (303)733-3319
Free: 800-722-4449
Format: Public Radio. **Owner:** Colorado Public Radio, at above address. **Key Personnel:** Andrew Shaw, Producer; Mike Flanagan, Prog. Dir.; Jim East, Sr. VP; Daniel Costello, Operations Mgr.; Jenny Gentry, Sr. VP of Fin. & Admin.; Max Wycisk, President; Mark Coulter, VP of Operations; Sean Nethery, Sr. VP. **Ad Rates:** Noncommercial; underwriting available. **URL:** http://www.cpr.org.

KPRH-FM - See Montrose, CO

5225 ■ KPRN-FM - 89.5
7409 S Alton Ct.
Centennial, CO 80112
Phone: (303)871-9191
Fax: (303)733-3319
Free: 800-722-4449
Format: News; Classical; Public Radio; Educational. **Networks:** National Public Radio (NPR); Public Radio International (PRI). **Owner:** Public Broadcasting of Colorado Inc., at above address. **Founded:** 1985. **Operating Hours:** Continuous. **ADI:** Grand Junction-Durango, CO. **Key Personnel:** Max Wycisk, President; Jenny Gentry, Exec. VP; Ed Trudeau, VP; Sean Nethery, VP, Comm., VP of Mktg.; Sue Coughlin, VP of Dev.; Bob Hensler, VP. **Wattage:** 19,830 ERP. **Ad Rates:** Underwriting available. **URL:** http://www.cpr.org.

KPRU-FM - See Grand Junction
KPYR-FM - See Craig
KVOD-AM - See Boulder

CHERRY HILLS VILLAGE

5226 ■ KNDZ-FM - 105.1
4915 S Vine St.
Cherry Hills Village, CO 80113
Phone: (425)466-4628
Format: Music of Your Life; Eighties. **Operating Hours:** Continuous. **Ad Rates:** Advertising accepted; rates available upon request.

5227 ■ KRPM-FM
4915 S Vine St.
Cherry Hills Village, CO 80113
Phone: (907)344-4045
Fax: (907)522-6053
Format: Classic Rock. **Wattage:** 100,000 ERP. **Ad Rates:** Noncommercial.

CHEYENNE WELLS

Cheyenne Co. Cheyenne Co. (EC).

Circulation: ★ = AAM; △ or • = BPA; ♦ = CAC; ❑ = VAC; ⊕ = PO Statement; ‡ = Publisher's Report; Boldface figures = sworn; Light figures = estimated.

5228 ■ Rebeltec Communications
185 S First East St.
Cheyenne Wells, CO 80810
Phone: (719)767-8902
Fax: (719)767-8906
Free: 866-879-7824
Email: tech@rebeltec.net
Cities Served: 24 channels. **URL:** http://www.rebeltec.net.

COLORADO SPRINGS

El Paso Co. El Paso Co. (EC). 68 m S of Denver. U.S. Air Force Academy. Colorado College. Union Printers' National Home. Health and Tourist resort. Sanatorium. Manufactures advertising film, granite, concrete, dairy products, brooms, novelties, chemicals, pottery, bricks, airplane engine mounts, machine tools, shell fuses, electric motors, gray and alloy castings, electronics, plastics, steel culverts. Chromium plating; meat packing; bookbinding; nuclear research.

5229 ■ Academy Spirit
Colorado Publishing Co.
31 E Platt, Ste. 300
Colorado Springs, CO 80903
Phone: (719)634-5905
Publisher's E-mail: csbj@csbj.com
Military tabloid for personnel of the United States Air Force Academy. **Freq:** Weekly (Fri.). **Print Method:** Web Offset. **Trim Size:** 11 1/4 x 17 1/4. **Cols./Page:** 6. **Col. Width:** 1 5/8 inches. **Col. Depth:** 16 inches. **Key Personnel:** Heidi Witherington, Manager, Advertising. **Alt. Formats:** PDF. **URL:** http://csmng.com/AcademySpirit. **Formerly**: The Falcon Flyer; Falconnews. **Remarks:** Accepts advertising. **Circ:** (Not Reported).

5230 ■ American Fencing
United States Fencing Association
4065 Sinton Rd., Ste. 140
Colorado Springs, CO 80907
Phone: (719)866-4511
Fax: (719)632-5737
Publisher's E-mail: info@usfencing.org
Magazine covering the sport of fencing. **Freq:** Quarterly. **Trim Size:** 8.5 x 11. **Key Personnel:** Cindy Bent Findlay, Editor. **ISSN:** 0002--8436 (print). **Subscription Rates:** Included in membership. **URL:** http://www.usfencing.org/page/show/704073-american-fencing-magazine. **Remarks:** Advertising accepted; rates available upon request. **Circ:** 80000.

5231 ■ Boundless
Focus on the Family
8605 Explorer Dr.
Colorado Springs, CO 80920
Fax: (719)548-5947
Free: 800-232-6459
Publisher's E-mail: pastors@fotf.org
Freq: Weekly. **Remarks:** Advertising not accepted. **Circ:** (Not Reported).

5232 ■ Breakaway
Focus on the Family
8605 Explorer Dr.
Colorado Springs, CO 80920
Fax: (719)548-5947
Free: 800-232-6459
Publisher's E-mail: pastors@fotf.org
Freq: Monthly. **Remarks:** Advertising not accepted. **Circ:** (Not Reported).

5233 ■ CBA Retailers+Resources
CBA: The Association for Christian Retail
1365 Garden of the Gods Rd., Ste. 105
Colorado Springs, CO 80907
Phone: (719)265-9895
Fax: (719)272-3510
Free: 800-252-1950
Publisher's E-mail: info@cbaonline.org
Magazine covering retail industry. **Freq:** Monthly. **Subscription Rates:** Included in membership. **Formerly**: Aspiring Retail. **Remarks:** Accepts advertising. **Circ:** (Not Reported).

5234 ■ Citizen
Focus on the Family
8605 Explorer Dr.
Colorado Springs, CO 80920
Fax: (719)548-5947
Free: 800-232-6459
Publisher's E-mail: pastors@fotf.org
Magazine focusing on family. **URL:** http://www.citizenlink.org/citizenmag/. **Circ:** 50000.

5235 ■ Clubhouse
Focus on the Family
8605 Explorer Dr.
Colorado Springs, CO 80920
Fax: (719)548-5947
Free: 800-232-6459
Publisher's E-mail: pastors@fotf.org
Freq: Monthly. **Subscription Rates:** $19.99 Individuals. **URL:** http://www.clubhousemagazine.com. **Remarks:** Accepts advertising. **Circ:** (Not Reported).

5236 ■ Clubhouse Jr.
Focus on the Family
8605 Explorer Dr.
Colorado Springs, CO 80920
Fax: (719)548-5947
Free: 800-232-6459
Publisher's E-mail: pastors@fotf.org
Freq: Monthly. **ISSN:** 0895--1136 (print). **Subscription Rates:** $14.99 Individuals. **URL:** http://www.clubhousejr.com. **Remarks:** Advertising not accepted. **Circ:** Controlled 88000.

5237 ■ Colorado Springs Independent
Colorado Springs Independent
235 S Nevada
Colorado Springs, CO 80903
Phone: (719)577-4545
Fax: (719)577-4107
Publisher's E-mail: newsroom@csindy.com
Community newspaper. **Freq:** Weekly. **Key Personnel:** Ralph Routon, Executive Editor; John Weiss, Publisher; Kirk Woundy, Editor-in-Chief. **Subscription Rates:** $20 Individuals /10 weeks for the Indy on Wednesdays and the Denver Post every Sunday; $104 Individuals /52 weeks for the Indy on Wednesdays and the Denver Post every Sunday. **URL:** http://www.csindy.com. **Remarks:** Accepts advertising. **Circ:** Combined 36300.

5238 ■ Focus on the Family Citizen
Focus on the Family
8605 Explorer Dr.
Colorado Springs, CO 80920
Fax: (719)548-5947
Free: 800-232-6459
Publisher's E-mail: pastors@fotf.org
Freq: Monthly. **Subscription Rates:** 19.95. **Remarks:** Advertising not accepted. **Circ:** (Not Reported).

5239 ■ Focus on the Family Clubhouse
Focus on the Family
8605 Explorer Dr.
Colorado Springs, CO 80920
Fax: (719)548-5947
Free: 800-232-6459
Publisher's E-mail: pastors@fotf.org
Consumer Christian magazine for children ages 8-12 years. **Freq:** Monthly. **Key Personnel:** Jesse Florea, Editor; Suzanne Hadley, Editor-in-Chief. **Subscription Rates:** $19.99 Individuals /year. **URL:** http://focusonthefamily.com; http://store.focusonthefamily.com/clubhouse-magazine. **Remarks:** Advertising not accepted. **Circ:** Paid 115000.

5240 ■ Focus on the Family Magazine Citizen
Focus on the Family
8605 Explorer Dr.
Colorado Springs, CO 80920
Fax: (719)548-5947
Free: 800-232-6459
Publisher's E-mail: pastors@fotf.org
Magazine containing marriage and parenting articles from a Christian perspective. **Freq:** Monthly. **Print Method:** Web offset. **Trim Size:** 8 x 10 1/2. **Cols./Page:** 3. **Col. Width:** 13 picas. **ISSN:** 0894--3346 (print). **Subscription Rates:** $19.95 Individuals. **URL:** http://www.focusonthefamily.com/socialissues/promos/subscribe-to-citizen-magazine. **Remarks:** Advertising not accepted. **Circ:** Free 2200000.

5241 ■ Fort Carson Mountaineer
Colorado Publishing Co.
31 E Platt, Ste. 300
Colorado Springs, CO 80903
Phone: (719)634-5905
Publisher's E-mail: csbj@csbj.com
Military tabloid for personnel of Fort Carson. **Founded:** 1941. **Freq:** Weekly (Fri.). **Print Method:** Offset. Accepts mats. **Trim Size:** 11 1/4 x 17 1/4. **Cols./Page:** 6. **Col. Width:** 1 5/8 inches. **Col. Depth:** 16 inches. **URL:** http://www.fortcarsonmountaineer.com/. **Ad Rates:** BW $1,550; 4C $1,733; PCI $17.75. **Remarks:** Accepts advertising. **Circ:** Free ‡23000.

5242 ■ The Gazette
The Gazette
30 E Pikes Peak Ave., Ste. 100
Colorado Springs, CO 80903
Phone: (719)632-5511
Free: 866-636-0289
Publisher's E-mail: dsteever@gazette.com
Community newspaper. **Freq:** Weekly. **Print Method:** Web offset. **Trim Size:** 9 7/8 x 15 3/4. **Cols./Page:** 4. **Col. Width:** 2 3/8 inches. **Col. Depth:** 15 3/4 inches. **Key Personnel:** Jeff Thomas, Editor, Vice President; Dan Steever, Publisher, phone: (719)636-0104. **Subscription Rates:** $6 Individuals archives - online access; $11 Individuals print and online; $5 Individuals print only; $3.99 Individuals e-Edition. **URL:** http://www.gazette.com. **Ad Rates:** BW $495. **Remarks:** Advertising accepted; rates available upon request. **Circ:** Controlled ‡2825.

5243 ■ Hispania
Hispania
PO Box 15116
Colorado Springs, CO 80935
Phone: (719)540-0220
Fax: (719)540-0599
Publisher's E-mail: editor@hispania-news.com
Community newspaper (English and Spanish). **Founded:** May 05, 1987. **Freq:** Weekly. **Key Personnel:** Robert L. Armendariz, Editor; William Green, Director, Marketing. **Subscription Rates:** $32 Individuals. **URL:** http://www.hispania-news.com/. **Circ:** Paid 2500, Free 7500.

5244 ■ InsideFlyer
Frequent Flyer Services
1930 Frequent Flyer Pt.
Colorado Springs, CO 80915-1500
Phone: (719)597-8889
Fax: (719)597-6855
Free: 800-209-2870
Publisher's E-mail: company@frequentflyerservices.com
Consumer magazine covering air travel for members of frequent flyer programs. **Freq:** Monthly. **Key Personnel:** Randy Petersen, Chief Executive Officer, President. **ISSN:** 1061--4494 (print). **URL:** http://frequentflyerservices.com/advertising. **Remarks:** Accepts advertising. **Circ:** (Not Reported).

5245 ■ InSite
Christian Camp and Conference Association
405 W Rockrimmon Blvd.
Colorado Springs, CO 80919
Phone: (719)260-9400
Religious magazine covering Christian camps and conferences. **Founded:** 1958. **Freq:** Bimonthly. **Print Method:** Offset. **Trim Size:** 8 3/8 x 10 7/8. **Cols./Page:** 3. **Col. Width:** 27 nonpareils. **Col. Depth:** 140 agate lines. **Key Personnel:** Martha Krienke, Editor. **ISSN:** 1094-3455 (print). **Subscription Rates:** $29.95 Non-members; $59.95 Out of country non-members. **URL:** http://www.ccca.org/ccca/InSite_Magazine1.asp. **Formerly**: Christian Camp & Conference Journal. **Ad Rates:** BW $2,545. **Remarks:** Accepts advertising. **Circ:** 8000.

5246 ■ Journal of Strength and Conditioning Research
National Strength and Conditioning Association
1885 Bob Johnson Dr.
Colorado Springs, CO 80906
Phone: (719)632-6722
Fax: (719)632-6367
Free: 800-815-6826
Publication E-mail: jscr@uconn.edu
Journal focusing on strength and conditioning in sport and exercise. **Freq:** Monthly. **Print Method:** Offset. **Trim Size:** 8 1/2 x 11. **Cols./Page:** 2. **Key Personnel:** T. Jeff Chandler, Editor-in-Chief; William J. Kraemer, PhD, Editor-in-Chief. **ISSN:** 1064--8011 (print); **EISSN:** 1533--4287 (electronic). **Subscription Rates:** $363 U.S., Canada, and Mexico; $849 Institutions U.S.; $377

Individuals UK/Australia; rest of the world; $876 Institutions UK/Australia; rest of the world; $862 Institutions, Canada and Mexico. **URL:** http://www.lww.com/Product/1064-8011; http://journals.lww.com/nsca-jscr/Pages/default.aspx. **Formerly**: Journal of Applied Sport Science Research. **Mailing address:** PO Box 908, Philadelphia, PA 19106-3621. **Ad Rates:** BW $565; 4C $925. **Remarks:** Advertising not accepted. **Circ:** Paid 13222.

5247 ■ League Peaks
Junior League of Colorado Springs
210 E Dale St., Ste. 200
Colorado Springs, CO 80903
Phone: (719)632-3855
Publisher's E-mail: office@jlcoloradosprings.org
Magazine containing articles and information of the happenings over the last year in the Junior League of Colorado Springs as well as the annual report. **Freq:** Annual. **Alt. Formats:** PDF. **URL:** http://www.jlcoloradosprings.org/?nd=media. **Remarks:** Accepts advertising. **Circ:** (Not Reported).

5248 ■ LifeWise
Focus on the Family
8605 Explorer Dr.
Colorado Springs, CO 80920
Fax: (719)548-5947
Free: 800-232-6459
Publisher's E-mail: pastors@fotf.org
Freq: Bimonthly. **Remarks:** Advertising not accepted. **Circ:** (Not Reported).

5249 ■ NJCAA Review
National Junior College Athletic Association
1631 Mesa Ave., Ste. B
Colorado Springs, CO 80906-2956
Phone: (719)590-9788
Fax: (719)590-7324
Sports and games magazine. **Freq:** 9/year September through May. **Print Method:** Offset. **Trim Size:** 8 3/8 x 11. **Cols./Page:** 2. **Col. Width:** 42 nonpareils. **Col. Depth:** 140 agate lines. **ISSN:** 0047--2956 (print). **Subscription Rates:** $45 Individuals /year; $5 Single issue. **URL:** http://www.njcaa.org/media/review/About_NJCAA_Review. **Formerly**: Juco Review. **Remarks:** Accepts advertising. **Circ:** 5000.

5250 ■ The Numismatist: For Collectors of Coins, Medals, Tokens and Paper Money
American Numismatic Association
818 N Cascade Ave.
Colorado Springs, CO 80903-3208
Fax: (719)634-4085
Free: 800-367-9723
Publisher's E-mail: ana@money.org
Freq: Monthly. **Print Method:** Offset. **Trim Size:** 7 3/8 x 9 1/4. **Cols./Page:** 3. **Col. Width:** 12 picas. **Col. Depth:** 46.5 picas. **Key Personnel:** David Truesdell, Manager, Sales, phone: (719)482-9847. **ISSN:** 0029--6090 (print). **Subscription Rates:** Included in membership. **URL:** http://www.money.org/the-numismatist. **Ad Rates:** BW $982. **Remarks:** Accepts advertising. **Circ:** Controlled ‡26000.

5251 ■ Organization Development Journal
International Society for Organization Development and Change
PO Box 50827
Colorado Springs, CO 80949
Publisher's E-mail: info@isodc.org
Contains articles on organization development for practitioners and academics. **Freq:** Quarterly. **ISSN:** 0889--6402 (print). **Subscription Rates:** $25 U.S.; Included in membership. **URL:** http://www.isodc.org/page-1730212. **Remarks:** Accepts advertising. **Circ:** 1000.

5252 ■ Plugged In
Focus on the Family
8605 Explorer Dr.
Colorado Springs, CO 80920
Fax: (719)548-5947
Free: 800-232-6459
Publisher's E-mail: pastors@fotf.org
A Catholic magazine designed to help equip parents, youth leaders, ministers, and teens with the essential tools that will enable then to understand, navigate and, impact the culture in which they live. **Freq:** Monthly. **Key Personnel:** Bob Smithouser, Editor; Steven Isaac, Editor; Adam R. Holz, Associate Editor. **Subscription Rates:** $24 Individuals; $1.67 Single issue. **URL:** http://www.pluggedinonline.com. **Remarks:** Advertising not accepted. **Circ:** (Not Reported).

5253 ■ Prorodeo Sports News: The Voice of ProRodeo
Professional Rodeo Cowboys Association
101 Pro Rodeo Dr.
Colorado Springs, CO 80919
Phone: (719)593-8840
Fax: (719)548-4876
Professional rodeo magazine. **Freq:** Biweekly. **Print Method:** Offset. **Trim Size:** 8 5/8 x 11 1/8. **Cols./Page:** 4. **Col. Width:** 2 1/3 inches. **Col. Depth:** 9 7/8 inches. **ISSN:** 0161--5815 (print). **URL:** http://www.prorodeo.com. **Remarks:** Accepts advertising. **Circ:** (Not Reported).

5254 ■ Racquetball
International Racquetball Federation
1631 Mesa Ave.
Colorado Springs, CO 80906
Phone: (719)433-2017
Publisher's E-mail: lstonge@internationalracquetball.com
Magazine containing articles regarding racquetball. **Freq:** Bimonthly. **ISSN:** 1060- 877X (print). **Subscription Rates:** Included in membership. **URL:** http://internationalracquetball.com. **Remarks:** Accepts advertising. **Circ:** 45000.

5255 ■ Racquetball Magazine
USA Racquetball
2812 W Colorado Ave., Ste. 200
Colorado Springs, CO 80904-2906
Phone: (719)635-5396
Fax: (719)635-0685
The official publication of the United States Racquetball Association. **Freq:** Quarterly. **Trim Size:** 8 3/8 x 10 7/8. **Key Personnel:** Steve Czarnecki, Executive Director. **ISSN:** 1060--877X (print). **Subscription Rates:** Included in membership. **URL:** http://www.teamusa.org/usa-racquetball/racquetball-magazine. **Remarks:** Accepts advertising. **Circ:** (Not Reported).

5256 ■ RESCUE Magazine
Association of Gospel Rescue Missions
7222 Commerce Center Dr., Ste. 120
Colorado Springs, CO 80919
Phone: (719)266-8300
Fax: (719)266-8600
Free: 800-473-7283
Publisher's E-mail: info@agrm.org
Freq: Bimonthly. **URL:** http://www.agrm.org/agrm/Publications1.asp. **Remarks:** Advertising not accepted. **Circ:** 4500.

5257 ■ Space Observer
Colorado Publishing Co.
31 E Platt, Ste. 300
Colorado Springs, CO 80903
Phone: (719)634-5905
Publisher's E-mail: csbj@csbj.com
Military newspaper (tabloid) for personnel at Peterson Air Force Base, NORAD, Space Command, Falcon A.F.B., and the Canadian Defense Forces. **Freq:** Weekly (Thurs.). **Print Method:** Web offset. **Trim Size:** 11 1/4 x 17 1/4. **Cols./Page:** 6. **Col. Width:** 1 5/8 inches. **Col. Depth:** 16 inches. **Key Personnel:** Ralph Routon, Executive Editor. **Alt. Formats:** PDF. **URL:** http://csmng.com/spaceobserver. **Remarks:** Accepts advertising. **Circ:** (Not Reported).

5258 ■ The Star: Magazine of the Mercedes-Benz Club of America
Mercedes-Benz Club of America
1907 Lelaray St.
Colorado Springs, CO 80909-2872
Phone: (719)633-6427
Fax: (719)633-9283
Free: 800-637-2360
Magazine covering the history, new models, events, and news about Mercedes-Benz autos; including technical information on maintenance, operation, and restoration. **Freq:** Bimonthly. **Print Method:** Offset. **Trim Size:** 8 3/8 x 10 7/8. **Cols./Page:** 3. **Col. Width:** 2 1/4 inches. **Col. Depth:** 10 inches. **Key Personnel:** Gary Anderson, Editor. **USPS:** 911-480. **Subscription Rates:** $45 Individuals; $55 Institutions, Canada other countries. **URL:** http://www.mbca.org/star-issues. **Ad Rates:** BW $1,829; 4C $2,437. **Remarks:** Accepts advertising. **Circ:** Paid ‡19735.

5259 ■ Strength and Conditioning Journal: The Professional Journal of the National Strength and Conditioning Association
National Strength and Conditioning Association
1885 Bob Johnson Dr.
Colorado Springs, CO 80906
Phone: (719)632-6722
Fax: (719)632-6367
Free: 800-815-6826
Peer-reviewed journal covering strength and conditioning research. **Freq:** Bimonthly. **Trim Size:** 8.5 x 10.88. **Key Personnel:** T. Jeff Chandler, Editor-in-Chief. **ISSN:** 1524--1602 (print); **EISSN:** 1533--4295 (electronic). **Subscription Rates:** $237 U.S., Canada, and Mexico; $297 Institutions; $246 Other countries; $317 Institutions, other countries. **URL:** http://journals.lww.com/nsca-scj/pages/default.aspx. **Formerly**: Strength and Conditioning; National Strength & Cond. Assoc. Journal. **Ad Rates:** BW $1,190; 4C $1,990. **Remarks:** Accepts advertising. **Circ:** Paid 28000.

5260 ■ SupportWorld
Help Desk Institute
121 S Tejon, Ste. 1100
Colorado Springs, CO 80903-2254
Phone: (719)955-8146
Fax: (719)955-8114
Free: 800-248-5667
Publisher's E-mail: support@thinkhdi.com
Magazine containing a broad array of topics related to technical support that may be of particular interest to customer service professionals, frontline technical support agents, desktop support professionals, external support professionals and service desk executives. **Freq:** 6/year. **Subscription Rates:** $79 Individuals online. **URL:** http://www.thinkhdi.com/topics/library/supportworld.aspx. **Remarks:** Accepts advertising. **Circ:** (Not Reported).

5261 ■ U.S.A. Table Tennis Magazine
U.S.A. Table Tennis
4065 Sinton Rd., Ste 120
Colorado Springs, CO 80907-5093
Phone: (719)866-4583
Fax: (719)632-6071
Publisher's E-mail: admin@usatt.org
Freq: Bimonthly. **ISSN:** 1089- 1870 (print). **USPS:** 942-0000. **Subscription Rates:** Included in membership. **URL:** http://www.teamusa.org/usa-table-tennis/magazine. **Remarks:** Accepts advertising. **Circ:** 7000.

5262 ■ U.S.A. Wrestler
U.S.A. Wrestling
6155 Lehman Dr.
Colorado Springs, CO 80918-3456
Phone: (719)598-8181
Fax: (719)598-9440
Freq: Bimonthly. **Subscription Rates:** $18 /year for nonmembers; free for members. **Remarks:** Accepts advertising. **Circ:** (Not Reported).

5263 ■ USA Table Tennis Magazine: The Official Magazine of USA Table Tennis
U.S.A. Table Tennis
4065 Sinton Rd., Ste 120
Colorado Springs, CO 80907-5093
Phone: (719)866-4583
Fax: (719)632-6071
Publisher's E-mail: admin@usatt.org
Magazine covering table tennis. **Freq:** Bimonthly. **Print Method:** Offset. **Trim Size:** 8 3/8 x 10. **Cols./Page:** 3. **Key Personnel:** Steve Hopkins, Editor-in-Chief; Marie Hopkins, Editor-in-Chief. **ISSN:** 1089--1870 (print). **URL:** http://www.teamusa.org/usa-table-tennis/magazine. **Formerly**: Table Tennis Topics; Spin; Table Tennis Today. **Ad Rates:** BW $550. **Remarks:** Accepts advertising. **Circ:** (Not Reported).

5264 ■ USA Ultimate Magazine
U.S.A. Ultimate
5825 Delmonico Dr., Ste. 350
Colorado Springs, CO 80919
Phone: (719)219-8322
Free: 800-872-4384
Publisher's E-mail: info@usaultimate.org

Circulation: ★ = AAM; △ or • = BPA; ♦ = CAC; ❑ = VAC; ⊕ = PO Statement; ‡ = Publisher's Report; Boldface figures = sworn; Light figures = estimated.

Magazine featuring reports, reviews, rules, championships and competitions, and team rankings and standings about the Ultimate sport. **Freq:** Quarterly. **Subscription Rates:** Included in membership. **URL:** http://www.usaultimate.org/multimedia/usa_ultimate_magazine. **Circ:** (Not Reported).

5265 ■ Volleyball USA
USA Volleyball
4065 Sinton Rd., Ste. 200
Colorado Springs, CO 80907
Phone: (719)228-6800
Fax: (719)228-6899
Publisher's E-mail: postmaster@usav.org
Freq: Quarterly. **Subscription Rates:** $10 /year; $24 outside US; included in membership dues. **Remarks:** Accepts advertising. **Circ:** 140000.

5266 ■ Wellbriety!
White Bison
5585 Erindale Dr., Ste. 203
Colorado Springs, CO 80918
Phone: (877)871-1495
Fax: (719)548-9407
Free: 877-871-1495
Publisher's E-mail: info@whitebison.org
Freq: Annual. **Alt. Formats:** PDF. **URL:** http://www.whitebison.org/wellbriety-online-magazine.php. **Remarks:** Advertising not accepted. **Circ:** (Not Reported).

5267 ■ HCJB-FM - 89.3
1065 Garden of the Gods Rd.
Colorado Springs, CO 80907
Phone: (719)590-9800
Fax: (719)590-9801
Free: 800-873-4859
Email: info@reachbeyond.org
Format: Religious. **Founded:** 1931. **Key Personnel:** Wayne Pederson, President. **Ad Rates:** Noncommercial. **URL:** http://www.reachbeyond.org.

5268 ■ KATC-FM - 95.1
6805 Corporate Dr., Ste. 130
Colorado Springs, CO 80919
Phone: (719)593-2700
Fax: (719)593-2727
Format: Country. **Owner:** Citadel Broadcasting Corp., 7201 W Lake Mead Blvd., Ste. 400, Las Vegas, NV 89128-8366, Ph: (702)804-5200, Fax: (702)804-8250. **ADI**: Colorado Springs-Pueblo, CO. **Key Personnel:** Scott Jones, Sales Mgr.; Bobby Irwin, Operations Mgr. **URL:** http://www.951Nashfm.com.

5269 ■ KBIQ-FM - 102.7
7150 Campus Dr., Ste. 150
Colorado Springs, CO 80920
Phone: (719)531-5438
Fax: (719)531-5588
Format: Contemporary Christian. **Operating Hours**: Continuous. **Key Personnel:** Jack Hamilton, Music Dir., jack@kbiqradio.com; Lance Montgomery, Dir. of Production, lance@kbiqradio.com; Kim Bratton, Bus. Mgr. **Wattage**: 57,000 ERP. **Ad Rates:** Advertising accepted; rates available upon request. **URL:** http://www.kbiqradio.com.

5270 ■ KCME-FM - 88.7
1921 N Weber St.
Colorado Springs, CO 80907
Phone: (719)578-5263
Free: 800-492-5263
Format: Classical; Big Band/Nostalgia; Jazz. **Owner:** Cheyenne Mountain Public Broadcast House, at above address, Colorado Springs, CO. **Founded:** 1977. **Operating Hours**: Continuous; 3% network, 97% local. **Key Personnel:** Jeanna Wearing, Gen. Mgr., genmanager@kcme.org; Brenda Bratton, Office Mgr., officemanager@kcme.org. **Wattage**: 13,000. **Ad Rates:** Noncommercial. **URL:** http://www.kcme.org.

5271 ■ KCMN-AM - 1530
5050 Edison Ave., Ste. 218
Colorado Springs, CO 80915
Phone: (719)570-1530
Format: Big Band/Nostalgia; Oldies. **Owner:** DJR Broadcasting, at above address. **Founded:** 1963. **Operating Hours**: Continuous. **ADI**: Colorado Springs-Pueblo, CO. **Wattage**: 15,000. **Ad Rates:** Noncommercial. Combined advertising rates available with KLZ, KLT.

5272 ■ KCSF-AM - 1300
6805 Corporate Dr., Ste. 130
Colorado Springs, CO 80919
Phone: (719)593-2700
Owner: Citadel Broadcasting Corp., 7201 W Lake Mead Blvd., Ste. 400, Las Vegas, NV 89128-8366, Ph: (702)804-5200, Fax: (702)804-8250. **ADI**: Colorado Springs-Pueblo, CO. **Wattage**: 5,000 ERP. **Ad Rates:** Accepts Advertising.

5273 ■ KDZA-FM - 107.9
2864 S Circle Dr., Ste. 300
Colorado Springs, CO 80906
Phone: (719)540-9200
Format: Oldies; Country. **Owner:** iHeartMedia Inc., 200 E Basse Rd., San Antonio, TX 78209, Ph: (210)832-3314. **Founded:** 1975. **Operating Hours**: Continuous. **ADI**: Colorado Springs-Pueblo, CO. **Wattage**: 100,000. **Ad Rates:** Advertising accepted; rates available upon request. $60-100 for 60 seconds. **URL:** http://www.z1079rocks.com.

5274 ■ KEPC-FM - 89.7
5675 S Academy Blvd.
Colorado Springs, CO 80906
Phone: (719)502-3131
Free: 800-456-6847
Format: Alternative/New Music/Progressive. **Owner:** Pikes Peak Community College, 5675 S Academy Blvd., Colorado Springs, CO 80906, Ph: (719)502-2000, Free: 866-411-7722. **Founded:** 1974. **Operating Hours**: Continuous. **Wattage**: 10,000. **Ad Rates:** Noncommercial. **URL:** http://www.ppcc.edu.

5275 ■ KGFT-FM - 100.7
7150 Campus Dr., Ste. 150
Colorado Springs, CO 80920
Phone: (719)531-5438
Fax: (719)531-5588
Format: Religious. **Simulcasts:** KZNT-AM. **Networks:** ESPN Radio; ABC. **Owner:** Salem Media Group Inc., 4880 Santa Rosa Rd., Camarillo, CA 93012, Ph: (805)987-0400, Fax: (805)384-4520. **Founded:** 1992. **Operating Hours**: Continuous. **ADI**: Colorado Springs-Pueblo, CO. **Key Personnel:** Carrie Lakey, Gen. Mgr.; Kim Bratton, Bus. Mgr., kbratton@kbiqradio.com. **Wattage**: 77,000 ERP. **Ad Rates:** Advertising accepted; rates available upon request. Combined advertising rates available with KBIQ-FM. **URL:** http://www.kgftradio.com.

5276 ■ KIBT-FM - 96.1
2864 S Circle Dr., Ste. 300
Colorado Springs, CO 80906
Phone: (719)540-9200
Fax: (719)579-0882
Format: Hip Hop; Top 40; Classic Rock. **Formerly**: KMOM-FM. **ADI**: Colorado Springs-Pueblo, CO. **Wattage**: 450. **URL:** http://www.beatcolorado.com.

5277 ■ KILO-FM - 94.3
1805 E Cheyenne Rd.
Colorado Springs, CO 80905
Phone: (719)633-5837
Fax: (719)634-5837
Free: 800-727-5456
Format: Album-Oriented Rock (AOR). **Founded:** 1966. **Operating Hours**: Continuous. **ADI**: Colorado Springs-Pueblo, CO. **Wattage**: 59,200. **Ad Rates:** Noncommercial. **URL:** http://www.kilo943.com.

5278 ■ KILO and KRXP - 103.9
1805 E Cheyenne Rd.
Colorado Springs, CO 80906
Phone: (719)634-4896
Fax: (719)634-5837
Format: Alternative/New Music/Progressive. **Networks:** Independent. **Founded:** 1979. **Formerly**: KCSJ-FM; KYZX-FM. **Operating Hours**: Continuous. **ADI**: Colorado Springs-Pueblo, CO. **Wattage**: 50,000. **Ad Rates:** Advertising accepted; rates available upon request. **URL:** http://www.1039rxp.com.

5279 ■ KKFM-FM - 98.1
6805 Corporate Dr., Ste. 130
Colorado Springs, CO 80919
Phone: (719)593-2700
Fax: (719)593-2727
Email: irwin@cumulus.com
Format: Classic Rock. **Networks:** ABC. **Owner:** Citadel Broadcasting Corp., 7201 W Lake Mead Blvd., Ste. 400, Las Vegas, NV 89128-8366, Ph: (702)804-5200, Fax: (702)804-8250. **Founded:** 1958. **Key Personnel:** Bobby Irwin, Operations Mgr., Prog. Dir., bobby.irwin@citcomm.com. **Wattage**: 71,000 ERP. **Ad Rates:** Advertising accepted; rates available upon request. Combined advertising rates available with KKMG-FM, KSPZ-FM, KVOR-AM, KTWK-AM. **URL:** http://www.kkfm.com.

5280 ■ KKLI-FM - 106.3
2864 S Cir. Dr., Ste. 150
Colorado Springs, CO 80906
Phone: (719)540-9200
Owner: iHeartMedia Inc., 200 E Basse Rd., San Antonio, TX 78209, Ph: (210)832-3314. **Wattage**: 1,600 ERP. **Ad Rates:** Accepts Advertising.

5281 ■ KKMG-FM - 98.9
6805 Corporate Center Dr., Ste. 130
Colorado Springs, CO 80919
Phone: (719)593-2700
Fax: (719)593-2727
Format: Top 40. **Networks:** Independent. **Owner:** Citadel Broadcasting Corp., 7201 W Lake Mead Blvd., Ste. 400, Las Vegas, NV 89128-8366, Ph: (702)804-5200, Fax: (702)804-8250. **Operating Hours**: Continuous. **ADI**: Colorado Springs-Pueblo, CO. **Wattage**: 57,000. **Ad Rates:** $75-150 per unit. Combined advertising rates available with KKFM-FM, KSPZ-FM, KVOR-AM, KTWK-AM. **URL:** http://www.989magicfm.com.

5282 ■ KKPK-FM - 92.9
6805 Corporate Dr., Ste. 130
Colorado Springs, CO 80919
Phone: (719)593-2700
Email: hookmeup@929peakfm.com
Format: Sports; News. **Owner:** Citadel Broadcasting Corp., 7201 W Lake Mead Blvd., Ste. 400, Las Vegas, NV 89128-8366, Ph: (702)804-5200, Fax: (702)804-8250. **Founded:** 1960. **ADI**: Colorado Springs-Pueblo, CO. **Key Personnel:** Bobby Irwin, Contact, bobby.irwin@citcomm.com. **Wattage**: 60,000 ERP. **Ad Rates:** Advertising accepted; rates available upon request. **URL:** http://www.929peakfm.com.

5283 ■ KKTV-TV - 11
3100 N Nevada Ave.
Colorado Springs, CO 80907
Phone: (719)634-2844
Fax: (719)632-0808
Format: Commercial TV. **Networks:** CBS. **Owner:** Gray Television Inc., 4370 Peachtree Rd. NE, No. 400, Atlanta, GA 30319-3054, Ph: (404)266-8333. **Founded:** 1952. **Operating Hours**: Continuous. **ADI**: Colorado Springs-Pueblo, CO. **Key Personnel:** Nick Matesi, News Dir.; Tim Merritt, Gen. Mgr.; Mark Doan, Chief Engineer. **Ad Rates:** $10-700 per unit. **URL:** http://www.kktv.com.

5284 ■ KRCC-FM - 91.5
912 N Weber St.
Colorado Springs, CO 80907
Phone: (719)473-4801
Fax: (719)473-7863
Free: 800-748-2727
Email: info@krcc.org
Format: News. **Networks:** National Public Radio (NPR); Public Radio International (PRI); Corporation for Public Broadcasting. **Owner:** Colorado College, 14 E Cache La Poudre St., Colorado Springs, CO 80903, Ph: (719)389-6000. **Founded:** 1951. **ADI**: Colorado Springs-Pueblo, CO. **Key Personnel:** Mike Procell, Operations Mgr., mike@krcc.org; Jeff Bieri, Program Mgr., jeff@krcc.org; Greg Bennett, Dir. of Production, greg@krcc.org; Joel Belik, Chief Engineer, joel@krcc.org; Mary Ellen Davis, Sales Mgr., maryellen@krcc.org. **Wattage**: 2,100 ERP. **Ad Rates:** Noncommercial. **URL:** http://www.krcc.org.

5285 ■ KRDO-AM - 1240
399 S Eighth St.
Colorado Springs, CO 80905
Phone: (719)632-1515
Email: krdonews@krdo.com
Format: News. **Networks:** ABC. **Owner:** News Press & Gazette Co., 825 Edmond St., Saint Joseph, MO. **Founded:** 1947. **Operating Hours**: Continuous; 88% network, 12% local. **ADI**: Colorado Springs-Pueblo, CO. **Key Personnel:** Tim Larson, Gen. Mgr., t.larson@krdo.com; Joe Reed, Chief Engineer, j.reed@krdo.com; Mike Lewis, Program Mgr., m.lewis@krdo.com. **Wattage**: 1,000. **Ad Rates:** Noncommercial. Combined advertis-

ing rates available with KRDO-FM, KSKX-FM. **URL:** http://www.krdo.com.

5286 ■ KRDO-FM - 105.5
399 S Eighth St.
Colorado Springs, CO 80905
Phone: (719)575-6285

Format: Jazz. **Networks:** ABC. **Owner:** WorldNow, 27-01 Queens Plz. N, Ste. 502, Long Island, NY 11101, Ph: (212)931-1200. **Founded:** 1973. **Formerly**: KWYD-FM; KHII-FM; KSKX-FM. **Operating Hours**: Continuous. **ADI**: Colorado Springs-Pueblo, CO. **Key Personnel:** Mike Lewis, Prog. Dir., m.lewis@krdo.com; Tim Larson, Gen. Mgr., t.larson@krdo.com; Michael Sipes, News Dir., m.sipes@krdo.com. **Wattage**: 490. **Ad Rates:** Advertising accepted; rates available upon request. **URL:** http://www.krdo.com.

5287 ■ KRDO-TV - 13
399 S 8th St.
Colorado Springs, CO 80905
Phone: (719)632-1515

Format: Commercial TV. **Networks:** ABC. **Owner:** Pike's Peak Broadcasting Co., at above address. **Founded:** 1953. **Operating Hours**: 18 hours Daily. **ADI**: Colorado Springs-Pueblo, CO. **Key Personnel:** Tim Larson, Gen. Mgr., t.larson@krdo.com; Michael Sipes, News Dir., m.sipes@krdo.com; Joe Reed, Chief Engineer, j.reed@krdo.com. **Wattage**: 282 KW. **Ad Rates:** Noncommercial. **URL:** http://www.krdo.com.

5288 ■ KRLJ-FM - 89.1
912 N Weber St.
Colorado Springs, CO 80903
Phone: (719)473-4801

Format: Public Radio; Music of Your Life; News; Talk; Information. **Operating Hours**: Continuous. **Key Personnel:** Delaney Utterback, Gen. Mgr., delaney@krcc.org; Mike Procell, Operations Mgr., mike@krcc.org; Jeff Bieri, Music Dir., jeff@krcc.org; Greg Bennett, Dir. of Production, greg@krcc.org; Mary Ellen Davis, Sales Mgr., maryellen@krcc.org; Eric Whitney, News Dir., eric@krcc.org; Joel Belik, Chief Engineer, joel@krcc.org. **Wattage**: 740 ERP. **Ad Rates:** Noncommercial. Underwriting available. **URL:** http://krcc.org.

5289 ■ KTLF-FM - 90.5
1665 Briargate Blvd., Ste. 100
Colorado Springs, CO 80920
Phone: (719)593-0600
Free: 855-593-0600

Format: Religious. **Simulcasts:** KTLC-FM. **Owner:** Educational Communications of Colorado Springs, at above address. **Founded:** 1989. **Operating Hours:** Continuous. **ADI**: Colorado Springs-Pueblo, CO. **Key Personnel:** Rick McConnell, Div. Mgr.; Marge Wallace, Office Mgr., marge@ktlf.org; Sharick Wade, Creative Dir., sharick@ktlf.org. **Wattage**: 20,000 ERP. **Ad Rates:** Noncommercial. **URL:** http://www.lightpraise.org.

5290 ■ KTPL-FM - 88.3
1665 Briargate Blvd., Ste. 100
Colorado Springs, CO 80920
Phone: (719)593-0600
Fax: (719)593-2399

Format: Contemporary Christian. **Founded:** Sept. 2008. **Key Personnel:** Sharick Wade, Dir. of Programs. **Ad Rates:** Noncommercial. **URL:** http://www.lightpraise.org.

K234AI-FM - See Las Vegas, NV

5291 ■ KVOR-AM - 740
6805 Corporate Dr., Ste. 130
Colorado Springs, CO 80919
Phone: (719)593-2700

Format: News; Talk. **Networks:** CBS; CNN Radio; Fox; ABC. **Owner:** Citadel Broadcasting Corp., 7201 W Lake Mead Blvd., Ste. 400, Las Vegas, NV 89128-8366, Ph: (702)804-5200, Fax: (702)804-8250. **Founded:** 1922. **Operating Hours**: Continuous. **ADI**: Colorado Springs-Pueblo, CO. **Key Personnel:** Charlie Stone, News Dir. **Wattage**: 3,300. **Ad Rates:** Advertising accepted; rates available upon request. KTWK-AM. **URL:** http://www.kvor.com.

5292 ■ KVUU-FM - 99.9
2864 S Circle Dr., Ste. 150
Colorado Springs, CO 80906
Phone: (719)540-9200

Format: Adult Contemporary. **Founded:** 1976. **Operating Hours**: Continuous. **ADI**: Colorado Springs-Pueblo, CO. **Wattage**: 67,400. **Ad Rates:** Advertising accepted; rates available upon request.

5293 ■ KWHS-TV - 51
1710 Briargate Blvd., Ste. 423
Colorado Springs, CO 80920
Phone: (719)228-0651

Founded: 1992. **ADI**: Colorado Springs-Pueblo, CO. **Key Personnel:** Dan Smith, Gen. Mgr. **URL:** http://www.mykwhs.com.

5294 ■ KXRM-TV - 21
560 Wooten Rd.
Colorado Springs, CO 80915
Phone: (719)596-2100
Fax: (719)591-4180

Format: Commercial TV. **Networks:** Fox. **Owner:** Sinclair Broadcast Group Inc., 10706 Beaver Dam Rd., Hunt Valley, MD 21030, Ph: (410)568-1500, Fax: (410)568-1533. **Founded:** 1985. **Operating Hours**: Continuous. **ADI**: Colorado Springs-Pueblo, CO. **Wattage**: 51,000 ERP H. **Ad Rates:** Advertising accepted; rates available upon request. **URL:** http://www.coloradoconnection.com.

5295 ■ KXTU-TV - 57
560 Wooten Rd.
Colorado Springs, CO 80915
Phone: (719)596-2100
Fax: (719)591-4180
URL: http://www.fox21news.com.

5296 ■ KZNT-AM - 1460
1750 Campus Dr., Ste. 150
Colorado Springs, CO 80920

Format: Talk; News. **Owner:** Salem Media Group Inc., 4880 Santa Rosa Rd., Camarillo, CA 93012, Ph: (805)987-0400, Fax: (805)384-4520. **Founded:** 2002. **Operating Hours**: 4 a.m.-7 p.m. **Key Personnel:** Eric Getzinger, Chief Sales Ofc.; Jon Cobb, Gen. Sales Mgr.; Julie Smith, Promotions Dir.; Jack Hamilton, Music Dir.; Kim Bratton, Bus. Mgr. **Ad Rates:** Advertising accepted; rates available upon request. **URL:** http://www.newstalk1460.com.

5297 ■ WAY-FM - 103.1
PO Box 64500
Colorado Springs, CO 80962
Phone: (719)533-0300
Free: 866-457-9293
Email: supportservices@wayfm.com

Format: Religious; Contemporary Christian. **Networks:** USA Radio. **Owner:** WAY-FM Media Group Inc., 5540 Tech Center Dr., Ste. 200, Colorado Springs, CO 80919, Ph: (719)533-0300. **Founded:** 1987. **Operating Hours**: Continuous; 90% network, 10% local. **Key Personnel:** Dusty Rhodes, Sr. VP; Lloyd Parker, COO; Bob Augsburg, CEO, President, Founder. **Wattage**: 50,000. **Ad Rates:** Noncommercial. **URL:** http://www.wayfm.com/contact-us.

CORTEZ

Montezuma Co. Montezuma Co. (SW). 45 m W of Durango. Tourism. Manufactures match sticks. Oil wells. Pine timber. Agriculture. Fruit, dairy. Livestock.

5298 ■ Cortez Journal
Animas Publishing Inc.
123 Roger Smith Ave.
Cortez, CO 81321
Phone: (970)565-8527
Fax: (970)565-8532

Community orientation. **Freq:** Semiweekly Tuesday and Friday. **Print Method:** Offset. **Cols./Page:** 6. **Col. Width:** 26 nonpareils. **Col. Depth:** 301 agate lines. **Key Personnel:** Russell Smyth, Managing Editor; Suzy Meyer, Publisher, Editor; Peggy Daves, Business Manager. **Subscription Rates:** $41 Individuals in Montezuma County, annual; $65 Out of area annual. **Formerly**: Montezuma Valley Journal. **Remarks:** Advertising accepted; rates available upon request. **Circ:** ‡6685.

5299 ■ Dolores Star
Animas Publishing Inc.
123 N Roger Smith Ave.
Cortez, CO 81321
Phone: (970)565-8527
Fax: (970)565-8532
Publication E-mail: dstar@hubwest.com

Community newspaper. **Freq:** Weekly (Thurs.). **Print Method:** Offset. **Cols./Page:** 4. **Col. Width:** 28 nonpareils. **Col. Depth:** 182 agate lines. **USPS:** 159-560. **Subscription Rates:** $41 Individuals in county; $65 Out of area. **URL:** http://www.cortezjournal.com; http://doloresstar.com/apps/pbcs.dll/section?category=ds. **Remarks:** Color advertising accepted; rates available upon request. **Circ:** (Not Reported).

5300 ■ KRTZ-FM - 98.7
2402 Hawkins St.
Cortez, CO 81321
Phone: (970)565-6565
Fax: (970)565-8567
Email: radio@krtzradio.com

Format: Adult Contemporary. **Founded:** 1981. **Operating Hours**: Continuous. **Wattage**: 27,000 ERP. **Ad Rates:** Advertising accepted; rates available upon request. $6.90-13.20 for 30 seconds; $8.40-16 for 60 seconds. **URL:** http://www.krtzradio.com.

5301 ■ KSJD-FM - 91.5
PO Box 116
Box 970
Cortez, CO 81321

Format: Alternative/New Music/Progressive; Contemporary Hit Radio (CHR). **Networks:** National Public Radio (NPR); American Public Radio (APR). **Owner:** Basin Area Voc-Technical School, at above address, Fax: (303)565-8457. **Founded:** 1990. **Operating Hours**: 6 a.m.-midnight, Mon.-Fri. **Wattage**: 150. **URL:** http://ksjd.org/contact-us.

CRAIG

Moffat Co. Moffat Co. (NW). 213 m NW of Denver. Creamery. Ships livestock. Oil, gas wells. Stock, grain farms.

5302 ■ Craig Daily Press
WorldWest L.L.C.
466 Yampa Ave.
Craig, CO 81625
Phone: (970)824-7031
Fax: (970)824-6810

Community newspaper. **Freq:** Daily. **Print Method:** Offset. **Cols./Page:** 5. **Col. Width:** 24 nonpareils. **Col. Depth:** 224 agate lines. **Key Personnel:** Joshua Roberts, Editor, phone: (970)875-1791; Amy Fontenot, Manager, Circulation, phone: (970)875-1785; Bryce Jacobson, Publisher, phone: (970)875-1788. **ISSN:** 1440--6000 (print). **USPS:** 144-060. **URL:** http://www.craigdailypress.com. **Formerly:** Northwest Colorado Daily Press. **Mailing address:** PO Box 5, Craig, CO 81626-0005. **Remarks:** Accepts advertising. **Circ:** (Not Reported).

5303 ■ KPYR-FM - 88.3
Bridges Broadcast Ctr.
7409 S Alton Ct.
Centennial, CO 80112
Phone: (303)871-9191
Fax: (303)733-3319
Free: 800-722-4449
Email: info@cpr.org

Format: News; Public Radio. **Owner:** Colorado Public Radio, at above address. **Key Personnel:** Mark Coulter, VP of Production; Dan Murphy, VP of HR; Max Wycisk, President; Sean Nethery, Sr. VP. **Wattage**: 250. **URL:** http://www.cpr.org.

5304 ■ KRAI-AM - 550
1111 W Victory Way
Craig, CO 81625
Phone: (970)824-6574
Fax: (970)826-4581
Email: 55country@krai.com

Format: Country. **Networks:** AP; CNN Radio. **Owner:** Wild West Radio Inc., at above address. **Founded:** 1948. **Operating Hours**: 5 a.m.-midnight. **ADI**: Denver (Steamboat Springs), CO. **Key Personnel:** Frank Hanel, Gen. Mgr., frank@krai.com. **Wattage**: 5,000. **Ad Rates:** Noncommercial. Combined advertising rates available with KRAI-FM, 55COUNTRY-AM. **URL:** http://www.krai.com.

CRESTED BUTTE

Gunnison Co. Gunnison Co. (W). 28 m N of Gunnison. Western State College. Tourism. Recreation and ski area.

Circulation: ★ = AAM; △ or • = BPA; ♦ = CAC; ❑ = VAC; ⊕ = PO Statement; ‡ = Publisher's Report; Boldface figures = sworn; Light figures = estimated.

5305 ■ Crested Butte Chronicle & Pilot
Crested Butte Chronicle and Pilot
301 Belleview Ave., Ste. 6A
Crested Butte, CO 81224
Phone: (970)349-0500
Fax: (970)349-9876
Newspaper. **Freq:** Weekly (Fri.). **Print Method:** Offset. **Cols./Page:** 5. **Col. Width:** 12 picas. **Col. Depth:** 15 inches. **Key Personnel:** Kimberly Metsch, Contact; Faith Gasparrini, Contact. **Subscription Rates:** $45 Individuals /year in county; $80 Two years in county; $49 Individuals /year out of county; $88 Two years out of county. **URL:** http://www.crestedbuttenews.com. **Mailing address:** PO Box 369, Crested Butte, CO 81224. **Remarks:** Accepts advertising. **Circ:** (Not Reported).

5306 ■ KBUT-FM - 90.3
508 Maroon Ave.
Crested Butte, CO 81224
Phone: (970)349-5225
Fax: (970)349-6440
Email: kbut@kbut.org
Format: News; Contemporary Hit Radio (CHR). **Owner:** Crested Butte Mountain Educational Radio Inc., 508 Maroon Ave., Crested Butte, CO 81224, Ph: (970)349-5225, Fax: (970)349-6440. **Founded:** 1986. **Operating Hours**: Continuous. **Key Personnel:** Chad Reich, Dir. of Programs, chad@kbut.org. **Wattage**: 1,000 ERP. **Ad Rates:** Accepts Advertising. **Mailing address:** PO Box 308, Crested Butte, CO 81224. **URL:** http://www.kbut.org.

CRESTONE

5307 ■ Desert Call
Spiritual Life Institute
c/o NADA Hermitage
PO Box 219
Crestone, CO 81131
Phone: (719)256-4778
Publisher's E-mail: nada@spirituallifeinstitute.org
Freq: Quarterly. **Print Method:** Offset. **Trim Size:** 8 1/2 x 11. **Cols./Page:** 2. **Col. Width:** 3 7/8 inches. **Col. Depth:** 9 1/2 inches. **ISSN:** 1076--304X (print). **Subscription Rates:** $20 Individuals 1 year, U.S.; $36 Individuals 2 years, U.S.; $28 Individuals 1 year, Canada; $50 Individuals 2 years, Canada; $38 Individuals 1 year, other countries; $64 Individuals 2 years, other countries. **Alt. Formats:** PDF. **URL:** http://www.spirituallifeinstitute.org/Publications%202.html. **Formerly**: Forefront. **Remarks:** Advertising not accepted. **Circ:** 3500, Paid 2200, Non-paid 200.

CRIPPLE CREEK

Teller Co. Teller Co. (C). 20 m SW of Colorado Springs. Residential.

5308 ■ Miniature Donkey Talk
International Miniature Donkey Registry
PO Box 982
Cripple Creek, CO 80813
Phone: (719)689-2904
Magazine featuring current news, training, health care, research and promotion information about donkeys. **Freq:** Quarterly. **Subscription Rates:** $15 Individuals online, email copy per year; $40 By mail printed per year. **Alt. Formats:** PDF. **URL:** http://www.web-donkeys.com/productsb.php?cat=6. **Remarks:** Accepts advertising. **Circ:** 5800.

5309 ■ Miniature Donkey Talk: The Talk of the Donkey World
Pheasant Meadow Farm
PO Box 982
Cripple Creek, CO 80813
Phone: (719)689-2904
Publication E-mail: minidonk@qis.net
Trade magazine covering animal health care, management, and training. **Freq:** Bimonthly. **Print Method:** Web offset. **Trim Size:** 7 3/4 x 10 3/4. **Cols./Page:** 2. **Col. Width:** 3 1/4 inches. **Col. Depth:** 9 1/4 inches. **Key Personnel:** Bonnie Gross, Editor. **ISSN:** 1058--7063 (print). **Subscription Rates:** $20 Individuals online only 1 year; $35 Two years online or by mail. **URL:** http://www.web-donkeys.com/products.php?cat=6. **Remarks:** Accepts advertising. **Circ:** (Not Reported).

DELTA

Delta Co. Delta Co. (W). 44 m SE of Grand Junction. Tannery; flour mills; cannery. Spruce, fir timber. Agriculture.

5310 ■ Delta County Independent
Leader Publishing Company Inc.
401 Meeker St.
Delta, CO 81416-1918
Fax: (970)874-4424
Local newspaper. **Freq:** Weekly (Wed.). **Print Method:** Offset. **Trim Size:** 12.5 x 22. **Cols./Page:** 6. **Col. Width:** 11 picas. **Col. Depth:** 21 inches. **Key Personnel:** Randy Sunderland, General Manager; Pat Sunderland, Managing Editor. **USPS:** 152-700. **Subscription Rates:** $29 Individuals print & online; $33 Individuals outside Delta or Montrose counties; $37 Other countries. **URL:** http://www.deltacountyindependent.com. **Remarks:** Accepts advertising. **Circ:** (Not Reported).

DENVER

Denver Co. Denver Co. (NC). The State Capital. 112 m N of Pueblo. University of Denver; law, theology, vocational and other colleges and private schools. U. S. Mint. Meat packing; oil refineries; brewery; coffee roasters; vegetable and fruit canneries; food processing; printing and publishing houses. Uranium market center. Mining and farming machinery, rubber goods, fabricated metal, chemical and allied stone and clay products, western clothing, transportation equipment, scientific instruments, feed, flour, luggage manufactured.

5311 ■ AHS Hernia
American Hernia Society
4582 S Ulster St., Ste. 201
Denver, CO 80237
Fax: (303)771-2550
Free: 866-798-5406
Publisher's E-mail: contact@americanherniasociety.org
Journal promoting research and teaching in the field of hernia. Containing clinical studies and basic research to the following: groin hernias, internal hernias, the abdominal wall (anterior and postero-lateral aspects), the diaphragm and the perineum. **Freq:** 5/year February, April, June, August and October. **ISSN:** 1265-4906 (print); **EISSN:** 1248-9204 (electronic). **Subscription Rates:** Included in membership; $384 Individuals. **URL:** http://americanherniasociety.org/members/journal-hernia/. **Remarks:** Accepts advertising. **Circ:** 1000.

5312 ■ American Journal of Orthopsychiatry
American Orthopsychiatric Association
PO Box 202798
Denver, CO 80220
Phone: (720)708-0187
Fax: (303)366-3471
Publisher's E-mail: americanortho@gmail.com
Journal on an interdisciplinary and interprofessional approach to mental health treatment. **Freq:** Quarterly. **Print Method:** Offset. **Trim Size:** 6 3/4 x 9 3/4. **Cols./Page:** 2. **Col. Width:** 29 nonpareils. **Col. Depth:** 112 agate lines. **Key Personnel:** Larry Smyth, Associate Editor; Oscar A. Barbarin, Editor; Gary B. Melton, PhD, Editor. **ISSN:** 0002--9432 (print). **Subscription Rates:** $90 Members domestic, student; $499 Institutions domestic; $126 Nonmembers domestic; $116 Members international; surface, student; $161 Nonmembers international; surface; $560 Institutions, other countries surface mail; $137 Members international; air mail, student; $580 Institutions, other countries air mail; $178 Nonmembers international; air mail. **URL:** http://www.aoatoday.com/Publications_AJO.html; http://www.apa.org/pubs/journals/ort/pricing.aspx. **Ad Rates:** BW $500. **Remarks:** Color advertising not accepted. **Circ:** ‡10000.

5313 ■ AORN Journal
Association of PeriOperative Registered Nurses
2170 S Parker Rd., Ste. 400
Denver, CO 80231
Phone: (303)755-6300
Fax: (800)847-0045
Free: 800-755-2676
Publication E-mail: aornjournal@aorn.org
Peer-reviewed journal publishing perioperative nurses and other health care professionals with practical and theoretical information. **Freq:** Monthly. **Print Method:** Web Offset. **Trim Size:** 8 3/8 x 10 7/8. **Cols./Page:** 2. **Col. Width:** 32 nonpareils. **Col. Depth:** 112 agate lines. **Key Personnel:** Zac Wiggy, Associate Editor; Joy Don Baker, Editor-in-Chief; Liz Cowperthwaite, Managing Editor. **ISSN:** 0001--2092 (print). **Subscription Rates:** $191 Individuals online and print; $246 Other countries online and print; $261 Canada online and print. **URL:** http://www.aorn.org/aorn-journal. **Remarks:** Advertising accepted; rates available upon request. **Circ:** (Not Reported).

5314 ■ Architecture and Design of the West
New West Publishing Inc.
10200 E Girard Bldg. B. Ste. 222
Denver, CO 80231
Phone: (303)751-0696
Fax: (303)751-6524
Magazine containing profiles of architects, designers and new products and ideas for the home and commercial environment. **Freq:** Quarterly. **Subscription Rates:** $22 Individuals 6 issue (1year); $42 Individuals 12 issues (2years); $62 Individuals 18 issues (3 years). **URL:** http://www.coloradoexpression.com/architecture-design. **Remarks:** Accepts advertising. **Circ:** (Not Reported).

5315 ■ The Argus
ANG Newspapers
101 W Colfax Ave., Ste. 950
Denver, CO 80202
Phone: (510)293-2733
Newspaper. **Freq:** Weekly. **URL:** http://www.insidebayarea.com/argus. **Remarks:** Accepts advertising. **Circ:** (Not Reported).

5316 ■ Asian Avenue Magazine
Asian Avenue Magazine Inc.
PO Box 221748
Denver, CO 80222
Phone: (303)937-6888
Fax: (303)750-8488
Magazine focusing on the Asian Pacific American community and culture. **Freq:** Monthly. **Key Personnel:** Yutai Christina Guo, Founder, Publisher; Annie Guo, President. **ISSN:** 1932--1449 (print). **Subscription Rates:** $25 Individuals; $40 Two years. **URL:** http://asianavemag.com. **Remarks:** Accepts advertising. **Circ:** (Not Reported).

5317 ■ AWWA Journal
American Water Works Association
6666 W Quincy Ave.
Denver, CO 80235
Phone: (303)794-7711
Fax: (303)347-0804
Free: 800-926-7337
Publisher's E-mail: service@awwa.org
Journal containing peer-reviewed research and technical articles and features of the best management practices, industry news, and current information on regulations affecting the water industry in the United States. **Freq:** Monthly. **ISSN:** 0003- 150X (print). **Subscription Rates:** included in membership dues. **Alt. Formats:** CD-ROM. **URL:** http://www.awwa.org/publications/journal-awwa.aspx. **Remarks:** Accepts advertising. **Circ:** (Not Reported).

5318 ■ Bible Advocate
Church of God - Seventh Day
PO Box 33677
Denver, CO 80233
Phone: (303)452-7973
Publication E-mail: bap.orders@cog7.org
Magazine encouraging Christian growth and offering biblical guidance. **Freq:** Bimonthly. **Print Method:** Offset. **Trim Size:** 83/8 x 10 7/8. **Cols./Page:** 3. **Col. Width:** 26 nonpareils. **Col. Depth:** 132 agate lines. **Key Personnel:** Calvin Burrell, Editor. **ISSN:** 0746--0104 (print). **Subscription Rates:** Free. **URL:** http://baonline.org. **Remarks:** Advertising not accepted. **Circ:** (Not Reported).

5319 ■ The Bloomsbury Review
The Bloomsbury Review
1553 Platte St., Ste. 206
Denver, CO 80202-1167
Phone: (303)455-3123
Fax: (303)455-7039
Publication E-mail: info@bloomsburyreview.com
Tabloid of book reviews, interviews with writers and poets, book-related essays, and original poetry. **Freq:** Quarterly. **Print Method:** Offset. **Trim Size:** 11 1/4 x 15

1/4. **Cols./Page:** 4. **Col. Width:** 14 picas. **Col. Depth:** 168 agate lines. **Key Personnel:** Marilyn Auer, Editor-in-Chief, Publisher. **ISSN:** 0276--1564 (print). **Subscription Rates:** $34 Canada; $46 Other countries; $20 Individuals /year; $35 Two years. **URL:** http://www.bloomsburyreview.com. **Remarks:** Advertising accepted; rates available upon request. **Circ:** Paid ‡5000, Controlled ‡30000.

5320 ■ Breakfast Serials: Good Books Unbound
Breakfast Serials Inc.
859 S York St.
Denver, CO 80209
Phone: (303)777-0538
Fax: (303)777-0478
Free: 888-827-9014
Magazine publishing original serial stories-novels written and illustrated by acclaimed writers and artists. **Key Personnel:** Sue Kassirer, Executive Editor; Linda Wright, Chief Executive Officer, Publisher. **Remarks:** Advertising not accepted. **Circ:** (Not Reported).

5321 ■ Cartography and Geographic Information Science
Cartography and Geographic Information Society
c/o Michael P. Finn, President
Box 25046, MS 510
Denver, CO 80225-0046
Publisher's E-mail: curtis.sumner@acsm.net
Scholarly journal for cartographers and geographic information systems professionals. **Freq:** 5/year. **Key Personnel:** Scott M. Freundschuh, Executive Editor. **ISSN:** 1523--0406 (print); **EISSN:** 1545--0465 (electronic). **Subscription Rates:** $201 Institutions online; $230 Institutions print and online. **Alt. Formats:** PDF. **URL:** http://www.cartogis.org/publications/journal.php. **Formerly:** The American Cartographer. **Remarks:** Advertising not accepted. **Circ:** (Not Reported).

5322 ■ Cement Americas
Mining Media Inc.
8751 E Hampden Ave., Ste. B-1
Denver, CO 80231
Phone: (303)283-0640
Fax: (303)283-0641
Publisher's E-mail: info@mining-media.com
Magazine providing comprehensive coverage of the North and South American cement markets from raw material extraction to delivery and transportation to end user. **Freq:** Quarterly. **Key Personnel:** Josephine Smith, Associate Editor; Steve Prokopy, Editor; Tom Judson, Manager, Sales; Mark Kuhar, Editor, phone: (330)722-4081. **Subscription Rates:** $81 Elsewhere. **URL:** http://cementamericas.com/magazine. **Ad Rates:** BW $2,945; 4C $3,870. **Remarks:** Accepts advertising. **Circ:** △**6960**.

5323 ■ The Charleston Advisor
The Charleston Advisor
6180 E Warren Ave.
Denver, CO 80222
Phone: (303)282-9706
Fax: (303)282-9743
Journal is concerned with reviewing of web products for information professionals. **Freq:** Quarterly. **Key Personnel:** Rebecca Lenzini, Editor-in-Chief, President, Publisher; George Machovec, Managing Editor. **ISSN:** 1525--4011 (print); **EISSN:** 1525--4003 (electronic). **Subscription Rates:** $295 Libraries; $495 Institutions. **Ad Rates:** 4C $1875. **Remarks:** Accepts advertising. **Circ:** (Not Reported).

5324 ■ The Clarion
2055 E Evans Ave.
Denver, CO 80208
Publication E-mail: abalakrishnan93@gmail.com
Collegiate newspaper. **Founded:** 1892. **Freq:** Weekly (Tues.). **Print Method:** Offset. **Cols./Page:** 4. **Col. Width:** 2 1/4 inches. **Col. Depth:** 16 inches. **Key Personnel:** Connor W. Davis, Editor-in-Chief. **URL:** http://duclarion.com. **Ad Rates:** GLR $.41; BW $525; PCI $7.50. **Remarks:** Accepts advertising. **Circ:** 1,000.

5325 ■ Coal Age
Mining Media Inc.
8751 E Hampden Ave., Ste. B-1
Denver, CO 80231
Phone: (303)283-0640
Fax: (303)283-0641
Publisher's E-mail: info@mining-media.com
Coal production magazine. **Founded:** 1916. **Freq:** Monthly. **Print Method:** Offset. **Trim Size:** 8 1/8 x 10 7/8. **Cols./Page:** 3. **Col. Width:** 2 3/16 inches. **Col. Depth:** 10 inches. **Key Personnel:** Steve Fiscor, Editor-in-Chief, phone: (904)721-2925, fax: (904)721-2930; Russ Carter, Managing Editor, phone: (801)943-9039; William M. Turley, Editor, phone: (630)585-7530. **ISSN:** 1040-7820 (print). **Subscription Rates:** Free. **URL:** http://www.coalage.com. **Formerly:** Coal. **Ad Rates:** BW $5060; 4C $6580. **Remarks:** Accepts advertising. **Circ:** ‡16,163.

5326 ■ Colorado Country Life
Colorado Rural Electric Association
5400 N Washington St.
Denver, CO 80216
Phone: (303)455-2700
Fax: (303)455-2807
Publication E-mail: mneeley@coloradocountrylife.org
Association journal. **Freq:** Monthly. **Print Method:** Offset. **Trim Size:** 8 1/8 x 10 7/8. **Cols./Page:** 3. **Col. Width:** 2 3/8 inches. **Col. Depth:** 10 inches. **Key Personnel:** Tom Compton, Board Member; Mona Neeley, Editor; Chris Morgan, President. **ISSN:** 1090--2503 (print). **USPS:** 469-400. **Subscription Rates:** $8. **URL:** http://www.coloradocountrylife.coop. **Ad Rates:** BW $2831.70; PCI $78.15. **Remarks:** Color advertising accepted; rates available upon request. **Circ:** 188145, Paid 186000.

5327 ■ Colorado Editor
Colorado Press Association
1120 Lincoln St., Suite 912
Denver, CO 80203
Phone: (303)571-5117
Fax: (303)571-1803
Publisher's E-mail: coloradopress@colopress.net
Regional newspaper on journalism. **Freq:** Monthly. **Print Method:** Offset. **Cols./Page:** 5. **Col. Width:** 12 picas. **Col. Depth:** 12 inches. **Key Personnel:** Samantha Johnston, Executive Director, phone: (303)571-1803. **ISSN:** 0162--0010 (print). **USPS:** 122-940. **URL:** http://www.coloradopressassociation.com/colorado-editor. **Remarks:** Accepts advertising. **Circ:** ‡1100.

5328 ■ Colorado Episcopalian
Episcopal Diocese of Colorado
1300 Washington St.
Denver, CO 80203-2008
Phone: (303)837-1173
Free: 800-446-3081
Publisher's E-mail: colorado@coloradodiocese.org
Religious tabloid. **Freq:** Quarterly. **Print Method:** Web offset. **Cols./Page:** 3. **Col. Width:** 3 1/4 inches. **Col. Depth:** 13 inches. **ISSN:** 0883--6728 (print). **USPS:** 123-000. **Subscription Rates:** Free. **Alt. Formats:** PDF. **URL:** http://www.coloradodiocese.org/Connect%20With%20Us/the-colorado-episcopalian.html. **Remarks:** Advertising not accepted. **Circ:** (Not Reported).

5329 ■ The Colorado Leader
The Colorado Leader
2150 S Bellaire St., Ste. 208
Denver, CO 80222
Phone: (303)922-0589
Publication E-mail: info@coloradoleader.com
Community newspaper. **Freq:** Weekly. **Print Method:** Offset. **Cols./Page:** 5. **Col. Width:** 22 nonpareils. **Col. Depth:** 217 agate lines. **Key Personnel:** Jim Eitzen, Owner, Publisher; Jayne Owston, Managing Editor. **Subscription Rates:** $45 Individuals. **URL:** http://www.coloradoleader.com. **Remarks:** Accepts advertising. **Circ:** (Not Reported).

5330 ■ Colorado Medicine
Colorado Medical Society
7351 Lowry Blvd., Ste. 110
Denver, CO 80230-6083
Phone: (720)859-1001
Fax: (720)859-7509
Free: 800-654-5653
Magazine publishing news for physicians in Colorado. **Freq:** Bimonthly. **Print Method:** Offset. **Trim Size:** 8 1/2 x 11. **Cols./Page:** 3. **Col. Width:** 26 nonpareils. **Col. Depth:** 133 agate lines. **Key Personnel:** Mike Campo, Contact; Alfred Gilchrist, Chief Executive Officer. **ISSN:** 0199--7343 (print). **Subscription Rates:** Included in membership. **URL:** http://www.cms.org/communications/colorado-medicine. **Mailing address:** PO Box 17550, Denver, CO 80217. **Remarks:** Accepts advertising. **Circ:** 7000.

5331 ■ Colorado Municipalities
Colorado Municipal League
1144 Sherman St.
Denver, CO 80203
Phone: (303)831-6411
Fax: (303)860-8175
Free: 866-578-0936
Publisher's E-mail: cml@cml.org
Magazine covering items of interest to local government in Colorado. **Freq:** Bimonthly February, April, June, August, October and December. **Print Method:** Offset. **Trim Size:** 8 1/4 x 10 3/4. **Cols./Page:** 3. **Col. Width:** 26 nonpareils. **Col. Depth:** 126 agate lines. **Key Personnel:** Traci Stoffel, Editor, phone: (303)831-6411. **USPS:** 123-140. **Subscription Rates:** $150 Individuals /year; $40 Individuals /year (for non-profits and government agencies); $25 Single issue. **URL:** http://www.cml.org/magazines. **Ad Rates:** 4C $850. **Remarks:** Advertising accepted; rates available upon request. **Circ:** Combined 5000.

5332 ■ Colorado Outdoors
Colorado Parks and Wildlife
6060 Broadway
Denver, CO 80216-1000
Phone: (303)297-1192
Publisher's E-mail: kay.knudsen@state.co.us
Regional publication. Hunting, fishing and watching wildlife. **Freq:** Bimonthly. **Print Method:** Offset. **Trim Size:** 8 1/2 x 11. **Cols./Page:** 2. **Col. Width:** 26 nonpareils. **Col. Depth:** 102 agate lines. **Key Personnel:** Jerry Neal, Editor. **ISSN:** 0010--1699 (print). **Subscription Rates:** $10.50 Individuals; $19 Two years; $13 Individuals combined. **URL:** http://coloradooutdoorsmag.com. **Remarks:** Advertising not accepted. **Circ:** (Not Reported).

5333 ■ Concrete Products
Mining Media Inc.
8751 E Hampden Ave., Ste. B-1
Denver, CO 80231
Phone: (303)283-0640
Fax: (303)283-0641
Publication E-mail: dmarsh@prismb2b.com
Magazine on concrete products and ready-mixed concrete. **Founded:** 1947. **Freq:** Monthly. **Print Method:** Web Offset. **Trim Size:** 7 7/8 x 10 3/4. **Cols./Page:** 3. **Col. Width:** 26 nonpareils. **Col. Depth:** 140 agate lines. **Key Personnel:** Don Marsh, Editor; Bill Green, Manager, Sales. **USPS:** 128-180. **Subscription Rates:** Free online; $96 Other countries print. **URL:** http://concreteproducts.com. **Ad Rates:** BW $3,800; 4C $4,750. **Remarks:** Advertising accepted; rates available upon request. **Circ:** Combined △**18500**.

5334 ■ Confetti
New West Publishing Inc.
10200 E Girard Bldg. B. Ste. 222
Denver, CO 80231
Phone: (303)751-0696
Fax: (303)751-6524
Magazine serving as a resource guide for great event planning and entertaining. From the best private dinner parties to the most elaborate corporate events. **Freq:** Annual. **Subscription Rates:** $22 Individuals 6 issues (1year); $42 Individuals 12 issues (2years); $62 Individuals 18 issues (3years). **URL:** http://www.coloradoexpression.com/confetti. **Remarks:** Accepts advertising. **Circ:** (Not Reported).

5335 ■ COPD: Journal of Chronic Obstructive Pulmonary Disease
Informa Healthcare
National Jewish Medical & Research Center
1400 Jackson St., Rm. K701b
Denver, CO 80206
Publisher's E-mail: healthcare.enquiries@informa.com
Journal publishing a wide range of research, reviews, case studies, and conference proceedings to promote advances in the pathophysiology, diagnosis, management, and control of lung and airway disease and inflammation. **Freq:** 6/year. **Key Personnel:** Vito Brusasco, Editor-in-Chief. **ISSN:** 1541--2555 (print); **EISSN:** 1541--2563 (electronic). **Subscription Rates:** $2531 Institutions online only; $2664 Institutions print & online.

Circulation: ★ = AAM; △ or • = BPA; ♦ = CAC; ❑ = VAC; ⊕ = PO Statement; ‡ = Publisher's Report; Boldface figures = swom; Light figures = estimated.

URL: http://www.tandfonline.com/toc/icop20/current#.Vm_949J94dU. **Circ:** 150.

5336 ■ Denver Catholic Register
Archdiocese of Denver
1300 S Steele St.
Denver, CO 80210
Phone: (303)722-4687
Publisher's E-mail: info@archden.org
Catholic newspaper (tabloid). **Freq:** Weekly (Wed.). **Print Method:** Offset. **Trim Size:** 10 1/4 x 14. **Cols./Page:** 6. **Col. Width:** 1 5/8 inches. **Col. Depth:** 14 inches. **USPS:** 557-020. **Subscription Rates:** Included in membership. **URL:** http://denvercatholic.org. **Remarks:** Accepts advertising. **Circ:** (Not Reported).

5337 ■ Denver Law
University of Denver Sturm College of Law
2255 E Evans Ave.
Denver, CO 80208
Phone: (303)871-6000
Fax: (303)871-6378
Publisher's E-mail: admissions@law.du.edu
Alumni magazine for the University of Denver's Sturm College of Law. **Freq:** Semiannual. **Subscription Rates:** Free to qualified subscribers. **URL:** http://www.law.du.edu/index.php/alumni/alumni-magazine. **Circ:** (Not Reported).

5338 ■ The Denver Post
The Denver Post L.L.C.
101 W Colfax Ave.
Denver, CO 80202-5315
Phone: (303)892-5000
Free: 888-454-9572
General newspaper. **Founded:** 1892. **Freq:** Daily. **Print Method:** Letterpress. **Trim Size:** 13 x 22. **Cols./Page:** 6. **Col. Width:** 2 1/16 inches. **Col. Depth:** 22 inches. **Key Personnel:** Gregory Moore, Editor, phone: (303)954-1400; William Dean Singleton, Chairman, Publisher. **URL:** http://www.denverpost.com. **Mailing address:** PO Box 719, Denver, CO 80201-0719. **Remarks:** Accepts advertising. **Circ:** Mon.-Fri. ★**264301**, Sat. ★**593747**, Sun. ★**725178**.

5339 ■ Denver Quarterly
Denver Quarterly
University of Denver
2199 S University Blvd.
Denver, CO 80208
Phone: (303)871-2892
Creative writing journal. **Freq:** Quarterly. **Print Method:** Offset. **Trim Size:** 6 x 9. **Cols./Page:** 1. **Col. Width:** 4 inches. **Col. Depth:** 6 1/4 inches. **Key Personnel:** Laird Hunt, Editor; Bin Ramke, Editor. **ISSN:** 0011--8869 (print). **Subscription Rates:** $25 Individuals /year; $35 Institutions /year; $50 Institutions 2 years; $40 Individuals 2 years; $10 Single issue. **URL:** http://www.du.edu/denverquarterly. **Remarks:** Accepts advertising. **Circ:** (Not Reported).

5340 ■ Denver Urban Spectrum
Echo Media
900 Circle 75 Pky., Ste. 1600
Atlanta, GA 30339
Phone: (770)955-3535
Fax: (770)955-3599
Publisher's E-mail: salesinfo@echo-media.com
Newspaper dedicated to Denver's multi-cultural interests. **Freq:** Monthly delivered every Wednesday. **Subscription Rates:** Free. **URL:** http://echomedia.com/medias/details/6137. **Remarks:** Accepts advertising. **Circ:** Free 25000.

5341 ■ Economics of Education Review
RELX Group P.L.C.
c/o Daniel Rees, Ed.-in-Ch.
Department of Economics
University of Colorado
Denver, CO 80217
Publisher's E-mail: amsterdam@relx.com
Journal dealing with development of sound theoretical, empirical and policy research. It acts as a forum for economists and scholars to exchange ideas and research methods in the field of education. **Freq:** 6/year. **Trim Size:** 7 1/2 x 10. **Cols./Page:** 2. **Col. Width:** 2 3/4 inches. **Col. Depth:** 7 1/2 inches. **Key Personnel:** Daniel Rees, Editor-in-Chief; E.R. Eide, Board Member. **ISSN:** 0272-7757 (print). **URL:** http://www.journals.elsevier.com/economics-of-education-review. **Remarks:** Advertising accepted; rates available upon request. **Circ:** (Not Reported).

5342 ■ EnCompass: The AAA Colorado Magazine
AAA Colorado Inc.
4100 E Arkansas Ave.
Denver, CO 80222
Phone: (303)753-8800
Fax: (888)228-4129
Free: 866-625-3601
Magazine for members of the Colorado American Automobile Association. Contains articles on domestic and foreign travel as well as automotive issues. **Freq:** 6/year. **Print Method:** Offset. **Trim Size:** 8 x 10 1/2. **Cols./Page:** 3. **Col. Width:** 2.125 inches. **Col. Depth:** 135 agate lines. **Key Personnel:** Keith Kaiser, Managing Director. **ISSN:** 0273--6772 (print). **URL:** http://www.colorado.aaa.com/encompass. **Formerly:** Rocky Mountain Motorist. **Ad Rates:** BW $9450. **Remarks:** Advertising accepted; rates available upon request. **Circ:** 370000.

5343 ■ Erosion Control Journal
International Erosion Control Association
3401 Quebec St., Ste. 3500
Denver, CO 80207
Phone: (303)640-7554
Fax: (866)308-3087
Free: 800-455-4322
Publisher's E-mail: ecinfo@ieca.org
Journal featuring information on preventive measures, minimization and control of soil erosion and its sediments. **Subscription Rates:** Included in membership. **URL:** http://www.ieca.org/Resources/ErosionControlJournal.asp. **Remarks:** Accepts advertising. **Circ:** (Not Reported).

5344 ■ 5280 Denver's Magazine
5280 Publishing Inc.
1515 Wazee St., Ste. 400
Denver, CO 80202
Phone: (303)832-5280
Fax: (303)832-0470
Free: 866-271-5280
Magazine focusing on the Mile-High City. **Freq:** Monthly. **Key Personnel:** Daniel Brogan, Founder, President, Editor-in-Chief; Maximillian Potter, Executive Editor; Lindsey B. Koehler, Managing Editor. **Subscription Rates:** $12 Individuals print; $24 Two years print; $36 Individuals print - three years. **URL:** http://www.5280.com. **Remarks:** Accepts advertising. **Circ:** (Not Reported).

5345 ■ FPA Journal of Financial Planning
Financial Planning Association
7535 E Hampden Ave., Ste. 600
Denver, CO 80231
Phone: (303)759-4900
Free: 800-322-4237
Publication E-mail: info@onefpa.org
Freq: Monthly. **Subscription Rates:** $139 U.S.; $164 Canada; $174 Other countries. **Alt. Formats:** PDF. **URL:** http://www.onefpa.org/journal/Pages/Subscribe.aspx. **Remarks:** Accepts advertising. **Circ:** ‡53000.

5346 ■ Highlander: An independent weekly student publication
Regis University
3333 Regis Blvd.
Denver, CO 80221-1099
Phone: (303)458-4126
Free: 800-568-8932
Publisher's E-mail: studentservices@regis.edu
Collegiate newspaper. **Freq:** Weekly during the academic year. **Print Method:** Offset. **Trim Size:** 11 x 17. **Cols./Page:** 5. **Col. Depth:** 1 3/4 inches. **Key Personnel:** Gina Nordini, Editor-in-Chief. **Subscription Rates:** Free. **URL:** http://ruhighlander.com. **Remarks:** Advertising accepted; rates available upon request. **Circ:** (Not Reported).

5347 ■ Human Development
Regis University
3333 Regis Blvd.
Denver, CO 80221-1099
Phone: (303)458-4126
Free: 800-568-8932
Publisher's E-mail: studentservices@regis.edu
Journal updating psychological, psychiatric, medical, and theological information needed by persons fostering the full human development of others. **Founded:** 1980. **Freq:** Quarterly. **Trim Size:** 8 1/4 x 11 in. **Cols./Page:** 2. **Key Personnel:** Robert M. Hamma, Editor-in-Chief; Loughlan Sofield, Senior Editor. **Subscription Rates:** $49 Individuals print & online; $39 Individuals online only; $6 Individuals single issue. **URL:** http://www.humandevelopmentmag.org. **Circ:** Paid ‡10000, Non-paid ‡300.

5348 ■ Human Rights & Human Welfare
University of Denver Josef Korbel School of International Studies Center on Rights Development
Aspen Hall, Rm. 730
2280 S Vine St.
Denver, CO 80210
Phone: (303)871-4610
Fax: (303)871-2124
Publisher's E-mail: cord.du@gmail.com
Journal that publishes literature dealing the areas of human rights, justice and welfare. **Freq:** Quarterly. **Key Personnel:** Daniel J. Whelan, Senior Editor; Jack Donelly, Board Member. **ISSN:** 1533--0834 (print). **URL:** http://www.du.edu/gsis/hrhw. **Circ:** (Not Reported).

5349 ■ Intermountain Jewish News
Intermountain Jewish News
1177 Grant St.
Denver, CO 80203
Phone: (303)861-2234
Fax: (303)832-6942
Publisher's E-mail: email@ijn.com
Jewish newspaper. **Freq:** Weekly. **Print Method:** Offset. **Trim Size:** 10 x 16. **Cols./Page:** 5. **Col. Width:** 11 1/2 picas. **Col. Depth:** 216 agate lines. **Key Personnel:** Miriam Goldberg, Editor, Publisher; Rabbi Hillel Goldberg, PhD, Executive Editor; Seiji Nagata, Manager, Production. **ISSN:** 0047--0511 (print). **Subscription Rates:** $62 Individuals print or online; $112 Two years; $31 Individuals online - 6 months. **URL:** http://www.ijn.com. **Remarks:** Accepts advertising. **Circ:** (Not Reported).

5350 ■ The Journal of Allergy and Clinical Immunology: The Official Publication of the American Academy of Allergy, Asthma and Immunology
Mosby Inc.
c/o Donald Y.M. Leung, Ed.-in-Ch.
National Jewish Medical & Research Center
1400 Jackson St., Ste. J324
Denver, CO 80206
Phone: (303)398-1963
Fax: (303)270-2269
Publication E-mail: jaci@njhealth.org
Journal for clinical allergists and immunologists, as well as dermatologists, internists, general practitioners, pediatricians, and otolaryngologists (ENT physicians) concerned with clinical manifestations of allergies in their practice. **Freq:** 13/yr. **Print Method:** Offset. **Trim Size:** 8 1/8 x 10 7/8. **Cols./Page:** 2. **Col. Width:** 3 and 4 inches. **Col. Depth:** 140 agate lines. **Key Personnel:** Joshua A. Boyce, MD, Associate Editor; Donald Y.M. Leung, MD, Editor-in-Chief; Fred Finkelman, MD, Associate Editor; Stanley J. Szefler, MD, Editor; William T. Shearer, MD, Associate Editor; Andrea J. Apter, MD, Associate Editor; David B. Peden, MD, Associate Editor. **ISSN:** 0091--6749 (print). **Subscription Rates:** $445 Individuals print + online; $598 Canada print + online; $581 Other countries print + online; $193 Students print + online; $261 Students, Canada print + online; $258 Students, other countries print + online. **URL:** http://www.jacionline.org. **Ad Rates:** BW $2285; 4C $1,860. **Remarks:** Accepts advertising. **Circ:** 6000.

5351 ■ Journal of the American Society of Farm Managers and Rural Appraisers
American Society of Farm Managers and Rural Appraisers
950 S Cherry St., Ste. 508
Denver, CO 80246-2664
Phone: (303)758-3513
Fax: (303)758-0190
Publisher's E-mail: info@asfmra.org
Journal providing a forum for those in the farm management, rural appraisal, and agricultural consulting fields to share experiences with others. **Freq:** Annual. **Subscription Rates:** Included in membership; $28 Nonmembers; $38 Other countries. **URL:** http://www.asfmra.org/ag-publications/journal-archives/. **Remarks:**

Advertising not accepted. **Circ:** (Not Reported).

5352 ■ Journal AWWA
American Water Works Association
6666 W Quincy Ave.
Denver, CO 80235
Phone: (303)794-7711
Fax: (303)347-0804
Free: 800-926-7337
Publisher's E-mail: service@awwa.org
Spanish and English language magazine covering the water works industry. **Freq:** Monthly. **Key Personnel:** Marcia Lacey, Editor; Laura High, Managing Editor; John Kayser, Director (Acting). **ISSN:** 0003--150X (print); **EISSN:** 1551--8833 (electronic). **URL:** http://www.awwa.org/publications/journal-awwa.aspx. **Remarks:** Advertising accepted; rates available upon request. **Circ:** (Not Reported).

5353 ■ Journal of Environmental & Engineering Geophysics
Environmental and Engineering Geophysical Society
1720 S Bellaire St., Ste. 110
Denver, CO 80222-4308
Phone: (303)531-7517
Fax: (303)820-3844
Publisher's E-mail: staff@eegs.org
Professional journal covering geoscience. **Freq:** Quarterly. **Key Personnel:** Janet E. Simms, Editor-in-Chief. **ISSN:** 1083--1363 (print). **Subscription Rates:** $90 Individuals; $50 Students. **URL:** http://jeeg.geoscienceworld.org; http://www.eegs.org/jeeg-current-issue. **Ad Rates:** BW $770. **Remarks:** Accepts advertising. **Circ:** 800, 600.

5354 ■ Journal of Environmental Health
National Environmental Health Association
720 S Colorado Blvd., Ste. 1000-N
Denver, CO 80246
Phone: (303)756-9090
Fax: (303)691-9490
Publisher's E-mail: staff@neha.org
Journal covering current issues, new researches, useful products and services, and employment opportunities in the field of environmental health. **Freq:** 10/year. **ISSN:** 0022- 0892 (print). **Subscription Rates:** $135 Individuals /year in U.S.; $160 Other countries /year; $250 Two years; $300 Two years Other Countries. **URL:** http://www.neha.org/JEH/. **Remarks:** Accepts advertising. **Circ:** 7,000.

5355 ■ Journal of Environmental Health: Dedicated to the Advancement of the Environmental Health Professional
National Environmental Health Association
720 S Colorado Blvd., Ste. 1000-N
Denver, CO 80246
Phone: (303)756-9090
Fax: (303)691-9490
Publisher's E-mail: staff@neha.org
Journal presenting environmental health and protection issues. **Freq:** 10/year. **Print Method:** Offset. **Trim Size:** 8 1/2 x 11. **Cols./Page:** 3. **Col. Width:** 13.5 picas. **Col. Depth:** 10 inches. **Key Personnel:** Kristen Ruby, Editor. **ISSN:** 0022--0892 (print). **Subscription Rates:** $135 Individuals 1 year; $160 Other countries 1 year; $250 Two years; $300 Other countries 2 years; $12 Single issue /issue. **URL:** http://www.neha.org/JEH. **Ad Rates:** BW $1130; 4C $1505. **Remarks:** Accepts advertising. **Circ:** Controlled 20000.

5356 ■ Journal of Sugar Beet Research
American Society of Sugar Beet Technologists
800 Grant St., Ste. 300
Denver, CO 80203
Phone: (303)832-4460
Peer-reviewed journal containing research development and latest information about sugar beet. **Freq:** Quarterly. **ISSN:** 0899--1502 (print). **Subscription Rates:** Included in membership. **Alt. Formats:** PDF. **URL:** http://assbt-jsbr.org. **Circ:** (Not Reported).

5357 ■ LA Voz Nueva: The Bilingual Voice of Colorado
La Voz Publishing Company Inc.
4047 Tejon St.
Denver, CO 80211
Phone: (303)936-8556
Fax: (720)889-2455
Publisher's E-mail: news@lavozcolorado.com
Bilingual Newspaper catering to the Hispanic community in Denver County, Colorado. **Freq:** Weekly (Wed.). **Key Personnel:** Pauline Rivera, Publisher. **Subscription Rates:** $12 Individuals. **URL:** http://www.lavozcolorado.com/. **Remarks:** Accepts advertising. **Circ:** Combined ♦**30000**.

5358 ■ Modern Drunkard
Modern Drunkard
135 W 3rd Ave.
Denver, CO 80223
Phone: (303)578-6363
Publisher's E-mail: sales@drunkard.com
Magazine that publishes humorous articles, essays, and interviews dealing with alcohol and alcohol consumption. **Freq:** 6/year. **Key Personnel:** Frank Kelly Rich, Editor, Publisher; Giles Humbert, III, Managing Editor. **Subscription Rates:** $29.99 U.S.; $34.99 Canada; $54.99 Other countries. **URL:** http://www.moderndrunkardmagazine.com. **Ad Rates:** 4C $985. **Remarks:** Accepts advertising. **Circ:** ‡20000.

5359 ■ Mountain Geologist
Rocky Mountain Association of Geologists
910 16th St., Ste. 1214
Denver, CO 80202
Phone: (303)573-8621
Fax: (303)628-0546
Publication E-mail: staff@rmag.org
Freq: Quarterly published; January, April, July and October of each year. **Key Personnel:** Barbara Luneau, Editor; Mark Longman, Editor. **ISSN:** 0027--254X (print). **Subscription Rates:** $15 limited past print issues. **URL:** http://www.rmag.org/i4a/pages/index.cfm?pageID=3345. **Remarks:** Accepts advertising. **Circ:** 2200, 2,200.

5360 ■ Mountain Living
1777 S Harrison St., Ste. 903
Denver, CO 80210
Phone: (303)248-2060
Fax: (303)248-2064
Consumer magazine for mountain living. **Freq:** 7/year. **Print Method:** Web Offset. **Trim Size:** 8 3/8 x 10 7/8. **Key Personnel:** Holly Scott, Publisher; Christine DeOrio, Editor-in-Chief. **ISSN:** 1088--6451 (print). **Subscription Rates:** $14.95 Individuals; $24.95 Two years; $38.95 Out of country; $72.95 Out of country 2 years. **URL:** http://www.mountainliving.com. **Ad Rates:** 4C $4,460. **Remarks:** Accepts advertising. **Circ:** Paid 19700, Non-paid 11300.

5361 ■ Museum Store
Museum Store Association
789 Sherman St., Ste. 600
Denver, CO 80203
Phone: (303)504-9223
Publisher's E-mail: info@museumdistrict.com
Freq: Quarterly. **Subscription Rates:** Included in membership i; $50 Individuals. **URL:** http://museumstoreassociation.org/learning/resources/museum-store-mag. **Remarks:** Advertising not accepted. **Circ:** 2,700.

5362 ■ National Civic Review
Jossey-Bass Publishers
National Civic League
1640 Logan St.
Denver, CO 80203
Phone: (303)571-4343
Fax: (303)571-4404
Publisher's E-mail: info@wiley.com
Journal on citizen democracy, state and local government. **Founded:** 1912. **Freq:** Quarterly. **Print Method:** Offset. **Trim Size:** 7 x 10. **Cols./Page:** 1. **Col. Width:** 6 inches. **Col. Depth:** 8 inches. **Key Personnel:** Michael McGrath, Editor. **ISSN:** 0027-9013 (print). **Subscription Rates:** $66 U.S., Canada, and Mexico print and online; $90 Elsewhere print and online; $243 Institutions print and online; $317 Institutions, other countries print and online. **URL:** http://www.wiley.com/WileyCDA/WileyTitle/productCd-NCR.html. **Remarks:** Advertising not accepted. **Circ:** ‡2250.

5363 ■ National Civic Review: Building Successful Communities
National Civic League
6000 E Evans Ave., Ste. 3-012
Denver, CO 80222
Phone: (303)571-4343
Freq: Quarterly. **ISSN:** 0027- 9013 (print). **Subscription Rates:** included in membership dues; $64 Individuals /year for nonmembers, print. **URL:** http://www.nationalcivicleague.org/national-civic-review. **Remarks:** Advertising not accepted. **Circ:** (Not Reported).

5364 ■ National Coalition Against Domestic Violence--Voice
National Coalition Against Domestic Violence
1 Broadway, Ste. B210
Denver, CO 80203
Phone: (303)839-1852
Fax: (303)831-9251
Publisher's E-mail: mainoffice@ncadv.org
Journal serves to challenge stereotypes of violence, challenges the systems and prejudices that contribute to violence, and presents distinctive, innovative, and tangible ways to end violence. **Freq:** Quarterly. **Subscription Rates:** Included in membership. **Alt. Formats:** PDF. **URL:** http://shop.ncadv.org/publications. **Remarks:** Accepts advertising. **Circ:** (Not Reported).

5365 ■ North American Mining
Mining Media Inc.
8751 E Hampden Ave., Ste. B-1
Denver, CO 80231
Phone: (303)283-0640
Fax: (303)283-0641
Publisher's E-mail: info@mining-media.com
Magazine reporting North American mining environmental and public policy issues. **Freq:** Bimonthly. **Print Method:** Web Offset. **Trim Size:** 8 x 10 3/4. **Cols./Page:** 3. **Key Personnel:** Peter Johnson, President, Publisher, phone: (303)283-0640, fax: (303)283-0641; Steve Fiscor, Editor-in-Chief, Vice President, phone: (904)721-2925, fax: (904)721-2930; Russ Carter, Managing Editor, phone: (801)943-9039. **ISSN:** 1047-7551 (print). **Subscription Rates:** $55 U.S.; $60 Canada; $85 Other countries. **Formerly:** Mining World News. **Ad Rates:** BW $1,870; 4C $2,250. **Remarks:** Accepts advertising. **Circ:** Paid ‡2000, Non-paid ‡5000.

5366 ■ Northwest Motor: Journal for the Automotive Industry
Automotive Counseling & Publishing Company Inc.
PO Box 18731
Denver, CO 80203
Fax: (303)765-4650
Free: 800-530-8557
Publisher's E-mail: edinfo@partsandpeople.com
Automotive Industry Trade Journal for NW & Alaska. **Freq:** Monthly. **Print Method:** Web offset. **Trim Size:** 10 9/16 x 13. **Cols./Page:** 4 and 4. **Col. Width:** 2 3/8 and 2 1/8 inches. **Col. Depth:** 11 10/16 inches. **Key Personnel:** Lance R. Buchner, President, Publisher. **ISSN:** 0029-3393 (print). **Subscription Rates:** $36 Individuals; Free to regional industry. **Ad Rates:** GLR $1495; BW $1495; 4C $1650. **Remarks:** Accepts advertising. **Circ:** Controlled △**12264**.

5367 ■ Out Front Colorado
Out Front Colorado
827 Grant St.
Denver, CO 80203
Phone: (303)778-7900
Fax: (303)778-7978
Newspaper. **Freq:** Biweekly. **Trim Size:** 10 1/4 x 13 1/2. **Key Personnel:** Greg Montoya, Editor-in-Chief; Matt Kailey, Managing Editor; Lynette Elliot, Manager, Sales. **URL:** http://www.outfrontonline.com/about-out-front-colorado. **Ad Rates:** BW $700; 4C $1,180. **Remarks:** Accepts advertising. **Circ:** Free 25000.

5368 ■ Pacific Coast Philology
Pacific Ancient and Modern Language Association
c/o Craig Svonkin, Executive Director
Metropolitan State College of Denver
Campus Box 32
Denver, CO 80217-3362
Publication E-mail: pcp@pamla.org
Peer-reviewed scholarly journal covering classical and modern languages, literatures and cultures. **Freq:** Semiannual. **Trim Size:** 6 x 9. **Key Personnel:** Roswitha Burwick, Editor; Friederike von Schwerin-High, Editor. **ISSN:** 0078--7469 (print). **URL:** http://www.pamla.org/pacific-coast-philology. **Mailing address:** PO Box 173362, Denver, CO 80217-3362. **Remarks:** Advertising not accepted. **Circ:** (Not Reported).

Circulation: ★ = AAM; △ or • = BPA; ♦ = CAC; ❑ = VAC; ⊕ = PO Statement; ‡ = Publisher's Report; Boldface figures = sworn; Light figures = estimated.

5369 ■ Park Science: Integrating research and resource management
U.S. National Park Service Natural Resource Information Division
PO Box 25287
Denver, CO 80225-0287
Bulletin reporting latest and ongoing natural and social science research, its implications for park planning and management, and its application in resource management. **Freq:** 3/year. **Key Personnel:** Jeff Selleck, Editor, phone: (305)369-2147. **ISSN:** 0735--9462 (print); **EISSN:** 1090--9966 (electronic). **URL:** http://www.nature.nps.gov/ParkScience. **Circ:** (Not Reported).

5370 ■ Parts & People
Automotive Counseling & Publishing Company Inc.
PO Box 18731
Denver, CO 80203
Fax: (303)765-4650
Free: 800-530-8557
Publisher's E-mail: edinfo@partsandpeople.com
Trade magazine covering the automotive parts and service industry in the Rocky Mountain, Midwestern, Northern California, River Valley, & Northwestern U.S. regions. **Freq:** Monthly. **Print Method:** Web Offset. **Cols./Page:** 4. **Col. Width:** 2 3/8 inches. **Col. Depth:** 11 5/8 inches. **Key Personnel:** Rob Merwin, Managing Editor; Lance Buchner, President, Publisher. **ISSN:** 1083--771X (print). **Subscription Rates:** Free to qualified subscribers. **URL:** http://www.partsandpeople.com. **Ad Rates:** BW $1,795; 4C $2,145. **Remarks:** Advertising accepted; rates available upon request. **Circ:** Combined 60000.

5371 ■ PATH Intl.'s Strides
Professional Association of Therapeutic Horsemanship International
PO Box 33150
Denver, CO 80221-6920
Phone: (303)452-1212
Fax: (303)252-4610
Free: 800-369-7433
Promotes training for recreation and rehabilitation through horseback riding. Provides information about riding for people with disabilities, including news of the Association and its operating groups, and a calendar of events. **Freq:** Quarterly. **Trim Size:** 8 1/2 x 11. **URL:** http://www.pathintl.org/resources-education/publications. **Formerly:** NARHA News; NARHA Strides. **Remarks:** Advertising accepted; rates available upon request. **Circ:** 4100.

5372 ■ Plastics Today
UBM Canon
3300 E 1st Ave., Ste. 370
Denver, CO 80206
Phone: (303)321-2322
Fax: (303)321-3552
Publisher's E-mail: ubmcanonconferences@ubm.com
Magazine for the plastics industry. **Founded:** 1925. **Freq:** Monthly. **Print Method:** Offset. **Trim Size:** 7 7/8 X 10 3/4. **Cols./Page:** 3. **Col. Width:** 2 3/16 inches. **Col. Depth:** 10 inches. **Key Personnel:** Matt Defosse, Editor-in-Chief; Tony Deligio, Senior Editor; Patrick Lundy, Publisher; John Clark, Senior Editor. **ISSN:** 0026-8275 (print). **Subscription Rates:** $59 Individuals; $99 Two years U.S. and possessions; $110 Canada; $199 Two years for Canada; $150 Other countries; $250 Two years; $199 Canada 2 years; $250 Other countries 2 years. **Online:** UBM Canon UBM Canon. **URL:** http://www.plasticstoday.com. **Formerly:** Modern Plastics Worldwide. **Ad Rates:** BW $8,590; 4C $2,570; BW $7,625. **Remarks:** Accepts advertising. **Circ:** △**39951**, △**43350**, Combined ‡79600.

5373 ■ Rock Products
Mining Media Inc.
8751 E Hampden Ave., Ste. B-1
Denver, CO 80231
Phone: (303)283-0640
Fax: (303)283-0641
Publication E-mail: info@rockproducts.com
Trade magazine focusing on the sand, gravel, crushed stone, cement, lime and gypsum industries. **Freq:** Monthly. **Print Method:** Web Offset. **Trim Size:** 7 7/8 x 10 3/4. **Cols./Page:** 3 and 2. **Col. Width:** 26 and 40 nonpareils. **Col. Depth:** 140 agate lines. **Key Personnel:** Mark S. Kuhar, Editor. **ISSN:** 0035--7464 (print). **URL:** http://www.rockproducts.com; http://www.mining-media.com/publications/rock-products.html. **Remarks:** Accepts advertising. **Circ:** Combined △**20000**.

5374 ■ Rocky Mountain Oil Journal
Rocky Mountain Oil Journal
701 S Logan St., Ste. 112
Denver, CO 80209-4169
Phone: (303)778-8661
Fax: (303)778-2351
Journal covering oil and gas development. **Freq:** Weekly. **Print Method:** Offset. **Cols./Page:** 4. **Col. Width:** 30 nonpareils. **Col. Depth:** 181 agate lines. **Key Personnel:** Jerry Davis, Publisher; Cody A. Huseby, Editor. **ISSN:** 0074--6803 (print). **Subscription Rates:** $169 Individuals 1 year (online only); $289 Individuals 1 year (online current issue plus previous year of article archives); $459 By mail 1 year (online current issue with previous year of article archives); $259 By mail; $339 By mail Canada; $339 By mail first class. **URL:** http://www.rmoj.com. **Formerly:** Montana Oil Journal. **Remarks:** Accepts advertising. **Circ:** 1100.

5375 ■ Sports Talk
American Chiropractic Association Council on Sports Injuries and Physical Fitness
c/o Carly May, Secretary
1720 S Bellaire St., Ste. 406
Denver, CO 80222
Phone: (303)758-1100
Publisher's E-mail: president@acasc.org
Freq: Quarterly. **Subscription Rates:** Included in membership. **Alt. Formats:** PDF. **URL:** http://www.acasc.org/sports-talk. **Remarks:** Advertising not accepted. **Circ:** (Not Reported).

5376 ■ State Legislatures: The National Magazine of State Government and Policy
National Conference of State Legislatures
7700 E 1st Pl.
Denver, CO 80230
Phone: (303)364-7700
Fax: (303)364-7800
Publication E-mail: magazine@ncsl.org
Magazine bringing a national perspective to state politics and government by tracking legislation and issues, examining innovations and ideas, monitoring trends and developments, and exploring operations and procedures in the 50 state legislatures. **Freq:** 10/year. **Print Method:** Offset. **Trim Size:** 8 1/2 x 10 7/8. **Cols./Page:** 3. **Col. Width:** 31 nonpareils. **Col. Depth:** 133 agate lines. **ISSN:** 0147--0641 (print). **Subscription Rates:** $49 Individuals; $82 Two years. **URL:** http://www.ncsl.org/bookstore/state-legislatures-magazine.aspx. **Ad Rates:** BW $3855; 4C $5295. **Remarks:** Advertising accepted; rates available upon request. **Circ:** Paid ‡25663.

5377 ■ University of Denver Water Law Review
Denver University College of Law
2255 E Evans Ave.
Denver, CO 80208
Phone: (303)871-6000
Fax: (303)871-6378
Legal magazine. **Freq:** Semiannual. **Print Method:** Offset. **Cols./Page:** 1. **Col. Width:** 54 nonpareils. **Col. Depth:** 112 agate lines. **Key Personnel:** Jennifer Najjar, Editor-in-Chief. **ISSN:** 0883--9409 (print). **Subscription Rates:** $40 Institutions /year; $20 Students /year; $25 Institutions single issue; $15 Students single issue. **URL:** http://duwaterlawreview.com. **Formerly:** Denver University Law Review: Water Law Review. **Remarks:** Advertising not accepted. **Circ:** (Not Reported).

5378 ■ Westword
Westword Corp.
PO Box 5970
Denver, CO 80217
Phone: (303)296-7744
Fax: (303)296-5416
Publication E-mail: denver.editorial@westword.com
Metro newsweekly. **Founded:** Sept. 1977. **Freq:** Weekly. **Trim Size:** 11 x 14. **Cols./Page:** 8. **Col. Width:** 10 21/32 inches. **Col. Depth:** 14 inches. **Key Personnel:** Patricia Calhoun, Editor. **Subscription Rates:** Free; $50 By mail. **URL:** http://www.westword.com. **Ad Rates:** BW $2,998; 4C $3,673.80; PCI $22. **Remarks:** Accepts advertising. **Circ:** Non-paid ★**105672**.

5379 ■ Zeitschrift fur Neuere Theologiegeschichte
Walter de Gruyter GmbH and Company KG
c/o Prof. Dr. Theodore M. Vial, Jr.
Iliff School of Theology
2201 S University Blvd.
Denver, CO 80210
Publisher's E-mail: info@degruyter.com
Journal focusing on history of theology since the enlightenment. **Freq:** Semiannual. **Print Method:** Offset. **Trim Size:** 12.5 x 22. **Cols./Page:** 6. **Col. Width:** 11 picas. **Col. Depth:** 21 inches. **Key Personnel:** Prof. Dr. Theodore M. Vial, Jr., Editor. **ISSN:** 0943--7592 (print); **EISSN:** 1612--9776 (electronic). **USPS:** 152-700. **Subscription Rates:** €197 Individuals print or online; $295 Institutions print or online; £148 Institutions print or online; €49 Individuals online; $74 Individuals online; £37 Individuals online; €197 Institutions print; $295 Institutions print; £148 Institutions print; €236 print and online - institution and individual; $354 print and online - institution and individual; £177 print and online - institution and individual. **URL:** http://www.degruyter.com/view/j/znth. **Ad Rates:** BW €350; 4C €750. **Remarks:** Accepts advertising. **Circ:** (Not Reported).

Cherry Creek Radio LLC - See Montrose

5380 ■ KALC-FM - 105.9
4700 S Syracuse St., Ste. 1050
Denver, CO 80237
Phone: (303)967-2700
Fax: (303)713-8744
Format: Adult Contemporary; Classic Rock; Album-Oriented Rock (AOR). **Owner:** Entercom Communications Corp., 401 City Ave., Ste. 809, Bala Cynwyd, PA 19004-1130, Ph: (610)660-5610, Fax: (610)660-5620; Clear Channel Communication, 101 Pine St., Dayton, OH 45402. **Founded:** 1959. **Formerly:** KXLT-FM. **Operating Hours:** Continuous. **ADI:** Denver (Steamboat Springs), CO. **Key Personnel:** Sam Hill, Music Dir.; Jeff Silver, Gen. Sales Mgr. **Wattage:** 100,000 ERP. **Ad Rates:** Noncommercial. $100-175 per unit. **URL:** http://www.alice1059.com.

KAVA-AM - See Pueblo

5381 ■ KAZY-FM - 106.7
4695 S Monaco St.
Denver, CO 80237
Phone: (918)664-4581
Format: Album-Oriented Rock (AOR). **Networks:** ABC. **Owner:** Summit Broadcasting Corp., 115 Perimeter Center Pl., Ste. 1150, Atlanta, GA 30346, Ph: (404)394-0707. **Founded:** 1972. **Formerly:** KLZ-FM. **Operating Hours:** Continuous; 5% network, 95% local. **ADI:** Denver (Steamboat Springs), CO. **Key Personnel:** Brian Taylor, Operations Mgr.; Beau Roberts, Music Dir.; Anne Millison, Promotions Dir.; Denny Moore, Gen. Sales Mgr; Berkley Silver, Contact; Lynn Sornsen, Contact; Rich Gerber, Contact; Jack Tyson, Contact. **Wattage:** 100,000. **Ad Rates:** $100-300 for 60 seconds. **URL:** http://kbpi.iheart.com.

5382 ■ KBCO-FM - 97.3
4695 S Monaco
Denver, CO 80237
Phone: (303)444-5600
Fax: (303)930-6890
Email: kbcostudioc@kbco.com
Format: Adult Album Alternative. **Networks:** Independent. **Owner:** iHeartMedia and Entertainment Inc. , 200 E Basse Rd., San Antonio, TX 78209, Ph: (210)822-2828. **Founded:** 1977. **Operating Hours:** Continuous. **Wattage:** 94,000. **Ad Rates:** $90-400 for 30 seconds. **URL:** http://www.kbco.com.

5383 ■ KBDI-TV - 12
2900 Welton St., 1st Fl.
Denver, CO 80205
Phone: (303)296-1212
Fax: (303)296-6650
Free: 800-727-8812
Format: Public TV. **Networks:** Public Broadcasting Service (PBS). **Owner:** Colorado Public Television, 2900 Welton St., Denver, CO 80205. **Founded:** 1978. **Operating Hours:** 12 hours Daily. **Key Personnel:** Scott Yates, Founder; Willard D. Rowland, Jr., President; Paula DeGroat, Bus. Mgr., Dir. of Fin.; Dominic Dezzutti, VP. **Local Programs:** *CIO*, Friday 12:15 p.m. **Wattage:** 229,000. **Ad Rates:** Noncommercial. **URL:** http://www.cpt12.org.

5384 ■ KBNO-AM - 1280
600 Grant St., Ste. 600
Denver, CO 80203
Phone: (303)733-5266
Fax: (303)733-5242
Format: Hispanic. **Networks:** CNN Radio. **Owner:** Latino Communications L.L.C., 3067 Waughtown St., Winston-Salem, NC 27107. **Founded:** 1954. **Operating Hours:** Continuous. **ADI:** Denver (Steamboat Springs), CO. **Local Programs:** *Por Las Tardes con Claudia Reyes,* Monday Tuesday Wednesday Thursday Friday Saturday 3:00 p.m. - 8:00 p.m. 11:00 a.m. - 3:00 p.m. **Wattage:** 5,000 Day and Night. **Ad Rates:** Noncommercial. **URL:** http://www.radioquebueno.com.

KCAP-AM - See Helena, MT

5385 ■ KCEC-TV - 50
777 Grant, Ste. 500
Denver, CO 80203
Phone: (303)832-0050
Format: Hispanic. **Networks:** Univision. **Owner:** Entravision, Golden Hills Broadcasting at above address. **Founded:** 1990. **Operating Hours:** Continuous. **ADI:** Denver (Steamboat Springs), CO. **Key Personnel:** Yrma Rico, Gen. Mgr., Contact, yrico@entravision.com; Sam Fuller, Gen. Sales Mgr., sfuller@entravision.com; Yrma Rico, Contact. **Wattage:** 2,500,000. **Ad Rates:** Advertising accepted; rates available upon request. **URL:** http://noticias.entravision.com/colorado/.

5386 ■ KCFR-AM - 1340
7409 S Alton Ct.
Centennial, CO 80112
Phone: (303)871-9191
Fax: (303)733-3319
Free: 800-722-4449
Email: news@cpr.org
Format: News. **Owner:** Public Broadcasting of Colorado Inc., at above address. **Key Personnel:** Bob Hensler, VP; Jenny Gentry, VP. **Ad Rates:** Noncommercial. **URL:** http://www.cpr.org.

5387 ■ KCKK-AM - 1510
1424 Larimer St., Ste. 100
Denver, CO 80202
Phone: (303)987-0937
Fax: (303)989-3987
Simulcasts: KYGO. **Owner:** Jefferson Pilot Communications Co., at above address. **Formerly:** KYGO-AM. **Key Personnel:** Renee Herlocker, Producer. **Ad Rates:** Advertising accepted; rates available upon request. **URL:** http://www.937therock.com.

5388 ■ KCNC-TV - 4
1044 Lincoln St.
Denver, CO 80203
Phone: (303)861-4444
Email: kcncnews@cbs.com
Format: News; Commercial TV. **Networks:** CBS. **Owner:** CBS Corp., 51 W 52nd St., New York, NY 10019-6188, Ph: (212)975-4321, Fax: (212)975-4516, Free: 877-227-0787. **Founded:** 1952. **ADI:** Denver (Steamboat Springs), CO. **Key Personnel:** John Montgomery, Mgr., jmontgomery@cbs.com. **Ad Rates:** Advertising accepted; rates available upon request. **URL:** http://denver.cbslocal.com.

5389 ■ KDDZ-AM
12136 W Bayaud Ave., Ste. 125
Lakewood, CO 80228
Phone: (303)783-0880
Owner: Radio Disney, 500 S Buena Vista St. MC 7663, Burbank, CA 91521-7716. **Ad Rates:** Advertising accepted; rates available upon request.

5390 ■ KDVR-TV - 31
100 E Speer Blvd.
Denver, CO 80203
Phone: (303)566-7600
Format: Commercial TV. **Networks:** Fox. **Owner:** Fox Television Stations Inc., 1211 Ave. of the Americas, 21st Fl., New York, NY 10036, Ph: (212)301-5400. **ADI:** Denver (Steamboat Springs), CO. **Wattage:** 1,000,000 ERP. **Ad Rates:** Advertising accepted; rates available upon request. **URL:** http://www.kdvr.com.

5391 ■ KFMD-FM - 95.7
4695 S Monaco St.
Denver, CO 80237
Phone: (303)713-8000
Format: Contemporary Hit Radio (CHR). **ADI:** Denver (Steamboat Springs), CO. **Key Personnel:** Lee Larsen, Contact. **Wattage:** 100,000. **URL:** http://957theparty.iheart.com/articles/contact-us-118412/station-and-contact-information-354651.

KGRZ-AM - See Missoula, MT

5392 ■ KHOW-AM - 630
4695 S Monaco St.
Denver, CO 80237
Phone: (303)713-8000
Email: internetsalesdenver@clearchannel.com
Format: Talk; News. **Networks:** Mutual Broadcasting System. **Founded:** 1925. **Operating Hours:** Continuous. **ADI:** Denver (Steamboat Springs), CO. **Wattage:** 5,000. **Ad Rates:** Noncommercial. **URL:** http://www.khow.com.

5393 ■ KIMN-FM - 100.3
720 S Colorado Blvd., Ste. 1200N
Denver, CO 80246
Phone: (303)832-5665
Format: Adult Contemporary. **Owner:** Wilks Broadcast Group L.L.C., 6470 E Johns Crossing, Ste. 450, Duluth, GA 30097, Ph: (678)240-8976, Fax: (678)240-8989. **ADI:** Denver (Steamboat Springs), CO. **Wattage:** 97,000. **Ad Rates:** Noncommercial. **URL:** http://www.mix100.com.

5394 ■ KJMN-FM - 92.1
777 Grant St., 5th Fl.
Denver, CO 80203
Phone: (303)832-0050
Fax: (303)721-1359
Format: Hispanic. **Owner:** Entravision Communications Corporation, 2425 Olympic Blvd., Ste. 6000 W, Santa Monica, CA 90404-4030, Ph: (310)447-3870, Fax: (310)447-3899. **ADI:** Denver (Steamboat Springs), CO. **Key Personnel:** Mario Carrera, Gen. Mgr. **URL:** http://www.entravision.com.

5395 ■ KJQY-FM - 95.5
4695 S Monaco St.
Denver, CO 80237
Phone: (719)545-2080
Fax: (719)543-9898
Format: Contemporary Hit Radio (CHR). **ADI:** Palm Springs, CA. **Key Personnel:** Olene Greenwood, Gen. Mgr. **Wattage:** 100,000.

5396 ■ KKFN-AM - 950
720 S Colorado Blvd., Ste. 1200N
Denver, CO 80246
Phone: (303)405-1100
Format: Sports. **Wattage:** 5,000. **Ad Rates:** Noncommercial. **URL:** http://www.altitudesports950.com.

5397 ■ KKHI-FM - 101.9
8975 E Kenyon Ave.
Denver, CO 80237-1836
Phone: (303)962-3560
Format: Jazz. **Owner:** Bustos Media, LLC, 3100 Fite Cir., Ste. 101, Sacramento, CA 95827. **Formerly:** KGDQ-FM. **ADI:** Denver (Steamboat Springs), CO.

KKXK-FM - See Montrose

5398 ■ KKZN-AM - 760
4695 S Monaco St.
Denver, CO 80237
Phone: (303)713-8000
Format: Talk. **ADI:** Denver (Steamboat Springs), CO. **Wattage:** 50,000. **Ad Rates:** Advertising accepted; rates available upon request. **URL:** http://www.realtalk760.com/main.html.

5399 ■ KLDV-FM - 91.1
PO Box 779002
Rocklin, CA 95677-9972
Fax: (916)251-1901
Free: 800-525-5683
Format: Contemporary Christian. **Owner:** Educational Media Foundation, PO Box 2098, Omaha, NE 68103-2098, Free: 800-434-8400. **Key Personnel:** Alan Mason, COO; Mike Novak, President, CEO. **Wattage:** 100,000. **URL:** http://www.klove.com.

5400 ■ KLWL-FM - 92.5
1560 Broadway, Ste. 1100
Denver, CO 80202
Phone: (303)832-5665
Format: Country. **ADI:** Denver (Steamboat Springs), CO. **Key Personnel:** Bill Gamble, Dir. of Programs, bill.gamble@cbsradio.com. **URL:** http://www.willie925.com/.

5401 ■ KLZ-AM - 560
2150 W 29th Ave., Ste. 300
Denver, CO 80211
Phone: (303)433-5500
Fax: (303)433-1555
Owner: Crawford Broadcasting Co., 725 Skippack St., Ste. 210, Blue Bell, PA 19422. **Operating Hours:** Continuous. **ADI:** Denver (Steamboat Springs), CO. **Wattage:** 5,000 ERP. **Ad Rates:** Accepts Advertising.

5402 ■ KMGH-TV - 7
123 Speer Blvd.
Denver, CO 80203-3417
Phone: (303)832-7777
Fax: (303)832-0119
Format: Commercial TV. **Networks:** ABC. **Owner:** The E. W. Scripps Co., 312 Walnut St., Cincinnati, OH 45202, Ph: (513)977-3000. **Founded:** 1954. **Formerly:** KLZ-TV. **Operating Hours:** Continuous. **ADI:** Denver (Steamboat Springs), CO. **Wattage:** 316,000. **Ad Rates:** Noncommercial. **URL:** http://www.thedenverchannel.com.

5403 ■ KNFO-FM - 106.1
1201 18th St., Ste. 200
Denver, CO 80202
Phone: (720)726-7777
Format: News; Talk; Sports. **Owner:** NRC Broadcasting Co., at above address. **Wattage:** 1,600 ERP. **URL:** http://alwaysmountaintime.com.

5404 ■ KNRV-AM - 1150
2821 S Parker Rd., Ste. 1205
Denver, CO 80014
Format: News; Information; Folk; Sports. **Owner:** New Radio Venture, at above address. **Wattage:** 10,000 ERP. **Ad Rates:** Advertising accepted; rates available upon request. **URL:** http://www.onda1150am.com/Mambo455/.

5405 ■ KOA-AM - 850
4695 S Monaco St.
Denver, CO 80237
Phone: (303)713-8000
Fax: (303)713-8735
Format: News; Talk. **Networks:** ABC; ESPN Radio. **Founded:** 1924. **Operating Hours:** Continuous. **Wattage:** 50,000. **Ad Rates:** Advertising accepted; rates available upon request. **URL:** http://www.850koa.com.

5406 ■ KOOL-FM - 94.5
1560 Broadway, Ste. 1100
Denver, CO 80202
Phone: (303)832-5665
Email: bozo@kool105.com
Format: Oldies. **Owner:** CBS Radio Inc., at above address. **ADI:** Phoenix (Kingman, Prescott), AZ. **Wattage:** 95,600. **Ad Rates:** Advertising accepted; rates available upon request. **URL:** http://www.kool105.com.

5407 ■ KOSI-FM - 101.1
4700 S Syracuse St., Ste. 1050
Denver, CO 80237-2713
Phone: (806)285-1011
Format: Adult Contemporary. **Owner:** Intercom Communications, 55 2nd St., 4th Fl., San Francisco, CA 94105. **Founded:** 1968. **Operating Hours:** Continuous. **ADI:** Denver (Steamboat Springs), CO. **Wattage:** 100,000. **Ad Rates:** Advertising accepted; rates available upon request. **URL:** http://www.kosi101.com/.

5408 ■ KPTT-FM - 95.7
4695 S Monaco St.
Denver, CO 80237
Phone: (303)713-8000
Format: Hip Hop; Urban Contemporary. **Networks:** ABC. **ADI:** Denver (Steamboat Springs), CO. **Wattage:** 100,000 ERP. **Ad Rates:** Advertising accepted; rates available upon request. **URL:** http://www.957theparty.com.

5409 ■ KQMT-FM - 99.5
4700 S Syracuse St., Ste. 1050
Denver, CO 80237
Phone: (303)967-2700
Format: Classic Rock. **Owner:** Entercom Communications Corp., 401 City Ave., Ste. 809, Bala Cynwyd, PA 19004-1130, Ph: (610)660-5610, Fax: (610)660-5620.

Circulation: ★ = AAM; △ or • = BPA; ♦ = CAC; ❑ = VAC; ⊕ = PO Statement; ‡ = Publisher's Report; Boldface figures = sworn; Light figures = estimated.

Founded: 1996. **Operating Hours:** Continuous. **ADI:** Denver (Steamboat Springs), CO. **Wattage:** 74,000. **Ad Rates:** Noncommercial. **URL:** http://www.995themountain.com.

5410 ■ KRFX-FM - 103.5
4695 S Monaco St.
Denver, CO 80237
Phone: (303)713-8000
Fax: (303)713-8743
Format: Classic Rock. **Founded:** 1945. **Formerly:** KOAQ-FM; KOA-FM. **Operating Hours:** Continuous. **ADI:** Denver (Steamboat Springs), CO. **Key Personnel:** Jack Evans, Contact. **Wattage:** 100,000. **Ad Rates:** Advertising accepted; rates available upon request. **URL:** http://www.krfx.com.

5411 ■ KRMA-TV - 6
1089 Bannock St.
Denver, CO 80204
Phone: (303)892-6666
Fax: (303)620-5600
Format: Public TV. **Networks:** Public Broadcasting Service (PBS). **Owner:** Rocky Mountain Public Broadcasting Network, Inc., at above address. **Founded:** Jan. 30, 1956. **Operating Hours:** 12 hours Daily; 65% network, 5% local and 30% syndication. **ADI:** Denver (Steamboat Springs), CO. **Key Personnel:** Doug Price, CEO; Donna Sanford, Contact. **Wattage:** 100,000. **Ad Rates:** Noncommercial. **URL:** http://www.rmpbs.org/home.

5412 ■ KTCL-FM - 93.3
4695 S Monaco St.
Denver, CO 80237
Phone: (303)713-8000
Format: Adult Contemporary; Adult Album Alternative. **Founded:** 1965. **Formerly:** KIIX-FM. **Operating Hours:** Continuous. **Wattage:** 71,000. **Ad Rates:** Noncommercial. **URL:** http://www.area93.com.

5413 ■ KTFD-TV - 14
777 Grant St., Ste. 500
Denver, CO 80203
Phone: (303)832-0050
Fax: (303)832-3410
Owner: Entravision Communications Corporation, 2425 Olympic Blvd., Ste. 6000 W, Santa Monica, CA 90404-4030, Ph: (310)447-3870, Fax: (310)447-3899. **Key Personnel:** Mario Carrera, Gen. Mgr. **URL:** http://www.entravision.com.

5414 ■ KUSA-TV - 9
500 Speer Blvd.
Denver, CO 80203
Phone: (303)871-9999
Format: Commercial TV. **Networks:** NBC. **Owner:** Multimedia Holdings Corp., at above address. **Formerly:** KBTV-TV. **Operating Hours:** Continuous. **ADI:** Denver (Steamboat Springs), CO. **Key Personnel:** Mark Cornetta, Gen. Mgr., President; Patti Dennis, News Dir., VP; Tim Ryan, Asst. Dir. **Ad Rates:** Advertising accepted; rates available upon request. **URL:** http://www.9news.com.

5415 ■ KUVO-FM - 89.3
2900 Welton St., Ste. 200
Denver, CO 80205
Phone: (303)480-9272
Email: info@kuvo.org
Format: Jazz; Public Radio. **Networks:** National Public Radio (NPR); Public Radio International (PRI); BBC World Service. **Owner:** Denver Educational Broadcasting Inc., 2900 Welton St., Ste. 200, Denver, CO 80205, Ph: (303)480-9272. **Founded:** 1985. **ADI:** Denver (Steamboat Springs), CO. **Key Personnel:** Carlos Lando, Gen. Mgr., carlos@kuvo.org; Arturo Gomez, Music Dir., arturo@kuvo.org; Victor Cooper, Production Mgr., victor@kuvo.org. **Wattage:** 22,500 ERP. **Mailing address:** PO Box 2040, Denver, CO 80201-2040. **URL:** http://www.kuvo.org.

5416 ■ KWOF-FM - 92.5
720 S Colorado Blvd., Ste. 1200 N
Denver, CO 80246
Phone: (303)832-5665
Format: Country. **Owner:** Wilks Broadcast Group L.L.C., 100 N Point Center E, Ste. 310, Alpharetta, GA 30022, Ph: (770)754-3211, Fax: (678)893-0123. **Formerly:** KWLI-FM. **Key Personnel:** Randy Shannon, Dir. of Programs. **Ad Rates:** Advertising accepted; rates available upon request. **URL:** http://www.925thewolf.com.

5417 ■ KXKL-FM - 105.1
1560 Broadway, Ste. 1100
Denver, CO 80202
Phone: (303)832-5665
Fax: (303)832-7000
Format: News; Music of Your Life. **Owner:** Wilks Broadcasting Group, LLC, 6470 E Johns Crossing, Ste. 450, Duluth, GA 30097, Ph: (678)240-8976, Fax: (678)240-8989; Chancellor, at above address. **Founded:** 1956. **Formerly:** KXKL-AM. **Operating Hours:** 8:00 a.m. - 4:00 p.m. Monday - Friday. **ADI:** Denver (Steamboat Springs), CO. **Wattage:** 100,000 ERP. **Ad Rates:** Advertising accepted; rates available upon request. **URL:** http://www.kool105.com.

5418 ■ KXPK-FM - 96.5
777 Grant St., 5th Fl.
Denver, CO 80203
Phone: (303)832-0050
Fax: (303)832-3410
Format: Hispanic. **Owner:** Entravision Communication Corp., 2425 Olympic Blvd. W, Ste. 6000, Santa Monica, CA 90404. **Operating Hours:** Continuous. **Wattage:** 100,000. **Ad Rates:** Advertising accepted; rates available upon request. **URL:** http://www.entravision.com.

5419 ■ KXRE-AM - 1490
600 Grant St., Ste. 600
Denver, CO 80203
Phone: (303)733-5266
Fax: (303)733-5242
Format: Hispanic. **ADI:** Denver (Steamboat Springs), CO. **URL:** http://www.radioquebueno.com.

KZMT-FM - See Helena, MT

DIVIDE

5420 ■ Giant Steps
Giant Schnauzer Club of America
c/o Cindy Wallace, Membership Chairperson
PO Box 967
Divide, CO 80814
Freq: Bimonthly. **Subscription Rates:** Included in membership. **Remarks:** Accepts advertising. **Circ:** (Not Reported).

DURANGO

La Plata Co. La Plata Co. (SW). 175 m SE of Grand Junction. Tourist resort. Gold, silver, lead, coal, uranium mines; oil, natural gas wells; pine timber; bottling works; nursery. Diversified farming. Hay, grain, fruit.

5421 ■ Cutthroat: A Journal of the Arts
Raven's Word Writers Center
PO Box 2414
Durango, CO 81302
Phone: (970)903-7914
Journal featuring poetry and short fiction. **Freq:** Annual. **Key Personnel:** Pamela Uschuk, Editor-in-Chief; Susan Foster, Managing Editor. **Subscription Rates:** $15 Single issue. **URL:** http://www.cutthroatmag.com. **Circ:** (Not Reported).

5422 ■ Durango Herald
The Durango Herald Inc.
1275 Main Ave.
Durango, CO 81301-5137
Phone: (970)247-3504
Fax: (970)259-5011
Free: 800-530-8318
Publisher's E-mail: herald@durangoherald.com
General newspaper. **Freq:** Daily. **Print Method:** Offset. **Trim Size:** 22 3/4 x 13 1/2. **Cols./Page:** 6. **Col. Width:** 25 nonpareils. **Col. Depth:** 294 agate lines. **Key Personnel:** Patrick Armijo, Editor, phone: (970)375-4553; Richard Ballantine, Publisher, phone: (970)375-4509; Sharon Hermes, Director, Marketing, phone: (970)375-4511; John Peel, Editor, phone: (970)375-4586. **USPS:** 162-960. **Subscription Rates:** $46 Individuals city delivery; Monday through Sunday; 13 weeks; $29 Individuals Saturday and Sunday; 13 weeks; $18 Individuals Sunday only; 13 weeks. **URL:** http://www.durangoherald.com. **Mailing address:** PO Box A-0950, Durango, CO 81301-0801. **Remarks:** Advertising accepted; rates available upon request. **Circ:** Mon.-Sat. ★**8196**, Sun. ★**8410**.

5423 ■ KDGO-AM - 1240
1315 Main Ave., No. 308
Durango, CO 81301-5156
Phone: (970)247-1240
Format: News; Talk. **Simulcasts:** KDGO-FM. **Networks:** Fox. **Owner:** Regional Radio, Inc., at above address, Fax: (303)247-1771. **Founded:** 1960. **ADI:** Grand Junction-Durango, CO. **Wattage:** 1,000. **Ad Rates:** Advertising accepted; rates available upon request. $5.75-7 for 30 seconds; $6.75-8 for 60 seconds. **URL:** http://www.kdgoradio.com/.

5424 ■ KDUR-FM - 91.9
1000 Rim Dr.
Durango, CO 81301
Phone: (970)247-7262
Email: kdur@fortlewis.edu
Format: Top 40; Contemporary Hit Radio (CHR); Alternative/New Music/Progressive. **Networks:** Pacifica. **Owner:** Fort Lewis College, at above address. **Founded:** 1975. **Operating Hours:** Continuous; 25% network, 75% local. **ADI:** Grand Junction-Durango, CO. **Key Personnel:** Wynn Harris, Contact; Bryant Liggett, Mgr., liggett_b@fortlewis.edu; Jennifer Cossey, Office Mgr., cossey_m@fortlewis.edu; Wynn Harris, Contact. **Wattage:** 150. **Ad Rates:** Noncommercial. $10 for 30 seconds. **URL:** http://www.kdur.org.

5425 ■ KIQX-FM - 101.3
190 Turner Dr., Ste. G
Durango, CO 81303
Phone: (970)259-4444
Fax: (970)247-1005
Email: sales@radiodurango.com
Format: Adult Contemporary. **Networks:** CBS. **Owner:** Four Corners Broadcasting L.L.C., 190 Turner Dr., Durango, CO 81303. **Founded:** 1981. **Operating Hours:** 5 a.m.-midnight; 2% network, 98% local. **ADI:** Grand Junction-Durango, CO. **Key Personnel:** Ward Holmes, Regional Mgr., ward@radiodurango.com; Kristin Dills, Bus. Mgr., kristin@radiodurango.com; Kim Emanual, Gen. Sales Mgr. **Wattage:** 100,000. **Ad Rates:** $9-13 for 30 seconds; $11-16 for 60 seconds. **URL:** http://www.radiodurango.com.

5426 ■ KIUP-AM - 930
190 Turner Dr., Ste. G
Durango, CO 81303
Phone: (970)259-4444
Fax: (970)247-1005
Email: sales@radiodurango.com
Format: Sports. **Networks:** CBS. **Owner:** Four Corners Broadcasting L.L.C., 190 Turner Dr., Durango, CO 81303. **Founded:** 1935. **Operating Hours:** Continuous; 35% network, 65% local. **ADI:** Albuquerque (Santa Fe & Hobbs), NM. **Key Personnel:** Ward Holmes, Regional Mgr.; Kristin Dills, Bus. Mgr., kristin@radiodurango.com; Kim Emanual, Gen. Sales Mgr. **Wattage:** 5,000. **Ad Rates:** $9.50-18.70 for 30 seconds; $11-18 for 60 seconds. Combined advertising rates available with KIQX-FM, KRSJ-FM. **URL:** http://www.radiodurango.com.

5427 ■ KPTE-FM - 92.9
1911 Main Ave., Ste. 100
Durango, CO 81301
Format: Adult Contemporary. **Wattage:** 9,200. **URL:** http://997thepoint.com.

5428 ■ KREZ-TV
4 Richmond Sq., Ste. 200
Providence, RI 02906
Phone: (970)259-6666
Email: krez@frontier.net
Networks: CBS. **Owner:** Lin of Colorado, LLC, at above address. **Founded:** 1963. **Wattage:** 46,000 ERP Horizonta. **Ad Rates:** $50-250 per unit. **URL:** http://www.krqe.com/fourcorners.

5429 ■ KRSJ-FM - 100.5
190 Turner Dr., Ste. G
Durango, CO 81303
Phone: (970)259-4444
Fax: (970)247-1005
Email: sales@radiodurango.com
Format: Country. **Networks:** CBS. **Owner:** Four Corners Broadcasting L.L.C., 190 Turner Dr., Durango, CO 81303. **Founded:** 1972. **Formerly:** KIUP-FM. **Operating Hours:** 19 hours Daily; 15% network, 85% local. **ADI:** Albuquerque (Santa Fe & Hobbs), NM. **Key**

Personnel: Kim Emanual, Sales Mgr.; Ward Holmes, Regional Mgr., ward@radiodurango.com; Kristin Dills, Bus. Mgr., kristin@radiodurango.com. **Wattage:** 100,000. **Ad Rates:** $8.50-16.50 for 30 seconds; $9.50-18.50 for 60 seconds. Combined advertising rates available with KIUP, KIQX. **URL:** http://www.radiodurango.com.

EADS

Kiowa Co. Kiowa Co. (E). 110 m E of Pueblo. Stock, grain, poultry. Milo maize. Natural gas.

5430 ■ Kiowa County Press
Kiowa County Press
1208 Maine St.
Eads, CO 81036-0248
Phone: (719)438-5800
Community newspaper. **Freq:** Weekly. **Print Method:** Offset & Digital. **Trim Size:** 8 x 10. **Cols./Page:** 4. **Col. Width:** 1.925 inches. **Col. Depth:** 10 INS. **ISSN:** 2959--4000 (print). **Alt. Formats:** PDF. **URL:** http://www.kiowacountypress.com. **Mailing address:** PO Box 248, Eads, CO 81036-0248. **Remarks:** Accepts classified advertising. **Circ:** Paid ‡1100, Free ‡50.

ENGLEWOOD

Arapahoe Co. Arapahoe Co. (C). 7 m S of Denver. Retail, industrial, professional city. Manufactures electronic components, steel structures, tools. Greenhouses.

5431 ■ Littleton Independent
Littleton Independent
9800 Mt. Pyramid Ct., Ste. 100
Englewood, CO 80112
Community newspaper. **Founded:** 1888. **Freq:** Weekly (Thurs.). **Print Method:** Offset. **Cols./Page:** 5. **Col. Width:** 9.5 picas. **Col. Depth:** 13 inches. **Key Personnel:** Jeremy Bangs, Managing Editor; Erin Addenbrooke, Manager, Sales. **Subscription Rates:** $30 Individuals home delivery, 12 months; $20 Individuals home delivery, senior rate, 12 months. **URL:** http://littletonindependent.net/. **Ad Rates:** SAU $12.25. **Remarks:** Accepts advertising. **Circ:** 3120.

5432 ■ Medical Problems of Performing Artists
Performing Arts Medicine Association
PO Box 117
Englewood, CO 80151
Phone: (303)808-5643
Free: 866-408-7069
Publisher's E-mail: editor@sciandmed.com
Peer-reviewed clinical medical journal covering etiology, diagnosis, and treatment of medical and psychological disorders and diseases related to the performing arts. **Freq:** Quarterly. **Trim Size:** 8 1/4 x 10 7/8. **Key Personnel:** Bronwen J. Ackermann, PhD, Editor. **ISSN:** 0885--1158 (print). **Subscription Rates:** $88 Individuals; $102 Other countries; $198.50 Institutions and library; $228 Institutions, other countries and library; $72 Individuals online only; Included in membership. **URL:** http://www.sciandmed.com/mppa/; http://www.artsmed.org/medical-problems-performing-artists-mppa-journal. **Ad Rates:** BW $640; 4C $900. **Remarks:** Advertising accepted; rates available upon request. **Circ:** Paid ‡1000.

5433 ■ Minerals and Metallurgical Processing
Society for Mining, Metallurgy, and Exploration
12999 E Adam Aircraft Cir.
Englewood, CO 80112
Phone: (303)948-4200
Fax: (303)973-3845
Free: 800-763-3132
Publication E-mail: publications@smenet.org
Peer-reviewed journal providing technical and research information on minerals and metallurgical processing. **Freq:** Quarterly February, May, August and November. **Print Method:** Offset. **Trim Size:** 8 1/8 x 10 7/8. **Cols./Page:** 2. **Col. Width:** 40 nonpareils. **Col. Depth:** 140 agate lines. **Key Personnel:** S. Komar Kawatra, Editor-in-Chief. **ISSN:** 0747--9182 (print). **Subscription Rates:** $129 Nonmembers print & online - SME; $129 Members print & online - affiliated organization; $629 Libraries print & online - institution; $169 Nonmembers print & online - individual and foreign; $159 Nonmembers print & online - individual and USA. **URL:** http://mmp.smenet.org. **Ad Rates:** BW $300; 4C $580. **Remarks:** Accepts advertising. **Circ:** ‡750.

5434 ■ Mining Engineering
Society for Mining, Metallurgy, and Exploration
12999 E Adam Aircraft Cir.
Englewood, CO 80112
Phone: (303)948-4200
Fax: (303)973-3845
Free: 800-763-3132
Publisher's E-mail: administration@smenet.org
Magazine for engineers and professionals engaged in exploration, underground and open pit mining, solution mining, rock mechanics, operations research, geological engineering, geohydrology, mineral processing, mineral, economics, and management. **Freq:** Monthly. **Print Method:** Offset. **Trim Size:** 8 1/8 x 10 7/8. **Cols./Page:** 3. **Col. Width:** 26 nonpareils. **Col. Depth:** 140 agate lines. **Key Personnel:** Steve Kral, Editor, phone: (303)948-4245; William M. Gleason, Senior Editor, phone: (303)948-4234; Georgene Renner, Senior Editor, phone: (303)948-4254. **ISSN:** 0026--5187 (print). **Subscription Rates:** $275 Nonmembers outside USA; $245 Individuals print and online. **URL:** http://me.smenet.org/index.cfm; http://me.smenet.org. **Ad Rates:** BW $4,930; 4C $5,860; BW $4500. **Remarks:** Accepts advertising. **Circ:** Paid 17000.

5435 ■ National Costumers Magazine
National Costumers Association
PO Box 3406
Englewood, CO 80155
Phone: (303)758-9611
Fax: (303)758-9616
Free: 800-NCA-1321
Publisher's E-mail: office@costumers.org
Magazine covering news and events of the organization, business tips, strategies and resources. **Freq:** Quarterly February,May,September and December. **Trim Size:** 8x11. **Subscription Rates:** Included in membership. **URL:** http://www.costumers.org/MembersOnly/TheCostumerMagazine.aspx. **Also known as:** The Costumers. **Ad Rates:** 4C $245; BW $160. **Remarks:** Accepts advertising. **Circ:** 600.

5436 ■ Nursing Administration Quarterly
Lippincott Williams and Wilkins
c/o Linda Pickett
Catholic Health Initiatives
198 Inverness Dr. W
Englewood, CO 80112
Publication E-mail: lindapickett@catholichealth.net
Peer-reviewed journal presenting information on the management of nursing services. **Freq:** Quarterly. **Print Method:** Offset. **Trim Size:** 7 x 10. **Cols./Page:** 2. **Col. Width:** 16 picas. **Col. Depth:** 45 picas. **Key Personnel:** Rhonda Anderson, Board Member; Kathleen D. Sanford, Editor-in-Chief; Beth L. Guthy, Publisher. **ISSN:** 0363--9568 (print); **EISSN:** 1550--5103 (electronic). **Subscription Rates:** $152 U.S.; $161 Canada and Mexico; $263 Other countries; $590 Institutions; $637 Institutions, Canada and Mexico; $774 Institutions, other countries; $91 U.S. in-training. **URL:** http://journals.lww.com/naqjournal/pages/default.aspx; http://www.lww.com/Product/0363-9568. **Ad Rates:** BW $1195; 4C $2520; BW $1100; 4C $1285. **Remarks:** Accepts advertising. **Circ:** Paid 1207, Non-paid 47, 1527.

5437 ■ Time Warner Cable
PO Box 6929
Englewood, CO 80155-6929
Phone: (303)799-9599
Fax: (303)649-8090
Free: 800-727-1855
Owner: Time Warner Cable, PO Box 6929, Englewood, CO 80155-6929, Ph: (303)799-9599, Fax: (303)649-8090, Free: 800-727-1855. **Formerly:** MetroVision Inc. **Key Personnel:** Henry Harris, President.

ERIE

5438 ■ Yellow Scene
Yellow Scene
PO Box 964
Erie, CO 80516
Phone: (303)828-2700
Fax: (720)239-1497
Publisher's E-mail: advertising@yellowscene.com
Magazine focusing on keeping up with a rapidly growing and increasing affluent North Metro population. **Freq:** Monthly. **Key Personnel:** Shavonne Blades, Publisher; Andra Coberly, Editor; Lacy Boggs, Associate Editor. **URL:** http://yellowscene.com/magazine. **Remarks:** Accepts advertising. **Circ:** ‡70000.

ESTES PARK

Larimer Co. Larimer Co. (N). 62 m NW of Denver. Estes Park eastern gateway to Rocky Mountain National Park resort region.

5439 ■ The Story Circle Journal
Story Circle Network
PO Box 1670
Estes Park, CO 80517-1670
Phone: (970)235-1477
Publisher's E-mail: storycircle@storycircle.org
Freq: Quarterly every March, June, September and December. **Subscription Rates:** Included in membership. **URL:** http://www.storycircle.org/journal.shtml. **Remarks:** Accepts advertising. **Circ:** (Not Reported).

5440 ■ Trail-Gazette
Estes Park Trail-Gazette
251 Moraine Ave.
Estes Park, CO 80517
Phone: (970)586-3356
Newspaper. **Freq:** Biweekly Wednesday, and Friday. **Print Method:** Offset. **Cols./Page:** 6. **Col. Width:** 12.3 picas. **Col. Depth:** 21 inches. **Key Personnel:** Mike Romero, Publisher; John Cordsen, Managing Editor. **Subscription Rates:** $45 Individuals in Larimer, Boulder & Weld Counties; $57 Elsewhere; $69 Out of state. **URL:** http://www.eptrail.com. **Mailing address:** PO Box 1707, Estes Park, CO 80517. **Remarks:** Accepts advertising. **Circ:** ‡5877.

5441 ■ KRBR-AM - 1470
184 E Elkhorn Ave., Ste. J
Estes Park, CO 80517
Phone: (970)586-9555
Fax: (970)586-9561
Email: kezestes@hotmail.com
Format: Information; News; Sports.

EVERGREEN

Jefferson Co. (NC). 29 m W of Denver. Residential.

5442 ■ The Canyon Courier
Landmark Community Newspapers L.L.C.
27902 Meadow Dr., Ste. 200
Evergreen, CO 80439
Phone: (303)674-5534
Publisher's E-mail: marketing@lcni.com
Community newspaper. **Freq:** Weekly. **Subscription Rates:** $32 Individuals online only; $55 Individuals print and online. **URL:** http://www.canyoncourier.com. **Remarks:** Accepts advertising. **Circ:** 8000.

5443 ■ Columbine Community Courier
Landmark Community Newspapers L.L.C.
27902 Meadow Drive, Suite 202
Evergreen, CO 80439
Phone: (303)674-5534
Publisher's E-mail: marketing@lcni.com
Community newspaper. **Freq:** Weekly. **Key Personnel:** Doug Bell, Editor, phone: (303)350-1039. **Subscription Rates:** $32 Individuals annual all access; $31 Individuals semi-annual all access; $14 Individuals quarterly all access. **URL:** http://www.columbinecourier.com. **Remarks:** Accepts advertising. **Circ:** (Not Reported).

5444 ■ High Timber Times
Evergreen Newspapers Inc.
27902 Meadow Dr., Ste. 200
Evergreen, CO 80439
Community newspaper. **Freq:** Weekly (Wed.). **Print Method:** Offset. **Cols./Page:** 4. **Col. Width:** 28 nonpareils. **Col. Depth:** 216 agate lines. **Key Personnel:** Doug Bell, Editor, phone: (303)350-1039. **Subscription Rates:** $36 Individuals /year in county; $38 Individuals /year out of county. **URL:** http://www.hightimbertimes.com. **Remarks:** Accepts advertising. **Circ:** (Not Reported).

5445 ■ 285 Hustler
Landmark Community Newspapers L.L.C.

Circulation: ★ = AAM; △ or • = BPA; ♦ = CAC; ❑ = VAC; ⊕ = PO Statement; ‡ = Publisher's Report; Boldface figures = sworn; Light figures = estimated.

27902 Meadow Drive, Suite 202
Evergreen, CO 80439
Phone: (303)838-5830
Publisher's E-mail: marketing@lcni.com
Community newspaper. **URL:** http://www.285hustler.com. **Formerly**: The Hustler. **Circ:** (Not Reported).

FLAGLER

Kit Carson Co. Kit Carson Co. (E). 110 m SE of Denver. Feed mill; bird seed packaging plant. Livestock, dairy, farms. Wheat, corn, barley, proso.

5446 ■ The Flagler News & Mile Saver Shopper
Flagler News
321 Main Ave.
Flagler, CO 80815
Phone: (719)765-4468
Fax: (719)765-4517
Publisher's E-mail: advertise@milesaver.com
Newspaper with a Republican orientation. **Freq:** Weekly (Thurs.). **Print Method:** Offset. **Cols./Page:** 5. **Col. Width:** 11 picas. **Col. Depth:** 15 inches. **Key Personnel:** Thomas E. Bredehoft, Publisher. **USPS:** 199-580. **URL:** http://www.milesaver.com. **Formerly**: The Flager News. **Mailing address:** PO Box 188, Flagler, CO 80815. **Ad Rates:** GLR $5.50; 4C $50; PCI $8.25. **Remarks:** Accepts advertising. **Circ:** Non-paid ‡14400, Paid ‡400.

FORT COLLINS

Larimer Co. Larimer Co. (N). 65 m N of Denver. Colorado State University. Manufactures sugar, flour, brick, tile, electronics, plastics, dental appliances, canned foods, machinery, beverages. Pine timber. Stock, grain, fruit, dairy farms. Sugar beets, lambs, alfalfa.

5447 ■ Across the Disciplines
WAC Clearinghouse
c/o Mike Palmquist, Ed.
Dept. of English, Eddy Hall Rm. 359
Colorado State University
Fort Collins, CO 80523
Phone: (970)491-3132
Academic journal that "provides CAC researchers, program designers, and teachers interested in using communication assignments and activities in their courses with a venue for scholarly debate about issues of disciplinarity and writing across the curriculum". **Key Personnel:** Michael Pemberton, Editor, phone: (912)871-1383, fax: (912)871-1902; Michael J. Cripps, Associate Editor, phone: (207)602-2908. **ISSN:** 1554--8244 (print). **Subscription Rates:** Free to qualified subscribers online. **URL:** http://wac.colostate.edu/atd/about.cfm. **Circ:** (Not Reported).

5448 ■ Catholic World Report
Ignatius Press
PO Box 1339
Fort Collins, CO 80522
Fax: (415)387-0896
Free: 800-651-1531
Publication E-mail: info@ignatius.com
Magazine covering stories about church, anti-Catholicism, and priest scandal. **Freq:** Monthly. **Key Personnel:** Joseph Fessio, Publisher; Carl E. Olson, Editor; Catherine Harmon, Managing Editor. **Subscription Rates:** $52.25 Individuals. **URL:** http://www.catholicworldreport.com/Default.aspx. **Remarks:** Accepts advertising. **Circ:** (Not Reported).

5449 ■ The Christian Chiropractor Journal
Christian Chiropractors Association Inc.
2550 Stover B-102
Fort Collins, CO 80525
Phone: (970)482-1404
Fax: (970)482-1538
Free: 800-999-1970
Journal containing information and edifying communiques of the association to its membership. **URL:** http://www.christianchiropractors.org/articles.htm. **Remarks:** Advertising not accepted. **Circ:** (Not Reported).

5450 ■ Colorado Review
Colorado State University Department of English
359 Eddy Hall
1773 Campus Delivery
Fort Collins, CO 80523
Phone: (970)491-6428
Publication E-mail: creview@colostate.edu
Magazine covering poetry, fiction, personal essay, and book reviews. **Freq:** 3/year. **Print Method:** Notch-bound paperback. **Trim Size:** 6 x 9 1/4. **Cols./Page:** 1. **Col. Width:** 4 inches. **Col. Depth:** 6 1/2 inches. **Key Personnel:** Sasha Steensen, Editor; Donald Revell, Editor; Stephanie G'Schwind, Editor. **ISSN:** 1046--3348 (print). **Subscription Rates:** $20 U.S. /year; $28 Canada /year; $44 Other countries /year; $19 Students /year. **URL:** http://coloradoreview.colostate.edu/colorado-review. **Formerly**: Colorado State Review. **Remarks:** Accepts advertising. **Circ:** (Not Reported).

5451 ■ The Earth Scientist
National Earth Science Teachers Association
PO Box 2716521
Fort Collins, CO 80527
Phone: (201)519-1071
Journal containing classroom activities, background science information for the Earth and space science teacher as well as news about NESTA programs and opportunities for teachers in the Earth and Space Sciences. **Freq:** Quarterly winter, spring, summer and fall. **Subscription Rates:** Included in membership. **Alt. Formats:** PDF. **URL:** http://www.nestanet.org/cms/content/publications/tes. **Remarks:** Accepts advertising. **Circ:** (Not Reported).

5452 ■ English Journal
National Council of Teachers of English
English Department
Colorado State University
1773 Campus Delivery
Fort Collins, CO 80523-1773
Phone: (970)491-6417
Fax: (970)491-3097
Publication E-mail: english-journal@colostate.edu
Journal for middle school and junior and senior high English teachers. Articles on the teaching of literature, language, and composition range from practical classroom techniques to theory and issues affecting the teacher and the student. **Freq:** 6/year Published September, November, January, March, May, and July. **Print Method:** Web. **Trim Size:** 8 1/2 x 11. **Cols./Page:** 3 and 2. **Col. Width:** 24 and 37 nonpareils. **Col. Depth:** 133 agate lines. **Key Personnel:** Theresa Kay, Associate Editor; Julie Gorlewski, Editor; David Gorlewski, Editor. **ISSN:** 0013--8274 (print). **Subscription Rates:** $75 Nonmembers; $25 Members; $12.50 Students; $12.50 Individuals emeritus. **URL:** http://www.ncte.org/journals/ej. **Ad Rates:** BW $2,000; 4C $3,000. **Remarks:** Accepts advertising. **Circ:** 16,000, 53,000, ‡18,000.

5453 ■ Fort Collins Coloradoan
Gannett Company Inc.
1300 Riverside Ave.
Fort Collins, CO 80524
Phone: (970)493-6397
General newspaper. **Freq:** Mon.-Sun. (morn.). **Print Method:** Offset. **Cols./Page:** 6. **Col. Width:** 24 nonpareils. **Col. Depth:** 301 agate lines. **Key Personnel:** Kevin Darst, Editor; Kathy Jack-Romero, President, Publisher. **Subscription Rates:** $16.47 Individuals 7 days a week/month; $11.27 Individuals Thursday to Sunday/month; $8.03 Individuals Sundays only/month. **URL:** http://www.gannett.com/brands; http://www.coloradoan.com. **Ad Rates:** SAU $16.67. **Remarks:** Accepts advertising. **Circ:** Mon.-Fri. ★**22279**, Sun. ★**26274**, Sat. ★**23117**.

5454 ■ Human Dimensions of Wildlife
Routledge
c/o Jerry J. Vaske, Co-Ed.-in-Ch.
Colorado State University
Department of Natural Resource Recreation & Tourism
244 Forestry Bldg.
Fort Collins, CO 80523
Publisher's E-mail: book.orders@tandf.co.uk
Journal covering wildlife, resource management and forestry. **Freq:** 6/year. **Trim Size:** 7 x 20. **Cols./Page:** 1. **Col. Width:** 7 inches. **Col. Depth:** 10 inches. **Key Personnel:** Michael J. Manfredo, Founder, Editor; Jerry J. Vaske, Editor-in-Chief. **ISSN:** 1087--1209 (print); **EISSN:** 1533--158X (electronic). **Subscription Rates:** $473 Institutions print & online; $414 Institutions online only; $219 Individuals print only. **URL:** http://www.tandfonline.com/toc/uhdw20/current#.UvSLMdIW2qY. **Remarks:** Accepts advertising. **Circ:** (Not Reported).

5455 ■ North Light
North Light Shop
4868 Innovation Dr., Bldg. 2
Fort Collins, CO 80525
Phone: (855)842-5267
Publication E-mail: nlbc@fwpubs.com
Magazine focusing on professional and amateur art. **Freq:** 14/yr. **Print Method:** Offset. **Cols./Page:** 4. **Col. Width:** 27 nonpareils. **Col. Depth:** 140 agate lines. **Key Personnel:** Jennifer Lepore, Editor. **Ad Rates:** BW $1,460; 4C $2,160. **Remarks:** Accepts advertising. **Circ:** Non-paid 68635.

5456 ■ Preventive Veterinary Medicine
Mosby Inc.
c/o M.D. Salman, Editor-in-Chief
Animal Population Health Institute
College of Veterinary Medicine & Biomedical Sciences
Colorado State University
Fort Collins, CO 80523-1644
Journal focusing on the epidemiology of domestic and wild animals, costs of epidemic and endemic diseases of animals, the latest methods in veterinary epidemiology, disease control or eradication by public veterinary services, relationships between veterinary medicine and animal production, and development of new techniques in diagnosing, recording, evaluating and controlling diseases in animal populations. **Freq:** 20/yr. **Key Personnel:** H.N. Erb, Associate Editor; M.D. Salman, Editor-in-Chief; M.G. Doherr, Associate Editor. **ISSN:** 0167--5877 (print). **Subscription Rates:** $3860.80 Institutions online; $3887 Institutions print. **URL:** http://www.journals.elsevier.com/preventive-veterinary-medicine. **Circ:** (Not Reported).

5457 ■ The Rocky Mountain Collegian
Colorado State University Center for Literary Publishing
Lory Student Ctr., Box 13
Fort Collins, CO 80523
Phone: (970)491-1146
Fax: (970)491-1690
Publisher's E-mail: news@collegian.com
Collegiate newspaper (broadsheet). **Freq:** Daily during academic year. **Print Method:** Offset. **Trim Size:** 11.6 1/4 x 21 1/2. **Cols./Page:** 6. **Col. Width:** 11 picas. **Col. Depth:** 21.5 inches. **Key Personnel:** Bailey Constas, Editor-in-Chief. **URL:** http://www.collegian.com. **Ad Rates:** BW $10. **Remarks:** Accepts advertising. **Circ:** Free ‡8000.

5458 ■ Ruminate Magazine
Ruminate
1041 N Taft Hill Rd.
Fort Collins, CO 80521
Magazine featuring short stories, creative non-fiction and visual art. **Freq:** Quarterly. **Key Personnel:** Brianna Van Dyke, Editor-in-Chief. **Subscription Rates:** $15 Individuals. **URL:** http://www.ruminatemagazine.org. **Remarks:** Accepts advertising. **Circ:** (Not Reported).

5459 ■ Southwestern Lore: Journal of Colorado Archaeology
Colorado Archaeological Society
PO Box 271735
Fort Collins, CO 80527-1735
Phone: (303)918-1236
Archaeology journal. **Freq:** Quarterly. **Key Personnel:** C.T. Hurst, Editor; Carolyn Bruce, Associate Editor; Michele Giometti, Treasurer, phone: (303)986-6307. **ISSN:** 0038-4844 (print). **Subscription Rates:** $15 Single issue CD-ROM; $4 Single issue plus $3.50 Postage & Handling. **Alt. Formats:** CD-ROM. **URL:** http://www.coloradoarchaeology.org/PUBLICATIONS/SouthwesternLore/swl.htm. **Ad Rates:** BW $125. **Remarks:** Accepts advertising. **Circ:** ‡800.

5460 ■ The Triangle of Mu Phi Epsilon
Mu Phi Epsilon International
PO Box 1369
Fort Collins, CO 80522-1369
Free: 888-259-1471
Publisher's E-mail: executiveoffice@muphiepsilon.org
Freq: Quarterly. **ISSN:** 0041- 2600 (print). **Alt. Formats:** Download; PDF. **URL:** http://www.muphiepsilon.org/readthetriangle. **Remarks:** Advertising not accepted. **Circ:** (Not Reported).

5461 ■ Tuberculosis
Mosby Inc.
Dept. of Microbiology

Veterinary College
Medicine & Biomedical Sciences
Colorado State University
Fort Collins, CO 80523-1677
Journal focusing on the latest research advances relevant to tuberculosis control and elimination. **Freq:** Bimonthly. **Key Personnel:** Patrick Brennan, Editor; Douglas Young, Editor; Brian Robertson, Editor. **ISSN:** 1472--9792 (print). **Subscription Rates:** $348 Individuals print and online; $295 Individuals online only. **URL:** http://www.tuberculosisjournal.com; http://www.journals.elsevier.com/tuberculosis. **Ad Rates:** BW $1134; 4C $2062. **Remarks:** Accepts advertising. **Circ:** ‡234.

5462 ■ Veterinary Clinics of North America: Equine Practice
Elsevier Inc.
c/o Prof. Simon A. Turner, Consulting Ed.
Dept. of Clinical Sciences
College of Veterinary Medicine & Biomedical Sciences
Colorado State University
Fort Collins, CO 80523
Publisher's E-mail: healthpermissions@elsevier.com
Journal reviewing current techniques, drugs, and diagnostic and treatment techniques in veterinary medicine. **Freq:** 3/year. **Print Method:** Offset. **Trim Size:** 6 x 9. **Cols./Page:** 2. **Col. Width:** 52 nonpareils. **Col. Depth:** 105 agate lines. **Key Personnel:** Prof. Simon A. Turner, Editor. **ISSN:** 0749-0739 (print). **Subscription Rates:** $365 Individuals print only; $1089.33 Individuals eJournal; $572 Institutions print only. **URL:** http://www.elsevier.com/journals/veterinary-clinics-of-north-america-equine-practice/0749-0739. **Circ:** (Not Reported).

5463 ■ KCSU-FM - 90.5
PO Box 13
Lory Student Ctr., Box 13
Fort Collins, CO 80523
Phone: (970)491-7611
Fax: (970)491-1690
Format: Alternative/New Music/Progressive; Educational. **Owner:** State Board of Agriculture, at above address. **Founded:** 1964. **Operating Hours:** Continuous. **ADI:** Denver (Steamboat Springs), CO. **Key Personnel:** Dan Allen, Station Mgr.; David Jarvis, Director. **Local Programs:** *The Training Show*, Monday 5:00 p.m. - 7:00 p.m. **Wattage:** 10,000. **Ad Rates:** Noncommercial. $10 per unit. Underwriting available for. **URL:** http://www.kcsufm.com.

5464 ■ KGCO-FM - 88.3
PO Box 779002
Rocklin, CA 95677-9972
Fax: (916)251-1901
Free: 800-525-LOVE
Email: info@klove.com
Format: Contemporary Christian. **Owner:** Educational Media Foundation, PO Box 2098, Omaha, NE 68103-2098, Free: 800-434-8400. **Formerly:** KLHV-FM. **Key Personnel:** Mike Novak, President; Alan Mason, COO. **URL:** http://www.klove.com.

5465 ■ KRFC-FM - 88.9
619 S College, No. 4
Fort Collins, CO 80524
Phone: (970)221-5065
Email: comments@krfcfm.org
Format: Public Radio. **Operating Hours:** Continuous. **Key Personnel:** Brian Hughes, Exec. Dir. **Wattage:** 010 ERP H; 3,000 ERP . **Ad Rates:** Noncommercial. Underwriting available. **URL:** http://www.krfcfm.org.

FORT MORGAN

Morgan Co. Morgan Co. (NE). 75 m NE of Denver. Manufactures modular homes; beet sugar processing; beef packing; nursery. Agriculture. Sugar beets, stock, corn, grain.

5466 ■ The Fort Morgan Times
Eastern Colorado Publishing Co.
329 Main St.
Fort Morgan, CO 80701
Phone: (970)867-5651
Fax: (970)867-7448
Newspaper with a community focus. **Founded:** 1884. **Freq:** Mon.-Sat. (eve.). **Print Method:** Offset. **Cols./Page:** 6. **Col. Width:** 25 nonpareils. **Col. Depth:** 301 agate lines. **Key Personnel:** Josephina Movsivais, Manager, Circulation; Julie Tonsing, Publisher. **USPS:** 205-940. **Subscription Rates:** $156 Individuals in county; $184.60 Out of area; $141.70 Individuals senior in county; $166.14 Out of area senior. **URL:** http://www.fortmorgantimes.com/contact_us/. **Ad Rates:** GLR $.66; BW $1,189.38; 4C $1,399.38; SAU $9.55. **Circ:** Mon.-Sat. ‡3202.

5467 ■ KBRU-FM - 101.7
PO Box 430
Fort Morgan, CO 80701
Phone: (970)867-5674
Fax: (970)842-1023
Format: Adult Contemporary. **Simulcasts:** KFTM. **Networks:** AP. **Founded:** 1979. **Operating Hours:** Continuous. **Key Personnel:** John Waters, Sports Dir.; Geoffrey Baumgartner, News Dir.; Roger Morgan, Dir. of Programs. **Wattage:** 3,000. **Ad Rates:** $7 for 30 seconds; $9 for 60 seconds. Combined advertising rates available with KSTC, KNNG.

5468 ■ KFTM-AM - 1400
16041 US Highway 34
Fort Morgan, CO 80701
Phone: (970)867-5674
Fax: (970)542-1023
Email: kftm@medialogicradio.com
Format: Adult Contemporary. **Networks:** AP. **Owner:** Media Logic L.L.C., 59 Wolf Rd., Albany 12205. **Founded:** 1949. **Operating Hours:** Continuous; 66.5% network, 33.5% local. **Key Personnel:** Scott Roberts, Dir. of Sales, Sports Dir.; Wayne Johnson, Gen. Mgr., Owner. **Local Programs:** *The Big Morning Show*, Monday Tuesday Wednesday Thursday Friday 6:00 a.m. - 10:00 a.m.; *Swap Shop*, Monday Tuesday Wednesday Thursday Friday 9:05 a.m. **Wattage:** 1,000. **Ad Rates:** Noncommercial. Combined advertising rates available with KATR-FM, KRDZ-AM, website. **Mailing address:** PO Box 430, Fort Morgan, CO 80701. **URL:** http://www.kftm.net.

5469 ■ KPRB-FM - 106.3
220 State St., Ste. 106
Fort Morgan, CO 80701
Phone: (970)867-7271
Free: 888-556-5747
Format: Adult Contemporary. **Owner:** Northeast Colorado Broadcasting, LLC, at above address. **Operating Hours:** Continuous. **Wattage:** 7,000. **Ad Rates:** Noncommercial. **URL:** http://www.ksir.com.

5470 ■ KSIR-AM - 1010
220 State St., Ste. 106
Fort Morgan, CO 80701
Phone: (970)867-7271
Free: 888-556-5747
Format: Sports; Agricultural. **Networks:** ABC. **Owner:** Northeast Colorado Broadcasting, LLC, at above address. **Founded:** 1977. **Operating Hours:** Continuous. **Local Programs:** *Cattleman's Corner*, Monday Tuesday Wednesday Thursday Friday 5:30 a.m. - 7:15 a.m.; *Noontime Farm Show*, Monday Tuesday Wednesday Thursday Friday 12:00 p.m.; *Horseman's Corner*, Saturday 9:00 a.m. - 10:00 a.m. **Wattage:** 25,000. **Ad Rates:** Noncommercial. **Mailing address:** PO Box 917, Fort Morgan, CO 80701. **URL:** http://www.ksir.com.

FOUNTAIN

El Paso Co. El Paso Co. (EC). 10 m SE of Colorado Springs. Nursery. Agriculture. Livestock, wheat, corn.

5471 ■ Fountain Valley News
Shopper Press Inc.
120 E Ohio
Fountain, CO 80817
Phone: (719)382-5611
Fax: (719)382-5614
Community newspaper. **Freq:** Weekly. **Print Method:** Offset. **Trim Size:** 11 x 17. **Cols./Page:** 7. **Col. Width:** 16 nonpareils. **Col. Depth:** 224 agate lines. **Key Personnel:** Karen Johnson, General Manager; Patricia St. Louis, Executive Editor. **ISSN:** 0747--1920 (print). **URL:** http://www.epcan.com. **Formerly:** The Advertiser/The Security Advertiser. **Ad Rates:** GLR $10/mm; BW $1,120; PCI $10. **Remarks:** Accepts advertising. **Circ:** (Not Reported).

FOWLER

Otero Co. Otero Co. (SE). On Arkansas River, 36 m E of Pueblo. Cannery; meat plant. Agriculture. Alfalfa, tomatoes, corn, beans.

5472 ■ Fowler Tribune
GateHouse Media Inc.
112 Cranston Ave.
Fowler, CO 81039
Phone: (719)263-5311
Newspaper. **Freq:** Weekly (Thurs.). **Print Method:** Offset. **Cols./Page:** 5. **Col. Width:** 24 nonpareils. **Col. Depth:** 210 agate lines. **Key Personnel:** Andrea Flores, Editor; Candi Hill, Publisher, phone: (719)384-1435; Pam Spitzer, Office Manager. **URL:** http://www.fowlertribune.com. **Ad Rates:** GLR $.47; BW $232; SAU $3.75; PCI $3.75. **Remarks:** Accepts advertising. **Circ:** ‡1200.

FRISCO

5473 ■ Summit Daily
Eagle Summit Publishing
331 W Main St.
Frisco, CO 80443
Phone: (970)668-3998
Publisher's E-mail: news@summitdaily.com
Community newspaper. **Freq:** Daily. **Print Method:** Web offset. **Trim Size:** 10.5 x 15.75. **Cols./Page:** 6. **Key Personnel:** Matt Sandberg, Publisher, phone: (970)668-4647; Maggie Butler, Director, Marketing, phone: (970)668-4649; Ben Trollinger, Managing Editor, phone: (970)668-4618. **Subscription Rates:** $3.50 Single issue; $30 Out of area 6 months; $40 Out of area; $40 Out of area 2 years; $30 Individuals in county; $40 By mail 2 years, In County. **URL:** http://www.summitdaily.com. **Remarks:** Accepts advertising. **Circ:** Free .

5474 ■ Copper Mountain Consolidated Metropolitan District
477 Copper Rd.
Frisco, CO 80443
Phone: (970)968-2537
Fax: (970)968-2932
Cities Served: subscribing households 920. **Mailing address:** PO Box 3002, Frisco, CO 80443. **URL:** http://www.coppermtnmetro.org.

5475 ■ KYSL-FM - 93.9
PO Box 27
Frisco, CO 80443
Phone: (970)513-9393
Email: support@krystal93.com
Format: Adult Contemporary. **Networks:** AP. **Owner:** Ann Penny Ogden. **Founded:** 1988. **Operating Hours:** Continuous. **Key Personnel:** Tom Fricke, Prog. Dir.; John O'Connor, Contact, john@krystal93.com; T.J. Sanders, Music Dir., feedback@krystal93.com. **Wattage:** 560. **Ad Rates:** $16-27 for 30 seconds; $20-35 for 60 seconds. **URL:** http://www.krystal93.com.

GLENWOOD SPRINGS

Garfield Co. Garfield Co. (W). 150 m W of Denver. Recreation area. Coal mines. Ranching.

5476 ■ KLXV-FM - 91.9
PO Box 779002
Rocklin, CA 95677-9972
Free: 800-525-5683
Format: Contemporary Christian. **Owner:** Educational Media Foundation, PO Box 2098, Omaha, NE 68103-2098, Free: 800-434-8400. **URL:** http://www.klove.com.

5477 ■ KMTS-FM - 99.1
3230-B S Glen Ave.
Glenwood Springs, CO 81601
Phone: (970)945-9124
Fax: (970)945-5409
Email: kmts@kmts.com
Format: Country. **Networks:** ABC; CNN Radio. **Founded:** 1977. **Formerly:** KGLS-FM. **Operating Hours:** Continuous. **Key Personnel:** Gabe Chenoweth, Gen. Mgr., gabe@kmts.com; Ron Milhorn, News Dir., cwbnews@kmts.com. **Wattage:** 10,000. **Ad Rates:** Noncommercial. Combined advertising rates available with KGLN-AM for 30 seconds. **URL:** http://www.kmts.com.

Circulation: ★ = AAM; △ or • = BPA; ♦ = CAC; ❑ = VAC; ⊕ = PO Statement; ‡ = Publisher's Report; Boldface figures = sworn; Light figures = estimated.

GOLDEN

Jefferson Co. Jefferson Co. (C). 15 m W of Denver. Colorado School of Mines. Coal, gold mines; clay pits. Porcelain; fire-brick; brewery. Truck, dairy, stock, poultry farms.

5478 ■ ACES Journal
Applied Computational Electromagnetics Society
Colorado School of Mines
310D Brown Bldg.
1610 Illinois St.
Golden, CO 80401
Phone: (408)646-1111
Fax: (408)646-0300
Freq: Monthly. **Subscription Rates:** free for members. **URL:** http://www.aces-society.org/journal.php. **Remarks:** Advertising not accepted. **Circ:** (Not Reported).

5479 ■ Advertising & Marketing Review
CSC Publishing
622 Gardenia Ct.
Golden, CO 80401
Phone: (303)277-9840
Publisher's E-mail: review@ad-mkt-review.com
Professional magazine covering advertising and marketing news in Colorado. **Freq:** Monthly. **Key Personnel:** Ken Custer, Editor. **ISSN:** 1528-6428 (print). **URL:** http://www.ad-mkt-review.com. **Ad Rates:** BW $1,000; 4C $1,100. **Remarks:** Accepts classified advertising. **Circ:** Combined 3000.

5480 ■ American Alpine Journal
American Alpine Club
710 10th St., Ste. 100
Golden, CO 80401
Phone: (303)384-0110
Fax: (303)384-0111
Publisher's E-mail: info@americanalpineclub.org
Journal of the American Alpine Club. **Freq:** Annual. **Key Personnel:** Erik Rieger, Editor. **Subscription Rates:** $34.95 Individuals 2015 issue - paperback; $14.95 Individuals 2015 issue - digital; Included in membership. **URL:** http://www.americanalpineclub.org/p/aaj. **Remarks:** Advertising not accepted. **Circ:** (Not Reported).

5481 ■ Body Sense
Associated Bodywork & Massage Professionals
25188 Genesee Trail Rd., Ste. 200
Golden, CO 80401
Phone: (303)674-8478
Free: 800-667-8260
Publisher's E-mail: expectmore@abmp.com
Magazine featuring up-to-date information on the latest trends in bodywork and skin care. **Freq:** Semiannual spring and autumn. **Key Personnel:** Leslie Young, Editor-in-Chief; Darren Buford, Managing Editor; Karrie Osborn, Editor. **Subscription Rates:** $1 Members. **URL:** http://www.abmp.com/body-sense-magazine. **Remarks:** Accepts advertising. **Circ:** 20000.

5482 ■ Creative Machine Embroidery
F+W
741 Corporate Cir., Ste. A
Golden, CO 80401
Phone: (303)215-5600
Magazine providing information on current trends, techniques, and step-by-step instructions to the home embroiderer. Includes detailed information, easy-to-read print and web formats. **Freq:** Bimonthly. **Key Personnel:** Ellen March, Editor-in-Chief. **Subscription Rates:** $22.95 Individuals; $28.95 Canada; $34.95 Other countries. **URL:** http://www.cmemag.com/index.html. **Ad Rates:** BW $2,285; 4C $53,530. **Remarks:** Accepts advertising. **Circ:** (Not Reported).

5483 ■ Creative Thought
Centers for Spiritual Living
573 Park Point Dr.
Golden, CO 80401
Phone: (720)496-1370
Fax: (303)526-0913
Freq: Monthly. **ISSN:** 1093--8761 (print). **URL:** http://csl.org/e-news/2014/pages/february-2014_communication.html. **Remarks:** Advertising not accepted. **Circ:** (Not Reported).

5484 ■ Golden Transcript
Mile High Newspapers Inc.
110 N Rubey Dr., Ste. 120
Golden, CO 80403
Phone: (303)279-5541
Fax: (303)279-7157
Publisher's E-mail: newsroom@milehighnews.com
Community newspaper. **Freq:** Weekly (Fri.). **Print Method:** Offset. **Cols./Page:** 5. **Col. Width:** 1 7/8 inches. **Col. Depth:** 14 inches. **Key Personnel:** Jerry Healey, Publisher. **ISSN:** 0746--6382 (print). **Subscription Rates:** $30 Individuals; $20 Individuals senior. **URL:** http://goldentranscript.net. **Formerly:** Colorado Transcript; Golden Daily Transcript. **Ad Rates:** GLR $.92; BW $1,716; 4C $1,592.80; SAU $14; PCI $14. **Remarks:** Accepts advertising. **Circ:** 3000.

5485 ■ Martial Arts Professional
National Association of Professional Martial Artists
14143 Denver West Pkwy., Ste. 100
Golden, CO 80401
Phone: (727)540-0500
Fax: (727)683-9581
Publisher's E-mail: info@napma.com
Freq: Monthly. **Subscription Rates:** Included in membership; $39.95 /year. **URL:** http://www.martialartsprofessional.com. **Remarks:** Accepts advertising. **Circ:** (Not Reported).

5486 ■ Massage & Bodywork: Nurturing Mind, Body & Spirit
Associated Bodywork & Massage Professionals
25188 Genesee Trail Rd., Ste. 200
Golden, CO 80401
Phone: (303)674-8478
Free: 800-667-8260
Publisher's E-mail: expectmore@abmp.com
Magazine covering research and information about massage. **Freq:** Bimonthly. **Trim Size:** 8 1/2 x 11 1/8. **Key Personnel:** Leslie Young, Editor-in-Chief; Darren Buford, Managing Editor; Amy Klein, Manager, Production. **ISSN:** 1544-8827 (print). **Subscription Rates:** included in membership dues. **URL:** http://www.massageandbodywork.com/. **Ad Rates:** BW $2,635; 4C $3,530. **Remarks:** Accepts advertising. **Circ:** 110000.

5487 ■ McCall's Quick Quilts
F+W
741 Corporate Cir., Ste. A
Golden, CO 80401
Publication E-mail: mcq@ckmedia.com quickquilts@emailcustomerservice.com
Magazine publishing beautifully photographed, well-designed quick and easy quilting projects with complete how-to instructions. Using the latest tools, fabrics and techniques, readers with beginning to intermediate skills can complete their quilting projects successfully. **Freq:** Bimonthly. **Key Personnel:** Beth Hayes, Editor-in-Chief. **Subscription Rates:** $16.98 Individuals; $35.94 Individuals newsstand price. **URL:** http://www.quickquilts.com. **Ad Rates:** 4C $2287. **Remarks:** Accepts advertising. **Circ:** (Not Reported).

5488 ■ McCall's Quilting
F+W
741 Corporate Cir., Ste. A
Golden, CO 80401
Phone: (303)278-1010
Magazine publishing a variety of well-designed complete how-to quilting projects, including bed-size quilts, wall hangings, wearables, and small projects, for readers of all skill levels. Features beautifully photographed settings to enhance each project, while detailed instructions use the latest techniques, as well as traditional methods for piecing and quilting, to guide the reader toward achieving rewarding, innovative creations. **Freq:** Bimonthly. **Key Personnel:** Beth Hayes, Editor-in-Chief; Sherri Bain Driver, Associate Editor. **Subscription Rates:** $16.98 Individuals. **URL:** http://www.mccallsquilting.com. **Ad Rates:** 4C $4055. **Remarks:** Accepts advertising. **Circ:** (Not Reported).

5489 ■ Mines Magazine
Colorado School of Mines Alumni Association
PO Box 1410
Golden, CO 80402
Phone: (303)273-3295
Fax: (303)273-3583
Free: 800-446-9488
Publication E-mail: magazine@mines.edu
Magazine containing news of alumni and campus research, feature stories related to school, for the Colorado School of Mines. **Founded:** Jan. 01, 1910. **Freq:** 3/yr (March, July, November). **Trim Size:** 8 3/8 x 10 5/8. **Key Personnel:** Karen Gilbert, Editor. **ISSN:** 0096-4859 (print). **Subscription Rates:** $35 Individuals; $45 Other countries. **URL:** http://minesmagazine.com/?CMSPAGE=magazine/. **Ad Rates:** BW $1,595; 4C $1,595. **Remarks:** Accepts advertising. **Circ:** ‡22500.

5490 ■ The Oredigger Newspaper: The Student Newspaper of Colorado School of Mines
Colorado School of Mines Arthur Lakes Library
1400 Illinois St.
Golden, CO 80401
Phone: (303)273-3911
Fax: (303)273-3199
Publication E-mail: oredig@mines.edu
Collegiate newspaper. **Freq:** Biweekly. **Print Method:** Web offset. **Trim Size:** 23 x 14. **Cols./Page:** 6. **Col. Width:** 2 inches. **Col. Depth:** 21 inches. **Key Personnel:** Ryan Browne, Editor-in-Chief; Robert Gill, Business Manager. **Subscription Rates:** $25.50 By mail within U.S. **URL:** http://www.oredigger.net. **Ad Rates:** BW $900; PCI $7. **Remarks:** Color advertising not accepted. **Circ:** Paid ‡500, Free ‡3000.

5491 ■ Paper Crafts
F+W
741 Corporate Cir., Ste. A
Golden, CO 80401
Phone: (303)215-5600
Magazine (formerly called Crafts) focusing on things that can be created from paper. Features a variety of new styles and techniques for making handmade greeting cards; gift wraps, bags, and tags; party decorations, invitations, and favors; plus unique home accents and gifts such as hand-embellished journals, frames, and shadowboxes. Columns include 101; Tips, Tools & Techniques; Gifts from the Heart; Paper Finishes; and Simple Sentiments. Also includes a complete supply list and sweepstakes. **Freq:** 8/year. **Key Personnel:** Jennifer Schaerer, Editor-in-Chief; Susan R. Opel, Editor. **URL:** http://www.papercraftsmag.com. **Remarks:** Accepts advertising. **Circ:** (Not Reported).

5492 ■ Renewable & Sustainable Energy Reviews
Elsevier
c/o Lawrence L. Kazmerski, Ed.-in-Ch.
National Renewable Energy Laboratory
1617 Cole Blvd.
Golden, CO 80401
Phone: (303)384-6600
Fax: (303)384-6604
Publisher's E-mail: t.reller@elsevier.com
Journal covering current advances in field of renewable and sustainable energy. **Freq:** 14/yr. **Print Method:** Web offset. **Trim Size:** 7 7/8 x 10 3/4. **Cols./Page:** 3. **Col. Width:** 13 picas. **Col. Depth:** 10 inches. **Key Personnel:** A.S. Bahaj, Associate Editor; A.S.A.C. Diniz, Associate Editor; Lawrence L. Kazmerski, Editor-in-Chief. **ISSN:** 1364--0321 (print). **Subscription Rates:** $281 Individuals print; $928.27 Institutions online; $2785 Institutions print. **URL:** http://www.journals.elsevier.com/renewable-and-sustainable-energy-reviews. **Circ:** (Not Reported).

5493 ■ Science of Mind
Centers for Spiritual Living
573 Park Point Dr.
Golden, CO 80401
Phone: (720)496-1370
Fax: (303)526-0913
Religious magazine on metaphysics and self-help. **Freq:** Monthly. **Print Method:** Offset. **Trim Size:** 5 3/8 x 7 3/4. **Cols./Page:** 2. **Col. Width:** 23 nonpareils. **Col. Depth:** 86 agate lines. **Key Personnel:** Claudia Abbott, Editor-in-Chief. **ISSN:** 0036--8458 (print). **Subscription Rates:** $29.95 Individuals; $36.95 Canada; $49.95 Other countries. **URL:** http://www.scienceofmind.com. **Ad Rates:** BW $1,650; 4C $2,920. **Remarks:** Accepts advertising. **Circ:** Paid ‡45000, Controlled ‡32495.

5494 ■ Wheat Ridge Transcript Newspaper
Mile High Newspapers Inc.
110 N Rubey Dr., Ste. 120
Golden, CO 80403
Phone: (303)279-5541
Fax: (303)279-7157
Publisher's E-mail: newsroom@milehighnews.com
Community newspaper. **Freq:** Weekly. **Print Method:** Web offset. **Cols./Page:** 5. **Col. Width:** 1 7/8 inches. **Col. Depth:** 14 inches. **Key Personnel:** Mikkel Kelly, Managing Editor; Jerry Healey, Publisher. **ISSN:** 1089-

9200 (print). **Subscription Rates:** $20 Individuals; $18 Individuals senior. **Formerly**: The Weekly Transcript; The Jefferson County Transcript. **Remarks:** Accepts advertising. **Circ:** ‡200,000.

GRANBY

Grand Co. Grand Co. (N). 32 m W of Boulder. Tourism. Cattle ranching; mining.

5495 ■ Sky-Hi News
Johnson Media Inc.
424 E Agate Ave.
Granby, CO 80446
Phone: (970)887-3334
Newspaper. **Freq:** Weekly (Thurs.). **Print Method:** Offset. **Cols./Page:** 4. **Col. Width:** 28 nonpareils. **Col. Depth:** 224 agate lines. **Key Personnel:** Matt Sandberg, Publisher; Drew Munro, Editor. **Subscription Rates:** $20 Individuals in county; $25 Out of country. **URL:** http://www.skyhidailynews.com. **Mailing address:** PO Box 409, Granby, CO 80446. **Ad Rates:** GLR $.34; BW $330; 4C $700. **Remarks:** Accepts advertising. **Circ:** Paid 4800.

GRAND JUNCTION

Mesa Co. Mesa Co. (W). 250 m W of Denver. Mountain resort, skiing, hunting, fishing. Electronics. Oil shale, uranium, coal, precious metals. Diversified farming. Fruit, truck crops.

5496 ■ The Business Times of Western Colorado
The Business Times of Western Colorado
609 N Ave., Ste. 2
Grand Junction, CO 81501
Phone: (970)424-5133
Publisher's E-mail: publisher@thebusinesstimes.com
Newspaper covering local business. **Freq:** Biweekly. **Key Personnel:** Craig Hall, Publisher; Phil Castle, Editor. **Subscription Rates:** $30 Individuals. **Formerly**: Grand Valley Business Times. **Remarks:** Advertising accepted; rates available upon request. **Circ:** ‡3000.

5497 ■ The Daily Sentinel
Daily Sentinel
734 S Seventh St.
Grand Junction, CO 81501
Phone: (970)242-5050
Publisher's E-mail: letters@gjsentinel.com
General newspaper. **Founded:** 1893. **Freq:** Daily (eve.). **Print Method:** Offset. **Cols./Page:** 6. **Col. Width:** 2 1/16 inches. **Col. Depth:** 21 inches. **Key Personnel:** Rev. Dennis Mitchell, Director, Advertising; Jay Seaton, Publisher. **Subscription Rates:** $117 Individuals home delivery (Mon.-Sun.); $54.60 Individuals home delivery (Wed.-Sun.); $57.20 Individuals home delivery (Sat. & Sun.); $260 Individuals mail 52 week (Mon.-Sun.); $78 Individuals mail 26 week (Wed.-Sun.). **URL:** http://www.gjsentinel.com/. **Feature Editors:** Ann Wright, *Features*, ann.wright@gjsentinel.com. **Circ:** Mon.-Sat. ★**30400**, Sun. ★**33843**.

5498 ■ GV Magazine
Grand Valley Magazine Inc.
2500 North Ave., Ste. 1
Grand Junction, CO 81501
Phone: (970)241-3310
Magazine featuring culture, landscape, and people of the Grand Valley and surrounding area on the Western Slope of Colorado. **Freq:** Monthly. **Key Personnel:** Krystyn Hartman, Publisher; Margaret Allyson, Editor; Kitty Nicholason, Art Director. **Subscription Rates:** $40 Individuals. **URL:** http://www.grandvalleymagazine.com. **Remarks:** Advertising accepted; rates available upon request. **Circ:** (Not Reported).

5499 ■ The Nickel Want Ads
Grand Junction Newspapers Inc.
1635 N First St.
Grand Junction, CO 81501
Phone: (970)242-5050
Community newspaper. **Freq:** Weekly. **Key Personnel:** Kari Fowler, General Manager. **URL:** http://nickads.com. **Remarks:** Accepts advertising. **Circ:** Combined 25000.

5500 ■ KAFM-FM - 88.1
1310 Ute Ave.
Grand Junction, CO 81501
Phone: (970)241-8801
Fax: (970)245-0995
Format: Jazz; Blues. **Owner:** Grand Valley Public Radio Inc., at above address. **Key Personnel:** Ryan Stringfellow, Exec. Dir., ryan@kafmradio.org. **Ad Rates:** Advertising accepted; rates available upon request. **URL:** http://www.kafmradio.org.

5501 ■ KBKL-FM - 107.9
315 Kennedy Ave.
Grand Junction, CO 81501
Phone: (970)242-7788
Format: Oldies. **Owner:** Cumulus Broadcasting Inc., 3280 Peachtree Rd. NW, Ste. 2300, Atlanta, GA 30305-2447, Ph: (404)949-0700, Fax: (404)949-0740. **Ad Rates:** Noncommercial. **URL:** http://www.kool1079.com.

5502 ■ KCIC-FM - 88.5
3102 E Rd.
Grand Junction, CO 81504
Fax: (970)434-8391
Format: Religious. **Networks:** Independent. **Founded:** 1979. **Operating Hours**: 6 am - 11 pm. **ADI**: Grand Junction-Durango, CO. **Wattage**: 450. **Ad Rates:** Noncommercial. **URL:** http://www.pearparkbaptistchurch.org/Pages/KCICFMRadio.aspx.

5503 ■ KDTA-AM - 1400
1354 E Sherwood Dr.
Grand Junction, CO 81501-7546
Phone: (303)874-4411
Format: Talk. **Key Personnel:** Ken Andrews, Mgr. **Ad Rates:** Noncommercial. **URL:** http://www.kjol.org.

5504 ■ KEKB-FM - 99.9
315 Kennedy Ave.
Grand Junction, CO 81501
Phone: (970)242-7788
Format: Country. **Owner:** Cumulus Broadcasting Inc., 3280 Peachtree Rd. NW, Ste. 2300, Atlanta, GA 30305-2447, Ph: (404)949-0700, Fax: (404)949-0740. **Founded:** 1998. **Formerly**: Jan Di Broadcasting, Inc. **Operating Hours**: Continuous. **Wattage**: 79,000. **Ad Rates:** $15-85 for 30 seconds. **URL:** http://www.kekbfm.com.

5505 ■ KEXO-AM - 1230
315 Kennedy Ave.
Grand Junction, CO 81501
Phone: (970)242-7788
Format: Sports. **Owner:** Cumulus Corporation, 315 Kennedy Ave., Grand Junction, CO 81501. **Founded:** 1948. **Operating Hours**: Continuous. **ADI**: Grand Junction-Durango, CO. **Ad Rates:** Advertising accepted; rates available upon request. **URL:** http://1230espn.com/.

5506 ■ KGLN-AM - 980
1360 E Sherwood Dr.
Grand Junction, CO 81501
Format: Talk. **Networks:** CNN Radio. **Operating Hours**: Continuous. **Key Personnel:** David Beck, Contact. **Wattage**: 1,000. **Ad Rates:** $12-20 for 30 seconds; $15-24 for 60 seconds. Combined advertising rates available with KMTS-FM: for 30 seconds for 60 seconds. **URL:** http://www.1100knzz.com.

5507 ■ KJCT-TV - 8
2531 Blichmann Ave.
Grand Junction, CO 81505
Phone: (970)245-8880
Email: promotions@kjct8.com
Format: News. **Owner:** Pike's Peak Broadcasting Co., at above address. **Operating Hours**: Continuous. **ADI**: Grand Junction-Durango, CO. **Key Personnel:** Jay Rademacher, Chief Engineer, jay.rademacher@kjct8.com; Dylan Hardy, Div. Mgr., dylan.hardy@kjct8.com. **Wattage**: 15,000 ERP. **Ad Rates:** Advertising accepted; rates available upon request. $10-500 for 30 seconds. **URL:** http://www.kjct8.com.

5508 ■ KJOL-AM - 620
1354 E Sherwood Dr.
Grand Junction, CO 81501-7546
Phone: (970)254-5565
Fax: (970)254-5550
Free: 866-532-5565
Email: info@kjol.org
Format: Contemporary Christian. **Operating Hours:** Continuous. **Key Personnel:** Kurt Neuswanger, Music Dir., kurt@kjol.org. **Wattage**: 080. **Ad Rates:** Noncommercial. **URL:** http://www.kjol.org.

5509 ■ KJOL-FM - 99.5
1354 E Sherwood Dr.
Grand Junction, CO 81501
Phone: (970)254-5565
Fax: (970)254-5550
Free: 866-532-5565
Email: info@kjol.org
Format: Contemporary Christian. **Networks:** Moody Broadcasting. **Founded:** 1982. **Operating Hours**: Continuous. **ADI**: Grand Junction-Durango, CO. **Key Personnel:** Ken Andrews, Station Mgr., ken@kjol.org; Kurt Neuswanger, Dept. Mgr. **Wattage**: 1,500 ERP. **URL:** http://www.kjol.org.

5510 ■ KJYE-FM - 92.3
1360 E Sherwood Dr.
Grand Junction, CO 81501
Phone: (970)254-2100
Fax: (970)245-7551
Format: Easy Listening. **Owner:** MBC Grand Broadcasting, 1360 E Sherwood Dr., Grand Junction, CO 81501. **Founded:** 1960. **Operating Hours**: Continuous. **ADI**: Grand Junction-Durango, CO. **Wattage**: 100,000 ERP. **Ad Rates:** Noncommercial.

5511 ■ KKCO-TV - 11
2531 Blichmann Ave.
Grand Junction, CO 81505
Phone: (970)243-1111
Fax: (970)243-1770
Email: news@nbc11news.com
Format: News. **Networks:** NBC. **Owner:** Gray Television Inc., 4370 Peachtree Rd. NE, No. 400, Atlanta, GA 30319-3054, Ph: (404)266-8333. **Founded:** July 19, 1996. **Operating Hours**: Continuous. **ADI**: Grand Junction-Durango, CO. **Key Personnel:** Amanda Wagner, News Dir., amanda.wagner@nbc11news.com; Dana McDonald, Gen. Mgr., dana.mcdonald@nbc11news.com; Scot Stewart, Promotions Mgr., scot.stewart@nbc11news.com. **Local Programs**: *11 News*, Monday Tuesday Wednesday Thursday Friday 5:30 a.m.; 10:00 p.m. **Wattage**: 155,000. **Ad Rates:** Noncommercial. KPYD-FM Telleride. **URL:** http://www.nbc11news.com.

5512 ■ KKNN-FM - 95.1
315 Kennedy Ave.
Grand Junction, CO 81501-7552
Phone: (970)242-7788
Format: Classic Rock. **Simulcasts:** WTHK, WCHR. **Owner:** Cumulus Broadcasting Inc., 3280 Peachtree Rd. NW, Ste. 2300, Atlanta, GA 30305-2447, Ph: (404)949-0700, Fax: (404)949-0740. **Founded:** 1985. **Formerly**: KKLY-FM. **Operating Hours**: 5:00 a.m. - 10:00 a.m. 3:00 p.m. - Midnight Monday - Friday,. **ADI**: Grand Junction-Durango, CO. **Key Personnel:** Kevin Wodlinger, Mktg. Mgr.; Mike Shafer, Operations Mgr. **Wattage**: 100,000 ERP. **Ad Rates:** Advertising accepted; rates available upon request. **URL:** http://95rockfm.com.

5513 ■ KLFV-FM - 90.3
PO Box 779002
Rocklin, CA 95677-9972
Fax: (916)251-1901
Free: 800-525-5683
Email: info@klove.com
Format: Contemporary Christian. **Owner:** Educational Media Foundation, PO Box 2098, Omaha, NE 68103-2098, Free: 800-434-8400. **ADI**: Grand Junction-Durango, CO. **Key Personnel:** Mike Novak, President, CEO; Alan Mason, COO. **Wattage**: 3,000. **URL:** http://www.klove.com.

5514 ■ KMGJ-FM - 93.1
1360 E Sherwood Dr.
Grand Junction, CO 81501
Phone: (970)254-2100
Email: 931magic@gmail.com
Format: Adult Contemporary. **Networks:** Independent. **Owner:** MBC Grand Broadcasting, 1360 E Sherwood Dr., Grand Junction, CO 81501. **Formerly**: KQIX-FM. **Operating Hours**: Continuous. **ADI**: Grand Junction-Durango, CO. **Wattage**: 100,000. **Ad Rates:** Noncommercial. **URL:** http://www.931magic.com.

5515 ■ KMOZ-FM - 100.7
1360 E Sherwood Dr.
Grand Junction, CO 81501-7546

Circulation: ★ = AAM; △ or • = BPA; ♦ = CAC; ❑ = VAC; ⊕ = PO Statement; ‡ = Publisher's Report; Boldface figures = sworn; Light figures = estimated.

Phone: (970)254-2121
Format: Country. **Ad Rates:** Noncommercial.

5516 ■ KMSA-FM - 91.3
1100 North Ave.
Grand Junction, CO 81501-3122
Phone: (970)248-1240
Format: Alternative/New Music/Progressive; Hip Hop. **Founded:** 1975. **Operating Hours:** Continuous. **ADI:** Grand Junction-Durango, CO. **Key Personnel:** Prof. Regis Tucci, Fac. Adv., rtucci@mesastate.edu. **Wattage:** 3,000. **Ad Rates:** Noncommercial. **URL:** http://kmsa913.com.

5517 ■ KMXY-FM - 104.3
315 Kennedy Ave.
Grand Junction, CO 81501
Phone: (970)242-7788
Fax: (970)243-0567
Format: Adult Contemporary. **Owner:** Cumulus Broadcasting Inc., 3280 Peachtree Rd. NW, Ste. 2300, Atlanta, GA 30305-2447, Ph: (404)949-0700, Fax: (404)949-0740. **URL:** http://www.coloradowest.com.

5518 ■ KNZZ-AM - 1100
1360 E Sherwood Dr.
Grand Junction, CO 81501
Phone: (970)254-2100
Format: News; Talk. **Networks:** CBS; ABC; Daynet. **Owner:** MBC Grand Broadcasting, 1360 E Sherwood Dr., Grand Junction, CO 81501. **Formerly:** KJYE. **Operating Hours:** Continuous. **ADI:** Grand Junction-Durango, CO. **Key Personnel:** David Beck, Contact. **Wattage:** 50,000 Day; 10,000 Night. **Ad Rates:** per unit. Combined advertising rates available with. **URL:** http://www.1100knzz.com.

5519 ■ KPRU-FM - 103.3
Bridges Broadcast Ctr.
7409 S Alton Ct.
Centennial, CO 80112
Fax: (303)733-3319
Free: 800-722-4449
Format: Classical. **Owner:** Colorado Public Radio, at above address. **Key Personnel:** Max Wycisk, President; Sean Nethery, Sr. VP; Mark Coulter, VP of Production; Dan Murphy, VP of HR. **Wattage:** 12,000. **URL:** http://www.cpr.org/listen/where.

5520 ■ KREG-TV - 3
345 Hillcrest Ave.
Grand Junction, CO 81501
Phone: (972)373-8800
Format: Commercial TV. **Networks:** CBS. **Owner:** Withers Broadcasting Companies, 1822 N Court St., Marion, IL 62959, Ph: (303)242-5000. **Operating Hours:** Continuous. **Key Personnel:** Matt Stubbs, Contact. **Wattage:** 16,100 H. **URL:** http://www.westernslopenow.com.

5521 ■ KREX-TV - 5
345 Hillcrest Dr.
Grand Junction, CO 81501
Phone: (970)242-5000
Fax: (970)242-0886
Format: Commercial TV. **Networks:** CBS. **Owner:** W. Russell Withers, Jr., at above address. **Founded:** 1954. **Operating Hours:** Continuous; 75% network, 25% local. **ADI:** Grand Junction-Durango, CO. **Key Personnel:** Randy Stone, Gen. Mgr.; Shelley Moore, Contact; David Lippman, Sports Dir. **Ad Rates:** $35-425 per unit. **URL:** http://www.krextv.com.

5522 ■ KRGS-AM - 690
751 Horizon Ct., No. 225
Grand Junction, CO 81506
Phone: (970)241-6460
Fax: (970)241-6452
Email: frank@wscradio.net
Format: News; Talk; Sports. **Networks:** Jones Satellite. **Owner:** Western Slope Communications, LLC, at above address. **Operating Hours:** Continuous. **Ad Rates:** Noncommercial. **URL:** http://www.wscradio.net/.

5523 ■ KRMJ-TV - 18
890 Hall Ave
Grand Junction, CO 81505
Phone: (970)245-1818
Networks: Public Broadcasting Service (PBS). **Owner:** Rocky Mountain Public Broadcasting Network Inc., 1089 Bannock St., Denver, CO 80204, Ph: (303)892-6666, Fax: (303)620-5600, Free: 800-274-6666. **Key Personnel:** David Miller, Chairperson; David Leonard, V. Chmn. of the Bd.; Michael Reynolds, Dir. of Production, michaelreynolds@rmpbs.org; Tom Craig, Chief Tech. Ofc., tomcraig@rmpbs.org. **URL:** http://www.rmpbs.org/.

5524 ■ KRYD-FM - 104.9
444 Seasons Dr.
Grand Junction, CO 81503
Phone: (970)263-4100
Fax: (970)263-9600
Email: studio@krydradio.com
Format: Album-Oriented Rock (AOR). **Owner:** Rocky III Investments, Inc., at above address. **Founded:** Oct. 29, 1997. **Operating Hours:** Continuous. **Wattage:** 24,000 ERP. **Ad Rates:** Noncommercial. **URL:** http://www.krydfm.com.

KSTR-FM - See Montrose

5525 ■ KTMM-AM - 1340
1360 E Sherwood Dr.
Grand Junction, CO 81501
Phone: (970)254-2100
Format: Sports; Talk. **Networks:** Fox. **Owner:** MBC Grand Broadcasting, 1360 E Sherwood Dr., Grand Junction, CO 81501. **Operating Hours:** Continuous. **ADI:** Grand Junction-Durango, CO. **Key Personnel:** Jim Davis, Contact; Jim Davis, Contact; Greg Wentzel, Contact; Reo VanGilder, Contact. **Wattage:** 1,000. **Ad Rates:** Noncommercial. **URL:** http://www.theteam1340.com.

5526 ■ K205CK-FM - 88.9
PO Box 391
Twin Falls, ID 83303
Fax: (208)736-1958
Free: 800-357-4226
Format: Religious; Contemporary Christian. **Owner:** CSN International, PO Box 391, Twin Falls, ID 83303, Ph: (208)736-1958, Fax: (208)736-1958, Free: 800-357-4226. **Key Personnel:** Kelly Carlson, Dir. of Engg.; Ray Gorney, Asst. Dir.; Don Mills, Music Dir., Prog. Dir. **URL:** http://www.csnradio.com.

5527 ■ KURA-FM - 105.7
751 Horizon Ct., Ste. 225
Grand Junction, CO 81506
Phone: (970)241-6460
Format: Country. **Simulcasts:** KAYW. **Founded:** 1987. **Operating Hours:** 6 a.m.-midnight. **Key Personnel:** John Ward, Gen. Mgr. **Wattage:** 60,000 Horizontal ER. **Ad Rates:** $6 for 30 seconds; $8.50 for 60 seconds. **URL:** http://wscradio.net.

5528 ■ KZKS-FM - 105.3
751 Horizon Ct., Ste. 225
Grand Junction, CO 81506
Phone: (970)241-6460
Format: Contemporary Hit Radio (CHR). **Networks:** Independent. **Owner:** Western Slope Communications, LLC, at above address. **Founded:** 1988. **Formerly:** KWWS-FM; KDBL-FM. **Operating Hours:** Continuous. **Key Personnel:** Katie Robley, Bus. Mgr.; Michael Johnson, Bus. Mgr., michael@range105.net. **Wattage:** 100,000. **Ad Rates:** $8-20 per unit. **URL:** http://wscradio.net/drive_105.htm.

GREELEY

Weld Co. Weld Co. (N). 50 m N of Denver. University of Northern Colorado and AIMS Junior College. Manufactures sugar, mobile homes, canned vegetables, butter, concrete products, machinery, potato sorters. Bottling works; meat packing plant; nursery; feed lots. Dairy products. Agriculture. Potatoes, sugar beets, alfalfa, grain, corn, beans.

5529 ■ The Fence Post
Greeley Publishing Co.
501 8th Ave.
Greeley, CO 80631
Phone: (970)352-0211
Farm and ranch magazine. **Freq:** Weekly (Mon.). **Print Method:** Offset. **Trim Size:** 8 x 10 3/4. **Cols./Page:** 4. **Col. Width:** 21 nonpareils. **Col. Depth:** 137 agate lines. **Key Personnel:** Nikki Work, Editor. **Subscription Rates:** $52 Individuals; $55 Two years. **URL:** http://www.thefencepost.com/. **Ad Rates:** BW $260; PCI $15. **Remarks:** Accepts advertising. **Circ:** Paid 30000.

5530 ■ The Greeley Tribune
Greeley Publishing Co.
501 8th Ave.
Greeley, CO 80631
Phone: (970)352-0211
General newspaper. **Freq:** Daily. **Print Method:** Offset. **Cols./Page:** 6. **Col. Width:** 25 nonpareils. **Col. Depth:** 301 agate lines. **Key Personnel:** Randy Bangert, Editor, phone: (970)392-4435; Bart Smith, Publisher, phone: (970)392-4403. **USPS:** 228-040. **Subscription Rates:** 13.25 print and online, monthly. **URL:** http://www.greeleytribune.com. **Remarks:** Advertising accepted; rates available upon request. **Circ:** Combined ‡19809, Combined ‡22633.

5531 ■ International Journal of Biological Macromolecules
Elsevier
c/o A. Dong, Ed.-in-Ch.
University of Northern Colorado
Department of Chemistry & Biochemistry
CB 98, Ross Hall 2576
Greeley, CO 80639
Publisher's E-mail: t.reller@elsevier.com
Journal featuring the structure of natural macromolecules includes biological interactions, molecular associations, and functional properties as well as related model systems, conformational studies, new techniques, and theoretical developments. **Freq:** Monthly. **Print Method:** Offset. **Trim Size:** 5 1/2 x 8 1/2. **Cols./Page:** 1. **Col. Width:** 50 nonpareils. **Col. Depth:** 100 agate lines. **Key Personnel:** A. Dong, Editor-in-Chief; J.F. Kennedy, Editor-in-Chief. **ISSN:** 0141--8130 (print). **Subscription Rates:** $301 Individuals print; $2366.40 Institutions online; $3550 Institutions print. **URL:** http://www.journals.elsevier.com/international-journal-of-biological-macromolecules. **Circ:** (Not Reported).

5532 ■ Journal of Musicological Research
Routledge
School of Music
Frasier Hall
University of Northern Colorado
CB 28
Greeley, CO 80639
Fax: (970)351-1923
Publisher's E-mail: book.orders@tandf.co.uk
Publication covering music. **Freq:** Quarterly. **Trim Size:** 6 x 9. **Key Personnel:** Mary Natvig, Editor; Jonathan Bellman, Board Member; Philip V. Bohlman, Board Member; Susan Youens, Board Member; Deborah Kauffman, Editor-in-Chief. **ISSN:** 0141--1896 (print); **EISSN:** 1547--7304 (electronic). **Subscription Rates:** $168 Individuals print only; $357 Institutions online only; $408 Institutions print & online. **URL:** http://www.tandfonline.com/toc/gmur20/current#.VH-0vNIW2qY. **Remarks:** Accepts advertising. **Circ:** (Not Reported).

5533 ■ The Mirror
Student Media Corp.
823 16th St.
Greeley, CO 80631
Phone: (970)392-9270
Fax: (970)392-9025
Publisher's E-mail: web@uncmirror.com
Collegiate newspaper. **Founded:** 1919. **Freq:** 3/week 11 3/8 x 13 1/2. **Print Method:** Offset. **Cols./Page:** 5. **Col. Width:** 10 inches. **Col. Depth:** 13 inches. **Subscription Rates:** $60 By mail. **URL:** http://www.uncmirror.com/. **Ad Rates:** GLR $4; BW $481.65; 4C $631.65; SAU $8.15; PCI $7.60. **Remarks:** Accepts advertising. **Circ:** Free ‡12000.

5534 ■ Technical Services Quarterly: New Trends in Computers, Automation & Advanced Technologies in the Technical Operation of Libraries & Information Centers
Routledge Journals Taylor & Francis Group
c/o James A. Michener Library
University of North Colorado
Greeley, CO 80639
New trends in Computers, Automation, and Advanced Technologies in the Technical Operation of Libraries and Information Centers. **Freq:** Quarterly. **Trim Size:** 6 x 8 3/8. **Cols./Page:** 1. **Col. Width:** 4 3/8 inches. **Col. Depth:** 7 1/8 inches. **Key Personnel:** Barry B. Baker, Board Member; Gary M. Pitkin, PhD, Editor-in-Chief; Glenda Ann Thornton, PhD, Board Member. **ISSN:** 0731--7131 (print); **EISSN:** 1555--3337 (electronic). **Subscription Rates:** $234 Individuals online only. **URL:** http://www.tandfonline.com/toc/wtsq20/current#.VGvyVNIW2qY. **Formerly:** Topics in Technical Services.

Ad Rates: BW $375; 4C $650. **Remarks:** Accepts advertising. **Circ:** (Not Reported).

5535 ■ Community Radio for Northern Colorado - 91.5
1901 56th Ave., Ste. 200
Greeley, CO 80634-2950
Phone: (970)378-2579
Free: 800-443-5862
Email: comment@kunc.org
Format: Public Radio. **Networks:** National Public Radio (NPR); BBC World Service. **Founded:** 1967. **Operating Hours**: Continuous. **Key Personnel:** Kirk Mowers, Operations Mgr., kirk.mowers@kunc.org; Brian Larson, Managing Ed; Neil Best, Contact, neil.best@kunc.org; Brian Larson, Contact. **Wattage**: 36,000 ERP. **Ad Rates:** Underwriting available. **URL:** http://www.kunc.org.

5536 ■ KFKA-AM - 1310
1002 31st Ave.
Greeley, CO 80634
Phone: (970)356-1310
Fax: (970)356-1214
Email: info@1310kfka.com
Format: News; Talk. **Founded:** 1870. **Key Personnel:** Troy Coverdale, News Dir. **Ad Rates:** Advertising accepted; rates available upon request. **URL:** http://www.1310kfka.com.

5537 ■ KGRE-AM - 1450
800 Eighth Ave., Ste. 304
Greeley, CO 80631
Phone: (970)356-1452
Format: Hispanic. **Networks:** Independent. **Owner:** Greeley Broadcasting Co., at above address. **Founded:** 1947. **Formerly**: KATR-AM. **Operating Hours:** Continuous. **Wattage**: 1,000. **Ad Rates:** Noncommercial. **URL:** http://www.tigrecolorado.com.

5538 ■ KJAC-FM
1901 56th Ave.
Greeley, CO 80634-2950
Phone: (303)296-7025
Fax: (303)296-7030
Format: Eclectic. **Owner:** NRC Broadcasting Co., at above address. **Wattage**: 50,000 ERP. **Ad Rates:** Advertising accepted; rates available upon request.

KPCR-FM - See Burlington, CO

GREENWOOD VILLAGE

5539 ■ ColoradoBiz
WiesnerMedia L.L.C.
6160 S Syracuse Way, Ste. 300
Greenwood Village, CO 80111
Phone: (303)662-5200
Business publication covering local issues. **Freq:** Monthly. **Print Method:** Web Offset. **Trim Size:** 8 3/8 x 10 7/8. **Key Personnel:** Dan Wiesner, Chief Executive Officer, Publisher; Mike Taylor, Managing Editor, phone: (303)662-5223. **ISSN:** 1523-6366 (print). **Subscription Rates:** $4 Single issue. **URL:** http://www.cobizmag.com. **Ad Rates:** BW $5,270; 4C $6,460. **Remarks:** Accepts advertising. **Circ:** (Not Reported).

5540 ■ Electronics Protection
Webcom Communications Corp.
7355 E Orchard Rd., Ste. 100
Greenwood Village, CO 80111
Phone: (720)528-3770
Fax: (720)528-3771
Free: 800-803-9488
Publisher's E-mail: general@webcomcommunications.com
Magazine for OEM engineers and product development professionals who work with electrical equipment in a variety of industries. **Freq:** Bimonthly. **Subscription Rates:** $60 Other countries. **URL:** http://www.equipmentprotectionmagazine.com. **Formerly**: Equipment Protection. **Remarks:** Accepts advertising. **Circ:** (Not Reported).

5541 ■ Fuel Cell
Webcom Communications Corp.
7355 E Orchard Rd., Ste. 100
Greenwood Village, CO 80111
Phone: (720)528-3770
Fax: (720)528-3771
Free: 800-803-9488
Publisher's E-mail: general@webcomcommunications.com
Trade publication covering development, integration, and applications of fuel cell technology. **Freq:** Bimonthly. **Subscription Rates:** $52 Other countries; $26 Students, other countries. **Remarks:** Accepts advertising. **Circ:** (Not Reported).

5542 ■ The Journal of Investment Consulting
Investment Management Consultants Association
5619 DTC Pky., Ste. 500
Greenwood Village, CO 80111
Phone: (303)770-3377
Fax: (303)770-1812
Publisher's E-mail: info@imca.org
Journal focusing on business consulting and researches, including commentary from academic authorities, industry leaders, and authors. **Freq:** Semiannual. **Key Personnel:** Debbie Nochlin, Managing Editor. **Subscription Rates:** $180 Nonmembers 1 year. **URL:** http://www.imca.org/pages/journal-investment-consulting. **Remarks:** Advertising not accepted. **Circ:** (Not Reported).

5543 ■ Magnetics Business & Technology
Webcom Communications Corp.
7355 E Orchard Rd., Ste. 100
Greenwood Village, CO 80111
Phone: (720)528-3770
Fax: (720)528-3771
Free: 800-803-9488
Publisher's E-mail: general@webcomcommunications.com
Trade publication for technical professionals who integrate or utilize magnetic technologies in their products and applications. **Freq:** Quarterly. **Key Personnel:** Heather Krier, Editor. **Subscription Rates:** $44 Individuals; $60 Other countries; Free to qualified subscribers. **URL:** http://www.magneticsmagazine.com/main. **Remarks:** Accepts advertising. **Circ:** (Not Reported).

5544 ■ Remote Site & Equipment Management
Webcom Communications Corp.
7355 E Orchard Rd., Ste. 100
Greenwood Village, CO 80111
Phone: (720)528-3770
Fax: (720)528-3771
Free: 800-803-9488
Publisher's E-mail: general@webcomcommunications.com
Tabloid newsmagazine for owners and operators of remotely-operated sites, facilities, and equipment. **Freq:** Bimonthly. **Key Personnel:** Nick Depperschmidt, Director; Jessi Albers, Director, Sales. **URL:** http://www.remotemagazine.com/main. **Ad Rates:** 4C $1500. **Remarks:** Accepts advertising. **Circ:** 20000.

5545 ■ Stitches Magazine
Intertec Publishing Corp.
5680 Greenwood Plaza Blvd., Ste. 100
Greenwood Village, CO 80111
Phone: (303)741-2901
Fax: (720)489-3101
Publication E-mail: stitches@asicentral.com
Trade and business magazine for commercial embroiderers. **Founded:** May 1987. **Freq:** 14/yr. **Print Method:** Offset. **Key Personnel:** Melinda Ligos, Editor-in-Chief; Joe Haley, Managing Editor. **ISSN:** 0899-5893 (print). **URL:** http://www.stitches.com. **Ad Rates:** 4C $5,341. **Remarks:** Accepts advertising. **Circ:** Combined 18302.

5546 ■ Western Livestock Journal
Crow Publications Inc.
7355 E Orchard Rd., Ste. 300
Greenwood Village, CO 80111
Phone: (303)722-7600
Fax: (303)722-0155
Free: 800-850-2769
Publication E-mail: editorial@wlj.net
Newspaper (tabloid) covering cattle industry and other livestock industry. **Freq:** Weekly. **Print Method:** Offset. **Trim Size:** 11 1/2 x 16 3/4. **Cols./Page:** 6. **Col. Width:** 19 nonpareils. **Col. Depth:** 224 agate lines. **Key Personnel:** Pete Crow, Publisher. **ISSN:** 0094--6710 (print). **Subscription Rates:** $50 Individuals; $75 Two years; $100 Individuals 3 years. **URL:** http://www.wlj.net. **Ad Rates:** BW $2280; 4C $450. **Remarks:** Accepts advertising. **Circ:** (Not Reported).

5547 ■ KEPN-AM - 1600
7800 E Orchard Rd., Ste. 400
Greenwood Village, CO 80111
Phone: (303)321-0950
Format: Sports. **Key Personnel:** Tim Spence, Contact, timothy.spence@lincolnfinancialmedia.com; Steven Price, Contact, steven.price@lincolnfinancialmedia.com.

KIDN-FM - See Hayden

KKTL-AM - See Casper, WY

KLDJ-FM - See Duluth, MN

5548 ■ KQKS-FM - 107.5
7800 E Orchard Rd., Ste. 400
Greenwood Village, CO 80111
Phone: (303)321-0950
Format: Hip Hop. **Key Personnel:** Cat Collins, Dir. of Programs, ccollins@ks1075.com; John Kage, Music Dir., jkage@ks1075.com. **Wattage**: 91,000. **Ad Rates:** Noncommercial. **URL:** http://www.ks1075.com.

5549 ■ KREC-FM
7400 E Orchard Rd.
Greenwood Village, CO 80111
Phone: (801)586-9812
Fax: (801)586-9889
Email: bh98@tcd.net
Format: Adult Contemporary. **Networks:** Unistar. **Owner:** Jeff and Pam Johnston, PO Box 1084, Parowan, UT 84761, Ph: (801)477-3442. **Founded:** 1988. **Key Personnel:** Rob Price, Dir. of Production. **Wattage**: 54,000 ERP. **Ad Rates:** $9.50-18 for 30 seconds; $15-35 for 60 seconds.

5550 ■ KRKY-AM
5670 Greenwood Plaza Blvd.
Greenwood Village, CO 80111
Phone: (303)887-2566
Fax: (303)887-3295
Format: Adult Contemporary; Country; Oldies. **Networks:** Satellite Music Network. **Founded:** 1986. **Wattage**: 4,500 Day; 121 Night. **Ad Rates:** $12 for 30 seconds; $15 for 60 seconds.

5551 ■ KSKE-FM - 104.7
5660 Greenwood Plaza Blvd., Ste. 490N
Greenwood Village, CO 80111
Phone: (720)726-7777
Format: Classic Rock. **Owner:** Vail/Aspen Broadcasting Ltd., at above address. **Founded:** 1974. **Operating Hours**: Continuous. **Key Personnel:** Terry Mathis, Gen. Mgr; Lisa Percell, Contact. **Wattage**: 100,000. **Ad Rates:** $25 per unit. **URL:** http://alwaysmountaintime.com/kske.

5552 ■ KWCD-FM - 107.3
7400 E Orchard Rd.
Greenwood Village, CO 80111
Owner: Westcom Communications Corp., at above address. **Founded:** 1984. **Formerly**: KOSZ-FM. **Key Personnel:** Laurie Cannon, Contact. **Wattage**: 4,200. **Ad Rates:** $20-35 per unit.

5553 ■ KWGN-TV - 2
6160 S Wabash Way
Greenwood Village, CO 80111
Phone: (303)740-2222
Email: sales@cw2.com
Format: Commercial TV. **Networks:** Warner Brothers Studios. **Owner:** The Tribune Media Co., 435 N Michigan Ave., Chicago, IL 60611-4066, Ph: (312)222-9100, Fax: (312)222-4206, Free: 800-874-2863. **Founded:** July 18, 1952. **Operating Hours**: Continuous; 100% local. **ADI**: Denver (Steamboat Springs), CO. **Key Personnel:** Beverly Martinez, Contact, bmartinez@cw2.com. **Ad Rates:** Advertising accepted; rates available upon request.

5554 ■ KWWW-FM
7400 E Orchard Rd.
Greenwood Village, CO 80111
Format: Adult Contemporary. **Founded:** Sept. 07, 2006. **Wattage**: 440 ERP.

5555 ■ KXDR-FM
7400 E Orchard Rd.
Greenwood Village, CO 80111
Format: Top 40. **Wattage**: 38,000 ERP. **Ad Rates:** Advertising accepted; rates available upon request.

Circulation: ★ = AAM; △ or • = BPA; ♦ = CAC; ❑ = VAC; ⊕ = PO Statement; ‡ = Publisher's Report; Boldface figures = sworn; Light figures = estimated.

5556 ■ KYGO-FM - 98.5
7800 E Orchard Rd.
Greenwood Village, CO 80111
Phone: (303)321-0950
Format: Contemporary Country. **Simulcasts:** KYGO-1. **Operating Hours**: Continuous; 100% local. **ADI**: Denver (Steamboat Springs), CO. **Key Personnel:** John Thomas, Dir. of Programs, jthomas@kygo.com; Garret Doll, Contact, gdoll@kygo.com. **Wattage**: 100,000. **Ad Rates:** Advertising accepted; rates available upon request. **URL:** http://www.kygo.com.

5557 ■ KZPH-FM - 106.7
7400 E Orchard Rd., Ste. 2800 N
Greenwood Village, CO 80111
Phone: (303)468-6500
Format: Classic Rock. **Networks:** ABC; Satellite Music Network. **Owner:** Sunbrook Communications, at above address. **Founded:** 1995. **Operating Hours**: Continuous. **Key Personnel:** Jim Senst, Gen. Mgr., jims@fisherwen.com; Dave Keefer, Dir. of Programs, dave@jazz-stream.com; Leona Frank, Sales Mgr., lfrank@fisherwen.com; Tera Hurd, Bus. Mgr., tera@fisherwen.com. **Wattage**: 5,000. **Ad Rates:** Advertising accepted; rates available upon request.

GUNNISON

Gunnison Co. Gunnison Co. (W). On Gunnison River, 125 m SE of Grand Junction. Western State College of Colorado. Resort. Pine timber. Hay, cattle.

5558 ■ Gunnison Country Times
Gunnison Country Times
218 N Wisconsin
Gunnison, CO 81230
Phone: (970)641-1414
Publisher's E-mail: editor@gunnisontimes.com
Community newspaper. **Freq:** Weekly (Wed.). **Print Method:** Offset. **Cols./Page:** 5. **Col. Width:** 1.904 inches. **Col. Depth:** 294 agate lines. **Key Personnel:** Chris Dickey, Owner, Publisher. **USPS:** 092-113. **Subscription Rates:** $41 Individuals; $53 Individuals out of county; $36 Individuals digital. **URL:** http://www.gunnisontimes.com. **Ad Rates:** GLR $.62; BW $720; 4C $900; PCI $10.80. **Remarks:** Accepts advertising. **Circ:** ‡4000.

5559 ■ KEJJ-FM - 98.3
PO Box 1288
Gunnison, CO 81230
Phone: (970)641-4000
Fax: (970)641-3300
Format: Adult Contemporary. **Networks:** Jones Satellite. **Founded:** 1980. **Formerly**: KGUC-FM; KKYY-FM; KPKE-AM 1490 1KW. **Operating Hours**: Continuous. **Wattage**: 25,000. **Ad Rates:** $10 for 30 seconds; $12 for 60 seconds. Combined advertising rates available with KPKB-AM.

5560 ■ KPKE-AM - 1490
PO Box 1288
Gunnison, CO 81230
Phone: (970)641-4000
Format: Oldies; Full Service. **Networks:** ABC; CBS. **Founded:** June 1960. **Formerly**: KGUC-AM-FM. **Operating Hours**: Continuous. **Key Personnel:** H. Rees, Gen. Mgr. **Wattage**: 1,000; 25,000 FM. **Ad Rates:** $8.50-15.50 for 30 seconds; for 60 seconds.

5561 ■ KSKE-AM - 610
1445 Hwy. 135 N
Gunnison, CO 81230
Phone: (303)476-1047
Fax: (303)949-6386
Format: Country; Adult Contemporary. **Networks:** Jones Satellite. **Owner:** Vail/Aspen Broadcasting Ltd., at above address. **Founded:** 1983. **Formerly**: KVMT-AM. **Operating Hours**: Continuous. **Key Personnel:** William Varecha, Gen. Mgr; Lisa Percell, Contact. **Wattage**: 5,000 day; 217 night. **Ad Rates:** $12 per unit. **URL:** http://www.kvleradio.com.

5562 ■ KWSB-FM - 91.1
Communication Arts, Languages, & Literature
Taylor Hall 116
Gunnison, CO 81231
Phone: (970)943-2025
Email: library@western.edu
Format: Eclectic; Educational. **Networks:** AP. **Founded:** 1968. **Operating Hours**: 6 a.m.-midnight. **Key Personnel:** Laura Anderson, Dir. of Programs, laura.anderson@western.edu; Terry Schliesman, Fac. Adv., Gen. Mgr., terry.schliesman@western.edu. **Wattage**: 100. **Ad Rates:** Noncommercial. **URL:** http://www.western.edu.

GYPSUM

5563 ■ KLRY-FM - 91.3
PO Box 779002
Rocklin, CA 95677-9972
Free: 800-525-5683
Format: Contemporary Christian. **Owner:** Educational Media Foundation, PO Box 2098, Omaha, NE 68103-2098, Free: 800-434-8400. **Key Personnel:** Alan Mason, COO; Mike Novak, President, CEO. **URL:** http://www.klove.com.

HAXTUN

Phillips Co. Phillips Co. (NE) 19 m NW of Holyoke. Residential.

5564 ■ The Haxtun-Fleming Herald
The Haxtun-Fleming Herald
217 S Colorado Ave.
Haxtun, CO 80731
Phone: (970)774-6118
Fax: (970)774-7690
Publication E-mail: news@hfherald.com
Community newspaper. **Freq:** Weekly. **Print Method:** Offset. **Trim Size:** Tabloid. **Cols./Page:** 5. **Col. Width:** 12 nonpareils. **Col. Depth:** 145 agate lines. **Key Personnel:** Candie Salyards, Owner, Publisher; Spring Atchinson, Owner, Publisher. **USPS:** 120-650. **Subscription Rates:** $35 Individuals; $40 Out of area. **URL:** http://www.hfherald.com. **Formerly**: The Haxtun Herald. **Mailing address:** PO Box 128, Haxtun, CO 80731. **Ad Rates:** GLR $.67; BW $379.20; 4C $414.20; PCI $5.40. **Remarks:** Accepts advertising. **Circ:** ‡1250.

HAYDEN

Routt Co. Routt Co. (NW). 22 m E of Steamboat Springs. Logging, sawmills. Dairy, stock, poultry, grain farms.

5565 ■ KIDN-FM
5670 Greenwood Plaza Blvd.
Greenwood Village, CO 80111
Phone: (303)870-0900
Fax: (303)870-0300
Format: Adult Contemporary; Alternative/New Music/Progressive. **Networks:** UPI. **Founded:** 1983. **Formerly**: KRDZ-FM; KKMX-FM. **Key Personnel:** Cliff Gardiner, President. **Wattage**: 6,000 ERP. **Ad Rates:** Advertising accepted; rates available upon request.

HIGHLANDS RANCH

5566 ■ Communications Engineering & Design: The Premier Magazine of Broadband Technology
Communications Engineering and Design
PO Box 266007
Highlands Ranch, CO 80163
Phone: (303)470-4800
Fax: (303)470-4890
Technical/business publication serving the engineering/management community within broadband/cable TV networks, telecommunications carriers, data and interactive networks. **Freq:** 10/year. **Print Method:** Offset. **Trim Size:** 8 1/4 x 10 3/4. **Cols./Page:** 3. **Col. Width:** 25 nonpareils. **Col. Depth:** 136 agate lines. **Key Personnel:** Brian Santo, Editor-in-Chief; Traci Patterson, Managing Editor. **ISSN:** 0191--5428 (print). **Subscription Rates:** $64 U.S.; $85 Canada; $92 Other countries; $116 Two years; $153 Two years in Canada; $166 Two years elsewhere. **URL:** http://www.cedmagazine.com. **Ad Rates:** BW $6325; 4C $8305. **Remarks:** Accepts advertising. **Circ:** △22,411.

5567 ■ Douglas County News Press/Highlands Ranch Herald
Colorado Community Media
9137 S Ridgeline Blvd., Ste. 210
Highlands Ranch, CO 80129
Phone: (303)566-4100
General newspaper. **Freq:** Weekly (Wed.). **Print Method:** Offset. **Cols./Page:** 6. **Col. Width:** 24 nonpareils. **Col. Depth:** 301 agate lines. **Key Personnel:** Erin Addenbrooke, Manager, Sales. **Subscription Rates:** $30 Individuals /year (home delivery); $20 Individuals /year (home delivery; senior rate). **URL:** http://douglascountynewspress.net. **Formerly**: Daily News Press. **Remarks:** Accepts advertising. **Circ:** (Not Reported).

5568 ■ Glass Art: The Magazine for the Art Glass Industry
Travin Inc.
PO Box 630377
Highlands Ranch, CO 80163-0377
Phone: (303)791-8998
Fax: (303)791-7739
Publisher's E-mail: info@glassartmagazine.com
Magazine featuring articles on hot and cold glass techniques, artists, studios, and industry news. **Freq:** 6/year. **Trim Size:** 8 3/8 x 10 7/8. **Col. Width:** 2 1/4 inches. **Col. Depth:** 9 7/8 inches. **Key Personnel:** Shawn Waggoner, Editor; Kevin Borgmann, Publisher. **ISSN:** 1068-2147 (print). **Subscription Rates:** $30 U.S., Canada, and Mexico print; $56 Other countries print; $26 Individuals digital; $30 U.S., Canada, and Mexico CD; $56 Other countries CD. **Alt. Formats:** CD-ROM. **URL:** http://www.glassartmagazine.com/glass-art-store/category/49-glass-art-issues. **Ad Rates:** BW $1,350; 4C $1,750. **Remarks:** Advertising accepted; rates available upon request. **Circ:** ***7000**.

HOLYOKE

Phillips Co. Phillips Co. (C). 48 m E of Sterling.

5569 ■ Holyoke Enterprise
Holyoke Enterprise
130 N Interocean
Holyoke, CO 80734
Phone: (970)854-2811
Fax: (970)854-2232
Community newspaper. **Freq:** Weekly (Thurs.). **Print Method:** Offset. **Cols./Page:** 6. **Col. Width:** 12 picas picas. **Col. Depth:** 21 inches. **Key Personnel:** Brenda Brandt, Owner, Publisher. **USPS:** 248-120. **Subscription Rates:** $29.50 Individuals online. **URL:** http://www.holyokeenterprise.com. **Mailing address:** PO Box 297, Holyoke, CO 80734. **Ad Rates:** SAU $7.40. **Remarks:** Accepts advertising. **Circ:** (Not Reported).

IDAHO SPRINGS

Clear Creek Co. Clear Creek Co. (C). 33 m W of Denver. Fishing and skiing resort. Gold, silver, lead, copper mines. Hot mineral springs.

5570 ■ The Clear Creek Courant
The Clear Creek Courant
1634 Miner St.
Idaho Springs, CO 80452-2020
Phone: (303)567-4491
Fax: (303)567-0520
Publisher's E-mail: courantEditor@evergreenco.com
Community newspaper (tabloid). **Freq:** Weekly (Wed.). **Print Method:** Offset. **Trim Size:** 11 1/2 x 16 3/4. **Cols./Page:** 5. **Col. Width:** 1 7/8 inches. **Col. Depth:** 16 inches. **Key Personnel:** Piper Maruskin, Manager, Circulation, phone: (303)350-1030; Doug Bell, Editor, phone: (303)350-1039. **USPS:** 052-610. **Subscription Rates:** $32 Individuals print and digital - annual; $21 Individuals print and digital - semiannual. **URL:** http://www.clearcreekcourant.com. **Mailing address:** PO Box 2020, Idaho Springs, CO 80452-2020. **Remarks:** Accepts advertising. **Circ:** Paid ‡2100.

5571 ■ Clear Creek Radio Inc. - 102.7
PO Box 1419
Idaho Springs, CO 80452
Phone: (303)567-4628
Format: News; Eclectic; Talk. **Operating Hours**: Continuous. **Key Personnel:** Greg Markle, Gen. Mgr. **Wattage**: 100 ERP. **Ad Rates:** Advertising accepted; rates available upon request. **URL:** http://www.clearcreekradio.com.

5572 ■ KYGT-FM - 102.7
PO Box 1419
Idaho Springs, CO 80452
Phone: (303)567-4628
Email: kygt66@msn.com
Format: Eclectic. **Owner:** Clear Creek Radio Inc., PO Box 1419, Idaho Springs, CO 80452, Ph: (303)567-4628. **Founded:** 1995. **Operating Hours**: Continuous. **Key Personnel:** Greg Markle, Gen. Mgr., President.

URL: http://www.clearcreekradio.com.

IGNACIO

La Plata Co. La Plata Co. (SW). 15 m SE of Durango.

5573 ■ KSUT-FM - 90.1
123 Capote Dr.
Ignacio, CO 81137
Phone: (970)563-0255
Format: Public Radio. **Networks:** National Public Radio (NPR); American Public Radio (APR). **Owner:** KUTE Inc., at above address. **Founded:** 1976. **Operating Hours**: Continuous; 50% network, 50% local. **Key Personnel:** Mike Santistevan, Dir. of Programs, mike@ksut.org; Stasia Lanier, Music Dir., stasia@ksut.org; Bruce Campbell, Dir. of Dev., bruce@ksut.org; Jennifer Simon, Dir. of Sales, jen@ksut.org. **Wattage**: 425. **Ad Rates:** Noncommercial; underwriting available. **Mailing address:** PO Box 737, Ignacio, CO 81137. **URL:** http://www.ksut.org.

JOHNSTOWN

Weld Co. Weld Co. (N). 18 m SW of Greeley. Agriculture. Cattle feeders and dairy operations. Sugar beets, grain, hay.

5574 ■ Johnstown Breeze
Johnstown Breeze
PO Box 400
Johnstown, CO 80534
Phone: (970)587-4525
Local newspaper. **Freq:** Weekly (Thurs.). **Print Method:** Offset. **Cols./Page:** 5. **Col. Width:** 11.5 picas. **Col. Depth:** 224 agate lines. **Subscription Rates:** $30 Students 9 months; $40 Individuals. **URL:** http://myjohnstownbreeze.com. **Ad Rates:** GLR $.48; BW $406.25; 4C $656.25; SAU $4; PCI $4.48. **Remarks:** Accepts advertising. **Circ:** 1900.

5575 ■ KHNC-AM - 1360
PO Box 1750
Johnstown, CO 80534
Free: 800-205-6245
Email: comments@americanewsnet.com
Format: News; Talk. **Wattage:** 10,000. **URL:** http://www.americanewsnet.com.

5576 ■ KTMG-AM - 1370
26886 Weld County Rd. 17
Johnstown, CO 80534
Phone: (303)769-4401
Fax: (303)769-4787
Format: Country; Agricultural. **Owner:** Gold Bar Broadcasting & Communications Inc., at above address. **Founded:** 1976. **Key Personnel:** Rick Martin, Contact; Michael Golden, News Dir.; John Turecek, President; Colleen Martin, Gen. Sales Mgr; Rick Martin, Contact. **Wattage**: 5,000 day; 160 night.

JULESBURG

Sedgwick Co. Sedgewick Co. (NE). On South Fork of Platte River, 135 m NE of Greeley. Manufactures beet sugar, fertilizer. Natural gas wells. Wheat, corn, beans.

5577 ■ Julesburg Advocate
Eastern Colorado Publishing Co.
108 Cedar St.
Julesburg, CO 80737
Phone: (970)474-3388
Fax: (970)474-3389
Publisher's E-mail: advertising@julesburgadvocate.com
Community newspaper. **Freq:** Weekly (Thurs.). **Print Method:** Offset. **Trim Size:** 13 x 21 1/2. **Cols./Page:** 6. **Col. Width:** 12.5 picas. **Col. Depth:** 301 agate lines. **Key Personnel:** Courtney Langmacher, Contact; Vickie Sandlin, Publisher, Editor. **USPS:** 230-160. **Subscription Rates:** $32 Individuals 1 year; $37 Out of area 1 year. **URL:** http://www.julesburgadvocate.com. **Ad Rates:** SAU $4.25; PCI $4.25. **Remarks:** Advertising accepted; rates available upon request. **Circ:** (Not Reported).

5578 ■ KJBL-FM - 96.5
205 Elm St.
Julesburg, CO 80737
Phone: (970)474-0953
Fax: (970)474-3414
Format: Oldies. **Key Personnel:** Bryan Loker, Gen. Mgr., openline@highplainsradio.net.

LA JUNTA

Otero Co. Otero Co. (SE). On Arkansas River, 65 m E of Pueblo. Cannery; grain mill and elevator; livestock sales rings. Agriculture. Sugar beets, melons, grain, cattle.

5579 ■ Ag Journal
Ag Journal
422 Colorado
La Junta, CO 81050
Phone: (719)384-1429
Publisher's E-mail: publisher@ljtdmail.com
Agricultural newspaper. **Freq:** Weekly. **Print Method:** Offset. **Cols./Page:** 4. **Key Personnel:** Candi Hill, Editor, Publisher, phone: (719)384-1453. **ISSN:** 0004--1890 (print). **Subscription Rates:** $35 Individuals; $58 Two years. **URL:** http://agjournalonline.com. **Mailing address:** PO Box 500, La Junta, CO 81050. **Ad Rates:** BW $870. **Remarks:** Accepts advertising. **Circ:** ‡10300.

5580 ■ La Junta Tribune-Democrat
GateHouse Media Inc.
422 Colorado Ave.
La Junta, CO 81050
Phone: (719)384-4475
General newspaper. **Freq:** Daily (eve.). **Print Method:** Offset. **Trim Size:** 11 3/8 x 14 1/2. **Cols./Page:** 5. **Col. Width:** 26 nonpareils. **Col. Depth:** 196 agate lines. **Key Personnel:** Candi Hill, Editor, Publisher, phone: (719)384-4475; Rita Ojeda, Contact, phone: (719)384-1437. **USPS:** 299-500. **Subscription Rates:** $115 Individuals 52 weeks. **URL:** http://www.lajuntatribunedemocrat.com. **Mailing address:** PO Box 500, La Junta, CO 81050. **Ad Rates:** BW $420; 4C $685; SAU $6. **Remarks:** Accepts advertising. **Circ:** ‡3787.

5581 ■ KBLJ-AM - 1400
116 Dalton
La Junta, CO 81050
Phone: (719)384-5456
Fax: (719)384-5450
Format: Oldies. **Key Personnel:** Delores Cox, Office Mgr. **Ad Rates:** Advertising accepted; rates available upon request. **Mailing address:** PO Box 485, La Junta, CO 81050. **URL:** http://www.myhometeamsports.com/radio.html.

5582 ■ KTHN-FM - 92.1
116 Dalton
La Junta, CO 81050
Phone: (719)384-5456
Fax: (719)384-5450
Format: Country. **Networks:** ABC. **Owner:** Cherry Creek Radio LLC, 501 S Cherry St., Ste. 480, Denver, CO 80246, Ph: (303)468-6500, Fax: (303)468-6555. **Founded:** 1974. **Formerly**: KBLJ-FM. **Operating Hours**: Continuous. **Key Personnel:** Pat Gittings, Gen. Mgr., pgittings@cherrycreekradio.com. **Wattage**: 3,000. **Ad Rates:** $10-36 for 60 seconds. Combined advertising rates available with KBLJ 1400 AM. **Mailing address:** PO Box 485, La Junta, CO 81050. **URL:** http://www.cherrycreekradio.com.

LAKE CITY

Hinsdale Co. Hinsdale Co. (SW). 60 m S.W. of Gunnison. Residential.

5583 ■ WAIR-FM - 104.9
148 E Grand River
Williamston, MI 48895
Free: 888-887-7139
Format: Music of Your Life. **Networks:** ABC. **Owner:** Superior Communications, Inc., at above address, White Plains, NY. **Founded:** 1988. **Operating Hours**: Continuous; 3% network, 97% local. **ADI**: Traverse City-Cadillac, MI. **Key Personnel:** Jenn Czelada, Contact. **Wattage**: 100,000. **Ad Rates:** $12-26 for 30 seconds; $19-33 for 60 seconds. **Mailing address:** PO Box 388, Williamston, MI 48895.

LAKEWOOD

Jefferson Co. Jefferson Co. (NC). 6 m SW of Denver. Residential. Commercial.

5584 ■ Community Pharmacist
ELF Publications Inc.
5285 W Louisiana Ave.
Lakewood, CO 80232-5976
Phone: (303)975-0075
Fax: (303)313-2183
Free: 800-922-8513
Publisher's E-mail: elfpub@qwest.net
National magazine addressing the professional and business needs, concerns and continuing education of retail pharmacists practicing in independent, chain and supermarket pharmacies. **Freq:** Bimonthly. **Print Method:** Offset web. **Trim Size:** 8 3/8 x 10 7/8. **Key Personnel:** Judith D. Lane, Publisher; Molley Casey, General Manager; John Nittoli, Sales Representative. **ISSN:** 1096--9179 (print). **URL:** http://www.elfpublications.com. **Formerly**: Southern Pharmacy Journal; Pharmacy West. **Ad Rates:** BW $4,900; 4C $1,500. **Remarks:** Accepts advertising. **Circ:** Controlled ‡34000.

5585 ■ HealthCare Distributor
ELF Publications Inc.
5285 W Louisiana Ave.
Lakewood, CO 80232-5976
Phone: (303)975-0075
Fax: (303)313-2183
Free: 800-922-8513
Publisher's E-mail: elfpub@qwest.net
Magazine covering the issues and opportunities facing companies that distribute pharmaceuticals, medical/surgical products, and other health-care goods and services. **Freq:** Bimonthly. **Print Method:** Web Offset. **Trim Size:** 8 3/8 x 10 7/8. **Cols./Page:** 3. **Col. Width:** 26 nonpareils. **Col. Depth:** 135 agate lines. **Key Personnel:** Judith D. Lane, Publisher; Molly Casey, General Manager. **ISSN:** 1096--9160 (print). **USPS:** 683-520. **Subscription Rates:** $29.95 U.S. per year; $80 Elsewhere per year. **URL:** http://www.elfpublications.com/Hamacher.html. **Formerly**: Wholesale Drugs Magazine. **Ad Rates:** BW $3900, full page; BW $2200, half page. **Remarks:** Accepts advertising. **Circ:** ‡7900.

5586 ■ Journal of the American Animal Hospital Association
American Animal Hospital Association
12575 W Bayaud Ave.
Lakewood, CO 80228-2021
Phone: (303)986-2800
Fax: (303)986-1700
Free: 800-252-2242
Publication E-mail: jaaha@aahanet.org
Scientific and educational journal that publishes information for the practice of small animal medicine and surgery. **Freq:** Bimonthly. **Print Method:** Web offset. **Trim Size:** 8 3/8 x 10 7/8. **Cols./Page:** 2. **Col. Width:** 21 picas. **Col. Depth:** 52 picas. **Key Personnel:** Dr. Lisa Fulton, Board Member; Dr. Lillian Aronson, Board Member; Dr. Rodney Bagley, Board Member; Dr. Kathleen Barrie, Board Member; Dr. Bonnie V. Beaver, Board Member; Dr. Ellen N. Behrend, Board Member; Dr. Joseph W. Bartges, Board Member; Alan H. Rebar, PhD, Editor-in-Chief. **ISSN:** 0587- 2871 (print). **Subscription Rates:** $149 U.S. and Canada print and online; $159 Other countries print and online; $107 Individuals online only; $107 U.S. and Canada print only; $117 Other countries print only; $495 Institutions online only. **URL:** http://www.aahanet.org/Library/JAAHA.aspx. **Remarks:** Accepts advertising. **Circ:** 13200, 13668.

5587 ■ Journal of Prenatal and Perinatal Psychology and Health
Association for Pre- and Perinatal Psychology and Health
PO Box 150966
Lakewood, CO 80215
Phone: (707)887-2838
Fax: (707)887-2838
Publisher's E-mail: consultant@birthpsychology.com
Freq: Quarterly. **Key Personnel:** Maureen Wolfe, PhD, Managing Editor, phone: (707)887-2838, fax: (707)887-2838. **ISSN:** 1097--8003 (print). **Subscription Rates:** $70 U.S. /year; $80 Other countries /year. **URL:** http://birthpsychology.com/journals. **Formerly**: Prenatal and Perinatal Psychology and Health. **Remarks:** Advertising not accepted. **Circ:** (Not Reported).

Circulation: ★ = AAM; △ or • = BPA; ♦ = CAC; ❏ = VAC; ⊕ = PO Statement; ‡ = Publisher's Report; Boldface figures = sworn; Light figures = estimated.

5588 ■ Journal of Veterinary Internal Medicine
American College of Veterinary Internal Medicine
1997 Wadsworth Blvd.
Lakewood, CO 80214-5293
Phone: (303)231-9933
Fax: (303)231-0880
Free: 800-245-9081
Publisher's E-mail: acvim@acvim.org
Medical journal covering large and small animal practice research. Official Publication of the American College of Veterinary Internal Medicine. **Freq:** Bimonthly. **Print Method:** Sheetfed offset. **Trim Size:** 8 1/8 x 11. **Key Personnel:** Stephen P. DiBartola, Editor-in-Chief; Kenneth W. Hinchcliff, Editor-in-Chief. **ISSN:** 0891-6640 (print); **EISSN:** 1939-1676 (electronic). **Subscription Rates:** $791 Institutions print plus online; $85 Individuals print plus online; $46 Students print plus online; $720 Institutions online. **URL:** http://onlinelibrary.wiley.com/journal/10.1111/(ISSN)1939-1676. **Ad Rates:** GLR $10; BW $595; 4C $1,420. **Remarks:** Accepts advertising. **Circ:** ‡3975.

5589 ■ Ski Patrol Magazine
National Ski Patrol System
133 S Van Gordon St., Ste. 100
Lakewood, CO 80228
Phone: (303)988-1111
Fax: (303)988-3005
Publisher's E-mail: nsp@nsp.org
Freq: 3/year. **ISSN:** 0890- 6076 (print). **Subscription Rates:** Included in membership; $15 Nonmembers /year. **Alt. Formats:** PDF. **URL:** http://www.nsp.org/press/spm.aspx. **Remarks:** Accepts advertising. **Circ:** 35000.

5590 ■ TRENDS Magazine
American Animal Hospital Association
12575 W Bayaud Ave.
Lakewood, CO 80228-2021
Phone: (303)986-2800
Fax: (303)986-1700
Free: 800-252-2242
Publisher's E-mail: info@aaha.org
Professional magazine covering the management of small animal veterinary practices. **Freq:** Monthly. **Print Method:** Web Offset. **Trim Size:** 8 3/8 x 10 7/8. **Cols./Page:** 3. **Key Personnel:** Constance Hardesty, Editor-in-Chief; Stephanie Pates, Manager, Sales. **ISSN:** 1062-8266 (print). **Subscription Rates:** $60 Individuals. **URL:** http://www.aaha.org/professional/resources/trends_magazine.aspx#gsc.tab=0. **Ad Rates:** BW $1,980; 4C $1,500. **Remarks:** Accepts advertising. **Circ:** 26000, 13000.

KDDZ-AM - See Denver

5591 ■ KVOD-FM - 88.1
180 S Garrison
Lakewood, CO 80226
Phone: (303)871-9191
Fax: (303)733-3319
Free: 800-722-4449
Email: news@cpr.org
Format: Classical. **Networks:** National Public Radio (NPR). **Owner:** Colorado Public Radio, at above address. **Founded:** 1970. **Operating Hours:** Continuous. **Key Personnel:** Andrew Shaw, Producer; Mark Coulter, VP of Operations; Daniel Costello, Operations Mgr.; Mike Flanagan, Prog. Dir.; Jim East, Sr. VP; Max Wycisk, President; Sue Coughlin, VP of Dev.; Jenny Gentry, Sr. VP of Fin. & Admin.; Sean Nethery, Sr. VP. **Local Programs**: *The Baroque Show*, Sunday 10:00 a.m. - 3:00 p.m. **Wattage**: 1,200 ERP. **Ad Rates:** Noncommercial. **URL:** http://www.cpr.org.

LAMAR

Prowers Co. Prowers Co (SE). 110 m E of Pueblo. Lamar Community College. Manufactures portable grinders, hydraulic cylinders, buses, oil, gas. Alfalfa meal and feed meal. Agriculture. Grain, wheat. Livestock feed yards.

5592 ■ KLMR-AM - 920
7350 US Hwy. 50
Lamar, CO 81052
Phone: (719)336-2206
Format: Country. **Networks:** ABC. **Owner:** Cherry Creek Radio LLC, 501 S Cherry St., Ste. 480, Denver, CO 80246, Ph: (303)468-6500, Fax: (303)468-6555. **Founded:** 1948. **Operating Hours**: Continuous. **Key Personnel:** Robert Townsend, Bus. Mgr.; Ty Harmon, News Dir., Prog. Dir.; Pat Gittings, Gen. Mgr. **Local Programs**: *Anything Goes*, Monday Tuesday Wednesday Thursday Friday 7:05 a.m. - 8:00 a.m. **Wattage**: 5,000 Day; 500 Night. **Ad Rates:** $9-12 for 30 seconds; $13-17 for 60 seconds. **URL:** http://www.myhometeamsports.com/KLMR.html.

5593 ■ KLMR-FM - 93.5
7350 US Hwy. 50
Lamar, CO 81052
Phone: (719)336-2206
Format: Adult Contemporary. **Owner:** Cherry Creek Radio LLC, 501 S Cherry St., Ste. 480, Denver, CO 80246, Ph: (303)468-6500, Fax: (303)468-6555. **Key Personnel:** Ty Harmon, Prog. Dir., Div. Dir.; Pat Gittings, Gen. Mgr.; Robert Townsend, Bus. Mgr. **Ad Rates:** Advertising accepted; rates available upon request. **Mailing address:** PO Box 890, Lamar, CO 81052. **URL:** http://www.myhometeamsports.com/KLMR.html.

5594 ■ KSNZ-FM - 93.3
7350 US Hwy. 50
Lamar, CO 81052
Phone: (719)336-2206
Email: klmr@hotmail.com
Format: Adult Contemporary. **Founded:** 1978. **Formerly**: KSNZ. **Operating Hours:** Continuous. **Key Personnel:** Russ Baldwin, Gen. Mgr.; Dex Allen, President. **Wattage**: 100,000. **Ad Rates:** $7 for 15 seconds; $10 for 30 seconds; $14 for 60 seconds. **URL:** http://www.myhometeamsports.com.

5595 ■ K211EI-FM - 90.1
PO Box 391
Twin Falls, ID 83303
Fax: (208)736-1958
Free: 800-357-4226
Format: Religious; Contemporary Christian. **Owner:** CSN International, PO Box 391, Twin Falls, ID 83303, Ph: (208)736-1958, Fax: (208)736-1958, Free: 800-357-4226. **Key Personnel:** Kelly Carlson, Dir. of Engg.; Ray Gorney, Asst. Dir.; Don Mills, Music Dir., Prog. Dir. **URL:** http://www.csnradio.com.

5596 ■ KVAY-FM - 105.7
PO Box 1176
Lamar, CO 81052
Phone: (719)336-8734
Fax: (719)336-5977
Email: deb@kvay.com
Format: Country. **Founded:** 1987. **Formerly**: KNIC-FM. **Operating Hours**: 5 a.m.- 5 a.m. **Key Personnel:** Debbie Ellis, Gen. Mgr. **Wattage**: 100,000. **Ad Rates:** Advertising accepted; rates available upon request. **URL:** http://www.kvay.com.

LAS ANIMAS

Bent Co. Bent Co. (NWC). 20 m E of La Junta. Oil and gas wells; agriculture.

5597 ■ Bent County Democrat
GateHouse Media Inc.
510 Carson Ave.
Las Animas, CO 81054
Phone: (719)456-1333
County newspaper. **Freq:** Weekly (Thurs.). **Print Method:** Offset. **Cols./Page:** 6. **Col. Width:** 2 1/16 inches. **Col. Depth:** 21 inches. **Key Personnel:** Candi Hill, Publisher, phone: (719)384-1435; Loreta Moss, Office Manager, phone: (719)456-1333. **URL:** http://www.bcdemocratonline.com. **Ad Rates:** GLR $5.75; BW $725; PCI $5.75. **Remarks:** Advertising accepted; rates available upon request. **Circ:** Paid ‡1200, Non-paid ‡800.

LIMON

Lincoln Co. Lincoln Co. (E). 74 SE of Denver. Agriculture. Wheat, livestock.

5598 ■ The Limon Leader
The Limon Leader
1062 Main St.
Limon, CO 80828
Phone: (719)775-2064
Publisher's E-mail: publisher@thelimonleader.com
Newspaper. **Freq:** Weekly (Thurs.). **Print Method:** Offset. **Cols./Page:** 6. **Col. Depth:** 21 inches. **USPS:** 313-360. **Subscription Rates:** $23 Individuals in Colorado; $28 Out of state. **URL:** http://www.thelimonleader.com. **Mailing address:** PO Box 1300, Limon, CO 80828. **Ad Rates:** BW $598.50; SAU $3.85. **Remarks:** Advertising accepted; rates available upon request. **Circ:** ‡2225.

5599 ■ K220IK-FM - 91.9
PO Box 391
Twin Falls, ID 83303
Fax: (208)736-1958
Free: 800-357-4226
Format: Religious; Contemporary Christian. **Owner:** CSN International, PO Box 391, Twin Falls, ID 83303, Ph: (208)736-1958, Fax: (208)736-1958, Free: 800-357-4226. **Key Personnel:** Mike Kestler, President; Don Mills, Music Dir., Prog. Dir. **URL:** http://www.csnradio.com.

LITTLETON

Douglas Co. Arapahoe Co. (NEC). 10 m S of Denver. Arapahoe Community College. Manufactures trucks, fire extinguishers; dynamite, precision instruments, electronic and photo equipment. Nurseries, foundry. Residential.

5600 ■ American Journal of Business Education
The Clute Institute for Academic Research
6901 S Pierce St., Ste. 239
Littleton, CO 80128
Phone: (303)904-4750
Publisher's E-mail: staff@cluteinstitute.com
Journal featuring articles relevant to the science and practice of teaching business courses and related administrative duties. **Key Personnel:** Cary Caro, Editor-in-Chief. **ISSN:** 1942--2504 (print); **EISSN:** 1942--2512 (electronic). **Subscription Rates:** $50 Individuals plus shipping fee for non-USA subscribers. **URL:** http://www.cluteinstitute.com/journals/american-journal-of-business-education-ajbe. **Circ:** (Not Reported).

5601 ■ American Journal of Engineering Education
The Clute Institute for Academic Research
6901 S Pierce St., Ste. 239
Littleton, CO 80128
Phone: (303)904-4750
Publisher's E-mail: staff@cluteinstitute.com
Journal focusing on focusing on practice, assessment and mainstreaming of innovative engineering education strategies. **Freq:** Semiannual June and December. **Key Personnel:** Bahram Asiabanpour, Editor-in-Chief. **ISSN:** 2153--2516 (print); **EISSN:** 2157--9644 (electronic). **URL:** http://www.cluteinstitute.com/journals/american-journal-of-engineering-education-ajee. **Circ:** (Not Reported).

5602 ■ American Journal of Health Sciences
The Clute Institute for Academic Research
6901 S Pierce St., Ste. 239
Littleton, CO 80128
Phone: (303)904-4750
Publisher's E-mail: staff@cluteinstitute.com
Journal featuring articles on the dissemination of health science practice, research, and education knowledge. **Key Personnel:** Suzanne J. Crouch, Editor-in-Chief. **ISSN:** 2156--7794 (print); **EISSN:** 2157--9636 (electronic). **Subscription Rates:** $50 Individuals plus shipping fee for non-USA subscribers. **URL:** http://www.cluteinstitute.com/journals/american-journal-of-health-sciences-ajhs. **Circ:** (Not Reported).

5603 ■ Colorado Key Magazine
Key Magazines Inc.
11609 Elk Head Range Rd.
Littleton, CO 80127
Phone: (303)971-0993
Publication E-mail: keytocolorado@comcast.net
Visitor's guide publication featuring coverage of events, dining, shopping, and more. **Freq:** Monthly. **Key Personnel:** Ted Trimble, Publisher. **URL:** http://keymagazine.com/colorado/index.html. **Remarks:** Accepts advertising. **Circ:** Combined **25000**.

5604 ■ Contemporary Issues in Education Research
The Clute Institute for Academic Research
6901 S Pierce St., Ste. 239
Littleton, CO 80128
Phone: (303)904-4750

Publisher's E-mail: staff@cluteinstitute.com
Journal containing information on college-level education and administration issues. **Freq:** Quarterly. **Key Personnel:** Dr. Nabi Bux Jumani, Advisor. **ISSN:** 1940--5847 (print); **EISSN:** 1941--756X (electronic). **Subscription Rates:** $50 Individuals /copy; Free online articles. **URL:** http://www.cluteinstitute.com/journals/contemporary-issues-in-education-research-cier. **Circ:** (Not Reported).

5605 ■ Economic Geology
Economic Geology Publishing Company Inc.
7811 Shaffer Pkwy.
Littleton, CO 80127
Phone: (720)981-7882
Fax: (720)981-7874
Publisher's E-mail: seg@segweb.org
Journal on geology and mining. **Founded:** 1905. **Freq:** semi-quarterly. **Print Method:** Letterpress and offset. **Trim Size:** 8 x 10 3/4. **Cols./Page:** 2. **Col. Width:** 56 nonpareils. **Col. Depth:** 100 agate lines. **Key Personnel:** Lawrence D. Meinert, Editor; Mabel J. Peterson, Managing Editor. **ISSN:** 0361-0128 (print). **URL:** http://www.editorialmanager.com/seg/; http://www.segweb.org/SEG/Publications/SEG/Publications.aspx. **Ad Rates:** BW $500. **Remarks:** Accepts advertising. **Circ:** 5000.

5606 ■ International Business & Economics Research Journal
The Clute Institute for Academic Research
6901 S Pierce St., Ste. 239
Littleton, CO 80128
Phone: (303)904-4750
Publisher's E-mail: staff@cluteinstitute.com
Applied business research journal. **Freq:** Monthly. **Print Method:** Offset. **Trim Size:** 7 1/4 x 10. **Cols./Page:** 2. **Col. Width:** 2 3/4 inches. **Col. Depth:** 7 3/4 inches. **Key Personnel:** Jason Stratton Davis, PhD, Managing Editor. **ISSN:** 1535--0754 (print); **EISSN:** 2157--9393 (electronic). **URL:** http://journals.cluteonline.com/index.php/IBER. **Ad Rates:** PCI $100. **Remarks:** Accepts advertising. **Circ:** Paid ‡300, Controlled ‡200.

5607 ■ International Journal of Management & Information Systems
The Clute Institute for Academic Research
6901 S Pierce St., Ste. 239
Littleton, CO 80128
Phone: (303)904-4750
Publisher's E-mail: staff@cluteinstitute.com
Journal featuring articles related to any aspect of international management. **Freq:** Quarterly January, April, July, and October. **Key Personnel:** Tom Seymour, PhD, Editor-in-Chief. **ISSN:** 1546--5748 (print); **EISSN:** 2157--9628 (electronic). **Subscription Rates:** $50 Individuals plus shipping fee for non-USA subscribers. **URL:** http://www.cluteinstitute.com/journals/international-journal-of-management-information-systems-ijmis. **Circ:** (Not Reported).

5608 ■ Journal of Applied Business Research
The Clute Institute for Academic Research
6901 S Pierce St., Ste. 239
Littleton, CO 80128
Phone: (303)904-4750
Publisher's E-mail: staff@cluteinstitute.com
Journal covering business and economic research. **Freq:** Bimonthly. **Print Method:** Offset. **Trim Size:** 7 1/4 x 10. **Cols./Page:** 2. **Col. Width:** 2 3/4 inches. **Col. Depth:** 7 3/4 inches. **Key Personnel:** Prof. Ronald C. Clute, Manager, Accounting; Dean R. Manna, Editor-in-Chief. **ISSN:** 0892--7626 (print); **EISSN:** 2157--8834 (electronic). **URL:** http://www.cluteinstitute.com/journals/journal-of-applied-business-research-jabr. **Remarks:** Advertising accepted; rates available upon request. **Circ:** (Not Reported).

5609 ■ Journal of Business Case Studies
The Clute Institute for Academic Research
6901 S Pierce St., Ste. 239
Littleton, CO 80128
Phone: (303)904-4750
Publisher's E-mail: staff@cluteinstitute.com
Journal containing case studies for use in business and economics courses. **Freq:** Monthly. **Key Personnel:** Darja Peljhan, Editor-in-Chief. **ISSN:** 1555--3353 (print); **EISSN:** 2157--8826 (electronic). **Subscription Rates:** $50 Individuals /copy; Free online articles. **URL:** http://www.cluteinstitute.com/journals/journal-of-business-case-studies-jbcs. **Remarks:** Advertising not accepted. **Circ:** (Not Reported).

5610 ■ Journal of Business & Economic Research
The Clute Institute for Academic Research
6901 S Pierce St., Ste. 239
Littleton, CO 80128
Phone: (303)904-4750
Publisher's E-mail: staff@cluteinstitute.com
Refereed academic journal covering business and economics. **Freq:** Quarterly January, April, July and October. **Print Method:** Offset. **Trim Size:** 7 1/4 x 10. **Cols./Page:** 2. **Col. Width:** 2 3/4 inches. **Col. Depth:** 7 3/4 inches. **Key Personnel:** Osamah Al-Khazali, PhD, Board Member. **ISSN:** 1542--4448 (print); **EISSN:** 2157--8893 (electronic). **URL:** http://www.cluteinstitute.com/journals/journal-of-business-economics-research-jber. **Remarks:** Advertising accepted; rates available upon request. **Circ:** (Not Reported).

5611 ■ Journal of College Teaching & Learning
The Clute Institute for Academic Research
6901 S Pierce St., Ste. 239
Littleton, CO 80128
Phone: (303)904-4750
Publisher's E-mail: staff@cluteinstitute.com
Refereed academic journal covering all areas of college level teaching, learning and administration. **Freq:** Quarterly January, April, July and October. **Print Method:** Offset. **Trim Size:** 7 1/4 x 10. **Cols./Page:** 2. **Col. Width:** 2 3/4 inches. **Col. Depth:** 7 3/4 inches. **Key Personnel:** Viviane Naimy, Advisor; Benton E. Miles, Advisor; Victor Selman, Advisor; Ronald C. Clute, Managing Editor; Jeanne L. Higbee, PhD, Editor-in-Chief. **ISSN:** 1544--0389 (print); **EISSN:** 2157--894X (electronic). **URL:** http://www.cluteinstitute.com/journals/journal-of-college-teaching-learning-tlc. **Remarks:** Advertising accepted; rates available upon request. **Circ:** (Not Reported).

5612 ■ Journal of Diversity Management
The Clute Institute for Academic Research
6901 S Pierce St., Ste. 239
Littleton, CO 80128
Phone: (303)904-4750
Publisher's E-mail: staff@cluteinstitute.com
Journal covering all types of diversity management issues. **Freq:** Quarterly. **Key Personnel:** Trudy Billion, Editor-in-Chief. **ISSN:** 1558--0121 (print); **EISSN:** 2157--9512 (electronic). **Subscription Rates:** $50 Individuals /copy. **URL:** http://www.cluteinstitute.com/journals/journal-of-diversity-management-jdm. **Circ:** (Not Reported).

5613 ■ Journal of International Education Research
The Clute Institute for Academic Research
6901 S Pierce St., Ste. 239
Littleton, CO 80128
Phone: (303)904-4750
Publisher's E-mail: staff@cluteinstitute.com
Journal covering all areas of college-level teaching methods, style, and administration. **Freq:** Monthly. **Key Personnel:** Ann T. Hilliard, Editor. **ISSN:** 2158--0979 (print); **EISSN:** 2158--0987 (electronic). **Subscription Rates:** $50 Individuals /copy - hardcopy; Free online - articles. **URL:** http://www.cluteinstitute.com/journals/journal-of-international-education-research-jier. **Formerly:** College Teaching Methods & Styles Journal. **Circ:** (Not Reported).

5614 ■ Journal of International Energy Policy
The Clute Institute for Academic Research
6901 S Pierce St., Ste. 239
Littleton, CO 80128
Phone: (303)904-4750
Publisher's E-mail: staff@cluteinstitute.com
Journal containing papers relevant to the understanding of international energy policy. **Key Personnel:** Jack R. Ethridge, Editor-in-Chief. **ISSN:** 2165--252X (print); **EISSN:** 2165--2538 (electronic). **Subscription Rates:** $50 Individuals plus shipping fee for non-USA subscribers. **URL:** http://www.cluteinstitute.com/journals/journal-of-international-energy-policy-jiep. **Circ:** (Not Reported).

5615 ■ Journal of Service Science
The Clute Institute for Academic Research
6901 S Pierce St., Ste. 239
Littleton, CO 80128
Phone: (303)904-4750
Publication E-mail: jss@savstate.edu
Journal covering the field of service science. **Freq:** Annual. **Key Personnel:** Harry Katzan, Jr., Editor, Founder; Donna Schaeffer, Managing Editor. **ISSN:** 1941--4722 (print); **EISSN:** 1941--4730 (electronic). **Subscription Rates:** $50 Individuals /copy. **URL:** http://www.cluteinstitute.com/journals/journal-of-service-science-jss. **Circ:** (Not Reported).

5616 ■ Journal of Sustainability Management
The Clute Institute for Academic Research
6901 S Pierce St., Ste. 239
Littleton, CO 80128
Phone: (303)904-4750
Publisher's E-mail: staff@cluteinstitute.com
Journal containing articles aiming to examine the best tools, theory, methodology and practical application of sustainability management. **Freq:** Annual December. **Key Personnel:** Cary Caro, Editor-in-Chief. **ISSN:** 2330--6866 (print); **EISSN:** 2330--6874 (electronic). **Subscription Rates:** $50 Individuals plus shipping fee for non-USA subscribers. **URL:** http://www.cluteinstitute.com/journals/journal-of-sustainability-management-jsm/. **Circ:** (Not Reported).

5617 ■ Rangeland Ecology and Management
Society for Range Management
6901 S Pierce St., Ste. 225
Littleton, CO 80128
Phone: (303)986-3309
Fax: (303)986-3892
Publisher's E-mail: info@rangelands.org
Freq: Bimonthly January, March, May, July, September and November. **Print Method:** Offset. **Trim Size:** 8 1/2 x 11. **Cols./Page:** 3 and 2. **Col. Width:** 26 and 41 nonpareils. **Col. Depth:** 133 agate lines. **Key Personnel:** Roger L. Sheley, Editor-in-Chief. **ISSN:** 1550--7424 (print); **EISSN:** 1551--5028 (electronic). **Subscription Rates:** Included in membership. **URL:** http://srm.allenpress.com/srm/JOURNALS.aspx. **Formerly:** Journal of Range Management. **Ad Rates:** BW $882; 4C $17,42. **Remarks:** Accepts advertising. **Circ:** 1083.

5618 ■ Review of Business Information Systems
The Clute Institute for Academic Research
6901 S Pierce St., Ste. 239
Littleton, CO 80128
Phone: (303)904-4750
Publisher's E-mail: staff@cluteinstitute.com
Accounting Information Systems magazine. **Freq:** Quarterly. **Print Method:** Offset. **Trim Size:** 7 1/4 x 10. **Cols./Page:** 2. **Col. Width:** 2 3/4 inches. **Col. Depth:** 7 3/4 inches. **Key Personnel:** Ronald C. Clute, PhD, Managing Editor. **ISSN:** 1534--665X (print); **EISSN:** 2157--9547 (electronic). **Subscription Rates:** $300 Institutions. **URL:** http://www.cluteinstitute.com/journals/review-of-business-information-systems-rbis/. **Formerly:** Review of Accounting Information Systems. **Ad Rates:** PCI $100. **Remarks:** Advertising accepted; rates available upon request. **Circ:** Paid ‡300, Controlled ‡50.

5619 ■ The Surgical Technologist
Association of Surgical Technologists
6 W Dry Creek Cir., Ste. 200
Littleton, CO 80120-8031
Phone: (303)694-9130
Fax: (303)694-9169
Free: 800-637-7433
Publisher's E-mail: memserv@ast.org
Medical and surgical journal. **Freq:** Monthly. **Print Method:** Offset. **Trim Size:** 8 3/8 x 10 7/8. **Cols./Page:** 3. **Col. Width:** 28 nonpareils. **Col. Depth:** 140 agate lines. **Key Personnel:** Karen Ludwig, Director. **ISSN:** 0164--4238 (print). **Subscription Rates:** $40 Individuals; $55 Other countries; Included in membership; $50 Nonmembers /year. **URL:** http://www.ast.org/Publications/The_Surgical_Technologist. **Ad Rates:** BW $560; 4C $1,160; BW $1635, full page; BW $926, half page. **Remarks:** Accepts advertising. **Circ:** Paid 16000, Non-paid 400, 18000.

LONGMONT

Boulder Co. Boulder Co. (N). 34 m NW of Denver. Electronics, food products, building and construction,

Circulation: ★ = AAM; △ or • = BPA; ♦ = CAC; ❑ = VAC; ⊕ = PO Statement; ‡ = Publisher's Report; Boldface figures = sworn; Light figures = estimated.

printing and publishing firms. Agriculture.

5620 ■ Daily Times-Call
Lehman Communications Corp.
PO Box 299
Longmont, CO 80502
Phone: (303)776-2244
Fax: (303)678-8615
Free: 800-796-8201
Publication E-mail: opinion@times-call.com
General newspaper. **Freq:** Daily and Sun. (morn.). **Print Method:** Offset. **Cols./Page:** 6. **Col. Width:** 26 nonpareils. **Col. Depth:** 301 agate lines. **Key Personnel:** John Vahlenkamp, Managing Editor; Tony Kindelspire, Editor; Dean Lehman, Publisher, fax: (303)684-5310. **URL:** http://www.timescall.com. **Ad Rates:** BW $2,483; 4C $3,003; PCI $19.25. **Remarks:** Accepts advertising. **Circ:** Mon.-Sat. ★**19817**, Sun. ★**21021**.

5621 ■ The Masonry Society Journal
The Masonry Society
105 S Sunset St., Ste. Q
Longmont, CO 80501-6172
Phone: (303)939-9700
Fax: (303)541-9215
Publisher's E-mail: info@masonrysociety.org
Freq: Annual. **ISSN:** 0741--1294 (print). **Subscription Rates:** $100 Nonmembers /year, within the U.S.A.; $115 Nonmembers /year, outside the U.S.A.; Included in membership. **Alt. Formats:** Electronic publishing. **URL:** http://www.masonrysociety.org/html/resources/journal. **Remarks:** Advertising not accepted. **Circ:** (Not Reported).

5622 ■ Renewal: A Journal for Waldorf Education
Association of Waldorf Schools of North America
515 Kimbark, Ste. 106
Longmont, CO 80501
Phone: (612)870-8310
Publisher's E-mail: awsna@awsna.org
Freq: Quarterly. **Subscription Rates:** $17 U.S.; $37 Other countries; $31 Two years U.S.; $41 U.S. 3 years. **URL:** http://waldorfeducation.org/RelId/624383/ISvars/default/Waldorf_Books_Resources.htm. **Ad Rates:** 4C $1,104; BW $920. **Remarks:** Accepts advertising. **Circ:** 22,000.

5623 ■ Comcast Communications
434 Kimbark St.
Longmont, CO 80501
Email: we_can_help@comcast.com
Owner: Comcast Corp., 1 Comcast Ctr., Philadelphia, PA 19103-2838, Ph: (215)665-1700, Fax: (215)981-7790, Free: 800-266-2278. **Founded:** 1982. **Formerly:** Scripps Howard Cable Co. **Key Personnel:** David L. Cohen, Exec. VP; Brian L. Roberts, CEO. **Cities Served:** Battlement Mesa, Berthoud, Fort Lupton, Lafayette, Louisville, Lovebud, Parachute, Parachute, Superior, Colorado: subscribing households 45,000; 60 channels; 4 community access channels; 168 hours per week community access programming. **URL:** http://www.comcast.com.

5624 ■ KGUD-FM - 90.7
PO Box 1534
Longmont, CO 80502
Phone: (303)485-9811
Format: Easy Listening. **Owner:** Longmont Community Radio, at above address. **Founded:** 1975. **Formerly:** KCDC-FM. **Operating Hours:** 100% local. 24 hrs. **Wattage:** 100. **Ad Rates:** Noncommercial. **URL:** http://www.kgud.org/local-events.

5625 ■ KREL-AM - 1580
614 Kimbark St.
Longmont, CO 80501
Phone: (303)776-2323
Fax: (303)776-1377
Owner: Pilgrim Communications II, at above address. **Founded:** 1975. **Formerly:** KWYD-AM; KKKK. **Operating Hours:** Continuous Daily; 60% network, 40% local. **Wattage:** 10,000 daytime 078 nighttime. **Ad Rates:** $12-15 per unit.

5626 ■ KSKE-AM - 1450
614 Kimbark St.
Longmont, CO 80501
Phone: (303)776-2323
Fax: (303)776-1377
Format: Talk. **Key Personnel:** Ron Nickell, Gen. Mgr., Sr. VP; Bill Schwamle, Operations Mgr., bill@rcnnetwork.com. **Ad Rates:** Advertising accepted; rates available upon request. **URL:** http://www.radiocoloradonetwork.com.

LOUISVILLE

Boulder Co. Boulder Co. (N). 15 m NW of Denver. Residential. Light manufacturing.

5627 ■ The Gottschee Tree
Gottscheer Heritage and Genealogy Association
PO Box 725
Louisville, CO 80027-0725
Freq: Quarterly. **Subscription Rates:** Included in membership. **Remarks:** Advertising not accepted. **Circ:** (Not Reported).

5628 ■ International Journal of Public Participation
International Association for Public Participation Practitioners
PO Box 270723
Louisville, CO 80027-5012
Publisher's E-mail: iap2hq@iap2.org
Freq: Semiannual. **URL:** http://www.iap2.org/page/187/?. **Remarks:** Advertising not accepted. **Circ:** (Not Reported).

5629 ■ Lightning Protection for Engineers
National Lightning Safety Institute
891 N Hoover Ave.
Louisville, CO 80027
Phone: (303)666-8817
Publication E-mail: media@lightningsafety.com
Publication providing lightning safety information for engineers. Describes approved air terminals, downconductors, shielding, bonding, surge suppression, detectors, and personal safety. **Freq:** Annual edition: 2016. **Subscription Rates:** $79.95 Individuals plus $5 for shipping and handling anywhere in the U.S. **URL:** http://www.lightningsafety.com/nlsi_bus/lp_for_eng_book.html. **Circ:** (Not Reported).

LOVELAND

Larimer Co. Larimer Co. (N). 50 m N of Denver. Residential and commercial. Tourism. Manufactures electronic cameras & film products, measuring devices, computers, water chemical equipment, farm machinery. Canneries; creamery. Agriculture. Sugar beets, corn, wheat, cattle.

5630 ■ Beadwork
Interweave Press L.L.C.
201 E 4th St.
Loveland, CO 80537-5601
Phone: (970)669-7672
Fax: (970)667-8317
Free: 800-272-2193
Publication E-mail: beadwork@interweave.com
Magazine for beadwork enthusiasts. **Freq:** 6/year. **Key Personnel:** Danielle Fox, Associate Editor; Jamie Bogner, Director, Editorial. **Subscription Rates:** $22.95 Individuals print ; $39.95 Two years print; $19.99 Individuals online. **URL:** http://www.beadingdaily.com/blogs/beadwork/default.aspx. **Remarks:** Accepts advertising. **Circ:** (Not Reported).

5631 ■ Children's Ministry Magazine: The Leading Resource for People who Serve Children in the Church
Group Publishing
1515 Cascade Ave.
Loveland, CO 80539-0481
Phone: (970)669-3836
Fax: (970)292-4373
Free: 800-447-1070
Publisher's E-mail: info@group.com
Easy-to-do programming ideas, resources and helpful information for those who work in the church with kids from birth to 6th grade. **Freq:** Bimonthly. **Trim Size:** 8 x 10. **Key Personnel:** Christine Yount, Editor. **ISSN:** 1054--1144 (print). **Subscription Rates:** $24.99 Individuals 6 Issues, print and digital; $47.59 Two years print and digital. **URL:** http://www.childrensministry.com. **Ad Rates:** BW $4,495. **Remarks:** Accepts advertising. **Circ:** Paid ‡50000.

5632 ■ Cloth Paper Scissors
Interweave Press L.L.C.
201 E 4th St.
Loveland, CO 80537-5601
Phone: (970)669-7672
Fax: (970)667-8317
Free: 800-272-2193
Publisher's E-mail: customerservice@interweave.com
Magazine for artists and crafters. **Freq:** Bimonthly. **Subscription Rates:** $7.99 Single issue print or digital; $29.95 Individuals. **URL:** http://www.interweavestore.com/mixed-media/mixed-media-magazines/mixed-media-magazines-cloth-paper-scissors. **Remarks:** Accepts advertising. **Circ:** (Not Reported).

5633 ■ Creative Jewelry
Interweave Press L.L.C.
201 E 4th St.
Loveland, CO 80537-5601
Phone: (970)669-7672
Fax: (970)667-8317
Free: 800-272-2193
Publisher's E-mail: customerservice@interweave.com
Magazine featuring quick and easy jewelry projects. **Freq:** Annual. **Key Personnel:** Linda Ligon, Founder. **Subscription Rates:** $14.95 Individuals. **Remarks:** Accepts advertising. **Circ:** (Not Reported).

5634 ■ Group Magazine
Group Publishing
1515 Cascade Ave.
Loveland, CO 80539-0481
Phone: (970)669-3836
Fax: (970)292-4373
Free: 800-447-1070
Publisher's E-mail: info@group.com
Magazine for youth ministers from all Christian denominations; deals with youth group philosophy, organization, activities, projects, programs, administration, workshop ideas, Bible studies, games, music, fund raising projects, service projects, resources, staff relationships and personal Christian growth. **Freq:** Bimonthly. **Print Method:** Heatset Web Offset. **Trim Size:** 8 x 10 3/4. **Cols./Page:** 4. **Col. Width:** 9.5 picas. **Col. Depth:** 47 picas. **Key Personnel:** Sophia Winter, Contact, fax: (970)292-4372; Tim Gilmour, Publisher; Thom Schultz, President. **ISSN:** 0163--8971 (print). **Subscription Rates:** $19.95 Individuals print and online. **URL:** http://youthministry.com/group-magazine; http://store.grouppublishing.com/OA_HTML/ibeCCtpltmDspRte.jsp?item=3165661. **Ad Rates:** BW $3,983. **Remarks:** Accepts advertising. **Circ:** ‡55000.

5635 ■ Knitscene
Interweave Press L.L.C.
201 E 4th St.
Loveland, CO 80537-5601
Phone: (970)669-7672
Fax: (970)667-8317
Free: 800-272-2193
Publisher's E-mail: customerservice@interweave.com
Magazine featuring knitting and crochet. **Freq:** Semiannual. **Subscription Rates:** $24 Individuals; $28 Canada; $35 Other countries. **URL:** http://www.knittingdaily.com/blogs/knitscenemagazine/default.aspx; http://www.interweave.com/magazines. **Remarks:** Accepts advertising. **Circ:** (Not Reported).

5636 ■ Loveland Daily Reporter-Herald
Lehman Communications Corp.
201 E Fifth St.
Loveland, CO 80537
Phone: (970)669-5050
Publisher's E-mail: hr@lehmancomm.com
General newspaper. **Freq:** Daily (morn.). **Print Method:** Offset. **Trim Size:** 13 x 21 1/2. **Cols./Page:** 6. **Col. Width:** 18 nonpareils. **Col. Depth:** 301 agate lines. **Key Personnel:** Jackie Hutchins, Editor. **Subscription Rates:** $216 By mail; $118.20 Individuals home delivery. **URL:** http://www.reporterherald.com. **Ad Rates:** BW $2,238.15; 4C $2,341.35; PCI $18.15. **Remarks:** Accepts advertising. **Circ:** Mon.-Sat. ★**17618**, Sun. ★**18042**.

5637 ■ Loving More Magazine
Loving More
PO Box 1658
Loveland, CO 80539
Phone: (970)667-5683
Freq: Annual. **ISSN:** 1523--5858 (print). **Subscription Rates:** Free. **Alt. Formats:** PDF. **URL:** http://lovemore.com/magazine. **Remarks:** Accepts advertising. **Circ:** (Not Reported).

5638 ■ PieceWork
Interweave Press L.L.C.
201 E 4th St.
Loveland, CO 80537-5601
Phone: (970)669-7672
Fax: (970)667-8317
Free: 800-272-2193
Publication E-mail: piecework@pcspublink.com
Magazine featuring jewelry design. **Freq:** 6/year. **Key Personnel:** Jeane Hutchins, Editor. **Subscription Rates:** $24 Individuals; $39 Two years. **URL:** http://www.needleworktraditions.com/magazines/piecework-magazine. **Remarks:** Accepts advertising. **Circ:** (Not Reported).

5639 ■ Spin-Off
Interweave Press L.L.C.
201 E 4th St.
Loveland, CO 80537-5601
Phone: (970)669-7672
Fax: (970)667-8317
Free: 800-272-2193
Publisher's E-mail: customerservice@interweave.com
Magazine for spinning enthusiasts. **Freq:** Quarterly. **Key Personnel:** Amy Clarke Moore, Editor. **Subscription Rates:** $26 Individuals; $39 Two years; $30 Canada; $31 Other countries; $47 Canada 2 years; $50 Other countries 2 years. **URL:** http://www.interweave.com/Magazines. **Remarks:** Accepts advertising. **Circ:** (Not Reported).

5640 ■ Step by Step Wire Jewelry
Interweave Press L.L.C.
201 E 4th St.
Loveland, CO 80537-5601
Phone: (970)669-7672
Fax: (970)667-8317
Free: 800-272-2193
Publisher's E-mail: customerservice@interweave.com
Magazine featuring jewelry making. **Freq:** Bimonthly. **Subscription Rates:** $22.95 U.S.; $39.95 Two years. **URL:** http://www.jewelrymakingdaily.com/blogs/stepbystepwirejewelry/default.aspx; http://www.interweavestore.com/jewelry/jewelry-magazines. **Remarks:** Accepts advertising. **Circ:** (Not Reported).

5641 ■ Tree-Ring Research
Tree-Ring Society
4624 Foothills Dr.
Loveland, CO 80537
Publisher's E-mail: trslori@gmail.com
Peer-reviewed journal publishing articles and research on growth rings of trees and the applications of tree-ring in a wide variety of fields. **Freq:** Semiannual. **Key Personnel:** Steven Leavitt, Editor. **ISSN:** 1536--1098 (print); **EISSN:** 2162--4585 (electronic). **URL:** http://www.treeringsociety.org/journal.html. **Formerly**: Tree-Ring Bulletin. **Remarks:** Advertising not accepted. **Circ:** 333.

5642 ■ KCOL-AM - 600
4270 Byrd Dr.
Loveland, CO 80538
Phone: (970)461-2560
Free: 866-888-5449
Format: News; Talk. **Networks:** ABC; Westwood One Radio. **Founded:** 1947. **Formerly:** 600 KIIX. **Operating Hours:** Continuous. **ADI:** Denver (Steamboat Springs), CO. **Key Personnel:** Mike Sanchez, Div. Dir.; Kathy Arias, Gen. Mgr.; Stu Haskell, Gen. Mgr. **Wattage:** 5,000. **Ad Rates:** $14-30 for 30 seconds; $18-35 for 60 seconds. Combined advertising rates available with 1410 KIIX, 96.1 FM KSME, 107.9 FM KPAW. **URL:** http://www.600kcol.com.

5643 ■ KIIX-AM - 1410
4270 Byrd Dr.
Loveland, CO 80538
Phone: (970)461-2560
Format: Country. **Owner:** iHeartMedia Inc., 200 E Basse Rd., San Antonio, TX 78209, Ph: (210)832-3314. **Founded:** 1959. **Operating Hours:** Continuous. **Key Personnel:** Stu Haskell, Div. Pres., stuhaskell@iheartmedia.com; Kathy Arias, Dir. of Sales, kathyarias@iheartmedia.com. **Wattage:** 1,000. **Ad Rates:** Advertising accepted; rates available upon request. Combined advertising rates available with KCOL, KPAW, KCOL-AM (1949-1999). **URL:** http://www.kiixcountry.iheart.com.

5644 ■ KOLZ-FM - 100.7
4270 Byrd Dr.
Loveland, CO 80538
Phone: (307)632-4400
Fax: (307)632-1818
Format: Country; News; Information. **Operating Hours:** 12:00 a.m. - 7:00 p.m. Monday - Saturday, 12:00 a.m. - 10:00 p.m. Sunday. **ADI:** Cheyenne, WY-Scottsbluff, NE (Sterling, CO). **Wattage:** 100,000. **Ad Rates:** Noncommercial; Advertising accepted; rates available upon request. **URL:** http://koltfm.iheart.com.

5645 ■ KPAW-FM - 107.9
4270 Byrd Dr.
Loveland, CO 80538
Phone: (970)461-2560
Free: 877-221-1079
Format: Classic Rock. **Owner:** Clear Channel Inc., 200 E Basse Rd., San Antonio, TX 78209, Ph: (612)336-9700, Fax: (612)336-9701. **Founded:** 1971. **Formerly:** KIMN-FM. **Operating Hours:** Continuous. **Key Personnel:** Stu Haskell, Gen. Mgr.; Mike Sanchez, Promotions Dir.; Kathy Arias, Gen. Mgr. **Wattage:** 100,000. **Ad Rates:** Advertising accepted; rates available upon request. Combined advertising rates available with KCOL-AM, KIIX-AM, KGLL. **URL:** http://www.1079thebear.com.

5646 ■ KSME-FM - 96.1
4270 Byrd Dr.
Loveland, CO 80538
Phone: (970)461-2560
Free: 877-498-9600
Format: Contemporary Hit Radio (CHR). **Owner:** iHeartMedia Inc., 200 E Basse Rd., San Antonio, TX 78209, Ph: (210)832-3314. **Key Personnel:** Stu Haskell, Gen. Mgr., stuhaskell@clearchannel.com; Mike Sanchez, Promotions Dir., mikesanchez2@clearchannel.com; Kathy Arias, Gen. Sales Mgr., kathyarias@clearchannel.com. **Wattage:** 100,000. **Ad Rates:** Advertising accepted; rates available upon request. **URL:** http://www.kissfmcolorado.com.

5647 ■ KXBG-FM - 97.9
4270 Byrd Dr.
Loveland, CO 80538
Phone: (970)461-2560
Format: Country; Adult Contemporary. **Formerly:** KQLF-FM. **Key Personnel:** Stu Haskell, Gen. Mgr., stuhaskell@clearchannel.com; Mike Sanchez, Promotions Dir., mikesanchez2@clearchannel.com; Kathy Arias, Sales Mgr., kathyarias@clearchannel.com. **Wattage:** 100,000. **URL:** http://www.bigcountry979.com//main.html.

MANCOS

Montezuma Co. Montezuma Co. (SW). 17 m E. of Cortez. Saw mills. Mining. Farming. Ranching.

5648 ■ The Mancos Times: Seaviril the Beautiful Mancos Valley
Animas Publishing Inc.
PO Box 987
Mancos, CO 81328-0987
Phone: (970)533-7766
Newspaper. **Freq:** Weekly (Wed.). **Print Method:** Offset. **Trim Size:** 11 x 17. **Cols./Page:** 5. **Col. Width:** 6 1/2 picas. **Col. Depth:** 16 inches. **Key Personnel:** Christine Brennan, Editor; Richard Ballantine, Publisher; Janice Hess, Advertising Representative. **Subscription Rates:** $15 Individuals. **Formerly**: The Mancos Times-Tribune. **Ad Rates:** GLR $.23; BW $414.40; 4C $684.40; SAU $5.18. **Remarks:** Accepts advertising. **Circ:** ‡992.

5649 ■ Tribal College Journal
Tribal College Journal of American Indian Higher Education
PO Box 720
Mancos, CO 81328
Phone: (970)533-9170
Fax: (970)533-9145
Publisher's E-mail: info@tribalcollegejournal.org
Journal covering American Indian higher education. **Freq:** Quarterly. **Key Personnel:** Rachael Marchbanks, Publisher; Marjane Ambler, Editor; Kim Cox, Coordinator, Advertising, phone: (970)533-9799. **ISSN:** 1052-5505 (print). **Subscription Rates:** $29 U.S. 1 year; $54 U.S. 2 years; C$44 Canada 1 year; C$84 Canada 2 years; $49 Other countries 1 year; $94 Other countries 2 years. **URL:** http://www.tribalcollegejournal.org. **Ad Rates:** BW $1,655. **Remarks:** Accepts advertising. **Circ:** 22000.

MONTE VISTA

Rio Grande Co. Rio Grande Co. (S).125m SW of Pueblo. Feed mill. Machine shops. Gold, silver mines. Spruce, pine timber. Dude ranches. Diversified farming, Potatoes, barley, lettuce, livestock.

5650 ■ Center Post-Dispatch
Valley Publishing
835 1st Ave.
Monte Vista, CO 81144
Phone: (719)852-3531
Fax: (719)852-3387
Community newspaper. **Freq:** Weekly (Wed.). **Print Method:** Offset. **Trim Size:** 10 1/2 x 16. **Cols./Page:** 5. **Col. Width:** 2 inches. **Col. Depth:** 16 inches. **Key Personnel:** Beth Cerny; Toni Steffens-Steward, Editor. **USPS:** 775-900. **Subscription Rates:** $34.75 By mail print; $46.75 Out of country mail, print; $34.75 Individuals mail-buddy plan, includes e-edition; $46.75 Out of area mail-buddy plan, includes e-edition; $34.75 Individuals e-edition; $46.75 Out of area e-edition. **Alt. Formats:** PDF. **URL:** http://www.centerpostdispatch.com/v2_main_page.php. **Mailing address:** PO Box 607, Monte Vista, CO 81144. **Remarks:** Accepts advertising. **Circ:** (Not Reported).

5651 ■ The Del Norte Prospector
Valley Publishing
835 1st Ave.
Monte Vista, CO 81144
Phone: (719)852-3531
Fax: (719)852-3387
Community newspaper. **Freq:** Weekly (Thurs.). **Print Method:** Offset. **Trim Size:** 10 1/2 x 16. **Cols./Page:** 5. **Col. Width:** 2 inches. **Col. Depth:** 16 inches. **Key Personnel:** Toni Steffens-Steward, Editor. **USPS:** 659-530. **Subscription Rates:** $34.75 By mail; $46.75 Out of area mail; $34.75 Individuals mail-buddy plan includes e-edition; $46.75 Out of area mail-buddy plan includes e-edition; $34.75 Individuals e-edition; $46.75 Out of area e-edition. **URL:** http://www.delnorteprospector.com/v2_main_page.php. **Mailing address:** PO Box 607, Monte Vista, CO 81144. **Remarks:** Accepts advertising. **Circ:** (Not Reported).

5652 ■ Mineral County Miner
Valley Publishing
835 1st Ave.
Monte Vista, CO 81144
Phone: (719)852-3531
Fax: (719)852-3387
Community newspaper. **Freq:** Weekly (Thurs.). **Print Method:** Offset. **Trim Size:** 10 1/2 x 16. **Cols./Page:** 5. **Col. Width:** 2 inches. **Key Personnel:** Toni Steffens-Steward, Editor, phone: (719)852-3531. **USPS:** 015-700. **Subscription Rates:** $34.75 By mail; $46.75 Out of area mail; $34.75 Individuals mail-buddy plan, includes e-edition; $46.75 Out of area mail-buddy plan, includes e-edition; $34.75 Individuals e-edition; $46.75 Out of area e-edition. **URL:** http://www.mineralcountyminer.com/v2_main_page.php. **Mailing address:** PO Box 607, Monte Vista, CO 81144. **Remarks:** Accepts advertising. **Circ:** (Not Reported).

5653 ■ The Monte Vista Journal
Valley Publishing
835 1st Ave.
Monte Vista, CO 81144
Phone: (719)852-3531
Fax: (719)852-3387
Newspaper. **Freq:** Weekly. **Print Method:** Offset. **Trim Size:** 10 1/2 x 16. **Cols./Page:** 5. **Col. Width:** 2 inches. **Col. Depth:** 16 inches. **Key Personnel:** Toni Steffens-Steward, Editor. **USPS:** 360-660. **Subscription Rates:** $46.75 By mail out of Valley - 12 months; $34.75 By mail 12 months; $46.75 Individuals out of Valley, e-edition only - 12 months; $34.75 Out of area e-edition only - 12 months. **URL:** http://www.montevistajournal.com. **Mailing address:** PO Box 607, Monte Vista, CO 81144. **Remarks:** Advertising accepted; rates available upon request. **Circ:** (Not Reported).

Circulation: ★ = AAM; △ or • = BPA; ♦ = CAC; ❑ = VAC; ⊕ = PO Statement; ‡ = Publisher's Report; Boldface figures = sworn; Light figures = estimated.

5654 ■ KSLV-AM - 1240
109 Adams St.
Monte Vista, CO 81144
Phone: (719)852-3581
Fax: (719)852-3583
Email: news@kslvradio.com
Format: Country. **Networks:** Jones Satellite. **Owner:** San Luis Valley Broadcasting Inc., at above address, Monte Vista, CO 81144. **Founded:** 1986. **Operating Hours**: Continuous; 92% network, 8% local. **ADI**: Colorado Springs-Pueblo, CO. **Key Personnel:** Gerald Vigil, Gen. Mgr., kslv@kslvradio.com; Linda Pacheco, News Dir., news@kslvradio.com; Jerry Medina, Dir. of Programs, horaslatina@kslvradio.com. **Wattage**: 1,000. **Mailing address:** PO Box 631, Monte Vista, CO 81144. **URL:** http://www.kslvradio.com.

5655 ■ KSLV-FM - 96.5
109 Adams St.
Monte Vista, CO 81144
Phone: (719)852-3581
Fax: (719)852-3583
Email: kslv@amigo.net
Format: Adult Contemporary. **Networks:** Jones Satellite. **Owner:** San Luis Valley Broadcasting Inc., at above address, Monte Vista, CO 81144. **Founded:** 1986. **Operating Hours**: Continuous; 97% network, 3% local. **ADI**: Colorado Springs-Pueblo, CO. **Key Personnel:** Gerald Vigil, Gen. Mgr., kslv@kslvradio.com; Linda Pacheco, News Dir., news@kslvradio.com; Jerry Medina, Prog. Dir., horaslatina@kslvradio.com. **Wattage:** 6,000. **Ad Rates:** Advertising accepted; rates available upon request. **Mailing address:** PO Box 631, Monte Vista, CO 81144. **URL:** http://www.kslvradio.com.

MONTROSE

Montrose Co. Montrose Co. (W). 59 m SE of Grand Junction. Black Canyon National Monument. Candy factory. Agriculture.

5656 ■ Montrose Daily Press
Montrose Daily Press
3684 N Townsend Ave.
Montrose, CO 81401
Phone: (970)249-3444
General newspaper. **Freq:** Daily (eve.). **Print Method:** Offset. **Cols./Page:** 6. **Key Personnel:** Phil Ashley, Manager, Circulation; Mike Easterling, Managing Editor; Francis Wick, Publisher. **Subscription Rates:** $128 Individuals Montrose home delivery; $180.50 By mail in State; $284.50 Out of state mail; $139.59 Out of area home delivery. **URL:** http://www.montrosepress.com. **Remarks:** Advertising accepted; rates available upon request. **Circ:** Mon.-Fri. ■ **5691**, Sun. ■ **5521**.

5657 ■ Cherry Creek Radio LLC
501 S Cherry St., Ste. 480
Denver, CO 80246
Phone: (303)468-6500
Fax: (303)468-6555
Format: News; Eclectic; Sports; Talk. **ADI**: Denver (Steamboat Springs), CO. **Key Personnel:** Travis L. Cronen, VP, Dir. of Operations, Dir. of Info. Technology, tcronen@cherrycreekradio.com; Kelley Cheatwood, Sr. VP, Regional Mgr., rcheatwood@cherrycreekradio.com. **URL:** http://www.cherrycreekradio.com.

5658 ■ KBNG-FM - 103.7
106 Rose Ln.
Montrose, CO 81401
Phone: (970)249-4546
Fax: (970)249-2229
Format: Adult Contemporary. **Owner:** Cherry Creek Radio LLC, 501 S Cherry St., Ste. 480, Denver, CO 80246, Ph: (303)468-6500, Fax: (303)468-6555. **Key Personnel:** Paul Orlando, Gen. Mgr., porlando@cherrycreekradio.com. **URL:** http://www.cherrycreekradio.com.

5659 ■ KKXK-FM - 94.1
501 S Cherry St., Ste. 480
Denver, CO 80246
Phone: (303)468-6500
Fax: (303)468-6555
Format: Country. **Networks:** ABC. **Owner:** Cherry Creek Radio LLC, 501 S Cherry St., Ste. 480, Denver, CO 80246, Ph: (303)468-6500, Fax: (303)468-6555. **Founded:** 1977. **Operating Hours**: Continuous; 50% network, 50% local. **Key Personnel:** Jay Austin, Gen. Mgr., jaustin@cherrycreekradio.com. **Wattage**: 100,000. **Ad Rates:** $19-25 for 30 seconds; $25-35 for 60 seconds. Combined advertising rates available with KUBC-AM. **URL:** http://www.cherrycreekradio.com.

5660 ■ KPRH-FM - 88.3
Bridges Broadcast Ctr.
7409 S Alton Ct.
Centennial, CO 80112
Fax: (303)733-3319
Free: 800-722-4449
Format: Public Radio. **Owner:** Colorado Public Radio, at above address. **Key Personnel:** Max Wycisk, President; Sean Nethery, Sr. VP; Mark Coulter, VP of Production; Dan Murphy, VP of HR. **Wattage**: 3,500. **URL:** http://www.cpr.org/listen/where.

5661 ■ KREY-TV - 10
500 Crescent Ct., Ste. 220
Dallas, TX 75201
Phone: (972)960-4848
Fax: (972)960-4899
Owner: Hoak Media Corp., 500 Crescent Ct., Ste. 220, Dallas, TX 75201, Ph: (972)960-4848, Fax: (972)960-4899. **Key Personnel:** Rich Adams, COO; Jim Hoax, Chairman.

5662 ■ KSTR-FM - 96.1
1360 E Sheerwood Dr.
Grand Junction, CO 81501
Phone: (970)254-2100
Format: Classic Rock. **Owner:** MBC Grand Broadcasting, 1360 E Sherwood Dr., Grand Junction, CO 81501. **Founded:** 1980. **Operating Hours**: Continuous. **Key Personnel:** Robert St. John, Contact; Robert St. John, Contact. **Wattage**: 91,000. **Ad Rates:** Advertising accepted; rates available upon request. **URL:** http://www.961kstr.com.

5663 ■ K213CK-FM - 90.5
PO Box 391
Twin Falls, ID 83303
Fax: (208)736-1958
Free: 800-357-4226
Format: Religious; Contemporary Christian. **Owner:** CSN International, PO Box 391, Twin Falls, ID 83303, Ph: (208)736-1958, Fax: (208)736-1958, Free: 800-357-4226. **Key Personnel:** Kelly Carlson, Dir. of Engg.; Ray Gorney, Asst. Dir.; Don Mills, Music Dir., Prog. Dir. **URL:** http://www.csnradio.com.

5664 ■ KUBC-AM - 580
PO Box 970
Montrose, CO 81402
Phone: (970)249-4546
Fax: (970)249-2229
Format: Country. **Networks:** ABC. **Owner:** Cherry Creek Radio LLC, 501 S Cherry St., Ste. 480, Denver, CO 80246, Ph: (303)468-6500, Fax: (303)468-6555. **Founded:** 1946. **Operating Hours**: Continuous. **Key Personnel:** Jay Austin, Gen. Mgr., jay@coloradoradio.com. **Local Programs:** *Greatest Sports Show on Earth*, Saturday 8:00 a.m. - 10:00 a.m. **Wattage**: 5,000. **Ad Rates:** Noncommercial. $11-19 for 30 seconds; $16-25 for 60 seconds. Combined advertising rates available with KKXK-FM. **URL:** http://www.coloradoradio.com.

MONUMENT

El Paso Co. El Paso Co. (EC). 22 m N. of Colorado Springs.

5665 ■ Tri-Lakes Cable
245 N Jefferson St.
Box 1929
Monument, CO 80132
Fax: (719)481-3030
Email: tlc2@tri-lakesonline.net
Owner: Pioneer Cable Inc., 10819 Airport Rd., Everett, WA 98204. **Founded:** 1982. **Key Personnel:** Rebecca Hendricks, Contact; Todd Lorenz, Contact. **Cities Served:** Gleneagle, Monument, Colorado: subscribing households 5,100; 54 channels. **URL:** http://tri-lakescares.org/about-tlc/employment.

NIWOT

5666 ■ Snow Board: Products, Places and Personalities
Storm Mountain Publishing
PO Box 789
Niwot, CO 80544
Phone: (303)834-9775
Fax: (303)834-9781
Magazine featuring information about products, places, and personalities related to snowboarding. **Freq:** Quarterly. **Key Personnel:** Chris Owen, Editor; Nate Deschenes, Senior Editor; Tawnya Schultz, Editor. **Subscription Rates:** $9.95 Individuals 1 year; $14.95 Individuals 2 years; $19.95 Individuals 3 years. **URL:** http://snowboardmag.com. **Ad Rates:** BW $7,350. **Remarks:** Accepts advertising. **Circ:** (Not Reported).

NORTHGLENN

Weld Co. Adams Co. (NEC). 11 m N of Denver. Residential.

5667 ■ Northglenn/Thornton Sentinel
Sentinel Publishing Co.
14305 E Alameda Ave., Second Fl.
Aurora, CO 80012
Phone: (303)750-7555
Fax: (303)750-7699
Publisher's E-mail: advertising@aurorasentinel.com
Community newspaper (tabloid). **Freq:** 3/week. **Print Method:** Offset. **Trim Size:** 11 3/8 x 13 3/4. **Cols./Page:** 5. **Col. Width:** 1 7/8 inches. **Col. Depth:** 13 1/2 inches. **Key Personnel:** Scott Perriman, Publisher; Barb Stolte, General Manager; Mikkel Kelly, Executive Editor. **Subscription Rates:** $20 Individuals 12 months; $60 Two years; $40 Two years senior rate. **URL:** http://northglenn-thorntonsentinel.com; http://northglenn-thorntonsentinel.com/news. **Ad Rates:** GLR $4.64; BW $4387.50; 4C $5487.50; PCI $65. **Remarks:** Accepts advertising. **Circ:** Combined 85,525.

OURAY

Ouray Co. Ouray Co. (SC). Zinc, silver, uranium and copper mining, hot springs.

5668 ■ Ouray County Plaindealer: The newspaper of record for the City of Ouray, Town of Ridgway and Ouray City
The Ridgway Sun
PO Box 607
Ouray, CO 81427
Phone: (970)325-4412
Publication E-mail: plaindealer@ouraynews.com
County newspaper (tabloid). **Freq:** Weekly (Wed.). **Print Method:** Offset. **Trim Size:** 10 1/4 x 16. **Cols./Page:** 6. **Col. Width:** 18 nonpareils. **Col. Depth:** 16 agate lines. **Key Personnel:** Alan Todd, Publisher, phone: (970)325-2838. **USPS:** 415-260. **Subscription Rates:** $55 Individuals print + online; $96 Two years print + online; $43 Individuals print; $78 Two years print; $48 Individuals online; $85 Two years online. **URL:** http://www.ouraynews.com. **Formerly**: Ouray County Plaindealer: The Newspaper That Refused to Die. **Ad Rates:** BW $480; 4C $768; PCI $6. **Remarks:** Accepts advertising. **Circ:** Paid ‡1025, Free ‡41.

5669 ■ KURA-FM - 98.9
400 7th Ave.
Ouray, CO 81427
Phone: (970)325-4505
Fax: (970)325-7343
Format: Eclectic. **Owner:** Ouray School District R-1, 400 7th Ave., Ouray, CO 81427, Ph: (970)325-4505, Fax: (970)325-7343. **Founded:** Jan. 2001. **Operating Hours**: Continuous. **Ad Rates:** Noncommercial; underwriting available. **URL:** http://ouray.k12.co.us/site.

PAGOSA SPRINGS

Archuleta Co. Archuleta Co. (S). On San Juan River, 60 m E of Durango. Tourism, Skiing, biggame hunting & fishing. Hot springs. Cattle

5670 ■ The Pagosa Springs Sun
The Pagosa Springs Sun
466 Pagosa St.
Pagosa Springs, CO 81147
Phone: (970)264-2100
Community newspaper. **Freq:** Weekly (Thurs.). **Print Method:** Offset. **Cols./Page:** 6. **Col. Width:** 2 1/32 inches. **Col. Depth:** 21 inches. **Key Personnel:** Shari Pierce, Manager, Advertising; Karl Isberg, Managing Editor; Terri House, Owner, Publisher, Editor. **Subscription Rates:** $25 Individuals print or online; $35 Out of state print and online. **URL:** http://www.pagosasun.com. **Mailing address:** PO Box 9, Pagosa Springs, CO

81147. **Ad Rates:** SAU $5.70; PCI $5.70. **Remarks:** Accepts advertising. **Circ:** Paid 4084.

5671 ■ KWUF-AM - 1400
PO Box 780
Pagosa Springs, CO 81147
Phone: (970)264-5983
Fax: (970)264-5129
Email: tradio@kwuf.com
Format: Country; Talk; Sports. **Networks:** CNN Radio; Westwood One Radio. **Founded:** 1975. **Formerly:** KPAG-AM. **Operating Hours:** Continuous. **Local Programs:** *Good Morning Pagosa*, Monday Tuesday Wednesday Thursday Friday 8:05 a.m. - 8:30 a.m.; *Community Clipboard*, Monday Tuesday Wednesday Thursday Friday 7:00 a.m. - 8:00 a.m.; *Tradio*, Monday Tuesday Wednesday Thursday Friday 11:05 a.m. - 11:35 a.m. **Wattage:** 1,000. **Ad Rates:** Noncommercial. Combined advertising rates available with KWUF-FM. **URL:** http://kwuf.com.

5672 ■ KWUF-FM - 106.1
PO Box 780
Pagosa Springs, CO 81147
Phone: (970)264-5983
Fax: (970)264-5129
Email: sales@kwuf.com
Format: Adult Contemporary; Oldies. **Networks:** CNN Radio; Westwood One Radio. **Operating Hours:** Continuous. **Wattage:** 500. **Ad Rates:** Advertising accepted; rates available upon request. **URL:** http://kwuf.com.

5673 ■ Rocky Mountain Cable
56 Talisman Dr., Ste. 200
Pagosa Springs, CO 81147
Free: 877-234-0102
Email: csr@usacommunications.tv
Cities Served: 48 channels. **URL:** http://usacommunications.tv.

PALISADE

Mesa Co. Mesa Co. (W). 15 m NE of Grand Junction. Residential. Recreation area. Mining. Agriculture.

5674 ■ The Palisade Tribune and Valley Report
Village Publishing Company Inc.
124 W. 3rd St
Palisade, CO 81526-0008
Phone: (970)464-5614
Publisher's E-mail: info@palisadetribune.com
Community newspaper. **Freq:** Weekly (Thurs.). **Print Method:** Offset. **Trim Size:** 11 1/2 x 17 1/2. **Cols./Page:** 5. **Col. Width:** 11.5 picas. **Col. Depth:** 16 inches. **Key Personnel:** Doug Freed, Publisher. **Subscription Rates:** $25 Individuals inside Mesa County; $30 Out of area; $35 Out of state; $0.50 Single issue. **Alt. Formats:** Microfilm. **URL:** http://www.palisadetribune.com. **Mailing address:** PO Box 162, Palisade, CO 81526-0008. **Ad Rates:** BW $840; 4C $1,025; PCI $10.50. **Remarks:** Advertising accepted; rates available upon request. **Circ:** Paid ‡1500.

PAONIA

Delta Co. Delta Co. (W). 28 m NE of Delta. Residential.

5675 ■ High Country News
High Country News
119 Grand Ave.
Paonia, CO 81428
Phone: (970)527-4898
Journal covering natural resource and environmental issues in the Western U.S. **Freq:** 22/yr. **Key Personnel:** Paul Larmer, Executive Director, Publisher; Kathy Martinez, Manager, Circulation; Cindy Wehling, Art Director; Denise Massart-Isaacson, Business Manager; Jodi Peterson, Managing Editor. **ISSN:** 1091--5657 (print). **Subscription Rates:** $37 Individuals 1 year (print and online); $15 Individuals 6 months (online only). **URL:** http://www.hcn.org. **Mailing address:** PO Box 1090, Paonia, CO 81428. **Remarks:** .65. **Circ:** Paid 24000.

5676 ■ KVMT-FM - 89.1
233 Grand Ave.
Paonia, CO 81428
Phone: (970)527-4866
Fax: (970)527-4865
Free: 866-KVN-FNOW
Format: Public Radio. **Founded:** Oct. 1979. **Key Personnel:** Jake Ryan, Producer; Jeff Reynolds, CMCA, AMS, Operations Mgr., jeff@kvnf.org. **Ad Rates:** Noncommercial; underwriting available. **Mailing address:** PO Box 1350, Paonia, CO 81428. **URL:** http://www.kvnf.org.

5677 ■ KVNF-FM - 90.9
233 Grand Ave.
Paonia, CO 81428
Phone: (970)527-4866
Fax: (970)527-4865
Format: Public Radio. **Networks:** National Public Radio (NPR); Public Radio International (PRI). **Founded:** 1979. **Operating Hours:** Continuous; 15% network, 85% local. **Key Personnel:** Jeff Reynolds, CMCA, AMS, Operations Mgr., jeff@kvnf.org; Candy Pennetta, Music Dir. **Wattage:** 3,000. **Ad Rates:** Underwriting available. **Mailing address:** PO Box 1350, Paonia, CO 81428. **URL:** http://www.kvnf.org.

PARKER

5678 ■ American Salers
American Salers Association
19590 E Main St., Ste. 202
Parker, CO 80138
Phone: (303)770-9292
Fax: (303)770-9302
Trade magazine for the livestock industry. Represents Salers cattle breed. Official publication of the American Salers Association. **Freq:** 5/year. **Key Personnel:** Dean Pike, Contact; Sherry Hartley, Office Manager; Sherry Doubet, Executive Vice President. **Subscription Rates:** Included in membership. **URL:** http://salersusa.org/media-room/magazine. **Remarks:** Accepts advertising. **Circ:** (Not Reported).

5679 ■ Authorship
National Writers Association
10940 S Parker Rd., No. 508
Parker, CO 80134
Phone: (303)841-0246
Fax: (303)841-2607
Publisher's E-mail: natlwritersassn@hotmail.com
Magazine for writers. **Freq:** Quarterly. **Print Method:** Offset. **Trim Size:** 8 1/4 x 11. **Cols./Page:** 3. **Col. Width:** 27 nonpareils. **Col. Depth:** 140 agate lines. **Key Personnel:** Sandy Whelchel, Editor. **ISSN:** 1097-9347 (print). **Subscription Rates:** $20 Individuals. **URL:** http://www.nationalwriters.com. **Ad Rates:** BW $300. **Remarks:** Accepts advertising. **Circ:** ‡4000.

5680 ■ Veterinary and Comparative Orthopaedics and Traumatology
Veterinary Orthopedic Society
PO Box 665
Parker, CO 80134
Phone: (720)335-6051
Publisher's E-mail: secretary@vosdvm.org
Freq: Quarterly. **Subscription Rates:** $66 Members. **URL:** http://vosdvm.org/veterinary-and-comparative-orthopaedics-and-traumatology/. **Remarks:** Advertising not accepted. **Circ:** (Not Reported).

PUEBLO

Pueblo Co. Pueblo Co. (SEC). On Arkansas River, 102 m S of Denver. University of Southern Colorado. Manufactures iron, steel, aluminum products, automotive pistons, storm sashes, plastic bags, windows, doors, auto trailers, brick, tile, lumber, compressed and liquified gases, dairy, concrete products. Clay pits. Stone quarries. Coal mines. Mineral insulation. Bottling works. Hatchery. Nursery.

5681 ■ The Colorado Tribune
Colorado Printing of Pueblo
447 Park Dr.
Pueblo, CO 81005
Phone: (719)561-4008
Fax: (719)561-4007
Publication E-mail: colotrib@coyotenet.net
Legal newspaper for Pueblo County. **Freq:** Weekly. **Print Method:** Offset. **Trim Size:** 10 3/16 x 15 1/4. **Cols./Page:** 5. **Col. Width:** 21 nonpareils. **Col. Depth:** 196 agate lines. **Key Personnel:** Jon F. Heaton, Editor, Publisher. **USPS:** 123-500. **Subscription Rates:** $24 Individuals in Pueblo County - print; $35 Out of area print; $44 Two years in Pueblo County - print; $65 Out of area 2 years - print. **URL:** http://www.tribuneusa.net. **Remarks:** Advertising accepted; rates available upon request. **Circ:** ‡374.

5682 ■ CSU-Pueblo Today
Colorado State University--Pueblo
2200 Bonforte Blvd.
Pueblo, CO 81001-4901
Phone: (719)549-2100
Fax: (719)549-2419
Publisher's E-mail: info@colostate-pueblo.edu
Collegiate newspaper. **Freq:** Weekly (Wed.) twice each academic year. **Print Method:** Offset. **Cols./Page:** 5. **Col. Width:** 26 nonpareils. **Col. Depth:** 182 agate lines. **Key Personnel:** Kelsey Brown, Manager, Advertising; Christy Wiabel, Editor-in-Chief. **URL:** http://csupueblotoday.com. **Formerly:** USC Today. **Ad Rates:** GLR $3.50; BW $150; PCI $3.50. **Circ:** (Not Reported).

5683 ■ The Pueblo Chieftain
Star-Journal Publishing Corp.
825 W Sixth St.
Pueblo, CO 81002
Phone: (719)544-3520
Publisher's E-mail: city@chieftain.com
General newspaper. **Freq:** Mon.-Sun. (morn.). **Print Method:** Offset. **Cols./Page:** 6. **Col. Width:** 25 nonpareils. **Col. Depth:** 300 agate lines. **Key Personnel:** Robert H. Rawlings, Publisher, Editor; Steve Henson, Managing Editor, phone: (719)404-2750. **Subscription Rates:** $358.80 By mail in Colorado - 52 weeks 7day; $404.30 By mail outside Colorado - 52 weeks 7day. **URL:** http://www.chieftain.com. **Remarks:** Advertising accepted; rates available upon request. **Circ:** Mon.-Sat. ★**47195**, Sun. ★**48667**.

5684 ■ KAVA-AM - 1480
600 Grant St., Ste. 600
Denver, CO 80203
Phone: (303)733-5266
Fax: (303)733-5242
Format: Hispanic. **Key Personnel:** Julie Scheff, Contact, julie@kbno.net. **Ad Rates:** Noncommercial. **URL:** http://www.radioquebueno.com.

5685 ■ KCFP-FM - 91.9
Bridges Broadcast Ctr.
7409 S Alton Ct.
Centennial, CO 80112
Phone: (303)871-9191
Fax: (303)733-3319
Free: 800-722-4449
Format: Classical. **Owner:** Public Broadcasting of Colorado Inc., at above address. **Founded:** 1994. **Key Personnel:** Max Wycisk, President; Jenny Gentry, VP of Fin., VP of Legal Affairs; Dan Murphy, VP of HR; Sue Coughlin, VP of Dev. **Ad Rates:** Noncommercial. **URL:** http://www.cpr.org.

5686 ■ KCSJ-AM - 590
106 W 24th St.
Pueblo, CO 81003
Phone: (719)542-0835
Fax: (719)543-9898
Format: News; Talk. **Networks:** ABC; Westwood One Radio. **Founded:** 1947. **Operating Hours:** Continuous Mon.-Fri. & Sun.; 12 a.m.-11 p.m. Sat. **Key Personnel:** Paul Kelley, Operations Mgr., paulkelley@clearchannel.com; Darci Ewell, Sr. VP. **Wattage:** 1,000. **Ad Rates:** Advertising accepted; rates available upon request. **URL:** http://www.590kcsj.com.

5687 ■ KGHF-AM - 1350
106 W 24th St.
Pueblo, CO 81003
Phone: (719)545-2080
Fax: (719)543-9898
Format: Sports. **Founded:** 1927. **Formerly:** KIDN-AM. **Operating Hours:** Continuous. **Key Personnel:** Scott Jones, Gen. Mgr., scottjones@clearchannel.com. **Wattage:** 5,000. **Ad Rates:** Advertising accepted; rates available upon request.

5688 ■ KKPC-AM - 1230
Bridges Broadcast Ctr.
7409 S Alton Ct.
Centennial, CO 80112
Fax: (303)733-3319
Free: 800-722-4449

Circulation: ★ = AAM; △ or • = BPA; ♦ = CAC; ❑ = VAC; ⊕ = PO Statement; ‡ = Publisher's Report; Boldface figures = sworn; Light figures = estimated.

Format: Public Radio. **Owner:** Colorado Public Radio, at above address. **Key Personnel:** Andrew Shaw, Producer; Sean Nethery, Sr. VP; Jenny Gentry, Sr. VP of Fin. & Admin.; Dan Murphy, VP of HR; Doug Clifton, Officer; Jim East, Sr. VP; Mark Coulter, VP of Production, VP of Operations; Max Wycisk, President; Daniel Costello, Operations Mgr. **URL:** http://www.cpr.org/listen/where.

5689 ■ KOAA-TV - 5
2200 7th Ave.
Pueblo, CO 81003
Phone: (719)544-5781
Format: Commercial TV. **Networks:** NBC. **Owner:** Cordillera Communications, 325 Cedar St., Saint Paul, MN 55101, Ph: (651)379-0050. **Founded:** 1953. **Operating Hours**: Continuous; 67% network, 33% local. **ADI**: Colorado Springs-Pueblo, CO. **Key Personnel:** Evie Hudson, Bus. Mgr., ehudson@koaa.com; Evan Pappas, Gen. Mgr.; Cindy Aubrey, News Dir., caubrey@koaa.com. **Wattage**: 100,000. **Ad Rates:** Advertising accepted; rates available upon request. **URL:** http://www.koaa.com.

5690 ■ KPHT 95.5 - 95.5
106 West 24th St.
Pueblo, CO 81003
Phone: (719)540-9200
Fax: (719)457-0109
Format: Oldies; Classic Rock. **Ad Rates:** Advertising accepted; rates available upon request. **URL:** http://www.kpht955.com.

5691 ■ KTPJ-FM - 103.5
3910 O'Neal Ave.
Pueblo, CO 81005
Format: Religious. **Key Personnel:** Dan Hewitt, Station Mgr., dhewitt@hewittcouch.com. **URL:** http://ktpj.org.

5692 ■ KTSC-FM - 89.5
2200 Bonforte Blvd.
Pueblo, CO 81001
Phone: (719)549-2820
Format: Album-Oriented Rock (AOR). **Networks:** Independent. **Operating Hours**: 18 hours weekdays; 12 hours Saturday and Sunday; 100% local. **ADI:** Colorado Springs-Pueblo, CO. **Key Personnel:** Dave Birks, Contact; Bonnie Chyco, Contact. **Wattage**: 10,000. **URL:** http://revolution89.com/contact.

5693 ■ KTSC-TV - 8
2200 Bonforte Blvd.
Pueblo, CO 81001
Phone: (719)543-8800
Format: Public TV. **Networks:** Public Broadcasting Service (PBS). **Owner:** Rocky Mountain Public Broadcasting Network Inc., 1089 Bannock St., Denver, CO 80204, Ph: (303)892-6666, Fax: (303)620-5600, Free: 800-274-6666. **Founded:** 1971. **Operating Hours**: Continuous; 95% network, 5% local. **ADI**: Colorado Springs-Pueblo, CO. **Key Personnel:** Wynona Sullivan, Contact; Michelle Regalado, Contact. **Local Programs**: *Homework Hotline*, Monday Tuesday Wednesday Thursday Friday 4:30 p.m. **Ad Rates:** $30 for 30 seconds. **URL:** http://www.rmpbs.org/home.

RAMAH

5694 ■ Your Piedmontese Voice
North American Piedmontese Cattle Association
1740 County Road 185
Ramah, CO 80832
Phone: (306)329-8600
Publisher's E-mail: napa@yourlink.ca
Magazine featuring beef production. **Freq:** Quarterly. **URL:** http://www.piedmontese.org/Your%20Piedmontese%20Voice.html. **Ad Rates:** BW $240. **Remarks:** Accepts advertising. **Circ:** (Not Reported).

RIDGWAY

5695 ■ The Ridgway Sun
The Ridgway Sun
609 Clinton St., Ste. 104
Ridgway, CO 81432
Phone: (970)626-5100
Publication E-mail: ridgwaysun@ouraynews.com
Tabloid covering community news. **Freq:** Weekly. **Print Method:** Offset. **Trim Size:** 10 1/4 x 13. **Cols./Page:** 6. **Col. Width:** 18 nonpareils. **Col. Depth:** 182 agate lines. **Key Personnel:** David Mullings, Publisher, phone: (970)325-2838. **USPS:** 557-510. **Subscription Rates:** $30 Individuals in Ouray, Montrose & San Juan counties; $36 Out of area. **URL:** http://www.ouraynews.com. **Mailing address:** PO Box 529, Ridgway, CO 81432. **Ad Rates:** BW $390; 4C $690; PCI $5. **Remarks:** Advertising accepted; rates available upon request. **Circ:** 1005.

SALIDA

Chaffee Co. Chaffee Co. (C). 75 m NW of Pueblo. Recreation, tourism, skiing. Bottling, sheet metal works. Limestone & molydenum mining. Calcium carbonate processing. Dairy, truck, poultry, cattle ranches.

5696 ■ Chaffee County Times
Arkansas Valley Publishing Co.
PO Box 189
Salida, CO 81201
Phone: (719)539-6691
Fax: (719)539-6630
Free: 866-539-1880
Community newspaper. **Freq:** Weekly (Thurs.). **Print Method:** Offset. **Trim Size:** 11 1/2 x 16. **Cols./Page:** 5. **Col. Width:** 12 picas. **Col. Depth:** 15.5 inches. **Key Personnel:** David Schiefelbein, Editor. **Subscription Rates:** $35 Individuals within Chaffee County; $43 Out of area; $7 Individuals /month; $2.50 Individuals 1 week; $25 Individuals 6 months; $43 Individuals 1 year. **URL:** http://www.chaffeecountytimes.com. **Ad Rates:** BW $448; 4C $596; PCI $5.60. **Remarks:** Advertising accepted; rates available upon request. **Circ:** ‡3000.

5697 ■ The Herald Democrat
Arkansas Valley Publishing Co.
PO Box 189
Salida, CO 81201
Phone: (719)539-6691
Fax: (719)539-6630
Free: 866-539-1880
Publication E-mail: allnews@leadvilleherald.com
Community newspaper. **Freq:** Weekly (Thurs.). **Key Personnel:** Stephanie Wagner, Manager, Advertising; Marcia Martinek, Editor; Merle Baranczyk, Publisher. **ISSN:** 0891-01197 (print). **USPS:** 241-100. **Subscription Rates:** $27 Individuals within lake County; $37 Out of area. **URL:** http://www.leadvilleherald.com. **Remarks:** Accepts classified advertising. **Circ:** (Not Reported).

5698 ■ The Mountain Mail
Arkansas Valley Publishing Co.
PO Box 189
Salida, CO 81201
Phone: (719)539-6691
Fax: (719)539-6630
Free: 866-539-1880
General newspaper. **Founded:** 1880. **Freq:** Daily 5/week (Mon.-Thur.). **Print Method:** Offset. **Trim Size:** 11 3/8 x 16 3/4. **Cols./Page:** 5. **Col. Width:** 25 nonpareils. **Col. Depth:** 15 1/2 inches. **Key Personnel:** Merle Baranczyk, Editor, Publisher; Sandra Christensen, Manager, Circulation, Manager, Subscriptions; Holly Russell, Web Administrator; Vickie Sue Vigil, Director, Advertising; Paul Goetz, Managing Editor. **Subscription Rates:** $27 Individuals 3 months; $45 Individuals 6 months; $24 Individuals 3 months; senior. **URL:** http://themountainmail.com/. **Remarks:** Accepts advertising. **Circ:** Paid ‡2900.

5699 ■ KBVC-FM - 104.1
7600 CR 120
Salida, CO 81201
Format: Country. **Owner:** Three Eagles Communications, 3800 Cornhusker Hwy., Lincoln, NE 68504, Ph: (402)466-1234, Fax: (402)467-4095. **Operating Hours:** Monday – Saturday ; 6:00 AM – Midnight;. **Key Personnel:** Gary Buchanan, President, COO; Dean Johnson, Station Mgr. **Wattage**: 600. **Ad Rates:** Advertising accepted; rates available upon request; Accepts classified advertising.

5700 ■ KHEN 106.9 FM - 106.9
124 E 3rd St.
Salida, CO 81201
Phone: (719)539-1069
Email: info@khen.org
Format: Alternative/New Music/Progressive. **Mailing address:** PO Box 596, Salida, CO 81201. **URL:** http://www.khen.org.

5701 ■ KSBV-FM - 93.7
735 Blake St.
Salida, CO 81201
Phone: (719)539-9377
Fax: (719)539-7904
Format: Classic Rock. **Operating Hours**: Continuous. **Key Personnel:** Marc Scott, Contact, ksbvradio@bresnan.net. **Wattage**: 1,000. **Ad Rates:** Noncommercial. **URL:** http://www.ksbv.net.

5702 ■ KVRH-FM - 92.3
7600 County Rd. 120
Salida, CO 81201
Phone: (719)539-2575
Fax: (719)539-4851
Format: Adult Contemporary. **Simulcasts:** KVRH-FM. **Owner:** Three Eagles Communications, 3800 Cornhusker Hwy., Lincoln, NE 68504, Ph: (402)466-1234, Fax: (402)467-4095. **Founded:** 1948. **Operating Hours**: Continuous. **Key Personnel:** Ron Gates, Gen. Mgr., ron@kvrh.com; Dean Johnson, Operations Mgr., dean@kvrh.com; Alan Baxter, News Dir., baxter@kvrh.com. **Wattage**: 13,500. **Ad Rates:** $8.80-10 for 30 seconds; $11-12.50 for 60 seconds. Combined advertising rates available with KVRH-FM. **URL:** http://www.kvrh.com.

SILVERTHORNE

5703 ■ Seminars in Vascular Surgery
Elsevier Inc.
c/o Robert B. Rutherford, MD, Ed.
0146 Springbeauty Dr., Mesa Cortina
Silverthorne, CO 80498
Publication E-mail: elspcs@elsevier.com
Journal for professionals involved with management of vascular disease. **Freq:** Quarterly. **Print Method:** Sheetfed Offset. **Trim Size:** 8 1/4 x 11. **Cols./Page:** 2. **Key Personnel:** Dr. Dennis Bandyk, Editor. **ISSN:** 0895--7967 (print). **Subscription Rates:** $428 Individuals; $266.93 Institutions eJournal; $998 print journal. **URL:** http://www.journals.elsevier.com/seminars-in-vascular-surgery. **Mailing address:** PO Box 23159, Silverthorne, CO 80498. **Ad Rates:** BW $1,180; 4C $1,380. **Remarks:** Accepts advertising. **Circ:** ‡520.

5704 ■ Viral Immunology
Mary Ann Liebert Inc., Publishers
c/o David Woodland, Editor-in-Chief
U.S. Highway 6, Ste. 200
Silverthorne, CO 80498
Phone: (970)262-1230
Fax: (970)262-1525
Publisher's E-mail: info@liebertpub.com
Peer-reviewed journal focusing on the growing body of research in viral immunology, clinical, veterinary and Laboratory Research. **Freq:** 10/year. **Trim Size:** 8 1/2 x 11. **Cols./Page:** 1. **Col. Width:** 36 picas. **Col. Depth:** 56 picas. **Key Personnel:** Ann M. Arvin, Board Member; David Woodland, Editor-in-Chief; Ian W. Lipkin, Board Member; Carol Shoshkes Reiss, Board Member. **ISSN:** 0882--8245 (print); **EISSN:** 1557--8976 (electronic). **Subscription Rates:** $749 Individuals USA (print and online); $744 Individuals online only; $916 Individuals other countries (print and online). **URL:** http://www.liebertpub.com/overview/viral-immunology/57. **Mailing address:** PO Box 1630, Silverthorne, CO 80498. **Remarks:** Accepts advertising. **Circ:** (Not Reported).

SIMLA

Elbert Co. Elbert Co. (EC). 43 m NE of Colorado Springs. Industry. Waterbeds. Grain, stock, poultry, dairy farms. Wheat, corn, beans.

5705 ■ Ranchland News
Lister Publishing
PO Box 307
Simla, CO 80835
Phone: (719)541-2288
Fax: (719)541-2289
Publication E-mail: ranchland@bigsandytelco.com
Community newspaper. **Freq:** Weekly (Thurs.). **Print Method:** Offset. **Trim Size:** 11 x 16. **Cols./Page:** 5. **Col. Width:** 11 1/2 picas. **Col. Depth:** 15 1/2 inches. **Key Personnel:** Fred Lister, Publisher; John Hill, Editor; Susan Lister, Publisher. **USPS:** 455-020. **Subscription Rates:** $25 Individuals in El Paso, Elbert, and Lincoln counties; $28 Elsewhere in Colorado; $30 Out of state. **URL:** http://www.ranchland-news.com. **Formerly**: Pikev-

iew Farmer, Raunchland News, and Simla Sun. **Ad Rates:** PCI $6.10. **Remarks:** Accepts advertising. **Circ:** 3800.

STEAMBOAT SPRINGS

Routt Co. Routt Co. (NW). 160 m NW of Denver. Ski Town, U.S.A. Tourist resort. Mineral springs. Coal mines. Agriculture. Grain farms, cattle.

5706 ■ Steamboat Magazine
Mac Media L.L.C.
Ski Town Publications, Inc.
1120 S. Lincoln Ave., Ste. F
Steamboat Springs, CO 80487
Phone: (970)871-9413
Fax: (970)871-1922
Lifestyle magazine about Vail and Beaver Creek, Colorado. **Freq:** Semiannual. **Print Method:** Web. **Trim Size:** 8 3/8 x 10 7/8. **Cols./Page:** 3. **Key Personnel:** Deborah Olsen, President, Publisher; Jennie Lay, Editor; Christina Freeman, Sales Executive, Editor. **Subscription Rates:** $17 U.S.; $31 Two years; $72 Other countries. **URL:** http://www.steamboatmagazine.com. **Formerly:** Colorado's Front Range Quarterly. **Remarks:** Advertising accepted; rates available upon request. **Circ:** Paid ‡3000, Controlled ‡17000.

5707 ■ Steamboat Pilot & Today
WorldWest L.L.C.
1901 Curve Plz.
Steamboat Springs, CO 80477
Phone: (970)879-1502
Fax: (970)879-2888
Community newspaper. **Freq:** Mon.-Sat. **Key Personnel:** Holly Hunter, Office Manager; Suzanne Schlicht, Chief Operating Officer, Publisher. **Subscription Rates:** $18 Individuals 52 issues; $24 Two years 104 issues. **URL:** http://steamboattoday.com/news/home. **Mailing address:** PO Box 774827, Steamboat Springs, CO 80477. **Remarks:** Accepts advertising. **Circ:** Mon.-Fri. ■ **9596**, Sat. ■ **7930**.

5708 ■ KBCR-FM
2550 Copper Ridge
Steamboat Springs, CO 80487
Phone: (303)879-2270
Fax: (303)879-1404
Format: Country. **Networks:** ABC. **Founded:** 1974. **Formerly:** KSBT-FM. **Key Personnel:** Tom Palmer, Gen. Mgr., trpalmer@aol.com. **Ad Rates:** $15-25 per unit.

5709 ■ KFMU-FM - 104.1
2955 Village Dr., Ste. 20
Steamboat Springs, CO 80477
Format: Classic Rock. **Networks:** CBS. **Operating Hours:** Continuous; 15% network, 85% local. **Wattage:** 1,400. **Ad Rates:** $16-36 per unit. **URL:** http://www.kfmuradio.com.

5710 ■ KLBV-FM - 89.3
PO Box 779002
Rocklin, CA 95677-9972
Fax: (916)251-1901
Free: 800-525-5683
Format: Contemporary Christian. **Owner:** Educational Media Foundation, PO Box 2098, Omaha, NE 68103-2098, Free: 800-434-8400. **ADI:** Denver (Steamboat Springs), CO. **Key Personnel:** Mike Novak, President, CEO; Alan Mason, COO. **Wattage:** 2,600. **URL:** http://www.klove.com.

5711 ■ KQZR-FM - 107.3
2955 Village Dr.
Steamboat Springs, CO 80477
Phone: (970)879-5368
Format: Classic Rock. **Owner:** NRC Broadcasting Mountain Group L.L.C., 130 Ski Hill Rd., Breckenridge, CO 80424, Ph: (970)453-2234. **Key Personnel:** John Johnston, Gen. Mgr., john@alwaysmountaintime.com. **Wattage:** 29,000. **URL:** http://www.alwaysmountaintime.com.

5712 ■ KRMR-FM - 107.3
2955 Village Dr., Ste. 20
Steamboat Springs, CO 80487
Phone: (970)879-5368
Format: Talk; Sports; Information; Eighties; Classic Rock. **Key Personnel:** Peter McMillan, Account Exec.; Cristin Frey, Account Exec.; Aurora Sidell, Account Exec.; David Wittlinger, Sales Mgr.; John Johnston, Dir. of Programs; Eli Campbell, Promotions Dir.; Julia Arrotti, Dir. of Programs. **Wattage:** 29,000 ERP. **Ad Rates:** Noncommercial; Advertising accepted; rates available upon request. **URL:** http://alwaysmountaintime.com/kqzr.

STERLING

Logan Co. Logan Co. (NE). 90 m NE of Greeley. Manufactures clothing, farm implements, sugar, beef processing plant. Alfalfa dehydrating. Diversified farming. Sugar beets, corn, wheat, beans.

5713 ■ Journal-Advocate
Digital First Media
PO Box 1272
Sterling, CO 80751
Phone: (970)522-1990
Fax: (970)522-2320
General newspaper. **Founded:** 1885. **Freq:** Daily (eve.) and Sat. (morn.). **Print Method:** Web offset. **Trim Size:** 13 3/4 x 21 1/2. **Cols./Page:** 6. **Col. Width:** 25 nonpareils. **Col. Depth:** 301 agate lines. **Key Personnel:** Julie Tonsing, Publisher. **USPS:** 285-760. **Subscription Rates:** $128 Individuals carrier routes; $140.39 Individuals motor routes; $186.86 Out of country; $72 Individuals online only. **URL:** http://www.journal-advocate.com. **Ad Rates:** GLR $88; BW $1,589.28; 4C $1,874.28; SAU $8.53; PCI $9.80. **Remarks:** Accepts advertising. **Circ:** Mon.-Sat. ‡3727.

5714 ■ The Lamar Ledger
Prairie Mountain Publishing Co.
504 N 3rd St.
Sterling, CO 80751
Phone: (970)522-1990
Fax: (970)522-2320
Newspaper with an independent orientation. **Founded:** Aug. 07, 1907. **Freq:** Sun. morning; Tue.-Fri. afternoon. **Print Method:** Offset. **Cols./Page:** 6. **Col. Width:** 26 nonpareils. **Col. Depth:** 294 agate lines. **Key Personnel:** Lance Maggart, Editor. **ISSN:** 5855-6000 (print). **Subscription Rates:** $56 Individuals. **URL:** http://www.lamarledger.com. **Formerly:** Lamar Daily News and Holly Chieftain. **Mailing address:** PO Box 1272, Sterling, CO 80751. **Ad Rates:** GLR $.47; BW $874.41; 4C $1,041.41; SAU $7.29; PCI $7.29. **Remarks:** Accepts advertising. **Circ:** Mon.-Fri. ★**2639**.

5715 ■ KATR-FM - 98.3
803 W Main St.
Sterling, CO 80751
Phone: (970)867-5674
Fax: (970)522-1322
Email: medialogic@kci.net
Format: Country. **Networks:** ABC; Brownfield; Jones Satellite. **Founded:** 1983. **Operating Hours:** Continuous. **Key Personnel:** Wayne Johnson, Gen. Mgr., Owner, wayne@kftm.net. **Wattage:** 100,000. **Ad Rates:** Advertising accepted; rates available upon request. KRD2. **URL:** http://www.katcountry983.com.

5716 ■ KLZV-FM - 91.3
PO Box 779002
Rocklin, CA 95677-9972
Free: 800-525-5683
Format: Contemporary Christian. **Owner:** Educational Media Foundation, PO Box 2098, Omaha, NE 68103-2098, Free: 800-434-8400. **URL:** http://www.klove.com.

5717 ■ KNNG-FM - 104.7
PO Box 830
Sterling, CO 80751
Phone: (970)522-1607
Fax: (970)522-1322
Email: knng@plains.net
Format: Country. **Simulcasts:** KSTC 5:45am-9am, 12pm-1pm. **Networks:** ABC. **Founded:** 1972. **Formerly:** KSTC-FM; KYOT-FM 1972. **Operating Hours:** Continuous. **ADI:** Denver (Steamboat Springs), CO. **Wattage:** 100,000. **Ad Rates:** $10-20 for 60 seconds. Combined advertising rates available with KSTC-AM, KNEC-FM.

5718 ■ KPMX-FM - 105.7
117 Main St.
Sterling, CO 80751
Phone: (970)522-4800
Fax: (970)522-3997
Email: kpmx@necolorado.com
Format: Contemporary Hit Radio (CHR). **Networks:** Jones Satellite; CNN Radio. **Founded:** 1983. **Formerly:** KMXX-FM. **Operating Hours:** Continuous. **ADI:** Denver (Steamboat Springs), CO. **Key Personnel:** Andy Rice, Contact; Theresa Leake, Sales Mgr., theresa@kpmx.com; Jim Jackson, Contact, jim@kpmx.com; Jim Jackson, Contact; Andy Rice, Contact. **Wattage:** 25,000. **Ad Rates:** $10-15 for 30 seconds; $15-20 for 60 seconds. **URL:** http://www.kpmx.com.

5719 ■ KSTC-AM - 1230
PO Box 830
Sterling, CO 80751
Phone: (970)522-1607
Fax: (970)522-1322
Format: Oldies. **Simulcasts:** 5:45-9am, 12:00-1pm. **Networks:** ABC. **Owner:** Arnold Broadcasting Inc., at above address. **Founded:** 1925. **Formerly:** KGEK. **Operating Hours:** Continuous. **ADI:** Cheyenne, WY-Scottsbluff, NE (Sterling, CO). **Wattage:** 1,000. **Ad Rates:** $10-20. Combined advertising rates available with KNNG-FM, KFTM-AM, KBRU-FM, KNEC-FM.

5720 ■ K203DD-FM - 88.5
PO Box 391
Twin Falls, ID 83303
Free: 800-357-4226
Format: Religious; Contemporary Christian. **Owner:** CSN International, PO Box 391, Twin Falls, ID 83303, Ph: (208)736-1958, Fax: (208)736-1958, Free: 800-357-4226.

STRASBURG

Adams & Arapahoe Co. (C) 5 m SE of Bennett. Residential. Home of Comanche Crossing. Museum and site where the rails first linked the east to the west.

5721 ■ Eastern Colorado News
Eastern Colorado News Inc.
1522 Main St.
Strasburg, CO 80136
Community newspaper. **Freq:** Weekly (Fri.). **Print Method:** Offset. **Cols./Page:** 4. **Col. Width:** 2 3/8 inches. **Key Personnel:** Douglas Claussen, Publisher. **USPS:** 165-666. **Subscription Rates:** $30 Individuals; $44 Out of state; $48 Out of area; $1 Single issue. **URL:** http://i-70scout.com/blog. **Ad Rates:** BW $633.60; 4C $825.60; PCI $9.90. **Remarks:** Accepts advertising. **Circ:** (Not Reported).

TELLURIDE

San Miguel Co. San Miguel Co. (SW). 87 m SE of Grand Junction. Tourist. Ski resort. Uranium mines. Ranching. Cattle and sheep.

5722 ■ Telluride Daily Planet
Telluride Daily Planet
307 E Colorado Ave.
Telluride, CO 81435
Phone: (970)728-9788
Fax: (970)728-8061
Publication E-mail: editor@telluridenews.com
General newspaper. **Freq:** Daily. **Key Personnel:** Katie Klingsporn, Editor; Andrew Mirrington, Publisher. **Subscription Rates:** $139 Individuals Friday only; $199 Individuals friday and sunday only. **URL:** http://www.telluridenews.com/. **Mailing address:** PO Box 2315, Telluride, CO 81435. **Remarks:** Accepts advertising. **Circ:** Non-paid 4500.

5723 ■ KOTO-FM - 91.7
207 N Pine St.
Telluride, CO 81435
Phone: (970)728-4333
Fax: (970)728-4326
Format: Full Service. **Networks:** National Public Radio (NPR). **Owner:** San Miguel Educational Fund, at above address, Telluride, CO. **Founded:** 1975. **Operating Hours:** Continuous; 10% network, 90% local. **Key Personnel:** Ben Kerr, Gen. Mgr., ben@koto.org; Suzanne Cheavens, VP, suzanne@koto.org; Kathryn Hurtley, Contact, khurtley@yahoo.com. **Wattage:** 3,000. **Ad Rates:** Noncommercial. **Mailing address:** PO Box 1069, Telluride, CO 81435. **URL:** http://www.koto.org.

THORNTON

Adams Co. Adams Co. (W). N of Denver.

Circulation: ★ = AAM; △ or • = BPA; ♦ = CAC; ❑ = VAC; ⊕ = PO Statement; ‡ = Publisher's Report; Boldface figures = sworn; Light figures = estimated.

5724 ■ The Professional Geologist
American Institute of Professional Geologists
12000 Washington St.
Thornton, CO 80241
Phone: (303)412-6205
Fax: (303)253-9220
Publisher's E-mail: aipg@aipg.org
Journal publishing scientific information in all areas of geology. **Freq:** Quarterly. **Key Personnel:** Robert A. Stewart, Editor. **ISSN:** 0279-0521 (print). **Subscription Rates:** $20 Members; $30 Nonmembers. **Alt. Formats:** PDF. **URL:** http://www.aipg.org/publications/TPGPublic.htm. **Remarks:** Accepts advertising. **Circ:** 5,672.

TRINIDAD

Las Animas Co. Las Animas Co. (SE). On Purgatory River, 85 m SW of La Junta. Manufactures butter, sausage. Coal mines. Natural gas. Pine, aspen timber. Dairy farms. Pinto beans, barley, oats.

5725 ■ Chronicle-News: Proudly Serving Southeastern Colorado and Northeastern New Mexico
The Shearman Group
200 Church St.
Trinidad, CO 81082-0763
Phone: (719)846-3311
Fax: (719)846-3612
Publication E-mail: cnadmanager@amigo.net
General newspaper. **Freq:** Daily (eve.). **Print Method:** Offset. **Trim Size:** 13 x 21 1/2. **Cols./Page:** 6. **Col. Width:** 2 inches. **Col. Depth:** 21 1/2 inches. **Key Personnel:** Aileen Hood, Publisher. **USPS:** 110-040. **Subscription Rates:** $5 Individuals 1 month; $15 Individuals 3 months; $30 Individuals 6 months; $60 Individuals 1 year. **URL:** http://www.thechronicle-news.com. **Ad Rates:** GLR $12.50; PCI $14.24. **Remarks:** Accepts advertising. **Circ:** (Not Reported).

5726 ■ KCRT-AM - 1240
100 Fisher Dr.
Trinidad, CO 81082
Phone: (719)846-3355
Free: 800-791-8028
Format: Country. **Networks:** ABC. **Operating Hours:** Continuous. **Key Personnel:** Bob Herrera, Contact. **Wattage:** 250. **Ad Rates:** $4-9 for 30 seconds; $5-11 per unit. **URL:** http://www.kcrtradio.com.

5727 ■ KCRT-FM - 92.5
100 Fisher Dr.
Trinidad, CO 81082
Phone: (719)846-3355
Fax: (719)846-4711
Free: 800-791-8028
Format: Adult Contemporary; Classical. **Networks:** ABC; Jones Satellite. **Owner:** Phillips Broadcasting Inc., at above address. **Founded:** 1981. **Operating Hours:** Continuous. **Wattage:** 15,000 ERP. **Ad Rates:** $6-11 for 30 seconds; $7-13 for 60 seconds. **URL:** http://kcrtradio.com.

USAF ACADEMY

5728 ■ Checkpoints
Association of Graduates of the United States Air Force Academy
3116 Academy Dr.
USAF Academy, CO 80840-4475
Phone: (719)472-0300
Fax: (719)333-4194
Publisher's E-mail: aog@aogusafa.org
Freq: Quarterly March, June, September and December. **ISSN:** 0274--7391 (print). **Subscription Rates:** Included in membership. **URL:** http://usafa.org/Membership/Checkpoints. **Remarks:** Accepts advertising. **Circ:** (Not Reported).

5729 ■ KAFA-FM - 97.7
3116 Academy Dr.
USAF Academy, CO 80840-4475
Phone: (719)333-5232
Email: aog@aogusafa.org
Format: Alternative/New Music/Progressive. **Owner:** United States Air Force Academy, c/o Lt Gen Michelle D. Johnson, Superintendent 2304 Cadet Dr., USAF Academy, CO 80840-5001, Ph: (719)333-1110, Free: 800-443-9266. **Founded:** 2008. **ADI:** Colorado Springs-Pueblo, CO. **Ad Rates:** Noncommercial. **URL:** http://www.usafa.org/kafa.aspx.

WALSENBURG

Huerfano Co. Huerfano Co. (S). 50 m S of Pueblo. Tourism. Timber. Stock, grain farms.

5730 ■ Huerfano World
Huerfano World
500 Main St.
Walsenburg, CO 81089
Phone: (719)738-1415
Publication E-mail: editor@huerfanojournal.com
Community newspaper. **Freq:** Weekly (Thurs.). **Print Method:** Offset. **Cols./Page:** 6. **Col. Width:** 26 nonpareils. **Col. Depth:** 294 agate lines. **Key Personnel:** Brian Orr, Publisher; Gretchen Sporleder Orr, Publisher. **Subscription Rates:** $40 Individuals; $3.99 Individuals per month. **URL:** http://huerfanojournal.com. **Mailing address:** PO Box 346, Walsenburg, CO 81089. **Ad Rates:** GLR $.50; BW $882; 4C $1,500; SAU $9.80; PCI $9.80. **Remarks:** Accepts advertising. **Circ:** Paid ‡2975, Free ‡25.

5731 ■ KSPK-FM - 102.3
516 Main St.
Walsenburg, CO 81089
Phone: (719)738-3636
Fax: (719)738-2010
Format: Country. **Networks:** ABC. **Owner:** Mainstreet Broadcasting Co., Inc., at above address, Walsenburg, CO 81089. **Founded:** Mar. 01, 1985. **Operating Hours:** Continuous; 80% network, 20% local. **ADI:** Colorado Springs-Pueblo, CO. **Key Personnel:** Paul Richards, Gen. Mgr., paul@kspk.com; Bryant Johnson, Sports Dir., bryant@kspk.com. **Wattage:** 100,000. **Ad Rates:** $10-17 for 30 seconds; $13-20 for 60 seconds. Combined advertising rates available with KSPK-TV. **URL:** http://www.kspk.com.

5732 ■ KSPK-TV
516 Main St.
Walsenburg, CO 81089
Phone: (719)738-3636
Owner: Mainstreet Broadcasting Co., Inc., at above address, Walsenburg, CO 81089.

WESTCLIFFE

Custer Co. Custer Co. (SC). 62 m W of Pueblo. Recreation area. Silver, lead mines. Stock farms. Hay, grain, cattle.

5733 ■ Wet Mountain Tribune
Little Publishing Company Inc.
PO Box 300
Westcliffe, CO 81252
Phone: (719)783-2361
Publication E-mail: editor@wetmountaintribune.com
Community newspaper. **Freq:** Weekly (Thurs.). **Print Method:** Offset. **Trim Size:** 10 1/8 x 16. **Cols./Page:** 6. **Col. Width:** 10 picas. **Col. Depth:** 224 agate lines. **Key Personnel:** James A. Little, Editor, Publisher; Constance Little, Editor; Dina Sockriter, Director, Advertising. **USPS:** 681-200. **Subscription Rates:** $28 Individuals in Custer & Fremont County; $39 Out of area; $175 Individuals first class. **URL:** http://wetmountaintribune.com. **Remarks:** Advertising accepted; rates available upon request. **Circ:** ‡2820.

5734 ■ KWMV-FM - 95.9
103 S 2nd St.,Ste. A
Westcliffe, CO 81252
Phone: (719)783-0987
Format: News; Information; Eclectic. **Wattage:** 094. **Mailing address:** PO Box 155, Westcliffe, CO 81252. **URL:** http://www.kwmv.org/home.asp.

WESTMINSTER

Jefferson Co. Adams Co. (NEC). 8m NW of Denver. Residential.

5735 ■ Apogee Photo Magazine
Apogee Photo Inc.
11749 Zenobia Loop
Westminster, CO 80031
Phone: (303)948-3539
Publisher's E-mail: info@apogeephoto.com
Consumer magazine covering photography for amateurs and professionals. **Freq:** Monthly. **Key Personnel:** Michael Fulks, Publisher; Susan Harris, Editor; Marla Meier, Director, Editorial. **Subscription Rates:** Free. **URL:** http://www.apogeephoto.com. **Remarks:** Advertising accepted; rates available upon request. **Circ:** 100000.

5736 ■ Bison World
National Bison Association
8690 Wolff Ct., No. 200
Westminster, CO 80031
Phone: (303)292-2833
Fax: (303)845-9081
Publisher's E-mail: info@bisoncentral.com
Magazine serving ranchers, farmers, and others interested in the American buffalo/bison. **Freq:** Quarterly. **Print Method:** Offset. **Trim Size:** 8 3/8 x 10 7/8. **Cols./Page:** 3. **Col. Width:** 27 nonpareils. **Col. Depth:** 136 agate lines. **Key Personnel:** David Carter, Executive Director; Jim Matheson, Assistant Director; Marilyn Wentz, Editor, Director, Advertising, fax: (303)845-9081. **ISSN:** 1056-2400 (print). **Subscription Rates:** $75 Individuals. **URL:** http://www.bisoncentral.com/advertising. **Ad Rates:** BW $1,105; 4C $1,305. **Remarks:** Accepts advertising. **Circ:** ‡2000.

5737 ■ Gelbvieh World: Official Publication of the American Gelbvieh Association
American Gelbvieh Association
10900 Dover St.
Westminster, CO 80021
Phone: (303)465-2333
Publisher's E-mail: info@gelbvieh.org
Magazine providing breed information to American Gelbvich Assn. members. **Freq:** Monthly (July/August issues combined). **Trim Size:** 8 1/4 x 11. **Key Personnel:** Lori Maude, Editor; Katie Danneman, Manager, Production. **Subscription Rates:** $35 Individuals; $65 Two years; $60 Canada and Mexico; $85 Other countries. **URL:** http://www.gelbvieh.org/communication/gelbviehworld.html. **Ad Rates:** BW $580; 4C $880; PCI $26. **Remarks:** Accepts advertising. **Circ:** 5000.

5738 ■ K57BT-TV
9020 Yates St.
Westminster, CO 80031
Phone: (303)650-5515
Owner: Trinity Broadcasting Network Inc., PO Box A, Santa Ana, CA 92711, Ph: (714)832-2950, Free: 888-731-1000. **Key Personnel:** Jim Riddle, Mgr. **URL:** http://www.tbn.org/index.php/9/2.html.

5739 ■ KPOF-AM - 910
3455 W 83rd Ave.
Westminster, CO 80031
Phone: (303)428-0910
Fax: (303)429-0910
Free: 800-748-1775
Email: info@am91.org
Format: Religious. **Networks:** Moody Broadcasting. **Owner:** Pillar of Fire, 1340 Sherman St., Denver, CO 80220, Ph: (303)839-1500. **Founded:** 1928. **Operating Hours:** Continuous. **Key Personnel:** Jack H. Pelon, Gen. Mgr; Ray Rogers, Contact. **Local Programs:** *Seeking Him*, Monday Tuesday Wednesday Thursday Friday 9:15 a.m. - 9:30 a.m. **Wattage:** 5,000 Day; 1,000 Night. **Ad Rates:** Noncommercial. **URL:** http://www.kpof.org.

WHEAT RIDGE

Jefferson Co. Jefferson Co. (NC). 5 m NW of Denver. Manufactures aluminum, containers, industrial supplies, office supplies. Nurseries, florists.

5740 ■ Applied Psychophysiology and Biofeedback Journal
Association for Applied Psychophysiology and Biofeedback
10200 W 44th Ave., Ste. 304
Wheat Ridge, CO 80033-2840
Phone: (303)422-8436
Free: 800-477-8892
Publisher's E-mail: info@aapb.org
Journal containing topics on the field of interrelationship of physiological systems, cognition, social and environmental parameters, and health. **Freq:** Quarterly. **URL:** http://www.aapb.org/i4a/pages/index.cfm?pageid=3313. **Circ:** (Not Reported).

5741 ■ Cognitive Science
Cognitive Science Society
10200 W 44th Ave., Ste. 304

Wheat Ridge, CO 80033-2840
Phone: (303)327-7547
Fax: (720)881-6101
Publisher's E-mail: info@cognitivesciencesociety.org
Journal containing articles, reviews, and new insights in the field of cognitive science, including artificial intelligence, linguistics, anthropology, psychology, neuroscience, philosophy, and education. **Freq:** Bimonthly. **Subscription Rates:** included in membership dues. **URL:** http://cognitivesciencesociety.org/journal_csj.html; http://csjarchive.cogsci.rpi.edu. **Remarks:** Advertising not accepted. **Circ:** (Not Reported).

5742 ■ New Perspectives
Association of Healthcare Internal Auditors
10200 W 44th Ave., Ste. 304
Wheat Ridge, CO 80033
Phone: (303)327-7546
Fax: (720)881-6101
Free: 888-ASK-AHIA
Publisher's E-mail: info@ahia.org
Freq: Quarterly. **Subscription Rates:** Included in membership; $65 Nonmembers. **URL:** http://www.ahia.org/news/new-perspectives. **Remarks:** Advertising accepted; rates available upon request. **Circ:** (Not Reported).

WHITEWATER

5743 ■ Journal of Pyrotechnics
Journal of Pyrotechnics Inc.
1775 Blair Rd.
Whitewater, CO 81527-9553
Phone: (970)245-0692
Fax: (970)245-0692
Technical journal covering pyrotechnics, fireworks, special effects, propellants, rocketry, and civilian pyrotechnics. **Freq:** Semiannual. **Print Method:** Laser. **Trim Size:** 8 x 11. **Cols./Page:** 2. **Col. Width:** 3 inches. **Col. Depth:** 9 inches. **ISSN:** 1082--3999 (print). **URL:** http://www.jpyro.com. **Remarks:** Accepts advertising. **Circ:** (Not Reported).

WINDSOR

Weld Co. Weld Co. (WC).

5744 ■ Adoption Today
Louis and Company Publishing
541 E Garden Dr., Ste. N
Windsor, CO 80550
Phone: (970)686-7412
Fax: (970)686-7412
Free: 888-924-6736
Publication E-mail: louis@adoptinfo.net
Magazine that publishes expert advice and articles about the experiences of adoptive families. **Freq:** Monthly. **Subscription Rates:** $14 Individuals digital. **URL:** http://www.adoptiontoday.com. **Circ:** (Not Reported).

5745 ■ Bertrand Russell Society Quarterly
Bertrand Russell Society
c/o Michael Berumen, Treasurer
37155 Dickerson Run
Windsor, CO 80550
Phone: (802)295-9058
Journal containing society news and proceedings, essays, discussions and reviews on all aspects of Bertrand Russell's life and works. **Freq:** Quarterly February, May, August, and November. **ISSN:** 1547--0334 (print). **Subscription Rates:** Included in membership; $20 Individuals. **URL:** http://www.lehman.edu/deanhum/philosophy/BRSQ. **Remarks:** Accepts advertising. **Circ:** (Not Reported).

5746 ■ EasyChair: EasyChair
EasyChair Media L.L.C.
800 3rd St.
Windsor, CO 80550
Fax: (800)438-2150
Free: 800-741-6308
Publisher's E-mail: info@easychairmedia.com
Magazine offers lifestyle and entertainment information for the various communities in Colorado. **Freq:** Quarterly. **Key Personnel:** Kristie Melendez, Contact. **Subscription Rates:** Free. **URL:** http://www.easychairmedia.com/. **Ad Rates:** 4C $4,495. **Remarks:** Accepts advertising. **Circ:** 200000.

5747 ■ Fostering Families Today
Louis and Company Publishing
541 E Garden Dr., Ste. N
Windsor, CO 80550
Phone: (970)686-7412
Fax: (970)686-7412
Free: 888-924-6736
Publication E-mail: louis@adoptinfo.net
Magazine that publishes articles and stories reflecting professional expertise and the perspective of foster and adopting parents. **Freq:** Bimonthly. **Subscription Rates:** $24.95 Individuals 1 year; $14 Individuals digital. **URL:** http://www.fosteringfamiliestoday.com/indexfft.html. **Circ:** (Not Reported).

5748 ■ International Journal of Construction Education and Research
Associated Schools of Construction
PO Box 29
Windsor, CO 80550-0029
Phone: (970)988-1130
Fax: (970)282-0396
Publisher's E-mail: info@ascweb.org
Peer-reviewed journal covering construction education and research. **Freq:** Quarterly. **Key Personnel:** Brian Moore, Editor; Salman Azhar, Phd, Associate Editor; John Schaufelberger, Associate Editor. **ISSN:** 1557--8771 (print); **EISSN:** 1550--3984 (electronic). **Subscription Rates:** $191 Individuals print (personal); $669 Institutions online; $765 Institutions print & online. **URL:** http://www.tandfonline.com/toc/uice20/current; http://www.tandfonline.com/loi/uice20. **Remarks:** Advertising not accepted. **Circ:** (Not Reported).

5749 ■ Windsor Beacon
Windsor Beacon
425 Main St.
Windsor, CO 80550
Phone: (970)686-9646
Fax: (970)686-9647
General newspaper. **Freq:** Weekly. **Cols./Page:** 6. **Col. Width:** 1.5625 inches. **Key Personnel:** David Persons, Editor; Jack Birne, Advertising Representative; Wilson Kim, Publisher. **USPS:** 068-626. **Subscription Rates:** $9.50 Individuals print (per month); $9.99 Individuals online (6 months). **URL:** http://www.coloradoan.com/windsor-beacon. **Remarks:** Advertising accepted; rates available upon request. **Circ:** Paid ‡3000.

5750 ■ Windsor Now
Greeley Publishing Co.
423 Main St.
Windsor, CO 80550
Community newspaper. **Freq:** Weekly (Sun.). **Key Personnel:** David Thiemann, Publisher, phone: (970)392-4430; T.M. Fasano, Reporter, phone: (970)392-5631. **URL:** http://www.mywindsornow.com. **Remarks:** Accepts advertising. **Circ:** Combined ‡7213.

5751 ■ KKQZ-FM - 94.3
600 Main St.
Windsor, CO 80550
Phone: (970)674-2700
Fax: (970)686-7491
Free: 800-595-2943
Format: Classic Rock; Album-Oriented Rock (AOR). **Owner:** Townsquare Media Inc., 2000 Fifth Third Ctr. 511 Walnut St., Cincinnati, OH 45202, Ph: (513)651-1190. **Operating Hours:** 5 a.m.- 7 p.m. **Key Personnel:** Ted Rose, Dir. of Programs; Mark Callaghan, Operations Mgr.; Pat Kelley, Gen. Mgr., pat.kelley@townsquaremedia.com; Justin Tyler, Mgr., justin.tyler@townsquaremedia.com. **URL:** http://www.943loudwire.com.

5752 ■ KMAX-FM - 94.3
600 Main St.
Windsor, CO 80550
Phone: (970)674-2700
Format: Classical. **Owner:** Townsquare Media Inc., 2324 Arkansas Blvd., Texarkana, AR 71854, Ph: (870)772-3771. **Key Personnel:** Pat Kelley, Gen. Mgr., pat.kelley@townsquaremedia.com; Justin Tyler, Mgr., justin.tyler@townsquaremedia.com. **URL:** http://www.943loudwire.com.

5753 ■ KRQU-FM - 102.9
600 Main St.
Windsor, CO 80550
Phone: (970)674-2700
Email: krqu@compuserve.com
Format: Classic Rock. **Owner:** Jerry Lundquist, at above address. **Founded:** 1982. **Key Personnel:** K.W. Gray-Bow, Operations Mgr.; Amy Isakson, Sales Mgr.; K.W. Graybow, Gen. Mgr. **Wattage:** 17,000 ERP. **Ad Rates:** $7 for 30 seconds; $9.50 for 60 seconds. Combined advertising rates available with KLDI-AM. **URL:** http://rock1029.com/help.

5754 ■ KTRR-FM - 102.5
600 Main St.
Windsor, CO 80550
Phone: (970)674-2700
Format: Soft Rock. **Wattage:** 17,000. **Ad Rates:** Noncommercial. **URL:** http://www.tri1025.com.

5755 ■ KUAD-FM - 99.1
600 Main St.
Windsor, CO 80550
Phone: (970)674-2700
Fax: (970)686-7491
Free: 800-500-2599
Format: Country. **Owner:** Townsquare Media Inc., 2000 Fifth Third Ctr. 511 Walnut St., Cincinnati, OH 45202, Ph: (513)651-1190. **Founded:** 1971. **Operating Hours:** Continuous; 100% local. **Key Personnel:** Justin Tyler, Mgr., justin.tyler@townsquaremedia.com; Pat Kelley, Gen. Mgr., pat.kelley@townsquaremedia.com; Brian Gary, Contact; Dave Jensen, Contact. **Wattage:** 100,000. **Ad Rates:** Noncommercial. **URL:** http://www.k99.com.

WOODLAND PARK

Teller Co. Teller Co. (C). 18 m NW of Colorado Springs. Recreation area. Ranches.

5756 ■ Elbert County News
Colorado Community Media
1200 East Hwy. 24
Woodland Park, CO 80863
Phone: (719)687-3006
Fax: (719)687-3009
Newspaper. **Freq:** Weekly (Thurs.). **Print Method:** Offset. **Cols./Page:** 6. **Col. Width:** 24 nonpareils. **Col. Depth:** 301 agate lines. **Subscription Rates:** $30 Individuals /year (home delivery); $20 Individuals /year (senior rate). **URL:** http://elbertcountynews.net. **Mailing address:** PO Box 340, Woodland Park, CO 80866. **Remarks:** Accepts advertising. **Circ:** (Not Reported).

WRAY

Yuma Co. Yuma Co. (EC). 65 m SE of Stirling.

5757 ■ KRDZ-AM - 1440
32992 U.S. Hwy. 34
Wray, CO 80758
Phone: (970)332-4171
Fax: (970)332-4172
Email: krdz@medialogicradio.com
Format: Classic Rock. **Networks:** ABC; Brownfield. **Operating Hours**: Continuous. **Wattage**: 5,000 Day; 212 Night. **Ad Rates:** Noncommercial. Combined advertising rates available with KATR FM. **Mailing address:** PO Box 354, Wray, CO 80758. **URL:** http://www.krdz.com.

YUMA

Yuma Co. Yuma Co. (WC). 43 m SE of Sterling. Grain farms.

5758 ■ Yuma Pioneer
Yuma Pioneer
1000 W 8th Ave.
Yuma, CO 80759
Phone: (970)848-2174
General interest community newspaper. **Freq:** Weekly (Thurs.). **Print Method:** Offset. **Trim Size:** 21 1/2 x 13 1/2. **Cols./Page:** 6. **Col. Width:** 13 picas. **Col. Depth:** 21 1/2 inches. **Key Personnel:** Tony Rayl, Editor. **Subscription Rates:** $30 Individuals print; $34 Out of state print; $30 Individuals online only. **URL:** http://www.yumapioneer.com. **Remarks:** Advertising accepted; rates available upon request. **Circ:** ‡2850.

5759 ■ K220IJ-FM - 91.9
PO Box 391
Twin Falls, ID 83303

Circulation: ★ = AAM; △ or • = BPA; ♦ = CAC; ❑ = VAC; ⊕ = PO Statement; ‡ = Publisher's Report; Boldface figures = sworn; Light figures = estimated.

Fax: (208)736-1958
Free: 800-357-4226
Format: Religious; Contemporary Christian. **Owner:** CSN International, PO Box 391, Twin Falls, ID 83303, Ph: (208)736-1958, Fax: (208)736-1958, Free: 800-357-4226. **Key Personnel:** Mike Kestler, President; Don Mills, Music Dir., Prog. Dir.; Ray Gorney, Asst. Dir.; Kelly Carlson, Dir. of Engg. **URL:** http://www.csnradio.com.

BERLIN

5760 ■ WERB 94.5FM - 94.5
139 Patterson Way
Berlin, CT 06037
Phone: (860)828-6577
Fax: (860)829-0526
Format: Full Service. **Owner:** Berlin Board of Education, 238 Kensington Rd., Berlin, CT 06037, Fax: (860)829-0832. **Ad Rates:** Noncommercial. **URL:** http://werb.berlinwall.org.

5761 ■ WPRX-AM
1253 Berlin Tpke.
Berlin, CT 06037
Phone: (860)727-0844
Fax: (860)727-0849
Key Personnel: P. Oscar Nieves, President. **Wattage:** 1,000 Day; 500 Night. **Ad Rates:** Advertising accepted; rates available upon request.

BETHEL

SW CT. Fairfield Co. 8 mi. S. of Brookfield. Residential.

5762 ■ East Coast Merchandiser
Sumner Communications Inc.
24 Stony Hill Rd.
Bethel, CT 06801
Phone: (203)748-2050
Fax: (203)830-2072
Free: 800-999-8281
Publisher's E-mail: nancy@sumnercom.com
Magazine publishing information about Flea Market and Swap Meet industry. **Freq:** Monthly. **Subscription Rates:** $30 Individuals. **URL:** http://www.wholesalecentral.com/SUM028/store.cfm?event=itemdetail&itemid=44. **Circ:** (Not Reported).

5763 ■ Experimental Mechanics
Society for Experimental Mechanics
7 School St.
Bethel, CT 06801-1405
Phone: (203)790-6373
Fax: (203)790-4472
Publisher's E-mail: sem@sem1.com
Archival journal for experimental mechanics focusing on techniques employed in the measurement of stresses and strains as applied to metals and other materials. **Freq:** 9/year. **Trim Size:** 8 1/8 x 10 7/8. **Cols./Page:** 2. **Col. Width:** 19 picas. **Col. Depth:** 58 picas. **Key Personnel:** Horacio D. Espinosa, Advisor, Board Member; Eric N. Brown, Associate Editor. **ISSN:** 0014--4851 (print); **EISSN:** 1741--2765 (electronic). **Subscription Rates:** $1355 Institutions print and online; €1124 Institutions print and online. **URL:** http://semimac.org/publications; http://www.springer.com/materials/mechanics/journal/11340. **Remarks:** Advertising not accepted. **Circ:** 4500.

5764 ■ Experimental Techniques: A Publication for the Practicing Engineer
Society for Experimental Mechanics
7 School St.
Bethel, CT 06801-1405
Phone: (203)790-6373
Fax: (203)790-4472
Publisher's E-mail: sem@sem1.com
Magazine on test techniques for solid mechanics programs. **Freq:** Bimonthly. **Print Method:** Offset. **Trim Size:** 8 1/8 x 10 7/8. **Cols./Page:** 3 and 2. **Col. Width:** 26 and 37 nonpareils. **Col. Depth:** 140 agate lines. **Key Personnel:** Tom Proulx, Publisher; Kristin B. Zimmerman, Associate Editor; Dahsin Liu, Associate Editor; Jason Blough, Associate Editor. **ISSN:** 0732--8818 (print); **EISSN:** 1747--1567 (electronic). **URL:** http://semimac.org/publications; http://onlinelibrary.wiley.com/journal/10.1111/(ISSN)1747-1567. **Remarks:** Advertising not accepted. **Circ:** ‡4380.

5765 ■ FleaMarketZone
Sumner Communications Inc.
24 Stony Hill Rd.
Bethel, CT 06801
Phone: (203)748-2050
Fax: (203)830-2072
Free: 800-999-8281
Publisher's E-mail: nancy@sumnercom.com
Magazine publishing information about Flea Market and Swap Meet industry. **Freq:** Monthly. **Key Personnel:** Brian Torreso, Associate Publisher; Gloria Mellinger, Editor-in-Chief. **Subscription Rates:** $30 Individuals; $7 Single issue. **URL:** http://fleamarketzone.com. **Remarks:** Accepts advertising. **Circ:** (Not Reported).

5766 ■ Independent Retailer
Sumner Communications Inc.
24 Stony Hill Rd.
Bethel, CT 06801
Phone: (203)748-2050
Fax: (203)830-2072
Free: 800-999-8281
Publisher's E-mail: nancy@sumnercom.com
Magazine publishing information for independent +retail store owners. **Freq:** Monthly. **Key Personnel:** Bill McNulty, Publisher; Woody Sumner, Publisher. **Subscription Rates:** $24 Individuals; $7 Single issue. **URL:** http://independentretailer.com. **Ad Rates:** 4C $1,125; 4C $975. **Remarks:** Accepts advertising. **Circ:** (Not Reported).

5767 ■ Midwest Merchandiser
Sumner Communications Inc.
24 Stony Hill Rd.
Bethel, CT 06801
Phone: (203)748-2050
Fax: (203)830-2072
Free: 800-999-8281
Publisher's E-mail: nancy@sumnercom.com
Magazine publishing information about Flea Market and Swap Meet Industry. **Freq:** Monthly. **Subscription Rates:** $30 Individuals 12 monthly issues, one year subscription. **URL:** http://www.wholesalecentral.com/SUM028/store.cfm?event=itemdetail&itemid=46. **Remarks:** Accepts advertising. **Circ:** (Not Reported).

5768 ■ Plastics Engineering
Society of Plastics Engineers
6 Berkshire Blvd., Ste. 306
Bethel, CT 06801
Phone: (203)775-0471
Fax: (203)775-8490
Plastics trade magazine. **Freq:** 10/year. **Print Method:** Web Offset. **Trim Size:** 8 1/8 x 10 3/4. **Cols./Page:** 3 and 2. **Col. Width:** 28 and 42 nonpareils. **Col. Depth:** 140 agate lines. **Key Personnel:** Daniel J. Domoff, Managing Editor, phone: (203)740-5429; Joseph Tomaszewski, Representative, Advertising and Sales. **ISSN:** 0091--9578 (print); **EISSN:** 1941--9635 (electronic). **Subscription Rates:** $142 Nonmembers; $242 Nonmembers outside North America; $180 Institutions corporate library; $280 Institutions corporate library outside North America; Included in membership included in membership dues; $160 Nonmembers. **URL:** http://plasticsengineering.org. **Ad Rates:** BW $4,300; 4C $7,200. **Remarks:** Accepts advertising. **Circ:** ***34000**.

5769 ■ Polymer Composites
Society of Plastics Engineers
6 Berkshire Blvd., Ste. 306
Bethel, CT 06801
Phone: (203)775-0471
Fax: (203)775-8490
Publisher's E-mail: info@wiley.com
Journal focusing on the fields of reinforced plastics and polymer composites. **Freq:** Monthly. **Trim Size:** 7 x 10. **Key Personnel:** Alan J. Lesser, Editor-in-Chief; Eric Baer, Advisor, Board Member. **ISSN:** 0272--8397 (print); **EISSN:** 1548--0569 (electronic). **Subscription Rates:** $2481 Institutions print or online; $2978 Institutions, Canada and Mexico print and online ; £1602 Institutions print and online (U.K.); €2026 Institutions print and online (Europe); $3137 Institutions, other countries print and online. **URL:** http://onlinelibrary.wiley.com/journal/10.1002/(ISSN)1548-0569; http://www.4spe.org/Resources/Content.aspx?ItemNumber=3913. **Ad Rates:** BW $757; 4C $1,009. **Remarks:** Accepts advertising. **Circ:** 420.

5770 ■ Western Merchandiser
Sumner Communications Inc.
24 Stony Hill Rd.
Bethel, CT 06801
Phone: (203)748-2050
Fax: (203)830-2072
Free: 800-999-8281
Publisher's E-mail: nancy@sumnercom.com
Magazine publishing information about Flea Market and Swap Meet industry. **Freq:** Monthly. **Subscription Rates:** $30 Individuals; $7 Single issue. **URL:** http://www.wholesalecentral.com/SUM028/store.cfm?event=itemdetail&itemid=48; http://www.wholesalecentral.com/SUM028/store.cfm?event=itemdetail&itemid=49. **Remarks:** Accepts advertising. **Circ:** (Not Reported).

BETHLEHEM

5771 ■ North American Archaeologist
Baywood Publishing Company Inc.
c/o Roger M. Moeller, Ed.
Archaeological Services
Bethlehem, CT 06751
Publisher's E-mail: info@baywood.com
Journal covering archaeological activity in the U.S., Canada, and northern Mexico. **Freq:** Quarterly. **Key**

Circulation: ★ = AAM; △ or • = BPA; ♦ = CAC; ❑ = VAC; ⊕ = PO Statement; ‡ = Publisher's Report; Boldface figures = sworn; Light figures = estimated.

Personnel: Roger M. Moeller, Editor; Anthony T. Boldurian, Editor. **ISSN:** 0197--6931 (print); **EISSN:** 1541--3543 (electronic). **Subscription Rates:** $143 Individuals print and online; $148 Institutions single issue; $493 Institutions online only; $537 Institutions print only; $548 Institutions print and online. **URL:** http://www.baywood.com/journals/PreviewJournals.asp?Id=0197-6931; http://us.sagepub.com/en-us/nam/north-american-archaeologist/journal202392. **Remarks:** Advertising not accepted. **Circ:** (Not Reported).

BLOOMFIELD

C. CT. Hartford Co. NNW of Hartford. Tobacco growing.

5772 ■ Academy Forum
American Academy of Psychoanalysis and Dynamic Psychiatry
1 Regency Dr.
Bloomfield, CT 06002
Fax: (860)286-0787
Free: 888-691-8281
Publisher's E-mail: info@aapdp.org
Magazine covering psychoanalysis and related topics. **Freq:** Semiannual. **Key Personnel:** Gerald P. Perman, MD, Editor; Ann Ruth Turkel, MD, Editor. **Subscription Rates:** $20 U.S. and Canada /year. **URL:** http://aapdp.org/index.php/publications/academy-forum. **Mailing address:** PO Box 30, Bloomfield, CT 06002-0030. **Remarks:** Advertising accepted; rates available upon request. **Circ:** (Not Reported).

5773 ■ The Catholic Transcript
The Catholic Transcript Inc.
467 Bloomfield Ave.
Bloomfield, CT 06002-2903
Phone: (860)286-2828
Fax: (860)726-0000
Publication E-mail: info@catholictranscript.org
Official newspaper of the Archdiocese of Hartford. **Freq:** Monthly fourth Wednesday of the month. **Print Method:** Offset. **Trim Size:** 11 3/8 x 17. **Cols./Page:** 5. **Col. Depth:** 16 inches. **Key Personnel:** Roberta Tuttle, Managing Editor; Jack Sheedy, Editor; David Q. Liptak, Executive Editor. **USPS:** 094-540. **Subscription Rates:** $12 Individuals 1 year. **Ad Rates:** BW $1,900; 4C $2,400; PCI $30. **Remarks:** Accepts advertising. **Circ:** 78000.

5774 ■ Journal of the American Academy of Psychiatry and the Law
American Academy of Psychiatry and the Law
1 Regency Dr.
Bloomfield, CT 06002-2310
Phone: (860)242-5450
Fax: (860)286-0787
Free: 800-331-1389
Publisher's E-mail: office@aapl.org
Journal covering forensic psychiatry. **Freq:** Quarterly. **Key Personnel:** Ezra E.H. Griffith, MD, Editor. **ISSN:** 1093--6793 (print). **URL:** http://www.jaapl.org. **Mailing address:** PO Box 30, Bloomfield, CT 06002. **Remarks:** Advertising not accepted. **Circ:** (Not Reported).

5775 ■ Psychodynamic Psychiatry
American Academy of Psychoanalysis and Dynamic Psychiatry
1 Regency Dr.
Bloomfield, CT 06002
Fax: (860)286-0787
Free: 888-691-8281
Publisher's E-mail: info@guilford.com
Journal providing forum for inquiry into all areas of human behavior. Offers stimulating insights into new biological, cultural, and other discoveries related to the human psyche and psychoanalysis. **Freq:** Quarterly. **Print Method:** Offset. **Trim Size:** 6 x 9. **Cols./Page:** 1. **Col. Width:** 72 nonpareils. **Col. Depth:** 42 picas. **Key Personnel:** Richard C. Friedman, MD, Editor; Cesar A. Alfonso, Editor; Gail W. Berry, Board Member; Matthew Tolchin, Board Member; Hrair M. Babikian, Board Member; Mariam C. Cohen, Board Member; Silvia Olarte, Board Member; Ann Ruth Turkel, Board Member; Roman N. Anshin, Board Member; Ronald Turco, Board Member. **ISSN:** 2162--2590 (print). **Subscription Rates:** $99 Individuals; $134 Other countries; $59.40 Students online only; $79 Members US, APA members. **URL:** http://www.guilford.com/journals/Psychodynamic-Psychiatry/Richard-Friedman/21622590; http://aapdp.org/index.php/publications/journal. **Formerly**: Journal of the American Academy of Psychoanalysis; Journal of the American Academy of Psychoanalysis and Dynamic Psychiatry. **Ad Rates:** BW $325. **Remarks:** Accepts advertising. **Circ:** 10000.

5776 ■ WDRC-AM - 1360
869 Blue Hills Ave.
Bloomfield, CT 06002
Phone: (860)243-1115
Fax: (860)286-8257
Format: Full Service; Information. **Simulcasts:** WMMW-AM. **Networks:** Independent. **Owner:** Buckley Broadcasting Corp. Inc., 166 W Putnam Ave., Greenwich, CT 06830-5241, Ph: (203)661-4309. **Founded:** 1922. **Operating Hours:** Continuous; 60% network, 40% local. **ADI:** Hartford-New Haven (New London), CT. **Wattage:** 5,000. **Ad Rates:** Advertising accepted; rates available upon request. Combined advertising rates available with WDRC-FM, WWCO-AM, WSNG-AM.

5777 ■ WDRC-FM - 102.9
869 Blue Hills Ave.
Bloomfield, CT 06002
Phone: (860)243-1115
Fax: (860)286-8257
Format: Classic Rock. **Owner:** Buckley Broadcasting Corp. Inc., 166 W Putnam Ave., Greenwich, CT 06830-5241, Ph: (203)661-4309. **Founded:** 1939. **Operating Hours:** Continuous. **Key Personnel:** Grahame Winters, Dir. of Programs, gwinters@drcfm.com. **Wattage:** 19,500 ERP. **Ad Rates:** WDRC-AM, WWCO-AM, WMMW-AM, WSNG-AM.

5778 ■ WMMW-AM - 1470
869 Blue Hills Ave.
Bloomfield, CT 06002
Phone: (860)243-1115
Fax: (860)286-8257
Format: Talk. **Wattage:** 2,500. **Ad Rates:** Noncommercial. **URL:** http://www.talkofconnecticut.com.

5779 ■ WSNG-AM - 610
869 Blue Hills Ave.
Bloomfield, CT 06002
Phone: (860)243-1115
Fax: (860)286-8257
Format: Adult Contemporary; Full Service; Talk; Information. **Networks:** Westwood One Radio; Mutual Broadcasting System; Talknet. **Owner:** Buckley Radio, at above address, Stratford, CT. **Founded:** 1948. **Formerly**: WTOR-AM. **Operating Hours:** Continuous; 5% network, 95% local. **Key Personnel:** Eric Fahnoe, Gen. Mgr., VP, efahnoe@drcfm.com; Laura Kittell, Operations Mgr., lkittell@drcfm.com; Grahame Winters, Dir. of Programs, gwinters@drcfm.com. **Wattage:** 1,000 Day; 500 Night. **Ad Rates:** Noncommercial.

5780 ■ WWCO-AM - 1240
869 Blue Hills Ave.
Bloomfield, CT 06002
Phone: (860)243-1115
Fax: (860)286-8257
Format: Adult Contemporary. **Networks:** CNN Radio. **Owner:** Buckley Broadcasting Corp. CT, 166 W Putnam Ave., Greenwich, CT 06830. **Founded:** 1946. **Operating Hours:** Continuous. **Key Personnel:** Grahame Winters, Dir. of Programs, gwinters@drcfm.com; Eric Fahnoe, Gen. Mgr., VP, efahnoe@drcfm.com; Laura Kittell, Operations Mgr., lkittell@drcfm.com. **Wattage:** 1,000. **Ad Rates:** $25-35 for 60 seconds. Combined advertising rates available with WDRC-AM, WSNG-AM.

BOLTON

5781 ■ The Community Voice Channel
105 Notch Rd.
Bolton, CT 06043
Phone: (860)645-1454
Email: bills@cvcct.org
Founded: 1991. **Formerly**: Eastern Connecticut TV. **Key Personnel:** Amy Heavisides, Production Mgr., cvc_production_manager@comcast.net. **Cities Served:** subscribing households 25,000. **URL:** http://www.cvcct.org.

BRANFORD

S. CT. New Haven Co. 7 mi. S. of New Haven.

5782 ■ Connecticut Parent Magazine
Connecticut Parent Magazine
420 E Main St., Ste. 18
Branford, CT 06405
Phone: (203)483-1700
Fax: (203)483-0522
Publication E-mail: editorial@ctparent.com
Parenting magazine. **Freq:** Monthly. **Trim Size:** 8 1/2 x 11. **Cols./Page:** 3. **Col. Width:** 2 3/8 inches. **Col. Depth:** 10 inches. **Key Personnel:** Joel D. MacClaren, Editor, Publisher; Joe Zibell, Associate Publisher. **Subscription Rates:** $24 Individuals third class. **Ad Rates:** BW $1,560; 4C $2,110. **Remarks:** Accepts advertising. **Circ:** (Not Reported).

BRIDGEPORT

SW CT. Fairfield Co. Port of entry on Long Island Sound, 56 mi. NE of New York. University of Bridgeport, Fairfield University, Sacred Heart University, Bridgeport Engineering Institute and Housatonic Community College. Manufactures electrical appliances, ammunition, firearms, airplane engines, jet engine components, cutlery, brake linings, adding machines, machine tools, sewing machines, helicopters, airplane and aircraft accessories, hardware, machinery, brass, steel, asbestos products, valves and fittings, textiles.

5783 ■ Casting World
Continental Communications
PO Box 1919
Bridgeport, CT 06601-1919
Phone: (203)377-5566
Fax: (203)377-7230
Magazine for users of ferrous and non-ferrous castings. **Freq:** Quarterly. **Print Method:** Offset. **Trim Size:** 11 x 14 3/4. **Cols./Page:** 5. **Col. Width:** 13 picas. **Col. Depth:** 10 inches. **Key Personnel:** W.W. Troland, Editor. **ISSN:** 0887--9060 (print). **Ad Rates:** BW $5,110; 4C $6,030. **Remarks:** Accepts advertising. **Circ:** Non-paid ‡77000.

5784 ■ Connecticut Post
Connecticut Post
410 State St.
Bridgeport, CT 06604
Phone: (203)333-0161
Fax: (203)367-8158
Publisher's E-mail: edit@ctpost.com
General newspaper. **Freq:** Mon.-Sun. (morn.). **Print Method:** Offset. **Trim Size:** 13 x 20 1/4. **Cols./Page:** 6. **Col. Width:** 12.4 picas. **Col. Depth:** 280 agate lines. **Key Personnel:** Jim Shay, Editor, phone: (203)330-6242; Gary Rogo, Editor, phone: (203)330-6223, fax: (203)334-6933; Patrick Quinn; Michael Daly, Editor, phone: (203)330-6394; Ted Tompkins, Assistant Managing Editor, phone: (203)330-6382; Tom Baden, Editor, phone: (203)330-6325; John DeAugustine, Publisher, phone: (203)330-6211. **Subscription Rates:** $3.50 Individuals per week; Thursday, Friday and Sunday; $6.50 Individuals per week, 7 days; $2.50 Individuals Sunday. **URL:** http://www.ctpost.com. **Formerly**: The Bridgeport Post. **Ad Rates:** GLR $2.35; PCI $30. **Remarks:** Accepts advertising. **Circ:** Mon.-Sat. 78455.

5785 ■ The Darien News
The Darien News
410 State St.
Bridgeport, CT 06604
Phone: (203)333-0161
Publication E-mail: jwolfe@scni.com
Newspaper covering Darien and McIntosh County. **Freq:** Daily. **Print Method:** Offset. **Cols./Page:** 6. **Col. Width:** 21 1/2 nonpareils. **Col. Depth:** 301 agate lines. **Key Personnel:** Ashley Varese, Editor, phone: (203)972-4405; Belinda Stasiukiewicz, Managing Editor, phone: (203)972-4401; Jon Chik, Editor, phone: (203)972-4402. **USPS:** 566-040. **Subscription Rates:** $3 Individuals /week (Thursday, Friday & Sunday); $5 Individuals /week (daily); $2.25 Individuals /week (Sunday only). **URL:** http://dariennewsonline.com. **Ad Rates:** GLR $.25; BW $516; 4C $876; SAU $4. **Remarks:** Accepts advertising. **Circ:** ‡3451.

5786 ■ Fairfield County Catholic
Fairfield County Catholic
238 Jewett Ave.
Bridgeport, CT 06606-2845
Publication E-mail: fcc@diobpt.org
Official newspaper of the Roman Catholic Diocese of Bridgeport, (Fairfield county), CT. **Freq:** Biweekly monthly in July/August. **Print Method:** Offset. **Trim**

Size: 10 1/2 x 15.5. **Cols./Page:** 5. **Col. Width:** 2 inches. **Col. Depth:** 15 1/2 inches. **Key Personnel:** Ralph Lazzaro, Manager, Advertising; Rev. William E. Lori, Publisher. **USPS:** 012-117. **Subscription Rates:** $20 Individuals within diocese; $50 Individuals outside diocese. **URL:** http://bridgeportdiocese.com/fcc. **Ad Rates:** GLR $2.50; BW $1,900; CNU $2; PCI $45. **Remarks:** Accepts advertising. **Circ:** ‡95000.

5787 ■ WCUM-AM - 1450
PO Box 3975
Bridgeport, CT 06605
Phone: (203)335-1450
Fax: (203)337-1220
Email: radiocumbre1450@aol.com
Format: Hispanic. **Networks:** Independent. **Owner:** Radio Cumbre Broadcasting Inc., at above address. **Founded:** 1941. **Formerly:** WJBX-AM. **Operating Hours:** Continuous. **ADI:** New York, NY. **Key Personnel:** Migdalia R. Colon, Contact. **Wattage:** 1,000. **Ad Rates:** $32-60 for 30 seconds; $50-75 for 60 seconds.

5788 ■ WDJZ-AM - 1530
211 State St., 3rd Fl.
Bridgeport, CT 06604
Phone: (203)368-4392
Fax: (203)367-4551
Email: wdjzradio@sbcglobal.net
Format: Gospel. **Networks:** Independent. **Owner:** Peoples Broadcast Network, at above address. **Founded:** 2001. **Operating Hours:** 6 a.m.-8 p.m. **Key Personnel:** Milford Edwards, Sr., Gen. Mgr.; Maria Miller, CEO, President; Thomas Hardy, Dir. of Sales. **Wattage:** 5,000. **Ad Rates:** Noncommercial. **URL:** http://www.wdjzradio.com.

5789 ■ WEBE-FM - 107.9
Two Lafayette Sq.
Bridgeport, CT 06604
Phone: (203)333-9108
Fax: (203)384-0600
Free: 800-932-3108
Email: contests@webe108.com
Format: Eighties. **Owner:** Cumulus Media Inc., 3280 Peachtree Rd. NW, Ste. 2300, Atlanta, GA 30305-2455, Ph: (404)949-0700, Fax: (404)949-0740. **Founded:** 1984. **Operating Hours:** Continuous. **Key Personnel:** Marnie Klebart, Sales Mgr., marnie.klebart@cumulus.com; Ann McManus, Gen. Mgr., ann.mcmanus@cumulus.com. **Wattage:** 50,000 ERP. **Ad Rates:** Noncommercial. **URL:** http://www.webe108.com.

5790 ■ WEDW-TV - 49
1049 Asylum Ave.
Hartford, CT 06105
Phone: (860)278-5310
Format: Public TV. **Simulcasts:** WEDH-TV. **Networks:** Public Broadcasting Service (PBS). **Owner:** Connecticut Public Broadcasting Network, 1049 Asylum Ave., Hartford, CT 06105-2432, Ph: (860)275-7550. **Operating Hours:** 6:45 a.m.-midnight. **ADI:** Hartford-New Haven (New London), CT. **Ad Rates:** Noncommercial. **URL:** http://www.cpbn.org/?cpbnnb_p=2&cpbnnb_t=4.

5791 ■ WICC-AM - 600
Two Lafayette Sq.
Bridgeport, CT 06604
Phone: (203)366-6000
Free: 800-922-6060
Format: News; Talk. **Owner:** Cumulus Media Inc., 3280 Peachtree Rd. NW, Ste. 2300, Atlanta, GA 30305-2455, Ph: (404)949-0700, Fax: (404)949-0740. **Founded:** 1926. **Operating Hours:** Continuous. **Key Personnel:** Marnie Klebart, Contact, marnie.klebart@cumulus.com. **Local Programs:** *The Clark Howard Show*, Monday Tuesday Wednesday Thursday Friday Monday Tuesday Wednesday Thursday Friday 1:00 p.m. - 4:00 p.m. 7:00 p.m. - 10:00 p.m.; *Oh Wow Oldies Show*, Saturday 7:00 p.m. - 12:00 a.m. **Wattage:** 1,000 Day; 500 Night. **Ad Rates:** Noncommercial. **URL:** http://www.wicc600.com.

5792 ■ WSAH-TV - 43
449 Broadway
New York, NY 10013
Phone: (212)966-1059
Owner: Multicultural Radio Broadcasting, Inc., at above address. **Key Personnel:** John Gabel, Contact, johng@mrbi.net.

BRISTOL

N. CT. Hartford Co. 18 mi. SW of Hartford. Manufactures ball bearings, springs, clocks, watches, timing devices, chemicals, metal shapes, electrical resistance coils, variable transformers, electronic devices, electrical component parts, brass and aluminum forgings, sheet metal, wire rods, glass cutters, paper boxes, dairy, screw machine products, wall box dimmers, sports equipment, electro plating, cutlery.

5793 ■ Acta Cardiologica: An International Journal of Cardiology the Official Journal of the Belgian Society of Cardiology
PEETERS-USA
70 Enterprise Dr., Ste. 2
Bristol, CT 06010
Publisher's E-mail: peeters@peeters-us.com
Peer-reviewed journal covering all aspects of cardiovascular disease. **Freq:** Bimonthly. **Print Method:** Offset. **Trim Size:** 8 1/4 x 11. **Cols./Page:** 3. **Col. Width:** 26 nonpareils. **Col. Depth:** 130 agate lines. **Key Personnel:** H. Ector, Editor; P. Unger, Editor; P. Lancelotti, Editor. **ISSN:** 0001-5385 (print). **Subscription Rates:** €85 Individuals. **URL:** http://poj.peeters-leuven.be/content.php?url=journal&journal_code=AC. **Remarks:** Advertising not accepted. **Circ:** (Not Reported).

5794 ■ Ancient Near Eastern Studies
PEETERS-USA
70 Enterprise Dr., Ste. 2
Bristol, CT 06010
Publisher's E-mail: peeters@peeters-us.com
Peer-reviewed journal covering articles on the languages and cultures of the ancient near east. **Freq:** Annual. **Key Personnel:** Antonio Sagona, Editor. **ISSN:** 1378--4641 (print); **EISSN:** 1783--1326 (electronic). **URL:** http://www.peeters-leuven.be/journoverz.asp?nr=1&number_of_volumes="0"; http://poj.peeters-leuven.be/content.php?url=journal&journal_code=ANES. **Remarks:** Advertising not accepted. **Circ:** (Not Reported).

5795 ■ ARAM Periodical
PEETERS-USA
70 Enterprise Dr., Ste. 2
Bristol, CT 06010
Publisher's E-mail: peeters@peeters-us.com
Peer-reviewed journal for Syro-mesopotamian studies. **Key Personnel:** Dr. Shafiq Abouzayd, Editor. **ISSN:** 0959--4213 (print); **EISSN:** 1783--1342 (electronic). **URL:** http://www.peeters-leuven.be/journoverz.asp?nr=68&number_of_volumes="0"; http://poj.peeters-leuven.be/content.php?url=journal&journal_code=ARAM. **Remarks:** Advertising not accepted. **Circ:** (Not Reported).

5796 ■ Bibliotheca Orientalis: Journal of the Dutch institute for the Near East
PEETERS-USA
70 Enterprise Dr., Ste. 2
Bristol, CT 06010
Publication E-mail: bior@hum.leidenuniv.nl
Journal covering bibliographical data on books published on the ancient and modern near east. **Freq:** 4/month. **Key Personnel:** D.J.W. Meijer, Editor; A. van der Kooij, Editor; M. Stol, Editor; R.E. Kon, Editor; J. de Roos, Editor. **ISSN:** 0006--1913 (print). **URL:** http://poj.peeters-leuven.be/content.php?url=journal&journal_code=BIOR. **Remarks:** Advertising not accepted. **Circ:** (Not Reported).

5797 ■ Caeculus: Papers on Mediterranean Archaeology and Greek and Roman Studies
PEETERS-USA
70 Enterprise Dr., Ste. 2
Bristol, CT 06010
Publisher's E-mail: peeters@peeters-us.com
Journal covering Mediterranean archaeology. **Key Personnel:** O.M. Van Nijf, Editor; M. Kleibrink, Editor; P.A.J. Attema, Editor; R.R. Nauta, Editor; M.A. Harder, Editor. **ISSN:** 1782--4907 (print); **EISSN:** 1783--1393 (electronic). **URL:** http://poj.peeters-leuven.be/content.php?url=journal&journal_code=CAE. **Remarks:** Advertising not accepted. **Circ:** (Not Reported).

5798 ■ Eastern Christian Art: In its Late Antique and Islamic Contexts
PEETERS-USA
70 Enterprise Dr., Ste. 2
Bristol, CT 06010
Publisher's E-mail: peeters@peeters-us.com
Journal devoted to studies in Christian art and archaeology in the Middle East. **Key Personnel:** Sofia Schaten, Board Member; Dr. Mat Immerzeel, Board Member; Dr. Gertrud J.M. van Loon, Board Member; Magda Laptas, Board Member; Dr. Bas ter Haar Romeny, Board Member. **ISSN:** 1781--0930 (print); **EISSN:** 1783--1415 (electronic). **URL:** http://poj.peeters-leuven.be/content.php?url=journal&journal_code=ECA. **Remarks:** Advertising not accepted. **Circ:** (Not Reported).

5799 ■ Ephemerides Theologicae Lovanienses: Louvain Journal of Theology and Canon Law
PEETERS-USA
70 Enterprise Dr., Ste. 2
Bristol, CT 06010
Publisher's E-mail: peeters@peeters-us.com
Journal covering theology and canon law. **Freq:** Quarterly. **Key Personnel:** L. Kenis, Board Member; J. Haers, Member; G. Van Belle, Board Member; E. Gaziaux, Board Member; E. Brito, Member; M. Lamberigts, Board Member. **ISSN:** 0013--9513 (print); **EISSN:** 1783--1423 (electronic). **URL:** http://poj.peeters-leuven.be/content.php?journal_code=ETL&url=journal; http://poj.peeters-leuven.be/content.php?url=journal&journal_code=ETL. **Remarks:** Advertising not accepted. **Circ:** (Not Reported).

5800 ■ ESPN The Magazine
ESPN Inc.
ESPN Plz.
Bristol, CT 06010
Phone: (860)766-2000
Fax: (860)585-2213
Free: 888-549-3776
Publisher's E-mail: espnpr@espn.com
Magazine covering sports of all types. **Freq:** Biweekly. **Subscription Rates:** $29.95 Individuals. **URL:** http://insider.espn.com/insider/espn-the-magazine. **Remarks:** Accepts advertising. **Circ:** (Not Reported).

5801 ■ Ethische Perspectieven
PEETERS-USA
70 Enterprise Dr., Ste. 2
Bristol, CT 06010
Publisher's E-mail: peeters@peeters-us.com
Journal focusing on ethical topics and applied ethics. **Key Personnel:** Bart Pattyn, Director. **ISSN:** 0778--6069 (print); **EISSN:** 1783--144X (electronic). **URL:** http://poj.peeters-leuven.be/content.php?url=journal&journal_code=EPN. **Remarks:** Advertising not accepted. **Circ:** (Not Reported).

5802 ■ Gentse Bijdragen tot de Interieurgeschiedenis
PEETERS-USA
70 Enterprise Dr., Ste. 2
Bristol, CT 06010
Publisher's E-mail: peeters@peeters-us.com
Journal covering archaeology, history of art and lectures held on the annual conference day of historical interior. **Key Personnel:** Prof. Anna Bergmans, Editor. **ISSN:** 0772--7151 (print); **EISSN:** 1783--1466 (electronic). **URL:** http://poj.peeters-leuven.be/content.php?url=journal&journal_code=GBI. **Remarks:** Advertising not accepted. **Circ:** (Not Reported).

5803 ■ L'information grammaticale
PEETERS-USA
70 Enterprise Dr., Ste. 2
Bristol, CT 06010
Publisher's E-mail: peeters@peeters-us.com
Journal covering archaeology in North Africa. **Key Personnel:** Roland Eluerd, Director. **ISSN:** 0222--9838 (print); **EISSN:** 1783--1601 (electronic). **URL:** http://poj.peeters-leuven.be/content.php?url=journal&journal_code=IG. **Remarks:** Advertising not accepted. **Circ:** (Not Reported).

5804 ■ Journal of Coptic Studies
PEETERS-USA
70 Enterprise Dr., Ste. 2
Bristol, CT 06010
Publisher's E-mail: peeters@peeters-us.com
Journal focusing on literature, history, art, archeology, and related subjects, during pre-modern era focusing on Coptic language only. **Freq:** Annual. **Key Personnel:** Dr. Karlheinz Schussler; A. Boud'hors, Editor. **ISSN:** 1016--5584 (print); **EISSN:** 1783--1512 (electronic). **URL:** http://poj.peeters-leuven.be/content.php?url=journal&journal_code=JCS. **Remarks:** Advertising ac-

Circulation: ★ = AAM; △ or • = BPA; ♦ = CAC; ❑ = VAC; ⊕ = PO Statement; ‡ = Publisher's Report; Boldface figures = sworn; Light figures = estimated.

cepted; rates available upon request. **Circ:** (Not Reported).

5805 ■ Journal of Eastern Christian Studies
PEETERS-USA
70 Enterprise Dr., Ste. 2
Bristol, CT 06010
Publisher's E-mail: peeters@peeters-us.com
Journal focusing on Eastern and Oriental Christian churches in the Middle East, Central and Eastern Europe. Covers classical, theological, historical and literary approaches; the perspectives of social sciences, such as anthropology and migration studies are emphasized. Journal published in connection with the Faculty of Theology and the Institute of Early Christian and Byzantine Studies at the Catholic University of Leuven. **Key Personnel:** W. van den Bercken, Board Member; J. Verheyden, Executive Editor. **ISSN:** 0009--5141 (print). **Subscription Rates:** €75 Individuals. **URL:** http://www.peeters-leuven.be/journoverz.asp?nr=50. **Circ:** (Not Reported).

5806 ■ Leuvense Bijdragen
PEETERS-USA
70 Enterprise Dr., Ste. 2
Bristol, CT 06010
Publisher's E-mail: peeters@peeters-us.com
Journal for studies in general linguistics, Germanic linguistics and Germanic philology. **Key Personnel:** L. Draye, Board Member; G. Claassens, Board Member; H. Cuyckens, Board Member. **ISSN:** 0024--1482 (print); **EISSN:** 1783--1598 (electronic). **Subscription Rates:** €60 Individuals. **URL:** http://www.peeters-leuven.be/journoverz.asp?nr=74&number_of_volumes="0"; http://poj.peeters-leuven.be/content.php?url=journal&journal_code=LB. **Remarks:** Advertising not accepted. **Circ:** (Not Reported).

5807 ■ Onoma
PEETERS-USA
70 Enterprise Dr., Ste. 2
Bristol, CT 06010
Publisher's E-mail: peeters@peeters-us.com
Peer-reviewed journal of onomastic sciences. **Key Personnel:** Elwys De Stefani, Editor-in-Chief. **ISSN:** 0078--463X (print); **EISSN:** 1783--1644 (electronic). **Subscription Rates:** €80 Individuals. **URL:** http://poj.peeters-leuven.be/content.php?url=journal&journal_code=ONO. **Remarks:** Advertising not accepted. **Circ:** (Not Reported).

5808 ■ Rocky Hill Post
Imprint Newspapers
99 Main St.
Bristol, CT 06010
Phone: (860)236-3571
Fax: (860)233-2080
Community newspaper. **Freq:** Weekly (Fri.). **Print Method:** Offset. **Cols./Page:** 4. **Col. Width:** 15 picas. **Col. Depth:** 16 inches. **Key Personnel:** Michael Schroeder, Owner, Publisher; Gary Curran, Manager, Advertising; Dave Warren, Executive Editor. **Subscription Rates:** $390 Individuals mail; $233.48 Individuals home delivery. **URL:** http://www.centralctcommunications.com/newbritainherald. **Circ:** (Not Reported).

5809 ■ Studia Rosenthaliana
PEETERS-USA
70 Enterprise Dr., Ste. 2
Bristol, CT 06010
Publisher's E-mail: peeters@peeters-us.com
Journal on history, culture and heritage of the Jews in Netherlands. **Key Personnel:** Dr. Emile G.L. Schrijver, Editor-in-Chief. **ISSN:** 1781--7838 (print); **EISSN:** 1783--1792 (electronic). **Subscription Rates:** €80 Individuals. **URL:** http://poj.peeters-leuven.be/content.php?url=journal&journal_code=SR; http://www.peeters-leuven.be/journoverz.asp?nr=69&number_of_volumes="0". **Remarks:** Advertising not accepted. **Circ:** (Not Reported).

5810 ■ Studies in Spirituality
PEETERS-USA
70 Enterprise Dr., Ste. 2
Bristol, CT 06010
Publication E-mail: sis@titusbrandsmainstituut.nl
Journal covering articles on spirituality and mysticism. **Key Personnel:** Kees Waaijman, Board Member; Hein Blommestijn, Board Member; Wendy Litjens, Board Member. **ISSN:** 0926--6453 (print); **EISSN:** 1783--1814 (electronic). **Subscription Rates:** €75 Individuals. **URL:** http://poj.peeters-leuven.be/content.php?url=journal&journal_code=SIS. **Remarks:** Advertising not accepted. **Circ:** (Not Reported).

BROOKFIELD

SW CT. Fairfield Co. 7 mi. N. of Danbury. Residential.

5811 ■ WINE-AM
1004 Federal Rd.
Brookfield, CT 06804-1123
Phone: (203)775-1212
Fax: (203)775-6452
Format: News. **Networks:** Connecticut Radio. **Owner:** Coumulus Media, 3280 Peachtree Rd., NW Ste. 2300, Atlanta, GA 30305. **Founded:** 1964. **Key Personnel:** Gary Starr, President; Pat Scully, News Dir. **Wattage:** 680 Day; 004 Night. **Ad Rates:** $15 for 30 seconds; $39 for 60 seconds. **URL:** http://940sportsradio.com/.

5812 ■ WRKI-FM - 95.1
1004 Federal Rd.
Brookfield, CT 06804
Phone: (203)775-1212
Format: Album-Oriented Rock (AOR). **Owner:** Cumulus Media Inc., 3280 Peachtree Rd. NW, Ste. 2300, Atlanta, GA 30305-2455, Ph: (404)949-0700, Fax: (404)949-0740. **Founded:** 1957. **Operating Hours:** Continuous. **Key Personnel:** Jason Finkelberg, Gen. Mgr. **Wattage:** 50,000. **Ad Rates:** Advertising accepted; rates available upon request. **URL:** http://www.i95rock.com.

CHESHIRE

S. CT. New Haven Co. 8 mi. SE of Waterbury. Manufactures stamped and pressed metals, wood products, machine tool accessories. Fruit, dairy, poultry, and bedding plant farms.

5813 ■ The Cheshire Herald
The True Publishing Co.
1079 S Main St.
Cheshire, CT 06410
Fax: (203)250-7145
Publication E-mail: news@cheshireherald.com
Community newspaper (tabloid). **Freq:** Weekly (Thurs.). **Print Method:** Offset. **Cols./Page:** 5. **Col. Width:** 2 inches. **Col. Depth:** 15 1/2 inches. **Key Personnel:** John Rook, Editor; Susan Keeney, Director, Advertising; Maureen Jakubisyn, Treasurer, Vice President; Joseph J. Jakubisyn, President, Publisher; Ellen Jarus Hanley, Assistant Editor. **USPS:** 102-760. **Subscription Rates:** $10 Individuals online only; $33 Individuals in New Haven County; $35 Out of country; $35 Individuals multiple address; $20 Students. **URL:** http://www.cheshireherald.com. **Ad Rates:** GLR $1.35; BW $749.35; 4C $175; PCI $12.40. **Remarks:** Accepts advertising. **Circ:** ‡7200.

5814 ■ Child Abuse & Neglect: The International Journal
RELX Group P.L.C.
c/o M. Roth, Mng. Ed.
220 Mansion Rd.
Cheshire, CT 06410-3404
Publisher's E-mail: amsterdam@relx.com
Journal emphasizing on all aspects of child abuse and neglect while concerned with prevention and treatment. **Freq:** Monthly. **Key Personnel:** C. Wekerle, Editor-in-Chief. **ISSN:** 0145--2134 (print). **Subscription Rates:** $360 Individuals print; $2359.33 Institutions eJournal; $2831 Institutions print. **URL:** http://www.journals.elsevier.com/child-abuse-and-neglect. **Circ:** (Not Reported).

CLINTON

S. CT. Middlesex Co. On Long Island Sound, 25 mi. E. of New Haven. Summer resort. Manufactures cosmetics, boats, plastics.

5815 ■ The Easley Progress
Heartland Publications
1 W Main St.
Clinton, CT 06413
Phone: (860)664-1075
Fax: (860)664-1085
Publication E-mail: brobinson@theeasleyprogress.com
Local newspaper. **Freq:** Weekly (Wed.). **Print Method:** Offset. **Trim Size:** 14 1/4 x 22 3/4. **Cols./Page:** 6. **Col. Width:** 24 nonpareils. **Col. Depth:** 297 agate lines. **Key Personnel:** Ben Robinson, Managing Editor; Bonnie Lesley, Contact. **USPS:** 164-220. **Subscription Rates:** $26 Individuals online only; 1 year; $13 Individuals online only; 6 months. **URL:** http://www.theeasleyprogress.com. **Ad Rates:** PCI $6.50. **Remarks:** Accepts advertising. **Circ:** (Not Reported).

5816 ■ Herald-Independent
Heartland Publications
1 W Main St.
Clinton, CT 06413
Phone: (860)664-1075
Fax: (860)664-1085
Local newspaper. **Founded:** 1844. **Freq:** Weekly (Thurs.). **Print Method:** Offset. **Trim Size:** 14 x 23. **Cols./Page:** 6. **Col. Width:** 12 picas. **Col. Depth:** 21.5 inches. **Key Personnel:** Denny Koenders, Publisher; James Denton, Editor, General Manager; Jill Cincotta, Reporter. **USPS:** 480-470. **Subscription Rates:** $132 Individuals. **URL:** http://www.heraldindependent.com/. **Formerly:** The News & Herald; The Fairfield Independent. **Ad Rates:** BW $875; 4C $995; SAU $6.75; PCI $6.75. **Remarks:** Advertising accepted; rates available upon request. **Circ:** Paid ‡5,295, Free ‡145.

5817 ■ The Pickens Sentinel
Heartland Publications
1 W Main St.
Clinton, CT 06413
Phone: (860)664-1075
Fax: (860)664-1085
Community newspaper. **Freq:** Weekly (Wed.). **Print Method:** Offset. **Trim Size:** 13 x 21. **Cols./Page:** 6. **Col. Width:** 12 picas. **Col. Depth:** 21 inches. **Key Personnel:** Todd Rainwater, Publisher; Sandy Foster, General Manager; Jason Evans, Editor. **Subscription Rates:** $22 Individuals home delivery; in county; $36 Out of area home delivery; $13 Individuals e-edition. **URL:** http://www.pickenssentinel.com. **Ad Rates:** GLR $.63; BW $1166.32; 4C $1351.37; PCI $8.45. **Remarks:** Advertising accepted; rates available upon request. **Circ:** ‡7,000.

COLLINSVILLE

5818 ■ The Door Opener: Connecticut's Holistic Health and Spirituality Resource Guide
An Open Door to the Inner Light Inc.
47 Maple Ave.
Collinsville, CT 06019-3013
Publication focusing on holistic health and spirituality classes and workshops in Connecticut, with 8-10 topic-focused articles per quarterly issue. **Freq:** Quarterly. **Col. Depth:** 9 1/2 inches. **Key Personnel:** Dory Dzinski, Editor, phone: (860)693-2840; Leanne Peters, Art Director; Jon Roe, Columnist. **ISSN:** 1069--6253 (print). **URL:** http://www.dooropenermagazine.com. **Ad Rates:** BW $360; 4C $560. **Remarks:** Accepts advertising. **Circ:** (Not Reported).

CORNWALL BRIDGE

5819 ■ NSCP Currents
National Society of Compliance Professionals
22 Kent Rd.
Cornwall Bridge, CT 06754
Phone: (860)672-0843
Fax: (860)672-3005
Freq: Monthly. **URL:** http://www.nscp.org/nscp-currents. **Remarks:** Accepts advertising. **Circ:** (Not Reported).

CROMWELL

NW CT. Middlesex Co.

5820 ■ Middlesex Magazine & Business Review
Middlesex County Chamber of Commerce
615 Main St.
Cromwell, CT 06416
Publisher's E-mail: info@middlesexchamber.com
Business journal/Consumer Mag. **Freq:** Monthly. **Print Method:** Offset. **Trim Size:** 8 x 10 1/2. **Cols./Page:** 3. **Col. Width:** 2 3/8 inches. **Col. Depth:** 9 1/2 inches. **Key Personnel:** Ron Nolan, Publisher, Contact; Clare Bearer, Publisher. **Subscription Rates:** $20. **Ad Rates:** BW $975. **Remarks:** Accepts advertising. **Circ:** Non-paid ‡7500.

DANBURY

SW CT. Fairfield Co. 21 mi. NW of Bridgeport. State College; State Trade School. Lake resort. Manufactures surgical instruments and supplies, electronic and railroad testing equipment, silverware, aluminum foil, aircraft parts, rubber tile, air conditioning equipment, steam generators, plastics, glue, textiles, ball and roller bearings, cardboard, fibre boxes. Agriculture. Dairying, poultry, truck farms.

5821 ■ Fly RC
Maplegate Media Group
42 Old Ridgebury Rd.
Danbury, CT 06810
Phone: (203)431-7787
Fax: (203)942-2983
Publication E-mail: editors@flyrc.com
Magazine featuring latest radio control products, technology and techniques. **Freq:** Monthly. **Key Personnel:** Tom Atwood, Editor-in-Chief. **Subscription Rates:** $19.95 Individuals print or online; $29.95 Canada print; $59.95 Other countries print. **URL:** http://www.flyrc.com. **Ad Rates:** 4C $500. **Remarks:** Accepts advertising. **Circ:** (Not Reported).

5822 ■ Journal of the Flagstaff Institute
World Economic Processing Zones Association
3 Bullet Hill Rd.
Danbury, CT 06811-2906
Phone: (203)798-9394
Fax: (203)798-9394
Publisher's E-mail: webmaster@wepza.org
Discusses free trade zones, free economic zones, development of a global market, and investment attraction in developing countries. **Freq:** Semiannual. **ISSN:** 0146--1958 (print). **Alt. Formats:** PDF. **URL:** http://www.wepza.org/flagstaff-journal-of-special-economic-zones. **Remarks:** Advertising not accepted. **Circ:** 150.

5823 ■ RC Driver
Maplegate Media Group
42 Old Ridgebury Rd.
Danbury, CT 06810
Phone: (203)431-7787
Fax: (203)942-2983
Publication E-mail: editorsinbox@rcdriver.com
Magazine for remote control car, buggy and truck enthusiasts. **Freq:** Monthly. **Trim Size:** 8 x 10 7/8. **Subscription Rates:** $19.95 Individuals print and online; $29.95 Canada print and online; $59.95 Other countries print and online; $19.95 Individuals online. **URL:** http://rcdriver.com. **Ad Rates:** 4C $600. **Remarks:** Accepts advertising. **Circ:** (Not Reported).

5824 ■ Robot
Maplegate Media Group
42 Old Ridgebury Rd.
Danbury, CT 06810
Phone: (203)431-7787
Fax: (203)942-2983
Publication E-mail: toma@botmag.com
Magazine for robot enthusiast and robot hobbyist. **Freq:** Bimonthly. **Key Personnel:** Tom Atwood, Editor-in-Chief; Erick Royer, Editor. **Subscription Rates:** $24.95 Individuals; $29.95 Canada; $39.95 Other countries; $42.95 Two years; $52.95 Canada two years; $72.95 Other countries two years; $59.95 U.S. 3 years; $74.95 Canada 3 years; $104.95 Other countries 3 years. **URL:** http://find.botmag.com. **Ad Rates:** 4C $600. **Remarks:** Accepts advertising. **Circ:** (Not Reported).

5825 ■ WDAQ-FM - 98.3
198 Main St.
Danbury, CT 06810
Phone: (203)744-4800
Fax: (203)778-4655
Format: Adult Contemporary. **Owner:** Berkshire Broadcasting Corp., at above address, Ph: (203)744-4800, Fax: (203)778-4655. **Founded:** 1954. **Operating Hours:** Continuous. **Key Personnel:** Mike Delpha, Sales Mgr., mikedelpha@98q.com. **Wattage:** 3,000. **Ad Rates:** Noncommercial. **URL:** http://www.98q.com.

5826 ■ WFAR-FM - 93.3
25 Chestnut St.
Danbury, CT 06810
Phone: (203)748-0001
Fax: (203)746-4262
Format: Ethnic; Religious. **Owner:** Danbury Community Radio, 25 Chestnut St., Danbury, CT 06810, Fax: (203)746-4262. **Founded:** 1981. **Operating Hours:** Continuous; 50% network, 50% local. **Key Personnel:** David Abrantes, Director; Helena Abrantes, Director; Elio Ferreira, Director. **Wattage:** 018. **Ad Rates:** Noncommercial. **URL:** http://radiofamilia.com.

5827 ■ WLAD-AM - 800
98 Mill Plain Rd.
Danbury, CT 06811
Phone: (203)744-4800
Fax: (203)778-4655
Email: news@wlad.com
Format: News; Sports; Talk. **Owner:** Berkshire Broadcasting Corp., at above address, Ph: (203)744-4800, Fax: (203)778-4655. **Founded:** 1947. **Operating Hours:** Continuous. **Key Personnel:** Mike Delpha, Sales Mgr., mikedelpha@98q.com. **Wattage:** 1,000 Day time; 286. **Ad Rates:** Advertising accepted; rates available upon request. **URL:** http://www.wlad.com.

5828 ■ WRNE-AM - 980
312 E Nine Mile Rd., Ste. 27
Pensacola, FL 32514-1475
Phone: (850)478-6000
Format: Urban Contemporary; Gospel; News; Talk; Contemporary Hit Radio (CHR). **Owner:** Media One Communications, Inc., at above address. **Founded:** 1957. **Formerly:** WFXP-AM. **Key Personnel:** Robert Hill, Gen. Mgr., hill@wrne980.com. **Ad Rates:** $16-25 for 30 seconds; $22-31 for 60 seconds. Combined advertising rates available with WBQP-TV. **URL:** http://choice980wrne.com.

5829 ■ WXCI-FM - 91.7
181 White St.
Danbury, CT 06810
Phone: (203)837-8387
Format: Alternative/New Music/Progressive. **Networks:** Independent. **Owner:** Campus Broadcast Assoc., at above address. **Founded:** 1973. **Formerly:** WSCT-FM. **Operating Hours:** 6 a.m.-2 a.m.; 100% local. **Key Personnel:** Nancy London, News Dir; Bill Repucci, Contact. **Wattage:** 3,000. **Ad Rates:** Noncommercial. **URL:** http://wxci.wcsu.edu.

DARIEN

SW CT. Fairfield Co. 3 mi. NE of Stamford. Residential.

5830 ■ ActionLine
Friends of Animals
777 Post Rd., Ste. 205
Darien, CT 06820
Phone: (203)656-1522
Fax: (203)656-0267
Magazine covering animal welfare issues. **Founded:** 1957. **Freq:** Quarterly. **ISSN:** 1072-2068 (print). **Subscription Rates:** $19.95 Nonmembers + shipping. **URL:** http://friendsofanimals.org/magazine. **Remarks:** Advertising not accepted. **Circ:** 160000.

5831 ■ The Darien Times
Hersam Acorn Newspapers L.L.C.
10 Corbin Dr., Fl. 3
Darien, CT 06820
Phone: (203)656-4230
Community newspaper. **Freq:** Weekly (Thurs.). **Key Personnel:** Steven Buono, Editor, phone: (203)656-4230; Susan Shultz, Editor. **URL:** http://www.darientimes.com. **Ad Rates:** 4C $550. **Remarks:** Advertising accepted; rates available upon request. **Circ:** Combined ‡6500.

5832 ■ Drug Benefit Trends
c/o Janice Zoeller, Ed.
CMP Health Care Media
330 Boston Post Rd.
Darien, CT 06820
Journal providing information for decision-making in managed health care, intended chiefly for medical directors, and pharmacy directors of managed care organizations. **Freq:** Monthly. **Key Personnel:** Janice Zoeller. **ISSN:** 1080-5826 (print). **Subscription Rates:** $95 Individuals residents, fellows, and students; $40 Libraries; $120 Other countries; $10 Single issue; $15 Single issue foreign countries. **URL:** http://www.medscape.com/viewpublication/90_about. **Mailing address:** PO Box 4027, Darien, CT 06820. **Circ:** (Not Reported).

5833 ■ Lamaze Para Padres
iVillage Parenting Network
Nine Old Kings Hwy. S
Darien, CT 06820
Phone: (203)656-3600
Fax: (203)656-2221
Consumer magazine covering prenatal education in Spanish. **Freq:** Quarterly at the end of March, June, Sept., and Dec. **Print Method:** Offset. **Trim Size:** 7 7/8 x 10 1/2. **Subscription Rates:** Free. **URL:** http://parenting.ivillage.com/pregnancy/plabor/0,,8pqpmcmg,00.html; http://lamaze.org. **Formerly:** Revista Lamaze Para Padres. **Ad Rates:** BW $44,975; 4C $60,025. **Remarks:** Accepts advertising. **Circ:** (Not Reported).

EAST HARTFORD

N. Ct. Hartford Co. 2 mi. E. of Hartford. Manufactures jet airplane engines, paper, stamping devices, furniture, confectionery, pickles. Bottling works. Dairy, stock, poultry farms.

5834 ■ The Gazette
The Gazette
1406 Main St.
East Hartford, CT 06108
Phone: (860)289-6468
Fax: (860)289-6469
Community newspaper. **Founded:** Oct. 1885. **Freq:** Weekly (Thurs.). **Print Method:** Offset. **Trim Size:** 10 3/8 x 12. **Cols./Page:** 5. **Col. Width:** 1 11/16 inches. **Col. Depth:** 12 inches. **Key Personnel:** Corinne Horan; William A. Doak, Editor; Nancy Phaneuf, Manager, Advertising. **ISSN:** 8750-9156 (print). **Subscription Rates:** $65.95 Individuals home delivery; 15 weeks; $129.95 Individuals home delivery; 31 weeks; $119.64 Individuals online; annual pre-paid. **URL:** http://thegazette.com/. **Ad Rates:** GLR $19.52; BW $720; 4C $795; SAU $15.05; PCI $19.52. **Remarks:** Accepts advertising. **Circ:** (Not Reported).

ENFIELD

N. CT. Hartford Co. 14 mi. N. of Hartford. Manufactures plastics, wood products, pumps, tools and dies, metal castings. Agriculture. Poultry, apples, potatoes.

5835 ■ WACC-FM - 107.7
170 Elm St.
Enfield, CT 06082 •
Phone: (860)253-3000
Free: 800-501-3967
Format: Public Radio. **Owner:** Asnuntuck Community College, 170 Elm St., Enfield, CT 06082, Ph: (860)253-3000, Fax: (860)253-3014, Free: 800-501-3967. **URL:** http://www.acc.commnet.edu.

ESSEX

S. Ct. Middlesex Co. 19 mi. SE of Middletown. Residential.

5836 ■ Power and Motoryacht
Active Interest Media
10 Bokum Rd.
Essex, CT 06426
Phone: (860)767-3200
Magazine for owners of large powerboats. **Freq:** Monthly. **Trim Size:** 7 7/8 x 10 3/4. **Cols./Page:** 3. **Key Personnel:** George Sass, Editor-in-Chief. **Subscription Rates:** $12 Individuals /year; $22 Two years. **URL:** http://www.powerandmotoryacht.com. **Remarks:** Accepts advertising. **Circ:** Controlled ‡157089, Paid ‡26343.

5837 ■ Soundings: Real Boats, Real Boaters
Dominion Enterprises
10 Bokum Rd.
Essex, CT 06426
Phone: (860)767-3200
Fax: (860)767-1048
Free: 800-444-7686
Publication E-mail: info@soundingspub.com
News magazine for recreational boaters. **Freq:** Monthly. **Print Method:** Offset. **Trim Size:** 10 3/4 x 14 1/2. **Cols./Page:** 4. **Key Personnel:** Paul Smith, Associate Editor. **USPS:** 527-030. **Subscription Rates:** $24.97 Individu-

Circulation: ★ = AAM; △ or • = BPA; ♦ = CAC; ❑ = VAC; ⊕ = PO Statement; ‡ = Publisher's Report; Boldface figures = sworn; Light figures = estimated.

als print only - 1 year; $15.99 Individuals digital only - 1 year; $40 Individuals print and digital - 1 year. **URL:** http://www.soundingsonline.com. **Formerly:** Soundings: The Nation's Boating Newspaper. **Ad Rates:** 4C $5,967. **Remarks:** Accepts advertising. **Circ:** Combined ‡40000.

5838 ■ Soundings Trade Only: Daily News for Marine Industry Professionals
Soundings Publications L.L.C.
10 Bokum Rd.
Essex, CT 06426
Phone: (860)767-3200
Fax: (860)767-0642
Free: 800-444-7686
Publication E-mail: ads@tradeonlytoday.com
Trade magazine for the recreational boating industry. **Freq:** Monthly. **Print Method:** Offset. **Trim Size:** 10 3/4 x 14 1/2. **Cols./Page:** 4. **Col. Width:** 14 picas. **Key Personnel:** Bill Sisson, Editor-in-Chief. **ISSN:** 0194--8366 (print). **Subscription Rates:** $9.95 Other countries digital; $45 Other countries print & online; Free to qualified subscribers; $41.95 Other countries print only. **URL:** http://www.tradeonlytoday.com. **Ad Rates:** BW $7,935, tabloid - full page; BW $4,260, magazine - full page; BW $2,340, 1/2 page island; BW $2,145, 1/2 magazine horizontal. **Remarks:** Accepts advertising. **Circ:** (Not Reported).

5839 ■ Woodshop News: The News Magazine for Professional Woodworkers
Dominion Enterprises
10 Bokum Rd.
Essex, CT 06426
Phone: (860)767-8227
Fax: (860)767-1048
Publication E-mail: info@woodshopnews.com
Newspaper (tabloid) focusing on people and businesses involved in woodworking. **Freq:** Monthly. **Print Method:** Offset. **Trim Size:** 10 3/4 x 13 1/2. **Cols./Page:** 4. **Col. Width:** 2 1/2 inches. **Col. Depth:** 13 inches. **Key Personnel:** Tod Riggio, Editor; Jennifer Hicks, Writer; Brian Caldwell, Writer. **ISSN:** 0894--5403 (print). **Subscription Rates:** $21.95 U.S. print only; $9.95 Individuals digital only; $30 U.S. print and digital; $33.95 Canada print; $40 Canada print & online; $35.95 Other countries print; $45 Other countries print & online. **URL:** http://www.woodshopnews.com. **Ad Rates:** BW $3,870; 4C $5,190. **Remarks:** Advertising accepted; rates available upon request. **Circ:** Paid 32000.

FAIRFIELD

SW CT. Fairfield Co. 4 mi. W. of Bridgeport. Fairfield University (Jesuit coed); Sacred Heart Univ. (Cath. coed). Manufactures batteries, chemicals, drugs, roller bearings, auto accessories, computer graphics, hardware, plastics, machine tools; cement products, wire, guns, boilers. Bottling works. Resort.

5840 ■ Fairfield Citizen-News
Brooks Community Newspapers Inc.
220 Carter Henry Dr.
Fairfield, CT 06824
Phone: (203)255-4561
Fax: (203)255-0456
Newspaper. **Founded:** 1964. **Freq:** Semiweekly (Wed. and Fri.). **Print Method:** Offset. **Cols./Page:** 5. **Col. Width:** 27 nonpareils. **Col. Depth:** 224 agate lines. **Key Personnel:** James Doody, Editor. **URL:** http://www.fairfieldcitizenonline.com. **Remarks:** Accepts advertising. **Circ:** (Not Reported).

5841 ■ Hitchcock Annual
Sacred Heart University College of Arts and Sciences
5151 Park Ave.
Fairfield, CT 06825
Phone: (203)371-7999
Scholarly journal covering film study and the work of director Alfred Hitchcock. **Freq:** Annual. **Print Method:** Photo Offset. **Trim Size:** 5 1/2 x 8 1/2. **Key Personnel:** Sidney Gottlieb, Editor. **ISSN:** 1062-5518 (print). **Ad Rates:** BW $100. **Remarks:** Advertising accepted; rates available upon request. **Circ:** Combined 1000.

WSHU-AM - See Westport

5842 ■ WSHU-FM - 91.1
5151 Park Ave.
Fairfield, CT 06825
Phone: (203)365-6604
Free: 800-937-6045
Format: Public Radio; Classical. **Owner:** Sacred Heart University, 5151 Park Ave., Fairfield, CT 06825, Ph: (203)371-7999. **Founded:** 1964. **Operating Hours:** Continuous. **Key Personnel:** Tom Kuser, Director, Contact; George Lombardi, Contact; Tom Kuser, Contact; Barbara Bashar, Contact; Paul Litwinovich, Contact; Gillian Anderson, Contact; Lori Miller, Contact; Janice Portentoso, Contact. **Wattage:** 20,000. **Ad Rates:** Noncommercial; underwriting available. **URL:** http://news.wshu.org/grids/wshufmgrid.php.

WSUF-FM - See Greenport, NY

5843 ■ WVOF-FM - 88.5
1703 N Benson Rd.
Barone Campus Ctr. Box
Fairfield, CT 06824
Phone: (203)254-4000
Fax: (203)254-4267
Format: Educational. **Owner:** Fairfield University, 1073 N Benson Rd., Fairfield, CT 06824, Ph: (203)254-4000. **Founded:** 1974. **Local Programs:** *Morning Ride*, Friday 10:00 a.m. - 12:00 p.m. **Wattage:** 100. **Ad Rates:** Noncommercial; underwriting available. **URL:** http://www.wvof.org.

FARMINGTON

WC CT. Hartford Co. Tunxis Community College. Residential.

5844 ■ Blood Pressure Monitoring
Lippincott Williams & Wilkins
c/o William B. White, MD, Editor-in-Chief
Section of Hypertension & Clinical Pharmacology
The School of Medicine, University of Connecticut Health Ctr.
263 Farmington Ave.
Farmington, CT 06032-3940
Phone: (860)679-2104
Fax: (860)679-1250
Peer-reviewed journal containing papers dealing with all aspects of manual, automated and ambulatory monitoring. **Freq:** Bimonthly. **Key Personnel:** Thomas G. Pickering, Editor; William B. White, MD, Editor-in-Chief; Phil Daly, Publisher. **ISSN:** 1359--5237 (print); **EISSN:** 1473--5725 (electronic). **Subscription Rates:** $563 U.S.; $591 Other countries; $2256 Institutions; $2241 Institutions, other countries; $287 Individuals in-training. **URL:** http://journals.lww.com/bpmonitoring/pages/default.aspx. **Remarks:** Accepts advertising. **Circ:** ‡136.

5845 ■ Journal of Personality
Wiley-Blackwell
University of Connecticut Health Ctr.
263 Farmington Ave.
Farmington, CT 06030-6325
Phone: (860)679-5466
Fax: (860)679-5464
Psychology journal. **Freq:** Bimonthly. **Print Method:** Offset. **Trim Size:** 6 x 9. **Cols./Page:** 1. **Col. Width:** 52 nonpareils. **Col. Depth:** 86 agate lines. **Key Personnel:** Charlotte N. Markey, Board Member; Patrick Markey, Board Member; Howard Tennen, Editor. **ISSN:** 0022--3506 (print); **EISSN:** 1467--6494 (electronic). **Subscription Rates:** $1463 Institutions online; £1249 Institutions online; €1585 Institutions online; $2447 Institutions online (rest of the world); $1756 Institutions print and online; £1499 Institutions print and online; €1902 Institutions print and online; $2937 Institutions, other countries print and online; $1463 Institutions print; £1249 Institutions print; €1585 Institutions print; $2447 Institutions, other countries print; $80 Students print and online; £79 Students print and online; €79 Students print and online (non euro zone); €117 Students print and online (euro zone); $79 Students print and online (rest of the world). **URL:** http://www.wiley.com/WileyCDA/WileyTitle/productCd-JOPY.html; http://onlinelibrary.wiley.com/journal/10.1111/(ISSN)1467-6494. **Ad Rates:** BW $300. **Remarks:** Call publisher for rates. **Circ:** ‡2000.

5846 ■ WRCH-FM - 100.5
10 Executive Dr.
Farmington, CT 06032
Phone: (860)284-9132
Format: Soft Rock. **Networks:** Independent. **Owner:** CBS Radio Inc., 40 W 57th St., New York, NY 10019, Ph: (212)846-3939, Fax: (212)315-2162. **Founded:** 1968. **Operating Hours:** Continuous. **ADI:** Hartford-New Haven (New London), CT. **Key Personnel:** Joseph Madden, Sales Mgr., joseph.madden@cbsradio.com; Allan Camp, Dir. of Programs, acamp@cbs.com. **Wattage:** 50,000. **Ad Rates:** Noncommercial. **URL:** http://wrch.cbslocal.com.

5847 ■ WTIC-AM - 1080
10 Executive Dr.
Farmington, CT 06032
Phone: (860)677-6700
Format: News; Talk; Contemporary Hit Radio (CHR). **Operating Hours:** Continuous. **Ad Rates:** Advertising accepted; rates available upon request.

5848 ■ WTIC-FM - 96.5
10 Executive Dr.
Farmington, CT 06032
Phone: (860)677-6700
Format: Adult Contemporary. **Networks:** CBS. **Owner:** CBS Corp., 51 W 52nd St., New York, NY 10019-6188, Ph: (212)975-4321, Fax: (212)975-4516, Free: 877-227-0787. **Operating Hours:** Continuous. **ADI:** Hartford-New Haven (New London), CT. **Key Personnel:** Geri DeRosa, Contact. **Wattage:** 50,000. **Ad Rates:** Advertising accepted; rates available upon request. **URL:** http://www.965tic.cbslocal.com.

5849 ■ WZMX-FM - 93.7
10 Executive Dr.
Farmington, CT 06032
Phone: (860)677-6700
Format: Adult Contemporary; Hip Hop; Blues. **Owner:** CBS Radio Inc., 1271 Avenue of the Americas, 44th Fl., New York, NY 10020-1401, Ph: (212)649-9600. **Founded:** 1939. **Formerly:** WLVH-FM. **Operating Hours:** Continuous. **Key Personnel:** Jason Ricketts, Sales Mgr., jason.ricketts@cbsradio.com. **Wattage:** 50,000. **Ad Rates:** Noncommercial. **URL:** http://hot937.cbslocal.com.

GEORGETOWN

SW CT. Fairfield Co. 12 mi. N. of Norwalk. Wire manufacturing.

5850 ■ Golf Range Magazine
Golf Range Association of America
PO Box 240
Georgetown, CT 06829-0240
Phone: (610)745-0862
Free: 800-541-1123
Magazine containing best practices, research and proven initiatives in golf range development and growth. **Freq:** Monthly. **Subscription Rates:** Included in membership. **URL:** http://golfrange.org. **Remarks:** Accepts advertising. **Circ:** 9200.

5851 ■ The Redding Pilot
Hersam Acorn Newspapers L.L.C.
PO Box 389
Georgetown, CT 06829
Community newspaper. **Freq:** Weekly (Thurs.). **Print Method:** Offset. **Cols./Page:** 6. **Col. Width:** 26 nonpareils. **Col. Depth:** 294 agate lines. **Key Personnel:** Kaitlin Bradshaw, Editor; Rocco Valluzzo, Editor. **Subscription Rates:** $39 Individuals; $45 Out of area. **URL:** http://www.thereddingpilot.com. **Ad Rates:** GLR $9.25; BW $1,103; 4C $450; PCI $8.75. **Circ:** Combined ‡1942.

GLASTONBURY

N. Ct. Hartford Co. 10 mi. SE of Hartford. Manufactures machine tools, tubing. Nursery; hatchery. Poultry, tobacco, vegetable, fruit farms.

5852 ■ Annals of Clinical Psychiatry
American Academy of Clinical Psychiatrists
PO Box 458
Glastonbury, CT 06033
Phone: (860)633-6023
Free: 866-668-9858
Publisher's E-mail: aacp@cox.net
Journal of the American Academy of Clinical Psychiatrists. **Freq:** Quarterly. **Key Personnel:** Donald W. Black, MD, Editor-in-Chief; Charles Rich, Editor-in-Chief. **ISSN:** 1040--1237 (print); **EISSN:** 1573--3238 (electronic). **URL:** http://www.tandfonline.com/toc/iacp20/current. **Circ:** (Not Reported).

5853 ■ The Glastonbury Citizen
Glastonbury Citizen Inc.
87 Nutmeg Ln.

Glastonbury, CT 06033-2314
Phone: (860)633-4691
Fax: (860)657-3258
Publication E-mail: citizen@snet.net
Community newspaper (tabloid). **Freq:** Weekly (Thurs.). **Print Method:** Offset. **Trim Size:** 11 x 17. **Cols./Page:** 4 and 8. **Col. Width:** 2 1/4 and 1 3/16 inches. **Col. Depth:** 15 1/2 and 15 1/2 inches. **Key Personnel:** Jim Hallas, Editor; Carole Saucier, Manager, Advertising. **Subscription Rates:** $25 Individuals; $28 Out of state; $22 Students. **URL:** http://www.glcitizen.com. **Formerly:** The Glastonbury Citizen: Rivereast News Bulletin. **Mailing address:** PO Box 373, Glastonbury, CT 06033-2314. **Ad Rates:** GLR $7; BW $1,364; PCI $11. **Remarks:** Accepts advertising. **Circ:** Combined ‡7792.

5854 ■ Rivereast News Bulletin
Glastonbury Citizen Inc.
87 Nutmeg Ln.
Glastonbury, CT 06033-2314
Phone: (860)633-4691
Fax: (860)657-3258
Publication E-mail: rivereast@snet.net
Community newspaper. **Freq:** Weekly (Fri.). **Print Method:** Offset. **Trim Size:** 8 1/2 x 11. **Cols./Page:** 4 and 8. **Col. Width:** 2 1/2 and 1 3/16 inches. **Col. Depth:** 15 1/2 and 15 1/2 inches. **Key Personnel:** James Hallas, Editor; Carole Saucier, Manager, Advertising. **Subscription Rates:** Free within circulation area; $100 Out of area outside circulation area. **URL:** http://www.glcitizen.com. **Mailing address:** PO Box 373, Glastonbury, CT 06033-2314. **Ad Rates:** GLR $.60; BW $1240; PCI $10. **Remarks:** Accepts advertising. **Circ:** Combined 27050.

5855 ■ WURH-FM - 104.1
131 New London Tpke., Ste. 101
Glastonbury, CT 06033
Phone: (860)657-1041
Fax: (860)657-1042
Email: requests@radio1041.fm
Format: Alternative/New Music/Progressive; Adult Album Alternative. **Owner:** Red Wolf Broadcasting Corp., 758 Colonel Ledyard Hwy., Ledyard, CT 06339, Ph: (860)464-1066. **Formerly**: WPHH-FM. **Operating Hours**: Continuous. **Wattage**: 50,000. **Ad Rates:** Advertising accepted; rates available upon request.

5856 ■ WXCT-AM - 990
131 New London Tpke., Ste. 101
Glastonbury, CT 06033
Phone: (860)883-4292
Email: info@talkradio990.com
Format: News; Talk; Sports; Information. **Networks:** Jones Satellite; Westwood One Radio. **Owner:** Davidson Media Group, at above address. **Founded:** 1969. **Formerly**: WNTY-AM. **Operating Hours**: Continuous. **Key Personnel:** Charlie Profit, Gen. Mgr. **Wattage**: 2,500. **Ad Rates:** Noncommercial.

GREENWICH

SW CT. Fairfield Co. 29 mi. NE of New York. Several private schools. Manufactures vacuum cleaners. Printing and publishing houses; engineering research.

5857 ■ Chief Executive
Chief Executive Group, LLC
1 Sound Shore Dr., Ste. 100
Greenwich, CT 06830
Phone: (203)930-2700
Fax: (203)930-2701
Publication E-mail: editorial@chiefexecutive.net
Business magazine for chief executives. **Freq:** 6/year. **Print Method:** Offset. **Trim Size:** 9 x 10 7/8. **Cols./Page:** 4. **Col. Width:** 22 nonpareils. **Col. Depth:** 145 agate lines. **Key Personnel:** Marshall Cooper, Chief Executive Officer, Publisher; Jennifer Pellet, Editor; J.P. Donlon, Editor-in-Chief. **Subscription Rates:** $99 U.S.; $198 Two years; $159 Other countries; $318 Other countries 2 years. **URL:** http://chiefexecutive.net/magazine. **Ad Rates:** BW $19,375; 4C $23,635. **Remarks:** Accepts advertising. **Circ:** Combined 170000.

5858 ■ KBAZ-FM
c/o Townsquare Media Inc.
Greenwich, CT 06830
Format: Alternative/New Music/Progressive. **Wattage**: 50,000 ERP.

5859 ■ KIKN-FM
c/o Townsquare Management Company LLC
Greenwich, CT 06830
Phone: (605)361-0300
Fax: (605)361-5410
Format: Country. **Key Personnel:** Don Jacobs, Gen. Mgr., don.jacobs@townsquaremedia.com; Jay Williams, Contact. **Wattage**: 100,000 ERP. **Ad Rates:** Noncommercial.

KIOO-FM - See Visalia, CA

KKBR-FM - See Los Alamos

5860 ■ KKPL-FM
c/o Townsquare Media Inc.
Greenwich, CT 06830
Format: Adult Album Alternative. **Wattage**: 50,000 ERP.

5861 ■ KNFM-FM
c/o Townsquare Management Company LLC
Greenwich, CT 06830
Format: Country. **Wattage**: 100,000 ERP. **Ad Rates:** Advertising accepted; rates available upon request.

5862 ■ KROF-AM - 960
240 Greenwich Ave.
Box 610
Greenwich, CT 06830
Phone: (318)893-2531
Fax: (318)893-2569
Format: Country; Cajun. **Networks:** Louisiana. **Founded:** 1948. **Operating Hours**: 6am - sunset. **ADI**: Lafayette, LA. **Wattage**: 1,000. **Ad Rates:** $12-17 for 30 seconds; $15-25 for 60 seconds.

KTRR-FM - See Loveland

5863 ■ KZRV-FM
c/o Townsquare Media Inc.
Greenwich, CT 06830
Format: Eighties. **Wattage**: 50,000 ERP. **Ad Rates:** Noncommercial.

5864 ■ WDKS-FM
c/o Townsquare Media Inc.
Greenwich, CT 06830
Phone: (812)425-4226
Fax: (812)421-0005
Format: Adult Contemporary; Contemporary Hit Radio (CHR). **Founded:** 1991. **Wattage**: 6,000 ERP. **Ad Rates:** Advertising accepted; rates available upon request.

5865 ■ WGCH-AM - 1490
71 Lewis St.
Greenwich, CT 06830-1490
Phone: (203)869-1490
Fax: (203)869-3636
Email: sales@wgch.com
Format: News; Talk. **Owner:** Greenwich Broadcasting Corp., at above address. **Founded:** 1964. **Operating Hours**: midnight to 11:00 p.m. **Key Personnel:** Tony Savino, News Dir., tony.savino@wgch.com; Bob Small, Operations Mgr., Traffic Mgr., bob.small@wgch.com; Elizabeth Kopyscinski, VP of Sales, liz.k@wgch.com. **Local Programs**: *The Ray Lucia Show*, Tuesday Tuesday Wednesday Thursday Friday Monday Tuesday Wednesday Friday 12:30 p.m. - 2:00 p.m. 6:30 p.m. - 8:00 p.m. 5:30 p.m. - 8:00 p.m.; *The Best of The Big Biz Show*, Saturday 12:00 a.m. - 1:00 a.m. **Ad Rates:** Advertising accepted; rates available upon request. **URL:** http://www.wgch.com.

5866 ■ WIYN-FM
c/o Townsquare Management Company LLC
Greenwich, CT 06830
Phone: (607)467-5400
Format: Soft Rock. **Networks:** Jones Satellite. **Owner:** Delaware County Broadcasting Corp., PO Box 58, Walton, NY 13856, Fax: (607)467-3175. **Founded:** 1991. **Key Personnel:** Amos F. Finch, Contact. **Wattage**: 770 ERP. **Ad Rates:** Advertising accepted; rates available upon request.

WLSP-AM - See Flint, MI

5867 ■ WOMI-AM
c/o Townsquare Media Inc.
Greenwich, CT 06830
Phone: (270)683-1558
Fax: (270)685-2500
Free: 800-666-1031
Format: News; Talk. **Networks:** NBC; CNN Radio. **Owner:** Regent Communicatons, Inc., Evansville, IN, Fax: (812)428-4021. **Founded:** 1938. **Key Personnel:** Lee Denney, News Dir. **Wattage**: 830. **Ad Rates:** $3.50-12 for 30 seconds; $5.50-14 for 60 seconds.

GROTON

SE CT. New London Co. On Thames River across from New London. Manufactures chemicals, machinery, submarines. Foundry; shipyards.

5868 ■ The Dolphin
Journal Register Inc.
Naval Submarine Base NLON PAO
Box 44
Groton, CT 06349-5044
Phone: (860)694-3514
Publication E-mail: dolphin@ctcentral.com
Military newspaper. **Freq:** Weekly. **Key Personnel:** Sheryl Walsh, Editor; Christina Lough, Assistant Editor. **URL:** http://www.dolphin-news.com/. **Remarks:** Accepts advertising. **Circ:** (Not Reported).

5869 ■ Journal of Experimental Marine Biology and Ecology
RELX Group P.L.C.
c/o S.E. Shumway, Ed.-in-Ch.
Dept. of Marine Sciences
University of Connecticut
1080 Shennecossett Rd.
Groton, CT 06340
Publisher's E-mail: amsterdam@relx.com
Journal devoted to biochemistry, physiology, behavior, and genetics of marine plants and animals in relation to their environment involving laboratory and field studies. **Freq:** 12/yr. **Key Personnel:** S.E. Shumway, Editor-in-Chief. **ISSN:** 0022--0981 (print). **Subscription Rates:** $8161 Institutions print; $6800.66 Institutions ejournal. **URL:** http://www.journals.elsevier.com/journal-of-experimental-marine-biology-and-ecology. **Circ:** (Not Reported).

GUILFORD

S. CT. New Haven Co. On Long Island Sound, 15 mi. E. of New Haven. Summer resort. Manufactures ferrous and non-ferrous metals, tracing and reproduction cloths, honing stones, boats. Oysters, lobster fisheries. Agriculture. Roses, poultry, apples.

5870 ■ WGRS-FM - 91.5
PO Box 920
Monroe, CT 06468
Phone: (203)268-9667
Email: music@wmnr.org
Format: Classical; Big Band/Nostalgia; Folk. **Owner:** Monroe Public Schools, 375 Monroe Tpke., Monroe, CT 06468, Ph: (203)452-2860. **Founded:** 1994. **Operating Hours**: Continuous. **Key Personnel:** Kurt Anderson, Gen. Mgr., kanderson@wmnr.org; Carol Babina, Asst. GM, Dir. of Dev., carol@babina.com; Jane Stadler, Dir. of Operations, jstadler@wmnr.org. **Wattage**: 3,100. **URL:** http://wmnr.org/web/home.

HAMDEN

S. CT. New Haven Co. 5 mi. N. of New Haven. Manufactures industrial machinery, precision tools, machine tools, paper products, communication equipment, cutlery, screw machine products, sewing machine parts, wood products, ceramics, automatic pistols, metal store fronts, structural steel fabricators, plastics, power transmission equipment, precision aircraft parts. Steel rolling mill.

5871 ■ The Hamden Journal
Hersam Acorn Newspapers L.L.C.
PO Box 187101
Hamden, CT 06518
Publication E-mail: info@thehamdenjournal.com
Community newspaper. **Freq:** Weekly (Wed.) published 1st and 3rd Fridays of the month. **Key Personnel:** Christopher D. LaTorraca, Founder, Publisher, phone: (203)438-1183. **URL:** http://www.thehamdenjournal.com/index.php/site/home; http://www.thehamdenjournal.com/index.php/archive. **Ad Rates:** $50-550, for single insertion; $55-600, for single insertion. BW $, for single insertion4C $, for single insertion. **Remarks:** Accepts advertising. **Circ:** (Not Reported).

Circulation: ★ = AAM; △ or • = BPA; ♦ = CAC; ❑ = VAC; ⊕ = PO Statement; ‡ = Publisher's Report; Boldface figures = sworn; Light figures = estimated.

5872 ■ New England Theatre Journal
New England Theatre Conference
215 Knob Hill Dr.
Hamden, CT 06518
Phone: (617)851-8535
Publisher's E-mail: mail@netconline.org
Journal containing articles and reviews of the New England Theatre Conference. **Freq:** Annual. **ISSN:** 1050--9720 (print). **URL:** http://www.netconline.org/netc-publications.php. **Remarks:** Accepts advertising. **Circ:** (Not Reported).

5873 ■ Rhode Island Beverage Journal
Rhode Island Beverage Journal Inc.
2508 Whitney Ave.
Hamden, CT 06518
Phone: (203)288-3375
Fax: (203)288-2693
Journal on beverage alcohol industry in Rhode Island. **Freq:** Monthly. **Trim Size:** 8 1/4 x 10 7/8. **Cols./Page:** 3. **Key Personnel:** Gerald P. Slone, Editor. **ISSN:** 0035--4562 (print). **Subscription Rates:** $35 Individuals; $60 Two years; $9 Single issue. **URL:** http://www.thebeveragejournal.com/rhodeisland. **Mailing address:** PO Box 185159, Hamden, CT 06518. **Ad Rates:** BW $396; 4C $865. **Remarks:** Accepts advertising. **Circ:** 140000.

5874 ■ WAVZ-AM - 1300
Radio Towers Pk.
495 Benham St.
Hamden, CT 06514
Phone: (203)281-9600
Format: Sports. **Networks:** Satellite Music Network. **Founded:** 1947. **Operating Hours**: Continuous. **ADI**: Hartford-New Haven (New London), CT. **Key Personnel:** Massimo Rosati, Dir. of Sales. **Wattage:** 1,000. **Ad Rates:** $8-40 for 30 seconds; $10-50 for 60 seconds. **URL:** http://www.espnradio1300.com.

5875 ■ WELI-AM - 960
495 Benham St.
Hamden, CT 06514
Phone: (203)288-9354
Fax: (203)407-4652
Email: comments@960weli.com
Format: News; Talk. **Networks:** Independent. **Founded:** 1937. **Operating Hours**: Continuous; 25% network, 75% local. **ADI:** Hartford-New Haven (New London), CT. **Key Personnel:** Massimo Rosati, Dir. of Sales; George Demaio, Contact. **Local Programs**: *Newsweek On-Air*, Sunday 6:00 a.m. - 7:00 a.m. **Wattage**: 5,000. **Ad Rates:** $20-175 for 60 seconds. WKCI-FM, WAVZ-AM. **URL:** http://www.960weli.com.

5876 ■ WKCI-FM - 101.3
495 Benham St.
Hamden, CT 06514
Phone: (203)281-9600
Format: Contemporary Hit Radio (CHR); Top 40. **Owner:** iHeartMedia Inc., 200 E Basse Rd., San Antonio, TX 78209, Ph: (210)832-3314. **Founded:** 1969. **Operating Hours**: 5:30 a.m. to midnight. **Key Personnel:** Massimo Rosati, Dir. of Sales. **Ad Rates:** Advertising accepted; rates available upon request. **URL:** http://www.kc101.com.

5877 ■ WQAQ-FM - 98.1
275 Mount Carmel Ave.
Hamden, CT 06518
Phone: (203)582-5278
Format: Full Service. **Owner:** Quinnipiac University, 275 Mt. Carmel Ave., Hamden, CT 06518, Ph: (203)582-8200, Free: 800-462-1944. **Founded:** 1969. **Operating Hours**: 7 a.m.-2 a.m. Mon.-Fri.; 9 a.m.-2 a.m. Sat. and Sun. **Wattage**: 010. **Ad Rates:** Noncommercial. **URL:** http://www.wqaq.com.

5878 ■ WQUN-AM - 1220
275 Mount Carmel Ave.
Hamden, CT 06518-1908
Phone: (203)582-8200
Free: 800-462-1944
Email: wqun@quinnipiac.edu
Format: News; Information; Music of Your Life. **Networks:** CBS; Jones Satellite; Music of Your Life/ Fairwest. **Owner:** Quinnipiac University, 275 Mt. Carmel Ave., Hamden, CT 06518, Ph: (203)582-8200, Free: 800-462-1944. **Founded:** 1960. **Formerly**: WXCT-AM; WNNR-AM. **Operating Hours**: Continuous. **ADI**: Hartford-New Haven (New London), CT. **Key Personnel:** Mark Thompson, Sr. VP. **Wattage**: 1,000 Day; 330 Night. **Ad Rates:** Advertising accepted; rates available upon request. **URL:** http://www.quinnipiac.edu.

HARTFORD

N. CT. Hartford Co. On Connecticut River, midway between Boston and New York. The State Capital. Trinity College; St. Joseph College; Hartford College; University of Hartford; law, theological, and private schools. Home of United Technologies. Economy consisting of manufacturing, trade, finance, insurance, real estate. Insurance Cowing region.

5879 ■ CBIA News: Journal of the Connecticut Business & Industry Association
CBIA
350 Church St.
Hartford, CT 06103-1126
Phone: (860)244-1900
Association journal for business management. **Freq:** 11/ year. **Print Method:** Offset. **Trim Size:** 8 1/2 x 11. **Cols./ Page:** 3. **Key Personnel:** Lesia Winiarskyj, Editor. **ISSN:** 0199--686X (print). **Subscription Rates:** $9 Members; $18 Members two years. **URL:** http://www5.cbia.com/cbianews. **Remarks:** Advertising not accepted. **Circ:** ‡11000.

5880 ■ Connecticut Housing Production and Permit Authorized Construction
State of Connecticut Department of Economic and Community Development
505 Hudson St.
Hartford, CT 06106
Phone: (860)270-8000
Publisher's E-mail: decd@ct.gov
Report on Connecticut housing permits authorized. **Freq:** Annual. **Key Personnel:** Kolie Sun Chang, Researcher, phone: (860)270-8167. **Subscription Rates:** Free. **Alt. Formats:** PDF. **Circ:** (Not Reported).

5881 ■ Connecticut Insurance Law Journal
University of Connecticut School of Law
45 Elizabeth St.
Hartford, CT 06105
Phone: (860)570-5100
Fax: (860)570-5153
Publisher's E-mail: admissions@law.uconn.edu
Journal containing articles on taxation and regulation of insurance companies. **Freq:** Semiannual. **Subscription Rates:** $28 Individuals domestic; $32 Individuals international; $15 Single issue special. **URL:** http://insurancejournal.org; http://www.law.uconn.edu/student-life-resources/law-review-journals/insurance-law-journal. **Circ:** (Not Reported).

5882 ■ Connecticut Jewish Ledger
Connecticut Jewish Ledger
36 Woodland St.
Hartford, CT 06105
Phone: (860)231-2424
Fax: (860)231-2485
Free: 800-286-6397
Publisher's E-mail: editorial@jewishledger.com
Jewish interest newspaper. **Freq:** Weekly (Fri.). **Print Method:** Offset. **Trim Size:** 11 x 13 1/2. **Cols./Page:** 5. **Col. Width:** 1 7/8 inches. **Col. Depth:** 13 inches. **Key Personnel:** Leslie Iarusso, Associate Publisher. **Subscription Rates:** $36 Individuals; $62 Two years. **URL:** http://www.jewishledger.com. **Ad Rates:** BW $1,885; PCI $39. **Remarks:** Advertising accepted; rates available upon request. **Circ:** ‡30000.

5883 ■ Connecticut Journal of International Law
University of Connecticut School of Law
45 Elizabeth St.
Hartford, CT 06105
Phone: (860)570-5100
Fax: (860)570-5153
Publisher's E-mail: admissions@law.uconn.edu
Journal containing articles on international law, comparative law, and the extraterritorial effect of United States law and policy. **Freq:** Semiannual. **URL:** http://www.cjil.org. **Circ:** (Not Reported).

5884 ■ Connecticut Public Interest Law Journal
University of Connecticut School of Law
45 Elizabeth St.
Hartford, CT 06105
Phone: (860)570-5100
Fax: (860)570-5153
Publication E-mail: cpilj@uconn.edu
Journal containing scholarly articles on public interest related issues. **Freq:** Semiannual. **Subscription Rates:** $20 Individuals. **URL:** http://cpilj.wordpress.com; http://www.law.uconn.edu/student-life-resources/law-review-journals/connecticut-public-interest-law-journal. **Circ:** (Not Reported).

5885 ■ Ecological Psychology
International Society for Ecological Psychology
c/o William M. Mace
Dept. of Psychology
Trinity College
300 Summit St.
Hartford, CT 06106-3100
Phone: (860)297-2343
Fax: (860)297-2538
Journal publishing articles that contribute to the understanding of psychological and behavioral processes as they occur within the ecological constraints of animal-environment systems. **Freq:** Quarterly. **ISSN:** 1040-7413 (print). **Subscription Rates:** Included in membership. **URL:** http://www.trincoll.edu/depts/ecopsyc/journal.html. **Remarks:** Advertising not accepted. **Circ:** 550.

5886 ■ Hartford Advocate
New Mass Media Inc.
121 Wawarme Ave., 1st Fl.
Hartford, CT 06114
Phone: (860)548-9300
Fax: (860)548-9335
News and arts alternative newspaper. **Freq:** Weekly. **Key Personnel:** Richard J. Daniels, Publisher. **URL:** http://www.ctnow.com/advocates. **Ad Rates:** SAU $37. **Remarks:** Advertising accepted; rates available upon request. **Circ:** ■ **45000.**

5887 ■ The Hartford Courant
The Tribune Media Co.
285 Broad St.
Hartford, CT 06105
Phone: (860)241-6200
Free: 800-524-4242
Publication E-mail: custserv@courant.com
General newspaper. **Freq:** Mon.-Sun. (morn.). **Print Method:** Offset. **Trim Size:** 13 1/2 x 21 3/4. **Cols./Page:** 6. **Col. Width:** 256 nonpareils. **Col. Depth:** 301 agate lines. **Key Personnel:** Richard J. Daniels, Publisher; Andrew Julien, Vice President, Editor; Christine Taylor, Editor. **Subscription Rates:** $3.99 Individuals /wk., Mon.-Sun.; print only; $2.99 Individuals /wk., Thurs.-Sun.; print only; $2.99 Individuals /wk., Sun.; print only; $2.50 Individuals /wk. for 52 wks.; online only; $2.75 Individuals /wk. for 26 wks.; online only; $2.99 Individuals /wk. for 13 wks.; online only; $1.50 Individuals Mon.-Sat.; newsstand only; $2.00 Individuals Sun.; newsstand only. **Online:** LexisNexis; The Tribune Media Co. The Tribune Media Co. **Alt. Formats:** Handheld. **URL:** http://www.courant.com; http://membership.courant.com. **Remarks:** Advertising accepted; rates available upon request. **Circ:** 40,000, Mon.-Fri. ***186518**, Sat. ***194718**, Sun. ***268573**.

5888 ■ Journal of Evolution and Technology
Institute for Ethics and Emerging Technologies
Williams 229B
Trinity College
300 Summit St.
Hartford, CT 06106
Phone: (860)297-2376
Publisher's E-mail: director@ieet.org
Journal covering issues relating to the future prospects of the human species and its descendants. **Key Personnel:** James Hughes, PhD, Associate Editor; Russell Blackford, PhD, Editor-in-Chief; Marcelo Rinesi, Managing Editor. **ISSN:** 1541--0099 (print). **URL:** http://www.jetpress.org. **Formerly**: The Journal of Transhumanism. **Circ:** (Not Reported).

5889 ■ The Mark Twain Annual
Mark Twain Circle of America
Saint Joseph University
Dept. of English

1678 Asylum Ave.
Hartford, CT 06117
Journal that publishes critical and pedagogical information on Mark Twain's work. **Freq:** Annual. **Key Personnel:** Ann Ryan, Editor; James Leonard, Managing Editor. **ISSN:** 1553--0981 (print); **EISSN:** 1756--2597 (electronic). **Subscription Rates:** $44 Individuals print; $88 Two years print; $43 Individuals electronic; $109 Institutions print; $218 Institutions print, 2 years. **URL:** http://www.psupress.org/journals/jnls_MTA.html. **Ad Rates:** BW $300. **Remarks:** Accepts advertising. **Circ:** (Not Reported).

5890 ■ The Muslim World
Hartford Seminary
77 Sherman St.
Hartford, CT 06105-2260
Phone: (860)509-9500
Fax: (860)509-9509
Publisher's E-mail: info@hartsem.edu
Journal of Islamic studies, addressing Christian-Muslim relations. **Freq:** Quarterly. **Key Personnel:** Steven Blackburn, Associate Editor; Dr. Yahya M. Michot, Editor; Nicolas Mumejian, Managing Editor. **ISSN:** 0027--4909 (print); **EISSN:** 1478--1913 (electronic). **Subscription Rates:** $51 Individuals print & online; $45 Students print & online; $430 Institutions print & online; $358 Institutions print or online; €58 Individuals print & online; $570 Institutions, other countries print & online; $475 Institutions, other countries print or online; £245 Institutions print or online; £294 Institutions print and online; £42 Individuals print and online; £28 Students print and online; €308 Institutions print or online; €370 Institutions print and online; $33 Members American Academy of Religion, America (print and online); $213 Members Association of British Theological and Philosophical Libraries, America (print and online); £28 Members American Academy of Religion, UK (print and online); £145 Members Association of British Theological and Philosophical Libraries, UK and Europe - nonEuro zone (print and online); €58 Individuals Europe - Euro zone (print and online); £28 Members American Academy of Religion, Europe - nonEuro zone (print and online); €45 Members American Academy of Religion, Europe - Euro zone (print and online); €216 Members Association of British Theological and Philosophical Libraries, Europe - Euro zone (print and online); €32 Students Europe - Euro zone (print and online); $101 Institutions developing world (print or online); $122 Institutions developing world (print and online); £28 Members American Academy of Religion, Developing World (print and online); £145 Members Association of British Theological and Philosophical Libraries, Developing World (print and online). **URL:** http://www.wiley.com/WileyCDA/WileyTitle/productCd-MUWO.html; http://www.hartsem.edu/macdonald-center/the-muslim-world-journal; http://onlinelibrary.wiley.com/journal/10.1111/(ISSN)1478-1913. **Remarks:** Accepts advertising. **Circ:** ‡1000, 1000.

5891 ■ The Muslim World
Hartford Seminary Duncan Black Macdonald Center for the Study of Islam and Christian-Muslim Relations
77 Sherman St.
Hartford, CT 06105
Phone: (860)509-9534
Fax: (860)509-9539
Publisher's E-mail: info@hartsem.edu
Journal of Islamic studies, addressing Christian-Muslim relations. **Freq:** Quarterly. **Key Personnel:** Steven Blackburn, Associate Editor; Dr. Yahya M. Michot, Editor; Nicolas Mumejian, Managing Editor. **ISSN:** 0027--4909 (print); **EISSN:** 1478--1913 (electronic). **Subscription Rates:** $51 Individuals print & online; $45 Students print & online; $430 Institutions print & online; $358 Institutions print or online; €58 Individuals print & online; $570 Institutions, other countries print & online; $475 Institutions, other countries print or online; £245 Institutions print or online; £294 Institutions print and online; £42 Individuals print and online; £28 Students print and online; €308 Institutions print or online; €370 Institutions print and online; $33 Members American Academy of Religion, America (print and online); $213 Members Association of British Theological and Philosophical Libraries, America (print and online); £28 Members American Academy of Religion, UK (print and online); £145 Members Association of British Theological and Philosophical Libraries, UK and Europe - nonEuro zone (print and online); €58 Individuals Europe - Euro zone (print and online); £28 Members American Academy of Religion, Europe - nonEuro zone (print and online); €45 Members American Academy of Religion, Europe - Euro zone (print and online); €216 Members Association of British Theological and Philosophical Libraries, Europe - Euro zone (print and online); €32 Students Europe - Euro zone (print and online); $101 Institutions developing world (print or online); $122 Institutions developing world (print and online); £28 Members American Academy of Religion, Developing World (print and online); £145 Members Association of British Theological and Philosophical Libraries, Developing World (print and online). **URL:** http://www.wiley.com/WileyCDA/WileyTitle/productCd-MUWO.html; http://www.hartsem.edu/macdonald-center/the-muslim-world-journal; http://onlinelibrary.wiley.com/journal/10.1111/(ISSN)1478-1913. **Remarks:** Accepts advertising. **Circ:** ‡1000, 1000.

5892 ■ The Trinity Tripod
Rare Reminders
Trinity College 702582
300 Summit St.
Hartford, CT 06106-3100
Publication E-mail: tripod@trincoll.edu
Collegiate newspaper. **Freq:** Weekly (Tues.). **Subscription Rates:** Free. **URL:** http://www.trinitytripod.com. **Ad Rates:** BW $432; CNU $432; PCI $7.26. **Remarks:** Accepts advertising. **Circ:** Paid 500, Free 3000.

5893 ■ Valley Advocate
New Mass Media Inc.
285 Broad St.
Hartford, CT 06115-2510
Phone: (860)548-9300
Alternative newsweekly. **Freq:** Weekly. **Key Personnel:** Tom Vannah; Kristin Palpini, Editor. **Remarks:** Accepts classified advertising. **Circ:** Free ■ **37928**.

5894 ■ Paradigm Communications Inc.
280 Trumbull St.
Hartford, CT 06103
Owner: Diversified Media Investors, at above address. **Founded:** 1979. **URL:** http://www.concord-sots.ct.gov/CONCORD/online?sn=InquiryServlet&eid=99.

5895 ■ WCCC-AM - 1290
1039 Asylum Ave.
Hartford, CT 06105
Phone: (860)525-1069
Format: Classical. **Owner:** Marlin Broadcasting, LLC, 32 Farfield St., Boston, MA 02116. **Founded:** 1947. **Operating Hours**: Continuous. **Key Personnel:** John Ramsey, Chief Tech. Ofc. **Ad Rates:** Advertising accepted; rates available upon request. **URL:** http://www.wccc.com.

5896 ■ WCCC-FM - 106.9
1039 Asylum Ave.
Hartford, CT 06105
Phone: (860)525-1069
Format: Classic Rock. **Owner:** Marlin Broadcasting L.L.C., at above address. **Founded:** 1947. **Operating Hours**: Continuous. **Ad Rates:** Noncommercial. **URL:** http://www.wccc.com.

5897 ■ WEDH-TV - 24
1049 Asylum Ave.
Hartford, CT 06105
Phone: (860)278-5310
Format: Public TV. **Simulcasts:** WEDN-TV. **Networks:** Public Broadcasting Service (PBS). **Owner:** Connecticut Public Broadcasting Network, 1049 Asylum Ave., Hartford, CT 06105-2432, Ph: (860)275-7550. **Founded:** 1962. **Operating Hours**: 6:45 a.m.-midnight Daily; 8 a.m.-midnight Sat.; 7:30 a.m.-midnight Sun. **ADI**: Hartford-New Haven (New London), CT. **Key Personnel:** Jerry Franklin, CFO. **Wattage**: 692 KW. **Ad Rates:** Noncommercial. **URL:** http://www.cpbn.org.

WEDN-TV - See Norwich

WEDW-FM - See Stamford

WEDW-TV - See Bridgeport

5898 ■ WEDY-TV - 65
1049 Asylum Ave.
Hartford, CT 06105
Phone: (860)275-7550
Format: Public TV. **Simulcasts:** WEDH-TV Hartford, CT. **Networks:** Public Broadcasting Service (PBS). **Owner:** Connecticut Public Broadcasting Network, 1049 Asylum Ave., Hartford, CT 06105-2432, Ph: (860)275-7550. **Founded:** 1962. **Operating Hours**: 7 a.m.-midnight Daily; 8 a.m.-midnight Sat. & Sun. **ADI**: Hartford-New Haven (New London), CT. **Key Personnel:** Jerry Franklin, President. **Local Programs**: *On The Record*, Friday. **Wattage**: 055 KW. **Ad Rates:** Advertising accepted; rates available upon request. **URL:** http://www.cpbn.org.

5899 ■ WHCN-FM - 105.9
10 Columbus Blvd.
Hartford, CT 06106
Phone: (860)723-6000
Format: Classic Rock. **Networks:** ABC. **Operating Hours**: Continuous. **ADI**: Hartford-New Haven (New London), CT. **Key Personnel:** Andrew Tartaglia, Sales Mgr., andrewtartaglia@clearchannel.com. **Wattage**: 50,000. **Ad Rates:** Advertising accepted; rates available upon request. **URL:** http://www.theriver1059.com.

5900 ■ WKSS-FM - 95.7
10 Columbus Blvd.
Hartford, CT 06106
Phone: (860)247-9570
Format: Contemporary Hit Radio (CHR). **Founded:** 1947. **Operating Hours**: Continuous. **ADI**: Hartford-New Haven (New London), CT. **Key Personnel:** Kelly Leclair, Sales Mgr., kellyleclair@clearchannel.com. **Wattage**: 50,000. **Ad Rates:** Advertising accepted; rates available upon request. **URL:** http://www.kiss957.com.

5901 ■ WMRQ-FM - 104.1
PO Box 31-1410
Newington Branch
Hartford, CT 06131
Phone: (860)657-1041
Fax: (860)657-1042
Format: Adult Contemporary. **Networks:** Fox. **Owner:** SFX Broadcasting, Inc., New York, NY, Ph: (212)980-4455, Fax: (212)735-3188. **Founded:** 1967. **Formerly**: WIOF-FM; WYSR-FM. **ADI**: Hartford-New Haven (New London), CT. **Wattage**: 14,000. **Ad Rates:** Advertising accepted; rates available upon request. **URL:** http://www.radio1041.fm/.

WNPR-FM - See Norwich

5902 ■ WPKT-FM - 90.5
1049 Asylum Ave.
Hartford, CT 06105
Phone: (860)275-7550
Format: Public Radio. **Owner:** Connecticut Public Broadcasting, 70 Audubon St., New Haven, CT 06510, Ph: (203)776-9677. **Founded:** 1978. **Operating Hours**: Continuous. **Key Personnel:** Jerry Franklin, President, CEO, jfranklin@cpbn.org. **Ad Rates:** Noncommercial. **URL:** http://www.cpbn.org.

5903 ■ WPOP-AM - 1410
10 Columbus Blvd.
Hartford, CT 06106
Phone: (860)723-6000
Format: Sports. **Networks:** ESPN Radio. **Owner:** iHeartMedia Inc., 200 E Basse Rd., San Antonio, TX 78209, Ph: (210)832-3314. **Founded:** 1935. **Formerly**: WNBC-AM. **Operating Hours**: Continuous; 5% network, 95% local. **ADI**: Hartford-New Haven (New London), CT. **Key Personnel:** Bob Cleaver, Sales Mgr. **Wattage**: 5,000. **Ad Rates:** Advertising accepted; rates available upon request. **URL:** http://www.foxsportsradio1410.com.

5904 ■ WQTQ-FM - 89.9
Weaver High School
415 Granby St.
Hartford, CT 06112
Phone: (860)695-1900
Fax: (860)243-2664
Email: wqtqfm@yahoo.com
Format: Eclectic; Educational; Gospel. **Networks:** UPI; American Urban Radio. **Owner:** Hartford Public Schools, 960 Main St., 8th Fl., Hartford, CT 06103. **Founded:** Sept. 1971. **Operating Hours**: Continuous. **ADI**: Hartford-New Haven (New London), CT. **Key Personnel:** Shirley J. Minnifield, Bus. Mgr.; Connie J. Coles, Gen. Mgr., Dir. of Programs. **Local Programs**: *Reggae Zone*, Saturday 5:00 p.m. - 8:00 p.m.; *Qute Club Classics*, Friday 6:00 p.m. - 8:00 p.m.; *Sundays With You*,

Circulation: ★ = AAM; △ or • = BPA; ♦ = CAC; ❑ = VAC; ⊕ = PO Statement; ‡ = Publisher's Report; Boldface figures = sworn; Light figures = estimated.

Sunday 12:00 p.m. - 4:00 p.m.; *Nite Traxx*, Monday Tuesday Wednesday Thursday Friday Saturday Sunday 12:00 a.m. - 6:00 a.m. **Wattage**: 115. **Ad Rates:** Noncommercial. **URL:** http://www.wqtqfm.com/wqtq/contact.htm.

WRLI-FM - See Southampton, NY

5905 ■ WRTC-FM - 89.3
300 Summit St.
Hartford, CT 06106
Phone: (860)297-2450
Format: Eclectic. **Owner:** Trinity College, 300 Summit St., Hartford, CT 06106, Ph: (860)297-2000, Fax: (860)297-5111. **Founded:** 1948. **Operating Hours**: Continuous. **ADI**: Hartford-New Haven (New London), CT. **Wattage**: 300. **Ad Rates:** Noncommercial. **URL:** http://www.wrtcfm.com.

5906 ■ WSGG-FM - 89.7
PO Box 4594
Hartford, CT 06147
Phone: (860)880-0225
Email: radioavivamiento@gmail.com
Format: Religious; Ethnic; Contemporary Hit Radio (CHR); Hispanic. **Owner:** Christian Radio, at above address. **Operating Hours**: Continuous. **Ad Rates:** Advertising accepted; rates available upon request. **URL:** http://www.avivamientofm.com.

5907 ■ WTIC-AM - 1080
1 Financial Plz.
Hartford, CT 06103
Phone: (203)522-1080
Fax: (203)549-3431
Format: Full Service. **Networks:** CBS. **Founded:** 1925. **Operating Hours**: Continuous. **ADI**: Hartford-New Haven (New London), CT. **Key Personnel:** Suzanne McDonald, Gen. Mgr.; Steve Salhancy, Dir. of Operations; Jenneen Hull, Asst. Dir. **Wattage**: 50,000.

5908 ■ WTIC-TV - 61
285 Broad St.
Hartford, CT 06115
Format: Commercial TV. **Networks:** Fox. **Owner:** The Tribune Media Co., 435 N Michigan Ave., Chicago, IL 60611-4066, Ph: (312)222-9100, Fax: (312)222-4206, Free: 800-874-2863. **Founded:** 1984. **Operating Hours**: Continuous. **ADI**: Hartford-New Haven (New London), CT. **Wattage**: 5,000,000. **Ad Rates:** Advertising accepted; rates available upon request. **URL:** http://www.ctnow.com.

5909 ■ WTXX-TV - 20
285 Broad St.
Hartford, CT 06115
Phone: (860)723-2190
Format: Commercial TV. **Networks:** Independent; United Paramount Network. **Owner:** The Tribune Media Co., 435 N Michigan Ave., Chicago, IL 60611-4066, Ph: (312)222-9100, Fax: (312)222-4206, Free: 800-874-2863. **Founded:** 1982. **Operating Hours**: Continuous. **ADI**: Hartford-New Haven (New London), CT. **Wattage**: 2,240. **Ad Rates:** Advertising accepted; rates available upon request. **URL:** http://ct.com.

5910 ■ WWYZ-FM - 92.5
10 Columbus Blvd.
Hartford, CT 06106
Phone: (860)723-6000
Format: Country. **Networks:** Westwood One Radio. **Founded:** 1961. **Formerly:** WATR-FM. **Operating Hours:** Continuous. **ADI**: Hartford-New Haven (New London), CT. **Key Personnel:** Bob Cleaver, Sales Mgr., bobcleaver@clearchannel.com. **Wattage**: 50,000. **Ad Rates:** Advertising accepted; rates available upon request. **URL:** http://www.country925.com.

HIGGANUM

5911 ■ Autism Spectrum Quarterly
Starfish Specialty Press L.L.C.
PO Box 799
Higganum, CT 06441-0799
Phone: (860)345-2155
Fax: (860)345-4471
Free: 877-782-7347
Publication E-mail: info@asquarterly.com
Magazine that includes scholarly content about autism as well as general interest features. **Freq:** Quarterly. **Key Personnel:** Diane Twachtman-Cullen, PhD, Editor-in-Chief; Jennifer Twachtman-Reilly, MS, Associate Editor. **ISSN:** 1551--448X (print). **Subscription Rates:** $34.95 Individuals shipping + handling; $64.90 Two years shipping + handling. **Ad Rates:** 4C $2,400. **Remarks:** Advertising accepted; rates available upon request. **Circ:** (Not Reported).

5912 ■ Differentiation
International Society of Differentiation
PO Box 55
Higganum, CT 06441
Fax: (860)838-4242
Publisher's E-mail: healthpermissions@elsevier.com
Journal focusing on cell biology. **Freq:** 10/year 6/year. **Key Personnel:** Colin Stewart, Editor-in-Chief; Nadia Rosenthal, Editor-in-Chief; Helen M. Blau, Senior Editor; Gerald R. Cunha, Senior Editor. **ISSN:** 0301--4681 (print). **Subscription Rates:** $2584.80 Institutions online; $2585 Institutions print; Included in membership. **URL:** http://www.journals.elsevier.com/differentiation; http://www.journals.elsevier.com/differentiation/#description. **Ad Rates:** BW $900. **Remarks:** Accepts advertising. **Circ:** (Not Reported).

5913 ■ Differentiation
Elsevier Inc.
1600 John F. Kennedy Blvd., Ste. 1800
Philadelphia, PA 19103-2899
Phone: (215)239-3900
Fax: (215)238-7883
Free: 800-523-1649
Publisher's E-mail: healthpermissions@elsevier.com
Journal focusing on cell biology. **Freq:** 10/year 6/year. **Key Personnel:** Colin Stewart, Editor-in-Chief; Nadia Rosenthal, Editor-in-Chief; Helen M. Blau, Senior Editor; Gerald R. Cunha, Senior Editor. **ISSN:** 0301--4681 (print). **Subscription Rates:** $2584.80 Institutions online; $2585 Institutions print; Included in membership. **URL:** http://www.journals.elsevier.com/differentiation; http://www.journals.elsevier.com/differentiation/#description. **Ad Rates:** BW $900. **Remarks:** Accepts advertising. **Circ:** (Not Reported).

LAKEVILLE

NW CT. Litchfield Co. 26 mi. NW of Torrington. Resort. Light manufacturing. Dairy, poultry, horse farms.

5914 ■ Lakeville Journal
The Lakeville Journal Company L.L.C.
33 Bissell St.
Lakeville, CT 06039-1688
Phone: (860)435-9873
Fax: (860)435-0146
Community newspaper. **Freq:** Weekly (Thurs.). **Print Method:** Offset. **Cols./Page:** 7. **Col. Width:** 25 nonpareils. **Col. Depth:** 294 agate lines. **Subscription Rates:** $53 Individuals in County; $60 Out of area; $28 Individuals online. **URL:** http://www.tricornernews.com/lakevillejournal. **Mailing address:** PO Box 1688, Lakeville, CT 06039-1688. **Remarks:** Accepts advertising. **Circ:** (Not Reported).

5915 ■ WQQQ-FM - 103.3
PO Box 446
Lakeville, CT 06039-0446
Phone: (860)435-3333
Fax: (860)435-3334
Email: info@wqqq.com
Format: Adult Contemporary; News; Classical; Talk. **Networks:** BBC World Service. **Owner:** Ridgefield Broadcasting Corp., at above address. **Founded:** 1994. **Operating Hours:** Continuous. **Key Personnel:** Dennis Jackson, Contact. **Wattage**: 1,500. **Ad Rates:** $15-23 for 30 seconds; $19-30 for 60 seconds. WRIP (FM), Windham, NY. **URL:** http://www.wqqq.com.

LEDYARD

5916 ■ WBMW-FM - 106.5
PO Box 357
Ledyard, CT 06339
Phone: (860)464-1066
Fax: (860)464-8143
Format: Adult Contemporary. **Owner:** Red Wolf Broadcasting Corp., 758 Colonel Ledyard Hwy., Ledyard, CT 06339, Ph: (860)464-1066. **Key Personnel:** John Fuller, Gen. Mgr., President, john@wbmw.com; Tim Burrows, Gen. Sales Mgr. **Ad Rates:** Advertising accepted; rates available upon request. **URL:** http://www.wbmw.com.

5917 ■ WWRX-FM - 107.7
PO Box 357
Ledyard, CT 06339
Phone: (860)464-1066
Fax: (860)464-8143
Format: Adult Contemporary. **Networks:** ABC. **Founded:** 1967. **Operating Hours:** Continuous. **ADI**: Providence, RI-New Bedford, MA. **Key Personnel:** John Fuller, Gen. Mgr., President; Tim Burrows, Gen. Sales Mgr.; Lori Robbins, Promotions Mgr. **Wattage**: 50,000. **Ad Rates:** $30-95 for 60 seconds. Combined advertising rates available with WFNX-FM Boston, WFEX-FM Manchester, WPHX-FM Portsmouth. **URL:** http://www.jammin1077.com.

LITCHFIELD

5918 ■ The Gardener: The Gardener
White Flower Farm
Rte. 63
Litchfield, CT 06759-1055
Free: 800-503-9624
Publisher's E-mail: custserv@whiteflowerfarm.com
Magazine covering gardening and horticulture. **Freq:** Bimonthly. **URL:** http://www.whiteflowerfarm.com/gardenwisdom-wisdom.html. **Mailing address:** PO Box 50, Litchfield, CT 06759-0050. **Remarks:** Advertising not accepted. **Circ:** (Not Reported).

5919 ■ WZBG-FM - 97.3
49 Commons Dr.
Litchfield, CT 06759-1497
Phone: (860)567-3697
Fax: (860)567-3292
Format: News; Country; Information. **Owner:** Local Boys & Girls Broadcasting Corp., at above address. **Founded:** July 1992. **Key Personnel:** Dale Jones, Prog. Dir., onair@wzbg.com. **Wattage**: 3,000 ERP. **Ad Rates:** Advertising accepted; rates available upon request. **Mailing address:** PO Box 1497, Litchfield, CT 06759-1497. **URL:** http://www.wzbg.com.

LOS ALAMOS

5920 ■ KKBR-FM
c/o Townsquare Media Inc.
Greenwich, CT 06830
Format: Album-Oriented Rock (AOR); Classical. **Founded:** 1956. **Key Personnel:** Bill Frost, Chief Engineer; Beth O'Leary, Contact. **Wattage**: 28,000 ERP.

LOVELAND

5921 ■ KTRR-FM
c/o Townsquare Media Inc.
Greenwich, CT 06830
Phone: (303)223-0435
Fax: (303)223-3857
Format: Adult Contemporary. **Owner:** Duchossois Comm. of Co. Inc., at above address. **Founded:** 1966. **Wattage**: 17,000 ERP. **Ad Rates:** $30 per unit.

MADISON

SE CT. New Haven Co. On Long Island Sound and Hammonasset River.

5922 ■ East Haven Courier
Shore Publishing L.L.C.
724 Boston Post Rd., Ste. 202
Madison, CT 06433
Phone: (203)245-1877
Fax: (203)245-9773
Publisher's E-mail: news@shorepublishing.com
Newspaper serving East Haven, Connecticut. **Col. Width:** 1.9 inches. **Key Personnel:** Brian Boyd, Editor; Robyn Collins, Publisher. **URL:** http://www.zip06.com/section/easthaven. **Mailing address:** PO Box 1010, Madison, CT 06443. **Ad Rates:** BW $800; 4C $1,100; PCI $14. **Remarks:** Accepts advertising. **Circ:** 10668.

5923 ■ Journal of Clinical Psychoanalysis
International Universities Press Inc.
59 Boston Post Rd.
Madison, CT 06443-1524
Journal exploring what really occurs in an analysis. **Freq:** Annual. **Trim Size:** 6 x 9. **Key Personnel:** Herbert M. Wyman, MD, Editor; Stephen M. Rittenberg, MD, Editor. **ISSN:** 1076--044X (print). **Subscription Rates:** $78 Individuals; $120 Institutions; $115 Other countries; $140

Institutions, other countries. **URL:** http://www.pep-web.org/toc.php?journal=jcp. **Ad Rates:** BW $580. **Remarks:** Accepts advertising. **Circ:** (Not Reported).

5924 ■ Journal of Geriatric Psychiatry
International Universities Press Inc.
59 Boston Post Rd.
Madison, CT 06443-1524
Publisher's E-mail: onlinelibrarysales@wiley.com
A multidisciplinary journal of mental health and aging. **Freq:** Monthly. **Key Personnel:** Margery Silver, Editor; Bennett Gurian, MD, Editor. **ISSN:** 0885--6230 (print); **EISSN:** 1099--1166 (electronic). **Subscription Rates:** $2875 Institutions USA, Canada, Mexico and rest of the world; £1470 Institutions UK; €1854 Institutions Euro; $3450 Institutions print and online - USA, Canada, Mexico and rest of the world; £1764 Institutions print and online - UK; €1854 Institutions print and online - Europe; $1740 Individuals print only - USA, Canada, Mexico, Europe and rest of the world; £883 Individuals print only - UK. **URL:** http://onlinelibrary.wiley.com/journal/10.1002/(ISSN)1099-1166. **Ad Rates:** BW $360. **Remarks:** Accepts advertising. **Circ:** (Not Reported).

5925 ■ Shore Line Times
Shore Publishing L.L.C.
724 Boston Post Rd., Ste. 202
Madison, CT 06433
Phone: (203)245-1877
Fax: (203)245-9773
Publisher's E-mail: news@shorepublishing.com
Newspaper. **Freq:** Semiweekly (Wed. and Sat.). **Print Method:** Offset. **Cols./Page:** 6. **Col. Width:** 9.6 picas. **Col. Depth:** 16 inches. **Key Personnel:** Susan Braden, Editor; John Slater, General Manager, phone: (203)752-2700. **Subscription Rates:** $39 Individuals in County; $57 Out of area. **URL:** http://shorelinetimes.com. **Mailing address:** PO Box 1010, Madison, CT 06443. **Ad Rates:** PCI $9.30. **Remarks:** Accepts advertising. **Circ:** Wed. ‡9548, Fri. ‡9548.

5926 ■ The Sound
Shore Publishing L.L.C.
724 Boston Post Rd., Ste. 202
Madison, CT 06433
Phone: (203)245-1877
Fax: (203)245-9773
Publisher's E-mail: news@shorepublishing.com
Community newspaper. **Freq:** Weekly. **Print Method:** Web. **Key Personnel:** Lisa Miksis, Publisher; Brian Boyd, Managing Editor; Dave Ellis, Manager, Advertising. **URL:** http://www.shorepublishing.com; http://www.shorepublishing.com/section/zip06details&town=The-Sound&details=morenews. **Mailing address:** PO Box 1010, Madison, CT 06443. **Ad Rates:** BW $800; 4C $1,000. **Remarks:** Accepts advertising. **Circ:** Combined 13765.

5927 ■ Wire Journal International
The Wire Association International, Inc.
71 Bradley Rd., Ste. 9
Madison, CT 06443-2662
Phone: (203)453-2777
Fax: (203)453-8384
Wire and cable manufacturing and fabricators magazine. **Freq:** Monthly. **Print Method:** Offset. **Trim Size:** 8 1/8 x 10 7/8. **Cols./Page:** 3. **Col. Width:** 26 nonpareils. **Col. Depth:** 140 agate lines. **Key Personnel:** Mark Marselli, Editor-in-Chief. **ISSN:** 0277--4275 (print). **Subscription Rates:** $95 Individuals. **URL:** http://www.wirenet.org/20-wai-article/158-wire-journal-international. **Ad Rates:** BW $2,270; 4C $925; PCI $170. **Remarks:** Accepts advertising. **Circ:** △**9778**, 10000.

MANCHESTER

N. CT. Hartford Co. 12 mi. E. of Hartford. Manufactures silk, rayon, paper, paper board, electrical instruments, soap, tools, reamers, friction clutches, reverse gears, parachutes. Nurseries. Dairy, tobacco farms.

5928 ■ American Period Furniture
Society of American Period Furniture Makers
c/o Bob Van Dyke
249 Spencer St.
Manchester, CT 06040
Publisher's E-mail: membership@sapfm.org
Journal containing how-to articles, biographies of important cabinetmakers, analyses of important pieces, and articles dealing with historical topics in period furniture making. **Freq:** Annual. **Subscription Rates:** Free for members. **URL:** http://www.sapfm.org/american-period-furniture. **Remarks:** Advertising not accepted. **Circ:** (Not Reported).

5929 ■ The Compendium
North American Sundial Society
27 Ninas Way - Humpton Run
Manchester, CT 06040-6388
Publisher's E-mail: nass_president@sundials.org
Freq: Quarterly. **ISSN:** 1074- 3197 (print). **Subscription Rates:** Included in membership. **Alt. Formats:** CD-ROM. **URL:** http://sundials.org/index.php/dial-resources/the-compendium; http://sundials.org/index.php/dial-resources/past-compendium-issues. **Remarks:** Advertising not accepted. **Circ:** (Not Reported).

5930 ■ WDZK-AM
160 Chapel Rd., Ste. 101
Manchester, CT 06040
Phone: (860)643-3912
Free: 877-870-5678
Owner: Radio Disney, 500 S Buena Vista St. MC 7663, Burbank, CA 91521-7716. **Ad Rates:** Advertising accepted; rates available upon request.

MERIDEN

S. CT. New Haven Co. 20 mi. S. of Hartford. Manufactures silverware, machine screws, lamps, plastics, electrical fixtures and appliances, auto parts, oil filters, automatic tools, telephones, switchboard equipment, airplane accessories, china, glassware, hardware.

5931 ■ Record-Journal
The Record-Journal Publishing Co.
11 Crown St.
Meriden, CT 06450
Phone: (203)235-1661
Publisher's E-mail: newsroom@record-journal.com
General newspaper. **Founded:** 1867. **Freq:** Daily and Sun. **Print Method:** Offset. **Cols./Page:** 6. **Col. Width:** 2 1/16 inches. **Col. Depth:** 21 1/2 inches. **Key Personnel:** Eliot C. White, Publisher, phone: (203)317-2350; Eric Cotton, Assistant Managing Editor, phone: (203)317-2344; Ralph Tomaselli, Editor, phone: (203)317-2220; David Pare, Manager, Circulation, Vice President, phone: (203)317-2407. **Subscription Rates:** $30.50 Individuals 1 month, print and online. **URL:** http://www.myrecordjournal.com. **Mailing address:** PO Box 915, Meriden, CT 06450. **Remarks:** Accepts advertising. **Circ:** Mon.-Sat. ‡18289, Sun. ‡19517.

5932 ■ WMMW-AM - 1470
900 E Main St.
Meriden, CT 06450
Format: Talk. **Networks:** Satellite Music Network. **Founded:** 1946. **Operating Hours:** Continuous. **Key Personnel:** Keith Dakin, Prog. Dir.; Stu Gorlick, Dir. of Sales, stu.gorlick@connoisseurct.com; John Voket, Exec. Dir., john.voket@connoisseurct.com; Kristin Okesson, Gen. Mgr., kristin.okesson@connoisseurct.com; Shannon Kinney, Sales Mgr., shannon.kinney@connoisseurct.com; Anthony Pescatello, Contact; Edward L. Diana, Contact. **Wattage:** 2,500 Day; Night. **Ad Rates:** Accepts Advertising. **URL:** http://www.talkofconnecticut.com.

MIDDLETOWN

S. CT. Middlesex Co. On Connecticut River, 15 mi. S. of Hartford. Wesleyan University (coed); Middlesex Community College (coed). Retail, commercial and insurance center. Manufactures jet aircraft engines, brake linings. automotive parts, chemicals, webbing, fabricated metals, textiles, marine and industrial hardware, leather gaskets, tools, dies, office supplies, corrugated cartons, packing machines, electronics, plastic products. Agriculture. Tobacco, apples, dairy products.

5933 ■ Choice: Current Reviews for Academic Libraries
Library and Information Technology Association
575 Main St., Ste. 300
Middletown, CT 06457
Phone: (860)347-6933
Publication E-mail: choicesubscriptions@brightkey.net
Reviews of scholarly publications for undergraduate libraries, special and public libraries, librarians, faculty, students, and scholars. **Freq:** Monthly (combined in July/Aug). **Key Personnel:** Mark Cummings, Editor, Publisher; Lisa M. Gross, Manager, Production, fax: (860)346-8586; Pamela Marino, Manager, Advertising and Sales. **ISSN:** 0009--4978 (print). **Subscription Rates:** $445 U.S.; $485 Canada and Mexico; $575 Other countries. **URL:** http://www.ala.org/acrl/choice. **Ad Rates:** BW $2,570; 4C $3,745. **Remarks:** Accepts advertising. **Circ:** (Not Reported).

5934 ■ Diaspora: A Journal of Transnational Studies
University of Toronto Press Journals Division
c/o Prof. Khachig Tololyan, Ed.
Wesleyan University
Middletown, CT 06459-0100
Publisher's E-mail: journals@utpress.utoronto.ca
Scholarly Journal covering the multidisciplinary study of the history, culture, social structure, politics, and economics of both traditional and recent diasporas. **Freq:** 3/year. **Print Method:** Offset. **Trim Size:** 6 x 9. **Key Personnel:** Khachig Tololyan, Editor. **ISSN:** 1044-2057 (print); **EISSN:** 1911-1568 (electronic). **Subscription Rates:** $85 Institutions, Canada print only; $42 Canada print only; $105 Institutions, other countries print. **URL:** http://www.utpjournals.com/diaspora/. **Ad Rates:** BW $395. **Remarks:** Accepts advertising. **Circ:** 500.

5935 ■ International Journal of Eating Disorders
John Wiley & Sons Inc.
c/o Ruth Striegel Weissman, PhD, Ed.-in-Ch.
Wesleyan University
Department of Psychology
207 High St.
Middletown, CT 06459-0408
Publisher's E-mail: info@wiley.com
Freq: 8/year. **Print Method:** Offset. **Trim Size:** 8 1/2 x 11 1/4. **Cols./Page:** 1. **Col. Width:** 84 nonpareils. **Col. Depth:** 140 agate lines. **Key Personnel:** Michael Strober, PhD, Board Member; Craig Johnson, PhD, Editor, Founder; Ruth Striegel Weissman, PhD, Editor-in-Chief. **ISSN:** 0276--3478 (print); **EISSN:** 1098--108X (electronic). **Subscription Rates:** $487 U.S., Canada, and Mexico print only; $544 Other countries print only; $3570 Institutions print or online (USA) online only (Canada & Mexico/other countries); $3688 Institutions, Canada and Mexico print only; £1806 Institutions UK; print only; €2416 Institutions Europe; print only; $3748 Institutions, other countries print only; $4284 Institutions print and online; $4426 Institutions, Canada and Mexico print and online; £2298 Institutions UK; print and online; €2900 Institutions Europe; print and online; $4209 Institutions, other countries print and online; £1824 Institutions UK; online only; €2302 Institutions Europe; online only; Included in membership. **URL:** http://onlinelibrary.wiley.com/journal/10.1002/(ISSN)1098-108X; http://www.wiley.com/WileyCDA/WileyTitle/productCd-EAT.html. **Ad Rates:** BW $1217; 4C $1545. **Remarks:** Accepts advertising. **Circ:** 8400.

5936 ■ Journal of Forensic Social Work
National Organization of Forensic Social Work
460 Smith St., Ste. K
Middletown, CT 06457
Phone: (860)613-0254
Free: 866-668-9858
Publication focusing on all aspects of forensic social work. **Key Personnel:** Paul Brady, Executive Director; Suzanne Dowling, MSW, President. **Remarks:** Advertising not accepted. **Circ:** (Not Reported).

5937 ■ The Wesleyan Argus
The Argus
45 Wyllys Ave., Ste. 91657
Middletown, CT 06459
Publication E-mail: argus@wesleyan.edu
Collegiate newspaper. **Freq:** Semiweekly during the school year. **Print Method:** Uses mats. Offset. **Cols./Page:** 5. **Col. Width:** 22 nonpareils. **Col. Depth:** 224 agate lines. **Key Personnel:** Gwendolyn Rosen, Editor-in-Chief. **USPS:** 674-680. **Subscription Rates:** $50 Individuals /semester; $80 Individuals /school year. **URL:** http://wesleyanargus.com. **Ad Rates:** GLR $1.50; PCI $6.75. **Remarks:** Accepts advertising. **Circ:** 3000.

Circulation: ★ = AAM; △ or • = BPA; ♦ = CAC; ❑ = VAC; ⊕ = PO Statement; ‡ = Publisher's Report; Boldface figures = sworn; Light figures = estimated.

5938 ■ Wesleyan: The University Magazine
Wesleyan University Science Library
265 Church St.
Middletown, CT 06459
Phone: (860)685-2860
University alumni magazine. **Freq:** Quarterly. **Print Method:** Offset. **Cols./Page:** 3 and 2. **Col. Width:** 27 and 41 nonpareils. **Col. Depth:** 130 agate lines. **Key Personnel:** William Holder, Editor; Cynthia Rockwell, Associate Editor. **USPS:** 674-760. **URL:** http://magazine.wesleyan.edu. **Remarks:** Advertising not accepted. **Circ:** Controlled 30000.

5939 ■ West Hartford News
Imprint Newspapers
386 Main St., 4th Fl.
Middletown, CT 06457
Phone: (860)347-3331
Fax: (860)347-4425
Publication E-mail: westhartfordnews@ctcentral.com
Community newspaper. **Freq:** Weekly (Thurs.). **Print Method:** Offset. **Cols./Page:** 6. **Col. Width:** 10 picas. **Col. Depth:** 16 inches. **Key Personnel:** Viktoria Sundqvist, Editor; Tom Wiley, Publisher, phone: (203)789-5205; John Gallacher, Director, Advertising. **ISSN:** 1057--1272 (print). **USPS:** 675-460. **Subscription Rates:** Free. **URL:** http://www.westhartfordnews.com. **Remarks:** Accepts advertising. **Circ:** (Not Reported).

5940 ■ WESU-FM - 88.1
45 Broad St., 2nd Fl.
Middletown, CT 06457
Phone: (860)685-7700
Fax: (860)704-0608
Email: wesu@wesufm.org
Format: Eclectic. **Owner:** Wesleyan Broadcasting Assoc., Inc., at above address. **Founded:** 1939. **Operating Hours:** Continuous. **Key Personnel:** Ben Michael, Gen. Mgr., generalmanager@wesufm.org. **Local Programs:** *Rumpus Room,* Monday 8:00 p.m. - 9:30 p.m.; *The Attention Deficit Disk Jockey,* Monday 9:30 p.m. - 11:00 p.m. **Wattage:** 6,000. **Ad Rates:** Noncommercial. **URL:** http://wesufm.org.

5941 ■ WIHS-FM - 104.9
1933 S Main St.
Middletown, CT 06457
Phone: (860)346-1049
Fax: (860)347-1049
Email: wihs@snet.net
Format: Religious. **Owner:** The Connecticut Radio Fellowship Inc., at above address. **Key Personnel:** Bill Bacon, President; John Barney, Director; Paul Kretschmer, News Dir. **Ad Rates:** Noncommercial. **URL:** http://www.wihsradio.org.

5942 ■ WLIS 1420-AM - 1420
PO Box 1150
Middletown, CT 06457
Phone: (860)388-1420
Fax: (860)347-7704
Free: 866-989-1975
Format: Adult Contemporary. **Simulcasts:** WMRD. **Networks:** CBS; CNN Radio; NBC. **Owner:** Crossroads Communications of Old Saybrook L.L.C., 777 River Rd., Middletown, CT 06457, Fax: (860)347-7704. **Founded:** 1956. **Operating Hours:** Continuous. **Key Personnel:** Don DeCesare, Gen. Mgr., President, Prog. Dir., don@wliswmrd.net. **Wattage:** 5,000. **Ad Rates:** $28-43 for 30 seconds; $33-48 for 60 seconds. Combined advertising rates available with WMRD. **Mailing address:** PO Box 1150, Middletown, CT 06457. **URL:** http://wliswmrd.net.

5943 ■ WMRD-AM - 1150
777 River Rd.
Middletown, CT 06457
Phone: (860)388-1420
Fax: (860)347-7704
Email: radio@wliswmrd.net
Format: News. **Simulcasts:** WUS-AM. **Networks:** CBS; CNN Radio; CRN International; Westwood One Radio. **Owner:** Crossroads Communications, L.L.C., 7120 S Lewis Ave., Ste. 210, Tulsa, OK 74136, Ph: (918)633-4397. **Founded:** Dec. 1950. **Formerly:** WCNX-AM. **Operating Hours:** Continuous. **Key Personnel:** Don DeCesare, Gen. Mgr., President, don@wliswmrd.net; Bob Muscatell, Director, bob@wliswmrd.net. **Wattage:** 2,500. **Ad Rates:** Noncommercial. WUS-AM OLD SAYBROOK, CT. **Mailing address:** PO Box 1150, Middletown, CT 06457. **URL:** http://wliswmrd.net.

MILFORD

S. CT. New Haven Co. On Long Island Sound, 9 mi. SW of New Haven. Summer resort. Manufactures ball point pens, aerosol pressure cans, razors, locks, brass goods, rivets, metal novelties, screws, machine parts and tools, auto and marine hardware, thermostats, electric motors.

5944 ■ JAX FAX Travel Marketing Magazine
Jet Airtransport Exchange Inc.
52 W Main St.
Milford, CT 06460-3310
Fax: (203)301-0250
Free: 800-952-9329
Publication E-mail: info@jaxfaxmagazine.com
Travel planning magazine for travel agents. **Founded:** 1973. **Freq:** Monthly. **Print Method:** Web offset. **Trim Size:** 8 1/8 x 10 7/8. **Cols./Page:** 2. **Col. Width:** 3 1/4 inches. **Col. Depth:** 10 inches. **Key Personnel:** Douglas S. Cooke, Publisher, Director, Editorial; Ryley Hartt, Editor. **ISSN:** 0148-9542 (print). **Subscription Rates:** $15 Individuals employed in the travel industry; $24 Two years employed in the travel industry; $38 Canada and Mexico employed in the travel industry. **URL:** http://www.jaxfax.com. **Ad Rates:** BW $4,903; 4C $4,552. **Remarks:** Accepts advertising. **Circ:** Paid ■ **23,172.**

5945 ■ Sustainable Communities Review
Environmental Alliance for Senior Involvement
PO Box 250
Milford, CT 06460-0250
Phone: (203)779-0024
Fax: (203)779-0025
Publisher's E-mail: easi@easi.org
Journal containing researches, news, and events in educating adults on how to preserve the environment. **Freq:** Biennial. **URL:** http://www.easi.org/publications/index.html. **Remarks:** Accepts advertising. **Circ:** (Not Reported).

5946 ■ WEZN-FM - 99.9
440 Wheelers Farms Rd., Ste. 302
Milford, CT 06461
Phone: (203)783-8200
Fax: (203)783-8383
Free: 800-330-9999
Format: Adult Contemporary. **Owner:** Cox Radio Inc., 6205 Peachtree Dunwood Rd., Atlanta, GA 30328-4524, Ph: (678)645-0000, Fax: (678)645-5002. **Founded:** 1973. **Operating Hours:** Continuous. **Key Personnel:** Steve Soyland, Dir. of Mktg.; John Voket, Div. Dir., john.voket@coxradio.com; Helaine Greenbaum, Sales Mgr., helaine.greenbaum@coxmg.com. **Ad Rates:** Advertising accepted; rates available upon request. **URL:** http://www.star999.com.

5947 ■ WFIF-AM - 1500
90 Kay Ave.
Milford, CT 06460-5421
Phone: (203)878-5915
Fax: (203)882-8756
Email: info@wfif.net
Format: Religious. **Networks:** USA Radio; Ambassador Inspirational Radio. **Owner:** Blount Communications Group, 8 Lawrence Rd., Derry, NH 03038, Ph: (603)437-9337, Fax: (603)434-1035. **Founded:** 1965. **Operating Hours:** Sunrise-sunset; 50% network, 50% local. **Wattage:** 5,000. **Ad Rates:** $10-12 for 30 seconds; $14-16 for 60 seconds. **URL:** http://www.lifechangingradio.com.

5948 ■ WPLR-FM - 99.1
440 Wheelers Farms Rd., Ste. 302
Milford, CT 06461
Phone: (203)783-8200
Fax: (203)783-8383
Format: Album-Oriented Rock (AOR). **Owner:** Cox Radio Inc., 6205 Peachtree Dunwood Rd., Atlanta, GA 30328-4524, Ph: (678)645-0000, Fax: (678)645-5002. **Founded:** 1944. **Operating Hours:** Continuous. **Key Personnel:** Keith Dakin, Prog. Dir.; Scott Laudani, Dir. of Programs, scott.laudani@coxradio.com; John Voket, Div. Dir., john.voket@connoisseurct.com; Kristin Okesson, Gen. Mgr., kristin.okesson@connoisseurct.com; Stu Gorlick, Dir. of Sales, stu.gorlick@connoisseurct.com. **Ad Rates:** Advertising accepted; rates available upon request. **URL:** http://www.wplr.com.

MONROE

SW CT. Fairfield Co. 12 mi. N. of Bridgeport.

5949 ■ Army Aviation Magazine: Official Publication of the Army Aviation Association of America (AAAA)
Army Aviation Association of America
593 Main St.
Monroe, CT 06468-2830
Phone: (203)268-2450
Fax: (203)268-5870
Publisher's E-mail: aaaa@quad-a.org
Army aviation magazine. **Freq:** Monthly. **Print Method:** Offset. **Trim Size:** 8 1/8 x 10 7/8. **Cols./Page:** 2. **Key Personnel:** Joseph Pisano, Sr., Editor; Anne Ewing, Manager, Production. **ISSN:** 0004--2484 (print). **Subscription Rates:** Included in membership. **URL:** http://www.armyaviationmagazine.com. **Ad Rates:** BW $6271; 4C $8157. **Remarks:** Accepts advertising. **Circ:** (Not Reported).

5950 ■ The Monroe Times
Monroe Publishing L.L.C.
110 Bart Rd.
Monroe, CT 06468-1117
Phone: (203)261-6517
Newspaper with an Independent orientation. **Freq:** Mon.-Sat. **Print Method:** Offset. **Cols./Page:** 6. **Col. Width:** 25 nonpareils. **Col. Depth:** 301 agate lines. **Key Personnel:** Connie Flint, Office Manager; Mary Jane Grenzow, Editor; Laura Hughes, Manager, Advertising. **Subscription Rates:** $175 Individuals print and online rate in Green County /year; $199 Out of area print and online /year; $179.45 Individuals online only. **URL:** http://www.themonroetimes.com. **Formerly:** Times, The Monroe Evening Times. **Ad Rates:** GLR $1.22; BW $1,758; 4C $1,983; PCI $10. **Remarks:** Advertising accepted; rates available upon request. **Circ:** Paid 6400.

WGRS-FM - See Guilford, CT

5951 ■ WGSK-FM - 90.1
PO Box 920
Monroe, CT 06468
Phone: (203)268-9667
Email: info@wmnr.org
Format: Classical. **Owner:** Monroe Board of Education, 375 Monroe Tpke., Monroe, CT 06468, Ph: (203)452-2860. **Operating Hours:** Continuous. **Key Personnel:** Kurt Anderson, Gen. Mgr., kanderson@wmnr.org; Carol Babina, Asst. GM, cbabina@wmnr.org; Jane Stadler, Dir. of Operations, jstadler@wmnr.org. **Wattage:** 077 ERP. **Ad Rates:** Noncommercial. **URL:** http://wmnr.org/web/home.

5952 ■ WMNR-FM - 88.1
PO Box 920
Monroe, CT 06468
Phone: (203)268-9667
Email: music@wmnr.org
Format: Classical; Big Band/Nostalgia. **Networks:** Independent. **Owner:** Monroe Public Schools, 375 Monroe Tpke., Monroe, CT 06468, Ph: (203)452-2860. **Operating Hours:** Continuous. **ADI:** New York, NY. **Key Personnel:** Kurt Anderson, Gen. Mgr., kanderson@wmnr.org; Carol Babina, Asst. GM, Dir. of Dev., carol@babina.com; Jane Stadler, Dir. of Operations, jstadler@wmnr.org. **Wattage:** 5,000. **Ad Rates:** Noncommercial. **URL:** http://wmnr.org/web/home.

WRXC-FM - See Shelton

NAUGATUCK

S. CT. New Haven Co. 5 mi. S. of Waterbury. Manufactures chemicals, malleable iron castings, candy, aeronautical parts and fabricated metal products.

5953 ■ WFNW-AM
700 Canal St.
Stamford, CT 06902
Format: Hispanic; Ethnic. **Founded:** 1961. **Wattage:** 3,500 Day; 350 Night.

5954 ■ WFNW-AM - 1380
175 Church St., 3rd Fl.
Naugatuck, CT 06770
Wattage: 3,500 Day Time/ 350 N.

NEW BRITAIN

N. CT. Hartford Co. 10 mi. SW of Hartford. Central Connecticut State College. Manufacturing.

5955 ■ The Bristol Press
The Bristol Press

One Court St.
New Britain, CT 06051
Phone: (860)584-0501
Fax: (860)584-2192
Publisher's E-mail: letters@bristolpress.com
General newspaper. **Freq:** Daily (eve.). **Print Method:** Offset. **Cols./Page:** 6. **Col. Width:** 25 nonpareils. **Col. Depth:** 301 agate lines. **Key Personnel:** Michael E. Schroeder, Publisher; Joseph Cannata, Jr., Manager, Circulation. **ISSN:** 0891--5563 (print). **Subscription Rates:** $252.20 Individuals home delivery; $390 By mail in State; $416 Out of state. **URL:** http://www.centralctcommunications.com/bristolpress. **Remarks:** Advertising accepted; rates available upon request. **Circ:** ‡10704.

5956 ■ Connecticut Bar Journal
Connecticut Bar Association
30 Bank St.
New Britain, CT 06050
Phone: (860)223-4400
Fax: (860)223-4488
Publisher's E-mail: msc@ctbar.org
Journal featureing articles on numerous legal topics. **Freq:** Quarterly. **Key Personnel:** James E. Wildes, Editor-in-Chief. **Subscription Rates:** Members free. **URL:** http://www.ctbar.org/?page=CTBarJournal. **Mailing address:** PO Box 350, New Britain, CT 06050. **Ad Rates:** BW $500. **Remarks:** Accepts advertising. **Circ:** (Not Reported).

5957 ■ The Herald
The Herald
1 Crt. St. 4th Fl.
New Britain, CT 06051
Phone: (860)225-4601
Fax: (860)229-5718
General newspaper. **Founded:** 1880. **Freq:** Mon.-Sat. **Print Method:** Offset. **Cols./Page:** 6. **Col. Width:** 25 nonpareils. **Col. Depth:** 301 agate lines. **USPS:** 377-920. **Subscription Rates:** $207.48 Individuals home delivery; $364 Individuals mail. **URL:** http://www.newbritainherald.com/. **Ad Rates:** GLR $23.11; BW $2535; 4C $2845; SAU $17.59; PCI $19.65. **Remarks:** Accepts advertising. **Circ:** Mon.-Sat. ★**12155**, Sun. ★**24238**.

5958 ■ Multicultural Perspectives
Routledge Journals Taylor & Francis Group
c/o Penelope L. Lisi, Ed.
Central Connecticut State University
Dept. of Educational Leadership
1615 Stanley St., Barnard Hall, Rm. 260
New Britain, CT 06050
Phone: (860)832-2137
Scholarly journal covering the philosophy of social justice, equity and inclusion for teachers, social scientists, those involved in multicultural education, and others. **Freq:** Quarterly. **Key Personnel:** Jill Aguilar, Associate Editor; Penelope L. Lisi, Editor; Bernard Beck, Associate Editor. **ISSN:** 1521--0960 (print); **EISSN:** 1532--7892 (electronic). **Subscription Rates:** $437 Institutions online only; $499 Institutions print and online; $83 Individuals print and online. **URL:** http://www.tandfonline.com/toc/hmcp20/current. **Ad Rates:** BW $500. **Remarks:** Accepts advertising. **Circ:** (Not Reported).

5959 ■ WFCS-FM - 107.7
1615 Stanley St.
New Britain, CT 06050
Phone: (860)832-1883
Email: wfcsgm@gmail.com
Format: Contemporary Hit Radio (CHR). **Networks:** Independent. **Founded:** 1950. **Formerly:** WTCC-AM. **Operating Hours:** Continuous; 100% local. **Key Personnel:** Salvatore Carchia, Contact. **Wattage:** 100. **Ad Rates:** Noncommercial. **URL:** http://ccsu.collegiatelink.net.

NEW CANAAN

SW CT. Fairfield Co. 5 mi. NW of Norwalk. Residential.

5960 ■ Nordstjernan
Nordstjernan Swedish News
PO Box 1710
New Canaan, CT 06840
Phone: (203)299-0380
Fax: (203)299-0381
Free: 800-827-9333
Publisher's E-mail: info@nordstjernan.com
Newspaper (tabloid; Swedish and English). Prints edition about Swedish industry. **Freq:** Weekly (Thurs.). **Print Method:** Offset. **Trim Size:** 9 7/8 x 14. **Cols./Page:** 5. **Col. Width:** 1 7/8 inches. **Col. Depth:** 14 inches. **Key Personnel:** Ulf E. Martensson, Editor. **ISSN:** 0895--2620 (print). **Subscription Rates:** $55 U.S. print; $99 Canada print; $167 Other countries print; $19.95 Individuals online; $39.95 Individuals print and online. **URL:** http://www.nordstjernan.com. **Also known as:** Swedish News. **Ad Rates:** BW $1280; PCI $21. **Remarks:** Color advertising not accepted. **Circ:** Paid ‡5000, Free ‡100.

5961 ■ WSLX-FM - 91.9
377 N Wilton Rd.
New Canaan, CT 06840
Phone: (203)966-5612
Fax: (203)972-3450
Email: info@stlukesct.org
Format: Classical; News. **Networks:** Independent. **Owner:** St. Luke's Foundation, 11327 Shaker Blvd., Ste. 600W, Cleveland, OH 44104. **Founded:** 1975. **Operating Hours:** 18 hours Daily; 100% local. **Key Personnel:** Jeffrey Kress, Contact; Troy Haynie, Contact. **Wattage:** 010. **Ad Rates:** Noncommercial. **URL:** http://www.stlukesct.org/schoollife/wslx.

NEW HAVEN

S. CT. New Haven Co. On Long Island Sound. Yale University (coed); divinity, pharmacy, physical education and other colleges; private schools. Industrial center. Trap rock quarries. Shipyard. Manufactures guns, ammunition, hardware, tools, rubber goods, toys, sewing machine attachments, lamps, clocks, watches, textiles, asbestos insulated wire, airplane parts, paper boxboard. Agriculture.

5962 ■ Agricultural and Forest Meteorology
RELX Group P.L.C.
c/o X. Lee, Ed.-in-Ch.
Yale University
School of Forestry & Environmental Studies
21 Sachem St.
New Haven, CT 06511
Publisher's E-mail: amsterdam@relx.com
Journal publishing original contributions on the interrelationship between meteorology and the fields of plant, animal and soil sciences, ecology, and biogeochemistry. Covers basic and applied scientific research connected with practical problems in agriculture, forestry, and natural ecosystems. **Founded:** 1964. **Freq:** 16/yr. **Key Personnel:** X. Lee, Editor-in-Chief; D. Aylor, Board Member; D. Baldocchi, Board Member; B.D. Amiro, Board Member. **ISSN:** 0168-1923 (print). **Subscription Rates:** $4306 Institutions print. **URL:** http://www.journals.elsevier.com/agricultural-and-forest-meteorology. **Circ:** (Not Reported).

5963 ■ American Journal of Science
American Journal of Science
210 Whitney Ave.
New Haven, CT 06520
Phone: (203)432-3131
Fax: (203)432-5668
Publication E-mail: ajs@yale.edu
Journal focusing on geology and the geological sciences. **Freq:** 10/year. **Trim Size:** 6 3/4 x 10. **Cols./Page:** 1. **Col. Width:** 54 nonpareils. **Col. Depth:** 102 agate lines. **Key Personnel:** Danny M. Rye, Editor; C. Page Chamberlain, Editor. **ISSN:** 0002--9599 (print). **Subscription Rates:** $80 Individuals; $230 Institutions; $40 Students. **URL:** http://www.ajsonline.org. **Mailing address:** PO Box 208109, New Haven, CT 06520. **Ad Rates:** BW $100. **Remarks:** Accepts advertising. **Circ:** 1300.

5964 ■ Behavioral and Brain Sciences
Cambridge University Press
c/o Prof. Paul Bloom, Co-Editor
PO Box 208205
New Haven, CT 06520-8205
Publisher's E-mail: newyork@cambridge.org
Peer-reviewed journal on psychology and neurosciences. **Freq:** Bimonthly. **Key Personnel:** Prof. Paul Bloom, Editor; Dr. Barbara L. Finlay, Editor. **ISSN:** 0140--525X (print). **Subscription Rates:** $1292 Institutions online only; £782 Institutions online only. **URL:** http://journals.cambridge.org/action/aboutTheJournal?jid=BBS. **Remarks:** Advertising accepted; rates available upon request. **Circ:** (Not Reported).

5965 ■ Cerebral Cortex
Oxford University Press
Dept. of Neurobiology
Yale University School of Medicine
333 Cedar St.
New Haven, CT 06510
Phone: (203)785-4808
Fax: (203)785-5263
Publisher's E-mail: uk@oup.com
Scholarly medical journal for neuroscientists and clinicians engaged in research or teaching of the cerebral cortex and related structures.Publishes papers on the development, organization, plasticity, and function of the cerebral cortex, including the hippocampus. **Freq:** Monthly. **Trim Size:** 7 x 10. **Cols./Page:** 2. **Col. Width:** 3 inches. **Col. Depth:** 9 inches. **Key Personnel:** Pasko Rakic, Editor-in-Chief; Patricia S. Goldman-Rakic, Editor, Founder. **ISSN:** 1047-3211 (print). **Subscription Rates:** £1709 Institutions print & online; $3247 Institutions print & online; €2563 Institutions print & online; £1211 Institutions online only; $2300 Institutions online only; €1816 Institutions online only; £1572 Institutions print only; $2987 Institutions print only; €2358 Institutions print only. **URL:** http://cercor.oxfordjournals.org/. **Ad Rates:** BW $415; 4C $1,065. **Remarks:** Accepts advertising. **Circ:** Paid 700.

5966 ■ Columbia: Knights of Columbus Magazine
Knights of Columbus
1 Columbus Plz.
New Haven, CT 06510
Phone: (203)752-4000
Free: 800-380-9995
Publisher's E-mail: info@kofc.org
International Catholic family magazine (French, Spanish, and English). **Freq:** Monthly. **Print Method:** Offset. **Trim Size:** 8 1/4 x 10 3/4. **Cols./Page:** 3. **Col. Width:** 13.5 picas. **Col. Depth:** 60 picas. **ISSN:** 0010--1869 (print). **Subscription Rates:** $6 Individuals; $11 Two years; $8 Other countries. **URL:** http://www.kofc.org/un/en/columbia/index.html. **Remarks:** Advertising not accepted. **Circ:** ‡1600000.

5967 ■ Connecticut Magazine
Connecticut Magazine
100 Gando Dr.
New Haven, CT 06513
Phone: (203)789-5300
Fax: (203)789-5255
Publisher's E-mail: advertising@connecticutmag.com
Magazine for Connecticut residents. Includes articles on politics, fashion, business, home interiors, restaurant reviews, the arts, and real estate. **Freq:** Monthly. **Print Method:** Web offset. **Trim Size:** 8 x 10 3/4. **Cols./Page:** 3. **Col. Width:** 27 nonpareils. **Col. Depth:** 140 agate lines. **Key Personnel:** Charles A. Monagan, Editor; Dale B. Salm, Managing Editor; Marisa B. Dragone, General Manager, phone: (203)789-5214. **ISSN:** 0889--7670 (print). **URL:** http://www.connecticutmag.com/Connecticut-Magazine/Magazine. **Ad Rates:** BW $7,885; 4C $11,585. **Remarks:** Accepts advertising. **Circ:** Paid ★**84,828**.

5968 ■ Econometric Theory
Cambridge University Press
c/o Peter C.B. Phillips, Ed.
Yale University
Cowles Foundation for Research in Economics
PO Box 208281
New Haven, CT 06520-8281
Publication E-mail: econometric.theory@yale.edu
Peer-reviewed journal on econometrics. **Freq:** Bimonthly. **Key Personnel:** Peter C.B. Phillips, Associate Editor; Peter Hansen, Editor. **ISSN:** 0266-4666 (print); **EISSN:** 1469-4360 (electronic). **Subscription Rates:** $45 Individuals article; $1209 Institutions online and print; $980 Institutions online only; £188 Individuals online and print; $321 Individuals online & print; £718 Institutions online & print; £580 Institutions online only; £30 Individuals article. **URL:** http://journals.cambridge.org/action/displayJournal?jid=ECT. **Ad Rates:** BW $885. **Circ:** ‡1000.

Circulation: ★ = AAM; △ or • = BPA; ♦ = CAC; ❑ = VAC; ⊕ = PO Statement; ‡ = Publisher's Report; Boldface figures = sworn; Light figures = estimated.

5969 ■ Eglute
Lithuanian-American Community Inc.
43 Anthony St.
New Haven, CT 06515
Phone: (203)415-7776
Fax: (703)773-1257
Publisher's E-mail: admin@lithuanian-american.org
Magazine featuring different topics for children who speak both Lithuanian and English, who live outside of Lithuania and who may or may not attend Lithuanian school and also for teachers who may use the content of journal as part of their lesson plan. **Freq:** 10/year. **URL:** http://eglute.org; http://lithuanian-american.org/m/explore-lac/publications. **Remarks:** Advertising not accepted. **Circ:** (Not Reported).

5970 ■ Fairfield County Weekly
New Mass Media Inc.
900 Chapel St., Ste. 1100
New Haven, CT 06510
Phone: (203)789-0010
Fax: (203)787-1418
Community newspaper covering investigative journalism. **Freq:** Weekly. **Key Personnel:** Joshua Mamis, Publisher; Susan Leighton, Director, Advertising; Sean Corbett, Editor. **URL:** http://www.ctnow.com/advocates. **Remarks:** Accepts classified advertising. **Circ:** ■ **30000**.

5971 ■ International Bulletin of Missionary Research
Overseas Ministries Study Center
490 Prospect St.
New Haven, CT 06511-2196
Phone: (203)624-6672
Fax: (203)865-2857
Publication E-mail: ibmr@omsc.org
Professional journal on Christian mission and cross-cultural ministries. Examines contemporary issues and developments in the Christian world mission, employing interdenominational, interdisciplinary, and international perspectives. **Freq:** Quarterly. **Print Method:** Offset. **Trim Size:** 8 1/2 x 10 7/8. **Cols./Page:** 2 and 3. **Col. Width:** 22 and 13 1/2 picas. **Col. Depth:** 140 agate lines. **Key Personnel:** J. Nelson Jennings, Editor; Jonathan Bonk, Editor; Daniel J. Nicholas, Managing Editor. **ISSN:** 0272--6122 (print). **Subscription Rates:** $31 Individuals print & online; $123 Students print & online - Theology Colleges & Seminaries Subscription; $158 Institutions e-access; $172 Institutions print; $175 Institutions print & online. **URL:** http://www.internationalbulletin.org. **Formerly**: Occasional Bulletin of Missionary Research. **Ad Rates:** BW $725. **Remarks:** Color advertising not accepted. **Circ:** (Not Reported).

5972 ■ Journal of Chemical Information and Modeling
American Chemical Society
c/o William L. Jorgensen, PhD, Ed.-in-Ch.
Dept. of Chemistry
Yale University
New Haven, CT 06520-8107
Phone: (203)432-4118
Publication E-mail: eic@jcim.acs.org jcics@yale.edu
Journal discussing on current advances in this area of research including programming innovations, software and book reviews to keep current with advances in this integral, multidisciplinary field. **Freq:** Monthly. **Print Method:** Offset. **Cols./Page:** 2. **Col. Width:** 36 nonpareils. **Col. Depth:** 136 agate lines. **Key Personnel:** Kenneth M. Merz, Jr., Editor-in-Chief. **ISSN:** 1549--9596 (print). **URL:** http://pubs.acs.org/journal/jcisd8. **Formerly:** Journal of Chemical Information and Computer Sciences. **Mailing address:** PO Box 208107, New Haven, CT 06520-8107. **Ad Rates:** BW $2035; 4C $2645. **Remarks:** Accepts advertising. **Circ:** ‡1700.

5973 ■ Journal of Clinical Gastroenterology
World Organization for Specialized Studies on Diseases of the Esophagus
c/o Martin H. Floch, MD, Editor-in-Chief
Yale University School of Medicine
Section of Digestive Diseases, LMP 1080
New Haven, CT 06520-8019
Phone: (203)855-0620
Fax: (203)855-0630
Publication E-mail: jcg@yale.edu
Peer-reviewed journal featuring original articles on the diagnosis of digestive diseases, treatment modalities, and surgical intervention. **Freq:** 10/year. **Print Method:** Sheetfed Offset. **Trim Size:** 8 1/8 x 10 7/8. **Key Personnel:** Nina Chang, Publisher; Martin H. Floch, MD, Editor-in-Chief. **ISSN:** 0192-0790 (print); **EISSN:** 1539-2031 (electronic). **Subscription Rates:** $554 Individuals; $1591 Institutions; $708 Other countries individual; $1542 Institutions, other countries; $272 Individuals in-training; $290 Other countries in-training. **URL:** http://journals.lww.com/jcge/pages/default.aspx; http://www.oeso.org; http://www.lww.com/Product/0192-0790. **Mailing address:** PO Box 208019, New Haven, CT 06520-8019. **Ad Rates:** BW $1,290; 4C $1,520. **Remarks:** Accepts advertising. **Circ:** 389.

5974 ■ Journal of Industrial Ecology
International Society for Industrial Ecology
Yale School of Forestry and Environmental Studies
Yale University
195 Prospect St.
New Haven, CT 06511-2189
Phone: (203)432-6953
Fax: (203)432-5556
Scholarly journal covering industrial ecology worldwide. **Freq:** Bimonthly. **Trim Size:** 7 x 10. **Key Personnel:** Reid Lifset, Editor-in-Chief; Helge Brattebo, Editor. **ISSN:** 1088--1980 (print); **EISSN:** 1530--9290 (electronic). **Subscription Rates:** $591 Institutions online only; £303 Institutions online only; €381 Institutions online only; £591 Institutions, other countries online only. **URL:** http://onlinelibrary.wiley.com/journal/10.1111/(ISSN)1530-9290; http://www.is4ie.org/jie. **Ad Rates:** BW $350. **Remarks:** Accepts advertising. **Circ:** Combined 1100.

5975 ■ Journal of Marine Research
Yale University
PO Box 208229
New Haven, CT 06520-8229
Phone: (203)432-1345
Peer-reviewed journal of interdisciplinary oceanographic research. **Freq:** Bimonthly. **Key Personnel:** Kenneth H. Brink, Editor; Peter J.S. Franks, Board Member; Steve Rintoul, Board Member. **ISSN:** 0022-2402 (print). **Subscription Rates:** $160 Individuals online; $185 Institutions libraries and agencies, for online and print. **URL:** http://peabody.yale.edu/scientific-publications/journal-marine-research/home. **Remarks:** Advertising not accepted. **Circ:** Paid 800.

5976 ■ Journal of Middle East Women's Studies
Indiana University Press
c/o Bonnie Rose Schulman, Mng. Ed.
Yale University, MacMillan Ctr.
34 Hillhouse Ave.
New Haven, CT 06520-8206
Publication E-mail: jmews@yale.edu
Peer-reviewed feminist journal focusing on gender studies, social sciences, and humanities. **Freq:** 3/year. **Key Personnel:** Marcia Inhorn, Editor. **ISSN:** 1552--5864 (print); **EISSN:** 1558--9579 (electronic). **URL:** http://www.jstor.org/journal/jmiddeastwomstud. **Mailing address:** PO Box 208206, New Haven, CT 06520-8206. **Circ:** (Not Reported).

5977 ■ Journal of Pediatric Endocrinology & Metabolism
Freund Publishing House Ltd.
Yale Child Health Research Ctr.
464 Congress Ave.
New Haven, CT 06520
Journal covering clinical investigations in pediatric endocrinology and basic research with relevance to clinical pediatric endocrinology and metabolism from all over the world. **Freq:** Monthly. **Print Method:** 8 1/4 x 10 3/4. **Key Personnel:** Prof. Z. Zadik, Editor-in-Chief. **ISSN:** 0334--018X (print). **Subscription Rates:** €1039 Institutions print; $1559 Institutions print; €1247 Institutions; $1873 Institutions. **URL:** http://www.degruyter.com/view/j/jpem. **Mailing address:** PO Box 208081, New Haven, CT 06520. **Ad Rates:** BW $1,200; 4C $2,400. **Remarks:** Accepts advertising. **Circ:** (Not Reported).

5978 ■ Journal of Sustainable Forestry
Taylor & Francis
c/o Graeme P. Berlyn, PhD, Ed.
Yale University School of Forestry
Greeley Mem. Lab
370 Prospect St.
New Haven, CT 06511
Publisher's E-mail: bookorders@dekker.com
Journal covering topics in biotechnology, physiology, silviculture, wood science, economics, forest management, political ecology, and community based management. **Freq:** 8/year. **Trim Size:** 6 x 8 3/8. **Key Personnel:** Graeme P. Berlyn, PhD, Editor; Ambrose O. Anoruo, Board Member. **ISSN:** 1054--9811 (print); **EISSN:** 1540--756X (electronic). **Subscription Rates:** $340 Individuals online only; $389 Individuals print & online; $980 Institutions online only; $1120 Institutions print & online. **URL:** http://www.tandfonline.com/toc/wjsf20/current. **Ad Rates:** BW $315; 4C $550. **Remarks:** Accepts advertising. **Circ:** 148.

5979 ■ Lituanus
Lithuanian-American Community Inc.
43 Anthony St.
New Haven, CT 06515
Phone: (203)415-7776
Fax: (703)773-1257
Publication E-mail: editor@lituanus.org
Peer-reviewed journal on the arts and sciences of Lithuania and the Baltic Topics of History, Linguistics, Art, Music, Political Science, Economics. **Freq:** Quarterly published in March, June, September and December. **Print Method:** Offset. **Trim Size:** 5 1/2 x 8 1/2. **Cols./Page:** 1. **Col. Width:** 47 nonpareils. **Col. Depth:** 95 agate lines. **Key Personnel:** Arvydas Tamulis, Director. **ISSN:** 0024--5089 (print). **Subscription Rates:** $30 Individuals print; $20 Individuals senior/student (print); $30 Other countries senior/student (print); $40 Institutions print; $20 Individuals online; $30 Institutions online. **URL:** http://www.lituanus.org/main.php?id=home. **Remarks:** Advertising not accepted. **Circ:** (Not Reported).

5980 ■ New Haven Register
New Haven Register
40 Sargent Dr.
New Haven, CT 06511
Phone: (203)789-5200
Free: 800-925-2509
Publisher's E-mail: letters@nhregister.com
General newspaper. **Freq:** Daily. **Print Method:** Offset. **Trim Size:** 13 x 21. **Cols./Page:** 6. **Col. Width:** 12.4 picas. **Col. Depth:** 21 inches. **Key Personnel:** Kevin Corrado, Publisher. **Subscription Rates:** $27.60 Individuals 7 daily, 4 weeks. **URL:** http://www.nhregister.com. **Remarks:** Accepts advertising. **Circ:** Mon.-Fri. ★**68905**, Sun. ★**100486**.

5981 ■ Pediatric and Developmental Pathology
Society for Pediatric Pathology
c/o Miguel Reyes-Mugica, Ed.-in-Ch.
Dept. of Pathology, Yale University School of Medicine
310 Cedar St.
Lauder Hall, LB20
New Haven, CT 06520-8023
Phone: (203)737-5383
Fax: (203)737-5388
Publication E-mail: peddev.path@yale.edu
Journal publishing peer-reviewed studies on pathophysiology of the developing human embryo, fetus, and child. Covers the variety of disorders of early development (including embryology, placentology, and teratology), gestational and perinatal diseases, and all diseases of childhood. **Freq:** Bimonthly. **Key Personnel:** Miguel Reyes-Mugica, Editor-in-Chief; Raj Kapur, Associate Editor. **ISSN:** 1093-5266 (print); **EISSN:** 1615-5742 (electronic). **Subscription Rates:** $350 Individuals print and online; $1200 Institutions print and online; $395 Other countries print and online; $1255 Institutions, other countries print and online. **URL:** http://www.pedpath.org/. **Remarks:** Advertising accepted; rates available upon request. **Circ:** (Not Reported).

5982 ■ Pensininkas
Lithuanian-American Community Inc.
43 Anthony St.
New Haven, CT 06515
Phone: (203)415-7776
Fax: (703)773-1257
Publisher's E-mail: admin@lithuanian-american.org
Magazine featuring different topics of Lithuanian senior citizens' interests. **Freq:** Bimonthly. **Alt. Formats:** Download; PDF. **URL:** http://lithuanian-american.org/m/explore-lac/publications/pensininkas. **Remarks:** Advertising not accepted. **Circ:** (Not Reported).

5983 ■ Seminars in Neurology
Thieme Medical Publishers, Inc.
c/o David Greer, Editor-in-Chief

15 York St.
New Haven, CT 06520
Publisher's E-mail: customerservice@thieme.com
Medical journal covering neurology. **Freq:** 6/year. **Trim Size:** 8 1/8 x 10 7/8. **Cols./Page:** 2. **Col. Width:** 38 nonpareils. **Col. Depth:** 133 agate lines. **Key Personnel:** Karen L. Roos, MD, Editor-in-Chief; David M. Greer, Editor-in-Chief. **ISSN:** 0271--8235 (print). **Subscription Rates:** $239 Individuals print and online; $1241 Institutions print and online; $135 Individuals resident rate. **URL:** http://www.thieme.com/books-main/neurology/product/2163-seminars-in-neurology. **Ad Rates:** BW $1455; 4C $1480. **Remarks:** Accepts advertising. **Circ:** Paid ‡2675.

5984 ■ Southern
Southern Connecticut State University Alumni Association
501 Crescent St.
New Haven, CT 06515
Phone: (203)392-6500
Publisher's E-mail: alumniinfo@southernct.edu
Freq: Semiannual. **URL:** http://www.southernct.edu/alumni/southern-magazine.html. **Remarks:** Advertising not accepted. **Circ:** (Not Reported).

5985 ■ Theater
Duke University Press
PO Box 208244
New Haven, CT 06520-8244
Phone: (203)432-1568
Fax: (203)432-8336
Publication E-mail: theater.magazine@yale.edu
Scholarly journal covering modern plays and theater. **Freq:** 3/year. **Trim Size:** 4 7/8 x 7 3/4. **Key Personnel:** Una Chaudhuri, Editor; Tom Sellar, Editor. **ISSN:** 0161--0775 (print); **EISSN:** 1527--196X (electronic). **Subscription Rates:** $30 Individuals; $20 Students copy of a valid student ID is required; $15 Individuals online only. **URL:** http://www.dukeupress.edu/Catalog/ViewProduct.php?productid=45632. **Ad Rates:** BW $350. **Remarks:** Accepts advertising. **Circ:** Combined 912.

5986 ■ Yale Alumni Magazine: The Oldest Independent Alumni Magazine in America
Yale Alumni Publications Inc.
PO Box 1905
New Haven, CT 06509-1905
Phone: (202)432-0645
Publication E-mail: yam@yale.edu
Magazine focusing on the achievements, issues, and problems of the university. **Freq:** Bimonthly. **Trim Size:** 8.375 x 10.875. **Key Personnel:** Kathrin Day Lassila, Editor; Theresa Holder, Business Manager; Mark Alden Branch, Executive Editor. **Subscription Rates:** $27.50 Individuals; $40 Other countries; $15.50 Students. **URL:** http://www.yalealumnimagazine.com. **Ad Rates:** BW $7415; 4C $11125. **Remarks:** Accepts classified advertising. **Circ:** △**136000**.

5987 ■ The Yale-China Health Journal
Yale-China Association
442 Temple St.
New Haven, CT 06520
Phone: (203)432-0884
Fax: (203)432-7246
Publisher's E-mail: yale-china@yale.edu
Journal focusing on internal migration and health in China. **Freq:** Annual. **Alt. Formats:** PDF. **URL:** http://www.yalechina.org/about/publications. **Mailing address:** PO Box 208223, New Haven, CT 06520. **Remarks:** Advertising not accepted. **Circ:** (Not Reported).

5988 ■ Yale Daily News
Yale Daily News Publishing Company Inc.
PO Box 209007
New Haven, CT 06520-9007
Phone: (203)432-2424
Fax: (203)432-7425
Publication E-mail: business@yaledailynews.com
Collegiate newspaper. **Freq:** Daily (morn.). **Print Method:** Offset. **Trim Size:** 13 x 21. **Cols./Page:** 6. **Col. Width:** 1.9 inches. **Col. Depth:** 21 inches. **Key Personnel:** Kyle Miller, Publisher; Abdullah Hanif, Publisher. **USPS:** 695-060. **Subscription Rates:** $20 Individuals. **URL:** http://yaledailynews.com. **Ad Rates:** BW $2,520; 4C $1,200; PCI $23.50. **Remarks:** Accepts advertising. **Circ:** Paid 1500.

5989 ■ The Yale Herald: An Undergraduate Publication
The Yale Herald
252 Park St.
New Haven, CT 06511
Phone: (203)432-7494
Collegiate newspaper. **Freq:** Weekly. **Trim Size:** 11.5 x 17. **Cols./Page:** 4. **Col. Width:** 2.5 INS. **Col. Depth:** 16 INS. **Key Personnel:** Tom Cusano, Editor-in-Chief; Rachel Strodel, Editor-in-Chief; Elizabeth Chrystal, Publisher. **Subscription Rates:** $45 Individuals. **URL:** http://yaleherald.com. **Ad Rates:** BW $625; 4C $900; PCI $4.37. **Remarks:** Advertising accepted; rates available upon request. **Circ:** (Not Reported).

5990 ■ Yale Human Rights and Development Law Journal
Yale University School of Law
127 Wall St.
New Haven, CT 06511
Phone: (203)432-4056
Publisher's E-mail: lawnfem@gmail.com
Journal covering writings that draw upon various academic disciplines, such as political science, public policy, economics, health and sociology. **Freq:** Annual. **Key Personnel:** Elizabeth Compa, Editor-in-Chief. **ISSN:** 1548--2596 (print). **URL:** http://www.law.yale.edu/academics/YHRDLJ.htm. **Mailing address:** PO Box 208215, New Haven, CT 06520-8215. **Circ:** (Not Reported).

5991 ■ The Yale Journal of Biology & Medicine
The Yale Journal of Biology and Medicine Inc.
300 George St., Ste. 773
New Haven, CT 06511
Phone: (203)737-2204
Fax: (203)737-2638
Publication E-mail: yjbm@yale.edu
Journal carrying original contributions, medical reviews, case reports, medical histories, biomedical symposia. **Freq:** Quarterly. **Key Personnel:** Michaela Panter, Editor-in-Chief; Alice Qinhua Zhou, Editor-in-Chief. **ISSN:** 0044-0086 (print). **Subscription Rates:** $150 Institutions electronic and print or print only; $120 Institutions online only; $155 Institutions, other countries electronic and print or print only; $50 Individuals online only; $75 Individuals electronic and print; $80 Other countries electronic and print. **URL:** http://www.med.yale.edu/yjbm. **Ad Rates:** BW $350. **Remarks:** Accepts advertising. **Circ:** ‡600.

5992 ■ Yale Journal of Health Policy, Law, and Ethics
Yale University
PO Box 208215
New Haven, CT 06520-8215
Phone: (203)436-0774
Publication E-mail: yjhple@yale.edu
Peer-reviewed journal covering legal and ethical issues as they relate to health and healthcare policy. **Freq:** Semiannual. **Key Personnel:** Maxwell Gregg Bloche, MD, Advisor, Board Member; Troyen A. Brennan, MD, Advisor, Board Member, phone: (917)732-8961; Scott Burris, Advisor, Board Member; Ruth R. Faden, PhD, Advisor, Board Member; Lori B. Andrews, Advisor, Board Member; George J. Annas, Advisor, Board Member; John D. Arras, PhD, Advisor, Board Member; James F. Childress, PhD, Advisor, Board Member; Prof. Robert A. Burt, Advisor, Board Member. **ISSN:** 1535--3532 (print). **Subscription Rates:** $29 Individuals; $39 Institutions; $18 Single issue back issue. **URL:** http://www.law.yale.edu/student-life/student-journals-and-publications/yjhple. **Remarks:** Accepts advertising. **Circ:** (Not Reported).

5993 ■ Yale Journal of International Law
Yale University School of Law
127 Wall St.
New Haven, CT 06511
Phone: (203)432-4056
Publisher's E-mail: lawnfem@gmail.com
Journal containing articles, essays, notes, and commentary on a wide range of subjects in the fields of international, transnational and comparative law. **Freq:** Semiannual. **Key Personnel:** Allison Day, Editor-in-Chief. **URL:** http://www.yjil.org. **Mailing address:** PO Box 208215, New Haven, CT 06520-8215. **Circ:** (Not Reported).

5994 ■ Yale Journal of Law and Feminism
Yale University School of Law
127 Wall St.
New Haven, CT 06511
Phone: (203)432-4056
Publisher's E-mail: lawnfem@gmail.com
Journal serving as a forum for the analysis of women's experience as affected by the law. **Freq:** Semiannual. **Key Personnel:** McKaye Neumeister, Editor-in-Chief; Janine Balekdjian, Managing Editor; Olivia Horton, Managing Editor; Michelle Cho, Editor. **ISSN:** 1043--9366 (print). **Subscription Rates:** $20 Individuals; $30 Institutions; $10 Single issue back issue; individual; $16 Single issue back issue; institution. **URL:** http://www.law.yale.edu/student-life/student-journals-and-publications/yale-journal-law-feminism. **Mailing address:** PO Box 208215, New Haven, CT 06520-8215. **Remarks:** Accepts advertising. **Circ:** (Not Reported).

5995 ■ Yale Journal of Law and the Humanities
Yale University School of Law
127 Wall St.
New Haven, CT 06511
Phone: (203)432-4056
Publisher's E-mail: lawnfem@gmail.com
Journal featuring articles on the intersections among law, the humanities, and the humanistic social sciences. **Freq:** Semiannual. **Subscription Rates:** $18 Individuals two issues; $10 Individuals back issues; $34 Institutions two issues; $18 Institutions back issues. **URL:** http://www.law.yale.edu/student-life/student-journals-and-publications/yale-journal-law-humanities. **Mailing address:** PO Box 208215, New Haven, CT 06520-8215. **Circ:** (Not Reported).

5996 ■ Yale Journal of Law and Technology
Yale University School of Law
127 Wall St.
New Haven, CT 06511
Phone: (203)432-4056
Publisher's E-mail: lawnfem@gmail.com
Journal containing articles on a very wide range of topics related to the intersection of law and technology. **Freq:** Semiannual. **Key Personnel:** Adam Adler, Editor-in-Chief. **URL:** http://yjolt.org. **Mailing address:** PO Box 208215, New Haven, CT 06520-8215. **Circ:** (Not Reported).

5997 ■ Yale Journal on Regulation
Yale University School of Law
127 Wall St.
New Haven, CT 06511
Phone: (203)432-4056
Publisher's E-mail: lawnfem@gmail.com
Journal covering different disciplines including law, business, economics and public policy. **Freq:** Semiannual. **Key Personnel:** Jaclyn Harris, Editor-in-Chief. **URL:** http://www.yalejreg.com. **Mailing address:** PO Box 208215, New Haven, CT 06520-8215. **Circ:** (Not Reported).

5998 ■ The Yale Law Journal
Yale Law Journal Co.
127 Wall St.
New Haven, CT 06520-8215
Phone: (203)432-1666
Publication E-mail: ylj@yalelawjournal.org
Professional law journal. **Founded:** 1891. **Freq:** 8/yr. **Print Method:** Letterpress. **Cols./Page:** 1. **Col. Width:** 57 nonpareils. **Col. Depth:** 105 agate lines. **Key Personnel:** Rachel Bayefsky, Editor-in-Chief. **Subscription Rates:** $55 Individuals; $87 Other countries Canada; $103 Other countries Asia; $79 Individuals Mexico. **URL:** http://www.yalelawjournal.org. **Ad Rates:** BW $175. **Remarks:** Accepts advertising. **Circ:** ‡4300.

5999 ■ The Yale Literary Magazine: An Undergraduate Publication
The Yale Literary Magazine
Woodbridge Hall
105 Wall St.
New Haven, CT 06511
Phone: (203)432-6602
Fax: (203)432-7307
Publisher's E-mail: secretary.office@yale.edu
Literary magazine. **Freq:** Semiannual. **Print Method:** Letterpress and offset. **Cols./Page:** 1. **Col. Width:** 60 nonpareils. **Col. Depth:** 112 agate lines. **Key Personnel:** Jake Orbison, Editor-in-Chief. **ISSN:** 0148--4605

Circulation: ★ = AAM; △ or • = BPA; ♦ = CAC; ❑ = VAC; ⊕ = PO Statement; ‡ = Publisher's Report; Boldface figures = sworn; Light figures = estimated.

(print). **Subscription Rates:** $15 Individuals; $35 Institutions; $30 Two years; $350 lifetime. **URL:** http://www.yale.edu/ylit. **Mailing address:** PO Box 208230, New Haven, CT 06520. **Remarks:** Advertising not accepted. **Circ:** Paid 130, Non-paid 2500.

6000 ■ Yale Scientific Magazine
Yale Scientific Publications Inc.
PO Box 204628
New Haven, CT 06520
Publisher's E-mail: ysm@yale.edu
Magazine on science and technology research at Yale. **Freq:** Quarterly. **Print Method:** Offset. **Trim Size:** 8 1/2 x 11 1/2. **Cols./Page:** 3. **Col. Width:** 2 1/4 inches. **Col. Depth:** 8 7/8 inches. **Key Personnel:** Rebecca Su, Editor-in-Chief. **ISSN:** 0091--0287 (print). **Subscription Rates:** $20 Individuals; $35 Two years. **URL:** http://www.yalescientific.org. **Remarks:** Accepts advertising. **Circ:** Paid ‡1900, Non-paid ‡3000.

6001 ■ WADS-AM - 690
PO Box 384
New Haven, CT 06513
Phone: (203)735-4606
Format: Adult Contemporary; Talk; Sports. **Networks:** Independent. **Founded:** 1956. **Operating Hours**: 5:30 a.m.-midnight. **Wattage:** 1,000.

6002 ■ WTNH-TV - 8
Eight Elm St.
New Haven, CT 06510
Phone: (203)784-8888
Fax: (203)789-2010
Format: Commercial TV. **Networks:** ABC. **Owner:** LIN TV Corp., One W Exchange St., Ste. 5A, Providence, RI 02903-1064, Ph: (401)454-2880, Fax: (401)454-6990. **Operating Hours**: Continuous. **ADI**: Hartford-New Haven (New London), CT. **Key Personnel:** Mark Higgins, Gen. Mgr., VP; Roger Megroz, Sales Mgr.; Paul Spingola, Dir. of Mktg., paul.spingola@wtnh.com. **Ad Rates:** Advertising accepted; rates available upon request. **URL:** http://www.wtnh.com.

6003 ■ WYBC-AM - 1340
142 Temple St., Ste. 203
New Haven, CT 06510
Phone: (203)776-4118
Email: info@wybc.com
Format: Educational. **Owner:** Yale Broadcasting Company Inc., 142 Temple St., Ste. 203, New Haven, CT 06510, Ph: (203)776-4118, Fax: (203)643-2079. **Key Personnel:** Sean Owczarek, Gen. Mgr.; Jesse Bradford, Dir. of Programs. **URL:** http://www.wybc.com.

6004 ■ WYBC-FM - 94.3
142 Temple St., Ste. 203
New Haven, CT 06510
Phone: (203)783-8200
Fax: (203)783-8383
Format: Urban Contemporary; Oldies; Blues. **Networks:** Satellite Music Network. **Owner:** Cox Radio Inc., 6205 Peachtree Dunwood Rd., Atlanta, GA 30328-4524, Ph: (678)645-0000, Fax: (678)645-5002. **Founded:** 1941. **Operating Hours**: Continuous. **Key Personnel:** Wayne Schmidt, Operations Mgr. **Wattage:** 3,000. **Ad Rates:** Advertising accepted; rates available upon request. **URL:** http://www.943wybc.com.

NEW LONDON

SE CT. New London Co. On Long Island Sound at mouth of Thames River, 14 mi. S. of Norwich. Port of entry with deep harbor. Naval Coast Guard Service Center. Connecticut College; Univ. of Conn. U. S. Coast Guard Academy. Private schools. Manufactures toothpaste and tube containers, printing presses, diesel, marine and turbine engines, submarines, chemicals, floor covering, bed springs, mattresses, textiles, gear cutters, corrugated paper containers, paper products, thread, soap, wooden cabinets, safety razors. Shipyards.

6005 ■ Catholic Digest: Faith and Family Living
Bayard Inc.
1 Montauk Ave., Ste. 200
New London, CT 06320
Phone: (860)437-3012
Fax: (800)572-0788
Free: 800-321-0411
General interest magazine for Catholics. **Freq:** Monthly. **Print Method:** Offset. **Trim Size:** 5 1/4 x 7 3/8. **Cols./Page:** 2. **Col. Width:** 13 picas. **Col. Depth:** 95 agate lines. **Key Personnel:** Valerie Westrate, Manager, Circulation; Danielle Bean, Editor-in-Chief; Sue Lachapelle, Account Executive; Bret D. Thomas, Chief Executive Officer, President; Paul Bourque, Director, Production. **ISSN:** 0008-7998 (print). **Subscription Rates:** $21.99 Individuals; $41.99 Two years; $59.99 Individuals 3 years. **URL:** http://www.catholicdigest.com; http://www.bayard-inc.com/links.php. **Ad Rates:** BW $12164. **Remarks:** Accepts advertising. **Circ:** Paid **★200,000**.

6006 ■ The College Voice
Connecticut College
270 Mohegan Ave.
New London, CT 06320
Phone: (860)447-1911
Publisher's E-mail: info@conncoll.edu
Collegiate newspaper. **Founded:** 1976. **Freq:** Weekly. **Print Method:** Offset. **Trim Size:** 13 x 20. **Cols./Page:** 6. **Col. Width:** 2.01 inches. **Col. Depth:** 238 agate lines. **Key Personnel:** Ayla Zuraw-Friedland, Editor-in-Chief. **Subscription Rates:** $50 Individuals. **URL:** http://thecollegevoice.org. **Ad Rates:** GLR $260. **Remarks:** Accepts advertising. **Circ:** Paid 2000.

6007 ■ The Connecticut College Journal
Connecticut College
270 Mohegan Ave.
New London, CT 06320
Phone: (860)447-1911
Publisher's E-mail: info@conncoll.edu
College newspaper. **Freq:** 3/year. **Subscription Rates:** Free all alumni, parents & friends of the College. **URL:** http://www.conncoll.edu/news/cc-magazine/#.VehPiyWqqko. **Remarks:** Advertising accepted; rates available upon request. **Circ:** (Not Reported).

6008 ■ Creative Catechist
Twenty-Third Publications
One Montauk Ave., Ste. 200
New London, CT 06320
Phone: (860)437-3012
Free: 800-321-0411
Publisher's E-mail: resources@pastoralplanning.com
Trade magazine used as a training vehicle by pastors for laypersons working with them as church educators. **Freq:** 7/year. **Print Method:** Offset. Uses mats. **Trim Size:** 8 1/4 x 11. **Cols./Page:** 3. **Col. Width:** 27 nonpareils. **Col. Depth:** 140 agate lines. **Key Personnel:** Robyn Lee, Editor. **ISSN:** 0034--401X (print). **Subscription Rates:** $24.95 Individuals 1 subscription; $20.95 Individuals 2-10 subscriptions; $17.95 Individuals 11-20 subscriptions. **URL:** http://www.rtjscreativecatechist.com. **Formerly**: Religion Teacher's Journal: The Magazine for Catechist Formation. **Ad Rates:** BW $2,155; 4C $3,265. **Remarks:** Accepts advertising. **Circ:** 24000.

6009 ■ The Day
Day Publishing Co.
47 Eugene O'Neill Dr.
New London, CT 06320-1231
Phone: (860)442-2200
Free: 800-542-3354
General newspaper. **Freq:** Mon.-Sun. (morn.). **Print Method:** Offset. **Trim Size:** 13 x 21. **Cols./Page:** 6. **Col. Width:** 2 1/16 inches. **Col. Depth:** 21 inches. **Key Personnel:** Timothy Dwyer, Executive Editor; Tim Cotter, Managing Editor. **Subscription Rates:** Included in membership. **URL:** http://www.theday.com. **Mailing address:** PO Box 1231, New London, CT 06320-1231. **Ad Rates:** GLR $.91; BW $3,507.84; 4C $4,157.84; PCI $15.70. **Remarks:** Accepts advertising. **Circ:** Mon.-Fri. **★28137**, Sun. **★29269**.

6010 ■ Jewish Leader
Jewish Federation of Eastern Connecticut
28 Channing St.
New London, CT 06320-5756
Phone: (860)442-8062
Fax: (860)443-4175
Magazine serving the Jewish community. **Freq:** Biweekly. **Print Method:** Offset. **Trim Size:** 10 x 16. **Cols./Page:** 5. **Col. Width:** 1 7/8 inches. **Col. Depth:** 196 agate lines. **Key Personnel:** Mimi Perl, Managing Editor. **Subscription Rates:** $15 Individuals. **URL:** http://sites.google.com/site/jfecsite/home/services. **Ad Rates:** GLR $.178; PCI $10. **Remarks:** Accepts advertising. **Circ:** 1600.

6011 ■ Today's Parish
Twenty-Third Publications
One Montauk Ave., Ste. 200
New London, CT 06320
Phone: (860)437-3012
Free: 800-321-0411
Publication E-mail: ttpubs@aol.com
Magazine which gives practical assistance in parish affairs for clergy, staff and lay workers in liturgy, music, education, computers, finance, administration and ministry in Catholic churches. **Freq:** 7/year. **Print Method:** Offset. **Trim Size:** 8 1/2 x 11. **Cols./Page:** 3. **Col. Width:** 26 nonpareils. **Col. Depth:** 140 agate lines. **Key Personnel:** Nick Wagner, Editor; Michelle kopfmann, Director, Advertising. **ISSN:** 0040--8459 (print). **Subscription Rates:** $24.95 Individuals. **URL:** http://www.todaysparish.com. **Ad Rates:** BW $1,265; 4C $1,595. **Remarks:** Advertising accepted; rates available upon request. **Circ:** Combined ‡32000.

6012 ■ WAXK-FM - 102.3
7 Governor Winthrop Blvd.
New London, CT 06320
Phone: (860)443-1980
Fax: (860)444-7970
Format: Alternative/New Music/Progressive. **Owner:** Citadel Broadcasting Corp., 7201 W Lake Mead Blvd., Ste. 400, Las Vegas, NV 89128-8366, Ph: (702)804-5200, Fax: (702)804-8250. **Wattage:** 3,000.

6013 ■ WCNI-FM
270 Mohegan Ave.
270 Mohegan Ave.
New London, CT 06320-4196
Phone: (860)439-2853
Fax: (860)439-2850
Format: Eclectic. **Founded:** 1974. **Ad Rates:** Noncommercial.

6014 ■ WKNL-FM - 100.9
89 Broad St.
New London, CT 06320
Phone: (860)447-8433
Format: Oldies. **ADI**: Hartford-New Haven (New London), CT. **Wattage**: 6,000. **Ad Rates:** Advertising accepted; rates available upon request.

6015 ■ WMOS-FM - 102.3
Seven Governor Winthrop Blvd.
New London, CT 06320
Phone: (860)443-1980
Fax: (860)444-7970
Free: 866-441-9653
Format: Classic Rock. **Owner:** Citadel Broadcasting Corp., 7201 W Lake Mead Blvd., Ste. 400, Las Vegas, NV 89128-8366, Ph: (702)804-5200, Fax: (702)804-8250. **Key Personnel:** Mark Stachowski, Dir. of Mktg., Mktg. Mgr., mark.stachowski@citcomm.com. **Ad Rates:** Noncommercial. **URL:** http://www.1023thewolf.com.

6016 ■ WPXQ-TV - 69
Three Shaws Cove, Ste. 226
New London, CT 06320
Phone: (860)775-6290
Fax: (860)440-2601
Email: deborahreed-iler@ionmedia.com
Ad Rates: Noncommercial. **URL:** http://www.ionmedianetworks.com.

6017 ■ WQGN-FM - 105.5
7 Governor Winthrop Blvd.
New London, CT 06320
Phone: (860)443-1055
Fax: (860)444-7970
Format: Top 40. **Networks:** ABC; Westwood One Radio. **Owner:** Citadel Broadcasting Corp., 7201 W Lake Mead Blvd., Ste. 400, Las Vegas, NV 89128-8366, Ph: (702)804-5200, Fax: (702)804-8250. **Founded:** 1971. **Formerly**: Q105. **Operating Hours**: Continuous. **Key Personnel:** Mark Stachowski, Contact, mark.stachowski@citcomm.com; Mark Stachowski, Contact, mark.stachowski@citcomm.com. **Wattage**: 3,000. **Ad Rates:** Advertising accepted; rates available upon request. **URL:** http://www.q105.fm.

6018 ■ WSUB-AM - 980
7 Governor Winthrop Blvd.
New London, CT 06320
Phone: (860)443-1980
Fax: (860)444-7970

Format: Hispanic. **Networks:** ABC; Talknet. **Owner:** Citadel Broadcasting Corp., 7201 W Lake Mead Blvd., Ste. 400, Las Vegas, NV 89128-8366, Ph: (702)804-5200, Fax: (702)804-8250. **Founded:** 1958. **Operating Hours**: Continuous. **Key Personnel:** Mark Stachowski, Contact, mark.stachowski@citcomm.com; Mark Stachowski, Contact, mark.stachowski@citcomm.com. **Wattage**: 1,000. **Ad Rates:** Noncommercial.

NEW MILFORD

NW CT. Litchfield Co. 16 mi. N. of Danbury. Manufactures disposable paper products, copper tubing, electronics equipment. Foundry. Summer resort. Dairy, poultry farms.

6019 ■ Anthropological Journal of European Cultures
Berghahn Journals
c/o Turpin North America
143 West St.
New Milford, CT 06776
Phone: (860)350-0041
Fax: (860)350-0039
Publisher's E-mail: berghahnjournalsus@turpin-distribution.com
Peer-reviewed journal featuring social and cultural transformations of contemporary European societies. **Freq:** Semiannual. **Key Personnel:** Ullrich Kockel, Editor; George Marcus, Board Member; Sharon Macdonald, Board Member. **ISSN:** 1755--2923 (print); **EISSN:** 1755--2931 (electronic). **Subscription Rates:** $211 Institutions print & online; £130 Institutions print & online; €162 Institutions print & online; $190 Institutions online only; £117 Institutions online only; €146 Institutions online only; $34.95 Individuals online only; £21.95 Individuals online only; €24.95 Individuals online only; $19.95 Students online only; £12.95 Students online only; €14.95 Students online only. **URL:** http://journals.berghahnbooks.com/ajec/index.php. **Remarks:** Accepts advertising. **Circ:** (Not Reported).

6020 ■ Anthropology in Action: Journal for Applied Anthropology in Policy and Practice
Berghahn Journals
c/o Turpin North America
143 West St.
New Milford, CT 06776
Phone: (860)350-0041
Fax: (860)350-0039
Publisher's E-mail: berghahnjournalsus@turpin-distribution.com
Peer-reviewed journal featuring the use of anthropology in all areas of policy and practice. **Freq:** 3/year. **Key Personnel:** Christine McCourt, Editor; Robert Simpson, Board Member. **ISSN:** 0967--201X (print); **EISSN:** 1752--2285 (electronic). **Subscription Rates:** $198 Institutions print & online; $60 Individuals print & online; $25 Students print & online; £118 Institutions print & online; £35 Individuals print & online; £15 Students print & online; €146 Institutions print & online; €42 Individuals print & online; €20 Students print & online; $169 Institutions online only. **URL:** http://journals.berghahnbooks.com/aia. **Remarks:** Accepts advertising. **Circ:** (Not Reported).

6021 ■ Anthropology of the Middle East
Berghahn Journals
c/o Turpin North America
143 West St.
New Milford, CT 06776
Phone: (860)350-0041
Fax: (860)350-0039
Publisher's E-mail: berghahnjournalsus@turpin-distribution.com
Peer-reviewed journal featuring anthropology in Middle East. **Freq:** Semiannual. **Key Personnel:** Soheila Shahshahani, Editor-in-Chief; Birgit Reinel, Managing Editor; Kamyar Abdi, Advisor. **ISSN:** 1746--0719 (print); **EISSN:** 1746--0727 (electronic). **Subscription Rates:** $252 Institutions print & online; £156 Institutions print & online; €191 Institutions print & online; $59 Individuals print only; £36 Individuals print only; €45 Individuals print only; $19.95 Students online only; £12.95 Students online only; €14.95 Students online only. **URL:** http://journals.berghahnbooks.com/ame. **Remarks:** Accepts advertising. **Circ:** (Not Reported).

6022 ■ Asia Pacific World
Berghahn Journals
c/o Turpin North America
143 West St.
New Milford, CT 06776
Phone: (860)350-0041
Fax: (860)350-0039
Publisher's E-mail: berghahnjournalsus@turpin-distribution.com
Peer-reviewed journal publishing information on social, political, cultural and economic development of the Asia Pacific region. **Freq:** Semiannual. **Key Personnel:** Malcolm J.M. Cooper, Editor-in-Chief. **ISSN:** 2042--6143 (print); **EISSN:** 2042--6151 (electronic). **Subscription Rates:** $212 Institutions print + online; £131 Institutions print + online; €151 Institutions print and online; $191 Institutions online only; £118 Institutions online only; €136 Institutions online only; $80 Individuals print and online; £49 Individuals print and online; €56 Individuals print and online; $35 Students online only; £21 Students online only; €24 Students online only. **Circ:** (Not Reported).

6023 ■ Critical Survey
Berghahn Journals
c/o Turpin North America
143 West St.
New Milford, CT 06776
Phone: (860)350-0041
Fax: (860)350-0039
Publisher's E-mail: webenquiry.uk@oup.com
Publication covering literature and ethnic, cultural and racial issues and studies. **Freq:** 3/year Spring, Summer and Winter. **Key Personnel:** Roger Ebbatson, Board Member, Editor; Graham Holderness, PhD, Editor; Catherine Belsey, Board Member; Richard H. King, Board Member; Peter Brooker, Board Member; Daniel Cordle, Board Member; Bryan Loughrey, Editor; Graham Holderness, Editor; Andrew Maunder, Editor. **ISSN:** 0011-1570 (print); **EISSN:** 1752-2293 (electronic). **Subscription Rates:** $221 Institutions print and online; £137 Institutions print and online; €164 Institutions print and online; $199 Institutions online only; £123 Institutions online only; €148 Institutions online only; $56 Individuals print only; £35 Individuals print only; €42 Individuals print only; $25 Students print only; £16 Students print only; €20 Students print only; $50 Individuals online. **URL:** http://journals.berghahnbooks.com/cs/; http://journals.berghahnbooks.com/cs/index.php. **Ad Rates:** BW $290, full page; BW £180, full page; BW $190, half page; BW £120, half page. **Remarks:** Accepts advertising. **Circ:** (Not Reported).

6024 ■ Durkheimian Studies
Berghahn Journals
c/o Turpin North America
143 West St.
New Milford, CT 06776
Phone: (860)350-0041
Fax: (860)350-0039
Publisher's E-mail: berghahnjournalsus@turpin-distribution.com
Journal featuring matters relating to Durkheim and his circle. **Freq:** Annual. **Key Personnel:** W. Watts Miller, Editor; K. Thompson, Board Member. **ISSN:** 1362--024X (print); **EISSN:** 1752--2307 (electronic). **Subscription Rates:** $68 Institutions print & online; £42 Institutions print & online; €52 Institutions print & online; $35 Individuals print only; £22 Individuals print only; €26 Individuals print only; $61 Institutions online only; £38 Institutions online only; €47 Institutions online only; $19.95 Students online only; £12.95 Students online only; €14.95 Students online only. **URL:** http://journals.berghahnbooks.com/ds. **Remarks:** Accepts advertising. **Circ:** (Not Reported).

6025 ■ Environment and Society: Advances in Research
Berghahn Journals
c/o Turpin North America
143 West St.
New Milford, CT 06776
Phone: (860)350-0041
Fax: (860)350-0039
Publisher's E-mail: berghahnjournalsus@turpin-distribution.com
Peer-reviewed journal covering research on environment and society. **Freq:** Annual. **Key Personnel:** Paige West, Editor; Dan Brockington, Editor. **ISSN:** 2150--6779 (print); **EISSN:** 2150--6787 (electronic). **Subscription Rates:** $179 Institutions print and online; $161 Institutions online only; $34.95 Individuals online only; $19.95 Students online only; £11 Institutions print and online; £100 Institutions online only; £21.95 Individuals online only; £12.95 Students online only; €135 Institutions print and online; €122 Institutions online only; €24.95 Individuals online only; €14.95 Students online only. **URL:** http://www.journals.berghahnbooks.com/environment-and-society; http://journals.berghahnbooks.com/environment-and-society. **Circ:** (Not Reported).

6026 ■ European Judaism: A Journal for the New Europe
Berghahn Journals
c/o Turpin North America
143 West St.
New Milford, CT 06776
Phone: (860)350-0041
Fax: (860)350-0039
Publication E-mail: european.judaism@lbc.ac.uk
Publication covering Judaism and religion in Europe. **Freq:** Semiannual Spring and Autumn. **Key Personnel:** Jonathan Magonet, Editor; Marion Berghahn, Board Member; Jenny Pizer, Managing Editor. **ISSN:** 0014--3006 (print); **EISSN:** 1752--2323 (electronic). **Subscription Rates:** $214 Institutions print & online; £133 Institutions print & online; €161 Institutions print & online; $193 Institutions online only; £120 Institutions online only; €145 Institutions online only; $34.95 Individuals online only; £21.95 Individuals online only; €24.95 Individuals online only; $19.95 Students online only; £12.95 Students online only; €14.95 Students online only. **URL:** http://journals.berghahnbooks.com/european-judaism/. **Ad Rates:** BW $190, full page; BW £120, full page; BW $120, half page; BW £175, half page. **Remarks:** Accepts advertising. **Circ:** (Not Reported).

6027 ■ German Politics and Society
Berghahn Journals
c/o Turpin North America
143 West St.
New Milford, CT 06776
Phone: (860)350-0041
Fax: (860)350-0039
Publication E-mail: gpsjournal@georgetown.edu
Peer-reviewed journal covering social and political issues in Germany. **Freq:** Quarterly Spring, Summer, Autumn, Winter. **Key Personnel:** Jeffrey J. Anderson, Editor; Eric Langenbacher, Managing Editor. **ISSN:** 1045--0300 (print); **EISSN:** 1558--5441 (electronic). **Subscription Rates:** $275 Institutions print & online; £171 Institutions print & online; €208 Institutions print & online; $248 Institutions online only; £154 Institutions online only; €188 Institutions online only; $34.95 Individuals online only; £21.95 Individuals online only; €24.95 Individuals online only; $19.95 Students online only; £12.95 Students online only; €14.95 Students online only. **URL:** http://journals.berghahnbooks.com/gps. **Remarks:** Advertising accepted; rates available upon request. **Circ:** (Not Reported).

6028 ■ International Journal of Social Quality
Berghahn Journals
c/o Turpin North America
143 West St.
New Milford, CT 06776
Phone: (860)350-0041
Fax: (860)350-0039
Publisher's E-mail: berghahnjournalsus@turpin-distribution.com
Journal covering issues in social science. **Freq:** Semiannual Summer and Winter. **Key Personnel:** Ka Lin, Editor; Prof. Ota De Leonardis, Advisor; Dr. Laurent Van Der Maesen, Board Member; Prof. Dave Gordon, Advisor. **ISSN:** 1757--0344 (print); **EISSN:** 1757--0352 (electronic). **Subscription Rates:** $216 Institutions print & online; £135 Institutions print & online; €168 Institutions print & online; $194 Institutions online only; £121 Institutions online only; €151 Institutions online only; $34.95 Individuals online only; £21.95 Individuals online only; €24.95 Individuals online only; $19.95 Students online only; £12.95 Students online only; €14.95 Students online only. **URL:** http://journals.berghahnbooks.com/ijsq. **Formerly**: European Journal of Social Quality. **Ad Rates:** BW $300, full page; BW

Circulation: ★ = AAM; △ or • = BPA; ♦ = CAC; ❑ = VAC; ⊕ = PO Statement; ‡ = Publisher's Report; Boldface figures = sworn; Light figures = estimated.

£160, full page; BW $200, half page; BW £100, half page. **Remarks:** Accepts advertising. **Circ:** (Not Reported).

6029 ■ Israel Studies Review: An Interdisciplinary Journal
Berghahn Journals
c/o Turpin North America
143 West St.
New Milford, CT 06776
Phone: (860)350-0041
Fax: (860)350-0039
Publisher's E-mail: berghahnjournalsus@turpin-distribution.com
Peer-reviewed journal featuring modern and contemporary Israel from the perspective of the social sciences, history, the humanities, and cultural studies. **Freq:** Semiannual. **Key Personnel:** Yoram Peri, Editor. **ISSN:** 2159--0370 (print); **EISSN:** 2159--0389 (electronic). **Subscription Rates:** $215 Institutions print & online; £134 Institutions print & online; €160 Institutions print & online; $194 Institutions online only; £120 Institutions online only; €144 Institutions online only. **URL:** http://journals.berghahnbooks.com/isr. **Formerly:** Israel Studies Forum. **Remarks:** Accepts advertising. **Circ:** (Not Reported).

6030 ■ Journal of Romance Studies
Berghahn Journals
c/o Turpin North America
143 West St.
New Milford, CT 06776
Phone: (860)350-0041
Fax: (860)350-0039
Publisher's E-mail: berghahnjournalsus@turpin-distribution.com
Journal featuring literature about romance. **Freq:** 3/year. **Key Personnel:** Bill Marshall, Managing Editor; Ruth Ben-Ghiat, Advisor. **ISSN:** 1473--3536 (print); **EISSN:** 1752--2331 (electronic). **Subscription Rates:** $234 Institutions print & online; £143 Institutions print & online; €179 Institutions print & online; $70 Individuals print only; £43 Individuals print only; €52 Individuals print only; $19.95 Students online only; £12.95 Students online only; €14.95 Students online only; $211 Institutions online only; £129 Institutions online only; €161 Institutions online only. **URL:** http://journals.berghahnbooks.com/jrs. **Remarks:** Accepts advertising. **Circ:** (Not Reported).

6031 ■ Nature and Culture
Berghahn Journals
c/o Turpin North America
143 West St.
New Milford, CT 06776
Phone: (860)350-0041
Fax: (860)350-0039
Publication E-mail: nature.culture@ufz.de
Peer-reviewed journal covering relationship between nature and culture. **Freq:** 3/year spring, summer, winter. **Key Personnel:** Jana Schoppe, Managing Editor; Sing C. Chew, Editor; Matthias Gross, Editor. **ISSN:** 1558--6073 (print); **EISSN:** 1558--5468 (electronic). **Subscription Rates:** $330 Institutions print & online; £190 Institutions print & online; €248 Institutions print & online; $297 Institutions online; £171 Institutions online; €223 Institutions online; $34.95 Individuals online; £21.95 Individuals online; €24.95 Individuals online; $19.95 Students online; £12.95 Students online; €14.95 Students online. **URL:** http://journals.berghahnbooks.com/nc. **Remarks:** Accepts advertising. **Circ:** (Not Reported).

6032 ■ Projections: The Journal for Movies and Mind
Berghahn Journals
c/o Turpin North America
143 West St.
New Milford, CT 06776
Phone: (860)350-0041
Fax: (860)350-0039
Publisher's E-mail: berghahnjournalsus@turpin-distribution.com
Peer-reviewed journal featuring the understanding of film. **Freq:** Semiannual. **Key Personnel:** Stephen Prince, Editor; Bruce Sklarew, Board Member; Richard Allen, Board Member. **ISSN:** 1934--9688 (print); **EISSN:** 1934--9696 (electronic). **Subscription Rates:** $219 Institutions print & online; £136 Institutions print & online; €164 Institutions print & online; $70 Individuals print only; £45 Individuals print only; €52 Individuals print only. **URL:** http://journals.berghahnbooks.com/proj. **Remarks:** Accepts advertising. **Circ:** (Not Reported).

6033 ■ Regions and Cohesion
Berghahn Journals
c/o Turpin North America
143 West St.
New Milford, CT 06776
Phone: (860)350-0041
Fax: (860)350-0039
Publisher's E-mail: berghahnjournalsus@turpin-distribution.com
Journal promoting comparative examination of human and environmental impacts of various aspects of regional integration across geographic areas, time periods, and policy arenas. **Freq:** 3/year spring, summer and winter. **Key Personnel:** Harlan Koff, Editor; Carmen Maganda, Editor. **ISSN:** 2152--906X (print); **EISSN:** 2152--9078 (electronic). **Subscription Rates:** $347 Institutions print + online; $314 Institutions online only; $34.95 Individuals online only; $19.95 Students online only; £215 Institutions print + online; £195 Institutions online only; £21.95 Individuals online only; £12.95 Students online only; €262 Institutions print + online; €236 Institutions online only; €24.95 Individuals online only; €14.95 Students online only. **URL:** http://www.journals.berghahnbooks.com/regions-and-cohesion; http://journals.berghahnbooks.com/regions-and-cohesion. **Circ:** (Not Reported).

6034 ■ Sartre Studies International: An Interdisciplinary Journal of Existentialism and Contemporary Culture
Berghahn Journals
c/o Turpin North America
143 West St.
New Milford, CT 06776
Phone: (860)350-0041
Fax: (860)350-0039
Publisher's E-mail: berghahnjournalsus@turpin-distribution.com
Publication covering philosophy and literature. **Freq:** Semiannual Spring and Winter. **Key Personnel:** David Drake, Board Member; Ronald Aronson, Editor; Bruce Baugh, Board Member. **ISSN:** 1357--1559 (print); **EISSN:** 1558--5476 (electronic). **Subscription Rates:** $198 Institutions print and online; £123 Institutions print and online; €150 Institutions print and online; $178 Institutions online only; £110 Institutions online only; €135 Institutions online only. **URL:** http://ournals.berghahnbooks.com/sartre-studies. **Remarks:** Accepts advertising. **Circ:** (Not Reported).

6035 ■ Sibirica: Interdisciplinary Journal of Siberian Studies
Berghahn Journals
c/o Turpin North America
143 West St.
New Milford, CT 06776
Phone: (860)350-0041
Fax: (860)350-0039
Publication E-mail: sibirica@abdn.ac.uk
Peer-reviewed journal featuring studies on Siberia. **Freq:** 3/year. **Key Personnel:** Alexander D. King, Managing Editor; David G. Anderson, Associate Editor; Mark Bassin, Board Member. **ISSN:** 1361--7362 (print); **EISSN:** 1476--6787 (electronic). **Subscription Rates:** $288 Institutions print & online; £175 Institutions print & online; €218 Institutions print & online; $58 Individuals print only; £35 Individuals print only; €44 Individuals print only. **URL:** http://journals.berghahnbooks.com/sib. **Remarks:** Accepts advertising. **Circ:** (Not Reported).

6036 ■ Social Analysis: The International Journal of Social and Cultural Practice
Berghahn Journals
c/o Turpin North America
143 West St.
New Milford, CT 06776
Phone: (860)350-0041
Fax: (860)350-0039
Publication E-mail: sa@uib.no
Peer-reviewed journal featuring critical and theoretical understanding of cultural, political, and social processes. **Freq:** Quarterly. **Key Personnel:** Bruce Kapferer, Editor-in-Chief; Bjorn Enge Bertelsen, Editor. **ISSN:** 0155--977X (print); **EISSN:** 1558--5727 (electronic). **Subscription Rates:** $362 Institutions print & online; £225 Institutions print & online; €275 Institutions print & online; $34.95 Individuals online only; £21.95 Individuals online only; €24.95 Individuals online only; $19.95 Students print only; £12.95 Students print only; €14.95 Students print only. **URL:** http://journals.berghahnbooks.com/sa. **Remarks:** Accepts advertising. **Circ:** (Not Reported).

6037 ■ Theoria: A Journal of Social and Political Theory
Berghahn Journals
c/o Turpin North America
143 West St.
New Milford, CT 06776
Phone: (860)350-0041
Fax: (860)350-0039
Publisher's E-mail: berghahnjournalsus@turpin-distribution.com
Peer-reviewed journal covering the humanities and political science. **Freq:** Quarterly March, June, September and December. **Key Personnel:** Barbara Adam, Consultant; Pal Ahluwalia, Consultant; Ronald Aronson, Consultant; Lawrence Hamilton, Editor-in-Chief; Peter Vale, Consultant; Lawrence Piper, Editor; Roger Deacon, Editor; Chris Allsobrook, Editor. **ISSN:** 0040--5817 (print); **EISSN:** 1558--5816 (electronic). **Subscription Rates:** $273 Institutions print and online; £160 Institutions print and online; €202 Individuals print and online; $245 Institutions online only; £144 Institutions online only; €182 Institutions online only; $34.95 Individuals online only; £21.95 Individuals online only; €24.95 Individuals online only; $19.95 Students online only; £12.95 Students online only; €41.95 Students online only. **URL:** http://www.berghahnjournals.com/view/journals/theoria/theoria-overview.xml; http://journals.berghahnbooks.com/theoria. **Remarks:** Accepts advertising. **Circ:** (Not Reported).

6038 ■ Transfers: Interdisciplinary Journal of Mobility Studies
Berghahn Journals
c/o Turpin North America
143 West St.
New Milford, CT 06776
Phone: (860)350-0041
Fax: (860)350-0039
Publisher's E-mail: berghahnjournalsus@turpin-distribution.com
Peer-reviewed journal publishing cutting-edge research on the processes, structures and consequences of the movement of people, resources and commodities. **Freq:** 3/year spring, summer and winter. **Key Personnel:** Gijs Mom, Editor-in-Chief. **ISSN:** 2045--4813 (print); **EISSN:** 2045--4821 (electronic). **Subscription Rates:** $218 Institutions print + online; $196 Institutions online only; $34.95 Individuals online only; $19.95 Students online only; £135 Institutions print + online; £121 Institutions online only; £21.95 Individuals online only; £12.95 Students online only; €165 Institutions print + online; €149 Institutions online only; €24.95 Individuals online only; €14.95 Students online only. **URL:** http://www.journals.berghahnbooks.com/transfers; http://journals.berghahnbooks.com/transfers. **Circ:** (Not Reported).

NEWINGTON

N. CT. Hartford Co. 5 mi. SW of Hartford. Manufactures dies and tools, chemicals, bolts, nuts and screws, aircraft engines, motor vehicle parts, concrete blocks, bricks, heating equipment.

6039 ■ QST
ARRL
225 Main St.
Newington, CT 06111-1494
Phone: (860)594-0200
Fax: (860)594-0259
Free: 888-277-5289
Publication E-mail: qst@arrl.org
Amateur radio magazine. **Freq:** Monthly. **Print Method:** Offset. **Trim Size:** 8 3/16 x 10 7/8. **Cols./Page:** 3. **Col. Width:** 27 nonpareils. **Col. Depth:** 140 agate lines. **Key Personnel:** Joel P. Kleinman, Managing Editor. **ISSN:** 0033--4812 (print). **Subscription Rates:** Included in membership. **URL:** http://www.arrl.org/qst. **Ad Rates:** BW $4,101; 4C $4,651. **Remarks:** Accepts advertising. **Circ:** ‡168975.

6040 ■ WRYM-AM - 840
1056 Willard Ave.
Newington, CT 06111

Phone: (860)666-0444
Email: wmartinez@wrym840.com
Format: Hispanic; News. **Networks:** CNN Radio. **Owner:** Hartford County Broadcasting Corp., at above address. **Founded:** 1961. **Operating Hours:** Continuous. **ADI:** Hartford-New Haven (New London), CT. **Key Personnel:** John Ramsey, Chief Engineer, john@ramseycommunications.com; Walter Martinez, Gen. Mgr., wmartinez@wrym840.com; Silvina Martinez, Traffic Mgr., smartinez@wrym840.com; Dina Casssarino, Bus. Mgr., dcassarino@wrym840.com; Darvin Garcia, Music Dir., rgarcia@wrym840.com. **Wattage:** 1,000. **Ad Rates:** $50-60 for 30 seconds; $70-80 for 60 seconds. **URL:** http://www.wrymradio.com.

NEWTOWN

SW CT. Fairfield Co. 9 mi. E. of Danbury. Manufactures rubber hose, plastic molding, scientific instruments, business forms, paper boxes, wire. Nursery. Dairy, poultry, fruit farms.

6041 ■ Antiques and the Arts Weekly
Bee Publishing Company Inc.
PO Box 5503
Newtown, CT 06470-5503
Phone: (203)426-3141
Fax: (203)426-5169
Publication E-mail: antiques@thebee.com
Magazine featuring antiques. **Freq:** Weekly. **Print Method:** Offset. **Trim Size:** 11 1/2 x 17. **Cols./Page:** 5. **Col. Width:** 10 1/2 inches. **Col. Depth:** 217 agate lines. **Key Personnel:** Scudder R. Smith, Editor; Dave Smith, Associate Editor. **Subscription Rates:** $87 U.S.; $320 Canada; $560 Other countries. **URL:** http://antiquesandthearts.com. **Ad Rates:** PCI $10.80. **Remarks:** Accepts advertising. **Circ:** Paid ‡24255, Non-paid ‡231.

6042 ■ Fine Cooking Magazine: For People Who Love To Cook
Taunton Press Inc.
63 S Main St.
Newtown, CT 06470
Phone: (203)426-8171
Fax: (203)426-3434
Free: 800-477-8727
Publisher's E-mail: booksales@taunton.com
Magazine focusing on food preparation. **Freq:** 6/year. **Trim Size:** 8 7/8 x 10 7/8. **Key Personnel:** Rebecca Freedman, Senior Editor; Sarah Breckenridge, Managing Editor. **ISSN:** 1072--5121 (print). **Subscription Rates:** $29.95 Individuals print & online or online only; $49.95 Two years print & online; $69.95 Individuals three years - print & online; $4.99 Individuals /month, online. **URL:** http://www.finecooking.com; http://www.finecookingmediakit.com; http://www.finecookingmediakit.com/magazine/index.php. **Mailing address:** PO Box 5506, Newtown, CT 06470. **Ad Rates:** BW $8,705; 4C $12,185. **Remarks:** Advertising accepted; rates available upon request. **Circ:** Paid ★**261547**.

6043 ■ Fine Gardening
Taunton Press Inc.
63 S Main St.
Newtown, CT 06470
Phone: (203)426-8171
Fax: (203)426-3434
Free: 800-477-8727
Publisher's E-mail: booksales@taunton.com
Hands-on magazine for avid gardeners of all skill levels. Filled with tips, ideas, information, and inspiration on garden design, gardening techniques, garden structures, and plants for the home landscape. **Freq:** 6/yr. **Print Method:** Web offset. **Trim Size:** 8 7/8 x 10 7/8. **Cols./Page:** 2 and 3. **Col. Width:** 3 1/8 and 2 inches. **Col. Depth:** 10.5 picas. **Key Personnel:** Greg Speichert, Publisher. **ISSN:** 0896--6281 (print). **Subscription Rates:** $29.95 U.S.; $49.95 Two years; $29.95 Individuals digital (1 year). **URL:** http://www.finegardening.com/. **Mailing address:** PO Box 5506, Newtown, CT 06470. **Ad Rates:** BW $7,330; 4C $10,110. **Remarks:** Accepts advertising. **Circ:** Paid ★**180423**.

6044 ■ Fine Homebuilding
Taunton Press Inc.
63 S Main St.
Newtown, CT 06470
Phone: (203)426-8171
Fax: (203)426-3434
Free: 800-477-8727
Publisher's E-mail: booksales@taunton.com
Magazine for builders, architects, designers, and owner-builders. **Freq:** 8/year. **Print Method:** Web offset. **Trim Size:** 8 7/8 x 10 7/8. **Cols./Page:** 2 and 3. **Col. Width:** 22 and 14 picas. **Col. Depth:** 9 3/4 inches. **Key Personnel:** Brian Pontolilo, Editor; Deb Silber, Managing Editor; Charles Bickford, Senior Editor; Justin Fink, Senior Editor. **ISSN:** 1096--360X (print). **Subscription Rates:** $37.95 U.S. print & online; $65.95 U.S. print & online - two years; $93.95 U.S. print & online - three years; $40.95 Canada print & online; $45.95 Other countries print & online; $39.95 Individuals online only. **URL:** http://www.finehomebuilding.com. **Mailing address:** PO Box 5506, Newtown, CT 06470. **Ad Rates:** BW $15,160; 4C $19,503. **Remarks:** Accepts advertising. **Circ:** Paid ★**2098282**.

6045 ■ Fine Woodworking
Taunton Press Inc.
63 S Main St.
Newtown, CT 06470
Phone: (203)426-8171
Fax: (203)426-3434
Free: 800-477-8727
Publisher's E-mail: booksales@taunton.com
Technical magazine for the amateur and professional woodworker. **Freq:** 7/year. **Print Method:** Offset. **Trim Size:** 8 1/2 x 11. **Cols./Page:** 2. **Key Personnel:** Timothy D. Schreiner, Publisher. **ISSN:** 0730--0271 (print). **Subscription Rates:** $34.95 U.S. print & online; $59.95 U.S. print & online - two years; $83.95 U.S. print & online - three years; $36.95 Canada print & online; $41.95 Other countries print & online; $34.95 Individuals online only. **URL:** http://www.finewoodworking.com. **Mailing address:** PO Box 5506, Newtown, CT 06470. **Ad Rates:** BW $13,335; 4C $18,205. **Remarks:** Accepts advertising. **Circ:** Paid ★**257316**.

6046 ■ Inspired House
Taunton Press Inc.
63 S Main St.
Newtown, CT 06470
Phone: (203)426-8171
Fax: (203)426-3434
Free: 800-477-8727
Publisher's E-mail: booksales@taunton.com
Magazine focusing on home decorating. **Freq:** Bimonthly. **Key Personnel:** Sheila Torres, Editor; Jeff Dwight, Director, Advertising; Mark Stiekman, Manager, Sales. **ISSN:** 1545--6536 (print). **URL:** http://www.taunton.com/inspiredhouse. **Mailing address:** PO Box 5506, Newtown, CT 06470. **Remarks:** Accepts advertising. **Circ:** (Not Reported).

6047 ■ LMT
LMT Communications Inc.
84 S Main St.
Newtown, CT 06470
Phone: (203)459-2888
Fax: (203)459-2889
Publisher's E-mail: info@lmtmag.com
Business strategies and marketing strategies magazine for dental laboratory owners and managers. **Freq:** 10/year. **Key Personnel:** Kim Molinaro Calabro, Managing Editor; Judy Fishman, President, Publisher; Maribeth Marsico, Senior Editor; Kelly Fessel-Carr, Associate Editor. **ISSN:** 8750--9539 (print). **Subscription Rates:** $35 Canada /year; $60 Canada two years; $65 Other countries /year; $17 U.S. /year. **URL:** http://www.lmtmag.com/about. **Ad Rates:** BW $4085; 4C $6625; PCI $85. **Remarks:** Accepts advertising. **Circ:** 18140.

6048 ■ The Newtown Bee
Bee Publishing Company Inc.
PO Box 5503
Newtown, CT 06470-5503
Phone: (203)426-3141
Fax: (203)426-5169
Publisher's E-mail: editor@thebee.com
Community newspaper. **Freq:** Weekly. **Print Method:** Offset. **Trim Size:** 17 x 23 1/2. **Cols./Page:** 9. **Col. Width:** 1 3/4 inches. **Col. Depth:** 20 1/2 inches. **Key Personnel:** Curtiss Clark, Editor; R. Scudder Smith, Publisher. **Subscription Rates:** $36 Individuals; $65 Two years. **URL:** http://newtownbee.com. **Remarks:** Accepts classified advertising. **Circ:** Paid ♦**6936**, Non-paid ♦**61**.

6049 ■ Threads
Taunton Press Inc.
63 S Main St.
Newtown, CT 06470
Phone: (203)426-8171
Fax: (203)426-3434
Free: 800-477-8727
Publisher's E-mail: booksales@taunton.com
Magazine for sewers, and quilters. Focus is on garment design, materials, and techniques. **Freq:** Bimonthly. **Print Method:** Offset. **Trim Size:** 8 7/8 x 10 7/8 in. **Cols./Page:** 3. **Col. Width:** 15 picas. **Col. Depth:** 7 inches. **Key Personnel:** Maria Taylor, Publisher. **ISSN:** 0882--7370 (print). **Subscription Rates:** $32.95 U.S. print & online; $54.95 U.S. print & online - two years; $78.95 U.S. print & online - 3/yr; $34.95 Canada print & online; $38.95 Other countries print & online; $32.95 Individuals online only. **URL:** http://www.threadsmagazine.com. **Mailing address:** PO Box 5506, Newtown, CT 06470. **Ad Rates:** BW $6,155; 4C $8,615; PCI $180. **Remarks:** Accepts advertising. **Circ:** ‡145000.

NORTH HAVEN

S. CT. New Haven Co. 6 mi. N. of New Haven. Chemical and aircraft plants.

6050 ■ Connecticut Medicine: The Journal of the Connecticut State Medical Society
Connecticut State Medical Society
East Bldg., 3rd Fl.
127 Washington Ave.
North Haven, CT 06473
Phone: (203)865-0587
Fax: (203)865-4997
Publisher's E-mail: membership@csms.org
Professional medical journal. **Freq:** Monthly 10/yr - combined issues June/July & Nov/Dec. **Print Method:** Web offset. **Trim Size:** 8 x 11. **Cols./Page:** 2. **Col. Width:** 19 picas. **Col. Depth:** 9 inches. **ISSN:** 0010-6178 (print). **URL:** http://www.csms.org/. **Ad Rates:** BW $395; 4C $1100. **Remarks:** Accepts advertising. **Circ:** 7,200.

6051 ■ National Catholic Register
Circle Media
432 Washington Ave.
North Haven, CT 06473
Fax: (203)230-3838
Free: 800-356-9916
Religious newspaper. **Freq:** Weekly (Sun.). **Print Method:** Offset. **Cols./Page:** 6. **Col. Width:** 26 nonpareils. **Col. Depth:** 287 agate lines. **Key Personnel:** Michael Warsaw, Publisher; Tom Wehner, Managing Editor. **ISSN:** 0027--8920 (print). **Subscription Rates:** $49.95 Individuals 1 year; $89.95 Two years; $3 Single issue. **URL:** http://www.ncregister.com. **Ad Rates:** GLR $2.36; BW $1890; 4C $2290; SAU $33; PCI $15. **Remarks:** Alcoholic beverages and tobacco products. **Circ:** Paid 15000, Free 453.

6052 ■ Probate Law Journal
Quinnipiac University School of Law
370 Bassett Rd.
North Haven, CT 06473
Phone: (203)582-3400
Fax: (203)582-3339
Free: 800-462-1944
Publisher's E-mail: law@quinnipiac.edu
Journal featuring articles on probate law, opinions from probate courts in Connecticut and other jurisdictions across the country. **Freq:** Quarterly. **Subscription Rates:** $36 Individuals /year. **URL:** http://www.qu.edu/probate-law-journal. **Circ:** (Not Reported).

NORWALK

SW CT. Fairfield Co. On Norwalk River, 45 mi. E. of New York. Manufactures pumps, textiles, astronomical instruments, electric signaling devices, air compressors, kitchen equipment, boats, stamped metal goods, neckties, wire cloth, cellophane, plastics, x-ray tubes, furniture, cosmetics, electronic equipment, office machines, duplicators, albums, and greeting cards. Oyster, lobster fisheries.

Circulation: ★ = AAM; △ or • = BPA; ♦ = CAC; ❑ = VAC; ⊕ = PO Statement; ‡ = Publisher's Report; Boldface figures = sworn; Light figures = estimated.

6053 ■ The AIDS Reader
UBM P.L.C.
535 Connecticut Ave., Ste. 300
Norwalk, CT 06854
Phone: (203)523-7020
Publisher's E-mail: communications@ubm.com
Monthly magazine helping clinicians improve the quality of life and treatment options for their HIV-positive patients. **Freq:** Monthly. **Key Personnel:** Bill Markowitz, Publisher, phone: (203)532-7059; John Hawes, Editor, phone: (203)662-6718; Joel E. Gallant, MD, Editor-in-Chief. **URL:** http://www.theaidsreader.com/home. **Circ:** 25759.

6054 ■ Alfred Hitchcock's Mystery Magazine
Penny Publications L.L.C.
6 Prowitt St.
Norwalk, CT 06855
Phone: (203)866-6688
Fax: (203)854-5962
Publisher's E-mail: corporatesales@pennypublications.com
Magazine for mystery enthusiasts. **Freq:** Monthly. **Print Method:** Offset. **Trim Size:** 5 1/4 x 8 5/16. **Cols./Page:** 1. **Col. Width:** 4 inches. **Col. Depth:** 7 inches. **ISSN:** 0002--5224 (print). **Subscription Rates:** $20.97 Individuals 6-months; $34.97 Individuals; $63.97 Two years; $93.97 Other countries two years; $49.97 Other countries; $28.47 Other countries 6-months. **URL:** http://www.themysteryplace.com/ahmm. **Remarks:** Accepts advertising. **Circ:** (Not Reported).

6055 ■ All-Star Tick Tock Word Seeks
Penny Publications L.L.C.
6 Prowitt St.
Norwalk, CT 06855
Phone: (203)866-6688
Fax: (203)854-5962
Publisher's E-mail: corporatesales@pennypublications.com
Magazine featuring word seeks for solvers who love to play against the clock. **Freq:** 6/year. **Key Personnel:** Peter Kanter, President. **Subscription Rates:** $19.97 Individuals; $36.97 Two years; $28.97 Other countries; $54.97 Other countries two years. **URL:** http://pennydellpuzzles.com/product.aspx?&p=MW. **Formerly**: Tick Tock Word Seeks. **Remarks:** Accepts advertising. **Circ:** (Not Reported).

6056 ■ Approved Easy & Fun Variety Puzzles
Penny Publications L.L.C.
6 Prowitt St.
Norwalk, CT 06855
Phone: (203)866-6688
Fax: (203)854-5962
Publisher's E-mail: corporatesales@pennypublications.com
Magazine featuring fun and relaxing puzzles. **Freq:** 6/year. **Key Personnel:** Peter Kanter, President. **Subscription Rates:** $23.97 Individuals. **URL:** http://pennydellpuzzles.com/product.aspx?c=easyvariety&p=ZG. **Formerly**: Easy & Fun Variety Puzzles and Games. **Remarks:** Accepts advertising. **Circ:** (Not Reported).

6057 ■ Approved Variety Puzzles
Penny Publications L.L.C.
6 Prowitt St.
Norwalk, CT 06855
Phone: (203)866-6688
Fax: (203)854-5962
Publisher's E-mail: corporatesales@pennypublications.com
Magazine featuring variety of puzzles. **Freq:** 6/year. **Key Personnel:** Peter Kanter, President. **Subscription Rates:** $24.97 Individuals. **URL:** http://pennydellpuzzles.com/product.aspx?c=crosswordsvarietysubscriptions&p=AX. **Remarks:** Accepts advertising. **Circ:** (Not Reported).

6058 ■ Arthritis Advisor
Belvoir Media Group L.L.C.
535 Connecticut Ave.
Norwalk, CT 06854-1631
Phone: (203)857-3100
Fax: (203)857-3013
Magazine featuring information for people with arthritis. **Freq:** Monthly. **Key Personnel:** Brian Donley, MD, Editor-in-Chief. **Subscription Rates:** $20 Individuals 12 months; $42 Other countries 12 months. **URL:** http://www.arthritis-advisor.com. **Mailing address:** PO Box 5656, Norwalk, CT 06856-5656. **Circ:** (Not Reported).

6059 ■ Aviation Consumer
Belvoir Media Group L.L.C.
P.O Box 5656
Norwalk, CT 06854
Free: 800-424-7887
Journal focusing on the evaluations of aircraft, avionics, accessories, and equipment. **Freq:** Monthly. **Key Personnel:** Larry Anglisano, Editor. **Subscription Rates:** $36 Individuals 6 issues - print; $34 Individuals online. **URL:** http://www.aviationconsumer.com. **Circ:** (Not Reported).

6060 ■ Beverage Dynamics: Wine, Beer & Spirits for Retail Decision Makers
Beverage Information Group
17 High St., 2nd Fl.
Norwalk, CT 06851
Phone: (203)855-8499
Trade magazine on beverage and food retail business. **Freq:** Bimonthly. **Print Method:** Offset. **Trim Size:** 8 x 10 7/8. **Cols./Page:** 2. **Key Personnel:** Richard Brandes, Editor; Tony Bongiovanni, Associate Publisher; Charlie Forman, Publisher, Senior Vice President. **ISSN:** 0024--4236 (print). **URL:** http://www.beveragedynamics.com. **Formerly:** Beverage & Food Dynamics; Liquor Store. **Ad Rates:** BW $16425; 4C $6750. **Remarks:** Accepts advertising. **Circ:** △**70040**, 24000.

6061 ■ Classic Variety Puzzles Plus Crosswords
Penny Publications L.L.C.
6 Prowitt St.
Norwalk, CT 06855
Phone: (203)866-6688
Fax: (203)854-5962
Publisher's E-mail: corporatesales@pennypublications.com
Magazine featuring mix of crossword and variety puzzles. **Freq:** 7/year. **Key Personnel:** Peter Kanter, President. **Subscription Rates:** $35.97 Individuals. **URL:** http://pennydellpuzzles.com/product.aspx?c=mixeddifficultycrosswordsvariety&p=CS. **Remarks:** Accepts advertising. **Circ:** (Not Reported).

6062 ■ Connecticut Cottages & Gardens
Cottages and Gardens Publications
142 East Ave., North Bldg., 2nd Fl.
Norwalk, CT 06851
Phone: (203)227-1400
Fax: (203)226-2824
Magazine that offers information for residents of Fairfield County, Connecticut. **Freq:** 11/year. **Key Personnel:** D.J. Carey, Director, Editorial. **Subscription Rates:** $49.95 Individuals. **Remarks:** Accepts advertising. **Circ:** Non-paid ★**40000**.

6063 ■ CTI
Technology Marketing Corp.
800 Connecticut Ave., 1st Fl.
Norwalk, CT 06854
Phone: (203)852-6800
Fax: (203)866-3326
Free: 800-243-6002
Publisher's E-mail: tmc@tmcnet.com
Trade magazine covering computer, network, and Internet telephony. **Freq:** 9/yr. **Key Personnel:** Tom Keating, Editor. **URL:** http://www.tmcnet.com/cti/sep/cti.htm. **Circ:** (Not Reported).

6064 ■ Customer
Technology Marketing Corp.
800 Connecticut Ave., 1st Fl.
Norwalk, CT 06854
Phone: (203)852-6800
Fax: (203)866-3326
Free: 800-243-6002
Publisher's E-mail: tmc@tmcnet.com
Publication covering issues in the telecommunications industry. **Freq:** Monthly. **Key Personnel:** Nadji Tehrani, Chairman, Chief Executive Officer, Editor-in-Chief, Founder; Richard Grigonis, Executive Editor; Tracey Schelmetic, Director, Editorial. **ISSN:** 1533-3078 (print). **URL:** http://www.customerzone360.com. **Formerly:** Customer Interaction Solutions. **Remarks:** Accepts advertising. **Circ:** (Not Reported).

6065 ■ Dell Crazy for Sudoku!
Penny Publications L.L.C.
6 Prowitt St.
Norwalk, CT 06855
Phone: (203)866-6688
Fax: (203)854-5962
Publisher's E-mail: corporatesales@pennypublications.com
Magazine featuring Sudoku puzzles with four difficulty levels. **Freq:** 9/year. **Subscription Rates:** $26.97 Individuals. **URL:** http://pennydellpuzzles.com/product.aspx?c=sudokusubscriptions&p=CFS. **Remarks:** Accepts advertising. **Circ:** (Not Reported).

6066 ■ Dell Fun Puzzles and Games for Kids
Penny Publications L.L.C.
6 Prowitt St.
Norwalk, CT 06855
Phone: (203)866-6688
Fax: (203)854-5962
Publisher's E-mail: corporatesales@pennypublications.com
Magazine featuring puzzles with Nickelodeon characters. **Freq:** 6/year. **Subscription Rates:** $5.95 Individuals. **URL:** http://pennydellpuzzles.com/product.aspx?c=varietyvaluepacks&p=NIKPK6. **Formerly**: Nickelodeon Fun Puzzles and Games. **Remarks:** Accepts advertising. **Circ:** (Not Reported).

6067 ■ Dell Fun-to-Solve Crosswords
Penny Publications L.L.C.
6 Prowitt St.
Norwalk, CT 06855
Phone: (203)866-6688
Fax: (203)854-5962
Publisher's E-mail: corporatesales@pennypublications.com
Magazine featuring combination of easy to medium crosswords. **Freq:** 6/year. **Subscription Rates:** $18.97 Individuals. **URL:** http://pennydellpuzzles.com/product.aspx?c=mediumcrosswords&p=FSX. **Remarks:** Accepts advertising. **Circ:** (Not Reported).

6068 ■ Dell Official Variety Puzzles
Penny Publications L.L.C.
6 Prowitt St.
Norwalk, CT 06855
Phone: (203)866-6688
Fax: (203)854-5962
Publisher's E-mail: corporatesales@pennypublications.com
Magazine covering quizzes, mazes, and word and number puzzles. **Freq:** 6/year. **Print Method:** Offset. **Trim Size:** 8 x 10 7/8. **Cols./Page:** 3. **Col. Width:** 2 1/4 inches. **Col. Depth:** 10 inches. **ISSN:** 0891-771X (print). **Subscription Rates:** $27.97 Individuals. **URL:** http://www.pennydellpuzzles.com/product.aspx?c=VarietySubscriptions&p=OVP. **Formerly**: Official Variety Puzzle & Word Games. **Remarks:** Accepts advertising. **Circ:** (Not Reported).

6069 ■ Dell Original Sudoku
Penny Publications L.L.C.
6 Prowitt St.
Norwalk, CT 06855
Phone: (203)866-6688
Fax: (203)854-5962
Publisher's E-mail: corporatesales@pennypublications.com
Magazine for beginners and more experienced Sudoku solvers. **Freq:** 8/year. **Subscription Rates:** $24.97 Individuals. **URL:** http://pennydellpuzzles.com/product.aspx?c=MediumSudoku&p=DOS. **Remarks:** Accepts advertising. **Circ:** (Not Reported).

6070 ■ Dell Pocket Crossword Puzzles
Penny Publications L.L.C.
6 Prowitt St.
Norwalk, CT 06855
Phone: (203)866-6688
Fax: (203)854-5962
Publisher's E-mail: corporatesales@pennypublications.com
Magazines dedicated to crossword puzzles. **Freq:** Monthly. **Print Method:** Heidelberg Cylinder Press adapted for zinc braille plates. **Trim Size:** 11 x 11 1/2. **Cols./Page:** 1. **Col. Width:** 9 inches. **Col. Depth:** 10 inches. **Subscription Rates:** $21.97 Individuals. **URL:** http://www.pennydellpuzzles.com/product.aspx?c=mediumcrosswords&p=PXP. **Formerly**: Pocket Cross-

word Puzzles. **Remarks:** Accepts advertising. **Circ:** (Not Reported).

6071 ■ Dell's Best All-Easy Crosswords
Penny Publications L.L.C.
6 Prowitt St.
Norwalk, CT 06855
Phone: (203)866-6688
Fax: (203)854-5962
Publisher's E-mail: corporatesales@pennypublications.com
Magazine featuring 100 fun and simple to solve crosswords. **Freq:** 6/year. **Subscription Rates:** $18.97 Individuals. **URL:** http://pennydellpuzzles.com/product.aspx?c=easycrosswords&p=AEX. **Formerly**: Dell All Easy Crosswords. **Remarks:** Accepts advertising. **Circ:** (Not Reported).

6072 ■ Dell's Best Easy Crosswords
Penny Publications L.L.C.
6 Prowitt St.
Norwalk, CT 06855
Phone: (203)866-6688
Fax: (203)854-5962
Publisher's E-mail: corporatesales@pennypublications.com
Magazine featuring collection of 100 easy to solve crosswords. **Freq:** 9/year. **Subscription Rates:** $26.97 Individuals. **URL:** http://pennydellpuzzles.com/product.aspx?c=crosswordssubscriptions&p=EXC. **Formerly**: Dell Easy Crossword Collection. **Remarks:** Accepts advertising. **Circ:** (Not Reported).

6073 ■ District Administration: Education, Trends, Issues Resources & Technology
Professional Media Group L.L.C.
488 Main Ave.
Norwalk, CT 06851
Phone: (203)663-0100
Product magazine for K-12 district leaders. **Freq:** Monthly. **Print Method:** Offset. **Trim Size:** 7 3/4 x 10 1/2. **Cols./Page:** 3. **Col. Width:** 12.5 picas. **Col. Depth:** 134 agate lines. **Key Personnel:** Daniel E. Kinnaman, President, Publisher; Joseph J. Hanson, Chairman of the Board, Chief Executive Officer. **ISSN:** 1082--5495 (print). **Subscription Rates:** Free to qualified subscribers. **URL:** http://www.districtadministration.com. **Remarks:** Advertising accepted; rates available upon request. **Circ:** (Not Reported).

6074 ■ E: The Environmental Magazine
Earth Action Network
28 Knight St.
Norwalk, CT 06851
Phone: (203)854-5559
Fax: (203)866-0602
Publication E-mail: info@emagazine.com
Clearinghouse of news, information and commentary on environmental issues. **Freq:** Bimonthly. **Print Method:** Web offset. **Trim Size:** 8 1/8 x 10 7/8. **Cols./Page:** 3. **Col. Width:** 2 1/8 inches. **Col. Depth:** 9 5/8 inches. **Key Personnel:** Doug Moss, Executive Director, Founder, Publisher; Brita Belli, Editor. **ISSN:** 1046-8021 (print). **Subscription Rates:** $24.95 Individuals; $34.95 Two years; $34.95 Canada; $64.95 Other countries. **URL:** http://www.emagazine.com. **Ad Rates:** GLR $3.15; BW $2,415; 4C $3,628; PCI $140. **Remarks:** Advertising accepted; rates available upon request. **Circ:** 56000.

6075 ■ Easy Crossword Express
Penny Publications L.L.C.
6 Prowitt St.
Norwalk, CT 06855
Phone: (203)866-6688
Fax: (203)854-5962
Publisher's E-mail: corporatesales@pennypublications.com
Magazine featuring quick and easy to solve crossword puzzles. **Freq:** 8/year. **Key Personnel:** Peter Kanter, President. **Subscription Rates:** $29.97 Individuals. **URL:** http://pennydellpuzzles.com/product.aspx?c=crosswordssubscriptions&p=ZX. **Remarks:** Accepts advertising. **Circ:** (Not Reported).

6076 ■ Event Design: For Builders of Events, Exhibits and Environments
Red 7 Media L.L.C.
10 Norden Pl.
Norwalk, CT 06855
Fax: (203)854-6735
Magazine focusing on information for designers and engineers of events, exhibits, and environments. **Freq:** 8/year. **Print Method:** 8 1/8 x 10 7/8. **Key Personnel:** Dan Hanover, Editor, Publisher. **URL:** http://www.eventmarketer.com. **Remarks:** Accepts advertising. **Circ:** (Not Reported).

6077 ■ Event Marketer
Red 7 Media L.L.C.
10 Norden Pl.
Norwalk, CT 06855
Fax: (203)854-6735
Magazine for brand-side event marketers and face-to-face media agency executives. **Freq:** 8/year. **Trim Size:** 8 1/8 x 10 7/8. **Key Personnel:** Chip Berry, Director, Advertising, phone: (732)359-6533; Dan Hanover, Editor, phone: (203)899-8446. **Subscription Rates:** $45 Individuals; $106 Canada and Mexico; $116 Other countries. **URL:** http://www.eventmarketer.com. **Ad Rates:** 4C $6,110. **Remarks:** Accepts advertising. **Circ:** Combined △**10000.**

6078 ■ Family Favorites Word Seek Puzzles
Penny Publications L.L.C.
6 Prowitt St.
Norwalk, CT 06855
Phone: (203)866-6688
Fax: (203)854-5962
Publisher's E-mail: corporatesales@pennypublications.com
Magazine containing over 100 large-type puzzles and primary word seek puzzles. **Freq:** Quarterly. **Subscription Rates:** $4.95 Single issue. **URL:** http://www.pennydellpuzzles.com/product.aspx?c=WordSeekSearchPuzzleBooks&p=WSFF. **Circ:** (Not Reported).

6079 ■ Family Variety Puzzles & Games Plus Crosswords
Penny Publications L.L.C.
6 Prowitt St.
Norwalk, CT 06855
Phone: (203)866-6688
Fax: (203)854-5962
Publisher's E-mail: corporatesales@pennypublications.com
Magazine featuring assortment of most popular variety puzzles. **Freq:** 6/year. **Key Personnel:** Peter Kanter, President. **Subscription Rates:** $25.97 Individuals. **URL:** http://pennydellpuzzles.com/product.aspx?c=crosswordsvarietysubscriptions&p=FX. **Formerly**: Family Variety and Crosswords. **Remarks:** Accepts advertising. **Circ:** (Not Reported).

6080 ■ Favorite Easy Crosswords
Penny Publications L.L.C.
6 Prowitt St.
Norwalk, CT 06855
Phone: (203)866-6688
Fax: (203)854-5962
Publisher's E-mail: corporatesales@pennypublications.com
Magazine featuring variety of easy to solve crossword puzzles. **Freq:** 6/year. **Key Personnel:** Peter Kanter, President. **Subscription Rates:** $22.97 Individuals. **URL:** http://pennydellpuzzles.com/product.aspx?c=crosswordssubscriptions&p=RX. **Remarks:** Accepts advertising. **Circ:** (Not Reported).

6081 ■ Favorite Fill-In
Penny Publications L.L.C.
6 Prowitt St.
Norwalk, CT 06855
Phone: (203)866-6688
Fax: (203)854-5962
Publisher's E-mail: corporatesales@pennypublications.com
Magazine featuring most popular variety Fill-Ins, ranging from easy to hard. **Freq:** 6/year. **Key Personnel:** Peter Kanter, President. **Subscription Rates:** $22.97 Single issue. **URL:** http://www.pennydellpuzzles.com/product.aspx?c=MediumFill-Ins&p=VF. **Formerly**: Favorite Fill-In Puzzles. **Remarks:** Accepts advertising. **Circ:** (Not Reported).

6082 ■ Folio: The Magazine for Magazine Management
Red 7 Media L.L.C.
10 Norden Pl.
Norwalk, CT 06855
Fax: (203)854-6735
Publishing industry trade magazine. **Freq:** Monthly plus four special reports printed in April, July, Sept., & Nov. **Print Method:** Offset. **Trim Size:** 8 1/2 x 11. **Cols./Page:** 3. **Col. Width:** 27 nonpareils. **Col. Depth:** 140 agate lines. **Key Personnel:** Tony Silber, General Manager, phone: (203)899-8424. **Subscription Rates:** Free to qualified subscribers. **URL:** http://www.foliomag.com/magazines. **Remarks:** Accepts advertising. **Circ:** (Not Reported).

6083 ■ Fun-to-Solve Easy Crosswords
Penny Publications L.L.C.
6 Prowitt St.
Norwalk, CT 06855
Phone: (203)866-6688
Fax: (203)854-5962
Publisher's E-mail: corporatesales@pennypublications.com
Magazine featuring puzzles with larger diagrams. **Freq:** 6/year. **Subscription Rates:** $18.97 Individuals. **URL:** http://pennydellpuzzles.com/product.aspx?c=easycrosswords&p=EXG. **Formerly**: Dell Easy Crosswords to Go!. **Remarks:** Accepts advertising. **Circ:** (Not Reported).

6084 ■ Garfield's Word Seeks
Penny Publications L.L.C.
6 Prowitt St.
Norwalk, CT 06855
Phone: (203)866-6688
Fax: (203)854-5962
Publisher's E-mail: corporatesales@pennypublications.com
Magazine featuring word seeks and puzzles with Garfield. **Freq:** 9/year. **Key Personnel:** Peter Kanter, President. **Subscription Rates:** $29.97 Individuals; $43.47 Other countries; $55.97 Two years; $82.97 Two years other countries. **URL:** http://pennydellpuzzles.com/product.aspx?c=MixedDifficultyWS&p=IW. **Remarks:** Accepts advertising. **Circ:** (Not Reported).

6085 ■ Good Time Crosswords
Penny Publications L.L.C.
6 Prowitt St.
Norwalk, CT 06855
Phone: (203)866-6688
Fax: (203)854-5962
Publisher's E-mail: corporatesales@pennypublications.com
Magazine featuring crossword from easy to hard levels. **Freq:** 6/year. **Key Personnel:** Peter Kanter, President. **Subscription Rates:** $29.97 Individuals; $31.97 Other countries; $42.97 Two years; $60.97 Two years other countries. **URL:** http://pennydellpuzzles.com/product.aspx?c=mediumcrosswords&p=GX. **Formerly**: Good Time Crossword Puzzles. **Remarks:** Accepts advertising. **Circ:** (Not Reported).

6086 ■ Good Time Easy Crosswords
Penny Publications L.L.C.
6 Prowitt St.
Norwalk, CT 06855
Phone: (203)866-6688
Fax: (203)854-5962
Publisher's E-mail: corporatesales@pennypublications.com
Magazine for crossword beginning solvers. **Freq:** 6/year. **Key Personnel:** Peter Kanter, President. **Subscription Rates:** $29.97 Individuals; $31.97 Other countries; $42.97 Two years; $60.97 Two years other countries. **URL:** http://pennydellpuzzles.com/product.aspx?c=easycrosswords&p=NX. **Formerly**: Nice & Easy Crosswords. **Remarks:** Accepts advertising. **Circ:** (Not Reported).

6087 ■ Good Time Variety Puzzles
Penny Publications L.L.C.
6 Prowitt St.
Norwalk, CT 06855
Phone: (203)866-6688
Fax: (203)854-5962
Publisher's E-mail: corporatesales@pennypublications.com
Magazine featuring relaxing variety puzzles. **Freq:** 8/year. **Key Personnel:** Peter Kanter, President. **Subscription Rates:** $31.97 Individuals; $82.97 Other

Circulation: ★ = AAM; △ or • = BPA; ♦ = CAC; ❑ = VAC; ⊕ = PO Statement; ‡ = Publisher's Report; Boldface figures = sworn; Light figures = estimated.

countries; $31.97 Two years; $58.97 Two years other countries. **URL:** http://pennydellpuzzles.com/product.aspx?c=easyvariety&p=GG. **Remarks:** Accepts advertising. **Circ:** (Not Reported).

6088 ■ Gun Tests
Belvoir Media Group L.L.C.
535 Connecticut Ave.
Norwalk, CT 06854-1631
Phone: (203)857-3100
Fax: (203)857-3013
Magazine featuring information and evaluation about handguns, rifles, shotguns, and shooting accessories. **Freq:** Monthly. **Key Personnel:** Todd Woodard, Editor. **Subscription Rates:** $24 Individuals print or online; $40 Two years. **URL:** http://www.gun-tests.com. **Mailing address:** PO Box 5656, Norwalk, CT 06856-5656. **Circ:** (Not Reported).

6089 ■ Hamptons Cottages & Gardens
Cottages and Gardens Publications
142 East Ave., North Bldg., 2nd Fl.
Norwalk, CT 06851
Phone: (203)227-1400
Fax: (203)226-2824
Magazine that offers information for residents of the Hamptons in Long Island. **Freq:** 7/year. **Key Personnel:** D.J. Carey, Director, Editorial; Pamela Eldridge, Publisher. **Subscription Rates:** $39.95 Individuals. **URL:** http://www.cottages-gardens.com/Hamptons-Cottages-Gardens. **Remarks:** Accepts advertising. **Circ:** ★**40000**.

6090 ■ The Hour
The Hour Publishing Co.
1 Selleck St.
Norwalk, CT 06855
Phone: (203)846-3281
General newspaper. **Freq:** Daily except major holidays. **Print Method:** Offset. **Trim Size:** 13 x 22 3/4. **Cols./Page:** 6. **Col. Width:** 24 nonpareils. **Col. Depth:** 297 agate lines. **Key Personnel:** Chet Valiante, Chief Operating Officer, Publisher, phone: (203)354-1010. **USPS:** 398-200. **Subscription Rates:** $247 Individuals; $50 Individuals online. **URL:** http://www.thehour.com. **Ad Rates:** GLR $2.34; BW $2,835; 4C $3,261; PCI $18.83. **Remarks:** Accepts advertising. **Circ:** Mon.-Sat. ★**14814**, Sun. ★**15200**.

6091 ■ IFR Refresher
Belvoir Media Group L.L.C.
535 Connecticut Ave.
Norwalk, CT 06854-1631
Phone: (203)857-3100
Fax: (203)857-3013
Journal focusing on reviews of IFR rules and procedures. **Freq:** Monthly. **Subscription Rates:** $24 Individuals; $36 Canada; $36 Other countries. **URL:** http://www.ifr-refresher.com. **Mailing address:** PO Box 5656, Norwalk, CT 06856-5656. **Circ:** (Not Reported).

6092 ■ Jewelers' Circular-Keystone
Reed Exhibitions
383 Main Ave.
Norwalk, CT 06851
Phone: (203)840-5404
Fax: (203)840-9404
Publisher's E-mail: rxinfo@reedexpo.co.uk
Retail jewelers trade magazine. **Freq:** Monthly. **Print Method:** Offset. **Trim Size:** 8.375 x 10.875. **Cols./Page:** 3 and 2. **Col. Width:** 13 and 20 picas. **Col. Depth:** 140 agate lines. **Key Personnel:** Donna Borrelli, Associate Publisher, phone: (646)783-3756; Victoria Gomelsky, Editor-in-Chief; Melissa Rose Bernardo, Managing Editor. **ISSN:** 0194-2905 (print). **Subscription Rates:** $39.95 Individuals; $109.95 Canada; $184.95 Other countries. **URL:** http://www.jckonline.com. **Ad Rates:** BW $7,900; 4C $11,390. **Remarks:** Accepts advertising. **Circ:** (Not Reported).

6093 ■ Large-Print Word Seek Puzzles
Penny Publications L.L.C.
6 Prowitt St.
Norwalk, CT 06855
Phone: (203)866-6688
Fax: (203)854-5962
Publisher's E-mail: corporatesales@pennypublications.com
Magazine featuring word seeks in large print. **Freq:** Quarterly. **Key Personnel:** Peter Kanter, President. **Subscription Rates:** $16.97 Individuals; $27.97 Other countries; $31.97 Two years; $47.97 Two years other countries. **URL:** http://pennydellpuzzles.com/product.aspx?c=mixeddifficultyws&p=KW. **Remarks:** Accepts advertising. **Circ:** (Not Reported).

6094 ■ Light Plane Maintenance
Belvoir Media Group L.L.C.
535 Connecticut Ave.
Norwalk, CT 06854-1631
Phone: (203)857-3100
Fax: (203)857-3013
Magazine featuring information about aircraft maintenance. **Freq:** Monthly. **Subscription Rates:** $19.97 Individuals 6 issues; $29.97 Other countries 6 issues; $29.97 Canada 6 issues. **URL:** http://www.lightplane-maintenance.com. **Mailing address:** PO Box 5656, Norwalk, CT 06856-5656. **Circ:** (Not Reported).

6095 ■ Little India
Little India
50 Washington St., Ste. 314
Norwalk, CT 06854
Phone: (212)560-0608
Fax: (212)560-0609
Publication E-mail: info@littleindia.com
Magazine for Asian Indian community. **Freq:** Monthly. **Print Method:** Web offset. **Trim Size:** 7.875 x 10.375. **Cols./Page:** 3. **Col. Width:** 2 inches. **Col. Depth:** 9 3/4 inches. **Key Personnel:** Achal Mehra, Editor. **ISSN:** 1552--449X (print). **URL:** http://www.littleindia.com. **Mailing address:** PO Box 1848, Torrington, CT 06790. **Remarks:** Accepts advertising. **Circ:** (Not Reported).

6096 ■ Living Without
Belvoir Media Group L.L.C.
535 Connecticut Ave.
Norwalk, CT 06854-1631
Phone: (203)857-3100
Fax: (203)857-3013
Magazine featuring dietary products. **Freq:** 6/yr. **Key Personnel:** Alicia Woodward, Managing Editor. **Subscription Rates:** $23 Individuals; $42 Two years. **URL:** http://www.livingwithout.com. **Mailing address:** PO Box 5656, Norwalk, CT 06856-5656. **Remarks:** Accepts advertising. **Circ:** (Not Reported).

6097 ■ Logic Lover's Logic Problems
Penny Publications L.L.C.
6 Prowitt St.
Norwalk, CT 06855
Phone: (203)866-6688
Fax: (203)854-5962
Publisher's E-mail: corporatesales@pennypublications.com
Magazine featuring logic puzzles. **Freq:** 6/year. **Subscription Rates:** $19.97 Individuals. **URL:** http://pennydellpuzzles.com/product.aspx?c=LogicMathSubscriptions&p=LOG. **Formerly:** Dell Logic Puzzles. **Remarks:** Accepts advertising. **Circ:** (Not Reported).

6098 ■ Logic Lover's Math and Logic Problems
Penny Publications L.L.C.
6 Prowitt St.
Norwalk, CT 06855
Phone: (203)866-6688
Fax: (203)854-5962
Publisher's E-mail: corporatesales@pennypublications.com
Magazine featuring math puzzles and logic problems. **Freq:** 6/year. **Subscription Rates:** $19.97 Individuals. **URL:** http://pennydellpuzzles.com/product.aspx?c=logicmathsubscriptions&p=DML. **Formerly:** Dell Math Puzzles and Logic Problems. **Remarks:** Accepts advertising. **Circ:** (Not Reported).

6099 ■ Master's Variety Puzzles
Penny Publications L.L.C.
6 Prowitt St.
Norwalk, CT 06855
Phone: (203)866-6688
Fax: (203)854-5962
Publisher's E-mail: corporatesales@pennypublications.com
Magazine featuring tough variety puzzles. **Freq:** Quarterly. **Key Personnel:** Peter Kanter, President. **Subscription Rates:** $18.97 Individuals; $26.97 Other countries; $34.97 Two years; $50.97 Two years other countries. **URL:** http://pennydellpuzzles.com/product.aspx?c=MixedDifficulty&p=MV. **Remarks:** Accepts advertising. **Circ:** (Not Reported).

6100 ■ Merit Variety Puzzles and Games
Penny Publications L.L.C.
6 Prowitt St.
Norwalk, CT 06855
Phone: (203)866-6688
Fax: (203)854-5962
Publisher's E-mail: corporatesales@pennypublications.com
Magazine featuring popular variety puzzles. **Freq:** 9/year. **Key Personnel:** Peter Kanter, President. **Subscription Rates:** $32.97 Individuals; $50.47 Other countries; $60.97 Two years; $96.97 Two years other countries. **URL:** http://pennydellpuzzles.com/product.aspx?c=MixedDifficulty&p=MG. **Remarks:** Accepts advertising. **Circ:** (Not Reported).

6101 ■ Modern Brewery Age Tabloid Edition
Business Journals Inc.
50 Day St.
Norwalk, CT 06854
Phone: (203)853-6015
Fax: (203)852-8175
Publisher's E-mail: bjisupport@busjour.com
Brewery industry tabloid. **Freq:** Weekly. **Key Personnel:** Peter Reid, Publisher, Editor, phone: (203)216-7488; Mac Brighton, Chairman, Chief Operating Officer; Britton Jones, Chief Executive Officer, President. **Subscription Rates:** $95 Individuals via email. **URL:** http://www.breweryage.com/tabloid. **Ad Rates:** BW $2,815; 4C $3,477. **Remarks:** Accepts advertising. **Circ:** ‡5181.

6102 ■ MR Magazine
Business Journals Inc.
50 Day St.
Norwalk, CT 06854
Phone: (203)853-6015
Fax: (203)852-8175
Publisher's E-mail: bjisupport@busjour.com
Journal focusing on menswear. **Key Personnel:** Stuart Nifoussi, Executive Vice President, Publisher, phone: (212)710-7407; Karen Alberg Grossman, Editor-in-Chief, phone: (212)710-7422; Elise Diamantini, Managing Editor, phone: (212)710-7429. **Subscription Rates:** $34 Individuals; $53 Two years; $63 Canada; $95 Canada two years; $102 Other countries airmail. **URL:** http://www.busjour.com/secure/mr/subscribe.php. **Ad Rates:** BW $9240; 4C $10685. **Remarks:** Accepts advertising. **Circ:** 13000.

6103 ■ Original Extreme Sudoku
Penny Publications L.L.C.
6 Prowitt St.
Norwalk, CT 06855
Phone: (203)866-6688
Fax: (203)854-5962
Publisher's E-mail: corporatesales@pennypublications.com
Magazine for Sudoku solvers who prefer a greater challenge. **Freq:** Quarterly. **Subscription Rates:** $16.97 Individuals. **URL:** http://pennydellpuzzles.com/product.aspx?c=sudokusubscriptions&p=DES. **Formerly:** Extreme Sudoku. **Remarks:** Accepts advertising. **Circ:** (Not Reported).

6104 ■ Original Logic Problems
Penny Publications L.L.C.
6 Prowitt St.
Norwalk, CT 06855
Phone: (203)866-6688
Fax: (203)854-5962
Publisher's E-mail: corporatesales@pennypublications.com
Magazine featuring assortment of stimulating logic problems. **Freq:** 6/year. **Key Personnel:** Peter Kanter, President. **Subscription Rates:** $22.97 Individuals; $34.97 Other countries; $41.97 Two years; $63.97 Two years other countries. **URL:** http://pennydellpuzzles.com/product.aspx?&p=OL. **Remarks:** Accepts advertising. **Circ:** (Not Reported).

6105 ■ Penny's Finest Favorite Word Seeks
Penny Publications L.L.C.
6 Prowitt St.
Norwalk, CT 06855
Phone: (203)866-6688
Fax: (203)854-5962
Publisher's E-mail: corporatesales@pennypublications.com

Magazine containing Word Seek and other puzzles. **Freq:** 6/year. **Subscription Rates:** $19.97 Individuals. **URL:** http://www.pennydellpuzzles.com/product.aspx?c=MixedDifficultyWS&p=RW. **Formerly**: Favorite Word Seek Puzzles. **Circ:** (Not Reported).

6106 ■ Penny's Finest Good Time Word Seeks
Penny Publications L.L.C.
6 Prowitt St.
Norwalk, CT 06855
Phone: (203)866-6688
Fax: (203)854-5962
Publisher's E-mail: corporatesales@pennypublications.com
Word puzzles magazine. **Freq:** 6/year. **Subscription Rates:** $22.97 Individuals. **URL:** http://www.pennydellpuzzles.com/product.aspx?c=MixedDifficultyWS&p=GW. **Formerly**: Good Time Word Seek Puzzles. **Circ:** (Not Reported).

6107 ■ Pocket Easy Crossword Puzzles
Penny Publications L.L.C.
6 Prowitt St.
Norwalk, CT 06855
Phone: (203)866-6688
Fax: (203)854-5962
Publisher's E-mail: corporatesales@pennypublications.com
Magazine featuring easy to solve crosswords. **Freq:** 6/year. **Subscription Rates:** $18.97 Individuals. **URL:** http://pennydellpuzzles.com/product.aspx?c=crosswordssubscriptions&p=EDX. **Formerly**: Dell Easy Does It Crosswords. **Remarks:** Accepts advertising. **Circ:** (Not Reported).

6108 ■ Puzzler's Sunday Crosswords
Penny Publications L.L.C.
6 Prowitt St.
Norwalk, CT 06855
Phone: (203)866-6688
Fax: (203)854-5962
Publisher's E-mail: corporatesales@pennypublications.com
Magazine for crossword lover who prefers themed crosswords. **Freq:** Quarterly. **Subscription Rates:** $14.97 Individuals. **URL:** http://pennydellpuzzles.com/product.aspx?c=MediumCrosswords&p=DXX. **Formerly**: Dell Crosswords Crosswords; Puzzler's Crosswords Crosswords. **Remarks:** Accepts advertising. **Circ:** (Not Reported).

6109 ■ Quick & Easy Crosswords
Penny Publications L.L.C.
6 Prowitt St.
Norwalk, CT 06855
Phone: (203)866-6688
Fax: (203)854-5962
Publisher's E-mail: corporatesales@pennypublications.com
Magazine featuring puzzles for beginners. **Freq:** 6/year. **Key Personnel:** Peter Kanter, President. **Subscription Rates:** $22.97 Individuals; $31.97 Other countries; $42.97 Two years; $60.97 Two years other countries. **URL:** http://pennydellpuzzles.com/product.aspx?&p=QX. **Remarks:** Accepts advertising. **Circ:** (Not Reported).

6110 ■ Solver's Choice Variety Puzzles
Penny Publications L.L.C.
6 Prowitt St.
Norwalk, CT 06855
Phone: (203)866-6688
Fax: (203)854-5962
Publisher's E-mail: corporatesales@pennypublications.com
Magazine featuring puzzles for younger and newer solvers. **Freq:** Quarterly. **Subscription Rates:** $17.97 Individuals. **URL:** http://pennydellpuzzles.com/product.aspx?c=mixeddifficulty&p=PVS. **Formerly**: Dell Pencil Puzzles Vacation Special. **Remarks:** Accepts advertising. **Circ:** (Not Reported).

6111 ■ Spotlight Movie & TV Word Seek
Penny Publications L.L.C.
6 Prowitt St.
Norwalk, CT 06855
Phone: (203)866-6688
Fax: (203)854-5962
Publisher's E-mail: corporatesales@pennypublications.com
Word seek magazine featuring entertainment stars, movies, and television shows. **Freq:** 6/year. **Subscription Rates:** $19.97 Individuals; $28.97 Other countries; $36.97 Two years; $54.97 Two years other countries. **URL:** http://pennydellpuzzles.com/product.aspx?&p=VW. **Formerly**: Movie & TV Word Seeks. **Remarks:** Accepts advertising. **Circ:** (Not Reported).

6112 ■ Spotlight Remember When Word Seek
Penny Publications L.L.C.
6 Prowitt St.
Norwalk, CT 06855
Phone: (203)866-6688
Fax: (203)854-5962
Publisher's E-mail: corporatesales@pennypublications.com
Magazine featuring variety of words seek puzzles with touch of the past. **Freq:** 8/year. **Key Personnel:** Peter Kanter, President. **Subscription Rates:** $23.97 Individuals. **URL:** http://pennydellpuzzles.com/product.aspx?c=wordseeksearchsubscriptions&p=NW. **Formerly**: Remember When Word Seek. **Remarks:** Accepts advertising. **Circ:** (Not Reported).

6113 ■ StateWays: The Beverage Alcohol Merchandising Magazine for the Control States
Beverage Information Group
17 High St., 2nd Fl.
Norwalk, CT 06851
Phone: (203)855-8499
Magazine devoted to issues concerning liquor control state systems. **Freq:** Bimonthly. **Print Method:** Offset. **Trim Size:** 8 x 10 7/8. **Cols./Page:** 3 and 2. **Col. Width:** 24 and 38 nonpareils. **Col. Depth:** 136 agate lines. **Key Personnel:** Richard Brandes, Editor; Tony Bongiovanni, Associate Publisher; Charlie Forman, Publisher, Senior Vice President. **URL:** http://stateways.com. **Ad Rates:** 4C $8235. **Remarks:** Accepts advertising. **Circ:** ‡8500.

6114 ■ Telemarketing & Call Center Solutions: The Magazine of Integrated Marketing
Technology Marketing Corp.
800 Connecticut Ave., 1st Fl.
Norwalk, CT 06854
Phone: (203)852-6800
Fax: (203)866-3326
Free: 800-243-6002
Publisher's E-mail: tmc@tmcnet.com
Magazine on telemarketing and business telecommunications technology. **Freq:** Monthly. **Print Method:** Offset. **Trim Size:** 8 1/4 x 11. **Cols./Page:** 3. **Col. Width:** 26 nonpareils. **Col. Depth:** 140 agate lines. **ISSN:** 0730-6156 (print). **Formerly**: Telemarketing. **Ad Rates:** BW $4,335; 4C $5,397. **Remarks:** Advertising accepted; rates available upon request. **Circ:** (Not Reported).

6115 ■ Totally Easy Sudoku
Penny Publications L.L.C.
6 Prowitt St.
Norwalk, CT 06855
Phone: (203)866-6688
Fax: (203)854-5962
Publisher's E-mail: corporatesales@pennypublications.com
Magazine for Sudoku novice. **Freq:** Quarterly. **Subscription Rates:** $14.97 Individuals. **URL:** http://pennydellpuzzles.com/product.aspx?c=EasySudoku&p=EFS. **Formerly**: Dell Easy Fast 'n' Fun Sudoku. **Remarks:** Accepts advertising. **Circ:** (Not Reported).

6116 ■ Tournament Variety Puzzles
Penny Publications L.L.C.
6 Prowitt St.
Norwalk, CT 06855
Phone: (203)866-6688
Fax: (203)854-5962
Publisher's E-mail: corporatesales@pennypublications.com
Magazine featuring different types of puzzle for solvers who loves a challenge. **Freq:** 4/yr. **Key Personnel:** Peter Kanter, President. **Subscription Rates:** $18.97 Individuals; $26.97 Other countries; $34.97 Two years; $50.97 Two years other countries. **URL:** http://pennydellpuzzles.com/product.aspx?c=mixeddifficulty&p=TG. **Formerly**: Master's Tournament Variety Puzzles. **Remarks:** Accepts advertising. **Circ:** (Not Reported).

6117 ■ Travel World News Magazine: The Magazine for Destination Travel Specialists
Travel Industry Network Inc.
28 Knight St.
Norwalk, CT 06851-4719
Phone: (203)286-6679
Fax: (203)286-6681
Publication E-mail: editor@travalworldnews.com
Magazine for the travel industry professional. **Freq:** Monthly. **Key Personnel:** Charles Gatt, Publisher; Carol A. Petro, Editor; Cindy Johnson, Manager, Circulation. **ISSN:** 1044--4602 (print). **Subscription Rates:** $25 By mail; $40 Canada; $60 Other countries. **URL:** http://www.travelworldnews.com. **Ad Rates:** GLR $890; BW $5,500; 4C $7,400. **Remarks:** Accepts advertising. **Circ:** (Not Reported).

6118 ■ Turbomachinery International
Business Journals Inc.
50 Day St.
Norwalk, CT 06854
Phone: (203)853-6015
Fax: (203)852-8175
Publisher's E-mail: bjisupport@busjour.com
Magazine for key management and engineering personnel in turbomachinery-using industries. Stimulates new approaches to energy conversion by providing technical concepts and details. **Freq:** Bimonthly. **Print Method:** Offset. **Trim Size:** 8 1/4 x 10 7/8. **Cols./Page:** 3. **Key Personnel:** Richard Zanetti, Publisher, phone: (203)663-7814; Peggy Eadie, Manager, Production, phone: (203)663-7838; Arthur Heilman, Manager, Circulation, phone: (203)663-7836; Kalyan Kalyanaraman, Executive Editor, phone: (203)663-7815. **ISSN:** 0149--4147 (print). **Subscription Rates:** $49 Individuals; $75 Two years; $75 Canada; $125 Canada for two years; $100 Other countries by airmail; $50 Individuals online only; $200 Institutions academic, online only. **URL:** http://turbomachinerymag.com/category/magazine. **Formerly**: Gas Turbine International. **Ad Rates:** BW $5,547; 4C $4,745; PCI $205. **Remarks:** Accepts advertising. **Circ:** (Not Reported).

6119 ■ Ultimate Favorite Variety Puzzles
Penny Publications L.L.C.
6 Prowitt St.
Norwalk, CT 06855
Phone: (203)866-6688
Fax: (203)854-5962
Publisher's E-mail: corporatesales@pennypublications.com
Magazine containing over 250 puzzles including Double Trouble, Alphabet Soup, Flower Power, and more. **Freq:** 8/year. **Subscription Rates:** $31.97 Individuals. **URL:** http://www.pennydellpuzzles.com/product.aspx?c=MixedDifficulty&p=RG. **Formerly**: Favorite Variety Puzzles and Games. **Remarks:** Accepts advertising. **Circ:** (Not Reported).

6120 ■ Whole Dog Journal
Belvoir Media Group L.L.C.
535 Connecticut Ave.
Norwalk, CT 06854-1631
Phone: (203)857-3100
Fax: (203)857-3013
Magazine covering various aspects of dog care and training. **Freq:** 13/yr. **Print Method:** Offset. **Cols./Page:** 6. **Col. Width:** 21 1/2 nonpareils. **Col. Depth:** 301 agate lines. **Key Personnel:** Nancy Kerns, Editor-in-Chief. **ISSN:** 8750--1740 (print). **Subscription Rates:** $20 Individuals 12 issues; $39 Other countries 12 issues; $30 Individuals 24 issues; $72 Other countries 24 issues. **URL:** http://www.whole-dog-journal.com. **Mailing address:** PO Box 5656, Norwalk, CT 06856-5656. **Remarks:** Advertising not accepted. **Circ:** (Not Reported).

6121 ■ World's Finest Variety Puzzles
Penny Publications L.L.C.
6 Prowitt St.
Norwalk, CT 06855
Phone: (203)866-6688
Fax: (203)854-5962
Publisher's E-mail: corporatesales@pennypublications.com
Magazine featuring cryptograms, code words, logic problems, and other word games. **Freq:** Quarterly. **Key Personnel:** Peter Kanter, President. **Subscription Rates:** $17.97 Individuals; $25.97 Other countries; $33.97 Two years; $49.97 Two years other countries. **URL:** http://pennydellpuzzles.com/product.aspx?&p=

Circulation: ★ = AAM; △ or • = BPA; ♦ = CAC; ❑ = VAC; ⊕ = PO Statement; ‡ = Publisher's Report; Boldface figures = sworn; Light figures = estimated.

WG. **Formerly**: Ultimate World's Finest Variety Puzzles. **Remarks:** Accepts advertising. **Circ:** (Not Reported).

6122 ■ WCTZ-FM - 96.7
444 Westport Ave., 3rd Fl.
Norwalk, CT 06851
Phone: (203)845-3030
Fax: (203)845-3097
Format: Adult Contemporary. **Owner:** Cox Radio Inc., 6205 Peachtree Dunwood Rd., Atlanta, GA 30328-4524, Ph: (678)645-0000, Fax: (678)645-5002. **Founded:** 1947. **Formerly**: WYRS-FM; KJAZ-FM; WKHL-FM. **Operating Hours**: Continuous. **Key Personnel:** Kristin Okesson, Gen. Mgr., VP, kristin.okesson@coxradio.com; Steve Soyland, Dir. of Mktg., Promotions Dir., steve.soyland@coxradio.com; Mike Raub, Asst. Mgr., mike.raub@coxradio.com; Shannon Kinney, Sales Mgr., shannon.kinney@coxradio.com; Keith Dakin, Operations Mgr., keith.dakin@coxradio.com; Steve Rugh, Dir. of Traffic, steve.rugh@coxradio.com. **Wattage**: 3,000. **Ad Rates:** $65-100 per unit.

6123 ■ WFOX-FM - 95.9
444 Westport Ave., 3rd Fl.
Norwalk, CT 06851
Phone: (203)783-8200
Fax: (203)783-8383
Format: Classic Rock. **Owner:** Cox Radio Inc., 6205 Peachtree Dunwood Rd., Atlanta, GA 30328-4524, Ph: (678)645-0000, Fax: (678)645-5002. **Founded:** 1975. **Formerly**: WDRN-FM; WEFX-FM. **Operating Hours**: Continuous. **Key Personnel:** John Voket, Gen. Mgr.; Steve Soyland, Div. Dir.; Kristin Okesson, Dir. of Sales, kristin.okesson@connoisseurct.com. **Wattage:** 3,000. **Ad Rates:** Noncommercial. **URL:** http://www.959thefox.com.

6124 ■ WNLK-AM - 1350
444 Westport Ave., 3rd Fl.
Norwalk, CT 06851
Phone: (203)845-3030
Fax: (203)845-3097
Format: News; Talk. **Owner:** Cox Radio Inc., 6205 Peachtree Dunwood Rd., Atlanta, GA 30328-4524, Ph: (678)645-0000, Fax: (678)645-5002. **Founded:** 1948. **Operating Hours**: Continuous; 5% network, 95% local. **Key Personnel:** Kristin Okesson, Gen. Mgr., VP, kristin.okesson@coxradio.com; Keith Dakin, Operations Mgr., keith.dakin@coxradio.com; Shannon Kinney, Sales Mgr., shannon.kinney@coxradio.com; Dawn Wachner, Promotions Mgr., dawn.wachner@coxradio.com; Jennifer Barbin, Director, jennifer.barbin@coxradio.com. **Wattage**: 1,000. **Ad Rates:** Advertising accepted; rates available upon request.

6125 ■ WSTC-AM - 1400
444 Westport Ave., 3rd Fl.
Norwalk, CT 06851
Phone: (203)845-3030
Fax: (203)845-3097
Format: News; Talk. **Networks:** ABC. **Owner:** Cox Radio Inc., 6205 Peachtree Dunwood Rd., Atlanta, GA 30328-4524, Ph: (678)645-0000, Fax: (678)645-5002. **Founded:** 1941. **Operating Hours**: Continuous. **Key Personnel:** Eric McDonald, Dir. of Programs, eric.mcdonald@coxradio.com; Dawn Wachner, Promotions Mgr., dawn.wachner@coxradio.com; Jennifer Barbin, Director, jennifer.barbin@coxradio.com. **Wattage**: 1,000. **Ad Rates:** $85-125 per unit.

6126 ■ W203BB-FM - 88.5
PO Box 391
Twin Falls, ID 83303
Fax: (208)736-1958
Free: 800-357-4226
Format: Religious; Contemporary Christian. **Owner:** CSN International, PO Box 391, Twin Falls, ID 83303, Ph: (208)736-1958, Fax: (208)736-1958, Free: 800-357-4226. **Key Personnel:** Ray Gorney, Dir. of Engg.; Kelly Carlson, Dir. of Engg.; Don Mills, Music Dir., Prog. Dir. **URL:** http://www.csnradio.com.

NORWICH

SE CT. New London Co. 15 mi. N. of New London. Residential.

6127 ■ Norwich Bulletin
Norwich Bulletin
66 Franklin St.
Norwich, CT 06360
Phone: (860)887-9211
Fax: (860)887-9666
Publisher's E-mail: news@norwichbulletin.com
General newspaper. **Founded:** 1791. **Freq:** Daily and Sun. **Print Method:** Offset. **Cols./Page:** 6. **Col. Width:** 2 inches. **Col. Depth:** 301 agate lines. **Key Personnel:** Dan Graziano, Director, Advertising; James Konrad, Executive Editor. **Subscription Rates:** $234 Individuals by mail; $260 Out of state by mail. **URL:** http://www.norwichbulletin.com. **Remarks:** Accepts advertising. **Circ:** Mon.-Fri. **★26252**, Sun. **★29332**, Sat. **★26545**.

6128 ■ Hall Communications Inc.
40 Cuprak Rd.
Norwich, CT 06360
Format: Contemporary Hit Radio (CHR); News; Country; Sports; Talk; Classic Rock; Information. **Networks:** ESPN Radio. **Founded:** 1964. **Ad Rates:** Accepts Advertising. **URL:** http://www.hallradio.com.

6129 ■ WCTY-FM - 97.7
40 Cuprak Rd.
Norwich, CT 06360-0551
Phone: (860)887-3511
Fax: (860)886-7649
Format: Country. **Networks:** ABC; CRN International; TNNR (The Nashville Network Radio). **Owner:** Hall Comunications Inc., 404 W Lime St., Lakeland, FL 33815-4651, Ph: (863)682-8184, Fax: (863)683-2409. **Founded:** 1968. **Operating Hours**: Continuous. **Key Personnel:** Andy Russell, Gen. Mgr., VP, arussell@hallradio.net; Jimmy Lane, Music Dir., jimmy@wcty.com; Dave Elder, Dir. of Programs, dave@wcty.com. **Wattage:** 3,000. **Ad Rates:** Noncommercial. Combined advertising rates available with WICH-AM, WKNL-FM, and WNLC-FM. **URL:** http://www.wcty.com.

6130 ■ WEDN-TV - 53
1049 Asylum Ave.
Hartford, CT 06105
Phone: (860)275-7550
Format: Public TV. **Simulcasts:** WEDH-TV. **Networks:** Public Broadcasting Service (PBS). **Owner:** Connecticut Public Broadcasting Network, 1049 Asylum Ave., Hartford, CT 06105-2432, Ph: (860)275-7550. **Founded:** 1962. **Operating Hours**: 6:45 a.m.-midnight Daily; 8 a.m.-midnight Sat.; 7:30 a.m.-midnight Sun. **ADI:** Hartford-New Haven (New London), CT. **Local Programs**: *On The Record*, Friday. **Wattage**: 802,000. **Ad Rates:** Advertising accepted; rates available upon request. **URL:** http://www.cpbn.org.

6131 ■ WICH-AM - 1310
PO Box 551
Norwich, CT 06360
Phone: (860)887-3511
Email: news@wich.com
Format: Adult Contemporary; Talk. **Key Personnel:** Andy Russell, Contact; Andy Russell, Contact. **Ad Rates:** Advertising accepted; rates available upon request. **URL:** http://www.wich.com.

6132 ■ WNPR-FM - 89.1
1049 Asylum Ave.
Hartford, CT 06105
Phone: (860)278-5310
Email: education@cpbn.org
Format: Public Radio. **Networks:** National Public Radio (NPR); Public Radio International (PRI). **Owner:** Connecticut Public Broadcasting Network, 1049 Asylum Ave., Hartford, CT 06105-2432, Ph: (860)275-7550. **Founded:** Sept. 19, 2006. **Operating Hours**: Continuous. **Key Personnel:** Lynn R. Fusco, Chairperson. **Wattage**: 5,100. **Ad Rates:** Noncommercial. **URL:** http://www.cpbn.org.

OLD GREENWICH

6133 ■ Greenwich Time
Hearst Connecticut Media Group
1445 E Putnam Ave.
Old Greenwich, CT 06870
Phone: (203)625-4400
General newspaper. **Freq:** Daily. **Print Method:** Offset. **Cols./Page:** 6. **Col. Width:** 2 1/16 inches. **Col. Depth:** 21 1/2 inches. **Key Personnel:** Thomas Mellana, Managing Editor, phone: (203)625-4470. **Online:** Hearst Connecticut Media Group Hearst Connecticut Media Group. **Alt. Formats:** Handheld. **URL:** http://www.greenwichtime.com. **Remarks:** Advertising accepted; rates available upon request. **Circ:** (Not Reported).

OLD LYME

SE CT. New London Co. Mouth of the Connecticut River on the Long Island Sound, 11 mi. SW of London. Residential.

6134 ■ Chihuahua Connection
Chihuahua Connection L.L.C.
PO Box 579
Old Lyme, CT 06371
Magazine focusing on Chihuahua breed. **Freq:** Bimonthly. **Trim Size:** 8.5 x 11. **Subscription Rates:** $29.95 Individuals regular; $45.95 Individuals first class; $49.95 Canada and Mexico; $59.95 Other countries. **URL:** http://newchihuahuaconnection.com. **Ad Rates:** BW $300. **Remarks:** Accepts advertising. **Circ:** (Not Reported).

OXFORD

6135 ■ La Catastrophe
Wreck and Crash Mail Society
c/o Ken Sanford
613 Championship Dr.
Oxford, CT 06478-128
Phone: (203)888-9237
Fax: (203)888-9237
Freq: Quarterly. **Subscription Rates:** Included in membership. **Remarks:** Advertising not accepted. **Circ:** (Not Reported).

6136 ■ North American Windpower
Zackin Publications Inc.
100 Willenbrock Rd.
Oxford, CT 06478
Phone: (203)262-4670
Publication E-mail: info@nawindpower.com
Magazine for professionals in the wind power industry. **Freq:** Monthly. **Trim Size:** 10 - 3/4 x 13 - 1/4. **Key Personnel:** Cheryl Samide, Manager, Accounting, Office Manager; Mark DelFranco, Editor; Michael Bates, Publisher. **Subscription Rates:** Free to wind industry professionals. **URL:** http://www.nawindpower.com/new_home.php. **Remarks:** Accepts advertising. **Circ:** ‡14000.

6137 ■ Secondary Marketing Executive: Journal of Mortgage Banking
Zackin Publications Inc.
100 Willenbrock Rd.
Oxford, CT 06478
Phone: (203)262-4670
Publisher's E-mail: info@zackin.com
Trade magazine (tabloid) covering the buying and selling of mortgages and mortgage servicing in the secondary market. **Freq:** Monthly. **Print Method:** Offset. **Trim Size:** 10 3/4 x 13 1/4. **Cols./Page:** 4. **Col. Width:** 13 3/5 picas. **Col. Depth:** 81 picas. **Key Personnel:** Cheryl Samide, Manager, Accounting, Office Manager; Vanessa Williams, Account Executive; Patrick Barnard, Editor; Paul Zackin, President. **ISSN:** 0891--2947 (print). **URL:** http://www.mortgageorb.com/online/issues/SME. **Remarks:** Advertising accepted; rates available upon request. **Circ:** (Not Reported).

6138 ■ Servicing Management: The Magazine for Loan Servicing Administrators
Zackin Publications Inc.
100 Willenbrock Rd.
Oxford, CT 06478
Phone: (203)262-4670
Publisher's E-mail: info@zackin.com
Trade magazine for mortgage professionals involved with mortgage loan servicing. **Freq:** Monthly. **Print Method:** Offset. **Trim Size:** 10 3/4 x 13 1/4. **Cols./Page:** 4. **Col. Width:** 2 1/4 inches. **Col. Depth:** 13 1/2 inches. **Key Personnel:** Vanessa Williams, Account Executive; Paul Zackin, President; Michael Bates, Publisher. **ISSN:** 1044-1077 (print). **Subscription Rates:** $48 Individuals; $72 Two years. **URL:** http://www.sm-online.com/sm/main.php. **Ad Rates:** BW $3395; 4C $4540. **Remarks:** Accepts advertising. **Circ:** Controlled 19000.

PAWCATUCK

6139 ■ WVVE-FM - 102.3
Liberty Street Ext.
Pawcatuck, CT 06379
Phone: (203)599-2214
Fax: (203)594-3568

Format: Oldies. **Networks:** AP; Connecticut Radio. **Owner:** Shoreline Communications, Inc., PO Box 97, Mystic, CT 06355, Ph: (203)447-1045. **Founded:** 1981. **Formerly**: WFAN-FM. **Operating Hours**: Continuous. **ADI**: Hartford-New Haven (New London), CT. **Key Personnel:** Richard Williams, Chief Engineer; Karen Perrin, Traffic Mgr.; Kevin O'Connor, Dir. of Programs; Bill Haberman, News Dir.; Robert Elmer, Gen. Sales Mgr; David J. Quinn, Contact; Karen A. Quinn, Contact. **Wattage**: 3,000. **Ad Rates:** $25.20-40.50 for 30 seconds; $28-45 for 60 seconds.

POMFRET

6140 ■ WBVC-FM - 91.1
398 Pomfret St.
Pomfret, CT 06258-0128
Phone: (860)963-6100
Email: techsupport@pomfretschool.org
Format: Eclectic. **Owner:** Pomfret School, 398 Pomfret St., Pomfret, CT 06258-0128, Ph: (860)963-6100. **Operating Hours**: Continuous. **Wattage**: 100. **URL:** http://www.pomfretschool.org.

PROSPECT

SC ST. New Haven Co. 3 mi. S. of Waterbury. Residential.

6141 ■ WJMJ-FM - 88.9
15 Peach Orchard Rd.
Prospect, CT 06712-1052
Phone: (860)242-8800
Free: 877-342-5956
Format: Classical; Easy Listening; Big Band/Nostalgia. **Networks:** ABC. **Owner:** Archdiocese of Hartford, 134 Farmington Ave., Hartford, CT 06105, Ph: (860)541-6491. **Founded:** 1976. **Operating Hours**: 5 a.m.-12 midnight. **Key Personnel:** Fr. John P. Gatzak, Gen. Mgr. **Wattage**: 6,200 ERP. **Ad Rates:** Noncommercial. **URL:** http://www.ortv.org.

PUTNAM

NE CT. Windham Co. On Quinnebaug River, 28 mi. NW of Providence, RI. Manufactures phonograph needles, paper boxes, shoes, novelties, pointed steel goods. Silk, woolen mills; foundry. Dairy, poultry, fruit farms.

6142 ■ WINY-AM - 1350
PO Box 231
Putnam, CT 06260
Phone: (860)928-1350
Email: info@winyradio.com
Format: Adult Contemporary. **Networks:** AP; Jones Satellite. **Owner:** Osbrey Broadcasting Co., at above address. **Founded:** 1953. **Operating Hours**: Continuous. **ADI**: Providence, RI-New Bedford, MA. **Key Personnel:** Karen Osbrey, Office Mgr., kareno@winyradio.com. **Local Programs**: *The Morning Show with Gary O*, Monday Tuesday Wednesday Thursday Friday 6:00 a.m. - 9:00 a.m. **Wattage**: 5,000. **Ad Rates:** $22-28 for 30 seconds. **URL:** http://www.winyradio.com.

REDDING

6143 ■ Antitrust Law Journal
American Bar Association
81 Seventy Acre Rd.
Redding, CT 06896
Phone: (203)938-8507
Fax: (203)938-2845
Publication E-mail: antitrust@att.net
Magazine for lawyers and legal professionals devoted exclusively to antitrust. **Freq:** 3/year. **Key Personnel:** Tina M. Miller, Executive Editor. **ISSN:** 0003--6056 (print). **Subscription Rates:** $30 /year for non-lawyers; $75 Individuals. **URL:** http://www.americanbar.org/groups/antitrust_law/publications/antitrust_law_journal.html. **Formerly**: Antitrust Law Magazine. **Remarks:** Advertising not accepted. **Circ:** Combined 10000.

6144 ■ Atomization and Sprays: Journal of the International Institute for Liquid Atomization & Spray Systems
Begell House Inc.
50 Cross Hwy.
Redding, CT 06896
Phone: (203)938-1300
Fax: (203)938-1304
Publisher's E-mail: orders@begellhouse.com
Journal publishing original papers reporting experimental and theoretical investigations of liquids and sprays. **Freq:** Monthly. **Print Method:** Offset. **Trim Size:** 7 x 10. **Cols./Page:** 1. **Col. Width:** 30 picas. **Col. Depth:** 47 picas. **Key Personnel:** Soo-Young No, Editor-in-Chief; Marco Marengo, Editor-in-Chief. **ISSN:** 1044--5110 (print); **EISSN:** 1936--2684 (electronic). **Subscription Rates:** $1855 Individuals; $1732 Individuals online; $1904 Individuals print and online; $1000 Individuals Archival Back Files 1 Year Lease. **URL:** http://www.begellhouse.com/journals/atomization-and-sprays.html. **Remarks:** Accepts advertising. **Circ:** (Not Reported).

6145 ■ Composites: Mechanics, Computations, Applications
Begell House Inc.
50 Cross Hwy.
Redding, CT 06896
Phone: (203)938-1300
Fax: (203)938-1304
Publisher's E-mail: orders@begellhouse.com
Journal featuring basic ideas in the mechanics of composite materials and structures between research workers and engineers. **Key Personnel:** Yuri G. Yanovsky, Editor-in-Chief. **ISSN:** 2152--2057 (print); **EISSN:** 2152--2073 (electronic). **Subscription Rates:** $1003 Individuals print + online; $975 Individuals print; $912 Individuals online. **URL:** http://www.begellhouse.com/journals/36ff4a142dec9609; http://www.begellhouse.com/journals/composites-mechanics-computations-applications-an-international-journal.html. **Circ:** (Not Reported).

6146 ■ Computational Thermal Sciences
Begell House Inc.
50 Cross Hwy.
Redding, CT 06896
Phone: (203)938-1300
Fax: (203)938-1304
Publisher's E-mail: orders@begellhouse.com
Journal focusing on the fundamental methods of thermodynamics, fluid mechanics, heat transfer and combustion. **Key Personnel:** Graham de Vahl Davis, Founder, Editor; Ivan Egorov, Editor-in-Chief; Darrell Pepper, Associate Editor. **ISSN:** 1940--2503 (print); **EISSN:** 1940--2554 (electronic). **Subscription Rates:** $950 Individuals print + online; $923 Individuals print; $864 Individuals online. **URL:** http://www.begellhouse.com/journals/648192910890cd0e; http://www.begellhouse.com/journals/computational-thermal-sciences.html. **Circ:** (Not Reported).

6147 ■ Critical Reviews in Therapeutic Drug Carrier Systems
Begell House Inc.
50 Cross Hwy.
Redding, CT 06896
Phone: (203)938-1300
Fax: (203)938-1304
Publisher's E-mail: orders@begellhouse.com
Journal covering life sciences, engineering, and technology. **Freq:** Bimonthly. **Print Method:** Offset. **Trim Size:** 7 x 10. **Cols./Page:** 1. **Col. Width:** 30 picas. **Col. Depth:** 46 picas. **Key Personnel:** Mandip Sachdeva, Editor-in-Chief; Dr. James Birchall, Associate Editor. **ISSN:** 0743--4863 (print); **EISSN:** 2162--660X (electronic). **Subscription Rates:** $1436 Individuals print only; $1368 Individuals online only; $1504 Individuals print and online; $1250 archival back files 1 year lease. **URL:** http://www.begellhouse.com/journals/critical-reviews-in-therapeutic-drug-carrier-systems.html. **Remarks:** Accepts advertising. **Circ:** Paid 500.

6148 ■ Ethics in Biology, Engineering and Medicine
Begell House Inc.
50 Cross Hwy.
Redding, CT 06896
Phone: (203)938-1300
Fax: (203)938-1304
Publisher's E-mail: orders@begellhouse.com
Peer-reviewed journal covering ethical issues on biomedical research and the development of new biomaterials, implants, devices and treatments. **Key Personnel:** Subrata Saha, Editor-in-Chief. **ISSN:** 2151--805X (print); **EISSN:** 2151--8068 (electronic). **Subscription Rates:** $918 Individuals print + online; $893 Individuals print; $834 Individuals online. **URL:** http://www.begellhouse.com/journals/6ed509641f7324e6; http://www.begellhouse.com/journals/ethics-in-biology-engineering-and-medicine.html. **Circ:** (Not Reported).

6149 ■ Forum on Immunopathological Diseases and Therapeutics
Begell House Inc.
50 Cross Hwy.
Redding, CT 06896
Phone: (203)938-1300
Fax: (203)938-1304
Publisher's E-mail: orders@begellhouse.com
Journal publishing articles on immunopathological diseases and therapeutics. **Key Personnel:** Benjamin Bonavida, Editor-in-Chief; Zouhair Atassi, Editor-in-Chief. **ISSN:** 2151--8017 (print); **EISSN:** 2151--8025 (electronic). **Subscription Rates:** $1058 Individuals print + online; $1027 Individuals print; $960 Individuals online. **URL:** http://www.begellhouse.com/journals/forum-on-immunopathological-diseases-and-therapeutics.html. **Circ:** (Not Reported).

6150 ■ Heat Exchanger Design Update
Begell House Inc.
50 Cross Hwy.
Redding, CT 06896
Phone: (203)938-1300
Fax: (203)938-1304
Publisher's E-mail: orders@begellhouse.com
Professional journal covering chemical and mechanical engineering. **Freq:** Quarterly. **Print Method:** Offset. **Trim Size:** 8 1/2 x 11. **Cols./Page:** 2. **Key Personnel:** Frank W. Schmidt, Editor; Jerry Taborek, Editor; Gian Piero Celata, Editor; Geoffrey F. Hewitt, Executive Editor; Kenneth J. Bell, Editor; David Butterworth, Editor; Clive F. Beaton, Editor. **ISSN:** 1074--7214 (print). **Subscription Rates:** $534 Institutions print. **URL:** http://www.begellhouse.com/journals/heat-exchanger-design-updates.html. **Remarks:** Advertising not accepted. **Circ:** Paid 100.

6151 ■ Heat Pipe Science and Technology
Begell House Inc.
50 Cross Hwy.
Redding, CT 06896
Phone: (203)938-1300
Fax: (203)938-1304
Publisher's E-mail: orders@begellhouse.com
Journal featuring the fundamentals, principles and technologies associated with the design and operation of heat pipes and thermosyphons. **Key Personnel:** Leonard L. Vasiliev, Editor-in-Chief; Marcia B.H. Mantelli, Editor-in-Chief. **ISSN:** 2151--7975 (print); **EISSN:** 2151--7991 (electronic). **Subscription Rates:** $857 Individuals print + online; $835 Individuals print; $780 Individuals online. **URL:** http://www.begellhouse.com/journals/4b0844fc3a2ef17f; http://www.begellhouse.com/journals/heat-pipe-science-and-technology.html. **Circ:** (Not Reported).

6152 ■ Hydrobiological Journal
Begell House Inc.
50 Cross Hwy.
Redding, CT 06896
Phone: (203)938-1300
Fax: (203)938-1304
Publisher's E-mail: orders@begellhouse.com
Translation of a periodical on freshwater biology. Original work and reviews on physiology, biochemistry, ecology and conservation of freshwater fish, invertebrates, vascular plants, and plankton, as well as biological effects of pollution of inland waters. **Freq:** 6/year. **Print Method:** Offset. **Cols./Page:** 1. **Col. Width:** 84 nonpareils. **Col. Depth:** 140 agate lines. **Key Personnel:** V.D. Romanenko, Editor-in-Chief. **ISSN:** 0018--8166 (print); **EISSN:** 1943--5991 (electronic). **URL:** http://www.begellhouse.com/journals/hydrobiological-journal.html. **Remarks:** Accepts advertising. **Circ:** 325.

6153 ■ International Journal on Algae
Begell House Inc.
50 Cross Hwy.
Redding, CT 06896
Phone: (203)938-1300
Fax: (203)938-1304
Publisher's E-mail: orders@begellhouse.com
Journal covering fundamental and applied aspects in algology. **Freq:** Quarterly. **Key Personnel:** Solomon

Circulation: ★ = AAM; △ or • = BPA; ♦ = CAC; ❑ = VAC; ⊕ = PO Statement; ‡ = Publisher's Report; Boldface figures = sworn; Light figures = estimated.

Wasser, Editor-in-Chief. **ISSN:** 1521--9429 (print); **EISSN:** 1940--4328 (electronic). **Subscription Rates:** $1398 Individuals print + online; $1358 Individuals print; $1268 Individuals online. **URL:** http://www.begellhouse.com/journals/7dd4467e7de5b7ef; http://www.begellhouse.com/journals/journal-on-algae.html. **Circ:** (Not Reported).

6154 ■ International Journal of Energetic Materials and Chemical Propulsion
Begell House Inc.
50 Cross Hwy.
Redding, CT 06896
Phone: (203)938-1300
Fax: (203)938-1304
Publisher's E-mail: orders@begellhouse.com
Journal promoting scientific investigation, technical advancements and information exchange on energetic materials and chemical propulsion. **Key Personnel:** Kenneth Kuo, Editor-in-Chief. **ISSN:** 2150--766X (print); **EISSN:** 2150--7678 (electronic). **Subscription Rates:** $1531 Individuals print + online; $1489 Individuals print; $1391 Individuals online. **URL:** http://www.begellhouse.com/journals/17bbb47e377ce023; http://www.begellhouse.com/journals/energetic-materials-and-chemical-propulsion.html. **Circ:** (Not Reported).

6155 ■ International Journal of Fluid Mechanics Research
Begell House Inc.
50 Cross Hwy.
Redding, CT 06896
Phone: (203)938-1300
Fax: (203)938-1304
Publisher's E-mail: orders@begellhouse.com
Journal publishing articles on fluid mechanics. **Key Personnel:** Victor Grinchenko, Editor-in-Chief. **ISSN:** 1064--2277 (print); **EISSN:** 2152--5102 (electronic). **Subscription Rates:** $2394 Individuals print + online; $2327 Individuals print; $2175 Individuals online. **URL:** http://www.begellhouse.com/journals/71cb29ca5b40f8f8; http://www.begellhouse.com/journals/fluid-mechanics-research.html. **Circ:** (Not Reported).

6156 ■ International Journal for Medicinal Mushrooms
Begell House Inc.
50 Cross Hwy.
Redding, CT 06896
Phone: (203)938-1300
Fax: (203)938-1304
Publisher's E-mail: orders@begellhouse.com
Journal publishing original research articles and critical reviews on medicinal mushrooms. **Key Personnel:** Solomon Wasser, Editor-in-Chief. **ISSN:** 1521--9437 (print); **EISSN:** 1940--4344 (electronic). **Subscription Rates:** $1396 Individuals print + online; $1358 Individuals print; $1267 Individuals online. **URL:** http://www.begellhouse.com/journals/708ae68d64b17c52; http://www.begellhouse.com/journals/medicinal-mushrooms.html. **Circ:** (Not Reported).

6157 ■ International Journal for Multiscale Computational Engineering
Begell House Inc.
50 Cross Hwy.
Redding, CT 06896
Phone: (203)938-1300
Fax: (203)938-1304
Publisher's E-mail: orders@begellhouse.com
Journal featuring the advancement of multiscale computational science and engineering. **Key Personnel:** Jacob Fish, Editor-in-Chief. **ISSN:** 1543--1649 (print); **EISSN:** 1940--4352 (electronic). **Subscription Rates:** $1644 Individuals print + online; $1600 Individuals print; $1527 Individuals online. **URL:** http://www.begellhouse.com/journals/61fd1b191cf7e96f; http://www.begellhouse.com/journals/multiscale-computational-engineering.html. **Circ:** (Not Reported).

6158 ■ International Journal of Physiology and Pathophysiology
Begell House Inc.
50 Cross Hwy.
Redding, CT 06896
Phone: (203)938-1300
Fax: (203)938-1304
Publisher's E-mail: orders@begellhouse.com
Journal publishing original papers on physiology, pathophysiology and experimental medicine. **Key Personnel:** Vadym Sagach, Editor-in-Chief. **ISSN:** 2155--014X (print); **EISSN:** 2155--0158 (electronic). **Subscription Rates:** $1003 Individuals print + online; $973 Individuals print; $911 Individuals online. **URL:** http://www.begellhouse.com/journals/6ec4ba27650016b1; http://www.begellhouse.com/journals/physiology-and-pathophysiology.html. **Circ:** (Not Reported).

6159 ■ International Journal for Uncertainty Quantification
Begell House Inc.
50 Cross Hwy.
Redding, CT 06896
Phone: (203)938-1300
Fax: (203)938-1304
Publisher's E-mail: orders@begellhouse.com
Journal featuring articles in the areas of analysis, modeling, design and control of complex systems in the presence of uncertainty. **Key Personnel:** Nicholas Zabaras, Editor-in-Chief; Dongbin Xiu, Associate Editor. **ISSN:** 2152--5080 (print); **EISSN:** 2152--5099 (electronic). **Subscription Rates:** $950 Individuals print + online; $924 Individuals print; $863 Individuals online. **URL:** http://www.begellhouse.com/journals/uncertainty-quantification.html; http://uncertainty-quantification.com. **Circ:** (Not Reported).

6160 ■ Journal of Automation and Information Sciences
Begell House Inc.
50 Cross Hwy.
Redding, CT 06896
Phone: (203)938-1300
Fax: (203)938-1304
Publisher's E-mail: orders@begellhouse.com
Journal for scientist and engineers concerned with automation control systems and information processing. Contains translations of Russian papers. **Freq:** Monthly. **Key Personnel:** N.V. Turovyerova, Associate Editor; Vsevold M. Kuntsevich, Editor-in-Chief. **ISSN:** 1064--2315 (print); **EISSN:** 2163--9337 (electronic). **Subscription Rates:** $2753 Individuals print only; $2572 Individuals online only; $2829 Individuals print + online; $1000 Individuals archival Back Files 1 Year Lease. **URL:** http://www.begellhouse.com/journals/automation-and-information-sciences.html. **Remarks:** Advertising not accepted. **Circ:** (Not Reported).

6161 ■ Journal of Enhanced Heat Transfer
Begell House Inc.
50 Cross Hwy.
Redding, CT 06896
Phone: (203)938-1300
Fax: (203)938-1304
Publisher's E-mail: orders@begellhouse.com
Journal relating to enhanced heat transfer in natural and forced convection of liquids and gases, boiling, condensation, and radiative heat transfer. **Freq:** Quarterly. **Key Personnel:** Ralph Webb, Editor, Founder; Raj M. Manglik, Editor-in-Chief. **ISSN:** 1065--5131 (print); **EISSN:** 1563--5074 (electronic). **Subscription Rates:** $971 Individuals print only; $907 Individuals online only; $996 Individuals print + online. **URL:** http://www.begellhouse.com/journals/enhanced-heat-transfer.html. **Circ:** (Not Reported).

6162 ■ Journal of Environmental Pathology, Toxicology and Oncology
Begell House Inc.
50 Cross Hwy.
Redding, CT 06896
Phone: (203)938-1300
Fax: (203)938-1304
Publisher's E-mail: orders@begellhouse.com
Journal covering research and reviews of factors and conditions that affect human and animal carcinogenesis. **Key Personnel:** Qian Peng, Editor-in-Chief. **ISSN:** 0731-8898 (print); **EISSN:** 2162-6537 (electronic). **Subscription Rates:** $1205 Individuals print + online. **URL:** http://www.begellhouse.com/journals/0ff459a57a4c08d0. **Circ:** (Not Reported).

6163 ■ Journal of Flow Visualization and Image Processing
Begell House Inc.
50 Cross Hwy.
Redding, CT 06896
Phone: (203)938-1300
Fax: (203)938-1304
Publisher's E-mail: orders@begellhouse.com
Peer-reviewed journal covering articles in the areas of flow visualization and image processing. **Freq:** Quarterly. **Key Personnel:** Sadanari Mochizuki, Advisor; Kenneth D. Kihm, Editor-in-Chief; Jean-Pierre Prenel, Advisor. **ISSN:** 1065--3090 (print); **EISSN:** 1940--4336 (electronic). **Subscription Rates:** $996 Individuals print + online; $949 Individuals print; $887 Individuals online. **URL:** http://www.begellhouse.com/journals/52b74bd3689ab10b; http://www.begellhouse.com/journals/flow-visualization-and-image-processing.html. **Circ:** (Not Reported).

6164 ■ Journal of Long-Term Effects of Medical Implants
Begell House Inc.
50 Cross Hwy.
Redding, CT 06896
Phone: (203)938-1300
Fax: (203)938-1304
Publisher's E-mail: orders@begellhouse.com
Peer-reviewed journal covering medical implants. **Key Personnel:** Subrata Saha, Editor-in-Chief. **ISSN:** 1050--6934 (print); **EISSN:** 1940--4379 (electronic). **Subscription Rates:** $1416 Individuals print + online; $1378 Individuals print; $1287 Individuals online. **URL:** http://www.begellhouse.com/journals/1bef42082d7a0fdf; http://www.begellhouse.com/journals/long-term-effects-of-medical-implants.html. **Circ:** (Not Reported).

6165 ■ Journal of Women and Minorities in Science and Engineering
Begell House Inc.
50 Cross Hwy.
Redding, CT 06896
Phone: (203)938-1300
Fax: (203)938-1304
Publisher's E-mail: orders@begellhouse.com
Peer-reviewed journal featuring innovative ideas and programs for classroom teachers, scientific studies, and formulation of concepts related to the education, recruitment, and retention of under-represented groups in science and engineering. **Key Personnel:** Kimberly D. Douglas-Mankin, Editor-in-Chief; Howard Adams, Associate Editor. **ISSN:** 1072--8325 (print); **EISSN:** 1940--431X (electronic). **Subscription Rates:** $349 Individuals print + online; $339 Individuals print; $318 Individuals online. **URL:** http://www.begellhouse.com/journals/00551c876cc2f027; http://www.begellhouse.com/journals/journal-of-women-and-minorities-in-science-and-engineering.html. **Circ:** (Not Reported).

6166 ■ Multiphase Science and Technology
Begell House Inc.
50 Cross Hwy.
Redding, CT 06896
Phone: (203)938-1300
Fax: (203)938-1304
Publisher's E-mail: orders@begellhouse.com
Journal covering multiphase science and technology. **Freq:** Quarterly. **Key Personnel:** Omar Matar, Editor-in-Chief; Jean-Marc Delhaye, Editor-in-Chief. **ISSN:** 0276--1459 (print); **EISSN:** 1943--6181 (electronic). **Subscription Rates:** $1155 Individuals print + online; $1123 Individuals print; $1051 Individuals online. **URL:** http://www.begellhouse.com/journals/5af8c23d50e0a883; http://www.begellhouse.com/journals/multiphase-science-and-technology.html. **Circ:** (Not Reported).

6167 ■ Nanomechanics Science and Technology: An International Journal
Begell House Inc.
50 Cross Hwy.
Redding, CT 06896
Phone: (203)938-1300
Fax: (203)938-1304
Publisher's E-mail: orders@begellhouse.com
Journal covering the areas of nano- and micromechanics. **Key Personnel:** Eduard E. Son, Editor-in-Chief; Yuri G. Yanovsky, Editor-in-Chief. **ISSN:** 1947--5748 (print); **EISSN:** 1947--5756 (electronic). **Subscription Rates:** $1057 Individuals print + online; $1028 Individuals print; $960 Individuals online. **URL:** http://www.begellhouse.com/journals/11e12455066dab5d; http://www.begellhouse.com/journals/nanomechanics-science-and-technology.html. **Circ:** (Not Reported).

6168 ■ Plasma Medicine
Begell House Inc.
50 Cross Hwy.
Redding, CT 06896
Phone: (203)938-1300
Fax: (203)938-1304
Publisher's E-mail: orders@begellhouse.com
Interdisciplinary journal providing emphasis on medicine, biology, plasma science and technology. **Key Personnel:** Alexander A. Fridman, Editor-in-Chief; Gary Friedman, Board Member. **ISSN:** 1947--5764 (print); **EISSN:** 1947--5772 (electronic). **Subscription Rates:** $936 Individuals print + online; $908 Individuals print; $850 Individuals online. **URL:** http://www.begellhouse.com/journals/5a5b4a3d419387fb; http://www.begellhouse.com/journals/plasma-medicine.html. **Circ:** (Not Reported).

6169 ■ Radio Physics and Radio Astronomy
Begell House Inc.
50 Cross Hwy.
Redding, CT 06896
Phone: (203)938-1300
Fax: (203)938-1304
Publisher's E-mail: orders@begellhouse.com
Journal publishing articles on investigations in present-day radio physics and electronic engineering, radio astronomy and astrophysics. **Key Personnel:** Leonid M. Lytvynenko, Editor-in-Chief. **ISSN:** 2152--274X (print); **EISSN:** 2152--2758 (electronic). **Subscription Rates:** $300 Individuals achival back files. **URL:** http://www.begellhouse.com/journals/6fd1549c0e2c05da; http://www.begellhouse.com/journals/radio-physics-and-radio-astronomy.html. **Circ:** (Not Reported).

6170 ■ Special Topics & Reviews in Porous Media: An International Journal
Begell House Inc.
50 Cross Hwy.
Redding, CT 06896
Phone: (203)938-1300
Fax: (203)938-1304
Publisher's E-mail: orders@begellhouse.com
Peer-reviewed journal covering research in fields related to porous media. **Key Personnel:** Kambiz Vafai, Editor-in-Chief. **ISSN:** 2151--4798 (print); **EISSN:** 2151--562X (electronic). **Subscription Rates:** $918 Individuals print + online; $892 Individuals print; $834 Individuals online. **URL:** http://www.begellhouse.com/journals/3d21681c18f5b5e7; http://www.begellhouse.com/journals/special-topics-and-reviews-in-porous-media.html. **Circ:** (Not Reported).

6171 ■ Telecommunications and Radio Engineering
Begell House Inc.
50 Cross Hwy.
Redding, CT 06896
Phone: (203)938-1300
Fax: (203)938-1304
Publisher's E-mail: orders@begellhouse.com
Journal covering telecommunications and radio engineering. **Key Personnel:** Anatoly Ivanovich Fisun, Editor-in-Chief; Vladimir M. Yakovenko, Editor-in-Chief. **ISSN:** 0040--2508 (print); **EISSN:** 1943--6009 (electronic). **Subscription Rates:** $4969 Individuals print + online; $4834 Individuals print; $4518 Individuals online. **URL:** http://www.begellhouse.com/journals/0632a9d54950b268; http://www.begellhouse.com/journals/telecommunications-and-radio-engineering.html. **Circ:** (Not Reported).

6172 ■ TsAGI Science Journal
Begell House Inc.
50 Cross Hwy.
Redding, CT 06896
Phone: (203)938-1300
Fax: (203)938-1304
Publisher's E-mail: orders@begellhouse.com
Journal covering the areas of mechanics, aviation and cosmonautics, industrial aerodynamic and hydrodynamics of rapid motion. **Freq:** Bimonthly. **Key Personnel:** Sergei Chernyshev, Editor-in-Chief; Ivan Egorov, Associate Editor. **ISSN:** 1948--2590 (print); **EISSN:** 1948--2604 (electronic). **Subscription Rates:** $1234 Individuals print + online; $1199 Individuals print; $1121 Individuals online. **URL:** http://www.begellhouse.com/journals/58618e1439159b1f; http://www.begellhouse.com/journals/tsagi-science-journal.html. **Circ:** (Not Reported).

RIDGEFIELD

SW CT. Fairfield Co. 9 mi. S. of Danbury. Summer resort. Pharmaceutical, geological and optical research.

6173 ■ The Amity Observer
Hersam Acorn Newspapers L.L.C.
16 Bailey Ave.
Ridgefield, CT 06877
Phone: (203)438-6544
Fax: (203)438-3395
Free: 800-372-2790
Community newspaper. **Freq:** Weekly (Wed.). **Key Personnel:** Thomas Nash, Publisher; Bettina Thiel, Editor. **Subscription Rates:** $29.50 Individuals; $46.75 Two years; $38 Out of area; $64 Out of area 2 years. **URL:** http://www.amityobserver.com. **Remarks:** Accepts advertising. **Circ:** ‡5189.

6174 ■ Bridgeport News
Hersam Acorn Newspapers L.L.C.
16 Bailey Ave.
Ridgefield, CT 06877
Phone: (203)438-6544
Fax: (203)438-3395
Free: 800-372-2790
Community newspaper. **Founded:** 1987. **Freq:** Weekly (Thurs.). **Print Method:** Offset. **Trim Size:** 13 x 22 1/2. **Cols./Page:** 6. **Col. Width:** 1 7/8 inches. **Col. Depth:** 21 inches. **Key Personnel:** Susan Chaves, Editor. **Subscription Rates:** $29.50 Individuals; $46.75 Two years; $38 Out of area; $64 Out of area 2 years. **URL:** http://www.thebridgeportnews.com. **Remarks:** Advertising accepted; rates available upon request. **Circ:** (Not Reported).

6175 ■ The Lewisboro Ledger
Hersam Acorn Newspapers L.L.C.
16 Bailey Ave.
Ridgefield, CT 06877
Phone: (203)438-6544
Fax: (203)438-3395
Free: 800-372-2790
Community newspaper. **Freq:** Weekly (Thurs.). **Print Method:** Offset. **Cols./Page:** 6. **Col. Width:** 2 1/16 inches. **Col. Depth:** 294 agate lines. **Key Personnel:** Thomas B. Nash, Publisher; Martin Hersam, Chief Operating Officer. **Subscription Rates:** $45 Individuals print; $60 Individuals print + online. **URL:** http://www.lewisboroledger.com. **Ad Rates:** BW $851; 4C $550; PCI $6.75. **Remarks:** Advertising accepted; rates available upon request. **Circ:** Combined ‡1603.

6176 ■ The Milford Mirror
Hersam Acorn Newspapers L.L.C.
16 Bailey Ave.
Ridgefield, CT 06877
Phone: (203)438-6544
Fax: (203)438-3395
Free: 800-372-2790
Community newspaper. **Freq:** Weekly (Wed.). **Key Personnel:** Jill Dion, Editor. **URL:** http://www.milfordmirror.com. **Remarks:** Accepts advertising. **Circ:** ‡3680.

6177 ■ Monroe Courier
Hersam Acorn Newspapers L.L.C.
16 Bailey Ave.
Ridgefield, CT 06877
Phone: (203)438-6544
Fax: (203)438-3395
Free: 800-372-2790
Community newspaper. **Freq:** Weekly (Thurs.). **Print Method:** Offset. **Trim Size:** 13 x 21 3/4. **Cols./Page:** 6. **Col. Width:** 1 7/8 inches. **Col. Depth:** 21 inches. **Key Personnel:** Kait Shea, Editor. **Subscription Rates:** $19 Individuals print only; $31 Two years print only; $38 Out of country; $64 Out of country 2 years. **URL:** http://www.monroecourier.com. **Ad Rates:** GLR $13.68; BW $1,724; 4C $2,124; PCI $16.85. **Remarks:** Accepts advertising. **Circ:** ‡2548.

6178 ■ New Canaan Advertiser
Hersam Acorn Newspapers L.L.C.
16 Bailey Ave.
Ridgefield, CT 06877
Phone: (203)438-6544
Fax: (203)438-3395
Free: 800-372-2790
Community newspaper. **Freq:** Weekly (Thurs.). **Print Method:** Offset. **Trim Size:** 17 x 22 3/4. **Cols./Page:** 9. **Col. Width:** 21 nonpareils. **Col. Depth:** 294 agate lines. **Key Personnel:** V. Donald Hersam, Jr., Publisher. **Subscription Rates:** $39 Individuals; $45 Individuals out of county; $70.20 Two years; $81 Two years out of county. **URL:** http://www.ncadvertiser.com. **Ad Rates:** GLR $.37; BW $926.10; 4C $1,826.10; PCI $5.40. **Remarks:** Accepts advertising. **Circ:** 4613.

6179 ■ The Ridgefield Press
Hersam Acorn Newspapers L.L.C.
16 Bailey Ave.
Ridgefield, CT 06877
Phone: (203)438-6544
Fax: (203)438-3395
Free: 800-372-2790
Community newspaper. **Freq:** Weekly (Thurs.). **Print Method:** Offset. **Cols./Page:** 6. **Col. Width:** 12 picas. **Col. Depth:** 21 inches. **Key Personnel:** Macklin K. Reid, Editor, phone: (203)894-3351; Jake Kara, Managing Editor. **USPS:** 465-860. **URL:** http://www.theridgefieldpress.com. **Circ:** (Not Reported).

6180 ■ The Sacred Octagon
New England M.G. "T" Register Limited
PO Box 1028
Ridgefield, CT 06877-9028
Phone: (802)434-8418
Fax: (203)261-9131
Freq: Bimonthly. **Subscription Rates:** Included in membership; $35 Nonmembers /year; $90 U.S. 1964-2004 CD-ROM; $110 Other countries 1964-2004 CD-ROM. **Alt. Formats:** CD-ROM. **URL:** http://www.nemgtr.org/our-magazine/the-sacred-octagon.html. **Remarks:** Accepts advertising. **Circ:** 9000.

6181 ■ Stratford Star
Hersam Acorn Newspapers L.L.C.
16 Bailey Ave.
Ridgefield, CT 06877
Phone: (203)438-6544
Fax: (203)438-3395
Free: 800-372-2790
Community newspaper. **Founded:** 1985. **Freq:** Weekly (Wed.). **Print Method:** Offset. **Trim Size:** 14 x 22 1/2. **Cols./Page:** 6. **Col. Width:** 1 3/8 inches. **Col. Depth:** 21 inches. **Key Personnel:** John Kovach, Editor; Nancy Doniger, Managing Editor. **Subscription Rates:** $29.50 Individuals; $46.75 Two years; $38 Out of area; $64 Out of area 2 years. **URL:** http://www.stratfordstar.com/about-us/. **Ad Rates:** GLR $.8; BW $1,263; 4C $1,863; SAU $11.23. **Circ:** 3802.

6182 ■ Trumbull Times
Hersam Acorn Newspapers L.L.C.
16 Bailey Ave.
Ridgefield, CT 06877
Phone: (203)438-6544
Fax: (203)438-3395
Free: 800-372-2790
Community newspaper. **Freq:** Weekly (Thurs.). **Print Method:** Offset. **Trim Size:** 14 x 22 1/2. **Cols./Page:** 6. **Col. Width:** 2 1/16 inches. **Col. Depth:** 21 inches. **Key Personnel:** Bill Bloxsom, Editor; Kate Czaplinski, Editor, phone: (203)402-2311. **Subscription Rates:** $19 Individuals; $31 Two years; $38 Out of area; $64 Out of area 2 years. **URL:** http://www.trumbulltimes.com. **Ad Rates:** BW $1,089.90; 4C $1,708.86; SAU $10. **Circ:** ‡4157.

6183 ■ The Valley Gazette
Hersam Acorn Newspapers L.L.C.
16 Bailey Ave.
Ridgefield, CT 06877
Phone: (203)438-6544
Fax: (203)438-3395
Free: 800-372-2790
Community newspaper. **Founded:** 1992. **Freq:** Weekly (Wed.). **Print Method:** Offset. **Key Personnel:** Susan Hunter, Editor; Donald Eng, Editor. **Subscription Rates:** $19 Individuals print only; $29 Individuals print and digital; $29.50 Out of area print only; $39.50 Out of area print and digital; $38 Out of country print only; $48 Out of country print and digital; $30 Out of country digital only. **URL:** http://www.thevalleygazette.com; http://www.hersamacorn.com. **Ad Rates:** GLR $18.79; BW $2,368; 4C $2,768. **Remarks:** Accepts advertising. **Circ:** ‡2250.

Circulation: ★ = AAM; △ or • = BPA; ♦ = CAC; ❑ = VAC; ⊕ = PO Statement; ‡ = Publisher's Report; Boldface figures = sworn; Light figures = estimated.

6184 ■ The Weston Forum
Hersam Acorn Newspapers L.L.C.
16 Bailey Ave.
Ridgefield, CT 06877
Phone: (203)438-6544
Fax: (203)438-3395
Free: 800-372-2790
Community newspaper. **Freq:** Weekly (Thurs.). **Cols./Page:** 6. **Col. Depth:** 2 1/16 inches. **Key Personnel:** Rocco Valluzzo, Editor; Patricia Gay, Editor. **URL:** http://www.thewestonforum.com. **Ad Rates:** BW $882; 4C $550; PCI $7. **Remarks:** Advertising accepted; rates available upon request. **Circ:** ‡1815.

ROCKY HILL

NC CT. Hartford Co. 7 mi. E. of New Britain.

6185 ■ Connecticut Pharmacist
Connecticut Pharmacists Association
35 Cold Spring Rd., Ste. 121
Rocky Hill, CT 06067-3161
Phone: (860)563-4619
Fax: (860)257-8241
Publisher's E-mail: members@ctpharmacists.org
Professional magazine. **Freq:** Quarterly. **Key Personnel:** Margherita R. Giuliano, RPh, Executive Vice President. **Ad Rates:** BW $450; 4C $1100. **Remarks:** Accepts advertising. **Circ:** Controlled 1500.

6186 ■ WFSB-TV - 3
333 Capital Blvd.
Rocky Hill, CT 06067
Phone: (860)728-3333
Fax: (860)247-8940
Format: Commercial TV. **Networks:** CBS. **Owner:** Meredith Corp., 1716 Locust St., Des Moines, IA 50309-3038, Ph: (515)284-3000. **Founded:** 1957. **Operating Hours**: Continuous. **ADI:** Hartford-New Haven (New London), CT. **Key Personnel:** Klarn DePalma, Gen. Mgr., VP; Dana Neves, News Dir. **Ad Rates:** Noncommercial. **URL:** http://www.wfsb.com.

SHELTON

SW CT. Fairfield Co. 10 mi. N. of Bridgeport. Manufactures tools, dies, office machines, iron and steel forging, steel and foam rubber products, electronic controls. Dairy, poultry farms.

6187 ■ American Laboratory News
International Scientific Communications Inc.
30 Controls Dr.
Shelton, CT 06484-0870
Phone: (650)243-5600
Fax: (203)926-9310
Publisher's E-mail: sales@americanlaboratory.com
Trade magazine for scientists. **Freq:** Monthly. **Print Method:** Offset. **Trim Size:** 10 7/8 x 14. **Cols./Page:** 4. **Col. Width:** 2 inches. **Col. Depth:** 12 7/8 inches. **Key Personnel:** Robert L. Stevenson, Editor. **ISSN:** 0044-7749 (print). **URL:** http://www.americanlaboratory.com/1413-Issues. **Ad Rates:** BW $8,000. **Remarks:** Accepts advertising. **Circ:** Non-paid 69625.

6188 ■ Military Retailer
MilitaryLife Publishing L.L.C.
4 Research Dr., Ste. 402
Shelton, CT 06484
Fax: (203)402-7201
Trade magazine for Defense Commissary Agency. **Freq:** Bimonthly. **Print Method:** Web offset. **Trim Size:** 8 1/8 x 10 7/8. **Cols./Page:** 2 and 3. **Col. Width:** 20 and 13 picas. **Col. Depth:** 56 and 56 picas. **Key Personnel:** Vincent Santoro, President, Publisher; Allen Harris, Manager, Production; Robin Donohoe, Associate Publisher. **ISSN:** 1058-8620 (print). **Subscription Rates:** Free. **URL:** http://www.militaryretailer.com. **Formerly**: Military Grocer. **Ad Rates:** 4C $3,455. **Remarks:** Advertising accepted; rates available upon request. **Circ:** Controlled 8000.

6189 ■ WRXC-FM - 90.1
PO Box 920
Monroe, CT 06468
Phone: (203)268-9667
Email: info@wmnr.org
Format: Classical. **Networks:** Independent. **Owner:** Monroe Public Schools, 375 Monroe Tpke., Monroe, CT 06468, Ph: (203)452-2860. **Founded:** 1982. **Operating Hours**: Continuous. **ADI:** New York, NY. **Key Personnel:** Jane Stadler, Dir. of Operations; Kurt Anderson, Gen. Mgr.; Carol Babina, Asst. GM, carol@babina.com. **Wattage:** 450. **Ad Rates:** Noncommercial. **URL:** http://wmnr.org/web/home.

SOMERS

NW CT. Tolland Co. E. of Enfield.

6190 ■ WDJW-FM
Ninth District Rd.
Somers, CT 06071
Phone: (860)749-0719
Format: Album-Oriented Rock (AOR); Top 40. **Founded:** 1986. **Key Personnel:** Peter Stone, Contact. **Ad Rates:** Noncommercial.

SOMERSVILLE

6191 ■ VHF-UHF Digest
Worldwide Television-FM DX Association
PO Box 501
Somersville, CT 06072-0501
Publisher's E-mail: support@wtfda.org
Freq: Monthly. **Key Personnel:** Mike Bugaj, Editor. **Subscription Rates:** Included in membership. **Alt. Formats:** PDF. **Remarks:** Accepts advertising. **Circ:** (Not Reported).

SOUTHBURY

SW CT. New Haven Co. 12 mi. SW of Waterbury. Residential.

6192 ■ MITA-TECH
Musical Instrument Technicians Association, International
c/o Fran Hellmann, Treasurer
376 Old Woodbury Rd.
Southbury, CT 06488
Freq: Quarterly. **URL:** http://mitatechs.org/node/916. **Remarks:** Accepts advertising. **Circ:** (Not Reported).

SOUTHINGTON

N. CT. Hartford Co. 7 mi. NW of Meriden. Manufactures hardware, tools, manifolds, forgings, airplane engines. Fruit, dairy, poultry farms. Apples, peaches.

6193 ■ The Observer
The Step Saver Inc.
213 Spring St.
Southington, CT 06489
Phone: (860)628-9645
Fax: (860)621-1841
Publisher's E-mail: info@stepsaver.com
Community newspaper. **Founded:** Dec. 1975. **Freq:** Weekly. **Print Method:** Offset. **Cols./Page:** 6. **Col. Width:** 12 picas. **Col. Depth:** 21 inches. **USPS:** 406-030. **Subscription Rates:** $90 Individuals; $55 Individuals 6 months. **URL:** http://www.theobserver.com/. **Ad Rates:** GLR $.29; BW $100; 4C $400; SAU $7.50. **Remarks:** Accepts advertising. **Circ:** (Not Reported).

SOUTHPORT

SW CT. Fairfield Co. 55 mi. E. of New York.

6194 ■ Gas Turbine World: Serving industrial and electric utility power engineers
Pequot Publishing Inc.
PO Box 447
Southport, CT 06890
Phone: (203)259-1812
Fax: (203)255-3313
Magazine containing technical and business information on the design application, operation, and maintenance of power plants for electrical generation, mechanical drive, oil and gas production and transmission, industrial process, CHP, and DHC applications. **Freq:** Bimonthly. **Print Method:** Web offset. **Trim Size:** 8 1/8 x 10 7/8. **Cols./Page:** 3. **Col. Width:** 2 1/16 inches. **Col. Depth:** 10 inches. **Key Personnel:** Victor de Biasi, Editor; Robert Farmer, Editor-in-Chief. **Subscription Rates:** $25 Single issue; $130 Individuals. **URL:** http://www.gasturbineworld.com. **Ad Rates:** BW $6,335; 4C $7885. **Remarks:** Accepts advertising. **Circ:** (Not Reported).

STAFFORD SPRINGS

N. CT. Tolland Co. 23 mi. NE of Hartford. Manufactures tools, dies, bottled soft drinks, chemicals. Woolens, worsted, cotton and silk mills.

6195 ■ Stafford Press
Stafford Press
Rt. 190
Stafford Springs, CT 06076
Newspaper. **Freq:** Weekly (Tues.). **Print Method:** Offset. **Cols./Page:** 6. **Col. Width:** 21 nonpareils. **Col. Depth:** 224 agate lines. **Key Personnel:** Thomas A. and Patrick Turley, Publisher. **URL:** http://www.staffordpress.com. **Remarks:** Accepts advertising. **Circ:** (Not Reported).

STAMFORD

SW CT. Fairfield Co. On Long Island Sound, 35 mi. NE of New York. Manufactures chemicals, electrical equipment, pharmaceuticals, cosmetics, aircraft, metals, machinery, die casting, textiles, printing and publishing. Chemical, electronic research laboratories.

6196 ■ The Advocate
Hearst Connecticut Media Group
9A Riverbend Dr. S
Stamford, CT 06907
Phone: (203)964-2200
Fax: (203)964-2345
General newspaper. **Founded:** 1829. **Freq:** Mon.-Sun. (morn.). **Print Method:** Offset. **Cols./Page:** 6. **Col. Width:** 2 1/16 inches. **Col. Depth:** 21 1/2 inches. **Key Personnel:** John Breunig, Editor; Henry Haitz, III, Publisher. **Subscription Rates:** $62.40 Individuals 13 weeks; $332.80 By mail 52 weeks. **URL:** http://www.stamfordadvocate.com; http://www.myhearstnewspaper.com/stamford. **Mailing address:** PO Box 9307, Stamford, CT 06907. **Ad Rates:** BW $4,687.54; 4C $5,112.54; SAU $43.95. **Circ:** Mon.-Fri. ★**23088**, Sat. ★**21269**, Sun. ★**24086**.

6197 ■ Global Custodian
Asset International Inc.
1055 Washington Blvd.
Stamford, CT 06901
Phone: (203)595-3200
Fax: (203)595-3201
Business journal for global investment and operations professionals. **Freq:** 5/year. **Key Personnel:** Giles Turner, Editor; Dominic Hobson, Executive Editor. **Subscription Rates:** £360 Individuals print only - 1 year; £530 Individuals print only - 2 years; £455 Individuals web only - 1 year; £755 Individuals web only - 2 years; £565 Individuals print+Web Package - 1 year; £834 Individuals print+Web Package - 2 years. **URL:** http://www.globalcustodian.com/magazine/magazine_index.aspx. **Ad Rates:** 4C $14,420, 4 color - full page; 4C $7,581, 4 color - half page; BW $8,189, full page; BW $4,635, half page. **Remarks:** Accepts advertising. **Circ:** 20000.

6198 ■ International Journal of Mineral Processing
RELX Group P.L.C.
c/o D.R. Nagaraj, Board Member
Cytec Industries Inc.
1937 W Main St.
Stamford, CT 06904
Phone: (203)321-2793
Fax: (203)321-2974
Publisher's E-mail: amsterdam@relx.com
Journal covering all aspects of the processing of solid-mineral materials. **Freq:** Monthly. **Key Personnel:** D.R. Nagaraj, Board Member. **ISSN:** 0301--7516 (print). **Subscription Rates:** $183 Individuals print; $1353 Institutions print; $1353.60 Institutions e-journal. **URL:** http://www.journals.elsevier.com/international-journal-of-mineral-processing. **Remarks:** Accepts advertising. **Circ:** (Not Reported).

6199 ■ Plan Sponsor: Insight on Plan Design & Investment Strategy
Asset International Inc.
1055 Washington Blvd.
Stamford, CT 06901
Phone: (203)595-3200
Fax: (203)595-3201
Trade magazine for pension fund and endowment executives. **Freq:** Monthly. **Print Method:** Web Offset. **Trim Size:** 8 1/4 x 10 7/8. **Key Personnel:** Alison Cooke Mintzer, Editor-in-Chief; Robert Jones, Advertising Representative. **Ad Rates:** BW $19,606. **Remarks:** Accepts advertising. **Circ:** 70,328.

6200 ■ The Sower
The Ukrainian Catholic Diocese of Stamford
14 Peveril Rd.
Stamford, CT 06902-3019
Phone: (203)324-7698
Fax: (203)967-9948
Publisher's E-mail: stamdevelop@yahoo.com
Official newspaper of Ukrainian Catholic Diocese of Stamford (Ukrainian and English). **Freq:** Monthly. **Print Method:** Offset. **Trim Size:** 11 1/2 x 17. **Cols./Page:** 4. **Col. Width:** 14.5 picas. **Col. Depth:** 16 inches. **Key Personnel:** Rev. Paul Chomnycky, OSBM, Publisher; Sr. Natalya Stoczanyn, SSMI, Editor-in-Chief. **ISSN:** 0896--6184 (print). **URL:** http://www.stamforddio.org/sower2016.html. **Remarks:** Advertising not accepted. **Circ:** Paid ‡8220, Non-paid ‡140.

6201 ■ Westport News
Brooks Community Newspapers Inc.
9A Riverbend Dr. S
Stamford, CT 06907
Phone: (203)964-2200
Fax: (203)964-2278
Community newspaper. **Founded:** 1964. **Freq:** Semi-weekly (Wed. and Fri.). **Print Method:** Dolwech. **Trim Size:** AS. **Cols./Page:** 5. **Col. Width:** 27 nonpareils. **Col. Depth:** 224 agate lines. **Key Personnel:** Eliot Schickler, Editor, phone: (203)255-4561; James Doody, Editor; Michelle McAbee, General Manager, phone: (203)750-5315. **URL:** http://www.westport-news.com. **Remarks:** Accepts advertising. **Circ:** (Not Reported).

6202 ■ Charter Communications Inc.
400 Atlantic St.
Stamford, CT 06901
Phone: (203)905-7801
Owner: Charter Communications Inc., 400 Atlantic St., Stamford, CT 06901, Ph: (203)905-7801; Charter Communications Inc., 400 Atlantic St., Stamford, CT 06901, Ph: (203)905-7801; Charter Communications Inc., 400 Atlantic St., Stamford, CT 06901, Ph: (203)905-7801; Charter Communications Inc., 400 Atlantic St., Stamford, CT 06901, Ph: (203)905-7801; Charter Communications Inc., 400 Atlantic St., Stamford, CT 06901, Ph: (203)905-7801; Charter Communications Inc., 400 Atlantic St., Stamford, CT 06901, Ph: (203)905-7801. **Founded:** 1999. **Key Personnel:** Neil Smit, CEO, President; Marwan Fawaz, Chief Tech. Ofc., Chief Tech. Ofc.; Jeffrey T. Fisher, CFO, Exec. VP; Scott Weber, Exec. VP; Tom Adams, Exec. VP; Don Detampel, Exec. VP; Rajive Johri, Contact; David C. Merritt, Contact; Marc B. Nathanson, Contact; Jo Allen Patton, Contact; Neil Smit, Contact; John H. Tory, Contact; Larry W. Wangberg, Contact; Lance W. Conn, Contact; Nathaniel A. Davis, Contact; Jonathan L. Dolgen, Contact; Robert P. May, Contact; Larry W. Conn, Contact. **Cities Served:** Amelia, Chauvin, Donner, Dulac, Gibson, Gibson, Houma, Montegut, Schriever, Theriot, Louisiana: subscribing households 5,700,000; 29 states in the U.S.; 320 channels; 1 community access channel; 17 hours per week community access programming. **URL:** http://www.charter.com.

6203 ■ WEDW-FM - 88.5
1049 Asylym Ave.
Hartford, CT 06105
Phone: (860)278-5310
Format: Public Radio. **Networks:** National Public Radio (NPR); American Public Radio (APR). **Owner:** Connecticut Public Broadcasting Network, 1049 Asylum Ave., Hartford, CT 06105-2432, Ph: (860)275-7550. **Founded:** 1991. **Operating Hours**: Continuous. **Wattage**: 5,000. **Ad Rates:** Noncommercial. **URL:** http://www.cpbn.org.

WFNW-AM - See Naugatuck

STEVENSON

6204 ■ Puppetry Journal
Puppeteers of America
336 Chestnut Hill Rd.
Stevenson, CT 06491
Phone: (860)462-8072
Publication E-mail: journal@puppeteers.org
Freq: Quarterly. **ISSN:** 0033--443X (print). **Subscription Rates:** Included in membership. **URL:** http://www.puppeteers.org/puppetry-journal. **Ad Rates:** BW $250; 4C $350. **Remarks:** Accepts advertising. **Circ:** (Not Reported).

STORRS

N. CT. Tollands Co. 8 mi. NW of Willmantic. University of Connecticut.

6205 ■ Biotropica
Association for Tropical Biology and Conservation
c/o Robin L. Chazdon, Executive Director
Dept. of Ecology and Evolutionary Biology, U-3043
75 N Eagleville Rd.
Storrs, CT 06269-3042
Journal focusing on original research on the ecology and conservation of tropical ecosystems and on the evolution, behavior, and ecology of tropical organisms. **Freq:** Bimonthly. **Key Personnel:** Jaboury Ghazoul, Editor; Emilio Bruna, Editor-in-Chief. **ISSN:** 0006--3606 (print); **EISSN:** 1744--7429 (electronic). **Subscription Rates:** $566 Institutions online only; £347 Institutions online only; €440 Institutions online only; $286 Institutions online only; Developing World; $678 Institutions, other countries online only. **URL:** http://onlinelibrary.wiley.com/journal/10.1111/(ISSN)1744-7429. **Ad Rates:** 4C $600. **Remarks:** Accepts advertising. **Circ:** (Not Reported).

6206 ■ The Daily Campus
University of Connecticut
1266 Storrs Rd.
Storrs, CT 06268
Phone: (860)486-3407
Collegiate newspaper. **Founded:** 1896. **Freq:** Daily (morn.) during the academic year. **Print Method:** Offset. **Trim Size:** 13 x 21. **Cols./Page:** 6. **Col. Width:** 2.15 inches. **Col. Depth:** 21 inches. **Key Personnel:** Kimberly Wilson, Editor-in-Chief, phone: (860)486-3407. **Subscription Rates:** $7 Individuals; $10 Individuals; $9 Individuals prepay; $6 Students; $6 Individuals on campus. **URL:** http://www.dailycampus.com. **Ad Rates:** GLR $5; BW $662; 4C $962; PCI $5.50. **Remarks:** Accepts advertising. **Circ:** Combined ‡20000.

6207 ■ Family Relations: Interdisciplinary Journal of Applied Family Studies
National Council on Family Relations
Human Development & Family Studies
University of Connecticut
Box U - 2058
Storrs, CT 06269-2058
Publisher's E-mail: info@ncfr.org
Publication for family practitioners and academics on relationships across the life cycle with implications for intervention, education and public policy. **Freq:** 5/yr. **Print Method:** Offset. **Trim Size:** 8 1/2 x 11. **Cols./Page:** 2. **Key Personnel:** Ronald M. Sabatelli Sabatelli, PhD, Editor; Jay Mancini, Board Member; Elaine Anderson, Board Member; Katherine Allen, Board Member; Sally Martin, Board Member; Larry Ganong, Board Member; Mark Fine, Board Member; Frank Fincham, Board Member. **ISSN:** 0197-6664 (print). **Subscription Rates:** $156 Individuals print + online; $66 Students print + online; £126 Other countries print + online; £63 Students, other countries print + online; €188 Individuals print + online; €94 Students print + online; $1532 Institutions print + online; $1276 Institutions print or online. **URL:** http://www.ncfr.org/fr; http://onlinelibrary.wiley.com/doi/10.1111/fare.2013.62.issue-1/issuetoc. **Formerly**: Family Relations: Journal of Applied Family of Child Studies. **Ad Rates:** BW $700. **Remarks:** Accepts advertising. **Circ:** 4060.

6208 ■ International Studies Quarterly
International Studies Association
337 Mansfield Rd., Unit 1013
Storrs, CT 06269-1013
Phone: (860)486-5850
Publisher's E-mail: journaladsusa@bos.blackwellpublishing.com
Freq: Quarterly. **Key Personnel:** Daniel H. Nexon, Editor; William R. Thompson, Board Member, Editor; Brett Ashley Leeds, Board Member. **ISSN:** 0020--8833 (print); **EISSN:** 1468--2478 (electronic). **URL:** http://www.isanet.org/Publications/ISQ. **Ad Rates:** BW $550. **Remarks:** Accepts advertising. **Circ:** (Not Reported).

6209 ■ International Studies Review
International Studies Association
337 Mansfield Rd., Unit 1013
Storrs, CT 06269-1013
Phone: (860)486-5850
Publisher's E-mail: journaladsusa@bos.blackwellpublishing.com
Journal focusing on international studies. **Freq:** Quarterly. **Key Personnel:** Laura Sjoberg, Editor-in-Chief; Mark A. Boyer, Board Member; Jennifer Sterling-Folker, Board Member. **ISSN:** 1521--9488 (print); **EISSN:** 1468--2486 (electronic). **Subscription Rates:** accessible only to members. **URL:** http://www.isanet.org/Publications/ISR. **Ad Rates:** BW $525; 4C $250. **Remarks:** Accepts advertising. **Circ:** (Not Reported).

6210 ■ Journal of the American Taxation Association
American Accounting Association
c/o John Phillips, Ed.
Scholarship of Business
University of Connecticut
2100 Hillside Rd., Unit 1041
Storrs, CT 06269-1041
Phone: (860)486-2789
Publication E-mail: jata@tuck.dartmouth.edu
Academic journal covering accounting and taxation. **Founded:** 1978. **Freq:** Semiannual (Spring and Fall) with a third conference supplement. **Trim Size:** 7 x 10. **Cols./Page:** 1. **Key Personnel:** Kenneth J. Klassen, Editor. **ISSN:** 0198-9073 (print). **Subscription Rates:** $120 Individuals print; $160 Individuals online from volume 21 to current issue; $175 Individuals online and print. **URL:** http://aaahq.org/ata/_ATAMenu/ATAPubJATA.html. **Ad Rates:** BW $375. **Remarks:** Accepts advertising. **Circ:** 1100.

6211 ■ The Linguistic Review
Walter de Gruyter GmbH and Company KG
c/o Harry van der Hulst, Ed.-in-Ch.
Dept. of Linguistics, U-1145
University of Connecticut, Oak Hall (E SSHB)
365 Fairfield Way
Storrs, CT 06269
Publisher's E-mail: info@degruyter.com
Peer-reviewed journal covering information on semantics, phonology, and morphology, within a framework of generative grammar and related disciplines. **Freq:** Quarterly. **Print Method:** Offset. **Trim Size:** 8 1/2 x 11. **Cols./Page:** 2. **Col. Width:** 42 nonpareils. **Col. Depth:** 140 agate lines. **Key Personnel:** Nancy Ritter, Managing Editor; Harry van der Hulst, Editor-in-Chief. **ISSN:** 0167--6318 (print); **EISSN:** 1613--3676 (electronic). **Subscription Rates:** €383 Institutions print or online; $574 Institutions print or online; £288 Institutions print or online; €99 Individuals online; $149 Individuals online; £75 Institutions online; €383 Individuals print; $574 Individuals print ; $288 Individuals print; €461 print and online - institution and individual; $690 print and online - institution and individual; £347 print and online - institution and individual. **URL:** http://www.degruyter.com/view/j/tlir. **Remarks:** Accepts advertising. **Circ:** (Not Reported).

STORRS MANSFIELD

6212 ■ Lit: Literature Interpretation Theory
Routledge
University of Connecticut
Department of English
215 Glenbrook Rd.
Storrs Mansfield, CT 06269-4025
Fax: (860)486-1530
Publisher's E-mail: book.orders@tandf.co.uk
Publication covering literature and writing. **Freq:** Quarterly. **Trim Size:** 6 x 9. **Key Personnel:** Dwight Codr, Editor; Regina Barreca, Editor; Margaret E. Mitchell, Editor. **ISSN:** 1043--6928 (print); **EISSN:** 1545--5866 (electronic). **Subscription Rates:** $207 Individuals print only; $668 Institutions online only; $763 Institutions print and online. **URL:** http://www.tandfonline.com/toc/glit20/current. **Mailing address:** PO Box 4025, Storrs Mansfield, CT 06269-4025. **Circ:** (Not Reported).

6213 ■ Sequential Analysis
Taylor & Francis Group Journals
c/o Nitis Mukhopadhyay, Editor-in-Chief
University of Connecticut
Dept. of Statistics
Storrs Mansfield, CT 06269-4120
Phone: (860)486-6144

Circulation: ★ = AAM; △ or • = BPA; ♦ = CAC; ❑ = VAC; ⊕ = PO Statement; ‡ = Publisher's Report; Boldface figures = sworn; Light figures = estimated.

Fax: (860)486-4113
Publisher's E-mail: customerservice@taylorandfrancis.com
Journal covering mathematical tools and concepts relating to sequential analysis. **Freq:** Quarterly. **Print Method:** Offset. **Trim Size:** 8 1/4 x 10 7/8. **Cols./Page:** 1. **Key Personnel:** Shelley Zacks, Associate Editor; Uttam Bandyopadhyay, Associate Editor; Linda J. Young, Associate Editor; Michael Baron, Associate Editor; Benzion Boukai, Associate Editor; Michael Woodroofe, Associate Editor; Dr. Makoto Aoshima, Associate Editor; Atanu Biswas, Associate Editor; Dr. Nitish Mukhopadhyay, Editor-in-Chief; Masafumi Akahira, Associate Editor. **ISSN:** 0747--4946 (print); **EISSN:** 1532--4176 (electronic). **Subscription Rates:** $474 Individuals print only; $2029 Institutions print & online; $1775 Institutions online only. **URL:** http://www.tandfonline.com/action/newsAndOffers?journalCode=lsqa#.VMm-gNLkjpo. **Mailing address:** PO Box 4120, Storrs Mansfield, CT 06269-4120. **Ad Rates:** BW $890; 4C $1,935. **Remarks:** Accepts advertising. **Circ:** Paid **325**.

6214 ■ Spectroscopy Letters: An International Journal for Rapid Communication
Taylor & Francis Online
c/o Robert G. Michel, Editor-in-Chief
University of Connecticut
Dept. of Chemical
55 N Eagleville Rd.
Storrs Mansfield, CT 06269
Publisher's E-mail: support@tandfonline.com
Professional Journal covering fundamental developments in spectroscopy. **Freq:** 10/year. **Print Method:** Offset. **Trim Size:** 8 1/4 x 10 7/8. **Cols./Page:** 1. **Key Personnel:** David J. Butcher, Associate Editor; Robert G. Michel, Editor-in-Chief; Xiandeng Dan Hou, Board Member. **ISSN:** 0038--7010 (print); **EISSN:** 1532--2289 (electronic). **Subscription Rates:** $873 Individuals print; $3459 Institutions online; $3953 Institutions print and online. **URL:** http://www.tandfonline.com/toc/lstl20/current#.Uvh0SWJLXIc. **Ad Rates:** BW $890; 4C $1,935. **Remarks:** Accepts advertising. **Circ:** Paid 325.

6215 ■ WHUS-FM - 91.7
Student Union Bldg., Rm. 412
2110 Hillside Rd., Unit 3008R
Storrs Mansfield, CT 06268-3008
Phone: (860)486-4007
Format: Eclectic. **Networks:** AP. **Founded:** 1956. **Operating Hours:** Continuous. **Wattage:** 4,400. **Ad Rates:** Noncommercial; underwriting available. **URL:** http://www.whus.org.

TOLLAND

6216 ■ International Journal of Instructional Media
Westwood Press Inc.
c/o Dr. Phillip J. Sleeman, Exec. Ed.
149 Goose Ln.
Tolland, CT 06084
Professional refereed journal featuring articles on instructional media and technology used in training, communication and distance education. **Freq:** Quarterly. **Print Method:** Offset. **Trim Size:** 6 x 9. **Cols./Page:** 1. **Key Personnel:** Dr. Phillip J. Sleeman, Executive Editor; Linda B. Sleeman, Associate Editor. **ISSN:** 0892-1815 (print). **Subscription Rates:** $245 Individuals includes shipping; $265 Other countries includes shipping. **URL:** http://www.adprima.com/ijim.htm. **Remarks:** Advertising not accepted. **Circ:** 2000.

TORRINGTON

NW CT. Litchfield Co. On Naugatuck River, 20 mi. N. of Waterbury. Manufactures industrial brushes, needles, bearings, universal joints, electronic computers, spring and mill machinery, venetian blinds, rotary pump, fans and blower wheels, castings, furniture, roller skates, sporting goods, machine screws and nuts, corrugated cardboard containers, lumber products, gaskets, textiles, hardware, tools.

6217 ■ Foothills Trader
Foothills Trader
PO Box 58
Torrington, CT 06790
Phone: (860)489-3121
Fax: (860)489-6790
Community shopper covering the area west of Hartford from Avon to the Massachusetts border, south to Bristol, and west to New York state line. **Freq:** Weekly (Mon.). **Print Method:** Offset. **Trim Size:** 10 1/2 x 12. **Cols./Page:** 6. **Col. Width:** 9.6 picas. **Col. Depth:** 12 inches. **Key Personnel:** Kevin Corrado, Publisher. **Subscription Rates:** Free. **URL:** http://www.foothillstrader.com. **Ad Rates:** GLR $6; BW $1,008. **Remarks:** Advertising accepted; rates available upon request. **Circ:** ‡52500.

6218 ■ The Register Citizen
Journal Register Inc.
190 Water St.
Torrington, CT 06790
Phone: (860)489-3121
Fax: (860)489-6790
Publication E-mail: editor@registercitizen.com
General newspaper. **Freq:** Daily. **Print Method:** Offset. **Trim Size:** 13 3/4 x 22 3/4. **Cols./Page:** 6. **Col. Width:** 12.3 picas. **Col. Depth:** 298 agate lines. **Key Personnel:** Kevin Corrado, Publisher. **USPS:** 634-200. **URL:** http://www.registercitizen.com. **Mailing address:** PO Box 58, Torrington, CT 06790. **Remarks:** Accepts advertising. **Circ:** (Not Reported).

TRUMBULL

SW CT. Fairfield Co. 5 mi. S. of Bridgeport. Manufactures electronic components, silver and plated ware. Residential.

6219 ■ The Bargain News
Bargain News L.L.C.
30 Nutmeg Dr.
Trumbull, CT 06611
Phone: (203)377-3000
Consumer weekly (tabloid) containing automotive classifieds and general news. **Freq:** Weekly. **Print Method:** Offset. **Trim Size:** 11 x 17. **Cols./Page:** 6. **Col. Width:** 10 picas. **Col. Depth:** 95.5 picas. **ISSN:** 7447--7353 (print). **Subscription Rates:** Free. **URL:** http://www.bargainnews.com. **Remarks:** Advertising accepted; rates available upon request. **Circ:** Paid 42000.

UNCASVILLE

6220 ■ WCSE-FM - 100.1
130 Sharp Hill Rd.
Uncasville, CT 06382
Phone: (860)848-1111
Email: info@wcse.org
Format: Contemporary Christian. **URL:** http://www.wcse.typepad.com.

UNIONVILLE

6221 ■ Acta Haematologica
S. Karger Publishers Inc.
26 W Avon Rd.
Unionville, CT 06085-1162
Phone: (860)675-7834
Fax: (203)675-7302
Free: 800-828-5479
Publisher's E-mail: karger@snet.net
Scientific medical journal on functional hematology. **Freq:** 8/year. **Print Method:** Offset. **Trim Size:** 210 x 280 mm. **Cols./Page:** 1. **Col. Width:** 99 nonpareils. **Col. Depth:** 155 agate lines. **Key Personnel:** I. Ben-Bassat, Editor-in-Chief; R.C. Tait, Associate Editor; M. Makris, Board Member. **ISSN:** 0001--5792 (print); **EISSN:** 1421--9662 (electronic). **Subscription Rates:** €2759 Institutions print & online Eurozone; 3090 FR Institutions print & online rest of Europe/other countries; $3323 Institutions print & online USA/Latin America; €1380 Individuals print & online Eurozone; 1605 FR Individuals print & online rest of Europe/other countries; $1662 Individuals print & online USA/Latin America. **URL:** http://www.karger.com/Journal/Home/223829. **Remarks:** Accepts advertising. **Circ:** (Not Reported).

6222 ■ American Journal of Nephrology
S. Karger Publishers Inc.
26 W Avon Rd.
Unionville, CT 06085-1162
Phone: (860)675-7834
Fax: (203)675-7302
Free: 800-828-5479
Publisher's E-mail: karger@snet.net
Peer-reviewed scientific medical journal focusing on timely topics in basic science with possible clinical applicability. **Freq:** Monthly. **Print Method:** Offset. **Trim Size:** 210 x 280 mm. **Cols./Page:** 1. **Col. Width:** 99 nonpareils. **Col. Depth:** 155 agate lines. **Key Personnel:** C. Abrass, Board Member; J. Arruda, III, Board Member; C.B. Langman, III, Board Member; M.R. Weir, Associate Editor; K. Abbott, Editor; R. Agarwal, Associate Editor; V. Bansal, III, Board Member; G. Bakris, III, Editor-in-Chief; J. Yee, Board Member. **ISSN:** 0250--8095 (print); **EISSN:** 1421-9670 (electronic). **Subscription Rates:** €4500 Institutions online only Eurozone; €4596 Institutions print only Eurozone; €5271 Institutions combined print & online Eurozone; $5510 Institutions online only USA/Latin America; $5666 Institutions print only USA/Latin America; $6493 Institutions combined print & online USA/Latin America; 5400 FR Institutions, other countries online only; 5568 FR Institutions, other countries print only; 6378 FR Institutions, other countries combined print & online; €900 Individuals online only Eurozone; €976.80 Individuals print only Eurozone; €1054.80 Individuals combined print & online Eurozone; $1102 Individuals online only USA/Latin America; $1226.80 Individuals print only USA/Latin America; $1322.80 Individuals combined print & online USA/Latin America; 1080 FR Other countries online only; 1214.40 FR Other countries print only; 1310.40 FR Other countries combined print & online. **URL:** http://www.karger.com/Journal/Home/223979. **Ad Rates:** BW $2,094. **Remarks:** Accepts advertising. **Circ:** 2200.

6223 ■ Annales Nestle
S. Karger Publishers Inc.
26 W Avon Rd.
Unionville, CT 06085-1162
Phone: (860)675-7834
Fax: (203)675-7302
Free: 800-828-5479
Publisher's E-mail: karger@snet.net
Journal covering developments in healthcare including sports medicine, genetic causes of mental handicaps, neuromuscular illnesses, and parenteral nutrition in the childhood. **ISSN:** 0517--8606 (print); **EISSN:** 1661--4011 (electronic). **URL:** http://www.karger.com/Journal/Home/231178. **Remarks:** Accepts advertising. **Circ:** (Not Reported).

6224 ■ Audiology and Neurotology: Basic Science and Clinical Research in the Auditory and Vestibular System and Diseases of the Ear
S. Karger Publishers Inc.
26 W Avon Rd.
Unionville, CT 06085-1162
Phone: (860)675-7834
Fax: (203)675-7302
Free: 800-828-5479
Publisher's E-mail: karger@snet.net
Scientific medical journal. **Freq:** 6/year. **Print Method:** Offset. **Trim Size:** 210 x 280 mm. **Cols./Page:** 1. **Col. Width:** 84 nonpareils. **Col. Depth:** 141 agate lines. **Key Personnel:** Jeffrey P. Harris, Editor-in-Chief. **ISSN:** 1420--3030 (print). **Subscription Rates:** €1767 Institutions print and online ; 1900 FR Institutions print and online; $1767 Institutions, other countries print and online. **URL:** http://www.karger.com/Journal/Home/224213. **Ad Rates:** BW $1,780. **Remarks:** Accepts advertising. **Circ:** 900.

6225 ■ Blood Purification
S. Karger Publishers Inc.
26 W Avon Rd.
Unionville, CT 06085-1162
Phone: (860)675-7834
Fax: (203)675-7302
Free: 800-828-5479
Publisher's E-mail: karger@snet.net
Medical journal on blood. **Freq:** 8/year. **Print Method:** Offset. **Trim Size:** 210 x 280 mm. **Cols./Page:** 1. **Col. Width:** 84 nonpareils. **Col. Depth:** 141 agate lines. **Key Personnel:** Claudio Ronco, Editor-in-Chief. **ISSN:** 0253--5068 (print); **EISSN:** 1421--9735 (electronic). **Subscription Rates:** €2945 Institutions print and online; $3546 Institutions print and online; 3298 FR Institutions, other countries print and online; €938 Individuals print and online; $1064 Individuals print and online; 989 FR Other countries print and online. **URL:** http://www.karger.com/Journal/Home/223997. **Ad Rates:** BW $1,780. **Remarks:** Accepts advertising. **Circ:** 1000.

6226 ■ Brain, Behavior and Evolution: Official Organ of the J.B. Johnston Club
S. Karger Publishers Inc.

26 W Avon Rd.
Unionville, CT 06085-1162
Phone: (860)675-7834
Fax: (203)675-7302
Free: 800-828-5479
Publisher's E-mail: karger@snet.net
Peer-reviewed scientific medical journal focusing on the morphology, physiology, and histochemistry of the nervous systems of vertebrates and invertebrates. **Freq:** 8/year. **Print Method:** Offset. **Trim Size:** 210 x 280 mm. **Cols./Page:** 1. **Col. Width:** 84 nonpareils. **Col. Depth:** 141 agate lines. **Key Personnel:** S.P. Collin, Board Member; Georg F. Striedter, Editor-in-Chief. **ISSN:** 0006--8977 (print). **Subscription Rates:** $2097.20 Individuals plus postage and handling; $2205.20 Individuals print and online; plus postage and handling; $2014 Individuals online; $4131 Institutions print plus postage and handling; $4735 Institutions print and online; plus postage and handling; $4027 Institutions online; 3745 FR Institutions, other countries online; 3857 FR Institutions, other countries print plus postage and handling; 4419 FR Institutions, other countries print and online; plus postage and handling; 1873 FR Other countries online (Individual); 1962 FR Other countries print plus postage and handling (Individual); 2058.60 FR Other countries print and online; plus postage and handling (Individual). **URL:** http://www.karger.com/Journal/Home/223831. **Ad Rates:** BW $2,094. **Remarks:** Accepts advertising. **Circ:** 800.

6227 ■ Cardiology: International Journal of Cardiovascular Medicine, Surgery and Pathology
S. Karger Publishers Inc.
26 W Avon Rd.
Unionville, CT 06085-1162
Phone: (860)675-7834
Fax: (203)675-7302
Free: 800-828-5479
Publisher's E-mail: karger@snet.net
Scientific medical journal. **Founded:** 1937. **Freq:** 12/yr. **Print Method:** Offset. **Trim Size:** 210 x 280 mm. **Cols./Page:** 1. **Col. Width:** 99 nonpareils. **Col. Depth:** 155 agate lines. **Key Personnel:** Jeffrey S. Borer, Editor-in-Chief; E. Abadie, Board Member; C.W. Akins, Board Member. **ISSN:** 0008-6312 (print). **Subscription Rates:** $907.80 Individuals includes postage and handlings; $3321 Individuals print and online; includes postage and handlings; $639 Individuals online; $4416 Institutions includes postage and handlings; $5055 Institutions print and online; includes postage and handlings; $4260 Institutions online. **URL:** http://www.karger.com/Journal/Home/223832. **Formerly:** Cardiologia. **Ad Rates:** BW $1,780. **Remarks:** Accepts advertising. **Circ:** 1000.

6228 ■ Caries Research: Journal of the European Organization for Caries Research (ORCA)
S. Karger Publishers Inc.
26 W Avon Rd.
Unionville, CT 06085-1162
Phone: (860)675-7834
Fax: (203)675-7302
Free: 800-828-5479
Publisher's E-mail: karger@snet.net
Professional journal. **Freq:** 6/year. **Print Method:** Offset. **Trim Size:** 210 x 280 mm. **Cols./Page:** 1. **Col. Width:** 84 nonpareils. **Col. Depth:** 141 agate lines. **Key Personnel:** D. Beighton, Editor-in-Chief; M. Barbour, Associate Editor; R.M. Duckworth, Associate Editor. **ISSN:** 0008--6568 (print); **EISSN:** 1421-976X (electronic). **Subscription Rates:** €1596 Institutions online Eurozone; €1644 Institutions print includes postage and handlings Eurozone; €1883 Institutions print and online; includes postage and handlings Eurozone; $1954 Institutions online only USA/Latin America; $2032 Institutions print includes postage and handlings USA/Latin America; $2325 Institutions print and online; includes postage and handlings USA/Latin America; 1915 FR Institutions, other countries online only; 1999 FR Institutions, other countries print includes postage and handlings; 2286 FR Institutions, other countries print and online; includes postage and handlings; €798 Individuals online Eurozone; €836.40 Individuals print includes postage and handlings Eurozone; €875.40 Individuals print and online; includes postage and handlings Eurozone; $977 Individuals online only USA/Latin America ; $1039.40 Individuals print includes postage and handlings USA/Latin America; $1087.40 Individuals print and online; includes postage and handlings USA/Latin America; 958 FR Other countries online only; 1025.20 FR Other countries print includes postage and handlings; 1073.20 FR Other countries print and online; includes postage and handlings. **URL:** http://www.karger.com/Journal/Home/224219. **Ad Rates:** BW $2,094. **Remarks:** Accepts advertising. **Circ:** 1450.

6229 ■ Cells Tissues Organs
S. Karger Publishers Inc.
26 W Avon Rd.
Unionville, CT 06085-1162
Phone: (860)675-7834
Fax: (203)675-7302
Free: 800-828-5479
Publisher's E-mail: karger@snet.net
Peer-reviewed scientific medical journal (English, French, and German). **Freq:** 12/yr. **Print Method:** Offset. **Trim Size:** 210 x 280 mm. **Cols./Page:** 1. **Col. Width:** 99 nonpareils. **Col. Depth:** 155 agate lines. **Key Personnel:** D. Newgreen, Associate Editor; Bader A. Leipzig, Board Member; H.W. Denker, Editor-in-Chief; A.W. English, Editor-in-Chief. **ISSN:** 1422--6405 (print); **EISSN:** 1422--6421 (electronic). **Subscription Rates:** €4187 Institutions print & online Eurozone; 5024 FR Institutions print & online rest of Europe; $5127 Institutions print & online USA/Latin America; €461 Individuals print & online Eurozone; 553 FR Individuals print and online rest of Europe; $564 Individuals print and online USA/Latin America; 553 FR Other countries print & online. **URL:** http://www.karger.com/Journal/Home/224197. **Formerly:** Acta Anatomica. **Remarks:** Accepts advertising. **Circ:** (Not Reported).

6230 ■ Cellular Physiology and Biochemistry: International Journal of Experimental Cellular Physiology, Biochemistry, and Pharmacology
S. Karger Publishers Inc.
26 W Avon Rd.
Unionville, CT 06085-1162
Phone: (860)675-7834
Fax: (203)675-7302
Free: 800-828-5479
Publisher's E-mail: karger@snet.net
Peer-reviewed medical journal on biochemistry. **Freq:** Monthly. **Print Method:** Offset. **Trim Size:** 210 x 297. **Cols./Page:** 1. **Col. Width:** 99 nonpareils. **Key Personnel:** W. Guggino, Managing Editor; F. Lang, Managing Editor. **ISSN:** 1015--8987 (print); **EISSN:** 1421--9778 (electronic). **Subscription Rates:** 3842 FR Institutions print or online; €2846 Institutions in Germany; print or online; $3590 Institutions print or online; 4226 FR Institutions combined print and online; €3130 Institutions in Germany; combined print and online; $3950 Institutions combined print and online. **URL:** http://www.karger.com/Journal/Home/224332. **Ad Rates:** BW $1,650. **Remarks:** Accepts advertising. **Circ:** ‡1450.

6231 ■ Cerebrovascular Diseases
S. Karger Publishers Inc.
26 W Avon Rd.
Unionville, CT 06085-1162
Phone: (860)675-7834
Fax: (203)675-7302
Free: 800-828-5479
Publisher's E-mail: karger@snet.net
Medical journal cerebrovascular research. **Freq:** Monthly. **Print Method:** Offset. **Trim Size:** 210 x 280. **Cols./Page:** 1. **Col. Width:** 99 nonpareils. **Key Personnel:** M.G. Hennerici, Editor-in-Chief; H. Adams, Board Member; J.P. Mohr, Associate Editor; R.H. Ackerman, Board Member; F. Aichner, Board Member; N. Bornstein, Board Member; M. Brainin, Board Member. **ISSN:** 1015--9770 (print); **EISSN:** 1421--9786 (electronic). **Subscription Rates:** 6048 FR Institutions online; 6162 FR Institutions print; 7069 FR Institutions combined print and online; 907 FR Individuals online; 998.20 FR Individuals print; 1094.20 FR Individuals combined print and online. **URL:** http://www.karger.com/Journal/Home/224153. **Ad Rates:** BW $2,094. **Remarks:** Accepts advertising. **Circ:** ‡4300.

6232 ■ Chemotherapy: International Journal of Experimental and Clinical Chemotherapy
S. Karger Publishers Inc.
26 W Avon Rd.
Unionville, CT 06085-1162
Phone: (860)675-7834
Fax: (203)675-7302
Free: 800-828-5479
Publisher's E-mail: karger@snet.net
Medical journal. **Freq:** 6/year. **Print Method:** Offset. **Trim Size:** 177 x 252 mm. **Cols./Page:** 1. **Col. Width:** 84 nonpareils. **Col. Depth:** 141 agate lines. **Key Personnel:** F. Sorgel, Editor-in-Chief. **ISSN:** 0009--3157 (print); **EISSN:** 1421--9794 (electronic). **Subscription Rates:** €2053 Institutions online Eurozone; €2101 Institutions print includes postage and handlings Eurozone; €2409 Institutions print and online; includes postage and handlings Eurozone; $2514 Institutions online only USA/Latin America; $2592 Institutions print includes postage and handlings USA/Latin America; $2969 Institutions print and online; includes postage and handlings USA/Latin America; 2464 FR Institutions, other countries online only; 2548 FR Institutions, other countries print includes postage and handlings; 2918 FR Institutions, other countries print and online; includes postage and handlings; €1027 Individuals online Eurozone; €1065.40 Individuals print includes postage and handlings Eurozone; €1104.40 Individuals print and online; includes postage and handlings Eurozone; $1257 Individuals online only USA/Latin America; $1319.40 Individuals print includes postage and handlings USA/Latin America; $1367.40 Individuals print and online; includes postage and handlings USA/Latin America; 1232 FR Other countries online only; 1299.20 FR Other countries print includes postage and handlings; 1347.20 FR Other countries print and online; includes postage and handlings. **URL:** http://www.karger.com/Journal/Home/223834. **Formerly:** Chemotherapia. **Ad Rates:** BW $2,094. **Remarks:** Accepts advertising. **Circ:** 800.

6233 ■ Current Urology
S. Karger Publishers Inc.
26 W Avon Rd.
Unionville, CT 06085-1162
Phone: (860)675-7834
Fax: (203)675-7302
Free: 800-828-5479
Publisher's E-mail: karger@snet.net
Peer-reviewed journal covering men's health issues including urologic diseases. **Freq:** Quarterly. **Print Method:** Offset. **Trim Size:** 210 x 280 mm. **Cols./Page:** 5. **Col. Width:** 12 1/16 inches. **Col. Depth:** 13 inches. **Key Personnel:** Shengtian Zhao, Editor-in-Chief. **ISSN:** 1661--7649 (print); **EISSN:** 1661--7657 (electronic). **URL:** http://www.karger.com/Journal/Home/231997. **Remarks:** Accepts advertising. **Circ:** (Not Reported).

6234 ■ Cytogenetics and Genome Research
S. Karger Publishers Inc.
26 W Avon Rd.
Unionville, CT 06085-1162
Phone: (860)675-7834
Fax: (203)675-7302
Free: 800-828-5479
Publisher's E-mail: karger@snet.net
Scientific medical journal (English, French, and German). **Freq:** Monthly. **Print Method:** Offset. **Trim Size:** 210 x 280 mm. **Cols./Page:** 1. **Col. Width:** 99 nonpareils. **Col. Depth:** 155 agate lines. **Key Personnel:** Michael Schmid, Editor-in-Chief; Linda A. Cannizzaro, Executive Editor, phone: (718)405-8103, fax: (718)931-3637; Martina Guttenbach, Managing Editor. **ISSN:** 1424--8581 (print). **Subscription Rates:** €3918 Individuals Print; €3918 Individuals online; Free online. **URL:** http://www.karger.com/Journal/Home/224037. **Formerly:** Cytogenetics and Cell Genetics. **Ad Rates:** BW $2,094. **Remarks:** Accepts advertising. **Circ:** 1300.

6235 ■ Dementia and Geriatric Cognitive Disorders
S. Karger Publishers Inc.
26 W Avon Rd.
Unionville, CT 06085-1162
Phone: (860)675-7834
Fax: (203)675-7302
Free: 800-828-5479
Publisher's E-mail: karger@snet.net
Medical journal. **Freq:** Monthly. **Print Method:** Offset. **Trim Size:** 210 x 280 mm. **Cols./Page:** 1. **Col. Width:** 99 nonpareils. **Key Personnel:** V. Chan-Palay, Editor-

Circulation: ★ = AAM; △ or • = BPA; ♦ = CAC; ❑ = VAC; ⊕ = PO Statement; ‡ = Publisher's Report; Boldface figures = sworn; Light figures = estimated.

in-Chief; P.G. Ince, Board Member; D.L. Bachman, Board Member; L. Gustafson, Board Member; S.E. Gandy, Board Member; C. Ballard, Board Member; J. Cummings, Board Member. **ISSN:** 1420--8008 (print); **EISSN:** 1421--9824 (electronic). **Subscription Rates:** 5599 FR Institutions online; 5713 FR Institutions print; 6553 FR Institutions combined print and online; 840 FR Individuals online; 931.20 FR Individuals print; 1027.20 FR Individuals combined print and online. **URL:** http://www.karger.com/Journal/Home/224226. **Formerly**: Dementia. **Ad Rates:** BW $2,094. **Remarks:** Accepts advertising. **Circ:** ‡1000.

6236 ■ Dermatology
S. Karger Publishers Inc.
26 W Avon Rd.
Unionville, CT 06085-1162
Phone: (860)675-7834
Fax: (203)675-7302
Free: 800-828-5479
Publisher's E-mail: karger@snet.net
Medical journal. **Freq:** 6/year. **Print Method:** Offset. **Trim Size:** 210 x 280 mm. **Cols./Page:** 1. **Col. Width:** 84 nonpareils. **Col. Depth:** 141 agate lines. **Key Personnel:** D. Lipsker, Associate Editor; Gregor B.E. Jemec, Editor-in-Chief. **ISSN:** 1018--8665 (print). **Subscription Rates:** €3013 Institutions Eurozone (print or online - includes postage & handling); €3457 Institutions Eurozone (print + online - includes postage & handling, online upgrade fee); 3344 FR Institutions rest of Europe (print or online - includes postage & handling); 3837 FR Institutions rest of Europe (print + online - includes postage & handling, online upgrade fee); $3654 Institutions U.S./Latin American (print or online - includes postage & handling); $4190 Institutions U.S./Latin American (print + online - includes postage & handling, online upgrade fee); 3371 FR Institutions, other countries print or online (includes postage & handling); 3864 FR Institutions, other countries print + online (includes postage & handling, online upgrade fee); €1523 Individuals Eurozone (print or online - includes postage & handling); €1563 Individuals Eurozone (print + online - includes postage & handling, online upgrade fee); 1690 FR Individuals rest of Europe (print or online - includes postage & handling); 1740 FR Individuals rest of Europe (print + online - includes postage & handling, online upgrade fee); $1852 Individuals U.S./Latin American (print or online - includes postage & handling); $1906 Individuals U.S./Latin American (print + online - includes postage & handling, online upgrade fee); 1711 FR Other countries print or online (includes postage & handling); 1761 FR Other countries print + online (includes postage & handling, online upgrade fee). **URL:** http://www.karger.com/Journal/Home/224164. **Formerly**: Dermatologische Zeitschrift'; Dermatologica. **Ad Rates:** BW $2094. **Remarks:** Accepts advertising. **Circ:** (Not Reported).

6237 ■ Developmental Neuroscience
S. Karger Publishers Inc.
26 W Avon Rd.
Unionville, CT 06085-1162
Phone: (860)675-7834
Fax: (203)675-7302
Free: 800-828-5479
Publisher's E-mail: karger@snet.net
Medical journal. **Freq:** Bimonthly. **Print Method:** Offset. **Trim Size:** 210 x 280 mm. **Cols./Page:** 1. **Col. Width:** 84 nonpareils. **Col. Depth:** 141 agate lines. **Key Personnel:** S.W. Levison, Editor-in-Chief; P.G. Bhide, Associate Editor. **ISSN:** 0378--5866 (print). **Subscription Rates:** €656 Institutions online Eurozone; €656 Institutions print Eurozone; €656 Institutions print and online; includes postage and handlings Eurozone. **URL:** http://www.karger.com/Journal/Home/224107. **Ad Rates:** BW $2,094. **Remarks:** Accepts advertising. **Circ:** 800.

6238 ■ Digestion
S. Karger Publishers Inc.
26 W Avon Rd.
Unionville, CT 06085-1162
Phone: (860)675-7834
Fax: (203)675-7302
Free: 800-828-5479
Publisher's E-mail: karger@snet.net
Medical journal. **Freq:** 8/year. **Print Method:** Offset. **Trim Size:** 210 x 280 mm. **Cols./Page:** 1. **Col. Width:** 84 nonpareils. **Col. Depth:** 141 agate lines. **Key Personnel:** B. Goke, Editor-in-Chief; Y. Shinomura, Editor-in-Chief; F. Kolligs, Managing Editor. **ISSN:** 0012--2823 (print); **EISSN:** 1421--9867 (electronic). **URL:** http://www.karger.com/Journal/Home/223838. **Formerly**: Archiv fur Verdauungskrankheiten'; Gastroenterologia. **Ad Rates:** BW $2,094. **Remarks:** Accepts advertising. **Circ:** 3600.

6239 ■ Digestive Diseases
S. Karger Publishers Inc.
26 W Avon Rd.
Unionville, CT 06085-1162
Phone: (860)675-7834
Fax: (203)675-7302
Free: 800-828-5479
Publisher's E-mail: karger@snet.net
Scientific medical journal. **Freq:** Bimonthly. **Print Method:** Offset. **Trim Size:** 210 x 280 mm. **Cols./Page:** 1. **Col. Width:** 84 nonpareils. **Col. Depth:** 141 agate lines. **Key Personnel:** Peter Malfertheiner, Editor-in-Chief. **ISSN:** 0257--2753 (print); **EISSN:** 1421--9875 (electronic). **URL:** http://www.karger.com/Journal/Home/224231. **Ad Rates:** BW $2,094. **Remarks:** Accepts advertising. **Circ:** 800.

6240 ■ Digestive Surgery
S. Karger Publishers Inc.
26 W Avon Rd.
Unionville, CT 06085-1162
Phone: (860)675-7834
Fax: (203)675-7302
Free: 800-828-5479
Publisher's E-mail: karger@snet.net
Scientific medical journal. **Freq:** Bimonthly. **Print Method:** Offset. **Trim Size:** 210 x 280 mm. **Cols./Page:** 1. **Col. Width:** 99 nonpareils. **Col. Depth:** 155 agate lines. **Key Personnel:** B. Gloor, Associate Editor; D.J. Gouma, Consultant; R. Parks, Associate Editor; H. Friess, Board Member; M. Pera, Associate Editor; J.V. Reynolds, Associate Editor; X. Rogiers, Associate Editor; C. Dervenis, Associate Editor; H.W. Tilanus, Editor; J.J.B. van Lanschot, Editor. **ISSN:** 0253--4886 (print); **EISSN:** 1421--9883 (electronic). **URL:** http://www.karger.com/Journal/Home/223996. **Ad Rates:** BW $2,094. **Remarks:** Accepts advertising. **Circ:** 2400.

6241 ■ European Neurology
S. Karger Publishers Inc.
26 W Avon Rd.
Unionville, CT 06085-1162
Phone: (860)675-7834
Fax: (203)675-7302
Free: 800-828-5479
Publisher's E-mail: karger@snet.net
Scientific medical journal. **Freq:** 12/yr. **Print Method:** Offset. **Trim Size:** 210 x 280 mm. **Cols./Page:** 1. **Col. Width:** 84 nonpareils. **Col. Depth:** 141 agate lines. **Key Personnel:** J. Bogousslavsky, Editor-in-Chief. **ISSN:** 0014--3022 (print); **EISSN:** 1421-9913 (electronic). **Subscription Rates:** €3283 Institutions online only Eurozone; €3379 Institutions print Eurozone; €3871 Institutions combined print & online Eurozone; $4019 Institutions online only USA/Latin America; $4175 Institutions print USA/Latin America; $4778 Institutions combined print & online USA/Latin America; 3939 FR Institutions, other countries online only; 4107 FR Institutions, other countries print; 4698 FR Institutions, other countries combined print & online; €657 Individuals online only Eurozone; €733.80 Individuals print Eurozone; €811.80 Individuals combined print & online Eurozone; $804 Individuals online only USA/Latin America; $928.80 Individuals print USA/Latin America; $1024.80 Individuals combined print & online USA/Latin America; 788 FR Other countries online only; 922.40 FR Other countries print only; 1018.40 FR Other countries combined print & online. **URL:** http://www.karger.com; http://www.karger.com/Journal/Home/223840. **Ad Rates:** BW $2,094. **Remarks:** Accepts advertising. **Circ:** 1100.

6242 ■ European Surgical Research
S. Karger Publishers Inc.
26 W Avon Rd.
Unionville, CT 06085-1162
Phone: (860)675-7834
Fax: (203)675-7302
Free: 800-828-5479
Publisher's E-mail: karger@snet.net
Scientific medical journal. **Freq:** 8/year. **Print Method:** Offset. **Trim Size:** 210 x 280 mm. **Cols./Page:** 1. **Col. Width:** 84 nonpareils. **Col. Depth:** 141 agate lines. **Key Personnel:** B. Vollmar, Editor-in-Chief. **ISSN:** 0014--312X (print); **EISSN:** 1421-9921 (electronic). **Subscription Rates:** €2306 Institutions online only Eurozone; €2370 Institutions print Eurozone; €2716 Individuals combined print & online Eurozone; $2823 Institutions online only USA/Latin America; $2927 Institutions print USA/Latin America; $3350 Institutions combined print & online USA/Latin America; 2767 FR Institutions, other countries online only; 2879 FR Institutions, other countries print; 3294 FR Institutions, other countries combined print & online; €692 Individuals online only Eurozone; €743.20 Individuals print Eurozone; €821.20 Individuals combined print & online Eurozone; $847 Individuals online only USA/Latin America; $930.20 Individuals print USA/Latin America; $1026.20 Individuals combined print & online USA/Latin America; 830 FR Other countries online only; 919.60 FR Other countries print; 1015.60 FR Other countries combined print & online. **URL:** http://www.karger.com; http://www.karger.com/Journal/Home/223841. **Ad Rates:** BW $2,094. **Remarks:** Accepts advertising. **Circ:** 1600.

6243 ■ Fetal Diagnosis and Therapy
S. Karger Publishers Inc.
26 W Avon Rd.
Unionville, CT 06085-1162
Phone: (860)675-7834
Fax: (203)675-7302
Free: 800-828-5479
Publisher's E-mail: karger@snet.net
Peer-reviewed scientific medical journal focusing on the fetus as a patient. **Freq:** 8/yr. **Print Method:** Offset. **Trim Size:** 210 x 280 mm. **Cols./Page:** 1. **Col. Width:** 84 nonpareils. **Col. Depth:** 177 agate lines. **Key Personnel:** E. Gratacos, Editor-in-Chief; F. Figueras, Associate Editor. **ISSN:** 1015--3837 (print); **EISSN:** 1421--9964 (electronic). **Subscription Rates:** €2417 Institutions online Eurozone; €2481 Institutions print includes postage and handlings Eurozone; €2844 Institutions print and online; includes postage and handlings Eurozone; $2959 Institutions online only USA/Latin America; $3063 Institutions print includes postage and handlings USA/Latin America; $3507 Institutions print and online; includes postage and handlings USA/Latin America; 2900 FR Institutions, other countries online only; 3012 FR Institutions, other countries print includes postage and handlings; 3447 FR Institutions, other countries print and online; includes postage and handlings; €967 Individuals online Eurozone; €1018.20 Individuals print includes postage and handlings Eurozone; €1096.20 Individuals print and online; includes postage and handlings Eurozone; $1184 Individuals online only USA/Latin America; $1267.20 Individuals print includes postage and handlings USA/Latin America; $1363.20 Individuals print and online; includes postage and handlings USA/Latin America; $1160 Other countries online only; $1249.60 Other countries print includes postage and handlings; $1345.60 Other countries print and online; includes postage and handlings. **URL:** http://www.karger.com; http://www.karger.com/Journal/Home/224239. **Formerly**: Fetal Therapy. **Ad Rates:** BW $2,094. **Remarks:** Accepts advertising. **Circ:** 950.

6244 ■ Folia Phoniatrica et Logopaedica
S. Karger Publishers Inc.
26 W Avon Rd.
Unionville, CT 06085-1162
Phone: (860)675-7834
Fax: (203)675-7302
Free: 800-828-5479
Publisher's E-mail: office@ialp.info
Medical journal (English, German and French). **Freq:** 6/year Bimonthly. **Print Method:** Offset. **Trim Size:** 210 x 280 mm. **Cols./Page:** 1. **Col. Width:** 84 nonpareils. **Key Personnel:** G. Weismer, Editor-in-Chief. **ISSN:** 1021--7762 (print); **EISSN:** 1421--9972 (electronic). **Subscription Rates:** €1228 Institutions online Eurozone; €1276 Institutions print includes postage and handlings Eurozone; €1460 Institutions print and online; includes postage and handlings Eurozone; $1504 Institutions online only USA/Latin America; $1582 Institutions print includes postage and handlings USA/Latin America; $1808 Institutions print and online; includes postage and handlings USA/Latin America; 1474 FR

Institutions, other countries online only; 1558 FR Institutions, other countries print includes postage and handlings; 1779 FR Institutions, other countries print and online; includes postage and handlings; €737 Individuals online Eurozone; €775.40 Individuals print includes postage and handlings Eurozone; €814.40 Individuals print and online; includes postage and handlings Eurozone; $902 Individuals online only USA/Latin America; $964.40 Individuals print includes postage and handlings USA/Latin America; $1012.40 Individuals print and online; includes postage and handlings USA/Latin America; 884 FR Other countries online only; 951.20 FR Other countries print includes postage and handlings; 999.20 FR Other countries print and online; includes postage and handlings; 968 FR Other countries print. **URL:** http://www.karger.com; http://www.karger.com/Journal/Home/224177. **Ad Rates:** BW $2,094. **Remarks:** Accepts advertising. **Circ:** 900.

6245 ■ Folia Primatologica: The Official Journal of the European Federation for Primatology
S. Karger Publishers Inc.
26 W Avon Rd.
Unionville, CT 06085-1162
Phone: (860)675-7834
Fax: (203)675-7302
Free: 800-828-5479
Publisher's E-mail: karger@snet.net
Peer-reviewed scientific journal focusing on primatology (English, German and French). **Freq:** Bimonthly. **Print Method:** Offset. **Trim Size:** 177 x 252 mm. **Cols./Page:** 1. **Col. Width:** 84 nonpareils. **Col. Depth:** 141 agate lines. **Key Personnel:** C. Harcourt, Assistant Editor; A.F. Dixson, Board Member; J. Fischer, Board Member; J. Ganzhorn, Board Member; T. Kimura, Board Member; R.H. Crompton, Editor-in-Chief; D.J. Chivers, Board Member. **ISSN:** 0015--5713 (print). **Subscription Rates:** €1184 Institutions online Eurozone; €1232 Institutions print includes postage and handlings Eurozone; €1410 Institutions print and online; includes postage and handlings Eurozone; $1450 Institutions online only USA/Latin America; $1528 Institutions print includes postage and handlings USA/Latin America; $1746 Institutions print and online; includes postage and handlings USA/Latin America; 1421 FR Institutions, other countries online only; 1505 FR Institutions, other countries print includes postage and handlings; 1718 FR Institutions, other countries print and online; includes postage and handlings; €592 Individuals online Eurozone; €630.40 Individuals print includes postage and handlings Eurozone; €669.40 Individuals print and online; includes postage and handlings Eurozone; $725 Individuals online only USA/Latin America; $787.40 Individuals print includes postage and handlings USA/Latin America; $835.40 Individuals print and online; includes postage and handlings USA/Latin America; 711 FR Other countries online only; 778.20 FR Other countries print includes postage and handlings; 826.20 FR Other countries print and online; includes postage and handlings. **URL:** http://www.karger.com/Journal/Home/223842. **Ad Rates:** BW $2,094. **Remarks:** Accepts advertising. **Circ:** 800.

6246 ■ Gerontology
S. Karger Publishers Inc.
26 W Avon Rd.
Unionville, CT 06085-1162
Phone: (860)675-7834
Fax: (203)675-7302
Free: 800-828-5479
Publisher's E-mail: karger@snet.net
Medical journal. **Founded:** 1957. **Freq:** 6/year. **Print Method:** Offset. **Trim Size:** 210 x 280 mm. **Cols./Page:** 1. **Col. Width:** 84 nonpareils. **Col. Depth:** 141 agate lines. **Key Personnel:** G. Wick, Editor-in-Chief. **ISSN:** 0304-324X (print). **Subscription Rates:** 1827 FR Institutions print or online, combined; $1864 Institutions print or online, combined; 914 FR Individuals print or online, combined; $932 Individuals print or online, combined. **URL:** http://www.karger.com; http://www.karger.com/Journal/Home/224091. **Formerly:** Gerontolgia Clinica. **Ad Rates:** BW $2,094. **Remarks:** Accepts advertising. **Circ:** 900.

6247 ■ Gynecologic and Obstetric Investigation
S. Karger Publishers Inc.
26 W Avon Rd.
Unionville, CT 06085-1162
Phone: (860)675-7834
Fax: (203)675-7302
Free: 800-828-5479
Publisher's E-mail: karger@snet.net
Scientific medical journal. **Freq:** 8/year. **Print Method:** Offset. **Trim Size:** 210 x 280 mm. **Cols./Page:** 1. **Col. Width:** 84 nonpareils. **Col. Depth:** 141 agate lines. **Key Personnel:** T.M. D'Hooghe, Editor-in-Chief. **ISSN:** 0378--7346 (print). **Subscription Rates:** €3527 Institutions online - Eurozone; €3584 Institutions print includes postage and handlings - Eurozone; €4113 Institutions print and online; includes postage and handlings - Eurozone; $3792 Institutions online only - USA/Latin America; $3870 Institutions print includes postage and handlings - USA/Latin America; $4439 Institutions print and online; includes postage and handlings - USA/Latin America; 3527 FR Institutions, other countries online only; 3611 FR Institutions, other countries print includes postage and handlings; 4140 FR Institutions, other countries print and online; includes postage and handlings; €1575 Individuals online only - Eurozone; €1615 Individuals print includes postage and handlings - Eurozone; €1655 Individuals print and online; includes postage and handlings Eurozone; $1896 Individuals online only - USA/Latin America; $1958.40 Individuals print includes postage and handlings - USA/Latin America; $1896.40 Individuals print and online; includes postage and handlings - USA/Latin America; 1764 FR Other countries online only; 1831.20 FR Other countries print includes postage and handlings; 1881.20 FR Other countries print and online; includes postage and handlings. **URL:** http://www.karger.com; http://www.karger.com/Journal/Home/223845. **Formerly:** Gynecologic Investigation. **Ad Rates:** BW $1,870. **Remarks:** Accepts advertising. **Circ:** 800.

6248 ■ Hormone Research in Paediatrics
S. Karger Publishers Inc.
26 W Avon Rd.
Unionville, CT 06085-1162
Phone: (860)675-7834
Fax: (203)675-7302
Free: 800-828-5479
Publisher's E-mail: karger@snet.net
Scientific medical journal. **Freq:** Monthly. **Print Method:** Offset. **Trim Size:** 210 x 280 mm. **Cols./Page:** 1. **Col. Width:** 84 nonpareils. **Col. Depth:** 141 agate lines. **Key Personnel:** P.E. Clayton, Associate Editor; S. Cianfarani, Editor-in-Chief. **ISSN:** 1663--2818 (print); **EISSN:** 1663--2826 (electronic). **Subscription Rates:** 4801 FR Institutions print and online - rest of Europe; $5256 Institutions print and online; 4855 FR Institutions, other countries print and online; 4325 FR Institutions print and online. **URL:** http://www.karger.com/Journal/Home/224036. **Formerly:** Hormone Research; Hormones. **Ad Rates:** BW $1,870. **Remarks:** Accepts advertising. **Circ:** 1750.

6249 ■ Human Heredity
S. Karger Publishers Inc.
26 W Avon Rd.
Unionville, CT 06085-1162
Phone: (860)675-7834
Fax: (203)675-7302
Free: 800-828-5479
Publisher's E-mail: karger@snet.net
Medical journal. **Freq:** Quarterly. **Print Method:** Offset. **Trim Size:** 210 x 280 mm. **Cols./Page:** 1. **Col. Width:** 84 nonpareils. **Col. Depth:** 141 agate lines. **Key Personnel:** M. Devoto, Editor; Katherine Montague, Director, Editorial. **ISSN:** 0001--5652 (print); **EISSN:** 1423-0062 (electronic). **Subscription Rates:** €3076 Institutions print and online; 3415 FR Institutions print and online - rest of Europe; $3731 Institutions print and online; 3442 FR Institutions print and online; €1397.20 Individuals print and online; 1557 FR Individuals print and online - rest of Europe; $1707.20 Individuals print and online; 1578.60 FR Other countries print and online. **URL:** http://www.karger.com/Journal/Guidelines/224250. **Formerly:** Acta Genetica et Statistica Medica. **Ad Rates:** BW $1,870. **Remarks:** Accepts advertising. **Circ:** 900.

6250 ■ International Archives of Allergy and Immunology
S. Karger Publishers Inc.
26 W Avon Rd.
Unionville, CT 06085-1162
Phone: (860)675-7834
Fax: (203)675-7302
Free: 800-828-5479
Publisher's E-mail: karger@snet.net
Scientific medical journal. **Freq:** Monthly. **Print Method:** Offset. **Trim Size:** 210 x 280 mm. **Cols./Page:** 1. **Col. Width:** 84 nonpareils. **Col. Depth:** 141 agate lines. **Key Personnel:** E. Jensen-Jarolim, Board Member; R. Valenta, Editor-in-Chief; H. Breiteneder, Board Member; M.D. Chapman, Board Member; R. Pawankar, Associate Editor; A. Radbruch, Associate Editor; K.T. HayGlass, Board Member; K. Blaser, Associate Editor. **ISSN:** 1018--2438 (print); **EISSN:** 1423--0097 (electronic). **Subscription Rates:** €4949 Institutions print & online Eurozone; 5543 FR Institutions print & online Rest of Europe/other countries; $5960 Institutions print & online USA/Latin America; €154 Individuals print & online Eurozone; 172 FR Individuals print & online Rest of Europe/other countries; $185 Individuals print & online USA/Latin America. **URL:** http://www.karger.com/Journal/Home/224161. **Formerly:** International Archives of Allergy and Applied Immunology. **Ad Rates:** BW $1780. **Remarks:** Accepts advertising. **Circ:** 1050.

6251 ■ Intervirology
S. Karger Publishers Inc.
26 W Avon Rd.
Unionville, CT 06085-1162
Phone: (860)675-7834
Fax: (203)675-7302
Free: 800-828-5479
Publisher's E-mail: karger@snet.net
Scientific medical journal. **Freq:** Bimonthly. **Print Method:** Offset. **Trim Size:** 210 x 280 mm. **Cols./Page:** 1. **Col. Width:** 84 nonpareils. **Col. Depth:** 141 agate lines. **Key Personnel:** J.-C. Manuguerra, Editor-in-Chief; U.G. Liebert, Board Member; T. Cunningham, Board Member; O. Hino, Board Member. **ISSN:** 0300--5526 (print); **EISSN:** 1423--0100 (electronic). **Subscription Rates:** €1829 Institutions print and online Eurozone; 2048 FR Institutions print and online rest of Europe/other countries; $2202 Institutions print and online USA/Latin America; €640 Individuals print and online Eurozone; 717 FR Individuals print and online rest of Europe/other countries; $771 Individuals print and online USA/Latin America. **URL:** http://www.karger.com/Journal/Home/224031. **Ad Rates:** BW $1780. **Remarks:** Accepts advertising. **Circ:** 800.

6252 ■ Journal of Molecular Microbiology and Biotechnology
S. Karger Publishers Inc.
26 W Avon Rd.
Unionville, CT 06085-1162
Phone: (860)675-7834
Fax: (203)675-7302
Free: 800-828-5479
Publisher's E-mail: karger@snet.net
Journal publishes original research papers from all areas of microbiology and biotechnology. **Freq:** 6/yr. **Trim Size:** 210 x 280 mm. **Key Personnel:** M.H. Saier, Jr., Editor-in-Chief; J. Deutscher, Senior Editor; F. Barras, Board Member. **ISSN:** 1464-1801 (print). **Subscription Rates:** 2562 FR Institutions print (Europe); $2634 Institutions print (USA/Latin America); 2589 FR Institutions print (all other regions); 1047.60 FR Individuals print (Europe); $1084 Individuals print (USA/Latin America); 1069.20 FR Individuals print (all other regions). **URL:** http://www.karger.com/Journal/Home/228391. **Ad Rates:** BW $2,094. **Remarks:** Accepts advertising. **Circ:** ‡600.

6253 ■ Journal of Nutrigenetics and Nutrigenomics
S. Karger Publishers Inc.
26 W Avon Rd.
Unionville, CT 06085-1162
Phone: (860)675-7834
Fax: (203)675-7302
Free: 800-828-5479
Publisher's E-mail: karger@snet.net
Journal covering genetic basis for the variable responses to diet and lifestyle factors in chronic conditions,

Circulation: ★ = AAM; △ or • = BPA; ♦ = CAC; ❑ = VAC; ⊕ = PO Statement; ‡ = Publisher's Report; Boldface figures = sworn; Light figures = estimated.

methods to assess gene-environment interactions, and other related topics. **Freq:** 6/year. **Trim Size:** 210 x 280 mm. **Key Personnel:** Jing X. Kang, Editor-in-Chief; Louis Perusse, Board Member; Marie-Claude Vohl, Board Member. **ISSN:** 1661--6499 (print); **EISSN:** 1661--6758 (electronic). **Subscription Rates:** €1459 Institutions print and online; $1761 Institutions print and online; 1620 FR Institutions print and online; €730 Individuals print and online; $881 Institutions print and online; 810 FR Individuals print and online; Included in membership. **URL:** http://www.karger.com/Journal/Home/232009. **Ad Rates:** BW 1780 FR; BW €1483; BW $2094. **Remarks:** Accepts advertising. **Circ:** (Not Reported).

6254 ■ Kidney and Blood Pressure Research
S. Karger Publishers Inc.
26 W Avon Rd.
Unionville, CT 06085-1162
Phone: (860)675-7834
Fax: (203)675-7302
Free: 800-828-5479
Publisher's E-mail: karger@snet.net
Scientific medical journal on the interdisciplinary approach to the mechanisms and regulation of renal functions. **Freq:** 6/year. **Print Method:** Offset. **Trim Size:** 210 x 280 mm. **Cols./Page:** 1. **Col. Width:** 84 nonpareils. **Col. Depth:** 140 agate lines. **Key Personnel:** C. Wanner, Board Member; F. Lang, Editor; A. Covic, Board Member; P. Kes; V. Tesar, Board Member; J. Floege, Board Member. **ISSN:** 1420--4096 (print); **EISSN:** 1423--0143 (electronic). **URL:** http://www.karger.com/Journal/Home/224258. **Formerly**: Renal Physiology and Biochemistry. **Ad Rates:** BW $1950. **Remarks:** Accepts advertising. **Circ:** 2700.

6255 ■ Medical Principles and Practice: International Journal of the Kuwait University Health Science Centre
S. Karger Publishers Inc.
26 W Avon Rd.
Unionville, CT 06085-1162
Phone: (860)675-7834
Fax: (203)675-7302
Free: 800-828-5479
Publisher's E-mail: karger@snet.net
Journal on recent advances made in basic medical sciences, clinical practice, and associated disciplines. **Freq:** Bimonthly. **Print Method:** Offset. **Trim Size:** 210 x 280 mm. **Key Personnel:** Azu Owunwanne, Editor-in-Chief; Ludmil Benov, Editor. **ISSN:** 1011--7571 (print); **EISSN:** 1423--0151 (electronic). **Subscription Rates:** $850 Individuals print or online; $944 Individuals print and online; $1698 Institutions print or online; $1866 Institutions print and online. **URL:** http://www.karger.com/Journal/Home/224259. **Ad Rates:** BW $1870. **Remarks:** Accepts advertising. **Circ:** 1950.

6256 ■ Neonatology: Fetal and Neonatal Research
S. Karger Publishers Inc.
26 W Avon Rd.
Unionville, CT 06085-1162
Phone: (860)675-7834
Fax: (203)675-7302
Free: 800-828-5479
Publisher's E-mail: karger@snet.net
Scientific medical journal. **Print Method:** Offset. **Trim Size:** 210 x 280 mm. **Cols./Page:** 1. **Col. Width:** 84 nonpareils. **Col. Depth:** 141 agate lines. **Key Personnel:** S. Andersson, Board Member; E. Bancalari, Board Member; W.A. Carlo, Board Member; M. Hallman, Board Member; M. Obladen, Board Member; E. Shinwell, Board Member; H.L Halliday, Editor-in-Chief; C.P Speer, Editor-in-Chief. **ISSN:** 1661--7800 (print); **EISSN:** 1661--7819 (electronic). **Subscription Rates:** €3004 Institutions print and online; $3617 Institutions print and online; $3364 Institutions, other countries print and online; €751 Individuals print and online; $904 U.S. print and online; $841 Individuals print and online. **URL:** http://www.karger.com/Journal/Home/224215. **Formerly**: Biology of the Neonate. **Ad Rates:** BW $1,780. **Remarks:** Accepts advertising. **Circ:** 900.

6257 ■ Nephron
S. Karger Publishers Inc.
26 W Avon Rd.
Unionville, CT 06085-1162
Phone: (860)675-7834
Fax: (203)675-7302
Free: 800-828-5479
Publisher's E-mail: karger@snet.net
Medical journal. **Freq:** Monthly. **Print Method:** Offset. **Trim Size:** 210 x 280 mm. **Cols./Page:** 1. **Col. Width:** 99 nonpareils. **Col. Depth:** 155 agate lines. **Key Personnel:** Bergamo A. Benigni, Editor-in-Chief. **ISSN:** 1660-8151 (print). **Subscription Rates:** $5733 Individuals print or online; $1405 Individuals print or online. **URL:** http://www.karger.com; http://www.karger.com/Journal/Home/223854. **Ad Rates:** BW $2,094. **Remarks:** Accepts advertising. **Circ:** 2600.

6258 ■ Nephron Clinical Practice
S. Karger Publishers Inc.
26 W Avon Rd.
Unionville, CT 06085-1162
Phone: (860)675-7834
Fax: (203)675-7302
Free: 800-828-5479
Publisher's E-mail: karger@snet.net
Journal provides readers with research and opinions on all aspects of clinical nephrology, dialysis and transplantation. **Freq:** Monthly. **Trim Size:** 210 x 280 mm. **Key Personnel:** Bergamo A. Benigni, Editor-in-Chief. **ISSN:** 1660-2110 (print). **Subscription Rates:** 532 FR Institutions print (Europe); $5889 Institutions print (USA/Latin America); 5786 FR Institutions print (all other regions); 1496.20 FR Individuals print (Europe); $1557.80 Individuals print (USA/Latin America); 1701.80 FR Individuals print (all other regions). **URL:** http://www.karger.com/Journal/Home/228539. **Ad Rates:** BW $1,040. **Remarks:** Accepts advertising. **Circ:** (Not Reported).

6259 ■ Neurodegenerative Diseases
S. Karger Publishers Inc.
26 W Avon Rd.
Unionville, CT 06085-1162
Phone: (860)675-7834
Fax: (203)675-7302
Free: 800-828-5479
Publisher's E-mail: karger@snet.net
Journal for the publication of advances in the understanding of neurodegenerative diseases, including Alzheimer disease, Parkinson's disease, amyotrophic lateral sclerosis, Huntington disease and related neurological and psychiatric disorders. **Freq:** 8/year. **Trim Size:** 210 x 280 mm. **Key Personnel:** C. Hock, Editor-in-Chief; R.M. Nitsch, Editor-in-Chief. **ISSN:** 1660-2854 (print). **Subscription Rates:** 2089 FR Institutions print (Europe); $2151 Institutions print (USA/Latin America); 2116 FR Institutions print (all other countries); 655.60 FR Individuals print (Europe); $684.40 Individuals print (USA/Latin America); 677.20 FR Individuals print (all other countries). **URL:** http://www.karger.com/Journal/Home/229093. **Ad Rates:** BW $1,780. **Remarks:** Accepts advertising. **Circ:** 800.

6260 ■ Neuroepidemiology
S. Karger Publishers Inc.
26 W Avon Rd.
Unionville, CT 06085-1162
Phone: (860)675-7834
Fax: (203)675-7302
Free: 800-828-5479
Publisher's E-mail: karger@snet.net
Expert findings on the etiology and distribution of neurological diseases. **Freq:** 8/year. **Print Method:** Offset. **Trim Size:** 210 x 280 mm. **Cols./Page:** 1. **Col. Width:** 84 nonpareils. **Col. Depth:** 140 agate lines. **Key Personnel:** D.A. Bennett, Associate Editor; E. Beghi, Associate Editor; V.L. Feigin, Editor-in-Chief. **ISSN:** 0251-5350 (print). **Subscription Rates:** 3298 FR Institutions print and online; $3365 Institutions print or online; 1154 FR Individuals print or online; $1178 Individuals print or online. **URL:** http://www.karger.com/Journal/Home/224263. **Ad Rates:** BW $2,094. **Remarks:** Accepts advertising. **Circ:** 800.

6261 ■ Neuroimmunomodulation
S. Karger Publishers Inc.
26 W Avon Rd.
Unionville, CT 06085-1162
Phone: (860)675-7834
Fax: (203)675-7302
Free: 800-828-5479
Publisher's E-mail: karger@snet.net
Official journal of the International Society for Neuroimmunomodulation. **Freq:** 6/year. **Trim Size:** 210 x 280 mm. **Key Personnel:** W. Savino, Editor; A. del Rey Marburg, Associate Editor. **ISSN:** 1021--7401 (print); **EISSN:** 1423--0216 (electronic). **Subscription Rates:** 2030 FR Institutions, other countries online; 711 FR Other countries online; 2114 FR Institutions, other countries print; 2419 FR Institutions, other countries print & online; 826.40 FR Other countries print; 880.40 FR Other countries print & online. **URL:** http://karger.com/Journal/Home/224176; http://www.isnim.org/journal. **Ad Rates:** BW $2,094. **Remarks:** Accepts advertising. **Circ:** 800.

6262 ■ Neuropsychobiology
S. Karger Publishers Inc.
26 W Avon Rd.
Unionville, CT 06085-1162
Phone: (860)675-7834
Fax: (203)675-7302
Free: 800-828-5479
Publisher's E-mail: karger@snet.net
Medical journal on the neurobiological approach to behavior and mental disorders. **Freq:** 8/year. **Print Method:** Offset. **Trim Size:** 210 x 280 mm. **Cols./Page:** 1. **Col. Width:** 99 nonpareils. **Col. Depth:** 155 agate lines. **Key Personnel:** P. Netter, Associate Editor; G. Erdmann, Board Member; W. Strik, Editor-in-Chief; T. Kinoshita, Associate Editor. **ISSN:** 0302--282X (print); **EISSN:** 1423--0224 (electronic). **Subscription Rates:** 3090 FR Institutions print or online; $3153 Institutions print or online; 1082 FR Individuals combined print and online, print or online; $1104 Individuals combined print and online, print or online. **URL:** http://www.karger.com/Journal/Home/224082. **Remarks:** Accepts advertising. **Circ:** 800.

6263 ■ Neurosignals
S. Karger Publishers Inc.
26 W Avon Rd.
Unionville, CT 06085-1162
Phone: (860)675-7834
Fax: (203)675-7302
Free: 800-828-5479
Publisher's E-mail: karger@snet.net
Medical journal. **Freq:** 4/yr. **Print Method:** Offset. **Trim Size:** 210 x 280 mm. **Cols./Page:** 1. **Col. Width:** 99 nonpareils. **Key Personnel:** Nancy Y. Ip, Editor-in-Chief; Yung Hou Wong, Associate Editor. **ISSN:** 1424--862X (print); **EISSN:** 1424--8638 (electronic). **Subscription Rates:** 1199 FR Institutions print or online; €959 Institutions in Germany; print or online; $1164 Institutions print or online; 1319 FR Institutions combined print and online; €1055 Institutions in Germany; combined print and online; $1281 Institutions combined print and online. **URL:** http://www.karger.com/Journal/Home/224154. **Formerly**: Biological Signals and Receptors. **Ad Rates:** BW $1,780. **Remarks:** Accepts advertising. **Circ:** 600.

6264 ■ Oncology
S. Karger Publishers Inc.
26 W Avon Rd.
Unionville, CT 06085-1162
Phone: (860)675-7834
Fax: (203)675-7302
Free: 800-828-5479
Publisher's E-mail: karger@snet.net
Peer-reviewed medical journal presenting experimental and clinical findings on cancer. **Founded:** 1948. **Freq:** 12/yr. **Print Method:** Offset. **Trim Size:** 210 x 280 mm. **Cols./Page:** 1. **Col. Width:** 99 nonpareils. **Col. Depth:** 155 agate lines. **Key Personnel:** D.L. Trump, Board Member; M. Markman, Editor-in-Chief; O. Hino, Editor. **ISSN:** 0030-2414 (print); **EISSN:** 1423-0232 (electronic). **Subscription Rates:** 3332 FR Institutions, other countries print or online; €2732 Institutions in Germany; print or online; $3332 Institutions print or online; 1666 FR Individuals combined print and online; €1366 Individuals in Germany; combined print and online; $1666 Institutions combined print and online. **URL:** http://www.karger.com/Journal/Home/223857. **Formerly**: Oncologia. **Also known as**: Oncology: International Journal for Cancer Research and Treatment. **Ad Rates:** BW $1,780. **Remarks:** Accepts advertising. **Circ:** 1300.

6265 ■ Ophthalmic Research
S. Karger Publishers Inc.
26 W Avon Rd.
Unionville, CT 06085-1162

Phone: (860)675-7834
Fax: (203)675-7302
Free: 800-828-5479
Publisher's E-mail: karger@snet.net
Research journal on ophthalmology. **Freq:** 8/year. **Print Method:** Offset. **Trim Size:** 210 x 280 mm. **Cols./Page:** 1. **Col. Width:** 84 nonpareils. **Col. Depth:** 140 agate lines. **Key Personnel:** Uwe Pleyer, Editor-in-Chief. **ISSN:** 0030--3747 (print); **EISSN:** 1423--0259 (electronic). **Subscription Rates:** 2054 FR Institutions print or online, combined; $2209 Institutions print or online, combined; 1027 FR Individuals print or online, combined ; $1105 Individuals print or online, combined. **URL:** http://www.karger.com/Journal/Home/223858. **Ad Rates:** BW $2094. **Remarks:** Accepts advertising. **Circ:** 800.

6266 ■ Ophthalmologica
S. Karger Publishers Inc.
26 W Avon Rd.
Unionville, CT 06085-1162
Phone: (860)675-7834
Fax: (203)675-7302
Free: 800-828-5479
Publisher's E-mail: karger@snet.net
Medical research journal (English, French, and German) on ophthalmology. **Freq:** 8/year. **Print Method:** Offset. **Trim Size:** 210 x 280 mm. **Cols./Page:** 1. **Col. Width:** 84 nonpareils. **Col. Depth:** 140 agate lines. **Key Personnel:** J. Cunha-Vaz, Editor. **ISSN:** 0030--3755 (print); **EISSN:** 1423--0267 (electronic). **Subscription Rates:** €2153 Institutions Europe/other countries (print or online); combined; $2315 Institutions USA (print or online); combined; $1157 Individuals USA (print or online); combined; €1077 Institutions Europe/other countries (print or online); combined. **URL:** http://www.karger.com/Journal/Home/224269. **Ad Rates:** BW $2094. **Remarks:** Accepts advertising. **Circ:** 1000.

6267 ■ ORL
S. Karger Publishers Inc.
26 W Avon Rd.
Unionville, CT 06085-1162
Phone: (860)675-7834
Fax: (203)675-7302
Free: 800-828-5479
Publisher's E-mail: karger@snet.net
Medical journal. **Freq:** 6/year. **Print Method:** Offset. **Trim Size:** 210 x 280 mm. **Cols./Page:** 1. **Col. Width:** 84 nonpareils. **Col. Depth:** 140 agate lines. **Key Personnel:** Bert W. O'Malley, Jr., Editor; Fernando L. Dias, Associate Editor; Wolfgang Arnold, Associate Editor; Y.A. Bayazit, Board Member; Jean-Philippe Guyot, Editor; Daqing Li, Editor; Hinrich Staecker, Associate Editor. **ISSN:** 0301--1569 (print); **EISSN:** 1423--0275 (electronic). **Subscription Rates:** 1683 FR Institutions print or online, combined; $1810 Institutions print or online, combined; $905 Individuals print or online, combined; 842 FR Individuals combined print & online. **URL:** http://www.karger.com/Journal/Home/224270. **Formerly**: Practica Oto-Rhino-Laryngologica. **Ad Rates:** BW 1780 FR; BW $2094. **Remarks:** Accepts advertising. **Circ:** 800.

6268 ■ Pathobiology
S. Karger Publishers Inc.
26 W Avon Rd.
Unionville, CT 06085-1162
Phone: (860)675-7834
Fax: (203)675-7302
Free: 800-828-5479
Publisher's E-mail: karger@snet.net
Scientific medical journal. **Freq:** Bimonthly. **Print Method:** Offset. **Trim Size:** 210 x 280 mm. **Cols./Page:** 1. **Col. Width:** 84 nonpareils. **Col. Depth:** 141 agate lines. **Key Personnel:** H. Denk, Board Member; P.L. Fernandez, Board Member; A. Horii, Board Member; A. Katalinic, Board Member; M. Reymond, Board Member; M. Werner, Board Member; Prof. W. Yasui, Editor; B. Borisch, Editor-in-Chief. **ISSN:** 1015--2008 (print); **EISSN:** 1423--0291 (electronic). **Subscription Rates:** €1779 Institutions online only Eurozone; €1827 Institutions print Eurozone; €2094 Institutions combined print & online Eurozone; $2179 Institutions online only USA/Latin America; $2257 Institutions print USA/Latin America; $2584 Individuals combined print & online USA/Latin America; 2135 FR Institutions, other countries online only; 2219 FR Institutions, other countries print; 2539 FR Institutions, other countries combined print & online; €445 Individuals online only Eurozone; €483.40 Individuals print Eurozone; €522.40 Individuals combined print & online Eurozone; $545 Individuals online only USA/Latin America; $607.40 Individuals print USA/Latin America; $655.40 Individuals combined print & online USA/Latin America; 534 FR Other countries online only; 601.20 FR Other countries print; 649.20 FR Other countries combined print & online. **URL:** http://www.karger.com; http://www.karger.com/Journal/Home/224272. **Formerly**: Schweizerische Zeitschrift fur allgemeine Pathologie und Bakteriologie; Pathologia et Microbiologia; Survey and Synthesis of Pathology Research. **Ad Rates:** BW $2094. **Remarks:** Accepts advertising. **Circ:** 800.

6269 ■ Pediatric Neurosurgery
S. Karger Publishers Inc.
26 W Avon Rd.
Unionville, CT 06085-1162
Phone: (860)675-7834
Fax: (203)675-7302
Free: 800-828-5479
Publisher's E-mail: karger@snet.net
Medical journal on neurosurgery. **Freq:** 6/year. **Print Method:** Offset. **Trim Size:** 210 x 280 mm. **Cols./Page:** 1. **Col. Width:** 99 nonpareils. **Col. Depth:** 155 agate lines. **Key Personnel:** David M. Frim, Advisor; J.G. McComb, Board Member. **ISSN:** 1016-2291 (print); **EISSN:** 1423-0305 (electronic). **Subscription Rates:** 2148 FR Institutions, other countries print and online; 1875 FR Institutions, other countries print or online; 1674 FR Institutions print or online, Euro zone; 1917 FR Institutions print and online, Euro zone; $2033 Institutions print or online; $2326 Institutions print and online. **URL:** http://www.karger.com/Journal/Home/224273. **Formerly**: Pediatric Neuroscience. **Ad Rates:** BW 1,780 FR. **Remarks:** Accepts advertising. **Circ:** 900.

6270 ■ Pharmacology
S. Karger Publishers Inc.
26 W Avon Rd.
Unionville, CT 06085-1162
Phone: (860)675-7834
Fax: (203)675-7302
Free: 800-828-5479
Publisher's E-mail: karger@snet.net
Medical journal on pharmacology. **Freq:** Monthly. **Print Method:** Offset. **Trim Size:** 210 x 280 mm. **Cols./Page:** 1. **Col. Width:** 84 nonpareils. **Col. Depth:** 140 agate lines. **Key Personnel:** L.Z. Benet, Board Member; A. Breckenridge, Board Member; S. Dhein, Board Member; M.L. Billingsley, Board Member; J. Donnerer, Editor; M. Hirafuji, Board Member; Y. Kamisaki, Board Member; N. Kaplowitz, Board Member; K. Maeyama, Editor. **ISSN:** 0031-7012 (print); **EISSN:** 1423-0313 (electronic). **Subscription Rates:** 3535 FR Institutions online only; 3649 FR Institutions print only; 4179 FR Institutions print and online; 1768 FR Individuals online only; 1859.20 FR Individuals print only; 1955.20 FR Individuals print and online. **URL:** http://www.karger.com/Journal/Home/224274. **Formerly**: Medicina Experimentis. **Ad Rates:** BW 1,780 FR. **Remarks:** Accepts advertising. **Circ:** 800.

6271 ■ Phonetica
S. Karger Publishers Inc.
26 W Avon Rd.
Unionville, CT 06085-1162
Phone: (860)675-7834
Fax: (203)675-7302
Free: 800-828-5479
Publisher's E-mail: karger@snet.net
Scientific medical journal focusing on spoken language research (English, French and German). **Freq:** Quarterly. **Print Method:** Offset. **Trim Size:** 177 x 252 mm. **Cols./Page:** 1. **Col. Width:** 84 nonpareils. **Col. Depth:** 140 agate lines. **Key Personnel:** Catherine T. Best, Editor; William J. Barry, Associate Editor. **ISSN:** 0031-8388 (print); **EISSN:** 1423-0321 (electronic). **Subscription Rates:** 1359 FR Institutions online only; 1397 FR Institutions print only; 1601 FR Institutions print and online; 340 FR Individuals online only; 370.40 FR Individuals print only; 420.40 FR Individuals print and online. **URL:** http://www.karger.com/Journal/Home/224275. **Ad Rates:** BW 1,780 FR. **Remarks:** Accepts advertising. **Circ:** 1100.

6272 ■ Psychopathology
S. Karger Publishers Inc.
26 W Avon Rd.
Unionville, CT 06085-1162
Phone: (860)675-7834
Fax: (203)675-7302
Free: 800-828-5479
Publisher's E-mail: karger@snet.net
Medical journal. **Freq:** 6/year. **Print Method:** Offset. **Trim Size:** 210 x 280 mm. **Cols./Page:** 1. **Col. Width:** 84 nonpareils. **Col. Depth:** 140 agate lines. **Key Personnel:** C. Mundt, Editor; S. Herpertz, Editor-in-Chief; W. Maier, Associate Editor; A. David, Associate Editor; M.F. Lenzenweger, Associate Editor; J. Parnas, Associate Editor. **ISSN:** 0254-4962 (print). **Subscription Rates:** $2254 Institutions combined, print or online; $323.60 Individuals combined, print or online. **URL:** http://www.karger.com/Journal/Home/224276. **Formerly**: Monatsschrift fur Psychiatrie und Neurologie'; Psychiatria Clinica. **Ad Rates:** BW 1,780 FR. **Remarks:** Accepts advertising. **Circ:** 800.

6273 ■ Psychotherapy and Psychosomatics
S. Karger Publishers Inc.
26 W Avon Rd.
Unionville, CT 06085-1162
Phone: (860)675-7834
Fax: (203)675-7302
Free: 800-828-5479
Publisher's E-mail: karger@snet.net
Medical journal. **Freq:** 6/year. **Print Method:** Offset. **Trim Size:** 210 x 280 mm. **Cols./Page:** 1. **Col. Width:** 84 nonpareils. **Col. Depth:** 140 agate lines. **Key Personnel:** G.A. Fava, Editor-in-Chief; C.D. Ryff, Board Member; C. Ruini, Assistant Editor; M.W. Otto, Board Member; S. Grandi, Board Member; E. Tomba, Assistant Editor; R. Balon, Board Member. **ISSN:** 0033-3190 (print). **Subscription Rates:** $2002 Institutions online or print, combined; $220.60 Individuals online or print, combined. **URL:** http://www.karger.com/Journal/Details/223864. **Formerly**: Acta Psychotherapeutica et Psychosomatica. **Ad Rates:** BW 1,780 FR. **Remarks:** Accepts advertising. **Circ:** 1050.

6274 ■ Public Health Genomics
S. Karger Publishers Inc.
26 W Avon Rd.
Unionville, CT 06085-1162
Phone: (860)675-7834
Fax: (203)675-7302
Free: 800-828-5479
Publisher's E-mail: karger@snet.net
Peer-reviewed medical journal covering medicine, genetics and society. **Freq:** 6/year. **Trim Size:** 210 x 280 mm. **Key Personnel:** A.M. Brand, Editor-in-Chief. **ISSN:** 1662--4246 (print); **EISSN:** 1662--8063 (electronic). **Subscription Rates:** 1671 FR Institutions print or online; €1492 Institutions in Germany; print or online; $1797 Institutions print or online; 1979 FR Institutions combined print and online; €1767 Institutions in Germany; combined print and online; $2145 Institutions combined print and online. **URL:** http://karger.com/Journal/Home/224224. **Formerly**: Community Genetics. **Ad Rates:** BW $1,780. **Remarks:** Accepts advertising. **Circ:** 800.

6275 ■ Respiration: International Journal of Thoracic Medicine
S. Karger Publishers Inc.
26 W Avon Rd.
Unionville, CT 06085-1162
Phone: (860)675-7834
Fax: (203)675-7302
Free: 800-828-5479
Publisher's E-mail: karger@snet.net
Peer-reviewed medical journal (English, French, German). **Freq:** Monthly. **Print Method:** Offset. **Trim Size:** 210 x 280 mm. **Cols./Page:** 1. **Col. Width:** 84 nonpareils. **Col. Depth:** 140 agate lines. **Key Personnel:** I.M. Adcock, Associate Editor; D. Bouros, Associate Editor. **ISSN:** 0025--7931 (print); **EISSN:** 1423--0356 (electronic). **Subscription Rates:** 2911 FR Institutions print or online; combined; $3130 Institutions print and online; combined; $163 Individuals other countries (print or online; combined); €146 Individuals Europe (print or online; combined); $175 Individuals USA (print or online; combined). **URL:** http://www.karger.com/Journal/Home/

Circulation: ★ = AAM; △ or • = BPA; ♦ = CAC; ❑ = VAC; ⊕ = PO Statement; ‡ = Publisher's Report; Boldface figures = sworn; Light figures = estimated.

224278. **Formerly**: Medicina Thoracalis. **Ad Rates:** BW $2094. **Remarks:** Accepts advertising. **Circ:** 1100.

6276 ■ Skin Pharmacology and Physiology: Journal of Pharmacological and Biophysical Research
S. Karger Publishers Inc.
26 W Avon Rd.
Unionville, CT 06085-1162
Phone: (860)675-7834
Fax: (203)675-7302
Free: 800-828-5479
Publisher's E-mail: karger@snet.net
Journal of pharmacological and biophysical research. **Freq:** Bimonthly. **Print Method:** Offset. **Trim Size:** 210 x 280 mm. **Key Personnel:** J. Lademann, Editor; E. Berardesca, Board Member; P.M. Elias, Associate Editor; N. Ahmad, Board Member; G.J. Nohynek, Associate Editor; J.M. Baron, Board Member. **ISSN:** 1660-5527 (print); **EISSN:** 1660-5535 (electronic). **Subscription Rates:** 1831 FR Institutions online; 1888 FR Institutions includes postage and handling; 2163 FR Institutions print and online; includes postage and handling; 916 FR Individuals online; 961.60 FR Individuals includes postage and handling; 1009.60 FR Individuals print and online; includes postage and handling. **URL:** http://www.karger.com/Journal/Home/224194. **Formerly**: Skin Pharmacology and Applied Skin Physiology. **Ad Rates:** BW $2,094. **Remarks:** Accepts advertising. **Circ:** 800.

6277 ■ Transfusion Medicine and Hemotherapy
S. Karger Publishers Inc.
26 W Avon Rd.
Unionville, CT 06085-1162
Phone: (860)675-7834
Fax: (203)675-7302
Free: 800-828-5479
Publisher's E-mail: karger@snet.net
Current concepts on immune regulation: impact on scientific and clinical aspects of immunohematology scientific and clinical aspects of immunohematology. **Freq:** Bimonthly. **Key Personnel:** P. Bugert, Associate Editor. **ISSN:** 1660-3796 (print). **Subscription Rates:** 318 FR Institutions print (Europe); $348 Institutions print (USA/Latin America); 345 FR Institutions print (all other regions); 318 FR Individuals print (Europe); $348 Individuals print (USA/Latin America); 345 FR Individuals print (all other regions). **URL:** http://www.karger.com/Journal/Home/224170. **Ad Rates:** BW $2,500. **Remarks:** Accepts advertising. **Circ:** ‡3000.

6278 ■ Urologia Internationalis
S. Karger Publishers Inc.
26 W Avon Rd.
Unionville, CT 06085-1162
Phone: (860)675-7834
Fax: (203)675-7302
Free: 800-828-5479
Publisher's E-mail: karger@snet.net
Medical practice-oriented research journal. **Freq:** 8/year. **Print Method:** Offset. **Trim Size:** 210 x 280 mm. **Cols./Page:** 1. **Col. Width:** 99 nonpareils. **Col. Depth:** 155 agate lines. **Key Personnel:** M. Porena, Editor; M.P. Wirth, Editor; D. Castro-Diaz, Editor; O.W. Hakenberg, Editor. **ISSN:** 004-2-1138 (print); **EISSN:** 1423--0399 (electronic). **Subscription Rates:** 4493 FR Institutions print and online - Europe; $4831 Institutions print and online; 4493 FR Institutions, other countries print and online; 2247 FR Individuals print and online - Europe; $2416 Individuals print and online; $2247 Other countries print and online. **URL:** http://www.karger.com/Journal/Home/224282. **Ad Rates:** BW $2094. **Remarks:** Accepts advertising. **Circ:** (Not Reported).

6279 ■ Verhaltenstherapie: Praxis, Forschung, Perspektiven
S. Karger Publishers Inc.
26 W Avon Rd.
Unionville, CT 06085-1162
Phone: (860)675-7834
Fax: (203)675-7302
Free: 800-828-5479
Publisher's E-mail: karger@snet.net
Medical journal (German). **Freq:** Quarterly. **Print Method:** Offset. **Trim Size:** 210 x 297 mm. **Cols./Page:** 1. **Col. Width:** 99 millimeters. **Key Personnel:** M. Linden, Editor-in-Chief. **ISSN:** 1016--6262 (print); **EISSN:** 1423--0402 (electronic). **Subscription Rates:** 196 FR Institutions online; 234 FR Institutions print; 297 FR Institutions combined print and online; 196 FR Individuals online; 234 FR Individuals print; 297 FR Individuals combined print and online. **URL:** http://www.karger.com/Journal/Home/224158. **Remarks:** Accepts advertising. **Circ:** ‡4000.

WALLINGFORD

SC CT. New Haven Co. 5 mi. S. of Meriden. Choate School. Summer theatre. Manufactures silverware, chemicals, fancy hardware, tools, measuring instruments, electronics, textile factories. Fruit orchards.

6280 ■ WWEB-FM - 89.9
333 Christian St.
Wallingford, CT 06492
Phone: (203)697-2000
Format: Full Service. **Networks:** Independent. **Owner:** Choate Rosemary Hall Foundation, 333 Christian St., Wallingford, CT 06492, Ph: (203)697-2418. **Founded:** 1969. **Operating Hours**: M-S 12:00-12:00. **Wattage:** 010. **Ad Rates:** Noncommercial. **URL:** http://www.choate.edu.

WASHINGTON DEPOT

6281 ■ Edible Nutmeg
Edible Communities Inc.
PO Box 308
Washington Depot, CT 06794
Phone: (860)868-2730
Publication E-mail: info@ediblenutmeg.com
Magazine featuring the local food of Connecticut. **Freq:** Quarterly. **Key Personnel:** Dana Jackson, Editor-in-Chief, Publisher. **Subscription Rates:** $28 Individuals. **URL:** http://ediblenutmegmagazine.com. **Ad Rates:** 4C $1850. **Remarks:** Advertising accepted; rates available upon request. **Circ:** (Not Reported).

WATERBURY

S. CT. New Haven Co. 21 mi. NW of New Haven. Center of the brass industry. Manufactures brass and copper goods, clocks, watches, buckles, buttons, chemicals, toys, tools, metal novelties, lighting fixtures, machine shop products. Foundry.

6282 ■ Republican-American
389 Meadow St.
Waterbury, CT 06712
Phone: (203)574-3636
General newspaper. **Freq:** Daily (morn.). **Print Method:** Offset. Uses mats. **Cols./Page:** 6. **Col. Width:** 12.5 picas. **Col. Depth:** 21 3/8 inches. **Key Personnel:** Susan Sprano, Director, Advertising; William J. Pape, II, Editor, Publisher. **Subscription Rates:** $26.13 Individuals Sunday and Thursday and online; $52 Individuals 7-day home delivery; $31.20 Individuals weekender (Thursday, Friday, Saturday and Sunday); $31.20 Individuals Monday thru Saturday. **URL:** http://www.rep-am.com. **Formerly**: Waterbury Republican-American. **Remarks:** Accepts advertising. **Circ:** Combined •195000.

6283 ■ WATR-AM - 1320
One Broadcast Ln.
Waterbury, CT 06706
Phone: (203)755-1121
Fax: (203)574-3025
Email: sales@watr.com
Format: News; Talk; Oldies. **Networks:** CBS. **Owner:** WATR Inc., at above address, Pioneer, CA. **Founded:** 1934. **Operating Hours**: Continuous. **ADI:** Hartford-New Haven (New London), CT. **Key Personnel:** Tom Chute, Gen. Mgr., Prog. Dir., tomchute@watr.com; Trish Torello, Sales Mgr., trishtorello@watr.com. **Wattage:** 5,000 Day; 1,000 Night. **Ad Rates:** $19-37 for 30 seconds; $22-40 for 60 seconds. **URL:** http://www.watr.com.

WATERFORD

SE CT. New London Co. 19 mi. S. of Montvilleo. Residential.

6284 ■ MetroCast
61 Myrock Ave.
Waterford, CT 06385
Free: 888-339-3605
Email: marketing@metrocast.com
Founded: 1973. **Formerly**: Eastern Connecticut Cable Television, Inc. **Cities Served:** East Lyme, Griswold, Griswold, Killingly, Montville, New London, Plainfield, Putnam, Sterling, Waterford, Connecticut: subscribing households 55,337; 185 channels; 1 community access channel; 35 hours per week community access programming. **URL:** http://www.metrocast.com.

WEST HARTFORD

N. CT. Hartford Co. Adjacent to Hartford. St. Joseph College (Cath. women), University of Connecticut. Residential. Planetarium; aquarium; publishing houses.

6285 ■ AES Epilepsia
American Epilepsy Society
342 N Main St., Ste. 301
West Hartford, CT 06117-2507
Phone: (860)586-7505
Fax: (860)586-7550
Publisher's E-mail: membership@aesnet.org
Freq: Monthly. **ISSN:** 0013--9580 (print); **EISSN:** 1528--1167 (electronic). **Subscription Rates:** Included in membership. **URL:** http://www.aesnet.org/professional_education/epilepsia; http://onlinelibrary.wiley.com/journal/10.1111/(ISSN)1528-1167. **Remarks:** Advertising not accepted. **Circ:** (Not Reported).

6286 ■ Autism Research
International Society for Autism Research
342 N Main St.
West Hartford, CT 06117-2507
Phone: (860)586-7575
Fax: (860)586-7550
Publisher's E-mail: info@autism-insar.org
Freq: Monthly Latest August 2016. **ISSN:** 1939--3792 (print); **EISSN:** 1939--3806 (electronic). **Subscription Rates:** $1628 U.S. and other countries institutional FTE - large: online only; $1357 U.S. and other countries institutional FTE - medium: online only; $1086 U.S. and other countries institutional FTE - small: online only; £1148 Institutions U.K. FTE - large: online only; £960 Institutions U.K. FTE - medium: online only; £768 Institutions U.K. FTE - small: online only; €1323 Institutions Euro zone FTE - large: online only; €1105 Institutions Euro zone FTE - medium: online only; €886 Institutions Euro zone FTE - small: online only. **URL:** http://onlinelibrary.wiley.com/journal/10.1002/(ISSN)1939-3806. **Remarks:** Advertising not accepted. **Circ:** (Not Reported).

6287 ■ Connecticut Jewish History
Jewish Historical Society of Greater Hartford
333 Bloomfield Ave.
West Hartford, CT 06117
Phone: (860)727-6171
Publisher's E-mail: jhsgh@jewishhartford.org
Journal containing informational about all aspects of Jewish history in Connecticut. **Freq:** Periodic. **Key Personnel:** Ms. Estelle Kafer, Executive Director. **Subscription Rates:** $31.85 Individuals volume 4; $21.27 Individuals volume 1-3. **URL:** http://www.jhsgh.org/books.html. **Circ:** (Not Reported).

6288 ■ Epilepsy Currents
American Epilepsy Society
342 N Main St., Ste. 301
West Hartford, CT 06117-2507
Phone: (860)586-7505
Fax: (860)586-7550
Publisher's E-mail: membership@aesnet.org
Freq: Bimonthly. **Key Personnel:** Michael A. Rogawski, Editor; Gregory K. Bergey, Editor. **ISSN:** 1535--7597 (print); **EISSN:** 1535--7511 (electronic). **Subscription Rates:** $198 U.S. and Canada; $265 Institutions, other countries. **URL:** http://www.aesnet.org/professional_education/epilepsy_currents; http://www.epilepsycurrents.org. **Remarks:** Accepts advertising. **Circ:** 3400.

6289 ■ Jewish Ledger
Jewish Ledger
740 N Main St., Ste. W
West Hartford, CT 06117
Fax: (860)231-2428
Free: 800-286-6397
Jewish newspaper. **Freq:** Weekly (Thurs.). **Print Method:** Offset. **Cols./Page:** 5. **Col. Width:** 24 nonpareils. **Col. Depth:** 224 agate lines. **Key Personnel:** Leslie Larusso, Associate Publisher; Stacey

Dresner, Editor. **Subscription Rates:** $36 Individuals; $62 Two years. **URL:** http://www.jewishledger.com. **Ad Rates:** BW $1885; 4C $2475. **Remarks:** Advertising accepted; rates available upon request. **Circ:** Paid ‡7000, Free ‡1000.

6290 ■ Neurotherapeutics
American Society for Experimental Neuro Therapeutics
342 N Main St.
West Hartford, CT 06117
Phone: (860)586-7570
Fax: (860)586-7550
Publisher's E-mail: info@asent.org
Freq: Quarterly. **Key Personnel:** Maral Mouradian, Editor-in-Chief. **ISSN:** 1933--7213 (print); **EISSN:** 1878--7479 (electronic). **Subscription Rates:** €502 Institutions print incl. free access or e-only; €602 Institutions print plus enhanced access; $617 Institutions print incl. free access or e-only; $740 Institutions print plus enhanced access. **URL:** http://www.springer.com/biomed/neuroscience/journal/13311; http://asent.org/neurotherapeuticsandreg. **Formerly**: NeuroRx. **Remarks:** Advertising not accepted. **Circ:** (Not Reported).

6291 ■ Peace & Change: A Journal of Peace Research
Peace History Society
c/o Kevin J. Callahan, President
University of Saint Joseph
1678 Asylum Ave.
West Hartford, CT 06117
Magazine publishing articles on peace-related topics such as peace movements and activism, conflict resolution, nonviolence, internationalism, race and gender issues, cross-cultural studies, economic development, the legacy of imperialism, and the post-Cold War upheaval. **Freq:** Quarterly. **Key Personnel:** Kevin Clements, Board Member; Sandi E. Cooper, Board Member; Mohammed Abu-Nimer, Board Member; Elavie Ndura-Ouedraogo, Board Member; Lee Smithey, Board Member. **ISSN:** 0149--0508 (print); **EISSN:** 1468--0130 (electronic). **Subscription Rates:** $549 Institutions print or online; £423 Institutions print or online; $827 Institutions, other countries print or online; $659 Institutions print and online; £508 Institutions print and online; $993 Institutions, other countries print and online; $125 Individuals print and online; £100 Other countries print and online; €536 Institutions print or online; €644 Institutions print and online; £100 Individuals print and online (UK and Europe non-Euro zone); €150 Individuals print and online (Europe - Euro zone). **URL:** http://onlinelibrary.wiley.com/journal/10.1111/(ISSN)1468-0130; http://www.peacehistorysociety.org/journal.php; http://www.peacejusticestudies.org/resources. **Remarks:** Accepts advertising. **Circ:** (Not Reported).

6292 ■ WVIT-TV - 30
1422 New Britain Ave.
West Hartford, CT 06110
Phone: (860)521-3030
Format: Commercial TV. **Networks:** NBC. **Owner:** NBC Universal Media L.L.C., 30 Rockefeller Plz., New York, NY 10112, Ph: (212)664-4444. **Founded:** 1953. **Formerly**: WNBC-TV; WKNB-TV; WHNB-TV. **Operating Hours**: Continuous. **ADI**: Hartford-New Haven (New London), CT. **Key Personnel:** David Doebler, Gen. Mgr., President; Ronni Attenello, Dir. of Programs. **Ad Rates:** Noncommercial. **URL:** http://www.nbcconnecticut.com.

6293 ■ WWUH-FM - 91.3
200 Bloomfield Ave.
West Hartford, CT 06117
Phone: (860)768-4703
Email: wwuh@hartford.edu
Format: Alternative/New Music/Progressive. **Owner:** University of Hartford, 200 Bloomfield Ave., West Hartford, CT 06117, Ph: (860)768-4100, Fax: (860)768-5220. **Founded:** 1968. **Key Personnel:** Susan Mullis, Dir. of Dev.; Steve Petke, Director, sdpetke@comcast.net; Mary Dowst, Bus. Mgr.; John Ramsey, Chief Engineer, Gen. Mgr., ramsey@hartford.edu; Peter Rost, Contact. **Ad Rates:** Noncommercial. **URL:** http://www.wwuh.org.

WEST HAVEN

S. CT. New Haven Co. Adjacent to New Haven. Residential. Summer resort. Manufactures aircraft parts, tools, gun parts, webbing, auto tires and tubes, fertilizer, perfumes, cellar and overhead doors, plastic, die castings, sheet metal and rubber products, elastic fabrics, pipe organs, rock drills, beer, and textiles.

6294 ■ Biological Psychiatry
Elsevier Inc.
Yale University School of Medicine & VA Connecticut Health-care products System
West Haven, CT 06516
Publication E-mail: biol.psych@utsouthwestern.edu
Journal reporting on research in biological psychiatry. **Freq:** Semimonthly 24/yr. **Trim Size:** 8 1/8 x 10 7/8. **Key Personnel:** Dennis S. Charney, MD, Board Member; John H. Krystal, Editor; E.S. Brown, MD, Board Member; C.S. Carter, MD, Editor. **ISSN:** 0006--3223 (print). **Subscription Rates:** $1398 Individuals U.S. (online and print); $284 Students U.S. (online and print); $1486 Other countries online and print; $304 Students, other countries online and print. **URL:** http://www.biologicalpsychiatryjournal.com. **Ad Rates:** BW $1,765. **Remarks:** Accepts advertising. **Circ:** 980.

6295 ■ WNHU-FM - 88.7
300 Boston Post Rd.
West Haven, CT 06516
Phone: (203)479-8807
Format: Alternative/New Music/Progressive; Oldies; Jazz. **Networks:** AP. **Owner:** University of New Haven, 300 Boston Post Rd., West Haven, CT 06516, Ph: (203)932-7000, Free: 800-342-5864. **Founded:** 1973. **Operating Hours:** Continuous. **Wattage:** 1,700. **Ad Rates:** Noncommercial. **URL:** http://www.wnhu.net.

WESTBROOK

S. CT. Middlesex Co. 6 mi. from Essex. Residential.

6296 ■ AllGreen
AllGreen Group L.L.C.
90 Knothe Rd.
Westbrook, CT 06498
Phone: (860)953-0455
Free: 888-845-7467
Magazine covering environmental news, events, and information for a greener way of living. **Freq:** Quarterly. **Key Personnel:** Michael J. Guinan, Publisher; Tara M. Cantore, Associate Editor; Carol A. Latter, Senior Editor. **Subscription Rates:** $9.95 Individuals. **URL:** http://allgreen.com/site. **Remarks:** Accepts advertising. **Circ:** (Not Reported).

WESTON

SW CT. Fairfield Co. 10 mi. W. of Bridgeport. Residential.

6297 ■ Modern Brewery Age
Business Journals Inc.
44 Indian Valley Rd.
Weston, CT 06883
Phone: (203)216-7488
Publisher's E-mail: bjisupport@busjour.com
Magazine for the wholesale and brewing industry. **Freq:** Bimonthly. **Key Personnel:** Mac R. Brighton, Chairman, Chief Operating Officer; Britton Jones, Chief Executive Officer, President; Peter V.K. Reid, Editor. **Subscription Rates:** $125 Individuals. **URL:** http://www.breweryage.com. **Ad Rates:** 4C $1,800. **Remarks:** Accepts advertising. **Circ:** (Not Reported).

WESTPORT

SW CT. Fairfield Co. On Saugatuck River, 3 mi. NE of Norwalk. Manufactures chemicals, liquid soaps, embalming fluid. Residential.

6298 ■ Fairfield Minuteman
Housatonic Publications
1175 Post Rd. E
Westport, CT 06880
Phone: (203)226-8877
Fax: (203)221-7540
Publication E-mail: news@fairfieldminuteman.com
Community newspaper. **Freq:** Weekly (Thurs.). **Subscription Rates:** $29.95 Individuals. **URL:** http://www.minutemannewscenter.com/fairfield. **Remarks:** Accepts classified advertising. **Circ:** Non-paid ‡22461.

6299 ■ Journal of Accounting, Auditing & Finance
Greenwood Publishing Group Inc.
PO Box 5007
Westport, CT 06881
Phone: (203)226-3571
Fax: (203)222-1502
Publisher's E-mail: customerservice@abc-clio.com
Journal focusing on the topics of accounting, auditing, and finance. **Freq:** Quarterly. **Key Personnel:** Kashi R. Balachandran, Editor-in-Chief, phone: (212)998-0029, fax: (212)995-4230. **ISSN:** 0148--558X (print); **EISSN:** 2160--4061 (electronic). **Subscription Rates:** $46 Individuals single print issue; $122 Institutions single print issue; $454 Institutions print and e-access; $499 Institutions current volume print & all online content; $452 Institutions e-access; $445 Institutions print only; $140 Individuals print only. **URL:** http://jaf.sagepub.com. **Remarks:** Advertising not accepted. **Circ:** (Not Reported).

6300 ■ KTCM-FM - 97.3
136 Main St., Ste. 202
Westport, CT 06880
Phone: (203)227-1978
Format: Contemporary Christian. **Owner:** Connoisseur Media L.L.C., 180 Post Rd., E, Ste. 201, Westport, CT 06880, Ph: (203)227-1978. **Operating Hours:** Continuous. **Wattage**: 12,000 ERP. **URL:** http://www.centralmoinfo.com.

6301 ■ WSHU-AM - 1260
5151 Park Ave.
Fairfield, CT 06825
Phone: (203)365-6604
Free: 800-365-2005
Format: News; Classical. **Networks:** USA Radio. **Founded:** 1959. **Formerly**: WMMM-AM. **Key Personnel:** Tom Kuser, Prog. Dir; George Lombardi, Contact; Barbara Bashar, Contact. **Local Programs:** *Acoustic-Connections*, Saturday 9:00 p.m. - 10:00 p.m. **Wattage:** 1,000. **URL:** http://news.wshu.org/grids/wshuamgrid.php.

6302 ■ WWPT-FM
Staples High School
70 North Ave.
Westport, CT 06880
Fax: (203)365-7669
Format: Eclectic. **Founded:** 1975. **Wattage**: 330 ERP. **Ad Rates:** Noncommercial.

WILLIMANTIC

NE CT. Windham Co. 30 mi. E. of Hartford. State College. Manufactures wire and cable, plastics, thread, non-woven fabric, braided fabric, insulation, mill and builders' supplies. Printing. Steel fabrication. Truck farms.

6303 ■ Campus Lantern: To Organize, Edit, and Publish a Student-Run Weekly Newspaper
Eastern Connecticut State University
83 Windham Street
Willimantic, CT 06226
Phone: (860)465-5000
Publisher's E-mail: webmaster@easternct.edu
College campus-oriented newspaper (tabloid). **Freq:** Weekly (Wed.). **Print Method:** Offset. **Cols./Page:** 5. **Col. Width:** 1 7/10 inches. **Col. Depth:** 11 1/2 inches. **Subscription Rates:** Free. **URL:** http://www.easternct.edu/studentactivities/clubs-orgs/club-index/campus-lantern. **Remarks:** Advertising accepted; rates available upon request. **Circ:** (Not Reported).

6304 ■ The Chronicle
The Chronicle
1 Chronicle Rd.
Willimantic, CT 06226-0148
Phone: (860)423-8466
Community newspaper. **Founded:** 1877. **Freq:** Daily. **Key Personnel:** Charles Ryan, Editor; Patrice Crosbie, Publisher, President. **Subscription Rates:** $177.61 Individuals e-edition. **URL:** http://thechronicle.com/index89.htm. **Mailing address:** PO Box 148, Willimantic, CT 06226-0148. **Remarks:** Accepts advertising. **Circ:** Combined ♦**6019**.

Circulation: ★ = AAM; △ or • = BPA; ♦ = CAC; ❑ = VAC; ⊕ = PO Statement; ‡ = Publisher's Report; Boldface figures = sworn; Light figures = estimated.

6305 ■ WECS-FM - 90.1
83 Windham St.
Willimantic, CT 06226
Phone: (860)465-5354
Fax: (860)465-5073
Format: Eclectic. **Networks:** National Public Radio (NPR). **Owner:** Eastern Connecticut State University, 83 Windham Street, Willimantic, CT 06226, Ph: (860)465-5000. **Founded:** 1982. **Operating Hours**: Continuous. **Key Personnel:** Phil Jackson, Promotions Dir.; Nathaniel Bishop, Music Dir. **Wattage**: 421. **Ad Rates:** Noncommercial. **URL:** http://www.easternct.edu.

6306 ■ WILI-AM - 1400
720 Main St.
Willimantic, CT 06226
Phone: (860)456-1111
Fax: (860)456-9501
Format: Full Service. **Networks:** ABC; Satellite Music Network; Westwood One Radio. **Founded:** 1957. **Operating Hours**: Continuous; 30% network, 70% local. **ADI**: Hartford-New Haven (New London), CT. **Key Personnel:** Jim Bohannon, Contact; Wayne Norman, Contact. **Wattage**: 1,000. **Ad Rates:** $26-31 for 30 seconds; $34-38 for 60 seconds. $26-$31 for 30 seconds; $34-$38 for 60 seconds. Combined advertising rates available with WILI-FM. **URL:** http://www.wili.com.

6307 ■ WILI-FM - 98.3
720 Main St.
Willimantic, CT 06226
Phone: (860)456-1400
Fax: (860)456-9501
Free: 888-456-1111
Format: Adult Contemporary; Contemporary Hit Radio (CHR). **Owner:** Nutmeg Broadcasting Co., 720 Main St., Willimantic, CT 06226, Ph: (860)456-1111, Fax: (860)456-9501. **Founded:** 1957. **Formerly**: WNOU-FM; WXLS-FM. **Operating Hours**: Continuous; 80% local, 20% network. **ADI:** Hartford-New Haven (New London), CT. **Key Personnel:** Mike Morrissette, Contact; Donna Evan, Sales Mgr., donna@wili.com; Mike Morrissette, Contact. **Wattage**: 3,000 ERP. **Ad Rates:** Noncommercial. WILI-AM. **URL:** http://www.wili.com.

WILTON

SW CT. Fairfield Co. 5 mi. N. of Norwalk. Residential. Manufactures optical and electronic equipment, golf clubs. Nurseries.

6308 ■ Architectural Designs
Architectural Designs Inc.
57 Danbury Rd.
Wilton, CT 06897
Phone: (262)521-4596
Fax: (203)761-8600
Free: 800-854-7852
Publisher's E-mail: info@architecturaldesigns.com
Consumer magazine offering over 200 house plans. **Freq:** Quarterly. **Ad Rates:** BW $2,195; 4C $2,395. **Remarks:** Accepts advertising. **Circ:** ‡20000000.

6309 ■ Die Cast X: The Ultimate Diecast Magazine
Air Age Publishing Inc.
88 Danbury Rd., Rte. 7
Wilton, CT 06897
Fax: (203)529-3010
Publication E-mail: dcxmagazine@airage.com
Magazine featuring diecast automotive. **Freq:** Quarterly. **Key Personnel:** Alan Paradise, Editor-in-Chief, phone: (619)504-8411. **Subscription Rates:** $14.95 Individuals print and online; $27.95 Two years print and online; $12.95 Individuals online only. **URL:** http://www.diecastxmagazine.com. **Remarks:** Accepts advertising. **Circ:** Paid 35174.

6310 ■ Flight Journal
Air Age Media
88 Danbury Rd.
Wilton, CT 06897
Phone: (203)431-9000
Fax: (203)529-3010
Free: 888-235-2021
Publication E-mail: flightjournal@airage.com
Aviation magazine featuring profiles of legendary aviators, as well as flight achievements, unexpected events and disasters. **Key Personnel:** Budd Davisson, Editor-in-Chief. **Subscription Rates:** $19.95 Individuals; $34.95 Two years; $25.95 Canada; $46.95 Canada two years; $31.95 Other countries; $58.95 Other countries two years. **URL:** http://www.flightjournal.com. **Remarks:** Accepts advertising. **Circ:** Paid ‡47164.

6311 ■ Model Airplane News: The World's Premier R/C Modeling Magazine
Air Age Publishing Inc.
88 Danbury Rd., Rte. 7
Wilton, CT 06897
Phone: (203)431-9000
Publisher's E-mail: production@airage.com
Magazine on radio-controlled model airplanes and helicopters. **Freq:** Monthly. **Print Method:** Offset. **Trim Size:** 8 1/4 x 10 7/8. **Cols./Page:** 3. **Col. Width:** 28 nonpareils. **Col. Depth:** 140 agate lines. **Key Personnel:** Debra Cleghorn, Executive Editor. **ISSN:** 0026--7295 (print). **Subscription Rates:** $24.95 Individuals /year (print and online); $39.95 Two years print and online. **URL:** http://www.modelairplanenews.com. **Remarks:** Advertising accepted; rates available upon request. **Circ:** (Not Reported).

6312 ■ Radio Control Car Action
Air Age Publishing Inc.
88 Danbury Rd., Rte. 7
Wilton, CT 06897
Phone: (203)431-9000
Fax: (203)529-3010
Publisher's E-mail: production@airage.com
Consumer magazine covering radio control automobile models. **Freq:** Monthly. **Trim Size:** 8 x 10 7/8. **Key Personnel:** Matt Higgins, Executive Editor. **Subscription Rates:** $24.95 Individuals print and online; $39.95 Two years print and online; $19.95 Individuals online only. **URL:** http://www.rccaraction.com. **Remarks:** Accepts advertising. **Circ:** Paid ‡64745.

6313 ■ Wilton Bulletin
Hersam Acorn Newspapers L.L.C.
644 Danbury Rd.
Wilton, CT 06897
Phone: (203)762-3866
Fax: (203)762-3120
Community newspaper. **Freq:** Weekly (Thurs.). **Print Method:** Offset. Uses mats. **Cols./Page:** 6. **Col. Width:** 12 picas. **Col. Depth:** 21 inches. **Key Personnel:** J.B. Cozens, Assistant Editor; Sally Sanders, Editor; Tim Murphy, Editor; Jeannette Ross, Editor. **USPS:** 685-780. **URL:** http://www.wiltonbulletin.com. **Ad Rates:** BW $1951; 4C $550. **Remarks:** Accepts advertising. **Circ:** Combined ‡2270.

6314 ■ American Cable Entertainment
5 River Rd., Nl. 311-15
Wilton, CT 06897-4097
Fax: (203)325-3110
Owner: American Cable Entertainment, at above address. **Founded:** 1994. **Formerly**: Simmons Communications Inc. **Key Personnel:** Bruce A. Armstrong, Contact; John Flanagan, Contact. **Cities Served:** subscribing households 76,200.

WNHI-FM - See Farmington, NH

WINDHAM

SW CT. Windham Co. Agriculture.

6315 ■ The Mailer Review
Norman Mailer Society
c/o David Light, Treasurer
75 Jennings Ln.
Windham, CT 06280
Publisher's E-mail: webmaster@mailerreview.org
Freq: Annual. **Subscription Rates:** Included in membership; $25 Single issue; $32 Other countries per issue. **URL:** http://medium.com/the-mailer-review. **Remarks:** Advertising not accepted. **Circ:** (Not Reported).

WINDSOR

C. CT. Hartford Co. Manufactures bricks. Machine shops; tobacco and truck farming.

6316 ■ LIMRA's MarketFacts: Marketing Magazine for Insurance Professionals
LIMRA International
300 Day Hill Rd.
Windsor, CT 06095
Phone: (860)688-3358
Fax: (860)298-9555
Free: 800-235-4672
Publisher's E-mail: customer.service@limra.com
Magazine covering the financial services and insurance industries. **Freq:** Quarterly. **Print Method:** Offset. **Trim Size:** 8 1/8 x 10 7/8. **Cols./Page:** 3. **Col. Width:** 13.5 picas. **Col. Depth:** 48 picas. **Key Personnel:** Wendy Weston, Editor-in-Chief. **ISSN:** 0889--0986 (print). **Subscription Rates:** $2000 Individuals nonmember. **URL:** http://www.limra.com/Posts/MarketFacts. **Ad Rates:** BW $5,000. **Remarks:** Accepts advertising. **Circ:** Paid ‡1700, Controlled ‡7500.

6317 ■ WKND-AM
544 Windsor Ave.
Windsor, CT 06095
Phone: (860)688-6221
Fax: (860)688-0711
Format: Full Service; Urban Contemporary. **Networks:** ABC. **Owner:** Freedom Communications of Connecticut, Inc., 360 Lexington Ave., New York, NY 10017, Ph: (646)227-1320, Fax: (646)227-1337. **Founded:** 1964. **Formerly**: WSOR-AM; WEHW-AM. **Key Personnel:** Thornton Anderson, Gen. Mgr. **Wattage**: 500 Day; 014 Night. **Ad Rates:** $50-100 for 60 seconds. **Mailing address:** PO Box 1480, Windsor, CT 06095.

WOODBURY

NW CT. Litchfield Co. 8 mi. SW of Waterbury. Residential.

6318 ■ Journal of the Iranian Chemical Society
Iranian Chemists' Association of the American Chemical Society
35 Meadowbrook Ln.
Woodbury, CT 06798
Phone: (203)573-3220
Fax: (203)573-3660
Publisher's E-mail: banijamali@ica-acs.org
Freq: Quarterly. **ISSN:** 1735--207X (print); **EISSN:** 1735--2428 (electronic). **Remarks:** Accepts advertising. **Circ:** (Not Reported).

6319 ■ Ski Area Management
Beardsley Publishing Corp.
45 Main St. N
Woodbury, CT 06798
Phone: (203)263-0888
Fax: (203)266-0452
Trade magazine covering ski area management. **Freq:** 6/year. **Key Personnel:** Olivia Rowan, Associate Publisher; Jennifer Rowan, Publisher; Sharon Walsh, Director, Advertising; Rick Kahl, Editor; Donna Jacobs, Vice President, Administration; Liz Eren, Assistant Editor, Web Administrator. **USPS:** 890-900. **Subscription Rates:** $59 Individuals; $69 Canada; $81 Other countries; $88 Individuals 2 years; $108 Canada 2 years; $132 Other countries 2 years; $110 Individuals 3 years; $140 Canada 3 years; $176 Other countries 3 years. **URL:** http://www.saminfo.com. **Mailing address:** PO Box 644, Woodbury, CT 06798. **Ad Rates:** BW $2,700; 4C $3,690. **Remarks:** Accepts advertising. **Circ:** (Not Reported).

6320 ■ Town Times
Prime Publishers Inc.
744 Main St. S, Ste. 90
Middle Quarter Mall
Woodbury, CT 06798
Phone: (203)263-2116
Fax: (203)266-0199
Community newspaper serving Washington, Bethlehem, Woodbury, Middlebury, Oxford, Naugatuck, Southbury, Roxbury, and Bridgewater, Connecticut. **Freq:** Weekly (Thurs.). **Print Method:** Offset. **Trim Size:** 11 x 16 1/2. **Cols./Page:** 5. **Col. Width:** 11 picas. **Col. Depth:** 210 agate lines. **Key Personnel:** Rudy Mazurosky, President, Publisher. **ISSN:** 0193--1474 (print). **USPS:** 635-480. **Subscription Rates:** $55 Individuals print or online. **URL:** http://www.primepublishers.com/towntimesnews. **Ad Rates:** GLR $1.33; 4C $1,764; SAU $18.62; PCI $13.58. **Remarks:** Voices and Voices Sunday-The Weekly Star. **Circ:** Thurs. ♦**15088**, Sun. ♦**37575**.

6321 ■ Voices
Prime Publishers Inc.
744 Main St. S, Ste. 90
Middle Quarter Mall
Woodbury, CT 06798

Phone: (203)263-2116
Fax: (203)266-0199

Community newspaper. **Founded:** 1972. **Freq:** Semi-weekly (Wed. and Sun.). **Print Method:** Offset. **Trim Size:** 11 1/2 x 16. **Cols./Page:** 5. **Col. Width:** 11.7 picas. **Col. Depth:** 210 agate lines. **Key Personnel:** Rudy Mazurosky, President, Publisher. **ISSN:** 0193-1474 (print). **Subscription Rates:** $55 Out of area mail delivery; Free part of the circulation area. **URL:** http://www.primepublishers.com/voicesnews. **Ad Rates:** GLR $1.33; BW $1,197; 4C $1,764; SAU $21.42; PCI $15.68. **Circ:** Paid ‡290, Free ‡31049, Combined ‡31339.

Circulation: ★ = AAM; △ or • = BPA; ♦ = CAC; ❑ = VAC; ⊕ = PO Statement; ‡ = Publisher's Report; Boldface figures = sworn; Light figures = estimated.

BEAR

6322 ■ Faire Magazine
Black Fox Designs
PO Box 1231
Bear, DE 19701
Magazine featuring Renaissance festival. **URL:** http://www.fairemagazine.com. **Remarks:** Accepts advertising. **Circ:** (Not Reported).

BETHANY BEACH

6323 ■ Delaware Wave
Gannett Newspaper Co.
Rte. 1 Lem Hichman Plz.
Bethany Beach, DE 19930
Phone: (302)537-1881
Fax: (302)537-9705
Community newspaper. **Founded:** 1987. **Freq:** Weekly (Wed.). **Print Method:** Photo offset. **Key Personnel:** Laren Hughes-Hall, Editor; Pat Purdum, General Manager. **Subscription Rates:** Free. **URL:** http://www.delmarvanow.com. **Also known as**: The Wave. **Mailing address:** PO Box 1420, Bethany Beach, DE 19930. **Ad Rates:** SAU $9.50. **Circ:** Combined ♦**18441**.

CAMDEN

6324 ■ Kleos
Alpha Phi Delta Fraternity
257 E Camden Wyoming Ave., Unit A
Camden, DE 19934
Phone: (302)531-7854
Publisher's E-mail: apdoffice@apd.org
Freq: 3/year. **Alt. Formats:** PDF. **URL:** http://www.apdfoundation.org/kleos/archive.html. **Remarks:** Advertising not accepted. **Circ:** 9500.

CLAYTON

6325 ■ Clayton Sun
GateHouse Media Inc.
224 E Glenwood Ave.
Smyrna, DE 19977
Community newspaper. **Freq:** Weekly (Thurs.). **Print Method:** Offset. **Cols./Page:** 6. **Col. Width:** 26 nonpareils. **Col. Depth:** 301 agate lines. **Key Personnel:** Keven Todd, Publisher; Ben Mace, Editor. **Subscription Rates:** $26 Individuals. **URL:** http://scsuntimes.com. **Ad Rates:** GLR $1.75; BW $2074.32; 4C $2334.32; SAU $16.08; PCI $16.08. **Remarks:** Accepts advertising. **Circ:** Free 31248.

DAGSBORO

6326 ■ Mediacom
32441 Royal Blvd.
Dagsboro, DE 19939
Phone: (302)732-6600
Fax: (302)732-6616
Free: 800-445-5562
Owner: American Cable Entertainment, 5 River Rd., NI. 311-15, Wilton, CT 06897-4097, Fax: (203)325-3110. **Founded:** 1968. **Formerly**: American Cable TV of Lower Delaware. **Cities Served:** Bethany Beach, Clarksville, Dagsboro, Frankford, Millville, Ocean View, Omar, Roxana, Roxana, Selbyville, Slaughter Beach, Delaware; Bishopville, Maryland; Sussex County, DE and Worcester County, MD.

DELAWARE CITY

6327 ■ Birding Magazine
American Birding Association
PO Box 744
Delaware City, DE 19706
Phone: (302)838-3660
Fax: (302)838-3651
Free: 800-850-2473
Publisher's E-mail: info@aba.org
Magazine of the American Birding Association that features articles on all aspects of birding, including field indentification, conservation, education, recent sightings, expert interviews, the latest electronic products, book reviews, and birding hotspots all over the world. **Freq:** Bimonthly. **Key Personnel:** Ted Floyd, Editor. **Subscription Rates:** Included in membership. **URL:** http://publications.aba.org. **Ad Rates:** 4C $2,345; BW $1,545. **Remarks:** Accepts advertising. **Circ:** 18000.

DOVER

C. DR. Kent Co. 42 mi. S. of Wilmington. The State Capital. State College, Wesley College, Delaware Technical and Community College. Manufactures dry and canned goods, processed chocolate, soft drinks, refrigerators, textiles, paper products, latex paint, brick. Dairy; foundry; bottling works; feed mill. Agriculture. Wheat, corn, vegetables, fruit.

6328 ■ American Mother Magazine
American Mothers Inc.
878 Walnut Shade Rd.
Dover, DE 19901
Phone: (302)697-6811
Fax: (302)674-1830
Free: 888-822-8486
Publication E-mail: trishrodriguez@aol.com
Consumer magazine covering parenting for women. **Freq:** Triennial. **Print Method:** professional printing company. **Trim Size:** 8 1/2 x 11. **Key Personnel:** Patricia Rodriguez, Publisher. **Subscription Rates:** Free. **Formerly**: American Mother. **Remarks:** Accepts advertising. **Circ:** Non-paid 4000.

6329 ■ Better Years
Dover Post Co.
1196 S Little Creek Rd.
Dover, DE 19901
Phone: (302)678-3616
Newspaper targeted to Delaware senior citizens. **Freq:** Monthly. **Key Personnel:** Bill Chanin, Executive Editor; Joe Amon, Publisher; Steve Baumer, Designer; John Wisniewski, Specialist, Circulation; Jason Brimmer, Editor; Bill Metten, Manager, Marketing and Sales; Alana K. Bower, Designer; Tracy H. Murdaugh, Coordinator; Jim Flood, Sr., Consultant; Rob Tornoe, Designer. **Remarks:** Accepts advertising. **Circ:** (Not Reported).

6330 ■ Delaware State News
Independent Newsmedia Inc.
110 Galaxy Dr.
Dover, DE 19903
Phone: (302)674-3600
Fax: (302)741-8261
Free: 800-282-8586
Publication E-mail: dsnnews@newszap.com
Community newspaper. **Founded:** 1953. **Freq:** Mon.-Sun. (morn.). **Print Method:** Offset. **Trim Size:** 12 1/2 x 22 1/2. **Cols./Page:** 6. **Col. Width:** 11 picas. **Col. Depth:** 21 1/2 inches. **USPS:** 152-160. **Subscription Rates:** $146 Individuals 1 year. **URL:** http://delaware.newszap.com. **Formed by the merger of**: The Daily Whale. **Ad Rates:** BW $3,695; 4C $4,740; PCI $28.64; BW $3,997; 4C $4,740; PCI $34.40. **Remarks:** Accepts advertising. **Circ:** Combined ‡11292, Combined ‡16023.

6331 ■ Dover Post
GateHouse Media Inc.
1196 S Little Creek Rd.
Dover, DE 19901
Community newspaper. **Freq:** Weekly. **Print Method:** Offset. **Trim Size:** 11 1/2 x 17. **Cols./Page:** 6. **Col. Width:** 9.5 picas. **Col. Depth:** 16 inches. **Key Personnel:** Keven Todd, Publisher. **URL:** http://www.doverpost.com. **Remarks:** Accepts advertising. **Circ:** (Not Reported).

6332 ■ Milford Chronicle
Independent Newsmedia Inc.
110 Galaxy Dr.
Dover, DE 19901
Phone: (302)674-3600
Fax: (302)760-7440
Free: 800-426-4192
Publisher's E-mail: help@newszap.com
Community newspaper. **Freq:** Weekly (Wed.). **Key Personnel:** Logan B. Anderson, Managing Editor. **Subscription Rates:** $26 Individuals e-subscription. **URL:** http://milfordchronicle.net. **Remarks:** Accepts advertising. **Circ:** Combined ♦**6389**.

6333 ■ Sun City West Independent
Independent Newsmedia Inc.
110 Galaxy Dr.
Dover, DE 19901
Phone: (302)674-3600
Fax: (302)760-7440
Free: 800-426-4192
Publication E-mail: wvnews@newszap.com
Community newspaper. **Freq:** Weekly (Wed.). **Subscription Rates:** $26 Individuals e-edition. **URL:** http://arizona.newszap.com/suncitywestindependent. **Remarks:** Accepts advertising. **Circ:** Non-paid ♦**14000**.

6334 ■ Surprise Independent
Independent Newsmedia Inc.
110 Galaxy Dr.
Dover, DE 19901
Phone: (302)674-3600
Fax: (302)760-7440
Free: 800-426-4192
Publication E-mail: wvnews@newszap.com
Community newspaper. **Freq:** Weekly (Wed.). **Key Personnel:** Julie Maurer, Editor; Ed Dulin, President, Chief Executive Officer. **Subscription Rates:** $26

Circulation: ★ = AAM; △ or • = BPA; ♦ = CAC; ❑ = VAC; ⊕ = PO Statement; ‡ = Publisher's Report; Boldface figures = sworn; Light figures = estimated.

Individuals e-subscription. **URL:** http://arizona.newszap.com/surpriseindependent. **Remarks:** Accepts advertising. **Circ:** Non-paid ♦**22025**.

6335 ■ WDOV-AM - 1410
1575 Mckee Rd., Ste. 206
Dover, DE 19904
Phone: (302)395-9800
Format: Talk; News; Sports. **Networks:** CNN Radio. **Owner:** iHeartMedia Inc., 200 E Basse Rd., San Antonio, TX 78209, Ph: (210)832-3314. **Founded:** 1956. **Operating Hours:** Continuous. **ADI:** Philadelphia, PA. **Key Personnel:** Chris Walus, Dept. Mgr. **Local Programs:** *Delaware Radio Magazine*, Sunday Saturday 6:00 a.m. - 7:00 a.m.; 9:00 a.m. - 10:00 a.m. 5:00 a.m. - 6:00 a.m. **Wattage:** 5,400. **Ad Rates:** Advertising accepted; rates available upon request. **URL:** http://www.wdov.com.

6336 ■ WIHW-FM - 96.1
401 Kesselring Ave.
Dover, DE 19904
Phone: (302)734-2410
Email: info@cbcofdover.com
Format: Religious. **Owner:** Capitol Baptist Church, 401 Kesselring Ave., Dover, DE 19904, Ph: (302)734-2410. **URL:** http://www.cbcofdover.com.

6337 ■ WTMC-AM - 1380
800 Bay Rd.
Dover, DE 19901
Phone: (302)760-2000
Fax: (302)739-2895
Format: Talk. **Owner:** Delaware Department of Transportation, 39 E Regal Blvd., Newark, DE 19713. **Key Personnel:** Michael Williams, Mgr. **Mailing address:** PO Box 778, Dover, DE 19903-0778. **URL:** http://www.deldot.org.

DOVER AFB

6338 ■ The Airlifter
U.S. Air Force Dover Air Force Base Library
263 Chad St.
Dover AFB, DE 19902-5262
Phone: (302)677-3680
Local military base newspaper. **Freq:** Weekly (Fri.). **Print Method:** Offset. **Trim Size:** 11 1/2 x 15. **Cols./Page:** 5. **Col. Width:** 11.5 picas. **Col. Depth:** 14 inches. **Subscription Rates:** Free. **URL:** http://airlifter.de.newsmemory.com. **Remarks:** Accepts advertising. **Circ:** (Not Reported).

GEORGETOWN

S DE. Sussex Co. 35 mi. S. of Dover. Saw mills. Food processing. Agriculture.

6339 ■ The News Journal
Gannett
132 E Market St.
Georgetown, DE 19947
General newspaper. **Founded:** 1871. **Freq:** Mon.-Sun. **Print Method:** Offset. **Cols./Page:** 6. **Col. Width:** 14 nonpareils. **Col. Depth:** 300 agate lines. **Subscription Rates:** $25.50 Individuals month (7 days a week); $19.50 Individuals month (Thursday, Friday, Saturday, Sunday); $15 Individuals month (Sundays). **URL:** http://www.delawareonline.com. **Ad Rates:** PCI $71.85. **Remarks:** Accepts advertising. **Circ:** Mon.-Sat. 121298, Sun. 142858.

6340 ■ WDTS-AM - 620
PO Box 610
Georgetown, DE 19947
Phone: (302)856-5400
Email: terry-info@dtcc.edu
Format: Alternative/New Music/Progressive. **Owner:** Delaware Technical and Community College, 21179 College Dr., Georgetown, DE 19947, Ph: (302)259-6160, Fax: (302)259-6767. **Operating Hours:** 8:30 a.m.-3:30 p.m., Daily; closed during summer semester. **Key Personnel:** Dr. Orlando J. George, Jr., President. **Wattage:** 090/CC. **Ad Rates:** Noncommercial. **URL:** http://www.dtcc.edu.

6341 ■ WGBG-FM - 98.5
20200 Dupont Blvd.
Georgetown, DE 19947
Phone: (302)856-2567
Free: 866-292-5483
Format: Classic Rock. **Owner:** Great Scott Broadcasting, at above address, VA, Ph: (610)326-4000. **Operating Hours:** 18 hours Daily. **Key Personnel:** Ron Stone, President, CEO. **Ad Rates:** Advertising accepted; rates available upon request. **URL:** http://www.bigclassicrock.com.

6342 ■ WJKI-FM - 103.5
20200 DuPont Blvd.
Georgetown, DE 19947
Phone: (302)856-2567
Fax: (302)856-7633
Email: sue@greatscottbroadcasting.com
Format: Classic Rock. **Owner:** Great Scott Broadcasting, at above address, VA, Ph: (610)326-4000. **Formerly:** WJNE-FM. **Key Personnel:** Jeff Evans, Dir. of Bus. Dev., Jeff@greatscottbroadcasting.com. **URL:** http://www.greatscottbroadcasting.com.

6343 ■ WJWL-AM
20200 Dupont Blvd.
Georgetown, DE 19947
Phone: (302)856-2567
Fax: (302)856-6839
Format: Big Band/Nostalgia. **Networks:** USA Radio; Music of Your Life/Fairwest. **Owner:** Great Scott Broadcasting, at above address, VA, Ph: (610)326-4000. **Founded:** 1951. **Formerly:** WSEA-AM; WSSR-AM. **Wattage:** 10,500 Day; 1,080 Ni.

6344 ■ WKDB-FM - 101.7
20200 DuPont Blvd.
Georgetown, DE 19947
Phone: (920)435-5200
Fax: (919)562-8632
Format: Top 40. **Owner:** Great Scott Broadcasting, at above address, VA, Ph: (610)326-4000. **Operating Hours:** Continuous. **Ad Rates:** Advertising accepted; rates available upon request. **URL:** http://www.greatscottbroadcasting.com.

WKHW-FM - See Pocomoke City, MD

WOCQ-FM - See Berlin, MD

6345 ■ WZBH-FM - 93.5
20200 Dupont Blvd.
Georgetown, DE 19947
Format: Classic Rock; Full Service. **Networks:** ABC. **Owner:** Great Scott Broadcasting, at above address, VA, Ph: (610)326-4000. **Founded:** 1969. **Wattage:** 50,000 ERP. **Ad Rates:** Accepts Advertising. **URL:** http://www.wzbhrocks.com.

6346 ■ WZEB-FM - 101.7
20200 DuPont Blvd.
Georgetown, DE 19947
Phone: (302)856-2567
Fax: (302)856-7633
Free: 866-320-9932
Format: Top 40. **Owner:** Great Scott Broadcasting, at above address, VA, Ph: (610)326-4000. **Key Personnel:** Bryan Shaw, Operator; Sue Timmons, Contact. **URL:** http://www.musicontheb.com.

HARRINGTON

S DE. Kent Co. 7 mi. W. of Milford.

6347 ■ Harrington Journal
Independent Newspapers Inc.
PO Box 239
Harrington, DE 19952
Phone: (302)674-3600
Fax: (302)741-8252
Newspaper on women's interests. **Freq:** Weekly (Wed.). **Print Method:** Offset. **Cols./Page:** 6. **Col. Width:** 17 nonpareils. **Col. Depth:** 294 agate lines. **Key Personnel:** Karen Welch, Contact; Michael Pelrine, Editor. **URL:** http://harringtonjournal.com. **Circ:** (Not Reported).

HOCKESSIN

6348 ■ Dissolution Technologies
Dissolution Technologies Inc.
9 Yorkridge Trl.
Hockessin, DE 19707
Phone: (302)235-0621
Fax: (443)946-1264
Journal publishing valuable information on dissolution testing by providing various topics on dissolution. **Freq:** Quarterly. **Key Personnel:** Vivian Gray, Managing Editor; Cynthia Brown, Editor. **ISSN:** 1521--298X (print). **URL:** http://www.dissolutiontech.com/DTresour/BackIssuefldr/BackIssuesfrmst.html. **Circ:** (Not Reported).

6349 ■ Hockessin Community News
GateHouse Media Inc.
24 W Main St.
Hockessin, DE 19709
Phone: (302)378-9531
Community newspaper. **Freq:** Weekly (Thurs.). **Key Personnel:** Jesse Chadderdon, Editor, phone: (302)239-0214. **URL:** http://www.hockessincommunitynews.com. **Ad Rates:** BW $461. **Remarks:** Accepts advertising. **Circ:** Combined 15987.

LEWES

S DE. Sussex Co. 5 mi. N. of Rehoboth Beach.

6350 ■ Air and Space
United States Ultralight Association
16192 Coastal Hwy.
Lewes, DE 19958
Phone: (717)339-0200
Publisher's E-mail: usua@usua.org
Magazine conveying the adventure of flight and space travel to an audience with a special interest in the history and technology of aerospace. **Freq:** Bimonthly. **Subscription Rates:** $22 U.S.; $28 Canada; $28 Other countries. **URL:** http://www.airspacemag.com. **Ad Rates:** BW $17,600. **Remarks:** Accepts advertising. **Circ:** (Not Reported).

6351 ■ Cape Gazette: Delaware's Cape Region
Cape Gazette
17585 Nassau Commons Blvd.
Lewes, DE 19958
Phone: (302)645-7700
Fax: (302)645-1664
Publisher's E-mail: newsroom@capegazette.com
Community newspaper. **Freq:** Weekly Tuesday and Friday. **Print Method:** Offset. **Cols./Page:** 5. **Col. Width:** 1 7/8 inches. **Key Personnel:** Trish Vernon, Editor; Dennis Forney, Publisher. **USPS:** 010-294. **Subscription Rates:** $25 Individuals Sussex, 6 months; $39 Individuals Sussex, 12 months; $70 Individuals Sussex, 24 months; $35 Individuals outside Sussex,6 months; $56 Individuals outside Sussex 12 months; $99 Individuals Sussex county , 24 months ; $23 Individuals Senior Sussex, 6 months; $37 Individuals Senior Sussex, 12 months; $68 Individuals Senior Sussex, 24 months; $33 Individuals senior outside Sussex, 16months; $54 Individuals senior outside Sussex, 12 months; $97 Individuals senior outside Sussex, 24 months; $49 Individuals Snowbird, 12 months; $97 Individuals Snowbird, 2 4 months; $39 Students 9 months. **URL:** http://capegazette.villagesoup.com. **Mailing address:** PO Box 213, Lewes, DE 19958. **Ad Rates:** GLR $.59; BW $623; SAU $8.30; PCI $8.30. **Remarks:** Accepts advertising. **Circ:** Paid ⊕**6000**.

6352 ■ Powered Sport Flying
United States Ultralight Association
16192 Coastal Hwy.
Lewes, DE 19958
Phone: (717)339-0200
Publisher's E-mail: usua@usua.org
Magazine covering powered paragliders, powered parachutes, ultralights, light sport aircraft, weight-shift control trikes and personal rotorcraft. **Freq:** Monthly. **Subscription Rates:** Included in membership; $36.95 U.S.; $48 Canada; $90 Other countries. **URL:** http://www.psfmagazine.com. **Formerly:** Ultraflight. **Ad Rates:** BW $515; 4C $825. **Remarks:** Accepts advertising. **Circ:** (Not Reported).

6353 ■ WGMD-FM - 92.7
31549 Dutton Ln.
Lewes, DE 19958
Phone: (302)945-2050
Fax: (302)945-3781
Free: 800-518-9292
Email: news@wgmd.com
Format: Full Service; Talk. **Networks:** Fox. **Founded:** 1980. **Operating Hours:** Continuous Monday – Friday; 12:00 a.m. - 10:00 p.m. Saturday – Sunday. **Key Personnel:** Sandy Christensen, Office Mgr., sandy@wgmd.com; Dan Gaffney, Dir. of Programs, dan@wgmd.com; Jared Morris, Contact, jared@wgmd.com. **Wattage:** 2,600 ERP. **Ad Rates:** Noncommercial; Advertising

accepted; rates available upon request. **Mailing address:** PO Box 530, Rehoboth Beach, DE 19971. **URL:** http://www.wgmd.com.

WRBG-FM - See Millsboro

MIDDLETOWN

6354 ■ Middletown Transcript
GateHouse Media Inc.
24 W Main St.
Middletown, DE 19709
Phone: (302)378-9531
Fax: (302)378-0114
Community newspaper. **Freq:** Weekly. **Print Method:** Offset. **Trim Size:** 11 1/2 x 17. **Cols./Page:** 6. **Col. Width:** 9.5 picas. **Col. Depth:** 16 inches. **Key Personnel:** Keven Todd, Publisher. **USPS:** 347-560. **Subscription Rates:** $19 By mail; $30 Out of country. **URL:** http://www.middletowntranscript.com. **Remarks:** Accepts advertising. **Circ:** (Not Reported).

MILFORD

S DE. Sussex Co. 60 mi. S. of Wilmington. Manufactures electronic equipment, cement blocks, bricks, garments, canned foods. Truck farms.

6355 ■ The Journal
Independent Newsmedia Inc.
37A N Walnut St.
Milford, DE 19963
Phone: (302)422-1200
Publisher's E-mail: help@newszap.com
Community newspaper. **Founded:** 1915. **Freq:** Weekly (Wed.). **Subscription Rates:** $26 Individuals e-subscription. **URL:** http://www.newszap.com/TheJournal/. **Remarks:** Accepts advertising. **Circ:** Paid ♦**392**.

6356 ■ The Sussex County Post
Independent Newspapers Inc.
37A N Walnut St.
Milford, DE 19963
Phone: (302)629-5505
Fax: (302)629-6700
Local newspaper. **Freq:** Weekly (Wed.). **Print Method:** Offset. **Trim Size:** 13.5 x 22.88. **Cols./Page:** 6. **Col. Width:** 24 nonpareils. **Col. Depth:** 301 agate lines. **URL:** http://sussexcountypost.com. **Ad Rates:** GLR $2; BW $1715.70; 4C $1915.70; PCI $13.30. **Remarks:** Accepts advertising. **Circ:** Wed. ♦**30000**.

6357 ■ WAFL-FM - 97.7
1666 Blairs Pond Rd.
Milford, DE 19963
Phone: (302)422-7575
Fax: (302)422-3069
Email: staff@eagle977.com
Format: Adult Contemporary. **Networks:** Independent. **Owner:** Delmarva Broadcasting Co., 2727 Shipley Rd., DE 19810. **Founded:** 1971. **Operating Hours**: Continuous; 100% local. **Wattage:** 6,000. **Ad Rates:** $36-42 for 30 seconds; $46-54 for 60 seconds. $25-$36 for 30 seconds; $32-$45 for 60 seconds. Combined advertising rates available with WYUS-AM. **URL:** http://www.eagle977.com.

6358 ■ WQJZ-FM - 97.1
1666 Blairs Pond Rd
Milford, DE 19963
Email: dtgm@wqjz.com
Format: Jazz; News; Information. **Owner:** Delmarva Broadcasting Co., 2727 Shipley Rd., DE 19810; Delmarva Broadcasting Co., 2727 Shipley Rd., Wilmington, DE 19803, Ph: (302)478-2700, Fax: (302)478-0100. **Founded:** 1994. **Operating Hours**: Continuous. **Key Personnel:** Michael Reath, Gen. Mgr., miker@radiocenter.com; Al Vincente, Gen. Mgr.; Joe Beail, Gen. Sales Mgr.; Joe Edwards, Operations Mgr. **Wattage**: 3,800. **Ad Rates:** Noncommercial; Advertising accepted; rates available upon request. **URL:** http://www.971thewave.com.

6359 ■ WXPZ-FM - 101.3
1666 Blairs Pond Rd.
Milford, DE 19963
Phone: (301)478-2700
Email: lightfm@wxpz.com
Format: Full Service. **Owner:** Samson Communications Inc., 241 Forsgate Dr., Ste. 209, Jamesburg, NJ 08831. **Founded:** 1990. **Key Personnel:** Denise Harper, Gen. Mgr., VP, Contact, dharper@wxpz.com; Denise Harper, Contact. **Wattage**: 3,000 ERP. **Ad Rates:** $18 for 30 seconds; $25 for 60 seconds. **URL:** http://www.cool1013.com.

6360 ■ WYUS-AM
1666 Blairpond Rd.
Milford, DE 19963
Phone: (302)422-7575
Fax: (302)422-3069
Format: Hispanic. **Owner:** Delmarva Broadcasting Co., 2727 Shipley Rd., DE 19810. **Founded:** 1953. **Formerly**: WTHD-AM. **Wattage**: 500 Day; 081 Night. **Ad Rates:** $15-25 for 30 seconds; $19-31 for 60 seconds. **Mailing address:** PO Box 808, Milford, DE 19963. **URL:** http://www.espn930.com.

MILLSBORO

S DE. Sussex Co. 13 mi. SW of Rehoboth Beach.

6361 ■ WRBG-FM - 106.5
23136 Prince George Dr.
Lewes, DE 19958-9342
Phone: (302)933-0385
Format: Public Radio. **Owner:** Joseph D'Alessandro, Not Available. **Operating Hours**: Continuous. **Key Personnel:** Joseph D'Alessandro, Owner; Olga D'Alessandro, Owner. **Ad Rates:** Noncommercial. **URL:** http://wrbg1079fm.com.

NEW CASTLE

N DE. New Castle Co. On Delaware River, 6 mi. S. of Wilmington. Tourism. National historic landmark. Manufactures fibre products, steel castings, furnaces, chemicals, cement blocks. Refineries.

6362 ■ WDSD-FM - 94.7
920 W Basin Rd., Ste. 400
New Castle, DE 19720
Phone: (302)395-9800
Free: 877-947-9373
Email: info@wdsd.com
Format: Country. **Owner:** iHeartMedia Inc., 200 E Basse Rd., San Antonio, TX 78209, Ph: (210)832-3314. **Founded:** 1956. **Key Personnel:** Chris Walus, Mktg. Mgr., chriswalus@iheartmedia.com; Martha Burns, Contact. **Ad Rates:** Noncommercial. **URL:** http://www.wdsd.com.

6363 ■ WILM-AM - 1450
920 W Basin Rd., Ste. 400
New Castle, DE 19720
Phone: (302)395-9800
Format: News. **Networks:** Fox; Wall Street Journal Radio. **Owner:** iHeartMedia Inc., 200 E Basse Rd., San Antonio, TX 78209, Ph: (210)832-3314. **Founded:** 1923. **Operating Hours**: Midnight - 10:00 p.m. **Key Personnel:** Bruce Elliot, Contact; Martha Burns, Contact, marthaburns@clearchannel.com. **Wattage**: 1,000. **Ad Rates:** Advertising accepted; rates available upon request. **URL:** http://www.wilm.com.

6364 ■ WRDX-FM - 92.9
920 W Basin Rd., Ste. 400
New Castle, DE 19720
Phone: (302)395-9800
Email: mail@wrdx.com
Format: Classic Rock. **Founded:** Sept. 16, 2006. **Wattage**: 50,000. **Ad Rates:** Noncommercial. **URL:** http://929tomfm.iheart.com.

6365 ■ WWTX-AM - 1290
920 W Basin Rd., Ste. 400
New Castle, DE 19720
Phone: (302)395-9800
Format: Sports. **Key Personnel:** Chris Walus, Mktg. Mgr. **Ad Rates:** Advertising accepted; rates available upon request. **URL:** http://www.foxsports1290am.com.

NEWARK

N DE. New Castle Co. 15 mi. SW of Wilmington. University of Delaware. Manufactures food, cosmetics, pharmaceuticals, fibre products, paper, chemical containers, automobiles, concrete blocks, buttons. Agriculture. Corn, wheat, apples.

6366 ■ Applicable Analysis
Taylor & Francis Group Journals
c/o Robert P. Gilbert, Ed.-in-Ch.
Dept. of Mathematical Sciences
University of Delaware
Newark, DE 19716
Publisher's E-mail: customerservice@taylorandfrancis.com
Journal associated with the International Society for Analysis, its applications and computation. **Freq:** Monthly. **Key Personnel:** Robert P. Gilbert, Editor-in-Chief; John Ball, Editor. **ISSN:** 0003--6811 (print); **EISSN:** 1563--504X (electronic). **Subscription Rates:** $8482 Institutions online only; $9693 Institutions print and online. **URL:** http://www.tandfonline.com/toc/gapa20/current. **Circ:** (Not Reported).

6367 ■ Business Ethics Quarterly
Philosophy Documentation Center
Alfred Lerner College of Business & Economics
University of Delaware
Newark, DE 19716
Phone: (302)831-4568
Publication E-mail: beqeditor@uncc.edu
Peer-reviewed scholarly journal covering business ethics studies. **Freq:** Quarterly. **Trim Size:** 6 x 9. **Key Personnel:** Gary R. Weaver, Associate Editor; Denis G. Arnold, Editor. **ISSN:** 1052--150X (print); **EISSN:** 2153--3326 (electronic). **Subscription Rates:** $185 Institutions; $470 Institutions online; $590 Institutions print and online; $100 Individuals; $40 Students and retirees. **URL:** http://secure.pdcnet.org/pdc/bvdb.nsf/journal?openform&journal=pdc_beq. **Remarks:** Accepts advertising. **Circ:** Paid 1000.

6368 ■ Composites Science and Technology
RELX Group P.L.C.
c/o T.W. Chou, Editor-in-Chief
Dept. of Mechanical Engineering
University of Delaware
Newark, DE 19716
Publisher's E-mail: amsterdam@relx.com
Journal covering the aspects of fundamental and applied science of engineering composites. **Freq:** 16/yr. **Key Personnel:** Tsu-Wei Chou, Editor-in-Chief; Y.W. Mai, Editor; K. Schulte, Editor. **ISSN:** 0266--3538 (print). **Subscription Rates:** $6412.66 Institutions online; $7695 Institutions print. **URL:** http://www.journals.elsevier.com/composites-science-and-technology. **Circ:** (Not Reported).

6369 ■ Delaware Medical Journal: Official Publication of the Medical Society of Delaware
Medical Society of Delaware
Iron Hill Corporate Center
900 Prides Crossing
Newark, DE 19713
Phone: (302)366-1400
Fax: (302)366-1354
Free: 800-348-6800
Medical journal. **Freq:** Monthly. **Print Method:** Offset. **Trim Size:** 8 1/2 x 11. **Cols./Page:** 2. **Col. Width:** 32 nonpareils. **Col. Depth:** 126 agate lines. **Key Personnel:** Peter V. Rocca, Editor-in-Chief. **ISSN:** 0011--7781 (print). **URL:** http://www.medsocdel.org/Communications/DelawareMedicalJournal.aspx. **Ad Rates:** BW $220; 4C $510. **Remarks:** Accepts advertising. **Circ:** Paid 1600.

6370 ■ Energy & Fuels
American Chemical Society
c/o Michael T. Klein, Ed.
University of Delaware
Department of Chemical Engineering
Newark, DE 19716
Publisher's E-mail: help@acs.org
Scientific journal dealing with chemistry of non-nuclear energy sources, including petroleum, coal, shale oil, tar sands, biomass, synfuels, C1 chemistry, organic geochemistry, applied catalysis, and combustion. **Freq:** Bimonthly. **Print Method:** Web offset. **Trim Size:** 8 3/16 x 11 1/4. **Cols./Page:** 3. **Col. Width:** 2 3/16 inches. **Col. Depth:** 10 inches. **Key Personnel:** Michael T. Klein, Editor-in-Chief; Dady B. Dadyburjor, Associate Editor. **ISSN:** 0887--0624 (print); **EISSN:** 1520--5029 (electronic). **Online:** American Chemical Society American Chemical Society. **URL:** http://pubs.acs.org/journal/enfuem. **Remarks:** Advertising accepted; rates available upon request. **Circ:** Paid 1000.

Circulation: ★ = AAM; △ or • = BPA; ♦ = CAC; ❑ = VAC; ⊕ = PO Statement; ‡ = Publisher's Report; Boldface figures = sworn; Light figures = estimated.

6371 ■ Journal of Adolescent & Adult Literacy
International Literacy Association
800 Barksdale Rd.
Newark, DE 19711-3204
Phone: (302)731-1600
Fax: (302)731-1057
Free: 800-336-7323
Publisher's E-mail: customerservice@reading.org
Scholarly journal of secondary and adult reading education. **Freq:** Bimonthly. **Print Method:** Offset. **Trim Size:** 8 3/8 x 10 7/8. **Cols./Page:** 3. **Col. Width:** 13.5 picas. **Key Personnel:** Margaret C. Hagood, Editor; Emily N. Skinner, Editor. **ISSN:** 1081--3004 (print); **EISSN:** 1936--2706 (electronic). **URL:** http://www.literacyworldwide.org/blog/literacy-daily/2012/10/05/new-editors-for-the-journal-of-adolescent-adult-literacy. **Formerly**: Journal of Reading. **Mailing address:** PO Box 8139, Newark, DE 19714-8139. **Ad Rates:** BW $750; 4C $1500. **Remarks:** Accepts advertising. **Circ:** ‡17000.

6372 ■ Journal of Field Ornithology
Association of Field Ornithologists
c/o Gregory Shriver, Treasurer
257 Townsend Hall
University of Delaware
Newark, DE 19717-2160
Phone: (302)831-1300
Publication E-mail: cs-journals@wiley.com
Freq: Quarterly. **Key Personnel:** Gary Ritchison, Editor. **ISSN:** 0273--8570 (print); **EISSN:** 1557--9263 (electronic). **Subscription Rates:** $468 Institutions print or online; $562 Institutions print and online; $103 Members Association of Field Ornithologists - print and online; £290 Institutions print or online; £348 Institutions print and online; £58 Members National Childrens' Bureau - print and online; €367 Institutions print or online; €441 Institutions print and online; €65 Members Association of Field Ornithologists - print and online; $564 Institutions, other countries print or online; $677 Institutions, other countries print and online; $468 Institutions print or online. **URL:** http://afonet.org/wp_english/journal; http://onlinelibrary.wiley.com/journal/10.1111/(ISSN)1557-9263. **Remarks:** Advertising accepted; rates available upon request. **Circ:** (Not Reported).

6373 ■ Journal of Seventeenth-Century Music
Society for Seventeenth-Century Music
c/o Maria Anne Purciello, Treasurer
University of Delaware
Department of Music
317 Amy E. du Pont Music Bldg.
Newark, DE 19716
Phone: (319)335-1622
Peer-reviewed journal providing a refereed forum for scholarly studies of the musical cultures of the seventeenth century. **Freq:** Annual. **Key Personnel:** Kelley Harness, Editor-in-Chief; Richard Charteris, Board Member. **ISSN:** 1089--747X (print). **URL:** http://sscm-jscm.org. **Remarks:** Advertising not accepted. **Circ:** (Not Reported).

6374 ■ Literacy Today
International Literacy Association
800 Barksdale Rd.
Newark, DE 19711-3204
Phone: (302)731-1600
Fax: (302)731-1057
Free: 800-336-7323
Publication E-mail: literacytoday@reading.org
Professional newspaper of the International Reading Association. **Freq:** Bimonthly. **Print Method:** Web offset. **Trim Size:** 10 1/2 x 14 1/2. **Cols./Page:** 4. **Col. Width:** 2 1/4 inches. **Col. Depth:** 13 inches. **Key Personnel:** John Micklos, Jr., Editor; Linda Hunter, Manager, Advertising. **ISSN:** 0737--4208 (print). **Subscription Rates:** $35 Individuals. **URL:** http://literacyworldwide.org/get-resources/em-literacy-today-em-magazine. **Formerly**: Reading Today. **Mailing address:** PO Box 8139, Newark, DE 19714-8139. **Remarks:** Advertising accepted; rates available upon request. **Circ:** (Not Reported).

6375 ■ Reading Research Quarterly
International Literacy Association
800 Barksdale Rd.
Newark, DE 19711-3204
Phone: (302)731-1600
Fax: (302)731-1057
Free: 800-336-7323
Publisher's E-mail: customerservice@reading.org
Educational journal with articles on theory and research in reading. **Freq:** Quarterly. **Print Method:** Offset. **Trim Size:** 8 3/8 x 10 7/8. **Key Personnel:** Susan Neuman, Editor; Linda Gambrell, Editor. **ISSN:** 0034--0553 (print); **EISSN:** 1936--2722 (electronic). **URL:** http://www.literacyworldwide.org/get-resources/journals. **Mailing address:** PO Box 8139, Newark, DE 19714-8139. **Ad Rates:** BW $825; 4C $1525. **Remarks:** Accepts advertising. **Circ:** ‡55000, 11000.

6376 ■ The Reading Teacher
International Literacy Association
800 Barksdale Rd.
Newark, DE 19711-3204
Phone: (302)731-1600
Fax: (302)731-1057
Free: 800-336-7323
Publisher's E-mail: customerservice@reading.org
Freq: 8/year. **Trim Size:** 8 3/8 x 10 7/8. **Key Personnel:** Diane Barone, Editor; Marla Mallette, Editor. **ISSN:** 0034--0561 (print); **EISSN:** 1936--2714 (electronic). **URL:** http://www.literacyworldwide.org/get-resources/journals; http://onlinelibrary.wiley.com/doi/10.1002/trtr.2015.69.issue-1/issuetoc. **Mailing address:** PO Box 8139, Newark, DE 19714-8139. **Ad Rates:** BW $1875; 4C $4025. **Remarks:** Accepts advertising. **Circ:** ‡55000.

6377 ■ The Review
University of Delaware
Newark, DE 19716
Phone: (302)831-2792
Publication E-mail: reviewud@yahoo.com
Collegiate newspaper (tabloid). **Founded:** 1882. **Freq:** Monthly. **Print Method:** Offset. **Cols./Page:** 5. **Col. Width:** 24 nonpareils. **Col. Depth:** 189 agate lines. **Key Personnel:** Johnnie Carrow, Director, Advertising. **Subscription Rates:** $40 Individuals; $5 Single issue per month. **URL:** http://www.udel.edu/TheReview/Rates.html; http://www.lib.udel.edu/digital/. **Ad Rates:** PCI $12. **Remarks:** Accepts advertising. **Circ:** Paid ‡11000.

6378 ■ WPA: Writing Program Administration
Council of Writing Program Administrators
c/o Michael McCamley, Secretary
212 Memorial Hall
University of Delaware
Newark, DE 19716
Freq: Semiannual. **Subscription Rates:** Included in membership. **Alt. Formats:** CD-ROM. **URL:** http://wpacouncil.org/node/1812. **Remarks:** Accepts advertising. **Circ:** (Not Reported).

6379 ■ WVUD-FM - 91.3
Perkins Student Ctr.
Newark, DE 19716
Phone: (302)831-2701
Fax: (302)831-1399
Format: Educational. **Owner:** University of Delaware, Newark, DE 19716, Ph: (302)831-2792. **Founded:** 1968. **Operating Hours**: Continuous. **Key Personnel:** Kevin Collins, Sports Dir., agerbosi@gmail.com; Dave MacKenzie, Chief Engineer, davemack@udel.edu; Steve Kramarck, Station Mgr., kramarck@udel.edu; Michele Ingari, Gen. Mgr., wvudgm@gmail.com; Kate Seymour, Promotions Dir., Dir. of Public Rel., wvudpr@gmail.com; Mike Tsarouhas, Dir. of Production, bcminch@udel.edu; Trish Saccomanno, Gen. Mgr., wvudmusic@gmail.com. **Ad Rates:** Noncommercial; underwriting available. **URL:** http://www.wvud.org.

OCEAN VIEW

6380 ■ WRKE-FM - 101.7
Q-Tone Broadcasting Corp.
63 Atlantic Ave.
Rte. 1, Box 24
Ocean View, DE 19970-9801
Phone: (302)539-2600
Format: Top 40. **Networks:** NBC. **Owner:** Q-Tone Broadcasting Corp., at above address. **Founded:** 1986. **Formerly**: WOVU-FM. **Operating Hours**: Continuous. **Key Personnel:** Anthony J. Quartarone, Gen. Mgr., Owner, VP; Charles A. Stephens, Coord.; Manuel Mena, Music Dir. **Wattage:** 3,000. **Ad Rates:** $16-24 for 30 seconds; $17-27 for 60 seconds.

REHOBOTH BEACH

S DE. Sussex Co. 5 mi. SE of Lewes.

6381 ■ Delaware Beach Life
Delaware Beach Life
PO Box 417
Rehoboth Beach, DE 19971
Phone: (302)227-9499
Publisher's E-mail: info@delawarebeachlife.com
Magazine covering coastal Delaware's culture and lifestyle. **Freq:** 8/year. **Key Personnel:** Terry Plowman, Editor, Publisher. **ISSN:** 1539--1655 (print). **Subscription Rates:** $18 Individuals; $45 Individuals Three years. **URL:** http://www.delawarebeachlife.com. **Remarks:** Advertising accepted; rates available upon request. **Circ:** (Not Reported).

SEAFORD

S DE. Sussex Co. On Nanticoke River, 20 mi. N. of Salisbury, MD. Manufactures nylon, baskets, boxes, crates, concrete blocks, feed, and garments. Truck and fruit farms.

6382 ■ Delmarva Real Estate
Independent Newsmedia Inc.
302 W Stein Hwy.
Seaford, DE 19973
Phone: (302)674-3600
Publisher's E-mail: help@newszap.com
Real estate guide focusing on Sussex County's resort industry and property markets. **Freq:** Monthly. **Key Personnel:** Ed Dulin, President, Chief Executive Officer. **Subscription Rates:** Free. **URL:** http://www.delmarvaclassifieds.newszap.com. **Mailing address:** PO Box 1130, Seaford, DE 19973. **Remarks:** Accepts advertising. **Circ:** Non-paid ♦**27500**.

SMYRNA

Clayton Sun - See Clayton

6383 ■ Smyrna/Clayton Sun-Times
GateHouse Media Inc.
224 E Glenwood Ave.
Smyrna, DE 19977-1080
Phone: (302)653-2083
Local newspaper (tabloid). **Freq:** Weekly (Wed.). **Print Method:** Offset. **Trim Size:** 11 1/2 x 17. **Cols./Page:** 6. **Col. Width:** 9.5 picas. **Col. Depth:** 16 inches. **Key Personnel:** Kevin Todd, Publisher; Ben Mace, Editor; Brigitte McKinney, Advertising Representative. **URL:** http://www.scsuntimes.com. **Formerly**: Smyrna Clayton Sun; Smyrna Times. **Remarks:** Accepts advertising. **Circ:** (Not Reported).

WILMINGTON

N DE. New Castle Co. On Delaware River, 25 mi. SW of Philadelphia. Brandywine College; Goldey Beacom College. Port of entry and important trading center. Manufactures chemicals, leather and rubber products, textiles, tile, floor coverings, cork products and railroad cars.

6384 ■ AAA World
AAA Mid-Atlantic
One River Pl.
Wilmington, DE 19801
Free: 888-222-8222
Publication for members of AAA. **Founded:** 1939. **Freq:** Bimonthly. **Print Method:** Offset. **Trim Size:** 8 x 10 1/2. **Cols./Page:** 3. **Col. Width:** 2 1/4 inches. **Col. Depth:** 9 3/4 inches. **URL:** http://midatlantic.aaa.com. **Formerly**: Spotlight; Spotlight on Travel; Car & Travel. **Ad Rates:** BW $13,787; 4C $17,877. **Remarks:** Accepts advertising. **Circ:** (Not Reported).

6385 ■ Cancer Cytopathology
American Society of Cytopathology
100 W 10th St., Ste. 605
Wilmington, DE 19801-6604
Phone: (302)543-6583
Fax: (302)543-6597
Journal containing studies regarding cytopathology, diagnosis, prevention and other relevant ideas about human cancer. **Freq:** Bimonthly. **URL:** http://www.cytopathology.org/cancer-cytopathology/. **Remarks:** Advertising not accepted. **Circ:** (Not Reported).

6386 ■ Canon
Collegiate Network
3901 Centerville Rd.
Wilmington, DE 19807

Phone: (302)652-4600
Fax: (302)652-1760
Free: 800-526-7022
Freq: 3/year each academic year. **Mailing address:** PO Box 45, Granada, Nicaragua. **Remarks:** Accepts advertising. **Circ:** 29000.

6387 ■ Continuity: A Journal of History
Intercollegiate Studies Institute
3901 Centerville Rd.
Wilmington, DE 19807-1938
Phone: (302)652-4600
Fax: (302)652-1760
Free: 800-526-7022
Publisher's E-mail: programs@isi.org
Freq: Semiannual. **ISSN:** 0277--1446 (print). **Mailing address:** PO Box 4431, Wilmington, DE 19807-1938. **Remarks:** Accepts advertising. **Circ:** (Not Reported).

6388 ■ Delaware Journal of Corporate Law
Widener University School of Law
4601 Concord Pke.
Wilmington, DE 19803
Phone: (302)477-2100
Fax: (302)477-2224
Publication E-mail: djcl@widener.edu
Professional journal covering corporate law. **Founded:** 1975. **Freq:** 3/yr. **Key Personnel:** Nicole Sciotto, Editor-in-Chief; Marisa Defeo, Managing Editor; Peter Tsoflias, Managing Editor. **Subscription Rates:** $50 Individuals; $20 Single issue; $63.70 Other countries. **URL:** http://www.djcl.org; http://law.widener.edu/campuslife/activitiesandorganizations/delawarejournalofcorporatelaw.aspx. **Mailing address:** PO Box 7474, Wilmington, DE 19803. **Ad Rates:** BW $425. **Remarks:** Accepts advertising. **Circ:** Paid 997.

6389 ■ Delaware Today
Delaware Today
3301 Lancaster Pke., Ste. 5-C
Wilmington, DE 19805-1436
Phone: (302)656-1809
Fax: (302)656-5843
Publisher's E-mail: sales@delawaretoday.com
Regional interest magazine. **Freq:** Monthly. **Print Method:** Offset. **Trim Size:** 8 3/16 x 10 7/8. **Cols./Page:** 3. **Col. Width:** 27 nonpareils. **Col. Depth:** 140 agate lines. **Key Personnel:** Robert F. Martinelli, President, Chief Executive Officer, Publisher; Maria Hess, Senior Editor, phone: (302)656-1809; Mark Nardone, Editor; Drew Ostroski, Managing Editor. **ISSN:** 1086--8380 (print). **Subscription Rates:** $14.97 Individuals print. **URL:** http://www.delawaretoday.com. **Ad Rates:** BW $2955; 4C $4085. **Remarks:** Accepts advertising. **Circ:** Combined ★**122187**.

6390 ■ Enterprise and Society: The International Journal of Business History
Business History Conference
c/o Hagley Museum and Library
PO Box 3630
Wilmington, DE 19807-0630
Phone: (302)658-2400
Fax: (302)655-3188
Journal covering scholarly research on the historical relations between businesses and their larger political, cultural, institutional, social, and economic contexts. **Freq:** Quarterly. **ISSN:** 1467-2227 (print); **EISSN:** 1467-2235 (electronic). **Subscription Rates:** Included in membership. **URL:** http://www.thebhc.org/enterprise-society; http://www.oxfordjournals.org/our_journals/entsoc/about.html. **Remarks:** Accepts advertising. **Circ:** (Not Reported).

6391 ■ The Intercollegiate Review: A Journal of Scholarship and Opinion
Intercollegiate Studies Institute
3901 Centerville Rd.
Wilmington, DE 19807-1938
Phone: (302)652-4600
Fax: (302)652-1760
Free: 800-526-7022
Publisher's E-mail: programs@isi.org
Contains articles for liberty-loving students at colleges across America. Includes introductions to the principles of liberty, current circumstances, and interviews with prominent professors. **Freq:** Semiannual. **ISSN:** 0020--5249 (print). **Subscription Rates:** $15 Individuals /year (print); $28 Two years /year; Included in membership. **URL:** http://home.isi.org/intercollegiate-review. **Mailing address:** PO Box 4431, Wilmington, DE 19807-1938. **Remarks:** Accepts advertising. **Circ:** (Not Reported).

6392 ■ Widener Journal of Law, Economics and Race
Widener University, Wilmington School of Law
4601 Concord Pke.
Wilmington, DE 19803-0474
Phone: (302)477-2703
Fax: (302)477-2224
Publisher's E-mail: lawadmissions@widener.edu
Journal providing a forum for in-depth analysis and academic discourse on issues involving the intersection of the law, race, and economics. **Freq:** Semiannual. **Key Personnel:** Jessica L. Santiago, Editor-in-Chief. **URL:** http://wjler.wordpress.com. **Mailing address:** PO Box 7474, Wilmington, DE 19803-0474. **Circ:** (Not Reported).

6393 ■ WDEL-AM - 1150
2727 Shipley Rd.
Wilmington, DE 19810
Phone: (302)478-2700
Fax: (302)478-0100
Email: wdelnews@wdel.com
Format: News; Talk. **Networks:** CBS. **Owner:** Delmarva Broadcasting Co., 2727 Shipley Rd., DE 19810. **Founded:** 1922. **Operating Hours**: Continuous. **Key Personnel:** Mark Weidel, Contact, mweidel@dbcmedia.com. **Wattage**: 5,000. **Ad Rates:** Advertising accepted; rates available upon request. **URL:** http://www.wdel.com.

6394 ■ WFAI-AM - 1510
704 King St., Ste. 604
Wilmington, DE 19801
Phone: (302)622-8895
Fax: (302)622-8678
Format: Religious; Talk; Gospel. **Networks:** ABC. **Owner:** Qc Communications, Inc., at above address. **Founded:** 1978. **Formerly**: WJIC-AM. **Operating Hours**: Sunrise-sunset; 100% local. **Key Personnel:** Manuel Mena, Dir. of Programs. **Wattage**: 2,500. **Ad Rates:** $24-26 for 30 seconds; $28-30 for 60 seconds. **URL:** http://www.faith1510.com.

6395 ■ WJBR-FM - 99.5
812 Philadelphia Pke., Ste. C
Wilmington, DE 19809
Phone: (302)765-1160
Free: 888-995-9527
Email: info@wjbr.com
Format: Adult Contemporary. **Networks:** Westwood One Radio; CNN Radio. **Owner:** Beasley Broadcast Group Inc., 3033 Riviera Dr., Ste. 200, Naples, FL 34103-2750, Ph: (239)263-5000, Fax: (239)263-8191. **Founded:** 1956. **Formerly**: WTUX-AM. **Operating Hours**: Continuous; 100% local. **ADI**: Philadelphia, PA. **Key Personnel:** Jane Bartsch, Gen. Mgr., VP, jbartsch@wjbr.com; Dan Sultzbach, Gen. Sales Mgr., dsultzbach@wjbr.com; Michelle Zeplin, Contact, michelle.zeplin@wjbr.com. **Wattage**: 50,000. **Ad Rates:** $50-120 per unit. **URL:** http://www.wjbr.com.

6396 ■ WJKS-FM - 101.7
First Federal Plz. Bldg.
704 King St., Ste. 604
Wilmington, DE 19801
Format: Hip Hop; Urban Contemporary. **Networks:** ABC. **Owner:** Qc Communications, Inc., at above address. **Founded:** 1972. **Operating Hours**: Mon. - Thur. - 6 a.m. to 2 a.m.; Fri. - Sun. 6 a.m. to 9.55. **Key Personnel:** Tony Quartarone, Gen. Sales Mgr., Owner, tonyq@wjks1017.com; Maria Sylvanus, Sales Mgr., marias@wjks1017.com. **Local Programs**: *The Doug Banks Morning Show*; *The Party Jam with Mellie Mel.* **Wattage**: 3,300. **Ad Rates:** $55-85 for 60 seconds. Combined advertising rates available with WNNN-AM. **URL:** http://www.wjks1017.com.

6397 ■ WMHS-FM - 88.1
301 McKennan's Church Rd.
Wilmington, DE 19808
Phone: (302)992-5520
Owner: Thomas McKean High School, 301 McKennans Church Rd., Wilmington, DE 19808, Ph: (302)992-5520, Fax: (302)992-5525. **Key Personnel:** Fran Kulas, Contact, francis.kulas@redclay.k12.de.us. **Wattage**: 088.

6398 ■ WMPH-FM - 91.7
Wilmington, DE 19809
Format: Eclectic. **Owner:** Brandywine School District, 1311 Brandywine Blvd., Wilmington, DE 19809, Ph: (302)793-5000. **Founded:** 1969. **Operating Hours**: Monday – Friday; 5:00 Am – 9:00 Am; 4:00 Pm – 7:00 Pm. **Wattage**: 100. **Ad Rates:** Noncommercial.

6399 ■ WSTW-FM - 93.7
2727 Shipley Rd.
Wilmington, DE 19810
Phone: (302)478-2700
Fax: (302)478-0100
Format: Adult Contemporary; Contemporary Hit Radio (CHR). **Networks:** Independent. **Owner:** Delmarva Broadcasting Co., 2727 Shipley Rd., DE 19810. **Founded:** 1950. **Operating Hours**: Continuous; 100% local. **ADI**: Philadelphia, PA. **Wattage**: 50,000. **Ad Rates:** Noncommercial. **URL:** http://www.wstw.com.

6400 ■ WXHL-FM - 89.1
2207 Concord Pke.
Wilmington, DE 19803
Phone: (302)731-0690
Fax: (302)738-3090
Free: 800-220-8078
Email: connect@myreachradio.com
Format: Contemporary Christian. **Owner:** Priority Radio Inc., at above address. **Ad Rates:** Noncommercial. **URL:** http://www.myreachradio.com.

6401 ■ WXJN-FM - 105.9
2727 Shipley Rd.
Wilmington, DE 19810
Phone: (410)219-3500
Fax: (410)548-1543
Format: Country. **Owner:** Delmarva Broadcasting Co., 2727 Shipley Rd., Wilmington, DE 19803, Ph: (302)478-2700, Fax: (302)478-0100. **Operating Hours**: Continuous. **Key Personnel:** Joe Edwards, Dir. of Programs. **Wattage**: 6,000. **URL:** http://www.catcountryradio.com.

WINTERTHUR

6402 ■ Winterthur Portfolio: A Journal of American Material Culture
The University of Chicago Press
5105 Kennett Pke. (Rt. 52)
Winterthur, DE 19735
Phone: (302)888-4615
Fax: (302)888-4870
Publisher's E-mail: custserv@press.uchicago.edu
Journal covering the history of American art and artifacts. **Freq:** 3/year. **Print Method:** Offset. **Trim Size:** 8 1/2 x 11. **Cols./Page:** 2. **Key Personnel:** Amy Earls, Managing Editor. **ISSN:** 0084--0416 (print). **URL:** http://www.journals.uchicago.edu/toc/wp/current. **Ad Rates:** BW $724. **Remarks:** Accepts advertising. **Circ:** ‡331.

YORKLYN

6403 ■ Britannia
Britannia.com L.L.C.
PO Box 136
Yorklyn, DE 19736
Phone: (610)388-6841
Fax: (610)388-1747
Publication E-mail: publish@britannia.com
Online magazine covering travel and tourism in the British Isles. **URL:** http://www.britannia.com/. **Remarks:** Accepts advertising. **Circ:** (Not Reported).

Circulation: ★ = AAM; △ or • = BPA; ♦ = CAC; ❑ = VAC; ⊕ = PO Statement; ‡ = Publisher's Report; Boldface figures = sworn; Light figures = estimated.

WASHINGTON

District of Columbia. On Potomac River, 38 mi. from Baltimore, 136 mi. from Philadelphia, 234 mi. from New York, 104 mi. from Richmond. Capitol of the United States. Eight bridges to suburban cities, Arlington, Alexandria, and Fairfax County in Virginia. George Washington, Georgetown, American, Catholic and Howard Universities; many other educational institutions. About 27 percent of Washington workers are employed by the Federal or District Government. United States Capitol and other Government buildings; National Cathedral. Has some of the finest libraries, museums, art galleries, historical shrines and memorials in the world. Draws a large number of tourists each year. Headquarters of many nonprofit organizations.

6404 ■ AAG Review of Books
American Association of Geographers
1710 16th St. NW
Washington, DC 20009
Phone: (202)234-1450
Fax: (202)234-2744
Publisher's E-mail: gaia@aag.org
Contains scholarly reviews of current books related to geography, public policy, and international affairs. **Freq:** Quarterly January, April, July and October. **Subscription Rates:** Included in membership. **URL:** http://www.aag.org/cs/publications/journals/rob. **Circ:** (Not Reported).

6405 ■ AARP Bulletin
AARP
601 E St. NW
Washington, DC 20049-0001
Phone: (202)434-3525
Free: 888-687-2277
Publisher's E-mail: member@aarp.org
Newspaper for mature Americans. **Freq:** Monthly latest issue: June 2015. **Print Method:** Rotogravure. **Trim Size:** 9 3/4 x 11 1/2. **Cols./Page:** 4. **Col. Width:** 27 nonpareils. **Col. Depth:** 133 agate lines. **Key Personnel:** Robert Wilson, Editor. **ISSN:** 1044-1123 (print). **Subscription Rates:** Included in membership. **Alt. Formats:** Download. **URL:** http://www.aarp.org/bulletin/. **Formerly**: HEALTHletter; AARP News Bulletins. **Remarks:** Advertising accepted; rates available upon request. **Circ:** Paid ★**22042940**.

6406 ■ AAUW Outlook
American Association of University Women
1111 16th St. NW
Washington, DC 20036-4809
Phone: (202)785-7700
Fax: (202)872-1425
Free: 800-326-2289
Publisher's E-mail: connect@aauw.org
Freq: Quarterly. **Key Personnel:** Jodi Lipson, Associate Director, Editor. **ISSN:** 0161--5661 (print). **Subscription Rates:** Included in membership. **Alt. Formats:** PDF. **URL:** http://www.aauw.org/who-we-are/outlookmag. **Formerly**: Graduate Women. **Ad Rates:** BW $4,500; PCI $125. **Remarks:** Accepts advertising. **Circ:** 100000.

6407 ■ ABA Consumer Credit Delinquency Bulletin
American Bankers Association
1120 Connecticut Ave. NW
Washington, DC 20036
Phone: (202)663-5071
Fax: (202)828-4540
Free: 800-226-5377
Publication E-mail: benchmarking@ABA.com
Publication that compares bank consumer loan delinquency rates and repossessions nationwide and by state. **Freq:** Quarterly. **Trim Size:** 8 1/2 x 11. **ISSN:** 1058--8841 (print). **Subscription Rates:** $260 Nonmembers list price; $260 Out of country; $135 Members. **URL:** http://www.aba.com/Products/Surveys/Pages/ss_delinquency.aspx. **Remarks:** Advertising not accepted. **Circ:** (Not Reported).

6408 ■ ABA Destinations
American Bus Association
111 K St. NE, 9th Fl.
Washington, DC 20002
Phone: (202)842-1645
Fax: (202)842-0850
Free: 800-283-2877
Publisher's E-mail: abainfo@buses.org
Freq: Bimonthly. **Subscription Rates:** $25 in U.S.; $30 in Canada. **URL:** http://www.buses.org/news-publications/destinations-magazine. **Remarks:** Accepts advertising. **Circ:** 6000.

6409 ■ Abstracts in Social Gerontology: Current Literature on Aging
EBSCO Information Services
National Council on the Aging
409 Third St. SW
Washington, DC 20024
Publication E-mail: advertising@sagepub.com
Annotated bibliography of books, journal articles, and documents relevant to social gerontology. **Freq:** Quarterly. **Print Method:** Offset. **Trim Size:** 5 1/4 x 8 1/2. **ISSN:** 1047--4862 (print). **URL:** http://www.ebscohost.com/academic/abstracts-in-social-gerontology. **Ad Rates:** BW $445. **Remarks:** Advertising accepted; rates available upon request. **Circ:** ‡350.

6410 ■ Academe: Bulletin of the AAUP
American Association of University Professors
1133 19th St. NW, Ste. 200
Washington, DC 20036
Phone: (202)737-5900
Fax: (202)737-5526
Publisher's E-mail: aaup@aaup.org
Higher education magazine for college and university professors. **Freq:** Bimonthly. **Print Method:** Offset. Uses mats. **Trim Size:** 8.25 x 10.875. **Cols./Page:** 3. **Col. Width:** 2 1/4 inches. **Col. Depth:** 9 3/4 inches. **ISSN:** 0190--2946 (print). **Subscription Rates:** $89 Individuals; $94 Other countries; $10 Included in membership single issue. **URL:** http://www.aaup.org/academe. **Ad Rates:** BW $3240; 4C $4555. **Remarks:** Accepts advertising. **Circ:** 40103, 46500.

6411 ■ Academic Medicine
Association of American Medical Colleges
655 K St. NW, Ste. 100
Washington, DC 20001-2399
Phone: (202)828-0400
Publisher's E-mail: amcas@aamc.org
Freq: Monthly. **ISSN:** 1040- 2446 (print). **Subscription Rates:** $253 Individuals; $556 Institutions other countries; $524 Institutions. **URL:** http://journals.lww.com/academicmedicine/Pages/InstructionsforAuthors.aspx; http://www.aamc.org/newsroom/news-pubs. **Remarks:** Accepts advertising. **Circ:** 6,000.

6412 ■ Academic Medicine
Association of American Medical Colleges
655 K St. NW, Ste. 100
Washington, DC 20001-2399
Phone: (202)828-0400
Publisher's E-mail: amcas@aamc.org
Peer-reviewed medical journal publishing scholarly and research articles on all aspects of the education of physicians. **Founded:** 1876. **Freq:** Monthly. **Print Method:** Offset. **Trim Size:** 8.5 x 11. **Cols./Page:** 2. **Col. Width:** 31 nonpareils. **Key Personnel:** Anne L. Farmakidis, Managing Editor; Steven L. Kanter, MD, Editor-in-Chief. **ISSN:** 0022-2577 (print). **Subscription Rates:** $253 Individuals; $524 Institutions; $154 Individuals in-training; $400 Other countries; $556 Institutions, other countries; $186 Other countries in-training. **URL:** http://journals.lww.com/academicmedicine/pages/default.aspx. **Remarks:** Accepts advertising. **Circ:** ‡5900.

6413 ■ The Academy TODAY
American Academy of Orthotists and Prosthetists
1331 H St. NW, Ste. 501
Washington, DC 20005
Phone: (202)380-3663
Fax: (202)380-3447
Freq: Quarterly. **URL:** http://www.oandp.org/academytoday/2016Jul. **Remarks:** Advertising not accepted. **Circ:** (Not Reported).

6414 ■ AcademyHealth Health Services Research
AcademyHealth
1666 K St. NW, Ste. 1100
Washington, DC 20036
Phone: (202)292-6700
Fax: (202)292-6800
Freq: Bimonthly. **ISSN:** 0017-9124 (print); **EISSN:** 1475-6773 (electronic). **Subscription Rates:** $1020 Institutions print or online; $1224 Institutions print and online; $159 Individuals print and online; $122 Members American Sociological Association (print and online). **URL:** http://www.hsr.org/; http://www.academyhealth.org/Publications/content.cfm?ItemNumber=2472&navItemNumber=536. **Remarks:** Advertising not accepted. **Circ:** (Not Reported).

6415 ■ ACC Docket: The Journal of the American Corporate Counsel Association
Association of Corporate Counsel
1025 Connecticut Ave. NW, Ste. 200
Washington, DC 20036
Phone: (202)293-4103
Fax: (202)293-4701

Circulation: ★ = AAM; △ or • = BPA; ♦ = CAC; ❑ = VAC; ⊕ = PO Statement; ‡ = Publisher's Report; Boldface figures = sworn; Light figures = estimated.

Professional journal covering law. **Freq:** 10/year. **Print Method:** Sheetfed offset. **Trim Size:** 8 1/4 x 11. **Cols./Page:** 2. **Col. Width:** 18 picas. **Col. Depth:** 52 picas. **Key Personnel:** Kim Howard, Publisher; Diane Rusignola, Assistant Editor; Kevin Buck, Chief Marketing Officer. **ISSN:** 0895--9544 (print). **Subscription Rates:** $335 U.S.; $350 Other countries; $170 Students law student. **URL:** http://www.acc.com/accdocket/themagazine.cfm. **Formerly**: ACCA Docket. **Ad Rates:** BW $3,250. **Remarks:** Accepts advertising. **Circ:** Paid ⊕**10500**, Combined 35000.

6416 ■ ACCEL
American College of Cardiology
2400 N St. NW
Washington, DC 20037
Phone: (202)375-6000
Fax: (202)375-7000
Free: 800-253-4636
Publisher's E-mail: resource@acc.org
Audio journal covering interviews with leaders in the field of cardiovascular medicine. **Freq:** Monthly. **Key Personnel:** Alfred Bove, MD, Editor-in-Chief. **Subscription Rates:** $399.89 Individuals online; $449.89 Individuals CD; $471.89 Canada CD; $519.89 Other countries CD. **Alt. Formats:** CD-ROM; Print. **URL:** http://www.audio-digest.org/cgi-bin/htmlos/current/ACCEL_landing.html. **Remarks:** Advertising not accepted. **Circ:** (Not Reported).

6417 ■ Access Management Journal
National Association of Healthcare Access Management
2025 M St. NW, Ste. 800
Washington, DC 20036-2422
Phone: (202)367-1125
Fax: (202)367-2125
Publisher's E-mail: info@naham.org
Freq: Quarterly. **ISSN:** 0894--1068 (print). **Subscription Rates:** Included in membership. **URL:** http://www.naham.org/?page=ArticleGuidelines. **Remarks:** Accepts advertising. **Circ:** (Not Reported).

6418 ■ ACE Presidency
American Council on Education
1 Dupont Cir. NW
Washington, DC 20036
Phone: (202)939-9300
Magazine covering critical issues that affect higher education leaders. **Freq:** Quarterly. **Subscription Rates:** $30 U.S. /year for members; $60 Other countries /year for members; $40 Nonmembers; $70 Nonmembers other countries. **URL:** http://www.acenet.edu/the-presidency/Pages/Summer-2014.aspx. **Remarks:** Advertising accepted; rates available upon request. **Circ:** (Not Reported).

6419 ■ ACOG Obstetrics and Gynecology
American Congress of Obstetricians and Gynecologists
409 12th St. SW
Washington, DC 20024-2188
Phone: (202)638-5577
Free: 800-673-8444
Publisher's E-mail: exbd@acog.org
Freq: Monthly. **ISSN:** 0029--7844 (print). **Subscription Rates:** Included in membership. **URL:** http://www.acog.org/About-ACOG/Green-Journal-Info. **Also known as:** The Green Journal. **Mailing address:** PO Box 70620, Washington, DC 20024-9998. **Remarks:** Accepts advertising. **Circ:** (Not Reported).

6420 ■ ACS Chemical Biology
American Chemical Society
1155 16th St. NW
Washington, DC 20036
Phone: (202)872-4600
Free: 800-227-5558
Publisher's E-mail: help@acs.org
Journal exploring cellular function from both chemical and biological perspectives. **Freq:** Monthly. **Print Method:** Offset. **Trim Size:** 8 x 10 3/4. **Cols./Page:** 3. **Col. Width:** 2 1/4 inches. **Col. Depth:** 10 inches. **Key Personnel:** Laura L. Kiessling, Editor-in-Chief. **ISSN:** 1554--8929 (print). **Subscription Rates:** Included in membership. **URL:** http://pubs.acs.org/journal/acbcct. **Circ:** (Not Reported).

6421 ■ ACS Sensors
American Chemical Society
1155 16th St. NW
Washington, DC 20036
Phone: (202)872-4600
Free: 800-227-5558
Publisher's E-mail: help@acs.org
Peer-reviewed journal containing research on all aspects of sensor science that selectively sense chemical or biological species or processes. **Freq:** Monthly. **EISSN:** 2379--3694 (electronic). **Subscription Rates:** $99 Members. **URL:** http://pubs.acs.org/journal/ascefj. **Circ:** (Not Reported).

6422 ■ ACTEC Journal
American College of Trust and Estate Counsel
901 15th St. NW, Ste. 525
Washington, DC 20005
Phone: (202)684-8460
Fax: (202)684-8459
Publisher's E-mail: info@actec.org
Professional journal covering changes in tax and nontax estate planning law for probate attorneys. **Freq:** Quarterly. **Key Personnel:** Edward Middleton Manigault, Associate Editor; Stephen R. Akers, Editor. **Subscription Rates:** Free ACTEC fellows. **URL:** http://www.actec.org/publications. **Formerly**: ACTEC Notes. **Remarks:** Advertising not accepted. **Circ:** (Not Reported).

6423 ■ Ad Astra
National Space Society
PO Box 98106
Washington, DC 20090-8106
Phone: (202)429-1600
Fax: (703)435-4390
Publication E-mail: adastra@nss.org
Freq: Quarterly. **Print Method:** Web offset. **Trim Size:** 8 1/4 x 10 7/8. **Cols./Page:** 3. **Key Personnel:** Katherine Brick, Editor. **ISSN:** 1041--102X (print). **Subscription Rates:** Included in membership included in membership dues; $35 Individuals; $3.50 Single issue for non members. **URL:** http://www.nss.org/adastra/. **Ad Rates:** BW $3000; 4C $3700. **Remarks:** Advertising accepted; rates available upon request. **Circ:** 30000.

6424 ■ Administrative Law Review
American Bar Association
Washington College of Law
American University
4801 Massachusetts Ave. NW, Ste. 622
Washington, DC 20016
Phone: (202)274-4000
Journal for lawyers and legal professionals dealing with the area of administrative law. **Freq:** Quarterly. **Key Personnel:** Stacy L.Z. Edwards, Editor-in-Chief; Keeley McCarty, Executive Editor; Brittany Ericksen, Managing Editor. **ISSN:** 0001--8368 (print). **Subscription Rates:** $40 Nonmembers /year, United States; $45 Nonmembers /year, outside United States and U.S. possessions; $10 Members /year (included in $35 dues); $3 Students /year (included in $10 dues); $10 Single issue. **Online:** LexisNexis; Westlaw; American University Washington College of Law American University Washington College of Law. **URL:** http://www.administrativelawreview.org; http://wcl.american.edu/journal/alr. **Remarks:** Advertising not accepted. **Circ:** (Not Reported).

6425 ■ The Advance
Council for Christian Colleges and Universities
321 8th St. NE
Washington, DC 20002
Phone: (202)546-8713
Fax: (202)546-8913
Publisher's E-mail: council@cccu.org
Magazine covering news and people of Christ-centered higher education. **Freq:** Semiannual spring and fall. **URL:** http://www.cccu.org/news/advance/Spring_2015. **Remarks:** Accepts advertising. **Circ:** (Not Reported).

6426 ■ Advances in Optics and Photonics
Optical Society of America
2010 Massachusetts Ave. NW
Washington, DC 20036
Phone: (202)223-8130
Fax: (202)223-1096
Publisher's E-mail: info@osa.org
Peer-reviewed journal featuring articles on optics and photonics technology. **Freq:** Quarterly. **Key Personnel:** Govind Agrawal, Editor-in-Chief. **EISSN:** 1943--8206 (electronic). **URL:** http://www.opticsinfobase.org/aop/home.cfm. **Circ:** (Not Reported).

6427 ■ Advancing Microelectronics
International Microelectronic and Packaging Society
611 2nd St. NE
Washington, DC 20002-4909
Phone: (202)548-4001
Fax: (202)548-6115
Free: 888-464-1066
Publisher's E-mail: modonoghue@imaps.org
Magazine covering information on technical and business-related information on the microelectronics and electronic packaging industries. **Freq:** 6/year January/February, March/April, May/June, July/August, September/October, and November/December. **Subscription Rates:** Included in membership; $75 Nonmembers print. **Alt. Formats:** PDF. **URL:** http://www.imaps.org/advancingmicro.htm. **Remarks:** Accepts advertising. **Circ:** (Not Reported).

6428 ■ Affordable Housing Finance
DoveTale Publishers
1 Thomas Cir. NW
Washington, DC 20005
Phone: (202)339-0744
Fax: (202)785-1974
Free: 877-275-8647
Publication E-mail: ahf@omeda.com
Journal providing information on financiers of affordable housing loans. **Freq:** 12/yr. **Key Personnel:** Robert M. Britt, Publisher. **Subscription Rates:** Free. **URL:** http://www.housingfinance.com/ahf/about.html. **Remarks:** Advertising accepted; rates available upon request. **Circ:** (Not Reported).

6429 ■ AfricaFocus
AfricaFocus
3509 Connecticut Ave. NW
Washington, DC 20008-2400
Newspaper focusing on topics of continent-wide concern with implications for international and U.S. policy. **Key Personnel:** William Minter, Editor. **Mailing address:** PO Box 540, Washington, DC 20008-2400. **Remarks:** Advertising not accepted. **Circ:** (Not Reported).

6430 ■ African Travel
Africa Travel Association
1100 17th St. NW, Ste. 1000
Washington, DC 20036
Phone: (202)835-1115
Fax: (202)835-1117
Free: 888-439-0478
Publisher's E-mail: info@africatravelassociation.org
Magazine featuring travel, tourism and transport to and within Africa. **Freq:** Quarterly. **URL:** http://www.africa-ata.org/bulletins.htm. **Remarks:** Accepts advertising. **Circ:** (Not Reported).

6431 ■ Afro-American Historical and Genealogical Society Journal
Afro-American Historical and Genealogical Society
PO Box 73067
Washington, DC 20056-3067
Phone: (202)234-5350
Publisher's E-mail: info@aahgs.org
Scholarly journal covering Afro-American history and genealogy. **Freq:** Semiannual. **Key Personnel:** Cassandra Davis, Editor. **URL:** http://www.aahgs.org/index.cfm?fuseaction=Page.ViewPage&pageId=590. **Remarks:** Advertising not accepted. **Circ:** Paid 910.

6432 ■ AFSCME Works: The Magazine of the American Federation of State, County and Municipal Employees, AFL-CIO
American Federation of State, County and Municipal Employees
1625 L St. NW
Washington, DC 20036-5687
Phone: (202)429-1000
Fax: (202)429-1293
Magazine providing news and features of concern to members of AFSCME. **Freq:** Quarterly. **Print Method:** Offset. **Trim Size:** 8 1/2 x 11. **Cols./Page:** 3. **Col. Width:** 14 picas. **Col. Depth:** 58 picas. **ISSN:** 1062--5992 (print). **URL:** http://www.afscme.org/news/publications/newsletters/works. **Formerly**: The Public Employee Magazine. **Remarks:** Advertising accepted; rates available upon request. **Circ:** ‡1400000.

6433 ■ AG Bell Volta Voices
Alexander Graham Bell Association for the Deaf and Hard of Hearing
3417 Volta Pl. NW
Washington, DC 20007
Phone: (202)337-5220

Publisher's E-mail: info@agbell.org

Freq: Quarterly. **Alt. Formats:** PDF. **URL:** http://www.agbell.org/Volta-Voices. **Remarks:** Accepts advertising. **Circ:** (Not Reported).

6434 ■ Agricultural Research
U.S. Government Publishing Office
732 N Capitol St. NW
Washington, DC 20401-0001
Phone: (202)512-1800
Fax: (202)512-2104
Free: 866-512-1800
Publisher's E-mail: contactcenter@gpo.gov
Research reports compiled by the U.S. Dept. of Agriculture. **Founded:** 1953. **Freq:** Bimonthly. **Print Method:** Offset. **Cols./Page:** 3. **Col. Width:** 28 nonpareils. **Col. Depth:** 126 agate lines. **Alt. Formats:** PDF. **URL:** http://www.ars.usda.gov/is/AR/. **Mailing address:** PO Box 979050, Saint Louis, MO 63197-9000. **Circ:** 1263.

6435 ■ AHIP Coverage
America's Health Insurance Plans
South Bldg., Ste. 500
601 Pennsylvania Ave. NW
Washington, DC 20004
Phone: (202)778-3200
Fax: (202)331-7487
Publisher's E-mail: ahip@ahip.org
Freq: Bimonthly. **Subscription Rates:** $60 /year. **URL:** http://www.ahipcoverage.org. **Remarks:** Advertising not accepted. **Circ:** (Not Reported).

6436 ■ AHLA Connections
American Health Lawyers Association
1620 Eye St. NW, 6th Fl.
Washington, DC 20006-4010
Phone: (202)833-1100
Fax: (202)833-1105
Freq: Monthly. **Subscription Rates:** Included in membership. **URL:** http://www.healthlawyers.org/News/Connections/Pages/default.aspx. **Remarks:** Advertising not accepted. **Circ:** (Not Reported).

6437 ■ Air Line Pilot
Air Line Pilots Association International
1625 Massachusetts Ave. NW
Washington, DC 20036
Phone: (703)689-2270
Publication E-mail: magazine@alpa.org
Magazine covering aviation industry trends and developments, flight technology, air safety; and pilot career matters. **Freq:** Monthly June and July is one issue. **Print Method:** Web offset. **Trim Size:** 8 1/4 x 10 7/8. **Cols./Page:** 3. **Col. Width:** 26 nonpareils. **Col. Depth:** 118 agate lines. **Key Personnel:** Pete Janhunen, Manager, Communications; Gary J. DiNunno, Editor-in-Chief. **ISSN:** 0002--242X (print). **URL:** http://www.alpa.org/news-and-events/air-line-pilot-magazine. **Remarks:** Accepts advertising. **Circ:** (Not Reported).

6438 ■ Air & Space
Smithsonian Institution Press
SI Building, Room 153, MRC 010
Washington, DC 20013-7012
Phone: (202)633-1000
Fax: (202)633-5285
Publisher's E-mail: info@si.edu
Magazine emphasizing the human stories as well as the technology of aviation and spaceflight. **Founded:** Apr. 1996. **Freq:** Bimonthly. **Key Personnel:** Linda Musser Shiner, Editor; Paul Hoversten, Executive Editor. **Subscription Rates:** $22 Individuals; $28 Canada; $28 Other countries. **URL:** http://www.airspacemag.com/. **Mailing address:** PO Box 37012, Washington, DC 20013-7012. **Ad Rates:** BW $15,285; 4C $22,815. **Remarks:** Accepts advertising. **Circ:** (Not Reported).

6439 ■ Alcohol Research and Health
U.S. Government Publishing Office
732 N Capitol St. NW
Washington, DC 20401-0001
Phone: (202)512-1800
Fax: (202)512-2104
Free: 866-512-1800
Publisher's E-mail: contactcenter@gpo.gov
Magazine presenting results of alcohol research. **Freq:** Quarterly. **Print Method:** Offset. **Cols./Page:** 2. **Col. Width:** 37 nonpareils. **Col. Depth:** 112 agate lines. **ISSN:** 6010-4319 (print). **Subscription Rates:** $33 Individuals; $12 Single issue; $16.80 Single issue in other countries; $33 Other countries. **URL:** http://bookstore.gpo.gov/products/sku/717-004-00000-1?ctid=. **Formerly:** Alcohol, Health and Research World. **Mailing address:** PO Box 979050, Saint Louis, MO 63197-9000. **Circ:** (Not Reported).

6440 ■ Alliance for Children & Families Magazine
Alliance for Strong Families and Communities
1020 19th St. NW, Ste. 500
Washington, DC 20036
Phone: (414)359-1040
Free: 800-221-3726
Magazine covering family issues. **Freq:** Quarterly. **Print Method:** offset. **Trim Size:** 8-1/2" x 11". **Key Personnel:** Nicole Klaas, Managing Editor. **Subscription Rates:** Included in membership. **URL:** http://www.alliance1.org/pubs/magazine. **Ad Rates:** 4C $2,000. **Remarks:** Accepts advertising. **Circ:** 13500, 350.

6441 ■ Almanac of Higher Education
National Education Association
1201 16th St. NW
Washington, DC 20036-3290
Phone: (202)833-4000
Fax: (202)822-7974
Publisher's E-mail: highered@nea.org
Journal covering issues in higher education. **Freq:** Annual. **ISSN:** 0743--670X (print). **Subscription Rates:** Included in membership. **Alt. Formats:** PDF. **URL:** http://www.nea.org/home/1819.htm. **Remarks:** Advertising not accepted. **Circ:** 85000, 85000.

6442 ■ Amber Waves: The Economics of Food, Farming, Natural Resources, and Rural America
United States Department of Agriculture
1400 Independence Ave. SW
Washington, DC 20250
Phone: (202)720-2791
Publication E-mail: amberwaveseditor@ers.usda.gov.
Trade publication on the economics of food, farming, natural resources, and rural America. **Freq:** Monthly. **Print Method:** Sheetfed. **Key Personnel:** Stephen Crutchfield, Board Member; Dale Simms, Managing Editor. **ISSN:** 1545--875X (print). **Online:** Gale GRP. **URL:** http://www.ers.usda.gov/amber-waves/about.aspx#.VfFbhdKqqko. **Remarks:** Advertising not accepted. **Circ:** (Not Reported).

6443 ■ The American Acupuncturist
American Association of Acupuncture and Oriental Medicine
PO Box 96503, No. 44144
Washington, DC 20090-6503
Fax: (866)455-7999
Free: 866-455-7999
Publisher's E-mail: info@aaaomonline.org
Freq: Quarterly. **Alt. Formats:** Electronic publishing. **URL:** http://www.aaaomonline.org/?page=ameracu. **Remarks:** Advertising not accepted. **Circ:** ‡7000.

6444 ■ American Annals of the Deaf
Conference of Educational Administrators Serving the Deaf
Gallaudet University Press
Denison House
Washington, DC 20002
Phone: (202)651-5488
Fax: (202)651-5489
Publisher's E-mail: valencia.simmons@gallaudet.edu
Journal focusing on education of the deaf. **Freq:** Quarterly. **Print Method:** Offset. Uses mats. **Trim Size:** 8 1/2 x 11. **Cols./Page:** 3. **Col. Width:** 42 nonpareils. **Col. Depth:** 121 agate lines. **Key Personnel:** Peter V. Paul, Editor, phone: (614)292-8059; Kathleen Arnos, Board Member; Thomas Allen, Board Member. **ISSN:** 0002--726X (print). **Subscription Rates:** $55 Individuals; $95 Institutions; $50 Members; $50 Students; $75 Other countries; $115 Institutions, other countries; $35 Individuals reference issue only. **URL:** http://gupress.gallaudet.edu/annals. **Ad Rates:** BW $435. **Remarks:** Accepts advertising. **Circ:** ‡3000.

6445 ■ American Antiquity
Society for American Archaeology
1111 14th St. NW, Ste. 800
Washington, DC 20005-5622
Phone: (202)789-8200
Fax: (202)789-0284
Publisher's E-mail: headquarters@saa.org
Journal on the archaeology of the New World. **Freq:** Quarterly. **Print Method:** Offset. **Trim Size:** 7 x 10. **Cols./Page:** 2. **Col. Width:** 16.5 picas. **Col. Depth:** 140 agate lines. **Key Personnel:** Robert L. Kelly, Editor. **ISSN:** 0002--7316 (print). **URL:** http://www.saa.org/AbouttheSociety/Publications/AmericanAntiquity.aspx. **Ad Rates:** BW $615. **Remarks:** Accepts advertising. **Circ:** ‡6600.

6446 ■ American Bicyclist
League of American Bicyclists
1612 K St. NW, Ste. 308
Washington, DC 20006-2849
Phone: (202)822-1333
Publisher's E-mail: bikeleague@bikeleague.org
Freq: Bimonthly. **Subscription Rates:** Included in membership. **Alt. Formats:** PDF. **Ad Rates:** 4C $1500. **Remarks:** Accepts advertising. **Circ:** 40000.

6447 ■ American Coal
American Coal Council
1101 Pennsylvania Ave. NW, Ste. 600
Washington, DC 20004
Phone: (202)756-4540
Fax: (202)756-7323
Publisher's E-mail: info@americancoalcouncil.org
Magazine featuring the latest information on energy/coal industry. **Freq:** Semiannual. **Key Personnel:** Jason Hayes, Editor. **URL:** http://www.americancoalcouncil.org/?page=mag. **Remarks:** Accepts advertising. **Circ:** (Not Reported).

6448 ■ American Criminal Law Review
Georgetown University Law Center
600 New Jersey Ave. NW
Washington, DC 20001
Phone: (202)662-9000
Publication E-mail: aclr@law.georgetown.edu
Periodical covering criminal law in the U.S. **Freq:** Quarterly. **Key Personnel:** Aiysha S. Hussain, Editor-in-Chief; Allison C. White, Managing Editor; Katherine S. Dumouchel, Editor. **ISSN:** 0164-0364 (print). **Subscription Rates:** $50 Individuals; $65 Other countries. **URL:** http://www.law.georgetown.edu/academics/law-journals/aclr/. **Circ:** (Not Reported).

6449 ■ American Educational Research Journal
American Educational Research Association
1430 K St. NW, Ste. 1200
Washington, DC 20005-2504
Phone: (202)238-3200
Fax: (202)238-3250
Publisher's E-mail: webmaster@aera.net
Educational research journal. **Freq:** Bimonthly. **Key Personnel:** Mark Berends, Editor. **ISSN:** 0002--8312 (print); **EISSN:** 1935--1011 (electronic). **Subscription Rates:** £44 Institutions print & e-access; £549 Institutions e-access; £598 Institutions print only; £610 Individuals print & e-access; £110 Institutions single issue; £10 Individuals single issue. **URL:** http://aer.sagepub.com. **Ad Rates:** BW $740; 4C $1185. **Remarks:** Color advertising not accepted. **Circ:** ‡19800.

6450 ■ American Educator
American Federation of Teachers
555 New Jersey Ave. NW
Washington, DC 20001
Phone: (202)879-4400
Publisher's E-mail: online@aft.org
Freq: Quarterly. **ISSN:** 0148--432X (print). **Subscription Rates:** Free. **Alt. Formats:** PDF. **URL:** http://www.aft.org/our-news/periodicals/american-educator. **Remarks:** Accepts advertising. **Circ:** (Not Reported).

6451 ■ American Forests
American Forests
1220 L St. NW, Ste. 750
Washington, DC 20005
Phone: (202)737-1944
Publisher's E-mail: info@americanforests.org
Magazine of trees and forests for people who know and appreciate the many benefits of trees. **Freq:** Quarterly. **Print Method:** Offset. **Trim Size:** 8 x 10 7/8. **Cols./Page:** 2. **Key Personnel:** Deborah Gangloff, Executive Director. **ISSN:** 0002--8541 (print). **URL:** http://www.americanforests.org/our-programs/american-forests-

Circulation: ★ = AAM; △ or • = BPA; ♦ = CAC; ❑ = VAC; ⊕ = PO Statement; ‡ = Publisher's Report; Boldface figures = sworn; Light figures = estimated.

publications/magazine. **Ad Rates:** BW $1372; 4C $2118. **Remarks:** Accepts advertising. **Circ:** ‡25000.

6452 ■ American Gas: The Monthly Magazine of the American Gas Association
American Gas Association
400 N Capitol St. NW
Washington, DC 20001
Phone: (202)824-7000
Magazine for gas distribution and transmission industry senior and mid-level executives focusing on business, legislative, regulatory, and technical issues. **Freq:** Monthly. **Print Method:** Web. **Trim Size:** 8 3/8 x 10 7/8. **Key Personnel:** Tracy Burleson, Director, Communications. **ISSN:** 0885--2413 (print). **Subscription Rates:** $59 U.S. and Canada; $110 Other countries. **URL:** http://www.aga.org/newsroom/american-gas-magazine; http://amgas.org. **Formerly:** AGA Monthly. **Ad Rates:** BW $4475. **Remarks:** Accepts advertising. **Circ:** (Not Reported).

6453 ■ The American Herald
American Heraldry Society
PO Box 96503
Washington, DC 20090-6503
Freq: Annual. **ISSN:** 1948-5611 (print); **EISSN:** 1948-9587 (electronic). **URL:** http://www.americanheraldry.org/pages/index.php?n=Publications.Journal. **Remarks:** Advertising not accepted. **Circ:** (Not Reported).

6454 ■ The American Historical Review: Journal of the American Historical Association
American Historical Association
400 A St. SE
Washington, DC 20003-3889
Phone: (202)544-2422
Fax: (202)544-8307
Publication E-mail: ahr@indiana.edu
Scholarly journal. **Freq:** 5/year (Feb., Apr., Jun., Oct., Dec.). **Print Method:** Offset. **Trim Size:** 7 1/4 x 10 1/4. **Cols./Page:** 2 and 1. **Col. Width:** 16.5 and 32 picas. **Col. Depth:** 52 and 52 picas. **Key Personnel:** Robert A. Schneider, Editor; Moureen Coulter, Editor. **ISSN:** 0002--8762 (print). **Subscription Rates:** Included in membership. **URL:** http://www.historians.org/publications-and-directories/american-historical-review. **Ad Rates:** BW $1115; 4C $1815. **Remarks:** Accepts advertising. **Circ:** Controlled ‡17094.

6455 ■ American Intellectual Property Law Association Quarterly Journal
George Washington University Law School
2000 H St. NW
Washington, DC 20052
Phone: (202)994-6261
Fax: (202)994-8980
Publisher's E-mail: jdadmit@law.gwu.edu
Journal presenting materials relating to intellectual property matters. **Freq:** Quarterly. **Key Personnel:** Joan E. Schaffner, Editor-in-Chief. **Subscription Rates:** $95 Libraries; $105 Individuals foreign; $25 Single issue. **URL:** http://www.aipla.org/learningcenter/library/books/qj/Pages/default.aspx. **Circ:** (Not Reported).

6456 ■ The American Interest: Policy, Politics & Culture
The American Interest
1730 Rhode Island Ave. NW, Ste. 707
Washington, DC 20036
Phone: (202)223-4408
Fax: (202)223-4489
Magazine exploring the theme of "America in the world" and presenting ideas from all points on the political spectrum. **Freq:** 6/year. **Key Personnel:** Charles Davidson, Chief Executive Officer, Publisher; Adam Garfinkle, Editor; Daniel Kennelly, Managing Editor. **Subscription Rates:** $81 Individuals /year; print + online; $2.99 Individuals /month; online only. **URL:** http://www.the-american-interest.com. **Remarks:** Accepts advertising. **Circ:** (Not Reported).

6457 ■ American Journal on Intellectual and Developmental Disabilities
American Association on Intellectual and Developmental Disabilities
501 3rd St. NW, Ste. 200
Washington, DC 20001
Phone: (202)387-1968
Fax: (202)387-2193
Freq: Bimonthly. **ISSN:** 1944- 7515 (print); **EISSN:** 1944-7558 (electronic). **Subscription Rates:** $420 /year. **URL:** http://aaidd.org/publications/journals#.VUizN47t2ko. **Ad Rates:** $315-1000, for display advertisng; $400-850. BW $, for display advertisng4C $. **Remarks:** Accepts display and classified advertising. **Circ:** 2055.

6458 ■ American Journal of International Law
American Society of International Law
2223 Massachusetts Ave. NW
Washington, DC 20008
Phone: (202)939-6000
Fax: (202)797-7133
Legal journal including research articles, current developments, judicial decisions, and book reviews written by leading scholars and practitioners of international law. **Freq:** Quarterly. **Print Method:** Offset. **Trim Size:** 6 7/8 x 10 1/4. **Cols./Page:** 1. **Col. Width:** 55 nonpareils. **Col. Depth:** 108 agate lines. **Key Personnel:** Prof. Jose Alvarez, Editor-in-Chief; Prof. Benedict Kingsbury, Editor-in-Chief. **ISSN:** 0002--9300 (print). **Subscription Rates:** $250 Nonmembers /year; $225 Nonmembers for electronic delivery plus $40 for shipping beyond US; Included in membership. **URL:** http://www.asil.org/resources/american-journal-international-law. **Ad Rates:** BW $460. **Remarks:** Accepts advertising. **Circ:** ‡6800, 6600.

6459 ■ American Journal of Obstetrics and Gynecology
Society for Maternal-Fetal Medicine
409 12th St. SW
Washington, DC 20024
Phone: (202)863-2476
Fax: (202)554-1132
Publication E-mail: usjcs@elsevier.com
Freq: Periodic 15/yr. **Print Method:** Offset. **Trim Size:** 8 1/8 x 10 7/8. **Cols./Page:** 2. **Col. Width:** 39 nonpareils. **Col. Depth:** 140 agate lines. **Key Personnel:** Ingrid E. Nygaard, MD, Editor-in-Chief; Roberto Romero, MD, Editor-in-Chief; Sandra Perrine, Managing Editor. **ISSN:** 0002--9378 (print). **Subscription Rates:** $430 Individuals print + online; $550 Other countries print + online; $199 Students print + online; $261 Students, other countries print + online. **URL:** http://www.ajog.org. **Ad Rates:** BW $4740; 4C $2815. **Remarks:** Accepts advertising. **Circ:** △43383.

6460 ■ American Journal of Preventive Medicine
Association for Prevention Teaching and Research
1001 Connecticut Ave. NW, Ste. 610
Washington, DC 20036
Phone: (202)463-0550
Fax: (202)463-0555
Free: 866-520-2787
Publisher's E-mail: info@aptrweb.org
Journal Covering basic and applied sciences that contribute to the promotion of health and the prevention of disease, disability, and premature death. **Freq:** Monthly. **Print Method:** Offset. **Trim Size:** 8 1/2 x 11. **Key Personnel:** Matthew L. Boulton, MD, Editor-in-Chief; R.B. Wallace, MD, Associate Editor; Jillian Morgan, Managing Editor. **ISSN:** 0749--3797 (print). **Subscription Rates:** $421 Other countries print and online; $393 Individuals print and online; $421 Canada print and online; Free to members. **URL:** http://www.ajpmonline.org; http://www.journals.elsevier.com/american-journal-of-preventive-medicine. **Ad Rates:** 4C $1,535. **Remarks:** Accepts advertising. **Circ:** Paid ‡2740.

6461 ■ American Journal of Public Health
American Public Health Association
800 I St. NW
Washington, DC 20001
Phone: (202)777-2742
Fax: (202)777-2534
Publisher's E-mail: comments@apha.org
Public health journal. **Freq:** Monthly. **Print Method:** Offset. **Trim Size:** 8 1/4 x 11. **Cols./Page:** 3. **ISSN:** 0090--0036 (print); **EISSN:** 1541--0048 (electronic). **Subscription Rates:** $515 Institutions print. **URL:** http://www.apha.org/publications-and-periodicals/american-journal-of-public-health. **Ad Rates:** GLR $3.50; BW $1500; 4C $3550. **Remarks:** Accepts advertising. **Circ:** (Not Reported).

6462 ■ American Mathematical Monthly
Mathematical Association of America
1529 18th St. NW
Washington, DC 20036-1358
Phone: (202)387-5200
Fax: (202)265-2384
Free: 800-741-9415
Publisher's E-mail: maahq@maa.org
A journal of mathematical exposition. Each issue includes articles on new developments on mathematical research, reviews of fields that are in interesting states of development, shorter mathematical notes that display interesting viewpoints on parts of mathematics. **Freq:** Monthly. **Print Method:** Offset. **Cols./Page:** 1. **Col. Width:** 65 nonpareils. **Col. Depth:** 115 agate lines. **Key Personnel:** Scott Chapman, Editor, phone: (936)294-1572, fax: (936)294-1882. **Subscription Rates:** Included in membership. **URL:** http://www.maa.org/press/periodicals/american-mathematical-monthly. **Ad Rates:** BW $1635. **Remarks:** Accepts advertising. **Circ:** ‡12000.

6463 ■ American Outlook
Hudson Institute
1201 Pennsylvania Ave. NW, Ste. 400
Washington, DC 20004
Phone: (202)974-2400
Fax: (202)974-2410
Publisher's E-mail: info@hudson.org
Magazine covering public policy in the U.S. **Freq:** Quarterly. **Key Personnel:** Jay F. Hein, Editor-in-Chief. **URL:** http://www.americanoutlook.org. **Remarks:** Advertising accepted; rates available upon request. **Circ:** (Not Reported).

6464 ■ The American Postal Worker
American Postal Workers Union
1300 L St. NW
Washington, DC 20005
Phone: (202)842-4250
AFL-CIO postal labor. **Freq:** Bimonthly. **Print Method:** Offset. **Trim Size:** 11 1/2 x 17. **Cols./Page:** 4. **Col. Width:** 33 nonpareils. **Col. Depth:** 187 agate lines. **ISSN:** 0044--7811 (print). **Subscription Rates:** Accessible only to members. **URL:** http://www.apwu.org/magazines. **Remarks:** Advertising not accepted. **Circ:** 300000.

6465 ■ American Psychologist
American Psychological Association
750 1st St. NE
Washington, DC 20002-4242
Phone: (202)336-5500
Free: 800-374-2721
Official journal of the association. Publishes empirical, theoretical, and professional articles. **Freq:** 9/year. **Key Personnel:** Anne E. Kazak, Editor-in-Chief. **ISSN:** 0003--066X (print); **EISSN:** 1935--990X (electronic). **Subscription Rates:** $1399 Institutions; $1509 Institutions, other countries; $1541 Institutions, other countries airmail. **URL:** http://www.apa.org/pubs/journals/amp. **Ad Rates:** BW $1440; 4C $2415. **Remarks:** Accepts advertising. **Circ:** ‡80000.

6466 ■ American Quarterly
American Studies Association
1120 19th St. NW, Ste. 301
Washington, DC 20036
Phone: (202)467-4783
Fax: (202)467-4786
Publication E-mail: american.quarterly@usc.edu
Journal on American culture. **Freq:** Quarterly. **Print Method:** Offset. **Trim Size:** 6 x 9. **Cols./Page:** 1. **Col. Width:** 26 picas. **Col. Depth:** 7 inches. **Key Personnel:** Cotten Seiler, Editor; Sarah Banet-Weiser, Editor; Jih-Fei Cheng, Managing Editor. **ISSN:** 0003--0678 (print); **EISSN:** 1080--6490 (electronic). **Subscription Rates:** $185 Institutions print; $370 Institutions print, 2 years; Included in membership; $38 Individuals. **URL:** http://www.press.jhu.edu/journals/american_quarterly/index.html; http://www.theasa.net/publications/page/american_quarterly; http://www.americanquarterly.org; http://muse.jhu.edu/journal/13. **Ad Rates:** BW $510, full page; BW $383, half page; BW $765, 2 page spread. **Remarks:** Accepts advertising. **Circ:** 4,513, 7,000.

6467 ■ American Review of Canadian Studies
Association for Canadian Studies in the United States
1740 Massachusetts Ave. NW, Nitze 516
Washington, DC 20036
Phone: (202)670-1424
Fax: (202)663-5717

Publisher's E-mail: info@acsus.org
Periodical covering the field of Canadian Studies. **Freq:** Quarterly. **Key Personnel:** David A. Rossiter, Editor; Catherine O'Mara Wallace, Managing Editor; Jeffrey Ayres, Associate Editor. **ISSN:** 0272--2011 (print); **EISSN:** 1943--9954 (electronic). **Subscription Rates:** $389 Institutions online only; $445 Institutions print and online. **URL:** http://www.tandfonline.com/toc/rarc20/current. **Remarks:** Accepts advertising. **Circ:** (Not Reported).

6468 ■ The American Scholar
The Phi Beta Kappa Society
1606 New Hampshire Ave. NW
Washington, DC 20009
Phone: (202)265-3808
Fax: (202)986-1601
Publisher's E-mail: info@pbk.org
Freq: Quarterly. **Print Method:** Web Offset. **Trim Size:** 6 7/8 x 10. **Cols./Page:** 2. **Col. Width:** 31 nonpareils. **Col. Depth:** 112 agate lines. **ISSN:** 0003--0937 (print). **Subscription Rates:** $31.99 Individuals print and online; $41.99 Canada print and online; $51.99 Other countries print and online. **URL:** http://theamericanscholar.org. **Ad Rates:** GLR $35; BW $730. **Remarks:** Advertising accepted; rates available upon request. **Circ:** ‡25000, 100000.

6469 ■ American Society for Microbiology News
American Society for Microbiology
1752 N St. NW
Washington, DC 20036-2904
Phone: (202)942-9207
Fax: (202)942-9333
Publisher's E-mail: service@asmusa.org
Freq: Monthly. **ISSN:** 0044--7897 (print). **URL:** http://asmscience.org/content/journal/microbe. **Remarks:** Accepts advertising. **Circ:** (Not Reported).

6470 ■ American Sociological Review
American Sociological Association
1430 K St. NW, Ste. 600
Washington, DC 20005
Phone: (202)383-9005
Fax: (202)638-0882
Publisher's E-mail: customer@asanet.org
Sociology journal. Focus is on issues with the most general bearing on the knowledge of society. **Freq:** Bimonthly February, April, June, August, October and December. **Print Method:** Offset. **Trim Size:** 6 3/4 x 9 7/8. **Cols./Page:** 2. **Col. Width:** 31 nonpareils. **Col. Depth:** 108 agate lines. **Key Personnel:** Omar Lizardo, Editor; Larry W. Isaac, Board Member; Tony N. Brown, Board Member. **ISSN:** 0003--1224 (print). **Subscription Rates:** $45 Members; $30 Students members; $630 Institutions print or online; $567 Institutions online only. **URL:** http://www.asanet.org/journals/asr/american_sociological_review.cfm. **Ad Rates:** BW $970. **Remarks:** Color advertising not accepted. **Circ:** ‡10000.

6471 ■ American Teacher
American Federation of Teachers
555 New Jersey Ave. NW
Washington, DC 20001
Phone: (202)879-4400
Publisher's E-mail: online@aft.org
Newspaper focusing on issues of education and the labor union. **Freq:** Monthly. **Print Method:** Offset. **Trim Size:** 8.38 x 10.88. **Cols./Page:** 5. **Col. Width:** 9.75 inches. **Col. Depth:** 169 agate lines. **Key Personnel:** Randi Weingarten, President. **ISSN:** 0003--1380 (print). **URL:** http://www.aft.org/periodical/american-teacher. **Ad Rates:** BW $12,320; 4C $15,000. **Remarks:** Accepts advertising. **Circ:** Paid ‡915000, 524700.

6472 ■ The American University Law Review
Joe Christensen Inc.
4801 Massachusetts Ave. NW, No. 621
Washington, DC 20016
Phone: (202)274-4433
Fax: (202)730-4703
Legal journal. **Freq:** Bimonthly. **Print Method:** Offset. **Trim Size:** 6 5/8 x 10. **Cols./Page:** 1. **Col. Width:** 57 nonpareils. **Col. Depth:** 112 agate lines. **Key Personnel:** Stephen M. Leblanc, Editor-in-Chief. **ISSN:** 0003--1453 (print). **Subscription Rates:** $45 Individuals domestic; $40 Individuals alumni; $50 Other countries; $25 Single issue. **URL:** http://www.wcl.american.edu/journal/lawrev/editors.cfm. **Ad Rates:** BW $100. **Remarks:** Accepts display advertising. **Circ:** Paid ‡570, Non-paid ‡700.

6473 ■ AMRPA
American Medical Rehabilitation Providers Association
c/o Carolyn C. Zollar, Vice President of Government Relations
1710 N St. NW
Washington, DC 20036
Phone: (202)223-1920
Fax: (202)223-1925
Free: 888-346-4624
Magazine covering insurance issues relevant to rehabilitation services. **Freq:** Monthly. **Subscription Rates:** free for members. **Alt. Formats:** PDF. **URL:** http://www.amrpa.org/Public/MagazineMain.aspx. **Remarks:** Advertising not accepted. **Circ:** (Not Reported).

6474 ■ Analyses of Social Issues and Public Policy
Society for the Psychological Study of Social Issues
208 I St. NE
Washington, DC 20002-4340
Phone: (202)675-6956
Fax: (202)675-6902
Free: 877-310-7778
Publisher's E-mail: customerservice@oxon.blackwellpublishing.com
Freq: Annual. **Key Personnel:** Heather Bullock, Editor-in-Chief. **ISSN:** 1529--7489 (print); **EISSN:** 1530--2415 (electronic). **URL:** http://onlinelibrary.wiley.com/journal/10.1111/(ISSN)1530-2415; http://www.spssi.org/index.cfm?fuseaction=page.viewpage&pageid=478. **Mailing address:** PO Box 1354, Oxford OX4 2ZG, United Kingdom. **Ad Rates:** 4C $335. **Remarks:** Accepts advertising. **Circ:** (Not Reported).

6475 ■ Annals of the Association of American Geographers
American Association of Geographers
1710 16th St. NW
Washington, DC 20009
Phone: (202)234-1450
Fax: (202)234-2744
Publisher's E-mail: gaia@aag.org
Geography journal. **Print Method:** Letterpress. **Trim Size:** 6 7/8 x 10. **Cols./Page:** 2. **Col. Width:** 35 nonpareils. **Col. Depth:** 115 agate lines. **Key Personnel:** Mark Fonstad, Editor; Mei-Po Kwan, Editor. **ISSN:** 0004--5608 (print); **EISSN:** 1467--8306 (electronic). **Subscription Rates:** Members free online access; $2979 Institutions online only; $3404 Institutions print and online. **URL:** http://www.aag.org/cs/publications/journals/annals; http://www.aag.org/cs/publications/annals; http://www.tandfonline.com/toc/raag20/current. **Also known as:** Annals of the AAG. **Ad Rates:** BW $675. **Remarks:** Accepts advertising. **Circ:** ‡8750.

6476 ■ Annual Energy Review
National Energy Information Center
Energy Information Administration, MS EI-30
1000 Independence Ave. SW
Washington, DC 20585
Phone: (202)586-8800
Fax: (202)586-0114
Publisher's E-mail: infoctr@eia.gov
Government publication covering energy and fuel data. **Founded:** May 1983. **Freq:** Annual. **URL:** http://www.eia.gov/totalenergy/data/annual/index.cfm. **Formerly:** Annual Report to Congress, Vol. II. **Remarks:** Advertising not accepted. **Circ:** (Not Reported).

6477 ■ Anthropological Quarterly
The George Washington University
1121 New Hampshire Ave., NW
Washington, DC 20037
Phone: (202)467-0867
Fax: (202)467-4283
Free: 800-321-6223
Publisher's E-mail: askncbe@ncbe.gwu.edu
Journal publishing articles, reviews, and lists of recently published books in all areas of socio-cultural anthropology. **Founded:** 1921. **Freq:** Quarterly. **Trim Size:** 7 1/2 x 9 1/2. **Cols./Page:** 2. **Col. Width:** 33 nonpareils. **Col. Depth:** 115 agate lines. **Key Personnel:** Roy Richard Grinker, Editor; Alexander S. Dent, Associate Editor; Stephen C. Lubkemann, Associate Editor. **ISSN:** 0003-5491 (print). **Subscription Rates:** $125 Individuals; $198 Institutions. **URL:** http://muse.jhu.edu/journals/anthropological_quarterly; http://aq.gwu.edu/. **Formerly:** Primitive Man. **Also known as:** AQ. **Remarks:** Accepts advertising. **Circ:** Paid ‡794, Non-paid ‡91.

6478 ■ Antimicrobial Agents and Chemotherapy
ASM Journals
1752 North St. NW
Washington, DC 20036
Phone: (202)737-3600
Fax: (202)942-9355
Publisher's E-mail: journals@asmusa.org
Journal devoted exclusively to all aspects of antimicrobial, antiviral, antiparasitic, and antimicrobial agents and chemotherapy. **Freq:** Monthly. **Print Method:** Offset. Uses mats. **Trim Size:** 8 1/8 x 10 7/8. **Cols./Page:** 2. **Col. Width:** 42 nonpareils. **Col. Depth:** 127 agate lines. **Key Personnel:** Henry F. Chambers, Editor; Paul G. Ambrose, Editor; Louis B. Rice, Editor-in-Chief. **ISSN:** 0066--4804 (print); **EISSN:** 1098--6596 (electronic). **Subscription Rates:** $796 Institutions online; 1-200 users; $1034 Institutions online; 201-1,500 users; $1346 Institutions online; 1,501-3,500 users. **URL:** http://aac.asm.org. **Ad Rates:** BW $1995. **Remarks:** Accepts advertising. **Circ:** Combined ‡11778.

6479 ■ Antimicrobial Agents and Chemotherapy
American Society for Microbiology
1752 N St. NW
Washington, DC 20036-2904
Phone: (202)942-9207
Fax: (202)942-9333
Publisher's E-mail: journals@asmusa.org
Journal devoted exclusively to all aspects of antimicrobial, antiviral, antiparasitic, and antimicrobial agents and chemotherapy. **Freq:** Monthly. **Print Method:** Offset. Uses mats. **Trim Size:** 8 1/8 x 10 7/8. **Cols./Page:** 2. **Col. Width:** 42 nonpareils. **Col. Depth:** 127 agate lines. **Key Personnel:** Henry F. Chambers, Editor; Paul G. Ambrose, Editor; Louis B. Rice, Editor-in-Chief. **ISSN:** 0066--4804 (print); **EISSN:** 1098--6596 (electronic). **Subscription Rates:** $796 Institutions online; 1-200 users; $1034 Institutions online; 201-1,500 users; $1346 Institutions online; 1,501-3,500 users. **URL:** http://aac.asm.org. **Ad Rates:** BW $1995. **Remarks:** Accepts advertising. **Circ:** Combined ‡11778.

6480 ■ APA Monitor
American Psychological Association
750 1st St. NE
Washington, DC 20002-4242
Phone: (202)336-5500
Free: 800-374-2721
Freq: Monthly. **ISSN:** 0001--2114 (print). **Subscription Rates:** Included in membership. **Remarks:** Accepts advertising. **Circ:** (Not Reported).

6481 ■ APARTMENT FINANCE TODAY
DoveTale Publishers
One Thomas Cir. NW, Ste. 600
Washington, DC 20005
Phone: (202)452-0800
Fax: (202)785-1974
Publisher's E-mail: hwmicustomerservice@hanleywood.com
Magazine featuring strategic financial decisions. **Freq:** Monthly. **Trim Size:** 8 x 10 1/2. **Key Personnel:** Rob Britt, Publisher. **Subscription Rates:** Free. **URL:** http://www.multifamilyexecutive.com/magazine/apartment-finance-today. **Ad Rates:** BW $6840; 4C $8285. **Remarks:** Accepts display and classified advertising. **Circ:** Combined ‡25000.

6482 ■ APIC American Journal of Infection Control
Association for Professionals in Infection Control and Epidemiology
1275 K St. NW, Ste. 1000
Washington, DC 20005-4006
Phone: (202)789-1890
Fax: (202)789-1899
Publisher's E-mail: info@apic.org
Freq: Monthly. **ISSN:** 0196--6553 (print). **Subscription Rates:** Included in membership print and online; $273 Nonmembers print and online (individuals and students); $351 Nonmembers print and online (Canada and other Countries; individuals and students); $232 Nonmembers

Circulation: ★ = AAM; △ or • = BPA; ♦ = CAC; ❑ = VAC; ⊕ = PO Statement; ‡ = Publisher's Report; Boldface figures = sworn; Light figures = estimated.

online only (U.S., Canada and other Countries, individuals and students). **URL:** http://www.apic.org/Professional-Practice/AJIC; http://www.apic.org/Member-Services/publications/AJIC. **Remarks:** Accepts advertising. **Circ:** (Not Reported).

6483 ■ Applied and Environmental Microbiology
ASM Journals
1752 North St. NW
Washington, DC 20036
Phone: (202)737-3600
Fax: (202)942-9355
Publisher's E-mail: journals@asmusa.org
Freq: Semimonthly. **Print Method:** Offset. Uses mats. **Trim Size:** 8 1/8 x 10 7/8. **Cols./Page:** 2. **Col. Width:** 42 nonpareils. **Col. Depth:** 127 agate lines. **Key Personnel:** Harold L. Drake, Editor-in-Chief. **ISSN:** 0099--2240 (print); **EISSN:** 1098--5336 (electronic). **Subscription Rates:** $1195 Institutions online; 1-200 users; $1552 Institutions online; 201-1,500 users; $2020 Institutions online;1,501-3.500 users. **URL:** http://aem.asm.org. **Ad Rates:** BW $1525; 4C $1010. **Remarks:** Accepts advertising. **Circ:** Combined ‡13507.

6484 ■ Applied and Environmental Microbiology
American Society for Microbiology
1752 N St. NW
Washington, DC 20036-2904
Phone: (202)942-9207
Fax: (202)942-9333
Publisher's E-mail: journals@asmusa.org
Freq: Semimonthly. **Print Method:** Offset. Uses mats. **Trim Size:** 8 1/8 x 10 7/8. **Cols./Page:** 2. **Col. Width:** 42 nonpareils. **Col. Depth:** 127 agate lines. **Key Personnel:** Harold L. Drake, Editor-in-Chief. **ISSN:** 0099--2240 (print); **EISSN:** 1098--5336 (electronic). **Subscription Rates:** $1195 Institutions online; 1-200 users; $1552 Institutions online; 201-1,500 users; $2020 Institutions online;1,501-3.500 users. **URL:** http://aem.asm.org. **Ad Rates:** BW $1525; 4C $1010. **Remarks:** Accepts advertising. **Circ:** Combined ‡13507.

6485 ■ Applied Optics
Optical Society of America
2010 Massachusetts Ave. NW
Washington, DC 20036
Phone: (202)223-8130
Fax: (202)223-1096
Publication E-mail: custserv@osa.org
Peer-reviewed journal covering all varieties and applications of optics including lasers, optical engineering, holography, quantum electronics, information processing, and meteorology. **Freq:** 36/yr. **Print Method:** Offset. **Trim Size:** 8 1/4 x 11 1/4. **Cols./Page:** 2. **Col. Width:** 40 nonpareils. **Col. Depth:** 140 agate lines. **Key Personnel:** Eugenio Mendez, Editor; Christopher Videll, Associate Director, phone: (202)416-1927; Ron Driggers, Editor-in-Chief. **ISSN:** 1559-128X (print); **EISSN:** 2155-3165 (electronic). **Subscription Rates:** $153 Individuals online only; $251 Members print and online; $471 Members Canada & Mexico, print and online; $736 Members Europe and Asia, print and online; $57 Students online only. **URL:** http://www.opticsinfobase.org/ao/home.cfm. **Remarks:** Advertising not accepted. **Circ:** 3200.

6486 ■ APS Observer
Association for Psychological Science
1800 Massachusetts Ave. NW, Ste. 402
Washington, DC 20036
Phone: (202)293-9300
Fax: (202)293-9350
Freq: Monthly. **ISSN:** 1050--4672 (print). **URL:** http://www.psychologicalscience.org/index.php/publications/observer. **Remarks:** Accepts advertising. **Circ:** (Not Reported).

6487 ■ APSA Perspectives on Politics
American Political Science Association
1527 New Hampshire Ave. NW
Washington, DC 20036-1206
Phone: (202)483-2512
Fax: (202)483-2657
Publisher's E-mail: apsa@apsanet.org
Freq: Quarterly March, June, September, December. **Key Personnel:** Jeffrey C. Isaac, Editor. **Subscription Rates:** Included in membership. **URL:** http://www.apsanet.org/perspectives. **Ad Rates:** BW $1,200. **Remarks:** Accepts advertising. **Circ:** 16000.

6488 ■ APWA Reporter
American Public Works Association
1275 K St. NW, Ste. 750
Washington, DC 20005
Phone: (202)408-9541
Fax: (202)408-9542
Publication E-mail: info@mohanna.com
Magazine reporting on public works. **Freq:** Monthly. **Print Method:** Offset. **Trim Size:** 8 1/8 x 10 7/8. **Cols./Page:** 3. **Col. Width:** 13 nonpareils. **Col. Depth:** 140 agate lines. **Key Personnel:** Kevin R. Clark, Editor. **ISSN:** 0092--4873 (print). **Subscription Rates:** Included in membership. **URL:** http://www.apwa.net/resources/reporter. **Remarks:** Advertising accepted; rates available upon request. **Circ:** (Not Reported).

6489 ■ Architect
DoveTale Publishers
1 Thomas Cir. NW
Washington, DC 20005
Phone: (202)339-0744
Fax: (202)785-1974
Free: 877-275-8647
Publisher's E-mail: hwmicustomerservice@hanleywood.com
Official publication of the American Institute of Architects. For architects, interior designers, engineers, and architectural students. **Founded:** Jan. 1913. **Freq:** Monthly. **Print Method:** Offset. **Trim Size:** 9 x 10 7/8. **Cols./Page:** 3. **Col. Width:** 2 1/2 inches. **Key Personnel:** Kriston Capps; Katie Gerfen; Ned Cramer, Editor-in-Chief; Greig O'Brien, Managing Editor; Dan Colunio, Publisher. **URL:** http://www.architectmagazine.com/. **Remarks:** Accepts advertising. **Circ:** 80000.

6490 ■ Architectural Lighting: The Lighting Specifiers Magazine
DoveTale Publishers
1 Thomas Cir. NW
Washington, DC 20005
Phone: (202)339-0744
Fax: (202)785-1974
Free: 877-275-8647
Publisher's E-mail: hwmicustomerservice@hanleywood.com
Magazine for professionals involved in the design, specification, and application of lighting. **Freq:** 7/year. **Print Method:** Web Offset. **Trim Size:** 8 1/8 x 10 7/8. **Cols./Page:** 2. **ISSN:** 0894-0436 (print). **USPS:** 000-846. **Subscription Rates:** $48 Individuals; $60 Canada; $96 Other countries. **URL:** http://www.archlighting.com/. **Remarks:** Accepts advertising. **Circ:** Non-paid 25000.

6491 ■ Archives of American Art Journal
Smithsonian Institution Archives of American Art
750 9th St. NW
Victor Bldg., Ste. 2200
Washington, DC 20013-7012
Phone: (202)633-7940
Fax: (202)633-7994
Scholarly journal covering American art history. **Freq:** Semiannual spring and fall. **Key Personnel:** Darcy Tell, Editor, phone: (202)633-7971; Jenifer Dismukes, Managing Editor. **Subscription Rates:** $30 Individuals online; $40 Individuals print and online. **Alt. Formats:** PDF. **URL:** http://www.aaa.si.edu/publications/journal. **Mailing address:** PO Box 37012, Washington, DC 20013-7012. **Remarks:** Advertising not accepted. **Circ:** (Not Reported).

6492 ■ Archon
Zeta Phi Beta Sorority, Inc.
1734 New Hampshire Ave. NW
Washington, DC 20009
Phone: (202)387-3103
Fax: (202)232-4593
Publisher's E-mail: info@zetaphibetasororityhq.org
College sorority magazine. Includes listing of employment opportunities. **Freq:** Semiannual. **URL:** http://www.zphib1920.org/. **Remarks:** Advertising not accepted. **Circ:** (Not Reported).

6493 ■ Arms Control Today
Arms Control Association
1313 L St. NW, Ste. 130
Washington, DC 20005
Phone: (202)463-8270
Fax: (202)463-8273
Publisher's E-mail: aca@armscontrol.org
Magazine focusing on arms control issues. **Freq:** 10/year. **Print Method:** Offset. **Trim Size:** 8 1/2 x 11. **Cols./Page:** 3. **Col. Width:** 28 nonpareils. **Col. Depth:** 98 agate lines. **Key Personnel:** Daniel Horner, Editor; Elisabeth Erickson, Managing Editor. **ISSN:** 0196--125X (print). **Subscription Rates:** $95 U.S. print + online; $115 Other countries print + online; $50 Individuals professional digital only. **URL:** http://www.armscontrol.org/act/current; http://legacy.armscontrol.org/act. **Ad Rates:** BW $400. **Remarks:** Accepts advertising. **Circ:** ‡3000, 1800.

6494 ■ Arts Link
Americans for the Arts
1000 Vermont Ave. NW, 6th Fl.
Washington, DC 20005
Phone: (202)371-2830
Fax: (202)371-0424
Freq: Quarterly. **Subscription Rates:** Included in membership. **URL:** http://www.americansforthearts.org/by-program/reports-and-data/research-studies-publications/americans-for-the-arts-publications/arts-link-magazine. **Remarks:** Advertising not accepted. **Circ:** (Not Reported).

6495 ■ ASAE Association Law and Policy
ASAE: The Center for Association Leadership
1575 I St. NW
Washington, DC 20005-1103
Phone: (202)371-0940
Fax: (202)371-8315
Free: 888-950-ASAE
Publisher's E-mail: asaeservice@asaecenter.org
Professional journal covering law issues. **Freq:** Monthly. **Key Personnel:** Joy Harper, Contact, phone: (202)626-2874; Joe Rominiecki, Contact, phone: (202)626-2734. **URL:** http://www.asaecenter.org. **Remarks:** Advertising not accepted. **Circ:** Non-paid 4000.

6496 ■ ASEE Prism
American Society for Engineering Education
1818 N St. NW, Ste. 600
Washington, DC 20036-2479
Phone: (202)331-3500
Publication E-mail: prism@asee.org
Professional magazine for educators in the field of engineering. **Freq:** 8/year. **Print Method:** Offset. **Trim Size:** 8 1/4 x 11. **Key Personnel:** Mark Matthews, Editor. **ISSN:** 1056--8077 (print). **USPS:** 000-7481. **Subscription Rates:** $225 Individuals domestic; $275 Other countries; $225 Libraries U.S. and Canada; included in membership dues. **URL:** http://www.asee.org/papers-and-publications/publications/prism; http://www.asee-prism.org. **Remarks:** Accepts advertising. **Circ:** 12000.

6497 ■ Aspen Idea
Aspen Institute
1 Dupont Cir. NW, Ste. 700
Washington, DC 20036-1133
Phone: (202)736-5800
Fax: (202)467-0790
Publisher's E-mail: info@aspenbsp.org
Freq: Semiannual. **URL:** http://www.aspeninstitute.org/about/#ideas. **Remarks:** Advertising not accepted. **Circ:** (Not Reported).

6498 ■ Association Management
ASAE: The Center for Association Leadership
1575 I St. NW
Washington, DC 20005-1103
Phone: (202)371-0940
Fax: (202)371-8315
Free: 888-950-ASAE
Publisher's E-mail: asaeservice@asaecenter.org
Freq: Monthly. **Subscription Rates:** Included in membership; $30 Nonmembers /year. **Alt. Formats:** CD-ROM. **URL:** http://www.asaecenter.org/resources. **Remarks:** Accepts advertising. **Circ:** (Not Reported).

6499 ■ ASTC Dimensions
Association of Science-Technology Centers
818 Connecticut Ave. NW, 7th Fl.
Washington, DC 20006
Phone: (202)783-7200
Fax: (202)783-7207
Publisher's E-mail: info@astc.org
Freq: Bimonthly. **ISSN:** 0895-7371 (print). **Subscription Rates:** $35 Students print in U.S.; $45 Students print outside U.S.; $60 Nonmembers print in U.S; $70 Nonmembers print outside U.S.; $35 Nonmembers

online; $29 Students online. **URL:** http://www.astc.org/pubs/dimensions.htm. **Ad Rates:** BW $1,500, member rate; BW $1,750, non-member rate. **Remarks:** Accepts advertising. **Circ:** 6000.

6500 ■ The Atlantic Monthly
The Atlantic Monthly Co.
600 NH Ave., NW
Washington, DC 20037
Phone: (202)266-6000
Fax: (202)266-6001
Publication E-mail: letters@theatlantic.com
General interest magazine. **Founded:** 1857. **Freq:** 10/year. **Print Method:** Offset. **Trim Size:** 8 1/16 x 10 7/8. **Cols./Page:** 3 and 2. **Col. Width:** 27 and 40 nonpareils. **Col. Depth:** 138 agate lines. **ISSN:** 0276-9077 (print). **Subscription Rates:** $24.50 Individuals 10 issues; $3.25 Canada per copy; $3.95 Other countries per copy. **Alt. Formats:** Handheld. **URL:** http://www.theatlantic.com/. **Formerly**: The Atlantic. **Remarks:** Accepts advertising. **Circ:** Paid **•462478**.

6501 ■ Austrian Information
Austrian Press and Information Service
3524 International Ct. NW
Washington, DC 20008
Phone: (202)895-6700
Fax: (202)895-6750
Publisher's E-mail: inbox@austria.org
Magazine covering Austria. **Freq:** 3/year. **Key Personnel:** Thorsten Eisingerich, Editor-in-Chief; Mr. Hannes Richter, Editor. **Subscription Rates:** Free. **URL:** http://www.austrianinformation.org; http://www.austria.org/austrianinformation. **Remarks:** Advertising not accepted. **Circ:** (Not Reported).

6502 ■ Aviation Week & Space Technology
The McGraw-Hill Companies Inc.
1200 G St. NW, Ste. 922
Washington, DC 20005
Phone: (202)383-2360
Fax: (202)383-2346
Publisher's E-mail: pbg.ecommerce_custserv@mcgraw-hill.com
Magazine serving the aviation and aerospace market worldwide. **Freq:** Weekly. **Print Method:** Offset. **Trim Size:** 7 7/8 x 10 7/8. **Cols./Page:** 3. **Col. Width:** 27 nonpareils. **Col. Depth:** 140 agate lines. **Key Personnel:** James R. Asker, Executive Editor; Joe Anselmo, Editor-in-Chief. **ISSN:** 0005--2175 (print). **Subscription Rates:** $79 Individuals digital and print; $59 Individuals all digital access; $99 Other countries digital and print. **URL:** http://aviationweek.com/aviation-week-space-technology. **Ad Rates:** BW $18,235; 4C $21,265. **Remarks:** Accepts advertising. **Circ:** Paid △**92312**.

6503 ■ Balance: The Source for Administrators in Long-Term Health Care
American College of Health Care Administrators
1101 Connecticut Ave. NW, Ste. 450
Washington, DC 20036
Phone: (202)536-5120
Fax: (866)874-1585
Publisher's E-mail: mgrachek@achca.org
Professional society magazine covering long-term care administration. **Founded:** July 1997. **Freq:** 6/year. **Print Method:** Web offset. **Trim Size:** 8 x 10 3/4. **Key Personnel:** Jan Lamoglia, Editor, Contact. **ISSN:** 1094-6195 (print). **Subscription Rates:** $80 Individuals. **Online:** CCI; Bell & Howell Information and Learning. **Alt. Formats:** Microform. **Formerly**: Journal of Long-Term Care Administration. **Mailing address:** PO Box 75060, Baltimore, MD 21275-5060. **Ad Rates:** BW $740; 4C $1,490. **Remarks:** Accepts display advertising. **Circ:** Combined 6900.

6504 ■ Bank Compliance Magazine
American Bankers Association
1120 Connecticut Ave. NW
Washington, DC 20036
Phone: (202)663-5071
Fax: (202)828-4540
Free: 800-226-5377
Publisher's E-mail: custserv@aba.com
Professional magazine covering issues for bankers. **Freq:** Bimonthly. **Trim Size:** 8 1/2 x 11. **Key Personnel:** Larry Price, Publisher. **Subscription Rates:** $300 Members domestic; $562.50 Members foreign; $450 Nonmembers domestic; $562.50 Nonmembers foreign. **URL:** http://www.aba.com/Products/bankcompliance/Pages/default.aspx. **Ad Rates:** BW $1,900; 4C $2,800. **Remarks:** Accepts advertising. **Circ:** 3000.

6505 ■ Bank Insurance and Securities Marketing
Bank Insurance and Securities Association
2025 M St. NW, Ste. 800
Washington, DC 20036-2422
Phone: (202)367-1111
Fax: (202)367-2111
Publisher's E-mail: bisa@bisanet.org
Magazine featuring successful bank programs, products, services, compliance issues, marketing, technology, legislative and regulatory developments. **Freq:** Quarterly. **Subscription Rates:** Included in membership. **URL:** http://www.bisanet.org/?page=BISAMagazine. **Remarks:** Accepts advertising. **Circ:** 22,500.

6506 ■ Behavioral Neuroscience
American Psychological Association
750 1st St. NE
Washington, DC 20002-4242
Phone: (202)336-5500
Free: 800-374-2721
Journal presenting research in the broad field of the biological bases of behavior. **Freq:** Bimonthly beginning in February. **Key Personnel:** Mark S. Blumberg, PhD, Editor; Ted Abel, Associate Editor; John H. Freeman, Associate Editor. **ISSN:** 0735--7044 (print); **EISSN:** 1939--0084 (electronic). **Subscription Rates:** $1794 Institutions U.S.; $1855 Institutions, other countries; $1875 Institutions, other countries air mail. **URL:** http://psycnet.apa.org/journals/bne; http://www.apa.org/pubs/journals/bne. **Ad Rates:** BW $260; 4C $975. **Remarks:** Accepts advertising. **Circ:** ‡500, 400.

6507 ■ Biblical Archaeology Review
Biblical Archaeology Society
4710 41st St. NW
Washington, DC 20016
Phone: (202)364-3300
Free: 800-221-4644
Publisher's E-mail: info@biblicalarchaeology.org
Magazine covering the study of the archaeology of bible lands. **Freq:** Bimonthly. **Print Method:** Offset. **Trim Size:** 8 1/4 x 10 7/8. **Cols./Page:** 3. **Col. Width:** 27 nonpareils. **Col. Depth:** 140 agate lines. **Key Personnel:** Hershel Shanks, Editor; Susan Laden, Publisher; Suzanne F. Singer, Editor. **ISSN:** 0098--9444 (print). **Subscription Rates:** $24.97 Individuals print. **URL:** http://www.biblicalarchaeology.org/magazine. **Ad Rates:** BW $2,590; 4C $3,090. **Remarks:** Accepts advertising. **Circ:** ‡175000.

6508 ■ Big Builder
DoveTale Publishers
1 Thomas Cir. NW
Washington, DC 20005
Phone: (202)339-0744
Fax: (202)785-1974
Free: 877-275-8647
Publisher's E-mail: hwmicustomerservice@hanleywood.com
Magazine featuring management, finance and operating concerns of largest builders in America. **Freq:** 16/yr. **Trim Size:** 8 1/2 x 10 7/8. **Key Personnel:** John McManus, Director, Editorial; Denise Dersin, Editor. **URL:** http://www.builderonline.com/big-builder. **Ad Rates:** 4C $7,870. **Remarks:** Accepts advertising. **Circ:** Combined ‡8500.

6509 ■ Biomedical Optics Express
Optical Society of America
2010 Massachusetts Ave. NW
Washington, DC 20036
Phone: (202)223-8130
Fax: (202)223-1096
Publisher's E-mail: info@osa.org
Peer-reviewed journal focusing on biomedical optics and biophotonics. **Freq:** Monthly. **Key Personnel:** Joseph Izatt, Editor-in-Chief; Gregory Faris, Editor; Sara Naughton, Managing Editor, phone: (202)416-1920. **EISSN:** 2156--7085 (electronic). **Subscription Rates:** online (open access). **URL:** http://www.osapublishing.org/boe/journal/boe/about.cfm. **Circ:** (Not Reported).

6510 ■ Black History Bulletin
Association for the Study of African-American Life and History
Howard Ctr.
2225 Georgia Ave. NW, Ste. 331
Washington, DC 20059
Phone: (202)238-5910
Fax: (202)986-1506
Publisher's E-mail: info@asalh.net
Magazine profiling black history through feature articles and biographies. **Founded:** 1937. **Freq:** Semiannual. **Trim Size:** 8 1/2 x 11. **Key Personnel:** Dr. Alicia L. Moore, Editor; Dr. La Vonne Neal, Editor. **ISSN:** 1938-6656 (print); **EISSN:** 2153--4810 (electronic). **Subscription Rates:** $25 Individuals; $35 Other countries; $50 Institutions; $70 Institutions, other countries. **URL:** http://www.asalh.org/bhb.html. **Formerly**: Negro History Bulletin. **Remarks:** Advertising not accepted. **Circ:** ‡10000.

6511 ■ Blood Advances
American Society of Hematology
2021 L St. NW, Ste. 900
Washington, DC 20036-4929
Phone: (202)776-0544
Fax: (202)776-0545
Open access journal that contains articles describing basic laboratory, translational, and clinical investigations in hematology and related sciences. **Subscription Rates:** Free. **URL:** http://www.bloodadvances.org. **Circ:** (Not Reported).

6512 ■ B'nai B'rith
B'nai B'rith International
1120 20th St. NW, Ste. 300 N
Washington, DC 20036
Phone: (202)857-6600
Free: 888-388-4224
Publication E-mail: bbm@bnaibrith.org
Presents information and analysis on topics of interest and concern to the international Jewish community. **Freq:** Quarterly. **Print Method:** Offset. **Trim Size:** 8 1/2 x 11. **Cols./Page:** 3. **Col. Width:** 28 nonpareils. **Col. Depth:** 140 agate lines. **Key Personnel:** Allan J. Jacobs, President. **ISSN:** 0279--3415 (print). **Subscription Rates:** Included in membership. **URL:** http://www.bnaibrith.org/bnai-brith-magazine.html. **Ad Rates:** 4C $4,000. **Remarks:** Accepts advertising. **Circ:** Paid ‡169434, Non-paid ‡2042.

6513 ■ Boma Magazine
Building Owners and Managers Association International
1101 15th St. NW, Ste. 800
Washington, DC 20005
Phone: (202)408-2662
Fax: (202)326-6377
Publication E-mail: bomamagazine@boma.org
Magazine on the commercial real estate industry. Contains news ad information on legislative, regulatory and codes activities, statistical trends and forecast. **Freq:** Bimonthly. **Print Method:** Offset. **Trim Size:** 7 7/8 x 10 7/8. **Cols./Page:** 2. **Col. Width:** 17 nonpareils. **Col. Depth:** 190 agate lines. **Key Personnel:** Lisa Prats, Publisher, Vice President; Laura Horsley, Editor. **ISSN:** 1532--4346 (print). **Subscription Rates:** $50 Members; $75 Nonmembers. **URL:** http://www.boma.org/research/newsroom/boma-magazine/Pages/default.aspx. **Formerly**: Skylines magazine. **Ad Rates:** $4940-5540, for ad size, full page; $1980-2215, for classified, 1/6 page; $1720-1930, for classified, 1/8 page(business card). BW $5,540. **Remarks:** Advertising accepted; rates available upon request. **Circ:** Paid ‡18000.

6514 ■ The Bond Lawyer
National Association of Bond Lawyers
601 13th St. NW, Ste. 800 S
Washington, DC 20005-3807
Phone: (202)503-3300
Fax: (202)637-0217
Freq: Quarterly. **Subscription Rates:** available to members only. **URL:** http://www.nabl.org. **Remarks:** Advertising not accepted. **Circ:** (Not Reported).

6515 ■ Braille Book Review
Library of Congress National Library Service for the Blind and Physically Handicapped
1291 Taylor St. NW
Washington, DC 20542-0002

Circulation: • = AAM; △ or • = BPA; ♦ = CAC; ❑ = VAC; ⊕ = PO Statement; ‡ = Publisher's Report; Boldface figures = sworn; Light figures = estimated.

Phone: (202)707-5100
Fax: (202)707-0712
Free: 800-424-8567
Publisher's E-mail: nls@loc.gov
Bibliography of publications for the visually and physically handicapped (braille and large print). **Freq:** Bimonthly. **Print Method:** Offset. **Trim Size:** 10 3/8 x 8 5/8. **Cols./Page:** 2. **Col. Width:** 42 nonpareils. **Col. Depth:** 99 agate lines. **ISSN:** 0006--873X (print). **Subscription Rates:** Free to registered patrons of NLS. **URL:** http://www.loc.gov/nls/bbr/index.html. **Remarks:** Advertising not accepted. **Circ:** Non-paid ‡15000.

6516 ■ The Bridge
National Academy of Engineering
500 5th St. NW
Washington, DC 20001
Phone: (202)334-3200
Fax: (202)334-2290
Journal of the National Academy of Engineering covering engineering and technology for members. **Freq:** Quarterly Spring, Summer, Fall, Winter. **Key Personnel:** Penelope Gibbs, Contact, phone: (202)334-1579. **URL:** http://www.nae.edu/Publications/Bridge.aspx. **Circ:** (Not Reported).

6517 ■ Brookings Papers on Economic Activity
Brookings Institution Press
1775 Massashusetts Ave. NW
Washington, DC 20036
Phone: (202)536-3600
Fax: (202)536-3623
Publication E-mail: brookingspapers@brookings.edu
Publication covering economics and business. **Freq:** Semiannual Spring and Fall. **Key Personnel:** David Romer, Editor; Justin Wolfers, Editor. **ISSN:** 0007-2303 (print). **Subscription Rates:** $110 Institutions; $124 Institutions, other countries; $70 Individuals; $84 Other countries; $60 Individuals; $74 Other countries; $100 Institutions. **Alt. Formats:** PDF. **URL:** http://www.brookings.edu/about/projects/bpea. **Remarks:** Advertising not accepted. **Circ:** 5500.

6518 ■ Brookings Papers on Economic Activity
Brookings Institution
1775 Massachusetts Ave. NW
Washington, DC 20036
Phone: (202)797-6210
Fax: (202)797-6133
Publication E-mail: brookingspapers@brookings.edu
Publication covering economics and business. **Freq:** Semiannual Spring and Fall. **Key Personnel:** David Romer, Editor; Justin Wolfers, Editor. **ISSN:** 0007-2303 (print). **Subscription Rates:** $110 Institutions; $124 Institutions, other countries; $70 Individuals; $84 Other countries; $60 Individuals; $74 Other countries; $100 Institutions. **Alt. Formats:** PDF. **URL:** http://www.brookings.edu/about/projects/bpea. **Remarks:** Advertising not accepted. **Circ:** 5500.

6519 ■ Brookings Papers on Education Policy
Brookings Institution Press
1775 Massashusetts Ave. NW
Washington, DC 20036
Phone: (202)536-3600
Fax: (202)536-3623
Publisher's E-mail: bibooks@brookings.edu
Journal dealing with all aspects of American education. **Freq:** Annual. **Key Personnel:** Tom Loveless, Editor; Frederick Hess, Editor. **Subscription Rates:** $36 Individuals; $30 /year for individuals (4th class); $36 /year for individuals (1st class); $46 /year for institutions (4th class); $52 /year for institutions (1st class). **URL:** http://www.brookings.edu/research/journals/2007/brookingspapersoneducationpolicy20062007. **Remarks:** Advertising not accepted. **Circ:** (Not Reported).

6520 ■ Brookings Trade Forum
Brookings Institution Press
1775 Massashusetts Ave. NW
Washington, DC 20036
Phone: (202)536-3600
Fax: (202)536-3623
Journal providing in-depth analysis available on issues in international trade. **Freq:** Annual. **Key Personnel:** Susan M. Collins, Editor; Carol Graham, Editor. **ISSN:** 1520--5479 (print). **Subscription Rates:** $50 Institutions; $36 Individuals; $57 Institutions, other countries; $43 Other countries; $30 Individuals paper text. **URL:** http://www.brookings.edu/research/journals/2008/brookingstradeforum2007. **Remarks:** Advertising not accepted. **Circ:** (Not Reported).

6521 ■ Brookings Trade Forum
Brookings Institution
1775 Massachusetts Ave. NW
Washington, DC 20036
Phone: (202)797-6210
Fax: (202)797-6133
Journal providing in-depth analysis available on issues in international trade. **Freq:** Annual. **Key Personnel:** Susan M. Collins, Editor; Carol Graham, Editor. **ISSN:** 1520--5479 (print). **Subscription Rates:** $50 Institutions; $36 Individuals; $57 Institutions, other countries; $43 Other countries; $30 Individuals paper text. **URL:** http://www.brookings.edu/research/journals/2008/brookingstradeforum2007. **Remarks:** Advertising not accepted. **Circ:** (Not Reported).

6522 ■ Brookings-Wharton Papers on Financial Services
Brookings Institution Press
1775 Massashusetts Ave. NW
Washington, DC 20036
Phone: (202)536-3600
Fax: (202)536-3623
Journal dealing with major financial issues. **Freq:** Annual. **Key Personnel:** Robert E. Litan, Editor; Richard Herring, Editor. **ISSN:** 1533--4430 (print). **Subscription Rates:** $48 Individuals print. **URL:** http://www.brookings.edu/research/journals/2004/brookingswhartonpapersonfinancialservices2004; http://fic.wharton.upenn.edu/fic/brookings.html. **Remarks:** Advertising not accepted. **Circ:** (Not Reported).

6523 ■ Brookings-Wharton Papers on Financial Services
Brookings Institution
1775 Massachusetts Ave. NW
Washington, DC 20036
Phone: (202)797-6210
Fax: (202)797-6133
Journal dealing with major financial issues. **Freq:** Annual. **Key Personnel:** Robert E. Litan, Editor; Richard Herring, Editor. **ISSN:** 1533--4430 (print). **Subscription Rates:** $48 Individuals print. **URL:** http://www.brookings.edu/research/journals/2004/brookingswhartonpapersonfinancialservices2004; http://fic.wharton.upenn.edu/fic/brookings.html. **Remarks:** Advertising not accepted. **Circ:** (Not Reported).

6524 ■ Brookings-Wharton Papers on Urban Affairs
Brookings Institution Press
1775 Massashusetts Ave. NW
Washington, DC 20036
Phone: (202)536-3600
Fax: (202)536-3623
Journal dealing with research on urban policy. **Freq:** Annual. **Key Personnel:** Janet Rothenberg Pack, Editor; Gary Burtless, Editor. **Subscription Rates:** $36 Individuals paperback. **URL:** http://www.brookings.edu/research/journals/0001/brookingswhartonpapersonurbanaffairs2009. **Remarks:** Advertising not accepted. **Circ:** (Not Reported).

6525 ■ Brookings-Wharton Papers on Urban Affairs
Brookings Institution
1775 Massachusetts Ave. NW
Washington, DC 20036
Phone: (202)797-6210
Fax: (202)797-6133
Journal dealing with research on urban policy. **Freq:** Annual. **Key Personnel:** Janet Rothenberg Pack, Editor; Gary Burtless, Editor. **Subscription Rates:** $36 Individuals paperback. **URL:** http://www.brookings.edu/research/journals/0001/brookingswhartonpapersonurbanaffairs2009. **Remarks:** Advertising not accepted. **Circ:** (Not Reported).

6526 ■ Builder Magazine
Building Systems Council
1201 15th St. NW
Washington, DC 20005
Free: 800-368-5242
Magazine providing information about the housing and light construction industry. **Freq:** Monthly. **Remarks:** Advertising not accepted. **Circ:** (Not Reported).

6527 ■ Building Safety Journal
International Code Council
500 New Jersey Ave. NW, 6th Fl.
Washington, DC 20001
Phone: (202)370-1800
Fax: (202)783-2348
Free: 888-422-7233
Journal covering construction and fire safety. **Freq:** Bimonthly. **Print Method:** Offset. **Cols./Page:** 6. **Col. Width:** 12 3/10 picas. **Col. Depth:** 301 agate lines. **Key Personnel:** Gregory A. Layne, Managing Editor; Trey Hughes, Manager; Sebastian Kunnappilly, Editor. **Subscription Rates:** $50 Individuals. **URL:** http://www.iccsafe.org/newsroom/Pages/default.aspx. **Remarks:** Accepts advertising. **Circ:** (Not Reported).

6528 ■ Bulletin of the American Astronomical Society
American Institute of Physics
c/o Kevin B. Marvel, Editor
2000 Florida Ave. NW, Ste. 400
Washington, DC 20009-1231
Phone: (202)328-2010
Fax: (202)234-2560
Publisher's E-mail: sales@aip.org
Journal presenting abstracts of meeting papers and obituaries. **Freq:** Quarterly. **Key Personnel:** Kevin B. Marvel, Executive Officer, Editor. **ISSN:** 0002--7537 (print). **Subscription Rates:** Free. **URL:** http://aas.org/publications/baas/baas-index. **Remarks:** Advertising not accepted. **Circ:** ‡1665.

6529 ■ Business Economics
National Association for Business Economics
1920 L St. NW, Ste. 300
Washington, DC 20036
Phone: (202)463-6223
Fax: (202)463-6239
Publisher's E-mail: nabe@nabe.com
Peer-reviewed professional Journal of the National Association of Business Economists covering topics such as macro and microeconomics, monetary and fiscal policy, business forecasting, international economics, and deregulation. **Freq:** Quarterly. **Print Method:** Sheetfed offset. **Trim Size:** 8 1/2 x 11. **Cols./Page:** 2. **Col. Width:** 40 nonpareils. **Col. Depth:** 138 agate lines. **Key Personnel:** Colette Brissett, Associate Director; Robert T. Crow, Editor; Tom Beers, Executive Director. **ISSN:** 0007--666X (print). **Subscription Rates:** Free. **URL:** http://www.nabe.com/NABE/Publications/Publications.aspx. **Remarks:** Accepts advertising. **Circ:** ‡3,600.

6530 ■ Business Woman
Business and Professional Women's Foundation
1030 15th St., NW, Ste. B1, No. 148
Washington, DC 20005
Phone: (202)293-1100
Fax: (202)861-0298
Publisher's E-mail: memberservices@bpwusa.org
Armenian and Russian language newspaper covering women in business. **Freq:** Quarterly Periodic. **ISSN:** 0027- 8831 (print). **Subscription Rates:** $12 /year; Free; Included in membership. **Alt. Formats:** PDF. **URL:** http://bpwfoundation.org. **Remarks:** Advertising accepted; rates available upon request. **Circ:** 80000, 99.

6531 ■ Business Woman
Business and Professional Women/U.S.A.
1620 Eye St. NW, Ste. 210
Washington, DC 20006
Phone: (202)293-1100
Fax: (202)861-0298
Free: 888-491-8833
Publisher's E-mail: memberservices@bpwusa.org
Armenian and Russian language newspaper covering women in business. **Freq:** Quarterly Periodic. **ISSN:** 0027- 8831 (print). **Subscription Rates:** $12 /year; Free; Included in membership. **Alt. Formats:** PDF. **URL:** http://bpwfoundation.org. **Remarks:** Advertising accepted; rates available upon request. **Circ:** 80000, 99.

6532 ■ Canadian Journal of Experimental Psychology
American Psychological Association
750 1st St. NE
Washington, DC 20002-4242
Phone: (202)336-5500
Free: 800-374-2721
Journal publishing research papers that advance

understanding of the field of experimental psychology. **Freq:** Quarterly. **Key Personnel:** Daniel Voyer, Associate Editor. **ISSN:** 1196-1961 (print). **Subscription Rates:** $92 Members; $116 Other countries members; $133 Nonmembers; $162 Other countries nonmembers; $360 Institutions; $409 Institutions, other countries. **URL:** http://www.apa.org/pubs/journals/cep/index.aspx. **Ad Rates:** 4C $1,225. **Remarks:** Accepts advertising. **Circ:** ‡500.

6533 ■ Cancer Nursing: An International Journal for Cancer Care
Lippincott Williams and Wilkins
c/o Pamela S. Hinds, PhD, Ed.-in-Ch.
Department of Nursing Research
Children's National Medical Center
111 Michigan Ave. NW, 6th Fl.
Washington, DC 20010
Phone: (202)476-4432
Publisher's E-mail: ronna.ekhouse@wolterskluwer.com
Medical journal covering problems arising in the care and support of cancer patients. **Freq:** Bimonthly. **Trim Size:** 7 3/4 x 10 3/4. **Key Personnel:** Pamela S. Hinds, PhD, Editor-in-Chief; Kathleen Phelan, Publisher; Carol Reed Ash, Editor. **ISSN:** 0162--220X (print); **EISSN:** 1538--9804 (electronic). **Subscription Rates:** $137 Individuals /year. **URL:** http://journals.lww.com/cancernursingonline/pages/default.aspx. **Ad Rates:** GLR $30; BW $2,170. **Remarks:** Accepts advertising. **Circ:** Paid ‡1045.

6534 ■ Capitol File
DLG Media Holdings L.L.C.
1301 Pennsylvania Ave. NW, Ste. 925
Washington, DC 20004
Phone: (202)293-8025
Fax: (202)293-8022
Publication E-mail: capitolfile@pubservice.com
Magazine covers upscale lifestyle & fashion in the Washington, DC region. **Freq:** Bimonthly. **Key Personnel:** Sarah Schaffer, Publisher; Kate Bennett, Editor-in-Chief; Wendie Pecharsky, Managing Editor. **ISSN:** 1557-2366 (print). **Subscription Rates:** $42 Individuals; $75 Two years. **URL:** http://capitolfile-magazine.com. **Formerly:** DC Style. **Ad Rates:** BW $18,025. **Remarks:** Accepts advertising. **Circ:** ★**50000**.

6535 ■ CAR Magazine
National Society of the Children of the American Revolution
1776 D St. NW, Rm. 224
Washington, DC 20006-5303
Phone: (202)638-3153
Fax: (202)737-3162
Publisher's E-mail: hq@nscar.org
Freq: Quarterly. **Subscription Rates:** $8 /year. **URL:** http://www.nscar.org/NSCAR/Sales/Magazine.aspx. **Remarks:** Accepts advertising. **Circ:** 5000.

6536 ■ Cardiovascular Revascularization Medicine
Elsevier
c/o Ron Waksman, MD, Editor-in-Chief
110 Irving St. NW, Ste. 4B-1
Washington, DC 20010
Publisher's E-mail: t.reller@elsevier.com
Journal focused on clinical investigations of revascularization therapies in cardiovascular medicine. **Freq:** 8/year. **Print Method:** Offset. **Trim Size:** 8 1/2 x 11. **Cols./Page:** 3. **Col. Width:** 14 picas. **Col. Depth:** 10 inches. **Key Personnel:** Ron Waksman, MD, Editor-in-Chief; Kenneth M. Kent, Associate Editor; Lowell F. Satler, Associate Editor. **ISSN:** 1553--8389 (print). **Subscription Rates:** $153 Individuals domestic; $180 Individuals other countries; $604 Institutions domestic; $689 Institutions, other countries. **URL:** http://www.journals.elsevier.com/cardiovascular-revascularization-medicine; http://www.cardiorevascmed.com. **Circ:** (Not Reported).

6537 ■ Career Outlook
U.S. Department of Labor Bureau of Labor Statistics
Postal Square Bldg.
2 Massachusetts Ave. NE
Washington, DC 20212-0001
Phone: (202)691-5200
Magazine providing occupational and employment information. **Freq:** Quarterly. **Print Method:** Letterpress. **Cols./Page:** 2. **Col. Width:** 40 nonpareils. **Col. Depth:** 128 agate lines. **Key Personnel:** Domingo Angeles, Managing Editor; Kathleen Green, Editor. **ISSN:** 0199--4786 (print). **Alt. Formats:** PDF. **URL:** http://www.bls.gov/careeroutlook. **Formerly:** Occupational Outlook Quarterly. **Remarks:** Advertising not accepted. **Circ:** Paid 7300.

6538 ■ Caring
National Association for Home Care and Hospice
228 7th St. SE
Washington, DC 20003
Phone: (202)547-7424
Fax: (202)547-3540
Publisher's E-mail: whho@nahc.org
Freq: Monthly. **Print Method:** Offset full-run. **Trim Size:** 8.125 x 10.875. **Cols./Page:** 2. **Col. Width:** 3 3/8 inches. **Col. Depth:** 9 1/2 inches. **Key Personnel:** Hubert H. Humphrey, Vice President; Val J. Halamandaris, President. **ISSN:** 0738--467X (print). **Subscription Rates:** included in membership dues. **URL:** http://www.nahc.org/caringmagazine/. **Ad Rates:** 4C $4,270. **Remarks:** Accepts advertising. **Circ:** Paid 30000.

6539 ■ Caring
World Homecare and Hospice Organization
228 7th St. SE
Washington, DC 20003
Phone: (202)547-7424
Fax: (202)547-3540
Publisher's E-mail: whho@nahc.org
Freq: Monthly. **Print Method:** Offset full-run. **Trim Size:** 8.125 x 10.875. **Cols./Page:** 2. **Col. Width:** 3 3/8 inches. **Col. Depth:** 9 1/2 inches. **Key Personnel:** Hubert H. Humphrey, Vice President; Val J. Halamandaris, President. **ISSN:** 0738--467X (print). **Subscription Rates:** included in membership dues. **URL:** http://www.nahc.org/caringmagazine/. **Ad Rates:** 4C $4,270. **Remarks:** Accepts advertising. **Circ:** Paid 30000.

6540 ■ The Carpenter
United Brotherhood of Carpenters and Joiners of America
101 Constituition Ave. NW
Washington, DC 20001
Phone: (202)546-6206
Fax: (202)547-8979
Publisher's E-mail: webmaster@carpenters.org
Official magazine of the Carpenters' Union. **Freq:** Bimonthly. **Print Method:** Offset. **Trim Size:** 8 5/16 x 11. **Cols./Page:** 3. **Col. Width:** 13 picas. **Col. Depth:** 58 picas. **Key Personnel:** Andris Silins, Editor. **ISSN:** 0008-6843 (print). **Subscription Rates:** $10 Individuals; $2 Single issue; free for members; $10 /year for nonmembers. **Alt. Formats:** PDF. **URL:** http://www.carpenters.org/; http://www.carpenters.org/Todays_UBC_Top_Nav/carpmag.aspx. **Ad Rates:** BW $11,400; 4C $19,950. **Remarks:** Accepts advertising. **Circ:** 473104, 630000.

6541 ■ CatComm Journal
Catalytic Communities
PO Box 42010
Washington, DC 20015-0610
Phone: (301)637-7360
Publisher's E-mail: info@catcomm.org
Journal containing information for community solution-sharing. **Subscription Rates:** Free. **Circ:** (Not Reported).

6542 ■ Catfish Processing
U.S. Department of Agriculture National Agricultural Statistics Service Agricultural Statistics Board
1400 Independence Ave. SW
Washington, DC 20250
Phone: (202)720-7017
Free: 800-727-9540
Publisher's E-mail: nass@nass.usda.gov
Provides basic processing data for the catfish industry. **Freq:** Monthly. **Circ:** (Not Reported).

6543 ■ Cathedral Age: Washington National Cathedral
Washington National Cathedral
3101 Wisconsin Ave. NW
Washington, DC 20016-5098
Phone: (202)537-6200
Fax: (202)364-6600
Publication E-mail: nca@cathedral.org
Magazine on activities at the Washington National Cathedral and other general religious topics. **Freq:** Quarterly. **Print Method:** Offset. **Trim Size:** 8 1/2 x 11. **Cols./Page:** 3. **Col. Width:** 13 INS. **Col. Depth:** 58 INS. **Key Personnel:** Craig Stapert, Contact. **ISSN:** 0008--7874 (print). **Subscription Rates:** Included in membership. **URL:** http://www.nationalcathedral.org/age. **Remarks:** Advertising not accepted. **Circ:** ‡36000.

6544 ■ Catheterization and Cardiovascular Interventions
Society for Cardiovascular Angiography and Interventions
1100 17th St. NW, Ste. 330
Washington, DC 20036
Phone: (202)741-9854
Fax: (800)863-5202
Free: 800-992-7224
Publisher's E-mail: info@wiley.com
Journal covering the broad field of cardiovascular diseases. **Freq:** 14/yr. **Print Method:** Offset. **Trim Size:** 8 1/4 x 11. **Key Personnel:** Christopher J. White, MD, Board Member; John P. Reilly, Board Member; Victor Samuel Lucas, Board Member; Gary M. Ansel, Board Member; Tyrone J. Collins, Board Member; Ziyad M. Hijazi, Editor. **ISSN:** 1522--1946 (print); **EISSN:** 1522--726X (electronic). **Subscription Rates:** $5602 Institutions online only; $6723 Institutions print and online; $5602 Institutions print only; $622 Individuals print only. **URL:** http://onlinelibrary.wiley.com/journal/10.1002/(ISSN)1522-726X; http://www.scai.org/CCI/default.aspx. **Ad Rates:** BW $1,241; 4C $1,150. **Remarks:** Accepts advertising. **Circ:** Paid 3261.

6545 ■ Catholic Biblical Quarterly
Catholic Biblical Association of America
Catholic University of America
433 Caldwell Hall
Washington, DC 20064
Phone: (202)319-5519
Fax: (202)319-4799
Publisher's E-mail: cba-office@cua.edu
Freq: Quarterly. **Print Method:** Offset. **Trim Size:** 6 x 9. **Cols./Page:** 1. **Col. Width:** 54 nonpareils. **Col. Depth:** 102 agate lines. **Key Personnel:** Leslie J. Hoppe, Editor. **ISSN:** 0008--7912 (print). **Subscription Rates:** $40 Individuals /year; $10 Single issue /issue. **URL:** http://catholicbiblical.org/publications/cbq. **Ad Rates:** BW $175. **Remarks:** Color advertising not accepted. **Circ:** 3900, 3800.

6546 ■ The Catholic Historical Review
Catholic University of America Press
620 Michigan Ave. NE, 240 Leahy Hall
Washington, DC 20064
Phone: (202)319-5052
Fax: (202)319-4985
Free: 800-537-5487
Magazine on all areas of church history. **Freq:** Quarterly. **Print Method:** Offset. **Trim Size:** 6 x 9. **Cols./Page:** 1. **Col. Width:** 53 nonpareils. **Col. Depth:** 93 agate lines. **Key Personnel:** Nelson Minnich, Editor; Robert Trisco, Associate Editor. **ISSN:** 0008--8080 (print); **EISSN:** 1534--0708 (electronic). **Subscription Rates:** $135 Institutions print or online; $60 Individuals print or online; $30 Students; $188 Institutions print & online; $20 Individuals single issue; $40 Institutions single issue. **URL:** http://cuapress.cua.edu/journals/CHR.cfm. **Ad Rates:** BW $150. **Remarks:** Accepts advertising. **Circ:** Paid ‡1600.

6547 ■ The Catholic Peace Voice
Pax Christi U.S.A.
415 Michigan Ave. NE, Ste. 240
Washington, DC 20017-4503
Phone: (202)635-2741
Publisher's E-mail: info@paxchristiusa.org
Covering the international Catholic peace movement. **Freq:** Quarterly. **Print Method:** Web press. **Trim Size:** 11 x 17. **Cols./Page:** 3. **Key Personnel:** Dave Robinson, Executive Director, phone: (814)453-4955; Johnny Zokovitch, Director, Programs, phone: (352)219-8419. **ISSN:** 0897-9545 (print). **Subscription Rates:** $20 Individuals. **URL:** http://www.paxchristiusa.org/. **Formerly:** Pax Christi USA Magazine; Pax Christi. **Remarks:** Accepts advertising. **Circ:** Paid 15000, Non-paid 10000.

6548 ■ Catholic Standard: Weekly Newspaper for the Archdiocese of Washington
Archdiocese of Washington
PO Box 4464

Circulation: ★ = AAM; △ or • = BPA; ♦ = CAC; ❑ = VAC; ⊕ = PO Statement; ‡ = Publisher's Report; Boldface figures = sworn; Light figures = estimated.

Washington, DC 20017-0260
Phone: (202)281-2410
Fax: (202)281-2408
Religious newspaper. **Freq:** Weekly. **Key Personnel:** Mark Zimmermann, Editor, phone: (202)281-2412. **ISSN:** 0411--2741 (print). **USPS:** 094-480. **Subscription Rates:** $30 Individuals; $20 Individuals senior; $65 Other countries; $56 Two years; $36 Two years senior. **URL:** http://cathstan.org. **Ad Rates:** GLR $30.90; BW $2,085.75; 4C $2,485.75. **Circ:** Mon.-Fri. ‡50000.

6549 ■ Catholic University Law Review
Catholic University Law Review
Columbus School of Law
The Catholic University of America
3600 John McCormack Rd. NE
Washington, DC 20064
Phone: (202)319-5159
Fax: (202)319-5246
Publication E-mail: cualawrev@gmail.com
Journal of legal scholarship. **Freq:** Quarterly. **Print Method:** Letterpress. **Cols./Page:** 1. **Col. Width:** 60 nonpareils. **Col. Depth:** 122 agate lines. **Key Personnel:** Alyssa King, Executive Editor. **ISSN:** 0008-8390 (print). **Subscription Rates:** $40 Individuals regular; $45 Individuals foreign; $130 Individuals sustaining contributor; $70 Individuals patron. **URL:** http://lawreview.law.edu. **Circ:** ‡1400.

6550 ■ Cato Journal
Cato Institute
1000 Massachusetts Ave. NW
Washington, DC 20001-5403
Phone: (202)842-0200
Fax: (202)842-3490
Publisher's E-mail: pr@cato.org
Journal covering public policy issues, right from environmental issues to monetary policy. **Freq:** 3/year. **Key Personnel:** Alan Peterson, Manager, Circulation; James A. Dorn, Editor. **ISSN:** 0273--3072 (print). **Subscription Rates:** $22 Individuals; $50 Institutions; $38 Individuals 2 years; $85 Institutions 2 years; $55 Individuals 3 years; $125 Institutions 3 years. **URL:** http://www.cato.org/cato-journal/winter-2016. **Ad Rates:** BW $180. **Remarks:** Accepts advertising. **Circ:** 3000.

6551 ■ CELE Exchange
OECD Washington Center
1776 I St. NW, Ste. 450
Washington, DC 20006
Phone: (202)785-6323
Fax: (202)315-2508
Free: 800-456-6323
Publisher's E-mail: washington.contact@oecd.org
Publication of the Organisation for Economic Cooperation and Development Programme on Education Building. **Freq:** 3/year. **ISSN:** 1018---9327 (print); **EISSN:** 2072--7925 (electronic). **Subscription Rates:** Free online editions. **URL:** http://www.oecd.org/edu/innovation-education/celeexchange.htm. **Formerly**: PEB Exchange. **Circ:** (Not Reported).

6552 ■ Chemical Engineering Education
American Society for Engineering Education
1818 N St. NW, Ste. 600
Washington, DC 20036-2479
Phone: (202)331-3500
Publisher's E-mail: board@asee.org
Freq: Quarterly February, May, August and November. **Key Personnel:** Tim Anderson, Editor. **URL:** http://www.asee.org/papers-and-publications/publications/division-publications#Chemical_Engineering_Education_Journal. **Remarks:** Advertising not accepted. **Circ:** (Not Reported).

6553 ■ Chemical & Engineering News
American Chemical Society
1155 16th St. NW
Washington, DC 20036
Phone: (202)872-4600
Free: 800-227-5558
Publisher's E-mail: help@acs.org
Magazine on chemical and engineering news. **Freq:** Weekly. **Key Personnel:** Rudy M. Baum, Editor-in-Chief. **ISSN:** 0009--2347 (print). **Online:** American Chemical Society American Chemical Society. **URL:** http://cen.acs.org/magazine.html. **Also known as:** Chemical & Engineering News--Facts and Figures Issue: The Newsmagazine of the Chemical World. **Ad Rates:** BW $11,440. **Remarks:** Accepts advertising. **Circ:** 146000, 150000.

6554 ■ Chemical Research in Toxicology
American Chemical Society
1155 16th St. NW
Washington, DC 20036
Phone: (202)872-4600
Free: 800-227-5558
Publisher's E-mail: help@acs.org
Journal providing a platform for the underlying chemical principles behind various toxicological reactions. **Freq:** Monthly. **Key Personnel:** Lawrence J. Marnett, PhD, Editor, phone: (615)343-7329, fax: (615)343-7534; Judy L. Bolton, Associate Editor. **ISSN:** 0893--228X (print). **Online:** American Chemical Society American Chemical Society. **URL:** http://pubs.acs.org/journal/crtoec. **Remarks:** Advertising accepted; rates available upon request. **Circ:** (Not Reported).

6555 ■ Chemical Reviews
American Chemical Society
1155 16th St. NW
Washington, DC 20036
Phone: (202)872-4600
Free: 800-227-5558
Publisher's E-mail: help@acs.org
Review journal on analytical, theoretical, and biological chemistry. **Freq:** Monthly. **Print Method:** Offset. **Trim Size:** 8 3/16 x 11 1/4. **Cols./Page:** 2. **Col. Width:** 32 nonpareils. **Col. Depth:** 119 agate lines. **Key Personnel:** Josef Michl, Editor; Huy Bertrand, Associate Editor. **ISSN:** 0009--2665 (print); **EISSN:** 1520--6890 (electronic). **Online:** American Chemical Society American Chemical Society. **Alt. Formats:** PDF. **URL:** http://pubs.acs.org/journal/chreay. **Remarks:** Advertising not accepted. **Circ:** (Not Reported).

6556 ■ Chemistry of Materials
American Chemical Society
1155 16th St. NW
Washington, DC 20036
Phone: (202)872-4600
Free: 800-227-5558
Publisher's E-mail: help@acs.org
Journal focusing on materials with a molecular-level perspective at the interface of chemistry, chemical engineering, and materials science. **Freq:** Monthly. **Key Personnel:** Peter D. Battle, Editor; Jean-Luc Bredas, Editor. **ISSN:** 0897--4756 (print). **Online:** American Chemical Society American Chemical Society. **URL:** http://pubs.acs.org/journal/cmatex. **Remarks:** Advertising accepted; rates available upon request. **Circ:** (Not Reported).

6557 ■ ChemMatters
American Chemical Society
1155 16th St. NW
Washington, DC 20036
Phone: (202)872-4600
Free: 800-227-5558
Publication E-mail: chemmatters@acs.org
Magazine for high school chemistry students. **Freq:** Quarterly October/November, December/January, February/March, and April/May. **Print Method:** Offset - 4 color. **Trim Size:** 8 1/2 x 11. **Cols./Page:** 3. **Key Personnel:** Terri Taylor, Editor; Carl Heltzel, Editor. **ISSN:** 0736--4687 (print). **Subscription Rates:** $16 Individuals; $30 Two years; $42 Individuals 3 years; $8 Individuals bulk; $15 Two years bulk; $21 Individuals 3 years, bulk. **URL:** http://www.acs.org/content/acs/en/education/resources/highschool/chemmatters.html. **Remarks:** Advertising not accepted. **Circ:** (Not Reported).

6558 ■ Child Welfare: Journal of Policy, Practice, and Program
Child Welfare League of America
1726 M St. NW, Ste. 500
Washington, DC 20036-4522
Phone: (202)688-4200
Fax: (202)833-1689
Publication E-mail: journal@cwla.org
Journal publishing articles on child welfare services. **Freq:** Bimonthly. **Print Method:** Offset. **Key Personnel:** Christine James-Brown, Chief Executive Officer, President. **ISSN:** 0009--4021 (print). **Subscription Rates:** $255 Nonmembers 2 years; $140 Nonmembers 1 year; Included in membership. **URL:** http://www.cwla.org/child-welfare-journal/. **Ad Rates:** GLR $25; BW $800; PCI $140. **Remarks:** Advertising accepted; rates available upon request. **Circ:** ‡7000.

6559 ■ Childhood Education: Infancy Through Early Adolescence
Association for Childhood Education International
1200 18th St. NW, Ste. 700
Washington, DC 20036
Phone: (202)372-9986
Fax: (202)372-9989
Free: 800-423-3563
Publisher's E-mail: headquarters@acei.org
Educational journal. **Freq:** Bimonthly. **Print Method:** Offset. **Trim Size:** 8 1/8 x 10 7/8. **Cols./Page:** 3. **Col. Width:** 13 picas. **Col. Depth:** 9 1/8 inches. **Key Personnel:** Paula Beckman, Board Member; Anne Watson Bauer, Editor; Bruce Herzig, Manager, Advertising. **ISSN:** 0009--4056 (print); **EISSN:** 2162--0725 (electronic). **Subscription Rates:** $197 Institutions print and online; $172 Institutions online only. **URL:** http://acei.org/childhood-education; http://www.tandfonline.com/action/pricing?journalCode=uced20#.VnATO9J962w. **Ad Rates:** BW $1100; 4C $1840. **Remarks:** Accepts classified advertising. **Circ:** Paid ‡4600.

6560 ■ Children & Schools: A Journal for Social Workers in Schools
National Association of Social Workers
750 1st St. NE, Ste. 800
Washington, DC 20002-4241
Phone: (202)408-8600
Fax: (202)336-8313
Free: 800-742-4089
Publisher's E-mail: membership@naswdc.org
Journal. **Freq:** Quarterly. **Print Method:** Offset. **Trim Size:** 7 1/4 x 10. **Cols./Page:** 2. **Col. Width:** 13.5 picas. **Col. Depth:** 48 picas. **Key Personnel:** William Meezan, Chairperson; Martell L. Teasley, PhD, Editor-in-Chief; Aaron M. Thompson, Board Member. **ISSN:** 1532--8759 (print); **EISSN:** 1545--682X (electronic). **Subscription Rates:** $92 Members print; $63 Students print; $117 Individuals print; $184 Institutions print; $160 Institutions online; $200 Institutions print & online. **URL:** http://www.naswpress.org/publications/journals/cs.html. **Formerly:** Social Work in Education. **Ad Rates:** BW $480. **Remarks:** Accepts advertising. **Circ:** 2400.

6561 ■ Children and Schools: A Journal of Social Work Practice
National Association of Social Workers
750 1st St. NE, Ste. 800
Washington, DC 20002-4241
Phone: (202)408-8600
Fax: (202)336-8313
Free: 800-742-4089
Publisher's E-mail: membership@naswdc.org
Freq: Quarterly. **ISSN:** 1532- 8759 (print). **Subscription Rates:** $66 Members online only; $88 Members print only; $112 Nonmembers print only; $190 Institutions print and online. **URL:** http://www.naswpress.org/publications/journals/cs.html. **Remarks:** Accepts advertising. **Circ:** 2300.

6562 ■ Children's Voice
Child Welfare League of America
1726 M St. NW, Ste. 500
Washington, DC 20036-4522
Phone: (202)688-4200
Fax: (202)833-1689
Publisher's E-mail: cwla@cwla.org
Magazine providing information on child welfare programs and policy developments. **Freq:** Bimonthly. **Print Method:** Sheetfed. **Trim Size:** 8 1/2 x 11. **Cols./Page:** 2. **Key Personnel:** Christine James-Brown, Chief Executive Officer, President; Rachel Adams, Editor-in-Chief. **ISSN:** 1057--736X (print). **URL:** http://www.cwla.org/childrens-voice. **Ad Rates:** BW $995; 4C $1,295. **Remarks:** Accepts advertising. **Circ:** 20000.

6563 ■ The China Business Review
U.S.-China Business Council
1818 N St. NW, Ste. 200
Washington, DC 20036
Phone: (202)429-0340
Fax: (202)775-2476
Publication E-mail: publications@uschina.org
Freq: Bimonthly. **Print Method:** Offset. **Trim Size:** 8 1/8 x 10 7/8. **Cols./Page:** 3. **Col. Width:** 26 nonpareils. **Col. Depth:** 137 agate lines. **Key Personnel:** Christina Nelson, Editor. **ISSN:** 0163--7169 (print). **Subscription Rates:** $100 Individuals print and online; $79 Individuals

online only; $69 Students online only; $149 /year in U.S. and Canada; $199 /year, international airmail. **URL:** http://www.chinabusinessreview.com. **Ad Rates:** BW $4,420; 4C $6,320. **Remarks:** Advertising accepted; rates available upon request. **Circ:** Paid 6900.

6564 ■ Chinese Journal of Geophysics
American Geophysical Union
2000 Florida Ave. NW
Washington, DC 20009-1277
Phone: (202)462-6900
Fax: (202)328-0566
Free: 800-966-2481
Publisher's E-mail: service@agu.org
Journal covering solid and applied geophysics, space and atmospheric physics, ocean physics and related fields. **Freq:** 6/year. **Key Personnel:** Liu Guang-Ding, Editor-in-Chief. **ISSN:** 0898--9591 (print); **EISSN:** 2326--0440 (electronic). **Subscription Rates:** $167 Institutions online only - large; £105 Institutions online only - large; €123 Institutions online only - large; $167 Institutions, other countries online only - large. **URL:** http://agupubs.onlinelibrary.wiley.com/agu/journal/10.1002/(ISSN)2326-0440. **Remarks:** Advertising not accepted. **Circ:** (Not Reported).

6565 ■ The Christian Post
The Christian Post
National Press Bldg.
529 14th St. NW, Ste. 440
Washington, DC 20045
Phone: (202)506-4706
Publication E-mail: editor@christianpost.com
Online news publication for Christians with a pan-denominational approach. **Freq:** Daily. **Key Personnel:** William C. Anderson, Chief Executive Officer, Publisher. **URL:** http://global.christianpost.com. **Remarks:** Accepts advertising. **Circ:** (Not Reported).

6566 ■ The Chronicle of Higher Education
The Chronicle
1255 23rd St. NW, 7th Fl.
Washington, DC 20037
Phone: (202)466-1000
Fax: (202)452-1033
Free: 800-290-5460
General newspaper. **Founded:** Jan. 04, 1877. **Freq:** Weekly. **Print Method:** Offset. **Cols./Page:** 6. **Col. Width:** 2 1/16 inches. **Col. Depth:** 21 inches. **Key Personnel:** Michael G. Riley, Editor-in-Chief; Jeffrey J. Selingo, Editor, phone: (202)466-1075. **USPS:** 684-960. **Subscription Rates:** $89 Individuals; $151 Two years. **URL:** http://chronicle.com/. **Remarks:** Advertising accepted; rates available upon request. **Circ:** (Not Reported).

6567 ■ The Chronicle of Higher Education
The Chronicle of Higher Education
Washington, DC 20037
Phone: (202)466-1000
Fax: (202)452-1033
Free: 800-728-2803
Higher education magazine (tabloid). **Founded:** Nov. 23, 1966. **Freq:** Weekly. **Print Method:** Offset. **Trim Size:** 11 3/8 x 15. **Cols./Page:** 5. **Col. Width:** 23 nonpareils. **Col. Depth:** 189 agate lines. **Key Personnel:** Michael G. Riley, Editor-in-Chief; Edward R. Weidlein, Editor. **ISSN:** 0009-5982 (print). **Subscription Rates:** $89 Individuals; $151 Two years. **URL:** http://chronicle.com; http://chronicle.com/section/Home/5. **Remarks:** Accepts advertising. **Circ:** Paid ★**83416**.

6568 ■ The Chronicle of Philanthropy: The Newspaper of the Non-Profit World
The Chronicle of Philanthropy
1255 23rd St. NW, Ste. 700
Washington, DC 20037
Phone: (202)466-1200
Fax: (202)466-2078
Publisher's E-mail: help@philanthropy.com
Magazine covering fundraising, philanthropy, and non-profit organizations. Includes information on tax rulings, new grants, and statistics, reports on grant makers, and profiles of foundations. **Freq:** 20/yr. **Key Personnel:** Gwen Gaiser, Director, Production; Erica Bergin, Manager, Sales; Ashley Page, Assistant Manager. **ISSN:** 1040--676X (print). **Subscription Rates:** $79 Individuals; $138 Two years. **URL:** http://philanthropy.com. **Ad Rates:** BW $7,060; 4C $8,680. **Remarks:** Accepts advertising. **Circ:** Paid ★**45000**.

6569 ■ Church & State
Americans United for Separation of Church and State
1901 L St. NW, Ste. 400
Washington, DC 20036-3564
Phone: (202)466-3234
Fax: (202)466-2587
Publisher's E-mail: americansunited@au.org
Magazine on church-state relations. **Freq:** 11/yr. **Print Method:** Offset. **Trim Size:** 8 3/8 x 10 7/8. **Cols./Page:** 3. **Col. Width:** 40 nonpareils. **Col. Depth:** 136 agate lines. **Key Personnel:** Rob Boston, Assistant Director; Barry Lynn, Executive Director. **ISSN:** 0009-6334 (print). **URL:** http://www.au.org/church-state. **Remarks:** Advertising not accepted. **Circ:** Paid ‡33,000, Controlled ‡2,600.

6570 ■ Cleaning & Restoration
Restoration Industry Association
2025 M St. NW, Ste. 800
Washington, DC 20036
Phone: (202)367-1180
Fax: (202)367-2180
Publisher's E-mail: info@restorationindustry.org
Journal covering drapery, rug, upholstery, and carpet cleaning; fire and water damage; and disaster restoration and mechanical systems cleaning and inspection. **Founded:** 1962. **Freq:** Monthly. **Print Method:** Offset. **Trim Size:** 8 1/2 x 11. **Cols./Page:** 3 and 2. **Col. Width:** 24 and 37 agate lines. **Col. Depth:** 122 agate lines. **Key Personnel:** Patricia L. Harman, Editor-in-Chief. **ISSN:** 0886-9901 (print). **Subscription Rates:** $69 Nonmembers; $79 Nonmembers Canada; $99 Nonmembers international; Included in membership. **URL:** http://www.restorationindustry.org/content/cr-magazine. **Formerly:** Voice. **Ad Rates:** BW $790; 4C $1,585. **Remarks:** Accepts advertising. **Circ:** ‡2600.

6571 ■ Clinical Chemistry: International Journal of Laboratory Medicine and Molecular Diagnostics
American Association for Clinical Chemistry
900 7th St., NW, Ste. 400
Washington, DC 20006
Fax: (202)887-0717
Free: 800-892-5093
Publication E-mail: clinchemed@aacc.org
Scholarly journal covering laboratory medicine worldwide. **Freq:** Monthly. **Print Method:** Web Offset. **Key Personnel:** Nader Rifai, PhD, Editor-in-Chief. **ISSN:** 0009--9147 (print). **Subscription Rates:** $414 Nonmembers print & online - USA; $630 Nonmembers print & online - elsewhere; $1330 Institutions print & online; $1572 Institutions, other countries print & online; $269 Individuals online only; $916 Institutions online only; Free to members. **Alt. Formats:** PDF. **URL:** http://www.clinchem.org; http://www.aacc.org/publications/clin_chem/Pages/default.aspx. **Remarks:** Advertising accepted; rates available upon request. **Circ:** Combined 18000.

6572 ■ Clinical Chemistry Journal
American Association for Clinical Chemistry
900 7th St., NW, Ste. 400
Washington, DC 20006
Fax: (202)887-0717
Free: 800-892-5093
Publisher's E-mail: custserv@aacc.org
Journal containing research studies in today's clinical laboratory practices. **Freq:** Monthly. **ISSN:** 0009- 9147 (print); **EISSN:** 1530- 8561 (electronic). **Subscription Rates:** $383 Nonmembers print and online (USA); $592 Nonmembers print and online (Elsewhere); Included in membership; $1266 Nonmembers print and online (USA, Institution); $1461 Nonmembers print and online (Elsewhere, Institution). **URL:** http://www.clinchem.org; http://www.aacc.org/publications/clinical-chemistry. **Ad Rates:** BW $2,620. **Remarks:** Accepts advertising. **Circ:** 6,027.

6573 ■ Clinical Journal of the American Society of Nephrology
American Society of Nephrology
1510 H St. NW, Ste. 800
Washington, DC 20005
Phone: (202)640-4660
Fax: (202)637-9793
Publisher's E-mail: email@asn-online.org
Freq: Monthly. **ISSN:** 1555- 9041 (print); **EISSN:** 1555-905X (electronic). **Subscription Rates:** $438 Nonmembers (print and online); $1000 Institutions (print and online) non-members; $847 Institutions (online only) non-members; $970 Institutions (print only) non-members; Included in membership. **URL:** http://cjasn.asnjournals.org/. **Ad Rates:** $990-2190; $995-2025. BW $4C $. **Remarks:** Accepts advertising. **Circ:** 13000.

6574 ■ Clinical Microbiology Reviews
ASM Journals
1752 North St. NW
Washington, DC 20036
Phone: (202)737-3600
Fax: (202)942-9355
Publisher's E-mail: journals@asmusa.org
Journal reviewing work in clinical microbiology field. **Freq:** Quarterly. **Print Method:** Offset. **Trim Size:** 8 1/8 x 10 7/8. **Cols./Page:** 2. **Col. Width:** 3 1/4 inches. **Col. Depth:** 9 1/2 inches. **Key Personnel:** Jo-Ane H. Young, Editor-in-Chief; Deirdre L. Church, Editor; Lynne S. Garcia, Editor; Peter B. Gillingan, Editor; Charles Brown, Editor. **ISSN:** 0893-8512 (print). **Subscription Rates:** $113 Members print; $151 Members print & online; $126 Members Canada, print; $164 Members Canada, print & online. **URL:** http://cmr.asm.org/. **Ad Rates:** BW $1,465; 4C $2,930. **Remarks:** Accepts advertising. **Circ:** Combined ‡12337.

6575 ■ Club Director
National Club Association
1201 15th St. NW, Ste. 450
Washington, DC 20005
Phone: (202)822-9822
Fax: (202)822-9808
Free: 800-625-6221
Publisher's E-mail: info@nationalclub.org
Magazine providing business, legal, legislative, policy and trend information for professional and volunteer private club leaders. **Freq:** Quarterly. **Print Method:** Web offset. **Trim Size:** 8.375 x 10.875. **Key Personnel:** Robert C. James, Executive Director. **Subscription Rates:** Members Only Resource. **URL:** http://www.nationalclub.org/knowledge_center/club_director. **Ad Rates:** BW $2,400. **Remarks:** Accepts advertising. **Circ:** (Not Reported).

6576 ■ Code of Federal Regulations
U.S. Government Publishing Office
732 N Capitol St. NW
Washington, DC 20401-0001
Phone: (202)512-1800
Fax: (202)512-2104
Free: 866-512-1800
Publisher's E-mail: contactcenter@gpo.gov
Journal on Federal regulations. **Founded:** 1977. **Freq:** Quarterly. **Print Method:** Irregular. **Cols./Page:** 2. **Col. Width:** 26 nonpareils. **Col. Depth:** 94 agate lines. **Subscription Rates:** $929 Individuals; $1300 Other countries. **URL:** http://www.gpoaccess.gov/cfr/index.html; http://www.gpo.gov/help/about_code_of_federal_regulations.htm. **Also known as:** CFR. **Mailing address:** PO Box 979050, Saint Louis, MO 63197-9000. **Circ:** (Not Reported).

6577 ■ CoED Journal
American Society for Engineering Education
1818 N St. NW, Ste. 600
Washington, DC 20036-2479
Phone: (202)331-3500
Publisher's E-mail: board@asee.org
Freq: Quarterly. **URL:** http://www.asee.org/papers-and-publications/publications/division-publications#Computers_in_Education_Journal. **Remarks:** Advertising not accepted. **Circ:** 1200.

6578 ■ College Mathematics Journal
Mathematical Association of America
1529 18th St. NW
Washington, DC 20036-1358
Phone: (202)387-5200
Fax: (202)265-2384
Free: 800-741-9415
Publisher's E-mail: maahq@maa.org
Journal providing articles for undergraduate college math students. **Freq:** 5/year. **Key Personnel:** Beverly Ruedi, Manager; Michael G. Henle, Editor. **ISSN:** 0746--8342 (print). **URL:** http://www.maa.org/publications/periodicals/college-mathematics-journal/the-college-

Circulation: ★ = AAM; △ or • = BPA; ♦ = CAC; ❑ = VAC; ⊕ = PO Statement; ‡ = Publisher's Report; Boldface figures = sworn; Light figures = estimated.

mathematics-journal. **Ad Rates:** BW $820. **Remarks:** Accepts advertising. **Circ:** Paid 8000.

6579 ■ College and University
American Association of Collegiate Registrars and Admissions Officers
1 Dupont Cir. NW, Ste. 520
Washington, DC 20036
Phone: (202)293-9161
Fax: (202)872-8857
Publisher's E-mail: membership@aacrao.org
Freq: Quarterly. **Key Personnel:** Daniel Bender, Board Member. **Subscription Rates:** Included in membership. **Alt. Formats:** PDF. **URL:** http://www.aacrao.org/resources/publications/college-university-journal-(c-u). **Remarks:** Accepts advertising. **Circ:** (Not Reported).

6580 ■ The Collegiate Scholar
National Society of Collegiate Scholars
2000 M St. NW, Ste. 600
Washington, DC 20036
Phone: (202)265-9000
Fax: (202)265-9200
Publisher's E-mail: nscs@nscs.org
Freq: Quarterly. **URL:** http://www.nscs.org/about/about-nscs/publications. **Remarks:** Advertising not accepted. **Circ:** (Not Reported).

6581 ■ Commercial Builder
National Association of Home Builders
1201 15th St. NW
Washington, DC 20005
Free: 800-268-5242
Publisher's E-mail: info@nahb.org
Magazine featuring commercial building industry. **Freq:** Quarterly. **Trim Size:** 10.875 X16.5. **Key Personnel:** Andrew Flank, Contact. **URL:** http://www.nahb.org. **Remarks:** Accepts advertising. **Circ:** (Not Reported).

6582 ■ CommonHealth
American International Health Alliance
1225 Eye St. NW, Ste. 205
Washington, DC 20005
Phone: (202)789-1136
Fax: (202)789-1277
Publisher's E-mail: info@aiha.com
Freq: Periodic. **Subscription Rates:** Free. **URL:** http://www.aiha.com/our-projects/project-archive/commonhealth. **Remarks:** Advertising not accepted. **Circ:** (Not Reported).

6583 ■ Communication, Culture, & Critique
International Communication Association
1500 21st St. NW
Washington, DC 20036
Phone: (202)955-1444
Fax: (202)955-1448
Publisher's E-mail: icahdq@icahdq.org
Subscription Rates: Free for members. **URL:** http://www.icahdq.org/pubs/journals.asp. **Mailing address:** PO Box 418950, Boston, MA 02241-8950. **Circ:** (Not Reported).

6584 ■ Communication Monographs
National Communication Association
1765 N St. NW
Washington, DC 20036
Phone: (202)464-4622
Fax: (202)464-4600
Publisher's E-mail: inbox@natcom.org
Communication journal focusing on scientific and empirical investigations of communication processes. **Freq:** Quarterly. **Print Method:** Letterpress. **Cols./Page:** 2. **Col. Width:** 30 nonpareils. **Col. Depth:** 112 agate lines. **Key Personnel:** Kory Floyd, Editor; Karen Ashcraft, Board Member. **ISSN:** 0363--7751 (print); **EISSN:** 1479--5787 (electronic). **Subscription Rates:** $409 Institutions print & online; $358 Institutions online only; $104 Individuals print. **URL:** http://www.tandfonline.com/toc/rcmm20/current. **Remarks:** Advertising accepted; rates available upon request. **Circ:** (Not Reported).

6585 ■ Communication Teacher
National Communication Association
1765 N St. NW
Washington, DC 20036
Phone: (202)464-4622
Fax: (202)464-4600
Publisher's E-mail: inbox@natcom.org
Freq: Quarterly. **Key Personnel:** Deanna Sellnow, Board Member; Cheri J. Simonds, Editor. **ISSN:** 1740--4622 (print); **EISSN:** 1740--4630 (electronic). **Subscription Rates:** $147 Institutions online only; $116 Individuals online only. **URL:** http://www.tandfonline.com/toc/rcmt20/current; http://www.natcom.org/journals; http://www.tandfonline.com/toc/rcmt20/current#.VOw3UnyUdGY. **Remarks:** Advertising accepted; rates available upon request. **Circ:** 1500.

6586 ■ Communication Theory
International Communication Association
1500 21st St. NW
Washington, DC 20036
Phone: (202)955-1444
Fax: (202)955-1448
Journal covering the theoretical development of communication from across a wide array of disciplines, such as communication studies, sociology, psychology, political science, cultural and gender studies, philosophy, linguistics, and literature. **Freq:** Quarterly. **Print Method:** Offset. **Trim Size:** 12.5 x 22. **Cols./Page:** 6. **Col. Width:** 11 picas. **Col. Depth:** 21 inches. **Key Personnel:** Karin Gwinn Wilkins, Editor; Angharad Valdivia, Board Member; Donnalyn Pompper, Board Member. **ISSN:** 1050--3293 (print); **EISSN:** 1468--2885 (electronic). **USPS:** 152-700. **Subscription Rates:** $85 Individuals print and online; £53 Other countries print and online; €77 Individuals print and online; £53 Individuals U.K, Europe (non-Euro zone) and Rest of the World - print and online. **URL:** http://onlinelibrary.wiley.com/journal/10.1111/%28ISSN%291468-2885; http://onlinelibrary.wiley.com/doi/10.1111/comt.2015.25.issue-1/issuetoc. **Ad Rates:** BW $445; SAU $5.25; PCI $4.95. **Remarks:** Accepts advertising. **Circ:** (Not Reported).

6587 ■ Communications Crossroads
United States Telecom Association
607 14th St. NW, Ste. 400
Washington, DC 20005
Phone: (202)326-7300
Fax: (202)326-7333
Freq: Quarterly. **Remarks:** Advertising not accepted. **Circ:** (Not Reported).

6588 ■ Communio-International Catholic Review
Communio-International Catholic Review
PO Box 4557
Washington, DC 20017
Phone: (202)526-0251
Fax: (202)526-1934
Publication E-mail: communio@aol.com
Journal on theology, philosophy, and culture promoting authentic renewal within the Catholic Church. **Freq:** Quarterly. **Key Personnel:** David L. Schindler, Editor; Emily Rielley, Managing Editor. **ISSN:** 0094-2065 (print). **Subscription Rates:** $40 Individuals; $25 Students; $70 Institutions. **URL:** http://www.communio-icr.com. **Ad Rates:** BW $300. **Remarks:** Accepts advertising. **Circ:** Paid ‡2500, Non-paid ‡150.

6589 ■ Community College Journal
American Association of Community Colleges
1 Dupont Cir. NW, Ste. 410
Washington, DC 20036-1145
Phone: (202)728-0200
Fax: (202)833-2467
Publisher's E-mail: aaccpub@pmds.com
Freq: Bimonthly. **Key Personnel:** Angel Royal, Editor. **ISSN:** 1067--1803 (print). **Subscription Rates:** $36 Individuals. **URL:** http://www.aacc.nche.edu/Publications/CCJ/Pages/default.aspx. **Ad Rates:** BW $3,615. **Remarks:** Accepts advertising. **Circ:** 12000.

6590 ■ Community College Times
American Association of Community Colleges
1 Dupont Cir. NW, Ste. 410
Washington, DC 20036-1145
Phone: (202)728-0200
Fax: (202)833-2467
Publisher's E-mail: aaccpub@pmds.com
Newspaper featuring college news and issues. **Freq:** Biweekly. **Key Personnel:** Matthew Dembicki, Editor, phone: (202)728-0200. **ISSN:** 8711--7189 (print). **Subscription Rates:** $54 Individuals; $63 Other countries. **URL:** http://www.ccdaily.com/Pages/Landing/Homepage.aspx; http://www.aacc.nche.edu/Publications/CCT/Pages/default.aspx. **Remarks:** Accepts advertising. **Circ:** 6000.

6591 ■ Community Colleges Journal
American Association of Community Colleges
1 Dupont Cir. NW, Ste. 410
Washington, DC 20036-1145
Phone: (202)728-0200
Fax: (202)833-2467
Publisher's E-mail: aaccpub@pmds.com
Educational magazine. **Freq:** 6/year. **Print Method:** Offset. **Trim Size:** 8.375 x 10.875. **Cols./Page:** 3. **Col. Width:** 26 nonpareils. **Col. Depth:** 130 agate lines. **Key Personnel:** Stella Perez, Editor. **ISSN:** 1067--1803 (print). **Subscription Rates:** $36 Nonmembers; $36 Members; Free online; members & journal subscribers. **URL:** http://www.aacc.nche.edu/Publications/CCJ/Pages/default.aspx. **Ad Rates:** BW $3,795; 4C $5,365. **Remarks:** Accepts advertising. **Circ:** Paid ‡12000.

6592 ■ Community and the Environment: Lessons from the Caribbean, 1994
Panos Institute
Webster House
1718 P St. NW, Ste. T-6
Washington, DC 20036
Phone: (202)429-0730
Fax: (202)483-3059
Publisher's E-mail: washington@panoscaribbean.org
Subscription Rates: $10 complete set; $3.95 each. **Remarks:** Advertising not accepted. **Circ:** (Not Reported).

6593 ■ Compassionate Action
Compassion Over Killing
PO Box 9773
Washington, DC 20016
Phone: (301)891-2458
Publisher's E-mail: info@cok.net
Magazine containing articles, news, lawsuits and cases filed, interviews, and vegetarian recipes promoting animal rights and vegetarian eating. **URL:** http://cok.net/about/enews. **Formerly:** The Abolitionist. **Remarks:** Advertising not accepted. **Circ:** (Not Reported).

6594 ■ Computational Seismology and Geodynamics
American Geophysical Union
2000 Florida Ave. NW
Washington, DC 20009-1277
Phone: (202)462-6900
Fax: (202)328-0566
Free: 800-966-2481
Publisher's E-mail: service@agu.org
Journal covering Russian translations of applications of modern mathematics and computer science to seismology and related earth science studies. **ISSN:** 0733--5792 (print). **URL:** http://www.agu.org/pubs/journals/translations/csg.shtml; http://publications.agu.org/books/computational-seismology-and-geodynamics. **Formerly:** Computational Seismology. **Remarks:** Advertising not accepted. **Circ:** (Not Reported).

6595 ■ Computer
IEEE - Computer Society
2001 L St. NW, Ste. 700
Washington, DC 20036-4928
Phone: (202)371-0101
Fax: (202)728-9614
Free: 800-678-4333
Publication E-mail: computer@computer.org
Trade magazine for the IEEE Computer Society. **Freq:** Monthly. **Trim Size:** 7 7/8 x 10 3/4. **Key Personnel:** Doris L. Carver, Editor-in-Chief; Ron Vetter, Editor-in-Chief. **ISSN:** 0018-9162 (print). **Subscription Rates:** $1650 Individuals online; $1730 Individuals online; $2160 Individuals print and online. **URL:** http://www.computer.org/portal/web/computer/home. **Ad Rates:** BW $8,700; 4C $1,300. **Remarks:** Accepts advertising. **Circ:** Combined 94000.

6596 ■ Computer Law Reporter
Computer Law Reporter Inc.
1601 Connecticut Ave. NW, No. 602
Washington, DC 20009
Phone: (202)462-5755
Fax: (202)328-2430
Publisher's E-mail: orders@lawreporters.com
Professional journal covering computer law, patent law, and trademark law. Available in print format or via e-mail. **Freq:** Monthly. **Print Method:** Photo offset. **Trim Size:** 8 1/2 x 11. **Cols./Page:** 2. **Col. Width:** 3 1/2 inches. **Col. Depth:** 8 inches. **Key Personnel:** John Noble, Editor.

ISSN: 0739--7771 (print). **Subscription Rates:** $3825 Individuals. **Available online. Alt. Formats:** PDF. **URL:** http://lawreporters.com/NewFiles/CLRx.html. **Remarks:** Advertising not accepted. **Circ:** (Not Reported).

6597 ■ Computers in Education Division
American Society for Engineering Education
1818 N St. NW, Ste. 600
Washington, DC 20036-2479
Phone: (202)331-3500
Publisher's E-mail: board@asee.org
Journal providing a broad-based forum for exchanging ideas in all areas that involve computers and computational tools for education in engineering, technology and computer science. **Freq:** Quarterly. **Subscription Rates:** $15 Individuals /year; $7.50 Students /year; $45 Institutions and libraries/year. **URL:** http://www.asee.org/papers-and-publications/publications/division-publications/computers-in-education-journal. **Remarks:** Advertising not accepted. **Circ:** (Not Reported).

6598 ■ Computing in Science and Engineering
IEEE - Computer Society
2001 L St. NW, Ste. 700
Washington, DC 20036-4928
Phone: (202)371-0101
Fax: (202)728-9614
Free: 800-678-4333
Publication E-mail: subs@aip.org
Magazine focusing on physics, medicine, astronomy and other hard sciences. **Freq:** 6/year. **Trim Size:** 7.785 x 10.75. **Key Personnel:** Isabel Beichi, Editor-in-Chief; Klaus Jurgen Bathe, Board Member; Isabel Beichl, Editor-in-Chief; Jim X. Chen, Associate Editor; John Rundle, Board Member; Douglass E. Post, Associate Editor; Charles J. Holland, Board Member; Rachel Kuske, Board Member; Michael W. Berry, Board Member. **ISSN:** 1521--9615 (print). **Subscription Rates:** Accessible only to members. **URL:** http://www.computer.org/web/computingnow/cise/about. **Formerly:** IEEE Computational Science and Engineering. **Remarks:** Advertising accepted; rates available upon request. **Circ:** (Not Reported).

6599 ■ Concrete Construction
DoveTale Publishers
1 Thomas Cir. NW
Washington, DC 20005
Phone: (202)339-0744
Fax: (202)785-1974
Free: 877-275-8647
Publisher's E-mail: hwmicustomerservice@hanleywood.com
Trade magazine that reaches companies involved in the design, placement, repair, specification, and utilization of concrete in the construction industry. **Freq:** Monthly. **Print Method:** Web offset/Perfect Bound. **Trim Size:** 8 x 10 1/2. **Key Personnel:** Chari O'Rourke, Manager, Circulation; Kate Hamilton, Managing Editor; Patrick J. Carroll, Group President; Vaughn Rockhold, Publisher; William D. Palmer, Jr., Editor-in-Chief; Joe Nasvik, Senior Editor. **ISSN:** 1051-5526 (print). **Subscription Rates:** $30 U.S. 1 year; $39 Canada 1 year; $93 Other countries 1 year; $46 U.S. 2 years; $64 Canada 2 years; $162 Other countries 2 years. **URL:** http://www.concreteconstruction.net. **Formerly**: Aberdeen's Concrete Construction. **Ad Rates:** BW $9,870; 4C $14,505. **Remarks:** Accepts advertising. **Circ:** Paid △**70000**.

6600 ■ Concrete & Masonry Construction Products
DoveTale Publishers
1 Thomas Cir. NW
Washington, DC 20005
Phone: (202)339-0744
Fax: (202)785-1974
Free: 877-275-8647
Publisher's E-mail: hwmicustomerservice@hanleywood.com
Publication that covers carpenter tips, tools, and up keep. **Freq:** Bimonthly. **Key Personnel:** Patrick J. Carroll, Executive Director; Kate Hamilton, Managing Editor; Joe Nasvik, Senior Editor. **Subscription Rates:** Free to qualified subscribers. **URL:** http://www.hanleywoodopportunities.com/Index.asp?Cat=cc&Pub=cmcp&Sect=Intro. **Ad Rates:** BW $3,930. **Remarks:** Accepts advertising. **Circ:** ‡30000.

6601 ■ CongressDaily/A.M.
National Journal Group Inc.
The Watergate
600 New Hampshire Ave. NW
Washington, DC 20037
Phone: (202)739-8400
Fax: (202)833-8069
Free: 800-613-6701
Publisher's E-mail: service@nationaljournal.com
Periodical covering news and other issues in the Federal Government. **Freq:** Daily. **URL:** http://www.nationaljournal.com/congressdaily. **Circ:** (Not Reported).

6602 ■ Congressional Record
U.S. Government Publishing Office
732 N Capitol St. NW
Washington, DC 20401-0001
Phone: (202)512-1800
Fax: (202)512-2104
Free: 866-512-1800
Publisher's E-mail: contactcenter@gpo.gov
Report on Congressional debates and other proceedings. **Founded:** 1873. **Freq:** Daily (when Congress is in session). **Print Method:** Letterpress. **Cols./Page:** 3. **Col. Width:** 27 nonpareils. **Col. Depth:** 129 agate lines. **ISSN:** 0363-7239 (print). **Subscription Rates:** $503 Individuals; $704.20 Other countries; $252 Single issue for six-month; $353.80 Other countries for six-month. **URL:** http://www.gpo.gov/fdsys/browse/collection.action?collectionCode=CREC. **Mailing address:** PO Box 979050, Saint Louis, MO 63197-9000. **Circ:** (Not Reported).

6603 ■ Conscience: The Newsjournal of Catholic Opinion
Catholics for Choice
1436 U St. NW, Ste. 301
Washington, DC 20009-3997
Phone: (202)986-6093
Fax: (202)332-7995
Publication E-mail: conscience@catholicforchoice.org
Journal devoted to the exploration of reproductive health and gender issues, with a focus on ethics and Catholicism.Contains in-depth, cutting-edge coverage of vital contemporary issues, including reproductive rights, sexuality and gender, feminism, the Religious Right, church and state and US politics. **Freq:** Quarterly. **Print Method:** Sheet Fed. **Trim Size:** 8 1/4 x 10 1/2. **Cols./Page:** 3. **Col. Width:** 2 1/8 inches. **Col. Depth:** 9 inches. **Key Personnel:** David Nolan, Editor; Jon O'Brien, Executive Editor. **ISSN:** 0740-6835 (print). **Subscription Rates:** $15 Individuals 1 year; $25 Two years; $25 Other countries 1 year; $40 Other countries 2 years; $6.50 Individuals back issues. **URL:** http://www.catholicsforchoice.org/about/conscience/current/default.asp; http://consciencemag.org. **Ad Rates:** BW $350, 2/3 page vertical; BW $275, 1/2 page vertical or horizontal; BW $225, 1/3 page vertical or horizontal; BW $175, 1/4 page. **Remarks:** Advertising accepted; rates available upon request. **Circ:** Combined 12500.

6604 ■ Construction Executive: The Magazine for the Business of Construction
Associated Builders and Contractors
440 1st St. NW, Ste. 200
Washington, DC 20001
Publisher's E-mail: gotquestions@abc.org
Magazine for contractors and subcontractors. Includes articles on national and regional construction news, construction management, project case histories, new products, building design, and legislative and regulatory updates. **Freq:** Monthly. **Print Method:** Web offset. **Trim Size:** 8 3/8 10 7/8. **Cols./Page:** 5. **Col. Width:** 25 nonpareils. **Col. Depth:** 139 agate lines. **Key Personnel:** Lisa A. Nardone, Editor-in-Chief. **ISSN:** 1544--3620 (print). **Subscription Rates:** $15 Members; $65 Nonmembers. **URL:** http://www.constructionexec.com. **Formerly**: Builder & Contractor; ABC Today. **Ad Rates:** BW $4,935; 4C $6,515. **Remarks:** Accepts advertising. **Circ:** 50000.

6605 ■ Construction & Modernization Report
American Hotel and Lodging Association
1250 I St. NW, Ste. 1100
Washington, DC 20005
Phone: (202)289-3100
Fax: (202)289-3199
Publication E-mail: membership@ahla.com
Lists new hotel/motel construction and renovation projects throughout the US and Canada. **Freq:** Monthly. **Subscription Rates:** Free members. **URL:** http://www.ahla.com. **Remarks:** Advertising not accepted. **Circ:** (Not Reported).

6606 ■ Consulting Psychology Journal: Practice and Research
American Psychological Association
750 1st St. NE
Washington, DC 20002-4242
Phone: (202)336-5500
Free: 800-374-2721
Psychology journal covering theoretical/conceptual, original research regarding consultation, reviews of research and literature in consultation practice and case studies. **Freq:** Quarterly. **Key Personnel:** Rodney L. Lowman, Editor; Clayton Aldefer, Board Member; Rob Kaiser, Editor. **ISSN:** 1065--9293 (print); **EISSN:** 1939--0149 (electronic). **Subscription Rates:** $518 Institutions; $567 Institutions, other countries; $582 Institutions, other countries air mail. **URL:** http://www.apa.org/pubs/journals/cpb/index.aspx. **Ad Rates:** BW $410; 4C $1,300. **Remarks:** Accepts advertising. **Circ:** 1200.

6607 ■ Contemporary Sociology
American Sociological Association
1430 K St. NW, Ste. 600
Washington, DC 20005
Phone: (202)383-9005
Fax: (202)638-0882
Publisher's E-mail: customer@asanet.org
Journal containing reviews of scholarly essays on sociology and related topics. **Freq:** Bimonthly. **Print Method:** Offset. **Trim Size:** 6 3/4 x 9 7/8. **Cols./Page:** 2. **Col. Width:** 2 5/8 inches. **Col. Depth:** 8 1/2 inches. **Key Personnel:** Alan Sica, Editor; Paul R. Amato, Board Member. **ISSN:** 0094--3061 (print). **Subscription Rates:** $45 Individuals ASA members; $30 Students ASA members; $478 Institutions (print/online); $430 Institutions (online); $20 Other countries postage outside the U.S./Canada. **URL:** http://www.asanet.org/journals/cs/cs.cfm. **Ad Rates:** BW $640; 4C $1,095. **Remarks:** Accepts advertising. **Circ:** ‡5000, 8000.

6608 ■ Contingencies
American Academy of Actuaries
1850 M St. NW, Ste. 300
Washington, DC 20036
Phone: (202)223-8196
Fax: (202)872-1948
Freq: Bimonthly. **Key Personnel:** Eric P. Harding, Editor; Laurie Young, Manager, Marketing. **ISSN:** 1048--9851 (print). **Subscription Rates:** Included in membership for members living in the U.S. or Canada; $24 Nonmembers in the U.S. and Canada; $33 Individuals living in other countries. **URL:** http://www.contingencies.org. **Ad Rates:** BW $3455; 4C $5595. **Remarks:** Accepts advertising. **Circ:** Combined △**29795**.

6609 ■ Contraception: An International Journal
Association of Reproductive Health Professionals
1300 19th St. NW, Ste. 200
Washington, DC 20036
Phone: (202)466-3825
Fax: (202)466-3826
Publisher's E-mail: arhp@arhp.org
Freq: Monthly. **Key Personnel:** Carolyn Westhoff, MD, Editor. **Subscription Rates:** $488 Individuals print and online; Included in membership. **URL:** http://www.arhp.org/publications-and-resources/contraception-journal; http://www.contraceptionjournal.org/. **Remarks:** Advertising not accepted. **Circ:** (Not Reported).

6610 ■ Cooperative Business Journal
National Cooperative Business Association
1401 New York Ave. NW, Ste. 1100
Washington, DC 20005
Phone: (202)638-6222
Fax: (202)638-1374
Trade magazine covering business. **Trim Size:** 11 x 17. **Key Personnel:** Kristina Klassen, Editor. **ISSN:** 0893-3391 (print). **Ad Rates:** GLR $7.50; BW $1,500; 4C $1,800. **Remarks:** Advertising accepted; rates available upon request. **Circ:** (Not Reported).

6611 ■ Cotton: Review of the World Situation
International Cotton Advisory Committee
1629 K St. NW, Ste. 702

Circulation: ★ = AAM; △ or • = BPA; ♦ = CAC; ❑ = VAC; ⊕ = PO Statement; ‡ = Publisher's Report; Boldface figures = sworn; Light figures = estimated.

Washington, DC 20006-1636
Phone: (202)463-6660
Fax: (202)463-6950
Publication E-mail: publications@icac.org
Freq: Bimonthly. **ISSN:** 0010- 9754 (print). **Subscription Rates:** $190 /year - hard copy; $160 /year - internet. **Alt. Formats:** PDF. **URL:** http://www.icac.org; http://www.icac.org/econ/Sources-of-Cotton-Statistics/Review. **Remarks:** Advertising not accepted. **Circ:** (Not Reported).

6612 ■ County News: The Voice of America's counties
National Association of Counties
25 Massachusetts Ave. NW, Ste. 500
Washington, DC 20001
Phone: (202)393-6226
Fax: (202)393-2630
Free: 888-407-6226
Publisher's E-mail: naco@naco.org
Newspaper focusing on county government for elected and appointed county officials. **Print Method:** Offset. **Trim Size:** 10 x 13. **Cols./Page:** 5. **Col. Width:** 2 inches. **Col. Depth:** 189 agate lines. **Key Personnel:** Tom Goodman, Director, Public Affairs; Bev Schlotterbeck, Associate Editor, phone: (202)942-4249. **ISSN:** 0744--9798 (print). **URL:** http://www.naco.org/news. **Ad Rates:** BW $3,629. **Remarks:** Accepts advertising. **Circ:** Paid 8000, Free 2500.

6613 ■ The CQ Researcher: Weekly Reports on Current Affairs
Congressional Roll Call
77 K St. NE, 8th Fl.
Washington, DC 20002-4681
Phone: (202)650-6500
Free: 800-432-2250
Publisher's E-mail: customerservice@cqrollcall.com
Magazine examining world affairs, science, and community welfare. **Freq:** Weekly. **Print Method:** Offset. **Key Personnel:** Tom Colin, Editor. **ISSN:** 1056--2036 (print). **Subscription Rates:** $1107 Individuals print. **URL:** http://www.cqpress.com/researcher; http://www.cqpress.com/product/Researcher-Reports-Only.html. **Formerly**: Editorial Research Reports. **Remarks:** Accepts advertising. **Circ:** Paid ‡5000.

6614 ■ CQ Weekly
Congressional Roll Call
77 K St. NE, 8th Fl.
Washington, DC 20002-4681
Phone: (202)650-6500
Free: 800-432-2250
Publisher's E-mail: customerservice@cqrollcall.com
Congressional and political news research service. **Freq:** Weekly (Sat.). **Print Method:** Offset. **Trim Size:** 8 1/2 x 11. **Cols./Page:** 2. **Col. Width:** 42 nonpareils. **Col. Depth:** 126 agate lines. **Key Personnel:** David Hawkings, Contact; Keith A. White. **Subscription Rates:** Free. **URL:** http://corporate.cqrollcall.com/products-services/cq-roll-call-insight-analysis; http://library.cqpress.com/cqweekly. **Formerly:** Congressional Quarterly Weekly Report. **Ad Rates:** BW $10,350; 4C $14,900. **Remarks:** Advertising accepted; rates available upon request. **Circ:** Paid △**14537**.

6615 ■ The Crescent
Phi Beta Sigma Fraternity
145 Kennedy St. NW
Washington, DC 20011-5294
Phone: (202)726-5434
Fax: (202)882-1681
Publisher's E-mail: info@phibetasigma1914.org
Journal containing articles, stories, concepts, researches and studies about the Phi Beta Sigma Fraternity. **Freq:** Semiannual. **Key Personnel:** Todd LeBon, Editor-in-Chief. **URL:** http://www.phibetasigma1914.org/category/the-crescent/. **Remarks:** Advertising not accepted. **Circ:** (Not Reported).

6616 ■ Criminology & Criminal Justice
American Bar Association Criminal Justice Section
1050 Connecticut Ave. NW, Ste. 400
Washington, DC 20036
Phone: (202)662-1500
Fax: (202)662-1501
Publisher's E-mail: sales@pfp.sagepub.com
Peer-reviewed journal focusing on the general field of criminal justice policy and practice. **Freq:** 5/year. **Key Personnel:** Sarah Armstrong, Editor; Alex Piquero, Advisor, Board Member; Gordon Hughes, Associate Editor; George Mair, Editor, Founder. **ISSN:** 1748--8958 (print); **EISSN:** 1748--8966 (electronic). **Subscription Rates:** $117 Individuals print; $955 Institutions e-access; $1040 Institutions print only; $1061 Institutions print and e-access; $32 Individuals single print; $229 Institutions single print; Included in membership. **URL:** http://crj.sagepub.com; http://www.britsoccrim.org/ccj. **Formerly:** Criminal Justice. **Remarks:** Accepts advertising. **Circ:** 9000.

6617 ■ Crisis Magazine
Morley Publishing Group Inc.
2100 M St., Ste. 170-339
Washington, DC 20037
Phone: (202)861-7790
Publication E-mail: mail@ampsinc.net
Magazine focusing on politics, culture, the arts, and the Church. **Freq:** Monthly 11/yr. **Trim Size:** 8 1/8 x 10 3/4. **Cols./Page:** 2. **Col. Depth:** 8 7/8 inches. **Key Personnel:** William Baer, Editor; Brian Saint-Paul, Editor, Publisher; Christopher O. Blum, PhD, Associate Editor; Chris Michalski, Editor. **ISSN:** 0084-1705 (print). **Subscription Rates:** $29.95 Individuals first class, airmail; $51.95 Other countries surface. **Alt. Formats:** Print. **URL:** http://www.crisismagazine.com. **Ad Rates:** PCI $25. **Remarks:** Accepts advertising. **Circ:** Paid 30000, Non-paid 2000.

6618 ■ Crisis: The Journal of Crisis Intervention and Suicide Prevention
International Association for Suicide Prevention
5221 Washington Ave. NW
Washington, DC 20015
Journal including life saving information for all those involved in crisis intervention and suicide prevention. **Freq:** Bimonthly. **Trim Size:** 210 x 277 mm. **Key Personnel:** Annette L. Beautrais, PhD, Editor, phone: 64 3 3720408; Diego De Leo, MD, Editor-in-Chief; J.F. Connolly, Board Member. **ISSN:** 0227--5910 (print); **EISSN:** 2151--2396 (electronic). **Subscription Rates:** $179 Individuals; €284 Individuals; £228 Individuals; $368 Institutions; €128 Institutions; £102 Institutions; $138 Members; €99 Members; £79 Members. **URL:** http://www.iasp.info/journal.php. **Remarks:** Accepts advertising. **Circ:** (Not Reported).

6619 ■ Crit
American Institute of Architecture Students
1735 New York Ave. NW, Ste. 300
Washington, DC 20006-5209
Phone: (202)626-7472
Fax: (202)626-7414
Publication E-mail: crit@aias.org
Journal featuring student's architectural work. **Freq:** Semiannual. **Key Personnel:** George Guarino, III, Editor-in-Chief. **Subscription Rates:** $50 U.S. and Canada; $100 Other countries. **URL:** http://aias.org/crit. **Circ:** (Not Reported).

6620 ■ Critical Half
Women for Women International
2000 M St. NW, Ste. 200
Washington, DC 20036
Phone: (202)737-7705
Fax: (202)737-7709
Publisher's E-mail: general@womenforwomen.org
Journal featuring various perspectives on economic, social and political issues as they relate to women in international development. **Freq:** Semiannual. **Alt. Formats:** PDF. **Mailing address:** PO Box 9224, Central Islip, NY 11722-9224. **Remarks:** Advertising not accepted. **Circ:** (Not Reported).

6621 ■ C.U.A. Magazine
Catholic University of America Office of Public Affairs
B15 Marist Hall
620 Michigan Ave. NE
Washington, DC 20064
Phone: (202)319-5600
Fax: (202)319-4440
Publisher's E-mail: cua-public-affairs@cua.edu
University magazine for alumni. **Founded:** 1989. **Freq:** 3/yr. **Key Personnel:** Ellen N. Woods, Managing Editor; Victor Nakas, Editor-in-Chief; Donna Hobson, Art Director. **Subscription Rates:** Free. **URL:** http://cuamagazine.cua.edu. **Remarks:** Advertising not accepted. **Circ:** Non-paid 60000.

6622 ■ Cued Speech Journal
National Cued Speech Association
1300 Pennsylvania Ave. NW, Ste. 190-713
Washington, DC 20004
Free: 800-459-3529
Publisher's E-mail: info@cuedspeech.com
Freq: Periodic. **URL:** http://www.cuedspeech.org/cued-speech/journal.php. **Remarks:** Advertising not accepted. **Circ:** (Not Reported).

6623 ■ Cultural Diversity and Ethnic Minority Psychology
American Psychological Association
750 1st St. NE
Washington, DC 20002-4242
Phone: (202)336-5500
Free: 800-374-2721
Journal focusing on the psychological effects of culture and ethnic heritage. **Freq:** Quarterly beginning in January. **Key Personnel:** Norweeta G. Milburn, PhD, Associate Editor; Richard Lee, Associate Editor. **ISSN:** 1099-9809 (print); **EISSN:** 1939-0106 (electronic). **Subscription Rates:** $71 Members; $71 Students; $126 Nonmembers; $557 Institutions; $95 Members international, surface; $95 Students, other countries surface; $155 Nonmembers international, surface; $606 Institutions, other countries surface; $109 Members airmail. **URL:** http://www.apa.org/pubs/journals/cdp/index.aspx. **Formerly:** Cultural Diversity and Mental Health. **Ad Rates:** BW $410; 4C $975. **Remarks:** Accepts advertising. **Circ:** 1,300.

6624 ■ CUR Quarterly
Council on Undergraduate Research
734 15th St. NW, Ste. 550
Washington, DC 20005-1013
Phone: (202)783-4810
Fax: (202)783-4811
Publisher's E-mail: cur@cur.org
Freq: Quarterly September, December, March, June. **ISSN:** 1072--5830 (print). **Subscription Rates:** included in membership dues; $42 Individuals; $87 Institutions for libraries. **URL:** http://www.cur.org/publications/curquarterly. **Remarks:** Accepts advertising. **Circ:** 3500.

6625 ■ Current Population Reports: Population Estimates & Projections, Series P-25
U.S. Government Publishing Office
732 N Capitol St. NW
Washington, DC 20401-0001
Phone: (202)512-1800
Fax: (202)512-2104
Free: 866-512-1800
Publisher's E-mail: contactcenter@gpo.gov
Current population data is derived from the Current Population Survey (CPS), primary task is to produce monthly statistics on unemployment and the labor force. **Freq:** Monthly. **Print Method:** Offset. Uses mats. **Cols./Page:** 2. **Col. Width:** 41 nonpareils. **Col. Depth:** 86 agate lines. **ISSN:** 0738--453X (print). **Subscription Rates:** $21 Individuals; $29.40 Other countries. **Alt. Formats:** PDF. **URL:** http://www.census.gov/main/www/cprs.html; http://www.census.gov/prod/www/population.html. **Mailing address:** PO Box 979050, Saint Louis, MO 63197-9000. **Circ:** (Not Reported).

6626 ■ Currents
Council for Advancement and Support of Education
1307 New York Ave. NW, Ste. 1000
Washington, DC 20005-4701
Phone: (202)328-2273
Free: 800-554-8536
Publisher's E-mail: membersupportcenter@case.org
Magazine covering fundraising techniques. **Founded:** Sept. 1975. **Freq:** Monthly. **Print Method:** Web offset. **Trim Size:** 8 1/4 x 11. **Cols./Page:** 3. **Col. Width:** 13.5 picas. **Col. Depth:** 9 inches. **Key Personnel:** Gayle Bennett, Editor, phone: (202)478-5665; Elizabeth Reilly, Editor-in-Chief, phone: (202)478-5648. **ISSN:** 0748-478X (print). **Subscription Rates:** $150 Nonmembers domestic; $220 Nonmembers 2 years, domestic; $180 Nonmembers international; $280 Nonmembers 2 years, international. **URL:** http://www.case.org/Publications_and_Products/2014/January_2014.html. **Remarks:** Accepts advertising. **Circ:** ★**15000**.

6627 ■ Custom Home Outdoors
Hanley Wood Media Inc.
1 Thomas Cir. NW, Ste. 600
Washington, WA 20005

Phone: (202)452-0800
Fax: (202)785-1974
Magazine featuring latest trends and products for building professionals. **Freq:** Quarterly. **Trim Size:** 8 x 10 1/2. **Key Personnel:** Jen Lash, Managing Editor; Amy Albert, Editor. **Subscription Rates:** $36 Individuals; $66 Canada; $192 Other countries. **URL:** http://www.customhomeonline.com/ch-outdoors. **Ad Rates:** 4C $7,000. **Remarks:** Accepts advertising. **Circ:** Combined △**25000.**

6628 ■ Dance/USA eJournal
Dance USA
1029 Vermont Ave. NW, Ste. 400
Washington, DC 20005
Phone: (202)833-1717
Fax: (202)833-2686
Publisher's E-mail: danceusa@danceusa.org
Freq: Quarterly. **Subscription Rates:** $40 U.S.; $50 Canada; $70 Other countries. **URL:** http://www.danceusa.org/publications. **Remarks:** Advertising not accepted. **Circ:** 1600.

6629 ■ DC
Modern Luxury Media
927 15th St. NW
Washington, DC 20005
Phone: (202)408-5665
Fax: (202)350-6333
Magazine covering affluent lifestyle in DC. **Freq:** 7/yr. **Subscription Rates:** $40 Individuals; $60 Two years. **URL:** http://digital.modernluxury.com/publication/?i=53669. **Remarks:** Accepts advertising. **Circ:** (Not Reported).

6630 ■ Defenders Magazine
Defenders of Wildlife
1130 17th St. NW
Washington, DC 20036
Phone: (202)682-9400
Free: 800-385-9712
Publisher's E-mail: defenders@mail.defenders.org
Wildlife conservation magazine. **Freq:** Quarterly. **Print Method:** Offset. **Trim Size:** 8 1/4 x 10 7/8. **Cols./Page:** 3. **Col. Width:** 30 nonpareils. **Col. Depth:** 132 agate lines. **Key Personnel:** Mark Cheater, Editor. **ISSN:** 0162--6337 (print). **Subscription Rates:** $3 Single issue. **URL:** http://www.defenders.org/defenders-magazine. **Ad Rates:** 4C $15,000. **Remarks:** Accepts advertising. **Circ:** (Not Reported).

6631 ■ Defense Technology International
The McGraw-Hill Companies Inc.
1200 G St. NW, Ste. 922
Washington, DC 20005
Phone: (202)383-2300
Publisher's E-mail: pbg.ecommerce_custserv@mcgraw-hill.com
Magazine that covers technologies in military and defense programs. **Freq:** Bimonthly. **Key Personnel:** Bill Sweetman, Editor-in-Chief; Sean Meade, Editor. **ISSN:** 1935-6269 (print). **Subscription Rates:** Free. **URL:** http://aviationweek.com/contact-aviation-week. **Remarks:** Accepts advertising. **Circ:** (Not Reported).

6632 ■ Del-Chem Bulletin
American Chemical Society Deleware Section
1155 16th St.
Washington, DC 20036
Phone: (202)992-4713
Magazine serving the chemical industry. **Freq:** Monthly. **Print Method:** Letterpress and offset. **Cols./Page:** 2. **Col. Width:** 28 nonpareils. **Col. Depth:** 112 agate lines. **Key Personnel:** Norman Henry, Manager, Advertising. **Alt. Formats:** PDF. **URL:** http://www.delawareacs.org/delchem-bulletin. **Ad Rates:** BW $194. **Remarks:** Accepts advertising. **Circ:** (Not Reported).

6633 ■ Demokratizatsiya: The Journal of Post-Soviet Democratization
George Washington University Institute for European, Russian and Eurasian Studies
1957 E St. NW, Ste. 412
Washington, DC 20052
Phone: (202)994-6340
Fax: (202)994-5436
Publisher's E-mail: customerservice@taylorandfrancis.com
Journal covering past and current political, economical, social, and legal changes and developments in the Soviet Union and its successor states. **Freq:** Quarterly. **Trim Size:** 6 x 9. **Col. Width:** 4 1/2 INS. **Col. Depth:** 7 INS. **Key Personnel:** Marshall Goldman, Executive Editor; Rachel Adams, Managing Editor; Christopher Marsh, Executive Editor. **ISSN:** 1074-6846 (print). **Subscription Rates:** $210 Institutions print and online; $62 Individuals online only; $65 Individuals print and online; $175 Institutions print or online. **URL:** http://www.gwu.edu/~ieresgwu/programs/demokratizatsiya.cfm. **Ad Rates:** BW $225. **Remarks:** Accepts advertising. **Circ:** Paid 513.

6634 ■ Design Lines Magazine
American Institute of Building Design
7059 Blair Rd. NW, Ste. 400
Washington, DC 20012
Phone: (202)750-4900
Fax: (866)204-0293
Free: 800-366-2423
Publisher's E-mail: info@aibd.org
Magazine focusing on issues, education, and events in the building design industry. **Freq:** Quarterly. **URL:** http://www.aibd.org/for_professionals/member_opportunities.php. **Circ:** (Not Reported).

6635 ■ Destinations: The Official Publication of the American Bus Association
American Bus Association
111 K St. NE, 9th Fl.
Washington, DC 20002
Phone: (202)842-1645
Fax: (202)842-0850
Free: 800-283-2877
Publisher's E-mail: abainfo@buses.org
Public. **Freq:** Bimonthly. **Print Method:** Offset. **Trim Size:** 8 1/2 x 11. **Cols./Page:** 3. **Key Personnel:** George Spencer, Senior Editor. **ISSN:** 0279--8468 (print). **Subscription Rates:** $25 Individuals; $30 Canada; $3 Single issue; $150 Institutions. **URL:** http://www.buses.org/News-Publications/Destinations-Magazine. **Ad Rates:** 4C $4,145. **Remarks:** Accepts advertising. **Circ:** ‡7500.

6636 ■ Developer
DoveTale Publishers
1 Thomas Cir. NW
Washington, DC 20005
Phone: (202)339-0744
Fax: (202)785-1974
Free: 877-275-8647
Publisher's E-mail: hwmicustomerservice@hanleywood.com
Magazine providing information on community creation, sustainable development and best use of land resources. **Freq:** Bimonthly. **Key Personnel:** Shabnam Mogharabi, Editor. **URL:** http://www.hanleywoodopportunities.com/Index.asp?Cat=mc&Pub=dev&Sect=Intro. **Remarks:** Accepts advertising. **Circ:** (Not Reported).

6637 ■ Developmental Psychology
American Psychological Association
750 1st St. NE
Washington, DC 20002-4242
Phone: (202)336-5500
Free: 800-374-2721
Journal presenting empirical contributions that advance knowledge and theory about human psychological growth and development from infancy to old age. **Freq:** Bimonthly beginning in January. **Print Method:** Offset. **Key Personnel:** Jacquelynne S. Eccles, Editor; Nameera Akhtar, Associate Editor. **ISSN:** 0012--1649 (print); **EISSN:** 1939--0599 (electronic). **Subscription Rates:** $195 Members domestic; $228 Members foreign, surface; $269 Members foreign, air mail; $158 Students domestic; $191 Students foreign, surface; $232 Students foreign, air mail; $527 Nonmembers domestic; $584 Nonmembers foreign, surface; $616 Nonmembers foreign, air mail; $1571 Institutions domestic; $1681 Institutions, other countries surface mail; $1713 Institutions, other countries air mail. **URL:** http://www.apa.org/pubs/journals/dev/index.aspx. **Ad Rates:** BW $335; 4C $975. **Remarks:** Accepts advertising. **Circ:** ‡1000.

6638 ■ Developments: The Voice of the Vacation Ownership Industry
American Resort Development Association
1201 15th St. NW, Ste. 400
Washington, DC 20005
Phone: (202)371-6700
Fax: (202)289-8544
Publisher's E-mail: customerservice@arda.org
Magazine for resort developers, suppliers, and related industries. **Freq:** 10/year. **Print Method:** Offset. **Trim Size:** 8.375 x 10.875. **Cols./Page:** 3. **Col. Width:** 2 5/16 inches. **Col. Depth:** 9 5/8 inches. **Key Personnel:** Kathryn Mullan, Editor, phone: (202)207-1075, fax: (202)289-8544. **URL:** http://www.arda.org/publications-resources/developmentsmagazine/overview.aspx. **Ad Rates:** 4C $4,025. **Remarks:** Accepts advertising. **Circ:** 13000.

6639 ■ Diplomatic List
U.S. Government Publishing Office
732 N Capitol St. NW
Washington, DC 20401-0001
Phone: (202)512-1800
Fax: (202)512-2104
Free: 866-512-1800
Publisher's E-mail: contactcenter@gpo.gov
Magazine listing foreign diplomats. **Founded:** 1977. **Freq:** Quarterly. **Print Method:** Letterpress. **Cols./Page:** 2. **Col. Width:** 37 nonpareils. **Col. Depth:** 123 agate lines. **ISSN:** 0012-3099 (print). **Subscription Rates:** $19 Individuals; $26.60 Other countries; $17 Single issue; $23.80 Single issue in other countries. **URL:** http://www.state.gov/s/cpr/rls/dpl/. **Mailing address:** PO Box 979050, Saint Louis, MO 63197-9000. **Circ:** (Not Reported).

6640 ■ Dispute Resolution Magazine
American Bar Association - Section of Dispute Resolution
1050 Connecticut NW, Ste. 400
Washington, DC 20036
Phone: (202)662-1680
Fax: (202)662-1683
Magazine featuring conferences, activities, technical services, articles, stories, and issues related to dispute resolution. **Freq:** Quarterly. **ISSN:** 0271--2709 (print). **Subscription Rates:** Included in membership; $30 Nonmembers /year; $8 Single issue back issue. **Alt. Formats:** PDF. **URL:** http://www.americanbar.org/groups/dispute_resolution/publications/dispute_resolutionmagazinearchives.html. **Remarks:** Advertising not accepted. **Circ:** (Not Reported).

6641 ■ Distance Education and Training Council News
Distance Education Accrediting Commission
1101 17th St. NW, Ste. 808
Washington, DC 20036
Phone: (202)234-5100
Fax: (202)332-1386
Publisher's E-mail: info@deac.org
Freq: Semiannual. **Alt. Formats:** PDF. **URL:** http://www.deac.org/Media-and-Events/DEAC-News-Room.aspx. **Remarks:** Advertising not accepted. **Circ:** (Not Reported).

6642 ■ Dreaming
American Psychological Association
750 1st St. NE
Washington, DC 20002-4242
Phone: (202)336-5500
Free: 800-374-2721
Professional journal publishing scholarly articles related to dreaming from any discipline and viewpoint. **Freq:** Quarterly. **Key Personnel:** Dierdre Barrett, PhD, Editor-in-Chief; Kelly Bulkeley, PhD, Senior Editor; Clara E. Hill, PhD, Senior Editor. **ISSN:** 1053-0797 (print); **EISSN:** 1573-3351 (electronic). **Subscription Rates:** $69 Members; $69 Students; $133 Nonmembers; $809 Institutions; $93 Members international, surface; $93 Students, other countries international, surface; $162 Nonmembers international, surface; $858 Institutions, other countries international, surface; $107 Members international, air mail; $107 Students, other countries international, air mail; $175 Nonmembers international, air mail; $873 Institutions international, air mail. **URL:** http://www.apa.org/pubs/journals/drm/index.aspx. **Ad Rates:** BW $275; 4C $1,175. **Remarks:** Accepts advertising. **Circ:** 100.

6643 ■ The Dupont Current
The Current Newspapers Inc.
5185 MacArthur Blvd. NW, Ste. 102
Washington, DC 20016-3349
Phone: (202)244-7223
Fax: (202)363-9850

Circulation: ★ = AAM; △ or • = BPA; ♦ = CAC; ❑ = VAC; ⊕ = PO Statement; ‡ = Publisher's Report; Boldface figures = sworn; Light figures = estimated.

Publisher's E-mail: newsdesk@currentnewspapers.com
Community newspaper. **Freq:** Weekly (Wed.). **Key Personnel:** Davis Kennedy, Editor, Publisher; Chris Kain, Managing Editor. **Subscription Rates:** $52 By mail. **URL:** http://www.currentnewspapers.com/. **Remarks:** Accepts advertising. **Circ:** Combined ■ **14074.**

6644 ■ Earth Ethics
Center for Respect of Life & Environment
2100 L St. NW
Washington, DC 20037
Phone: (202)778-6133
Fax: (202)778-6138
Publication E-mail: info@crle.org
Freq: Semiannual. **Subscription Rates:** $3 Single issue. **URL:** http://crle.org/publications.asp. **Remarks:** Advertising not accepted. **Circ:** (Not Reported).

6645 ■ Earth in Space
American Geophysical Union
2000 Florida Ave. NW
Washington, DC 20009-1277
Phone: (202)462-6900
Fax: (202)328-0566
Free: 800-966-2481
Publication E-mail: publications@agu.org
Freq: 9/year. **ISSN:** 1040- 3124 (print). **Subscription Rates:** $12 /year plus postage, outside U.S. **URL:** http://publications.agu.org/journals/earth-and-space-science/. **Remarks:** Advertising not accepted. **Circ:** (Not Reported).

6646 ■ EBRI Issue Brief
Employee Benefit Research Institute
1100 13th St. NW, Ste. 878
Washington, DC 20005-4051
Phone: (202)659-0670
Fax: (202)775-6312
Publisher's E-mail: info@ebri.org
Publication printing summaries and reports on benefit topics (covers one topic per issue). **Freq:** Monthly. **ISSN:** 0887--137X (print). **Subscription Rates:** $199 Individuals hard copy; annual; $89 Individuals PDF; annual. **URL:** http://www.ebri.org/publications/ib. **Remarks:** Advertising not accepted. **Circ:** (Not Reported).

6647 ■ Eco-Structure
DoveTale Publishers
1 Thomas Cir. NW
Washington, DC 20005
Phone: (202)339-0744
Fax: (202)785-1974
Free: 877-275-8647
Publication E-mail: ecos@omeda.com
Magazine that features articles about environmentally-friendly buildings and structures. **Freq:** Quarterly. **Key Personnel:** Ned Cramer, Director, Editorial; Patrick J. Carroll, Group President; Russell S. Ellis, Publisher. **Subscription Rates:** Free. **URL:** http://www.ecobuildingpulse.com/toc/eco-structure-magazine.aspx. **Remarks:** Accepts advertising. **Circ:** Combined △**88449.**

6648 ■ Ecological Restoration
Society for Ecological Restoration International
1133 15th St. NW, Ste. 300
Washington, DC 20005
Phone: (202)299-9518
Fax: (270)626-5485
Publisher's E-mail: info@ser.org
Trim Size: 8 1/2 x 11. **Key Personnel:** Steven N. Handel, PhD, Editor. **ISSN:** 1543-4060 (print). **Alt. Formats:** PDF. **URL:** http://www.ser.org/resources/resources-detail-view/ecological-restoration-a-means-of-conserving-biodiversity-and-sustaining-livelihoods. **Formerly**: Restoration and Management Notes. **Ad Rates:** BW $415. **Remarks:** Advertising not accepted. **Circ:** Paid ‡2200.

6649 ■ Economic Development Journal
International Economic Development Council
734 15th St. NW, Ste. 900
Washington, DC 20005
Phone: (202)223-7800
Fax: (202)223-4745
Journal featuring in-depth articles on important programs, projects, and trends in the economics of the United States and around the world. **Freq:** Quarterly. **Subscription Rates:** Included in membership. **Alt. Formats:** PDF. **URL:** http://www.iedconline.org/web-pages/resources-publications/economic-development-journal. **Mailing address:** PO Box 75219, Baltimore, MD 21275-9219. **Remarks:** Advertising not accepted. **Circ:** (Not Reported).

6650 ■ Economic Policy Reforms
OECD Washington Center
1776 I St. NW, Ste. 450
Washington, DC 20006
Phone: (202)785-6323
Fax: (202)315-2508
Free: 800-456-6323
Publisher's E-mail: washington.contact@oecd.org
Periodical providing an overview of structural policy development in Organisation for Economic Cooperation and Development countries. **Freq:** Annual. **ISSN:** 1813-2715 (print); **EISSN:** 1813-2723 (electronic). **Subscription Rates:** €56 Individuals ebook; $78 Individuals ebook; £50 Individuals ebook; ¥7200 Individuals ebook; $1000 Individuals ebook. **Alt. Formats:** E-book; PDF. **URL:** http://www.oecd-ilibrary.org/economics/economic-policy-reforms_18132723. **Circ:** (Not Reported).

6651 ■ EcuLink
National Council of the Churches of Christ in the USA
110 Maryland Ave. NE, Ste. 108
Washington, DC 20002-5603
Phone: (202)544-2350
Fax: (212)543-1297
Free: 800-379-7729
Publication E-mail: staff@eculink.org
Freq: Monthly. **Subscription Rates:** Free. **URL:** http://eculink.org/home/; http://www.ncccusa.org/news/. **Remarks:** Advertising not accepted. **Circ:** 150000.

6652 ■ Educational Evaluation and Policy Analysis
American Educational Research Association
1430 K St. NW, Ste. 1200
Washington, DC 20005-2504
Phone: (202)238-3200
Fax: (202)238-3250
Publisher's E-mail: webmaster@aera.net
Educational evaluation and policy analysis journal. **Freq:** Quarterly. **Print Method:** Sheetfed offset. **Trim Size:** 6 3/4 x 10. **Cols./Page:** 2. **Col. Width:** 32 nonpareils. **Col. Depth:** 116 agate lines. **Key Personnel:** Mark Berends, Editor. **ISSN:** 0162--3737 (print); **EISSN:** 1935--1062 (electronic). **Subscription Rates:** £249 Institutions print & e-access; £244 Institutions print; £38 Individuals print & e-access; £67 Institutions single print; £12 Single issue print. **URL:** http://www.aera.net/Publications/Journals/iEducationalEvaluationandPolicyAnaysisi/tabid/12608/Default.aspx; http://www.sagepub.com/journalsProdDesc.nav?prodId=Journal201852. **Ad Rates:** BW $945; 4C $1,275. **Remarks:** Accepts advertising. **Circ:** Paid ‡3160.

6653 ■ Educational Researcher
American Educational Research Association
1430 K St. NW, Ste. 1200
Washington, DC 20005-2504
Phone: (202)238-3200
Fax: (202)238-3250
Publisher's E-mail: webmaster@aera.net
Educational research journal. **Freq:** 9/year. **Trim Size:** 8 1/2 x 10. **Key Personnel:** Carolyn D. Herrington, Editor, phone: (850)645-8711; Vivian L. Gadsden, Editor, phone: (215)573-3528. **ISSN:** 0013--189X (print); **EISSN:** 1935--102X (electronic). **Subscription Rates:** £326 Institutions print and e-access; £293 Institutions e-access; £319 Institutions print only; £38 Individuals print and e-access. **URL:** http://www.aera.net/Publications/Journals/iEducationalResearcheri/tabid/12609/Default.aspx; http://www.sagepub.com/journals/Journal201856. **Ad Rates:** BW $1,895. **Remarks:** Accepts advertising. **Circ:** ‡23610.

6654 ■ eg Magazine
Society for Environmental Graphic Design
1900 L St. NW, Ste. 710
Washington, DC 20036
Phone: (202)638-5555
Publisher's E-mail: segd@segd.org
Publication that covers environmental graphics, exhibit and industrial design, architecture, interiors, landscape architecture, and communication arts. **Freq:** Quarterly. **Key Personnel:** Pat Matson Knapp, Editor-in-Chief, phone: (513)751-1383. **URL:** http://segd.org/egMagazine. **Formerly**: SEGDesign. **Remarks:** Accepts advertising. **Circ:** Paid ‡3000.

6655 ■ El Latino
El Latino
2370 Chaplain St. NW, Ste. B
Washington, DC 20009-2670
Phone: (202)232-0447
Fax: (202)265-4848
Community newspaper (Spanish). **Founded:** 1977. **Freq:** Daily. **Print Method:** Web offset. **Key Personnel:** Martin Sanders, Editor; Varsi Padayachee, Publisher; Sandra Aceuedo, Manager, Advertising. **Subscription Rates:** Free; $16 By mail. **Ad Rates:** BW $980. **Remarks:** Accepts advertising. **Circ:** Paid ‡1150, Free ‡23850.

6656 ■ El Pregonero
Ministerio Hispano
145 Taylor St. NE
Washington, DC 20017
Phone: (202)281-2406
Fax: (202)281-2408
Newspaper that features local, national, and international news coverage (Spanish). **Freq:** Weekly (Thurs.). **Cols./Page:** 5. **Col. Width:** 1 7/8 inches. **Col. Depth:** 13 1/2 inches. **Key Personnel:** Thomas H. Schmidt, Publisher. **Subscription Rates:** Free. **URL:** http://www.elpregonero.org. **Remarks:** Accepts advertising. **Circ:** (Not Reported).

6657 ■ Elections Insight
Business-Industry Political Action Committee
888 16th St. NW, Ste. 305
Washington, DC 20006-4103
Phone: (202)833-1880
Fax: (202)833-2338
Publisher's E-mail: info@bipac.org
Freq: Semimonthly. **Subscription Rates:** free. **URL:** http://www.bipac.org/page.asp?g=ppg&content=eis&parent=bipac. **Remarks:** Advertising not accepted. **Circ:** (Not Reported).

6658 ■ Elements: An International Magazine of Mineralogy, Geochemistry, and Petrology
Geochemical Society
5241 Broad Branch Rd. NW
Washington, DC 20015-1305
Phone: (202)545-6946
Publisher's E-mail: gsoffice@geochemsoc.org
Freq: Bimonthly. **ISSN:** 1811- 5209 (print). **Subscription Rates:** included in membership dues. **URL:** http://www.geochemsoc.org/publications/elementsmagazine/; http://www.elementsmagazine.org/archives/. **Remarks:** Accepts advertising. **Circ:** 10,000.

6659 ■ ELI Environmental Forum
Environmental Law Institute
2000 L St. NW, Ste. 620
Washington, DC 20036
Phone: (202)939-3824
Journal publishing articles on environmental law and policy. **Freq:** Bimonthly. **Subscription Rates:** Included in membership. **URL:** http://www.eli.org/the-environmental-forum. **Remarks:** Accepts advertising. **Circ:** 4000.

6660 ■ Emotion
American Psychological Association
750 1st St. NE
Washington, DC 20002-4242
Phone: (202)336-5500
Free: 800-374-2721
Publisher's E-mail: info@sitag.ch
Journal discussing different aspects of emotional reactions in humans. **Freq:** Bimonthly beginning in February. **Key Personnel:** David DeSteno, Editor. **ISSN:** 1528-3542 (print); **EISSN:** 1931-1516 (electronic). **Subscription Rates:** $99 Individuals; $45 Students; $149 Nonmembers individual domestic; $999 Institutions; $125 Members international, surface; $71 Students, other countries surface; $184 Nonmembers international, surface; $1060 Institutions, other countries surface; $146 Members international, airmail; $92 Students, other countries airmail. **URL:** http://www.apa.org/journals/emo.html. **Ad Rates:** BW $350; 4C $975. **Remarks:** Accepts advertising. **Circ:** 600.

6661 ■ Employment and Earnings
U.S. Government Publishing Office
732 N Capitol St. NW

Washington, DC 20401-0001
Phone: (202)512-1800
Fax: (202)512-2104
Free: 866-512-1800
Publisher's E-mail: contactcenter@gpo.gov
Publication covering employment and economics. **Founded:** 1969. **Freq:** Monthly. **ISSN:** 0013-6840 (print). **Subscription Rates:** $53 Individuals; $74.20 Other countries; $27 Single issue; $37.80 Other countries single copy. **Alt. Formats:** PDF. **URL:** http://www.bls.gov/opub/ee/home.htm. **Mailing address:** PO Box 979050, Saint Louis, MO 63197-9000. **Circ:** (Not Reported).

6662 ■ Endocrine News
Endocrine Society
2055 L St. NW, Ste. 600
Washington, DC 20036
Phone: (202)971-3636
Fax: (202)736-9705
Free: 888-363-6274
Publisher's E-mail: societyservices@endocrine.org
Freq: Monthly. **Subscription Rates:** Included in membership. **Alt. Formats:** PDF. **URL:** http://www.endocrine.org/endocrine-press/endocrine-news. **Remarks:** Accepts advertising. **Circ:** (Not Reported).

6663 ■ Endocrine Reviews: A Publication of the Endocrine Society
Endocrine Society
2055 L St. NW, Ste. 600
Washington, DC 20036
Phone: (202)971-3636
Fax: (202)736-9705
Free: 888-363-6274
Publisher's E-mail: societyservices@endocrine.org
Peer-reviewed medical journal providing in-depth information on cutting-edge issues in all facets of endocrinology. **Freq:** Bimonthly. **Print Method:** Web Offset. **Trim Size:** 8 3/8 x 10 7/8. **Cols./Page:** 2. **Col. Width:** 32 nonpareils. **Col. Depth:** 119 agate lines. **Key Personnel:** Leonard Wartofsky, Editor-in-Chief. **ISSN:** 0163--769X (print); **EISSN:** 1945--7189 (electronic). **Subscription Rates:** $135 Members print and online; $549 Nonmembers print and online; $10 Members online only, in-training. **URL:** http://press.endocrine.org/journal/edrv. **Remarks:** Advertising accepted; rates available upon request. **Circ:** Combined ‡4000.

6664 ■ Endocrinology
Endocrine Society
2055 L St. NW, Ste. 600
Washington, DC 20036
Phone: (202)971-3636
Fax: (202)736-9705
Free: 888-363-6274
Publisher's E-mail: societyservices@endocrine.org
Freq: Monthly. **Print Method:** Web Offset. **Trim Size:** 8 3/8 x 10 7/8. **Cols./Page:** 2. **Col. Width:** 32 nonpareils. **Col. Depth:** 119 agate lines. **Key Personnel:** Andrea C. Gore, Editor-in-Chief. **ISSN:** 0013--7227 (print); **EISSN:** 1945--7170 (electronic). **Subscription Rates:** $225 Members print and online; $919 Nonmembers print and online; Free online. **URL:** http://press.endocrine.org/journal/endo. **Ad Rates:** BW $1740. **Remarks:** Advertising accepted; rates available upon request. **Circ:** Paid ‡3500.

6665 ■ Energy Prices and Taxes: Quarterly Statistics
OECD Washington Center
1776 I St. NW, Ste. 450
Washington, DC 20006
Phone: (202)785-6323
Fax: (202)315-2508
Free: 800-456-6323
Publication E-mail: sourceoced@oecd.org stats@iea.org
Tabloid presenting energy price and tax information. **Freq:** Quarterly. **Print Method:** Offset. **Trim Size:** 7 7/8 x 10 5/8. **ISSN:** 0256--2332 (print); **EISSN:** 1609--6835 (electronic). **Subscription Rates:** $618 Individuals print and online; €470 Individuals print and online; £375 Individuals print and online; ¥58000 Individuals print and online. **Alt. Formats:** PDF. **URL:** http://www.oecd-ilibrary.org/energy/energy-prices-and-taxes_16096835. **Remarks:** Advertising not accepted. **Circ:** (Not Reported).

6666 ■ The Engineering Economist
American Society for Engineering Education
1818 N St. NW, Ste. 600
Washington, DC 20036-2479
Phone: (202)331-3500
Publisher's E-mail: customerservice@taylorandfrancis.com
Journal covering capital investment analysis, cost estimation and accounting, cost of capital, design economics, economic decision analysis, education, policy analysis, and research and development. **Freq:** Quarterly. **Key Personnel:** Dr. Joseph C. Hartman; Phil Jones, Editor; Jerome P. Lavelle, Board Member; Joseph Hartman, Editor-in-Chief; Thomas O. Boucher, Editor-in-Chief. **ISSN:** 0013--791X (print); **EISSN:** 1547--2701 (electronic). **Subscription Rates:** $113 Individuals print only; $191 Institutions online only; $218 Institutions print and online. **URL:** http://www.tandfonline.com/toc/utee20/current; http://www.iienet2.org/details.aspx?id=1486; http://www.asee.org/papers-and-publications/publications/division-publications#The_Engineering_Economist. **Remarks:** Advertising not accepted. **Circ:** (Not Reported).

6667 ■ EOS
American Geophysical Union
2000 Florida Ave. NW
Washington, DC 20009-1277
Phone: (202)462-6900
Fax: (202)328-0566
Free: 800-966-2481
Publication E-mail: eos@agu.org
Professional newspaper containing refereed articles on current geophysical/planetary sciences research and on the relationship of geophysics to social and political questions. **Freq:** Weekly (Tues.). **Key Personnel:** Barbara T. Richman, Editor; Wendy S. Gordon, Editor. **ISSN:** 0096--3941 (print); **EISSN:** 2324--9250 (electronic). **Subscription Rates:** Free online. **URL:** http://onlinelibrary.wiley.com/journal/10.1002/(ISSN)2324-9250/homepage/ProductInformation.html. **Ad Rates:** GLR $9; BW $5,500; 4C $1,400; PCI $75. **Remarks:** Advertising accepted; rates available upon request. **Circ:** 53000.

6668 ■ EPA Administrative Law Reporter
EPA Administrative Law Reporter
1601 Connecticut Ave. NW, Ste. 602
Washington, DC 20009
Phone: (202)462-5755
Fax: (202)328-2430
Professional journal covering environmental law. Available in print format or via e-mail. **Freq:** Monthly. **Trim Size:** 8 1/2 x 11. **Cols./Page:** 2. **Col. Width:** 2 1/2 inches. **Col. Depth:** 8 inches. **Key Personnel:** Mark Cohen, Editor. **ISSN:** 1072--8635 (print). **Subscription Rates:** $3820 Individuals /year. **Available online. URL:** http://lawreporters.com/NewFiles/EPAALRx.html. **Remarks:** Advertising not accepted. **Circ:** (Not Reported).

6669 ■ EPI Journal
Economic Policy Institute
1225 Eye St. NW, Ste. 600
Washington, DC 20005
Phone: (202)775-8810
Fax: (202)775-0819
Free: 800-374-4844
Publisher's E-mail: epi@epi.org
Publishes articles on economic policy. **Subscription Rates:** Included in membership. **Alt. Formats:** PDF. **URL:** http://www.epi.org/types/epi-journal. **Remarks:** Advertising not accepted. **Circ:** (Not Reported).

6670 ■ Ethics: An International Journal of Social, Political, and Legal Philosophy
The University of Chicago Press
Georgetown University
New North 215
Washington, DC 20057
Phone: (202)687-4739
Fax: (202)687-4367
Publication E-mail: ethicsjournal@georgetown.edu
Journal. **Freq:** Quarterly. **Print Method:** Offset. **Trim Size:** 6 x 9. **Cols./Page:** 1. **Col. Width:** 54 nonpareils. **Col. Depth:** 106 agate lines. **Key Personnel:** Martha C. Nussbaum, Board Member; Donald C. Hubin, Associate Editor; Daniel Hausman, Associate Editor; David Copp, Board Member; David Miller, Associate Editor; Henry S. Richardson, Editor; Catherine Galko Campbell, Managing Editor. **ISSN:** 0014--1704 (print); **EISSN:** 1539--297X (electronic). **Subscription Rates:** $58 Individuals print and electronic; $50 Individuals electronic only; $51 Individuals print only; $29 Students electronic only; $47 Individuals special APA, print and electronic; $116 Two years individual, print and electronic; $100 Two years individual, electronic only; $102 Two years individual, print only; $94 Two years special APA, print and electronic; $58 Two years student, electronic only. **URL:** http://www.journals.uchicago.edu/journals/et/pr/141020. **Ad Rates:** BW $690. **Remarks:** Accepts advertising. **Circ:** ‡1443.

6671 ■ Eukaryotic Cell
American Society for Microbiology
1752 N St. NW
Washington, DC 20036-2904
Phone: (202)942-9207
Fax: (202)942-9333
Publisher's E-mail: service@asmusa.org
Journal featuring reports of research on simple eukaryotic microorganisms. **Freq:** Monthly. **Key Personnel:** Aaron P. Mitchell, Editor-in-Chief; N. Louise Glass, Editor; Geraldine Butler, Editor. **ISSN:** 1535--9778 (print); **EISSN:** 1535--9786 (electronic). **URL:** http://ec.asm.org. **Remarks:** Accepts advertising. **Circ:** (Not Reported).

6672 ■ Eurasian Geography and Economics
Taylor and Francis Group PLC
1750 Massachusetts Ave. NW
Washington, DC 20036-1903
Publisher's E-mail: enquiries@taylorandfrancis.com
Journal covering geography and economics of Asiatic, Russia and European countries. **Freq:** 6/year. **Key Personnel:** Anders Aslund, Editor; Clifton W. Pannell, Editor; Alexander B. Murphy, Editor. **ISSN:** 1538--7216 (print); **EISSN:** 1938--2863 (electronic). **Subscription Rates:** $835 Institutions online; $955 Institutions online and print; $171 Individuals print only. **URL:** http://www.tandfonline.com/toc/rege20/current#.VIGAWu-BIPM. **Circ:** (Not Reported).

6673 ■ Executive Intelligence Review
EIR News Service
PO Box 17390
Washington, DC 20041
Phone: (703)777-9451
Professional magazine covering economics. **Freq:** Weekly. **Key Personnel:** Susan Welsh, Associate Editor; Marsha Freeman, Director, Advertising; Lyndon H. LaRauche, Jr., Editor-in-Chief. **ISSN:** 0273-6314 (print). **Subscription Rates:** $396 Individuals; $10 Single issue; $360 Individuals online only /year. **Alt. Formats:** PDF. **URL:** http://www.larouchepub.com/eiw/index.html; http://www.larouchepub.com. **Remarks:** Accepts advertising. **Circ:** Combined ⊕**15000**.

6674 ■ Experimental Biology and Medicine
Society for Experimental Biology and Medicine
3220 N St. NW, No. 179
Washington, DC 20007-2829
Phone: (201)962-3519
Fax: (201)962-3522
Publisher's E-mail: ed@sebm.org
Journal covering multidisciplinary and interdisciplinary research in the biomedical sciences. Also covering topics on anatomy, biochemistry and molecular biology, cell and developmental biology, endocrinology and nutrition, immunology, neuroscience, pharmacology and toxicology, physiology, and translational research. **Freq:** Monthly. **Print Method:** Offset. **Trim Size:** 10 3/4 x 13. **Cols./Page:** 5. **Col. Width:** 10.75 picas. **Col. Depth:** 13 inches. **Key Personnel:** Steven R. Goodman, PhD, Editor-in-Chief; Michael J. Friedlander, Associate Editor. **ISSN:** 1535--3702 (print); **EISSN:** 1535--3699 (electronic). **Subscription Rates:** $1274 Institutions print + online; $1147 Institutions e-access; $403 Individuals print + online; $149 Institutions single issue; $29 Individuals single issue. **URL:** http://ebm.sagepub.com. **Ad Rates:** BW £650. **Remarks:** Accepts advertising. **Circ:** (Not Reported).

6675 ■ Experimental and Clinical Psychopharmacology
American Psychological Association
750 1st St. NE
Washington, DC 20002-4242
Phone: (202)336-5500

Circulation: ⋆ = AAM; △ or • = BPA; ♦ = CAC; ❑ = VAC; ⊕ = PO Statement; ‡ = Publisher's Report; Boldface figures = sworn; Light figures = estimated.

Free: 800-374-2721
Journal including articles related to psychoactive drugs. **Freq:** Bimonthly beginning in February. **Key Personnel:** Suzette M. Evans, Editor. **ISSN:** 1064-1297 (print); **EISSN:** 1936-2293 (electronic). **Subscription Rates:** $92 Members; $38 Students; $125 Nonmembers; $746 Institutions; $118 Members surface; $64 Students surface; $160 Nonmembers surface individual; $807 Institutions surface; $139 Members airmail; $85 Students airmail. **URL:** http://www.apa.org/pubs/journals/pha/index.aspx. **Ad Rates:** BW $275; 4C $975. **Remarks:** Accepts advertising. **Circ:** 200.

6676 ■ FAA Safety Briefing
DOT/FAA
800 Independence Ave. SW
Washington, DC 20591
Free: 866-835-5322
Magazine containing aviation safety information. **Freq:** 6/year. **Print Method:** Web. **Trim Size:** 8 1/2 x 11. **Cols./Page:** 3. **Col. Width:** 30 nonpareils. **Col. Depth:** 136 agate lines. **ISSN:** 1057--9648 (print). **Subscription Rates:** $21 U.S.; $29.40 Other countries; $8 Single issue; $11.20 Other countries single issue. **URL:** http://www.faa.gov/news/safety_briefing. **Formerly:** FAA Aviation News: A DOT/Flight Standards Safety Publication. **Remarks:** Advertising not accepted. **Circ:** Paid 18000, Controlled 13000.

6677 ■ False Claims Act and Qui Tam Quarterly Review
Taxpayers Against Fraud Education Fund
1220 19th St. NW, Ste. 501
Washington, DC 20036-2497
Phone: (202)296-4826
Publisher's E-mail: info@taf.org
Journal analyzing court opinions, judgments, settlements and trends from the past. **Freq:** Quarterly. **Alt. Formats:** PDF. **URL:** http://www.taf.org/publications/quarterly-review/archive-public. **Remarks:** Advertising not accepted. **Circ:** (Not Reported).

6678 ■ Families, Systems & Health: The Journal of Collaborative Healthcare
American Psychological Association
750 1st St. NE
Washington, DC 20002-4242
Phone: (202)336-5500
Free: 800-374-2721
Peer-reviewed multidisciplinary journal publishing clinical research, training, and theoretical contributions in areas of families and health, with particular focus on collaborative family healthcare. **Freq:** Quarterly beginning in March. **Print Method:** Perfect Bound. **Trim Size:** 6 x 10. **Key Personnel:** Donald A. Bloch, Editor, Founder; Todd M. Edwards, PhD, Associate Editor; Colleen T. Fogarty. **ISSN:** 1091--7527 (print). **Subscription Rates:** $491 Institutions domestic; $540 Institutions, other countries surface; $555 Institutions, other countries air mail; $185 Individuals domestic; $214 Individuals International (surface); $227 Individuals International (air mail). **URL:** http://www.apa.org/pubs/journals/fsh/index.aspx. **Formerly:** Family Systems Medicine. **Ad Rates:** BW $200; 4C $1,175. **Remarks:** Accepts advertising. **Circ:** 200.

6679 ■ Family Systems: A Journal of Natural Systems Thinking in Psychiatry and the Sciences
Bowen Center for the Study of the Family
4400 MacArthur Blvd. NW, Ste. 103
Washington, DC 20007
Phone: (202)965-4400
Fax: (202)965-1765
Publisher's E-mail: info@thebowencenter.org
Professional journal covering biology and family behavior and evolution. **Freq:** Semiannual. **Print Method:** Offset. **Trim Size:** 7 x 10. **Cols./Page:** 1. **Col. Width:** 4 1/2 inches. **Col. Depth:** 8 1/8 inches. **Key Personnel:** Robert J. Noone, Editor; Ruth Riley Sagar, Managing Editor. **ISSN:** 1070--0609 (print). **Subscription Rates:** $50 Individuals; $60 Out of state; $95 Institutions. **Alt. Formats:** PDF. **URL:** http://thebowencenter.org/miva/merchant.mvc?Screen=CTGY&Store_Code=TBC&Category_Code=FSJ. **Remarks:** Advertising not accepted. **Circ:** Combined 680.

6680 ■ FAS Public Interest Report
Federation of American Scientists
1725 DeSales St. NW, 6th Fl.
Washington, DC 20036
Phone: (202)546-3300
Publisher's E-mail: fas@fas.org
Freq: Quarterly. **Subscription Rates:** $50 Individuals /year. **Alt. Formats:** PDF. **URL:** http://fas.org/publications/public-interest-reports/. **Remarks:** Advertising not accepted. **Circ:** 5,000.

6681 ■ FASTrack
Fund for American Studies
1706 New Hampshire Ave. NW
Washington, DC 20009
Phone: (202)986-0384
Fax: (202)986-0390
Publisher's E-mail: info@tfas.org
Magazine featuring news on programs, alumni and upcoming events. **Freq:** Quarterly. **URL:** http://www.tfas.org/Page.aspx?pid=1804. **Remarks:** Advertising not accepted. **Circ:** (Not Reported).

6682 ■ FBI Law Enforcement Bulletin
U.S. Federal Bureau of Investigation
935 Pennsylvania Ave., NW
Washington, DC 20535-0001
Phone: (202)324-3000
Publication E-mail: leb@fbiacademy.edu
Trade magazine covering law enforcement. **Freq:** Monthly. **Cols./Page:** 3. **Col. Width:** 13 picas. **Col. Depth:** 50 picas. **Key Personnel:** John E. Ott, Editor. **ISSN:** 0014-5688 (print). **Subscription Rates:** $53 Individuals; $74.20 Other countries. **URL:** http://www.fbi.gov/stats-services/publications/law-enforcement-bulletin/leb. **Remarks:** Advertising not accepted. **Circ:** Controlled 45000.

6683 ■ Federal Circuit Bar Journal
Federal Circuit Bar Association
1620 I St. NW, Ste. 801
Washington, DC 20006-4033
Phone: (202)466-3923
Fax: (202)833-1061
Freq: Quarterly. **Subscription Rates:** Included in membership. **URL:** http://www.fedcirbar.org/Resources/Publications/Journal; http://thefcbj.org. **Remarks:** Advertising not accepted. **Circ:** (Not Reported).

6684 ■ Federal Circuit Bar Journal
George Washington University Law School
2000 H St. NW
Washington, DC 20052
Phone: (202)994-6261
Fax: (202)994-8980
Freq: Quarterly. **Subscription Rates:** Included in membership. **URL:** http://www.fedcirbar.org/Resources/Publications/Journal; http://thefcbj.org. **Remarks:** Advertising not accepted. **Circ:** (Not Reported).

6685 ■ Federal Communications Law Journal
George Washington University Law School
2000 H St. NW
Washington, DC 20052
Phone: (202)994-6261
Fax: (202)994-8980
Publication E-mail: fclj@law.gwu.edu
Journal featuring articles, book reviews, student notes, and commentaries focusing on domestic and international communications issues. **Freq:** 3/year. **Subscription Rates:** $30 U.S.; $40 Canada and Mexico; $50 Other countries; $15 Canada and Mexico single issue; $20 Other countries single issue; $15 Single issue Domestic, Canada & Mexico; $20 Single issue International. **URL:** http://fclj.org. **Remarks:** Advertising not accepted. **Circ:** (Not Reported).

6686 ■ Federal Register
U.S. Government Publishing Office
732 N Capitol St. NW
Washington, DC 20401-0001
Phone: (202)512-1800
Fax: (202)512-2104
Free: 866-512-1800
Publisher's E-mail: contactcenter@gpo.gov
Publication providing information on regulations and legal notices issued by federal agencies. **Freq:** Daily. **Print Method:** Letterpress. **Cols./Page:** 3. **Col. Width:** 25 nonpareils. **Col. Depth:** 126 agate lines. **ISSN:** 0097-6326 (print). **Subscription Rates:** $464.50 Individuals for six-month; $650.30 Other countries for six-month; $1300.60 Other countries; $929 Individuals. **URL:** http://www.gpo.gov/fdsys/browse/collection.action?collectionCode=FR. **Mailing address:** PO Box 979050, Saint Louis, MO 63197-9000. **Circ:** (Not Reported).

6687 ■ The Federalist Paper
Federalist Society for Law and Public Policy Studies
1776 I St. NW, Ste. 300
Washington, DC 20006
Phone: (202)822-8138
Fax: (202)296-8061
Publisher's E-mail: info@fed-soc.org
Magazine featuring reviews of many programs and publications the Federalist Society has sponsored through various divisions and special projects over the past months. **Freq:** Quarterly. **Subscription Rates:** Included in membership. **Alt. Formats:** PDF. **URL:** http://www.fed-soc.org/publications/type/the-federalist-paper; http://www.fed-soc.org/publications/page/the-federalist-paper. **Remarks:** Advertising not accepted. **Circ:** (Not Reported).

6688 ■ Fellowship of Catholic Scholars Quarterly
The Fellowship of Catholic Scholars
c/o William L. Saunders, Esq., President
655 15th St., Ste. 410
Washington, DC 20005-5709
Phone: (202)289-1478
Publisher's E-mail: webcoordinator@catholicscholars.org
Journal containing articles regarding Fellowship of Catholic Scholars and some relevant ideas about Jesus Christ. **Freq:** Quarterly. **Subscription Rates:** Included in membership. **Alt. Formats:** Download; PDF. **URL:** http://www.catholicscholars.org/QuarterlyList.php. **Remarks:** Advertising not accepted. **Circ:** 1600.

6689 ■ 50 Housing Magazine
National Association of Home Builders
1201 15th St. NW
Washington, DC 20005
Free: 800-268-5242
Publisher's E-mail: info@nahb.org
Magazine featuring housing industry. **Freq:** Quarterly. **Key Personnel:** Harris Floyd, Contact. **Subscription Rates:** $95 Members; $114 Nonmembers. **URL:** http://www.nahb.org/reference_list.aspx?sectionID=470. **Circ:** 20000.

6690 ■ Financial Market Trends
OECD Washington Center
1776 I St. NW, Ste. 450
Washington, DC 20006
Phone: (202)785-6323
Fax: (202)315-2508
Free: 800-456-6323
Publisher's E-mail: washington.contact@oecd.org
Publication containing analyses and examinations of financial market developments in OECD countries. **Freq:** Semiannual. **Print Method:** Offset. **ISSN:** 0378--651X (print). **URL:** http://www.oecd.org/finance/financial-markets/financialmarkettrends-oecdjournal.htm. **Remarks:** Advertising not accepted. **Circ:** (Not Reported).

6691 ■ Financial Statistics
OECD Washington Center
1776 I St. NW, Ste. 450
Washington, DC 20006
Phone: (202)785-6323
Fax: (202)315-2508
Free: 800-456-6323
Publisher's E-mail: washington.contact@oecd.org
Magazine providing statistics on financial markets and balances in OECD countries. **Freq:** Monthly. **Print Method:** Offset. **ISSN:** 0304--3371 (print). **URL:** http://www.oecd.org/std/fin-stats. **Remarks:** Advertising not accepted. **Circ:** (Not Reported).

6692 ■ First Amendment Studies
National Communication Association
1765 N St. NW
Washington, DC 20036
Phone: (202)464-4622
Fax: (202)464-4600
Publisher's E-mail: inbox@natcom.org
Contains original essays that make a significant contribution to theory and/or policy on all aspects of free speech. **Freq:** Semiannual. **ISSN:** 2168--9725 (print); **EISSN:** 2168--9733 (electronic). **Subscription Rates:** $43

Individuals print only; $135 Institutions online only; $154 Institutions print and online. **URL:** http://www.tandfonline.com/toc/rfsy20/current. **Formerly:** Free Speech Yearbook; Speech Association of America: Committee on Freedom of Speech - Yearbook. **Circ:** (Not Reported).

6693 ■ Fishery Bulletin
U.S. Government Publishing Office
732 N Capitol St. NW
Washington, DC 20401-0001
Phone: (202)512-1800
Fax: (202)512-2104
Free: 866-512-1800
Publisher's E-mail: contactcenter@gpo.gov
Bulletin publishing original research on all aspects of fishery science. **Freq:** Quarterly. **Print Method:** Letterpress. **Cols./Page:** 2. **Col. Width:** 34 nonpareils. **Col. Depth:** 112 agate lines. **Key Personnel:** Sharyn Matriotti, Managing Editor, phone: (206)526-5403; Kathryn Dennis, Associate Editor; Richard D. Brodeur, PhD, Member. **Subscription Rates:** $32 Individuals; $44.80 Other countries. **URL:** http://fishbull.noaa.gov. **Mailing address:** PO Box 979050, Saint Louis, MO 63197-9000. **Circ:** (Not Reported).

6694 ■ Flightlog
Association of Flight Attendants - CWA
501 3rd St. NW
Washington, DC 20001
Phone: (202)434-1300
Free: 800-424-2401
Publisher's E-mail: info@afacwa.org
Freq: Quarterly. **ISSN:** 0164--8689 (print). **Alt. Formats:** PDF. **URL:** http://www.afacwa.org/flightlog. **Remarks:** Accepts advertising. **Circ:** (Not Reported).

6695 ■ The Foggy Bottom Current
The Current Newspapers Inc.
5185 MacArthur Blvd. NW, Ste. 102
Washington, DC 20016-3349
Phone: (202)244-7223
Fax: (202)363-9850
Publisher's E-mail: newsdesk@currentnewspapers.com
Community newspaper. **Freq:** Weekly (Wed.). **Key Personnel:** Davis Kennedy, Editor, Publisher; Chris Kain, Managing Editor. **Subscription Rates:** $52 By mail. **URL:** http://www.currentnewspapers.com/. **Remarks:** Accepts advertising. **Circ:** Combined ■ **2400**.

6696 ■ Food and Drug Law Journal
Food and Drug Law Institute
1155 15th St. NW, Ste. 910
Washington, DC 20005-2706
Phone: (202)371-1420
Fax: (202)371-0649
Free: 800-956-6293
Publisher's E-mail: service@fdli.org
Freq: Quarterly. **ISSN:** 0015- 6361 (print). **Subscription Rates:** $299 Members; $379 Nonmembers. **URL:** http://www.fdli.org/products-services/publications/food-and-drug-law-journal. **Remarks:** Advertising not accepted. **Circ:** 1100.

6697 ■ Foreign Policy
Carnegie Endowment for International Peace
1779 Massachusetts Ave. NW
Washington, DC 20036-2103
Phone: (202)483-7600
Fax: (202)483-1840
Publisher's E-mail: info@carnegieendowment.org
Magazine publishing articles on U.S. foreign policy. **Founded:** 1970. **Freq:** Bimonthly. **Trim Size:** 8 1/8 x 10 3/4. **Cols./Page:** 2. **Col. Width:** 8 1/8 inches. **Col. Depth:** 10 7/8 inches. **Key Personnel:** Susan Glasser, Editor-in-Chief; Blake Hounshell, Managing Editor. **ISSN:** 0015-7228 (print). **Subscription Rates:** $59.99 Individuals print & online. **URL:** http://www.foreignpolicy.com/. **Remarks:** Accepts advertising. **Circ:** △**101208**.

6698 ■ Foreign Policy in Focus
Institute for Policy Studies
1301 Connecticut Ave. NW, Ste. 600
Washington, DC 20036
Phone: (202)234-9382
Publisher's E-mail: info@ips-dc.org
Periodical covering U.S. foreign policy. **Freq:** Bimonthly. **Print Method:** online only. **Key Personnel:** Emira Woods, Director; John Feffer, Director. **URL:** http://fpif.org. **Remarks:** Advertising not accepted. **Circ:** Free 11000.

6699 ■ Foreign Service Journal
American Foreign Service Association
2101 E St. NW
Washington, DC 20037
Phone: (202)338-4045
Fax: (202)338-6820
Publisher's E-mail: member@afsa.org
Covers foreign policy and professional issues; includes book and periodical reviews, obituaries, and association newsletter. **Freq:** 10/year. **ISSN:** 0146--3543 (print). **Subscription Rates:** $50 Individuals domestic mailing - one year; $86 Other countries air mailing - one year; $68 Other countries surface mailing - one year; $30 Students domestic mailing - one year; $66 Students, other countries air mailing - one year; $48 Students, other countries surface mailing - one year. **URL:** http://www.afsa.org/foreign-service-journal. **Ad Rates:** $2350-2710. 4C $. **Remarks:** Accepts advertising. **Circ:** Combined 18500.

6700 ■ Foreign Service Journal: The Magazine for Foreign Affairs Professionals
American Foreign Service Association
2101 E St. NW
Washington, DC 20037
Phone: (202)338-4045
Fax: (202)338-6820
Publication E-mail: journal@afsa.org
Magazine guiding professionals in foreign affairs (State Department, AID, USIA). **Freq:** 10/year monthly but January-February and July-August issues combined. **Print Method:** Offset. **Trim Size:** 8 1/2 x 11. **Cols./Page:** 3. **Col. Width:** 31 nonpareils. **Col. Depth:** 136 agate lines. **Key Personnel:** Shawn Dorman, Editor-in-Chief. **ISSN:** 0146--3543 (print). **Subscription Rates:** $50 Individuals; $30 Students. **URL:** http://www.afsa.org/foreign_service_journal.aspx. **Ad Rates:** BW $1,795; 4C $2,555. **Remarks:** Accepts advertising. **Circ:** Combined ‡17500.

6701 ■ Forum Journal
National Trust for Historic Preservation
2600 Virginia Ave. NW, Ste. 1100
Washington, DC 20037
Phone: (202)588-6000
Fax: (202)588-6038
Free: 800-944-6847
Publisher's E-mail: info@savingplaces.org
Journal covering real estate and preservation revolving funds across the country. **Freq:** Bimonthly. **URL:** http://www.preservationnation.org/forum. **Remarks:** Advertising not accepted. **Circ:** (Not Reported).

6702 ■ The Forum Magazine
National Forum for Black Public Administrators
777 N Capitol St. NE, Ste. 550
Washington, DC 20002
Phone: (202)408-9300
Fax: (202)408-8558
Freq: Quarterly. **Trim Size:** 8.5 x 11. **URL:** http://www.nfbpa.org/i4a/pages/index.cfm?pageid=3325. **Remarks:** Accepts advertising. **Circ:** (Not Reported).

6703 ■ Framework
Steel Framing Alliance
25 Massachusetts Ave. NW, Ste. 800
Washington, DC 20001-7400
Phone: (202)452-1039
Fax: (202)452-1039
Publisher's E-mail: membership@steelframing.org
Journal featuring information about steel framing industry. **Freq:** Quarterly. **Key Personnel:** Sarah Humphreys, Editor. **Alt. Formats:** PDF. **URL:** http://www.steelframing.org/framework.html. **Remarks:** Advertising not accepted. **Circ:** (Not Reported).

6704 ■ Franchising World
International Franchise Association
1900 K St., NW Ste. 700
Washington, DC 20006
Phone: (202)628-8000
Fax: (202)628-0812
Publisher's E-mail: ifa@franchise.org
Trade magazine covering topics of interest to franchise company executives and the business world. **Freq:** Monthly. **Print Method:** Offset. **Trim Size:** 8 3/8 x 10 7/8. **Cols./Page:** 3. **Col. Width:** 13.5 picas. **Col. Depth:** 203 agate lines. **Key Personnel:** Stephen J. Caldeira, President, Chief Executive Officer. **ISSN:** 1041--7311 (print). **URL:** http://www.franchise.org/franchising-world-digital-version. **Ad Rates:** BW $3,185; 4C $4,550. **Remarks:** Accepts advertising. **Circ:** Paid ‡233, ‡10063.

6705 ■ Futures Industry
Futures Industry Association
2001 Pennsylvania Ave. NW, Ste. 600
Washington, DC 20006
Phone: (202)466-5460
Publisher's E-mail: info@fia.org
Magazine highlighting analysis, proprietary statistics, and interviews of professionals and senior executives in the financial services industry. **Freq:** 5/year. **Subscription Rates:** free for qualified individuals. **URL:** http://fimag.fia.org. **Remarks:** Accepts advertising. **Circ:** (Not Reported).

6706 ■ Gallaudet Today
Gallaudet University Alumni Association
c/o Gallaudet University
800 Florida Ave. NE
Washington, DC 20002
Phone: (202)651-5060
Fax: (202)651-5062
Publisher's E-mail: alumni.relations@gallaudet.edu
Freq: Semiannual. **Subscription Rates:** $15 Individuals /year in U.S.; $25 Individuals /year outside U.S. **Alt. Formats:** PDF. **URL:** http://www.gallaudet.edu/university_communications/gallaudet_today_newsletter.html. **Remarks:** Advertising not accepted. **Circ:** (Not Reported).

6707 ■ Gender Issues
Springer Science + Business Media LLC
School of Public Affairs
Dept. of Justice, Law, & Society
American University
4400 Massachusetts Ave. NW
Washington, DC 20016-8043
Publisher's E-mail: service-ny@springer.com
Journal covering basic and applied research on the relationships between men and women, socialization, personality, behaviour, roles, and statuses throughout the world. **Freq:** Quarterly. **Key Personnel:** J.M. Simons-Rudolph, Editor-in-Chief; A.P. Simons-Rudolph, Editor-in-Chief. **ISSN:** 1098-092X (print); **EISSN:** 1936-4717 (electronic). **Subscription Rates:** €433 Institutions print including free access or e-only; €520 Institutions print plus enhanced access; $596 Institutions print including free access or e-only; $715 Institutions print plus enhanced access; €63.02 Individuals. **URL:** http://www.springer.com/social+sciences/journal/12147. **Ad Rates:** BW $300. **Remarks:** Accepts advertising. **Circ:** Paid ‡700.

6708 ■ Geochemistry, Geophysics, Geosystems
American Geophysical Union
2000 Florida Ave. NW
Washington, DC 20009-1277
Phone: (202)462-6900
Fax: (202)328-0566
Free: 800-966-2481
Publication E-mail: g-cubed@agu.org
Journal covering research in geochemistry and geophysics. **Freq:** Monthly. **Key Personnel:** Thorsten Becker, Editor-in-Chief, phone: (213)740-8365, fax: (213)740-6244. **ISSN:** 1525--2027 (print). **Subscription Rates:** $1490 Institutions large, online. **URL:** http://agupubs.onlinelibrary.wiley.com/agu/journal/10.1002/(ISSN)1525-2027/. **Circ:** (Not Reported).

6709 ■ GeoHumanities
American Association of Geographers
1710 16th St. NW
Washington, DC 20009
Phone: (202)234-1450
Fax: (202)234-2744
Publisher's E-mail: gaia@aag.org
Contains articles that cover conceptual and methodological debates in geography and the humanities. **Freq:** Semiannual June and December. **Subscription Rates:** Included in membership. **URL:** http://www.aag.org/cs/publications/journals/gh. **Circ:** (Not Reported).

6710 ■ The George Washington Law Review
The George Washington Law Review

Circulation: ★ = AAM; △ or • = BPA; ♦ = CAC; ❑ = VAC; ⊕ = PO Statement; ‡ = Publisher's Report; Boldface figures = sworn; Light figures = estimated.

1919 Pennsylvania Ave., Ste. M25
Washington, DC 20006
Phone: (202)994-4610
Fax: (202)994-4609
Publication E-mail: gwlr@gwu.edu
Collective law journal. **Freq:** Annual. **Print Method:** Offset. Uses mats. **Cols./Page:** 1. **Col. Width:** 55 nonpareils. **Col. Depth:** 115 agate lines. **Key Personnel:** Dane P. Shikman, Editor-in-Chief. **ISSN:** 0016-8076 (print). **Subscription Rates:** $46 Individuals; $46 Libraries; $51 Other countries; $44 Elsewhere. **URL:** http://www.gwlr.org. **Ad Rates:** BW $200. **Remarks:** Accepts advertising. **Circ:** ‡2000.

6711 ■ The Georgetown Current
The Current Newspapers Inc.
5185 MacArthur Blvd. NW, Ste. 102
Washington, DC 20016-3349
Phone: (202)244-7223
Fax: (202)363-9850
Publisher's E-mail: newsdesk@currentnewspapers.com
Community newspaper. **Freq:** Weekly (Wed.). **Key Personnel:** Davis Kennedy, Editor, Publisher; Chris Kain, Managing Editor. **Subscription Rates:** $52 Individuals. **URL:** http://www.currentnewspapers.com/power.html. **Remarks:** Accepts advertising. **Circ:** (Not Reported).

6712 ■ Georgetown Immigration Law Journal
Georgetown University Law Center
600 New Jersey Ave. NW
Washington, DC 20001
Phone: (202)662-9000
Publisher's E-mail: admis@law.georgetown.edu
Journal focusing on the advancement of legal knowledge in the field of immigration law. **Freq:** Quarterly. **Key Personnel:** Jennifer Bartlett, Editor-in-Chief. **ISSN:** 0891--4371 (print). **Subscription Rates:** $35 Individuals domestic. **URL:** http://www.law.georgetown.edu/academics/law-journals/gilj. **Circ:** (Not Reported).

6713 ■ Georgetown Journal of Gender and the Law
Georgetown University Law Center
600 New Jersey Ave. NW
Washington, DC 20001
Phone: (202)662-9000
Publication E-mail: genderjournal@law.georgetown.edu
Journal addressing the impact of gender, sexuality, and race on both the theory and practice of law. **Freq:** 3/year. **Key Personnel:** Noah Butsch Baron, Editor-in-Chief. **ISSN:** 1525- 6146 (print). **Subscription Rates:** $35 Individuals domestic. **URL:** http://www.law.georgetown.edu/academics/law-journals/gender/index.cfm. **Circ:** (Not Reported).

6714 ■ Georgetown Journal of History
Georgetown University
37th & O St. NW
Washington, DC 20057
Phone: (202)687-0100
Freq: Semiannual. **URL:** http://georgetownhistoryjournal.org. **Circ:** (Not Reported).

6715 ■ Georgetown Journal of International Law
Georgetown University Law Center
600 New Jersey Ave. NW
Washington, DC 20001
Phone: (202)662-9000
Publication E-mail: gjil@law.georgetown.edu
Professional journal covering international law. **Freq:** Quarterly. **Key Personnel:** Luke Engan, Managing Editor; Yolande Bornik Hanlan, Editor; John Dalebroux, Executive Editor; Allison Clark Ambrose, Editor-in-Chief; Amanda Wall, Senior Editor. **ISSN:** 0023--9208 (print). **Subscription Rates:** $55 Individuals; $70 Other countries. **URL:** http://www.law.georgetown.edu/academics/law-journals/gjil/index.cfm. **Formerly:** Law and Policy in International Business. **Also known as:** Journal of Law and Policy in International Business. **Remarks:** Accepts advertising. **Circ:** (Not Reported).

6716 ■ Georgetown Journal of International Law
Georgetown University Law Center
600 New Jersey Ave. NW
Washington, DC 20001
Phone: (202)662-9000
Publisher's E-mail: admis@law.georgetown.edu
Journal covering a diverse range of material in the fields of public international law, private international law, transnational law, foreign relations law and comparative law. **Freq:** Quarterly. **Key Personnel:** Sean Topping, Editor-in-Chief. **ISSN:** 0023--9208 (print). **Subscription Rates:** $55 Individuals domestic; $70 Individuals foreign. **URL:** http://law.georgetown.edu/academics/law-journals/gjil. **Circ:** (Not Reported).

6717 ■ Georgetown Journal of Law and Modern Critical Race Perspectives
Georgetown University Law Center
600 New Jersey Ave. NW
Washington, DC 20001
Phone: (202)662-9000
Publication E-mail: gjil@law.georgetown.edu
Journal containing legal scholarship on race and identity. **Freq:** Semiannual. **Key Personnel:** Katherine McInnis, Editor-in-Chief. **ISSN:** 1946--3154 (print). **Subscription Rates:** $30 Individuals. **URL:** http://www.law.georgetown.edu/academics/law-journals/mcrp. **Circ:** (Not Reported).

6718 ■ Georgetown Journal of Law & Public Policy
Georgetown University Law Center
600 New Jersey Ave. NW
Washington, DC 20001
Phone: (202)662-9000
Publisher's E-mail: admis@law.georgetown.edu
Journal focusing on conservative, libertarian and natural law thought. **Freq:** Semiannual. **Key Personnel:** Isaiah Peterson, Editor-in-Chief. **ISSN:** 1536--5077 (print). **Subscription Rates:** $40 Individuals. **URL:** http://www.law.georgetown.edu/academics/law-journals/gjlpp/index.cfm. **Circ:** (Not Reported).

6719 ■ Georgetown Journal of Legal Ethics
Georgetown University Law Center
600 New Jersey Ave. NW
Washington, DC 20001
Phone: (202)662-9000
Publication E-mail: gjle@law.georgetown.edu
Journal serving as the main forum for the discussion and development of the most compelling and pertinent issues currently affecting both the Bench and the Bar. **Freq:** Quarterly. **Key Personnel:** Meg Parker, Editor-in-Chief. **ISSN:** 1041- 5548 (print). **Subscription Rates:** $50 Individuals. **URL:** http://www.law.georgetown.edu/academics/law-journals/gjle/index.cfm. **Circ:** (Not Reported).

6720 ■ Georgetown Journal on Poverty Law and Policy
Georgetown University Law Center
600 New Jersey Ave. NW
Washington, DC 20001
Phone: (202)662-9000
Publisher's E-mail: admis@law.georgetown.edu
Journal covering on poverty issues. **Freq:** 3/year. **Key Personnel:** Anna Kent, Editor-in-Chief. **ISSN:** 1524--3974 (print). **Subscription Rates:** $35 Individuals domestic; $45 Individuals foreign. **URL:** http://www.law.georgetown.edu/academics/law-journals/poverty/index.cfm. **Circ:** (Not Reported).

6721 ■ Georgetown Law Journal
Georgetown University Law Center
600 New Jersey Ave. NW
Washington, DC 20001
Phone: (202)662-9000
Publisher's E-mail: admis@law.georgetown.edu
Journal containing articles and essays concerning all areas of the law. **Freq:** 6/year. **Key Personnel:** V. Noah Gimbel, Editor-in-Chief. **ISSN:** 0016--8092 (print). **Subscription Rates:** $60 Individuals domestic; $75 Individuals foreign. **URL:** http://georgetownlawjournal.org. **Circ:** (Not Reported).

6722 ■ Georgetown Magazine
Georgetown University
37th & O St. NW
Washington, DC 20057
Phone: (202)687-0100
Magazine for alumni, parents, faculty, and staff of Georgetown University. **Freq:** Bimonthly. **Print Method:** Offset. **Cols./Page:** 2 and 3. **Col. Width:** 13 and 20 nonpareils. **Col. Depth:** 54 picas. **Key Personnel:** Jeff Donahoe, Editor. **ISSN:** 0745--9009 (print). **URL:** http://alumni.georgetown.edu/alumni-stories?f[0]=field_category%3A1606. **Remarks:** Advertising not accepted. **Circ:** 140000.

6723 ■ The Georgetown Voice
Georgetown University
37th & O St. NW
Washington, DC 20057
Phone: (202)687-0100
Collegiate newspaper. **Freq:** Weekly (Thurs.). **Print Method:** Offset. **Trim Size:** 13 x 20. **Cols./Page:** 4. **Col. Width:** 2.5 inches. **Key Personnel:** Tim Shine; Sean Quigley; Connor Jones, Editor-in-Chief. **URL:** http://www.georgetownvoice.com. **Ad Rates:** BW $400, full page ad, back cover; 4C $600, full page ad, back cover; PCI $12. **Circ:** ‡6000.

6724 ■ The Gerontologist
Gerontological Society of America
1220 L St. NW, Ste. 901
Washington, DC 20005-4001
Phone: (202)842-1275
Freq: Bimonthly. **ISSN:** 0016- 9013 (print); **EISSN:** 1758-5341 (electronic). **Subscription Rates:** $421 Institutions print and online; £280 Institutions print and online. **URL:** http://gerontologist.oxfordjournals.org. **Remarks:** Accepts advertising. **Circ:** 7,400.

6725 ■ Gerontology & Geriatrics Education
Gerontological Society of America
1220 L St. NW, Ste. 901
Washington, DC 20005-4001
Phone: (202)842-1275
Journal presenting practical curriculum information for educators, trainers, and supervisors in the aging field. **Freq:** Quarterly. **Print Method:** Offset. **Trim Size:** 6 x 8 3/8. **Cols./Page:** 1. **Col. Width:** 51 nonpareils. **Col. Depth:** 95 agate lines. **Key Personnel:** Kelly Niles-Yokum, Managing Editor; Pearl M. Mosher-Ashley, PhD, Editor. **ISSN:** 0270--1960 (print); **EISSN:** 1545--3847 (electronic). **Subscription Rates:** $148 Individuals online only; $160 Individuals print & online; $810 Institutions online only; $926 Institutions print & online. **URL:** http://www.tandfonline.com/toc/wgge20/current. **Ad Rates:** BW $315; 4C $550. **Remarks:** Accepts advertising. **Circ:** ‡407.

6726 ■ GFWC Clubwoman Magazine
General Federation of Women's Clubs
1734 N St. NW
Washington, DC 20036-2990
Phone: (202)347-3168
Fax: (202)835-0246
Publisher's E-mail: gfwc@gfwc.org
Magazine covering women's clubs news and community service projects. **Freq:** Bimonthly. **Print Method:** Offset. **Trim Size:** 8 1/4 x 10 7/8. **Cols./Page:** 3. **Col. Width:** 2 1/8 inches. **Col. Depth:** 9 5/8 inches. **ISSN:** 0745--2209 (print). **Subscription Rates:** $10 Individuals. **URL:** http://www.gfwc.org/news-publications/clubwoman-magazine. **Ad Rates:** BW $850; 4C $1,350. **Remarks:** Accepts advertising. **Circ:** ‡18000.

6727 ■ Gifted Child Quarterly
National Association for Gifted Children
1331 H St. NW, Ste. 1001
Washington, DC 20005
Phone: (202)785-4268
Fax: (202)785-4248
Publisher's E-mail: nagc@nagc.org
Peer-reviewed professional journal covering education for gifted students. **Freq:** Quarterly. **Trim Size:** 8 1/2 x 11. **Cols./Page:** 2. **Key Personnel:** Del Siegle, Editor. **ISSN:** 0016--9862 (print); **EISSN:** 1934--9041 (electronic). **Subscription Rates:** £149 Institutions e-access; £163 Institutions print; £166 Institutions print and e-access; £45 Institutions single print. **URL:** http://www.nagc.org/resources-publications/nagc-publications/gifted-child-quarterly; http://gcq.sagepub.com. **Ad Rates:** BW $700. **Remarks:** Advertising accepted; rates available upon request. **Circ:** Paid 6500.

6728 ■ Global Biogeochemical Cycles
American Geophysical Union
2000 Florida Ave. NW
Washington, DC 20009-1277
Phone: (202)462-6900
Fax: (202)328-0566
Free: 800-966-2481
Publication E-mail: gbc@agu.org

Journal focused on global change involving the geosphere and biosphere, marine, hydrologic, atmospheric, extraterrestrial, geologic & biologic. **Freq:** Monthly. **Key Personnel:** Eric Sundquist, Editor; Philip Boyd, Associate Editor; George C. Hurtt, Associate Editor. **ISSN:** 0886--6236 (print); **EISSN:** 1944--9224 (electronic). **Subscription Rates:** $1211 U.S. and other countries online - large; $812 U.S. and other countries online - medium; $546 U.S. and other countries online - small; £764 Institutions online - large; £513 Institutions online - medium; £345 Institutions online - small; €886 Institutions online - large; €594 Institutions online - medium; €401 Institutions online - small. **URL:** http://agupubs.onlinelibrary.wiley.com/agu/journal/10.1002/(ISSN)1944-9224. **Circ:** (Not Reported).

6729 ■ Good Medicine
Physicians Committee for Responsible Medicine
5100 Wisconsin Ave. NW, Ste. 400
Washington, DC 20016
Phone: (202)686-2210
Fax: (202)686-2216
Free: 866-416-PCRM
Publisher's E-mail: pcrm@pcrm.org
Freq: Quarterly. **Key Personnel:** Neal D. Barnard, MD, Editor-in-Chief; Doug Hall, Managing Editor; Michael Keevican, Editor; Carrie Clyne, Editor. **Subscription Rates:** Included in membership. **URL:** http://www.pcrm.org/media/good-medicine. **Remarks:** Advertising not accepted. **Circ:** (Not Reported).

6730 ■ Governing Magazine: The Magazine of States and Localities
Times Publishing Co.
1100 Connecticut Ave. NW, Ste. 1300
Washington, DC 20036
Phone: (202)862-8802
Fax: (202)862-0032
Free: 800-944-0922
Publisher's E-mail: custserv@sptimes.com
Magazine serving the public sector of federal, state and local government. **Freq:** Monthly. **Print Method:** Web offset. **Trim Size:** 8 1/4 x 10 7/8. **Key Personnel:** Peter Harkness, Columnist. **Subscription Rates:** $19.95 Individuals; $34.95 Two years. **URL:** http://www.governing.com. **Ad Rates:** BW $15,950; 4C $16,850. **Remarks:** Accepts advertising. **Circ:** Controlled 86000.

6731 ■ Government Executive
National Journal Group Inc.
The Watergate
600 New Hampshire Ave. NW
Washington, DC 20037
Phone: (202)739-8400
Fax: (202)833-8069
Free: 800-613-6701
Publisher's E-mail: service@nationaljournal.com
Magazine for government executives. **Freq:** Monthly. **Print Method:** Offset. **Trim Size:** 8 3/16 x 10 7/8. **Cols./Page:** 3. **Col. Width:** 27 nonpareils. **Col. Depth:** 140 agate lines. **Key Personnel:** Susan Fourney, Managing Editor; Katherine McIntire Peters, Executive Editor; Tom Shoop, Editor-in-Chief. **ISSN:** 0017--2626 (print). **URL:** http://www.govexec.com/magazine. **Remarks:** Accepts advertising. **Circ:** (Not Reported).

6732 ■ gradPSYCH
American Psychoanalytic Association
750 First St. NE
Washington, DC 20002-4242
Phone: (202)336-5500
Publisher's E-mail: info@apsa.org
Freq: Quarterly January, March, September and November. **Key Personnel:** Rhea K. Farberman, Publisher; Jamie Chamberlin, Assistant Managing Editor; Dana Schwartz, Assistant Editor; Sara Martin, Editor; Malcolm McGaughy, Art Director; Christopher Munsey, Writer; Michael Price, Writer; Erika Packard, Writer. **Subscription Rates:** Included in membership for graduate student affiliate members; $17.50 Members; $35 Nonmembers; $16 Institutions discounted rate for a minimum order of 25. **URL:** http://www.apa.org/gradpsych. **Ad Rates:** BW $2,910; BW $2,985. **Remarks:** Accepts display and classified advertising. **Circ:** 25000.

6733 ■ Graphic Communicator
Graphic Communications Conference of the International Brotherhood of Teamsters
25 Louisiana Ave. NW
Washington, DC 20001
Phone: (202)624-6800
Trade newspaper of the Graphic Communications International Union. **Freq:** Quarterly. **Print Method:** Offset. **Trim Size:** 11 x 16. **Cols./Page:** 4. **Col. Width:** 14.5 picas. **Col. Depth:** 74 picas. **ISSN:** 0746--3626 (print). **USPS:** 410-750. **URL:** http://teamster.org/divisions/graphics-communications/graphic-communicator-archive. **Formerly:** GraphiCommunicator. **Remarks:** Advertising not accepted. **Circ:** ‡140000.

6734 ■ Grassroots Development
Inter-American Foundation
1331 Pennsylvania Ave. NW, Ste. 1200 N
Washington, DC 20004-1766
Phone: (202)360-4530
Fax: (703)306-4365
Publisher's E-mail: inquiries@iaf.gov
Journal publishing the experiences of recipients of IAF funds. **Key Personnel:** Paula Durbin, Managing Editor. **Alt. Formats:** PDF. **URL:** http://www.iaf.gov/resources/publications/2015-stories-of-sustainability. **Circ:** (Not Reported).

6735 ■ Green American
Green America
1612 K St. NW, Ste. 600
Washington, DC 20006-2810
Fax: (202)331-8166
Free: 800-584-7336
Publisher's E-mail: info@coopamerica.org
Freq: Bimonthly. **ISSN:** 0885- 9930 (print). **Subscription Rates:** Included in membership. **URL:** http://www.greenamerica.org/pubs/greenamerican/index.cfm. **Remarks:** Accepts advertising. **Circ:** 50000.

6736 ■ Green Guide
National Geographic Society
1145 17th St. NW
Washington, DC 20036-4688
Phone: (202)862-8638
Free: 800-373-1717
Magazine covering stories on healthy, green living. **URL:** http://www.thegreenguide.com. **Remarks:** Accepts advertising. **Circ:** 25,000.

6737 ■ The Greenpeace Quarterly
Greenpeace U.S.A.
702 H St. NW, Ste. 300
Washington, DC 20001
Phone: (202)462-1177
Fax: (202)462-4507
Free: 800-722-6995
Publisher's E-mail: info@wdc.greenpeace.org
Magazine covering environmental issues and the activities of Greenpeace. **Freq:** Quarterly. **Print Method:** Web Offset. **Trim Size:** 8 1/8 x 10 7/8. **Cols./Page:** 3. **Col. Width:** 2 1/16 inches. **Col. Depth:** 9 5/8 inches. **Key Personnel:** David Barre, Contact; John Passacantando, Executive Director; Anastasia Pfarr, Managing Editor. **ISSN:** 0899-0190 (print). **Alt. Formats:** PDF. **URL:** http://www.greenpeace.org/international/en/about/greenpeace-quarterlies/. **Remarks:** Advertising not accepted. **Circ:** Paid ‡400000.

6738 ■ Group Dynamics: Theory, Research, and Practice
American Psychological Association
750 1st St. NE
Washington, DC 20002-4242
Phone: (202)336-5500
Free: 800-374-2721
Journal discussing the impact of being a part of a group upon individuals in a variety of settings. **Freq:** Quarterly beginning in March. **Key Personnel:** Craig D. Parks, Board Member; Cheri L. Marmarosh, Associate Editor; Bryan L. Bonner, Associate Editor. **ISSN:** 1089-2699 (print); **EISSN:** 1930-7802 (electronic). **Subscription Rates:** $71 Members domestic students, affiliate; $126 Nonmembers domestic; $524 Institutions domestic; $95 Members students, affiliate, surface; $155 Nonmembers foreign, surface; $573 Institutions, other countries surface freight; $109 Members students, affiliate, air mail; $168 Nonmembers air mail; $588 Institutions, other countries air mail. **URL:** http://www.apa.org/pubs/journals/gdn/index.aspx. **Ad Rates:** BW $275; 4C $975. **Remarks:** Accepts advertising. **Circ:** 400.

6739 ■ Guild of Natural Science Illustration
Guild of Natural Science Illustrators
PO Box 652
Ben Franklin Station
Washington, DC 20044
Phone: (301)309-1514
Journal publishing articles of interest to natural science illustrators. **Freq:** Quarterly. **Subscription Rates:** Included in membership. **URL:** http://www.gnsi.org/resources/publications/journal-natural-science-illustration. **Remarks:** Advertising not accepted. **Circ:** (Not Reported).

6740 ■ The GW Hatchet
Hatchet Publications Inc.
2140 G St. NW
Washington, DC 20037
Collegiate newspaper (tabloid). **Freq:** Semiweekly (Mon. and Thurs.). **Print Method:** Offset. **Trim Size:** 10 13/16 x 14. **Cols./Page:** 6. **Col. Width:** 24 nonpareils. **Col. Depth:** 192.5 agate lines. **Key Personnel:** Brianna Gurciullo, Editor-in-Chief. **URL:** http://www.gwhatchet.com. **Ad Rates:** BW $900; 4C $1,200; SAU $10.75; PCI $16.50. **Remarks:** Accepts advertising. **Circ:** Mon.-Thurs. 12000.

6741 ■ G.W. Review
George Washington University
The Marvin Ctr.
800 21st St. NW
Washington, DC 20052
Literary review magazine. **Freq:** Semiannual. **Key Personnel:** Darci Frinquelli, Editor-in-Chief; Kelli Leubben, Editor; Laura Feigin, Managing Editor. **URL:** http://www.gwu.edu/student-publications. **Mailing address:** Box 20B, Washington, DC 20052. **Circ:** (Not Reported).

6742 ■ HAC Rural Voices
Housing Assistance Council
1025 Vermont Ave. NW, Ste. 606
Washington, DC 20005
Phone: (202)842-8600
Fax: (202)347-3441
Publisher's E-mail: hac@ruralhome.org
Freq: Quarterly. **ISSN:** 1093- 8044 (print). **Subscription Rates:** $16 /year; $4 single copy. **URL:** http://www.ruralhome.org/sct-information/rural-voices. **Remarks:** Advertising not accepted. **Circ:** (Not Reported).

6743 ■ Health Promotion Practice
Society for Public Health Education
10 G St. NE, Ste. 605
Washington, DC 20002-4242
Phone: (202)408-9804
Fax: (202)408-9815
Publisher's E-mail: sales@pfp.sagepub.com
Peer-reviewed journal focusing on the practical application of health promotion and education. **Freq:** Bimonthly Quarterly. **Key Personnel:** Jesus Ramirez-Valles, PhD, Editor-in-Chief. **ISSN:** 1524--8399 (print); **EISSN:** 1552--6372 (electronic). **Subscription Rates:** $202 Individuals print only; $743 Institutions e-access; $809 Institutions print only; $826 Institutions print and e-access; $44 Individuals single print; $151 Institutions single print; Included in membership. **URL:** http://us.sagepub.com/en-us/nam/health-promotion-practice/journal201271; http://www.sophe.org/Health_Promotion_Practice.cfm. **Ad Rates:** BW $1120; 4C $1100. **Remarks:** Accepts advertising. **Circ:** (Not Reported).

6744 ■ Health Psychology
American Psychological Association
750 1st St. NE
Washington, DC 20002-4242
Phone: (202)336-5500
Free: 800-374-2721
Journal exploring the relationship between behavioral principles and physical health. **Freq:** Monthly beginning in January. **Print Method:** Offset. **Key Personnel:** Anne Kazak, Editor; Anne E. Kazak, Editor; Belinda Borrelli, Associate Editor; Annmarie Cano, Associate Editor. **ISSN:** 0278-6133 (print); **EISSN:** 1930-7810 (electronic). **Subscription Rates:** $133 Members domestic, students; $290 Nonmembers domestic; $1177 Institutions domestic; $166 Members outside U.S., students, surface; $347 Nonmembers outside U.S., surface; $1287 Institutions, other countries surface; $207 Members outside U.S., students, air mail; $379 Nonmembers outside U.S., air mail; $1319 Institutions, other

Circulation: ★ = AAM; △ or • = BPA; ♦ = CAC; □ = VAC; ⊕ = PO Statement; ‡ = Publisher's Report; Boldface figures = sworn; Light figures = estimated.

countries air mail; $129 Members domestic; $162 Members surface; $203 Members airmail; $129 Students domestic; $162 Students surface; $203 Students airmail; $276 Individuals non members, domestic; $333 Individuals non members, surface; $365 Individuals non members, air mail; $1076 Institutions domestic; $1186 Institutions surface; $1218 Institutions airmail. **URL:** http://www.apa.org/pubs/journals/hea/index.aspx; http://www.apa.org/pubs/journals/hea/; http://www.health-psych.org/ResourcesJournal.cfm. **Ad Rates:** BW $485; 4C $1,460. **Remarks:** Accepts advertising. **Circ:** 4100, 3800, 9500.

6745 ■ Health & Social Work: A Journal of the National Association of Social Workers
National Association of Social Workers
750 1st St. NE, Ste. 800
Washington, DC 20002-4241
Phone: (202)408-8600
Fax: (202)336-8313
Free: 800-742-4089
Publication E-mail: press@naswdc.org
Journal on social work practices in the health field. **Freq:** Quarterly. **Print Method:** Offset. **Trim Size:** 7 x 10. **Cols./Page:** 2. **Col. Width:** 17 picas. **Col. Depth:** 53 picas. **Key Personnel:** Stephen H. Gorin, PhD, Editor-in-Chief; Samuel S. Flint, Board Member. **ISSN:** 0360--7283 (print); **EISSN:** 1545--6854 (electronic). **Subscription Rates:** $92 Members print only; $63 Students print only; $117 Nonmembers print only; $184 Institutions print only; $200 Institutions print and online; $160 Institutions online only; $69 Members online only. **URL:** http://www.naswpress.org/publications/journals/hsw.html; http://hsw.oxfordjournals.org. **Ad Rates:** BW $525. **Remarks:** Accepts advertising. **Circ:** 2500.

6746 ■ Hematology: American Society of Hematology Education Program Book
American Society of Hematology
2021 L St. NW, Ste. 900
Washington, DC 20036-4929
Phone: (202)776-0544
Fax: (202)776-0545
Journal providing continuing medical education for physicians. **Freq:** Annual. **Print Method:** Offset. **Cols./Page:** 6. **Col. Width:** 25 nonpareils. **Col. Depth:** 301 agate lines. **Key Personnel:** Linda J. Burns, MD, Executive Editor. **ISSN:** 1520--4391 (print). **Subscription Rates:** $100 Members; $175 Nonmembers. **URL:** http://asheducationbook.hematologylibrary.org. **Circ:** (Not Reported).

6747 ■ The Hill
The Hill
1625 K St. NW, Ste. 900
Washington, DC 20006-1606
Phone: (202)628-8500
Fax: (202)628-8503
Free: 800-284-3437
Publisher's E-mail: ads@thehill.com
Newspaper covering Capitol Hill. **Founded:** Sept. 1994. **Freq:** 4/week. **Key Personnel:** Hugo Gurdon, Editor-in-Chief, phone: (202)628-8501; Bob Cusack, Managing Editor. **ISSN:** 1521-1568 (print). **Subscription Rates:** $225 Individuals print only; $415 Two years print only; $365 Canada print only; $730 Other countries print only; $150 Students print only; $600 Students, other countries print only; $235 Students, Canada print only; $695 Canada 2 years; print only; $1425 Other countries 2 years; print only; $175 Individuals 1 year; online only; $300 U.S. print and online; $365 Canada print and online; $730 Other countries print and online. **URL:** http://thehill.com. **Remarks:** Accepts classified advertising. **Circ:** 21,000.

6748 ■ History of Psychology
American Psychological Association
750 1st St. NE
Washington, DC 20002-4242
Phone: (202)336-5500
Free: 800-374-2721
Peer-reviewed journal featuring articles addressing all aspects of psychology's past and its interrelationship with the many contexts within which it has emerged and been practiced. **Freq:** Quarterly. **Key Personnel:** Mitchell G. Ash, Editor; Wade E. Pickren, PhD, Editor. **ISSN:** 1093--4510 (print); **EISSN:** 1939--0610 (electronic). **Subscription Rates:** $666 Institutions; $715 Institutions, other countries; $730 Institutions, other countries by air mail. **URL:** http://www.apa.org/pubs/journals/hop/index.aspx. **Ad Rates:** BW $350; 4C $975; BW $335. **Remarks:** Accepts advertising. **Circ:** 500.

6749 ■ Home Design Journal
American Institute of Building Design
7059 Blair Rd. NW, Ste. 400
Washington, DC 20012
Phone: (202)750-4900
Fax: (866)204-0293
Free: 800-366-2423
Publisher's E-mail: info@aibd.org
Remarks: Advertising not accepted. **Circ:** (Not Reported).

6750 ■ The Howard Journal of Communications
Routledge
c/o Carolyn A. Stroman, Ed.-in-Ch.
Department of Communication & Culture
Howard University
Washington, DC 20059
Publisher's E-mail: book.orders@tandf.co.uk
Examines ethnicity, gender, and culture as domestic and international communication concerns. **Freq:** Quarterly. **Print Method:** Offset. **Key Personnel:** Carolyn A. Stroman, Editor-in-Chief; William J. Starosta, Associate Editor; Ronald Jackson, II, Associate Editor; Anne M. Nicotera, Associate Editor; Clint Wilson, II, Associate Editor; Richard Allen, Board Member; Carolyn Calloway-Thomas, Reviewer; Brenda Allen, Board Member. **ISSN:** 1064--6175 (print); **EISSN:** 1096--4649 (electronic). **Subscription Rates:** $138 Individuals print only; $436 Institutions online only; $498 Institutions print and online. **URL:** http://www.tandfonline.com/toc/uhjc20/current. **Remarks:** Accepts advertising. **Circ:** (Not Reported).

6751 ■ Howard Law Journal
Howard University School of Law
2900 Van Ness St. NW
Washington, DC 20008
Phone: (202)806-8000
Publisher's E-mail: admissions@law.howard.edu
Journal promoting the civil and human rights of all people. **Freq:** 3/year. **Key Personnel:** Jacqueline C. Young, Director. **Subscription Rates:** $34 Individuals domestic; $44 Individuals international. **URL:** http://www.law.howard.edu/229. **Circ:** (Not Reported).

6752 ■ The HOYA: Georgetown's Newspaper of Record Since 1920
Georgetown University
37th & O St. NW
Washington, DC 20057
Phone: (202)687-0100
Collegiate newspaper. **Freq:** Semiweekly during the academic year. **Print Method:** Offset. **Trim Size:** 13 3/8 x 20. **Cols./Page:** 6. **Col. Width:** 14 picas. **Col. Depth:** 20 inches. **URL:** http://www.thehoya.com. **Remarks:** Advertising accepted; rates available upon request. **Circ:** Paid ‡500, Free ‡8400.

6753 ■ Human Events: Leading the Conservative Movement
Eagle Publishing Inc.
300 New Jersey Ave., NW, Ste. 500
Washington, DC 20001
Phone: (202)216-0600
Publisher's E-mail: info@eaglepub.com
Foreign and domestic political news tabloid. **Freq:** Weekly. **Print Method:** Offset. **Trim Size:** 11 1/2 x 14. **Cols./Page:** 4. **Col. Width:** 27 nonpareils. **Col. Depth:** 176 agate lines. **Key Personnel:** Allan H. Ryskind, Editor; Jason Mattera, Editor; Thomas S. Winter, Editor-in-Chief. **ISSN:** 0018--7194 (print). **URL:** http://www.humanevents.com. **Ad Rates:** BW $1,995. **Remarks:** Accepts advertising. **Circ:** ‡72000.

6754 ■ Human Rights Brief
American University Washington College of Law
4801 Massachusetts Ave. NW
Washington, DC 20016
Phone: (202)274-4000
Fax: (202)274-4005
Publication E-mail: hrbrief@wcl.american.edu
Journal dedicated to international human rights and humanitarian law and provides concise legal analysis of complex human rights issues. **Founded:** 1994. **Freq:** 3/year. **Key Personnel:** Diana Damschroder, Editor-in-Chief. **URL:** http://www.wcl.american.edu/hrbrief. **Circ:** (Not Reported).

6755 ■ Human Rights Magazine
American Bar Association Section of Civil Rights and Social Justice
1050 Connecticut Ave. NW, Ste. 400
Washington, DC 20036
Phone: (202)662-1030
Fax: (202)662-1031
Free: 800-285-2221
Publisher's E-mail: irr@americanbar.org
Freq: Quarterly. **Subscription Rates:** Included in membership; $18 Nonmembers. **URL:** http://www.americanbar.org/publications/human_rights_magazine_home.html. **Remarks:** Advertising not accepted. **Circ:** (Not Reported).

6756 ■ The Humanist: A Magazine of Critical Inquiry and Social Concern
American Humanist Association
1777 T St. NW
Washington, DC 20009-7102
Phone: (202)238-9088
Fax: (202)238-9003
Free: 800-837-3792
Publisher's E-mail: aha@americanhumanist.org
Magazine presenting a secular and naturalistic approach to philosophy, science, and broad areas of personal and social concern. Focuses on humanistic ideas, developments, and revolutions. **Freq:** Bimonthly. **Print Method:** Offset. Uses mats. **Trim Size:** 8 1/4 x 10 3/4. **Cols./Page:** 3 and 2. **Col. Width:** 27 and 42 nonpareils. **Col. Depth:** 135 agate lines. **Key Personnel:** Jennifer Bardi, Editor, phone: (202)238-9088, fax: (202)238-9003. **ISSN:** 0018--7399 (print). **URL:** http://thehumanist.com. **Remarks:** Accepts advertising. **Circ:** (Not Reported).

6757 ■ Humanities
National Endowment for the Humanities
400 7th St. SW
Washington, DC 20506
Phone: (202)606-8400
Free: 800-634-1121
Publisher's E-mail: info@neh.gov
Freq: Quarterly. **Subscription Rates:** $25 Individuals; $9 Single issue local; $12 Single issue foreign. **URL:** http://www.neh.gov/humanities. **Remarks:** Advertising not accepted. **Circ:** (Not Reported).

6758 ■ ICSID Review: Foreign Investment Law Journal
Johns Hopkins University Press
1818 H St., NW
Washington, DC 20433
Publisher's E-mail: webmaster@jhupress.jhu.edu
Law journal focusing on foreign investment issues. **Freq:** 3/year. **Print Method:** Offset. **Trim Size:** 7 x 10. **Cols./Page:** 1. **Col. Width:** 26 picas. **Col. Depth:** 7 inches. **Key Personnel:** Meg Kinnear, Editor-in-Chief. **ISSN:** 0258--3690 (print); **EISSN:** 2049--1999 (electronic). **Subscription Rates:** $88 Individuals print; $223 Institutions online; $257 Institutions print; $279 Institutions print + online. **URL:** http://icsidreview.oxfordjournals.org. **Remarks:** Accepts advertising. **Circ:** (Not Reported).

6759 ■ IEEE Annals of the History of Computing
IEEE - Computer Society
2001 L St. NW, Ste. 700
Washington, DC 20036-4928
Phone: (202)371-0101
Fax: (202)728-9614
Free: 800-678-4333
Publisher's E-mail: help@computer.org
Journal covering history of computing. **Freq:** Quarterly. **Key Personnel:** Sandy Brown, Manager, Business Development. **ISSN:** 1058--6180 (print). **Subscription Rates:** $69 Members professional; $20 Members student; $29.99 Individuals digital. **URL:** http://www.computer.org/portal/web/computingnow/annals; http://www.computer.org/web/computingnow/annals. **Remarks:** Advertising accepted; rates available upon request. **Circ:** (Not Reported).

6760 ■ IEEE Computer Graphics and Applications
IEEE - Computer Society
2001 L St. NW, Ste. 700
Washington, DC 20036-4928
Phone: (202)371-0101
Fax: (202)728-9614
Free: 800-678-4333

Publisher's E-mail: help@computer.org
Magazine addressing the interests and needs of professional designers and users of computer graphics hardware, software, and systems. **Freq:** Bimonthly. **Print Method:** Offset. **Trim Size:** 7 7/8 x 10 3/4. **Cols./Page:** 2. **ISSN:** 0272--1716 (print). **Subscription Rates:** $39 Individuals professional; $20 Students; $29.99 Individuals online; $69 Members professional (print only). **URL:** http://www.computer.org/web/computingnow/cga; http://www.ieee.org/membership-catalog/productdetail/showProductDetailPage.html?product=PER306-ELE&refProd=MEMC016. **Ad Rates:** BW $1,130; 4C $1,830. **Remarks:** Accepts advertising. **Circ:** **2250**, 1993.

6761 ■ IEEE Design and Test
IEEE - Computer Society
2001 L St. NW, Ste. 700
Washington, DC 20036-4928
Phone: (202)371-0101
Fax: (202)728-9614
Free: 800-678-4333
Publisher's E-mail: help@computer.org
Magazine on computer design and testing. **Freq:** Bimonthly. **Print Method:** Offset. **Trim Size:** 7 7/8 x 10 3/4. **Cols./Page:** 2. **Col. Width:** 26 nonpareils. **Col. Depth:** 138 agate lines. **Key Personnel:** Andre Ivanov, Editor-in-Chief. **ISSN:** 2168--2356 (print). **Subscription Rates:** $20 Members; $146 Nonmembers. **Alt. Formats:** CD-ROM. **URL:** http://www.computer.org/web/computingnow/designandtest. **Formerly:** IEEE Design and Test of Computers. **Ad Rates:** BW $490; 4C $700; PCI $96. **Remarks:** Accepts advertising. **Circ:** Paid 1565.

6762 ■ IEEE Intelligent Systems
IEEE - Computer Society
2001 L St. NW, Ste. 700
Washington, DC 20036-4928
Phone: (202)371-0101
Fax: (202)728-9614
Free: 800-678-4333
Publisher's E-mail: help@computer.org
Freq: 6/year. **ISSN:** 1541--1672 (print). **Subscription Rates:** $69 Members professional; $29.99 Individuals online; $20 Members society member. **URL:** http://www.computer.org/portal/web/computingnow/intelligentsystems. **Remarks:** Accepts advertising. **Circ:** (Not Reported).

6763 ■ IEEE Intelligent Systems: High-Impact, Cutting-Edge Theory and Applications
IEEE - Computer Society
2001 L St. NW, Ste. 700
Washington, DC 20036-4928
Phone: (202)371-0101
Fax: (202)728-9614
Free: 800-678-4333
Publisher's E-mail: help@computer.org
Peer-reviewed journal covering artificial intelligence, and intelligent systems. **Freq:** Bimonthly. **Trim Size:** 7 7/8 x 10 3/4. **Cols./Page:** 3. **Col. Width:** 13 picas. **Col. Depth:** 54 picas. **Key Personnel:** Fei-Yue Wang, Editor-in-Chief. **ISSN:** 1541-1672 (print). **Subscription Rates:** $69 Members; $20 Students. **URL:** http://www.computer.org/web/computingnow/intelligentsystems. **Formerly:** IEEE Expert. **Ad Rates:** BW $1,130; 4C $1,830. **Remarks:** Accepts advertising. **Circ:** **2239**.

6764 ■ IEEE Internet Computing
IEEE - Computer Society
2001 L St. NW, Ste. 700
Washington, DC 20036-4928
Phone: (202)371-0101
Fax: (202)728-9614
Free: 800-678-4333
Publisher's E-mail: help@computer.org
Freq: Bimonthly. **Subscription Rates:** $99 Members professional member; $35 Students online; $69 Members society member; $1275 Individuals print; $1594 Individuals print & online; $1110 Individuals online. **URL:** http://www.computer.org/portal/web/computingnow/internetcomputing. **Remarks:** Accepts advertising. **Circ:** (Not Reported).

6765 ■ IEEE Internet Computing: Engineering and Applying the Internet
IEEE - Computer Society
2001 L St. NW, Ste. 700
Washington, DC 20036-4928
Phone: (202)371-0101
Fax: (202)728-9614
Free: 800-678-4333
Publisher's E-mail: help@computer.org
Trade magazine covering the Internet, including process mining, e-commerce, and context-aware computing. **Freq:** Bimonthly. **Trim Size:** 7 7/8 x 10 3/4. **Key Personnel:** Linda World, Editor; Michael Rabinovich, Editor-in-Chief; Robin Baldwin, Managing Editor. **ISSN:** 1089--7801 (print). **Subscription Rates:** $9.99 Single issue; $1110 Nonmembers online only; $1594 Nonmembers online and print; $1275 Nonmembers print only; $69 Members professional member (print and online); $20 Members student member (print and online); $39 Members sponsoring society member (print and online); $99 Members professional member (print only); $35 Members student member (print only); $69 Members sponsoring society member (print only). **URL:** http://www.computer.org/web/computingnow/internetcomputing. **Ad Rates:** BW $1360; 4C $1810. **Remarks:** Accepts advertising. **Circ:** Paid **3655**.

6766 ■ IEEE Pervasive Computing
IEEE - Computer Society
2001 L St. NW, Ste. 700
Washington, DC 20036-4928
Phone: (202)371-0101
Fax: (202)728-9614
Free: 800-678-4333
Publisher's E-mail: help@computer.org
Magazine that covers developments in pervasive, mobile, and ubiquitous computing to developers, researchers, and educators who want to keep abreast of rapid technology change. **Freq:** Quarterly. **Trim Size:** 7 7/8 x 10 3/4. **Key Personnel:** Roy Want, Editor-in-Chief; M. Satyanarayanan, Editor-in-Chief. **Subscription Rates:** $69 Members professional; $20 Members student; $770 Individuals digital; $885 Individuals print. **URL:** http://www.computer.org/portal/web/computingnow/pervasivecomputing. **Ad Rates:** BW $1130; 4C $1830. **Remarks:** Accepts advertising. **Circ:** **1757**, 1639.

6767 ■ IEEE Security & Privacy Magazine
IEEE - Computer Society
2001 L St. NW, Ste. 700
Washington, DC 20036-4928
Phone: (202)371-0101
Fax: (202)728-9614
Free: 800-678-4333
Publisher's E-mail: help@computer.org
Journal that aims to explore role and importance of networked infrastructure and developing lasting security solutions. **Freq:** Bimonthly. **Key Personnel:** Carl E. Landwehr, Editor-in-Chief; Marc Donner, Associate Editor; Bret Michael, Associate Editor; Georgann Carter, Manager, Marketing; Steve Woods, Managing Editor. **Subscription Rates:** $69 Members professional; $20 Students; $820 Individuals digital; $940 Individuals print. **URL:** http://www.computer.org/portal/web/computingnow/securityandprivacy. **Ad Rates:** BW $1,600; 4C $2,300. **Remarks:** Accepts advertising. **Circ:** 9268.

6768 ■ IEEE Software: Building the Community of Leading Software Practitioners
IEEE - Computer Society
2001 L St. NW, Ste. 700
Washington, DC 20036-4928
Phone: (202)371-0101
Fax: (202)728-9614
Free: 800-678-4333
Publication E-mail: software@computer.org
Magazine covering the computer software industry for the community of leading software practitioners. **Freq:** Bimonthly. **Key Personnel:** Forrest Shull, Editor-in-Chief. **ISSN:** 0740--7459 (print). **Subscription Rates:** $69 Individuals print and online; professional member; $20 Students print and online. **URL:** http://www.computer.org/web/computingnow/software. **Ad Rates:** BW $2,000; 4C $2,450. **Remarks:** Accepts advertising. **Circ:** (Not Reported).

6769 ■ IEEE Spectrum
Institute of Electrical and Electronics Engineers USA
2001 L St. NW, Ste. 700
Washington, DC 20036-4910
Phone: (202)785-0017
Fax: (202)785-0835
Publisher's E-mail: ieeeusa@ieee.org
Magazine for the scientific and engineering professional. Provides information on developments and trends in engineering, physics, mathematics, chemistry, medicine/biology, and the nuclear sciences. **Freq:** Monthly. **Print Method:** Web Offset. **Trim Size:** 7 7/8 x 10 1/2. **Cols./Page:** 3 and 2. **Col. Width:** 2 3/16 and 3 1/4 inches. **Col. Depth:** 10 inches. **Key Personnel:** James Vick, Publisher, phone: (212)419-7767, fax: (212)419-7589; Elizabeth A. Bretz, Managing Editor; Glenn Zorpette, Executive Editor; Robert T. Ross, Business Manager; Susan Hassler, Editor-in-Chief. **ISSN:** 0018--9235 (print). **URL:** http://advertise.ieee.org/products/ieee-spectrum/ieee-spectrum-magazine. **Ad Rates:** BW $9975; 4C $11575. **Remarks:** Accepts advertising. **Circ:** ‡394540.

6770 ■ IEEE Transactions on Computers
IEEE - Computer Society
2001 L St. NW, Ste. 700
Washington, DC 20036-4928
Phone: (202)371-0101
Fax: (202)728-9614
Free: 800-678-4333
Publisher's E-mail: help@computer.org
Magazine on computers. **Freq:** Monthly. **Key Personnel:** Elisardo Antelo, Associate Editor. **ISSN:** 0018--9340 (print). **Subscription Rates:** $2465 Individuals electronic; $3080 Individuals electronic, abstract, CD-ROM; $80 Members electronic, abstract, CD-ROM, professional; $25 Members electronic, abstract, CD-ROM, students. **Alt. Formats:** CD-ROM; Electronic publishing. **URL:** http://www.computer.org/portal/web/tc; http://www.computer.org/web/tc. **Remarks:** Accepts advertising. **Circ:** (Not Reported).

6771 ■ IEEE Transactions on Dependable and Secure Computing
IEEE - Computer Society
2001 L St. NW, Ste. 700
Washington, DC 20036-4928
Phone: (202)371-0101
Fax: (202)728-9614
Free: 800-678-4333
Publisher's E-mail: help@computer.org
Journal that publishes archival research results focusing on research into foundations, methodologies, and mechanisms that support the achievement of systems and networks that are dependable and secure to the desired degree without compromising performance. **Freq:** 3/year. **Key Personnel:** Ravi Sandhu, Editor-in-Chief. **ISSN:** 1545--5971 (print). **Subscription Rates:** $410 Institutions electronic; $515 Institutions electronic, abstract & CD-ROM; $67 Members electronic, abstract & CD-ROM; $19 Students electronic, abstract & CD-ROM. **URL:** http://ieeexplore.ieee.org/xpl/RecentIssue.jsp?punumber=8858; http://www.computer.org/portal/web/tdsc. **Remarks:** Accepts advertising. **Circ:** (Not Reported).

6772 ■ IEEE Transactions on Education
IEEE - Education Society
c/o IEEE
2001 L St. NW, Ste. 700
Washington, DC 20036-4910
Phone: (202)785-0017
Fax: (202)785-0835
Publisher's E-mail: i.engelson@ieee.org
Freq: Quarterly. **Key Personnel:** Jeffrey E. Froyd, Editor-in-Chief. **ISSN:** 0018--9359 (print). **URL:** http://ieeexplore.ieee.org/xpl/RecentIssue.jsp?punumber=13; http://ieee-edusociety.org/publications/publications. **Mailing address:** IEEE Admission and AdvancementPO Box 6804, Piscataway, NJ 08855-6804. **Remarks:** Accepts advertising. **Circ:** (Not Reported).

6773 ■ IEEE Transactions on Haptics
IEEE - Computer Society
2001 L St. NW, Ste. 700
Washington, DC 20036-4928
Phone: (202)371-0101
Fax: (202)728-9614
Free: 800-678-4333
Publisher's E-mail: help@computer.org
Journal addressing the science, technology and applications associated with information acquisition and object manipulation through touch. **Freq:** Quarterly. **Trim Size:**

Circulation: ★ = AAM; △ or • = BPA; ♦ = CAC; ❑ = VAC; ⊕ = PO Statement; ‡ = Publisher's Report; Boldface figures = sworn; Light figures = estimated.

8 x 11. **Key Personnel:** J. Edward Colgate, Editor-in-Chief. **ISSN:** 1939--1412 (print). **URL:** http://ieeexplore.ieee.org/xpl/RecentIssue.jsp?reload=true&punumber=4543165. **Remarks:** Advertising not accepted. **Circ:** (Not Reported).

6774 ■ IEEE Transactions on Knowledge & Data Engineering
IEEE - Computer Society
2001 L St. NW, Ste. 700
Washington, DC 20036-4928
Phone: (202)371-0101
Fax: (202)728-9614
Free: 800-678-4333
Publication E-mail: tkde@computer.org
Magazine providing an international and interdisciplinary forum to publish results on research, design, and development of data engineering methodologies, strategies, and systems. **Freq:** Monthly. **Trim Size:** 8 1/4 x 11. **Cols./Page:** 2. **Col. Width:** 21 picas. **Col. Depth:** 10 inches. **Key Personnel:** Beng Chin Ooi, Editor-in-Chief; Jian Pei, Editor-in-Chief. **ISSN:** 1041--4347 (print). **Subscription Rates:** $85 professional; $28 Students; $55 sponsoring society; $1710 Institutions electronic; $1881 Institutions electronic, abstract, CD-ROM; $83 Members electronic, abstract, CD-ROM, professional; $27 Members electronic, abstract, CD-ROM, student. **URL:** http://www.computer.org/web/tkde. **Remarks:** Accepts advertising. **Circ:** 6000.

6775 ■ IEEE Transactions on Mobile Computing
IEEE - Computer Society
2001 L St. NW, Ste. 700
Washington, DC 20036-4928
Phone: (202)371-0101
Fax: (202)728-9614
Free: 800-678-4333
Publication E-mail: tmc@computer.org
Journal that publishes archival research results related to mobility of users, systems, data, and computing. **Freq:** Monthly. **Key Personnel:** Prasant Mohapatra, Editor-in-Chief. **ISSN:** 1536--1233 (print). **Subscription Rates:** $1095 Institutions online; $1370 Institutions electronic, abstract & CD-ROM; $72 Members electronic, abstract & CD-ROM; $21 Students electronic, abstract & CD-ROM. **URL:** http://ieeexplore.ieee.org/xpl/RecentIssue.jsp?punumber=7755; http://www.computer.org/portal/web/tmc. **Remarks:** Accepts advertising. **Circ:** (Not Reported).

6776 ■ IEEE Transactions on NanoBioscience
IEEE - Computer Society
2001 L St. NW, Ste. 700
Washington, DC 20036-4928
Phone: (202)371-0101
Fax: (202)728-9614
Free: 800-678-4333
Publisher's E-mail: help@computer.org
Journal that reports on original, innovative and interdisciplinary work on all aspects of molecular systems, cellular systems, and tissues including molecular electronics. **Freq:** 4/yr. **Key Personnel:** Henry Hess, Editor-in-Chief, phone: (212)854-7749; Parag Katira, Managing Editor. **ISSN:** 1536--1241 (print). **URL:** http://tnb.embs.org; http://ieeexplore.ieee.org/xpl/RecentIssue.jsp?punumber=7728. **Remarks:** Accepts advertising. **Circ:** (Not Reported).

6777 ■ IEEE Transactions on Parallel and Distributed Systems
IEEE - Computer Society
2001 L St. NW, Ste. 700
Washington, DC 20036-4928
Phone: (202)371-0101
Fax: (202)728-9614
Free: 800-678-4333
Publisher's E-mail: help@computer.org
Journal on computers mainly dealing with multiple-processor systems. **Freq:** Monthly. **Key Personnel:** David A. Bader, Editor-in-Chief. **ISSN:** 1045--9219 (print). **Subscription Rates:** $1790 Individuals electronic; $2240 Institutions electronic, abstract, CD-ROM; $70 Members electronic, abstract, CD-ROM, professional; $20 Members electronic, abstract, CD-ROM, student. **Alt. Formats:** CD-ROM. **URL:** http://www.computer.org/portal/web/tpds; http://www.computer.org/web/tpds. **Remarks:** Accepts advertising. **Circ:** (Not Reported).

6778 ■ IEEE Transactions on Pattern Analysis and Machine Intelligence
IEEE - Computer Society
2001 L St. NW, Ste. 700
Washington, DC 20036-4928
Phone: (202)371-0101
Fax: (202)728-9614
Free: 800-678-4333
Publication E-mail: tpami@computer.org
Journal covering research results in statistical and structural pattern recognition; image analysis; computational models of vision; computer vision systems; enhancement, restoration, segmentation, feature extraction, shape and texture analysis; applications of pattern analysis in medicine, industry, government, and the arts and sciences; artificial intelligence, knowledge representation, logical and probabilistic inference, learning, speech recognition, character and text recognition, syntactic and semantic processing, understanding natural language, expert systems, and specialized architectures for such processing. **Freq:** Monthly. **Key Personnel:** David A. Forsyth, Editor-in-Chief. **ISSN:** 0162--8828 (print). **Subscription Rates:** $129 Members print and online (professional); $49 Members print and online (student); $3788 Individuals print and online; $3030 Individuals print; $2635 Individuals online. **Alt. Formats:** CD-ROM. **URL:** http://www.computer.org/portal/web/tpami; http://www.computer.org/web/tpami. **Remarks:** Accepts advertising. **Circ:** (Not Reported).

6779 ■ IEEE Transactions on Services Computing
IEEE - Computer Society
2001 L St. NW, Ste. 700
Washington, DC 20036-4928
Phone: (202)371-0101
Fax: (202)728-9614
Free: 800-678-4333
Publication E-mail: tsc@computer.org
Journal focusing on any computing or software aspect of the science and technology related to services innovation research and development. **Freq:** 6/year. **Key Personnel:** Ling Liu, Editor-in-Chief. **ISSN:** 1939--1374 (print). **Subscription Rates:** $435 Individuals online; $76 Members professional; $23 Members students. **URL:** http://www.computer.org/portal/web/tsc. **Circ:** (Not Reported).

6780 ■ IEEE Transactions on Software Engineering
IEEE - Computer Society
2001 L St. NW, Ste. 700
Washington, DC 20036-4928
Phone: (202)371-0101
Fax: (202)728-9614
Free: 800-678-4333
Publication E-mail: tse@computer.org
Journal on software engineering. **Freq:** Monthly. **Key Personnel:** Matthew B. Dwyer, Editor-in-Chief. **ISSN:** 0098--5589 (print). **Subscription Rates:** $2110 Individuals online; $2640 Individuals online, abstract, CD-ROM; $75 Members online, abstract, CD-ROM (professional); $23 Members online, abstract, CD-ROM (student). **Alt. Formats:** CD-ROM. **URL:** http://www.computer.org/portal/web/tse; http://www.computer.org/web/tse. **Remarks:** Accepts advertising. **Circ:** (Not Reported).

6781 ■ ILAR e-Journal
The National Academies of Sciences, Engineering, Medicine Division on Earth and Life Studies Institute for Laboratory Animal Research
500 5th St. NW
Washington, DC 20001
Phone: (202)334-2590
Fax: (202)334-1687
Freq: Quarterly. **ISSN:** 1930- 6180 (print). **Subscription Rates:** $109 Individuals print only; $66 Students; $1134 Institutions print and online; $54 Single issue. **URL:** http://ilarjournal.oxfordjournals.org/; http://dels.nas.edu/global/ilar/Ilar-Journal. **Remarks:** Advertising not accepted. **Circ:** (Not Reported).

6782 ■ ILSA Journal of International and Comparative Law
International Law Students Association
701 13th St. NW, 6th Fl.
Washington, DC 20005
Phone: (202)729-2470
Fax: (202)639-9355
Publication E-mail: ilsa.journal.novasoutheastern@gmail.com
Freq: 3/year. **Key Personnel:** Ronald Smith, Editor-in-Chief. **Subscription Rates:** $30 Individuals; $35 Other countries; $12.50 U.S. ILSA Members; $15 Other countries ILSA Members. **URL:** http://www.ilsa.org/publications/journal-of-intl-a-comparative-law. **Remarks:** Advertising not accepted. **Circ:** (Not Reported).

6783 ■ IMF Economic Review
Palgrave Macmillan
c/o Tracey Lookadoo, Ed. Asst.
Research Dept.
700 19th St.
Washington, DC 20431
Phone: (202)623-5866
Fax: (202)589-5866
Publication E-mail: imf_er@imf.org
Peer-reviewed journal featuring articles in the field of economics. **Freq:** Quarterly. **Key Personnel:** Pierre-Olivier Gourinchas, Editor; M. Ayhan Kose, Board Member. **ISSN:** 2041--4161 (print); **EISSN:** 2041--417X (electronic). **Subscription Rates:** $119 Individuals print & online; £77 Individuals Europe and rest of the world; £171 Individuals print. **URL:** http://www.palgrave-journals.com/imfer/index.html. **Circ:** (Not Reported).

6784 ■ Independent Banker
Independent Community Bankers of America
1615 L St. NW, Ste. 900
Washington, DC 20036
Phone: (202)659-8111
Fax: (202)659-3604
Free: 800-422-8439
Publication E-mail: magazine@icba.org
Freq: Monthly. **Print Method:** Letterpress and offset. **Trim Size:** 8 1/4 x 10 7/8. **Cols./Page:** 3. **Col. Width:** 26 nonpareils. **Col. Depth:** 120 agate lines. **Key Personnel:** Ellen Ryan, Editor; Rachael Solomon, Director, Sales. **ISSN:** 0019--3674 (print). **Subscription Rates:** $75 Nonmembers /year; Included in membership; $20 Members /year. **URL:** http://independentbanker.org; http://www.icba.org/publications/index.cfm?ItemNumber=16256&navItemNumber=183940; http://www.icba.org/publications/index2.cfm?ItemNumber=4172. **Ad Rates:** BW $1690; 4C $2590. **Remarks:** Accepts advertising. **Circ:** ‡13,500.

6785 ■ Independent School
National Association of Independent Schools
1129 20th St. NW, Ste. 800
Washington, DC 20036-3425
Phone: (202)973-9700
Fax: (888)316-3862
Publisher's E-mail: membership@nais.org
Freq: Quarterly. **Key Personnel:** Michael Brosnan, Editor. **Subscription Rates:** $54 Nonmembers; $32 Members; $52 Members Canada and Mexico; $72 Nonmembers Canada and Mexico; $60 Members Outside North America; $84 Nonmembers Outside North America. **URL:** http://www.nais.org/Magazines-Newsletters/ISMagazine/Pages/Issues/Education-and-the-Brain.aspx. **Remarks:** Accepts advertising. **Circ:** (Not Reported).

6786 ■ India Post
The India Study Circle for Philately
PO Box 7326
Washington, DC 20044-7326
Phone: (202)564-6876
Fax: (202)565-2441
Freq: Quarterly. **Subscription Rates:** Included in membership. **URL:** http://www.indiastudycircle.org/india-post.html. **Remarks:** Accepts advertising. **Circ:** (Not Reported).

6787 ■ Infection and Immunity
ASM Journals
1752 North St. NW
Washington, DC 20036
Phone: (202)737-3600
Fax: (202)942-9355
Publisher's E-mail: journals@asmusa.org
Freq: Monthly. **Print Method:** Offset. Uses mats. **Trim Size:** 8 1/8 x 10 7/8. **Cols./Page:** 2. **Col. Width:** 42 nonpareils. **Col. Depth:** 127 agate lines. **Key Personnel:** Ferric C. Fang, PhD, Editor-in-Chief. **ISSN:** 0019-9567 (print); **EISSN:** 1098--5522 (electronic). **Subscription Rates:** $122 Members online only; $855 Institutions online only, for sites with 1-200 authorized users; $1109

Institutions online only, for sites with 201-1,500 authorized users; $1442 Institutions online only, for sites with 1,501-3,500 authorized users. **URL:** http://iai.asm.org. **Ad Rates:** $1335-1465, full page; $935-1005, 1/2 page; $625-680, 1/4 page; $2670-5860, insert. **Remarks:** Accepts advertising. **Circ:** Combined ‡12923.

6788 ■ Infection and Immunity
American Society for Microbiology
1752 N St. NW
Washington, DC 20036-2904
Phone: (202)942-9207
Fax: (202)942-9333
Publisher's E-mail: journals@asmusa.org
Freq: Monthly. **Print Method:** Offset. Uses mats. **Trim Size:** 8 1/8 x 10 7/8. **Cols./Page:** 2. **Col. Width:** 42 nonpareils. **Col. Depth:** 127 agate lines. **Key Personnel:** Ferric C. Fang, PhD, Editor-in-Chief. **ISSN:** 0019--9567 (print); **EISSN:** 1098--5522 (electronic). **Subscription Rates:** $122 Members online only; $855 Institutions online only, for sites with 1-200 authorized users; $1109 Institutions online only, for sites with 201-1,500 authorized users; $1442 Institutions online only, for sites with 1,501-3,500 authorized users. **URL:** http://iai.asm.org. **Ad Rates:** $1335-1465, full page; $935-1005, 1/2 page; $625-680, 1/4 page; $2670-5860, insert. **Remarks:** Accepts advertising. **Circ:** Combined ‡12923.

6789 ■ Inorganic Chemistry
American Chemical Society
1155 16th St. NW
Washington, DC 20036
Phone: (202)872-4600
Free: 800-227-5558
Publisher's E-mail: help@acs.org
Fundamental studies in all phases of inorganic chemistry. **Freq:** 3/year. **Print Method:** Offset. **Trim Size:** 8 3/16 x 11 1/4. **Cols./Page:** 2. **Col. Width:** 36 nonpareils. **Col. Depth:** 126 agate lines. **Key Personnel:** Allan L. Balch, Associate Editor; William B. Tolman, Editor-in-Chief. **ISSN:** 0020--1669 (print); **EISSN:** 1520--510X (electronic). **Online:** American Chemical Society American Chemical Society. **URL:** http://pubs.acs.org/journal/inocaj. **Ad Rates:** BW $2,520; 4C $3,275. **Remarks:** Accepts advertising. **Circ:** ‡3000.

6790 ■ Intellectual and Developmental Disabilities
American Association on Intellectual and Developmental Disabilities
501 3rd St. NW, Ste. 200
Washington, DC 20001
Phone: (202)387-1968
Fax: (202)387-2193
Freq: Bimonthly. **Trim Size:** 8 3/4 x 11 1/4. **Key Personnel:** Glenn T. Fujiura, Editor; Dianne L. Ferguson, Associate Editor. **ISSN:** 1934--9556 (print). **URL:** http://aaiddjournals.org. **Formerly:** Mental Retardation. **Ad Rates:** $290-975, for display advertising; $400-850. BW $975; BW $, for display advertising4C $. **Remarks:** Accepts display and classified advertising. **Circ:** Paid 5000, 2115.

6791 ■ Internal Revenue Bulletin
U.S. Government Publishing Office
732 N Capitol St. NW
Washington, DC 20401-0001
Phone: (202)512-1800
Fax: (202)512-2104
Free: 866-512-1800
Publisher's E-mail: contactcenter@gpo.gov
Tax news bulletin. **Founded:** 1922. **Freq:** Weekly. **Print Method:** Letterpress. **Cols./Page:** 3. **Col. Width:** 27 nonpareils. **Col. Depth:** 126 agate lines. **ISSN:** 0020-5761 (print). **Subscription Rates:** $7.50 Single issue; $10.50 Other countries single copy. **URL:** http://www.irs.gov/app/picklist/list/internalRevenueBulletins.html. **Mailing address:** PO Box 979050, Saint Louis, MO 63197-9000. **Circ:** (Not Reported).

6792 ■ The International Economy: The Magazine of International Economic Policy
The International Economy Publications Inc.
888 16 St. NW, Ste. 740
Washington, DC 20006
Phone: (202)861-0791
Fax: (202)861-0790
Publication E-mail: editor@international-economy.com
Magazine. **Freq:** Quarterly. **Key Personnel:** David Hale, Executive Editor; Angela C. Wikes, Managing Editor; David Smick, Editor, Founder, Publisher. **ISSN:** 0898--4336 (print). **Subscription Rates:** $72 Individuals; $120 Two years; $87 U.S. and Canada 1st class delivery - 1 year; $135 U.S. and Canada 1st class delivery - 2 year; $132 Other countries airmail - 1 year; $180 Other countries airmail - 2 years. **URL:** http://www.international-economy.com. **Ad Rates:** BW $2,750; 4C $3,750; PCI $133. **Remarks:** Advertising accepted; rates available upon request. **Circ:** Paid 2000.

6793 ■ International Educator
NAFSA: Association of International Educators
1307 New York Ave. NW, 8th Fl.
Washington, DC 20005-4701
Phone: (202)737-3699
Fax: (202)737-3657
Freq: Bimonthly. **Subscription Rates:** $40 Individuals; $55 Canada; $72 Elsewhere. **URL:** http://www.nafsa.org/Find_Resources/Publications/Periodicals/International_Educator/International_Educator_Archives. **Remarks:** Accepts advertising. **Circ:** (Not Reported).

6794 ■ International Fire Fighter
International Association of Fire Fighters
1750 New York Ave. NW, Ste. 300
Washington, DC 20006-5395
Phone: (202)737-8484
Fax: (202)737-8418
Union tabloid. **Freq:** Bimonthly. **Print Method:** Offset. **Trim Size:** 11 1/2 x 15 1/2. **Cols./Page:** 4. **Col. Width:** 14 picas. **Col. Depth:** 84 picas. **Key Personnel:** Craig Renfro, Director, Advertising, phone: (972)416-9782; Jane Blume, Managing Editor; Harold A. Schaitberger, Editor. **ISSN:** 0020--6773 (print). **URL:** http://www.iaff.org/mag. **Remarks:** Advertising not accepted. **Circ:** Non-paid 195000, 267000.

6795 ■ International Journal of Engineering Education
American Society for Engineering Education
1818 N St. NW, Ste. 600
Washington, DC 20036-2479
Phone: (202)331-3500
Publisher's E-mail: board@asee.org
Journal for engineering education. **Freq:** Quarterly. **Key Personnel:** Michael C. Loui, Editor. **ISSN:** 1069--4730 (print); **EISSN:** 2168--9830 (electronic). **Subscription Rates:** $648 Institutions print and online ; £411 Institutions print and online; €476 Institutions print and online; $648 Institutions, other countries print and online; $540 Institutions print or online; £342 Institutions print or online; €396 Institutions print or online; $540 Institutions, other countries print or online. **URL:** http://www.asee.org/papers-and-publications/publications/jee. **Remarks:** Advertising not accepted. **Circ:** (Not Reported).

6796 ■ International Journal of Government Auditing
U.S. Government Accountability Office
441 G St. NW
Washington, DC 20548
Phone: (202)512-3000
Publication E-mail: intosaijournal@gao.gov
Financial management journal printed in Arabic, French, German, Spanish, and English. **Founded:** 1974. **Freq:** Quarterly. **Print Method:** Letterpress. **Trim Size:** 8 1/2 x 11. **ISSN:** 0047-0724 (print). **Subscription Rates:** $5 Individuals. **URL:** http://www.intosaijournal.org/. **Remarks:** Advertising not accepted. **Circ:** (Not Reported).

6797 ■ The International Journal of Marine and Coastal Law
Koninklijke Brill NV
c/o Prof. David Freestone, Ed.-in-Ch.
Lobingier Visiting Professor
The George Washington University
Washington, DC 20052
Publisher's E-mail: brillonline@brill.com
Journal covering all aspects of marine and coastal law worldwide. **Freq:** Quarterly. **Print Method:** Offset. **Key Personnel:** David Freestone, LLB, LLD, LLM, Editor-in-Chief, Professor, phone: (202)994-8763, fax: (202)994-5614. **ISSN:** 0927--3522 (print); **EISSN:** 1571--8085 (electronic). **Subscription Rates:** €832 Institutions online only; $1133 Institutions online only; €915 Institutions print only; $1246 Institutions print only; €998 Institutions print and online; $1359 Institutions print and online; €193 Individuals online or print; $254 Individuals online or print. **URL:** http://www.brill.com/international-journal-marine-and-coastal-law. **Circ:** (Not Reported).

6798 ■ The International Journal for Not-for-Profit Law
International Center for Not-for-Profit Law
1126 16th St. NW, Ste. 400
Washington, DC 20036-4837
Phone: (202)452-8600
Fax: (202)452-8555
Publisher's E-mail: infoicnl@icnl.org
Journal focusing on global civil society. Addresses issues affecting the legal environment. **Freq:** Quarterly. **Key Personnel:** Stephen Bates, Editor; Douglas Rutzen, Senior Editor; Stephan Klingelhofer, Editor. **ISSN:** 1833--2595 (print). **Subscription Rates:** Free e-book. **Alt. Formats:** E-book. **URL:** http://www.icnl.org/research/journal. **Remarks:** Advertising not accepted. **Circ:** (Not Reported).

6799 ■ International Journal of Play Therapy
American Psychological Association
750 1st St. NE
Washington, DC 20002-4242
Phone: (202)336-5500
Free: 800-374-2721
Journal for mental health professionals specializing on play therapy. **Freq:** Quarterly. **Key Personnel:** Franc Hudspeth, PhD, Editor. **ISSN:** 1555-6824 (print); **EISSN:** 1939-0629 (electronic). **Subscription Rates:** $65 Members; $89 Other countries members; $65 Students; $454 Institutions; $518 Institutions, other countries by mail; $120 Nonmembers; $149 Other countries nonmembers. **URL:** http://www.apa.org/pubs/journals/pla/index.aspx. **Ad Rates:** 4C $975; BW $450. **Remarks:** Accepts advertising. **Circ:** ‡6000.

6800 ■ International Journal of Stress Management
American Psychological Association
750 1st St. NE
Washington, DC 20002-4242
Phone: (202)336-5500
Free: 800-374-2721
Journal publishing peer-reviewed original articles including empirical, theoretical, review and historical articles on stress management. **Freq:** Quarterly. **Key Personnel:** Sharon Glazer, PhD, Editor; David B. Barker, Board Member. **ISSN:** 1072--5245 (print); **EISSN:** 1573--3424 (electronic). **Subscription Rates:** $903 Institutions; $952 Institutions, other countries; $967 Institutions, other countries by air mail. **URL:** http://www.apa.org/pubs/journals/str/index.aspx. **Ad Rates:** 4C $975; BW $275. **Remarks:** Accepts advertising. **Circ:** 300.

6801 ■ International Legal Materials
American Society of International Law
2223 Massachusetts Ave. NW
Washington, DC 20008
Phone: (202)939-6000
Fax: (202)797-7133
Documentary journal includes treaties, national legislation, national and international judicial decisions, and reports and resolutions of international organizations. **Freq:** Bimonthly. **Print Method:** Offset. **Trim Size:** 8 1/2 x 11. **Key Personnel:** Djurdja Lazic, Managing Editor. **ISSN:** 0020-7829 (print). **Subscription Rates:** $150 Members print; $285 Nonmembers online access only; $305 Nonmembers; Included in membership online. **URL:** http://www.asil.org/resources/international-legal-materials. **Ad Rates:** BW $350. **Remarks:** Accepts advertising. **Circ:** Paid 2111.

6802 ■ International Perspectives in Psychology: Research, Practice, Consultation
APA Division 52: International Psychology
750 1st St. NE
Washington, DC 20002-4242
Phone: (202)336-6013
Free: 800-374-2721
Publisher's E-mail: apadivision52@gmail.com
Journal publishing research that examines human behavior and experiences around the globe from a psychological perspective. **Freq:** Quarterly January, April, July and October. **Key Personnel:** Judith L. Gibbons, Editor. **ISSN:** 2157--3883 (print); **EISSN:** 2157--3891 (electronic). **Subscription Rates:** $560 Institutions; $609 Institutions, other countries; $133 Individuals;

Circulation: ★ = AAM; △ or • = BPA; ♦ = CAC; ❑ = VAC; ⊕ = PO Statement; ‡ = Publisher's Report; Boldface figures = sworn; Light figures = estimated.

$162 Individuals international. **URL:** http://www.apa.org/pubs/journals/ipp. **Ad Rates:** BW $335, full page. **Remarks:** Accepts advertising. **Circ:** 700.

6803 ■ International Trade by Commodity Statistics
OECD Washington Center
1776 I St. NW, Ste. 450
Washington, DC 20006
Phone: (202)785-6323
Fax: (202)315-2508
Free: 800-456-6323
Publisher's E-mail: washington.contact@oecd.org
Magazine on the value of trade flows of OECD countries. **Freq:** 5/year. **ISSN:** 1028--8376 (print); **EISSN:** 2074--4005 (electronic). **URL:** http://www.oecd-ilibrary.org/trade/data/international-trade-by-commodity-statistics_itcs-data-en. **Formerly:** Foreign Trade by Commodities, Series C. **Remarks:** Advertising not accepted. **Circ:** (Not Reported).

6804 ■ International Urogynecology Journal
American Urogynecologic Society
2025 M St. NW, Ste. 800
Washington, DC 20036-2422
Phone: (301)273-0570
Fax: (301)273-0778
Publisher's E-mail: info@augs.org
Freq: Monthly. **URL:** http://www.springer.com/medicine/gynecology/journal/192; http://www.augs.org/p/cm/ld/fid=64. **Remarks:** Accepts advertising. **Circ:** (Not Reported).

6805 ■ The InTowner Newspaper
The InTowner Newspaper
1730-B Corcoran St. NW
Washington, DC 20009
Phone: (202)234-1717
Community newspaper providing local news for residents of downtown neighborhoods. **Freq:** Monthly. **Print Method:** Offset. **Trim Size:** 11 1/4 x 15. **Cols./Page:** 4. **Col. Width:** 2 1/4 inches. **Col. Depth:** 13 7/8 inches. **Key Personnel:** P.L. Wolf, Managing Editor, Publisher. **ISSN:** 0887--9400 (print). **URL:** http://intowner.com/archive-back-issue-pdf-documents. **Ad Rates:** BW $1,050. **Remarks:** Accepts advertising. **Circ:** 30000.

6806 ■ Investment Laws of the World
International Centre for Settlement of Investment Disputes
1818 H St. NW
Washington, DC 20433
Phone: (202)458-1534
Fax: (202)522-2615
Publisher's E-mail: icsidsecretariat@worldbank.org
Subscription Rates: $1345 Individuals available from Oxford University Press.; $2690 Individuals also be ordered as a set with Investment Treaties. **URL:** http://icsid.worldbank.org/apps/ICSIDWEB/resources/Pages/Investment-Laws-of-the-World.aspx. **Remarks:** Advertising not accepted. **Circ:** (Not Reported).

6807 ■ The Ironworker
International Association of Bridge, Structural, Ornamental and Reinforcing Iron Workers
1750 New York Ave. NW, Ste. 400
Washington, DC 20006
Phone: (202)383-4800
Fax: (202)638-4856
Publication E-mail: iwmagazine@iwintl.org
Magazine reporting industry news for ironworkers. **Freq:** Monthly. **Print Method:** Offset. **Trim Size:** 8 1/2 x 11. **Key Personnel:** Scott Malley, Editor. **ISSN:** 0021--163X (print). **Subscription Rates:** $5 Individuals. **Alt. Formats:** PDF. **URL:** http://www.ironworkers.org; http://www.ironworkers.org/news-magazine/ironworker-magazine. **Remarks:** Advertising not accepted. **Circ:** (Not Reported).

6808 ■ IT Professional
IEEE - Computer Society
2001 L St. NW, Ste. 700
Washington, DC 20036-4928
Phone: (202)371-0101
Fax: (202)728-9614
Free: 800-678-4333
Publisher's E-mail: help@computer.org
Trade magazine for information technology professionals. **Freq:** Bimonthly. **Trim Size:** 7 7/8 x 10 3/4. **Key Personnel:** Simon Liu, Editor-in-Chief; Philip A. Laplante, Associate Editor. **ISSN:** 1520--9202 (print). **URL:** http://www.computer.org/portal/web/computingnow/itpro. **Remarks:** Accepts advertising. **Circ:** (Not Reported).

6809 ■ Italian America
Order Sons of Italy in America
219 E St. NE
Washington, DC 20002
Phone: (202)547-2900
Fax: (202)546-8168
Free: 800-552-OSIA
Publisher's E-mail: nationaloffice@osia.org
Magazine featuring issues regarding Italian Americans' culture, history, contributions and traditions. **Freq:** Quarterly. **Subscription Rates:** $20 U.S.; $30 Other countries. **URL:** http://www.osia.org/ia-magazine/about-ia.php. **Ad Rates:** 4C $2,500. **Remarks:** Accepts advertising. **Circ:** (Not Reported).

6810 ■ ITE Journal
Institute of Transportation Engineers
1627 Eye St. NW, Ste. 600
Washington, DC 20006
Phone: (202)785-0060
Fax: (202)785-0609
Publisher's E-mail: ite_staff@ite.org
Technical magazine focusing on the plan, design, and operation of surface transportation systems. **Freq:** Monthly. **Print Method:** Web offset. **Trim Size:** 8.25 x 10.875. **Cols./Page:** 3. **Col. Width:** 13 picas. **Col. Depth:** 130 agate lines. **ISSN:** 0162--8178 (print). **Subscription Rates:** $100 Individuals; $150 Other countries. **URL:** http://www.ite.org/itejournal. **Ad Rates:** BW $1,850; 4C $3,150. **Remarks:** Accepts advertising. **Circ:** Paid ‡18330.

6811 ■ The Jewish Veteran: National Publication of the Jewish War Veterans of the USA
Jewish War Veterans of the United States of America
1811 R St. NW
Washington, DC 20009
Phone: (202)265-6280
Fax: (202)234-5662
Publication E-mail: jwv@jwv.org
Jewish magazine providing valuable information on various topics such as Jewish issues, foreign policy, veterans affairs, military history, JWV news and Museum News. **Freq:** Quarterly. **Print Method:** Offset. **Trim Size:** 8 3/8 x 10 3/4. **Cols./Page:** 3. **Col. Width:** 26 nonpareils. **Col. Depth:** 154 agate lines. **Key Personnel:** Cheryl Waldman, Managing Editor. **ISSN:** 0047--2018 (print). **Alt. Formats:** PDF. **URL:** http://www.jwv.org/communications/the_jewish_veteran. **Remarks:** Advertising accepted; rates available upon request. **Circ:** Paid 40000, Non-paid 5000.

6812 ■ JIAPAC
International Association of Providers of AIDS Care
2200 Pennsylvania Ave., NW, 4th Fl. E
Washington, DC 20037
Phone: (202)507-5899
Fax: (202)315-3651
Publisher's E-mail: iapac@iapac.org
Freq: Bimonthly. **ISSN:** 1081- 454X (print). **Subscription Rates:** £261 Institutions print + online; £63 Individuals print only. **URL:** http://jia.sagepub.com. **Remarks:** Accepts advertising. **Circ:** 9000.

6813 ■ JOCEPS
Chi Eta Phi Sorority
3029 13th St. NW
Washington, DC 20009
Phone: (202)232-3858
Fax: (202)232-3460
Publisher's E-mail: chietaphi@verizon.net
Freq: Annual. **Subscription Rates:** For members and subscribers only. **URL:** http://www.chietaphi.com/index.php?option=com_wrapper&view=wrapper&Itemid=121. **Remarks:** Accepts advertising. **Circ:** 4000.

6814 ■ Journal of the AACAP
American Academy of Child and Adolescent Psychiatry
3615 Wisconsin Ave. NW
Washington, DC 20016-3007
Phone: (202)966-7300
Fax: (202)966-2891
Publisher's E-mail: communications@aacap.org
Freq: Monthly. **ISSN:** 0890--8567 (print). **Subscription Rates:** Included in membership; $339 Individuals in U.S. (online and print); $223 Students in U.S. (online and print). **URL:** http://www.jaacap.com. **Remarks:** Accepts display advertising. **Circ:** (Not Reported).

6815 ■ Journal of Abnormal Psychology
American Psychological Association
750 1st St. NE
Washington, DC 20002-4242
Phone: (202)336-5500
Free: 800-374-2721
Journal presenting articles on basic research and theory in the broad field of abnormal behavior. **Freq:** Quarterly. **Key Personnel:** Sherryl H. Goodman, Editor; Deanna M. Barch, Editor; Timothy A. Brown, Associate Editor. **ISSN:** 0021--843X (print); **EISSN:** 1939--1846 (electronic). **Subscription Rates:** $898 Individuals; $975 Other countries; $999 By mail international. **URL:** http://www.apa.org/pubs/journals/abn. **Ad Rates:** BW $390; 4C $975. **Remarks:** Accepts advertising. **Circ:** ‡1300, 6,000.

6816 ■ Journal of the Afro-American Historical and Genealogical Society
Afro-American Historical and Genealogical Society
PO Box 73067
Washington, DC 20056-3067
Phone: (202)234-5350
Publisher's E-mail: info@aahgs.org
Freq: Semiannual. **Subscription Rates:** Included in membership. **URL:** http://www.aahgs.org/index.cfm?fuseaction=Page.ViewPage&pageId=590. **Remarks:** Accepts advertising. **Circ:** 800.

6817 ■ Journal of Agricultural, Biological and Environmental Statistics
International Biometric Society
1444 I St. NW, Ste. 700
Washington, DC 20005
Phone: (202)712-9049
Fax: (202)216-9646
Publication E-mail: jabes.editor@gmail.com
Journal contributing to the development and use of statistical methods in the agricultural, biological and environmental sciences. **Freq:** Quarterly. **Key Personnel:** Linda Young, Business Manager; Montse Fuentes, Editor-in-Chief. **ISSN:** 1085--7117 (print); **EISSN:** 1537--2693 (electronic). **Subscription Rates:** €63.02 Individuals; $308 Institutions print + free access; $370 Institutions print + enhanced access; €230 Institutions print + free access; €276 Institutions print + enhanced access. **Available online. URL:** http://www.biometricsociety.org/publications/jabes; http://www.amstat.org/publications/journals.cfm; http://www.springer.com/statistics/life+sciences,+medicine+%26+health/journal/13253. **Remarks:** Accepts advertising. **Circ:** (Not Reported).

6818 ■ Journal of Agricultural and Food Chemistry
American Chemical Society
1155 16th St. NW
Washington, DC 20036
Phone: (202)872-4600
Free: 800-227-5558
Publisher's E-mail: help@acs.org
Journal covering the applications of chemistry to agriculture and food products. **Freq:** Weekly. **Print Method:** Offset. **Cols./Page:** 2. **Col. Width:** 36 nonpareils. **Col. Depth:** 140 agate lines. **Key Personnel:** Thomas F. Hofmann, Editor-in-Chief. **ISSN:** 0021--8561 (print). **URL:** http://pubs.acs.org/journal/jafcau. **Ad Rates:** BW $2,520; 4C $3,275. **Remarks:** Accepts advertising. **Circ:** ‡2900.

6819 ■ Journal of the Alliance of Black School Educators
National Alliance of Black School Educators
310 Pennsylvania Ave. SE
Washington, DC 20003
Phone: (202)608-6310
Fax: (202)608-6319
Free: 800-221-2654
Publication E-mail: jabse@nabse.org
Journal containing myriad of conceptual and empirical articles that contribute to knowledge and ideas in the quest for excellence in educating and facilitating quality education for all students, particularly students of African descent. **URL:** http://www.nabse.org/publications.html. **Formerly:** NABSE Journal. **Remarks:** Advertising not accepted. **Circ:** (Not Reported).

6820 ■ Journal of Allied Health
Association of Schools of Allied Health Professions

122 C St. NW, Ste. 650
Washington, DC 20001
Phone: (202)237-6481
Journal covering medical education. **Freq:** Quarterly. **Key Personnel:** Mike Bokulich, Contact, phone: (610)660-8097. **URL:** http://www.asahp.org/publications/journal-of-allied-health. **Ad Rates:** BW $640; 4C $900. **Remarks:** Accepts advertising. **Circ:** (Not Reported).

6821 ■ Journal of the American Institute for Conservation
American Institute for Conservation of Historic & Artistic Works
1156 15th St. NW, Ste. 320
Washington, DC 20005
Phone: (202)452-9545
Fax: (202)452-9328
Publisher's E-mail: info@conservation-us.org
Peer-reviewed journal covering field of conservation and preservation of historic and cultural works. **Freq:** Quarterly. **Key Personnel:** Julio M. Del Hoyo-Melendez, Editor-in-Chief. **ISSN:** 0197--1360 (print); **EISSN:** 1945--2330 (electronic). **Subscription Rates:** $350 Institutions online; $396 Institutions online and print. **URL:** http://www.conservation-us.org/publications-resources/periodicals/jaic#.Vlafytlwrlc; http://www.tandfonline.com/loi/yjac20#.VsFhhbR962w. **Ad Rates:** BW $520; 4C $1,220. **Remarks:** Advertising accepted; rates available upon request. **Circ:** 3600.

6822 ■ Journal of the American Society of Nephrology
American Society of Nephrology
1510 H St. NW, Ste. 800
Washington, DC 20005
Phone: (202)640-4660
Fax: (202)637-9793
Publisher's E-mail: email@asn-online.org
Freq: Monthly. **ISSN:** 1046- 6673 (print); **EISSN:** 1533-3450 (electronic). **Subscription Rates:** $590 Individuals (print and online); $1963 Institutions non-members (print and online); $1788 Institutions non-members (online only); $1852 Institutions non-members (print only); Included in membership. **URL:** http://jasn.asnjournals.org/. **Ad Rates:** $990-2190; 995-2205. BW $4C. **Remarks:** Accepts advertising. **Circ:** 13000.

6823 ■ Journal of Applied Communication Research
National Communication Association
1765 N St. NW
Washington, DC 20036
Phone: (202)464-4622
Fax: (202)464-4600
Freq: Quarterly. **Print Method:** Offset. **Key Personnel:** Michele H. Jackson, Editor. **ISSN:** 0090-9882 (print); **EISSN:** 1479--5752 (electronic). **USPS:** 147-95752. **Subscription Rates:** $116 Individuals print; $124 Individuals online; $394 Institutions online; $450 Institutions print & online; $113 online only. **URL:** http://www.tandfonline.com/toc/rjac20/current#.VMsQpNIwrfJ; http://www.natcom.org; http://www.natcom.org/journals; http://www.tandfonline.com/toc/rjac20/current#.Vcv3DnGqqko; http://www.tandfonline.com/toc/rjac20/current#.VOw5SnyUdGY. **Ad Rates:** BW $200. **Remarks:** Accepts advertising. **Circ:** (Not Reported).

6824 ■ Journal of Applied Psychology
American Psychological Association
750 1st St. NE
Washington, DC 20002-4242
Phone: (202)336-5500
Free: 800-374-2721
Journal presenting research on applications of psychology in work settings such as industry, correction systems, government, and educational institutions. **Freq:** Bimonthly. **Key Personnel:** Winfred Arthur, Jr., Editor; Jennifer M. George, Editor; Gilad Chen, Editor. **ISSN:** 0021--9010 (print); **EISSN:** 1939--1854 (electronic). **Subscription Rates:** $1299 Institutions; $1409 Institutions, other countries; $1441 Institutions, other countries by mail. **URL:** http://www.apa.org/pubs/journals/apl/index.aspx. **Ad Rates:** BW $390; 4C $975. **Remarks:** Accepts advertising. **Circ:** ‡1300.

6825 ■ Journal of Applied Testing Technology
Association of Test Publishers
South Bldg., Ste. 900
601 Pennsylvania Ave. NW
Washington, DC 20004-3647
Phone: (717)755-9747
Free: 866-240-7909
Journal containing articles related to technological applications and advances in educational and psychological measurement. **Freq:** Annual. **Subscription Rates:** Free. **URL:** http://www.jattjournal.com; http://www.testpublishers.org/journal-of-applied-testing-technology c. **Remarks:** Advertising not accepted. **Circ:** (Not Reported).

6826 ■ Journal of Architectural Education
Association of Collegiate Schools of Architecture
1735 New York Ave. NW, 3rd Fl.
Washington, DC 20006
Phone: (202)785-2324
Fax: (202)628-0448
Publisher's E-mail: academicviprequests@informa.com
Scholarly journal covering architectural education. **Freq:** Semiannual Quarterly fall and spring. **Trim Size:** 8 1/2 x 11. **Key Personnel:** Jerry Portwood, Managing Editor; George Dodds, Executive Editor; Marc Neveu, Executive Editor; Kevin Mitchell, Managing Editor. **ISSN:** 1046--4883 (print); **EISSN:** 1531--314X (electronic). **Subscription Rates:** $600 Institutions online only; $686 Institutions print and online; $86 Individuals print and online. **URL:** http://www.tandfonline.com/toc/rjae20/current#.Uw1dCeOSxWU; http://onlinelibrary.wiley.com/journal/10.1111/(ISSN)1531-314X; http://www.jaeonline.org. **Ad Rates:** BW $375. **Remarks:** Accepts advertising. **Circ:** Combined 500, 3500.

6827 ■ Journal of the Association for Communication Administration
Association for Communication Administration
1765 N St.
Washington, DC 20036
Phone: (202)464-4622
Fax: (202)464-4600
Publisher's E-mail: ebruner@natcom.org
Communication administration magazine. **Founded:** 1972. **Freq:** 3/year. **Print Method:** Offset. **Trim Size:** 6 1/2 x 10. **Key Personnel:** Ronald Applbaum, Editor; Ellie Bruner, Contact. **ISSN:** 0360-0939 (print). **Subscription Rates:** $75; $60 Libraries; $18 Single issue. **Formerly:** ACA Bulletin. **Ad Rates:** BW $150. **Remarks:** Accepts advertising. **Circ:** ‡400.

6828 ■ Journal of Association Leadership
ASAE: The Center for Association Leadership
1575 I St. NW
Washington, DC 20005-1103
Phone: (202)371-0940
Fax: (202)371-8315
Free: 888-950-ASAE
Publisher's E-mail: asaeservice@asaecenter.org
Subscription Rates: $30 Members; $45 Nonmembers. **URL:** http://www.asaecenter.org/resources. **Remarks:** Advertising not accepted. **Circ:** (Not Reported).

6829 ■ Journal of the Association of Proposal Management Professionals
Association of Proposal Management Professionals
c/o Rick Harris, Executive Director
20 F St. NW, 7th Fl.
Washington, DC 20001
Phone: (240)646-7075
Free: 866-466-APMP
Publisher's E-mail: apmpinfo@apmp.org
Journal covering case studies about business development and proposal management. **Freq:** Semiannual. **Key Personnel:** Rick Harris, Executive Director. **URL:** http://www.apmp.org/?page=PubsHome. **Remarks:** Accepts advertising. **Circ:** (Not Reported).

6830 ■ Journal of Bacteriology
ASM Journals
1752 North St. NW
Washington, DC 20036
Phone: (202)737-3600
Fax: (202)942-9355
Publisher's E-mail: journals@asmusa.org
Freq: Semimonthly. **Print Method:** Offset. Uses mats. **Trim Size:** 8 1/8 x 10 7/8. **Cols./Page:** 2. **Col. Width:** 42 nonpareils. **Col. Depth:** 127 agate lines. **Key Personnel:** Thomas J. Silhavy, Editor-in-Chief. **ISSN:** 0021--9193 (print); **EISSN:** 1098--5530 (electronic). **Subscription Rates:** $1365 Institutions online only, for sites with 1-200 authorized users; $1776 Institutions online only, for sites with 201-1,500 authorized users; $2307 Institutions online only, for sites with 1,501-3,500 authorized users. **URL:** http://jb.asm.org. **Ad Rates:** $1295-1425, full page; $910-975, 1/2 page; $605-660, 1/4 page; $2590-5700, insert. BW $, full pageBW $, 1/2 pageBW $, 1/4 page. **Remarks:** Advertising accepted; rates available upon request. **Circ:** Combined ‡14293.

6831 ■ Journal of Bacteriology
American Society for Microbiology
1752 N St. NW
Washington, DC 20036-2904
Phone: (202)942-9207
Fax: (202)942-9333
Publisher's E-mail: journals@asmusa.org
Freq: Semimonthly. **Print Method:** Offset. Uses mats. **Trim Size:** 8 1/8 x 10 7/8. **Cols./Page:** 2. **Col. Width:** 42 nonpareils. **Col. Depth:** 127 agate lines. **Key Personnel:** Thomas J. Silhavy, Editor-in-Chief. **ISSN:** 0021--9193 (print); **EISSN:** 1098--5530 (electronic). **Subscription Rates:** $1365 Institutions online only, for sites with 1-200 authorized users; $1776 Institutions online only, for sites with 201-1,500 authorized users; $2307 Institutions online only, for sites with 1,501-3,500 authorized users. **URL:** http://jb.asm.org. **Ad Rates:** $1295-1425, full page; $910-975, 1/2 page; $605-660, 1/4 page; $2590-5700, insert. BW $, full pageBW $, 1/2 pageBW $, 1/4 page. **Remarks:** Advertising accepted; rates available upon request. **Circ:** Combined ‡14293.

6832 ■ Journal of Bone and Mineral Research: The Official Journal of the American Society for Bone and Mineral Research
American Society for Bone and Mineral Research
2025 M St. NW, Ste. 800
Washington, DC 20036-3309
Phone: (202)367-1161
Fax: (202)367-2161
Publisher's E-mail: asbmr@asbmr.org
Medical research journal covering the pathophysiology and treatment of disorders of bone and mineral metabolism. **Freq:** Monthly. **Print Method:** Offset. **Trim Size:** 8 3/8 x 10 7/8. **Cols./Page:** 2. **Col. Width:** 19 picas. **Col. Depth:** 54 picas. **Key Personnel:** Thomas L. Clemens, Editor; Juliet E. Compston, Editor-in-Chief. **ISSN:** 0884--0431 (print); **EISSN:** 1523--4681 (electronic). **Subscription Rates:** $1038 Institutions print or online; $1246 Institutions print and online; $719 Individuals print or online; $792 Individuals print and online. **Alt. Formats:** CD-ROM. **URL:** http://www.asbmr.org/Publications/JBMR/default.aspx. **Ad Rates:** BW $1514; 4C $1207. **Remarks:** Accepts advertising. **Circ:** 3837.

6833 ■ Journal of Business Cycle Measurement and Analysis
OECD Washington Center
1776 I St. NW, Ste. 450
Washington, DC 20006
Phone: (202)785-6323
Fax: (202)315-2508
Free: 800-456-6323
Publisher's E-mail: washington.contact@oecd.org
Journal publishing information on the theory and operation of business and economic cycle research. **Freq:** 3/yr. **Key Personnel:** Michael Graff, Editor-in-Chief; Gerd Ronning, Board Member; Marco Malgarini, Board Member; Ataman Ozyildirim, Board Member. **ISSN:** 1995-2880 (print); **EISSN:** 1995-2899 (electronic). **URL:** http://www.oecd-ilibrary.org/economics/oecd-journal-journal-of-business-cycle-measurement-and-analysis_19952899. **Circ:** (Not Reported).

6834 ■ Journal of Chemical & Engineering Data
American Chemical Society
1155 16th St. NW
Washington, DC 20036
Phone: (202)872-4600
Free: 800-227-5558
Publisher's E-mail: help@acs.org
Journal sharing information from research on the physical, thermodynamic, and transport properties of organic and inorganic compounds and their mixtures, including systems of biomechanical interest. Also providing global standards on symbols, terminology, and units of measurement required for the explicit reporting of experimental data. **Freq:** Monthly. **Key Personnel:** Robert Chirico,

Circulation: ★ = AAM; △ or • = BPA; ♦ = CAC; ❑ = VAC; ⊕ = PO Statement; ‡ = Publisher's Report; Boldface figures = sworn; Light figures = estimated.

Associate Editor; Joan F. Brennecke, Editor-in-Chief. **ISSN:** 0021--9568 (print). **Subscription Rates:** $1273 Institutions; $1405 Institutions, other countries; $37 /year for members; $395 /year for nonmembers. **URL:** http://pubs.acs.org/journal/jceaax. **Ad Rates:** BW $1840; 4C $2295. **Remarks:** Accepts advertising. **Circ:** (Not Reported).

6835 ■ Journal of Chemical Theory and Computation
American Chemical Society
1155 16th St. NW
Washington, DC 20036
Phone: (202)872-4600
Free: 800-227-5558
Publisher's E-mail: help@acs.org
Journal presenting new theories, methodology, and/or important applications in quantum chemistry, molecular dynamics, and statistical mechanics. **Freq:** Bimonthly. **Key Personnel:** William L. Jorgensen, Editor; Gustavo E. Scuseria, Editor. **ISSN:** 1549--9618 (print); **EISSN:** 1549--9626 (electronic). **Subscription Rates:** $1367 Institutions North America; $1499 Institutions, other countries. **URL:** http://pubs.acs.org/journal/jctcce. **Ad Rates:** BW $2035; 4C $2645. **Remarks:** Accepts advertising. **Circ:** (Not Reported).

6836 ■ Journal of Classification
Classification Society
c/o Beth Ayers, Secretary/ Treasurer
American Institutes for Research
1000 Thomas Jefferson St. NW
Washington, DC 20007
Journal of the Classification Society of North America. **Freq:** Semiannual. **Key Personnel:** Willem J. Heiser, Editor-in-Chief. **ISSN:** 0176--4268 (print); **EISSN:** 1432--1343 (electronic). **Subscription Rates:** €753 Institutions print incl. free access or e-only; $541 Institutions print incl. free access or e-only ; $649 Institutions print plus enhanced access. **URL:** http://www.springer.com/statistics/statistical+theory+and+methods/journal/357. **Remarks:** Advertising not accepted. **Circ:** (Not Reported).

6837 ■ Journal of Cleaner Production
National Pollution Prevention Roundtable
50 F St. NW, Ste. 350
Washington, DC 20001-1770
Phone: (202)299-9701
Publisher's E-mail: t.reller@elsevier.com
Journal devoted to encourage industrial innovation, implementation of prevention oriented governmental policies and education programs. **Freq:** 60/yr. **Key Personnel:** Don Huisingh, Editor-in-Chief; M. Overcash, Board Member; L. Stone, Board Member; H. Schnitzer, Board Member; D. Mebratu, Board Member; C. Luttropp, Board Member. **ISSN:** 0959--6526 (print). **Subscription Rates:** $351 Individuals print; $729.60 Institutions online; $2188 Institutions print. **URL:** http://www.journals.elsevier.com/journal-of-cleaner-production. **Mailing address:** PO Box 945, New York, NY 10159-0945. **Remarks:** Advertising not accepted. **Circ:** (Not Reported).

6838 ■ Journal of Clinical Endocrinology and Metabolism
Endocrine Society
2055 L St. NW, Ste. 600
Washington, DC 20036
Phone: (202)971-3636
Fax: (202)736-9705
Free: 888-363-6274
Publisher's E-mail: societyservices@endocrine.org
Freq: Monthly. **ISSN:** 0021-972X (print); **EISSN:** 1945-7197 (electronic). **Subscription Rates:** Included in membership. **URL:** http://press.endocrine.org/journal/jcem. **Remarks:** Accepts advertising. **Circ:** (Not Reported).

6839 ■ Journal of Clinical Microbiology
ASM Journals
1752 North St. NW
Washington, DC 20036
Phone: (202)737-3600
Fax: (202)942-9355
Publisher's E-mail: journals@asmusa.org
Freq: Monthly. **Print Method:** Offset. Uses mats. **Trim Size:** 8 1/8 x 10 7/8. **Cols./Page:** 2. **Col. Width:** 42 nonpareils. **Col. Depth:** 127 agate lines. **Key Personnel:** Alexander J. McAdam, Editor-in-Chief. **ISSN:** 0095--1137 (print); **EISSN:** 1098--660X (electronic). **Subscription Rates:** $740 Institutions online only, for sites with 1-200 authorized users; $963 Institutions online only, for sites with 201-1,500 authorized users; $1251 Institutions online only, for sites with 1,501-3,500 authorized users. **URL:** http://jcm.asm.org. **Ad Rates:** $1875-2225, full page; $1290-1510, 1/2 page; $1010-1060, 1/4 page; $3750-8900, insert. BW $2,225; 4C $1,840. **Remarks:** Accepts advertising. **Circ:** Combined ‡13221.

6840 ■ Journal of Clinical Microbiology
American Society for Microbiology
1752 N St. NW
Washington, DC 20036-2904
Phone: (202)942-9207
Fax: (202)942-9333
Publisher's E-mail: journals@asmusa.org
Freq: Monthly. **Print Method:** Offset. Uses mats. **Trim Size:** 8 1/8 x 10 7/8. **Cols./Page:** 2. **Col. Width:** 42 nonpareils. **Col. Depth:** 127 agate lines. **Key Personnel:** Alexander J. McAdam, Editor-in-Chief. **ISSN:** 0095--1137 (print); **EISSN:** 1098--660X (electronic). **Subscription Rates:** $740 Institutions online only, for sites with 1-200 authorized users; $963 Institutions online only, for sites with 201-1,500 authorized users; $1251 Institutions online only, for sites with 1,501-3,500 authorized users. **URL:** http://jcm.asm.org. **Ad Rates:** $1875-2225, full page; $1290-1510, 1/2 page; $1010-1060, 1/4 page; $3750-8900, insert. BW $2,225; 4C $1,840. **Remarks:** Accepts advertising. **Circ:** Combined ‡13221.

6841 ■ Journal of Coatings Technology and Research: The Leading Technical Journal of the Industry
American Coatings Association
1500 Rhode Island Ave. NW
Washington, DC 20005
Phone: (202)462-6272
Fax: (202)462-8549
Publisher's E-mail: members@paint.org
Journal containing reports of research in paint and coatings technology. **Freq:** Bimonthly. **Print Method:** Offset. **Trim Size:** 8 1/4 x 11. **Cols./Page:** 3 and 2. **Col. Width:** 26 and 40 nonpareils. **Col. Depth:** 140 agate lines. **Key Personnel:** Dr. Mark E. Nichols, Editor-in-Chief; Dr. Ray A. Dickie, Editor. **ISSN:** 1547--0091 (print); **EISSN:** 1935--3804 (electronic). **Subscription Rates:** $768 Nonmembers print or online; $922 Nonmembers print and online; Included in membership. **URL:** http://www.springer.com/materials/surfaces+interfaces/journal/11998. **Formerly:** Journal of Coatings Technology. **Ad Rates:** BW $2075; 4C $3285. **Remarks:** Accepts advertising. **Circ:** (Not Reported).

6842 ■ The Journal of College and Character
NASPA - Student Affairs Administrators in Higher Education
111 K St. NE, 10th Fl.
Washington, DC 20002
Phone: (202)265-7500
Publisher's E-mail: office@naspa.org
Journal focusing on character development in college. **Freq:** Quarterly. **Key Personnel:** Dr. Jon C. Dalton, Editor; Dr. Pamela C. Crosby, Editor. **ISSN:** 2194--587X (print); **EISSN:** 1940--1639 (electronic). **Subscription Rates:** $140 Individuals print only (year 2015); $94 Individuals print and online (year 2016); $193 Institutions online; $220 Institutions print and online. **URL:** http://www.naspa.org/publications/journals/journal-of-college-and-character; http://www.tandfonline.com/toc/ujcc20/current. **Circ:** (Not Reported).

6843 ■ Journal of College and University Law
National Association of College and University Attorneys
1 Dupont Cir., Ste. 620
Washington, DC 20036
Phone: (202)833-8390
Fax: (202)296-8379
Publisher's E-mail: nacua@nacua.org
Legal journal covering law and education. **Freq:** 3/year. **Trim Size:** 6 3/4 x 10. **Cols./Page:** 1. **Col. Width:** 4 5/8 inches. **Col. Depth:** 8 inches. **Key Personnel:** John H. Robinson, Contact. **ISSN:** 0093--8688 (print). **Subscription Rates:** $75 Nonmembers /year; $37.50 Members /year; Free online subscription for members; $29.50 Single issue; $85 Individuals international. **URL:** http://www.nacua.org; http://www3.nd.edu/~jcul; http://www3.nd.edu/~jcul/subscriptions_online.html. **Remarks:** Advertising not accepted. **Circ:** Paid 248.

6844 ■ Journal of Communication
International Communication Association
1500 21st St. NW
Washington, DC 20036
Phone: (202)955-1444
Fax: (202)955-1448
Publisher's E-mail: icahdq@icahdq.org
Scholarly journal focusing on the communications field. **Freq:** Bimonthly Quarterly. **Print Method:** Offset. **Trim Size:** 6 7/8 x 9 3/4. **Cols./Page:** 1. **Col. Width:** 5 inches. **Col. Depth:** 7 3/4 inches. **Key Personnel:** Joseph Cappella, Board Member; Travis Dixon, Board Member; Silvio Waisbord, Editor. **ISSN:** 0021--9916 (print); **EISSN:** 1460--2466 (electronic). **Subscription Rates:** $119 Individuals print and online; £86 Individuals print and online - UK, Europe (non-euro zone) and ROW; €127 Individuals print and online; $80 Students print and online; £57 Students print and online - UK, Europe (non-euro zone) and ROW; Included in membership. **URL:** http://onlinelibrary.wiley.com/journal/10.1111/(ISSN)1460-2466; http://www.icahdq.org/pubs/journals.asp. **Mailing address:** PO Box 418950, Boston, MA 02241-8950. **Ad Rates:** BW $556. **Remarks:** Color advertising not accepted. **Circ:** Paid ‡6200.

6845 ■ Journal of Comparative Psychology
American Psychological Association
750 1st St. NE
Washington, DC 20002-4242
Phone: (202)336-5500
Free: 800-374-2721
Journal publishing original empirical and theoretical research from a comparative perspective on the behavior, cognition, perception, and social relationships of diverse species. **Freq:** Quarterly. **Key Personnel:** David F. Bjorklund, Editor; Josep Call, Editor; Irene M. Pepperberg, Associate Editor; Gordon M. Burghardt, PhD, Editor. **ISSN:** 0735--7036 (print); **EISSN:** 1939--2087 (electronic). **Subscription Rates:** $636 Institutions; $685 Institutions, other countries; $700 Institutions, other countries air mail. **URL:** http://www.apa.org/pubs/journals/com/index.aspx. **Ad Rates:** 4C $975; BW $275. **Remarks:** Accepts advertising. **Circ:** 200.

6846 ■ Journal of Computer-Mediated Communication
International Communication Association
1500 21st St. NW
Washington, DC 20036
Phone: (202)955-1444
Fax: (202)955-1448
Publisher's E-mail: consumers@wiley.com
Publishes scholarship on computer-mediated communication. **Freq:** Quarterly. **EISSN:** 1083--6101 (electronic). **Subscription Rates:** $1950 Institutions print and online; £1192 Institutions print and online; €1514 Institutions print and online; $2328 Institutions, other countries print and online; $1625 Institutions Online only; £993 Institutions online only; €1261 Institutions online only; $1940 Institutions, other countries Online only; Included in membership. **URL:** http://www.icahdq.org/pubs/jnlcomcomm.asp; http://onlinelibrary.wiley.com/journal/10.1111/(ISSN)1083-6101. **Remarks:** Advertising not accepted. **Circ:** (Not Reported).

6847 ■ Journal of Consulting and Clinical Psychology
American Psychological Association
750 1st St. NE
Washington, DC 20002-4242
Phone: (202)336-5500
Free: 800-374-2721
Freq: Monthly. **Print Method:** Offset. **Trim Size:** 8 1/4 x 11. **Cols./Page:** 2. **Col. Width:** 47 nonpareils. **Col. Depth:** 127 agate lines. **Key Personnel:** Arthur M. Nezu, Editor. **ISSN:** 0022--006X (print); **EISSN:** 1939--2117 (electronic). **Subscription Rates:** $160 Individuals print, for associate and affiliate APA members, U.S.; $108 Individuals print, for student affiliate members, U.S.; $360 Individuals print, nonmembers, U.S.; $1399 Institutions print, U.S.; $193 Individuals print, for associate and affiliate APA members, other countries (surface mail); $141 Individuals print, for student affiliate members, other countries (surface mail); $417 Nonmembers print, other countries (surface mail); $1509 Institutions, other countries print, (surface mail); $234 Individuals print, for associate and affiliate APA members, other

countries (air mail); $182 Individuals print, for student affiliate members, other countries (air mail); $449 Individuals print, nonmembers (air mail); $1541 Institutions print, (air mail). **URL:** http://www.apa.org/pubs/journals/ccp. **Ad Rates:** BW $425; 4C $975. **Remarks:** Accepts advertising. **Circ:** ‡1600.

6848 ■ Journal of Contemporary Health Law and Policy
Catholic University of America Columbus School of Law
3600 John McCormack Rd., NE
Washington, DC 20064
Phone: (202)319-5140
Publisher's E-mail: admissions@law.edu
Journal covering in-depth legal analysis of the recent trends in modern health care, issues involving the relationship of the life sciences to the social sciences and humanities, bioethics, and ethical, economic, philosophical and social aspects of medical practice and the delivery of health care systems. **Freq:** Annual. **Key Personnel:** Elizabeth Papoulakos, Editor-in-Chief. **Subscription Rates:** $20 U.S.; $23 Other countries. **URL:** http://jchlp.law.edu; http://scholarship.law.edu/jchlp. **Circ:** (Not Reported).

6849 ■ Journal of Continuing Education in the Health Professions
Alliance for Continuing Education in the Health Professions
2025 M St. NW, Ste. 800
Washington, DC 20036
Phone: (202)367-1151
Fax: (202)367-2151
Publisher's E-mail: acehp@acehp.org
Journal covering information on health care performance through education, advocacy and collaboration. **Freq:** Quarterly. **Key Personnel:** Curtis Olson, PhD. **Subscription Rates:** $89.25 for nonmembers in U.S. and Canada (individual); $139.75 for nonmembers in U.S. and Canada (institution); $121.50 for nonmembers outside U.S. and Canada (individual); $177.40 for nonmembers outside U.S. and Canada (institution). **URL:** http://www.acehp.org/p/cm/ld/fid=10; http://www.sacme.org/Publications#JCEHP. **Remarks:** Advertising not accepted. **Circ:** (Not Reported).

6850 ■ Journal of Counseling Psychology
American Psychological Association
750 1st St. NE
Washington, DC 20002-4242
Phone: (202)336-5500
Free: 800-374-2721
Journal presenting empirical studies about counseling processes and interventions, theoretical articles about counseling, and studies dealing with evaluation of counseling applications and programs. **Freq:** 6/year. **Print Method:** Offset. **Trim Size:** 8 1/4 x 11. **Cols./Page:** 2. **Col. Width:** 46 nonpareils. **Col. Depth:** 126 agate lines. **Key Personnel:** Terence J. G. Tracey, Editor; Patricia A. Frazier, Editor; William T. Hoyt, Editor. **ISSN:** 0022--0167 (print); **EISSN:** 1939--2168 (electronic). **Subscription Rates:** $649 Institutions; $710 Institutions, other countries; $730 Institutions, other countries by airmail. **URL:** http://www.apa.org/pubs/journals/cou. **Ad Rates:** BW $440; 4C $975. **Remarks:** Accepts advertising. **Circ:** ‡2000.

6851 ■ Journal of Democracy
National Endowment for Democracy
1025 F St. NW, Ste. 800
Washington, DC 20004-1432
Phone: (202)378-9700
Fax: (202)378-9407
Publisher's E-mail: info@ned.org
Journal covering democratic regimes and movements around the world. **Freq:** Quarterly. **Trim Size:** 6 x 9. **Key Personnel:** Nancy Bermeo, Board Member; Yun-Han Chu, Board Member; Brent Kallmer, Managing Editor; Shaul Bakhash, Board Member; Daniel Brumberg, Board Member; Joao Carlos Espada, Board Member; Marc F. Plattner, Editor; Laurence Whitehead, Board Member; Larry Diamond, Editor. **ISSN:** 1045--5736 (print); **EISSN:** 1086--3214 (electronic). **Subscription Rates:** $45 Individuals print; $50 Individuals online; $170 Institutions print online; $81 Individuals print; 2 years; $48.13 Individuals online; 2 years; $340 Institutions print; 2 years. **URL:** http://www.journalofdemocracy.org. **Ad Rates:** BW $400, full page; BW $300, half page. **Remarks:** Accepts advertising. **Circ:** 1750, 5000.

6852 ■ Journal of Dental Education
American Dental Education Association
655 K St. NW, Ste. 800
Washington, DC 20001
Phone: (202)289-7201
Fax: (202)289-7204
Publisher's E-mail: membership@adea.org
Peer-reviewed journal for scholarly research and reviews on dental education. **Freq:** Monthly. **Print Method:** Offset. **Trim Size:** 8 1/4 x 11. **Cols./Page:** 2. **Col. Width:** 19 picas. **Col. Depth:** 54 picas. **Key Personnel:** Dr. Nadeem Karimbux, Editor. **ISSN:** 0022--0337 (print); **EISSN:** 1930--7837 (electronic). **Subscription Rates:** $160 U.S.; $190 Canada; $220 Other countries; online is free. **URL:** http://www.jdentaled.org. **Ad Rates:** BW $710; 4C $1,560. **Remarks:** Accepts advertising. **Circ:** Paid ‡3900, Controlled ‡195.

6853 ■ Journal of Diversity in Higher Education
American Psychological Association
750 1st St. NE
Washington, DC 20002-4242
Phone: (202)336-5500
Free: 800-374-2721
Journal publishing research findings, theory and promising practices in higher education. **Freq:** Quarterly. **Key Personnel:** Roger L. Worthington, Editor; Jeni Hart, Associate Editor. **ISSN:** 1938--8926 (print); **EISSN:** 1938--8934 (electronic). **Subscription Rates:** $74 Members; $98 Other countries members, surface; $112 Other countries members, air mail; $133 Nonmembers; $162 Other countries non-members, surface; $175 Other countries non-members, air mail; $74 Students; $98 Other countries students, surface; $112 Other countries students, air mail; $582 Institutions; $631 Institutions, other countries surface; $646 Institutions, other countries air mail. **URL:** http://www.apa.org/pubs/journals/dhe/index.aspx. **Ad Rates:** 4C $975; BW $350. **Remarks:** Accepts advertising. **Circ:** ‡500.

6854 ■ Journal of the DMA Nonprofit Federation
DMA Nonprofit Federation
1615 L St. NW, Ste. 1100
Washington, DC 20036
Phone: (202)861-2427
Journal providing useful information in enhancing member's knowledge base of the nonprofit sector. **Freq:** 3/year January, April and September. **Subscription Rates:** Free for members and corporate partners; $35 Nonmembers /year. **Alt. Formats:** CD-ROM. **URL:** http://www.nonprofitfederation.org/the-journal/. **Ad Rates:** BW $595, full page; BW $315, half page. **Remarks:** Accepts advertising. **Circ:** 4000.

6855 ■ Journal of Education for International Development: A Professional Online Journal for Practitioners
Educational Quality Improvement Program
1300 Pennsylvania Ave. NW
Washington, DC 20523
Phone: (202)712-0222
Fax: (202)216-3381
Publication E-mail: jeid@air.org
Journal devoted to the improvement of education policies supporting long term learning for the sustainable economic growth and poverty alleviation in under developed countries. **Key Personnel:** Keri Culver, Editor. **ISSN:** 1554--2262 (print). **URL:** http://www.equip123.net/JEID/default.htm. **Circ:** (Not Reported).

6856 ■ Journal of Educational and Behavioral Statistics
American Educational Research Association
1430 K St. NW, Ste. 1200
Washington, DC 20005-2504
Phone: (202)238-3200
Fax: (202)238-3250
Publisher's E-mail: webmaster@aera.net
Scholarly journal for applied statisticians in educational or behavioral research. Published jointly with the American Statistical Association. **Freq:** Bimonthly. **Trim Size:** 6 x 9. **Key Personnel:** Daniel McCaffrey, Editor. **ISSN:** 1076--9986 (print); **EISSN:** 1935--1054 (electronic). **Subscription Rates:** £46 Individuals print + online; £359 Institutions print only; £366 Institutions print + online. **Alt. Formats:** PDF. **URL:** http://jeb.sagepub.com; http://ojs.aera.net/journals/index.php/jebs; http://www.aera.net/tabid/12610/Default.aspx. **Remarks:** Accepts advertising. **Circ:** (Not Reported).

6857 ■ Journal of Educational Psychology
American Psychological Association
750 1st St. NE
Washington, DC 20002-4242
Phone: (202)336-5500
Free: 800-374-2721
Journal presenting articles dealing with learning, especially as related to instruction, development, and adjustment. **Freq:** 8/year. **Print Method:** Offset. **Trim Size:** 8 1/4 x 11. **Cols./Page:** 2. **Col. Width:** 46 nonpareils. **Col. Depth:** 126 agate lines. **Key Personnel:** Jill Fitzgerald, Associate Editor; Steve Graham, Editor; Steven Graham, Editor. **ISSN:** 0022--0663 (print); **EISSN:** 1939--2176 (electronic). **Subscription Rates:** $899 Institutions; $976 Institutions, other countries; $1000 Institutions, other countries air mail. **URL:** http://www.apa.org/pubs/journals/edu. **Ad Rates:** BW $390; 4C $975. **Remarks:** Accepts advertising. **Circ:** ‡1300, 5,500.

6858 ■ Journal of Energy and Environmental Law
George Washington University Law School
2000 H St. NW
Washington, DC 20052
Phone: (202)994-6261
Fax: (202)994-8980
Publisher's E-mail: jdadmit@law.gwu.edu
Journal covering articles across the full range of environmental issues, but focuses on the intersections between energy, environment, and climate law, recognizing the increasing importance of these areas in producing more sustainable environmental outcomes. **Freq:** 3/year. **Key Personnel:** Addison Miller, Editor-in-Chief. **Subscription Rates:** $30 Individuals. **URL:** http://gwujeel.wordpress.com. **Circ:** (Not Reported).

6859 ■ Journal of Engineering Education
American Society for Engineering Education
1818 N St. NW, Ste. 600
Washington, DC 20036-2479
Phone: (202)331-3500
Publisher's E-mail: board@asee.org
Freq: Quarterly. **Key Personnel:** Michael C. Loui, Dr., Editor. **ISSN:** 1069--4730 (print); **EISSN:** 2168--9830 (electronic). **Subscription Rates:** $648 Institutions print and online; £411 Institutions print and online; €476 Institutions print and online; $648 Institutions, other countries print and online; $540 Institutions print or online; £342 Institutions print or online; €396 Institutions print or online; $540 Institutions, other countries print or online. **URL:** http://www.asee.org/papers-and-publications/publications/jee; http://onlinelibrary.wiley.com/journal/10.1002/(ISSN)2168-9830. **Remarks:** Accepts advertising. **Circ:** Combined 12000.

6860 ■ Journal of Engineering Technology
American Society for Engineering Education
1818 N St. NW, Ste. 600
Washington, DC 20036-2479
Phone: (202)331-3500
Publisher's E-mail: board@asee.org
Peer-reviewed journal covering the field of engineering technology. **Freq:** Semiannual spring and fall. **ISSN:** 0747--9964 (print). **Subscription Rates:** $25 Individuals; $35 Other countries. **URL:** http://www.asee.org/papers-and-publications/publications/division-publications#Journal_of_Engineering_Technology; http://www.engtech.org/jet. **Remarks:** Advertising not accepted. **Circ:** (Not Reported).

6861 ■ Journal of Experimental Psychology:Animal Learning and Cognition
American Psychological Association
750 1st St. NE
Washington, DC 20002-4242
Phone: (202)336-5500
Free: 800-374-2721
Journal presenting experimental studies on the basic mechanisms of perception, learning, motivation, and performance, especially in non-human animals. **Freq:** Quarterly. **Key Personnel:** Ralph R. Miller, Editor. **ISSN:** 2329--8456 (print); **EISSN:** 2329--8464 (electronic). **Subscription Rates:** $606 Institutions; $655 Institu-

Circulation: ⋆ = AAM; △ or • = BPA; ♦ = CAC; ❑ = VAC; ⊕ = PO Statement; ‡ = Publisher's Report; Boldface figures = sworn; Light figures = estimated.

tions, other countries; $670 Institutions, other countries air mail. **URL:** http://www.apa.org/pubs/journals/xan. **Formerly**: Journal of Experimental Psychology: Animal Behavior Processes. **Ad Rates:** BW $260; 4C $975. **Remarks:** Accepts advertising. **Circ:** ‡200.

6862 ■ Journal of Experimental Psychology: Human Perception and Performance
American Psychological Association
750 1st St. NE
Washington, DC 20002-4242
Phone: (202)336-5500
Free: 800-374-2721
Journal presenting studies of perception, verbal and motor performance, and related cognitive processes in humans. **Freq:** Monthly. **Print Method:** Offset. **Trim Size:** 8 1/4 x 11. **Cols./Page:** 2. **Col. Width:** 46 nonpareils. **Col. Depth:** 126 agate lines. **Key Personnel:** James T. Enns, Editor. **ISSN:** 0096--1523 (print); **EISSN:** 1939--1277 (electronic). **Subscription Rates:** $1789 Institutions; $1899 Institutions, other countries; $1931 Institutions, other countries air mail. **URL:** http://www.apa.org/pubs/journals/xhp. **Ad Rates:** BW $335; 4C $975. **Remarks:** Accepts advertising. **Circ:** ‡600, 1800.

6863 ■ Journal of Experimental Psychology: Learning, Memory, and Cognition
American Psychological Association
750 1st St. NE
Washington, DC 20002-4242
Phone: (202)336-5500
Free: 800-374-2721
Journal presenting experimental studies on fundamental encoding, transfer, memory, and cognitive processes in human behavior. **Freq:** Monthly. **Print Method:** Offset. **Trim Size:** 8 1/4 x 11. **Cols./Page:** 2. **Col. Width:** 46 nonpareils. **Col. Depth:** 126 agate lines. **Key Personnel:** Randi C. Martin, PhD, Editor; Robert L. Greene, Editor. **ISSN:** 0278--7393 (print); **EISSN:** 1939--1285 (electronic). **Subscription Rates:** $1789 Institutions; $1899 Institutions, other countries; $1931 Institutions, other countries air mail. **URL:** http://www.apa.org/pubs/journals/xlm. **Ad Rates:** BW $335; 4C $975. **Remarks:** Accepts advertising. **Circ:** ‡500, 3,600.

6864 ■ Journal of Experimental Psychology: Applied
American Psychological Association
750 1st St. NE
Washington, DC 20002-4242
Phone: (202)336-5500
Free: 800-374-2721
Journal publishing original empirical investigations in experimental psychology that bridge practically oriented problems and psychological theory. **Freq:** Quarterly. **Key Personnel:** Neil Brewer, Editor; Mary Hegarty, Associate Editor; Walter R. Boot, Board Member. **ISSN:** 1076--898X (print); **EISSN:** 1939--2192 (electronic). **Subscription Rates:** $61 Members; $85 Members international surface; $99 Members international airmail; $38 Students; $62 Students, other countries surface; $76 Students, other countries airmail; $125 Nonmembers; $154 Nonmembers international surface mail; $167 Nonmembers international airmail; $456 Institutions; $505 Institutions; $520 Institutions, other countries. **URL:** http://www.apa.org/pubs/journals/xap/index.aspx. **Ad Rates:** 4C $975; BW $350. **Remarks:** Accepts advertising. **Circ:** 500.

6865 ■ Journal of Experimental Psychology: General
American Psychological Association
750 1st St. NE
Washington, DC 20002-4242
Phone: (202)336-5500
Free: 800-374-2721
Psychology journal publishing articles describing empirical work that bridges the traditional interests of two or more communities of psychology. **Freq:** Bimonthly. **Key Personnel:** Isabelle Gauthier, Editor; Tim Curran, Associate Editor; Klaus Fiedler, Associate Editor. **ISSN:** 0096--3445 (print); **EISSN:** 1939--2222 (electronic). **Subscription Rates:** $164 Members; $197 Members international, surface; $238 Members international, air mail; $123 Students; $156 Students, other countries surface; $197 Students, other countries airmail; $411 Nonmembers; $468 Nonmembers international, surface; $500 Nonmembers international, airmail; $1897 Institutions; $2007 Institutions; $2039 Institutions international, airmail. **URL:** http://www.apa.org/pubs/journals/xge/index.aspx. **Ad Rates:** 4C $975; BW $350. **Remarks:** Accepts advertising. **Circ:** 700.

6866 ■ Journal of Gender, Social Policy & the Law
American University Washington College of Law
4801 Massachusetts Ave. NW
Washington, DC 20016
Phone: (202)274-4000
Fax: (202)274-4005
Publication E-mail: wcljournalcoordinator@wcl.american.edu
Journal featuring gender issues and feminist legal studies. **Freq:** 3/year. **Key Personnel:** Madeline Dang, Editor-in-Chief. **Subscription Rates:** $15 Students; $35 Individuals; $40 Other countries. **URL:** http://www.wcl.american.edu/journal/genderlaw/. **Circ:** (Not Reported).

6867 ■ Journal of Gender, Social Policy, and the Law
American University Washington College of Law
4801 Massachusetts Ave. NW
Washington, DC 20016
Phone: (202)274-4000
Fax: (202)274-4005
Publisher's E-mail: deans-office@wcl.american.edu
Journal focusing on gender and social policy issues. **Key Personnel:** Jesse Weinstein, Editor-in-Chief. **Subscription Rates:** $15 Students; $35 Individuals; $40 Other countries; $50 Individuals friend of journal. **URL:** http://www.wcl.american.edu/journal/genderlaw. **Circ:** (Not Reported).

6868 ■ Journal of General Internal Medicine
Society of General Internal Medicine
2501 M St. NW, Ste. 575
Washington, DC 20037
Phone: (202)887-5150
Free: 800-822-3060
Journal on general internal medicine. **Freq:** Monthly. **Trim Size:** 8 1/4 x 11. **Key Personnel:** Richard L. Kravitz, MD, Editor-in-Chief; Mitchell D. Feldman, MD, Editor-in-Chief. **ISSN:** 0884--8734 (print). **Subscription Rates:** €586 Institutions print incl. free access or e-only; €703 Institutions print incl. enhanced access; Included in membership. **URL:** http://www.springer.com/medicine/internal/journal/11606; http://www.sgim.org/jgim-home. **Ad Rates:** BW $1685; 4C $1300. **Remarks:** Advertising accepted; rates available upon request. **Circ:** 2800.

6869 ■ Journal of Geography
National Council for Geographic Education
1775 Eye St. NW, Ste. 1150
Washington, DC 20006-2435
Phone: (202)587-5727
Fax: (202)618-6249
Publisher's E-mail: support@tandfonline.com
Journal for geography instructors at all educational levels. **Freq:** 6/year. **Print Method:** Letterpress and offset. **Trim Size:** 8 1/2 x 11. **Cols./Page:** 2. **Col. Width:** 40 nonpareils. **Col. Depth:** 133 agate lines. **Key Personnel:** Dr. Jerry T. Mitchell, Editor; Owen Dwyer, Associate Editor. **ISSN:** 0022--1341 (print); **EISSN:** 1752--6868 (electronic). **Subscription Rates:** $306 Institutions online only; $350 Institutions print and online. **URL:** http://www.ncge.org/journal-of-geography. **Ad Rates:** BW $450; 4C $1,500. **Remarks:** Accepts advertising. **Circ:** ‡2600.

6870 ■ Journal of Health Administration Education
Association of University Programs in Health Administration
1730 M St. NW, Ste. 407
Washington, DC 20036
Phone: (202)763-7283
Fax: (202)894-0941
Publisher's E-mail: aupha@aupha.org
Peer-reviewed journal covering health administration education. **Freq:** Quarterly. **Key Personnel:** Lydia Middleton, Contact, phone: (703)894-0940, fax: (703)894-0941. **Subscription Rates:** $120 Individuals; $25 Members; $30 Nonmembers. **URL:** http://www.aupha.org/publications/journalofhealthadministrationeducation. **Remarks:** Advertising not accepted. **Circ:** (Not Reported).

6871 ■ Journal of Health and Life Sciences Law
American Health Lawyers Association
1620 Eye St. NW, 6th Fl.
Washington, DC 20006-4010
Phone: (202)833-1100
Fax: (202)833-1105
Professional journal covering healthcare issues and cases and their impact on the health care arena. **Freq:** 3/year. **Key Personnel:** Cynthia F. Wisner, Editor-in-Chief. **ISSN:** 1942--4736 (print). **Subscription Rates:** $179 Nonmembers; Included in membership. **URL:** http://www.healthlawyers.org/find-a-resource/news/healthlawjournal/Pages/default.aspx. **Formerly**: Journal of Health and Hospital Law. **Remarks:** Advertising not accepted. **Circ:** (Not Reported).

6872 ■ Journal of Housing and Community Development
National Association of Housing and Redevelopment Officials
630 Eye St. NW
Washington, DC 20001-3736
Phone: (202)289-3500
Fax: (202)289-8181
Free: 877-866-2476
Publisher's E-mail: nahro@nahro.org
Housing and community development information for association members, practitioners in the field, and academicians. **Freq:** Bimonthly. **Print Method:** Offset. **Trim Size:** 8 1/2 x 11. Offset. **Cols./Page:** 3. **Col. Width:** 13 picas. **Col. Depth:** 58 picas. **Key Personnel:** Sylvia Gimenez, Managing Editor, phone: (202)289-3500. **Subscription Rates:** $25 Members; $45 Nonmembers; $45.50 Other countries. **URL:** http://www.nahro.org/housing-journal. **Formerly**: Journal of Housing. **Mailing address:** PO Box 90487, Washington, DC 20090. **Ad Rates:** BW $4,240; 4C $6,140. **Remarks:** Advertising accepted; rates available upon request. **Circ:** Non-paid 13000, 13000.

6873 ■ Journal of Human Rights and Civil Society
Protection Project
1717 Massachusetts Ave. NW
Washington, DC 20036
Phone: (202)256-7520
Journal containing original, unpublished scholarly articles, essays, book reviews, interviews, and annotated bibliographies, associated with human rights and civil society development and non-governmental activities and other related topics. **URL:** http://www.protectionproject.org/publications. **Remarks:** Advertising not accepted. **Circ:** (Not Reported).

6874 ■ The Journal of Indo-European Studies
Institute for the Study of Man
1133 13th St. NW, Ste. C2
Washington, DC 20005
Phone: (202)371-2700
Fax: (202)371-1523
Freq: Annual. **Print Method:** Offset. **Trim Size:** 6 x 9. **Cols./Page:** 1. **Col. Width:** 50 nonpareils. **Col. Depth:** 98 agate lines. **Key Personnel:** Karlene Jones-Bley, Editor; J.P. Mallory, Editor. **ISSN:** 0092--2323 (print). **Subscription Rates:** $188 Institutions print or online; $218 Institutions, other countries print only; $248 Institutions print and online; $278 Institutions, other countries print and online; $60 Individuals print only; $90 Other countries. **URL:** http://www.jies.org. **Ad Rates:** BW $250. **Remarks:** Accepts advertising. **Circ:** (Not Reported).

6875 ■ Journal of Industrial Engineering Design
American Society for Engineering Education
1818 N St. NW, Ste. 600
Washington, DC 20036-2479
Phone: (202)331-3500
Publisher's E-mail: board@asee.org
Journal focusing on dissemination and discussion of the capstone design course in industrial engineering. **Freq:** Quarterly. **Key Personnel:** Michael C. Loui, Dr., Editor. **ISSN:** 1069--4730 (print); **EISSN:** 2168--9830 (electronic). **Subscription Rates:** $509 Institutions print or online; $611 Institutions print and online. **Circ:** (Not Reported).

6876 ■ Journal of Insurance Fraud in America
Coalition Against Insurance Fraud

1012 14th St. NW, Ste. 200
Washington, DC 20005
Phone: (202)393-7330
Publisher's E-mail: info@insurancefraud.org
Journal containing latest fraud trends, investigations of emerging scams, notable fraud cases, and sometimes-controversial opinions on fraud issues. **Freq:** Quarterly. **URL:** http://www.insurancefraud.org/JIFA.htm. **Remarks:** Advertising not accepted. **Circ:** (Not Reported).

6877 ■ Journal of International Business Studies
Journal of International Business Studies
3240 Prospect St. NW
Washington, DC 20007
Phone: (202)944-3755
Fax: (202)944-3762
Publisher's E-mail: jibs@msb.edu
Scholarly business journal, covering topics from e-commerce to foreign markets. **Freq:** 9/year. **Key Personnel:** John Cantwell, Editor-in-Chief. **ISSN:** 0047--8210 (print); **EISSN:** 1478--6990 (electronic). **Subscription Rates:** $572 Institutions print; £356 Institutions, other countries; £356 Institutions print; $137 Individuals print + online; £219 Individuals print + online. **URL:** http://www.palgrave-journals.com/jibs/index.html; http://aib.msu.edu/jibs. **Remarks:** Advertising accepted; rates available upon request. **Circ:** Paid 4200.

6878 ■ Journal of International Economic Law
Oxford University Press
c/o Georgetown University Law Center
600 New Jersey Ave. NW
Washington, DC 20001
Publisher's E-mail: webenquiry.uk@oup.com
Journal covering to encourage thoughtful and scholarly attention to a very broad range of subjects that concern the relation of law to international economic activity by providing the major English language medium for publication of high-quality manuscripts relevant to the endeavors of scholars, government officials, legal professionals and others with the emphasis on fundamental, long-term, systemic problems and possible solutions, in the light of empirical observations and experience, as well as theoretical and multi-disciplinary approaches. **Freq:** Quarterly. **Key Personnel:** Chris Brummer, Editor-in-Chief; Joost Pauwelyn, Editor-in-Chief; Frederick Abbott, Board Member; Kenneth W. Abbott, Board Member; Dukgeun Ahn, Board Member; Alan O. Sykes, Associate Editor; Marco Bronckers, Associate Editor; William J. Davey, Associate Editor; Ernst-Ulrich Petersmann, Associate Editor; Jagdish Bhagwati, Board Member. **ISSN:** 1369-3034 (print); **EISSN:** 1464-3758 (electronic). **Subscription Rates:** $726 Institutions print and online; $581 Institutions online only; $668 Institutions print only; $187 Individuals print; $84 Students print; $150 Members print. **URL:** http://jiel.oxfordjournals.org/. **Remarks:** Advertising accepted; rates available upon request. **Circ:** (Not Reported).

6879 ■ The Journal of International Security Affairs
Jewish Institute for National Security Affairs
1101 14th St. NW, Ste. 1110
Washington, DC 20005
Phone: (202)667-3900
Fax: (202)667-0601
Publisher's E-mail: info@jinsa.org
Freq: Semiannual. **Key Personnel:** Ilan Berman, Editor. **ISSN:** 1532--4060 (print). **URL:** http://www.securityaffairs.org. **Remarks:** Accepts advertising. **Circ:** 5000.

6880 ■ Journal on Jewish Aging
Association of Jewish Aging Services
2519 Connecticut Ave. NW
Washington, DC 20008
Phone: (202)543-7500
Publisher's E-mail: info@ajas.org
Freq: Semiannual. **Subscription Rates:** $72 /year. **Remarks:** Accepts advertising. **Circ:** (Not Reported).

6881 ■ Journal of Legal Education
Association of American Law Schools
1614 20th St. NW
Washington, DC 20009-1001
Phone: (202)296-8851
Fax: (202)296-8869
Publisher's E-mail: aals@aals.org
Journal containing ideas and information about legal education and related matters, including but not limited to the legal profession, legal theory, and legal scholarship. **Freq:** Quarterly. **ISSN:** 0022--2208 (print). **Subscription Rates:** $50 U.S.; $50 Other countries; $18 Single issue. **URL:** http://www.swlaw.edu/jle; http://swlaw.edu/jle; http://jle.aals.org/home. **Remarks:** Advertising not accepted. **Circ:** (Not Reported).

6882 ■ Journal of Medicinal Chemistry
American Chemical Society
1155 16th St. NW
Washington, DC 20036
Phone: (202)872-4600
Free: 800-227-5558
Publisher's E-mail: help@acs.org
Research journal covering relationship of chemistry to biological activity. **Freq:** Semimonthly Biweekly. **Print Method:** Offset. **Trim Size:** 8 3/16 x 11 1/4. **Cols./Page:** 2. **Col. Width:** 37 nonpareils. **Col. Depth:** 98 agate lines. **Key Personnel:** Gunda I. George, Editor, phone: (612)624-6184, fax: (202)513-8609. **ISSN:** 0022--2623 (print). **Subscription Rates:** $2562 Institutions print edition; $2826 Institutions, other countries print edition; $58 Members /year; $790 Nonmembers /year. **URL:** http://pubs.acs.org/journal/jmcmar. **Ad Rates:** BW $2,520; 4C $3,275. **Remarks:** Accepts advertising. **Circ:** ‡4400.

6883 ■ Journal of Microbiology and Biology Education
American Society for Microbiology
1752 N St. NW
Washington, DC 20036-2904
Phone: (202)942-9207
Fax: (202)942-9333
Publisher's E-mail: service@asmusa.org
Journal focusing on research in microbiology education. **Freq:** Annual. **Key Personnel:** Dr. Samantha Elliott, Editor-in-Chief. **ISSN:** 1935--7885 (print). **URL:** http://jmbe.asm.org/index.php/jmbe; http://www.asm.org/index.php/education/education-board/22-education/7830-journal-of-microbiology-biology-education-editorial-committee. **Formerly:** Microbiology Education. **Ad Rates:** BW $450. **Remarks:** Accepts advertising. **Circ:** (Not Reported).

6884 ■ Journal of Microelectronics and Electronic Packaging
International Microelectronic and Packaging Society
611 2nd St. NE
Washington, DC 20002-4909
Phone: (202)548-4001
Fax: (202)548-6115
Free: 888-464-1066
Publisher's E-mail: modonoghue@imaps.org
Freq: Quarterly. **Subscription Rates:** $75 Members printed edition; $35 Members CD-ROM edition; $175 Nonmembers printed edition; $75 Nonmembers CD-ROM edition. **Alt. Formats:** CD-ROM. **URL:** http://www.imaps.org/jmep/index.htm. **Remarks:** Advertising not accepted. **Circ:** (Not Reported).

6885 ■ Journal of the Middle East and Africa
Association for the Study of the Middle East and Africa
2100 M St. NW, No. 170-291
Washington, DC 20037
Phone: (202)429-8860
Publisher's E-mail: info@asmeascholars.org
Freq: Quarterly. **ISSN:** 2152--0844 (print); **EISSN:** 2152--0852 (electronic). **Subscription Rates:** Included in membership; $81 Individuals print only; $284 Institutions online only; $325 Institutions print and online. **URL:** http://tandfonline.com/toc/ujme20/current#.U-ioXnKSwX2. **Remarks:** Advertising not accepted. **Circ:** (Not Reported).

6886 ■ Journal of Museum Education
Museum Education Roundtable
PO Box 15727
Washington, DC 20003
Publication E-mail: info@mer-online.org
Journal covering museum education practice and theory. **Freq:** 3/year. **Key Personnel:** Cynthia Robinson, Editor-in-Chief. **ISSN:** 1059--8650 (print). **Subscription Rates:** Included in membership. **URL:** http://museumeducation.info/jme. **Remarks:** Advertising not accepted. **Circ:** (Not Reported).

6887 ■ Journal of the National Association for Alternative Certification
National Association for Alternative Certification
PO Box 5750
Washington, DC 20016
Phone: (202)277-3600
Fax: (202)403-3545
Publisher's E-mail: info@alternativecertification.org
Freq: Semiannual fall and spring. **Key Personnel:** Brian R. Evans, Managing Editor. **Subscription Rates:** Included in membership. **Alt. Formats:** PDF. **URL:** http://www.alt-teachercert.org/journal.asp; http://www.jnaac.com/index.php/JNAAC. **Remarks:** Advertising not accepted. **Circ:** (Not Reported).

6888 ■ Journal of the National Grants Management Association
National Grants Management Association
2100 M St. NW, Ste. 170
Washington, DC 20037
Phone: (202)308-9443
Publisher's E-mail: info@ngma.org
Peer-reviewed journal discussing important issues in the field of grant management. **Freq:** Semiannual. **Subscription Rates:** Included in membership. **Remarks:** Advertising not accepted. **Circ:** (Not Reported).

6889 ■ Journal of National Security Law & Policy
Georgetown University Law Center
600 New Jersey Ave. NW
Washington, DC 20001
Phone: (202)662-9000
Publisher's E-mail: admis@law.georgetown.edu
Journal covering articles exclusively to national security law and policy. **Freq:** 3/year. **Key Personnel:** William C. Banks, Editor-in-Chief. **ISSN:** 1553--3158 (print). **Subscription Rates:** $35 Individuals. **URL:** http://jnslp.com. **Ad Rates:** 4C $1,500; BW $1,000. **Remarks:** Accepts advertising. **Circ:** (Not Reported).

6890 ■ The Journal of Negro Education
Howard University School of Education
2900 Van Ness St. NW
Washington, DC 20008
Phone: (202)806-8120
Fax: (202)806-8434
Publication E-mail: journalnegroed@gmail.com
Peer-reviewed educational research journal devoted to black and minority education. **Freq:** Quarterly. **Print Method:** Letterpress. **Trim Size:** 7 x 10. **Cols./Page:** 1. **Col. Width:** 5 1/2 inches. **Col. Depth:** 7 1/2 inches. **Key Personnel:** Dr. Ivory A. Toldson, Editor-in-Chief. **ISSN:** 0022--2984 (print). **Subscription Rates:** $75 Individuals; $130 Two years; $125 Institutions; $215 Institutions 2 years; $45 Individuals student, retired; $70 Two years student, retired; $20 Single issue back-issues. **URL:** http://www.journalnegroed.org. **Ad Rates:** BW $500. **Remarks:** Color advertising not accepted. **Circ:** Paid ‡2300, Controlled ‡100.

6891 ■ The Journal of Neuroscience: The Official journal of the Society for Neuroscience
Society for Neuroscience
1121 14th St. NW, Ste. 1010
Washington, DC 20005
Phone: (202)962-4000
Medical journal.Publishes papers on a broad range of topics of general interest to those working on the nervous system. **Freq:** Weekly except for the last two weeks of December. **Print Method:** Offset. **Trim Size:** 8 1/8 x 1o 7/8. **Cols./Page:** 2. **Col. Width:** 32 nonpareils. **Col. Depth:** 119 agate lines. **Key Personnel:** John H.R. Maunsell, Editor-in-Chief; David Fitzpatrick, Senior Editor. **ISSN:** 0270--6474 (print); **EISSN:** 1529--2401 (electronic). **Subscription Rates:** $1185 Members; $895 Students; $2950 Institutions single site; $1180 Institutions multi-site (academic); $1770 Institutions multi-site (corporate). **URL:** http://www.jneurosci.org. **Ad Rates:** BW $1,005; 4C $1,085. **Remarks:** Accepts advertising. **Circ:** Paid ‡3341, Non-paid ‡303.

6892 ■ Journal of Neuroscience, Psychology, and Economics
Association for NeuroPsychoEconomics
c/o Catherine Wattenberg
750 1st St. NE
Washington, DC 20002
Publisher's E-mail: info@neuropsychoeconomics.org

Circulation: ★ = AAM; △ or • = BPA; ♦ = CAC; ❑ = VAC; ⊕ = PO Statement; ‡ = Publisher's Report; Boldface figures = sworn; Light figures = estimated.

Freq: Quarterly. **Key Personnel:** Prof. Daniel Houser, Editor. **ISSN:** 1937- 321X (print); **EISSN:** 2151-318X (electronic). **Subscription Rates:** Included in membership. **URL:** http://www.jnpe.org/front_content.php?idcat=5; http://www.apa.org/pubs/journals/npe/index.aspx. **Ad Rates:** BW $275, full page. **Remarks:** Accepts advertising. **Circ:** (Not Reported).

6893 ■ Journal of Obstetric, Gynecologic and Neonatal Nursing
Association of Women's Health, Obstetric and Neonatal Nurses
2000 L St. NW, Ste. 740
Washington, DC 20036-4912
Phone: (202)261-2400
Fax: (202)728-0575
Free: 800-673-8499
Publisher's E-mail: journaladsusa@bos.blackwellpublishing.com
Journal covering trends, policies, and research. Official publication of the Association of Women's Health, Obstetric, and Neonatal Nurses. **Freq:** Bimonthly. **Print Method:** Web Offset. **Trim Size:** 8 3/8 x 10 7/8. **Cols./Page:** 2. **Col. Width:** 39 nonpareils. **Col. Depth:** 140 agate lines. **Key Personnel:** Angela Hartley, Managing Editor; Nancy K. Lowe, PhD, Editor; Marily Stringer, PhD, Associate Editor. **ISSN:** 0884--2175 (print); **EISSN:** 1552--6909 (electronic). **Subscription Rates:** $149 Individuals; $134 Other countries. **URL:** http://www.awhonn.org/?AWHONNJournals; http://www.jognn.org. **Remarks:** Accepts advertising. **Circ:** Paid 19990.

6894 ■ Journal of Occupational Health Psychology
American Psychological Association
750 1st St. NE
Washington, DC 20002-4242
Phone: (202)336-5500
Free: 800-374-2721
Journal discussing job-related emotional and health issues. **Freq:** Quarterly beginning in January. **Trim Size:** 7 x 10. **Key Personnel:** Joseph J. Hurell, Jr., Editor; Leslie Hammer, Board Member; Pamela Perrewe, Board Member. **ISSN:** 1076-8998 (print); **EISSN:** 1939-1307 (electronic). **Subscription Rates:** $71 Members; $71 Students; $126 Nonmembers; $574 Institutions; $95 Members international, surface; $95 Students, other countries surface; $155 Nonmembers international, surface; $623 Institutions, other countries surface; $109 Members international, airmail; $109 Students, other countries airmail. **URL:** http://www.apa.org/pubs/journals/ocp/index.aspx. **Ad Rates:** BW $275; 4C $975. **Remarks:** Accepts advertising. **Circ:** 300.

6895 ■ Journal of Optical Communications and Networking
Optical Society of America
2010 Massachusetts Ave. NW
Washington, DC 20036
Phone: (202)223-8130
Fax: (202)223-1096
Publisher's E-mail: info@osa.org
Freq: Monthly. **Key Personnel:** Patrick Iannone, Editor; Ori Gerstel, Editor. **ISSN:** 1943--0620 (print); **EISSN:** 1943--0639 (electronic). **URL:** http://www.opticsinfobase.org/jocn/journal/jocn/about.cfm. **Formed by the merger of:** Journal on Selected Areas in Communications; Journal of Optical Networking. **Remarks:** Advertising not accepted. **Circ:** 8000.

6896 ■ Journal of Optical Communications and Networking
Optical Fiber Communication Conference and Exhibition
2010 Massachusetts Ave. NW
Washington, DC 20036
Phone: (202)416-1435
Publisher's E-mail: info@osa.org
Freq: Monthly. **Key Personnel:** Patrick Iannone, Editor; Ori Gerstel, Editor. **ISSN:** 1943--0620 (print); **EISSN:** 1943--0639 (electronic). **URL:** http://www.opticsinfobase.org/jocn/journal/jocn/about.cfm. **Formed by the merger of:** Journal on Selected Areas in Communications; Journal of Optical Networking. **Remarks:** Advertising not accepted. **Circ:** 8000.

6897 ■ Journal of the Optical Society of America A
Optical Society of America
2010 Massachusetts Ave. NW
Washington, DC 20036
Phone: (202)223-8130
Fax: (202)223-1096
Publication E-mail: jamss@osa.org
Freq: Monthly. **Print Method:** Offset. **Trim Size:** 8 1/4 x 11 1/4. **Cols./Page:** 2. **Col. Width:** 38 nonpareils. **Col. Depth:** 123 agate lines. **Key Personnel:** P. Scott Carney, Editor; Alexine Hart, Managing Editor; Nicole Williams-Jones, Coordinator; Franco Gori, Editor-in-Chief. **ISSN:** 1084--7529 (print); **EISSN:** 1520--8532 (electronic). **Subscription Rates:** $2873 Institutions print and online, U.S.; $2963 Institutions print and online; Canada and South America; $3053 Institutions print and online; Europe and Asia; $2239 Institutions online only. **URL:** http://www.osapublishing.org/josaa/home.cfm. **Formerly:** Journal of the Optical Society of America A: Optics and Image Science. **Remarks:** Advertising not accepted. **Circ:** Paid 2200.

6898 ■ Journal of the Optical Society of America B: Optical Physics
Optical Society of America
2010 Massachusetts Ave. NW
Washington, DC 20036
Phone: (202)223-8130
Fax: (202)223-1096
Publication E-mail: jbmss@osa.org
Freq: Monthly. **Print Method:** Offset. **Trim Size:** 8 1/4 x 11. **Cols./Page:** 2. **Col. Width:** 38 nonpareils. **Col. Depth:** 123 agate lines. **Key Personnel:** Alexine Hart, Managing Editor, phone: (202)416-1923; Richard Averitt, Editor; Maria Bondani, Editor; Henry M. Van Driel, Editor-in-Chief. **ISSN:** 0740--3224 (print); **EISSN:** 1520--8540 (electronic). **Subscription Rates:** $2239 Institutions online; $2873 Institutions print and online; $2963 Institutions Canada & South America, print and online; $3053 Institutions Europe/Asia, print and online; $2790 Individuals print + online. **URL:** http://www.opticsinfobase.org/josab/Issue.cfm; http://www.opticsinfobase.org/josab/journal/josab/about.cfm. **Remarks:** Advertising not accepted. **Circ:** (Not Reported).

6899 ■ Journal of the Optical Society of America B: Optical Physics
Optical Fiber Communication Conference and Exhibition
2010 Massachusetts Ave. NW
Washington, DC 20036
Phone: (202)416-1435
Publication E-mail: jbmss@osa.org
Freq: Monthly. **Print Method:** Offset. **Trim Size:** 8 1/4 x 11. **Cols./Page:** 2. **Col. Width:** 38 nonpareils. **Col. Depth:** 123 agate lines. **Key Personnel:** Alexine Hart, Managing Editor, phone: (202)416-1923; Richard Averitt, Editor; Maria Bondani, Editor; Henry M. Van Driel, Editor-in-Chief. **ISSN:** 0740--3224 (print); **EISSN:** 1520--8540 (electronic). **Subscription Rates:** $2239 Institutions online; $2873 Institutions print and online; $2963 Institutions Canada & South America, print and online; $3053 Institutions Europe/Asia, print and online; $2790 Individuals print + online. **URL:** http://www.opticsinfobase.org/josab/Issue.cfm; http://www.opticsinfobase.org/josab/journal/josab/about.cfm. **Remarks:** Advertising not accepted. **Circ:** (Not Reported).

6900 ■ Journal of Optical Technology
Optical Fiber Communication Conference and Exhibition
2010 Massachusetts Ave. NW
Washington, DC 20036
Phone: (202)416-1435
Publisher's E-mail: sales@aip.org
Russian journal on optics and space translated to English. **Freq:** Monthly. **Key Personnel:** A.S. Tibilov, Editor-in-Chief. **ISSN:** 1070--9762 (print); **EISSN:** 1091--0786 (electronic). **URL:** http://www.osapublishing.org/jot/journal/jot/about.cfm. **Formerly:** Soviet Journal of Optical Technology. **Remarks:** Advertising not accepted. **Circ:** ‡470.

6901 ■ The Journal of Organic Chemistry
American Chemical Society
1155 16th St. NW
Washington, DC 20036
Phone: (202)872-4600
Free: 800-227-5558
Publication E-mail: joc@chem.utah.edu
Periodical offering critical accounts of original work and interpretive reviews of existing data that present new viewpoints in organic and bioorganic chemistry. **Freq:** Semimonthly. **Key Personnel:** Katie Turner, Editor; Tamara Hanna, Managing Editor; C. Dale Poulter, Editor-in-Chief, phone: (801)581-3368, fax: (202)513-8639. **ISSN:** 0022--3263 (print); **EISSN:** 1520--6904 (electronic). **Subscription Rates:** $125 Individuals print and online; $145 Other countries; $3295 Institutions; $3595 Institutions, other countries. **URL:** http://pubs.acs.org/journal/joceah. **Ad Rates:** BW $3920; 4C $5095. **Remarks:** Accepts advertising. **Circ:** 7,500.

6902 ■ Journal of Palestine Studies
University of California Press - Journals and Digital Publishing Division
Institute for Palestine Studies
3501 M Street NW
Washington, DC 20007
Publication E-mail: jps@palestine-studies.org
North American journal covering Palestinian affairs and the Arab-Israeli conflict; including comprehensive information on the region's political, religious, and cultural concerns. **Freq:** Quarterly. **Key Personnel:** Linda Butler, Associate Editor; Rashid I. Khalidi, Editor; Ussama Makdisi, Member; Joseph Massad, Member; Salim Tamari, Member. **ISSN:** 0377--919X (print); **EISSN:** 1533--8614 (electronic). **Subscription Rates:** $50 Individuals /yr. online ; $65 Individuals /yr. online & print; $20 Individuals /issue; $35 Students /yr. online& print; $30 Students online ; $83 Institutions single issue. **Alt. Formats:** Electronic publishing. **URL:** http://jps.ucpress.edu. **Remarks:** Accepts advertising. **Circ:** 2050, 4000.

6903 ■ Journal of Personality and Social Psychology
American Psychological Association
750 1st St. NE
Washington, DC 20002-4242
Phone: (202)336-5500
Free: 800-374-2721
Journal presenting research in three major areas: attitudes and social cognition; interpersonal relations and group processes; and personality processes and individual differences. **Freq:** Monthly. **Print Method:** Offset. **Trim Size:** 8 1/4 x 11. **Cols./Page:** 2. **Col. Width:** 46 nonpareils. **Col. Depth:** 126 agate lines. **Key Personnel:** Eliot R. Smith, Editor; Laura A. King, Editor; Jeffry A. Simpson, PhD, Editor. **ISSN:** 0022--3514 (print); **EISSN:** 1939--1315 (electronic). **Subscription Rates:** $273 Members domestic; $306 Members foreign, surface; $347 Members foreign, air mail; $221 Students domestic; $254 Students foreign, surface; $295 Students foreign, air mail; $737 Nonmembers domestic; $794 Nonmembers foreign surface; $826 Nonmembers foreign, air mail; $2660 Institutions domestic; $2770 Institutions, other countries surface mail; $2802 Institutions, other countries air mail. **URL:** http://www.apa.org/pubs/journals/psp/index.aspx. **Ad Rates:** BW $375; 4C $1,350. **Remarks:** Accepts advertising. **Circ:** ‡1500, 5800.

6904 ■ Journal of Physician Assistant Education
Physician Assistant Education Association
655 K St. NW, Ste. 700
Washington, DC 20001-2385
Phone: (703)548-5538
Publisher's E-mail: info@paeaonline.org
Peer-reviewed journal containing ethically produced, scholarly manuscripts germane to PA educators and by providing a forum for the sharing of ideas and innovations that will enhance the education of PA students. **Freq:** Quarterly. **Key Personnel:** David P. Asprey, PhD, PA-C, Editor-in-Chief. **ISSN:** 1941--9430 (print); **EISSN:** 1941--9449 (electronic). **URL:** http://journals.lww.com/jpae/pages/default.aspx. **Ad Rates:** BW $1000, full page; 4C $1000, full page - four color; BW $680, half page; 4C $680, half page - four color. **Remarks:** Accepts advertising. **Circ:** (Not Reported).

6905 ■ Journal of Professional Nursing
American Association of Colleges of Nursing
1 Dupont Cir. NW, Ste. 530
Washington, DC 20036
Phone: (202)463-6930

Fax: (202)785-8320
Publisher's E-mail: info@aacn.nche.edu
Freq: Bimonthly. **ISSN:** 8755--7223 (print). **Subscription Rates:** Included in membership. **URL:** http://www.aacn.nche.edu/publications/jpn. **Ad Rates:** BW $1,170. **Remarks:** Accepts advertising. **Circ:** ‡1044.

6906 ■ Journal of Prosthetics and Orthotics
American Academy of Orthotists and Prosthetists
1331 H St. NW, Ste. 501
Washington, DC 20005
Phone: (202)380-3663
Fax: (202)380-3447
Publisher's E-mail: ronna.ekhouse@wolterskluwer.com
Industry publication provides information concerning the latest research and clinical thinking in orthotics and prosthetics, including information on new devices, fitting techniques and patient management experiences. **Freq:** Quarterly. **Key Personnel:** Steven A. Gard, Editor-in-Chief. **ISSN:** 1040--8800 (print). **Subscription Rates:** $197 Individuals 1 year; $554 Institutions 1 year; $269 Canada and Mexico 1 year; $670 Institutions, Canada and Mexico 1 year; $285 Other countries 1 year; $686 Institutions, other countries 1 year. **URL:** http://www.oandp.org/jpo. **Mailing address:** PO Box 908, Philadelphia, PA 19106-3621. **Remarks:** Accepts advertising. **Circ:** (Not Reported).

6907 ■ Journal of Proteome Research
American Chemical Society
1155 16th St. NW
Washington, DC 20036
Phone: (202)872-4600
Free: 800-227-5558
Publisher's E-mail: help@acs.org
Journal that covers information concerning systems-oriented, global protein analysis and function, emphasizing the synergy between physical and life sciences. **Freq:** Monthly. **Key Personnel:** William S. Hancock, Editor-in-Chief, phone: (617)373-4881, fax: (202)513-8698. **ISSN:** 1535--3893 (print); **EISSN:** 1535--3907 (electronic). **Subscription Rates:** Included in membership. **URL:** http://pubs.acs.org/journals/jprobs. **Ad Rates:** BW $3,645; 4C $4,745. **Remarks:** Accepts advertising. **Circ:** (Not Reported).

6908 ■ Journal of Psychosocial Oncology
Routledge Journals Taylor & Francis Group
102 Shahan Hall
Washington, DC 20064
Phone: (202)319-5454
Provide psychosocial services to cancer patients, their families, and their caregivers. **Freq:** Quarterly. **Print Method:** Offset. **Trim Size:** 6 x 8 3/8. **Key Personnel:** Karen Kayser, Editor-in-Chief. **ISSN:** 0734--7332 (print); **EISSN:** 1540--7586 (electronic). **Subscription Rates:** $225 Individuals online only; $1305 Institutions online only; $257 Individuals print and online; $1491 Institutions print and online; $83 Members. **URL:** http://www.tandfonline.com/toc/wjpo20/current; http://www.aosw.org/publications-media/journal-of-psychosocial-oncology. **Remarks:** Accepts advertising. **Circ:** Paid 1002.

6909 ■ Journal of Psychotherapy Integration
American Psychological Association
750 1st St. NE
Washington, DC 20002-4242
Phone: (202)336-5500
Free: 800-374-2721
Psychotherapy integration is an approach to treatment that goes beyond any single theory or set of techniques. The history of the psychotherapy integration movement is described, along with several approaches to integration that have been developed. **Freq:** Quarterly. **Key Personnel:** Jack C. Anchin, PhD, Associate Editor; Diane B. Arnkoff, PhD, Board Member; Arthur C. Bohart, PhD, Board Member; Louis G. Castonguay, PhD, Board Member; Andres J. Consoli, PhD, Board Member; Guillem Feixias, PhD, Board Member; David M. Allen, MD, Associate Editor. **ISSN:** 1053--0479 (print); **EISSN:** 1573--3696 (electronic). **Subscription Rates:** $1022 Institutions; $1071 Institutions, other countries; $1086 Institutions, other countries by air mail. **URL:** http://www.apa.org/pubs/journals/int/index.aspx. **Ad Rates:** BW $250; 4C $1,225. **Remarks:** Advertising accepted; rates available upon request. **Circ:** 450, 1000.

6910 ■ Journal of Public Affairs Education
Network of Schools of Public Policy, Affairs, and Administration
1029 Vermont Ave. NW, Ste. 1100
Washington, DC 20005-3517
Phone: (202)628-8965
Fax: (202)626-4978
Publisher's E-mail: naspaa@naspaa.org
Journal covering public administration issues. **Freq:** Quarterly. **Key Personnel:** David Schultz, Editor-in-Chief. **ISSN:** 1523--6803 (print). **Subscription Rates:** $125 Institutions; $50 Individuals; $40 Students. **Alt. Formats:** PDF. **URL:** http://www.naspaa.org/initiatives/jpae/jpae.asp. **Circ:** (Not Reported).

6911 ■ Journal of Public Management and Social Policy
Conference of Minority Public Administrators
1120 G St. NW, Ste. 700
Washington, DC 20005
Freq: Semiannual. **ISSN:** 1080--8523 (print). **Subscription Rates:** $140 Institutions; $40 Individuals. **URL:** http://www.jpmsp.com. **Remarks:** Advertising not accepted. **Circ:** (Not Reported).

6912 ■ Journal of Research in Childhood Education
Association for Childhood Education International
1200 18th St. NW, Ste. 700
Washington, DC 20036
Phone: (202)372-9986
Fax: (202)372-9989
Free: 800-423-3563
Publisher's E-mail: headquarters@acei.org
Journal covering education research. **Freq:** Quarterly. **Print Method:** Offset. **Trim Size:** 6 7/8 x 9 7/8. **Key Personnel:** Jeff Leonard, Advertising Executive, phone: (215)675-9208. **ISSN:** 0256--8543 (print); **EISSN:** 2150--2641 (electronic). **Subscription Rates:** Included in membership. **URL:** http://acei.org/journal-of-research-in-childhood-education. **Ad Rates:** BW $250. **Remarks:** Accepts advertising. **Circ:** 2000.

6913 ■ Journal of Research of the National Institute of Standards and Technology
U.S. Government Publishing Office
732 N Capitol St. NW
Washington, DC 20401-0001
Phone: (202)512-1800
Fax: (202)512-2104
Free: 866-512-1800
Publisher's E-mail: contactcenter@gpo.gov
Journal containing information on metrology in physics, chemistry, engineering, and computer sciences. **Freq:** 6/year. **Print Method:** Letterpress. **Cols./Page:** 2. **Col. Width:** 40 nonpareils. **Col. Depth:** 122 agate lines. **Key Personnel:** Robert A. Dragoset, Executive Editor; Robert L. Watters, Jr. **ISSN:** 0160--1741 (print). **Subscription Rates:** Free. **URL:** http://www.nist.gov/nvl/jres.cfm. **Mailing address:** PO Box 979050, Saint Louis, MO 63197-9000. **Circ:** (Not Reported).

6914 ■ Journal of Social, Political & Economic Studies
Council for Social and Economic Studies
1133 13th St. NW
Washington, DC 20005
Phone: (202)371-2700
Fax: (202)371-1523
Publication E-mail: socecon@aol.com
Peer-reviewed journal on current and international social, political, and economic issues. **Freq:** Quarterly. **Print Method:** Offset. **Trim Size:** 6 x 9. **Cols./Page:** 1. **Col. Width:** 50 nonpareils. **Col. Depth:** 98 agate lines. **Key Personnel:** Prof. Roger Pearson, PhD, Editor; Prof. Dwight D. Murphey, Associate Editor. **ISSN:** 0193--5941 (print). **Subscription Rates:** $55.50 Individuals print; $75.50 Other countries print; $148 Libraries print; $178 Libraries print - non - U.S.; $228 Libraries printed and electronic version; $248 Libraries printed and electronic - non - U.S.; $168 Libraries online only. **URL:** http://www.jspes.org; http://www.jspes.org/subscribe.html. **Mailing address:** PO Box 34143, Washington, DC 20043. **Remarks:** Accepts advertising. **Circ:** 1060.

6915 ■ Journal of the Student National Medical Association
Student National Medical Association
5113 Georgia Ave. NW
Washington, DC 20011-3921
Phone: (202)882-2881
Fax: (202)882-2886
Publisher's E-mail: operations@snma.org
Freq: Quarterly. **Subscription Rates:** included in membership dues; $30 Nonmembers. **Alt. Formats:** CD-ROM; Magnetic tape. **URL:** http://www.snma.org/?pID=30. **Remarks:** Advertising not accepted. **Circ:** 20000.

6916 ■ Journal of Teacher Education
American Association of Colleges for Teacher Education
1307 New York Ave. NW, Ste. 300
Washington, DC 20005-4721
Phone: (202)293-2450
Fax: (202)457-8095
Publisher's E-mail: aacte@aacte.org
Freq: 5/year. **ISSN:** 0022- 4871 (print). **Subscription Rates:** $136 Institutions single print; $33 Individuals single print. **URL:** http://aacte.org/resources/journal-of-teacher-education; http://jte.sagepub.com. **Remarks:** Advertising not accepted. **Circ:** (Not Reported).

6917 ■ Journal of Veterinary Medical Education
Association of American Veterinary Medical Colleges
1101 Vermont Ave. NW, Ste. 301
Washington, DC 20005
Phone: (202)371-9195
Fax: (202)842-0773
Freq: Quarterly. **Key Personnel:** Dr. Daryl Buss, Editor-in-Chief. **ISSN:** 0748--321X (print); **EISSN:** 1943--7218 (electronic). **Subscription Rates:** $180 Individuals print only; $103 Individuals online only; $220 Individuals print and online; $412 Institutions Tier 1 - print only; $304 Institutions Tier 1 - online only; $582 Institutions Tier 2 - online only; $461 Institutions Tier 1 - print and online. **URL:** http://www.aavmc.org/publications/journal-of-veterinary-medical-education.aspx; http://jvme.utpjournals.press/loi/jvme. **Ad Rates:** BW $550. **Remarks:** Accepts advertising. **Circ:** (Not Reported).

6918 ■ Journal of Virology
ASM Journals
1752 North St. NW
Washington, DC 20036
Phone: (202)737-3600
Fax: (202)942-9355
Publisher's E-mail: journals@asmusa.org
Journal on viruses of bacteria, plants, and animals. **Freq:** Semimonthly. **Print Method:** Offset. Uses mats. **Trim Size:** 8 1/8 x 10 7/8. **Cols./Page:** 2. **Col. Width:** 42 nonpareils. **Col. Depth:** 127 agate lines. **Key Personnel:** Rozanne M. Sandri-Goldin, Editor-in-Chief. **ISSN:** 0022--538X (print). **Subscription Rates:** $564 Members print; $732 Canada members; $516 Other countries online; members. **URL:** http://jvi.asm.org. **Ad Rates:** BW $1,485; 4C $2,980. **Remarks:** Accepts advertising. **Circ:** Combined ‡12323.

6919 ■ The Journals of Gerontology: Series A
Gerontological Society of America
1220 L St. NW, Ste. 901
Washington, DC 20005-4001
Phone: (202)842-1275
Freq: Monthly. **Print Method:** Web offset. **Trim Size:** 8 3/8 x 10 7/8. **Cols./Page:** 2. **Col. Width:** 30 nonpareils. **Col. Depth:** 116 agate lines. **Key Personnel:** Rafael de Cabo, PhD, Editor; Stephen Kritchevsky, PhD, Editor. **ISSN:** 1079--5006 (print); **EISSN:** 1758--535X (electronic). **Subscription Rates:** £785 Institutions print and online; $1170 Institutions print and online; €1170 Institutions print and online. **URL:** http://biomedgerontology.oxfordjournals.org. **Formerly:** Journal of Gerontology. **Ad Rates:** BW $1605; 4C $2675. **Remarks:** Accepts advertising. **Circ:** Paid ‡2350.

6920 ■ The Journals of Gerontology, Series B
Gerontological Society of America
1220 L St. NW, Ste. 901
Washington, DC 20005-4001
Phone: (202)842-1275
Freq: Bimonthly. **ISSN:** 1079- 5014 (print); **EISSN:** 1758-5368 (electronic). **Subscription Rates:** $833 print and online; £554 print and online. **URL:** http://psychsocgerontology.oxfordjournals.org. **Remarks:** Accepts advertising. **Circ:** 6000.

Circulation: ★ = AAM; △ or • = BPA; ♦ = CAC; ❑ = VAC; ⊕ = PO Statement; ‡ = Publisher's Report; Boldface figures = sworn; Light figures = estimated.

6921 ■ Journeyman Roofer and Waterproofer
United Union of Roofers Waterproofers and Allied Workers
1660 L St. NW, Ste. 800
Washington, DC 20036-5646
Phone: (202)463-7663
Fax: (202)463-6906
Publisher's E-mail: roofers@unionroofers.com
Trade journal. **Freq:** Quarterly. **Subscription Rates:** Included in membership; $6 Individuals. **Alt. Formats:** PDF. **URL:** http://www.unionroofers.com/Who-We-Are/Publications.aspx. **Formerly**: Journeyman Roofer. **Remarks:** Advertising not accepted. **Circ:** 23000.

6922 ■ The JSEA Bulletin
Association of Jesuit Colleges and Universities
1016 16th St. NW, Ste. 200
Washington, DC 20036
Phone: (202)667-3888
Fax: (202)387-6305
Newsletter reporting events of interest to Ignatian educators and others outside of Jesuit schools. **Founded:** 1923. **Freq:** 7/year. **Print Method:** Offset. **Cols./Page:** 6. **Col. Width:** 25 nonpareils. **Col. Depth:** 301 agate lines. **Key Personnel:** James A. Stoeger, President. **URL:** http://www.jsea.org/resources/bulletin-magisine. **Remarks:** Accepts advertising. **Circ:** (Not Reported).

6923 ■ Kennedy Institute of Ethics Journal
Joseph P. and Rose F. Kennedy Institute of Ethics
Healy Hall, 4th Fl.
Georgetown University
37th & O Sts. NW
Washington, DC 20057
Phone: (202)687-8099
Publisher's E-mail: littlem@georgetown.edu
Freq: Quarterly. **Trim Size:** 6 3/4 x 10. **Cols./Page:** 1. **Col. Width:** 4 3/4 inches. **Col. Depth:** 7 1/2 inches. **Key Personnel:** Rebecca Kukla, PhD, Editor-in-Chief; Dan W. Brock, PhD, Board Member; Lisa Sowle Cahill, PhD, Board Member; Arthur Caplan, PhD, Board Member; Alexander M. Capron, Board Member; Bernard Lo, MD, Board Member; James Childress, PhD, Board Member. **ISSN:** 1054--6863 (print); **EISSN:** 1086--3249 (electronic). **Subscription Rates:** $210 Institutions print; $420 Institutions print, 2 years. **Alt. Formats:** PDF. **URL:** http://kiej.georgetown.edu. **Ad Rates:** BW $325. **Remarks:** Accepts advertising. **Circ:** 1008.

6924 ■ Kennedy Institute of Ethics Journal
Georgetown University Joseph and Rose Kennedy Institute of Ethics
Healey Hall, 4th Fl.
Washington, DC 20057
Phone: (202)687-8099
Fax: (202)687-8089
Publisher's E-mail: littlem@georgetown.edu
Freq: Quarterly. **Trim Size:** 6 3/4 x 10. **Cols./Page:** 1. **Col. Width:** 4 3/4 inches. **Col. Depth:** 7 1/2 inches. **Key Personnel:** Rebecca Kukla, PhD, Editor-in-Chief; Dan W. Brock, PhD, Board Member; Lisa Sowle Cahill, PhD, Board Member; Arthur Caplan, PhD, Board Member; Alexander M. Capron, Board Member; Bernard Lo, MD, Board Member; James Childress, PhD, Board Member. **ISSN:** 1054--6863 (print); **EISSN:** 1086--3249 (electronic). **Subscription Rates:** $210 Institutions print; $420 Institutions print, 2 years. **Alt. Formats:** PDF. **URL:** http://kiej.georgetown.edu. **Ad Rates:** BW $325. **Remarks:** Accepts advertising. **Circ:** 1008.

6925 ■ Kidney News
American Society of Nephrology
1510 H St. NW, Ste. 800
Washington, DC 20005
Phone: (202)640-4660
Fax: (202)637-9793
Publisher's E-mail: email@asn-online.org
Freq: Monthly. **Alt. Formats:** PDF. **URL:** http://www.asn-online.org/publications/kidneynews/. **Remarks:** Accepts advertising. **Circ:** 18,000.

6926 ■ Kiplinger's Personal Finance
Kiplinger Washington Editors Inc.
1100 13th St. NW, Ste. 750
Washington, DC 20005
Phone: (202)887-6400
Free: 800-554-0155
Publisher's E-mail: sub.services@kiplinger.com
Personal finance magazine featuring new and existing products and services providing information on investments, insurance, taxes, home ownership, recreation, education, automobiles, healthcare, and career and retirement planning. **Founded:** 1947. **Freq:** Monthly. **Print Method:** Offset. **Trim Size:** 8 x 10 13/16. **Cols./Page:** 3. **Col. Width:** 13 picas. **Col. Depth:** 140 agate lines. **Key Personnel:** Alex McKenna, Publisher, phone: (212)398-6321. **ISSN:** 0009-143X (print). **Subscription Rates:** $12 Individuals digital issue; $1 Single issue. **Alt. Formats:** Handheld. **URL:** http://www.kiplinger.com. **Formerly**: Changing Times. **Ad Rates:** GLR $58.30; BW $18,000; 4C $25,500. **Remarks:** Accepts advertising. **Circ:** Paid ★**790,068**, Paid ★**631,403**.

6927 ■ Korea's Economy
Korea Economic Institute
1800 K St. NW, Ste. 1010
Washington, DC 20006
Phone: (202)464-1982
Fax: (202)464-1987
Publisher's E-mail: info@keia.org
Freq: Annual. **ISSN:** 0894- 6302 (print). **URL:** http://www.keia.org/page/korea%E2%80%99s-economy. **Remarks:** Advertising not accepted. **Circ:** (Not Reported).

6928 ■ Land Development
National Association of Home Builders
1201 15th St. NW
Washington, DC 20005
Free: 800-268-5242
Publisher's E-mail: info@nahb.org
Magazine featuring land development industry. **Freq:** Quarterly. **Trim Size:** 8.25 x 11. **Key Personnel:** Daisy Linda Kone, Contact. **Subscription Rates:** $32.99 Members; $38.99 Nonmembers. **Alt. Formats:** E-book. **URL:** http://ebooks.builderbooks.com/product/land-development. **Remarks:** Accepts advertising. **Circ:** (Not Reported).

6929 ■ Landscape Architecture: The Magazine of the American Society of Landscape Architects
American Society of Landscape Architects
636 Eye St. NW
Washington, DC 20001-3736
Phone: (202)898-2444
Fax: (202)898-1185
Free: 888-999-2752
Publisher's E-mail: info@asla.org
Professional magazine covering land planning and design. **Freq:** Monthly. **Print Method:** Offset. **Trim Size:** 8 1/2 x 11. **Key Personnel:** Mark Frieden, Manager, Advertising and Sales; Lisa Speckhardt, Managing Editor; Christopher McGee, Art Director; Daniel Jost, Editor, Writer; Shelly Neill, Manager, Production; Bradford McKee, Editor; Lisa Schultz, Associate Editor. **ISSN:** 0023--8031 (print). **Subscription Rates:** $59 Nonmembers; $99 Other countries; $118 Two years; $198 Other countries 2 years. **URL:** http://landscapearchitecturemagazine.org. **Ad Rates:** 4C $9,800. **Remarks:** Accepts advertising. **Circ:** Paid ★**22700**.

6930 ■ Landscape Architecture Magazine
American Society of Landscape Architects
636 Eye St. NW
Washington, DC 20001-3736
Phone: (202)898-2444
Fax: (202)898-1185
Free: 888-999-2752
Publisher's E-mail: info@asla.org
Freq: Monthly. **ISSN:** 0023-- 8031 (print). **Subscription Rates:** $59 Individuals one year; print only; $118 Individuals two years; print only; $99 Other countries one year; individuals; print only; $198 Other countries two years; individuals; print only; $44.25 Individuals one year; online only; $88.50 Individuals two years; online only; $89 Individuals one year; print + online; $178 Individuals two years; print + online; $129 Other countries one year; individuals; print + online; $258 Other countries two years; individuals; print + online; $5.50 Single issue members; print only; $9 Single issue non-members; print only; $5.25 Single issue online only; $118 Institutions one year; print only; $236 Institutions two years; print only; $158 Other countries one year; institutions; print only; $316 Other countries two years; institutions; print only; $88 Institutions one year; online only; $177 Institutions two years; online only; $178 Institutions one year; institutions; print + online; $356 Institutions two years; institutions; print + online; $218 Other countries one year; institutions; print + online; $436 Other countries two years; institutions; print + online; $9 Single issue institutions; print only. **URL:** http://landscapearchitecturemagazine.org. **Remarks:** Accepts advertising. **Circ:** 25000.

6931 ■ Latin American Antiquity
Society for American Archaeology
1111 14th St. NW, Ste. 800
Washington, DC 20005-5622
Phone: (202)789-8200
Fax: (202)789-0284
Publication E-mail: publications@saa.org
Journal covering the archaeology of Mesoamerica, Central and South America, and the Caribbean (English and Spanish). **Freq:** Quarterly. **Print Method:** Offset. **Trim Size:** 7 x 10. **Cols./Page:** 2. **Col. Width:** 16.5 picas. **Col. Depth:** 140 agate lines. **Key Personnel:** Christopher A. Pool, Editor, phone: (859)257-2793; Gabriela Urunuela Y Ladron de Guevara, Editor. **ISSN:** 1045-6635 (print). **Subscription Rates:** $25 Members; $50 Individuals; $115 for nonmembers, institutional subscribers. **URL:** http://www.saa.org/AbouttheSociety/Publications/LatinAmericanAntiquity/tabid/127/Default.aspx. **Ad Rates:** BW $244. **Remarks:** Advertising accepted; rates available upon request. **Circ:** ‡1600.

6932 ■ Law and Human Behavior
American Psychological Association
750 1st St. NE
Washington, DC 20002-4242
Phone: (202)336-5500
Free: 800-374-2721
Scholarly journal covering research on psychology-law topics including jury decision-making, eyewitness identification, expert witnesses, and mental health. **Freq:** Bimonthly. **Key Personnel:** Margaret Bull Kovera, Editor. **ISSN:** 0147--7307 (print); **EISSN:** 1573--661X (electronic). **Subscription Rates:** $1969 U.S.; $2030 Other countries; $2050 Other countries air mail. **URL:** http://www.apa.org/pubs/journals/lhb. **Ad Rates:** BW $485. **Remarks:** Accepts advertising. **Circ:** Combined ⊕**3000**.

6933 ■ Leader's Edge
Council of Insurance Agents & Brokers
701 Pennsylvania Ave. NW, Ste. 750
Washington, DC 20004-2608
Phone: (202)783-4400
Fax: (202)783-4410
Publisher's E-mail: ciab@ciab.com
Magazine featuring latest industry news and market trends worldwide, focusing on issues of importance to commercial insurance brokers, including legal and legislative issues, international regulation and business, management tools and tips, technology, carrier news and even insurance humor. **Freq:** 10/year. **Subscription Rates:** Included in membership; $100 Nonmembers in U.S.; $175 Nonmembers outside U.S. **URL:** http://leadersedgemagazine.com. **Remarks:** Accepts advertising. **Circ:** (Not Reported).

6934 ■ The Leadership Exchange
NASPA - Student Affairs Administrators in Higher Education
111 K St. NE, 10th Fl.
Washington, DC 20002
Phone: (202)265-7500
Publisher's E-mail: office@naspa.org
Freq: Quarterly. **Subscription Rates:** $41 Members; $50 Nonmembers. **URL:** http://www.naspa.org/publications/books/leadership-exchange-magazine. **Remarks:** Advertising not accepted. **Circ:** (Not Reported).

6935 ■ Leadership: The Magazine for Volunteer Association Leaders
ASAE: The Center for Association Leadership
1575 I St. NW
Washington, DC 20005-1103
Phone: (202)371-0940
Fax: (202)371-8315
Free: 888-950-ASAE
Publisher's E-mail: asaeservice@asaecenter.org
Freq: Annual. **Subscription Rates:** $6.50 Members /issue; $13.60 Nonmembers /issue. **Remarks:** Accepts advertising. **Circ:** (Not Reported).

6936 ■ LeadingAge
LeadingAge
2519 Connecticut Ave. NW

Washington, DC 20008-1520
Phone: (202)783-2242
Fax: (202)783-2255
Publisher's E-mail: info@leadingage.org
Magazine featuring leadership, excellence and innovation in aging services. **Freq:** Bimonthly. **Subscription Rates:** Included in membership. **URL:** http://www.leadingage.org/LeadingAge_magazine.aspx. **Formerly**: FutureAge. **Remarks:** Accepts advertising. **Circ:** (Not Reported).

6937 ■ Liberal Education
Association of American Colleges and Universities
1818 R St. NW
Washington, DC 20009
Phone: (202)387-3760
Publication E-mail: pub_desk@aacu.nw.dc.us
Freq: Quarterly. **Print Method:** Offset. **Trim Size:** 8 1/2 x 11. **Cols./Page:** 2. **Col. Width:** 48 nonpareils. **Col. Depth:** 134 agate lines. **Key Personnel:** Debra Humphreys, Vice President, Communications and Public Affairs; David Tritelli, Editor, Senior Editor. **ISSN:** 0024--1822 (print). **Subscription Rates:** $10 Members single; $14 Nonmembers single; $60 Libraries /year; $50 Individuals /year. **URL:** http://www.aacu.org/liberaleducation; http://www.aacu.org/liberaleducation/index.cfm. **Remarks:** Advertising not accepted. **Circ:** Paid ‡900, Controlled ‡4000, 8000.

6938 ■ The Link, APSCU
Association of Private Sector Colleges and Universities
1101 Connecticut Ave. NW, Ste. 900
Washington, DC 20036
Phone: (202)336-6700
Fax: (202)336-6828
Free: 866-711-8574
Publisher's E-mail: apscu@apscu.org
Freq: Quarterly. **URL:** http://www.career.org/knowledge-center/publications/the-link. **Remarks:** Accepts advertising. **Circ:** 1400.

6939 ■ Literary Imagination
Association of Literary Scholars, Critics, and Writers
Marist Hall
The Catholic University of America
620 Michigan Ave. NE
Washington, DC 20064
Phone: (202)319-5650
Fax: (202)319-5650
Publisher's E-mail: uk@oup.com
Journal covering academic literary study. **Freq:** 3/year. **Key Personnel:** Archie Burnett, Editor; Saskia Hamilton, Editor. **ISSN:** 1523--9012 (print); **EISSN:** 1752--6566 (electronic). **Subscription Rates:** $165 Institutions online; $190 Institutions print; $206 Institutions print and online; $119 Individuals print. **URL:** http://litimag.oxfordjournals.org. **Remarks:** Accepts advertising. **Circ:** (Not Reported).

6940 ■ Lodging
American Hotel & Lodging Educational Foundation
1250 I St. NW, Ste. 1100
Washington, DC 20005-3931
Phone: (202)289-3180
Fax: (202)289-3199
Publisher's E-mail: foundation@ahlef.org
Freq: Monthly. **Remarks:** Accepts advertising. **Circ:** 40000.

6941 ■ LSA Journal
Linguistic Society of America
Archibald A. Hill
522 21st St. NW, Ste. 120
Washington, DC 20006-5012
Phone: (202)835-1714
Fax: (202)835-1717
Freq: published as necessary. **URL:** http://www.linguisticsociety.org/lsa-publications. **Circ:** (Not Reported).

6942 ■ LUNGhealth
American Lung Association in the District of Columbia
1301 Pennsylvania Ave. NW
Washington, DC 20004
Phone: (202)785-3355
Fax: (202)452-1805
Free: 800-548-8252
Publisher's E-mail: lungdc@lunginfo.org
Magazine containing research and studies regarding lung health and other related ideas. **Freq:** Quarterly. **Remarks:** Advertising not accepted. **Circ:** (Not Reported).

6943 ■ Main Economic Indicators
OECD Washington Center
1776 I St. NW, Ste. 450
Washington, DC 20006
Phone: (202)785-6323
Fax: (202)315-2508
Free: 800-456-6323
Publisher's E-mail: washington.contact@oecd.org
Report graphing changes in the economies of OECD member countries. **Freq:** Monthly. **Print Method:** Offset. **Trim Size:** 7 7/8 x 10 5/8. **Cols./Page:** 1. **Col. Width:** 84 nonpareils. **Col. Depth:** 133 agate lines. **ISSN:** 2219--4991 (print). **Subscription Rates:** $980 Individuals print & online; €735 Individuals print & online; £585 Individuals print & online; ¥93800 Individuals print & online; $625 Individuals online only; £378 Individuals online only; €477 Individuals online only. **Alt. Formats:** Database. **URL:** http://www.oecd-ilibrary.org/economics/main-economic-indicators_22195009. **Also known as**: Principaux indicateurs economiques. **Remarks:** Advertising not accepted. **Circ:** (Not Reported).

6944 ■ Main Science & Technology Indicators
OECD Washington Center
1776 I St. NW, Ste. 450
Washington, DC 20006
Phone: (202)785-6323
Fax: (202)315-2508
Free: 800-456-6323
Publisher's E-mail: washington.contact@oecd.org
Magazine examining resources devoted to research and development, and the output and impact of scientific and technological activity. **Freq:** Semiannual. **Print Method:** Offset. **ISSN:** 2304--2761 (print); **EISSN:** 2304--277X (electronic). **Alt. Formats:** Database. **URL:** http://www.oecd-ilibrary.org/science-and-technology/main-science-and-technology-indicators_2304277x; http://www.oecd.org/sti/msti.htm. **Remarks:** Advertising not accepted. **Circ:** (Not Reported).

6945 ■ Majallat al-Dirasat al-Filastiniyah
Institute for Palestine Studies
3501 M St. NW
Washington, DC 20007
Phone: (202)342-3990
Fax: (202)342-3927
Publisher's E-mail: ipsdc@palestine-studies.org
Journal covering the latest developments in Palestinian and Arab-Israeli affairs. **Founded:** 1990. **Freq:** Quarterly. **Key Personnel:** Dr. Ahmed Samih Khalidi, Contact. **Subscription Rates:** $30 Members; $20 Students; $50 Institutions. **URL:** http://www.palestine-studies.org. **Circ:** (Not Reported).

6946 ■ The Mankind Quarterly
Scott-Townsend Publishers
PO Box 34143
Washington, DC 20043
Phone: (202)371-2700
Fax: (202)371-1523
Publisher's E-mail: socecon@aol.com
Anthropology journal. **Founded:** 1961. **Freq:** Quarterly. **Print Method:** Offset. **Trim Size:** 8 1/2 x 6. **Cols./Page:** 1. **Col. Width:** 50 nonpareils. **Col. Depth:** 98 agate lines. **Key Personnel:** Brunetto Chiarelli, Contact; Peter Boev, Contact; Richard Lynn, Contact. **ISSN:** 0025-2344 (print). **Subscription Rates:** $55.50 Individuals print; $75.50 Other countries print; $148 Libraries print; $168 Libraries non-U.S., print; $208 Libraries print & electronic; $228 Libraries non-U.S., print & electronic; $168 Libraries electronic only. **URL:** http://www.mankindquarterly.org. **Ad Rates:** BW $200. **Remarks:** Accepts advertising. **Circ:** Paid ‡985, Non-paid ‡35.

6947 ■ Marine Technology Society Journal: The International, Interdisciplinary Journal Devoted to Ocean and Marine Engineering, Science and Policy
Marine Technology Society
1100 H St. NW, Ste. LL100
Washington, DC 20005
Phone: (202)717-8705
Fax: (202)347-4302
Publisher's E-mail: membership@mtsociety.org
Covering marine technology, ocean science, marine policy and education. **Freq:** 6/year. **Print Method:** Offset. **Trim Size:** 8 1/2 x 11. **Cols./Page:** 2. **Col. Width:** 42 nonpareils. **Col. Depth:** 136 agate lines. **Key Personnel:** Justin Manley, Board Member, Editor; Amy Morgante, Managing Editor; Richard Lawson, Executive Director. **ISSN:** 0025--3324 (print). **Subscription Rates:** $445 Institutions online only; $470 Institutions print and online; $140 U.S. print only; $155 Canada print only; $210 Other countries print only. **URL:** http://www.mtsociety.org/MTS_Journal_public/home.aspx. **Ad Rates:** 4C $725; BW $551.25. **Remarks:** color advertisements accepted only for cover. **Circ:** ‡3500.

6948 ■ Masonry Construction
DoveTale Publishers
1 Thomas Cir. NW
Washington, DC 20005
Phone: (202)339-0744
Fax: (202)785-1974
Free: 877-275-8647
Publisher's E-mail: hwmicustomerservice@hanleywood.com
Trade magazine. **Freq:** 10/yr. **Key Personnel:** Chari O'Rourke, Manager, Circulation; Shelby O. Mitchell, Managing Editor; Richard Yelton, Coordinator, Events. **ISSN:** 0898-6088 (print). **Subscription Rates:** $30 U.S.; $93 Other countries includes airmail; $39 Canada and Mexico; $64 Canada and Mexico 2 year; $162 Other countries 2 year, includes airmail; $46 U.S. 2 year. **URL:** http://www.masonryconstruction.com. **Formerly**: Aberdeen's Magazine of Masonry Construction. **Ad Rates:** BW $5,755; 4C $7,370. **Remarks:** Accepts advertising. **Circ:** Paid 27000.

6949 ■ Math Horizons
Mathematical Association of America
1529 18th St. NW
Washington, DC 20036-1358
Phone: (202)387-5200
Fax: (202)265-2384
Free: 800-741-9415
Publication E-mail: mathhorizons@maa.org
Magazine covering career guidance, essays, puzzles and articles on contemporary mathematics. **Freq:** Quarterly. **Key Personnel:** Steve Abbott, Editor; Bruce Torrence, Editor; David Richeson, Editor. **Subscription Rates:** $20 Members; $11 Students; $54 Nonmembers. **Alt. Formats:** Electronic publishing. **URL:** http://www.maa.org/press/periodicals/math-horizons. **Remarks:** Accepts advertising. **Circ:** (Not Reported).

6950 ■ Mathematics Magazine
Mathematical Association of America
1529 18th St. NW
Washington, DC 20036-1358
Phone: (202)387-5200
Fax: (202)265-2384
Free: 800-741-9415
Publisher's E-mail: maahq@maa.org
Magazine featuring informal mathematical articles and notes designed to appeal to faculty and students at the undergraduate level. Also contains a problems section, a reviews section, a news and letters section featuring early publication of problems and solutions from Olympiads and Putnam Competitions. **Freq:** 5/year. **Print Method:** Offset. **Cols./Page:** 1. **Col. Width:** 65 nonpareils. **Col. Depth:** 115 agate lines. **Key Personnel:** Walter Stromquist, Editor. **ISSN:** 0025--570X (print). **URL:** http://www.maa.org/publications/periodicals/mathematics-magazine. **Ad Rates:** BW $770; BW $820. **Remarks:** Accepts advertising. **Circ:** ‡8400.

6951 ■ Mediterranean Quarterly
Duke University Press
Mediterranean Affairs, Inc.
National Press Bldg., Ste. 984
14th & F St. NW
Washington, DC 20045
Phone: (202)662-7655
Fax: (202)662-7656
Publication E-mail: medquarterly@aol.com
Scholarly journal covering the Mediterranean region. **Freq:** Quarterly. **Key Personnel:** Selwa Roosevelt, Senior Editor. **ISSN:** 1047--4552 (print); **EISSN:** 1527--1935 (electronic). **Subscription Rates:** $30 Individuals; $16 Students a copy of a valid student ID is required. **URL:** http://www.dukeupress.edu/Mediterranean-Quarterly; http://mq.dukejournals.org. **Ad Rates:** BW

Circulation: ★ = AAM; △ or • = BPA; ♦ = CAC; ❑ = VAC; ⊕ = PO Statement; ‡ = Publisher's Report; Boldface figures = sworn; Light figures = estimated.

$250. **Remarks:** Accepts advertising. **Circ:** (Not Reported).

6952 ■ Metro Weekly
Jansi L.L.C.
1012 14th St. NW, Ste. 209
Washington, DC 20005
Phone: (202)638-6830
Fax: (202)638-6831
Publisher's E-mail: editor@metroweekly.com
Entertainment magazine for the gay and lesbian community. **Freq:** Weekly (Thurs.). **Key Personnel:** Randy Shulman, Editor-in-Chief, Publisher; Sean Bugg, Writer. **URL:** http://www.metroweekly.com. **Remarks:** Accepts advertising. **Circ:** (Not Reported).

6953 ■ Microbe Magazine
American Society for Microbiology
1752 N St. NW
Washington, DC 20036-2904
Phone: (202)942-9207
Fax: (202)942-9333
Publisher's E-mail: service@asmusa.org
Magazine of the American Society for Microbiology. **Freq:** Monthly. **Print Method:** Offset. **Trim Size:** 11 3/8 x 14 1/2. **Cols./Page:** 5. **Col. Width:** 27 nonpareils. **Col. Depth:** 189 agate lines. **Key Personnel:** Patrick N. Lacey, Managing Editor; Michael I. Goldberg, Executive Director; Moselio Schaechter, Board Member; Jonathan R. Beckwith, Board Member; Simon Silver, Board Member; Fernando Baquero, Board Member; Alan Weiner, Board Member. **ISSN:** 1558--7452 (print). **URL:** http://www.asmscience.org/content/journal/microbe. **Ad Rates:** BW $3,095. **Remarks:** Accepts advertising. **Circ:** ‡28893.

6954 ■ Microbiology and Molecular Biology Reviews
ASM Journals
1752 North St. NW
Washington, DC 20036
Phone: (202)737-3600
Fax: (202)942-9355
Publisher's E-mail: journals@asmusa.org
Broad-based review journal covering microbiology, immunology, and molecular and cellular biology. **Freq:** Quarterly. **Print Method:** Offset. Uses mats. **Trim Size:** 8 1/8 x 10 7/8. **Cols./Page:** 2. **Col. Width:** 42 nonpareils. **Col. Depth:** 127 agate lines. **Key Personnel:** Diana Downs, PhD, Editor-in-Chief; Stephen D. Bell, Editor. **ISSN:** 1092--2172 (print); **EISSN:** 1098--5557 (electronic). **Subscription Rates:** $138 Members print, U.S.; $146 Members Canada; $150 Other countries members; $722 Institutions online; $1213 Institutions print, U.S.; $1225 Institutions print, Canada; $1229 Institutions print, Europe; $1234 Institutions print, Latin America, rest of world; $85 Members online, worldwide; $147 Members print, Europe; $149 Members print, Latin America; $150 Members print, rest of the world. **Alt. Formats:** CD-ROM. **URL:** http://mmbr.asm.org. **Formerly:** Microbiological Reviews. **Ad Rates:** BW $1,840; 4C $3,160. **Remarks:** Advertising accepted; rates available upon request. **Circ:** Combined ‡18628, 11944.

6955 ■ Microbiology and Molecular Biology Reviews
American Society for Microbiology
1752 N St. NW
Washington, DC 20036-2904
Phone: (202)942-9207
Fax: (202)942-9333
Publisher's E-mail: journals@asmusa.org
Broad-based review journal covering microbiology, immunology, and molecular and cellular biology. **Freq:** Quarterly. **Print Method:** Offset. Uses mats. **Trim Size:** 8 1/8 x 10 7/8. **Cols./Page:** 2. **Col. Width:** 42 nonpareils. **Col. Depth:** 127 agate lines. **Key Personnel:** Diana Downs, PhD, Editor-in-Chief; Stephen D. Bell, Editor. **ISSN:** 1092--2172 (print); **EISSN:** 1098--5557 (electronic). **Subscription Rates:** $138 Members print, U.S.; $146 Members Canada; $150 Other countries members; $722 Institutions online; $1213 Institutions print, U.S.; $1225 Institutions print, Canada; $1229 Institutions print, Europe; $1234 Institutions print, Latin America, rest of world; $85 Members online, worldwide; $147 Members print, Europe; $149 Members print, Latin America; $150 Members print, rest of the world. **Alt. Formats:** CD-ROM. **URL:** http://mmbr.asm.org. **Formerly:** Microbiological Reviews. **Ad Rates:** BW $1,840; 4C $3,160. **Remarks:** Advertising accepted; rates available upon request. **Circ:** Combined ‡18628, 11944.

6956 ■ The Middle East Journal
Middle East Institute
1761 N St. NW
Washington, DC 20036
Phone: (202)785-1141
Fax: (202)331-8861
Publication E-mail: mej@mei.edu
Provides original and objective research and analysis, as well as source material, on the social, political, and economic aspects of the Middle East. **Freq:** Quarterly. **Print Method:** Offset. **Trim Size:** 6 1/2 x 9 1/2. **Cols./Page:** 1. **Col. Width:** 30 nonpareils. **Col. Depth:** 96 agate lines. **Key Personnel:** Michael Collins Dunn, Editor; Jacob Passel, Managing Editor. **ISSN:** 0026--3141 (print). **Subscription Rates:** $15 Individuals single issue; C$17 Individuals single issue; Included in membership. **Online:** Ingenta PLC. **URL:** http://www.mei.edu/middle-east-journal. **Ad Rates:** BW $1,000. **Remarks:** Advertising accepted; rates available upon request. **Circ:** Paid ‡2000.

6957 ■ Middle East Report
Middle East Research and Information Project
1344 T St. NW, No. 1
Washington, DC 20009
Phone: (202)223-3677
Fax: (202)223-3604
Freq: Quarterly. **ISSN:** 0899- 2851 (print). **Subscription Rates:** $42 U.S. and Canada; $60 Other countries; $77 Two years; $116 Other countries 2 years; $180 Institutions; $210 Institutions, other countries; $350 Institutions 2 years; $409 Institutions, other countries 2 years. **Alt. Formats:** Electronic publishing. **URL:** http://www.merip.org/mer. **Remarks:** Accepts advertising. **Circ:** 6000.

6958 ■ Middle East Research & Information Project
Middle East Research and Information Project
1344 T St. NW, No. 1
Washington, DC 20009
Phone: (202)223-3677
Fax: (202)223-3604
Publication focusing on Middle Eastern politics and societal issues. **Freq:** Quarterly. **Trim Size:** 8 1/4 x 10 3/4. **Key Personnel:** Joel Beinin, Editor; Chris Toensing, Executive Director. **ISSN:** 0899--2851 (print). **Subscription Rates:** $42 U.S. and Canada 1 year; $77 U.S. and Canada 2 years; $60 Other countries 1 year; $116 Other countries 2 years; $180 Institutions U.S and Canada, 1 year; $350 Institutions U.S and Canada, 2 years; $210 Institutions, other countries 1 year; $409 Institutions, other countries 2 years. **URL:** http://www.merip.org. **Remarks:** Advertising not accepted. **Circ:** 4000.

6959 ■ Military Law Review
U.S. Government Publishing Office
732 N Capitol St. NW
Washington, DC 20401-0001
Phone: (202)512-1800
Fax: (202)512-2104
Free: 866-512-1800
Publisher's E-mail: contactcenter@gpo.gov
Designed for use by military attorneys in connection with their official duties. Provides a forum for those interested in military law to share the products of their experience and research. **Freq:** Quarterly. **Print Method:** Letterpress. **Cols./Page:** 1. **Col. Width:** 50 nonpareils. **Col. Depth:** 96 agate lines. **ISSN:** 0026--4040 (print). **Subscription Rates:** $20 Individuals; $28 Other countries; $18 Single issue; $25.20 Other countries single copy. **Alt. Formats:** PDF. **URL:** http://www.loc.gov/rr/frd/Military_Law/Military-Law-Review-home.html. **Mailing address:** PO Box 979050, Saint Louis, MO 63197-9000. **Circ:** (Not Reported).

6960 ■ Mississippi Press
Newhouse Newspapers
1101 Connecticut Ave. NW, Ste. 300
Washington, DC 20036
Phone: (202)383-7850
General newspaper. **Freq:** Daily (eve.). **Print Method:** Offset. **Cols./Page:** 6. **Col. Width:** 2 1/16 inches. **Col. Depth:** 21 1/4 inches. **Key Personnel:** Ricky Matthews, Publisher; Gareth Clary, Executive Editor; Gary Raskett, Manager, Circulation. **Subscription Rates:** $9 Individuals per month. **URL:** http://www.gulflive.com/mississippipress/. **Ad Rates:** BW $1637.10; 4C $1902.10; SAU $12.84. **Remarks:** Accepts advertising. **Circ:** Mon.-Fri. ★**18,212**, Sun. ★**18,352**, Sat. ★**16,921**.

6961 ■ Molecular Endocrinology
Endocrine Society
2055 L St. NW, Ste. 600
Washington, DC 20036
Phone: (202)971-3636
Fax: (202)736-9705
Free: 888-363-6274
Publication E-mail: steveh@scherago.com
Peer-reviewed medical journal covering molecular biology for medical professionals. **Freq:** Monthly. **Print Method:** Web Offset. **Trim Size:** 8 3/8 x 10 7/8. **Cols./Page:** 2. **Key Personnel:** Stephen R. Hammes, PhD, Editor-in-Chief. **ISSN:** 0888--8809 (print); **EISSN:** 1944--9917 (electronic). **Subscription Rates:** $1775 Institutions online only; Included in membership. **URL:** http://press.endocrine.org/journal/mend. **Remarks:** Advertising accepted; rates available upon request. **Circ:** (Not Reported).

6962 ■ Moment Magazine: The Magazine of Jewish Culture and Opinion
Jewish Educational Ventures Inc.
4115 Wisconsin Ave. NW, Ste. 102
Washington, DC 20016
Phone: (202)363-6422
Fax: (202)362-2514
Free: 800-777-1005
Publication E-mail: editor@momentmag.com
Magazine for the Jewish community. **Freq:** Bimonthly. **Print Method:** Offset. **Trim Size:** 8 1/8 x 10 7/8. **Cols./Page:** 3. **Col. Width:** 16.5 picas. **Col. Depth:** 9 3/4 inches. **Key Personnel:** Nadine Epstein, Editor, Publisher. **ISSN:** 0099--0280 (print). **Subscription Rates:** $19.97 Individuals; $34.97 Out of country; $31.97 Two years; $61.97 Out of country 2 years. **URL:** http://www.momentmag.com. **Ad Rates:** BW $1200; 4C $1600. **Remarks:** Accepts advertising. **Circ:** ‡40000.

6963 ■ Monitor on Psychology
American Psychological Association
750 First St. NE
Washington, DC 20002-4242
Phone: (202)336-5600
Magazine of the APA. Reports on the science, profession, and social responsibility of psychology, including latest legislative developments affecting mental health, education, and research support. **Freq:** Monthly 1st week of the month of issue. **Print Method:** heatset web offset. **Trim Size:** 8 1/4 x 10 7/8. **ISSN:** 1529--4978 (print). **Subscription Rates:** $50 Nonmembers; $103 Individuals foreign, surface freight; $131 Individuals foreign, air mail; $93 Institutions; $195 Institutions surface freight; $223 Institutions air freight; $20 Single issue; Included in membership APA members and students. **URL:** http://www.apa.org/monitor. **Ad Rates:** BW $7995; 4C $1200. **Remarks:** Accepts advertising. **Circ:** Combined ‡96000.

6964 ■ Monthly Catalog of U.S. Government Publications
U.S. Government Publishing Office
732 N Capitol St. NW
Washington, DC 20401-0001
Phone: (202)512-1800
Fax: (202)512-2104
Free: 866-512-1800
Publisher's E-mail: contactcenter@gpo.gov
Bibliographic records of U.S. Government information products. Use it to link to Federal agency online resources or identify materials distributed to Federal depository libraries. **Freq:** Monthly. **Print Method:** Letterpress. **Cols./Page:** 2. **Col. Width:** 38 nonpareils. **Col. Depth:** 118 agate lines. **ISSN:** 0362--6830 (print). **Subscription Rates:** $65 Individuals; $81.25 Other countries; $6 Single issue; $7.50 Single issue in other countries. **URL:** http://catalog.gpo.gov/F?RN=472317236. **Mailing address:** PO Box 979050, Saint Louis, MO 63197-9000. **Circ:** (Not Reported).

6965 ■ Monthly Energy Review
U.S. Government Publishing Office
732 N Capitol St. NW
Washington, DC 20401-0001
Phone: (202)512-1800
Fax: (202)512-2104
Free: 866-512-1800

Publisher's E-mail: contactcenter@gpo.gov
Publication covering the petroleum, energy and mining industries. **Freq:** Monthly. **ISSN:** 0095--7356 (print). **Subscription Rates:** $147 Individuals; $205.80 Other countries; $27 Single issue; $37.80 Other countries single copy. **Alt. Formats:** PDF. **URL:** http://www.eia.doe.gov/emeu/mer/contents.html. **Mailing address:** PO Box 979050, Saint Louis, MO 63197-9000. **Circ:** (Not Reported).

6966 ■ Monthly Labor Review
U.S. Government Publishing Office
732 N Capitol St. NW
Washington, DC 20401-0001
Phone: (202)512-1800
Fax: (202)512-2104
Free: 866-512-1800
Publisher's E-mail: contactcenter@gpo.gov
Publication reporting on labor issues. Features reviews of developments in industrial relations, book reviews, and current labor statistics. **Founded:** 1915. **Freq:** Monthly. **Print Method:** Letterpress. **Cols./Page:** 2. **Col. Width:** 40 nonpareils. **Col. Depth:** 128 agate lines. **Key Personnel:** Terry L. Schau, Managing Editor; Michael D. Levi, Editor-in-Chief; William Parks, II, Executive Editor. **ISSN:** 0098-1818 (print). **Subscription Rates:** $49 Individuals; $68.60 Other countries; $15 Single issue; $21 Other countries single copy. **URL:** http://www.bls.gov/mlr. **Mailing address:** PO Box 979050, Saint Louis, MO 63197-9000. **Circ:** (Not Reported).

6967 ■ Monthly Statistics of International Trade
OECD Washington Center
1776 I St. NW, Ste. 450
Washington, DC 20006
Phone: (202)785-6323
Fax: (202)315-2508
Free: 800-456-6323
Publisher's E-mail: washington.contact@oecd.org
Statistical report on foreign trade of OECD countries. **Freq:** Monthly. **Print Method:** Offset. **Trim Size:** 7 7/8 x 10 5/8. **Cols./Page:** 1. **Col. Width:** 84 nonpareils. **Col. Depth:** 133 agate lines. **ISSN:** 1607--0623 (print); **EISSN:** 2074--398X (electronic). **Subscription Rates:** €158 Individuals online; $200 Individuals online; £124 Individuals online; ¥22500 Individuals online. **URL:** http://www.oecd-ilibrary.org/trade/data/monthly-statistics-of-international-trade_msit-data-en. **Formerly**: Monthly Statistics of Foreign Trade. **Circ:** (Not Reported).

6968 ■ Mortgage Banking Magazine: The Magazine of Real Estate Finance
Mortgage Bankers Association
1919 M St. NW, 5th Fl.
Washington, DC 20036
Phone: (202)557-2700
Free: 800-793-6222
Publisher's E-mail: membership@mba.org
Magazine of the real estate finance industry. **Freq:** Monthly. **Print Method:** Offset. **Trim Size:** 8 1/2 x 10 7/8. **Cols./Page:** 3. **Col. Width:** 26 nonpareils. **Col. Depth:** 140 agate lines. **Key Personnel:** Janet Hewitt, Editor-in-Chief; Barbara Van Allen, Publisher; Lesley Hall, Editor. **ISSN:** 0730--0212 (print). **USPS:** 446-910. **Subscription Rates:** $80 Members; $95 Nonmembers; $150 Two years members; $180 Two years nonmembers. **URL:** http://www.mortgagebankingmagazine.com. **Remarks:** Accepts advertising. **Circ:** Paid ★**9801**.

6969 ■ Mortgage Banking: The Magazine of Real Estate Finance
Mortgage Bankers Association
1919 M St. NW, 5th Fl.
Washington, DC 20036
Phone: (202)557-2700
Free: 800-793-6222
Publisher's E-mail: membership@mba.org
Freq: Monthly. **ISSN:** 0027--1241 (print). **Alt. Formats:** Download; PDF. **URL:** http://www.mba.org/news-research-and-resources/newsroom/mortgage-banking-magazine. **Remarks:** Advertising accepted; rates available upon request. **Circ:** (Not Reported).

6970 ■ MTS Journal
Marine Technology Society
1100 H St. NW, Ste. LL100
Washington, DC 20005
Phone: (202)717-8705
Fax: (202)347-4302
Publisher's E-mail: membership@mtsociety.org
Freq: Quarterly. **ISSN:** 0025- 3324 (print). **Subscription Rates:** $445 Institutions online only; $470 Institutions print and online; $210 Institutions print only within the USA (includes shipping). **URL:** http://www.mtsociety.org/MTS_Journal_public/. **Remarks:** Accepts advertising. **Circ:** 3,400.

6971 ■ Multifamily Executive
Hanley Wood Media Inc.
1 Thomas Cir. NW, Ste. 600
Washington, WA 20005
Phone: (202)452-0800
Fax: (202)785-1974
Magazine for multifamily housing market. **Freq:** Monthly. **Trim Size:** 8 x 10 7/8. **Key Personnel:** Rob Britt, Publisher; Jerry Ascierto, Editor-in-Chief; Warren Nesbitt, Group President. **Subscription Rates:** Free. **URL:** http://www.mfemediakit.com; http://www.multifamilyexecutive.com. **Ad Rates:** 4C $8690. **Remarks:** Accepts advertising. **Circ:** Combined △**20700**.

6972 ■ Multinational Monitor
Essential Information
PO Box 19405
Washington, DC 20036
Phone: (202)387-8030
Publication E-mail: monitor@essential.org
Magazine reporting on the impact of multinational corporations on labor, Third World development, women, and politics. **Freq:** Monthly. **Print Method:** Offset. **Trim Size:** 8 1/2 x 11. **Cols./Page:** 2. **Key Personnel:** Robert Weissman, Editor. **ISSN:** 0197--4637 (print). **Subscription Rates:** $19.95 Individuals for new subscribers; $34.95 Individuals non profit orgs.; $44.95 Individuals business; $29.95 Canada and Mexico for new subscribers; $45 Canada and Mexico nonprofit orgs.; $55 Canada and Mexico business; $45 Out of country for new subscribers; $50 Out of country nonprofit orgs.; $60 Out of country business; $50 Two years. **URL:** http://www.multinationalmonitor.org. **Ad Rates:** BW $700. **Remarks:** Accepts advertising. **Circ:** Paid ‡10000, Non-paid ‡2000.

6973 ■ Musical Mainstream
Library of Congress National Library Service for the Blind and Physically Handicapped
1291 Taylor St. NW
Washington, DC 20542-0002
Phone: (202)707-5100
Fax: (202)707-0712
Free: 800-424-8567
Publication E-mail: nlsm@loc.gov
General music magazine available only in braille and large print, and on audiotape. **Freq:** Quarterly. **Print Method:** Offset. **Cols./Page:** 2. **Col. Width:** 72 nonpareils. **Col. Depth:** 146 agate lines. **Key Personnel:** John S. Hanson, Editor, phone: (202)707-9254. **ISSN:** 0364--7501 (print). **Alt. Formats:** Braille; Large print. **URL:** http://www.loc.gov/nls/music/circular5.html. **Remarks:** Advertising not accepted. **Circ:** Non-paid ‡3600.

6974 ■ Nabe Outlook
National Association for Business Economics
1920 L St. NW, Ste. 300
Washington, DC 20036
Phone: (202)463-6223
Fax: (202)463-6239
Publisher's E-mail: nabe@nabe.com
Journal of National Association for Business Economists. **Freq:** Quarterly. **Key Personnel:** Tom Beers, Executive Director. **URL:** http://www.nabe.com. **Formerly**: Nabe Quarterly Surveys. **Remarks:** Advertising not accepted. **Circ:** (Not Reported).

6975 ■ NAHC Caring
National Association for Home Care and Hospice
228 7th St. SE
Washington, DC 20003
Phone: (202)547-7424
Fax: (202)547-3540
Publisher's E-mail: hospice@nahc.org
Magazine featuring cutting-edge trends in home care and hospice. **Freq:** Monthly. **ISSN:** 0738--467X (print). **URL:** http://www.nahc.org/caringmagazine; http://digitalcaringmagazine.nahc.org. **Remarks:** Accepts advertising. **Circ:** (Not Reported).

6976 ■ Nano Letters: A Journal Dedicated to Nanoscience and Nanotechnology
American Chemical Society
1155 16th St. NW
Washington, DC 20036
Phone: (202)872-4600
Free: 800-227-5558
Publication E-mail: nanoletters@chemistry.harvard.edu
Journal that reports on theory and practice of nanoscience and nanotechnology. **Freq:** Monthly. **Key Personnel:** A. Paul Alivisatos, Editor; Charles M. Lieber, Editor. **ISSN:** 1530--6984 (print); **EISSN:** 1530--6992 (electronic). **Subscription Rates:** Included in membership. **URL:** http://pubs.acs.org/journal/nalefd. **Circ:** (Not Reported).

6977 ■ NASPA Journal About Women in Higher Education
NASPA - Student Affairs Administrators in Higher Education
111 K St. NE, 10th Fl.
Washington, DC 20002
Phone: (202)265-7500
Publisher's E-mail: office@naspa.org
Freq: Semiannual. **ISSN:** 1940- 7882 (print). **Subscription Rates:** $50 Members; $75 Nonmembers. **URL:** http://www.naspa.org/publications/books/naspa-journal-about-women-in-higher-education. **Remarks:** Advertising not accepted. **Circ:** (Not Reported).

6978 ■ NASW News
National Association of Social Workers
750 1st St. NE, Ste. 800
Washington, DC 20002-4241
Phone: (202)408-8600
Fax: (202)336-8313
Free: 800-742-4089
Publisher's E-mail: membership@naswdc.org
Newspaper providing information for practitioners, administrators, researchers, faculty and students. **Freq:** 10/year. **ISSN:** 0027- 6022 (print). **Subscription Rates:** Included in membership; $20 /year for student members; $35 Individuals /year for nonmembers; $35 Institutions. **URL:** http://www.naswpress.org/publications/news/index.html; http://www.socialworkers.org. **Remarks:** Accepts advertising. **Circ:** (Not Reported).

6979 ■ National Alliance
National Alliance of Postal and Federal Employees
1628 11th St. NW
Washington, DC 20001-5008
Phone: (202)939-6325
Fax: (202)939-6392
Publisher's E-mail: info@napfe.org
Magazine for postal and federal employees. **Freq:** Monthly. **Print Method:** Offset. **Trim Size:** 8 1/2 x 11. **Cols./Page:** 3. **Col. Width:** 28 nonpareils. **Col. Depth:** 133 agate lines. **Key Personnel:** James M. McGee, President; Ernestine Taylor, Editor. **ISSN:** 0027--8513 (print). **Subscription Rates:** $20 Individuals; $2 Single issue; $20 /year; $2 /copy. **Alt. Formats:** PDF. **URL:** http://www.napfe.com/page.php?pid=41. **Remarks:** Accepts advertising. **Circ:** ‡14700, 15000.

6980 ■ National Council
National Council for Behavioral Health
1400 K St. NW, Ste. 400
Washington, DC 20005
Phone: (202)684-7457
Publisher's E-mail: communications@thenationalcouncil.org
Freq: Quarterly. **URL:** http://www.thenationalcouncil.org/consulting-best-practices/magazine/. **Remarks:** Advertising not accepted. **Circ:** (Not Reported).

6981 ■ National Environmental Enforcement Journal
National Association of Attorneys General
2030 M St. NW, 8th Fl.
Washington, DC 20036
Phone: (202)326-6000
Publisher's E-mail: feedback@naag.org
Trade journal covering law and environmental enforcement. **Freq:** 24/yr. **Key Personnel:** Paula Cotter, Editor. **URL:** http://www.naag.org/neej.php. **Remarks:** Advertising not accepted. **Circ:** Controlled 750.

6982 ■ The National Fragile X Foundation Quarterly
National Fragile X Foundation

Circulation: ★ = AAM; △ or • = BPA; ♦ = CAC; ❑ = VAC; ⊕ = PO Statement; ‡ = Publisher's Report; Boldface figures = sworn; Light figures = estimated.

2100 M St. NW, Ste. 170
Washington, DC 20037-1233
Fax: (202)747-6208
Free: 800-688-8765
Publisher's E-mail: natlfx@fragilex.org
Freq: Quarterly. **Subscription Rates:** included in membership dues. **Mailing address:** PO Box 302, Washington, DC 20037. **Remarks:** Advertising not accepted. **Circ:** 3500.

6983 ■ National Geographic Adventure
National Geographic Society
1145 17th St. NW
Washington, DC 20036-4688
Phone: (202)862-8638
Free: 800-373-1717
Consumer magazine covering sports, fitness, travel, recreation and leisure. **Freq:** Bimonthly. **ISSN:** 1523--6226 (print). **Subscription Rates:** $12 Individuals digital; $15 Individuals print; $19 Individuals print & online. **URL:** http://www.nationalgeographic.com/adventure; http://www.nationalgeographic.com/adventure/0603/features/peru.html. **Remarks:** Accepts advertising. **Circ:** Paid ★506835.

6984 ■ National Geographic: Official Journal of the National Geographic Society
National Geographic Society
1145 17th St. NW
Washington, DC 20036-4688
Phone: (202)862-8638
Free: 800-373-1717
Magazine designed to teach individuals about history, culture, the environment, science, and themselves. **Freq:** Monthly. **Print Method:** Offset. **Trim Size:** 6 3/4 x 10. **Cols./Page:** 2. **Col. Width:** 32 nonpareils. **Col. Depth:** 122 agate lines. **Key Personnel:** Laurin Ensslin, Manager. **ISSN:** 0027--9358 (print). **Subscription Rates:** $15 Individuals. **URL:** http://www.nationalgeographic.com. **Remarks:** Accepts advertising. **Circ:** Paid ★5431117.

6985 ■ National Geographic Traveler
National Geographic Society
1145 17th St. NW
Washington, DC 20036-4688
Phone: (202)862-8638
Free: 800-373-1717
Publication E-mail: traveler@ngs.org
Travel magazine emphasizing practical information about U.S. and foreign destinations. **Freq:** Bimonthly. **Print Method:** Web Offset. **Trim Size:** 8 x 10 1/2. **Cols./Page:** 4. **Col. Width:** 15 picas. **Col. Depth:** 57 picas. **Key Personnel:** Keith Bellows, Editor-in-Chief. **ISSN:** 0747--0932 (print). **Subscription Rates:** $10 Individuals print; $15 Individuals print + ipad edition; $8 Individuals digital only. **URL:** http://travel.nationalgeographic.com/travel/traveler-magazine. **Ad Rates:** BW $75,600; 4C $84,000. **Remarks:** Accepts advertising. **Circ:** Paid 742575, 700000.

6986 ■ National Grange-Journal of Proceedings
National Grange
1616 H St. NW
Washington, DC 20006
Phone: (202)628-3507
Fax: (202)347-1091
Free: 888-447-2643
Publisher's E-mail: info@nationalgrange.org
Freq: Annual. **URL:** http://www.nationalgrange.org/journal-of-proceedings. **Remarks:** Advertising not accepted. **Circ:** (Not Reported).

6987 ■ The National Interest
National Interest Inc.
1615 L St. NW, Ste. 1250
Washington, DC 20036
Free: 800-344-7952
Publication E-mail: editor@nationalinterest.org
Journal covering foreign policy. **Founded:** 1985. **Freq:** Bimonthly. **Print Method:** Web. **Trim Size:** 7 x 10. **Cols./Page:** 2. **Col. Width:** 2 3/4 inches. **Col. Depth:** 10 inches. **Key Personnel:** Robert Merry, Editor; Paul Saunders, Associate Publisher; Dimitri K. Simes, Chief Executive Officer, Publisher. **ISSN:** 0884-9382 (print). **Subscription Rates:** $29.95 Individuals print; $39.95 Two years print; $19.95 Individuals electronic edition; $24.95 Two years electronic edition; $49.95 Other countries print; $79.95 Other countries 2 years; print. **URL:** http://www.nationalinterest.org. **Ad Rates:** BW $1,000. **Remarks:** Advertising accepted; rates available upon request. **Circ:** (Not Reported).

6988 ■ National Jesuit News
National Jesuit News
1424 16th St. NW, Ste. 300
Washington, DC 20036
Fax: (202)328-9212
Publisher's E-mail: outreach@jesuit.org
Newspaper reporting on the activities of American Jesuits and national and international issues affecting their ministries. **Founded:** 1971. **Freq:** Monthly. **Print Method:** Offset. **Trim Size:** 11 1/4 x 14 5/8. **Cols./Page:** 4. **Col. Width:** 15 picas. **Col. Depth:** 13 3/8 inches. **Key Personnel:** Kaitlyn McCarthy, Editor; Tricia Steadman Jump, Managing Editor. **ISSN:** 0199-0284 (print). **URL:** http://www.jesuit.org/. **Circ:** Non-paid ‡6000.

6989 ■ National Journal: The Weekly on Politics and Government
National Journal Group Inc.
The Watergate
600 New Hampshire Ave. NW
Washington, DC 20037
Phone: (202)739-8400
Fax: (202)833-8069
Free: 800-613-6701
Publisher's E-mail: service@nationaljournal.com
National news magazine. **Freq:** Weekly. **Print Method:** Offset. **Trim Size:** 8 1/2 x 11. **Cols./Page:** 3. **Col. Width:** 25 nonpareils. **Col. Depth:** 126 agate lines. **Key Personnel:** Amanda Cormier, Managing Editor; Tim Grieve, Editor-in-Chief, President; Richard Just, Editor; Kristin Roberts, Managing Editor; Bob Moser, Senior Editor; Ronald Brownstein, Director, Editorial; Ron Fournier, Director, Editorial, Columnist. **ISSN:** 0360--4217 (print). **Subscription Rates:** $1499 Individuals. **URL:** http://www.nationaljournal.com. **Ad Rates:** BW $11,760; 4C $16,500. **Remarks:** Accepts advertising. **Circ:** (Not Reported).

6990 ■ National Parks: The Magazine of the National Parks and Conservation Association
National Parks Conservation Association
777 6th St. NW, Ste. 700
Washington, DC 20036
Phone: (202)223-6722
Fax: (202)454-3333
Free: 800-628-7275
Publication E-mail: npmag@npca.org
Magazine on issues affecting our National Parks. **Freq:** Quarterly. **Print Method:** Web offset. **Trim Size:** 8 x 10 1/2. **Cols./Page:** 2. **Col. Width:** 13.5 picas. **Col. Depth:** 127 agate lines. **Key Personnel:** Tom Kiernan, President. **ISSN:** 0276--8186 (print). **Subscription Rates:** $15 Individuals introductory offer; Included in membership. **URL:** http://www.npca.org/news/magazine. **Ad Rates:** BW $11,500; 4C $14,700. **Remarks:** Accepts advertising. **Circ:** Paid 348951.

6991 ■ National Prison Project Journal
American Civil Liberties Union National Prison Project
915 15th St. NW, 7th Fl.
Washington, DC 20005
Phone: (202)393-4930
Fax: (202)393-4931
Freq: Semiannual. **ISSN:** 0748--2655 (print). **Subscription Rates:** $35 /year for non-inmates; $2 /year for inmates. **URL:** http://www.aclu.org/national-prison-project-journal-spring-summer-2012. **Remarks:** Advertising not accepted. **Circ:** (Not Reported).

6992 ■ National Tax Journal
National Tax Association
725 15th St. NW, No. 600
Washington, DC 20005-2109
Phone: (202)737-3325
Fax: (202)737-7308
Publication E-mail: ntj@rice.edu
Freq: Quarterly March, June, September and December. **Key Personnel:** William M. Gentry, Editor; Rosanne Altshuler, Advisor; Dorey Zodrow, Managing Editor; William M. Gentry, Editor. **ISSN:** 0028--0283 (print). **Subscription Rates:** $110 Individuals /year; $350 Libraries /year; $365 Libraries /year - foreign; $120 Other countries /year. **URL:** http://www.ntanet.org/publications/national-tax-journal.html; http://ntanet.org/publications/national-tax-journal.html. **Remarks:** Advertising not accepted. **Circ:** 3500.

6993 ■ National Trust Forum: The Journal of the National Trust for Historic Preservation
National Trust for Historic Preservation
2600 Virginia Ave. NW, Ste. 1100
Washington, DC 20037
Phone: (202)588-6000
Fax: (202)588-6038
Free: 800-944-6847
Publication E-mail: forum@nthp.org
Journal covering historic preservation. **Freq:** Quarterly. **Print Method:** Offset Press. **Trim Size:** 6 x 9. **Key Personnel:** Stephanie Meeks, President; Alison Hinchman, Program Manager; Valecia Crisafulli, Director; Byrd Wood, Manager; Priya Chhaya, Assistant; Nicole Vann, Administrator; Ron Woods, Business Manager. **ISSN:** 0893--9403 (print). **USPS:** 001-715. **Subscription Rates:** $115 Individuals; $140 Individuals international; $95 Individuals non-U.S. addresses only; $75 Students proof of current, full-time student status require. **URL:** http://www.preservationnation.org. **Formerly:** Historic Preservation Forum. **Remarks:** Advertising not accepted. **Circ:** Paid 4000.

6994 ■ Nation's Building News
Nations Building News
1201 15th St. NW
Washington, DC 20005
Phone: (202)266-8200
Fax: (202)266-8400
Free: 800-368-5242
Publication E-mail: editor@nationsbuildingnews.com
Trade magazine (tabloid) covering home building and all related industries. **Founded:** 1985. **Freq:** Weekly (Mon.). **Print Method:** Offset. **Trim Size:** 10 1/4 x 14. **Cols./Page:** 4. **Col. Width:** 27 nonpareils. **Col. Depth:** 196 agate lines. **ISSN:** 8750-6580 (print). **URL:** http://www.nahb.org/page.aspx/category/sectionID=191. **Ad Rates:** BW $3,800; 4C $4,880. **Remarks:** Accepts advertising. **Circ:** Non-paid 235000.

6995 ■ The Nation's Health
American Public Health Association
800 I St. NW
Washington, DC 20001
Phone: (202)777-2742
Fax: (202)777-2534
Publisher's E-mail: comments@apha.org
Public health policy, research and legislation news. **Freq:** 10/year with combined issues in May/June and November/December. **Print Method:** Offset. **Trim Size:** Tabloid. **Cols./Page:** 5. **Col. Width:** 1 5/8 inches. **Col. Depth:** 76 picas. **Key Personnel:** Ashell R. Alston, Director, Advertising, phone: (202)777-2470; Michele Late, Executive Editor, phone: (202)777-2438; Charlotte Tucker, Senior Editor. **ISSN:** 0028--0496 (print). **Subscription Rates:** $78 U.S. and Canada print only; $109 U.S. and Canada print + online; $161 Institutions print + online, U.S./canada; $99 Individuals online only; $125 U.S. and Canada online only; $130 Institutions online only; $94 Institutions, other countries print; $125 Other countries print & online; $177 Institutions, other countries print & online. **URL:** http://thenationshealth.aphapublications.org. **Remarks:** Accepts advertising. **Circ:** Combined ‡28000, 33000.

6996 ■ Nature
Nature Publishing Group
968 National Press Bldg.
529 14 St. NW
Washington, DC 20045-1938
Phone: (202)737-2355
Fax: (202)628-1609
Publisher's E-mail: registration@natureny.com
International Journal of Science. **Founded:** Nov. 04, 1869. **Freq:** Weekly. **Print Method:** Web Offset. **Trim Size:** 8 1/4 x 11. **Cols./Page:** 5. **Col. Width:** 2 3/8 inches. **ISSN:** 0028-0836 (print). **Subscription Rates:** $199 Individuals print and online; $338 Two years print and online. **URL:** http://www.nature.com/nature/index.html. **Remarks:** Accepts advertising. **Circ:** 52836, ‡65955.

6997 ■ Naval Aviation News
U.S. Government Publishing Office
Dept. of the Navy, Naval Historical Ctr.
Naval Warfare Division
Washington Navy Yard
1242 10th St. SE
Washington, DC 20374-5059

Publisher's E-mail: contactcenter@gpo.gov
Magazine presenting articles on all phases of Navy and Marine air activity. **Founded:** 1927. **Freq:** Bimonthly. **Print Method:** Letterpress and Offset. Uses mats. **Cols./Page:** 3. **Col. Width:** 26 nonpareils. **Col. Depth:** 116 agate lines. **ISSN:** 0028-1417 (print). **Subscription Rates:** $23 Individuals. **Alt. Formats:** PDF. **URL:** http://www.history.navy.mil/nan/backissues/newbackissues.htm. **Circ:** (Not Reported).

6998 ■ Navy Medicine
U.S. Government Publishing Office
732 N Capitol St. NW
Washington, DC 20401-0001
Phone: (202)512-1800
Fax: (202)512-2104
Free: 866-512-1800
Publisher's E-mail: contactcenter@gpo.gov
Medical journal (military). **Freq:** Quarterly. **Print Method:** Letterpress. **Cols./Page:** 2. **Col. Width:** 40 nonpareils. **Col. Depth:** 112 agate lines. **ISSN:** 0895--8211 (print). **Subscription Rates:** $26 Individuals; $6.50 U.S. single copy; $9.10 Other countries single copy. **URL:** http://bookstore.gpo.gov/products/sku/708-054-00000-3. **Mailing address:** PO Box 979050, Saint Louis, MO 63197-9000. **Remarks:** Accepts advertising. **Circ:** (Not Reported).

6999 ■ NCBW Forum
National Center for Bicycling and Walking
1612 K St. NW, Ste. 802
Washington, DC 20006
Phone: (202)223-3621
Publisher's E-mail: info@bikewalk.org
Freq: Quarterly. **URL:** http://www.bikewalk.org/forum.php. **Remarks:** Advertising not accepted. **Circ:** (Not Reported).

7000 ■ NCGR Journal
National Council for GeoCosmic Research
c/o Alvin Burns, Executive Secretary
1351 Maryland Ave. NE, Apt. B
Washington, DC 20002-4439
Technical journal covering cosmology and astrology. **Freq:** Semiannual. **Print Method:** Offset. **Trim Size:** 8 1/2 x 11. **Cols./Page:** 2. **Col. Width:** 3 1/4 inches. **Col. Depth:** 9 1/4 inches. **Key Personnel:** Arlene Nimark, Manager, Advertising, phone: (718)377-0482; Ronnie Gale Dreyer, Editor, phone: (212)799-9187. **ISSN:** 1080-6423 (print). **Subscription Rates:** $7 Single issue back issue depending on size; $10 Single issue back issue depending on size. **URL:** http://www.geocosmic.org; http://geocosmic.org/publications/journals. **Ad Rates:** BW $350. **Remarks:** Accepts advertising. **Circ:** Paid 3100.

7001 ■ NCVC Networks
National Center for Victims of Crime
2000 M St. NW, Ste. 480
Washington, DC 20036
Phone: (202)467-8700
Fax: (202)467-8701
Freq: Quarterly. **Subscription Rates:** included in membership dues; $5 for nonmembers. **Alt. Formats:** PDF. **URL:** http://identitytheftnetwork.org/. **Remarks:** Advertising not accepted. **Circ:** (Not Reported).

7002 ■ NEA News
OECD Washington Center
1776 I St. NW, Ste. 450
Washington, DC 20006
Phone: (202)785-6323
Fax: (202)315-2508
Free: 800-456-6323
Publisher's E-mail: washington.contact@oecd.org
Journal of the Organisation for Economic Cooperation and Development Nuclear Energy Agency. **Freq:** Semiannual. **Key Personnel:** William D. Magwood, Editor. **ISSN:** 1605-9581 (print). **Subscription Rates:** £31 Individuals. **URL:** http://www.oecd-nea.org/nea-news. **Circ:** (Not Reported).

7003 ■ NEA Today
National Education Association
1201 16th St. NW
Washington, DC 20036-3290
Phone: (202)833-4000
Fax: (202)822-7974
Education magazine. **Freq:** 8/year. **Print Method:** Offset. **Trim Size:** 10 x 14. **Cols./Page:** 4. **Col. Width:** 28 nonpareils. **Col. Depth:** 187 agate lines. **Key Personnel:** Steven Grant, Editor. **Subscription Rates:** Included in membership; $50 Nonmembers /year. **URL:** http://www.nea.org/home/1814.htm; http://neatoday.org. **Ad Rates:** BW $33,035; 4C $37,795; PCI $895. **Remarks:** Accepts advertising. **Circ:** 2700000, 2400000, 2700000.

7004 ■ Neuropsychology
American Psychological Association
750 1st St. NE
Washington, DC 20002-4242
Phone: (202)336-5500
Free: 800-374-2721
Journal focusing on basic and clinical research, the integration of basic and applied findings, and improving practice in the field of neuropsychology. **Freq:** Bimonthly beginning in January. **Key Personnel:** Gregory G. Brown, Editor; Vicki Anderson, Associate Editor. **ISSN:** 0894-4105 (print); **EISSN:** 1931-1559 (electronic). **Subscription Rates:** $120 Members domestic; $72 Students domestic; $240 Nonmembers domestic; $699 Institutions domestic; $148 Members outside U.S., surface; $100 Students, other countries surface; $282 Nonmembers outside U.S., surface; $776 Institutions, other countries surface; $176 Members outside U.S., air mail; $128 Students outside U.S., airmail; $304 Nonmembers outside U.S., airmail; $800 Institutions, other countries air mail. **URL:** http://www.apa.org/pubs/journals/neu/index.aspx. **Ad Rates:** BW $410; 4C $1,385. **Remarks:** Accepts advertising. **Circ:** 2100.

7005 ■ New Directions for Evaluation
American Evaluation Association
2025 M St. NW, Ste. 800
Washington, DC 20036
Phone: (202)367-1166
Fax: (202)367-2166
Publisher's E-mail: info@eval.org
Journal featuring all aspects of evaluation with an emphasis on presenting timely and thoughtful reflections on leading-edge issues of evaluation theory, practice, methods, the profession and the organizational, cultural and societal context within which evaluation occurs. **Freq:** Quarterly. **Key Personnel:** Paul R. Brandon, Editor-in-Chief, phone: (808)956-4928. **Subscription Rates:** Included in membership. **URL:** http://www.eval.org/p/cm/ld/fid=48. **Remarks:** Advertising not accepted. **Circ:** (Not Reported).

7006 ■ The New Republic: A Journal of Politics and the Arts
The New Republic L.L.C.
1331 H St. NW, Ste. 700
Washington, DC 20005
Phone: (202)508-4444
Fax: (202)628-9380
Free: 800-827-1289
Publication E-mail: tnrcustserv@cdsfulfillment.com
Journal featuring current events comments and reviews. **Freq:** Weekly. **Print Method:** Offset. **Trim Size:** 8 x 10 1/2. **Cols./Page:** 3. **Col. Width:** 2 1/4 inches. **Col. Depth:** 134 agate lines. **Key Personnel:** Martin Peretz, Editor-in-Chief; Franklin Foer, Editor; Richard Just, Editor. **ISSN:** 0028--6583 (print). **Subscription Rates:** $19.97 Individuals 1 year; $14.97 Individuals 6 months; $34.97 Two years. **URL:** http://www.newrepublic.com. **Ad Rates:** BW $7,980; 4C $9,960. **Remarks:** Accepts advertising. **Circ:** ‡51757.

7007 ■ The News Media & the Law
Reporters Committee for Freedom of the Press
1156 15th St. NW, Ste. 1250
Washington, DC 20005-1779
Phone: (202)795-9300
Free: 800-336-4243
Publisher's E-mail: info@rcfp.org
Freq: Quarterly Winter, Spring, Summer, Fall. **Print Method:** Offset. **Trim Size:** 8 1/8 x 10 7/8. **Cols./Page:** 3. **Col. Width:** 13.5 picas. **Col. Depth:** 693 picas. **Key Personnel:** Lucy A. Dalglish, Contact; Gregg Leslie, Executive Director; Nicole Lozare, Managing Editor. **ISSN:** 0149--0737 (print). **Subscription Rates:** Free. **Alt. Formats:** PDF. **URL:** http://www.rcfp.org/magazine-archive. **Remarks:** Advertising not accepted. **Circ:** Paid ‡1000, Non-paid ‡1000, 2,000.

7008 ■ NICLC Perspective on Aging
National Institute on Community-Based Long-Term Care
National Council on Aging
1901 L St. NW, 4th Fl.
Washington, DC 20036
Phone: (202)479-1200
Fax: (202)479-0735
Publisher's E-mail: cha@ncoa.org
Freq: Periodic. **URL:** http://nihseniorhealth.gov/longtermcare/planningforlongtermcare/01.html. **Remarks:** Advertising not accepted. **Circ:** (Not Reported).

7009 ■ The Northwest Current
The Current Newspapers Inc.
5185 MacArthur Blvd. NW, Ste. 102
Washington, DC 20016-3349
Phone: (202)244-7223
Fax: (202)363-9850
Publication E-mail: current@crols.com
Community newspaper. **Freq:** Weekly (Wed.). **Print Method:** Offset. **Cols./Page:** 5. **Col. Width:** 11.5 picas. **Col. Depth:** 13 inches. **URL:** http://www.currentnewspapers.com/archiveweek.php?n=1&year=2013. **Remarks:** Advertising accepted; rates available upon request. **Circ:** (Not Reported).

7010 ■ Nurse Leader
American Organization of Nurse Executives
Two City Ctr., Ste. 400
800 10th St. NW
Washington, DC 20001
Phone: (202)626-2240
Fax: (202)638-5499
Publisher's E-mail: support@elsevier.com
Journal publishing articles on the vision, skills, and tools needed by nurses currently aspiring to leadership positions. **Freq:** Bimonthly. **Print Method:** Sheetfed. **Trim Size:** 8 1/8 x 10 7/8. **Key Personnel:** Roxane B. Spitzer, PhD, Editor-in-Chief; Mary C. Tonges, Board Member; Frank Shaffer, Board Member; Katherine Vestal, Board Member; Rhonda Anderson, Board Member; Jim Cato, Board Member; Lisa Johnson, Manager. **ISSN:** 1541--4612 (print). **Subscription Rates:** $102 Individuals online and print; $164 Canada online and print; $152 Other countries online and print; $85 Individuals online only. **URL:** http://www.nurseleader.com; http://www.journals.elsevier.com/nurse-leader. **Ad Rates:** BW $1,505; 4C $1,620. **Remarks:** Advertising accepted; rates available upon request. **Circ:** ‡7595, 8700.

7011 ■ Nursing for Women's Health
Association of Women's Health, Obstetric and Neonatal Nurses
2000 L St. NW, Ste. 740
Washington, DC 20036-4912
Phone: (202)261-2400
Fax: (202)728-0575
Free: 800-673-8499
Publisher's E-mail: customerservice@awhonn.org
Freq: Bimonthly. **Key Personnel:** Mary C. Brucker, Editor. **ISSN:** 1751--4851 (print); **EISSN:** 1751--486X (electronic). **URL:** http://onlinelibrary.wiley.com/journal/10.1111/(ISSN)1751-486X/issues. **Remarks:** Accepts advertising. **Circ:** 24000.

7012 ■ Nutrition Reviews
International Life Sciences Institute
1156 15th Street NW, Ste. 200
Washington, DC 20005
Phone: (202)659-0074
Fax: (202)659-3859
Publisher's E-mail: info@ilsi.org
Journal providing information on developments in nutrition, dietetics, food science, and nutrition science policy. **Founded:** 1942. **Freq:** Monthly. **Print Method:** Offset. **Trim Size:** 8 1/6 x 11. **Cols./Page:** 2. **Col. Width:** 32 nonpareils. **Col. Depth:** 112 agate lines. **Key Personnel:** Naomi Fukagawa, MD, Editor-in-Chief; Allison Worden, Managing Editor. **ISSN:** 0029-6643 (print). **Subscription Rates:** $237 Individuals print + online; $496 Institutions print + online; $430 Institutions online; €230 Individuals European, print + online; £398 Institutions European, print + online; €346 Institutions European, online; £154 Other countries print + online; $611 Institutions, other countries print + online; $532 Institutions, other countries online. **URL:** http://www.ilsi.org/Pages/

Circulation: ★ = AAM; △ or • = BPA; ♦ = CAC; ❑ = VAC; ⊕ = PO Statement; ‡ = Publisher's Report; Boldface figures = sworn; Light figures = estimated.

NutritionReviews.aspx; http://onlinelibrary.wiley.com/journal/10.1111/(ISSN)1753-4887. **Remarks:** Advertising accepted; rates available upon request. **Circ:** ‡6,500.

7013 ■ OD Practitioner
Organization Development Network
2025 M St. NW, Ste. 800
Washington, DC 20036
Phone: (202)367-1127
Fax: (202)367-2127
Publisher's E-mail: odnetwork@odnetwork.org
Journal containing information for OD practitioners. **Freq:** Quarterly. **Key Personnel:** John Vogelsang, Editor-in-Chief; Marilyn Blair, Contact. **URL:** http://www.odnetwork.org/?. **Ad Rates:** BW $1,500. **Remarks:** Accepts advertising. **Circ:** (Not Reported).

7014 ■ OD Seasonings
Organization Development Network
2025 M St. NW, Ste. 800
Washington, DC 20036
Phone: (202)367-1127
Fax: (202)367-2127
Publisher's E-mail: odnetwork@odnetwork.org
Journal containing articles that clearly express a point of view or document significant learning based on many years of relevant practice, offering less experienced practitioners the benefit of a well-integrated, deeply experienced professional perspective. **Freq:** Quarterly. **Subscription Rates:** for members only. **URL:** http://www.odnetwork.org/page/SamplesSeasons/OD-Seasonings-Samples.htm. **Remarks:** Advertising not accepted. **Circ:** (Not Reported).

7015 ■ OECD Economic Outlook
OECD Washington Center
1776 I St. NW, Ste. 450
Washington, DC 20006
Phone: (202)785-6323
Fax: (202)315-2508
Free: 800-456-6323
Publisher's E-mail: washington.contact@oecd.org
Periodical publishing projections of the Economics Department of the Organisation for Economic Cooperation and Development. **Freq:** Semiannual. **ISSN:** 0474--5574 (print). **Subscription Rates:** €72 Individuals ebook; $105 Individuals ebook; £65 Individuals ebook; ¥8700 Individuals ebook; $1300 Individuals ebook. **Alt. Formats:** E-book; PDF. **URL:** http://www.oecdbookshop.org/en/browse/title-detail/OECD-Economic-Outlook-Volume-2015-Issue-1/?K=5JZ0ZBPLMMXS. **Circ:** (Not Reported).

7016 ■ OECD Economic Studies
OECD Washington Center
1776 I St. NW, Ste. 450
Washington, DC 20006
Phone: (202)785-6323
Fax: (202)315-2508
Free: 800-456-6323
Publisher's E-mail: washington.contact@oecd.org
Journal containing articles on macroeconomics and economic policy in international and national settings. **Freq:** Semiannual. **Print Method:** Offset. **ISSN:** 1995--2856 (print); **EISSN:** 1995--2848 (electronic). **URL:** http://www.oecd-ilibrary.org/economics/oecd-journal-economic-studies_19952856. **Remarks:** Advertising not accepted. **Circ:** (Not Reported).

7017 ■ OECD Economic Surveys
OECD Washington Center
1776 I St. NW, Ste. 450
Washington, DC 20006
Phone: (202)785-6323
Fax: (202)315-2508
Free: 800-456-6323
Publisher's E-mail: washington.contact@oecd.org
Journal containing annual reviews of member countries' economies. **Freq:** 18/yr. **ISSN:** 0376-6438 (print). **Subscription Rates:** €805 Individuals online access plus print; $1060 Individuals online access plus print; £635 Individuals online access plus print; ¥102000 Individuals online access plus print; $13290 Individuals online access plus print. **Alt. Formats:** PDF. **URL:** http://www.oecdbookshop.org/oecd/display.asp?k=sub-10011s1&CID=&LANG=EN&ds=%20oecdeconomicsurveys. **Circ:** (Not Reported).

7018 ■ OECD Journal on Budgeting
OECD Washington Center
1776 I St. NW, Ste. 450
Washington, DC 20006
Phone: (202)785-6323
Fax: (202)315-2508
Free: 800-456-6323
Publisher's E-mail: washington.contact@oecd.org
Journal providing information on institutional budgeting and allocation and management of resources. **Freq:** 3/year. **Key Personnel:** Jon R. Blondal, Editor-in-Chief. **ISSN:** 1608-7143 (print); **EISSN:** 1681-2336 (electronic). **Subscription Rates:** €259 Individuals print and online; $344 Individuals print and online; £207 Individuals print and online; ¥36300 Individuals print and online; $4340 Individuals print and online. **Alt. Formats:** PDF. **URL:** http://www.oecd.org/gov/budgeting/oecdjournalonbudgeting.htm; http://www.oecd-ilibrary.org/governance/oecd-journal-on-budgeting_16812336. **Circ:** (Not Reported).

7019 ■ The Officer
Reserve Officers Association
1 Constitution Ave. NE
Washington, DC 20002
Phone: (202)479-2200
Fax: (202)547-1641
Free: 800-809-9448
Publisher's E-mail: info@roa.org
Magazine for active and reserve officers of all uniformed services. **Freq:** 10/year. **Print Method:** Web offset. **Trim Size:** 8 1/4 x 10 3/4. **Cols./Page:** 3. **Col. Width:** 13.5 picas. **Col. Depth:** 58 picas. **Key Personnel:** Maj. Gen. David Brokel, Executive Director, phone: (202)646-7705; Chris Prawdzik, Editor. **ISSN:** 0030--0268 (print). **Subscription Rates:** $12 Individuals; $1.15 Single issue. **URL:** http://www.roa.org/publications. **Ad Rates:** BW $3,825; 4C $5,500; PCI $110. **Remarks:** Accepts advertising. **Circ:** 65000, 80000.

7020 ■ OPASTCO Roundtable: The Magazine of Ideas for Small Telephone Companies
Organization for the Promotion and Advancement of Small Telecommunications Companies
2020 K St. NW, 7th Fl.
Washington, DC 20006
Phone: (202)659-5990
Publisher's E-mail: mks@opastco.org
Freq: Quarterly. **Subscription Rates:** included in membership dues; $14 /year for additional subscriptions; $27 /year for nonmembers. **Remarks:** Accepts advertising. **Circ:** 3000.

7021 ■ Optics Express: The International Electronic Journal of Optics
Optical Society of America
2010 Massachusetts Ave. NW
Washington, DC 20036
Phone: (202)223-8130
Fax: (202)223-1096
Publisher's E-mail: info@osa.org
Peer-reviwed journal focusing on advances in the field of optical science and technology. **Freq:** Biweekly. **Key Personnel:** Andrew M. Weiner, Editor-in-Chief; Sharon Jeffress, Managing Editor, phone: (202)416-1448. **ISSN:** 1094--4087 (print). **URL:** http://www.osapublishing.org/oe/home.cfm. **Circ:** (Not Reported).

7022 ■ Optics Letters
Optical Society of America
2010 Massachusetts Ave. NW
Washington, DC 20036
Phone: (202)223-8130
Fax: (202)223-1096
Publisher's E-mail: info@osa.org
Technical journal covering research in optical science. **Freq:** Semimonthly. **Print Method:** web offset. **Trim Size:** 8 1/4 x 11 1/8. **Key Personnel:** Xi-Cheng Zhang, Editor-in-Chief. **ISSN:** 0146--9592 (print); **EISSN:** 1539--4794 (electronic). **URL:** http://www.osa.org/en-us/publications; http://www.osapublishing.org/ol/home.cfm. **Remarks:** Advertising not accepted. **Circ:** (Not Reported).

7023 ■ Optics & Photonics News
Optical Society of America
2010 Massachusetts Ave. NW
Washington, DC 20036
Phone: (202)223-8130
Fax: (202)223-1096
Publication E-mail: opn@osa.org
Magazine covering the field of optics and photonics from theory to instrumentation and systems applications; research, industry trends; fiber optics, laser research and applications. **Founded:** 1975. **Freq:** Monthly. **Print Method:** Offset. **Trim Size:** 8.125 x 10.875. **Cols./Page:** 3. **Col. Width:** 26 nonpareils. **Col. Depth:** 140 agate lines. **Key Personnel:** Elizabeth Nolan, Publisher; Christine E. Folz, Managing Editor. **ISSN:** 1047-6938 (print). **Subscription Rates:** Included in membership. **URL:** http://www.osa-opn.org. **Formerly:** Optics News. **Ad Rates:** BW $2,900; 4C $4,900. **Remarks:** Accepts advertising. **Circ:** △**16000**.

7024 ■ Origins CNS Documentary Service
Catholic News Service
3211 4th St. NE
Washington, DC 20017
Phone: (202)541-3250
Fax: (202)541-3255
Publisher's E-mail: cns@catholicnews.com
Freq: Periodic. **Subscription Rates:** $99 /year, online; $114 /year, print and online. **URL:** http://www.originsonline.com/thisweek1.htm. **Remarks:** Advertising not accepted. **Circ:** (Not Reported).

7025 ■ OSA Journals
Optical Society of America
2010 Massachusetts Ave. NW
Washington, DC 20036
Phone: (202)223-8130
Fax: (202)223-1096
Publisher's E-mail: info@osa.org
Journal covering scholarly research about optics and photonics. **URL:** http://www.osapublishing.org. **Remarks:** Advertising not accepted. **Circ:** (Not Reported).

7026 ■ PA Times
American Society for Public Administration
1370 Rhode Island Ave. NW, Ste. 500
Washington, DC 20036
Phone: (202)393-7878
Fax: (202)638-4952
Publisher's E-mail: info@aspanet.org
Public administration newspaper (tabloid). **Freq:** Semiweekly. **Print Method:** Offset. **Trim Size:** 11 1/2 x 15. **Cols./Page:** 4. **Col. Width:** 28 nonpareils. **Col. Depth:** 185 agate lines. **Key Personnel:** Bruce Perlman, Editor-in-Chief. **ISSN:** 0149--8797 (print). **Subscription Rates:** $50 Nonmembers; $75 Nonmembers other countries. **URL:** http://www.aspanet.org/public; http://patimes.org. **Ad Rates:** BW $1,050; 4C $300. **Remarks:** Accepts advertising. **Circ:** 13500.

7027 ■ PaleoAnthropology Journal
Paleoanthropology Society
810 E St. SE
Washington, DC 20003
Journal containing articles, book reviews, and the abstracts of the annual meetings of the society. **Freq:** Annual. **Subscription Rates:** Free. **Alt. Formats:** PDF. **URL:** http://www.paleoanthro.org/journal. **Circ:** (Not Reported).

7028 ■ Paleoceanography
American Geophysical Union
2000 Florida Ave. NW
Washington, DC 20009-1277
Phone: (202)462-6900
Fax: (202)328-0566
Free: 800-966-2481
Publication E-mail: paleoceanography@agu.org
Journal focused on reconstructions of past conditions and processes of change as recorded in sediments deposited in water. **Freq:** Monthly. **Key Personnel:** Christopher D. Charles, Editor; Rainer Zahn, Editor; Min-Te Chen, Associate Editor. **ISSN:** 0883--8305 (print); **EISSN:** 1944--9186 (electronic). **Subscription Rates:** $1042 U.S. and other countries online - large; $691 U.S. and other countries online - medium; £657 Institutions online - large; £437 Institutions online - medium; £300 Institutions online - small; €762 Institutions online - large; €506 Institutions online - medium; €347 Institutions online - small. **URL:** http://agupubs.onlinelibrary.wiley.com/agu/journal/10.1002/(ISSN)1944-9186. **Remarks:** Advertising not accepted. **Circ:** (Not Reported).

7029 ■ Parenting for High Potential
National Association for Gifted Children
1331 H St. NW, Ste. 1001
Washington, DC 20005

Phone: (202)785-4268
Fax: (202)785-4248
Publisher's E-mail: nagc@nagc.org
Consumer magazine covering parenting issues. **Freq:** Quarterly. **Print Method:** Web offset. **Trim Size:** 8.5 x 11. **Key Personnel:** Kathleen Nilles. **Subscription Rates:** Included in membership. **Alt. Formats:** PDF. **URL:** http://www.nagc.org/parenting-high-potential; http://www.nagc.org/resources-publications/nagc-publications/parenting-high-potential. **Ad Rates:** BW $900; 4C $1,500. **Remarks:** Accepts advertising. **Circ:** Combined 15000.

7030 ■ Parking Magazine: A Publication of the National Parking Association
National Parking Association
1112 16th St. NW, Ste. 840
Washington, DC 20036
Phone: (202)296-4336
Fax: (202)296-3102
Free: 800-647-7275
Publisher's E-mail: info@weareparking.org
Parking industry magazine. **Freq:** 10/year. **Print Method:** Sheetfed offset. **Trim Size:** 8 1/4 x 11. **Cols./Page:** 4. **Col. Depth:** 9 3/4 inches. **ISSN:** 0031--2193 (print). **Subscription Rates:** $125 Individuals /year - print and digital; $165 Other countries /year - print and digital; $99 Individuals /year - digital only. **URL:** http://weareparking.org/?page=Parking_Magazine. **Ad Rates:** BW $1,400; 4C $2,100. **Remarks:** Accepts advertising. **Circ:** 5000.

7031 ■ Parks
National Park Foundation
1110 Vermont Ave. NW, Ste. 200
Washington, DC 20005
Phone: (202)796-2500
Fax: (202)796-2509
Publisher's E-mail: ask-npf@nationalparks.org
Freq: Quarterly. **Remarks:** Advertising not accepted. **Circ:** (Not Reported).

7032 ■ Party Politics: An International Journal for the Study of Political Parties and Political Organizations
American Political Science Association
1527 New Hampshire Ave. NW
Washington, DC 20036-1206
Phone: (202)483-2512
Fax: (202)483-2657
Peer-reviewed journal covering the character and organization of political parties and the various national political systems worldwide. **Freq:** Bimonthly January, March, May, July, September, November. **Key Personnel:** Paul Webb, Editor, phone: 44 0 1273877796; Kenneth Janda, Editor, fax: (847)491-8985; David M. Farrell, Editor; Prof. Aleks Szczerbiak, Associate Editor, phone: 44 0 1273678443, fax: 44 0 1273678571. **ISSN:** 1354--0688 (print); **EISSN:** 1460--3683 (electronic). **Subscription Rates:** £66 Individuals print only; £733 Institutions e-access (content through 1998); £765 Institutions e-access; £833 Institutions print only; £850 Institutions print & e-access; £850 Institutions e-access plus backfile (all online content); £935 Institutions combined plus backfile (current volume print & all online content); £14 Individuals single print issue; £153 Institutions single print issue. **Online:** Sage Publications Ltd. Sage Publications Ltd. **URL:** http://ppq.sagepub.com. **Ad Rates:** BW £650. **Remarks:** Advertising accepted; rates available upon request. **Circ:** (Not Reported).

7033 ■ Passenger Transport: The Weekly Newspaper of the Public Transportation Industry
American Public Transportation Association
1300 I St. NW, Ste. 1200 E
Washington, DC 20005
Phone: (202)496-4800
Fax: (202)496-4324
Publisher's E-mail: info@apta.com
Newspaper covering the public transit industry in the U.S. and Canada. **Freq:** Weekly. **Print Method:** Offset. **Trim Size:** 10 5/8 x 14. **Cols./Page:** 4. **Col. Width:** 28 nonpareils. **Col. Depth:** 139 agate lines. **Key Personnel:** Jack Gonzalez, Director, Marketing and Sales, phone: (202)496-4824; Susan Berlin, Senior Editor, phone: (202)496-4847. **ISSN:** 0364--345X (print). **Subscription Rates:** $75 Individuals; $125 Two years; $87 Other countries. **URL:** http://www.apta.com/passengertransport/Pages/default.aspx. **Ad Rates:** GLR $7.75; BW $2,360; 4C $3,375; PCI $67. **Remarks:** Classified line rate 8.40 member (9.60 non-member). **Circ:** Paid 4535, Free 401, 5000.

7034 ■ Peace & Change: A Journal of Peace Research
Peace and Justice Studies Association
1421 37th St. NW, Ste. 130
Washington, DC 20057
Magazine publishing articles on peace-related topics such as peace movements and activism, conflict resolution, nonviolence, internationalism, race and gender issues, cross-cultural studies, economic development, the legacy of imperialism, and the post-Cold War upheaval. **Freq:** Quarterly. **Key Personnel:** Kevin Clements, Board Member; Sandi E. Cooper, Board Member; Mohammed Abu-Nimer, Board Member; Elavie Ndura-Ouedraogo, Board Member; Lee Smithey, Board Member. **ISSN:** 0149--0508 (print); **EISSN:** 1468--0130 (electronic). **Subscription Rates:** $549 Institutions print or online; £423 Institutions print or online; $827 Institutions, other countries print or online; $659 Institutions print and online; £508 Institutions print and online; $993 Institutions, other countries print and online; $125 Individuals print and online; £100 Other countries print and online; €536 Institutions print or online; €644 Institutions print and online; £100 Individuals print and online (UK and Europe non-Euro zone); €150 Individuals print and online (Europe - Euro zone). **URL:** http://onlinelibrary.wiley.com/journal/10.1111/(ISSN)1468-0130; http://www.peacehistorysociety.org/journal.php; http://www.peacejusticestudies.org/resources. **Remarks:** Accepts advertising. **Circ:** (Not Reported).

7035 ■ Peanut Stocks and Processing
U.S. Department of Agriculture National Agricultural Statistics Service
1400 Independence Ave. SW
Washington, DC 20250
Free: 800-727-9540
Publisher's E-mail: nass@nass.usda.gov
Publication providing information on Peanut Stocks and Processing. **Freq:** Monthly. **Subscription Rates:** Free. **Alt. Formats:** PDF. **URL:** http://usda.mannlib.cornell.edu/MannUsda/viewDocumentInfo.do?documentID=1118. **Circ:** (Not Reported).

7036 ■ Peer Review
Association of American Colleges and Universities
1818 R St. NW
Washington, DC 20009
Phone: (202)387-3760
Freq: Quarterly. **Key Personnel:** Shelley Johnson Carey, Editor. **ISSN:** 1541--1389 (print). **Subscription Rates:** $10 Single issue for nonmembers; $8 Single issue for members; $45 Libraries; $35 Individuals. **Alt. Formats:** E-book. **URL:** http://www.aacu.org/peerreview. **Remarks:** Advertising not accepted. **Circ:** (Not Reported).

7037 ■ Persist
National Conference on Public Employee Retirement Systems
444 N Capitol St. NW, Ste. 630
Washington, DC 20001
Phone: (202)624-1456
Fax: (202)624-1439
Free: 877-202-5706
Publisher's E-mail: info@ncpers.org
Subscription Rates: accessible only to members. **URL:** http://www.ncpers.org/persist. **Remarks:** Advertising not accepted. **Circ:** (Not Reported).

7038 ■ Personality and Social Psychology Review
Society for Personality and Social Psychology
1660 L St. NW, No. 1000
Washington, DC 20036
Phone: (202)524-6545
Publisher's E-mail: spspinfo@spsp.org
Freq: Quarterly. **Trim Size:** 8 1/2 x 11. **Key Personnel:** Monica Biernat, Editor. **ISSN:** 1088--8683 (print); **EISSN:** 1532--7957 (electronic). **Subscription Rates:** $432 Institutions combined (print & e-access); $475 Institutions combined plus backfile; $389 Institutions e-access; $423 Institutions print only; $78 Individuals combined (print & e-access); $116 Institutions single print; $25 Individuals single print; included in membership dues; $129 /year for individuals, print & online; $677 /year for institutions, print & online; $42 Single issue /issue for individuals; $186 Single issue /issue for institutions. **URL:** http://psr.sagepub.com; http://www.spsp.org/?page=Publications; http://www.spsp.org/?page=pspr; http://www.sagepub.com/journalsProdDesc.nav?ct_p=subscribe&prodId=Journal201783. **Ad Rates:** BW $515; 4C $995. **Remarks:** Accepts advertising. **Circ:** (Not Reported).

7039 ■ Perspectives on Politics
American Political Science Association
1527 New Hampshire Ave. NW
Washington, DC 20036-1206
Phone: (202)483-2512
Fax: (202)483-2657
Publication E-mail: perspectives@apsanet.org
Peer-reviewed journal that aims to connect research findings, conceptual innovations, or theoretical developments to real problems of politics. **Freq:** Quarterly. **Key Personnel:** James Moskowitz, Managing Editor; Prof. Jeffrey C. Isaac, Editor. **ISSN:** 1537--5927 (print); **EISSN:** 1541--0986 (electronic). **Subscription Rates:** sold as part of a joint subscription. **Online:** Cambridge University Press Cambridge University Press. **URL:** http://journals.cambridge.org/action/displayJournal?jid=PPS; http://www.apsanet.org/perspectives. **Remarks:** Advertising accepted; rates available upon request. **Circ:** 16000.

7040 ■ Perspectives on Psychological Science
Association for Psychological Science
1800 Massachusetts Ave. NW, Ste. 402
Washington, DC 20036
Phone: (202)293-9300
Fax: (202)293-9350
Publisher's E-mail: info@sagepub.in
Journal publishing articles on latest advances in the entire field of psychology. Includes articles on related areas in other behavioral and social sciences and neuroscience. **Freq:** Bimonthly. **Key Personnel:** Bethany A. Teachman, Associate Editor. **ISSN:** 1745--6916 (print); **EISSN:** 1745--6924 (electronic). **Subscription Rates:** $293 Institutions single print issue. **URL:** http://pps.sagepub.com; http://www.psychologicalscience.org/index.php/publications/journals/perspectives; http://www.sagepub.in/journals/Journal201964?q=Science%20%20Technology%20and&prodTypes=Journals&subject=K00&fs=1&fs=1. **Remarks:** Advertising accepted; rates available upon request. **Circ:** (Not Reported).

7041 ■ Petroleum Supply Monthly
National Energy Information Center
Energy Information Administration, MS EI-30
1000 Independence Ave. SW
Washington, DC 20585
Phone: (202)586-8800
Fax: (202)586-0114
Publication E-mail: infoctr@eia.doe.gov
Web-only publication covering the petroleum industry. **Freq:** Monthly. **Print Method:** Web. **ISSN:** 0733--0553 (print). **Alt. Formats:** PDF. **URL:** http://www.eia.gov/petroleum/supply/monthly. **Circ:** (Not Reported).

7042 ■ Pi Sigma Alpha Undergraduate Journal of Politics
Pi Sigma Alpha
1527 New Hampshire Ave. NW
Washington, DC 20036
Phone: (202)349-9285
Publisher's E-mail: office@pisigmaalpha.org
Freq: Semiannual spring and fall. **Key Personnel:** Jane Dixon. **ISSN:** 1556- 2034 (print). **URL:** http://www.psajournal.org. **Remarks:** Advertising not accepted. **Circ:** 750.

7043 ■ Plating & Surface Finishing: The Official Publication of the National Association for Surface Finishing
American Electroplaters and Surface Finishers Society
1155 15th St. NW, Ste. 500
Washington, DC 20005
Phone: (202)457-8404
Fax: (202)530-0659
Magazine. **Freq:** Monthly. **Print Method:** Web press. **Trim Size:** 8 1/8 x 11. **Cols./Page:** 3. **Col. Width:** 26

Circulation: ★ = AAM; △ or • = BPA; ♦ = CAC; ❑ = VAC; ⊕ = PO Statement; ‡ = Publisher's Report; Boldface figures = sworn; Light figures = estimated.

nonpareils. **Col. Depth:** 140 agate lines. **Key Personnel:** Cheryl Clark, Manager, Advertising; John Flatley, Publisher. **ISSN:** 0360--3164 (print). **Subscription Rates:** $130 Individuals; $210 Other countries includes shipping & handling; $20 Single issue back issue. **URL:** http://www.nasf.org. **Ad Rates:** BW $1,010; 4C $3,600; PCI $50. **Remarks:** Accepts advertising. **Circ:** Paid ‡508.

7044 ■ Policy and Internet
Policy Studies Organization
1527 New Hampshire Ave. NW
Washington, DC 20036
Fax: (202)483-2657
Freq: Quarterly. **EISSN:** 1944--2866 (electronic). **Subscription Rates:** $406 U.S., Canada, and Mexico online only - institution; £257 Institutions online only; €297 Institutions online only. **URL:** http://onlinelibrary.wiley.com/journal/10.1002/(ISSN)1944-2866; http://www.ipsonet.org/publications/journals/policy-and-internet. **Circ:** (Not Reported).

7045 ■ Policy and Practice: The Magazine of the American Public Human Services Association
American Public Human Services Association
1133 19th St. NW, Ste. 400
Washington, DC 20036-3631
Phone: (202)682-0100
Fax: (202)289-6555
Publisher's E-mail: pubs@aphsa.org
Magazine focusing on current issues and future trends in the public human services. **Freq:** Bimonthly. **Print Method:** Offset. **Trim Size:** 8 1/4 x 10 7/8. **ISSN:** 1942--6828 (print). **Subscription Rates:** $400 Individuals; $475 Other countries; $65 Single issue back issue; $75 Other countries single issue, back issue. **URL:** http://www.aphsa.org/content/APHSA/en/resources/PUBLICATIONS/POLICY_AND_PRACTICE.html. **Remarks:** Accepts advertising. **Circ:** (Not Reported).

7046 ■ Policy Studies Journal
Policy Studies Organization
1527 New Hampshire Ave. NW
Washington, DC 20036
Fax: (202)483-2657
Publication E-mail: psj@bushschool.tamu.edu
Journal devoted to political and social science and applications to public policy issues at all levels of government. **Freq:** Quarterly. **Print Method:** Offset. **Trim Size:** 10 x 7. **Cols./Page:** 1. **Col. Width:** 57 nonpareils. **Col. Depth:** 108 agate lines. **Key Personnel:** Peter de Leon, Board Member. **ISSN:** 0190--292X (print); **EISSN:** 1541--0072 (electronic). **Subscription Rates:** $2088 Institutions online only; £1535 Institutions online only, United Kingdom; €1951 Institutions online only, Euro zone; $3004 Institutions, other countries online only. **URL:** http://onlinelibrary.wiley.com/journal/10.1111/(ISSN)1541-0072; http://www.ipsonet.org/publications/journals/policy-studies-journal. **Remarks:** Accepts advertising. **Circ:** (Not Reported).

7047 ■ Population Bulletin
Population Reference Bureau
1875 Connecticut Ave. NW, Ste. 520
Washington, DC 20009-5728
Fax: (202)328-3937
Free: 800-877-9881
Publisher's E-mail: popref@prb.org
Journal on population studies. **Freq:** Quarterly. **Print Method:** Offset. **Trim Size:** 7 x 9 1/4. **Cols./Page:** 2. **Col. Width:** 28 nonpareils. **Col. Depth:** 100 agate lines. **Key Personnel:** Mary Mederios Kent, Editor. **ISSN:** 0032--468X (print). **URL:** http://www.prb.org. **Remarks:** Advertising not accepted. **Circ:** ‡5000, 4500.

7048 ■ Population Connection: Magazine of the International Civil Aviation Organization
Population Connection
2120 L St. NW, Ste. 500
Washington, DC 20037
Phone: (202)332-2200
Fax: (202)332-2302
Free: 800-767-1956
Publication E-mail: info@populationconnection.org
Magazine promoting a sustainable balance of population, resources, and the environment. **Freq:** Quarterly. **Trim Size:** 11 x 14. **Key Personnel:** Marian Starkey, Director, Communications. **ISSN:** 0199-0071 (print). **URL:** http://www.populationconnection.org/. **Formerly:** The ZPG Reporter. **Mailing address:** PO Box 97129, Washington, DC 20077. **Remarks:** Advertising not accepted. **Circ:** Paid 75000.

7049 ■ Population Health Management
DMAA: The Care Continuum Alliance
701 Pennsylvania Ave. NW, Ste. 700
Washington, DC 20004-2694
Phone: (202)737-5980
Fax: (202)478-5113
Publisher's E-mail: dmaa@dmaa.org
Journal providing comprehensive, authoritative strategies for improving the systems and policies that affect health care quality, access, and outcomes, ultimately improving the health of an entire population. **Freq:** Bimonthly. **Subscription Rates:** Included in membership. **URL:** http://www.populationhealthalliance.org/pha/our-journal.html. **Formerly:** Disease Management. **Remarks:** Accepts advertising. **Circ:** (Not Reported).

7050 ■ Postal Record
National Association of Letter Carriers
100 Indiana Ave. NW
Washington, DC 20001-2144
Phone: (202)393-4695
Publication E-mail: postalrecord@nalc.org
Magazine for active and retired letter carriers. **Freq:** Monthly. **Print Method:** Web press. **Trim Size:** 8 1/4 x 11. **Cols./Page:** 3. **Col. Width:** 26 nonpareils. **Col. Depth:** 133 agate lines. **Key Personnel:** Frederic V. Rolando, President. **ISSN:** 0032--5376 (print). **Subscription Rates:** Included in membership. **URL:** http://www.nalc.org/news/the-postal-record. **Remarks:** Advertising not accepted. **Circ:** Non-paid ‡298000, 310000.

7051 ■ Practicing OD
Organization Development Network
2025 M St. NW, Ste. 800
Washington, DC 20036
Phone: (202)367-1127
Fax: (202)367-2127
Publisher's E-mail: odnetwork@odnetwork.org
Freq: Bimonthly. **Subscription Rates:** for members only. **URL:** http://www.odnetwork.org/?CurrentIssuePOD. **Remarks:** Advertising not accepted. **Circ:** (Not Reported).

7052 ■ Preservation
National Trust for Historic Preservation
2600 Virginia Ave. NW, Ste. 1100
Washington, DC 20037
Phone: (202)588-6000
Fax: (202)588-6038
Free: 800-944-6847
Publisher's E-mail: info@savingplaces.org
Magazine featuring historic preservation. **Freq:** Bimonthly. **Print Method:** Web offset. **Trim Size:** 8 1/8 x 10 1/2. **Cols./Page:** 3. **Col. Width:** 34 nonpareils. **Col. Depth:** 210 agate lines. **Key Personnel:** Dennis Hockman, Editor-in-Chief; Beth Caudell Siegel, Manager, Production. **ISSN:** 0032--7735 (print). **Subscription Rates:** Included in membership. **URL:** http://www.preservationnation.org/magazine. **Formerly:** Historic Preservation News. **Ad Rates:** 4C $14,830. **Remarks:** Accepts classified advertising. **Circ:** ★185000, 250000.

7053 ■ The Presidency: The Magazine for Higher Education Leaders
American Council on Education
1 Dupont Cir. NW
Washington, DC 20036
Phone: (202)939-9300
Magazine publishes articles on issues affecting higher education leadership; provides a forum for the presentation of ideas and information for college and university presidents. **Freq:** Quarterly. **Print Method:** Offset. **Trim Size:** 8 3/8 x 10 7/8. **Cols./Page:** 3. **Col. Width:** 26 nonpareils. **Col. Depth:** 140 agate lines. **ISSN:** 0013--1873 (print). **Subscription Rates:** $70 Other countries; $40 Nonmembers; $30 Members. **URL:** http://www.acenet.edu/the-presidency/Pages/Fall-2014.aspx. **Formerly:** Educational Record. **Ad Rates:** BW $1,275; 4C $1,775. **Remarks:** Accepts advertising. **Circ:** Paid ‡1150, Non-paid ‡6350.

7054 ■ Privacy Journal
Center for Democracy and Technology
1401 K St. NW, Ste. 200
Washington, DC 20005
Phone: (202)637-9800
Fax: (202)637-0968
Publisher's E-mail: press@cdt.org
Freq: Monthly. **Remarks:** Advertising not accepted. **Circ:** (Not Reported).

7055 ■ The Professional Geographer
Wiley-Blackwell
1710 Sixteenth St., NW
Association of American Geographers
San Diego State University
Washington, DC 20009-3198
Phone: (202)234-1450
Fax: (202)234-2744
Publisher's E-mail: customerservice@oxon.blackwellpublishing.com
Geographical journal. **Freq:** Quarterly. **Print Method:** Offset. **Trim Size:** 6 x 9. **Cols./Page:** 1. **Col. Width:** 29 nonpareils. **Col. Depth:** 43 agate lines. **Key Personnel:** Robin Maier, Editor; Barney Warf, Editor; Thomas Hodler, Editor. **ISSN:** 0033--0124 (print). **Online:** OARE. **URL:** http://www.aag.org/cs/publications/journals/pg. **Remarks:** Accepts advertising. **Circ:** (Not Reported).

7056 ■ Professional Psychology: Research and Practice
American Psychological Association
750 1st St. NE
Washington, DC 20002-4242
Phone: (202)336-5500
Free: 800-374-2721
Publication E-mail: subscriptions@apa.org
Journal presenting articles on techniques and practices used in the application of psychology, including applications of research, standards of practice, interprofessional relations, delivery of services, and training. **Freq:** Bimonthly beginning in February. **Key Personnel:** Norman Abeles, PhD, Editor; Mary Beth Kenkel, PhD, Editor; Michael C. Roberts, PhD, Editor; Ronald T. Brown, Editor. **ISSN:** 0735--7028 (print); **EISSN:** 1939--1323 (electronic). **Subscription Rates:** $64 Members domestic; $90 Members foreign, surface; $111 Members foreign, air mail; $59 Students domestic; $85 Students foreign, surface; $106 Students foreign, air mail; $197 Nonmembers domestic; $232 Nonmembers foreign, surface; $249 Nonmembers foreign, air mail; $751 Institutions domestic; $812 Institutions, other countries surface mail; $832 Institutions, other countries air mail. **URL:** http://www.apa.org/pubs/journals/pro/index.aspx. **Ad Rates:** BW $450; 4C $1,425. **Remarks:** Accepts advertising. **Circ:** ‡4500.

7057 ■ Professional Report
Society of Industrial and Office Realtors
1201 New York Ave. NW, Ste. 350
Washington, DC 20005-6126
Phone: (202)449-8200
Fax: (202)216-9325
Publisher's E-mail: membership@sior.com
Trade magazine for commercial real estate brokerage. **Founded:** Jan. 1991. **Freq:** Quarterly. **Trim Size:** 8 1/2 x 11. **Cols./Page:** 2 and 3. **Col. Width:** 4 1/4 and 2 1/2 inches. **Col. Depth:** 9 1/2 and 9 1/2 inches. **USPS:** 324-270. **Subscription Rates:** Members free; $35 Nonmembers additional for one Member/Candidate is included in dues; $45 Nonmembers within USA; $55 Nonmembers outside USA. **URL:** http://www.sior.com/resources/professional-report-magazine. **Ad Rates:** BW $1,620; 4C $1,360. **Remarks:** Accepts advertising. **Circ:** Paid 3500.

7058 ■ Professional Report of Industrial and Office Real Estate
Society of Industrial and Office Realtors
1201 New York Ave. NW, Ste. 350
Washington, DC 20005-6126
Phone: (202)449-8200
Fax: (202)216-9325
Publisher's E-mail: membership@sior.com
Freq: Quarterly. **Subscription Rates:** Included in membership; $45 Nonmembers /year in U.S.; $55 Nonmembers /year outside U.S. **URL:** http://www.sior.com/resources/professional-report-magazine. **Remarks:** Accepts advertising. **Circ:** 3000.

7059 ■ ProSales
DoveTale Publishers
1 Thomas Cir. NW
Washington, DC 20005
Phone: (202)339-0744

Fax: (202)785-1974
Free: 877-275-8647
Publisher's E-mail: hwmicustomerservice@hanleywood.com
Trade publication covering construction and retail sales. **Founded:** 1989. **Freq:** Monthly. **Print Method:** Web Offset. **Trim Size:** 8 1/4 x 11 1/8. **Cols./Page:** 3. **Key Personnel:** Mark Taussig, Publisher; Johanna Daproza, Manager, Production; Craig Webb, Editor. **ISSN:** 1055-3444 (print). **Subscription Rates:** $36 Individuals; $66 Canada; $192 Other countries airmail delivery; $69 Two years. **URL:** http://www.prosalesmediakit.com. **Ad Rates:** BW $5,100; 4C $11,295; PCI $135. **Remarks:** Accepts advertising. **Circ:** Combined △**36320.**

7060 ■ Protecting Children
American Humane Association
1400 16th St. NW, Ste. 360
Washington, DC 20036
Phone: (818)501-0123
Free: 800-227-4645
Publisher's E-mail: info@americanhumane.org
Peer-reviewed journal covering broad range of child welfare topics. **Freq:** Quarterly. **ISSN:** 0893--4231 (print). **Subscription Rates:** Included in membership; $40 Libraries /year; $10 Nonmembers each. **URL:** http://www.americanhumane.org/children/professional-resources/protecting-children-journal. **Remarks:** Advertising not accepted. **Circ:** (Not Reported).

7061 ■ Provider: For Long Term Care Professionals
American Health Care Association
1201 L St. NW
Washington, DC 20005
Phone: (202)842-4444
Fax: (202)842-3860
Publication E-mail: sales@ahca.org
Provider Magazine. **Freq:** Monthly. **Print Method:** Web offset. **Trim Size:** 8 1/8 x 10 7/8. **Cols./Page:** 3. **Col. Width:** 13 picas. **Col. Depth:** 58 picas. **Key Personnel:** Joanne Erickson, Editor-in-Chief. **ISSN:** 0360--4069 (print). **Subscription Rates:** Free to qualified long-term and post-acute care professionals.; $48 U.S.; $61 Canada and Mexico; $85 Other countries. **URL:** http://www.providermagazine.com. **Formerly**: American Health Care Association Journal. **Ad Rates:** BW $4,320; 4C $1,365; PCI $150. **Remarks:** Accepts advertising. **Circ:** 24000.

7062 ■ PS: Political Science & Politics
American Political Science Association
1527 New Hampshire Ave. NW
Washington, DC 20036-1206
Phone: (202)483-2512
Fax: (202)483-2657
Publication E-mail: ps@apsanet.org
Peer-reviewed journal focusing on contemporary politics, teaching and the discipline. **Freq:** Quarterly Current Issue: Volume 48, Issue 01. **Print Method:** Web press. **Trim Size:** 8 1/2 x 11. **Cols./Page:** 3. **Key Personnel:** Robert J.P. Hauck, Editor. **ISSN:** 1049--0965 (print). **Subscription Rates:** Included in membership. **URL:** http://www.apsanet.org/PS. **Remarks:** Advertising accepted; rates available upon request. **Circ:** ‡16000.

7063 ■ PsycCRITIQUES: APA Review of Books
American Psychological Association
750 1st St. NE
Washington, DC 20002-4242
Phone: (202)336-5500
Free: 800-374-2721
Journal presenting critical reviews of books, films, tapes, and other media representing a cross section of psychological literature. **Freq:** Weekly. **Key Personnel:** Robert Sternberg, Editor. **ISSN:** 1554-0138 (print). **URL:** http://www.apa.org/pubs/databases/psyccritiques/index.aspx. **Formerly**: Contemporary Psychology. **Remarks:** Accepts advertising. **Circ:** ‡3400.

7064 ■ Psychoanalytic Psychology
American Psychological Association
750 1st St. NE
Washington, DC 20002-4242
Phone: (202)336-5500
Free: 800-374-2721
Journal publishing original contributions that reflect and broaden the interaction between psychoanalysis and psychology. **Freq:** Quarterly. **Key Personnel:** Elliot Jurist, PhD, Editor; Ricardo C. Ainslie, Board Member. **ISSN:** 0736-9735 (print); **EISSN:** 1939-1331 (electronic). **Subscription Rates:** $69 Members; $93 Members international surface; $107 Members international airmail; $69 Students; $93 Students, other countries surface; $107 Students, other countries airmail; $120 Nonmembers; $149 Nonmembers international surface; $162 Nonmembers international airmail; $711 Institutions; $760 Institutions international surface; $775 Institutions international airmail. **URL:** http://www.apa.org/pubs/journals/pap/index.aspx. **Ad Rates:** 4C $1,400. **Remarks:** Accepts advertising. **Circ:** 3000.

7065 ■ Psychological Assessment
American Psychological Association
750 1st St. NE
Washington, DC 20002-4242
Phone: (202)336-5500
Free: 800-374-2721
Journal presenting original empirical articles concerning clinical assessment and evaluations. **Freq:** Monthly. **Key Personnel:** Cecil R. Reynolds, PhD, Editor; Yossef S. Ben-Porath, Editor. **ISSN:** 1040--3590 (print); **EISSN:** 1939--134X (electronic). **Subscription Rates:** $160 Members domestic; $193 Members foreign, surface; $234 Members foreign, air mail; $87 Students domestic; $120 Students foreign, surface; $161 Students foreign, air mail; $290 Nonmembers domestic; $347 Nonmembers foreign, surface; $379 Nonmembers foreign, air mail; $725 Institutions domestic; $835 Institutions, other countries surface mail; $867 Institutions, other countries air mail. **URL:** http://www.apa.org/pubs/journals/pas/index.aspx. **Ad Rates:** BW $425; 4C $975. **Remarks:** Accepts advertising. **Circ:** Paid ‡1900, 6700.

7066 ■ Psychological Bulletin
American Psychological Association
750 1st St. NE
Washington, DC 20002-4242
Phone: (202)336-5500
Free: 800-374-2721
Journal presenting comprehensive and integrative reviews and interpretations of critical substantive and methodological issues and practical problems from all the diverse areas of psychology. **Freq:** Bimonthly. **Key Personnel:** Stephen P. Hinshaw, Editor; Dolores Albarracin, Editor. **ISSN:** 0033--2909 (print); **EISSN:** 1939--1455 (electronic). **Subscription Rates:** $160 Members domestic; $193 Members foreign, surface; $234 Members foreign, air mail; $87 Students domestic; $120 Students foreign, surface; $161 Students foreign, air mail; $290 Nonmembers domestic; $347 Nonmembers foreign, surface; $379 Nonmembers foreign, air mail; $1199 Institutions domestic; $1309 Institutions surface mail; $1341 Institutions air mail. **URL:** http://www.apa.org/pubs/journals/bul. **Ad Rates:** BW $375; 4C $1,350. **Remarks:** Accepts advertising. **Circ:** ‡1400, 7700.

7067 ■ Psychological Methods
American Psychological Association
750 1st St. NE
Washington, DC 20002-4242
Phone: (202)336-5500
Free: 800-374-2721
Journal presenting articles related to research methods and outcomes in the field of psychology. **Freq:** Quarterly beginning in March. **Trim Size:** 8 1/2 x 11. **Key Personnel:** Scott E. Maxwell, PhD, Editor; Lisa Harlow, Editor; Keith A. Markus, Editor. **ISSN:** 1082-989X (print); **EISSN:** 1939-1463 (electronic). **Subscription Rates:** $62 Members domestic; $41 Students domestic; $138 Nonmembers domestic; $593 Institutions domestic; $86 Members international, surface; $167 Nonmembers international, surface; $642 Institutions, other countries surface; $100 Members international, airmail; $65 Students surface mail; $642 Institutions surface mail; $79 Students air mail; $180 Nonmembers air mail; $657 Institutions air mail. **URL:** http://www.apa.org/pubs/journals/met/index.aspx. **Ad Rates:** BW $410; 4C $975. **Remarks:** Accepts advertising. **Circ:** 1,200.

7068 ■ Psychological Review
American Psychological Association
750 1st St. NE
Washington, DC 20002-4242
Phone: (202)336-5500
Free: 800-374-2721
Journal presenting articles that make theoretical contributions to all areas of scientific psychology. **Freq:** Bimonthly. **Key Personnel:** Charles S. Carver, Editor; Keith J. Holyoak, Editor. **ISSN:** 0033--295X (print); **EISSN:** 1939--1471 (electronic). **Subscription Rates:** $102 Members domestic; $128 Members foreign, surface; $149 Members foreign, air mail; $72 Students domestic; $98 Students foreign, surface; $119 Students foreign, air mail; $240 Nonmembers domestic; $275 Nonmembers foreign, surface; $292 Nonmembers foreign, air mail; $983 Institutions domestic; $1044 Institutions, other countries; $1064 Institutions, other countries. **URL:** http://www.apa.org/pubs/journals/rev/index.aspx. **Ad Rates:** BW $375; 4C $1,350. **Remarks:** Accepts advertising. **Circ:** ‡1400.

7069 ■ Psychological Science
Association for Psychological Science
1800 Massachusetts Ave. NW, Ste. 402
Washington, DC 20036
Phone: (202)293-9300
Fax: (202)293-9350
Scientific research journal of the American Psychological Society. **Freq:** Bimonthly. **Key Personnel:** D. Stephen Lindsay, Editor-in-Chief; Michele Nathan, Managing Editor. **ISSN:** 0956--7976 (print); **EISSN:** 1467--9280 (electronic). **Subscription Rates:** $8968 Institutions print and online; $9865 Institutions current volume print & all online content; $8071 Institutions online; $293 Single issue institutions; $8890 Institutions online, content through 1998; $8789 Institutions print only. **URL:** http://pss.sagepub.com; http://www.cpsbeijing.org/en/journals.php; http://www.psychologicalscience.org. **Remarks:** Accepts advertising. **Circ:** 15000.

7070 ■ Psychological Science in the Public Interest
Association for Psychological Science
1800 Massachusetts Ave. NW, Ste. 402
Washington, DC 20036
Phone: (202)293-9300
Fax: (202)293-9350
Journal providing definitive assessments of topics where psychological science may have the potential to inform and improve the lives of individuals and the well-being of society. **Freq:** 3/year. **Key Personnel:** Wendy M. Williams, Board Member; Elizabeth F. Loftus, Board Member; Valerie F. Reyna, Editor. **ISSN:** 1529-1006 (print); **EISSN:** 1539-6053 (electronic). **URL:** http://www.wiley.com. **Remarks:** Accepts advertising. **Circ:** (Not Reported).

7071 ■ Psychological Services
American Psychological Association
750 1st St. NE
Washington, DC 20002-4242
Phone: (202)336-5500
Free: 800-374-2721
Journal of the Division of Psychologists in Public Service, publishing data-based articles on the broad range of psychological services. **Freq:** Quarterly. **Key Personnel:** Patrick H. DeLeon, Editor; Gary R. VandenBos, Managing Editor. **ISSN:** 1541--1559 (print); **EISSN:** 1939--148X (electronic). **Subscription Rates:** $655 Institutions; $704 Institutions, other countries; $719 Institutions, other countries airmail; $76 Members; $100 Members international by surface; $114 Members international by airmail; $76 Students; 100 Students international by surface; 114 Students international by airmail; $139 Nonmembers; $168 Nonmembers international by surface; $181 Nonmembers international by airmail. **URL:** http://www.apa.org/pubs/journals/ser/index.aspx. **Ad Rates:** 4C $975; BW $350. **Remarks:** Accepts advertising. **Circ:** 900.

7072 ■ Psychology of Addictive Behaviors
American Psychological Association
750 1st St. NE
Washington, DC 20002-4242
Phone: (202)336-5500
Free: 800-374-2721
Journal including original research related to the psychological aspects of addictive behaviors, such as alcoholism, drug abuse, eating disorders, and other compulsive behaviors. **Freq:** Quarterly. **Print Method:** Offset. **Trim Size:** 6 3/4 x 10. **Cols./Page:** 2. **Col. Width:** 16 picas. **Col. Depth:** 50 picas. **Key Personnel:**

Circulation: ★ = AAM; △ or • = BPA; ♦ = CAC; ❑ = VAC; ⊕ = PO Statement; ‡ = Publisher's Report; Boldface figures = sworn; Light figures = estimated.

Stephen A. Maisto, PhD, Editor; Antonia Abbey, Editor; Kate Carey, Editor. **ISSN:** 0893--164X (print); **EISSN:** 1939--1501 (electronic). **Subscription Rates:** $1049 U.S.; $1126 Other countries; $1150 By mail international, air mail. **URL:** http://www.apa.org/pubs/journals/adb. **Ad Rates:** BW $410; 4C $975. **Remarks:** Advertising accepted; rates available upon request. **Circ:** Paid ‡1,600, ‡1,400, 1500.

7073 ■ Psychology of Addictive Behaviors
APA Division 50: Society of Addiction Psychology
750 1st St. NE
Washington, DC 20002-4242
Phone: (202)216-7602
Journal including original research related to the psychological aspects of addictive behaviors, such as alcoholism, drug abuse, eating disorders, and other compulsive behaviors. **Freq:** Quarterly. **Print Method:** Offset. **Trim Size:** 6 3/4 x 10. **Cols./Page:** 2. **Col. Width:** 16 picas. **Col. Depth:** 50 picas. **Key Personnel:** Stephen A. Maisto, PhD, Editor; Antonia Abbey, Editor; Kate Carey, Editor. **ISSN:** 0893--164X (print); **EISSN:** 1939--1501 (electronic). **Subscription Rates:** $1049 U.S.; $1126 Other countries; $1150 By mail international, air mail. **URL:** http://www.apa.org/pubs/journals/adb. **Ad Rates:** BW $410; 4C $975. **Remarks:** Advertising accepted; rates available upon request. **Circ:** Paid ‡1,600, ‡1,400, 1500.

7074 ■ Psychology and Aging
American Psychological Association
750 1st St. NE
Washington, DC 20002-4242
Phone: (202)336-5500
Free: 800-374-2721
Journal presenting original articles on adult development and aging. Represents both research and practice on the subject of psychogerontology. **Freq:** 8/year. **Key Personnel:** Paul Duberstein, Associate Editor; Cheryl Grady, Associate Editor. **ISSN:** 0882--7974 (print); **EISSN:** 1939--1498 (electronic). **Subscription Rates:** $120 Members domestic; $148 Members foreign, surface freight; $176 Members foreign, air freight; $72 Students domestic; $100 Students foreign, surface freight; $128 Students foreign, air freight; $240 Nonmembers domestic; $282 Nonmembers foreign, surface freight; $304 Nonmembers foreign, air freight; $849 Institutions domestic; $926 Institutions, other countries surface mail; $950 Institutions, other countries air mail. **URL:** http://www.apa.org/pubs/journals/pag/index.aspx. **Ad Rates:** BW $375; 4C $975. **Remarks:** Accepts advertising. **Circ:** ‡1500.

7075 ■ Psychology of Men & Masculinity
American Psychological Association
750 1st St. NE
Washington, DC 20002-4242
Phone: (202)336-5500
Free: 800-374-2721
Freq: Quarterly. **Trim Size:** 7 x 10. **Key Personnel:** Ronald F. Levant, Editor; Ronald F. Levant, PhD, Editor; William Ming Liu, Associate Editor. **ISSN:** 1524-9220 (print); **EISSN:** 1939-151X (electronic). **Subscription Rates:** $71 Members; $126 Nonmembers; $574 Institutions; $95 Members international, surface; $155 Nonmembers international, surface; $623 Institutions, other countries surface; $109 Members international, airmail; Included in membership. **Alt. Formats:** PDF. **URL:** http://www.apa.org/pubs/journals/men/index.aspx; http://www.division51.org/publications/PMM.htm. **Ad Rates:** BW $350; 4C $975. **Remarks:** Accepts advertising. **Circ:** 600.

7076 ■ Psychology of Men & Masculinity
APA Division 51: Society for the Psychological Study of Men and Masculinity
750 1st St. NE
Washington, DC 20002-4241
Free: 800-336-6013
Freq: Quarterly. **Trim Size:** 7 x 10. **Key Personnel:** Ronald F. Levant, Editor; Ronald F. Levant, PhD, Editor; William Ming Liu, Associate Editor. **ISSN:** 1524-9220 (print); **EISSN:** 1939-151X (electronic). **Subscription Rates:** $71 Members; $126 Nonmembers; $574 Institutions; $95 Members international, surface; $155 Nonmembers international, surface; $623 Institutions, other countries surface; $109 Members international, airmail; Included in membership. **Alt. Formats:** PDF. **URL:** http://www.apa.org/pubs/journals/men/index.aspx; http://www.division51.org/publications/PMM.htm. **Ad Rates:** BW $350; 4C $975. **Remarks:** Accepts advertising. **Circ:** 600.

7077 ■ Psychology, Public Policy, and Law
American Psychological Association
750 1st St. NE
Washington, DC 20002-4242
Phone: (202)336-5500
Free: 800-374-2721
Journal covering psychology issues as they relate to public policies and law formation and implementation. **Freq:** Quarterly. **Key Personnel:** Michael E. Lamb, Editor; J. Lawrence Aber, Board Member. **ISSN:** 1076-8971 (print); **EISSN:** 1939-1528 (electronic). **Subscription Rates:** $62 Members; $41 Students; $138 Nonmembers; $754 Institutions; $86 Members international, surface; $65 Students, other countries surface; $167 Nonmembers international, surface; $803 Institutions, other countries surface; $100 Members international, airmail; $79 Students, other countries airmail. **URL:** http://www.apa.org/pubs/journals/law/index.aspx. **Ad Rates:** BW $350; 4C $975. **Remarks:** Accepts advertising. **Circ:** 900.

7078 ■ Psychology of Religion and Spirituality
American Psychological Association
750 1st St. NE
Washington, DC 20002-4242
Phone: (202)336-5500
Free: 800-374-2721
Publishes peer-reviewed, original articles related to psychological aspects of religion and spirituality. **Freq:** Quarterly. **Key Personnel:** Ralph L. Piedmont, Editor; Chris J. Boyatzis, Associate Editor. **ISSN:** 1941--1022 (print); **EISSN:** 1943--1562 (electronic). **Subscription Rates:** $617 U.S.; $666 Other countries; $681 Other countries air mail. **URL:** http://www.apa.org/pubs/journals/rel/index.aspx. **Ad Rates:** BW $575; 4C $975. **Remarks:** Accepts advertising. **Circ:** ‡1000.

7079 ■ Psychology of Violence
American Psychological Association
750 1st St. NE
Washington, DC 20002-4242
Phone: (202)336-5500
Free: 800-374-2721
Multidisciplinary research journal concerning topics on the psychology of violence and extreme aggression. **Freq:** Quarterly. **Key Personnel:** Sherry Hamby, Editor; Carlos A. Cuevas, Editor. **ISSN:** 2152--0828 (print); **EISSN:** 2152--081X (electronic). **Subscription Rates:** $74 Members; $98 Members other countries, surface; $112 Members other countries, air mail; $133 Nonmembers; $162 Nonmembers other countries, surface; $175 Nonmembers other countries, air mail; $74 Students; $98 Students other Countries, surface; $112 Students other Countries, air mail; $617 Institutions; $666 Institutions, other countries surface; $681 Institutions, other countries air mail. **URL:** http://www.apa.org/pubs/journals/vio/index.aspx. **Ad Rates:** 4C $975; BW $275. **Remarks:** Accepts advertising. **Circ:** ‡200.

7080 ■ Psychotherapy
American Psychological Association
750 1st St. NE
Washington, DC 20002-4242
Phone: (202)336-5500
Free: 800-374-2721
Journal publishing articles relevant to the field of psychotherapy. **Freq:** Quarterly. **Key Personnel:** Mark J. Hilsenroth, Editor; Jesse J. Owens, Associate Editor. **ISSN:** 0033-3204 (print); **EISSN:** 1939-1536 (electronic). **Subscription Rates:** $77 Members; $77 Students; $150 Nonmembers; $465 Institutions; $101 Members international; surface; $101 Students, other countries international; surface; $179 Nonmembers international; surface; $514 Institutions, other countries international; surface; $115 Members international; airmail; $115 Students, other countries international; airmail; $192 Nonmembers international; airmail; $529 Institutions international; airmail. **URL:** http://www.apa.org/pubs/journals/pst/index.aspx. **Ad Rates:** 4C $1,400. **Remarks:** Accepts advertising. **Circ:** 3000.

7081 ■ Psychotherapy Networker
Psychotherapy Networker
5135 MacArthur Blvd. NW
Washington, DC 20016
Phone: (202)537-8950
Fax: (202)537-6869
Free: 888-851-9498
Publisher's E-mail: customersupport@pesi.com
Freq: Bimonthly. **ISSN:** 1535--573X (print). **Subscription Rates:** $18 U.S. /year; $34 Two years; $24 U.S. and other countries. **URL:** http://www.psychotherapynetworker.org. **Ad Rates:** $330-4220. 4C $. **Remarks:** Accepts display advertising. **Circ:** (Not Reported).

7082 ■ PsycSCAN: Applied Psychology
American Psychological Association
750 1st St. NE
Washington, DC 20002-4242
Phone: (202)336-5500
Free: 800-374-2721
Journal presenting abstracts from subscriber-selected journals in the area of applied psychology. **Founded:** 1981. **ISSN:** 0271-7506 (print). **Subscription Rates:** $35 Members; $59 Nonmembers. **URL:** http://www.apa.org/pubs/databases/psycinfo/psycscan.aspx. **Circ:** ‡1400.

7083 ■ PsycSCAN: Behavior Analysis & Therapy
American Psychological Association
750 1st St. NE
Washington, DC 20002-4242
Phone: (202)336-5500
Free: 800-374-2721
Journal on basic and applied behavior analysis. Developed jointly by APA and Division of Experimental Analysis of Behavior (Division 25). **Freq:** Monthly. **ISSN:** 1078-3946 (print). **Subscription Rates:** $39 Members Associate and Affiliate; $69 Nonmembers. **URL:** http://www.apa.org/pubs/databases/psycscans/index.aspx. **Remarks:** Accepts advertising. **Circ:** Paid 1200.

7084 ■ PsycSCAN: Clinical Psychology
American Psychological Association
750 1st St. NE
Washington, DC 20002-4242
Phone: (202)336-5500
Free: 800-374-2721
Journal presenting abstracts from subscriber-selected journals in the area of developmental psychology. **Freq:** Monthly. **ISSN:** 0197-1484 (print). **Subscription Rates:** $1299 Institutions. **URL:** http://www.apa.org/pubs/databases/psycinfo/psycscan.aspx. **Remarks:** Accepts advertising. **Circ:** ‡2785.

7085 ■ PsycSCAN: Learning Disabilities and Mental Retardation
American Psychological Association
750 1st St. NE
Washington, DC 20002-4242
Phone: (202)336-5500
Free: 800-374-2721
Journal presenting abstracts from subscriber-selected journals in the area of learning disabilities, mental retardation, and communication disorders. **Print Method:** Offset. **ISSN:** 0730--1928 (print). **Subscription Rates:** $39 Members; $69 Nonmembers. **URL:** http://www.apa.org/pubs/databases/psycinfo/psycscan.aspx. **Circ:** ‡900.

7086 ■ Public Administration Review
American Society for Public Administration
1370 Rhode Island Ave. NW, Ste. 500
Washington, DC 20036
Phone: (202)393-7878
Fax: (202)638-4952
Publisher's E-mail: info@aspanet.org
Public administration journal. **Freq:** Bimonthly. **Print Method:** Offset. **Trim Size:** 6 1/2 x 9. **Cols./Page:** 2. **Col. Width:** 38 nonpareils. **Col. Depth:** 125 agate lines. **Key Personnel:** James L. Perry, Editor-in-Chief. **ISSN:** 0033--3352 (print); **EISSN:** 1540--6210 (electronic). **USPS:** 154-06210. **Subscription Rates:** $629 Institutions U.S., print + online; £624 Institutions U.K., print + online; $524 Institutions U.S., print or online; €660 Institutions European, print or online; £520 Institutions print or online; $1017 Institutions, other countries print or online; $1221 Institutions, other countries print & online. **URL:** http://www.aspanet.org/public; http://www.blackwellpublishing.com/journal.asp?ref=0033-3352. **Remarks:** Accepts advertising. **Circ:** ‡16000, 13000.

7087 ■ Public Contract Law Journal
American Bar Association
c/o Patricia H. Wittie, Ed.-in-Ch.
Wittie, Letsche & Waldo LLP
915 15th St. NW, 2nd Flr.
Washington, DC 20005
Phone: (202)464-9353
Publication E-mail: pwittie@wlw-lawfirm.com
Contains articles on laws on all phases of federal, state, and local procurement. **Freq:** Quarterly. **Trim Size:** 6 x 9. **Cols./Page:** 1. **Key Personnel:** Kathryn E. Swisher; Patricia H. Wittie, Editor-in-Chief. **ISSN:** 0033-3341 (print). **Subscription Rates:** $90 Individuals; $15 Single issue for back issues; plus 3.95 shipping and handling; $100 Other countries; Included in membership. **URL:** http://www.pclj.org; http://www.americanbar.org/publications/public_contract_law_jrnl.html. **Circ:** (Not Reported).

7088 ■ Public Contract Law Journal
George Washington University Law School
2000 H St. NW
Washington, DC 20052
Phone: (202)994-6261
Fax: (202)994-8980
Journal presenting scholarly analyses and insight into issues affecting the broad scope of public contract and grant law. **Freq:** Quarterly. **Key Personnel:** Amy Novak Fuentes, Editor-in-Chief. **Subscription Rates:** $90 Individuals; $100 Other countries. **URL:** http://pclj.org. **Circ:** (Not Reported).

7089 ■ Public Health Reports
Association of Schools and Programs of Public Health
1900 M St. NW, Ste. 710
Washington, DC 20036
Phone: (202)296-1099
Fax: (202)296-1252
Publisher's E-mail: info@asph.org
Freq: 6/year. **Subscription Rates:** $200 Members /year; $250 Nonmembers /year. **URL:** http://www.publichealthreports.org. **Remarks:** Advertising not accepted. **Circ:** (Not Reported).

7090 ■ Public Management
International City/County Management Association
777 N Capitol St. NE, Ste. 500
Washington, DC 20002-4201
Phone: (202)289-4262
Fax: (202)962-3500
Free: 800-745-8780
Publisher's E-mail: customerservices@icma.org
Magazine for local government administrators. **Founded:** 1919. **Freq:** 11/yr. **Print Method:** Sheet-fed Offset. **Trim Size:** 8 1/4 x 10 7/8. **Cols./Page:** 3 and 2. **Col. Width:** 26 and 40 nonpareils. **Col. Depth:** 116 agate lines. **ISSN:** 0033-3611 (print). **Subscription Rates:** $46 Nonmembers; $62 Other countries. **URL:** http://www.icma.org/pm. **Also known as**: PM. **Ad Rates:** BW $2,388; 4C $1,100. **Remarks:** Advertising accepted; rates available upon request. **Circ:** ‡10000.

7091 ■ Public Understanding of Science
Council of Scientific Society Presidents
1155 16th St. NW
Washington, DC 20036
Phone: (202)872-6230
Publisher's E-mail: info@sciencepresidents.org
Peer-reviewed journal covering all aspects of the interrelationships between science (including technology and medicine) and the public. **Freq:** 8/year. **Key Personnel:** Martin Bauer, Editor. **ISSN:** 0963--6625 (print); **EISSN:** 1361--6609 (electronic). **Subscription Rates:** £58 Individuals print; £825 Institutions online; £899 Institutions print; £917 Institutions print and online; £9 Individuals single print; £124 Institutions single print. **URL:** http://pus.sagepub.com. **Remarks:** Accepts advertising. **Circ:** (Not Reported).

7092 ■ Public Works
Hanley Wood Media Inc.
1 Thomas Cir. NW, Ste. 600
Washington, WA 20005
Phone: (202)452-0800
Fax: (202)785-1974
Trade magazine covering the public works industry nationwide for city, county, and state. **Freq:** 13/yr. **Key Personnel:** Victoria K. Sicaras, Managing Editor, phone: (773)824-2504; Stephanie Johnston, Editor-in-Chief, phone: (773)824-2507; Jeff Stockman, Manager, Circulation. **ISSN:** 0033-3840 (print). **Subscription Rates:** $60 Individuals; $75 Canada; $90 Other countries; $110 Two years; $137.50 Two years Canada; $165 Two years International. **URL:** http://www.pwmag.com. **Ad Rates:** BW $6,820; 4C $1,760. **Remarks:** Accepts advertising. **Circ:** △**65000**.

7093 ■ Quarterly Journal of Speech
National Communication Association
1765 N St. NW
Washington, DC 20036
Phone: (202)464-4622
Fax: (202)464-4600
Publisher's E-mail: inbox@natcom.org
Freq: Quarterly February, May, August and November. **Print Method:** Offset. **Trim Size:** 7 x 10. **Cols./Page:** 2. **Col. Width:** 30 nonpareils. **Col. Depth:** 119 agate lines. **Key Personnel:** John Louis Lucaites, Board Member; Barbara Biesecker, Editor. **ISSN:** 0033--5630 (print); **EISSN:** 1479--5779 (electronic). **Subscription Rates:** $96 Individuals print; $382 Institutions online; $437 Institutions print and online; $91 Individuals print. **URL:** http://www.natcom.org/journaleditors/#QJS; http://www.tandfonline.com/toc/rqjs20/.VBeQPZTWIdU; http://www.tandfonline.com/loi/rqjs20#.V1kBmtKrTcv. **Remarks:** Accepts advertising. **Circ:** (Not Reported).

7094 ■ Quarterly National Accounts
OECD Washington Center
1776 I St. NW, Ste. 450
Washington, DC 20006
Phone: (202)785-6323
Fax: (202)315-2508
Free: 800-456-6323
Publisher's E-mail: washington.contact@oecd.org
Report compiling income statistics on U.S. and 11 other OECD countries. **Freq:** Quarterly. **Print Method:** Offset. **Trim Size:** 7 7/8 x 10 5/8. **Cols./Page:** 1. **Col. Width:** 84 nonpareils. **Col. Depth:** 133 agate lines. **ISSN:** 0257--7801 (print); **EISSN:** 1609--7629 (electronic). **URL:** http://www.oecd-ilibrary.org/economics/quarterly-national-accounts_16097629;jsessionid=2wn30lgi1vr3o.x-oecd-live-03. **Remarks:** Advertising not accepted. **Circ:** (Not Reported).

7095 ■ Quotarian
Quota International
1420 21st St. NW
Washington, DC 20036-5901
Phone: (202)331-9694
Fax: (202)331-4395
Publication E-mail: staff@quota.org
Member magazine for non-profit international service organization. **Freq:** Semiannual. **Trim Size:** 8 x 11. **Key Personnel:** Kathleen W. Treiber, Executive Director; Nancy Fitzpatrick, Deputy Director. **ISSN:** 0747-2072 (print). **URL:** http://www.quota.org/member-center/publications/. **Formerly**: Quota Connection. **Remarks:** Accepts advertising. **Circ:** Controlled ⊕**8322**.

7096 ■ Radio Science
American Geophysical Union
2000 Florida Ave. NW
Washington, DC 20009-1277
Phone: (202)462-6900
Fax: (202)328-0566
Free: 800-966-2481
Publication E-mail: radioscience@agu.org
Peer-reviewed journal covering scientific contributions on all aspects of electromagnetic phenomena related to physical problems. **Freq:** Bimonthly. **Key Personnel:** Richard F. Bradley, Associate Editor; Aria Abubakar, Associate Editor; Paul S. Cannon, Editor-in-Chief. **ISSN:** 0048--6604 (print); **EISSN:** 1944--799X (electronic). **Subscription Rates:** $1103 U.S. and other countries large: online; $752 U.S. and other countries medium: online; $498 U.S. and other countries small: online; £697 Institutions large: online; £475 Institutions medium: online; £315 Institutions small: online; €806 Institutions large: online; €550 Institutions medium: online; €365 Institutions small: online. **URL:** http://agupubs.onlinelibrary.wiley.com/agu/journal/10.1002/(ISSN)1944-799X. **Remarks:** Advertising not accepted. **Circ:** (Not Reported).

7097 ■ Rails to Trails
Rails-to-Trails Conservancy
Duke Ellington Bldg., 5th Fl.
2121 Ward Ct. NW
Washington, DC 20037
Phone: (202)331-9696
Fax: (202)223-9257
Publisher's E-mail: media@railstotrails.org
Magazine containing interesting articles about rails to trails stories and experiences. **Freq:** Quarterly. **Key Personnel:** Amy Kapp, Editor-in-Chief. **ISSN:** 1523--4126 (print). **Subscription Rates:** Included in membership. **URL:** http://www.railstotrails.org/magazine. **Circ:** (Not Reported).

7098 ■ Real Estate Finance Today
Mortgage Bankers Association
1919 M St. NW, 5th Fl.
Washington, DC 20036
Phone: (202)557-2700
Free: 800-793-6222
Publisher's E-mail: membership@mba.org
Tabloid tracing economic trends and government actions that affect mortgage lenders. **Freq:** Weekly. **Print Method:** Offset. **Trim Size:** 10 x 15. **Cols./Page:** 4. **Col. Width:** 14.4 picas. **Col. Depth:** 189 agate lines. **Key Personnel:** Marshall Taylor, Editor, fax: (202)429-9524; Peter House, Director, Advertising, phone: (202)861-1946. **ISSN:** 0742--0021 (print). **Subscription Rates:** $98 Individuals. **Ad Rates:** GLR $10; BW $2,185; 4C $2,860; PCI $55. **Remarks:** Accepts advertising. **Circ:** Paid ‡7000, Non-paid ‡1000.

7099 ■ Regardie's Washington: The Business of Washington
Regardie's Inc.
1010 Wisconsin Ave. NW, No. 600
Washington, DC 20007
Phone: (202)342-0410
Fax: (202)342-0515
Business magazine covering the metropolitan Washington area. **Freq:** Monthly. **Print Method:** Offset. **Trim Size:** 8 1/4 x 11. **Cols./Page:** 3. **Col. Width:** 2 1/4 inches. **Col. Depth:** 9 3/4 inches. **Key Personnel:** Brian Kelly, Editor; Michael A. DeSimone, Publisher. **ISSN:** 0279--5965 (print). **Subscription Rates:** $48 Individuals. **Ad Rates:** BW $4,098; 4C $5,275. **Remarks:** Accepts advertising. **Circ:** Paid 12721, Non-paid 42305.

7100 ■ The Register Report
Council for the National Register of Health Service Providers in Psychology, Inc.
1200 New York Ave. NW, Ste. 800
Washington, DC 20005
Phone: (202)783-7663
Fax: (202)347-0550
Freq: Semiannual. **URL:** http://www.nationalregister.org/publications/the-register-report. **Remarks:** Advertising not accepted. **Circ:** (Not Reported).

7101 ■ Regulation: Cato Review of Business & Government
Cato Institute
1000 Massachusetts Ave. NW
Washington, DC 20001-5403
Phone: (202)842-0200
Fax: (202)842-3490
Publisher's E-mail: pr@cato.org
Magazine publishing articles on government regulation. **Freq:** Quarterly. **Print Method:** Offset. **Trim Size:** 8 1/2 x 11. **Cols./Page:** 2. **Col. Width:** 3 3/4 inches. **Col. Depth:** 10 inches. **Key Personnel:** Thomas A. Firey, Managing Editor, phone: (202)218-4636; Peter Van Doren, Editor, phone: (202)789-5200; Edward H. Crane, Publisher; Alan Peterson, Manager, Circulation. **ISSN:** 0147--0590 (print). **Subscription Rates:** $20 Individuals; $35 Two years; $50 Individuals 3 years; $40 Institutions and libraries; $70 Two years institutions and libraries; $100 Institutions 3 years; libraries and institutions. **URL:** http://www.cato.org/regulation/summer-2016. **Ad Rates:** BW $650; 4C $800. **Remarks:** Accepts advertising. **Circ:** Paid 1500, Controlled 7000.

7102 ■ Rehabilitation Psychology
American Psychological Association
750 1st St. NE
Washington, DC 20002-4242
Phone: (202)336-5500
Free: 800-374-2721
Peer-reviewed journal addressing the psychosocial and behavioral aspects of rehabilitation in a wide range of settings and from a variety of perspectives, including

Circulation: ★ = AAM; △ or • = BPA; ♦ = CAC; ❑ = VAC; ⊕ = PO Statement; ‡ = Publisher's Report; Boldface figures = sworn; Light figures = estimated.

psychology, medicine, law, and social work. **Freq:** Quarterly issuance: February, May, August and November. **Print Method:** Offset. **Trim Size:** 6 x 9. **Cols./Page:** 1. **Col. Width:** 4 1/4 inches. **Col. Depth:** 7 inches. **Key Personnel:** Janet E. Farmer, Editor; Maria T. Schultheis, Associate Editor; Stephen T. Wegener, Editor; Bruce Caplan, PhD, Editor; Timothy R. Elliott, PhD, Consultant, Editor. **ISSN:** 0090--5550 (print); **EISSN:** 1939--1544 (electronic). **Subscription Rates:** $726 U.S.; $775 Other countries; $790 Other countries airmail. **URL:** http://www.apa.org/pubs/journals/rep. **Ad Rates:** BW $410; 4C $975. **Remarks:** Accepts advertising. **Circ:** 1600, ‡1400.

7103 ■ Relief Report: A Regulatory Relief Update from the National Center for Public Policy Research
National Center for Public Policy Research
20 F St. NW, Ste. 700
Washington, DC 20001
Phone: (202)507-6398
Publication E-mail: reliefreport@nationalcenter.org
Periodical covering government regulation. **Freq:** Monthly. **Key Personnel:** David Ridenour, Editor, phone: (202)371-1400. **URL:** http://www.nationalcenter.org. **Remarks:** Advertising not accepted. **Circ:** (Not Reported).

7104 ■ Remodeling
DoveTale Publishers
1 Thomas Cir. NW
Washington, DC 20005
Phone: (202)339-0744
Fax: (202)785-1974
Free: 877-275-8647
Publication E-mail: rm@omeda.com
Trade magazine for the professional remodeling industry. **Freq:** Monthly. **Print Method:** Offset. **Trim Size:** 8 x 10 1/2. **Cols./Page:** 3. **Col. Width:** 13 picas. **Col. Depth:** 58 picas. **Key Personnel:** Craig Webb, Editor-in-Chief. **ISSN:** 0885--8039 (print). **Subscription Rates:** $24.95 Individuals. **URL:** http://www.remodeling.hw.net. **Ad Rates:** 4C $17,285. **Remarks:** Accepts advertising. **Circ:** (Not Reported).

7105 ■ Replacement Contractor
DoveTale Publishers
1 Thomas Cir. NW
Washington, DC 20005
Phone: (202)339-0744
Fax: (202)785-1974
Free: 877-275-8647
Publisher's E-mail: hwmicustomerservice@hanleywood.com
Magazine for contractors engaged in roofing, siding, decking and window replacement. **Freq:** Quarterly. **Key Personnel:** Rick Strachan, Publisher. **URL:** http://www.hanleywoodopportunities.com/Index.asp?Cat=rr&Pub=rplco&Sect=Intro. **Remarks:** Accepts advertising. **Circ:** ‡16500.

7106 ■ Report from the Capital
Baptist Joint Committee for Religious Liberty
200 Maryland Ave. NE
Washington, DC 20002
Phone: (202)544-4226
Fax: (202)544-2094
Publisher's E-mail: bjc@BJConline.org
Freq: 10/year latest issue: May 2015. **ISSN:** 0346--0661 (print). **Subscription Rates:** Free. **Alt. Formats:** PDF. **URL:** http://bjconline.org/report-from-the-capital. **Remarks:** Advertising not accepted. **Circ:** (Not Reported).

7107 ■ Research Management Review
National Council of University Research Administrators
1015 18th St. NW, Ste. 901
Washington, DC 20036-5273
Phone: (202)466-3894
Fax: (202)223-5573
Journal providing a forum for the dissemination of knowledge about the study and practice of the research administration profession. **Freq:** Semiannual. **Key Personnel:** Jo Ann Smith, Editor. **Subscription Rates:** Included in membership. **URL:** http://www.ncura.edu/PublicationsStore/ResearchManagementReview.aspx. **Remarks:** Advertising not accepted. **Circ:** (Not Reported).

7108 ■ Research & Practice for Persons with Severe Disabilities
TASH
2013 H St. NW
Washington, DC 20006
Phone: (202)540-9020
Fax: (202)540-9019
Publisher's E-mail: info@tash.org
Journal featuring the works of emerging authors and researchers with topics such as inclusive education, augmentative and alternative communication, supported living, customized employment, and self-advocacy. **Freq:** Quarterly. **Subscription Rates:** Included in membership. **URL:** http://tash.org/publications/research-practice-persons-severe-disabilities. **Remarks:** Advertising not accepted. **Circ:** (Not Reported).

7109 ■ Residential Architect
Hanley Wood Media Inc.
1 Thomas Cir. NW, Ste. 600
Washington, WA 20005
Phone: (202)452-0800
Fax: (202)785-1974
Magazine for architects, designers, and building professionals. **Freq:** Quarterly. **Trim Size:** 9 x 10 7/8. **Key Personnel:** Marni Coccaro, Manager, Production; Ned Cramer, Director, Editorial. **Subscription Rates:** $39.95 Individuals; $66 Canada; $132.50 Other countries. **URL:** http://www.residentialarchitect.com; http://www.hanleywood.com/products/magazines-digital-editions. **Ad Rates:** 4C $9090. **Remarks:** Accepts advertising. **Circ:** Combined △**20000**.

7110 ■ The Review of Communication
National Communication Association
1765 N St. NW
Washington, DC 20036
Phone: (202)464-4622
Fax: (202)464-4600
Publisher's E-mail: book.orders@tandf.co.uk
Freq: Quarterly. **Key Personnel:** James Chesebro, Board Member; Raymie McKerrow, Board Member. **EISSN:** 1535--8593 (electronic). **Subscription Rates:** $330 Institutions online only; Included in membership. **URL:** http://www.tandfonline.com/toc/rroc20/current; http://www.natcom.org/journals.aspx. **Remarks:** Accepts advertising. **Circ:** (Not Reported).

7111 ■ Review of Educational Research
American Educational Research Association
1430 K St. NW, Ste. 1200
Washington, DC 20005-2504
Phone: (202)238-3200
Fax: (202)238-3250
Publisher's E-mail: webmaster@aera.net
Journal of reviews of research literature relating to education. **Freq:** Quarterly. **Print Method:** Web offset. **Trim Size:** 6 x 9. **Cols./Page:** 1. **Col. Width:** 54 nonpareils. **Col. Depth:** 98 agate lines. **Key Personnel:** Frank C. Worrell, Editor; Zeus Leonardo, Editor. **ISSN:** 0034--6543 (print); **EISSN:** 1935--1046 (electronic). **URL:** http://www.aera.net/Publications/Journals/Review-of-Educational-Research. **Remarks:** Accepts advertising. **Circ:** ‡18400.

7112 ■ Review of Environmental Economics and Policy
Association of Environmental and Resource Economists
c/o Dr. Alan J. Krupnick, President
1616 P St. NW, Ste. 600
Washington, DC 20036
Phone: (202)328-5125
Fax: (202)939-3460
Publisher's E-mail: info@aere.org
Freq: Semiannual. **Key Personnel:** Charles D. Kolstad, Editor. **ISSN:** 1750--6816 (print); **EISSN:** 1750--6824 (electronic). **Subscription Rates:** £129 Individuals print; $217 Individuals print; €193 Individuals print; £133 Institutions online; $223 Institutions online; €197 Institutions online; £153 Institutions print; $256 Institutions print; €227 Institutions print and online; £167 Institutions print and online; $278 Institutions print and online; €247 Institutions print and online; £167 corporate - online; $278 corporate - online; €247 corporate - online; £191 corporate - print; $320 corporate - print; €284 corporate - print; £209 corporate - print and online; $348 corporate - print and online; €309 corporate - print and online. **URL:** http://www.aere.org/journals; http://reep.oxfordjournals.org. **Remarks:** Advertising not accepted. **Circ:** (Not Reported).

7113 ■ Review of General Psychology
American Psychological Association
750 1st St. NE
Washington, DC 20002-4242
Phone: (202)336-5500
Free: 800-374-2721
Journal including a wide variety of psychological research-related articles. **Freq:** Quarterly. **Key Personnel:** Gerianne M. Alexander, Editor. **ISSN:** 1089-2680 (print). **Subscription Rates:** $71 Members; $71 Students; $126 Nonmembers; $581 Institutions; $95 Members international, surface; $95 Students, other countries surface; $155 Nonmembers international, surface; $630 Institutions, other countries surface; $109 Members international, airmail; $109 Students, other countries airmail. **URL:** http://www.apa.org/pubs/journals/gpr/index.aspx. **Ad Rates:** BW $410; 4C $975. **Remarks:** Accepts advertising. **Circ:** 1000.

7114 ■ Review of Metaphysics
Philosophy Education Society
The Catholic University of America
223 Aquinas Hall
Washington, DC 20064
Phone: (202)635-8778
Fax: (202)319-4484
Free: 800-255-5924
Publisher's E-mail: mail@reviewofmetaphysics.org
Journal containing philosophical articles, abstracts, book reviews, announcements, and annual notices. **Freq:** Quarterly September, December, March, and June. **Print Method:** Offset. **Trim Size:** 4 5/8 x 7 3/4. **Cols./Page:** 1. **Col. Width:** 55 nonpareils. **Col. Depth:** 103 agate lines. **Key Personnel:** Blaise Blain, Managing Editor; Dr. Jude P. Dougherty, Editor; Michael Staron, Editor. **ISSN:** 0034--6632 (print). **Subscription Rates:** $40 Individuals; $60 Other countries; $100 Institutions; $120 Institutions, other countries; $25 Students; $45 Other countries students; $15 Single issue back issue. **URL:** http://www.reviewofmetaphysics.org. **Remarks:** Accepts advertising. **Circ:** Paid 1300.

7115 ■ Review of Research in Education
American Educational Research Association
1430 K St. NW, Ste. 1200
Washington, DC 20005-2504
Phone: (202)238-3200
Fax: (202)238-3250
Publisher's E-mail: webmaster@aera.net
Journal providing an overview and descriptive analysis of selected topics of relevant research literature through critical and synthesizing essays. **Freq:** Annual. **ISSN:** 0091--732X (print); **EISSN:** 1935--1038 (electronic). **URL:** http://www.aera.net/Publications/Journals/ReviewofResearchinEducation/tabid/12612/Default.aspx. **Remarks:** Advertising not accepted. **Circ:** (Not Reported).

7116 ■ Revista Panamericana de Salud Publica
Pan American Health Organization Foundation
1889 F St. NW, Ste. 312
Washington, DC 20006
Phone: (202)974-3416
Fax: (202)974-3636
Publication E-mail: publiper@paho.org
Multilingual public health journal providing information on medical and health progress in America. **Founded:** 1997. **Freq:** Monthly. **Print Method:** Offset. **Trim Size:** 8 1/2 x 11. **Cols./Page:** 3. **Col. Width:** 43.5 nonpareils. **Key Personnel:** Carlos Campbell, Board Member; Susana Belmartino, Board Member; Celia Maria de Almeida, Board Member. **ISSN:** 1020-4989 (print); **EISSN:** 1680-5348 (electronic). **Subscription Rates:** $44 Individuals electronic; $81 Two years electronic; $72 Institutions electronic; $133 Institutions two years, electronic; Free print. **URL:** http://journal.paho.org/; http://www.scielosp.org/scielo.php?script=sci_serial&pid=1020-4989&lng=en&n rm=iso. **Mailing address:** PO Box 27733, Washington, DC 20038-7733. **Remarks:** Accepts advertising. **Circ:** ‡12000.

7117 ■ RMRScience
U.S. Forest Service Rocky Mountain Research Station
1400 Independence Ave. SW
Washington, DC 20250-1111
Free: 800-832-1355
Publication E-mail: rmrspubrequest@fs.fed.us
Science newsletter covering natural resources research in the western U.S. **Freq:** Biennial. **Key Personnel:**

Rick Fletcher, Editor, phone: (970)295-5920. **Subscription Rates:** Free. **URL:** http://www.fs.fed.us. **Formerly**: Forestry Research West. **Remarks:** Advertising not accepted. **Circ:** Controlled 2000.

7118 ■ Roll Call
Roll Call Inc.
77 K St. NE, 8th Fl
Washington, DC 20001
Phone: (202)650-6621
Free: 800-824-6819
Publisher's E-mail: customerservice@cqrollcall.com
Contains the news of Congress from a unique insider perspective. **Founded:** June 16, 1955. **Freq:** Daily Mon.- Thurs. **Print Method:** Offset. **Trim Size:** 10.5 x 15. **Cols./Page:** 4. **Col. Width:** 2.25 picas. **Col. Depth:** 14 inches. **Key Personnel:** Scott Montgomery, Editor; Kate Ackley, Writer; Morton M. Kondracke, Senior Editor; Katie Smith, Managing Editor. **ISSN:** 0035-788X (print). **Subscription Rates:** Free online access to paid order print edition; $350 Individuals online. **URL:** http://www.rollcall.com. **Ad Rates:** BW $11,220; 4C $12,900. **Remarks:** Accepts advertising. **Circ:** 19069.

7119 ■ Rural Matters
Rural Community Assistance Partnership
1701 K St. NW, Ste. 700
Washington, DC 20006
Phone: (202)408-1273
Fax: (202)408-8165
Free: 800-321-7227
Publisher's E-mail: info@rcap.org
Magazine publishing information about environmental and infrastructure development issues facing rural communities. **Freq:** Published several times per year - from three to six issues. **Subscription Rates:** Free. **URL:** http://www.rcap.org/RuralMatters. **Remarks:** Accepts advertising. **Circ:** 7800.

7120 ■ Russia Business Watch
U.S.-Russia Business Council
1110 Vermont Ave. NW, Ste. 350
Washington, DC 20005
Phone: (202)739-9180
Fax: (202)659-5920
Publisher's E-mail: info@usrbc.org
Magazine publishing latest commercial and political developments in U.S.-Russian relations. **Freq:** Quarterly. **Key Personnel:** Svetlana Minjack, Editor. **Alt. Formats:** PDF. **URL:** http://www.usrbc.org/resources/russiabusinesswatch/article/3929. **Remarks:** Accepts advertising. **Circ:** (Not Reported).

7121 ■ Russian Language Journal
American Councils for International Education
1828 L St. NW, Ste. 1200
Washington, DC 20036-5136
Phone: (202)833-7522
Fax: (202)833-7523
Publication E-mail: rlj@actr.org
Freq: Annual. **Key Personnel:** William P. Rivers, Editor. **ISSN:** 0036--0252 (print). **Subscription Rates:** $50 U.S. and Canada for Institutions and Libraries; $65 Other countries for Institutions and Libraries. **URL:** http://rlj.americancouncils.org. **Remarks:** Accepts advertising. **Circ:** (Not Reported).

7122 ■ SAA Archaeological Record
Society for American Archaeology
1111 14th St. NW, Ste. 800
Washington, DC 20005-5622
Phone: (202)789-8200
Fax: (202)789-0284
Publication E-mail: publications@saa.org
Professional magazine covering archaeology for members. **Freq:** 5/year. **Key Personnel:** Anna Marie Prentiss, Editor. **ISSN:** 1532-7299 (print). **Subscription Rates:** Free. **Alt. Formats:** PDF. **URL:** http://www.saa.org/AbouttheSociety/Publications/TheSAAArchaeologicalRecord/tabid/64/Default.aspx. **Ad Rates:** 4C $687. **Remarks:** Accepts advertising. **Circ:** 8000, 6600.

7123 ■ The SAIS Review
Johns Hopkins University Press
1619 Massachusetts Ave., NW
Washington, DC 20036
Publication E-mail: saisreview@sais-jhu.edu
Scholarly journal covering international affairs. **Freq:** Semiannual. **ISSN:** 0036-0775 (print); **EISSN:** 1088-3142 (electronic). **Subscription Rates:** $110 Institutions print; $35 Individuals print; $63 Two years individual; $40 Individuals online. **URL:** http://www.press.jhu.edu/journals/sais_review. **Ad Rates:** BW $275. **Remarks:** Accepts advertising. **Circ:** Combined 294.

7124 ■ Salary Survey
National Association for Business Economics
1920 L St. NW, Ste. 300
Washington, DC 20036
Phone: (202)463-6223
Fax: (202)463-6239
Publisher's E-mail: nabe@nabe.com
Publication that provides data on income levels by educational attainment, industry and location. **Freq:** Biennial. **Key Personnel:** Tomas Beers, Executive Director. **Subscription Rates:** $250 Nonmembers. **URL:** http://www.nabe.com/surveys. **Remarks:** Advertising not accepted. **Circ:** (Not Reported).

7125 ■ Sales & Marketing Ideas
National Association of Home Builders
1201 15th St. NW
Washington, DC 20005
Free: 800-268-5242
Publisher's E-mail: info@nahb.org
Trade magazine for sales and marketing professionals in the home building industry. **Freq:** Bimonthly. **Print Method:** Offset. **Trim Size:** 8 1/2 x 11. **Key Personnel:** Steve Bunce, Contact; Joseph Mcgaw, Contact. **Subscription Rates:** $70 Nonmembers; $59 Members. **URL:** http://www.nahb.org/sitecore/commerce/products/NAHB/2014/12/23/11/56/NSMC%20Magazine%20Subscription%20-%2030.aspx?code=30&sc_lang=en. **Remarks:** Accepts advertising. **Circ:** 3745.

7126 ■ Saving Land
Land Trust Alliance
1660 L St. NW, Ste. 1100
Washington, DC 20036
Phone: (202)638-4725
Fax: (202)638-4730
Publisher's E-mail: info@lta.org
Freq: Quarterly. **ISSN:** 2159- 2918 (print). **Subscription Rates:** Included in membership. **Circ:** (Not Reported).

7127 ■ School Psychology Quarterly
American Psychological Association
750 1st St. NE
Washington, DC 20002-4242
Phone: (202)336-5500
Free: 800-374-2721
Journal covering school psychology. **Freq:** Quarterly. **Trim Size:** 6 x 9. **Key Personnel:** Shane Jimerson, Editor. **ISSN:** 1045--3830 (print); **EISSN:** 1939--1560 (electronic). **Subscription Rates:** $635 Institutions U.S; $684 Institutions international; $699 Institutions international (airmail). **URL:** http://www.apa.org/pubs/journals/spq/index.aspx. **Formerly**: Professional School Psychology. **Ad Rates:** 4C $975; BW $425. **Remarks:** Accepts advertising. **Circ:** 1700.

7128 ■ SCHS Journal of Supreme Court History
Supreme Court Historical Society
Opperman House
224 E Capitol St. NE
Washington, DC 20003
Phone: (202)543-0400
Fax: (202)547-7730
Free: 888-539-4438
Publisher's E-mail: suggestions@supremecourthistory.org
Journal dedicated to the collection and preservation of the history of the Supreme Court of the United States, and to expanding public awareness of that history and heritage. **Freq:** 3/year March, July and November. **Key Personnel:** Melvin I. Urofsky, Editor. **ISSN:** 1059--4329 (print); **EISSN:** 1540--5818 (electronic). **Subscription Rates:** $236 Institutions print or online; $284 Institutions print and online; £183 Institutions print or online; £220 Institutions print and online; €231 Institutions print or online; €278 Institutions print and online; $352 Institutions, other countries print or online; $453 Institutions, other countries print and online. **URL:** http://supremecourthistory.org/pub_journal_archive.html; http://onlinelibrary.wiley.com/journal/10.1111/(ISSN)1540-5818. **Remarks:** Accepts advertising. **Circ:** (Not Reported).

7129 ■ Science Books & Films: A Critical Review Journal for all Sciences and all Ages
American Association for the Advancement of Science
1200 New York Ave. NW
Washington, DC 20005
Phone: (202)326-6400
Publication E-mail: sb&f@aaas.org
Professional journal reviewing science books, AV materials, and software made for general audiences, teachers, and students from kindergarten to college. **Freq:** Bimonthly. **Print Method:** Offset. **Trim Size:** 8 1/2 x 11. **Cols./Page:** 3. **Key Personnel:** Maria Sosa, Editor-in-Chief; Ann M. Williams, Art Director; Heather Malcomson, Editor. **ISSN:** 0098--342X (print). **Subscription Rates:** $45 Individuals; $85 Two years. **URL:** http://www.sbfonline.com. **Ad Rates:** BW $900; 4C $1,800. **Remarks:** Accepts advertising. **Circ:** 5000.

7130 ■ Science News: The Weekly Newsmagazine of Science
Society for Science and the Public
1719 N St. NW
Washington, DC 20036
Phone: (202)785-2255
Free: 800-552-4412
Publication E-mail: scinews@sciencenews.org
Reports on new findings in physical, biological and behavioral sciences. **Freq:** Biweekly. **Print Method:** Web offset. **Trim Size:** 8.125 x 10.5. **Cols./Page:** 3. **Key Personnel:** Tom Siegfried, Editor; Eva Emerson, Editor-in-Chief; Elizabeth Marincola, President, Publisher. **ISSN:** 0036--8423 (print). **Subscription Rates:** Included in membership. **URL:** http://www.sciencenews.org. **Remarks:** Advertising accepted; rates available upon request. **Circ:** 130000.

7131 ■ The Scottish Rite Journal
Supreme Council of the 33rd Degree
1733 Sixteenth St., NW
Washington, DC 20009-3103
Phone: (202)777-3152
Fax: (202)464-0487
Publisher's E-mail: council@scottishrite.org
Masonic magazine. **Freq:** Bimonthly. **Print Method:** Offset. **Trim Size:** 8 x 10 3/4. **Cols./Page:** 2. **Col. Width:** 25 nonpareils. **Col. Depth:** 85 agate lines. **Key Personnel:** S. Brent Morris, Managing Editor. **ISSN:** 1076--8572 (print). **Subscription Rates:** $15 Individuals; $37 Other countries; $2.50 Individuals masonic windows; $3 Single issue. **URL:** http://scottishrite.org/about/media-publications/journals. **Remarks:** Accepts advertising. **Circ:** Non-paid ‡400000.

7132 ■ Scrap Magazine
Institute of Scrap Recycling Industries
1615 L St. NW, Ste. 600
Washington, DC 20036-5610
Phone: (202)662-8500
Fax: (202)626-0900
Publisher's E-mail: isri@isri.org
Magazine providing articles and columns to member professionals that will help increase the profitability of their businesses for their process, broker, and consume scrap commodities. **Freq:** Bimonthly. **Subscription Rates:** free for members. **URL:** http://www.isri.org/news-publications/scrap-magazine. **Remarks:** Advertising not accepted. **Circ:** (Not Reported).

7133 ■ Section 504 Compliance Handbook
Thompson Publishing Group Inc.
Government Information Services
Education Funding Research Council
1725 K St. NW, Ste. 700
Washington, DC 20006
Fax: (800)999-5661
Free: 800-677-3789
Publisher's E-mail: service@thompson.com
Magazine covering new developments in disability law. **Freq:** Monthly. **Key Personnel:** Ruth Fink, Advisor; Stephan Hamlin-Smith, Advisor; Bruce Hunter, Advisor. **Subscription Rates:** $349 Individuals. **Remarks:** Advertising not accepted. **Circ:** (Not Reported).

7134 ■ Secular World
Atheist Alliance International
1777 T St. NW
Washington, DC 20009-7102

Circulation: ★ = AAM; △ or • = BPA; ♦ = CAC; ❑ = VAC; ⊕ = PO Statement; ‡ = Publisher's Report; Boldface figures = sworn; Light figures = estimated.

Publisher's E-mail: info@atheistalliance.org
Magazine comprising of topics, studies, and researches about atheism. **Freq:** Quarterly. **Subscription Rates:** Included in membership. **URL:** http://www.atheistalliance.org/secular-world.html. **Remarks:** Advertising not accepted. **Circ:** (Not Reported).

7135 ■ Secure Retirement, The Newsmagazine for Mature Americans
National Committee to Preserve Social Security and Medicare
10 G St. NE, Ste. 600
Washington, DC 20002
Phone: (202)216-0420
Fax: (202)216-0446
Free: 800-966-1935
Publisher's E-mail: webmaster@ncpssm.org
Magazine for senior citizens and others interested in politics and government and how they affect senior concerns and issues. **Freq:** 6/year. **Print Method:** Offset. **Trim Size:** 8 1/2 x 10 1/2. **Cols./Page:** 3. **Col. Width:** 2 1/4 inches. **Col. Depth:** 10 inches. **Key Personnel:** Denise Fremeau, Editor, phone: (202)822-9459; Jack McDavitt, Director, Publications, phone: (202)467-9030. **ISSN:** 1069-6911 (print). **Subscription Rates:** $1.25 Single issue. **Alt. Formats:** PDF. **Formerly**: Saving Social Security. **Ad Rates:** BW $27980; 4C $36300. **Remarks:** Accepts advertising. **Circ:** Paid 2097766, Non-paid 31410.

7136 ■ Security and Defense Studies Review: Interdisciplinary Journal of the Center for Hemispheric Defense Studies
National Defense University
Bldg. 62
300 5th Ave. SW
Washington, DC 20319-5066
Phone: (202)685-4700
Multi-lingual scholarly journal that publishes articles related to security and defense topics in the Western Hemisphere. **Freq:** Semiannual. **Key Personnel:** Richard D. Downie, PhD, Editor. **ISSN:** 1533--2535 (print). **Subscription Rates:** Free. **Circ:** (Not Reported).

7137 ■ Segunda Juventud
AARP
601 E St. NW
Washington, DC 20049-0001
Phone: (202)434-3525
Free: 888-687-2277
Publication E-mail: segundajuventud@aarp.org
Newspaper offering information for health, money, travel, and lifestyle for retired Hispanic people. **Freq:** Bimonthly. **ISSN:** 1539-0179 (print). **Subscription Rates:** $13 Individuals. **URL:** http://www.aarpsegundajuventud.org/english/index.html. **Remarks:** Accepts advertising. **Circ:** (Not Reported).

7138 ■ Shakespeare Quarterly
Johns Hopkins University Press
Editor of Shakespeare Quarterly
201 E Capitol St., SE
Washington, DC 20003-1094
Publication E-mail: sq@folger.edu
Refereed journal committed to publishing articles in the vanguard of Shakespeare studies, notes that bring to light new information on Shakespeare and his age, issue and exchange sections on the latest research and debates, theater reviews of significant Shakespeare productions, and book reviews to keep readers current with Shakespeare criticism and scholarship. **Founded:** 1950. **Freq:** Quarterly. **Print Method:** Offset. **Trim Size:** 6 7/8 x 10. **Cols./Page:** 1. **Col. Width:** 30 picas. **Col. Depth:** 46.5 picas. **Key Personnel:** Gail Kern Paster, Editor; William H. Sherman, Board Member; Jonathan Gil Harris, Associate Editor; Mimi Godfrey, Managing Editor; Barbara A. Mowat, Editor. **ISSN:** 0037-3222 (print). **Subscription Rates:** $45 Individuals; $160 Institutions; $34 Individuals for print; $105 Institutions for print or online; $147 Institutions for print and online; $29 Students. **URL:** http://www.folger.edu/template.cfm?cid=542; http://www.press.jhu.edu/journals/shakespeare_quarterly/index.html. **Ad Rates:** BW $325. **Remarks:** Color advertising not accepted. **Circ:** Paid ‡3400, Non-paid ‡250.

7139 ■ Share the Word
Paulist Evangelization Ministries
3031 4th St. NE
Washington, DC 20017
Phone: (202)832-5022
Fax: (202)269-0209
Publisher's E-mail: info@pemdc.org
Catholic magazine reflecting upon the Sunday and daily lectionary readings, with articles on spirituality, evangelism, and scripture. **Freq:** Bimonthly 7/year. **ISSN:** 0199-5049 (print). **Subscription Rates:** $17.50 /year; $31.50 /2 years; $42 /3 years. **URL:** http://www.pemdc.org. **Ad Rates:** BW $900. **Remarks:** Accepts advertising. **Circ:** Paid ‡17500, 20000.

7140 ■ Sheet Metal Workers' Journal
International Association of Sheet Metal, Air, Rail and Transportation Workers
1750 New York Ave. NW, 6th Fl.
Washington, DC 20006
Phone: (202)783-5880
Publisher's E-mail: info@smwia.org
Freq: Bimonthly. **ISSN:** 1528--2805 (print). **Subscription Rates:** $7.50 Members. **Remarks:** Advertising not accepted. **Circ:** (Not Reported).

7141 ■ Shofar
BBYO, Inc.
800 8th St. NW
Washington, DC 20001
Phone: (202)857-6633
Fax: (202)857-6568
Publisher's E-mail: info@bbyo.org
Jewish youth newspaper. **Freq:** Quarterly. **Print Method:** Offset. **Cols./Page:** 4. **Col. Width:** 28 nonpareils. **Col. Depth:** 205 agate lines. **ISSN:** 0745--9327 (print). **URL:** http://bbyo.org/blog/shofar. **Remarks:** Accepts advertising. **Circ:** ‡30000.

7142 ■ Sign Language Studies
Gallaudet University Press
800 Florida Ave. NE
Washington, DC 20002-3695
Phone: (202)651-5488
Fax: (202)651-5489
Publisher's E-mail: gupress@gallaudet.edu
Magazine concerning the use of primary and alternative sign languages.Publishes scholarly research on Sign Languages and other nonvocal means of communication. **Freq:** Quarterly. **Key Personnel:** Ceil Lucas, Editor. **ISSN:** 0302--1475 (print). **Subscription Rates:** $55 Individuals; $95 Institutions; $50 Students. **URL:** http://gupress.gallaudet.edu/SLS.html. **Remarks:** Advertising not accepted. **Circ:** (Not Reported).

7143 ■ SIRC Review
Styrene Information and Research Center
910 17th St. NW, 5th Fl.
Washington, DC 20006
Phone: (202)787-5996
Publisher's E-mail: sirc@styrene.org
Freq: Periodic. **URL:** http://styrene.org/the-sirc-review-journal. **Remarks:** Advertising not accepted. **Circ:** (Not Reported).

7144 ■ Sister 2 Sister
Sister 2 Sister Inc.
PO Box 41148
Washington, DC 20018
Consumer magazine covering entertainment for a black audience. **Freq:** Monthly. **Key Personnel:** Jamie Foster-Brown, Publisher; Lorenzo Brown, Managing Editor; Ericka Boston, Senior Editor. **Subscription Rates:** $14.98 Individuals 1 year; $24 Individuals 2 years. **URL:** http://www.s2smagazine.com. **Ad Rates:** BW $11,050; 4C $12,350. **Remarks:** Advertising accepted; rates available upon request. **Circ:** Paid ★184944.

7145 ■ Smithsonian Magazine
Smithsonian Magazine
PO Box 37012
MRC 513
Washington, DC 20013-7012
Phone: (202)633-6090
Free: 800-766-2149
General interest magazine. **Freq:** 11/year. **Print Method:** Offset. **Trim Size:** 8 x 10 7/8. **Cols./Page:** 3. **Col. Width:** 2 1/4 inches. **Col. Depth:** 140 agate lines. **Key Personnel:** Jennifer Hicks, Publisher, phone: (212)916-1338; Carey Winfrey, Editor; Alison McLean, Managing Editor. **ISSN:** 0037--7333 (print). **Subscription Rates:** $25 Canada; $38 Other countries; $12 U.S. **URL:** http://www.smithsonianmag.com; http://www.smithsonianmag.com/?no-ist. **Ad Rates:** BW $89,845; 4C $131,640. **Remarks:** Accepts advertising. **Circ:** Paid 2000000.

7146 ■ Social Work
National Association of Social Workers
750 1st St. NE, Ste. 800
Washington, DC 20002-4241
Phone: (202)408-8600
Fax: (202)336-8313
Free: 800-742-4089
Publisher's E-mail: membership@naswdc.org
Freq: Quarterly. **ISSN:** 0037- 8046 (print). **Subscription Rates:** Included in membership; $196 Institutions print and online; $111 Individuals /year for nonmembers; print only; $244 /year for corporate; print and online. **URL:** http://www.naswpress.org/publications/journals/sw.html. **Remarks:** Accepts advertising. **Circ:** (Not Reported).

7147 ■ Social Work: Journal of the National Association of Social Workers
National Association of Social Workers
750 1st St. NE, Ste. 800
Washington, DC 20002-4241
Phone: (202)408-8600
Fax: (202)336-8313
Free: 800-742-4089
Publisher's E-mail: membership@naswdc.org
Journal for social workers. **Freq:** Quarterly. **Print Method:** Offset. **Trim Size:** 7 1/4 x 10. **Cols./Page:** 2. **Col. Width:** 17 picas. **Col. Depth:** 50 picas. **Key Personnel:** William Meezan, Chairperson; Monit Cheung, Board Member; Tricia B. Bent-Goodley, PhD, Editor-in-Chief. **ISSN:** 0037--8046 (print). **Subscription Rates:** $117 Individuals print; $189 Institutions print; $164 Institutions online; $206 Institutions print & online. **URL:** http://www.naswpress.org/publications/journals/sw.html. **Ad Rates:** BW $1465. **Remarks:** Accepts advertising. **Circ:** 148000.

7148 ■ Social Work Research
National Association of Social Workers
750 1st St. NE, Ste. 800
Washington, DC 20002-4241
Phone: (202)408-8600
Fax: (202)336-8313
Free: 800-742-4089
Publisher's E-mail: membership@naswdc.org
Research journal for social workers. **Freq:** Quarterly. **Print Method:** Offset. **Trim Size:** 7 1/4 x 10. **Cols./Page:** 2. **Col. Width:** 16 picas. **Col. Depth:** 53 picas. **Key Personnel:** James Herbert Williams, PhD, MSW, Editor-in-Chief; Philip Hong, Board Member; William Meezan, Chairperson. **ISSN:** 1070--5309 (print); **EISSN:** 1545--6838 (electronic). **Subscription Rates:** $92 Members print; $117 Individuals print; $184 Institutions print; $200 Institutions print and online; $160 Institutions online. **URL:** http://www.naswpress.org/publications/journals/swr.html. **Formerly**: Social Work Research & Abstracts. **Ad Rates:** BW $465. **Remarks:** Accepts advertising. **Circ:** Paid 2500, 2200.

7149 ■ Sociological Methodology
American Sociological Association
1430 K St. NW, Ste. 600
Washington, DC 20005
Phone: (202)383-9005
Fax: (202)638-0882
Publisher's E-mail: customer@asanet.org
Scholarly publication covering methods of research in the social sciences, including conceptualizations and modeling, research design, data collection, and related issues. **Freq:** Annual August. **Key Personnel:** Tim Futing Liao, Editor; Lisa Savage, Managing Editor; Tim Liao, Editor. **ISSN:** 0081--1750 (print); **EISSN:** 1467--9531 (electronic). **Subscription Rates:** $45 Members; $30 Students; $425 Institutions print/online; $383 Institutions online only. **URL:** http://www.asanet.org/journals/sm/sm.cfm. **Remarks:** Advertising not accepted. **Circ:** (Not Reported).

7150 ■ Sociology of Education
American Sociological Association
1430 K St. NW, Ste. 600
Washington, DC 20005
Phone: (202)383-9005
Fax: (202)638-0882
Publication E-mail: edu-soe@uiowa.edu
International journal on studies of education and human social development by social science scholars. **Freq:** Quarterly January, April, July and October. **Key Person-**

nel: John Robert Warren, Editor. **ISSN:** 0038--0407 (print). **Subscription Rates:** $45 Members /year; $30 Students members; $402 Institutions online only; $446 Institutions print and online. **URL:** http://www.asanet.org/journals/soe/soe.cfm. **Ad Rates:** BW $350. **Remarks:** Accepts advertising. **Circ:** ‡2500.

7151 ■ Socius: Sociological Research for a Dynamic World
American Sociological Association
1430 K St. NW, Ste. 600
Washington, DC 20005
Phone: (202)383-9005
Fax: (202)638-0882
Publisher's E-mail: customer@asanet.org
Journal providing an online forum for the dissemination of peer-reviewed researches and public debates. **Key Personnel:** Lisa A. Keister, Editor. **ISSN:** 2378--0231 (print). **URL:** http://www.asanet.org/journals/socius.cfm. **Circ:** (Not Reported).

7152 ■ Sojourners: Faith, Politics, and Culture
Sojourners
3333 14th St. NW, Ste. 200
Washington, DC 20010
Phone: (202)328-8842
Fax: (202)328-8757
Free: 800-714-7474
Publisher's E-mail: sojourners@sojo.net
Independent, ecumenical Christian magazine which analyzes faith, politics, and culture from a progressive, justice-oriented perspective. **Freq:** Monthly. **Key Personnel:** Rose Marie Berger, Associate Editor; Jim Rice, Editor; Jim Wallis, President, Editor-in-Chief. **ISSN:** 0364--2097 (print). **Subscription Rates:** $39.95 Individuals; $49.95 Canada; $59.95 Other countries. **URL:** http://sojo.net. **Ad Rates:** BW $1,845; 4C $2,055. **Remarks:** Accepts advertising. **Circ:** Paid ‡600000, Non-paid ‡3000.

7153 ■ Space Weather: The International Journal of Research and Applications
American Geophysical Union
2000 Florida Ave. NW
Washington, DC 20009-1277
Phone: (202)462-6900
Fax: (202)328-0566
Free: 800-966-2481
Publisher's E-mail: service@agu.org
Peer-reviewed journal offering information on space weather and its impact on telecommunications, electric power, and satellite navigation. **Freq:** Monthly. **Key Personnel:** Howard Singer, Editor; Delores J. Knipp, Editor-in-Chief. **ISSN:** 1542--7390 (print); **EISSN:** 1542--7390 (electronic). **Subscription Rates:** $727 U.S. and other countries online - large; £458 Institutions online - large; €532 Institutions online - large; $498 U.S. and other countries online - medium; £315 Institutions online - medium; €365 Institutions online - medium; $341 U.S. and other countries online - small; £216 Institutions online - small; €249 Institutions online - small. **URL:** http://www.agu.org/journals/spaceweather; http://agupubs.onlinelibrary.wiley.com/agu/journal/10.1002/(ISSN)1542-7390. **Remarks:** Accepts advertising. **Circ:** (Not Reported).

7154 ■ SPEC Kit
Association of Research Libraries
21 Dupont Cir. NW, Ste. 800
Washington, DC 20036-1543
Phone: (202)296-2296
Fax: (202)872-0884
Publisher's E-mail: webmgr@arl.org
Survey report pertaining to research library management practices. **Freq:** 6/year. **Trim Size:** 8 1/2 x 11. **Key Personnel:** Lee Anne George, Officer. **ISSN:** 0160--3582 (print). **Subscription Rates:** $400 Individuals collection full access; $50 Individuals kit full access. **URL:** http://www.arl.org/publications-resources; http://www.arl.org/publications-resources/search-publications/term/summary/50. **Formerly**: Systems & Procedures Exchange Center (SPEC) Kit. **Remarks:** Advertising not accepted. **Circ:** Paid 550, Non-paid 10.

7155 ■ The Special Educator e-Journal
National Association of Special Education Teachers
1250 Connecticut Ave. NW, Ste. 200
Washington, DC 20036
Free: 800-754-4421
Publisher's E-mail: contactus@naset.org
Freq: Monthly. **Subscription Rates:** Included in membership. **Alt. Formats:** PDF. **URL:** http://www.naset.org/520.0.html. **Remarks:** Advertising accepted; rates available upon request. **Circ:** (Not Reported).

7156 ■ Spiritual Life: A Quarterly of Contemporary Spirituality
Discalced Carmelite Friars
2131 Lincoln Rd. NE
Washington, DC 20002
Fax: (202)832-5711
Catholic journal of spirituality. **Freq:** Quarterly. **Print Method:** Offset. **Trim Size:** 6 x 9. **Cols./Page:** 1. **Col. Width:** 54 nonpareils. **Col. Depth:** 98 agate lines. **Key Personnel:** Edward O'Donnell, Editor. **ISSN:** 0038--7630 (print). **Subscription Rates:** $3.50 Single issue 5 back issues; Free online. **URL:** http://spiritual-life.org. **Remarks:** Advertising not accepted. **Circ:** 12000.

7157 ■ SPLC Report
Student Press Law Center
1608 Rhode Island Ave. NW, Ste. 211
Washington, DC 20036
Phone: (202)785-5450
Fax: (202)822-5045
Report summarizing current cases, legislation and controversies involving student press rights. **Freq:** 3/year 3/yr. **Key Personnel:** Frank LoMonte, Executive Director. **URL:** http://www.splc.org/news/report.asp. **Remarks:** Advertising not accepted. **Circ:** (Not Reported).

7158 ■ Stability Operations Magazine
International Stability Operations Association
2025 M St. NW, Ste. 800
Washington, DC 20036
Phone: (202)367-1153
Fax: (202)367-2153
Publisher's E-mail: ISOA@stability-operations.org
Magazine containing studies of the private sector's role in peace and stability operations. **Freq:** Bimonthly. **Subscription Rates:** $30 U.S.; $35 Other countries; $15 registered friend; Free online. **URL:** http://www.stability-operations.org/?page=SOmagazine; http://www.stability-operations.org/?page=pubsarchive. **Formerly**: Journal of International Peace Operations. **Remarks:** Accepts advertising. **Circ:** 15000.

7159 ■ Stars & Stripes
Stars & Stripes
529 14th St. NW, Ste. 350
Washington, DC 20045-1301
Phone: (312)763-0900
Fax: (312)763-0890
Publisher's E-mail: news@stripes.com
U.S. Department of Defense-authorized newspaper for the overseas United States military community. Provides commercially available U.S. and world news as well as objective staff-produced stories relevant to the military community. **Freq:** Daily. **Key Personnel:** Max D. Lederer, Jr., Publisher. **Subscription Rates:** $39.99 Individuals online. **URL:** http://www.stripes.com. **Remarks:** Advertising accepted; rates available upon request. **Circ:** (Not Reported).

7160 ■ Statistics of Income SOI Bulletin
U.S. Government Publishing Office
732 N Capitol St. NW
Washington, DC 20401-0001
Phone: (202)512-1800
Fax: (202)512-2104
Free: 866-512-1800
Publisher's E-mail: contactcenter@gpo.gov
Publication covering financial and economic statistics and business. **Freq:** Quarterly Winter, Spring, Summer and Fall. **ISSN:** 0730--0743 (print). **Mailing address:** PO Box 979050, Saint Louis, MO 63197-9000. **Circ:** (Not Reported).

7161 ■ STORES Magazine
National Retail Federation
1101 New York Ave. NW
Washington, DC 20005
Phone: (202)783-7971
Fax: (202)737-2849
Free: 800-673-4692
Freq: Monthly. **ISSN:** 0039--1867 (print). **Subscription Rates:** $120 /year. **URL:** http://nrf.com/connect-us/stores-magazine. **Ad Rates:** BW $8,995. **Remarks:** Accepts advertising. **Circ:** 35000.

7162 ■ Stores: The Magazine for Retail Decision Makers
NRF Enterprises Inc.
325 Seventh St. NW, Ste. 1100
Washington, DC 20004
Phone: (202)783-7971
Fax: (202)737-2849
Free: 800-673-4692
Publisher's E-mail: press@nrf.com
Magazine for retail traders. **Freq:** Monthly. **Print Method:** Offset. **Trim Size:** 8 x 10 1/2. **Cols./Page:** 3. **Col. Width:** 26 nonpareils. **Col. Depth:** 140 agate lines. **Key Personnel:** Susan Reda, Editor. **ISSN:** 0039--1867 (print). **Subscription Rates:** Included in membership. **URL:** http://nrf.com/connect-us/stores-magazine. **Remarks:** Accepts advertising. **Circ:** Paid ‡42858.

7163 ■ Structure Magazine
American Council of Engineering Companies
1015 15th St. NW, 8th Fl.
Washington, DC 20005-2605
Phone: (202)347-7474
Fax: (202)898-0068
Publisher's E-mail: acec@acec.org
Magazine focused on providing tips, tools, techniques, and innovative concepts for structural engineers. **Freq:** Annual. **Print Method:** Offset. **Trim Size:** 8 3/8 x 10 7/8. **Cols./Page:** 6. **Col. Width:** 1 3/4 inches. **Col. Depth:** 21 1/2 inches. **Key Personnel:** Christine M. Sloat, PE, Editor, Publisher; Nikki M. Alger, Associate Editor; Jeanne Vogelzang, Executive Editor; Robert Fullmer, Graphic Designer; Chuck Minor, Manager, Advertising. **ISSN:** 0969--2126 (print). **Subscription Rates:** $65 Nonmembers for U.S. residents; $35 Students; $90 Canada; $125 Other countries; $90 Students other countries. **URL:** http://www.structuremag.org; http://www.acec.org/case/news/publications. **Ad Rates:** 4C $4,300. **Remarks:** Advertising accepted; rates available upon request. **Circ:** ‡33043.

7164 ■ Studies in Conflict and Terrorism
Routledge
c/o Bruce Hoffman, Editor-in-Chief
Georgetown University
214 3600 N St. NW
Washington, DC 20057
Publisher's E-mail: book.orders@tandf.co.uk
Journal publishing research on all forms of conflict and terrorism. **Freq:** 12/yr. **Print Method:** Offset. **Trim Size:** 7 x 10. **Cols./Page:** 1. **Col. Width:** 32 picas. **Col. Depth:** 51 picas. **Key Personnel:** Dr. Bruce Hoffman, Editor-in-Chief; Ami Pedahzur, Associate Editor; Michael L.R. Smith, Associate Editor; George K. Tanham, Editor, Founder; Peter Bergen, Board Member; Rogelio Alonso, Board Member; Peter Chalk, Associate Editor; Seth Jones, Board Member; David W. Brannan, Board Member; Gavin Cameron, Editor; Bruce Hoffman, Editor-in-Chief. **ISSN:** 1057--610X (print); **EISSN:** 1521--0731 (electronic). **Subscription Rates:** $612 Individuals print only; $1556 Institutions online only; $1778 Institutions print and online. **URL:** http://www.tandfonline.com/toc/uter20/current. **Remarks:** on request. **Circ:** 850.

7165 ■ Suicide and Life-Threatening Behavior
American Association of Suicidology
5221 Wisconsin Ave. NW
Washington, DC 20015
Phone: (202)237-2280
Fax: (202)237-2282
Journal containing issues on suicidology employing biological, statistical and sociological approach. **Freq:** Bimonthly. **ISSN:** 0363- 0234 (print). **Subscription Rates:** Included in membership. **URL:** http://www.suicidology.org/resources/sltb. **Remarks:** Accepts advertising. **Circ:** (Not Reported).

7166 ■ Sulphur in Agriculture
The Sulphur Institute
1020 19th St. NW, Ste. 520
Washington, DC 20036
Phone: (202)331-9660
Fax: (202)293-2940
Publisher's E-mail: sulphur@sulphurinstitute.org
Journal covering the use of sulphur in agriculture. **Freq:** Semiannual. **ISSN:** 0160--0680 (print). **Remarks:** Advertising not accepted. **Circ:** (Not Reported).

Circulation: ★ = AAM; △ or • = BPA; ♦ = CAC; ☐ = VAC; ⊕ = PO Statement; ‡ = Publisher's Report; Boldface figures = sworn; Light figures = estimated.

7167 ■ Sustainable Development Law & Policy
American University Washington College of Law
4801 Massachusetts Ave. NW
Washington, DC 20016
Phone: (202)274-4000
Fax: (202)274-4005
Publication E-mail: sdlp@wcl.american.edu
Journal that focuses on the tension between environmental sustainability, economic development, and human welfare. **Freq:** 3/yr. **Key Personnel:** Veronica Kennedy, Editor-in-Chief. **ISSN:** 1552-3721 (print). **URL:** http://www.wcl.american.edu/org/sustainabledevelopment/. **Remarks:** Accepts advertising. **Circ:** (Not Reported).

7168 ■ SWHR Journal of Women's Health
Society for Women's Health Research
1025 Connecticut Ave. NW, Ste. 601
Washington, DC 20036
Phone: (202)223-8224
Fax: (202)833-3472
Publisher's E-mail: info@swhr.org
Journal comprising of review papers, columns, articles, and researches about topics and issues affecting women, procedures and protocols for the diseases, and diagnosis and care for women's health. **Freq:** Monthly. **Subscription Rates:** $567 U.S. print and online; $941 Out of country print and online; $489 Individuals online only. **URL:** http://www.liebertpub.com/JWH. **Remarks:** Advertising not accepted. **Circ:** (Not Reported).

7169 ■ Talking Book Topics
Library of Congress National Library Service for the Blind and Physically Handicapped
1291 Taylor St. NW
Washington, DC 20542-0002
Phone: (202)707-5100
Fax: (202)707-0712
Free: 800-424-8567
Publisher's E-mail: nls@loc.gov
Catalog of audio books and magazines available to the blind and disabled people through free program administered by the Library of Congress. Recorded, online, and diskette editions also available. **Freq:** Bimonthly. **Print Method:** Offset. **Trim Size:** 8 1/2 x 11. **Cols./Page:** 2. **Col. Width:** 42 nonpareils. **Col. Depth:** 99 agate lines. **Key Personnel:** Jean M. Moss, Project Manager. **ISSN:** 0039--9183 (print). **Subscription Rates:** Free. **Alt. Formats:** PDF. **URL:** http://loc.gov/nls/tbt/index.html. **Remarks:** Advertising not accepted. **Circ:** Free ‡286000.

7170 ■ The Tax Executive
Tax Executives Institute
1200 G St. NW, Ste. 300
Washington, DC 20005
Phone: (202)638-5601
Publisher's E-mail: asktei@tei.org
Professional journal covering business tax issues. **Freq:** Bimonthly. **Key Personnel:** Timothy McCormally, Executive Director; Christine Hayes, Director, Publications. **ISSN:** 0040-0025 (print). **Subscription Rates:** $120 Single issue. **URL:** http://www.tei.org/; http://www.tei.org/news/Pages/The-Tax-Executive-Feature-Articles.aspx. **Ad Rates:** BW $975; 4C $1,775. **Remarks:** Accepts advertising. **Circ:** Paid 7,000, 5800.

7171 ■ The Tax Lawyer
American Bar Association
740 15th St. NW
Washington, DC 20005-1019
Phone: (202)662-1000
Tax law. **Freq:** Quarterly. **Print Method:** Offset. **Trim Size:** 6 x 9. **Cols./Page:** 1. **Col. Width:** 54 nonpareils. **Col. Depth:** 104 agate lines. **Key Personnel:** Jeffrey Reed, Editor-in-Chief. **ISSN:** 0040--005X (print). **Subscription Rates:** Included in membership; $83 Nonmembers; $40 Single issue back issues and individual copies. **URL:** http://www.americanbar.org/groups/taxation/publications/tax_lawyer_home.html. **Remarks:** Advertising not accepted. **Circ:** Paid 20,000, Non-paid 1,800.

7172 ■ Teaching Sociology
American Sociological Association
1430 K St. NW, Ste. 600
Washington, DC 20005
Phone: (202)383-9005
Fax: (202)638-0882
Publisher's E-mail: customer@asanet.org
Journal with research articles, teaching tips, and reports on teaching sociology. **Freq:** Quarterly. **Key Personnel:** Kathleen Lowney, Editor. **ISSN:** 0092--055X (print). **Subscription Rates:** $45 Members; $446 Institutions print + online; $30 Students members; $402 Institutions online; $20 Individuals for postage outside US and Canada. **URL:** http://asanet.org/journals/ts/ts.cfm?CFID=17796732&CFTOKEN=25767131. **Ad Rates:** BW $400; 4C $1,020. **Remarks:** Color advertising not accepted. **Circ:** ‡2400, 2000.

7173 ■ The Teamster
Graphic Communications Conference of the International Brotherhood of Teamsters
25 Louisiana Ave. NW
Washington, DC 20001
Phone: (202)624-6800
Labor union magazine. **Freq:** Quarterly. **Print Method:** Web. **Trim Size:** 8 1/2 x 11. **Cols./Page:** 3. **Col. Width:** 13 picas. **Col. Depth:** 133 agate lines. **ISSN:** 1083--2394 (print). **Alt. Formats:** PDF. **URL:** http://teamster.org/magazine. **Formerly**: The New Teamster; The International Teamster. **Remarks:** Advertising not accepted. **Circ:** ‡1760000.

7174 ■ Tectonics
American Geophysical Union
2000 Florida Ave. NW
Washington, DC 20009-1277
Phone: (202)462-6900
Fax: (202)328-0566
Free: 800-966-2481
Publication E-mail: tect@agu.org
Scientific journal covering tectonics and earth sciences. **Freq:** Bimonthly. **Key Personnel:** Rebecca Bendick, Associate Editor. **ISSN:** 0278--7407 (print); **EISSN:** 1944--9194 (electronic). **Subscription Rates:** $485 U.S. and other countries small; online only; £306 Institutions small; online only; €355 Institutions small; online only; $716 U.S. and other countries medium; online only; £452 Institutions medium; online only; €523 Institutions medium; online only; $1066 U.S. and other countries large; online only; £674 Institutions large; online only; €780 Institutions large; online only; $910 U.S., Canada, and Mexico small medium and large; print only; $910 Institutions small medium and large; print only (rest of America). **URL:** http://agupubs.onlinelibrary.wiley.com/agu/journal/10.1002/(ISSN)1944-9194. **Remarks:** Advertising not accepted. **Circ:** (Not Reported).

7175 ■ Telemedicine and e-Health Journal
American Telemedicine Association
1100 Connecticut Ave. NW, Ste. 540
Washington, DC 20036
Phone: (202)223-3333
Fax: (202)223-2787
Publisher's E-mail: info@americantelemed.org
Freq: Quarterly. **Subscription Rates:** $130 Members /year, print and online; $87 Members /year, online only. **URL:** http://www.americantelemed.org/about-telemedicine/outside-resources/telemedicine-journals#.VpCM8rariko. **Remarks:** Advertising not accepted. **Circ:** (Not Reported).

7176 ■ Television & Cable Factbook
Warren Communications News Inc.
2115 Ward Ct. NW
Washington, DC 20037
Phone: (202)872-9200
Fax: (202)318-8350
Free: 800-771-9202
Publisher's E-mail: info@warren-news.com
Publication focusing on television, cable, and support industries. **Founded:** 1945. **Freq:** Annual. **Print Method:** Offset. **Trim Size:** 8 1/2 x 11. **Cols./Page:** 4. **Key Personnel:** Robert T. Dwyer, Senior Editor; Michael C. Taliaferro, Managing Editor; Paul Warren, Publisher; Daniel Warren, Editor, President. **Subscription Rates:** $945 Individuals print. **URL:** http://www.warren-news.com/factbook.htm. **Ad Rates:** BW $2,800; 4C $5,300. **Remarks:** Advertising accepted; rates available upon request. **Circ:** (Not Reported).

7177 ■ Text and Performance Quarterly
National Communication Association
1765 N St. NW
Washington, DC 20036
Phone: (202)464-4622
Fax: (202)464-4600
Publisher's E-mail: inbox@natcom.org
Scholarly journal covering communication and performance. **Freq:** Quarterly January, April, July, October. **Print Method:** Offset. **Cols./Page:** 1. **Key Personnel:** Heidi Rose, Associate Editor; Bruce Henderson, Associate Editor. **ISSN:** 1046--2937 (print); **EISSN:** 1479--5760 (electronic). **Subscription Rates:** $109 Individuals print only; $389 Institutions online only; $445 Institutions print & online. **URL:** http://www.natcom.org/journals.aspx; http://www.tandfonline.com/toc/rtpq20/current#.VOw7NHyUdGY. **Remarks:** Accepts advertising. **Circ:** 1500.

7178 ■ The Thomist: A Speculative Quarterly Review
Dominican Fathers, Province of St. Joseph
487 Michigan Ave. NE
Washington, DC 20017
Phone: (202)495-3866
Publication E-mail: thomist@thomist.org
Journal promoting inquiry into contemporary philosophical and theological questions. **Freq:** Quarterly. **Trim Size:** 6 x 9. **Cols./Page:** 1. **Key Personnel:** Joseph Torchia, OP, Editor. **ISSN:** 0040-6325 (print). **Subscription Rates:** $30 Individuals print; $35 Individuals print + online; $45 Out of country print; $50 Out of country print + online; $20 Individuals online; $15 Single issue; $55 Individuals religious houses and seminaries; $70 Individuals college & university, print & online. **URL:** http://www.thomist.org. **Remarks:** Accepts advertising. **Circ:** Paid 1000, Controlled 50.

7179 ■ Thought & Action: The NEA Higher Education Journal
National Education Association
1201 16th St. NW
Washington, DC 20036-3290
Phone: (202)833-4000
Fax: (202)822-7974
Publisher's E-mail: highered@nea.org
Journal covering higher education. **Freq:** Annual. **Key Personnel:** Mary Ellen Flannery, Editor. **URL:** http://www.nea.org/home/1821.htm. **Remarks:** Advertising not accepted. **Circ:** Paid 80000.

7180 ■ Title News
American Land Title Association
1800 M St. NW, Ste. 300S
Washington, DC 20036-5828
Phone: (202)296-3671
Fax: (202)223-5843
Free: 800-787-ALTA
Publisher's E-mail: service@alta.org
Magazine containing information and articles about the land title industry as well as general business articles on subjects that affect everyone in the real estate industry. **Freq:** Monthly. **Subscription Rates:** Included in membership. **URL:** http://www.alta.org/publications/titlenews/2016_archive.cfm. **Remarks:** Accepts advertising. **Circ:** (Not Reported).

7181 ■ Tools of the Trade
Hanley Wood Media Inc.
1 Thomas Cir. NW, Ste. 600
Washington, WA 20005
Phone: (202)452-0800
Fax: (202)785-1974
Magazine featuring tools for commercial and residential construction. **Freq:** Bimonthly. **Trim Size:** 8 x 10 1/2. **Key Personnel:** Mark Taussig, Publisher; Rick Schwolsky, Editor-in-Chief; Katy Tomasulo, Managing Editor; David Frane, Editor. **Subscription Rates:** $36 Individuals; $66 Canada; $192 Other countries; $70 Two years. **URL:** http://www.toolsofthetrade.net; http://www.hanleywood.com/products/magazines-digital-editions. **Ad Rates:** 4C $12110. **Remarks:** Accepts advertising. **Circ:** Combined 65,010.

7182 ■ The Tower
The Tower
127 Pryzbyla Center
Catholic University of America
620 Michigan Ave., NE
Washington, DC 20064
Phone: (202)319-5778
Fax: (202)319-6675
Publisher's E-mail: editor@cuatower.com
University newspaper. **Founded:** 1922. **Freq:** Weekly. **Cols./Page:** 5. **Col. Width:** 1.798 inches. **Col. Depth:** 13 inches. **Key Personnel:** Liz Grden, Editor-in-Chief. **Subscription Rates:** Free on campus. **URL:** http://www.

cuatower.com. **Ad Rates:** GLR $10; BW $422.50; 4C $225; PCI $8.25. **Remarks:** Accepts advertising. **Circ:** Free 5000.

7183 ■ Transactions on Education
IEEE - Education Society
c/o IEEE
2001 L St. NW, Ste. 700
Washington, DC 20036-4910
Phone: (202)785-0017
Fax: (202)785-0835
Publication E-mail: informs@informs.org
Freq: Quarterly. **ISSN:** 0018--9359 (print). **Subscription Rates:** Currently, free of charge, however, may adopt a small subscription fee to become self-sustaining.; Included in membership. **URL:** http://pubsonline.informs.org/journal/ited; http://ieeexplore.ieee.org/xpl/aboutJournal.jsp?punumber=13. **Remarks:** Advertising not accepted. **Circ:** (Not Reported).

7184 ■ Treasury Bulletin
U.S. Government Publishing Office
732 N Capitol St. NW
Washington, DC 20401-0001
Phone: (202)512-1800
Fax: (202)512-2104
Free: 866-512-1800
Publication E-mail: treasury.bulletin@fms.treas.gov
Bulletin featuring articles and analyses on Treasury issues and statistics of Federal financial operations and international monetary activity. **Founded:** 1939. **Freq:** Quarterly. **Print Method:** Letterpress. **Cols./Page:** 2. **Col. Width:** 40 nonpareils. **Col. Depth:** 112 agate lines. **Key Personnel:** LaDonna Cooley, Contact, phone: (202)874-9939; Bertha Butts, Contact, phone: (202)874-9938; Darcy Howe, Contact, phone: (202)874-9942. **ISSN:** 0041-2155 (print). **Subscription Rates:** $46 Individuals; $64.40 Other countries. **Alt. Formats:** PDF. **URL:** http://fms.treas.gov/bulletin/overview.html. **Mailing address:** PO Box 979050, Saint Louis, MO 63197-9000. **Remarks:** Advertising not accepted. **Circ:** 594.

7185 ■ Treaties and Other International Acts Series
U.S. Government Publishing Office
732 N Capitol St. NW
Washington, DC 20401-0001
Phone: (202)512-1800
Fax: (202)512-2104
Free: 866-512-1800
Publisher's E-mail: contactcenter@gpo.gov
Text of agreements entered into by the U.S. and other nations. **Freq:** Periodic. **Print Method:** Letterpress. **Cols./Page:** 1. **Col. Width:** 53 nonpareils. **Col. Depth:** 98 agate lines. **Subscription Rates:** $164 Individuals; $230 Other countries. **URL:** http://www.state.gov/s/l/treaty/tias. **Mailing address:** PO Box 979050, Saint Louis, MO 63197-9000. **Circ:** 126.

7186 ■ Tree Farmer: The Guide to Sustaining America's Family Forests
American Forest Foundation
2000 M St. NW, Ste. 550
Washington, DC 20036
Phone: (202)765-3660
Fax: (202)827-7924
Publisher's E-mail: info@forestfoundation.org
Journal covering sustainable forestry for private forest landowners in the U.S. **Freq:** Quarterly. **ISSN:** 1553--7749 (print). **URL:** http://www.forestfoundation.org/woodland-tree-farmer-dwight-judy-batt. **Ad Rates:** BW $1410; 4C $2464. **Remarks:** Accepts advertising. **Circ:** Non-paid 8000, Paid 8000, 65000, ‡15000.

7187 ■ Trends in Organized Crime
International Association for the Study of Organized Crime
1919 Connecticut Ave. NW
Washington, DC 20009
Publisher's E-mail: service-ny@springer.com
Provides information and analysis about organized crime. Reports on international efforts to anticipate the development of organized criminal activities and to devise strategies to counter them. **Freq:** Quarterly. **Key Personnel:** Jeff McIllwain, Associate Editor; Klaus V. Lampe, Editor-in-Chief. **ISSN:** 1084--4791 (print). **Subscription Rates:** €490 Institutions print incl. free access or e-only; $588 Institutions print plus enhanced access. **URL:** http://www.springer.com/social+sciences/criminology/journal/12117. **Ad Rates:** BW $200. **Remarks:** Advertising not accepted. **Circ:** Paid ‡300.

7188 ■ Trial Magazine
American Association for Justice
777 6th St. NW, Ste. 200
Washington, DC 20001
Phone: (202)965-3500
Free: 800-424-2725
Publisher's E-mail: help@justice.org
Consumer magazine about the law. **Freq:** Monthly. **Print Method:** Litho and web press. **Trim Size:** 8 1/4 x 10 7/8. **Key Personnel:** Anne Grant, Editor. **ISSN:** 0897--1056 (print). **URL:** http://www.justice.org/node/17576. **Remarks:** Advertising accepted; rates available upon request. **Circ:** (Not Reported).

7189 ■ Trustee Quarterly
Association of Community College Trustees
1101 17th St. NW, Ste. 300
Washington, DC 20036
Phone: (202)775-4667
Fax: (202)223-1297
Publisher's E-mail: acctinfo@acct.org
Freq: Quarterly. **Subscription Rates:** Included in membership. **URL:** http://www.acct.org/news/trustee-quarterly. **Circ:** (Not Reported).

7190 ■ Trusteeship
Association of Governing Boards of Universities and Colleges
1133 20th St. NW, Ste. 300
Washington, DC 20036
Phone: (202)296-8400
Fax: (202)223-7053
Publisher's E-mail: membership@agb.org
Freq: Bimonthly. **URL:** http://agb.org/trusteeship. **Remarks:** Advertising not accepted. **Circ:** 32000.

7191 ■ 21st Century Science & Technology
21st Century Science Associates Inc.
PO Box 16285
Washington, DC 20041
Phone: (703)777-6943
Fax: (703)771-9214
Publication E-mail: tcs@mediasoft.net
Science magazine. **Founded:** 1988. **Freq:** Quarterly. **Print Method:** Offset. **Trim Size:** 8 1/4 x 10 1/2. **Cols./Page:** 3. **Col. Depth:** 9 inches. **ISSN:** 0895-6420 (print). **Subscription Rates:** $25 Individuals online; 6 issues; $48 Individuals online; 12 issues; $5 Single issue online. **URL:** http://www.21stcenturysciencetech.com. **Formerly:** Fusion. **Ad Rates:** BW $1,000; 4C $1,500. **Remarks:** Accepts advertising. **Circ:** (Not Reported).

7192 ■ U.S. News & World Report
U.S. News & World Report Inc.
1050 Thomas Jefferson St. NW
Washington, DC 20007
Phone: (202)955-2000
Fax: (202)955-2506
National and international news magazine. **Founded:** 1933. **Freq:** Weekly. **Print Method:** Offset. **Trim Size:** 8 x 10 1/2. **Cols./Page:** 3. **Col. Width:** 27 nonpareils. **Col. Depth:** 140 agate lines. **Key Personnel:** Elizabeth Putze, Director, Public Relations, phone: (202)955-2136; Kerry F. Dyer, Publisher, phone: (212)967-8770; Mortimer B. Zuckerman, Chairman, Editor-in-Chief. **Subscription Rates:** $9.99 Individuals on the apple ipad; $9.95 Individuals on nook. **Alt. Formats:** Handheld. **URL:** http://www.usnews.com. **Remarks:** Accepts advertising. **Circ:** Paid ★**2021485**.

7193 ■ United States Tax Court Reports
U.S. Government Publishing Office
732 N Capitol St. NW
Washington, DC 20401-0001
Phone: (202)512-1800
Fax: (202)512-2104
Free: 866-512-1800
Publisher's E-mail: contactcenter@gpo.gov
Publication consolidating decisions for a month. **Freq:** Monthly. **Print Method:** Letterpress. **Trim Size:** 24. **Cols./Page:** 1. **Col. Width:** 54 nonpareils. **Col. Depth:** 98 agate lines. **ISSN:** 8755--6294 (print). **Subscription Rates:** $70 Individuals; $98 Other countries; $11 Single issue; $15.40 Other countries Single issue. **URL:** http://bookstore.gpo.gov/products/sku/728-001-00000-3?ctid=1409; http://bookstore.gpo.gov/catalog/laws-regulations/court-cases-documents-us-tax-court/tax-court-reports. **Mailing address:** PO Box 979050, Saint Louis, MO 63197-9000. **Circ:** (Not Reported).

7194 ■ Upscale Remodeling
Hanley Wood Media Inc.
1 Thomas Cir. NW, Ste. 600
Washington, WA 20005
Phone: (202)452-0800
Fax: (202)785-1974
Magazine for remodelers who are looking for new ideas, products, and inspiration. **Key Personnel:** Rick Strachan, Publisher; Lauren Hunter, Assistant Editor; Holly Miller, Director, Marketing; Craig Webb, Editor-in-Chief. **Subscription Rates:** $24.95 Individuals; $39.95 Individuals Canada; $192 Individuals international. **URL:** http://www.remodeling.hw.net/upscale/. **Ad Rates:** 4C $5,100. **Remarks:** Accepts advertising. **Circ:** 12500.

7195 ■ Urban Land Magazine
Urban Land Institute
2001 L St. NW
Washington, DC 20036
Phone: (202)624-7000
Fax: (202)624-7140
Publication E-mail: urbanland@uli.org
Professional magazine for land use and development practitioners. **Freq:** Monthly 11/yr. **Trim Size:** 8 7/8 x 10 7/8. **Key Personnel:** Elizabeth Razzi, Editor-in-Chief. **ISSN:** 0042-0891 (print). **Subscription Rates:** Included in membership. **URL:** http://urbanland.uli.org; http://uli.org/publications/urban-land-magazine. **Ad Rates:** BW $4,990; 4C $6,465. **Remarks:** Advertising accepted; rates available upon request. **Circ:** Paid 37000, 13000.

7196 ■ UTC Journal
Utilities Telecom Council
1129 20th St. NW, Ste. 350
Washington, DC 20036
Phone: (202)872-0030
Fax: (202)872-1331
Journal containing case studies, research, regulatory-related news, and emerging technologies articles about the issues, challenges, and opportunities in the Information and Communication Technology (ICT) and critical infrastructure professionals at energy and water organizations across North America. **Freq:** Quarterly. **URL:** http://www.utc.org/utc-journal. **Remarks:** Advertising not accepted. **Circ:** (Not Reported).

7197 ■ The Venture Capital Review
National Venture Capital Association
25 Massachusetts Avenue NW, Ste. 730
Washington, DC 20001
Phone: (202)864-5920
Fax: (202)864-5930
Freq: Annual. **Subscription Rates:** free. **Alt. Formats:** PDF. **Remarks:** Advertising not accepted. **Circ:** (Not Reported).

7198 ■ The Veterans Advocate
National Veterans Legal Services Program
PO Box 65762
Washington, DC 20035
Phone: (202)265-8305
Publication E-mail: tva@nvlsp.org
Journal containing articles for service officers, attorneys and others who assist veterans and their families on how to claim VA benefits. **Freq:** Quarterly. **ISSN:** 1046--3429 (print). **URL:** http://www.nvlsp.org/store/the-veterans-advocate-one-year-subscription-vol-24-year-2013. **Remarks:** Advertising not accepted. **Circ:** (Not Reported).

7199 ■ Vientiane Times
Vientiane Times
c/o Embassy of the Lao People's Democratic Republic
2222 S St. NW
Washington, DC 20008
Phone: (202)332-6416
Fax: (202)332-4923
Publisher's E-mail: embasslao@gmail.com
Newspaper. **Freq:** Daily and Sat. (morn.). **ISSN:** 1607--663X (print). **URL:** http://www.vientianetimes.org.la. **Remarks:** Accepts advertising. **Circ:** (Not Reported).

7200 ■ Virtual Journal for Biomedical Optics
Optical Society of America
2010 Massachusetts Ave. NW
Washington, DC 20036

Circulation: ★ = AAM; △ or • = BPA; ♦ = CAC; ❑ = VAC; ⊕ = PO Statement; ‡ = Publisher's Report; Boldface figures = sworn; Light figures = estimated.

Phone: (202)223-8130
Fax: (202)223-1096
Publisher's E-mail: info@osa.org
Peer-reviewed journal covering research involving the interface between light and medicine or biology. **Freq:** Monthly. **Key Personnel:** Andrew Dunn, Editor; Anthony Durkin, Editor. **ISSN:** 1931--1532 (print). **Subscription Rates:** $94 Individuals regular; $35 Members PDF. **Alt. Formats:** PDF. **URL:** http://www.opticsinfobase.org/vjbo/virtual_issue.cfm. **Remarks:** Advertising not accepted. **Circ:** (Not Reported).

7201 ■ Voice of Ataturk
Atatürk Society of America
4731 Massachusetts Ave. NW
Washington, DC 20016
Phone: (202)362-7173
Publisher's E-mail: info@ataturksociety.org
Journal containing historical and political stories pertaining to Ataturk. **Freq:** Quarterly. **ISSN:** 1544--0966 (print). **Alt. Formats:** PDF. **URL:** http://ataturksociety.org/voice-of-ataturk. **Remarks:** Advertising not accepted. **Circ:** (Not Reported).

7202 ■ The Volta Review
Alexander Graham Bell Association for the Deaf and Hard of Hearing
3417 Volta Pl. NW
Washington, DC 20007
Phone: (202)337-5220
Publication E-mail: mfelzien@agbell.org
Scholarly journal relating to the field of deafness. **Freq:** 3/year. **Print Method:** Offset. **Trim Size:** 6 x 9. **Cols./Page:** 1. **Col. Width:** 54 nonpareils. **Col. Depth:** 105 agate lines. **ISSN:** 0042--8639 (print). **Subscription Rates:** Included in membership. **URL:** http://www.listeningandspokenlanguage.org/thevoltareview. **Ad Rates:** BW $800. **Remarks:** Accepts advertising. **Circ:** ‡4400, 5500, 4000.

7203 ■ Volta Voices
Alexander Graham Bell Association for the Deaf and Hard of Hearing
3417 Volta Pl. NW
Washington, DC 20007
Phone: (202)337-5220
Publisher's E-mail: info@agbell.org
Magazine providing news and feature articles of interest to the deaf and hearing impaired-child, parent, adult and professional. **Freq:** Bimonthly. **Print Method:** Offset. **Trim Size:** 8 x 10 3/4. **ISSN:** 1074--8016 (print). **URL:** http://www.agbell.org/Tertiary.aspx?id=1226. **Formerly:** Newsounds, Our Kids Magazine. **Ad Rates:** BW $1,200; 4C $2,494. **Remarks:** Accepts advertising. **Circ:** Paid ⊕**4400**, 5000.

7204 ■ Warrior Citizen
Office of the Chief, Army Reserve
2400 Army Pentagon
Washington, DC 20310
Free: 888-550-ARMY
Military magazine. **Freq:** Quarterly. **Print Method:** Offset. **Cols./Page:** 3. **Col. Width:** 26 nonpareils. **Col. Depth:** 120 agate lines. **ISSN:** 0004--2579 (print). **URL:** http://www.usar.army.mil/Featured/Warrior-Citizen. **Formerly:** Army Reserve Magazine. **Circ:** (Not Reported).

7205 ■ The Washington Blade
The Washington Blade
1408 U St. NW
Washington, DC 20009
Phone: (202)797-7000
Publication E-mail: news@washblade.com
Tabloid presenting gay and lesbian community and national news. **Freq:** Weekly (Fri.). **Print Method:** Web offset. **Trim Size:** 9 3/4 x 13 1/2. **Cols./Page:** 4. **Col. Width:** 14 picas. **Col. Depth:** 13 1/4 inches. **Key Personnel:** Joshua Lynsen, Editor; Kevin Naff, Editor. **ISSN:** 0278--9892 (print). **Subscription Rates:** $195 Individuals residential; $475 Institutions. **URL:** http://washingtonblade.com. **Remarks:** Accepts advertising. **Circ:** (Not Reported).

7206 ■ Washington Business Journal
American City Business Journals Inc.
1555 Wilson Blvd., Ste. 400
Arlington, VA 22209-2405
Phone: (703)258-0800
Fax: (703)258-0802
Publication E-mail: washington@bizjournals.com
Metropolitan business newspaper (tabloid). **Freq:** Weekly. **Print Method:** Offset. **Cols./Page:** 4. **Col. Width:** 27 nonpareils. **Col. Depth:** 196 agate lines. **Key Personnel:** Robert J. Terry, Managing Editor, phone: (703)258-0821; Doug Fruehling, Editor-in-Chief, phone: (703)258-0820; Chuck Springston, Editor, phone: (703)258-0824. **ISSN:** 0737-3147 (print). **Subscription Rates:** $103 Individuals print and online; $103 Individuals online only; $4.99 Single issue PDF. **Alt. Formats:** PDF. **URL:** http://www.bizjournals.com/washington. **Remarks:** Advertising accepted; rates available upon request. **Circ:** (Not Reported).

7207 ■ Washington City Paper
Creative Loafing
1400 Eye St., NW, Ste. 900
Washington, DC 20005
Phone: (202)332-2100
Fax: (202)332-8500
Alternative newspaper. **Freq:** Weekly (Thurs.). **Key Personnel:** Amy Austin, Publisher, phone: (202)650-6922; Michael Schaffer, Editor, phone: (202)650-6949; Mike Madden, Editor, phone: (202)650-6939. **Subscription Rates:** Free. **URL:** http://clatl.com/atlanta/ArticleArchives?tag=Washington-City-Paper. **Remarks:** Accepts advertising. **Circ:** Free ■ **66408**, Free ‡73000.

7208 ■ Washington DC Beverage Journal
Beverage Journal Inc.
PO Box 159
Hampstead, MD 21074-0159
Phone: (410)796-5455
Fax: (410)796-5511
Publisher's E-mail: spatten@beerwineliquor.com
Trade publication for the beer, wine and liquor industry in Washington, DC. **Freq:** Monthly. **Print Method:** Offset. **Trim Size:** 8.375 x 10.875. **Cols./Page:** 3. **Col. Width:** 2 3/8 inches. **Col. Depth:** 10 inches. **Key Personnel:** Stephen A. Patten, Associate Publisher. **USPS:** 783-300. **Subscription Rates:** $36 Individuals 12 issues - hard copy includes electronic access. **URL:** http://www.beerwineliquor.com. **Ad Rates:** BW $500, full page; BW $300, half page; BW $200, 1/3 page; BW $150, 1/4 page; BW $100, 1/6 page. **Remarks:** Accepts advertising. **Circ:** 5478.

7209 ■ The Washington Examiner
Journal Newspapers
1015 15th St. NW, Ste. 500
Washington, DC 20005
Phone: (202)903-2000
General newspaper. **Freq:** Daily except Saturdays. **Print Method:** Offset. **Cols./Page:** 6. **Col. Width:** 26 nonpareils. **Col. Depth:** 301 agate lines. **Key Personnel:** Hugo Gurdon, Director, Editorial; Philip Klein, Managing Editor; Michael Phelps, President, Publisher; Stephen G. Smith, Editor. **ISSN:** 0162--2080 (print). **Subscription Rates:** $400 Out of area; Free to qualified subscribers online. **URL:** http://washingtonexaminer.com. **Remarks:** Accepts advertising. **Circ:** Mon. ‡96304, Tues. ‡96869, Wed. ‡98375, Thurs. ‡288811, Fri. ‡132294.

7210 ■ Washington Frederick News-Post
Echo Media
900 Circle 75 Pky., Ste. 1600
Atlanta, GA 30339
Phone: (770)955-3535
Fax: (770)955-3599
Publisher's E-mail: salesinfo@echo-media.com
Community newspaper. **Freq:** Daily and Sun. **Subscription Rates:** Free. **URL:** http://echomedia.com/medias/details/5204. **Remarks:** Accepts advertising. **Circ:** Paid 32400, Paid 29000.

7211 ■ Washington History
Historical Society of Washington, D.C.
801 K St. NW
Washington, DC 20001
Phone: (202)249-3955
Fax: (202)417-3823
Publisher's E-mail: info@historydc.org
Freq: Semiannual. **ISSN:** 1042- 9719 (print). **Subscription Rates:** $40 Individuals. **URL:** http://www.dchistory.org/publications/washington-history/. **Remarks:** Advertising not accepted. **Circ:** 2500.

7212 ■ The Washington Informer
The Washington Informer
3117 Martin Luther King Jr. Ave. SE
Washington, DC 20032
Phone: (202)561-4100
Fax: (202)574-3785
Publisher's E-mail: news@washingtoninformer.com
Newspaper (tabloid) serving Washington's metropolitan area black community. **Freq:** Weekly (Thurs.). **Print Method:** Offset. **Cols./Page:** 5. **Col. Width:** 2 1/16 inches. **Col. Depth:** 13 inches. **Key Personnel:** Denise Rolark Barnes, Publisher; Ron Burke, Manager, Advertising. **Subscription Rates:** $45 Individuals; $60 Two years. **URL:** http://www.washingtoninformer.com. **Ad Rates:** GLR $1.28; BW $1,170; 4C $2,325; PCI $18. **Remarks:** Accepts advertising. **Circ:** 15750.

7213 ■ The Washington Lawyer: Official Journal of the District of Columbia Bar
District of Columbia Bar
1101 K St. NW, Ste. 200
Washington, DC 20005-4210
Phone: (202)737-4700
Free: 877-333-2227
Publisher's E-mail: memberservices@dcbar.org
Forum for articles and news items for the Washington legal community. **Freq:** 11/yr; latest edition 2014. **Key Personnel:** Dominick Alcid, Contact; Latisha McKoy, Contact; Tim Wells, Managing Editor. **ISSN:** 0890--8761 (print). **URL:** http://www.dcbar.org/bar-resources/publications/washington-lawyer. **Formerly:** District Lawyer. **Ad Rates:** BW $5,100; 4C $7,400. **Remarks:** Accepts advertising. **Circ:** Paid 90000.

7214 ■ Washington Life
Washington Life
2301 Tracy Pl. NW
Washington, DC 20008
Phone: (202)745-9788
Fax: (202)745-9268
Publisher's E-mail: info@washingtonlife.com
Lifestyle magazine. **Freq:** Monthly. **Key Personnel:** Michael M. Clements, Executive Editor; Nancy Reynolds Bagley, Editor-in-Chief; Karin Tanabe, Managing Editor. **Subscription Rates:** $79.95 Individuals; $140 Two years; $210 Individuals three years. **URL:** http://www.washingtonlife.com. **Remarks:** Accepts advertising. **Circ:** △**60000**.

7215 ■ Washington Monthly: In-depth Coverage of Government, Politics, Media, and Culture
Washington Monthly
1200 18th St. NW, Ste. 330
Washington, DC 20036
Phone: (202)955-9010
Fax: (202)955-9011
Publisher's E-mail: successes@washingtonmonthly.com
Political and public policy opinion magazine. **Freq:** 6/year. **Print Method:** Offset. **Trim Size:** 7 1/2 x 10 3/4. **Cols./Page:** 2. **Col. Width:** 18 picas. **Col. Depth:** 57 picas. **Key Personnel:** Paul Glastris, Editor-in-Chief; Diane Straus Tucker, Publisher; Amy M. Stackhouse, Managing Editor. **ISSN:** 0043--0633 (print). **Subscription Rates:** $29.95 Individuals; $52 Two years; $72 Individuals three years. **URL:** http://washingtonmonthly.com. **Ad Rates:** BW $1,425; 4C $2,800. **Circ:** Paid 24000, Non-paid 1500.

7216 ■ The Washington National Opera Magazine
Washington National Opera
2600 Virgina Ave., Ste. 301
Washington, DC 20037
Phone: (202)295-2400
Fax: (202)295-2479
Publisher's E-mail: info@dc-opera.org
Magazine presenting background information on opera productions presented at Kennedy Center by the Washington Opera. **Freq:** 5/year. **Print Method:** Web offset. **Trim Size:** 8 1/2 x 11. **Cols./Page:** 3. **Key Personnel:** Mark J. Weinstein, Executive Director; Kenneth R. Feinberg, President. **ISSN:** 5147-1000 (print). **URL:** http://www.kennedy-center.org/wno/index. **Formerly:** The Washington Opera Magazine. **Ad Rates:** BW $2,999; 4C $3,889. **Remarks:** Accepts advertising. **Circ:** Controlled 30000.

7217 ■ The Washington Post
Nash Holdings LLC
1150 15th St., NW
Washington, DC 20071
Phone: (202)334-6000
Free: 800-627-1150
General newspaper. **Freq:** Mon.-Sun. (morn.). **Print Method:** Letterpress and Offset Uses mats. **Cols./Page:** 6. **Col. Width:** 26 nonpareils. **Col. Depth:** 308 agate lines. **Key Personnel:** Fred Ryan, Publisher; Martin Baron, Executive Editor; Kevin Merida, Managing Editor. **Subscription Rates:** $99 Individuals /yr.; national edition; $149 Individuals /yr.; national and Washington D.C. edition. **Online:** ProQuest L.L.C. ProQuest L.L.C.; LexisNexis; Westlaw; Nash Holdings LLC Nash Holdings LLC. **Alt. Formats:** Handheld. **URL:** http://www.washingtonpost.com. **Ad Rates:** BW $45,531; 4C $49,769; PCI $586. **Remarks:** Accepts advertising. **Circ:** 1000000.

7218 ■ The Washington Quarterly
Taylor & Francis Online
Center for Strategic & International Studies
1800 K St., NW, Ste. 400
Washington, DC 20006
Phone: (202)887-0200
Fax: (202)775-3199
Publication E-mail: twq@csis.org
Journal of international affairs focusing on the full set of political, economic, and security issues related to the international engagement of the United States and their policy implications. **Freq:** Quarterly. **Print Method:** Offset. **Trim Size:** 6 3/4 x 10. **Cols./Page:** 2. **Col. Width:** 30 nonpareils. **Col. Depth:** 98 agate lines. **Key Personnel:** Alex T.J. Lennon, Editor-in-Chief; Walter Laqueur, Chairman; Karen Donfried, Board Member; Yoichi Funabashi, Board Member; Robin Niblett, Board Member. **ISSN:** 0163-660X (print); **EISSN:** 1530-9177 (electronic). **Subscription Rates:** $76 Individuals print and online; $486 Institutions online only; $555 Institutions print and online; $72 Individuals print only; $463 Institutions print only. **URL:** http://csis.org/program/washington-quarterly. **Ad Rates:** BW $400. **Remarks:** Accepts advertising. **Circ:** Paid ‡3300, Non-paid ‡250.

7219 ■ Washington Report on Middle East Affairs
American Educational Trust
1902 18th St. NW
Washington, DC 20009
Phone: (202)939-6050
Fax: (202)265-4574
Free: 800-368-5788
Publisher's E-mail: letters@wrmea.org
Freq: 9/year. **Subscription Rates:** $29 Individuals / year - print and digital; $10 Individuals /year - digital only; $44 Individuals /year - print, voices and digital; $55 Two years /year - print and digital; $85 Two years /year - print , voices and digital. **URL:** http://www.wrmea.org. **Mailing address:** PO Box 53062, Washington, DC 20009. **Ad Rates:** BW $700; 4C $1100. **Remarks:** Accepts advertising. **Circ:** 30000.

7220 ■ The Washington Times
3600 New York Ave. NE
Washington, DC 20002
Phone: (202)636-3000
Newspaper with a Republican orientation. **Freq:** Mon.-Sun. (morn.). **Print Method:** Offset. **Trim Size:** 14 x 22 3/4. **Cols./Page:** 6. **Col. Width:** 24 nonpareils. **Col. Depth:** 294 agate lines. **Key Personnel:** Christopher Dolan, Managing Editor, phone: (202)636-3183; John Solomon, Editor, phone: (202)636-2916; Ian Bishop, Editor, phone: (202)636-4719. **ISSN:** 0732-8494 (print). **Subscription Rates:** $45 Individuals 12 weeks; Mon.-Fri.; print only; $90 Individuals 24 weeks; Mon.-Fri.; print only; $195 Individuals 52 weeks; Mon.-Fri.; print only; 39.99 /yr.; Mon.-Sun.; national edition; digital only; 5.99 /mo.; Mon.-Sun.; national edition; digital only; 2.99 /wk.; Mon.-Sun.; national edition; digital only. **Online:** ProQuest L.L.C. **Alt. Formats:** Handheld. **URL:** http://www.washingtontimes.com. **Ad Rates:** PCI $92. **Remarks:** Accepts advertising. **Circ:** Mon.-Fri. ★**98031**, Sat. ★**80437**, Sun. ★**39478**.

7221 ■ Washingtonian Magazine
Washington Magazine Inc.
1828 L St. NW, Ste. 200
Washington, DC 20036
Phone: (202)296-3600
Publication E-mail: editorial@washingtonian.com
Metropolitan interest magazine. **Freq:** Monthly. **Print Method:** Offset. **Trim Size:** 8 1/4 x 10 7/8. **Cols./Page:** 3. **Col. Width:** 2 1/4 inches. **Col. Depth:** 10 inches. **Key Personnel:** Sherri Dalphonse, Senior Editor; John A. Limpert, Editor; Catherine Merrill Williams, President, Publisher. **ISSN:** 0043--0897 (print). **Subscription Rates:** $29.95 Individuals 12 issues; $49.95 Two years 24 issues; $19.99 Individuals digital only. **Alt. Formats:** Handheld. **URL:** http://www.washingtonian.com/index.php. **Ad Rates:** BW $12,975; 4C $19,895. **Remarks:** Accepts advertising. **Circ:** Paid ★**139595**.

7222 ■ Water Resources Research
American Geophysical Union
2000 Florida Ave. NW
Washington, DC 20009-1277
Phone: (202)462-6900
Fax: (202)328-0566
Free: 800-966-2481
Publication E-mail: wrr@agu.org
Interdisciplinary sciences journal containing original contributions on physical, chemical, biological, and sociological aspects of water science as well as water law. **Freq:** Monthly. **Key Personnel:** Alberto Montanari, Editor-in-Chief; Praveen Kumar, Editor-in-Chief, phone: (217)333-4688; Ronald C. Griffin, Editor, phone: (979)845-7049; Hoshin Gupta, Editor, phone: (520)626-9712. **ISSN:** 004-3-1397 (print); **EISSN:** 1944--7973 (electronic). **Subscription Rates:** $1079 Institutions FTE - small online; £681 Institutions FTE - small online; €788 Institutions FTE - small online; $1610 Institutions FTE - medium: online only; £1017 Institutions FTE - medium: online only; €1176 Institutions FTE - medium: online only; $2421 Institutions FTE - Large: Online Only; £1526 Institutions FTE - large: online only; €1683 Institutions FTE - large: online only; $2094 U.S., Canada, and Mexico FTE - Small: Print Only; $2094 U.S., Canada, and Mexico FTE - medium: print only; $2094 Institutions FTE - large: print only (rest of America). **URL:** http://publications.agu.org/journals; http://wrr-submit.agu.org/cgi-bin/main.plex. **Remarks:** Advertising not accepted. **Circ:** (Not Reported).

7223 ■ WCET Journal
World Council of Enterostomal Therapists
1000 Potomac St. NW, Ste. 108
Washington, DC 20007
Phone: (202)567-3030
Fax: (202)833-3636
Journal featuring works of researchers and practitioners in the field of enterostomal therapy. **Freq:** Quarterly. **Key Personnel:** Elizabeth A. Ayello, Editor. **Subscription Rates:** Included in membership. **URL:** http://www.wcetn.org/journal. **Circ:** (Not Reported).

7224 ■ Weekly Compilation of Presidential Documents
U.S. Government Publishing Office
732 N Capitol St. NW
Washington, DC 20401-0001
Phone: (202)512-1800
Fax: (202)512-2104
Free: 866-512-1800
Publisher's E-mail: contactcenter@gpo.gov
Publication containing transcripts of the President's news conferences, messages to Congress, public speeches and statements, and other presidential materials released by the White House. **Freq:** 52/yr. **Print Method:** Offset. **Cols./Page:** 2. **Col. Width:** 29 nonpareils. **Col. Depth:** 227 agate lines. **ISSN:** 0511--4187 (print). **Alt. Formats:** PDF. **URL:** http://www.gpo.gov/fdsys/browse/collection.action?collectionCode=CPD. **Mailing address:** PO Box 979050, Saint Louis, MO 63197-9000. **Remarks:** Advertising not accepted. **Circ:** (Not Reported).

7225 ■ The Weekly Standard
The Weekly Standard
1152 15th St., NW, Ste. 200
Washington, DC 20036
Phone: (386)597-4378
Fax: (202)293-4901
Free: 800-283-2014
Publisher's E-mail: editor@weeklystandard.com
News and opinion magazine covering political issues. **Freq:** Weekly. **Trim Size:** 8 x 10.5. **Key Personnel:** Terry Eastland, Publisher; William Kristol, Editor; Nicholas H.B. Swezey, Director, Advertising. **ISSN:** 1083--3013 (print). **Subscription Rates:** $36 Individuals 24 issues; $64 Individuals 48 issues. **URL:** http://www.weeklystandard.com. **Ad Rates:** 4C $9625. **Remarks:** Advertising accepted; rates available upon request. **Circ:** Combined ⊕**85895**.

7226 ■ Weston A. Price Foundation Journal: Nutrient Deficiencies
Weston A. Price Foundation
4200 Wisconsin Ave. NW, PMB 106-380
Washington, DC 20016
Phone: (202)363-4394
Fax: (202)363-4396
Publisher's E-mail: info@westonaprice.org
Freq: Quarterly. **URL:** http://www.westonaprice.org/journals. **Circ:** (Not Reported).

7227 ■ The Wilson Quarterly
Woodrow Wilson International Center for Scholars
1 Woodrow Wilson Plz.
1300 Pennsylvania Ave. NW
Washington, DC 20004-3027
Phone: (202)691-4000
Fax: (202)691-4001
Publication E-mail: wq@wilsoncenter.org
News magazine on the world of ideas. Covers world affairs, history, art, theater, television, and popular culture. **Freq:** Quarterly. **Print Method:** Offset. **Key Personnel:** James H. Carman, Managing Editor; Suzanne Napper, Director, Business Development; Steven Lagerfeld, Editor. **ISSN:** 0363-3276 (print). **Subscription Rates:** $24.95 Individuals; $39.95 Other countries; $20 /year in U.S.; $35 /year outside U.S. **URL:** http://www.wilsonquarterly.com; http://www.wilsoncenter.org/publications. **Remarks:** Accepts advertising. **Circ:** Paid ‡60000, 60000.

7228 ■ Wise Traditions in Food, Farming, and the Healing Arts
Weston A. Price Foundation
4200 Wisconsin Ave. NW, PMB 106-380
Washington, DC 20016
Phone: (202)363-4394
Fax: (202)363-4396
Publisher's E-mail: info@westonaprice.org
Freq: Quarterly. **Subscription Rates:** Included in membership. **URL:** http://www.westonaprice.org/journals. **Remarks:** Accepts advertising. **Circ:** 2600.

7229 ■ The World & I: The Magazine for Serious Readers
News World Communications Inc.
3600 New York Ave. NE
Washington, DC 20002-1947
Phone: (202)636-3000
Fax: (202)269-1245
Publication E-mail: education@worldandi.com
Encyclopedic journal including world news; developments in science, the arts, and philosophy; book reviews; photo essays. **Freq:** Monthly. **Print Method:** Offset. **Trim Size:** 7 1/2 x 10 1/8. **Cols./Page:** 3. **Col. Width:** 2 1/4 inches. **Col. Depth:** 8 3/4 inches. **Key Personnel:** Charles Kim, Publisher; Steve Osmond, Editor. **ISSN:** 5669--8721 (print). **Subscription Rates:** $36 Individuals /year; $32 Individuals 6 months; $12 Individuals 1 month; $6 Individuals 1 day. **URL:** http://www.worldandi.com. **Remarks:** Advertising accepted; rates available upon request. **Circ:** (Not Reported).

7230 ■ World Report
Volunteers in Overseas Cooperative Assistance - USA
50 F St. NW, Ste. 1000
Washington, DC 20001
Phone: (202)469-6000
Fax: (202)469-6257
Free: 800-929-8622
Publisher's E-mail: webmaster@acdivoca.org
Magazine containing technical approaches to development issues around the world. **Freq:** Semiannual. **Subscription Rates:** Free. **Alt. Formats:** PDF. **URL:** http://www.acdivoca.org/site/ID/resources_worldreport. **Remarks:** Advertising not accepted. **Circ:** (Not Reported).

Circulation: ★ = AAM; △ or • = BPA; ♦ = CAC; ❑ = VAC; ⊕ = PO Statement; ‡ = Publisher's Report; Boldface figures = sworn; Light figures = estimated.

7231 ■ WorldView: The Magazine of the National Peace Corps Association
National Peace Corps Association
1900 L St. NW, Ste. 610
Washington, DC 20036
Phone: (202)293-7728
Fax: (202)293-7554
Publisher's E-mail: npca@peacecorpsconnect.org
Magazine covering news and commentary about the Peace Corps World. **Freq:** Quarterly. **Trim Size:** 8 1/8 x 10 3/4. **Key Personnel:** Erica Burman, Editor. **URL:** http://www.peacecorpsconnect.org/cpages/worldview. **Remarks:** Accepts advertising. **Circ:** (Not Reported).

7232 ■ Young Children
National Association for the Education of Young Children
1313 L St. NW, Ste. 500
Washington, DC 20005
Phone: (202)232-8777
Fax: (202)328-1846
Free: 800-424-2460
Freq: 5/year. **ISSN:** 0044--0728 (print). **Subscription Rates:** Included in membership; $70 Individuals; $110 Institutions; $90 Other countries; $140 Institutions, other countries. **URL:** http://www.naeyc.org/yc. **Ad Rates:** BW $3000. **Remarks:** Accepts advertising. **Circ:** 115000.

7233 ■ Young Children: The Journal of the National Association for the Education of Young Children
National Association for the Education of Young Children
1313 L St. NW, Ste. 500
Washington, DC 20005
Phone: (202)232-8777
Fax: (202)328-1846
Free: 800-424-2460
Publication E-mail: editorial@naeyc.org
Peer-reviewed professional journal focusing on issues in the field of early childhood education. **Freq:** 5/year. **Print Method:** Heatset web. **Trim Size:** 8 3/8 x 10 7/8. **Cols./Page:** 3 and 2. **Col. Width:** 28 and 42 nonpareils. **Col. Depth:** 134 agate lines. **ISSN:** 0044--0728 (print). **Subscription Rates:** $70 Individuals; $110 Institutions; $100 Other countries; $140 Institutions, other countries. **URL:** http://www.naeyc.org/yc. **Ad Rates:** BW $3,000; 4C $4,250. **Remarks:** Accepts advertising. **Circ:** 90000.

7234 ■ Youth Today: The Newspaper on Youth Work
American Association of Children's Residential Centers
1331 H St. NW, Ste. 701
Washington, DC 20005
Phone: (202)785-0764
National newspaper focusing on out-of-school programs and services in operation in the U.S. Plus reports on news, policy formulation, decision-making and emerging technology affecting youth-serving agencies. **Freq:** Bimonthly. **Print Method:** Offset. **Trim Size:** 9 1/2 x 13 1/2. **Cols./Page:** 4. **Col. Width:** 2.25 inches. **Col. Depth:** 12.5 inches. **Key Personnel:** John Fleming, Editor-in-Chief; Ryan Schill, Assistant Editor. **ISSN:** 1089-6724 (print). **Subscription Rates:** $65 Individuals. **URL:** http://www.youthtoday.org. **Ad Rates:** BW $2,335. **Remarks:** Advertising accepted; rates available upon request. **Circ:** Paid 5000, 10000.

7235 ■ Zero to Three
Zero to Three: National Center for Infants, Toddlers and Families
1255 23rd St. NW, Ste. 350
Washington, DC 20037
Phone: (202)638-1144
Fax: (202)638-0851
Freq: Bimonthly 6/yr. **ISSN:** 0736- 8086 (print). **Subscription Rates:** $59 /year (online only); $79 U.S. /year, outside U.S. (online and print); $99 Canada for two years; $139 U.S. /year, outside U.S. (online and print); $169 Canada for two years; $15 Single issue. **Remarks:** Advertising not accepted. **Circ:** 7400.

7236 ■ ZooGoer
Friends of the National Zoo
3001 Connecticut Ave. NW
Washington, DC 20008
Phone: (202)633-3038
Publication E-mail: zoogoer@fonz.org
Magazine for members of Friends of the National Zoo. **Freq:** Bimonthly. **Print Method:** Web offset. **Trim Size:** 8 3/8 x 10 7/8. **Cols./Page:** 3. **Key Personnel:** Cindy Han, Editor. **ISSN:** 0163--416X (print). **Subscription Rates:** Included in membership. **URL:** http://nationalzoo.si.edu/joinfonz/join/green-zoogoer.cfm. **Mailing address:** PO Box 37012, Washington, DC 20013-7012. **Remarks:** Accepts advertising. **Circ:** (Not Reported).

7237 ■ KBLR-TV - 39
300 New Jersey Ave. NW, Ste. 700
Washington, DC 20001
Phone: (702)258-0039
Fax: (702)258-0556
Format: Commercial TV; Hispanic. **Networks:** Telemundo. **Founded:** 1989. **Operating Hours:** on air 24 hrs./Business offices 8:30 am - 5:00 pm M-F. **Key Personnel:** Scott Gentry, Gen. Mgr. **Wattage:** 13,000. **Ad Rates:** $25-300 for 30 seconds.

7238 ■ KFRO-AM - 1370
1155 Connecticut Ave. NW
Washington, DC 20036
Phone: (202)861-0870
Email: kfro@kfro.com
Format: News; Talk; Sports; Adult Contemporary. **Networks:** CBS; Texas State. **Owner:** Voice of Longview, Inc., at above address. **Founded:** 1935. **Operating Hours:** Continuous. **ADI:** Tyler-Longview-Jacksonville, TX. **Key Personnel:** Ed Cearley, Gen. Mgr. **Wattage:** 1,000. **Ad Rates:** $15-85. Combined advertising rates available with KYKX-FM.

7239 ■ KIDZ-TV - 54
Covington & Burling
Washington, DC 20001-4956
Fax: (202)662-5552
Email: kidz@kidzfox.com
Format: Commercial TV. **Networks:** Fox. **Owner:** Sage Broadcasting Corp., 406 S Irving, San Angelo, TX 76903. **Founded:** Feb. 14, 1992. **Key Personnel:** William Carter, Gen. Mgr., President, carter@foxsanangelo.com; Jack Smith, Sales Mgr.; Erica Villanueva, Traffic Mgr. **Wattage:** 12,000 ERP. **Ad Rates:** $200 per unit.

7240 ■ KIKK-AM
1725 Desales St. N
Washington, DC 20036-4426
Phone: (713)881-5100
Format: News. **Networks:** CBS. **Owner:** CBS Radio Inc., 1271 Avenue of the Americas, 44th Fl., New York, NY 10020-1401, Ph: (212)649-9600. **Founded:** 1959. **Wattage:** 250 Day. **Ad Rates:** Noncommercial.

7241 ■ KNAZ-TV - 2
7950 Jones Branch Dr.
Washington, DC 20001-4956
Fax: (602)526-8110
Format: Commercial TV. **Networks:** NBC. **Owner:** Grand Canyon Television Co., Inc., 2525 W Camelback Rd., No. 800, Phoenix, AZ 85016. **Founded:** 1969. **Formerly:** KOAI-TV. **Operating Hours:** Continuous. **ADI:** Flagstaff, AZ. **Key Personnel:** Dan Robbins, Contact; Nick Matesi, Contact; Stan Koplowitz, Gen. Sales Mgr; Dan Robbins, Contact; Nick Matesi, Contact; Michele Madril, Contact. **Wattage:** 100,000. **Ad Rates:** $25-200 for 30 seconds.

7242 ■ KRAK-AM
1725 Desales St. N
Washington, DC 20036-4426
Format: Big Band/Nostalgia. **Owner:** Infinity Radio, Inc, at above address. **Wattage:** 700 Day; 500 Night.

7243 ■ KSTS-TV - 48
1299 Pennsylvania Ave. NW, 9th Fl.
Washington, DC 20004
Phone: (202)637-4535
Format: Commercial TV; Hispanic. **Networks:** Telemundo. **Owner:** NBC Telemundo License Co., at above address. **Operating Hours:** Continuous. **ADI:** San Francisco-Oakland-San Jose. **Key Personnel:** Paul Niedermeyer, Contact. **Ad Rates:** Noncommercial.

7244 ■ KTVD-TV - 20
1 City Ctr., 850 10th St. NW
Washington, DC 20001-4956
Phone: (303)792-2020
Fax: (303)790-4633
Format: Commercial TV. **Networks:** United Paramount Network. **Owner:** FRFQ Fychaner, at above address. **Founded:** 1988. **Operating Hours:** Continuous. **ADI:** Denver (Steamboat Springs), CO. **Key Personnel:** Greg Armstrong, Gen. Mgr; Linda Larney, Contact. **Wattage:** 5,000,000. **Mailing address:** PO Box 6522, Centennial, CO 80111.

7245 ■ KVEA-TV - 52
300 New Jersey Ave. NW, Ste. 700
Washington, DC 20001
Phone: (720)726-7770
Format: Commercial TV. **Networks:** Telemundo. **Owner:** Telemundo Group, Miami, at above address, Ph: (818)502-5800. **Founded:** 1985. **Operating Hours:** Continuous; 75% network, 25% local. **ADI:** Los Angeles (Corona & San Bernardino), CA. **Key Personnel:** Karen Harmon, Controller; Juan Carlos Aviles, Contact. **Ad Rates:** $100-1800 per unit. **URL:** http://www.telemundo52.com.

7246 ■ KZZO-FM
1725 Desales St. N
Washington, DC 20036-4426
Format: Adult Contemporary; Contemporary Hit Radio (CHR). **Networks:** Independent. **Owner:** Taber Communications, 8445 Camino Santa Fe, San Diego, CA 92121. **Wattage:** 115,000 ERP. **Ad Rates:** $13-17.19 for 60 seconds.

7247 ■ MIX-FM - 102.3
4400 Jenifer St. NW
Washington, DC 20015
Phone: (202)686-3100
Free: 800-727-1073
Format: Eclectic; News. **Simulcasts:** 90.8FM. **Operating Hours:** Continuous. **Key Personnel:** Cathy J. Whissel, Contact, cathy.j.whissel@abc.com. **Ad Rates:** Advertising accepted; rates available upon request. **URL:** http://www.mix1073.com.

7248 ■ VOA Albanian - 9460
330 Independence Ave. SW
Washington, DC 20237
Phone: (202)382-5494
Email: shqip@voanews.com
Format: News; Information; Educational. **Owner:** Voice of America, 330 Independence Ave., SW, Washington, DC 20237, Ph: (202)203-4959, Fax: (202)203-4960. **Operating Hours:** 0500-0530. **URL:** http://www.voanews.com.

7249 ■ VOA Creole - 21555
330 Independence Ave. SW, Rm. 3520
Washington, DC 20237
Phone: (202)382-7027
Fax: (202)619-0601
Email: creole-service@voanews.com
Format: News; Information; Educational. **Owner:** Voice of America, 330 Independence Ave., SW, Washington, DC 20237, Ph: (202)203-4959, Fax: (202)203-4960. **Operating Hours:** 2100-2130. **URL:** http://www.voanews.com/creole.

7250 ■ VOA Indonesia - 9890
330 Independence Ave. SW, Ste. 2711
Washington, DC 20237
Phone: (202)382-5800
Fax: (202)619-1461
Email: voaindonesia@voanews.com
Format: News; Information; Educational. **Owner:** Voice of America, 330 Independence Ave., SW, Washington, DC 20237, Ph: (202)203-4959, Fax: (202)203-4960. **Operating Hours:** 1130-1230. **URL:** http://www.voaindonesia.com.

7251 ■ Voice of America - 11905
330 Independence Ave., SW
Washington, DC 20237
Phone: (202)203-4959
Fax: (202)203-4960
Email: horn@voanews.com
Format: News; Information; Educational. **Operating Hours:** 1800-1900. **URL:** http://www.voanews.com.

7252 ■ WAMU-FM - 88.5
4400 Massachusetts Ave. NW
Washington, DC 20016-8082
Phone: (202)885-1200
Free: 800-433-8850
Email: feedback@wamu.org
Format: Country. **Networks:** National Public Radio (NPR); BBC World Service. **Founded:** 1961. **Operating Hours:** Continuous. **ADI:** Washington, DC. **Key Personnel:** Walt Gillette, Dir. of Dev.; Mark McDonald, Dir. of Programs. **Local Programs:** *The Kojo Nnamdi Show*, Monday Tuesday Wednesday Thursday 12:00 p.m. -

1:00 p.m.; *Diane Rehm Show*, Monday Tuesday Wednesday Thursday 10:00 a.m. - 12:00 p.m.; *Metro Connection*, Friday Saturday 1:00 p.m. 7:00 a.m. **Wattage**: 50,000 ERP. **Ad Rates:** Advertising accepted; rates available upon request. **URL:** http://wamu.org.

7253 ■ Washington Cable
700 7th St. S
Washington, DC 20024
Phone: (202)646-1600
Fax: (202)479-4396
Founded: 1979. **Key Personnel:** Perry Klein, VP. **Cities Served:** Washington, District of Columbia; Fairfax, Virginia: subscribing households 2,000; 30 channels; 1 community access channel. **URL:** http://www.washcable.tv/contact_us.

7254 ■ WBAV-AM - 1600
2175 K St. NW, Ste. 350
Washington, DC 20037
Email: feedback@v1019.com
Format: Gospel. **Networks:** Satellite Music Network. **Founded:** 1942. **Formerly**: WGIV-AM. **Operating Hours**: Continuous; 100% network. **ADI**: Charlotte (Hickory), NC. **Key Personnel:** Wayne K. Brown, Gen. Mgr., wkb1008@aol.com; Deborah Kwei, Sales Mgr. **Wattage**: 1,000. **Ad Rates:** $5-20 per unit. Combined advertising rates available with WPEG-FM and WBAV-FM.

7255 ■ WBFS-TV - 33
1725 Desales St. N
Washington, DC 20036-4426
Phone: (305)621-3333
Fax: (305)628-3448
Format: Commercial TV. **Networks:** Independent; United Paramount Network. **Founded:** 1982. **Key Personnel:** Bill Ballard, Contact; Bill Ballard, Contact; Bernie Diaz, Contact. **Wattage**: 1,000,000 ERP.

7256 ■ WBZW-FM - 93.7
1725 Desales St. NW, Ste. 501
2nd Fl., Foster Plz. 5
Washington, DC 20036-4426
Phone: (202)457-4505
Format: Contemporary Hit Radio (CHR). **Owner:** CBS Radio Inc., 1271 Avenue of the Americas, 44th Fl., New York, NY 10020-1401, Ph: (212)649-9600. **Formerly**: WTZN-FM. **Ad Rates:** Advertising accepted; rates available upon request.

7257 ■ WCSP-FM - 90.1
400 N Capitol St. NW, Ste. 650
Washington, DC 20001
Phone: (202)737-3220
Free: 877-662-7726
Format: News; Talk; Information. **Owner:** National Cable Satellite Corp., at above address. **Founded:** Mar. 1979. **Operating Hours**: Continuous. **Key Personnel:** Rob Kennedy, Co-CEO, President. **URL:** http://www.c-span.org.

7258 ■ WDCA-TV - 20
5151 Wisconsin Ave. NW
Washington, DC 20016
Format: Commercial TV. **Networks:** United Paramount Network. **Owner:** Fox TV Stations, at above address. **Founded:** Apr. 1966. **Operating Hours**: Continuous. **ADI**: Washington, DC. **Wattage**: 4,000,000. **Ad Rates:** Noncommercial. **URL:** http://www.my20dc.com.

7259 ■ WDCW-TV - 50
2121 Wisconsin Ave. NW, Ste. 350
Washington, DC 20007
Phone: (202)965-5050
Fax: (202)965-0050
Founded: 1995. **Formerly**: WBDC-TV. **Ad Rates:** Advertising accepted; rates available upon request. **URL:** http://dcw50.com.

7260 ■ WFED-AM - 1050
3400 Idaho Ave. NW
Washington, DC 20016
Phone: (202)895-5086
Fax: (202)895-5144
Format: News; Talk. **Owner:** Bonneville International Corp., 55 North 300 West, Salt Lake City, UT 84101-3502, Ph: (801)575-7500. **Operating Hours**: Continuous. **Key Personnel:** Lisa Wolfe, Dir. of Programs, lwolfe@federalnewsradio.com; Joel Oxley, Gen. Mgr., joxley@federalnewsradio.com. **Wattage**: 1,000. **Ad Rates:** Advertising accepted; rates available upon request. **URL:** http://www.federalnewsradio.com.

7261 ■ WFTY-TV - 50
2121 Wisconsin Ave. NW, Ste. 350
Washington, DC 20007
Phone: (202)965-5050
Format: Commercial TV. **Networks:** Independent. **Founded:** 1986. **Formerly:** WCQR-TV. **Operating Hours**: 6:30 a.m.-6:00 a.m. **ADI**: Washington, DC. **Key Personnel:** Don Hazen, Production Mgr.; Curtis Garris, Chief Engineer; Andy Ockershausen, Gen. Mgr.; Terri Bornstein, Gen. Sales Mgr; Michelle Dowd, Contact; Andy Zmindinski, Contact. **URL:** http://dcw50.com.

7262 ■ WGTB-FM - 92.3
Georgetown University
432 Leavey Ctr.
Washington, DC 20057
Email: events@georgetownradio.com
Format: Eclectic; Folk; Hip Hop; Classical; Information; Oldies; Album-Oriented Rock (AOR). **Founded:** 1946. **Operating Hours**: Continuous. **Key Personnel:** Daniel Cook, Gen. Mgr., wgtb.gm@gmail.com; John Kenchelian, Sports Dir., wgtb.sports@gmail.com. **Wattage**: 6,700. **Ad Rates:** Noncommercial; underwriting available. **URL:** http://www.georgetownradio.com.

7263 ■ WGYM-AM - 1580
1201 Connecticut Ave. NW
Washington, DC 20036
Email: sportsteam@prodigy.net
Format: News; Talk; Sports. **Owner:** Access 1 Communications, 11 Pennsylvania Plz., New York, NY 10001. **Formerly**: WONZ-AM. **Operating Hours**: Continuous. **ADI**: Philadelphia, PA. **Key Personnel:** Dick Irland, Gen. Mgr.; Cindy Hesley, Sales Mgr.; Jackson T. Chase, Operations Mgr. **Wattage**: 1,000 Watts. **Ad Rates:** Advertising accepted; rates available upon request; Noncommercial. $25-50 for 60 seconds.

7264 ■ WHUR-FM - 96.3
529 Bryant St. NW
Washington, DC 20059
Phone: (202)806-3500
Fax: (800)221-9487
Format: Urban Contemporary; Adult Contemporary; Hip Hop; Oldies; Blues; Gospel. **Networks:** ESPN Radio; Fox; CNN Radio; ABC. **Owner:** Howard University, 2400 6th St. NW, Washington, DC 20059, Ph: (202)806-6100. **Founded:** 1971. **Operating Hours**: Continuous. **ADI**: Washington, DC. **Wattage**: 16,500 ERP. **Ad Rates:** Advertising accepted; rates available upon request. **URL:** http://www.whur.com.

7265 ■ WHUT-TV - 32
2222 4th St. NW
Washington, DC 20059
Phone: (202)806-3200
Format: Public TV. **Networks:** Public Broadcasting Service (PBS). **Owner:** Howard University Board of Trustees, 2400 Sixth St. NW, Washington, DC 20059. **Founded:** 1980. **Formerly**: WHMM-TV. **Operating Hours**: 8 a.m-12:30 a.m.; 60% network, 40% local. **ADI**: Washington, DC. **Ad Rates:** Noncommercial. **URL:** http://www.whut.org.

7266 ■ WJZW-FM - 105.9
4400 Jenifer St. NW
Washington, DC 20015-2113
Phone: (202)686-3100
Format: Jazz. **Networks:** Independent. **Owner:** Citadel Broadcasting Corp., 7201 W Lake Mead Blvd., Ste. 400, Las Vegas, NV 89128-8366, Ph: (702)804-5200, Fax: (702)804-8250. **Founded:** 1958. **Formerly**: WCXR-FM. **Operating Hours**: Continuous. **Local Programs**: *Spectrum*, Sunday 6:00 a.m. - 7:00 a.m. **Wattage**: 28,000. **Ad Rates:** Advertising accepted; rates available upon request. **URL:** http://www.smoothjazz1059.com.

7267 ■ WMAL-AM - 630
4400 Jenifer St. NW
Washington, DC 20015
Phone: (202)686-3100
Free: 888-630-9625
Format: News; Talk. **Networks:** ABC. **Owner:** Citadel Broadcasting Corp., 7201 W Lake Mead Blvd., Ste. 400, Las Vegas, NV 89128-8366, Ph: (702)804-5200, Fax: (702)804-8250. **Founded:** 1925. **Operating Hours**: Continuous. **ADI**: Washington, DC. **Key Personnel:** Jeff Boden, Contact, jeff.boden@citcomm.com. **Wattage**: 10,000 Day; 5,000 Ni. **Ad Rates:** Advertising accepted; rates available upon request. **URL:** http://www.wmal.com.

7268 ■ WMAL 105.9 FM - 105.9
4400 Jenifer St. NW
Washington, DC 20015
Phone: (202)895-2432
Format: Classic Rock. **Owner:** Citadel Broadcasting Corp., 7201 W Lake Mead Blvd., Ste. 400, Las Vegas, NV 89128-8366, Ph: (702)804-5200, Fax: (702)804-8250. **Formerly**: WVRX-FM. **URL:** http://www.wmal.com.

7269 ■ WPFW-FM - 89.3
2390 Champlain St. NW
2nd Fl., Washington City Paper Bldg.
Washington, DC 20009
Phone: (202)588-0999
Fax: (202)588-0561
Format: Jazz; Ethnic; News. **Networks:** Pacifica. **Owner:** Pacifica Foundation, 1925 Martin Luther King Jr. Way, Berkeley, CA 94704-1037, Ph: (510)849-2590. **Founded:** 1949. **Operating Hours**: Continuous. **ADI**: Washington, DC. **Key Personnel:** Gerrie Mahdi, Office Mgr., mahdi_gerrie@wpfw.org; Tiffany Jordan, Dir. of Dev., jordan_tiffany@wpfw.org; Gloria Minott, Dir. Pub. Aff., minott_gloria@wpfw.org; Bobby Hill, Contact, stitt_katea@wpfw.org. **Wattage**: 50,000. **Ad Rates:** Noncommercial. **URL:** http://www.wpfwfm.org.

7270 ■ WPGC-FM - 95.5
4200 Parliament Pl., Ste. 300
Lanham, MD 20706
Phone: (301)918-0955
Fax: (301)441-9555
Format: Hip Hop; Contemporary Hit Radio (CHR); Urban Contemporary. **Owner:** CBS Radio, New York, NY, Ph: (614)249-7676, Fax: (614)249-6995. **Founded:** 1959. **Operating Hours**: Continuous. **Key Personnel:** Sam Rogers, Sales Mgr. **Wattage**: 50,000. **Ad Rates:** Advertising accepted; rates available upon request. **URL:** http://wpgc.cbslocal.com/about-sunni.

7271 ■ WPXB-TV - 60
300 New Jersey Ave. NW, Ste. 700
Washington, DC 20001
Phone: (202)524-6401
Format: Commercial TV. **Networks:** Independent. **Owner:** Paxon Communications Inc., at above address. **Founded:** 1987. **Formerly**: WGOT-TV. **Operating Hours**: Continuous. **ADI**: Boston-Worcester,MA-Derry-Manchester,NH. **Key Personnel:** Lon Mirolli, Gen. Mgr., Contact; Lorrae Jones, Bus. Mgr.; David Raymond, Chief Engineer; Doreen Warchal, Dir. of Programs; Don Hill, Operations Mgr; Lon Mirolli, Contact. **Wattage**: 1,400,000. **Ad Rates:** $100-700 per unit. **URL:** http://www.telemundoboston.com.

7272 ■ WRC-TV - 4
4001 Nebraska Ave. NW
Washington, DC 20016
Phone: (202)885-4000
Format: Commercial TV. **Networks:** NBC. **Owner:** General Electric Co., 3135 Easton Tpke., Fairfield, CT 06828-0001, Ph: (203)373-2211, Fax: (203)373-3131. **Operating Hours**: Continuous. **ADI**: Washington, DC. **Ad Rates:** Advertising accepted; rates available upon request. **URL:** http://www.nbcwashington.com.

7273 ■ WRQX-FM - 107.3
4400 Jenifer St. NW
Washington, DC 20015
Phone: (202)686-3100
Free: 800-727-1073
Format: Adult Contemporary. **Networks:** ABC. **Owner:** Cumulus Media Inc., 3280 Peachtree Rd. NW, Ste. 2300, Atlanta, GA 30305-2455, Ph: (404)949-0700, Fax: (404)949-0740. **Founded:** 1948. **Formerly**: WMAL-FM. **Operating Hours**: Continuous. **ADI**: Washington, DC. **Wattage**: 50,000. **Ad Rates:** Noncommercial. **URL:** http://www.dcs1073.com.

7274 ■ WSCV-TV - 51
1299 Pennsylvania Ave. NW, 9th Fl.
Washington, DC 20004
Phone: (202)637-4535
Format: Commercial TV. **Networks:** Telemundo. **Owner:** NBC Telemundo License Co., at above address.

Circulation: ★ = AAM; △ or • = BPA; ♦ = CAC; ❑ = VAC; ⊕ = PO Statement; ‡ = Publisher's Report; Boldface figures = sworn; Light figures = estimated.

Operating Hours: 20 hours Daily. **ADI**: Miami (Ft. Lauderdale), FL. **Key Personnel:** Manuel J. Calvo, Contact; Ramon Pineda, Contact; Jose Franchi, Contact. **Wattage**: 8,400,000. **Ad Rates:** Noncommercial.

7275 ■ WTOP-AM - 1500
3400 Idaho Ave. NW
Washington, DC 20016-3046
Phone: (202)895-5000
Free: 877-222-1035
Email: kking@wtop.com
Format: News; Sports; Information. **Owner:** Bonneville International Corp., 55 North 300 West, Salt Lake City, UT 84101-3502, Ph: (801)575-7500. **Founded:** 1926. **ADI:** Washington, DC. **Key Personnel:** Joel Oxley, Gen. Mgr., Sr. VP, joxley@wtop.com; Skip Quast, Sales Mgr., squast@wtop.com. **Wattage**: 50,000. **Ad Rates:** Advertising accepted; rates available upon request. **URL:** http://www.wtop.com.

7276 ■ WTOP-FM - 103.5
3400 Idaho Ave. NW
Washington, DC 20016
Phone: (202)895-5000
Email: kking@wtop.com
Format: News. **Networks:** NBC. **Owner:** Bonneville International Corp., 55 North 300 West, Salt Lake City, UT 84101-3502, Ph: (801)575-7500. **Founded:** 1947. **ADI:** Washington, DC. **Key Personnel:** Joel Oxley, Gen. Mgr. **Wattage:** 3,000. **Ad Rates:** Advertising accepted; rates available upon request. **URL:** http://www.wtop.com.

7277 ■ WTTG-TV - 5
5151 Wisconsin Ave. NW
Washington, DC 20016
Phone: (202)244-5151
Format: News. **Networks:** Fox. **Owner:** Fox Television Stations Inc., 1211 Ave. of the Americas, 21st Fl., New York, NY 10036, Ph: (212)301-5400. **Operating Hours:** Continuous. **Ad Rates:** Noncommercial. **URL:** http://www.myfoxdc.com.

7278 ■ WTWP-AM - 1500
3400 Idaho Ave. NW
Washington, DC 20016
Phone: (651)642-4334
Format: News. **Owner:** Graham Holdings Co., 1300 N 17th St., 17th Fl., Arlington, VA 22209, Ph: (703)345-6300. **Operating Hours:** Continuous. **Ad Rates:** Advertising accepted; rates available upon request. **URL:** http://federalnewsradio.com.

7279 ■ WUSA-TV - 9
4100 Wisconsin Ave. NW
Washington, DC 20016
Phone: (206)895-5999
Fax: (202)244-1547
Free: 877-333-4926
Email: 9news@wusa9.com
Format: Commercial TV. **Networks:** CBS. **Owner:** Gannett Company Inc., 7950 Jones Branch Dr., McLean, VA 22107-0150, Ph: (703)854-6089. **Operating Hours**: Continuous. **ADI**: Washington, DC. **Wattage**: 52,000 ERP. **Ad Rates:** Advertising accepted; rates available upon request. **URL:** http://www.wusa9.com.

7280 ■ WWJ-AM - 950
1725 Desales St. NW, Ste. 501
Washington, DC 20036-4426
Format: News.

ALACHUA

7281 ■ Back to Godhead
International Society for Krishna Consciousness
PO Box 430
Alachua, FL 32616
Magazine containing topics concerned with the philosophy of Bhakti, Yoga, Vegetarianism, Karma, Reincarnation and the activities of ISKCON. **Freq:** Monthly. **Subscription Rates:** $19.95 U.S.; $37.95 U.S. 2 years; $23.95 Canada; $44.95 Canada 2 years; $29.95 Other countries; $56.95 Other countries 2 years. **URL:** http://backtogodhead.in; http://btg.krishna.com. **Remarks:** Advertising not accepted. **Circ:** (Not Reported).

ALTAMONTE SPRINGS

EC FL. Seminole Co. 10 mi. NE of Orlando.

7282 ■ ASCnet Quarterly
Applied Client Network
801 Douglas Ave., Ste. 205
Altamonte Springs, FL 32714
Phone: (407)869-0404
Fax: (407)869-0418
Free: 800-605-1045
Publisher's E-mail: registration@ascnet.org
Professional magazine covering technical information, association news, and industry information for insurance professionals. **Freq:** Quarterly. **Subscription Rates:** $24 Individuals. **URL:** http://www.ascnet.org/AM/Template.cfm?Section=About. **Ad Rates:** BW $1499.50. **Remarks:** Advertising accepted; rates available upon request. **Circ:** 5000.

7283 ■ Florida Monthly Magazine
Florida Media Inc.
999 Douglas Ave., Ste. 3301
Altamonte Springs, FL 32714
Phone: (407)816-9596
Fax: (407)816-9373
Publisher's E-mail: editorial@floridamagazine.com
Statewide lifestyle magazine. **Freq:** Monthly. **Print Method:** Web Offset. **Trim Size:** 8 x 10 7/8. **Cols./Page:** 3. **Col. Width:** 13 picas. **Col. Depth:** 10 inches. **Key Personnel:** Douglas E. Cifers, Publisher. **ISSN:** 0888-9600 (print). **Subscription Rates:** $21.95 Individuals; $37.95 Two years; $66 Other countries. **URL:** http://www.floridamagazine.com. **Formerly**: Florida Living. **Ad Rates:** BW $4,552; 4C $6,935. **Remarks:** Accepts advertising. **Circ:** Paid ‡211412.

7284 ■ Internal Auditor
Institute of Internal Auditors
247 Maitland Ave.
Altamonte Springs, FL 32701-4201
Phone: (407)937-1111
Fax: (407)937-1101
Publication E-mail: iaonline@theiia.org
Internal auditing. **Freq:** Bimonthly. **Print Method:** Offset. **Trim Size:** 8 x 10 7/8. **Cols./Page:** 3. **Col. Width:** 28 nonpareils. **Col. Depth:** 140 agate lines. **Key Personnel:** Tim McCollum, Assistant Managing Editor; Gretchen Gorfine, Manager, Production; David Salierno, Managing Editor; Anne Millage, Editor-in-Chief. **ISSN:** 0020--5745 (print). **Subscription Rates:** $75 U.S. and Canada print and online; $135 U.S. and Canada two years, print and online; $99 Other countries print and online; $183 Other countries two years, print and online; $60 Individuals /year - online. **URL:** http://iaonline.theiia.org. **Ad Rates:** BW $2,718; 4C $4,919. **Remarks:** Accepts advertising. **Circ:** 68000.

7285 ■ Journal of Paralegal Education and Practice
American Association for Paralegal Education
222 S Westmonte Dr., Ste. 101
Altamonte Springs, FL 32714
Phone: (407)774-7880
Fax: (407)774-6440
Publisher's E-mail: info@aafpe.org
Journal covering paralegal practice and education. **Freq:** Annual. **Remarks:** Advertising accepted; rates available upon request. **Circ:** (Not Reported).

7286 ■ Pageantry
Pageantry, Talent and Entertainment Services Inc.
PO Box 160307
Altamonte Springs, FL 32716-0307
Phone: (407)260-2262
Fax: (407)260-5131
Trade magazine covering the pageant, fashion, talent and modeling industries. **Freq:** Quarterly. **Print Method:** Web offset. **Trim Size:** 8 3/8 x 10 7/8. **Cols./Page:** 3. **Col. Width:** 2 7/16 inches. **Col. Depth:** 10 1/8 inches. **Key Personnel:** Ashley Burns, Editor; Carl Dunn, Chief Executive Officer, Director, Marketing. **ISSN:** 1075--3133 (print). **Subscription Rates:** $18 Individuals /year; $30 Two years. **URL:** http://www.pageantrymagazine.com. **Remarks:** Accepts advertising. **Circ:** (Not Reported).

7287 ■ WBZW-AM - 1520
1188 Lake View Dr.
Altamonte Springs, FL 32714
Phone: (407)682-9494
Format: Public Radio; Talk; News; Information. **Owner:** Salem Media Group Inc., 4880 Santa Rosa Rd., Camarillo, CA 93012, Ph: (805)987-0400, Fax: (805)384-4520. **Operating Hours**: Continuous. **Wattage**: 5,000 Day; 350 Night. **URL:** http://www.1520wbzw.com.

7288 ■ WDYZ-AM - 990
1188 Lake View Dr.
Altamonte Springs, FL 32714
Phone: (407)618-1773
Format: Educational. **URL:** http://lanueva990.com.

7289 ■ WHIM-AM - 1520
1188 Lake View Dr.
Altamonte Springs, FL 32714
Phone: (407)682-9494
Fax: (407)682-7005
Format: Religious. **Networks:** Independent. **Owner:** Pennsylvania Media Associates Inc., at above address. **Founded:** 1964. **Operating Hours**: Continuous; 75% satellite; 25% local, or syndicated tape pro. **Key Personnel:** Allan Dempsey, Contact; Joe Ferraro, Div. Dir., joef@salemorlando.com; David Koon, Gen. Mgr.; Lou Mueller, Chief Engineer; Allan Dempsey, Contact. **Wattage:** 5,000; 350 Night. **Ad Rates:** Advertising accepted; rates available upon request. **URL:** http://www.wtln.com.

7290 ■ WNUE-FM - 98.1
523 Douglas Ave.
Altamonte Springs, FL 32714
Phone: (407)332-0098
Format: Hispanic. **Ad Rates:** Noncommercial. **URL:** http://www.salsa981.com.

7291 ■ WORL-AM - 660
1188 Lake View Dr.
Altamonte Springs, FL 32714
Phone: (407)682-9494
Fax: (407)682-7005
Format: News; Talk. **Owner:** Salem Media Group Inc., 4880 Santa Rosa Rd., Camarillo, CA 93012, Ph: (805)987-0400, Fax: (805)384-4520. **Operating Hours**: Continuous. **Wattage**: 3,500 Day; 1,000. **Ad Rates:** Accepts Advertising. **URL:** http://www.660theanswer.com.

7292 ■ WOTF-TV - 43
523 Douglas Ave.
Altamonte Springs, FL 32714
Fax: (407)774-3384
Owner: Entravision Communications Corporation, 2425 Olympic Blvd., Ste. 6000 W, Santa Monica, CA 90404-4030, Ph: (310)447-3870, Fax: (310)447-3899. **URL:** http://www.entravision.com.

7293 ■ WPOZ-FM - 88.3
1065 Rainer Dr.
Altamonte Springs, FL 32714-3847
Phone: (407)869-8000
Free: 800-525-8887
Format: Contemporary Christian. **Key Personnel:** Jim Hoge, CEO, Founder, President; Dean O. Neal, Gen. Mgr., Prog. Dir., VP; Carol Ellingson, Promotions Dir.; Judy Wise, Office Mgr.; Mark Chambers, Chief Engineer. **Ad Rates:** Advertising accepted; rates available upon request. **URL:** http://www.zradio.org.

7294 ■ WRMQ-AM - 1140
1355 E Altamonte Dr.
Altamonte Springs, FL 32701
Phone: (407)830-0800
Fax: (407)260-6100
Email: info@rejoice1140.com
Format: Gospel; Hispanic. **Networks:** Sun Radio; CNN Radio. **Owner:** Q-Broadcasting Corp., at above address; Florida Broadcasters, at above address. **Founded:** 1985. **Formerly**: WONQ-AM. **Operating Hours**: Sunrise-sunset. **ADI**: Orlando-Daytona Beach-Melbourne, FL. **Wattage**: 5,000. **Ad Rates:** Noncommercial. $12-15 for 15 seconds; $19-22 for 30 seconds; $24-26 for 60 seconds.

7295 ■ WTLN-AM - 950
1188 Lake View Dr.
Altamonte Springs, FL 32714
Phone: (407)682-9494
Email: wtln@salemorlando.com
Format: Religious. **Owner:** TM2 Inc., at above address. **Founded:** 1968. **Key Personnel:** Lou Mueller, Chief Engineer, rfamfm@earthlink.net; Allan Dempsey, Dir. of Programs, alland@salemorlando.com; David Koon, Gen. Mgr., david.koon@salemorlando.com. **Wattage**: 12,000Daytime;5,000 N. **Ad Rates:** Accepts Advertising. **URL:** http://www.wtln.com.

Circulation: ★ = AAM; △ or • = BPA; ♦ = CAC; ❑ = VAC; ⊕ = PO Statement; ‡ = Publisher's Report; Boldface figures = sworn; Light figures = estimated.

7296 ■ WVEN-TV - 26
523 Douglas Ave.
Altamonte Springs, FL 32714
Phone: (407)774-2626
Fax: (407)774-3384
Owner: Entravision Communications Corporation, 2425 Olympic Blvd., Ste. 6000 W, Santa Monica, CA 90404-4030, Ph: (310)447-3870, Fax: (310)447-3899. **Key Personnel:** Lilly Gonzalez, Div. Pres.; Antonio Guernica, Gen. Mgr., VP, guernica@entravision.com. **URL:** http://www.wventv.com.

ALVA

7297 ■ National Roster
Society of the 3rd Infantry Division
c/o Kathleen M. Daddato, Membership Chairperson
22511 N River Rd.
Alva, FL 33920-3358
Phone: (239)728-2475
Freq: Triennial. **Subscription Rates:** Included in membership. **Alt. Formats:** Magnetic tape. **Remarks:** Advertising not accepted. **Circ:** 3500.

APOPKA

EC FL. Orange Co. 10 mi. NW of Orlando. Nurseries. Citrus fruit, poultry and truck farms.

7298 ■ The Apopka Chief
Apopka Chief
439 W Main St.
Apopka, FL 32712
Phone: (407)886-2777
Fax: (407)889-4121
Publisher's E-mail: news@theapopkachief.com
Community newspaper. **Freq:** Weekly. **Key Personnel:** John Ricketson, Publisher; John Peery, Editor; Richard Corbeil, Columnist. **USPS:** 545-440. **Subscription Rates:** $25 Individuals. **URL:** http://theapopkachief.com. **Ad Rates:** GLR $7; BW $903; 4C $1,038; SAU $7; PCI $7. **Remarks:** Accepts advertising. **Circ:** Paid 3700.

7299 ■ Bow & Swing
Bow N Spring
34 E Main St.
Apopka, FL 32703
Phone: (407)886-7151
Fax: (407)886-8464
Trade magazine covering square and round dancing in Florida. **Freq:** Monthly. **Print Method:** Offset. **Trim Size:** 5 x 8. **Cols./Page:** 2. **Key Personnel:** Bill Boyd, Associate Editor; Randy Boyd, Editor. **Subscription Rates:** $15 Individuals 1 year; $25 Two years. **URL:** http://bow-n-swing.com. **Remarks:** Accepts advertising. **Circ:** (Not Reported).

7300 ■ Critical Reviews in Plant Sciences
Taylor & Francis Group Journals
c/o Dennis Gray, Ed.
University of Florida, Mid-Florida Research & Education Center
Institute of Food & Agricultural Sciences
2725 Binion Rd.
Apopka, FL 32703-8504
Publisher's E-mail: customerservice@taylorandfrancis.com
Journal focusing on plant science. **Freq:** Bimonthly. **Key Personnel:** Dennis Gray, Editor-in-Chief; Robert Trigiano, Editor-in-Chief; Rattan Lal, Advisor; B.V. Conger, Editor; Schuyler S. Korban, Advisor. **ISSN:** 0735--2689 (print); **EISSN:** 1549--7836 (electronic). **Subscription Rates:** $1802 Institutions print and online; $1577 Institutions online only; $254 Individuals print only. **URL:** http://www.tandfonline.com/toc/bpts20/current. **Circ:** (Not Reported).

7301 ■ Journal of Applied Research in Clinical and Experimental Therapeutics
Therapeutic Solutions L.L.C.
PO Box 2083
Apopka, FL 32704-2083
Phone: (267)566-0270
Fax: (407)880-1418
Publisher's E-mail: jhulbig@aol.com
Journal that aims to provide accurate, timely and cost efficient solutions in medical publishing and customized medical communications. **Freq:** Quarterly. **Key Personnel:** Emily King, Editor; Jim Jenkins, Publisher; Bob Issler, Managing Director. **Subscription Rates:** $39 U.S.; $49 Canada and Mexico; $65 Other countries; $69 Two years; $89 Canada and Mexico two years; $121 Other countries two years. **URL:** http://www.jrnlappliedresearch.com. **Circ:** (Not Reported).

7302 ■ The Planter Newspaper
The Planter Newspaper
400 N Park Ave.
Apopka, FL 32712
Phone: (407)886-2777
Fax: (407)889-4121
Publisher's E-mail: news@apopkachief.fdn.com
Local newspaper. **Freq:** Weekly (Fri.). **Print Method:** Offset. **Cols./Page:** 6. **Col. Width:** 26 nonpareils. **Col. Depth:** 301 agate lines. **Key Personnel:** John E. Ricketson, Publisher; John R. Peery, Editor; Jacquelyne Trefcer, Manager, Advertising. **Subscription Rates:** $18 Individuals 52 weeks; $23 Out of country. **URL:** http://theapopkachief.com. **Ad Rates:** GLR $9; BW $1,401; 4C $1,296; SAU $9; PCI $9. **Remarks:** Accepts advertising. **Circ:** (Not Reported).

ARCADIA

SW FL. DeSoto Co. 50 mi. E. of Sarasota. Manufactures electrical transformers. Phosphate mining. Citrus fruit, cattle.

7303 ■ WFLN-AM - 1480
201 Asbury St.
Arcadia, FL 34266
Phone: (863)993-1480
Fax: (863)993-1489
Email: wflnradio@aol.com
Format: News; Talk. **Owner:** Integrity Radio of Florida, LLC, at above address. **Operating Hours:** Continuous. **Key Personnel:** George S. Kalman, President. **Wattage:** 1,000. **Ad Rates:** Advertising accepted; rates available upon request. **URL:** http://www.wflnradio.com.

7304 ■ WZTK-AM - 1480
201 Asbury St.
Arcadia, FL 34266
Phone: (863)993-1480
Fax: (863)993-1489
Format: Talk; News; Contemporary Christian; Sports. **Networks:** CBS. **Owner:** Heartland Broadcasting Corp., at above address. **Founded:** 1955. **Formerly:** WAPG-AM; WKGF-AM. **Operating Hours:** Continuous. **Key Personnel:** Hal Kneller, Consultant; Bill Noel, Gen. Mgr.; Ron Brown, Sales Mgr. **Wattage:** 1,000. **Ad Rates:** for 30 seconds; $15 for 60 seconds. Combined advertising rates available with WZZS-FM, WZSP-FM. **URL:** http://www.wflnradio.com.

AUBURNDALE

C FL. Polk Co. 41 mi. NE of Tampa.

7305 ■ WTWB-AM - 1570
127 Glenn Rd.
Auburndale, FL 33823
Phone: (863)968-1570
Email: laraza1570@gmail.com
Format: Contemporary Christian; Talk; Hispanic. **Networks:** ABC. **Owner:** La Raza Media Group L.L.C., at above address. **Founded:** 1956. **Operating Hours:** Continuous. **ADI:** Tampa-St. Petersburg (Lakeland, Sarasota), FL. **Local Programs:** *Los Corridos De La Raza*, Monday Tuesday Wednesday Thursday Friday 6:00 p.m. - 8:00 p.m. **Wattage:** 5,000. **Ad Rates:** Noncommercial. **URL:** http://www.laraza1570.com.

AVE MARIA

7306 ■ Legatus Magazine
Legatus
5072 Annunciation Cir., Ste. 202
Ave Maria, FL 34142
Phone: (239)867-4900
Fax: (239)867-4198
Publisher's E-mail: legatusinquiry@legatus.org
Freq: Monthly. **Subscription Rates:** Included in membership. **URL:** http://legatus.org/category/features. **Remarks:** Accepts advertising. **Circ:** 5000.

AVENTURA

7307 ■ Aventura Magazine: The Haute Luxe-Life
Discover Magazine Inc.
20533 Biscayne Blvd., Ste. 126
Aventura, FL 33180
Phone: (305)932-2400
Fax: (305)466-9285
Publisher's E-mail: info@aventuramagazine.com
Consumer magazine covering regional lifestyle and entertainment. **Freq:** 11/year. **Print Method:** web. **Trim Size:** 8 1/2 x 11. **URL:** http://www.aventuramagazine.com. **Formerly:** Discover Aventura. **Ad Rates:** 4C $3900. **Remarks:** Accepts advertising. **Circ:** Combined 35000.

7308 ■ Bachow & Associates Inc.
21200 NE 38th Ave., Ste. 2101
Aventura, FL 33180
Phone: (610)660-4900
Fax: (610)660-4930
Email: info@bachow.com
Founded: 1985. **Cities Served:** Area in Mississippi. **URL:** http://www.bachow.com.

AVON PARK

C FL. Highlands Co. 43 mi. SE of Lakeland. South Florida Junior College. Citrus packing plants; bottling works. Timber. Citrus, stock, truck farms.

7309 ■ Florida Fireman
Florida State Firefighters' Association
2450 US Highway 27 S
Avon Park, FL 33825
Phone: (863)453-4817
Fax: (863)453-7450
Free: 800-883-4817
Publisher's E-mail: administration@fsfa.com
Magazine for fire fighters. **Freq:** Monthly. **Print Method:** Letterpress and offset. **Cols./Page:** 3. **Col. Width:** 28 nonpareils. **Col. Depth:** 140 agate lines. **Subscription Rates:** Included in membership. **URL:** http://fsfa.com/about-us. **Ad Rates:** BW $245. **Remarks:** Accepts advertising. **Circ:** ‡5900.

BAKER

7310 ■ WTJT 90.1 FM - 90.1
957 Hwy. C 4A
Baker, FL 32531
Phone: (850)537-2009
Fax: (850)537-8010
Email: wtjtradio@yahoo.com
Format: Gospel; Bluegrass; Country. **Wattage:** 50,000 ERP. **Mailing address:** PO Box 189, Baker, FL 32531. **URL:** http://www.wtjt901fm.com.

BALDWIN

7311 ■ WHJX-FM - 105.7
5634 Normandy Blvd.
Jacksonville, FL 32205
Phone: (904)781-4321
Format: Tejano; Ethnic; Hispanic. **Owner:** Tama Broadcasting, Inc., 5207 Washington Blvd., Tampa, FL 33619, Ph: (813)620-1300, Fax: (813)628-0713. **Operating Hours:** Continuous. **Key Personnel:** Dr. Glenn W. Cherry, Chmn. of the Bd., CEO, President. **Wattage:** 25,000. **Ad Rates:** Advertising accepted; rates available upon request. **URL:** http://www.wjgmradio.com.

BARTOW

C FL. Polk Co. 12 mi. SE of Lakeland. Fruit and vegetable shipping. Phosphate mines. Citrus fruit, cattle, and truck farms.

7312 ■ The Polk County Democrat
Frisbie Publishing
PO Box 120
Bartow, FL 33831
Phone: (863)533-4183
Fax: (863)533-0402
Publication E-mail: polkdemo@aol.com
Community newspaper. **Freq:** Semiweekly (Mon. and Thurs.). **Print Method:** Web Offset. **Trim Size:** 16 x 22 3/4. **Cols./Page:** 7. **Col. Width:** 2 1/16 inches. **Col. Depth:** 21 inches. **Key Personnel:** Jim Gouvellis, Publisher; Peggy Kehoe, Managing Editor. **ISSN:** 1522--

0354 (print). **Subscription Rates:** $47.99 Individuals; $59.20 Out of country; $64.80 Out of state. **URL:** http://www.polkcountydemocrat.com. **Remarks:** Accepts advertising. **Circ:** Paid ♦**2100**, Free ♦**1457**, Combined ♦**3557**.

7313 ■ WWBF-AM - 1130
1130 Radio Rd.
Bartow, FL 33830
Phone: (863)533-0744

Format: Oldies. **Networks:** CNN Radio; Jones Satellite; Motor Racing. **Owner:** Thornburg Communications Inc., at above address, Bartow, FL 33830-7600. **Founded:** 1969. **Formerly**: WPUL-AM. **Operating Hours**: Continuous; 75% network, 25% local. **ADI**: Tampa-St. Petersburg (Lakeland, Sarasota), FL. **Wattage**: 2,500 Day; 500 Night. **Ad Rates:** $10-13 for 30 seconds; $15-21 for 60 seconds. **URL:** http://wwbf.com.

BELLE GLADE

Palm Beach Co Palm Beach Co. Palm Beach Co. (NW). On SE shore of Lake Okeechobee. Palm Beach Co. (SE). 20 m W of West Palm Beach.

7314 ■ WBGF-FM - 93.5
715 State Rd.
Box 1505
Belle Glade, FL 33430
Phone: (561)627-9966
Fax: (561)627-9993

Format: Classic Rock; News. **Networks:** ABC. **Founded:** 1951. **Formerly**: WSWN-FM. **Operating Hours**: Continuous. **Wattage**: 15,500 ERP. **Ad Rates:** $5-10 for 30 seconds; $7.50-15 for 60 seconds. **URL:** http://935thebar.com/.

7315 ■ WSWN-AM
2001 State Rd. 715
Belle Glade, FL 33430
Phone: (561)996-2063
Fax: (561)996-1852

Format: Urban Contemporary. **Networks:** ABC; Florida Radio. **Founded:** 1947. **Wattage**: 1,000 Day; 022 Night. **Ad Rates:** $11.75-15 for 30 seconds; $14.75-22.50 for 60 seconds. **Mailing address:** PO Box 1505, Belle Glade, FL 33430.

BELLEVIEW

NC FL. Marion Co. 11 mi. S. of Ocala.

7316 ■ Voice of South Marion
Voice of South Marion
5513 SE 113th St.
Belleview, FL 34420
Phone: (352)245-3161
Publication E-mail: vosminfo@aol.com

Community newspaper. **Freq:** Weekly (Thurs.). **Print Method:** Offset. **Trim Size:** 10 x 14. **Cols./Page:** 4. **Col. Width:** 28 nonpareils. **Col. Depth:** 196 agate lines. **Subscription Rates:** $15 Individuals online - 1 year; $25 Individuals print and online - 1 year; $20 Individuals print only; $9 Individuals online - 6 months; $13.50 Individuals print and online - 6 months. **Alt. Formats:** Electronic publishing. **URL:** http://www.thevosm.com; http://www.thevosm.net/37350/2119/1/voice-of-southmariononline-edition. **Mailing address:** PO Box 700, Belleview, FL 34421. **Ad Rates:** BW $140; PCI $5. **Remarks:** Accepts advertising. **Circ:** 2800.

BEVERLY HILLS

7317 ■ The Visitor
Landmark Community Newspapers L.L.C.
4 Beverly Hills Blvd.
Beverly Hills, FL 34464-0850
Phone: (352)746-4292
Publisher's E-mail: marketing@lcni.com

Community newspaper. **URL:** http://www.lcni.com/properties/florida/visitor.htm. **Mailing address:** PO Box 640-850, Beverly Hills, FL 34464-0850. **Circ:** (Not Reported).

BIG PINE KEY

Monroe Co. (S). One of the Florida Keys, just below Marathon.

7318 ■ WWUS-FM - 104.1
30336 Overseas Hwy.
Big Pine Key, FL 33043
Phone: (305)872-9100
Fax: (305)872-1603

Format: Oldies. **Networks:** CNN Radio. **Owner:** Vox Communications Group. **Founded:** 1980. **Operating Hours**: Continuous. **Key Personnel:** Kevin LeRoux, Gen. Mgr., kevinleroux@bellsouth.net; Bill Becker, News Dir., news@us1radio.com. **Wattage**: 100,000. **Ad Rates:** Noncommercial. **URL:** http://www.us1radio.com.

BLOUNTSTOWN

Calhoun Co. Calhoun Co. (NW). 10 m S of Calhoun.

7319 ■ The County Record
The County Record
PO Box 366
Blountstown, FL 32424
Phone: (850)674-5041
Fax: (850)674-5008
Publisher's E-mail: subscriptions@thecountyrecord.net

Community newspaper. **Freq:** Weekly (Thurs.). **Print Method:** Web offset. **Cols./Page:** 6. **Col. Width:** 2 inches. **Col. Depth:** 21 1/2 inches. **USPS:** 110-810. **Subscription Rates:** $21 Individuals; $26 Out of area. **URL:** http://www.thecountyrecord.net. **Formerly**: Blounstown County Record. **Ad Rates:** BW $3.75; SAU $3.75. **Remarks:** Accepts advertising. **Circ:** 3000.

7320 ■ WPHK-FM - 102.7
269 Kelly Ave.
Blountstown, FL 32424
Phone: (850)674-5101
Fax: (850)674-2965

Owner: Blountstown Communications Inc., at above address. **Founded:** 1973. **Formerly**: WRTM-FM. **Wattage**: 13,000. **Ad Rates:** $18-24 for 30 seconds; $23-29 for 60 seconds.

7321 ■ WYBT-AM - 1000
20872 Kelly Ave.
Blountstown, FL 32424
Phone: (850)674-5101
Fax: (850)674-2965

Format: Full Service. **Owner:** Blountstown Communication Inc., at above address. **Founded:** 1962. **Formerly**: WKMK-AM. **Operating Hours**: Sunrise-sunset. **Wattage**: 1,000. **Ad Rates:** $13-16 for 30 seconds; $15-20 for 60 seconds. **URL:** http://www.wybtradio.

BOCA RATON

SE FL. Palm Beach Co. On Atlantic Ocean, 25 mi. S. of West Palm Beach. Florida Atlantic University; College of Boca Raton. Computer center. Truck, poultry, and dairy farms.

7322 ■ Applause
Solution Technology Inc.
1101 S Rogers Cir., Ste. 14
Boca Raton, FL 33487-2749
Phone: (561)241-3210
Fax: (561)997-6518
Publisher's E-mail: sales@stiscan.com

Members magazine containing programming information and features for WHYY-FM and WHYY-TV. **Freq:** Monthly. **Trim Size:** 6 x 10 3/4. **Key Personnel:** Mary Eileen O'Connor, Editor; Nessa R. Forman, Executive Editor; Anna Christopher, Assistant Editor; Monica L. McGeary, Editor. **ISSN:** 1090-3526 (print). **Available online. Remarks:** Advertising not accepted. **Circ:** Controlled 125000.

7323 ■ Boca Raton Magazine: Florida At Its Best
JES Publishing Corp.
6413 Congress Ave., Ste. 100
Boca Raton, FL 33487-0820
Phone: (561)997-8683
Fax: (561)997-8909
Free: 877-553-5363
Publication E-mail: magazine@bocamag.com

Publication showcases life in Southern Florida; includes features on food, fashion, interior design, the arts, entertainment, and travel. **Freq:** Bimonthly. **Print Method:** Offset. **Trim Size:** 8 3/8 x 10 7/8. **Cols./Page:** 3. **Col. Width:** 13.5 picas. **Col. Depth:** 58.5 picas. **Key Personnel:** Marie Speed, Editor-in-Chief; Kevin Kaminski, Editor. **ISSN:** 0740--2856 (print). **Subscription Rates:** $17.95 Individuals; $24.95 Two years; $33.95 Individuals 3 years. **URL:** http://www.bocamag.com. **Formerly**: Florida Style. **Mailing address:** PO Box 820, Boca Raton, FL 33487-0820. **Ad Rates:** BW $3,490; 4C $4,520. **Remarks:** Accepts advertising. **Circ:** Paid ‡16331, Non-paid ‡3993.

7324 ■ The Boca Raton News
Boca Raton News
1141 S Rogers Cir., Ste. 7
Boca Raton, FL 33487
Phone: (561)893-6400
Fax: (561)893-6674
Publisher's E-mail: service@bocanews.com

General newspaper. **Founded:** 1955. **Freq:** Mon.-Sun. (morn.). **Print Method:** Offset. **Cols./Page:** 6. **Col. Width:** 2 inches. **Key Personnel:** John Johnston, Managing Editor. **Subscription Rates:** $21.45 Individuals 3-month; $37.70 Individuals 6-month; $65 Individuals. **URL:** http://www.bocanews.com/. **Formerly**: The News; Delray Beach News. **Ad Rates:** SAU $14.25. **Remarks:** Accepts advertising. **Circ:** (Not Reported).

7325 ■ Cavallino: The Journal of Ferrari History
Cavallino Inc.
PO Box 810819
Boca Raton, FL 33481
Phone: (561)994-1345
Fax: (561)994-9473
Free: 800-306-6937
Publisher's E-mail: cavallinosubs@hotmail.com

Magazine for Ferrari enthusiasts. **Freq:** Bimonthly. **Print Method:** Offset. **Trim Size:** 8 1/8 x 10 7/8. **Subscription Rates:** $46 Individuals; $85 Two years; $76 Canada; $145 Two years; $86 Other countries; $165 Two years. **URL:** http://www.cavallino.com. **Ad Rates:** 4C $1,495. **Remarks:** Accepts advertising. **Circ:** (Not Reported).

7326 ■ Corporate & Incentive Travel
Coastal Communications Corp.
2700 N Military Trl., Ste. 120
Boca Raton, FL 33431-6394
Phone: (561)989-0600
Fax: (561)989-9509

Magazine for corporate executives with the responsibility for site selection, staging and planning meetings, incentive travel programs, conferences, and conventions. **Freq:** Monthly. **Print Method:** Offset. **Trim Size:** 8.125 x 10.875. **Cols./Page:** 3. **Col. Width:** 2 1/8 inches. **Col. Depth:** 10 inches. **Key Personnel:** Harvey Grotsky, Editor-in-Chief, Publisher; Susan Wyckoff Fell, Managing Editor; Susan S. Gregg, Managing Editor; Mitch D. Miller, Creative Director. **ISSN:** 0739--1587 (print). **Subscription Rates:** Free. **URL:** http://www.themeetingmagazines.com/corporate-incentive-travel/. **Ad Rates:** 4C $13,845, full page - 4 color; 4C $12,615, full page - 2 color; BW $11,275, full page. **Remarks:** Accepts advertising. **Circ:** 40000.

7327 ■ The Family Journal: Counseling and Therapy for Couples and Families
International Association for Marriage and Family Counselors
c/o Dr. Paul Peluso, President
Bldg. 47, Rm. 270
Dept. of Counselor Education
Florida Atlantic University
777 Glades Rd.
Boca Raton, FL 33431-0991
Phone: (561)297-3625
Publisher's E-mail: sales@pfp.sagepub.com

Journal focusing on the theory, research, and practice of counseling with couples and families from a family systems perspective. **Freq:** Quarterly. **Key Personnel:** Jill D. Duba, Editor; Stephen Southern, Editor. **ISSN:** 1066--4807 (print); **EISSN:** 1552--3950 (electronic). **Subscription Rates:** $146 Individuals print; $899 Institutions e-access; $979 Institutions print; $999 Institutions print and e-access; $47 Individuals single issue; $269 Institutions single issue. **URL:** http://tfj.sagepub.com; http://www.iamfconline.org/public/department26.cfm. **Remarks:** Accepts advertising. **Circ:** 10000.

7328 ■ Gifts & Decorative Accessories
SANDOW

Circulation: ⋆ = AAM; △ or • = BPA; ♦ = CAC; ❑ = VAC; ⊕ = PO Statement; ‡ = Publisher's Report; Boldface figures = sworn; Light figures = estimated.

3651 NW 8th Ave.
Boca Raton, FL 33431
Phone: (561)961-7600
Publisher's E-mail: info@sandow.com
International magazine for retailers of gifts, greeting cards, decorative accessories, and stationery-related merchandise. **Freq:** 10/year. **Print Method:** Offset. **Trim Size:** 7 7/8 x 10 1/2. **Key Personnel:** Caroline Kennedy, Editor-in-Chief, phone: (917)934-2876; Nancy Wolkow, Publisher, phone: (917)934-2889. **Subscription Rates:** $49.99 U.S.; $149.99 Other countries. **Online:** SANDOW SANDOW. **URL:** http://www.giftsanddec.com/. **Formerly**: Playthings. **Ad Rates:** BW $6,790; 4C $8,860. **Remarks:** Advertising accepted; rates available upon request. **Circ:** Combined 27000.

7329 ■ Home Textiles Today
SANDOW
3651 NW 8th Ave.
Boca Raton, FL 33431
Phone: (561)961-7600
Publisher's E-mail: info@sandow.com
Business and fashion magazine of the home textiles industry. Intended for senior management, buyers, and home fashion coordinators in all retail channels of home textiles distribution. **Freq:** Monthly. **Print Method:** Offset. **Trim Size:** 10.5 x 13.5. **Cols./Page:** 5. **Col. Width:** 23 nonpareils. **Col. Depth:** 196 agate lines. **Key Personnel:** Warren Shoulberg, Director, Editorial, Publisher, phone: (646)805-0226; Jennifer Marks, Editor-in-Chief, phone: (732)204-2012. **ISSN:** 0195--3187 (print). **URL:** http://www.hometextilestoday.com. **Ad Rates:** BW $6,450; 4C $7,500. **Remarks:** Accepts advertising. **Circ:** Controlled ‡7200.

7330 ■ Hotel & Resort Industry
Coastal Communications Corp.
2700 N Military Trl., Ste. 120
Boca Raton, FL 33431-6394
Phone: (561)989-0600
Fax: (561)989-9509
Magazine for headquarters executives, owners, operations management, specifiers, and purchasing directors in hotels, resorts, motels, and motor inns. **Freq:** Monthly. **Print Method:** Offset. **Trim Size:** 8 1/8 x 10 7/8. **Cols./Page:** 3. **Col. Width:** 27 nonpareils. **Col. Depth:** 98 agate lines. **Key Personnel:** Stefani O'Connor, Editor-in-Chief; Walter Pierce, Publisher. **ISSN:** 0149--3639 (print). **Ad Rates:** BW $5,620; 4C $6,860. **Remarks:** Accepts advertising. **Circ:** Controlled ‡49494.

7331 ■ Insurance & Financial Meetings Management
Coastal Communications Corp.
2700 N Military Trl., Ste. 120
Boca Raton, FL 33431-6394
Phone: (561)989-0600
Fax: (561)989-9509
Trade magazine covering the insurance industry for professionals responsible for meeting destination; site selection; convention and incentive travel programs. **Freq:** Bimonthly. **Print Method:** Web Offset. **Trim Size:** 8 1/8 x 10 7/8. **Cols./Page:** 3. **Col. Width:** 2 1/8 inches. **Col. Depth:** 10 inches. **Key Personnel:** Harvey Grotsky, Editor-in-Chief, Publisher, President, Chief Executive Officer; Susan Wyckoff Fell, Managing Editor; Mitch D. Miller, Creative Director. **ISSN:** 1078--7666 (print). **URL:** http://www.themeetingmagazines.com/insurance-financial-meetings-management/insurance-advertise. **Formerly**: Insurance Meetings & Incentives; Insurance Meetings Management. **Ad Rates:** BW $1,575; 4C $4,590. **Remarks:** Accepts advertising. **Circ:** 5000.

7332 ■ Jazziz
JAZZIZ Magazine Inc.
PO Box 880189
Boca Raton, FL 33488
Phone: (561)893-6868
Fax: (561)893-6867
Publisher's E-mail: mail@jazziz.com
Music magazine focusing on all aspects of improvisational and instrumental music for sophisticated listeners. Comes monthly with audio and multimedia CD featuring new, classic and exclusive music. **Freq:** Monthly. **Print Method:** Offset. **Trim Size:** 8 1/2 x 10 1/2. **Cols./Page:** 3. **Col. Width:** 2 1/8 inches. **Col. Depth:** 9 1/4 inches. **Key Personnel:** Lori Blum Fagien, Publisher; Michael Fagien, Publisher. **ISSN:** 0074--5885 (print). **Subscription Rates:** $59.95 Individuals; C$69.99 Canada and Mexico; $79.99 Other countries. **URL:** http://jazziz.com/magazine. **Remarks:** Accepts advertising. **Circ:** Paid ‡150000, Non-paid ‡65000.

7333 ■ Journal of the Fantastic in the Arts
International Association for the Fantastic in the Arts
1279 W Palmetto Park Rd., Unit 272285
Boca Raton, FL 33427
Publisher's E-mail: iafareg@gmail.com
Freq: Quarterly. **Subscription Rates:** $35 Individuals; $35 Institutions; $50 Other countries individual and institution. **URL:** http://www.fantastic-arts.org/jfa. **Remarks:** Accepts advertising. **Circ:** (Not Reported).

7334 ■ Journal of Public Budgeting, Accounting & Financial Management
PrAcademics Press
21760 Mountain Sugar Ln.
Boca Raton, FL 33433
Publisher's E-mail: info@pracademics.com
Journal covering theories and practices in the fields of public budgeting, governmental accounting, and financial management. **Freq:** Quarterly. **Key Personnel:** Khi V. Thai, Editor; Howard A. Frank, Managing Editor. **ISSN:** 1096--3367 (print); **EISSN:** 1945--1814 (electronic). **Subscription Rates:** $400 Individuals print or online; $500 Institutions print or online; $700 Individuals print and online; $900 Institutions print and online. **URL:** http://pracademics.com/index.php/jpbafm. **Circ:** (Not Reported).

7335 ■ Journal of Public Procurement
PrAcademics Press
21760 Mountain Sugar Ln.
Boca Raton, FL 33433
Publisher's E-mail: info@pracademics.com
Peer-reviewed journal dedicated to the study of public procurement. **Freq:** Quarterly. **Key Personnel:** Khi V. Thai, PhD, Editor-in-Chief. **ISSN:** 1535-0118 (print); **EISSN:** 2150-6930 (electronic). **Subscription Rates:** $700 Individuals print and online; $900 Institutions print and online; $400 Individuals print or online; $500 Institutions print or online. **URL:** http://pracademics.com/index.php/jopp. **Circ:** (Not Reported).

7336 ■ Luxe
SANDOW
3651 NW 8th Ave.
Boca Raton, FL 33431
Phone: (561)961-7600
Publication E-mail: editorial@luxemagazine.com
Magazine featuring home design, architecture and decor for homes in Colorado. **Freq:** Quarterly. **Subscription Rates:** $34.95 Individuals. **URL:** http://www.luxesource.com. **Remarks:** Accepts advertising. **Circ:** (Not Reported).

7337 ■ New Beauty
SANDOW
3651 NW 8th Ave.
Boca Raton, FL 33431
Phone: (561)961-7600
Publisher's E-mail: info@sandow.com
Magazine covering plastic surgery, dermatology, and cosmetic dentistry. **Freq:** Quarterly. **ISSN:** 1556--4878 (print). **Subscription Rates:** $29.95 Individuals. **URL:** http://www.newbeauty.com. **Remarks:** Accepts advertising. **Circ:** (Not Reported).

7338 ■ Powerline Magazine
Electrical Generating Systems Association
1650 S Dixie Hwy., Ste. 400
Boca Raton, FL 33432
Phone: (561)750-5575
Fax: (561)395-8557
Publisher's E-mail: e-mail@egsa.org
Trade magazine for the on-site power generating industry. **Freq:** Bimonthly. **Print Method:** Offset. **Trim Size:** 8.375 x 10.875. **Subscription Rates:** Free to qualified subscribers; $5 Single issue. **Alt. Formats:** PDF. **URL:** http://www.egsa.org/Publications/PowerlineMagazine.aspx; http://www.egsa.org/Publications/PowerlineMagazine/Archives.aspx. **Formerly**: Powerline. **Ad Rates:** BW $1645; 4C $820. **Remarks:** Accepts advertising. **Circ:** (Not Reported).

7339 ■ Simply The Best Magazine: South Florida Life Style
Good Press Publishing
301 Yamato Rd., Ste. 1240
Boca Raton, FL 33431
Magazine covering high-end lifestyle in South Florida. **Freq:** Bimonthly. **Key Personnel:** Adam Goodkin, Publisher. **Subscription Rates:** $21 Individuals. **URL:** http://www.simplythebestmagazine.com. **Ad Rates:** 4C $3,175. **Remarks:** Accepts advertising. **Circ:** (Not Reported).

7340 ■ Sports & Entertainment Today
SET Magazine Inc.
20283 State Rd. 7, Ste. 300
Boca Raton, FL 33431
Magazine featuring lifestyles of the nation's top athletes and entertainers. **Freq:** Quarterly. **Key Personnel:** Danisha Rolle, Founder, Publisher. **URL:** http://setmagazine.com. **Remarks:** Advertising accepted; rates available upon request. **Circ:** (Not Reported).

7341 ■ ZOOMER
AgeVenture
19432 Preserve Dr.
Boca Raton, FL 33498
Phone: (561)866-8251
Publisher's E-mail: zoomer@demko.com
Magazine featuring research, retirement trends, and advances in medical sciences that help humans stay youthful longer. **Key Personnel:** Dr. David J. Demko, PhD, Editor-in-Chief. **ISSN:** 1088--5889 (print). **URL:** http://demko.com/Zoomer/ZoomerMagazine.htm. **Circ:** (Not Reported).

7342 ■ WHSR-AM - 980
1650 S Dixie Hwy., Fifth Fl.
Boca Raton, FL 33432
Phone: (561)997-0074
Fax: (561)997-0476
Format: Ethnic; World Beat; News. **Key Personnel:** Bob Morency, Gen. Mgr., morencybob@aol.com; Duff Lindsey, Operations Mgr. **Ad Rates:** Noncommercial. **URL:** http://www.whsrradio.com.

7343 ■ WSBR-AM - 740
1650 S Dixiw Hwy., 5th Fl.
Boca Raton, FL 33432
Phone: (561)997-0074
Fax: (561)997-0476
Format: Talk. **Networks:** ABC; Unistar. **Owner:** Beasley Broadcast Group Inc., 3033 Riviera Dr., Ste. 200, Naples, FL 34103-2750, Ph: (239)263-5000, Fax: (239)263-8191. **Founded:** 1965. **Operating Hours**: Continuous. **Key Personnel:** Bob Morency, Gen. Mgr., morencybob@aol.com; Duff Lindsey, Operations Mgr., duff@bbgiboca.com. **Wattage:** 2,500 Day; 940 Night. **Ad Rates:** Advertising accepted; rates available upon request. **URL:** http://www.wsbrradio.com.

7344 ■ WWNN-AM - 980
1650 S Dixie Hwy., 5th Fl.
Boca Raton, FL 33432
Phone: (561)997-0074
Fax: (561)997-0476
Founded: 1987. **Formerly**: WBSS-AM; WWHR-AM. **Operating Hours**: Continuous; 90% network, 10% local. **ADI**: Miami (Ft. Lauderdale), FL. **Key Personnel:** Bob Morency, Gen. Mgr.; Duff Lindsey, Operations Mgr., Prog. Dir; Joseph Nuckols, Contact. **Wattage**: 5,000. **URL:** http://whsrradio.com.

BOKEELIA

7345 ■ The Pine Island Eagle
Breeze Publishing Co.
10700 Stringfellow Rd.
Bokeelia, FL 33922
Phone: (239)283-2022
Publisher's E-mail: customerservice@breezenewspapers.com
Community newspaper. **Freq:** Weekly (Wed.). **Print Method:** Offset. **Cols./Page:** 6. **Col. Depth:** 16 inches. **Key Personnel:** Charlene Russ, Representative, Advertising and Sales; Valarie Harring, Executive Editor; Marianne Paton, Editor. **Subscription Rates:** $12 By mail 3 months; $24 By mail 6 months; $40 By mail 12 months. **URL:** http://pineisland-eagle.com. **Remarks:** Accepts advertising. **Circ:** Free ‡8500.

BONIFAY

Holmes Co. Holmes Co. (SE). 96 m ENE of Pensacola. Timber, diversified farming.

7346 ■ Holmes County Advertiser
Freedom Communications Inc.
112 E Virginia Ave.
Bonifay, FL 32425
Phone: (850)547-9414
Fax: (850)547-9418
Publisher's E-mail: info@freedom.com
Community newspaper. **Founded:** 1892. **Freq:** Weekly (Wed.). **Print Method:** Offset. **Cols./Page:** 6. **Col. Width:** 12 picas. **Col. Depth:** 21 inches. **Key Personnel:** Jay Felsberg, Editor; Nicole Barefield, Publisher, phone: (850)638-0212. **Subscription Rates:** $29 Individuals; $39 Out of area. **URL:** http://www.chipleypaper.com. **Mailing address:** PO Box 67, Bonifay, FL 32425. **Ad Rates:** BW $441; 4C $841; SAU $5.50; PCI $3.50. **Remarks:** Accepts advertising. **Circ:** Free ‡4200.

7347 ■ WJED-FM - 91.1
PO Box 527
Bonifay, FL 32425
Owner: Kingswood University, 26 Western St., Sussex, NB, Canada E4E 1E6, Ph: (506)432-4400, Fax: (506)432-4444, Free: 888-432-4444. **Wattage:** 700.

BONITA SPRINGS

Lee Co. (S). 22 m S of Ft. Myers on Gulf Coast.

7348 ■ Cultic Studies Review: An Internet Journal of Research, News & Opinion
International Cultic Studies Association
PO Box 2265
Bonita Springs, FL 34133
Phone: (239)514-3081
Fax: (305)393-8193
Publisher's E-mail: mail@icsamail.com
Online journal covering cults and related groups. **Freq:** Annual. **Key Personnel:** Carmen Almendros, PhD, Contact; Sandy Andron, PhD, Contact; Marybeth Ayella, Contact. **ISSN:** 1539--1052 (print). **Subscription Rates:** $45 Individuals print only; $20 Individuals online only. **URL:** http://www.icsahome.com/memberelibrary/csr. **Formed by the merger of:** Cultic Studies Journal; The Cult Observer. **Remarks:** Advertising not accepted. **Circ:** (Not Reported).

7349 ■ Hi-Tech Home
BBS Press Service Inc.
PO Box 367209
Bonita Springs, FL 34136
Phone: (239)992-0397
Professional operators of online services, web site designers, etc. **Freq:** 1-3 times weekly. **Print Method:** Online. **Subscription Rates:** Free. **Remarks:** Advertising not accepted. **Circ:** Controlled ‡45000.

7350 ■ Riding Instructor
American Riding Instructors Association
28801 Trenton Ct.
Bonita Springs, FL 34134-3337
Phone: (239)948-3232
Fax: (239)948-5053
Publisher's E-mail: riding-instructor@comcast.net
Freq: Quarterly. **URL:** http://www.riding-instructor.com/aria-membership. **Remarks:** Advertising not accepted. **Circ:** (Not Reported).

7351 ■ WGUF-FM - 98.9
10915 K-Nine Dr.
Bonita Springs, FL 34135
Phone: (239)495-8383
Format: News; Talk. **Key Personnel:** Roger Harris, Regional Mgr., rharris@rendabroadcasting.com. **Ad Rates:** Advertising accepted; rates available upon request. **URL:** http://www.wguf989.com.

7352 ■ WJGO-FM - 102.9
10915 K-Nine Dr.
Bonita Springs, FL 34135
Format: Eclectic. **Owner:** Renda Broadcasting Corp., 900 Parish St., 4th Fl., Pittsburgh, PA 15220, Ph: (412)875-1800, Fax: (412)875-1801. **Key Personnel:** Ryan Sherwin, Dir. of Mktg., rsherwin@rendabroadcasting.com. **URL:** http://www.1029bobfm.com.

7353 ■ WSGL-FM - 104.7
10915 K-Nine Dr.
Bonita Springs, FL 34135
Phone: (239)495-8383
Owner: Renda Broadcasting Corp., 900 Parish St., 4th Fl., Pittsburgh, PA 15220, Ph: (412)875-1800, Fax: (412)875-1801. **Operating Hours**: Monday-Friday8:30a.m. to 5:30p.m. **Key Personnel:** Randy Savage, Prog. Dir.; Ryan Sherwin, Dir. of Mktg. **Wattage**: 20,000. **Ad Rates:** Advertising accepted; rates available upon request.

7354 ■ WWGR-FM - 101.9
10915 K-Nine Dr.
Bonita Springs, FL 34135-6802
Phone: (239)495-8383
Format: Country. **Networks:** Independent. **Owner:** Renda Broadcasting Corp., at above address. **Founded:** 1969. **Formerly**: WHEW-FM. **Operating Hours**: Continuous. **ADI**: Fort Myers-Naples, FL. **Key Personnel:** Randy Savage, Dir. of Programs; Roger Harris, Contact, rharris@rendabroadcasting.com; Ryan Sherwin, Dir. of Mktg; Julio Gonzalez, Contact. **Wattage**: 100,000. **Ad Rates:** $8.25-10.50 for 15 seconds; $26-35 for 30 seconds; $34-47 for 60 seconds. **URL:** http://www.gatorcountry1019.com.

BOYNTON BEACH

Palm Beach Co. Palm Beach Co. (SE). 10 m N of Delray Beach.

7355 ■ WRMB-FM - 89.3
1511 W Boynton Beach Blvd.
Boynton Beach, FL 33436
Phone: (561)737-9762
Fax: (561)737-9899
Email: wrmb@moody.edu
Format: Religious. **Networks:** Moody Broadcasting. **Owner:** The Moody Bible Institute of Chicago, 820 N Lasalle St., Chicago, IL 60610, Ph: (312)329-4000, Free: 800-356-6639. **Founded:** 1979. **Operating Hours**: Continuous; 36% network, 64% local. **Key Personnel:** Jennifer Epperson, Station Mgr., wrmb@moody.edu. **Wattage**: 100,000. **Ad Rates:** Noncommercial. **URL:** http://www.moodyradiosouthflorida.fm.

7356 ■ WXEL-FM - 90.7
3401 S Congress Ave.
Boynton Beach, FL 33426
Phone: (561)737-8000
Fax: (561)369-3067
Email: info@wxel.org
Format: Public Radio. **Networks:** National Public Radio (NPR); Public Radio International (PRI). **Owner:** Barry Telecommunications, Inc., at above address. **Founded:** 1969. **Formerly**: WHRS-FM. **Operating Hours**: Continuous. **ADI**: West Palm Beach-Ft. Pierce-Vero Beach, FL. **Key Personnel:** Linda Bevilacqua, Sr., Chairman. **Wattage**: 25,000. **Ad Rates:** Noncommercial. **URL:** http://www.wxel.org.

7357 ■ WXEL-TV - 42
3401 S Congress Ave.
Boynton Beach, FL 33426
Phone: (561)737-8000
Fax: (561)369-3067
Email: info@wxel.org
Format: Public TV. **Networks:** Public Broadcasting Service (PBS). **Owner:** Barry Telecommunications, Inc., at above address. **Founded:** 1982. **Formerly**: WHRS-TV. **Operating Hours**: Continuous. **ADI**: West Palm Beach-Ft. Pierce-Vero Beach, FL. **Key Personnel:** Linda Bevilacqua, Chairman. **Ad Rates:** Noncommercial. **URL:** http://www.wxel.org.

BRADENTON

WC FL. Manatee Co. On Manatee River, 41 mi. S. of Tampa. Fruit and vegetable shipping; grapefruit cannery; bottling works; crate mill. Winter resort. Pine timber. Diversified farming.

7358 ■ Advanced Diver Magazine
Advanced Diver Magazine
327 Snapdragon Loop
Bradenton, FL 34212
Phone: (941)748-3483
Publisher's E-mail: advdvrmag@aol.com
Magazine covering underwater world. **Freq:** Quarterly. **Key Personnel:** Curt Bowen, Owner, Publisher; Linda Bowen, Owner, Publisher. **Subscription Rates:** $25 Individuals; $50 Two years; $50 Canada and Mexico; $100 Canada and Mexico 2 years; $60 Other countries; $120 Other countries 2 years; $7.50 Single issue. **URL:** http://www.advanceddivermagazine.com. **Remarks:** Accepts advertising. **Circ:** (Not Reported).

7359 ■ Bradenton Herald
McClatchy Newspapers Inc.
1111 3rd Ave., W
Bradenton, FL 34205
Phone: (941)748-0411
Publisher's E-mail: pensions@mcclatchy.com
General newspaper. **Founded:** 1922. **Freq:** Daily. **Print Method:** Offset. **Trim Size:** 13 x 21 1/4. **Cols./Page:** 6. **Col. Width:** 2 1/32 inches. **Col. Depth:** 297 agate lines. **Key Personnel:** Terry Tramell, Manager, Circulation; Joan Krauter, Executive Editor, Vice President. **Subscription Rates:** $1.49 Individuals /week,print and digital; $.99 Individuals /month,digital only; $98.95 Individuals annual, digital only. **Alt. Formats:** Handheld. **URL:** http://www.bradenton.com. **Remarks:** Accepts advertising. **Circ:** Mon.-Fri. ★**39135**, Sun. ★**45925**.

7360 ■ NAHI Forum
National Association of Home Inspectors
4426 5th St. W
Bradenton, FL 34207
Phone: (941)462-4265
Fax: (941)896-3187
Free: 800-448-3942
Publisher's E-mail: info@nahi.org
Freq: Quarterly. **Subscription Rates:** Included in membership. **URL:** http://www.nahi.org/education/forum-magazine/. **Remarks:** Accepts advertising. **Circ:** 1400.

7361 ■ WJIS-FM - 88.1
6469 Parkland Dr.
Sarasota, FL 34243
Phone: (941)753-0401
Fax: (941)753-2963
Free: 800-456-8910
Email: thejoyfm@thejoyfm.com
Format: Contemporary Christian. **Owner:** WJIS FM Radio, 6469 Parkland Dr., Sarasota, FL 34243, Ph: (941)753-0401, Fax: (941)753-2963. **Founded:** 1986. **Operating Hours**: Continuous. **ADI**: Tampa-St. Petersburg (Lakeland, Sarasota), FL. **Key Personnel:** Curt Baker, Contact; Johanna Antes, Director; Karen Rutherford, Office Mgr.; Jeff MacFarlane, Gen. Mgr., jeff@thejoyfm.com. **Wattage**: 100,000. **Ad Rates:** Noncommercial. **URL:** http://www.florida.thejoyfm.com.

7362 ■ WWPR-AM - 1490
5910 Cortez Rd. W, No. 130
Bradenton, FL 34210
Phone: (941)761-8843
Fax: (941)761-8683
Email: manager@1490wwpr.com
Format: Oldies; Talk. **Operating Hours**: Continuous. **Key Personnel:** Valerie Silver, Contact. **Wattage**: 800. **Ad Rates:** for 30 seconds; for 60 seconds. **URL:** http://www.1490wwpr.com.

BRANFORD

Suwannee Co. Suwannee Co. (S). 23 m S of Live Oak.

7363 ■ The Branford News
Branford News Inc.
PO Box 148
Branford, FL 32008
Phone: (386)935-1427
Publication E-mail: branfordnews@alltel.net
Community newspaper. **Freq:** Weekly (Thurs.). **Print Method:** Offset. **Cols./Page:** 9. **Col. Width:** 2 inches. **Col. Depth:** 21 1/2 inches. **Key Personnel:** Myra Regan, Publisher; Monja Slater, Director, Advertising. **USPS:** 063-280. **Subscription Rates:** $16 Individuals home delivery; $23 Out of area home delivery. **URL:** http://www.suwanneedemocrat.com. **Ad Rates:** BW $470.85; PCI $5.85. **Remarks:** Accepts advertising. **Circ:** Paid ‡2000.

BRONSON

7364 ■ Levy County Journal
Levy County Journal
440 S Ct. St.
Bronson, FL 32621-6518
Phone: (352)486-2312
Fax: (352)486-5042
Community newspaper. **Freq:** Weekly (Thurs.). **Print**

Circulation: ★ = AAM; △ or • = BPA; ♦ = CAC; ❑ = VAC; ⊕ = PO Statement; ‡ = Publisher's Report; Boldface figures = sworn; Light figures = estimated.

Method: Offset. **Cols./Page:** 7. **Col. Width:** 2 inches. **Col. Depth:** 21 inches. **Key Personnel:** Kathy Hilliard, Editor. **USPS:** 310-708. **Subscription Rates:** $25 Individuals in Levy County; $30 Individuals Florida; $35 Individuals outside Florida. **Mailing address:** PO Box 159, Bronson, FL 32621-6518. **Ad Rates:** PCI $1.50. **Remarks:** Accepts advertising. **Circ:** Paid 1100.

BROOKSVILLE

WC FL. Hernando Co. 50 mi. N. of Tampa. Manufactures electronic components and furniture. Citrus fruit, poultry, and stock farms. Horse breeding.

7365 ■ Hernando Today
Hernando Today
15299 Cortez Blvd.
Brooksville, FL 34613
Phone: (352)544-5200
Community newspaper. **Founded:** 1987. **Freq:** Mon.-Sat. **Key Personnel:** Duane Chichester, General Manager, Publisher, phone: (352)544-5204; Brenda Milton, Manager, Advertising, phone: (352)544-5261; Denise Nohejl, Office Manager, phone: (352)544-5206. **ISSN:** 0000-6285 (print). **Subscription Rates:** $36 Individuals Wednesday - Sunday; $130 By mail 52 weeks. **URL:** http://hernandotoday.com. **Formerly:** Green Sheet. **Ad Rates:** GLR $1.39; BW $2,142; 4C $2,507; SAU $17; PCI $11.75. **Remarks:** Accepts advertising. **Circ:** Free ‡12000, Paid ‡15000.

7366 ■ National Cockatiel Society Journal
National Cockatiel Society
c/o Deb Dollar, Treasurer
PO Box 12058
Brooksville, FL 34603-2058
Publisher's E-mail: NCSTreasury@aol.com
Journal consisting of news and information, photos and stories, advice columns, avian recipes and humor for cockatiel owners, exhibitors and breeders. **Freq:** Bimonthly. **Subscription Rates:** Included in membership. **URL:** http://www.cockatiels.org/join-ncs. **Remarks:** Accepts advertising. **Circ:** (Not Reported).

7367 ■ WKFL-AM - 1170
PO Box 1424
Brooksville, FL 34605
Phone: (352)330-4033
Email: wkfl1170am@yahoo.com
Format: Gospel; Religious. **Ad Rates:** Advertising accepted; rates available upon request.

7368 ■ WWJB-AM - 1450
55 W Fort Dade Ave.
Brooksville, FL 34601
Phone: (352)796-7469
Fax: (352)796-5074
Free: 888-613-2050
Format: News; Talk; Sports. **Networks:** ABC. **Owner:** Hernando Broadcasting Co., at above address. **Founded:** 1958. **Operating Hours:** Continuous. **Wattage:** 1,000. **Ad Rates:** Noncommercial. **Mailing address:** PO Box 1507, Brooksville, FL 34605. **URL:** http://www.jbnewsradio.com.

BUNNELL

NE FL. Flagler Co. 65 mi. SE of Jacksonville. Pine, cypress timber. Agriculture. Citrus fruits, corn, vegetables.

7369 ■ Flagler Pennysaver
Volusia Pennysaver Inc.
2729 E Moody Blvd.
Bunnell, FL 32110
Phone: (386)677-4262
Publisher's E-mail: flagleri@psavers.com
Shopper. **Freq:** Weekly (Wed.). **Key Personnel:** Melinda Marchione, Manager, Sales; Pat Waterman, Manager, General Sales; Jon Riddell, Manager, Circulation. **URL:** http://www.floridapennysavers.com/SiteDefault.aspx?edition=FL. **Ad Rates:** 4C $100; 4C $115, back page; 4C $115, 1-color; 4C $150, 2-color; 4C $185, full color. **Remarks:** Accepts advertising. **Circ:** ‡38,500, ‡39,629.

WJBT-FM - See Green Cove Springs

7370 ■ WNZF-AM - 1550
2405 E Moody Blvd., Ste. 402
Bunnell, FL 32110-5994
Phone: (386)437-1992
Fax: (386)437-8728
Format: News; Talk; Sports. **Key Personnel:** David Ayers, Gen. Mgr., david@wnzf.com; Ron Charles, News Dir., ron@wnzf.com; Marc Gilliland, Operations Mgr., marc@wnzf.com; David Ayres, Gen. Mgr. **URL:** http://www.wnzf.com.

7371 ■ WNZF-FM - 106.3
2405 E Moody Blvd., Ste. 402
Bunnell, FL 32110-5994
Phone: (386)437-1992
Format: News; Talk; Sports. **Key Personnel:** David Ayres, Sales Mgr.; Ron Charles, Traffic Mgr., Chief Engineer, ron@wnzf.com; Marc Gilliland, News Dir., marc@wnzf.com. **URL:** http://www.wnzf.com.

7372 ■ WSJF-FM - 105.5
2405 E Moody Blvd., Ste. 402
Bunnell, FL 32110
Phone: (386)437-8728
Format: Jazz; Oldies. **Key Personnel:** Annie Ashe, Contact; Brian Culbertson, Contact. **Wattage:** 17,000 ERP. **Ad Rates:** Advertising accepted; rates available upon request. **URL:** http://www.flaglerbroadcasting.com.

BUSHNELL

C FL. Sumter Co. 63 mi. NE of Tampa. Agriculture. Cattle, tomatoes, cucumbers, watermelons.

7373 ■ Sumter County Times
Landmark Community Newspapers L.L.C.
204 E McCollum Ave.
Bushnell, FL 33513
Phone: (352)793-2161
Publisher's E-mail: marketing@lcni.com
Community newspaper. **Freq:** Weekly (Thurs.). **Print Method:** Offset. **Cols./Page:** 6. **Col. Width:** 1.83 inches. **Col. Depth:** 1 inches. **Key Personnel:** Bob Reichman, Editor; Brenda Locklear, Administrator, Writer; Tricia Marks, General Manager; Mike Taylor, Manager, Advertising and Sales; Amanda Mims, Writer. **Subscription Rates:** $25 Individuals print and online; $15 Individuals 6 months; print and online. **URL:** http://www.sumtercountytimes.com. **Ad Rates:** GLR $1; BW $1,118; 4C $1,418; PCI $6.52. **Remarks:** Accepts advertising. **Circ:** ‡5500.

7374 ■ WKFL-AM
PO Box 1000
Bushnell, FL 33513
Phone: (352)793-9535
Format: Oldies. **Networks:** NBC; Unistar; Mutual Broadcasting System. **Owner:** StarStrip Communications, Inc., at above address, Ph: (904)357-1240. **Founded:** 1989. **Key Personnel:** Jim Johnson, Contact; Roberta Johnson, Contact; Frank Strand, Contact. **Wattage:** 1,000 Day. **Ad Rates:** $7-14 for 30 seconds; $9-16 for 60 seconds. **URL:** http://www.1170radio.com/.

CALLAHAN

NE FL. Nassau Co. 20 mi. NW of Jacksonville. Pine, cypress timber. Manufactures veneer. Naval stores. Diversified farming. Poultry, livestock, potatoes, truck crops.

7375 ■ Nassau County Record
Nassau County Record
617317 Brandies Ave.
Callahan, FL 32011
Phone: (904)879-2727
Fax: (904)879-5155
Publication E-mail: nassctyrec@aol.com
Community newspaper. **Freq:** Weekly (Thurs.). **Print Method:** Offset. **Cols./Page:** 6. **Col. Width:** 27 nonpareils. **Col. Depth:** 301 agate lines. **Key Personnel:** Foy Maloy, Publisher; Mike Hankins, Director, Advertising; Amanda Bishop, Editor, Manager. **USPS:** 371-640. **Subscription Rates:** $22.50 Individuals in Nassau County; $35 Out of area; $25 Individuals online only; $7 Individuals online - 1 month access. **URL:** http://www.nassaucountyrecord.com. **Mailing address:** PO Box 609, Callahan, FL 32011. **Ad Rates:** GLR $.29; BW $580.50; SAU $4.25; PCI $4.50. **Remarks:** Accepts advertising. **Circ:** ‡5000.

CAPE CORAL

S FL. Lee Co. 10 mi. SW of Fort Myers.

7376 ■ American Dancer Magazine
U.S.A. Dance
PO Box 152988
Cape Coral, FL 33915-2988
Fax: (239)573-0946
Free: 800-447-9047
Publisher's E-mail: central-office@usadance.org
Magazine covering competition results, letters, financial and developmental reports, calendar of events, and articles relating to ballroom dance. **Freq:** 6/year. **Key Personnel:** Angela F. Prince, Publisher, Editor-in-Chief. **Subscription Rates:** Included in membership; $25 Nonmembers within USA. **URL:** http://www.usadance.org/news/american-dancer. **Formerly:** Amateur Dancers. **Remarks:** Advertising accepted; rates available upon request. **Circ:** (Not Reported).

7377 ■ American Dancers
U.S.A. Dance
PO Box 152988
Cape Coral, FL 33915-2988
Fax: (239)573-0946
Free: 800-447-9047
Publisher's E-mail: central-office@usadance.org
Freq: 6/year. **Subscription Rates:** included in membership dues; $25 Nonmembers. **URL:** http://www.usadance.org/news/our-publications. **Remarks:** Accepts advertising. **Circ:** 23000.

7378 ■ The Cape Coral Daily Breeze
Breeze Publishing Co.
2510 Del Prado Blvd.
Cape Coral, FL 33904
Phone: (239)574-1110
Publisher's E-mail: customerservice@breezenewspapers.com
General newspaper. **Freq:** Daily. **Print Method:** Offset. **Cols./Page:** 8. **Col. Width:** 9 picas. **Col. Depth:** 21 1/2 inches. **Key Personnel:** Scott Blonde, Publisher; Jim Linette, Editor; Renee Brown, Manager, Advertising and Sales; Chris Strine, Editor; Valarie Harring, Executive Editor. **Subscription Rates:** $8.00 Individuals 3 months, home delivery; $14.00 Two years 6 months,mail(usps); 26.66 12 months, mail(usps). **URL:** http://www.cape-coral-daily-breeze.com. **Ad Rates:** PCI $4.95. **Remarks:** Accepts advertising. **Circ:** ‡5500.

7379 ■ Fort Myers Beach Bulletin
Breeze Newspapers
2510 Del Prado Blvd.
Cape Coral, FL 33904
Phone: (239)574-1110
Publisher's E-mail: customerservice@breezenewspapers.com
Arts and entertainment. **Freq:** Weekly (Fri.). **Print Method:** Offset. **Trim Size:** 10 3/8 x 16. **Cols./Page:** 6. **Col. Width:** 1 5/8 inches. **Col. Depth:** 16 inches. **Key Personnel:** Melissa Schneider, Editor; Robert Petcher, Editor; Vickie Jones, Account Executive. **Subscription Rates:** Included in membership; $40 By mail; $24 By mail 6 months; $12 By mail 3 months. **URL:** http://fortmyersbeachtalk.com. **Ad Rates:** GLR $1.25; BW $888; 4C $1,038; PCI $4.25. **Remarks:** Accepts advertising. **Circ:** Paid ‡16000, Free ‡14500.

7380 ■ The Founders Journal
Founders Ministries
PO Box 150931
Cape Coral, FL 33915
Phone: (941)772-1400
Fax: (941)772-1400
Publisher's E-mail: founders@founders.org
Publication of the Founders Ministries. **Freq:** Quarterly. **Key Personnel:** Thomas K. Ascol, PhD, Editor. **Subscription Rates:** Free in PDF format; $1.99 Single issue. **Alt. Formats:** E-book; PDF. **URL:** http://founders.org/journal. **Remarks:** Advertising not accepted. **Circ:** Paid 1000.

7381 ■ Lee County Shopper
Breeze Publishing Co.
2510 Del Prado Blvd.
Cape Coral, FL 33904
Phone: (239)574-1110
Publisher's E-mail: customerservice@breezenewspapers.com
Shopper. **Freq:** Weekly (Wed.). **Print Method:** Offset. **Cols./Page:** 6. **Col. Width:** 20 nonpareils. **Col. Depth:** 224 agate lines. **Key Personnel:** Scott Blonde, Publisher. **Subscription Rates:** $90 By mail 2 days per week; $12 By mail Saturday only. **URL:** http://www.leecountyshopper.com. **Ad Rates:** GLR $.992; BW

$1,334.40; 4C $1,554.40; PCI $13.90. **Remarks:** Accepts advertising. **Circ:** Free 105000.

7382 ■ WFTX-TV - 36
621 SW Pine Island Rd.
Cape Coral, FL 33991
Email: news@fox4now.com
Format: Commercial TV. **Networks:** Fox. **Owner:** Journal Broadcast Group Inc., 1533 Amherst Rd., Knoxville, TN 37909. **Founded:** 1986. **Formerly:** Wabash Valley Broadcasting, Inc. **Operating Hours:** 6 a.m.-2 a.m. **ADI:** Fort Myers-Naples, FL. **Key Personnel:** Judy Kenney, Gen. Mgr., VP, jkenney@fox4now.com; Mike Mayne, VP, Gen. Mgr., mmayne@fox4now.com. **Ad Rates:** Advertising accepted; rates available upon request. **URL:** http://www.fox4now.com.

CEDAR KEY

7383 ■ Cedar Key Beacon
Cedar Key Beacon
PO Box 532
Cedar Key, FL 32625-0532
Phone: (352)543-5701
Fax: (352)543-5928
Community newspaper covering local news, travel, outdoor, and tourism. **Freq:** Weekly (Thurs.). **Cols./Page:** 6. **Col. Width:** 1 5/8 inches. **Subscription Rates:** $27 Individuals print and online - annual; $16.20 Individuals print and online - semi annual; $10 Individuals print and online - quarterly. **URL:** http://www.cedarkeybeacon.com. **Remarks:** Accepts classified advertising. **Circ:** Controlled 1500.

CHIEFLAND

Levy Co. Levy Co. (NW). 5 m N of Bronson.

7384 ■ Chiefland Citizen
Chiefland Citizen
624 W Park Ave.
Chiefland, FL 32626
Phone: (904)493-4796
Fax: (904)493-9336
Community newspaper. **Freq:** Weekly (Thurs.). **Trim Size:** 14 3/4 x 22 3/4. **Cols./Page:** 7. **Col. Width:** 1 13/16 inches. **Col. Depth:** 21 1/2 inches. **Key Personnel:** Lou Elliott Jones, Editor. **Remarks:** Accepts advertising. **Circ:** 4200.

7385 ■ CommuniComm Services
PO Box 182245
Columbus, OH 43218
Free: 800-392-2662
Founded: 1930. **Cities Served:** 35 channels. **URL:** http://www.netcommander.com.

7386 ■ WLQH-AM - 940
12750 Old Fanning Springs Rd.
Chiefland, FL 32626
Phone: (727)410-1642
Fax: (727)937-8390
Format: Information; Full Service. **Simulcasts:** WZCC. **Owner:** Dix Communications, at above address. **Founded:** 1967. **Ad Rates:** Advertising accepted; rates available upon request. $5-10 for 30 seconds; $7.50-10 for 60 seconds. **URL:** http://www.classichits933.com/.

7387 ■ WTBH-FM
PO Box 1730
Chiefland, FL 32644
Phone: (904)493-2650
Fax: (904)493-7352
Free: 800-344-9824
Format: Religious. **Owner:** Long Pond Baptist Church, at above address. **Founded:** 1988. **Wattage:** 3,000 ERP.

CHIPLEY

NW FL. Washington Co. 36 mi. S. of Dothan, AL. Manufactures lumber, spools. Agriculture. Cotton, peanuts, watermelons.

7388 ■ Washington County News
Washington County News
PO Box 627
Chipley, FL 32428
Phone: (850)638-0212
Publisher's E-mail: news@chipleypaper.com
Community newspaper. **Founded:** 1924. **Freq:** Semiweekly (Mon. and Thurs.). **Print Method:** Offset. **Cols./Page:** 6. **Col. Width:** 24 nonpareils. **Col. Depth:** 301 agate lines. **Key Personnel:** Brenda Taylor, Contact; Nicole Barefield, Publisher. **URL:** http://www.chipleypaper.com. **Remarks:** Advertising accepted; rates available upon request. **Circ:** (Not Reported).

7389 ■ WBGC-AM
1513 South Blvd.
Chipley, FL 32428
Phone: (850)638-0234
Fax: (850)638-4333
Format: Oldies. **Networks:** UPI; Florida Radio. **Founded:** 1956. **Key Personnel:** Emory W. Wells, Engg. Mgr. **Wattage:** 1,000. **Ad Rates:** Advertising accepted; rates available upon request.

CHULUOTA

7390 ■ Groomer to Groomer
American Mobile Groomers Association
1777 Brumley Rd.
Chuluota, FL 32766
Phone: (717)691-3388
Publisher's E-mail: director@americanmobilegroomer.com
Magazine featuring information about pet-care industry. **Freq:** 9/year. **Key Personnel:** Todd Shelly, Editor. **Subscription Rates:** Included in membership. **URL:** http://groomertogroomer.com. **Ad Rates:** BW $2,230; 4C $3,370. **Remarks:** Advertising not accepted. **Circ:** ‡20,000.

CLEARWATER

WC FL. Pinellas Co. On Gulf of Mexico, 25 mi. W. of Tampa. Tourist resort. Fishing. Citrus fruit, flowers.

7391 ■ Consumer Finance Law Quarterly Report
Conference on Consumer Finance Law
PO Box 17981
Clearwater, FL 33762
Phone: (405)208-5198
Publication E-mail: ccflqr@okcu.edu
Law journal publishing legal developments in the consumer financial services industry. **Freq:** Quarterly. **ISSN:** 0883--4555 (print). **Subscription Rates:** Included in membership; $50 Nonmembers. **URL:** http://www.ccflonline.org/report.cfm. **Remarks:** Accepts advertising. **Circ:** 1,200.

7392 ■ Jewish Press of Pinellas County
Jewish Press Group of Tampa Bay Inc.
PO Box 6970
Clearwater, FL 33758
Phone: (727)535-4400
Fax: (727)530-3039
Publisher's E-mail: info@jewishpresstampabay.com
Jewish community newspaper. **Freq:** Biweekly. **Print Method:** Offset. **Cols./Page:** 5. **Col. Width:** 2 inches. **Col. Depth:** 15 3/4 inches. **Key Personnel:** Jim Dawkins, Publisher. **Alt. Formats:** PDF. **URL:** http://www.jewishpresspinellas.com. **Ad Rates:** BW $895; PCI $16. **Remarks:** Accepts advertising. **Circ:** Controlled 4900.

7393 ■ Jewish Press of Tampa
Jewish Press Group of Tampa Bay Inc.
PO Box 6970
Clearwater, FL 33758
Phone: (727)535-4400
Fax: (727)530-3039
Publisher's E-mail: info@jewishpresstampabay.com
Jewish community newspaper. **Freq:** Biweekly. **Print Method:** Offset. **Cols./Page:** 5. **Col. Width:** 2 inches. **Col. Depth:** 15 3/4 inches. **Key Personnel:** Jim Dawkins, Manager, Advertising, Publisher; Karen Dawkins, Managing Editor. **ISSN:** 3763--1792 (print). **URL:** http://www.jewishpresstampabay.com. **Ad Rates:** BW $895; PCI $16. **Remarks:** Accepts advertising. **Circ:** Controlled 7000.

7394 ■ Journal of the American College of Nutrition
American College of Nutrition
300 S Duncan Ave., Ste. 225
Clearwater, FL 33755
Phone: (727)446-6086
Fax: (727)446-6202
Publication E-mail: jacn@wayne.edu
Freq: Bimonthly. **Print Method:** Offset. **Trim Size:** 8 1/4 x 10 7/8. **Cols./Page:** 2. **Col. Width:** 18 picas. **Col. Depth:** 53 picas. **Key Personnel:** Greg Reed, Managing Editor; John J. Cunningham, PhD, Editor-in-Chief. **ISSN:** 0731--5724 (print); **EISSN:** 1541--1087 (electronic). **Subscription Rates:** $226 Individuals print only; $473 Institutions online only; $540 Institutions print & online; included in membership dues. **Available online. URL:** http://www.jacn.org. **Ad Rates:** BW $700; BW $1,000; 4C $2,000. **Remarks:** Accepts advertising. **Circ:** 1150, 1300.

7395 ■ Space Energy Journal
Space Energy Association
PO Box 1136
Clearwater, FL 33757-1136
Phone: (954)749-6553
Journal covering research and development in the advanced energy field. **Freq:** Quarterly. **Key Personnel:** Jim Kettner. **Subscription Rates:** $35 Members U.S (/ year); $40 Canada and Mexico (/ year); $50 Other countries (/ year). **URL:** http://keelynet.com/sea.htm. **Remarks:** Advertising not accepted. **Circ:** 275.

7396 ■ Value Retail News
International Council of Shopping Centers
2519 N McMullen Booth Rd., Ste. 510-356
Clearwater, FL 33761
Phone: (727)781-7557
Fax: (732)694-1753
Publisher's E-mail: icsc@icsc.org
Trade magazine. **Freq:** 10/year. **Print Method:** Sheetfed offset. **Trim Size:** 9 1/2 x 13. **Cols./Page:** 4. **Col. Width:** 1 7/8 inches. **Col. Depth:** 11 3/4 inches. **Key Personnel:** Patricia Norins, Publisher; Sally Stephenson, Contact, phone: (847)835-1617, fax: (847)835-5196. **Subscription Rates:** $99 Members; $144 Nonmembers; $175 Out of country. **Alt. Formats:** PDF. **URL:** http://valueretailnews.com. **Ad Rates:** BW $3135; 4C $1105. **Remarks:** Accepts advertising. **Circ:** ‡5000.

7397 ■ WCLF-TV - 22
PO Box 6922
Clearwater, FL 33758
Phone: (727)535-5622
Fax: (727)531-2497
Free: 800-229-0059
Networks: Christian Television. **Owner:** Christian Television Network Inc., 6922 142nd Ave, Largo, FL 33771, Ph: (727)535-5622, Fax: (727)531-2497. **Founded:** 1979. **Operating Hours:** Continuous; 65% network, 35% local. **ADI:** Tampa-St. Petersburg (Lakeland, Sarasota), FL. **Key Personnel:** Robert R. D'Andrea, President. **Local Programs:** *Gospel Voice*, Sunday Saturday 12:30 a.m. 11:30 p.m.; 9:30 p.m.; *The Good Life*, Monday Friday 3:00 a.m. 8:30 p.m.; *We Got Next*, Saturday 11:00 p.m. **Ad Rates:** Noncommercial. **URL:** http://www.ctnonline.com.

7398 ■ WTAN-AM - 1340
706 N Mrytle Ave.
Clearwater, FL 33755
Phone: (727)441-3000
Email: lola@tantalk1340.com
Format: Talk. **Networks:** USA Radio; Westwood One Radio. **Owner:** Drenick Communication, at above address. **Founded:** 1948. **Operating Hours:** Continuous. 100% local. **ADI:** Tampa-St. Petersburg (Lakeland, Sarasota), FL. **Key Personnel:** Lola Jean, Contact, lola@tantalk1340.com. **Local Programs:** *Original Gospel Explosion*, Sunday 8:00 a.m. - 9:00 a.m.; 10:00 a.m. - 10:30 a.m. **Wattage:** 1,000. **Ad Rates:** $39 for 30 seconds; $59 for 60 seconds. **URL:** http://www.tantalk1340.com.

7399 ■ WZHR 1400-AM - 1400
706 N Myrtle Ave.
Clearwater, FL 33755
Phone: (352)567-1009
Format: Talk. **Founded:** Sept. 07, 2006. **Ad Rates:** Advertising accepted; rates available upon request. **URL:** http://wzhr.tantalk1340.com.

CLEARWATER BEACH

Pinellas Co. (WC). 18 m NW of St. Petersburg. Resort.

Circulation: ★ = AAM; △ or • = BPA; ♦ = CAC; ❑ = VAC; ⊕ = PO Statement; ‡ = Publisher's Report; Boldface figures = sworn; Light figures = estimated.

7400 ■ The Journal of NEAFCS
National Extension Association of Family and Consumer Sciences
140 Island Way, Ste. 316
Clearwater Beach, FL 33767
Phone: (561)477-8100
Fax: (561)910-0896
Freq: Annual. **Alt. Formats:** PDF. **URL:** http://www.neafcs.org/journal-of-neafcs. **Remarks:** Advertising not accepted. **Circ:** (Not Reported).

CLEWISTON

SC FL. Hendry Co. On Lake Okeechobee, 55 mi. W. of West Palm Beach. Raw sugar, mills. Agriculture. Sugar cane, beans, tomatoes, watermelons, cucumbers. Beef cattle.

7401 ■ Clewiston News: Serving America's Sweetest Town
Independent Newsmedia Inc.
820 W Sugarland Hwy., Ste. 5
Clewiston, FL 33440
Phone: (863)983-9148
Publisher's E-mail: help@newszap.com
Newspaper. **Freq:** Weekly (Thurs.). **Print Method:** Offset. **Cols./Page:** 6. **Col. Width:** 12 nonpareils. **Col. Depth:** 301 agate lines. **USPS:** 117-920. **Subscription Rates:** $26 Individuals online; $39 Individuals print. **URL:** http://theclewistonnews.com. **Ad Rates:** BW $415; 4C $655; PCI $10.26. **Remarks:** Accepts advertising. **Circ:** ‡7500.

7402 ■ Glades County Democrat
Glades County Democrat
820 W Sugarland Hwy., Ste. 5
Clewiston, FL 33440
Fax: (866)399-5253
Community newspaper. **Freq:** Weekly (Thurs.). **Print Method:** Offset. **Cols./Page:** 6. **Col. Width:** 12 nonpareils. **Col. Depth:** 301 agate lines. **Key Personnel:** Katrina Elsken, Executive Editor. **ISSN:** 0745--4120 (print). **URL:** http://gladesdemocrats.org. **Ad Rates:** BW $185; SAU $6.13. **Remarks:** Accepts advertising. **Circ:** ‡7500.

7403 ■ WAFC-AM - 590
530 E Alverdez Ave.
Clewiston, FL 33440
Format: Hispanic. **Owner:** Glades Media Group, 2105 West Immokalee Dr., Immokalee, FL 34142, Ph: (239)657-9210, Fax: (239)658-6109. **Key Personnel:** KC Kelly, Gen. Mgr., kc@gladesmedia.com. **URL:** http://www.radiofiesta.com.

7404 ■ WAFC-FM - 106.1
116 Commercio St.
Clewiston, FL 33440
Phone: (863)983-5900
Email: robbiec@gate.net
Format: News. **Owner:** Glades Media Company, at above address; Robert Castellanos, at above address, Clewiston, FL 33440. **Founded:** 1979. **Operating Hours**: Continuous - Mponday - Friday. **Key Personnel:** Brian Johnson, Contact, brian@gladesmedia.com; Liza Flores, Gen. Mgr., liza@gladesmedia.com; Paul Danitz, Sales Mgr., paul@gladesmedia.com; Brian Johnson, Contact, brian@gladesmedia.com. **Wattage**: 12,500 ERP. **Ad Rates:** $13-18 for 60 seconds; $11.75-16.95 per unit. Combined advertising rates available with WAFC-AM. **Mailing address:** PO Box 2109, Clewiston, FL 33440. **URL:** http://www.wafcfm.com.

COCOA

7405 ■ Sociological Spectrum: The Official Journal of the Mid-South Sociological Association
Routledge
c/o Olivia Metott, Managing Editor
University of Central Florida
Department of Sociology
1519 Clearlake Rd., Bldg. 3 Ste. 283
Cocoa, FL 32922
Publisher's E-mail: book.orders@tandf.co.uk
Journal publishing papers and applied research in sociology, social psychology, anthropology, and political science. **Freq:** 6/year. **Print Method:** Offset. **Trim Size:** 6 x 9. **Cols./Page:** 1. **Col. Width:** 52 nonpareils. **Col. Depth:** 101 agate lines. **Key Personnel:** John Lynxwiler, Board Member; Olivia Metott, Managing Editor, phone: (321)433-7882, fax: (321)433-7912. **ISSN:** 0273--2173 (print); **EISSN:** 1521--0707 (electronic). **Subscription Rates:** $457 Individuals print only; $891 Institutions online only; $1018 Institutions print and online. **URL:** http://www.tandfonline.com/toc/usls20/current. **Remarks:** Accepts advertising. **Circ:** (Not Reported).

7406 ■ WEFS-TV - 68
1519 Clearlake Rd.
Cocoa, FL 32922
Phone: (321)433-7110
Format: Educational. **Networks:** Public Broadcasting Service (PBS). **Owner:** Eastern Florida State College, 3865 N Wickham Rd., Melbourne, FL 32935, Ph: (321)632-1111, Free: 888-747-2802. **Founded:** 1988. **Formerly**: WRES-TV; WBCC-TV. **Operating Hours**: 18 hours Daily. **ADI**: Orlando-Daytona Beach-Melbourne, FL. **Wattage**: 60,000. **Ad Rates:** Noncommercial.

7407 ■ WJFP-FM - 91.1
1150 W King St.
Cocoa, FL 32922
Phone: (321)632-1000
Free: 800-957-9537
Email: info@wjfp.com
Format: Information. **ADI**: West Palm Beach-Ft. Pierce-Vero Beach, FL. **Wattage**: 100,000 ERP. **URL:** http://www.wjfp.com/.

7408 ■ WMIE-FM
1150 W King St.
Cocoa, FL 32922-8618
Phone: (321)632-1000
Format: Religious. **Owner:** Last Harvest - The Outreach, 1813 Eldorado Dr., Garland, TX 75042, Ph: (214)703-0505. **Founded:** 1984. **Key Personnel:** Ray Kassis, Gen. Mgr. **Ad Rates:** Accepts Advertising. **URL:** http://www.wmiefm.com.

7409 ■ WWBC-AM - 1510
1150 W King St.
Cocoa, FL 32922-8618
Phone: (321)632-1000
Owner: Astro Enterprises, at above address. **Founded:** 1965. **Key Personnel:** Waylon Duff, Contact. **Wattage**: 50,000 Daytime; 250. **Ad Rates:** $6.50 for 30 seconds; $11.50 for 60 seconds. $6.50 for 30 seconds; $11.50 for 60 seconds. Combined advertising rates available with WMIE-FM. **URL:** http://www.1510wwbc.com/.

COCONUT GROVE

Dade Co. (SE). South suburban section of Miami.

7410 ■ WSBS-TV - 22
2601 S Bayshore Dr.
Coconut Grove, FL 33133
Phone: (305)441-6901
Fax: (305)444-2171
Owner: Spanish Broadcasting System Inc., Pablo Raul Alarcon Media Ctr., 7007 NW 77th Ave., Miami, FL 33166, Ph: (305)441-6901, Fax: (305)883-3375. **URL:** http://www.spanishbroadcasting.com.

CORAL GABLES

S FL. Dade Co. On Atlantic Ocean at mouth of Biscayne Bay. University of Miami. Resort. Manufactures cosmetics, garments, furniture, fertilizer, radio equipment, paper boxes, fiberglass boats.

7411 ■ Alpha-1-To-One Magazine
Alpha-1 Foundation
3300 Ponce de Leon Blvd.
Coral Gables, FL 33134
Phone: (305)567-9888
Fax: (305)567-1317
Free: 877-228-7321
Publisher's E-mail: info@alpha-1foundation.org
Freq: 3/year. **Alt. Formats:** PDF. **URL:** http://www.alpha1.org/Alphas-Friends-Family/Publications/Alpha-1-To-One-Magazine. **Circ:** (Not Reported).

7412 ■ Awards Quarterly
American Orchid Society
10901 Old Cutler Rd.
Coral Gables, FL 33156
Phone: (305)740-2010
Fax: (305)740-2011
Publisher's E-mail: theaos@aos.org
Freq: Quarterly. **ISSN:** 0747- 3109 (print). **Subscription Rates:** $45 Members; $65 Nonmembers; $50 Members other countries; $70 Nonmembers other countries. **Remarks:** Advertising not accepted. **Circ:** (Not Reported).

7413 ■ The Caribbean Travel Planner
Caribbean Hotel and Tourism Association
2655 Le Jeune Rd., Ste. 910
Coral Gables, FL 33134
Phone: (305)443-3040
Fax: (305)675-7977
Publisher's E-mail: events@caribbeanhotelandtourism.com
Freq: Semiannual. **Subscription Rates:** $4.99 plus shipping and handling. **Remarks:** Advertising not accepted. **Circ:** (Not Reported).

7414 ■ James Joyce Literary Supplement
University of Miami Department of English
1252 Memorial Dr., Ashe Bldg., Rm. 321
Coral Gables, FL 33146
Phone: (305)284-2182
Fax: (305)284-5635
Publication E-mail: jjls.english@miami.edu
Scholarly journal covering the works of James Joyce and his contemporaries. **Freq:** Semiannual usually in December and May. **Trim Size:** 11 x 17. **Key Personnel:** Joseph Mendes, Managing Editor. **ISSN:** 0899-3114 (print). **Subscription Rates:** $16 Individuals; $18 Institutions; $18 Individuals outside countries; $20 Institutions, other countries. **URL:** http://www.as.miami.edu/english/publications/james-joyce-literary-supplement. **Ad Rates:** BW $500. **Remarks:** Accepts advertising. **Circ:** Combined 475.

7415 ■ Latin American Politics and Society
University of Miami School of International Studies
1000 Memorial Dr., Rm. 22 Ferre Bldg.
Coral Gables, FL 33124-3010
Phone: (305)284-4303
Fax: (305)284-4406
Publisher's E-mail: questions@rienner.com
Journal on Latin American politics and society. **Freq:** Quarterly. **Print Method:** Offset. **Trim Size:** 6 x 9. **Cols./Page:** 1. **Col. Width:** 50 nonpareils. **Col. Depth:** 100 agate lines. **Key Personnel:** William C. Smith, Editor; Eleanor Lahn, Managing Editor. **ISSN:** 1531--426X (print); **EISSN:** 1548--2456 (electronic). **Subscription Rates:** $819 Institutions print or online; $682 Institutions print or online; $36 Students print & online; $64 Individuals print & online. **URL:** http://onlinelibrary.wiley.com/journal/10.1111/(ISSN)1548-2456. **Mailing address:** P.O. Box 248123, Coral Gables, FL 33124-3010. **Circ:** Paid 1300, Controlled 202.

7416 ■ The Miami Hurricane
University of Miami
1320 S Dixie Hwy.
Coral Gables, FL 33124
Phone: (305)284-2211
Collegiate newspaper. **Freq:** Semiweekly during the academic year. **Print Method:** Offset. **Cols./Page:** 6. **Col. Width:** 24 nonpareils. **Col. Depth:** 315 agate lines. **Key Personnel:** Alexa Lopez, Editor-in-Chief; Isabel Gonzalez, Business Manager. **URL:** http://www.themiamihurricane.com. **Ad Rates:** BW $780; 4C $1130. **Remarks:** Accepts advertising. **Circ:** Free ‡10000.

7417 ■ Orchids - The Magazine of the American Orchid Society
American Orchid Society
10901 Old Cutler Rd.
Coral Gables, FL 33156
Phone: (305)740-2010
Fax: (305)740-2011
Publisher's E-mail: theaos@aos.org
Freq: Monthly. **Subscription Rates:** Included in membership. **URL:** http://www.aos.org/Default.aspx?id=704. **Remarks:** Accepts advertising. **Circ:** (Not Reported).

7418 ■ Res Ipsa Loquitur: The Official Newspaper of the University of Miami School of Law
University of Miami School of Law
1311 Miller Dr.
Coral Gables, FL 33146
Phone: (305)284-2339
Fax: (305)284-3084
Publisher's E-mail: cle@law.miami.edu
Collegiate newspaper for the law school. **Freq:** Biweekly.

Print Method: Offset. **Trim Size:** 11 x 16. **Cols./Page:** 4. **Col. Width:** 25 nonpareils. **Col. Depth:** 224 agate lines. **Key Personnel:** Eduardo Aybar-Landrau, Editor-in-Chief; Phillip Hoffman, Managing Editor. **Subscription Rates:** Free. **Formerly**: The Slip Sheet. **Ad Rates:** BW $130; 4C $500; PCI $15. **Remarks:** Accepts advertising. **Circ:** Free 1500.

7419 ■ WAMR-FM - 107.5
Annex Bldg.
800 Douglas Rd., Ste. 111
Coral Gables, FL 33134
Phone: (305)447-1140
Format: Adult Contemporary; Ethnic; Hispanic. **Owner:** Univision Communications, Inc., at above address. **Founded:** 1971. **Formerly**: WQBA-FM. **Operating Hours**: Continuous. **ADI**: Miami (Ft. Lauderdale), FL. **Key Personnel:** Claudia Puig, Gen. Mgr.; Sam Potter, Operations Mgr.

7420 ■ WAQI-AM - 710
800 Douglas Road Annex Bldg., Ste. 111
800 Douglas Rd.
Coral Gables, FL 33134
Phone: (305)445-4040
Fax: (305)443-3601
Format: Talk; News. **Owner:** Univision Communications, Inc., at above address. **Founded:** 1985. **Operating Hours**: Continuous; 100% local. **ADI**: Miami (Ft. Lauderdale), FL. **Key Personnel:** Armando Perz-Roura, Dir. of Programs. **Wattage**: 50,000. **URL:** http://www.radiomambi710.univision.com.

7421 ■ WCMQ-FM - 92.3
1001 Ponce de Leon Blvd.
Coral Gables, FL 33133
Phone: (305)533-9200
Fax: (305)205-5228
Format: Hispanic. **Owner:** Spanish Broadcasting System Inc., Pablo Raul Alarcon Media Ctr., 7007 NW 77th Ave., Miami, FL 33166, Ph: (305)441-6901, Fax: (305)883-3375. **ADI**: Miami (Ft. Lauderdale), FL. **Key Personnel:** Jackie Nosti, Gen. Mgr., VP. **Ad Rates:** Noncommercial.

7422 ■ WQBA-AM - 1140
800 Douglas Road Annex Bldg., Ste. 111
Coral Gables, FL 33134
Format: Hispanic. **Key Personnel:** Claudia Puig, Gen. Mgr.; Monica Rabassa, Promotions Dir.; Yvette Sanguily, Gen. Sales Mgr. **Ad Rates:** Noncommercial. **URL:** http://www.univisionamerica.univision.com.

7423 ■ WRTO-FM - 98.3
Annex Bldg., Ste. 111
800 Douglas Rd.
Coral Gables, FL 33134
Phone: (305)447-1140
Format: Hispanic. **Key Personnel:** Claudia Puig, Gen. Mgr.; Monica Rabassa, Promotions Dir.; Maritza Cano, Gen. Sales Mgr. **Ad Rates:** Noncommercial. **URL:** http://www.mix983.univision.com.

7424 ■ WVUM-FM - 90.5
PO Box 248191
Coral Gables, FL 33124
Email: underwriting@wvum.org
Format: Alternative/New Music/Progressive; Educational. **Networks:** Independent. **Owner:** University of Miami, 1320 S Dixie Hwy., Coral Gables, FL 33124, Ph: (305)284-2211. **Founded:** 1968. **Operating Hours**: Continuous; 100% local. **Key Personnel:** Amber Robertson, Gen. Mgr.; Kevin Mason, Dir. of Programs; Laura Sutnick, Music Dir.; Isabella Douzoglou, Promotions Dir. **Wattage**: 1,500. **Ad Rates:** Noncommercial. **URL:** http://www.wvum.org.

CORAL SPRINGS

S FL. Broward Co. 38 mi. N. of Miami.

7425 ■ Advanced Cable Communications
12409 NW 35th St.
Coral Springs, FL 33065
Phone: (954)753-0100
Email: info@advancedcable.net
Owner: Schurz Communications Inc., 1301 E Douglas Rd., Mishawaka, IN 46545, Ph: (574)247-7237. **Founded:** 1975. **Formerly**: Cable TV of Coral Springs. **Cities Served:** Coral Springs, Weston, Florida: subscribing households 50,000; 200 channels; 1 community access channel. **URL:** http://www.advancedcable.net.

CRESTVIEW

NW FL. Okaloosa Co. 45 mi. NE of Pensacola. Sawmills. Ships pecans. Diversified agriculture. Cattle, cotton, corn.

7426 ■ WAAZ-FM - 104.7
PO Box 267
Crestview, FL 32536
Phone: (850)682-4623
Fax: (850)685-5232
Email: waazwjsb@earthlink.net
Owner: Crestview Broadcasting Company Inc., at above address. **Founded:** 1965. **Wattage**: 100,000.

7427 ■ WJSB-AM
PO Box 267
Crestview, FL 32536
Phone: (850)682-4623
Fax: (850)682-5232
Email: waazwjsb@earthlink.net
Owner: Crestview Broadcasting Company Inc., at above address. **Founded:** 1954.

7428 ■ WXEI-FM
3497 Melissa Ln.
Crestview, FL 32539
Format: Contemporary Christian; News; Talk. **Owner:** X-Static Enterprises, at above address. **Founded:** 2001. **Key Personnel:** Jon Arthur, Gen. Mgr. **Ad Rates:** Noncommercial.

CROSS CITY

Dixie Co. Dixie Co. (NW). 10 m NE of Shamrock.

7429 ■ Dixie County Advocate
Dixie County Advocate
174 NE 351 Hwy.
Cross City, FL 32628
Phone: (352)498-3312
Community newspaper. **Freq:** Weekly (Thurs.). **Print Method:** Offset. **Cols./Page:** 7. **Col. Width:** 11 picas. **Col. Depth:** 21 1/2 inches. **Key Personnel:** Katherine McKinney, Editor. **USPS:** 158-760. **Mailing address:** PO Box 5030, Cross City, FL 32628. **Ad Rates:** GLR $2; BW $906; 4C $1,06; SAU $6; CNU $5; PCI $6; PCI $5. **Remarks:** Accepts advertising. **Circ:** ‡3500.

CRYSTAL RIVER

W FL. Citrus Co. 35 mi. SW of Ocala.

7430 ■ Citrus County Chronicle
Landmark Community Newspapers L.L.C.
1624 N Meadowcrest Blvd.
Crystal River, FL 34429
Phone: (352)563-6363
Fax: (352)563-5665
Free: 888-852-2340
Publisher's E-mail: marketing@lcni.com
General newspaper. **Freq:** Daily. **Print Method:** Offset. Uses mats. **Cols./Page:** 6. **Col. Width:** 12.3 picas. **Col. Depth:** 21 1/2 inches. **Key Personnel:** Gerard Mulligan, Publisher; Charlie Brennan, Editor, phone: (352)563-3225; Trina Murphy, Director, Advertising. **Subscription Rates:** $11.44 Individuals 7-day delivery - premium subscription; $6.75 Individuals Fri, Sat & Sun delivery without viewfinder; $3.98 Individuals Sunday only delivery without viewfinder. **URL:** http://www.chronicleonline.com. **Ad Rates:** BW $1,548; 4C $1,798; SAU $12. **Remarks:** Accepts advertising. **Circ:** Controlled ‡25906, Sun. ★**32170**, Sat. ★**27508**.

7431 ■ WHGN-FM - 91.9
PO Box 8889
Saint Petersburg, FL 33738
Phone: (727)391-9994
Fax: (727)397-6425
Free: 800-551-9537
Format: Contemporary Christian; Talk. **Owner:** Moody Radio, 820 N La Salle Blvd., Chicago, IL 60610, Ph: (312)329-4000, Free: 800-356-6639.

7432 ■ WRGO-FM - 102.7
1929 NW Hwy. 19
Crystal River, FL 34428
Phone: (352)795-1027
Fax: (352)795-0002
Format: Oldies. **Owner:** Pamal Broadcasting, Ltd., 715 Rte. 52, Beacon, NY 12508, Ph: (845)838-6000. **Key Personnel:** Ben Hill, Gen. Mgr. **Ad Rates:** Noncommercial.

7433 ■ WYFE-FM - 100.9
11530 Carmel Commons Blvd.
Charlotte, NC 28226
Phone: (704)523-5555
Free: 800-888-7077
Email: bbn@bbnmedia.org
Format: Gospel; Religious. **Networks:** Bible Broadcasting. **Owner:** Bible Broadcasting Network Inc., 11530 Carmel Commons Blvd., Charlotte, NC 28226, Ph: (704)523-5555, Free: 800-888-7077. **Founded:** 1988. **Formerly**: WFCE-FM. **Operating Hours**: Continuous; 93% network, 7% local. **Wattage**: 60,000. **Ad Rates:** Noncommercial. **Mailing address:** PO Box 7300, Charlotte, NC 28241. **URL:** http://www.bbnradio.org.

DADE CITY

WC FL. Pasco Co. 30 mi. NW of Lakeland. Manufactures concrete water pipes, lumber. Citrus fruit, truck, and poultry farms.

7434 ■ Pasco Shopper
Sunpress Publications Inc.
13032 U.S Hwy. 301
Dade City, FL 33525
Phone: (352)567-5639
Fax: (352)567-5640
Publication E-mail: info@pasconews.com
Shopper. **Freq:** Weekly (Wed.). **Print Method:** Offset. **Trim Size:** 10 x 16 1/2. **Cols./Page:** 6. **Col. Width:** 10 picas. **Col. Depth:** 16 inches. **Subscription Rates:** Free. **Alt. Formats:** Electronic publishing. **URL:** http://pascoshoppingguide.com. **Ad Rates:** GLR $.49; BW $603.90; 4C $703.90; PCI $8.34. **Remarks:** Accepts advertising. **Circ:** Wed. ‡31300.

7435 ■ WDCF-AM - 1350
37905 WDCF Dr.
Dade City, FL 33525
Phone: (727)441-3311
Format: Talk; Music of Your Life; Sports. **Networks:** NBC; Florida Radio. **Owner:** Wagenvoord Advertising Group, Inc., at above address. **Founded:** 1954. **Operating Hours**: Continuous; 25% network, 75% local. **Wattage**: 1,000 day; 500 night. **Ad Rates:** Advertising accepted; rates available upon request. $5.95-10.95 for 60 seconds. **URL:** http://wdcf.tantalk1340.com/.

DAVIE

Broward Co. Broward Co. (SE). 5 m W of Hollywood.

7436 ■ Journal of International Agricultural and Extension Education
Association for International Agricultural and Extension Education
c/o Anita Zavodska, Treasurer
School of Professional and Career Education
Barry University
4900 S University Dr., Ste. 203-205
Davie, FL 33328
Professional journal covering agricultural education worldwide. **Freq:** 3/year spring, summer and fall. **Key Personnel:** Brenda Seevers, Dr., Executive Editor; Brenda Seevers, Executive Director; Amy Harder, Managing Editor; Benjamin Swan, Associate Editor. **ISSN:** 1077--0755 (print). **Subscription Rates:** $70 Individuals; $150 Libraries; $150 Individuals agencies. **Alt. Formats:** PDF. **URL:** http://www.aiaee.org/index.php/journal. **Remarks:** Advertising not accepted. **Circ:** (Not Reported).

7437 ■ The Observer
Broward Community College
3501 SW Davie Rd.
Davie, FL 33314
Publication E-mail: observer@mail.broward.edu
Collegiate newspaper (tabloid). **Founded:** 1986. **Freq:** Biweekly. **Print Method:** Offset. **Trim Size:** 10 1/4 x 16. **Cols./Page:** 5. **Col. Width:** 11.5 picas. **Col. Depth:** 224 agate lines. **Key Personnel:** Jennifer Shapiro, Contact. **Subscription Rates:** Free. **URL:** http://www.broward.edu/observer_BCC/. **Formed by the merger of**: The Polaris; The Phoenix; New Horizons. **Ad Rates:** BW

Circulation: ★ = AAM; △ or • = BPA; ♦ = CAC; ❏ = VAC; ⊕ = PO Statement; ‡ = Publisher's Report; Boldface figures = sworn; Light figures = estimated.

$400; 4C $700; PCI $10. **Remarks:** Accepts advertising. **Circ:** Free 10000.

7438 ■ WAVS-AM - 1170
6360 SW 41st Pl.
Davie, FL 33314
Phone: (954)792-1170
Fax: (954)581-6441
Free: 888-854-9660
Email: info@wavs1170.com
Format: Ethnic. **Founded:** 1987. **Operating Hours:** Continuous. **ADI:** Miami (Ft. Lauderdale), FL. **Key Personnel:** Dean Hooper, Station Mgr.; Winston Barnes, News Dir., newsguywb@hotmail.com. **Wattage:** 5,000. **Ad Rates:** Advertising accepted; rates available upon request. **URL:** http://www.wavs1170.com.

DAYTONA BEACH

E FL. Volusia Co. On Halifax River, 91 mi. S. of Jacksonville. Bethune Cookman College; Embry-Riddle Aeronautical University; Daytona Beach Community College. Summer and winter resort. Sport and commercial fishing. Stock car racing. Agriculture. Citrus fruit, truck crops.

7439 ■ Advances and Applications in Fluid Mechanics
Pushpa Publishing House
c/o Prof. Shahrdad G. Sajjadi, Ed.-in.-Ch.
Department of Mathematics
Embry-Riddle Aeronautical University
600 S Clyde Morris Blvd.
Daytona Beach, FL 32114
Publisher's E-mail: arun@pphmj.com
Journal covering fields of fluid mechanics. **Freq:** Quarterly. **Key Personnel:** Prof. Shahrdad G. Sajjadi, Editor-in-Chief. **ISSN:** 0973--4686 (print). **Subscription Rates:** €345 Institutions print + online; $465 Institutions print + online; €295 Institutions print + online; $345 Institutions print + online; Rs 6000 Institutions print + online. **URL:** http://www.pphmj.com/journals/aafm.htm. **Circ:** (Not Reported).

7440 ■ Flagler/Palm Coast News-Tribune
News-Journal Corp.
901 Sixth St.
Daytona Beach, FL 32117
Phone: (386)252-1511
Publisher's E-mail: ron.wallace@news-jrnl.com
Newspaper with a Democratic orientation. **Freq:** Semiweekly. **Print Method:** Offset. **Trim Size:** 13 3/4 x 22. **Cols./Page:** 6. **Col. Width:** 23 nonpareils. **Col. Depth:** 294 agate lines. **Key Personnel:** Mac Thrower, Editor, phone: (386)681-2248; Pat Winston, Office Manager, phone: (386)681-2465; Derek Catron, Assistant Managing Editor, Team Leader, phone: (386)681-2289; Cory Lancaster, Managing Editor, phone: (386)681-2440; Michael Redding, Chief Executive Officer, Publisher; Mike Baskin, Director, Advertising. **URL:** http://www.news-journalonline.com. **Remarks:** Accepts advertising. **Circ:** 10500.

7441 ■ The News-Journal: The Independent Voice of Volusia and Flagler Counties
News-Journal Corp.
901 Sixth St.
Daytona Beach, FL 32117
Phone: (386)252-1511
Publisher's E-mail: ron.wallace@news-jrnl.com
Newspaper with a Democratic orientation. **Freq:** Mon.-Sun. (morn.). **Print Method:** Offset. **Trim Size:** 13 3/4 x 22. **Cols./Page:** 6. **Col. Width:** 26 nonpareils. **Col. Depth:** 294 agate lines. **Key Personnel:** Pat Winston, Office Manager; Michael Redding, Chief Executive Officer, Publisher; Mike Baskin, Director, Advertising; Cory Lancaster, Managing Editor, phone: (386)681-2440; Kathy Kelly, Assistant Managing Editor, phone: (386)681-2281; Nick Klasne, Assistant Managing Editor, phone: (386)681-2422; Cal Massey, Managing Editor, phone: (386)681-2468; Chris Seymour, Managing Editor, phone: (386)681-2242. **USPS:** 149-820. **Subscription Rates:** $15.17 Individuals weekend - print; $13 Individuals Sunday only - print; $10.95 Individuals digital only. **URL:** http://www.news-journalonline.com. **Ad Rates:** BW $7,660.80; 4C $9,285.80; SAU $60.80; BW $8,637.30; 4C $10,262.30. **Remarks:** Accepts advertising. **Circ:** Mon.-Fri. ★**98393**, Sun. ★**116922**, Sat. ★**104313**.

7442 ■ Public Safety Communications
APCO International Inc.
351 N Williamson Blvd.
Daytona Beach, FL 32114-1112
Phone: (386)322-2500
Fax: (386)322-2501
Free: 888-272-6911
Public safety communications magazine. **Freq:** Monthly. **Print Method:** Web offset. **Trim Size:** 7 3/4 x 10 3/4. **Cols./Page:** 3. **Col. Width:** 28 nonpareils. **Col. Depth:** 140 agate lines. **Key Personnel:** George S. Rice, Jr., Executive Director; Courtney McCarron, Contact. **ISSN:** 1526--1646 (print). **Subscription Rates:** Included in membership. **URL:** http://www.apcointl.org. **Formerly:** APCO BULLETIN. **Ad Rates:** BW $3,105; 4C $4,375. **Remarks:** Accepts advertising. **Circ:** 12678.

7443 ■ WCEU-TV - 15
1200 W International Speedway Blvd.
Daytona Beach, FL 32114
Phone: (386)506-4415
Networks: Public Broadcasting Service (PBS). **Owner:** Daytona Beach College. **Founded:** 1987. **Operating Hours:** 6 a.m. - 1:00 a.m. **ADI:** Orlando-Daytona Beach-Melbourne, FL. **Wattage:** 708,000. **Ad Rates:** Noncommercial.

7444 ■ WDSC-TV - 15
1200 W International Speedway Blvd.
Daytona Beach, FL 32114
Phone: (386)506-3000
Free: 800-638-9238
Owner: Daytona State College, 1200 W International Speedway Blvd., Daytona Beach, FL 32114, Ph: (386)506-3000. **URL:** http://www.wdsctv.org.

7445 ■ WERU-FM - 104.7
600 S Clyde Morris Blvd.
600 S Clyde Morris Blvd.
Student Center, 2nd Fl.
Daytona Beach, FL 32114
Phone: (904)226-7056
Fax: (904)226-6083
Email: weru_radio@cts.db.erau.edu
Format: Educational. **Owner:** Embry-Riddle Aeronautical University, at above address. **Key Personnel:** Jesse Lesperance, Chairman, Chief Engineer, Gen. Mgr.; Will Robertson, Gen. Mgr.; David Moroni, Dir. of Info. Svcs., News Dir., Bus. Mgr.; Tim McGrath, Promotions Dir.; Andrew Peng, Chief Engineer; David Yarwood, Dir. of Programs; Ron West, Training Mgr.; Greg Huston, Chairman; Travis Sauder, Bus. Mgr.; Peter Richardson, Music Dir. **Ad Rates:** $50-150 for 30 seconds. **URL:** http://www.wikd1025.com.

7446 ■ WKRO-FM - 93.1
126 W International Speedway Blvd.
Daytona Beach, FL 32114
Phone: (386)255-9300
Format: Country. **Founded:** Sept. 07, 2006. **Key Personnel:** Donna Fillion, Sales Mgr., donna@whog.fm. **Ad Rates:** Noncommercial. **URL:** http://www.931coast.com.

7447 ■ WROD-AM - 1340
100 Marina Point Dr.
Daytona Beach, FL 32114
Phone: (386)253-0000
Fax: (386)255-3178
Format: Music of Your Life. **Networks:** ABC. **Owner:** Gore-Overgaard Broadcasting Inc., at above address. **Founded:** 1947. **Operating Hours:** Continuous; 40% network, 60% local. **ADI:** Orlando-Daytona Beach-Melbourne, FL. **Wattage:** 1,000. **Ad Rates:** $25-35 for 30 seconds; $30-40 for 60 seconds. **URL:** http://www.wrodradio.com.

7448 ■ WZDQ-FM - 102.3
126 W International Speedway Blvd.
Daytona Beach, FL 32114
Phone: (731)427-9616
Fax: (731)424-2473
Format: Adult Contemporary. **Owner:** Thomas Media Broadcast Center, at above address. **Operating Hours:** Continuous. **ADI:** Jackson, TN. **Key Personnel:** Shane Connor, Dir. of Programs, sconnor@wwyn.fm; Jeff Jones, Advertising Mgr., jjones@96kix.fm. **Wattage:** 6,000. **Ad Rates:** Advertising accepted; rates available upon request.

DEERFIELD BEACH

SE FL. Broward Co. 5 mi. N. of Pompano Beach.

7449 ■ Counselor: The Magazine for Addiction Professionals
Health Communications Inc.
3201 SW 15th St.
Deerfield Beach, FL 33442
Phone: (954)360-0909
Fax: (954)360-0034
Free: 800-441-5569
Publisher's E-mail: cs@hcibooks.com
Professional journal for counselors, program directors, clinical supervisors, and treatment specialists working in alcohol and drug counseling programs. **Freq:** Bimonthly. **Print Method:** Sheetfed Full Run. **Trim Size:** 8 3/8 x 10 7/8. **Key Personnel:** Gary Seidler, Executive Editor; Robert Ackerman, Editor; Tonya Woodworth, Associate Editor; Ann Gossy, Executive Editor. **ISSN:** 1047--7314 (print). **Subscription Rates:** $9.95 Individuals /year, online only; $25.95 U.S. /year, print and online; $14.95 Individuals /year, tablet and mobile. **URL:** http://www.counselormagazine.com. **Formerly:** Professional Counselor; The NAADAC Counselor. **Ad Rates:** BW $2,514; 4C $3,905. **Remarks:** Accepts advertising. **Circ:** 21000.

7450 ■ Journal of the International Society of Sports Nutrition
International Society of Sports Nutrition
c/o Jose Antonio, Founder
4511 NW 7th St.
Deerfield Beach, FL 33442
Fax: (561)239-1754
Publisher's E-mail: issn.sports.nutrition@gmail.com
Peer-reviewed journal that covers supplementation, exercise metabolism, and scientific policies related to sports nutrition. **Freq:** Semiannual. **Key Personnel:** Richard B. Kreider, PhD, Editor-in-Chief; Dr. Bill Campbell, Associate Editor; Dr. Douglas S. Kalman, Editor-in-Chief; Mike Greenwood, PhD, Associate Editor; Craig E. Broeder, PhD, Board Member; Conrad Earnest, PhD, Board Member; Roger Harris, PhD, Board Member; Mr. Anthony L. Almada, Board Member. **ISSN:** 1550--2783 (print). **Subscription Rates:** Free. **URL:** http://www.jissn.com. **Remarks:** Advertising not accepted. **Circ:** (Not Reported).

7451 ■ South Florida Parenting
South Florida Parenting Inc.
1701 Green Rd., Ste. B
Deerfield Beach, FL 33064
Phone: (954)747-3050
Free: 800-244-8447
Parenting magazine. **Freq:** Monthly. **Trim Size:** 8 1/4 x 10 1/4. **Cols./Page:** 3. **Key Personnel:** Lisa Goodlin, Publisher; Angela Bartalone, Contact. **Subscription Rates:** Free. **URL:** http://www.sun-sentinel.com/features/south-florida-parenting. **Ad Rates:** BW $2,055; 4C $3,360. **Remarks:** Accepts advertising. **Circ:** Free ■ **90000**.

DEFUNIAK SPRINGS

Walton Co. (NW). 30 m SW of Bonifay.

7452 ■ The Herald Breeze
The Herald Breeze
PO Box 1546
DeFuniak Springs, FL 32435-7546
Phone: (850)892-3232
Fax: (850)892-2270
Publisher's E-mail: candaces91@gmail.com
Community newspaper. **Freq:** Weekly. **Print Method:** Offset. **Trim Size:** 14 x 23. **Cols./Page:** 6. **Col. Width:** 12 picas. **Col. Depth:** 21 inches. **Key Personnel:** Bruce Collier, Editor; Gary Woodham, Advertising Representative, Publisher. **Subscription Rates:** $39 Individuals; $45 Out of state. **URL:** http://defuniakherald.com. **Ad Rates:** BW $504; PCI $4. **Remarks:** Accepts advertising. **Circ:** Paid 877, Free 3500.

DEFUNIAK SPRINGS

7453 ■ Bright House Networks
94 Walton Rd.
Defuniak Springs, FL 32433
Key Personnel: Robert Miron, Chairman, CEO; Steve Miron, President. **Cities Served:** 59 channels. **URL:** http://brighthouse.com.

7454 ■ WAKJ-FM - 91.3
295 Hwy. 90 W
Defuniak Springs, FL 32435
Phone: (850)892-2107
Email: wakjradio@gmail.com
Format: Contemporary Christian; Religious. **Key Personnel:** Jesse Knapp, Station Mgr. **Mailing address:** PO Box 128, Defuniak Springs, FL 32435. **URL:** http://wakjradio.com.

7455 ■ WWEO-FM
86 N Davis Ln.
Defuniak Springs, FL 32433
Phone: (850)892-6226
Email: weochurch@earthlink.net
Format: Religious; Contemporary Christian. **Owner:** World Evangelism Outreach Church, PO Box 72, Winona, MS 38967. **Founded:** 1983. **Wattage:** 026 ERP. **Ad Rates:** Underwriting available. **URL:** http://www.weo1039.org.

7456 ■ WZEP-AM - 1460
449 N 12th St.
Defuniak Springs, FL 32433
Phone: (850)892-3158
Fax: (850)892-9675
Email: wzep@wzep1460.com
Format: Sports; News; Country; Talk; Information. **Owner:** Walton County Broadcasting Inc., at above address. **Founded:** 1955. **Key Personnel:** Kevin Chilcutt, News Dir.; Art Dees, Gen. Mgr., artnmarty@wzep1460.com. **Local Programs:** *Hi Neighbor*, Monday Tuesday Wednesday Thursday Friday 6:00 a.m. - 9:00 a.m. **Wattage:** 10,000 Day; 186 Nigh. **Ad Rates:** Advertising accepted; rates available upon request. **URL:** http://www.wzep1460.com.

DELAND

E FL. Volusia Co. 23 mi. SW of Daytona Beach. Stetson University. Winter resort. Manufactures cabinets, hypodermic needles, boats. Bottling works; lumber mill; fruit packing. Poultry, truck, dairy, and citrus fruit farms.

7457 ■ Financial Services Review: The Journal of Individual Financial Management
Cadmus Journal Services
c/o Stuart Michelson, Editor
421 N. Woodland Blvd., Unit 8398
Deland, FL 32723-8421
Journal that covers personal finance. **Freq:** Quarterly. **Key Personnel:** Vickie Bajtelsmit, Board Member; Stephen Horan, Board Member; Andrew L. Somers, Board Member; Walter Woerheide, Board Member; John Nofsinger, Board Member; Robert Brooks, Board Member; Dale Domian, Board Member; Stuart Michelson, Editor. **ISSN:** 1057--0810 (print). **Subscription Rates:** Included in membership. **URL:** http://academyfinancial.org/financial-services-review. **Ad Rates:** BW $200. **Remarks:** Advertising accepted; rates available upon request. **Circ:** Paid 500.

DELAND

7458 ■ West Volusia Pennysaver
Volusia Pennysaver Inc.
245 S Woodland Blvd.
DeLand, FL 32720
Phone: (386)736-2880
Fax: (386)736-3587
Publication E-mail: wvpsco@psavers.com
Shopper. **Freq:** Semiweekly (Wed. and Sat.). **Print Method:** Offset. **Cols./Page:** 7. **Col. Width:** 8 picas. **Col. Depth:** 11.5 inches. **Key Personnel:** Clarrisa Williams, Manager; John Shaw, Manager, Circulation. **Subscription Rates:** Free. **URL:** http://www.floridapennysavers.com//GetPennysaver.aspx?edition=WV; http://www.floridapennysavers.com//SiteDefault.aspx?edition=WV. **Formerly:** De Land Pennysaver. **Ad Rates:** GLR $.82; BW $897; 4C $300; PCI $14.75. **Remarks:** Accepts advertising. **Circ:** Wed. 52053, Sat. 51785.

DELAND

E FL. Volusia Co. 23 mi. SW of Daytona Beach. Stetson University. Winter resort. Manufactures cabinets, hypodermic needles, boats. Bottling works; lumber mill; fruit packing. Poultry, truck, dairy, and citrus fruit farms.

7459 ■ WMOB-AM - 1360
316 E Taylor Rd.
Deland, FL 32724
Phone: (716)748-0815
Format: Religious. **Owner:** Theodore "Buddy" Tucker, at above address. **Founded:** 1961. **Operating Hours:** 5 a.m.-1 a.m. **ADI:** Mobile, AL-Pensacola, FL. **Key Personnel:** Buddy Tucker, Contact. **Wattage:** 9,000 KW. **Mailing address:** PO Box 63, Mobile, AL 36601. **URL:** http://www.buddytuckerassociation.org.

DELAND

7460 ■ WYND-AM - 1310
316 E Taylor Rd.
DeLand, FL 32724
Phone: (386)734-1310
Format: Religious; News; Talk. **Founded:** 1956. **Wattage:** 5,000 Day; 095 Night. **Ad Rates:** Noncommercial.

DELRAY BEACH

SE FL. Palm Beach Co. On Atlantic Ocean, 17 mi. S. of West Palm Beach. Tourist resort. Nurseries. Agriculture.

7461 ■ Made in U.S.A.
Made in U.S.A. Industries
777 E Atlantic Ave.
Delray Beach, FL 33483
Phone: (561)279-2855
Publisher's E-mail: info@usa-c.com
Magazine covering products manufactured in the United States. **Freq:** Bimonthly. **Key Personnel:** Adam Reiser, Contact. **URL:** http://www.certified.bz/index.php/certification/2016-06-02-15-54-39. **Remarks:** Accepts advertising. **Circ:** (Not Reported).

DESTIN

NW FL. Okaloosa Co. 6 mi. S. of Fort Walton Beach. Tourist resort.

7462 ■ The Destin Log
Halifax Media Holdings L.L.C.
PO Box 339
Destin, FL 32540
Phone: (850)837-2828
Publisher's E-mail: support@halifaxmediagroup.com
Newspaper. **Freq:** Semiweekly. **Print Method:** Offset. **Cols./Page:** 6. **Col. Width:** 25 nonpareils. **Col. Depth:** 301 agate lines. **Key Personnel:** William Hatfield, Editor, phone: (850)654-8448; Billy Kirk, Director, Advertising; Belinda Martinez, Office Manager, phone: (850)654-8424. **Subscription Rates:** $38.68 Individuals in County; $48.90 Out of area by mail. **URL:** http://thedestinlog.com. **Ad Rates:** 4C $450. **Remarks:** Accepts advertising. **Circ:** (Not Reported).

7463 ■ WMXZ-FM - 103.1
743 Harbor Blvd., Ste. 6
Destin, FL 32541
Phone: (850)654-1000
Format: Top 40.

DORAL

7464 ■ El Nuevo Herald
Miami Herald Media Co.
One Herald Plz.
Doral, FL 33172
Free: 800-843-4372
Publication E-mail: perspectiva@elherald.com
Spanish-language newspaper. **Freq:** Mon.-Sun. (morn.). **Print Method:** Offset. **Trim Size:** 13 x 22 1/2. **Cols./Page:** 6. **Col. Width:** 2 1/16 inches. **Col. Depth:** 22 1/2 inches. **Subscription Rates:** $4.99 Individuals /month (Saturday and Sunday); $8 Individuals 7 days. **URL:** http://www.elnuevoherald.com/. **Formerly:** El Miami Herald. **Ad Rates:** GLR $42; BW $5,231.25; 4C $6,181.25; SAU $36.25. **Remarks:** Accepts advertising. **Circ:** Mon.-Fri. ★**85534**, Sat. ★**94457**.

7465 ■ Herald Values
Miami Herald Media Co.
One Herald Plz.
Doral, FL 33172
Free: 800-843-4372
Shopping guide. **Freq:** Weekly (Thurs.). **Circ:** Free ■ **864897**.

7466 ■ The Miami Herald
Miami Herald Media Co.
One Herald Plz.
Doral, FL 33172
Free: 800-843-4372
General newspaper. **Freq:** Daily. **Print Method:** Letterpress, Offset, and Flexography. **Cols./Page:** 6. **Col. Width:** 22.5 nonpareils. **Col. Depth:** 315 agate lines. **ISSN:** 0898--865X (print). **Subscription Rates:** $3.99 Individuals /month (Sunday only); $10.99 Individuals /month (Thursday to Sunday). **Online:** ProQuest L.L.C.; McClatchy Newspapers Inc. McClatchy Newspapers Inc. **URL:** http://www.miamiherald.com. **Formerly:** The Miami Evening Record. **Remarks:** Accepts advertising. **Circ:** (Not Reported).

DUNNELLON

Marion Co. Marion Co. (NC). 10 m SW of Ocala.

7467 ■ Riverland News
Landmark Community Newspapers L.L.C.
20441 E Pennsylvania Ave.
Dunnellon, FL 34432
Phone: (352)489-2731
Publisher's E-mail: marketing@lcni.com
Community newspaper. **Freq:** Weekly (Thurs.). **URL:** http://www.riverlandnews.com. **Remarks:** Accepts advertising. **Circ:** (Not Reported).

7468 ■ South Marion Citizen
Landmark Community Newspapers L.L.C.
20441 E. Pennsylvania Avenue
Dunnellon, FL 34432
Phone: (352)854-3986
Publisher's E-mail: marketing@lcni.com
Community newspaper. **Freq:** Weekly (Fri.). **URL:** http://www.smcitizen.com. **Remarks:** Accepts advertising. **Circ:** ‡15000.

7469 ■ WRLE-FM
3092 Harbor Hills Rd.
Dunnellon, FL 34431
Phone: (352)489-7614
Email: wrle949@netzero.com
Format: Easy Listening. **Wattage:** 072 ERP. **Ad Rates:** Noncommercial.

EAST PALATKA

7470 ■ Grape Times
Florida Grape Growers Association
111 Yelvington Rd., Ste. 1
East Palatka, FL 32131
Phone: (386)329-0318
Fax: (386)329-1262
Publisher's E-mail: admin@fgga.org
Magazine for wine enthusiasts and those working in wineyards and wineries. **Freq:** Bimonthly. **Key Personnel:** Bob Paulish, President, phone: (813)633-8692. **URL:** http://fgga.org. **Circ:** 200.

EASTPOINT

7471 ■ WOYS-FM - 100.5
108 Island Dr.
Eastpoint, FL 32328
Phone: (850)670-8450
Fax: (850)670-5686
Format: Adult Contemporary. **Owner:** Oyster Radio Inc., at above address. **Key Personnel:** Michael Allen, Dir. of Programs, manager@oysterradio.com; Kate Gomes, Office Mgr., kgomes@oysterradio.com. **Ad Rates:** Advertising accepted; rates available upon request. **URL:** http://www.oysterradio.com.

EDGEWATER

7472 ■ WKTO-FM - 88.9
900 Old Mission Rd.
New Smyrna Beach, FL 32168
Phone: (386)427-1095
Email: info@wkto.net
Format: Religious. **Founded:** 1998. **Key Personnel:** Carol Henry, Gen. Mgr., carol@wkto.net. **Wattage:** 29,000. **URL:** http://www.wkto.net.

ENGLEWOOD

SW FL. Sarasota & Charlotte Co. On Gulf of Mexico and Lemon Bay, 30 mi. S. of Sarasota. Tourist resort.

Circulation: ★ = AAM; △ or • = BPA; ♦ = CAC; ❑ = VAC; ⊕ = PO Statement; ‡ = Publisher's Report; Boldface figures = sworn; Light figures = estimated.

Boat yard. Boating and fishing. Citrus fruit farms.

7473 ■ Englewood Sun Herald
Englewood Sun Herald
120 W Dearborn St.
Englewood, FL 34223
Newspaper. **Freq:** 3/week. **Print Method:** Offset. **Cols./Page:** 6. **Col. Width:** 26 nonpareils. **Col. Depth:** 301 agate lines. **Key Personnel:** David Dunn-Rankin, President, Publisher; Glen Dickerson, Director, Advertising; John Hackworth, Managing Editor. **Subscription Rates:** $400.40 Individuals 52 weeks; $200.20 Individuals 26 weeks; $100.10 Individuals 13 weeks. **URL:** http://yoursun.com/csp/mediapool/sites/SunNews/Englewood/index.csp. **Ad Rates:** BW $1,064.70; 4C $1,294.70; SAU $8.45. **Remarks:** Accepts advertising. **Circ:** ‡4500.

7474 ■ The Florida Humanist
Florida Humanist Association
PO Box 808
Englewood, FL 34295-0808
Publisher's E-mail: info@floridahumanist.org
Journal containing news and thoughts of the Humanists of Florida Association. **Freq:** Quarterly. **Subscription Rates:** Free. **URL:** http://floridahumanist.org. **Remarks:** Accepts advertising. **Circ:** (Not Reported).

7475 ■ WENG-AM - 1530
1355 S River Rd.
Englewood, FL 34223
Phone: (941)474-3231
Fax: (941)475-2205
Free: 888-434-1530
Email: info@wengradio.com
Format: News; Talk. **Networks:** Florida Radio. **Owner:** Viper Communications, 11A Commerce Way, Totowa, NJ 07512, Free: 800-494-1240. **Founded:** 1964. **Operating Hours**: Sunrise - Sunset. **Key Personnel:** Kenneth Birdsong, Gen. Mgr., kenb@wengradio.com. **Wattage**: 1,000 Day; 001 Night. **Ad Rates:** Advertising accepted; rates available upon request. **URL:** http://www.wengradio.com.

7476 ■ WSEB-FM - 91.3
135 W Dearborn St.
Englewood, FL 34223
Phone: (941)475-9732
Email: comments@wsebfm.com
Format: Religious. **Networks:** Voice of Christian Youth America. **Owner:** Suncoast Educational Broadcasting Corp., at above address. **Founded:** 1989. **Operating Hours**: Continuous; 40% network, 60% local. **Wattage**: 62,000. **Ad Rates:** Noncommercial. **URL:** http://www.wsebfm.com.

ESTERO

Lee Co. (SW). 10 m SW of Ft. Myers.

7477 ■ WJBX-FM - 99.3
20125 S Tamiami Trl.
Estero, FL 33928
Phone: (239)495-2100
Format: Alternative/New Music/Progressive. **Networks:** AP. **Owner:** Beasley Broadcast Group Inc., 3033 Riviera Dr., Ste. 200, Naples, FL 34103-2750, Ph: (239)263-5000, Fax: (239)263-8191. **Founded:** 1983. **Operating Hours**: Continuous. **Key Personnel:** Robert Hallman, Dir. of Sales, robert.hall@bbgi.com. **Wattage:** 50,000. **Ad Rates:** Advertising accepted; rates available upon request. **URL:** http://www.96krock.com.

7478 ■ WJPT-FM - 106.3
20125 S Tamiami Trl.
Estero, FL 33928
Phone: (239)390-3535
Format: Oldies. **Key Personnel:** Brad Beasley, Dir. of Mktg., Mktg. Mgr., brad@bbswfl.com. **Ad Rates:** Advertising accepted; rates available upon request. **URL:** http://sunny1063.com/streamer.

7479 ■ WRXK-FM - 96.1
20125 S Tamiami Trl.
Estero, FL 33928
Phone: (239)495-2100
Format: Classic Rock. **Networks:** ABC. **Owner:** Beasley Broadcast Group Inc., 3033 Riviera Dr., Ste. 200, Naples, FL 34103-2750, Ph: (239)263-5000, Fax: (239)263-8191. **Founded:** 1976. **Formerly:** WLEQ-FM. **Operating Hours:** Continuous; 3% network, 97% local. **Key Personnel:** Brad Beasley, Gen. Mgr., brad@bbgi.com; Robert Hallman, Dir. of Sales, robert.hallman@bbgi.com. **Local Programs:** *Stan & Haney*, Monday Tuesday Wednesday Thursday Friday 2:00 p.m. - 6:00 p.m. **Wattage:** 100,000. **Ad Rates:** Noncommercial. **URL:** http://www.96krock.com.

7480 ■ WWCN-AM - 770
20125 S Tamiami Trl.
Estero, FL 33928
Phone: (239)495-2100
Format: Sports. **Owner:** Beasley Broadcast Group Inc., 3033 Riviera Dr., Ste. 200, Naples, FL 34103-2750, Ph: (239)263-5000, Fax: (239)263-8191. **Operating Hours:** Continuous. **Key Personnel:** Robert Hallman, Gen. Mgr., robert.hallman@bbgi.com; Brad Beasley, Dir. of Mktg., Mktg. Mgr., brad@bbswfl.com; John Cassio, Dir. of Programs, johnjcassio@aol.com. **Ad Rates:** Advertising accepted; rates available upon request. **URL:** http://993espn.com.

7481 ■ WXKB-FM - 103.9
20125 S Tamiami Trl.
Estero, FL 33928
Phone: (239)495-2100
Email: brad@bbgi.com
Format: Top 40; Hip Hop; Urban Contemporary. **Owner:** Beasley Broadcast Group Inc., 3033 Riviera Dr., Ste. 200, Naples, FL 34103-2750, Ph: (239)263-5000, Fax: (239)263-8191. **Operating Hours:** Continuous. **Ad Rates:** Advertising accepted; rates available upon request. **URL:** http://www.b1039.com.

EUSTIS

Lake Co. Lake Co. (NC). 5 m NW of Mt. Dora.

7482 ■ The New Calliope
Clowns of America International
PO Box 122
Eustis, FL 32727-0122
Phone: (352)357-1676
Free: 877-816-6941
Publisher's E-mail: coaioffice@aol.com
Freq: 6/year. **Subscription Rates:** Included in membership. **URL:** http://www.coai.org/?page=Calliope. **Remarks:** Accepts advertising. **Circ:** 6000.

FERNANDINA BEACH

NE FL. Nassau Co. On Amelia Island, 25 mi. NE of Jacksonville. Manufactures wood pulp, fish oil, meal fertilizer. Shrimp packing. Shrimp, oyster, fisheries; pine timber.

7483 ■ News-Leader: Florida's Oldest Weekly Newspaper
News-Leader
511 Ash St.
Fernandina Beach, FL 32034
Phone: (904)261-3696
Fax: (904)261-3698
Publisher's E-mail: editor2@fbnewsleader.com
Newspaper. **Freq:** Weekly. **Print Method:** Offset. **Cols./Page:** 6. **Col. Width:** 2 1/16 inches. **Col. Depth:** 21 1/2 inches. **Key Personnel:** Mike Hankins, Director, Advertising; Michael Parnell, Editor; Foy Maloy, Publisher. **Subscription Rates:** $40 Individuals print and online; $71.99 Out of country print and online; $49.99 Individuals online only. **URL:** http://www.fbnewsleader.com. **Mailing address:** PO Box 16766, Fernandina Beach, FL 32035. **Remarks:** Accepts advertising. **Circ:** Wed. 10068.

FORT LAUDERDALE

S FL. Broward Co. On Atlantic Ocean, 25 mi. N. of Miami. Broward Community College; Fort Lauderdale College of Business and Finance. Tourist resort. Manufactures cement products, fertilizer, mattresses, furniture, aircraft fittings, electronic equipment, fibre glass, chemicals, plastics, aluminum and concrete products, boats.

7484 ■ American Swimming Magazine
American Swimming Coaches Association
5101 NW 21st Ave., Ste. 530
Fort Lauderdale, FL 33309
Phone: (954)563-4930
Fax: (954)563-9813
Free: 800-356-2722
Publisher's E-mail: asca@swimmingcoach.org
Freq: 6/year. **Subscription Rates:** Included in membership Accessible only to members. **URL:** http://swimmingcoach.org/publications/american-swimming-magazine. **Remarks:** Advertising not accepted. **Circ:** (Not Reported).

7485 ■ Boat International USA
Boat International Group
101 NE 3rd Ave., Ste. 1220
Fort Lauderdale, FL 33301
Phone: (954)522-2441
Fax: (954)522-2240
Publisher's E-mail: info@boatinternational.co.uk
Magazine covering luxury yacht in North America. **Freq:** 10/year. **Trim Size:** 223 x 275 mm. **Key Personnel:** Tim Thomas, Editor; Tony Harris, Chief Executive Officer, Publisher; Ben Farnborough, Contact. **URL:** http://boatinternationalmedia.com/mags/mag02.htm. **Remarks:** Accepts advertising. **Circ:** Combined 43525.

7486 ■ City Link
Sun Sentinel
200 E Las Olas Blvd.
Fort Lauderdale, FL 33301
Phone: (954)356-4144
Fax: (954)356-4559
Free: 877-732-3786
Publisher's E-mail: sfeedback@sun-sentinel.com
Alternative local newspaper. **Freq:** Weekly. **Print Method:** Offset. **Cols./Page:** 5. **Col. Width:** 1 inches. **Col. Depth:** 12 inches. **Key Personnel:** Jake Cline, Editor; Dan Sweeney, Associate Editor; Laura Kokus, Editor; T.M. Shine, Reporter. **URL:** http://www.southflorida.com. **Formerly:** XS Magazine. **Ad Rates:** BW $2,574; 4C $3,174; PCI $42. **Remarks:** Advertising accepted; rates available upon request. **Circ:** Non-paid ‡53000, Non-paid ‡142200, Non-paid ‡315000.

7487 ■ Countdown
JDRF South Florida Chapter
3411 NW 9th Ave., Ste. 701
Fort Lauderdale, FL 33309-5946
Phone: (954)565-4775
Fax: (954)565-4767
Publisher's E-mail: southflorida@jdrf.org
Magazine containing information on diabetes research. **Freq:** Quarterly. **URL:** http://www.jdrf.org. **Circ:** (Not Reported).

7488 ■ Goldfish Report
Goldfish Society of America
PO Box 551373
Fort Lauderdale, FL 33355-1373
Publisher's E-mail: info@goldfishsociety.org
Freq: Bimonthly. **Subscription Rates:** Included in membership. **Alt. Formats:** PDF. **URL:** http://www.goldfishsociety.org/the_report.html. **Remarks:** Accepts advertising. **Circ:** 1000.

7489 ■ The Gourmet Retailer Magazine
Specialty Media Inc.
3230 W Commercial Blvd., No. 250
Fort Lauderdale, FL 33309-3451
Phone: (305)893-8771
Fax: (305)893-8783
Magazine covering upscale cookware and the specialty food industry. **Freq:** 7/year 5/yr. **Print Method:** Web offset. **Trim Size:** 8 1/8 x 10 7/8. **Cols./Page:** 3. **Key Personnel:** Edward Loeb, Publisher; Jeff Friedman, Publisher, Vice President; Anna Wolfe, Editor-in-Chief. **Subscription Rates:** $24. **URL:** http://www.gourmetretailer.com/index.html; http://www.gourmetretailer.com. **Ad Rates:** 4C $3595; BW $2772. **Remarks:** Accepts advertising. **Circ:** Combined 32000.

7490 ■ International Journal of Doctoral Studies
Informing Science Institute
Nova Southeastern University
Fort Lauderdale, FL 33314-7796
Peer-reviewed journal focusing on theory practice, innovation and research of all aspects of doctoral studies. **Freq:** Annual. **Key Personnel:** Michael Jones, Editor-in-Chief. **ISSN:** 1556--8881 (print); **EISSN:** 1556--8873 (electronic). **Subscription Rates:** Free online. **URL:** http://www.informingscience.org/Journals/IJDS/Overview. **Circ:** (Not Reported).

7491 ■ International Journal of Motorcycle Studies
Nova Southeastern University
c/o Suzanne Ferriss, Editor

3301 College Ave.
Fort Lauderdale, FL 33314
Phone: (954)262-8219
Fax: (954)262-3881
Publication E-mail: ijms@nova.edu
Journal focusing on motorcycling culture. **Freq:** Semiannual spring and fall. **Key Personnel:** Suzanne Ferriss, Editor, phone: (954)262-8219, fax: (954)262-3881. **ISSN:** 1931--275X (print). **URL:** http://motorcyclestudies.org. **Remarks:** Accepts advertising. **Circ:** (Not Reported).

7492 ■ Internet Journal of Allied Health Sciences and Practice
Nova Southeastern University
3301 College Ave.
Fort Lauderdale, FL 33314
Phone: (305)475-7300
Free: 800-541-6682
Peer-reviewed, scholarly on-line journal dedicated to the exploration of allied health professional practice and education utilizing modern technologies for communication. **Freq:** Quarterly. **Key Personnel:** Dr. Richard E. Davis, Editor-in-Chief, phone: (954)262-1200; Dr. Guy M. Nehrenz, Managing Editor, Publisher. **ISSN:** 1540--580X (print). **Subscription Rates:** Free. **URL:** http://ijahsp.nova.edu. **Remarks:** Accepts advertising. **Circ:** (Not Reported).

7493 ■ Journal of Child and Adolescent Substance Abuse
Routledge Journals Taylor & Francis Group
c/o Vincent B. VanHasselt, PhD, Co-Ed.
Nova Southeastern University
Center for Psychological Studies
3301 College Ave.
Fort Lauderdale, FL 33314
Journal covering strategies for chemically dependent adolescents and their families. **Freq:** 6/year. **Trim Size:** 6 x 8 3/8. **Key Personnel:** Vincent B. VanHasselt, PhD, Editor; Brad Donohue, Editor. **ISSN:** 1067-828X (print); **EISSN:** 1547-0652 (electronic). **Subscription Rates:** $165 Individuals online only; $182 Individuals print + online; $678 Institutions online only; $775 Institutions print + online. **URL:** http://www.tandfonline.com/loi/wcas20#.Ve6YntKqqko; http://www.tandfonline.com/toc/wcas20/current#.Ve6YmtKqqko. **Ad Rates:** BW $315; 4C $550. **Remarks:** Accepts advertising. **Circ:** Paid 325.

7494 ■ Journal of Creativity in Mental Health
The Haworth Press Inc.
Center for Psychological Studies
Nova Southeastern University
3301 College Ave.
Fort Lauderdale, FL 33314
Phone: (954)262-3093
Fax: (954)202-3093
Publisher's E-mail: getinfo@haworthpress.com
Journal for private practice psychotherapists. **Freq:** Quarterly. **Trim Size:** 6 x 8 3/8. **Key Personnel:** Thelma Duffey, PhD, Editor. **ISSN:** 1540--1383 (print); **EISSN:** 1540--1391 (electronic). **Subscription Rates:** $99 Individuals online only; $349 Institutions online only; $104 Individuals print and online; $398 Institutions print and online. **URL:** http://www.tandfonline.com/toc/wcmh20/current#.VePxsyWqqko. **Formerly:** Psychotherapy in Private Practice; Journal of Psychotherapy in Independent Practice: Innovations In Clinical Methods and Assessment, Consultation and Practice Management. **Ad Rates:** BW $300; BW $315; 4C $550. **Remarks:** Accepts advertising. **Circ:** 399.

7495 ■ Journal of Swimming Research
American Swimming Coaches Association
5101 NW 21st Ave., Ste. 530
Fort Lauderdale, FL 33309
Phone: (954)563-4930
Fax: (954)563-9813
Free: 800-356-2722
Publisher's E-mail: asca@swimmingcoach.org
Freq: Annual. **Key Personnel:** Joel M. Stager, PhD, Board Member; Jan Prins, Ph.D., Editor. **Alt. Formats:** PDF. **URL:** http://swimmingcoach.org/journal/. **Remarks:** Advertising not accepted. **Circ:** (Not Reported).

7496 ■ MSFocus
Multiple Sclerosis Foundation
6520 N Andrews Ave.
Fort Lauderdale, FL 33309-2130
Phone: (954)776-6805
Fax: (954)938-8708
Free: 800-225-6495
Publisher's E-mail: admin@msfocus.org
Freq: Quarterly. **Key Personnel:** Terry Schenker, Manager; Christopher Paine, Coordinator. **Subscription Rates:** Free. **URL:** http://msfocus.org/msf-publications.aspx. **Remarks:** Accepts advertising. **Circ:** (Not Reported).

7497 ■ New Times Broward-Palm Beach
New Times Broward-Palm Beach
PO Box 14128
Fort Lauderdale, FL 33302-4128
Phone: (954)233-1600
Fax: (954)233-1521
Community newspaper. **Freq:** Weekly. **Key Personnel:** Adam Simon, Publisher; Chuck Strouse, Editor. **URL:** http://www.browardpalmbeach.com. **Remarks:** Accepts advertising. **Circ:** (Not Reported).

7498 ■ Porthole: The International Cruise Magazine
Porthole Cruise Magazine
6261 NW 6th Way, Ste. 100
Fort Lauderdale, FL 33309-3403
Phone: (954)377-7777
Fax: (954)377-7000
Free: 888-774-4768
Consumer magazine covering travel and tourism. **Freq:** Bimonthly. **Key Personnel:** Bill Panoff, Chief Executive Officer, President; Jodi Ornstein, Editor; Jeffrey Laign, Director, Editorial. **ISSN:** 1070-9479 (print). **Subscription Rates:** $19.99 Individuals; $29.99 Two years; $15.99 Individuals digital only. **URL:** http://www.porthole.com. **Ad Rates:** BW $4,680; 4C $5,200. **Remarks:** Accepts advertising. **Circ:** (Not Reported).

7499 ■ The Sanford Herald
Sanford Herald
1429 N Federal Hwy.
Fort Lauderdale, FL 33304
Phone: (954)778-0751
Fax: (954)323-9408
General newspaper. **Founded:** Dec. 1930. **Freq:** Daily except Mondays & Christmas Day. **Print Method:** Offset. **Trim Size:** 13 3/4 x 21 1/2. **Cols./Page:** 6. **Col. Width:** 25 nonpareils. **Col. Depth:** 301 agate lines. **Key Personnel:** Bill Horner, III, Publisher, phone: (919)718-1234; Billy Liggett, Editor, phone: (919)718-1226; Gina Eaves, Director, Advertising, phone: (919)718-1259. **Subscription Rates:** $41.25 Individuals E-Edition and tube-delivery; 3 months; $48 Individuals mail; 3 months; $192 By mail; $153 Individuals e-edition & throw-out delivery; $165 Individuals e-edition & tube-delivery. **URL:** http://www.sanfordherald.com. **Ad Rates:** BW $383.50; 4C $1198.50; SAU $6.50. **Remarks:** Accepts advertising. **Circ:** ★**9,048**, Sun. ★**8,834**.

7500 ■ Southern Boating: The South's Largest Boating Magazine
Southern Boating and Yachting Inc.
330 N Andrews Ave.
Fort Lauderdale, FL 33301
Phone: (954)522-5515
Fax: (954)522-2260
Sporting magazine for boating enthusiasts. **Freq:** Monthly. **Print Method:** Web offset. **Trim Size:** 8 1/8 x 10 3/4. **Cols./Page:** 3 and 2. **Col. Width:** 12 and 18 picas. **Col. Depth:** 9 1/2 inches. **Key Personnel:** Louisa Rudeen Beckett, Editor; Skip Allen, Jr., Editor; Vincent Scutellaro, Director, Advertising. **ISSN:** 0192--3579 (print). **Subscription Rates:** $25 Individuals; $55 Canada; $55 Other countries; $38 Two years; $98 Canada two years; $98 Other countries two years. **URL:** http://southernboating.com. **Ad Rates:** BW $2,670; 4C $3,915. **Remarks:** Advertising accepted; rates available upon request. **Circ:** Paid ‡19804, Non-paid ‡9567.

7501 ■ Sun-Sentinel
Sun Sentinel
200 E Las Olas Blvd.
Fort Lauderdale, FL 33301
Phone: (954)356-4144
Fax: (954)356-4559
Free: 877-732-3786
Publisher's E-mail: sfeedback@sun-sentinel.com
Newspaper. **Founded:** 1960. **Freq:** Daily. **Print Method:** Offset. **Cols./Page:** 6. **Col. Width:** 25 nonpareils. **Col. Depth:** 297 agate lines. **Key Personnel:** Dana Banker, Editor; Anne Vasquez, Editor; Arnold Rosenberg, Editor; Kathy Laughlin, Editor; Antonio Fins, Contact. **URL:** http://www.sun-sentinel.com/. **Ad Rates:** BW $3,870; 4C $5,015. **Remarks:** Accepts advertising. **Circ:** Mon.-Sat. ★**208073**, Sun. ★**289682**.

7502 ■ Today's Caregiver
Caregiver Media Group
3350 Griffin Rd.
Fort Lauderdale, FL 33312
Phone: (954)893-0550
Fax: (954)893-1779
Publisher's E-mail: editor@caregiver.com
Magazine providing information, support, and guidance for family and professional caregivers. **Freq:** Bimonthly. **Key Personnel:** Gary Barg, Editor-in-Chief. **Subscription Rates:** $18 Individuals; $32 Two years. **URL:** http://www.caregiver.com; http://www.caregiver.com/magazine/index.htm. **Circ:** (Not Reported).

7503 ■ The Voice: Medical Case Management - Physical Rehabilitation Newspaper
The Voice of Florida
PO Box 030397
Fort Lauderdale, FL 33303-0397
Phone: (954)463-5556
Fax: (954)463-2674
Publication E-mail: voicehab@gate.net
Paper for persons with disabilities and referral resources. **Founded:** 1987. **Freq:** Monthly. **Print Method:** Web. **Trim Size:** 10 x 14. **Cols./Page:** 4. **Col. Width:** 2 7/16 inches. **Col. Depth:** 14 inches. **Key Personnel:** Ray Brasted, Editor. **Subscription Rates:** $25 Individuals. **URL:** http://www.voicepaper.com/. **Formerly:** The Voice. **Ad Rates:** BW $1,195; 4C $1,600. **Remarks:** Accepts advertising. **Circ:** (Not Reported).

7504 ■ Westside Gazette
Westside Gazette
PO Box 5304
Fort Lauderdale, FL 33310
Phone: (954)525-1489
Fax: (954)525-1861
Publication E-mail: wgazette@thewestsidegazette.com
Black community newspaper. **Freq:** Weekly (Thurs.). **Print Method:** Offset. **Cols./Page:** 6. **Col. Width:** 24 nonpareils. **Col. Depth:** 294 agate lines. **Key Personnel:** Bobby R. Henry, Sr., Publisher. **URL:** http://thewestsidegazette.com. **Ad Rates:** GLR $.75; SAU $10.50. **Remarks:** Accepts advertising. **Circ:** Paid ‡7000, Free ‡14500.

7505 ■ Yachts International
Active Interest Media
1850 SE 17th. St., Ste. 310
Fort Lauderdale, FL 33316
Phone: (954)761-8777
Fax: (954)761-8890
Publisher's E-mail: admin@aimmedia.com
Magazine featuring yachts. **Freq:** 7/year. **Key Personnel:** Karlene Pack, President, Vice President; Cecile Gauert, Editor. **Subscription Rates:** $24.95 Individuals; $44.95 Canada two years; $104.95 Two years international; $54.95 Other countries. **URL:** http://www.yachtsinternational.com; http://www.activeinterestmedia.com/magazines.html. **Remarks:** Accepts advertising. **Circ:** ‡51486.

7506 ■ WDZL-TV - 39
500 E Broward Blvd., Ste. 800
Fort Lauderdale, FL 33394
Phone: (954)925-3939
Format: News. **Owner:** The Tribune Media Co., 435 N Michigan Ave., Chicago, IL 60611-4066, Ph: (312)222-9100, Fax: (312)222-4206, Free: 800-874-2863. **Founded:** 1982. **Operating Hours:** Continuous. **Key Personnel:** Jeanette Jordan, Dir. Pub. Aff.; Harvey Cohen, Gen. Mgr.; Gary Zenobi, Gen. Sales Mgr.; Alan Rosenfeld, Sales Mgr.; Ed Perl, Sales Mgr.; Diana Swords, Program Mgr.; Eric Berkowitz, Dir. of Creative Svcs.; Mark Ryan, Controller; Steve Ellis, Chief Engineer; Jeff Eggleston, Operations Mgr. **Wattage:** 5,000,000. **URL:** http://sflcw.com.

7507 ■ WFLL-AM - 1400
4431 Rock Island Rd.
Fort Lauderdale, FL 33319
Phone: (954)731-1855

Circulation: ★ = AAM; △ or • = BPA; ♦ = CAC; ❑ = VAC; ⊕ = PO Statement; ‡ = Publisher's Report; Boldface figures = sworn; Light figures = estimated.

Format: Sports. **Owner:** James Crystal Licenses, Inc., at above address, Dallas, TX 75207. **Operating Hours:** Continuous. **Ad Rates:** Advertising accepted; rates available upon request.

7508 ■ WFTL-AM - 1400
2100 NW 21st Ave.
Fort Lauderdale, FL 33310
Phone: (305)485-4111
Fax: (305)484-0225
Format: Talk. **Networks:** CNN Radio. **Owner:** Tri-Talk Radio, L.C., at above address. **Founded:** 1946. **Operating Hours:** Continuous; 2% network, 98% local. **Key Personnel:** John King, Operations Mgr.; Steve Kane, Dir. of Programs. **Wattage:** 1,000. **Mailing address:** PO Box 100819, Fort Lauderdale, FL 33310.

7509 ■ WREH-FM - 90.5
2701 W Cypress Creek Rd.
Fort Lauderdale, FL 33309
Email: info@reachfm.org
Format: Religious; Contemporary Christian; Talk. **Owner:** Reach Communications Inc., 2746 Bristol Way, Redwood City, CA 94061, Ph: (650)701-0776. **Operating Hours:** Continuous. **Ad Rates:** Noncommercial; underwriting available. **URL:** http://www.reachfm.org.

7510 ■ WSFL-TV - 39
200 E Las Olas Blvd., 11th Fl.
Fort Lauderdale, FL 33301
Phone: (954)627-7300
Fax: (954)355-5200
Founded: Oct. 1982. **Formerly:** WBZL-TV. **Ad Rates:** Advertising accepted; rates available upon request. **URL:** http://www.southflorida.com.

7511 ■ WYBP-FM - 90.3
5555 N Federal Hwy.
Fort Lauderdale, FL 33308
Phone: (954)776-7705
Fax: (954)771-2633
Email: info@gracefmradio.com
Format: Religious; Contemporary Christian. **Formerly:** WAFG-FM. **Operating Hours:** 18 hours Daily. **Key Personnel:** Dolores King St. George, Gen. Mgr., dolores@gracefmradio.com; Lesley Hurst, Dir. of Programs, lesley@gracefmradio.com. **Ad Rates:** Advertising accepted; rates available upon request. **Mailing address:** PO Box 15008, Fort Lauderdale, FL 33318. **URL:** http://www.gracefmradio.com.

FORT MEADE

C FL. Polk Co. 50 mi. SE of Tampa. Phosphate mining. Citrus growing and processing. Cattle.

7512 ■ The Fort Meade Leader
Frisbie Publishing
214 W Broadway, Ste. B
Fort Meade, FL 33841
Phone: (863)533-0402
Fax: (863)285-7634
Publication E-mail: news@fortmeadeleader.com
Local newspaper. **Freq:** Semiweekly Tuesday and Friday. **Print Method:** Offset. **Trim Size:** 16 x 22 3/4. **Cols./Page:** 7. **Col. Width:** 2 1/8 inches. **Col. Depth:** 21 inches. **Key Personnel:** Aileen Hood, General Manager; Jim Gouvellis, Publisher; Brian Ackley, Editor. **USPS:** 907-620. **Subscription Rates:** $47.99 Individuals; $91.19 Two years; $59.20 Out of country; $112.48 Out of country two years; $64.80 Out of state; $123.12 Out of state two years. **URL:** http://fortmeadeleader.com. **Ad Rates:** BW $767; SAU $5.55. **Remarks:** Accepts advertising. **Circ:** Paid ‡850, Free ‡10, Combined ‡860.

FORT MYERS

S FL. Lee Co. On Caloosahatchee River, 120 mi. SE of Tampa. Edison Community College. Resort area. Manufactures trailers, boats, surgical and medical supplies, lumber, cigars, electronic equipment. Ships fruit and vegetables.

7513 ■ Doctor's Life
Island Coast Media
PO Box 61726
Fort Myers, FL 33906
Phone: (239)246-7460
Publisher's E-mail: chris.bergman@islandcoastmedia.com
Magazine for doctors. **Freq:** Monthly. **Key Personnel:** Ruth Marshall, Editor; Chris Bergman, Publisher. **URL:** http://doctorslifemag.com. **Remarks:** Advertising accepted; rates available upon request. **Circ:** (Not Reported).

7514 ■ Shore and Beach
American Shore & Beach Preservation Association
5460 Beaujolais Ln.
Fort Myers, FL 33919
Phone: (239)489-2616
Fax: (239)362-9771
Publisher's E-mail: managing@asbpa.org
Freq: Quarterly. **ISSN:** 0037- 4237 (print). **Subscription Rates:** included in membership dues. **URL:** http://asbpa.org/publications/pubs_S_and_B.htm. **Remarks:** Accepts advertising. **Circ:** 800.

7515 ■ SignCraft: The guide to profitable and creative sign production
Signcraft Publishing Co.
10271 Deer Run Farms Rd.
Fort Myers, FL 33966
Phone: (239)939-4644
Fax: (239)939-0607
Free: 800-204-0204
Publication E-mail: signcraft@signcraft.com
Trade magazine. **Freq:** 7/year. **Print Method:** Web offset. **Trim Size:** 9 x 10 7/8. **Cols./Page:** 3. **Col. Width:** 28 nonpareils. **Col. Depth:** 140 agate lines. **Key Personnel:** Bill McIltrot, Contact; Michell Sutton, Contact. **ISSN:** 0270--4757 (print). **Subscription Rates:** $39 Individuals; $69 Two years; $49 Other countries; $91 Other countries 2 years. **URL:** http://signcraft.com. **Mailing address:** PO Box 60031, Fort Myers, FL 33966. **Ad Rates:** BW $3,586; 4C $4,486. **Remarks:** Accepts advertising. **Circ:** Paid 12763.

7516 ■ WAKS-FM - 103.9
3440 Marinatown Ln., No. 102
Fort Myers, FL 33903
Format: Adult Contemporary. **Networks:** Independent. **Owner:** WRCC Partners, at above address. **Founded:** 1975. **Operating Hours:** Continuous. **Key Personnel:** Dick Parrish, Gen. Mgr; Cara Cameron, Contact. **Wattage:** 50,000.

7517 ■ WARO-FM - 94.5
2824 Palm Beach Blvd.
Fort Myers, FL 33916
Phone: (239)334-1111
Fax: (239)479-5535
Format: Classic Rock. **Owner:** Meridian Broadcasting, Inc., at above address. **Operating Hours:** Continuous. **ADI:** Fort Myers-Naples, FL. **Wattage:** 100,000. **Ad Rates:** Noncommercial. **URL:** http://www.classicrock945.com.

7518 ■ WAYJ-FM - 88.7
1860 Boy Scout Dr., Ste. 202
Fort Myers, FL 33907
Free: 888-936-1929
Email: supportservices@wayfm.com
Format: Religious. **Owner:** WAY-FM Media Group Inc., 5540 Tech Center Dr., Ste. 200, Colorado Springs, CO 80919, Ph: (719)533-0300. **Founded:** 1980. **ADI:** Fort Myers-Naples, FL. **Key Personnel:** Jeff Taylor, Contact; Jeff Taylor, Contact; Kristen Pell, Contact; Steve Shore, Contact. **Mailing address:** PO Box 61275, Fort Myers, FL 33906. **URL:** http://www.wayfm.com.

7519 ■ WBBH-TV - 2
3719 Central Ave.
Fort Myers, FL 33901
Phone: (239)939-2020
Format: News. **Networks:** NBC. **Owner:** Waterman Broadcasting Corp., 3719 Central Ave., Fort Myers, FL 33901. **Founded:** 1968. **Operating Hours:** Continuous. **ADI:** Fort Myers-Naples, FL. **Key Personnel:** Deborah Abbot, Dir. of Programs; Darrel Adams, News Dir., Div. Mgr.; Bob Beville, Sales Mgr.; Steven Pontius, Exec. VP, Gen. Mgr. **Ad Rates:** Noncommercial. **URL:** http://www.nbc-2.com.

7520 ■ WBTT-FM - 105.5
13320 Metro Pky., Ste. 1
Fort Myers, FL 33966
Phone: (239)225-4300
Format: Contemporary Hit Radio (CHR). **ADI:** Fort Myers-Naples, FL. **Wattage:** 28,500. **Ad Rates:** Noncommercial. **URL:** http://www.1055thebeat.com.

7521 ■ WCKT-FM - 107.1
13320 Metro Pky., Ste. 1
Fort Myers, FL 33966
Format: Country. **ADI:** Fort Myers-Naples, FL. **Wattage:** 100,000. **Ad Rates:** Advertising accepted; rates available upon request. **URL:** http://www.catcountry1071.com.

7522 ■ WCRM-AM - 1350
3548 Canal St.
Fort Myers, FL 33916
Phone: (239)332-1350
Format: Gospel; Hispanic. **Networks:** CNN Radio. **Founded:** 1964. **Operating Hours:** Continuous. **ADI:** Fort Myers-Naples, FL. **Key Personnel:** Dr. Mario Garcia, President, pastormario@vidaradionetwork.com. **Local Programs:** *Musica con Vida*. **Wattage:** 2,000. **Ad Rates:** Advertising accepted; rates available upon request.

7523 ■ WCVU-FM - 104.9
13320 Metro Pky., Ste. 1
Fort Myers, FL 33966
Phone: (239)225-4300
Format: Easy Listening. **Wattage:** 6,000. **URL:** http://www.wcvu.com.

7524 ■ WGCU-FM - 90.1
10501 FGCU Blvd. S
Fort Myers, FL 33965
Phone: (239)590-2300
Fax: (239)590-2310
Email: wgcunews@wgcu.org
Format: Jazz; News; Classical; Public Radio. **Networks:** National Public Radio (NPR); Public Broadcasting Service (PBS). **Owner:** Florida Board of Regents, at above address. **Founded:** 1983. **Formerly:** WSFP-AM. **Operating Hours:** Continuous; 34% network, 66% local. **ADI:** Fort Myers-Naples, FL. **Key Personnel:** Valerie Alker, Producer, valker@fgcu.edu; Johnson Rick, Gen. Mgr., rjohnson@wgcu.org; Luc Martin, Operations Mgr., lamartin@fgcu.edu. **Wattage:** 100,000. **Ad Rates:** Noncommercial. **URL:** http://wgcu.org/programs/changes-fm-lineup.

7525 ■ WGCU-TV - 30
10501 FGCU Blvd. S
Fort Myers, FL 33965
Email: wgcusales@wgcu.org
Format: Public TV. **Networks:** Public Broadcasting Service (PBS). **Owner:** Florida Golf Coast University, at above address, Fort Myers, FL 33965-6565. **Founded:** 1983. **Formerly:** WSFP-TV. **Operating Hours:** Continuous; 95% network, 5% local. **ADI:** Fort Myers-Naples, FL. **Key Personnel:** Rick Johnson, Gen. Mgr; Terry Brennen, Contact. **Ad Rates:** Noncommercial. **URL:** http://www.wgcu.org.

7526 ■ WINK-FM - 96.9
2824 Palm Beach Blvd.
Fort Myers, FL 33916-1590
Format: Adult Contemporary. **Owner:** Fort Myers Broadcasting Co., 2824 Palm Beach Blvd., Fort Myers, FL 33916. **Founded:** 1964. **Operating Hours:** Continuous. **ADI:** Fort Myers-Naples, FL. **Key Personnel:** Wayne Simons, Gen. Mgr., VP, wayne.simons@fmbcmail.com. **Wattage:** 100,000. **Ad Rates:** Noncommercial. **URL:** http://www.969morefm.com.

7527 ■ WINK-TV - 11
2824 Palm Beach Blvd.
Fort Myers, FL 33916-1590
Phone: (239)334-1111
Email: golfdoctor@winknews.com
Format: News. **Networks:** CBS. **Owner:** Fort Myers Broadcasting Co., 2824 Palm Beach Blvd., Fort Myers, FL 33916. **Founded:** Mar. 18, 1954. **ADI:** Fort Myers-Naples, FL. **Key Personnel:** Greg Stetson, Contact, greg.stetson@winktv.com. **Local Programs:** *WINK News at 6pm*; *Wink News at 5pm*; *Late Late Show*; *WINK News at 5:30pm*; *WINK News at 11*; *WINK News at 7pm*. **Wattage:** 1,000,000 ERP. **Ad Rates:** Advertising accepted; rates available upon request. **URL:** http://www.winknews.com.

7528 ■ WJBX-FM - 99.3
12995 S Cleveland Ave., Ste. 258
Fort Myers, FL 33907
Phone: (813)275-9980
Fax: (813)275-5611

Format: Adult Contemporary; Soft Rock. **Owner:** Justice Broadcasting, at above address. **Founded:** 1984. **Formerly**: WQEZ-FM. **Operating Hours**: Continuous; 100% local. **Key Personnel:** Ann Wells, Dir. of Traffic; Andy Frame, Dir. of Programs; Sherri Griswold, Gen. Sales Mgr.; Dean Tyler, Dir. of Programs; Carol K. Cook, Contact; Jennifer Vaughn, Contact. **Wattage**: 50,000. **Ad Rates:** $30-60 per unit.

7529 ■ WJYO-FM - 91.5
PO Box 61721
Fort Myers, FL 33906
Phone: (239)274-9150
Email: info@kingdom.fm
Format: Religious; Contemporary Christian. **Owner:** Airwaves for Jesus Inc., at above address. **Operating Hours**: Continuous. **Key Personnel:** Art Ramos, President. **Wattage**: 3,000 ERP. **Ad Rates:** Noncommercial; underwriting available. **URL:** http://www.kingdom.fm.

7530 ■ WMYR-AM
2835 Hanson St.
Fort Myers, FL 33916
Phone: (239)332-2102
Fax: (239)332-3135
Free: 888-EARS-018
Owner: Starboard Network, Inc., at above address. **Founded:** 1952. **Wattage**: 5,000. **Ad Rates:** $20 for 15 seconds; $25 for 30 seconds; $35 for 60 seconds.

7531 ■ WNOG-AM
2824 Palm Beach Blvd.
Fort Myers, FL 33916
Phone: (239)337-2346
Fax: (239)332-0767
Format: Talk; News. **Networks:** CBS. **Owner:** Meridian Broadcasting, Inc., 2824 Palm Blvd., Fort Myers, FL 33916. **Founded:** 1954. **Key Personnel:** Randy Marsh, Program Mgr. **Wattage**: 5,000.

7532 ■ WOLZ-FM - 95.3
13320 Metro Pkwy., Ste. 1
Fort Myers, FL 33966
Phone: (239)225-4300
Fax: (239)225-4410
Format: Adult Contemporary. **Founded:** 1987. **Formerly**: WFJY-FM. **Operating Hours**: 6 a.m.-10 a.m. **Key Personnel:** Sherri Carlson, Gen. Mgr. **Wattage**: 79,000. **Ad Rates:** Noncommercial. **URL:** http://www.953theriver.com.

7533 ■ WTLQ-AM - 1240
2824 Palm Beach Blvd.
Fort Myers, FL 33916
Phone: (239)334-1111
Format: Talk. **Networks:** CNN Radio. **Owner:** Fort Meyers Broadcasting Co., at above address. **Operating Hours**: Continuous. **ADI**: Fort Myers-Naples, FL. **Wattage**: 1,000. **Ad Rates:** Noncommercial. **URL:** http://www.winknews.com/contact.

7534 ■ WUSV-FM - 98.5
2824 Palm Beach Blvd.
Fort Myers, FL 33916
Phone: (239)337-2346
Fax: (239)479-5553
Owner: Meridian Broadcasting, 333 8th St. S, Naples, FL 34102. **Wattage**: 18,500. **Ad Rates:** Advertising accepted; rates available upon request.

7535 ■ WXNX-FM - 93.7
2824 Palm Beach Blvd.
Fort Myers, FL 33916
Phone: (239)334-1111
Fax: (239)479-5535
Email: randy.marsh@mbimail.com
Format: Adult Contemporary. **Owner:** Meridian Broadcasting, Inc., at above address. **Formerly**: WPRW-FM; WTLT-FM. **Operating Hours**: Continuous. **ADI**: Fort Myers-Naples, FL. **Key Personnel:** Jim Schwartzel, Contact; Jim Schwartzel, Contact. **Wattage**: 6,000. **Ad Rates:** Advertising accepted; rates available upon request. **URL:** http://93x.fm.

7536 ■ WZJZ-FM - 100.1
13320 Metro Pkwy., Ste. 1
Fort Myers, FL 33966
Phone: (239)225-4300
Format: Jazz. **Operating Hours**: Continuous. **Ad Rates:** Advertising accepted; rates available upon request. **URL:** http://www.y100florida.com.

7537 ■ WZVN-TV - 7
3719 Central Ave.
Fort Myers, FL 33901
Phone: (239)939-2020
Fax: (239)936-7771
Format: News. **Networks:** ABC. **Owner:** Waterman Broadcasting Corp., 3719 Central Ave., Fort Myers, FL 33901. **Operating Hours**: Continuous. **Key Personnel:** Kevin Henry, Sales Mgr.; Deborah Abbott, News Dir., dabbott@water.net; Darrel Adams, Promotions Dir., Mktg. Mgr., News Dir., darrel.adams@water.net; Steven Pontius, Gen. Mgr., CFO, spontius@water.net; Bob Hannon, Exec. VP, bhannon@water.net; Bob Beville, HR Mgr., bobb@water.net. **Ad Rates:** Noncommercial. **URL:** http://www.abc-7.com.

FORT PIERCE

SE FL. St. Lucie Co. On Atlantic Ocean, 58 mi. N. of West Palm Beach. Indian River Community College. Resort. Manufactures barrels, beverages, fertilizer, boats, lumber. Fruit canning. Fisheries. Citrus fruits, beans, cucumbers, tomatoes.

7538 ■ International Journal of Applied Philosophy
Philosophy Documentation Center
c/o Elliot D. Cohen, Ed.
Indian River Station College
3209 Virginia Ave.
Fort Pierce, FL 34981-5596
Publication E-mail: ijapsubmissions@gmail.com
Peer-reviewed scholarly journal covering philosophy in the areas of education, business, law, government, health care, psychology, science, and the environment. **Freq:** Semiannual. **Key Personnel:** Elliot D. Cohen, Editor. **ISSN:** 0739--098X (print); **EISSN:** 2153--6910 (electronic). **Subscription Rates:** $64 Institutions print only; $33 Individuals print only; $32 Institutions single/back issues; $17 Individuals single/back issues; $40 Individuals online only; $192 Institutions online only; $53 Individuals print and online; $230 Institutions print and online. **URL:** http://www.pdcnet.org/pdc/bvdb.nsf/journal?openform&journal=pdc_ijap; http://www.pdcnet.org/ijap. **Remarks:** Accepts advertising. **Circ:** (Not Reported).

7539 ■ WAVW-FM - 101.7
PO Box 39
Fort Pierce, FL 34954
Phone: (772)335-9300
Fax: (561)335-3291
Free: 800-562-WAVW
Format: Country. **Owner:** Clear Channel Radio, Inc., San Antonio, TX. **Founded:** 1973. **Operating Hours**: Continuous. **ADI**: West Palm Beach-Ft. Pierce-Vero Beach, FL. **Key Personnel:** Mark Bass, Mktg. Mgr., markbass@clearchannel.com; Layne Ryan, Dir. of Sales, layneryan@clearchannel.com; Mike Michaels, Operations Mgr., mikemichaels@clearchannel.com; Heath West, Dir. of Programs, heathwest@clearchannel.com; Carla Wooten, Traffic Mgr., carlawooten@clearchannel.com. **Wattage**: 6,000. **Ad Rates:** $40 for 30 seconds; $45 for 60 seconds.

7540 ■ WBOF-FM - 105.9
3794 Oleander Ave.
Fort Pierce, FL 34982
Format: Religious. **Owner:** Faith Baptist Church, 3607 Oleander Ave., Fort Pierce, FL 34982, Ph: (772)461-3607, Fax: (772)461-4732. **ADI**: West Palm Beach-Ft. Pierce-Vero Beach, FL. **Key Personnel:** Mike Schneider, Station Mgr., mike@wbofradio.com. **Wattage**: 094 ERP. **URL:** http://www.wbofradio.com.

7541 ■ WJNX-AM - 1330
4100 Metzger Rd.
Fort Pierce, FL 34947
Phone: (772)464-1330
Email: radio@lagigante1330.com
Format: Hispanic; News; Talk. **Ad Rates:** Advertising accepted; rates available upon request. **URL:** http://www.lagigante1330.com.

7542 ■ WPSL-AM - 1590
4100 Metzger Rd.
Fort Pierce, FL 34947
Phone: (772)340-1590
Format: Talk; Sports. **Networks:** CBS; ABC; ESPN Radio. **Founded:** 1985. **Operating Hours**: Continuous. **Key Personnel:** Carol Wyatt, Contact, carol@wpls.com. **Local Programs**: *Bone Talk*, Wednesday 10:00 a.m. - 11:00 a.m.; *World of Nutrition*, Thursday 10:00 a.m. - 11:00 a.m.; *Swap Shop*, Saturday Sunday 9:00 a.m. - 10:00 a.m.; *Hammock Creek Golf Show*; *Treasure Coast Health Week*, Monday 10:00 a.m. - 11:00 a.m.; *Cindy's Health Beat and Where to Eat!*, Saturday 11:00 a.m. - 12:00 p.m. **Wattage**: 5,000 Day; 063 Night. **Ad Rates:** Combined advertising rates available with WIRA. **URL:** http://www.wpsl.com.

7543 ■ WQCS-FM - 88.9
3209 Virginia Ave.
Fort Pierce, FL 34981
Phone: (772)465-8989
Fax: (772)462-4743
Free: 888-286-8936
Email: info@wqcs.org
Format: Public Radio; Classical. **Networks:** National Public Radio (NPR); AP; American Public Radio (APR). **Owner:** Indian River Community College. **Founded:** 1982. **Operating Hours**: Continuous. **ADI**: West Palm Beach-Ft. Pierce-Vero Beach, FL. **Key Personnel:** Madison Hodges, Mgr., mhodges@wqcs.org; Randy Murdock, Chief Engineer, rmurdock@wqcs.org; Joe Lenartiene, Operations Mgr., jlenarti@wqcs.org. **Wattage**: 100,000 ERP. **Ad Rates:** Noncommercial. Underwriting available. **URL:** http://www.wqcs.org.

7544 ■ WSTU-AM - 1450
4100 Metzger Rd.
Fort Pierce, FL 34947
Format: News; Talk. **Ad Rates:** Noncommercial. **URL:** http://www.wstu1450.com.

7545 ■ WTCE-TV - 21
3601 N 25th St.
Fort Pierce, FL 34946
Phone: (772)489-2701
Owner: Community Educational Television, Inc., PO Box A, Santa Ana, CA 92711, Ph: (714)832-2950. **Wattage**: 1,000,000.

7546 ■ WTSM-FM - 93.5
5057 Turnpike Feeder Rd.
Fort Pierce, FL 34951

FORT WALTON BEACH

NW FL. Okaloosa Co. On Gulf of Mexico, 40 mi. E. of Pensacola. Center of Emerald Coast. Tourist resort.

7547 ■ WFFY-FM - 92.1
111 Ferry Rd.
Fort Walton Beach, FL 32548
Format: Hip Hop. **Owner:** Qantum Communications, Inc., at above address. **URL:** http://q92online.com.

7548 ■ WFTW-AM - 1260
225 NW Hollywood Blvd.
Fort Walton Beach, FL 32548
Phone: (850)664-1260
Format: News; Talk; Information. **Networks:** ABC. **Owner:** Cumulus Media Inc., 3280 Peachtree Rd. NW, Ste. 2300, Atlanta, GA 30305-2455, Ph: (404)949-0700, Fax: (404)949-0740. **Founded:** 1953. **Operating Hours**: Continuous. **Wattage**: 2,500 Day; 131 Night. **URL:** http://www.wftw.com.

7549 ■ WKSM-FM - 99.5
225 NW Hollywood Blvd.
Fort Walton Beach, FL 32548
Phone: (850)243-3699
Fax: (850)243-6806
Email: frunch@wksm.com
Format: Classic Rock. **Founded:** 1965. **Operating Hours**: Continuous. **Wattage**: 50,000 ERP. **Ad Rates:** Advertising accepted; rates available upon request. Combined advertising rates available with WFTW-AM, WYZB-FM, WNCV-FM, and WZNS-FM. **URL:** http://www.wksm.com.

7550 ■ WMMK-FM - 92.1
PO Box 921
Fort Walton Beach, FL 32549-0921
Format: Oldies. **Owner:** Emerald Coast Radio Corp., at above address, Ph: (904)664-2400, Fax: (904)664-2552. **Founded:** 1981. **Operating Hours**: Continuous; 100% local. **Key Personnel:** Ron Hale, Sr., Gen. Mgr.; Dean Crumly, Dir. of Programs; Skip Davis, Music Dir. **Watt-**

Circulation: ⋆ = AAM; △ or • = BPA; ♦ = CAC; ❑ = VAC; ⊕ = PO Statement; ‡ = Publisher's Report; Boldface figures = sworn; Light figures = estimated.

age: 25,000. **Ad Rates:** $19-39 per unit.

7551 ■ WNCV-FM - 93.3
225 NW Hollywood Blvd.
Fort Walton Beach, FL 32548
Phone: (850)243-7676
Format: Adult Contemporary. **Owner:** Cumulus Broadcasting Inc., 3280 Peachtree Rd. NW, Ste. 2300, Atlanta, GA 30305-2447, Ph: (404)949-0700, Fax: (404)949-0740. **Wattage:** 50,000 ERP. **Ad Rates:** Advertising accepted; rates available upon request. **URL:** http://www.wncv.com.

7552 ■ WPSM-FM - 91.1
233 N Hill Ave.
Fort Walton Beach, FL 32548
Phone: (850)244-7667
Fax: (850)244-3254
Email: info@wpsm.com
Format: Contemporary Christian. **Founded:** 1985. **Operating Hours:** Continuous; 2% network, 98% local. **Wattage:** 5,000. **URL:** http://www.wpsm.com.

7553 ■ WRKN-FM - 100.3
21 Miracle Strip Pky.
Fort Walton Beach, FL 32548
Phone: (850)244-1400
Fax: (850)243-1471
Format: Classic Rock. **Operating Hours:** Continuous. **Ad Rates:** Advertising accepted; rates available upon request.

7554 ■ WTKE-FM - 100.3
21 Miracle Strip Pkwy.
Fort Walton Beach, FL 32548
Phone: (850)244-1400
Fax: (850)243-1471
Format: News; Sports; Talk. **Operating Hours:** Continuous. **Wattage:** 3,000. **Ad Rates:** Advertising accepted; rates available upon request. **URL:** http://theticketsportsnetwork.com.

7555 ■ WYZB-FM - 105.5
225 NW Hollywood Blvd.
Fort Walton Beach, FL 32548
Phone: (850)244-1055
Format: Contemporary Country. **Founded:** Sept. 07, 2006. **Ad Rates:** Noncommercial. **URL:** http://www.wyzb.com.

7556 ■ WZNS-FM - 96.5
225 NW Hollywood Blvd.
Fort Walton Beach, FL 32548
Phone: (850)243-7676
Format: Alternative/New Music/Progressive. **Owner:** Cumulus Broadcasting Inc., 3280 Peachtree Rd. NW, Ste. 2300, Atlanta, GA 30305-2447, Ph: (404)949-0700, Fax: (404)949-0740. **Key Personnel:** Melissa Campbell, Contact, melissa.campbell@cumulus.com; Melissa Campbell, Contact, melissa.campbell@cumulus.com. **URL:** http://www.z96.com.

GAINESVILLE

N FL. Alachua Co. 72 mi. SW of Jacksonville. University of Florida; Sante Fe Community College. Manufactures electronics, sporting goods, sailboats, heavy equipment. Corn, soybeans, sunflower seeds.

7557 ■ Agricultural and Human Values: Journal of the Agriculture, Food, and Human Values Society
Springer Netherlands
c/o Richard P. Haynes, Founding Ed.
Dept. of Philosophy
University of Florida
Gainesville, FL 32611
Journal covering ethical, social, and biological understanding of agriculture. **Freq:** Quarterly. **Key Personnel:** Harvey S. James, Jr., Editor-in-Chief; Carol J. Pierce Colfer, Editor; David Barling, Board Member; Jane Adams, Board Member; Laura B. DeLind, Board Member; David Cleveland, Board Member; Margaret Grossman, Board Member; Richard P. Haynes, Editor, Founder. **ISSN:** 0889--048X (print); **EISSN:** 1572--8366 (electronic). **Subscription Rates:** $734 Institutions print incl. free access or e-only ; $881 Institutions print plus enhanced access ; €695 Institutions print incl. free access or e-only ; €834 Institutions print plus enhanced access. **URL:** http://link.springer.com/journal/10460. **Remarks:** Accepts advertising. **Circ:** (Not Reported).

7558 ■ Chemical Engineering Education Journal
American Society for Engineering Education
c/o Chemical Engineering Department
University of Florida
Gainesville, FL 32611-6005
Phone: (352)392-0861
Fax: (352)392-0861
Publication E-mail: cee@che.ufl.edu
Journal serves engineering, mathematics, science, and computer science educators interested in improving instruction through computing. **Freq:** Quarterly. **Print Method:** Offset. **Trim Size:** 11 3/8 x 15. **Cols./Page:** 4. **Key Personnel:** Lynn Heasley, Managing Editor; Phillip C. Wankat, Editor. **Subscription Rates:** $30 Members /yr; $100 Individuals all others; $26 Individuals 2-4 bulk rates; $24 Individuals 5-9 bulk rates; $19 Individuals 10-14; $17 Individuals additional. **Alt. Formats:** PDF. **URL:** http://www.che.ufl.edu/cee; http://www.asee.org/papers-and-publications/publications/division-publications#Chemical_Engineering_Education_Journal. **Circ:** (Not Reported).

7559 ■ Critical Reviews in Solid State and Materials Sciences
Taylor & Francis Group Journals
c/o Wolfgang Sigmund, Editor
University of Florida
Dept. of Materials Science & Engineering
Gainesville, FL 32611-6400
Publisher's E-mail: customerservice@taylorandfrancis.com
Journal covering topics in solid state materials properties, processing, and applications. **Freq:** 6/year. **Key Personnel:** Joseph E. Greene, Board Member; Buddy D. Ratner, Board Member; Takuo Sugano, Board Member; Paul Holloway, Board Member; Wolfgang Sigmund, Editor; Siegfried Hofmann, Board Member; Jerry M. Woodall, Board Member; Jan-Eric Sundgren, Board Member; Hendrik C. Swart, Board Member. **ISSN:** 1040--8436 (print); **EISSN:** 1547--6561 (electronic). **Subscription Rates:** $1624 Institutions print and online; $1421 Institutions online only; $289 Individuals print only. **URL:** http://www.tandfonline.com/toc/bsms20/current. **Mailing address:** PO Box 116400, Gainesville, FL 32611-6400. **Circ:** (Not Reported).

7560 ■ Current Protein & Peptide Science
Bentham Science Publishers Ltd.
Dept. of Biochemistry & Molecular Biology
University of Florida, College of Medicine
Gainesville, FL 32610-0245
Publisher's E-mail: subscriptions@benthamscience.org
Journal presenting summaries of specific aspects of research involving proteins, peptides, and interactions between the enzymes, especially proteases; the binding interactions of hormones and their receptors; the properties of transcription factors and other molecules that regulate gene expression; the reactions leading to the immune response; the process of signal transduction; the structure and function of proteins involved in the cytoskeleton and molecular motors; the properties of membrane channels and transporters; and the generation and storage of metabolic energy. **Freq:** 8/year. **Key Personnel:** Ben M. Dunn, Editor-in-Chief. **ISSN:** 1389--2037 (print); **EISSN:** 1875--5550 (electronic). **Subscription Rates:** $330 Individuals print; $1540 print and online - academic; $1400 print or online - academic; $3050 print and online - corporate; $250 print and online - corporate. **URL:** http://benthamscience.com/journals/current-protein-and-peptide-science. **Mailing address:** PO Box 100245, Gainesville, FL 32610-0245. **Ad Rates:** BW $700; 4C $900. **Remarks:** Accepts advertising. **Circ:** ‡800.

7561 ■ Education Finance and Policy
The MIT Press
PO Box 117140
Gainesville, FL 32611-7140
Phone: (352)392-5017
Fax: (352)392-7860
Publication E-mail: efp@cba.ufl.edu
Journal devoted to examining the policy implications, scholarly basis, and operational practices on which the financing of education institutions and systems is based. **Freq:** Quarterly. **Key Personnel:** Amy Ellen Schwartz, PhD, Editor; Thomas A. Downes, Board Member; Dan Goldhaber, Board Member. **ISSN:** 1557--3060 (print); **EISSN:** 1557--3079 (electronic). **Subscription Rates:** $140 Nonmembers print & online; $125 Nonmembers online; $374 Institutions print & online, nonmembers; $324 Institutions online, nonmembers. **URL:** http://www.mitpressjournals.org/loi/edfp. **Ad Rates:** BW $350. **Remarks:** Accepts advertising. **Circ:** 650.

7562 ■ Florida Journal of International Law
University of Florida College of Law Holland Law Center
309 Village Dr.
Gainesville, FL 32611
Phone: 352 273-0890
Fax: 352 392-4087
Publication E-mail: fjil@law.ufl.edu
Scholarly journal covering issues dealing with international law. **Freq:** 3/year. **Key Personnel:** Victoria A. Redd, Editor. **ISSN:** 0882--6420 (print). **Subscription Rates:** $45 Individuals domestic; $50 Other countries; $15 Single issue domestic orders; $20 Single issue other countries. **URL:** http://fjil.org. **Ad Rates:** BW $350. **Remarks:** Accepts advertising. **Circ:** Combined 285.

7563 ■ Florida Journal of International Law
University of Florida Fredric G. Levin College of Law
309 Village Dr.
Gainesville, FL 32611
Phone: (352)273-0890
Fax: (352)392-4087
Publisher's E-mail: admissions@law.ufl.edu
Journal covering articles devoted to timely discussion of prescient international legal issues. **Freq:** 3/year. **Key Personnel:** Sumer C. Thomas, Editor-in-Chief. **Subscription Rates:** $45 U.S.; $50 Other countries; $15 Single issue domestic; $20 Single issue international. **URL:** http://fjil.org. **Mailing address:** PO Box 117621, Gainesville, FL 32611-7621. **Circ:** (Not Reported).

7564 ■ FloridAgriculture
Florida Farm Bureau Federation
PO Box 147030
Gainesville, FL 32614-7030
Phone: (352)378-8100
Newspaper for members of the Florida Farm Bureau Federation. **Freq:** Monthly. **Print Method:** Offset. **Trim Size:** 10 1/4 x 13 1/2. **Cols./Page:** 4. **Col. Width:** 28 nonpareils. **Col. Depth:** 182 agate lines. **Key Personnel:** G.B. Crawford, Assistant Editor, phone: (352)374-1517; Ed Albanesi, Editor, phone: (352)374-1521; Joey Mazzaferro, Manager, Advertising, phone: (352)374-1523. **ISSN:** 0015--3869 (print). **Subscription Rates:** $3.25 Members. **URL:** http://floridagriculture.org. **Ad Rates:** BW $2,950; 4C $3,969. **Remarks:** Accepts advertising. **Circ:** Combined ‡145000.

7565 ■ Gainesville Magazine: The Best of the University City
Gainesville Life Magazine
2700 SW 13th St.
Gainesville, FL 32608
Phone: (325)378-1411
Publisher's E-mail: letters@gainesville.com
Magazine covering things to do in Gainesville, Georgia. **Freq:** Bimonthly. **Key Personnel:** Jacki Levine, Editor; James Doughton, Publisher. **URL:** http://www.gainesville.com/section/magazine; http://www.gainesville.com/section/gmag; http://www.gainesville.com/magazine. **Ad Rates:** BW $1,275; 4C $1,628. **Remarks:** Accepts advertising. **Circ:** (Not Reported).

7566 ■ The Gainesville Sun
The Gainesville Sun
PO Box 147147
Gainesville, FL 32614-7147
Phone: (352)378-1411
Fax: (352)338-3128
Free: 800-443-9493
Publisher's E-mail: online@gvillesun.com
General newspaper. **Freq:** Daily. **Print Method:** Offset. **Trim Size:** 13 3/4 x 22. **Cols./Page:** 6. **Col. Width:** 2 1/16 inches. **Col. Depth:** 21 inches. **Key Personnel:** Jacki Levine, Managing Editor, phone: (352)374-5040; Jim Osteen, Executive Editor, phone: (352)374-5035; Ron Cunningham, Editor, phone: (352)374-5075; James E. Doughton, Publisher, phone: (352)374-5001. **ISSN:** 0163--4925 (print). **Subscription Rates:** $18.37 Individuals 7 day print and digital; monthly; $13.60 Individuals Thursday through Sunday; $11.90 Individuals digital only. **URL:** http://gainesville.com. **Remarks:** Accepts advertising. **Circ:** Mon.-Fri. ★**44658**, Sun. ★**49179**, Sat. ★**44250**.

7567 ■ Genetic Testing and Molecular Biomarkers
Mary Ann Liebert Inc., Publishers
c/o Kenneth I. Berns, MD, Ed.-in-Ch.
Department of Molecular Genetics & Microbiology
College of Medicine
University of Florida
1600 SW Archer Rd., R-254
Gainesville, FL 32610-0266
Phone: (352)273-8072
Fax: (352)273-7994
Publisher's E-mail: info@liebertpub.com
Medical journal devoted to all aspects of human genetic disease testing. **Freq:** Monthly. **Print Method:** Offset. **Trim Size:** 8 1/2 x 11. **Cols./Page:** 2. **Col. Width:** 3 1/4 inches. **Col. Depth:** 9 1/2 inches. **Key Personnel:** Michele Caggana, Board Member; Kenneth I. Berns, MD, Editor-in-Chief. **ISSN:** 1945--0265 (print); **EISSN:** 1945--0257 (electronic). **Subscription Rates:** $995 Individuals print and online; $1337 Other countries print and online; $954 Individuals online only; $2043 Institutions print and online; $2451 Institutions, other countries print and online; $1807 Institutions print only; $2078 Institutions, other countries print only; $1964 Institutions online only. **URL:** http://www.liebertpub.com/overview/genetic-testing-and-molecular-biomarkers/18. **Formerly:** Genetic Testing. **Mailing address:** PO Box 100266, Gainesville, FL 32610-0266. **Ad Rates:** BW $1,075; 4C $1,825. **Remarks:** Accepts advertising. **Circ:** (Not Reported).

7568 ■ ImageTexT: Interdisciplinary Comics Studies
University of Florida
4008 Turlington Hall
Gainesville, FL 32611-7310
Publication E-mail: imagetext@gmail.com
Peer-reviewed open access journal dedicated to furthering comics scholarship. **Freq:** 3/year. **Key Personnel:** Dr. Donald Ault, Editor, Founder; Anastacia Ulanowicz, Associate Editor. **ISSN:** 1549--6732 (print). **Subscription Rates:** Free to qualified subscribers online. **URL:** http://www.english.ufl.edu/imagetext. **Circ:** (Not Reported).

7569 ■ The Independent Florida Alligator
Campus Communications Inc.
1105 W University Ave.
Gainesville, FL 32601
Collegiate newspaper. **Founded:** Oct. 1906. **Freq:** Weekly Mon.-Fri.(morn.) except during holidays & exam periods. **Print Method:** Offset. **Trim Size:** 11 x 14. **Cols./Page:** 5. **Col. Width:** 2 1/16 inches. **Col. Depth:** 13 inches. **Key Personnel:** Elizabeth Behrman, Editor; Shaun O'Connor, Director, Advertising. **ISSN:** 0015-3877 (print). **Subscription Rates:** $40 Individuals; $35 Individuals fall & spring; $10 Individuals summer. **URL:** http://www.alligator.org. **Formerly**: The University News,. **Mailing address:** PO Box 14257, Gainesville, FL 32601. **Ad Rates:** 4C $235; PCI $40.25. **Remarks:** Accepts advertising. **Circ:** Free ‡35000.

7570 ■ Journal of the American Society of Nephrology: Official Journal of the American Society of Nephrology
Lippincott Williams and Wilkins
3324 W University Ave.
PMB No. 269
Gainesville, FL 32607
Phone: (352)335-1100
Fax: (352)335-8100
Publisher's E-mail: ronna.ekhouse@wolterskluwer.com
Journal covering kidney functions and renal diseases. **Freq:** Monthly 2 issues in October. **Print Method:** Offset. **Trim Size:** 8 1/8 x 10 7/8. **Key Personnel:** Bonnie O'Brien, Managing Editor; Susan Quaggin, MD, Editor; Eric G. Neilson, MD, Editor-in-Chief. **ISSN:** 1046--6673 (print); **EISSN:** 1533--3450 (electronic). **Subscription Rates:** $2022 Nonmembers print and online - institution; $1842 Nonmembers online only - institution; $1908 Nonmembers print only - institution; $546 Individuals online only. **URL:** http://jasn.asnjournals.org. **Ad Rates:** BW $1,465; 4C $1,905. **Remarks:** Accepts advertising. **Circ:** 12596.

7571 ■ Journal of Family Issues
SAGE Publications Inc.
c/o Constance Shehan, Ed.
Dept. of Sociology, University of Florida
3219 Turlington Hall
Gainesville, FL 32611
Publication E-mail: advertising@sagepub.com
Family studies journal. **Founded:** 1980. **Freq:** 14/year. **Print Method:** Offset. **Trim Size:** 5 1/2 x 8 1/2. **Cols./Page:** 1. **Col. Width:** 50 nonpareils. **Col. Depth:** 100 agate lines. **Key Personnel:** Constance Shehan, Editor. **ISSN:** 0192-513X (print); **EISSN:** 1552-5481 (electronic). **Subscription Rates:** $1852 Individuals print & e-access; $2037 Institutions combined (print & e-access); $1667 Institutions e-access; $1852 Institutions backfile lease, combined plus backfile, print; $2468 Institutions e-access (content through 1998); $1815 Institutions print; $185 Individuals print only; $143 Institutions single print; $17 Individuals single print. **URL:** http://www.sagepub.com/journals/Journal200912. **Mailing address:** PO Box 117330, Gainesville, FL 32611. **Ad Rates:** BW $605; 4C $1080. **Remarks:** Accepts advertising. **Circ:** Paid ‡800.

7572 ■ Journal of Law and Public Policy
University of Florida College of Law Holland Law Center
309 Village Dr.
Gainesville, FL 32611
Phone: 352 273-0890
Fax: 352 392-4087
Publisher's E-mail: admissions@law.ufl.edu
Scholarly journal covering law and public policy. **Freq:** 3/year. **Print Method:** Hard Copy. **Key Personnel:** Stephanie Moncada, Editor-in-Chief. **ISSN:** 1047--8035 (print). **Subscription Rates:** $55 Individuals domestic; $60 Other countries. **URL:** http://www.ufjlpp.org. **Ad Rates:** BW $350. **Remarks:** Accepts advertising. **Circ:** Paid 225.

7573 ■ Journal of Medical Systems
Springer Netherlands
c/o Ralph R. Grams, Ed.-in-Ch.
Journal of Medical Systems
2025 NW 24th St.
Gainesville, FL 32605
Journal focusing on physicians' office administration and hospital systems. **Freq:** Bimonthly. **Print Method:** Letterpress. **Trim Size:** 7 x 10. **Cols./Page:** 1. **Col. Width:** 54 nonpareils. **Col. Depth:** 103 agate lines. **Key Personnel:** Ralph R. Grams, Founder, Editor. **ISSN:** 0148-5598 (print); **EISSN:** 1573-689X (electronic). **Subscription Rates:** €2046 Institutions print or online. **URL:** http://link.springer.com/journal/10916; http://www.springer.com/new+%26+forthcoming+titles+(default)/journal/10916. **Ad Rates:** 4C $1200; BW $1308. **Remarks:** Accepts advertising. **Circ:** (Not Reported).

7574 ■ Journal for the Study of Religion, Nature and Culture
Equinox Publishing Ltd.
PO Box 117410
Gainesville, FL 32611-7410
Phone: (352)392-1625
Fax: (352)392-7395
Publisher's E-mail: info@equinoxpub.com
Journal covering relationship between religion and ecology. **Freq:** Quarterly. **Key Personnel:** Bron Taylor, Editor. **ISSN:** 1749--4907 (print). **URL:** http://www.equinoxpub.com/index.php/JSRNC. **Remarks:** Accepts advertising. **Circ:** (Not Reported).

7575 ■ Polyhedron
RELX Group P.L.C.
c/o G. Christou, Editor
Department of Chemistry
University of Florida
Gainesville, FL 32611-7200
Publisher's E-mail: amsterdam@relx.com
Journal publishing fundamental, experimental and theoretical work in areas of inorganic chemistry. **Freq:** 18/yr. **Key Personnel:** G. Christou, Editor; C.E. Housecroft, Editor. **ISSN:** 0277--5387 (print). **Subscription Rates:** $4251.47 Institutions eJournal; $12757 Institutions print. **URL:** http://www.journals.elsevier.com/polyhedron. **Mailing address:** PO Box 117200, Gainesville, FL 32611-7200. **Circ:** (Not Reported).

7576 ■ Republican Liberty
Republican Liberty Caucus
2508 S.W. 35th Place No. 41
Gainesville, FL 32608
Phone: (904)378-1548
Fax: (904)337-9888
Free: 800-RLC-9660
Publication E-mail: afn14454@afn.org 76025.1244@compuserve.com
Magazine covering the libertarian Republican movement. Contains reviews, satire, letters, and articles. **Freq:** Bimonthly 6/year. **Trim Size:** 8-1/2 x 11. **Key Personnel:** Mike Holmes, Contact; Phil Blumel, Contact. **Subscription Rates:** $20 Individuals; Free for sample copy; included in membership dues. **Remarks:** Advertising not accepted. **Circ:** Paid 600, Non-paid 100.

7577 ■ Research in Human Development
Society for the Study of Human Development
c/o Monika Ardelt, Executive Secretary
University of Florida
PO Box 117330
Gainesville, FL 32611-7330
Publisher's E-mail: book.orders@tandf.co.uk
Journal seeks to promote a more inclusive, integrative, and interdisciplinary approach to the study of human development across the entire life span. **Freq:** Quarterly. **Key Personnel:** Jacquelynne S. Eccles, Board Member; Carolyn Aldwin, Editor. **ISSN:** 1542-7609 (print); **EISSN:** 1542- 7617 (electronic). **Subscription Rates:** $431 Institutions online; $493 Institutions print and online; $93 Individuals print and online; $432 Institutions online only; free for members. **URL:** http://www.tandfonline.com/toc/hrhd20/current#.VH6iPdKUflc; http://support.sshdonline.org/journal; http://www.tandfonline.com/toc/hrhd20/current. **Ad Rates:** BW $375. **Remarks:** Accepts advertising. **Circ:** (Not Reported).

7578 ■ Subtropics
University of Florida
Gainesville, FL 32611
Phone: (352)392-3261
Publisher's E-mail: webmaster@ufl.edu
Journal publishing best fiction, non-fiction and poetry. **Freq:** 3/yr. **Key Personnel:** David Leavitt, Editor; Mark Mitchell, Managing Editor. **ISSN:** 1559--0704 (print). **Subscription Rates:** $21 Individuals; $36 Two years; $36 Libraries and institution. **URL:** http://subtropics.english.ufl.edu. **Circ:** (Not Reported).

7579 ■ Surgery for Obesity and Related Diseases
American Society for Metabolic and Bariatric Surgery
100 SW 75th St., Ste. 201
Gainesville, FL 32607-5776
Phone: (352)331-4900
Fax: (352)331-4975
Journal publishing articles on the effects of surgically induced weight loss on obesity physiological, psychiatric and social co-morbidities. **Freq:** Bimonthly. **Print Method:** Web offset. **Trim Size:** 8 X 10 3/4. **Key Personnel:** Harvey J. Sugerman, Editor-in-Chief; Marc Bessler, MD, Board Member; Angelica Kerr, Managing Editor; Preston Carter, MD, Associate Editor. **ISSN:** 1550--7289 (print). **Subscription Rates:** $261 Individuals print and online ; $274 Other countries print and online. **URL:** http://www.soard.org; http://www.journals.elsevier.com/surgery-for-obesity-and-related-diseases/; http://asmbs.org/professional-education/soard. **Ad Rates:** BW $1340; 4C $1005. **Remarks:** Accepts advertising. **Circ:** ‡2305.

7580 ■ Tropical Lepidoptera Research
Association for Tropical Lepidoptera
PO Box 141210
Gainesville, FL 32614-1210
Fax: (352)373-3249
Publisher's E-mail: troplep@gmail.com
Peer-reviewed journal publishing scientific articles on tropical species lepidoptera. **Freq:** Semiannual. **ISSN:** 1941-7659 (print). **URL:** http://www.troplep.org/tl.htm. **Remarks:** Advertising not accepted. **Circ:** 1200.

7581 ■ University of Florida Journal of Law and Public Policy
University of Florida Fredric G. Levin College of Law
309 Village Dr.
Gainesville, FL 32611
Phone: (352)273-0890
Fax: (352)392-4087
Publisher's E-mail: admissions@law.ufl.edu
Journal fostering contemporary discourse on judicial decisions, legislation, law reform, and other legal and social issues facing public policy decision-makers. **Freq:**

Circulation: ★ = AAM; △ or • = BPA; ♦ = CAC; ❑ = VAC; ⊕ = PO Statement; ‡ = Publisher's Report; Boldface figures = sworn; Light figures = estimated.

3/year. **Key Personnel:** Amy Lee, Editor-in-Chief. **Subscription Rates:** $55 Individuals domestic; $60 Individuals international. **URL:** http://www.ufjlpp.org. **Mailing address:** PO Box 117621, Gainesville, FL 32611-7621. **Circ:** (Not Reported).

7582 ■ University of Florida Today Magazine: University of Florida Alumni Association Magazine
University of Florida Alumni Association
1938 W University Ave.
Gainesville, FL 32603
Phone: (352)392-1905
Fax: (352)846-3636
Free: 888-352-5866
Publisher's E-mail: ufalum@ufalumni.ufl.edu
Collegiate magazine for members of the alumni association. **Freq:** Quarterly. **Print Method:** DTP Web. **Trim Size:** 9 x 10 7/8. **Cols./Page:** 3. **Col. Width:** 27 nonpareils. **Col. Depth:** 126 agate lines. **Key Personnel:** Cinnamon Bair, Editor, phone: (352)846-2818. **Subscription Rates:** $ Included in membership. **Remarks:** Accepts advertising. **Circ:** Controlled ‡50000.

7583 ■ Utopian Studies
Society for Utopian Studies
c/o Dr. Phillip E. Wegner, Membership Chairman
Dept. of English
University of Florida
Gainesville, FL 32611-7310
Phone: (352)392-6650
Freq: Semiannual. **ISSN:** 1045--991X (print); **EISSN:** 2154--9648 (electronic). **Subscription Rates:** $51 Individuals print - 1 year; $102 Two years print; $50 Individuals online; $131 Institutions print - 1 year; $262 Institutions print - 2 years. **URL:** http://utopian-studies.org/journal; http://www.psupress.org/journals/jnls_utopian_studies.html. **Mailing address:** c/o Dr. Phillip E. Wegner, Membership ChairmanPO Box 117310, Gainesville, FL 32611-7310. **Remarks:** Accepts advertising. **Circ:** 370.

7584 ■ Cox Cable-University City
3218 SW 35th Blvd.
Gainesville, FL 32608
Phone: (904)377-1741
Fax: (904)378-2790
Owner: Cox Cable Communications, at above address, Ph: (404)843-5000, Fax: (401)828-3835. **Founded:** 1965. **URL:** http://www.cox.com.

7585 ■ 97.3 The SKY / WSKY - 97.3
3600 NW 43rd St., Ste. B
Gainesville, FL 32606
Phone: (352)377-0985
Format: News; Talk. **Owner:** Entercom Communications Corp., 401 City Ave., Ste. 809, Bala Cynwyd, PA 19004-1130, Ph: (610)660-5610, Fax: (610)660-5620. **Founded:** 1998. **Formerly:** WGGG-FM. **Operating Hours:** Continuous. **ADI:** Gainesville (Ocala), FL. **Key Personnel:** Shaun Buford, Gen. Mgr. **Wattage:** 50,000. **Ad Rates:** Advertising accepted; rates available upon request. **URL:** http://www.thesky973.com.

7586 ■ WBXY-FM - 99.5
4424 NW 13th St., Ste. C-5
Gainesville, FL 32609
Phone: (352)375-1317
Fax: (352)375-6961
Format: Adult Contemporary; Talk; News. **Owner:** Asterisk Communications Inc., at above address. **Key Personnel:** John Starr, Contact, sales@thestar.fm. **Ad Rates:** Advertising accepted; rates available upon request.

7587 ■ WCJB-TV - 20
6220 NW 43rd St.
Gainesville, FL 32653
Phone: (352)377-2020
Format: News; Sports. **Networks:** ABC; NBC. **Owner:** Diversified Broadcasting Inc., at above address. **Founded:** Apr. 07, 1971. **Operating Hours:** 6 a.m.-1:30 a.m. weekdays; 6 a.m.-2:30 a.m. Fri. and Sat. **ADI:** Gainesville (Ocala), FL. **Wattage:** 2,800,000. **Ad Rates:** Advertising accepted; rates available upon request. **URL:** http://www.wcjb.com.

7588 ■ WDVH-FM - 101.7
3135 SE 27th St.
Gainesville, FL 32641
Phone: (352)313-3150
Fax: (352)313-3166
Free: 888-974-4265
Format: Country. **Owner:** Pamal Broadcasting, Ltd., 715 Rte. 52, Beacon, NY 12508, Ph: (845)838-6000. **Key Personnel:** Ben Hill, Gen. Mgr.

WFVR-AM - See Valdosta, GA

7589 ■ WGFL-TV - 4
1703 NW 80th Blvd.
Gainesville, FL 32606
Phone: (352)332-1128
URL: http://www.mygtn.tv.

7590 ■ WGGG-AM
900 NW 8th Ave.
Gainesville, FL 32601
Phone: (352)732-2010
Format: News; Talk; Sports. **Networks:** Sun Radio; Mutual Broadcasting System; NBC. **Founded:** 1947. **Key Personnel:** Mike Jurian, Contact. **Wattage:** 1,000. **Ad Rates:** $15-60 per unit. **URL:** http://www.floridasportstalk.fm/.

7591 ■ WGOT-FM - 94.7
PO Box 14012
Gainesville, FL 32604
Phone: (352)519-4680
Email: info@wgot.org
Format: Eclectic; Talk. **URL:** http://www.wgot.org.

7592 ■ WHHZ-FM - 100.5
100 NW 76th Dr., Ste. 2
Gainesville, FL 32607
Phone: (352)313-3150
Fax: (352)313-3166
Format: Country. **Operating Hours:** Continuous. **Key Personnel:** Kevin McKay, Prog. Dir., kevin.mangan@marcradio.com. **Wattage:** 44,000 ERP. **Ad Rates:** Advertising accepted; rates available upon request. **URL:** http://www.1005thebuzz.com.

7593 ■ WJUF-FM - 90
PO Box 118405
Gainesville, FL 32611
Phone: (352)392-5200
Fax: (352)392-5741
Format: Classical; Public Radio. **Founded:** 1981. **Ad Rates:** Advertising accepted; rates available upon request. **URL:** http://www.wuftfm.org.

7594 ■ WKTK-FM - 98.5
3600 NW 43rd St., Ste. B
Gainesville, FL 32606-8127
Phone: (352)377-0985
Fax: (352)377-1884
Free: 800-882-7798
Format: Adult Contemporary. **Owner:** Entercom Gainesville, LLC, at above address, Bala Cynwyd, PA. **Founded:** Apr. 01, 1986. **Formerly:** WRYO-FM. **Operating Hours:** Continuous. **ADI:** Gainesville (Ocala), FL. **Wattage:** 100,000. **Ad Rates:** Advertising accepted; rates available upon request. **URL:** http://www.ktk985.com.

7595 ■ WKZY-FM - 106.9
100 NW 76th Dr., Ste. 2
Gainesville, FL 32607
Phone: (352)313-3150
Fax: (352)313-3199
Format: Adult Contemporary. **Key Personnel:** Matt Derrick, Dir. of Programs, mderrick@sunshinebroadcasting.com; Kevin Mckay, Music Dir., kmangan@sunshinebroadcasting.com; Tom Machnik, Sales Mgr., tmachnik@sunshinebroadcasting.com. **Wattage:** 100,000. **Ad Rates:** Noncommercial. **URL:** http://www.1069thepulse.com.

7596 ■ WLUS-AM - 980
100 NW 76th Dr., Ste. 2
Gainesville, FL 32607
Phone: (321)377-2882
Format: Middle-of-the-Road (MOR); Talk; Contemporary Hit Radio (CHR). **Networks:** ABC; Precision Racing; AP. **Owner:** Radio Disney, 500 S Buena Vista St. MC 7663, Burbank, CA 91521-7716; Pamal, 6 Johnson Rd., Latham, NY 12110, Ph: (518)786-6600. **Founded:** 1954. **Formerly:** WDVH-AM; WMGI-AM. **Operating Hours:** Continuous. **ADI:** Gainesville (Ocala), FL. **Key Personnel:** Karl Kaufmann, Gen. Sales Mgr.; Wayne Irwin, Chief Engineer; Jim Brand, Dir. of Programs; Douglas Gillen, President; Jeri Banta, Dir. of Programs. **Wattage:** 5,000/nite 166 watts. **Ad Rates:** Advertising accepted; rates available upon request. $18-21 for 30 seconds; $24-28 for 60 seconds. Combined advertising rates available with WDJY-FM. **URL:** http://www.iamcountryradio.com.

7597 ■ WRUF-AM - 850
1885 Stadium Rd., University of Florida
Gainesville, FL 32604
Phone: (352)392-8255
Free: 877-392-8255
Format: News; Sports. **Owner:** University of Florida, Gainesville, FL 32611, Ph: (352)392-3261. **Founded:** 1928. **ADI:** Gainesville (Ocala), FL. **Key Personnel:** Steve Russell, Sports Dir. **Wattage:** 5,000. **Ad Rates:** Combined advertising rates available with WRUF-FM. **Mailing address:** PO Box 118405, Gainesville, FL 32611. **URL:** http://www.wruf.com/the-larry-vettel-show.

7598 ■ WRUF-FM - 103.7
PO Box 14444
Gainesville, FL 32604-2444
Phone: (352)392-5551
Fax: (352)392-0519
Format: Sports; News; Country. **Networks:** ESPN Radio. **Owner:** Alan Gray, at above address; University of Florida, Gainesville, FL 32611, Ph: (352)392-3261. **Founded:** 1948. **Operating Hours:** Continuous. **ADI:** Gainesville (Ocala), FL. **Local Programs:** *Breaking and Entering*; *The 90's at Noon.* **Wattage:** 100,000 ERP. **Ad Rates:** Accepts Advertising. **URL:** http://1037thegator.com.

7599 ■ WTMG-FM - 101.3
100 NW 76th Dr., Ste. 2
Gainesville, FL 32607
Phone: (352)313-3101
Fax: (352)313-3166
Email: acarter@magic1013.com
Format: Blues. **Ad Rates:** Advertising accepted; rates available upon request. **URL:** http://www.magic1013.com.

7600 ■ WUFT-FM - 89
PO Box 118405
Gainesville, FL 32611
Fax: (352)392-5741
Format: Public Radio. **Simulcasts:** WJUF-FM. **Networks:** National Public Radio (NPR); American Public Radio (APR). **Owner:** University of Florida, Gainesville, FL 32611, Ph: (352)392-3261. **Founded:** 1981. **Operating Hours:** Continuous; 40% network, 60% local. **Key Personnel:** Larry Dankner, Contact, ldankner@wruf.com; Richard Drake, Contact, rdrake@wuft.org; Tom Krynski, Contact, tkrynski@wruf.com; Larry Dankner, Contact, ldankner@wruf.com; Richard Drake, Contact, rdrake@wuft.org; Tom Krynski, Contact, tkrynski@wruf.com; Forrest Smith, Contact, dschermer@wuft.org; Melanie Perry, Contact, mperry@wuft.org; Tim Kinney, Contact, tkinney@wuft.org. **Local Programs:** *Conner Calling*, Friday 1:00 p.m. - 2:00 p.m.; *Only A Game*, Saturday 7:00 a.m.; 7:00 p.m.; *Sikorski's Attic.* **Wattage:** 100,000. **Ad Rates:** Noncommercial. **URL:** http://www.wuftfm.org.

7601 ■ WUFT-TV - 5
1200 Weimer Hall
Gainesville, FL 32611
Phone: (352)392-5551
Fax: (352)392-5731
Format: News. **Networks:** Public Broadcasting Service (PBS). **Owner:** University of Florida, Gainesville, FL 32611, Ph: (352)392-3261. **Founded:** 1958. **Operating Hours:** Continuous. **ADI:** Gainesville (Ocala), FL. **Key Personnel:** Mark Leeps, News Dir., mleeps@wuft.org. **Wattage:** 100,000. **Ad Rates:** Noncommercial. **Mailing address:** PO Box 118405, Gainesville, FL 32611. **URL:** http://www.wuft.org.

7602 ■ WXJZ-FM - 100.9
4424 NW 13th St., Ste. C-5
Gainesville, FL 32609
Phone: (352)375-1317
Fax: (352)375-6961
Format: Jazz; News. **Owner:** Asterisk Communications Inc., 2848 E Oakland Park Blvd., Fort Lauderdale, FL 33306. **Operating Hours:** Continuous. **Key Personnel:** John Starr, Contact, johnstarr@wxjz.fm. **Ad Rates:** Advertising accepted; rates available upon request.

7603 ■ WYFB-FM - 90.5
11530 Carmel Commons Blvd.
Charlotte, NC 28226
Phone: (704)523-5555
Free: 800-888-7077
Email: bbn@bbnmedia.org
Format: Religious. **Networks:** Bible Broadcasting; AP. **Owner:** Bible Broadcasting Network Inc., 11530 Carmel Commons Blvd., Charlotte, NC 28226, Ph: (704)523-5555, Free: 800-888-7077. **Founded:** 1985. **Operating Hours**: Continuous; 90% network, 10% local. **Wattage**: 100,000. **Ad Rates:** Noncommercial. **URL:** http://www.bbnradio.org.

7604 ■ WYKS-FM - 105.3
7120 SW 24th Ave.
Gainesville, FL 32607
Phone: (352)331-2200
Fax: (352)331-0401
Free: 800-330-1053
Format: Contemporary Hit Radio (CHR); Top 40. **Networks:** AP. **Founded:** 1970. **Operating Hours**: Continuous. **ADI**: Gainesville (Ocala), FL. **Key Personnel:** Doug Gillen, Gen. Mgr., doug@kiss1053.com; Ryan Dupree, Dir. of Production, ryan@kiss1053.com; Christian Chase, Gen. Mgr. of Sales & Mktg., christian@kiss1053.com. **Wattage**: 3,000. **Ad Rates:** $15-40 for 30 seconds. **URL:** http://www.kiss1053.com.

GAINSVILLE

7605 ■ Paleobiology
Paleontological Society
Florida Museum of Natural History
Dickinson Hall
University of Florida
Gainsville, FL 32611-7800
Publication E-mail: paleobiology@flmnh.ufl.edu
Freq: Quarterly. **Key Personnel:** Bruce MacFadden, Editor; Douglas Jones, Editor, phone: (352)273-1902; Jonathan Bloch, Editor, phone: (352)273-1938. **ISSN:** 0094-8373 (print). **Subscription Rates:** $55 Members regular - electonic only; $50 Members retired - electonic only; $30 Members student and spouse of member - electonic only; $200 Institutions; $75 Members Regular - print only; $65 Members retired - print only; $8.50 Members back issue; $16 Nonmembers back issue; included in membership dues. **URL:** http://www.paleosoc.org/paleobio.htm; http://www.psjournals.org. **Mailing address:** PO Box 117800, Gainsville, FL 32611-7800. **Ad Rates:** BW $500, full page; BW $250, half page. **Remarks:** Accepts advertising. **Circ:** 2100.

GOLDENROD

7606 ■ Florida Specifier
National Technical Communications Company Inc.
PO Box 2175
Goldenrod, FL 32733
Phone: (407)671-7777
Fax: (407)671-7757
Free: 800-881-6822
Publisher's E-mail: info@enviro-net.com
Tabloid on environmental aspects in Florida. **Freq:** Monthly. **Print Method:** Offset. **Trim Size:** 11 1/4 x 17. **Cols./Page:** 4. **Col. Width:** 27 nonpareils. **Col. Depth:** 224 agate lines. **Key Personnel:** Mike Eastman, Editor. **ISSN:** 0740--1973 (print). **Subscription Rates:** $24.95 Individuals. **URL:** http://enviro-net.com/about-us/florida-specifier. **Remarks:** Accepts advertising. **Circ:** Controlled 10500.

GOULDS

7607 ■ WRTO-FM
Miami, FL
Phone: (305)445-4040
Format: Adult Contemporary. **Networks:** UPI. **Founded:** 1986. **Wattage**: 100,000 ERP. **Ad Rates:** $125 for 30 seconds; $150 for 60 seconds.

GRACEVILLE

NW FL. Jackson Co. 20 mi. S. of Dothan, AL. Lumber mills, cotton ginning. Agriculture. Cotton, watermelons, peanuts.

7608 ■ The Graceville News
The Graceville News
PO Box 187
Graceville, FL 32440
Phone: (904)263-6015
Fax: (904)263-1042
Publisher's E-mail: gvnews@wfeca.net
Community newspaper. **Freq:** Weekly (Thurs.). **Print Method:** Offset. **Cols./Page:** 6. **Col. Width:** 24 nonpareils. **Col. Depth:** 126 agate lines. **Key Personnel:** Ferrin Cox, Publisher; Sharon Taylor, Editor. **Subscription Rates:** $16 Individuals; $14 senior citizens. **Ad Rates:** SAU $2.67. **Remarks:** Accepts advertising. **Circ:** ‡1750.

7609 ■ WFBU-FM - 94.7
5400 College Dr.
Graceville, FL 32440
Phone: (850)263-9328
Format: Religious; Contemporary Christian. **Owner:** The Baptist College of Florida, at above address. **Operating Hours**: 6 a.m. to 7:55 p.m. Mon.-Fri.;7 a.m to 11:55 a.m. Sat. **Wattage**: 100. **Ad Rates:** Noncommercial. **URL:** http://www.wfbu.com.

GREEN COVE SPRINGS

NE FL. Clay Co. On St. Johns River, 26 mi. S. of Jacksonville. Health resort. Commercial and sport fishing.

7610 ■ WAYR-AM - 550
2500 Russell Rd.
Green Cove Springs, FL 32043
Phone: (904)272-1111
Fax: (904)284-2501
Free: 866-353-9297
Format: Religious. **Networks:** Voice of Christian Youth America. **Owner:** Good Tidings Trust, Inc., at above address. **Founded:** 1960. **Operating Hours**: Continuous; 10% network, 90% local. **ADI**: Jacksonville (Brunswick), FL. **Wattage**: 5,000 Day; 500 Night. **Ad Rates:** Noncommercial. **URL:** http://www.550.wayradio.org.

7611 ■ WAYR-FM - 90.7
2500 Russell Rd.
Green Cove Springs, FL 32043
Format: Religious. **Founded:** Sept. 07, 2006. **URL:** http://www.wayradio.org/.

7612 ■ WJBT-FM - 92.7
2405 E Moody Blvd., Ste. 402
Bunnell, FL 32110
Phone: (386)437-1992
Fax: (386)437-8728
Networks: CBS. **Founded:** 1978. **Key Personnel:** Bruce Demps, Gen. Mgr., VP; Nate Bell, Dir. of Programs. **Wattage**: 5,300 ERP. **Ad Rates:** Accepts Advertising. **URL:** http://www.flaglerbroadcasting.com.

GRETNA

7613 ■ WGWD-FM - 93.3
100A N Madison
Quincy, FL 32351
Phone: (904)627-7086
Fax: (904)627-3422
Format: Country. **Founded:** 1989. **Operating Hours**: Continuous. **ADI**: Tampa-St. Petersburg (Lakeland, Sarasota), FL. **Key Personnel:** Tony Woods, Dir. of Programs; Monte Bitner, Contact, monbit@aol.com. **Wattage**: 25,000. **Ad Rates:** $12.50-17.50 for 60 seconds. **Mailing address:** PO Box 919, Quincy, FL 32351.

GULF BREEZE

NW FL. Santa Rosa Co. On Gulf of Mexico, 3 mi. S. of Pensacola.

7614 ■ Russia & Eurasia Military Review Annual
Academic International Press
PO Box 1111
Gulf Breeze, FL 32562-1111
Phone: (850)932-5479
Fax: (850)934-0953
Publisher's E-mail: info@ai-press.com
Professional publication covering military developments in Russia and other former Soviet Union states. **Freq:** Annual. **Trim Size:** 6 x 9. **Key Personnel:** Theodore Karasik, Editor. **Subscription Rates:** $80 Individuals subscription; $100 Individuals non-subscription. **URL:** http://www.ai-press.com/SAFRA.html. **Remarks:** Advertising not accepted. **Circ:** (Not Reported).

7615 ■ WPAN-TV - 53
155 Middle Plantation Ln.
Gulf Breeze, FL 32561
Phone: (904)243-0000
Format: Commercial TV. **Networks:** Independent. **Owner:** John Franklin Ministries Inc., 3950 Hwy. 98W, Navarre, FL 32566. **Key Personnel:** John L. Franklin, Gen. Mgr. **Wattage**: 33,500 ERP.

7616 ■ W205AS-FM - 88.9
PO Box 391
Twin Falls, ID 83303
Fax: (208)736-1958
Free: 800-357-4226
Format: Religious; Contemporary Christian. **Owner:** CSN International, PO Box 391, Twin Falls, ID 83303, Ph: (208)736-1958, Fax: (208)736-1958, Free: 800-357-4226. **URL:** http://www.csnradio.com.

GULFPORT

WC FL. Pinellas Co. Directly W. of St. Petersburg.

7617 ■ Journal for International Aging Law and Policy
Stetson University College of Law
1401 61st St. S
Gulfport, FL 33707
Phone: (727)562-7802
Fax: (727)343-0136
Publisher's E-mail: lawadmit@law.stetson.edu
Journal addressing a wide range of topics involving the elderly, both domestically and internationally. **Freq:** Semiannual. **Key Personnel:** Caitlein J. Jammo, Editor-in-Chief. **URL:** http://www.stetson.edu/law/agingjournal. **Circ:** (Not Reported).

7618 ■ Journal for International Wildlife Law and Policy
Stetson University College of Law
1401 61st St. S
Gulfport, FL 33707
Phone: (727)562-7802
Fax: (727)343-0136
Publisher's E-mail: lawadmit@law.stetson.edu
Journal covering articles related to wildlife law and policy. **Freq:** Quarterly. **Key Personnel:** Jessica Beaulieu, Editor. **ISSN:** 1388--0292 (print); **EISSN:** 1548--1476 (electronic). **Subscription Rates:** $185 Individuals print ; $324 Individuals online; $370 Individuals print and online. **URL:** http://www.tandfonline.com/toc/uwlp20/current#.Ve_pt9Kqqkp. **Circ:** (Not Reported).

HAINES CITY

C FL. Polk Co. 20 mi. NE of Lakeland. Citrus fruit canning and packing. Fruit, truck, stock farms.

7619 ■ WLVF-FM - 90.3
810 E Hinson Ave.
Haines City, FL 33844
Phone: (863)422-5175
Fax: (863)422-0110
Free: 888-422-9583
Format: Gospel. **Networks:** USA Radio. **Owner:** Landmark Baptist Church, 2020 Hinson Ave., Haines City, FL 33844, Ph: (941)422-2037, Fax: (941)422-8290. **Founded:** 1986. **Operating Hours**: Continuous. **Key Personnel:** Lewis Cruz, Station Mgr., lewis@gospel903.com; Bobby Ogden, Contact. **Local Programs**: *The Peoples Gospel Hour*, Sunday 4:00 p.m. - 4:30 p.m. **Wattage**: 1,200. **Ad Rates:** Noncommercial. **URL:** http://www.gospel903.org.

HALLANDALE BEACH

7620 ■ WIMX-FM
134 S Dixie Hwy., Ste. 206
Hallandale Beach, FL 33009
Phone: (305)935-0002
Format: Urban Contemporary. **Owner:** Urban Radio Broadcasting, LLC, 134 S Dixie Hwy., Ste. 206, Hallandale Beach, FL 33009, Ph: (786)787-0404, Fax: (786)787-0405. **Wattage**: 3,500 ERP. **Ad Rates:** Advertising accepted; rates available upon request.

Circulation: ★ = AAM; △ or • = BPA; ♦ = CAC; ❑ = VAC; ⊕ = PO Statement; ‡ = Publisher's Report; Boldface figures = sworn; Light figures = estimated.

HERNANDO

7621 ■ WRZN-AM - 720
3988 N Roscoe Rd.
Hernando, FL 34442
Phone: (352)726-7221
Fax: (352)726-3172
Format: Adult Contemporary. **Networks:** Satellite Music Network. **Owner:** Pamal Broadcasting, Ltd., 715 Rte. 52, Beacon, NY 12508, Ph: (845)838-6000. **Founded:** 1989. **Operating Hours:** 6 a.m.-12 midnight. **ADI:** Gainesville (Ocala), FL. **Key Personnel:** Ben Hill, Gen. Mgr.; Jim Brand, Dir. of Programs. **Wattage:** 10,000 Day; 250 Night. **Ad Rates:** Noncommercial.

HIALEAH

S FL. Dade Co. On Miami Canal, 7 mi. NW of Miami. Hialeah Park Race Track. Manufactures furniture, chemicals, machinery, glass, textiles, aluminum, concrete, paper, food, leather, electronic products, boats, plastics.

7622 ■ Oscar Aguero Ministry Inc.
6050 West 20th Ave.
Hialeah, FL 33016
Phone: (305)826-5555
Fax: (305)819-9896
Free: 888-848-4455
URL: http://www.oscaragueroministry.com.

7623 ■ WRFM-AM - 830
8080 W Flagler St., Ste. 3-E
Miami, FL 33144
Phone: (305)264-1100
Fax: (305)266-9919
Format: Ethnic; Hispanic; Sports; News; Talk. **Networks:** CBS. **Owner:** Interamerican Broadcasting, Inc., at above address. **Founded:** 1987. **Operating Hours:** Continuous. **ADI:** Miami (Ft. Lauderdale), FL. **Key Personnel:** Adib Eden, Jr., Gen. Mgr., President; Elisabeth Eden, Music Dir.; Alberto Sabina, VP of Mktg. **Wattage:** 1,000. **Ad Rates:** $20-35 for 15 seconds; $35-50 for 30 seconds; $45-75 for 60 seconds.

HIALEAH GARDENS

7624 ■ WJWN-TV - 38
13001 NW107th Ave.
Hialeah Gardens, FL 33018-1104
Phone: (809)765-1810
Format: Commercial TV. **Networks:** Independent. **Founded:** 1987. **Key Personnel:** Haydee Diaz, Contact. **Wattage:** 700,000 ERP.

7625 ■ WKPV-TV - 20
13001 NW107th Ave.
Hialeah Gardens, FL 33018-1104
Phone: (809)767-8055
Format: Commercial TV. **Networks:** Independent. **Owner:** Multi-Media Television, at above address. **Founded:** 1985. **Wattage:** 700,000 ERP.

HIGH SPRINGS

N FL. Alachua Co. On Santa Fe River, 22 mi. NW of Gainesville. Manufactures plastic pipe, transformers, air compressors. Phosphate mine. Tobacco, watermelons, peanuts.

7626 ■ Communicomm Services
17774 NW US Hwy. 441
High Springs, FL 32643
Free: 800-881-9740
Owner: James Cable L.L.C., 38710 Woodward Ave., Ste. 180, Bloomfield Hills, MI 48304-5073, Ph: (248)647-1080. **Formerly:** Cable Florida. **Cities Served:** Alachua, Branford, Chiefland, Cross City, Hawthorne, High Springs, McIntosh, Micanopy, Orange Lake, Reddick, Steinhatchee, Florida: subscribing households 6,800; Municipal/Marion County.; 50 channels; 1 community access channel; 168 hours per week community access programming. **URL:** http://www.netcommander.com/.

HOBE SOUND

7627 ■ VASCULAR
International Society for Vascular Surgery
10062 SE Osprey Point Dr.
Hobe Sound, FL 33455
Phone: (631)993-4321
Publisher's E-mail: isvs@isvs.com
Freq: Bimonthly. **Key Personnel:** Kenneth Ouriel, MD, Editor-in-Chief. **Subscription Rates:** Included in membership. **URL:** http://www.isvs.com/Journal.aspx. **Remarks:** Accepts advertising. **Circ:** (Not Reported).

HOLLISTER

7628 ■ WIYD-AM - 1260
PO Box 913
Hollister, FL 32147
Phone: (386)325-5177
Format: Country; Contemporary Country. **Networks:** ABC; Florida Radio; Motor Racing. **Owner:** Hall Broadcasting Co., at above address. **Founded:** 1947. **Formerly:** WWPF-AM. **Operating Hours:** Continuous. **Wattage:** 1,000. **Ad Rates:** $8-10 for 30 seconds; $10-15 for 60 seconds.

HOLLY HILL

E FL. Volusia Co. 2 mi. N. of Daytona Beach.

7629 ■ Grassroots Motorsports: The Hardcore Sports Car Magazine
Motorsport Marketing Inc.
915 Ridgewood Ave.
Holly Hill, FL 32117
Phone: (386)239-0523
Fax: (386)239-0573
Free: 888-676-9747
Magazine covering the entire world of amateur motorsports, from autocrossing to rallying and racing. **Freq:** 8/yr. **Key Personnel:** Tim Suddard, Publisher; Marjorie Suddard, General Manager; David S. Wallens, Director, Editorial. **Subscription Rates:** $10 U.S. 6 months; $19.99 U.S. 1 year; $14 Canada 6 months; $27.99 Canada 1 year; $26 Other countries 6 months; $51.99 Other countries 1 year. **URL:** http://grassrootsmotorsports.com. **Ad Rates:** BW $1,700. **Remarks:** Accepts advertising. **Circ:** (Not Reported).

7630 ■ WAPN-FM - 91.5
1508 State Ave.
Holly Hill, FL 32117
Phone: (386)677-4272
Fax: (386)677-7095
Email: wapn@wapn.net
Format: Religious. **Owner:** Public Radio Inc., at above address. **Founded:** 1985. **Operating Hours:** Continuous. **ADI:** Orlando-Daytona Beach-Melbourne, FL. **Key Personnel:** Machelle L. Vallance, Prog. Dir., machelle@wapn.net. **Wattage:** 1,800. **Ad Rates:** Noncommercial. **URL:** http://www.wapn.net.

HOLLYWOOD

S FL. Broward Co. On Atlantic Ocean and Intracoastal Waterway, 20 mi. N. of Miami. Resort. Race tracks. Boating and water skiing. Manufactures concrete blocks, furniture, electronic equipment, game equipment, aluminum castings, plastics, jewelry, boats.

7631 ■ Community News
Community News Publishing Co.
6836 Stirling Rd.
Hollywood, FL 33024
Phone: (954)963-4000
Fax: (954)964-2000
Community newspaper (tabloid). **Founded:** 1921. **Freq:** Weekly (Wed.). **Print Method:** Offset. **Trim Size:** 10 1/8 x 16. **Cols./Page:** 5 and 6. **Col. Width:** 1 7/8 inches and 20 9.5 nonpareils picas. **Col. Depth:** 16 and 224 16 inches. **Key Personnel:** Roger Clark, Publisher; Victor R. Ketchman, Publisher; C.R. Bockskopf, Editor; R.J. Huneke, Jr., Publisher. **Subscription Rates:** $104 Free to qualified subscribers; $104 By mail; Free; $65 Individuals. **Ad Rates:** PCI $30; GLR $2; BW $838.50; PCI $6.50. **Remarks:** Accepts advertising. **Circ:** Free ‡30000.

7632 ■ Journal of the American Academy of Business, Cambridge
American Academy of Business, Cambridge
6051 N Ocean Dr., No. 506
Hollywood, FL 33019
Fax: (866)724-9117
Publisher's E-mail: drsenguder@aol.com
Journal that publishes papers of business academicians and business professionals in a varied business disciplines. **Freq:** Semiannual. **Key Personnel:** Dr. Stewart L. Tubbs, Advisor. **ISSN:** 1540--7780 (print). **Subscription Rates:** $382 U.S.; $396 Other countries. **URL:** http://www.jaabc.com/journal.htm. **Remarks:** Advertising not accepted. **Circ:** (Not Reported).

7633 ■ Journal of Forensic Identification
International Association for Identification
2131 Hollywood Blvd., Ste. 403
Hollywood, FL 33020
Phone: (954)589-0628
Fax: (954)589-0657
Journal covering forensic identification. **Freq:** Quarterly. **Key Personnel:** Alan McRoberts, Editor, phone: (909)587-8337, fax: (909)587-8347. **ISSN:** 0895--173X (print). **Subscription Rates:** $175 Individuals North America; $205 Institutions library, North America; $235 Institutions outside North America; Included in membership. **URL:** http://www.theiai.org/publications/jfi.php; http://www.theiai.org/publications. **Remarks:** Advertising not accepted. **Circ:** 7000.

7634 ■ Labmedica
GLOBETECH Publishing Inc.
450 N Park Rd.
Unit 503
Hollywood, FL 33021
Phone: (954)893-0003
Fax: (954)893-0038
Publisher's E-mail: info@globetech.net
Professional magazine for managers of all kinds of laboratories. **Freq:** Bimonthly. **Trim Size:** 11 x 15 3/4. **Cols./Page:** 4. **Col. Width:** 244 INS. **Col. Depth:** 14 1/2 INS. **Subscription Rates:** Included in membership. **URL:** http://www.labmedica.com. **Ad Rates:** BW $4,750; 4C $6,350. **Remarks:** Accepts advertising. **Circ:** Combined △**24000**.

7635 ■ Le Soleil de la Floride: Florida's Unique French Newspaper
Worldwide Publications No. 1 Inc.
2117 Hollywood Blvd.
Hollywood, FL 33020
Phone: (954)922-1800
Newspaper (tabloid) featuring Florida attractions for vacationing Canadians (French). **Freq:** Monthly. **Print Method:** Offset. **Cols./Page:** 7. **Col. Width:** 1 5/16 inches. **Col. Depth:** 11 1/4 inches. **Key Personnel:** Yves Beauchamp, Editor; Denyse Chartrand, Associate Editor, Executive Vice President; Barry Sacharow, Editor. **ISSN:** 0835--1805 (print). **Subscription Rates:** Free. **URL:** http://www.lesoleildelafloride.com/index.php/fr. **Ad Rates:** GLR $1.60; BW $1,000; 4C $1,500; PCI $22.40. **Remarks:** 1.60. **Circ:** Free 350000, Controlled 150000.

7636 ■ Life Extension
Life Extension Foundation
c/o Burton and Co.
3107 Stirling Rd., Ste. 105
Hollywood, FL 33021
Phone: (954)766-8433
Fax: (954)761-9199
Free: 800-544-4440
Publisher's E-mail: customerservice@lifeextension.com
Magazine focusing on health, wellness and nutrition. Also providing scientific information on anti-aging therapies. **Freq:** Monthly. **Print Method:** Web Offset. **Trim Size:** 8.375 x 10.875. **Key Personnel:** Jason W. Morrison, Contact. **Subscription Rates:** Free. **URL:** http://www.lifeextension.com/Magazine/2016. **Ad Rates:** 4C $7500. **Remarks:** Accepts advertising. **Circ:** 320000.

7637 ■ Mergers & Acquisitions: The Dealmaker's Journal
Association for Corporate Growth South Florida
414 S 57 Ave.
Hollywood, FL 33081
Phone: (561)682-1637
Publisher's E-mail: sdp@tfn.com
Financial magazine containing data, reports and roundtable discussions on the M&A field, and articles covering international and "leading edge" issues. **Freq:** Bimonthly. **Print Method:** Offset. **Trim Size:** 11 1/4 x 15. **Cols./Page:** 3 and 2. **Col. Width:** 26 and 42 nonpareils. **Col. Depth:** 136 agate lines. **Key Personnel:** Mary Kathleen Flynn, Editor-in-Chief. **ISSN:** 0026-0010 (print). **Subscription Rates:** $995 Individuals print and online. **Available online. URL:** http://www.themiddlemarket.com. **Ad Rates:** BW $6395; 4C $7993; PCI $175. **Remarks:** Accepts advertising. **Circ:** ‡30,500.

7638 ■ Phi Delta Epsilon News and Scientific Journal
Phi Delta Epsilon International Medical Fraternity
1005 N Northlake Dr.
Hollywood, FL 33019
Phone: (786)302-1120
Fax: (786)472-7133
Publisher's E-mail: phide@phide.org
Journal containing information and insights about the area of Medicine, its branches, and how it affects the people and the society. **Freq:** Quarterly. **Subscription Rates:** Included in membership. **Remarks:** Advertising not accepted. **Circ:** (Not Reported).

7639 ■ PlantFinder
Betrock Information Systems Inc.
7770 Davie Rd. Ext.
Hollywood, FL 33024
Phone: (954)981-2821
Fax: (954)981-2823
Free: 800-627-3819
Publisher's E-mail: betrock@betrock.com
Trade magazine for the nursery industry. **Freq:** Monthly. **Print Method:** Offset. **Trim Size:** 5 1/2 x 8 1/2. **Cols./Page:** 2. **Key Personnel:** Irv Betrock, President, Publisher. **Subscription Rates:** $20 Single issue; $60 Single issue international; $89.95 Individuals. **URL:** http://www.plantfinder.com. **Ad Rates:** GLR $2.50; BW $1,050; 4C $2,000. **Remarks:** Advertising accepted; rates available upon request. **Circ:** Paid ‡4500, Non-paid ‡12350.

7640 ■ Retail Environment
Association for Retail Environments
4651 Sheridan St., Ste. 470
Hollywood, FL 33021
Phone: (954)893-7300
Fax: (954)893-7500
Publisher's E-mail: are@retailenvironments.org
Freq: Bimonthly. **Subscription Rates:** free for members. **URL:** http://www.retailenvironments.org/retail-environments-magazine-2/; http://www.retailenvironments-digital.org/retailenvironments/. **Remarks:** Accepts advertising. **Circ:** (Not Reported).

7641 ■ Seminole Tribune
Seminole Tribune
6300 Stirling Rd.
Hollywood, FL 33024
Phone: (954)966-6300
Free: 800-683-7800
Community newspaper. **Freq:** Biweekly. **ISSN:** 0891--8252 (print). **Subscription Rates:** $35 Individuals 1 year. **URL:** http://www.semtribe.com/SeminoleTribune/AboutUs.aspx. **Circ:** 4000.

7642 ■ Welding and Gases Today
Gases and Welding Distributors Association
1 Oakwood Blvd., Ste. 195
Hollywood, FL 33020
Phone: (954)367-7728
Fax: (954)367-7790
Free: 844-251-3219
Publisher's E-mail: gawda@gawda.org
Freq: Quarterly. **Subscription Rates:** included in membership dues; $195 /year for nonmembers. **URL:** http://www.weldingandgasestoday.org. **Remarks:** Advertising not accepted. **Circ:** (Not Reported).

7643 ■ WEDR-FM - 99.1
2741 N 29th Ave.
Hollywood, FL 33020
Phone: (305)444-4404
Format: Urban Contemporary; Adult Contemporary. **Networks:** Independent. **Owner:** Cox Radio Inc., 6205 Peachtree Dunwood Rd., Atlanta, GA 30328-4524, Ph: (678)645-0000, Fax: (678)645-5002. **Founded:** 1963. **Operating Hours**: Continuous. **ADI**: Miami (Ft. Lauderdale), FL. **Key Personnel:** Derrick Baker, Dir. of Programs, derrick.baker@coxmg.com. **Wattage**: 70,000. **Ad Rates:** Advertising accepted; rates available upon request. **URL:** http://www.wedr.com.

7644 ■ WFLC-FM - 97.3
2741 N 29th Ave.
Hollywood, FL 33020
Phone: (305)444-4404
Fax: (954)847-3201
Free: 866-227-9730
Format: Adult Contemporary. **Networks:** Independent. **Owner:** Cox Radio Inc., 6205 Peachtree Dunwood Rd., Atlanta, GA 30328-4524, Ph: (678)645-0000, Fax: (678)645-5002. **Founded:** 1963. **Formerly**: WAIA-FM; WGTR-FM. **Operating Hours**: Continuous; 100% local. **ADI**: Miami (Ft. Lauderdale), FL. **Wattage**: 100,000. **Ad Rates:** $200-300 per unit. **URL:** http://www.hits973.com.

7645 ■ WHDR-FM - 93.1
2741 N 29th Ave.
Hollywood, FL 33020
Phone: (305)444-4404
Format: Album-Oriented Rock (AOR). **Owner:** Cox Radio, 1611 S Main St., Dayton, OH 45409, Free: 888-802-6964. **Operating Hours**: Continuous. **Key Personnel:** Marc Telsey, Gen. Sales Mgr., marc.telsey@coxradio.com; Kevin Vargas, Dir. of Programs, kevin.vargas@coxradio.com; Derick Pitts, Mgr., derick.pitts@coxradio.com; Ryan Sherwin, Promotions Mgr., ryan.sherwin@coxradio.com. **Ad Rates:** Advertising accepted; rates available upon request.

7646 ■ WHQT-FM - 105.1
2741 N 29th Ave.
Hollywood, FL 33020
Phone: (305)444-4404
Fax: (954)584-7117
Format: Adult Contemporary. **Key Personnel:** Jerry Rushin, Mktg. Mgr., VP, jerry.rushin@coxradio.com; Janine Dupont, Promotions Dir., janine.dupont@coxradio.com; Phil Michaels-Trueba, Dir. of Programs, pmt@coxradio.com; Susan Isreal, Sales Mgr., susan.isreal@coxradio.com. **Ad Rates:** Advertising accepted; rates available upon request. **URL:** http://www.hot105fm.com.

7647 ■ WTMI-FM - 93.1
2741 N 29th Ave.
Hollywood, FL 33020
Phone: (305)444-4404
Format: Classical; Jazz. **Networks:** Concert Music Network (CMN). **Founded:** 1971. **Formerly**: WKAT-FM. **Operating Hours**: Continuous. **Key Personnel:** John Burkavage, Gen. Mgr.; Lyn Farmer, Dir. of Programs; Woody Tanger, CEO; Todd Tanger, Gen. Sales Mgr. **Wattage**: 100,000. **URL:** http://www.easy93.com.

HOMESTEAD

S FL. Dade Co. 28 mi. SW of Miami. Homestead Air Force Base. Fertilizer factory. Citrus fruit, truck farms. Tomatoes, okra, beans, squash, potatoes.

7648 ■ South Dade News Leader
South Dade News Leader
15 NE 1st Rd.
Homestead, FL 33030
Phone: (305)245-2311
Fax: (305)248-0596
General newspaper. **Freq:** Weekly. **Print Method:** Offset. **Cols./Page:** 6. **Col. Width:** 25 nonpareils. **Col. Depth:** 21.5 inches. **Subscription Rates:** $8.99 Individuals monthly. **URL:** http://southdadenewsleader.com. **Ad Rates:** GLR $6.60; BW $800; 4C $960; PCI $19.60. **Remarks:** Accepts advertising. **Circ:** 24000.

7649 ■ WKLG-FM - 102.1
1460 Jefferson Dr., Unit F
Homestead, FL 33034
Phone: (305)246-1123
Format: Adult Contemporary. **Networks:** ABC. **Owner:** WKLG Inc., 1460 Jefferson Dr., Unit F, Homestead, FL 33034. **Founded:** 1984. **Operating Hours**: Continuous. **ADI**: Miami (Ft. Lauderdale), FL. **Wattage**: 50,000. **Ad Rates:** $45-50 for 30 seconds; $75-80 for 60 seconds. **URL:** http://wklginc.com.

7650 ■ WWWK-FM - 105.5
27501 S Dixie Hwy., Ste. 208
Homestead, FL 33032
Phone: (305)398-3362
Format: Full Service. **Operating Hours**: Continuous. **Key Personnel:** Gilda Fernandez, Contact, gilda@myradioexito.com. **Wattage**: 50,000 ERP. **Ad Rates:** Accepts Advertising. **URL:** http://www.myradioexito.com.

HOMOSASSA

7651 ■ WEKJ-FM - 103.1
8145 W Pebble Ln.
Homosassa, FL 34448
Phone: (352)422-2918
Email: wekjfm@yahoo.com
Format: Religious. **Owner:** Christian Radio Network, 25 Beverly Ct, Homosassa, FL 34446-4248. **Key Personnel:** Peter Swartz, Station Mgr.

7652 ■ WXCV-FM - 95.3
4554 S Suncoast Blvd.
Homosassa, FL 34446
Phone: (352)628-4444
Fax: (352)628-4450
Email: citrus95@xtalwind.net
Format: Adult Contemporary; Top 40. **Owner:** WGUL-FM, Inc., at above address. **Founded:** 1983. **Operating Hours**: Continuous. **Wattage**: 6,000 ERP. **Ad Rates:** $17-23 per unit. **URL:** http://www.citrus95radio.com/.

IMMOKALEE

7653 ■ WAFZ-AM - 1490
2105 W Immokalee Dr.
Immokalee, FL 34142
Phone: (239)657-9210
Fax: (239)658-6109
Format: Ethnic; Religious. **Owner:** Glades Media Group, 530 E Alverdez Ave., Clewiston, FL 33440, Ph: (863)983-5900. **Key Personnel:** Paul Danitz, Dir. of Sales, paul@gladesmedia.com. **Ad Rates:** Noncommercial. **URL:** http://www.wafz.com.

JACKSONVILLE

NE FL. Duval Co. Located on Atlantic Ocean an equal distance from Miami and Atlanta. Edward Waters College; Jones College; Jacksonville University; Florida Junior College at Jacksonville. Center of commerce, finance and insurance with three large naval facilities.

7654 ■ American Shipper
American Shipper
200 W Forsyth St., Ste. 1000
Jacksonville, FL 32202
Phone: (904)355-2601
Fax: (904)791-8836
Free: 800-874-6422
Transportation and shipping magazine. **Freq:** Monthly. **Cols./Page:** 2. **Col. Width:** 41 nonpareils. **Key Personnel:** Eric S. Kulisch, Editor, phone: (703)723-2833; Eric Johnson, Director, Research, phone: (562)366-4384; Christopher Gillis, Editor, phone: (202)620-1625; Hayes H. Howard, Chief Executive Officer, Publisher. **ISSN:** 0160--225X (print). **Subscription Rates:** $180 Individuals print and online. **URL:** http://americanshipper.com. **Ad Rates:** BW $3,650; 4C $4,830. **Remarks:** Accepts advertising. **Circ:** (Not Reported).

7655 ■ Avian Diseases
American Association of Avian Pathologists
12627 San Jose Blvd., Ste. 202
Jacksonville, FL 32223-8638
Phone: (904)425-5735
Fax: (281)664-4744
Publisher's E-mail: aaap@aaap.info
Professional journal covering case reports related to avian diseases. **Freq:** Quarterly. **Key Personnel:** B.R. Charlton, Editor. **ISSN:** 0005-2086 (print). **Subscription Rates:** $40 Individuals + S & H; included in membership dues; $335 /year for nonmembers in U.S.; $360 /year for nonmembers outside U.S. **URL:** http://www.aaap.info/aviandiseases. **Ad Rates:** GLR $67. **Remarks:** Advertising accepted; rates available upon request. **Circ:** 1400, 1800.

7656 ■ The Breast Journal
Wiley-Blackwell
c/o Shahla Masood, MD, Editor-in-Chief
Dept. of Pathology
University of Florida Health Science Ctr.
655 W 8th St.
Jacksonville, FL 32209-6511
Journal focusing on all facets of research, diagnosis, and treatment of breast disease. **Freq:** Bimonthly. **Key Personnel:** Karen Earick, Managing Editor; Shahla Masood, MD, Editor-in-Chief. **ISSN:** 1075--122X (print); **EISSN:** 1524--4741 (electronic). **Subscription Rates:** $1022 Institutions print & online; £826 Institutions print & online; €1048 Institutions print & online; $1617 Institutions, other countries print & online; $307 Individuals print & online; £264 Other countries print & online; €395

Circulation: ★ = AAM; △ or • = BPA; ♦ = CAC; ❑ = VAC; ⊕ = PO Statement; ‡ = Publisher's Report; Boldface figures = sworn; Light figures = estimated.

Individuals print & online; $113 Students print & online; £106 Students, other countries print & online; €161 Students print & online. **URL:** http://onlinelibrary.wiley.com/journal/10.1111/(ISSN)1524-4741; http://www.asbd.org/login/index.cfm?destURL=%2Fmembers%2Fbreast_journal%2Ecfm. **Remarks:** Accepts advertising. **Circ:** (Not Reported).

7657 ■ Engineering and Mining Journal
Mining Media Inc.
c/o Steve Fiscor, VP & Editorial Dir.
11555 Central Pkwy., Ste. 401
Jacksonville, FL 32224
Publisher's E-mail: info@mining-media.com
Provides professionals in metallic and nonmetallic ores and minerals industries with news and technical economic information. **Freq:** Monthly. **Print Method:** Web Offset. **Trim Size:** 8 7/8 x 10 3/4. **Cols./Page:** 2 and 3. **Col. Width:** 45 and 26 nonpareils. **Col. Depth:** 140 agate lines. **Key Personnel:** Steve Fiscor, Director, Editorial, Vice President, phone: (904)721-2925, fax: (904)721-2930; Russ Carter, Managing Editor. **ISSN:** 0095--8948 (print). **Subscription Rates:** Free. **Online:** Mining Media Inc. Mining Media Inc. **URL:** http://www.mining-media.com/publications/engineering-and-mining-journal.html. **Also known as**: EMJ. **Ad Rates:** BW $5,060; 4C $6,580. **Remarks:** Accepts advertising. **Circ:** △**20008**.

7658 ■ Florida Baptist Witness
Florida Baptist Witness
PO Box 10289
Jacksonville, FL 32247-0289
Phone: (904)596-3165
Fax: (904)346-0696
Free: 800-226-8584
Publisher's E-mail: info@gofbw.com
Baptist newspaper. **Freq:** Semimonthly. **Print Method:** Offset. **Trim Size:** 11 x 17. **Cols./Page:** 5. **Col. Width:** 2 inches. **Col. Depth:** 16 inches. **Key Personnel:** James A. Smith, Sr., Executive Editor; Joni B. Hannigan, Managing Editor; John C. Hannigan, Business Manager. **USPS:** 700-940. **Subscription Rates:** $24.95 Individuals; $17.95 Individuals club/group of 10; $11.50 Individuals active resident family churches. **URL:** http://www.gofbw.com. **Ad Rates:** BW $3,160; PCI $40. **Remarks:** Color advertising accepted; rates available upon request. **Circ:** Paid ‡42000.

7659 ■ Folio Weekly
Folio Weekly
9456 Phillips Hwy., Ste. 11
Jacksonville, FL 32256
Phone: (904)260-9770
Fax: (904)260-9773
Publisher's E-mail: mail@folioweekly.com
Magazine featuring news, commentary, and information on events and happenings in the Greater Jacksonville area. **Freq:** Weekly (Tues.). **Print Method:** Web offset. **Trim Size:** 10 1/2 x 13 1/2. **Key Personnel:** Sam Taylor, Publisher. **URL:** http://www.folioweekly.com. **Remarks:** Accepts advertising. **Circ:** Free ■ **43291**.

7660 ■ Jacksonville Magazine
White Publishing Co.
1261 King St.
Jacksonville, FL 32204
Fax: (904)389-3628
Publisher's E-mail: mail@jacksonvillemag.com
City lifestyle magazine. **Founded:** 1983. **Freq:** Monthly. **Print Method:** Offset. **Trim Size:** 8 1/4 x 11. **Cols./Page:** 3. **Col. Width:** 14.5 picas. **Col. Depth:** 10 inches. **Key Personnel:** Virginia Chamlee, Managing Editor; Joseph White, Editor, Publisher. **ISSN:** 0885-4769 (print). **Subscription Rates:** $18.95 Individuals; $26.95 Two years; $35.95 Individuals three years. **URL:** http://jacksonvillemag.com. **Formerly**: Jacksonville Today. **Ad Rates:** BW $1,170; 4C $3,435. **Remarks:** Accepts advertising. **Circ:** 22000.

7661 ■ Journal of Academic and Business Ethics
Academic and Business Research Institute
PO Box 350997
Jacksonville, FL 32235-0997
Phone: (904)435-4330
Publication E-mail: editorial.staff@aabri.com
Journal containing information on the ethical issues of business and education. **Key Personnel:** Dr. Gina Almerico, Editor. **ISSN:** 2327--7114 (print); **EISSN:** 1941--336X (electronic). **URL:** http://www.aabri.com/jabe.html. **Remarks:** Advertising not accepted. **Circ:** (Not Reported).

7662 ■ Journal of Behavioral Studies in Business
Academic and Business Research Institute
PO Box 350997
Jacksonville, FL 32235-0997
Phone: (904)435-4330
Publication E-mail: editorial.staff@aabri.com
Journal containing manuscripts of behavioral studies in business related disciplines. **Key Personnel:** Dr. Michael Adams, Editor. **ISSN:** 2327--7114 (print); **EISSN:** 1941--5508 (electronic). **URL:** http://www.aabri.com/jbsb.html. **Remarks:** Advertising not accepted. **Circ:** (Not Reported).

7663 ■ Journal of Finance and Accountancy
Academic and Business Research Institute
PO Box 350997
Jacksonville, FL 32235-0997
Phone: (904)435-4330
Publication E-mail: editorial.staff@aabri.com
Journal containing studies related to financial and accounting topics in business and education. **Key Personnel:** Dr. Walter Moore, Editor. **ISSN:** 2327--5383 (print); **EISSN:** 1948--3015 (electronic). **URL:** http://aabri.com/jfa.html. **Circ:** (Not Reported).

7664 ■ Journal of Instructional Pedagogies
Academic and Business Research Institute
PO Box 350997
Jacksonville, FL 32235-0997
Phone: (904)435-4330
Publication E-mail: editorial.staff@aabri.com
Journal containing manuscripts related to teaching techniques and education issues. **Key Personnel:** Dr. Raymond Papp, Editor. **ISSN:** 1941--3394 (print); **EISSN:** 2327--5324 (electronic). **URL:** http://www.aabri.com/jip.html. **Circ:** (Not Reported).

7665 ■ Journal of International Business and Cultural Studies
Academic and Business Research Institute
PO Box 350997
Jacksonville, FL 32235-0997
Phone: (904)435-4330
Publication E-mail: editorial.staff@aabri.com
Journal containing manuscripts related to international business and cultural relations issues. **Key Personnel:** Dr. Frank LaPira, Editor. **ISSN:** 2327--5391 (print); **EISSN:** 1941--5087 (electronic). **URL:** http://www.aabri.com/jibcs.html. **Remarks:** Advertising not accepted. **Circ:** (Not Reported).

7666 ■ Journal of Laparoendoscopic and Advanced Surgical Techniques
Mary Ann Liebert Inc., Publishers
c/o Daniel C. Smith, MD, Editor-in-Chief
Dept. of Surgery
Mayo Clinic
4500 San Pablo Rd.
Jacksonville, FL 32224
Publication E-mail: jlastedit@me.com
Peer-reviewed journal focusing on surgical techniques and advanced surgical technologies. **Freq:** 18/yr. **Print Method:** Offset. **Trim Size:** 8 1/2 x 11. **Cols./Page:** 1. **Col. Width:** 36 picas. **Col. Depth:** 50 picas. **Key Personnel:** C. Daniel Smith, Editor-in-Chief; Thom E. Lobe, Editor, phone: (515)241-5926, fax: (515)241-4127; Laura Neuberger, MD, Managing Editor, phone: (443)567-2533. **ISSN:** 1092--6429 (print); **EISSN:** 1557--9034 (electronic). **Subscription Rates:** $2022 Individuals print and online; $2492 Other countries print and online; $1946 Institutions online. **URL:** http://www.liebertpub.com/overview/journal-of-laparoendoscopicbr--and-advanced-surgical-techniquesbr--and-part-b-videoscopy/36. **Formerly**: Journal of Laparoendoscopic Surgery. **Remarks:** Accepts advertising. **Circ:** (Not Reported).

7667 ■ Journal of Management and Marketing Research
Academic and Business Research Institute
PO Box 350997
Jacksonville, FL 32235-0997
Phone: (904)435-4330
Publication E-mail: editorial.staff@aabri.com
Journal containing manuscripts related to management and marketing issues. **Key Personnel:** Dr. Erika Matulich, Editor. **ISSN:** 1941--3408 (print); **EISSN:** 2327--5340 (electronic). **URL:** http://www.aabri.com/jmmr.html. **Circ:** (Not Reported).

7668 ■ Journal of Singing
National Association of Teachers of Singing
9957 Moorings Dr., Ste. 401
Jacksonville, FL 32257
Phone: (904)992-9101
Fax: (904)262-2587
Publisher's E-mail: info@nats.org
Journal covering information in all aspect of singing. **Freq:** 5/year. **Key Personnel:** Richard Sjoerdsma. **Subscription Rates:** $55 Individuals; $85 Other countries; $30 Students; $60 Institutions; $85 Institutions. **URL:** http://www.nats.org/cgi/page.cgi/about_journal_singing.html. **Remarks:** Accepts advertising. **Circ:** (Not Reported).

7669 ■ Journal of Technology Research
Academic and Business Research Institute
PO Box 350997
Jacksonville, FL 32235-0997
Phone: (904)435-4330
Publication E-mail: editorial.staff@aabri.com
Journal containing manuscripts related to information and instructional technology issues. **Key Personnel:** Dr. Phillip D. Coleman, Editor. **ISSN:** 1941--3416 (print); **EISSN:** 2327--5359 (electronic). **URL:** http://www.aabri.com/jtr.html. **Circ:** (Not Reported).

7670 ■ 904: Northeast Florida's Business & Executive Life Authority
White Publishing Co.
1261 King St.
Jacksonville, FL 32204
Fax: (904)389-3628
Publisher's E-mail: mail@jacksonvillemag.com
Business periodical featuring business-related articles focusing on high-profile executives and business managers. **Freq:** 6/year. **Key Personnel:** Joseph White, Editor. **Subscription Rates:** $9.04 Individuals 1 year; $17.08 Individuals 2 years; $25.12 Individuals 3 years. **URL:** http://www.jacksonvillemag.com/904-magazine. **Ad Rates:** 4C $2400. **Remarks:** Accepts advertising. **Circ:** 12500.

7671 ■ The Religious Herald
Baptist News Global
PO Box 23769
Jacksonville, FL 32241-3769
Free: 800-340-6626
Publication E-mail: news@religiousherald.org
News journal for Virginia Baptists. **Freq:** Bimonthly. **Print Method:** Web Press. **Trim Size:** 11 1/2 x 15. **Cols./Page:** 4. **Col. Width:** 2 1/4 inches. **Col. Depth:** 13 1/2 inches. **Key Personnel:** Jim White, Editor; Robert Dilday, Associate Editor; Barbara Francis, Manager, Advertising. **ISSN:** 0738--7318 (print). **URL:** http://www.religiousherald.org. **Remarks:** Accepts advertising. **Circ:** (Not Reported).

7672 ■ Research in Higher Education Journal
Academic and Business Research Institute
PO Box 350997
Jacksonville, FL 32235-0997
Phone: (904)435-4330
Publication E-mail: editorial.staff@aabri.com
Journal containing manuscripts about higher education. **Key Personnel:** Judith Bazler, Editor. **ISSN:** 1941--3432 (print); **EISSN:** 2327--7092 (electronic). **URL:** http://www.aabri.com/rhej.html. **Circ:** (Not Reported).

7673 ■ Southern Genealogists Exchange Quarterly
Southern Genealogist's Exchange Society
PO Box 7728
Jacksonville, FL 32238-7728
Genealogical and historical magazine. **Founded:** 1957. **Freq:** Quarterly. **Print Method:** electronic mimeograph. **Trim Size:** 8 1/2 x 11. **Cols./Page:** 1. **Key Personnel:** Nadine C. Ferguson, Editor, phone: (904)388-8959; Shirley Douglas, Recording Secretary, phone: (904)771-0810; Mary Rudd, Corresponding Secretary, phone: (904)387-0728; Jon R. Ferguson, President, phone: (904)388-8959. **ISSN:** 0584-4487 (print). **Subscription Rates:** $20 Individuals; $6 Single issue. **Remarks:** Accepts advertising. **Circ:** Controlled 300.

7674 ■ WAPE-FM - 95.1
8000 Belfort Pky.
Jacksonville, FL 32256
Phone: (904)245-8500
Fax: (904)245-8501
Free: 800-475-9595
Format: Contemporary Hit Radio (CHR). **Networks:** Independent. **Owner:** Cox Radio Inc., 6205 Peachtree Dunwood Rd., Atlanta, GA 30328-4524, Ph: (678)645-0000, Fax: (678)645-5002. **Founded:** 1968. **Operating Hours**: Continuous; 100% local. **ADI**: Jacksonville (Brunswick), FL. **Wattage**: 100,000. **Ad Rates:** $70-280 for 60 seconds. WFYV-FM, WKQL-FM, WMXQ-FM, WOKV-AM. **URL:** http://www.wape.com.

7675 ■ WCGL-AM - 1360
3890 Dunn Ave., Ste. 804
Jacksonville, FL 32218
Phone: (904)766-9955
Fax: (904)765-9214
Format: Gospel. **Owner:** JBD Communications. **Founded:** 1948. **Operating Hours**: Sunrise-sunset. **ADI**: Jacksonville (Brunswick), FL. **Key Personnel:** Kelvin Postell, Contact. **Wattage**: 5,000 Day; 089 Night. **Ad Rates:** Advertising accepted; rates available upon request. **URL:** http://www.wcgl1360.com.

7676 ■ WCRJ-FM - 88.1
7235 Bonneval Rd.
Jacksonville, FL 32256
Phone: (904)641-9626
Format: Contemporary Christian; Country. **Networks:** Independent. **Owner:** Hoker Broadcasting, 901 Main St., Dallas, TX 75202, Ph: (214)747-2925. **Founded:** 1984. **Operating Hours**: Continuous. **ADI**: Jacksonville (Brunswick), FL. **Key Personnel:** Linda Byrd, Contact; Linda Byrd, Contact. **Wattage**: 100,000. **Ad Rates:** Advertising accepted; rates available upon request. $36-104 for 30 seconds; $45-130 for 60 seconds. **URL:** http://ilovethepromise.com.

7677 ■ WCWJ-TV - 17
9117 Hogan Rd.
Jacksonville, FL 32216
Phone: (904)641-1700
Format: Commercial TV; News; Sports; Contemporary Christian. **Networks:** Warner Brothers Studios. **Owner:** Media General Inc., 333 E Franklin St., Richmond, VA 23219, Ph: (804)649-6000, Fax: (502)259-5537. **Founded:** 1966. **Formerly**: WJKS-TV; WJWB-TV. **Operating Hours**: Continuous. **ADI**: Jacksonville (Brunswick), FL. **Key Personnel:** Marc Hefner, Gen. Mgr., VP. **Wattage**: 4,700,000. **Ad Rates:** Advertising accepted; rates available upon request. **URL:** http://www.mycw17.com.

7678 ■ WEJZ-FM - 96.1
6440 Atlantic Blvd.
Jacksonville, FL 32211
Phone: (904)727-9696
Fax: (904)721-9322
Format: Adult Contemporary. **Networks:** Independent. **Owner:** Renda Broadcasting of Jacksonville, 900 Parish St., 4th Fl., Pittsburgh, PA 15220, Ph: (412)875-1800, Fax: (412)875-1801. **Founded:** 1949. **Operating Hours**: Continuous. **ADI**: Jacksonville (Brunswick), FL. **Key Personnel:** Bill Reese, Gen. Sales Mgr., breese@rendabroadcasting.com; Chuck Beck, News Dir., cbeck@rendabroadcasting.com; Jim Byard, Gen. Mgr., jbyard@rendabroadcasting.com. **Wattage**: 100,000. **Ad Rates:** $140-250 per unit. Combined advertising rates available with WWRR-FM. **URL:** http://www.wejz.com.

7679 ■ WFKS-FM - 97.9
11700 Central Pkwy.
Jacksonville, FL 32224
Phone: (904)636-0507
Free: 800-725-9990
Format: Contemporary Hit Radio (CHR); Country. **Founded:** 1981. **Formerly**: WNFI-FM. **Operating Hours**: Continuous. **ADI**: Jacksonville (Brunswick), FL. **Wattage**: 50,000 ERP. **Ad Rates:** Noncommercial; Advertising accepted; rates available upon request. **URL:** http://www.979kissfm.com.

7680 ■ WFOX-TV - 30
11700 Central Pkwy., Ste. 2
Jacksonville, FL 32224
Phone: (904)996-0400
Format: Public TV. **Networks:** Fox. **Founded:** 1981. **Formerly**: WAWS-TV. **Operating Hours**: Continuous. **ADI**: Jacksonville (Brunswick), FL. **Key Personnel:** Tim Ford, Bus. Mgr. **Ad Rates:** Advertising accepted; rates available upon request. **URL:** http://www.actionnewsjax.com.

7681 ■ WFXJ-AM - 930
11700 Central Pky.
Jacksonville, FL 32224
Phone: (904)636-0507
Fax: (904)636-7971
Format: Sports. **Operating Hours**: Continuous. **ADI**: Jacksonville (Brunswick), FL. **Key Personnel:** Aaron Wilborn, Gen. Mgr. **Wattage**: 5,000 ERP. **Ad Rates:** Noncommercial.

7682 ■ WFYV-FM - 104.5
8000 Belfort Pky.
Jacksonville, FL 32256-6971
Phone: (904)245-8500
Fax: (904)245-8501
Format: News. **Owner:** Cox Radio Inc., 6205 Peachtree Dunwood Rd., Atlanta, GA 30328-4524, Ph: (678)645-0000, Fax: (678)645-5002. **Founded:** 1979. **Operating Hours**: Continuous. **ADI**: Jacksonville (Brunswick), FL. **Ad Rates:** Advertising accepted; rates available upon request. $90-325 for 60 seconds.

WHJX-FM - See Baldwin, FL

7683 ■ WIOJ-AM - 1010
9090 Hogan Rd.
Jacksonville, FL 32216-4648
Phone: (904)641-1010
Fax: (904)641-1022
Format: Contemporary Christian. **Networks:** Sun Radio; USA Radio. **Owner:** McEntee Broadcasting of Florida, Inc., at above address. **Founded:** 1946. **Operating Hours**: Continuous. **Wattage**: 10,000. **Ad Rates:** Noncommercial. **URL:** http://www.1010xl.com/contact-us.

7684 ■ WJAX-AM - 1220
5353 Arlington Expy.
Jacksonville, FL 32211-5588
Email: wktz@jones.edu
Format: Big Band/Nostalgia. **Networks:** CNN Radio. **Owner:** Jones College Radio, 1195 Edgewood Ave. S, Jacksonville, FL 32205, Ph: (904)743-1122, Fax: (800)331-0176. **Founded:** 1964. **Operating Hours**: Continuous. **ADI**: Jacksonville (Brunswick), FL. **Key Personnel:** Kenneth L. Jones, Gen. Mgr., kjones@jones.edu; Tom Buetow, Music Dir., Program Mgr., tbuetow@jones.edu. **Wattage**: 1,000. **Ad Rates:** Advertising accepted; rates available upon request. **URL:** http://wktz.jones.edu/Broadcast/wjax_radio.htm.

7685 ■ WJAX-TV - 47
11700 Central Pky., No. 2
Jacksonville, FL 32224
Phone: (904)996-0400
Networks: United Paramount Network. **Owner:** Newport Television, LLC, 460 Nichols Rd., Ste. 250, Kansas City, MO 64112, Ph: (816)751-0200, Fax: (816)751-0250. **Formerly**: WNFT-TV; WTEV-TV. **Operating Hours**: Continuous. **ADI**: Jacksonville (Brunswick), FL. **Key Personnel:** Brad Raney, Sales Mgr., braney@actionnewsjax.com. **Ad Rates:** Noncommercial. **URL:** http://www.placestogoinjacksonville.com.

7686 ■ WJBC-FM - 91.7
5634 Normandy Blvd.
Jacksonville, FL 32205
Phone: (904)781-4321
Format: Religious; Southern Gospel. **Key Personnel:** Dr. Rodney Kelley, Pastor. **Wattage**: 32,000. **URL:** http://www.westjaxbaptist.org.

7687 ■ WJCT-FM - 89.9
100 Festival Park Ave.
Jacksonville, FL 32202
Phone: (904)353-7770
Email: audienceservices@wjct.org
Format: Public Radio. **Networks:** National Public Radio (NPR); Public Broadcasting Service (PBS); Public Radio International (PRI); American Public Radio (APR). **Owner:** WJCT Public Broadcasting, 100 Festival Park Ave., Jacksonville, FL 32202, Ph: (904)353-7770. **Founded:** 1972. **Operating Hours**: Continuous. **ADI**: Jacksonville (Brunswick), FL. **Key Personnel:** Michael Boylan, President, CEO, mboylan@wjct.org. **Wattage**: 98,000 ERP. **Ad Rates:** Advertising accepted; rates available upon request. **URL:** http://www.wjct.org.

7688 ■ WJCT-TV - 7
100 Festival Park Ave.
Jacksonville, FL 32202-1309
Phone: (904)353-7770
Format: Public TV. **Networks:** Public Broadcasting Service (PBS). **Owner:** WJCT Public Broadcasting, 100 Festival Park Ave., Jacksonville, FL 32202, Ph: (904)353-7770. **Founded:** 1958. **Operating Hours**: Continuous; 80% network, 20% local. **ADI**: Jacksonville (Brunswick), FL. **Key Personnel:** Michael Boylan, CEO, President, mboylan@wjct.org. **Local Programs**: *The NewsHour*; *Bill Moyers Journal*; *NOW on PBS*. **Ad Rates:** Noncommercial. **URL:** http://www.wjct.org.

7689 ■ WJEB-TV - 59
3101 Emerson Expy.
Jacksonville, FL 32207
Phone: (904)399-8413
Fax: (904)399-8423
Email: prayer@wjeb.org
Founded: May 14, 1991. **URL:** http://www.wjeb.org.

7690 ■ WJGL-FM - 96.9
8000 Belfort Pky., Ste. 100
Jacksonville, FL 32256
Phone: (904)245-8500
Fax: (904)245-8501
Format: Oldies. **Owner:** Cox Radio Inc., 6205 Peachtree Dunwood Rd., Atlanta, GA 30328-4524, Ph: (678)645-0000, Fax: (678)645-5002. **Operating Hours**: Continuous. **Key Personnel:** Todd Shannon, Dir. of Operations, Prog. Dir., todd.shannon@coxradio.com. **Ad Rates:** Advertising accepted; rates available upon request. **URL:** http://www.969theeagle.com.

7691 ■ WJXR-FM - 92.1
PO Box 1
Jacksonville, FL 32234
Format: Commercial TV. **Networks:** ABC. **Owner:** WJXR Inc., 28 W Macclenny Ave., Ste. 9, Macclenny, FL 32063, Ph: (904)259-2292. **Founded:** 1978. **Formerly**: WBKF-FM. **Operating Hours**: Continuous; 5% network, 95% local. **ADI**: Jacksonville (Brunswick), FL. **Key Personnel:** Greg Perich, Gen. Mgr., Owner; Sarah Perich, Owner. **Local Programs**: *Bargain Channel*. **Wattage**: 25,000. **Ad Rates:** Noncommercial. **URL:** http://www.wjxr.com.

7692 ■ WJXT-TV - 4
4 Broadcast Pl.
Jacksonville, FL 32207
Phone: (904)399-4000
Networks: CBS. **Owner:** Graham Media Group Inc., 550 W Lafayette Blvd., Detroit, MI 48226. **Founded:** 1949. **Formerly**: WMBR-TV. **Operating Hours**: Continuous; 60% network, 40% local. **ADI**: Jacksonville (Brunswick), FL. **Key Personnel:** Kathryn Bonfield, News Dir., kbonfield@wjxt.com. **Wattage**: 100 KW. **Ad Rates:** Advertising accepted; rates available upon request. **URL:** http://www.news4jax.com.

7693 ■ WJXX-TV - 25
1070 E Adams St.
Jacksonville, FL 32202
Phone: (904)354-1212
Email: news@firstcoastnews.com
Networks: ABC. **Owner:** Tegna Inc., 7950 Jones Branch Dr., McLean, VA 22107-0150, Ph: (703)854-6089. **Founded:** 1997. **Key Personnel:** Dodie Cantrell-Bickley, Gen. Mgr., President, dcantrell@firstcoastnews.com; Mike Garber, News Dir., mgarber@firstcoastnews.com. **Ad Rates:** Advertising accepted; rates available upon request. **URL:** http://www.firstcoastnews.com.

7694 ■ WKQL-FM - 96.9
8000 Belfort Pky., Ste. 100
Jacksonville, FL 32256
Email: oldies@cool969.com
Format: News; Sports. **Networks:** Independent. **Owner:** Cox Radio Inc., 6205 Peachtree Dunwood Rd., Atlanta, GA 30328-4524, Ph: (678)645-0000, Fax: (678)645-5002. **Formerly**: WAIV-FM. **Operating Hours**: 8:30 a.m. - 5:30 p.m. Monday - Friday. **ADI**: Jacksonville (Brunswick), FL. **Key Personnel:** Angie Pinto, Promotions Dir.; Cat Thomas, Operations Mgr.; Heather White, News Dir. **Wattage**: 98,000. **Ad Rates:** Advertising accepted; rates

Circulation: ★ = AAM; △ or • = BPA; ♦ = CAC; ❑ = VAC; ⊕ = PO Statement; ‡ = Publisher's Report; Boldface figures = sworn; Light figures = estimated.

available upon request. $75-160 per unit. **URL:** http://www.969theeagle.com.

7695 ■ WKTZ-FM - 90.9
5353 Arlington Expy.
Jacksonville, FL 32211
Phone: (904)371-1184
Fax: (904)743-4446
Free: 800-331-0176
Email: wktz@jones.edu
Format: Easy Listening. **Networks:** AP. **Owner:** Jones College Radio, 1195 Edgewood Ave. S, Jacksonville, FL 32205, Ph: (904)743-1122, Fax: (800)331-0176. **Founded:** 1964. **Operating Hours:** Continuous. **ADI:** Jacksonville (Brunswick), FL. **Key Personnel:** Kenneth Jones, Gen. Mgr., kjones@jones.edu; Tom Buetow, Music Dir., Program Mgr., tbuetow@jones.edu. **Wattage:** 50,000. **Ad Rates:** Noncommercial. **URL:** http://wktz.jones.edu/WKTZ-FM.htm.

7696 ■ WMUV-FM - 100.7
6440 Atlantic Blvd.
Jacksonville, FL 32211
Phone: (904)727-9696
Fax: (904)721-9322
Format: Country. **Owner:** Renda Broadcasting Corp., at above address. **Operating Hours:** Continuous. **Key Personnel:** Bill Reese, Gen. Mgr., breese@rendabroadcasting.com; Charlie Jennings, Gen. Sales Mgr., cjennings@rendabroadcasting.com; Chuck Beck, Dir. of Programs, cbeck@rendabroadcasting.com; Kimberly Homitz, Bus. Mgr., khomitz@rendabroadcasting.com. **Ad Rates:** Advertising accepted; rates available upon request.

7697 ■ WMXQ-FM - 102.9
8000 Belfort Pky.
Jacksonville, FL 32256
Phone: (904)245-8500
Fax: (904)245-8501
Format: Alternative/New Music/Progressive. **Networks:** Independent. **Owner:** Cox Radio Inc., 6205 Peachtree Dunwood Rd., Atlanta, GA 30328-4524, Ph: (678)645-0000, Fax: (678)645-5002. **Founded:** 1965. **Formerly:** WIVY-FM. **Operating Hours:** Continuous; 100% local. **ADI:** Jacksonville (Brunswick), FL. **Key Personnel:** Matt Urban, Contact; Matt Urban, Contact. **Wattage:** 98,000. **Ad Rates:** Advertising accepted; rates available upon request. per unit. **URL:** http://www.x1029.com.

7698 ■ WNCM-FM - 88.1
2361 Cortez Rd.
Jacksonville, FL 32246
Phone: (904)641-9626
Fax: (904)645-9626
Format: Religious; Contemporary Christian. **Networks:** Sun Radio. **Owner:** New Covenant Educational Ministries, at above address. **Founded:** 1984. **Operating Hours:** Continuous. **ADI:** Jacksonville (Brunswick), FL. **Key Personnel:** Calvin Grabau, Contact; Calvin Grabau, Contact. **Wattage:** 1,000. **Ad Rates:** $12 for 30 seconds; $15 for 60 seconds. **URL:** http://www.riverradio.org.

7699 ■ WOKV-AM - 690
8000 Belfort Pky., Ste. 100
Jacksonville, FL 32256
Phone: (904)245-8500
Fax: (904)245-8501
Format: News; Talk. **Owner:** Cox Radio Inc., 6205 Peachtree Dunwood Rd., Atlanta, GA 30328-4524, Ph: (678)645-0000, Fax: (678)645-5002. **Key Personnel:** Mike Dorwart, Dir. of Programs, mike.dorwart@coxradio.com; Rich Jones, News Dir., rich.jones@coxradio.com. **Ad Rates:** Noncommercial. **URL:** http://www.wokv.com.

7700 ■ WOKV-FM - 106.5
8000 Belfort Pky., Ste. 100
Jacksonville, FL 32256
Phone: (904)245-8500
Fax: (904)245-8501
Format: News; Talk; Information. **Owner:** Cox Radio Inc., 6205 Peachtree Dunwood Rd., Atlanta, GA 30328-4524, Ph: (678)645-0000, Fax: (678)645-5002. **Operating Hours:** Continuous. **Key Personnel:** Mike Dorwart, Dir. of Programs, mike.dorwart@coxradio.com; Rich Jones, News Dir., rich.jones@coxradio.com. **Ad Rates:** Advertising accepted; rates available upon request. **URL:** http://www.wokv.com.

7701 ■ WPLA-FM - 107.3
11700 Central Pky.
Jacksonville, FL 32224
Phone: (904)737-0107
Format: Alternative/New Music/Progressive. **Key Personnel:** Neal Sharpe, Dir. of Programs, nealsharpe@clearchannel.com. **Wattage:** 50,000. **Ad Rates:** Noncommercial. **URL:** http://www.1069planetradio.com.

7702 ■ WQIK-FM - 99.1
11700 Central Pky.
Jacksonville, FL 32224
Phone: (904)388-3699
Email: jaxhr@clearchannel.com
Format: Contemporary Country. **Networks:** ABC. **Founded:** 1954. **Operating Hours:** Continuous. **ADI:** Jacksonville (Brunswick), FL. **Key Personnel:** Gail Austin, Dir. of Programs, gailaustin@clearchannel.com; Stephanie Lee, Promotions Dir., stephanielee@clearchannel.com. **Wattage:** 100,000. **Ad Rates:** Advertising accepted; rates available upon request. **URL:** http://www.991wqik.com.

7703 ■ WROS-AM - 1050
5590 Rio Grande Ave.
Jacksonville, FL 32254
Phone: (904)353-1050
Fax: (904)353-7076
Email: studiob@wros.net
Format: Religious; Sports; Talk; News; Southern Gospel. **Networks:** ABC; Mutual Broadcasting System; Westwood One Radio; Independent. **Owner:** Metropolitan Radio Group, Inc., 154 Greenbridge Rd., Ozark, MO 65721, Ph: (417)581-5595, Fax: (417)581-5596, Free: 800-961-5595; Jacor Communications, Inc., 1300 PNC Ctr., 201 E 5th St. 1300 Central Trust Center, Cincinnati, OH 45202, Ph: (513)621-1300; The Rose of Jacksonville. **Founded:** 1980. **Operating Hours:** 6:00 a.m. - 7:30 p.m. Monday – Sunday. **ADI:** Jacksonville (Brunswick), FL. **Key Personnel:** Larry Stevens, Dir. of Programs, Contact; Elwyn Hall, Gen. Mgr.; Dean Hall, VP; Robyne Hall, Contact; Berneida Owens, Contact; Larry Stevens, Contact. **Wattage:** 5,000 Day;013 Night. **Ad Rates:** Advertising accepted; rates available upon request. $30 for 30 seconds; for 30 seconds; $25 for 30 seconds; for 40 seconds; $35 for 60 seconds; for 60 seconds. **URL:** http://wros.net.

7704 ■ WSOL-FM - 101.5
11700 Central Pky.
Jacksonville, FL 32224
Phone: (904)636-0507
Format: Adult Contemporary. **Owner:** Jacor Broadcasting Co., Columbus, OH, Ph: (614)249-7676. **Founded:** 1966. **Operating Hours:** Continuous. **ADI:** Jacksonville (Brunswick), FL. **Key Personnel:** Sandra Rockwell, Contact. **Wattage:** 100,000 ERP. **URL:** http://v1015.iheart.com/articles/contact-wsol-488710.

7705 ■ WSOS-FM - 94.1
6440 Atlantic Blvd.
Jacksonville, FL 32211
Owner: Renda Broadcasting Corp., at above address. **Founded:** 1982. **Wattage:** 5,500. **Ad Rates:** $20 for 30 seconds; $25 for 60 seconds.

7706 ■ WSVE-AM
4343 Spring Grove St.
Jacksonville, FL 32209-3629
Phone: (904)768-1211
Founded: 1982. **Formerly:** WEXI-AM. **Key Personnel:** Emily Timmons, Contact. **Ad Rates:** $20 for 30 seconds; $35 for 60 seconds. **URL:** http://www.well.com/~irw/stations/wslm.html.

7707 ■ WTLV-TV - 12
1070 E Adams St.
Jacksonville, FL 32202
Phone: (904)354-1212
Format: Commercial TV; News; Sports. **Networks:** NBC. **Owner:** Gannett Company Inc., 7950 Jones Branch Dr., McLean, VA 22107-0150, Ph: (703)854-6089. **Founded:** 1957. **Operating Hours:** Continuous. **ADI:** Jacksonville (Brunswick), FL. **Key Personnel:** Bonnie Solloway, Prod. Mgr., bsolloway@firstcoastnews.com. **Wattage:** 53,300 ERP Horizonta. **Ad Rates:** Advertising accepted; rates available upon request. **URL:** http://www.firstcoastnews.com.

7708 ■ W217BL-FM - 91.3
PO Box 391
Twin Falls, ID 83303
Fax: (208)736-1958
Free: 800-357-4226
Format: Religious; Contemporary Christian. **Owner:** CSN International, PO Box 391, Twin Falls, ID 83303, Ph: (208)736-1958, Fax: (208)736-1958, Free: 800-357-4226. **Key Personnel:** Ray Gorney, Asst. Dir.; Kelly Carlson, Dir. of Engg. **URL:** http://www.csnradio.com.

7709 ■ W229AH-FM - 93.7
PO Box 391
Twin Falls, ID 83303
Fax: (208)736-1958
Free: 800-357-4226
Format: Religious; Contemporary Christian. **Owner:** CSN International, PO Box 391, Twin Falls, ID 83303, Ph: (208)736-1958, Fax: (208)736-1958, Free: 800-357-4226. **URL:** http://www.csnradio.com.

7710 ■ WXXJ-FM - 102.9
8000 Belfort Pky., Ste. 100
Jacksonville, FL 32256
Phone: (904)245-8500
Fax: (904)245-8501
Format: Alternative/New Music/Progressive. **Owner:** Cox Radio Inc., 6205 Peachtree Dunwood Rd., Atlanta, GA 30328-4524, Ph: (678)645-0000, Fax: (678)645-5002. **URL:** http://www.x1029.com.

7711 ■ WZAZ-AM - 1400
4190 Belfort Rd., Ste. 450
Jacksonville, FL 32216
Phone: (904)470-4707
Format: Gospel. **Networks:** CBS; ABC. **Owner:** Titus Broadcasting Inc. **Founded:** 1984. **Formerly:** WERD-AM; UNC Media of Jacksonville. **Operating Hours:** Continuous. **ADI:** Jacksonville (Brunswick), FL. **Key Personnel:** Yolanda Hooper, Station Mgr., manager@wzaz.com. **Wattage:** 1,000. **Ad Rates:** Advertising accepted; rates available upon request. **URL:** http://www.gospelam1400.com.

7712 ■ WZNZ-AM - 1460
11700 Central Pky.
Jacksonville, FL 32224
Phone: (904)997-1880
Fax: (904)997-7740
Format: Sports. **Networks:** Business Radio; ABC. **Owner:** Concord Media Group, 11521 Inn Fields Dr., Odessa, FL 33556, Ph: (813)926-9001. **Operating Hours:** Continuous. **ADI:** Jacksonville (Brunswick), FL. **Key Personnel:** Jon Bosworth, Gen. Mgr., JBosworth@1065thepromise.com. **Wattage:** 5,000. **Ad Rates:** Advertising accepted; rates available upon request.

JACKSONVILLE BEACH

NE FL. Duval Co. 15 mi. E. of Jacksonville. Beach resort.

7713 ■ Beaches Leader
Community Newspapers Inc.
1114 Beach Blvd.
Jacksonville Beach, FL 32250-3404
Phone: (904)249-9033
Fax: (909)249-1501
Publisher's E-mail: dnesmith@cninewspapers.com
Newspaper serving Atlantic Beach, Jacksonville Beach, Neptune Beach, Mayport and Ponte Vedra Beach, Florida. **Freq:** Semiweekly. **Key Personnel:** Kathleen Feindt Bailey, Senior Editor; Steve Fouraker, Manager, Circulation. **Subscription Rates:** $32 Individuals; $60 Out of area; $55 Two years; $45 Individuals online. **URL:** http://www.beachesleader.com. **Remarks:** Accepts advertising. **Circ:** Paid 9200.

7714 ■ WQOP-AM - 1460
PO Box 51585
Jacksonville Beach, FL 32240
Phone: (904)241-3311
Email: queenofpeaceradio@yahoo.com
Format: Religious. **Ad Rates:** Noncommercial. **URL:** http://www.qopradio.com.

JASPER

N FL. Hamilton Co. 90 mi. W. of Jacksonville. Manufactures textiles, industrial coatings, steel fabrication, lumber, fertilizer, feed. Phosphate mines. Cotton, corn, tobacco, truck farms.

7715 ■ Jasper News
Community Newspaper Holdings Inc.
105 NE 2nd Ave.
Jasper, FL 32052
Phone: (386)792-2487
Publication E-mail: jaspernews1@windstream.net
Newspaper serving Jasper, Florida. **Key Personnel:** Myra Regan, Publisher. **Subscription Rates:** $18 Individuals in county delivery; $26 Out of area. **URL:** http://www.suwanneedemocrat.com/jasper. **Remarks:** Accepts advertising. **Circ:** (Not Reported).

JUPITER

SE FL. Palm Beach Co. 18 mi. N. of West Palm Beach.

7716 ■ Geotextiles and Geomembranes
International Geosynthetics Society
1934 Commerce Ln., Ste. 4
Jupiter, FL 33458
Phone: (561)768-9489
Fax: (561)828-7618
Publisher's E-mail: IGSsec@geosyntheticssociety.org
Journal publishing information on geotextiles and geomembranes. **URL:** http://www.geosyntheticssociety.org/Resources.aspx?pg=Journals. **Remarks:** Advertising not accepted. **Circ:** (Not Reported).

KEY BISCAYNE

S FL. Dade Co. 6 mi. S. of Miami Beach.

7717 ■ The Islander News: The Life and Times of Key Biscayne, Florida
Islander News
104 Crandon Blvd., Ste. 301
Key Biscayne, FL 33149
Phone: (305)361-3333
Publisher's E-mail: info@islandernews.com
Community newspaper. **Freq:** Weekly (Thurs.). **Print Method:** Offset. **Trim Size:** 11 1/4 x 17 1/2. **Cols./Page:** 4. **Col. Width:** 2 3/8 inches. **Col. Depth:** 10 inches. **USPS:** 007-287. **Subscription Rates:** $50.44 Individuals. **URL:** http://www.islandernews.com/97503/2383/1/online-edition. **Ad Rates:** BW $880; PCI $20. **Remarks:** Accepts advertising. **Circ:** Paid ‡3900.

KEY LARGO

Monroe Co. (SE). 5 m N of Tavernier.

7718 ■ Catamaran Sailor
Catamaran Sailor Magazine
PO Box 2060
Key Largo, FL 33037
Phone: (305)451-3287
Fax: (305)453-0255
Free: 866-451-3287
Publisher's E-mail: info@catsailor.com
Newspaper for catamaran sailors. **Freq:** 8/yr. **Print Method:** Webpress. **Trim Size:** 8 1/2 x 11. **Cols./Page:** 3. **Col. Width:** 2 1/4 inches. **Subscription Rates:** $40 Individuals. **URL:** http://www.catsailor.com. **Ad Rates:** PCI $15. **Remarks:** Advertising accepted; rates available upon request. **Circ:** Paid 2000, Non-paid 2000.

KEY WEST

S FL. Monroe Co. On Gulf of Mexico, 153 mi. S. of Miami. Florida Keys Community College. Tourist resort. Fisheries. Shrimp factories; sponge industry; bottling works.

7719 ■ Cancer Biotherapy and Radiopharmaceuticals
Mary Ann Liebert Inc., Publishers
c/o Robert K. Oldham, MD, Ed.
3428 N Roosevelt Blvd.
Key West, FL 33040
Phone: (305)294-1706
Publisher's E-mail: info@liebertpub.com
Peer-reviewed journal covering cutting-edge biotherapy and innovative investigations of methods to improve cancer therapy. **Freq:** 10/year. **Print Method:** Offset. **Trim Size:** 8 x 11. **Cols./Page:** 2. **Col. Width:** 3 inches. **Col. Depth:** 9 1/2 inches. **Key Personnel:** Jim Xiang, MD, Board Member; Jens Atzpodien, PhD, Associate Editor; Robert K. Oldham, MD, Editor. **ISSN:** 1084-9785 (print); **EISSN:** 1557-8852 (electronic). **Subscription Rates:** $1241 Individuals print and online; $1571 Other countries print and online; $1094 Individuals online only; $2931 Institutions print and online; $3370 Institutions, other countries print and online; $2651 Institutions print only; $3049 Institutions, other countries print only; $2791 Institutions online only. **URL:** http://www.liebertpub.com/overview/cancer-biotherapy-and-radiopharmaceuticals/8. **Formed by the merger of:** "Cancer Biotherapy and Antibody, Immunoconjuates, and Radiopharmaceuticals". **Ad Rates:** BW $1,095; 4C $1,845. **Remarks:** Accepts advertising. **Circ:** (Not Reported).

7720 ■ Forward Pass
International Women's Flag Football Association
25 A 7th Ave.
Key West, FL 33040
Phone: (305)293-9315
Fax: (305)293-9315
Free: 888-464-9332
Publisher's E-mail: iwffa@iwffa.com
Magazine containing articles about the International Women's Flag Football Association. **Freq:** Semiannual. **Subscription Rates:** Included in membership. **Alt. Formats:** Download. **URL:** http://www.iwffa.com/index.php/iwffa-media/forward-pass-new. **Remarks:** Accepts advertising. **Circ:** (Not Reported).

7721 ■ Key West Citizen: Monroe County's Only Daily Newspaper
Cooke Communications L.L.C.
3420 Northside Dr.
Key West, FL 33040
Phone: (305)292-7777
Fax: (305)295-8004
Publication E-mail: support@keysnews.com
Local newspaper. **Freq:** Daily. **Print Method:** Offset. **Trim Size:** 13 x 21 1/2. **Cols./Page:** 9. **Col. Width:** 26 nonpareils. **Col. Depth:** 301 agate lines. **Key Personnel:** John McCormick, Chief Technology Officer; Paul Clarin, Publisher. **USPS:** 294-240. **Subscription Rates:** $90 Individuals electronic edition only; $12 Individuals 1 month; $48 Individuals 6 months, electronic edition only; $30 Individuals 3 months; $1.25 Single issue Sunday; $150 Two years electronic edition only. **URL:** http://keysnews.com; http://cookecommunications.com. **Ad Rates:** PCI $21.20. **Remarks:** Accepts advertising. **Circ:** Mon.-Sat. ★**10028**, Sun. ★**10872**.

7722 ■ Rocky Mount Telegram
Cooke Communications L.L.C.
3420 Northside Dr.
Key West, FL 33040
Phone: (305)292-7777
Fax: (305)295-8004
Publisher's E-mail: sales@keysnews.com
General newspaper. **Freq:** Daily. **Key Personnel:** Mark Wilson, Publisher, phone: (252)407-9967; Ross Chandler, Editor; Jeff Herrin, Editor, phone: (252)407-9943. **Subscription Rates:** $12 Individuals EZ pay/month; $145 Individuals 12 months; $74 Individuals 6 months. **URL:** http://www.rockymounttelegram.com. **Ad Rates:** BW $1,680, full page; BW $935, half page. **Remarks:** Accepts advertising. **Circ:** (Not Reported).

7723 ■ WEOW-FM - 92.7
5450 MacDonald Ave., Ste. 10
Key West, FL 33040
Phone: (305)296-7511
Fax: (305)296-0358
Format: Contemporary Hit Radio (CHR). **Networks:** CBS; Westwood One Radio. **Founded:** 1967. **Operating Hours:** Continuous; 100% local. **Wattage:** 100,000. **Ad Rates:** $16-40 for 30 seconds; $18-50 for 60 seconds. Combined advertising rates available with WAIL, WKEY, WKWF. **URL:** http://www.weow927.com.

7724 ■ WIIS-FM - 106.9
1075 Duval St., Ste. C17
Key West, FL 33040
Phone: (305)292-1071
Format: Alternative/New Music/Progressive. **Operating Hours:** Continuous. **Local Programs:** *Reggae Sundays Show*, Sunday 10:00 a.m. - 4:00 p.m. **Wattage:** 5,700. **Ad Rates:** Noncommercial. **URL:** http://island107.com.

7725 ■ WKEY-FM - 93.5
5450 MacDonald Ave., Ste. 10
Key West, FL 33040
Phone: (305)296-7511
Fax: (305)296-0358
Format: Adult Contemporary. **Networks:** Independent. **Owner:** Clear Channel Communication, Inc., 200 E Basse Rd., San Antonio, TX 78209, Ph: (210)822-2828, Fax: (210)822-2828. **Founded:** 1986. **Operating Hours:** Continuous. **Key Personnel:** Mark Mills, Sales Mgr.; Geri Luer, Bus. Mgr. **Wattage:** 33,000. **Ad Rates:** for 30 seconds; $21-38 for 60 seconds. Combined advertising rates available with WEOW, WKWF, WAIL, WAVK, WKZY, WCTH, WFKZ. **URL:** http://www.themixofoldies.com.

7726 ■ WKIZ-AM - 1500
PO Box 6621
Key West, FL 33041
Phone: (305)293-9536
Fax: (305)296-0358
Format: Talk; Sports. **Networks:** CBS; Florida Radio; American Information Radio (AIN); Mutual Broadcasting System. **Founded:** 1959. **Operating Hours:** Continuous. **Key Personnel:** Mark Mills, Sales Mgr. **Wattage:** 500. **Ad Rates:** Advertising accepted; rates available upon request; Noncommercial. $11-25 for 30 seconds; $13-25 for 60 seconds.

7727 ■ WKWR-FM - 90.1
PO Box 2098
Omaha, NE 68103
Free: 800-525-5683
Email: info@klove.com
Format: Contemporary Christian. **Owner:** Educational Media Foundation, 5700 W Oaks Blvd., CA 95765, Free: 800-800434-8400. **URL:** http://www.klove.com.

7728 ■ WOZN-FM - 98.7
PO Box 14369
Tallahassee, FL 32317-4369
Fax: (305)293-9654
Format: Album-Oriented Rock (AOR). **Owner:** Key West Communications Inc., 411 E Huntington Dr., Ste. 117, Arcadia, CA 91006, Ph: (626)701-4100, Fax: (626)574-7407. **Founded:** 1986. **Operating Hours:** Continuous. **ADI:** Miami (Ft. Lauderdale), FL. **Key Personnel:** Bruce Timm, President; Daniel P. Amann, Dir. of Production. **Wattage:** 100,000. **Ad Rates:** $10-16 for 15 seconds; $12-18 for 30 seconds; $14-20 for 60 seconds.

7729 ■ W220DF-FM - 91.9
PO Box 391
Twin Falls, ID 83303
Fax: (208)736-1958
Free: 800-357-4226
Format: Religious; Contemporary Christian. **Owner:** CSN International, PO Box 391, Twin Falls, ID 83303, Ph: (208)736-1958, Fax: (208)736-1958, Free: 800-357-4226. **URL:** http://www.csnradio.com.

KEYSTONE HEIGHTS

Clay Co. Clay Co. (NE). 20 m SE of Starke.

7730 ■ Lake Region Monitor
Bradford County Telegraph
7380 State Road 21
Keystone Heights, FL 32656
Phone: (352)473-2210
Publication E-mail: lrmonitor@bellsouth.net
Community newspaper. **Freq:** Weekly (Thurs.). **Cols./Page:** 6. **Col. Width:** 12 picas. **Col. Depth:** 21 inches. **Subscription Rates:** $39 Individuals; $20 Individuals 6 months. **URL:** http://www.bctelegraph.com. **Ad Rates:** BW $517; PCI $4.1. **Remarks:** Advertising accepted; rates available upon request. **Circ:** 2300.

KISSIMMEE

C FL. Osceola Co. On Lake Tohopekalige, 8 mi. E. of Walt Disney World. Plastic factory. Sawmills. Boat building. Naval stores. Fruit, cattle, beans, potatoes.

7731 ■ Florida Cattleman and Livestock Journal
Florida Cattlemen's Association
800 Shakerag Rd.
Kissimmee, FL 34744
Phone: (407)846-6221
Fax: (407)933-8209
Publisher's E-mail: info@floridacattlemen.org
Livestock news. **Freq:** Monthly. **Print Method:** Offset. **Trim Size:** 8.375 x 10.875. **Cols./Page:** 3. **Col. Width:** 26 nonpareils. **Col. Depth:** 140 agate lines. **Key**

Circulation: ★ = AAM; △ or • = BPA; ♦ = CAC; ❑ = VAC; ⊕ = PO Statement; ‡ = Publisher's Report; Boldface figures = sworn; Light figures = estimated.

Personnel: Barbara Starcher Bird, Editor, Manager, Production; Jim Handley, Managing Editor. **ISSN:** 0015--3958 (print). **Subscription Rates:** Included in membership. **URL:** http://www.floridacattlemen.org/magazine. **Mailing address:** PO Box 421929, Kissimmee, FL 34742-1929. **Ad Rates:** BW $650; 4C $300; PCI $40. **Remarks:** Accepts advertising. **Circ:** 5000, 5000.

7732 ■ The Journal of Osceola County Business
Kissimmee - Osceola County Chamber of Commerce
1425 E Vine St.
Kissimmee, FL 34744-3621
Phone: (407)847-3174
Fax: (407)870-8607
Publisher's E-mail: info@kissimmeechamber.com
Freq: Bimonthly. **Remarks:** Advertising not accepted. **Circ:** (Not Reported).

7733 ■ Osceola Shopper
Florida Sun Publications
108 Church St.
Kissimmee, FL 34741
Shopper. **Freq:** Weekly (Wed.). **Print Method:** Photo Offset. **Trim Size:** 11 1/2 x 15 1/2. **Key Personnel:** Marvin Cortner, Editor, phone: (407)846-7600; Ellen Johnston, Manager, Production; Kathy Beckham, Manager, Circulation. **Subscription Rates:** Free. **Ad Rates:** GLR $1,735; 4C $250. **Remarks:** Accepts advertising. **Circ:** (Not Reported).

LABELLE

7734 ■ WBIY-FM - 88.3
PO Box 2507
LaBelle, FL 33935
Phone: (305)826-5555
Fax: (305)819-9896
Format: Religious. **Owner:** Oscar Aguero Ministry Inc., 6050 West 20th Ave., Hialeah, FL 33016, Ph: (305)826-5555, Fax: (305)819-9896, Free: 888-848-4455. **URL:** http://www.oscaragueroministry.com.

LAKE ALFRED

7735 ■ Bulletin of Environmental Contamination and Toxicology
Springer Science + Business Media LLC
c/o Herbert N. Nigg, PhD, Ed.-in-Ch.
University of Florida
700 Experiment Station Rd.
Lake Alfred, FL 33850
Publisher's E-mail: service-ny@springer.com
Peer-reviewed journal covering toxicants and environmental interests. **Freq:** Monthly. **Print Method:** Offset. **Trim Size:** 6 1/2 x 9 1/2. **Cols./Page:** 1. **Col. Width:** 60 nonpareils. **Col. Depth:** 117 agate lines. **Key Personnel:** Herbert N. Nigg, PhD, Editor-in-Chief; John Hylin, PhD, Editor, Founder. **ISSN:** 0007--4861 (print); **EISSN:** 1432--0800 (electronic). **Subscription Rates:** €125.21 Individuals online only. **URL:** http://springer.com/environment/pollution+and+remediation/journal/128. **Remarks:** Advertising accepted; rates available upon request. **Circ:** Combined **1100**.

LAKE CITY

N FL. Columbia Co. 60 mi. W. of Jacksonville. Lake City Community College. Manufactures turpentine, mobile homes, lumber. Poultry and stock.

7736 ■ Lake City Reporter
Community Newspapers Inc.
180 E Duval St.
Lake City, FL 32055
Phone: (386)754-0418
Publisher's E-mail: dnesmith@cninewspapers.com
Newspaper (Democratic). **Freq:** Daily (morn.). **Print Method:** Offset. **Cols./Page:** 6. **Col. Width:** 26 nonpareils. **Col. Depth:** 301 agate lines. **Key Personnel:** Robert Bridges, Editor, phone: (386)754-0428; Tim Kirby, Director, Sports, phone: (386)754-0421; Todd Wilson, Publisher, phone: (386)754-0418. **Subscription Rates:** $83.46 Individuals 1 year (print and online); $48.79 Individuals 24 weeks (print and online); $26.32 Individuals 12 weeks (print and online); $9.63 Individuals 4 weeks (print and online). **URL:** http://www.lakecityreporter.com; http://www.cninewspapers.com/publications. **Mailing address:** PO Box 1709, Lake City, FL 32056-1709. **Remarks:** Accepts advertising. **Circ:** ★8500.

7737 ■ WCJX-FM - 106.5
5348 NW Hwy. 41
Lake City, FL 32055
Phone: (386)755-9259
Email: wcjxaudio@gmail.com
Format: Classic Rock. **Owner:** Black Crow Media, Not Available. **Operating Hours:** Continuous. **Ad Rates:** Advertising accepted; rates available upon request. **URL:** http://www.northflatoday.com.

7738 ■ WDSR-AM - 1340
2485 S Marion Ave.
Lake City, FL 32025
Phone: (386)752-1340
Format: Sports; Talk. **Networks:** CBS. **Founded:** 1946. **Operating Hours:** Continuous; 100% network. **Key Personnel:** Cesta Newman, Contact; John Newman, Contact. **Wattage:** 1,000. **Ad Rates:** $8-12 for 30 seconds; $10-15 for 60 seconds. Combined advertising rates available with WNFB. **URL:** http://www.northfloridanow.com.

7739 ■ WJTK-FM - 96.5
229 SW Main Blvd.
Lake City, FL 32025
Phone: (386)758-9696
Email: news@965wjtk.com
Format: Talk; News. **Key Personnel:** Ken Allen, Contact, gary@965wjtk.com; Cesta Newman, Contact, cesta@965wjtk.com; Bill Madden, Contact, johnnewman@mix943.com; Ken Allen, Contact, gary@965wjtk.com. **Ad Rates:** Advertising accepted; rates available upon request. **URL:** http://www.northfloridanow.com.

7740 ■ WNFB-FM - 94.3
2485 S Marion Ave.
Lake City, FL 32025
Phone: (386)961-9494
Format: Adult Contemporary. **Networks:** CBS; Florida Radio. **Founded:** 1969. **Operating Hours:** Continuous; 100% local. **Key Personnel:** Cesta Newman, Contact; John Newman, Contact, johnnewman@mix943.com; Barry Cole, Contact. **Wattage:** 50,000. **Ad Rates:** $15-24 for 30 seconds; $20-32 for 60 seconds. Combined advertising rates available with WDSR-AM. **URL:** http://www.northfloridanow.com.

7741 ■ WQLC-FM - 102.1
9206 W US Hwy. 90
Lake City, FL 32055
Fax: (818)957-0035
Format: Country; Oldies; News. **Operating Hours:** Continuous. **Ad Rates:** Advertising accepted; rates available upon request. **URL:** http://www.powercountry102.com.

7742 ■ W23AQ - 23
PO Box A
Santa Ana, CA 92711
Phone: (714)832-2950
Free: 888-731-1000
Owner: Trinity Broadcasting Network Inc., PO Box A, Santa Ana, CA 92711, Ph: (714)832-2950, Free: 888-731-1000. **URL:** http://www.tbn.org.

LAKE MARY

Seminole Co. Seminole Co. (NC). 2 m W of Sanford.

7743 ■ Charisma: Life in the Spirit
Charisma Media
600 Rinehart Rd.
Lake Mary, FL 32746
Phone: (407)333-0600
Fax: (407)333-7100
Free: 800-749-6500
Publication E-mail: charisma@strang.com
Religious magazine on Christian life. **Freq:** Monthly. **Print Method:** Offset. **Trim Size:** 8 x 10 1/2. **Cols./Page:** 3. **Col. Width:** 27 nonpareils. **Col. Depth:** 140 agate lines. **Key Personnel:** Stephen Strang, Publisher; Jimmy Stewart, Managing Editor; Marcus Yoars, Editor; J. Lee Grady, Editor. **ISSN:** 0895--156X (print). **Subscription Rates:** $15 Individuals 12 issues; $25 Individuals 24 issues; $36 Individuals 36 issues. **URL:** http://www.charismamedia.com/index.php/magazines/charisma; http://www.charismamag.com. **Remarks:** Accepts advertising. **Circ:** Combined 220000.

7744 ■ Christian Retailing
Charisma Media
600 Rinehart Rd.
Lake Mary, FL 32746
Phone: (407)333-0600
Fax: (407)333-7100
Free: 800-749-6500
Publisher's E-mail: info@charismamedia.com
Tabloid on retailing Christian merchandise. **Freq:** 20/yr. **Print Method:** Offset. **Trim Size:** 10 3/4 x 14. **Cols./Page:** 4. **Col. Width:** 2.25 picas. **Col. Depth:** 14 inches. **Key Personnel:** Eric Tiansay, Editor; Christine D. Johnson, Editor; Dave Condiff, Director, Advertising, Publisher. **ISSN:** 0027--6782 (print). **Subscription Rates:** $40 Individuals; $65 Canada; $80 Other countries. **URL:** http://www.christianretailing.com. **Remarks:** Accepts advertising. **Circ:** Controlled ‡10500.

7745 ■ Ministry Today
Charisma Media
600 Rinehart Rd.
Lake Mary, FL 32746
Phone: (407)333-0600
Fax: (407)333-7100
Free: 800-749-6500
Publication E-mail: ministrytoday@strang.com
Consumer magazine covering Christianity. **Freq:** 6/year. **Trim Size:** 8 x 10 1/2. **Key Personnel:** Stephen Strang, Publisher; Valerie G. Lowe, Managing Editor. **Subscription Rates:** $15 Individuals 1 year; $25 Individuals 2 years; $25 Individuals 3 Years of Ministry Today - SPECIAL OFFER: Same price as 2 years!. **URL:** http://www.ministrytodaymag.com. **Remarks:** Accepts advertising. **Circ:** Combined 125000.

7746 ■ SpiritLed Woman
Charisma Media
600 Rinehart Rd.
Lake Mary, FL 32746
Phone: (407)333-0600
Fax: (407)333-7100
Free: 800-749-6500
Publisher's E-mail: info@charismamedia.com
Consumer magazine covering Christianity and women. **Freq:** Monthly. **Key Personnel:** Brenda J. Davis, Editor; Joy F. Strang, Publisher. **Subscription Rates:** $12 Individuals 1 year; $24 Individuals 2 years; $36 Individuals 3 years. **URL:** http://www.charismamag.com/life/women. **Remarks:** Accepts advertising. **Circ:** (Not Reported).

7747 ■ Vida Cristiana
Charisma Media
600 Rinehart Rd.
Lake Mary, FL 32746
Phone: (407)333-0600
Fax: (407)333-7100
Free: 800-749-6500
Publication E-mail: vida@strang.com
Consumer magazine covering Christianity in Spanish. **Freq:** 6/year. **Key Personnel:** Rebeccah Barker, Manager, Sales; Tessie Guell de Devore, Publisher. **Subscription Rates:** $10 Individuals; $15 Single issue print and digital. **URL:** http://vidacristiana.com. **Remarks:** Accepts advertising. **Circ:** (Not Reported).

7748 ■ WHLV-TV - 52
31 Skyline Dr.
Lake Mary, FL 32746
Email: cr@tbn.org
Networks: Christian Television. **Owner:** Trinity Broadcasting Network Inc., PO Box A, Santa Ana, CA 92711, Ph: (714)832-2950, Free: 888-731-1000. **Founded:** 1982. **Formerly:** WTGL-TV. **Operating Hours:** Continuous Sat.-Thurs.; 1 a.m.-6 a.m. Fri. **ADI:** Orlando-Daytona Beach-Melbourne, FL. **Key Personnel:** Mark Reynolds, Div. Dir; Mark Reynolds, Contact. **Wattage:** 5,000,000. **Ad Rates:** $100 for 30 seconds; $160 for 60 seconds. **URL:** http://www.tbn.org.

7749 ■ WKTS-FM
1307 S International Pky.
Lake Mary, FL 32746-1414
Phone: (407)833-9600
Email: thebridgefm@yahoo.com
Format: Religious; Contemporary Christian. **Owner:** Foothills Broadcasting, Inc., at above address. **Ad Rates:** Underwriting available.

7750 ■ WOFL-TV - 35
35 Skyline Dr.
Lake Mary, FL 32746
Phone: (407)644-3535
Format: Commercial TV; News. **Networks:** Fox. **Owner:** Fox Television Station Inc., 1211 Ave. of the Americas, New York, NY 10036. **Founded:** 1979. **Operating Hours**: Continuous. **Ad Rates:** Advertising accepted; rates available upon request. **URL:** http://www.myfoxorlando.com.

7751 ■ WOGX-TV - 51
35 Skyline Dr.
Lake Mary, FL 32746
Phone: (407)644-3535
Format: Commercial TV. **Networks:** Fox. **Owner:** Fox Television, Inc., 1999 S Bundy Dr., Los Angeles, CA 90025, Ph: (310)584-2000. **Founded:** 1983. **Operating Hours**: Continuous. **ADI**: Gainesville (Ocala), FL. **Wattage**: 2,750,000. **Ad Rates:** $30-1100 per unit. **URL:** http://www.wogx.com.

7752 ■ WRBW-TV - 65
35 Skyline Dr.
Lake Mary, FL 32746
Phone: (407)644-3535
Format: Commercial TV. **Networks:** United Paramount Network. **Owner:** Fox Television, Inc., 1999 S Bundy Dr., Los Angeles, CA 90025, Ph: (310)584-2000. **Founded:** 1993. **Operating Hours**: Continuous. **Wattage**: 20,000. **Ad Rates:** Noncommercial. **URL:** http://www.my65orlando.com.

LAKE WALES

C FL. Polk Co. 30 mi. SE of Lakeland. Tourist resort. Ships citrus fruits. Manufactures boats, fertilizer, mattresses, concrete products, ceramic tile, canned fruits and vegetables. Citrus fruit packed; grapefruit cannery. Agriculture. Oranges, grapefruit, cattle.

7753 ■ The Lake Wales News
Sun Coast Media Group Inc.
140 E Stuart Ave.
Lake Wales, FL 33853
Phone: (863)676-3467
Fax: (863)678-1297
Community newspaper. **Freq:** Weekly. **Print Method:** Offset. **Trim Size:** 16 1/8 x 22. **Cols./Page:** 7. **Col. Width:** 25 nonpareils. **Col. Depth:** 21 inches. **Key Personnel:** Jim Gouvellis, Publisher; Jeff Roslow, Editor. **USPS:** 302-900. **Subscription Rates:** $47.99 Individuals home delivery; $59.20 Out of country; $64.80 Out of state. **URL:** http://lakewalesnews.com. **Remarks:** Accepts advertising. **Circ:** Paid ‡2963.

7754 ■ WIPC-AM
630 Mountain Lake Cutoff Rd.
Lake Wales, FL 33859
Phone: (863)676-8842
Fax: (863)679-9395
Format: Hispanic. **Founded:** 1951. **Formerly**: WKZJ-AM. **Wattage**: 1,000 Day; 500 Night. **Ad Rates:** $18-22 for 30 seconds; $24-29 for 60 seconds.

LAKE WORTH

SE FL. Palm Beach Co. Adjoins West Palm Beach on the south. Manufactures storage batteries, chemicals, paint. Nurseries. Winter resort.

7755 ■ Polo Magazine
United States Polo Association
9011 Lake Worth Rd.
Lake Worth, FL 33467
Free: 800-232-8772
Publisher's E-mail: info@newportrotary.org
Freq: Annual. **URL:** http://www.clubrunner.ca/CPrg/DxProgramHome/programhome.aspx?cid=4861&pid=46497&sid=66776. **Remarks:** Advertising not accepted. **Circ:** (Not Reported).

7756 ■ Polo Magazine
Rotary Club of Newport
PO Box 164
Newport, RI 02840-0002
Phone: (401)847-6340
Fax: (401)847-8476
Publisher's E-mail: info@newportrotary.org
Freq: Annual. **URL:** http://www.clubrunner.ca/CPrg/DxProgramHome/programhome.aspx?cid=4861&pid=46497&sid=66776. **Remarks:** Advertising not accepted. **Circ:** (Not Reported).

7757 ■ Polo Players Edition
United States Polo Association
9011 Lake Worth Rd.
Lake Worth, FL 33467
Free: 800-232-8772
Magazine containing feature articles, tournament reports, current events, and Polo Association news. **Freq:** Monthly. **Print Method:** Offset. **Trim Size:** 8 1/2 x 10 3/4. **Cols./Page:** 3. **Col. Width:** 28 nonpareils. **Col. Depth:** 138 agate lines. **Key Personnel:** Gwen Rizzo, Editor. **ISSN:** 1096--2255 (print). **Subscription Rates:** $45 Individuals; $78 Two years. **URL:** http://www.poloplayersedition.com. **Formerly:** Polo. **Ad Rates:** 4C $1640. **Remarks:** Accepts advertising. **Circ:** ‡7000.

7758 ■ Prison Legal News: Dedicated to Protecting Human Rights
Prison Legal News
PO Box 1151
Lake Worth, FL 33466
Phone: (561)360-2523
Fax: (866)735-7136
Publisher's E-mail: info@prisonlegalnews.org
Magazine covering news relating to prisoners' rights. **Freq:** Monthly. **Print Method:** Offset. **Trim Size:** 8 1/2 x 11. **Cols./Page:** 3. **Col. Width:** 2 1/4 inches. **Col. Depth:** 7 1/2 inches. **Key Personnel:** Alex Friedmann, Associate Editor; Paul Wright, Editor. **ISSN:** 1075--7678 (print). **Subscription Rates:** $30 Individuals 1 Year Print Subscription for Incarcerated Individuals.; $35 Individuals 1 Year Print Subscription for Non-Incarcerated Individuals.; $90 Institutions 1 Year Print Subscription for Legal Institutions.; $60 Individuals 2 Year Print Subscription for Incarcerated Individuals.; $70 Individuals 2 Year Print Subscription for Non-Incarcerated Individuals.; $180 Institutions 2 Year Print Subscription for Legal Institutions. **URL:** http://www.prisonlegalnews.org. **Formerly**: Prisoners' Legal News. **Ad Rates:** BW $7,520. **Remarks:** Accepts advertising. **Circ:** Paid 5000, Non-paid 250.

7759 ■ Psychology and Marketing
John Wiley & Sons Inc.
c/o Ronald Jay Cohen, PhD, Ed.-in-Ch.
Bldg. A-4, Ste. 224
8927 Hypoluxo Rd.
Lake Worth, FL 33467
Phone: (954)567-8530
Publisher's E-mail: info@wiley.com
Journal providing a forum for collaboration between psychologists and market researchers. Devoted exclusively to understanding the nature and operation of psychological principles as they apply to market strategies. **Founded:** 1984. **Freq:** Monthly. **Print Method:** Offset. **Trim Size:** 7 1/4 x 10 1/4. **Cols./Page:** 1. **Col. Width:** 72 nonpareils. **Col. Depth:** 126 agate lines. **Key Personnel:** Ronald Jay Cohen, PhD, Editor-in-Chief; Rajan Nataraajan, PhD, Executive Editor, phone: (334)844-2450, fax: (334)844-4032; Astrid Keel, PhD, Editor; Neal Roese, PhD, Board Member; Michelle Roehm, PhD, Board Member; Donald H. Hantula, PhD, Board Member. **ISSN:** 0742-6046 (print); **EISSN:** 1520-6793 (electronic). **Subscription Rates:** $2615 Institutions print with online; $2179 Institutions print or online. **URL:** http://onlinelibrary.wiley.com/journal/10.1002/(ISSN)1520-6793. **Ad Rates:** BW $772; 4C $1,009; SAU $420. **Remarks:** Accepts advertising. **Circ:** Paid 5600.

7760 ■ WPBR 96.1FM - 1340
1776 Lake Worth, Ste. 201
Lake Worth, FL 33460
Phone: (561)641-8882
Fax: (561)533-0607
Format: Talk. **Networks:** Mutual Broadcasting System. **Founded:** 1988. **Operating Hours**: Continuous. **ADI**: West Palm Beach-Ft. Pierce-Vero Beach, FL. **Wattage**: 1,000. **Ad Rates:** $16-44 for 30 seconds; $20-55 for 60 seconds. **URL:** http://sakpase.fm.

LAKELAND

C FL. Polk Co. 32 mi. E. of Tampa. Florida Southern College. Manufactures fertilizer, beverages, batteries, furniture, food machinery, ceramic tile. Phosphate mines. Citrus fruit packing and canning. Fruit, truck, poultry farms.

7761 ■ The Ledger
The Ledger
300 W Lime St.
Lakeland, FL 33815
Phone: (863)802-7323
Free: 888-431-7323
Publication E-mail: voice@theledger.com
General newspaper. **Founded:** 1924. **Freq:** Daily. **Print Method:** Offset. **Trim Size:** 17 x 24. **Cols./Page:** 6. **Col. Width:** 25 nonpareils. **Col. Depth:** 301 agate lines. **Key Personnel:** Lenore Devore, Editor, phone: (863)802-7501. **Subscription Rates:** $14.65 Individuals 7 day, monthly. **URL:** http://www.theledger.com/apps/pbcs.dll/frontpage. **Mailing address:** PO Box 408, Lakeland, FL 33802. **Remarks:** Accepts advertising. **Circ:** Mon.-Fri. ***54991**, Sun. ***70617**, Sat. ***54933**.

7762 ■ Managerial and Decision Economics
John Wiley & Sons Inc.
c/o Antony W. Dnes, Ed.-in-Ch.
Barney Barnett School of Business and Free Enterprise
Florida Southern College
Lakeland, FL 33801
Publisher's E-mail: info@wiley.com
Academic journal dealing with the analysis of economic issues. **Freq:** 8/year. **Key Personnel:** Antony Dnes, Editor-in-Chief; Roger Clarke, Board Member; Mark A. Cohen, Board Member; William S. Comanor, Board Member; Warren R. Hughes, Board Member; Gordon R. Foxall, Board Member; Edward P. Lazear, Board Member. **ISSN:** 0143--6570 (print); **EISSN:** 1099--1468 (electronic). **Subscription Rates:** $2846 Institutions online or print - USA/Canada & Mexico/ROW; $3416 Institutions print & online - USA/Canada & Mexico/ROW; $552 Individuals print - USA/Canada & Mexico/Europe/ROW; £1454 Institutions online or print - UK; £1745 Institutions print & online - UK; €1837 Institutions online or print - Europe; €2205 Institutions print & online - Europe. **URL:** http://onlinelibrary.wiley.com/journal/10.1002/(ISSN)1099-1468; http://authorservices.wiley.com/bauthor/Aims_scope.asp?ref=0143-6570&site=1. **Remarks:** Accepts advertising. **Circ:** (Not Reported).

7763 ■ Osceola News-Gazette
Florida Sun Publications
7060 Havertys Way
Lakeland, FL 33805
Phone: (863)583-1202
Community newspaper. **Freq:** Semiweekly (Thurs. & Sat.). **Print Method:** Offset. **Trim Size:** 13 x 20 1/2. **Cols./Page:** 8. **Col. Width:** 18 nonpareils. **Col. Depth:** 287 agate lines. **Key Personnel:** Matt Plocha, Publisher; Kathy Beckham, Manager, Circulation. **ISSN:** 1060--1244 (print). **USPS:** 513-540. **URL:** http://www.aroundosceola.com. **Remarks:** Accepts advertising. **Circ:** Combined ‡86000.

7764 ■ The Southern
Florida Southern College
111 Lake Hollingsworth Dr.
Lakeland, FL 33801
Phone: (863)680-4111
Collegiate newspaper. **Founded:** 1923. **Freq:** Biweekly. **Print Method:** Letterpress and offset. **Cols./Page:** 5. **Col. Width:** 11 picas. **Col. Depth:** 90 picas. **Subscription Rates:** $5 Individuals. **URL:** http://www.fscsouthern.com/. **Ad Rates:** BW $375; PCI $5. **Remarks:** Accepts advertising. **Circ:** Free ‡2500.

7765 ■ Water Flying
Seaplane Pilots Association
3859 Laird Blvd.
Lakeland, FL 33811
Phone: (863)701-7979
Publisher's E-mail: spa@seaplanes.org
Freq: Bimonthly. **ISSN:** 0733--1754 (print). **Subscription Rates:** Included in membership; $17.50 Nonmembers. **URL:** http://www.seaplanes.org/Water-Flying-Magazine.html. **Remarks:** Accepts advertising. **Circ:** (Not Reported).

7766 ■ Cablevision of Central Florida
5735 S Florida Ave.
Box 6220
Lakeland, FL 33807
Phone: (813)644-6149
Owner: American TV & Communications Corp., at above address. **Founded:** 1983.

Circulation: ★ = AAM; △ or • = BPA; ♦ = CAC; ❑ = VAC; ⊕ = PO Statement; ‡ = Publisher's Report; Boldface figures = sworn; Light figures = estimated.

7767 ■ Hall Comunications Inc.
404 W Lime St.
Lakeland, FL 33815-4651
Phone: (863)682-8184
Fax: (863)683-2409
Ad Rates: Advertising accepted; rates available upon request. **URL:** http://www.hallradio.com.

7768 ■ WLKF-AM - 1430
404 W Lime St.
Lakeland, FL 33815
Phone: (863)682-8184
Fax: (863)683-2409
Format: News; Talk. **Networks:** NBC; ABC. **Founded:** 1936. **Formerly:** WLAK-AM. **Operating Hours:** Continuous. **Key Personnel:** Jessica Brown, Dir. Pub. Aff.; Nancy Cattarius, Gen. Mgr.; Andrea Oliver, Dir. Pub. Aff. **Wattage:** 5,000-Day; 1,000-Night. **Ad Rates:** Advertising accepted; rates available upon request. **URL:** http://www.wlkf.com.

7769 ■ WONN-AM - 1230
404 W Lime St.
Lakeland, FL 33815
Phone: (863)682-8184
Free: 800-582-0201
Format: Oldies. **Networks:** CNN Radio. **Founded:** 1949. **Operating Hours:** Continuous; 10% network, 90% local. **ADI:** Tampa-St. Petersburg (Lakeland, Sarasota), FL. **Key Personnel:** Nancy Cattarius, Gen. Mgr.; Mike James, Prog. Dir.; Andrea Oliver, Dir. Pub. Aff., News Dir. **Wattage:** 1,000. **Ad Rates:** Noncommercial. **URL:** http://www.wonn.com.

7770 ■ WPCV-FM - 97.5
404 W Lime St.
Lakeland, FL 33815
Phone: (863)682-8184
Fax: (863)683-2409
Free: 800-227-9797
Format: Country. **Founded:** 1973. **Formerly:** WINT-FM. **Operating Hours:** Continuous. **Key Personnel:** Mike James, Dir. of Programs; Jessica Brown, Promotions Dir.; Andrea Oliver, Dir. Pub. Aff., News Dir. **Wattage:** 100,000. **Ad Rates:** Advertising accepted; rates available upon request. **URL:** http://www.wpcv.com.

7771 ■ WTXR-FM
PO Box 7217
Lakeland, FL 33807
Format: Religious. **Founded:** Nov. 08, 1997. **Wattage:** 400 ERP. **Ad Rates:** Noncommercial.

7772 ■ WWAB-AM - 1330
1203 W Chase St.
Lakeland, FL 33802-0065
Phone: (863)682-2998
Format: Gospel; Blues. **Founded:** 1957. **ADI:** Tampa-St. Petersburg (Lakeland, Sarasota), FL. **Wattage:** 1,000 Daytime; 118 N. **Ad Rates:** $10 for 30 seconds; $15 for 60 seconds. **Mailing address:** PO Box 65, Lakeland, FL 33802-0065. **URL:** http://wwab1330.net/.

7773 ■ WWRZ-FM - 98.3
404 W Lime St.
Lakeland, FL 33815
Phone: (863)682-8184
Fax: (863)683-2409
Free: 866-601-1629
Format: Adult Contemporary. **Founded:** 1990. **Key Personnel:** Mike James, Div. Dir. **Wattage:** 50,000. **Ad Rates:** Advertising accepted; rates available upon request. **URL:** http://www.max983fm.com.

LAND O LAKES

7774 ■ Birding Business
Longdown Management Inc.
PO Box 1440
Land O Lakes, FL 34639
Phone: (813)995-2804
Fax: (813)996-7620
Publisher's E-mail: editor@birdingbusiness.com
Business magazine providing the latest news and information about the bird feeding industry. **Freq:** Quarterly. **Key Personnel:** Raymond W. David, Publisher; Felix Schilling, Associate Publisher; Sharon Stiteler, Editor. **Subscription Rates:** $22 Individuals. **URL:** http://www.birdingbusiness.com/. **Remarks:** Advertising accepted; rates available upon request. **Circ:** (Not Reported).

LARGO

WC FL. Pinellas Co. 12 mi. NW of St. Petersburg. Small Industries. Nurseries.

7775 ■ WIXL-AM - 1190
800 8th Ave. SE
Largo, FL 33771
Phone: (813)281-1040
Email: kevinbaldinger@espn1080.com
Networks: ABC; Business Radio. **Owner:** Genesis Communications, 2110 Powers Ferry Rd., Ste. 290, Atlanta, GA 30339-5062, Ph: (678)324-0170, Fax: (404)324-0174. **Founded:** 1977. **Formerly:** WAJL. **Operating Hours:** Sunrise-sunset. **ADI:** Orlando-Daytona Beach-Melbourne, FL. **Key Personnel:** Bruce Maduri, Gen. Mgr., Owner, ceo@radiogenesis.com; Kevin J. Baldinger, News Dir. **Wattage:** 5,000. **Ad Rates:** $50-75 per unit. Combined advertising rates available with WHOO-AM. **URL:** http://www.newstalkflorida.com.

WVUP-TV - See Tallahassee

LECANTO

7776 ■ WIFL-FM - 104.3
5399 W Gulf to Lake Hwy.
Lecanto, FL 34461
Phone: (352)436-1043
Email: wow104@gmail.com
Format: Adult Contemporary; Contemporary Hit Radio (CHR); Talk. **Owner:** Nature Coast Broadcasting Inc., at above address. **Founded:** Oct. 01, 1996. **Operating Hours:** Continuous. **Key Personnel:** Lisa Cupelli, Dir. of Operations, lisacupelli@yahoo.com; Sab Cupelli, Owner. **Wattage:** 4,400. **Ad Rates:** Advertising accepted; rates available upon request. **URL:** http://www.keysports1043.com.

7777 ■ WYKE-TV - 47
5399 W Gulf to Lake Hwy.
Lecanto, FL 34461
Phone: (352)527-2341
Fax: (352)746-6514
Free: 888-377-0340
Email: tvproduction@keytrainingcenter.org
Format: News; Sports. **Operating Hours:** Continuous. **Wattage:** 15,000 ERP. **Ad Rates:** Advertising accepted; rates available upon request. **URL:** http://www.wyke47.com.

LEESBURG

C FL. Lake Co. 40 mi. NW of Orlando. Lake-Sumter Community College. Manufactures concrete products, mobile homes. Packs citrus fruit. Fishing resort. Truck and citrus farms.

7778 ■ Daily Commercial
Halifax Media Holdings L.L.C.
Daytona Beach, FL 32119
Phone: (386)265-6700
Fax: (386)265-6750
Publisher's E-mail: support@halifaxmediagroup.com
General newspaper. **Freq:** Daily. **Print Method:** Offset. **Cols./Page:** 6. **Col. Width:** 26 nonpareils. **Col. Depth:** 301 agate lines. **Key Personnel:** Frank Jolley, Editor, phone: (352)365-8268; Tom Mcniff, Executive Editor. **Subscription Rates:** $165.25 Individuals 7 day daily; $103.20 Individuals weekend only - Friday, Saturday, Sunday; $79.21 Individuals Sunday only; $437.19 By mail 7 day daily; $165.44 By mail Sunday only. **URL:** http://www.dailycommercial.com. **Remarks:** Accepts advertising. **Circ:** (Not Reported).

7779 ■ Leesburg Lakeshore Mobile Home Park
1208 N Lee St.
Leesburg, FL 34748
Email: llmhp@aol.com
Owner: Sally .musso, at above address. **Founded:** 1947. **Key Personnel:** Sally Reeves, Partner. **Cities Served:** subscribing households 184. **URL:** http://leesburglakeshoremhc.com/.

7780 ■ WLBE-AM - 790
32900 Radio Rd.
Leesburg, FL 34788
Phone: (352)787-7900
Fax: (352)787-1402
Format: Information; News. **Owner:** WLBE Radio Inc., 32900 Radio Rd., Leesburg, FL 34788, Ph: (352)787-7900. **Founded:** 1947. **Wattage:** 5,000. **URL:** http://www.my790am.com.

LEHIGH ACRES

S FL. Lee Co. 12 mi. E. of Fort Myers. Semi retirement community.

7781 ■ Lehigh Acres News Star
News-Press Publications Inc.
1280 Lee Blvd.
Lehigh Acres, FL 33936
Phone: (239)369-2191
Community newspaper. **Founded:** Feb. 15, 1962. **Freq:** 2/week. **Print Method:** Offset. **Cols./Page:** 6. **Col. Width:** 11 picas. **Col. Depth:** 21.5 inches. **Key Personnel:** Gene Shue, Director, Finance, phone: (239)335-0374; Casey Logan, Editor, phone: (239)344-4721; Mei-Mei Chan, Publisher, phone: (239)335-0277; Michelle Hudson, Editor, phone: (239)344-4883. **Subscription Rates:** $16.31 Individuals month; daily; $11.96 Individuals month; weekends; $8.70 Individuals month; Sunday & Holiday. **URL:** http://www.news-press.com/section/NEWS0103. **Formerly:** News-Star. **Remarks:** Accepts advertising. **Circ:** Paid 8393, Free 6889.

LITHIA

7782 ■ Farm and Ranch News
Farm & Ranch News
PO Box 160
Lithia, FL 33547-0160
Publication E-mail: farmranchnews@aol.com
Trade publication covering agribusiness issues for commercial farmers and ranchers. **Freq:** Monthly. **Print Method:** Web offset. **Trim Size:** 11 x 13 3/4. **Cols./Page:** 6. **Col. Width:** 1 7/8 inches. **Col. Depth:** 12 inches. **Key Personnel:** George Parker, Jr., Editor, phone: (813)737-6397. **USPS:** 111-230. **Subscription Rates:** $12.50 Individuals in Florida; $15 Out of state. **Ad Rates:** BW $440; 4C $540; PCI $7.50. **Remarks:** Accepts advertising. **Circ:** Paid 6000, Controlled 13000.

LIVE OAK

Suwannee Co. Suwannee Co. (NC). 20 m NW of Lake City.

7783 ■ The Jasper News
Live Oak Publications
211 Howard St. E
Live Oak, FL 32064
Publication E-mail: jaspernews1@alltel.net
Local newspaper. **Founded:** 1870. **Freq:** Weekly (Thurs.). **Print Method:** Offset. **Trim Size:** 13 x 21 1/2. **Cols./Page:** 6. **Col. Width:** 2 inches. **Col. Depth:** 21 1/2 inches. **Key Personnel:** Jeff Waters, Editor. **Subscription Rates:** $18 Individuals; $25 Out of area. **URL:** http://www.suwanneedemocrat.com/news/jasper_news/. **Ad Rates:** GLR $8.50; SAU $6.25; PCI $6.37. **Remarks:** Accepts advertising. **Circ:** Paid 2100, Free 300.

7784 ■ Live Oak Suwannee Democrat
Live Oak Publications
211 Howard St. E
Live Oak, FL 32064
Community newspaper. **Freq:** Semiweekly (Wed. and Fri.). **Print Method:** Offset press. **Cols./Page:** 6. **Col. Width:** 12 picas. **Col. Depth:** 21 1/2 inches. **Key Personnel:** Myra Regan, Publisher. **URL:** http://www.suwanneedemocrat.com. **Remarks:** Accepts advertising. **Circ:** 5500.

7785 ■ WLVO-FM - 106.1
PO Box 1061
Live Oak, FL 32064-1061
Phone: (386)364-1061
Format: Classic Rock. **Owner:** Leon F. Pettersen, Not Available. **Founded:** Sept. 01, 1998. **Operating Hours:** Continuous. **Ad Rates:** Noncommercial.

7786 ■ WOLR-FM - 91.3
PO Box 1448
Live Oak, FL 32064
Phone: (386)362-3042
Owner: WOLR 91.3 FM Inc., at above address. **Founded:** 1986. **Wattage:** 18,000. **Ad Rates:** Noncommercial.

7787 ■ WORL-FM
PO Box 1448
Live Oak, FL 32064

Ad Rates: Noncommercial.

7788 ■ WQHL-AM - 1250
1305 Helvenston St.
Live Oak, FL 32060
Phone: (386)362-1250
Email: wqhlaudio@gmail.com
Format: Oldies. **Networks:** ABC; ESPN Radio. **Owner:** RTG Radio, LLC, 126 W International SpeedWestay Blvd., Daytona Beach, FL 32114. **Founded:** 1949. **Formerly:** WNER-AM. **Operating Hours:** Continuous; 10% local, 90% network. **ADI:** Tallahassee, FL-Thomasville (Bainbridge), GA. **Wattage:** 1,000. **Ad Rates:** $3 for 15 seconds; $5 for 30 seconds; $8 for 60 seconds. Combined advertising rates available with WQHL-FM and WCJX-FM. **URL:** http://www.wqhl981.com.

7789 ■ WQHL-FM
1305 E Helvenston St.
Live Oak, FL 32064
Phone: (386)362-1250
Format: News; Talk. **Networks:** ABC. **Owner:** RTG Media, at above address. **Founded:** 1973. **Key Personnel:** Kickin Kevin, Contact; Jake Rhodes, Contact; Gail Taylor, Contact, deanb@wqhlcountry.com; Road Dog Russell Howard, Contact. **Wattage:** 50,000 ERP. **Ad Rates:** Advertising accepted; rates available upon request. $5-5.88 for 15 seconds; $10-12 for 30 seconds; $18-21 for 60 seconds. **URL:** http://wqhl981.com.

LONG BOAT KEY

7790 ■ The East County Observer
The Observer Group Inc.
5570 Gulf of Mexico Dr.
Long Boat Key, FL 34228
Phone: (941)366-5509
Fax: (941)383-7193
Publication E-mail: eastcountynews@yourobserver.com eastcountyletters@yourobserver.com
Community newspaper. **Freq:** Weekly (Thurs.). **Key Personnel:** Matt Walsh, Editor, Chief Executive Officer; Jen Blanco, Editor. **URL:** http://www.yourobserver.com/east-county. **Remarks:** Accepts advertising. **Circ:** Combined ■ **18033**.

7791 ■ The Longboat Observer
The Observer Group Inc.
5570 Gulf of Mexico Dr.
Long Boat Key, FL 34228
Phone: (941)366-5509
Fax: (941)383-7193
Publisher's E-mail: longboatnews@yourobserver.com
Community newspaper serving the island of Longboat Key, the surrounding islands of Lido Key, Bird Key, St. Armands Key, and Anna Maria Island, and areas of Sarasota and Bradenton. **Freq:** Weekly (Thurs.). **Key Personnel:** Matt Walsh, Chief Executive Officer, Editor; Lisa Walsh, Vice President, Chief Marketing Officer; Jessica Luck, Executive Editor. **URL:** http://www.yourobserver.com/e-editions?publication=12&date%5Bvalue%5D%5Byear%5D=2016. **Remarks:** Accepts advertising. **Circ:** Free ■ **12937**, Paid ■ **724**, Combined ■ **13661**.

7792 ■ The Sarasota Observer
The Observer Group Inc.
5570 Gulf of Mexico Dr.
Long Boat Key, FL 34228
Phone: (941)366-5509
Fax: (941)383-7193
Publication E-mail: sarasotanews@yourobserver.com sarasotaletters@yourobserver.com
Community newspaper. **Freq:** Weekly (Thurs.). **Key Personnel:** Lisa Walsh, Vice President, Chief Marketing Officer; Matt Walsh, Editor, Chief Executive Officer; Jessica Luck, Executive Editor. **URL:** http://www.yourobserver.com/news/sarasota/Front-Page/. **Remarks:** Accepts advertising. **Circ:** Combined ■ **31,000**.

LONGWOOD

Seminole Co. Seminole Co. (C). 10 m N of Orlando.

7793 ■ Bull & Bear Financial Report
Bull & Bear Financial Newspaper
PO Box 917179
Longwood, FL 32791
Fax: (407)682-6170
Free: 800-336-2855
Newspaper featuring a comprehensive digest of what the top performing investment advisory newsletters are recommending as well as general financial news. Includes articles pertaining to listed stocks, precious metals, stocks, mutual funds, economy, domestic and international stock markets and personal finance. **Freq:** Monthly. **Print Method:** Web offset. **Cols./Page:** 4. **Col. Width:** 14.5 picas. **Col. Depth:** 15.5 inches. **Key Personnel:** Valerie Waters, Manager, Advertising; David J. Robinson, Editor. **ISSN:** 0319--1362 (print). **Subscription Rates:** $44 Individuals; $69 Two years. **URL:** http://www.thebullandbear.com. **Ad Rates:** BW $3,268; 4C $4,404; PCI $70. **Remarks:** Accepts advertising. **Circ:** (Not Reported).

7794 ■ La Opinion Contigo
ImpreMedia L.L.C.
685 S Ronald Reagan Blvd.
Longwood, FL 32750
Phone: (407)767-0070
Newspaper serving the Hispanic community in Los Angeles, California. **Freq:** Weekly (Sat.). **Key Personnel:** Monica Lozano, Publisher; Bill Elliot, Director, Advertising; Jim Pellegrino, Manager, Circulation. **URL:** http://www.laopinion.com. **Remarks:** Accepts advertising. **Circ:** Non-paid ♦**255091**.

7795 ■ La Prensa Newspaper
ImpreMedia L.L.C.
685 S Ronald Reagan Blvd.
Longwood, FL 32750
Phone: (407)767-0070
Newspaper (tabloid) serving the Hispanic community of Central and South Florida (Spanish). **Freq:** Weekly (Thurs.). **Print Method:** Offset. **Trim Size:** 11 1/2 x 17. **Cols./Page:** 5. **Col. Width:** 2 1/16 inches. **Col. Depth:** 16 inches. **Key Personnel:** Tino Duran, Publisher. **URL:** http://laprensafl.com. **Ad Rates:** BW $1,360; 4C $1,660; SAU $17. **Remarks:** Accepts advertising. **Circ:** Non-paid ‡34139.

7796 ■ La Opinion
ImpreMedia L.L.C.
685 S Ronald Reagan Blvd.
Longwood, FL 32750
Phone: (407)767-0070
General newspaper (Spanish). **Freq:** Mon.-Sun. (morn.). **Print Method:** Offset. **Cols./Page:** 6. **Col. Width:** 12 picas. **Col. Depth:** 294 agate lines. **Key Personnel:** Jose I. Lozano, Contact; Monica Lozano, Chief Executive Officer, Executive Editor. **URL:** http://www.laopinion.com. **Ad Rates:** GLR $34.96; BW $4510; 4C $5429.89. **Remarks:** Accepts advertising. **Circ:** Mon.-Fri. ★**121026**, Sat. ★**101412**, Sun. ★**58985**.

LUTZ

7797 ■ Florida Entomologist: An International Journal of the Americas
Florida Entomological Society
PO Box 1007
Lutz, FL 33548-1007
Phone: (813)903-9234
Fax: (813)979-4908
Publisher's E-mail: flaentsoc@gmail.com
Peer-reviewed entomological journal containing abstracts (English and Spanish). **Freq:** Quarterly. **Print Method:** Offset. **Trim Size:** 7 x 10. **Cols./Page:** 2. **Key Personnel:** Dr. Waldemar Klassen, Editor; Teresa DuChene, Business Manager. **ISSN:** 0015--4040 (print); **EISSN:** 1938--5102 (electronic). **Subscription Rates:** $50 Nonmembers; $15 Single issue; $50 Institutions; $20 Students; $40 Members; $15 Elsewhere. **URL:** http://www.fcla.edu/FlaEnt. **Remarks:** Advertising not accepted. **Circ:** ‡1000.

MACCLENNY

7798 ■ The Baker County Press
The Baker County Press
104 S Fifth St.
Macclenny, FL 32063
Phone: (904)259-2400
Local newspaper. **Freq:** Weekly (Thurs.). **Print Method:** Offset. **Cols./Page:** 6. **Col. Width:** 27 nonpareils. **Col. Depth:** 301 agate lines. **Key Personnel:** Karin Thomas, Office Manager; Jessica Prevatt, Director, Advertising, Director, Production. **Subscription Rates:** $25 Individuals. **URL:** http://bakercountypress.com. **Mailing address:** PO Box 598, Macclenny, FL 32063. **Remarks:** Accepts advertising. **Circ:** (Not Reported).

MADISON

N FL. Madison Co. 28 mi. S. of Valdosta, GA. Sawmills. Agriculture. Tobacco, cotton, corn, peaches, watermelons, cattle and hogs.

7799 ■ Madison Magazine
Madison County Chamber of Commerce
248 SW Range Ave.
Madison, FL 32340
Phone: (850)973-2788
Fax: (850)973-8864
Free: 877-272-3642
Publisher's E-mail: chamber@madisonfl.org
Magazine containing information about the community of Madison County, Fl. **Freq:** Periodic. **Alt. Formats:** PDF. **URL:** http://www.madisonfl.org; http://madisonfl.org/magazine_archive.php. **Mailing address:** PO Box 817, Madison, FL 32340. **Remarks:** Advertising not accepted. **Circ:** (Not Reported).

7800 ■ WMAF-AM - 1230
PO Box 621
Madison, FL 32341
Phone: (850)973-3233
Fax: (850)973-3097
Format: Country. **URL:** http://www.radiowmaf.com.

MAITLAND

EC FL. Orange Co. 5 mi. N. of Orlando.

7801 ■ WEBG-FM - 100.3
2500 Maitland Center Pky., Ste. 401
Maitland, FL 32751
Phone: (407)916-7800
Free: 888-978-1003
Format: Oldies. **ADI:** Orlando-Daytona Beach-Melbourne, FL. **Key Personnel:** Linda Byrd, Gen. Mgr.; Raymond Torres, Dir. of Programs; Suheiley Gonzales, Promotions Dir. **Wattage:** 100,000. **URL:** http://www.rumba100.com/main.html.

7802 ■ WFLF-AM - 540
2500 Maitland Center Pkwy.
Maitland, FL 32751
Phone: (407)916-7800
Format: News; Talk. **Operating Hours:** Continuous. **ADI:** Orlando-Daytona Beach-Melbourne, FL. **Key Personnel:** Mark McCauley, Sales Mgr., markmccauley@clearchannel.com. **Wattage:** 50,000 ERP. **Ad Rates:** Advertising accepted; rates available upon request. **URL:** http://www.1025wfla.com.

7803 ■ WGMF-FM - 107.7
2500 Maitland Center Pkwy., Ste. 401
Maitland, FL 32751
Phone: (407)916-7800
Fax: (407)916-0329
Free: 888-978-1077
Format: Eclectic. **Operating Hours:** Continuous. **URL:** http://www.magic107.com.

7804 ■ WJRR-FM - 101.1
2500 Maitland Center Pky., No. 401
Maitland, FL 32751
Phone: (407)916-1011
Free: 888-978-1011
Format: Album-Oriented Rock (AOR). **Networks:** Independent. **Owner:** iHeartMedia Inc., 200 E Basse Rd., San Antonio, TX 78209, Ph: (210)832-3314. **Founded:** 1985. **Formerly:** WCKS-FM; WSTF-FM. **Operating Hours:** Continuous. **Key Personnel:** Rick Everett, Prog. Dir. **Wattage:** 100,000. **Ad Rates:** Advertising accepted; rates available upon request. **URL:** http://www.wjrr.com.

7805 ■ WLOQ-FM - 107.7
2301 Lucien Way, Ste. 180
Maitland, FL 32751
Phone: (407)647-5557
Fax: (407)647-4495
Format: Jazz; Sports. **Owner:** Gross Communications Corp., at above address, MAITLAND, FL. **Founded:** 1966. **Operating Hours:** Continuous. **Key Personnel:** Raymond Torres, Prog. Dir.; Laura Kam, Mgr. **Ad Rates:** Advertising accepted; rates available upon request.

Circulation: ★ = AAM; △ or • = BPA; ♦ = CAC; ❑ = VAC; ⊕ = PO Statement; ‡ = Publisher's Report; Boldface figures = sworn; Light figures = estimated.

URL: http://www.wloqradio.com.

7806 ■ WMGF-FM - 107.7
2500 Maitland Center Pky., Ste. 401
Maitland, FL 32751
Phone: (407)916-7800
Free: 888-978-1077
Format: Adult Contemporary; Soft Rock. **Networks:** NBC. **Founded:** 1966. **Operating Hours:** Continuous. **Key Personnel:** Laura Kam, Promotions Mgr., laurakam@ccorlando.com. **Wattage:** 100,000. **Ad Rates:** Advertising accepted; rates available upon request. **URL:** http://www.magic107.com.

7807 ■ WRUM-FM - 100.3
2500 Maitland Center Pky., Ste. 401
Maitland, FL 32751
Phone: (407)916-1003
Fax: (407)916-0329
Free: 888-978-1003
Format: Hispanic. **Founded:** 1971. **Operating Hours:** Continuous. **Key Personnel:** Raymond Torres, Dir. of Programs, raymondtorres@rumba100.com. **Wattage:** 100,000. **Ad Rates:** $40-225 per unit. **URL:** http://www.rumba100.com.

7808 ■ WTKS-FM - 104.1
2500 Maitland Center Pky., Ste. 401
Maitland, FL 32751
Phone: (407)916-1041
Fax: (407)916-7511
Free: 888-978-1041
Format: Talk; Alternative/New Music/Progressive. **Ad Rates:** Noncommercial. **URL:** http://www.realradio.fm.

7809 ■ WXXL-FM - 106.7
2500 Maitland Center Pky., Ste. 401
Maitland, FL 32751-7407
Phone: (407)916-7800
Format: Contemporary Hit Radio (CHR). **Networks:** Independent. **Founded:** 1990. **Formerly:** WCAT-FM. **Operating Hours:** Continuous. **Key Personnel:** Linda Byrd, Gen. Mgr. **Wattage:** 100,000. **Ad Rates:** Advertising accepted; rates available upon request. **URL:** http://www.xl1067.com//main.html.

7810 ■ WYGM-AM - 740
2500 Maitland Centre Pkwy., Ste. 401
Maitland, FL 32751
Phone: (407)916-7800
Free: 800-729-8255
Format: Sports. **Formerly:** WQTM-AM. **Ad Rates:** Noncommercial. **URL:** http://www.740thegame.com.

MARATHON

S FL. Monroe Co. On Gulf of Mexico, 45 mi. NE of Key West. Fisheries. Tourist resort.

7811 ■ WFFG-AM
Boot Key Rd., No. 1
Marathon, FL 33050
Phone: (305)743-5563
Fax: (305)743-9441
Free: 800-944-9334
Format: Talk; Sports; News. **Networks:** People's Network; NBC; Westwood One Radio; Meadows Racing. **Owner:** Mr. Joseph Nascone, PO Box 500940, Marathon, FL 33050. **Founded:** 1962. **Key Personnel:** John Perry, Operations Mgr; J. Nascone, Contact. **Wattage:** 2,500.

7812 ■ WGMX-FM - 94.3
PO Box 500940
Marathon, FL 33050
Phone: (305)743-5563
Fax: (305)743-9441
Free: 800-944-9334
Format: Adult Contemporary. **Networks:** Independent; Westwood One Radio; NBC. **Owner:** Mr. Joseph Nascone, PO Box 500940, Marathon, FL 33050. **Founded:** 1976. **Formerly:** WMUM-FM. **Operating Hours:** Continuous. **ADI:** Tampa-St. Petersburg (Lakeland, Sarasota), FL. **Key Personnel:** John Perry, Dir. of Operations; J. Nascone, Contact. **Wattage:** 50,000.

7813 ■ WKYZ-FM - 101.3
1 Boot Key
Marathon, FL 33050
Email: sales@conchrepublicgroup.com
Format: Classic Rock. **Owner:** Glades Media Group, 530 E Alverdez Ave., Clewiston, FL 33440, Ph: (863)983-5900. **Mailing address:** PO Box 500940, Marathon, FL 33050. **URL:** http://www.keystv.com.

MARCO ISLAND

S FL. Collier Co. On Gulf of Mexico, 45 mi. S. of Fort Myers.

7814 ■ Marco Island
Marco Island Area Chamber of Commerce
1102 N Collier Blvd.
Marco Island, FL 34145
Phone: (239)394-7549
Fax: (239)394-3061
Free: 800-788-6272
Freq: 3/year. **URL:** http://www.marcoreview.com. **Remarks:** Advertising not accepted. **Circ:** (Not Reported).

MARGATE

S FL. Broward Co. 10 mi. NE of Fort Lauderdale.

7815 ■ Dealer Communicator
Fichera Publications
441 S State Rd.7, Ste. 14
Margate, FL 33068
Trade journal (tabloid) for the printing industry. **Freq:** Monthly. **Print Method:** Offset. Uses mats. **Trim Size:** 11 x 17. **Cols./Page:** 4. **Col. Width:** 29 nonpareils. **Col. Depth:** 196 agate lines. **Key Personnel:** Mike O. Fichera, President, Publisher; Patricia Leavitt, Vice President. **URL:** http://www.dealercommunicator.com. **Remarks:** Accepts advertising. **Circ:** (Not Reported).

MARIANNA

NW FL. Jackson Co. On Chipola River, 60 mi. NW of Tallahassee. Chipola Junior College. Recreation area. Manufactures furniture, textiles, commercial laundry equipment. Limestone quarries. Agriculture.

7816 ■ National Driller
BNP Media
National Driller
4636 Hwy. 90 E, Ste. P
Marianna, FL 32446
Publisher's E-mail: asm@halldata.com
Publication covering the construction, petroleum, and energy industries. **Freq:** Monthly. **Key Personnel:** Lisa Schroeder, Managing Editor, phone: (630)694-4349, fax: (248)786-1446; Dan Murfey, Publisher, phone: (248)244-1277, fax: (248)244-3913; Dean Laramore, Manager, Advertising and Sales, fax: (248)502-2047; Greg Ettling, Editor, phone: (847)387-9391, fax: (248)502-1005; Teresa Owens, Manager, Circulation, phone: (847)763-9534, fax: (847)763-9538; Carrie Cypert, Director, Production, phone: (248)786-1688, fax: (248)502-1020. **ISSN:** 1527--1501 (print). **Subscription Rates:** Free to qualified subscribers. **URL:** http://www.nationaldriller.com; http://www.nationaldriller.com/publications/3. **Ad Rates:** BW $3,925, full page; BW $3,371, 2/3 page; BW $2,840, junior page; BW $2,795, 1/2 page horizontal; BW $2,315, 1/3 page; BW $2,105, 1/4 page; BW $1,610, 1/6 page. **Remarks:** Accepts advertising. **Circ:** Combined △**20000**.

7817 ■ WAYP-FM - 88.3
653 W 23rd St., No. 251
Panama City, FL 32405
Free: 888-422-9293
Format: Contemporary Christian. **Owner:** WAY-FM Media Group Inc., 5540 Tech Center Dr., Ste. 200, Colorado Springs, CO 80919, Ph: (719)533-0300. **Key Personnel:** Bob Augsburg, President, Founder; Lloyd Parker, COO; Craig Vinson, Dir. of Operations; Steve Young, Gen. Mgr. **Mailing address:** PO Box 4188, Tallahassee, FL 32315. **URL:** http://www.wayp.wayfm.com.

7818 ■ WJAQ-FM - 100.9
PO Box 569
Marianna, FL 32447
Phone: (850)482-3046
Fax: (850)482-3049
Format: Country. **Networks:** ABC. **Founded:** 1964. **Operating Hours:** Continuous. **ADI:** Tallahassee, FL-Thomasville (Bainbridge), GA. **Wattage:** 6,000. **Ad Rates:** $10-30 for 30 seconds. WTOT-AM, WTOT-FM.

7819 ■ WJNF-FM - 88.3
2914 Jefferson St.
Marianna, FL 32447
Phone: (850)526-4477
Fax: (850)526-1831
Format: Religious. **Networks:** Moody Broadcasting; Ambassador Inspirational Radio. **Owner:** Marianna Educational Broadcast Foundation Inc. **Founded:** May 1985. **Operating Hours:** Continuous. **Key Personnel:** Shellie Hollis, CFO, shellie@wjnf.org. **Wattage:** 25,000. **Ad Rates:** Noncommercial.

7820 ■ WTOT-AM - 980
4376 Lafayette St.
Marianna, FL 32447
Phone: (850)482-3046
Format: Country. **Simulcasts:** WTUT-FM. **Networks:** ABC. **Founded:** 1958. **Operating Hours:** Continuous. **ADI:** Tallahassee, FL-Thomasville (Bainbridge), GA. **Wattage:** 1,000. **Ad Rates:** $9-12 for 30 seconds; $13-17 for 60 seconds. Combined advertising rates available with; WJAQ-FM, WTUT-FM. **Mailing address:** PO Box 569, Marianna, FL 32447.

7821 ■ WTYS-AM - 1340
2725 Jefferson St.
Marianna, FL 32448
Phone: (850)482-2131
Fax: (850)526-3687
Email: wtysradio@embarqmail.com
Format: Gospel. **Simulcasts:** WBNF-FM. **Networks:** Westwood One Radio; NBC. **Owner:** James L. Adams, Jr. **Founded:** 1948. **Operating Hours:** Continuous. **ADI:** Dothan, AL. **Key Personnel:** Skip Taylor, Contact. **Local Programs:** *Country Classified*, Monday Tuesday Wednesday Thursday Friday 8:00 a.m. - 9:00 a.m.; *Skip Taylor Show*, Monday Tuesday Wednesday Thursday Friday 10:00 a.m. - 1:00 p.m. **Wattage:** 1,000. **Ad Rates:** Noncommercial. Combined advertising rates available with WBNF-FM. **URL:** http://www.wtys.cc.

7822 ■ WTYS-FM - 94.1
PO Box 777
Marianna, FL 32447
Phone: (850)482-2131
Fax: (850)526-3687
Email: wtysradio@embarqmail.com
Format: Gospel. **Networks:** Westwood One Radio; Florida Radio. **Owner:** James L. Adams, Jr. **Founded:** Aug. 1995. **Formerly:** WBNF-FM. **Operating Hours:** Continuous. **Key Personnel:** James L. Adams, Jr., Owner. **Wattage:** 4,400. **Ad Rates:** Noncommercial. **URL:** http://www.wtys.cc.

MEDLEY

7823 ■ El Nuevo Zol 106.7 FM - 106.7
7007 NW 77 Ave.
Medley, FL 33166
Phone: (305)550-9106
Format: Hispanic. **Networks:** Independent. **Owner:** Spanish Broadcasting System Inc., Pablo Raul Alarcon Media Ctr., 7007 NW 77th Ave., Miami, FL 33166, Ph: (305)441-6901, Fax: (305)883-3375. **Formerly:** WTPX-FM; WRMA-FM. **Operating Hours:** Continuous. **ADI:** Miami (Ft. Lauderdale), FL. **Wattage:** 100,000. **URL:** http://www.romancefm.com.

MELBOURNE

E FL. Brevard Co. On Indian River and Atlantic Ocean, 35 mi. S. of Kennedy Space Center. Florida Institute of Technology. Resort. Aerospace industry. Manufactures electronic components. Citrus fruit, vegetables.

7824 ■ Florida Today
Gannett Company Inc.
PO Box 419000
Melbourne, FL 32941-9000
Phone: (321)242-3500
General newspaper. **Founded:** Mar. 21, 1966. **Freq:** Mon.-Sun. (morn.). **Print Method:** Offset. Uses mats. **Cols./Page:** 6. **Col. Width:** 11 picas. **Col. Depth:** 21 inches. **Key Personnel:** Jeff Kiel, Publisher. **Subscription Rates:** $25.48 Individuals month; 7 days a week. **URL:** http://www.floridatoday.com. **Feature Editors:** Suzy Fleming Leonard, *Features*, phone: (321)242-3614, sleonard@floridatoday.com. **Ad Rates:** GLR $3.95; BW $119.04; 4C $2,050; SAU $43.10; PCI $36.75. **Remarks:** Accepts advertising. **Circ:** Mon.-Fri. ★**72838**, Sun. ★**100176**, Sat. ★**79305**.

7825 ■ International Journal of Stochastic Analysis
Hindawi Publishing Corp.

c/o Jewgeni H. Dshalalow, Editorial Board
Dept. of Mathematical Sciences
Florida Institute of Technology
Melbourne, FL 32901-6975
Publication E-mail: ijsa@hindawi.com
Peer-reviewed journal publishing Research articles on theory and applications of stochastic analysis, nonlinear analysis, and stochastic models. **Key Personnel:** Jewgeni H. Dshalalow, Board Member. **ISSN:** 2090--3332 (print); **EISSN:** 2090--3340 (electronic). **Subscription Rates:** $195 Individuals print. **URL:** http://www.hindawi.com/journals/ijsa. **Formerly**: The Journal of Applied Mathematics & Stochastic Analysis. **Remarks:** Accepts advertising. **Circ:** (Not Reported).

7826 ■ Journal of Cross-Cultural Psychology
International Association for Cross-Cultural Psychology
c/o William Gabrenya, Secretary General
Florida Institute of Technology
School of Psychology
150 W University Blvd.
Melbourne, FL 32901
Phone: (310)825-7526
Publisher's E-mail: sales@pfp.sagepub.com
Cross-cultural psychology journal. **Freq:** 10/year January , February , April , May , June , July , August , September , October and November. **Print Method:** Offset. **Trim Size:** 7 x 10. **Cols./Page:** 1. **Col. Width:** 50 nonpareils. **Col. Depth:** 100 agate lines. **Key Personnel:** David Matsumoto, Editor; Walter J. Lonner, Editor, Founder; David R. Matsumoto, Editor; Juri Allik, Associate Editor; Deborah L. Best, Editor; Cindy Gallois, Editor; Junko Tanaka-Matsumi, Associate Editor; Walter Lonner, Founder, Senior Editor. **ISSN:** 0022--0221 (print); **EISSN:** 1552--5422 (electronic). **Subscription Rates:** $1648 Institutions print & e-access; $1813 Institutions print & all online content; $1483 Institutions e-access; $3353 Institutions backfile purchase, e-access (1998); $1615 Institutions print only; $191 Individuals print only; $178 Institutions single print; $25 Individuals single print. **URL:** http://jcc.sagepub.com. **Ad Rates:** BW $875; 4C $1110. **Remarks:** Accepts advertising. **Circ:** (Not Reported).

7827 ■ Journal of Nano Education
American Scientific Publishers
c/o Dr. Kurt Winkelmann, Editor-in-Chief
Department of Chemistry
Florida Institute of Technology
150 W University Blvd.
Melbourne, FL 32901
Phone: (321)674-7376
Fax: (321)674-8951
Publisher's E-mail: order@aspbs.com
Peer-reviewed journal covering nanoscale science, technology, engineering, and medical education. **Freq:** Semiannual. **Key Personnel:** Dr. Kurt Winkelmann, Editor-in-Chief, phone: (321)674-7376, fax: (321)674-8951; Dr. K. Eric Drexler, Board Member. **Subscription Rates:** $200 Individuals; $250 Other countries; $500 Institutions; $600 Institutions, other countries. **URL:** http://www.aspbs.com/jne. **Remarks:** Accepts advertising. **Circ:** (Not Reported).

7828 ■ Model Yachting
American Model Yachting Association
c/o Michelle Dannenhoffer, Secretary
PO Box 360374
Melbourne, FL 32936-0374
Free: 888-237-9524
Publisher's E-mail: membership@theamya.org
Magazine consisting of articles, racing rules explanations, regatta reports, class news and tips with detailed photos and drawings, and organizational conferences, and events. **Freq:** Quarterly. **Trim Size:** 8 1/2 x 11. **Subscription Rates:** Included in membership. **URL:** http://www.theamya.org/my. **Remarks:** Accepts advertising. **Circ:** 1600.

7829 ■ KFTE-FM
c/o Jay Meyers
Melbourne, FL 32935
Phone: (337)235-9636
Fax: (337)234-7360
Format: Alternative/New Music/Progressive. **Wattage:** 25,000 ERP. **Ad Rates:** Noncommercial.

7830 ■ WAOA-FM - 107.1
1800 W Hibiscus Blvd., Ste. 138
Melbourne, FL 32901
Phone: (321)984-1000
Format: Contemporary Hit Radio (CHR). **Networks:** Independent. **Owner:** Cumulus Media Inc., 3280 Peachtree Rd. NW, Ste. 2300, Atlanta, GA 30305-2455, Ph: (404)949-0700, Fax: (404)949-0740. **Founded:** 1971. **Operating Hours**: Continuous; 3% network, 97% local. **ADI**: Orlando-Daytona Beach-Melbourne, FL. **Key Personnel:** Gary Mertins, Contact, gary.mertins@cumulus.com. **Wattage**: 100,000. **Ad Rates:** Advertising accepted; rates available upon request. **URL:** http://www.wa1a.com.

7831 ■ WCIF-FM - 106.3
PO Box 366
Melbourne, FL 32902-0366
Phone: (321)725-9243
Free: 877-725-9243
Email: info@wcif.com
Format: Religious. **Owner:** First Baptist Church of Melbourne, 3301 Dairy Rd., Melbourne, FL 32904. **Founded:** 1980. **Operating Hours**: Continuous. **ADI**: Orlando-Daytona Beach-Melbourne, FL. **Key Personnel:** Lee Martinez, Gen. Mgr. **Wattage** 4,200. **Ad Rates:** Noncommercial. **URL:** http://www.wcif.citymax.com/page/page/4105093.htm.

7832 ■ WFIT-FM - 89.5
150 W University Blvd.
Melbourne, FL 32901
Phone: (321)674-8140
Format: Jazz; Public Radio. **Networks:** National Public Radio (NPR). **Owner:** Florida Institute of Technology, 150 W University Blvd., Melbourne, FL 32901, Ph: (321)674-8000. **Founded:** 1975. **Operating Hours**: Continuous. **Key Personnel:** Todd Kennedy, Dir. of Programs, tkennedy@fit.edu; Terri L. Wright, Gen. Mgr., twright@fit.edu. **Wattage**: 4,600. **Ad Rates:** Noncommercial. **URL:** http://www.wfit.org.

7833 ■ WFKS-FM - 95.1
1388 S Babcock St.
Melbourne, FL 32901
Free: 800-242-0100
Format: Contemporary Hit Radio (CHR). **Owner:** iHeartMedia Inc., 200 E Basse Rd., San Antonio, TX 78209, Ph: (210)832-3314. **Formerly**: WBVD-FM. **ADI**: Orlando-Daytona Beach-Melbourne, FL. **Wattage**: 6,000. **Ad Rates:** Noncommercial. **URL:** http://www.mykiss951.com.

7834 ■ WHKR-FM - 102.7
1800 W Hibiscus Blvd., Ste. 138
Melbourne, FL 32901
Phone: (321)984-1000
Format: Country. **Owner:** Cumulus Media Inc., 3280 Peachtree Rd. NW, Ste. 2300, Atlanta, GA 30305-2455, Ph: (404)949-0700, Fax: (404)949-0740. **Ad Rates:** Noncommercial. **URL:** http://www.nashfm1027.com.

7835 ■ WINT-AM - 1560
1800 W Hibiscus Blvd., Ste. 138
Melbourne, FL 32901
Phone: (321)984-1000
Fax: (321)724-1565
Format: Oldies. **Owner:** Cumulus Broadcasting Inc., 3280 Peachtree Rd. NW, Ste. 2300, Atlanta, GA 30305-2447, Ph: (404)949-0700, Fax: (404)949-0740.

7836 ■ WLRQ-FM - 99.3
1388 S Babcock St.
Melbourne, FL 32901-3009
Phone: (321)821-7100
Fax: (321)733-0904
Format: Adult Contemporary; Jazz. **Networks:** CNN Radio. **Owner:** iHeartMedia Inc., 200 E Basse Rd., San Antonio, TX 78209, Ph: (210)832-3314. **Founded:** 1959. **Formerly:** WEZY-FM. **Operating Hours**: Continuous; 2% network, 98% local. **Key Personnel:** Michael W. Lowe, Dir. of Programs, michaellowe@clearchannel.com; Laurie Reid, HR Mgr., lauriereid@clearchannel.com. **Wattage**: 50,000. **Ad Rates:** $15-65 per unit. **URL:** http://www.literock993.com.

7837 ■ WMEL-AM - 920
2020 W Eau Gallie Blvd., Ste. 103
Melbourne, FL 32935
Phone: (321)757-7717
Format: News; Talk; Sports. **Owner:** Twin Towers Broadcasting, at above address. **Operating Hours**: Continuous. **Key Personnel:** John Harper, Gen. Mgr., jharper@920wmel.com; Vernon Harper, Sales Mgr., vern@920wmel.com; Mark Pence, Dir. of Pub. Prog. & Svcs., mark@920wmel.com. **Wattage**: 5,000. **Ad Rates:** Advertising accepted; rates available upon request. **URL:** http://www.divinemercyradio.com.

7838 ■ WMEL-FM - 920
2020 W Eau Gallie Blvd., Ste 103
Twin Towers Broadcasting
1800 Turtlemound Rd.
Melbourne, FL 32935
Phone: (321)757-7717
Format: News; Talk; Sports. **Wattage:** 5,000 Watts. **Ad Rates:** Advertising accepted; rates available upon request. **URL:** http://www.divinemercyradio.com.

7839 ■ WMMB-AM - 1240
1388 S Babcock St.
Melbourne, FL 32901
Phone: (321)821-7100
Fax: (321)733-0904
Format: News; Talk. **Networks:** ABC; Mutual Broadcasting System; Florida Radio. **Founded:** 1947. **Operating Hours**: Continuous; 8% network, 92% local. **ADI**: Orlando-Daytona Beach-Melbourne, FL. **Key Personnel:** Ken Holiday, Dir. of Operations, kenholiday@clearchannel.com. **Wattage**: 1,000. **Ad Rates:** Advertising accepted; rates available upon request. **URL:** http://www.wmmbam.com/main.html.

MIAMI

S FL. Dade Co. On Biscayne Bay, 355 mi. S. of Jacksonville. Miami Christian University; Miami-Dade Community College; Barry College. Winter and summer resort. Shipyards. Manufactures airplane parts, canned fruits and vegetables, furniture, mattresses, garments, pharmaceuticals, paint, fertilizers, cement, plastics, electronic components, cigars, water heaters, leather products.

7840 ■ Air Cargo Focus
Cargo Network Services Corp.
703 Waterford Way, Ste. 680
Miami, FL 33126
Phone: (786)413-1000
Fax: (786)413-1005
Publisher's E-mail: cassusaserviceteam@cnsc.us
Trade magazine covering air cargo. **Freq:** Quarterly. **URL:** http://www.cnsc.net/publications/Pages/focus.aspx. **Formerly**: CNS Focus. **Remarks:** Accepts advertising. **Circ:** Non-paid 7000.

7841 ■ Airliners: The World's Airline Magazine
Airliners Publications Holdings L.L.C.
6355 NW 36 St., Ste. 600
Miami, FL 33166-7027
Phone: (786)264-6692
Free: 800-875-6711
Publisher's E-mail: subscriptions@airliners.tv
Magazine for airliner professionals. Includes news, air transport trends, travel adventures, nostalgia, humor, and photography. **Freq:** Bimonthly. **Trim Size:** 8 1/2 x 11. **Cols./Page:** 3. **Col. Width:** 2 1/4 inches. **Key Personnel:** Dwayne Darnell, Managing Editor; Vito La Forgia, Publisher. **ISSN:** 0896--6575 (print). **Subscription Rates:** $49.95 Two years USA Media Mail; $58.95 Two years Canada; $74.95 Two years Mexico, Central and South America, Carribean; $77.95 Two years Europe, Africa, Middle East, Australia, NZ, Japan, Asia. **URL:** http://www.airliners.tv. **Ad Rates:** GLR $14; BW $1180; 4C $1780. **Remarks:** Accepts advertising. **Circ:** ‡35,000.

7842 ■ Audubon
Audubon Florida
4500 Biscayne Blvd., Ste. 205
Miami, FL 33137
Phone: (305)371-6399
Fax: (305)371-6398
Publication E-mail: editor@audubon.org
Freq: Bimonthly. **Key Personnel:** David Siedeman, Editor-in-Chief. **ISSN:** 0097--7136 (print). **Subscription Rates:** Included in membership; $20 Nonmembers. **URL:** http://www.audubonmagazine.org. **Ad Rates:** 4C $47,450, full page; 4C $28,470, half page; BW $28,700,

Circulation: ★ = AAM; △ or • = BPA; ♦ = CAC; ❑ = VAC; ⊕ = PO Statement; ‡ = Publisher's Report; Boldface figures = sworn; Light figures = estimated.

full page; BW $17,220, half page. **Remarks:** Accepts advertising. **Circ:** (Not Reported).

7843 ■ BRL Memorandum
Braille Revival League
c/o Paul Edwards, President
20330 NE 20th Ct.
Miami, FL 33179-2202
Phone: (305)692-9206
Freq: Quarterly Winter, Spring, Summer, Fall. **URL:** http://www.braillerevivalleague.org/memorandum.php. **Remarks:** Advertising not accepted. **Circ:** (Not Reported).

7844 ■ Buenhogar
Editorial Televisa
6355 NW 36th St.
Miami, FL 33166-7099
Phone: (305)871-6400
Fax: (305)871-4939
Magazine for the homemaker featuring articles of general interest and entertainment (Spanish). **Founded:** 1965. **Freq:** 12/year. **Print Method:** Offset. **Trim Size:** 8 5/8 x 10 7/8. **Cols./Page:** 3. **Col. Width:** 13.5 picas. **Col. Depth:** 59.5 picas. **Key Personnel:** Mirta Blanco, Editor; Enrique J. Perez, Director, Advertising and Sales; Mario A. Freude, Vice President, Sales. **Subscription Rates:** $24.95 Individuals; $2.95 Single issue. **URL:** http://www.almacenesbuenhogar.com/. **Ad Rates:** BW $1,200; 4C $1,600. **Remarks:** Accepts advertising. **Circ:** ‡18449.

7845 ■ Bulletin of Marine Science
Rosenstiel School of Marine and Atmospheric Science
4600 Rickenbacker Cswy.
Miami, FL 33149-1098
Phone: (305)421-4000
Fax: (305)421-4711
Publisher's E-mail: dean@rsmas.miami.edu
Professional journal covering marine science. **Freq:** Quarterly. **Key Personnel:** Su Sponaugle, Associate Editor; Felicia C. Coleman, Associate Editor; Peter B. Ortner, Associate Editor; Joseph E. Serafy, Editor. **ISSN:** 0007--4977 (print); **EISSN:** 1553--6955 (electronic). **Subscription Rates:** $825 Individuals print and online; $645 Individuals online only. **Alt. Formats:** CD-ROM; PDF. **URL:** http://www.rsmas.miami.edu/bms. **Circ:** (Not Reported).

7846 ■ Casa & Estilo Internacional: Su Mejor Guia De Diseno, Arte Y Estilo De Vida
Casa Estilo International
12182 SW 128th St.
Miami, FL 33186
Phone: (305)378-4466
Fax: (305)378-9951
Free: 800-848-0466
Home design and lifestyle magazine. Also featuring interior design projects, home furnishings, decoration and fine art, and lifestyles. **Freq:** Bimonthly. **Print Method:** Offset. **Trim Size:** 8 3/8 x 10 7/8. **Key Personnel:** Jose Alfonso Nino, Editor-in-Chief; Ugo Campello, Editor; Joel Pinto, Director, Advertising. **Subscription Rates:** $29.94 Individuals; $59.88 Two years; $4.99 Single issue. **Ad Rates:** BW $4,500; 4C $4,500. **Remarks:** Accepts advertising. **Circ:** (Not Reported).

7847 ■ Cell Transplantation: The Regenerative Medicine Journal
Cognizant Communications Corp.
c/o Camillo Ricordi, Co-Ed.-in-Ch.
Diabetes Research Institute
University of Medicine
1450 NW 10th Ave., No. R134
Miami, FL 33136
Publisher's E-mail: cogcomm@aol.com
Peer-reviewed journal covering subject of cell transplantation and its application to human diseases. **Freq:** Monthly. **Key Personnel:** Shinn-Zong Lin, Editor-in-Chief; Camillo Ricordi, Editor-in-Chief. **ISSN:** 0963--6897 (print); **EISSN:** 1555--3892 (electronic). **Subscription Rates:** $1200 Institutions online & hard copy; $240 Members online & hard copy. **URL:** http://www.cognizantcommunication.com/journal-titles/cell-transplantation. **Remarks:** Accepts advertising. **Circ:** (Not Reported).

7848 ■ Coral Gables News
Community Newspapers
6796 S W 62 Ave.
Miami, FL 33143
Phone: (305)669-7030
Fax: (305)662-6980
Publisher's E-mail: sales@communitynewspapers.com
Community newspaper (tabloid). **Freq:** Weekly. **Print Method:** Offset. **Trim Size:** 10 1/4 x 17. **Cols./Page:** 6. **Col. Width:** 1 1/2 inches. **Col. Depth:** 16 inches. **Key Personnel:** David Berkowitz, Editor. **Subscription Rates:** $12 Individuals. **URL:** http://communitynewspapers.com/coralgables. **Ad Rates:** GLR $.72; BW $1,350; 4C $2,400; PCI $13.50. **Remarks:** Accepts advertising. **Circ:** ‡9000.

7849 ■ Cormac McCarthy Journal
The Cormac McCarthy Society
13850 SW 100th Ave.
Miami, FL 33176-6717
Publisher's E-mail: info@cormacmccarthy.com
Journal containing articles, notes, and reviews related to Cormac McCarthy's novels, dramas, and screenplays; the film adaptations of his work; and other appropriate scholarly materials. **Freq:** Annual. **Key Personnel:** John Wegner, Editor. **Subscription Rates:** $13.50 Members; $15 Nonmembers. **URL:** http://journals.tdl.org/cormacmccarthy/index.php/cormacmccarthy. **Remarks:** Advertising not accepted. **Circ:** (Not Reported).

7850 ■ Cosmopolitan en Espanol
Editorial Televisa
6355 NW 36th St.
Miami, FL 33166-7099
Phone: (305)871-6400
Fax: (305)871-4939
Magazine for the young modern Hispanic woman; covering fashion, relationships, travel, entertainment, and career (Spanish). **Freq:** Monthly. **Print Method:** Offset. **Trim Size:** 8 x 10 7/8. **Cols./Page:** 3. **Col. Width:** 13 picas. **Col. Depth:** 58.5 picas. **Key Personnel:** Carlos Castro, Director; Eugenio Lopez Negrete, Director General. **Subscription Rates:** $378 Individuals. **URL:** http://cosmoenespanol.com. **Ad Rates:** BW $2,250; 4C $3,000. **Remarks:** Accepts advertising. **Circ:** Paid ★225000.

7851 ■ The Counter Terrorist: Official Journal of the Homeland Security Professional
Security Solutions International
13155 SW 134th St., Ste. 103
13155 SW 134th St., Ste. 204
Miami, FL 33186
Fax: (786)573-2090
Free: 866-573-3999
Publisher's E-mail: cgraham@thecounterterroristmag.com
Magazine featuring technical information to combat terrorism at home and abroad. **Freq:** Bimonthly. **Key Personnel:** Chris Graham, Editor. **Subscription Rates:** $34.99 Individuals /year. **URL:** http://www.thecounterterroristmag.com. **Ad Rates:** 4C $4746. **Remarks:** Accepts advertising. **Circ:** (Not Reported).

7852 ■ Daily Business Review
ALM Media Properties L.L.C.
1 SE 3rd Ave., Ste. 900
Miami, FL 33131
Phone: (305)377-3721
Fax: (305)347-8474
Free: 877-256-2472
Publication E-mail: review@floridabiz.com
Daily newspapers covering business, real estate and law in South Florida. **Founded:** 1926. **Freq:** Daily. **Print Method:** Offset. **Trim Size:** 11 3/8 x 15. **Cols./Page:** 4. **Col. Width:** 2 3/8 inches. **Col. Depth:** 15 inches. **Key Personnel:** Jay Rees, Executive Editor, phone: (305)347-6627; David Lyons, Editor-in-Chief, phone: (305)347-6694; Jeff Fried, Chief Financial Officer, Chief Operating Officer, phone: (305)347-6615. **ISSN:** 0888-0263 (print). **USPS:** 344-300. **Subscription Rates:** $29.99 Individuals /month (digital + print); $24.99 Individuals /month (digital access); $179. **Alt. Formats:** Diskette. **URL:** http://www.alm.com/publications/daily-business-review; http://www.floridabiz.com; http://DailyBusinessReview.com. **Formerly**: Miami Review. **Ad Rates:** BW $300; 4C $850; BW $2,684; 4C $3,484. **Remarks:** Accepts advertising. **Circ:** Paid 10184, Controlled 286, Non-paid 53.

7853 ■ El Faro
Asociación Filatélica Salvadoreña
c/o Pierre Cahen
PO Box 02-5364
Miami, FL 33102
Publisher's E-mail: sfes-aces@elsalvadorphilately.org
Freq: Quarterly. **Subscription Rates:** Included in membership. **Remarks:** Accepts advertising. **Circ:** 100.

7854 ■ Florida Architecture: Florida's Luxury Building Design Magazine
Florida Architecture Inc.
8485 SW 168th Ter.
Miami, FL 33157
Phone: (305)251-2510
Fax: (305)251-8899
Publisher's E-mail: info@facorp.com
Magazine featuring beautiful homes built in the state of Florida, or any other state in the country. **Freq:** Semiannual. **Trim Size:** 9 5/8 x 13 1/4. **Key Personnel:** Olivia Hammar, Publisher. **Subscription Rates:** $36 Individuals; $21 Single issue; $18 Individuals two or more editions. **URL:** http://www.facorp.com. **Remarks:** Accepts advertising. **Circ:** (Not Reported).

7855 ■ Harper's Bazaar en Espanol
Editorial Televisa
6355 NW 36th St.
Miami, FL 33166-7099
Phone: (305)871-6400
Fax: (305)871-4939
Hispanic edition of Harper's Bazaar (Spanish). **Freq:** Monthly 8/yr. **Print Method:** Offset. **Trim Size:** 8 5/8 x 10 7/8. **Cols./Page:** 3. **Col. Width:** 14 picas. **Col. Depth:** 60 picas. **URL:** http://www2.esmas.com. **Ad Rates:** BW $800; 4C $1,200. **Remarks:** Accepts advertising. **Circ:** (Not Reported).

7856 ■ Home Miami
Bonnier Corp.
4040 NE 2nd Ave., Ste. 313
Miami, FL 33137
Phone: (305)673-2112
Publication E-mail: info@homemia.com
Magazine featuring home design and architecture in Miami. **Freq:** 11/yr. **Trim Size:** 9 x 10 7/8. **Key Personnel:** Beth Dunlop, Editor-in-Chief; Shamus Hillier, Publisher; Megan Aquilina, Managing Editor. **Subscription Rates:** $28 Individuals; $50 Two years. **URL:** http://www.bonniercorp.com/brands/Home-Miami.html. **Remarks:** Accepts advertising. **Circ:** 30000.

7857 ■ International Journal of Dental Anthropology
Syllaba Press
1900 NW 97th Ave., Ste. 722-4586
Miami, FL 33172
Publisher's E-mail: legal@syllabapress.com
Journal covering treatment topics, focusing on the clinical, bioanthropological, bioarchaeological, genetic and evolutionary aspects. **Freq:** Semiannual January and July. **Key Personnel:** Carlos David Rodriguez Florez, Editor; Ernesto Leon Rodriguez, Contact. **ISSN:** 0124--7336 (print). **URL:** http://www.syllabapress.com/productos/index.html. **Circ:** (Not Reported).

7858 ■ International Journal of Hydrogen Energy
International Association for Hydrogen Energy
5794 SW 40 St., No. 303
Miami, FL 33155
Publisher's E-mail: amsterdam@relx.com
Freq: 48/yr. **Key Personnel:** E.A. Veziroglu, Editor-in-Chief; F. Barbir, Editor; John W. Sheffield, Associate Editor. **ISSN:** 0360--3199 (print). **Subscription Rates:** $4805.60 Institutions online, access for 5 users and access to 4 years of archives; $4805 Institutions print. **URL:** http://www.journals.elsevier.com/international-journal-of-hydrogen-energy. **Mailing address:** PO Box 152, 1043 NX Amsterdam, Netherlands. **Remarks:** Accepts advertising. **Circ:** (Not Reported).

7859 ■ Interval World
Interval International
6262 Sunset Dr.
Miami, FL 33143-4843
Phone: (305)666-1884
Fax: (305)667-5321
Free: 800-843-8843
Subscription Rates: Included in membership. **URL:** http://www.intervalworld.com/web/my/info/planning/magazine. **Mailing address:** PO Box 431920, Miami, FL 33243-1920. **Remarks:** Advertising not accepted. **Circ:** (Not Reported).

7860 ■ Japan Studies Review
Florida International University Modesto A. Maidique Campus
11200 SW 8th St.
Miami, FL 33199
Phone: (305)348-1914
Fax: (305)348-6586
Publication E-mail: asian@fiu.edu
Peer-reviewed journal covering Japan studies. **Freq:** Annual. **Key Personnel:** Steven Heine, Editor; Yumiko Hulvey, Advisor; John A. Tucker, Editor. **ISSN:** 1550-0713 (print). **Subscription Rates:** $35 Individuals. **Alt. Formats:** PDF. **URL:** http://asian.fiu.edu/projects-and-grants/japan-studies-review. **Remarks:** Accepts advertising. **Circ:** (Not Reported).

7861 ■ Journal of the ISTH
InterAmerican Society for Tropical Horticulture
Fairchild Tropical Garden Research Ctr.
11935 Old Cutler Rd.
Miami, FL 33156
Phone: (305)667-1651
Fax: (305)665-8032
Journal containing articles on tropical horticulture. **Freq:** Annual. **ISSN:** 2237--4256 (print); **EISSN:** 2237--4264 (electronic). **URL:** http://www.iasth.org/internas/publications.html. **Formerly:** Proceedings of the Inter-american Society for Tropical Horticulture. **Remarks:** Advertising not accepted. **Circ:** (Not Reported).

7862 ■ Journal of the Society of Laparoendoscopic Surgeons
Society of Laparoendoscopic Surgeons
7330 SW 62nd Pl., Ste. 410
Miami, FL 33143-4825
Phone: (305)665-9959
Publisher's E-mail: info@sls.org
Freq: Quarterly. **ISSN:** 1086- 8089 (print). **Subscription Rates:** included in membership dues. **URL:** http://jsls.sls.org. **Remarks:** Accepts advertising. **Circ:** 8000.

7863 ■ Kendall Gazette
Community Newspapers
6796 S W 62 Ave.
Miami, FL 33143
Phone: (305)669-7030
Fax: (305)662-6980
Publisher's E-mail: sales@communitynewspapers.com
Community newspaper (tabloid). **Freq:** 3/week. **Print Method:** Offset. **Trim Size:** 10 1/4 x 16. **Cols./Page:** 6. **Col. Width:** 19 nonpareils. **Col. Depth:** 238 agate lines. **Key Personnel:** David Berkowitz, Editor; Grant Miller, Publisher, phone: (305)669-7355. **URL:** http://communitynewspapers.com/kendall-gazette. **Remarks:** Accepts advertising. **Circ:** (Not Reported).

7864 ■ Key Biscayne Magazine: Island Living at Its Finest
TAGMedia Inc.
1818 SW 1st Ave., Ste. 801
Miami, FL 33129
Phone: (305)854-4794
Fax: (305)854-4529
Lifestyle and entertainment magazine for South Florida residents and visitors. **Freq:** 9/year. **Key Personnel:** Alexander Avila, Publisher, phone: (305)776-7161; Jorge Arauz, Editor. **URL:** http://keybiscaynemag.com/?q=keybiscayne. **Remarks:** Accepts advertising. **Circ:** Combined ‡15000.

7865 ■ Latin Finance
World Publications Service
1101 Brickell Ave., Ste. N-1200
Miami, FL 33131
Phone: (305)416-5261
Fax: (305)416-5286
Magazine providing coverage of new debt and capital market activities in Latin America. **Freq:** Monthly. **Key Personnel:** James Crombie, Editor, phone: (212)224-3052; James Norton, Associate Publisher, phone: (305)428-6273; Patricia Arcic, Manager, Circulation, phone: (305)428-6290. **Subscription Rates:** $495 Individuals. **URL:** http://www.latinfinance.com. **Ad Rates:** 4C $16,500. **Remarks:** Accepts advertising. **Circ:** (Not Reported).

7866 ■ Latin Trade
Latin Trade
Brickell Bay Office Tower
1001 Brickell Bay Dr., Ste. 2700
Miami, FL 33131
Phone: (305)749-0880
Fax: (786)513-2407
Publisher's E-mail: info@latintrade.com
Trade publication featuring business news and analysis on Latin America and the Caribbean. **Freq:** Monthly. **Print Method:** Web Offset. **Trim Size:** 8 1/8 x 10 7/8. **ISSN:** 1087--0857 (print). **Subscription Rates:** $499 Individuals. **URL:** http://latintrade.com. **Formerly:** U.S./Latin Trade. **Remarks:** Accepts advertising. **Circ:** (Not Reported).

7867 ■ Libre
LIBRE
2700 SW 8 St.
Miami, FL 33135
Phone: (305)643-4888
Fax: (305)649-2767
Publisher's E-mail: info@lincoln-marti.com
Community newspaper (tabloid, Spanish). **Freq:** Weekly. **Print Method:** Offset. **Trim Size:** 10 x 16 1/2. **Cols./Page:** 6. **Key Personnel:** Demetrio Alberto Perez, Jr., Director. **Formerly:** El Matancero Libre. **Remarks:** Advertising accepted; rates available upon request. **Circ:** Paid 2000, Free 8000.

7868 ■ MADDvocate
Mothers Against Drunk Driving - Miami-Dade County
7700 N Kendall Dr., Ste. 803
Miami, FL 33156
Phone: (305)273-3744
Magazine featuring information about victims and survivors of drunk driving crashes and those who work with crash victims. **Freq:** Semiannual. **URL:** http://www.madd.org/media-center/publications/maddvocate.html. **Remarks:** Advertising not accepted. **Circ:** (Not Reported).

7869 ■ Miami New Times: Miami's News and Arts Weekly
Village Voice Media
2800 Biscayne Blvd.
Miami, FL 33137
Phone: (305)576-8000
Fax: (305)571-7677
Publisher's E-mail: sthrahser@villagevoice.com
Alternative Weekly. **Founded:** 1987. **Freq:** Weekly (Thurs.). **Print Method:** Offset. **Trim Size:** 10 x 12 7/8. **Cols./Page:** 8. **Col. Width:** 1 1/16 inches. **Col. Depth:** 10 inches. **Key Personnel:** Nadine DeMarco, Manager, Operations; Richard Lynch, Manager, Circulation; Chuck Strouse, Editor. **URL:** http://www.miaminewtimes.com. **Formerly:** New Times of Miami; New Times. **Remarks:** Accepts advertising. **Circ:** (Not Reported).

7870 ■ The Miami Times
The Miami Times
900 NW 54th St.
Miami, FL 33127
Phone: (305)694-6210
Fax: (305)694-6211
Publisher's E-mail: info@miamitimesonline.com
Black community newspaper. **Print Method:** Offset. **Trim Size:** 13 3/4 x 22. **Cols./Page:** 6. **Col. Width:** 2 1/16 inches. **Col. Depth:** 21 inches. **USPS:** 344-340. **URL:** http://miamitimesonline.com. **Ad Rates:** BW $4183. **Remarks:** Accepts advertising. **Circ:** (Not Reported).

7871 ■ Miami Today: The Newspaper for the Future of Miami
Today Enterprises Inc.
710 Brickell Ave.
Miami, FL 33131
Phone: (305)358-2663
Newspaper (tabloid) covering business and community information targeted to the upper management levels. **Freq:** Weekly (Thurs.). **Print Method:** Offset. **Trim Size:** 11 1/4 x 17 1/2. **Cols./Page:** 5. **Col. Width:** 12.5 picas. **Col. Depth:** 16 inches. **Key Personnel:** Michael Lewis, Editor. **USPS:** 012-964. **Subscription Rates:** $145 By mail print; $210 Two years print; $180 Individuals print and online. **URL:** http://www.miamitodaynews.com. **Remarks:** Accepts classified advertising; Advertising accepted; rates available upon request. **Circ:** (Not Reported).

7872 ■ Palmetto Bay News
Community Newspapers
6796 S W 62 Ave.
Miami, FL 33143
Phone: (305)669-7030
Fax: (305)662-6980
Publisher's E-mail: sales@communitynewspapers.com
Community newspaper (tabloid). **Freq:** Weekly. **Print Method:** Offset. **Trim Size:** 10 1/4 x 16. **Cols./Page:** 6. **Col. Width:** 19 nonpareils. **Col. Depth:** 238 agate lines. **Key Personnel:** Grant Miller, Publisher; David Berkowitz, Editor. **URL:** http://communitynewspapers.com/palmetto-bay. **Formerly:** Homestead-Florida City News. **Ad Rates:** GLR $3. **Remarks:** #3. **Circ:** Free 6000.

7873 ■ Pinecrest Tribune
Community Newspapers
6796 S W 62 Ave.
Miami, FL 33143
Phone: (305)669-7030
Fax: (305)662-6980
Publisher's E-mail: sales@communitynewspapers.com
Community newspaper. **Freq:** Bimonthly. **Print Method:** Offset. **Key Personnel:** Grant Miller, Publisher. **URL:** http://www.communitynewspapers.com/category/pinecrest. **Ad Rates:** BW $1,300. **Remarks:** Advertising accepted; rates available upon request. **Circ:** Controlled ‡15000.

7874 ■ SOBeFit
MPG Publishing
1201 Brickell Ave., Ste. 320
Miami, FL 33131
Phone: (305)375-9595
Fax: (305)375-9596
Publisher's E-mail: questions@sobefitmagazine.com
Magazine focusing on fitness, nutrition, health, and sports. **Freq:** Bimonthly. **Trim Size:** 9 x 10.875. **Key Personnel:** Marta Montenegro, Editor-in-Chief, Publisher, Founder, Chief Executive Officer; Annette Kidd, Manager, Sales; Chan Tran, Managing Editor. **URL:** http://www.sobefitmagazine.com. **Remarks:** Accepts advertising. **Circ:** (Not Reported).

7875 ■ South Miami News
Community Newspapers
6796 S W 62 Ave.
Miami, FL 33143
Phone: (305)669-7030
Fax: (305)662-6980
Publisher's E-mail: sales@communitynewspapers.com
Community newspaper (tabloid). **Freq:** Weekly. **Print Method:** Offset. **Trim Size:** 10 1/4 x 16. **Cols./Page:** 6. **Col. Width:** 19 nonpareils. **Col. Depth:** 238 agate lines. **Key Personnel:** Michael Miller, Publisher. **URL:** http://communitynewspapers.com/south-miami. **Ad Rates:** GLR $.72; BW $1,350; 4C $2,400; PCI $13.50. **Remarks:** Accepts advertising. **Circ:** ‡8000.

7876 ■ Tecnologia del Plastico
B2B Portales
6355 NW 36 St., Ste. 408
Miami, FL 33126
Phone: (305)448-6875
Fax: (305)448-9942
Publication E-mail: adomador@b2bportales.com
Plastics industry magazine. Coverage includes makers, suppliers, and users of machinery, raw materials, molds, injection, extrusion, blow molding, thermoforming transformation, plastics products, and packaging. **Freq:** Monthly. **Print Method:** Web Offset. **Trim Size:** 8 1/4 x 10 7/8. **Cols./Page:** 3. **Col. Width:** 13 picas. **Key Personnel:** Alfredo Domador, Vice President, Operations; Terry Beirne, Publisher; Miguel Garzon, Vice President. **Alt. Formats:** PDF. **URL:** http://www.plastico.com. **Ad Rates:** BW $4,370; 4C $5,515; PCI $135. **Remarks:** Accepts advertising. **Circ:** Controlled 15109.

7877 ■ Tequesta: The Journal of the Historical Association of Southern Florida
History Miami
101 W Flagler St.
Miami, FL 33130
Phone: (305)375-1492
Fax: (305)375-1609
Publisher's E-mail: e.info@historymiami.org
Journal covering local history. **Freq:** Annual. **Remarks:** Advertising not accepted. **Circ:** Paid 3600.

7878 ■ Tropical Fruit News
Miami Rare Fruit Council International

Circulation: ★ = AAM; △ or • = BPA; ♦ = CAC; ❑ = VAC; ⊕ = PO Statement; ‡ = Publisher's Report; Boldface figures = sworn; Light figures = estimated.

14735 SW 48 Ter.
Miami, FL 33185-4066
Phone: (305)554-1333
Magazine publishing information about rare and tropical fruits. **Freq:** 6/year. **ISSN:** 1075-6108 (print). **Subscription Rates:** Included in membership; $4.95 Nonmembers. **URL:** http://tropicalfruitnews.org/?page_id=61. **Remarks:** Accepts advertising. **Circ:** 1000.

7879 ■ TV y Novelas
Editorial Televisa
6355 NW 36th St.
Miami, FL 33166-7099
Phone: (305)871-6400
Fax: (305)871-4939
Magazine covering the spanish-language soap operas lifestyles of entertainers; including photos and interviews (Spanish). **Founded:** 1982. **Freq:** Semimonthly 26/yr. **Print Method:** Offset. **Trim Size:** 7 3/4 x 10 11/16. **Cols./Page:** 3. **Col. Width:** 13 picas. **Col. Depth:** 58.5 picas. **Subscription Rates:** $31.95 Individuals; $69 Canada. **URL:** http://www.tvynovelas.com/. **Ad Rates:** 4C $3,100. **Remarks:** Accepts advertising. **Circ:** Paid **★122709.**

7880 ■ TV y Novelas
Editorial Televisa
6355 NW 36th St.
Miami, FL 33166-7099
Phone: (305)871-6400
Fax: (305)871-4939
Magazine covering the spanish-language soap operas lifestyles of entertainers; including photos and interviews (Spanish). **Founded:** 1982. **Freq:** Semimonthly 26/yr. **Print Method:** Offset. **Trim Size:** 7 3/4 x 10 11/16. **Cols./Page:** 3. **Col. Width:** 13 picas. **Col. Depth:** 58.5 picas. **Subscription Rates:** $31.95 Individuals; $69 Canada. **URL:** http://www.esmas.com/televisahome/ventas/programacion/. **Ad Rates:** BW $2,325; 4C $3,100. **Remarks:** Accepts advertising. **Circ:** Paid **★122709.**

7881 ■ Welding Journal
American Welding Society
8669 NW 36th St., Ste. 130
Miami, FL 33166-6672
Phone: (305)443-9353
Free: 800-443-9353
Trade magazine. **Freq:** Monthly. **Print Method:** Offset. **Trim Size:** 8 1/8 x 10 7/8. **Cols./Page:** 3. **Col. Width:** 26 nonpareils. **Col. Depth:** 140 agate lines. **Key Personnel:** Rob Saltzstein, Director, Sales; Lea Garrigan badwy, Representative, Advertising and Sales; Tania Lyter, Coordinator, Advertising. **ISSN:** 0043--2296 (print). **Subscription Rates:** Included in membership. **URL:** http://app.aws.org/wj. **Ad Rates:** BW $5740; 4C $1295; PCI $140. **Remarks:** Accepts advertising. **Circ:** 71000.

7882 ■ World Industrial Reporter
B2B Portales
6355 NW 36 St., Ste. 408
Miami, FL 33126
Phone: (305)448-6875
Fax: (305)448-9942
World-wide industrial manufacturing magazine (tabloid) (English, Arabic, Spanish). **Freq:** 9/year. **Print Method:** Offset. **Cols./Page:** 4. **Col. Width:** 26 nonpareils. **Col. Depth:** 206 agate lines. **ISSN:** 0043--8561 (print). **URL:** http://www.reporteroindustrial.com. **Also known as:** Reportero Industrial. **Ad Rates:** BW $8260. **Remarks:** Accepts advertising. **Circ:** ‡37,107.

Spanish Broadcasting System Inc. - See Ponce

7883 ■ Sunbeam Television Corp. - 7
1401 79th Street Cswy.
Miami, FL 33141-4104
Format: News. **Networks:** Fox; Independent. **Founded:** 1962. **Operating Hours:** Continuous. **ADI:** Miami (Ft. Lauderdale), FL. **Key Personnel:** Cyndi Feinstein, Gen. Sales Mgr., cfeinstein@wsvn.com. **Ad Rates:** Noncommercial. **URL:** http://www.wsvn.com.

7884 ■ WACC-AM - 830
1779 NW 28th St.
Miami, FL 33142
Email: rmcid@paxcc.org
Format: Ethnic; World Beat. **Owner:** Pax Catholic Communications, at above address, Ph: (305)638-9729, Fax: (305)636-3976. **Operating Hours:** Continuous. **Ad Rates:** Advertising accepted; rates available upon request. **URL:** http://www.paxcc.org.

7885 ■ WAXY-AM - 790
20450 NW 2nd Ave.
Miami, FL 33169
Phone: (305)521-5100
Format: Sports; Talk. **Networks:** AP. **Owner:** Lincoln Financial Media Co., 1615 Murray Canyon Rd., San Diego, CA 92108. **Founded:** 1960. **Operating Hours:** Continuous. **ADI:** Miami (Ft. Lauderdale), FL. **Key Personnel:** Howard Davis, Station Mgr., hdavis@790theticket.com; Marc Hochman, Dir. of Programs, mhochman@790theticket.com; Miguel Escobar, Promotions Dir., miguel@790theticket.com. **Wattage:** 25,000. **Ad Rates:** $15-220 per unit. **URL:** http://www.waxy.com.

7886 ■ WDNA-FM - 88.9
2921 Coral Way
Miami, FL 33145
Phone: (305)662-8889
Fax: (305)446-1132
Email: info@wdna.org
Format: Public Radio; Jazz. **Networks:** BBC World Service; Public Radio International (PRI). **Owner:** Bascomb Memorial Broadcasting Foundation. **Founded:** 1971. **Operating Hours:** Continuous; 100% local. **Key Personnel:** Michael Valentine, Music Dir.; Cecil B. Persaud, President; Howard Duperly, Mktg. & Sales Mgr. **Wattage:** 7,400. **Ad Rates:** Advertising accepted; rates available upon request. **URL:** http://www.wdna.org.

7887 ■ WIOB-FM
7007 NW 77th Ave.
Miami, FL 33166
Phone: (809)832-1150
Format: Easy Listening; Hispanic. **Founded:** 1947. **Wattage:** 50,000 ERP.

7888 ■ WKAT-AM - 1036
5757 Blue Lagoon Dr.,Ste.450
Miami, FL 33126
Phone: (305)541-2365
Email: info@broadwaychurch.net
Format: Sports; Contemporary Christian. **Owner:** Salem Media Group Inc., 4880 Santa Rosa Rd., Camarillo, CA 93012, Ph: (805)987-0400, Fax: (805)384-4520. **Founded:** 1937. **Operating Hours:** Midnight - 11.30 p.m. **ADI:** Miami (Ft. Lauderdale), FL. **Key Personnel:** Mike Castillo, Dir. of Dev., mcastillo@salemmiami.com. **Wattage:** 10,000 Day time; 050. **URL:** http://1360wkat.com.

7889 ■ WKCP-FM - 89.7
480 Cedar St.
Saint Paul, MN 55101
Free: 800-562-8440
Email: mail@americanpublicmedia.org
Format: Classical. **Networks:** USA Radio. **Founded:** Aug. 1970. **Formerly:** WMCU-FM. **Operating Hours:** Continuous. **Key Personnel:** Tim Roesler, Sr. VP of Bus. Dev.; Bill Davis, Div. Pres., Co-CEO; Bill Kling, President; Dave Murphy, President. **Wattage:** 100,000. **Ad Rates:** Noncommercial. **URL:** http://www.americanpublicmedia.org.

7890 ■ WKIS-FM - 99.9
194 NW 187 St.
Miami, FL 33169
Phone: (305)654-1700
Fax: (305)654-1715
Format: Country. **Owner:** Beasley Broadcast Group Inc., 3033 Riviera Dr., Ste. 200, Naples, FL 34103-2750, Ph: (239)263-5000, Fax: (239)263-8191. **Founded:** 1965. **Formerly:** WKQS-FM. **Operating Hours:** Continuous. **Key Personnel:** Ken Boesen, Dir. of Programs; Carole Bowen, Gen. Sales Mgr.; Joe Bell, Gen. Mgr. **Local Programs:** *Kiss Country*, Friday 6:00 p.m. - 8:00 p.m. **Wattage:** 100,000. **Ad Rates:** $75-300 for 60 seconds. **URL:** http://www.wkis.com.

7891 ■ WLRN-FM - 91.3
172 NE 15th St.
Miami, FL 33132
Phone: (305)995-1717
Fax: (305)995-2299
Email: info@wlrn.org
Format: Public Radio; News; Talk. **Networks:** National Public Radio (NPR); Public Radio International (PRI). **Founded:** 1948. **Operating Hours:** Continuous. **ADI:** Miami (Ft. Lauderdale), FL. **Key Personnel:** John LaBonia, Gen. Mgr. **Wattage:** 100,000. **Ad Rates:** Noncommercial. **URL:** http://wlrn.org.

7892 ■ WLRN-TV - 17
172 NE 15th St.
Miami, FL 33132
Phone: (305)995-1717
Email: info@wlrn.org
Format: Public TV. **Networks:** Public Broadcasting Service (PBS). **Owner:** WLRN Public Radio and Television, at above address, Miami, FL 33132. **Founded:** 1969. **Operating Hours:** Continuous. **ADI:** Miami (Ft. Lauderdale), FL. **Key Personnel:** Tom Hudson, VP; John LaBonia, Gen. Mgr. **Ad Rates:** Noncommercial. **URL:** http://www.wlrn.org.

7893 ■ WLTV-TV - 23
9405 NW 41st
Miami, FL 33178
Phone: (305)471-4145
Fax: (305)471-3906
Format: Commercial TV. **Networks:** Univision. **Owner:** Univision Television Group Inc., 605 3rd Ave., 12th Fl., New York, NY 10158-0180, Ph: (212)455-5200, Fax: (212)867-6710. **Founded:** 1971. **Operating Hours:** 21 hours daily; 80% network, 20% local. **ADI:** Miami (Ft. Lauderdale), FL. **Key Personnel:** Stephanie Kontzamanys, Sales Mgr.; Matt Boxer, Sales Mgr.; Marilyn Hansen, Gen. Sales Mgr. **Ad Rates:** $190-4000 per unit. **URL:** http://www.univision.com/miami/wltv.

7894 ■ WLYF-FM - 101.5
20450 NW 2nd Ave.
Miami, FL 33169-2505
Fax: (305)652-1015
Free: 877-790-1015
Format: Soft Rock; Adult Contemporary. **Founded:** 1970. **Operating Hours:** Continuous. **Wattage:** 100,000. **Ad Rates:** Advertising accepted; rates available upon request. Combined advertising rates available with WMXJ-FM. **URL:** http://www.litemiami.com.

7895 ■ WMEG-FM
7007 NW 77TH Ave.
42 Calle Frances
Miami, FL 33166
Email: mega@megaestacion.com
Format: Contemporary Hit Radio (CHR). **Networks:** Independent. **Owner:** Spanish Broadcasting System Inc., Pablo Raul Alarcon Media Ctr., 7007 NW 77th Ave., Miami, FL 33166, Ph: (305)441-6901, Fax: (305)883-3375. **Founded:** 1965. **Formerly:** WXRF-FM; WSRA-FM. **Key Personnel:** Joseph A. Garcia, Contact; Raymond Totti, Contact; Luis Diaz Albertini, Contact. **Wattage:** 24,500 ERP. **Ad Rates:** $75-99 for 15 seconds; $101-132 for 30 seconds; $177-231 for 60 seconds.

7896 ■ WMKL-FM - 91.9
PO Box 561832
Miami, FL 33256-1832
Phone: (305)662-7736
Fax: (305)251-2293
Format: Contemporary Christian. **Owner:** Call Communication Group Inc., Not Available. **Key Personnel:** Rob Robbins, PhD, Gen. Mgr., President. **Wattage:** 50,000. **URL:** http://www.callfm.com.

7897 ■ WMXJ-FM - 102.7
20450 NW 2nd Ave.
Miami, FL 33169
Phone: (305)521-5100
Fax: (305)652-1888
Free: 800-226-1027
Format: Oldies. **Networks:** Independent. **Owner:** Lincoln Financial Media Co., 1615 Murray Canyon Rd., San Diego, CA 92108. **Founded:** 1985. **Operating Hours:** Continuous; 100% local. **ADI:** Miami (Ft. Lauderdale), FL. **Key Personnel:** Bill Stedman, Dir. of Programs, bill.stedman@lincolnfinancialmedia.com; Connie Estopinan-Collova, Promotions Dir., cestopinan@wmxj.com; Daryl Leoce, Sales Mgr., dleoce@wmxj.com. **Wattage:** 100,000. **Ad Rates:** $50-400 per unit. **URL:** http://www.magicmiami.com.

7898 ■ WMYM-AM - 990
2525 Ponce De Leon Blvd.
Miami, FL 33134
Free: 888-327-7018
Format: Contemporary Hit Radio (CHR). **Ad Rates:** Noncommercial.

7899 ■ WNMA-AM - 1210
7250 NW 58th St.
Miami, FL 33166
Format: Hispanic. **Owner:** Multicultural Radio Broadcasting Inc., 27 William St., 11th Fl., New York, NY 10005, Ph: (212)966-1059, Fax: (212)966-9580. **Founded:** 1962. **Key Personnel:** John Gabel, Contact, johng@mrbi.net. **URL:** http://www.mrbi.net.

7900 ■ WOCN-AM - 1450
350 NE 71st St.
Miami, FL 33138
Phone: (305)759-7280
Fax: (305)759-2276
Format: Hispanic; News; Talk. **Networks:** Independent. **Founded:** 1984. **Operating Hours**: Continuous; 100% local. **ADI**: Miami (Ft. Lauderdale), FL. **Key Personnel:** Michel Silva, Gen. Sales Mgr.; Casey Ghee, Production Mgr.; Lynore Clarke, Bus. Mgr., Traffic Mgr. **Wattage**: 1,000. **Ad Rates:** $65 for 60 seconds.

7901 ■ WOQI-FM - 93.3 MHz
7007 NW 77th Ave.
Miami, FL 33166
Fax: (305)883-3375
Email: coqi@coqui.net
Format: Hispanic; News. **Networks:** Independent; ABC. **Owner:** WPAB, Inc., at above address. **Founded:** 1969. **Formerly**: WPAB-FM. **ADI**: Ponce, Puerto Rico. **Key Personnel:** Angie Santiago, Operations Mgr.; Edwin Berrios, Music Dir. **Wattage**: 14,500 ERP. **Ad Rates:** $12 for 15 seconds; $15 for 30 seconds; $20 for 60 seconds. **URL:** http://www.spanishbroadcasting.com.

7902 ■ WPAT-FM
7007 NW 77TH Ave.
Miami, FL 33166
Phone: (201)345-9300
Fax: (201)471-1386
Format: Easy Listening. **Networks:** Independent. **Founded:** 1957. **Wattage**: 5,400 ERP.

7903 ■ WPBT-TV - 2
PO Box 610002
Miami, FL 33261-0002
Phone: (305)949-8321
Fax: (305)944-4211
Format: Public TV. **Networks:** Public Broadcasting Service (PBS). **Owner:** Community Television Foundation of South Florida Inc., at above address, Miami, FL 33261. **Founded:** Aug. 12, 1955. **Operating Hours**: Continuous. **ADI**: Miami (Ft. Lauderdale), FL. **Key Personnel:** James Patterson, Chairman. **Local Programs**: *Fight in the Fields*; *The First Measured Century*; *From Swastika to Jim Crow*; *Prince Among Slaves*; *Global Connections*; *Hopes on the Horizon*; *In the Mix*; *PBS Digital TV*; *Illicit: The Dark Trade*; *America Responds*; *Arguing the World*; *The Black Press*; *Blueprint America*; *Changing Stages*; *Conscience and the Constitution*; *Culture Shock*; *Destination America*; *Do You Speak American?*; *Rick Steves' Europe*; *Router Workshop*; *Rudy Maxa's World*, Saturday 10:00 a.m. - 12:00 p.m.; *Stage on Screen*; *Standard Deviants TV*; *Taxi Dreams*; *The U.S. - Mexican War*, *Well-Founded Fear*, *Your Life, Your Money*; *The New Americans*; *Eyes On The Prize*; *Faith and Reason*; *A Falconer's Memoir*, *For Gold and Glory*; *The Farmer's Wife*; *Good War and Those Who Refused to Fight It*; *Great Projects: The Building of America*; *The Greeks: Crucible of Civilization*; *Healthcare Crisis: Who's at Risk?*; *American Storytellers: The Sensible Thing*; *Secret Files Of The Inquisition*. **Wattage**: 100 KW. **Ad Rates:** $650 for 30 seconds. **URL:** http://www.wpbt2.org/.

7904 ■ WPIK-FM - 102.5
1730 NW 79TH Ave.
Miami, FL 33126
Phone: (305)593-5333
Format: Top 40. **Owner:** Summerland Media, LLC, at above address, Doral, FL. **Operating Hours**: Continuous. **Key Personnel:** Lilliam M. Sierra, Gen. Mgr., lsierra@myradioritmo.com; Pepin Navarro, News Dir., Prog. Dir., pepin@myradioritmo.com. **Ad Rates:** Advertising accepted; rates available upon request.

7905 ■ WPLG-TV - 10
3900 Biscayne Blvd.
Miami, FL 33137
Phone: (954)364-2500
Format: News; Sports. **Networks:** ABC. **Founded:** 1967. **ADI**: Miami (Ft. Lauderdale), FL. **Wattage**: 34,000 Horizontal. E. **Ad Rates:** Accepts Advertising. **URL:** http://www.local10.com.

7906 ■ WPOW-FM - 96.5
194 NW 187th St.
Miami, FL 33169
Phone: (305)654-1700
Fax: (305)654-1715
Format: Contemporary Hit Radio (CHR). **Owner:** Beasley Broadcast Group Inc., 3033 Riviera Dr., Ste. 200, Naples, FL 34103-2750, Ph: (239)263-5000, Fax: (239)263-8191. **Founded:** 1985. **Operating Hours**: Continuous. **ADI**: Miami (Ft. Lauderdale), FL. **Key Personnel:** John Jaras, Gen. Sales Mgr.; Ruben Perez, Promotions Dir. **Wattage**: 100,000. **Ad Rates:** Advertising accepted; rates available upon request. **URL:** http://www.power96.com.

7907 ■ WPXM-TV - 35
13801 NW 14th St.
Sunrise, FL 33323
Phone: (954)703-1921
Fax: (954)858-1848
Key Personnel: Brandon Burgess, Chairman, CEO. **URL:** http://www.ionmedia.tv.

7908 ■ WQAM-AM - 560
194 NW 187th St.
Miami, FL 33169
Phone: (305)654-1700
Fax: (305)770-1456
Format: Sports. **Networks:** ESPN Radio. **Owner:** Beasley Broadcast Group Inc., 3033 Riviera Dr., Ste. 200, Naples, FL 34103-2750, Ph: (239)263-5000, Fax: (239)263-8191. **Founded:** 1921. **Operating Hours**: Continuous. **Key Personnel:** George Corso, Chief Engineer, george@wqam.com; Josh Darrow, Dir. of Programs, joshd@wqam.com; Lee Feldman, Dir. of Programs, Promotions Dir., lee.feldman@wqam.com. **Local Programs:** *Weekly Fisherman*; *Dolphins Tonight*. **Wattage**: 5,000. **Ad Rates:** Noncommercial. **URL:** http://www.wqam.com.

WRFM-AM - See Hialeah

7909 ■ WRGP-FM - 88.1
11200 SW 8th St.
11200 SW 8th St.
Miami, FL 33199
Phone: (305)348-3071
Format: Eclectic. **Founded:** Sept. 13, 2006. **Key Personnel:** Pablo Penton, Gen. Mgr., pablo.penton@fiusm.com. **Ad Rates:** Advertising accepted; rates available upon request. **URL:** http://www.fiu.edu.

7910 ■ WRHC-AM - 1550
330 SW 27th Ave., Ste. 207
Miami, FL 33135
Phone: (305)541-3300
Email: info@cadenaazul.com
Format: Hispanic; News; Talk. **Networks:** Independent. **Owner:** WRHC Broadcasting Corp., at above address, Miami, FL 33135. **Founded:** 1963. **Operating Hours**: Continuous. **Key Personnel:** Jorge A. Rodriguez, President. **Wattage**: 45,000. **Ad Rates:** Advertising accepted; rates available upon request. Combined advertising rates available with WWFE-670 AM. **URL:** http://www.cadenaazul.com.

WRTO-FM - See Goulds

7911 ■ WSUA-AM - 1260
2100 Coral Way
Miami, FL 33145
Phone: (305)285-1260
Email: info@caracol1260.com
Format: News; Talk. **Networks:** Independent. **Founded:** 1996. **Operating Hours**: Continuous; 100% local. **Wattage**: 5,000. **Ad Rates:** $120 for 60 seconds. **URL:** http://www.caracol1260.com.

7912 ■ WTVJ-TV - 6
15000 SW 27th St.
Miami, FL 33128
Phone: (305)379-6666
Format: Commercial TV. **Networks:** NBC. **Founded:** 1949. **Operating Hours**: Continuous. **ADI**: Miami (Ft. Lauderdale), FL. **Key Personnel:** Paul Russell, Contact; Donald V. Browne, Contact; Barry Allenuck, Contact; Karla Nelson, Contact; Carol DeVane, Contact; Donald Ramsey, Contact; Paul Russell, Contact. **Wattage**: 100 kw. **Ad Rates:** $100-12000 per unit. **URL:** http://www.nbcmiami.com.

7913 ■ WWFE-AM - 670
330 SW 27th Ave., 2nd Fl.
Miami, FL 33135
Phone: (305)541-3300
Fax: (305)541-2013
Email: info@lapoderosa.com
Format: Hispanic. **Founded:** 1988. **Operating Hours**: Continuous. **ADI**: Miami (Ft. Lauderdale), FL. **Key Personnel:** Jorge A. Rodriguez, President; Ana Vidal Rodriguez, VP. **Wattage**: 050. **URL:** http://www.lapoderosa.com.

7914 ■ WXDJ-FM - 95.7
3191 Coral Way, Ste. 1000
Miami, FL 33145
Phone: (305)447-9595
Fax: (305)448-4735
Format: Hispanic. **Networks:** Independent. **Founded:** 1987. **Operating Hours**: Continuous; 100% local. **ADI**: Miami (Ft. Lauderdale), FL. **Key Personnel:** Kymm Abrahamson, Gen. Mgr.; Maggie Rodriguez, Gen. Sales Mgr.; Jesus Salas, Dir. of Production. **Wattage**: 100,000.

WZNT-FM - See San Juan

MIAMI BEACH

S FL. Dade Co. 3 mi. SE of Miami. Summer and winter resort.

7915 ■ Caesars Player
Onboard Media Inc.
1691 Michigan Ave., Ste. 600
Miami Beach, FL 33139
Free: 855-438-0587
Publisher's E-mail: press@onboard.com
Official publication of Caesar's Palace hotels, casinos, and resorts. **Freq:** 3/yr. **Trim Size:** 10 x 12. **Key Personnel:** Rod Musum, Executive Director, Publisher, phone: (305)772-6543; Ryan Slattery, Managing Editor, phone: (702)212-5690. **Ad Rates:** BW $18,687; 4C $19,750. **Remarks:** Accepts advertising. **Circ:** ‡4965990.

7916 ■ El Paracaidista: La guia del recien llegado y de todos
Clave Corp.
1745 Blarritz Dr.
Miami Beach, FL 33141
Phone: (786)553-4008
Fax: (305)866-9033
Publication E-mail: info@elparacaidista.com
Hispanic community newspaper. **Freq:** Monthly. **Print Method:** Photo offset. **Key Personnel:** Ira Guevara, Editor. **Subscription Rates:** $35 Individuals. **URL:** http://www.elparacaidista.com/. **Mailing address:** PO Box 416501, Miami Beach, FL 33141. **Remarks:** Accepts advertising. **Circ:** Non-paid ♦**19994**.

7917 ■ Informedica Journal: Informedica Journal
Medical Informatics Foundation
9 Island Ave., Apt. 609
Miami Beach, FL 33139
Online journal dedicated to the study of the subjects relative to medical information science, New Technologies of the Information & Comunicaciones (NTIC) and its application in the field of the health. Includes articles in English, Spanish, and Portuguese. **Key Personnel:** Dr. Nora Oliveri, Director, Editorial. **ISSN:** 1540--4471 (print). **Subscription Rates:** Free online. **Circ:** (Not Reported).

7918 ■ Ocean Drive Magazine
Niche Media L.L.C.
404 Washington Ave., Ste. 650
Miami Beach, FL 33139
Phone: (305)532-2544
Fax: (305)532-4366
Fashion magazine. **Freq:** 10/year. **Key Personnel:** Suzy Buckley, Editor-in-Chief; John Heinz, Managing Editor; Courtland Lantaff, Publisher. **Subscription Rates:** $70 Individuals; $125 Two years. **URL:** http://oceandrive.com. **Circ:** ⋆**50000**.

Circulation: ⋆ = AAM; △ or • = BPA; ♦ = CAC; ❑ = VAC; ⊕ = PO Statement; ‡ = Publisher's Report; Boldface figures = sworn; Light figures = estimated.

MIAMI GARDENS

7919 ■ St. Thomas Law Review
St. Thomas University School of Law
16401 NW 37th Ave.
Miami Gardens, FL 33054
Phone: (305)628-6546
Free: 800-367-9010
Publication E-mail: lawrev@stu.edu
Legal journal. **Freq:** 3/yr. **Key Personnel:** Michael A. Vera, Editor-in-Chief; Jenkins Chan, Managing Editor; Maureen Budlong, Office Manager. **Subscription Rates:** $27.50 Individuals; $10 Single issue; $38 Other countries. **URL:** http://www.stthomaslawreview.org. **Remarks:** Advertising not accepted. **Circ:** Paid ‡234.

MIAMI LAKES

7920 ■ Recommend: The Travel Agent Market
Worth International Communications Corp.
5979 NW 151 St., Ste. 120
Miami Lakes, FL 33014
Travel industry magazine. **Freq:** Monthly. **Print Method:** Offset. **Trim Size:** 8 1/8 x 10 7/8. **Cols./Page:** 3. **Col. Width:** 2 1/4 inches. **Col. Depth:** 10 inches. **Key Personnel:** Paloma Villaverde de Rico, Editor-in-Chief. **ISSN:** 0034--1452 (print). **Subscription Rates:** Free to industry affiliate. **URL:** http://www.recommend.com. **Ad Rates:** 4C $14280. **Remarks:** Accepts advertising. **Circ:** (Not Reported).

MIAMI SHORES

Dade Co. Dade Co. (NE). 9 m N of Miami.

7921 ■ Barry Magazine
University Relations
11300 NE 2nd Ave.
Miami Shores, FL 33161-6695
Phone: (305)899-3188
Fax: (305)899-3186
Free: 800-756-6000
Publication E-mail: admissions@mail.barry.edu
Collegiate magazine. **Founded:** 1994. **Freq:** Semiannual. **Print Method:** Web Offset. **Trim Size:** 8 1/2 x 10 7/8. **Key Personnel:** Mike Laderman, Publisher, Executive Director, phone: (305)899-3189; Paige Stein, Managing Editor; Jeremy Jones, Editor. **URL:** http://www.barry.edu/barrymagazine. **Formerly:** The Flame. **Remarks:** Advertising not accepted. **Circ:** Non-paid 40000.

MIDWAY

7922 ■ WTLH-TV - 49
950 Commerce Blvd.
Midway, FL 32343
Phone: (850)576-4990
Format: Commercial TV. **Networks:** Fox. **Founded:** 1989. **Operating Hours:** 5:30 a.m. Monday - 1 a.m. Sunday. **ADI:** Tallahassee, FL-Thomasville (Bainbridge), GA. **Key Personnel:** Dan Mecca, Gen. Mgr.; Nathan Mears, Sales Mgr., nmears@newagemediatv.com; Doris Jones, Bus. Mgr; Sue Schultz, Contact. **URL:** http://www.myfoxtallahassee.com.

MILTON

NW FL. Santa Rosa Co. On Blackwater River, 25 mi. NE of Pensacola. Naval stores, lumber, chemical, fiber industries. Pine timber. Agriculture. Cotton, corn, soybeans.

7923 ■ Santa Rosa Free Press
Santa Rosa Press Gazette
6629 SW Elva St.
Milton, FL 32570
Phone: (850)623-2120
Fax: (850)623-2007
Publication E-mail: news@srpressgazette.com
Community newspaper serving Santa Rosa County. **Freq:** Weekly (Wed.). **Print Method:** Offset. **Cols./Page:** 9. **Col. Width:** 17 nonpareils. **Col. Depth:** 301 agate lines. **Key Personnel:** Bill Gamblin, Editor; Jim Fletcher, Publisher. **Subscription Rates:** $31.92 By mail; $48 Out of area mail. **URL:** http://srpressgazette.com. **Ad Rates:** GLR $.429; BW $1,102.25; 4C $1,458.25; PCI $9.25. **Remarks:** Accepts advertising. **Circ:** Free ‡21500.

7924 ■ WEBY-AM - 1330
7179 Printers Alley
Milton, FL 32583
Phone: (850)983-2242
Fax: (850)983-3231
Email: weby@1330weby.com
Format: News; Talk. **Operating Hours:** 6.00 a.m.-12.00 p.m. **Key Personnel:** Anthony Daughtery, Producer; Mike Bates, Contact, mikebates@1330weby.com. **Wattage:** 25,000. **Ad Rates:** Noncommercial. **Mailing address:** PO Box 4430 , Milton, FL 32572. **URL:** http://www.1330weby.com.

7925 ■ WTKE-AM - 1490
6583 Berryhill Rd.
Milton, FL 32570
Phone: (850)623-1400
Format: Oldies. **Founded:** 1989. **Formerly:** WCKC-AM; WECM-AM. **Operating Hours:** Continuous. **Key Personnel:** Michael Pfost, President. **Wattage:** 1,000. **Ad Rates:** $5 for 30 seconds; $8 for 60 seconds. Combined advertising rates available with WTGF-FM.

MIRAMAR

Broward Co. Broward Co. (SE). 20 m W of Hallandale.

7926 ■ WHYI-FM - 100.7
7601 Riviera Blvd.
Miramar, FL 33023
Phone: (954)862-3102
Format: Contemporary Hit Radio (CHR). **Networks:** Independent. **Owner:** iHeartMedia Inc., 200 E Basse Rd., San Antonio, TX 78209, Ph: (210)832-3314. **Founded:** 1960. **Operating Hours:** Continuous. **ADI:** Miami (Ft. Lauderdale), FL. **Wattage:** 100,000. **Ad Rates:** $100-400 for 60 seconds. **URL:** http://www.y100.com.

7927 ■ WINZ-AM - 940
7601 Riviera Blvd.
Miramar, FL 33023
Phone: (954)862-2000
Fax: (954)862-4013
Format: News; Talk. **Networks:** ABC. **Founded:** 1946. **Operating Hours:** Continuous. **Key Personnel:** Gary Reyes, Contact, greyes@ccmiami.com. **Wattage:** 50,000. **Ad Rates:** Advertising accepted; rates available upon request. **URL:** http://www.940winz.com.

7928 ■ WIOD-AM - 610
7601 Riviera Blvd.
Miramar, FL 33023-6574
Phone: (954)862-2000
Fax: (954)862-4010
Format: News; Talk. **Networks:** AP; ABC. **Founded:** 1926. **Operating Hours:** Continuous. **Key Personnel:** Brian Olson, Gen. Mgr. **Wattage:** 10,000. **Ad Rates:** Noncommercial.

7929 ■ WLVE-FM - 93.9
7601 Riviera Blvd.
Miramar, FL 33023-6574
Phone: (954)862-2000
Format: Jazz. **Simulcasts:** WWLV-FM. **Networks:** Independent. **Founded:** 1955. **Formerly:** WWWL-FM. **Operating Hours:** Continuous; 100% local. **Key Personnel:** Greg Alexander, Gen. Sales Mgr. **Wattage:** 98,000. **Ad Rates:** Advertising accepted; rates available upon request.

7930 ■ WMGE-FM - 94.9
7601 Riviera Blvd.
Miramar, FL 33023
Phone: (954)862-2000
Format: Hispanic. **Founded:** Sept. 07, 2006. **Ad Rates:** Advertising accepted; rates available upon request. **URL:** http://www.mega949.com.

7931 ■ WMIB-FM - 103.5
7601 Riviera Blvd.
Miramar, FL 33023
Phone: (954)862-2000
Format: Urban Contemporary. **Operating Hours:** 18 hours Daily. **Ad Rates:** Advertising accepted; rates available upon request.

7932 ■ WPLL-FM - 103.5
7601 Riviera Blvd.
Miramar, FL 33023-6574
Format: Adult Contemporary. **Owner:** ION Media Networks Inc., 601 Clearwater Park Rd., West Palm Beach, FL 33401-6233, Ph: (561)659-4122, Fax: (561)659-4252. **Founded:** 1959. **Formerly:** WSHE-FM. **Operating Hours:** 0% network, 100% local. **ADI:** Miami (Ft. Lauderdale), FL. **Key Personnel:** Ronna Woulfe, Gen. Mgr., VP; Dave Stewart, Dir. of Programs; Roger Koch, Gen. Sales Mgr.; Terri Lynn, Dir. Pub. Aff. **Wattage:** 100,000.

7933 ■ WZTA-FM - 94.9
7601 Riviera Blvd.
Miramar, FL 33023-6574
Phone: (954)862-2000
Format: Alternative/New Music/Progressive. **Networks:** Independent. **Owner:** iHeartMedia Inc., 200 E Basse Rd., San Antonio, TX 78209, Ph: (210)832-3314. **Operating Hours:** Continuous. **Key Personnel:** Nicole Covar, Contact. **Wattage:** 98,000. **Ad Rates:** Advertising accepted; rates available upon request. **URL:** http://www.big1059.com.

NAPLES

S FL. Collier Co. On Gulf of Mexico, 30 mi. S. of Fort Myers. Resort. Shrimp fisheries. Agriculture.

7934 ■ Ave Maria Law Review
Ave Maria School of Law
1025 Commons Cir.
Naples, FL 34119
Phone: (239)687-5300
Fax: (239)352-2890
Publication E-mail: lawreview@avemarialaw.edu
Journal offers information to research law with a catholic perspective. **Freq:** Semiannual. **Key Personnel:** James W. Devine, Editor-in-Chief; Dylan M. Marck, Managing Editor. **URL:** http://lr.avemarialaw.edu/Home/issues. **Remarks:** Advertising not accepted. **Circ:** (Not Reported).

7935 ■ Gulfshore Life Magazine: The Magazine of Southwest Florida
Gulfshore Media Inc.
3560 Kraft Rd., Ste. 301
Naples, FL 34105
Phone: (239)449-4111
Fax: (239)449-4163
Lifestyle magazine. **Freq:** Monthly 10/yr. (combined issues July/August/September). **Print Method:** Webb. **Trim Size:** 8 3/8 x 10 7/8. **Cols./Page:** 3. **Col. Width:** 42 picas. **Col. Depth:** 60.3 picas. **Key Personnel:** Pam Daniel, Director, Editorial, Vice President; Dan Denton, President, Publisher; David Sendler, Editor-in-Chief. **ISSN:** 0745--0079 (print). **Subscription Rates:** $16.95 Individuals; $26.95 Two years; $36.95 Individuals 3 years. **URL:** http://gulfshorelife.com. **Ad Rates:** BW $1,800; 4C $2,500. **Remarks:** Accepts advertising. **Circ:** Non-paid ■ **11906**, Paid ■ **7666**, Combined ■ **19572**.

7936 ■ International Law Journal
Ave Maria School of Law
1025 Commons Cir.
Naples, FL 34119
Phone: (239)687-5300
Fax: (239)352-2890
Publication E-mail: InternationalLawJournal@avemarialaw.edu
Journal containing articles that address issues in international law, from a natural law perspective. **Freq:** Annual. **Key Personnel:** Kate Lloyd, Editor-in-Chief. **URL:** http://ilj.avemarialaw.edu. **Circ:** (Not Reported).

7937 ■ Journal of Thermal Stresses
Taylor & Francis Group Journals
c/o Richard B. Hetnarski, Editor-in-Chief
St. Raphael, Unit 1209
7117 Pelican Bay Blvd.
Naples, FL 34108
Publisher's E-mail: customerservice@taylorandfrancis.com
Journal publishing refereed articles on theoretical and industrial applications of thermal stress. **Freq:** Monthly. **Print Method:** Offset. **Trim Size:** 7 x 10. **Cols./Page:** 1. **Col. Width:** 60 nonpareils. **Col. Depth:** 112 agate lines. **Key Personnel:** Louis G. Hector, Jr., Board Member; Bruno A. Boley, Board Member; J.R. Barber, Board Member; Reza M. Eslami, Board Member; Fumihiro Ashida, Board Member; Dorin Iesan, Board Member; David H. Allen, Board Member; Fazil Erdogan, Board Member; Richard B. Hetnarski, Editor-in-Chief. **ISSN:** 0149--5739 (print); **EISSN:** 1521--074X (electronic). **Subscription Rates:** $2335 Individuals print only; $4643 Institutions print and online; $4062 Institutions

online. **URL:** http://www.tandfonline.com/toc/uths20/current. **Remarks:** Accepts advertising. **Circ:** ‡308.

7938 ■ Link
Distributor's Link Inc.
4297 Corporate Sq.
Naples, FL 34104
Phone: (239)643-2713
Fax: (239)643-5220
Free: 800-356-1639
Trade magazine for the fastener industry. **Founded:** 1975. **Freq:** Quarterly. **Key Personnel:** Leo J. Coar, Editor; Tracey Lumia, Manager, Marketing and Sales; Maryann Marzocchi, Vice President, Advertising, Vice President, Sales. **Subscription Rates:** $50 Individuals; $60 Canada and Mexico; $70 Other countries. **URL:** http://www.linkmagazine.com. **Remarks:** Advertising accepted; rates available upon request. **Circ:** Paid 13000.

7939 ■ Naples Daily News
Collier County Publishing Co.
1100 Immokalee Rd.
Naples, FL 34110
Phone: (239)213-6000
Free: 877-263-6047
Publisher's E-mail: news@naplesnews.com
General newspaper. **Freq:** Daily. **Print Method:** Offset. **Cols./Page:** 6. **Col. Width:** 25 nonpareils. **Col. Depth:** 22 1/4 inches. **Key Personnel:** Eric Strachan, Managing Editor; Phil Lewis, Editor; Chris Doyle, President, Publisher. **URL:** http://naplesnews.com. **Remarks:** Accepts advertising. **Circ:** ★**59079**, ★**45227**, Combined ★**70995**, Combined ★**60232**.

7940 ■ Naples Guide
Naples Guide
990 1st Ave. S, Ste. 201
Naples, FL 34102-6122
Publication E-mail: info@naplesguide.com
Magazine covering arts, entertainment, shopping, dining, beauty, health, home and garden, and real estate in Naples, FL, and the surrounding areas. **Freq:** Monthly. **Print Method:** Web. **Trim Size:** 5 1/2 x 8 1/2. **Cols./Page:** 2. **Col. Width:** 13 picas. **Col. Depth:** 45 picas. **URL:** http://naplesguide.com. **Ad Rates:** BW $1,295; 4C $1,760. **Remarks:** Accepts advertising. **Circ:** Controlled ‡270000.

7941 ■ Natural Awakenings
Natural Awakenings Publishing Corp.
4933 Tamiami Trl., Ste. 200
Naples, FL 34103
Phone: (239)434-9392
Fax: (239)434-9513
Publisher's E-mail: franchiseinfo@naturalawakeningsmag.com
Magazine featuring nutrition, fitness, creative expression, personal growth, and sustainable living. **Key Personnel:** Sharon Bruckman, Chief Executive Officer. **URL:** http://www.naturalawakeningsmag.com. **Circ:** (Not Reported).

7942 ■ Southeast Food Service News
Southeast Publishing Company Inc.
c/o Elliott Fischer, Marketing Director
8805 Tamiami Trail N, No. 301
Naples, FL 34108
Phone: (239)514-1258
Magazine (tabloid) serving the food industry. **Freq:** Monthly. **Print Method:** Offset-Web. **Trim Size:** 10 1/2 x 13. **Cols./Page:** 4. **Col. Width:** 1 3/4 inches. **Col. Depth:** 13 3/4 inches. **Key Personnel:** Elliott Fischer, Director, Marketing; John P. Hayward, Account Executive, Editor. **ISSN:** 0199--2805 (print). **Subscription Rates:** $36 Individuals; $5 Single issue; $59 Individuals directory issue. **URL:** http://sfsn.com. **Ad Rates:** GLR $50; BW $2799; 4C $995; PCI $60. **Remarks:** Accepts advertising. **Circ:** Combined ‡17426.

7943 ■ Beasley Broadcasting Group Inc.
3033 Riviera Dr., Ste. 200
Naples, FL 34103
Phone: (239)263-5000
URL: http://bbgi.com.

7944 ■ Beasley Broadcasting of Naples Florida
3033 Riviera Dr., Ste. 200
Naples, FL 34103
Phone: (239)263-5000
Fax: (239)263-8191
URL: http://bbgi.com.

7945 ■ Continental Cablevision
PO Box 413018
Naples, FL 34101-3018
Phone: (941)793-9600
Fax: (941)793-1317
Owner: US West Media, at above address. **Founded:** 1967. **Key Personnel:** Ken Fuchs, District Mgr.; Larry Hoepfner, Dir. of Mktg.; David Elliot, Dir. of Sales. **Cities Served:** Everglades City, Ft. Myers, Naples, Sanibel, Florida: subscribing households 130,000; 50 channels; 1 community access channel; 168 hours per week community access programming.

7946 ■ Jones Intercable
PO Box 413018
Naples, FL 34101-3018
Owner: Jones Intercable Inc., 9697 E Mineral Ave., Englewood, CO 80112-3446, Ph: (303)792-3111, Fax: (303)790-0533. **Founded:** 1961. **Formerly:** Southern Cablevision. **Key Personnel:** Gary McDonald, Gen. Mgr.; Beverly Wall, Mktg. Mgr.; Gregg Wood, Chief Engineer; Paul Gregg, Sales Mgr; Kristine Flint, Contact. **Cities Served:** Briarcliff, East Lee County, Fort Myers, Gateway, Iona, South Fort Myers, Florida: subscribing households 45,000; Lee County; 61 channels; 1 community access channel; 16 hours per week community access programming.

7947 ■ WAFZ-FM - 92.1
2105 W Immokalee Dr.
Naples, FL 34120
Phone: (239)657-9210
Fax: (239)658-6109
Format: Ethnic; Religious. **Owner:** Glades Media Group, 530 E Alverdez Ave., Clewiston, FL 33440, Ph: (863)983-5900. **Key Personnel:** Paul Danitz, Sales Mgr., paul@gladesmedia.com. **Ad Rates:** Advertising accepted; rates available upon request. **URL:** http://www.wafz.com.

7948 ■ WAVV-FM - 101.1
11800 Tamiami Trl. E
Naples, FL 34113
Phone: (239)793-1011
Fax: (941)793-7000
Free: 877-310-9288
Format: Easy Listening. **Networks:** AP. **Owner:** Alpine Broadcasting Corp., 11800 Tamiami Trl. E, Naples, FL 34113, Ph: (239)793-1011, Fax: (239)793-7000, Free: 800-310-9288. **Founded:** 1987. **Operating Hours:** Continuous. **ADI:** Fort Myers-Naples, FL. **Key Personnel:** Walt Tiburski, Gen. Mgr., w.tiburski@wavv101.com; Al Baxa, Chief Engineer, albaxa@wavv101.com. **Wattage:** 100,000. **Ad Rates:** $46-77 for 30 seconds; $53-89 for 60 seconds. **URL:** http://www.wavv101.com.

7949 ■ WSGL-FM - 103.1
2640 Golden Gate Pkwy, Ste. 316
Naples, FL 34105-3203
Phone: (239)435-9100
Fax: (239)793-7329
Free: 800-349-1031
Format: Adult Contemporary. **Networks:** Independent. **Owner:** Renda Broadcasting Corp., at above address. **Founded:** 1980. **Operating Hours:** Continuous; 100% local. **ADI:** Fort Myers-Naples, FL. **Key Personnel:** David Rosato, Gen. Sales Mgr.; Janet Manzelli, News Dir.; Marty Simpson, Music Dir.; Chuck Thomas, Director; Bill Berry, Gen. Mgr.; Randy Savage, Dir. of Programs. **Wattage:** 14,000. **Ad Rates:** $20-34 per unit.

7950 ■ W16CJ - 16
PO Box A
Santa Ana, CA 92711
Phone: (714)832-2950
Free: 888-731-1000
Owner: Trinity Broadcasting Network Inc., PO Box A, Santa Ana, CA 92711, Ph: (714)832-2950, Free: 888-731-1000. **URL:** http://www.tbn.org.

7951 ■ WSRX-FM - 89.5
3805 The Lord's Way
Naples, FL 34114
Phone: (239)775-8950
Fax: (239)774-5889
Format: Contemporary Christian. **Key Personnel:** Curt Baker, Director; Michael Shelley, Gen. Mgr. **Ad Rates:** Noncommercial.

NEW PORT RICHEY

WC FL. Pasco Co. 18 mi. N. of Clearwater. Citrus fruit.

7952 ■ The PSQH
American Board of Quality Assurance and Utilization Review Physicians
6640 Congress St.
New Port Richey, FL 34653
Phone: (727)569-0195
Fax: (727)569-0195
Free: 800-998-6030
Publisher's E-mail: abqaurp@abqaurp.org
Journal covering a broad range of safety and quality topics. **Freq:** Bimonthly. **ISSN:** 1553--6637 (print). **Subscription Rates:** $27 /year; $39 Two years; $47 Canada and Mexico /year; $67 Other countries /year; $59 Canada and Mexico 2 years; $79 Other countries 2 years. **URL:** http://psqh.com. **Remarks:** Accepts advertising. **Circ:** (Not Reported).

NEW SMYRNA BEACH

E FL. Volusia Co. On North Indian River, 14 mi. S. of Daytona Beach. Tourist resort. Shrimp and crab fisheries. Citrus fruit.

7953 ■ Mature Fitness
American Senior Fitness Association
PO Box 2575
New Smyrna Beach, FL 32170
Phone: (386)423-6634
Fax: (877)365-3048
Free: 888-689-6791
Publisher's E-mail: asfa@seniorfitness.net
Magazine featuring the newest in senior strength training, aerobic choreography, seated exercise, and programming for special conditions. **Freq:** Quarterly. **URL:** http://www.seniorfitness.net/sfamag.htm. **Remarks:** Advertising not accepted. **Circ:** (Not Reported).

7954 ■ New Smyrna Pennysaver
Volusia Pennysaver Inc.
223A Canal St.
New Smyrna Beach, FL 32168
Phone: (386)423-2300
Fax: (386)426-2807
Shopper. **Freq:** Weekly (Wed.). **Print Method:** Offset. **Trim Size:** 11 x 13 3/4. **Cols./Page:** 6. **Col. Width:** 18 nonpareils. **Col. Depth:** 182 agate lines. **Key Personnel:** Sharon Farmer, Manager, Sales; John Shaw, Manager, Circulation. **Subscription Rates:** Free. **URL:** http://floridapennysavers.com/GetPennysaver.aspx?edition=NS. **Ad Rates:** GLR $647.40; BW $631.80; 4C $827.40; PCI $8.30. **Circ:** 27600.

7955 ■ The Observer
The Observer
318 Flagler Ave.
New Smyrna Beach, FL 32169
Phone: (386)427-1000
General newspaper. **Founded:** 1913. **Freq:** Semiweekly. **Key Personnel:** Myriah Chandler, Contact. **USPS:** 382-200. **Subscription Rates:** $29.95 Individuals in county mail delivery; $39.95 Individuals out-of-county mail delivery; $9.95 Individuals online only. **URL:** http://www.sevobserver.com/index.php?option=com_content&view=frontpage&Item id=1. **Formerly:** News & Observer. **Ad Rates:** GLR $.70; SAU $9.22. **Remarks:** Accepts advertising. **Circ:** Combined ★**452078**.

7956 ■ ORL-Head and Neck Nursing
Society of Otorhinolaryngology and Head-Neck Nurses
207 Downing St.
New Smyrna Beach, FL 32168
Phone: (386)428-1695
Fax: (386)423-7566
Publisher's E-mail: info@sohnnurse.com
Freq: Quarterly. **Alt. Formats:** PDF. **URL:** http://sohnnurse.com/publications-and-resources/publications/orl-journal. **Remarks:** Accepts advertising. **Circ:** 1500.

WKTO-FM - See Edgewater

NOKOMIS

SW FL. Sarasota Co. 20 mi. S. of Sarasota.

7957 ■ Aquatic Therapy and Fitness Research Journal
Aquatic Exercise Association

Circulation: ★ = AAM; △ or • = BPA; ♦ = CAC; ❑ = VAC; ⊕ = PO Statement; ‡ = Publisher's Report; Boldface figures = sworn; Light figures = estimated.

201 Tamiami Trl. S, Ste. 3
Nokomis, FL 34275-3198
Phone: (941)486-8600
Fax: (941)486-8820
Free: 888-232-9283
Publisher's E-mail: info@aeawave.com
Freq: Semiannual. **Subscription Rates:** Included in membership. **Alt. Formats:** Download; PDF. **URL:** http://aeawave.com/Portals/2/GENERAL%20FILES/2013ConfPosterSessions.pdf; http://aeawave.com/PublicPages/Research/ResearchResources.aspx. **Mailing address:** PO Box 1609, Nokomis, FL 34274-1609. **Remarks:** Advertising not accepted. **Circ:** 1000.

7958 ■ Communications News: Solutions for Today's Networking Decision Makers
Nelson Publishing Inc.
2500 Tamiami Trl. N
Nokomis, FL 34275
Phone: (941)966-9521
Fax: (941)966-2590
Magazine featuring networking communications technology applications. **Freq:** Monthly. **Print Method:** Offset. **Trim Size:** 8 x 10 3/4. **Cols./Page:** 3 and 2. **Col. Width:** 26 and 40 nonpareils. **Col. Depth:** 140 agate lines. **Key Personnel:** Vern Nelson, Publisher. **ISSN:** 0010--3632 (print). **URL:** http://www.comnews.com. **Ad Rates:** BW $9195; 4C $2130. **Remarks:** Accepts advertising. **Circ:** △**85,000**.

7959 ■ EE Evaluation Engineering: The Magazine of Electronic Evaluation & Test
Nelson Publishing Inc.
2500 Tamiami Trl. N
Nokomis, FL 34275
Phone: (941)966-9521
Fax: (941)966-2590
Trade magazine covering electronic engineering, evaluation and test. **Freq:** Monthly. **Print Method:** Offset. **Trim Size:** 7 3/4 x 10 3/4. **Cols./Page:** 3 and 2. **Col. Width:** 26 and 40 nonpareils. **Col. Depth:** 140 agate lines. **Key Personnel:** Janelle Hartman, Publisher, phone: (941)388-7050; Paul Milo, Director, Editorial, phone: (941)966-9521; Michael Hughes, Associate Editor, phone: (805)529-6790. **ISSN:** 0149--0370 (print). **Subscription Rates:** Free. **URL:** http://www.evaluationengineering.com. **Ad Rates:** BW $8,214; 4C $7,271. **Remarks:** Accepts advertising. **Circ:** Non-paid △**46026**.

7960 ■ Health Management Technology: The Source for Information Systems Solutions
Nelson Publishing Inc.
2500 Tamiami Trl. N
Nokomis, FL 34275
Phone: (941)966-9521
Fax: (941)966-2590
Business magazine for healthcare information systems professionals and managers. **Freq:** Monthly. **Trim Size:** 3/8 x 10 7/8. **Cols./Page:** 3. **Col. Width:** 27 nonpareils. **Col. Depth:** 134 agate lines. **Key Personnel:** Kris Russell, Publisher, phone: (941)388-7050. **ISSN:** 1074--4770 (print). **Subscription Rates:** Free to qualified subscribers. **URL:** http://www.healthmgttech.com. **Ad Rates:** BW $5224; 4C $995. **Remarks:** Accepts advertising. **Circ:** ■ **40206**.

7961 ■ Medical Laboratory Observer
Nelson Publishing Inc.
2500 Tamiami Trl. N
Nokomis, FL 34275
Phone: (941)966-9521
Fax: (941)966-2590
Magazine for clinical laboratory professionals. **Freq:** Monthly. **Print Method:** Web offset. **Trim Size:** 7 3/4 x 10 3/4. **Cols./Page:** 3. **Col. Width:** 2 1/4 inches. **Col. Depth:** 10 inches. **Key Personnel:** Alan Lenhoff, Editor; Kristine Russell, Publisher, Executive Editor, President. **USPS:** 060-930. **Subscription Rates:** Free to qualified clinical laboratory professionals. **URL:** http://www.mlo-online.com. **Remarks:** Advertising accepted; rates available upon request. **Circ:** △**48043**.

7962 ■ Modern Applications News: The Metalworking Idea Magazine
Nelson Publishing Inc.
2500 Tamiami Trl. N
Nokomis, FL 34275
Phone: (941)966-9521
Fax: (941)966-2590
Publisher's E-mail: informatie@tmg.nl
Trade magazine covering metalworking engineering, design, and manufacturing. **Founded:** 1967. **Freq:** Monthly. **Print Method:** Web Offset. **Trim Size:** 7 3/4 x 10 3/4. **Cols./Page:** 3 and 2. **Col. Width:** 26 and 40 nonpareils. **Col. Depth:** 140 agate lines. **Key Personnel:** Vern Nelson, Publisher. **URL:** http://www.modernapplicationsnews.com; http://www.nelsonpub.com. **Also known as:** MAN. **Mailing address:** PO Box 376, 1000 EB Amsterdam, Netherlands. **Ad Rates:** BW $5,775; 4C $1,365. **Remarks:** Accepts advertising. **Circ:** Paid ‡25000.

7963 ■ Tooling & Production: Providing Solutions for Metalworking Manufacturers
Nelson Publishing Inc.
2500 Tamiami Trl. N
Nokomis, FL 34275
Phone: (941)966-9521
Fax: (941)966-2590
Magazine concerning metalworking. **Freq:** Bimonthly 24 issues per year. **Print Method:** Offset. **Trim Size:** 8 x 10 3/4. **Cols./Page:** 3. **Col. Width:** 26 nonpareils. **Col. Depth:** 144 agate lines. **Key Personnel:** Vern Nelson, Publisher, Director, Editorial. **USPS:** 633-440. **Subscription Rates:** Free. **URL:** http://www.manufacturingcenter.com; http://www.toolingandproduction.com. **Formerly:** Tooling & Production: The Manufacturing Magazine. **Ad Rates:** BW $4,485; 4C $995. **Remarks:** Accepts advertising. **Circ:** △**60000**.

NORTH MIAMI

Dade Co Dade Co. Dade Co. (N). Suburb of Miami.

7964 ■ FIU Hospitality Review
Florida International University Chaplin School of Hospitality & Tourism Management
3000 NE 151st St.
North Miami, FL 33181
Phone: (305)919-4500
Fax: (305)919-4555
Publisher's E-mail: hospitality@fiu.edu
Trade journal covering hospitality management. **Freq:** Biennial. **Trim Size:** 7 x 10. **Key Personnel:** Mike Hampton, Publisher; Randall S. Upchurch, Editor-in-Chief; Catherine Curtis, Managing Editor. **ISSN:** 0739--7011 (print). **Subscription Rates:** $150 Institutions /year; $150 Individuals /year. **URL:** http://digitalcommons.fiu.edu/hospitalityreview. **Remarks:** Accepts advertising. **Circ:** Controlled 7,000.

7965 ■ WLQY-AM - 1320
1055 NE 125 St.
North Miami, FL 33161
Format: Hispanic. **Owner:** Entravision Communications Corporation, 2425 Olympic Blvd., Ste. 6000 W, Santa Monica, CA 90404-4030, Ph: (310)447-3870, Fax: (310)447-3899. **Founded:** 1953. **Operating Hours:** Continuous. **ADI:** Miami (Ft. Lauderdale), FL. **Key Personnel:** Rick Santos, Gen. Mgr. **Wattage:** 5,000. **Ad Rates:** $55-90 for 60 seconds. **URL:** http://www.entravision.com.

7966 ■ WMBM-AM - 1490
13242 NW 7th Ave.
North Miami, FL 33168
Phone: (305)769-1100
Fax: (305)769-9975
Free: 800-721-9626
Email: wmbm@wmbm.com
Format: Gospel. **Networks:** American Urban Radio; Westwood One Radio. **Owner:** New Birth Broadcasting Corp. **Founded:** Mar. 1995. **Operating Hours:** Continuous. **Key Personnel:** Bishop Victor T. Curry, Gen. Mgr., President, vcurry@wmbm.com; Greg Cooper, Div. Dir., gcooper@wmbm.com; Shayla Forde, Bus. Mgr., sforde@wmbm.com; Rev. C.J. Kelly, Asst. GM, ckelly@wmbm.com; Jose Miller, Producer, jmiller@wmbm.com. **Local Programs:** *Tuesday Talk*, Tuesday 9:30 a.m. - 12:00 p.m. **Wattage:** 1,000. **Ad Rates:** $70-85 for 30 seconds; $98-160 for 60 seconds. **URL:** http://www.wmbm.com.

NORTH MIAMI BEACH

S FL. Dade Co. 10 mi. N. of Miami. Marinas. Tourist resort. Light manufacturing.

7967 ■ WSRF-AM - 1580
1510 NE 162 St.
North Miami Beach, FL 33162
Phone: (305)945-1580
Fax: (305)947-8050
Email: info@wsrf.com
Format: Full Service; Talk. **Networks:** Independent. **Founded:** 1955. **Operating Hours:** Continuous. **ADI:** Miami (Ft. Lauderdale), FL. **Wattage:** 10,000 Day; 1,500 Nig. **Ad Rates:** Advertising accepted; rates available upon request. $75 for 30 seconds; $75 for 60 seconds. **URL:** http://www.wsrf.com.

NORTH PALM BEACH

SE FL. Palm Beach Co. 8 mi. N. of Palm Beach. Commercial area.

7968 ■ Archival Issues
Midwest Archives Conference
631 US Highway 1, Ste. 400
North Palm Beach, FL 33408-4618
Publisher's E-mail: membership@midwestarchives.org
Professional journal covering issues and problems confronting the contemporary archivist. **Freq:** Semiannual. **Key Personnel:** Barbara Floyed, Chairperson. **ISSN:** 1067--4993 (print). **Subscription Rates:** $35 Individuals print; $80 Institutions print; $90 Canada print; $100 Other countries print; included in membership dues. **URL:** http://www.midwestarchives.org/archival-issues. **Remarks:** Advertising accepted; rates available upon request. **Circ:** (Not Reported).

7969 ■ Consulting Psychology Journal
Society of Consulting Psychology
c/o Debra Nolan, CAE
631 US Highway 1, Ste., 400
North Palm Beach, FL 33408
Free: 800-440-4066
Freq: Quarterly. **ISSN:** 1065--9293 (print); **EISSN:** 1939--0149 (electronic). **Subscription Rates:** $133 Individuals; $488 Institutions. **URL:** http://www.apa.org/pubs/journals/cpb/index.aspx. **Remarks:** Advertising accepted; rates available upon request. **Circ:** 1300.

7970 ■ Gridiron Strategies
L.C. Clark Publishing Company Inc.
840 US Hwy. 1, Ste. 330
North Palm Beach, FL 33408-3874
Phone: (561)627-3393
Fax: (561)694-6578
Free: 800-537-4271
Publisher's E-mail: jmoody@lcclark.com
Magazine dedicated to football coaching. **Freq:** Bimonthly. **Print Method:** Offset. **Trim Size:** 6 7/8 x 10. **Cols./Page:** 2. **Col. Width:** 2 2/3 inches. **Col. Depth:** 8 1/2 inches. **Key Personnel:** Rex Lardner, Editor; Charlotte Vann, Manager, Circulation; John Gallup, Publisher. **ISSN:** 1074-3529 (print). **Subscription Rates:** $44.95 Individuals North America; $79.95 Two years; $66.95 Other countries; $123.95 Two years foreign. **URL:** http://www.gridironstrategies.com/. **Mailing address:** PO Box 13079, North Palm Beach, FL 33408-3874. **Remarks:** Advertising accepted; rates available upon request. **Circ:** (Not Reported).

7971 ■ Undersea & Hyperbaric Medicine
Undersea and Hyperbaric Medical Society
631 US Highway 1, Ste. 307
North Palm Beach, FL 33408
Phone: (919)490-5140
Fax: (919)490-5149
Free: 877-533-8467
Publisher's E-mail: uhms@uhms.org
Scientific journal covering diving physiology and clinical hyperbaric medicine. **Freq:** Bimonthly. **Trim Size:** 8 1/2 x 11. **Cols./Page:** 2. **Key Personnel:** Renee Duncan, Managing Editor; George Mychaskiw, Editor-in-Chief. **ISSN:** 1066--2936 (print). **Subscription Rates:** $200 Individuals; $250 Nonmembers. **URL:** http://www.uhms.org. **Formerly**: Undersea Biomedical Research. **Remarks:** Advertising not accepted. **Circ:** Controlled 2200.

7972 ■ WGBZ-FM - 105.5
11675 Lost Tree Way N
North Palm Beach, FL 33408
Phone: (609)484-8444
Fax: (609)646-6331
Email: info@993thebuzz.com
Format: Blues. **Owner:** Equity Communications, at

above address. **Wattage**: 3,300. **Ad Rates:** Noncommercial.

7973 ■ WZBZ-FM
c/o Stephen F. Gormley
North Palm Beach, FL 33408
Email: info@993thebuzz.com
Format: Top 40. **Founded:** Sept. 07, 2006. **Wattage:** 3,000 ERP.

OCALA

NC FL. Marion Co. 38 mi. S. of Gainesville. Central Florida Community College. Limestone and phosphate mines. Vegetables, melons.

7974 ■ Maestrino
Leopold Stokowski Club
3900 SE 33 Ave.
Ocala, FL 34480
Freq: Semiannual. **Subscription Rates:** Included in membership. **Remarks:** Accepts advertising. **Circ:** 2000.

7975 ■ Ocala Magazine
Ocala Magazine
743 SE Fort King St.
Ocala, FL 34471
Phone: (352)622-2995
Fax: (352)622-9200
Publisher's E-mail: letters@ocalamagazine.com
Lifestyle magazine in the heart of Florida. **Trim Size:** 9 x 10.875. **Subscription Rates:** $30 Individuals; $50 Two years. **URL:** http://ocalamagazine.com. **Ad Rates:** 4C $3,600. **Remarks:** Accepts display advertising. **Circ:** Paid ‡27000.

7976 ■ Ocala Star-Banner
Star Banner
2121 SW 19th Ave. Rd.
Ocala, FL 34471
Phone: (352)867-4020
Fax: (352)867-4018
Free: 800-541-2171
Publisher's E-mail: customerservice@starbanner.com
General newspaper. **Freq:** Daily. **Print Method:** Offset. **Trim Size:** 13 x 21 1/2. **Cols./Page:** 6. **Col. Width:** 26 nonpareils. **Col. Depth:** 301 agate lines. **Key Personnel:** Allen Parsons, Publisher, phone: (325)867-4020; Bill Hayter, Manager, Circulation, phone: (352)867-4172. **Subscription Rates:** $18.19 7 day print and digital; monthly; 14.24 Thursday through Sunday; 11.90 digital only. **URL:** http://ocala.com/apps/pbcs.dll/frontpage. **Remarks:** Accepts advertising. **Circ:** Mon.-Fri. ★**45424**, Sun. ★**50185**, Sat. ★**46994**.

7977 ■ Cox Communications
1749 W Siliver Spring Blvd.
Ocala, FL 34478
Phone: (352)237-1111
Fax: (352)237-6706
Founded: 1978. **Formerly**: Cox Cable Ocala. **Key Personnel:** Kathy Grimes, Gen. Mgr., VP; Barbara Searle, Dir. of Operations; Jim Warner, Dir. of Mktg. **Cities Served:** Ocala, Silver Springs, Florida: subscribing households 31,000; 38 channels; 2 community access channels. **URL:** http://www.cox.com/residential/home.html.

7978 ■ WGGG-AM
2325 NE 2ND St., Ste. 5
Ocala, FL 34470
Format: Sports. **Founded:** Sept. 07, 2006. **Wattage:** 1,000.

7979 ■ WHIJ-FM - 88.1
6469 Parkland Dr.
Sarasota, FL 34243
Phone: (941)753-0401
Fax: (941)753-2963
Free: 800-456-8910
Format: Contemporary Christian. **Owner:** Radio Training Network, PO Box 7217, Lakeland, FL 33813, Ph: (863)644-3464. **URL:** http://www.thejoyfm.com.

WJUS-AM - See Marion, AL

7980 ■ WMFQ-FM - 92.9
3357 SW Seventh St.
Ocala, FL 34474
Phone: (352)732-0079
Fax: (352)622-6675
Format: Oldies. **Owner:** Asterisk Communications Inc., at above address. **Founded:** 1965. **Operating Hours**: Continuous; 100% local. **ADI**: Gainesville (Ocala), FL. **Key Personnel:** Bill Barr, Dir. of Programs. **Wattage**: 50,000. **Ad Rates:** Advertising accepted; rates available upon request. Combined advertising rates available with WTRS, WYGC. **URL:** http://www.radio92q.com.

7981 ■ WMOP-AM - 900
2320 NE 2nd St., Ste. 5
Ocala, FL 34470
Phone: (352)732-2010
Format: Sports; Talk. **Networks:** ESPN Radio. **Owner:** Florida Sports Talk Inc., at above address, Ocala, FL 34470. **Founded:** 1953. **Operating Hours**: Continuous; 5% network, 95% local. **ADI**: Gainesville (Ocala), FL. **Key Personnel:** Jeff Frances, Contact; Tom Scmitz, Contact. **Wattage**: 2,700 Day; 023 Night. **Ad Rates:** Noncommercial. **URL:** http://www.floridasportstalk.fm.

7982 ■ WNDD-FM - 95.5
3602 NE 20th Pl.
Ocala, FL 34470
Phone: (352)622-9500
Format: Classic Rock. **Operating Hours**: Continuous. **Key Personnel:** Jim Robertson, Gen. Mgr., VP; Cheree Carr, Traffic Mgr., ccarr@windwogksales.com. **Wattage**: 3,000. **Ad Rates:** Advertising accepted; rates available upon request. **URL:** http://www.windfm.com.

7983 ■ WNDT-FM - 92.5
3602 NE 20th Pl.
Ocala, FL 34470
Phone: (352)622-9500
Format: Classic Rock; Soft Rock. **Key Personnel:** Jim Robertson, Gen. Mgr., VP; Bob Kassi, Sales Mgr., rkassi@windwogksales.com; Cheree Carr, Traffic Mgr., ccarr@windwogksales.com. **URL:** http://share.yes.com.

7984 ■ WOCA-AM - 1370
3100 SW College Rd., Ste. 199
Ocala, FL 34474
Phone: (352)351-8000
Fax: (352)240-3858
Email: woca@woca.com
Format: News; Talk. **Networks:** ABC. **Owner:** Westshore Broadcasting Inc., at above address. **Founded:** 1957. **Operating Hours**: 6 a.m.-8 p.m.; 65% network, 35% local. **Local Programs:** *AM Ocala Live!*, Monday Tuesday Wednesday Thursday Friday 7:00 a.m. - 12:00 p.m. **Wattage**: 5,000. **Ad Rates:** $15-17 for 30 seconds; $25-30 for 60 seconds. **Mailing address:** PO Box 1056, Ocala, FL 34478-1056. **URL:** http://www.thesource1370.com.

7985 ■ WOGK-FM - 93.7
3602 NE 20th Pl.
Ocala, FL 34470-4957
Phone: (352)622-5600
Fax: (352)622-7822
Format: Country. **Owner:** Dix Communications, 212 E Liberty St., Wooster, OH 44691, Ph: (330)264-1125. **Founded:** 1985. **Operating Hours**: Continuous. **ADI**: Gainesville (Ocala), FL. **Key Personnel:** Jim Robertson, Gen. Mgr., VP, dbrobertso@aol.com; Bob Kassi, Sales Mgr., rkassi@windwogksales.com; Emily Carey, Bus. Mgr., ecarey@windwogksales.com; Cheree Carr, Traffic Mgr., ccarr@windwogksales.com. **Wattage**: 100,000. **Ad Rates:** $35-80 per unit. **URL:** http://www.937kcountry.com.

7986 ■ WTMC-AM - 1290
3621 NW 10th St.
Ocala, FL 34475
Fax: (352)622-8648
Email: am1290@aol.com
Format: News; Talk. **Networks:** CNN Radio. **Owner:** News, at above address. **Founded:** 1939. **Operating Hours**: Continuous; 90% network/10% local. **ADI**: Gainesville (Ocala), FL. **Key Personnel:** Gin Swab, News Dir.; Ken Jones, Sales Mgr., Contact; Ken Jones, Contact; Larry Whitler, Contact. **Wattage**: 5,000 day; 1,000 night. **Ad Rates:** $9-11.25 for 30 seconds; $11.50-14 for 60 seconds.

7987 ■ WTRS-FM - 102.3
3357 SW 7th St.
Ocala, FL 34474
Phone: (352)867-1023
Fax: (352)622-6675
Free: 888-450-1023
Format: Contemporary Country; Country. **Networks:** Independent. **Founded:** 1969. **Operating Hours**: Continuous. **ADI**: Gainesville (Ocala), FL. **Wattage**: 50,000. **Ad Rates:** $30-45 for 30 seconds; $35-50 for 60 seconds. Combined advertising rates available with WMFQ, WYGC.

7988 ■ WYFZ-FM - 91.3
11530 Carmel Commons Blvd.
Charlotte, NC 28226
Phone: (704)523-5555
Free: 800-888-7077
Format: Religious. **Owner:** Bible Broadcasting Network Inc., 11530 Carmel Commons Blvd., Charlotte, NC 28226, Ph: (704)523-5555, Free: 800-888-7077. **Founded:** Nov. 18, 2005. **Wattage**: 900. **Mailing address:** PO Box 7300, Charlotte, NC 28241. **URL:** http://www.bbnradio.org.

OCOEE

Orange Co. Orange Co. (NC). 20 m NW of Orlando.

7989 ■ WOKB-AM
50 S Clarke Rd.
Ocoee, FL 34761
Phone: (407)523-2770
Fax: (407)523-2888
Format: Gospel; Hispanic. **Networks:** ABC; Spanish Information Service. **Owner:** Rama Communications, Inc., 4938 W Colonial Dr., Orlando, FL 32808. **Founded:** 1980. **Key Personnel:** Pedro Sanchez, Dir. of Programs. **Wattage**: 10,000 Day; 1,000 Ni. **Ad Rates:** $40 for 30 seconds; $10-15 for 30 seconds; $50 for 60 seconds; $19-26 for 60 seconds.

7990 ■ WUNA-AM
749 S Bluford Ave.
Ocoee, FL 34761
Phone: (407)656-9823
Fax: (407)656-2092
Format: Religious. **Networks:** Christian Broadcasting (CBN). **Owner:** N & S Partnership, Inc., at above address. **Founded:** 1952. **Formerly**: WXIV-AM; WVCF-AM. **Key Personnel:** Sylvia Burdick, Contact; David Dillingham, Contact; Theresa Wingard, Contact; Ray Kiser, Contact. **Wattage**: 1,000 Day; 071 Night.

ODESSA

7991 ■ World Wide Shipping
World Wide Shipping Guide Inc.
16302 Byrnwyck Ln.
Odessa, FL 33556-2807
Phone: (813)920-4788
Fax: (813)920-8268
Publisher's E-mail: info@wwship.com
Magazine reporting trends, developments, and government regulations effecting the shipping business. Serves ports, carriers, shippers, forwarders, customs brokers, distributors, agents, stevedores, terminal operators, and logistics providers. **Freq:** 8/year. **Print Method:** Offset. **Trim Size:** 8 3/8 x 10 7/8. **Cols./Page:** 3. **Col. Width:** 26 nonpareils. **Col. Depth:** 140 agate lines. **Key Personnel:** Lee Di Paci, President; Bob DiPaci, Publisher; Steve Rigo, Director, Advertising; Barbara Edwards, Editor. **ISSN:** 1060--7900 (print). **Formerly**: World Ports -- American Seaports; American Seaports; WWS/World Ports. **Ad Rates:** BW $3000; 4C $1100. **Remarks:** Accepts advertising. **Circ:** 24700.

OKEECHOBEE

EC FL. Okeechobee Co. At head of Lake Okeechobee, 60 mi. NW of West Palm Beach. Vegetable canning and packing plants. Commercial fishing. Agriculture. Cattle and dairy farms.

7992 ■ Okeechobee News
Independent Newsmedia Inc.
107 SW 17th St.
Okeechobee, FL 34974
Phone: (863)763-3134
Publication E-mail: okeenews@okeechobee.com
Community newspaper. **Freq:** Triweekly Wednesday, Friday, and Sunday. **Print Method:** Offset Uses mats. **Trim Size:** 10 X 11.125. **Cols./Page:** 6. **Col. Width:** 1.833 inches. **Col. Depth:** 301 agate lines. **USPS:** 406-160. **Subscription Rates:** $72 Individuals print or

Circulation: ★ = AAM; △ or • = BPA; ♦ = CAC; ❑ = VAC; ⊕ = PO Statement; ‡ = Publisher's Report; Boldface figures = sworn; Light figures = estimated.

online; $130 By mail print only. **URL:** http://florida.newszap.com/okeechobeenews. **Ad Rates:** GLR $696; BW $2,307; 4C $2,707; PCI $17.88. **Remarks:** Accepts advertising. **Circ:** Sun. ‡4000.

7993 ■ WOKC-AM - 1570
210 W North Park St.
Okeechobee, FL 34972
Phone: (863)467-1570
Format: Country. **Networks:** NBC. **Owner:** Glades Media Group, 530 E Alverdez Ave., Clewiston, FL 33440, Ph: (863)983-5900. **Founded:** 1962. **Operating Hours:** 6 a.m.-11 p.m. **Key Personnel:** Wayne Cunningham, Gen. Mgr., wayne@gladesmedia.com. **Local Programs:** *The Country Store*, Monday Tuesday Wednesday Thursday Friday 9:30 a.m. - 10:00 a.m.; 3:30 p.m. - 4:00 p.m.; *AM 1570 Morning Show*, Monday Tuesday Wednesday Thursday Friday 7:00 a.m. - 11:00 a.m. **Wattage:** 1,000. **Ad Rates:** $12 per unit. **URL:** http://www.wokc.com.

7994 ■ WOKC-FM - 103.1
210 NW Park St.
Okeechobee, FL 34972
Phone: (863)467-1570
Format: Country. **Networks:** NBC. **Founded:** 1965. **Formerly:** WLMC-FM. **Operating Hours:** 6 a.m.-11 p.m. **Key Personnel:** Al Stokes, Contact; Diane Kinchen, Contact. **Wattage:** 3,000. **Ad Rates:** $10-13 for 60 seconds. **URL:** http://www.wokc.com.

OLDSMAR

WC FL. Pinellas Co. 15 mi. NW of Tampa.

7995 ■ Photoshop User
National Association of Photoshop Professionals
333 Douglas Rd. E
Oldsmar, FL 34677-2922
Phone: (813)433-5005
Fax: (813)433-5015
Free: 800-738-8513
Freq: 10/year. **Subscription Rates:** Included in membership. **Alt. Formats:** Download. **URL:** http://kelbyone.com/magazine. **Remarks:** Advertising not accepted. **Circ:** (Not Reported).

7996 ■ WPSO-AM - 1500
109 Bayview Blvd., Ste. A
Oldsmar, FL 34677
Phone: (813)814-7575
Email: wpso@wpso.com
Format: Ethnic; Religious. **Owner:** ASA Broadcasting Inc., at above address. **Founded:** 1963. **Operating Hours:** Sunrise-sunset. **Key Personnel:** Sotirios Agelatos, Contact. **Wattage:** 250. **Ad Rates:** for 30 seconds; for 60 seconds. **URL:** http://www.wpso.com.

7997 ■ WZRA-TV - 48
109 Bayview Blvd. S, Ste. A
Oldsmar, FL 34677
Phone: (727)725-5555
Fax: (813)855-4100
Email: info@wzra48.com
Key Personnel: Sotirios Angelatos, Gen. Mgr.; Angelo Angelatos, Operations Mgr., angelos@wpso.com. **URL:** http://wpso.com.

ORANGE CITY

EC FL. Volusia Co. 12 mi. N. of Sanford.

7998 ■ St. John's Pennysaver
Volusia Pennysaver Inc.
1109 Saxon Blvd.
Orange City, FL 32763
Phone: (386)774-2817
Publisher's E-mail: wvpsoa@psavers.com
Shopper. **Freq:** Weekly (Thurs.). **Key Personnel:** Jon Riddell, Manager, Circulation. **Subscription Rates:** Free. **Ad Rates:** BW $705.90; 4C $885.90; PCI $7. **Remarks:** Accepts advertising. **Circ:** Thurs. 12000.

ORANGE PARK

7999 ■ Better Software
Software Quality Engineering
340 Corporate Way, Ste. 300
Orange Park, FL 32073-6214
Phone: (904)278-0524
Fax: (904)278-4380
Free: 888-268-8770
Publication E-mail: info@bettersoftware.com
Magazine focusing on the needs of improving quality throughout the software development lifecycle. **Freq:** Quarterly. **Key Personnel:** Holly Bourquin, Director. **URL:** http://www.techwell.com/better-software-magazine. **Circ:** (Not Reported).

8000 ■ PileDriver
Pile Driving Contractors Association
33 Knight Boxx Rd., Ste. 1
Orange Park, FL 32065
Phone: (904)215-4771
Fax: (904)215-2977
Free: 888-311-7322
Publisher's E-mail: info@piledrivers.org
Magazine containing articles, features, news and events of the trends, equipment rentals and sales, project spotlights, member profiles and milestones related to the piling industry. **Freq:** Quarterly. **URL:** http://www.piledrivers.org/publications. **Mailing address:** PO Box 66208, Orange Park, FL 32065. **Remarks:** Accepts advertising. **Circ:** (Not Reported).

8001 ■ The Veteran Voice
The Veteran Voice Inc.
71 Hialeah Dr.
Orange Park, FL 32073
Phone: (904)276-7927
Fax: (904)298-3706
Newspaper serving veterans, active duty and retired military. **Freq:** Monthly. **Trim Size:** 10 x 13. **Key Personnel:** Regina McKenzie, Publisher. **Subscription Rates:** $19.26 Individuals; $28.76 Two years. **URL:** http://www.veteranvoice.com. **Ad Rates:** BW $555. **Remarks:** Accepts advertising. **Circ:** (Not Reported).

8002 ■ W300AS-FM - 107.9
PO Box 391
Twin Falls, ID 83303
Fax: (208)736-1958
Free: 800-357-4226
Format: Religious; Contemporary Christian. **Owner:** CSN International, PO Box 391, Twin Falls, ID 83303, Ph: (208)736-1958, Fax: (208)736-1958, Free: 800-357-4226. **URL:** http://www.csnradio.com.

ORLANDO

EC FL. Orange Co. 100 mi. NE of Tampa. University of Central Florida; Orlando Naval Training Center. Walt Disney World. Manufactures electronics, weapons systems, missiles. Citrus fruit and truck farms.

8003 ■ American Journal of Mediation
American College of Civil Trial Mediators
20 N Orange Ave., Ste. 704
Orlando, FL 32801
Phone: (407)843-8878
Fax: (407)843-1996
Publisher's E-mail: acctm@acctm.org
Journal of the American College of Civil Trial Mediators. **URL:** http://www.americanjournalofmediation.com. **Circ:** (Not Reported).

8004 ■ Art Calendar: The Business Magazine for Visual Artists
Art Calendar
1500 Park Center Dr.
Orlando, FL 32835
Publication E-mail: info@artcalendar.com
Business magazine for visual artists. **Freq:** Monthly. **Print Method:** Offset. **Trim Size:** 8 3/8 x 10 7/8. **Cols./Page:** 3. **Col. Width:** 2.25 inches. **Col. Depth:** 9.8 inches. **Key Personnel:** Kim Hall, Editor, phone: (407)563-7057, fax: (407)563-7099; David Trask, Publisher, Specialist, Advertising and Sales, phone: (407)515-2603. **ISSN:** 0893--3901 (print). **Subscription Rates:** $37 Individuals; $59 Two years; $85 Other countries; $155 Other countries 2 years; $65 Canada; $115 Canada 2 years. **Ad Rates:** BW $1,200; 4C $1,900. **Remarks:** Accepts advertising. **Circ:** Paid 12000.

8005 ■ The Augustan Omnibus
Augustan Society
PO Box 771267
Orlando, FL 32877-1267
Phone: (407)745-0848
Fax: (321)206-6313
Publisher's E-mail: hq@augustansociety.org
Freq: Semiannual. **ISSN:** 0004-7988 (print). **Subscription Rates:** $18 Members. **URL:** http://www.augustansociety.org/cpage.php?pt=63. **Remarks:** Accepts advertising. **Circ:** 200.

8006 ■ Baby Couture
Medina Favis Publishing L.L.C.
PO Box 772246
Orlando, FL 32837
Lifestyle magazine featuring children's fashion and beauty that provides fresh outlook on parenting. **Trim Size:** 9 x 10 7/8. **Key Personnel:** Kariz Medina-Favis, Editor-in-Chief, Founder. **Subscription Rates:** $15 Individuals; $27 Two years. **URL:** http://bc-mag.com. **Ad Rates:** BW $7,350; 4C $10,500. **Remarks:** Accepts advertising. **Circ:** 100000.

8007 ■ Chestnut Tree
Pierre Chastain Family Association
c/o David Long, Vice President
2796 Vine St.
Orlando, FL 32806
Phone: (407)894-8454
Freq: Quarterly January, April, July and October. **Subscription Rates:** included in membership dues; $6 back issue. **URL:** http://www.pierrechastain.com/content/pubs.html. **Remarks:** Advertising not accepted. **Circ:** 400.

8008 ■ Child and Family Law Journal
Barry University Dwayne O. Andreas School of Law
6441 E Colonial Dr.
Orlando, FL 32807
Phone: (321)206-5600
Fax: (321)206-5620
Free: 800-756-6000
Publication E-mail: CFLJ@barry.edu
Journal incorporating scholarly articles discussing all topics related to child and family law,. **URL:** http://www.barry.edu/law/future-students/academic-program/child-family-law.html. **Circ:** (Not Reported).

8009 ■ Child Neuropsychology
Psychology Press
c/o Michael Westerveld, PhD, Ed.
Florida Physicians Medical Group
Adanson Ave.
Orlando, FL 32804
Journal focusing on neuropsychological evaluation of children and adolescents in terms of information processing mechanisms, the impact of injury or disease on neuropsychological functioning, behavioral cognitive and pharmacological approaches to treatment/intervention, psychosocial correlates of neuropsychological dysfunction, definitive normative, reliability, and validity studies of psychometric and other procedures applied. **Freq:** 8/year. **Key Personnel:** Jacobus Donders, PhD, Associate Editor; Michael Westerveld, PhD, Editor. **ISSN:** 0929--7049 (print); **EISSN:** 1744--4136 (electronic). **Subscription Rates:** $502 Individuals print; $1339 Institutions online; $1530 Institutions print and online. **URL:** http://www.tandfonline.com/toc/ncny20/current. **Remarks:** Advertising accepted; rates available upon request. **Circ:** (Not Reported).

8010 ■ Design, The Journal of the Society for News Design
Society for News Design
424 E Central Blvd., Ste. 406
Orlando, FL 32801
Phone: (407)420-7748
Fax: (407)420-7697
Freq: Quarterly. **ISSN:** 1520--4243 (print). **URL:** http://www.snd.org/2016/03/design-journal-a-look-inside. **Remarks:** Accepts advertising. **Circ:** (Not Reported).

8011 ■ Faulkner Journal
University of Central Florida - Department of English
12790 Aquarius Agora Dr.
Orlando, FL 32816
Phone: (407)823-5596
Fax: (407)823-3300
Publication E-mail: faulknerjournal@gmail.com
Peer-reviewed journal publishing life and works of William Faulkner. **Founded:** 1985. **Freq:** Semiannual. **Trim Size:** 6 x 9. **Key Personnel:** Michael Zeitlin, Advisor, Board Member; Martin Kreiswirth, Editor; Susan V. Donaldson, Associate Editor; John T. Matthews, Associate Editor; Dawn Trouard, Executive Editor. **ISSN:** 0884-2949 (print). **Subscription Rates:** $20 U.S., Canada,

and Mexico; $30 Libraries continental U.S., Canada, and Mexico; $28 Other countries individuals; $38 Institutions, other countries. **URL:** http://www.english.ucf.edu/faulkner. **Mailing address:** PO Box 161346, Orlando, FL 32816-1346. **Remarks:** Advertising not accepted. **Circ:** (Not Reported).

8012 ■ Financial Ops
International Accounts Payable Professionals
615 E Colonial Dr.
Orlando, FL 32803
Phone: (407)351-3322
Fax: (407)895-5031
Free: 877-885-IAPP
Publisher's E-mail: jo.laborde@financialops.org
Freq: Quarterly. **Subscription Rates:** Included in membership. **Formerly:** AP Matters. **Remarks:** Advertising not accepted. **Circ:** (Not Reported).

8013 ■ The Florida Catholic
The Florida Catholic Newspaper
50 E Robinson St.
Orlando, FL 32801
Phone: (407)373-0075
Free: 888-275-9953
Official newspaper (tabloid) of the Diocese of Orlando. **Freq:** Semimonthly. **Print Method:** Offset. **Cols./Page:** 5. **Col. Width:** 11.3 picas. **Col. Depth:** 12.5 inches. **Key Personnel:** Denise O'Toole, Managing Editor; Christopher Gunty, Associate Publisher; Tammy Osborne, Manager, Circulation. **Subscription Rates:** $20 Individuals e-edition; $26 Individuals print ; $35 Individuals print and e-edition; $32 Two years out of state; $49 Two years in-state. **Ad Rates:** BW $250. **Remarks:** Accepts advertising. **Circ:** Combined ⊕**320000**.

8014 ■ Florida Realtor
Florida Realtors
7025 Augusta National Dr.
Orlando, FL 32822-5017
Phone: (407)438-1400
Fax: (407)438-1411
Publisher's E-mail: support@floridarealtors.org
Real estate magazine. **Freq:** 10/year. **Print Method:** Web offset. **Trim Size:** 8 x 10 3/4. **Cols./Page:** 3. **Col. Width:** 14 picas. **Col. Depth:** 140 agate lines. **ISSN:** 0199--5839 (print). **Subscription Rates:** $24.95 Individuals; $42.95 Other countries. **URL:** http://floridarealtors.org/FLRealtorMagazine/index.cfm. **Ad Rates:** BW $3,740; 4C $4,680. **Remarks:** Accepts advertising. **Circ:** Combined ★**105908**.

8015 ■ Florida Review
University of Central Florida - Department of English
12790 Aquarius Agora Dr.
Orlando, FL 32816
Phone: (407)823-5596
Fax: (407)823-3300
Publication E-mail: flreview@mail.ucf.edu
Literary magazine covering fiction, nonfiction and poetry. **Freq:** Semiannual. **Print Method:** Offset. **Trim Size:** 6 x 9. **Key Personnel:** Jocelyn Bartkevicius, Editor-in-Chief; Russ Kesler, Editor; Nathan Holic, Editor; Kirsten Holt, Managing Editor. **ISSN:** 0742--2466 (print). **Subscription Rates:** $15 Individuals 1 year; $25 Two years; $8 Single issue; $20 Libraries institutions - 1 year; $30 Libraries institutions - 2 years. **URL:** http://floridareview.cah.ucf.edu. **Mailing address:** PO Box 161346, Orlando, FL 32816-1346. **Remarks:** Accepts advertising. **Circ:** (Not Reported).

8016 ■ Florida Sun Review
Florida Sun Review
2700 Catalina Dr.
Orlando, FL 32805-5808
Phone: (407)423-1156
Fax: (407)849-1286
Publisher's E-mail: sunreview@aol.com
African American-oriented publication. **Freq:** Weekly (Thurs.). **Print Method:** Offset. **Trim Size:** 10 x 16. **Cols./Page:** 6. **Col. Width:** 1 5/8 inches. **Key Personnel:** James A. Madison, Publisher; Jessie Hewett, Manager, Circulation; S. Timothy Johnson, Director, Advertising. **Subscription Rates:** $39 Individuals delivery, online; $69 Two years delivery, online. **URL:** http://www.floridasunreview.com. **Remarks:** Advertising accepted; rates available upon request. **Circ:** (Not Reported).

8017 ■ Golfweek: Golf's News Leader
Golfweek
1500 Park Ctr. Dr.
Orlando, FL 32835
Phone: (407)563-7000
Fax: (407)563-7077
Journal of record for competitive golf. Delivers the most complete news and information about the game, the people and the industry, to golf's most important audience. **Freq:** Weekly. **Print Method:** Offset. **Trim Size:** 10 x 11 7/8. **Cols./Page:** 4. **Col. Width:** 56 inches. **Col. Depth:** 13 1/2 inches. **Key Personnel:** Craig Horan, Managing Editor; Jeff Babineau, Editor, Vice President. **ISSN:** 0745--7464 (print). **Subscription Rates:** $44.95 Individuals print and online; $34.95 Individuals print or online; $10 Individuals online. **URL:** http://golfweek.com. **Ad Rates:** BW $16,412; 4C $27,426. **Remarks:** Accepts advertising. **Circ:** 155000.

8018 ■ IEEE Aerospace and Electronic Systems Magazine
IEEE - Communications Society
c/o Teresa Pace Editor-in-Chief
12601 Research Pkwy.
Orlando, FL 32826
Phone: (407)207-1900
Technical magazine providing information to electronic and aerospace electronic systems engineers. **Freq:** Monthly. **Print Method:** Offset. **Trim Size:** 8 1/2 x 11. **Cols./Page:** 2. **Col. Width:** 24 picas. **Col. Depth:** 58 picas. **Key Personnel:** David Dobson; Teresa Pace, PhD EE, Editor-in-Chief. **ISSN:** 0885--8985 (print). **URL:** http://ieeexplore.ieee.org/xpl/RecentIssue.jsp?punumber=62. **Remarks:** Advertising not accepted. **Circ:** Paid ‡11500, Non-paid ‡500.

8019 ■ International Journal of Accounting Information Systems
Elsevier
c/o Steve G. Sutton, Editor
Dixon School of Accounting
4000 Central Florida Blvd.
Orlando, FL 32816
Publisher's E-mail: t.reller@elsevier.com
Journal examining the rapidly evolving relationship between accounting and information technology. **Freq:** Quarterly. **Print Method:** Offset. **Trim Size:** 5 x 12 1/2. **Cols./Page:** 5. **Col. Width:** 11.5 picas. **Col. Depth:** 12 1/2 inches. **Key Personnel:** E. Boritz, Board Member; J. Dillard, Board Member; A.I. Nicolaou, Board Member. **ISSN:** 1467--0895 (print). **Subscription Rates:** $146 Individuals print; $257.60 Institutions online; $774 Institutions print. **URL:** http://www.journals.elsevier.com/international-journal-of-accounting-information-systems. **Remarks:** Advertising not accepted. **Circ:** (Not Reported).

8020 ■ Numerical Functional Analysis and Optimization: An International Journal
Taylor & Francis Group Journals
c/o M.Z. Nashed, Ed.-in-Ch.
Dept. of Mathematics
University of Central Florida
Orlando, FL 32816-1364
Publisher's E-mail: customerservice@taylorandfrancis.com
Journal examining the development & applications of functional analysis & operator theoretic methods in numerical analysis, approximation theory, optimization, control & systems theory. **Freq:** 12/yr. **Print Method:** Offset. **Trim Size:** 8 1/4 x 10 7/8. **Cols./Page:** 1. **Col. Width:** 72 nonpareils. **Col. Depth:** 126 agate lines. **Key Personnel:** M. Brokate, Board Member; W. Freeden, Board Member; P.L. Butzer, Board Member; X. Chen, Board Member; R.P. Gilbert, Board Member; C. De Mol, Board Member; F. Altomare, Board Member; M. Bardi, Board Member; V. Barbu, Board Member; M.Z. Nashed, Editor-in-Chief. **ISSN:** 0163-0563 (print). **Subscription Rates:** $1038 Individuals print only; $3564 Institutions online only; $4073 Institutions print & online. **URL:** http://www.tandfonline.com/toc/lnfa20/current#.VdGbQ--BkpR. **Mailing address:** PO Box 161364, MAP 209, Orlando, FL 32816-1364. **Ad Rates:** BW $890; 4C $1,935. **Remarks:** Accepts advertising. **Circ:** 400.

8021 ■ Optometry and Vision Science
American Academy of Optometry
2909 Fairgreen St.
Orlando, FL 32803
Phone: (321)710-3937
Fax: (407)893-9890
Free: 800-969-4226
Publisher's E-mail: aaoptom@aaoptom.org
Optometry journal. **Freq:** Monthly Bimonthly. **Print Method:** Offset. **Trim Size:** 8 1/8 x 10 7/8. **Cols./Page:** 1. **Col. Width:** 58 nonpareils. **Col. Depth:** 110 agate lines. **Key Personnel:** Michael D. Twa, Editor-in-Chief; Anthony J. Adams, Editor. **ISSN:** 1040--5488 (print); **EISSN:** 1538--9235 (electronic). **Subscription Rates:** $550 Individuals online only; $894 Institutions online only; $1046 Institutions, Canada and Mexico online only; $1062 Institutions, other countries online only; Included in membership. **URL:** http://journals.lww.com/optvissci/Pages/default.aspx; http://www.aaopt.org/section/OVS. **Ad Rates:** BW $490; 4C $1140. **Remarks:** Accepts advertising. **Circ:** Paid ‡4800, Non-paid ‡50.

8022 ■ The Orlando Sentinel
Orlando Sentinel Media Group
633 N Orange Ave.
Orlando, FL 32801
Phone: (407)420-5000
Publisher's E-mail: feedback@orlandosentinel.com
General newspaper. **Founded:** June 06, 1876. **Freq:** Mon.-Sun. (morn.). **Print Method:** Offset. **Cols./Page:** 6. **Col. Width:** 1.83 inches. **Col. Depth:** 294 agate lines. **Key Personnel:** Charlotte H. Hall, Editor, Vice President, phone: (407)420-5195; Manning Pynn, Editor, phone: (407)650-6410; Jane Healy, Editor, phone: (407)420-5406. **Subscription Rates:** $29.98 Individuals home delivery; 13 weeks. **URL:** http://www.orlandosentinel.com. **Ad Rates:** GLR $22.90; BW $37,485; 4C $40,698; PCI $297.50. **Remarks:** Accepts advertising. **Circ:** Paid ★**325078**.

8023 ■ The Orlando Times
The Orlando Times
4403 Vineland Rd., Ste. B-5
Orlando, FL 32811
Phone: (407)841-3052
Fax: (407)849-0434
Publisher's E-mail: news@orlando-times.com
Black community newspaper. **Freq:** Weekly (Thurs.). **Key Personnel:** Dr. Calvin Collins, Jr., Publisher. **Subscription Rates:** $46 Individuals /year; $51 Out of state /year; $24 Individuals six months. **Mailing address:** PO Box 555339, Orlando, FL 32855-5339. **Ad Rates:** BW $14; 4C $484; SAU $6; PCI $14. **Remarks:** Advertising accepted; rates available upon request. **Circ:** 11000.

8024 ■ Pegasus
University of Central Florida Alumni Association
12676 Gemini Blvd. N
Orlando, FL 32816-0046
Phone: (407)823-2586
Fax: (407)823-0172
Free: 800-330-2586
Publisher's E-mail: knights@ucfalumni.com
Magazine featuring publications by the University of Central Florida Alumni Association. **Freq:** Bimonthly. **URL:** http://www.ucfalumni.com/pegasus. **Mailing address:** PO Box 160046, Orlando, FL 32816-0046. **Ad Rates:** 4C $3,900. **Remarks:** Accepts advertising. **Circ:** (Not Reported).

8025 ■ Theoretical Issues in Ergonomics Science
Taylor and Francis Group PLC
c/o Waldemar Karwowski, Ed.
Industrial Engineering & Management Systems
University of Central Florida
Orlando, FL 32816-2993
Publisher's E-mail: enquiries@taylorandfrancis.com
Journal covering science and philosophy of human factors and ergonomics. **Freq:** Bimonthly. **Key Personnel:** Waldemar Karwowski, Editor-in-Chief; Tadeusz Marek, Board Member; William S. Marras, Board Member; Gavriel Salvendy, Board Member; Sebastiano Bagnara, Associate Editor. **ISSN:** 1463--922X (print); **EISSN:** 1464--536X (electronic). **Subscription Rates:** $1078 Institutions online only; $548 Individuals online. **URL:** http://www.tandfonline.com/toc/ttie20/current. **Circ:** (Not Reported).

8026 ■ Worldwide Challenge
Campus Crusade for Christ International
100 Lake Hart Dr.
Orlando, FL 32832

Circulation: ★ = AAM; △ or • = BPA; ♦ = CAC; ❑ = VAC; ⊕ = PO Statement; ‡ = Publisher's Report; Boldface figures = sworn; Light figures = estimated.

Free: 888-278-7233
Religious magazine. **Freq:** Bimonthly. **Print Method:** Offset. **Trim Size:** 8 1/2 x 10 3/4. **Cols./Page:** 3. **Col. Width:** 27 nonpareils. **Col. Depth:** 133 agate lines. **ISSN:** 0746--9241 (print). **URL:** http://www.cru.org/about/worldwide-challenge-magazine.html. **Ad Rates:** 4C $2,772. **Remarks:** Accepts advertising. **Circ:** 85000.

8027 ■ WACX-TV - 55
PO Box 608040
Orlando, FL 32860
Phone: (407)263-4040
Free: 800-578-9494
Format: Commercial TV. **Founded:** 1982. **Formerly:** WIYE-TV. **Operating Hours:** Continuous; 50% network, 25% local. **ADI:** Orlando-Daytona Beach-Melbourne, FL. **Wattage:** 5,000,000. **Ad Rates:** $25-75 for 30 seconds. **URL:** http://wacxtv.com.

8028 ■ WAMT-AM - 1190
1160 S Semoran Blvd., Ste. A
Orlando, FL 32807
Phone: (407)380-9255
Fax: (407)382-7565
Free: 888-300-3776
Format: Talk. **Networks:** CNN Radio. **Operating Hours:** Continuous. **Key Personnel:** Sabrina Lavender, Contact, sabrinalavender@radiogenesis.com. **Wattage:** 10,000. **Ad Rates:** Advertising accepted; rates available upon request.

8029 ■ WBZS-AM - 1270
PO Box 547857
Orlando, FL 32854-7857
Phone: (407)297-1115
Fax: (407)299-2808
Format: News; Information. **Networks:** CBS; Business Radio. **Owner:** S.E. Broadcasting, at above address. **Founded:** 1957. **Formerly:** WORL-AM. **Operating Hours:** Continuous; 50% network, 50% local. **ADI:** Orlando-Daytona Beach-Melbourne, FL. **Key Personnel:** Tony Betros, Dir. of Programs; Dave Elliott, Gen. Sales Mgr. **Wattage:** 5,000.

8030 ■ WCFB-FM - 94.5
4192 John Young Pkwy.
Orlando, FL 32804
Phone: (321)281-2000
Format: Adult Contemporary. **Networks:** Independent. **Owner:** Cox Radio Inc., 6205 Peachtree Dunwood Rd., Atlanta, GA 30328-4524, Ph: (678)645-0000, Fax: (678)645-5002. **Founded:** 1952. **Formerly:** WWLV-FM. **Operating Hours:** Continuous; 100% local. **ADI:** Orlando-Daytona Beach-Melbourne, FL. **Key Personnel:** Amelia Moore, Mktg. Mgr., Promotions Mgr., amelia.moore@coxradio.com. **Wattage:** 100,000. **Ad Rates:** $100 per unit. **URL:** http://www.star945.com.

8031 ■ WDBO-AM - 580
4192 N John Young Pky.
Orlando, FL 32804
Phone: (321)281-2000
Fax: (407)297-0156
Email: news@news965.com
Format: Talk; News. **Networks:** ABC. **Owner:** Cox Radio Inc., 6205 Peachtree Dunwood Rd., Atlanta, GA 30328-4524, Ph: (678)645-0000, Fax: (678)645-5002. **Founded:** 1924. **Operating Hours:** Continuous. **ADI:** Orlando-Daytona Beach-Melbourne, FL. **Key Personnel:** Jimmy Farrell, Gen. Sales Mgr., Mktg. Mgr., jimmy.farrell@coxradio.com; Steve Holbrook, Contact, steve.holbrook@coxradio.com. **Wattage:** 50,000. **URL:** http://www.news965.com.

8032 ■ WFTV-TV - 9
490 E S St.
Orlando, FL 32801
Phone: (407)841-9000
Networks: ABC. **Owner:** Cox Enterprises Inc., 6205 Peachtree Dunwoody Rd., Atlanta, GA 30328, Ph: (678)645-0000, Fax: (678)645-1079. **Founded:** 1958. **Operating Hours:** Continuous; 41% network, 59% local. **ADI:** Orlando-Daytona Beach-Melbourne, FL. **Local Programs:** *Eyewitness News.* **Ad Rates:** $75-4000 per unit. **URL:** http://www.wftv.com.

8033 ■ WHOO-AM - 990
1160 S Semoran Blvd., Ste. A
Orlando, FL 32807
Phone: (407)380-9255
Fax: (407)382-7565
Format: Big Band/Nostalgia. **Networks:** ABC; Satellite Music Network. **Founded:** 1952. **Operating Hours:** Continuous. **ADI:** Orlando-Daytona Beach-Melbourne, FL. **Key Personnel:** Kelly McGrath, Exec. VP, kelleymcgrath@radiogenesis.com; Brad James, VP. **Wattage:** 50,000. **Ad Rates:** Noncommercial.

8034 ■ WHTQ-FM - 96.5
4192 John Young Pky.
Orlando, FL 32804
Phone: (321)281-2000
Fax: (407)422-0917
Format: Classic Rock. **Networks:** NBC. **Owner:** Cox Radio Inc., 6205 Peachtree Dunwood Rd., Atlanta, GA 30328-4524, Ph: (678)645-0000, Fax: (678)645-5002. **Founded:** 1952. **Operating Hours:** Continuous. **Key Personnel:** Scott Buckley, Promotions Dir., scott.buckley@coxradio.com; Fleetwood Gruver, Dir. of Programs, fleetwood.gruver@coxradio.com; Debbie Morel, Gen. Mgr., debbie.morel@coxradio.com. **Wattage:** 100,000. **Ad Rates:** Noncommercial.

WITX-FM - See Beaver Falls, PA

8035 ■ WJHM-FM - 101.9
1800 Pembrook Dr., Ste. 400
Orlando, FL 32810
Phone: (407)919-0102
Free: 877-919-0102
Format: Urban Contemporary; Hip Hop. **Owner:** CBS Radio Inc., 40 W 57th St., New York, NY 10019, Ph: (212)846-3939, Fax: (212)315-2162. **Founded:** 1988. **Formerly:** WCFI-FM. **Operating Hours:** Continuous; 3% network, 100% local. **ADI:** Orlando-Daytona Beach-Melbourne, FL. **Key Personnel:** Paul Diaz, Dir. of HR. **Wattage:** 61,000. **Ad Rates:** Noncommercial. **URL:** http://www.1019ampradio.cbslocal.com.

8036 ■ WKMG-TV - 6
4466 John Young Pky.
Orlando, FL 32804
Phone: (407)521-1200
Format: News; Sports. **Networks:** CBS. **Owner:** Post Newsweek Stations, 550 W Lafayette Blvd., Detroit, MI 48226-3140, Ph: (313)222-0444. **Founded:** 1954. **Formerly:** WDBO-TV; WCPX-TV. **Operating Hours:** Continuous. **ADI:** Orlando-Daytona Beach-Melbourne, FL. **Wattage:** 944,000. **Ad Rates:** Accepts Advertising. **URL:** http://www.local6.com.

8037 ■ WMFE-FM - 90.7
11510 E Colonial Dr.
Orlando, FL 32817
Phone: (407)273-2300
Email: wmfe@wmfe.org
Format: Classical; News. **Founded:** Sept. 14, 2006. **Ad Rates:** Noncommercial. **URL:** http://www.wmfe.org.

8038 ■ WMFE-TV - 24
11510 E Colonial Dr.
Orlando, FL 32817
Phone: (407)273-2300
Format: Public TV. **Networks:** CBS; ABC. **Owner:** Community Communications Inc., One Canal St., Lawrence, MA 01840, Free: 888-869-4595. **Founded:** Mar. 1965. **Operating Hours:** 7:15 a.m.-midnight. **Ad Rates:** Noncommercial. **URL:** http://www.wmfe.org.

8039 ■ WMMO-FM - 98.9
4192 John Young Pky.
Orlando, FL 32804
Phone: (321)281-2000
Fax: (407)536-2556
Format: Adult Contemporary. **Owner:** Cox Radio Inc., 6205 Peachtree Dunwood Rd., Atlanta, GA 30328-4524, Ph: (678)645-0000, Fax: (678)645-5002. **Founded:** 1990. **Operating Hours:** Continuous. **Key Personnel:** Fleetwood Gruver, Dir. of Programs, fleetwood.gruver@coxradio.com; Chris Ganoudis, Gen. Sales Mgr., chris.ganoudis@coxradio.com. **Wattage:** 44,000. **Ad Rates:** Advertising accepted; rates available upon request. **URL:** http://www.wmmo.com.

8040 ■ WOCL-FM - 105.9
1800 Pembrook Dr., Ste. 400
Orlando, FL 32810
Phone: (407)919-1059
Free: 877-919-1059
Format: Alternative/New Music/Progressive. **Networks:** Independent. **Owner:** CBS Radio Inc., 1271 Avenue of the Americas, 44th Fl., New York, NY 10020-1401, Ph: (212)649-9600. **Founded:** 1986. **Operating Hours:** Continuous; 100% local. **ADI:** Orlando-Daytona Beach-Melbourne, FL. **Key Personnel:** Lydia Frost, Sales Mgr., lydia.frost@cbsradio.com; Angela Schlesman, Div. Dir., angela.schlesman@cbsradio.com; Rick Stacy, Prog. Dir., rick@sunny1059.com. **Wattage:** 100,000. **Ad Rates:** Advertising accepted; rates available upon request. **URL:** http://www.1059sunnyfm.cbslocal.com/about.

8041 ■ WOMX-FM - 105.1
1800 Pembrook Dr., Ste. 400
Orlando, FL 32810
Phone: (407)919-1051
Free: 877-919-1051
Format: Adult Contemporary. **Owner:** CBS Radio Inc., 1271 Avenue of the Americas, 44th Fl., New York, NY 10020-1401, Ph: (212)649-9600. **Founded:** 1967. **Operating Hours:** Continuous. **ADI:** Orlando-Daytona Beach-Melbourne, FL. **Key Personnel:** Angela Schlesman, Promotions Dir., angela@mix1051.com. **Wattage:** 100,000. **Ad Rates:** Noncommercial. **URL:** http://www.mix1051.cbslocal.com.

8042 ■ WOPX-TV - 56
7091 Grand National Dr., Ste. 100
Orlando, FL 32819
Format: Public TV; Information. **Networks:** Independent. **Owner:** ION Media Networks, at above address. **Founded:** 1985. **Formerly:** WAKY-TV; WIRB-TV. **Operating Hours:** Continuous. **ADI:** Orlando-Daytona Beach-Melbourne, FL. **Key Personnel:** Brandon Burgess, Chairman, CEO. **Wattage:** 1,000,000 ERP Horizo. **Ad Rates:** Accepts Advertising. **URL:** http://www.ionmedianetworks.com.

8043 ■ WPRD-AM - 1440
222 Hazard St.
Orlando, FL 32804-3030
Phone: (407)841-8282
Fax: (407)841-8250
Email: wprd1440@hotmail.com
Format: News. **Networks:** CNN Radio. **Owner:** JandV Communications Inc. **Founded:** 1954. **Operating Hours:** Continuous. **Wattage:** 5,000 Day; 1,000 Night. **Ad Rates:** Noncommercial. **URL:** http://www.wprd.com.

8044 ■ WPYO-FM - 95.3
4192 John Young Pkwy.
Orlando, FL 32804
Phone: (321)281-2000
Fax: (407)290-1302
Format: Contemporary Hit Radio (CHR). **Owner:** Cox Radio Inc., 6205 Peachtree Dunwood Rd., Atlanta, GA 30328-4524, Ph: (678)645-0000, Fax: (678)645-5002. **Ad Rates:** Advertising accepted; rates available upon request. **URL:** http://www.power953.com.

8045 ■ WRDQ-TV - 27
490 E South St.
Orlando, FL 32801
Phone: (407)841-9000
Key Personnel: Mario Mendoza, Contact, mario.mendoza@wrdq.com. **URL:** http://www.wftv.com.

8046 ■ WRLZ-AM
6101 Hoffner Ave.
Orlando, FL 32822
Phone: (407)345-0700
Email: info@radioluz1270.com
Format: Hispanic. **Key Personnel:** Dr. Nino Gonzalez, President. **Wattage:** 25,000 Day; 5,000 Ni. **Ad Rates:** Noncommercial.

8047 ■ WSDO-AM - 1400
222 Hazard St.
Orlando, FL 32804-3030
Phone: (407)841-8282
Fax: (407)841-8250
Owner: JandV Communications Inc. **Founded:** 1947. **Formerly:** WTRR-AM; WNSI-AM. **Wattage:** 1,000. **Ad Rates:** $12-26 for 30 seconds.

8048 ■ WUCF-FM - 89.9
Communication Bldg. 75, Ste. 130
12405 Aquarius Agora Dr.
Orlando, FL 32816-8040
Phone: (407)823-0899
Format: Jazz. **Networks:** Public Radio International (PRI); National Public Radio (NPR). **Owner:** University of Central Florida, 4000 Central Florida Blvd, Orlando, FL 32816, Ph: (407)823-2000. **Founded:** 1977. **Operating Hours:** Continuous. **Key Personnel:** Kayonne Riley,

Gen. Mgr., kriley@mail.ucf.edu; Bruce Doerle, Dir. of Engg., bdoerle@mail.ucf.edu; Patricia Stucky, Office Mgr., pstucky@mail.ucf.edu. **Local Programs**: *Drivetime Jazz*, Monday Tuesday Wednesday Thursday Friday 6:00 a.m. - 10:00 a.m.; *Jazzworks*, Monday Tuesday Wednesday Thursday Friday Saturday Sunday, 12:00 a.m. - 6:00 a.m. and 8:00 p.m. - 12:00 a.m. 12:00 a.m. - 7:00 a.m. and 3:00 p.m. - 7:00 p.m. 12:00 am. - 7:00 a.m. and 11:00 p.m. - 12:00 a.m. **Wattage**: 360 horizontal ERP; 5,600 Vertical ERP. **Ad Rates:** Noncommercial. **Mailing address:** PO Box 162199, Orlando, FL 32816-2199. **URL:** http://www.wucf.org.

8049 ■ WWKA-FM - 92
4192 John Young Pky.
Orlando, FL 32804
Phone: (407)298-9292
Fax: (407)299-4947
Format: Country. **Networks:** Independent. **Owner:** Cox Radio Inc., 6205 Peachtree Dunwood Rd., Atlanta, GA 30328-4524, Ph: (678)645-0000, Fax: (678)645-5002. **Founded:** Jan. 1983. **Operating Hours**: Continuous; 100% local. **ADI:** Orlando-Daytona Beach-Melbourne, FL. **Key Personnel:** Len Shackelford, Dir. of Programs, len.shackelford@coxmediagroup.com. **Wattage:** 100,000. **Ad Rates:** Advertising accepted; rates available upon request. **URL:** http://www.k923orlando.com.

8050 ■ WWNZ-AM - 740
3500 W Colonial Dr., Ste. 400
Orlando, FL 32808-7960
Phone: (407)299-7400
Fax: (407)290-2879
Format: Talk. **Networks:** CBS. **Founded:** 1947. **Formerly**: WKIS-AM. **Operating Hours**: Continuous. **Key Personnel:** Matt Mills, Gen. Mgr.; Allen Wilkerson, Dir. of Programs; Karen Kgos, Gen. Sales Mgr. **Wattage:** 50,000.

ORMOND BEACH

E FL. Volusia Co. 7 mi. N. of Daytona Beach. Tourist resort.

8051 ■ Daytona Pennysaver
Volusia Pennysaver Inc.
454 S Yonge St.
Ormond Beach, FL 32174
Phone: (386)677-4262
Publication E-mail: daytona.pennysaver@psavers.com
Community shopper. **Freq:** Weekly (Wed.). **Print Method:** Tabloid. Offset. Uses mats. **Cols./Page:** 6. **Col. Width:** 21 nonpareils. **Col. Depth:** 182 agate lines. **Key Personnel:** Leonard A. Marsh, General Manager; John Riddell, Manager, Circulation. **URL:** http://floridapennysavers.com/SiteDefault.aspx?edition=DB. **Ad Rates:** GLR $.50; SAU $8. **Remarks:** Accepts advertising. **Circ:** Controlled ‡67700.

PACE

8052 ■ WMEZ-FM - 94.1
6085 Quintette Rd.
Pace, FL 32571
Phone: (850)932-0941
Fax: (850)478-3971
Free: 888-741-0941
Format: Adult Contemporary; Soft Rock. **Networks:** Westwood One Radio. **Owner:** Pamal Broadcasting, Ltd., 715 Rte. 52, Beacon, NY 12508, Ph: (845)838-6000. **Founded:** Dec. 01, 2000. **Operating Hours**: Continuous. **Wattage**: 100,000. **Ad Rates:** $50-90 per unit. **URL:** http://www.softrock941.com.

8053 ■ WOW-FM
4000 Highway 90
Pace, FL 32571
Phone: (402)390-2059
Fax: (402)390-0540
Format: Country. **Networks:** ABC. **Founded:** 1959. **Wattage**: 100,000 ERP.

8054 ■ WTGF-FM - 90.5
4670 Hwy. 90
Pace, FL 32571
Phone: (850)994-3747
Email: wtgf@bellsouth.net
Format: Religious; Gospel. **Founded:** 1992. **Operating Hours**: Continuous. **Wattage**: 25,000. **URL:** http://www.truthradiofm.org.

8055 ■ WXBM-FM - 102.7
6085 Quintette Rd.
Pace, FL 32571
Phone: (850)310-9102
Format: Country. **Networks:** Mutual Broadcasting System. **Owner:** Pamal Broadcasting, Ltd., 715 Rte. 52, Beacon, NY 12508, Ph: (845)838-6000. **Founded:** 1964. **Operating Hours**: Continuous. **Key Personnel:** Dave Collins, Contact, dcollins@wxbm.com; Dave Collins, Contact, dcollins@wxbm.com; Marty White, Contact, marty@wxbm.com; Lynn West, Contact, lynn@wxbm.com. **Wattage**: 100,000. **Ad Rates:** Advertising accepted; rates available upon request. **URL:** http://www.nashpensacola.com.

PALATKA

NE FL. Putnam Co. On St. Johns River, 52 mi. S. of Jacksonville. Saint Johns River Community College. Fisheries. Lumber. Citrus fruit.

8056 ■ Palatka Daily News
Palatka Daily News
1825 St. Johns Ave.
Palatka, FL 32177
Phone: (386)312-5200
Fax: (386)312-5209
Free: 888-843-6501
General newspaper. **Freq:** Triweekly. **Print Method:** Offset. **Cols./Page:** 6. **Key Personnel:** Rusty Starr, Publisher; Mary Kaye Wells, Director, Advertising; Larry Sullivan, Editor; Mike Reynolds, Manager, Circulation. **USPS:** 418-500. **Subscription Rates:** $93.68 Individuals home delivery; $119.35 By mail; $111.54 Out of state by mail. **URL:** http://palatkadailynews.com. **Remarks:** Accepts advertising. **Circ:** Mon.-Fri. ‡11733.

8057 ■ Putnam Pennysaver
Volusia Pennysaver Inc.
930 Hwy. 19 S
Palatka, FL 32178
Phone: (386)328-4649
Publication E-mail: putnamps@psavers.com
Shopper serving Putnam County and adjacent communities. **Freq:** Weekly (Wed.). **Print Method:** Offset. **Trim Size:** 11 x 14. **Cols./Page:** 6. **Col. Width:** 1 1/2 inches. **Col. Depth:** 13 inches. **URL:** http://floridapennysavers.com/SiteDefault.aspx?edition=PP. **Mailing address:** PO Box 220, Palatka, FL 32178. **Ad Rates:** BW $460.20; 4C $640.20; PCI $5.90. **Remarks:** Accepts advertising. **Circ:** 24500.

8058 ■ WHIF-FM - 91.3
201 S Palm Ave.
Palatka, FL 32177
Phone: (386)325-3334
Fax: (386)325-0934
Format: Contemporary Christian. **Founded:** 1996. **Key Personnel:** Robin Robinson, Station Mgr. **Ad Rates:** Advertising accepted; rates available upon request. **URL:** http://www.whif.org.

8059 ■ WPLK-AM - 800
1428 St. Johns Ave.
Palatka, FL 32177
Format: Music of Your Life; Gospel. **Networks:** ABC. **Owner:** Radio Palatka Inc., at above address. **Founded:** 1947. **Operating Hours**: Continuous; 10% network, 90% local. **Key Personnel:** Wayne Bullock, Gen. Mgr.; Susan Player, Traffic Mgr., Office Mgr. **Wattage**: 1,000 Day; 334 Night. **Ad Rates:** $10-15 for 30 seconds; $15-20 for 60 seconds. **URL:** http://www.wplk.com.

PALM BAY

Brevard Co. Brevard Co. (EC). 3 m S of Melbourne.

8060 ■ WEJF-FM
2824 Palm Bay Rd.
Palm Bay, FL 32905
Phone: (321)267-3000
Fax: (321)264-9370
Format: Gospel; Religious. **Ad Rates:** Noncommercial. **URL:** http://www.wejf.net/.

PALM BEACH

SE FL. Palm Beach Co. Across Lake Worth from West Palm Beach. Resort area.

8061 ■ Naples Illustrated: The Magazine of Gracious Living
Palm Beach Media Group
PO Box 3344
Palm Beach, FL 33480
Phone: (561)659-0210
Fax: (561)659-1736
Magazine about lifestyle and entertainment in the Naples area. **Freq:** 10/year. **Key Personnel:** Kaleigh Grover, Publisher. **Subscription Rates:** $34.95 Individuals; $48.95 Two years; $17 Individuals renewal; $27 Two years renewal. **Alt. Formats:** PDF. **URL:** http://www.naplesillustrated.com. **Remarks:** Accepts advertising. **Circ:** ‡26000.

8062 ■ Palm Beach Society Magazine
Palm Beach Society Magazine
240 Worth Ave.
Palm Beach, FL 33480
Phone: (561)659-5555
Fax: (561)655-6209
Publication E-mail: info@pbsociety.com
Society magazine. **Freq:** Weekly from mid-October to mid-April. **Print Method:** Offset. **Trim Size:** 9.625 x 13.5. **Cols./Page:** 5. **Col. Width:** 1 11/16 inches. **Col. Depth:** 12 inches. **ISSN:** 1045--7259 (print). **Subscription Rates:** $45 Individuals 24 issues; $5 Single issue back issue (+ shipping and handling). **URL:** http://pbsociety.com/Home.html. **Formerly**: The Social Pictorial. **Ad Rates:** GLR $13; BW $1000; 4C $1,600; PCI $13. **Remarks:** Advertising accepted; rates available upon request. **Circ:** 5000, 20,000.

PALM BEACH GARDENS

Palm Beach Co.

8063 ■ African American Golfer's Digest
Professional Golfers' Association of America
100 Avenue of the Champions
Palm Beach Gardens, FL 33418-3653
Phone: (561)624-8400
Magazine publishing golf related stories and information for African American golfers. **Freq:** Quarterly. **Key Personnel:** Debert C. Cook, Publisher. **Subscription Rates:** $18 Individuals. **URL:** http://www.africanamericangolfersdigest.com. **Remarks:** Accepts classified advertising. **Circ:** (Not Reported).

8064 ■ NADOHE Journal of Diversity in Higher Education
National Association of Diversity Officers in Higher Education
4440 PGA Blvd., Ste. 600
Palm Beach Gardens, FL 33410
Phone: (561)472-8479
Fax: (561)472-8401
Publisher's E-mail: info@nadohe.org
Freq: Quarterly Volume 2016. **ISSN:** 1938--8926 (print); **EISSN:** 1938--8934 (electronic). **Subscription Rates:** $74 Members; $133 Nonmembers; $582 Institutions; $24 Members individual; $182 Members institution. **URL:** http://nadohe.org/journal. **Remarks:** Advertising not accepted. **Circ:** (Not Reported).

8065 ■ WPBF-TV - 25
3970 RCA Blvd., Ste. 7007
Palm Beach Gardens, FL 33410
Phone: (561)694-2525
Fax: (561)627-6738
Format: Commercial TV. **Networks:** ABC. **Owner:** Hearst Television Inc., 300 W 57th St., New York, NY 10019-3741, Ph: (212)887-6800, Fax: (212)887-6855. **Operating Hours**: Continuous. **Key Personnel:** Ryan Rothstein, Gen. Sales Mgr., rrothstein@hearst.com. **Wattage:** 1,000,000 ERP. **Ad Rates:** Advertising accepted; rates available upon request. **URL:** http://www.wpbf.com/index.html.

PALM CITY

E FL. Martin Co. 2 mi. SW of Stuart.

8066 ■ WCNO-FM - 89.9
2960 SW Mapp Rd.
Palm City, FL 34990
Phone: (772)221-1100
Fax: (772)221-8716
Free: 888-221-8990
Email: wcno@wcno.com

Circulation: ★ = AAM; △ or • = BPA; ♦ = CAC; ❑ = VAC; ⊕ = PO Statement; ‡ = Publisher's Report; Boldface figures = sworn; Light figures = estimated.

Format: Religious; Contemporary Christian. **Owner:** FamilyNet, at above address. **Founded:** Apr. 09, 1990. **Operating Hours**: Continuous; 100% local. **ADI:** West Palm Beach-Ft. Pierce-Vero Beach, FL. **Key Personnel:** Ray Kassis, Owner; Tom Craton, Contact. **Wattage**: 100,000. **Ad Rates:** Noncommercial. **URL:** http://www.wcno.com.

PALM COAST

Flagler Co.

8067 ■ Create & Decorate
All American Crafts Inc.
PO Box 422414
Palm Coast, FL 32142
Phone: (386)246-0189
Free: 800-940-6594
Publisher's E-mail: readersvc@allamericancrafts.com
Magazine focusing on craft and decorating projects. **Freq:** Bimonthly. **Key Personnel:** Darren S. Cohen, Publisher; Beverly Hotz, Editor; Marie-Claire Macdonald, Director, Marketing. **Subscription Rates:** $19.97 Individuals; $33.97 Canada; $40.97 Other countries; $34.97 Two years; $62.97 Canada two years; $76.97 Other countries two years. **URL:** http://createanddecorate.com. **Remarks:** Accepts advertising. **Circ:** (Not Reported).

8068 ■ Fantastic Flagler
Flagler County Palm Coast Chamber of Commerce
20 Airport Rd., Ste. C
Palm Coast, FL 32164
Phone: (386)437-0106
Fax: (386)437-5700
Publisher's E-mail: info@flaglerchamber.org
Magazine containing general information about the community, business information and a visitor's guide to Flagler County. **Freq:** Annual. **URL:** http://ww.flaglerchamber.org/pages/fantastic-flagler. **Remarks:** Accepts advertising. **Circ:** 12000.

8069 ■ Poets & Writers Magazine
Poets and Writers
PO Box 422460
Palm Coast, FL 32142
Phone: (386)246-0106
Publication E-mail: editor@pw.org
Magazine containing essays, interviews with writers, news and comment on publishing, political issues, and practical topics of interest to writers. Includes coverage of grants and awards, deadlines for applications, and calls for manuscript submissions. **Founded:** 1972. **Freq:** Bimonthly. **Print Method:** Offset. **Trim Size:** 7 3/4 x 10. **Cols./Page:** 3. **Col. Width:** 3 inches. **Col. Depth:** 9 3/16 inches. **Key Personnel:** Kevin Larimer, Editor; Suzanne Pettypiece, Managing Editor; Elliot Figman, Executive Director. **ISSN:** 0891-6136 (print). **Subscription Rates:** $15.95 Individuals; $25.95 Two years; $25.95 Canada; $45.95 Canada two years; $31.95 Other countries; $57.95 Other countries two years. **URL:** http://www.pw.org/magazine. **Formerly**: Coda: Poets & Writers Newsletter. **Ad Rates:** BW $1,695; 4C $2,415. **Remarks:** Accepts advertising. **Circ:** 60000, 70000.

8070 ■ Quilter's Newsletter Magazine
F+W
PO Box 433054
Palm Coast, FL 32143-3054
Free: 800-477-6089
Publication E-mail: qnewsletter@palmcoastd.com
Magazine for dedicated quilters, featuring industry news, high quality features on contemporary and historical quiltmaking, the latest in quilting techniques, and product news. Every issue contains complete instructions for several quilt projects, top-quality photography of the finest quilts being made today, book and Web site reviews, and popular and entertaining columns. **Freq:** 10/year. **Key Personnel:** Bill Gardner, Editor-in-Chief; Mary Kate Karr-Petras, Associate Editor. **Subscription Rates:** $17.97 Individuals; $12.97 Individuals. **URL:** http://www.quiltersnewsletter.com/index.html. **Ad Rates:** 4C $5,032. **Remarks:** Accepts advertising. **Circ:** (Not Reported).

8071 ■ Quiltmaker: Step-by-Step Patterns, Tips & Techniques
F+W
PO Box 433054
Palm Coast, FL 32143-3054
Phone: (386)597-4387
Publication E-mail: editor@quiltmaker.com
Step-by-step, how-to-quilt magazine targeted to the beginning and intermediate quilter. Devoted to helping people of all skill levels make quilts successfully. Publication rates the complexity of each project; features a variety of styles and techniques; provides clear and accurate yardages, instructions, tips and shortcuts; shows additional colorways, and reviews products of interest to quiltmakers. **Freq:** Bimonthly. **Key Personnel:** Carolyn Beam, Editor. **Subscription Rates:** $17.97 Individuals print; $13.97 Individuals online; $31.97 Canada print and online; $25.97 Individuals print and online. **URL:** http://www.quiltmaker.com. **Ad Rates:** 4C $3562. **Remarks:** Accepts advertising. **Circ:** (Not Reported).

8072 ■ Sailing World: The Authority on Performance Sailing
Bonnier Corp.
PO Box 420235
Palm Coast, FL 32142-0235
Publication E-mail: editor@sailingworld.com
Magazine on performance sailing. **Freq:** 8/year. **Print Method:** Web Offset. **Trim Size:** 8 x 10 3/4. **Cols./Page:** 2 and 4. **Col. Width:** 21 and 27 nonpareils. **Col. Depth:** 140 agate lines. **Key Personnel:** Sally Helme, Publisher, phone: (401)845-4405. **Subscription Rates:** $19.97 U.S.; $31.97 Canada; $43.97 Other countries. **URL:** http://www.sailingworld.com. **Formerly**: Yacht Racing and Cruising. **Ad Rates:** 4C $10,425. **Remarks:** Accepts advertising. **Circ:** Paid ‡47500.

8073 ■ Vegetarian Times
Active Interest Media
PO Box 420235
Palm Coast, FL 32142-0235
Free: 877-717-8923
Publication E-mail: editor@vegetariantimes.com
Magazine devoted to plant-based foods and related topics such as health, fitness, and the environment. **Freq:** 9/year. **Trim Size:** 8 x 10 1/2. **Key Personnel:** Cynthia Lyons, Director, Production; Mark Stokes, Manager, Production; Bill Harper, Publisher, phone: (310)356-2270. **Subscription Rates:** $14.95 Individuals; $26.95 Canada 9 issues; $47.95 Canada 18 issues; $38.95 Other countries 9 issues; $71.95 Other countries 18 issues. **URL:** http://www.vegetariantimes.com; http://www.aimmedia.com/vt.html. **Ad Rates:** BW $19,195; 4C $21,815. **Remarks:** Accepts advertising. **Circ:** Paid ***212007**.

8074 ■ Palm Coast Cablevision Ltd.
211 St. Joe Plaza Dr.
Palm Coast, FL 32137
Fax: (904)445-5434
Formerly: Palm Cable Inc. **Key Personnel:** Rosa Rosas, Gen. Mgr., rrosas@kingwoodcable.com. **Cities Served:** Volusia, Colorado; Palm Coast, Florida: subscribing households 10,000; 65 channels; 1 community access channel. **URL:** http://search.sunbiz.org/Inquiry/CorporationSearch/SearchResultDetail?inquirytype=EntityName&directionType=Initial&searchNameOrder=PALMCOASTCABLEVISION%20P960000875260&aggregateId=domp-p96000087526-ac96ab6b-3810-45e9-a21d-1438cdb37585&searchTerm=Palm%20Coast%20C.

PALM HARBOR

8075 ■ Algebras, Groups & Geometries
Hadronic Press Inc.
35246 US 19 N, Ste. 215
Palm Harbor, FL 34684
Phone: (727)934-9593
Fax: (727)934-9275
Publisher's E-mail: info@hadronicpress.com
Scholarly journal covering mathematics for graduate and post graduate students. **Freq:** Quarterly. **Trim Size:** 7 /14 x 9. **Key Personnel:** L.P. Horwitz, Board Member; Prof. Ruggero Maria Santilli, Editor-in-Chief, Founder. **ISSN:** 0741--9937 (print). **Alt. Formats:** Download; PDF. **URL:** http://www.hadronicpress.com. **Remarks:** Advertising not accepted. **Circ:** Paid 200.

8076 ■ Hadronic Journal
Hadronic Press Inc.
35246 US 19 N, Ste. 215
Palm Harbor, FL 34684
Phone: (727)934-9593
Fax: (727)934-9275
Publisher's E-mail: info@hadronicpress.com
Scholarly journal covering physics for graduate and post-graduate students. **Freq:** Bimonthly. **Trim Size:** 7 1/4 x 9. **Key Personnel:** G.H.A. Cole, Board Member; T.L. Gill, Board Member; G.-C. Cavalleri, Board Member; L.P. Horwitz, Board Member; E. Recami, Board Member; A.O.E. Animalu, Board Member; D.P. Bhattacharyya, Board Member; Prof. Ruggero Maria Santilli, Editor-in-Chief, Founder; M. Saleem, Board Member. **ISSN:** 0162--5519 (print). **Alt. Formats:** Download; PDF. **URL:** http://www.hadronicpress.com. **Remarks:** Advertising not accepted. **Circ:** Paid 150.

8077 ■ Hadronic Journal Supplement
Hadronic Press Inc.
35246 US 19 N, Ste. 215
Palm Harbor, FL 34684
Phone: (727)934-9593
Fax: (727)934-9275
Publisher's E-mail: info@hadronicpress.com
Scholarly journal covering physics for graduate and post-graduate students. **Freq:** Quarterly. **Trim Size:** 7 1/4 x 9. **Key Personnel:** Prof. Ruggero Maria Santilli, Editor-in-Chief, Founder; A.O. Animalu, Board Member. **ISSN:** 0882--5396 (print). **Alt. Formats:** PDF. **URL:** http://www.hadronicpress.com. **Remarks:** Advertising not accepted. **Circ:** Paid 100.

8078 ■ WGHR-FM - 106.3
35048 US Highway, 19 N
Palm Harbor, FL 34684
Free: 888-311-1063
Email: staff@trueoldies1063.com
Format: Oldies. **Simulcasts:** WGUL-AM. **Networks:** AP. **Owner:** WGUL-FM, Inc., at above address. **Founded:** 1985. **Formerly**: WGUL-FM; WJQB-FM. **Operating Hours:** Continuous; 40% network, 60% local. **Key Personnel:** Steve Schurdell, Partner; Cem Maier, Gen. Sales Mgr. **Wattage**: 25,000. **Ad Rates:** $50-60 for 30 seconds; $80-100 for 60 seconds. Combined advertising rates available with WGUL-AM, WUGL-AM. **URL:** http://www.greatesthits106.com.

PANAMA CITY

NW FL. Bay Co. On St. Andrews Bay and Gulf of Mexico, 98 mi. E. of Pensacola. Gulf Coast Community College. Resort area. Manufactures boats, concrete products, lumber, textiles, auto disc pads, and beverages.

8079 ■ News Herald
Freedom Communications Inc.
501 W 11th St.
Panama City, FL 32401
Phone: (850)747-5000
Fax: (850)747-5097
Publisher's E-mail: info@freedom.com
Community newspaper. **Founded:** 1936. **Freq:** Mon.-Sun. (morn.). **Print Method:** Offset. **Trim Size:** 9 1/2 x 11. **Cols./Page:** 6. **Col. Width:** 25 1/2 nonpareils. **Col. Depth:** 301 agate lines. **Key Personnel:** Mike Cazalas, Managing Editor; Karen Hanes, Publisher. **USPS:** 419-560. **Subscription Rates:** $167.88 Individuals Daily home delivery; $312 Individuals mail; $356.20 Out of state mail. **Alt. Formats:** Handheld. **URL:** http://www.freedom.com. **Ad Rates:** GLR $.52; BW $1,475.76; 4C $1,925.76; SAU $11.44. **Remarks:** Accepts advertising. **Circ:** Mon.-Sat. **♦21158**, Sun. **♦27885**.

8080 ■ WAVK-FM - 105.5
PO Box 27761
Panama City, FL 32411
Phone: (412)370-4143
Format: Adult Contemporary. **Networks:** Satellite Music Network. **Owner:** Vox Communications, at above address. **Founded:** 1985. **Formerly**: WPLC-FM. **Operating Hours**: Continuous; 80% network, 20% local. **Key Personnel:** Shannon Butler, Gen. Sales Mgr., shannon2@safari.net. **Wattage**: 26,000. **Ad Rates:** $6-8 for 30 seconds; $6-10 for 60 seconds. Combined advertising rates available with WKRY, WFKZ, WKEZ, WAIL, WKWF, WEDW.

WAYP-FM - See Marianna

8081 ■ WBPC-FM - 95.1
700 W 23rd St., Ste. E-40
Panama City, FL 32405

Phone: (850)235-2195
Fax: (850)235-2795
Format: Classic Rock; News; Oldies. **Owner:** Bay Broadcasting, Mile 2 Alaska Peninsula Hwy., Naknek, AK 99633. **Operating Hours:** Continuous. **Key Personnel:** Rhonda Sheffield, Bus. Mgr., rfsheffield@beach951.com. **Wattage:** 21,000 ERP. **Ad Rates:** Advertising accepted; rates available upon request. **Mailing address:** PO Box 27272, Panama City, FL 32405. **URL:** http://www.beach951.com.

8082 ■ WDIZ-AM - 590
1834 Lisenby Ave.
Panama City, FL 32405-3713
Phone: (850)769-1408
Fax: (850)769-0659
Format: Sports. **ADI:** Panama City, FL. **Ad Rates:** Noncommercial. **URL:** http://Www.img.ccrd.clearchannel.com.

8083 ■ WEBZ-FM - 93.5
1834 Lisenby Ave.
Panama City, FL 32405
Phone: (850)769-1408
Format: Contemporary Hit Radio (CHR). **ADI:** Panama City, FL. **Wattage:** 50,000. **Ad Rates:** Noncommercial. **URL:** http://www.clearchannel.com.

8084 ■ WFBX-FM - 94.5
1834 Lisenby Ave.
Panama City, FL 32405
Phone: (918)664-4581
Format: Album-Oriented Rock (AOR). **Founded:** Sept. 15, 2006. **ADI:** Panama City, FL. **Key Personnel:** Jay Cruze, Dir. of Programs, jay@945wfla.com. **Wattage:** 100,000 ERP. **Ad Rates:** Noncommercial. **URL:** http://945wfla.iheart.com.

8085 ■ WFSG-TV - 4
1600 Red Barber Plz.
Tallahassee, FL 32310
Phone: (850)487-3170
Fax: (850)487-3093
Email: mail@wfsu.org
Simulcasts: WFSU-TV Tallahassee, FL. **Networks:** Public Broadcasting Service (PBS). **Owner:** Florida State University, 600 W College Ave., Tallahassee, FL 32306, Ph: (850)644-2525, Fax: (850)645-0108. **Founded:** Nov. 1988. **Operating Hours:** 5 a.m.-11:00 p.m. **ADI:** Panama City, FL. **Key Personnel:** Patrick Keating, Gen. Mgr., pkeating@mailer.fsu.edu; Denison Graham, Dir. of Fin., dgraham@admin.fsu.edu. **Local Programs:** *Florida Face to Face,* Monday Tuesday Wednesday Thursday Friday Saturday Sunday Sunday 6:00 a.m.; 6:00 p.m. 11:30 a.m. **Ad Rates:** Noncommercial. **URL:** http://www.wfsu.org.

8086 ■ WFSY-FM - 98.5
1834 Lisenby Ave.
Panama City, FL 32405
Phone: (850)769-1408
Fax: (850)769-0659
Free: 866-985-9379
Email: help@sunny985.com
Format: Adult Contemporary. **Networks:** ABC. **Founded:** 1986. **Formerly:** WGNE-FM. **Operating Hours:** Continuous; 1% network, 99% local. **ADI:** Panama City, FL. **Key Personnel:** Michael Reineri, Gen. Mgr. **Wattage:** 100,000. **Ad Rates:** $20-38 for 30 seconds; $25-47.50 for 60 seconds. **URL:** http://www.sunny985.com.

8087 ■ WILN-FM - 105.9
7106 Laird St., Ste. 102
Panama City, FL 32405
Phone: (850)230-5855
Format: Contemporary Hit Radio (CHR). **Owner:** Magic Broadcasting II, at above address. **Founded:** 1985. **Operating Hours:** Continuous; 100% local. **ADI:** Panama City, FL. **Wattage:** 50,000. **Ad Rates:** $25 per unit. **URL:** http://www.island106.com.

8088 ■ WKGC-AM - 1480
5230 W Hwy. 98
Panama City, FL 32401
Phone: (850)873-3500
Email: info@visitpanamacitybeach.com
Format: Eclectic. **Owner:** Gulf Coast State College, 5230 W Highway 98, Panama City, FL 32401-1041, Ph: (850)769-1551, Fax: (850)913-3319, Free: 800-311-3685. **Founded:** 1968. **Operating Hours:** Continuous. **Ad Rates:** Advertising accepted; rates available upon request. **URL:** http://www.visitpanamacitybeach.com/beachflagiframe.cfm?small=1.

8089 ■ WKGC-FM - 90.7
5230 W Hwy. 98
Panama City, FL 32401
Phone: (850)873-3500
Format: Eclectic. **Owner:** Gulf Coast State College, 5230 W Highway 98, Panama City, FL 32401-1041, Ph: (850)769-1551, Fax: (850)913-3319, Free: 800-311-3685. **Founded:** 1968. **Operating Hours:** Continuous. **Ad Rates:** Advertising accepted; rates available upon request.

8090 ■ WLTG-AM - 1430
3216 West Hwy., 390 No. B
Panama City, FL 32405-2718
Format: Information; News; Talk; Sports. **Networks:** Precision Racing. **Owner:** Hour Group Broadcasting, Inc., PO Box 15635, Panama City, FL 32406. **Founded:** 1949. **Formerly:** WPCF-AM. **Operating Hours:** Continuous. **ADI:** Panama City, FL. **Key Personnel:** Peggy Gay, Contact. **Wattage:** 5,000. **Ad Rates:** Advertising accepted; rates available upon request. **URL:** http://www.1430newstalk.com/.

8091 ■ WMBB-TV - 13
613 Harrison Ave.
Panama City, FL 32401
Phone: (850)769-2313
Fax: (850)769-8231
Email: info@visitpanamacitybeach.com
Format: Commercial TV. **Networks:** ABC. **Owner:** Hoak Media Corp., 500 Crescent Ct., Ste. 220, Dallas, TX 75201, Ph: (972)960-4848, Fax: (972)960-4899. **Founded:** 1973. **Formerly:** WDTB-TV. **Operating Hours:** Continuous; 75% network, 25% local. **ADI:** Panama City, FL. **Wattage:** 316. **Ad Rates:** Advertising accepted; rates available upon request. **URL:** http://www.visitpanamacitybeach.com.

8092 ■ WPAP-FM - 92.5
1834 Lisenby Ave.
Panama City, FL 32405
Phone: (850)769-1408
Fax: (850)769-0659
Free: 866-925-9727
Email: help@925wpap.com
Format: Country. **Networks:** Independent. **Operating Hours:** Continuous; 100% local. **ADI:** Panama City, FL. **Key Personnel:** Michael Reineri, Gen. Mgr. **Wattage:** 100,000. **Ad Rates:** $36-60 for 30 seconds; $40-70 for 60 seconds. **URL:** http://www.925wpap.com.

8093 ■ WPBH-FM - 99.3
1834 Lisenby Ave.
Panama City, FL 32405
Phone: (850)769-1408
Email: request@993thebeat.com
Format: Hip Hop; Blues. **Owner:** iHeartMedia Inc., 200 E Basse Rd., San Antonio, TX 78209, Ph: (210)832-3314. **Key Personnel:** Todd Berry, Dir. of Programs, toddberry@clearchannel.com. **Ad Rates:** Advertising accepted; rates available upon request.

8094 ■ WPGX-TV - 28
28 Corporate Pk.
700 W 23rd St.
Panama City, FL 32406-6028
Phone: (904)784-0028
Fax: (904)784-1773
Format: Commercial TV. **Networks:** Fox. **Founded:** 1988. **ADI:** Panama City, FL. **Key Personnel:** Mike Harding, Contact. **Wattage:** 24,100 ERP. **Mailing address:** PO Box 16028, Panama City, FL 32406-6028.

8095 ■ WTBB-FM - 97.7
7106 Laird St., Ste. 102
Panama City, FL 32408
Phone: (850)230-5855
Format: Album-Oriented Rock (AOR). **Owner:** Styles Media Group LLC, 7106 Laird St., Ste.102, Panama City, FL 32408-7622, Ph: (850)230-5855, Fax: (850)230-6988. **Founded:** 1983. **Operating Hours:** Continuous. **ADI:** Panama City, FL. **Key Personnel:** Kim Styes, Mgr. **Wattage:** 100,000. **Ad Rates:** $20 per unit. Combined advertising rates available with WILN-FM. **URL:** http://www.iam97x.com.

8096 ■ W34DH - 34
PO Box A
Santa Ana, CA 92711
Phone: (714)832-2950
Free: 888-731-1000
Owner: Trinity Broadcasting Network Inc., PO Box A, Santa Ana, CA 92711, Ph: (714)832-2950, Free: 888-731-1000. **URL:** http://www.tbn.org.

8097 ■ W204CD-FM - 88.7
PO Box 391
Twin Falls, ID 83303
Fax: (208)736-1958
Free: 800-357-4226
Format: Religious; Contemporary Christian. **Owner:** CSN International, PO Box 391, Twin Falls, ID 83303, Ph: (208)736-1958, Fax: (208)736-1958, Free: 800-357-4226.

8098 ■ WVVE-FM - 100.1
7106 Laird St., Ste. 102
Panama City, FL 32405
Phone: (850)230-5855
Fax: (850)230-6988
Format: Adult Contemporary. **Owner:** Magic Broadcasting L.L.C., 7106 Laird St., Panama City, FL 32408, Ph: (850)230-5855. **Operating Hours:** 18 hours Daily. **Key Personnel:** Joan Williams, Contact, jwilliams@magicbroadcasting.net; Joan Williams, Contact, jwilliams@magicbroadcasting.net. **Ad Rates:** Advertising accepted; rates available upon request.

PANAMA CITY BEACH

8099 ■ WASJ-FM - 105.1
118 Gwyn Dr.
Panama City Beach, FL 32408
Phone: (850)234-8858
Fax: (850)234-6592
Format: Adult Contemporary; Oldies; Eighties. **Key Personnel:** Melissa Miller, Dir. of Programs, melissamiller@panamacityradio.com. **URL:** http://www.bobatthebeach.com.

8100 ■ WJHG-TV - 7
8195 Front Beach Rd.
Panama City Beach, FL 32407
Phone: (850)234-7777
Fax: (850)233-6647
Format: Commercial TV. **Networks:** NBC. **Owner:** Gray Television Inc., 4370 Peachtree Rd. NE, No. 400, Atlanta, GA 30319-3054, Ph: (404)266-8333. **Founded:** 1953. **Formerly:** WJDM-TV. **Operating Hours:** Continuous. **ADI:** Panama City, FL. **Key Personnel:** Scott Rossman, Sports Dir., scott.rossman@wjhg.com. **Ad Rates:** Advertising accepted; rates available upon request. **URL:** http://www.wjhg.com.

8101 ■ WPFM-FM - 107.9
118 Gwyn Dr.
Panama City Beach, FL 32408
Phone: (850)234-8858
Fax: (850)234-6592
Format: Contemporary Hit Radio (CHR). **Networks:** Independent. **Owner:** Root Communications, Ltd., at above address. **Founded:** 1963. **Operating Hours:** Continuous; 100% local. **ADI:** Panama City, FL. **Key Personnel:** Mike Stone, Contact; Charlie Wooten, Contact; Thomas DiBacco, Contact. **Wattage:** 100,000. **Ad Rates:** $14-20 for 30 seconds; $16-30 for 60 seconds. $10-$14 for 30 seconds; $12-$16 for 60 seconds. Combined advertising rates available with WDRK-FM. **URL:** http://hot1079pc.com.

8102 ■ WYOO-FM - 101.1
7106 Laird St., Ste. 102
Panama City Beach, FL 32408
Phone: (850)230-5855
Fax: (850)230-6988
Format: Talk. **Ad Rates:** Noncommercial.

PARRISH

8103 ■ PENnant
Pen Collectors of America
PO Box 705
Parrish, FL 34219
Phone: (920)809-5182
Magazine featuring in-depth articles about the history and restoration of pens, about modern pens, information

Circulation: ★ = AAM; △ or • = BPA; ♦ = CAC; ❑ = VAC; ⊕ = PO Statement; ‡ = Publisher's Report; Boldface figures = sworn; Light figures = estimated.

about Internet sites, letters to the editor, reviews of pen reference books, information about local clubs and more. **Freq:** 3/year. **Key Personnel:** Richard Jarvis, Managing Editor. **Alt. Formats:** PDF. **URL:** http://www.pencollectorsofamerica.com/component/docman/cat_view/78-pennant-archive?Itemid=. **Remarks:** Accepts advertising. **Circ:** (Not Reported).

PEMBROKE PARK

Broward Co. Broward Co.

8104 ■ WHFT-TV - 45
3324 Pembroke Rd.
Pembroke Park, FL 33021
Phone: (954)962-1700
Fax: (954)962-2817
Free: 888-731-1000
Format: Religious. **Founded:** 1980. **Formerly:** WFCB-TV. **Key Personnel:** Elizabeth M. Crespo, Contact. **Wattage:** 1,000,000 ERP. **Ad Rates:** Accepts Advertising.

PEMBROKE PINES

8105 ■ WIRP-FM - 88.3
19620 Pines Blvd., Ste. 114
Pembroke Pines, FL 33029
Phone: (954)438-8830
Email: info@lanuevafm.net
Format: Hispanic. **Operating Hours:** Continuous. **Ad Rates:** Advertising accepted; rates available upon request. **URL:** http://www.lanuevafm.net/cms.

PENSACOLA

NW FL. Escambia Co. On Pensacola Bay, 7 mi. from Gulf of Mexico, 61 mi. SE of Mobile, AL. Pensacola Junior College; University of West Florida; U.S. Naval Air Station. Port of entry with deep harbor and considerable commerce. Manufactures boats, nylon, chemicals, cottonseed oil, lumber, fertilizer, furniture, beverages, and paper products.

8106 ■ The Chronicle/Women's Dental Journal
American Association of Women Dentists
7794 Grow Dr.
Pensacola, FL 32514
Fax: (850)484-8762
Free: 800-920-2293
Publisher's E-mail: info@aawd.org
Freq: Bimonthly. **Subscription Rates:** Included in membership; $30 Nonmembers. **Alt. Formats:** PDF. **URL:** http://www.aawd.org. **Remarks:** Accepts advertising. **Circ:** 19000.

8107 ■ Electronic Government: An International Journal
Inderscience Publishers
c/o Dr. June Wei, Ed.-in-Ch.
College of Business, Bldg. 76, Rm. 116
University of West Florida
11000 University Pky.
Pensacola, FL 32514
Publication E-mail: info@inderscience.com
Peer-reviewed journal publishing articles on present current practice and research in the area of e-government. **Freq:** Quarterly. **Key Personnel:** Dr. June Wei, Editor-in-Chief; Prof. Dr. Sang M. Lee, Senior Editor. **ISSN:** 1740--7494 (print); **EISSN:** 1740--7508 (electronic). **Subscription Rates:** $928 Individuals print + online; $685 Individuals print or online for 1 user. **URL:** http://www.inderscience.com/jhome.php?jcode=eg. **Circ:** (Not Reported).

8108 ■ Environmental Toxicology and Chemistry
Society of Environmental Toxicology and Chemistry
229 S Baylen St., 2nd Fl.
Pensacola, FL 32502
Phone: (850)469-1500
Fax: (888)296-4136
Publisher's E-mail: setac@setac.org
Freq: Monthly. **ISSN:** 1552- 8618 (print). **Subscription Rates:** Included in membership. **Alt. Formats:** CD-ROM. **URL:** http://www.setac.org/?page=SETACJournals. **Remarks:** Accepts advertising. **Circ:** (Not Reported).

8109 ■ The Escambia Sun-Press
Escambia Sun-Press Inc.
605 S Old Corry Field Rd.
Pensacola, FL 32507
Phone: (850)456-3121
Fax: (850)456-0103
Publisher's E-mail: esp@escambiasunpress.com
Local newspaper. **Freq:** Weekly. **Print Method:** Offset. **Cols./Page:** 9. **Col. Width:** 10.5 picas. **Col. Depth:** 21 inches. **Subscription Rates:** $17.20 Individuals Escambia County; $22.57 Individuals Santa Rosa and Okaloosa counties; $27.95 Individuals other locations in Florida and other states. **URL:** http://escambiasunpress.com. **Ad Rates:** PCI $4.50. **Remarks:** Accepts advertising. **Circ:** 3500.

8110 ■ Integrated Environmental Assessment and Management
Society of Environmental Toxicology and Chemistry
229 S Baylen St., 2nd Fl.
Pensacola, FL 32502
Phone: (850)469-1500
Fax: (888)296-4136
Publisher's E-mail: setac@setac.org
Journal publishing critical reviews, original research, brief communications, policy analyses, case studies and special series that focus on bridging the gap between scientific research and the application of sound science in decision making, regulation and environmental management. **Freq:** Quarterly. **ISSN:** 1551-3777 (print); **EISSN:** 1551-3793 (electronic). **Subscription Rates:** $753 Institutions online only. **URL:** http://www.setac.org/?page=SETACJournals; http://onlinelibrary.wiley.com/journal/10.1002/(ISSN)1551-3793/homepage/ProductInformation.html. **Remarks:** Accepts advertising. **Circ:** (Not Reported).

8111 ■ International Journal of Electronic Finance
Inderscience Publishers
c/o Dr. June Wei, Senior Editor
College of Business
University of West Florida, Bldg. 76, Rm. 116
11000 University Pky.
Pensacola, FL 32514
Publisher's E-mail: editor@inderscience.com
Journal covering electronic finance. **Freq:** Quarterly. **Key Personnel:** Dr. June Wei, Senior Editor; Dr. Cheng Few Lee, Board Member; Dr. Philip Tsang, Board Member; Dr. Binshan Lin, Board Member; Dr. Stuart J. Barnes, Board Member; Dr. Chang E. Koh, Board Member. **ISSN:** 1746--0069 (print); **EISSN:** 1746--0077 (electronic). **Subscription Rates:** $685 Individuals print or online; $928 Individuals online and print. **URL:** http://www.inderscience.com/jhome.php?jcode=ijef. **Circ:** (Not Reported).

8112 ■ International Journal of Mobile Communications
Inderscience Publishers
c/o Dr. June Wei, Ed.-in-Ch.
University of West Florida
Department of Management & Management Information Systems, College of Business
Bldg. 76 Rm. 116, 11000 University Pky.
Pensacola, FL 32514
Publication E-mail: info@inderscience.com
Journal publishing articles that present current practice and theory of mobile communications, mobile technology, and mobile commerce applications. **Freq:** 6/year. **Key Personnel:** Dr. June Wei, Editor-in-Chief; Prof. Dr. Sang M. Lee, Senior Editor; Prof. Dong-Her Shih, Associate Editor. **ISSN:** 1470--949X (print); **EISSN:** 1741--5217 (electronic). **Subscription Rates:** $820 Individuals print or online for 1 user; $1394 Individuals online only for 2-3 users; $1147 Individuals print and online; $2050 Individuals online only for 4-5 users; $2665 Individuals online only for 6-7 users; $3239 Individuals online only for 8-9 users; $3772 Individuals online only for 10-14 users; $4305 Individuals online only for 15-19 users; $4084 Individuals online only for 20+ users. **URL:** http://www.inderscience.com/jhome.php?jcode=ijmc. **Circ:** (Not Reported).

8113 ■ Pensacola History Illustrated
Pensacola Historical Society
PO Box 12866
Pensacola, FL 32502
Phone: (850)595-5985
Fax: (850)595-5989
Publisher's E-mail: phstaff@pensacolahistory.org
Journal covering local history. **Freq:** Semiannual. **Print Method:** Offset. **Trim Size:** 8 1/2 x 11. **Cols./Page:** 2. **Col. Width:** 3 1/4 inches. **Col. Depth:** 9 1/2 inches. **ISSN:** 1082-5193 (print). **Subscription Rates:** $4 Individuals back issues. **URL:** http://www.pensacolahistory.org. **Formerly:** Echo and Pensacola Historical Society Quarterly. **Remarks:** Advertising not accepted. **Circ:** Controlled 700.

8114 ■ Pensacola Voice
Pensacola Voice
213 E Yonge St.
Pensacola, FL 32503
Phone: (850)434-6963
Publisher's E-mail: info@pensacolavoice.com
Black community newspaper. **Freq:** Weekly. **Cols./Page:** 6. **Col. Width:** 2 inches. **Col. Depth:** 21 inches. **Key Personnel:** LaDonna Spivey, Consultant; Jacqueline Miles, Editor. **Ad Rates:** BW $2105.28; 4C $2505.58; PCI $16.32. **Remarks:** Accepts advertising. **Circ:** ‡35896.

8115 ■ Teaching and Learning in Nursing
Organization for Associate Degree Nursing
7794 Grow Dr.
Pensacola, FL 32514
Fax: (850)484-8762
Free: 877-966-6236
Publisher's E-mail: t.reller@elsevier.com
Journal devoted to associate degree nursing education and practice. **Freq:** Monthly. **Print Method:** Sheetfed. **Trim Size:** 8 x 10 3/4. **Cols./Page:** 1. **Col. Width:** 50 nonpareils. **Col. Depth:** 100 agate lines. **Key Personnel:** Tracey Siegel, Editor. **ISSN:** 1557--3087 (print). **Subscription Rates:** $106 U.S. online and print; $90 U.S. and other countries online; $152 Canada online and print; $148 Other countries online and print. **URL:** http://www.jtln.org; http://www.journals.elsevier.com/teaching-and-learning-in-nursing. **Mailing address:** PO Box 945, New York, NY 10159-0945. **Remarks:** Accepts advertising. **Circ:** (Not Reported).

8116 ■ WASG-AM - 540
2070 N Palafox St.
Pensacola, FL 32501-2145
Phone: (850)434-1230
Format: Gospel; Religious; Talk. **Owner:** 550 AM, Inc., at above address. **Founded:** 1981. **Operating Hours:** Continuous. **ADI:** Mobile, AL-Pensacola, FL. **Wattage:** 2,500 Daytime; 019 Ni. **Ad Rates:** Advertising accepted; rates available upon request. $12.50-20 for 30 seconds; $20-25 for 60 seconds. **URL:** http://www.wasg.net.

8117 ■ WBSR-AM - 1450
1601 N Pace Blvd.
Pensacola, FL 32505
Phone: (850)438-4982
Fax: (850)607-8114
Free: 855-444-3776
Format: Contemporary Hit Radio (CHR). **Networks:** Unistar; CNN Radio. **Owner:** WBSR Radio, at above address. **Founded:** 1946. **Operating Hours:** Continuous. **Key Personnel:** Mike Carr, Sales Mgr; Mary Gilbert, Contact. **Wattage:** 1,000. **URL:** http://www.espnpcola.com.

8118 ■ WCOA-AM - 1370
6565 N W St.
Pensacola, FL 32505
Phone: (850)478-6011
Fax: (850)478-3971
Format: News; Talk. **Networks:** ABC. **Owner:** Cumulus Broadcasting Inc., 3280 Peachtree Rd. NW, Ste. 2300, Atlanta, GA 30305-2447, Ph: (404)949-0700, Fax: (404)949-0740. **Founded:** 1926. **Operating Hours:** Continuous. **ADI:** Mobile, AL-Pensacola, FL. **Wattage:** 5,000. **Ad Rates:** Advertising accepted; rates available upon request. **URL:** http://www.wcoapensacola.com.

8119 ■ WDWR-AM - 1230
PO Box 866
Pensacola, FL 32591
Phone: (850)438-7667
Email: info@divinewordradio.com
Format: Contemporary Christian. **Owner:** Divine Word Communications, PO Box 866, Pensacola, FL 32591, Ph: (850)438-7667. **URL:** http://www.divinewordradio.com.

8120 ■ WEAR-TV - 3
4990 Mobile Hwy.
Pensacola, FL 32506

Phone: (850)456-3333
Free: 866-856-9327
Email: news@weartv.com
Format: News. **Networks:** ABC. **Owner:** Sinclair Broadcast Group Inc., 10706 Beaver Dam Rd., Hunt Valley, MD 21030, Ph: (410)568-1500, Fax: (410)568-1533. **Founded:** 1953. **Operating Hours**: 12 a.m. - 11 p.m. **ADI**: Tampa- St. Petersburg (Lakeland, Sarasota),FL. **Key Personnel:** Deb Currie, Gen. Sales Mgr., dcurrie@weartv.com; Dan Shugart, Sports Dir., dshugart@weartv.com. **Wattage**: 100,000 visual. **Ad Rates:** Advertising accepted; rates available upon request. **URL:** http://www.weartv.com.

8121 ■ WEGS-FM
1836 Olive Rd.
Pensacola, FL 32514
Phone: (850)473-4465
Format: Religious. **Founded:** 1975. **Wattage**: 20,000 ERP. **Ad Rates:** Noncommercial. **URL:** http://www.917online.com.

8122 ■ WFGX-TV - 35
35 4990 Mobile Hwy.
Pensacola, FL 32506
Phone: (850)456-3333
Fax: (850)445-0159
Free: 866-856-9327
Owner: Sinclair Broadcast Group Inc., 10706 Beaver Dam Rd., Hunt Valley, MD 21030, Ph: (410)568-1500, Fax: (410)568-1533. **Founded:** Sept. 07, 2006. **Key Personnel:** Deb Currie, Gen. Sales Mgr. **URL:** http://www.wfgxtv.com/sections/station.

8123 ■ WHBR-TV - 33
6500 Pensacola Blvd.
Pensacola, FL 32505-1704
Phone: (850)473-8633
Fax: (850)473-8631
Free: 800-533-9427
Email: info@whbr.org
Format: Religious. **Networks:** Christian Television. **Owner:** Christian Television Corp. of Pensacola/Mobile Inc., at above address. **Founded:** 1986. **Operating Hours**: Continuous. **ADI**: Mobile, AL-Pensacola, FL. **Key Personnel:** David Mayo, Station Mgr. **Wattage**: 3,000,000. **Ad Rates:** $232-561 per unit. **URL:** http://www.whbr.org/watch-now.html.

8124 ■ WJLQ-FM - 100.7
6565 N West St., Ste. 270
Pensacola, FL 32505
Phone: (850)478-6011
Fax: (850)478-3971
Free: 888-476-1007
Format: Contemporary Hit Radio (CHR); Top 40. **Owner:** Cumulus Broadcasting Inc., 3280 Peachtree Rd. NW, Ste. 2300, Atlanta, GA 30305-2447, Ph: (404)949-0700, Fax: (404)949-0740. **Founded:** 1966. **Operating Hours**: Continuous. **ADI**: Mobile, AL-Pensacola, FL. **Key Personnel:** Monte Saunders, Office Mgr.; Terry Simmons, Dir. of Programs; Marcia Knight, Traffic Mgr. **Wattage**: 100,000. **Ad Rates:** $25-57 for 30 seconds; $30-63 for 60 seconds.

8125 ■ WJTC-TV - 44
6706-A Plantation Rd.
Pensacola, FL 32504
Phone: (251)602-1500
Fax: (251)602-1547
Format: Commercial TV; News; Sports. **Networks:** Independent; Fox; CBS; NBC; Univision; ABC. **Founded:** 1984. **Operating Hours**: Continuous. **ADI**: Mobile, AL-Pensacola, FL. **Key Personnel:** Cathy Gretencord, Contact. **Wattage**: 1,000,000 ERP Horizo. **Ad Rates:** Advertising accepted; rates available upon request. $15-130 per unit. **URL:** http://utv44.com/.

8126 ■ WKGT-FM - 105.1
312 E 9 Mile Rd., Ste. 27
Pensacola, FL 32514-1475
Phone: (904)474-1099
Fax: (904)474-0709
Format: Big Band/Nostalgia; Middle-of-the-Road (MOR). **Networks:** Satellite Music Network. **Founded:** 1988. **Operating Hours**: Continuous. **ADI**: Mobile, AL-Pensacola, FL. **Key Personnel:** Richard I. Lott, President; Mark Jay, Operations Mgr.; Jack Hixon, Sales Mgr. **Wattage**: 6,000. **Ad Rates:** $10.50-14 for 30 seconds; $15-20 for 60 seconds.

8127 ■ WNRP-AM - 1620
7251 Plantation Rd.
Pensacola, FL 32504
Phone: (850)262-6000
Fax: (850)494-0778
Email: news@newsradio1620.com
Format: News; Talk. **Networks:** Fox; ABC. **Owner:** ADX Communications of Escambia L.L.C., at above address. **Operating Hours**: Continuous. **Key Personnel:** Mary Hoxeng, Gen. Mgr., mhoxeng@newsradio1620.com; Jeff Wayne, Mktg. Mgr., jwayne@newsradio1620.com; Mary Hoxeng, Contact. **Wattage**: 10,000 Day 1,000 Nig. **Ad Rates:** Advertising accepted; rates available upon request. **URL:** http://www.newsradio1620.com.

8128 ■ WNVY-AM - 1070
2070 N Palafox Rd.
Pensacola, FL 32501
Phone: (850)432-3658
Format: Gospel. **Owner:** Wilkins Communications Network Inc., 292 S Pine St., Spartanburg, SC 29302, Ph: (864)585-1885, Fax: (864)597-0687, Free: 888-989-2299. **Key Personnel:** Jessica Jordan, Station Mgr. **Wattage**: 15,000. **URL:** http://www.wilkinsradio.com.

8129 ■ WNWF-AM - 1120
PO Box 9414
Pensacola, FL 32513
Phone: (850)324-1210
Format: News; Talk. **Operating Hours**: 13 hours Daily. **Key Personnel:** Steve Williams, News Dir., steve@fox1120.com. **Ad Rates:** Advertising accepted; rates available upon request.

8130 ■ WPCS-FM - 89.5
Rejoice Broadcast Network
Pensacola, FL 32523
Phone: (850)479-6570
Email: rbn@rejoice.org
Format: Religious. **Founded:** June 1971. **Ad Rates:** Noncommercial. **URL:** http://www.rejoice.org.

8131 ■ WPNN-AM - 790
3801 N Pace Blvd.
Pensacola, FL 32505
Phone: (850)433-1141
Format: News. **Operating Hours**: Continuous. **Ad Rates:** Advertising accepted; rates available upon request. **URL:** http://www.talk790.com.

WRNE-AM - See Danbury, CT

8132 ■ WRRX-FM - 106.1
6565 NW St.
Pensacola, FL 32505
Phone: (850)478-6011
Fax: (850)478-3971
Format: Urban Contemporary. **Owner:** Cumulus Media Inc., 3280 Peachtree Rd. NW, Ste. 2300, Atlanta, GA 30305-2455, Ph: (404)949-0700, Fax: (404)949-0740. **Operating Hours**: Continuous. **Key Personnel:** James Alexander, CPBE, CBNT, Program Mgr.; Linda Moorer, Promotions Dir.; John Lewis, Gen. Sales Mgr., Mktg. Mgr.; Monte Saunders, Bus. Mgr. **Wattage**: 3,000. **Ad Rates:** Advertising accepted; rates available upon request. **URL:** http://www.mymagic106.com.

8133 ■ WSRE-TV - 23
1000 College Blvd.
Pensacola, FL 32504-8910
Phone: (850)484-1200
Fax: (850)484-1255
Free: 800-239-9773
Email: questions@wsre.org
Format: Public TV. **Networks:** Public Broadcasting Service (PBS). **Owner:** Pensacola State College, 1000 College Blvd., Pensacola, FL 32504, Ph: (850)484-1000, Fax: (850)595-8485, Free: 888-897-3605. **Founded:** 1967. **Operating Hours**: Continuous. **ADI**: Mobile, AL-Pensacola, FL. **Key Personnel:** James Roy, Traffic Mgr.; Sandy Cesaretti Ray, Dir. of Engg. **Wattage**: 1,000,000 ERP H. **Ad Rates:** Noncommercial. Underwriting available. **URL:** http://www.wsre.org.

8134 ■ WSWL-AM - 790
3801 N Pace Blvd.
Pensacola, FL 32505
Format: Talk. **Formerly**: WPFA-AM. **Operating Hours**: Continuous. **Key Personnel:** Don Schroeder, Contact. **Wattage**: 1,000. **Ad Rates:** $10-35 for 30 seconds; $20-40 for 60 seconds. **URL:** http://talk790.com.

8135 ■ WTKX-FM - 101.5
6485 N Pensacola Blvd.
Pensacola, FL 32505
Phone: (850)473-0400
Free: 888-357-7625
Format: Album-Oriented Rock (AOR). **Networks:** Independent. **Founded:** 1971. **Operating Hours**: Continuous; 100% local. **ADI**: Mobile, AL-Pensacola, FL. **Key Personnel:** Ronnie Bloodworth, Gen. Mgr., ronniebloodworth@iheartmedia.com. **Wattage**: 100,000. **Ad Rates:** Advertising accepted; rates available upon request. **URL:** http://www.tk101.com.

8136 ■ WUWF-FM - 88.1
11000 University Pky.
Pensacola, FL 32514
Phone: (850)474-2787
Free: 800-239-9893
Email: wuwf@wuwf.org
Format: Public Radio; News. **Networks:** National Public Radio (NPR); BBC World Service. **Owner:** University of West Florida, 11000 University Pky., Pensacola, FL 32514, Ph: (850)474-2000, Fax: (850)474-3360, Free: 866-931-4872. **Founded:** 1981. **Operating Hours**: Continuous. **ADI**: Mobile, AL-Pensacola, FL. **Key Personnel:** Lynne Marshall, Promotions Dir., lynne@wuwf.org; Sandra Averhart, News Dir., sandra@wuwf.org; Dave Dunwoody, Asst. Dir., dave@wuwf.org; Dale Riegle, Tech. Dir., dale@wuwf.org; Joe Vincenza, Prog. Dir., Station Mgr., joe@wuwf.org; Trish Allison, Contact, trish@wuwf.org; Enid Sisskin, Contact, enid@wuwf.org. **Local Programs**: *Acoustic Interlude*, Sunday 4:00 p.m. **Wattage**: 100,000 ERP. **Ad Rates:** Accepts Advertising. **URL:** http://www.wuwf.org.

8137 ■ WYCL-FM - 107.3
6485 Pensacola Blvd.
Pensacola, FL 32505
Phone: (850)473-0400
Format: Oldies. **Founded:** 1996. **Formerly**: WOWW-FM. **Operating Hours**: Continuous. **Key Personnel:** Melissa Sirorski, Contact, melissamack@clearchannel.com. **Wattage**: 100,000. **Ad Rates:** Advertising accepted; rates available upon request. Combined advertising rates available with WTKX-FM. **URL:** http://www.1073now.com//main.html.

8138 ■ WYCT-FM - 98.7
7251 Plantation Rd.
Pensacola, FL 32504
Phone: (850)494-2800
Fax: (850)494-0778
Free: 866-899-1987
Format: Country. **Key Personnel:** Mary Hoxeng, Gen. Mgr., mhoxeng@catcountry987.com; Chris Phillips, Sales Mgr., cphillips@catcountry987.com. **Ad Rates:** Noncommercial. **URL:** http://www.catcountry987.com.

PERRY

N FL. Taylor Co. 52 mi. SE of Tallahassee. Manufactures lumber, forestry products, marine products, pyrotechnics, snack foods. Commercial fishing. Stock and poultry farms. Tobacco, peanuts, potatoes.

8139 ■ Perry News-Herald
Perry Newspapers Inc.
123 S Jefferson St.
Perry, FL 32347
Phone: (850)584-5513
Fax: (850)838-1566
Publisher's E-mail: newsdesk@perrynewspapers.com
Community newspaper serving Taylor County. **Freq:** Weekly (Fri.). **Print Method:** Offset. **Cols./Page:** 6. **Col. Width:** 23 nonpareils. **Col. Depth:** 301 agate lines. **ISSN:** 0747--2358 (print). **Subscription Rates:** $35 Individuals; $49 Out of area; $18 Individuals 6 months; $25 Out of area 6 months. **URL:** http://perrynewspapers.com. **Ad Rates:** BW $896.55; PCI $10.29. **Remarks:** Accepts advertising. **Circ:** 5346.

8140 ■ WPRY-AM - 1400
872 Hwy. 27 E
Perry, FL 32347
Phone: (850)223-1400
Fax: (850)223-3501

Circulation: ★ = AAM; △ or • = BPA; ♦ = CAC; ❑ = VAC; ⊕ = PO Statement; ‡ = Publisher's Report; Boldface figures = sworn; Light figures = estimated.

Format: Oldies. **Simulcasts:** WNFK-FM. **Networks:** ABC. **Founded:** 1953. **Operating Hours:** Continuous. **Wattage:** 1,000. **Ad Rates:** Advertising accepted; rates available upon request.

PLANT CITY

WC FL. Hillsborough Co. 22 mi. E. of Tampa. Manufactures mobile homes, fertilizer, crates, boxes, and concrete blocks. Agriculture. Cattle, strawberries, citrus fruits, vegetables.

8141 ■ World Softball
International Softball Federation
1900 S Park Rd.
Plant City, FL 33563
Phone: (813)864-0100
Fax: (813)864-0105
Publisher's E-mail: info@isfsoftball.org
Magazine containing articles about the development of softball around the world and its recognition anywhere. Highlighting championships, games, interviews, news and notes. **Freq:** 3/year. **Subscription Rates:** $7.50 /issue. **Alt. Formats:** PDF. **URL:** http://www.isfsoftball.org/english/communication/magazine.asp. **Remarks:** Advertising not accepted. **Circ:** (Not Reported).

POLK CITY

8142 ■ The Water Skier
U.S.A. Water Ski
1251 Holy Cow Rd.
Polk City, FL 33868
Phone: (863)324-4341
Fax: (863)325-8259
Free: 800-533-2972
Publication E-mail: satkinson@usawaterski.org
Freq: 6/year. **Print Method:** Offset. **Trim Size:** 8 3/8 x 10 7/8. **Cols./Page:** 3. **Col. Width:** 13 picas. **Col. Depth:** 57 picas. **Key Personnel:** Lynn Novakofski, Graphic Designer; Scott Atkinson, Editor. **ISSN:** 0049--7002 (print). **Subscription Rates:** Included in membership. **Alt. Formats:** PDF. **URL:** http://usawaterski.org/pages/wsextramenu.htm. **Ad Rates:** $1850-2060; $1200-1340. BW $1340; 4C $2060; PCI $80; 4C $BW $. **Remarks:** Accepts advertising. **Circ:** ‡20000.

POMPANO BEACH

S FL. Broward Co. On Atlantic Ocean, 9 mi. N. of Fort Lauderdale. Resort area. Light industry and manufacturing. Manufactures boats, computer-related products, concrete products, lighting fixtures, venetian blinds, metal awnings. Agriculture. Citrus fruits, vegetables.

8143 ■ Margate/Coconut Creek Forum
Forum Publishing Group Inc.
1701 Green Rd., Ste. B
Pompano Beach, FL 33064
Fax: (954)429-1207
Free: 800-275-8820
Publisher's E-mail: sales@atlanticsyndication.com
Community newspaper (tabloid). **Freq:** Weekly (Thurs.). **Print Method:** Offset. **Cols./Page:** 6. **Col. Width:** 1 5/8 inches. **Col. Depth:** 16 inches. **Key Personnel:** Robert S. Morrison, Director; William Stinehart, Jr., Director; William A. Osborn, Director; Dudley S. Taft, Director; Jeffrey Chandler, Director; Dennis J. FitzSimons, Director; Enrique Hernandez, Jr., Director; Christopher J. Reyes, Director; Betsy D. Holden, Director; Roger Goodan, Director. **Subscription Rates:** Free. **URL:** http://sun-sentinel.com/sfl-fpg_margateforum-story.html. **Ad Rates:** PCI $20.80. **Remarks:** Accepts advertising. **Circ:** (Not Reported).

8144 ■ Media One
141 NW 16th St.
Box 1689
Pompano Beach, FL 33061
Phone: (305)946-7011
Fax: (305)782-5781
Owner: Continental Cablevision Inc., The Pilot House, Lewis Wharf, Boston, MA 02110, Ph: (617)742-9500. **Founded:** 1975. **Formerly:** Continental Cablevision. **Cities Served:** subscribing households 180,000.

8145 ■ WFTL-AM - 850
2100 Park Central N, Ste. 100
Pompano Beach, FL 33064
Phone: (954)315-1515
Fax: (954)315-1555
Format: News; Talk; Sports. **Owner:** James Crystal Radio, Inc., at above address. **Operating Hours:** Continuous. **Ad Rates:** Advertising accepted; rates available upon request. **URL:** http://www.850wftl.com.

PONCE

8146 ■ Spanish Broadcasting System Inc.
Pablo Raul Alarcon Media Ctr., 7007 NW 77th Ave.
Miami, FL 33166
Phone: (305)441-6901
Fax: (305)883-3375
Email: sbscontact@sbscorporate.com
Format comprises ethnic programming. **Format:** News. **Founded:** 1983. **Key Personnel:** Raul Alarcon, Jr., CEO, President, Chairman; Joseph A. Garcia, CFO, Sr. Exec. VP, Chief Adm. Ofc., Secretary. **Ad Rates:** Advertising accepted; rates available upon request. **URL:** http://www.spanishbroadcasting.com.

PONTE VEDRA BEACH

8147 ■ Actuarial Digest
Actuarial Digest
PO Box 1127
Ponte Vedra Beach, FL 32004
Trade magazine for actuarial professionals. **Freq:** Quarterly. **Print Method:** Web offset. **Trim Size:** 8 1/2 x 11. **Key Personnel:** Gene Hubbard, Editor. **Subscription Rates:** $24 Individuals U.S. only; $6 Single issue. **URL:** http://www.theactuarialdigest.com. **Ad Rates:** BW $1,995; 4C $2,695. **Remarks:** Accepts advertising. **Circ:** Controlled 15000.

8148 ■ Digital Output
Digital Output
6000A Sawgrass Village Ctr., Ste. 1
Ponte Vedra Beach, FL 32082-5061
Trade magazine covering electronic communications and digital equipment for commercial printers, specialty printers, advertising agencies and others. **Freq:** Monthly. **Key Personnel:** Cassandra Carnes, Associate Editor; Dana Bussiere, Art Director. **URL:** http://www.digitaloutput.net; http://rockportpubs.com/trade-publications. **Ad Rates:** BW $4430; 4C $5440; PCI $250. **Remarks:** Advertising accepted; rates available upon request. **Circ:** △22500.

PORT CHARLOTTE

Charlotte Co. (SW). 2 m NW of Punta Gorda.

8149 ■ The Charlotte Sun Herald
Sun Coast Media Group Inc.
23170 Harborview Rd.
Port Charlotte, FL 33980
Phone: (941)206-1000
Fax: (941)629-2085
General newspaper. **Freq:** Daily. **Print Method:** Offset. **Trim Size:** 22 x 27 1/2. **Cols./Page:** 6. **Col. Width:** 2 1/16 inches. **Col. Depth:** 290 1/2 agate lines. **Key Personnel:** David Dunn-Rankin, President, Publisher, phone: (941)206-1003; Derek Dunn-Rankin, Chief Executive Officer, phone: (941)206-1001; Chris Porter, Editor, phone: (941)206-1134; John Hackworth, Managing Editor, phone: (941)206-1147. **Subscription Rates:** $232.93 Individuals 52 weeks; $133.19 Individuals 26 weeks; $74.02 Individuals 13 weeks. **URL:** http://www.yoursun.com/csp/mediapool/sites/SunNews/PortCharlotte/index.csp. **Ad Rates:** SAU $9.60. **Remarks:** Accepts advertising. **Circ:** (Not Reported).

8150 ■ North Port Sun Herald
Sun Coast Media Group Inc.
23170 Harborview Rd.
Port Charlotte, FL 33980
Phone: (941)206-1000
Fax: (941)629-2085
Community newspaper. **Freq:** Daily. **Print Method:** Offset. **Cols./Page:** 6. **Col. Width:** 2 1/16 inches. **Col. Depth:** 21 inches. **Key Personnel:** David Dunn-Rankin, President, Publisher. **Subscription Rates:** $400.40 Individuals 52 weeks; $200.20 Individuals 26 weeks; $100.10 Individuals 13 weeks. **URL:** http://www.yoursun.com; http://yoursun.com/csp/mediapool/sites/SunNews/NorthPort/index.csp. **Ad Rates:** BW $831.60; 4C $1,061.60; SAU $7.75. **Remarks:** Accepts advertising. **Circ:** Paid 3200, Free 5000.

8151 ■ WBCG-FM - 98.9
24100 Tiseo Blvd., No. 10
Port Charlotte, FL 33980
Phone: (941)206-9890
Format: Adult Contemporary. **URL:** http://www.989myfm.com.

8152 ■ WKII-AM - 1070
24100 Tiseo Blvd., Ste. 10
Port Charlotte, FL 33980
Phone: (941)206-1188
Format: News; Music of Your Life. **Networks:** CNN Radio. **Owner:** Clear Channel Communications, Inc., San Antonio, TX, Ph: (214)866-8000, Fax: (214)866-8008. **Founded:** 1986. **Key Personnel:** Steve Johnson, Gen. Sales Mgr. **Wattage:** 1,800 KW. **Ad Rates:** $11-40 per unit. **URL:** http://1070nbcsports.iheart.com.

8153 ■ W17CK - 17
PO Box A
Santa Ana, CA 92711
Phone: (714)832-2950
Free: 888-731-1000
Owner: Trinity Broadcasting Network Inc., PO Box A, Santa Ana, CA 92711, Ph: (714)832-2950, Free: 888-731-1000. **URL:** http://www.tbn.org.

8154 ■ WVIJ-FM - 91.7
3279 Sherwood Rd.
Port Charlotte, FL 33980
Phone: (941)624-5000
Fax: (775)243-0586
Email: wvij@wvij.com
Format: Contemporary Christian; Religious. **Networks:** USA Radio. **Owner:** Port Charlotte Educational Broadcasting Foundation Inc., 3279 Sherwood Rd., Port Charlotte, FL 33980. **Founded:** 1987. **Operating Hours:** Continuous; 25% network, 75% local. **Key Personnel:** Dan Kolenda, Contact. **Wattage:** 2,000. **Ad Rates:** Noncommercial. **URL:** http://wvij.com/www.wvij.com/Home.html.

PORT ORANGE

E FL. Volusia Co. 10 mi. S. of Daytona Beach.

8155 ■ The Journal of the Bromeliad Society
Bromeliad Society International
c/o Jay Thurrott, President
713 Breckenridge Dr.
Port Orange, FL 32127
Publication E-mail: editor@bsi.org
Publications on botany and gardening. **Freq:** Bimonthly. **Print Method:** Offset. **Trim Size:** 6 x 9. **Key Personnel:** David H. Benzing, Advisor; Gregory K. Brown, Advisor. **ISSN:** 0090--8738 (print). **Subscription Rates:** Included in membership Free. **URL:** http://bsi.org/publications/journal.html. **Formerly:** Bromeliad Society Journal. **Ad Rates:** BW $125, Full page - One issue; 4C $200, Full page - One issue; BW $70, Half page - One issue; 4C $100, Half page - One issue; BW $45, Quarter page - One issue; 4C $60, Quarter page - One issue; BW $25, Eighth page - One issue; 4C $40, Eighth page - One issue. **Remarks:** Accepts advertising. **Circ:** Combined 1700, 1600.

8156 ■ WJLH-FM - 90.3
c/o Cornerstone Ministry
4295 Ridgewood Ave.
Port Orange, FL 32127
Phone: (386)756-9094
Fax: (386)760-7107
Format: Religious. **Founded:** 1989. **Key Personnel:** Bill Powell, Gen. Mgr., President. **Ad Rates:** Advertising accepted; rates available upon request. **URL:** http://www.cornerstoneministry.org.

8157 ■ WJLU-FM - 89.7
c/o Cornerstone Ministry
4295 Ridgewood Ave.
Port Orange, FL 32127
Format: Religious. **Founded:** Oct. 07, 1989. **Key Personnel:** Bill Powell, Gen. Mgr., President. **Ad Rates:** Noncommercial. **URL:** http://www3.wjlu.org:81.

8158 ■ WMFJ-AM - 1450
4295 Ridgewood Ave.
Port Orange, FL 32127
Phone: (386)756-9094
Free: 800-756-9094
Format: Contemporary Christian. **Founded:** 1935. **Operating Hours:** Continuous. **Key Personnel:** Bill Powell,

Gen. Mgr; William A. Leisner, Contact. **Wattage:** 1,000. **Ad Rates:** $5-12 for 30 seconds; $7-15 for 60 seconds. **URL:** http://wjlu.org.

PORT RICHEY

Pasco Co. Pasco Co. (WC). 2 m W of Land O'Lakes.

8159 ■ Suncoast News
Suncoast News
8609 Regency Park Blvd.
Port Richey, FL 34668
Phone: (727)815-1000
Community newspaper. **Freq:** Semiweekly (Wed. and Sat.). **Print Method:** Offset. **Cols./Page:** 5. **Col. Width:** 20 nonpareils. **Col. Depth:** 238 agate lines. **Key Personnel:** Robert Hibbs, Editor. **URL:** http://suncoastnews.com. **Remarks:** Advertising accepted; rates available upon request. **Circ:** Wed. ■ **89452**, Sat. ■ **115284**.

8160 ■ WLPJ-FM - 91.5
6214 Springer Dr.
Port Richey, FL 34668
Phone: (727)848-9150
Fax: (727)848-1233
Format: Contemporary Christian. **Simulcasts:** WJIS-Sarasota. **Owner:** Radio Training Network, PO Box 7217, Lakeland, FL 33813, Ph: (863)644-3464. **Founded:** 1985. **Operating Hours:** Continuous. **Key Personnel:** Johanna Antes, Director; Carmen Brown, Dir. of Programs; Jeff MacFarlane, Gen. Mgr.; Karen Rutherford, Office Mgr; Bill Harrier, Contact. **Wattage:** 16,500. **Ad Rates:** Noncommercial. **URL:** http://www.thejoyfm.com.

PORT SAINT JOE

NW FL. Gulf Co. On Gulf of Mexico, 37 mi. SE of Panama City. Resort. Pine timber. Manufactures paper, sawmill products, and chemicals.

8161 ■ The Star
Freedom Communications Inc.
Port City Shopping Ctr.
135 Hwy. 98
Port Saint Joe, FL 32456
Phone: (850)227-1278
Publication E-mail: thestar@pcnh.com
Newspaper. **Founded:** 1937. **Freq:** Weekly. **Print Method:** Offset. **Trim Size:** 6 x 21. **Cols./Page:** 6. **Col. Width:** 1.8125 inches. **Col. Depth:** 308 agate lines. **USPS:** 518-880. **Subscription Rates:** $23 Individuals in County; $33 Out of area; $15 Out of country. **URL:** http://www.starfl.com. **Ad Rates:** PCI $7.90. **Remarks:** Accepts advertising. **Circ:** ‡5075.

8162 ■ WOCY-FM - 106.5
200-B Reid Ave.
Port Saint Joe, FL 32456
Phone: (850)705-1065
Fax: (850)670-5686
Owner: Oyster Radio Inc., at above address. **Founded:** 1988. **Formerly:** WOYS-FM. **Wattage:** 100,000. **Ad Rates:** Noncommercial.

PORT SAINT LUCIE

8163 ■ WCZR-FM
3771 SE Jennings Rd.
Port Saint Lucie, FL 34952
Phone: (561)616-6600
Fax: (561)616-6677
Format: Talk. **Key Personnel:** Mark S. Bass, Gen. Mgr. **Wattage:** 4,200 ERP. **URL:** http://wzzr.iheart.com.

8164 ■ WFLM-FM - 104.7
6803 S Federal Hwy.
Port Saint Lucie, FL 34952
Phone: (772)460-9356
Format: Blues. **Ad Rates:** Noncommercial. **URL:** http://www.1047theflame.com.

8165 ■ WIRA-AM - 1400
6803 S Federal Hwy.
Port Saint Lucie, FL 34952
Phone: (772)461-6622
Format: Religious; Information. **Owner:** Midway Broadcasting Corp., 1000 E 87th St., Chicago, IL 60619, Ph: (773)721-2271. **Founded:** 1946. **Operating Hours:** Continuous. **Wattage:** 1,000. **Ad Rates:** $28-32 for 30 seconds; $38-45 for 60 seconds. **URL:** http://wira1400am.com.

8166 ■ WLYX-FM - 96.7
595 SE Nome Dr.
Port Saint Lucie, FL 34984
Phone: (770)491-7748
Format: Adult Contemporary; Urban Contemporary; Blues. **Operating Hours:** Continuous. **Ad Rates:** Advertising accepted; rates available upon request.

8167 ■ WQOL-FM - 103.7
3771 SE Jennings Rd.
Port Saint Lucie, FL 34952
Phone: (772)335-9300
Free: 800-486-0103
Format: Oldies; News. **Founded:** 1986. **Operating Hours:** Continuous. **ADI:** West Palm Beach-Ft. Pierce-Vero Beach, FL. **Key Personnel:** John Hunt, Gen. Mgr. **Wattage:** 50,000 ERP. **Ad Rates:** Advertising accepted; rates available upon request. **URL:** http://oldies1037fm.iheart.com.

8168 ■ WSYR-FM - 94.7
PO Box 0093
Port Saint Lucie, FL 34985
Phone: (772)335-9300
Format: Adult Contemporary. **Key Personnel:** Katerina Perez, Contact. **URL:** http://www.clearchannel.com.

PUNTA GORDA

SW FL. Charlotte Co. On Charlotte Harbor Bay, 23 mi. NW of Fort Myers. Retirement Area. Yachting and fishing resort. Agriculture.

8169 ■ WCCF-AM - 1580
4810 Deltona Dr.
Punta Gorda, FL 33950
Phone: (941)206-1188
Format: Talk; Full Service. **Owner:** Clear Channel Communications Inc., at above address, Ph: (210)822-2828, Fax: (210)822-2299. **Founded:** 1961. **Operating Hours:** Continuous. **Wattage:** 1,250. **Ad Rates:** Advertising accepted; rates available upon request. $25.00 for 60 seconds. **URL:** http://www.wccfam.com.

8170 ■ WIKX-FM
4810 Deltona Dr.
Punta Gorda, FL 33950
Phone: (941)639-1188
Fax: (941)639-6742
Free: 800-749-9290
Format: Country. **Networks:** ABC. **Founded:** 1982. **Formerly:** WQLM-FM. **Key Personnel:** Michael Moody, Gen. Mgr. **Wattage:** 100,000 ERP. **Ad Rates:** $45.00 per unit. **URL:** http://kixcountry929.iheart.com.

8171 ■ WRXY-TV - 49
40000 Horseshoe Rd.
Punta Gorda, FL 33982
Phone: (293)543-7200
Fax: (293)543-6800
Format: Commercial TV. **Operating Hours:** Continuous. **Key Personnel:** Ronald Davis, Contact. **Wattage:** 1,000,000 H. **URL:** http://www.ctn10.com.

QUINCY

NW FL. Gadsden Co. 26 mi. W. of Tallahassee. SManufactures wire, lumber, furniture, tobacco. Bottling works. Diversified agriculture.

8172 ■ Gadsden County Times
Gadsden County Times
15 S Madison St.
Quincy, FL 32351-3137
Phone: (850)627-7649
Fax: (850)627-7191
Publisher's E-mail: gm@gadcotimes.com
Community newspaper. **Freq:** Weekly (Thurs.). **Print Method:** Offset. **Cols./Page:** 6. **Col. Width:** 26 nonpareils. **Col. Depth:** 285 agate lines. **Key Personnel:** Cheri Harris, Editor. **Subscription Rates:** $30 Individuals print and online. **URL:** http://www.gadcotimes.com. **Ad Rates:** GLR $.42; BW $704.34; 4C $854.34; PCI $5.74. **Remarks:** Accepts advertising. **Circ:** 6500.

WGWD-FM - See Gretna

RIVERVIEW

Hillsborough Co. (WC). 8 m SE of Tampa.

8173 ■ Sources: The Journal of Underwater Education
National Association of Underwater Instructors
9030 Camden Field Pkwy.
Riverview, FL 33578
Phone: (813)628-6284
Fax: (813)628-8253
Free: 800-553-6284
Publisher's E-mail: nauihq@naui.org
Scuba diving magazine covering policy, standards, procedures, diver education, and business of diver education. **Freq:** Quarterly. **Print Method:** Offset. **Trim Size:** 8 1/2 x 11. **Cols./Page:** 3. **Col. Width:** 14 picas. **Col. Depth:** 9 3/4 inches. **Key Personnel:** Peter Oliver, Editor; Jim Bram, President. **ISSN:** 3596--1806 (print). **Subscription Rates:** $107 Nonmembers; Included in membership. **URL:** http://www.naui.org. **Formerly:** NDA News. **Ad Rates:** BW $885; 4C $1,635. **Remarks:** Accepts advertising. **Circ:** Paid ‡14000, Controlled ‡1000.

ROCKLEDGE

8174 ■ Clinical Neuropathology
Dustri-Verlag Inc.
Swiss Point Office Bldg.
2990 S Fiske Blvd.
Rockledge, FL 32955
Phone: (321)960-9342
Fax: (321)414-0219
Publisher's E-mail: info@dustri.com
Publication covering recent developments in clinical neuropathology. **Freq:** Bimonthly. **ISSN:** 0722--5091 (print). **Subscription Rates:** $306 Individuals print or online; $378 Institutions print or online; $262 Individuals print. **URL:** http://www.dustri.com/nc/journals-in-english/mag/clinical-neuropathology.html. **Circ:** (Not Reported).

8175 ■ IMSA Journal
International Municipal Signal Association
597 Haverty Ct., Ste. 100
Rockledge, FL 32955
Phone: (321)392-0500
Fax: (321)806-1400
Free: 800-723-4672
Public safety field. **Freq:** 6/year. **Print Method:** Offset. **Trim Size:** 8 1/2 x 11. **Cols./Page:** 3. **Col. Width:** 28 nonpareils. **Col. Depth:** 140 agate lines. **Key Personnel:** Marilyn Lawrence, Editor. **URL:** http://www.imsasafety.org/journal/ma10.htm. **Ad Rates:** BW $440; 4C $920. **Remarks:** Accepts advertising. **Circ:** 3220.

ROTONDA WEST

8176 ■ MacAlasdair Clan Journal
Clan McAlister of America
c/o Robert W. McAlister, Membership Chairman
208 Annapolis Ln.
Rotonda West, FL 33947
Phone: (941)698-1112
Publisher's E-mail: president@clancalister.org
Freq: Quarterly. **Subscription Rates:** $10 Individuals back issues. **URL:** http://www.clanmcalister.org/backissues.html. **Remarks:** Advertising not accepted. **Circ:** (Not Reported).

RUSKIN

8177 ■ The Observer News
The Observer News
210 Woodland Estates Blvd. SW
Ruskin, FL 33570
Phone: (813)645-3111
Fax: (813)645-4118
Newspaper. **Freq:** Weekly (Thurs.). **Print Method:** Offset. **Cols./Page:** 5. **Col. Width:** 1 7/8 inches. **Col. Depth:** 16 INS. **Key Personnel:** Wes Mullins, Publisher. **URL:** http://www.observernews.net. **Formerly:** The Shopper Observer News. **Ad Rates:** GLR $9; BW $600; 4C $750; PCI $15. **Remarks:** Accepts advertising. **Circ:** Free 21000.

8178 ■ The Sun
Sunbelt Newspapers Inc.
3036 College Ave.
Ruskin, FL 33570
Phone: (813)645-6858
Fax: (813)645-1297
Community newspaper. **Founded:** 1922. **Freq:** Weekly (Wed.). **Print Method:** Offset. **Trim Size:** 5 x 15. **Cols./**

Circulation: ★ = AAM; △ or • = BPA; ♦ = CAC; ❑ = VAC; ⊕ = PO Statement; ‡ = Publisher's Report; Boldface figures = sworn; Light figures = estimated.

Page: 6 and 5. **Col. Width:** 9 picas and 20 nonpareils. **Col. Depth:** 301 and 238 agate lines. **Key Personnel:** B.W. Clements, Editor. **Subscription Rates:** Free. **Formerly:** Sunbelt Publilshing Co. **Ad Rates:** GLR $.70; BW $638; 4C $938; SAU $4.95; PCI $4.95; GLR $2.87; BW $1,021.50; 4C $1,271.50; PCI $13.60. **Remarks:** Accepts advertising. **Circ:** ‡5000.

SAINT AUGUSTINE

NE FL. St. Johns Co. On Matanzas Bay, 38 mi. SE of Jacksonville. Oldest permanent settlement in North America, founded 1565. Winter and summer resort.

8179 ■ Flagler College Magazine
Flagler College
74 King St.
Saint Augustine, FL 32084
Phone: (904)829-6481
Free: 800-304-4208
Publisher's E-mail: admissions@flagler.edu
An alumni magazine for Flagler College. **Freq:** Semiannual. **Subscription Rates:** Free to qualified subscribers. **URL:** http://www.flagler.edu/news-events/flagler-college-magazine/flagler-college-magazine. **Circ:** (Not Reported).

8180 ■ The Florida Anthropologist
Florida Anthropological Society
c/o Pat Balanzategui, Secretary
PO Box 1135
Saint Augustine, FL 32085
Journal focusing on anthropology and archaeology. **Freq:** Quarterly. **Print Method:** Letterpress and offset. **Trim Size:** 8 1/2 x 11. **Cols./Page:** 2. **Col. Width:** 56 nonpareils. **Col. Depth:** 102 agate lines. **Key Personnel:** Jeffrey P. Du Vernay, PhD, Editor; Julie Rogers Saccente, Editor. **ISSN:** 0015--3893 (print). **Alt. Formats:** PDF. **URL:** http://fasweb.org/publications. **Ad Rates:** BW $100. **Remarks:** Accepts advertising. **Circ:** ‡950.

8181 ■ The National Culinary Review
American Culinary Federation
180 Center Place Way
Saint Augustine, FL 32095
Fax: (904)824-4468
Free: 800-624-9458
Publisher's E-mail: acf@acfchefs.net
Trade magazine covering food and cooking. Includes articles on food, drink, and menu trends; recipes; personal and professional development; and management. **Freq:** 10/year. **Print Method:** Heat set web offset. **Trim Size:** 8 3/8 x 10 7/8. **Key Personnel:** Kay Orde, Editor. **ISSN:** 0747--7716 (print). **Subscription Rates:** $60 Individuals print, U.S.; $200 Individuals print, other countries; $20 Individuals online. **URL:** http://www.acfchefs.org/Content/NavigationMenu2/About/Media/Publications/default.htm; http://www.acfchefs.org/ACF/About/Media/Publications/ACF/About/Media/Publications/. **Ad Rates:** BW $3,355; 4C $4,355. **Remarks:** Accepts advertising. **Circ:** (Not Reported).

8182 ■ The St. Augustine Record
Morris Communications Company L.L.C.
One News Pl.
Saint Augustine, FL 32086
Phone: (904)829-6562
Fax: (904)819-3557
Publisher's E-mail: allaccessprogram@morris.com
General newspaper. **Freq:** Daily. **Print Method:** Offset. **Cols./Page:** 6. **Col. Width:** 12.5 picas. **Col. Depth:** 21 inches. **Key Personnel:** Craig Richardson, Editor. **URL:** http://staugustine.com; http://www.morris.com/divisions/daily-newspapers/st-augustine-record. **Remarks:** Accepts advertising. **Circ:** Mon.-Fri. ‡19000.

8183 ■ Sound Truth Magazine
Clearer Vision Ministries
251B San Marco Ave.
Saint Augustine, FL 32084
Phone: (904)201-1358
Publisher's E-mail: info@clearervisionministries.org
Freq: Bimonthly. **URL:** http://www.clearervisionministries.org/ministry.html. **Mailing address:** PO Box 297, Saint Augustine, FL 32085-0297. **Remarks:** Accepts advertising. **Circ:** 100.

8184 ■ WAOC-AM - 1420
567 Lewis Point Road Ext.
Saint Augustine, FL 32086-5222
Format: Sports; Information. **Networks:** CBS. **Owner:** Shull Broadcasting Co., Inc., at above address, Ph: (904)797-4444, Fax: (904)797-3446. **Founded:** 1957. **Operating Hours:** 6:00 a.m. - 1:30 a.m. Monday - Friday, 9:00 a.m. - 10:00 a.m Saturday, 10:00 a.m. - Noon Sunday. **Wattage:** 2,000. **Ad Rates:** $14-18 for 60 seconds. Combined advertising rates available with WFOY-AM. **URL:** http://965sports.com.

8185 ■ WFCF-FM - 88.5
PO Box 1027
Saint Augustine, FL 32085-1027
Phone: (904)819-6449
Email: wfcf@flagler.edu
Format: Educational. **Owner:** Flagler College, 74 King St., Saint Augustine, FL 32084, Ph: (904)829-6481, Free: 800-304-4208. **Operating Hours:** Continuous. **Key Personnel:** Daniel O. McCook, Station Mgr. **Wattage:** 10,000. **Ad Rates:** Noncommercial. **URL:** http://www.flagler.edu/campus-life/campus-facilities/wfcf.html.

8186 ■ WFOY-AM - 1240
527 Lewis Point Rd.
Saint Augustine, FL 32086
Phone: (904)797-1955
Founded: 1936. **Wattage:** 500. **Ad Rates:** $14-18 for 60 seconds. **Mailing address:** PO Box 3847, Saint Augustine, FL 32085.

SAINT GEORGE ISLAND

8187 ■ Journal of the National Collegiate Honors Council
National Collegiate Honors Council
c/o Ada Long, Ed.
316 Cook St.
Saint George Island, FL 32328-2453
Phone: (850)927-3776
Publisher's E-mail: nchc@unl.edu
Scholarly journal covering honors education. **Freq:** Semiannual. **Print Method:** Perfect Binding. **Trim Size:** 6 x 9. **Key Personnel:** Ada Long, Editor; Dail Mullins, Jr., Editor. **ISSN:** 1559- 0151 (print). **Subscription Rates:** $25 Members; $45 Nonmembers. **Alt. Formats:** PDF. **URL:** http://nchchonors.org/nchc-publications; http://digitalcommons.unl.edu/nchcjournal. **Remarks:** Advertising not accepted. **Circ:** Non-paid 990.

SAINT PETERSBURG

WC FL. Pinellas Co. On Pinellas Peninsula between Tampa Bay and Gulf of Mexico, 22 mi. SW of Tampa. Eckerd College; Saint Petersburg Junior College. Tourist resort. Yachting and sport-fishing center. Ships fruit and vegetables.

8188 ■ The duPont Registry: A Buyer's Gallery of Fine Automobiles
duPont Publishing Inc.
3051 Tech Dr.
Saint Petersburg, FL 33716
Phone: (727)573-9339
Free: 800-233-1731
Glossy, full-color magazine featuring the finest classic, luxury, and exotic cars in the world for sale. **Freq:** Monthly. **Print Method:** Offset. **Trim Size:** 8 x 10 7/8. **Key Personnel:** Ron Barreto, Contact. **ISSN:** 0890--362X (print). **Subscription Rates:** $49.95 Individuals 12 issues; $79.95 Individuals 24 issues; $99.95 Individuals 36 issues. **URL:** http://www.dupontregistry.com. **Remarks:** Accepts advertising. **Circ:** Paid 105037.

8189 ■ The duPont Registry: A Buyer's Gallery of Fine Boats
duPont Publishing Inc.
3051 Tech Dr.
Saint Petersburg, FL 33716
Phone: (727)573-9339
Free: 800-233-1731
Magazine featuring worldwide luxury homes for sale. **Freq:** Monthly. **Print Method:** Web Offset. **Trim Size:** 8 x 10 7/8. **Cols./Page:** 2. **ISSN:** 1091--6482 (print). **Subscription Rates:** $15.95 Individuals; $26.95 Two years. **URL:** http://www.dupontregistry.com/boats. **Ad Rates:** 4C $4,995. **Remarks:** Accepts advertising. **Circ:** Paid 22000, Controlled 28000.

8190 ■ The duPont Registry: A Buyer's Gallery of Fine Homes
duPont Publishing Inc.
3051 Tech Dr.
Saint Petersburg, FL 33716
Phone: (727)573-9339
Free: 800-233-1731
Magazine featuring worldwide luxury sail and sport boats for sale. **Freq:** Bimonthly. **Print Method:** Web offset. **Trim Size:** 8 x 10 7/8. **Cols./Page:** 2. **ISSN:** 1091--6474 (print). **Subscription Rates:** $29.95 Individuals; $49.95 Two years. **URL:** http://www.dupontregistry.com/homes. **Remarks:** Accepts advertising. **Circ:** Paid 16000, Controlled 38000.

8191 ■ Fish and Wildlife Research Institute Technical Reports
Florida Fish and Wildlife Conservation Commission
Fish and Wildlife Research Institute
100 8th Ave. SE
Saint Petersburg, FL 33701-5020
Phone: (727)896-8626
Scientific journal covering marine resource topics, especially marine resource management. **Freq:** Irregular. **Print Method:** Sheetfed offset. **Trim Size:** 8 1/2 x 11. **Cols./Page:** 2. **Col. Width:** 20 picas. **Col. Depth:** 54 picas. **ISSN:** 1092--194X (print). **URL:** http://myfwc.com/research/publications/scientific/technical-reports. **Formerly:** Florida Marine Research Institute Technical Reports. **Remarks:** Advertising not accepted. **Circ:** Non-paid 600.

8192 ■ Florida Marine Research Publications
Florida Fish and Wildlife Conservation Commission
Fish and Wildlife Research Institute
100 8th Ave. SE
Saint Petersburg, FL 33701-5020
Phone: (727)896-8626
Scientific journal covering marine resource topics. **Freq:** Irregular. **Print Method:** Sheetfed Offset. **Trim Size:** 8 1/2 x 11. **Cols./Page:** 2. **Col. Width:** 20 picas. **Col. Depth:** 54 picas. **Key Personnel:** James F. Quinn, Jr., Contact; Llyn French, Contact. **ISSN:** 0095--0157 (print). **Alt. Formats:** PDF. **URL:** http://myfwc.com/research; http://myfwc.com/research/publications. **Remarks:** Advertising not accepted. **Circ:** Non-paid 600.

8193 ■ Florida Trend
Trend Magazines Inc.
490 1st Ave. S, 8th Fl.
Saint Petersburg, FL 33701-4223
Phone: (727)821-5800
Fax: (727)822-5083
Publication E-mail: custrelations@floridatrend.com
Business. **Freq:** Monthly. **Print Method:** Offset. **Trim Size:** 8 1/8 x 10 7/8. **Cols./Page:** 3. **Col. Width:** 13.5 picas. **Col. Depth:** 60 agate lines. **Key Personnel:** Mark R. Howard, Executive Editor; Lynn Lotkowictz, Director, Advertising, phone: (727)892-2612; Andrew P. Corty, President, Publisher. **ISSN:** 0015--4326 (print). **Subscription Rates:** $24.98 Individuals print and online; $14.98 Individuals print or online. **Online:** Trend Magazines Inc. Trend Magazines Inc. **URL:** http://floridatrend.com. **Remarks:** Advertising accepted; rates available upon request. **Circ:** ‡58829.

8194 ■ Grand Magazine
Grand Media L.L.C.
4791 Baywood Point Dr. S
Saint Petersburg, FL 33711
Free: 866-327-9039
Publisher's E-mail: info@grandmagazine.com
Magazine covering affluent neighborhoods in Waterloo region, including features on local cuisine, decor, fashion, fitness, and travel. **Key Personnel:** Cristine Crosby, Founder, Publisher. **URL:** http://www.grandmagazine.com/news. **Remarks:** Accepts advertising. **Circ:** (Not Reported).

8195 ■ Journal of Global Drug Policy and Practice
Institute on Global Drug Policy
Journal of Global Drug Policy and Practice
2600 9th St. N, Ste. 200
Saint Petersburg, FL 33704-2744
Phone: (727)828-0211
Fax: (727)828-0210
Publisher's E-mail: info@globaldrugpolicy.org
Journal publishing articles on drug policy issues and articles on providing drug policy recommendations. **Freq:** Quarterly. **Key Personnel:** Eric Voth, Editor. **ISSN:** 1934--4708 (print). **URL:** http://www.globaldrugpolicy.

org. **Remarks:** Accepts advertising. **Circ:** (Not Reported).

8196 ■ Journal of Mass Media Ethics: Exploring Questions of Media Morality
Routledge Journals Taylor & Francis Group
c/o Jay Black, Founding Co-Ed., Emeritus
Journalism & Media Studies
University of South Florida
140 Seventh Ave. S
Saint Petersburg, FL 33701-5016
Journal focusing on mass media ethics and morality among academic and professional groups. **Freq:** Quarterly. **Key Personnel:** Wendy N. Wyatt, Editor; Jay Black, Editor, Founder; Lee Wilkins, Board Member. **ISSN:** 0890--0523 (print). **Subscription Rates:** $68 Individuals print only; $71 Individuals print and online; $237 Individuals online only. **URL:** http://www.tandfonline.com/toc/hmme20/current. **Ad Rates:** BW $300. **Remarks:** Accepts advertising. **Circ:** (Not Reported).

8197 ■ Memoirs of the Hourglass Cruises
Florida Fish and Wildlife Conservation Commission
Fish and Wildlife Research Institute
100 8th Ave. SE
Saint Petersburg, FL 33701-5020
Phone: (727)896-8626
Scientific journal covering marine resource and marine research topics. **Freq:** Irregular. **Print Method:** Sheetfed Offset. **Trim Size:** 8 1/4 x 10 3/4. **Cols./Page:** 1. **Col. Width:** 39 picas. **Col. Depth:** 54 picas. **ISSN:** 0085--0683 (print). **URL:** http://myfwc.com/research/publications/scientific/hourglass-cruises. **Remarks:** Advertising not accepted. **Circ:** Non-paid 600.

8198 ■ Motorcycle Events Magazine
Motorcycle Events Association
3221 Tyrone Blvd. N
Saint Petersburg, FL 33710
Phone: (727)343-1049
Fax: (727)344-0327
Free: 866-203-4485
Publication E-mail: info@motorcycleevents.com
Consumer magazine covering motorcycle events and travel in the U.S. for motorcyclists. **Freq:** Quarterly. **ISSN:** 1099--0100 (print). **URL:** http://www.motorcycleevents.com/magazine. **Remarks:** Advertising accepted; rates available upon request. **Circ:** Controlled 100000.

8199 ■ tbt: Tampa Bay Times
Times Publishing Co.
490 First Ave. S
Saint Petersburg, FL 33701
Phone: (727)893-8111
Fax: (727)893-8675
Free: 800-333-7505
Publisher's E-mail: custserv@sptimes.com
Community newspaper. **Freq:** Daily. **Key Personnel:** Joe DeLuca, Publisher; Neville Green, Editor; Dawn Phillips, Manager, Advertising. **Subscription Rates:** Free. **URL:** http://www.tampabay.com/tbt/. **Mailing address:** PO Box 1121, Saint Petersburg, FL 33731-1121. **Remarks:** Accepts advertising. **Circ:** Mon.-Thurs. ♦**67471**, Fri. ♦**102133**.

8200 ■ Women's Running
Wet Dog Media Inc.
1499 Beach Dr. SE, Ste. B
Saint Petersburg, FL 33701
Phone: (727)502-9202
Fax: (727)824-0859
Magazine covering women's fitness and sports. **Freq:** 10/year. **Key Personnel:** Dawna Stone, President, Publisher. **Subscription Rates:** $19.95 Individuals U.S.; $33.95 Canada; $54.95 Elsewhere includes postage. **URL:** http://womensrunning.competitor.com. **Formerly:** Her Sports. **Remarks:** Accepts advertising. **Circ:** (Not Reported).

8201 ■ WDUV-FM - 105.5
11300 4th St. N, Ste. 300
Saint Petersburg, FL 33716
Phone: (727)579-2000
Fax: (727)579-2662
Free: 888-723-9388
Email: 1055comments@coxtampa.com
Format: Adult Contemporary. **Owner:** Cox Radio Inc., 6205 Peachtree Dunwood Rd., Atlanta, GA 30328-4524, Ph: (678)645-0000, Fax: (678)645-5002. **Founded:** 1963. **Operating Hours**: Continuous. **ADI**: Tampa-St. Petersburg (Lakeland, Sarasota), FL. **Wattage**: 100,000. **Ad Rates:** $125-250 for 60 seconds. **URL:** http://www.wduv.com.

8202 ■ WECX-FM - 99.9
4200 54th Ave. S
Saint Petersburg, FL 33711
Phone: (813)864-8419
Email: wecx@eckerd.edu
Format: Alternative/New Music/Progressive. **Founded:** 1977. **Operating Hours**: Continuous. **Ad Rates:** Noncommercial. **URL:** http://wecx.eckerd.edu.

8203 ■ WFTI-FM - 91.7
290 Hegenberger Rd.
Oakland, CA 94621
Free: 800-543-1495
Email: info@familyradio.org
Format: Religious. **Owner:** Family Station, Inc., 1350 S Loop Rd., Ste. 130, Alameda, CA 94502. **Founded:** 1958. **Ad Rates:** Advertising accepted; rates available upon request. **URL:** http://www.familyradio.org.

WHGN-FM - See Crystal River

8204 ■ WHPT-FM - 102.5
11300 Fourth St. N, Ste. 300
Saint Petersburg, FL 33716
Phone: (727)579-2000
Fax: (727)579-2271
Free: 800-771-1025
Format: Adult Contemporary; Album-Oriented Rock (AOR). **Networks:** Independent. **Owner:** Cox Radio Inc., 6205 Peachtree Dunwood Rd., Atlanta, GA 30328-4524, Ph: (678)645-0000, Fax: (678)645-5002. **Founded:** 1973. **Formerly**: WAVE-FM. **Operating Hours**: Continuous. **ADI**: Tampa-St. Petersburg (Lakeland, Sarasota), FL. **Key Personnel:** Jason Meder, Gen. Sales Mgr., jason.meder@coxradio.com. **Wattage**: 100,000. **Ad Rates:** $175-250 per unit. **URL:** http://www.theboneonline.com.

8205 ■ WKES-FM - 91.1
PO Box 8889
Saint Petersburg, FL 33738
Phone: (727)391-9994
Fax: (727)397-6425
Free: 800-551-9537
Email: moodyradiooffice@moody.edu
Format: Religious. **Founded:** 1961. **Key Personnel:** Ron Maxwell, Producer; Pierre Chestang, Div. Dir., pierre.chestang@moody.edu. **Ad Rates:** Noncommercial. **URL:** http://www.moodyradioflorida.fm.

8206 ■ WLKT-TV - 62
PO Box 11566
Saint Petersburg, FL 33733-1566
Format: Commercial TV. **Networks:** Independent. **Founded:** 1988. **ADI**: Lexington, KY. **Key Personnel:** Tom Watson, Gen. Mgr.

8207 ■ WLLD-FM - 94.1
9721 Executive Center Dr., Ste. 200
Saint Petersburg, FL 33702
Phone: (727)578-9941
Free: 888-429-0941
Format: Blues; Rap. **Owner:** CBS Radio Inc., 1271 Avenue of the Americas, 44th Fl., New York, NY 10020-1401, Ph: (212)649-9600. **Key Personnel:** Tom Davis, Promotions Dir., tom.davis@bbgi.com; Ken Denton, Contact, ken.denton@cbsradio.com. **Ad Rates:** Advertising accepted; rates available upon request. **URL:** http://wild941.com.

8208 ■ WLVU-FM - 97.1
11300 4th St. N, Ste. 300
Saint Petersburg, FL 33716
Phone: (813)845-1063
Fax: (727)579-2662
Format: Middle-of-the-Road (MOR). **Networks:** Fox; ABC. **Founded:** 1979. **ADI**: Tampa-St. Petersburg (Lakeland, Sarasota), FL. **Key Personnel:** Frank Ferreri, Gen. Mgr. **Wattage**: 11,500 ERP. **Ad Rates:** Accepts Advertising. **URL:** http://www.97xonline.com.

8209 ■ WPOI-FM - 101.5
11300 4th St. N, Ste. 300
Saint Petersburg, FL 33716
Phone: (727)579-2000
Free: 877-999-1015
Format: Eighties. **Owner:** Cox Radio Inc., 6205 Peachtree Dunwood Rd., Atlanta, GA 30328-4524, Ph: (678)645-0000, Fax: (678)645-5002. **Key Personnel:** Keith Lawless, VP, keith.lawless@coxradio.com. **Ad Rates:** Advertising accepted; rates available upon request. **URL:** http://www.hot1015tampabay.com.

8210 ■ WQYK-AM - 1010
9721 Executive Center Dr. N, Ste. 200
Saint Petersburg, FL 33702
Phone: (727)579-1925
Format: Sports. **Networks:** Westwood One Radio. **Owner:** CBS Radio Inc., 1271 Avenue of the Americas, 44th Fl., New York, NY 10020-1401, Ph: (212)649-9600. **Operating Hours**: Continuous; 100% local. **ADI**: Tampa-St. Petersburg (Lakeland, Sarasota), FL. **Key Personnel:** Mike Culotta, Operations Mgr., mculotta@cbs.com. **Wattage**: 50,000. **Ad Rates:** Advertising accepted; rates available upon request. **URL:** http://www.tampa.cbslocal.com.

8211 ■ WQYK-FM - 99.5
9721 Executive Center Dr. N, No. 200
Saint Petersburg, FL 33702
Phone: (727)579-1925
Fax: (727)563-8202
Free: 800-992-1099
Email: dmckay@wqyk.com
Format: Country. **Networks:** Independent. **Owner:** CBS Radio Inc., at above address. **Operating Hours**: Continuous; 100% local. **ADI**: Tampa-St. Petersburg (Lakeland, Sarasota), FL. **Wattage**: 100,000. **Ad Rates:** Advertising accepted; rates available upon request. **URL:** http://wqyk.com.

8212 ■ WRBQ-FM - 104.7
9721 Executive Center Dr. N, Ste. 200
Saint Petersburg, FL 33702
Phone: (727)579-1925
Fax: (727)579-8888
Format: Full Service. **Networks:** ABC. **Owner:** Cbs Radio Stations Inc, at above address. **Founded:** 1954. **Formerly**: WPKM-FM. **Operating Hours**: 8:30 a.m. - 5:30 p.m. Monday - Friday. **ADI**: Tampa-St. Petersburg (Lakeland, Sarasota), FL. **Wattage**: 55,000 ERP. **Ad Rates:** Advertising accepted; rates available upon request. **URL:** http://tampabaysq105.com/index.php.

8213 ■ WSJT-FM - 94.1
9721 Executive Center Dr. N, Ste. 200
Saint Petersburg, FL 33702-2439
Fax: (727)568-9758
Format: Adult Contemporary. **Networks:** Independent; Westwood One Radio. **Owner:** CBS Corp., 51 W 52nd St., New York, NY 10019-6188, Ph: (212)975-4321, Fax: (212)975-4516, Free: 877-227-0787. **Founded:** 1967. **Operating Hours**: Continuous. **ADI**: Tampa-St. Petersburg (Lakeland, Sarasota), FL. **Key Personnel:** Bob Neumann, Dir. of Programs, bob.neumann@cbsradio.com. **Wattage**: 100,000. **Ad Rates:** $125-175 for 30 seconds; $150-200 for 60 seconds. Combined advertising rates available with WHNZ, WHPT, WZTM, WRBQ-AM, WRBQ-FM, WSSR, WILV. **URL:** http://cbsplay987.wordpress.com.

8214 ■ WSOR-FM - 90.9
PO Box 8889
Saint Petersburg, FL 33738
Phone: (727)391-9994
Fax: (727)397-6425
Free: 800-551-9537
Format: Religious. **Networks:** USA Radio. **Owner:** Moody Broadcasting Network, 820 N La Salle Blvd., Chicago, IL 60610, Ph: (312)329-4300, Fax: (312)329-4339, Free: 800-356-6639. **Founded:** 1971. **Operating Hours**: Continuous. **ADI**: Fort Myers-Naples, FL. **Key Personnel:** Pierre Chestang, Station Mgr., pierre.chestang@moody.edu; Ron Maxwell, Dir. of Programs. **Wattage**: 36,000. **Ad Rates:** Noncommercial. **URL:** http://www.moodyradioflorida.fm.

8215 ■ WSUN-FM - 97.1
11300 4th St. N, Ste. 300
Saint Petersburg, FL 33716
Phone: (727)579-2000
Fax: (727)579-2271
Free: 877-327-9797

Circulation: ★ = AAM; △ or • = BPA; ♦ = CAC; ❑ = VAC; ⊕ = PO Statement; ‡ = Publisher's Report; Boldface figures = swom; Light figures = estimated.

Format: Alternative/New Music/Progressive. **Owner:** Cox Radio Inc., 6205 Peachtree Dunwood Rd., Atlanta, GA 30328-4524, Ph: (678)645-0000, Fax: (678)645-5002. **Operating Hours:** Continuous. **Key Personnel:** Aaron Miller, Gen. Sales Mgr., aaron.miller@coxradio.com. **Ad Rates:** Advertising accepted; rates available upon request. **URL:** http://www.97xonline.com.

8216 ■ W36CO - 36
PO Box A
Santa Ana, CA 92711
Phone: (714)832-2950
Free: 888-731-1000
Owner: Trinity Broadcasting Network Inc., PO Box A, Santa Ana, CA 92711, Ph: (714)832-2950, Free: 888-731-1000. **URL:** http://www.tbn.org.

8217 ■ WTIS-AM - 1110
311 112th Ave. N
Saint Petersburg, FL 33716
Phone: (727)576-2234
Fax: (727)577-3814
Format: Religious; Talk; Contemporary Christian; Gospel. **Owner:** Westshore Broadcasting Inc., at above address. **Founded:** 1946. **Operating Hours:** Sunrise-sunset. **ADI:** Tampa-St. Petersburg (Lakeland, Sarasota), FL. **Key Personnel:** Mike Smith, Contact. **Wattage:** 10,000 KW. **Ad Rates:** Advertising accepted; rates available upon request. $30 per unit. **URL:** http://wtis1110.com/.

8218 ■ WTOG-TV - 44
365 105th Ter. NE
Saint Petersburg, FL 33716
Phone: (727)576-4444
Fax: (727)577-3799
Email: wtogmcr@gmail.com
Format: Commercial TV. **Networks:** United Paramount Network. **Owner:** CBS Corp., 51 W 52nd St., New York, NY 10019-6188, Ph: (212)975-4321, Fax: (212)975-4516, Free: 877-227-0787. **Founded:** 1968. **Operating Hours:** Continuous; 100% local. **ADI:** Tampa-St. Petersburg (Lakeland, Sarasota), FL. **Key Personnel:** Stephen Tolomeo, Traffic Mgr.; Stan Gill, VP, Gen. Mgr. **Wattage:** 600,000. **Ad Rates:** Advertising accepted; rates available upon request. **URL:** http://www.cwtampa.cbslocal.com.

8219 ■ WTSP-TV - 10
11450 Gandy Blvd.
Saint Petersburg, FL 33702
Phone: (727)577-1010
Fax: (727)576-6924
Format: News. **Networks:** CBS. **Owner:** Gannett Broadcasting, 7950 Jones Branch Dr., McLean, VA 22107-0150, Ph: (703)854-6000. **Founded:** 1965. **Operating Hours:** Continuous. **Key Personnel:** Stephen Ross, Owner. **Wattage:** 300 ERP. **Ad Rates:** Advertising accepted; rates available upon request. **URL:** http://www.wtsp.com.

8220 ■ WWMI-AM - 1380
11300 N 4th St., Ste. 143
Saint Petersburg, FL 33716
Phone: (727)577-2815
Format: Educational. **Owner:** Radio Disney, 500 S Buena Vista St. MC 7663, Burbank, CA 91521-7716.

8221 ■ WWRM-FM - 94.9
11300 Fourth St. N, Ste. 300
Saint Petersburg, FL 33716
Phone: (727)579-2000
Fax: (727)579-2271
Free: 800-850-0949
Email: 949comments@coxtampa.com
Format: Adult Contemporary. **Owner:** Cox Radio Inc., 6205 Peachtree Dunwood Rd., Atlanta, GA 30328-4524, Ph: (678)645-0000, Fax: (678)645-5002. **Formerly:** WWBA-FM. **Operating Hours:** Continuous; 100% local. **ADI:** Tampa-St. Petersburg (Lakeland, Sarasota), FL. **Key Personnel:** Howard Tuuri, VP of Sales, howard.tuuri@coxradio.com. **Wattage:** 100,000. **Ad Rates:** Advertising accepted; rates available upon request. **URL:** http://www.mymagic949.com.

8222 ■ WXGL-FM - 107.3
11300 4th St. N, Ste. 300
Saint Petersburg, FL 33716
Phone: (727)579-2000
Fax: (727)579-2271
Email: 1073comments@coxtampa.com
Format: Classic Rock. **Owner:** Cox Radio Inc., 6205 Peachtree Dunwood Rd., Atlanta, GA 30328-4524, Ph: (678)645-0000, Fax: (678)645-5002. **Operating Hours:** Continuous. **Key Personnel:** Jason Meder, Contact, jason.meder@coxradio.com; Jason Meder, Contact, jason.meder@coxradio.com. **Ad Rates:** Advertising accepted; rates available upon request. **URL:** http://www.1073theeagle.com.

8223 ■ WXGL-107.3 Eagle - 107.3
11300 Fourth St., N, Ste. 300
Saint Petersburg, FL 33716
Phone: (727)579-2000
Fax: (727)579-2271
Email: 1073comments@coxtampa.com
Format: Adult Contemporary; Classical. **Owner:** Rovi Corp., 100 Phoenix Drive, Suite 201, Ann Arbor, MI 48108-2202, Ph: (734)887-5600, Fax: (734)827-2492. **Formerly:** WBBY-FM. **Key Personnel:** Julia Hughes, Contact, jhughes@macrovision.com. **URL:** http://www.1073theeagle.com.

8224 ■ WYUU-FM - 92.5
9721 Executive Center Dr. N, Ste. 200
Saint Petersburg, FL 33702
Phone: (727)576-9250
Free: 866-932-9250
Format: Hispanic. **Networks:** Independent. **Owner:** Cbs Radio Stations Inc, at above address. **Formerly:** WXCR-FM. **Operating Hours:** Continuous. **ADI:** Tampa-St. Petersburg (Lakeland, Sarasota), FL. **Wattage:** 50,000. **Ad Rates:** Advertising accepted; rates available upon request. **URL:** http://925maxima.com.

SAN JUAN

8225 ■ WZNT-FM
7007 NW 77th Ave.
Miami, FL 33166
Phone: (809)720-5001
Fax: (809)720-2126
Format: Top 40; Hispanic. **Founded:** 1959. **Key Personnel:** Carlos Alvarez, Sales Mgr.; Pedro Arroyo, Music Dir., Prog. Dir. **Wattage:** 28,000 ERP. **Ad Rates:** $42-50 for 15 seconds; $63-74 for 30 seconds; $105-121 for 60 seconds.

SANFORD

EC FL. Seminole Co. On St. Johns River, 22 mi. N. of Orlando. Manufactures electronic components, boats, boat accessories, mobile homes, attache cases. Agriculture. Celery, vegetables, citrus fruits.

8226 ■ NTM@Work
New Tribes Mission
1000 E 1st St.
Sanford, FL 32771-1441
Phone: (407)323-3430
Publisher's E-mail: ntm@ntm.org
Freq: Quarterly. **Subscription Rates:** Free. **URL:** http://usa.ntm.org/ntm-at-work. **Remarks:** Advertising not accepted. **Circ:** (Not Reported).

8227 ■ Tabletalk
Ligonier Ministries Inc.
421 Ligonier Ct.
Sanford, FL 32771
Phone: (407)333-4244
Free: 800-435-4343
Publisher's E-mail: admissions@ligonier.org
Magazine featuring theological articles and biblical studies. **Freq:** Monthly. **Key Personnel:** R.C. Sproul, Executive Editor; Burk Parsons, Editor. **ISSN:** 1064--881X (print). **USPS:** 009-013. **Subscription Rates:** $23 Individuals /year; $39 Individuals 2 years; $49 Individuals 3 years. **URL:** http://www.ligonier.org/tabletalk. **Remarks:** Advertising not accepted. **Circ:** (Not Reported).

SANIBEL

S FL. Lee Co. On the Gulf of Mexico, 20 mi. SW of Fort Myers.

8228 ■ Island Reporter
Island Reporter
2340 Periwinkle Pl.
Sanibel, FL 33957
Phone: (239)472-1587
Local newspaper. **Freq:** Weekly (Fri.). **Print Method:** Offset. **Cols./Page:** 6. **Col. Width:** 20 nonpareils. **Col. Depth:** 224 agate lines. **Key Personnel:** Jeff Lysiak, Executive Editor. **Subscription Rates:** $40 By mail weekly. **URL:** http://islandreporter.com. **Mailing address:** PO Box 809, Sanibel, FL 33957. **Ad Rates:** GLR $.22; BW $6,966; 4C $846; PCI $7.25. **Remarks:** Accepts advertising. **Circ:** 8500.

8229 ■ The Nautilus
Bailey-Matthews Shell Museum
3075 Sanibel-Captiva Rd.
Sanibel, FL 33957-3111
Phone: (239)395-2233
Fax: (239)395-6706
Free: 888-679-6450
Publisher's E-mail: shell@shellmuseum.org
Peer-reviewed journal publishing articles on diverse aspects of the biology, ecology, and systematics of mollusks. **Freq:** Quarterly. **Trim Size:** 8 1/2 x 11. **Cols./Page:** 2. **Col. Width:** 36 nonpareils. **Col. Depth:** 96 agate lines. **Key Personnel:** Linda Kramer, Managing Editor; Dr. Jose H. Leal, Editor. **ISSN:** 0028--1344 (print). **Subscription Rates:** $60 Individuals; $97 Institutions yearly; $70 Individuals outside U.S., mail delivery; $88 Individuals outside U.S., air delivery; $107 Institutions outside U.S., mail delivery; $125 Institutions outside U.S., air delivery; $30 Individuals back issues. **URL:** http://shellmuseum.org/nautilus/index.html. **Remarks:** Advertising not accepted. **Circ:** ‡700.

SANTA ROSA BEACH

8230 ■ The Walton Sun
Halifax Media Holdings L.L.C.
5597 Hwy. 98 W
Santa Rosa Beach, FL 32459
Phone: (850)267-4555
Fax: (850)267-0929
Publisher's E-mail: support@halifaxmediagroup.com
Newspaper serving the Walton County in Florida. **Freq:** Weekly. **Key Personnel:** William Hatfield, Editor, phone: (850)654-8440; Matt Algarin, Director, Editorial. **Subscription Rates:** Free. **URL:** http://www.waltonsun.com. **Mailing address:** PO Box 2263, Santa Rosa Beach, FL 32459. **Remarks:** Accepts advertising. **Circ:** Free 12000.

8231 ■ WSBZ-FM - 106.3
1306 Bay Dr.
Santa Rosa Beach, FL 32459
Phone: (850)267-3279
Fax: (850)231-1775
Format: Jazz. **Ad Rates:** Advertising accepted; rates available upon request. **URL:** http://www.seabreeze.fm.

8232 ■ WTHA-FM
PO Box 4727
Santa Rosa Beach, FL 32459
Founded: 2003. **Ad Rates:** Advertising accepted; rates available upon request.

SARASOTA

SW FL. Sarasota Co. On Sarasota Bay, 52 mi. S. of Tampa. Winter and summer resort. Manufactures mobile homes and electronic parts. Citrus fruit and celery farms.

8233 ■ Accounting Horizons
American Accounting Association
5717 Bessie Dr.
Sarasota, FL 34233-2399
Phone: (941)921-7747
Fax: (941)923-4093
Publisher's E-mail: info@aaahq.org
Publication covering the banking, finance, and accounting industries. **Freq:** Quarterly. **Trim Size:** 7 x 10. **Key Personnel:** Paul A. Griffin, Editor; Arnold M. Wright, Editor. **ISSN:** 0888--7993 (print); **EISSN:** 1558--7975 (electronic). **URL:** http://aaahq.org/Research/AAA-Journals/Accounting-Horizons. **Ad Rates:** BW $800, full page; BW $550, half page - horizontal. **Remarks:** Accepts advertising. **Circ:** 5500.

8234 ■ The Accounting Review
American Accounting Association
5717 Bessie Dr.
Sarasota, FL 34233-2399
Phone: (941)921-7747
Fax: (941)923-4093
Publication E-mail: tar@mccombs.utexas.edu
Accounting education, research, financial reporting, and book reviews. Includes job postings of organizations seeking to hire accounting professionals. **Freq:**

Bimonthly. **Print Method:** Offset. **Trim Size:** 7 x 10. **Cols./Page:** 1. **Col. Depth:** 110 agate lines. **Key Personnel:** Prof. John Harry Evans, III, Senior Editor; Michael L. Ettredge, Editor; Prof. Stephen Zeff, Editor, phone: (713)348-6066. **ISSN:** 0001--4826 (print); **EISSN:** 1558--7967 (electronic). **URL:** http://aaahq.org/research/aaa-journals/the-accounting-review. **Ad Rates:** BW $850. **Remarks:** Accepts advertising. **Circ:** 8500.

8235 ■ ATA Journal of Legal Tax Research
American Accounting Association
5717 Bessie Dr.
Sarasota, FL 34233-2399
Phone: (941)921-7747
Fax: (941)923-4093
Publisher's E-mail: info@aaahq.org
Journal that offers information and research articles tax law. **Freq:** Annual. **Key Personnel:** Anthony P. Curatola, Editor. **ISSN:** 1543--866X (print). **URL:** http://aaapubs.org/loi/jltr. **Circ:** (Not Reported).

8236 ■ Auditing: A Journal of Practice & Theory
American Accounting Association
5717 Bessie Dr.
Sarasota, FL 34233-2399
Phone: (941)921-7747
Fax: (941)923-4093
Publisher's E-mail: info@aaahq.org
Trade journal covering the practice and theory of auditing for accounting professionals. **Freq:** Quarterly. **Cols./Page:** 2. **Col. Width:** 16 picas. **Col. Depth:** 49 picas. **Key Personnel:** Jean Bedard, Contact, phone: (418)656-7055; Jeff Cohen, Editor. **ISSN:** 0278--0380 (print); **EISSN:** 1558--7991 (electronic). **URL:** http://aaajournals.org/loi/ajpt. **Ad Rates:** BW $400. **Remarks:** Accepts advertising. **Circ:** Paid 2000.

8237 ■ Aviation Safety
Belvoir Media Group L.L.C.
7820 Holiday Dr. S, Ste. 315
Sarasota, FL 34231
Magazine featuring information about risk management and accident prevention. **Freq:** Monthly. **Key Personnel:** Joseph E. Burnside, Editor-in-Chief. **Subscription Rates:** $29.95 Individuals 6 issues - print; $27.95 Individuals online. **URL:** http://www.aviationsafetymagazine.com. **Circ:** (Not Reported).

8238 ■ Behavioral Research in Accounting
American Accounting Association
5717 Bessie Dr.
Sarasota, FL 34233-2399
Phone: (941)921-7747
Fax: (941)923-4093
Publisher's E-mail: info@aaahq.org
Academic journal covering research in accounting. **Freq:** Semiannual. **Trim Size:** 6 x 9. **Cols./Page:** 1. **Key Personnel:** Prof. Rick Hatfield, Editor. **ISSN:** 1050-4753 (print); **EISSN:** 1558-8009 (electronic). **URL:** http://aaajournals.org/loi/bria. **Ad Rates:** BW $400. **Remarks:** Accepts advertising. **Circ:** Paid 1400.

8239 ■ Biz941
CurtCo Media Labs L.L.C.
330 S Pineapple Ave., Ste. 205
Sarasota, FL 34236
Phone: (941)487-1100
Free: 800-881-2394
Publisher's E-mail: webfeedback@curtco.com
Magazine covering the growth in the Sarasota/Manatee market. **Freq:** Monthly. **Key Personnel:** Kay Kipling, Senior Editor; Susan Burns, Editor. **URL:** http://www.biz941.com. **Ad Rates:** BW $2,400; 4C $2,900. **Remarks:** Accepts advertising. **Circ:** (Not Reported).

8240 ■ Designfax: Technology for OEM Design Engineers
Nelson Publishing Inc.
c/o Mike Foley, Editor
2477 Stickney Point Rd., Ste. 221B
Sarasota, FL 34231
Phone: (941)388-7050
Trade journal serving OEM design engineers in all market niches. **Freq:** Weekly (Tues.) 48/year. **Print Method:** Offset. **Cols./Page:** 1. **Col. Width:** 52 nonpareils. **Col. Depth:** 91 agate lines. **Key Personnel:** Vern Nelson, Publisher; Mike Foley, Editor; John Holmes, Manager, Sales, phone: (847)364-7441, fax: (847)364-9170. **ISSN:** 0163--6669 (print). **URL:** http://www.designfax.net/web/home.php. **Ad Rates:** BW $5,370; 4C $6,800. **Remarks:** Accepts advertising. **Circ:** Non-paid 108919.

8241 ■ Healthcare Purchasing News: Business News and Analysis for Purchasing Decision-Makers
Nelson Publishing Inc.
2477 Stickney Point Rd., Ste. 315B
Sarasota, FL 34231
Phone: (941)927-9345
Fax: (941)927-9588
Publication E-mail: krussell@hpnonline.com
Magazine for healthcare material management, central services, operating room and infection control professionals, and others involved in supply chain issues with hospitals and outpatient settings. **Freq:** Monthly. **Print Method:** Web Offset. **Trim Size:** 8 1/4 x 11. **Cols./Page:** 4. **Col. Width:** 28 nonpareils. **Col. Depth:** 140 agate lines. **Key Personnel:** Susan Cantrell, Editor, phone: (615)356-6440; Rick Dana Barlow, Senior Editor; Jeannie Akridge, Managing Editor; Kristine Russell, Publisher. **ISSN:** 0278--4799 (print). **Subscription Rates:** $72 U.S.; $110 Canada; $130 Other countries. **URL:** http://www.hpnonline.com. **Formerly:** HPN; Hospital Purchasing News. **Feature Editors:** Julie Williamson, phone: (480)373-8999, jewilliamson@qwest.net. **Ad Rates:** BW $5,356; 4C $1,250. **Remarks:** Advertising accepted; rates available upon request. **Circ:** Non-paid △**33175**.

8242 ■ Journal of Information Systems
American Accounting Association
5717 Bessie Dr.
Sarasota, FL 34233-2399
Phone: (941)921-7747
Fax: (941)923-4093
Publisher's E-mail: info@aaahq.org
Journal covering high technology, banking and finance. **Freq:** 3/year. **Trim Size:** 7 x 10. **Key Personnel:** Mary Curtis, Senior Editor. **ISSN:** 0888--7985 (print); **EISSN:** 1558--7959 (electronic). **Subscription Rates:** $136 Individuals print only. **URL:** http://aaajournals.org/loi/isys. **Ad Rates:** BW $350. **Remarks:** Accepts advertising. **Circ:** 900.

8243 ■ Pelican Press
The Observer Group Inc.
1970 Main St.
Sarasota, FL 34236
Phone: (941)366-3468
Fax: (941)362-4808
Publication E-mail: pelicanpressrelease@jcpgroup.com
Community newspaper (tabloid) serving Sarasota and coastal regions. **Freq:** Weekly. **Print Method:** Offset. **Trim Size:** 10 7/8 x 16 1/2. **Cols./Page:** 6. **Col. Width:** 9.5 picas. **Col. Depth:** 217 agate lines. **Key Personnel:** Matt Walsh, Editor; Rachel Hackney, Managing Editor. **URL:** http://www.yourobserver.com/news/siesta-key/Front-Page. **Ad Rates:** BW $1,012; 4C $1,427; PCI $12. **Remarks:** Accepts advertising. **Circ:** Paid ‡800, Free ‡23500.

8244 ■ Pointer Points
American Pointer Club
c/o Paul Wessberg, Membership Chairman
4485 N Lake Dr.
Sarasota, FL 34232
Phone: (412)343-9169
Magazine containing information on breeding and proper management of purebred pointers, as well as the latest dog shows and field trials of the American Pointer Club. **Freq:** Bimonthly. **Subscription Rates:** Members free; $10 Members extra copy; $40 Nonmembers U.S.; $65 Nonmembers other countries; $7.50 advertisers extra copy. **URL:** http://www.americanpointerclub.org/ppmag.shtml. **Ad Rates:** BW $65, members; BW $78.95, nonmembers; 4C $200, members; 4C $250, nonmembers. **Remarks:** Accepts advertising. **Circ:** (Not Reported).

8245 ■ Practical Sailor
Belvoir Media Group L.L.C.
c/o Darrell Nicholson, Ed.-in-Ch.
7820 S Holiday Dr., Ste. 315
Sarasota, FL 34231
Journal focusing on evaluations of sailing gear and equipment. **Freq:** 7/year. **Key Personnel:** Darrell Nicholson, Editor-in-Chief. **Subscription Rates:** $19.97 Individuals print & online; $39.94 Two years print & online; $34 Individuals online. **URL:** http://www.practical-sailor.com. **Circ:** (Not Reported).

8246 ■ Sarasota Herald-Tribune
The New York Times Co.
1741 Main St.
Sarasota, FL 34236
Phone: (941)953-7755
Fax: (941)361-4880
Publisher's E-mail: national@nytimes.com
General newspaper. **Freq:** Monthly. **Print Method:** Offset. **Cols./Page:** 6. **Col. Width:** 26 nonpareils. **Col. Depth:** 294 agate lines. **Key Personnel:** Diane McFarlin, Publisher. **Subscription Rates:** $11.90 Individuals online only. **URL:** http://heraldtribune.com. **Remarks:** Accepts advertising. **Circ:** Mon.-Sat. ★**99839**, Sun. ★**118704**.

8247 ■ Sarasota Magazine
Gulfshore Media L.L.C.
330 S Pineapple Ave., Ste. 205
Sarasota, FL 34236
Phone: (941)487-1100
Fax: (941)365-7272
Free: 800-881-2394
Publisher's E-mail: subscriptions@sarasotamagazine.com
Business publication covering Sarasota and Manatee County inserted into monthly city magazine. **Freq:** 11/year. **Print Method:** Offset. **Cols./Page:** 3. **Col. Width:** 27 nonpareils. **Col. Depth:** 137 agate lines. **Key Personnel:** Diana Riser, Associate Publisher; Ilene Denton, Director, Marketing and Business Development; Pam Daniel, Contact. **Subscription Rates:** $17.95 Individuals; $28.95 Two years; $38.95 Individuals 3 years. **URL:** http://sarasotamagazine.com. **Ad Rates:** BW $1,200; 4C $1,800. **Remarks:** Accepts advertising. **Circ:** Combined ‡25000.

8248 ■ SEE Emerald Coast
Miles Media Group Inc.
6751 Professional Pky. W
Sarasota, FL 34240-8443
Phone: (941)342-2300
Free: 800-683-0010
Consumer magazine covering visitor information and travel. **Freq:** 3/yr. **Trim Size:** 5 1/1 x 8 1/4. **URL:** http://www.see-florida.com/emerald-coast. **Remarks:** Accepts advertising. **Circ:** △**600000**.

8249 ■ SEE Florida Keys
Miles Media Group Inc.
6751 Professional Pky. W
Sarasota, FL 34240-8443
Phone: (941)342-2300
Free: 800-683-0010
Tourist magazine for the Florida Keys. **Freq:** Semiannual. **Print Method:** Web Offset. **Trim Size:** 5 1/4 x 8 1/4. **Cols./Page:** 2. **Col. Width:** 13 picas. **Col. Depth:** 41 picas. **Subscription Rates:** Free. **URL:** http://www.see-florida.com/florida-keys; http://www.see-florida.com/guides/florida-keys. **Formerly:** The Keys Guide. **Ad Rates:** 4C $5,850. **Remarks:** Accepts advertising. **Circ:** Non-paid △**600000**.

8250 ■ SEE Sarasota, Bradenton, Venice & Gulf Coast Islands Magazine
Miles Media Group Inc.
6751 Professional Pky. W
Sarasota, FL 34240-8443
Phone: (941)342-2300
Free: 800-683-0010
Consumer travel guides. **Freq:** Annual. **Subscription Rates:** Free. **URL:** http://www.see-florida.com/sarasota-bradenton. **Formerly:** SEE Beaches. **Ad Rates:** 4C $570. **Remarks:** Accepts advertising. **Circ:** Non-paid 500000.

8251 ■ Sharing the Practice
Academy of Parish Clergy
2249 Florinda St.
Sarasota, FL 34231
Phone: (941)922-8633
Freq: Quarterly. **ISSN:** 0193--8274 (print). **Subscription Rates:** Included in membership. **Remarks:** Accepts advertising. **Circ:** 300.

Circulation: ★ = AAM; △ or • = BPA; ♦ = CAC; ❑ = VAC; ⊕ = PO Statement; ‡ = Publisher's Report; Boldface figures = sworn; Light figures = estimated.

8252 ■ Swimmer
United States Masters Swimming
1751 Mound St., Ste. 201
Sarasota, FL 34236
Phone: (941)256-8767
Fax: (941)556-7946
Free: 800-550-7946
Magazine providing leading-edge information that supports a healthy lifestyle, including tips on cross-training, general fitness and health, and products geared towards swimmers. **Freq:** Bimonthly. **Print Method:** Web offset. **Subscription Rates:** accessible only to members. **URL:** http://www.usms.org/myusms/mag/index.php. **Ad Rates:** BW $3,130. **Remarks:** Accepts advertising. **Circ:** (Not Reported).

8253 ■ WAQV-FM - 90.9
6469 Parkland Dr.
Sarasota, FL 34243
Phone: (941)753-0401
Fax: (941)753-2963
Free: 800-456-8910
Email: thejoyfm@thejoyfm.com
Format: Contemporary Christian. **Owner:** The JOY FM, 6469 Parkland Dr. , Sarasota, FL 34243, Ph: (941)753-0401, Fax: (941)753-2963. **Key Personnel:** Jeff MacFarlane, Gen. Mgr., jeff@thejoyfm.com; Mary Douglas, Promotions Dir., mary@thejoyfm.com. **Ad Rates:** Noncommercial. **URL:** http://www.thejoyfm.com.

8254 ■ WBRD-AM - 1420
2101 Hammock Pl.
Sarasota, FL 34235
Fax: (941)752-4794
Format: News; Talk. **Networks:** ABC. **Owner:** Birach Broadcasting Corp., at above address. **Founded:** 1957. **Operating Hours**: Continuous. **Wattage**: 2,500. **Ad Rates:** $10-40 for 30 seconds; $15-60 for 60 seconds. $10-$40 for 30 seconds; $15-$60 for 60 seconds. Combined advertising rates available with WDUV-FM.

8255 ■ WCTQ-FM - 106.5
1779 Independence Blvd.
Sarasota, FL 34234
Phone: (941)552-4800
Free: 888-329-1065
Format: Country. **Networks:** NBC. **Founded:** 1974. **Operating Hours**: Continuous; 5% network, 95% local. **ADI**: Tampa-St. Petersburg (Lakeland, Sarasota), FL. **Key Personnel:** Heidi Decker, Dir. of Programs, heidi@1065ctq.com. **Wattage:** 25,000. **Ad Rates:** $75-100 for 30 seconds; $75-125 for 60 seconds. Combined advertising rates available with WSRZ, WAMR-AM, WDDV, WYNF. **URL:** http://www.1065ctq.com.

8256 ■ WDDV-AM - 1450
1779 Independence Blvd.
Sarasota, FL 34234
Phone: (941)552-4800
Fax: (941)552-4900
Free: 888-599-1079
Format: Adult Contemporary. **Networks:** NBC; CBS; Westwood One Radio; ESPN Radio. **Owner:** iHeartMedia Inc., 200 E Basse Rd., San Antonio, TX 78209, Ph: (210)832-3314. **Founded:** 1960. **Formerly**: WAMR-AM. **Operating Hours**: Continuous. **Key Personnel:** Bryan Kelly, Dir. of Sales, bryan@doveradio.com; Peter Norden, Gen. Mgr; JJ Paone, Contact, jj@dovaradio.com. **Wattage:** 5,000. **Ad Rates:** Advertising accepted; rates available upon request; Noncommercial. **URL:** http://www.sunnyradioam.com//main.html.

8257 ■ WDDV-FM - 92.1
1779 Independence Blvd.
Sarasota, FL 34234
Phone: (918)664-4581
Format: Soft Rock; News; Country; Information. **Operating Hours**: 12:00 a.m.-7:00 p.m. Monday-friday; 12:00 a.m.-4:00 p.m. Saturday; 12:00 a.m.-9:00 a.m. Sunday. **Wattage**: 11,500. **Ad Rates:** Noncommercial; Advertising accepted; rates available upon request. **URL:** http://921ctq.iheart.com.

WHIJ-FM - See Ocala

WJIS-FM - See Bradenton

8258 ■ WSDV-AM - 1450
1779 Independence Blvd.
Sarasota, FL 34234
Phone: (941)552-4800
Free: 888-599-1079
Format: Big Band/Nostalgia; Oldies. **Owner:** Clear Channel Communication, Inc., 200 E Basse Rd., San Antonio, TX 78209, Ph: (210)822-2828, Fax: (210)822-2828. **Key Personnel:** Drew Thomas, Dir. of Programs. **Ad Rates:** Advertising accepted; rates available upon request. **URL:** http://www.sunnyradioam.com//main.html.

8259 ■ WSLR-FM - 96.5
252 Kumaquat Ct.
Sarasota, FL 34236
Phone: (941)894-6469
Email: info@wslr.org
Format: News; Information. **Founded:** 2005. **Key Personnel:** Arlene Sweeting, Station Mgr.; Tom Walker, Chmn. of the Bd. **Mailing address:** PO Box 2540, Sarasota, FL 34230. **URL:** http://wslr.org.

8260 ■ WSRZ-FM - 108
1779 Independence Blvd.
Sarasota, FL 34234
Phone: (941)552-4800
Free: 888-599-1079
Format: Oldies. **Networks:** Independent. **Owner:** iHeartMedia Inc., 200 E Basse Rd., San Antonio, TX 78209, Ph: (210)832-3314. **Founded:** 1986. **Operating Hours**: Continuous. **Key Personnel:** Bryan Kelly, Dir. of Sales, bryan@wsrz.com. **Wattage:** 46,000. **Ad Rates:** $20-100 per unit; per unit. Combined advertising rates available with WYNF-FM, WSPB-AM. **URL:** http://www.wsrz.com.

8261 ■ WTMY-AM - 1280
2101 Hammock Pl.
Sarasota, FL 34236
Fax: (941)955-9062
Format: Talk. **Networks:** Business Radio. **Owner:** Polnet Communications, Ltd., at above address. **Founded:** Dec. 02, 1961. **Operating Hours**: Continuous. **Wattage**: 500 Day; 340 Night. **Ad Rates:** Noncommercial. Combined advertising rates available with WBRD-AM; WRXB-AM. **URL:** http://www.wtmy.com.

8262 ■ WTZB-FM - 105.9
1779 Independence Blvd.
Sarasota, FL 34234
Phone: (941)552-4800
Free: 800-820-2899
Format: Album-Oriented Rock (AOR). **Ad Rates:** Advertising accepted; rates available upon request. **URL:** http://www.1059thebuzz.com.

8263 ■ WWSB-TV - 7
1477 10th St.
Sarasota, FL 34236-4046
Phone: (941)923-8840
Fax: (941)923-8709
Format: News; Sports; Information. **Networks:** ABC. **Founded:** 1971. **Formerly**: WXLT-TV. **Operating Hours**: Continuous. **ADI**: Tampa-St. Petersburg (Lakeland, Sarasota), FL. **Key Personnel:** Jack Dillon, Dir. of Engg., jdillon@wwsb.tv; Manny Calvo, Gen. Mgr., generalmanager@wwsb.tv; Jeff Benninghoff, Station Mgr.; Vann Smith, Gen. Sales Mgr., vsmith@wwsb.tv; Julie Shaffer, Sales Mgr., jshaffer@wwsb.tv; Jason Wildenstein, Operations Mgr., operations@wwsb.tv. **Wattage**: 90,000. **Ad Rates:** Advertising accepted; rates available upon request. **URL:** http://www.mysuncoast.com.

8264 ■ WYFO-FM - 97.3
11530 Carmel Commons Blvd.
Charlotte, NC 28226
Phone: (704)523-5555
Free: 800-888-7077
Format: Gospel; Religious. **Owner:** Bible Broadcasting Network Inc., 11530 Carmel Commons Blvd., Charlotte, NC 28226, Ph: (704)523-5555, Free: 800-888-7077. **Founded:** Nov. 07, 1989. **Wattage**: 25,000. **URL:** http://www.bbnradio.org.

SEBRING

S FL. Highlands Co. On Lake Jackson, 70 mi. SE of Tampa. Agriculture. Citrus fruit, cattle, and truck farms.

8265 ■ The News-Sun
The News-Sun
207 Cir. Park Dr.
Sebring, FL 33870
Phone: (863)385-6155
Fax: (863)385-1954
Newspaper with a focus on community news and events. **Founded:** 1927. **Freq:** 3/week (Wed., Fri. & Sun.). **Print Method:** Offset. Uses mats. **Cols./Page:** 6. **Col. Width:** 21 nonpareils. **Col. Depth:** 301 agate lines. **Subscription Rates:** $77.28 Individuals 12 months, home delivery; $114.75 By mail 12 months,in state; $130.98 Out of state 12 months. **URL:** http://www.newssun.com. **Remarks:** Accepts advertising. **Circ:** (Not Reported).

8266 ■ Cohan Radio Group Inc.
3750 US Highway 27 N
Sebring, FL 33870
Phone: (863)382-9999
Fax: (863)382-1982
Format: Adult Contemporary; Oldies; Country; Talk. **Founded:** 1998. **Key Personnel:** Peter Coughlin, President. **Ad Rates:** Advertising accepted; rates available upon request. **URL:** http://www.cohanradiogroup.com.

8267 ■ W51DY - 51
PO Box A
Santa Ana, CA 92711
Phone: (714)832-2950
Free: 888-731-1000
Email: comments@tbn.org
Owner: Trinity Broadcasting Network Inc., PO Box A, Santa Ana, CA 92711, Ph: (714)832-2950, Free: 888-731-1000. **URL:** http://www.tbn.org.

8268 ■ WITS-AM - 1340
The Cohan Radio Group, 3750 US 27 N
3750 US 27 N
Sebring, FL 33870
Phone: (863)382-9999
Fax: (863)382-1982
Email: cohanradiogroup@htn.net
Format: Oldies. **Founded:** 1981. **Key Personnel:** Peter Coughlin, Prog. Dir. **Ad Rates:** Noncommercial. **URL:** http://www.cohanradiogroup.com.

8269 ■ WJCM-AM - 1050
3750 US 27 N, Ste. 1
Sebring, FL 33870
Phone: (863)382-9999
Email: cohanradiogroup@htn.net
Format: Oldies; Soft Rock. **Networks:** ABC; Florida Radio; Jones Satellite. **Founded:** 1950. **Operating Hours:** Continuous; 16% network, 84% local. **ADI**: Tampa-St. Petersburg (Lakeland, Sarasota), FL. **Key Personnel:** Peter Coughlin, Station Mgr.; Don Ray, Operations Mgr. **Wattage**: 5,000 day; 1,000 night. **Ad Rates:** Noncommercial. $10-20 for 30 seconds; $12-24 for 60 seconds. **URL:** http://www.cohanradiogroup.com.

8270 ■ WWLL-FM - 105.7
3750 US 27 N
Sebring, FL 33870
Phone: (863)382-9999
Fax: (863)382-1982
Format: Adult Contemporary. **Owner:** Cohan Radio Group Inc., 3750 US Highway 27 N, Sebring, FL 33870, Ph: (863)382-9999, Fax: (863)382-1982. **Founded:** 1967. **Formerly**: WYMR; WCAC. **Operating Hours**: Continuous. **Wattage**: 20,000 C-003. **Ad Rates:** Combined advertising rates available with WWOJ-FM; WWTK-AM; WITS-AM; WJCM-AM. **URL:** http://www.lite1057fm.com.

8271 ■ WWOJ-FM - 99.1
3750 U.S. 27 N
Sebring, FL 33870
Phone: (863)385-9910
Email: cohanradiogroup@htn.net
Format: Country. **Networks:** ABC. **Owner:** Cohan Radio Group Inc., 3750 US Highway 27 N, Sebring, FL 33870, Ph: (863)382-9999, Fax: (863)382-1982. **Founded:** 1980. **Operating Hours:** Continuous; 1% network, 99% local. **ADI**: Tampa-St. Petersburg (Lakeland, Sarasota), FL. **Key Personnel:** Peter Coughlin, Contact, President; Pete Coughlin, Contact. **Wattage**: 25,000 ERP. **Ad Rates:** Advertising accepted; rates available upon request. Combined advertising rates available with WWLL-FM; WWTK-AM; WITS-AM; WJCM-AM. **URL:** http://www.oj991.com.

SEMINOLE

8272 ■ Curriculum and Teaching Dialogue
American Association for Teaching and Curriculum
c/o Lynne Bailey, Executive Secretary

5640 Seminole Blvd.
Seminole, FL 33772
Journal containing conference papers, researches, book reviews, and columns about the study of teaching and curriculum. **Freq:** Semiannual. **Key Personnel:** Christy Moroye, Editor. **URL:** http://aatchome.org/journal-information. **Remarks:** Advertising not accepted. **Circ:** (Not Reported).

8273 ■ The Scottish Banner
The Scottish Banner
No. 271, 13799 Pk. Blvd.
Seminole, FL 33776
Fax: (727)595-2572
Free: 866-544-5157
Publisher's E-mail: mail@scottishbanner.com
Fraternal newspaper (tabloid). **Freq:** Monthly. **Key Personnel:** Valerie Cairney, Editor, Publisher. **ISSN:** 0707--073X (print). **Subscription Rates:** A$45 Individuals in Australia; A$85 Two years in Australia; A$60 Individuals in New Zealand; A$99 Two years in New Zealand; $40 Canada 1 year; C$76 Two years Canada. **Remarks:** Accepts advertising. **Circ:** (Not Reported).

SOUTH DAYTONA

Volusia Co. Volusia Co. (NE). 4 m S of Daytona Beach.

8274 ■ WPUL-AM - 1590
PO Box 4010
South Daytona, FL 32121-4010
Phone: (386)492-2907
Format: News; Sports; Talk; Gospel. **Networks:** CBS. **Founded:** 1988. **Formerly:** WZIP-AM. **Operating Hours:** Continuous Monday - Friday, 6:00 a.m. - 12:00 a.m. Saturday, 5:00 a.m. - 11:00 p.m. Sunday. **Key Personnel:** Charles W. Cherry, Gen. Mgr., Station Mgr. **Ad Rates:** $18 for 30 seconds; for 60 seconds. **URL:** http://www.wpul1590.com/.

8275 ■ WSBB-AM - 1230
2400 Ridgewood Ave., Ste. 52
South Daytona, FL 32119
Phone: (835)428-9091
Email: wsbb@volusia.com
Format: Sports; Information; News; Talk; Jazz. **Networks:** Westwood One Radio. **Owner:** Brian Tolby, at above address. **Founded:** 1951. **Operating Hours:** Continuous. **Wattage:** 1,000. **Ad Rates:** $28 for 30 seconds; $36 for 60 seconds. **URL:** http://www.myam1230.com.

SOUTH MIAMI

Dade Co Dade Co. Dade Co. (SE). 7 m SW of Miami. Ships fruit and truck crops.

8276 ■ Aroideana
International Aroid Society
PO Box 43-1853
South Miami, FL 33143
Magazine covering gardening. **Freq:** Annual. **Key Personnel:** Dr. Thomas B. Croat, Editor; Dr. Derek Burch, Editor. **ISSN:** 0197-4033 (print). **Subscription Rates:** Included in membership. **URL:** http://www.aroid.org/aroideana/. **Remarks:** Advertising accepted; rates available upon request. **Circ:** 550.

8277 ■ Today's Grocer
Florida Grocer Publications Inc.
PO Box 430760
South Miami, FL 33243-0760
Free: 800-440-3067
Publisher's E-mail: contact@todaysgrocer.com
Trade journal serving the Florida food industry. **Freq:** Monthly. **Print Method:** Offset. Uses mats. **Trim Size:** 13 x 20.5. **Cols./Page:** 6. **Col. Width:** 1 1/8 inches. **Col. Depth:** 20.5 inches. **USPS:** 432-630. **URL:** http://todaysgrocer.com. **Formerly:** Florida Grocer. **Ad Rates:** BW $2,800; 4C $3,400. **Remarks:** Accepts advertising. **Circ:** Controlled ‡19500.

SPARR

8278 ■ The International Permaculture Solutions Journal
Yankee Permaculture Publications
PO Box 69
Sparr, FL 32192
Publisher's E-mail: yankeeperm@aol.com
Journal covering the environment and permaculture. **Founded:** 1983. **Freq:** Irregular. **ISSN:** 1046-8366 (print). **Subscription Rates:** $27.50 Individuals. **URL:** http://www.barkingfrogspermaculture.org/publications.htm. **Formerly**: The International Permaculture Species Yearbook. **Remarks:** Advertising not accepted. **Circ:** (Not Reported).

STARKE

8279 ■ Bradford County Telegraph
Bradford County Telegraph
131 W Call St.
Starke, FL 32091
Phone: (904)964-6305
Fax: (904)964-8628
Publisher's E-mail: editor@bctelegraph.com
Community newspaper. **Freq:** Weekly (Thurs.). **Cols./Page:** 6. **Col. Width:** 12 picas. **Col. Depth:** 21 inches. **Subscription Rates:** $39 Individuals; $20 Individuals 6 months. **URL:** http://www.bctelegraph.com. **Mailing address:** PO Box A, Starke, FL 32091. **Ad Rates:** BW $687; PCI $5.45. **Remarks:** Advertising accepted; rates available upon request. **Circ:** 5825.

8280 ■ WEAG-AM - 1490
1421 S Water St.
Starke, FL 32091-4508
Phone: (904)964-5001
Format: Country. **Founded:** 1957. **Operating Hours**: Continuous. **Wattage**: 1,000. **Ad Rates:** Noncommercial. **URL:** http://www.weagchuckkramer.com.

8281 ■ WEAG-FM - 106.3
1421 S Water St.
Starke, FL 32091
Phone: (904)964-5001
Free: 800-457-6647
Format: Country. **Ad Rates:** Advertising accepted; rates available upon request. **URL:** http://weagchuckkramer.com.

8282 ■ WTLG-FM - 88.3
PO Box 2440
Tupelo, MS 38803
Phone: (662)844-8888
Email: faq@afa.net
Format: Religious. **Owner:** American Family Radio, at above address.

STUART

E FL. Martin Co. On St. Lucie River, 38 mi. N. of West Palm Beach. Tourist resort. Commercial fishing.

8283 ■ Florida Sportsman
Wickstrom Publishers
2700 S Kanner Hwy.
Stuart, FL 34994
Phone: (772)219-7400
Fax: (772)219-6900
Free: 800-274-6386
Boating, fishing, camping, hunting, and conservation magazine. **Freq:** Monthly. **Print Method:** Offset. **Trim Size:** 8 1/4 x 10 7/8. **Cols./Page:** 3. **Col. Width:** 27 nonpareils. **Col. Depth:** 140 agate lines. **Key Personnel:** Jeff Weakley, Editor; Karl Wickstrom, Editor-in-Chief, Founder; Blair Wickstrom, Publisher; David Conway, Managing Editor. **ISSN:** 0015--3885 (print). **Subscription Rates:** $21 Individuals print and online. **Remarks:** Accepts advertising. **Circ:** Paid ★**116432**.

8284 ■ JOY: The Journal of Yoga
GodConsciousness.com
4002 Lincoln St. SE
Stuart, FL 34997
Publication E-mail: journalofyoga@gmail.com
Journal that aims to serve the global community and educational institutions throughout the world in furthering understanding of yoga. **Freq:** Semiannual. **Key Personnel:** Douglas J. Phillips, II, Editor. **ISSN:** 1541--5910 (print). **URL:** http://www.journalofyoga.org. **Circ:** (Not Reported).

8285 ■ The Stuart News
Scripps Treasure Coast Newspapers
PO Box 9009
Stuart, FL 34995-9009
Publisher's E-mail: feedback@tcpalm.com
General newspaper. **Freq:** Mon.-Sun. (morn.). **Print Method:** Offset. **Trim Size:** 13 3/4 x 22 3/4. **Cols./Page:** 6. **Col. Width:** 24 nonpareils. **Col. Depth:** 301 agate lines. **Key Personnel:** Thomas E. Weber, Jr., Editor; Greg Anderson, Director, Advertising, phone: (561)221-4275; Rebecca Freeman, Business Manager, phone: (561)221-4131, fax: (561)221-4132. **Subscription Rates:** $79.80 Individuals. **URL:** http://www.tcpalm.com. **Ad Rates:** GLR $5.89; BW $3,148.89; 4C $480; PCI $24.41. **Remarks:** Accepts advertising. **Circ:** Mon.-Fri. ★**94956**, Sun. ★**106504**, Sat. ★**93439**.

8286 ■ WHLG-FM - 101.3
1670 NW Federal Hwy.
Stuart, FL 34994
Phone: (772)344-1999
Format: Adult Contemporary. **Key Personnel:** Larry McKay, Prog. Dir., larry@coast1013.com; Chet Tart, Dir. of Sales, ctart@coast1013.com. **Wattage:** 7,000. **URL:** http://www.coast1013.com.

8287 ■ WSTU-AM - 1450
1000 NW Alice Ave.
Stuart, FL 34994
Phone: (772)220-9788
Fax: (772)340-3245
Format: News; Sports; Religious; Information. **Networks:** ABC. **Owner:** MMM Broadcasting, Inc., 6699 N Federal Hwy., Boca Raton, FL 33487. **Founded:** 1969. **Operating Hours**: Continuous. **Key Personnel:** Tom Teter, Contact. **Wattage**: 1,000 KW. **Ad Rates:** Accepts Advertising. **URL:** http://www.wstu1450.com.

8288 ■ WWFR-FM - 91.7
290 Hegenberger Rd.
Oakland, CA 94621
Free: 800-543-1495
Email: info@familyradio.org
Format: Religious. **Owner:** Family Stations Inc., 290 Hegenberger Rd., Oakland, CA 94621, Free: 800-543-1495. **URL:** http://www.familyradio.org.

SUNRISE

Broward Co. Broward Co. (NE). Suburb of Ft. Lauderdale.

8289 ■ The Broward Informer: Condo Informer Travel Magazine- Broward Informer Travel
The Broward Informer
PO Box 451527
Sunrise, FL 33345
Phone: (954)370-6009
Publication E-mail: informar@comcast.net
Local with emphasis on travel and consumer protection, and seniors' affairs news. **Freq:** Biweekly. **Print Method:** Offset. Accepts mats. **Trim Size:** 10 1/4 x 16. **Cols./Page:** 6. **Col. Width:** 1 9/16 inches. **Col. Depth:** 16 inches. **Key Personnel:** Mayda Mangerian, Publisher; Michael Gains, Office Manager. **URL:** http://browardinformer.com/index86.htm. **Formerly**: Broward Sunrise Informer; Sunrise News; Condo Informer. **Ad Rates:** GLR $10; BW $900; PCI $10. **Remarks:** Accepts advertising. **Circ:** Paid ‡2000, Free ‡80000.

8290 ■ WKPX-FM - 88.5
8000 NW 44th St.
Sunrise, FL 33351
Phone: (954)572-1321
Fax: (954)572-1344
Format: Eclectic; Album-Oriented Rock (AOR); Alternative/New Music/Progressive. **Founded:** Feb. 1983. **Ad Rates:** Noncommercial. **URL:** http://www.wkpx.freeservers.com.

WPXM-TV - See Miami

8291 ■ WPXP-TV - 67
13801 NW 14th St.
Sunrise, FL 33323
Phone: (954)703-1921
Fax: (954)858-1848
URL: http://www.ionmedianetworks.com.

TALLAHASSEE

N FL. Leon Co. 160 mi. NW of Jacksonville. State Capital. Florida State University; Florida Agricultural and Mechanical University. Manufactures lumber, boats, pine extracts pulpwood, feed, insecticides, and pre-stressed concrete. Diversified agriculture.

Circulation: ★ = AAM; △ or • = BPA; ♦ = CAC; ❑ = VAC; ⊕ = PO Statement; ‡ = Publisher's Report; Boldface figures = sworn; Light figures = estimated.

8292 ■ Argia
Dragonfly Society of the Americas
c/o Jerrell Daigle, Treasurer
2067 Little River Ln.
Tallahassee, FL 32311
Journal covering Odonata and odonatologists. **Freq:** Quarterly. **Key Personnel:** Thomas Donnelly, Editor. **ISSN:** 1061--8503 (print). **Subscription Rates:** $25 Institutions. **URL:** http://www.odonatacentral.org/index.php/IssueAction.getAll; http://odonatacentral.org/index.php/IssueAction.getAll. **Circ:** 400.

8293 ■ Association Source
Florida Society of Association Executives
2410 Mahan Dr., Ste. 2
Tallahassee, FL 32308
Phone: (850)222-7994
Fax: (850)222-6350
Publisher's E-mail: fsae@fsae.org
Magazine containing feature articles on Florida Society of Association Executives' management and meeting plans. **Freq:** Bimonthly January/February and November/December combined. **Print Method:** Saddle stitched. **Trim Size:** 7 1/2 x 10. **ISSN:** 1066-8691 (print). **URL:** http://www.fsae.org/reachourmembers/sourcemagazine. **Ad Rates:** BW $1,125; 4C $2025. **Remarks:** Accepts advertising. **Circ:** (Not Reported).

8294 ■ Bulletin of American Odonatology
Dragonfly Society of the Americas
c/o Jerrell Daigle, Treasurer
2067 Little River Ln.
Tallahassee, FL 32311
ISSN: 1061- 3781 (print). **Remarks:** Advertising not accepted. **Circ:** (Not Reported).

8295 ■ Capital Outlook
Capitol Outlook
225 E Jennings St.
Tallahassee, FL 32301-4425
Black community newspaper. **Freq:** Weekly. **Cols./Page:** 6. **Col. Depth:** 21 1/2 INS. **Key Personnel:** Roosevelt Wilson, Editor; Cather Wilson, General Manager; Vaughn Wilson, Manager, Advertising; Martha Washington, Manager, Circulation; Van Wilson, Business Manager; Stephanie Lambert, Associate Editor. **Subscription Rates:** $40 Individuals. **URL:** http://capitaloutlook.com. **Ad Rates:** GLR $9; BW $1,548. **Remarks:** Accepts advertising. **Circ:** 11333.

8296 ■ CLA Journal: Official Publication of the College Language Association
College Language Association
c/o Yakini B. Kemp, Treasurer
PO Box 38515
Tallahassee, FL 32315
Phone: (850)599-3737
Fax: (850)561-2976
Journal containing articles on language and literature. **Freq:** Quarterly Sept., Dec., Mar., and June. **Print Method:** Offset. **Trim Size:** 6 x 9. **Cols./Page:** 1. **Col. Width:** 54 nonpareils. **Col. Depth:** 94 agate lines. **Key Personnel:** Cason L. Hill, Editor. **ISSN:** 0007--8549 (print). **Subscription Rates:** $80 Nonmembers libraries; $82.50 Nonmembers Canada; libraries; $93 Other countries non-members; libraries; $42.75 Single issue special issue; included in membership dues; $43.75 /copy for special issue. **URL:** http://www.clascholars.org/cla-journal. **Ad Rates:** BW $300. **Remarks:** Color advertising not accepted. **Circ:** Paid ‡1,500, Controlled ‡10, 1,700.

8297 ■ Elder Update
Florida Department of Elder Affairs
4040 Esplanade Way
Tallahassee, FL 32399-7016
Phone: (850)414-2000
Fax: (850)414-2004
Free: 800-963-5337
Publication E-mail: eueditor@elderaffairs.org
Newspaper (tabloid) providing Florida's senior citizens with consumer information. **Freq:** Bimonthly. **Print Method:** Offset. **Trim Size:** 11 1/4 x 13 5/8. **Cols./Page:** 4. **USPS:** 403-710. **Subscription Rates:** Free. **Alt. Formats:** PDF. **URL:** http://elderaffairs.state.fl.us/doea/elder_update.php. **Formerly**: The Senior Consumer. **Remarks:** Advertising not accepted. **Circ:** Free ‡80000.

8298 ■ The Famuan
Florida A&M University
510 Orr Dr., Ste. 3081
Tallahassee, FL 32307
College newspaper. **Freq:** Weekly. **Print Method:** Offset. **Trim Size:** 11 1/2 x 17 1/2. **Cols./Page:** 5. **Col. Width:** 26 nonpareils. **Col. Depth:** 196 agate lines. **Key Personnel:** Jordan Calver, Managing Editor; Caryn Wilson, Editor-in-Chief. **URL:** http://thefamuanonline.com. **Ad Rates:** GLR $1; BW $448; PCI $8. **Remarks:** Accepts advertising. **Circ:** Free ‡3400.

8299 ■ FJA Journal
Florida Justice Association
218 S Monroe St.
Tallahassee, FL 32301
Phone: (850)224-9403
Fax: (850)224-4254
Publisher's E-mail: info@floridajusticeassociation.org
Journal containing case law updates, commentaries and articles of interest to the trial bar. **Freq:** Monthly. **Key Personnel:** Kenneth D. Kranz, Editor-in-Chief. **Subscription Rates:** $300 Individuals. **Formerly**: Academy of Florida Trial Lawyers Journal. **Remarks:** Accepts advertising. **Circ:** 5500.

8300 ■ Florida Banking
Florida Bankers Association
1001 Thomasville Rd., Ste. 201
Tallahassee, FL 32303-6267
Phone: (850)224-2265
Publisher's E-mail: info@floridabankers.com
Trade journal for Florida bankers. **Freq:** 11/year. **Key Personnel:** Alejandro Sanchez, Chief Executive Officer, President; Kristi Wagner, Contact. **URL:** http://www.omagdigital.com/publication/?i=290011&page=1. **Formerly**: Banking Today; Florida Banker. **Mailing address:** PO Box 1360, Tallahassee, FL 32302. **Ad Rates:** BW $1,145. **Remarks:** Accepts advertising. **Circ:** (Not Reported).

8301 ■ The Florida Bar Journal
The Florida Bar
651 E Jefferson St.
Tallahassee, FL 32399-2300
Phone: (850)561-5685
Publisher's E-mail: clemail@flabar.org
Legal journal. **Freq:** Monthly. **Print Method:** Web Offset. **Trim Size:** 8 3/8 x 10 7/8. **Cols./Page:** 3. **Col. Width:** 13.5 picas. **Col. Depth:** 58 picas. **Key Personnel:** Randy Traynor, Director, Advertising. **ISSN:** 0015--3915 (print). **Subscription Rates:** $50 Individuals; $120 Individuals 3 years. **URL:** http://floridabar.org/DIVCOM/JN/JNJournal01.nsf. **Ad Rates:** BW $2,987; 4C $2,960; CNU $2,243; PCI $2,893. **Remarks:** Accepts advertising. **Circ:** ‡68945.

8302 ■ Florida CPA Today
Florida Institute of Certified Public Accountants
325 W College Ave.
Tallahassee, FL 32301
Phone: (850)224-2727
Fax: (850)222-8190
Free: 800-342-3197
Publication E-mail: msc@ficpa.org
Magazine covering issues relating to Florida's CPA Profession. **Freq:** Bimonthly. **Key Personnel:** Kathryn Anderson, Chief Accounting Officer, Chief Executive Officer, Executive Director; Drew Miller, Manager, Sales. **Subscription Rates:** Included in membership. **URL:** http://www.ficpa.org/Content/Members/Tools/Publications/FCT.aspx. **Mailing address:** PO Box 5437, Tallahassee, FL 32314. **Ad Rates:** BW $2,423; 4C $3,315. **Remarks:** Accepts advertising. **Circ:** Controlled 18500.

8303 ■ Florida Engineering Society Journal
Florida Engineering Society
125 S Gadsden St.
Tallahassee, FL 32301
Phone: (850)224-7121
Fax: (850)222-4349
Publication E-mail: fes@fleng.org
Freq: Monthly. **Print Method:** Offset. **Trim Size:** 8 1/2 x 11. **Cols./Page:** 3. **Col. Width:** 2 3/8 inches. **Col. Depth:** 10 inches. **Key Personnel:** Allen Douglas, Executive Director; Kathy Roland, Communications Specialist. **ISSN:** 0015--4032 (print). **Subscription Rates:** $50 Nonmembers; Included in membership. **URL:** http://fleng.org/pubs.cfm. **Mailing address:** PO Box 750, Tallahassee, FL 32302-0750. **Ad Rates:** BW $1,185; 4C $785. **Remarks:** Accepts advertising. **Circ:** Paid ‡5000, 4800.

8304 ■ Florida Field Naturalist
Florida Ornithological Society
1503 Wekewa Nene
Tallahassee, FL 32301
Phone: (850)559-2192
Peer-reviewed journal focusing on field biology and natural history. **Freq:** Quarterly. **Print Method:** Offset. **Trim Size:** 6 x 9. **Cols./Page:** 1. **Col. Width:** 45 nonpareils. **Col. Depth:** 75 agate lines. **Key Personnel:** Scott Robinson, Editor. **ISSN:** 0738--999X (print). **Subscription Rates:** Included in membership. **URL:** http://fosbirds.org/content/florida-field-naturalist. **Ad Rates:** BW $100. **Remarks:** Color advertising not accepted. **Circ:** ‡575.

8305 ■ Florida Market Bulletin
Florida Department of Agriculture & Consumer Services
Capitol Plz., Level 10
400 S Monroe St.
Tallahassee, FL 32399-0800
Phone: (850)410-3800
Free: 800-435-7352
Agricultural publication. **Freq:** Monthly. **USPS:** 330-180. **Subscription Rates:** Free. **URL:** http://www.freshfromflorida.com/Divisions-Offices/Marketing-and-Development/Agriculture-Industry/Florida-Market-Bulletin. **Remarks:** Accepts classified advertising. **Circ:** Controlled ‡20000.

8306 ■ Florida Music Director
Florida Music Educators Association
402 Office Plaza Dr.
Tallahassee, FL 32301
Phone: (850)878-6844
Fax: (850)942-1793
Free: 800-301-3632
Music magazine. **Freq:** 10/year. **Print Method:** Offset. **Trim Size:** 8 1/2 x 11. **Cols./Page:** 3. **Col. Width:** 28 nonpareils. **Col. Depth:** 140 agate lines. **Key Personnel:** Kathleen Sanz, Executive Director; Val Anderson, Director, Operations. **ISSN:** 0046--4155 (print). **Subscription Rates:** $27 Individuals; $2.50 Single issue. **URL:** http://flmusiced.org/fmd/magazine_demographics.html; http://fmea.flmusiced.org/publications/florida-music-director. **Ad Rates:** BW $699; 4C $950. **Remarks:** Accepts advertising. **Circ:** Paid ‡4500.

8307 ■ Florida Psychologist
Florida Psychological Association
408 Office Plaza Dr.
Tallahassee, FL 32301
Phone: (850)656-2222
Fax: (850)344-9085
Membership magazine for psychologists. **Freq:** 3/year 3/yr. **Print Method:** Offset. **Trim Size:** @eig. **Subscription Rates:** Members free. **Ad Rates:** BW $425. **Remarks:** Accepts advertising. **Circ:** Controlled 1800, 1,650.

8308 ■ Florida Truck News
Florida Trucking Association
350 E College Ave.
Tallahassee, FL 32301-1565
Phone: (850)222-9900
Fax: (850)222-9363
Publisher's E-mail: info@fltrucking.org
Trucking industry association magazine. **Freq:** Quarterly. **Print Method:** Offset. **Trim Size:** 8 1/2 x 11. **Cols./Page:** 3 and 2. **Col. Width:** 26 and 42 nonpareils. **Col. Depth:** 140 agate lines. **Key Personnel:** Ken Armstrong, PhD, President, Chief Executive Officer. **ISSN:** 0015--4334 (print). **URL:** http://fltrucking.org/florida-truck-news. **Ad Rates:** BW $1375; 4C $1475; PCI $35. **Remarks:** Accepts advertising. **Circ:** Paid ‡1600, Controlled ‡800.

8309 ■ Focal Point
Professional Opticians of Florida
1947 Greenwood Dr.
Tallahassee, FL 32303
Phone: (850)201-2622
Fax: (850)201-2947
Free: 800-972-2698
Publication E-mail: info@pof.org
Trade magazine for licensed opticians. **Freq:** Quarterly. **Print Method:** saddle-stitched. **Trim Size:** 8 1/4 x 10 7/8. **URL:** http://www.pof.org. **Ad Rates:** GLR $133; BW

$275; 4C $664. **Remarks:** Accepts advertising. **Circ:** 1200.

8310 ■ Independent Dealer
Florida Independent Automobile Dealers Association
1840 Fiddler Ct.
Tallahassee, FL 32308
Phone: (850)385-2712
Fax: (850)385-3251
Free: 800-237-0448
Publisher's E-mail: info@fiada.com
Freq: Monthly. **Trim Size:** 8 1/2 x 11. **Subscription Rates:** Included in membership. **URL:** http://www.fiada.com/?page=Magazine. **Ad Rates:** BW $500; 4C $1,075. **Remarks:** Accepts advertising. **Circ:** (Not Reported).

8311 ■ International Artist
Portrait Society of America
1349 E Lafayette St.
Tallahassee, FL 32301
Fax: (850)222-7890
Free: 877-772-4321
Publisher's E-mail: info@portraitsociety.org
Magazine containing information highlighting events and artistic accomplishments, articles on the personal and artistic development of contemporary luminaries of the art world and step-by-step- illustrated demonstrations by acclaimed artists from around the globe. **Freq:** Bimonthly. **Subscription Rates:** Included in membership. **URL:** http://www.portraitsociety.org/#!subscriptions/c1qs5. **Mailing address:** PO Box 11272, Tallahassee, FL 32302. **Remarks:** Advertising not accepted. **Circ:** (Not Reported).

8312 ■ Journal of the Assembly for Expanded Perspectives on Learning
Florida State University
600 W College Ave.
Tallahassee, FL 32306
Phone: (850)644-2525
Fax: (850)645-0108
Journal covering perspectives of learning involving expanded concepts of language. Topics include intuition, inspiration, insight, imagery, meditation, silence, archetypes, emotion, attitudes, values, spirituality, motivation, body wisdom, and felt sense. **Key Personnel:** Joonna Smitherman Trapp, Editor; Bradley Peters, Editor. **URL:** http://www.sworps.tennessee.edu/aepl/html/jaepl.htm. **Remarks:** Advertising not accepted. **Circ:** (Not Reported).

8313 ■ The Journal of Dental Technology
National Association of Dental Laboratories
325 John Knox Rd., No. L103
Tallahassee, FL 32303
Fax: (850)222-0053
Free: 800-950-1150
Publisher's E-mail: nadl@nadl.org
Journal containing technical articles and quizzes. **ISSN:** 0746- 8962 (print). **Subscription Rates:** Included in membership; $85. **URL:** http://nadl.org/store/product.cfm?product=283. **Remarks:** Accepts advertising. **Circ:** (Not Reported).

8314 ■ Journal of Dental Technology
National Association of Dental Laboratories
325 John Knox Rd., No. L103
Tallahassee, FL 32303
Fax: (850)222-0053
Free: 800-950-1150
Publisher's E-mail: nadl@nadl.org
Magazine on dental laboratory technology and management. **Founded:** 1954. **Freq:** 9/yr. **Print Method:** Offset. **Trim Size:** 8 1/4 x 10 7/8. **Cols./Page:** 2 and 3. **Col. Width:** 16 nonpareils. **Col. Depth:** 112 agate lines. **Key Personnel:** Cassandra Corcoran, Editor; Lisa Kamper, Publisher. **ISSN:** 1088-3118 (print). **Subscription Rates:** Free to member (first copy); $85 Individuals bulk; $110 Other countries bulk; $45 Members bulk; $10 Single issue. **URL:** http://www.jdtunbound.com. **Ad Rates:** GLR $150; BW $2,900; 4C $4,500. **Remarks:** Accepts advertising. **Circ:** 4500.

8315 ■ Journal of Drug Issues
Journal of Drug Issues
College of Criminology and Criminal Justice
Florida State University
634 West Call St.
Tallahassee, FL 32306
Phone: (850)644-7368
Fax: (850)644-9614
Professional publication covering mental health, psychology and law. **Freq:** Quarterly. **Key Personnel:** Nicole Piquero, Editor. **ISSN:** 002-2-0426 (print); **EISSN:** 1945--1369 (electronic). **Subscription Rates:** $350 Institutions print and e-access; $381 Institutions e-access; $415 Institutions print only; $423 Institutions print & e-access; $114 Individuals single print issue; $114 Institutions single print issue. **URL:** http://jod.sagepub.com. **Circ:** (Not Reported).

8316 ■ Journal of Insurance Regulation
National Association of Insurance Commissioners
c/o Cassandra Cole, Editor
Department of Risk Management/Insurance, Real Estate, and Legal Studies
College of Business
Florida State University
821 Academic Way
Tallahassee, FL 32306-1110
Forum for research and public policy analysis of topics dealing with the control of insurance companies/markets by regulatory bodies. **Freq:** Quarterly. **Print Method:** Offset. **Trim Size:** 6 x 9. **Cols./Page:** 1. **Col. Width:** 4 inches. **Col. Depth:** 7 inches. **Key Personnel:** Cassandra Cole, Editor. **ISSN:** 0736--248X (print). **URL:** http://www.naic.org/prod_serv_jir.htm. **Remarks:** Advertising not accepted. **Circ:** (Not Reported).

8317 ■ Journal of Land Use and Environmental Law
Florida State University College of Law
425 W Jefferson St.
Tallahassee, FL 32306-1601
Phone: (850)644-3400
Fax: (850)644-5487
Publisher's E-mail: admissions@law.fsu.edu
Journal covering articles related to land use and environmental law. **Freq:** Semiannual. **Key Personnel:** Stephanie Schwarz, Editor-in-Chief. **ISSN:** 0892--4880 (print). **Subscription Rates:** $30 Individuals; $15 Single issue. **URL:** http://www.law.fsu.edu/co-curriculars/jluel. **Circ:** (Not Reported).

8318 ■ Journal of Planning Education and Research
Association of Collegiate Schools of Planning
6311 Mallard Trace Dr.
Tallahassee, FL 32312
Phone: (850)385-2054
Fax: (850)385-2084
Journal covering planning education. **Freq:** Quarterly. **Key Personnel:** Luci Yamamoto, Managing Editor. **ISSN:** 0739--456X (print); **EISSN:** 1552--6577 (electronic). **Subscription Rates:** £84 Individuals print; £261 Institutions e-access; £284 Institutions print; £290 Institutions print and all online content; £319 Institutions current volume print and all online content; £376 Institutions e-access (content through 1998); £27 Individuals single print issue; £78 Institutions single print issue. **URL:** http://www.acsp.org/?page=PubsJPER; http://jpe.sagepub.com; http://tp://intl-jpe.sagepub.com. **Remarks:** Advertising not accepted. **Circ:** (Not Reported).

8319 ■ Journal of Religious Ethics
Wiley-Blackwell
c/o John Kelsay
Journal of Religious Ethics, Department of Religion
Florida State University
Dodd Hall M05
Tallahassee, FL 32306-1520
Phone: (850)644-2154
Fax: (850)644-7225
Publisher's E-mail: info@wiley.com
Journal on religious ethics. **Freq:** Quarterly. **Key Personnel:** John Kelsay, Board Member; Sumner B. Twiss, Board Member; Aline Kalbian, Editor. **ISSN:** 0384--9694 (print); **EISSN:** 1467--9795 (electronic). **Subscription Rates:** $61 Individuals print + online; £60 Individuals print + online; €90 Individuals print + online; $549 Institutions, other countries print + online. **URL:** http://onlinelibrary.wiley.com/journal/10.1111/(ISSN)1467-9795. **Ad Rates:** BW $530. **Remarks:** Advertising accepted; rates available upon request. **Circ:** ‡1400.

8320 ■ Journal of Sport & Exercise Psychology
Human Kinetics Inc.
c/o Robert C. Eklund, Editor
Florida State University
Educational Psychology & Learning Systems
3204K Stone Bldg.
Tallahassee, FL 32306
Phone: (850)645-2909
Fax: (850)644-8776
Publication E-mail: jsep@coe.fsu.edu
Journal of research and theory in sport and exercise psychology. **Freq:** Bimonthly February, April, June, August, October, and December. **Trim Size:** 8.5 x 11. **Key Personnel:** Robert C. Eklund, PhD, Editor; Fuzhong Li, Associate Editor; Alan L. Smith, Board Member. **ISSN:** 0895--2779 (print); **EISSN:** 1543--2904 (electronic). **Subscription Rates:** $129 Individuals online and print; $748 Institutions online and print; $198 Students online and print; $99 Individuals online only; $74 Students online only; $587 Institutions online only. **URL:** http://journals.humankinetics.com/jsep; http://www.humankinetics.com/journals. **Ad Rates:** BW $399. **Remarks:** Accepts advertising. **Circ:** (Not Reported).

8321 ■ Journal of Transnational Law and Policy
Florida State University College of Law
425 W Jefferson St.
Tallahassee, FL 32306-1601
Phone: (850)644-3400
Fax: (850)644-5487
Publisher's E-mail: admissions@law.fsu.edu
Journal providing a scholarly forum for discussion of legal developments in the world community. **Freq:** Annual. **Key Personnel:** Nicholas Giovanni Bush, Editor-in-Chief. **ISSN:** 1067--8182 (print). **Subscription Rates:** $20 U.S.; $21 Canada; $22 Other countries. **URL:** http://www.law.fsu.edu/co-curriculars/jtlp. **Circ:** (Not Reported).

8322 ■ New Directions in Institutional Research
Association for Institutional Research
1435 E Piedmont Dr., Ste. 211
Tallahassee, FL 32308
Phone: (850)385-4155
Fax: (850)385-5180
Publisher's E-mail: air@airweb.org
Journal focusing on topics related to institutional research, planning, or higher education management. **Freq:** Quarterly. **Subscription Rates:** $341 U.S., Canada, and Mexico online; $410 U.S. print and online ; $450 Canada and Mexico print and online ; £257 Institutions print and online ; €324 Institutions print and online; £176 Institutions online; €222 Institutions online; $341 U.S. print ; $381 Canada and Mexico print ; £214 Institutions print ; €270 Institutions print ; $415 Institutions print, ROW; $89 U.S. and other countries online ; £46 Individuals online ; €58 Individuals online ; $98 U.S., Canada, and Mexico print and online ; £61 Individuals print and online ; €77 Individuals print and online ; $122 Individuals print and online, ROW ; $89 U.S., Canada, and Mexico print ; £56 Individuals print ; €72 Individuals print ; $113 Individuals print, ROW. **URL:** http://www.airweb.org/eAIR/journalnews/Pages/NewDirectionsforIR.aspx. **Remarks:** Advertising not accepted. **Circ:** (Not Reported).

8323 ■ Quality Cities
Florida League of Cities, Inc.
301 S Bronough St., Ste. 300
Tallahassee, FL 32301
Phone: (850)222-9684
Fax: (850)222-3806
Free: 800-342-8112
Magazine covering issues of interest to Florida's municipal officials. **Freq:** 6/year. **Print Method:** Offset. **Trim Size:** 8 1/2 x 11. **Cols./Page:** 3. **Col. Width:** 13 picas. **Col. Depth:** 56 picas. **Key Personnel:** Beth Dolan, Editor. **ISSN:** 0892--4171 (print). **Subscription Rates:** $20 Nonmembers; $10 Members; $4 Single issue. **URL:** http://floridaleagueofcities.com/Publications.aspx?CNID=182. **Mailing address:** PO Box 1757, Tallahassee, FL 32302-1757. **Ad Rates:** BW $500; 4C $500; PCI $30. **Remarks:** Accepts advertising. **Circ:** Combined ‡4000.

8324 ■ Real Estate Economics
American Real Estate and Urban Economics Association

Circulation: ★ = AAM; △ or • = BPA; ♦ = CAC; ❑ = VAC; ⊕ = PO Statement; ‡ = Publisher's Report; Boldface figures = sworn; Light figures = estimated.

The Center for Real State Education and Research
821 Academic Way, 223 RBB
Tallahassee, FL 32306-1110
Phone: (850)644-7898
Fax: (850)644-4077
Free: 866-273-8321
Professional journal to promote communication between academic researchers and industry professionals in real estate from the American Real Estate and Urban Economics Association. **Freq:** Quarterly. **Key Personnel:** Crocker Liu, Board Member; Walter Torous, Board Member; Edward Coulson, Board Member; Sumit Agarwal, Editor. **ISSN:** 1080--8620 (print); **EISSN:** 1540--6229 (electronic). **Subscription Rates:** Included in membership. **URL:** http://www.areuea.org/publications/ree. **Mailing address:** PO Box 3061110, Tallahassee, FL 32306-1110. **Remarks:** Accepts advertising. **Circ:** (Not Reported).

8325 ■ Relay Magazine
Florida Municipal Electric Association
417 E College Ave.
Tallahassee, FL 32301-1523
Phone: (850)224-3314
Fax: (850)224-2831
Publication E-mail: relay@publicpower.com
Trade magazine covering the electric utility industry in Florida. **Freq:** Quarterly. **Key Personnel:** Garnie Holmes, Jr., Editor-in-Chief. **URL:** http://relaymagazine.org; http://publicpower.com/relay-pdf-archive. **Mailing address:** PO Box 10114, Tallahassee, FL 32302-2114. **Remarks:** Accepts advertising. **Circ:** (Not Reported).

8326 ■ Research in Higher Education
Association for Institutional Research
1435 E Piedmont Dr., Ste. 211
Tallahassee, FL 32308
Phone: (850)385-4155
Fax: (850)385-5180
Publisher's E-mail: air@airweb.org
Journal containing peer-reviewed articles intended for those concerned with the functioning of postsecondary education, including two-year and four-year colleges, universities, and graduate and professional schools. **Freq:** Bimonthly. **URL:** http://www.airweb.org/eAIR/journalnews/Pages/JournalNewsRIHE.aspx. **Remarks:** Advertising not accepted. **Circ:** (Not Reported).

8327 ■ Social Theory and Practice: An International and Interdisciplinary Journal of Social Philosophy
Florida State University Department of Philosophy
151 Dodd Hall
Tallahassee, FL 32306-1500
Phone: (850)644-1483
Fax: (850)644-3832
Publication E-mail: order@pdcnet.org
Scholarly journal of social philosophy. **Freq:** Quarterly January, April, July, October. **Print Method:** Offset. **Trim Size:** 6 x 9 1/4. **Cols./Page:** 1. **Col. Width:** 4 1/2 inches. **Col. Depth:** 7 1/4 inches. **Key Personnel:** Joshua Gert, Member; John Kelsay, Member; Elizabeth Anderson, Advisor, Board Member; Margaret Dancy, Managing Editor; Victoria Costa, Member. **ISSN:** 0037--802X (print). **URL:** http://stp.philosophy.fsu.edu. **Remarks:** Accepts advertising. **Circ:** (Not Reported).

8328 ■ The Southeast Review
Florida State University Creative Writing Program
405 Williams Bldg.
Tallahassee, FL 32306-1580
Phone: (850)644-4230
Fax: (850)644-0811
Publication E-mail: southeastreview@gmail.com
Magazine featuring literary fiction, creative non-fiction, poetry and art. **Freq:** 2/yr. **Key Personnel:** Katie Cortese, Editor. **Subscription Rates:** $15 Individuals; $27 Other countries; $8 Single issue. **URL:** http://southeastreview.org. **Circ:** (Not Reported).

8329 ■ Surveying and Land Information Science
American Association for Geodetic Surveying
c/o Ronnie Taylor
2905 Carnaby Ct.
Tallahassee, FL 32309-2537
Phone: (850)933-9155
Publication E-mail: ilse@acsm.net
Scholarly journal for surveying and land information systems professionals. **Freq:** Quarterly. **Print Method:** Offset, sheetfed. **Trim Size:** 8 1/4 x 10 7/8. **Cols./Page:** 2. **Col. Width:** 18.5 picas. **Key Personnel:** Dr. Charles Ghilani, Editor-in-Chief. **ISSN:** 1538--1242 (print); **EISSN:** 1559--7202 (electronic). **URL:** http://www.acsm.net. **Formerly:** Surveying and Mapping. **Ad Rates:** BW $890; 4C $850. **Remarks:** Accepts advertising. **Circ:** 5500, 4500, Paid 6500.

8330 ■ The Tallahassee Advertiser
The Tallahassee Advertiser
3471 Monroe St., Unit A
Tallahassee, FL 32303
Phone: (850)574-0520
Publisher's E-mail: ads@tallyads.com
Local community newspaper. **Print Method:** Offset. **Trim Size:** 11.25 x 12. **Cols./Page:** 6. **Col. Width:** 1 9/16 inches. **Col. Depth:** 12 inches. **ISSN:** 0744--4400 (print). **URL:** http://recycler.com/tallyads. **Remarks:** Accepts advertising. **Circ:** Paid 8120, Free 1880.

8331 ■ Tallahassee Democrat
Tallahassee Media Group
277 N Magnolia Dr.
Tallahassee, FL 32301
Phone: (850)599-2100
Free: 800-999-2271
Publication E-mail: tallahasseedemocrat@gannett.com
General newspaper. **Freq:** Daily. **Print Method:** Offset. **Trim Size:** 13 11/16 x 22 3/4. **Cols./Page:** 6. **Col. Width:** 2 1/16 inches. **Col. Depth:** 21 1/2 inches. **Key Personnel:** Skip Foster, President, Publisher, phone: (850)599-2126; Bill Taylor, General Manager, phone: (850)599-2337; Rebeccah Lutz, Managing Editor, phone: (850)599-2391; William Hatfield, Executive Editor, phone: (850)599-2177. **ISSN:** 0738-5153 (print). **Subscription Rates:** $11.16 Individuals /mo.; Sun.; print + online; $13.96 Individuals /mo.; Fri.-Sun.; print + online; $20.46 Individuals /mo.; Mon.-Sun.; print + online; $12 Individuals /mo.; Mon.-Sun.; online only. **Online:** Tallahassee Media Group Tallahassee Media Group; Gannett Company Inc. Gannett Company Inc. **Alt. Formats:** Handheld. **URL:** http://www.tallahassee.com. **Remarks:** Accepts advertising. **Circ:** Mon.-Fri. ***39762**, Sun. ***49627**, Sat. ***41641**.

8332 ■ Tallahassee Magazine
Rowland Publishing Inc.
1932 Miccosukee Rd.
Tallahassee, FL 32308
Phone: (850)878-0554
Fax: (850)656-1871
Publisher's E-mail: info@rowlandpublishing.com
Magazine focusing on lifestyles in Tallahassee, FL. **Freq:** Bimonthly. **Key Personnel:** Kim Howes, Chief Operating Officer; Brian E. Rowland, President, Publisher; Rosanne Dunkelberger, Editor. **Subscription Rates:** $30 Individuals; $45 Two years. **URL:** http://www.tallahasseemagazine.com. **Ad Rates:** BW $1560; 4C $1940. **Remarks:** Advertising accepted; rates available upon request. **Circ:** 89700.

8333 ■ Today's FDA
Florida Dental Association
1111 E Tennessee St.
Tallahassee, FL 32308-6914
Phone: (850)681-3629
Fax: (850)561-0504
Free: 800-877-9922
Publication E-mail: fda@floridadental.org
Professional journal for members of Florida Dental Association. **Founded:** 1989. **Freq:** Bimonthly. **Print Method:** Sheetfed. **Trim Size:** 8 3/8 x 10 7/8. **Cols./Page:** 2. **Key Personnel:** David Higgins, Contact, fax: (850)681-3629. **ISSN:** 1048-5317 (print). **URL:** http://www.floridadental.org/todays-fda. **Formerly:** Florida Dental Journal; Dental Times Dispatch. **Ad Rates:** GLR $30; BW $560; 4C $1,400. **Remarks:** Accepts advertising. **Circ:** 7500.

8334 ■ WAIB-FM - 103.1
3000 Olson Rd.
Tallahassee, FL 32308
Format: Country. **Networks:** AP. **Owner:** Opus Broadcasting, 511 Rossanley Dr., Medford, OR 97501. **Founded:** 1976. **Formerly:** WTHZ-FM; WUMX-FM. **Operating Hours:** Continuous. **ADI:** Tallahassee, FL-Thomasville (Bainbridge), GA. **Key Personnel:** Darren Stephens, Dir. of Programs. **Wattage:** 420,000 ERP. **Ad Rates:** $75 for 30 seconds. **URL:** http://1031thewolf.com.

8335 ■ WAKU-FM - 94.1
3225 Hartsfield Rd.
Tallahassee, FL 32303
Phone: (850)926-8000
Fax: (850)562-2730
Format: Contemporary Christian. **Key Personnel:** Doug Apple, Gen. Mgr., dougapple@wave94.com. **Ad Rates:** Noncommercial. **URL:** http://www.wave94.com.

8336 ■ WANK-FM - 99.9
3000 Olson Rd.
Tallahassee, FL 32308
Phone: (850)386-8004
Fax: (850)422-1897
Format: Oldies. **Owner:** Opus Broadcasting, 511 Rossanley Dr., Medford, OR 97501. **URL:** http://www.999hank.fm.

8337 ■ WANM-FM - 90.5
510 Orr Dr., Ste. 3056
Tallahassee, FL 32304
Phone: (850)599-8448
Fax: (850)561-2829
Format: Urban Contemporary; Full Service. **Owner:** Florida A&M University, 1601 S Martin L. King Jr. Blvd., FL 32307. **Founded:** Jan. 23, 1976. **Operating Hours:** Continuous. **Key Personnel:** Keith Miles, Gen. Mgr.; Cynthia Fields, Asst. GM, Bus. Mgr. **Wattage:** 1,600. **URL:** http://www.famu.edu/?a=famcast.

8338 ■ WAY-FM - 88.1
2199 B N Monroe St.
Tallahassee, FL 32303
Free: 888-422-9293
Email: supportservices@wayfm.com
Format: Contemporary Christian. **Owner:** WAY-FM Media Group Inc., 5540 Tech Center Dr., Ste. 200, Colorado Springs, CO 80919, Ph: (719)533-0300. **Key Personnel:** Bob Augsburg, President, Founder; Lloyd Parker, COO; Steve Young, Contact; Craig Vinson, Contact. **Ad Rates:** Noncommercial; underwriting available. **URL:** http://www.wayfm.com.

8339 ■ WBWT-FM - 100.7
325 John Knox Rd., Bldg. G
Tallahassee, FL 32303
Phone: (850)422-3107
Format: Urban Contemporary. **Founded:** Sept. 15, 2006. **ADI:** Tallahassee, FL-Thomasville (Bainbridge), GA. **Key Personnel:** Jeff Horn, Dir. of Programs, jeffhorn@clearchannel.com; Lisa Rice, Mktg. Mgr., VP. **Wattage:** 11,500. **Ad Rates:** Noncommercial. **URL:** http://www.mix1071.com/.

8340 ■ WBZE-FM - 98.9
3411 W Tharpe St.
Tallahassee, FL 32303
Phone: (850)201-3000
Fax: (850)205-3711
Format: Adult Contemporary; Gospel. **Networks:** ESPN Radio. **Owner:** Cumulus Media Inc., 3280 Peachtree Rd. NW, Ste. 2300, Atlanta, GA 30305-2455, Ph: (404)949-0700, Fax: (404)949-0740; Cumulus Broadcasting Inc., 3280 Peachtree Rd. NW, Ste. 2300, Atlanta, GA 30305-2447, Ph: (404)949-0700, Fax: (404)949-0740. **Founded:** 1962. **Formerly:** HVS Partners; WBGM-AM. **Operating Hours:** Continuous. **ADI:** Tallahassee, FL-Thomasville (Bainbridge), GA. **Wattage:** 100,000. **Ad Rates:** Noncommercial; Advertising accepted; rates available upon request. WHBX. **URL:** http://www.cocanet.org.

8341 ■ WCTV-TV - 6
1801 Halstead Blvd.
Tallahassee, FL 32309
Phone: (850)893-6666
Email: sales@wctv.tv
Format: Commercial TV. **Networks:** CBS. **Owner:** Gray Television Inc., 4370 Peachtree Rd. NE, No. 400, Atlanta, GA 30319-3054, Ph: (404)266-8333. **Founded:** Sept. 15, 1955. **Operating Hours:** Continuous. **ADI:** Tallahassee, FL-Thomasville (Bainbridge), GA. **Key Personnel:** Nick Waller, Gen. Mgr. **Wattage:** 1,000,000 ERP H. **Ad Rates:** Advertising accepted; rates available upon request. **URL:** http://www.wctv.tv.

8342 ■ WCVC-AM
117 1/2 Henderson Rd.
Tallahassee, FL 32312-2337
Phone: (850)386-1330

Founded: 1953. **ADI**: Tallahassee, FL-Thomasville (Bainbridge), GA. **Key Personnel:** Alan McCall, Operations Mgr; Erwin O'Connor, Contact. **Local Programs**: *Gospel Memories*, Saturday 10:00 a.m. - 11:00 a.m. **Ad Rates:** $10 for 30 seconds; $13 for 60 seconds.

8343 ■ WEGT-FM - 99.9
3000 Olson Rd.
Tallahassee, FL 32308
Phone: (850)386-8004
Fax: (850)422-1897
Email: 999hankfm@gmail.com
Format: Classic Rock. **Owner:** Opus Broadcasting of Tallahassee, at above address. **Operating Hours**: Continuous. **Ad Rates:** Advertising accepted; rates available upon request. **URL:** http://www.999hank.fm/home.php.

8344 ■ WFLA-FM - 100.7
325-G John Knox Rd.
Tallahassee, FL 32303
Phone: (850)422-3107
Free: 866-927-8477
Format: Talk; Sports; News. **Owner:** iHeartMedia Inc., 200 E Basse Rd., San Antonio, TX 78209, Ph: (210)832-3314. **Operating Hours**: Continuous. **Key Personnel:** Matt Millar, Dir. of Programs, mattmillar@clearchannel.com. **Ad Rates:** Advertising accepted; rates available upon request. **URL:** http://www.wflafm.com.

8345 ■ WFLP-FM
Department Of Transportation
MS 90
Tallahassee, FL 32399-0450
Phone: (850)245-2555
Fax: (850)245-2572
Format: Information; Educational. **Wattage**: 100 ERP. **Ad Rates:** Underwriting available.

8346 ■ WFRF-AM - 1070
PO Box 181000
Tallahassee, FL 32318-0009
Fax: (850)201-1071
Format: Gospel; Religious. **Owner:** Faith Radio Network Inc., PO Box 181000, Tallahassee, FL 32318, Ph: (850)201-1070, Fax: (850)201-1071, Free: 877-801-1070. **Founded:** July 1997. **Operating Hours**: Continuous. **Ad Rates:** Noncommercial. **URL:** http://www.faithradio.us.

8347 ■ WFRF-FM - 105.7
PO Box 181000
Tallahassee, FL 32318-0009
Fax: (818)775-4664
Free: 800-486-1806
Format: Religious; Contemporary Christian; News; Gospel. **Owner:** Faith Radio Network Inc., PO Box 181000, Tallahassee, FL 32318, Ph: (850)201-1070, Fax: (850)201-1071, Free: 877-801-1070. **Operating Hours**: Continuous. **Ad Rates:** Noncommercial; underwriting available. **URL:** http://www.faithradio.us.

WFSG-TV - See Panama City

8348 ■ WFSQ-FM - 91.5
1600 Red Barber Plz.
Tallahassee, FL 32310
Phone: (850)487-3086
Fax: (850)487-2611
Email: fprn@wfsu.org
Format: Classical; Information; Public Radio. **Networks:** National Public Radio (NPR); Public Radio International (PRI). **Owner:** Florida State University, 600 W College Ave., Tallahassee, FL 32306, Ph: (850)644-2525, Fax: (850)645-0108. **Founded:** 1990. **Formerly**: WFSU-FM. **Operating Hours**: Continuous. **Key Personnel:** Tom Flanigan, News Dir., tflanigan@fsu.edu; Andy Hanus, Dir. of Engg., ahanus@mailer.fsu.edu; John Kwak, Dir. of Dev., john_kwak@wfsu.org; Patrick Keating, Gen. Mgr., pkeating@mailer.fsu.edu; Caroline Austin, Station Mgr., caustin@mailer.fsu.edu; Crystal Cumbo, Mgr., ccumbo@fsu.edu; Krysta Brown, News Dir., kjbrown@fsu.edu. **Local Programs**: *Perspectives*, Thursday 11:00 a.m. - 12:00 p.m. **Wattage**: 100,000. **Ad Rates:** Noncommercial. **URL:** http://news.wfsu.org.

8349 ■ WFSU-TV - 11
1600 Red Barber Plz.
Tallahassee, FL 32310
Phone: (850)487-3170
Fax: (850)487-3093
Email: mail@wfsu.org
Format: Public TV. **Networks:** Public Broadcasting Service (PBS). **Owner:** Florida State University, 600 W College Ave., Tallahassee, FL 32306, Ph: (850)644-2525, Fax: (850)645-0108. **Founded:** 1960. **Operating Hours**: 24-hours a day; High Definition for 12-hours a day. **ADI**: Tallahassee, FL-Thomasville (Bainbridge), GA. **Key Personnel:** Patrick Keating, Gen. Mgr., pkeating@mailer.fsu.edu; Denison Graham, Dir. of Fin., dgraham@admin.fsu.edu; Mike Dunn, Dir. of Production, mdunn@fsu.edu. **Ad Rates:** Noncommercial. **URL:** http://www.wfsu.org.

8350 ■ WFSW-FM - 89.1
1600 Red Barber Plz.
Tallahassee, FL 32310
Phone: (850)487-3086
Fax: (850)487-2611
Format: Public Radio; News; Talk. **Operating Hours**: Continuous. **Key Personnel:** Tom Flanigan, News Dir., tflanigan@fsu.edu. **Ad Rates:** Noncommercial; underwriting available. **URL:** http://news.wfsu.org.

8351 ■ WGLF-FM - 104.1
3411 W Tharpe St.
Tallahassee, FL 32303
Phone: (850)201-3000
Format: Classic Rock. **Networks:** Independent. **Owner:** Cumulus Media Inc., 3280 Peachtree Rd. NW, Ste. 2300, Atlanta, GA 30305-2455, Ph: (404)949-0700, Fax: (404)949-0740. **Founded:** 1969. **Operating Hours**: Continuous. **Wattage**: 100,000. **Ad Rates:** $40-60 per unit. **URL:** http://www.gulf104.com.

8352 ■ WHBX-FM - 96.1
3411 W Tharpe St.
Tallahassee, FL 32303
Phone: (850)201-3000
Format: Urban Contemporary. **Networks:** ABC. **Owner:** Cumulus Media Inc., 3280 Peachtree Rd. NW, Ste. 2300, Atlanta, GA 30305-2455, Ph: (404)949-0700, Fax: (404)949-0740. **Founded:** 1981. **Formerly**: WTMG-FM. **Operating Hours**: Continuous. **ADI**: Tallahassee, FL-Thomasville (Bainbridge), GA. **Local Programs**: *Tom Joyner*, Monday Tuesday Wednesday Thursday Friday Saturday 6:00 a.m. - 10:00 a.m. **Wattage**: 36,000. **Ad Rates:** Noncommercial. Combined advertising rates available with WBZE, WWLD, WGLF. **URL:** http://www.961jamz.com.

8353 ■ WHTF-FM - 104.9
3000 Olson Rd.
Tallahassee, FL 32308
Phone: (850)386-8004
Fax: (850)422-1897
Format: Top 40. **Founded:** Sept. 07, 2006. **URL:** http://www.hot1049.com.

8354 ■ WJZT-FM - 97.9
435 St. Francis St.
Tallahassee, FL 32301
Phone: (850)561-8400
Format: Jazz; Oldies. **Key Personnel:** Christopher Cooper, Gen. Mgr., ccooper@wjztfm.com. **Ad Rates:** Advertising accepted; rates available upon request. **URL:** http://www.espntallahassee.com.

8355 ■ WKVH-FM - 91.9
PO Box 2098
Omaha, NE 68103
Free: 800-525-5683
Format: Contemporary Christian. **Owner:** Educational Media Foundation, 5700 W Oaks Blvd., CA 95765, Free: 800-800434-8400. **Founded:** 2005. **URL:** http://www.klove.com.

8356 ■ WMLO-FM - 104.9
3360 Capital Cir. N
Tallahassee, FL 32308
Phone: (904)668-6600
Fax: (904)422-1070
Free: 800-560-5448
Email: wompam@weir.net
Format: Adult Contemporary. **Networks:** Wall Street Journal Radio; CNN Radio. **Owner:** Ed Winton, at above address. **Founded:** 1987. **Operating Hours**: Continuous. **ADI**: Tallahassee, FL-Thomasville (Bainbridge), GA. **Key Personnel:** Linda Winton, Gen. Mgr. **Wattage**: 50,000. **Ad Rates:** $18-38 per unit.

8357 ■ WNLS-AM - 1270
325 John Knox Rd., Bldg. G
325 John Knox Rd.
Tallahassee, FL 32303
Phone: (850)422-3107
Format: Sports; News; Talk. **Networks:** Fox; ABC. **Founded:** 1935. **Operating Hours**: Continuous. **ADI**: Tallahassee, FL-Thomasville (Bainbridge), GA. **Key Personnel:** Matt Millar, Dir. of Programs, mattmillar@clearchannel.com; Jason Sauer, Promotions Dir., jasonsauer@clearchannel.com. **Wattage**: 5,000. **Ad Rates:** Noncommercial. Combined advertising rates available with WTNT-FM, WXSR-FM, WOKL-FM, WTLY-FM. **URL:** http://www.myfm943.com.

WOZN-FM - See Key West

8358 ■ WQTL-FM
3000 Olson Rd.
Tallahassee, FL 32308
Phone: (419)523-4020
Fax: (419)523-6460
Format: Contemporary Hit Radio (CHR). **Owner:** Media Management Group, 6321 La Pas Trl., No. 250, Indianapolis, IN 46268-2514. **Founded:** 1976. **Formerly**: WPNM-FM. **Key Personnel:** K.C. Allen, Contact; Gary Rivers, Contact. **Wattage**: 2,250 ERP. **Ad Rates:** $6.50-17.50 for 10 seconds; $13-35 for 60 seconds.

8359 ■ WTAL-AM - 1450
1363 E Tennessee St.
Tallahassee, FL 32308
Phone: (850)877-0105
Fax: (850)877-5110
Email: wtal@wtal1450.com
Format: Talk. **Networks:** Sun Radio. **Founded:** 1935. **Operating Hours**: 5:30 a.m.-midnight; 95% network, 5% local. **ADI**: Tallahassee, FL-Thomasville (Bainbridge), GA. **Key Personnel:** Ronald Holmes, VP. **Wattage**: 1,000. **Ad Rates:** $7-10 for 30 seconds; $9-12.50 for 60 seconds. **URL:** http://www.wtal1450.com.

8360 ■ WTLY-FM - 107.1
325 John Knox Rd., Bldg. G
Tallahassee, FL 32303
Phone: (850)422-3107
Format: Adult Contemporary. **Founded:** Sept. 07, 2006. **Key Personnel:** John Hunt, Gen. Mgr.; Jeff Horn, Dir. of Programs, jeffhorn@clearchannel.com. **Wattage**: 100,000. **Ad Rates:** Advertising accepted; rates available upon request. **URL:** http://www.kissfm1071.com.

8361 ■ WTNT-FM - 94.9
325 John Knox Rd., Bldg. G
Tallahassee, FL 32303
Phone: (850)422-3107
Format: Country. **Networks:** Independent. **Founded:** 1967. **Operating Hours**: Continuous; 100% local. **ADI**: Tallahassee, FL-Thomasville (Bainbridge), GA. **Key Personnel:** Chuck Redden, Station Mgr.; Jason Taylor, Director; Jeff Horn, Dir. of Programs, jeff@949tnt.com; Woody Hayes, Contact. **Wattage**: 100,000. **Ad Rates:** $60-70 for 60 seconds. **URL:** http://www.949tnt.com//main.html.

8362 ■ WTWC-TV - 40
8440 Deerlake S
Tallahassee, FL 32312
Phone: (850)893-4140
Fax: (850)893-6974
Format: Commercial TV. **Networks:** NBC. **Operating Hours**: Continuous. 22. **ADI**: Tallahassee, FL-Thomasville (Bainbridge), GA. **Wattage**: 3,100,000. **Ad Rates:** $10-14 per unit. **URL:** http://www.wtwc40.com.

8363 ■ W283AW-FM - 104.5
PO Box 391
Twin Falls, ID 83303
Fax: (208)736-1958
Free: 800-357-4226
Format: Religious; Contemporary Christian. **Owner:** CSN International, PO Box 391, Twin Falls, ID 83303, Ph: (208)736-1958, Fax: (208)736-1958, Free: 800-357-4226. **URL:** http://www.csnradio.com.

8364 ■ WTXL-TV - 27
8927 Thomasville Rd.
Tallahassee, FL 32312
Fax: (850)893-3127
Format: Commercial TV. **Networks:** ABC. **Owner:** Media Venture Management, Inc, at above address.

Circulation: ★ = AAM; △ or • = BPA; ♦ = CAC; ❑ = VAC; ⊕ = PO Statement; ‡ = Publisher's Report; Boldface figures = sworn; Light figures = estimated.

Founded: 1976. **Formerly:** WECA-TV. **ADI:** Tallahassee, FL-Thomasville (Bainbridge), GA. **Wattage:** 1,000,000 ERP Horizon. **Ad Rates:** Advertising accepted; rates available upon request. $20-2000 per unit. **URL:** http://www.wtxl.com.

8365 ■ WUJC-FM - 91.1
PO Box 391
Twin Falls, ID 83303
Fax: (208)736-1958
Free: 800-357-4226
Format: Religious; Contemporary Christian. **Owner:** CSN International, PO Box 391, Twin Falls, ID 83303, Ph: (208)736-1958, Fax: (208)736-1958, Free: 800-357-4226. **Key Personnel:** Mike Kestler, Contact. **URL:** http://www.csnradio.com.

8366 ■ WUTL-FM - 106.1
3000 Olson Rd.
Tallahassee, FL 32308
Phone: (850)386-8004
Format: Talk; Oldies. **Owner:** Opus Broadcasting of Tallahassee, at above address. **Operating Hours:** 16 hours Daily. **Ad Rates:** Advertising accepted; rates available upon request. **URL:** http://www.1061thepath.com.

8367 ■ WVFS-FM - 89.7
420 Diffenbaugh
Tallahassee, FL 32306-1550
Phone: (850)644-3871
Format: Educational. **Owner:** Florida State University Board of Regents, at above address. **Founded:** July 1987. **Operating Hours:** Continuous. **Key Personnel:** Misha H. Laurents, PhD, Gen. Mgr., Prog. Dir., misha@wvfs.fsu.edu. **Local Programs:** *Sunday Morning Blues*, Sunday 10:00 a.m.; *Undaground Railroad*, Saturday 5:00 p.m.; *Your Voice*, Monday 6:00 p.m. **Wattage:** 2,700. **Ad Rates:** Noncommercial; underwriting available. $8-10 per unit. **URL:** http://www.wvfs.fsu.edu.

8368 ■ WVUP-TV - 45
6922 142nd Ave.
Largo, FL 33771
Phone: (727)535-5622
Fax: (727)531-2497
Owner: Christian Television Network Inc., 6922 142nd Ave, Largo, FL 33771, Ph: (727)535-5622, Fax: (727)531-2497. **URL:** http://www.wvup.net.

8369 ■ WWLD-FM - 102.3
3411 W Tharpe St.
Tallahassee, FL 32303
Phone: (850)201-3000
Fax: (406)721-5734
Format: Hip Hop; Urban Contemporary; Blues. **Owner:** Cumulus Broadcasting Inc., 3280 Peachtree Rd. NW, Ste. 2300, Atlanta, GA 30305-2447, Ph: (404)949-0700, Fax: (404)949-0740. **Operating Hours:** Continuous. **Ad Rates:** Advertising accepted; rates available upon request. **URL:** http://www.blazin1023.com.

8370 ■ WXSR-FM - 101.5
325 John Knox Rd., Bldg. G
Tallahassee, FL 32303
Phone: (850)422-3107
Format: Adult Album Alternative. **Networks:** Westwood One Radio. **Owner:** iHeartMedia Inc., 200 E Basse Rd., San Antonio, TX 78209, Ph: (210)832-3314. **Founded:** 1990. **Operating Hours:** Continuous. **ADI:** Tallahassee, FL-Thomasville (Bainbridge), GA. **Key Personnel:** Jason Sauer, Promotions Dir., jasonsauer@clearchannel.com. **Wattage:** 50,000. **Ad Rates:** Advertising accepted; rates available upon request. **URL:** http://www.x1015.com//main.html.

TAMPA

WC FL. Hillsborough Co. At head of Hillsboro Bay, 24 mi. from Gulf of Mexico. University of Tampa; University of South Florida; Florida College. Mac Dill A.F.B. Resort area. Leading port in shipping phosphate and citrus fruit. Manufactures cigars, fertilizer, feed, cement, beverages, clothing, paint, glass, chemicals, aluminum products, and pharmaceuticals. Fruit and vegetable packing and canning.

8371 ■ AAA Going Places
AAA Auto Club South
1515 N Westshore Blvd.
Tampa, FL 33607-4505
Phone: (813)289-5000
Fax: (813)288-7263
Magazine for auto club members and the travel market. **Freq:** Bimonthly. **Print Method:** Offset. **Trim Size:** 8 x 10 1/2. **Cols./Page:** 3. **Col. Width:** 2 3/16 inches. **Col. Depth:** 9 3/8 inches. **Key Personnel:** Phyllis W. Zeno, Editor; Sandra Klim, Editor. **Subscription Rates:** Free. **URL:** http://aaagoingplaces.com/map.asp. **Ad Rates:** BW $36,488; 4C $39,900. **Remarks:** Accepts advertising. **Circ:** Paid ★2424248.

8372 ■ AAKP RENALIFE
American Association of Kidney Patients
1440 Bruce B. Downs Blvd.
Tampa, FL 33613
Fax: (813)636-8122
Free: 800-749-2257
Publication E-mail: info@aakp.org
Magazine covering news and information for kidney patients. **Freq:** Bimonthly 6/yr; every January, March, May, July, September and November. **Trim Size:** 8.5 x 11. **Key Personnel:** Jerome Bailey, Editor; Emily Carbone, Associate Editor. **Subscription Rates:** Included in membership; $10 Nonmembers. **URL:** http://www.aakp.org/education/magazines/item/renalife.html?category_id=26. **Formerly:** Renalife Bulletin. **Ad Rates:** BW $1,650; 4C $2,450. **Remarks:** Advertising accepted; rates available upon request. **Circ:** 20000, Paid 24000.

8373 ■ The American Journal of Clinical Medicine
American Association of Physician Specialists, Inc.
5550 W Executive Dr., Ste. 400
Tampa, FL 33609
Phone: (813)433-2277
Fax: (813)830-6599
Freq: Quarterly. **URL:** http://www.aapsus.org/journals. **Remarks:** Accepts advertising. **Circ:** (Not Reported).

8374 ■ BICSI News
BICSI
8610 Hidden River Pky.
Tampa, FL 33637-1000
Phone: (813)979-1991
Fax: (813)971-4311
Free: 800-242-7405
Publisher's E-mail: bicsi@bicsi.org
Freq: Bimonthly. **Subscription Rates:** Included in membership. **URL:** http://www.bicsi.org/double.aspx?l=1760,1754&r=1756,1758. **Remarks:** Advertising accepted; rates available upon request. **Circ:** (Not Reported).

8375 ■ BizEd: The Leading Voice of Business Education
Association to Advance Collegiate Schools of Business
777 S Harbour Island Blvd., Ste. 750
Tampa, FL 33602
Phone: (813)769-6500
Fax: (813)769-6559
Publisher's E-mail: events@aacsb.edu
Magazine covering trends in business education. **Freq:** Bimonthly. **Print Method:** Web Offset. **Trim Size:** 8.375 x 10.75. **Key Personnel:** Tricia Bisoux, Editor; Sharon Shinn, Editor, phone: (314)961-0677. **ISSN:** 1537--338X (print). **Subscription Rates:** $35 U.S. print and online; $45 Canada print and online; $55 Other countries print and online; $25 Individuals online only. **URL:** http://www.bizedmagazine.com. **Ad Rates:** BW $4,690; 4C $6,090. **Remarks:** Accepts advertising. **Circ:** 15000.

8376 ■ blu Tampa Bay
Rain Publishing Group
708 Harbour Post Dr.
Tampa, FL 33602
Phone: (813)600-4000
Fax: (813)600-4001
Free: 888-600-4005
Publication E-mail: info@blutampabay.com
Magazine featuring luxury and lifestyle in Tampa Bay. **Freq:** Quarterly. **Trim Size:** 10 x 12. **Subscription Rates:** $24.95 Individuals 1 year; $39.95 Two years. **URL:** http://www.thetampamagazine.com. **Remarks:** Accepts advertising. **Circ:** (Not Reported).

8377 ■ Cancer Control: Journal of the Moffitt Cancer Center
H. Lee Moffitt Cancer Center & Research Institute
12902 Magnolia Dr.
Tampa, FL 33612
Phone: (813)745-4673
Free: 800-456-3434
Publication E-mail: ccjournal@moffitt.org
Peer-reviewed professional journal covering cancer. **Freq:** Quarterly. **Key Personnel:** John Horton, Editor. **ISSN:** 1073--2748 (print). **URL:** http://moffitt.org/publications/cancer-control-journal. **Ad Rates:** BW $2850; 4C $4375. **Remarks:** Accepts advertising. **Circ:** 13000.

8378 ■ Computer-Aided Design and Applications
CAD Solutions
18002 Richmond Place Dr., Ste. 2224
Tampa, FL 33647
Peer-reviewed journal that publishes reports of new applications in computer design and uses for existing applications in computer aided design. **Freq:** Bimonthly. **Key Personnel:** Les A. Piegl, Editor-in-Chief; Robert Joan-Arinyo, Associate Editor. **EISSN:** 1686--4360 (electronic). **Subscription Rates:** $656 Institutions online. **URL:** http://www.cadanda.com; http://www.tandfonline.com/loi/tcad20#.Uv9Tb2JLVWU. **Remarks:** Advertising not accepted. **Circ:** (Not Reported).

8379 ■ Creative Loafing Tampa
Creative Loafing
1911 N 13th St., Ste. W200
Tampa, FL 33605
Phone: (813)739-4800
Fax: (813)739-4801
Alternative newspaper. **Freq:** Weekly (Wed.). **Key Personnel:** David Warner, Editor-in-Chief; James Howard, Publisher. **Subscription Rates:** Free. **URL:** http://cltampa.com. **Remarks:** Accepts advertising. **Circ:** Free ■ **49454**.

8380 ■ Daytona Times: East Central Florida's Black Voice
Daytona Times Inc.
5207 Washington Blvd.
Tampa, FL 33619
Free: 877-352-4455
Publication E-mail: editor@daytontimes.com
Black community newspaper. **Freq:** Weekly (Thurs.). **Print Method:** Offset. **Cols./Page:** 6. **Col. Width:** 2 1/16 inches. **Col. Depth:** 21 inches. **Key Personnel:** Charles W. Cherry, II, Publisher. **Subscription Rates:** $59 Individuals. **URL:** http://daytonatimes.com. **Ad Rates:** GLR $.82; BW $2,397.78; 4C $2,647.78; PCI $19.03. **Remarks:** Accepts advertising. **Circ:** ‡20150.

8381 ■ Disaster Safety Review
Insurance Institute for Business & Home Safety
4775 E Fowler Ave.
Tampa, FL 33617
Phone: (813)286-3400
Fax: (813)286-9960
Publisher's E-mail: info@ibhs.org
Journal publishing scientific research to identify and promote effective actions that strengthen homes, businesses and communities against natural disasters and other causes of loss. **Freq:** Quarterly. **Key Personnel:** Candance Iskowitz, Editor. **Subscription Rates:** Included in membership. **URL:** http://disastersafety.org/ibhs-studies-reports/disaster-safety-review. **Remarks:** Advertising not accepted. **Circ:** 3,000.

8382 ■ FDCC Quarterly
Federation of Defense and Corporate Counsel
11812 N 56th St.
Tampa, FL 33617
Phone: (813)983-0022
Fax: (813)988-5837
Freq: Quarterly. **Subscription Rates:** $34 /year for university law libraries; $40 /year all others. **Alt. Formats:** Download; PDF. **URL:** http://www.thefederation.org/process.cfm?pageid=2054. **Remarks:** Advertising not accepted. **Circ:** (Not Reported).

8383 ■ 5.0 Mustangs and Super Fords
TEN: The Enthusiast Network
9036 Brittany Way
Tampa, FL 33619
Publication E-mail: 5mustang@emailcustomerservice.com inquiries@automotive.com
Magazine publishing for 5.0 liter and mod-motor enthusiasts seeking maximum performance from their Mustangs. Features new product evaluations, performance how-tos, technical advice, new-car drive reports, and the latest innovations in street and strip

performance. Provides feature articles on late-model Mustangs. **Freq:** Monthly. **URL:** http://www.mustangandfords.com/50-mustang-super-fords-magazine/. **Remarks:** Accepts advertising. **Circ:** (Not Reported).

8384 ■ Financial Management: The Journal of the Financial Management Association
Financial Management Association International
College of Business Administration
University of South Florida
4202 E Fowler Ave., BSN 3416
Tampa, FL 33620-5500
Phone: (813)974-2084
Fax: (813)974-3318
Publication E-mail: fma@coba.usf.edu
Journal covering business, economics, finance and management. **Freq:** Quarterly. **Print Method:** Offset. **Trim Size:** 8 1/4 x 10 7/8. **Cols./Page:** 2. **Col. Width:** 38 nonpareils. **Col. Depth:** 118 agate lines. **Key Personnel:** Raghu Rau, Editor; Dr. Marc Lipson, Editor. **ISSN:** 004-6-3892 (print); **EISSN:** 1755--053X (electronic). **Subscription Rates:** $471 Institutions online only; $566 Institutions print and online; $511 Other countries online only; $614 Other countries print and online. **URL:** http://fma.org/Publications/FM/FMIndex.htm. **Ad Rates:** BW $500. **Remarks:** Accepts advertising. **Circ:** ‡12000.

8385 ■ Florida Sentinel-Bulletin
Florida Sentinel-Bulletin
2207-21st Ave.
Tampa, FL 33605
Phone: (813)248-1921
Black community newspaper (tabloid). **Freq:** Semi-weekly Tues. and Fri. **Print Method:** Offset. **Trim Size:** 10 x 15. **Cols./Page:** 5. **Col. Width:** 2 inches. **Col. Depth:** 15 inches. **Key Personnel:** Blythe C. Andrews, Jr., Chairman; Sybil K. Andrews, Publisher; Gwen Hayes, Editor. **Subscription Rates:** $44 By mail 6 months; $87 By mail 1 year. **URL:** http://flsentinel.com. **Mailing address:** PO Box 3363, Tampa, FL 33605. **Ad Rates:** GLR $.72; PCI $10. **Remarks:** Color advertising not accepted. **Circ:** ‡23345.

8386 ■ Free Press
Free Press Publishing Co.
1010 W Cass St.
Tampa, FL 33606
Phone: (813)254-5888
Community newspaper. **Founded:** 1911. **Freq:** Weekly. **Print Method:** Offset. **Cols./Page:** 8. **Col. Width:** 9.5 picas. **Col. Depth:** 20 inches. **Subscription Rates:** $20 Individuals. **Alt. Formats:** PDF. **URL:** http://4freepress.com; http://4freepress.com/newspaper-archive. **Circ:** ‡1040.

8387 ■ La Gaceta
La Gaceta Publishing Inc.
3210 7th Ave. E
Tampa, FL 33603
Phone: (813)248-3921
Fax: (813)247-5357
Publication E-mail: lagaceta@tampabay.rr.com
Community newspaper (Spanish, English, Italian). **Freq:** Weekly (Fri.). **Print Method:** Offset. **Cols./Page:** 5. **Col. Width:** 22 nonpareils. **Col. Depth:** 231 agate lines. **Key Personnel:** Patrick Manteiga, Editor, Publisher; Angie Manteiga, Associate Publisher; Alberto dela Rosa, Contact. **USPS:** 299-240. **Subscription Rates:** $35 Individuals; $65 Two years; $40 Out of area; $75 Out of area two years; $45 Out of country. **URL:** http://lagacetanewspaper.com. **Ad Rates:** BW $701.25; 4C $1,126.25; PCI $8.50. **Remarks:** Accepts advertising. **Circ:** ‡18079.

8388 ■ Georgetown Journal of History
Phi Alpha Theta
University of South Florida
4202 E Fowler Ave., SOC107
Tampa, FL 33620-8100
Fax: (813)974-8215
Free: 800-394-8195
Freq: Semiannual. **URL:** http://georgetownhistoryjournal.org. **Circ:** (Not Reported).

8389 ■ Go For A Ride
Savidge Publishing
14907 W Hardy Dr.
Tampa, FL 33613
Phone: (813)505-5119
Magazine focusing on motorcycle community. **Freq:** Monthly. **Subscription Rates:** $40 Individuals. **URL:** http://www.gofarmag.com. **Remarks:** Accepts advertising. **Circ:** (Not Reported).

8390 ■ HAWKEYE
Hillsborough Community College
PO Box 31127
Tampa, FL 33631
Phone: (813)253-7000
Collegiate newspaper. **Founded:** 1969. **Freq:** Monthly. **Print Method:** Offset. **Trim Size:** 10 x 16. **Cols./Page:** 4. **Col. Width:** 14 picas. **Col. Depth:** 16 inches. **Key Personnel:** Emily Duren, Editor-in-Chief. **Subscription Rates:** Free. **URL:** http://www.hawkeyenews.net. **Remarks:** Accepts advertising. **Circ:** Free ‡5000.

8391 ■ The Historian
Wiley-Blackwell
University of South Florida
Dept. of History
4202 E Fowler Ave., SOC107
Tampa, FL 33620
Phone: (813)974-4674
Fax: (813)974-8215
Publication E-mail: historian@cas.usf.edu
Journal focusing on contemporary and relevant historical scholarship. **Freq:** Quarterly. **Key Personnel:** Kees Boterbloem, Editor. **ISSN:** 0018-2370 (print); **EISSN:** 1540-6563 (electronic). **Subscription Rates:** $60 Individuals print & online; $269 Institutions print & online; £188 Institutions print or online; $224 Institutions U.S. print or online; £54 Individuals print & online; €80 Individuals print & online; £226 Institutions print & online. **URL:** http://www.wiley.com/WileyCDA/WileyTitle/productCd-HISN.html. **Ad Rates:** BW $500. **Remarks:** Accepts advertising. **Circ:** (Not Reported).

8392 ■ Ice World
International Packaged Ice Association
238 E Davis Blvd., Ste. 213
Tampa, FL 33606
Phone: (813)258-1690
Journal publishing articles, calendar of events, regional association news and industry updates. **Freq:** Quarterly. **URL:** http://www.packagedice.org/publications.html. **Remarks:** Advertising not accepted. **Circ:** (Not Reported).

8393 ■ Journal of Applied Finance
Financial Management Association International
College of Business Administration
University of South Florida
4202 E Fowler Ave., BSN 3416
Tampa, FL 33620-5500
Phone: (813)974-2084
Fax: (813)974-3318
Publisher's E-mail: fma@coba.usf.edu
Journal for financial practice and education developments. **Freq:** Semiannual spring and fall. **Trim Size:** 7.5 x 9.5. **Key Personnel:** Eric Ball, Editor; Josh Rosett, Editor, phone: (909)607-3625; Richard Smith, Editor, phone: (951)827-3554. **ISSN:** 1534--6668 (print). **URL:** http://69.175.2.130/~finman/Publications/JAF.htm. **Formerly:** Financial Practice and Education. **Remarks:** Advertising not accepted. **Circ:** (Not Reported).

8394 ■ Journal of Behavioral Health Services & Research
Springer Science + Business Media LLC
Colorado of Behavioral & Community Science and Public Health
University of South Florida
13301 Bruce B. Downs Blvd.
Tampa, FL 33612
Publisher's E-mail: service-ny@springer.com
Peer-reviewed journal on the organization, financing, delivery, and outcome of behavioral health services. **Founded:** 1972. **Freq:** Quarterly. **Trim Size:** 7 x 10. **Key Personnel:** Dr. Bruce Lubotsky Levin, Editor-in-Chief. **ISSN:** 1094-3412 (print). **Subscription Rates:** €337 Institutions print or online; €404 Institutions print & enchanced access. **URL:** http://jbhsr.fmhi.usf.edu; http://www.springer.com/public+health/journal/11414; http://link.springer.com/journal/11414. **Formerly:** Journal of Mental Health Administration. **Ad Rates:** BW $250. **Remarks:** Accepts advertising. **Circ:** (Not Reported).

8395 ■ Journal of Chemical Ecology: Official Journal of the International Society of Chemical Ecology
Springer Netherlands
c/o John T. Romeo, Ed.-in-Ch.
Dept. of Biology
University of South Florida
Tampa, FL 33620-5200
Scientific research journal. **Freq:** Monthly. **Print Method:** Offset. **Trim Size:** 6 x 9. **Cols./Page:** 1. **Col. Width:** 54 nonpareils. **Col. Depth:** 103 agate lines. **Key Personnel:** Jeff Aldrich, Board Member; Jocelyn G. Millar, Board Member; Tetsu Ando, Board Member; Stephen Foster, Associate Editor; Jeremy N. McNeil, Board Member; Heidi Appel, Board Member; John T. Romeo, Editor-in-Chief. **ISSN:** 0098--0331 (print); **EISSN:** 1573--1561 (electronic). **Subscription Rates:** €2544 Institutions print including free access or e-only; €3053 Institutions print plus enhanced access. **URL:** http://www.springer.com/life+sciences/ecology/journal/10886; http://link.springer.com/journal/10886. **Remarks:** Advertising accepted; rates available upon request. **Circ:** (Not Reported).

8396 ■ The Journal of Craniofacial Surgery: An International Journal dedicated to the Art and Science essential to the Practice of Craniofacial Surgery and Pediatric Plastic Surgery
Lippincott Williams and Wilkins
c/o Mutaz B. Habal MD, Ed.-in-Ch.
6358 Maclaurin Dr.
Tampa, FL 33647-1164
Publisher's E-mail: ronna.ekhouse@wolterskluwer.com
Medical journal concerning the field of facial skeletal surgery. Peer review for the state of the art in patient care and research. **Freq:** Bimonthly. **Print Method:** Offset. **Trim Size:** 8 1/8 x 10 7/8. **Cols./Page:** 2. **Col. Width:** 3 3/8 inches. **Col. Depth:** 10 inches. **Key Personnel:** Mutaz B. Habal, MD, Editor-in-Chief; Ali Gavenda, Publisher. **ISSN:** 1049--2275 (print). **Subscription Rates:** $1325 U.S., Canada, and Mexico print, 1 year; $1349 Other countries print, 1 year; $2423 Institutions print, 1 year; $2214 Institutions, Canada and Mexico print, 1 year; $2238 Institutions, other countries print, 1 year; $548 U.S. in-training; $523 Canada and Mexico in-training; $572 Other countries in-training. **URL:** http://lww.com/Product/1049-2275. **Formerly:** Journal of Craniofacial Surgery. **Remarks:** Accepts advertising. **Circ:** (Not Reported).

8397 ■ Journal for Ecumenical Studies
North American Academy of Ecumenists
3838 W Cypress St.
Tampa, FL 33607
Phone: (813)435-5335
Publisher's E-mail: members@naae.net
Journal covering scholarly articles in the field of dialogue across lines of religious difference. **Freq:** Quarterly. **Subscription Rates:** $45 Individuals; $25 Students; $105 Institutions. **URL:** http://www.journal.jesdialogue.org; http://naae.net/site/?page_id=27. **Remarks:** Advertising not accepted. **Circ:** (Not Reported).

8398 ■ Journal of Emergencies, Trauma, and Shock
Medknow Publications Private Ltd.
Global Emergency Medical Sciences
University of South Florida-Emergency Medicine
1 Davis Blvd., Ste. 504
Davis Island
Tampa, FL 33606
Publication E-mail: editor@onlinejets.org
Peer-reviewed journal of the INDO-US Emergency and Trauma Collaborative. **Freq:** Quarterly. **Key Personnel:** Sagar Galwankar, Executive Editor. **ISSN:** 0974--2700 (print). **Subscription Rates:** Rs 1500 Individuals print only; Rs 2500 Institutions print only; Rs 3200 Institutions print and online; Rs 1900 Individuals print and online; $469 Single issue individuals; $781 Single issue institution. **URL:** http://www.onlinejets.org. **Remarks:** Accepts advertising. **Circ:** (Not Reported).

8399 ■ Journal of Orthopaedic Trauma
Orthopaedic Trauma Association
c/o Roy Sanders, MD, Editor-in-Chief
5 Tampa General Circle, Ste. No. 710
Tampa, FL 33606
Phone: (813)253-2068
Fax: (813)558-6912

Circulation: ★ = AAM; △ or • = BPA; ♦ = CAC; ❑ = VAC; ⊕ = PO Statement; ‡ = Publisher's Report; Boldface figures = sworn; Light figures = estimated.

Publication E-mail: editor@jotonline.org
Freq: Monthly. **Print Method:** Sheetfed Offset. **Trim Size:** 8 1/8 x 10 7/8. **Key Personnel:** Roy Sanders, MD, Editor-in-Chief; Marcia Serepy, MD, Publisher. **ISSN:** 0890-5339 (print); **EISSN:** 1531-2291 (electronic). **Subscription Rates:** $686 Individuals; $1534 Institutions; $289 Individuals in-training; $822 Other countries individual; $1604 Institutions, other countries; $321 Other countries in-training; $656 Individuals; $763 Canada and Mexico; $786 Other countries; $1401 Institutions U.S.A; $1581 Institutions, Canada and Mexico; $275 U.S. in-training; $283 Canada and Mexico in-training; $306 Other countries in-training. **URL:** http://journals.lww.com/jorthotrauma/pages/default.aspx; http://www.lww.com/Product/0890-5339; http://ota.org/research/journal-of-orthopaedic-trauma/. **Ad Rates:** BW $1540; 4C $1790. **Remarks:** Accepts advertising. **Circ:** 2,300.

8400 ■ Journal of Pharmaceutical Innovation
International Society for Pharmaceutical Engineering
600 N Westshore Blvd., Ste. 900
Tampa, FL 33609-1114
Phone: (813)960-2105
Fax: (813)264-2816
Publisher's E-mail: ask@ispe.org
Freq: Quarterly Bimonthly. **Key Personnel:** James K. Drennen, III, Editor-in-Chief; Emanuel Diliberto, Editor. **ISSN:** 1872--5120 (print); **EISSN:** 1939--8042 (electronic). **Subscription Rates:** $652 Institutions print including free access or e-only. **URL:** http://www.springer.com/biomed/pharmaceutical+science/journal/12247. **Remarks:** Accepts advertising. **Circ:** (Not Reported).

8401 ■ Kidney Beginnings: The Magazine
American Association of Kidney Patients
1440 Bruce B. Downs Blvd.
Tampa, FL 33613
Fax: (813)636-8122
Free: 800-749-2257
Publisher's E-mail: info@aakp.org
Freq: Quarterly in February, May, August and November. **Subscription Rates:** Included in membership. **URL:** http://www.aakp.org/magazines/kidney-beginnings.html. **Remarks:** Accepts advertising. **Circ:** 60,000.

8402 ■ The Member's Guide
Florida State Golf Association
12630 Telecom Dr.
Tampa, FL 33637
Phone: (813)632-3742
Fax: (813)910-2129
Magazine covering for the Florida State Golf Association. **Freq:** Annual. **Subscription Rates:** Free. **URL:** http://www.fsga.org/sections/Clubs/FSGA-Club-Membership/55. **Remarks:** Accepts advertising. **Circ:** (Not Reported).

8403 ■ Mustang & Fords
RentPath Inc.
9036 Brittany Way
Tampa, FL 33619
Publication E-mail: modifiedmustangsandfords@emailcustomerservice.com
Magazine featuring a variety of Mustang events and other car-related activities across the country. **Freq:** Monthly. **Print Method:** Web Offset. **Trim Size:** 7 7/8 x 10 1/2. **Key Personnel:** Sandy Patterson, Specialist, Advertising and Sales, phone: (813)675-3477. **ISSN:** 1059--5368 (print). **Subscription Rates:** $19.97 Individuals; $29.97 Two years; $31.97 Canada; $53.97 Canada 2 years; $43.97 Other countries; $77.97 Other countries 2 years. **URL:** http://www.mustangandfords.com. **Circ:** (Not Reported).

8404 ■ Mustang Monthly
RentPath Inc.
9036 Brittany Way
Tampa, FL 33619
Publication E-mail: mustangmonthly@emailcustomerservice.com inquiries@automotive.com
Specialized automobile magazine for Mustang vehicle owners and enthusiasts. **Freq:** Monthly. **Key Personnel:** Sandy Patterson, Contact, phone: (813)675-3477. **URL:** http://www.mustangmonthly.com. **Remarks:** Accepts advertising. **Circ:** (Not Reported).

8405 ■ Nonlinear Studies
International Federation of Nonlinear Analysts
c/o Dr. Rebecca Wooten, Vice President/Treasurer
University of South Florida, CMC 319
4202 E Fowler Ave.
Tampa, FL 33620
Remarks: Advertising not accepted. **Circ:** (Not Reported).

8406 ■ Oracle
University of South Florida
4202 E Fowler Ave.
Tampa, FL 33620
Phone: (813)974-2011
Fax: (813)974-9689
Publisher's E-mail: admissions@grad.usf.edu
Collegiate newspaper. **Founded:** Sept. 06, 1966. **Freq:** Daily Mon.-Thu. **Print Method:** Offset. **Trim Size:** 5 x 13. **Cols./Page:** 5. **Col. Width:** 19 nonpareils. **Col. Depth:** 224 agate lines. **URL:** http://www.usforacle.com. **Ad Rates:** PCI $12.50; BW $900; 4C $1,350. **Remarks:** Accepts advertising. **Circ:** Combined 12800.

8407 ■ Outdoor Life
Time4 Media
PO Box 60001
Tampa, FL 33660-0001
Free: 800-365-1580
Publication E-mail: olmagazine@aol.com
Outdoor sports magazine. **Freq:** Monthly. **Print Method:** Offset. **Trim Size:** 7 7/8 x 10 3/4. **Cols./Page:** 3. **Col. Width:** 28 nonpareils. **Col. Depth:** 143 agate lines. **Key Personnel:** Todd W. Smith, Editor-in-Chief; Anthony Licata, Director, Editorial; Gerry Bethge, Editor. **Subscription Rates:** $10 Individuals; $15 Two years; C$26 Canada; $42 Other countries. **URL:** http://www.outdoorlife.com. **Ad Rates:** BW $53800; 4C $78000. **Remarks:** Accepts advertising. **Circ:** Paid ★750000.

8408 ■ Perspectives on Science: Historical, Philosophical, Social
The MIT Press
c/o Alex Levine, Ed.
University of South Florida
Dept. of Philosophy
4202 E Fowler Ave., FAO 226
Tampa, FL 33620-7926
Phone: (813)974-0126
Fax: (813)974-5914
Publication E-mail: pos@cas.usf.edu
Peer-reviewed journal devoted to studies of the sciences that integrate historical, philosophical, and sociological perspectives. Interdisciplinary approach is intended to foster a more comprehensive understanding of the sciences and the contexts in which they develop. Contributions to the journal include theoretical essays, case studies, and review essays. **Freq:** Quarterly. **Key Personnel:** Prof. Roger Ariew, Editor; Richard M. Burian, Advisor, Editor; Mordechai Feingold, Editor; Jed Z. Buchwald, Associate Editor; Joseph C. Pitt, Associate Editor. **ISSN:** 1063--6145 (print); **EISSN:** 1530--9274 (electronic). **Subscription Rates:** $57 Individuals online only; $269 Institutions online only; $29 Students online only. **URL:** http://www.mitpressjournals.org/loi/posc. **Ad Rates:** BW $350. **Remarks:** Accepts advertising. **Circ:** 350.

8409 ■ Pharmaceutical Engineering
International Society for Pharmaceutical Engineering
600 N Westshore Blvd., Ste. 900
Tampa, FL 33609-1114
Phone: (813)960-2105
Fax: (813)264-2816
Publisher's E-mail: ask@ispe.org
Freq: Bimonthly. **Print Method:** Offset. **Trim Size:** 8 3/8 x 10 7/8. **Cols./Page:** 2 and 3. **Col. Width:** 39 and 24 nonpareils. **Col. Depth:** 140 agate lines. **Key Personnel:** Gloria N. Hall, Editor, Director; Gloria Hall, Director, Editor. **ISSN:** 0273--8139 (print). **Subscription Rates:** Included in membership. **URL:** http://www.pharmaceuticalengineering.org; http://www.ispe.org/pharmaceutical-engineering-magazine/about-pe. **Ad Rates:** BW $4650; 4C $6280. **Remarks:** Accepts advertising. **Circ:** 30000.

8410 ■ Physician Executive
American Association for Physician Leadership
400 N Ashley Dr., Ste. 400
Tampa, FL 33602
Fax: (813)287-8993
Free: 800-562-8088
Publisher's E-mail: acpe@acpe.org
Focuses on health care management and medical management for physician executives. **Freq:** Bimonthly. **Print Method:** Offset. **Trim Size:** 8 1/2 x 11. **Cols./Page:** 3. **Col. Width:** 27 nonpareils. **Col. Depth:** 140 agate lines. **Key Personnel:** Bill Steiger, Editor. **ISSN:** 0898--2759 (print). **Subscription Rates:** $100 Individuals; $120 Other countries nonmembers; Included in membership. **URL:** http://www.physicianleaders.org/news/journals/plj; http://www.physicianleaders.org/shop/journals/plj. **Formerly**: Physician Executive Journal of Medical Management. **Ad Rates:** BW $3,000, full page; BW $1,800, half page horizontal; BW $1,200, half page vertical. **Remarks:** Accepts display advertising. **Circ:** Paid ‡300, Controlled ‡13000, 10000.

8411 ■ Sociology of Religion
Association for the Sociology of Religion
University of South Florida
Dept. of Sociology
4202 E Fowler Ave.
Tampa, FL 33620
Phone: (813)974-2758
Fax: (813)974-6455
Journal containing topics regarding to the sociological study of religion. **Freq:** Quarterly. **Key Personnel:** Gerardo Marti, Editor. **ISSN:** 1069-4404 (print); **EISSN:** 1759-8818 (electronic). **Subscription Rates:** £140 Institutions print and online; £112 Institutions online; £129 Institutions print; $211 Institutions print and online; $169 Institutions online; $194 Institutions print; €193 Institutions print and online; €155 Institutions online; €178 Institutions print; £47 Individuals print; $69 Individuals print; €64 Individuals print. **Alt. Formats:** CD-ROM. **URL:** http://socrel.oxfordjournals.org. **Remarks:** Accepts advertising. **Circ:** (Not Reported).

8412 ■ Southern Living: Lifestyle Magazine of the Changing South
Southern Progress Corp.
PO Box 62120
Tampa, FL 33662-2120
Free: 800-272-4101
Publication E-mail: southernliving@customersvc.com
Magazine featuring food, homes, garden, travel, and features edited for southern tastes. **Freq:** Monthly. **Print Method:** Offset. **Trim Size:** 8 3/8 x 10 1/2. **Cols./Page:** 3. **Col. Width:** 31 nonpareils. **Col. Depth:** 140 agate lines. **Key Personnel:** Greg Schumann, Publisher. **ISSN:** 0038--4305 (print). **Subscription Rates:** $35 Two years; $19.95 Individuals; $1.54 Single issue. **URL:** http://www.southernliving.com. **Ad Rates:** BW $129100; 4C $170000. **Remarks:** Accepts advertising. **Circ:** Paid ★2800000.

8413 ■ Stock Car Racing
The Enthusiast Network
9036 Brittany Way
Tampa, FL 33619
Phone: (813)675-3500
Fax: (813)675-3559
Magazine covering stock car racing. **Founded:** 1966. **Freq:** Monthly. **Print Method:** Offset. **Trim Size:** 8 1/8 x 10 3/4. **Cols./Page:** 3. **Col. Width:** 27 nonpareils. **Col. Depth:** 140 agate lines. **Key Personnel:** Larry Cothren, Editor; C.J. Baker, Publisher. **ISSN:** 0734-7340 (print). **Subscription Rates:** $15 Individuals; $22 Two years. **Available online. URL:** http://www.stockcarracing.com/. **Ad Rates:** BW $7,010; 4C $11,375. **Remarks:** Advertising accepted; rates available upon request. **Circ:** Paid 225117.

8414 ■ Tampa Review: Literary Journal of The University of Tampa
University of Tampa Press
401 W Kennedy Blvd.
Tampa, FL 33606
Phone: (813)253-6266
Fax: (813)258-7593
Literary magazine publishing poetry, fiction, nonfiction and art. **Freq:** Semiannual. **Key Personnel:** Richard Mathews, Editor; Yuly Restrepo, Editor. **ISSN:** 0896--064X (print). **Subscription Rates:** $22 Individuals /year; 2 issues; $40 Two years 4 issues; $14.95 Single issue. **URL:** http://www.ut.edu/tampareview/trmain.aspx. **Remarks:** Advertising not accepted. **Circ:** Paid 650.

The Temple Terrace Beacon - See Temple Terrace

8415 ■ Vette Magazine
RentPath Inc.
9036 Brittany Way
Tampa, FL 33619

Publication E-mail: inquiries@automotive.com
Forum for Corvette owners regarding automobile technical and hobbies. **Freq:** Monthly. **Key Personnel:** Sandy Patterson, Publisher, phone: (813)675-3477. **ISSN:** 0195--1661 (print). **Subscription Rates:** $32.95 U.S.; $44.95 Canada; $56.95 Other countries. **URL:** http://www.superchevy.com/vette-magazine. **Formerly**: Corvette Fever. **Remarks:** Accepts advertising. **Circ:** (Not Reported).

8416 ■ AM 1150 WTMP - 96.1
407 N Howard Ave.
Tampa, FL 33606
Phone: (813)259-9867
Fax: (813)254-9867
Format: Blues. **Owner:** Tama Broadcasting, Inc., at above address. **Operating Hours**: Continuous. **Ad Rates:** Advertising accepted; rates available upon request. **URL:** http://www.am1150wtmp.com.

8417 ■ Jones Intercable, Inc.
4400 W Martin Luther King Jr. Blvd.
Tampa, FL 33607
Phone: (813)877-6805
Fax: (813)875-2507
Owner: Jones Intercable, Inc., Gerogetown, CO. **Founded:** 1983.

8418 ■ WAMA-AM - 1550
PO Box 151300
Tampa, FL 33684-1300
Format: Hispanic. **Networks:** UPI. **Owner:** ZGS Broadcasting Holdings, Inc., at above address. **Founded:** 1961. **Operating Hours**: 6 a.m.-midnight. **ADI**: Tampa-St. Petersburg (Lakeland, Sarasota), FL. **Key Personnel:** Manuel Enrique Semprit, Station Mgr. **Wattage**: 10,000. **Ad Rates:** $28-34 for 30 seconds; $32-41 for 60 seconds.

8419 ■ WBUL-AM - 1620
4202 E Fowler Ave., Ste. CIS1040
Tampa, FL 33620
Phone: (813)974-4906
Fax: (813)974-2592
Format: News; Talk; Country; Sports. **Owner:** University of South Florida Student Government, 4202 E Fowler Ave., Tampa, FL 33620, Ph: (813)974-4014. **Operating Hours:** Continuous. **Ad Rates:** Noncommercial. **URL:** http://bullsradio.org.

8420 ■ WBVM-FM - 90.5
717 S Dale Mabry Hwy.
Tampa, FL 33609
Phone: (813)289-8040
Fax: (813)282-3580
Free: 800-223-9286
Email: contact@spiritfm905.com
Format: Contemporary Christian. **Owner:** The Diocese of St. Petersburg, 6363 9th Ave. N, Saint Petersburg, FL 33710, Ph: (727)344-1611, Fax: (727)345-2143. **Founded:** 1985. **Operating Hours**: Continuous. **ADI**: Tampa-St. Petersburg (Lakeland, Sarasota), FL. **Wattage**: 74,500 ERP. **Ad Rates:** Noncommercial. **URL:** http://www.spiritfm905.com.

8421 ■ WDAE-AM - 620
4002 W Gandy Blvd.
Tampa, FL 33611
Phone: (813)832-1000
Fax: (813)839-0234
Free: 888-546-4620
Format: Sports. **Networks:** ESPN Radio. **Owner:** iHeartMedia Inc., 200 E Basse Rd., San Antonio, TX 78209, Ph: (210)832-3314. **Founded:** 1922. **Operating Hours**: 50% network, 50% local. **ADI**: Tampa-St. Petersburg (Lakeland, Sarasota), FL. **Key Personnel:** Sam Nein, Gen. Mgr. **Wattage**: 5,000. **Ad Rates:** Advertising accepted; rates available upon request. **URL:** http://www.620wdae.com.

8422 ■ WEDU-TV - 3
1300 North Blvd.
Tampa, FL 33607
Fax: (208)736-1958
Free: 800-357-4226
Format: Public TV; News. **Networks:** Public Broadcasting Service (PBS). **Owner:** Florida West Coast Public Broadcasting, Inc., Berkman Family Broadcast Ctr., 1300 N Blvd., Tampa, FL 33607-5699. **Founded:** 1956. **Operating Hours**: Continuous. **ADI**: Tampa-St. Petersburg (Lakeland, Sarasota), FL. **Key Personnel:** Frank Wolynski, Chief Engineer; Leah Rickenbacker, Contact. **Wattage**: 25,000 ERP Circular. **Ad Rates:** Noncommercial; Advertising accepted; rates available upon request. Underwriting available. **URL:** http://csnradio.com.

8423 ■ WFLA-AM - 970
4002 W Gandy Blvd.
Tampa, FL 33611
Phone: (813)832-1000
Fax: (813)837-0300
Format: News; Talk. **Networks:** ABC. **Owner:** iHeartMedia Inc., 200 E Basse Rd., San Antonio, TX 78209, Ph: (210)832-3314. **Founded:** 1924. **Operating Hours**: Continuous. **Key Personnel:** Sam Nein, Gen. Mgr. **Wattage**: 25,000 Day 11,600 Night. **Ad Rates:** $250-400 for 60 seconds. **URL:** http://www.970wfla.com.

8424 ■ WFLA-TV - 8
200 S Parker St.
Tampa, FL 33606
Phone: (813)228-8888
Email: news@wfla.com
Format: News. **Networks:** NBC. **Owner:** Media General Communications Holdings L.L.C., 333 E Franklin St., Richmond, VA 23219, Ph: (804)649-6000. **Operating Hours**: Continuous. **ADI**: Tampa-St. Petersburg (Lakeland, Sarasota), FL. **Wattage**: 32,000 ERP. **Ad Rates:** Advertising accepted; rates available upon request. **Mailing address:** PO Box 1410 , Tampa, FL 33601. **URL:** http://www.wfla.com.

8425 ■ WFTS-TV - 28
4045 N Himes Ave.
Tampa, FL 33607
Phone: (813)354-2828
Free: 877-833-2828
Format: Commercial TV. **Networks:** ABC. **Owner:** The E. W. Scripps Co., 312 Walnut St., Cincinnati, OH 45202, Ph: (513)977-3000. **Founded:** 1981. **Operating Hours**: Continuous. **ADI**: Tampa-St. Petersburg (Lakeland, Sarasota), FL. **Key Personnel:** Matt Brown, News Dir. **Ad Rates:** Advertising accepted; rates available upon request. **URL:** http://www.abcactionnews.com.

8426 ■ WFTT-TV - 50
2610 W Hillsborough Ave.
Tampa, FL 33614
Phone: (813)872-6262
Fax: (813)998-3600
Key Personnel: Lily Gonzalez, Gen. Mgr. **URL:** http://www.entravision.com.

8427 ■ WFUS-FM - 103.5
4002 W Gandy Blvd.
Tampa, FL 33611
Phone: (813)832-1000
Fax: (813)832-1090
Free: 888-405-1035
Format: Country. **Key Personnel:** Travis Daily, Dir. of Programs; Rebecca Kaplan, Promotions Dir. **Ad Rates:** Advertising accepted; rates available upon request. **URL:** http://www.us1035.com.

8428 ■ WGUL-AM - 860
5211 W Laurel St., Ste. A
Tampa, FL 33607
Format: Talk. **Simulcasts:** WGUL-FM. **Networks:** AP. **Owner:** Salem Broadcasting, at above address. **Founded:** 1985. **Operating Hours:** 12:01 a.m.-9 p.m. **Key Personnel:** Christopher Gould, Sr., Gen. Mgr.; Barb Yoder, Gen. Sales Mgr.; Michael Serio, Operations Mgr.; Rey Noriega, Bus. Mgr., Traffic Mgr. **Wattage**: 5,000. **Ad Rates:** $50-60 for 30 seconds; $80-100 for 60 seconds. WGUL-FM, WLSS-AM, WXOV-FM, WXOF-FM. **URL:** http://www.860wgul.townhall.com.

8429 ■ WHBO-AM - 1470
4300 W Cypress St., Ste. 1040
Tampa, FL 33607
Phone: (813)281-1040
Format: Sports; News. **Operating Hours**: Continuous. **Key Personnel:** Donna Peterson, Contact; Donna Peterson, Contact. **Ad Rates:** Advertising accepted; rates available upon request.

8430 ■ WHNZ-AM - 1250
4002 W Gandy Blvd.
Tampa, FL 33611
Phone: (813)832-1000
Fax: (813)837-0300
Format: Talk. **Networks:** CBS; Westwood One Radio. **Founded:** 1941. **Operating Hours**: Continuous; 70% network, 30% local. **Key Personnel:** Sam Nein, Gen. Mgr. **Wattage**: 25,000 Day; 5,900 Night. **Ad Rates:** $50-100 for 60 seconds. Combined advertising rates available with WFLA, WDAE.

8431 ■ WLCC-AM - 760
3514 W Arch St.
Tampa, FL 33607
Phone: (813)871-1819
Fax: (813)871-1155
Format: Ethnic; World Beat. **Ad Rates:** Advertising accepted; rates available upon request.

8432 ■ WLSS-AM - 930
5211 W Laurel St., Ste. A
Tampa, FL 33607
Phone: (941)363-0930
Fax: (813)639-1272
Format: Talk; News. **Simulcasts:** WGUL-AM, WGUL-FM. **Owner:** Salem Media Group Inc., 4880 Santa Rosa Rd., Camarillo, CA 93012, Ph: (805)987-0400, Fax: (805)384-4520. **Founded:** 1949. **Formerly**: WKXY-AM. **Operating Hours**: Continuous. **ADI**: Tampa-St. Petersburg (Lakeland, Sarasota), FL. **Key Personnel:** Christopher Gould, Sr., Gen. Mgr., cgould@saletampa.com; Joe Weaver, Operations Mgr., jweaver@salemtampa.com; Barb Yoder, Gen. Sales Mgr., barb@saletampa.com; Bill Carl, Dir. of Production, bcarl@saletampa.com. **Wattage**: 5,000 Day; 2,500 Night. **Ad Rates:** Advertising accepted; rates available upon request. Combined advertising rates available with WGUL-AM, WGUL-FM. **URL:** http://www.wlssradio.com.

8433 ■ WMGG-AM
PO Box 25434
Tampa, FL 33622
Phone: (813)871-1819
Format: Classical. **Owner:** Mega Communications, at above address. **Wattage**: 5,000 Day; 500 Night. **Ad Rates:** Advertising accepted; rates available upon request.

8434 ■ WMNF-FM - 88.5
1210 E Martin Luther King Blvd.
Tampa, FL 33603-4417
Phone: (813)238-8001
Fax: (813)238-1802
Email: wmnf@wmnf.org
Format: Contemporary Hit Radio (CHR). **Networks:** National Public Radio (NPR). **Owner:** Nathan B. Stubblefield Foundation. **Founded:** 1979. **Operating Hours**: Continuous; 10% network, 90% local. **Key Personnel:** Randy Wynne, Dir. of Programs, randy@wmnf.org; Lee Courtney, Music Dir., flee@wmnf.org; Jim Bennett, Station Mgr., jimb@wmnf.org; Mercedes Skelton, Bus. Mgr., mercedes@wmnf.org; Rob Lorei, Dir. Pub. Aff., News Dir., rob@wmnf.org; Bill Brown, Chief Engineer. **Local Programs**: *Morning Show*, Monday Tuesday Wednesday Thursday Friday 6:00 a.m. - 9:00 a.m.; *Freak Show*, Tuesday 7:00 p.m. - 9:00 p.m.; *Women's Show*. **Wattage**: 70,000. **Ad Rates:** Noncommercial. **URL:** http://www.wmnf.org.

8435 ■ WMOR-TV - 32
7201 E Hillsborough Ave.
Tampa, FL 33610
Fax: (813)626-1961
Format: Commercial TV. **Owner:** Hearst Television Inc., 300 W 57th St., New York, NY 10019-3741, Ph: (212)887-6800, Fax: (212)887-6855. **Founded:** 1986. **Formerly**: WWWB-TV. **Operating Hours**: Continuous. **ADI**: Tampa-St. Petersburg (Lakeland, Sarasota), FL. **Key Personnel:** Pam Barber, Account Exec., pbarber@hearst.com. **Wattage**: 5,000,000. **Ad Rates:** Noncommercial. **URL:** http://www.mor-tv.com.

8436 ■ WMTX-FM - 100.7
4002 W Gandy Blvd.
Tampa, FL 33611
Phone: (813)832-1000
Fax: (813)832-1090
Format: Adult Contemporary. **Founded:** 1947. **Formerly**: WAKS; WUSA-FM; WNLT-FM; WSSR-FM. **ADI**: Tampa- St. Petersburg (Lakeland, Sarasota),FL. **Wattage**: 96,000. **Ad Rates:** Advertising accepted; rates available upon request. $300-400 for 60 seconds; $250-

Circulation: ★ = AAM; △ or • = BPA; ♦ = CAC; ❑ = VAC; ⊕ = PO Statement; ‡ = Publisher's Report; Boldface figures = sworn; Light figures = estimated.

350 per unit. **URL:** http://tampabaysmix.iheart.com.

8437 ■ WQBN-AM - 1300
5203 N Armenia Ave.
Tampa, FL 33603
Phone: (813)871-1333
Fax: (813)876-1333
Format: Hispanic. **Founded:** 1950. **Operating Hours:** Continuous. **ADI:** Tampa-St. Petersburg (Lakeland, Sarasota), FL. **Wattage:** 5,000 Day; 160 Night. **Ad Rates:** $45-60 for 30 seconds; $30-65 for 60 seconds.

8438 ■ WSMR-FM - 89.1
4202 E Fowler Ave., Ste. TVB100
Tampa, FL 33620-6870
Phone: (941)906-9767
Free: 866-906-9767
Format: Religious. **Owner:** Northwestern College Radio, 3003 Snelling Ave. N, Saint Paul, MN 55113, Ph: (651)631-5100, Free: 800-692-4020. **Key Personnel:** Susan Geiger, Prog. Dir.; Russell Gant, Music Dir.; Jorge Cunha, Dir. of Production; Sheila Rue, Prog. Dir., srue@wusf.org; Brian Best, Contact; Sandy James, Contact, sandy@life891.com. **Ad Rates:** Noncommercial. **URL:** http://www.wusf.usf.edu.

8439 ■ WTAM-TV - 30
3301 Barham Blvd., Ste. 200
Los Angeles, CA 90068
Owner: Lotus Communications, at above address. **Key Personnel:** John Paley, VP; Howard A. Kalmenson, CEO, President; William H. Shriftman, Sr. VP. **URL:** http://www.wtam.com.

8440 ■ WTBN-AM - 570
5211 W Laurel St.
Tampa, FL 33607
Phone: (813)349-8231
Fax: (813)639-1272
Free: 877-943-9673
Format: Religious. **Key Personnel:** Christopher Gould, Sr., Gen. Mgr., cgould@salemtampa.com. **Ad Rates:** Advertising accepted; rates available upon request. **URL:** http://www.bayword.com.

8441 ■ WTMP-AM - 1150
407 N Howard Ave., Ste. 200
Tampa, FL 33606
Phone: (813)259-9867
Format: Gospel; Hip Hop; Talk. **Owner:** Tama Broadcasting, Inc., at above address. **Founded:** 1954. **Operating Hours:** Continuous Monday - Friday, 5:00 a.m. - 9:00 p.m. Saturday, Continuous Sunday. **ADI:** Tampa-St. Petersburg (Lakeland, Sarasota), FL. **Wattage:** 5,000. **Ad Rates:** Advertising accepted; rates available upon request. $45-95 for 30 seconds; $55-150 for 60 seconds. **URL:** http://am1150wtmp.com.

8442 ■ WTTA-TV - 38
7622 Bald Cypress Pl.
Tampa, FL 33614
Phone: (813)886-9882
Fax: (813)880-8154
Format: Commercial TV. **Networks:** Independent; Florida Contemporary Radio. **Owner:** Bay Television Inc., at above address, Tampa, FL. **Founded:** 1985. **Operating Hours:** Continuous. **ADI:** Tampa-St. Petersburg (Lakeland, Sarasota), FL. **URL:** http://www.mytvtampabay.com.

8443 ■ WTVT-TV - 13
3213 W Kennedy Blvd.
Tampa, FL 33609
Phone: (813)870-9611
Fax: (813)875-8329
Format: News. **Networks:** Fox. **Owner:** Fox Television Stations Inc., 1211 Ave. of the Americas, 21st Fl., New York, NY 10036, Ph: (212)301-5400. **Founded:** 1955. **Operating Hours:** Continuous. **Wattage:** 318. **Ad Rates:** Advertising accepted; rates available upon request. **URL:** http://www.myfoxtampabay.com.

8444 ■ WUSF-TV - 16
4202 E Fowler Ave., TVB100
Tampa, FL 33620-6902
Phone: (813)974-8700
Fax: (813)974-5016
Free: 800-741-9090
Email: info@wusf.org
Format: Public TV. **Networks:** Public Broadcasting Service (PBS). **Owner:** University of South Florida, 4202 E Fowler Ave., Tampa, FL 33620, Ph: (813)974-2011, Fax: (813)974-9689. **Founded:** 1966. **Operating Hours:** Continuous. **ADI:** Tampa-St. Petersburg (Lakeland, Sarasota), FL. **Key Personnel:** Jorge Cunha, Dir. of Production, jcunha@wusf.org; Susan Geiger, Dir. of Programs, sgeiger@wusf.org. **Wattage:** 1,200,000. **Ad Rates:** Underwriting available. **URL:** http://www.wusf.usf.edu.

8445 ■ WVEA-TV - 62
2610 W Hillsborough Ave.
Tampa, FL 33614
Phone: (813)872-6262
Fax: (813)998-3600
Format: Commercial TV. **Networks:** Univision. **Owner:** Entravision Communications Corporation, 2425 Olympic Blvd., Ste. 6000 W, Santa Monica, CA 90404-4030, Ph: (310)447-3870, Fax: (310)447-3899. **Founded:** May 03, 1991. **Operating Hours:** Continuous. **ADI:** Tampa-St. Petersburg (Lakeland, Sarasota), FL. **Wattage:** 5,000,000. **Ad Rates:** Advertising accepted; rates available upon request. **URL:** http://www.wveatv.com.

8446 ■ WWBA-AM
PO Box 25434
Tampa, FL 33622
Phone: (813)281-1040
Fax: (813)281-1948
Free: 877-355-1040
Format: News; Talk. **Founded:** Sept. 07, 2006. **Wattage:** 50,000 Day; 1,000 Ni. **Ad Rates:** Advertising accepted; rates available upon request.

8447 ■ WXTB-FM - 97.8
4002 W Gandy Blvd.
Tampa, FL 33611
Phone: (813)832-1000
Free: 800-737-0098
Format: Album-Oriented Rock (AOR). **Founded:** 1967. **Formerly:** WKRL-FM. **Operating Hours:** Continuous. **ADI:** Tampa-St. Petersburg (Lakeland, Sarasota), FL. **Key Personnel:** Double Down, Dir. of Programs, doubledown@98rock.com. **Wattage:** 100,000. **Ad Rates:** Advertising accepted; rates available upon request. **URL:** http://www.98rock.com.

TARPON SPRINGS

WC FL. Pinellas Co. On Gulf of Mexico, 27 mi. NW of Tampa. Winter tourist resort. Manufactures clothing, chemicals, and boats. Sponge industry center.

8448 ■ Journal of Consumer Affairs
American Council on Consumer Interests
PO Box 2528
Tarpon Springs, FL 34688-2528
Phone: (727)940-2658
Scholarly journal covering research in consumerism. **Freq:** 3/year spring, summer, fall. **Key Personnel:** Sharon Tennyson, Editor. **ISSN:** 0022--0078 (print); **EISSN:** 1745--6606 (electronic). **Online:** Wiley Online Library. **URL:** http://www.consumerinterests.org/journal. **Remarks:** Advertising not accepted. **Circ:** (Not Reported).

8449 ■ Music and Sound Journal
Independent Music Retailers Association
912 Carlton Rd.
Tarpon Springs, FL 34689
Phone: (727)938-0571
Freq: Bimonthly. **ISSN:** 1042--0649 (print). **Subscription Rates:** $35 /year. **Remarks:** Accepts advertising. **Circ:** (Not Reported).

TAVARES

8450 ■ WKIQ-AM - 1240
14624 US Hwy. 441
Tavares, FL 32778-4315
Phone: (352)357-1240
Fax: (352)357-4250
Format: Talk; News; Sports. **Networks:** NBC; People's Network; Westwood One Radio. **Owner:** Rama Communications, Inc., at above address. **Founded:** 1942. **Formerly:** WLCF-AM; WEUS-AM; WWLB-AM. **Operating Hours:** Continuous. **Key Personnel:** Carl Christianson, Contact. **Wattage:** 790. **Ad Rates:** Advertising accepted; rates available upon request. $5-14 for 30 seconds. **URL:** http://www.graveline.com.

TAVERNIER

8451 ■ Florida Keys Keynoter
Keynoter Publishing Company Inc.
PO Box 1197
Tavernier, FL 33070
Phone: (305)852-3216
Community newspaper (tabloid). **Freq:** Semiweekly (Wed. and Sat.). **Print Method:** Letterpress and flexo. **Trim Size:** 10 1/4 x 12.85. **Cols./Page:** 5. **Col. Width:** 11.6 picas. **Col. Depth:** 12.85 inches. **Key Personnel:** Carter Townshend, Manager, Circulation; Larry Kahn, Editor; Todd Swift, Manager, Production. **ISSN:** 8756--6427 (print). **Subscription Rates:** $54.23 Individuals home delivery (Monroe County only); $98.12 By mail in state; $92.56 Out of state mail delivery. **URL:** http://www.keysnet.com/archive. **Remarks:** Accepts advertising. **Circ:** (Not Reported).

8452 ■ Free Press
Free Press
91731 Overseas Hwy.
Tavernier, FL 33070
Phone: (305)853-7277
Fax: (305)853-0556
Publisher's E-mail: freepress@keysnews.com
Community newspaper of general interest for the Florida Keys. **Founded:** Jan. 1987. **Freq:** Weekly (Wed.). **Print Method:** Web Offset. **Trim Size:** 11 x 12 1/2. **Cols./Page:** 5. **Col. Width:** 22 1/2 nonpareils. **Col. Depth:** 224 agate lines. **Key Personnel:** Paul Clarin, Publisher; Vicki Heddings, Office Manager; Dan Campbell, Managing Editor. **Subscription Rates:** $240 By mail; $102 Individuals home delivery; $90 Individuals online; $150 Two years online. **URL:** http://keysnews.com. **Ad Rates:** BW $546.25; PCI $10.50. **Remarks:** Accepts advertising. **Circ:** Free ‡12800, 14000.

8453 ■ Keynoter
Keynoter
PO Box 1197
Tavernier, FL 33070
Phone: (305)852-3216
Publication E-mail: keynoter@kiwanis.org
Magazine of the high school service organization Key Club International. **Founded:** 1946. **Freq:** Bimonthly. **Key Personnel:** Larry Kahn, Editor; Todd Swift, Manager, Production. **USPS:** 584-680. **Subscription Rates:** $54.23 Individuals home delivery within Monroe County; $64.84 Individuals mail delivery; $60.32 Out of state mail delivery. **URL:** http://www.keysnet.com/. **Remarks:** Accepts advertising. **Circ:** Paid 190000.

8454 ■ WAIL-FM - 99.5
5450 McDonald Ave., Ste. 10
Tavernier, FL 33070
Phone: (305)294-2523
Fax: (305)296-0358
Email: wail995@flkeysmedia.com
Format: Album-Oriented Rock (AOR); Classic Rock. **Networks:** Independent. **Owner:** iHeartMedia Inc., 200 E Basse Rd., San Antonio, TX 78209, Ph: (210)832-3314. **Founded:** 1981. **Formerly:** WVFK-FM. **Operating Hours:** Continuous; 100% local. **Wattage:** 100,000. **Ad Rates:** Noncommercial. **URL:** http://www.wail995.com.

8455 ■ WCTH-FM - 100.3
93351 Overseas Hwy.
Tavernier, FL 33070
Phone: (305)852-9085
Format: Country. **Wattage:** 100,000. **Ad Rates:** Advertising accepted; rates available upon request. **URL:** http://www.thundercountry.com.

8456 ■ WFKZ-FM - 103.1
93351 Overseas Hwy.
Tavernier, FL 33070
Phone: (305)852-9085
Fax: (305)852-2304
Format: Classic Rock. **Owner:** Clear Channel Radio, 200 E Basse Rd., San Antonio, TX 78209, Ph: (210)822-2828, Fax: (210)832-3428. **Founded:** 1983. **Operating Hours:** Continuous. **ADI:** Miami (Ft. Lauderdale), FL. **Key Personnel:** Scott Hamilton, Contact. **Wattage:** 50,000. **Ad Rates:** $22-26 for 30 seconds; $26-34 for 60 seconds. **URL:** http://www.sun103.com.

8457 ■ WKEZ-FM - 96.9
93351 Overseas Hwy.
Tavernier, FL 33070

Phone: (305)852-9085
Fax: (305)852-2304
Format: Easy Listening. **Key Personnel:** Randall Perry, Chief Engineer, randallperry@clearchannel.com; Mark Mills, Mktg. Mgr., VP, markmills@clearchannel.com. **Wattage:** 25,000. **Ad Rates:** Noncommercial.

TEMPLE TERRACE

8458 ■ The Temple Terrace Beacon
The Temple Terrace Beacon
PO Box 271880
Tampa, FL 33688-1880
Phone: (813)963-1918
Fax: (813)963-3910
Community newspaper. **Freq:** Weekly. **Cols./Page:** 6. **Col. Width:** 1 9/16 inches. **Col. Depth:** 16 inches. **Key Personnel:** Anne McKenna, Editor, Contact. **Subscription Rates:** Free; $60 By mail. **URL:** http://digitalcollections.hcplc.org/cdm/landingpage/collection/p16054coll7; http://templeterrace.com/409/Library-Archives. **Ad Rates:** PCI $8.40. **Remarks:** Accepts advertising. **Circ:** Free 10000.

THE VILLAGES

8459 ■ The Villages Daily Sun
The Villages Daily Sun
1100 Main St.
The Villages, FL 32159-7719
Phone: (352)753-1119
General newspaper. **Freq:** Daily. **Print Method:** Web offset. **Key Personnel:** Matt Fry, Associate Editor; Larry D. Croom, Director, Editorial; Meta Minton, Managing Editor. **URL:** http://www.thevillagesdailysun.com. **Remarks:** Accepts advertising. **Circ:** Mon.-Fri. ***35808**, Sun. ***36610**, Sat. ***35663**.

TITUSVILLE

E FL. Brevard Co. On Indian River, 42 mi. E. of Orlando. Resort area. Kennedy Space Center. Citrus fruit farms.

8460 ■ The Chief of Police
National Association of Chiefs of Police
6350 Horizon Dr.
Titusville, FL 32780
Phone: (321)264-0911
Publisher's E-mail: policeinfo@aphf.org
Publishing articles focusing on promotional exams, profiles of commanders of elite units, legal decisions, profiles of County Sheriffs and heads of security firms. **Freq:** Bimonthly. **URL:** http://www.aphf.org/thechief.html. **Ad Rates:** BW $1,400; 4C $1,940. **Remarks:** Accepts advertising. **Circ:** 7,000.

8461 ■ Shutterbug
Source Interlink Media L.L.C.
PO Box 7
Titusville, FL 32781
Phone: (321)269-3212
Fax: (321)225-3146
Publication E-mail: editorial@shutterbug.com
Photography magazine. **Freq:** Monthly. **Print Method:** Offset. **Trim Size:** 8 x 10.875. **Cols./Page:** 4. **Col. Width:** 22 nonpareils. **Col. Depth:** 182 agate lines. **Key Personnel:** Keith Pray, Publisher; Joanne George, Advertising Representative, phone: (321)225-3130. **ISSN:** 0895--321X (print). **Subscription Rates:** $17.95 Individuals; $32.95 Two years; $41.93 Canada; $29.93 Other countries. **URL:** http://www.shutterbug.com. **Ad Rates:** BW $6,115; 4C $9,093. **Remarks:** Accepts advertising. **Circ:** Paid ***110000**.

8462 ■ WKSG-FM - 89.5
1403 Indian River Ave.
Titusville, FL 32780
Phone: (352)369-8950
Fax: (352)369-1109
Format: Contemporary Christian. **Owner:** Daystar Public Radio, INC, at above address. **Founded:** 1998. **Operating Hours:** Continuous. **Wattage:** 30,000. **Ad Rates:** Noncommercial. **URL:** http://www.cflradio.net.

8463 ■ WPGS-AM - 840
805 N Dixie Ave.
Titusville, FL 32796
Email: bob@cflradio.net
Format: Hispanic; News; Sports; Religious. **Simulcasts:** WNTF 1580. **Owner:** WPGS Inc., at above address. **Founded:** 1984. **Formerly:** WNUY-AM. **Operating Hours:** Daytime. **Key Personnel:** Ed Shiflett, Chief Engineer, Operations Mgr. **Wattage:** 1,000. **Ad Rates:** Noncommercial. Combined advertising rates available with WNTF 1580 AM. **URL:** http://www.cflradio.net.

8464 ■ WPIO-FM - 89.3
PO Box 1831
Titusville, FL 32780
Email: ashley.godsquad@gmail.com
Format: Religious. **Founded:** Sept. 14, 2006. **Ad Rates:** Noncommercial.

TRENTON

N FL. Gilchrist Co. 30 mi. W. of Gainesville. Naval stores. Saw, grist mills. Agriculture.

8465 ■ WYNY-AM - 1240
8749 SW 25th Ave.
Trenton, FL 32693
Phone: (352)463-1345
Fax: (352)463-9966
Format: Country. **Owner:** Pamal Broadcasting, Ltd., 715 Rte. 52, Beacon, NY 12508, Ph: (845)838-6000. **Key Personnel:** Ben Hill, Gen. Mgr.; Jeanie Edwards, Sales Mgr.; Jim Brand, Dir. of Programs. **Mailing address:** PO Box 1430, Trenton, FL 32693.

VALPARAISO

Okaloosa Co. Okaloosa Co. (NW). 2 m N of Elgin Air Force Base.

8466 ■ Valparaiso Communication Systems
465 Valparaiso Pky.
Valparaiso, FL 32580
Phone: (850)729-5404
Fax: (850)678-4553
Owner: City of Valparaiso, at above address. **Founded:** 1976. **Key Personnel:** Burt B. Bennett, Contact. **Cities Served:** Valparaiso, Florida: subscribing households 1620; 72 channels; 1 community access channel; 168 hours per week community access programming. **URL:** http://www.valp.tv.

VALRICO

8467 ■ Design Cost Data: Cost Estimating Magazine for Design and Construction
DC and D Technologies Inc.
PO Box 948
Valrico, FL 33595-0948
Phone: (813)662-6830
Fax: (813)662-6793
Free: 800-533-5680
Publication E-mail: webmaster@dcd.com
Publication providing real cost data case studies of various types completed around the country for design and building professionals. **Freq:** Bimonthly. **Print Method:** Web offset. **Trim Size:** 8 x 10 3/4. **Cols./Page:** 3. **Col. Width:** 2 1/4 inches. **Col. Depth:** 10 inches. **Key Personnel:** Barbara Castelli, President, Publisher; David Castelli, Vice President. **ISSN:** 0739--3946 (print). **Subscription Rates:** $149 Individuals one year; $239 Two years; $174.80 Canada and Mexico one year; $274.80 Canada and Mexico two year. **URL:** http://www.dcd.com/departments.htm. **Ad Rates:** BW $1,945; 4C $1945. **Remarks:** Accepts advertising. **Circ:** Controlled ‡9600.

VENICE

SW FL. Sarasota Co. On Gulf of Mexico, 18 mi. S. of Sarasota. Resort area.

8468 ■ Florida Mariner: The Boater's Guide to Florida
Florida Mariner
PO Box 1220
Venice, FL 34284
Phone: (941)488-9307
Fax: (941)488-9309
Free: 800-615-5089
Recreational boats, related products and services magazine. **Freq:** Biweekly. **Subscription Rates:** free online subscription. **URL:** http://www.floridamariner.com/. **Formerly:** Gulf Mariner; Gulf/Atlantic Mariner. **Ad Rates:** BW $1,099; 4C $1,354. **Remarks:** Accepts advertising. **Circ:** Paid 332, Free 23500.

8469 ■ The Seed Pod
American Hibiscus Society
PO Box 1580
Venice, FL 34284-1580
Phone: (941)627-1332
Publication E-mail: seedpod@americanhibiscus.org
Professional horticultural magazine covering Hibiscus care and showing. **Freq:** Quarterly. **Print Method:** Offset. **Trim Size:** 5 x 8. **Key Personnel:** Rita Hall, Vice President, Editor. **ISSN:** 0745- 3590 (print). **USPS:** 687-170. **Subscription Rates:** included in membership dues. **URL:** http://www.americanhibiscus.org/theseedpod.htm. **Ad Rates:** BW $100; 4C $350. **Remarks:** Accepts advertising. **Circ:** Controlled 1200, 2000.

VERO BEACH

E FL. Indian River Co. On Indian River, 72 mi. N. of West Palm Beach. Winter resort. Citrus fruit.

8470 ■ Gridiron Greats
Bigg Publishing
5082 4th Ln.
Vero Beach, FL 32968
Phone: (772)563-0425
Publication E-mail: gridirongreats@aol.com
Magazine that covers the history of American sports and the collection of sports memorabilia. **Freq:** Quarterly. **Trim Size:** 7.25 x 9.75. **Key Personnel:** Bob Swick, Publisher, Editor. **Subscription Rates:** $29.95 Individuals; $44 Canada; $8 Single issue. **URL:** http://www.gridirongreats.net. **Ad Rates:** BW $230. **Remarks:** Accepts advertising. **Circ:** (Not Reported).

8471 ■ Journal of Medical Entomology
Entomological Society of America
c/o Walter J. Tabachnick, Ed.-in-Ch.
Florida Medical Entomology Lab.
Vero Beach, FL 32962
Publisher's E-mail: esa@entsoc.org
Journal on systematic and biology of insects, acarines and other arthropods of public health and veterinary significance. **Freq:** Bimonthly. **Print Method:** Offset. **Trim Size:** 7 x 10. **Cols./Page:** 2. **Col. Width:** 17 picas. **Col. Depth:** 52 picas. **Key Personnel:** Alan Kahan, Managing Editor; Walter J. Tabachnick, Editor-in-Chief. **ISSN:** 0022--2585 (print). **Subscription Rates:** $258 Individuals print; $206 Individuals online; $504 Institutions print; $437 Institutions online; $548 Institutions print and online; £136 Individuals print; £109 Individuals online; £264 Institutions print; £229 Institutions online; £287 Institutions print and online; €203 Individuals print; €163 Individuals online; €396 Institutions print; €345 Institutions online; €431 Institutions print and online. **URL:** http://www.entsoc.org/Pubs/Periodicals/JME. **Remarks:** Accepts advertising. **Circ:** 600.

8472 ■ KBIF-AM - 900
1000 Olde Doubloon Dr.
Vero Beach, FL 32963
Owner: Gore-Overgaard Broadcasting Inc., at above address. **Founded:** 1954. **Operating Hours:** Continuous. **Key Personnel:** Michele Her, Contact, michele@kbif900am.com. **Wattage:** 1,000 Day Time/500 N. **Ad Rates:** Advertising accepted; rates available upon request; Accepts classified advertising.

8473 ■ KIRV-AM - 1510
1000 Olde Doubloon Dr.
Vero Beach, FL 32963
Phone: (559)222-0900
Fax: (559)222-1573
Email: kbifkirv@aol.com
Format: Contemporary Christian; Talk. **Operating Hours:** Sunrise-sunset. **Wattage:** 10,000. **Ad Rates:** Advertising accepted; rates available upon request. **URL:** http://www.1510kirv.com.

8474 ■ WGYL-FM - 93.7
1235 16th St.
Vero Beach, FL 32960
Phone: (772)794-7748
Fax: (772)562-4747
Free: 877-937-9393
Format: Adult Contemporary. **Networks:** ABC. **Owner:** Vero Beach Broadcasters L.L.C. **Founded:** Dec. 18, 1970. **Operating Hours:** Continuous. **Key Personnel:** Jim Davis, Gen. Mgr., jimd@wgylfm.com. **Wattage:**

Circulation: ★ = AAM; △ or • = BPA; ♦ = CAC; ❑ = VAC; ⊕ = PO Statement; ‡ = Publisher's Report; Boldface figures = sworn; Light figures = estimated.

50,000. **Ad Rates:** Advertising accepted; rates available upon request. WTTB-AM. **URL:** http://www.thebreeze.fm.

8475 ■ WJKD-FM - 99.7
1235 16th St.
Vero Beach, FL 32960
Phone: (772)567-0937
Fax: (772)562-4747
Free: 866-930-5225
Email: contest@997jackfm.com
Format: News. **Owner:** Vero Beach FM Radio Partnership, Not Available. **ADI:** West Palm Beach-Ft. Pierce-Vero Beach, FL. **Key Personnel:** Jim Davis, Gen. Mgr., jimd@wgylfm.com; Karen Franke, Prog. Dir., karen_franke@bellsouth.net. **Wattage:** 50,000 ERP. **Ad Rates:** Noncommercial. **URL:** http://www.997jackfm.com.

8476 ■ WOSN-FM - 97.1
1235 16th St.
Vero Beach, FL 32960
Phone: (772)567-0937
Fax: (772)562-4747
Free: 800-896-1669
Email: anniversary@wosnfm.com
ADI: West Palm Beach-Ft. Pierce-Vero Beach, FL. **Key Personnel:** Jim Davis, Gen. Mgr., jimd@wgylfm.com. **Wattage:** 23,000 ERP. **Ad Rates:** Accepts Advertising. **URL:** http://www.wosnfm.com.

8477 ■ WSCF-FM - 91.9
9055 Americana Rd.
Vero Beach, FL 32966
Free: 800-780-0919
Format: Contemporary Christian. **Wattage:** 15,500. **Ad Rates:** Noncommercial. **URL:** http://www.wscf.com.

8478 ■ WTTB-AM - 1490
1235 16th St.
Vero Beach, FL 32960
Phone: (772)567-0937
Fax: (772)562-4747
Format: News; Talk; Sports. **Networks:** ABC. **Owner:** Vero Beach Broadcasters L.L.C. **Founded:** 1954. **Operating Hours:** Continuous. **ADI:** West Palm Beach-Ft. Pierce-Vero Beach, FL. **Key Personnel:** Karen Franke, Gen. Mgr., Dir. of Engg., Dir. of Sales. **Local Programs:** *Cindy's Health Beat and Where to Eat!*, Saturday 11:00 a.m. - 12:00 p.m. **Wattage:** 1,000. **Ad Rates:** Advertising accepted; rates available upon request. $10 for 60 seconds. **URL:** http://www.wttbam.com.

8479 ■ WWCI-TV - 10
525 - 1St St.
Vero Beach, FL 32962-3632
Phone: (772)978-0023
Fax: (772)978-0053
Wattage: 3,000 ERP.

WAUCHULA

C FL. Hardee Co. 40 mi. S. of Lakeland. Parks. Truck, fruit, stock farms. Citrus groves.

8480 ■ WAUC-AM
1310 S Florida Ave.
Wauchula, FL 33873
Phone: (863)767-0919
Fax: (863)773-2032
Email: waucradiostation@earthlink.com
Format: Top 40; Agricultural; Sports. **Networks:** Florida Radio; Satellite Music Network. **Owner:** Marvina Enterprises, Inc., at above address. **Founded:** 1958. **Wattage:** 5,000 Day; 500 Night. **Ad Rates:** $6-10 for 30 seconds; $10-15 for 60 seconds.

WELLINGTON

8481 ■ The Town Crier
The Town Crier
12794 W Forest Hill Blvd., Ste. 31
Wellington, FL 33414
Phone: (561)793-7606
Fax: (561)793-6090
Shopper. **Founded:** May 13, 1933. **Freq:** Weekly (Mon.). **Print Method:** Offset. **Cols./Page:** 6. **Col. Width:** 24 nonpareils. **Col. Depth:** 231 agate lines. **Key Personnel:** Barry S. Manning, Publisher; Joshua I. Manning, Executive Editor. **Subscription Rates:** Free to those who request it. **URL:** http://gotowncrier.com/. **Remarks:** Advertising accepted; rates available upon request. **Circ:** Free 72000.

WEST PALM BEACH

SE FL. Palm Beach Co. On Lake Worth opposite Palm Beach, with bridge connections. Port of entry with deep harbor. Resort area. Commercial fisheries. Manufactures data processing systems, aircraft engines and parts, electronic components, transistors, tools and dies, furniture, mattresses, aluminum doors, and concrete products.

8482 ■ Ancestry
Palm Beach County Genealogical Society
3650 Summit Blvd.
West Palm Beach, FL 33416
Phone: (561)616-3455
Publisher's E-mail: ancestry@gensocofpbc.org
Genealogical magazine. **Freq:** Quarterly published in January, April, July and October. **Print Method:** Camera ready copy. **Trim Size:** 8 1/2 x 11. **Key Personnel:** Majorie W. Nelson, Specialist, Circulation, phone: (561)737-7707. **ISSN:** 1527--8581 (print). **Subscription Rates:** $20 Nonmembers; Included in membership. **URL:** http://www.gensocofpbc.org/cpage.php?pt=46. **Mailing address:** PO Box 17617, West Palm Beach, FL 33416. **Remarks:** Accepts advertising. **Circ:** Combined 400, 350.

8483 ■ Medical Tourism Magazine
Medical Tourism Association
10130 Northlake Blvd., Ste. 214-315
West Palm Beach, FL 33412
Phone: (561)791-2000
Publication E-mail: info@medicaltourismmag.com
Magazine focusing on issues affecting the Medical Tourism industry and the quality of healthcare overseas. **Freq:** Monthly. **Trim Size:** 8 1/2 x 11. **Key Personnel:** Renee-Marie Stephano, Editor-in-Chief. **Subscription Rates:** Included in membership; $100 Nonmembers. **URL:** http://www.medicaltourismmag.com. **Ad Rates:** BW $3,000. **Remarks:** Accepts advertising. **Circ:** (Not Reported).

8484 ■ Palm Beach Daily News
Palm Beach Newspapers Inc.
2751 S Dixie Hwy.
West Palm Beach, FL 33405
Phone: (561)820-4100
Free: 800-926-7678
General newspaper. **Freq:** Mon.-Sun. (morn.) except biweekly (Thursday and Sunday) from the first Sunday in May to the first Sunday in October. **Print Method:** Offset. **Trim Size:** 13 x 22 1/2. **Cols./Page:** 6. **Col. Width:** 2 1/16 inches. **Col. Depth:** 22 1/2 inches. **Key Personnel:** Joyce Reingold, Editor. **USPS:** 418-660. **Subscription Rates:** $9.99 Individuals unlimited digital access. **URL:** http://palmbeachdailynews.com. **Ad Rates:** GLR $46.91; BW $63.32; 4C $7,677. **Remarks:** Accepts advertising. **Circ:** Paid ‡6040, Free ‡908.

8485 ■ Palm Beach Illustrated
Palm Beach Media Group
1000 N Dixie Hwy., Ste. C
West Palm Beach, FL 33401
Lifestyle publication covering travel, fashion, design, real estate and social for Palm Beach, FL. **Freq:** 11/year. **Print Method:** Web offset. **Trim Size:** 8 1/8 x 10 7/8. **Cols./Page:** 3. **ISSN:** 1047--5575 (print). **Subscription Rates:** $39.95 Individuals; $59.95 Two years. **URL:** http://www.palmbeachillustrated.com; http://www.palmbeachmedia.com/illustrateds#PBI. **Remarks:** Accepts advertising. **Circ:** Paid **★23500**, ‡30000.

8486 ■ The Palm Beach Post
Cox Media Group Inc.
2751 S Dixie Hwy.
West Palm Beach, FL 33405
Free: 800-926-POST
General newspaper. **Freq:** Mon.-Sun. (morn.). **Print Method:** Offset. **Trim Size:** 13 1/2 x 23 9/16. **Cols./Page:** 6. **Col. Width:** 2.17 inches. **Col. Depth:** 22 1/2 inches. **Key Personnel:** Clay Clifton, Director; Tim Burke, Publisher. **Online:** LexisNexis; Cox Media Group Inc. Cox Media Group Inc. **Alt. Formats:** Handheld. **URL:** http://palmbeachpost.com. **Ad Rates:** GLR $77.35; BW $10,442.25; 4C $12,196.25. **Remarks:** Accepts advertising. **Circ:** Mon.-Fri. **★164474**, Sun. **★195608**, Sat. **★163087**.

8487 ■ QCWA Journal
Quarter Century Wireless Association
12967 N Normandy Way
West Palm Beach, FL 33410-1412
Phone: (352)425-1097
Journal promoting interest in amateur radio communications and in the advancement of electronics. **Freq:** Monthly. **Subscription Rates:** Free visually impaired paid up members. **URL:** http://www.qcwa.org/journal.htm. **Remarks:** Advertising not accepted. **Circ:** (Not Reported).

8488 ■ UCWA Quarterly Journal: The Journal of the QCWA Organization
Quarter Century Wireless Association
12967 N Normandy Way
West Palm Beach, FL 33410-1412
Phone: (352)425-1097
Radio and TV magazine. **Freq:** Monthly. **Print Method:** Offset. **Cols./Page:** 1. **Col. Width:** 90 nonpareils. **Col. Depth:** 140 agate lines. **Key Personnel:** Doug Walbrdige, Editor, phone: (978)985-5814; Amber Pelletier, Editor. **Subscription Rates:** Included in membership. **URL:** http://www.qcwa.org/journal.htm. **Formerly:** QCWA News. **Remarks:** Advertising accepted; rates available upon request. **Circ:** 10000.

8489 ■ Vive
Vive Magazine
400 Executive Center Dr., Ste. 106
West Palm Beach, FL 33401
Publication E-mail: vive@vivemagazine.com
Lifestyle magazine for women living in Florida. **Subscription Rates:** $12.95 Individuals; $21.95 Two years; $29.95 Individuals three years; $4.95 Single issue. **URL:** http://www.vivemagazine.com. **Remarks:** Accepts advertising. **Circ:** (Not Reported).

8490 ■ Tele-Media Corporation
2200 N Florida Mango Rd., Ste. 302
West Palm Beach, FL 33409
Phone: (407)683-1414

8491 ■ WAY-FM - 88.1
800 Northpoint Pkwy., Ste. 881
West Palm Beach, FL 33407
Phone: (561)881-1929
Free: 877-919-2559
Format: Contemporary Christian. **Owner:** Way-FM Network, PO Box 64500, Colorado Springs, CO 80962, Free: 877-702-9293. **Founded:** 1987. **Key Personnel:** Bob Augsburg, Founder; Jim Marshall, Gen. Mgr. **Ad Rates:** Noncommercial. **URL:** http://www.wayfm.com.

8492 ■ WBWP-TV - 57
7354 Central Industrial Park Dr.
West Palm Beach, FL 33404
Phone: (305)441-6901
Fax: (866)269-1521
Format: Commercial TV. **Owner:** Spanish Broadcasting System Inc., Pablo Raul Alarcon Media Ctr., 7007 NW 77th Ave., Miami, FL 33166, Ph: (305)441-6901, Fax: (305)883-3375. **Founded:** 1983. **ADI:** West Palm Beach-Ft. Pierce-Vero Beach, FL. **Wattage:** 15,000 ERP. **Ad Rates:** Advertising accepted; rates available upon request. **URL:** http://wbwp57.com.

8493 ■ WBZT-AM - 1230
3071 Continental Dr.
West Palm Beach, FL 33407
Phone: (561)616-6646
Format: Talk. **Networks:** ABC. **Owner:** iHeartMedia Inc., 200 E Basse Rd., San Antonio, TX 78209, Ph: (210)832-3314. **Founded:** 1947. **Formerly:** WPCK-AM; WPBG-AM; WIRK-AM. **Operating Hours:** Continuous. **ADI:** West Palm Beach-Ft. Pierce-Vero Beach, FL. **Key Personnel:** John Hunt, Gen. Mgr. **Wattage:** 5,000. **Ad Rates:** Noncommercial. **URL:** http://www.wbzt.com.

8494 ■ WCLB-FM - 95.5
901 N Point Pky., Ste. 201
West Palm Beach, FL 33407
Phone: (561)838-4300
Fax: (561)838-4357
Format: Country. **Operating Hours:** Continuous. **ADI:** West Palm Beach-Ft. Pierce-Vero Beach, FL. **Key Personnel:** Chet Tart, Gen. Mgr.; Eric Chaney, Dir. of Programs; David Nau, Promotions Dir. **Wattage:** 100,000.

8495 ■ WDBF-AM - 1420
613 Sunny Lane Ct.
Box 1420
West Palm Beach, FL 33415
Phone: (561)642-2783

Email: wjbw@wjbw.com
Format: Big Band/Nostalgia; Jazz. **Networks:** CBS. **Owner:** Vic Knight, at above address. **Founded:** 1952. **Operating Hours:** Continuous. **Key Personnel:** Paul Dunn; George Mills, Gen. Mgr. **Wattage:** 5,000. **Ad Rates:** Combined advertising rates available with WJBW-FM. **URL:** http://universo1420.com.

8496 ■ WDJA-AM - 1420
2341 S Military Trl.
West Palm Beach, FL 33415
Phone: (561)278-1420
Format: News. **URL:** http://universo1420.com.

8497 ■ WEAT-AM - 850
2406 S Congress Ave.
West Palm Beach, FL 33406
Fax: (561)965-1102
Format: News; Sports. **Networks:** AP; CBS. **Founded:** 1948. **Operating Hours:** Continuous. **ADI:** West Palm Beach-Ft. Pierce-Vero Beach, FL. **Wattage:** 5,000 Day; 1,000 Night. **Ad Rates:** Combined advertising rates available with WOLL-FM, WKGR-FM.

8498 ■ WEAT-FM - 104.3
701 Northpoint Pkwy., Ste. 500
West Palm Beach, FL 33407
Phone: (561)616-4600
Format: Adult Contemporary. **Networks:** Independent. **Founded:** 1969. **Operating Hours:** Continuous. **ADI:** West Palm Beach-Ft. Pierce-Vero Beach, FL. **Wattage:** 100,000. **Ad Rates:** Noncommercial. **URL:** http://www.sunny1079.com.

8499 ■ WEFL-AM - 760
2090 Palm Beach Lakes Blvd., Ste. 701
West Palm Beach, FL 33409
Phone: (561)697-8353
Fax: (561)697-8525
Free: 888-760-3776
Format: Sports. **Key Personnel:** Evan Cohen, Contact, ecohen@espn760.com. **Ad Rates:** Noncommercial. **URL:** http://www.espn760.com.

8500 ■ WFAY-TV - 62
601 Clearwater Park Rd.
West Palm Beach, FL 33401
Phone: (561)682-4206
Format: Commercial TV. **Networks:** Fox. **Founded:** 1985. **Formerly:** WFCT-TV. **Operating Hours:** 20 hours Daily. **Key Personnel:** Jim Thrash, Gen. Mgr; Peggy Dill, Contact. **Wattage:** 1,000,000. **Ad Rates:** $40-700 for 30 seconds; $80-1400 for 60 seconds.

8501 ■ WFGC-TV - 61
1900 S Congress Ave., Ste. A
West Palm Beach, FL 33406
Phone: (561)642-3361
Fax: (561)967-5961
Email: gm@wfgc.com
Owner: Christian Television Network Inc., 6922 142nd Ave, Largo, FL 33771, Ph: (727)535-5622, Fax: (727)531-2497. **Key Personnel:** Mike Gonzalez, Gen. Mgr. **URL:** http://www.wfgctelevision.com.

8502 ■ WFLX-TV - 29
1100 Banyan Blvd.
West Palm Beach, FL 33401
Phone: (561)845-2929
Fax: (561)863-1238
Free: 888-369.4762
Email: share@wflx.com
Networks: Fox. **Owner:** Raycom Media Inc., 201 Monroe St., RSA Twr., 20th Fl., Montgomery, AL 36104-3731, Ph: (334)206-1400. **Founded:** 1982. **Operating Hours:** Continuous. **ADI:** West Palm Beach-Ft. Pierce-Vero Beach, FL. **Wattage:** 5,000,000. **Ad Rates:** Noncommercial. **URL:** http://www.wflx.com.

8503 ■ WIPX-TV - 63
601 Clearwater Park Rd.
West Palm Beach, FL 33401
Phone: (317)842-0063
Fax: (317)594-0630
Email: wiib@iquest.net
Format: Commercial TV. **Networks:** Independent. **Owner:** Channel 63, Inc., 2000 W 41st St., Baltimore, MD 21211, Ph: (410)467-4545. **Founded:** 1988. **Operating Hours:** 8:00 a.m. - 2:00 a.m. **Key Personnel:** Brian Bonested, Chief Engineer; Jenessa Denniston, Contact; Jenessa Denniston, Contact. **Wattage:** 165,000 H. **Ad Rates:** $10 per unit. **URL:** http://www.iontelevision.com.

8504 ■ WIRK-FM - 107.9
701 Northpoint Pkwy., Ste. 500
West Palm Beach, FL 33407
Phone: (561)686-9505
Free: 855-400-9475
Format: Country. **Owner:** CBS Corp., 51 W 52nd St., New York, NY 10019-6188, Ph: (212)975-4321, Fax: (212)975-4516, Free: 877-227-0787. **Founded:** 1965. **Operating Hours:** Continuous. **ADI:** West Palm Beach-Ft. Pierce-Vero Beach, FL. **Key Personnel:** Kailey Mills, Promotions Dir. **Wattage:** 100,000. **URL:** http://www.wirk.com.

8505 ■ WJNO-AM - 1290
3071 Continental Dr.
West Palm Beach, FL 33407
Phone: (561)616-6600
Format: News; Big Band/Nostalgia. **Networks:** ABC. **Operating Hours:** Continuous. **ADI:** Miami (Ft. Lauderdale), FL. **Key Personnel:** Brian Mudd, Dir. of Programs, brianmudd@clearchannel.com; AL Baker, Operations Mgr; Tim Reever, Contact, timreever@clearchannel.com; Geraldo Arriaga, Contact, geraldoarriaga@clearchannel.com. **Wattage:** 25,000 day; 1,000 night. **Ad Rates:** Advertising accepted; rates available upon request. Combined advertising rates available with WDJA, West Palm Beach, WFTL, Fort Lauderdale. **URL:** http://www.wjno.com.

8506 ■ WKGR-FM - 98.7
3071 Continental Dr.
West Palm Beach, FL 33407-3274
Phone: (561)616-6677
Free: 866-880-9870
Format: Classic Rock. **Networks:** Independent. **Founded:** 1961. **Operating Hours:** Continuous. **ADI:** West Palm Beach-Ft. Pierce-Vero Beach, FL. **Key Personnel:** Tim Frater, Promotions Dir; Geraldo Arriaga, Contact. **Wattage:** 100,000. **Ad Rates:** Advertising accepted; rates available upon request. **URL:** http://www.gaterrocks.com.

8507 ■ WLDI-FM - 95.5
3071 Continental Dr.
West Palm Beach, FL 33407
Phone: (561)616-6600
Free: 866-550-9550
Format: Contemporary Hit Radio (CHR); Alternative/New Music/Progressive. **Owner:** Clear Channel Communication, Inc., 200 E Basse Rd., San Antonio, TX 78209, Ph: (210)822-2828, Fax: (210)822-2828. **Key Personnel:** Geraldo Arriaga, Contact, geraldoarriaga@clearchannel.com; Aaron Wilbourne, Contact, wendydarby@clearchannel.com. **Ad Rates:** Noncommercial. **URL:** http://www.wild955.com.

8508 ■ WMBX-FM - 102.3
701 Northpoint Pky., Ste. 500
West Palm Beach, FL 33407
Free: 800-969-1023
Format: Rap; Hip Hop; Blues. **Founded:** 1980. **Formerly:** WHLG-FM. **Operating Hours:** Continuous. **ADI:** West Palm Beach-Ft. Pierce-Vero Beach, FL. **Key Personnel:** Kailey Mills, Promotions Dir., kailey.mills@cbsradio.com. **Wattage:** 50,000. **Ad Rates:** Advertising accepted; rates available upon request. **URL:** http://www.thex1023.com.

8509 ■ WOLL-FM - 105.5
3071 Continental Dr.
West Palm Beach, FL 33407
Phone: (561)616-6600
Free: 888-415-1055
Format: Oldies. **Networks:** Independent. **Founded:** 1971. **Operating Hours:** Continuous. **Key Personnel:** John Hunt, Gen. Mgr. **Wattage:** 6,000. **Ad Rates:** Advertising accepted; rates available upon request. Combined advertising rates available with WBZT-AM, WKGR-FM. **URL:** http://www.1055online.com.

8510 ■ WPBZ-FM - 103.1
701 Northpoint Pky., Ste. 500
West Palm Beach, FL 33407
Phone: (561)686-9505
Format: Alternative/New Music/Progressive; Album-Oriented Rock (AOR). **Owner:** CBS Radio Inc., 40 W 57th St., New York, NY 10019, Ph: (212)846-3939, Fax: (212)315-2162. **Key Personnel:** Benjamin Hill, Gen. Mgr., benjamin.hill@cbsradio.com; Melissa Sorrentino, Promotions Mgr., melissaleigh.sorrentino@cbsradio.com; Ross Mahoney, Music Dir., ross.mahoney@cbsradio.com. **Ad Rates:** Noncommercial.

8511 ■ WPEC-TV - 12
1100 Fairfield Dr.
West Palm Beach, FL 33407
Phone: (561)844-1212
Fax: (561)842-1212
Free: 800-310-9732
Email: newstips@cbs12.com
Format: Commercial TV. **Networks:** CBS. **Owner:** Freedom Broadcasting of Florida, Inc., at above address, Santa Ana, CA 92701. **Founded:** 1955. **Operating Hours:** Continuous. **ADI:** West Palm Beach-Ft. Pierce-Vero Beach, FL. **Key Personnel:** Carl Pugliese, Sales Mgr. **Wattage:** 316,000. **Ad Rates:** $25-3000 per unit. **URL:** http://www.cbs12.com.

8512 ■ WPOM-AM - 1600
2475 Mercer Ave., Ste. 104
West Palm Beach, FL 33401
Phone: (561)242-8155
Fax: (561)623-7668
Format: Educational; Country. **Founded:** 1958. **Operating Hours:** Continuous. **Wattage:** 5,000 Day; 4,700 Nig. **Ad Rates:** $30-60 per unit. **URL:** http://www.radiovisionmedia.com.

8513 ■ WPTV-TV - 5
1100 Banyan Blvd.
West Palm Beach, FL 33401
Phone: (561)655-5455
Fax: (561)653-5719
Email: newstips@wptv.com
Format: Commercial TV. **Networks:** NBC. **Owner:** Scripps TV Station Group, 312 Walnut St., Cincinnati, OH 45201. **Founded:** Aug. 22, 1954. **Operating Hours:** Continuous. **ADI:** West Palm Beach-Ft. Pierce-Vero Beach, FL. **Key Personnel:** Steve Wasserman, Gen. Mgr., VP. **Wattage:** 100 KW. **Ad Rates:** Noncommercial. **URL:** http://www.wptv.com.

8514 ■ WPXE-TV - 55
601 Clearwater Park Rd.
West Palm Beach, FL 33401
Phone: (414)657-9453
Fax: (414)656-7664
Format: Commercial TV. **Networks:** Independent. **Founded:** 1988. **Formerly:** WHKE-TV. **Operating Hours:** Continuous. **ADI:** Milwaukee (Kenosha & Racine), WI. **Key Personnel:** Randall Harris, Gen. Mgr. **Wattage:** 5,000,000.

8515 ■ WRLX-FM - 92.1
3071 Continental Dr.
West Palm Beach, FL 33407
Phone: (561)616-6600
Free: 866-310-9210
Format: Easy Listening; Full Service; Hip Hop; Country; Talk; Classic Rock. **Founded:** 1978. **Formerly:** WNGS-FM. **Operating Hours:** Continuous. **ADI:** West Palm Beach-Ft. Pierce-Vero Beach, FL. **Key Personnel:** Bill Brady, Contact, billbrady@clearchannel.com. **Wattage:** 7,200 ERP. **Ad Rates:** Advertising accepted; rates available upon request. **URL:** http://www.921wrlx.com/main.html.

8516 ■ WRMF-FM - 97.9
701 Northpoint Pkwy., Ste. 500
West Palm Beach, FL 33407
Free: 877-979-9763
Format: Adult Contemporary. **Networks:** Independent. **Owner:** Cobalt Operating L.L.C., at above address, Midland, TX 79705. **Founded:** 1957. **Operating Hours:** Continuous. **ADI:** West Palm Beach-Ft. Pierce-Vero Beach, FL. **Key Personnel:** Erika Ewald, Dir. of Mktg., erika@wrmf.com; Bob Neumann, Dir. of Programs, bob@wrmf.com; Stacy DelValle, Gen. Sales Mgr., stacydelvalle@wrmf.com. **Wattage:** 100,000. **Ad Rates:** Advertising accepted; rates available upon request. **URL:** http://www.wrmf.com.

8517 ■ WTCN-TV - 43
1100 Fairfield Dr.
West Palm Beach, FL 33407
URL: http://www.my15wtcn.com.

Circulation: ★ = AAM; △ or • = BPA; ♦ = CAC; ❑ = VAC; ⊕ = PO Statement; ‡ = Publisher's Report; Boldface figures = swom; Light figures = estimated.

8518 ■ WTVX-TV - 34
1700 Palm Beach Lakes Blvd., Ste. 150
West Palm Beach, FL 33401
Phone: (561)681-3434
Fax: (561)684-9193
Email: info@wtvx.com
Format: Commercial TV. **Networks:** United Paramount Network. **Owner:** Four Points Media Group, LLC, at above address. **Founded:** Apr. 05, 1966. **Operating Hours:** 6 a.m.-2 a.m. **ADI:** West Palm Beach-Ft. Pierce-Vero Beach, FL. **Wattage:** 5,000,000. **Ad Rates:** Advertising accepted; rates available upon request.

8519 ■ W203AY-FM - 88.5
PO Box 391
Twin Falls, ID 83303
Fax: (208)736-1958
Free: 800-357-4226
Format: Religious; Contemporary Christian. **Owner:** CSN International, PO Box 391, Twin Falls, ID 83303, Ph: (208)736-1958, Fax: (208)736-1958, Free: 800-357-4226. **Key Personnel:** Kelly Carlson, Dir. of Engg.; Ray Gorney, Asst. Dir. **URL:** http://www.csnradio.com.

8520 ■ WWHB-TV - 48
1700 Palm Beach Lakes Blvd., Ste. 150
West Palm Beach, FL 33401
Phone: (561)681-3434
Fax: (561)684-9193
Owner: Four Points Media Group, LLC, at above address. **URL:** http://www.azteca48.com.

8521 ■ WWRF-AM - 1380
2326 S Congress Ave.
West Palm Beach, FL 33406
Phone: (561)721-9950
Format: Hispanic. **Networks:** CNN Radio. **Founded:** 1959. **Formerly:** WLVS-AM; WLIZ-AM. **Operating Hours:** Continuous; 100% local. **ADI:** West Palm Beach-Ft. Pierce-Vero Beach, FL. **Key Personnel:** Brian Johnson, VP; Paul Danitz, Office Mgr. **Local Programs:** *Radio Fiesta*. **Wattage:** 1,000. **Ad Rates:** Noncommercial. Combined advertising rates available with WAFC/Clewiston; WAFZ/Ft. Myers-Naples, Fl. **URL:** http://www.la1380.com.

8522 ■ WWRF-FM - 96.9
2326 S Congress Ave., Ste. 2A
West Palm Beach, FL 33406
Phone: (561)721-9950
Fax: (561)721-9973
Email: info@gladesmedia.com
Format: Hispanic. **Owner:** Glades Media Group, 530 E Alverdez Ave., Clewiston, FL 33440, Ph: (863)983-5900. **Key Personnel:** Liza Flores, Gen. Mgr. **URL:** http://www.gladesmedia.com.

8523 ■ WYPX-TV - 55
601 Clearwater Park Rd.
West Palm Beach, FL 33401
Phone: (561)682-4206
Email: wypx@pax.net
Format: Commercial TV. **Owner:** ION Media Networks Inc., 601 Clearwater Park Rd., West Palm Beach, FL 33401-6233, Ph: (561)659-4122, Fax: (561)659-4252. **Founded:** 1987. **Formerly:** WOCD-TV. **Operating Hours:** Continuous. **Key Personnel:** Charmaine Ushkow, cushkow@pax.net; Renee Osterlitz, Traffic Mgr., rosterlitz@pax.net; Chris Iorio, Production Mgr., ciorio@pax.net. **Wattage:** 5,000,000. **Ad Rates:** $25-150 for 30 seconds.

8524 ■ WZZR-FM - 94.3
3071 Continental Dr.
West Palm Beach, FL 33407
Phone: (561)616-6600
Fax: (561)616-6653
Format: Talk. **Wattage:** 50,000. **Ad Rates:** Noncommercial; Advertising accepted; rates available upon request.

WILDWOOD

8525 ■ U.S. Marine Corps Combat Correspondents Association--Annual Conference Journal
United States Marine Corps Combat Correspondents Association
110 Fox Ct.
Wildwood, FL 34785
Publisher's E-mail: usmccca@cfl.rr.com
Freq: Annual. **Subscription Rates:** included in membership dues. **Remarks:** Accepts advertising. **Circ:** 2000.

WILLISTON

N FL. Levy Co. 20 mi. S. of Gainesville.

8526 ■ Williston Pioneer Sun-News
Landmark Community Newspapers L.L.C.
607 South West 1st Avenue
Williston, FL 32696
Phone: (352)528-3343
Publisher's E-mail: marketing@lcni.com
Community newspaper. **Subscription Rates:** $27 Individuals annual all access; $17 Individuals semi-annual all access; $10 Individuals quarterly all access. **URL:** http://www.willistonpioneer.com. **Remarks:** Accepts advertising. **Circ:** (Not Reported).

WIMAUMA

8527 ■ Cablevision Industries Inc.
10902 Bill Tucker Rd.
Wimauma, FL 33598
Phone: (813)633-1455
Fax: (813)634-3865
Owner: Cablevision Industries Inc., 1 Cablevision Center, Liberty, NY 12754, Ph: (914)292-7550. **Founded:** 1957. **Cities Served:** Palmetto, Florida: subscribing households 21,939; Hillsborough County, Manatez County, MacDill Air Force Base; 43 channels.

WINTER HAVEN

Polk Co. Polk Co. (C). 14 m E of Lakeland. Winter resort. Cypress Gardens. Manufactures citrus by-products, alcohol, molasses, feed, nutfood products, cigars, roofing, paper boxes, fertilizer. Crate, planing mills; sheet metal, bottling works; fruit packing and canning. Nurseries. Citrus fruit groves.

8528 ■ Journal of Food Science
Institute of Food Technologists
PO Box 3065
Winter Haven, FL 33885-3065
Phone: (941)293-6519
Fax: (941)299-8244
Publisher's E-mail: info@ift.org
Journal containing original research papers and articles relating to food science. **Freq:** Bimonthly Latest Edition: Volume 78 Issue 10 (October 2013). **Print Method:** Offset. **Trim Size:** 8 1/2 x 11. **Cols./Page:** 2. **Col. Width:** 21 picas. **Col. Depth:** 59 picas. **Key Personnel:** Bob Swientek, Director, Publications; E. Allen Foegeding, Editor-in-Chief. **ISSN:** 0022--1947 (print). **Subscription Rates:** $110 Members online; $150 Members online & print; $25 Students; £508 Nonmembers institutions, print & online (UK). **URL:** http://www.ift.org/knowledge-center/read-ift-publications/journal-of-food-science.aspx. **Remarks:** Advertising not accepted. **Circ:** ‡10550, ‡300.

8529 ■ Newschief
The New York Times Co.
455 Sixth St. NW
Winter Haven, FL 33881
Phone: (863)401-6900
Fax: (863)401-6999
Publisher's E-mail: national@nytimes.com
Community newspaper. **Freq:** Weekly (Thurs.). **Print Method:** Offset. **Trim Size:** 12 3/4 x 21 1/2. **Cols./Page:** 6. **Col. Width:** 2 inches. **Col. Depth:** 21 1/2 inches. **Key Personnel:** Bill Blocher, Managing Editor, phone: (863)401-6973; Jeff Amero, Manager, Circulation. **USPS:** 586-700. **Subscription Rates:** $10.2† Individuals print and digital; $9.95 Individuals digital ledger and news chief. **Alt. Formats:** Handheld. **URL:** http://www.newschief.com. **Formerly:** Auburndale Star. **Ad Rates:** GLR $.45; BW $516; 4C $900; PCI $3.85. **Remarks:** Advertising accepted; rates available upon request. **Circ:** Combined 2104.

8530 ■ WHNR-AM - 1360
1505 Dundee Rd.
Winter Haven, FL 33884
Phone: (863)299-1141
Fax: (863)293-6397
Owner: La Poderosa L.L.C. **Wattage:** 5,000 Day; 2,500 Night.

WINTER PARK

Orange Co. Orange Co. (EC). 3 m NE of Orlando. Residential. Rollins College. U.S. Navy training center. Tourist resort.

8531 ■ American Photo
Bonnier Corp.
460 N Orlando Ave., Ste. 200
Winter Park, FL 32789
Phone: (407)628-4802
Fax: (407)628-7061
Publisher's E-mail: mobileapps@bonniercorp.com
Photography magazine. **Freq:** Bimonthly. **Print Method:** Offset. **Trim Size:** 9 x 10 7/8. **Cols./Page:** 3. **Col. Width:** 26 nonpareils. **Col. Depth:** 138 agate lines. **Key Personnel:** Jeffrey Roberts, Publisher, Vice President. **Subscription Rates:** $22 Two years; $14 Individuals. **URL:** http://www.bonnier.com/English-tags/American-Photo/; http://www.popphoto.com/tags/american-photo. **Ad Rates:** BW $24,710; 4C $39,425. **Remarks:** Accepts advertising. **Circ:** Paid ‡175000.

8532 ■ ATV Rider
Bonnier Corp.
460 N Orlando Ave., Ste. 200
Winter Park, FL 32789
Phone: (407)628-4802
Fax: (407)628-7061
Publisher's E-mail: mobileapps@bonniercorp.com
Magazine featuring all-terrain vehicles, as well as utility, hunting and sporting areas. Includes articles on selecting, buying, equipping and using ATVs, as well as comprehensive product listings that include descriptions, specifications, prices and photos of virtually every ATV available. Other informative features include: new model tests, bolt-ons and accessories reference guide; safety and riding tips; and ATV travel. **Freq:** Monthly. **Subscription Rates:** $24.95 Individuals; $14.97 Individuals 6 issues; $36.95 Canada; $20.97 Canada 6 issues; $48.95 Other countries; $26.97 Other countries 6 issues. **URL:** http://www.bonniercorp.com/atv-rider. **Remarks:** Accepts advertising. **Circ:** (Not Reported).

8533 ■ Baggers
Bonnier Corp.
460 N Orlando Ave., Ste. 200
Winter Park, FL 32789
Phone: (407)628-4802
Fax: (407)628-7061
Publisher's E-mail: mobileapps@bonniercorp.com
Performance magazine for Harley-Davidson and American V-twin motorcycle enthusiasts. Features detailed articles covering the latest performance and cosmetic modifications for both the novice and the expert owner. Also includes detailed, step-by-step, technical package; comprehensive road tests; in-depth apparel and accessory evaluations; exciting event coverage; and outstanding bike features. **Freq:** Monthly. **Key Personnel:** David Roe, Associate Publisher, phone: (310)265-1876. **Subscription Rates:** $19.97 Individuals; $29.97 Two years; $31.97 Canada; $53.97 Canada 2 years; $43.97 Other countries; $77.97 Other countries 2 years. **URL:** http://www.baggersmag.com. **Formerly:** Hot Rod Bikes. **Remarks:** Accepts advertising. **Circ:** Paid ★75361.

8534 ■ Boating Life: The Authority on Recreational Boating
Bonnier Corp.
460 N Orlando Ave., Ste. 200
Winter Park, FL 32789
Phone: (407)628-4802
Fax: (407)628-7061
Publisher's E-mail: mobileapps@bonniercorp.com
Consumer magazine covering boating for vessels under 36 feet long. **Freq:** 10/year. **Print Method:** Perfect Bound. **Trim Size:** 8 1/8 x 10 3/4. **Key Personnel:** John McEver, Publisher, phone: (407)571-4682; Randy Vance, Editor-in-Chief. **Subscription Rates:** $12 U.S. 10 issues 1 year; $22 Canada 10 issues 1 year; $32 Other countries 10 issues 1 year. **URL:** http://www.boatingmag.com. **Ad Rates:** BW $8,650; 4C $12,995. **Remarks:** Accepts advertising. **Circ:** Paid 162402.

8535 ■ Conceive
Bonnier Corp.
460 N Orlando Ave., Ste. 200
Winter Park, FL 32789
Phone: (407)628-4802
Fax: (407)628-7061

Publisher's E-mail: mobileapps@bonniercorp.com
Magazine offers information on how to increase fertility and better conceive children. **Freq:** Quarterly. **Key Personnel:** Beth Weinhouse, Director, Editorial; Emily Kruckemyer, Managing Editor. **Subscription Rates:** $11.20 Individuals; $22.40 Two years; $24 Canada; $32 Other countries. **Remarks:** Accepts advertising. **Circ:** (Not Reported).

8536 ■ Deer and Turkey Show Previews
Bonnier Corp.
460 N Orlando Ave., Ste. 200
Winter Park, FL 32789
Phone: (407)628-4802
Fax: (407)628-7061
Publisher's E-mail: mobileapps@bonniercorp.com
Five magazines on 5 deer and turkey hunting shows. **Freq:** 1/yr, 5 different states, 1 issue/state. **Print Method:** Offset. **Trim Size:** 8 3/8 x 10 7/8. **Cols./Page:** 2 and 3. **Col. Width:** 3 1/3 and 2 1/4 inches. **Col. Depth:** 10 inches. **Key Personnel:** Jake Steingraeber, Executive Director. **Subscription Rates:** Free. **URL:** http://www.deerinfo.com. **Formerly:** Deer Show Previews. **Ad Rates:** BW $3,629; 4C $4,894. **Remarks:** Advertising accepted; rates available upon request. **Circ:** Controlled 150000.

8537 ■ Destination Weddings & Honeymoons
Bonnier Corp.
460 N Orlando Ave., Ste. 200
Winter Park, FL 32789
Phone: (407)628-4802
Fax: (407)628-7061
Publisher's E-mail: mobileapps@bonniercorp.com
Magazine featuring destinations for wedding or honeymoon. **Freq:** Bimonthly. **Key Personnel:** Susan Moynihan, Editor-in-Chief; Carol Johnson, Publisher, phone: (908)221-9122. **Subscription Rates:** $19.97 Individuals; $28.97 Canada. **URL:** http://www.destinationweddingmag.com; http://www.bonniercorp.com/brands/Destination-Weddings-Honeymoons.html. **Ad Rates:** 4C $14,675. **Remarks:** Accepts advertising. **Circ:** 100000.

8538 ■ Dirt Rider
Bonnier Corp.
460 N Orlando Ave., Ste. 200
Winter Park, FL 32789
Phone: (407)628-4802
Fax: (407)628-7061
Publication E-mail: inquiries@automotive.com
Off-road motorcycle magazine. **Freq:** Monthly. **Print Method:** Offset. **Trim Size:** 7 7/8 x 10 1/2. **Key Personnel:** Damian Ercole, Publisher, phone: (212)915-4404. **Subscription Rates:** $12 Individuals; $22 Canada; $32 Other countries. **Alt. Formats:** Handheld. **URL:** http://www.bonniercorp.com/dirt-rider; http://www.dirtrider.com. **Remarks:** Advertising accepted; rates available upon request. **Circ:** Paid **★174650**.

8539 ■ Florida Grower
Meister Media Worldwide
1555 Howell Branch Rd., No. C-204
Winter Park, FL 32789
Phone: (407)539-6552
Fax: (407)539-6544
Publisher's E-mail: info@meistermedia.com
Agricultural magazine. **Freq:** Monthly. **Print Method:** Offset. **Trim Size:** 8 1/2 x 11. **Cols./Page:** 3. **Col. Width:** 27 nonpareils. **Col. Depth:** 140 agate lines. **Key Personnel:** Frank Giles, Editor, phone: (407)539-6552; Paul Rusnak, Managing Editor; Joseph Monahan, Publisher. **ISSN:** 0015--4091 (print). **URL:** http://meistermedia.com/publications/florida-grower. **Formerly:** Florida Grower & Rancher. **Ad Rates:** GLR $4.70; PCI $66. **Remarks:** Advertising accepted; rates available upon request. **Circ:** (Not Reported).

8540 ■ Florida Roofing Magazine
FRSA
4111 Metric Dr., Ste. 6
Winter Park, FL 32792
Phone: (407)671-3772
Fax: (407)679-0010
Publication E-mail: bbp1@floridaroof.com
Roofing, sheet metal, and air conditioning magazine. **Freq:** Monthly. **Print Method:** Offset. **Trim Size:** 8 1/4 x 11. **Cols./Page:** 3 and 2. **Col. Width:** 27 and 40 nonpareils. **Col. Depth:** 140 agate lines. **Key Personnel:** Bonnie B. Pierce, Editor, phone: (407)671-3772; Alberto E. Duenas, Contact. **ISSN:** 0191--4618 (print). **URL:** http://floridaroof.com/florida-roofing-magazine. **Formerly:** Florida Forum. **Ad Rates:** BW $1968; 4C $2768; PCI $30. **Remarks:** Accepts advertising. **Circ:** Controlled ‡4500.

8541 ■ Florida Travel & Life
Bonnier Corp.
460 N Orlando Ave., Ste. 200
Winter Park, FL 32789
Phone: (407)628-4802
Fax: (407)628-7061
Publisher's E-mail: mobileapps@bonniercorp.com
Magazine featuring Florida and its destinations. **Freq:** 7/year. **Trim Size:** 8 7/8 X 10 7/8. **Key Personnel:** Laura Walker, Publisher; Patricia Letakis, Editor-in-Chief; Susan Friedman, Senior Editor. **Subscription Rates:** $11.97 Individuals + one copy; $19.97 Canada; $35.97 Other countries. **URL:** http://www.bonniercorp.com/brands/Florida-Travel-Life.html; http://www.floridatravellife.com. **Ad Rates:** 4C $11,790. **Remarks:** Accepts advertising. **Circ:** 103389.

8542 ■ Flying
Bonnier Corp.
460 N Orlando Ave., Ste. 200
Winter Park, FL 32789
Phone: (407)628-4802
Fax: (407)628-7061
Publisher's E-mail: mobileapps@bonniercorp.com
General aviation magazine. **Freq:** Monthly. **Print Method:** Offset. **Trim Size:** 7 7/8 x 10 1/2. **Cols./Page:** 3. **Col. Width:** 27 nonpareils. **Col. Depth:** 140 agate lines. **Key Personnel:** Robert Goyer, Editor-in-Chief. **Subscription Rates:** $14 Individuals print; $22 Two years print; $29 Canada print; $44 Other countries print. **URL:** http://www.flyingmag.com. **Ad Rates:** GLR $32; BW $14,915; 4C $22,385. **Remarks:** Accepts advertising. **Circ:** Paid **★226000**.

8543 ■ Garden Design
Bonnier Corp.
460 N Orlando Ave., Ste. 200
Winter Park, FL 32789
Phone: (407)628-4802
Fax: (407)628-7061
Publisher's E-mail: mobileapps@bonniercorp.com
Magazine on garden design, featuring individual gardens, design trend stories, design history, profiles, horticulture coverage, and book reviews. **Freq:** Quarterly. **Print Method:** Offset. **Trim Size:** 8 7/8 x 10 7/8. **Key Personnel:** Bill Marken, Editor-in-Chief; Sarah Kinbar, Editor; Jamie Burris, Publisher. **ISSN:** 0733--4923 (print). **Subscription Rates:** $45 U.S.; $56 Canada. **URL:** http://www.gardendesign.com. **Ad Rates:** BW $21,560; 4C $31,730. **Remarks:** Accepts advertising. **Circ:** Paid **★253561**.

8544 ■ The Hemingway Review
Hemingway Foundation and Society
c/o Gail Sinclair
Rollins College
1000 Holt Ave. 2770
Winter Park, FL 32789
Publisher's E-mail: webmaster@jhupress.jhu.edu
Academic journal covering the work and life of Ernest Hemingway. **Freq:** Semiannual. **Print Method:** Photo offset. **Trim Size:** 6 x 9. **Key Personnel:** Susan F. Beegel, Editor. **ISSN:** 0276--3362 (print); **EISSN:** 1548--4815 (electronic). **URL:** http://muse.jhu.edu/journal/275; http://hemingwaysociety.org/?page_id=10. **Formerly:** Hemingway Notes. **Remarks:** Accepts advertising. **Circ:** Combined 1000, 1150.

8545 ■ Islands Magazine: An International Magazine
Islands Publishing Co.
460 North Orlando Ave., Ste. 200
Winter Park, FL 32789
Publication E-mail: editor@islands.com
Publication on islands of the world and traveling. **Freq:** 10/year. **Print Method:** Print/Web. **Trim Size:** 8 3/8 x 10 1/2. **Cols./Page:** 3. **Col. Width:** 25 nonpareils. **Col. Depth:** 133 agate lines. **Key Personnel:** Eddy Patricelli, Editor-in-Chief. **ISSN:** 0745--7847 (print). **Subscription Rates:** $21.97 Two years U.S.; $14.97 Individuals U.S.; $23.97 Canada; $32.97 Other countries. **URL:** http://www.islands.com. **Remarks:** Accepts advertising. **Circ:** Paid 200000.

8546 ■ Marlin: The International Sportingfishing Magazine
Bonnier Corp.
460 N Orlando Ave., Ste. 200
Winter Park, FL 32789
Phone: (407)628-4802
Fax: (407)628-7061
Publication E-mail: editor@marlinmag.com
Covers offshore sport-fishing for billfish and other large pelagics. **Freq:** 8/year. **Print Method:** Web Offset. **Trim Size:** 8 1/8 x 10 3/4. **Cols./Page:** 3. **Col. Width:** 2 3/16 inches. **Col. Depth:** 10 inches. **Key Personnel:** Natasha Lloyd, Publisher, phone: (954)760-4602; Dave Ferrell, Editor; Scott Shane, Editor-in-Chief; David Ritchie, Director, Editorial. **ISSN:** 0749--2006 (print). **Subscription Rates:** $21 U.S.; $39 Canada; $57 Other countries. **URL:** http://www.marlinmag.com; http://www.bonniercorp.com/marlin. **Remarks:** Accepts advertising. **Circ:** (Not Reported).

8547 ■ Motorcycle Cruiser
Bonnier Corp.
460 N Orlando Ave., Ste. 200
Winter Park, FL 32789
Phone: (407)628-4802
Fax: (407)628-7061
Publication E-mail: motorcyclecruiser@emailcustomerservice.com inquiries@automotive.com
Magazine catering to mature, affluent motorcyclists (those less concerned about top speed, but very passionate about personalization) who prefer the laidback styling and ergonomics of modern cruisers. Offers readers examples and information about choices such as bolt-on accessories, painting techniques and even fabrication, in addition to advice on performance enhancements. Issues feature comprehensive road tests and comparisons of new models as well as features on the people, destinations and events that make riding a cruiser such a unique experience. Includes regular departments, which focus on riding techniques, new accessories and apparel, how-to marketplace and tech guides and in-depth product comparisons. **Freq:** Bimonthly. **Subscription Rates:** $14.97 Individuals; $38.97 Canada; $62.97 Other countries. **URL:** http://www.motorcyclecruiser.com. **Remarks:** Accepts advertising. **Circ:** (Not Reported).

8548 ■ Motorcyclist
Bonnier Corp.
460 N Orlando Ave., Ste. 200
Winter Park, FL 32789
Phone: (407)628-4802
Fax: (407)628-7061
Publication E-mail: inquiries@automotive.com
Motorcycle magazine. Includes road tests, technical competition. **Freq:** Monthly. **Print Method:** Offset. **Trim Size:** 7 7/8 x 10 1/2. **Key Personnel:** Marty Estes, Publisher, phone: (310)531-9857. **ISSN:** 0027--2205 (print). **Subscription Rates:** $10 Individuals; $22 Canada; $34 Other countries. **URL:** http://www.motorcyclistonline.com. **Remarks:** Accepts advertising. **Circ:** Paid **★240046**.

8549 ■ Ornamental Outlook: Growing the Florida Landscape
Meister Media Worldwide
1555 Howell Branch Rd., Ste. C-204
Winter Park, FL 32789-1170
Phone: (407)539-6552
Fax: (407)539-6544
Publisher's E-mail: info@meistermedia.com
Trade magazine for the environmental horticulture industry. **Freq:** Monthly. **Trim Size:** 8 1/2 x 11. **Cols./Page:** 3. **Col. Width:** 28 nonpareils. **Col. Depth:** 182 agate lines. **Key Personnel:** Joe W. Monahan, Publisher; Michael L. DeLuca, President; Paul Rusnak, Managing Editor. **Ad Rates:** BW $1,840. **Remarks:** Advertising accepted; rates available upon request. **Circ:** (Not Reported).

8550 ■ Relevant: God, Life, Progressive Culture
Relevant Media Group
900 Orange Ave.
Winter Park, FL 32789
Phone: (407)660-1411
Publisher's E-mail: info@relevantmediagroup.com

Circulation: ★ = AAM; △ or • = BPA; ♦ = CAC; ❑ = VAC; ⊕ = PO Statement; ‡ = Publisher's Report; Boldface figures = sworn; Light figures = estimated.

Magazine for contemporary Christian young adults. Covers faith, career, relationships, music, and progressive culture. **Freq:** Bimonthly. **Key Personnel:** Maya Strang, Contact; Roxanne Wieman, Director, Editorial; Cameron Strang, Publisher. **Subscription Rates:** $12 U.S. print and online; $20 Canada print and online; $26 Other countries print and online. **URL:** http://www.relevantmagazine.com. **Remarks:** Accepts advertising. **Circ:** (Not Reported).

8551 ■ Salt Water Sportsman
Bonnier Corp.
460 N Orlando Ave., Ste. 200
Winter Park, FL 32789
Phone: (407)628-4802
Fax: (407)628-7061
Publisher's E-mail: mobileapps@bonniercorp.com
Consumer magazine covering marine sport fishing. **Freq:** 10/year. **Key Personnel:** John Brownlee, Editor-in-Chief; Glenn Law, Senior Editor; Dave Morel, Publisher; Nick Honachefsky, Managing Editor. **Subscription Rates:** $18 10 issues. **Alt. Formats:** PDF. **URL:** http://www.bonniercorp.com/salt-water-sportsman; http://www.saltwatersportsman.com. **Remarks:** Accepts advertising. **Circ:** Paid **★172460**.

8552 ■ The Sandspur
Rollins College
1000 Holt Ave.
Winter Park, FL 32789
Phone: (407)646-2000
Collegiate newspaper. **Freq:** Weekly. **Print Method:** Offset. **Trim Size:** 11 x 16. **Cols./Page:** 5. **Col. Width:** 22 nonpareils. **Col. Depth:** 217 agate lines. **Key Personnel:** Jennifer Stull, Editor-in-Chief; Shannon Lynch, Managing Editor; Jeanna Kim, Business Manager. **Subscription Rates:** $10 Individuals. **URL:** http://thesandspur.org. **Ad Rates:** BW $600; 4C $850; PCI $8. **Remarks:** Accepts advertising. **Circ:** 2000.

8553 ■ Sport Diver
Bonnier Corp.
460 N Orlando Ave., Ste. 200
Winter Park, FL 32789
Phone: (407)628-4802
Fax: (407)628-7061
Publisher's E-mail: mobileapps@bonniercorp.com
Consumer magazine covering scuba diving. **Freq:** Monthly. **Subscription Rates:** $29 Individuals; $41 Canada; $62 Other countries. **URL:** http://www.sportdiver.com; http://www.worldpub.net/brands/SportDiver.html. **Ad Rates:** BW $15,705; 4C $23,095. **Remarks:** Accepts advertising. **Circ:** Paid ‡175000.

8554 ■ Sport Fishing
Bonnier Corp.
460 N Orlando Ave., Ste. 200
Winter Park, FL 32789
Phone: (407)628-4802
Fax: (407)628-7061
Publisher's E-mail: mobileapps@bonniercorp.com
Magazine about saltwater fishing. **Freq:** 9/year. **Print Method:** Web Offset. **Trim Size:** 8 1/8 x 10 3/4. **Cols./Page:** 3. **Col. Width:** 2 3/16 inches. **Col. Depth:** 10 inches. **Key Personnel:** Scott Salyers, Publisher; Chris Woodward, Editor; Dave Morel, Publisher; Stephanie Pancratz, Managing Editor. **ISSN:** 0896--7369 (print). **Subscription Rates:** $9.97 Individuals; $37.97 Other countries; $23.97 Canada. **URL:** http://www.bonniercorp.com/sport-fishing; http://www.sportfishingmag.com. **Ad Rates:** BW $13635; 4C $19485. **Remarks:** Accepts advertising. **Circ:** Paid **★148830**.

8555 ■ Sport Rider
Bonnier Corp.
460 N Orlando Ave., Ste. 200
Winter Park, FL 32789
Phone: (407)628-4802
Fax: (407)628-7061
Publication E-mail: inquiries@automotive.com sportrider@emailcustomerservice.com
Magazine focusing on the world of sportbikes. Celebrates high-performance street bikes, racing motorcycles and high-performance riding. Staff editors and contributors are serious sportbike riders' and accomplished racers. Pairs coverage of advanced-technology sporting machines with a focus on the skills and attitude needed to ride them responsibly. **Freq:** 8/year. **Key Personnel:** Marty Estes, Publisher, phone: (310)531-9857. **Subscription Rates:** $14 Individuals; $24 Canada; $34 Other countries. **URL:** http://www.sportrider.com. **Remarks:** Accepts advertising. **Circ:** Paid **★86097**.

8556 ■ Super Streetbike
Bonnier Corp.
460 N Orlando Ave., Ste. 200
Winter Park, FL 32789
Phone: (407)628-4802
Fax: (407)628-7061
Publisher's E-mail: mobileapps@bonniercorp.com
Street bike magazine featuring profiles, photographs, equipment reports, technical articles, modification tips, and motorcycle reviews. **Freq:** Monthly. **Print Method:** Offset. **Cols./Page:** 3. **Col. Width:** 27 nonpareils. **Col. Depth:** 140 agate lines. **Key Personnel:** Dave Sonsky, Editor-in-Chief; Marty Estes, Publisher, phone: (310)531-9857. **Subscription Rates:** $18 Individuals; $28 Two years; $30 Canada; $42 Other countries. **URL:** http://www.superstreetbike.com/index.html; http://www.sourceinterlinkmedia.com/motorcycle/superstreetbike/. **Remarks:** Accepts advertising. **Circ:** Combined **★35298**.

8557 ■ Wake Boarding
Bonnier Corp.
460 N Orlando Ave., Ste. 200
Winter Park, FL 32789
Phone: (407)628-4802
Fax: (407)628-7061
Publisher's E-mail: mobileapps@bonniercorp.com
Consumer magazine covering the water sport, wake boarding. **Freq:** 8/year. **Key Personnel:** Shawn Perry. **Subscription Rates:** $14.97 Individuals; $28.97 Canada; $42.97 Other countries. **URL:** http://www.wakeboardingmag.com. **Ad Rates:** 4C $9,875. **Remarks:** Accepts advertising. **Circ:** Paid 50000.

8558 ■ Waterski
Bonnier Corp.
460 N Orlando Ave., Ste. 200
Winter Park, FL 32789
Phone: (407)628-4802
Fax: (407)628-7061
Publication E-mail: editor@waterskimag.com
Magazine on waterskiing. **Freq:** 6/year. **Print Method:** Web offset. **Trim Size:** 8 1/8 x 10 3/4. **Cols./Page:** 3. **Col. Width:** 2 3/16 inches. **Col. Depth:** 10 inches. **Key Personnel:** Todd Ristorcelli, Editor. **ISSN:** 0883--7813 (print). **Subscription Rates:** $14.97 Individuals 6 issues. **URL:** http://www.waterskimag.com. **Formerly:** World Waterskiing. **Remarks:** Accepts advertising. **Circ:** (Not Reported).

8559 ■ Windsurfing
Bonnier Corp.
460 N Orlando Ave., Ste. 200
Winter Park, FL 32789
Phone: (407)628-4802
Fax: (407)628-7061
Publisher's E-mail: mobileapps@bonniercorp.com
Windsurfing magazine. **Freq:** 8/yr. **Print Method:** Offset. **Cols./Page:** 3. **Col. Width:** 26 nonpareils. **Col. Depth:** 140 agate lines. **Key Personnel:** David Combe, Publisher, phone: (503)417-7934; Josh Sampiero, Editor; Amanda Harris, Manager. **Subscription Rates:** $9.97 Individuals; $15.97 Canada; $24.97 Other countries. **URL:** http://www.bonniercorp.com/brands/WindSurfing.html. **Ad Rates:** BW $3,595; 4C $5,385. **Remarks:** Accepts advertising. **Circ:** (Not Reported).

8560 ■ WESH-TV - 2
1021 N Wymore Rd.
Winter Park, FL 32789
Phone: (407)645-2222
Format: Commercial TV. **Networks:** NBC. **Founded:** 1956. **Operating Hours**: Continuous. **ADI**: Orlando-Daytona Beach-Melbourne, FL. **Key Personnel:** James J. Carter, Gen. Mgr., President. **Wattage**: 100. **Ad Rates:** Noncommercial. **URL:** http://www.wesh.com.

8561 ■ WKCF-TV - 18
1021 N Wymore Rd.
Winter Park, FL 32789
Phone: (407)645-2222
Email: emailnews@wesh.com
Format: Commercial TV. **Owner:** Emmis Communications Corp., One Emmis Plz., 40 Monument Cir., Ste. 700, Indianapolis, IN 46204-3011, Ph: (317)266-0100. **Founded:** 1988. **Operating Hours**: 9 a.m.-5 p.m. **ADI**: Orlando-Daytona Beach-Melbourne, FL. **Key Personnel:** Michelle Bell, Contact, mdbell@hearst.com. **Ad Rates:** Noncommercial. **URL:** http://www.wesh.com.

8562 ■ WPRK-FM - 91.5
1000 Holt Ave., Ste. 2771
Winter Park, FL 32789
Phone: (407)646-2241
Email: wprkfm@rollins.edu
Format: Eclectic. **Owner:** Rollins College, 1000 Holt Ave., Winter Park, FL 32789, Ph: (407)646-2000. **Founded:** 1952. **Operating Hours**: Continuous. **Key Personnel:** Jerrid Kalakay, Gen. Mgr., jkalakay@rollins.edu. **Wattage**: 1,300. **Ad Rates:** Noncommercial; underwriting available. **URL:** http://www.rollins.edu/student-affairs/community/student-media.html.

YULEE

Nassau Co. (NE). 8 m SW of Fernandiana Beach.

8563 ■ Journal of Zoo and Wildlife Medicine
American Association of Zoo Veterinarians
581705 White Oak Rd.
Yulee, FL 32097
Phone: (904)225-3275
Fax: (904)225-3289
Publisher's E-mail: Admin@aazv.org
Journal covering research findings, clinical observations, and case reports in the field of veterinary medicine dealing with captive and freeranging wild animals. **Freq:** Quarterly. **ISSN:** 1042--7260 (print); **EISSN:** 1937--2825 (electronic). **Subscription Rates:** Included in membership. **URL:** http://zoowildlifejournal.com; http://www.aazv.org/?page=A8. **Ad Rates:** BW $705; 4C $800. **Remarks:** Accepts advertising. **Circ:** (Not Reported).

ZOLFO SPRINGS

8564 ■ WZSP-FM - 105.3
7891 US Hwy. 17 S
Zolfo Springs, FL 33890
Phone: (863)494-1053
Fax: (863)494-4443
Format: Hispanic. **Key Personnel:** Sherry Good, Bus. Mgr., sherry@lazeta.fm. **URL:** http://www.lazeta.fm.

8565 ■ WZZS-FM - 106.9
7981 US Higway 17 S
Zolfo Springs, FL 33890
Wattage: 5,000.

ALBANY

SW GA. Dougherty Co. On Flint River, 89 mi. SE of Columbus. Albany State College; Albany Junior College. Manufactures cottonseed oil, house trailers, farm implements, and fertilizer. Lumber mills; bottling works; meat packing; peanuts, pecan shelling. Radium spring. Pine timber. Agriculture. Pecans, peanuts, cotton.

8566 ■ The Albany Herald
The Albany Herald
PO Box 48
Albany, GA 31702-0048
Phone: (229)888-9300
Fax: (229)438-3200
Free: 800-234-3725
Daily newspaper. **Founded:** 1891. **Freq:** Daily (morn.). **Print Method:** Offset. **Trim Size:** 13 1/2 x 22 3/4. **Cols./Page:** 6. **Col. Width:** 26 nonpareils. **Col. Depth:** 301 agate lines. **Key Personnel:** John H. Hetzler, Publisher, phone: (229)888-9319; Jim Hendricks, Editor, phone: (229)888-9352; Danny Carter, Managing Editor, phone: (229)888-9346. **USPS:** 012-320. **Subscription Rates:** $182.95 Individuals 1 year. **URL:** http://www.albanyherald.com. **Ad Rates:** GLR $23.25; BW $2999.25; 4C $3396.25; SAU $16.98; PCI $23.25. **Remarks:** Accepts advertising. **Circ:** Combined ‡13,584, Combined ‡16,579.

8567 ■ Business Magazine
Albany Area Chamber of Commerce
225 W Broad Ave.
Albany, GA 31721
Phone: (229)434-8700
Fax: (229)434-8716
Free: 800-475-8700
Magazine containing information regarding Albany-Daugherty County, GA chamber activities and items of interest to businesses. **Freq:** Bimonthly. **Key Personnel:** Catherine Glover, Chief Executive Officer, President. **USPS:** 886-680. **Subscription Rates:** $50 Individuals. **URL:** http://www.albanyga.com/. **Circ:** (Not Reported).

8568 ■ ASU-TV
504 College Dr.
Albany, GA 31705
Phone: (229)430-4600
Owner: Albany State University, 504 College Dr., Albany, GA 31705, Ph: (229)430-4600.

8569 ■ Gray Television Inc.
126 N Washington St.
Albany, GA 31701
Format: News. **Networks:** Fox; CBS; NBC; ABC. **URL:** http://www.gray.tv.

8570 ■ WALB-TV - 10
1709 Stuart Ave.
Albany, GA 31706-3130
Phone: (229)446-1010
Fax: (229)446-4000
Email: publicfile@walb.com
Format: Commercial TV. **Networks:** NBC. **Owner:** Raycom Media Inc., 201 Monroe St., RSA Twr., 20th Fl., Montgomery, AL 36104-3731, Ph: (334)206-1400. **Founded:** Apr. 15, 1954. **Operating Hours:** 6:30 a.m.-2 a.m. **ADI:** Albany (Valdosta & Cordele), GA. **Key Personnel:** Jim Wilcox, Gen. Mgr., jim.wilcox@walb.com; Rick Williams, News Dir., rick.williams@walb.com. **Local Programs:** *Dialogue*; *Today in Georgia*, Monday Tuesday Wednesday Thursday Friday 5:00 a.m. - 7:00 a.m. **Ad Rates:** Advertising accepted; rates available upon request. **Mailing address:** PO Box 3130, Albany, GA 31706-3130. **URL:** http://www.walb.com.

8571 ■ WALG-AM - 1590
1104 W Broad Ave.
Albany, GA 31707-4340
Format: News. **Owner:** Cumulus Media Inc., 3280 Peachtree Rd. NW, Ste. 2300, Atlanta, GA 30305-2455, Ph: (404)949-0700, Fax: (404)949-0740. **Founded:** 1940. **ADI:** Albany (Valdosta & Cordele), GA. **Ad Rates:** Advertising accepted; rates available upon request. **URL:** http://www.1590walg.com/.

8572 ■ WASU-FM - 92.7
504 College Dr.
Albany, GA 31705
Phone: (229)430-4600
Email: radio@asurams.edu
Format: Talk; Jazz; Hip Hop. **Owner:** Albany State University, 504 College Dr., Albany, GA 31705, Ph: (229)430-4600. **Operating Hours:** Continuous. **Key Personnel:** Bernard Adusei, Dir. of Production, bernard.adusei@asurams.edu. **Wattage:** 100. **URL:** http://www.asurams.edu/wasu-fm-927.

8573 ■ WAZE-FM - 92.1
PO Box 4876
Albany, GA 31706
Phone: (912)888-9292
Format: Adult Contemporary; Oldies. **Networks:** Independent. **Founded:** 1969. **Formerly:** WHIA-FM; WDWA-FM. **Operating Hours:** Continuous; 100% local. **ADI:** Albany (Valdosta & Cordele), GA. **Key Personnel:** John Thacker, Gen. Mgr.; Valerie Ransom, Sales Mgr.; Carol Ward, Operations Mgr. **Wattage:** 3,000. **Ad Rates:** Advertising accepted; rates available upon request.

8574 ■ WEGC-FM - 107.7
1104 W Broad Ave.
Albany, GA 31707
Phone: (229)888-5000
Free: 888-633-5452
Format: Adult Contemporary; Soft Rock. **ADI:** Albany (Valdosta & Cordele), GA. **Key Personnel:** April Bailey, Bus. Mgr., april.bailey@cumulus.com. **URL:** http://www.mix1077albany.com.

8575 ■ WFXL-TV - 31
PO Box 4050
Albany, GA 31706
Phone: (229)435-3100
Format: News. **Networks:** Fox. **Owner:** Barrington Broadcasting Corp., 650 E Algonquin Rd., Schaumburg, IL 60173. **Founded:** 1982. **Formerly:** WTSG-TV. **Operating Hours:** Continuous. **Key Personnel:** Terry Graham, News Dir., tgraham@wfxl.com. **Ad Rates:** Advertising accepted; rates available upon request. **URL:** http://www.mysouthwestga.com.

8576 ■ WGPC-AM - 1450
1104 W Broad Ave.
Albany, GA 31707
Phone: (229)888-5000
Format: Sports; News. **Owner:** Cumulus Broadcasting Inc., 3280 Peachtree Rd. NW, Ste. 2300, Atlanta, GA 30305-2447, Ph: (404)949-0700, Fax: (404)949-0740. **Founded:** 1933. **Operating Hours:** Continuous. **ADI:** Albany (Valdosta & Cordele), GA. **Wattage:** 1,000.

8577 ■ WHKV-FM - 106.1
PO Box 779002
Rocklin, CA 95677-9972
Free: 800-525-5683
Format: Contemporary Christian. **Owner:** Educational Media Foundation, PO Box 2098, Omaha, NE 68103-2098, Free: 800-434-8400. **URL:** http://www.klove.com.

8578 ■ WJIZ-FM - 96.3
809 South Westover Blvd.
Albany, GA 31707
Phone: (229)439-9704
Format: Urban Contemporary; Blues; Hip Hop. **Wattage:** 100,000. **Ad Rates:** Advertising accepted; rates available upon request. **URL:** http://www.wjiz.com.

8579 ■ WJYZ-AM - 960
809 S Westover Blvd.
Albany, GA 31707
Phone: (229)439-9704
Fax: (229)439-1509
Format: Gospel. **Key Personnel:** Jackie Toye, Gen. Sales Mgr., jackietoye@clearchannel.com. **Ad Rates:** Noncommercial. **URL:** http://www.wjyz.com.

8580 ■ WKAK-FM - 101.7
Dunbar Ln., POB W
Albany, GA 31702
Phone: (912)436-7233
Fax: (912)888-6018
Format: Contemporary Country. **Networks:** ABC. **Owner:** Radio One: WKAK Inc., at above address. **Founded:** 1972. **Operating Hours:** Continuous. **ADI:** Albany (Valdosta & Cordele), GA. **Key Personnel:** Bob Roddy, Gen. Mgr.; Dave Cobb, Sales Mgr. **Wattage:** 3,000.

8581 ■ WMRZ-FM - 98.1
809 S Westover Blvd.
Albany, GA 31707
Phone: (229)439-9704
Format: Urban Contemporary; Contemporary Hit Radio (CHR); Oldies. **Key Personnel:** Jackie Toye, Contact, jackietoye@clearchannel.com; Jackie Toye, Contact, jackietoye@clearchannel.com. **URL:** http://www.kissalbany.com.

8582 ■ WNUQ-FM - 102.1
1104 W Broad Ave.
Albany, GA 31707
Phone: (229)888-1021
Format: Adult Contemporary. **Owner:** Cumulus Broadcasting Inc., 3280 Peachtree Rd. NW, Ste. 2300, Atlanta, GA 30305-2447, Ph: (404)949-0700, Fax: (404)949-0740. **ADI:** Albany (Valdosta & Cordele), GA. **Key Personnel:** April Bailey, Bus. Mgr., april.bailey@cumulus.com; Roger Russell, Dir. of Production, roger.

Circulation: ★ = AAM; △ or • = BPA; ♦ = CAC; ❑ = VAC; ⊕ = PO Statement; ‡ = Publisher's Report; Boldface figures = sworn; Light figures = estimated.

russell@cumulus.com. **URL:** http://www.1021NashIcon.com.

8583 ■ WOBB-FM - 100.3
809 S Westover Blvd.
Albany, GA 31707
Phone: (229)439-9704
Free: 800-567-1003
Founded: 1970. **Operating Hours**: Continuous. **ADI**: Albany (Valdosta & Cordele), GA. **Wattage**: 100,000 ERP. **Ad Rates:** Advertising accepted; rates available upon request. **URL:** http://www.b100wobb.com.

8584 ■ WQVE-FM - 101.7
1104 W Broad Ave.
Albany, GA 31707-4340
Phone: (229)888-5000
Fax: (229)888-6018
Format: Blues. **Networks:** ABC. **Owner:** Cumulus Media Inc., 3280 Peachtree Rd. NW, Ste. 2300, Atlanta, GA 30305-2455, Ph: (404)949-0700, Fax: (404)949-0740. **Founded:** 1976. **Formerly**: WOFF-FM. **Operating Hours**: Continuous; 75% Local 25% Network. **ADI**: Albany (Valdosta & Cordele), GA. **Wattage**: 6,000. **Ad Rates:** Advertising accepted; rates available upon request. **URL:** http://www.wqvealbany.com.

8585 ■ W34CZ - 34
PO Box A
Santa Ana, CA 92711
Phone: (714)832-2950
Free: 888-731-1000
Owner: Trinity Broadcasting Network Inc., PO Box A, Santa Ana, CA 92711, Ph: (714)832-2950, Free: 888-731-1000.

8586 ■ WUNV-FM - 91.7
300 Pine Ave.
Albany, GA 31701
Phone: (229)420-3210
Free: 800-222-4788
Email: ask@gpb.org
Format: Public Radio. **Owner:** Georgia Public Telecommunications Commission, 260 14th St. NW, Atlanta, GA 30318, Ph: (404)685-4788, Free: 800-222-6006. **Key Personnel:** Bob Olive, Gen. Mgr. **Wattage**: 3,000. **Ad Rates:** Noncommercial. **URL:** http://www.gpb.org.

8587 ■ WVAG-TV - 44
415 Pine Ave., Ste. 100
Albany, GA 31701
Phone: (229)985-1340
Email: wgvp@wgvp.com
Format: Commercial TV. **Networks:** United Paramount Network. **Owner:** Hutchens Communications, inc., at above address. **Founded:** 1980. **Formerly**: WVGA-TV; WGVP-TV. **Operating Hours**: Continuous. **Key Personnel:** Brad Stromman, Chief Engineer; Don Meinke, CEO, Gen. Mgr., don@wvagtv.com; Bobby McCready, Chief Engineer, bobby@wvagtv.com; Gilda Lieghter, Bus. Mgr., gilda@wvagtv.com; Pamela Griffin, Bus. Mgr. **Wattage**: 001.008 million. **Ad Rates:** $20-250 for 30 seconds. **URL:** http://www.wswg.tv.

8588 ■ WZBN-FM
302 Adkins St.
Albany, GA 31705
Phone: (229)435-9961
Format: Top 40; Blues. **Owner:** Cumulus Broadcasting Inc., 3280 Peachtree Rd. NW, Ste. 2300, Atlanta, GA 30305-2447, Ph: (404)949-0700, Fax: (404)949-0740. **Wattage**: 6,000 ERP. **Ad Rates:** Advertising accepted; rates available upon request.

8589 ■ WZIQ-FM - 106.5
PO Box 510
Appling, GA 30802
Phone: (706)309-9610
Fax: (706)309-9669
Free: 800-926-4669
Format: Religious. **Owner:** Good News Network, PO Box 428, Manassas, VA 20108, Ph: (703)392-4118, Free: 866-466-3639. **URL:** http://www.gnnradio.org/common/content.asp?PAGE=398.

ALMA

SE GA. Bacon Co. 65 mi. NW of Brunswick. Manufactures carpet fiber, clothing, optical lenses, manufactured homes. Agriculture. Tobacco, soybean, corn, wheat. Blueberries, peaches. Cattle, swine.

8590 ■ Alma Times
The Alma Times
402 W 12th St.
Alma, GA 31510
Phone: (912)632-7201
Fax: (912)632-4156
Publication E-mail: mail@thealmatimes.com
Local newspaper. **Freq:** Weekly (Thurs.). **Print Method:** Offset. **Cols./Page:** 6. **Col. Width:** 21 1/2 nonpareils. **Col. Depth:** 301 agate lines. **Key Personnel:** Cheryl Williams, President; Robert Williams, Jr., Publisher; Jerry Hudson, Editor. **Subscription Rates:** $25 Individuals in Bacon County; $35 Out of area. **URL:** http://thealmatimes.com. **Formerly**: Alma Times-Statesman. **Mailing address:** PO Box 428, Alma, GA 31510. **Ad Rates:** GLR $.23; BW $483.75; 4C $633.75. **Remarks:** Accepts advertising. **Circ:** ‡3200.

8591 ■ Dixie Cable TV
PO Box 97
Alma, GA 31510
Phone: (912)632-4241
Fax: (912)632-4519
Key Personnel: Teddy Solomon, President, tsolomon@accessatc.net; Kevin Brooks, Mgr., kbrooks@accessatc.net. **Cities Served:** subscribing households 1,802.

ALPHARETTA

NW GA. Fulton Co. 20 mi. N. of Atlanta. Residential. Light industry.

8592 ■ Alpharetta Neighbor
Neighbor Newspapers Inc.
10930 Crabapple Rd., Ste. 9
Roswell, GA 30075
Phone: (770)993-7400
Fax: (770)518-6062
Community newspaper. **Freq:** Weekly (Wed.). **Print Method:** Offset. **Cols./Page:** 6. **Col. Width:** 26 nonpareils. **Col. Depth:** 301 agate lines. **Key Personnel:** Wade Stephens, Director, Advertising, phone: (770)428-9411. **USPS:** 071-770. **Subscription Rates:** $112.00 Individuals 1 year. **URL:** http://www.mdjonline.com/neighbor_newspapers. **Ad Rates:** GLR $.99; BW $1793; 4C $2118; SAU $13.90. **Remarks:** Accepts advertising. **Circ:** Non-paid ♦**11805**.

8593 ■ Attachment Parenting: The Journal of Attachment Parenting International
Attachment Parenting International
PO Box 4615
Alpharetta, GA 30023
Fax: (800)850-8320
Publisher's E-mail: development@attachmentparenting.org
Freq: Annual. **Subscription Rates:** Included in membership. **URL:** http://www.attachmentparenting.org/journalofattachmentparenting. **Remarks:** Accepts advertising. **Circ:** (Not Reported).

8594 ■ Point Of Purchase
VNU Business Publications USA
1145 Sanctuary Pkwy., Ste. 355
Alpharetta, GA 30004
Phone: (770)569-1540
Fax: (770)569-5105
Free: 800-241-9034
Industry publication providing news, market trends, issues, research, and analysis on the point of purchase industry from the perspective of brand marketers and retailers. **Freq:** 12/year. **Print Method:** Web offset. **Trim Size:** 8 x 10 3/4. **Key Personnel:** Heather Rhodes, Manager, Circulation, phone: (800)933-8202, fax: (770)777-8770; Murray Kasmenn, Publisher, phone: (800)933-8202, fax: (770)777-8696; Robyn Wesley, Contact. **ISSN:** 1085--5009 (print). **Subscription Rates:** $75 U.S.; $85 Canada; $95 Other countries surface; $190 Other countries airmail. **URL:** http://www.popmag.com. **Ad Rates:** BW $3,360; 4C $4,485. **Remarks:** Accepts advertising. **Circ:** Controlled 19500.

8595 ■ Professional Sports Wives
Professional Sports Wives Association
Bldg. 1, 6th Fl.
13010 Morris Rd.
Alpharetta, GA 30004
Publisher's E-mail: advertising@prosportswives.com
Magazine for the wives of professional sports players. **Freq:** Quarterly. **Key Personnel:** Mike Pitts, Associate Publisher, phone: (770)619-0383; Angela Shipp, Managing Editor, phone: (770)619-0383; Gena James Pitts, Editor-in-Chief, Publisher, phone: (770)619-0383. **Subscription Rates:** $39.99 Individuals. **Remarks:** Accepts advertising. **Circ:** (Not Reported).

8596 ■ Johnson Media Inc.
2475 Northwinds Parkway, Suite 200
Alpharetta, GA 30009
Phone: (404)487-6010
Fax: (404)487-6010
Founded: 2000. **URL:** http://www.johnsonmedia.com.

8597 ■ KBTE-FM - 104.9
100 N Point Ctr. E, Ste. 310
Alpharetta, GA 30022
Format: Hip Hop. **Owner:** Wilks Broadcast Group L.L.C., 6470 E Johns Crossing, Ste. 450, Duluth, GA 30097, Ph: (678)240-8976, Fax: (678)240-8989. **Key Personnel:** Jeff Wilks, CEO. **URL:** http://www.1049thebeat.com.

8598 ■ WNGT-TV - 48
11770 Haynes Bridge Rd., Ste. 205
Alpharetta, GA 30004
Free: 800-808-0130
Email: info@wngt.com
Founded: Sept. 07, 2006. **Ad Rates:** Advertising accepted; rates available upon request. **URL:** http://wmnttv.com.

AMERICUS

SW GA. Sumter Co. 35 mi. N. of Albany. Georgia Southwestern College. Manufactures metal products, cottonseed oil, light fixtures, furniture, textiles. Vegetable packing. Pine timber. Agriculture. Cotton, fruit, peanuts, livestock.

8599 ■ Americus Times-Recorder
South Georgia Media Group
101 Hwy. 27th E
Americus, GA 31709
Phone: (229)924-2751
Fax: (229)928-6344
Daily newspaper. **Founded:** 1879. **Freq:** Bimonthly Tues. - Fri. & Sunday mornings. **Key Personnel:** Beth Alston, Executive Editor. **Subscription Rates:** $10 Individuals. **URL:** http://www.sgaonline.com; http://www.americustimesrecorder.com. **Remarks:** Accepts advertising. **Circ:** Combined 7000.

8600 ■ Journal of Third World Studies
Association of Third World Studies
PO Box 1232
Americus, GA 31709
Phone: (318)797-5349
Fax: (318)795-4203
Scholarly journal covering Third World problems, issues, and developments. **Freq:** Semiannual. **Key Personnel:** Dr. Harold Isaacs, Editor. **ISSN:** 8755--3449 (print). **Subscription Rates:** $60 Individuals; $30 Single issue; Included in membership. **URL:** http://apps.gsw.edu/atws/journal.htm. **Ad Rates:** BW $250. **Remarks:** Accepts advertising. **Circ:** Paid 815, 900.

8601 ■ WBJY-FM - 89.3
PO Box 3206
Tupelo, MS 38803
Format: Religious. **Owner:** American Family Association, at above address. **Wattage**: 65,000. **Ad Rates:** Noncommercial. **URL:** http://www.afa.net.

8602 ■ WDEC-FM - 94.7
PO Box 727
Americus, GA 31709
Phone: (229)924-6500
Fax: (229)928-2337
Format: Adult Contemporary. **Networks:** ABC. **Owner:** Sumter Broadcasting Co. Inc. **Founded:** 1968. **Operating Hours**: Continuous. **ADI**: Columbus, GA (Opelika, AL). **Key Personnel:** Steve Lashley, Gen. Mgr., stevelashley@mchsi.com; Donnie McCrary, News Dir., doones1974@live.com; Thurston Clary, Dir. of Programs, tclary@mchsi.com. **Wattage**: 25,000. **Ad Rates:** $10.80-20.30 for 30 seconds; $13.40-24.60 for 60 seconds. **URL:** http://www.americusradio.com.

8603 ■ WFRP-FM - 88.7
290 Hegenberger Rd.
Oakland, CA 94621
Free: 800-543-1495
Email: info@familyradio.org

Format: Religious. **Owner:** Family Stations Inc., 290 Hegenberger Rd., Oakland, CA 94621, Free: 800-543-1495. **URL:** http://www.familyradio.org.

8604 ■ WISK-AM
PO Box 727
Americus, GA 31709
Fax: (912)928-2337
Format: Talk; News. **Networks:** ABC; Georgia Radio. **Owner:** Sumter Broadcasting Co. Inc. **Founded:** 1962. **Key Personnel:** Donnie McCrary, News Dir., doones74@hotmail.com. **Wattage:** 2,500 Day.

8605 ■ WISK-FM - 98.7
1028 Adderton St.
Americus, GA 31709
Phone: (912)924-6500
Fax: (912)928-2337
Format: Country. **Networks:** ABC; Gannett News. **Owner:** Sumter Broadcasting Co. Inc. **Founded:** 1973. **Formerly:** WPUR-FM. **Operating Hours:** continuous. **ADI:** Columbus, GA (Opelika, AL). **Key Personnel:** Steve Lashley, Gen. Mgr. **Wattage:** 25,000. **Mailing address:** PO Box 727, Americus, GA 31709. **URL:** http://www.americusradio.com.

APPLING

8606 ■ WBLR-FM - 1430
PO Box 510
Appling, GA 30802
Phone: (706)309-9610
Fax: (706)309-9669
Free: 800-926-4669
Format: Ethnic; Religious. **Owner:** Good News Network, PO Box 428, Manassas, VA 20108, Ph: (703)392-4118, Free: 866-466-3639. **Ad Rates:** Noncommercial. **URL:** http://www.gnnradio.org.

WGPH-FM - See Vidalia

8607 ■ WJDS-FM - 88.7
PO Box 510
Appling, GA 30802
Phone: (706)309-9610
Fax: (706)309-9669
Free: 800-926-4669
Format: Hispanic. **Owner:** Good News Network, PO Box 428, Manassas, VA 20108, Ph: (703)392-4118, Free: 866-466-3639. **Founded:** 1999. **Operating Hours:** Continuous. **Wattage:** 1,000. **Ad Rates:** Noncommercial. **URL:** http://www.gnnradio.org.

8608 ■ WKTM-FM - 106.1
PO Box 510
Appling, GA 30802
Phone: (706)309-9610
Fax: (706)309-9669
Free: 800-926-4669
Format: Hispanic. **Owner:** Good News Network, PO Box 428, Manassas, VA 20108, Ph: (703)392-4118, Free: 866-466-3639. **Operating Hours:** Continuous. **ADI:** Macon, GA. **Wattage:** 6,000. **Ad Rates:** Noncommercial. Combined advertising rates available with WBLR and WQRX. **URL:** http://www.gnnradio.org.

WLGP-FM - See Harkers Island, NC

8609 ■ WLPE-FM - 91.7
PO Box 510
Appling, GA 30802
Phone: (706)309-9610
Fax: (706)309-9669
Free: 800-926-4669
Email: ctbarinowski@comcast.net
Format: Religious. **Owner:** Good News Network, PO Box 428, Manassas, VA 20108, Ph: (703)392-4118, Free: 866-466-3639. **URL:** http://www.gnnradio.org.

WLPG-FM - See Florence, SC

WLPT-FM - See Jesup

8610 ■ WPMA-FM - 102.7
PO Box 510
Appling, GA 30802
Phone: (706)309-9610
Fax: (706)309-9669
Free: 800-926-4669
Email: music@gnnradio.org
Format: Religious. **Owner:** Good News Network, PO Box 428, Manassas, VA 20108, Ph: (703)392-4118, Free: 866-466-3639. **URL:** http://www.gnnradio.org.

8611 ■ WPWB-FM - 90.5
PO Box 510
Appling, GA 30802
Phone: (706)309-9610
Fax: (706)309-9669
Free: 800-926-4669
Format: Religious. **Owner:** Good News Network, PO Box 428, Manassas, VA 20108, Ph: (703)392-4118, Free: 866-466-3639. **URL:** http://www.gnnradio.org.

8612 ■ WQRX-AM - 870
PO Box 510
Appling, GA 30802
Phone: (706)309-9610
Fax: (706)309-9669
Free: 800-926-4669
Format: Hispanic; Religious. **Networks:** USA Radio. **Owner:** Good News Network, PO Box 428, Manassas, VA 20108, Ph: (703)392-4118, Free: 866-466-3639. **Founded:** 1986. **Operating Hours:** Sunrise-sunset. **Wattage:** 10,000. **Ad Rates:** Advertising accepted; rates available upon request. **URL:** http://www.gnnradio.org.

8613 ■ WWGF-FM - 107.5
PO Box 510
Appling, GA 30802
Phone: (706)309-9610
Fax: (706)309-9669
Free: 800-926-4669
Format: Religious. **Owner:** Good News Network, PO Box 428, Manassas, VA 20108, Ph: (703)392-4118, Free: 866-466-3639. **URL:** http://www.gnnradio.org.

WZIQ-FM - See Albany

ASHBURN

8614 ■ The Wiregrass Farmer
Ashburn Newspapers
109 Gordon St.
Ashburn, GA 31714
Phone: (229)567-3655
Fax: (229)567-4402
Publisher's E-mail: wiregrassfarmer@yahoo.com
Community newspaper. **Freq:** Weekly (Wed.). **Cols./Page:** 6. **Col. Width:** 12 inches. **Col. Depth:** 21 1/2 inches. **USPS:** 687-460. **Subscription Rates:** $36 Individuals /year (in County, print and online); $44 Individuals /year (other Georgia counties,print and online); $50 Out of state /year (print and online); $24 Individuals /year (online); $12 Individuals six months (online). **URL:** http://www.thewiregrassfarmer.com/2717/1330/1/this-weeks-issue. **Ad Rates:** GLR $6.50; BW $645; 4C $75; PCI $4.10. **Remarks:** Accepts advertising. **Circ:** 3000.

ATHENS

NE GA. Clarke Co. On Oconee River, 70 mi. NE of Atlanta. University of Georgia; U.S. Navy Supply Corps School. Manufactures fertilizer, textiles, clocks, transformers, electronics, cottonseed products, furniture. Timber. Food and poultry processing center. Agriculture producing and marketing center. Livestock, poultry farms.

8615 ■ Athens Banner Herald
Morris Communications Company L.L.C.
One Press Pl.
Athens, GA 30601
Phone: (706)549-0123
Fax: (706)543-5234
Publisher's E-mail: allaccessprogram@morris.com
General newspaper. **Freq:** Daily (eve.), Sat. and Sun. (morn.). **Print Method:** Offset. **Cols./Page:** 6. **Col. Width:** 24 nonpareils. **Col. Depth:** 301 agate lines. **Key Personnel:** Windy Harrell, Administrative Assistant, phone: (706)208-2202; Margaret W. Blanchard, Editor, phone: (706)208-2330; Scott Morrissey, Publisher; Melissa Hanna, Executive Editor, phone: (706)208-2220; Dennis McCraven, Manager, Production. **Subscription Rates:** $9.88 Individuals /month, print and online. **URL:** http://onlineathens.com; http://morris.com/divisions/daily-newspapers/athens-banner-herald. **Ad Rates:** SAU $10.97. **Remarks:** Accepts advertising. **Circ:** Mon.-Fri. ★**26515**, Sun. ★**30888**, Sat. ★**26151**.

8616 ■ Cashiers Crossroads Chronicle
Community Newspapers Inc.
297 Prince Ave., Ste. 14
Athens, GA 30601-2475
Phone: (706)548-0010
Fax: (706)548-0808
Free: 800-226-0692
Publisher's E-mail: dnesmith@cninewspapers.com
Newspaper serving Cashiers, Glenville, Sapphire and Tuckasegee, North Carolina. **Freq:** Weekly (Wed.). **Key Personnel:** Mike Henry, Publisher; Kelly Donaldson, Editor. **Subscription Rates:** $28 Individuals; $47 Out of area; $7 Individuals online. **URL:** http://www.crossroadschronicle.com. **Mailing address:** PO Box 792, Athens, GA 30603-0792. **Ad Rates:** 4C $200. **Remarks:** Accepts advertising. **Circ:** Paid 3200.

8617 ■ COGEL Guardian
Council on Governmental Ethics Laws
PO Box 81237
Athens, GA 30608
Phone: (706)548-7758
Fax: (706)548-7079
Publisher's E-mail: director@cogel.org
Freq: Quarterly. **Subscription Rates:** Included in membership. **Remarks:** Advertising not accepted. **Circ:** (Not Reported).

8618 ■ Communications in Soil Science and Plant Analysis
Taylor & Francis Group Journals
c/o Dr. Harry A. Mills, Exec. Ed.
183 Paradise Blvd., Ste. 108
Athens, GA 30607
Publication E-mail: communsoilsci@aol.com
Journal on soil chemistry, fertility, soil testing, soil crop nutrition, plant analysis, plant physiology, and liming. **Freq:** 22/yr. **Print Method:** Offset. **Trim Size:** 8 1/4 x 10 7/8. **Cols./Page:** 1. **Col. Width:** 54 nonpareils. **Col. Depth:** 103 agate lines. **Key Personnel:** Gretchen Bryson, Assistant Editor; Eric H. Simonne, Board Member; Dr. Harry A. Mills, Executive Editor. **ISSN:** 0010--3624 (print); **EISSN:** 1532-2416 (electronic). **Subscription Rates:** $1055 Individuals print only; $4177 Institutions online only; $4774 Institutions print and online. **URL:** http://www.tandfonline.com/toc/lcss20/current#.VGs3azQwrld. **Remarks:** Accepts advertising. **Circ:** ‡800.

8619 ■ Crossroads Chronicle
Community Newspapers Inc.
297 Prince Ave., Ste. 14
Athens, GA 30601-2475
Phone: (706)548-0010
Fax: (706)548-0808
Free: 800-226-0692
Publication E-mail: news@crossroadschronicle.com
Community newspaper. **Freq:** Weekly (Wed.). **Cols./Page:** 6. **Col. Width:** 2 1/16 inches. **Col. Depth:** 21 1/2 inches. **Key Personnel:** Kelly Donaldson, Editor; Mike Henry, Publisher. **Subscription Rates:** $30 Individuals print and online; $49 Out of area print and online; $7 Individuals online only. **URL:** http://www.crossroadschronicle.com. **Formerly:** Cashiers Chronicle. **Mailing address:** PO Box 792, Athens, GA 30603-0792. **Ad Rates:** 4C $180. **Remarks:** Accepts advertising. **Circ:** Paid ‡3200.

8620 ■ Ethics & the Environment
Indiana University Press
c/o Victoria Davion, Ed.
University of Georgia
Dept. of Philosophy
Athens, GA 30602-1627
Journal focusing on all aspects of environmental management, education, and ethics. **Freq:** Semiannual. **Key Personnel:** Victoria Davion, Editor; Melissa Link, Managing Editor. **ISSN:** 1085-6633 (print); **EISSN:** 1535-5306 (electronic). **Subscription Rates:** $43.50 Individuals print and online; $39.50 Individuals print only; $37.50 Individuals online only. **URL:** http://www.jstor.org/action/showPublication?journalCode=ethicsenviro. **Circ:** (Not Reported).

8621 ■ Fire Mark Circle of the Americas--Journal
Fire Mark Circle of the Americas
1010 Allgood Rd.
Athens, GA 30606-5367
Publisher's E-mail: information@firemarkcircle.org

Circulation: ★ = AAM; △ or • = BPA; ♦ = CAC; ❑ = VAC; ⊕ = PO Statement; ‡ = Publisher's Report; Boldface figures = sworn; Light figures = estimated.

Freq: Annual. **Subscription Rates:** Included in membership. **Remarks:** Advertising not accepted. **Circ:** (Not Reported).

8622 ■ Flagpole Magazine
Flagpole Magazine
112 S Foundry St.
Athens, GA 30601
Phone: (706)549-9523
Fax: (706)548-8981
Publisher's E-mail: ads@flagpole.com
Magazine covering the arts, entertainment, politics, and news in Athens, GA; also reports on the international music scene. **Freq:** Weekly (Wed.). **Print Method:** Web press. **Trim Size:** 11 3/8 x 15. **Cols./Page:** 4. **Col. Width:** 2 3/8 inches. **Col. Depth:** 13 inches. **Key Personnel:** Alicia Nickles, Director, Advertising, Publisher; Pete McCommons, Editor, Publisher; Larry Tenner, Director, Production. **Subscription Rates:** Free. **URL:** http://flagpole.com. **Mailing address:** PO Box 1027, Athens, GA 30601. **Remarks:** Accepts advertising. **Circ:** (Not Reported).

8623 ■ Georgia Business and Economic Conditions
University of Georgia Terry College of Business
Brooks Hall
310 Herty Dr.
Athens, GA 30602-6269
Phone: (706)542-8100
Fax: (706)542-3835
Publisher's E-mail: help@terry.uga.edu
Journal publishing information on business and economic research. **Freq:** Quarterly. **Print Method:** Offset. **Trim Size:** 8 1/2 x 11. **Cols./Page:** 2. **Col. Width:** 38 nonpareils. **Col. Depth:** 112 agate lines. **Key Personnel:** Lorena M. Akioka, Senior Editor, phone: (706)425-2961; Jeffrey Humphreys, Director, phone: (706)425-2962. **ISSN:** 0297--3857 (print). **Subscription Rates:** Free. **Alt. Formats:** PDF. **URL:** http://terry.uga.edu/about/centers-institutes/selig/gbec. **Remarks:** Advertising not accepted. **Circ:** Free ‡2000.

8624 ■ Georgia Business and Economic Conditions
University of Georgia Selig Center for Economic Growth
c/o Dr. Jeffrey M. Humphreys, Director
110 E Clayton St.
Athens, GA 30602
Phone: (706)542-4085
Publisher's E-mail: help@terry.uga.edu
Journal publishing information on business and economic research. **Freq:** Quarterly. **Print Method:** Offset. **Trim Size:** 8 1/2 x 11. **Cols./Page:** 2. **Col. Width:** 38 nonpareils. **Col. Depth:** 112 agate lines. **Key Personnel:** Lorena M. Akioka, Senior Editor, phone: (706)425-2961; Jeffrey Humphreys, Director, phone: (706)425-2962. **ISSN:** 0297--3857 (print). **Subscription Rates:** Free. **Alt. Formats:** PDF. **URL:** http://terry.uga.edu/about/centers-institutes/selig/gbec. **Remarks:** Advertising not accepted. **Circ:** Free ‡2000.

8625 ■ Georgia Journal of International and Comparative Law
University of Georgia School of Law
225 Herty Dr.
Athens, GA 30602-6012
Phone: (706)542-5191
Fax: (706)542-5556
Journal serving as forum for academic discussion on global legal issues, theories and developments. **Freq:** 3/year. **Key Personnel:** Cory Lyn Takeuchi, Editor-in-Chief. **URL:** http://digitalcommons.law.uga.edu/gjicl. **Circ:** (Not Reported).

8626 ■ Georgia Law Review
University of Georgia School of Law
225 Herty Dr.
Athens, GA 30602-6012
Phone: (706)542-5191
Fax: (706)542-5556
Publication E-mail: galrev@uga.edu
Professional journal covering law. **Freq:** Quarterly. **Key Personnel:** Jerrod Michael Lukacs, Editor-in-Chief; Kathleen Hart, Contact; Andrew J. Tuck, Contact. **Subscription Rates:** $34 Individuals domestic; $40 Individuals foreign. **URL:** http://georgialawreview.org. **Remarks:** Advertising not accepted. **Circ:** (Not Reported).

8627 ■ Georgia Magazine
University of Georgia Public Affairs Division
Hodgson Oil Bldg., Ste. 200 N
286 Oconee St.
Athens, GA 30602-1999
Phone: (706)542-8083
Magazine serving the interests of university alumni. **Freq:** Quarterly. **Print Method:** Offset Web. **Trim Size:** 8 3/8 x 10 7/8. **Cols./Page:** 3. **Col. Width:** 27 nonpareils. **Col. Depth:** 140 agate lines. **Key Personnel:** Kelly Simmons, Editor; Lindsay Bland Robinson, Art Director; Allyson Mann, Managing Editor; Fran Burke, Office Manager. **ISSN:** 0016--8130 (print). **Subscription Rates:** $35 Individuals. **URL:** http://ugamagazine.uga.edu. **Formerly:** Georgia Alumni Record. **Ad Rates:** BW $5175; 4C $2065. **Remarks:** Accepts advertising. **Circ:** 150000.

8628 ■ Georgia Music News
Georgia Music Educators Association
University of Georgia
School of Music
Athens, GA 30602
Phone: (706)542-3737
Fax: (706)542-2773
Music education journal. **Freq:** Quarterly. **Print Method:** Offset. **Trim Size:** 8 1/2 x 11. **Cols./Page:** 3. **Col. Width:** 28 nonpareils. **Col. Depth:** 140 agate lines. **Key Personnel:** Mary Leglar, Editor. **ISSN:** 0046--5789 (print). **URL:** http://www.gmea.org/georgia-music-news. **Ad Rates:** BW $400. **Remarks:** Accepts advertising. **Circ:** 3200.

8629 ■ The Georgia Review
The Georgia Review
706A Main Library, 320 S Jackson St., The University of Georgia
Athens, GA 30602-9009
Phone: (706)542-3481
Fax: (706)542-0047
Free: 800-542-3481
Publisher's E-mail: garev@uga.edu
Magazine featuring poetry, fiction, essays, and reviews--as well as a visual art portfolio, usually in full color. **Freq:** Quarterly. **Print Method:** Offset. **Trim Size:** 6 3/4 x 10. **Cols./Page:** 1. **Col. Width:** 28 picas. **Col. Depth:** 42 picas. **Key Personnel:** Brenda Keen, Business Manager; Stephen Corey, Editor; Jenny Gropp Hess, Managing Editor. **ISSN:** 0016--8386 (print). **Subscription Rates:** $40 Individuals print or online; $70 Two years print or online; $50 Individuals print only; $30 Individuals online only. **URL:** http://garev.uga.edu. **Ad Rates:** BW $350. **Remarks:** Color advertising not accepted. **Circ:** (Not Reported).

8630 ■ Journal of Biomolecular Techniques
Association of Biomolecular Resource Facilities
c/o Ron Orlando PhD, Co-Ed.-in-Ch.
The University of Georgia
315 Riverbend Rd.
Athens, GA 30602-4712
Publisher's E-mail: abrf@abrf.org
Peer-reviewed journal covering biotechnology research and other issues for professionals in biotechnology research and service. **Freq:** Quarterly. **Key Personnel:** Ron Orlando, PhD, Editor-in-Chief. **ISSN:** 1524--0215 (print). **Subscription Rates:** Free. **Alt. Formats:** PDF. **URL:** http://jbt.abrf.org/jbt-static/index.cfm/page/author_instructions.htm. **Remarks:** Accepts advertising. **Circ:** (Not Reported).

8631 ■ Journal of Corporate Finance
RELX Group P.L.C.
c/o A. Poulsen, Ed.
Terry College of Business
University of Georgia
531 Brooks Hall
Athens, GA 30602
Publication E-mail: jcf@terry.uga.edu
Journal looking into issues of corporate finance. **Freq:** 6/year. **Key Personnel:** J.M. Netter, Editor; A. Poulsen, Editor. **ISSN:** 0929--1199 (print). **Subscription Rates:** $91 Individuals print; $959 Institutions print; $800 Institutions ejournal. **URL:** http://www.journals.elsevier.com/journal-of-corporate-finance. **Circ:** (Not Reported).

8632 ■ Journal of Higher Education Outreach and Engagement
University of Georgia Institute of Higher Education
Meigs Hall
Athens, GA 30602-6772
Phone: (706)542-3464
Fax: (706)542-7588
Publisher's E-mail: web@ihe.uga.edu
Journal covering higher education outreach and engagement for scholars, practitioners, and professionals. **Freq:** Semiannual Quarterly. **Print Method:** soft cover. **Trim Size:** 6 x 9. **Key Personnel:** Trish Kalivoda, Editor, phone: (706)542-3946, fax: (706)542-6278; Gwen Moss, Business Manager; Katie Fite, Assistant; Julia Mills, Assistant. **ISSN:** 1534-6102 (print). **Subscription Rates:** $60 Individuals; $95 Other countries; $30 Students; $65 Students, other countries; $100 Institutions; $199 Institutions, other countries. **URL:** http://openjournals.libs.uga.edu/index.php/jheoe. **Formerly:** Journal of Public Service and Outreach. **Remarks:** Advertising not accepted. **Circ:** (Not Reported).

8633 ■ Journal of Intellectual Property Law
University of Georgia School of Law
225 Herty Dr.
Athens, GA 30602-6012
Phone: (706)542-5191
Fax: (706)542-5556
Journal focusing exclusively to the field of intellectual property law. **Freq:** Semiannual. **Key Personnel:** Emily Nicole Evans, Editor-in-Chief. **Subscription Rates:** $30 Individuals domestic; $40 Individuals foreign. **URL:** http://www.law.uga.edu/jipl; http://digitalcommons.law.uga.edu/jipl. **Circ:** (Not Reported).

8634 ■ Journal of Luminescence
RELX Group P.L.C.
c/o R.S. Meltzer, Ed.
Dept. of Physics & Astronomy
University of Georgia
Athens, GA 30602
Publisher's E-mail: amsterdam@relx.com
Journal covering the electronic excited state of molecular, ionic and covalent systems, whether crystalline, amorphous, or liquid. **Freq:** 12/yr. **Key Personnel:** R.S. Meltzer, Associate Editor. **ISSN:** 0022--2313 (print). **Subscription Rates:** $4838 Institutions print; $4031.33 Institutions ejournal. **URL:** http://www.journals.elsevier.com/journal-of-luminescence. **Circ:** (Not Reported).

8635 ■ Journal of Plant Nutrition
Taylor & Francis Group Journals
c/o Harry A. Mills, Exec. Ed.
183 Paradise Blvd., Ste. 104
Athens, GA 30607
Publisher's E-mail: customerservice@taylorandfrancis.com
Journal exploring the influence of currently known essential and nonessential elements on plant physiology and growth. **Freq:** 14/yr. **Key Personnel:** A.V. Barker, Board Member; Gretchen Bryson, Associate, Executive Editor; Harry A. Mills, Executive Editor. **ISSN:** 0190--4167 (print); **EISSN:** 1532--4087 (electronic). **Subscription Rates:** $4639 Institutions print and online; $4059 Institutions online only; $744 Individuals print only. **URL:** http://tandfonline.com/toc/lpla20/current. **Remarks:** Advertising accepted; rates available upon request. **Circ:** (Not Reported).

8636 ■ News Photographer Magazine
National Press Photographers Association
120 Hooper St.
Athens, GA 30602
Publisher's E-mail: info@nppa.org
Freq: 10/year. **Subscription Rates:** $48 U.S.; $60 Canada; $65 Other countries. **URL:** http://nppa.org/magazine. **Remarks:** Accepts advertising. **Circ:** 11000.

8637 ■ The Red and Black
The Red and Black Publishing Co.
540 Baxter St.
Athens, GA 30605
Phone: (706)433-3000
Fax: (706)433-3033
College newspaper for University of Georgia students and faculty. **Founded:** 1892. **Freq:** Mon.-Fri. (during academic year). **Print Method:** Offset. **Cols./Page:** 6. **Col. Width:** 21 nonpareils. **Col. Depth:** 301 agate lines. **Key Personnel:** Polina Marinova, Editor-in-Chief; Alex Laughlin, Officer, Recruiting; Julia Carpenters, Manag-

ing Editor. **Subscription Rates:** $95 Individuals semester; $195 Individuals. **URL:** http://www.redandblack.com. **Ad Rates:** BW $2066.40; PCI $20. **Remarks:** Accepts advertising. **Circ:** Combined 18,000.

8638 ■ Southeastern Journal of Music Education
University of Georgia Hugh Hodgson School of Music
250 River Rd.
Athens, GA 30602
Phone: (706)542-3737
Fax: (706)542-2773
Professional journal covering music education and music research. **Freq:** Annual. **Print Method:** Photo offset. **Key Personnel:** Mary A. Leglar, Associate Director. **ISSN:** 1047--9635 (print). **Alt. Formats:** PDF. **URL:** http://www.uga.edu. **Remarks:** Advertising not accepted. **Circ:** Paid 300.

8639 ■ Sylvania Telephone
Community Newspapers Inc.
297 Prince Ave., Ste. 14
Athens, GA 30601-2475
Phone: (706)548-0010
Fax: (706)548-0808
Free: 800-226-0692
Publisher's E-mail: dnesmith@cninewspapers.com
Community newspaper. **Freq:** Weekly (Thurs.). **Print Method:** Offset. **Cols./Page:** 6. **Col. Width:** 24 nonpareils. **Col. Depth:** 2 1/2 inches. **Key Personnel:** Enoch Autry, Editor. **Subscription Rates:** $37.45 Individuals; $58.85 Two years; $42.80 Elsewhere in Georgia; $53.50 Out of state. **URL:** http://sylvaniatelephone.com. **Mailing address:** PO Box 792, Athens, GA 30603-0792. **Ad Rates:** GLR $4; BW $648. 90; PCI $5.15. **Remarks:** Accepts advertising. **Circ:** 5061.

8640 ■ The Verse: Book of Interviews
Wave Books
c/o Brian Henry
Dept. of English, UGA
Athens, GA 30602
Publisher's E-mail: info@wavepoetry.com
Consumer magazine covering poetry worldwide. **Freq:** Annual. **Key Personnel:** Brian Henry, Editor; Andrew Zawacki, Editor. **Subscription Rates:** $16 Individuals. **URL:** http://www.wavepoetry.com/products/the-verse-book-of-interviews. **Circ:** (Not Reported).

8641 ■ Charter Communications
495 Hawthorne Ave., Ste. 102
Athens, GA 30606
Phone: (706)543-6585
Fax: (706)354-8027
Free: 800-955-7766
Owner: Charter Communications Inc., 400 Atlantic St., Stamford, CT 06901, Ph: (203)905-7801. **Founded:** 1964. **Formerly:** TCI Cablevision of Georgia. **Cities Served:** subscribing households 47,164. **URL:** http://www.charter.com/f.

8642 ■ WGAU-AM - 1340
850 Bobbin Mill Rd.
Athens, GA 30606
Phone: (706)549-6222
Format: News; Talk; Information. **Owner:** Southern Broadcasting, at above address. **Founded:** 1938. **Operating Hours:** Continuous. **Key Personnel:** Matt Caesar, Dir. of Programs. **Wattage:** 1,000. **Ad Rates:** $25 for 30 seconds; $30 for 60 seconds. **URL:** http://www.wgauradio.com.

8643 ■ WNGC-FM - 106.1
850 Bobbin Mill Rd.
Athens, GA 30606
Phone: (706)549-6222
Format: Country. **Networks:** NBC; Unistar. **Owner:** Cox Radio Inc., 6205 Peachtree Dunwood Rd., Atlanta, GA 30328-4524, Ph: (678)645-0000, Fax: (678)645-5002. **Founded:** 1969. **Formerly:** WGAU-FM. **Operating Hours:** Continuous; 100% local. **ADI:** Atlanta (Athens & Rome), GA. **Key Personnel:** Pete de Graaff, Dir. of Programs, pete.degraaff@coxradio.com; Tim Bryant, News Dir. **Wattage:** 100,000. **Ad Rates:** $50 for 30 seconds; $60 for 60 seconds. Combined advertising rates available with WGAU-AM. **URL:** http://www.1061wngc.com.

8644 ■ W201BJ-FM - 88.1
PO Box 391
Twin Falls, ID 83303
Fax: (208)736-1958
Free: 800-357-4226
Format: Religious; Contemporary Christian. **Owner:** CSN International, PO Box 391, Twin Falls, ID 83303, Ph: (208)736-1958, Fax: (208)736-1958, Free: 800-357-4226. **URL:** http://www.csnradio.com.

8645 ■ WUOG-FM - 90.5
102 Tate Student Ctr.
Athens, GA 30602
Phone: (706)542-4567
Format: Educational; Full Service. **Owner:** University of Georgia, at above address. **Founded:** Oct. 16, 1972. **ADI:** Atlanta (Athens & Rome), GA. **Wattage:** 26,000 ERP. **URL:** http://wuog.org.

8646 ■ WXAG-AM - 1470
855 Sunset Dr., Ste. 16
Athens, GA 30606
Phone: (706)552-1470
Fax: (706)425-0847
Format: Gospel; Full Service; Educational; Urban Contemporary; Talk. **Simulcasts:** WXAG-FM. **Networks:** American Urban Radio. **Founded:** 1982. **Operating Hours:** Continuous. **ADI:** Atlanta (Athens & Rome), GA. **Key Personnel:** Lee King, Contact. **Wattage:** 1,000. **Ad Rates:** $8 for 15 seconds; $10 for 30 seconds; $12.50 for 60 seconds. **URL:** http://www.1470wxag.com.

8647 ■ WXKT-FM - 100.1
850 Bobbin Mill
Athens, GA 30606
Phone: (706)678-7100
Fax: (706)678-1925
Owner: Southern Broadcasting, at above address. **Founded:** 1970. **Formerly:** WLOV-FM. **ADI:** Augusta, GA. **Wattage:** 3,000. **Ad Rates:** $5.50 for 30 seconds; $8 for 60 seconds.

ATLANTA

NE GA. Fulton Co. 60 mi. SW of Athens. The State Capital. Georgia State University; Georgia Institute of Technology; Emory University; Atlanta University; other colleges and private schools. Finance, transportation, distribution and telephone communication center. Manufactures batteries, textiles, fertilizers, furniture, chemicals, cottonseed oil, flour,building products. Printing and publishing; automobile, aircraft assembly plants.

8648 ■ ACS Combinatorial Science
American Chemical Society
c/o M.G. Finn, Editor-in-Chief
Georgia Institute of Technology
School of Chemistry and Biochemistry; School of Biology
901 Atlantic Dr. NW
Atlanta, GA 30332-0400
Phone: (404)385-0906
Fax: (404)385-0973
Publisher's E-mail: help@acs.org
Journal covering combinatorial chemistry for chemists, scientists, and related professionals. **Freq:** Bimonthly. **Print Method:** Web offset. **Trim Size:** 8-3/16 x 10-7/8. **Key Personnel:** Anthony W. Czarnik, Editor, Founder; M.G. Finn, Editor-in-Chief. **ISSN:** 2156--8952 (print); **EISSN:** 2156--8944 (electronic). **URL:** http://pubs.acs.org/loi/acsccc. **Formerly:** Journal of Combinatorial Chemistry. **Remarks:** Accepts advertising. **Circ:** (Not Reported).

8649 ■ ACS Medicinal Chemistry Letters
American Chemical Society
c/o Prof. Dennis C. Liotta, Ed.-in-Ch.
Cherry Logan Emerson Hall
Department of Chemistry
Emory University
Atlanta, GA 30322
Phone: (404)727-6602
Publisher's E-mail: help@acs.org
Peer-reviewed journal publishing research articles on medicinal chemistry. **Key Personnel:** Prof. Dennis C. Liotta, Editor-in-Chief, phone: (404)727-6602. **ISSN:** 1948--5875 (print). **URL:** http://pubs.acs.org/journal/amclct. **Remarks:** Accepts advertising. **Circ:** (Not Reported).

8650 ■ Adelphean
Alpha Delta Pi
1386 Ponce de Leon Ave. NE
Atlanta, GA 30306
Phone: (404)378-3164
Publisher's E-mail: info@alphadeltapi.com
Fraternal magazine. **Freq:** Quarterly. **Key Personnel:** Jennifer McGhee Siler, Editor. **URL:** http://www.alphadeltapi.org/Page/Adelphean. **Remarks:** Advertising not accepted. **Circ:** (Not Reported).

8651 ■ Adult Education Quarterly
American Association for Adult and Continuing Education
Bldg. 14, Ste. 100
1827 Powers Ferry Rd.
Atlanta, GA 30339
Phone: (678)271-4319
Fax: (678)229-2777
Publisher's E-mail: sales@pfp.sagepub.com
Journal focusing on the understanding and practice of adult and continuing education. Published in association with the American Association for Adult and Continuing Education. **Freq:** Quarterly. **Key Personnel:** Leona M. English, Editor; Ashley Gleiman, Assistant Editor; Lisa R. Merriweather, Editor. **ISSN:** 0741--7136 (print); **EISSN:** 1552--3047 (electronic). **Subscription Rates:** $472 Institutions print & e-access; $519 Institutions current volume print & all online content; $472 Institutions backfile lease, e-access plus backfile (online); $1736 Institutions backfile purchase, e-access (content through 1998); $463 Institutions print only; $127 Institutions single print; $35 Individuals single print. **Online:** SAGE Publications Inc. SAGE Publications Inc. **URL:** http://aeq.sagepub.com; http://intl-aeq.sagepub.com online; http://us.sagepub.com/en-us/nam/adult-education-quarterly/journal200765. **Ad Rates:** BW $725. **Remarks:** Accepts advertising. **Circ:** (Not Reported).

Adult 55 Communities - See Philadelphia, PA

8652 ■ Adult Learning
American Association for Adult and Continuing Education
Bldg. 14, Ste. 100
1827 Powers Ferry Rd.
Atlanta, GA 30339
Phone: (678)271-4319
Fax: (678)229-2777
Freq: Quarterly. **Key Personnel:** Mary V. Alfred, Editor. **ISSN:** 1045--1595 (print); **EISSN:** 2162--4070 (electronic). **Subscription Rates:** Included in membership; $286 Institutions print and online; $257 Institutions online; $280 Institutions print; $34 Individuals print; $77 Institutions single print issue; $11 Individuals single print issue. **URL:** http://alx.sagepub.com; http://us.sagepub.com/en-us/nam/adult-learning/journal202126. **Ad Rates:** BW $725. **Remarks:** Accepts advertising. **Circ:** (Not Reported).

8653 ■ Adult Learning Quarterly
American Association for Adult and Continuing Education
Bldg. 14, Ste. 100
1827 Powers Ferry Rd.
Atlanta, GA 30339
Phone: (678)271-4319
Fax: (678)229-2777
Peer-reviewed journal publishing research on basic education on literacy. **Freq:** Quarterly February, May, August, and November. **Key Personnel:** Mary V. Alfred, Editor. **ISSN:** 1045--1595 (print); **EISSN:** 2162--4070 (electronic). **Remarks:** Advertising accepted; rates available upon request. **Circ:** (Not Reported).

8654 ■ AirTran GO
Echo Media
900 Circle 75 Pky., Ste. 1600
Atlanta, GA 30339
Phone: (770)955-3535
Fax: (770)955-3599
Publisher's E-mail: salesinfo@echo-media.com
Flight magazine. **Freq:** Monthly. **Remarks:** Advertising not accepted. **Circ:** 1,200,000.

8655 ■ American Baptist Quarterly
American Baptist Historical Society
3001 Mercer University Dr.,
Atlanta, GA 30341
Phone: (678)547-6680

Circulation: ★ = AAM; △ or • = BPA; ♦ = CAC; ❑ = VAC; ⊕ = PO Statement; ‡ = Publisher's Report; Boldface figures = sworn; Light figures = estimated.

Fax: (678)547-6682
Free: 800-222-3872
Magazine covering theology, history, containing Baptist religious material, with book reviews. **Freq:** Quarterly. **ISSN:** 0745-3698 (print). **Subscription Rates:** $50 U.S. churches, institutions, individual; $15 Single issue current issue, back issue; $30 /year (student rate). **URL:** http://abhsarchives.org/publications/american-baptist-quarterly. **Formerly**: Foundations. **Mailing address:** PO Box 851, Valley Forge, PA 19482-0851. **Ad Rates:** BW $100. **Remarks:** Accepts advertising. **Circ:** (Not Reported).

8656 ■ American Journal of Transplantation
Wiley-Blackwell
c/o Allan D. Kirk, Ed.-in-Ch.
Division of of Transplantation/Department of Surgery
Emory University
101 Woodruff Cir., 5105 WMB
Atlanta, GA 30322
Phone: (404)727-1400
Fax: (404)712-7575
Publisher's E-mail: customerservice@oxon.blackwellpublishing.com
Journal focusing on new high quality data in organ and tissue transplantation and the related sciences. **Freq:** Monthly. **Key Personnel:** Allan D. Kirk, Editor-in-Chief; Jonathan S. Bromberg, Editor; Guiseppe Remuzzi, Editor. **ISSN:** 1600--6135 (print); **EISSN:** 1600--6143 (electronic). **Subscription Rates:** $2878 Institutions print or online; £1711 Institutions print or online, UK; €2175 Institutions print or online, Europe; $3351 Institutions, other countries print or online; $3454 Institutions print and online; £2054 Institutions print and online, UK; €2610 Institutions print and online, Europe; $4022 Institutions, other countries print and online; $830 Individuals online only; £497 Individuals online only - UK, Europe (non-euro zone) and rest of the world; €743 Individuals online only, Europe; $874 Individuals print and online; £522 Individuals print and online - UK, Europe (non-euro zone) and rest of the world; €784 Individuals print and online, Europe. **URL:** http://onlinelibrary.wiley.com/journal/10.1111/(ISSN)1600-6143. **Remarks:** Accepts advertising. **Circ:** (Not Reported).

8657 ■ American Profile
Echo Media
900 Circle 75 Pky., Ste. 1600
Atlanta, GA 30339
Phone: (770)955-3535
Fax: (770)955-3599
Publisher's E-mail: salesinfo@echo-media.com
Magazine devoted to family affairs. **Founded:** Apr. 2000. **Freq:** 52/yr. **URL:** http://www.echo-media.com/mediaDetail.php?ID=971. **Circ:** 530,400,000.

8658 ■ Art Papers Magazine
Art Papers Inc.
1083 Austin Ave. NE, Ste. 206
Atlanta, GA 30307
Phone: (404)588-1837
Fax: (678)999-7002
Publisher's E-mail: info@artpapers.org
Magazine featuring articles on contemporary art and artists, reviews, newsbriefs, letters, and a classified listing section. **Freq:** Bimonthly. **Print Method:** Web offset. **Trim Size:** 8 x 11. **Col. Width:** 3 1/2 inches. **Col. Depth:** 10 inches. **Key Personnel:** Victoria Camblin, Editor. **ISSN:** 1524--9581 (print). **Subscription Rates:** $35 U.S.; $30 Students museum member; $65 Two years; $45 Canada and Mexico; $75 Other countries airmail; $10 Single issue U.S; $12 Single issue other country. **URL:** http://www.artpapers.org. **Formerly**: Art Papers. **Mailing address:** PO Box 5748, Atlanta, GA 30307. **Ad Rates:** BW $1400; 4C $1700. **Remarks:** Advertising accepted; rates available upon request. **Circ:** 180000.

8659 ■ Arthritis Care and Research
American College of Rheumatology
2200 Lake Blvd. NE
Atlanta, GA 30319
Phone: (404)633-3777
Fax: (404)633-1870
Publisher's E-mail: arhp@rheumatology.org
Freq: Monthly. **Key Personnel:** Marian T. Hannan, Editor. **ISSN:** 2151--464X (print); **EISSN:** 2151--4658 (electronic). **URL:** http://www.rheumatology.org/Learning-Center/Publications-News/Journals/AC-R; http://onlinelibrary.wiley.com/journal/10.1002/(ISSN)2151-4658. **Remarks:** Accepts advertising. **Circ:** (Not Reported).

8660 ■ Arthritis and Rheumatology
American College of Rheumatology
2200 Lake Blvd. NE
Atlanta, GA 30319
Phone: (404)633-3777
Fax: (404)633-1870
Publisher's E-mail: arhp@rheumatology.org
Freq: 28/yr. **Key Personnel:** Richard J. Bucala, Editor-in-Chief. **ISSN:** 2326--5191 (print); **EISSN:** 2326--5205 (electronic). **Subscription Rates:** $2328 Institutions print and online; $2756 Institutions, Canada and Mexico print and online; £1517 Institutions print and online; €1917 Institutions print and online; $2970 Institutions, other countries print and online; $1940 Institutions print or online; $1940 Institutions, Canada and Mexico print or online; £992 Institutions print or online; €1252 Institutions print or online; $1940 Institutions, other countries print or online. **URL:** http://www.rheumatology.org/Learning-Center/Publications-News/Journals/A-R. **Remarks:** Accepts advertising. **Circ:** (Not Reported).

8661 ■ Arthritis Today
Arthritis Foundation
1330 Peachtree St. NE, 6th Fl.
Atlanta, GA 30309
Phone: (404)872-7100
Freq: 6/year Bimonthly Monthly Biweekly latest issue: 2015. **ISSN:** 0890--1120 (print). **Subscription Rates:** $12.95 U.S. /year; $18.95 Canada /year; $20.95 Other countries /year ; $21.95 U.S. 2 years; $33.95 Canada 2 years; $37.95 Other countries 2 years; $29.95 U.S. 3 years; $47.95 Canada 3 years; $53.95 Other countries 3 years; included in membership dues; $3.99 for nonmembers; included in membership dues; $21.95 Two years; $33.95 Two years Canada; $37.95 Two years other countries; Included in membership. **Alt. Formats:** Download. **URL:** http://www.arthritis.org/arthritis-today-magazine; http://www.arthritistoday.org; http://www.arthritistoday.org/tools-and-resources/arthritis-today-magazine. **Ad Rates:** $5605-24230, for full page-1/6 page; $10635-29370, for 2 colors, ful page-1/6 page; $12455-34745, for four color, ful page-1/6 page; $39885-41835, for 2nd-4th covers. BW $, for full page-1/6 pageBW $24,230, full page; BW $14,630, half page; 4C $29,370, full page - two color; 4C $17,375, half page - two color; 4C $34,745, full page - four color; 4C $20,915, half page - four color. **Remarks:** Accepts advertising. **Circ:** 700000.

8662 ■ ASHRAE Journal
American Society of Heating, Refrigerating and Air-Conditioning Engineers
1791 Tullie Cir. NE
Atlanta, GA 30329
Phone: (404)636-8400
Fax: (404)321-5478
Free: 800-527-4723
Publisher's E-mail: ashrae@ashrae.org
Magazine for the heating, refrigeration, and air conditioning trade. **Freq:** Monthly. **Print Method:** Web Offset. **Trim Size:** 8 3/16 x 10 7/8. **Cols./Page:** 3 and 2. **Col. Width:** 26 and 40 nonpareils. **Col. Depth:** 140 agate lines. **Key Personnel:** Fred Turner, Editor; Sarah Foster, Managing Editor. **ISSN:** 0001--2491 (print). **Subscription Rates:** $197 Institutions U.S. and Canada; $249 Institutions, other countries. **URL:** http://ashrae.org/resources--publications/ashrae-journal/ashrae-journal. **Ad Rates:** BW $8055; 4C $1415. **Remarks:** Accepts advertising. **Circ:** (Not Reported).

8663 ■ Atlanta Business Chronicle
Atlanta Business Chronicle
3384 Peachtree Rd. NE, Ste. 900
Atlanta, GA 30326
Phone: (404)249-1000
Fax: (404)249-1048
Publisher's E-mail: atlanta@bizjournals.com
Local business newspaper. **Freq:** Weekly. **Print Method:** Web Offset. **Trim Size:** 11 3/8 x 16. **Cols./Page:** 4. **Col. Width:** 2 1/4 inches. **Col. Depth:** 14 inches. **Key Personnel:** David Allison, Editor, phone: (404)249-1039; Ed Baker, Publisher. **ISSN:** 0164--8071 (print). **Subscription Rates:** $96 Individuals. **URL:** http://www.bizjournals.com/atlanta. **Ad Rates:** 4C $9499. **Remarks:** Accepts advertising. **Circ:** (Not Reported).

8664 ■ Atlanta Clipper Magazine
Echo Media
900 Circle 75 Pky., Ste. 1600
Atlanta, GA 30339
Phone: (770)955-3535
Fax: (770)955-3599
Publisher's E-mail: salesinfo@echo-media.com
Magazine devoted to local retail advertising. **Freq:** Monthly. **URL:** http://echomedia.com/medias/details/818. **Remarks:** Accepts advertising. **Circ:** (Not Reported).

8665 ■ Atlanta Daily World
Atlanta Daily World
3485 N Desert Dr.
Atlanta, GA 30344
Phone: (404)761-1114
Fax: (404)761-1164
Publisher's E-mail: publisher@atlantadailyworld.com
Black community newspaper. **Freq:** Weekly (Thurs.). **Print Method:** Offset. **Cols./Page:** 6. **Col. Width:** 1 5/8 inches. **Col. Depth:** 21 inches. **Key Personnel:** Michelle Gipson, Director, Advertising; Mr. Alexis Scott, Chief Executive Officer, Publisher. **Ad Rates:** GLR $.70; BW $2800; 4C $670; PCI $22.22; 4C $33.92. **Remarks:** Accepts advertising. **Circ:** ‡10000.

8666 ■ Atlanta Homes and Lifestyles
Network Communications Inc.
1100 Johnson Ferry Rd.
Center 2, Ste. 595
Atlanta, GA 30342
Phone: (404)252-6670
Fax: (404)252-6673
Magazine on shelter and design topics, gardening, remodeling and entertaining. **Freq:** Monthly. **Print Method:** Web offset. **Trim Size:** 8 3/8 x 10 7/8. **Cols./Page:** 3. **Col. Width:** 13.5 picas. **Col. Depth:** 132 agate lines. **Key Personnel:** Clinton Ross Smith, Director, Editorial; Gina Christman, Publisher. **ISSN:** 0887--1523 (print). **Subscription Rates:** $51 Canada and Mexico; $75 Two years Canada & Mexico; $27 Individuals; $47 Two years. **Ad Rates:** BW $5,325; 4C $7,285. **Remarks:** Accepts advertising. **Circ:** (Not Reported).

8667 ■ The Atlanta Inquirer
The Atlanta Inquirer
PO Box 92367
Atlanta, GA 30314-0367
Phone: (404)523-6086
Fax: (404)523-6088
Publication E-mail: news@atlinq.com
Black community newspaper. Distributed each Thursday with a Saturday publication date. **Freq:** Weekly (Thurs.). **Key Personnel:** John B. Smith, Sr., Chief Executive Officer, President, Publisher; Sallie Pope-Howard, Office Manager; David T. Stokes, Associate Editor; Herbert Linsey, Manager, Circulation; John B. Smith, Jr., Chief Operating Officer, Editor. **Subscription Rates:** $28 Individuals /year; $52.50 Two years; $78.75 Individuals three years. **URL:** http://www.atlinq.com. **Remarks:** Accepts advertising. **Circ:** Paid 61000.

8668 ■ The Atlanta Journal and Constitution
Cox Newspapers Inc.
6205 Peachtree Dunwoody Rd.
Atlanta, GA 30328-4524
Phone: (678)645-0000
Fax: (678)645-5002
General newspaper. **Founded:** June 16, 1868. **Freq:** Mon.-Sun. (morn.). **Print Method:** Offset. **Cols./Page:** 6. **Col. Width:** 25 nonpareils. **Col. Depth:** 297 agate lines. **Key Personnel:** Kevin Riley, Editor, phone: (404)526-2161; Michael Joseph, Publisher, phone: (404)526-5893. **ISSN:** 0093-1179 (print). **USPS:** 256-020. **Subscription Rates:** $119.99 Individuals Mon.-Sun.; home delivery; $99.99 Individuals Sat.-Sun.; home delivery; $74.99 Individuals Sunday only; home delivery. **Online:** LexisNexis. **Alt. Formats:** Handheld. **URL:** http://www.ajc.com. **Formed by the merger of**: The Atlanta Journal; The Atlanta Constitution. **Feature Editors:** Sheila Reed, *Garden/Home*, phone: (404)526-5485, fax: (404)526-5509, sreed@ajc.com; Frank Rizzo, *Features*, phone: (404)526-5494, fax: (404)526-5509, frizzo@ajc.com; Bob Longino, *Features*, phone: (404)526-5430, fax: (404)526-5590, blongino@ajc.com; Howard Pousner, , phone: (404)526-5479, fax: (404)526-5509, hpousner@ajc.com; Susan Puckett, *Food*, phone: (404)526-5443, fax: (404)526-5509, spuckett@ajc.com; Nick Tate, , phone: (404)526-5671, fax: (404)526-5509,

ntate@ajc.com; Kathy Janich, *Entertainment*, phone: (404)526-5971, fax: (404)526-5509, kjanich@ajc.com; Ron Feinberg, , phone: (404)526-5491, fax: (404)526-5509, rfeinberg@ajc.com; Eleanor Ringel, , phone: (404)526-5468, fax: (404)526-5509, eringel@ajc.com; Jennifer Hill, , phone: (404)526-5869, fax: (404)614-2764, jhill@ajc.com. **Remarks:** Accepts advertising. **Circ:** Mon.-Fri. ★**326907**, Sat. ★**329765**, Sun. ★**497149**.

8669 ■ Atlanta Magazine
Emmis Publishing Corp.
260 Peachtree St., Ste. 300
Atlanta, GA 30303
Phone: (404)527-5500
Fax: (404)527-5575
City magazine. **Founded:** 1961. **Freq:** Monthly. **Print Method:** Offset. **Trim Size:** 8 X 10 7/8. **Cols./Page:** 3. **Col. Width:** 2.25 picas. **Col. Depth:** 10 inches. **ISSN:** 0004-6701 (print). **Subscription Rates:** $14.99 Individuals print only; $28 Two years print only; $40 Individuals print only, 3 years. **URL:** http://www.atlantamagazine.com; http://www.emmis.com/property/publishing-atlanta-magazine/. **Ad Rates:** BW $5455; 4C $7180. **Remarks:** Accepts advertising. **Circ:** Combined ‡65,415, ‡68,000.

8670 ■ Atlanta Parent
Atlanta Parent Inc.
2346 Perimeter Pk., Dr.
Atlanta, GA 30341
Phone: (770)454-7599
Fax: (770)454-7699
Publisher's E-mail: atlantaparent@atlantaparent.com
Parenting magazine. **Freq:** Monthly. **Key Personnel:** Liz White, Publisher. **Subscription Rates:** Free; $30 Individuals first class subscription. **URL:** http://www.atlantaparent.com. **Ad Rates:** BW $2500; 4C $2950. **Remarks:** Accepts advertising. **Circ:** ‡100000.

8671 ■ Atlanta Savings & Values
Echo Media
900 Circle 75 Pky., Ste. 1600
Atlanta, GA 30339
Phone: (770)955-3535
Fax: (770)955-3599
Publisher's E-mail: salesinfo@echo-media.com
Newspaper covering variety of advertising. **Freq:** Weekly 52/yr. **URL:** http://echomedia.com/medias/details/2330. **Remarks:** Accepts advertising. **Circ:** (Not Reported).

8672 ■ The Atlanta Voice
Atlanta Voice
633 Pryor St. SW
Atlanta, GA 30312
Phone: (404)524-6426
Fax: (404)523-7853
Publisher's E-mail: info@theatlantavoice.com
Black community newspaper. **Freq:** Weekly. **Key Personnel:** Janis Ware, Publisher; Stan Washington, Editor; James Washington, General Manager. **Ad Rates:** GLR $6.50; BW $2194; 4C $500. **Remarks:** Accepts advertising. **Circ:** ♦**30000**.

8673 ■ The Atlantan
Modern Luxury Media
3280 Peachtree Rd., Ste. 2300
Atlanta, GA 30305
Phone: (404)443-1180
Fax: (404)443-6199
Magazine featuring affluent lifestyle in Atlanta. **Freq:** 7/yr. **Key Personnel:** Chris C. Van Duyne, Publisher; Nancy Staab, Editor-in-Chief. **Subscription Rates:** $40 Individuals; $60 Two years. **URL:** http://www.modernluxury.com/the-atlantan. **Remarks:** Accepts advertising. **Circ:** (Not Reported).

8674 ■ The Atlantan Brides
Modern Luxury Media
3340 Peachtree Rd. NE, Ste. 1425
Atlanta, GA 30326-1077
Phone: (404)443-0004
Fax: (404)443-6199
Magazine featuring the latest trends in wedding arrangements. **Freq:** Semiannual. **Key Personnel:** Phebe Wahl, Editor-in-Chief; Spencer Beck, Director, Editorial; Chris C. Van Duyne, Publisher. **Subscription Rates:** $20 Individuals; $35 Two years. **URL:** http://www.modernluxury.com/the-atlantan. **Remarks:** Accepts advertising. **Circ:** (Not Reported).

8675 ■ Atlantic Economic Journal
International Atlantic Economic Society
229 Peachtree St. NE, Ste. 650
Atlanta, GA 30303
Phone: (404)965-1555
Fax: (404)965-1556
Publisher's E-mail: iaes@iaes.org
Professional journal covering economics. **Freq:** Quarterly. **Print Method:** Offset. **Trim Size:** 5 x 7. **Key Personnel:** Katherine S. Virgo, Managing Editor; Milton H. Marquis, Board Member. **ISSN:** 0197-4254 (print). **URL:** http://www.iaes.org/publications/atlantic-economic-journal. **Ad Rates:** BW $525. **Remarks:** Accepts advertising. **Circ:** (Not Reported).

8676 ■ AUC Digest
Atlanta University Center
156 Mildred St.
Atlanta, GA 30314
Phone: (404)523-5148
Fax: (404)525-7377
Collegiate newspaper (tabloid). **Founded:** 1973. **Freq:** Weekly (Mon.). **Print Method:** Offset. **Cols./Page:** 4. **Col. Width:** 27 nonpareils. **Col. Depth:** 196 agate lines. **Subscription Rates:** $42 Individuals. **URL:** http://aucdigest.com. **Mailing address:** PO Box 92527, Atlanta, GA 30314. **Ad Rates:** GLR $.70; BW $587. **Remarks:** Accepts advertising. **Circ:** Paid ‡100, Non-paid ‡20,000.

8677 ■ Barbers Only Magazine: Lifestyle of the Barber Professional
Barbers Only Magazine
PO Box 1248
Atlanta, GA 30301
Phone: (678)458-5117
Publication E-mail: info@barbersonlymagazine.com
Magazine featuring shops, styles, hair cutting techniques, and the latest barber products used by the best barber technicians in the world. **Freq:** Bimonthly. **Trim Size:** 8.5 x 11. **Key Personnel:** B.G. Cutta, Contact; Vinny Barberino, Contact; Craig Logan, Director, Education. **URL:** http://barbersonlymagazine.com. **Remarks:** Accepts advertising. **Circ:** (Not Reported).

8678 ■ Beckett Hockey Card Plus
Echo Media
900 Circle 75 Pky., Ste. 1600
Atlanta, GA 30339
Phone: (770)955-3535
Fax: (770)955-3599
Publisher's E-mail: salesinfo@echo-media.com
Sports magazine. **Freq:** Quarterly. **URL:** http://echomedia.com/medias/details/10344. **Remarks:** Advertising not accepted. **Circ:** 40000.

8679 ■ Bee Culture
American Beekeeping Federation
3525 Piedmont Rd., Bldg. 5, Ste. 300
Atlanta, GA 30305
Phone: (404)760-2875
Fax: (404)240-0998
Publisher's E-mail: info@abfnet.org
Magazine featuring articles, advice and information for every level beekeeper, from not-yet-started to the commercial operator. Highlights ways on how to keep bees, make your own equipment, new products on the market, national honey report and honey market surveys. **Freq:** Monthly. **Subscription Rates:** $25 /year, print; $47.50 Other countries /year, print; $88 Other countries 24 months, print; $15 /year, online. **URL:** http://www.beeculture.com; http://www.abfnet.org/?24. **Remarks:** Advertising not accepted. **Circ:** (Not Reported).

8680 ■ Being Single Magazine
Echo Media
900 Circle 75 Pky., Ste. 1600
Atlanta, GA 30339
Phone: (770)955-3535
Fax: (770)955-3599
Publisher's E-mail: salesinfo@echo-media.com
Single lifestyle magazine for African-Americans. **Freq:** Bimonthly. **URL:** http://www.echo-media.com/medias/details/4537/being+single+magazine. **Remarks:** Accepts advertising. **Circ:** 300000.

8681 ■ Blender
Echo Media
900 Circle 75 Pky., Ste. 1600
Atlanta, GA 30339
Phone: (770)955-3535
Fax: (770)955-3599
Publisher's E-mail: salesinfo@echo-media.com
Magazine covering big-personality music and pop-culture. **Freq:** 11/year. **URL:** http://echomedia.com/medias/details/5261. **Remarks:** Advertising not accepted. **Circ:** 9900000.

8682 ■ Bluff Magazine: The Thrill of Poker
Bluff Media
1200 Lake Hearn Dr., Ste. 450
Atlanta, GA 30319
Fax: (404)250-1943
Publisher's E-mail: support@bluffmagazine.com
Magazine for poker enthusiasts. **Freq:** Monthly. **Key Personnel:** Matthew Parvis. **Subscription Rates:** $24.99 Individuals; $34.99 Canada; $44.99 Other countries. **URL:** http://www.bluff.com. **Remarks:** Accepts advertising. **Circ:** (Not Reported).

Boston Magazine's Concierge - See Boston, MA

Boston Magazine's Elegant Wedding - See Boston, MA

Boston Metro - See Boston, MA

8683 ■ Bride's Receptions
Echo Media
900 Circle 75 Pky., Ste. 1600
Atlanta, GA 30339
Phone: (770)955-3535
Fax: (770)955-3599
Publisher's E-mail: salesinfo@echo-media.com
Magazine covering latest wedding dress styles and fashionable rings, to reception advice and honeymoon suggestions. **Freq:** Annual. **URL:** http://echomedia.com/medias/details/10381. **Remarks:** Advertising not accepted. **Circ:** 600000.

8684 ■ CA: A Cancer Journal for Clinicians
American Cancer Society
250 Williams St. NW
Atlanta, GA 30303-1002
Free: 800-227-2345
Original peer-reviewed articles on all aspects of cancer management. **Freq:** Bimonthly. **Trim Size:** 8 1/8 x 10 7/8. **Key Personnel:** Otis Webb Brawley, MD, Editor-in-Chief; Ted Gansler, MD, Editor. **ISSN:** 0007--9235 (print); **EISSN:** 1542--4863 (electronic). **Subscription Rates:** Free. **Online:** Wiley Online Library Wiley Online Library. **URL:** http://www.cacancerjournal.org. **Mailing address:** PO Box 22478, Oklahoma City, OK 73123. **Ad Rates:** BW $5340; 4C $1450. **Remarks:** Accepts advertising. **Circ:** 95000, 76617.

8685 ■ Cancer
American Cancer Society
250 Williams St. NW
Atlanta, GA 30303-1002
Free: 800-227-2345
Publication E-mail: canceredoff@cancer.org
Journal publishing peer-reviewed original articles related to cancer. **Freq:** Biweekly. **Trim Size:** 8 1/8 x 10 7/8. **Key Personnel:** Fadlo Khuri, MD, Editor-in-Chief; Henry Friedman, MD, Editor; Carissa A. Gilman, Managing Editor. **ISSN:** 0008- 543X (print); **EISSN:** 1097- 0142 (electronic). **Subscription Rates:** $1075 Institutions online only; $1075 Institutions, Canada and Mexico online only; £551 Institutions online only, for UK; €695 Institutions online only, Euro zone; $1075 Institutions, other countries online only; $1075 Institutions print only; $1225 Institutions, Canada and Mexico print only; £673 Institutions print only, for UK; €850 Institutions print only, Euro zone; $1315 Institutions, other countries print only; $1290 Institutions print and online; $1578 Institutions, Canada and Mexico print and online; £808 Institutions print and online, for UK; €1020 Institutions print and online, Euro zone; $1570 Institutions, other countries print and online. **URL:** http://onlinelibrary.wiley.com/journal/10.1002/(ISSN)1097-0142. **Mailing address:** PO Box 22478, Oklahoma City, OK 73123. **Ad Rates:** $600-900, for full page; $422-630, for 1/2 page; $274-410, for 1/4 page. BW $, for full pageBW $, for 1/2 pageBW $, for 1/4 pageBW $2456; 4C $1339. **Remarks:** Accepts advertising. **Circ:** 2,035, 8,251.

8686 ■ Chamblee De Kalb Neighbor
Neighbor Newspapers Inc.
3060 Mercer University Dr., Ste. 210
Atlanta, GA 30341

Circulation: ★ = AAM; △ or • = BPA; ♦ = CAC; ❑ = VAC; ⊕ = PO Statement; ‡ = Publisher's Report; Boldface figures = sworn; Light figures = estimated.

Phone: (770)993-7400
Fax: (770)993-7400
Publication E-mail: dekalb@neighbornewspapers.com
Community newspaper. **Freq:** Weekly (Wed.). **Print Method:** Offset. **Cols./Page:** 6. **Col. Width:** 26 nonpareils. **Col. Depth:** 301 agate lines. **Key Personnel:** Otis A. Brumby, Jr., Publisher; Otis Brumby, III, General Manager. **USPS:** 951-740. **Subscription Rates:** $135.68 By mail outside the delivery area; $72.08 By mail outside the delivery area; 6 months; $36.57 By mail outside the delivery area; 3 months. **URL:** http://www.mdjonline.com/neighbor_newspapers/dekalb. **Ad Rates:** GLR $.97; BW $1741.50; 4C $2066.50; SAU $13.50. **Circ:** (Not Reported).

Chicago Catolico - See Chicago, IL

Cincinnati Reach - See Cincinnati, OH

8687 ■ Clark Atlanta University Magazine
Clark Atlanta University
223 James P. Brawley Dr. SW
Atlanta, GA 30314
Phone: (404)880-8000
Publisher's E-mail: info@cau.edu
College alumni magazine. **Freq:** Monthly. **URL:** http://www.atlantamagazine.com. **Circ:** (Not Reported).

Columbus Paper Mint - See Columbus, OH

8688 ■ Computer Networks
Elsevier
c/o I.F. Akyildiz, Ed.-in-Ch.
Georgia Institute of Technology
School of Electrical & Computer Engineering
777 Atlantic Dr. NW
Atlanta, GA 30302
Publisher's E-mail: t.reller@elsevier.com
Journal focused on computer communications networking area. **Founded:** Nov. 11, 1976. **Freq:** 18/yr. **Print Method:** Offset. **Trim Size:** 8 3/8 x 10 7/8. **Cols./Page:** 2. **Col. Width:** 3 1/2 inches. **Col. Depth:** 10 inches. **Key Personnel:** I.F. Akyildiz, Editor-in-Chief; H. Rudin, Editor-in-Chief. **ISSN:** 1389-1286 (print). **Subscription Rates:** $3327 Institutions print; $3327.20 Institutions ejournal. **URL:** http://www.journals.elsevier.com/computer-networks. **Circ:** (Not Reported).

8689 ■ Conversations
Conversations
McCarty Bldg.
2055 Mount Paran Rd. NW
Atlanta, GA 30327
Phone: (404)835-6128
Publication E-mail: conversations@psy.edu
Christian journal. **Freq:** Semiannual. **Trim Size:** 8 1/2 x 11. **Key Personnel:** Joannah M. Sadler, Managing Editor; Gary W. Moon, Editor, Founder. **Subscription Rates:** $32 Individuals print; $38 Canada print; $47 Other countries print; $25 Individuals online; $50 Institutions print (plus shipping). **URL:** http://conversationsjournal.com. **Ad Rates:** BW $500. **Remarks:** Accepts advertising. **Circ:** 6000.

8690 ■ Corporate Real Estate Executive
CoreNet Global
133 Peachtree St. NE, Ste. 3000
Atlanta, GA 30303-1815
Phone: (404)589-3200
Fax: (404)589-3201
Free: 800-726-8111
Real estate deal-making techniques magazine. **Freq:** 9/yr. **Print Method:** Offset. **Trim Size:** 8 1/2 x 11. **Cols./Page:** 4. **Col. Width:** 14 picas. **Col. Depth:** 10 inches. **Key Personnel:** Kathleen B. Dempsey, Editor. **ISSN:** 1042--9115 (print). **Ad Rates:** BW $3,225; 4C $4,820. **Remarks:** Advertising accepted; rates available upon request. **Circ:** Paid 3800.

8691 ■ Cotton & Quail Antique Gazette
Echo Media
900 Circle 75 Pky., Ste. 1600
Atlanta, GA 30339
Phone: (770)955-3535
Fax: (770)955-3599
Publisher's E-mail: salesinfo@echo-media.com
Newspaper covering antiques and collectibles in the southwestern U.S. **Founded:** 1988. **Freq:** Monthly. **Trim Size:** 11 1/2 x 13 1/2. **Key Personnel:** Linda Kunkel, Editor. **URL:** http://www.echo-media.com/mediaDetail.php?ID=10170. **Ad Rates:** 4C $670. **Remarks:** Accepts advertising. **Circ:** Combined 189600.

8692 ■ Creative Loafing Atlanta
Creative Loafing
384 Northyards Blvd., Ste. 600
Atlanta, GA 30313
Phone: (404)688-5623
Fax: (404)614-3599
Alternative news weekly newspaper (tabloid). **Freq:** Weekly. **Print Method:** Offset. **Trim Size:** 10 x 12 7/8. **Cols./Page:** 4. **Col. Width:** 2.3125 inches. **Col. Depth:** 11.25 inches. **Key Personnel:** Eric Celeste, Editor-in-Chief; Chris Mihal, Creative Director; Sharry Smith, Publisher. **URL:** http://clatl.com. **Remarks:** Accepts advertising. **Circ:** ■ **100000**, ■ **90000**.

8693 ■ Criminal Justice Review
SAGE Publications Inc.
Georgia State University
Atlanta, GA 30302-4018
Phone: (404)413-1041
Fax: (404)413-1030
Publisher's E-mail: sales@pfp.sagepub.com
Peer-reviewed journal presenting a broad perspective on criminal justice issues within the domestic United States. **Freq:** Quarterly. **Key Personnel:** Leah E. Daigle, Editor. **ISSN:** 0734--0168 (print); **EISSN:** 1556--3839 (electronic). **Subscription Rates:** £30 Individuals print; £248 Institutions e-access; £270 Institutions print ; £276 Institutions print and e-access; £10 Individuals single print; £74 Institutions single print. **URL:** http://cjr.sagepub.com. **Mailing address:** PO Box 4018, Atlanta, GA 30302-4018. **Remarks:** Accepts advertising. **Circ:** (Not Reported).

8694 ■ David Atlanta
Echo Media
1874 Piedmont Ave., Ste. 490D
Atlanta, GA 30324
Phone: (404)418-8901
Fax: (404)889-8679
Publisher's E-mail: salesinfo@echo-media.com
Magazine catering to the gay communities in the southeast. **Freq:** Weekly 52/yr. **Key Personnel:** David Thompson, Publisher. **URL:** http://davidatlanta.com. **Remarks:** Accepts advertising. **Circ:** (Not Reported).

Denver Urban Spectrum - See Denver, CO

8695 ■ Departures
Echo Media
900 Circle 75 Pky., Ste. 1600
Atlanta, GA 30339
Phone: (770)955-3535
Fax: (770)955-3599
Publisher's E-mail: salesinfo@echo-media.com
Flight magazine. **Freq:** 8/year. **URL:** http://www.echo-media.com/medias/details/4089/departures. **Remarks:** Accepts advertising. **Circ:** 900000.

8696 ■ Dwell
Echo Media
900 Circle 75 Pky., Ste. 1600
Atlanta, GA 30339
Phone: (770)955-3535
Fax: (770)955-3599
Publisher's E-mail: salesinfo@echo-media.com
Magazine covering articles on interior design, including innovative design and architecture. **Freq:** 8/year. **URL:** http://echomedia.com/medias/details/5998. **Remarks:** Accepts advertising. **Circ:** 26000000.

The East Cobb Neighbor - See Cobb

8697 ■ Econometric Reviews
Taylor & Francis Group Journals
c/o Esfandiar Maasoumi, Ed.
Department of Economics
Emory University
Atlanta, GA 30322
Publisher's E-mail: customerservice@taylorandfrancis.com
Journal focusing on econometrics. **Freq:** 8/year. **Key Personnel:** Esfandiar Maasoumi, Editor; Badi H. Baltagi, Associate Editor; James Heckman, Associate Editor; Qi Li, Associate Editor; Amos Golan, Associate Editor; Alastair Hall, Associate Editor. **ISSN:** 0747--4938 (print); **EISSN:** 1532--4168 (electronic). **Subscription Rates:** $2971 Institutions print and online; $2600 Institutions online only; $685 Individuals print only. **URL:** http://www.tandfonline.com/toc/lecr20/current. **Circ:** (Not Reported).

8698 ■ Emerging Infectious Diseases
U.S. Department of Health and Human Services
Centers for Disease Control and Prevention National Center for Emerging and Zoonotic Infectious Diseases
1600 Clifton Rd. NE, Mail Stop D-76
Atlanta, GA 30333
Free: 800-232-4636
Publisher's E-mail: cdcinfo@cdc.gov
Medical journal covering infectious diseases. **Freq:** Monthly. **Key Personnel:** Joseph E. McDade, PhD, Editor, Founder; Polyxeni Potter, Managing Editor; Peter D. Drotman, MD, Editor-in-Chief. **ISSN:** 1080--6040 (print). **URL:** http://wwwnc.cdc.gov/eid. **Remarks:** Advertising not accepted. **Circ:** 2500.

8699 ■ Emory Law Journal
Emory University School of Law
1301 Clifton Rd. NE
Atlanta, GA 30322-2770
Phone: (404)727-6816
Publisher's E-mail: lawcommunications@emory.edu
Journal containing articles regarding general and public law. **Freq:** 6/year. **Key Personnel:** Matthew B. Johnson, Editor-in-Chief. **ISSN:** 0094--4076 (print). **Subscription Rates:** $40 Individuals; $45 Other countries; $36 Individuals agent; $40.50 Other countries agent; $12 Single issue domestic; $20 Single issue foreign. **URL:** http://law.emory.edu/elj. **Circ:** (Not Reported).

8700 ■ Emory Magazine
Emory University
1762 Clifton Rd.
Atlanta, GA 30322
Publication E-mail: eurec@emory.edu
Magazine for university alumni. **Freq:** Quarterly. **Print Method:** Web offset. **Trim Size:** 8 1/2 x 11. **Cols./Page:** 3 and 2. **Col. Width:** 13 and 20 nonpareils. **Col. Depth:** 147 agate lines. **Key Personnel:** Mary J. Loftus, Associate Editor; Paige P. Parvin, Editor. **ISSN:** 0013--6727 (print). **URL:** http://emory.edu/EMORY_MAGAZINE/issues/2013/autumn/index.html. **Remarks:** Advertising accepted; rates available upon request. **Circ:** Non-paid ‡78000.

8701 ■ The Emory Wheel
Emory University
201 Dowman Dr.
Atlanta, GA 30322
Phone: (404)727-6123
Collegiate newspaper (tabloid). **Freq:** Weekly (Wed.). **Print Method:** Offset. **Trim Size:** 11 1/2 x 15. **Cols./Page:** 5. **Col. Width:** 22 nonpareils. **Col. Depth:** 196 agate lines. **Key Personnel:** Evan Mah, Editor-in-Chief; Roshani Chokshi, Managing Editor; Ariana Skibell, Executive Editor. **Subscription Rates:** Free. **URL:** http://emorywheel.com. **Ad Rates:** PCI $8. **Remarks:** Accepts advertising. **Circ:** 5000, 4000.

8702 ■ Energy Engineering Journal
Association of Energy Engineers
3168 Mercer University Dr.
Atlanta, GA 30341
Phone: (770)447-5083
Journal covering a variety of energy management, building systems, HVAC, lighting, financing, performance contracting, energy efficiency, smart metering, distributed generation, plant engineering, facility management, energy service, and energy procurement issues. **Freq:** Bimonthly. **ISSN:** 0199--8595 (print); **EISSN:** 1546-0118 (electronic). **Subscription Rates:** Included in membership; $414 Nonmembers Individual (print); $435 Individuals print; $506 Institutions online; $578 Institutions print and online. **URL:** http://www.aeecenter.org/i4a/pages/index.cfm?pageid=3284#Publications. **Remarks:** Accepts advertising. **Circ:** (Not Reported).

8703 ■ Farmers & Consumers Market Bulletin
Georgia Department of Agriculture
19 Martin Luther King Jr. Dr., SW
Atlanta, GA 30334
Phone: (404)656-3600
Free: 800-282-5852
Publisher's E-mail: farmtax@agr.georgia.gov
State agriculture and consumer newspaper. **Freq:** Biweekly. **Print Method:** Web offset. **Trim Size:** 11 1/4 x 15. **Cols./Page:** 5. **Col. Width:** 22 nonpareils. **Col. Depth:** 215 agate lines. **Key Personnel:** Carlton Moore, Editor, phone: (404)656-3682; Randy L. Cox, Managing Editor. **ISSN:** 0889--5619 (print). **Subscription Rates:** $20 Out of state; $10 Individuals to Georgia residents;

$5 Individuals online only. **URL:** http://agr.georgia.gov/market-bulletin.aspx. **Remarks:** Advertising accepted; rates available upon request. **Circ:** Free 205428.

8704 ■ Florida Pennysaver
Cox Newspapers Inc.
6205 Peachtree Dunwoody Rd.
Atlanta, GA 30328-4524
Phone: (678)645-0000
Fax: (678)645-5002
Newspaper covering the news and events in Palm Beach, Florida. **Remarks:** Accepts advertising. **Circ:** (Not Reported).

8705 ■ Forest Landowner
Forest Landowners Association
900 Circle 75 Pkwy., Ste. 205
Atlanta, GA 30339
Phone: (404)325-2954
Fax: (404)325-2955
Free: 800-325-2954
Publisher's E-mail: info@forestlandowners.com
Forestry magazine. **Freq:** 6/year. **Print Method:** Offset. **Trim Size:** 8.375 x 10.75. **Cols./Page:** 3. **Col. Width:** 28 nonpareils. **Col. Depth:** 133 agate lines. **Key Personnel:** Sarah Sturm, Editor. **ISSN:** 0015--7406 (print). **Subscription Rates:** Included in membership; $59 Individuals. **URL:** http://forestlandowners.com/?50; http://forestlandowners.com/?302. **Formerly**: Forest Farmer Magazine. **Ad Rates:** BW $1241; 4C $2100, full page; PCI $131. **Remarks:** Accepts advertising. **Circ:** 8500.

8706 ■ The Freeman: Ideas on Liberty and Notes from FEE
Foundation for Economic Education
1718 Peachtree Rd. NE, Ste. 300
Atlanta, GA 30309
Phone: (404)554-9980
Fax: (404)393-3142
Free: 800-960-4333
Publication E-mail: freeman@fee.org
Magazine containing commentary concerning free market, limited government and private property. **Freq:** Monthly. **Print Method:** Web Offset. **Trim Size:** 6 3/4 x 10. **Cols./Page:** 2. **Col. Width:** 31 nonpareils. **Col. Depth:** 118 agate lines. **ISSN:** 0016--0652 (print). **Subscription Rates:** $50 Individuals. **URL:** http://fee.org/the-freeman. **Ad Rates:** BW $800. **Remarks:** Accepts advertising. **Circ:** 31000.

8707 ■ From a Women's Perspective
Women's Entrepreneurial Opportunity Project, Inc.
250 Georgia Ave., Ste. 213
Atlanta, GA 30312
Phone: (404)681-2497
Fax: (404)681-2499
Publisher's E-mail: women@weop.org
Magazine focusing on issues that matter to women. **Freq:** Annual. **URL:** http://www.weop.org/#!our-story/c1iqw; http://fawpmagazine.wordpress.com/. **Ad Rates:** BW $1,500, back cover page; BW $450, half page. **Remarks:** Accepts advertising. **Circ:** (Not Reported).

8708 ■ Georgia Bar Journal
State Bar of Georgia
104 Marietta St. NW, Ste. 100
Atlanta, GA 30303
Phone: (404)527-8700
Fax: (404)527-8717
Free: 800-334-6865
Law journal. **Freq:** 6/year February, April, June, August, October and December. **Print Method:** Offset. **Trim Size:** 8.375 x 10.875. **Cols./Page:** 3. **Col. Width:** 27 nonpareils. **Col. Depth:** 133 agate lines. **Key Personnel:** Cliff Brashier, Executive Director; Jennifer Mason, Contact. **Alt. Formats:** PDF. **URL:** http://gabar.org/newsandpublications/georgiabarjournal/index.cfm. **Ad Rates:** BW $1738; 4C $2781. **Remarks:** Accepts advertising. **Circ:** 32000.

8709 ■ Georgia Tech Alumni Magazine
Georgia Tech Alumni Association
190 N Ave. NW
Atlanta, GA 30313
Phone: (404)894-2391
Free: 800-482-5867
Publication E-mail: editor@alumni.gatech.edu
Alumni magazine covering management of technology. **Freq:** Quarterly. **Print Method:** Web. **Trim Size:** 8 1/8 x 10 7/8. **Key Personnel:** Joseph P. Irwin, Publisher; Van Jensen, Editor. **ISSN:** 1061-9747 (print). **URL:** http://gtalumnimag.com. **Ad Rates:** BW $2,000; 4C $2,750. **Remarks:** Accepts advertising. **Circ:** Paid 33000.

8710 ■ The Gladewater Mirror
Cox Enterprises Inc.
6205 Peachtree Dunwoody Rd.
Atlanta, GA 30328
Phone: (678)645-0000
Fax: (678)645-1079
Publisher's E-mail: contactus@coxinc.com
Community newspaper. **Freq:** Weekly (Wed.). **Print Method:** Offset. **Cols./Page:** 6. **Col. Width:** 24 nonpareils. **Col. Depth:** 296 agate lines. **Key Personnel:** Jim Bardwell, Publisher; Tiffany Hobbs, Office Manager. **URL:** http://www.gladewatermirror.com. **Mailing address:** PO Box 105357, Atlanta, GA 30348-5357. **Ad Rates:** GLR $.28; BW $394; SAU $4; PCI $6. **Remarks:** Accepts advertising. **Circ:** ‡1900.

8711 ■ Golf Illustrated
Echo Media
900 Circle 75 Pky., Ste. 1600
Atlanta, GA 30339
Phone: (770)955-3535
Fax: (770)955-3599
Publisher's E-mail: salesinfo@echo-media.com
Magazine covering golf instructions. **Freq:** Bimonthly. **URL:** http://www.echo-media.com/medias/details/5872/golf+illustrated. **Remarks:** Accepts advertising. **Circ:** 100000.

Harte-Hanks Pennysaver - See Los Angeles, CA

8712 ■ Health Education Research
Oxford University Press
c/o Dr. Michael P. Eriksen, Ed.-in-Ch.
Georgia State University
Institute of Public Health
Atlanta, GA 30302-3995
Publisher's E-mail: webenquiry.uk@oup.com
Journal covering issues involved in health education and promotion worldwide. **Freq:** Bimonthly. **Print Method:** Web offset. **Trim Size:** 8 1/4 x 10 7/8. **Cols./Page:** 3. **Col. Width:** 2 1/4 inches. **Col. Depth:** 10 inches. **Key Personnel:** D.S. Leathar, Editor, Founder; Dr. Michael P. Eriksen, Executive Editor; P. Aggleton, Associate Editor; J. Allegrante, Board Member; T. Baranowski, Board Member; J.M. Bernhardt, Board Member; S.B. Fawcett, Board Member. **ISSN:** 0268--1153 (print); **EISSN:** 1465--3648 (electronic). **Subscription Rates:** $1587 Institutions print and online; $1985 print and online (corporate); $534 Individuals print; $213 Students print. **URL:** http://her.oxfordjournals.org/. **Mailing address:** PO Box 3995, Atlanta, GA 30302-3995. **Remarks:** Accepts advertising. **Circ:** (Not Reported).

8713 ■ Healthcare Marketing Report
HMR Publications Group Inc.
3180 Presidential Dr., Ste. K
Atlanta, GA 30340
Phone: (770)457-6106
Fax: (770)457-4606
Publisher's E-mail: info@hmrpublicationsgroup.com
Newspaper covering health care marketing in the U.S. **Founded:** 1982. **Freq:** Monthly. **Print Method:** web offset. **Trim Size:** 8 1/2 x 11. **Cols./Page:** 3. **Col. Width:** 2-1/4 inches. **Col. Depth:** 10 inches. **Key Personnel:** Richard Cohen, Editor, phone: (404)377-6131; Jan Michael Lok, Publisher, phone: (770)457-6106. **Subscription Rates:** $235 Individuals; $275 Other countries. **URL:** http://www.hmrpublicationsgroup.com/. **Ad Rates:** BW $700. **Remarks:** Accepts advertising. **Circ:** (Not Reported).

8714 ■ Heartland Real Estate Business
France Publications Inc.
3500 Piedmont Rd., Ste. 415
Atlanta, GA 30305
Phone: (404)832-8262
Fax: (404)832-8260
Publication E-mail: heartland@francepublications.com
Magazine that covers the latest news, developments and trends in commercial real estate in the Midwest. **Freq:** Monthly. **Key Personnel:** Coleman Wood, Editor; Matt Valley, Editor; Scott France, Publisher, phone: (404)832-8262, fax: (404)832-8260. **ISSN:** 1542--8311 (print). **Subscription Rates:** $65 Individuals; $112 Two years. **URL:** http://rebusinessonline.com/magazines/heartland-real-estate-business; http://www.heartlandrebusiness.com/subscribe.html. **Ad Rates:** BW $3,760; 4C $995. **Remarks:** Accepts advertising. **Circ:** (Not Reported).

8715 ■ Herbs for Health
Echo Media
900 Circle 75 Pky., Ste. 1600
Atlanta, GA 30339
Phone: (770)955-3535
Fax: (770)955-3599
Publisher's E-mail: salesinfo@echo-media.com
Magazine covering topics ranging from recent scientific research to consumer guides, medicinal recipes, and legislative updates. **Freq:** Bimonthly. **URL:** http://echomedia.com. **Circ:** 222000.

8716 ■ Hogan's Alley: The Magazine of the Cartoon Arts
Hogan's Alley
PO Box 47684
Atlanta, GA 30362
Publisher's E-mail: sales@cagle.com
Journal covering comics, editorial cartoons, and animated entertainment. **Freq:** Quarterly. **Print Method:** Offset. **Trim Size:** 8 3/8 x 10 3/4. **Cols./Page:** 3. **Col. Width:** 2.25 inches. **Col. Depth:** 9 1/2 inches. **Key Personnel:** Tom Heintjes, Editor. **ISSN:** 1074--7354 (print). **Subscription Rates:** $24 Individuals 1 year, print only. **URL:** http://cartoonician.com. **Remarks:** Accepts advertising. **Circ:** (Not Reported).

8717 ■ Human and Ecological Risk Assessment
Taylor & Francis Group Journals
c/o Barry L. Johnson, Editor
Rollins School of Public Health
Emory University
2618 Riverglenn Cir.
Atlanta, GA 30338-5947
Publisher's E-mail: customerservice@taylorandfrancis.com
Journal focusing on human and/or ecological risk assessment and related fields; including exposure assessment, environmental fate assessment, hazard assessment, risk management, and more. **Freq:** 8/year. **Key Personnel:** Barry L. Johnson, Editor; Ann Bostrom, Associate Editor; Bruce K. Hope, Board Member; David Gaylor, Board Member; Morris Maslia, Board Member; James R. Clark, Board Member; Christopher M. Teaf, Associate Editor. **ISSN:** 1080--7039 (print); **EISSN:** 1549--7860 (electronic). **Subscription Rates:** $357 Individuals print only; $1482 Institutions online only; $1694 Institutions print and online. **URL:** http://tandfonline.com/toc/bher20/current. **Circ:** (Not Reported).

8718 ■ HVAC&R Research
American Society of Heating, Refrigerating and Air-Conditioning Engineers
1791 Tullie Cir. NE
Atlanta, GA 30329
Phone: (404)636-8400
Fax: (404)321-5478
Free: 800-527-4723
Publisher's E-mail: ashrae@ashrae.org
Trade journal covering research and development in heating, refrigeration and air-conditioning engineering. **Freq:** 8/year. **Cols./Page:** 1. **Key Personnel:** Prof. J. Steven Brown, Associate Editor; Prof. Shinsuke Kato, PhD, Associate Editor; Prof. Bjarne W. Olesen, PhD, Associate Editor; James E. Braun, PhD, Associate Editor; Richard Radermacher, PhD, Editor. **ISSN:** 1078--9669 (print). **Subscription Rates:** $98 Members online; $319 Members print and online; $97 Single issue. **URL:** http://www.ashrae.org/publications/page/544. **Formerly:** International Journal of Heating, Ventilating, Air-Conditioning and Refrigeration Research. **Remarks:** Advertising not accepted. **Circ:** (Not Reported).

8719 ■ IAQ Applications
American Society of Heating, Refrigerating and Air-Conditioning Engineers
1791 Tullie Cir. NE
Atlanta, GA 30329
Phone: (404)636-8400
Fax: (404)321-5478

Circulation: • = AAM; △ or • = BPA; ♦ = CAC; ❑ = VAC; ⊕ = PO Statement; ‡ = Publisher's Report; Boldface figures = sworn; Light figures = estimated.

Free: 800-527-4723
Publisher's E-mail: ashrae@ashrae.org
Freq: Quarterly. **Subscription Rates:** $8 PDF copy. **Alt. Formats:** PDF. **Remarks:** Advertising not accepted. **Circ:** (Not Reported).

8720 ■ Information and Organization
Elsevier
c/o L. Mathiassen, Senior Editor
Georgia State University
Department of Computer Information Systems
Atlanta, GA 30302-4015
Publisher's E-mail: t.reller@elsevier.com
Journal covers advances in information and communication technologies. **Freq:** Quarterly. **Key Personnel:** Kalle Lyytinen, Senior Editor; Richard J. Boland, Jr., Senior Editor; M. Newman, Senior Editor; Claude M. Boudreau, Board Member; F. Collopy, Board Member; E. Trauth, Senior Editor; Daniel Robey, Editor-in-Chief; B.S. Butler, Board Member. **ISSN:** 1471--7727 (print). **Subscription Rates:** $426.13 Institutions online; $1278 Institutions print. **URL:** http://www.journals.elsevier.com/information-and-organization. **Mailing address:** PO Box 4015, Atlanta, GA 30302-4015. **Circ:** (Not Reported).

8721 ■ Inside SEMC: quarterly news magazine
Southeastern Museums Conference
PO Box 550746
Atlanta, GA 30355-3246
Phone: (404)814-2048
Fax: (404)814-2031
Publisher's E-mail: membershipservices@semcdirect.net
Magazine containing information from the Southeastern Museums Conference, including current events and state museums updates. **Freq:** Quarterly. **Trim Size:** 8 1/2 x 11. **URL:** http://www.semcdirect.net/page-706788?. **Ad Rates:** BW $1,825. **Remarks:** Accepts advertising. **Circ:** 3800.

8722 ■ InStyle Weddings
Echo Media
900 Circle 75 Pky., Ste. 1600
Atlanta, GA 30339
Phone: (770)955-3535
Fax: (770)955-3599
Publisher's E-mail: salesinfo@echo-media.com
Magazine providing latest wedding styles for all budgets, focusing on basic wedding etiquettes. **Freq:** Monthly. **URL:** http://echomedia.com/medias/details/5216. **Remarks:** Accepts advertising. **Circ:** 1700000.

8723 ■ International Advances in Economic Research
International Atlantic Economic Society
229 Peachtree St. NE, Ste. 650
Atlanta, GA 30303
Phone: (404)965-1555
Fax: (404)965-1556
Publisher's E-mail: iaes@iaes.org
Professional publication covering economics research worldwide. **Freq:** Quarterly. **Print Method:** Offset. **Trim Size:** 5 x 7. **Key Personnel:** Reinhard Neck, Board Member; Walid Hejazi, Board Member; Katherine S. Virgo, Editor, Editor-in-Chief; Paul Hettler, Board Member; Richard J. Cebula, Board Member; Nicholas Apergis, Board Member. **ISSN:** 1083--0898 (print). **Subscription Rates:** Included in membership. **Alt. Formats:** CD-ROM. **URL:** http://iaes.org/international-advances-in-economic-research. **Ad Rates:** BW $300. **Remarks:** Advertising accepted; rates available upon request. **Circ:** (Not Reported).

8724 ■ International Criminal Justice Review
SAGE Publications Inc.
Georgia State University
Atlanta, GA 30302-4018
Phone: (404)413-1040
Fax: (404)413-1030
Publication E-mail: icjr@gsu.edu
Journal presenting system-wide trends and problems on crime and justice throughout the world. **Freq:** Quarterly. **Key Personnel:** Scott Jacques, Editor. **ISSN:** 1057--5677 (print); **EISSN:** 1556--3855 (electronic). **Subscription Rates:** £30 Individuals print only; £212 Institutions e-access; £230 Institutions print only; £235 Institutions print and e-access; £10 Individuals single print; £63 Institutions single print. **URL:** http://icj.sagepub.com; http://uk.sagepub.com/en-gb/asi/international-criminal-justice-review/journal201727. **Mailing address:** PO Box 4018, Atlanta, GA 30302-4018. **Remarks:** Advertising accepted; rates available upon request. **Circ:** (Not Reported).

8725 ■ International Journal of Bioinformatics Research and Applications
Inderscience Publishers
c/o Prof. Yi Pan, Ed.-in-Ch.
Georgia State University
Dept. of Computer Science
34 Peachtree St., Ste. 1450
Atlanta, GA 30302-4110
Publication E-mail: info@inderscience.com
Journal aiming to develop, promote and coordinate the development and practice of bioinformatics and computational biology. **Freq:** 6/year. **Key Personnel:** Prof. Yi Pan, Editor-in-Chief. **ISSN:** 1744--5485 (print); **EISSN:** 1744--5493 (electronic). **Subscription Rates:** $820 Individuals print or online for 1 user; $1147 Individuals print + online. **URL:** http://www.inderscience.com/jhome.php?jcode=ijbra. **Circ:** (Not Reported).

8726 ■ InTouch Weekly
Echo Media
900 Circle 75 Pky., Ste. 1600
Atlanta, GA 30339
Phone: (770)955-3535
Fax: (770)955-3599
Publisher's E-mail: salesinfo@echo-media.com
Hollywood entertainment magazine. **Freq:** Weekly 52/yr. **URL:** http://echomedia.com/medias/details/4331. **Remarks:** Accepts advertising. **Circ:** 27,300,000.

8727 ■ J-14 Magazine
Echo Media
900 Circle 75 Pky., Ste. 1600
Atlanta, GA 30339
Phone: (770)955-3535
Fax: (770)955-3599
Publisher's E-mail: salesinfo@echo-media.com
Magazine for teenagers. **Freq:** 10/year. **URL:** http://echomedia.com/medias/details/4269. **Remarks:** Accepts advertising. **Circ:** 4000000.

8728 ■ JB Dollar Stretcher Magazine
Echo Media
900 Circle 75 Pky., Ste. 1600
Atlanta, GA 30339
Phone: (770)955-3535
Fax: (770)955-3599
Publisher's E-mail: salesinfo@echo-media.com
Glossy coupon magazine. **Freq:** 10/year. **Subscription Rates:** By mail. **URL:** http://echomedia.com/medias/details/11862. **Remarks:** Accepts advertising. **Circ:** (Not Reported).

8729 ■ John Marshall Law Journal
Atlanta's John Marshall Law School
1422 W Peachtree St. NW
Atlanta, GA 30309
Phone: (678)916-2600
Fax: (404)873-3802
Publisher's E-mail: admissions@johnmarshall.edu
Journal focusing on areas of law that have a direct impact on the state and the nation. **Freq:** Semiannual. **Key Personnel:** Brandy Porter, Editor-in-Chief. **URL:** http://www.johnmarshall.edu/ajmls-students/student-services/john-marshall-law-journal. **Circ:** (Not Reported).

8730 ■ Journal of the Association for Information Systems
Association for Information Systems
Computer Information Systems Dept.
J. Mack Robinson College of Business
Georgia State University
35 Broad St., Ste. 917
Atlanta, GA 30303
Phone: (404)413-7445
Publisher's E-mail: office@aisnet.org
Journal publishing scholarship in the field of information systems. **Freq:** Periodic. **ISSN:** 1536-9323 (print). **Subscription Rates:** Included in membership; $40 Nonmembers; $135 Libraries. **URL:** http://aisel.aisnet.org/jais/. **Mailing address:** PO Box 2712, Atlanta, GA 30301-2712. **Remarks:** Advertising not accepted. **Circ:** (Not Reported).

8731 ■ Journal of Biblical Literature
Society of Biblical Literature
Luce Ctr.
825 Houston Mill Rd.
Atlanta, GA 30329
Phone: (404)727-3100
Fax: (404)727-3101
Publication E-mail: sblorders@aidcvt.com
Freq: Quarterly. **Print Method:** Offset. **Trim Size:** 6 x 9. **Cols./Page:** 1. **Col. Width:** 54 nonpareils. **Col. Depth:** 96 agate lines. **Key Personnel:** James C. VanderKam, Editor. **ISSN:** 0021--9231 (print); **EISSN:** 1934--3876 (electronic). **Subscription Rates:** Included in membership online only; $295 Institutions print & online; $220 Institutions print or online; $55 Members print only. **URL:** http://sbl-site.org/publications/journals_jbl_noLogin.aspx. **Ad Rates:** BW $600; 4C $400. **Remarks:** Accepts advertising. **Circ:** 3000, 9000.

8732 ■ Journal of Individual Psychology: The Journal of Adlerian Theory, Research, and Practice
University of Texas Press Studies in Latin American Popular Culture
GSU Educational Research Bureau
Atlanta, GA 30302-3977
Phone: (404)413-8090
Publisher's E-mail: utpress@uts.cc.utexas.edu
Journal covering Adlerian practices, principles and theoretical development in the field of psychology. Journal of the North American Society of Adlerian Psychology. **Freq:** Quarterly. **Trim Size:** 6 x 9. **Key Personnel:** Roy M. Kern, Editor; Bill Curlette, Editor. **ISSN:** 1522--2527 (print). **Subscription Rates:** $60 Individuals USA; $80 Individuals Canada; $87 Individuals international; $256 Institutions USA; $276 Institutions, Canada; $283 Institutions, other countries. **URL:** http://www.utexas.edu/utpress/journals/jip.html. **Mailing address:** PO Box 3977, Atlanta, GA 30302-3977. **Remarks:** Accepts advertising. **Circ:** (Not Reported).

8733 ■ Journal of the Medical Association of Georgia
Medical Association of Georgia
1849 The Exchange, Ste. 200
Atlanta, GA 30339-2027
Phone: (678)303-9290
Fax: (678)303-3732
Free: 800-282-0224
Publication E-mail: aboltz@mag.org
Medical journal. **Freq:** Quarterly. **Print Method:** Offset. **Trim Size:** 8 1/4 x 11. **Cols./Page:** 3. **Col. Width:** 39 nonpareils. **Col. Depth:** 133 agate lines. **Key Personnel:** Stanley W. Sherman, MD, Editor. **ISSN:** 0025--7028 (print). **Subscription Rates:** Included in membership. **URL:** http://mag.org/resources/journal. **Ad Rates:** BW $1450; 4C $1825. **Remarks:** Accepts advertising. **Circ:** 8000, 7500.

8734 ■ Journal of Nursing Measurement
Springer Publishing Co.
c/o Ora L. Strickland, PhD, Sen. Ed.
Nell Hodgson Woodruff School of Nursing
Emory University
Atlanta, GA 30322
Phone: (404)727-7941
Fax: (404)727-0536
Publisher's E-mail: cs@springerpub.com
Scholarly journal covering tools, approaches, or procedures for the measurement of variables for nursing practice, education, health and research. **Freq:** 3/year. **Trim Size:** 7 x 10. **Cols./Page:** 1. **Col. Width:** 5 inches. **Col. Depth:** 10 inches. **Key Personnel:** Janice L. Hinkle, PhD, Editor-in-Chief. **ISSN:** 1063--3749 (print); **EISSN:** 1945--7049 (electronic). **Subscription Rates:** $188 Individuals print and online; $240 Other countries print and online; $461 Institutions print and online; $545 Institutions, other countries print and online. **URL:** http://www.springerpub.com/journal-of-nursing-measurement.html. **Ad Rates:** BW $415; 4C $2,515. **Remarks:** Accepts advertising. **Circ:** Combined 400.

8735 ■ Journal of Physical Activity and Health
Human Kinetics Inc.
c/o Jennifer M. Hootman, Editor.-in-Chief Emeriti
Division of Adult & Community Health
National Center for Chronic Disease Prevention & Health Promotion
4770 Buford Hwy. NE, MS K5
Atlanta, GA 30341-3717
Publisher's E-mail: info@hkusa.com
Interdisciplinary journal for researchers in fields of chronic disease (e.g., cancer, heart disease, mental health, weight control, neurologic deficits, etc.), where physical activity may play a role in prevention, treat-

ment, or rehabilitation. Publishes original research and review papers examining the relationship between physical activity and health and studying physical activity as an exposure, as well as an outcome. Publishes articles examining how physical activity influences all aspects of health. **Freq:** 8/year. **Print Method:** Offset. **Trim Size:** 8 1/2 x 11. **Key Personnel:** Jennifer M. Hootman, Editor-in-Chief; Harold W. Kohl, III, Editor-in-Chief; Loretta DiPietro, Editor-in-Chief. **ISSN:** 1543--3080 (print). **Subscription Rates:** $179 Individuals online and print; $144 Students online and print; $139 Individuals online; $104 Students online; $1149 Institutions online and print; $979 Institutions online. **URL:** http://journals.humankinetics.com/JPAH. **Circ:** (Not Reported).

8736 ■ KNOW Atlanta Magazine: The Premier Relocation Guide
New South Publishing Inc.
9040 Roswell Rd., Ste. 210
Atlanta, GA 30350
Phone: (770)650-1102
Fax: (770)650-2848
Relocation guide about Atlanta. **Freq:** Quarterly. **Print Method:** Web Offset. **Trim Size:** 81/8 x 10 7/8. **Cols./Page:** 3. **Col. Width:** 1 3/4 inches. **Col. Depth:** 10 inches. **Key Personnel:** Larry Lebovitz, President; Lindsay Field, Editor. **URL:** http://www.knowatlanta.com. **Ad Rates:** BW $4,640; 4C $5,800. **Remarks:** Accepts advertising. **Circ:** Controlled ⊕**48000**.

8737 ■ Lake Travis View
Cox Newspapers Inc.
6205 Peachtree Dunwoody Rd.
Atlanta, GA 30328-4524
Phone: (678)645-0000
Fax: (678)645-5002
Newspaper covering the news and events in Austin, Texas. **Freq:** Weekly (Thurs.). **Key Personnel:** Ed Allen, Editor, phone: (512)912-2502. **Subscription Rates:** Free. **URL:** http://www.statesman.com/s/news/local/lake-travis-view. **Remarks:** Accepts advertising. **Circ:** (Not Reported).

8738 ■ Landover-New Carrollton Gazette
Echo Media
900 Circle 75 Pky., Ste. 1600
Atlanta, GA 30339
Phone: (770)955-3535
Fax: (770)955-3599
Publisher's E-mail: salesinfo@echo-media.com
Community newspaper. **Freq:** Weekly (Thurs.). **Key Personnel:** Alison Walker, Assistant Managing Editor, phone: (240)473-7544, fax: (240)473-7501. **Subscription Rates:** Free. **URL:** http://echomedia.com/medias/details/7796. **Remarks:** Accepts advertising. **Circ:** Free ■ **24922**.

8739 ■ The Leader
CoreNet Global
133 Peachtree St. NE, Ste. 3000
Atlanta, GA 30303-1815
Phone: (404)589-3200
Fax: (404)589-3201
Free: 800-726-8111
Publication E-mail: leader@corenetglobal.org
Professional magazine for the corporate real estate industry. **Freq:** Bimonthly 6/yr. **Trim Size:** 9 x 10.875. **Key Personnel:** Tim Venable, Vice President. **Subscription Rates:** $75 Individuals; $85 Canada; $95 Individuals outside North America; Free for members. **URL:** http://www2.corenetglobal.org/learning/publications/the_leader.vsp. **Ad Rates:** BW $5,900. **Remarks:** Accepts advertising. **Circ:** Controlled 8000.

8740 ■ LOMA Resource
LOMA
6190 Powers Ferry Rd., Ste. 600
Atlanta, GA 30339
Phone: (770)951-1770
Fax: (770)984-6422
Free: 800-ASK-LOMA
Publication E-mail: resource@loma.org
Life insurance industry management magazine. **Freq:** Monthly. **Print Method:** Offset. **Trim Size:** 8 1/8 x 10 7/8. **Cols./Page:** 3. **Col. Width:** 13 picas. **Col. Depth:** 60 picas. **Key Personnel:** Ron Clark, Director, Advertising, phone: (770)984-3718. **Subscription Rates:** $75 Nonmembers print version; $100 Nonmembers Canada and overseas. **URL:** http://www.loma.org/Resource. **Ad Rates:** BW $3700; 4C $1380. **Remarks:** Accepts advertising. **Circ:** Non-paid 18,960, 18,225, 18,000.

Los Angeles Watts Times - See Los Angeles, CA

8741 ■ Main Street Values
Echo Media
900 Circle 75 Pky., Ste. 1600
Atlanta, GA 30339
Phone: (770)955-3535
Fax: (770)955-3599
Publisher's E-mail: salesinfo@echo-media.com
Newspaper covering local retail and service oriented advertisers. **Freq:** Monthly. **Subscription Rates:** By mail. **URL:** http://echomedia.com/medias/details/828. **Remarks:** Accepts advertising. **Circ:** (Not Reported).

8742 ■ Marshall News Messenger
Cox Newspapers Inc.
6205 Peachtree Dunwoody Rd.
Atlanta, GA 30328-4524
Phone: (678)645-0000
Fax: (678)645-5002
General newspaper. **Freq:** Daily and Sun. (eve.). **Print Method:** Offset. **Cols./Page:** 6. **Col. Width:** 22 nonpareils. **Col. Depth:** 301 agate lines. **Key Personnel:** Jerry Pye, Publisher, phone: (903)927-5977; Johnnie Fancher, Advertising Executive, phone: (903)927-5986. **Subscription Rates:** $132 Individuals Tuesday - Sunday, home delivery; $180 Individuals Tuesday - Sunday, by mail; $156 Individuals Tuesday - Sunday, home delivery + E-edition. **URL:** http://www.marshallnewsmessenger.com. **Ad Rates:** BW $873.33; 4C $1,048.33; SAU $8.40. **Remarks:** Accepts advertising. **Circ:** Mon.-Fri. 6853, Sun. 7238.

8743 ■ Mathematical Programming
Springer-Verlag GmbH & Company KG
c/o Alexander Shapiro, Editor-in-Chief
Georgia Tech
School of Industrial and Systems Engineering
765 Ferst Dr.
Atlanta, GA 30332-0205
Publisher's E-mail: customerservice@springer.com
Journal concerned with all aspects of mathematical programming such as linear, nonlinear, integer and stochastic programming, computational testing, techniques for formulating and applying mathematical programming models, unconstrained optimization, convexity and the theory of polyhedra, and control and game theory. **Freq:** Semiannual. **Key Personnel:** S.J. Wright, Associate Editor; Alexander Shapiro, Editor-in-Chief. **ISSN:** 0025--5610 (print); **EISSN:** 1436--4646 (electronic). **Subscription Rates:** $772 Institutions print including free access or e-only; $926 Institutions print plus enhanced access; €792 Institutions print including free access or e-only; €950 Institutions print plus enhanced access. **URL:** http://www.springer.com/mathematics/journal/10107; http://link.springer.com/journal/10107. **Remarks:** Advertising accepted; rates available upon request. **Circ:** (Not Reported).

8744 ■ Medicinal Research Reviews
John Wiley & Sons Inc.
c/o Binghe Wang, Editor-in-Chief
Georgia State University
Department of Chemistry
Atlanta, GA 30302-4098
Publisher's E-mail: info@wiley.com
Review journal embracing all aspects of research and addressing the study of disease states and the consequent development of therapeutic agents. Features developments in specific areas of medicinal research, including a total review of the history leading up to the introduction of a new pharmaceutical. **Freq:** Bimonthly. **Print Method:** Offset. **Trim Size:** 7 1/4 x 10 1/4. **Cols./Page:** 1. **Col. Width:** 78 nonpareils. **Col. Depth:** 140 agate lines. **Key Personnel:** Binghe Wang, Editor-in-Chief; George DeStevens, Editor, Founder; Dhiren R. Thakker, Board Member; Erik De Clercq, Board Member; Rodolfo Paoletti, Board Member; Teruna Siahaan, Board Member; Gunda Georg, Board Member; W.L.F. Armarego, Board Member; Wayne Brouillette, Board Member. **ISSN:** 0198--6325 (print); **EISSN:** 1098--1128 (electronic). **Subscription Rates:** $3360 Institutions print or online; $4032 Institutions print and online; $3360 Institutions, Canada and Mexico online only; $4139 Institutions, Canada and Mexico print and online; $3449 Institutions, Canada and Mexico print only; £1717 Institutions online only; £2141 Institutions print and online; £1784 Institutions print only; €2168 Institutions online only; €2705 Institutions print and online; €2254 Institutions print only; $3360 Institutions, other countries online only; $4192 Institutions, other countries print and online; $3493 Institutions, other countries print only. **URL:** http://onlinelibrary.wiley.com/journal/10.1002/(ISSN)1098-1128; http://www.wiley.com/WileyCDA/WileyTitle/productCd-MED.html. **Mailing address:** PO Box 4098, Atlanta, GA 30302-4098. **Ad Rates:** BW $795; 4C $1040. **Remarks:** Accepts advertising. **Circ:** 3850.

8745 ■ Morbidity and Mortality Weekly Report: Morbidity and Mortality Weekly Report
Centers for Disease Control and Prevention Office of Scientific and Health Communications
2900 Woodcock Blvd.
Atlanta, GA 30341
Phone: (404)639-3311
Fax: (888)232-6348
Free: 800-232-4636
Publisher's E-mail: cdcinfo@cdc.gov
Magazine focusing on public health problems and diseases. **Freq:** Weekly (Fri.). **Trim Size:** 5 15/16 x 8 1/2. **Key Personnel:** Ron Moolenaar, MD, Editor-in-Chief. **ISSN:** 0149--2195 (print); **EISSN:** 1545--861X (electronic). **Alt. Formats:** PDF. **URL:** http://www.cdc.gov/mmwr/index2016.html. **Formerly:** MMWR. **Remarks:** Advertising not accepted. **Circ:** Combined 44000.

8746 ■ Mundo Hispanico
Mundo Hispanico
PO Box 13808
Atlanta, GA 30324-0808
Phone: (404)881-0441
Fax: (404)881-6085
Publication E-mail: editorial@mundohispanico.com
Newspaper (tabloid) for the Hispanic community (English and Spanish). **Freq:** Weekly. **Key Personnel:** Anibal Torres, Director, Publisher; Gerard Delaney, General Manager; Rodrigo Cervantes, Editor. **ISSN:** 1051--4147 (print). **URL:** http://mundohispanico.com. **Formerly:** Mundo Hispanico Inc. **Ad Rates:** GLR $18.83; BW $50; 4C $450; PCI $17.50. **Remarks:** Advertising accepted; rates available upon request. **Circ:** Combined 57500.

8747 ■ Net News: Official Publication of the Atlanta Lawn Tennis Association (ALTA)
New South Publishing Inc.
9040 Roswell Rd., Ste. 210
Atlanta, GA 30350
Phone: (770)650-1102
Fax: (770)650-2848
Tennis news magazine. **Freq:** Bimonthly. **Print Method:** Web Offset. **Trim Size:** 8 1/8 x 10 7/8. **Cols./Page:** 3. **Key Personnel:** John Hanna, Publisher, phone: (770)650-1102. **Subscription Rates:** Free to paying members. **URL:** http://www.netnewsmag.com/web. **Remarks:** Accepts advertising. **Circ:** (Not Reported).

New Orleans Homes & Lifestyles - See New Orleans, LA

8748 ■ The North Stoddard Countian: A Compilation of the Bloomfield Vindicator and the Advance Statesman
Echo Media
900 Circle 75 Pky., Ste. 1600
Atlanta, GA 30339
Phone: (770)955-3535
Fax: (770)955-3599
Publisher's E-mail: salesinfo@echo-media.com
Newspaper with an Independent orientation. **Founded:** 1877. **Freq:** Weekly (Wed.). **Print Method:** Offset. **Cols./Page:** 6. **Col. Width:** 12.5 picas. **Col. Depth:** 21 inches. **Key Personnel:** Michael Puffer, Chief Executive Officer. **Subscription Rates:** Free. **URL:** http://www.echo-media.com/MediaDetailNP.asp?IDNumber=5685. **Formed by the merger of:** The Bloomfield Vindicator. **Formerly:** The Vindicator. **Remarks:** Accepts advertising. **Circ:** Mon.-Fri. ‡2300.

8749 ■ Northside Neighbor
Neighbor Newspapers Inc.
5290 Roswell Rd. NW, Ste. M
Atlanta, GA 30342
Phone: (404)256-3100
Fax: (404)256-3292
Publication E-mail: nside@neighbornewspapers.com

Circulation: ★ = AAM; △ or • = BPA; ♦ = CAC; ❑ = VAC; ⊕ = PO Statement; ‡ = Publisher's Report; Boldface figures = sworn; Light figures = estimated.

Community newspaper. **Freq:** Weekly (Wed.). **Print Method:** Offset. **Cols./Page:** 6. **Col. Width:** 26 nonpareils. **Col. Depth:** 301 agate lines. **Key Personnel:** Everett Catts, Editor. **USPS:** 865-620. **URL:** http://www.mdjonline.com/neighbor_newspapers/northside_sandy_springs. **Ad Rates:** BW $3434; 4C $3784; SAU $17.10; PCI $27.75. **Remarks:** Accepts advertising. **Circ:** ‡28200.

8750 ■ Oral History Review
Oral History Association
c/o Gayle Knight, Program Associate
Dept. of History
Georgia State University
Atlanta, GA 30302-4117
Phone: (404)413-5751
Fax: (404)413-6384
Publisher's E-mail: oha@gsu.edu
Scholarly journal of the Oral History Association covering oral history of people who have participated in important political, cultural, and economic social developments in modern times. **Freq:** Semiannual. **Trim Size:** 6 x 9. **Key Personnel:** Kathryn Nasstrom, Editor-in-Chief; Doug Boyd, Editor. **ISSN:** 0094--0798 (print); **EISSN:** 1533--8592 (electronic). **Subscription Rates:** £112 Institutions online only; $174 Institutions online only; €151 Institutions online only; £129 Institutions print only; $200 Institutions print only; €174 Institutions print only; £141 Institutions print and online; $218 Institutions print and online; €189 Institutions print and online; Included in membership. **URL:** http://ohr.oxfordjournals.org; http://www.oralhistory.org/publications/oral-history-review. **Mailing address:** c/o Gayle Knight, Program AssociatePO Box 4117, Atlanta, GA 30302-4117. **Ad Rates:** BW $325. **Remarks:** Accepts advertising. **Circ:** 1065.

8751 ■ Performance Management Ezine
Aubrey Daniels International
3344 Peachtree Rd. NE, Ste. 1050
Atlanta, GA 30326-1436
Phone: (678)904-6140
Fax: (678)904-6141
Free: 800-223-6191
Publisher's E-mail: info@aubreydaniels.com
Magazine promoting improved productivity and performance through use of applied behavioral analysis. **Freq:** Monthly. **Key Personnel:** Aubrey Daniels, Founder. **ISSN:** 0734--029X (print). **URL:** http://www.pmezine.com. **Formerly:** Performance Management Magazine. **Remarks:** Advertising not accepted. **Circ:** 3000.

Performances Magazine - See Los Angeles, CA

8752 ■ The Pflugerville Pflag
Cox Newspapers Inc.
6205 Peachtree Dunwoody Rd.
Atlanta, GA 30328-4524
Phone: (678)645-0000
Fax: (678)645-5002
Community newspaper. **Freq:** Weekly (Thurs.). **Print Method:** Offset. **Cols./Page:** 5. **Col. Width:** 1 7/8 inches. **Col. Depth:** 11 1/2 inches. **Key Personnel:** Keith Tooley, Publisher; Mark Loyd, Editor. **ISSN:** 0892--1105 (print). **URL:** http://www.coxmediagroup.com/austin/solutions. **Feature Editors:** Monica DiSchiano, *Features*, sports@pflugervillepflag.com. **Ad Rates:** GLR $.60; BW $506.25; 4C $606.25; PCI $8.10. **Remarks:** Accepts advertising. **Circ:** ‡4000.

Phoenix Clipper Marketplace - See Phoenix, AZ

Phoenix Saguaro Gold - See Phoenix, AZ

Phoenix TV y Mas - See Phoenix, AZ

8753 ■ Pink
Pink Magazine
790 Marietta St. NW
Atlanta, GA 30318
Phone: (404)574-5353
Publication E-mail: info@littlepinkbook.com
Magazine for professional women. **Freq:** 7/yr. **Key Personnel:** Cynthia Good, Chief Executive Officer, Editor. **Subscription Rates:** $15 U.S.; $35 Canada; $49 Other countries. **URL:** http://www.littlepinkbook.com. **Remarks:** Accepts advertising. **Circ:** (Not Reported).

Pomona Civil Citizen's Journal - See Los Angeles, CA

8754 ■ Prion
Taylor & Francis Online
Dept. of Biology
Georgia Institute of Technology
Atlanta, GA 30332
Publisher's E-mail: support@tandfonline.com
Peer-reviewed journal focusing on protein folding and misfolding, assembly disorders and structural inheritance. **Freq:** 6/year. **Key Personnel:** Richard A. Rachubinski, Board Member; Greenfield Sluder, Board Member; Sven J. Saupe, Board Member; Adriano Aguzzi, Board Member; Dr. Yury Chernoff, Editor-in-Chief; Brian S. Cox, Board Member; Michael Sherman, Board Member; Stanley Prusiner, Board Member; Douglas M. Cyr, Board Member. **ISSN:** 1933--6896 (print); **EISSN:** 1933--690X (electronic). **Subscription Rates:** $74 Institutions online and print; $65 Individuals online only; $1080 Institutions online and print; $945 Institutions online only. **URL:** http://www.tandfonline.com/loi/kprn20#.VzaLYTWrQdU. **Circ:** (Not Reported).

8755 ■ Puppetry International
Union Internationale de la Marionnette
1404 Spring St. NW
Atlanta, GA 30309
Phone: (404)881-5110
Fax: (404)873-9907
Publisher's E-mail: unima@mindspring.com
Freq: Semiannual. **Key Personnel:** Andrew Periale, Editor. **Subscription Rates:** Included in membership; $5.95 Individuals newsstand price; $3 Individuals /back issue. **URL:** http://www.unima-usa.org/puppetry-international. **Ad Rates:** BW $350. **Remarks:** Accepts advertising. **Circ:** 5000.

8756 ■ Quest
Informa UK Ltd.
c/o Mike W. Metzler, Editor
Dept. of Kinesiology and Health
Georgia State University
30 Courtland St., SE
Atlanta, GA 30303
Phone: (404)413-8373
Fax: (404)413-8053
Publisher's E-mail: marketing.enquiries@informa.com
Journal featuring articles that examine critical issues facing today's physical education faculty and students. **Founded:** 1949. **Freq:** Quarterly February, May, August, November. **Print Method:** Offset. **Trim Size:** 6 x 9. **Key Personnel:** Mike W. Metzler. **ISSN:** 0033-6297 (print). **Subscription Rates:** $84 Individuals print and online; $379 Institutions print and online. **Ad Rates:** BW $300. **Remarks:** Accepts advertising. **Circ:** (Not Reported).

8757 ■ R&R TV
Echo Media
900 Circle 75 Pky., Ste. 1600
Atlanta, GA 30339
Phone: (770)955-3535
Fax: (770)955-3599
Publisher's E-mail: salesinfo@echo-media.com
TV magazine for the US military market. **Freq:** Monthly. **URL:** http://echomedia.com/medias/details/2639. **Remarks:** Advertising not accepted. **Circ:** 792000.

8758 ■ Review of Biblical Literature
Society of Biblical Literature
Luce Ctr.
825 Houston Mill Rd.
Atlanta, GA 30329
Phone: (404)727-3100
Fax: (404)727-3101
Publisher's E-mail: sblexec@sbl-site.org
Journal containing reviews of books in biblical studies and related fields. **Freq:** Annual Weekly Annual: print edition weekly: electronic. **Subscription Rates:** Free. **URL:** http://www.bookreviews.org/; http://www.sbl-site.org/educational/researchtools.aspx. **Remarks:** Accepts advertising. **Circ:** 9000.

8759 ■ The Round Rock Leader
Cox Media Group Inc.
6205 Peachtree Dunwoody Rd.
Atlanta, GA 30328
Phone: (678)645-0000
Fax: (678)645-5002
Community newspaper. **Freq:** 3/week Tuesday, Thursday and Saturday. **Print Method:** Offset. **Cols./Page:** 6. **Col. Width:** 12.5 picas. **Col. Depth:** 21 inches. **Key Personnel:** Brad Stutzman, Editor; Marcial Guajardo, Managing Editor. **ISSN:** 0164-9124 (print). **Subscription Rates:** $54.60 Individuals; $78 Out of country. **URL:** http://www.statesman.com/s/news/local/round-rock-leader. **Remarks:** Accepts advertising. **Circ:** (Not Reported).

8760 ■ Sandy Springs Neighbor
Neighbor Newspapers Inc.
5290 Roswell Rd. NW, Ste. M
Atlanta, GA 30342
Phone: (404)256-3100
Fax: (404)256-3292
Publication E-mail: nside@neighbornewspapers.com
Community newspaper. **Freq:** Weekly (Wed.). **Key Personnel:** Otis A. Brumby, Jr., Publisher. **Subscription Rates:** Free. **URL:** http://neighbornewspapers.com/nni_al?neighbor=sandy. **Remarks:** other Neighbor Newspapers. **Circ:** ‡10150.

8761 ■ Science and Technology for the Built Environment
American Society of Heating, Refrigerating and Air-Conditioning Engineers
1791 Tullie Cir. NE
Atlanta, GA 30329
Phone: (404)636-8400
Fax: (404)321-5478
Free: 800-527-4723
Publisher's E-mail: ashrae@ashrae.org
Freq: Semiannual June and December. **ISSN:** 1078--9669 (print). **Subscription Rates:** $318 Institutions online copy; $363 Institutions print and online. **Alt. Formats:** CD-ROM. **URL:** http://www.ashrae.org/resources--publications/hvac-r-research. **Formerly:** International Journal of HUAC&R Research. **Remarks:** Advertising not accepted. **Circ:** 60000.

8762 ■ Selden/Farmingville Suffolk Life
Echo Media
900 Circle 75 Pky., Ste. 1600
Atlanta, GA 30339
Phone: (770)955-3535
Fax: (770)955-3599
Community newspaper. **Freq:** Weekly (Wed.). **Print Method:** Offset. **Trim Size:** 10 1/2 x 14. **Cols./Page:** 8. **Col. Width:** 10 picas. **Col. Depth:** 200 agate lines. **Subscription Rates:** Free. **URL:** http://www.echo-media.com/MediaDetailNP.asp?IDNumber=9211. **Ad Rates:** GLR $1.19; SAU $23.85; PCI $121.93. **Remarks:** Accepts advertising. **Circ:** Mon.-Fri. 13100.

8763 ■ SkyWest Magazine
Echo Media
900 Circle 75 Pky., Ste. 1600
Atlanta, GA 30339
Phone: (770)955-3535
Fax: (770)955-3599
Publisher's E-mail: salesinfo@echo-media.com
Flight magazine. **Freq:** 6/year. **Remarks:** Accepts advertising. **Circ:** 516,000.

The Smyrna Neighbor - See Smyrna

8764 ■ Social Psychology Quarterly
American Sociological Association
Emory University
Dept. of Sociology
1555 Dickey Dr.
Atlanta, GA 30322
Publication E-mail: spq@emory.edu
Journal on society's impact on the individual and on individual interaction in small groups and communities. **Freq:** Quarterly March, June, September, December. **Print Method:** Offset. **Trim Size:** 6 3/4 x 9 7/8. **Cols./Page:** 2. **Col. Width:** 27 nonpareils. **Col. Depth:** 112 agate lines. **ISSN:** 0190--2725 (print). **Subscription Rates:** $45 Members /year; $30 Students members; $446 Institutions print and online; $402 Institutions online only. **URL:** http://www.asanet.org/journals/spq/index.cfm. **Formerly:** Sociometry; Social Psychology. **Ad Rates:** BW $540; 4C $1,115. **Remarks:** Accepts advertising. **Circ:** ‡2300, 3500.

8765 ■ South Atlantic Review
South Atlantic Modern Language Association
Georgia State University
941 Langdale Hall
38 Peachtree Ctr. Ave.
Atlanta, GA 30303
Phone: (404)413-5817
Fax: (404)413-5830
Publication E-mail: sar@samla.org

Freq: Quarterly. **Print Method:** Offset. **Trim Size:** 6 x 9. **Cols./Page:** 1. **Col. Width:** 50 nonpareils. **Col. Depth:** 112 agate lines. **Key Personnel:** R. Barton Palmer, Editor. **ISSN:** 0277--335X (print); **EISSN:** 2325--7970 (electronic). **Subscription Rates:** $60 Individuals; $80 Institutions; $80 Libraries; $35 Students. **URL:** http://samla.memberclicks.net/sar. **Formerly**: South Atlantic Bulletin. **Mailing address:** PO Box 3968, Atlanta, GA 30302-3968. **Ad Rates:** BW $150; BW $125. **Remarks:** Advertising accepted; rates available upon request. **Circ:** Paid ‡1300, Non-paid ‡200.

8766 ■ South Cobb Neighbor
Echo Media
900 Circle 75 Pky., Ste. 1600
Atlanta, GA 30339
Phone: (770)955-3535
Fax: (770)955-3599
Publisher's E-mail: salesinfo@echo-media.com
Community newspaper. **Freq:** Weekly (Thurs.). **Subscription Rates:** Free. **URL:** http://www.echo-media.com/mediaDetail.php?ID=4307. **Remarks:** Accepts advertising. **Circ:** Non-paid ♦**20,275**.

8767 ■ Southern Changes
Southern Regional Council
133 Carnegie Way, NW, Ste. 900
Atlanta, GA 30303-1024
Publisher's E-mail: info@southerncouncil.org
Journal covering the politics, history, literature, racial, social and economic conditions of the South. Includes book reviews. **Freq:** Quarterly. **Trim Size:** 8 x 10 3/4. **Cols./Page:** 2. **Col. Width:** 3 1/2 inches. **Col. Depth:** 9 inches. **Key Personnel:** Allen Tullos, Editor; Wendy S. Johnson, Publisher. **ISSN:** 0193--2446 (print). **Subscription Rates:** $75 Institutions; $30 Individuals; Included in membership. **URL:** http://www.southerncouncil.org/publication.html. **Ad Rates:** BW $350. **Remarks:** Accepts advertising. **Circ:** Combined 5000.

8768 ■ Southern Spaces
Emory University
201 Dowman Dr.
Atlanta, GA 30322
Phone: (404)727-6123
Journal that publishes contextual materials on the South that use ideas of place and space as organizing principles. **Freq:** Continuous. **Key Personnel:** Katie Rawson; Sarah Melton, Assistant Managing Editor; Allen Tullos, Senior Editor; Jesse P. Karlsberg, Managing Editor. **ISSN:** 1551--2754 (print). **Subscription Rates:** Free. **URL:** http://www.southernspaces.org. **Remarks:** Accepts advertising. **Circ:** (Not Reported).

8769 ■ Southface Journal of Sustainable Building
Southface Energy Institute
241 Pine St. NE
Atlanta, GA 30308
Phone: (404)872-3549
Fax: (404)872-5009
Publisher's E-mail: socialmedia@southface.org
Freq: Quarterly. **Subscription Rates:** included in membership dues. **URL:** http://www.southface.org/learning-center/library/. **Remarks:** Accepts advertising. **Circ:** 3000.

8770 ■ The Spenser Review
International Spenser Society
Dept. of English
Emory University
Callaway Ste. N302
537 Kilgo Cir.
Atlanta, GA 30322
Journal containing single reviews and essay-reviews and reports of topics in and around Edmund Spenser studies with abstracts of articles and essays in collections, CFPs and announcements of conferences, and the text of the annual Hugh McLean memorial lecture from the International Spenser Society luncheon at the MLA. **Freq:** 3/year winter (January 31), spring-summer (May 30), and fall (September 30). **Key Personnel:** David Lee Miller, Editor. **Subscription Rates:** Included in membership; $14 U.S. and Canada for nonmembers; $19 Other countries for nonmembers. **URL:** http://www.english.cam.ac.uk/spenseronline/review. **Also known as**: Spenser Online. **Remarks:** Advertising not accepted. **Circ:** (Not Reported).

8771 ■ Strategic Planning for Energy and the Environment
Association of Energy Engineers
3168 Mercer University Dr.
Atlanta, GA 30341
Phone: (770)447-5083
Magazine on energy and environmental planning. **Freq:** Quarterly. **Print Method:** Offset. **Cols./Page:** 1. **Col. Width:** 52 nonpareils. **Col. Depth:** 98 agate lines. **Key Personnel:** Wayne C. Turner, PhD, Editor. **ISSN:** 1048--5236 (print); **EISSN:** 1546--0126 (electronic). **Subscription Rates:** $375 Individuals print only; $399 Institutions online only; $456 Institutions print & online. **URL:** http://www.fairmontpress.com; http://www.tandfonline.com/toc/ustp20/current#.VOvNcHyUfIc; http://www.aeecenter.org/i4a/pages/index.cfm?pageid=3284#Publications; http://www.tandfonline.com/action/pricing?journalCode=ustp20#.Vc3aQ9L7JFI. **Ad Rates:** BW $600. **Remarks:** Accepts advertising. **Circ:** Paid 8600.

8772 ■ Sun Life Magazine
Echo Media
900 Circle 75 Pky., Ste. 1600
Atlanta, GA 30339
Phone: (770)955-3535
Fax: (770)955-3599
Publisher's E-mail: salesinfo@echo-media.com
Community magazine reflecting the lifestyle and activities of residents of the retirement communities in the N.W. Valley of Phoenix area. **Freq:** 9/yr (September through May). **Print Method:** Offset. **Trim Size:** 8 1/4 x 10 3/4. **Cols./Page:** 2 and 3. **Col. Width:** 20.5 and 13.5 picas. **Col. Depth:** 9 3/4 inches. **Subscription Rates:** $22 Individuals. **URL:** http://www.echo-media.com/MediaDetail.asp?IDNumber=6143. **Formerly**: Sun Cities Life. **Ad Rates:** BW $1,615; 4C $1,990. **Remarks:** Accepts advertising. **Circ:** 45000.

8773 ■ The Technique: The South's Liveliest College Newspaper
Georgia Institute of Technology
North Ave.
Atlanta, GA 30332
Phone: (404)894-2000
Collegiate newspaper. **Freq:** Weekly (Fri.). **Print Method:** Offset. **Trim Size:** 5 x 15. **Cols./Page:** 5. **Col. Width:** 25 nonpareils. **Col. Depth:** 192 agate lines. **Key Personnel:** Vivian Fan, Managing Editor; Kamna Bohra, Editor-in-Chief; Mike Donohue, Business Manager. **URL:** http://nique.net. **Ad Rates:** PCI $12. **Remarks:** Accepts advertising. **Circ:** ‡7000.

8774 ■ Texas Mint Family Living
Echo Media
900 Circle 75 Pky., Ste. 1600
Atlanta, GA 30339
Phone: (770)955-3535
Fax: (770)955-3599
Publisher's E-mail: salesinfo@echo-media.com
Magazine on family living. **Freq:** Bimonthly. **Remarks:** Accepts advertising. **Circ:** (Not Reported).

8775 ■ Texas Neighbors Farm Bureau Magazine
Echo Media
900 Circle 75 Pky., Ste. 1600
Atlanta, GA 30339
Phone: (770)955-3535
Fax: (770)955-3599
Publisher's E-mail: salesinfo@echo-media.com
Magazine focusing on general interest publications. **Freq:** Quarterly. **Subscription Rates:** By mail. **Remarks:** Advertising not accepted. **Circ:** (Not Reported).

8776 ■ Texas Real Estate Business
France Publications Inc.
3500 Piedmont Rd., Ste. 415
Atlanta, GA 30305
Phone: (404)832-8262
Fax: (404)832-8260
Magazine that covers the latest news, developments and trends in commercial real estate in Texas. **Freq:** Monthly. **Key Personnel:** Daniel Beaird, Editor; John Nelson, Associate Editor; Scott France, Publisher. **Subscription Rates:** $64 Individuals; $110 Two years. **URL:** http://rebusinessonline.com/magazines/texas-real-estate-business; http://www.texasrebusiness.com/subscribe.html. **Ad Rates:** BW $3,135; 4C $500. **Remarks:** Accepts advertising. **Circ:** (Not Reported).

8777 ■ Textile World
Billian Publishing Inc. and Trans World Publishing Inc.
2100 River Edge Pky., Ste. 1200
Atlanta, GA 30328
Free: 800-533-8484
International magazine on textile manufacturing and man-made fiber products. **Freq:** Monthly. **Print Method:** Offset. **Trim Size:** 8 x 10 3/4. **Cols./Page:** 3. **Col. Width:** 24 nonpareils. **Col. Depth:** 123 agate lines. **Key Personnel:** James M. Borneman, Editor-in-Chief; Jennifer Dennard, Managing Editor; Robert S. Reichard, Editor. **ISSN:** 0040--5213 (print). **Subscription Rates:** Free to qualified subscribers. **URL:** http://textileworld.com. **Remarks:** Advertising accepted; rates available upon request. **Circ:** Paid 617, Controlled 31803.

8778 ■ Textiles Panamericanos
Billian Publishing Inc. and Trans World Publishing Inc.
2100 River Edge Pky., Ste. 1200
Atlanta, GA 30328
Free: 800-533-8484
Textile manufacturing magazine. Printed in Spanish. (Latin American circulation.). **Freq:** Bimonthly. **Print Method:** Offset. **Trim Size:** 8 x 10 3/4. **Cols./Page:** 3. **Col. Width:** 26 nonpareils. **Col. Depth:** 140 agate lines. **ISSN:** 0049--3570 (print). **Subscription Rates:** Free to qualified subscribers. **URL:** http://textilespanamericanos.com. **Ad Rates:** BW $3,620; 4C $5,590; PCI $100. **Remarks:** Accepts advertising. **Circ:** Controlled 13000.

8779 ■ Today's Insurance Professionals
International Association of Insurance Professionals
Bldg. 5, Ste. 300
3525 Piedmont Rd.
Atlanta, GA 30305
Phone: (404)789-3153
Fax: (404)240-0998
Free: 800-766-6249
Publisher's E-mail: membership@iaip-ins.org
Magazine on insurance and professional development topics for men and women in the risk and insurance field. **Freq:** Quarterly. **Print Method:** Offset. **Trim Size:** 8 3/8 x 10 7/8. **Cols./Page:** 3. **Key Personnel:** Melissa Cobbs, Director, Communications, Editor. **ISSN:** 1538--0963 (print). **Subscription Rates:** $5 Individuals. **Alt. Formats:** PDF. **URL:** http://naiw.site-ym.com/store/ViewProduct.aspx?id=251211. **Formerly**: Today's Insurance Woman. **Remarks:** Accepts advertising. **Circ:** (Not Reported).

8780 ■ Transformations: Liberal Arts in the Digital Age
Associated Colleges of the South
1975 Century Blvd. NE, Ste. 10
Atlanta, GA 30345
Phone: (404)636-9533
Fax: (404)636-9558
Academic journal discussing digital information literacy. **Key Personnel:** Bob Johnson, Managing Editor; Terry Metz, Managing Editor. **ISSN:** 1545--9284 (print). **Circ:** (Not Reported).

8781 ■ Travel 50 & Beyond Magazine
Echo Media
900 Circle 75 Pky., Ste. 1600
Atlanta, GA 30339
Phone: (770)955-3535
Fax: (770)955-3599
Publisher's E-mail: salesinfo@echo-media.com
Magazine focusing on new vacation ideas, providing timely information on vacations preferred by travelers in the age group of fifty years and above. **Freq:** Quarterly. **Remarks:** Accepts advertising. **Circ:** (Not Reported).

8782 ■ TravelGirl: Inspiration for Today's Women
TravelGirl Inc.
3508 Broad St.
Atlanta, GA 30341
Phone: (770)451-9399
Fax: (770)454-6366
Publication E-mail: editor@travelgirlinc.com
Travel magazine for women. **Freq:** Bimonthly. **Key Personnel:** Stephanie Oswald, Editor-in-Chief; Renee Werbin, Publisher; Robyn Werbin, Vice President. **ISSN:** 1554--6047 (print). **Subscription Rates:** $17.95 Individuals; $32.95 Two years; $5.99 Single issue. **URL:** http://www.travelgirlinc.com. **Remarks:** Accepts advertising. **Circ:** (Not Reported).

Circulation: ★ = AAM; △ or • = BPA; ♦ = CAC; ❑ = VAC; ⊕ = PO Statement; ‡ = Publisher's Report; Boldface figures = sworn; Light figures = estimated.

8783 ■ VOX
VOX Teen Communications
229 Peachtree St. NE, Ste. 725
Atlanta, GA 30303
Phone: (404)614-0040
Newspaper published by Youth Communication: Metro Atlanta, containing articles written by teens for their peers. **Founded:** 1995. **Freq:** 5/yr. **Key Personnel:** Richard L. Eldredge, Senior Editor, Coordinator. **Subscription Rates:** Free to youth; $25 Individuals. **URL:** http://www.voxteencommunications.org. **Remarks:** Accepts advertising. **Circ:** (Not Reported).

8784 ■ La Voz de Houston Newspaper
Echo Media
900 Circle 75 Pky., Ste. 1600
Atlanta, GA 30339
Phone: (770)955-3535
Fax: (770)955-3599
Publisher's E-mail: salesinfo@echo-media.com
Spanish newspaper. **Freq:** Weekly. **Print Method:** Offset. **Trim Size:** 12 7/8 x 22. **Cols./Page:** 6. **Col. Width:** 12 inches. **Col. Depth:** 21 inches. **Subscription Rates:** Free. **URL:** http://lavoztx.com. **Remarks:** Accepts advertising. **Circ:** (Not Reported).

Washington Frederick News-Post - See Washington, DC

8785 ■ Welcome to Europe/Best of the Pacific
Echo Media
900 Circle 75 Pky., Ste. 1600
Atlanta, GA 30339
Phone: (770)955-3535
Fax: (770)955-3599
Publisher's E-mail: salesinfo@echo-media.com
Magazine for military personnel recently relocated to Europe. **Freq:** 3/year. **URL:** http://echomedia.com/medias/details/2658. **Remarks:** Advertising not accepted. **Circ:** 120000.

8786 ■ Western Real Estate Business: Connecting Real Estate in the West
France Publications Inc.
3500 Piedmont Rd., Ste. 415
Atlanta, GA 30305
Phone: (404)832-8262
Fax: (404)832-8260
Magazine that covers the latest news, developments and trends in commercial real estate in the western states. **Freq:** Monthly. **Key Personnel:** Nellie Day, Editor. **ISSN:** 1547--965X (print). **Subscription Rates:** $67 Individuals; $116 Two years. **URL:** http://rebusinessonline.com/magazines/western-real-estate-business; http://www.westernrebusiness.com. **Ad Rates:** BW $3,760; 4C $995. **Remarks:** Accepts advertising. **Circ:** (Not Reported).

8787 ■ Westlake Picayune
Cox Enterprises Inc.
6205 Peachtree Dunwoody Rd.
Atlanta, GA 30328
Phone: (678)645-0000
Fax: (678)645-1079
Publisher's E-mail: contactus@coxinc.com
Newspaper covering Eanes Independent School District. **Freq:** Weekly (Thurs.). **Print Method:** Offset. **Trim Size:** 11 1/2 x 14. **Cols./Page:** 5. **Col. Width:** 2 1/16 inches. **Col. Depth:** 13 11/16 inches. **Key Personnel:** Ed Allen, Editor; Jay Plotkin, Publisher. **ISSN:** 0745--581X (print). **URL:** http://www.statesman.com/s/news/local/westlake-picayune. **Mailing address:** PO Box 105357, Atlanta, GA 30348-5357. **Ad Rates:** BW $602; 4C $902; PCI $9.25. **Remarks:** Accepts advertising. **Circ:** ‡3000.

8788 ■ The Westville Reporter
Echo Media
900 Circle 75 Pky., Ste. 1600
Atlanta, GA 30339
Phone: (770)955-3535
Fax: (770)955-3599
Publisher's E-mail: salesinfo@echo-media.com
Community newspaper. **Freq:** Weekly (Sun.). **Print Method:** Offset. **Cols./Page:** 6. **Col. Width:** 12 picas. **Col. Depth:** 21 1/2 inches. **Key Personnel:** Michael Puffer, Chief Executive Officer, phone: (770)955-3535. **USPS:** 681-060. **URL:** http://echomedia.com/medias/details/5885/westville+reporter. **Remarks:** Accepts advertising. **Circ:** Sun. 1317.

8789 ■ Where to Retire Magazine
Echo Media
900 Circle 75 Pky., Ste. 1600
Atlanta, GA 30339
Phone: (770)955-3535
Fax: (770)955-3599
Publisher's E-mail: salesinfo@echo-media.com
Magazine designed to help pre-retirees plan and make a successful retirement move. **Freq:** Bimonthly. **Remarks:** Advertising not accepted. **Circ:** 1,200,000.

8790 ■ Women's Health Weekly
NewsRX
2727 Paces Ferry Rd. SE, Ste. 2-440
Atlanta, GA 30339
Phone: (770)507-7777
Fax: (770)435-6800
Free: 800-726-4550
Publisher's E-mail: techsupport@newsrx.com
Publication covering health issues for women. **Freq:** Weekly. **Key Personnel:** Susan Hasty, Publisher, phone: (770)507-7777, fax: (770)435-6800. **ISSN:** 1078-7240 (print); **EISSN:** 1532-4729 (electronic). **Subscription Rates:** $2295 Other countries Online Access & E-mail Delivery; $2295 U.S. and Canada print; $2525 U.S. and Canada print and online; $2495 Other countries print; $2755 Other countries print and online. **URL:** http://www.newsrx.com/NewsRxCorp. **Circ:** (Not Reported).

8791 ■ Cox Enterprises Inc.
6205 Peachtree Dunwoody Rd.
Atlanta, GA 30328
Phone: (678)645-0000
Fax: (678)645-1079
Email: contactus@coxinc.com
Owner: Cox Communications Inc., 1400 Lake Hearn Dr., Atlanta, GA 30319-1464, Ph: (404)843-5000, Free: 866-456-9944. **Founded:** 1898. **Formerly:** Dimension Cable. **Key Personnel:** John Michael Dyer, CEO, President; James C. Kennedy, Chairman; Leigh Scott, Sr. VP of Real Estate. **Cities Served:** Aliso Viejo, Irvine, Ladera Ranch, Laguna Beach, Laguna Hills, Laguna Nigel, Laguna Nigel, Mission Viejo, Newport Coast, Orange, California: subscribing households 1,300,000; San Juan Capistrano and County of Orange.; 200 channels; 1 community access channel; 25 hours per week community access programming. **Mailing address:** PO Box 105357, Atlanta, GA 30348-5357. **URL:** http://www.coxenterprises.com.

8792 ■ KARX-FM - 95.7
3280 Peachtree Rd., Ste. 2300
Atlanta, GA 30305
Phone: (806)342-5200
Format: Classic Rock. **Networks:** AP. **Founded:** 1992. **Operating Hours:** Continuous. **ADI:** Amarillo, TX. **Key Personnel:** David Bell, Dir. of Programs; Tim Guentz, Chief Engineer; Bill Lacy, Station Mgr. **Wattage:** 100,000. **URL:** http://www.957nashicon.com.

8793 ■ KOQL-FM
3280 Peachtree Rd. N
Atlanta, GA 30305
Format: Top 40. **Wattage:** 69,000 ERP. **Ad Rates:** Noncommercial.

8794 ■ KPUR-FM
3280 Peachtree Rd. N
Atlanta, GA 30305
Phone: (806)371-9797
Fax: (806)371-9129
Format: Oldies. **Networks:** Satellite Music Network; Westwood One Radio. **Owner:** Westwind Broadcasting, Inc., at above address. **Founded:** 1985. **Key Personnel:** Keith Adams, Gen. Mgr. **Wattage:** 6,000 ERP. **Ad Rates:** $15-40 per unit.

8795 ■ KQSM-FM
3280 Peachtree Rd. N
Atlanta, GA 30305
Email: requests@sam98.com
Format: Country. **Wattage:** 7,600 ERP.

8796 ■ KZRA-AM - 1590
3280 Peachtree Rd. NW, Ste. 2300
Atlanta, GA 30305
Phone: (404)949-0700
Format: Hispanic. **Owner:** Hochman Communications, Inc., at above address. **Operating Hours:** Continuous. **Key Personnel:** Mariposa Salas, Contact; Miguel Ramirez, Contact. **Wattage:** 2,500. **Ad Rates:** Advertising accepted; rates available upon request. $15 for 30 seconds; $20 for 60 seconds.

8797 ■ WABE-FM - 90.1
740 Bismark Rd., NE
Atlanta, GA 30324
Phone: (678)686-0321
Email: memberservices@wabe.org
Format: Public Radio; Classical. **Networks:** National Public Radio (NPR); Public Broadcasting Service (PBS). **Owner:** Atlanta Public Schools, 130 Trinity Ave., Atlanta, GA 30303, Ph: (404)802-3500. **Founded:** 1948. **ADI:** Atlanta (Athens & Rome), GA. **Key Personnel:** Doug Guthrie, Sr. VP; Jared Blass, Contact, jblass@pba.org. **Local Programs:** *Between the Lines*, Friday 7:00 p.m. **Wattage:** 100,000 ERP. **Ad Rates:** Noncommercial. Underwriting available. **URL:** http://www.wabe.org.

8798 ■ WABR-FM - 91.1
260 14th St. NW
Atlanta, GA 30318
Phone: (404)685-4788
Free: 800-222-6006
Format: Classical. **Owner:** Georgia Public Broadcasting, 260 14th St. NW, Atlanta, GA 30318, Ph: (404)685-2400, Free: 800-222-6006. **Ad Rates:** Noncommercial. **URL:** http://www.gpb.org.

8799 ■ WAEC-AM - 860
1465 Northside Dr., Ste. 218
Atlanta, GA 30318
Phone: (404)355-8600
Format: Religious. **Networks:** Independent. **Owner:** Beasley Broadcast Group Inc., 3033 Riviera Dr., Ste. 200, Naples, FL 34103-2750, Ph: (239)263-5000, Fax: (239)263-8191. **Founded:** 1978. **Operating Hours:** Continuous. **ADI:** Atlanta (Athens & Rome), GA. **Key Personnel:** Chris Edmonds, Gen. Mgr. **Wattage:** 5,000. **Ad Rates:** $30-45 for 30 seconds; $40-55 for 60 seconds. WWWE. **URL:** http://www.love860.com.

8800 ■ WAFS-AM - 1190
2970 Peachtree Rd., Ste. 700
Atlanta, GA 30305
Phone: (404)995-7300
Format: Religious. **Networks:** USA Radio; Moody Broadcasting. **Founded:** 1989. **Operating Hours:** Sunrise-sunset. **ADI:** Atlanta (Athens & Rome), GA. **Key Personnel:** Kevin Isaacs, Contact, kevini@salematlanta.com; Chris Anderson, CEO. **Wattage:** 25,000. **Ad Rates:** Noncommercial. **URL:** http://www.biz1190.com.

8801 ■ WAGA-TV - 5
1551 Briarcliff Rd. NE
Atlanta, GA 30306
Fax: (404)724-4426
Format: News. **Networks:** Fox. **Owner:** Fox Television Stations Inc., 1999 S Bundy Dr., Los Angeles, CA 90025-5235, Ph: (310)584-2000. **Founded:** 1949. **Operating Hours:** Continuous. **Wattage:** 100,000. **Ad Rates:** Advertising accepted; rates available upon request. **URL:** http://www.myfoxatlanta.com.

8802 ■ WALR-AM - 1340
780 Johnson Ferry Rd. NE, 5th Fl.
Atlanta, GA 30342
Phone: (404)688-0068
Format: Country. **Owner:** Dickey Broadcasting Company, at above address. **Ad Rates:** Advertising accepted; rates available upon request. **URL:** http://www.680thefan.com.

8803 ■ WALR-FM - 104.1
1601 W Peachtree St.
Atlanta, GA 30309
Phone: (404)897-7500
Fax: (404)897-7363
Format: Adult Contemporary; Urban Contemporary. **Networks:** ABC. **Owner:** Cox Radio Inc., 6205 Peachtree Dunwood Rd., Atlanta, GA 30328-4524, Ph: (678)645-0000, Fax: (678)645-5002. **Founded:** 1986. **Operating Hours:** Continuous. **ADI:** Atlanta (Athens & Rome), GA. **Key Personnel:** Tony Kidd, Mktg. Mgr., VP, tony.kidd@coxradio.com; Clarence Natto, Promotions Mgr., clarence.natto@coxradio.com. **Local Programs:** *Youngblood*, Saturday 7:00 a.m. - 12:00 p.m.; *Lost In The 80's*, Sunday 11:00 p.m. **Wattage:** 50,000. **Ad Rates:** Advertising accepted; rates available upon request. **URL:** http://www.kiss104fm.com.

8804 ■ WAOK-AM - 1380
1201 Peachtree St., Ste. 800
Atlanta, GA 30361
Phone: (404)898-8900
Fax: (404)898-8900
Format: News; Talk. **Simulcasts:** Bev Smith Show - Natl Synd. **Networks:** NBC. **Owner:** CBS Radio Inc., 1271 Avenue of the Americas, 44th Fl., New York, NY 10020-1401, Ph: (212)649-9600. **Founded:** 1954. **Operating Hours**: Continuous. **Key Personnel:** Mary Johnson, Contact, maryjohnson@maryjohnson.com; Mary Johnson, Contact, maryjohnson@maryjohnson.com. **Wattage**: 5,000. **Ad Rates:** Advertising accepted; rates available upon request. Combined advertising rates available with WVWW-FM. **URL:** http://www.atlanta.cbslocal.com.

8805 ■ WATL-TV - 36
7950 Jones Branch Dr.
McLean, VA 22107
Format: News. **Networks:** Warner Brothers Studios. **Owner:** Pacific and Southern Co., Inc., at above address. **Founded:** 1969. **Operating Hours**: 6 a.m.-2 a.m. Daily; 2 a.m.-6 a.m. Tue.-Sat. **Wattage**: 2,030,000 video; 204,500 audio. **Ad Rates:** Advertising accepted; rates available upon request. **URL:** http://www.myatltv.com.

WATY-FM - See Folkston

8806 ■ WBTS-FM - 95.5
1601 W Peachtree St.
Atlanta, GA 30309
Phone: (404)897-7500
Format: Contemporary Hit Radio (CHR); News; Talk. **Owner:** Cox Radio Inc., 6205 Peachtree Dunwood Rd., Atlanta, GA 30328-4524, Ph: (678)645-0000, Fax: (678)645-5002. **Founded:** 1961. **Operating Hours**: Sunrise-sunset. **Key Personnel:** Tony Kidd, VP, tony.kidd@cox.com. **Wattage**: 1,000. **Ad Rates:** $1.75 for 15 seconds; $2.25 for 30 seconds; $3 for 60 seconds. **URL:** http://www.cox.com.

WBZN-FM - See Old Town, ME

8807 ■ WBZY-FM - 105.3
1819 Peachtree Rd. NE, Ste. 700
Atlanta, GA 30309
Phone: (404)607-1336
Format: Hispanic. **ADI:** Atlanta (Athens & Rome), GA. **Wattage**: 2,150. **Ad Rates:** Noncommercial. **URL:** http://www.1053elpatron.com.

WCES-TV - See Augusta

8808 ■ WCFO-AM - 1160
1100 Spring St., Ste. 610
Atlanta, GA 30309
Phone: (404)681-9307
Fax: (404)870-8859
Email: listeners@newstalk1160.com
Format: News; Talk. **Operating Hours**: 6:00 a.m. - Midnight. **Key Personnel:** Jeff Davis, Gen. Mgr., VP, jeffdavis@newstalk1160.com. **Wattage**: 50,000 Day; 160 Nigh. **URL:** http://www.newstalk1160.com.

8809 ■ WCLK-FM - 91.9
111 James P. Brawley Dr. SW
Atlanta, GA 30314
Phone: (404)880-8284
Fax: (404)880-8869
Email: wclkfm@cau.edu
Format: Jazz. **Networks:** National Public Radio (NPR). **Founded:** 1974. **Operating Hours**: Continuous. **ADI**: Atlanta (Athens & Rome), GA. **Key Personnel:** Wendy Williams, Gen. Mgr.; Aaron Cohen, Dir. of Programs; Tammy Nobles, Contact, tnobles@cau.edu. **Wattage**: 480 ERP. **Ad Rates:** Noncommercial. Underwriting available. **URL:** http://www.wclk.com.

8810 ■ WCNN-AM - 680
780 Johnson Ferry Rd. NE, 5th Fl.
Atlanta, GA 30342
Phone: (404)688-0068
Format: Talk; Sports. **Owner:** Dickey Broadcasting Company, at above address. **Founded:** 1967. **Formerly**: WGTW-AM. **Operating Hours**: Continuous. **ADI**: Atlanta (Athens & Rome), GA. **Key Personnel:** Jim Mahanay, Operations Mgr., cwheat@680thefan.com. **Wattage**: 50,000. **Ad Rates:** $25-125 per unit. **URL:** http://www.680thefan.com.

8811 ■ WDWD-AM - 590
900 Cir. 75 Pky., Ste. 1320
Atlanta, GA 30339
Phone: (770)541-7472
Free: 877-870-5678
Format: Eclectic. **Networks:** ABC. **Founded:** 1938. **Operating Hours**: Continuous; 100% local. **Wattage**: 5,000. **Ad Rates:** Advertising accepted; rates available upon request. Combined advertising rates available with WYAY-FM.

8812 ■ WFOM-AM - 1230
3535 Piedmont Rd., Bldg. 14, Ste. 1200
Atlanta, GA 30305
Phone: (404)688-0068
Format: Talk; Sports. **Networks:** Business Radio. **Owner:** Dickey Broadcasting Company, at above address. **Operating Hours**: 2 a.m.-6 a.m. **Key Personnel:** David Dickey, Gen. Mgr., President; Jim Mahanay, Operations Mgr., jimmahanay@680thefan.com. **Wattage**: 1,000 KW. **Ad Rates:** $12-16 for 30 seconds; $15-20 for 60 seconds. **URL:** http://www.680thefan.com.

8813 ■ WFSH-FM - 104.7
2970 Peachtree Rd. NW, Ste. 700
Atlanta, GA 30305
Phone: (404)741-1047
Fax: (404)816-0748
Format: Contemporary Christian. **Wattage**: 24,000 ERP. **Ad Rates:** Noncommercial. **URL:** http://www.thefishatlanta.com.

8814 ■ WGCL-TV - 46
425 14th St. NW
Atlanta, GA 30318
Fax: (404)327-3004
Format: Commercial TV. **Networks:** CBS. **Owner:** Meredith Corp., 1716 Locust St., Des Moines, IA 50309-3038, Ph: (515)284-3000. **Founded:** 1971. **Formerly**: WGNX-TV; WANX-TV. **Operating Hours**: Continuous. **ADI**: Atlanta (Athens & Rome), GA. **Key Personnel:** Kirk Black, Sr., Gen. Mgr., VP, kirk.black@cbsatlanta.com; Eric Ludgood, News Dir., eric.ludgood@cbsatlanta.com; James Estes, Operations Mgr., james.estes@cbsatlanta.com. **Ad Rates:** Advertising accepted; rates available upon request. **URL:** http://www.cbs46.com.

8815 ■ WGKA-AM - 920
2970 Peachtree Rd., NW, Ste. 700
Atlanta, GA 30305
Phone: (404)995-7300
Email: myopinioncounts@920wgka.com
Format: Talk; News. **Owner:** Salem Media of Georgia Inc., 4880 Santa Rosa Rd.,Ste. 300, Camarillo, CA 93012-0958, Ph: (805)987-0400. **Founded:** 1955. **Operating Hours**: Continuous. **ADI**: Atlanta (Athens & Rome), GA. **Key Personnel:** Jeff Carter, Operations Mgr., jeff@920wgka.com; Mike Moran, Gen. Mgr., mikem@thefishatlanta.com. **Local Programs**: *Health Talk Atlanta*; *The Bob & Rodman Home Show*, Saturday 9:00 a.m. - 11:00 am. **Wattage**: 14,000. **Ad Rates:** $28-48 for 30 seconds; $35-60 for 60 seconds. **URL:** http://am920theanswer.com.

8816 ■ WGST-AM - 640
1819 Peachtree Rd. NE, Ste. 700
Atlanta, GA 30309
Phone: (404)367-9478
Format: Talk; News. **Networks:** ABC; CBS. **Owner:** iHeartMedia Inc., 200 E Basse Rd., San Antonio, TX 78209, Ph: (210)832-3314. **Operating Hours**: Continuous; 35% network, 65% local. **ADI**: Atlanta (Athens & Rome), GA. **Wattage**: 50,000. **Ad Rates:** Noncommercial. **URL:** http://www.640wgst.com.

8817 ■ WGTV-TV - 8
260 14th St. NW
Atlanta, GA 30318
Phone: (404)685-2389
Free: 800-222-4788
Email: ask@gpb.org
Format: Public TV. **Networks:** Public Broadcasting Service (PBS); Georgia Public Television. **Owner:** Georgia Public Broadcasting, 260 14th St. NW, Atlanta, GA 30318, Ph: (404)685-2400, Free: 800-222-6006. **Founded:** 1967. **Formerly**: WABW. **Operating Hours**: midnight. **ADI**: Albany (Valdosta & Cordele), GA. **Key Personnel:** Tiffany Brown Rideaux, Contact. **Ad Rates:** Noncommercial. **URL:** http://www.gpb.org.

8818 ■ WHHY-FM
3280 Peachtree Rd. N
Atlanta, GA 30305
Phone: (334)240-9274
Email: Y102requests@atscumulus.com
Format: Top 40; Contemporary Hit Radio (CHR). **Owner:** Cumulus Media Inc., 3280 Peachtree Rd. NW, Ste. 2300, Atlanta, GA 30305-2455, Ph: (404)949-0700, Fax: (404)949-0740. **Founded:** 1962. **Wattage**: 100,000 ERP. **Ad Rates:** $20-55 for 30 seconds; $30-65 for 60 seconds.

8819 ■ WHSC-AM
3280 Peachtree Rd. N
Atlanta, GA 30305
Phone: (803)332-8101
Format: Contemporary Country. **Networks:** South Carolina News. **Founded:** 1946. **Key Personnel:** Howard Garland, Contact. **Wattage**: 5,000 Day; 473 Night. **Ad Rates:** $4.50 for 15 seconds; $5.50-5.95 for 30 seconds; $6.50-7.25 for 60 seconds.

8820 ■ WIBR-AM
3280 Peachtree Rd. N
Atlanta, GA 30305
Phone: (504)292-9556
Fax: (504)291-6420
Format: Sports. **Owner:** Don Nelson, at above address. **Founded:** 1947. **Formerly**: WCLA-AM. **ADI**: Baton Rouge, LA. **Key Personnel:** Don Nelson, Contact; Greg Weston, Dir. of Programs; Lew Campbell, Contact; Don Nelson, Contact. **Wattage**: 5,000 Day; 1,000 Nig.

8821 ■ WIFN-AM
780 Johnson Ferry Rd. N
Atlanta, GA 30342
Phone: (810)765-8893
Fax: (810)765-8894
Email: wifn@aol.com
Format: News; Talk. **Networks:** Mutual Broadcasting System; ABC. **Owner:** Barr/Schremp Communications, at above address. **Founded:** 1951. **Formerly**: WDOG-AM; WSMA-AM. **Key Personnel:** David Barr, Dir. of Sales, Gen. Mgr., Operations Mgr. **Wattage**: 1,000. **Ad Rates:** $9-13 for 10 seconds; $11-15 for 30 seconds; $13-17 for 60 seconds.

8822 ■ WIGO-AM - 1340
780 Johnson Ferry Rd. NE, 5th Fl.
Atlanta, GA 30342
Phone: (404)688-0068
Format: Sports. **Owner:** Allied Media of Georgia, at above address. **Founded:** 1965. **Operating Hours**: Continuous; 5% network, 95% local. **ADI**: Atlanta (Athens & Rome), GA. **Key Personnel:** Roger Amato, CEO; Al Parks, Gen. Mgr. **Wattage**: 1,000 KW. **URL:** http://atlantassportsstation.com.

8823 ■ WIOV-AM
3280 Peachtree Rd. N
Atlanta, GA 30305
Phone: (717)738-1661
Fax: (800)500-1051
Format: Country; Sports. **Networks:** ESPN Radio; Meadows Racing. **Owner:** Brill Media Corp., Evansville, IN, Ph: (812)423-6002; Cumulus Media Inc., 3280 Peachtree Rd. NW, Ste. 2300, Atlanta, GA 30305-2455, Ph: (404)949-0700, Fax: (404)949-0740. **Founded:** 1955. **Formerly**: WGSA-AM; WAGO-AM. **Key Personnel:** Mitch Carroll, Gen. Mgr. **Wattage**: 1,000. **Ad Rates:** Advertising accepted; rates available upon request. $30-40 per unit.

8824 ■ WJAD-FM - 103.5
3280 Peachtree Rd. NW, Ste. 2300
Atlanta, GA 30305
Phone: (229)888-7625
Format: Classic Rock. **Owner:** Cumulus Broadcasting Inc., 3280 Peachtree Rd. NW, Ste. 2300, Atlanta, GA 30305-2447, Ph: (404)949-0700, Fax: (404)949-0740. **URL:** http://www.rock103albany.com.

WJSP-TV - See Columbus

8825 ■ WJZZ-FM - 107.5
101 Marietta St., 12th Fl.
Atlanta, GA 30303
Phone: (404)765-9750
Fax: (404)688-7686
Format: Jazz. **Ad Rates:** Noncommercial. **URL:** http://www.1075wjzz.com.

Circulation: ★ = AAM; △ or • = BPA; ♦ = CAC; □ = VAC; ⊕ = PO Statement; ‡ = Publisher's Report; Boldface figures = sworn; Light figures = estimated.

8826 ■ WKHX-FM - 101.5
210 Interstate N Pky., 1st Fl.
Atlanta, GA 30339
Phone: (404)521-1015
Format: Contemporary Country. **Networks:** NBC. **Owner:** Citadel Broadcasting Corp., 7201 W Lake Mead Blvd., Ste. 400, Las Vegas, NV 89128-8366, Ph: (702)804-5200, Fax: (702)804-8250. **Founded:** 1950. **Operating Hours**: Continuous. **ADI**: Atlanta (Athens & Rome), GA. **Wattage**: 100,000 ERP. **Ad Rates:** Advertising accepted; rates available upon request. **URL:** http://www.wkhx.com.

8827 ■ WKIN-AM - 1320
3280 Peachtree Rd. NW, Ste. 2300
Atlanta, GA 30305
Phone: (404)949-0700
Email: wjcwwkin@preferred.com
Format: Country. **Networks:** AP. **Owner:** Citadel Broadcasting Corp., 7201 W Lake Mead Blvd., Ste. 400, Las Vegas, NV 89128-8366, Ph: (702)804-5200, Fax: (702)804-8250. **Founded:** 1951. **Operating Hours**: Continuous. **Key Personnel:** Jeff Hall, News Dir.; Bob Lawrence, Contact, bob.lawrence@citcomm.com; Bob Lawrence, Contact, bob.lawrence@citcomm.com. **Wattage**: 5,000 Day; 500 Night. **Ad Rates:** Noncommercial. **Mailing address:** PO Box 8668, Gray, TN 37615.

WLCL-FM - See Sellersburg, IN

8828 ■ WLFF-FM - 95.3
3280 Peachtree Rd. N
Atlanta, GA 30305
Phone: (765)474-1410
Fax: (765)474-3442
Owner: Artistic Media Media Partners Inc., 5520 E 75th St., Indianapolis, IN 46250. **Founded:** 1967. **Formerly**: WLZR-FM; WWET-FM; WKJM-FM; WEZV-FM. **Wattage**: 6,000. **Ad Rates:** $14 for 30 seconds; $16 for 60 seconds. WAZY FM, WSHP FM.

8829 ■ WMGL-FM - 101.7
3280 Peachtree Rd. NW, Ste. 2300
Atlanta, GA 30305
Format: Urban Contemporary. **Ad Rates:** Noncommercial.

8830 ■ WMLB-AM - 1690
1110 Spring St., Ste. 610
Atlanta, GA 30309
Phone: (404)681-9307
Fax: (404)870-8859
Format: Eclectic. **Owner:** JW Broadcasting L.L.C., at above address. **Operating Hours**: 7.00 a.m.-9.30 p.m. **Wattage**: 10,000. **Ad Rates:** Advertising accepted; rates available upon request. $12 for 30 seconds; $20 for 60 seconds. **URL:** http://www.1690wmlb.com.

8831 ■ WNAM-AM - 1280
3280 Peachtree Rd. NW, Ste. 2300
Atlanta, GA 30305
Phone: (920)727-2045
Fax: (920)722-0211
Format: Big Band/Nostalgia. **Networks:** ABC. **Owner:** Value Radio Corp., at above address, Fax: (414)236-1040. **Founded:** 1948. **Operating Hours**: Continuous; 5% network, 95% local. **ADI**: Green Bay-Appleton (Suring), WI. **Key Personnel:** Bill Mann, Gen. Mgr.; Eric James, Promotions Dir.; Ron Ross, Dir. of Programs. **Wattage**: 5,000. **Ad Rates:** $18 for 60 seconds.

8832 ■ WNIV-AM - 970
2970 Peachtree Rd. NW
Atlanta, GA 30305
Phone: (404)995-7300
Format: Talk; Religious. **Simulcasts:** WLTA-AM. **Owner:** Salem Media Group Inc., 4880 Santa Rosa Rd., Camarillo, CA 93012, Ph: (805)987-0400, Fax: (805)384-4520. **Founded:** May 17, 1988. **Operating Hours**: Continuous. **Key Personnel:** Adam Asher, Station Mgr. **Wattage**: 5,000. **Ad Rates:** $30-75 per unit. **URL:** http://www.wniv.com.

8833 ■ WNNX-FM - 100.5
780 Johnson Ferry Rd. NE, 5th Fl.
Atlanta, GA 30342
Phone: (404)741-7625
Format: Album-Oriented Rock (AOR). **Owner:** Cumulus Broadcasting Inc., 3280 Peachtree Rd. NW, Ste. 2300, Atlanta, GA 30305-2447, Ph: (404)949-0700, Fax: (404)949-0740. **Founded:** Oct. 1993. **Formerly**: WAPW-FM. **Operating Hours**: Continuous; 3% network, 97% local. **Wattage**: 100,000 ERP. **Ad Rates:** Advertising accepted; rates available upon request. **URL:** http://www.atlantasrockstation.com.

8834 ■ WPBA-TV - 30
740 Bismark Rd. NE
Atlanta, GA 30324
Phone: (678)686-0321
Format: Public TV. **Networks:** Public Broadcasting Service (PBS). **Owner:** Atlanta Educational Telecommunications Collaborative, Inc., at above address, Atlanta, GA. **Founded:** 1958. **Operating Hours**: 5 a.m.-4:30 a.m. **ADI**: Atlanta (Athens & Rome), GA. **Key Personnel:** Milton C. Clipper, Jr., CEO, President; John Weatherford, Gen. Mgr., Sr. VP. **Wattage**: 100,000. **Ad Rates:** $175-250 per unit. **URL:** http://www.pba.org.

8835 ■ WPCH-FM - 94.9
1819 Peachtree Rd., Ste. 700
Atlanta, GA 30309
Phone: (404)875-8080
Format: Music of Your Life. **Networks:** Independent. **Owner:** Clear Channel Communications Inc., at above address, Ph: (210)822-2828, Fax: (210)822-2299. **Founded:** 1972. **ADI**: Atlanta (Athens & Rome), GA. **Key Personnel:** Jason Mosher, Sales Mgr., jasonmosher@clearchannel.com. **Wattage**: 78,000 ERP. **Ad Rates:** Advertising accepted; rates available upon request. **URL:** http://949thebull.iheart.com.

8836 ■ WQXI-AM - 790
3340 Peachtree Rd. NE, Ste. 1430
Atlanta, GA 30326
Phone: (404)237-0079
Email: promotions@790thezone.com
Format: Sports; Talk. **Owner:** Jefferson Pilot Communications Co., at above address. **Founded:** 1947. **Operating Hours**: Continuous. **Key Personnel:** Andrew Saltzman, Founder, President; Matt Edgar, Dir. of Programs; Chris Young, Gen. Sales Mgr.; Cody Hicks, Dir. of Mktg., Promotions Dir.; Neal Maziar, Gen. Mgr., VP. **Wattage**: 28,000 Day; 1,000 Night. **URL:** http://lincolnfi.pro.poola.tritondigitalcms.com.

8837 ■ WRAD-AM - 1460
3280 Peachtree Rd., Ste. 2300
Atlanta, GA 30305
Phone: (540)639-2461
Fax: (540)639-1725
Format: Oldies. **Networks:** CNN Radio. **Owner:** WRAD Broadcasting Co., at above address. **Founded:** 1940. **Operating Hours**: Continuous. **Key Personnel:** Robert Travis, Contact. **Wattage**: 20,000 ERP. **Ad Rates:** $8-15 for 30 seconds; $10-15 for 60 seconds. **URL:** http://www.1460wrad.com.

8838 ■ WRAS-FM - 88.5
PO Box 4048
Atlanta, GA 30302-4048
Phone: (404)413-9727
Format: Alternative/New Music/Progressive. **Networks:** ABC. **Owner:** Georgia State University, 33 Gilmer st., Atlanta, GA 30302-3965, Ph: (404)413-2000. **Founded:** 1971. **Operating Hours**: Continuous. **ADI**: Atlanta (Athens & Rome), GA. **Key Personnel:** Paul Alberto, Dean; Dale Palmer, Asst. VP of Mktg.; Jeff Walker, Operations Mgr., jeffwalker@gsu.edu; Wayne Reed, Asst. VP; Linda Nelson, Asst. VP; Beth Jones, Asst. VP of HR; John Clark, Assoc. VP. **Wattage**: 100,000. **Ad Rates:** Noncommercial. **URL:** http://www.gsu.edu.

8839 ■ WREK-FM - 91.1
350 Ferst Dr. NW, Ste. 2224
Atlanta, GA 30332-0630
Phone: (404)894-2468
Fax: (404)894-6872
Email: general.manager@wrek.org
Format: Eclectic; Information; Sports. **Owner:** Georgia IST of Technology - Radio Communications Board, at above address. **Founded:** 1968. **Operating Hours**: Continuous. **ADI**: Atlanta (Athens & Rome), GA. **Key Personnel:** Curtis Stephens, Music Dir.; Adam Lawrence, Gen. Mgr. **Wattage**: 100,000. **Ad Rates:** Noncommercial. Underwriting available. **URL:** http://www.wrek.org.

8840 ■ WRFG-FM - 89.3
1083 Austin Ave. NE
Atlanta, GA 30307-1940
Phone: (404)523-3471
Email: info@wrfg.org
Format: Eclectic; Ethnic. **Networks:** Pacifica. **Owner:** Radio Free Georgia Broadcasting Foundation Inc. **Founded:** 1973. **Operating Hours**: Continuous; 95% local. **Key Personnel:** Wanique Shabazz, Dir. of Operations, wanique@wrfg.org. **Local Programs**: *Good Morning Blues*, Monday Tuesday Wednesday Thursday Friday 6:00 a.m. - 10:00 a.m.; *Soul Rhapsody*, Monday Tuesday Wednesday Thursday Friday 10:00 a.m. - 12:00 p.m.; *Zydeco Show*, Sunday 1:00 p.m. - 3:00 p.m. **Wattage**: 100,000. **Ad Rates:** Noncommercial; underwriting available. **URL:** http://www.wrfg.org.

8841 ■ WSB-AM - 750
1601 W Peachtree St.
Atlanta, GA 30309
Phone: (404)897-7500
Fax: (404)897-7363
Format: Talk; News. **Networks:** AP. **Owner:** Cox Radio Inc., 6205 Peachtree Dunwood Rd., Atlanta, GA 30328-4524, Ph: (678)645-0000, Fax: (678)645-5002. **Founded:** 1922. **Operating Hours**: Continuous. **Key Personnel:** Pete Spriggs, Dir. of Programs; Condace Pressley, Operations Mgr. **Local Programs**: *The Clark Howard Show*, Monday Tuesday Wednesday Thursday Friday 8:00 p.m. - 10:00 p.m.; *Atlanta's Morning News*, Monday Tuesday Wednesday Thursday Friday 4:30 a.m. - 9:00 a.m.; *The Neal Boortz Radio Show*, Monday Tuesday Wednesday Thursday Friday 8:45 a.m. **Wattage**: 50,000. **Ad Rates:** Advertising accepted; rates available upon request. **URL:** http://www.wsbradio.com.

8842 ■ WSB-FM - 98.5
1601 W Peachtree St.
Atlanta, GA 30309
Phone: (404)897-7500
Format: Adult Contemporary. **Simulcasts:** WNGC. **Owner:** Cox Radio Inc., 6205 Peachtree Dunwood Rd., Atlanta, GA 30328-4524, Ph: (678)645-0000, Fax: (678)645-5002. **Founded:** 1948. **ADI**: Atlanta (Athens & Rome), GA. **Wattage**: 100,000 ERP. **Ad Rates:** Advertising accepted; rates available upon request. **URL:** http://b985.com.

8843 ■ WSB-TV - 2
1601 W Peachtree St. NE
Atlanta, GA 30309
Phone: (404)897-7000
Fax: (404)897-7339
Email: talk2us@wsbtv.com
Format: Commercial TV. **Networks:** ABC. **Owner:** Cox Enterprises Inc., 6205 Peachtree Dunwoody Rd., Atlanta, GA 30328, Ph: (678)645-0000, Fax: (678)645-1079. **Founded:** 1948. **Operating Hours**: Continuous. **ADI**: Atlanta (Athens & Rome), GA. **Key Personnel:** Greg Stone, Gen. Mgr., VP; Josh Eure, Contact. **Ad Rates:** Advertising accepted; rates available upon request. **URL:** http://www.wsbtv.com.

8844 ■ WSTR-FM - 94.1
3350 Peachtree Rd. NE, Ste. 1800
Atlanta, GA 30326
Phone: (404)261-2970
Fax: (404)365-9026
Format: Contemporary Hit Radio (CHR); Top 40. **Networks:** Independent. **Owner:** Lincoln Financial Media Co., 1615 Murray Canyon Rd., San Diego, CA 92108. **Founded:** 1966. **Formerly**: WQXI-FM. **Operating Hours**: Continuous. **ADI**: Atlanta (Athens & Rome), GA. **Wattage**: 100,000. **Ad Rates:** Noncommercial. **URL:** http://www.star94.com.

W264AK-FM - See Toledo, OH

8845 ■ W229AG-FM - 93.7
PO Box 391
Twin Falls, ID 83303
Fax: (208)736-1958
Free: 800-357-4226
Format: Religious; Contemporary Christian. **Owner:** CSN International, PO Box 391, Twin Falls, ID 83303, Ph: (208)736-1958, Fax: (208)736-1958, Free: 800-357-4226.

8846 ■ WUBL-FM - 94.9
1819 Peachtree Rd., Ste. 700
Atlanta, GA 30309
Phone: (404)741-0949
Email: cherylervin@clearchannel.com
Format: Sports; Contemporary Hit Radio (CHR). **Owner:** iHeartMedia Inc., 200 E Basse Rd., San Antonio, TX 78209, Ph: (210)832-3314. **Operating**

Hours: Continuous. **Ad Rates:** Advertising accepted; rates available upon request. **URL:** http://www.949thebull.com.

8847 ■ WUPA-TV - 69
2700 NE Expy., Bldg. A
Atlanta, GA 30345
Phone: (404)325-6969
Format: Commercial TV. **Networks:** United Paramount Network. **Owner:** CBS Corp., 51 W 52nd St., New York, NY 10019-6188, Ph: (212)975-4321, Fax: (212)975-4516, Free: 877-227-0787. **Founded:** 1981. **Formerly**: WVEU-TV. **Operating Hours**: Continuous. **ADI**: Atlanta (Athens & Rome), GA. **Wattage**: 2,630. **Ad Rates:** $50-3500 per unit. **URL:** http://cwatlanta.cbslocal.com.

WVAN-TV - See Savannah

8848 ■ WVEE-FM - 103.3
1201 Peachtree St., Ste. 800
Atlanta, GA 30361
Phone: (404)898-8900
Format: Urban Contemporary. **Networks:** NBC. **Owner:** CBS Radio Inc., 40 W 57th St., New York, NY 10019, Ph: (212)846-3939, Fax: (212)315-2162. **Founded:** 1948. **Operating Hours**: Continuous. **ADI**: Atlanta (Athens & Rome), GA. **Key Personnel:** Reggie Rouse, Dir. of Programs. **Wattage**: 100,000. **Ad Rates:** $300-800 for 60 seconds. **URL:** http://www.v103.cbslocal.com.

8849 ■ WWLG-FM - 96.7
1819 Peachtree Rd., Ste. 700
Atlanta, GA 30309
Phone: (918)664-4581
Format: Country. **Formerly**: WLTM-FM. **Operating Hours**: Continuous. **Key Personnel:** Jason Mosher, Sales Mgr., jasonmosher@clearchannel.com; Melissa Forrest, Gen. Mgr. **Ad Rates:** Advertising accepted; rates available upon request. **URL:** http://radio1057.iheart.com.

8850 ■ WWUF-FM - 97.7
1350 Paces Forest Dr.
Atlanta, GA 30301
Phone: (912)285-0977
Format: Classic Rock; Information. **Owner:** Mattox Broadcasting, Inc., at above address. **Founded:** 1986. **Formerly**: WMUI-FM. **Wattage**: 6,000 ERP. **Ad Rates:** $8 for 30 seconds; $10.30-12.60 for 60 seconds. **URL:** http://waycrossradio.com/977.

8851 ■ WWVA-FM - 105.7
1819 Peachtree St., Ste. 700
Atlanta, GA 30309
Phone: (404)875-8080
Format: World Beat; Ethnic. **Owner:** iHeartMedia Inc., 200 E Basse Rd., San Antonio, TX 78209, Ph: (210)832-3314. **Operating Hours**: Continuous. **Ad Rates:** Advertising accepted; rates available upon request. **URL:** http://www.iheart.com.

8852 ■ WWWE-AM - 1100
1465 Northside Dr., Ste. 218
Atlanta, GA 30318
Phone: (404)591-6736
Format: Hispanic. **Owner:** Beasley Broadcast Group Inc., 3033 Riviera Dr., Ste. 200, Naples, FL 34103-2750, Ph: (239)263-5000, Fax: (239)263-8191. **ADI**: Atlanta (Athens & Rome), GA. **Ad Rates:** Advertising accepted; rates available upon request.

8853 ■ WWWQ-FM - 100.5
780 Johnson Ferry Rd., 5th Fl.
Atlanta, GA 30342
Phone: (404)497-4700
Format: Top 40. **Owner:** Cumulus Broadcasting Inc., 3280 Peachtree Rd. NW, Ste. 2300, Atlanta, GA 30305-2447, Ph: (404)949-0700, Fax: (404)949-0740. **Key Personnel:** Gary Lewis, Gen. Mgr., gary.lewis@cumulus.com; Rob Roberts, Dir. of Programs, rob.roberts@cumulus.com; Vickki Shelton, Gen. Sales Mgr., vickki.shelton@cumulus.com. **Ad Rates:** Advertising accepted; rates available upon request.

WXGA-TV - See Waycross

8854 ■ WXIA-TV - 11
One Monroe Pl. NE
Atlanta, GA 30324
Phone: (404)892-1611
Fax: (404)881-0675
Format: Commercial TV. **Networks:** NBC. **Owner:** Gannett Company Inc., 7950 Jones Branch Dr., McLean, VA 22107-0150, Ph: (703)854-6089. **Founded:** 1951. **Formerly**: WQXI-TV. **Operating Hours**: Continuous. **ADI**: Atlanta (Athens & Rome), GA. **Key Personnel:** Bob Walker, Gen. Mgr., President. **Ad Rates:** Noncommercial. **URL:** http://www.11alive.com.

8855 ■ WXRS-AM - 1590
PO Box 5356
Atlanta, GA 31107-5356
Phone: (404)432-1450
Fax: (912)237-3559
Owner: RadioJones, LLC, at above address, Ph: (404)254-2911. **Founded:** 1978. **Wattage**: 2,500 Day; 023 Night. **Ad Rates:** $4.30 for 30 seconds; $9.50 for 60 seconds.

WXRS-FM - See Swainsboro, GA

8856 ■ WYAI-FM - 104.1
1601 W Peachtree St. NE
Atlanta, GA 30309
Phone: (404)897-7500
Fax: (404)956-0498
Format: News. **Owner:** NewCity Communications, Inc., at above address. **Founded:** 1947. **Operating Hours**: Continuous. **Key Personnel:** Bob Green, Gen. Mgr.; Ken Christiansen, Gen. Sales Mgr; Jamie Slone, Contact. **Wattage**: 100,000 ERP. **Ad Rates:** Accepts Advertising. **URL:** http://www.kiss104fm.com.

8857 ■ WYAY-FM - 106.7
210 Interstate North Pky., 1st Fl.
Atlanta, GA 30339
Phone: (404)521-1067
Format: Oldies. **Networks:** ABC. **Owner:** Citadel Broadcasting Corp., 7201 W Lake Mead Blvd., Ste. 400, Las Vegas, NV 89128-8366, Ph: (702)804-5200, Fax: (702)804-8250. **Operating Hours**: Continuous; 100% local. **Key Personnel:** Mary Gordon, Gen. Sales Mgr., mary.gordon@citcomm.com. **Wattage**: 99,000. **Ad Rates:** Advertising accepted; rates available upon request. Combined advertising rates available with WKHX-FM.

8858 ■ WYZE-AM - 1480
1111 Blvd. S
Atlanta, GA 30312
Phone: (404)622-7802
Format: Music of Your Life; News; Information. **Owner:** WYZE Radio, Inc., 1111 Boulevard S, Atlanta, GA 30312. **Founded:** 1967. **Operating Hours**: Continuous. **ADI**: Atlanta (Athens & Rome), GA. **Key Personnel:** Donald Cochran, Dir. of Programs; Cynthia Waters, Contact; Eli Smith, Contact. **Wattage**: 10,000. **Ad Rates:** Advertising accepted; rates available upon request. $14-28 for 30 seconds; $20-30 for 60 seconds. **URL:** http://wyzeradio.com/.

8859 ■ WZGC-FM - 92.9
1201 Peachtree St., Ste. 800
Atlanta, GA 30361
Phone: (404)898-8900
Owner: CBS Radio Inc., 1271 Avenue of the Americas, 44th Fl., New York, NY 10020-1401, Ph: (212)649-9600. **Founded:** 1965. **ADI**: Atlanta (Athens & Rome), GA. **Wattage**: 64,000 ERP. **Ad Rates:** Accepts Advertising. **URL:** http://www.929dave.fm.

AUGUSTA

E. GA. Richmond Co. On Savannah River, at head of navigation on Georgia/South Carolina border. Medical College of Georgia; Augusta College; Paine College (black); Georgia School of Dentistry. Manufactures textiles, vehicles, plastics, brick, tile, pharmaceuticals, cottonseed oil, paper products, chemicals, fertilizers. Timber. Kaolin deposits.

8860 ■ The Augusta Chronicle
The Augusta Chronicle
725 Broad St.
Augusta, GA 30901
Phone: (706)724-0851
Fax: (706)823-3345
Free: 866-249-8223
Publisher's E-mail: newsroom@augustachronicle.com
Daily newspaper. **Freq:** Mon.-Sun. **Print Method:** Offset. **Cols./Page:** 6. **Col. Width:** 24 nonpareils. **Col. Depth:** 301 agate lines. **Key Personnel:** Michael Ryan, Editor; Alan English, Executive Editor. **Subscription Rates:** $192 Individuals seven days, home delivery; $135 Individuals Friday, Saturday and Sundays (home delivery). **URL:** http://chronicle.augusta.com. **Remarks:** Accepts advertising. **Circ:** Mon.-Fri. ⋆**61,784**, Sat. ⋆**66,571**, Sun. ⋆**76,745**.

8861 ■ Barrel Horse News
National Barrel Horse Association
725 Broad St.
Augusta, GA 30901
Phone: (706)722-7223
Freq: Monthly. **Key Personnel:** Patty Tiberg, Publisher; Bonnie Wheatley, Editor. **Subscription Rates:** $23.95 U.S.; $40 Two years; $43.95 Canada; $80 Canada two years; $63.95 Other countries; $120 Other countries two years. **URL:** http://barrelhorses.com. **Mailing address:** PO Box 1988, Augusta, GA 30903. **Remarks:** Accepts advertising. **Circ:** (Not Reported).

8862 ■ Best Read Guide New Hampshire
Best Read Guide
725 Broad St.
Augusta, GA 30901
Fax: (706)836-3596
Magazine offering tourism information on the state of New Hampshire including attractions, lodging, dining, etc. **Freq:** Quarterly. **Key Personnel:** Mitch Hanson, Contact, phone: (603)651-7477; Dick St. Onge, Contact, phone: (603)651-8580. **Subscription Rates:** $20 Individuals; $3 Single issue. **Remarks:** Accepts advertising. **Circ:** (Not Reported).

8863 ■ Best Read Guide Smoky Mountains
Best Read Guide
725 Broad St.
Augusta, GA 30901
Fax: (706)836-3596
Publication E-mail: contact@bestreadguidesmokymountains.com
Magazine offering tourism information on the Smoky Mountains including attractions, lodging, dining, etc. **Freq:** Monthly. **Subscription Rates:** $20 Individuals; $3 Single issue. **URL:** http://www.smokymountainsbestreadguide.com. **Remarks:** Accepts advertising. **Circ:** 1000000.

8864 ■ Gray's Sporting Journal
Morris Communications Company L.L.C.
735 Broad St.
Augusta, GA 30901
Publisher's E-mail: allaccessprogram@morris.com
Gray's explores the sophisticated outdoor adventurer's world of hunting, fishing and conservation through literature, fine sporting photography, art and travel. **Freq:** 7/year. **Print Method:** Web Offset. **Trim Size:** 8 1/8 x 10 7/8. **Cols./Page:** 2. **Col. Width:** 35 nonpareils. **Col. Depth:** 9 5/16 inches. **Key Personnel:** James R. Babb, Editor; Russ Lumpkin, Managing Editor; Mike Floyd, Manager, Advertising, phone: (706)823-3729. **ISSN:** 0273-6691 (print). **Subscription Rates:** $39.95 U.S.; $59.95 Canada; $79.95 Other countries; $73.90 Two years; $113.90 Canada 2 years; $153.90 Other countries 2 years. **URL:** http://www.grayssportingjournal.com; http://www.morris.com/divisions/magazine-publishing/grays-sporting-journal. **Ad Rates:** BW $3,780; 4C $4,990. **Remarks:** Accepts advertising. **Circ:** Paid ⋆**29,155**.

8865 ■ The Journal of ECT
International Society for ECT and Neurostimulation
c/o Vaughn McCall, Editor-in-Chief
Dept. of Psychiatry & Health Behavior
Georgia Health Sciences University
The Stoney (EG Building), 997 St. Sebastian Way
Augusta, GA 30912
Publisher's E-mail: contact@isen-ect.org
Peer-reviewed journal covering all aspects of contemporary ECT, reporting on major clinical and research developments worldwide. **Freq:** Quarterly 4/year. **Print Method:** Sheetfed Offset. **Trim Size:** 8 1/8 x 10 7/8. **Key Personnel:** Natalie McGroarty, Publisher; Vaughn McCall, Editor-in-Chief. **ISSN:** 1095-0680 (print); **EISSN:** 1533-4112 (electronic). **Subscription Rates:** $486 Individuals; $1400 Institutions; $144 Individuals in-training; $609 Other countries individual; $1502 Institutions, other countries. **URL:** http://journals.lww.com/ectjournal/pages/default.aspx; http://www.lww.com/Product/1095-0680. **Formerly**: Convulsive Therapy. **Ad**

Circulation: ⋆ = AAM; △ or • = BPA; ♦ = CAC; ❑ = VAC; ⊕ = PO Statement; ‡ = Publisher's Report; Boldface figures = sworn; Light figures = estimated.

Rates: BW $1,070; 4C $1,485. **Remarks:** Accepts advertising. **Circ:** 421.

8866 ■ Laboratory Investigation
Lippincott Williams and Wilkins
Laboratory Investigation
United States & Canadian Academy of Pathology
3643 Walton Way Ext.
Augusta, GA 30909
Phone: (770)559-3569
Fax: (706)733-8033
Publication E-mail: labinvest@pathology.ufl.edu
Pathology journal.Publishes original manuscripts and review articles in the broad area of translational and basic research as is related to experimental pathology. **Freq:** Monthly. **Key Personnel:** Gene P. Siegal, PhD, Editor-in-Chief; Sylvia L. Asa, MD, Associate Editor; Robert W. Hardy, PhD, Associate Editor; Catherine M. Ketcham, PhD, Managing Editor. **ISSN:** 0023--6837 (print); **EISSN:** 1530--0307 (electronic). **Subscription Rates:** $401 Individuals print and online; $363 Individuals online only; €457 Individuals print and online - Europe; €411 Individuals online only - Europe; ¥78100 Individuals print and online - Japan; ¥70300 Individuals online only - Japan; £294 Other countries print and online - UK/Rest of the world; £265 Other countries online only - UK/Rest of the world; $91 Members print and online; $34 Members print and online - junior; $34 Members online only; €430 Individuals print and online - for all European countries (excluding the UK); €388 Individuals online only - for all European countries (excluding the UK); ¥73500 Individuals print and online - for Japan; ¥66200 Individuals online only - for Japan. **URL:** http://www.nature.com/labinvest/index.html; http://www.nature.com/labinvest/subscribe.html. **Remarks:** Accepts advertising. **Circ:** (Not Reported).

8867 ■ MCG Today
Medical College of Georgia - Division of University Advancement
Alumni Ctr., Fl-1000
1120 15th St.
Augusta, GA 30912
Phone: (706)721-4001
Free: 800-869-1113
Magazine for Medical College of Georgia. **Freq:** Quarterly. **Key Personnel:** Damon Cline, Editor. **URL:** http://www.gru.edu/mcg. **Circ:** (Not Reported).

8868 ■ MCG Tomorrow
Medical College of Georgia - Division of University Advancement
Alumni Ctr., Fl-1000
1120 15th St.
Augusta, GA 30912
Phone: (706)721-4001
Free: 800-869-1113
Magazine highlighting advances in thematic areas of cancer, cardiovascular disease, diabetes/obesity, infection/inflammation, and neurological disease. **Freq:** Annual. **Key Personnel:** Christine Hurley Deriso, Editor, phone: (706)721-2124, fax: (706)721-6397. **Circ:** (Not Reported).

8869 ■ Where Las Vegas Quick Guide
Best Read Guide
725 Broad St.
Augusta, GA 30901
Fax: (706)836-3596
Magazine offering tourism information on the city of Las Vegas including attractions, lodging, dining, etc. **Freq:** Monthly. **Trim Size:** 4 x 7. **Key Personnel:** Courtney Fuhrmann, Publisher. **URL:** http://www.wheretraveler.com/las-vegas. **Formerly:** Best Read Guide Las Vegas. **Remarks:** Accepts advertising. **Circ:** (Not Reported).

8870 ■ KCMJ-AM - 1270
725 Broad St.
Augusta, GA 30901
Phone: (706)724-0851
Free: 706-724-0851
Format: Oldies; Big Band/Nostalgia. **Owner:** Morris Desert Media. **Founded:** 1946. **Formerly:** Westminster Broadcasting Corp. **Operating Hours:** Continuous. **ADI:** Palm Springs, CA. **Key Personnel:** Bruce Johnson, Gen. Mgr. **Wattage:** 10,000. **Ad Rates:** Noncommercial. **URL:** http://www.morris.com.

KEAG-FM - See Anchorage, AK

KSAJ-FM - See Abilene, TX

8871 ■ WAGT-TV - 26
905 Broad St.
Augusta, GA 30901
Phone: (706)826-0026
Fax: (706)724-7491
Email: info@schurz.com
Format: Commercial TV. **Networks:** NBC. **Owner:** Schurz Communications and Co., 1301 E Douglas Rd., Mishawaka, IN 46545, Ph: (574)247-7237, Fax: (574)247-7238. **Founded:** 1968. **Operating Hours:** 6 a.m.-2:15 weekdays; 6 a.m.-1 a.m. Saturday and Sunday. **ADI:** Augusta, GA. **Key Personnel:** Mike Bell, Gen. Mgr.; Marilyn Brock, Bus. Mgr.; Pete Michenfelder, Gen. Sales Mgr. **Ad Rates:** Advertising accepted; rates available upon request. **URL:** http://www.schurz.com.

8872 ■ WAJY-FM - 102.7
4051 Jimmie Dyess Pky.
Augusta, GA 30909
Phone: (239)263-5000
Format: Adult Contemporary. **Networks:** CBS. **Founded:** 1989. **ADI:** Augusta, GA. **Key Personnel:** Brian Fawcett, Gen. Mgr., Contact; Ken Seigler, Dir. of Programs; Brian Fawcett, Contact. **Wattage:** 4,300 ERP. **Ad Rates:** $16 for 30 seconds; $20 for 60 seconds. **URL:** http://1027wgus.com.

8873 ■ WBBQ-AM - 1340
2743 Perimeter Pky., Bldg. 100, Ste. 300
Augusta, GA 30909
Phone: (706)396-6000
Fax: (706)396-6010
Email: info@csra.clearchannel.com
Format: Sports. **Founded:** 1946. **Operating Hours:** Continuous. **ADI:** Augusta, GA. **Key Personnel:** Cynthia Robinson, Bus. Mgr., cynthiarobinson@clearchannel.com; Lee Reynolds, Dir. of Programs, lee@wbbq.com; John Patrick, Mgr., johnmpatrick@clearchannel.com. **Wattage:** 1,000. **Ad Rates:** $34-120 for 30 seconds; $42-150 for 60 seconds. **URL:** http://foxsportsaugusta.iheart.com.

8874 ■ WBBQ-FM - 104.3
2743 Perimeter Parkway Bldg. 100, Ste. 300
Augusta, GA 30909
Phone: (706)396-6000
Format: Adult Contemporary; News. **Simulcasts:** WBBQ-AM. **Networks:** ABC. **Owner:** iHeartMedia Inc., 200 E Basse Rd., San Antonio, TX 78209, Ph: (210)832-3314. **Founded:** 1947. **Operating Hours:** Continuous; 5% network, 95% local. **ADI:** Augusta, GA. **Key Personnel:** Ivy Elam, Div. Pres., ivyelam@clearchannel.com; Cliff Bennett, Promotions Dir., cliffbennett@clearchannel.com. **Wattage:** 100,000. **Ad Rates:** $65-150 per unit. Combined advertising rates available with WBBQ-AM. **URL:** http://www.wbbq.com.

8875 ■ WCES-TV - 20
260 Fourteenth St. N
1540 Stewart Ave. SW
Atlanta, GA 30318-5360
Phone: (404)756-4700
Fax: (404)756-4713
Free: 800-222-6006
Format: Public TV. **Networks:** Public Broadcasting Service (PBS); Georgia Public Television. **Owner:** Georgia Public Telecommunications Commission, at above address. **Founded:** 1966. **Key Personnel:** Kent Steele, Dir. of Programs; Richard E. Ottinger, Contact; Frank Bugg, Contact; Al Korn, Contact; Carolyn F. Kowalski, Contact. **Wattage:** 7,900 ERP. **Ad Rates:** Noncommercial.

8876 ■ WCHZ-FM - 95.1
4051 Jimmie Dyess Pky.
Augusta, GA 30909
Phone: (706)396-7000
Fax: (706)396-7100
Format: Classic Rock. **Owner:** Beasley Broadcast Group Inc., 3033 Riviera Dr., Ste. 200, Naples, FL 34103-2750, Ph: (239)263-5000, Fax: (239)263-8191. **ADI:** Augusta, GA. **Key Personnel:** Chuck Williams, Dir. of Programs, chuck@95rock.com. **Ad Rates:** Advertising accepted; rates available upon request. **URL:** http://www.95rock.com.

8877 ■ WDRR-FM - 93.9
4051 Jimmie Dyess Pky.
Augusta, GA 30909
Phone: (706)396-7000
Fax: (706)396-7100
Format: Adult Contemporary; Eclectic. **Owner:** Beasley Broadcast Group Inc., 3033 Riviera Dr., Ste. 200, Naples, FL 34103-2750, Ph: (239)263-5000, Fax: (239)263-8191. **Founded:** Sept. 16, 2006. **Operating Hours:** Continuous. **Key Personnel:** Kent Murphy, Sales Mgr., kmurphy@bbgi.com; Chris O'Kelley, Operations Mgr., chris.okelley@bbgi.com. **Wattage:** 023. **Ad Rates:** Noncommercial. **URL:** http://ilovebobfm.com.

8878 ■ WFAM-AM - 1050
552 Laney-Walker Ext.
Augusta, GA 30901
Phone: (706)722-6077
Email: info@wilkinsradio.com
Format: Religious; Talk; Gospel. **Owner:** Wilkins Communications Network Inc., 292 S Pine St., Spartanburg, SC 29302, Ph: (864)585-1885, Fax: (864)597-0687, Free: 888-989-2299. **Founded:** 1960. **Operating Hours:** Continuous; 30% network, 70% local. **ADI:** Augusta, GA. **Key Personnel:** Bob Wilkins, Div. Dir.; Greg Garrett, Asst. Dir., glg@wilkinsradio.com. **Wattage:** 5,000. **Ad Rates:** Noncommercial. **URL:** http://www.wilkinsradio.com.

8879 ■ W58CZ - 58
PO Box A
Santa Ana, CA 92711
Phone: (714)832-2950
Free: 888-731-1000
Email: comments@tbn.org
Owner: Trinity Broadcasting Network Inc., PO Box A, Santa Ana, CA 92711, Ph: (714)832-2950, Free: 888-731-1000. **URL:** http://www.tbn.org.

8880 ■ WFXG-TV - 54
3933 Washington Rd.
Augusta, GA 30907
Phone: (706)650-5400
Fax: (706)650-8411
Ad Rates: Noncommercial. **URL:** http://www.wfxg.com.

8881 ■ WGAC-AM - 580
4051 Jimmie Dyess Pkwy.
Augusta, GA 30909
Phone: (706)863-5800
Format: News; Talk. **Networks:** CBS. **Founded:** 1970. **Operating Hours:** Continuous. **Key Personnel:** Harley Drew, Dir. of Programs; Mary Liz Nolan, Contact, maryliz@wgac.com. **Wattage:** 5,000. **Ad Rates:** $9-21 for 15 seconds; $10-24 for 30 seconds; $11-30 for 60 seconds. **URL:** http://www.wgac.com.

8882 ■ WGAC-FM - 93.1
4051 Jimmie Dyess Pky.
Augusta, GA 30909
Phone: (706)863-5800
Fax: (706)396-7000
Format: News; Talk. **Owner:** Beasley Broadcast Group Inc., 3033 Riviera Dr., Ste. 200, Naples, FL 34103-2750, Ph: (239)263-5000, Fax: (239)263-8191. **ADI:** Augusta, GA. **Key Personnel:** Harley Drew, Contact, harley@wgac.com; Harley Drew, Contact, harley@wgac.com. **Ad Rates:** Advertising accepted; rates available upon request. **URL:** http://www.wgac.com.

8883 ■ WGOR-FM - 93.9
4051 Jimmie Dyess Pky.
Augusta, GA 30909
Format: Oldies. **Networks:** CNN Radio. **Founded:** 1983. **Formerly:** WMTZ-FM. **Operating Hours:** Continuous. **ADI:** Augusta, GA. **Key Personnel:** Harley Drew, Contact; Kent Dunn, Gen. Mgr; Harley Drew, Contact. **Wattage:** 14,500 ERP. **Ad Rates:** Advertising accepted; rates available upon request. **URL:** http://ilovebobfm.com.

8884 ■ WHHD-FM - 98.3
4051 Jimmie Dyess Pky.
Augusta, GA 30909
Phone: (706)396-7000
Format: Contemporary Hit Radio (CHR). **Owner:** Beasley Broadcast Group Inc., 3033 Riviera Dr., Ste. 200, Naples, FL 34103-2750, Ph: (239)263-5000, Fax: (239)263-8191. **Operating Hours:** Continuous. **Key Personnel:** Kent Murphy, Sales Mgr., kmurphy@wgac.com. **Ad Rates:** Advertising accepted; rates available

upon request. **URL:** http://www.hd983.com.

8885 ■ WIBL-FM - 102.3
2743 Perimeter Pky., Bldg. 100, Ste. 300
Augusta, GA 30909
Phone: (706)396-6000
Format: Country. **Networks:** Jones Satellite. **Owner:** Clear Channel Radio, 200 E Basse Rd., San Antonio, TX 78209, Ph: (210)822-2828, Fax: (210)832-3428. **Founded:** 1989. **Formerly**: WTHQ. **Operating Hours**: Continuous. **Key Personnel:** Cliff Bennett, Promotions Dir., cliffbennett@clearchannel.com; Ivy Elam, Div. Pres., ivyelam@clearchannel.com. **Wattage**: 6,000. **Ad Rates:** Advertising accepted; rates available upon request. **URL:** http://www.eagle102.com.

8886 ■ WJBF-TV - 6
PO Box 1404
Augusta, GA 30903-1404
Phone: (706)722-6664
Email: investigate@wjbf.com
Format: Commercial TV. **Networks:** ABC. **Owner:** Media General Broadcast Group, 333 E Franklin St., Richmond, VA 23219, Ph: (804)887-5000. **Founded:** 1953. **ADI**: Augusta, GA. **Key Personnel:** Bill Stewart, Gen. Mgr.; Cary Hale, Chief Engineer. **Local Programs**: *WJBF-TV News Channel 6*. **Wattage**: 1,000,000 ERP H. **Ad Rates:** Accepts Advertising. **URL:** http://www2.wjbf.com.

8887 ■ WKSP-FM - 96.3
2743 Perimeter Pkwy., Bldg. 100, Ste. 300
Augusta, GA 30909
Phone: (706)396-6000
Fax: (706)396-6010
Email: augustapsa@clearchannel.com
Format: Blues; Hip Hop. **Key Personnel:** Ivy Elam, Gen. Mgr.; Cliff Bennett, Div. Dir., cliffbennett@iheartmedia.com. **Wattage**: 25,200. **Ad Rates:** Advertising accepted; rates available upon request. **URL:** http://www.963kissfm.com.

8888 ■ WKZK-AM
PO Box 1454
Augusta, GA 30903
Phone: (706)738-9191
Fax: (706)481-8442
Format: Gospel. **Networks:** American Urban Radio. **Owner:** Gospel Radio, Inc., at above address. **Founded:** 1982. **Formerly**: WFNL-AM. **Key Personnel:** Garfield Turner, Gen. Sales Mgr., Prog. Dir. **Local Programs**: *New Covenant Church*, Sunday 9:30 a.m. - 10:00 a.m.; *Tower of Refuge*, Monday Tuesday Wednesday Thursday Friday 10:30 a.m. **Wattage**: 4,000 Day; 027 Night. **Ad Rates:** $9 for 30 seconds; $18 for 60 seconds.

8889 ■ WPJK-AM - 1580
2358 Amsterdam Dr.
Augusta, GA 30906
Phone: (706)793-8084
Format: Religious. **Networks:** USA Radio. **Founded:** 1986. **Formerly**: WBLO-AM. **Operating Hours**: Sunrise-sunset. **Key Personnel:** Bose Gowdy, Gen. Mgr. **Wattage**: 1,000. **Ad Rates:** $4-13 for 60 seconds.

8890 ■ WPRW-FM - 107.7
2743 Perimeter Parkway Bldg. 100, Ste. 300
Augusta, GA 30909
Phone: (706)396-6000
Format: Hip Hop; Blues; Urban Contemporary. **Operating Hours:** Continuous. **Key Personnel:** Minnesota Fattz, Dir. of Programs, minnesotafattz@power107.net; Cher Best, Promotions Dir., cherbest@clearchannel.com; Ivy Elam, Div. Pres., ivyelam@clearchannel.com. **Ad Rates:** Advertising accepted; rates available upon request. **URL:** http://www.power107.net.

8891 ■ WRDW-AM - 1630
4051 Jimmie Dyess Pky.
Augusta, GA 30907
Format: Sports; News; Talk. **Owner:** Beasley Broadcast Group Inc., 3033 Riviera Dr., Ste. 200, Naples, FL 34103-2750, Ph: (239)263-5000, Fax: (239)263-8191. **Founded:** 1930. **Operating Hours**: Continuous. **ADI**: Augusta, GA. **Key Personnel:** Ashley Brown, Contact, ab@wrdwam.com. **Wattage**: 5,000. **Ad Rates:** $15-25 for 30 seconds; $20-30 for 60 seconds. **URL:** http://www.wrdwam.com.

8892 ■ WRMK-FM - 100.3
400 Warren Rd.
Augusta, GA 30907
Phone: (706)739-0022
Fax: (706)739-0229
Email: office@goodnewsaugusta.com
Format: Religious; Contemporary Christian. **Owner:** Good News Church, 135 Wildwood Dr., Saint Augustine, FL 32086, Ph: (904)819-0064. **Operating Hours**: Continuous. **Wattage**: 047. **Ad Rates:** Noncommercial; underwriting available. **URL:** http://www.goodnewsaugusta.com.

8893 ■ WSGF-AM - 1340
2743 Perimeter Pky., Bldg. 100, Ste. 300
Bldg. 100, Ste. 300
Augusta, GA 30909
Phone: (918)664-4581
Format: Gospel; Religious; Contemporary Christian. **Operating Hours:** Continuous. **Key Personnel:** Rob Collins, Dir. of Programs, robcollins@clearchannel.com; Jerome Turner, Gen. Sales Mgr., jerometurner@clearchannel.com. **Ad Rates:** Advertising accepted; rates available upon request. **URL:** http://foxsportsaugusta.iheart.com.

8894 ■ WTHB-AM
PO Box 1584
Augusta, GA 30903-1584
Phone: (803)279-2330
Fax: (803)279-8149
Format: Gospel. **Networks:** ABC; CBS. **Owner:** Radio One Licenses L.L.C., 1010 Wayne Ave., 14th Fl., Silver Spring, MD 20910. **Founded:** 1960. **ADI**: Augusta, GA. **Key Personnel:** Carroll Redd, Contact. **Wattage**: 5,000 Day; 011 Night.

8895 ■ WYNF-AM - 1380
2743 Perimeter Pkwy.
Bldg. 100, Ste. 300
Augusta, GA 30909
Phone: (706)396-6000
Fax: (706)396-6010
Email: augustapsa@clearchannel.com
Format: Sports. **Operating Hours**: Continuous. **Key Personnel:** Ivy Elam, Gen. Sales Mgr., ivyelam@clearchannel.com. **Ad Rates:** Advertising accepted; rates available upon request. **URL:** http://www.foxsportsaugusta.com.

8896 ■ WZNY-FM - 105.7
2743 Perimeter Pky., Bldg. 100, Ste. 300
Augusta, GA 30909
Phone: (918)664-4581
Networks: ABC. **Founded:** 1980. **Formerly**: WYMX-FM. **Operating Hours**: 12:00 a.m.- 7:00 p.m. Monday-Saturday;12:00 a.m.- 10:00 p.m. Sunday. **ADI**: Augusta, GA. **Key Personnel:** Cliff Bennett, Exec. Dir., cliffbennett@iheartmedia.com; Cynthia Robinson, Bus. Mgr., cynthiarobinson@iheartmedia.com; Birnie Florie, Mgr.; Bruce Stevens, Music Dir., Program Mgr.; Jon Brewster, Sales Mgr. **Wattage**: 100,000. **Ad Rates:** $8-67 for 30 seconds; $10-84 for 60 seconds. **URL:** http://bull1057.iheart.com.

AUSTELL

Douglas Co.

8897 ■ The Owner's Perspective
Construction Owners Association of America
5000 Austell Powder Springs Rd., Ste. 217
Austell, GA 30106
Phone: (770)433-0820
Fax: (404)577-3551
Free: 800-994-2622
Publisher's E-mail: coaa@coaa.org
Magazine featuring news and information to owners and developers across the county. **Freq:** Semiannual. **Subscription Rates:** Included in membership. **URL:** http://www.coaa.org/Owner-Resources/Owners-Perspective-en. **Remarks:** Accepts advertising. **Circ:** 25000.

8898 ■ WAOS-AM - 1600
5815 Westside Rd.
Austell, GA 30106-3179
Phone: (770)944-0900
Fax: (770)944-9794
Format: Hispanic. **Networks:** Independent. **Owner:** La Favorita, Inc., 60 Main St., East Rockaway, NY 11518. **Founded:** 1964. **Formerly**: WJYA-AM; WLKQ-AM. **Operating Hours**: Sunrise-sunset; network news. **Wattage**: 5,000. **Ad Rates:** $30 for 30 seconds; $40 for 60 seconds.

8899 ■ WLBA-AM - 1130
5815 Westside Rd.
Austell, GA 30106
Phone: (770)944-0900
Fax: (770)944-9794
Owner: La Favorita, Inc., 60 Main St., East Rockaway, NY 11518. **Founded:** 1957. **Formerly**: WNRJ-AM. **ADI**: Gainesville (Ocala), FL. **Ad Rates:** Accepts Advertising. **URL:** http://www.radiolafavorita.com/.

8900 ■ WXEM-AM - 1460
5815 Westside Rd.
Austell, GA 30106
Phone: (770)944-0900
Fax: (770)944-9794
Format: Hispanic. **Owner:** La Favorita, Inc., 60 Main St., East Rockaway, NY 11518.

BAINBRIDGE

SW GA. Decatur Co. On Flint River, 67 mi. SW of Albany. Fuller's earth mines. Manufactures bottle washing machinery, crates, boxes, asphalt, molded plastics, automotive ignition harnesses, lumber, mattresses, polypropylene fabrics. Tobacco packing; pecans shelling; cotton ginning. Pine timber. Diversified farming.

8901 ■ The Post-Searchlight
The Bainbridge Post-Searchlight Inc.
301 N Crawford St.
Bainbridge, GA 39817
Phone: (229)246-2827
Fax: (229)246-7665
Publisher's E-mail: news@thepostsearchlight.com
Newspaper. **Freq:** Semiweekly (Wed. and Sat.). **Print Method:** Offset. **Trim Size:** 13 3/4 x 22 3/4. **Cols./Page:** 6. **Col. Width:** 12.5 nonpareils. **Col. Depth:** 301 agate lines. **Key Personnel:** Jeff Findley, Publisher; Justin Schuver, Managing Editor. **USPS:** 439-920. **Subscription Rates:** $37 Individuals 1 year delivery; $30 Individuals 1 year senior delivery; $43 Individuals 1 year local mail out; $53 Individuals 1 year out of town mail. **URL:** http://thepostsearchlight.com. **Remarks:** Advertising accepted; rates available upon request. **Circ:** ‡7500.

8902 ■ The Post-Searchlight Extra
The Bainbridge Post-Searchlight Inc.
301 N Crawford St.
Bainbridge, GA 39817
Phone: (229)246-2827
Fax: (229)246-7665
Publisher's E-mail: news@thepostsearchlight.com
Shopper. **Freq:** Semiweekly (Wed. and Sat.). **Print Method:** Offset. **Cols./Page:** 6. **Col. Width:** 25 nonpareils. **Col. Depth:** 301 agate lines. **Key Personnel:** Jeff Findley, Publisher; Carol Heard, Managing Editor; Mark Pope, General Manager. **URL:** http://thepostsearchlight.com. **Ad Rates:** GLR $.31; BW $461. **Remarks:** Accepts advertising. **Circ:** Paid ‡7500.

8903 ■ WBGE-FM - 101.9
521 S Scott St.
Bainbridge, GA 39819
Phone: (229)246-7776
Format: Adult Contemporary; Soft Rock; Religious. **Key Personnel:** Bradley Warren, Contact, bradley@live1019.com. **Ad Rates:** Noncommercial. **URL:** http://www.sowegalive.com.

8904 ■ WKLD-FM - 97.7
1425 M L King Jr. Dr.
Bainbridge, GA 39817
Phone: (205)625-3333
Owner: Blount County Broadcasting System, at above address. **Founded:** 1968. **Wattage**: 4,000. **Ad Rates:** $4-8 for 30 seconds; $6-10 for 60 seconds. $3-$7 for 30 seconds; $4-$8 for 60 seconds. Combined advertising rates available with WCRL-AM.

8905 ■ WMGR-AM - 930
306 Boulevard Dr.
Bainbridge, GA 39819
Phone: (229)246-1650
Fax: (229)246-1403
Format: Oldies. **Networks:** ABC. **Founded:** 1946. **Operating Hours**: Continuous. **ADI**: Tallahassee, FL-

Circulation: ★ = AAM; △ or • = BPA; ♦ = CAC; ❑ = VAC; ⊕ = PO Statement; ‡ = Publisher's Report; Boldface figures = sworn; Light figures = estimated.

Thomasville (Bainbridge), GA. **Wattage**: 5,000. **Ad Rates:** Noncommercial. **URL:** http://www.wmgr.net.

8906 ■ WMGR-FM - 97.3
203 W Shotwell St.
Bainbridge, GA 39819
Phone: (229)246-1650
Fax: (229)246-1403
Format: Contemporary Hit Radio (CHR). **Founded:** 1960. **Operating Hours**: Continuous. **ADI**: Albany (Valdosta & Cordele), GA. **Local Programs**: *True Oldies Channel*. **Wattage**: 100,000. **Ad Rates:** $32 for 30 seconds; $42 for 60 seconds. **URL:** http://www.wmgr.net.

8907 ■ WMGR-TV - 22
306 Boulevard Dr.
Bainbridge, GA 39819-3996
URL: http://www.wmgr.net.

BARNESVILLE

W. GA. Lamar Co. 45 mi. S. of Atlanta. Manufactures tire fabrics, childrens clothing, wood products, lumber. Flour mill. Agriculture. Cotton, peaches, pecans, soybeans.

8908 ■ The Herald-Gazette
The Herald-Gazette
509 Greenwood St.
Barnesville, GA 30204
Fax: (770)358-0756
Local newspaper. **Founded:** 1869. **Freq:** Weekly. **Print Method:** Offset. **Cols./Page:** 6. **Col. Width:** 28 nonpareils. **Col. Depth:** 298 agate lines. **Key Personnel:** Walter Geiger, Publisher; Missy Ware, Office Manager; Sherri Ellington, Writer. **USPS:** 506-810. **Subscription Rates:** $25 Individuals in country; $40 Out of state; $35 Individuals mixed Georgia. **URL:** http://www.barnesville.com. **Circ:** ‡5000.

8909 ■ WBAF-AM - 1090
645 Forsyth St.
Barnesville, GA 30204
Phone: (770)358-1090
Fax: (770)358-1090
Format: Country; Religious. **Networks:** Georgia Radio; NBC. **Owner:** Barnesville Broadcasting Inc., at above address. **Founded:** 1966. **Operating Hours**: Sunrise-sunset; 10% network, 10% local, 80% other. **Key Personnel:** Ken Green, News Dir; Charles Waters, Contact. **Wattage**: 1,000. **Ad Rates:** $3.50 for 30 seconds; $5 for 60 seconds.

BAXLEY

SE GA. Appling Co. 45 mi. N. of Waycross. Manufactures mobile homes, garments, steel fabricated buildings, lumber. Naval stores. Truck, stock farms. Cotton, tobacco, blueberries, vegetables.

8910 ■ The Baxley News-Banner: Bipartisan
The Baxley News-Banner
PO Box 410
Baxley, GA 31515
Phone: (912)367-2468
Fax: (912)367-0277
Publication E-mail: mail@baxleynewsbanner.com
Newspaper with a Bipartisan orientation. **Freq:** Weekly (Wed.). **Print Method:** Offset. **Trim Size:** 14 x 22 1/2. **Cols./Page:** 6. **Col. Width:** 24 nonpareils. **Col. Depth:** 301 agate lines. **Key Personnel:** Matt Gardner, General Manager; Cindy Rogers, Office Manager; Jamie Gardner, Editor. **USPS:** 385-960. **Subscription Rates:** $30 Individuals online; $55 Individuals print & online. **URL:** http://baxleynewsbanner.com. **Remarks:** Advertising accepted; rates available upon request. **Circ:** ‡4600.

8911 ■ ATC BroadBand
371 W Parker St.
Baxley, GA 31513
Phone: (912)705-5000
Fax: (912)705-2959
Free: 800-540-6480
Email: sales@atcbroadband.com
Cities Served: 109 channels. **URL:** http://www.atcbroadband.com.

8912 ■ WBYZ-FM - 94.5
4005 Golden Isles Pky.
Baxley, GA 31515-0390
Phone: (912)367-3000
Format: Country. **Networks:** ABC. **Owner:** South Georgia Broadcasters Inc., at above address. **Founded:** 1954. **Operating Hours**: Continuous. **ADI**: Albany (Valdosta & Cordele), GA. **Wattage**: 100,000. **Ad Rates:** Noncommercial. **Mailing address:** PO Box 390, Baxley, GA 31515-0390. **URL:** http://www.wbyz94.com.

8913 ■ WUFE-AM - 1260
PO Box 390
Baxley, GA 31515
Phone: (912)367-3000
Fax: (912)367-9779
Format: Contemporary Christian. **Networks:** ABC. **Owner:** South Georgia Broadcasters Inc., at above address. **Founded:** 1954. **Operating Hours**: 6:00 a.m.-6:00 p.m. **ADI**: Savannah, GA. **Wattage**: 5,000. **Ad Rates:** $4 for 30 seconds; $6 for 60 seconds.

BETHLEHEM

8914 ■ WIMO-AM - 1300
PO Box 565
Bethlehem, GA 30620
Phone: (770)867-1300
Fax: (678)963-5483
Founded: 1952. **Ad Rates:** Noncommercial.

BLACKSHEAR

SE GA. Pierce Co. 8 mi. NE of Waycross. Utility-Industrial Park. Naval store industries. Manufactures fertilizer, lumber products, textiles, knives. Yellow pine timber. Agriculture. Tobacco, corn. pecans, livestock.

8915 ■ The Blackshear Times
The Blackshear Times
113 S Central Ave.
Blackshear, GA 31516
Phone: (912)449-6693
Fax: (912)449-1719
Publication E-mail: mail@theblackineartimes.com
Community newspaper. **Freq:** Weekly (Tues.). **Print Method:** Offset. **Cols./Page:** 6. **Col. Width:** 1.83 inches. **Col. Depth:** 294 agate lines. **Key Personnel:** Cheryl Williams, Associate Publisher; Robert M. Williams, Jr., Editor; Sandy Chancey, General Manager. **Subscription Rates:** $30 Individuals; $35 Out of area; $57 Two years; $67 Out of area 2 years. **URL:** http://theblackineartimes.com. **Ad Rates:** GLR $.25; BW $516; 4C $716; PCI $6.50. **Remarks:** Accepts advertising. **Circ:** 3600.

8916 ■ ATC Broadband
3349 Hwy. 84 W, Ste. 104
Blackshear, GA 31516
Phone: (912)449-5443
Fax: (912)449-2602
Free: 877-217-2842
Email: info@atc.cc
Cities Served: 104 channels. **URL:** http://www.atcbroadband.com.

8917 ■ WKUB-FM
2132 Highway 84
Blackshear, GA 31516
Phone: (912)449-3391
Fax: (912)449-6284
Email: wkub@almatel.net
Format: Country. **Networks:** ABC. **Owner:** Mattox Broadcasting, Inc., at above address. **Founded:** 1979. **Key Personnel:** Ray Williamson, Contact. **Wattage**: 50,000 ERP. **Ad Rates:** $12-16 for 30 seconds; $14-18 for 60 seconds.

BLAIRSVILLE

N. GA. Union Co. 85 mi. NE of Atlanta. Timber. Farming. Industrial.

8918 ■ North Georgia News
North Georgia News
266 Cleveland St.
Blairsville, GA 30514
Phone: (706)745-6343
Fax: (706)745-1830
Publisher's E-mail: northgeorgianews@hotmail.com
Newspaper. **Freq:** Weekly (Wed.). **Print Method:** Offset. **Cols./Page:** 6. **Col. Width:** 27 nonpareils. **Col. Depth:** 301 agate lines. **Key Personnel:** Norman Cooper, Editor; Kenneth West, Publisher; Justin Owenby, Director, Advertising. **Subscription Rates:** $35 Other countries; $3 Single issue; Free online only. **URL:** http://nganews.com. **Mailing address:** PO Box 2029 , Blairsville, GA 30514. **Ad Rates:** GLR $.17; BW $330.24; 4C $500; SAU $5.50; PCI $3.25. **Remarks:** Accepts advertising. **Circ:** Paid ‡9700, Free ‡5000.

BLAKELY

SW GA. Early Co. 50 mi. W. of Albany. Manufactures metal, paper products, textiles, farming machinery, truck trailers.Grist mills. Pine, hardwood timber. Agriculture. Cotton, peanuts, corn.

8919 ■ Early County News
The Early County News
529 College St.
Blakely, GA 39823
Phone: (229)723-4376
Fax: (229)723-6097
Publisher's E-mail: news@earlycountynews.com
Community newspaper. **Freq:** Weekly (Thurs.). **Print Method:** Offset. **Cols./Page:** 6. **Col. Width:** 25 nonpareils. **Col. Depth:** 301 agate lines. **Key Personnel:** William Fleming, Publisher; Judy Fleming, General Manager; Brenda Wall, Associate Editor. **ISSN:** 1640--6000 (print). **Subscription Rates:** $26.75 Individuals print & online; $48.68 Out of area print & online; $55.64 Individuals online only; $26.75 Out of area online only; $22.47 Individuals print & online (senior); $39.06 Out of area print & online (senior); $48.15 Two years print & online; $86.67 Out of area 2 years (print & online). **URL:** http://earlycountynews.com. **Ad Rates:** GLR $.25; BW $451.50; 4C $851.50; SAU $3.50. **Remarks:** Accepts advertising. **Circ:** ‡3,900.

8920 ■ Southern Festivals: The South's Festival Newspaper
Southern Festivals
PO Box 390
Blakely, GA 21723
Fax: (229)723-2779
Free: 800-558-3378
A statewide newspaper covering travel and tourism. **Freq:** Bimonthly. **Trim Size:** 10 x 13 1/2. **Cols./Page:** 5. **Col. Width:** 1 7/8 inches. **Key Personnel:** Jim Taylor, Contact. **URL:** http://www.southfest.com/index.html. **Remarks:** Accepts advertising. **Circ:** (Not Reported).

BLUE RIDGE

SC GA. Fannin Co.

8921 ■ The News Observer
The News Observer
5748 Appalachian Hwy.
Blue Ridge, GA 30513
Phone: (706)632-2019
Fax: (706)632-2577
Publisher's E-mail: news@thenewsobserver.com
Community newspaper. **Founded:** 1990. **Freq:** Weekly (Wed.). **Print Method:** Offset. **Trim Size:** 13 x 21 1/2. **Cols./Page:** 6. **Col. Width:** 12.5 picas. **Subscription Rates:** $25. **URL:** http://www.thenewsobserver.com. **Formerly**: The Observer. **Mailing address:** PO Box 989, Blue Ridge, GA 30513. **Ad Rates:** BW $735.30; 4C $1,000.30; PCI $6.71. **Remarks:** Accepts advertising. **Circ:** 10200.

8922 ■ WPPL-FM - 103.9
333 W Highland St.
Blue Ridge, GA 30513
Phone: (706)632-9775
Fax: (706)632-5922
Free: 888-632-9775
Format: Country. **Networks:** Georgia Radio; Satellite Music Network; Meadows Racing; Precision Racing. **Founded:** 1971. **Operating Hours**: Sun-Sat 6 a.m.-10 p.m. **Key Personnel:** Vicky Pulliam, Station Mgr. **Wattage**: 6,000. **Ad Rates:** $20-25 per unit. **URL:** http://www.mountaincountryradio.com.

8923 ■ W203BA-FM - 88.5
PO Box 391
Twin Falls, ID 83303
Fax: (208)736-1958
Free: 800-357-4226
Format: Religious; Contemporary Christian. **Owner:** CSN International, PO Box 391, Twin Falls, ID 83303, Ph: (208)736-1958, Fax: (208)736-1958, Free: 800-357-4226. **Key Personnel:** Kelly Carlson, Dir. of Engg.; Ray Gorney, Asst. Dir. **URL:** http://www.csnradio.com.

BOGART

NC GA. Oconee Co. 10 mi. W. of Athens.

8924 ■ WMSL-FM
2121 Ruth Jackson Blvd.
Bogart, GA 30622
Phone: (770)725-8890
Fax: (678)753-0088
Email: gm@wmsl.fm
Format: Religious. **Wattage:** 20,000 ERP.

BREMEN

SE GA. NW GA. Haralson Co Haralson Co. 40 mi. W. of Atlanta 5 mi. NE of Waco.

8925 ■ WGMI-AM - 1440
613 Tallapoosa St.
Bremen, GA 30110
Phone: (770)537-0840
Fax: (770)406-2324
Email: wgmi1440@yahoo.com
Format: Contemporary Christian; Gospel. **Networks:** Country Gold. **Owner:** Garner Ministries, Inc., 23 Eden Dr., Danbury, CT 06810, Ph: (203)778-4444, Fax: (203)797-0702. **Founded:** 1957. **Formerly:** WSLE-AM; WBKI-AM. **Key Personnel:** Scott Garner, Contact. **Wattage:** 2,500 Daytime;062 Nig. **Ad Rates:** $6-10 for 30 seconds; $14 for 60 seconds. **URL:** http://www.1440thetrain.com.

BRUNSWICK

SE GA. Glynn Co. 60 mi. N. of Jacksonville. Seaport. Tourism. Manufactures plastics, sheet rock, turpentine, resin, lumber, paint, steam boilers, caustic soda, chlorine. Seafood and auto processing. Shrimp fisheries. Pine timber.

8926 ■ The Brunswick News
Brunswick News Publishing Co.
PO Box 1557
Brunswick, GA 31521
Phone: (912)265-8320
Fax: (912)264-4973
Publisher's E-mail: editor@thebrunswicknews.com
General newspaper. **Freq:** Mon.-Sat. **Print Method:** Offset. **Cols./Page:** 6. **Col. Width:** 2 1/16 inches. **Col. Depth:** 21 inches. **Key Personnel:** Amy Carter, Editor; Ron Maulden, General Manager; Kerry Klumpe, Managing Editor. **USPS:** 068-180. **Subscription Rates:** $119.32 Individuals; $99.44 By mail. **URL:** http://www.thebrunswicknews.com. **Ad Rates:** GLR $9.52; 4C $1484.52; SAU $9.52; PCI $9.52; BW $1199.52. **Remarks:** Advertising accepted; rates available upon request. **Circ:** ‡16,284, ‡16,284.

8927 ■ WGIG-AM - 1440
3833 US Hwy. 82
Brunswick, GA 31523
Phone: (912)267-1025
Format: News; Talk; Sports. **Networks:** ABC. **Owner:** Qantum Communications, Inc., at above address. **ADI:** Jacksonville (Brunswick), FL. **Wattage:** 5,000 Day; 1,000 Nig. **Ad Rates:** Noncommercial. **URL:** http://www.1440wgig.iheart.com.

8928 ■ WHFX-FM - 107.7
3833 US Higway 82
Brunswick, GA 31523
Format: Classic Rock. **Owner:** Qantum Communications, Inc., at above address. **Founded:** 1972. **Operating Hours:** Continuous. **Wattage:** 50,000. **Ad Rates:** Noncommercial; Advertising accepted; rates available upon request. $20-25 for 30 seconds; $25-40 for 60 seconds.

8929 ■ WRJY-FM - 104.1
185 Benedict Rd.
Brunswick, GA 31520
Phone: (912)261-1000
Fax: (912)265-8391
Format: Country. **Owner:** Golden Isles Broadcasting, at above address. **Key Personnel:** Joe Willie Sousa, Gen. Mgr., joewilliesousa@goldenislesbroadcasting.com; Jack Edwards, Operations Mgr., Prog. Dir., jackedwards@goldenislesbroadcasting.com; Everett Armstrong, Bus. Mgr., everett@goldenislesbroadcasting.com. **URL:** http://goldenislesbroadcasting.com.

8930 ■ WSFN-AM - 790
7515 Blythe Island Hwy.
Brunswick, GA 31523
Phone: (912)264-6251
Fax: (912)264-9991
Format: Sports. **Networks:** CNN Radio; ABC; ESPN Radio. **Owner:** MarMac Communication, 7515 Blythe Island Hwy., Brunswick, GA 31523-6261. **Formerly:** WPIQ-AM. **Operating Hours:** Continuous. **Key Personnel:** Gary Marmitt, Owner. **Wattage:** 615. **Ad Rates:** Noncommercial.

8931 ■ W33AL - 33
PO Box A
Santa Ana, CA 92711
Phone: (714)832-2950
Free: 888-731-1000
Owner: Trinity Broadcasting Network Inc., PO Box A, Santa Ana, CA 92711, Ph: (714)832-2950, Free: 888-731-1000. **URL:** http://www.tbn.org.

8932 ■ W218BK-FM - 91.5
PO Box 391
Twin Falls, ID 83303
Fax: (208)736-1958
Free: 800-357-4226
Format: Religious; Contemporary Christian. **Owner:** CSN International, PO Box 391, Twin Falls, ID 83303, Ph: (208)736-1958, Fax: (208)736-1958, Free: 800-357-4226. **Key Personnel:** Ray Gorney, Asst. Dir.; Kelly Carlson, Dir. of Engg. **URL:** http://www.csnradio.com.

8933 ■ WXMK-FM - 105.9
185 Benedict Rd.
Brunswick, GA 31520
Phone: (912)261-1000
Fax: (912)265-8391
Format: Top 40. **Key Personnel:** Bryan Steele, Gen. Mgr. **Wattage:** 25,000. **Ad Rates:** Noncommercial. **URL:** http://www.magic1059.com.

WYNR-FM - See Waycross

BUFORD

NC GA. Hall Co. 15 mi. N. of Swannee.

8934 ■ W201CC-FM - 88.1
PO Box 391
Twin Falls, ID 83303
Fax: (208)736-1958
Free: 800-357-4226
Format: Religious; Contemporary Christian. **Owner:** CSN International, PO Box 391, Twin Falls, ID 83303, Ph: (208)736-1958, Fax: (208)736-1958, Free: 800-357-4226. **Key Personnel:** Kelly Carlson, Dir. of Engg.; Ray Gorney, Asst. Dir. **URL:** http://www.csnradio.com.

CAIRO

SW GA. Grady Co. 6 mi. E. of Whigham. Residential.

8935 ■ Cairo Messenger
Cairo Messenger Inc.
PO Box 30
Cairo, GA 39828-0030
Phone: (229)377-2032
Fax: (229)377-4640
Publisher's E-mail: news@cairomessenger.com
Community newspaper. **Freq:** Weekly (Wed.). **Print Method:** Offset. **Cols./Page:** 6. **Col. Width:** 12.04 picas. **Col. Depth:** 21 inches. **USPS:** 888-260. **Subscription Rates:** $21.40 Individuals in Grady County; $19.26 Individuals senior citizen; $29.96 Individuals in Georgia; $26.96 Individuals in Georgia (senior citizen); $32 Out of state; $28.80 Out of state senior citizen. **URL:** http://www.cairomessenger.com. **Remarks:** Accepts advertising. **Circ:** (Not Reported).

8936 ■ WGRA-AM - 790
1809 Hwy. 84 W
Cairo, GA 39828
Phone: (229)377-4392
Fax: (229)377-4564
Email: info@wgra.net
Format: News; Talk. **Key Personnel:** Jeff Lovett, Contact, jeff@wgra.net; Norman Pyles, Contact, norman@wgra.net. **Wattage:** 1,000. **Mailing address:** PO Box 120, Cairo, GA 39828. **URL:** http://www.wgra.net.

CALHOUN

NW GA. Gordon Co. 60 mi. N. of Atlanta. Manufactures carpets, rugs, ball bearings, concrete mixers, outboard motors. Lumber. Agriculture. Corn, hay. Poultry.

8937 ■ The Calhoun Times
News Publishing Co.
215 W Line St.
Calhoun, GA 30701-1815
Phone: (706)629-2231
Fax: (706)625-0899
Newspaper with a Democratic orientation. **Founded:** 1870. **Freq:** Semiweekly (Wed. and Sat.). **Print Method:** Offset. **Cols./Page:** 6. **Col. Width:** 21 nonpareils. **Col. Depth:** 301 agate lines. **Key Personnel:** Billy Steele, Manager, Advertising; Brandi Owczarz, Editor. **URL:** http://www.northwestgeorgianews.com/calhoun_times/. **Ad Rates:** BW $867; 4C $905; PCI $11.99. **Remarks:** Accepts advertising. **Circ:** Paid ‡7930.

8938 ■ WEBS-AM - 1030
PO Box 1299
Calhoun, GA 30703
Phone: (706)629-1110
Format: News; Oldies; Sports; Classic Rock. **Simulcasts:** WEBS-FM. **Owner:** Radio WEBS, Inc., at above address. **Founded:** 1966. **Wattage:** 5,000 Daytime; 003 Nigh. **Ad Rates:** Advertising accepted; rates available upon request. $8 for 30 seconds; $10 for 60 seconds. **URL:** http://webscalhoun.com/.

8939 ■ WJTH-AM - 900
PO Box 1119
Calhoun, GA 30703
Phone: (706)629-6397
Format: Country. **Networks:** ABC. **Founded:** 1977. **Operating Hours:** Continuous; 2% network, 98% local. **ADI:** Atlanta (Athens & Rome), GA. **Key Personnel:** Sam Thomas, Gen. Mgr., sthomas@wjth.com; Gloria Cooley, Sales Mgr., gloriajcooley@att.net; Keith Thomas, Dir. of Traffic, Prog. Dir. **Wattage:** 1,000. **Ad Rates:** $11.80-12.95 for 30 seconds; $15.10-16.20 for 60 seconds. **URL:** http://wjth.com.

8940 ■ WLOJ-FM - 102.9
255 Conference Rd. N
Calhoun, GA 30701
Format: Religious; News; Talk; Contemporary Christian. **Operating Hours:** Continuous. **URL:** http://www.lifetalk.net/stationInfo.html?id=6.

CAMILLA

SW GA. Mitchell Co. 26 mi. S. of Albany. Manufactures fertilizer, cottonseed oil, textiles. Poultry and peanut processing; lumber mills. Pine timber. Stock, cattle, poultry, truck farms. Cotton, corn, soybeans, peanuts, pecans.

8941 ■ WCLB-AM - 1400
Drawer 113
Camilla, GA 31730
Phone: (912)336-5614
Format: Classic Rock. **Networks:** ABC. **Owner:** McMinn Communications, 1107 S Congress Pky., Athens, TN 37303. **Founded:** 1954. **Operating Hours:** 6 a.m.-10 p.m.; 5% network, 95% local. **ADI:** Columbus, GA (Opelika, AL). **Key Personnel:** Ed McMinn, Contact; Jerry White, Contact. **Wattage:** 1,000. **Ad Rates:** $8.75 for 30 seconds.

CANTON

NW GA. Cherokee Co. On Etowah River, 35 mi. NW of Atlanta. Cotton mills. Chicken processing plants. Pine, poplar timber. Agriculture. Corn, poultry, livestock.

8942 ■ Cherokee Tribune
Neighbor Newspapers Inc.
521 E Main St.
Canton, GA 30114
Phone: (770)479-1441
Community newspaper covering for Cherokee County, Georgia. **Freq:** Daily. **Key Personnel:** Wade Stephens, Vice President, Advertising, phone: (770)428-9411; Otis A. Brumby, Jr., Publisher. **Subscription Rates:** $1 Individuals /week (home delivery & online); $1.02 Individuals /week (online only). **URL:** http://www.cherokeetribune.com/. **Remarks:** Accepts advertising. **Circ:** ‡6800.

Circulation: ★ = AAM; △ or • = BPA; ♦ = CAC; ❑ = VAC; ⊕ = PO Statement; ‡ = Publisher's Report; Boldface figures = sworn; Light figures = estimated.

8943 ■ Circuits Assembly: The Journal for Surface Mount and Electronics Assembly
UP Media Group Inc.
PO Box 470
Canton, GA 30169
Phone: (404)661-0349
Serves the PCB assembly marketplace. **Freq:** Monthly. **Print Method:** Offset. **Trim Size:** 8 x 10 3/4. **Cols./Page:** 3 and 2. **Col. Width:** 26 and 40 nonpareils. **Col. Depth:** 140 agate lines. **Key Personnel:** Mike Buetow, Editor-in-Chief, phone: (617)327-4702; Chelsey Drysdale, Senior Editor; Pete Waddell, President, Publisher. **ISSN:** 1070--4779 (print). **URL:** http://www.circuitsassembly.com/ca; http://upmediagroup.com/publications.shtml. **Remarks:** Advertising accepted; rates available upon request. **Circ:** Combined ‡32000.

8944 ■ WCHK-AM
2203 Wynnton Rd.
Columbus, GA 31902
Phone: (706)576-5360
Fax: (770)479-1134
Format: News; Oldies. **Networks:** Georgia Radio; USA Radio. **Owner:** Davis Broadcasting of Atlanta, LLC, at above address. **Founded:** 1957. **Wattage:** 10,000 Day; 500 Nigh. **Ad Rates:** $10-15 for 30 seconds; $15-20 for 60 seconds.

8945 ■ WNSY-FM - 100.1
2189 Marietta Hwy.
Canton, GA 30114
Phone: (770)720-0110
Fax: (770)479-1134
Format: Hispanic. **Owner:** Davis Broadcasting of Atlanta L.L.C., 2203 Wynnton Rd., Columbus, GA 31902. **Key Personnel:** Rebecca Johnston, Gen. Mgr. **Wattage:** 25,000. **Ad Rates:** Noncommercial.

CARROLLTON

W. GA. Carroll Co. 50 mi. SW of Atlanta. West Georgia College; Carroll County Area Voc-Tech.; John Tanner State Park. Fishing, boating and swimming. Manufactures wire and cable products, auto body parts, stainless steel pipes & tubing, textiles.

8946 ■ Peregrinations
International Society for the Study of Pilgrimage Art
324 Humanities Hall
Art Dept.
University of West Georgia
Carrollton, GA 30118
Phone: (770)836-4532
Fax: (770)836-4392
Journal that examines pilgrimage art and architecture. **Freq:** Periodic. **Key Personnel:** Sarah Blick, Editor-in-Chief; Rita Tekippe, Executive Editor. **ISSN:** 1554--8678 (print). **URL:** http://peregrinations.kenyon.edu. **Remarks:** Advertising not accepted. **Circ:** (Not Reported).

8947 ■ The Times-Georgian
The Times-Georgian
901 Hay's Mill Rd.
Carrollton, GA 30117
Phone: (770)834-6631
Publication E-mail: publisher@times-georgian.com
General newspaper. **Freq:** Tues.-Sun. **Print Method:** Offset. **Cols./Page:** 6. **Col. Width:** 25 nonpareils. **Col. Depth:** 301 agate lines. **Key Personnel:** Leonard Woolsey, Publisher; John Knoll, Manager, Circulation. **Subscription Rates:** $4.30 Individuals /week. **URL:** http://times-georgian.com. **Remarks:** Advertising accepted; rates available upon request. **Circ:** Combined ★15868.

8948 ■ Transactions of the Charles S. Peirce Society: A Quarterly Journal in American Philosophy
Charles S. Peirce Society
University of West Georgia
Philosophy Program
1601 Maple St.
Carrollton, GA 30118
The premier journal specializing in the history of American philosophy. **Freq:** Quarterly. **Cols./Page:** 1. **Col. Width:** 84 nonpareils. **Col. Depth:** 140 agate lines. **Key Personnel:** Cornelis de Waal, Editor-in-Chief. **ISSN:** 0009--1774 (print); **EISSN:** 1558--9578 (electronic). **Subscription Rates:** $44 U.S.; $88 Two years; $85 Institutions. **URL:** http://peircesociety.org/transactions.html. **Remarks:** Accepts advertising. **Circ:** (Not Reported).

8949 ■ WBTR-FM - 92.1
102 Parkwood Cir.
Carrollton, GA 30117
Phone: (770)834-9685
Fax: (770)830-1027
Format: Country. **Simulcasts:** WLBB-AM, WKNG-AM, KISS-FM, WWGA-FM. **Owner:** Georgia Radio, at above address. **Founded:** 1964. **Wattage:** 580 ERP. **Ad Rates:** $9-12 for 30 seconds; $11-15 for 60 seconds. **URL:** http://www.b92country.com/.

8950 ■ WCKS-FM - 102.7
102 Parkwood Cir.
Carrollton, GA 30117
Phone: (770)834-5477
Fax: (770)830-1027
Format: Adult Contemporary. **Operating Hours:** Continuous. **Key Personnel:** Steve Gradick, Owner; Michael Vincent, Dir. of Production, production@wcks.com. **Wattage:** 1,650. **Ad Rates:** Noncommercial. **URL:** http://www.gradickcommunications.com.

8951 ■ WLBB-AM - 1330
808 Newnan Rd.
Carrollton, GA 30117
Phone: (678)601-1330
Fax: (678)601-8256
Format: Talk; News. **Networks:** Independent. **Owner:** WYAI Inc., 102 Parkwood Cir., Carrollton, GA 30117. **Founded:** 1947. **Operating Hours:** Daytime; 100% local. **ADI:** Atlanta (Athens & Rome), GA. **Key Personnel:** Steve Gradick, Contact, steve1027@aol.com; Michael Vincent, Dir. of Production; Steve Gradick, Contact, steve1027@aol.com. **Wattage:** 1,000. **Ad Rates:** Noncommercial. **URL:** http://www.gradickcommunications.com.

8952 ■ WPPI-AM - 1330
808 Newnan Rd.
Carrollton, GA 30117
Phone: (404)832-1330
Format: Adult Contemporary; Oldies; Talk. **Networks:** NBC. **Owner:** W.P. Johnson, at above address. **Founded:** 1974. **Operating Hours:** 6 a.m.-midnight; 15% network, 85% local. **Key Personnel:** Gordon Staples, Contact. **Wattage:** 500. **Ad Rates:** $3.75-6 for 30 seconds; $5-7 for 60 seconds. **URL:** http://ecorp.sos.ga.gov/BusinessSearch/BusinessInformation?businessId=1028907&businessType=Domestic%20Profit%20Corporation.

CARTERSVILLE

NW GA. Bartow Co. 40 mi. NW of Atlanta. Manufactures plastic bags. Carpet and knitting mills. Limestone, barium, iron ore, manganese mines; pine timber. Livestock.

8953 ■ The Daily Tribune News
Cartersville Newspapers
251 S Tenn. St.
Cartersville, GA 30120-0070
Fax: (770)382-2711
General newspaper. **Freq:** Weekly (Tues.). **Print Method:** Offset. **Trim Size:** 14 x 22 3/4. **Cols./Page:** 6. **Col. Width:** 26 nonpareils. **Col. Depth:** 301 agate lines. **USPS:** 146-740. **Subscription Rates:** $98.95 Individuals print only; $99.95 Individuals print by carrier + e-edition; $99.95 Individuals print by mail + e-edition; $169.95 Out of country print by mail + e-edition; $207.95 Out of state print by mail + e-edition. **Alt. Formats:** CD-ROM. **URL:** http://daily-tribune.com. **Remarks:** Advertising accepted; rates available upon request. **Circ:** 102000.

8954 ■ WBHF-AM - 1450
1410 Hwy. 411 N
Cartersville, GA 30121
Phone: (770)321-6400
Free: 800-888-1047
Format: Full Service. **Networks:** Fox. **Founded:** 1946. **Operating Hours:** 6:00a.m-3:00p.m Monday-Friday,6:00a.m-5:30p.m Saturday-Sunday. **Wattage:** 1,000 Daytime;1,000. **Ad Rates:** Accepts Advertising. **URL:** http://www.wbhf1450.com/.

8955 ■ WCCV-FM - 91.7
779 S Erwin St.
Cartersville, GA 30120-1000
Phone: (770)387-0917
Fax: (770)387-2856
Free: 800-387-0917
Email: onair@ibn.org
Format: Religious. **Networks:** Ambassador Inspirational Radio; SkyLight Satellite. **Owner:** Immanuel Broadcasting Network, 779 S Erwin St., Cartersville, GA 30120, Ph: (770)387-0917, Fax: (770)387-2856. **Founded:** 1983. **Operating Hours:** 95% local, 5% network. **Key Personnel:** Ed Tuten, Founder. **Wattage:** 7,300. **Ad Rates:** Underwriting available. **Mailing address:** PO Box 1000, Cartersville, GA 30120-1000. **URL:** http://www.ibn.org.

8956 ■ WYXC-AM - 1270
1410 Hwy. 411 NE
Cartersville, GA 30120
Phone: (770)334-8302
Format: News; Talk. **Networks:** Fox; Westwood One Radio. **Owner:** Clarion Communications Inc., 83 Clerkenwell Rd. 83 Clerkenwell Road, London EC1R 5AR, United Kingdom, Ph: 44 20 747-909-10. **Founded:** 1961. **Operating Hours:** Continuous; 85% network, 15% local. **ADI:** Atlanta (Athens & Rome), GA. **Wattage:** 2,000 005 Day; 187 sunset. **Ad Rates:** $10 for 30 seconds; $12 for 60 seconds. **Mailing address:** PO Box 200399, Cartersville, GA 30120.

CEDARTOWN

NW GA. Polk Co. 40 mi. SW of Rome.

8957 ■ The Cedartown Standard
News Publishing Co.
213 Main St.
Cedartown, GA 30125
Phone: (706)291-6397
Fax: (706)234-6478
Community newspaper. **Freq:** Semiweekly Tues. and Thurs. **Print Method:** Offset. **Trim Size:** 13 3/4 x 22 3/4. **Cols./Page:** 6. **Col. Width:** 2 1/16 inches. **Col. Depth:** 21 1/4 inches. **Key Personnel:** Lowell Vickers, Editor. **URL:** http://www.northwestgeorgianews.com/polkfishwrap/news/cedartown; http://www.npco.com. **Remarks:** Accepts advertising. **Circ:** Paid ‡3400.

8958 ■ WGAA-AM - 1340
413 Lakeview Dr.
Cedartown, GA 30125
Phone: (770)748-1340
Fax: (770)748-4539
Email: info@wgaaradio.com
Format: Country; Adult Contemporary; Religious. **Networks:** NBC. **Owner:** Burgess Broadcasting Corp., 413 Lakeview Dr , Cedartown, GA 30125-2020. **Founded:** 1941. **Operating Hours:** Continuous. **Local Programs:** *Andrew Carter in the Morning*, Monday Tuesday Wednesday Thursday Friday Saturday Sunday 6:30 a.m.; 7:30 a.m.; 8:30 a.m. 7:30 a.m.; 8:30 a.m. 7:30 a.m. - 7:45 a.m. **Wattage:** 1,000. **Ad Rates:** $7.50-12.50 for 30 seconds; $8.50-13.50 for 60 seconds. **Mailing address:** PO Box 167, Cedartown, GA 30125. **URL:** http://www.wgaaradio.com.

CHATSWORTH

NW GA. Murray Co. 38 mi. SE of Chattanooga, TN. Summer resort. Manufactures textiles, talc products. Talc mines; pine timber. Agriculture. Corn, cotton, hay.

8959 ■ Chatsworth Times
Walls Newspapers
PO Box 130
Chatsworth, GA 30705
Phone: (706)695-4646
Publication E-mail: news@chatsworthtimes.com
Newspaper. **Freq:** Weekly (Thurs.). **Print Method:** Offset. **Cols./Page:** 6. **Col. Width:** 21 nonpareils. **Col. Depth:** 287 agate lines. **Key Personnel:** Lorri Harrison, Editor, General Manager. **Subscription Rates:** $21.95 Individuals; $35 Out of area. **URL:** http://chatsworthtimes.com. **Ad Rates:** BW $586.95; 4C $786.95; SAU $6; PCI $4.55. **Remarks:** Accepts advertising. **Circ:** Paid 5400.

8960 ■ WNGH-TV - 18
2765 Fort Mountain Park Rd.
Chatsworth, GA 30705
Phone: (404)685-2389
Free: 800-222-4788
Email: ask@gpb.org
Owner: Georgia Public Broadcasting, 260 14th St. NW, Atlanta, GA 30318, Ph: (404)685-2400, Free: 800-222-

6006. **URL:** http://www.gpb.org.

CLARKESVILLE

NE GA. Habersham Co. 80 mi. NE of Atlanta. Saw, planing, grist, knitting mills; poultry processing plant. Manufactures electrical products, furniture, textiles. Walnut, pine timber. Fruit, truck farms. Peaches, apples, beans.

8961 ■ WCHM-AM - 1490
683 Grant St., Ste.U.
Clarkesville, GA 30523
Format: Southern Gospel. **Networks:** USA Radio. **Founded:** 1975. **Formerly**: WLTA-AM. **Operating Hours**: Continuous; 5% network, 95% local. **Wattage**: 1,000. **Ad Rates:** $9.75 for 30 seconds; $10 for 60 seconds. **URL:** http://www.wchmradio.com/.

CLAXTON

SE GA. Evans Co. 50 mi. W. of Savannah. Residential.

8962 ■ The Claxton Enterprise
The Claxton Enterprise Inc.
PO Box 218
Claxton, GA 30417
Phone: (912)739-2132
Fax: (912)739-2140
Local newspaper. **Freq:** Weekly (Wed.). **Print Method:** Offset. **Cols./Page:** 6. **Col. Width:** 26 nonpareils. **Col. Depth:** 294 agate lines. **Key Personnel:** Pamela A. Peace, Publisher; Mitchell E. Peace, Publisher. **Subscription Rates:** $30 Individuals in state, print and online; $7 Individuals online access only. **URL:** http://claxtonenterprise.com. **Mailing address:** PO Box 218, Claxton, GA 30417. **Ad Rates:** BW $504; 4C $629; PCI $5.75. **Remarks:** Accepts advertising. **Circ:** ‡3500.

8963 ■ WCLA-AM - 1470
316 N River St.
Claxton, GA 30417
Phone: (912)739-9252
Format: Oldies. **Networks:** Georgia Radio; ABC. **Founded:** 1958. **Operating Hours**: Continuous. **ADI**: Savannah, GA. **Wattage**: 1,000 Day; 260 Night. **Ad Rates:** $6-8 for 30 seconds; $9-10 for 60 seconds. Combined advertising rates available with WCLA-FM. **URL:** http://www.wclaradio.net.

8964 ■ WMCD-FM - 100.1
6316 Peake Rd.
Macon, GA 31210
Phone: (912)764-5446
Fax: (912)764-8827
Format: Adult Contemporary. **Networks:** Independent. **Owner:** Georgia Eagle Broadcasting, Inc., at above address. **Founded:** 1967. **Operating Hours**: Continuous; 100% local. **ADI**: Savannah, GA. **Wattage**: 50,000. **Ad Rates:** $12-14 per unit. Combined advertising rates available with WUNS-AM, WSYL-AM, WZBX-FM.

CLAYTON

NE GA. Rabun Co. 45 mi. NE of Gainesville. Tourist resort. Skiing, whitewater rafting. Manufactures textiles, fabricated metal products, carpets. Saw mills. Pine, hardwood timber. Agriculture.

8965 ■ The Clayton Tribune: Serving Rabun County, Georgia
Community Newspapers Inc.
120 N Main St.
Clayton, GA 30525
Phone: (706)782-3312
Fax: (706)782-4230
Publication E-mail: thetribune@theclaytontribune.com
Community newspaper. **Freq:** Weekly (Thurs.). **Print Method:** Offset. **Trim Size:** 13 x 21 1/4. **Cols./Page:** 6. **Col. Depth:** 21.5 picas. **Key Personnel:** Blake Spurney, Editor. **Subscription Rates:** $30 Individuals in county (print and online); $37 Out of country print and online; $30 Out of country online only. **URL:** http://theclaytontribune.com. **Mailing address:** PO Box 425, Clayton, GA 30525. **Remarks:** Advertising accepted; rates available upon request. **Circ:** Paid 6500.

CLEVELAND

NE GA. White Co. 30 mi. N. of Clermont.

8966 ■ White County News
White County News
13 E Jarrard St.
Cleveland, GA 30528
Publication E-mail: publisher@whitecountynews.net
Community newspaper. **Freq:** Weekly (Thurs.). **Print Method:** Offset. **Cols./Page:** 6. **Col. Width:** 12 picas. **Col. Depth:** 21 1/2 inches. **Key Personnel:** Billy Chism, Publisher. **USPS:** 682-400. **URL:** http://www.whitecountynews.net. **Ad Rates:** PCI $3.55. **Remarks:** Accepts advertising. **Circ:** 7000.

8967 ■ White County News-Telegraph
Community Newspapers Inc.
13 E Jarrard St.
Cleveland, GA 30528
Phone: (706)865-4718
Fax: (706)865-3048
Publisher's E-mail: dnesmith@cninewspapers.com
Newspaper serving White County, Georgia. **Freq:** Weekly (Thurs.). **Key Personnel:** Billy Chism, Editor, Publisher. **Subscription Rates:** $30 Individuals in White County; $40 Out of area; $50 Out of state; $7 Individuals online - monthly. **URL:** http://www.whitecountynewstelegraph.com. **Remarks:** Accepts advertising. **Circ:** Paid 6000.

8968 ■ WRWH-AM - 1350
PO Box 181
Cleveland, GA 30528
Phone: (706)865-3181
Fax: (706)865-0421
Email: info@wrwh.com
Format: Country; Talk. **Founded:** 1958. **Operating Hours**: 6 a.m.-Sunrise-sunset. **ADI**: Atlanta (Athens & Rome), GA. **Local Programs**: *Swap Shop*. **Wattage**: 1,000. **Ad Rates:** Noncommercial. **URL:** http://www.wrwh.com.

COBB

8969 ■ The East Cobb Neighbor
Echo Media
900 Circle 75 Pky., Ste. 1600
Atlanta, GA 30339
Phone: (770)955-3535
Fax: (770)955-3599
Publisher's E-mail: salesinfo@echo-media.com
Community newspaper. **Freq:** Daily. **Print Method:** Offset. **Cols./Page:** 6. **Col. Width:** 26 nonpareils. **Col. Depth:** 301 agate lines. **USPS:** 398-050. **Subscription Rates:** Free. **URL:** http://echomedia.com/medias/details/4305/east+cobb+neighbor. **Ad Rates:** GLR $1.05; BW $1902.75; 4C $2192.75; SAU $14.75. **Remarks:** Accepts advertising. **Circ:** Free 41950.

COCHRAN

C. GA. Bleckley Co. 40 mi. S. of Macon. Manufactures textiles, fluorescent lighting fixtures. Planing mill; cotton ginning. Pine timber. Agriculture. Cotton, corn, peaches, peanuts.

8970 ■ WMUM-FM - 89.7
243 Carey Salem Rd.
Cochran, GA 31014
Free: 800-222-4788
Email: ask@gpb.org
Format: Public Radio. **Owner:** Georgia Public Broadcasting, 260 14th St. NW, Atlanta, GA 30318, Ph: (404)685-2400, Free: 800-222-6006. **Formerly**: WDCO-FM. **Key Personnel:** Nancy G. Hall, Exec. Dir; Randy Cranford, Contact. **URL:** http://www.gpb.org.

8971 ■ WMUM-TV - 29
243 Carey Salem Rd.
Cochran, GA 31014
Phone: (478)934-3095
Free: 800-222-4788
Email: ask@gpb.org
Owner: Georgia Public Broadcasting, 260 14th St. NW, Atlanta, GA 30318, Ph: (404)685-2400, Free: 800-222-6006. **Key Personnel:** Randy Cranford, Contact. **URL:** http://www.gpb.org.

COLQUITT

SW GA. Miller Co. 30 mi. N. of Decatur. Cotton ginning. Manufactures timber, fertilizer, plaster. Dairy, stock, poultry farms. Cotton, corn, peanuts.

8972 ■ Miller County Liberal
Miller County Liberal
157 E Main St.
Colquitt, GA 39837
Phone: (229)758-5549
Fax: (229)758-5540
Publisher's E-mail: millercountyliberal@gmail.com
Newspaper with a Democratic orientation. **Freq:** Weekly. **Print Method:** offset. **Trim Size:** 13 3/4 x 21 1/2. **Cols./Page:** 6. **Col. Width:** 12 picas. **Col. Depth:** 21.5 inches. **Key Personnel:** Betty Jo Toole, General Manager; Terry Toole, Editor; Wanda Griffin, Director, Advertising. **USPS:** 349-700. **Subscription Rates:** $21.40 Individuals print or online; $36.92 Out of area print; $42.80 Individuals print and online; $58.32 Out of area print and online. **URL:** http://millercountyliberal.com. **Ad Rates:** GLR $4.50; BW $580; 4C $718; SAU $4.50; PCI $4.50. **Remarks:** Accepts advertising. **Circ:** ‡2900.

COLUMBUS

W. GA. Muscogee Co. On Chattahoochee River, at head of navigation, 95 mi. SW of Atlanta. U.S. Infantry School. Convention & trade center. Historic district. Manufactures textiles, fiber bags, hand tools, electric capacitors, brick. Iron works; foundries; machine shops; bottling works; meat packing.

8973 ■ ACResolution
Association for Conflict Resolution
c/o Cheryl L. Jamison, J.D., Executive Director
1639 Bradley Park Dr., Ste. 500-142
Columbus, GA 31904
Phone: (202)780-5999
Fax: (703)435-4390
Professional journal covering conflict resolution. **Freq:** Quarterly. **Key Personnel:** Susan Summers Raines, Editor-in-Chief; Sharon Pickett, Associate. **Subscription Rates:** $6.40 Individuals print and digital; $2 Individuals online. **URL:** http://imis100us2.com/acr/ACR/Publications/ACResolution_Magazine/ACR/Publications/ACResolution_Magazine.aspx?hkey=3d69e2af-e6f2-4c3f-a531-75503a96ef26. **Ad Rates:** BW $1,200. **Remarks:** Accepts advertising. **Circ:** Combined 10000.

8974 ■ Cavalry and Armor Journal
U.S. Cavalry & Armor Association
3100 Gentian Blvd., Ste. 17B
Columbus, GA 31907
Phone: (706)563-5714
Publisher's E-mail: caa1@cavalryarmor.com
Journal containing recorded step-by-step change in warfare by horse to warfare by machine. **Freq:** Quarterly. **ISSN:** 1942- 8790 (print). **Subscription Rates:** Included in membership. **URL:** http://www.cavalryandarmor.com/Journal/USCavalryArmorJournal.aspx. **Remarks:** Accepts advertising. **Circ:** 5500.

8975 ■ Columbus Ledger-Enquirer
McClatchy Newspapers Inc.
17 W 12th St.
Columbus, GA 31901
Phone: (706)571-8565
Fax: (706)576-6290
Free: 800-282-7859
Publisher's E-mail: pensions@mcclatchy.com
General newspaper. **Freq:** Daily. **Print Method:** Offset. **Cols./Page:** 6. **Col. Width:** 25 nonpareils. **Col. Depth:** 301 agate lines. **Key Personnel:** Joseph Kieta, Executive Editor; Rodney Mahone, President, Publisher. **URL:** http://ledger-enquirer.com; http://mcclatchy.com/2006/06/09/353/ledger-enquirer.html. **Remarks:** Advertising accepted; rates available upon request. **Circ:** Mon.-Fri. 26223, Sun. 34427.

8976 ■ The Columbus Times
Columbus Times
PO Box 2845
Columbus, GA 31902
Phone: (706)324-2404
Fax: (706)596-0657
Publication E-mail: info@columbustimes.com
Black community newspaper. **Freq:** Weekly (Wed.). **Print Method:** Offset. Broadsheet. **Trim Size:** 13 x 21 1/2. **Cols./Page:** 6. **Col. Width:** 2 1/16 inches. **Col. Depth:** 21 1/2 inches. **Key Personnel:** Ophelia Devore Mitchell, Publisher; Petra Gertjegerdes, Managing Editor; Helmut Gertjegerdes, Managing Editor. **Subscription Rates:** $108.13 Individuals 1 year; $1 Single issue.

Circulation: ★ = AAM; △ or • = BPA; ♦ = CAC; ❑ = VAC; ⊕ = PO Statement; ‡ = Publisher's Report; Boldface figures = sworn; Light figures = estimated.

URL: http://columbustimes.com. **Ad Rates:** BW $1,733.76; 4C $2,048.76; SAU $15.69. **Remarks:** Accepts advertising. **Circ:** ‡20000.

8977 ■ DRESS: The Journal of The Costume Society of America
Costume Society of America
PO Box 852
Columbus, GA 31902-0852
Phone: (706)615-2851
Free: 800-CSA-9447
Publisher's E-mail: national.office@costumesocietyamerica.com
Journal covering all areas of study of dress, with scholarly emphasis on history and preservation. **Freq:** Semiannual 1 to 2 issues per year. **Key Personnel:** Christina Bates, Editor. **ISSN:** 0361--2112 (print); **EISSN:** 2042--1729 (electronic). **Subscription Rates:** Included in membership; $295 Institutions print + online; $263 Institutions online only. **URL:** http://costumesocietyamerica.com/publications/dress; http://www.tandfonline.com/loi/ydre20#.VxIn3tJ962w. **Remarks:** Advertising not accepted. **Circ:** (Not Reported).

8978 ■ Journal of Athletic Training
National Athletic Trainers' Association
c/o Hughston Sports Medicine Foundation
6262 Veterans Pky.
Columbus, GA 31908
Phone: (706)494-3345
Fax: (706)494-3348
Professional journal for athletic trainers, coaches, and physicians, focusing on sports medicine. **Freq:** Bimonthly. **Print Method:** Sheetfed offset. **Trim Size:** 8 1/2 x 11. **Cols./Page:** 3. **Col. Width:** 28 nonpareils. **Col. Depth:** 131 agate lines. **Key Personnel:** Craig Denegar, PhD, Editor-in-Chief. **ISSN:** 1062- 6050 (print); **EISSN:** 1938--162X (electronic). **Subscription Rates:** $267 Institutions; $303 Institutions Canada and other countries; $128 U.S. and other countries. **URL:** http://www.nata.org/news-publications/publications; http://natajournals.org. **Ad Rates:** BW $2,125; 4C $3,138. **Remarks:** Accepts advertising. **Circ:** 18000, 18000.

8979 ■ Journal of Technology in Counseling
Columbus State University
4225 University Ave.
Columbus, GA 31907
Phone: (706)507-8800
Fax: (706)569-3168
Free: 866-264-2035
Journal providing information about convergence of technology and the counseling field. **Freq:** Annual. **Key Personnel:** Marty Jencius, PhD, Editor; Michael Baltimore, PhD, Editor. **Circ:** (Not Reported).

8980 ■ Private Varnish
American Association of Private Railroad Car Owners, Inc.
PO Box 6307
Columbus, GA 31917-6307
Phone: (706)326-6262
Publisher's E-mail: ExecDirector@aaprco.com
Freq: 3/year. **Subscription Rates:** $30 U.S.; $33 Other countries; $7.50 Single issue; $56 U.S. 2 years; $62 Other countries 2 years. **URL:** http://www.aaprco.com/private_varnish/varnish.html. **Remarks:** Accepts advertising. **Circ:** 3000.

8981 ■ TeleCable of Columbus Inc.
6700 Macon Rd.
Columbus, GA 31907
Phone: (706)569-5900
Fax: (706)568-8270
Owner: Telecable Corp., 799 Waterside Dr., No. 900, Norfolk, VA 23510-3306, Ph: (804)624-5000, Fax: (804)624-5079. **Founded:** 1970. **Cities Served:** Muscogee County.

8982 ■ WAGH-FM - 101.3
1501 13th Ave.
Columbus, GA 31901
Phone: (706)576-3000
Fax: (706)576-3010
Format: Urban Contemporary. **Owner:** iHeartMedia Inc., 200 E Basse Rd., San Antonio, TX 78209, Ph: (210)832-3314. **ADI:** Columbus, GA (Opelika, AL). **Key Personnel:** Jennifer Newman, Gen. Mgr., jennifernewman@clearchannel.com. **Wattage:** 6,000. **Ad Rates:** Noncommercial. **URL:** http://www.mymagic101.com//main.html.

8983 ■ WBFA-FM - 98.3
1501 13th Ave.
Columbus, GA 31901
Phone: (706)576-3000
Fax: (706)576-3010
Format: Urban Contemporary. **Owner:** iHeartMedia Inc., 200 E Basse Rd., San Antonio, TX 78209, Ph: (210)832-3314. **ADI:** Columbus, GA (Opelika, AL). **Key Personnel:** Jim Martin, Gen. Mgr. **Wattage:** 6,000. **Ad Rates:** Noncommercial. **URL:** http://www.thebeatcolumbus.com.

8984 ■ WBOJ-FM - 103.7
1820 Wynnton Rd.
Columbus, GA 31906
Format: Contemporary Christian. **Owner:** River City Broadcasting, 1820 Wynnton Rd., Columbus, GA 31906-2930. **Key Personnel:** Brian Waters, Dir. of Programs, brian@1037lite.fm. **Ad Rates:** Advertising accepted; rates available upon request. **URL:** http://www.1037lite.fm.

8985 ■ WCGQ-FM - 107.3
1820 Wynnton Rd.
Columbus, GA 31904
Phone: (706)327-1217
Fax: (706)596-4600
Format: Adult Contemporary. **Owner:** Alvicente, at above address. **Founded:** 1973. **Operating Hours**: Continuous. **ADI:** Columbus, GA (Opelika, AL). **Key Personnel:** Helen Neal, Dir. of Sales, hneal@pmbradio.com; Dave Arwood, Contact, dave@q1073.com. **Wattage**: 100,000. **Ad Rates:** $30-50 for 30 seconds; $36-60 for 60 seconds. $25-$45 for 30 seconds; $35-$55 for 60 seconds. Combined advertising rates available with WRCG-AM. **URL:** http://www.q1073.com.

WCHK-AM - See Canton, GA

8986 ■ WDAK-AM
1501 13th Ave.
Columbus, GA 31904-2847
Phone: (706)596-3000
Format: Sports; Talk. **Networks:** ABC; NBC; ESPN Radio. **Founded:** 1940. **Wattage**: 4,000 Day; 038 Night. **Ad Rates:** $15 for 30 seconds; $20 for 60 seconds. **URL:** http://newsradio540.iheart.com/.

8987 ■ WFRC-FM - 90.5
290 Hegenberger Rd.
Oakland, CA 94621
Free: 800-543-1495
Email: info@familyradio.org
Format: Religious. **Owner:** Family Stations Inc., 290 Hegenberger Rd., Oakland, CA 94621, Free: 800-543-1495. **Ad Rates:** Noncommercial. **URL:** http://www.familyradio.org.

8988 ■ WFXE-FM - 104.9
2203 Wynnton Rd.
Columbus, GA 31902
Phone: (706)576-3565
Fax: (706)576-3683
Format: Urban Contemporary; Hip Hop; Blues. **Owner:** Davis Broadcasting Inc., 2203 Wynnton Rd., Columbus, GA 31906. **Operating Hours**: Continuous. **Ad Rates:** Advertising accepted; rates available upon request.

8989 ■ WGSY-FM - 100.1
1501 13th Ave.
Columbus, GA 31901
Phone: (706)576-3000
Format: Adult Contemporary. **Networks:** ABC. **Owner:** iHeartMedia Inc., 200 E Basse Rd., San Antonio, TX 78209, Ph: (210)832-3314. **Founded:** 1971. **Operating Hours**: Continuous; 100% local. **ADI:** Columbus, GA (Opelika, AL). **Key Personnel:** Brian Thomas, Dir. of Programs; Jennifer Newman, Gen. Mgr., jennifernewman@iheartmedia.com. **Wattage:** 6,000. **Ad Rates:** Advertising accepted; rates available upon request. **URL:** http://www.sunny100.com.

8990 ■ WIOL-FM - 95.7
2203 Wynnton Rd.
Columbus, GA 31906-2531
Phone: (706)576-3565
Fax: (706)576-3683
Free: 888-SAY-ESPN
Format: Adult Contemporary. **Key Personnel:** Carl Conner, VP of Operations, cconner@dbicolumbus.com.

8991 ■ WJSP-TV - 28
260 14TH St. N
1540 Stewart Ave. SW
Atlanta, GA 30318-5360
Phone: (404)756-4700
Fax: (404)756-4713
Free: 800-222-6006
Format: Public TV. **Networks:** Public Broadcasting Service (PBS); Georgia Public Television. **Owner:** Georgia Public Telecommunications Commission, at above address. **Founded:** 1964. **Key Personnel:** Kent Steele, Dir. of Programs; Richard E. Ottinger, Contact; Frank Bugg, Contact; Al Korn, Contact. **Wattage:** 177,000 ERP. **Ad Rates:** Noncommercial.

8992 ■ WKCN-FM - 99.3
1820 Wynnton Rd.
Columbus, GA 31906
Phone: (706)327-1217
Fax: (706)596-4600
Format: Country. **Owner:** Abg Georgia Licenses, LLC, at above address, Columbus, GA. **Key Personnel:** Helen Neal, Dir. of Sales, hneal@pmbradio.com; Brian Thomas, Contact, bthomas@pmbradio.com; Brian Thomas, Contact, bthomas@pmbradio.com. **Ad Rates:** Noncommercial. **URL:** http://www.kissin993.com.

8993 ■ WKZJ-FM - 92.7
2203 Wynnton Rd.
Columbus, GA 31906
Phone: (706)576-3565
Fax: (706)576-3683
Format: Blues. **Owner:** Davis Broadcasting Inc., 2203 Wynnton Rd., Columbus, GA 31906. **Key Personnel:** Michael Soul, Dir. of Programs. **URL:** http://www.k927.com.

8994 ■ WLTZ-TV - 38
6140 Buena Vista Rd.
Columbus, GA 31907
Phone: (706)561-3838
Email: wltz@wltz.com
Format: Commercial TV. **Networks:** NBC. **Founded:** 1970. **Operating Hours**: Continuous. **ADI**: Columbus, GA (Opelika, AL). **Key Personnel:** Drew Rhodes, Gen. Mgr., drhodes@wltz.com; Fred Steppe, Gen. Sales Mgr., fsteppe@wltz.com. **Local Programs**: *Last Call with Carson Daly*, Monday Tuesday Wednesday Thursday Friday 1:35 p.m. **Wattage**: 1,070,000. **Ad Rates:** Advertising accepted; rates available upon request. Combined advertising rates available with WBG-Warner Bros. Off. **URL:** http://www.wltz.com.

8995 ■ WRAK-FM - 97.3
1501 13th Ave.
Columbus, GA 31901
Phone: (706)576-3000
Fax: (706)576-3005
Format: Adult Contemporary. **Key Personnel:** Kurt Baker, Dir. of Programs, kurt@clearchannel.com. **Wattage:** 100,000.

8996 ■ WRBL-TV - 3
1350 13th Ave.
Columbus, GA 31901
Phone: (706)323-3333
Fax: (706)327-6655
Email: news@wrbl.com
Format: Commercial TV. **Networks:** CBS. **Owner:** Media General Inc., 333 E Franklin St., Richmond, VA 23219, Ph: (804)649-6000, Fax: (502)259-5537. **Founded:** 1953. **Operating Hours**: Continuous. **ADI**: Columbus, GA (Opelika, AL). **Wattage**: 1,000,000 ERP H. **Ad Rates:** Advertising accepted; rates available upon request. **URL:** http://www.wrbl.com.

8997 ■ WRCG-AM - 1420
1820 Wynnton Rd.
Columbus, GA 31906
Phone: (706)327-1217
Format: News; Talk; Sports. **Ad Rates:** Advertising accepted; rates available upon request. **URL:** http://www.am1420wrcg.com.

8998 ■ WRLD-FM - 95.3
1820 Wynnton Rd.
Columbus, GA 31906
Phone: (706)327-1217
Fax: (706)596-4600
Email: digital@pmbradio.com

Format: Oldies. **Owner:** McClure Broadcasting Group. **Founded:** 1993. **Operating Hours:** Continuous. **Key Personnel:** Helen Neal, Dir. of Sales, hneal@archwaybroadcasting.com. **Wattage:** 25,000. **Ad Rates:** Noncommercial. **URL:** http://www.boomer953.com.

8999 ■ WSTH-FM - 106.1
1501 13th Ave.
Columbus, GA 31901
Phone: (706)576-3000
Fax: (706)576-3005
Free: 800-445-4106
Format: Country. **Networks:** ABC. **Founded:** 1986. **Formerly:** WRFS-FM. **Operating Hours:** Continuous. **ADI:** Columbus, GA (Opelika, AL). **Key Personnel:** Jennifer Newman, Gen. Mgr., Mktg. Mgr., jennifermnewman@clearchannel.com. **Wattage:** 100,000. **Ad Rates:** $35-58 for 60 seconds. Combined advertising rates available with WDAK, WRFS. **URL:** http://www.mysouth1061.com.

9000 ■ WTVM-TV - 9
PO Box 1848
Columbus, GA 31902
Phone: (706)494-5400
Fax: (706)322-7527
Format: Commercial TV. **Networks:** ABC. **Owner:** Raycom Media Inc., 201 Monroe St., RSA Twr., 20th Fl., Montgomery, AL 36104-3731, Ph: (334)206-1400. **Founded:** Oct. 06, 1953. **Operating Hours:** Continuous. **ADI:** Columbus, GA (Opelika, AL). **Key Personnel:** Lee Brantley, Gen. Mgr. **Ad Rates:** Advertising accepted; rates available upon request. **URL:** http://www.wtvm.com.

9001 ■ WVRK-FM - 102.9
1501 13th Ave.
Columbus, GA 31901
Phone: (706)576-3000
Fax: (706)576-3010
Format: Classic Rock; Album-Oriented Rock (AOR). **Owner:** iHeartMedia Inc., 200 E Basse Rd., San Antonio, TX 78209, Ph: (210)832-3314; Cumulus Broadcasting Inc., 3280 Peachtree Rd. NW, Ste. 2300, Atlanta, GA 30305-2447, Ph: (404)949-0700, Fax: (404)949-0740. **Operating Hours:** Continuous. **Key Personnel:** Jennifer Newman, Gen. Mgr. **Wattage:** 100,000. **Ad Rates:** Noncommercial. **URL:** http://www.rock103columbus.com.

9002 ■ WXTX-TV - 54
PO Box 12188
Columbus, GA 31917
Phone: (706)494-5458
Fax: (706)327-0179
Format: Commercial TV. **Networks:** Fox; ABC. **Founded:** 1983. **Operating Hours:** Continuous. **ADI:** Columbus, GA (Opelika, AL). **Key Personnel:** Nicole Bussey, Contact. **Ad Rates:** Advertising accepted; rates available upon request. **URL:** http://www.wxtx.com.

COMMERCE

NE GA. Jackson Co. 18 mi. N. of Athens. Manufactures textiles, hydraulic pumps, electronic products, cotton goods, lumber. Farming. Peach orchards.

9003 ■ The Commerce News
Jackson Herald Inc.
1672 S Broad St.
Commerce, GA 30529
Phone: (706)335-2927
Fax: (706)335-4531
Community newspaper. **Founded:** 1875. **Freq:** Weekly (Wed.). **Print Method:** Offset. Uses mats. **Cols./Page:** 6. **Col. Width:** 26 nonpareils. **Col. Depth:** 294 agate lines. **Subscription Rates:** $19.75 Individuals in Jackson or adjoining counties; $17.75 Individuals with senior discount; $38.85 Individuals other in State of Georgia; $36.85 Individuals other in State of Georgia with senior discount; $44.50 Out of state; $42.50 Out of state with senior discount; $42.20 Individuals military with APO address. **URL:** http://www.mainstreetnews.com. **Mailing address:** PO Box 459, Commerce, GA 30529. **Ad Rates:** BW $599.85; PCI $4.65. **Remarks:** Color advertising accepted; rates available upon request. **Circ:** ‡4600.

9004 ■ WJJC-AM - 1270
PO Box 379
Commerce, GA 30529
Phone: (706)335-3155
Fax: (706)335-1905
Email: wjjc@windstream.net
Format: Country; Southern Gospel; Information; Sports. **Networks:** NBC; Georgia Radio. **Founded:** 1957. **Operating Hours:** Continuous; 8% network, 92% local. **ADI:** Atlanta (Athens & Rome), GA. **Key Personnel:** Rob Jordan, Gen. Mgr. **Local Programs:** *Trading Post*, Monday Tuesday Wednesday Thursday Friday 12:30 p.m. - 1:00 p.m. **Wattage:** 5,000. **Ad Rates:** $7-10 for 30 seconds; $8-10 for 60 seconds. **URL:** http://www.wjjc.net.

CONYERS

NC GA. Rockdale Co. 20 mi. SE of Atlanta. Manufactures tires, mattresses, business forms, fluorescent fixtures, food products, fabricated steel, aluminum screens, awnings, clothing, plastics. Meat packing plant. Pine timber. Agriculture.

9005 ■ Rockdale Citizen
Rockdale Citizen
969 S Main St.
Conyers, GA 30012
Phone: (770)483-7108
General newspaper. **Freq:** Daily (eve.). **Print Method:** Offset. **Cols./Page:** 6. **Col. Width:** 24 nonpareils. **Col. Depth:** 301 agate lines. **Key Personnel:** Alice Queen, Executive Editor, phone: (770)483-7108; J.K. Murphy, Publisher. **Subscription Rates:** $89 Individuals; $236.47 Out of country. **URL:** http://rockdalecitizen.com. **Ad Rates:** SAU $4.60. **Remarks:** Accepts advertising. **Circ:** Paid ♦**3097**, Paid ♦**5013**.

9006 ■ WPBS-AM
c/o Jeffrey L. Timmons, Esq.
Lawrenceville, GA 30043
Phone: (404)932-5006
Fax: (770)483-1099
Format: Gospel. **Owner:** Pacificstar Media Corp., at above address. **Founded:** 1979. **Formerly:** WTPO-AM. **Wattage:** 50,000 Day; 5,500 CH. **Ad Rates:** $25 for 30 seconds; $50 for 60 seconds.

CORDELE

SWC GA. Crisp Co. 65 mi. S. of Macon. Manufactures phosphate, lumber, fertilizer, textiles, air conditioners, concrete products, foundry products, feeds. Timber. Diversified farming. Cotton, peanuts, pecans, watermelons.

9007 ■ Cordele Dispatch
McLeansboro Times-Leader
306 13th Ave. W
Cordele, GA 31015-1058
Phone: (912)273-2277
General newspaper. **Founded:** 1908. **Freq:** Daily (eve.). **Print Method:** Offset. **Trim Size:** 13 x 21 1/2. **Cols./Page:** 6. **Col. Width:** 2 1/16 inches. **Col. Depth:** 301 agate lines. **Key Personnel:** Peggy King, Publisher; Chris Mann, Manager, Advertising. **Subscription Rates:** $87.10 Individuals home delivery; $5.40 Individuals. **URL:** http://www.cordeledispatch.com. **Mailing address:** PO Box 1058, Cordele, GA 31015-1058. **Ad Rates:** GLR $0.58; BW $1,056.51; 4C $1,286.51; SAU $8.19. **Remarks:** Accepts advertising. **Circ:** ‡6000.

9008 ■ WAEF-FM - 90.3
PO Drawer 2440
Tupelo, MS 38803
Phone: (662)844-8888
Format: Contemporary Christian. **Owner:** American Family Association, at above address. **URL:** http://www.afa.net.

9009 ■ WKKN-FM - 98.3
PO Box 460
Cordele, GA 31015-0460
Phone: (912)276-0306
Fax: (912)276-0073
Format: Country. **Networks:** NBC; Georgia Radio. **Owner:** Silverstar Communications, Inc., at above address. **Founded:** 1940. **Formerly:** WFAV-FM. **Operating Hours:** 5% network, 95% local. **ADI:** Atlanta (Athens & Rome), GA. **Key Personnel:** Jim Jennings, Gen. Mgr., VP; Royce Plummer, Sales Mgr.; Roy Walsh, Dir. of Programs. **Wattage:** 3,000. **Ad Rates:** $9.59 for 30 seconds; $11.50 for 60 seconds.

9010 ■ WSST-TV - 55
112 7th St. S
Cordele, GA 31015
Phone: (229)273-0001
Fax: (229)273-8894
Format: Commercial TV. **Owner:** Sunbelt-South Tele-Communications, Ltd., at above address. **Founded:** June 01, 1987. **Operating Hours:** Continuous. **ADI:** Albany (Valdosta & Cordele), GA. **Key Personnel:** Philip Streetman, Gen. Mgr. **Local Programs:** *South Georgia Sunrise*, Monday Tuesday Wednesday Thursday Friday 6:00 a.m. **Wattage:** 100,000. **Ad Rates:** Noncommercial. **Mailing address:** PO Box 917, Cordele, GA 31015. **URL:** http://www.wsst51.com.

CORNELIA

NE GA. Habersham Co. 5 mi. W. of Mt. Airy.

9011 ■ The Northeast Georgian
Community Newspapers Inc.
2440 Old Athens Hwy.
Cornelia, GA 30531
Phone: (706)778-4215
Fax: (706)778-4114
Publisher's E-mail: dnesmith@cninewspapers.com
Community newspaper. **Freq:** Semiweekly. **Print Method:** Offset. **Cols./Page:** 6. **Col. Width:** 12 picas. **Col. Depth:** 21 1/2 inches. **Key Personnel:** Lane Gresham, Managing Editor; Alan NeSmith, Publisher. **Subscription Rates:** $7 Individuals /month (online); $30 Individuals /year (online); $30 By mail /year in Habersham, Banks, White or Stephens Counties; $40 By mail /year (print); $50 By mail /year outside Georgia. **URL:** http://www.thenortheastgeorgian.com; http://www.cninewspapers.com/publications. **Formerly:** Cornelia Northeast Georgian. **Mailing address:** PO Box 1555, Cornelia, GA 30531. **Remarks:** Advertising accepted; rates available upon request. **Circ:** 10000.

9012 ■ WCON-AM - 1450
540 N Main St.
Cornelia, GA 30531
Phone: (706)778-2241
Fax: (706)778-0576
Email: wcon@windstream.net
Format: Country. **Networks:** ABC. **Owner:** Habersham Broadcasting Company Inc., 540 N Main St., Cornelia, GA 30531, Ph: (706)778-2241 , Fax: (706)778-0576. **Founded:** 1953. **Operating Hours:** Continuous. **Key Personnel:** Bobbie C. Foster, Gen. Mgr., President, bobbiefoster@windstream.net. **Wattage:** 1,000. **Ad Rates:** Noncommercial. **Mailing address:** PO Box 100, Cornelia, GA 30531. **URL:** http://www.wconfm.com.

9013 ■ WCON-FM - 99.3
540 N Main St.
Cornelia, GA 30531
Phone: (706)778-2241
Fax: (706)778-0576
Email: wcon@windstream.net
Format: Country. **Simulcasts:** WCON-AM. **Networks:** ABC; Georgia Radio. **Owner:** Habersham Broadcasting Company Inc., 540 N Main St., Cornelia, GA 30531, Ph: (706)778-2241 , Fax: (706)778-0576. **Founded:** 1965. **Operating Hours:** Continuous. **Key Personnel:** Bobbie C. Foster, Gen. Mgr., President. **Wattage:** 50,000. **Ad Rates:** $7-9 for 15 seconds; $9-12 for 30 seconds; $11-14 for 60 seconds. **Mailing address:** PO Box 100, Cornelia, GA 30531. **URL:** http://www.wconfm.com.

COVINGTON

NC GA. Newton Co. 36 mi. SE of Atlanta. Manufactures automotive moulding, industrial adhesive, corrugated boxes, wire screening, olefin fiber, plastic bags and foam products. Pine, oak, poplar timber. Diversified farming.

9014 ■ Covington News
Covington Newspaper Company Inc.
1166 Usher St.
Covington, GA 30014
Phone: (770)787-6397
Fax: (770)786-6451
Publisher's E-mail: news@covnews.com

Circulation: ★ = AAM; △ or • = BPA; ♦ = CAC; ❑ = VAC; ⊕ = PO Statement; ‡ = Publisher's Report; Boldface figures = sworn; Light figures = estimated.

Community newspaper. **Freq:** Triweekly. **Print Method:** Offset. **Cols./Page:** 6. **Col. Width:** 26 nonpareils. **Col. Depth:** 301 agate lines. **Key Personnel:** T. Pat Cavanaugh, General Manager; Charles Hill Morris, Publisher; Gabriel Khouli, Editor. **Subscription Rates:** $2.99 Individuals full online access on auto pay; $27.82 Individuals 6 months web and print delivered; $55 Individuals 1 year web and print delivered; $77.04 Individuals 1 year web and print mailed; $5 Individuals print edition on auto pay. **URL:** http://covnews.com. **Ad Rates:** BW $896.55; 4C $1,271.55; PCI $7.90. **Remarks:** Accepts advertising. **Circ:** ‡7450.

9015 ■ Newton Citizen
Stamats Business Media
7121 Turner Lake Rd.
Covington, GA 30014
Phone: (770)787-7303
Publisher's E-mail: info@stamatsbusinessmedia.com
Community newspaper. **Freq:** Tue.-Fri. **Key Personnel:** Alice Queen, Executive Editor. **Subscription Rates:** $26 Individuals Sunday only, home delivery; $135 Individuals Tuesday-Friday and Sunday, home delivery. **URL:** http://www.newtoncitizen.com. **Remarks:** Accepts advertising. **Circ:** Paid ♦**2322**.

9016 ■ City of Covington CATV
2194 Emory St.
Covington, GA 30014
Owner: City of Covington, Covington, GA. **Founded:** 1980. **Cities Served:** subscribing households 11,002. **URL:** http://www.cityofcovington.org/departmentsnew/customer_service/Pages/default.aspx.

CUMMING

N. GA. Forsyth Co. 35 mi. N. of Atlanta. Residential.

9017 ■ The American Surgeon
Southeastern Surgical Congress
115 Samaritan Dr., No. 200
Cumming, GA 30040
Phone: (678)965-2422
Fax: (678)965-2278
Free: 800-558-8958
Publisher's E-mail: sesc@sesc.org
Journal publishing original papers on the advancement of surgery. **Freq:** Monthly. **Print Method:** Sheetfed offset. **Trim Size:** 8 1/8 x 11. **Cols./Page:** 2. **Col. Width:** 39 nonpareils and 7 inches. **Col. Depth:** 140 agate lines and 10 inches. **Key Personnel:** Dr. Talmadge A. Bowden, Jr., Contact; J. David Richardson, MD, Editor-in-Chief; Marcia E. Serepy, Publisher; Monica Brent, Editor. **ISSN:** 0003-1348 (print). **Subscription Rates:** $575 Individuals print; $695 Institutions print. **URL:** http://sesc.org/american-surgeon-journal/subscribe. **Ad Rates:** BW $610; 4C $1,460; BW $1,000; 4C $2,000; BW $1,200; 4C $2,500. **Remarks:** Accepts advertising. **Circ:** ‡5789, Controlled 3250, 3,250.

9018 ■ Forsyth County News
Forsyth County News
302 Veterans Memorial Blvd.
Cumming, GA 30040
Phone: (770)887-3126
Fax: (770)889-6017
Publisher's E-mail: circ@forsythnews.com
Community newspaper. **Freq:** Triweekly (Wed., Fri., Sun.). **Print Method:** Offset. Uses sheets. **Cols./Page:** 6. **Col. Width:** 26 nonpareils. **Col. Depth:** 301 agate lines. **Key Personnel:** Kevin Atwill, Editor; Ryan Garmon, Director, Advertising. **Subscription Rates:** $5.99 Individuals online only (1 month subscription); $7.99 Individuals print only (1 month subscription); $9.99 Out of country (1 month subscription); $99 Individuals annual subscription; $59 Institutions 6 month subscription. **URL:** http://forsythnews.com. **Ad Rates:** BW $1449; 4C $1674; SAU $11.50. **Remarks:** Advertising accepted; rates available upon request. **Circ:** (Not Reported).

9019 ■ WGTA-AM - 950
6320 Sunbriar Dr.
Cumming, GA 30040
Phone: (678)772-7038
Format: Country; Hispanic. **Networks:** NBC; Georgia Radio; Westwood One Radio. **Owner:** Azteca Communications Inc., 705 Green Pastures Dr., Kyle, TX 78640. **Founded:** 1950. **Operating Hours:** Continuous. **ADI:** Atlanta (Athens & Rome), GA. **Wattage:** 5,000. **Ad Rates:** $5 for 15 seconds; $7-9 for 30 seconds; $8-10 for 60 seconds.

9020 ■ WWEV-FM - 91.5
PO Box 248
Cumming, GA 30028
Phone: (770)781-9150
Fax: (770)781-5003
Free: 800-522-9150
Email: info@victory915.com
Format: Religious; Contemporary Christian. **Networks:** USA Radio. **Owner:** Curriculum Development Foundation, 1705 Sawnee Dr, Cumming, GA 30040-4473, Ph: (770)781-9150. **Founded:** 1981. **Operating Hours:** Continuous; 100% local. **ADI:** Atlanta (Athens & Rome), GA. **Key Personnel:** Ray Haynes, Promotions Dir., Traffic Mgr., ray@wwev.org. **Local Programs:** *Weekend Top 20 Countdown*. **Wattage:** 9,000. **Ad Rates:** Noncommercial. **URL:** http://victory915.com.

DAHLONEGA

C. GA. Lumpkin Co. North Georgia College. Gold mining, trading, and poultry production.

9021 ■ The Dahlonega Nugget
Community Newspapers Inc.
1074 Morrison Moore Pkwy.
Dahlonega, GA 30533
Phone: (706)864-3613
Fax: (706)864-4360
Publisher's E-mail: dnesmith@cninewspapers.com
Local newspaper. **Freq:** Weekly (Wed.). **Print Method:** Offset. **Cols./Page:** 6. **Col. Width:** 12.2 picas. **Col. Depth:** 21 1/2 inches. **Key Personnel:** Wayne Knuckles, Editor. **Subscription Rates:** $29 Individuals online (1 year); $7 Individuals online (1 month); $29 Individuals print and online (1 year); $39 Out of country print and online (1 year); $49 Out of state print and online (1 year). **URL:** http://thedahloneganugget.com. **Mailing address:** PO Box 36, Dahlonega, GA 30533. **Remarks:** Advertising accepted; rates available upon request. **Circ:** Paid ‡5600.

9022 ■ Journal of the Antique Telescope Society
Antique Telescope Society
c/o Walter Breyer, PhD, Secretary
1878 Robinson Rd.
Dahlonega, GA 30533
Covers the history of the telescope. **Freq:** 3-4/yr. **Subscription Rates:** Included in membership. **URL:** http://webari.com/oldscope/atspages/atsfaq02.htm. **Remarks:** Advertising not accepted. **Circ:** (Not Reported).

9023 ■ WDGR-AM
Radio Rd.
Dahlonega, GA 30533
Phone: (404)864-4477
Fax: (404)446-5981
Format: Adult Contemporary; Oldies. **Networks:** NBC; Georgia Radio. **Founded:** 1982. **Formerly:** WAAH-AM. **Key Personnel:** Phil Castleberry, Gen. Mgr. **Wattage:** 10,000 Day; 2,500 CH. **Ad Rates:** $4-5.75 for 30 seconds; $5-6.75 for 60 seconds. **Mailing address:** PO Box 1210, Dahlonega, GA 30533.

9024 ■ WKHC-FM - 104.3
1376 Ben Higgins Rd.
Dahlonega, GA 30533
Phone: (706)265-9221
Email: wkhc@alltel.net
Format: Country. **Networks:** ABC. **Owner:** Ridgeline Communications, LLC, at above address. **Founded:** Dec. 16, 1996. **Operating Hours:** Continuous. **Wattage:** 6,000. **Ad Rates:** Advertising accepted; rates available upon request. $15 for 30 seconds; $18 for 60 seconds. **URL:** http://thunder1043fm.com.

DALLAS

C. GA. Paulding Co. 30 mi. WNW of Atlanta. Lumber and cotton mills.

9025 ■ WDPC-AM
226 Professional Ct.
Dallas, GA 30132
Format: Country. **Networks:** Satellite Music Network. **Founded:** 1979. **Key Personnel:** Paul Carden, Contact. **Wattage:** 5,000 Day; 3,200 CH. **Mailing address:** PO Box 166, Dallas, GA 30132. **URL:** http://wordchristianbroadcasting.com/.

DALTON

NW GA. Whitfield Co. 30 mi. SE of Chattanooga, TN. Manufactures carpets, lumber, concrete blocks, septic tanks, tile, textiles. Talc mines. Pine, oak timber. Agriculture. Cotton, corn, poultry.

9026 ■ The Daily Citizen
Community Newspaper Holdings Inc.
308 S Thornton Ave.
Dalton, GA 30720
Phone: (706)217-6397
Newspaper serving northwest Georgia. **Freq:** Daily. **Key Personnel:** Tim Rogers, Editor, phone: (706)272-7735; William H. Bronson, III, Publisher, phone: (706)272-7700; Gary Jones, Director, Advertising, phone: (706)272-7731. **Subscription Rates:** $167.16 By mail; $129 Individuals carrier. **URL:** http://www.daltondailycitizen.com. **Remarks:** Accepts advertising. **Circ:** Mon.-Sat. ★**11162**, Sun. ★**10524**.

9027 ■ Eller Chronicles
Eller Family Association
c/o Edward K. Eller, Secretay/Treasurer
3009 E Walnut Ave.
Dalton, GA 30721
Journal consisting of researches and stories about the Eller family history. **Freq:** Quarterly February, May, August and November. **Remarks:** Advertising not accepted. **Circ:** 300.

9028 ■ WBAC-AM
PO Box 1284
Dalton, GA 30722-1284
Phone: (423)242-7656
Fax: (423)472-5290
Email: news@wbacradio.com
Format: Full Service; Talk; News; Sports. **Networks:** Mutual Broadcasting System; Unistar; Tennessee Radio; ABC. **Owner:** J.L. Brewer Broadcasting of Cleveland, at above address; Brewer Broadcasting Corp., 1305 Carter St., Chattanooga, TN 37402, Ph: (423)265-9494, Fax: (423)266-2335. **Founded:** 1945. **Formerly:** WDNT-AM. **Key Personnel:** Cordel A. Whitlock, Contact. **Wattage:** 1,000. **Ad Rates:** Advertising accepted; rates available upon request. $4.55-5.50 for 15 seconds; $5.95-7 for 30 seconds; $6.90-8 for 60 seconds.

9029 ■ WBLJ-AM - 1230
613 Silver Cir.
Dalton, GA 30721
Phone: (706)279-1230
Format: News; Talk. **Networks:** CBS. **Founded:** 1940. **Operating Hours:** Continuous; 100% network. **ADI:** Chattanooga (Cleveland), TN. **Key Personnel:** Patty Scoggins, Contact, pscoggins@ngaradio.com; Deborah Parker, Contact, dparker@ngaradio.com. **Wattage:** 1,000. **Ad Rates:** $12-18 for 30 seconds; $24 for 60 seconds. **URL:** http://www.wblj1230.com.

9030 ■ WDAL-AM - 1430
613 Silver Cir.
Dalton, GA 30722
Phone: (706)278-5511
Fax: (706)226-8766
Founded: 1953. **Formerly:** WRCD-AM; WLSQ-AM. **Key Personnel:** Mark Cooper, Gen. Mgr., VP. **Wattage:** 2,500 Daytime;072 Nig. **Ad Rates:** $8 for 30 seconds; $14 for 60 seconds. **URL:** http://www.clearchannel.com.

9031 ■ WDNN-TV - 10
101 S Spencer St.
Dalton, GA 30721
Phone: (706)278-9713
Fax: (706)278-7950
Email: info@wdnntv.com
Founded: 1989. **Mailing address:** PO Box 1740, Dalton, GA 30722. **URL:** http://www.wdnntv.com.

9032 ■ WQMT-FM
PO Box 1284
Dalton, GA 30722-1284
Phone: (706)278-9950
Fax: (706)287-9917
Format: Country. **Networks:** CBS. **Founded:** 1977. **Wattage:** 16,500 ERP. **Ad Rates:** Noncommercial.

9033 ■ WYYU-FM - 104.5
613 Silver Cir.
Dalton, GA 30721
Phone: (706)278-5511
Fax: (706)226-8766

Email: mix1045@ngaradio.com
Format: Adult Contemporary; News; Sports. **Networks:** CBS; Westwood One Radio. **Key Personnel:** Patty Scoggins, Contact, pscoggins@ngaradio.com; Deborah Parker, Contact, dparker@ngaradio.com; Lisa Griffin, Contact, lgriffin@ngaradio.com. **Wattage:** 6,000. **URL:** http://www.mixx1045.com.

DANIELSVILLE

NE GA. Madison Co. 16 mi. NE of Athens. Farming. Dairy, poultry products.

9034 ■ W209BJ-FM - 89.7
PO Box 391
Twin Falls, ID 83303
Free: 800-357-4226
Format: Religious; Contemporary Christian. **Owner:** CSN International, PO Box 391, Twin Falls, ID 83303, Ph: (208)736-1958, Fax: (208)736-1958, Free: 800-357-4226. **URL:** http://www.csnradio.com.

DAWSON

C. GA. Terrell Co. 22 mi. NW of Albany. Lumber, peanuts.

9035 ■ The Dawson News
The Dawson News
139 W Lee St.
Dawson, GA 39842
Phone: (229)995-2175
Fax: (229)995-2176
Publisher's E-mail: editor@dawsonnews.com
Community newspaper. **Freq:** Weekly. **Print Method:** Offset. **Trim Size:** 13 x 21 1/2. **Cols./Page:** 6. **Col. Width:** 2 1/8 inches. **Col. Depth:** 21 inches. **Key Personnel:** Stephanie Griffin, Editor; Jennifer Lyness, Director, Advertising. **USPS:** 149-480. **Subscription Rates:** $45 Individuals 104 weeks (print and online); $25 Individuals 52 weeks (print and online); $40 Individuals 52 weeks of print and online outside Dawson County; $50 Individuals 52 weeks of print and online outside Georgia. **URL:** http://dawsonnews.com. **Remarks:** Advertising accepted; rates available upon request. **Circ:** ‡2800.

DAWSONVILLE

N. GA. Dawson Co. 22 mi. NW of Gainesville. North Georgia College; Gainesville Junior College; Lanier Tech. Blackburn State Park. Camping, fishing, swimming. Manufactures carpet yarn, textiles. Book binding; feed mill; newspaper, commercial printing.

9036 ■ Dawson News & Advertiser: Dawson's County's Oldest and Most Read Newspaper
Community Newspapers Inc.
40 N Hwy. 9N
Dawsonville, GA 30534
Phone: (706)265-2345
Fax: (706)265-7842
Publication E-mail: news@dawsonadvertiser.com
Community newspaper. **Freq:** Weekly (Wed.). **Print Method:** Web. **Trim Size:** 11 x 16. **Cols./Page:** 6. **Col. Width:** 12.4 picas. **Col. Depth:** 21 1/2 inches. **Key Personnel:** Alan NeSmith, Publisher. **USPS:** 149-420. **Formerly:** Dawson County Advertiser & News. **Mailing address:** PO Box 225, Dawsonville, GA 30534. **Remarks:** Advertising accepted; rates available upon request. **Circ:** Paid ‡3000.

DECATUR

NWC GA. DeKalb Co. Adjacent to Atlanta. Agnes Scott College (women); Columbia Theological Seminary. Residential. Dairy, poultry, truck farms.

9037 ■ Agnes Scott The Magazine
Agnes Scott College
141 E College Ave.
Decatur, GA 30030
Phone: (404)471-6000
Free: 800-868-8602
Publication E-mail: alumnae@agnesscott.edu
College alumnae magazine. **Freq:** Semiannual. **Print Method:** Sheetfed Offset. **Trim Size:** 8 3/8 x 10 7/8. **Cols./Page:** 4. **Col. Width:** 1 inches. **Col. Depth:** 8 1/4 inches. **Key Personnel:** Jennifer Bryon Owen, Contact; Susan Soper, Editor. **Alt. Formats:** PDF. **URL:** http://www.agnesscott.edu/alumnae/publications.html; http://www.agnesscott.edu/news/agnes-scott-publications.html. **Formerly:** Agnes Scott Quarterly. **Remarks:** Advertising not accepted. **Circ:** Non-paid 15000.

9038 ■ Homily Service
Taylor & Francis Group Journals
c/o Sarah Webb Phillips, Editor
801 Pinetree Dr.
Decatur, GA 30030
Publication E-mail: homilyservice@nc.rr.com
Journal for those who use and study the church's lectionary. Journal of the Liturgical Conference. **Freq:** 4/yr. **Key Personnel:** Sarah Webb Phillips, Editor; Byron E. Anderson, Board Member; Todd Johnson, Vice President. **ISSN:** 0732-1872 (print); **EISSN:** 1547-3562 (electronic). **Subscription Rates:** £81 Institutions print and online; £77 Institutions online only; $136 Institutions print and online; $128 Institutions online only. **URL:** http://www.tandf.co.uk/journals/titles/07321872.asp. **Circ:** (Not Reported).

9039 ■ The Journal of Pastoral Care and Counseling: A Professional Publication in pastoral Care, Counseling and Education
Journal of Pastoral Care Publications Inc.
1549 Clairmont Rd., Ste. 103
Decatur, GA 30033-4635
Phone: (404)320-0195
Fax: (404)320-0849
Publisher's E-mail: office@jpcp.org
Religious magazine. **Freq:** Quarterly. **Print Method:** Letterpress and offset. **Trim Size:** 6 x 9. **Cols./Page:** 1. **Col. Width:** 51 nonpareils. **Col. Depth:** 101 agate lines. **Key Personnel:** Orlo C. Strunk, Jr., Managing Editor; Rabbi Terry Bard, Managing Editor. **ISSN:** 1542--3050 (print); **EISSN:** 2167--776X (electronic). **Subscription Rates:** £28 Individuals online only; £42 Individuals print only; £130 Individuals print and online; £167 Institutions online only; £181 Institutions print only; £185 Institutions print and online; £186 Institutions All online content; £439 Institutions E-access (Content through 1998); £14 Individuals single print issue; £50 Institutions single print issue. **URL:** http://www.jpcp.org. **Formerly:** The Journal of Pastoral Care. **Ad Rates:** BW $600. **Remarks:** Accepts advertising. **Circ:** Paid ‡9000.

9040 ■ Paste
Paste Media Group L.L.C.
PO Box 1606
Decatur, GA 30031
Phone: (404)664-4320
Fax: (404)377-4508
Free: 866-370-9067
Publisher's E-mail: news@pastemagazine.com
Music magazine. **Freq:** 11/yr (December/January issues combined). **Trim Size:** 8 x 10.875. **Key Personnel:** Mark DiCristina, Coordinator; Palmer Houchins, Coordinator, Marketing. **ISSN:** 1540-3106 (print). **Subscription Rates:** $19.95 Individuals; $39.90 Two years; $50 Other countries; $25 Canada and Mexico. **URL:** http://www.pastemagazine.com. **Remarks:** Accepts advertising. **Circ:** Paid 205000.

9041 ■ The Profile
Agnes Scott College
141 E College Ave.
Decatur, GA 30030
Phone: (404)471-6000
Free: 800-868-8602
Publisher's E-mail: info@agnesscott.edu
Collegiate newspaper. **Founded:** 1916. **Freq:** Biweekly. **Print Method:** Web Press. **Trim Size:** 11 x 14. **Cols./Page:** 5. **Col. Width:** 22 nonpareils. **Col. Depth:** 210 agate lines. **URL:** http://ascprofile.com. **Ad Rates:** BW $100; PCI $4.10. **Remarks:** Accepts advertising. **Circ:** Paid ‡75, Free ‡925.

9042 ■ Young Horizons Indigo
Young Horizons Indigo
PO Box 371595
Decatur, GA 30037
Phone: (404)241-5003
Newsmagazine for parents and teachers of African-American youth containing articles of general interest. **Freq:** Monthly. **Print Method:** Newsprint & Web. **Cols./Page:** 4. **Col. Width:** 2 3/8 INS. **Key Personnel:** Terry Williams, Executive Director, Founder, Senior Editor. **Subscription Rates:** $5 Individuals. **URL:** http://younghorizonsonline.com. **Ad Rates:** BW $1,350; 4C $1,800. **Remarks:** Advertising accepted; rates available upon request. **Circ:** Paid 18000, 54000.

9043 ■ WHSG-TV - 63
1550 Agape Way
Decatur, GA 30035
Phone: (404)288-1156
Owner: Trinity Broadcasting Network Inc., PO Box A, Santa Ana, CA 92711, Ph: (714)832-2950, Free: 888-731-1000. **URL:** http://www.tbn.org.

9044 ■ WXLL-AM - 1310
4287 Memorial Dr.
Suite H
Decatur, GA 30032
Phone: (404)299-8933
Fax: (404)288-4697
Format: Religious. **Networks:** Independent. **Owner:** Margery J. Watson, at above address. **Founded:** 1964. **Operating Hours:** Daytime. **Key Personnel:** Margary J. Watson, Gen. Mgr. **Wattage:** 500. **Ad Rates:** $12-24 for 30 seconds; $15-30 for 60 seconds.

DEMOREST

9045 ■ WPPR-FM - 88.3
The Swanson Ctr.
365 College Dr., Ste. 112
Demorest, GA 30535
Phone: (706)778-8500
Free: 800-222-4788
Email: ask@gpb.org
Format: Public Radio. **Owner:** Georgia Public Broadcasting, 260 14th St. NW, Atlanta, GA 30318, Ph: (404)685-2400, Free: 800-222-6006. **Key Personnel:** Candice Felice, Contact. **URL:** http://www.gpb.org/radio/stations/wppr.

DORAVILLE

DeKalb Co.

9046 ■ WFTD-AM - 1080
PO Box 48122
Doraville, GA 30362
Fax: (404)424-9853
Format: Contemporary Christian; Talk. **Networks:** USA Radio. **Founded:** 1987. **Operating Hours:** Daytime. **ADI:** Atlanta (Athens & Rome), GA. **Wattage:** 10,000.

DOUGLAS

S. GA. Coffee Co. 36 mi. NW of Waycross. South Georgia College. Manufactures mobile homes, farm machinery, concrete, lumber, turpentine, ice, asphalt, feed. Bottling works; garment plants; printers; poultry & egg processing. Timber. Agriculture. Tobacco, poultry, peanuts, corn, swine, cattle.

9047 ■ The Douglas Shopper
Coffee County News and Shopper Inc.
404 N Peterson Ave.
Douglas, GA 31533
Phone: (912)384-9112
Fax: (912)384-4220
Shopper. **Freq:** Weekly (Tues.). **Print Method:** Offset. **Trim Size:** 10 1/2 x 15. **Cols./Page:** 6. **Col. Width:** 9 picas. **Col. Depth:** 15 inches. **Subscription Rates:** Free. **URL:** http://yourdouglasshopper.com. **Mailing address:** PO Box 390, Douglas, GA 31533. **Ad Rates:** GLR $1; BW $450; 4C $550; PCI $5. **Remarks:** Accepts advertising. **Circ:** Free ‡19259.

9048 ■ Charter Communications
1007 Madison Ave. S
Douglas, GA 31533-3129
Free: 888-438-2427
Owner: Charter Communications Inc., 400 Atlantic St., Stamford, CT 06901, Ph: (203)905-7801. **Founded:** May 1994. **Key Personnel:** Neil Smit, CEO, President. **Cities Served:** subscribing households 6,200. **URL:** http://www.charter.com.

9049 ■ WDMG-AM
1931 Georgia Hwy. 32 E
Douglas, GA 31533
Phone: (912)389-0995
Fax: (912)383-8552
Format: News; Talk; Sports; Classic Rock. **Networks:** USA Radio; Gannett News. **Owner:** RTG Media, at above address. **Founded:** 1947. **Key Personnel:** Bob

Circulation: ★ = AAM; △ or • = BPA; ♦ = CAC; ❑ = VAC; ⊕ = PO Statement; ‡ = Publisher's Report; Boldface figures = sworn; Light figures = estimated.

Ganzak, President, wdmg@amfm.com. **Wattage**: 5,000. **Ad Rates:** $8-22 for 30 seconds; $12-30 for 60 seconds.

9050 ■ WDMG-FM - 97.7
1931 Georgia Hwy. 32 E
Douglas, GA 31533
Phone: (229)423-2077
Fax: (229)386-9866
Format: Adult Contemporary. **Networks:** USA Radio; Gannett News. **Owner:** Broadcast South, LLC, 509 S Columbia Ave., Douglas, GA 31533, Ph: (912)389-0995, Fax: (912)383-8552. **Operating Hours**: Continuous. **ADI**: Savannah, GA. **Key Personnel:** John Higgs, Gen. Mgr., broadcastsouth@windstream.net. **Wattage**: 3,500. **Ad Rates:** Noncommercial. Combined advertising rates available with WDMG-AM.

9051 ■ WOKA-AM - 1310
1310 W Walker St.
Douglas, GA 31533
Phone: (912)384-8153
Fax: (912)383-6328
Free: 866-576-1067
Format: Religious. **Networks:** NBC; Georgia Radio. **Owner:** Coffee County Broadcasters Inc., 1030 Oakdale St, Manchester, TN 37355-5618, Ph: (931)723-3869. **Operating Hours**: 6 a.m.-sundown; 4% network, 96% local. **ADI**: Albany (Valdosta & Cordele), GA. **Wattage**: 100,000. **Ad Rates:** $4.50-5.65 for 30 seconds; $5.50-6.65 for 60 seconds. **URL:** http://www.dixiecountry.com.

9052 ■ WOKA-FM - 106.7
1310 W Walker St.
Douglas, GA 31533
Phone: (912)384-8153
Fax: (912)383-6328
Free: 866-576-1067
Format: Country. **Networks:** NBC; Georgia Radio. **Owner:** Coffee County Broadcasters Inc., 1030 Oakdale St, Manchester, TN 37355-5618, Ph: (931)723-3869. **Founded:** 1962. **Operating Hours**: Continuous; 4% network, 96% local. **ADI**: Albany (Valdosta & Cordele), GA. **Wattage**: 100,000. **Ad Rates:** $10 for 30 seconds; $12 for 60 seconds. Combined advertising rates available with WOKA-AM. **URL:** http://www.tunein.com.

9053 ■ WPNG-FM - 101.9
509 S Columbia Ave.
Douglas, GA 31533
Free: 877-611-1019
Email: shine@broadcastsouth.com
Owner: Broadcast South, LLC, 509 S Columbia Ave., Douglas, GA 31533, Ph: (912)389-0995, Fax: (912)383-8552. **Wattage**: 13,000. **Ad Rates:** Advertising accepted; rates available upon request. **URL:** http://www.shine1019.fm.

9054 ■ WVOH-FM - 93.5
1931 Georgia Hwy. 32 E
Douglas, GA 31533
Phone: (912)345-9350
Fax: (912)383-8552
Email: TheEagle@broadcastsouth.com
Format: Adult Contemporary; Oldies. **Networks:** NBC; Georgia Radio. **Owner:** Broadcast South, LLC, 509 S Columbia Ave., Douglas, GA 31533, Ph: (912)389-0995, Fax: (912)383-8552. **Founded:** 1976. **Operating Hours**: Continuous; 50% network, 50% local. **Key Personnel:** John I. Hulett, Contact; Wilbur G. Heath, Contact; Bruce Bostwick, Contact; Joan Davis, Contact. **Wattage**: 50,000 ERP. **Ad Rates:** $4.00-12.00 for 30 seconds; $6.00-14.00 for 60 seconds; $4.50 for 60 seconds. **URL:** http://www.935theeagle.com.

DOUGLASVILLE

W. GA. Douglas Co. 20 mi. W. of Atlanta. Chemical research. Manufactures textile products, metal fabrication. Asphalt refinery; lumber mills; quarries. Pine, hardwood timber.

9055 ■ WDCY-AM
8451 S Cherokee Blvd., Ste. B
Douglasville, GA 30134-2520
Phone: (770)920-1520
Format: Gospel; Southern Gospel. **Owner:** Word Christian Broadcasting Inc., 8451 Earl D. Lee Blvd., Ste. B, Douglasville, GA 30134, Ph: (770)920-1520. **Founded:** 1963. **Formerly**: WDGL-AM. **Key Personnel:** Sandy Johns, Dir. of Programs. **Wattage**: 2,500 Day; 800 CH. **URL:** http://wordchristianbroadcasting.com.

9056 ■ WDPC-AM - 1500
8451 S Cherokee Blvd., Ste. B
Douglasville, GA 30134
Phone: (770)920-1520
Format: Religious. **Founded:** Sept. 07, 2006. **Ad Rates:** Advertising accepted; rates available upon request. **URL:** http://www.wordchristianbroadcasting.com.

9057 ■ WNEA-AM - 1300
8451 S Cherokee Blvd., Ste. B
Douglasville, GA 30134
Phone: (770)920-1520
Format: Gospel. **Networks:** NBC; Georgia Radio. **Owner:** Word Christian Broadcasting Inc., 8451 Earl D. Lee Blvd., Ste. B, Douglasville, GA 30134, Ph: (770)920-1520. **Founded:** 1962. **Operating Hours**: Mon-Sun 6am-sunset; 20-30% network 70-80%. **Wattage**: 1,000. **Ad Rates:** $5.50-6.75 for 30 seconds; $5-8 for 60 seconds. **URL:** http://wordchristianbroadcasting.com.

9058 ■ Wometco Cable
5979 Fairburn Rd.
Douglasville, GA 30134
Phone: (404)942-0010
Fax: (404)949-7010
Owner: Wometco Cable Corp., 9500 S Dadeland Blvd., Ste. 800, Miami, FL 33156, Ph: (305)662-2205, Fax: (305)662-7015. **Founded:** Aug. 1978. **Cities Served:** Douglasville, Lithia Springs, Georgia: subscribing households 17,450; 56 channels; 1 community access channel.

9059 ■ Word Christian Broadcasting Inc.
8451 Earl D. Lee Blvd., Ste. B
Douglasville, GA 30134
Phone: (770)920-1520
Format: Contemporary Christian. **Networks:** Christian Broadcasting (CBN). **URL:** http://www.wordchristianbroadcasting.com.

DU PONT

9060 ■ WBTY-FM - 105.5
PO Box 9
Du Pont, GA 31630
Phone: (912)487-3412
Fax: (912)487-3414
Format: Classic Rock. **Founded:** 1979. **Operating Hours**: Continuous. **Key Personnel:** Nancy Strickland, Mgr. **Wattage**: 3,000. **Ad Rates:** $2.50 for 30 seconds; $4.75 for 60 seconds.

DUBLIN

C. GA. Laurens Co. On Oconee River, 50 mi. SE of Macon. Manufactures furniture, textiles, carpets, aluminum products, fertilizer, lumber, farm implements. Meat packing; recycling plant; cotton warehouses. Timber. Agriculture. Cotton.

9061 ■ The Courier Herald
Courier Herald
115 S Jefferson St.
Dublin, GA 31021
Phone: (478)272-5522
Fax: (478)272-2189
Free: 800-833-2504
Publication E-mail: news@courier-herald.com
General newspaper. **Founded:** 1930. **Freq:** Daily (eve.) and Sat. (morn.). **Print Method:** Offset. **Cols./Page:** 6. **Col. Width:** 25 nonpareils. **Col. Depth:** 301 agate lines. **Key Personnel:** Pam Burney, Director, Advertising; Cheryl Gay, Manager, Circulation; Griffin Lovett, Publisher; DuBose Porter, Chief Executive Officer. **Subscription Rates:** $112 Individuals online; $57 Individuals 6 months; online; $29 Individuals 3 months; online; $10 Individuals 1 month; online. **URL:** http://www.courier-herald.com. **Ad Rates:** GLR $2; BW $1,290; 4C $1,530; SAU $11.85; PCI $10. **Remarks:** Accepts classified advertising. **Circ:** Mon.-Sat. 11000.

9062 ■ WAWH-FM - 88.3
PO Box 3206
Tupelo, MS 38803
Format: Religious. **Owner:** American Family Association, at above address. **Founded:** 1987. **Ad Rates:** Advertising accepted; rates available upon request. **URL:** http://tunein.com.

9063 ■ WKKZ-FM - 92.7
Glenwood Rd.
Box 967
Dublin, GA 31040-0967
Phone: (478)272-9270
Fax: (478)275-3592
Format: Adult Contemporary; News; Sports; Information. **Founded:** 1964. **Formerly**: WXLI-FM. **Key Personnel:** Mike Kirby, Contact; Ray Beck, Mgr; Mike Kirby, Contact. **Wattage**: 50,000. **Ad Rates:** Advertising accepted; rates available upon request. $8-14 for 30 seconds; $12-16 for 60 seconds. **URL:** http://www.wkkz927.com/.

9064 ■ WMCG-FM
PO Box 130
Dublin, GA 31040-0130
Phone: (912)365-7788
Fax: (912)365-7799
Format: Country. **Networks:** ABC. **Founded:** 1982. **Wattage**: 49,000 ERP. **Ad Rates:** $3-8.50 for 30 seconds; $3.63-11.50 for 60 seconds. **URL:** http://1049wmcg.com.

9065 ■ WMLT-AM - 1330
PO Box 130
Dublin, GA 31040
Phone: (478)272-4422
Fax: (478)275-4657
Format: Urban Contemporary; Gospel. **Networks:** ABC; Georgia Radio. **Owner:** State Broadcasting Corp., at above address, Dublin, GA. **Founded:** 1945. **Operating Hours**: Continuous; 40% network, 60% local. **Key Personnel:** Robert Whitt, Operations Mgr., rickhumphrey@wqzy.com; Yvonne Lamb Castillo, Dir. of Pub. Prog. & Svcs., publicservice@1330wmlt.com; Rick Humphrey, Gen. Mgr., rickhumphrey@wqzy.com. **Wattage**: 5,000. **Ad Rates:** $4.60-7.25 for 30 seconds; $5.70-9 for 60 seconds. **URL:** http://969thebuzz.com.

9066 ■ WQIL-FM - 101.3
807 Bellevue Ave
Dublin, GA 31021
Format: Gospel. **URL:** http://www.wqilfm.com.

9067 ■ WQZY-FM - 95.9
807 Bellevue Ave.
Dublin, GA 31021
Phone: (478)272-4422
Format: Country. **Networks:** NBC. **Founded:** 1976. **Operating Hours**: Continuous; 5% network, 95% local. **ADI:** Macon, GA. **Key Personnel:** Robert Whitt, Operations Mgr., robert@wqzy.com. **Wattage**: 100,000. **Ad Rates:** Noncommercial. **URL:** http://www.wqzy.com.

9068 ■ WXLI-AM
PO Box 967
Box 967
Dublin, GA 31040
Phone: (912)272-4282
Fax: (912)275-3592
Format: Contemporary Country. **Networks:** CBS. **Founded:** 1958. **Key Personnel:** Mike Kirby, Gen. Mgr. **Wattage**: 700. **Ad Rates:** $5-9 for 30 seconds; $7-11 for 60 seconds.

9069 ■ WZOB-AM - 1250
PO Box 967
Dublin, GA 31021
Phone: (256)845-2810
Fax: (256)845-7521
Format: Country. **Networks:** CNN Radio; Alabama Radio (ALANET). **Owner:** Central Broadcasting Company L.L.C., at above address. **Founded:** 1950. **Operating Hours**: Continuous. **Wattage**: 5,000 Day; 122 Night.

DULUTH

NW GA. Gwinnett Co.

9070 ■ The Christian Index
The Christian Index
6405 Sugarloaf Pky.
Duluth, GA 30097
Phone: (770)936-5590
Free: 877-424-6339
News magazine for the Georgia Baptist Convention. **Freq:** Biweekly. **Print Method:** Letterpress and offset. **Trim Size:** 10 x 14. **Cols./Page:** 5. **Col. Width:** 1 7/8 inches. **Col. Depth:** 13 1/2 inches. **Key Personnel:** Donna Ward, Coordinator, Advertising, phone: (770)936-5591; Joe Westbury, Managing Editor; Gerald Harris, Editor. **ISSN:** 0362--0832 (print). **Subscription Rates:**

$12 Individuals; $20 Two years; $6 Individuals online only. **URL:** http://christianindex.org. **Ad Rates:** GLR $5; BW $1754; 4C $2185; PCI $30. **Remarks:** Accepts advertising. **Circ:** Paid 35000.

9071 ■ Computers, Materials & Continua
Tech Science Press
5805 State Bridge Rd., Ste. G108
Duluth, GA 30097-8220
Phone: (678)392-3239
Fax: (678)922-2259
Publisher's E-mail: sale@techscience.com
Journal covering results of research in engineering and science disciplines. Some of the areas of interest including computer modeling & simulation; analysis and synthesis of engineered structural and functional materials, biomaterials, smart materials and structures, solid and fluid mechanics, micro-electromechanical systems, nano-electromechanical systems, nano-micro-macro-level coupled modeling, nano-structured composites, chemo-mechanical engineering in biosystems. **Freq:** 18/yr. **Key Personnel:** Prof. Raimund Rolfes, Board Member; Prof. Weinong Chen, Board Member; Dr. Vinod Tewary, Board Member. **ISSN:** 1546--2218 (print); **EISSN:** 1546--2226 (electronic). **Subscription Rates:** $3000 Individuals print & online. **URL:** http://www.techscience.com/cmc/index.html. **Remarks:** Advertising not accepted. **Circ:** (Not Reported).

9072 ■ Inside Gwinnett
Gwinnett Chamber of Commerce
6500 Sugarloaf Pky.
Duluth, GA 30097
Phone: (770)232-3000
Magazine of the Gwinnett Chamber of Commerce. **Freq:** Quarterly. **Subscription Rates:** Free. **URL:** http://www.gwinnettchamber.org; http://www.insidegwinnett.com. **Remarks:** Accepts advertising. **Circ:** (Not Reported).

9073 ■ Journal of African Business
African Business Alliance
5805 State Bridge Rd., Ste. G255
Duluth, GA 30097
Phone: (770)409-8780
Fax: (678)605-0271
Publisher's E-mail: info@aballiance.org
Freq: 3/year. **Trim Size:** 6 x 8 3/8. **Key Personnel:** Samuel Bonsu, Editor-in-Chief. **ISSN:** 1522--8916 (print); **EISSN:** 1522--9076 (electronic). **Subscription Rates:** $158 Individuals online only; $211 Individuals print and online; $638 Institutions online only; $729 Institutions print and online. **URL:** http://www.tandfonline.com/toc/wjab20/current. **Ad Rates:** BW $315; 4C $550. **Remarks:** Accepts advertising. **Circ:** (Not Reported).

9074 ■ Molecular & Cellular Biomechanics
Tech Science Press
5805 State Bridge Rd., Ste. G108
Duluth, GA 30097-8220
Phone: (678)392-3239
Fax: (678)922-2259
Publisher's E-mail: sale@techscience.com
Journal that aims to facilitate the studies of the mechanics of biomolecules including proteins and nucleic acid and the mechanics of single cells, and their interactions with extracellular matrix. **Freq:** Quarterly. **Key Personnel:** Dalin Tang, Editor-in-Chief; Prof. Pin Tong, Editor. **ISSN:** 1556--5297 (print); **EISSN:** 1556--5300 (electronic). **URL:** http://www.techscience.com/mcb. **Formerly**: Mechanics & Chemistry of Biosystems. **Circ:** (Not Reported).

9075 ■ Structural Integrity & Durability
Tech Science Press
5805 State Bridge Rd., Ste. G108
Duluth, GA 30097-8220
Phone: (678)392-3239
Fax: (678)922-2259
Publication E-mail: sale@techscience.com
Journal that publishes original research papers, communications, and review articles related to structural integrity and durability. **Freq:** Quarterly. **Key Personnel:** Satya N. Atluri, Editor. **ISSN:** 1551--3750 (print). **Subscription Rates:** $262.50 Individuals. **Alt. Formats:** PDF. **URL:** http://www.techscience.com/books/sid_hc.html. **Remarks:** Advertising not accepted. **Circ:** (Not Reported).

9076 ■ WPLO-AM
239 Ezzard S
Duluth, GA 30097
Phone: (770)237-9897
Fax: (770)237-8769
Format: Hispanic. **Founded:** 1954. **Formerly**: WLAW-AM. **Wattage:** 1,500 Day; 225 Night. **Ad Rates:** $25-45 for 30 seconds; $25-35 for 30 seconds; $45-70 for 60 seconds.

DUNWOODY

NW GA. DeKalb Co. 22 mi. N. of Atlanta.

9077 ■ The Chattahoochee Review
Georgia Perimeter College
2101 Womack Rd.
Dunwoody, GA 30338-4435
Phone: (770)274-5000
Fax: (770)551-7447
Publisher's E-mail: gpccr@gpc.edu
Literary review. **Freq:** Quarterly. **Print Method:** Offset. **Trim Size:** 6 x 9. **Cols./Page:** 1. **Key Personnel:** Anna Schachner, Editor. **ISSN:** 0741--9155 (print). **Subscription Rates:** $16 By mail 1 year; $30 By mail 2 years. **URL:** http://thechattahoocheereview.gpc.edu. **Remarks:** Advertising not accepted. **Circ:** (Not Reported).

9078 ■ Journal of Travel Medicine
International Society of Travel Medicine
1200 Ashwood Pky., Ste. 310
Dunwoody, GA 30338-4767
Phone: (404)373-8282
Fax: (404)373-8283
Publisher's E-mail: istm@istm.org
Freq: Bimonthly. **ISSN:** 1195--1982 (print); **EISSN:** 1708--8305 (electronic). **Subscription Rates:** £216 Individuals online, UK; £346 Individuals online, non-UK; $411 Individuals online, non-UK; €324 Individuals online, non-UK. **URL:** http://www.istm.org/journaloftravelmedicine; http://jtm.oxfordjournals.org. **Remarks:** Accepts advertising. **Circ:** (Not Reported).

EAST POINT

NW GA. Fulton Co. 5 mi. S. of Atlanta. Manufactures textiles, paint, glass, paper products, fertilizer, chemicals, concrete products, machinery, auto batteries. Agriculture. Cotton, corn, dairying.

9079 ■ WAEN-TV
3105 Washington Rd.
East Point, GA 30344
Phone: (404)477-0300
Format: Hip Hop; Classic Rock. **Ad Rates:** Accepts Advertising. **URL:** http://www.waen.tv.

EASTMAN

C. GA. Dodge Co. 52 mi. SE of Macon. Tobacco, timber, cotton, corn.

9080 ■ The Times Journal
Rosebud Publishing
PO Box 4189
Eastman, GA 31023
Phone: (478)374-5562
Fax: (478)374-3464
Publication E-mail: timejnl@bellsouth.net
Community newspaper. **Founded:** 1872. **Freq:** Weekly. **Print Method:** Offset. **Cols./Page:** 6. **Col. Width:** 12 picas. **Col. Depth:** 21 inches. **Key Personnel:** Barbara Williams, Managing Editor; Don Richardson, Associate Editor; Neal Minor, Manager, Sales; Nancy Dawson, Manager, Advertising and Sales. **Subscription Rates:** $21 Individuals in Dodge County; $30 Out of state; $26 Out of area. **URL:** http://thetimesjnl.tripod.com. **Formerly**: Times Journal Spotlight. **Ad Rates:** GLR $.30; BW $529.20; 4C $769.20; PCI $4.20. **Remarks:** Accepts advertising. **Circ:** ‡4,950.

9081 ■ WUFF-AM
PO Box 4097
Box 4097
Eastman, GA 31023
Phone: (478)374-3437
Fax: (478)374-3585
Format: Country. **Networks:** NBC. **Owner:** Dodge Broadcasting, Inc., at above address, Ph: (912)374-3438. **Founded:** 1961. **Formerly**: WPFE-AM. **Key Personnel:** Joy Henderson, Contact. **Wattage:** 2,500 Day. **Ad Rates:** $4 for 30 seconds; $5 for 60 seconds.

9082 ■ WUFF-FM - 97.5
PO Box 4097
Eastman, GA 31023
Phone: (478)374-3437
Fax: (478)374-3585
Format: Country. **Key Personnel:** Wanda Lancaster, Gen. Mgr., wanda@wolfcountry975.com; Quint Bush, Prog. Dir., quint@wolfcountry975.com; Greg Grantham, Sales Mgr., greg@wolfcountry975.com. **Wattage:** 6,000. **Ad Rates:** Noncommercial. **URL:** http://www.wolfcountry975.com.

EATONTON

C. GA. Putnam Co. 41 mi. NE of Macon. Resort. Manufactures feed, mobile homes. Dairying. Timber. Diversified farming. Horses, cattle.

9083 ■ The Eatonton Messenger
Smith Communications L.L.C.
100 N Jefferson Ave.
Eatonton, GA 31024
Phone: (706)485-3501
Fax: (706)485-4166
General newspaper. **Freq:** Weekly (Thurs.). **Print Method:** Offset. **Cols./Page:** 6. **Subscription Rates:** $35 Individuals Georgia; $55 Out of state; $30 Individuals 1 year; online; $45 Out of country. **URL:** http://www.msgr.com. **Ad Rates:** PCI $900. **Circ:** Paid ‡5600.

9084 ■ CommuniComm Services
PO Box 3310
Eatonton, GA 31024
Phone: (337)436-5538
Free: 800-239-5367
Cities Served: Westlake, Louisiana; 44 channels. **URL:** http://www.netcommander.com.

9085 ■ Plantation Cablevision
865 Harmony Rd.
Eatonton, GA 31024
Phone: (706)485-7740
Free: 877-830-5454
Email: feedback@plantationcable.net
Founded: 1989. **Key Personnel:** Roslyn Hooks, Contact; Chris Byrd, Contact. **Cities Served:** 80 channels. **URL:** http://www.plantationcable.net.

ELBERTON

NE GA. Elbert Co. 70 mi. NW of Augusta. Extensive granite works. Manufactures lumber, silk, cotton, cottonseed products, tools. Granite quarries; pine, oak timber. Agriculture. Cotton, corn, oats.

9086 ■ The Elberton Star & Examiner
Community Newspapers Inc.
25 N Public Sq.
Elberton, GA 30635-0280
Phone: (706)283-8500
Fax: (706)283-9700
Publisher's E-mail: dnesmith@cninewspapers.com
Community newspaper. **Freq:** Weekly (Wed.). **Print Method:** Offset. Uses mats. **Cols./Page:** 6. **Col. Width:** 24 3/4 nonpareils. **Col. Depth:** 297 1/2 agate lines. **Key Personnel:** Mark Berryman, Managing Editor; Gary Jones, Publisher; Ryne Daniels, Director, Sports. **ISSN:** 8750--6734 (print). **Subscription Rates:** $30 Individuals in county - print and online; $60 Two years print and online; $7 Individuals 1 month - online only; $34 Out of country print and online; $42 Out of state print and online. **URL:** http://elberton.com. **Formerly**: The Gilbert County Examiner; The Elberton Star. **Mailing address:** PO Box 280, Elberton, GA 30635-0280. **Ad Rates:** 4C $80. **Remarks:** Accepts advertising. **Circ:** Wed. ‡4400.

9087 ■ The Graniteer Magazine
Elberton Granite Association
1 Granite Plz.
Elberton, GA 30635
Phone: (706)283-2551
Fax: (706)283-6380
Publisher's E-mail: granite@egaonline.com
Magazine featuring news on memorial industry with a focus on Elberton firms. **Freq:** Quarterly. **Subscription Rates:** Included in membership. **URL:** http://egaonline2008.weborizon.net. **Mailing address:** PO Box 640, Elberton, GA 30635. **Remarks:** Advertising not accepted. **Circ:** 11,000.

Circulation: ★ = AAM; △ or • = BPA; ♦ = CAC; ❑ = VAC; ⊕ = PO Statement; ‡ = Publisher's Report; Boldface figures = sworn; Light figures = estimated.

9088 ■ WEHR-FM - 105.1
14 S Public Sq., Ste. 200
Elberton, GA 30635
Phone: (706)213-1051
Fax: (706)213-6955
Email: todays105@dj.net
Format: Adult Contemporary. **Networks:** ABC. **Owner:** Chase Broadcasting Inc., at above address. **Founded:** May 1998. **Formerly**: WDDA-FM. **Operating Hours**: Continuous. **Key Personnel:** Scott Smith, Gen. Mgr., todays105@dj.net. **Ad Rates:** $8 for 30 seconds; $10 for 60 seconds.

9089 ■ WSGC-AM - 1400
562 Jones St.
Elberton, GA 30635
Phone: (706)213-1051
Email: wsgc@elbertonradio.com
Format: Oldies. **Founded:** 1947. **Key Personnel:** Carl Pundt, Gen. Mgr., VP. **Mailing address:** PO Box 340, Elberton, GA 30635. **URL:** http://www.wsgcradio.com.

9090 ■ WWRK-FM - 92.1
PO Box 340
Elberton, GA 30635-0340
Phone: (706)283-1714
Fax: (706)283-8710
Format: Contemporary Country. **Networks:** Jones Satellite. **Founded:** 1972. **Formerly**: WSGC-FM. **Operating Hours**: Continuous; 40% network, 60% local. **Key Personnel:** Mickey Palmer, Contact; Scott Smith, Music Dir.; Mel Stovall, News Dir.; Nate Hirsch, President; Mickey Palmer, Contact. **Wattage**: 3,000. **Ad Rates:** $5 for 15 seconds; $7 for 30 seconds; $8.50 for 60 seconds.

ELLIJAY

N. GA. Gilmer Co. 65 mi. N. of Atlanta. Resort. Poultry processing. Pine, oak timber. Farming. Corn, cabbage, apples.

9091 ■ Times-Courier
Times-Courier Pub.
PO Box 1076
Ellijay, GA 30540
Phone: (706)635-4313
Fax: (706)635-7006
Publisher's E-mail: online@timescourier.com
Community newspaper. **Founded:** 1875. **Freq:** Weekly (Wed.). **Print Method:** Offset. **Trim Size:** 13 x 22. **Cols./Page:** 6. **Col. Width:** 10.5 picas. **Col. Depth:** 21 inches. **Key Personnel:** George N. Bunch, III, Associate Publisher, General Manager, phone: (706)635-4313; Kathy Aker, Representative, Advertising and Sales. **USPS:** 639-280. **Subscription Rates:** $24 Individuals in Gilmer, Fannin and Pickens counties; $24 Individuals in Dawson and Murray counties; $28 Out of area. **URL:** http://timescourier.com. **Ad Rates:** GLR $5.95; BW $749.70; 4C $1,004.50; SAU $5.95; PCI $5.95. **Remarks:** Advertising accepted; rates available upon request. **Circ:** Paid 6,850.

EVANS

9092 ■ Columbia County News Times
The Columbia County News Times
4272 Washington Rd., Ste. 3B
Evans, GA 30809
Phone: (706)868-1222
Fax: (706)823-6062
Publisher's E-mail: cnt@newstimesonline.com
Community newspaper. **Freq:** Semiweekly (Wed. and Sun.). **Print Method:** Offset. **Cols./Page:** 6. **Col. Width:** 11.625 inches. **Col. Depth:** 21 inches. **Key Personnel:** Barry L. Paschal, Publisher; Suzanne Liverett, Office Manager. **USPS:** 124-100. **URL:** http://newstimes.augusta.com. **Formerly**: Columbia News/Martinez-Evans Times. **Ad Rates:** GLR $.32; BW $619.20. **Remarks:** Accepts advertising. **Circ:** Wed. 18000, Sun. 26000.

9093 ■ Modern Pathology: The Official Journal of the United States and Canadian Academy of Pathology (USCAP)
Nature Publishing Group
c/o Catherine Ketcham, PhD, Managing Editor
United States & Canadian Academy of Pathology
404 Town Park Blvd., Ste. 201
Evans, GA 30809
Phone: (770)559-3569
Publisher's E-mail: registration@natureny.com
Journal of The United States-Canadian Academy of Pathology, Inc. devoted to the continuing education of practicing pathologists. **Freq:** Monthly. **Key Personnel:** John N. Eble, MD, Editor-in-Chief; Catherine Ketcham, PhD, Managing Editor, phone: (770)559-3569. **ISSN:** 0893--3952 (print); **EISSN:** 1530--0285 (electronic). **Subscription Rates:** $558 Individuals print and online - The Americas ; $490 Individuals online only - The Americas ; €576.29 Individuals print and online - Europe; €520.13 Individuals online only - Europe; ¥98600 Individuals print and online - Japan; ¥88800 Individuals online only - Japan; £372 Other countries print and online - UK/ROW; £335 Other countries online only - UK/ROW. **URL:** http://www.nature.com/modpathol/index.html. **Remarks:** Accepts classified advertising. **Circ:** Paid ‡5,514, Non-paid ‡87.

FAYETTEVILLE

C. GA. Fayette Co.

9094 ■ The Citizen
Fayette Publishing Inc.
310-B N Glynn St.
Fayetteville, GA 30214
Phone: (770)719-1880
Publication E-mail: editor@thecitizennews.com
Community newspaper. **Founded:** 1996. **Freq:** Weekly (Wed.). **URL:** http://www.thecitizennews.com/. **Remarks:** Accepts advertising. **Circ:** Non-paid ♦**23432**.

9095 ■ The Citizen--Coweta Edition
Fayette Publishing Inc.
310-B N Glynn St.
Fayetteville, GA 30214
Phone: (770)719-1880
Community newspaper. **Freq:** Weekly (Fri.). **Key Personnel:** Cal Beverly, Publisher, Editor. **URL:** http://www.thecitizen.com. **Remarks:** Accepts advertising. **Circ:** Non-paid ♦**7912**.

9096 ■ The Citizen-Peachtree/Tyrone
Fayette Publishing Inc.
310-B N Glynn St.
Fayetteville, GA 30214
Phone: (770)719-1880
Community newspaper. **Freq:** Weekly (Sat.). **Key Personnel:** Cal Beverly, Publisher, Editor. **URL:** http://thecitizen.com. **Remarks:** Accepts advertising. **Circ:** Non-paid ♦**11944**.

9097 ■ Fayette Daily News
Fayette Newspapers Inc.
210 Jeff Davis Pl.
Fayetteville, GA 30214
Phone: (770)461-6317
Fax: (770)460-8172
Community newspaper. **Freq:** Daily. **Print Method:** Offset. **Trim Size:** 13 x 21 1/2. **Cols./Page:** 6. **Col. Width:** 2 1/8 inches. **Col. Depth:** 21 1/2 inches. **Key Personnel:** Martha Barksdale, Managing Editor; Geneva Weaver, Publisher. **ISSN:** 5818-6957 (print). **Subscription Rates:** $31.80 Individuals Fayette County; $28.62 Individuals senior citizens in Fayette County; $58.30 Individuals Georgia; $52.47 Individuals senior citizens in Georgia; $75 Out of state; $67.50 Out of state senior citizens. **URL:** http://www.fayettedailynews.com/. **Mailing address:** PO Box 96, Fayetteville, GA 30214. **Ad Rates:** GLR $.24; BW $445.05; 4C $815.05; SAU $3.60. **Remarks:** Accepts advertising. **Circ:** ‡9100.

9098 ■ WFDR-AM - 1370
185 Melody Ln.
Fayetteville, GA 30215
Phone: (678)860-1504
Owner: Ploener Radio Group, LLC, at above address. **Founded:** Mar. 1983. **Formerly**: WQCK-AM; WVFJ-AM. **Key Personnel:** Rick Davison, Contact, rdavison@wvfj.com. **Wattage:** 2,300 Day;028 Night. **Ad Rates:** Accepts Advertising. **URL:** http://wfdram1370.com.

FITZGERALD

S. GA. Irwin Co. 152 mi. S. of Atlanta. Manufactures carpet yarn, mobile homes, automotive batteries, irrigation equipment, aluminum casting, concrete products. Peanut processing; garment factories; sawmills; meat packing plant; metal works. Diversified farming.

9099 ■ The Herald-Leader: Telling Fitzgerald Stories since 1895
Pryor Publications Inc.
202 E Central Ave.
Fitzgerald, GA 31750
Phone: (229)423-9331
Fax: (229)423-6533
Community newspaper. **Founded:** 1892. **Freq:** Weekly (Wed.) (Sunday and Wed.). **Print Method:** Offset. **Cols./Page:** 6. **Col. Width:** 24 nonpareils. **Col. Depth:** 301 agate lines. **Key Personnel:** Tim Anderson, Editor, Publisher; Becky Anderson, Manager, Advertising. **USPS:** 001-729. **Subscription Rates:** $25 Individuals Ben Hill & adjoining counties (print and online); $45 Two years Ben Hill & adjoining counties (print and online); $35 Individuals elsewhere in Georgia (print and online); $65 Two years elsewhere in Georgia (print and online); $45 Out of state (print and online); $85 Out of state 2 years (print and online); $35 Out of state online; $65 Out of state 2 years online. **URL:** http://www.herald-leader.net/. **Formerly**: The Herald-Democrat. **Ad Rates:** GLR $.25; BW $677; 4C $882; SAU $5.25. **Remarks:** .25. **Circ:** Combined 5000.

FOLKSTON

SE GA. Charlton Co. 35 mi. S. of Waycross. Manufactures staves, textiles, lumber, turpentine. Pine, hardwood timber. Titanium mining. Cattle and hogs. Agriculture. Tobacco, cotton, corn.

9100 ■ WATY-FM - 91.3
260 14th St. NW
Atlanta, GA 30318
Phone: (404)685-2400
Free: 800-222-4788
Format: Public Radio. **Owner:** Georgia Public Broadcasting, 260 14th St. NW, Atlanta, GA 30318, Ph: (404)685-2400, Free: 800-222-6006. **Founded:** Nov. 06, 1997. **Key Personnel:** Tiffany Brown Rideaux, Contact. **Wattage**: 600 ERP. **Ad Rates:** Noncommercial. **URL:** http://www.gpb.org.

FOREST PARK

9101 ■ The Henry Neighbor
Neighbor Newspapers Inc.
5442 Frontage Rd., Ste. 130
Forest Park, GA 30297
Phone: (404)363-8484
Fax: (404)363-0212
Publication E-mail: smetro@neighbornewspapers.com
Community newspaper. **Freq:** Weekly (Thurs.). **Print Method:** Offset. **Cols./Page:** 6. **Col. Width:** 26 nonpareils. **Col. Depth:** 301 agate lines. **Key Personnel:** Otis Brumby, III, General Manager. **USPS:** 405-570. **Subscription Rates:** $135.68 By mail outside of delivery area; $72.08 By mail 6 months, outside of delivery area; $36.57 By mail 3 months, outside of delivery area. **URL:** http://www.mdjonline.com/neighbor_newspapers. **Ad Rates:** GLR $.77; BW $1393; 4C $1683; SAU $10.80. **Remarks:** Accepts advertising. **Circ:** Thurs. ♦**15604**.

9102 ■ The South Fulton Neighbor
Neighbor Newspapers Inc.
5442 Frontage Rd., Ste. 130
Forest Park, GA 30297-2516
Phone: (404)363-8484
Fax: (404)363-0212
Community newspaper. **Freq:** Weekly (Thurs.). **Print Method:** Offset. **Cols./Page:** 6. **Col. Width:** 26 nonpareils. **Col. Depth:** 301 agate lines. **USPS:** 951-940. **URL:** http://www.mdjonline.com/neighbor_newspapers/south_metro. **Ad Rates:** GLR $1.22; BW $2206; 4C $2531; SAU $17.10. **Remarks:** Accepts advertising. **Circ:** Wed. ♦**24063**.

FORSYTH

C. GA. Monroe Co. 25 mi. NW of Macon. Tift College of Mercer University (women). Textiles, lumber and wood products.

9103 ■ Monroe County Reporter
Monroe County Reporter
50 N Jackson St.
Forsyth, GA 31029
Phone: (478)994-2358
Fax: (478)994-2359

Newspaper. **Freq:** Weekly (Wed.). **Print Method:** Offset. **Cols./Page:** 6. **Col. Width:** 27 nonpareils. **Col. Depth:** 301 agate lines. **Key Personnel:** Will Davis, Editor; Carolyn Martel, Manager, Advertising; Trellis Grant, Business Manager. **Subscription Rates:** $35 Individuals in county; $10 Individuals per month. **URL:** http://mymcr.net. **Mailing address:** PO Box 795, Forsyth, GA 31029. **Ad Rates:** 4C $250, process color; 4C 100, spot color. **Remarks:** Accepts advertising. **Circ:** 4000.

FORT BENNING

W. GA. Chattahoochee Co. 8 mi. S. of Columbus.

9104 ■ Armor
Maneuver Center of Excellence
1 Karker St., McGinnis-Wickam Hall, Ste. W-141
Fort Benning, GA 31905
Phone: (706)545-2011
Military news magazine. **Freq:** Annual. **Print Method:** Letterpress and offset. **Trim Size:** 8 1/4 x 11. **Cols./Page:** 3. **Col. Width:** 41 nonpareils. **Col. Depth:** 133 agate lines. **Key Personnel:** Vivian Oertle, Contact, phone: (502)624-2610. **ISSN:** 0004-2420 (print). **Subscription Rates:** $27 Individuals. **URL:** http://www.knox.army.mil; http://www.benning.army.mil/armor/eARMOR. **Remarks:** Advertising not accepted. **Circ:** Paid 7000, Non-paid 7000.

FORT GAINES

9105 ■ WJWV-FM - 90.9
210 Washington St., Ste. 3
Fort Gaines, GA 39851
Phone: (229)768-2631
Free: 800-222-4788
Email: ask@gpb.org
Format: Public Radio. **Owner:** Georgia Public Broadcasting, 260 14th St. NW, Atlanta, GA 30318, Ph: (404)685-2400, Free: 800-222-6006. **Key Personnel:** Ellen Reinhardt, Host. **URL:** http://www.gpb.org.

FORT GORDON

E. GA. Richmond Co. SW of Augusta.

9106 ■ Army Communicator: Voice of the Signal Regiment
U.S. Army Signal Regiment
Public Affairs Office
Darling Hall, Bldg. 33720, Ste. 382
307 Chamberlain Ave.
Fort Gordon, GA 30905-5730
Phone: (706)791-6844
Publication E-mail: aceditor@conus.army.mil
Magazine providing information technology to the Signal Regiment and industry partners, allied signal services, other U.S. armed forces, ROTC and JROTC cadets. **Freq:** Quarterly. **Print Method:** Offset. **Trim Size:** 8 1/2 x 11. **Cols./Page:** 3. **Col. Width:** 15 picas. **Col. Depth:** 64 picas. **Key Personnel:** Janet A. McElmurray, Editor-in-Chief. **ISSN:** 0362--5745 (print). **Subscription Rates:** Free. **Remarks:** Advertising not accepted. **Circ:** Controlled ‡5000.

9107 ■ The Signal
Citizen Newspapers
Public Affairs Office, Bldg. 29801, Rm. 209
520 Chamberlain Ave.
Fort Gordon, GA 30905-5735
Military and community newspaper. **Founded:** 1892. **Freq:** Weekly. **Print Method:** Offset. **Trim Size:** 11 1/2. **Cols./Page:** 6. **Col. Width:** 26 nonpareils. **Col. Depth:** 301 agate lines. **Key Personnel:** Bonnie K. Taylor, General Manager; Larry Edmond, Editor; Bonnie Heater, Writer. **Subscription Rates:** $20 Individuals by post; $26 Individuals combo print and internet; $40 Individuals; $33 Out of country; $47 Individuals combo print and internet; $40 Out of country; $54 Individuals combo print and internet. **URL:** http://www.fortgordonsignal.com. **Formerly**: The Semaphore. **Ad Rates:** GLR $.70; BW $1229; 4C $1569; SAU $9.75; PCI $9.75. **Remarks:** Accepts advertising. **Circ:** ‡16,000, ‡12,000.

FORT VALLEY

C. GA. Peach Co. 29 mi. SW of Macon. Fort Valley State College (black). Manufactures cottonseed oil, baskets, farm implements, chemicals, ventilating fans, truck and bus bodies. Pine timber. Agriculture. Peaches, corn, grain, asparagus.

9108 ■ Camellia Journal
American Camellia Society
Massee Lane Gardens
100 Massee Ln.
Fort Valley, GA 31030
Phone: (478)967-2358
Fax: (478)967-2083
Free: 877-422-6355
Publisher's E-mail: ask@americancamellias.org
Journal featuring full-color photographs and informative articles on camellias and camellia-related events. **Freq:** Quarterly. **Subscription Rates:** Included in membership. **Alt. Formats:** PDF. **URL:** http://www.americancamellias.com/about-american-camellia-society/publications-library/the-camellia-journal; http://www.americancamellias.com/about-american-camellia-society/publications-library. **Remarks:** Advertising not accepted. **Circ:** (Not Reported).

9109 ■ The Leader Tribune
Peach Publishing Company Inc.
109 Anderson Ave.
Fort Valley, GA 31030
Phone: (478)825-2432
Fax: (478)825-4130
Publication E-mail: news@theleadertribune.net
Newspaper covering Harper and Eastern Beaver Counties in Oklahoma. **Freq:** Weekly (Wed.). **Print Method:** Web press. **Cols./Page:** 6. **Col. Width:** 2 1/8 12.4 inches picas. **Col. Depth:** 21 1/2 inches. **Key Personnel:** Victor Kulkosky, Editor; Sonya Harris, Editor; Jerry Anderson, Publisher; Darla Hollon, Manager, Advertising. **ISSN:** 8750--250X (print). **USPS:** 307-740. **Subscription Rates:** $20.50; $21.50 Out of state. **Formerly:** Fort Valley Leader-Tribune. **Mailing address:** PO Box 1060, Fort Valley, GA 31030. **Ad Rates:** PCI $4.50; GLR $8; BW $907. **Remarks:** Accepts advertising. **Circ:** Combined ‡12200.

GAINESVILLE

N. GA. Hall Co. 48 mi. NE of Atlanta. Brenau College (women); Gainesville Junior College. Manufactures textiles, furniture, gasoline turbine engines, nylon thread, bricks. Poultry, egg production and processing plant. Hardwood timber. Agriculture.

9110 ■ Merrick Herald Life
L & M Publications Inc.
PO Box 3273
Gainesville, GA 30501
Phone: (770)532-5610
Fax: (770)532-5667
Community newspaper. **Freq:** Weekly (Thurs.). **Print Method:** Offset. **Cols./Page:** 4. **Col. Width:** 2 1/4 inches. **Col. Depth:** 14 inches. **Key Personnel:** Linda Laursen Toscano, Publisher; Paul Laursen, Editor. **USPS:** 340-100. **URL:** http://www.liherald.com/merrick. **Formerly**: Merrick Life. **Remarks:** Accepts advertising. **Circ:** (Not Reported).

9111 ■ Shelby Report of the Southeast
Shelby Publishing Company Inc.
517 Green St. NW
Gainesville, GA 30501
Phone: (770)534-8380
Publisher's E-mail: admin@shelbypublishing.com
Retail and wholesale food trade newspaper. **Freq:** Monthly. **Print Method:** Offset. **Trim Size:** 11 1/8 x 15. **Cols./Page:** 5. **Col. Width:** 11 nonpareils. **Col. Depth:** 196 agate lines. **Key Personnel:** Ron Johnston, President, Publisher; Penny Smith, Director. **ISSN:** 0194--1968 (print). **Subscription Rates:** $42 Individuals; $70 Two years; $85 Individuals 3 years. **URL:** http://www.theshelbyreport.com/about. **Ad Rates:** BW $3725; 4C $1200; PCI $70. **Remarks:** Accepts advertising. **Circ:** 15066.

9112 ■ Shelby Report of the Southwest
Shelby Publishing Company Inc.
517 Green St. NW
Gainesville, GA 30501
Phone: (770)534-8380
Publisher's E-mail: admin@shelbypublishing.com
Retail and wholesale food trade newspaper. **Freq:** Monthly. **Print Method:** Offset. **Trim Size:** 11 1/8 x 15. **Cols./Page:** 5. **Col. Width:** 11 picas. **Col. Depth:** 13 7/8 inches. **Key Personnel:** Penny Smith, Director; Lorrie Griffith, Editor; Ron Johnston, President, Publisher. **ISSN:** 0192-916X (print). **USPS:** 054-710. **Subscription Rates:** $36 Individuals; $60 Two years; $75 three years. **URL:** http://www.theshelbyreport.com/southwest. **Ad Rates:** BW $3,725; 4C $1,200; PCI $70. **Remarks:** Advertising accepted; rates available upon request. **Circ:** Paid ‡1846, Controlled ‡20357, Non-paid ‡3638.

9113 ■ Sunbelt Foodservice
Shelby Publishing Company Inc.
517 Green St. NW
Gainesville, GA 30501
Phone: (770)534-8380
Publisher's E-mail: admin@shelbypublishing.com
Trade newspaper (tabloid) covering the food industry geared toward restaurant operators. **Freq:** Monthly. **Print Method:** Offset. **Trim Size:** 8 1/4 x 11. **Cols./Page:** 4. **Col. Width:** 11 picas. **Col. Depth:** 10 inches. **Key Personnel:** Ron Johnston, President, Publisher; Lorrie Griffith, Editor; Karen Cooper, Manager, Operations. **Subscription Rates:** $36 Individuals; $60 Two years; $75 Individuals three years. **URL:** http://www.sunbeltfoodservice.com. **Ad Rates:** BW $2076; 4C $1200; PCI $60. **Remarks:** Accepts advertising. **Circ:** Combined 28066.

9114 ■ The Times
The Times
345 Green St. NW
Gainesville, GA 30501
Phone: (770)532-1234
Free: 800-395-5005
Publisher's E-mail: life@gainesvilletimes.com
General newspaper in print and online. **Founded:** 1947. **Freq:** Daily Sunday through Friday. **Print Method:** Offset. **Trim Size:** 12 1/2 x 21 1/2. **Cols./Page:** 6. **Col. Width:** 1.833 inches. **Col. Depth:** 301 agate lines. **USPS:** 212-860. **Subscription Rates:** $169 Individuals home delivery. **URL:** http://www.gainesvilletimes.com/index.shtml. **Ad Rates:** GLR $2.06; BW $5,314.80; 4C $5,709.80; SAU $10 x 21.5; PCI $26.56. **Remarks:** Advertising accepted; rates available upon request. **Circ:** Mon.-Sat. 21153, Sun. 25200.

9115 ■ Wantagh-Seaford Citizen
L & M Publications Inc.
PO Box 3273
Gainesville, GA 30501
Phone: (770)532-5610
Fax: (770)532-5667
Publisher's E-mail: mclark@thebooklm.com
Community newspaper. **Freq:** Weekly (Thurs.). **Print Method:** Offset. **Cols./Page:** 4. **Col. Width:** 2 1/4 inches. **Col. Depth:** 14 inches. **Key Personnel:** Linda Laursen Toscano, Publisher; Paul Laursen, Editor. **USPS:** 665-800. **Subscription Rates:** $18 Individuals. **URL:** http://merricklife.com. **Ad Rates:** GLR $1.05; BW $562.80; SAU $13.30; PCI $11.61. **Remarks:** other Life newspapers. **Circ:** Thurs. 3,125.

9116 ■ WBCX-FM - 89.1
500 Washington St. SE
Gainesville, GA 30501
Phone: (770)538-4744
Fax: (770)538-4701
Free: 800-252-5119
Email: info@brenau.edu
Format: Eclectic. **Networks:** Jones Satellite; Public Radio International (PRI). **Owner:** Brenau University, 500 Washington St. SE, Gainesville, GA 30501, Ph: (770)534-6299. **Founded:** 1976. **Operating Hours**: Continuous; satellite/local. **ADI**: Atlanta (Athens & Rome), GA. **Key Personnel:** Prof. David Morrison, VP of Commercial Dev., dmorrison@brenau.edu; Matt Thomas, VP of Rel., mthomas@brenau.edu; Kristina Rhoades, Gen. Mgr., krhoades@brenau.edu. **Wattage**: 835. **Ad Rates:** Noncommercial. **URL:** http://www.brenau.edu/about/wbcx.

9117 ■ WDUN-AM - 550
1102 Thompson Bridge Rd.
Gainesville, GA 30501
Email: sales@jacobsmedia.net
Format: News; Talk. **Networks:** ABC. **Owner:** Jacobs Media Corp., 30300 Telegraph Rd., Ste. 240, Bingham Farms, MI 48025. **Founded:** 1949. **Operating Hours**: Continuous; 25% network, 75% local. **Key Personnel:** Bill Maine, Contact, bill.maine@jacobsmedia.net. **Local Programs**: *Martha Zoller Show.* **Wattage**: 10,000 day; 2,500 night. **Ad Rates:** $12-29 for 30 seconds; $22-39

Circulation: ★ = AAM; △ or • = BPA; ♦ = CAC; ❑ = VAC; ⊕ = PO Statement; ‡ = Publisher's Report; Boldface figures = sworn; Light figures = estimated.

for 60 seconds. **Mailing address:** PO Box 10, Gainesville, GA 30501. **URL:** http://www.wdun.com/shows.

9118 ■ WDUN-FM - 102.9
1102 Thompson Bridge Rd. NE
Gainesville, GA 30501
Phone: (770)532-9921
Fax: (770)532-0459
Format: News; Talk. **Owner:** Jacobs Media Corp., 30300 Telegraph Rd., Ste. 240, Bingham Farms, MI 48025. **Founded:** 1990. **Operating Hours:** Continuous. **Key Personnel:** Rebecca Cameron, Dir. of Traffic. **Wattage:** 16,000. **Ad Rates:** $10-30 for 30 seconds; $15-35 for 60 seconds. **URL:** http://www.wdun.com/shows.

9119 ■ WGGA-AM - 1240
1102 Thompson Bridge Rd. N
Gainesville, GA 30501
Phone: (770)532-9921
Email: info@jacobsmedia.net
Format: Sports; News; Talk; Information. **Simulcasts:** WDUN. **Networks:** CBS. **Owner:** Jacobs Media Corp., 30300 Telegraph Rd., Ste. 240, Bingham Farms, MI 48025. **Founded:** 1941. **Operating Hours:** Continuous. **ADI:** Gainesville (Ocala), FL. **Key Personnel:** Jean Pethel, Sales Mgr., jean.pethel@jacobsmedia.net. **Wattage:** 1,000 KW. **Ad Rates:** Advertising accepted; rates available upon request. **URL:** http://www.wdun.com.

9120 ■ WGTJ-AM - 1330
PO Box 907038
Gainesville, GA 30501
Phone: (770)297-7485
Fax: (770)297-8030
Free: 866-876-WGTJ
Email: mail@glory1330.com
Format: Religious. **Founded:** Sept. 12, 2006. **Ad Rates:** Noncommercial. **URL:** http://www.glory1330.com.

9121 ■ WHOD-AM - 1230
324 Bradford St. NW
Gainesville, GA 30501
Phone: (918)481-1700
Fax: (918)481-5363
Format: Sports. **Owner:** Capital Assets, Inc., 8002 S 101st East Ave., Tulsa, OK 74133. **Founded:** 1950. **Operating Hours:** Continuous. **Key Personnel:** Dave Hedrick, Mgr.; Bob Summer, Dir. of Programs. **Wattage:** 1,000. **Ad Rates:** $5 for 30 seconds; $7 for 60 seconds. **URL:** http://www.capitalassetsok.com.

9122 ■ WKZD-AM - 1330
1864 Thompson Bridge Rd.
Gainesville, GA 30501
Phone: (770)531-1330
Fax: (770)718-0551
Format: Adult Contemporary; Oldies. **Networks:** CNN Radio. **Owner:** Georgia Mountains Communications, Inc., PO Box 2255, Gainesville, GA 30503. **Founded:** 1986. **Operating Hours:** 6 a.m.-sunset; 100% local. **ADI:** Atlanta (Athens & Rome), GA. **Key Personnel:** Sam Davis, Dir. of Programs; Mike Wofford, Sports Dir.; Dave Puckett, Station Mgr.; Carol McAboy, News Dir. **Wattage:** 1,000. **Ad Rates:** $7.50 for 30 seconds; $10 for 60 seconds.

9123 ■ W204BN-FM - 88.7
PO Box 391
Twin Falls, ID 83303
Fax: (208)736-1958
Free: 800-357-4226
Format: Religious; Contemporary Christian. **Owner:** CSN International, PO Box 391, Twin Falls, ID 83303, Ph: (208)736-1958, Fax: (208)736-1958, Free: 800-357-4226. **Key Personnel:** Kelly Carlson, Dir. of Engg.; Ray Gorney, Asst. Dir. **URL:** http://www.csnradio.com.

GLENNVILLE

SE GA. Tattnall Co. 20 mi. S. of Collins. Residential. Import and export industry. Rotary mowers.

9124 ■ Glennville Sentinel
Glennville Sentinel
105 W Barnard St.
Glennville, GA 30427
Phone: (912)654-2515
Fax: (912)654-2527
Publisher's E-mail: editor@glennvillesentinel.net
Community newspaper. **Freq:** Weekly (Wed.). **Cols./Page:** 6. **Col. Width:** 2 inches. **Col. Depth:** 21 inches. **Key Personnel:** Sarah McCleod, Assistant Editor; Pamela S. Waters, Editor; Hunter McCumber, Manager, Production. **ISSN:** 2199--0000 (print). **Subscription Rates:** $26.75 Individuals in Georgia; $32.10 Out of state. **URL:** http://www.glennvillesentinel.net. **Mailing address:** PO Box 218, Glennville, GA 30427. **Ad Rates:** PCI $5. **Remarks:** Accepts classified advertising. **Circ:** Paid ⊕**4300**.

9125 ■ WOAH-FM
25 Bristle Cone Dr.
Savannah, GA 31419
Phone: (912)408-1063
Format: Urban Contemporary. **Owner:** Broadcast Executives Corp., at above address. **Founded:** 1977. **Formerly:** WCGN FM. **Wattage:** 4,000 ERP. **Ad Rates:** $7-10 per unit.

GRAY

C. GA. Jones Co. 14 mi. NE of Macon. Agriculture. Corn, cotton, peaches.

9126 ■ The Jones County News
The Jones County News
PO Box 1538
Gray, GA 31032
Phone: (478)986-3929
Fax: (478)986-1935
Publisher's E-mail: articles@jcnews.com
Local newspaper. **Freq:** Weekly (Thurs.). **Print Method:** Offset. **Cols./Page:** 6. **Col. Width:** 24 nonpareils. **Col. Depth:** 301 agate lines. **Key Personnel:** Josh Lurie, Publisher; Debbie Lurie-Smith, Editor. **Subscription Rates:** $37 Individuals neighboring Jones County - print and online; $54 Out of area print and online; $65 Out of state print and online; $20 Individuals online; $42 Individuals neighboring Jones county - print and online. **URL:** http://jcnews.com. **Ad Rates:** GLR $.18; BW $332.80; PCI $2.60. **Remarks:** Accepts advertising. **Circ:** 4500.

GREENSBORO

NE GA. Greene Co. 30 mi. S. of Athens. Residential.

9127 ■ Crawfordville Advocate-Democrat
Cache Valley Publishing L.L.C.
107 N Main St.
Greensboro, GA 30642-1143
Phone: (706)453-7988
Fax: (706)453-2311
Community newspaper. **Freq:** Weekly. **Cols./Page:** 6. **Col. Width:** 2 inches. **Col. Depth:** 21 inches. **Subscription Rates:** $5 Individuals. **Ad Rates:** GLR $2.50; PCI $6.40. **Remarks:** Accepts advertising. **Circ:** Paid 790, Free 10.

9128 ■ WDDK-FM - 103.9
1271-B E Broad St.
Greensboro, GA 30642
Phone: (706)453-4140
Fax: (706)453-7179
Format: Full Service; Information. **Networks:** ABC. **Founded:** 1980. **Operating Hours:** Continuous. **Key Personnel:** Chip Lyness, Contact, chip@dock1039.com. **Wattage:** 5,300 ERP. **Ad Rates:** $3.40-7.40 for 30 seconds; $5-9 for 60 seconds. **URL:** http://dock1039.com.

GRIFFIN

W. GA. Spalding Co. 40 mi. S. of Atlanta. Manufactures textiles. Fruit, dairy farms. Cotton, peppers, wheat.

9129 ■ Griffin Daily News
Griffin Daily News
1403 North Expy., Ste. J
Griffin, GA 30223
Phone: (770)227-3276
Fax: (770)412-1678
Newspaper with a Democratic orientation. **Freq:** Mon.-Sat. (eve.). **Print Method:** Offset. **Cols./Page:** 6. **Col. Width:** 2 inches. **Col. Depth:** 301 agate lines. **Key Personnel:** Joy Gaddy, Director, Advertising; David Clevenger, Publisher; Tim Daly, Managing Editor. **Subscription Rates:** $3.70 Individuals /week. **URL:** http://griffindailynews.com. **Mailing address:** PO Box M, Griffin, GA 30224. **Remarks:** Advertising accepted; rates available upon request. **Circ:** Mon.-Sat. ★**6936**, Sun. ★**6246**.

9130 ■ WHIE-AM
PO Box G
Griffin, GA 30224-0010
Phone: (770)227-9451
Fax: (770)227-8822
Format: Country; News; Talk. **Founded:** 1952. **Key Personnel:** Fred Watkins, Contact. **Wattage:** 5,000 Day; 083 Night.

9131 ■ WKEU-AM - 1450
1000 Memorial Dr.
Griffin, GA 30224
Phone: (770)227-5507
Fax: (770)229-2291
Format: Sports; News. **Networks:** ABC; Westwood One Radio. **Founded:** 1934. **Operating Hours:** Continuous. **Wattage:** 1,000. **Mailing address:** PO Box 997, Griffin, GA 30224. **URL:** http://www.wkeuradio.com.

9132 ■ WKEU-FM - 88.9
1000 Memorial Dr.
Griffin, GA 30224
Phone: (770)227-5507
Fax: (770)229-2291
Format: News; Sports. **Networks:** ABC. **Owner:** WKEU Radio, 1000 Memorial Dr., Griffin, GA 30224, Ph: (770)227-5507, Fax: (770)229-2291. **Founded:** 1966. **Wattage:** 5,000 ERP. **Mailing address:** PO Box 997, Griffin, GA 30224. **URL:** http://www.wkeuradio.com.

9133 ■ WKEU Radio
1000 Memorial Dr.
Griffin, GA 30224
Phone: (770)227-5507
Fax: (770)229-2291
Email: wkeu@aol.com
Format: Talk; Information. **Operating Hours:** Continuous. **Mailing address:** PO Box 997, Griffin, GA 30224. **URL:** http://www.wkeuradio.com.

9134 ■ WMVV-FM - 90.7
PO Box 2020
Griffin, GA 30224
Phone: (770)229-2020
Email: contactus@newlife.fm
Format: Religious. **Key Personnel:** Joe Emert, President; Jenny Emert, Bus. Mgr.; Jim Stewart, Dir. of Operations. **URL:** http://www.wmvv.com.

HARTWELL

NE GA. Hart Co. 21 mi. E. of Anderson, SC. Recreational area. Manufactures textiles, flour. Textile plant. Agriculture. Cotton, grain, clover, poultry, livestock.

9135 ■ The Hartwell Sun
Community Newspapers Inc.
8 Benson St.
Hartwell, GA 30643
Phone: (706)376-8025
Fax: (706)376-3016
Publication E-mail: hartwellsun@hartcom.net
Newspaper. **Freq:** Weekly (Thurs.). **Print Method:** Offset. **Cols./Page:** 6. **Col. Width:** 21 1/2 nonpareils. **Col. Depth:** 301 agate lines. **Key Personnel:** John Brasier, Editor; Peggy Vickery, General Manager; Robert Rider, Publisher. **Subscription Rates:** $28 Individuals; $56 Two years; $30 Out of country; $43 Out of state. **URL:** http://thehartwellsun.com. **Mailing address:** PO Box 700, Hartwell, GA 30643. **Ad Rates:** 4C $250; PCI $9.63. **Remarks:** Accepts advertising. **Circ:** Paid ‡5600.

9136 ■ Hart Cable TV
196 N Forest Ave.
Hartwell, GA 30643
Phone: (706)376-4701
Free: 800-276-3925
Cities Served: 108 channels. **Mailing address:** PO Box 388, Hartwell, GA 30643. **URL:** http://www.hartcom.webs.com.

9137 ■ WKLY-AM - 980
PO Box 636
Hartwell, GA 30643
Phone: (706)376-2233
Fax: (706)376-3100
Format: Country. **Networks:** CNN Radio; Georgia Radio. **Owner:** WKLY AM-980, PO Box 636, Hartwell, GA 30643, Ph: (706)3762233, Fax: (706)376-3100. **Founded:** 1947. **Operating Hours:** 15 hours Daily. **Key Personnel:** Bryan Hicks, Station Mgr., bryanhicks@wklyradio.com. **Wattage:** 1,000 Day; 149 Night. **Ad**

Rates: $7-8 for 30 seconds; $14-16 for 60 seconds. **URL:** http://www.wklyradio.com.

9138 ■ WLHR-FM - 92.1
12715 Augusta Rd.
Lavonia, GA 30553
Phone: (706)356-0921
Fax: (706)356-5921
Email: wlhr@gacaradio.com
Format: News; Sports. **Owner:** Georgia-Carolina Radiocasting Company L.L.C. **Founded:** 2008. **Key Personnel:** Daniel Brown, Gen. Mgr., VP. **URL:** http://www.921wlhr.com.

HAZLEHURST

SE GA. Jeff Davis Co. 50 mi. N. of Waycross. Manufactures carpet backing, sporting goods, textiles, refrigeration filter dryer, tobacco and naval stores industries. Yellow pine timber. Agriculture. Tobacco, cotton, corn.

9139 ■ Jeff Davis Ledger
Jeff Davis Ledger
PO Box 460
Hazlehurst, GA 31539
Publisher's E-mail: news@jdledger.com
Community newspaper. **Freq:** Weekly (Wed.). **Print Method:** Offset. **Cols./Page:** 6. **Col. Width:** 26 nonpareils. **Col. Depth:** 294 agate lines. **Subscription Rates:** $30 Individuals. **URL:** http://www.jdledger.com/v2/content.aspx?IsHome=1&MemberID=1284&ID=1941. **Ad Rates:** GLR $.33; BW $504; SAU $4.50. **Remarks:** Accepts advertising. **Circ:** ‡3800.

HELEN

9140 ■ WZGA-FM - 92.9
PO Box 256
Helen, GA 30545
Phone: (706)878-1051
Format: Sports; News; Information; Classic Rock. **Owner:** Sorenson Southeast Radio L.L.C., at above address. **Operating Hours:** Continuous. **ADI:** Atlanta (Athens & Rome), GA. **Ad Rates:** Advertising accepted; rates available upon request.

HIAWASSEE

N. GA. Towns Co. 90 mi. NE of Atlanta. Hardwood timber. Diversified farming. Corn, wheat, apples.

9141 ■ Towns County Herald
Towns County Herald
PO Box 365
Hiawassee, GA 30546
Phone: (706)896-4454
Publisher's E-mail: tcherald@windstream.net
Community newspaper. **Freq:** Weekly (Thurs.). **Print Method:** Offset. **Cols./Page:** 6. **Col. Width:** 24 nonpareils. **Col. Depth:** 301 agate lines. **Key Personnel:** Charles Duncan, Editor. **Subscription Rates:** $20 Individuals; $30 Other countries; Free online. **URL:** http://www.townscountyherald.net. **Ad Rates:** GLR $.17; BW $419.25; 4C $919.25; PCI $4. **Remarks:** Accepts advertising. **Circ:** ‡3500.

HINESVILLE

SE GA. Liberty Co. 35 mi. SW of Savannah. Fort Steward. Manufactures paper. Timber.

9142 ■ The Coastal Courier
The Coastal Courier
125 S Main St.
Hinesville, GA 31310
Phone: (912)876-0156
Fax: (912)368-6329
Newspaper. **Founded:** 1871. **Freq:** 3/week. **Print Method:** Offset. **Trim Size:** 13 x 21 1/2. **Cols./Page:** 6. **Col. Width:** 24 nonpareils. **Col. Depth:** 301 agate lines. **Key Personnel:** S. Marshall Griffin, Publisher; Kathryn Fox, General Manager. **USPS:** 311-680. **Subscription Rates:** $44 Individuals Liberty and Long County; $60 Individuals Georgia; $75 Individuals outside Georgia. **URL:** http://www.coastalcourier.com. **Ad Rates:** GLR $.34; BW $826.89; SAU $6.41. **Remarks:** Advertising accepted; rates available upon request. **Circ:** 5500.

9143 ■ WBAW-FM - 99.1
321 Fraser Dr.
Hinesville, GA 31313
Format: Adult Contemporary. **Networks:** Mutual Broadcasting System; South Carolina News. **Founded:** 1966. **Operating Hours:** 5 a.m.-midnight. **Key Personnel:** Joe Wilder, President; Drew Wilder, Gen. Mgr.; Steve Brown, Dir. of Programs; B.J. Funderburk, Dir. of Traffic. **Wattage:** 25,000. **Ad Rates:** $3-5 for 15 seconds; $5-9 for 30 seconds; $8.75-16.50 for 60 seconds.

9144 ■ WGML-AM
308 Rolland St.
Hinesville, GA 31310-0615
Phone: (912)368-3210
Fax: (912)368-4191
Format: Ethnic; Religious. **Owner:** Powerhouse of Deliverance Church, Inc., at above address. **Founded:** 1958. **Wattage:** 250 Day; 076 Night. **Ad Rates:** $5.50-8 for 30 seconds; $6-12 for 60 seconds.

HIRAM

The Paulding Neighbor - See Paulding

HOMERVILLE

S. GA. Clinch Co. 26 mi. W. of Waycross. Manufactures plastic and metal containers. Lithography. Pine timber.

9145 ■ Clinch County News
Clinch County News
113 E Dame Ave.
Homerville, GA 31634
Phone: (912)487-5337
Fax: (912)487-3227
Community newspaper. **Freq:** Weekly (Thurs.). **Print Method:** Offset. **Cols./Page:** 8. **Col. Width:** 21 nonpareils. **Col. Depth:** 294 agate lines. **Key Personnel:** Bonnie Whitley, Manager, Production; A.I. Robbins, III, Editor, Publisher; Carolyn Burtchaell, Business Manager. **Subscription Rates:** $30 Individuals in Clinch County, printed newspaper; $38 Out of area; $45 Individuals print and online; $33 Individuals online. **URL:** http://www.theclinchcountynews.com/4021/1340/1/this-weeks-issue-(home-page)pdf. **Mailing address:** PO Box 377, Homerville, GA 31634. **Ad Rates:** GLR $.14. **Remarks:** Accepts advertising. **Circ:** (Not Reported).

IRWINTON

C. GA. Wilkinson Co. 30 mi. SE of Macon. Pine timber; kaolin deposits. Agriculture.

9146 ■ WVKX-FM
PO Box 569
Irwinton, GA 31042
Phone: (912)946-3445
Fax: (912)946-2406
Format: Urban Contemporary; Blues. **Owner:** Wilkinson Broadcasting, at above address. **Key Personnel:** James Thomas, Coord.; Stan Carter, Gen. Mgr. **Wattage:** 6,000 ERP. **Ad Rates:** $16 for 30 seconds; $20 for 60 seconds.

JACKSON

C. GA. Butts Co. 45 mi. SE of Atlanta. Sheet metal fabrication. Timber. Cattle farms.

9147 ■ Jackson Progress-Argus
Jackson Progress-Argus
129 S Mulberry St.
Jackson, GA 30233
Phone: (770)775-3107
Fax: (770)775-3855
Newspaper. **Freq:** Weekly (Wed.). **Print Method:** Offset. **Cols./Page:** 6. **Col. Width:** 12 picas. **Col. Depth:** 21 1/2 inches. **Key Personnel:** Marshall Avett, Publisher; Stewart Voegtlin, Editor. **USPS:** 272-140. **Subscription Rates:** $36 Individuals one year, home delivery. **URL:** http://www.jacksonprogress-argus.com. **Ad Rates:** BW $1006.20; 4C $300; PCI $7.80. **Remarks:** Accepts advertising. **Circ:** ‡4100.

9148 ■ WJGA-FM - 92.1
PO Box 878
Jackson, GA 30233
Phone: (770)775-3151
Fax: (770)775-3153
Email: wkkp1410@charter.net
Format: Adult Contemporary; Urban Contemporary. **Simulcasts:** Channel 10 & 20. **Networks:** Independent. **Owner:** Earnhart Broadcasting Co., Inc., 940 Brownlee Rd, Jackson, GA 30233, Ph: (770)775-3151. **Founded:** 1967. **Operating Hours:** Continuous. **Key Personnel:** Donald Earnhart, Owner. **Wattage:** 3,000. **Ad Rates:** $15 for 30 seconds; $20 for 60 seconds. WKKP.

JASPER

N. GA. Pickens Co. 50 mi. N. of Atlanta. Manufactures shoes, industrial rubber products. Marble mining and processing. Agriculture.

9149 ■ Pickens County Progress
Pickens County Progress
PO Box 67
Jasper, GA 30143
Phone: (706)253-2457
Publication E-mail: progress@ellijay.com
Newspaper with a Democratic orientation. **Freq:** Weekly (Thurs.). **Print Method:** Offset. **Cols./Page:** 6. **Col. Width:** 20 nonpareils. **Col. Depth:** 294 agate lines. **Subscription Rates:** $36.96 Individuals In Pickens, Gilmer, Cherokee, Dawson and Gordon Counties, print and online; $46.59 Individuals All Other GA Counties, print and online; $51.94 Out of state print and online; $28 online. **URL:** http://www.pickensprogressonline.com. **Ad Rates:** BW $630. **Remarks:** Accepts advertising. **Circ:** ‡7000.

9150 ■ WLJA-FM
134 S Main St.
Jasper, GA 30143
Phone: (678)454-9552
Fax: (678)454-3950
Format: Country; Gospel. **Networks:** USA Radio; Georgia Radio. **Owner:** Tri-State Communications, Inc., PO Box 738, Palo Cedro, CA 96073. **Founded:** 1985. **Formerly:** WLEJ-FM. **Key Personnel:** Byron Dobbs, Contact. **Wattage:** 19,000 ERP. **Ad Rates:** $12 for 30 seconds; $15 for 60 seconds.

9151 ■ WPGY-AM
134 S Main St.
Jasper, GA 30143
Phone: (706)276-2016
Fax: (706)635-1018
Format: Oldies. **Networks:** USA Radio; Georgia Radio. **Owner:** Tri-State Communications, Inc., PO Box 738, Palo Cedro, CA 96073. **Formerly:** WLEJ-AM. **Wattage:** 500 Day. **Ad Rates:** Advertising accepted; rates available upon request.

9152 ■ WYYZ-AM - 1490
268 Hood Rd.
Jasper, GA 30143
Phone: (706)692-4100
Fax: (706)692-4012
Email: wyyz_1490am@yahoo.com
Format: Country; Gospel; Classic Rock. **Networks:** USA Radio. **Operating Hours:** Continuous. **Local Programs:** *Gospel Music*, Sunday 12:00 p.m. - 1:00 p.m.; 1:30 p.m. - 7:00 a.m. **Wattage:** 1,000. **Ad Rates:** Noncommercial. **URL:** http://www.wyyzradio.com.

JEFFERSON

NE GA. Jackson Co. 65 mi. SE of Macon. Cotton mills. Dairy products. Agriculture. Soybeans, corn, cattle, poultry.

9153 ■ Banks County News
MainStreet Newspapers Inc.
33 Lee St.
Jefferson, GA 30549
Phone: (706)367-5233
Fax: (706)367-8056
Newspaper. **Freq:** Weekly. **Print Method:** Web offset. **Cols./Page:** 6. **Col. Width:** 27 nonpareils. **Col. Depth:** 301 agate lines. **Key Personnel:** Helen Buffington, Editor. **Subscription Rates:** $25 Individuals. **URL:** http://www.mainstreetnews.com. **Mailing address:** PO Box 908, Jefferson, GA 30549. **Ad Rates:** GLR $2.20. **Remarks:** Accepts advertising. **Circ:** Paid 3500.

9154 ■ The Jackson Herald
MainStreet Newspapers Inc.
33 Lee St.
Jefferson, GA 30549
Phone: (706)367-5233
Fax: (706)367-8056
Newspaper with an independent orientation. **Founded:** June 1875. **Freq:** Weekly. **Print Method:** Web offset. **Cols./Page:** 6. **Col. Width:** 27 nonpareils. **Col. Depth:**

Circulation: ★ = AAM; △ or • = BPA; ♦ = CAC; ❑ = VAC; ⊕ = PO Statement; ‡ = Publisher's Report; Boldface figures = sworn; Light figures = estimated.

301 agate lines. **Subscription Rates:** $25.00 Individuals 1 year,newspaper delivery,email updates,and e-edition, or with auto renewal; $75.00 Individuals 3 years. **URL:** http://www.mainstreetnews.com. **Mailing address:** PO Box 908, Jefferson, GA 30549. **Ad Rates:** GLR $5.60; PCI $3.50. **Remarks:** Accepts advertising. **Circ:** Paid 8000.

9155 ■ The News-Messenger
Main Street Newspapers Inc.
33 Lee St.
Jefferson, GA 30549
Phone: (706)367-5233
Fax: (706)367-8056
Publication E-mail: news@newsmessenger.net
General newspaper. **Founded:** 1869. **Freq:** Semiweekly (Wed. and Sat.). **Print Method:** Offset. **Cols./Page:** 6. **Col. Width:** 25 nonpareils. **Col. Depth:** 301 agate lines. **Key Personnel:** Tonya Hall Bowyer, Managing Editor; Rhonda Fleming, Manager, Advertising. **USPS:** 016-490. **Subscription Rates:** $29.99 Individuals; $33 Elsewhere; $37 Out of state. **URL:** http://www.mainstreetnewspapers.com/. **Mailing address:** PO Box 908, Jefferson, GA 30549. **Ad Rates:** BW $1,200.31; 4C $1,450; SAU $9.31. **Circ:** Paid ‡9500.

JESUP

SE GA. Wayne Co. 40 mi. NE of Waycross. Manufactures lumber, turpentine, textiles, furniture. Timber. Grain, truck, poultry, stock farms. Tobacco, corn.

9156 ■ The Press-Sentinel
The Press-Sentinel
252 W Walnut St.
Jesup, GA 31598
Phone: (912)427-3757
Fax: (912)427-4092
Publisher's E-mail: thepress@bellsouth.net
General newspaper. **Freq:** Semiweekly (Wed. and Sun.). **Print Method:** Offset. **Trim Size:** 14 x 22 3/4. **Cols./Page:** 6. **Col. Width:** 12.25 picas. **Col. Depth:** 301 agate lines. **Key Personnel:** Drew Davis, Editor; Eric Denty, Publisher. **Subscription Rates:** $42 Individuals Wayne County Resident; $46 Out of area; $49 Out of state; $35 Wayne County Resident- 62 and Older. **URL:** http://www.thepress-sentinel.com. **Ad Rates:** BW $690.15; 4C $990.15; SAU $5.35; PCI $9.75. **Remarks:** Accepts advertising. **Circ:** 7200.

9157 ■ WIFO-FM
PO Box 647
Jesup, GA 31598-0647
Phone: (912)427-3712
Fax: (912)530-7717
Format: Country. **Networks:** ABC; Georgia Radio. **Founded:** 1968. **Wattage:** 25,000 ERP. **Ad Rates:** $9.41 for 30 seconds; $13.53 for 60 seconds. **URL:** http://wifo1055.wix.com.

9158 ■ WLOP-AM
PO Box 647
Jesup, GA 31545
Phone: (912)427-3711
Fax: (912)530-7717
Format: Country. **Networks:** ABC; Georgia Radio. **Founded:** 1949. **Wattage:** 5,000 Day; 035 Night. **Ad Rates:** $9.41 for 30 seconds; $13.53 for 60 seconds.

9159 ■ WLPT-FM - 88.3
PO Box 510
Appling, GA 30802
Phone: (706)309-9610
Fax: (706)309-9669
Free: 800-926-4669
Format: Religious. **Owner:** Good News Network, PO Box 428, Manassas, VA 20108, Ph: (703)392-4118, Free: 866-466-3639. **URL:** http://www.gnnradio.org.

JONESBORO

NWC GA. Clayton Co. 15 mi. S. of Atlanta. Manufactures furniture, machinery, hardware, dies, sheet metal, concrete, wood products.

9160 ■ Clayton News Daily
Triple Crown Media Inc.
PO Box 368
Jonesboro, GA 30237
Phone: (770)478-5753
General newspaper. **Freq:** Mon.-Sat. **Print Method:** Offset. **Cols./Page:** 6. **Col. Width:** 24 nonpareils. **Col. Depth:** 301 agate lines. **Key Personnel:** Donna Sanders, Business Manager; Bonnie Pratt, Publisher; Daniel Lenz, Manager, Information Technology; Gary Toohey, Manager. **Subscription Rates:** $49 one year home delivery; $46 one year home delivery (gift). **URL:** http://www.news-daily.com. **Remarks:** Accepts advertising. **Circ:** Fri. ♦6657.

9161 ■ News Daily
Star Media Group
PO Box 368
Jonesboro, GA 30237
Phone: (770)478-5753
Fax: (770)473-9032
Publisher's E-mail: editor@canadianimmigrant.ca
Newspaper serving Clayton County, Georgia. **Freq:** Daily Monday through Friday. **Key Personnel:** Bonnie Pratt, Publisher; Donna Sanders, Business Manager; Chet Fuller, Managing Editor. **Subscription Rates:** $49 Individuals. **URL:** http://www.news-daily.com. **Remarks:** Accepts advertising. **Circ:** (Not Reported).

9162 ■ Wometco Cable
6435 Tara Blvd., Ste. 22
Jonesboro, GA 30236
Phone: (404)340-0030
Fax: (404)471-6639
Owner: U.S. West, at above address. **Cities Served:** subscribing households 45,000.

KENNESAW

Cobb Co.

9163 ■ Bright Side: Cobb County Community Newspapers
Bright Side
PO Box 935
Kennesaw, GA 30156
Phone: (770)423-9555
Publisher's E-mail: brightnews@aol.com
Community newspaper. **Freq:** Monthly. **Key Personnel:** Carol Thompson, Publisher, phone: (770)423-9555. **URL:** http://brightsidenewspapernews.com. **Ad Rates:** BW $1150. **Remarks:** Accepts advertising. **Circ:** (Not Reported).

KINGSLAND

SE GA. Camden Co. 36 mi. NE of Jacksonville, FL. Navy submarine base. Chemical factory. Timber. Agriculture. Stock, poultry, dairying.

9164 ■ WKBX-FM - 106.3
111 N Grove Blvd.
Kingsland, GA 31548
Phone: (912)729-6000
Fax: (912)729-4106
Format: Country; News. **Networks:** ABC. **Owner:** Radio Kings Bay Inc., 111 N Grove Blvd., Kingsland, GA 31548, Ph: (912)729-6000. **Founded:** 1987. **Operating Hours:** Controlled. **ADI:** Jacksonville (Brunswick), FL. **Local Programs:** *Great Country Music*, Tuesday Wednesday Thursday Friday 6:00 a.m. - 10:00 a.m. **Wattage:** 6,000. **Ad Rates:** $5-12.50 for 30 seconds; $7-16.50 for 60 seconds. **URL:** http://www.kbay1063.com.

LA FAYETTE

C. GA. Walker Co. 18 mi. WSW of Dalton. Agricultural trading center, textile mills.

9165 ■ Walker County Messenger
News Publishing Co.
102 N Main St.
La Fayette, GA 30728
Phone: (706)638-1859
Fax: (706)638-7045
Publication E-mail: walkercountymessenger@walkermessenger.com
County newspaper. **Freq:** Semiweekly (Wed. and Fri.). **Print Method:** Offset. **Trim Size:** 13 3/4 x 22 3/4. **Cols./Page:** 6. **Col. Width:** 2 1/16 inches. **Col. Depth:** 21 1/4 inches. **Key Personnel:** Don Stilwell, Publisher; Angie Clark, Manager, Advertising; Scott Herpst, Editor; Josh O'Bryant, Reporter. **URL:** http://www.northwestgeorgianews.com/catwalkchatt/news/obits. **Ad Rates:** BW $867; 4C $1117; SAU $7.13; PCI $7.76. **Remarks:** Accepts advertising. **Circ:** (Not Reported).

9166 ■ WQCH-AM - 1590
PO Box 746
La Fayette, GA 30728
Phone: (706)638-3276
Fax: (706)638-3896
Email: info@wqch.net
Format: Country. **Owner:** Radix Broadcasting, Inc., 801 Warthen St, La Fayette, GA 30728, Ph: (706)638-3276. **Founded:** 1954. **Formerly:** WLFA-AM. **Operating Hours:** 6 a.m.-sundown; 2% network, 98% local. **ADI:** Chattanooga (Cleveland), TN. **Key Personnel:** Rich Gwyn, Gen. Mgr. **Wattage:** 5,000. **Ad Rates:** Noncommercial. **URL:** http://www.wqch.net.

LAGRANGE

9167 ■ WCAG-TV - 33
200 Fort Dr.
LaGrange, GA 30240
Phone: (706)845-8833
Operating Hours: Continuous. **URL:** http://wcag-tv33.net.

9168 ■ WLAG-AM - 1240
304 E Broome St.
LaGrange, GA 30240
Phone: (706)845-1023
Format: Sports; Talk. **Simulcasts:** WELR-AM. **Networks:** ABC; People's Network; ESPN Radio. **Owner:** Eagle's Nest Inc., 112 E 9th Ave., Winfield, KS 67156, Ph: (620)229-8282, Fax: (620)229-8236. **Founded:** 1941. **Operating Hours:** Continuous. **Key Personnel:** Jim Vice, Contact. **Wattage:** 1,000. **Ad Rates:** Advertising accepted; rates available upon request. **URL:** http://www.eagle1023.com.

9169 ■ WOAK-FM - 90.9
1921 Hamilton Rd.
LaGrange, GA 30241
Phone: (706)884-2950
Format: Contemporary Christian. **Networks:** USA Radio. **Owner:** Oakside Baptist Church, 1921 Hamilton Rd., Lagrange, GA 30241, Ph: (706)882-7728. **Founded:** 1984. **Operating Hours:** Continuous. **Wattage:** 3,400. **Ad Rates:** Noncommercial. **URL:** http://www.woak.org.

9170 ■ WTRP-AM - 620
1695 E University Dr.
Auburn, AL 36830
Phone: (706)884-7022
Format: Sports; News; Oldies. **Owner:** Tiger Communication, Inc., at above address. **Founded:** 1953. **Operating Hours:** Continuous. **Wattage:** 2,500. **Ad Rates:** Advertising accepted; rates available upon request. $5.40-8.60 for 30 seconds; $5.90-8.90 for 60 seconds. **URL:** http://wtrp620.com/.

LAKELAND

C. Ga. Lanier Co. 20 mi. NE of Valdosta. Agricultural market.

9171 ■ WJEM-AM - 1150
PO Box 5883
Lakeland, GA 31635
Phone: (229)241-9797
Fax: (229)253-1133
Format: Southern Gospel. **Simulcasts:** with WVCM-FM. **Networks:** NBC. **Owner:** WJEM, Inc., at above address. **Founded:** 1955. **Formerly:** WVCM-FM. **Operating Hours:** 6 a.m.-8 p.m.; 8% network, 92% local. **ADI:** Albany (Valdosta & Cordele), GA. **Wattage:** 5,000. **Ad Rates:** $9-21.50 for 30 seconds; $11-26.50 for 60 seconds.

LAVONIA

9172 ■ Carnesville Gumlog Cable TV
1591 S Fairview Rd.
Lavonia, GA 30553
Phone: (706)356-1714
Key Personnel: John W. Williamson, Jr., President. **Cities Served:** 82 channels. **URL:** http://tvlistings.aol.com.

WLHR-FM - See Hartwell

LAWRENCEVILLE

NC GA. Gwinnett Co. 30 mi. NE of Atlanta. Industrial and research parks. Manufactures telephone cables, satellite components, missile systems, color video display terminals & television sets, insulated entry doors and windows, micro-measuring devices, garments, leather goods. Steel & aluminum fabrication. Farming.

9173 ■ Gwinnett Daily Post
Gray Television Inc.
PO Box 603
Lawrenceville, GA 30046-0603
Phone: (770)963-9205
Publisher's E-mail: advertising@gwinnettdailypost.com
Community newspaper. **Freq:** 6/week. **Print Method:** Offset. **Trim Size:** 13 x 21. **Cols./Page:** 6. **Col. Width:** 2 1/16 inches. **Col. Depth:** 21 inches. **Key Personnel:** J.K. Murphy, Publisher; Todd Cline, Editor. **ISSN:** 1086--0096 (print). **USPS:** 921-980. **Subscription Rates:** $150 Individuals for 52 weeks; mail; all other zip codes; $116.22 Individuals for 26 weeks; mail; all other zip codes; $70.73 Individuals for 13 weeks; mail; all other zip codes. **URL:** http://www.gwinnettdailypost.com. **Formerly:** Gwinnett Home Weekly; Gwinnett Post-Tribune. **Remarks:** Advertising accepted; rates available upon request. **Circ:** Mon.-Sat. ♦**60181**, Sun. ♦**102754**.

9174 ■ Ornamental and Miscellaneous Metal Fabricator
National Ornamental & Miscellaneous Metals Association
PO Box 492167
Lawrenceville, GA 30049
Fax: (888)279-7994
Free: 888-516-8585
Publication E-mail: fabricator@nomma.org
Magazine for ornamental and miscellaneous metals fabrication industry. **Freq:** Bimonthly. **Trim Size:** 8 1/4 x 10 7/8. **Cols./Page:** 3. **Key Personnel:** Todd Daniel, Executive Director. **ISSN:** 0191--5940 (print). **Subscription Rates:** $44 Other countries /year; $78 Two years; $10 Individuals back issue, online; $30 U.S., Canada, and Mexico /year; $50 Two years; Included in membership. **URL:** http://nomma.org/?page=83. **Ad Rates:** BW $1385; 4C $1590. **Remarks:** Accepts advertising. **Circ:** Combined ‡8000.

WPBS-AM - See Conyers, GA

LEESBURG

9175 ■ Lee County Ledger
Lee County Ledger
126 4th St.
Leesburg, GA 31763
Phone: (912)759-2413
Fax: (912)759-6599
Publisher's E-mail: jim@leecountyledger.com
Community newspaper. **Freq:** Weekly. **USPS:** 470-310. **Subscription Rates:** $20 Individuals; $25 Other countries. **URL:** http://www.leecountyledger.com. **Mailing address:** PO Box 715, Leesburg, GA 31763. **Ad Rates:** GLR $2.70; BW $348.30; 4C $100; PCI $3. **Remarks:** Accepts advertising. **Circ:** (Not Reported).

LESLIE

9176 ■ Citizens Cable TV
PO Box 465
Leslie, GA 31764
Phone: (229)853-1600
Free: 866-341-3050
Cities Served: Crisp County, Drayton, Lake Blackshear, Lilly, Plains, Smithville, Smithville, Warwick, Worth County, Georgia; 42 channels. **URL:** http://www.citizenscatv.com.

LILBURN

NW GA. Gwinnett Co. 20 mi. NE of Atlanta. Residential.

9177 ■ Distributed Generation and Alternative Energy Journal
Fairmont Press Inc.
700 Indian Trl.
Lilburn, GA 30047-3724
Phone: (770)925-9388
Fax: (770)381-9865
Publisher's E-mail: info@fairmontpress.com
Journal designed to fill the needs of engineers and executives involved in the assessment, planning, implementation and management of cogeneration projects. **Founded:** 1985. **Freq:** Quarterly. **ISSN:** 1545-3669 (print); **EISSN:** 2156-6550 (electronic). **Subscription Rates:** $357 Individuals print only; $380 Institutions online only; $434 Institutions print and online. **URL:** http://www.fairmontpress.com; http://www.tandfonline.com/pricing/journal/ucgn21#.VFzFxdIW2qY. **Formerly:** Cogeneration and Competitive Power Journal; Cogeneration and Distributed Generation Journal. **Ad Rates:** BW $600. **Remarks:** Accepts advertising. **Circ:** Paid 2200.

9178 ■ Energy Engineering
Fairmont Press Inc.
700 Indian Trl.
Lilburn, GA 30047-3724
Phone: (770)925-9388
Fax: (770)381-9865
Publisher's E-mail: info@fairmontpress.com
Engineering trade journal. **Founded:** 1904. **Freq:** 6/year. **Print Method:** Offset. **Cols./Page:** 1. **Col. Width:** 52 nonpareils. **Col. Depth:** 98 agate lines. **Key Personnel:** Wayne C. Turner, PhD, Editor. **ISSN:** 0199-8595 (print); **EISSN:** 1546-0118 (electronic). **Subscription Rates:** $435 Individuals print only; $578 Institutions print & online; $506 Institutions online only. **URL:** http://www.fairmontpress.com; http://www.tandfonline.com/action/pricing?journalCode=uene20#.VFzHKNIW2qY. **Ad Rates:** BW $600. **Remarks:** Accepts advertising. **Circ:** Paid 9000.

9179 ■ Strategic Planning for Energy and the Environment
Fairmont Press Inc.
700 Indian Trl.
Lilburn, GA 30047-3724
Phone: (770)925-9388
Fax: (770)381-9865
Magazine on energy and environmental planning. **Freq:** Quarterly. **Print Method:** Offset. **Cols./Page:** 1. **Col. Width:** 52 nonpareils. **Col. Depth:** 98 agate lines. **Key Personnel:** Wayne C. Turner, PhD, Editor. **ISSN:** 1048--5236 (print); **EISSN:** 1546--0126 (electronic). **Subscription Rates:** $375 Individuals print only; $399 Institutions online only; $456 Institutions print & online. **URL:** http://www.fairmontpress.com; http://www.tandfonline.com/toc/ustp20/current#.VOvNcHyUfIc; http://www.aeecenter.org/i4a/pages/index.cfm?pageid=3284#Publications; http://www.tandfonline.com/action/pricing?journalCode=ustp20#.Vc3aQ9L7JFI. **Ad Rates:** BW $600. **Remarks:** Accepts advertising. **Circ:** Paid 8600.

LINCOLNTON

9180 ■ Lincolnton Journal
Lincolnton Journal
PO Box 399
Lincolnton, GA 30817
Phone: (706)359-3229
Community newspaper. **Freq:** Weekly (Thurs.). **Cols./Page:** 6. **Col. Width:** 12.5 picas. **Col. Depth:** 21 inches. **Key Personnel:** Sparky Newsome, Editor; Teri Eno, Managing Editor. **USPS:** 313-660. **Subscription Rates:** $25 Individuals Lincoln county, print; $40 Individuals Lincoln county, online and print; $30 Individuals Lincoln county, online only; $30 Out of area print; $40 Out of area online and print; $30 Out of area online only. **URL:** http://www.lincolnjournalonline.com. **Remarks:** Accepts advertising. **Circ:** 2300.

LITHONIA

NWC GA. DeKalb Co. 11 mi. SE of Decatur.

9181 ■ WFXM-FM - 100.1
6070 Rock Springs Rd.
Lithonia, GA 30038
Phone: (912)745-3301
Fax: (912)742-8299
Format: Urban Contemporary. **Networks:** American Urban Radio; Mutual Broadcasting System. **Owner:** Roberts Communications Inc., 64 Commercial St., Rochester, NY 14614. **Founded:** 1973. **Formerly:** WFNE-FM. **Operating Hours:** Continuous. **Key Personnel:** Albert E. Smith, Gen. Mgr.; George Threatt, Operations Mgr.; Sharon Wilson, Traffic Mgr.; Patricia Glass, Sales Mgr.; Wanda Harvey, Office Mgr. **Wattage:** 3,000.

LOOKOUT MOUNTAIN

9182 ■ WELF-TV - 23
384 S Campus Rd.
Lookout Mountain, GA 30750
Phone: (706)820-1663
Owner: Trinity Broadcasting Network Inc., PO Box A, Santa Ana, CA 92711, Ph: (714)832-2950, Free: 888-731-1000. **Key Personnel:** Onya Richter, Mgr. **URL:** http://www.tbn.org.

LOUISVILLE

C. GA. Jefferson Co. 40 mi. SW of Augusta. Lumber, peanuts, cotton.

9183 ■ News & Farmer & Wadley Herald/The Jefferson Reporter
Fall Line Publishing Inc.
PO Box 487
Louisville, GA 30434
Phone: (478)625-7722
Fax: (478)625-8816
Publisher's E-mail: news@thenewsandfarmer.com
Local newspaper. **Freq:** Weekly. **Print Method:** Offset. **Trim Size:** 14 x 22 1/2. **Cols./Page:** 6. **Col. Width:** 12.3 picas. **Col. Depth:** 21 inches. **Key Personnel:** David Irwin, Director, Advertising; Carol McLeod, Writer; Parish Howard, Editor, Publisher. **USPS:** 385-380. **Subscription Rates:** $29.16 Individuals; $27 Individuals senior; $37.80 Individuals elsewhere in Georgia; $35.64 Individuals senior citizen elsewhere in Georgia; $40 Out of state. **URL:** http://www.thenewsandfarmer.com/. **Ad Rates:** GLR $5; BW $5; 4C $730; PCI $7.50. **Remarks:** Accepts advertising. **Circ:** Paid ‡4400, Free ‡65.

9184 ■ WPEH-AM - 1420
PO Box 425
Louisville, GA 30434
Phone: (478)625-7248
Format: Country; Oldies. **Simulcasts:** WPEH-FM. **Networks:** CNN Radio. **Owner:** Peach Broadcasting Co., Inc., at above address. **Founded:** 1960. **Operating Hours:** 6 a.m.-midnight; 10% network, 90% local. **ADI:** Augusta, GA. **Wattage:** 1,000. **Ad Rates:** Noncommercial.

9185 ■ WPEH-FM
PO Box 425
Louisville, GA 30434
Format: Oldies. **Networks:** CNN Radio. **Owner:** Peach Broadcasting Co., Inc., at above address. **Founded:** 1971. **Wattage:** 6,000 ERP. **Ad Rates:** $6-7.50 for 30 seconds; $7.50-10 for 60 seconds.

LUMBER CITY

9186 ■ WMOC-FM - 88.7
414 Renwick St.
Lumber City, GA 31549
Format: Religious; Gospel. **Operating Hours:** Continuous. **Wattage:** 50,000. **Ad Rates:** Advertising accepted; rates available upon request. **Mailing address:** PO Box 520, Lumber City, GA 31549.

LYONS

NE GA SC GA. Toombs Co Toombs Co. 72 mi. W. of Savannah 5 mi. SE of Vidalia. Lumber and agriculture.

9187 ■ WBBT-AM
Attn: Ray Bilbrey
Lyons, GA 30436
Phone: (912)526-8122
Fax: (912)526-8123
Format: Oldies; Talk. **Networks:** NBC; Georgia Radio. **Owner:** Harry H. Thompson Jr., at above address, Fax: (912)526-9155. **Founded:** 1959. **Key Personnel:** Ray Bilbrey, Contact; Tony Deloach, Contact; Heather Freeland, Contact; Earl Averett, Contact; Peggy Spikes, Contact. **Wattage:** 1,000. **Ad Rates:** $2.75-4 for 30 seconds; $3.75-5 for 60 seconds.

9188 ■ WLYU-FM
Attn: Ray Bilbrey
Lyons, GA 30436
Phone: (912)526-8122
Fax: (912)526-8123
Format: Contemporary Country. **Networks:** NBC. **Owner:** Harry H. Thompson Jr., at above address, Fax: (912)526-9155. **Founded:** 1989. **Key Personnel:** Ray

Circulation: ★ = AAM; △ or • = BPA; ♦ = CAC; ❑ = VAC; ⊕ = PO Statement; ‡ = Publisher's Report; Boldface figures = sworn; Light figures = estimated.

Bilbrey, Contact; Tony DeLoach, Contact; Heather Freeland, Contact; Earl Averett, Contact; Peggy Spikes, Contact. **Wattage:** 6,000 ERP. **Ad Rates:** $4.25-6.95 for 30 seconds; $5.25-6.50 for 60 seconds.

MACON

C. GA. Jones Co. On Ocmulgee River, 92 mi. SE of Atlanta. Wesleyan College (women); Mercer University; Macon Junior College. Kaolin, fuller's earth mines; timber. Peach production center. Manufactures wood furniture, linens, cotton yarns, cigarettes, brick & cement block, processed poultry, boxes, container board.

9189 ■ The Cluster
Mercer University
1501 Mercer University Dr.
Macon, GA 31207
Phone: (478)301-2700
Free: 800-837-2911
Publisher's E-mail: info@mercer.edu
Newspaper featuring university contributors, alumni news, faculty news, and general information. **Freq:** Bimonthly. **Cols./Page:** 2. **Col. Width:** 36 nonpareils. **Col. Depth:** 136 agate lines. **Key Personnel:** Emily Farlow, Editor-in-Chief. **URL:** http://mercercluster.com; http://www.mercer.edu. **Formerly:** The Mercer Spirit. **Ad Rates:** BW $250; BW $400. **Remarks:** Accepts advertising. **Circ:** Paid ‡30000, 1300.

9190 ■ Georgia Farm Bureau News: The Voice of Georgia Farmers
Georgia Farm Bureau
1620 Bass Rd.
Macon, GA 31209
Phone: (478)474-8411
Free: 800-633-5432
Publisher's E-mail: websites@gfb.org
Magazine featuring news of Georgia. **Freq:** 6/year. **Print Method:** Offset. **Trim Size:** 8 1/4 x 10 3/8. **Key Personnel:** Jennifer Whittaker, Editor; Paul Beliveau, Contact. **ISSN:** 0735--696X (print). **Subscription Rates:** $15 Nonmembers. **URL:** http://www.gfb.org/media. **Mailing address:** PO Box 7068, Macon, GA 31209. **Remarks:** Accepts advertising. **Circ:** 62000.

9191 ■ Journal of Southern Legal History
Mercer University Walter F. George School of Law
1021 Georgia Ave.
Macon, GA 31207
Phone: (478)301-2605
Fax: (478)301-2989
Publisher's E-mail: admissions@law.mercer.edu
Journal depicting the history of law, the legal culture and profession, and the courts, including federal courts, in Georgia, South Carolina, North Carolina, Virginia, West Virginia, Maryland, Delaware, Kentucky, Tennessee, Alabama, Florida, Mississippi, Arkansas, Missouri, Louisiana, and Texas. **Freq:** Annual. **Key Personnel:** Stuart E. Walker, Editor-in-Chief. **URL:** http://law.mercer.edu/academics/journals/jslh/jslh.cfm. **Circ:** (Not Reported).

9192 ■ Macon Magazine
Macon Magazine Inc.
2208 Ingleside Ave.
Macon, GA 31204
Phone: (478)746-7779
Fax: (478)743-4608
Publisher's E-mail: advertising@maconmagazine.com
Magazine covering local history, arts and cultural events, homes and real estate developments plus the people and places that make Central Georgia unique. **Freq:** Bimonthly. **Key Personnel:** James Palmer, Editor; Jodi Palmer, Editor. **Subscription Rates:** $18 Individuals; $25 Two years; $35 Individuals three years. **URL:** http://maconmagazine.com. **Circ:** (Not Reported).

9193 ■ The Mercer Cluster
The Mercer Cluster
1400 Coleman Ave.
Macon, GA 31207-0001
Phone: (478)301-5335
Fax: (478)301-2700
Collegiate newspaper. **Freq:** Bimonthly. **Print Method:** Offset. Uses mats. **Trim Size:** 11 1/4 x 15. **Cols./Page:** 5. **Col. Width:** 24 nonpareils. **Col. Depth:** 196 agate lines. **Key Personnel:** Conner Wood, Editor-in-Chief. **URL:** http://mercercluster.com. **Ad Rates:** GLR $10; BW $350; SAU $3.50; PCI $8. **Remarks:** Accepts advertising. **Circ:** Free ‡1300.

9194 ■ Mercer Law Review
Mercer University
1501 Mercer University Dr.
Macon, GA 31207
Phone: (478)301-2700
Free: 800-837-2911
Publication E-mail: lawreview@law.mercer.edu
Journal on law. **Founded:** 1949. **Freq:** Quarterly. **Key Personnel:** Bowen Reichert, Editor-in-Chief; Jennifer R. Findley, Editor-in-Chief. **Subscription Rates:** $40 Individuals; $15 Single issue. **URL:** http://law.mercer.edu/academics/journals/lawreview/. **Remarks:** Accepts advertising. **Circ:** (Not Reported).

9195 ■ Mercer Lawyer
Mercer University
1501 Mercer University Dr.
Macon, GA 31207
Phone: (478)301-2700
Free: 800-837-2911
Publisher's E-mail: info@mercer.edu
Journal covering legal education. **Freq:** Semiannual spring and fall. **Subscription Rates:** Free. **Alt. Formats:** PDF. **URL:** http://law.mercer.edu/alumni/mercerlawyer. **Circ:** (Not Reported).

9196 ■ The Pilot Log
Pilot International
102 Preston Ct.
Macon, GA 31210-5768
Phone: (478)477-1208
Fax: (478)477-6978
Publication E-mail: pilotlog@pilothq.org
Magazine for Pilot International, a civic service organization for executives and professionals. **Freq:** Quarterly. **Print Method:** Web. **Trim Size:** 8 1/2 x 11. **Cols./Page:** 3. **Key Personnel:** Donna Ham, Editor. **ISSN:** 1045--179X (print). **USPS:** 433-020. **Subscription Rates:** $10 U.S.; $15 Other countries outside north America. **URL:** http://www.pilotinternational.org/Home. **Remarks:** Accepts advertising. **Circ:** Controlled ‡15000.

9197 ■ The Telegraph
McClatchy Newspapers Inc.
487 Cherry St.
Macon, GA 31201
Phone: (478)744-4200
Free: 800-342-5845
Publication E-mail: letters@macontel.com
General newspaper. **Founded:** 1826. **Freq:** Daily. **Print Method:** Flexographic. **Cols./Page:** 6. **Col. Width:** 26 nonpareils. **Col. Depth:** 301 agate lines. **Key Personnel:** Donald W. Bailey, Publisher; Sherrie Marshall, Editor, Vice President. **URL:** http://www.mcclatchy.com/2006/06/09/358/the-telegraph.html. **Formerly:** The Macon Telegraph. **Mailing address:** P.O. Box 4167, Macon, GA 31208. **Remarks:** Accepts advertising. **Circ:** Mon.-Fri. **★53311**, Sun. **★67771**.

9198 ■ WAYS-AM - 1500
544 Mulberry St., Ste. 500
Macon, GA 31201
Phone: (478)746-6286
Format: Sports. **Networks:** CBS. **Owner:** Cumulus Broadcasting Inc., 3280 Peachtree Rd. NW, Ste. 2300, Atlanta, GA 30305-2447, Ph: (404)949-0700, Fax: (404)949-0740. **Operating Hours:** Continuous. **ADI:** Macon, GA. **Ad Rates:** Advertising accepted; rates available upon request. **URL:** http://www.waysam.com.

9199 ■ WBKG-FM - 88.9
PO Box 3206
Tupelo, MS 38803
Owner: American Family Radio, at above address. **Key Personnel:** Rick Robertson, Contact. **Wattage:** 5,500. **Ad Rates:** Noncommercial.

9200 ■ WBML-AM
6174 Highway 57
Macon, GA 31217
Phone: (912)743-5453
Fax: (912)743-9265
Format: Religious; Gospel. **Networks:** UPI. **Owner:** David Rodgers, at above address. **Founded:** 1941. **Key Personnel:** Orvil Nichols, Contact; Michael Mimbs, Contact. **Wattage:** 15,000 Day; 500 Nigh. **Ad Rates:** $5-9 for 30 seconds; $7-14 for 60 seconds.

9201 ■ WBNM-AM - 1120
RR 006, PO Box 735
Macon, GA 31201-9580
Phone: (912)745-1077
Fax: (912)742-2293
Email: jion@jion.com
Format: News; Talk. **Networks:** Business Radio. **Owner:** Quality Broadcasting, Inc., at above address. **Operating Hours:** Continuous; 75% network, 25% local. **ADI:** Macon, GA. **Key Personnel:** Bob Davis, Operations Mgr., Prog. Dir.; Howard Ebo, Sales Mgr.; Lisa Bacarro, Office Mgr. **Wattage:** 10,000. **Ad Rates:** $19.50-25 for 60 seconds.

9202 ■ WDDO-AM - 1240
544 Mulberry St., 5th Fl.
Macon, GA 31201
Phone: (478)746-6286
Format: Gospel. **Networks:** Fox. **Owner:** Cumulus Media Inc., 3280 Peachtree Rd. NW, Ste. 2300, Atlanta, GA 30305-2455, Ph: (404)949-0700, Fax: (404)949-0740. **Founded:** 1940. **ADI:** Macon, GA. **Ad Rates:** Advertising accepted; rates available upon request. **URL:** http://www.wddoam.com.

9203 ■ WDEN-AM - 1500
544 Mulberry St., Ste. 500
Macon, GA 31201
Phone: (478)746-6286
Format: Country. **Simulcasts:** WDEN-FM. **Networks:** NBC. **Owner:** Cumulus Broadcasting Inc., 3280 Peachtree Rd. NW, Ste. 2300, Atlanta, GA 30305-2447, Ph: (404)949-0700, Fax: (404)949-0740. **Founded:** 1967. **Operating Hours:** Sunrise-sunset. **ADI:** Macon, GA. **Wattage:** 1,000. **Ad Rates:** Noncommercial. WDEN-FM. **URL:** http://www.wden.com.

9204 ■ WDEN-FM - 99.1
544 Mulberry St., Ste. 500
Macon, GA 31201-8258
Phone: (478)746-6286
Format: Country. **Simulcasts:** WDEN-AM. **Networks:** Westwood One Radio. **Owner:** Cumulus Broadcasting Inc., 3280 Peachtree Rd. NW, Ste. 2300, Atlanta, GA 30305-2447, Ph: (404)949-0700, Fax: (404)949-0740. **Founded:** 1968. **Operating Hours:** Continuous; 10% network, 90% local. **ADI:** Macon, GA. **Key Personnel:** Bobby Reed, Contact; Bobby Reed, Contact. **Wattage:** 100,000. **Ad Rates:** $45-130 per unit. Combined advertising rates available with WDEN-AM/FM. **URL:** http://www.wden.com.

9205 ■ WEBL-FM - 102.5
7080 Industrial Hwy.
Macon, GA 31216
Phone: (478)781-1063
Fax: (478)784-2635
Format: Country. **ADI:** Macon, GA. **Key Personnel:** Bill Clark, Dir. of Mktg., Mktg. Mgr.; John Lund, Operations Mgr.; Mark Cooper, Dir. of Sales; Melissa Stinebaugh, Bus. Mgr.; James Gay, Chief Engineer. **Wattage:** 4,000. **Ad Rates:** Noncommercial. **URL:** http://www.bull1025.com.

9206 ■ WGXA-TV - 24
599 Martin Luther King Jr. Blvd.
Macon, GA 31201
Phone: (478)745-2424
Format: News. **Networks:** Fox; ABC. **Owner:** Piedmont Television Holdings L.L.C., 7621 Little Ave., Ste. 506, Charlotte, NC 28226-8404. **Founded:** 1982. **Operating Hours:** Continuous; 25% network, 75% local. **Wattage:** 1,290,000. **Ad Rates:** Advertising accepted; rates available upon request. **URL:** http://www.wgxa.tv.

9207 ■ WHTA-FM - 107.9
101 Marietta St., 12th Fl.
Macon, GA 31201
Phone: (404)765-9750
Fax: (404)688-7686
Format: Blues; Hip Hop. **Operating Hours:** Continuous. **Key Personnel:** Tim Davies, Gen. Mgr. **Wattage:** 27,000 ERP. **Ad Rates:** Noncommercial. **URL:** http://www.hotspotatl.com.

9208 ■ WIBB-AM - 1280
369 2nd St.
Macon, GA 31208
Phone: (912)742-2505
Format: Urban Contemporary; Gospel. **Key Personnel:** Albert E. Smith, Gen. Mgr.; Patricia Glass, Gen. Sales

Mgr.; Jess Branson, Sales Mgr.; George Threatt, Operations Mgr. **Wattage**: 5,000. **Mailing address:** PO Box 4527, Macon, GA 31208.

9209 ■ WIBB-FM - 97.9
7080 Industrial Hwy.
Macon, GA 31216
Phone: (478)781-1063
Format: Blues; Hip Hop. **Owner:** iHeartMedia Inc., 200 E Basse Rd., San Antonio, TX 78209, Ph: (210)832-3314. **Operating Hours**: Continuous. **ADI**: Macon, GA. **Key Personnel:** James Gay, Promotions Dir.; Thomas Bacote, Prog. Dir.; Melissa Stinebaugh, Prog. Dir.; Brent Henslee, Dir. of Programs. **Wattage:** 10,500 ERP. **Ad Rates:** Noncommercial. **URL:** http://www.wibb.com.

9210 ■ WIFN-FM - 105.5
544 Mulberry St., Ste. 500
Macon, GA 31201
Phone: (478)746-6286
Fax: (478)745-2078
Format: Sports. **Networks:** Mutual Broadcasting System. **Owner:** Cumulus Broadcasting Inc., 3280 Peachtree Rd. NW, Ste. 2300, Atlanta, GA 30305-2447, Ph: (404)949-0700, Fax: (404)949-0740. **Founded:** 1984. **Operating Hours**: Continuous. **ADI:** Macon, GA. **Wattage:** 100,000. **Ad Rates:** Noncommercial.

9211 ■ WLCG-AM - 1280
7080 Industrial Hwy.
Macon, GA 31216
Phone: (478)781-1063
Fax: (478)781-6711
Format: Gospel. **Key Personnel:** Bill Clark, Gen. Mgr. **Wattage**: 5,000.

9212 ■ WLZN-FM - 92.3
Cumulus Media-Macon
544 Mulberry St., 5th Fl.
Macon, GA 31201
Phone: (478)746-6286
Format: Urban Contemporary. **Owner:** Cumulus Broadcasting Inc., 3280 Peachtree Rd. NW, Ste. 2300, Atlanta, GA 30305-2447, Ph: (404)949-0700, Fax: (404)949-0740. **Operating Hours**: Continuous. **Key Personnel:** Gentleman George, Contact. **Ad Rates:** Advertising accepted; rates available upon request. **URL:** http://www.blazin923.com.

9213 ■ WMAC-AM - 940
544 Mulberry St., Ste. 500
Macon, GA 31201
Phone: (478)746-6286
Fax: (912)752-1339
Format: News; Talk; Sports. **Networks:** ABC. **Owner:** Cumulus Broadcasting Inc., 3280 Peachtree Rd. NW, Ste. 2300, Atlanta, GA 30305-2447, Ph: (404)949-0700, Fax: (404)949-0740. **Founded:** 1922. **Formerly**: WMAZ-AM. **Operating Hours**: Continuous. **ADI**: Macon, GA. **Wattage**: 50,000. **Ad Rates:** Advertising accepted; rates available upon request. **URL:** http://www.wmac-am.com.

9214 ■ WMAZ-TV - 13
1314 Gray Hwy.
Macon, GA 31211
Phone: (478)752-1313
Fax: (478)752-1331
Email: eyewitnessnews@13wmaz.com
Format: Commercial TV. **Networks:** CBS. **Owner:** Gannett Company Inc., 7950 Jones Branch Dr., McLean, VA 22107-0150, Ph: (703)854-6089. **Founded:** 1953. **Operating Hours**: Continuous. **ADI**: Macon, GA. **Key Personnel:** Jeff Dudley, Gen. Mgr. **Wattage**: 52,600 ERP H. **Ad Rates:** Advertising accepted; rates available upon request. **URL:** http://www.13wmaz.com.

WMCD-FM - See Claxton, GA

9215 ■ WMGB-FM - 93.7
544 Mulberry St., 5th Fl.
Macon, GA 31201
Phone: (478)646-9510
Format: Contemporary Hit Radio (CHR). **Networks:** Westwood One Radio. **Owner:** Cumulus Broadcasting Inc., 3280 Peachtree Rd. NW, Ste. 2300, Atlanta, GA 30305-2447, Ph: (404)949-0700, Fax: (404)949-0740. **Operating Hours**: Continuous. **ADI**: Macon, GA. **Wattage**: 46,000. **Ad Rates:** Noncommercial. **URL:** http://www.allthehitsb951.com.

9216 ■ WMGT-TV - 41
301 Poplar St.
Macon, GA 31201
Phone: (478)745-4141
Fax: (478)742-2626
Email: news@41nbc.com
Format: Commercial TV. **Networks:** NBC. **Founded:** Dec. 19, 1968. **Operating Hours**: Continuous. Sun.-Thur.; 5 a.m.-3 a.m. Fri.-Sat. **ADI**: Macon, GA. **Key Personnel:** Derek Brown, Gen. Mgr., dbrown@41nbc.com; Brandon Long, News Dir., blong@41nbc.com. **URL:** http://www.41nbc.com.

9217 ■ WPEZ-FM - 93.7
544 Mulberry St., Ste. 500
Macon, GA 31201
Phone: (478)646-9370
Format: Adult Contemporary. **Networks:** Unistar; Westwood One Radio. **Owner:** Cumulus Broadcasting Inc., 3280 Peachtree Rd. NW, Ste. 2300, Atlanta, GA 30305-2447, Ph: (404)949-0700, Fax: (404)949-0740. **Founded:** 1973. **Operating Hours**: Continuous. **ADI**: Macon, GA. **Key Personnel:** Victoria Fowler, Dir. of Mktg., Promotions Dir., victoria.fowler@cumulus.com; Bobby Reed, Operations Mgr., bobby.reed@cumulus.com; Brian Roberts, Dir. of Programs, brian.roberts@cumulus.com. **Wattage**: 100,000. **Ad Rates:** $45-105 for 30 seconds; $60-140 for 60 seconds. **URL:** http://www.z937.com.

9218 ■ WPGA-AM
1691 Forsyth St.
Macon, GA 31201
Phone: (478)745-5858
Fax: (478)745-0500
Format: Eclectic. **Networks:** ABC. **Owner:** Radio Perry Inc., at above address. **Founded:** 1955. **Wattage:** 2,600 Day; 080 Night. **Ad Rates:** $20-25 for 30 seconds; $25-30 for 60 seconds.

9219 ■ WPGA-FM - 100.9
533 Cherry St.
Macon, GA 31201
Phone: (478)508-7096
Format: Adult Contemporary; Oldies. **Networks:** ABC. **Owner:** Citadel Broadcasting Corp., 7201 W Lake Mead Blvd., Ste. 400, Las Vegas, NV 89128-8366, Ph: (702)804-5200, Fax: (702)804-8250. **Founded:** 1966. **Operating Hours**: Continuous. **Key Personnel:** Peter Stewart, Contact; Tom Kennedy, Contact; Brian Kane, Contact. **Wattage**: 33,000 ERP. **Ad Rates:** Advertising accepted; rates available upon request. **URL:** http://thecreekfm.com.

9220 ■ WPGA-TV - 58
1691 Forsyth St.
Macon, GA 31201
Phone: (478)745-5858
Fax: (478)745-5800
Key Personnel: Lowell Register, President, lowell@wpga.tv; Debbie R. Hart, Gen. Mgr., dhart@wpga.tv; Janice Register, Contact, janice@wpga.tv. **Ad Rates:** Advertising accepted; rates available upon request. **URL:** http://www.wpga58.com.

9221 ■ WQBZ-FM - 106
7080 Industrial Hwy.
Macon, GA 31216
Phone: (478)781-1063
Fax: (478)781-6711
Format: Album-Oriented Rock (AOR). **Owner:** iHeartMedia Inc., 200 E Basse Rd., San Antonio, TX 78209, Ph: (210)832-3314. **Founded:** 1981. **Operating Hours**: Continuous; 100% local. **ADI**: Macon, GA. **Key Personnel:** James Gay, CEO; Melissa Stinebaugh, Chief Engineer; Thomas Bacote, Prog. Dir. **Wattage**: 50,000. **Ad Rates:** $50-110 per unit. Combined advertising rates available with WIBB-FM; WRBV-FM; WLCG-AM; WRNC-AM, WELV-FM. **URL:** http://www.q106.fm//main.html.

9222 ■ WRBV-FM - 101.7
7080 Industrial Hwy.
Macon, GA 31216
Phone: (478)781-1063
Format: Adult Contemporary; Urban Contemporary. **Operating Hours**: Continuous. **Key Personnel:** Melissa Stinebaugh, Bus. Mgr.; James Gay, Chief Engineer. **Ad Rates:** Advertising accepted; rates available upon request. **URL:** http://www.v1017.com.

9223 ■ W203BH-FM - 88.5
PO Box 391
Twin Falls, ID 83303
Fax: (208)736-1958
Free: 800-357-4226
Format: Religious; Contemporary Christian. **Owner:** CSN International, PO Box 391, Twin Falls, ID 83303, Ph: (208)736-1958, Fax: (208)736-1958, Free: 800-357-4226. **URL:** http://www.csnradio.com.

9224 ■ WYFK-FM - 104.3
11530 Carmel Commons Blvd.
Charlotte, NC 28226
Phone: (704)523-5555
Free: 800-888-7077
Format: Gospel; Religious. **Networks:** Bible Broadcasting. **Owner:** Bible Broadcasting Network Inc., 11530 Carmel Commons Blvd., Charlotte, NC 28226, Ph: (704)523-5555, Free: 800-888-7077. **Founded:** 1987. **Operating Hours**: Continuous; 97.5% network, 2.5% local. **Key Personnel:** Dr. Lowell Davey, President. **Wattage**: 50,000. **Ad Rates:** Noncommercial. **URL:** http://www.bbnradio.org.

9225 ■ WYNF-FM - 96.5
7080 Industrial Hwy.
Macon, GA 31216
Phone: (478)781-1063
Fax: (478)781-6711
Format: Alternative/New Music/Progressive; Country. **Owner:** Clear Channel Communications, 50 E River Center Blvd., Covington, KY 41011, Ph: (606)655-2261, Fax: (606)655-9395. **Key Personnel:** Bill Clark, Gen. Mgr.; Erich West, News Dir. **Wattage**: 8,000 ERP. **Ad Rates:** Advertising accepted; rates available upon request. **URL:** http://965thebull.iheart.com/articles/macon-employment-and-eeo-107157/eeo-10219293.

MARIETTA

NW GA. Cobb Co. 20 mi. NW of Atlanta. Southern Technical Institute, Kennesaw College. Aircraft plant. Manufactures textiles, furniture, chemicals, marble, plastics, paper products. Metal and food processing.

9226 ■ AKFCF Quarterly
Lionheart Publishing Inc.
506 Roswell St., Ste. 220
Marietta, GA 30060
Phone: (770)431-0867
Fax: (770)432-6969
Free: 888-303-5639
Publisher's E-mail: lpi@lionhrtpub.com
Magazine devoted to the needs of KFC franchisees. **Freq:** Quarterly. **Key Personnel:** Dale Black, President, phone: (308)381-1415; Michelle Hunt, Editor; Kevin Schlutz, Secretary, phone: (319)728-3283, fax: (319)728-2940; Dave Evans, Treasurer, phone: (781)982-0755, fax: (781)982-9904. **ISSN:** 1071--9873 (print). **Subscription Rates:** Included in membership. **Alt. Formats:** PDF. **URL:** http://www.akfcf.com/akfcf-quarterly.html; http://www.lionhrtpub.com/adinfo/akfcfmkmain.html. **Ad Rates:** BW $2,404; 4C $2,758. **Remarks:** Accepts advertising. **Circ:** (Not Reported).

9227 ■ Analytics
Lionheart Publishing Inc.
506 Roswell St., Ste. 220
Marietta, GA 30060
Phone: (770)431-0867
Fax: (770)432-6969
Free: 888-303-5639
Publisher's E-mail: lpi@lionhrtpub.com
Magazine featuring mathematical analysis. **Freq:** Bimonthly. **Key Personnel:** Peter Horner, Editor. **URL:** http://analytics-magazine.org. **Remarks:** Accepts advertising. **Circ:** (Not Reported).

9228 ■ Andalusian
Lionheart Publishing Inc.
506 Roswell St., Ste. 220
Marietta, GA 30060
Phone: (770)431-0867
Fax: (770)432-6969
Free: 888-303-5639
Publisher's E-mail: lpi@lionhrtpub.com
Magazine containing articles on educating the public about horses of Andalusian breed. **Freq:** Quarterly. **Sub-**

Circulation: ★ = AAM; △ or • = BPA; ♦ = CAC; ❑ = VAC; ⊕ = PO Statement; ‡ = Publisher's Report; Boldface figures = sworn; Light figures = estimated.

scription Rates: Included in membership. **URL:** http://lionheartpub.com/Andalusian. **Ad Rates:** 4C $500; BW $350. **Remarks:** Accepts advertising. **Circ:** (Not Reported).

9229 ■ Bartow Neighbor
Neighbor Newspapers Inc.
580 S Fairground St.
Marietta, GA 30060
Publication E-mail: bartow@mdjonline.com
Community newspaper. **Freq:** Weekly (Wed.). **Key Personnel:** Otis Brumby, Jr., Publisher; Otis Brumby, III, General Manager. **Subscription Rates:** $135.68 By mail outside of delivery area; $72.08 By mail 6 months, outside of delivery area; $36.57 By mail 3 months, outside of delivery area. **URL:** http://neighbornewspapers.com/nni_al?neighbor=bartow. **Remarks:** Accepts advertising. **Circ:** ‡15125.

9230 ■ Comic Shop News
Comic Shop News
c/o Cliff Biggers
2770 Carillon Crossing
Marietta, GA 30066
Publisher's E-mail: wbatty@csnsider.com
Newspaper for comic book store owners and management. **Freq:** Weekly. **Print Method:** Web. **URL:** http://www.csnsider.com. **Remarks:** Accepts advertising. **Circ:** Combined 60000.

9231 ■ The International Journal of Aviation Psychology
Association for Aviation Psychology
PO Box 671393
Marietta, GA 30066
Freq: Quarterly. **Key Personnel:** Richard S. Jensen, Executive Editor; Hans-Juergen Hoermann, Associate Editor. **ISSN:** 1050--8414 (print); **EISSN:** 1532--7108 (electronic). **Subscription Rates:** $96 Individuals print and online; $271 Individuals online only; included in membership dues; $87 Individuals print and online; $890 Institutions print and online. **URL:** http://www.tandfonline.com/toc/hiap20/current; http://www.tandfonline.com/toc/hiap20/.U33C6NIW2qY. **Ad Rates:** BW $350. **Remarks:** Accepts advertising. **Circ:** (Not Reported).

9232 ■ Johns Creek Neighbor
Neighbor Newspapers Inc.
580 S Fairground St.
Marietta, GA 30060
Community newspaper. **Freq:** Weekly (Wed.). **Key Personnel:** Otis A. Brumby, Jr., Publisher. **Subscription Rates:** $112.00 Individuals 1 year. **URL:** http://neighbornewspapers.com/nni_al?neighbor=johns&leaderboardtop=257&leaderboardbot=258&pillowtop=394&pillowbot=260&tt=261&box=262. **Remarks:** Accepts advertising. **Circ:** Non-paid ♦**9939**.

9233 ■ Marietta Daily Journal
Neighbor Newspapers Inc.
PO Box 449
Marietta, GA 30061
Phone: (770)428-9411
Community newspaper. **Founded:** 1866. **Freq:** Mon.-Sun. (morn.). **Print Method:** Offset. **Cols./Page:** 6. **Col. Width:** 26 nonpareils. **Col. Depth:** 301 agate lines. **Key Personnel:** Otis Brumby, III, General Manager. **Subscription Rates:** $112 Individuals. **URL:** http://www.mdjonline.com. **Ad Rates:** GLR $1; BW $1,806; 4C $2,116; PCI $14. **Remarks:** Accepts advertising. **Circ:** Mon.-Sat. 19800.

9234 ■ Marietta Daily Journal
Neighbor Newspapers Inc.
580 S Fairground St.
Marietta, GA 30060
Community newspaper for Cobb County, Georgia. **Freq:** Daily and Sun. **Key Personnel:** Bill Kinney, Associate Editor; Billy Mitchell, Managing Editor. **Subscription Rates:** $2.12 Individuals /week (home delivery & online); $1.92 Individuals /week (online only). **URL:** http://www.mdjonline.com/. **Remarks:** Accepts advertising. **Circ:** Mon.-Sat. ★**19800**.

9235 ■ Markee 2.0
Lionheart Publishing Inc.
506 Roswell St., Ste. 220
Marietta, GA 30060
Phone: (770)431-0867
Fax: (770)432-6969
Free: 888-303-5639
Publication E-mail: markee@markeemag.com
Magazine for the film and video industry across the US. **Freq:** Monthly. **Print Method:** Offset. **Trim Size:** 8 3/8 x 10 7/8. **Cols./Page:** 3. **Col. Width:** 2 1/4 INS. **Col. Depth:** 9 5/8 INS. **Key Personnel:** Tom Inglesby, Editor, Associate Publisher. **ISSN:** 1073-8924 (print). **Subscription Rates:** Free qualified industry professionals; $34 Individuals; $60 Canada and Mexico; $120 Other countries. **URL:** http://markeemagazine.com. **Formerly:** Florida Marquee; Markee Southeast; Markee: America's Magazine for Regional Film & Video Production. **Ad Rates:** 4C $4,000. **Remarks:** Accepts advertising. **Circ:** (Not Reported).

9236 ■ Masonry Design
Lionheart Publishing Inc.
506 Roswell St., Ste. 220
Marietta, GA 30060
Phone: (770)431-0867
Fax: (770)432-6969
Free: 888-303-5639
Publisher's E-mail: lpi@lionhrtpub.com
Magazine featuring materials, trends, and technologies for masonry projects. **Freq:** Quarterly. **Trim Size:** 8 3/8 x 10 7/8. **Key Personnel:** Cory Sekine-Pettite, Editor. **Subscription Rates:** Free to qualified subscribers. **URL:** http://masonrydesignmagazine.com. **Ad Rates:** BW $675. **Remarks:** Accepts advertising. **Circ:** (Not Reported).

9237 ■ Milton Neighbor
Neighbor Newspapers Inc.
580 S Fairground St.
Marietta, GA 30060
Community newspaper. **Freq:** Weekly (Wed.). **Key Personnel:** Otis A. Brumby, Jr., Publisher. **Subscription Rates:** $112.00 Individuals 1 year. **URL:** http://neighbornewspapers.com/nni_al?neighbor=milton&leaderboardtop=263&leaderboardbot=264&pillowtop=396&pillowbot=266&tt=267&box=268. **Remarks:** Accepts advertising. **Circ:** Non-paid ♦**5176**.

9238 ■ New Jersey CPA
Lionheart Publishing Inc.
506 Roswell St., Ste. 220
Marietta, GA 30060
Phone: (770)431-0867
Fax: (770)432-6969
Free: 888-303-5639
Publisher's E-mail: lpi@lionhrtpub.com
Magazine covering articles in auditing, financial planning, forensic accounting, industry, tax and technology for certified public accountants. **Freq:** Bimonthly. **Key Personnel:** David Plaskow, Editor. **Subscription Rates:** Included in membership. **URL:** http://www.lionhrtpub.com/New-Jersey-CPA-Magazine. **Ad Rates:** BW $2220. **Remarks:** Accepts advertising. **Circ:** 16000.

9239 ■ North Cobb Neighbor
Neighbor Newspapers Inc.
580 S Fairground St.
Marietta, GA 30060
Community newspaper. **Freq:** Weekly (Thurs.). **Key Personnel:** Otis A. Brumby, Jr., Publisher; Matthew Heck, Manager, Circulation. **Subscription Rates:** $135.68 Out of area. **URL:** http://www.neighbornewspapers.com/. **Remarks:** Accepts advertising. **Circ:** Non-paid ♦**23201**.

9240 ■ OR/MS Today
Lionheart Publishing Inc.
506 Roswell St., Ste. 220
Marietta, GA 30060
Phone: (770)431-0867
Fax: (770)432-6969
Free: 888-303-5639
Publisher's E-mail: lpi@lionhrtpub.com
Membership magazine of the Institute for Operations Research and the Management Sciences for upper management professionals and academicians in the field of operations research and management science. **Freq:** Bimonthly. **Print Method:** Web Offset. **Trim Size:** 8 1/8 x 10 7/8. **Key Personnel:** Alan Brubaker, Art Director, phone: (770)431-0867; Peter Horner, Editor, phone: (770)587-3172, fax: (770)587-3172. **Subscription Rates:** $62 Individuals individual; $79 Canada and Mexico individual; $85 Other countries. **URL:** http://www.orms-today.org/ormsmain.shtml. **Ad Rates:** GLR $26; BW $1,997; 4C $2,785. **Remarks:** Accepts advertising. **Circ:** Combined 14268.

9241 ■ Patient Safety & Quality Healthcare
Lionheart Publishing Inc.
506 Roswell St., Ste. 220
Marietta, GA 30060
Phone: (770)431-0867
Fax: (770)432-6969
Free: 888-303-5639
Publisher's E-mail: lpi@lionhrtpub.com
Publication that provides information about patient safety and quality healthcare for patients, doctors, hospital administrators, and others in the healthcare industry. **Freq:** Monthly. **Key Personnel:** John Llewellyn, Publisher, phone: (770)431-0867; Susan C. Carr, Editor, phone: (978)287-0195. **Subscription Rates:** $16 Individuals 1 year. **URL:** http://www.psqh.com. **Ad Rates:** GLR $26; BW $1785. **Remarks:** Accepts advertising. **Circ:** (Not Reported).

9242 ■ Paulding Neighbor
Neighbor Newspapers Inc.
580 S Fairground St.
Marietta, GA 30060
Publication E-mail: paulding@neighbornewspapers.com
Community newspaper. **Freq:** Weekly (Thurs.). **Key Personnel:** Otis Brumby, Jr., Publisher; Otis Brumby, III, General Manager. **Subscription Rates:** $135.68 By mail outside of delivery area; $72.08 By mail 6 months, outside of delivery area; $36.57 By mail 3 months, outside of delivery area. **URL:** http://neighbornewspapers.com/nni_al?neighbor=paulding&leaderboardtop=287&leaderboardbot=288&pillowtop=398&pillowbot=290&tt=291&box=292. **Remarks:** Accepts advertising. **Circ:** Non-paid ♦**23951**.

9243 ■ Southern Jewish History
Southern Jewish Historical Society
PO Box 71601
Marietta, GA 30007-1601
Publisher's E-mail: info@jewishsouth.org
Freq: Annual. **Key Personnel:** Mark K Bauman, Editor. **Subscription Rates:** $15 Members; $20 Individuals; $40 Institutions; Included in membership. **URL:** http://www.jewishsouth.org/about-southern-jewish-history. **Remarks:** Accepts advertising. **Circ:** (Not Reported).

9244 ■ Tipularia: A Botanical Magazine
Georgia Botanical Society
c/o Anita Reeves, Membership Chair
2718 Stillwater Lake Ln.
Marietta, GA 30066
Phone: (770)827-5186
Publisher's E-mail: members@gabotsoc.org
Journal magazine covering botany in Georgia. **Freq:** Annual. **Trim Size:** 6 x 9. **Cols./Page:** 2. **Col. Width:** 2 3/8 inches. **Col. Depth:** 7 7/8 inches. **Key Personnel:** Brad Sanders, Editor, phone: (706)548-6446; Richard Ware, Editor. **ISSN:** 1090--1876 (print). **Subscription Rates:** $10 Single issue Back issues post-1991 issues; Included in membership; $6 Single issue 1991 and before Back issues. **URL:** http://www.gabotsoc.org/?page_id=7. **Remarks:** Advertising not accepted. **Circ:** (Not Reported).

9245 ■ The Truth at Last: News Suppressed by the Daily Press
Stormfront
PO Box 1211
Marietta, GA 30061
Right-wing segregationist newspaper. **Freq:** Monthly. **Print Method:** Offset. **Cols./Page:** 5. **Col. Width:** 22 nonpareils. **Col. Depth:** 193 agate lines. **Key Personnel:** Dr. Edward R. Fields, Editor. **Subscription Rates:** $18 Individuals. **URL:** http://www.stormfront.org/truth_at_last. **Remarks:** Advertising not accepted. **Circ:** Paid ‡30000, Free ‡12000.

9246 ■ Upscale Magazine: What Successful People Read
Upscale Communications
2141 Powers Ferry Rd.
Marietta, GA 30067
Phone: (770)988-0015
Periodical covering entertainment and lifestyle. **Freq:** Bimonthly. **Print Method:** Web offset. **Trim Size:** 8 1/8 x 11. **Key Personnel:** Tiffany Anderson, Contact. **ISSN:** 1047--2592 (print). **Subscription Rates:** $14.99 Individuals; $23.95 Two years. **Formerly:** Upscale: The Suc-

cessful Black Magazine. **Ad Rates:** BW $8460; 4C $12842. **Remarks:** Accepts advertising. **Circ:** Controlled ‡182476.

9247 ■ Vinings Neighbor
Neighbor Newspapers Inc.
580 S Fairground St.
Marietta, GA 30060
Community newspaper. **Freq:** Weekly (Wed.). **Key Personnel:** Otis A. Brumby, Jr., Publisher. **Subscription Rates:** Free. **URL:** http://neighbornewspapers.com/nni_al?neighbor=vinings&leaderboardtop=239&leaderboardbot=240&pillowtop=402&pillowbot=242&tt=243&box=244. **Remarks:** other Neighbor Newspapers. **Circ:** ‡18050.

9248 ■ Prime Star Inc.
4516 Ashmore Cir. N
Marietta, GA 30066-1613
Formerly: GCTV. **Key Personnel:** William R. Proud, Contact. **Cities Served:** subscribing households 206,000. **URL:** http://ecorp.sos.ga.gov/BusinessSearch/BusinessInformation?businessId=844192&businessType=Domestic%20Profit%20Corporation.

9249 ■ WGHR-FM - 100.7
1100 S Marietta Pky.
Marietta, GA 30060
Email: admissions@spsu.edu
Format: News; Top 40. **Owner:** Kennesaw State University, 1100 S Marietta Pky., Marietta, GA 30060, Ph: (470)578-6000. **Founded:** 1972. **Operating Hours**: Continuous. **Wattage**: 017 ERP. **URL:** http://www.spsu.edu.

9250 ■ WPXA-TV - 14
200 Cobb Pky. N, Ste. 110
Marietta, GA 30062
Phone: (404)528-1400
Fax: (404)528-1403
Email: wpxa@pax.net
Format: Commercial TV. **Owner:** Paxson Communications of Atlanta, 200 N Cobb Pkwy., Ste. 114, Marietta, GA 30062. **Founded:** 1988. **Formerly**: WTLK-TV. **Operating Hours**: Continuous. **ADI**: Atlanta (Athens & Rome), GA. **Key Personnel:** Jack Crumpier, Gen. Mgr., jackcrumpier@pax.net. **URL:** http://www.ionmedianetworks.com.

MATTHEWS

9251 ■ WACG-FM - 90.7
2316 Miller Place Rd.
Matthews, GA 30818
Phone: (706)737-1661
Format: News; Classical; Public Radio; Jazz. **Networks:** National Public Radio (NPR); Public Radio International (PRI). **Owner:** Georgia Public Radio, 260 14Th St. NW, Atlanta, GA 30318, Ph: (404)685-2400, Free: 800-222-6006. **Founded:** June 02, 1970. **Operating Hours**: Continuous; 90% network, 10% local. **ADI**: Augusta, GA. **Wattage**: 30,000. **Ad Rates:** Noncommercial. **URL:** http://www.gpb.org.

MCDONOUGH

NWC GA. Henry Co. 28 mi. S. of Atlanta. Residential. Manufactures television sets, lawn mowers, textiles. Agriculture.

9252 ■ Premiere Cable Communications
PO Box 959
31 Griffin St.
McDonough, GA 30253
Phone: (404)957-1526
Fax: (404)954-4574
Free: 800-800-9904
Owner: Masada Corp., 2160 Highland Ave. S, Ste. 100., Birmingham, AL 35205, Ph: (205)558-4688. **Key Personnel:** Greg Orr, VP.

9253 ■ WKKP-AM
12 N Cedar St.
McDonough, GA 30253
Phone: (770)775-3151
Fax: (770)775-3153
Format: Middle-of-the-Road (MOR); Adult Contemporary; Oldies; News. **Networks:** Independent. **Owner:** Henry Co. Radio Co., Inc., at above address. **Founded:** 1979. **Formerly**: WZAL-AM. **Wattage**: 2,500 Day; 058 Night. **Ad Rates:** $5-6 for 30 seconds; $7-8 for 60 seconds. **Mailing address:** PO Box 351, McDonough, GA 30253.

MCRAE

SC GA. Telfair Co. 65 mi. SE of Macon. Manufactures cottonseed oil, lumber, lawn mowers, textiles. Pine and hardwood timber. Agriculture. Cotton, dewberries, watermelons.

9254 ■ The Telfair Enterprise
Telfair Enterprise
31 W Oak St.
McRae, GA 31055
Phone: (229)868-6015
Fax: (229)868-5486
Publication E-mail: telfairenterprise@windstream.net
Newspaper with Democratic orientation. **Freq:** Weekly (Wed.). **Print Method:** Offset. **Trim Size:** 7 1/4 x 11 1/2. **Cols./Page:** 6. **Col. Width:** 2 inches. **Col. Depth:** 21 1/2 inches. **Key Personnel:** Eric R. Denty, Publisher; Don Richard, Editor; Donna J. Bell, General Manager. **USPS:** 537-220. **Subscription Rates:** $28 Individuals in county; $26 Individuals senior citizens; $35 Elsewhere in Georgia; $38 Out of state. **URL:** http://www.thetelfairenterprise.com. **Mailing address:** PO Box 269, McRae, GA 31055. **Ad Rates:** GLR $4; BW $580.50; 4C $780.50; SAU $5; PCI $3. **Remarks:** Advertising accepted; rates available upon request. **Circ:** ‡3400.

METTER

E. GA. Candler Co. 60 mi. NW of Savannah. Manufactures lumber, fertilizer manufactured. Cotton ginning; naval stores. Agriculture. Cotton, tobacco stock.

9255 ■ The Metter Advertiser
Snell Publications Inc.
15 S Rountree
Metter, GA 30439
Phone: (912)685-6566
Fax: (912)685-4901
Publication E-mail: news@metteradvertiser.com
Local newspaper. **Freq:** Weekly (Wed.). **Print Method:** Offset. **Cols./Page:** 6. **Col. Width:** 26 nonpareils. **Col. Depth:** 294 agate lines. **Key Personnel:** Carvy Snell, Editor. **USPS:** 410-910. **Subscription Rates:** $32.40 Individuals in county; $36.72 Individuals other Georgia county; $41.04 Out of state; $32.40 Out of state online only. **URL:** http://www.metteradvertiser.com. **Ad Rates:** GLR $5; PCI $4.60. **Remarks:** Advertising accepted; rates available upon request. **Circ:** ‡2966.

9256 ■ WBMZ-FM - 103.7
PO Box 238
Metter, GA 30439
Phone: (912)685-2136
Fax: (912)685-2137
Free: 888-644-7079
Format: Classical. **Simulcasts:** WHCG-AM. **Networks:** Georgia Radio; Westwood One Radio; Gannett News; NBC. **Founded:** 1971. **Formerly**: WQKK-FM; WHCG-FM. **Operating Hours**: Continuous. **Key Personnel:** Jimmy Page, Gen. Mgr., jpage@wbmzfm.com; Steve Lawson, Operations Mgr., slawson@wbmzfm.com. **Wattage**: 6,000. **Ad Rates:** $6-8 for 30 seconds; $8-10 for 60 seconds. WHCG-FM, WMAC-AM.

9257 ■ WHCG-AM - 1360
PO Box 238
Metter, GA 30439
Owner: Radio Metter Inc., at above address. **Founded:** 1961. **Ad Rates:** $6 for 30 seconds; $8 for 60 seconds.

MILLEDGEVILLE

C. GA. Baldwin Co. On Oconee River, 33 mi. NE of Macon. Georgia College at Milledgeville; Georgia Military College. Tile, clay products plants; lumber, knitting and spinning (yarn) mills; bottling works. Manufactures pharmaceuticals, mobile homes, airplane parts. Pine and hardwood timber. Dairy, truck, poultry farms.

9258 ■ Georgia College & State University Connection: A Publication for Alumni and Friends of GC&SU
Georgia College Alumni Association
231 W Hancock St.
Milledgeville, GA 31061
Phone: (478)445-5004
Free: 800-342-0471
Publication E-mail: connection@gcsu.edu
University magazine. **Freq:** Quarterly. **Key Personnel:** Kyle Brogdon, Editor. **URL:** http://civil.aalto.fi/en/research/transportation. **Formerly**: Georgia College Connection'. **Remarks:** Advertising not accepted. **Circ:** Free ‡23000.

9259 ■ The Union-Recorder
Community Newspaper Holdings Inc.
165 Garrett Way
Milledgeville, GA 31061
Phone: (478)452-0567
Local newspaper. **Freq:** Daily Tues.-Sat. (morn.). **Print Method:** Offset. **Trim Size:** 13 3/4 x 22 3/4. **Cols./Page:** 6. **Col. Width:** 2 1/16 inches. **Col. Depth:** 21 1/2 inches. **Key Personnel:** Keith Barlow, Publisher, phone: (478)453-1441; Lynda Jackson, Business Manager, phone: (478)453-1442; Erin Simmons, Director, Advertising, phone: (478)453-1437. **Subscription Rates:** $8.99 total access per month; $7.99 digital access per month. **URL:** http://www.unionrecorder.com. **Ad Rates:** GLR $1.75; BW $1329; 4C $1579; SAU $11.25; PCI $7.65. **Remarks:** Accepts advertising. **Circ:** 8500.

9260 ■ WGUR-FM - 88.9
Georgia College & State University
231 W Hancock St.
Milledgeville, GA 31061
Phone: (478)445-5004
Free: 800-342-0471
Format: Top 40; Alternative/New Music/Progressive. **Owner:** Georgia College & State University, 231 W Hancock St., Milledgeville, GA 31061, Ph: (478)445-2774, Free: 800-342-0471. **Founded:** 1970. **Formerly**: WXGC-FM. **Operating Hours**: 7:30 a.m.-11 p.m. **ADI**: Macon, GA. **Wattage**: 010. **Ad Rates:** Advertising accepted; rates available upon request. **URL:** http://www.gcsu.edu.

9261 ■ WKZR-FM - 102.3
1250 W Charlton St.
Milledgeville, GA 31061
Phone: (478)452-0586
Format: Country; Full Service. **Networks:** ABC. **Owner:** WMVG, Inc., 1250 W Charlton St, Milledgeville, GA 31061, Ph: (478)452-0586. **Founded:** 1966. **Formerly**: WMVG-FM. **Operating Hours**: Continuous; 10% network, 90% local. **Wattage**: 3,300. **Ad Rates:** $10-17 for 30 seconds; $14-20 for 60 seconds. Combined advertising rates available with WMVG. **URL:** http://www.country102fm.com.

9262 ■ WSKS-FM - 97.7
PO Box 832
Milledgeville, GA 31061-0832
Phone: (912)453-9406
Fax: (912)453-9770
Format: Contemporary Hit Radio (CHR). **Networks:** Satellite Music Network. **Owner:** Alexander Mitchell Communications Corp., at above address. **Founded:** 1988. **Operating Hours**: Continuous; 70% network, 30% local. **Key Personnel:** James A. Karrh, Gen. Mgr.; John W. Ferguson, Dir. of Programs; Steven M. Layne, Contact. **Wattage**: 3,000. **Ad Rates:** $8-10 for 30 seconds.

9263 ■ W201BN-FM - 88.1
PO Box 391
Twin Falls, ID 83303
Fax: (208)736-1958
Free: 800-357-4226
Format: Religious; Contemporary Christian. **Owner:** CSN International, PO Box 391, Twin Falls, ID 83303, Ph: (208)736-1958, Fax: (208)736-1958, Free: 800-357-4226. **URL:** http://www.csnradio.com.

9264 ■ WYIS-AM - 1410
200 N Jefferson St. NE
Milledgeville, GA 31061-3418
Phone: (229)868-5611
Fax: (229)868-7552
Email: star1027@alltel.net
Format: Adult Contemporary. **Owner:** Cinecom Broadcasting Systems, Inc., at above address. **Founded:** 1957. **Formerly**: WDAX-AM. **Operating Hours**: Continuous. **Wattage**: 1,000.

MILLEN

EC GA. Jenkins Co. 20 mi. E. of Herndon.

Circulation: ★ = AAM; △ or • = BPA; ♦ = CAC; ❑ = VAC; ⊕ = PO Statement; ‡ = Publisher's Report; Boldface figures = sworn; Light figures = estimated.

9265 ■ Millen News
The Millen News
856E Cotton Ave.
Millen, GA 30442
Phone: (478)982-5460
Fax: (478)982-1785
Community newspaper. **Freq:** Weekly. **Print Method:** Offset. **Cols./Page:** 6. **Col. Width:** 12.5 picas. **Col. Depth:** 21 1/2 inches. **Key Personnel:** Deborah Bennett, Editor; Roy F. Chalker, Jr., Publisher. **URL:** http://www.themillennews.com. **Ad Rates:** BW $483.75; 4C $823.75; PCI $6.35. **Remarks:** Accepts advertising. **Circ:** Mon.-Fri. ‡2200.

MONROE

NC GA. Walton Co. 45 mi. E. of Atlanta. Manufactures textiles, china products, plastic pipe, fertilizer, cottonseed oil. Poultry, egg processing plant. Agriculture. Cotton, corn, poultry, dairy and beef cattle.

9266 ■ The Loganville Tribune
Southern Newspapers Inc.
124 N Broad St.
Monroe, GA 30655
Phone: (770)267-8371
Fax: (770)267-7780
Community newspaper. **Freq:** Weekly (Fri.). **Key Personnel:** David Clemons, Editor, Publisher, phone: (770)267-2443; Brian Arrington, Managing Editor, phone: (770)267-2492. **Subscription Rates:** $60 Individuals; $70 By mail. **URL:** http://waltontribune.com/loganville/. **Remarks:** Accepts advertising. **Circ:** Paid ♦**1231**.

9267 ■ Walton Tribune/Advertiser
Walton Tribune/Advertiser
124 N Broad
Monroe, GA 30655-0808
Phone: (770)267-8371
Fax: (770)267-7780
Publisher's E-mail: tribstaff@waltontribune.com
Community newspaper. **Freq:** Semiweekly (Wed. and Sun.). **Print Method:** Offset. **Cols./Page:** 6. **Col. Width:** 20 nonpareils. **Col. Depth:** 301 agate lines. **Key Personnel:** Lisa J. Owens, Business Manager; Brian Arrington, Editor. **Subscription Rates:** $67 Individuals; $70 By mail. **URL:** http://www.waltontribune.com. **Mailing address:** PO Box 808, Monroe, GA 30655-0808. **Ad Rates:** SAU $7; PCI $7. **Remarks:** Color advertising accepted; rates available upon request. **Circ:** Wed. ‡5036, Sun. ‡5036.

9268 ■ Monroe Utilities Network
215 N Broad St.
Monroe, GA 30655
Phone: (770)267-3429
Fax: (770)267-3698
Email: comments@monroeutilities.net
Founded: Feb. 1972. **Key Personnel:** Mark S. Ennis, Gen. Mgr., mennis@mwlgc.com; Debbie Kirk, Contact. **Cities Served:** Bostwick, Good Hope, Monroe, Social Circle, Georgia: subscribing households 5,971; 69 channels; 1 community access channel; 168 hours per week community access programming. **URL:** http://www.monroega.com.

9269 ■ WMOQ-FM
PO Box 649
Monroe, GA 30655
Phone: (770)464-3521
Format: Country. **Wattage**: 3,000 ERP. **Ad Rates:** Advertising accepted; rates available upon request.

MONTICELLO

NC GA. Jasper Co. 38 mi. N. of Macon. Manufactures forest products, plywood, feed, fertilizer. Pine timber. Agriculture. Poultry, dairy farms. Soybeans, corn, cattle.

9270 ■ The Monticello News
The Monticello News
PO Box 30
Monticello, GA 31064
Publication E-mail: news@themonticellonews.com
Community newspaper. **Freq:** Weekly (Thurs.). **Print Method:** Offset. **Cols./Page:** 6. **Col. Width:** 12 picas. **Col. Depth:** 301 agate lines. **Key Personnel:** Kathy Mudd, Editor. **USPS:** 361-640. **URL:** http://themonticellonews.com/index1.htm. **Ad Rates:** GLR $5.25; BW $495; 4C $545; SAU $4.50; PCI $3.85. **Remarks:** Accepts advertising. **Circ:** ‡3100.

MOULTRIE

S. GA. Colquitt Co. 65 mi. NE of Tallahassee, FL. Manufactures textiles, lumber, mobile homes, aluminum cans, cottonseed oil, fertilizer. Carpet yarn spinning; die casting; pork packing plant. Agriculture. Tobacco, peanuts, livestock, grains, vegetables.

9271 ■ Moultrie Observer
Community Newspaper Holdings Inc.
PO Box 2349
Moultrie, GA 31776
Phone: (229)985-4545
Fax: (229)985-3569
General newspaper. **Founded:** 1905. **Freq:** Mon.-Sat. (morn.). **Print Method:** Offset. **Cols./Page:** 6. **Col. Width:** 24 nonpareils. **Col. Depth:** 301 agate lines. **Key Personnel:** Dwain Walden, Managing Editor, Publisher; Shawn Highsmith, Manager, Circulation. **Subscription Rates:** $10.99 total access per month; $9.99 digital access per month. **URL:** http://www.moultrieobserver.com. **Ad Rates:** SAU $6.82. **Remarks:** Accepts advertising. **Circ:** 7306.

9272 ■ WMTM-AM
PO Box 788
Moultrie, GA 31776
Phone: (912)985-1300
Fax: (912)890-0905
Format: Gospel. **Networks:** ABC. **Owner:** Colquitt Broadcasting Company, LLC, at above address, Free: 888-985-9400. **Founded:** 1953. **Key Personnel:** Jim Turner, Contact; Jim Lane, Music Dir; Jim Turner, Contact. **Wattage**: 5,000 Day; 060 Night. **Ad Rates:** $6 for 30 seconds; $8 for 60 seconds.

9273 ■ WMTM-FM - 93.9
PO Box 788
Moultrie, GA 31776
Phone: (229)985-1300
Fax: (229)890-0905
Format: Oldies. **Simulcasts:** WMTM-AM. **Networks:** CNN Radio; ABC. **Owner:** Colquitt Broadcasting Company, LLC, at above address, Free: 888-985-9400. **Founded:** 1964. **Operating Hours**: Continuous. **Wattage**: 100,000. **Ad Rates:** Noncommercial.

MOUNTAIN CITY

9274 ■ The Foxfire Magazine
Foxfire Fund Inc.
PO Box 541
Mountain City, GA 30562-0541
Phone: (706)746-5828
Fax: (706)746-5829
Publisher's E-mail: foxfire@foxfire.org
Magazine focusing on the Appalachian culture, written and edited by Appalachian high school students. **Freq:** Semiannual. **Trim Size:** 10 1/2 x 7 3/4. **Cols./Page:** 2. **Col. Width:** 3 inches. **Col. Depth:** 8 inches. **ISSN:** 0015--9220 (print). **Subscription Rates:** $12.95 Individuals; $35 Other countries; $7 Single issue. **URL:** http://www.foxfirefund.org/the-magazine.html. **Formerly**: Foxfire. **Remarks:** Advertising not accepted. **Circ:** 3000.

9275 ■ WALH-AM - 1340
Hwy. 441 N
Box F
Mountain City, GA 30562
Phone: (706)746-2256
Fax: (706)746-2259
Format: Easy Listening. **Simulcasts:** WISB-AM (1400), WYHG-AM (770). **Networks:** USA Radio; ABC; Meadows Racing. **Owner:** Tugart Properties, LLC, at above address, Toccoa, GA. **Founded:** 1986. **Operating Hours**: Continuous. **Wattage**: 1,000. **Ad Rates:** Noncommercial.

NASHVILLE

S. GA. Berrien Co. 117 mi. SE of Macon. Manufactures automotive parts, carpet backing, feed, boats. Textile mill. Tobacco warehouse. Screen printing. Pine timber. Agriculture. Corn, tobacco, peanuts, cotton.

9276 ■ The Berrien Press
The Berrien Press
PO Box 455
Nashville, GA 31639
Phone: (229)686-3523
Fax: (229)686-7771
Publication E-mail: theberrienpress@alltel.net
Community newspaper. **Freq:** Weekly (Wed.). **Print Method:** Offset. **Cols./Page:** 6. **Col. Width:** 12 picas. **Col. Depth:** 21.5 inches. **Key Personnel:** Donald Boyd, Editor; Debbie Cole, Assistant Editor; Jonna Exum, General Manager. **URL:** http://www.theberrienpress.com/sub/account_login.asp. **Ad Rates:** BW $567; 4C $627; SAU $5. **Remarks:** Accepts advertising. **Circ:** ‡4200.

NEWNAN

W. GA. Coweta Co. 40 mi. SW of Atlanta. Manufactures safety goggles, textiles, aluminum products, concrete blocks, tanks, plastics, lumber. Agriculture. Cotton, dairy products, corn, peanuts.

9277 ■ The Newnan Times-Herald
The Newnan Times-Herald
PO Box 1052
Newnan, GA 30264
Phone: (770)253-1576
Community newspaper. **Freq:** Daily. **Print Method:** Offset. **Cols./Page:** 6. **Col. Width:** 24 nonpareils. **Col. Depth:** 301 agate lines. **Key Personnel:** William W. Thomasson, President; Lamar Truitt, Manager, Advertising. **ISSN:** 0883--2536 (print). **Subscription Rates:** $132.68 Individuals in Coweta County; $245 Out of area. **URL:** http://www.times-herald.com. **Remarks:** Accepts advertising. **Circ:** Paid 12033.

9278 ■ WCOH-AM - 1400
154 Boone Dr.
Newnan, GA 30263
Phone: (770)683-7234
Fax: (770)683-9846
Email: onair@wcoh.com
Format: Sports; News; Talk. **Founded:** 1947. **Operating Hours**: Continuous. **Wattage**: 1,000. **Ad Rates:** Advertising accepted; rates available upon request. **URL:** http://www.wcoh.com.

9279 ■ WMGP-FM - 98.1
154 Boone Dr.
Newnan, GA 30263
Phone: (770)683-7234
Format: Adult Contemporary. **Owner:** iHeartMedia Inc., 200 E Basse Rd., San Antonio, TX 78209, Ph: (210)832-3314. **Operating Hours**: Continuous. **Wattage**: 25,000. **Ad Rates:** Advertising accepted; rates available upon request. **URL:** http://www.magic981.com.

9280 ■ WVCC-AM - 720
154 Boone Dr.
Newnan, GA 30263
Phone: (770)683-7234
Format: News; Talk. **Formerly**: WGSE-AM. **Operating Hours**: 6:00 a.m. - 9:00 p.m. Monday - Saturday; 8:00 a.m. - 9:00 p.m. Sunday. **Key Personnel:** Glenn Beck, Contact; Rush Limbaugh, Contact; Sean Hannity, Contact. **Ad Rates:** Advertising accepted; rates available upon request. **URL:** http://www.720thevoice.com/.

NORCROSS

NC GA. Gwinnett Co. 15 mi. N. of Atlanta. Manufactures cables, plastic, fabricated metal products. Diversified farming. Cotton, corn, cattle.

9281 ■ Better Crops with Plant Food
International Plant Nutrition Institute
3500 Parkway Ln., Ste. 550
Norcross, GA 30092-2844
Phone: (770)447-0335
Fax: (770)448-0439
Publisher's E-mail: info@ipni.net
Agricultural magazine. **Freq:** Quarterly. **Print Method:** Offset. **Trim Size:** 6 x 9. **Cols./Page:** 1 and 2. **Col. Width:** 68 and 32 nonpareils. **Col. Depth:** 105 agate lines. **ISSN:** 0006--0089 (print). **URL:** http://ipni.net/publication/bettercrops.nsf. **Circ:** Paid ‡50, Non-paid ‡16,000.

9282 ■ Bowhunter
Outdoor Sportsman Group
Publication E-mail: bowhunter@emailcustomerservice.com
Magazine focusing on archery hunting. Provides readers with the latest advice on how to use bowhunting tackle and techniques, tips on the best bowhunting locations in North America, insights to the hottest new products on the market, an insider's understanding of

various topics and issues important to bowhunters, hunting adventures in pursuit of the world's most popular game animals, and more. Includes features, columns, and essays on the bowhunting experience. **Freq:** 9/yr. **Key Personnel:** Jeff Millar, Manager, Advertising and Sales, phone: (717)695-8081; Jeff Waring, Publisher, phone: (717)695-8080; Dwight Schuh, Editor. **Subscription Rates:** $10 Individuals; $18 Two years; $23 Canada; $44 Canada 2 years; $25 Other countries; $48 Other countries 2 years. **URL:** http://www.bowhunter.com. **Remarks:** Accepts advertising. **Circ:** Paid ⋆**154093**.

9283 ■ The Engineering Economist
Institute of Industrial and Systems Engineers
3577 Parkway Ln., Ste. 200
Norcross, GA 30092
Phone: (770)449-0460
Fax: (770)441-3295
Free: 800-494-0460
Publisher's E-mail: customerservice@taylorandfrancis.com
Journal covering capital investment analysis, cost estimation and accounting, cost of capital, design economics, economic decision analysis, education, policy analysis, and research and development. **Freq:** Quarterly. **Key Personnel:** Dr. Joseph C. Hartman; Phil Jones, Editor; Jerome P. Lavelle, Board Member; Joseph Hartman, Editor-in-Chief; Thomas O. Boucher, Editor-in-Chief. **ISSN:** 0013--791X (print); **EISSN:** 1547--2701 (electronic). **Subscription Rates:** $113 Individuals print only; $191 Institutions online only; $218 Institutions print and online. **URL:** http://www.tandfonline.com/toc/utee20/current; http://www.iienet2.org/details.aspx?id=1486; http://www.asee.org/papers-and-publications/publications/division-publications#The_Engineering_Economist. **Remarks:** Advertising not accepted. **Circ:** (Not Reported).

9284 ■ Firearms News
RentPath Inc.
3585 Engineering Dr., Ste. 100
Norcross, GA 30092-2831
Phone: (678)421-3000
Free: 800-216-1423
Gun sales magazine for collectors, dealers and hunters. **Freq:** 3/month. **Trim Size:** 11 x 13. **Cols./Page:** 5. **Col. Width:** 2 inches. **Col. Depth:** 12.25 inches. **Key Personnel:** Robert W. Hunnicutt, Editor. **ISSN:** 0049--0415 (print). **Subscription Rates:** $25 U.S. 30 issues (print or online); $31 U.S. 30 issues (print and online); $38 Canada 30 issues (print); $25 Canada 30 issues (online); $44 Canada 30 issues (print and online); $40 Other countries 30 issues (print); $25 Other countries 30 issues (online); $46 Other countries 30 issues (print and online). **URL:** http://www.firearmsnews.com. **Formerly**: Shotgun News: The World's Largest Gun Sales Publication. **Remarks:** Accepts advertising. **Circ:** Paid ⋆**112302**.

9285 ■ Gun Dog
RentPath Inc.
3585 Engineering Dr., Ste. 100
Norcross, GA 30092-2831
Phone: (678)421-3000
Free: 800-216-1423
Hunting magazine focusing on the use of dogs in the sport. **Freq:** Bimonthly. **Print Method:** Offset. **Trim Size:** 8 1/4 x 10 7/8. **Cols./Page:** 2 and 3. **Col. Width:** 3 1/2 inches. **Col. Depth:** 2.25 inches. **Key Personnel:** Aaron Decker, Director, Editorial; Rick Van Etten, Editor. **ISSN:** 0279--5086 (print). **Subscription Rates:** $19 Individuals print and online; $14 Individuals print or online. **Ad Rates:** BW $2,875; 4C $3,885; PCI $105. **Remarks:** Advertising accepted; rates available upon request. **Circ:** Paid ⋆**46102**.

9286 ■ Hot Bike: The Harley-Davidson Enthusiasts' Magazine
RentPath Inc.
3585 Engineering Dr., Ste. 100
Norcross, GA 30092-2831
Phone: (678)421-3000
Free: 800-216-1423
Magazine for motorcycle enthusiasts interested in high performance. **Freq:** 13/yr. **Print Method:** Web Offset. **Trim Size:** 8 x 10 7/8. **Cols./Page:** 3. **Col. Width:** 28 nonpareils. **Col. Depth:** 140 agate lines. **Key Personnel:** David Roe, Associate Publisher. **ISSN:** 8750--3212 (print). **Subscription Rates:** $19.97 Individuals 1 year; $29.97 Two years. **Ad Rates:** BW $5,285; 4C $7,050. **Remarks:** Accepts advertising. **Circ:** Paid ⋆**122566**.

9287 ■ Industrial Management
Institute of Industrial and Systems Engineers
3577 Parkway Ln., Ste. 200
Norcross, GA 30092
Phone: (770)449-0460
Fax: (770)441-3295
Free: 800-494-0460
Publisher's E-mail: executiveoffices@iienet.org
Trade publication covering industrial management. **Freq:** Bimonthly 6/year. **Key Personnel:** Michael Hughes, Contact. **ISSN:** 0019-8471 (print). **Subscription Rates:** Free members; $145 Nonmembers U.S; $179 Other countries. **URL:** http://www.iienet2.org/Details.aspx?id=652; http://www.iienet2.org/details.aspx?id=1486. **Remarks:** Advertising not accepted. **Circ:** (Not Reported).

9288 ■ Iowa Game & Fish
RentPath Inc.
3585 Engineering Dr., Ste. 100
Norcross, GA 30092-2831
Phone: (678)421-3000
Free: 800-216-1423
Magazine covering hunting and fishing in Iowa. Also covering environmental and conservation issues. **Freq:** Monthly. **Print Method:** Offset. **Trim Size:** 13 x 21 1/2. **Cols./Page:** 6. **Col. Width:** 29 nonpareils. **Col. Depth:** 294 agate lines. **Key Personnel:** Peter Gross, Publisher, phone: (678)589-2007; Ken Dunwoody, Director, Editorial. **ISSN:** 8750-2038 (print). **USPS:** 241-780. **URL:** http://www.gameandfishmag.com/midwest/iowa. **Remarks:** Accepts advertising. **Circ:** (Not Reported).

9289 ■ Journal of Engineering for Gas Turbines and Power
International Gas Turbine Institute
6525 The Corners Pky., Ste. 115
Norcross, GA 30092
Phone: (404)847-0072
Fax: (404)847-0151
Publisher's E-mail: igti@asme.org
Peer-reviewed journal on power engineering. **Freq:** Monthly. **Print Method:** Offset. **Trim Size:** 8 1/4 x 11 1/4. **Cols./Page:** 2. **Col. Width:** 39 nonpareils. **Col. Depth:** 210 agate lines. **Key Personnel:** David Wisler, Editor. **ISSN:** 0742--4795 (print). **Subscription Rates:** $931 Institutions print and online. **URL:** http://gasturbinespower.asmedigitalcollection.asme.org/journal.aspx. **Remarks:** Advertising not accepted. **Circ:** 2224.

9290 ■ Jp Magazine
RentPath Inc.
3585 Engineering Dr., Ste. 100
Norcross, GA 30092-2831
Phone: (678)421-3000
Free: 800-216-1423
Consumer magazine for Jeep owners and enthusiasts. **Freq:** Monthly. **Key Personnel:** Steve VonSeggern, Contact, phone: (949)705-3179. **Remarks:** Accepts advertising. **Circ:** Combined 80000.

9291 ■ Muscle Car Review
RentPath Inc.
3585 Engineering Dr., Ste. 100
Norcross, GA 30092-2831
Phone: (678)421-3000
Free: 800-216-1423
Consumer magazine covering automobiles. **Key Personnel:** Drew Hardin, Editor; Jim Foos, Publisher. **Circ:** (Not Reported).

9292 ■ Petersen's Hunting
RentPath Inc.
3585 Engineering Dr., Ste. 100
Norcross, GA 30092-2831
Phone: (678)421-3000
Free: 800-216-1423
Publication E-mail: hunting@emailcustomerservice.com
Sport hunting magazine. **Freq:** 11/year. **Print Method:** Offset. **Trim Size:** 7 7/8 x 10 1/2. **Key Personnel:** Kevin E. Steele, Publisher. **Subscription Rates:** $11 Individuals print or digital; $12 Individuals print & digital. **URL:** http://www.petersenshunting.com. **Remarks:** Accepts advertising. **Circ:** Paid ⋆**364902**.

9293 ■ Registered Rep.: The Source for Investment Professionals
Primedia Business
3585 Engineering Dr., Ste. 100
Norcross, GA 30092
Phone: (678)421-3000
Free: 800-216-1423
Magazine providing comprehensive coverage of securities industry trends directly affecting the job performance and productivity of retail stockbrokers. **Founded:** Sept. 1976. **Freq:** Monthly. **Print Method:** Web Offset. **Trim Size:** 7 3/4 x 10 3/4. **Cols./Page:** 3. **Col. Width:** 2 1/8 inches. **Col. Depth:** 10 inches. **Key Personnel:** Rich Santos, Publisher, phone: (212)204-4227. **ISSN:** 0193-1865 (print). **URL:** http://registeredrep.com/. **Formerly**: Registered Representative. **Ad Rates:** BW $16,936; 4C $19,445; PCI $232. **Remarks:** Accepts advertising. **Circ:** Controlled 93800.

9294 ■ Rocky Mountain Construction
ACP/CMP Group
30 Technology Pkwy. S, Ste. 100
Norcross, GA 30092
Magazine serving the construction industry of America's mountain regions. Topics covered include heavy engineering, building, landscaping, soil conservation, mining, and logging and federal, state, county, and city projects. Includes weekly construction reports. **Freq:** Semimonthly. **Print Method:** Offset. Uses mats. **Trim Size:** 7 7/8 x 10 1/2. **Cols./Page:** 3 and 2. **Col. Width:** 26 and 40 nonpareils. **Col. Depth:** 140 agate lines. **USPS:** 468-980. **URL:** http://rockymountainconstruction.acppubs.com. **Ad Rates:** BW $16,260; 4C $19,760; PCI $32. **Remarks:** Accepts advertising. **Circ:** Paid 53, Controlled 8792.

9295 ■ SAIL: Largest Circulation Sailing Magazine in the World
RentPath Inc.
3585 Engineering Dr., Ste. 100
Norcross, GA 30092-2831
Phone: (678)421-3000
Free: 800-216-1423
SAIL is a magazine for sailors of all types, cruisers and racers with both large boats and small, all of whom are actively involved in the development of their sailing skills. Articles cover cruising, racing, sail trim, hull and sail design, rigging, spinnaker handling, wind and water conditions, etc. The focus is on the practical considerations of choosing and owning sailboats, gear, and equipment and getting more enjoyment from sailing in general. **Freq:** Monthly. **Print Method:** Offset. **Trim Size:** 7 7/8 x 10 3/4. **Key Personnel:** Peter Nielsen, Editor-in-Chief, phone: (617)720-8601; David Schmidt, Senior Editor, phone: (617)720-8624. **Subscription Rates:** $15 Individuals 12 issues; $25 Two years 24 issues. **URL:** http://www.sailmagazine.com. **Ad Rates:** BW $16,060; 4C $22,960. **Remarks:** Accepts advertising. **Circ:** Paid ‡105305.

9296 ■ Site Selection Magazine
Conway Data Inc.
6625 The Corners Parkway, Ste. 200
Norcross, GA 30092-3334
Phone: (770)446-6996
Fax: (770)263-8825
Publisher's E-mail: info@conway.com
Magazine on real estate and site selectors. **Freq:** Bimonthly. **Print Method:** Offset. **Trim Size:** 8 1/8 x 10 7/8. **Cols./Page:** 3. **Col. Width:** 26 nonpareils. **Col. Depth:** 140 agate lines. **Key Personnel:** Julie Clarke, Manager, Circulation; Adam Bruns, Managing Editor; Ronald J. Starner, Executive Vice President; John McCurry, Senior Editor; Mark Arend, Editor-in-Chief. **ISSN:** 1080--7799 (print). **URL:** http://www.siteselection.com. **Ad Rates:** BW $8,355; 4C $2400. **Remarks:** Accepts advertising. **Circ:** 44000.

9297 ■ SuperFord.org
RentPath Inc.
3585 Engineering Dr., Ste. 100
Norcross, GA 30092-2831
Phone: (678)421-3000
Free: 800-216-1423
Ford automaker's information and entertainment newsletter. **Subscription Rates:** Included in membership. **URL:** http://www.superford.org. **Remarks:** Accepts advertising. **Circ:** (Not Reported).

Circulation: ⋆ = AAM; △ or • = BPA; ♦ = CAC; ❑ = VAC; ⊕ = PO Statement; ‡ = Publisher's Report; Boldface figures = sworn; Light figures = estimated.

9298 ■ Truck Trend
RentPath Inc.
3585 Engineering Dr., Ste. 100
Norcross, GA 30092-2831
Phone: (678)421-3000
Free: 800-216-1423
Publication E-mail: inquiries@automotive.com
Consumer magazine covering light trucks. **Freq:** Bimonthly. **Key Personnel:** Alan Reed, Contact, phone: (310)531-5970. **ISSN:** 1094--4370 (print). **Subscription Rates:** $25.94 Individuals 6 issues; $53.88 Individuals 12 issues. **URL:** http://www.trucktrend.com. **Remarks:** Accepts advertising. **Circ:** (Not Reported).

9299 ■ Trucker's Connection
Trucker's Connection Inc.
5960 Crooked Creek Rd., Ste. 15
Norcross, GA 30092
Trade magazine for over-the-road, long haul truck operators. **Freq:** Monthly. **Key Personnel:** Mark Schiffmacher, Chief Executive Officer; Megan Cullingford, Editor, phone: (678)325-1022. **Subscription Rates:** $26.95 Individuals; $45 Canada; $90 Other countries. **URL:** http://www.truckersconnection.com. **Remarks:** Accepts advertising. **Circ:** (Not Reported).

9300 ■ Trusts and Estates: Essential Information and strategies for Advisors to the Wealthy
Primedia Business
3585 Engineering Dr., Ste. 100
Norcross, GA 30092
Phone: (678)421-3000
Free: 800-216-1423
Financial, wealth management, estate planning, and investment magazine. Covers charitable giving, insurance, retirement benefits, industry software and technology, valuation and appraisal of assets, intergenerational wealth transfer, private banking, and multidisciplinary practice issues. **Freq:** Monthly. **Print Method:** Offset. **Trim Size:** 7 3/4 x 10 3/4. **Cols./Page:** 3. **Col. Width:** 2 1/8 inches. **Col. Depth:** 10 inches. **Key Personnel:** Carolyn Chandler, Associate Editor, phone: (212)204-4225; John Herr, Director, phone: (212)204-4216; Thomas Albano, Art Director, phone: (212)204-4214; Rorie Sherman, Editor-in-Chief, phone: (212)204-4229; Carolyn A. Chandler, Associate Editor; Rich Santos, Publisher, phone: (212)204-4227. **ISSN:** 0041--3682 (print). **Subscription Rates:** $199 Individuals; $229 Canada; $249 Other countries. **URL:** http://wealthmanagement.com/te-home. **Ad Rates:** BW $4,828; 4C $6,381. **Remarks:** Accepts advertising. **Circ:** (Not Reported).

9301 ■ The Weekly
The Weekly
Peachtree Cor.
Norcross, GA 30010-1141
Phone: (770)446-2364
Publisher's E-mail: weeklypub1@comcast.net
Community newspaper. **Founded:** Oct. 30, 1996. **Freq:** Weekly. **Print Method:** Online. **Key Personnel:** Gay Wiley Shook, Editor; Ronald E. Shook, Publisher. **URL:** http://theweekly.com. **Mailing address:** PO Box 921141, Norcross, GA 30010-1141. **Remarks:** Accepts advertising. **Circ:** (Not Reported).

9302 ■ Wildfowl
RentPath Inc.
3585 Engineering Dr., Ste. 100
Norcross, GA 30092-2831
Phone: (678)421-3000
Free: 800-216-1423
Magazine covering the sport of duck and goose hunting. **Founded:** 1986. **Freq:** Bimonthly 7/yr. **Print Method:** Offset. **Trim Size:** 8 1/4 x 10 7/8. **Cols./Page:** 2 and 3. **Col. Width:** 3 1/2 inches. **Col. Depth:** 2.25 inches. **Key Personnel:** Paul Wait, Editor. **ISSN:** 0886-0637 (print). **Subscription Rates:** $19 Individuals print and online; $14 Individuals print or online. **URL:** http://www.wildfowlmag.com. **Ad Rates:** BW $3,260; 4C $4,420. **Remarks:** Accepts advertising. **Circ:** Paid ★**40104**.

9303 ■ WATC-TV - 57
1862 Enterprise Dr.
Norcross, GA 30093
Phone: (770)300-9828
Fax: (770)300-9838
Email: contact@watc.tv
Format: Educational. **Owner:** Community Television, Inc., at above address, Santa Cruz, CA. **Founded:** 1984. **Operating Hours**: Continuous. **ADI:** Atlanta (Athens & Rome), GA. **Local Programs:** *Atlanta Live*, Monday Tuesday Wednesday Thursday Friday 7:00 p.m. - 8:30 p.m.; *Transforming Truth*, Sunday Tuesday 11:00 a.m. 6:00 p.m.; *Music City Gospel Showcase*; *Breaking Barriers*; *The Gravedigger Show*, Saturday 4:30 p.m.; *God's True Worshippers*; *Transforming Truth*; *Restoring The Years*, Tuesday Thursday Friday Sunday 6:30 p.m. 10:30 a.m.; *Living In Victory*, Sunday 7:30 p.m. - 8:00 p.m.; *Babbie's House*, Monday Tuesday Wednesday Thursday Friday 4:00 p.m.; *Friends & Neighbors*, Monday Tuesday Wednesday Thursday Friday Saturday 6:30 a.m.; 4:30 p.m. 8:30 a.m.; *Gospel Touch*. **Wattage:** 1,700,000. **Ad Rates:** Noncommercial. **URL:** http://watc.tv/atlantalive.

9304 ■ WTBS-TV - 17
5675 Jimmy Carter Blvd., Ste. 740
Norcross, GA 30071
Email: info@wtbs26.com
Networks: Independent. **Owner:** Turner Broadcasting System Inc., One CNN Ctr., Atlanta, GA 30303, Ph: (404)827-1700, Fax: (404)827-2437. **Founded:** 1976. **Operating Hours**: Continuous. **ADI**: Atlanta (Athens & Rome), GA. **Ad Rates:** Noncommercial. **URL:** http://www.wtbs26.com.

OCILLA

S. Ga. Irwin Co. 50 mi. N. of Valdosta. Manufactures cottonseed oil, lumber, turpentine. Meat curing plant. Pine timber. Stock, poultry farms. Cotton, corn, peanuts.

9305 ■ Ocilla Star
Star
102 E Fourth St.
Ocilla, GA 31774
Phone: (229)468-5433
Fax: (229)468-5045
Newspaper with a Democratic orientation. **Founded:** 1903. **Freq:** Weekly (Wed.). **Print Method:** Offset. **Cols./Page:** 6. **Col. Width:** 21 1/2 nonpareils. **Col. Depth:** 298 agate lines. **Subscription Rates:** $36 Individuals in Country; $44 Out of country; $50 Out of state. **URL:** http://www.theocillastar.com/. **Formerly**: Star. **Mailing address:** PO Box 25, Ocilla, GA 31774. **Ad Rates:** BW $483.75; 4C $608.75; SAU $3; PCI $3. **Remarks:** Accepts advertising. **Circ:** 2300.

OXFORD

9306 ■ Oxford Journal of Anthropology
Oxford College of Emory University History and Social Sciences Division
100 Hamill St.
Oxford, GA 30054
Phone: (770)784-8888
Peer-reviewed journal covering research in anthropology as part of undergraduate studies of Department of Anthropology at Oxford College of Emory University. **Freq:** Annual. **Key Personnel:** Beth Haines, Managing Editor, phone: (770)784-8380; Wendy Dirks, Editor-in-Chief, phone: (770)784-8349. **Circ:** (Not Reported).

PARROTT

9307 ■ WACS-TV - 25
585 TV Tower Rd.
Parrott, GA 39877
Phone: (229)623-4883
Free: 800-222-4788
Email: ask@gpb.org
Format: Public TV. **Networks:** Public Broadcasting Service (PBS); Georgia Public Television. **Owner:** Georgia Public Broadcasting, 260 14th St. NW, Atlanta, GA 30318, Ph: (404)685-2400, Free: 800-222-6006. **Founded:** 1967. **Operating Hours**: 6 a.m.-midnight; 100% local. **ADI:** Columbus, GA (Opelika, AL). **Key Personnel:** Eddie Miller, Contact. **Ad Rates:** Noncommercial. **URL:** http://www.gpb.org.

PAULDING

9308 ■ The Paulding Neighbor
Neighbor Newspapers Inc.
4471 Jimmy Lee Smith Pky., Ste. 200 & 201C
Hiram, GA 30141
Phone: (770)445-0565
Publication E-mail: paulding@neighbornewspapers.com
Community newspaper. **Founded:** 1978. **Freq:** Weekly (Thurs.). **Print Method:** Offset. **Cols./Page:** 6. **Col. Depth:** 301 agate lines. **Key Personnel:** Tom Spigolon, Editor; Otis Brumby, III, General Manager. **USPS:** 406-910. **Subscription Rates:** $135.68 By mail outside the delivery area; $72.08 By mail outside the delivery area; 6 months; $36.57 By mail outside the delivery area; 3 months. **URL:** http://neighbornewspapers.com/; http://www.neighbornewspapers.com/nni_al?neighbor=paulding. **Ad Rates:** GLR $.58; BW $1,367.40; 4C $1,334.90; SAU $9; PCI $10.60. **Remarks:** Accepts advertising. **Circ:** Thurs. ♦**23874**.

PEACHTREE CITY

W. GA. Fayette Co. 25 mi. SW of Atlanta. Commercial and industrial areas. McIntosh Trail.

9309 ■ Aglaia
Phi Mu Fraternity
400 Westpark Dr.
Peachtree City, GA 30269
Phone: (770)632-2090
Fax: (770)632-2136
Publisher's E-mail: info@phimu.org
Magazine highlighting current events, news, alumnae achievements and success stories of the sorority. **Freq:** Quarterly. **Key Personnel:** Jackie Gilpin Isaacson, Editor. **Subscription Rates:** Members free. **URL:** http://digitaleditions.sheridan.com/publication/?m=22639&l=1. **Remarks:** Advertising not accepted. **Circ:** 100000.

9310 ■ Aglaia: The National Magazine for the Women of Phi Mu
Phi Mu
400 Westpark Dr.
Peachtree City, GA 30269
Phone: (770)632-2090
Fax: (770)632-2136
Publication E-mail: aglaia@phimu.org
College sorority magazine. **Freq:** Continuous. **Key Personnel:** Jackie Isaacson, Editor, Director, Communications, Editor. **Subscription Rates:** Included in membership. **URL:** http://www.phimu.org/alumnae/benefitsofphimu. **Circ:** 100000.

9311 ■ Contemporary Impressions
American Print Alliance
302 Larkspur Turn
Peachtree City, GA 30269-2210
Freq: Semiannual. **Subscription Rates:** $39 Nonmembers; $32 Members; $56 Institutions; $19 Students. **URL:** http://www.printalliance.org/alliance/al_subscribe.html. **Remarks:** Advertising not accepted. **Circ:** (Not Reported).

9312 ■ Contemporary Impressions: The Journal of the American Print Alliance
American Print Alliance
302 Larkspur Turn
Peachtree City, GA 30269-2210
Journal of critical writings on prints, computer prints, paperworks, and artists' books; includes one original print each year. **Freq:** Semiannual. **Key Personnel:** Carol Pulin, PhD, Director. **ISSN:** 1066--9434 (print). **Subscription Rates:** $39 Individuals; $32 Members; $56 Institutions; $19 Students. **URL:** http://www.printalliance.org; http://www.printalliance.org/alliance/al_subscribe.html. **Remarks:** Advertising accepted; rates available upon request. **Circ:** (Not Reported).

PEACHTREE CORNERS

9313 ■ PPSA Quarterly Review
Pulp and Paper Safety Association
15 Technology Pky. S
Peachtree Corners, GA 30092-8200
Phone: (770)209-7300
Publisher's E-mail: info@ppsa.org
Freq: Quarterly. **Subscription Rates:** Included in membership. **Alt. Formats:** PDF. **Remarks:** Advertising not accepted. **Circ:** (Not Reported).

9314 ■ TAPPI JOURNAL
Technical Association of the Pulp and Paper Industry
15 Technology Pky. S, Ste. 115
Peachtree Corners, GA 30092
Phone: (770)446-1400
Publisher's E-mail: outreach@tappi.org
Magazine on pulp and paper research, production, conversion, and packaging. **Freq:** Monthly. **Print**

Method: Offset. **Trim Size:** 8 1/8 x 10 7/8. **Cols./Page:** 3 and 2. **Col. Width:** 26 and 39 nonpareils. **Col. Depth:** 140 agate lines. **Key Personnel:** Monica Shaw, Director, Editorial. **ISSN:** 0734--1415 (print). **Subscription Rates:** $132 Members print + electronic; $29 By mail electronic; $14 Out of country electronic; $262 Nonmembers electronic; $376 Nonmembers print + electronic; free with membership. **URL:** http://www.tappi.org/Publications-Standards/TAPPI-Journal/Index. **Remarks:** Advertising accepted; rates available upon request. **Circ:** (Not Reported).

PELHAM

SW GA. Mitchell Co. 25 mi. NW of Thomasville. Residential.

9315 ■ WABW-TV - 14
4966 Hwy. 93
Pelham, GA 31779
Phone: (229)794-6501
Free: 800-222-4788
Email: ask@gpb.org
Owner: Georgia Public Broadcasting, 260 14th St. NW, Atlanta, GA 30318, Ph: (404)685-2400, Free: 800-222-6006. **Key Personnel:** Irmgard Jones, Contact. **URL:** http://www.gpb.org.

PERRY

9316 ■ AgAir Update: Ag Aviation's Newspaper
AgAir Update
475 Myrtle Field Rd.
Perry, GA 31069
Phone: (478)987-2250
Fax: (478)352-0025
Free: 888-987-2250
Publication serving the agricultural aircraft and the agricultural aviation industry. **Freq:** Monthly. **Key Personnel:** Bill Lavender, Editor; Ernest Eggler, Advertising Executive. **Subscription Rates:** $39 Individuals; $70 Two years; $19.95 Individuals 6 months. **URL:** http://www.agairupdate.com/. **Mailing address:** PO Box 850, Perry, GA 31069. **Remarks:** Accepts advertising. **Circ:** Combined ‡3000.

9317 ■ The Houston Home Journal
The Houston Home Journal
PO Box 1910
Perry, GA 31069
Phone: (478)987-1823
Publication E-mail: hhj@evansnewspapers.com
Community newspaper. **Freq:** Semiweekly. **Key Personnel:** Cheri Adams, Assistant; Daniel F. Evans, Editor; Kerri Wright, Accountant. **ISSN:** 1526--7393 (print). **Subscription Rates:** $25 Individuals online, 1 year; $60 Individuals print and online, 1 year (In County); $70 Out of state print and online, 1 year; $50 Individuals print and online, 1 year (In County), senior; 60 Out of state print and online, 1 year, senior; $30 Individuals print, 6 months (In County); $50 Individuals print, 1 year (In County); $45 Individuals print, 1 year (In County), senior; $60 Out of state print, 1 year. **URL:** http://hhjonline.com. **Formerly**: Houston Times-Journal; The Perry Times. **Remarks:** Accepts advertising. **Circ:** 8900.

9318 ■ WXKO-AM - 1150
PO Box 1410
Perry, GA 31069
Phone: (478)825-1150
Fax: (478)827-1273
Format: Religious; Ethnic. **Owner:** Roberts Communications Inc., 64 Commercial St., Rochester, NY 14614. **Founded:** 1951. **Formerly**: WFPM-AM. **Operating Hours**: 6 a.m.-sunset. **ADI**: Macon, GA. **Key Personnel:** Wanda Harvey, Office Mgr.; Sharon Wilson, Traffic Mgr.; Jarrett Reagan, Operations Mgr.; Rudy Carson, Sales Mgr.; Patricia Glass, Sales Mgr.; George Threatt, Operations Mgr. **Wattage**: 1,000 day; 072 night.

POOLER

9319 ■ Journal of Aesthetics and Art Criticism
American Society for Aesthetics
PO Box 915
Pooler, GA 31322
Phone: (912)748-9524
Publisher's E-mail: secretary-treasurer@aesthetics-online.org
Freq: Quarterly. **ISSN:** 0021- 8529 (print). **Subscription Rates:** $263 Institutions print or online; $316 Institutions print + online. **URL:** http://onlinelibrary.wiley.com/journal/10.1111/%28ISSN%291540-6245. **Remarks:** Accepts advertising. **Circ:** 1500.

QUITMAN

9320 ■ WSFB-AM
PO Box 632
Quitman, GA 31643-0632
Phone: (229)263-4373
Fax: (229)263-7693
Format: Contemporary Country; Soft Rock; Gospel; Easy Listening. **Networks:** Georgia Radio; NBC. **Owner:** Jim S. Chion, Rt. 2, Box 533, Tallahassee, FL 32311, Ph: (904)878-5746. **Founded:** 1957. **Key Personnel:** Jim S. Chion, Contact. **Wattage:** 1,000. **Ad Rates:** $4.90 for 30 seconds; $4.60-6.95 for 60 seconds.

REIDSVILLE

SE GA. Tattnall Co. 60 mi. W. of Savannah. Naval stores; cotton ginning. Pine timber. Agriculture. Tobacco, cotton, sweet potatoes.

9321 ■ The Tattnall Journal
The Tattnall Journal
PO Box 278
Reidsville, GA 30453
Phone: (912)557-6761
Fax: (912)557-4132
Publication E-mail: mail@tattnalljournal.com
Newspaper with Democratic orientation. **Freq:** Weekly (Thurs.). **Print Method:** Offset. **Cols./Page:** 6. **Col. Width:** 21 nonpareils. **Col. Depth:** 294 agate lines. **Key Personnel:** Russell J. Rhoden, Owner, Publisher; Allison Cobb, Editor; Lillian Durrence, General Manager. **URL:** http://www.tattnalljournal.com. **Circ:** ‡4100.

9322 ■ WRBX-FM - 104.1
125 Friar Tuck Cir.
Reidsville, GA 30453
Phone: (912)557-4140
Fax: (912)557-4140
Email: wrbx@wrbxfm.com
Format: Southern Gospel. **Founded:** 1994. **Operating Hours:** 6:05 a.m. - 9:05 p.m. Monday - Friday; 8:05 a.m. - 11:00 p.m. Saturday; 8:05 a.m. - 6:30 p.m. Sunday. **Key Personnel:** Keith Register, Gen. Mgr. **Wattage:** 4,900 ERP. **Ad Rates:** Advertising accepted; rates available upon request. **URL:** http://wrbxfm.com.

9323 ■ WTNL-AM - 1390
PO Box 69
Reidsville, GA 30453
Phone: (912)557-4140
Fax: (912)557-4140
Email: wrbxwtnl@windstream.net
Format: Southern Gospel. **Networks:** USA Radio. **Founded:** 1976. **Operating Hours:** 6:00 a.m.-5:30 p.m. **Key Personnel:** Keith Register, Dept. Head. **Wattage:** 500. **Ad Rates:** $3-4 for 30 seconds. **URL:** http://www.wrbx.org.

REYNOLDS

9324 ■ Flint Cable TV
PO Box 669
Reynolds, GA 31076
Phone: (478)847-3101
Fax: (478)847-2010
Free: 855-593-3278
Founded: Sept. 06, 2006. **Cities Served:** 33 channels. **URL:** http://flintrvr.com.

RICHLAND

SW GA. Stewart Co. 38 mi. SE of Columbus. Lumber mill; box factories. Pine, hardwood timber. Dairy, poultry, fruit farms. Pecans, peanuts, cotton, corn.

9325 ■ Stewart-Webster Journal: Serving Georgia's Fastest Growing Tourist Area
Star Mercury Publishing Co.
106 Broad St.
Richland, GA 31825-0250
Phone: (229)887-3674
Fax: (229)887-2800
Publication E-mail: swjpc@bellsouth.net
Community newspaper. **Freq:** Weekly (Thurs.). **Print Method:** Offset. **Trim Size:** 6 x 21 1/2. **Cols./Page:** 6. **Col. Width:** 20 nonpareils. **Col. Depth:** 21.5 agate lines. **Key Personnel:** Ron Provencher, Publisher, Contact; Linda Provencher, Editor, phone: (912)887-3675. **Subscription Rates:** $21 Individuals; $28 Other countries; $38 Out of state; $23 Individuals; $30 Other countries. **URL:** http://www.swjpc.com/v2/content.aspx?IsHome=1&MemberID=1279&ID=1884; http://www.swjpc.com/1884/1279/1/online-edition-pages. **Mailing address:** PO Box 250, Richland, GA 31825-0250. **Ad Rates:** GLR $.14; 4C $614.40; SAU $4; PCI $4; BW $516. **Remarks:** Accepts advertising. **Circ:** ‡3000.

RINCON

9326 ■ Effingham Herald
Effingham Herald
586 S Columbia Ave., Ste. 13
Rincon, GA 31326
Phone: (912)826-5012
Fax: (912)826-0381
Newspaper. **Founded:** 1908. **Freq:** Semiweekly Tues. & Fri. **Print Method:** Offset. **Trim Size:** 6 x 21 1/2. **Cols./Page:** 6. **Col. Width:** 26 nonpareils. **Col. Depth:** 294 agate lines. **Subscription Rates:** $35 Individuals; $9.75 Institutions for 3 months; $18.50 Individuals for 6 months. **URL:** http://www.effinghamherald.net/. **Formerly**: Herald; The Effingham Herald. **Ad Rates:** GLR $.28; BW $945; 4C $1,095; SAU $7.50; PCI $7.50. **Remarks:** Advertising accepted; rates available upon request. **Circ:** 4300.

WSLT-FM - See Statesboro, GA

RINGGOLD

9327 ■ Catoosa County News
Catoosa County News
7513 Nashville St.
Ringgold, GA 30736
Community newspaper. **Freq:** Weekly (Wed.). **Key Personnel:** Don Stilwell, Publisher; Becky McDaniel, Editor. **Subscription Rates:** $26.75 Individuals Catoosa County; $41.60 Individuals Georgia; $40 Individuals outside Georgia. **URL:** http://www.northwestgeorgianews.com/catwalkchatt/news/catoosa/. **Ad Rates:** BW $95; 4C $250; SAU $4.20; PCI $10.81. **Remarks:** Advertising accepted; rates available upon request. **Circ:** Mon.-Fri. ★**17419**.

9328 ■ The Northeast Square Dancer Magazine
E & PJ Enterprises
782 Jays Way
Ringgold, GA 30736
Phone: (706)935-5605
Publication E-mail: nsd@squaredance.ws
Hobby magazine containing articles, dates and location of dances, festivals, conventions, workshops, and meetings for square, round, clogging, and country/western dancers. Available online only. **Founded:** Aug. 1951. **Freq:** Monthly. **Key Personnel:** Ed Juaire, Editor; Pat Juaire, Manager, Advertising. **ISSN:** 1044-2928 (print). **Alt. Formats:** Download. **URL:** http://www.squaredance.ws/. **Remarks:** Accepts advertising. **Circ:** ‡4000.

RIVERDALE

SW GA. Clayton Co. 14 mi. S. of Atlanta.

9329 ■ Fashion Insider
Fashion Insider
1313 Revelstoke Cove
Riverdale, GA 30296
Publication E-mail: info@thefashioninsider.com
Magazine featuring the latest news on fashion, beauty, and accessories. **Key Personnel:** Marcellous Jones, Editor-in-Chief. **URL:** http://www.thefashioninsider.com. **Circ:** (Not Reported).

ROBINS AFB

9330 ■ Citizen Airman: The Official Magazine of the Air Force Reserve
Air Force Reserve Command
255 Richard Ray Blvd., Ste. 137
255 Richard Ray Blvd., Ste. 137
Robins AFB, GA 31098
Phone: (478)327-1770

Circulation: ★ = AAM; △ or • = BPA; ♦ = CAC; ❑ = VAC; ⊕ = PO Statement; ‡ = Publisher's Report; Boldface figures = sworn; Light figures = estimated.

Fax: (478)327-0878
Official Magazine of the Air Force Reserve. **Freq:** Bi-monthly February, April, June, August, October and December. **Print Method:** Offset. Uses mats. **Trim Size:** 8 1/8 x 10 7/8. **Cols./Page:** 3. **Col. Width:** 13.6 picas. **Col. Depth:** 9 3/4 inches. **Key Personnel:** Cliff Tyler, Managing Editor; Bo Joyner, Associate Editor. **ISSN:** 0887--9680 (print). **Subscription Rates:** $19 Individuals; $26.60 Other countries; Free to reservists, individual mobilization augmentees, members of the active Guard and Reserve and air reserve technicians. **URL:** http://www.citamn.afrc.af.mil. **Formerly**: The Air Reservist. **Remarks:** Advertising not accepted. **Circ:** Controlled 65000.

9331 ■ Robins Rev-Up
The Daily Sun
Robins Office of Public Affairs
620 9th St., Bldg. 905
Robins AFB, GA 31098
Phone: (478)468-2137
Fax: (478)468-9597
Military newspaper (tabloid). **Freq:** Weekly (Fri.). **Print Method:** Offset. **Trim Size:** 11 3/4 x 14. **Cols./Page:** 5. **Col. Width:** 2 1/16 inches. **Col. Depth:** 13 inches. **Key Personnel:** Lanorris Askew, Editor, phone: (478)472-0806. **Alt. Formats:** PDF. **URL:** http://www.robins.af.mil/library/rev.asp. **Ad Rates:** BW $1609; 4C $1804; SAU $12.43; PCI $12.43. **Remarks:** Accepts advertising. **Circ:** Free ‡20000.

ROCKMART

NW GA. Polk Co. 10 mi. E. of Cedartown.

9332 ■ WZOT-AM - 1220
602 Elm St.
Rockmart, GA 30153
Phone: (770)684-7848
Fax: (770)748-1549
Format: Gospel. **Networks:** NBC; CNN Radio. **Formerly**: WPLK-AM. **Operating Hours**: 6 a.m.-8 p.m.; 10% network, 90% local. **Wattage**: 500. **Ad Rates:** $5.25-8 for 30 seconds; $6.75-10 for 60 seconds. **URL:** http://pro.wzot-am.tritonflex.com/page.php?page_id=86.

ROME

NW GA. Floyd Co. On Coosa River, 68 mi. NW of Atlanta. Museums, Berry Waterwheel. Shorter College; Floyd Junior College; Berry College. Pine, hardwood timber; stone quarry. Manufactures tiles, plastic products, cotton textiles, steel wire, furniture, woodwork, fertilizer, flour, valves, hand trucks, aluminum die casting, lumber, boxes, paper, paper products, transformers, carpets, carpet yarn. Agriculture.

9333 ■ Magnolia
News Publishing Co.
305 E 6th Ave.
Rome, GA 30161
Fax: (706)232-9632
Magazine featuring women of Northwest Georgia. **Key Personnel:** Charlotte Atkins, Editor; Mike Schuttinga, Director, Advertising. **Subscription Rates:** Free. **URL:** http://magnoliawoman.com. **Remarks:** Accepts advertising. **Circ:** (Not Reported).

9334 ■ Rome News-Tribune
News Publishing Co.
PO Box 1633
Rome, GA 30161
Phone: (706)290-5252
General newspaper. **Freq:** Daily (morn.). **Print Method:** Offset. **Trim Size:** 13 3/4 x 22 3/4. **Cols./Page:** 6. **Col. Width:** 2 1/16 inches. **Col. Depth:** 21 1/4 inches. **Key Personnel:** Charlotte Atkins, Editor; Otis Raybon, Publisher; Mike Schuttinga, Director, Advertising; Jamie Bennett, Manager, Circulation; Dan Montgomery, Manager, Circulation; Joe Morgan, Business Manager. **USPS:** 470-320. **URL:** http://www.northwestgeorgianews.com/rome. **Ad Rates:** GLR $1.20; BW $2139; 4C $2464; SAU $16.78; PCI $19.33. **Remarks:** Accepts advertising. **Circ:** Mon.-Sat. ★**17419**, Sun. ★**18153**.

9335 ■ WGPB-FM - 97.7
415 E 3rd Ave.
Rome, GA 30161-3241
Phone: (706)204-2276
Free: 800-222-4788
Email: ask@gpb.org
Format: Public Radio. **Owner:** Georgia Public Broadcasting, 260 14th St. NW, Atlanta, GA 30318, Ph: (404)685-2400, Free: 800-222-6006. **Key Personnel:** Ellen Reinhardt, Contact; John Sepulvado, Contact. **URL:** http://www.gpb.org.

9336 ■ WKCX-FM - 97.7
710 Turner McCall Blvd.
Rome, GA 30165
Phone: (706)291-9766
Fax: (706)291-9706
Email: mills@k98radio.com
Format: Adult Contemporary. **Networks:** CNN Radio; Jones Satellite. **Owner:** Briar Creek Broadcasting Corp., at above address. **Founded:** 1966. **Operating Hours**: Continuous. **ADI**: Atlanta (Athens & Rome), GA. **Key Personnel:** Mills Fitzner, Gen. Mgr. **Wattage**: 25,000 ERP. **Ad Rates:** Noncommercial. **Mailing address:** PO Box 1546, Rome, GA 30165.

9337 ■ WLAQ-AM - 1410
Two Mt. Alto Rd. SW
Rome, GA 30165-4142
Phone: (706)232-7767
Email: wlaq@comcast.net
Format: News; Talk; Sports. **Networks:** CBS. **Owner:** Cripple Creek Broadcasting Co., 2 Mount Alto Rd. SW, Rome, GA 30165-4142. **Founded:** 1947. **Operating Hours**: 5 a.m.-1 a.m. Mon.-Fri.; 6 a.m.-midnight Sun. **ADI**: Atlanta (Athens & Rome), GA. **Key Personnel:** Jerry Lee, Chairman. **Wattage**: 1,000. **Ad Rates:** $4.75-5.25 for 15 seconds; $7.50-12 for 30 seconds; $8.50-13 for 60 seconds. **URL:** http://www.wlaq1410.com.

9338 ■ WQTU-FM - 102.3
20 John Davenport Dr.
Rome, GA 30165
Phone: (706)291-9496
Email: sales@q102rome.com
Format: Adult Contemporary. **Networks:** Independent. **Founded:** 1946. **Formerly**: WRGA-FM. **Operating Hours**: Continuous; 100% local. **ADI**: Atlanta (Athens & Rome), GA. **Key Personnel:** Kevin Daniels, Dir. of Programs, kevind@rrpga.com; Cheryl Scott, Mgr.; Rick Bradley, Dir. of Production, rickb@rrpga.com; Randy Quick, Gen. Mgr., randyq@south107.com. **Wattage**: 1,100. **Ad Rates:** $18-30 for 60 seconds. Combined advertising rates available with WRGA-AM and WTSH-FM. **URL:** http://www.q102rome.com.

9339 ■ WRGA-AM - 1470
20 John Davenport Dr.
Rome, GA 30165
Phone: (706)291-9496
Email: news@wrgarome.com
Format: News; Talk. **Networks:** ABC. **Founded:** 1929. **Operating Hours**: Continuous. **ADI**: Atlanta (Athens & Rome), GA. **Key Personnel:** Randy Quick, Gen. Mgr., randyq@south107.com; Cheryl Scott, Bus. Mgr., cheryls@south107.com; Clarke Johnson, Prog. Dir., clarkej@south107.com. **Wattage**: 5,000. **Ad Rates:** Advertising accepted; rates available upon request. **URL:** http://www.wrganews.com.

9340 ■ WROM-AM - 710
1105 Calhoun Ave.
Rome, GA 30161
Phone: (706)234-7171
Fax: (706)234-8043
Format: Religious; Southern Gospel. **Owner:** LGV Broadcasting, Inc., at above address. **Founded:** 1946. **Operating Hours**: Sunrise-sunset. **ADI**: Atlanta (Athens & Rome), GA. **Key Personnel:** Robert Vines, Sales Mgr., Owner. **Wattage**: 1,000. **Ad Rates:** $8-10 for 30 seconds; $10-15 for 60 seconds.

9341 ■ WSRM-FM - 95.3
20 John Davenport Dr.
Rome, GA 30165
Phone: (706)291-9496
Email: news@wrgarome.com
Format: News; Talk. **Key Personnel:** Randy Quick, Gen. Mgr., randyq@south107.com; Kevin Daniels, Operations Mgr. **URL:** http://www.wrgarome.com.

9342 ■ WTSH-AM - 1360
20 John Davenport Dr.
Rome, GA 30165
Phone: (706)291-9496
Email: sales@south107.com
Format: News; Sports. **Networks:** NBC; Unistar. **Owner:** Radio Data Group, Inc., 2070 Chain Bridge Rd., Ste. 105, Vienna, VA 22182, Ph: (703)748-2800, Fax: (703)748-2133. **Founded:** 1964. **Formerly**: WIYN-AM. **Operating Hours**: 6 a.m.-6 p.m.; 20% network; 80% local. **ADI**: Atlanta (Athens & Rome), GA. **Key Personnel:** Randy Quick, Gen. Mgr., randyq@south107.com; Tony McIntosh, Gen. Sales Mgr., tonym@south107.com. **Wattage**: 500. **Ad Rates:** Noncommercial. **URL:** http://www.south107.com.

9343 ■ WTSH-FM - 107.1
20 John Davenport Dr.
Rome, GA 30165
Phone: (706)291-9496
Email: sales@south107.com
Format: Country. **Networks:** Unistar. **Owner:** Southern Broadcasting, at above address. **Founded:** 1962. **Formerly**: WIYN-FM. **Operating Hours**: Continuous. **ADI**: Atlanta (Athens & Rome), GA. **Key Personnel:** Randy Quick, Gen. Mgr., randyq@south107.com. **Wattage**: 50,000. **Ad Rates:** Advertising accepted; rates available upon request. **URL:** http://www.south107.com.

ROSWELL

Fulton Co.

Alpharetta Neighbor - See Alpharetta

9344 ■ Atlanta Tribune: The Magazine
L & L Communications Inc.
875 Old Roswell Rd., Ste. C-100
Roswell, GA 30076-1660
Phone: (770)587-0501
Fax: (770)642-6501
Publisher's E-mail: info@atlantatribune.com
Minority business magazine. **Freq:** Monthly. **Print Method:** Web offset. **Trim Size:** 7 x 10. **Cols./Page:** 4. **Col. Width:** 2 1/4 inches. **Col. Depth:** 10 inches. **Key Personnel:** Patricia Lottier, Publisher; Kamille D. Whittaker, Associate Editor; Katrice L. Mines, Editor. **Subscription Rates:** $50 Individuals /year. **Ad Rates:** 4C $5000. **Remarks:** Accepts advertising. **Circ:** ‡35000.

9345 ■ Pro Trucker
Ramp Publishing Group
PO Box 549
Roswell, GA 30077-0549
Free: 800-878-0311
Trucking industry magazine. **Freq:** Monthly. **Key Personnel:** Andy Shefsky, Publisher. **Ad Rates:** BW $3,495; 4C $3,595. **Remarks:** Accepts advertising. **Circ:** (Not Reported).

9346 ■ Roswell Neighbor
Neighbor Newspapers Inc.
10930 Crabapple Rd., Ste. 9
Roswell, GA 30075
Phone: (770)993-7400
Fax: (770)518-6062
Publication E-mail: nfulton@neighbornewspapers.com
Community newspaper. **Freq:** Weekly (Wed.). **Key Personnel:** Otis A. Brumby, Jr., Publisher; Otis Brumby, III, General Manager. **URL:** http://neighbornewspapers.com/nni_al?neighbor=roswell&leaderboardtop=251&leaderboardbot=252&pillowtop=399&pillowbot=254&tt=255&box=256. **Remarks:** Accepts advertising. **Circ:** Non-paid ‡19457.

ROYSTON

NE GA. Madison Co. 9 mi. S. of Carnesville.

9347 ■ WBIC-AM - 810
259 Turner St.
Royston, GA 30662
Phone: (706)246-0059
Fax: (706)245-0890
Email: studio@familycountry.com
Format: Talk. **Networks:** CBS. **Owner:** Oconee River Broadcasting, LLC, 1720 Epps Bridge Pky., Ste. 108-303, Athens, GA 30606. **Founded:** 1970. **Formerly**: WBLW-AM. **Operating Hours**: Continuous. **Key Personnel:** KJ Allen, Gen. Mgr., kjallen@familycountry.com; Lynn Woodall, Sales Mgr., Office Mgr., lynn@familycountry.com. **Wattage**: 230 KW. **Ad Rates:** $5 for 30 seconds; $7 for 60 seconds. **URL:** http://newstalk810.com.

SAINT MARYS

9348 ■ Tribune & Georgian
Community Newspapers Inc.
PO Box 6960
Saint Marys, GA 31558
Phone: (912)882-4927
Fax: (912)882-6519
Publisher's E-mail: dnesmith@cninewspapers.com
Community newspaper. **Founded:** 1950. **Freq:** Weekly (Thurs.). **Print Method:** Offset. **Cols./Page:** 6. **Col. Width:** 11 picas. **Col. Depth:** 21 1/2 inches. **Key Personnel:** Emily Heglund, Editor; Jill Helton, Publisher; Brad Spaulding, Director, Marketing. **Subscription Rates:** $29.99 Individuals in county; $59.99 Out of area; $54.98 Two years In-County. **URL:** http://www.tribune-georgian.com. **Formerly**: Camden County Tribune; Southeast Georgian. **Remarks:** Advertising accepted; rates available upon request. **Circ:** Wed. ‡8000, Fri. ‡7000.

9349 ■ WECC-FM - 89.3
5465 Hwy. 40 E
Saint Marys, GA 31558
Fax: (912)882-9322
Email: mail@thelighthousefm.org
Format: Religious. **Key Personnel:** Paul Hafer, Gen. Mgr., President, paul@thelighthousefm.org; Mark McMillan, Operations Mgr., mark@thelighthousefm.org. **Ad Rates:** Noncommercial. **URL:** http://www.thelighthousefm.org.

SAINT SIMONS ISLAND

E. GA. Glynn Co. Island off E. coast of Glynn Co.

9350 ■ KSNX-FM - 93.5
130 Hampton Point Dr.
Saint Simons Island, GA 31522-3031
Phone: (813)948-2554
Format: Oldies. **Owner:** Petracom of Holbrook L.L.C., at above address. **Operating Hours**: Continuous. **Key Personnel:** Bob Funk, Gen. Sales Mgr. **Wattage:** 25,000. **Ad Rates:** Advertising accepted; rates available upon request.

SANDERSVILLE

EC GA. Washington Co. 45 mi. NE of Macon.

9351 ■ Northland Communications Corp.
125 Church St., Ste. F
Sandersville, GA 31082
Phone: (478)552-2905
Fax: (478)552-0532
Formerly: Northland Cable Television. **Cities Served:** 35 channels. **Mailing address:** PO Box 1118, Sandersville, GA 31082.

9352 ■ WSNT-AM - 1490
PO Box 150
Sandersville, GA 31082
Phone: (478)552-5182
Fax: (478)553-0800
Email: info@waco100fm.com
Format: Sports. **Networks:** ESPN Radio. **Owner:** WSNT, Inc., at above address. **Founded:** 1960. **Operating Hours:** Continuous; 90% network, 10% local. **ADI**: Macon, GA. **Wattage**: 1,000. **Ad Rates:** $5-10 for 30 seconds; $7.50-12.50 for 60 seconds.

9353 ■ WSNT-FM - 99.9
312 Morningside Dr.
Sandersville, GA 31082
Phone: (478)552-5182
Fax: (478)553-0800
Format: Country. **Networks:** ABC. **Founded:** 1956. **Operating Hours**: Continuous; 90% network, 10% local. **ADI:** Macon, GA. **Key Personnel:** Richard Lee, Dir. of Programs. **Wattage**: 6,000. **Ad Rates:** Noncommercial. CBR WSNT-AM. **Mailing address:** PO Box 150, Sandersville, GA 31082. **URL:** http://www.waco100dev.cogentes.com.

SAVANNAH

SE GA. Chatham Co. On Savannah River, 18 mi. from Atlantic Ocean, 254 mi. SE of Atlanta. Port of entry. Armstrong State College; Savannah State College; Savannah College of Art and Design. Resort. Restored historic district. Shipyards. Fisheries. Timber. Cotton and naval stores market. Manufactures airplanes, injection molded plastics, plywood, sugar, table top conveyors, lumber, fertilizer, paper bags, cottonseed products, roofing metal, steel products, fuel oil, paint, rosin oils, burlap and bagging, asphalt, wire fencing, gypsum products.

9354 ■ The Georgia Historical Quarterly
Georgia Historical Society
104 W Gaston St.
Savannah, GA 31401
Phone: (912)651-2125
Fax: (912)651-2831
Free: 877-424-4789
Historical magazine. **Freq:** Quarterly. **Print Method:** Uses mats. Letterpress and offset. **Cols./Page:** 1. **Col. Width:** 51 nonpareils. **Col. Depth:** 91 agate lines. **Key Personnel:** Dr. Glenn McNair, Editor, phone: (740)427-5325; Stan Deaton, Managing Editor. **ISSN:** 0016--8297 (print). **URL:** http://georgiahistory.com/publications-scholarship/the-georgia-historical-quarterly. **Ad Rates:** BW $300. **Remarks:** Accepts advertising. **Circ:** ‡3500.

9355 ■ Inhalation Toxicology
Taylor & Francis Inc.
c/o Donald E. Gardner, PhD, Ed.-in-Ch.
11 Monastery Rd. W
Savannah, GA 31411
Publisher's E-mail: academicviprequests@informa.com
Peer-reviewed journal promoting an improved understanding of the respiratory system in disease and health and health risk associated with airborne chemicals. **Freq:** 14 issues published per year. **Print Method:** Offset. **Trim Size:** 7 x 10. **Key Personnel:** Donald E. Gardner, PhD, Editor-in-Chief; Dr. Mitchell Cohen, Associate Editor. **ISSN:** 0895--8378 (print); **EISSN:** 1091--7691 (electronic). **Subscription Rates:** $3149 Institutions online; $3315 Institutions print and online. **URL:** http://www.tandfonline.com/toc/iiht20/current. **Remarks:** Accepts advertising. **Circ:** (Not Reported).

9356 ■ The Riverbank News
Morris Newspaper of California
27 Abercorn St.
Savannah, GA 31401
Phone: (912)233-1281
Fax: (912)232-4639
Newspaper. **Freq:** Weekly (Wed.). **Print Method:** Offset. **Cols./Page:** 8. **Col. Width:** 1 1/2 inches. **Col. Depth:** 21 inches. **Key Personnel:** Marg Jackson, Editor. **Subscription Rates:** $31 Individuals; $26 Individuals senior citizens; $38 Out of country plus postage; $46 Two years; $38 Two years senior citizens. **URL:** http://www.theriverbanknews.com. **Remarks:** Advertising accepted; rates available upon request. **Circ:** 1300.

9357 ■ Savannah Jewish News
Savannah Jewish Federation
5111 Abercorn St.
Savannah, GA 31405
Phone: (912)355-8111
Jewish newspaper covering local, national, and world news. **Freq:** 10/year. **Print Method:** Offset. **Trim Size:** 10 x 14. **Cols./Page:** 4. **Col. Width:** 14 picas. **Col. Depth:** 12 3/4 agate lines. **Subscription Rates:** Free. **URL:** http://www.savj.org/savannah-jewish-news. **Ad Rates:** BW $600; SAU $18. **Remarks:** Accepts advertising. **Circ:** ‡1700.

9358 ■ Savannah Morning News
Savannah Morning News
PO Box 1088
Savannah, GA 31402-1088
Phone: (912)236-0271
Fax: (912)525-0796
Publication E-mail: letted@savannahnow.com
General newspaper. **Freq:** Mon.-Sun. **Print Method:** Offset. **Cols./Page:** 6. **Col. Width:** 24 nonpareils. **Col. Depth:** 301 agate lines. **Key Personnel:** Michael Traynor, Publisher, phone: (912)652-0268; Gale Baldwin, Managing Editor, phone: (912)652-0300; Richard Reeves, Director, Advertising, phone: (912)652-0243; Susan Catron, Executive Editor, phone: (912)652-0327; Chris Thompson, Administrator, phone: (912)652-0301. **Subscription Rates:** $18.63 Individuals /month - 7 Day Delivery; $12.94 Individuals /month - 3 Day Delivery; $11.63 Individuals /month - Sunday Only Delivery; $99.50 Individuals online only. **URL:** http://www.savannahnow.com. **Remarks:** Accepts advertising. **Circ:** Mon.-Fri. ⋆**52422**, Sun. ⋆**65475**, Sat. ⋆**51484**.

9359 ■ The Savannah Tribune
Savannah Tribune Inc.
1805 Martin Luther King, Jr. Blvd.
Savannah, GA 31401
Phone: (912)233-6128
Fax: (912)233-6140
Black community newspaper. **Freq:** Weekly (Wed.). **Print Method:** Offset. **Trim Size:** 13 x 21 1/2. **Cols./Page:** 6. **Col. Width:** 2 inches. **Col. Depth:** 21 1/2 inches. **Key Personnel:** Shirley B. James, Editor; Marius Davis, Managing Editor. **ISSN:** 1086--2285 (print). **Alt. Formats:** PDF. **Ad Rates:** GLR $.86; PCI $15. **Remarks:** Accepts advertising. **Circ:** Paid ‡8000, Free ‡8000.

9360 ■ The South
Bad Ink
116-A Bull St.
Savannah, GA 31401
Phone: (912)236-5501
Fax: (912)236-5524
Publication E-mail: info@thesouthmag.com
Lifestyle magazine. **Freq:** Bimonthly. **Key Personnel:** Michael Brooks, Creative Director, Publisher; Lauren Hunsberger, Managing Editor. **Subscription Rates:** $19.99 Individuals 1 year; $29 Individuals 2 years; $4.95 Individuals 1 year, digital. **URL:** http://thesouthmag.com. **Remarks:** Advertising accepted; rates available upon request. **Circ:** 20000.

9361 ■ Southern Poetry Review
Armstrong State University
11935 Abercorn St.
Savannah, GA 31419-1909
Phone: (912)344-2576
Fax: (912)344-3417
Free: 800-633-2349
Publisher's E-mail: admissions.info@armstrong.edu
Journal covering poetry and literature worldwide. **Freq:** Semiannual. **Trim Size:** 6 x 9. **Cols./Page:** 1. **Key Personnel:** Robert Parham, M.A., Editor; James Smith, Associate Editor; Tony Morris, Managing Editor. **ISSN:** 0038--447X (print). **Subscription Rates:** $18 Institutions; $14 Individuals; $7 Single issue. **Alt. Formats:** Microform. **URL:** http://southernpoetryreview.org. **Remarks:** Advertising not accepted. **Circ:** Controlled 1000.

9362 ■ WAEV-FM - 97.3
245 Alfred St.
Savannah, GA 31408
Phone: (912)964-7794
Free: 800-543-3548
Email: info@973kissfm.com
Format: Contemporary Hit Radio (CHR). **Networks:** Unistar. **Owner:** iHeartMedia Inc., 200 E Basse Rd., San Antonio, TX 78209, Ph: (210)832-3314. **Founded:** 1978. **Operating Hours**: Continuous; 1% network, 99% local. **ADI**: Savannah, GA. **Wattage**: 100,000. **Ad Rates:** $30-70 per unit. Combined advertising rates available with WYKZ. **URL:** http://www.973kissfm.com//main.html.

9363 ■ WBMQ-AM - 630
PO Box 876
Savannah, GA 31498-6901
Phone: (912)897-1529
Fax: (912)897-9795
Format: Talk; Sports; Oldies. **Networks:** CBS. **Owner:** Radio Southeast, at above address. **Founded:** 1939. **Formerly**: WKBX-AM. **Operating Hours**: Continuous. **ADI**: Savannah, GA. **Wattage**: 5,000. **Ad Rates:** $7-12 for 30 seconds; $9-16 for 60 seconds.

9364 ■ WEAS-AM - 900
214 Television Cir.
Savannah, GA 31406
Email: thefan@weas.com
Format: Sports. **Founded:** 1950. **ADI:** Savannah, GA. **Key Personnel:** M.B. Rivers, President; Rick Whitson, Gen. Mgr.; Ray Williams, Operations Mgr. **Wattage**: 4,350 day; 152 night. **Ad Rates:** $7-10 for 30 seconds; $9-12 for 60 seconds. **URL:** http://www.900theticket.com.

9365 ■ W43CT - 43
PO Box A
Santa Ana, CA 92711
Phone: (714)832-2950
Free: 888-731-1000

Circulation: ⋆ = AAM; △ or • = BPA; ♦ = CAC; ❑ = VAC; ⊕ = PO Statement; ‡ = Publisher's Report; Boldface figures = sworn; Light figures = estimated.

Email: comments@tbn.org
Owner: Trinity Broadcasting Network Inc., PO Box A, Santa Ana, CA 92711, Ph: (714)832-2950, Free: 888-731-1000. **URL:** http://www.tbn.org.

9366 ■ WGCO-FM - 98.3
401 Mall Blvd., Ste. 101 D
Savannah, GA 31406
Phone: (912)351-9830
Fax: (912)352-4821
Free: 866-465-0983
Format: Oldies. **Owner:** Adventure Radio Group, 401 Mall Blvd., Ste. 101D, Savannah, GA 31406. **Founded:** 1973. **Operating Hours:** Continuous. **ADI:** Savannah, GA. **Key Personnel:** Claire Beverly, News Dir., cbeverly@adventureradio.fm; Jon Robbins, Operations Mgr., jrobbins@adventureradio.fm; Mark Halverson, Dir. of Mktg., Mktg. Mgr., mhalverson@adventureradio.fm. **Wattage:** 100,000. **Ad Rates:** $30-50 for 30 seconds; $30-50 for 60 seconds. **URL:** http://www.983hank.com.

9367 ■ WGSA-TV - 13
401 Mall Blvd., Ste. 201-B
Savannah, GA 31406
Phone: (912)692-8000
Fax: (912)692-0400
Format: Commercial TV. **Networks:** United Paramount Network. **Owner:** Southern TV Corp., 401 Mall Blvd., Ste. 201-B, Savannah, GA 31406, Ph: (912)692-8000, Fax: (912)692-0400. **Founded:** 1991. **Formerly:** WUBI-TV. **Operating Hours:** Continuous. **ADI:** Savannah, GA. **Key Personnel:** Dan L. Johnson, CEO, danjohnson@wssa.tv. **Wattage:** 1,000,000. **Ad Rates:** Advertising accepted; rates available upon request. **URL:** http://www.wgsa.tv.

9368 ■ WHCJ-FM - 90.3
PO Box 20484
Savannah, GA 31404
Phone: (912)358-4233
Email: whcj@savannahstate.edu
Format: Public Radio; Eclectic; Educational. **Owner:** Savannah State University, 3219 College St., Savannah, GA 31404, Ph: (912)358-4338, Fax: (912)356-2998. **Founded:** 1975. **Operating Hours:** Continuous. **ADI:** Savannah, GA. **Key Personnel:** Grace Curry, Asst. Dir. **Wattage:** 6,000. **Ad Rates:** Noncommercial. **URL:** http://www.savannahstate.edu/academic-affairs/whcj-contact.shtml.

9369 ■ WIXV-FM - 95.5
PO Box 876
Savannah, GA 31401
Phone: (912)961-9000
Fax: (912)961-7070
Format: Album-Oriented Rock (AOR); News. **Simulcasts:** WCBS. **Networks:** CNN Radio. **Owner:** Radio Southeast, at above address. **Founded:** 1972. **Formerly:** WSGF-FM. **Operating Hours:** Continuous. **ADI:** Savannah, GA. **Key Personnel:** Jay Sinclair, Music Dir. **Wattage:** 98,000 ERP. **Ad Rates:** Advertising accepted; rates available upon request. $40-55 per unit. **URL:** http://www.rockofsavannah.net/.

9370 ■ WIZA-AM - 1450
234 Falligant Ave
Savannah, GA 31410
Phone: (912)236-9926
Fax: (912)236-3832
Format: Religious. **Networks:** ABC. **Owner:** Inter-Urban Broadcasting, 8701 S Kimbark, Chicago, IL 60619, Ph: (312)374-9200. **Founded:** 1988. **Formerly:** WSAI-AM. **Operating Hours:** Continuous; 20% network, 80% local. **Wattage:** 1,000. **Ad Rates:** $10-19 for 30 seconds; $12-24 for 60 seconds. **Mailing address:** PO Box 858, Waycross, GA 31502. **URL:** http://ecorp.sos.ga.gov/BusinessSearch/BusinessInformation?businessId=1747609&businessType=Domestic%20Limited%20Liability%20Company.

9371 ■ WJCL-FM - 96.5
214 Television Cir.
Savannah, GA 31406
Phone: (912)961-9000
Fax: (912)961-6000
Free: 866-999-9650
Format: Country. **Owner:** Cumulus Broadcasting Inc., 3280 Peachtree Rd. NW, Ste. 2300, Atlanta, GA 30305-2447, Ph: (404)949-0700, Fax: (404)949-0740. **Founded:** 1972. **Operating Hours:** Continuous. **ADI:** Savannah, GA. **Wattage:** 100,000. **Ad Rates:** Noncommercial. **URL:** http://www.nashfm965.com.

9372 ■ WJCL-TV - 22
1375 Chatham Pkwy., 3rd Fl.
Savannah, GA 31405
Phone: (912)925-0022
Fax: (912)921-2235
Networks: ABC. **Owner:** New Vision Television, Inc., 11766 Wilshire Blvd., Ste. 405, Los Angeles, CA 90025, Ph: (310)478-3200, Fax: (310)478-3222. **Founded:** 1970. **Operating Hours:** Continuous. **ADI:** Savannah, GA. **Key Personnel:** Jason Usry, Dir. of Mktg., jusry@thecoastalsource.com. **Wattage:** 3,800,000 ERP. **Ad Rates:** Noncommercial. **URL:** http://wjcl.com.

9373 ■ WLFS-FM - 91.9
5859 Abercorn Rd., Ste. 3
Savannah, GA 31405
Phone: (912)353-9226
Fax: (912)353-9325
Format: Contemporary Christian. **Owner:** Radio Training Network, PO Box 7217, Lakeland, FL 33813, Ph: (863)644-3464. **URL:** http://www.hisradio.com.

9374 ■ WLVH-FM - 101.1
245 Alfred St.
Savannah, GA 31408
Phone: (912)964-7794
Fax: (912)964-9414
Format: Urban Contemporary. **URL:** http://www.love1011.com.

9375 ■ WLXP-FM - 88.1
PO Box 2118
Omaha, NE 68172
Free: 888-937-2471
Email: info@air1.com
Format: Contemporary Christian. **Owner:** Educational Media Foundation, 2351 Sunset Blvd., Ste. 170-218, Rocklin, CA 95677, Ph: (800)434-8400. **Key Personnel:** Dan Antonelli, Director; Emanuel J. Kallina, II, Director; Mike Novak, President; Larry Moody, Director; Alan Mason, COO. **URL:** http://www.air1.com.

9376 ■ WNMT-AM - 1520
217 E 65th St.
Savannah, GA 31405-5308
Phone: (912)354-4601
Format: Country. **Networks:** Georgia Radio. **Founded:** 1968. **Operating Hours:** 14 hrs. Daily; 15% network, 85% local. **ADI:** Savannah, GA. **Wattage:** 1,000. **Ad Rates:** $5-15 per unit.

WOAH-FM - See Glennville, GA

9377 ■ WQBT-FM - 94.1
245 Alfred St.
Savannah, GA 31408
Email: info@941thebeat.com
Format: Hip Hop; Blues; Urban Contemporary. **Operating Hours:** Continuous. **Ad Rates:** Advertising accepted; rates available upon request. **URL:** http://www.941thebeat.com.

9378 ■ WRHQ-FM - 105.3
1102 E 52nd St.
Savannah, GA 31404
Phone: (912)234-1053
Fax: (912)354-6600
Email: qualityrock@wrhq.com
Format: Classic Rock; Adult Contemporary. **Owner:** Thoroughbred Communications, Inc., at above address. **Founded:** 1991. **Operating Hours:** Continuous. **ADI:** Savannah, GA. **Key Personnel:** Jerry Rogers, Gen. Mgr. **Wattage:** 25,000. **Ad Rates:** Advertising accepted; rates available upon request. $5-25 per unit. **URL:** http://www.wrhq.com.

9379 ■ WSAV-TV - 3
1430 E Victory Dr.
Savannah, GA 31404
Phone: (912)651-0300
Email: hotline@wsav.com
Format: News. **Networks:** NBC. **Owner:** Media General Communications Inc., 333 E Franklin St., Richmond, VA 23219, Ph: (804)887-5000. **Founded:** 1956. **Operating Hours:** Continuous. **ADI:** Savannah, GA. **Wattage:** 100,000 ERP H. **Ad Rates:** Advertising accepted; rates available upon request. **URL:** http://www.wsav.com.

9380 ■ WSEG-AM - 1400
PO Box 60999
Savannah, GA 31420
Phone: (912)920-4441
Fax: (912)264-9991
Format: Oldies. **Networks:** Westwood One Radio. **Wattage:** 650.

9381 ■ WSOK-AM - 1230
245 Alfred St.
Savannah, GA 31408
Phone: (912)947-1230
Fax: (912)964-9414
Email: info@1230wsok.com
Format: Gospel. **Networks:** American Urban Radio; ABC. **Operating Hours:** Continuous; 16% network, 84% local. **ADI:** Savannah, GA. **Key Personnel:** Daniel Frazier, Contact, daniel@1230wsok.com; E. Larry McDuffie, Contact, elarry@1230wsok.com; J. Vernard Flowers, Contact, jflowers@clearchannel.com. **Wattage:** 5,000. **Ad Rates:** $25-44 for 30 seconds. **URL:** http://www.1230wsok.com.

9382 ■ WSSJ-FM - 100.1
6203 Abercorn St., Ste. 213
Savannah, GA 31405
Phone: (912)691-1934
Format: Adult Contemporary; Jazz. **Key Personnel:** Camellia Pflum, Gen. Mgr.; Joel Widdows, Operations Mgr. **Wattage:** 50,000.

9383 ■ WSVH-FM - 91.1
12 Ocean Science Cir.
Savannah, GA 31411
Phone: (912)598-3300
Format: Public Radio; Classical; Jazz. **Networks:** National Public Radio (NPR); Public Radio International (PRI); Peach State Public Radio. **Owner:** Georgia Public Broadcasting, 260 14th St. NW, Atlanta, GA 30318, Ph: (404)685-2400, Free: 800-222-6006. **Founded:** 1981. **Operating Hours:** Continuous; 50% network, 50% local. **ADI:** Savannah, GA. **Wattage:** 100,000. **Ad Rates:** Noncommercial. **URL:** http://www.gpb.org.

9384 ■ WTGS-TV - 28
10001 Abercorn St.
Savannah, GA 31406
Phone: (912)925-0022
Fax: (912)921-2235
Format: Commercial TV. **Networks:** Fox; Independent. **Founded:** 1984. **Operating Hours:** Continuous. **ADI:** Savannah, GA. **Wattage:** 1,000. **Ad Rates:** Advertising accepted; rates available upon request. **URL:** http://www.wjcl.com.

9385 ■ WTHG-FM - 104.7
6203 Abercorn St., Ste. 101
Savannah, GA 31405
Phone: (912)921-7222
Format: Eighties; Oldies. **Founded:** 1992. **Wattage:** 12,000. **Ad Rates:** Advertising accepted; rates available upon request.

9386 ■ WTOC-TV - 11
PO Box 8086
Savannah, GA 31412
Phone: (912)234-1111
Fax: (912)238-5133
Email: publicfile@wtoc.com
Format: Commercial TV. **Networks:** CBS. **Owner:** Raycom Media Inc., 201 Monroe St., RSA Twr., 20th Fl., Montgomery, AL 36104-3731, Ph: (334)206-1400. **Founded:** 1954. **Operating Hours:** Continuous. **ADI:** Savannah, GA. **Key Personnel:** Bill Cathcart, Gen. Mgr., VP, bill.cathcart@wtoc.com; Randy Peltier, Gen. Sales Mgr., rpeltier@wtoc.com; Jan Smith, News Dir., janetsmith@wtoc.com. **URL:** http://www.wtoc.com.

9387 ■ W206AT-FM - 89.1
PO Box 391
Twin Falls, ID 83303
Fax: (208)736-1958
Free: 800-357-4226
Format: Religious; Contemporary Christian. **Owner:** CSN International, PO Box 391, Twin Falls, ID 83303, Ph: (208)736-1958, Fax: (208)736-1958, Free: 800-357-4226. **Key Personnel:** Kelly Carlson, Dir. of Engg.; Ray Gorney, Asst. Dir. **URL:** http://www.csnradio.com.

9388 ■ WTYB-FM - 103.9
214 Television Cir.
Savannah, GA 31406

Format: Urban Contemporary. **Owner:** Cumulus Broadcasting Inc., 3280 Peachtree Rd. NW, Ste. 2300, Atlanta, GA 30305-2447, Ph: (404)949-0700, Fax: (404)949-0740. **Key Personnel:** Doug Davis, Dir. of Programs, doug.davis@cumulus.com. **Ad Rates:** Advertising accepted; rates available upon request. **URL:** http://www.magic1039fm.com.

9389 ■ WUBB-FM - 106.9
401 Mall Blvd., Ste. 101 D
Savannah, GA 31406
Phone: (912)351-9830
Fax: (912)352-4821
Format: Country. **Formerly:** WGZR-FM. **Operating Hours:** 18 hours Daily. **Key Personnel:** Tim Leary, Contact; Christine Manzione, Contact. **Ad Rates:** Advertising accepted; rates available upon request. **URL:** http://www.bob1069.com.

9390 ■ WVAN-TV - 9
260 14TH St. N
1540 Stewart Ave. SW
Atlanta, GA 30318-5360
Phone: (404)756-4700
Free: 800-222-6006
Format: Public TV. **Networks:** Public Broadcasting Service (PBS); Georgia Public Television. **Owner:** Georgia Public Telecommunications Commission, at above address. **Founded:** 1963. **ADI:** Savannah, GA. **Key Personnel:** Kent Steele, Dir. of Programs; Richard E. Ottinger, Contact; Frank Bugg, Contact; Al Korn, Contact. **Wattage:** 20,000 ERP. **Ad Rates:** Noncommercial.

9391 ■ WWIO-FM - 88.9
13040 Abercorn St., Ste. 8
Savannah, GA 31411
Phone: (912)344-3565
Fax: (912)344-3411
Free: 800-673-7332
Email: ask@gpb.org
Format: Public Radio. **Owner:** Georgia Public Broadcasting, 260 14th St. NW, Atlanta, GA 30318, Ph: (404)685-2400, Free: 800-222-6006. **Key Personnel:** Eric Nauert, Station Mgr., enauert@gpb.org; Russell Wells, Operations Mgr., rwells@gpb.org; Orlando Montoya, Producer, omontoya@gpb.org; Bethany Ford, Music Dir., bford@gpb.org. **Wattage:** 100,000. **Ad Rates:** Noncommercial. **URL:** http://www.gpb.org.

9392 ■ WYFS-FM - 89.5
11530 Carmel Commons Blvd.
Charlotte, NC 28226
Phone: (704)523-5555
Free: 800-888-7077
Format: Religious. **Networks:** Bible Broadcasting. **Owner:** Bible Broadcasting Network Inc., 11530 Carmel Commons Blvd., Charlotte, NC 28226, Ph: (704)523-5555, Free: 800-888-7077. **Founded:** Nov. 10, 1986. **Operating Hours:** Continuous; 97.5% network, 2.5% local. **Wattage:** 100,000. **Ad Rates:** Noncommercial. **Mailing address:** PO Box 7300, Charlotte, NC 28241-7300. **URL:** http://www.bbnradio.org.

9393 ■ WYKZ-FM - 98.7
245 Alfred St.
Savannah, GA 31408
Phone: (912)964-9870
Fax: (912)964-9414
Free: 866-762-0987
Email: info@987theriver.com
Format: Adult Contemporary. **Networks:** CNN Radio. **Founded:** 1954. **Formerly:** WQLO-FM. **Operating Hours:** Continuous; 100% local. **ADI:** Savannah, GA. **Key Personnel:** Mark Robertson, Contact, mark@987theriver.com. **Wattage:** 100,000. **Ad Rates:** $25-36 for 30 seconds; $25-30 for 60 seconds. **URL:** http://www.987theriver.com//main.html.

9394 ■ WZAT-FM - 102.2
214 Television Cir.
Savannah, GA 31406
Phone: (404)949-0700
Format: Contemporary Hit Radio (CHR). **Networks:** NBC; ABC. **Founded:** 1971. **Operating Hours:** Continuous. **Wattage:** 100,000. **Ad Rates:** $11-60 for 30 seconds; $13-72 for 60 seconds. **URL:** http://www.savannahnashicon.com.

SCOTTDALE

9395 ■ WGFS-AM - 1430
3589 N Decatur Rd.
Scottdale, GA 30079
Format: Easy Listening; Religious. **Networks:** CBS; Georgia Radio. **Owner:** Multicultural Radio Broadcasting Inc., 27 William St., 11th Fl., New York, NY 10005, Ph: (212)966-1059, Fax: (212)966-9580. **Founded:** 1946. **Operating Hours:** Continuous. **Wattage:** 5,000. **Ad Rates:** $8-12.50 for 30 seconds; $10-15 for 60 seconds.

SENOIA

9396 ■ WEKS-FM - 92.5
120 Village Cir.
Senoia, GA 30276
Phone: (770)599-1923
Email: info@925fmthebear.com
Format: Country. **Networks:** Meadows Racing; Precision Racing. **Owner:** Spalding Broadcasting, Inc., 1523 Kell Ln Ste 1, Griffin, GA 30224, Ph: (770)412-8700. **Founded:** Dec. 31, 1995. **Operating Hours:** Continuous. **Wattage:** 25,000. **Ad Rates:** Advertising accepted; rates available upon request. **URL:** http://www.925fmthebear.com.

SMYRNA

Cobb Co.

9397 ■ The Georgia Bulletin
Roman Catholic Archdiocese of Atlanta
2401 Lake Park Dr. SE
Smyrna, GA 30080
Phone: (404)920-7430
Religious newspaper (tabloid) for the Catholic Archdiocese of Atlanta. **Freq:** Biweekly every Thursday. **Print Method:** Offset. **Trim Size:** 10 1/4 x 13 1/2. **Col. Depth:** 196 agate lines. **Key Personnel:** Gretchen Keiser, Editor; Mary Anne Castranio, Executive Editor; Tom Aisthorpe, Manager, Advertising. **Subscription Rates:** $23 Individuals; Included in membership. **URL:** http://georgiabulletin.org. **Ad Rates:** BW $1920; 4C $2170; PCI $14. **Remarks:** Accepts advertising. **Circ:** 72,000.

9398 ■ The Smyrna Neighbor
Echo Media
900 Circle 75 Pky., Ste. 1600
Atlanta, GA 30339
Phone: (770)955-3535
Fax: (770)955-3599
Publisher's E-mail: salesinfo@echo-media.com
Community newspaper. **Freq:** Weekly (Thurs.). **Print Method:** Offset. **Cols./Page:** 6. **Col. Width:** 26 nonpareils. **Col. Depth:** 301 agate lines. **USPS:** 925-860. **Subscription Rates:** Free. **URL:** http://www.echo-media.com/mediaDetail.php?ID=4306. **Ad Rates:** GLR $.82; BW $1483.50; 4C $1773.50; SAU $11.50. **Circ:** Mon.-Fri. 10000.

9399 ■ WAZX-AM - 1550
1800 Lake Park Dr., Ste. 99
Smyrna, GA 30080
Phone: (770)436-6171
Fax: (770)436-0100
Format: Hispanic; Public Radio. **Networks:** CNN Radio. **Owner:** Ga-Mex Broadcasting, Inc., at above address. **Operating Hours:** Continuous. **ADI:** Atlanta (Athens & Rome), GA. **Key Personnel:** Javier Macias, President. **Wattage:** 50,000 Day; 800 Night. **Ad Rates:** Noncommercial. Combined advertising rates available with WAZX, WGTA, WCOC.

SNELLVILLE

9400 ■ W213BE-FM - 90.5
PO Box 391
Twin Falls, ID 83303
Fax: (208)736-1958
Free: 800-357-4226
Format: Religious; Contemporary Christian. **Owner:** CSN International, PO Box 391, Twin Falls, ID 83303, Ph: (208)736-1958, Fax: (208)736-1958, Free: 800-357-4226. **URL:** http://www.csnradio.com.

SOCIAL CIRCLE

9401 ■ WKUN-AM - 1580
1081 N Cherokee Rd.
Social Circle, GA 30025
Phone: (770)267-6558
Fax: (770)267-0341
Format: Gospel. **Owner:** B.R. Anderson Sr., at above address, Ph: (770)267-0923, Fax: (706)342-8135. **Founded:** 1971. **Operating Hours:** Sunrise-sunset. **ADI:** Atlanta (Athens & Rome), GA. **Key Personnel:** Mickey Palmer, Gen. Mgr. **Wattage:** 1,000. **Ad Rates:** $7 for 30 seconds; $10 for 60 seconds.

SOPERTON

SE GA. Treutlen Co. 70 mi. SE of Macon. Turpentine distillery; carpetbacking factory; cotton ginning; printing plants. Pine timber. Agriculture. Cotton, corn, tobacco.

9402 ■ The Soperton News
Herald Publishing Company
115 S Jefferson St.
Dublin, GA 31021
Phone: (478)272-5522
Fax: (478)272-2189
Free: 800-833-2504
Publisher's E-mail: weeklies@courier-herald.com
Community newspaper. **Freq:** Weekly (Wed.). **Print Method:** Offset. **Cols./Page:** 6. **Col. Width:** 25 nonpareils. **Col. Depth:** 294 agate lines. **Key Personnel:** Du Bose S. Porter, Editor, phone: (912)272-5522. **URL:** http://heraldpublishingcompany.com/pages/home_soperton. **Mailing address:** Drawer B, CSS, Dublin, GA 31040. **Ad Rates:** GLR $.27; BW $645; 4C $965; SAU $1.68; PCI $5. **Remarks:** Advertising accepted; rates available upon request. **Circ:** 2050.

9403 ■ The Soperton News
Soperton News Building
2nd Main St.
Soperton, GA 30457
Phone: (912)529-6624
Fax: (912)529-5399
Publisher's E-mail: weeklies@courier-herald.com
Community newspaper. **Freq:** Weekly (Wed.). **Print Method:** Offset. **Cols./Page:** 6. **Col. Width:** 25 nonpareils. **Col. Depth:** 294 agate lines. **Key Personnel:** Du Bose S. Porter, Editor, phone: (912)272-5522. **URL:** http://heraldpublishingcompany.com/pages/home_soperton. **Mailing address:** Drawer B, CSS, Dublin, GA 31040. **Ad Rates:** GLR $.27; BW $645; 4C $965; SAU $1.68; PCI $5. **Remarks:** Advertising accepted; rates available upon request. **Circ:** 2050.

STATESBORO

E. GA. Bulloch Co. 50 mi. W. of Savannah. Georgia Southern College. Manufactures iron castings, textiles, shears, plastic products. Lumber mills. Cold storage; peanut and pecan plants. Agriculture. Soybeans, corn, peanuts, tobacco, livestock, forestry.

9404 ■ The George-Anne
Georgia Southern University
F.I. Williams Ctr., Rm. 2023
Georgia South University
Statesboro, GA 30460
Phone: (912)681-5246
Fax: (912)478-7113
Publication E-mail: gaeditor@georgiasouthern.edu
Collegiate newspaper. **Freq:** Mon., Tue., Wed., Thu. **Print Method:** Offset. **Trim Size:** 13 3/4 x 22 3/4. **Cols./Page:** 6. **Col. Width:** 12 picas. **Col. Depth:** 21 inches. **Key Personnel:** Lauren Gorla, Editor-in-Chief. **Subscription Rates:** Free. **URL:** http://thegeorgeanne.com. **Ad Rates:** 4C $273. **Remarks:** Accepts advertising. **Circ:** Free ‡5000.

9405 ■ Statesboro Herald: Statesboro Herald
Statesboro Publishing Company Inc.
1 Proctor St., Herald Sq.
Statesboro, GA 30458
Phone: (912)764-9031
Fax: (912)489-8181
General newspaper. **Freq:** Daily. **Print Method:** offset. **Trim Size:** 12 1/2 x 22. **Key Personnel:** Jim Healy, Manager, Operations, phone: (912)489-9402; Jan Melton, Director, Advertising, phone: (912)489-9401; Randy Morton, Publisher, phone: (912)489-9431; Darrell

Circulation: ★ = AAM; △ or • = BPA; ♦ = CAC; ❑ = VAC; ⊕ = PO Statement; ‡ = Publisher's Report; Boldface figures = sworn; Light figures = estimated.

Elliott, Manager, Circulation, phone: (912)489-9425; Pam Pollard, Manager, Advertising, phone: (912)489-9420. **Subscription Rates:** $75 Individuals digital. **URL:** http://www.statesboroherald.com. **Remarks:** Accepts advertising. **Circ:** 8000.

9406 ■ Northland Cable TV
32 E Vine
Statesboro, GA 30458
Phone: (912)489-8715
Fax: (912)489-5479
Email: service@yournorthland.com
Owner: Northland Communications Corp., Nine Boardwalk Pl., Seneca, SC 29678, Ph: (864)882-0002. **Founded:** Sept. 01, 2006. **Cities Served:** Brooklet, Statesboro, Georgia: subscribing households 8,500; 48 channels; 1 community access channel. **Mailing address:** PO Box 407, Statesboro, GA 30459. **URL:** http://www.yournorthland.com.

9407 ■ W48BH - 48
PO Box A
Santa Ana, CA 92711
Phone: (714)832-2950
Free: 888-731-1000
Email: comments@tbn.org
Owner: Trinity Broadcasting Network Inc., PO Box A, Santa Ana, CA 92711, Ph: (714)832-2950, Free: 888-731-1000. **URL:** http://www.tbn.org.

9408 ■ WPMX-FM - 102.9
561 E Olliff St.
Statesboro, GA 30458
Phone: (912)764-5446
Format: Sports. **Owner:** Georgia Eagle Broadcasting, Inc., at above address.

9409 ■ WSLT-FM - 99
265 Cantebury St.
Rincon, GA 31326
Phone: (706)396-7000
Fax: (706)396-7092
Format: Adult Contemporary. **Owner:** Salt and Light Communication, Inc., at above address, Ph: (803)279-2099. **Founded:** Mar. 1993. **Formerly:** WCNA-FM. **Operating Hours:** Continuous. **ADI:** Augusta, GA. **Wattage:** 6,000. **Ad Rates:** Noncommercial. **URL:** http://www.wslt.com/.

9410 ■ WWNS-AM - 1240
PO Box 958
Statesboro, GA 30459
Phone: (912)764-5446
Fax: (912)764-8827
Free: 800-595-7525
Email: wwnswmcd@enia.net
Format: Talk; News; Information. **Networks:** CBS. **Owner:** Radio Statesboro, Inc., at above address. **Founded:** 1946. **Operating Hours:** Continuous. **Key Personnel:** Nate Hirsch, Gen. Mgr.; Ted Byrne, News Dir.; Buddy Horne, Dir. of Programs. **Wattage:** 710 KW. **Ad Rates:** Advertising accepted; rates available upon request. $8-10 per unit. **URL:** http://www.radiostatesboro.com.

STOCKBRIDGE

9411 ■ Human Ecologist
Human Ecology Action League
PO Box 509
Stockbridge, GA 30281
Phone: (770)389-4519
Fax: (770)389-4520
Publisher's E-mail: healnatnl@aol.com
Freq: Quarterly March, June, September, December. **Alt. Formats:** PDF. **URL:** http://www.healnatl.org/artical_index.html. **Remarks:** Accepts advertising. **Circ:** (Not Reported).

9412 ■ The Human Ecologist
Human Ecology Action League of Mississippi
PO Box 509
Stockbridge, GA 30281
Phone: (770)389-4519
Fax: (770)389-4520
Publisher's E-mail: healnatnl@aol.com
Magazine containing current articles and publications dealing with environmental issues. **Freq:** Quarterly. **Subscription Rates:** $20 Individuals. **URL:** http://www.healnatl.org. **Ad Rates:** BW $410. **Remarks:** Accepts advertising. **Circ:** (Not Reported).

SUMMERVILLE

NW GA. Chattooga Co. 9 mi. E. of Menlo. Residential.

9413 ■ The Summerville News
ESPY Pub. Co.
20 Wildlife Lake Rd.
Summerville, GA 30747
Phone: (706)857-2494
Fax: (706)857-2393
Publication E-mail: admin@thesummervillenews.com sumnews@aol.com
Local newspaper. **Freq:** Weekly (Thurs.). **Print Method:** Offset. **Cols./Page:** 8. **Col. Width:** 21 nonpareils. **Col. Depth:** 301 agate lines. **Key Personnel:** David T. Espy, General Manager; Greg Espy, Manager, Production, Contact; Winston E. Espy, Editor; Gene Espy, Editor; Jimmy Espy, Contact. **Subscription Rates:** $10.60 Individuals. **URL:** http://thesummervillenews.com/index.php?option=com_frontpage&Itemid=1. **Mailing address:** PO Box 310, Summerville, GA 30747. **Ad Rates:** GLR $.19; PCI $3; BW $516. **Remarks:** Accepts advertising. **Circ:** ‡7850, ‡7850.

9414 ■ WZQZ-AM - 1180
10143 Commerce St.
Summerville, GA 30747
Phone: (706)857-5555
Fax: (706)859-1195
Email: wzqz@alltel.net
Format: Music of Your Life. **Founded:** Sept. 07, 2006. **Operating Hours:** 6 a.m.-10 p.m. Daily. **URL:** http://chattooga1180.com/index.php?option=com_frontpage&Itemid=1.

SUWANEE

9415 ■ The Chi Phi Chakett
Chi Phi
1160 Satellite Blvd.
Suwanee, GA 30024
Phone: (404)231-1824
Free: 800-849-1824
Publisher's E-mail: chiphi@chiphi.org
Freq: Quarterly. **Subscription Rates:** Free for members. **Remarks:** Advertising not accepted. **Circ:** (Not Reported).

9416 ■ Gwinnett Parents
Gwinnett Parents Magazine
3651 Peachtree Pkwy., Ste. 325
Suwanee, GA 30024
Publication E-mail: editor@gwinnettparents.com
Magazine that publishes information of interest to parents of Gwinnett County, Georgia. **Freq:** Monthly. **URL:** http://www.gwinnettparents.com. **Remarks:** Accepts advertising. **Circ:** (Not Reported).

9417 ■ WLKQ-FM - 102.3
1176 Satellite Blvd., Ste. 200
Suwanee, GA 30024
Phone: (770)623-8772
Fax: (770)623-4722
Format: Oldies. **Networks:** Mutual Broadcasting System; Georgia Radio. **Owner:** Davis Broadcasting Inc., 2203 Wynnton Rd., Columbus, GA 31906. **Founded:** 1970. **Formerly:** WGCO-FM. **Operating Hours:** Continuous; 5% network, 95% local. **ADI:** Atlanta (Athens & Rome), GA. **Key Personnel:** Al Garner, Gen. Sales Mgr. **Wattage:** 3,300. **Ad Rates:** $26 for 30 seconds; for 60 seconds. **URL:** http://www.laraza1023.com/inicio.

SWAINSBORO

E. GA. Emanuel Co. 65 mi. SW of Augusta. Manufactures lumber, lawn mowers, electrical equipment, feed, textiles. Pine timber. Agriculture. Cotton, corn, tobacco.

9418 ■ The Blade Plus
Forest-Blade Publishing Inc.
416 W Moring St.
Swainsboro, GA 30401
Phone: (478)237-9971
Fax: (478)237-9451
Publisher's E-mail: graphics@forest-blade.com
Newspaper. **Freq:** Weekly. **Print Method:** Offset. **Cols./Page:** 6. **Col. Width:** 28 nonpareils. **Col. Depth:** 301 agate lines. **Key Personnel:** Wally Gallian, Publisher; Gail Williamson, General Manager. **Subscription Rates:** $38 Individuals in state; $49 Out of state. **URL:** http://www.forest-blade.com. **Ad Rates:** GLR $.27; BW $538.02; 4C $666.02; SAU $3.92; PCI $7.99. **Remarks:** Advertising accepted; rates available upon request. **Circ:** Paid 9985.

9419 ■ Northland Cable Television
123 Roger Shaw St.
Swainsboro, GA 30401
Phone: (478)237-6434
Fax: (478)237-9569
Cities Served: 71 channels. **Mailing address:** PO Box 417, Swainsboro, GA 30401. **URL:** http://www.northlandcabletv.com.

9420 ■ WXRS-FM - 100.5
PO Box 5356
Atlanta, GA 31107-5356
Phone: (478)237-1590
Fax: (478)237-3559
Format: Contemporary Country. **Networks:** Fox; NewsTalk Radio. **Owner:** RadioJones, LLC, at above address, Ph: (404)254-2911. **Founded:** 1982. **Wattage:** 3,000 ERP. **Ad Rates:** Advertising accepted; rates available upon request. $10-20 per unit. Combined advertising rates available with WELT-FM, WJAT-AM, WXRS-AM. **URL:** http://www.wxrs.com.

TALLAPOOSA

NW GA. Haralson Co. 10 mi. S. of Buchanan.

9421 ■ WKNG-AM - 1060
One Golf Course Rd.
Tallapoosa, GA 30176
Phone: (770)574-1060
Fax: (770)574-1062
Format: Country. **Networks:** ABC; Georgia Radio. **Owner:** Gradick Communication, at above address, Ph: (770)214-8989, Fax: (770)830-1027. **Founded:** 1976. **Operating Hours:** Sunrise-sunset. **Key Personnel:** Michael Vincent, Dir. of Production. **Wattage:** 50,000. **Ad Rates:** $11 for 30 seconds; $15 for 60 seconds. **URL:** http://www.gradickcommunications.com.

TENNILLE

9422 ■ WJFL-FM - 101.9
5440 Tennille-Oconee Rd.
Tennille, GA 31089
Phone: (478)553-1019
Fax: (478)553-1123
Format: Adult Contemporary. **Operating Hours:** Continuous. **Key Personnel:** Michael Cowan, Dir. of Sales, Gen. Mgr.; Andrea Turner, Office Mgr., Prog. Dir. **Ad Rates:** Noncommercial. **Mailing address:** PO Box 36, Tennille, GA 31089. **URL:** http://www.wjfl.com.

THOMASTON

C. GA. Upson Co. 38 mi. W. of Macon. Textiles, lumber, fruit farms.

9423 ■ Thomaston Times
Thomaston Publishing Co.
PO Box 430
Thomaston, GA 30286
Phone: (706)647-5414
Fax: (706)647-2833
Community newspaper. **Freq:** Triweekly (Mon., Wed., Fri.). **Print Method:** Offset. **Trim Size:** 22 3/4 x 14. **Cols./Page:** 6. **Col. Width:** 11.6 picas. **Col. Depth:** 21 1/2 inches. **Key Personnel:** Chris Smith, Publisher; Kim Madlom, Editor; Elmo Jackson, General Manager; Kim Miller, Contact. **URL:** http://thomastontimes.com. **Ad Rates:** GLR $2.08; BW $728.85; 4C $1028.85; PCI $5.65. **Remarks:** Accepts advertising. **Circ:** 6700.

9424 ■ WTGA-AM - 1590
208 S Center St.
Thomaston, GA 30286
Phone: (706)647-7121
Fax: (706)647-7122
Format: Adult Contemporary. **Ad Rates:** Noncommercial. **URL:** http://www.fun101fm.com.

9425 ■ WTGA-FM - 101.1
208 S Center St.
Thomaston, GA 30286
Phone: (706)647-7121
Fax: (706)647-7122
Format: Full Service. **Simulcasts:** WTGA-AM 1590. **Founded:** 1982. **Operating Hours:** Continuous. **Key**

Personnel: David Piper, Contact. **Wattage:** 1,250.

THOMASVILLE

SW GA. Thomas Co. 35 mi. N. of Tallahassee, FL. Historic sites. Winter resort. Famous for its roses and annual Rose Festival. Manufactures meat products, mattresses, mobile homes, elastics, paint, carbide drill bits, jet engines blades, aluminum windows, furniture, plastics, rubber, fertilizers, pipe, thread. Sawmills; silica sand mining. Diversified farming. Tobacco, corn, soybeans, watermelon, peanuts, mixed vegetables, livestock.

9426 ■ Thomasville Times-Enterprise
Community Newspaper Holdings Inc.
PO Box 650
Thomasville, GA 31799
Phone: (229)226-2400
Fax: (229)228-5863
Newspaper serving Thomasville, Georgia area. **Key Personnel:** Mark Lastinger, Managing Editor; Norman Bankston, Publisher; Chris White, Director, Advertising. **URL:** http://www.timesenterprise.com. **Remarks:** Accepts advertising. **Circ:** Mon.-Sat. ★**8250**, Sun. ★**8228**.

9427 ■ DWSBX-AM - 1020
131 Doe Run Cir.
Thomasville, GA 31757
Phone: (229)233-6153
Email: woody@rockmewoody.com
Format: Hispanic; Classic Rock. **Networks:** SkyLight Satellite. **Owner:** Georgia Triangle Broadcasting, Not Available. **Founded:** June 04, 1982. **Formerly:** WJEP-AM; WSBX-AM. **Operating Hours:** 7:30 a.m.-5:30 p.m; 25% network, 75% local. **ADI:** Tallahassee, FL-Thomasville (Bainbridge), GA. **Wattage:** 10,000. **Ad Rates:** Noncommercial. for 30 seconds; for 60 seconds.

9428 ■ WHGH-AM
PO Box 6880
Thomasville, GA 31758
Phone: (229)228-4124
Fax: (229)225-9508
Format: Urban Contemporary. **Networks:** American Urban Radio. **Owner:** Gross Broadcasting Co., PO BOX 2218, Thomasville, GA 31799, Fax: (912)228-9508. **Founded:** 1986. **Key Personnel:** Moses L. Gross, Gen. Mgr; Raymond Johnson, Contact. **Wattage:** 10,000 Day. **Ad Rates:** $8.50-9.50 for 30 seconds; $8-8.50 for 60 seconds.

9429 ■ WPAX-AM - 1240
117 Remington Ave.
Thomasville, GA 31792
Phone: (229)226-1240
Fax: (229)226-1361
Format: Adult Contemporary; Middle-of-the-Road (MOR). **Simulcasts:** Sundays 6-11am "Gospeltime". **Networks:** CBS; Georgia Radio. **Owner:** Len Robinson Enterprises Inc., at above address. **Founded:** 1922. **Operating Hours:** Continuous; 55% local. **ADI:** Tallahassee, FL-Thomasville (Bainbridge), GA. **Key Personnel:** Len Robinson, Contact, lenrob@rose.net. **Wattage:** 1,000. **Ad Rates:** for 30 seconds; $15 for 60 seconds. Combined advertising rates available with WTUF-FM. **URL:** http://www.wpaxradio.com.

9430 ■ WSTT-AM - 730
730 AM 2194 US 319 S
Thomasville, GA 31792
Phone: (912)228-7302
Format: Gospel; Talk; Sports. **Founded:** 1948. **Operating Hours:** 5:30 a.m. - 11 p.m. **ADI:** Tallahassee, FL-Thomasville (Bainbridge), GA. **Key Personnel:** Rick Warren, Contact. **Wattage:** 5,000 Day; 027 Night. **Ad Rates:** $6 for 30 seconds; $8 for 60 seconds. **URL:** http://www.wstt730.com.

9431 ■ W22BP - 22
PO Box A
Santa Ana, CA 92711
Phone: (714)832-2950
Free: 888-731-1000
Owner: Trinity Broadcasting Network Inc., PO Box A, Santa Ana, CA 92711, Ph: (714)832-2950, Free: 888-731-1000. **URL:** http://www.tbn.org.

9432 ■ W216BQ-FM - 91.1
PO Box 391
Twin Falls, ID 83303
Fax: (208)736-1958
Free: 800-357-4226
Format: Religious; Contemporary Christian. **Owner:** CSN International, PO Box 391, Twin Falls, ID 83303, Ph: (208)736-1958, Fax: (208)736-1958, Free: 800-357-4226. **URL:** http://www.csnradio.com.

THOMSON

E. GA. McDuffie Co. 35 mi. W. of Augusta. Manufactures lumber, cottonseed oil, fertilizer, textiles. Pine, hardwood timber. Agriculture. Cotton, corn, potatoes.

9433 ■ McDuffie Progress
McDuffie Progress
101 Church St.
Thomson, GA 30824
Phone: (706)595-1601
Fax: (706)597-8974
Community newspaper. **Print Method:** Offset. **Trim Size:** 13 x 21 1/2. **Cols./Page:** 6. **Col. Width:** 2 1/16 inches. **Col. Depth:** 21 1/2 inches. **Key Personnel:** Dick Mitchell, Consultant; Wayne Parham, Editor. **USPS:** 335-140. **Subscription Rates:** $33 Individuals McDuffie County. **URL:** http://mcduffieprogress.com. **Mailing address:** PO Box 1090, Thomson, GA 30824. **Ad Rates:** GLR $.33; BW $85; 4C $180; CNU $4; PCI $6. **Remarks:** Accepts advertising. **Circ:** 4500.

9434 ■ WTHO-FM - 101.7
788 Cedar Rock Rd.
Thomson, GA 30824
Phone: (706)595-5122
Fax: (706)595-3021
Format: Country. **Networks:** NBC; Georgia Radio. **Owner:** Camellia City Communication, Inc., at above address, Thomson, GA 30824. **Founded:** 1971. **Operating Hours:** Continuous. **ADI:** Augusta, GA. **Key Personnel:** Steve Ferguson, Dir. of Programs, wthomusic@classicsouth.net; Donna Branch, News Dir., wthonews@classicsouth.net. **Wattage:** 6,000. **Ad Rates:** $5.20-12 for 30 seconds; $6.95-17.15 for 60 seconds. **URL:** http://www.wtho.com.

9435 ■ WTWA-AM - 1240
PO Box 900
Thomson, GA 30824
Phone: (706)595-1561
Fax: (706)595-3021
Format: Big Band/Nostalgia. **Networks:** Westwood One Radio; Georgia Radio. **Owner:** Camellia City Communication, Inc., at above address, Thomson, GA 30824. **Founded:** 1948. **Operating Hours:** Continuous. **ADI:** Augusta, GA. **Wattage:** 1,000. **Ad Rates:** $3.60-9.15 for 30 seconds; $5.15-13.05 for 60 seconds. WTHO-FM.

TIFTON

S. GA. Tift Co. 40 mi. E. of Albany. Abraham Baldwin College. Coastal Plain Experiment Station. Manufactures lumber, aluminum products, refrigerator coils, textiles, plastics, concrete, and pipes. Cotton, saw, peanut mills; bottling, brick works; tobacco market. Tomato, cabbage plants shipped. Timber. Diversified farming. Tobacco, peanuts.

9436 ■ Southeastern Peanut Farmer
Southeastern Peanut Farmer Federation
PO Box 967
Tifton, GA 31793
Phone: (229)386-3470
Fax: (229)386-3501
Publisher's E-mail: don@gapeanuts.com
Magazine for peanut growers. **Freq:** 6/year. **Print Method:** Offset. **Trim Size:** 8 1/2 x 11. **Cols./Page:** 4. **Key Personnel:** Joy Carter, Editor, phone: (229)386-3690. **ISSN:** 0038--3694 (print). **URL:** http://www.sepfonline.com; http://southernpeanutfarmers.org. **Circ:** (Not Reported).

9437 ■ The Tifton Gazette
The Tifton Gazette
211 N Tift Ave.
Tifton, GA 31794
Phone: (229)382-4321
Fax: (229)387-7322
General newspaper. **Founded:** 1888. **Print Method:** Offset. **Cols./Page:** 6. **Col. Width:** 26 nonpareils. **Col. Depth:** 301 agate lines. **Key Personnel:** Frank Sayles, Jr., Publisher; Rachel Wainwright, Manager, Circulation; Fred Buescher, Director, Advertising. **Subscription Rates:** $10 Individuals. **URL:** http://www.tiftongazette.com. **Mailing address:** PO Box 708, Tifton, GA 31794. **Remarks:** Advertising accepted; rates available upon request. **Circ:** 9,880.

9438 ■ WPLH-FM - 103.1
2802 Moore Hwy.
Tifton, GA 31793
Phone: (229)391-4977
Format: Contemporary Hit Radio (CHR). **Owner:** Abraham Baldwin Agricultural College, 2802 Moore Hwy., Tifton, GA 31793, Ph: (229)391-5001, Free: 800-733-3653. **Founded:** 1988. **Formerly:** WABR-FM. **Operating Hours:** Continuous. **Key Personnel:** Keith Perry, Fac. Adv., kperry@abac.edu. **Wattage:** 250. **Ad Rates:** Noncommercial. **URL:** http://www.abac.edu.

9439 ■ W33BX - 33
PO Box A
Santa Ana, CA 92711
Phone: (714)832-2950
Free: 888-731-1000
Owner: Trinity Broadcasting Network Inc., PO Box A, Santa Ana, CA 92711, Ph: (714)832-2950, Free: 888-731-1000. **URL:** http://www.tbn.org.

9440 ■ WTIF-AM - 1340
PO Box 968
Tifton, GA 31793
Phone: (912)382-1340
Fax: (912)386-8658
Owner: Three Trees Communications, Inc., at above address. **Founded:** 1957. **Key Personnel:** David Haire, News Dir. **Wattage:** 1,000. **Ad Rates:** $4.20-6.50 for 15 seconds; $6.20-8.50 for 30 seconds; $7.20-9.50 for 60 seconds. **URL:** http://www.107.wtif.com.

TOCCOA

NE GA. Stephens Co. 100 mi. NE of Atlanta. Toccoa Falls. Manufactures furniture, carpet yarn, textiles, caskets, foundry products, paints, plastics, small appliances. Metalworking. Agriculture. Poultry, livestock.

9441 ■ The Toccoa Record
The Toccoa Record Co.
P.O Drawer 1069
Toccoa, GA 30577
Phone: (706)886-9476
Fax: (706)886-2161
Publication E-mail: toccoarecord@windstream.net
Newspaper. **Print Method:** Offset. **Cols./Page:** 6. **Col. Width:** 26 nonpareils. **Col. Depth:** 301 agate lines. **Key Personnel:** Teresa Thacker, Contact; Tom Law, Publisher; Jessica Waters, Editor. **USPS:** 632-120. **Subscription Rates:** $25 Individuals in Stephens County; $34 Out of area; $42 Out of state. **URL:** http://thetoccoarecord.com. **Ad Rates:** PCI $12.55. **Remarks:** Accepts advertising. **Circ:** 7100.

9442 ■ Northland Cable Television
119 Falls Rd.
Toccoa, GA 30577
Phone: (706)886-2727
Fax: (706)886-0144
Mailing address: PO Box 1667, Toccoa, GA 30577.

9443 ■ WNEG-AM - 630
145 N Alexander St.
Toccoa, GA 30577
Phone: (706)886-2191
Fax: (706)282-0189
Email: wneg@windstream.net
Format: Oldies. **Networks:** CBS; Westwood One Radio. **Founded:** 1956. **Operating Hours:** Continuous; 75% local; 25% network. **ADI:** Greenville-Spartanburg, SC-Asheville, NC. **Key Personnel:** Phil Hobbs, Gen. Mgr., VP, hobbs@gacaradio.com; Ken Brady, Sales Mgr., kbrady@gacaradio.com; Charlie Bauder, News Dir., cbauder@gacaradio.com; Connie Gaines, Operations Mgr., cgaines@gacaradio.com. **Wattage:** 500 Daytime. **Ad Rates:** $8-9 for 15 seconds; $9-10 for 30 seconds; $12-13 for 60 seconds. **Mailing address:** PO Box 1159, Toccoa, GA 30577. **URL:** http://www.wnegradio.com.

9444 ■ WNEG-TV - 32
597 Big A Rd.
Toccoa, GA 30577
Phone: (301)570-5922

Circulation: ★ = AAM; △ or • = BPA; ♦ = CAC; ❑ = VAC; ⊕ = PO Statement; ‡ = Publisher's Report; Boldface figures = sworn; Light figures = estimated.

Networks: CBS. **Owner:** Media General Inc., 333 E Franklin St., Richmond, VA 23219, Ph: (804)649-6000, Fax: (502)259-5537. **Founded:** 1984. **Operating Hours:** Continuous. **ADI:** Greenville-Spartanburg, SC-Asheville, NC. **Key Personnel:** Jeff Dantre, News Dir.; Cody Chaffins, Sports Dir.; Jimmy Sanders, Station Mgr. **Wattage:** 647,000 visual; 120,000 audio. **Ad Rates:** $20-75 for 30 seconds. **URL:** http://www.wgtatv.com.

9445 ■ WRBN-FM - 104.1
233 Big A Rd.
Toccoa, GA 30577
Phone: (706)297-7264
Fax: (706)297-7266
Email: sutton@gacaradio.com
Format: Adult Contemporary. **Networks:** ABC; Meadows Racing; Precision Racing; Gannett News. **Owner:** Georgia-Carolina Radiocasting Co., 233 Big A Rd., Toccoa, GA 30577, Ph: (706)297-7264, Fax: (706)297-7266. **Founded:** 1989. **Formerly**: WQXJ-FM. **Operating Hours**: Continuous. **ADI:** Atlanta (Athens & Rome), GA. **Key Personnel:** Dick Mangrum, News Dir.; Chad Dorsett, News Dir.; Debbie Lyles, Office Mgr.; Doug Stephens, Mgr.; John Hubbard, Office Mgr.; Douglas M. Sutton, Jr., CEO, President; Connie Gaines, Operations Mgr.; George Young, Operations Mgr.; Keith Giles, News Dir.; Charlie Bauder, News Dir.; Benita Snyder, Office Mgr. **Wattage**: 6,000. **Ad Rates:** Noncommercial. **URL:** http://www.gacaradio.com.

TOCCOA FALLS

Stephens Co.

WEPC-FM - See Belton, SC

9446 ■ WLET-AM - 1420
Falls Rd.
Toccoa Falls, GA 30598
Phone: (706)886-6831
Fax: (706)282-6090
Free: 800-251-8326
Email: wlet@toccoafalls.edu
Format: Talk; Information; Gospel. **Owner:** Toccoa Falls College, 107 Kincaid Dr., Toccoa Falls, GA 30598-9602, Ph: (706)886-6831, Free: 888-785-5624. **Founded:** 1941. **Formerly**: WRLC-AM. **Operating Hours**: Continuous. **ADI:** Greenville-Spartanburg, SC-Asheville, NC. **Wattage:** 5,000 Day 073 Night. **Ad Rates:** $5-6 for 30 seconds; $6-8 for 60 seconds. **URL:** http://www.wletradio.org/.

9447 ■ WRAF-FM - 90.9
PO Box 780
Toccoa Falls, GA 30598
Fax: (706)282-6090
Free: 800-251-8326
Email: radio@myfavoritestation.net
Format: Religious. **Networks:** Sun Radio. **Owner:** Toccoa Falls College, 107 Kincaid Dr., Toccoa Falls, GA 30598-9602, Ph: (706)886-6831, Free: 888-785-5624. **Founded:** 1980. **Operating Hours**: Continuous. **Key Personnel:** Lillian Cash, Contact, lcash@tfc.edu. **Local Programs**: *Walk in the Word*, Saturday 1:00 a.m.; *Just Thinking*, Monday Tuesday Wednesday Thursday Friday 9:30 p.m.; *'Round the Country*, Monday Tuesday Wednesday Thursday Friday 12:00 p.m. - 1:30 p.m. **Wattage**: 100,000 Horizontal ERP; 96,000 Vertical ERP. **Ad Rates:** Advertising accepted; rates available upon request. **URL:** http://www.toccoafallsradio.org.

9448 ■ WTFH-FM - 89.9
PO Box 780
Toccoa Falls, GA 30598
Fax: (706)282-6090
Free: 800-251-8326
Email: radio@myfavoritestation.net
Format: Religious. **URL:** http://www.wrafradio.org.

TRENTON

NW GA. Dade Co. 15 mi. NW of Lafayette. Residential.

9449 ■ The Dade County Sentinel
The Sentinel
9481 Hwy. 11
Trenton, GA 30752
Phone: (706)657-6182
Fax: (706)657-4970
Publication E-mail: editor@dadesentinel.com
Community newspaper. **Freq:** Weekly (Wed.). **Print Method:** Offset. **Cols./Page:** 6. **Col. Width:** 23 nonpareils. **Col. Depth:** 301 agate lines. **Subscription Rates:** $26.50 Individuals local combo; print and online; 1 year; $33 Out of area print and online; 1 year; $21.50 Individuals print only; 1 year; $28 Out of area print only; 1 year. **URL:** http://www.dadesentinel.com/v2/content.aspx?IsHome=1&MemberID=1338&module=Page&ID=2868. **Ad Rates:** GLR $5.50; BW $709.50; 4C $959.50; PCI $5.50. **Remarks:** Accepts advertising. **Circ:** ‡3850.

9450 ■ WBDX-FM - 102.7
5512 Ringgold Rd., Ste. 214
Chattanooga, TN 37412
Phone: (423)892-1200
Free: 877-262-5103
Email: info@j103.com
Format: Contemporary Christian. **Owner:** Partners for Christian Media, Inc., 2288 Gumbarell Rd., Ste. 111, Chattanooga, TN 37421, Fax: (423)892-1633. **Key Personnel:** Bob Lubell, Founder, President; Justin Wade, Dir. of Programs. **Wattage:** 320 Watts. **Ad Rates:** Noncommercial. **Mailing address:** PO Box 9396, Chattanooga, TN 37412. **URL:** http://www.j103.com.

9451 ■ WKWN-AM - 1420
12544 N Main St.
Trenton, GA 30752
Phone: (706)657-7594
Format: Oldies; Religious. **Networks:** CNN Radio. **Owner:** Dade County Broadcasting, Inc., at above address, Trenton, GA, Fax: (706)657-6767. **Founded:** 1982. **Formerly**: WADX-AM. **Operating Hours**: Continuous. **Key Personnel:** Evan Stone, Owner. **Wattage**: 2,500 Day; 112 Night. **Ad Rates:** $4-7 for 30 seconds. **Mailing address:** PO Box 829, Trenton, GA 30752.

TUCKER

NW GA. De Kalb Co. 20 mi. N. of Atlanta. Residential.

9452 ■ GEORGIA Magazine: Official Publication of Georgia Electric Membership Corporation
Georgia Electric Membership Corp.
2100 E Exchange Pl., Ste. 510
Tucker, GA 30084
Phone: (770)270-6950
Fax: (770)270-6995
Free: 800-544-4362
Publisher's E-mail: info@georgiaemc.com
General interest magazine for and about Georgians. **Freq:** Monthly. **Print Method:** Offset. **Trim Size:** 8 x 10 1/2. **Cols./Page:** 3. **Col. Width:** 28 nonpareils. **Col. Depth:** 140 agate lines. **Key Personnel:** Ann Orowski, Editor, phone: (770)270-6951; Jennifer Hewett, Managing Editor, phone: (770)270-6952; Victoria De Castro, Associate Editor. **ISSN:** 1061--5822 (print). **Subscription Rates:** $10 Individuals; $16 Two years. **URL:** http://georgiamagazine.org. **Mailing address:** PO Box 1707, Tucker, GA 30085-1707. **Ad Rates:** BW $5730; 4C $6230. **Circ:** ‡500,000, Paid ‡516,000.

9453 ■ Prick Magazine
Chuck B., Inc.
PO Box 381
Tucker, GA 30085
Phone: (770)723-9824
Fax: (770)723-0751
Publisher's E-mail: chuckb@prickmag.net
Magazine providing information on tattoos. **Freq:** Quarterly. **Print Method:** Offset. **Trim Size:** 11 x 14 1/2. **Cols./Page:** 5. **Col. Width:** 11 picas. **Col. Depth:** 230 agate lines. **Key Personnel:** Charles D. Brank, Chief Executive Officer, Editor-in-Chief, Publisher. **ISSN:** 0744--0618 (print). **URL:** http://www.prickmag.net. **Remarks:** Accepts advertising. **Circ:** (Not Reported).

TYRONE

9454 ■ The JOY FM 93.3 - 93.3
1175 Senoia Rd.
Tyrone, GA 30290
Phone: (770)487-4500
Format: Contemporary Christian. **Owner:** Provident Broadcasting Co., 120 Peachtree East Shopping Ctr, Peachtree City, GA 30269, Ph: (770)487-4500. **Founded:** 1981. **Operating Hours:** Continuous. **Key Personnel:** Johanna Antes, Div. Dir; Don Schaeffer, Contact; John Zeiler, Contact, john@wvfj.com. **Wattage**: 38,000. **Ad Rates:** Noncommercial. **URL:** http://georgia.thejoyfm.com.

VALDOSTA

SE GA. Lowndes Co. 45 mi. E. of Thomasville. Valdosta State College. Manufactures boats, batteries, lumber, agricultural chemicals. Pecan shelling; food processing; paper mills; naval stores; concrete pipe, paperboard, garment and mobile homes factories. Pine, hardwood timber. Diversified farming. Tobacco, vegetables, watermelons, peanuts.

9455 ■ Snake Nation Review
Snake Nation Press
110 W Force St.
Valdosta, GA 31601
Publication E-mail: rgeorge@snakenationpress.org
Journal covering fiction, poetry and art. **Key Personnel:** Jean Arambula, Editor. **Remarks:** Accepts advertising. **Circ:** Controlled 700.

9456 ■ Southern Communication Journal
Southern States Communication Association
c/o Dr. Carl M. Cates, Executive Director
Valdosta State University
1500 N Patterson St.
Valdosta, GA 31698
Phone: (229)333-5832
Fax: (229)245-3799
Journal for speech, communication and mass communication professionals and educators. **Freq:** Quarterly. **Print Method:** Offset. Uses mats. **Trim Size:** 8 x 11. **Cols./Page:** 1. **Col. Width:** 48 nonpareils. **Col. Depth:** 98 agate lines. **Key Personnel:** J.D. Ragsdale, Editor. **ISSN:** 1041-794X (print). **URL:** http://www.ssca.net/scj. **Formerly**: Southern Speech Communication Journal. **Remarks:** Advertising accepted; rates available upon request. **Circ:** Paid ‡2650, Non-paid ‡50, 2600.

9457 ■ The Spectator
Valdosta State University
1500 N Patterson St.
Valdosta, GA 31698
Phone: (229)333-5800
Fax: (229)333-5482
Free: 800-618-1878
Publication E-mail: vsuspectator@yahoo.com
University newspaper. **Founded:** 1930. **Freq:** Weekly (Thurs.). **Key Personnel:** Will Lewis, Editor-in-Chief. **URL:** http://www.vsuspectator.com/. **Ad Rates:** BW $795; 4C $405; PCI $6.50. **Remarks:** Advertising accepted; rates available upon request. **Circ:** Free 13243.

9458 ■ The Valdosta Daily Times
Community Newspaper Holdings Inc.
PO Box 968
Valdosta, GA 31603
Phone: (229)244-1880
Fax: (229)244-2560
General newspaper. **Freq:** Mon.-Sun. (morn.). **Print Method:** Offset. **Cols./Page:** 6. **Col. Width:** 2 1/8 inches. **Col. Depth:** 21 1/2 inches. **Key Personnel:** Nick Kazi, Manager, Circulation; Mae Stokes, Director, Advertising; Jeff Masters, Publisher. **Subscription Rates:** $12.99 Individuals online only; $15.99 Individuals full access. **URL:** http://valdostadailytimes.com. **Ad Rates:** GLR $.68; BW $1,235; 4C $1,585; PCI $9.57. **Remarks:** Accepts advertising. **Circ:** Mon.-Sat. ★**14179**, Sun. ★**16097**.

9459 ■ WAFT-FM - 101.1
215 Waft Hill Ln.
Valdosta, GA 31602
Phone: (229)244-5180
Fax: (229)242-8808
Free: 888-923-8101
Email: mail@waft.org
Format: Religious. **Owner:** Christian Radio Fellowship Inc., 215 Waft Hill Ln., Valdosta, GA 31602, Fax: (229)242-8808, Free: 888-923-8101. **Founded:** 1971. **Operating Hours**: Continuous. **ADI:** Albany (Valdosta & Cordele), GA. **Key Personnel:** Bill Tidwell, Contact; Bill Tidwell, Contact; Terry Tidwell, Contact. **Wattage**: 100,000. **Ad Rates:** Noncommercial. **URL:** http://www.waft.org.

9460 ■ WDDQ-FM - 92.1
3766 Old Clyattville Rd.
Valdosta, GA 31601
Phone: (229)219-7080

Email: guestservices@wild-adventure.com
Format: Information; Sports; Talk. **Founded:** 1979. **Operating Hours**: Continuous; 100% local. **Wattage**: 2,600 ERP. **Ad Rates:** Advertising accepted; rates available upon request. **URL:** http://talk921.com.

9461 ■ WFVR-AM - 910
4908-6 NW 34th St.
Gainesville, FL 32605
Phone: (904)376-4442
Fax: (904)372-5338
Format: Country. **Networks:** NBC. **Founded:** 1951. **ADI**: Gainesville (Ocala), FL. **Key Personnel:** Alan Murray, Gen. Mgr; C.H. Fletcher, Contact. **Wattage**: 5,000.

9462 ■ WGOV-AM - 950
Highway 84 W
Valdosta, GA 31601
Phone: (912)242-4513
Fax: (912)247-7676
Format: Urban Contemporary. **Networks:** ABC. **Owner:** Gram Corp., 2973 US 84 W, Valdosta, GA 31601, Ph: (229)242-2210. **Founded:** 1940. **Operating Hours**: Continuous; 100% local. **ADI**: Tallahassee, FL-Thomasville (Bainbridge), GA. **Key Personnel:** Lamar Freeman, Dir. of Programs. **Wattage**: 5,000 Day; 1,000 Night. **Ad Rates:** $7-18 for 30 seconds; $11-28 for 60 seconds. WAAC-FM.

9463 ■ WHBS-AM - 1400
PO Box 1305
Valdosta, GA 31603
Email: whbsam1400@hotmail.com
Format: Religious. **Owner:** Christ In You The Hope of Glory Church, Inc., at above address. **Operating Hours**: 7 a.m. to 4 p.m. Mon.-Fri.;8.30 a.m to 12 p.m. Sat.-Sun. **Key Personnel:** Pastor Franklin Walden, Jr., Gen. Mgr.; Sandra Barnes, Station Mgr.

9464 ■ WKAA-FM - 99.5
1711 Ellis Dr.
Valdosta, GA 31601
Phone: (229)244-8642
Fax: (229)242-7620
Format: Country. **Networks:** Jones Satellite. **Owner:** Black Crow Media, Not Available. **Founded:** 1982. **Formerly**: WSPX-FM. **Operating Hours**: Continuous. **ADI**: Albany (Valdosta & Cordele), GA. **Key Personnel:** Kim Pelkowski, Gen. Mgr., kpelkowski@blackcrow.fm; Jim Morgan, Contact, cwhittle@blackcrow.fm. **Wattage**: 3,000. **Ad Rates:** $6 for 30 seconds; $10 for 60 seconds. **URL:** http://www.valdostatoday.com.

9465 ■ WQPW-FM - 95.7
1711 Ellis Dr.
Valdosta, GA 31601
Phone: (229)244-8642
Format: Adult Contemporary. **Networks:** Independent. **Founded:** 1977. **Formerly**: WLGA-FM. **Operating Hours**: Continuous; 100% local. **ADI**: Albany (Valdosta & Cordele), GA. **Wattage**: 50,000. **Ad Rates:** $24-42 for 60 seconds. **URL:** http://www.mykixcountry.com.

9466 ■ WSTI-FM - 105.3
1711 Ellis Dr.
Valdosta, GA 31601
Phone: (229)244-8642
Fax: (229)242-7620
Email: cgibson@blackcrow.fm
Format: Urban Contemporary; Blues. **Owner:** RTG Media, at above address. **Founded:** 1986. **Operating Hours**: Continuous. **ADI**: Albany (Valdosta & Cordele), GA. **Key Personnel:** Clarke Johnson, Operations Mgr., cjohnson@blackcrow.fm. **Wattage**: 3,000. **Ad Rates:** $12-20 for 30 seconds; $15-25 for 60 seconds. WXHT-FM. **URL:** http://www.valdostatoday.com/star1053.html.

9467 ■ WTHV-AM - 810
4198 Rebecca Cir.
Valdosta, GA 31606
Phone: (229)245-9848
Format: Gospel. **Founded:** Sept. 07, 2006. **Wattage**: 2,500.

9468 ■ WVDA-FM - 88.5
PO Box 2118
Omaha, NE 68103-2118
Free: 888-937-2471
Format: Contemporary Christian. **Owner:** Educational Media Foundation, 2351 Sunset Blvd., Ste. 170-218, Rocklin, CA 95677, Ph: (800)434-8400. **URL:** http://www.air1.com.

9469 ■ WVGA-FM
1711 Ellis Dr.
Valdosta, GA 31601
Phone: (229)244-8642
Fax: (229)242-7620
Format: Talk; News. **Owner:** Radio Data Group, Inc., 2070 Chain Bridge Rd., Ste. 105, Vienna, VA 22182, Ph: (703)748-2800, Fax: (703)748-2133. **Wattage**: 10,000 ERP. **Ad Rates:** Advertising accepted; rates available upon request. **URL:** http://valdostatoday.com.

9470 ■ WVLD-AM - 1450
1711 Ellis Dr.
Valdosta, GA 31601
Phone: (229)244-8642
Format: Sports; News; Talk. **Networks:** Precision Racing; Gannett News; CBS. **Owner:** Valdosta Media Service, at above address. **Founded:** 1959. **Operating Hours**: Continuous. **ADI**: Tallahassee, FL-Thomasville (Bainbridge), GA. **Key Personnel:** John Rodriguez, Contact. **Wattage**: 1,000. **Ad Rates:** $3.75-10.70 for 30 seconds; $4.75-13.30 for 60 seconds. Underwriting available. **URL:** http://rock1069.com.

9471 ■ WVLD-FM - 106.9
1711 Ellis Dr.
Valdosta, GA 31601
Phone: (229)244-8642
Fax: (229)242-7620
Format: Full Service. **ADI**: Albany (Valdosta & Cordele), GA. **Wattage**: 860. **Ad Rates:** Advertising accepted; rates available upon request.

9472 ■ WVVS-FM - 90.9
1500 N Patterson St.
Valdosta, GA 31698
Phone: (229)333-5662
Format: Alternative/New Music/Progressive; Urban Contemporary. **Owner:** Valdosta State University, 1500 N Patterson St., Valdosta, GA 31698, Ph: (229)333-5800, Fax: (229)333-5482, Free: 800-618-1878. **Founded:** 1971. **Operating Hours**: Continuous. **ADI**: Albany (Valdosta & Cordele), GA. **Key Personnel:** Daniel Oakes, Station Mgr. **Wattage**: 5,300. **Ad Rates:** Noncommercial. **URL:** http://www.valdosta.edu/vsu/stuorg/V91//index.html.

9473 ■ WWET-FM - 91.7
100 E Central Ave.
Valdosta, GA 31603
Phone: (229)333-5154
Free: 800-222-4788
Email: ask@gpb.org
Format: Public Radio. **Owner:** Georgia Public Broadcasting, 260 14th St. NW, Atlanta, GA 30318, Ph: (404)685-2400, Free: 800-222-6006. **Key Personnel:** Carl Smith, Contact. **URL:** http://www.gpb.org.

9474 ■ WWRQ-FM - 107.7
1711 Ellis Dr.
Valdosta, GA 31601
Phone: (229)244-8642
Format: Album-Oriented Rock (AOR). **Networks:** ABC. **Founded:** 1992. **Operating Hours**: Continuous. **ADI**: Albany (Valdosta & Cordele), GA. **Key Personnel:** Al Brooks, Gen. Mgr.; Scott James, Dir. of Programs. **Wattage**: 25,000. **Ad Rates:** $14-20 for 30 seconds; $16-25 for 60 seconds. $14-$20 for 30 seconds; $16-$25 for 60 seconds. **URL:** http://thebeat1079.com.

VIDALIA

SE GA. Toombs Co. 82 mi. W. of Savannah. Residential.

9475 ■ Northland Cable Television
320 Commerce Way
Vidalia, GA 30474
Phone: (912)537-3200
Fax: (912)537-7395
Founded: Sept. 06, 2006. **Cities Served:** 75 channels. **Mailing address:** PO Box 547, Vidalia, GA 30474. **URL:** http://www.northlandcabletv.com.

9476 ■ W14CQ - 14
PO Box A
Santa Ana, CA 92711
Phone: (714)832-2950
Free: 888-731-1000
Owner: Trinity Broadcasting Network Inc., PO Box A, Santa Ana, CA 92711, Ph: (714)832-2950, Free: 888-731-1000.

9477 ■ WGPH-FM - 91.5
PO Box 510
Appling, GA 30802
Phone: (706)309-9610
Fax: (706)309-9669
Free: 800-926-4669
Format: Contemporary Christian. **Owner:** Good News Network, PO Box 428, Manassas, VA 20108, Ph: (703)392-4118, Free: 866-466-3639. **Founded:** 1989. **Operating Hours**: Continuous. **Wattage**: 50,000. **Ad Rates:** Noncommercial. **URL:** http://www.gnnradio.org.

9478 ■ WTCQ-FM - 97.7
1501 Mt. Vernon Rd.
Vidalia, GA 30474
Phone: (912)537-9202
Fax: (912)537-4477
Free: 800-374-5888
Format: Adult Contemporary. **Networks:** ABC. **Owner:** Vidalia Communications Corp., Not Available. **Founded:** 1969. **Operating Hours**: Continuous. **ADI**: Savannah, GA. **Key Personnel:** Zack Fowler, Station Mgr., zfowler@vidaliacommunications.com; Marvin McIntyre, Contact. **Local Programs:** *ABC Morning Sports*, Monday Tuesday Wednesday Tuesday Friday 6:30 a.m.; *Classic Cuts At Lunch*, Monday Tuesday Wednesday Thursday Friday 11:00 a.m.; 12:30 p.m. **Wattage**: 6,000. **Ad Rates:** $3.50-5.50 for 30 seconds; $5-7 for 60 seconds. **Mailing address:** PO Box 900, Vidalia, GA 30474. **URL:** http://www.southeastgeorgiatoday.com/wtcq/index.htm.

9479 ■ WVOP-AM - 970
1501 Mt. Vernon Rd.
Vidalia, GA 30474
Phone: (912)537-9202
Format: News; Talk. **Networks:** ABC. **Owner:** Vidalia Communications Corp., Not Available. **Founded:** 1946. **Operating Hours**: Continuous. **ADI**: Savannah, GA. **Key Personnel:** Zack Fowler, Station Mgr., zfowler@vidaliacommunications.com; Joyce Foskey, Office Mgr., jfoskey@vidaliacommunications.com; Marvin McIntyre, Contact. **Wattage**: 5,000. **Ad Rates:** $3.50-5.50 for 30 seconds; $5-7 for 60 seconds. **Mailing address:** PO Box 900, Vidalia, GA 30474. **URL:** http://www.southeastgeorgiatoday.com.

9480 ■ WYUM-FM - 101.7
1501 Mt. Vernon Rd.
Vidalia, GA 30474
Phone: (912)537-9202
Format: Country. **Owner:** Vidalia Communications Corp., Not Available. **Key Personnel:** Zack Fowler, Mgr.; Dorothy Davis, Traffic Mgr.; Joyce Foskey, Office Mgr. **Mailing address:** PO Box 900, Vidalia, GA 30474. **URL:** http://www.southeastgeorgiatoday.com.

VILLA RICA

W. GA. Douglas Co. 25 mi. W. of Atlanta. Residential.

9481 ■ Villa Rican
Villa Rican
901 Hays Mill Rd.
Villa Rica, GA 30180
Phone: (770)834-6631
Newspaper. **Freq:** Weekly (Thurs.). **Print Method:** Offset. **Cols./Page:** 6. **Col. Width:** 26 nonpareils. **Col. Depth:** 301 agate lines. **Key Personnel:** Spencer Crawford, Editor; Leonard Woolsey, Publisher; David Bragg, Director, Advertising. **Subscription Rates:** $2.14 Individuals /day. **URL:** http://times-georgian.com/villarican. **Ad Rates:** GLR $4.25; BW $503.10; 4C $40; SAU $3.90; PCI $5. **Remarks:** Color advertising accepted; rates available upon request. **Circ:** 2000.

WALESKA

9482 ■ W214AS-FM - 90.7
PO Box 391
Twin Falls, ID 83303
Fax: (208)736-1958
Free: 800-357-4226
Format: Religious; Contemporary Christian. **Owner:** CSN International, PO Box 391, Twin Falls, ID 83303, Ph: (208)736-1958, Fax: (208)736-1958, Free: 800-357-

Circulation: ★ = AAM; △ or • = BPA; ♦ = CAC; ❑ = VAC; ⊕ = PO Statement; ‡ = Publisher's Report; Boldface figures = sworn; Light figures = estimated.

4226. **URL:** http://www.csnradio.com.

WARM SPRINGS

9483 ■ WJSP-FM - 88.1
609 White House Pkwy.
Warm Springs, GA 31830
Phone: (706)655-2145
Free: 800-222-4788
Format: Public Radio. **Networks:** Public Broadcasting Service (PBS); National Public Radio (NPR). **Owner:** Georgia Public Broadcasting, 260 14th St. NW, Atlanta, GA 30318, Ph: (404)685-2400, Free: 800-222-6006. **Founded:** 1985. **Operating Hours:** 6 a.m.-midnight. **Wattage:** 100,000. **Ad Rates:** Advertising accepted; rates available upon request. **URL:** http://www.gpb.org.

9484 ■ WWGC-FM - 90.7
609 White House Pky.
Warm Springs, GA 31830
Phone: (404)685-2400
Email: wwgc@westga.edu
Format: Public Radio; Jazz. **Networks:** Public Radio International (PRI); National Public Radio (NPR); Peach State Public Radio. **Owner:** State University of West Georgia, 1601 Maple St., Carrollton, GA 30118-0001, Ph: (678)839-5000. **Founded:** 1973. **Operating Hours:** 6 a.m.-midnight; 40% local. **Wattage:** 500. **Ad Rates:** Noncommercial. **URL:** http://www.gpb.org.

WARNER ROBINS

C. GA. Houston Co. 17 mi. S. of Macon. Robin Air Force Base. Machine shop. Manufactures aircraft parts. Agriculture. Soybeans, peaches, peanuts.

9485 ■ Journal of Special Education Leadership
Council of Administrators of Special Education
Osigian Office Ctre.
101 Katelyn Cir., Ste. E
Warner Robins, GA 31088
Phone: (478)333-6892
Fax: (478)333-2453
Journal covering programs and developments affecting the special education field. **Freq:** Semiannual. **Key Personnel:** Mary Lynn Boscardin, Editor. **Subscription Rates:** Included in membership. **URL:** http://csef.air.org/publications/related/jsel/jsel.html; http://www.casecec.org/resources/jsel.asp. **Remarks:** Advertising accepted; rates available upon request. **Circ:** 5300, 5300.

9486 ■ WRCC-FM - 101.7
2052 Watson Blvd.
Box 5051
Warner Robins, GA 31099
Phone: (912)922-2222
Fax: (912)929-4487
Format: Country. **Networks:** Jones Satellite. **Founded:** 1966. **Formerly:** WRBN-FM; WPPR-FM. **Operating Hours:** Continuous. **Key Personnel:** Janiz Arnold, Contact; Vernon Arnold, Gen. Mgr; Janiz Arnold, Contact. **Wattage:** 6,000. **Ad Rates:** $10 for 30 seconds; $18 for 60 seconds.

9487 ■ WRWR-AM - 1350
1350 Radio Loop
Warner Robins, GA 31088
Phone: (478)923-3416
Fax: (478)923-3236
Format: Big Band/Nostalgia; Talk; News. **Formerly:** WNNG-AM. **Key Personnel:** Cecil Staton, President, cecilstaton@georgiaeaglemedia.com. **Ad Rates:** Noncommercial.

9488 ■ W202BA-FM - 88.3
PO Box 391
Twin Falls, ID 83303
Fax: (208)736-1958
Free: 800-357-4226
Format: Religious; Contemporary Christian. **Owner:** CSN International, PO Box 391, Twin Falls, ID 83303, Ph: (208)736-1958, Fax: (208)736-1958, Free: 800-357-4226. **Key Personnel:** Kelly Carlson, Dir. of Engg.; Ray Gorney, Asst. Dir. **URL:** http://www.csnradio.com.

WASHINGTON

NE GA. Wilkes Co. 40 mi. S. of Athens. Historic sites, museums. Manufactures fibre glass fabrics, polyethylene film, textiles. Pine, hardwood timber. Agriculture. Dairy, beef, poultry, cornmeal.

9489 ■ News-Reporter
News-Reporter
116 W Robert Toombs Ave.
Washington, GA 30673
Phone: (706)678-2636
Fax: (706)678-3857
Publisher's E-mail: editor@news-reporter.com
Local newspaper. **Founded:** 1912. **Freq:** Weekly (Thurs.). **Print Method:** Offset. **Cols./Page:** 6. **Col. Width:** 27 nonpareils. **Col. Depth:** 301 agate lines. **Key Personnel:** Sparky Newsome, Editor; Teri Eno, Manager, Circulation; Mary Newsome, Managing Editor. **Subscription Rates:** $26 Individuals in Wilkes County; $41 Out of area; $33 Individuals online. **URL:** http://www.news-reporter.com. **Mailing address:** PO Box 340, Washington, GA 30673. **Ad Rates:** GLR $.20; BW $245.10. **Remarks:** Accepts advertising. **Circ:** 4,900.

9490 ■ WLOV-AM - 1370
823 Berkshire Dr.
Washington, GA 30673
Phone: (706)678-0100
Format: Sports. **Founded:** 1955. **Operating Hours:** 7:00 a.m. - 7:00 p.m. network. **Wattage:** 1,000. **Ad Rates:** $5.50 for 30 seconds; $8 for 60 seconds. **URL:** http://wlovradio.com/.

WATKINSVILLE

9491 ■ Oconee Enterprise
Oconee Enterprise
PO Box 535
Watkinsville, GA 30677-0535
Phone: (706)769-5175
Fax: (706)769-8532
Publisher's E-mail: oconeeenterprise@mindspring.com
Community newspaper. **Freq:** Weekly (Thurs.). **Print Method:** Offset. **Trim Size:** 6 x 21 1/2. **Cols./Page:** 6. **Col. Width:** 13 1/2 agate lines. **Col. Depth:** 21 1/2 nonpareils. **Key Personnel:** Vinnie Williams, Publisher; Maridee Williams, Director, General Manager; Blake Giles, Editor. **USPS:** 402-720. **Subscription Rates:** $19 Individuals in Oconee County; $36 Two years in Oconee County; $22 Individuals in Georgia; $42 Two years in Georgia; $24 Out of state; $46 Out of state 2 years. **URL:** http://www.oconeeenterprise.com. **Ad Rates:** GLR $6.90; BW $1,102.50; 4C $956.60; PCI $6.60. **Remarks:** Accepts advertising. **Circ:** (Not Reported).

9492 ■ WGMG-FM - 102.1
1010 Tower Pl.
Watkinsville, GA 30677
Phone: (706)549-6222
Fax: (706)546-0441
Format: Adult Contemporary. **Key Personnel:** Kobe Fargo, Dir. of Programs, kobe.fargo@coxradio.com; Scott Smith, Gen. Mgr., VP, scott.smith@coxradio.com; Tim Bryant, News Dir., tim.bryant@coxradio.com. **Ad Rates:** Noncommercial. **URL:** http://www.magic1021.com.

9493 ■ WPUP-FM - 100.1
1010 Tower Pl.
Watkinsville, GA 30677
Phone: (706)549-6222
Fax: (706)546-0441
Format: Contemporary Hit Radio (CHR); Top 40. **Owner:** Southern Broadcasting, at above address. **Founded:** 1988. **Operating Hours:** Continuous. **Key Personnel:** Scott Smith, Gen. Mgr., VP; Evan Delany, Music Dir.; Kobe Fargo, Dir. of Programs, kobe.fargo@coxradio.com. **Wattage:** 25,000. **Ad Rates:** $23.50 for 30 seconds; $27 for 60 seconds. **URL:** http://www.powerathens.com.

9494 ■ WRFC-AM - 960
1010 Tower Pl.
Watkinsville, GA 30677
Phone: (706)549-6222
Format: Talk; News. **Networks:** ABC; ESPN Radio; CBS. **Owner:** Cox Radio Inc., 6205 Peachtree Dunwood Rd., Atlanta, GA 30328-4524, Ph: (678)645-0000, Fax: (678)645-5002. **Founded:** 1948. **Operating Hours:** Continuous; 50% network, 50% local. **Key Personnel:** David Johnston, Dir. of Programs, david.johnston@coxradio.com; Lynda Brame, Sales Mgr., lynda.brame@coxradio.com. **Wattage:** 5,000. **Ad Rates:** Noncommercial. **URL:** http://www.960theref.com.

WAYCROSS

SE GA. Ware Co. 90 mi. SW of Savannah. Manufactures caskets, footwear, mobile homes, cigars, furniture, rubber products, textiles. Meat packing, cold storage plants; naval stores. Pine, cypress, gum timber. Diversified farming. Tobacco, corn.

9495 ■ Waycross Journal Herald
Waycross Journal Herald
400 Isabella St.
Waycross, GA 31501
Phone: (912)283-2244
Publisher's E-mail: circulation@wjhnews.com
Newspaper with Democratic orientation. **Freq:** Mon.-Sat. (eve.). **Print Method:** Offset. **Trim Size:** 12 x 20. **Cols./Page:** 6. **Col. Width:** 24 nonpareils. **Col. Depth:** 301 agate lines. **Key Personnel:** Jack Williams, III, Editor; Roger Williams, Publisher; Gary Griffin, Managing Editor. **ISSN:** 6702--2000 (print). **Subscription Rates:** $11.50 Individuals home delivery; $10.50 Individuals online delivery; $14.50 Individuals home delivery and online. **URL:** http://wjhnews.com. **Remarks:** Accepts advertising. **Circ:** (Not Reported).

9496 ■ Mediastream
126 Havanna Ave.
Waycross, GA 31501
Phone: (912)283-2332
Formerly: Waycross Cable Co. **Cities Served:** Ware and Brantley counties.; 149 channels. **URL:** http://www.mediastreamus.com.

9497 ■ WASW-FM - 91.9
PO Box 3206
Tupelo, MS 38803
Format: Religious. **Founded:** Feb. 1991. **Key Personnel:** Rick Robertson, Contact; Rick Robertson, Contact. **URL:** http://www.afa.net.

9498 ■ WAYX-AM - 1230
1766 Memorial Dr., Ste. 1
Waycross, GA 31501
Phone: (912)283-3518
Email: newstalk1230@wayx.net
Format: News; Talk. **Owner:** Satilla Broadcast Properties, LLC, at above address. **Formerly:** WWGA-AM. **Operating Hours:** Continuous. **Wattage:** 1,000. **Ad Rates:** Advertising accepted; rates available upon request. **URL:** http://www.wayx.net/.

9499 ■ W45CU - 45
PO Box A
Santa Ana, CA 92711
Phone: (714)832-2950
Free: 888-731-1000
Email: comments@tbn.org
Owner: Trinity Broadcasting Network Inc., PO Box A, Santa Ana, CA 92711, Ph: (714)832-2950, Free: 888-731-1000. **URL:** http://www.tbn.org.

9500 ■ WXGA-TV - 8
c/o WGTV-TV
1540 Stewart Ave. SW
Atlanta, GA 30310
Phone: (404)685-2400
Fax: (404)685-4788
Format: Public TV. **Networks:** Public Broadcasting Service (PBS); Georgia Public Television. **Owner:** Georgia Public Telecommunications, at above address. **Founded:** 1961. **Key Personnel:** Kent Steele, Dir. of Programs; Richard E. Ottinger, Contact; Frank Bugg, Contact; Al Korn, Contact. **Wattage:** 35,300 ERP. **Ad Rates:** Noncommercial. **URL:** http://www.gpb.org/.

9501 ■ WXVS-FM - 90.1
6443 TV Rower Rd.
Waycross, GA 31501
Phone: (912)338-5200
Free: 800-222-4788
Email: ask@gpb.org
Format: Public Radio. **Owner:** Georgia Public Broadcasting, 260 14th St. NW, Atlanta, GA 30318, Ph: (404)685-2400, Free: 800-222-6006. **Operating Hours:** Continuous. **Key Personnel:** Charles W. Kurtz, Contact. **Ad Rates:** Noncommercial; underwriting available. **URL:** http://www.gpb.org.

9502 ■ WYNR-FM - 102.5
3833 US Hwy. 82
Brunswick, GA 31523
Phone: (912)267-1025

Fax: (912)264-5462
Format: Country. **Owner:** Qantum Communications, Inc., at above address. **URL:** http://www.1025wynr.net.

WAYNESBORO

E. GA. Burke Co. 30 mi. S. of Augusta. Cotton and lumber mills; garment, steel, and metal factories. Nuclear generating plant. Timber. Agriculture. Cotton, corn, soybeans, peanuts.

9503 ■ The True Citizen
Citizen Newspapers
PO Box 948
Waynesboro, GA 30830
Community newspaper. **Freq:** Weekly (Wed.). **Print Method:** Offset. **Trim Size:** 11 1/2 x 21 1/2. **Cols./Page:** 6. **Col. Width:** 26 nonpareils. **Col. Depth:** 301 agate lines. **Key Personnel:** Roy F. Chalker, Editor; Bonnie K. Taylor, General Manager. **Subscription Rates:** $18.90 Individuals online only; $29.10 Individuals with free 1 year online; $35 Individuals contiguous counties; $44.30 Out of area; $55 Out of state. **URL:** http://www.thetruecitizen.com. **Ad Rates:** GLR $.38; BW $630; 4C $10; SAU $.55; PCI $7.06. **Remarks:** Accepts advertising. **Circ:** ‡5,400.

9504 ■ WYFA-FM - 107.1
11530 Carmel Commons Blvd.
Charlotte, NC 28226
Phone: (704)523-5555
Free: 800-888-7077
Format: Religious. **Networks:** Bible Broadcasting. **Owner:** Bible Broadcasting Network Inc., 11530 Carmel Commons Blvd., Charlotte, NC 28226, Ph: (704)523-5555, Free: 800-888-7077. **Founded:** 1985. **Operating Hours:** Continuous; 99% network, 1% local. **Wattage:** 25,000. **Ad Rates:** Noncommercial. **Mailing address:** PO Box 7300, Charlotte, NC 28241. **URL:** http://www.bbnradio.org.

WEST POINT

WC GA. Troup Co. 2 mi. E. of Lanett.

9505 ■ WCJM-FM - 100.9
915 Veteran's Pkwy.
Opelika, AL 36803-2329
Phone: (706)645-2991
Fax: (706)645-3364
Format: Country. **Networks:** CBS. **Owner:** Quantum of Auburn License Company L.L.C., at above address. **Founded:** 1958. **Operating Hours:** Continuous; 50% network, 50% local. **Key Personnel:** Ben Taylor, Dir. of Sales, ben.taylor@qantumofauburn.com. **Wattage:** 6,000. **Ad Rates:** $6 for 15 seconds; $8 for 30 seconds; $12 for 60 seconds. **URL:** http://www.wcjmthebull.com.

9506 ■ WOW!
1241 O.G. Skinner Dr.
West Point, GA 31833-1789
Phone: (706)645-8553
Fax: (706)645-0148
Free: 877-KNO-LOGY
Founded: 1994. **Formerly:** Cable Alabama Corp.; Verizon Americast; PCL Cable; Knology Inc. **Key Personnel:** Richard Luke, Ph.D., Chief Tech. Ofc.; Debbie Schmidt, Systems Mgr., debra.schmidt@knology.com. **Cities Served:** subscribing households 8,100. **URL:** http://www.knology.com.

WINDER

NE GA. Barrow Co. 20 mi. W. of Athens. Manufactures furniture, textiles, fiberglass, railroad cars, rugs, fertilizer. Poultry processing, seed cleaning plants. Agriculture. Cotton, corn, vegetables, chickens and cattle.

9507 ■ The Barrow County News
Swartz-Morris Media Inc.
189 W Athens St.
Winder, GA 30680
Phone: (770)408-0272
Fax: (770)867-1034
Publisher's E-mail: debbie@barrowcountynews.com
Local newspaper. **Freq:** Semiweekly (Wed. and Sun.). **Print Method:** Offset. **Cols./Page:** 6. **Col. Width:** 1.75 inches. **Col. Depth:** 294 agate lines. **Key Personnel:** Debbie Burgamy, Publisher. **Subscription Rates:** $19.26 Individuals home delivery; 6 months; $32.10 Out of area mail delivery; 12 months; $40 Individuals home delivery; 12 months; $31 Other countries mail delivery; 6 months. **Formerly:** The Winder News. **Remarks:** Accepts advertising. **Circ:** (Not Reported).

9508 ■ The Barrow County Shopper
Swartz-Morris Media Inc.
189 W Athens St.
Winder, GA 30680
Phone: (770)408-0272
Fax: (770)867-1034
Publisher's E-mail: debbie@barrowcountynews.com
Shopper guide. **Founded:** 1984. **Freq:** Weekly (Wed.). **Print Method:** Photo offset. **Cols./Page:** 6. **Col. Width:** 11.625 inches. **Col. Depth:** 21 inches. **Key Personnel:** Debbie Burgamy, Publisher; LeAnne Akin, Editor; JoAnn Craven, Manager, Circulation. **Subscription Rates:** Free. **URL:** http://www.barrowcountynews.com/. **Formerly:** The Advantage. **Ad Rates:** BW $1,663.20; 4C $190; PCI $13.20. **Remarks:** Accepts advertising. **Circ:** (Not Reported).

9509 ■ WYFW-FM - 89.5
11530 Carmel Commons Blvd.
Charlotte, NC 28226
Phone: (704)523-5555
Free: 800-888-7077
Format: Middle-of-the-Road (MOR); Religious. **Networks:** Bible Broadcasting. **Owner:** Bible Broadcasting Network Inc., 11530 Carmel Commons Blvd., Charlotte, NC 28226, Ph: (704)523-5555, Free: 800-888-7077. **Founded:** 1987. **Operating Hours:** Continuous. **Wattage:** 6,000. **Ad Rates:** Noncommercial. **Mailing address:** PO Box 7300, Charlotte, NC 28241-7300. **URL:** http://www.bbnradio.org.

WOODSTOCK

NW GA. Cherokee Co. 33 mi. N. of Atlanta. Residential.

9510 ■ GWPCA Wire News
German Wirehaired Pointer Club of America
c/o Erika Brown, Treasurer
236 Park Ave.
Woodstock, GA 30188-4274
Phone: (770)591-4329
Publisher's E-mail: gwpca.mail@gmail.com
Freq: Quarterly. **Subscription Rates:** Included in membership. **URL:** http://www.gwpca.com/WireNews.html. **Ad Rates:** 4C $175; BW $75. **Remarks:** Accepts advertising. **Circ:** (Not Reported).

9511 ■ Journal of Human Service Education: A Journal of the National Organization for Human Services
National Organization for Human Services
5431 Old Hwy. 5, Ste. 206, No. 214
Woodstock, GA 30188
Phone: (770)924-8899
Fax: (678)494-5076
Free: 800-597-2306
Publisher's E-mail: info@nationalhumanservices.org
Professional journal covering human services education. **Freq:** Annual. **Key Personnel:** Dr. Edward Neukrug, Editor; Dr. Tammi Milliken, Editor. **URL:** http://www.nationalhumanservices.org/journal-of-human-services. **Remarks:** Accepts advertising. **Circ:** (Not Reported).

9512 ■ The Royal Cross
Order of the Daughters of the King
101 Weatherstone Dr., Ste. 870
Woodstock, GA 30188
Phone: (770)517-8552
Fax: (770)517-8066
Publisher's E-mail: dok1885@doknational.org
Magazine containing articles, news, stories, and organizational events of the Order of the Daughters of the King. **Freq:** Quarterly. **Alt. Formats:** PDF. **URL:** http://www.doknational.com/royal_cross.html. **Remarks:** Advertising not accepted. **Circ:** (Not Reported).

WRIGHTSVILLE

EC GA. Johnson Co. 56 mi. E. of Macon. Manufactures textiles. Agriculture. Cotton, corn, soybeans, peanuts, wheat. Livestock.

9513 ■ The Wrightsville Headlight
The Sandersville Georgian Inc.
102 W Elm St.
Wrightsville, GA 31096
Phone: (706)846-3188
Publication E-mail: headlight@washeme.net
Community newspaper. **Freq:** Weekly (Thurs.). **Print Method:** Offset. **Cols./Page:** 6. **Col. Width:** 12 picas. **Col. Depth:** 21 inches. **Ad Rates:** BW $581; 4C $881; SAU $4.50; PCI $4.50. **Remarks:** Accepts advertising. **Circ:** ‡2200.

YOUNG HARRIS

NE GA. Towns Co. 10 mi. W. of Hiawassee.

9514 ■ WYHG-AM - 770
1352 Main St., Ste. 6
Young Harris, GA 30582
Phone: (706)379-9770
Format: Oldies. **Simulcasts:** WLSB, WALH. **Networks:** ABC. **Founded:** 1984. **Formerly:** WZEL-AM; WZCM-AM. **Operating Hours:** Sunrise-sunset. **Wattage:** 750. **Ad Rates:** Noncommercial. Combined advertising rates available with WLBB, WALH.

ZEBULON

W. GA. Pike Co. 12 mi. S. of Griffin. Residential. Agricultural.

9515 ■ Pike County Journal-Reporter
Hometown News Corp.
PO Box 789
Zebulon, GA 30295
Phone: (770)567-3446
Fax: (770)567-8814
Publisher's E-mail: news@barnesville.com
Community newspaper. **Freq:** Weekly (Wed.). **Print Method:** Offset. **Cols./Page:** 6. **Col. Width:** 27 nonpareils. **Col. Depth:** 301 agate lines. **Key Personnel:** Walter Geiger, Publisher; Rachel McDaniel, Editor, Reporter; Jennifer Taylor, Office Manager. **Subscription Rates:** $25 Individuals in County; $30 Out of area; $35 Out of state. **URL:** http://www.pikecountygeorgia.com. **Ad Rates:** GLR $.17; SAU $6. **Remarks:** Accepts advertising. **Circ:** ‡3,000.

Circulation: ★ = AAM; △ or • = BPA; ♦ = CAC; ❑ = VAC; ⊕ = PO Statement; ‡ = Publisher's Report; Boldface figures = sworn; Light figures = estimated.

ASAN

9516 ■ KTWG-AM - 801
1868 Halsey Dr.
Asan, Guam 96922-1505
Phone: (671)477-5894
Fax: (671)477-6411
Email: ktwg@twr.hafa.net.gu
Format: Contemporary Christian; Full Service. **Owner:** Trans World Radio, PO Box 8700, Cary, NC 27512, Ph: (919)460-3700, Fax: (919)460-3702, Free: 800-456-7897. **Founded:** 1975. **Operating Hours:** 5 a.m.-11 p.m. **ADI:** Agana, Guam. **Key Personnel:** Nate McGurk, Station Mgr.; Wally Hollis, Music Dir.; Jeff Nelson, Mgr. of Public Rel.; Rich Fuller, Mgr. of Public Rel. **Wattage:** 10,000. **Ad Rates:** Underwriting available. **URL:** http://www.ktwg.com.

BARRIGADA

9517 ■ KHMG-FM
PO Box 23189
Barrigada, Guam 96921
Phone: (671)477-6341
Fax: (671)477-7136
Email: khmg@harvestministries.net
Format: Religious. **Owner:** Harvest Christian Academy, 1000 N Randall Rd., Elgin, IL 60123. **Founded:** Mar. 26, 1996. **Key Personnel:** Rev. Dan Pelletier, President, pastor@harvestministries.net; John Collier, VP, johnc@who.net. **Wattage:** 8,000 ERP. **Ad Rates:** Noncommercial.

DEDEDO

9518 ■ KUAM-AM - 610
600 Harmon Loop Rd., Ste. 102
Dededo, Guam 96912
Phone: (671)635-5837
Email: lyndae@isla61.com
Format: Talk; Album-Oriented Rock (AOR). **Networks:** CBS; NBC. **Owner:** Calvo Enterprises Inc., 138 Martyr St., Guam 96910. **Founded:** Mar. 14, 1954. **Operating Hours:** Sunrise-sunset. **ADI:** Agana, Guam. **Key Personnel:** Robert Clarke, Chief Engineer, robert@kuam.com; Joey Calvo, Gen. Mgr., jcalvo@kuam.com; James Castro, Station Mgr., jcastro@kuam.com; Lynda Evangelista, Program Mgr., lyndae@isla61.com. **Wattage:** 10,000. **Ad Rates:** $36-52 for 30 seconds; $57.60-83.20 for 60 seconds. **URL:** http://www.kuam.com.

9519 ■ KUAM-TV - 8
600 Harmon Loop Rd., Ste. 102
Dededo, Guam 96912
Phone: (671)635-5837
Format: News. **Networks:** NBC. **Owner:** Calvo Enterprises, Inc., 138 Martyr St., Hagatna, Guam 96910. **Founded:** 1956. **Key Personnel:** Joey Calvo, Gen. Mgr., jcalvo@kuam.com; James Castro, Station Mgr., jcastro@kuam.com; Krista Gaza, Gen. Sales Mgr., kgaza@kuam.com; Robert Clarke, Chief Engineer, robert@kuam.com. **Wattage:** 3,500 ERP H. **Ad Rates:** Advertising accepted; rates available upon request. **URL:** http://www.kuam.com.

HAGATNA

9520 ■ KGUM-AM
111 W Chalan Santo Papa, Ste. 800
Hagatna, Guam 96910
Phone: (671)477-5700
Format: News; Talk. **Owner:** Sorensen Media Group, 111 Chalan Santo Papa St., Ste. 800, Hagatna, Guam 96910, Ph: (671)477-5700, Fax: (671)477-3982. **Key Personnel:** Rex Sorensen, Chairman, CEO, rex@spbguam.com. **Wattage:** 10,000.

9521 ■ KOKU-FM - 100
107 Julale Ctr.
424 W O'Brien Dr.
Hagatna, Guam 96910
Phone: (671)477-1003
Fax: (671)472-7663
Email: marketing@hitradio100.com
Format: Contemporary Hit Radio (CHR). **Ad Rates:** Advertising accepted; rates available upon request. **URL:** http://www.hitradio100.com.

9522 ■ KPXP-FM - 99.5
111 Chalan Santo Papa, Ste. 800
Hagatna, Guam 96910
Phone: (671)477-5700
Fax: (671)477-3982
Format: News; Information; Contemporary Hit Radio (CHR). **Owner:** Sorensen Media Group, 111 Chalan Santo Papa St., Ste. 800, Hagatna, Guam 96910, Ph: (671)477-5700, Fax: (671)477-3982. **Founded:** Dec. 20, 1992. **Operating Hours:** Continuous.

9523 ■ KRSI-FM - 97.9
111 Chalan Santo Papa, Ste. 800
Hagatna, Guam 96910
Phone: (671)477-5700
Fax: (671)477-3982
Format: Oldies; Classical. **Owner:** Sorensen Media Group, 111 Chalan Santo Papa St., Ste. 800, Hagatna, Guam 96910, Ph: (671)477-5700, Fax: (671)477-3982.

9524 ■ KZGZ-FM - 97.5
111 Chalan Santo Papa, Ste. 800
Hagatna, Guam 96910
Phone: (671)477-5700
Fax: (671)477-3982
Format: Adult Contemporary. **Owner:** Sorensen Media Group, 111 Chalan Santo Papa St., Ste. 800, Hagatna, Guam 96910, Ph: (671)477-5700, Fax: (671)477-3982. **Key Personnel:** Rex Sorensen, Chmn. of the Bd., CEO. **Wattage:** 40,000. **URL:** http://www.sorensenmediagroup.com/power98.

MANGILAO

9525 ■ KPRG-FM - 89.3
UOG Station
303 University Dr.
Mangilao, Guam 96923
Phone: (671)734-8930
Fax: (671)734-2958
Format: Public Radio. **Owner:** Guam Educational Radio Foundation. **Founded:** Jan. 28, 1994. **Operating Hours:** Continuous except Wed, Fri 12 a.m. - 9 p.m. **Key Personnel:** Joanne F. Barta, Founder; George J. Boughton, Founder; George M. Butler, Founder; Ted Carol, Founder; Michael McCarthy, Founder. **Ad Rates:** Noncommercial; underwriting available. **URL:** http://www.kprgfm.com.

TAMUNING

9526 ■ KIJI-FM - 104.3
543A Top Plaza Bldg.
N Marine Corps Dr.
Tamuning, Guam 96913
Phone: (671)478-0104
Fax: (671)647-7840
Format: Oldies. **Owner:** Choice Broadcasting L.L.C.

AIEA

9527 ■ KLHT-AM - 1040
98-1016 Komo Mai Dr.
Aiea, HI 96701
Phone: (808)524-1040
Fax: (808)487-1040
Format: Religious. **Networks:** Independent. **Owner:** Calvary Chapel of Honolulu, 98-1016 Komo Mai Dr., Aiea, HI 96701, Ph: (808)524-0844, Fax: (808)275-5193. **Founded:** 1985. **Formerly:** KIFH-AM. **Operating Hours:** Continuous. **ADI:** Honolulu, HI. **Wattage:** 10,000. **Ad Rates:** $15-20 for 30 seconds; $25 for 60 seconds. **URL:** http://www.klight.org.

CAMP H M SMITH

9528 ■ Asia-Pacific Defense Forum
U.S. Pacific Command
PO Box 64031
Camp H M Smith, HI 96861-4031
Phone: (808)477-1341
Fax: (808)477-6247
Publication E-mail: apdforum@apan-info.net
Professional magazine for members of the militaries of all nations in the Asia-Pacific region. **Freq:** Quarterly. **Trim Size:** 8 1/4 x 10 1/2. **Cols./Page:** 3. **Key Personnel:** Andrea Davis, Editor-in-Chief; Thomas Black, Program Manager, phone: (808)477-0760, fax: (808)477-1471. **URL:** http://apdforum.com. **Remarks:** Advertising not accepted. **Circ:** Non-paid 27000.

ELEELE

S HI. Kauai Co. S. coast of Kauai Island, E. of Hanapepe.

9529 ■ KUAI-AM - 570
4271 Halenani St.
Eleele, HI 96705
Phone: (808)245-9527
Founded: 1965. **Wattage:** 1,000. **Ad Rates:** $18-25 for 30 seconds; $22-30 for 60 seconds.

HANALEI

9530 ■ KAQA-FM - 90.9
PO Box 825
Hanalei, HI 96714
Phone: (808)826-7774
Fax: (808)826-7977
Free: 866-275-1112
Email: kkcr@kkcr.org
Format: Educational. **Networks:** Pacifica. **Owner:** Kekahu Foundation Inc., at above address. **Founded:** 1993. **Operating Hours:** 5 a.m. to 12 p.m. **Wattage:** 1,000. **Ad Rates:** Noncommercial. **URL:** http://www.kkcr.org.

9531 ■ KKCR-FM - 90.9
PO Box 825
Hanalei, HI 96714
Free: 866-275-1112
Email: kkcr@kkcr.org
Format: Eclectic. **Networks:** Pacifica. **Owner:** Kekahu Foundation Inc., at above address. **Founded:** 1993. **Operating Hours:** 5 a.m. to 12 p.m. **Key Personnel:** Dean Rogers, Gen. Mgr; Ken Jannelli, Contact, ken@kkcr.org. **Local Programs:** *Island Roots*, Tuesday 12:00 p.m. - 2:00 p.m. **Wattage:** 1,000. **Ad Rates:** Noncommercial. **URL:** http://www.kkcr.org.

HILO

SE HI. Hawaii Co. On NE coast of the Island of Hawaii. Port of entry. Tourist resort. This is the most tropical of the islands and the only one with an active volcano. Agriculture. Sugar cane, coffee, vegetables, orchids, tropical flowers, papaya, macadamia nuts. Tuna, mullet fisheries.

9532 ■ Hawaii Tribune-Herald
Stephens Media L.L.C.
PO Box 767
Hilo, HI 96721
Phone: (808)935-6621
Fax: (808)969-9100
Publisher's E-mail: sfrederick@stephensmedia.com
General newspaper. **Freq:** Daily and Sun. (morn.). **Print Method:** Offset. **Cols./Page:** 6. **Col. Width:** 25 nonpareils. **Col. Depth:** 301 agate lines. **Key Personnel:** David Bock, Editor; Ted Dixon, Publisher; Alice Sledge, Director, Advertising. **Subscription Rates:** $13.50 Individuals /month; $40.50 Individuals 3 months; $81 Individuals 6 months; $162 Individuals /year. **URL:** http://www.hawaiitribune-herald.com. **Ad Rates:** SAU $13.75. **Remarks:** Advertising accepted; rates available upon request. **Circ:** Paid ♦**16,155**, Paid ♦**20,379**.

9533 ■ KANO-FM - 91.1
738 Kaheka St.
Honolulu, HI 96814
Phone: (808)955-8821
Fax: (808)946-3863
Email: mail@hawaiipublicradio.org
Format: Public Radio. **Owner:** Hawaii Public Radio, 738 Kaheka St., Honolulu, HI 96814, Ph: (808)955-8821, Fax: (808)946-3863. **Key Personnel:** Michael Titterton, President; Bill Dorman, News Dir., news@hawaiipublicradio.org; Charles Husson, Dir. of Operations, chusson@hawaiipublicradio.org; Gene Schiller, Music Dir., gschiller@hawaiipublicradio.org. **Ad Rates:** Noncommercial. **URL:** http://www.hawaiipublicradio.org.

9534 ■ KCIF-FM - 90.3
PO Box 1066
Hilo, HI 96721
Phone: (808)935-7434
Fax: (808)961-6022
Format: Religious. **Networks:** SkyLight Satellite. **Owner:** Hilo Christian Broadcasting Corp., PO Box 1066, Hilo, HI 96721, Ph: (808)982-4536. **Founded:** Sept. 01, 1995. **Operating Hours:** Continuous. **Wattage:** 5,000. **Ad Rates:** Noncommercial. **URL:** http://www.kcifhawaii.org.

9535 ■ KGMD-TV - 9
420 Waiakamilo Rd., Ste. 205
Honolulu, HI 96817
Phone: (808)847-3246
Fax: (808)845-3616
Format: Commercial TV. **Simulcasts:** KGMD-TV, Hilo, HI. **Networks:** CBS. **Owner:** Raycom Media Inc., 201 Monroe St., RSA Twr., 20th Fl., Montgomery, AL 36104-3731, Ph: (334)206-1400. **Formerly:** KGMB-TV. **ADI:** Honolulu, HI. **Ad Rates:** Advertising accepted; rates available upon request. **URL:** http://www.hawaiinewsnow.com.

9536 ■ KHBC-AM - 1060
688 Kinoole St., Ste. 112
Hilo, HI 96720
Phone: (808)365-5181
Format: Adult Contemporary. **Founded:** May 01, 1936. **Key Personnel:** Buddy Gordon, Gen. Mgr., buddy@khbcradio.com; Stephanie Salazar, News Dir., news@khbcradio.com; Brad Freeman, Dir. of Production, Music Dir., prod@khbcradio.com.

9537 ■ KHBC-FM - 92.7
688 Kino'ole St., Ste. 112
Hilo, HI 96720-3877
Phone: (208)837-4104
Format: Adult Contemporary. **Owner:** Parrott Broadcasting, at above address. **Founded:** May 25, 1989. **Wattage:** 7,500. **Ad Rates:** Advertising accepted; rates available upon request.

9538 ■ KHHB-TV
305 Wailuku Dr., Ste. 5
Hilo, HI 96720
Phone: (808)930-8690
Email: info@khhb.tv
URL: http://www.khhb.tv/home.html.

9539 ■ KHLO-AM - 850
913 Kanuelehua
Hilo, HI 96720-5116
Phone: (808)961-0651
Format: Sports. **Owner:** Pacific Radio Group Inc., 311 Ano S, Kahului, HI 96732. **Founded:** 1950. **Operating Hours:** Continuous. **Wattage:** 5,000. **Ad Rates:** $6-12 for 30 seconds; $10-16 for 60 seconds. **URL:** http://www.espnhawaii.com.

9540 ■ KHWI-FM - 92.1
688 Kino'ole St., Ste. 112
Hilo, HI 96720-3877
Free: 800-365-5181
Format: Full Service. **Owner:** Parrott Broadcasting Ltd. Partnership, at above address. **Founded:** 1988. **ADI:** Honolulu, HI. **Wattage:** 4,500. **Ad Rates:** Advertising accepted; rates available upon request.

9541 ■ KILE-AM - 1560
5353 W Alabama St., Ste. 415
Houston, TX 77056
Format: Sports. **Owner:** Fred R and Evelyn K Morton, at above address. **Founded:** 1922. **Operating Hours:** Monday,Wednesday 12 am-9 pm ; Tuesday,12 am- 8 pm ; Thursday,,staurday,Sunday 12 am-10 pm ; Friday 12 am-11 pm. **Wattage:** 15,000 N; 46,000 D. **Ad Rates:** $17-32 for 60 seconds. **URL:** http://www.sbnation1560.com.

9542 ■ KIPA-AM
688 Kinoole S
Hilo, HI 96720

Circulation: • = AAM; △ or • = BPA; ♦ = CAC; ❑ = VAC; ⊕ = PO Statement; ‡ = Publisher's Report; Boldface figures = sworn; Light figures = estimated.

Phone: (808)935-6858
Fax: (808)969-7949
Format: Middle-of-the-Road (MOR). **Networks:** NBC. **Owner:** Skynet Communications, Inc., at above address. **Founded:** 1947. **Wattage:** 5,000. **Ad Rates:** Advertising accepted; rates available upon request.

9543 ■ KKBG-FM - 97.9
913 Kanoelehua Ave.
Hilo, HI 96720
Phone: (808)961-0651
Fax: (808)934-8088
Format: News; Sports; Information. **Owner:** Pacific Radio Group, Inc., 913 Kanoelehua Ave., Hilo, HI 96720, Ph: (808)961-0651. **Founded:** 1979. **Operating Hours:** 6:00 a.m. - 7:00 p.m. Monday - Friday, 10:00 a.m. - 3:00 p.m. Saturday - Sunday. **Key Personnel:** Rodney Pacheco, Contact. **Wattage:** 51,000 ERP. **Ad Rates:** $21-29; $22-35 for 30 seconds; $19-25 for 60 seconds. **URL:** http://www.kbigfm.com/.

9544 ■ KNWB-FM - 97.1
1145 Kilauea Ave.
Hilo, HI 96720
Phone: (808)296-2971
Fax: (808)935-7761
Format: Oldies. **Operating Hours:** 6 a.m. - 12 a.m. **Wattage:** 38,000. **Ad Rates:** Advertising accepted; rates available upon request. **URL:** http://www.b97hawaii.com.

9545 ■ KPUA-AM - 670
1145 Kilauea Ave.
Hilo, HI 96720
Phone: (808)935-5461
Fax: (808)935-7761
Email: news@kpua.net
Format: News; Information; Talk. **Networks:** CBS; Westwood One Radio; Wall Street Journal Radio; ESPN Radio. **Owner:** New West Broadcasting Corp., 1145 Kilauea Ave., Hilo, HI 96720, Ph: (808)935-5461, Fax: (808)935-7761. **Founded:** 1932. **Operating Hours:** Continuous. **Local Programs:** *The Community Forum*, Wednesday. **Wattage:** 10,000. **Ad Rates:** $11-15 for 30 seconds; $14-19 for 60 seconds. $11-$15 for 30 seconds; $14-$19 for 60 seconds. Combined advertising rates available with KWXX-FM. **URL:** http://www.kpua.net.

9546 ■ KPVS-FM - 95.9
913 Kanoelehua Ave.
Hilo, HI 96720
Phone: (808)961-0651
Fax: (808)935-0396
Email: studio@nativefm.com
Format: Contemporary Hit Radio (CHR). **Owner:** Pacific Radio Group Inc., 311 Ano S, Kahului, HI 96732. **Key Personnel:** Chuck Bergson, Co-CEO, President. **URL:** http://www.nativefm.com/.

9547 ■ K201FQ-FM - 88.1
PO Box 391
Twin Falls, ID 83303
Fax: (208)736-1958
Free: 800-357-4226
Format: Religious; Contemporary Christian. **Owner:** CSN International, PO Box 391, Twin Falls, ID 83303, Ph: (208)736-1958, Fax: (208)736-1958, Free: 800-357-4226. **Key Personnel:** Mike Kestler, Contact; Don Mills, Music Dir., Prog. Dir. **URL:** http://www.csnradio.com.

9548 ■ KWXX-FM - 94.7
1145 Kilauea Ave.
Hilo, HI 96720
Phone: (808)935-5461
Fax: (808)935-7761
Email: sales@kwxx.com
Format: Reggae; Hawaiian. **Networks:** CBS. **Owner:** New West Broadcasting Corp., 1145 Kilauea Ave., Hilo, HI 96720, Ph: (808)935-5461, Fax: (808)935-7761. **Founded:** 1984. **Operating Hours:** Continuous. **Local Programs:** *Top 5 at 5*, Monday Tuesday Wednesday Thursday Friday 5:00 p.m.; *Traffic Jam 'n' Jokes*, Monday Tuesday Wednesday Thursday Friday 4:00 p.m. - 5:00 p.m.; *The Lunchtime Kalabash*, Monday Tuesday Wednesday Thursday Friday 12:00 p.m. - 1:00 p.m.; *Alana I Kai Hikina*, Sunday 4:00 p.m. - 7:00 p.m. **Wattage:** 51,000. **Ad Rates:** $18 for 30 seconds; $20 for 60 seconds. KPUA-AM. **URL:** http://www.kwxx.com.

HONOLULU

SC HI. Honolulu Co. On Oahu Island. University of Hawaii. State capital. Tourist resort. Principal port and business center of the islands. Major military installations. Oil refining. Wood carvings. Pineapple canneries; sugar industries; fish packing and canning. Manufactures fertilizer, cement, concrete products, steel bars, flour, soap, garments, awnings, tents, beverages.

9549 ■ Adaptive Behavior
International Society for Adaptive Behavior
University of Hawaii at Manoa
Dept. of Psychology
2430 Campus Rd.
Honolulu, HI 96822
Phone: (808)956-6727
Fax: (808)956-4700
Publisher's E-mail: sales@pfp.sagepub.com
Peer-reviewed journal focusing on adaptive behavior in animals and autonomous artificial systems. **Freq:** Bimonthly. **Key Personnel:** Ezequiel Di Paolo, Editor; Joanna J. Bryson, Associate Editor; Randall D. Beer, Associate Editor; Peter M. Todd, Associate Editor. **ISSN:** 1059--7123 (print); **EISSN:** 1741--2633 (electronic). **Subscription Rates:** £451 Institutions e-access; £491 Institutions print only; £501 Institutions print and e-access; £90 Institutions single print issue; $767 Institutions content through 1998; $768 Institutions e-access; $836 Institutions print; $853 Institutions print and online; $853 Institutions all online content; $938 Institutions current volume print & all online content; $153 Institutions single issue. **URL:** http://adb.sagepub.com. **Ad Rates:** BW £600. **Remarks:** Accepts advertising. **Circ:** (Not Reported).

9550 ■ Ala Moana Shopping Center Magazine
This Week Publications
130 Iolana Pl.
Honolulu, HI 96819-2234
Phone: (808)834-5813
Free: 877-255-8532
Bilingual magazine covering the Ala Moana Shopping Center open-air shopping mall for visitors (English and Japanese). Features news about shopping and dining. **Freq:** Monthly. **Trim Size:** 8 1/2 x 11. **Key Personnel:** Jasmine Lombardi, Editor-in-Chief. **URL:** http://www.alamoanacenter.com/Events/Ala-Moana-Magazine.aspx. **Remarks:** Advertising accepted; rates available upon request. **Circ:** 41600.

9551 ■ Asian-Pacific Law and Policy Journal
University of Hawaii - Manoa William S. Richardson School of Law
2515 Dole St.
Honolulu, HI 96822-2350
Phone: (808)956-7966
Fax: (808)956-3813
Publisher's E-mail: lawadm@hawaii.edu
Journal containing articles on legal issues in Asia and the Pacific Rim. **Freq:** Semiannual. **Key Personnel:** Grace Magruder, Editor-in-Chief. **URL:** http://www.hawaii.edu/aplpj. **Circ:** (Not Reported).

9552 ■ Asian Theater Journal
University of Hawaii Press
2840 Kolowalu St.
Honolulu, HI 96822-1888
Phone: (808)956-8255
Fax: (808)988-6052
Publisher's E-mail: uhpbooks@hawaii.edu
Journal focusing on the modern and traditional forms of performing arts in Asia. **Freq:** Semiannual March & September. **Trim Size:** 7 x 10. **Key Personnel:** Cindy Chun, Editor; Kathy Foley, Editor. **ISSN:** 0742--5457 (print); **EISSN:** 1527--2109 (electronic). **Subscription Rates:** $40 Individuals 1 year; $72 Two years; $25 Single issue; $160 Institutions 1 year; $288 Institutions 2 years; $85 Single issue institution. **URL:** http://www.uhpress.hawaii.edu/t-asian-theatre-journal.aspx; http://www.uhpress.hawaii.edu/p-8511-asian-theatre-journal.aspx?journal=1. **Ad Rates:** BW $200. **Remarks:** Accepts advertising. **Circ:** Paid 450.

9553 ■ Bamboo Ridge: Journal of Hawai'i Literature and Arts
Bamboo Ridge Press
PO Box 61781
Honolulu, HI 96839-1781
Phone: (808)626-1481
Fax: (808)626-1481
Publisher's E-mail: brinfo@bambooridge.com
Journal covering Hawaii's literary scene. **Freq:** Semiannual. **Print Method:** Offset. **Trim Size:** 6 x 9. **Key Personnel:** Eric Chock, Editor; Darrel Lum, Editor; Joy Kobayashi-Cintron, Contact. **ISSN:** 0733--0308 (print). **Subscription Rates:** $30 Individuals 2-issue; $60 Individuals 4-issue; $90 Individuals 6-issue. **URL:** http://www.bambooridge.com. **Ad Rates:** BW $150. **Remarks:** Advertising accepted; rates available upon request. **Circ:** ‡500.

9554 ■ Biography: An Interdisciplinary Quarterly
University of Hawaii Press
Ctr. for Biographical Research
Dept. of English
University of Hawaii
1733 Donaghho Rd.
Honolulu, HI 96822
Publisher's E-mail: uhpbooks@hawaii.edu
Journal acting as a forum for learned articles dealing with life-writing. **Freq:** Quarterly. **Print Method:** Offset. **Trim Size:** 6 x 9. **Cols./Page:** 1. **Col. Width:** 26 picas. **Col. Depth:** 46.5 picas. **Key Personnel:** Miriam Fuchs, Editor; George Simson, Editor, Founder; Craig Howes, Editor; Marie-Jose Fassiotto, Editor; Lanning Lee, Coordinator; Stanley Schab, Managing Editor. **ISSN:** 0162--4962 (print); **EISSN:** 1529--1456 (electronic). **Subscription Rates:** $40 Individuals /year; $72 Individuals two years; $15 Individuals single issue; $100 Institutions /year; $180 Institutions two years; $30 Institutions single issue. **URL:** http://www.uhpress.hawaii.edu/t-biography.aspx. **Ad Rates:** BW $200. **Remarks:** Accepts advertising. **Circ:** Paid ‡250.

9555 ■ Buddhist-Christian Studies
University of Hawaii Press
2840 Kolowalu St.
Honolulu, HI 96822-1888
Phone: (808)956-8255
Fax: (808)988-6052
Publisher's E-mail: uhpbooks@hawaii.edu
Journal focusing on Buddhism and Christianity and their historical and contemporary interrelationships. **Freq:** Annual November. **Trim Size:** 6 x 9. **Key Personnel:** Terry Muck, Editor; Rebecca Clifford, Managing Editor. **ISSN:** 0882--0945 (print); **EISSN:** 1527--9472 (electronic). **Subscription Rates:** $30 Individuals 1 year; $54 Two years; $60 Institutions 1 year; $108 Institutions 2 years. **URL:** http://www.uhpress.hawaii.edu/t3-buddhist-christian-studies.aspx; http://www.uhpress.hawaii.edu/p-8513-buddhist-christian-studies.aspx?journal=1. **Ad Rates:** BW $200. **Remarks:** Accepts advertising. **Circ:** Paid 330.

9556 ■ Building Management Hawaii
Trade Publishing Co.
287 Mokauea St.
Honolulu, HI 96819
Phone: (808)848-0711
Fax: (808)841-3053
Free: 800-234-5619
Publisher's E-mail: advertising@tradepublishing.com
Magazine covering maintenance and building management. **Freq:** Bimonthly. **Cols./Page:** 3. **Col. Width:** 13 picas. **Col. Depth:** 57 picas. **Key Personnel:** Aimee Harris, Editor. **Subscription Rates:** $25 Individuals Hawaii; $30 Individuals U.S. Mainland; $45 Other countries. **URL:** http://www.buildingmanagementhawaii.com. **Ad Rates:** BW $995; 4C $1,665. **Remarks:** Advertising accepted; rates available upon request. **Circ:** Non-paid 4700.

9557 ■ China Review International: A Journal of Reviews of Scholarly Literature in Chinese Studies
University of Hawaii Press
c/o Benjamin Hoffman, Mng. Ed.
Center for Chinese Studies, University of Hawaii
1890 East West Rd.
Honolulu, HI 96822-2318
Publisher's E-mail: uhpbooks@hawaii.edu
Journal presenting reviews of important current publications relating to China. **Freq:** Quarterly March, June, September, December. **Trim Size:** 7 x 10. **Cols./Page:** 1. **Col. Width:** 30 picas. **Col. Depth:** 48 picas. **Key Personnel:** Cindy Chun, Editor; Roger T. Ames, Editor; Benjamin Hoffman, Managing Editor. **ISSN:** 1069--5834

(print); **EISSN:** 1527--9367 (electronic). **Subscription Rates:** $30 Individuals 1 year - PDF; $54 Two years PDF; $13 Single issue PDF; $50 Institutions 1 year - PDF; $90 Institutions 2 years - PDF; $18 Single issue institution - PDF; $100 Individuals 1 year - print; $180 Two years print; $30 Single issue print. **Alt. Formats:** PDF. **URL:** http://www.uhpress.hawaii.edu/t-china-review-international.aspx; http://www.uhpress.hawaii.edu/p-8525-china-review-international.aspx?journal=1. **Ad Rates:** BW $200. **Remarks:** Accepts advertising. **Circ:** Paid 315.

9558 ■ Computer Applications in Engineering Education
John Wiley & Sons Inc.
c/o Magdy F. Iskander, Ed.
Director, Hawaii Center for Advanced Communications
College of Engineering, University of Hawaii at Manoa
2540 Dole St., Holmes Hall 483
Honolulu, HI 96822
Publisher's E-mail: info@wiley.com
Journal publishing articles relating to the innovative use of computers in education, especially in the engineering curriculum. **Freq:** Quarterly. **Trim Size:** 7 x 10. **Key Personnel:** Magdy F. Iskander, Editor; Hojjat Adeli, Board Member; William G. Gray, Board Member. **ISSN:** 1061--3773 (print); **EISSN:** 1099--0542 (electronic). **Subscription Rates:** $1545 Institutions online or print - USA online only - Canada & Mexico/ROW; $1854 Institutions print and online; $1601 Institutions, Canada and Mexico print only; $1910 Institutions, Canada and Mexico print & online; £790 Institutions online only - UK; £1000 Institutions print & online - UK; £833 Institutions print only - UK; €998 Institutions online only - Europe; €1263 Institutions print & online - Europe; €1052 Institutions print only - Europe; $1938 Institutions, other countries print & online ; $1629 Institutions, other countries print only; $80 Individuals print only - personal or students in USA/Canada & Mexico; $108 Individuals print only - personal or students in UK/Europe/ROW. **URL:** http://onlinelibrary.wiley.com/doi/10.1002/cae.v22.1/issuetoc. **Ad Rates:** BW $757; 4C $1,009. **Remarks:** Accepts advertising. **Circ:** 4550.

9559 ■ The Contemporary Pacific: A Journal of Island Affairs
University of Hawaii Press
1890 E W Rd.
Center for Pacific Island Studies
University of Hawaii at Manoa
Honolulu, HI 96822
Publication E-mail: muse@muse.jhu.edu uhtcp@hawaii.edu
Journal covering a wide range of current issues and events in the Pacific islands. **Founded:** 1989. **Freq:** Semiannual. **Print Method:** Offset. **Trim Size:** 7 x 10. **Key Personnel:** Cindy Chun, Editor; Jan Rensel, Managing Editor; Prof. Terence A. Wesley-Smith, PhD, Editor. **ISSN:** 1043-898X (print). **Subscription Rates:** $35 Individuals /year, TCP; $100 Institutions /year, TCP; $124 Institutions /year, TCP, international; $63 Individuals /two years, TCP; $100 Single issue /year, TCP. **URL:** http://www.uhpress.hawaii.edu/t-the-contemporary-pacific.aspx. **Ad Rates:** BW $200. **Remarks:** Accepts advertising. **Circ:** Paid 368.

9560 ■ Contrast Magazine
Contrast Magazine L.L.C.
PO Box 372031
Honolulu, HI 96837
Publisher's E-mail: info@contrastmagazine.com
Lifestyle magazine. **Freq:** Quarterly. **Key Personnel:** Mark Kushimi, Editor-in-Chief; Race Skelton, Publisher; Daniel Ikaika Ito, Editor. **Subscription Rates:** Free. **URL:** http://contrastmagazine.com. **Remarks:** Advertising accepted; rates available upon request. **Circ:** 20000.

9561 ■ Ethnobotany Research and Applications: A Journal of Plants, People, and Applied Research
University of Hawaii National Foreign Language Resource Center
1859 East-West Rd., No. 106
Honolulu, HI 96822-2322
Phone: (808)956-9424
Fax: (808)956-5983
Publisher's E-mail: nflrc@hawaii.edu
Peer-reviewed open access journal devoted to the rapid dissemination of current research in ethnobotany. **Freq:** Irregular. **Key Personnel:** Will McClatchey, Senior Editor; Han Lau, Managing Editor; Kim Bridges, Editor. **ISSN:** 1547--3465 (print). **Subscription Rates:** Free to qualified subscribers online. **URL:** http://www.ethnobotanyjournal.org; http://scholarspace.manoa.hawaii.edu/handle/10125/31. **Circ:** (Not Reported).

9562 ■ Hawaii
Hawaii Magazine
1000 Bishop St., Ste. 405
Honolulu, HI 96813
Phone: (808)537-9500
Fax: (808)537-6455
Publisher's E-mail: letters@hawaiimagazine.com
Consumer magazine covering Hawaii. **Freq:** Bimonthly. **Subscription Rates:** $15 Individuals. **URL:** http://www.hawaiimagazine.com/. **Remarks:** Accepts advertising. **Circ:** Paid ‡68000.

9563 ■ Hawaii Bar Journal
Grass Shack Productions
1111 Nuuanu Ave., Ste. 212
Honolulu, HI 96817
Phone: (808)521-1929
Fax: (808)521-6931
Publication E-mail: edracers@aol.com
Legal journal containing Hawaii State Bar news and articles for Hawaii attorneys. **Freq:** Monthly. **Print Method:** Offset. **Trim Size:** 8 1/8 x 10 7/8. **Cols./Page:** 3. **Col. Width:** 2.5 inches. **Col. Depth:** 8 inches. **Key Personnel:** Paulette Suwa, Managing Editor; Carol K. Muranaka, Editor, phone: (808)539-2877, fax: (808)539-2883; Mary Grace Flores, Assistant Managing Editor. **Subscription Rates:** $50 Individuals; $60 Other countries; $3 Single issue. **URL:** http://hsba.org/HSBA/News___Events/Hawaii_Bar_Journal.aspx?WebsiteKey=11fe7c6a-afa1-44dc-868d-d7d25627e91f. **Formerly:** Hawaii Bar News. **Ad Rates:** GLR $6; BW $1095; 4C $585. **Remarks:** Accepts advertising. **Circ:** Paid 5400, Non-paid 500.

9564 ■ Hawaii Beverage Guide
Hawaii Beverage Guide
1311 Kapiolani Blvd., Ste. 401
Honolulu, HI 96814
Phone: (808)591-0049
Publisher's E-mail: publisher@hawaiibevguide.com
Magazine for the beverage industry; including brand index, local and national news, product and special events promotion, and government agency releases. **Freq:** Monthly. **Print Method:** Offset. **Trim Size:** 8 1/2 x 11. **Cols./Page:** 3. **Col. Width:** 28 nonpareils. **Col. Depth:** 140 agate lines. **Key Personnel:** Christopher Teves, President, Publisher. **USPS:** 018-010. **Subscription Rates:** $41.88 U.S. 1-Year Subscription; $78.53 Two years 1-Time Order; $10 Single issue; $115.18 Individuals 3 years. **URL:** http://www.hawaiibevguide.com. **Ad Rates:** BW $792; 4C $1500. **Remarks:** Accepts advertising. **Circ:** ‡2,000.

9565 ■ Hawaii Business
PacificBasin Communications
1000 Bishop St., Ste. 405
Honolulu, HI 96813
Phone: (808)537-9500
Fax: (808)537-6455
Publication E-mail: hbeditorial@pacificbasin.net
Business magazine for business personnel in Hawaii. **Founded:** 1955. **Freq:** Monthly. **Print Method:** Web. **Trim Size:** 8 1/8 x 10 7/8. **Cols./Page:** 3. **Col. Width:** 2 3/16 inches. **Col. Depth:** 140 agate lines. **Key Personnel:** David Tumilowicz, Publisher, phone: (808)534-7535; Steve Petranik, Editor, phone: (808)534-7584; Jason Ubay, Managing Editor; Dennis Hollier, Senior Editor, phone: (808)534-7129; Chuck Tindle, Manager, Circulation, phone: (808)534-7521; Bobby Senaha, Director, Advertising, phone: (808)534-7575. **ISSN:** 0440-5056 (print). **Subscription Rates:** $29.95 Individuals 12 issues; $49.95 Individuals 24 issues; $59.95 Individuals 36 issues. **URL:** http://www.hawaiibusiness.com. **Ad Rates:** BW $2495; 4C $3095. **Remarks:** Advertising accepted; rates available upon request. **Circ:** (Not Reported).

9566 ■ Hawaii Catholic Herald
Hawaii Catholic Herald
1184 Bishop St.
Honolulu, HI 96813-2858
Phone: (808)585-3300
Fax: (808)585-3381
Free: 800-530-1790
Publication E-mail: pdownes@rcchawaii.org
Official newspaper (tabloid) of the Roman Catholic Diocese of Honolulu, HI. **Freq:** 26/yr. **Print Method:** Offset. **Trim Size:** 10 1/4 x 14 1/2. **Cols./Page:** 5. **Col. Width:** 1 7/8 inches. **Col. Depth:** 15 inches. **Key Personnel:** Patrick Downes, Editor; Donna Ann Aquino, Manager, Circulation; Bishop Larry Silva, Publisher, phone: (808)585-3346. **ISSN:** 1045--3636 (print). **Subscription Rates:** $24 Individuals in Hawaii; $26 Individuals in Mainland; $30 Other countries. **Ad Rates:** GLR $.35; PCI $16.80. **Remarks:** Accepts advertising. **Circ:** ‡16000.

9567 ■ Hawaii Crop Weather
U.S. Department of Agriculture National Agricultural Statistics Service - Hawaii Field Office
300 Ala Moana Blvd., Ste. 7-118
Honolulu, HI 96850
Phone: (808)522-8080
Fax: (844)332-7146
Publisher's E-mail: nass-hi@nass.usda.gov
Government Report. **Freq:** Weekly (Mon.). **Print Method:** Offset. **Cols./Page:** 1. **Col. Width:** 84 nonpareils. **Col. Depth:** 133 agate lines. **Subscription Rates:** $15 Individuals. **URL:** http://www.nass.usda.gov/Statistics_by_State/Hawaii/Publications/Crop_Progress_&_Condition. **Mailing address:** PO Box 50026, Honolulu, HI 96850. **Remarks:** Advertising not accepted. **Circ:** (Not Reported).

9568 ■ Hawaii Hochi
Hawaii Hochi Ltd.
917 Kokea St.
Honolulu, HI 96817-4528
Phone: (808)845-2255
Fax: (808)841-1357
Publisher's E-mail: editorial@thehawaiihochi.com
Japanese language newspaper for Japanese Americans in Hawaii. **Freq:** Mon.-Sat. **URL:** http://www.thehawaiihochi.com. **Ad Rates:** BW $1876.88; 4C $2294.88. **Remarks:** Accepts advertising. **Circ:** Combined 8000.

9569 ■ Hawaii Hospitality
Trade Publishing Co.
287 Mokauea St.
Honolulu, HI 96819
Phone: (808)848-0711
Fax: (808)841-3053
Free: 800-234-5619
Publisher's E-mail: advertising@tradepublishing.com
Magazine of the Hawaii Hotel and Lodging Association. **Freq:** Bimonthly Quarterly. **Key Personnel:** Faith Freitas, Sales Representative; Barry Redmayne, Publisher. **Subscription Rates:** $25 Individuals Hawaii; $30 Out of state; $45 Other countries. **URL:** http://www.hawaiihospitalityonline.com; http://www.hawaiihospitalityonline.com/about.html. **Remarks:** Accepts advertising. **Circ:** (Not Reported).

9570 ■ Hawaii Journal of Medicine and Public Health
Hawaii Medical Journal
1360 S Beretania St., Ste. 200
Honolulu, HI 96814
Phone: (808)536-7702
Publication E-mail: info@hawaiimedicaljournal.org
Peer-reviewed medical journal. **Freq:** Monthly. **Key Personnel:** Kalani S. Brady, MD, Editor; Norman Goldstein, MD, Editor; Dr. Frank L. Tabrah, Board Member; John Breinich, PhD, Board Member; Russell T. Stodd, Editor. **ISSN:** 2165--8218 (print); **EISSN:** 2165--8242 (electronic). **URL:** http://hjmph.org. **Formed by the merger of:** Hawaii Medical Journal; Hawaii Journal of Public Health. **Ad Rates:** 4C $850. **Remarks:** Accepts advertising. **Circ:** (Not Reported).

9571 ■ Hawaii Pacific Review
Hawaii Pacific University
1164 Bishop St.
Honolulu, HI 96813
Phone: (808)544-0200
Fax: (808)544-0862
Publication E-mail: hpreview@hpu.edu
Literary magazine containing short stories, poetry, and personal essays. **Freq:** Annual. **Print Method:** Perfect bound. **Trim Size:** 6 x 9. **Key Personnel:** Tyler McMa-

Circulation: ★ = AAM; △ or • = BPA; ♦ = CAC; ❑ = VAC; ⊕ = PO Statement; ‡ = Publisher's Report; Boldface figures = sworn; Light figures = estimated.

hon, Editor. **ISSN:** 1047--4331 (print). **Subscription Rates:** $5 Single issue back issue (print). **Alt. Formats:** Print. **URL:** http://hawaiipacificreview.org. **Remarks:** exchange basis only. **Circ:** Non-paid 500.

9572 ■ Hawaii Realtor Journal
Hawaii Association of Realtors
1259 A ala St., Ste. 300
Honolulu, HI 96817
Phone: (808)733-7060
Fax: (808)737-4977
Free: 888-737-9070
Publisher's E-mail: har@hawaiirealtors.com
Real estate tabloid. **Freq:** Semimonthly. **Cols./Page:** 5. **Col. Width:** 11 1/2 picas. **Col. Depth:** 14 3/4 inches. **Key Personnel:** Denise Motohiro, Contact; Nancy Donahue-Jones, Chief Executive Officer. **Subscription Rates:** Included in membership. **URL:** http://www.hawaiirealtors.com/membership. **Ad Rates:** BW $1,205; 4C $1,435. **Remarks:** Accepts advertising. **Circ:** 8500.

9573 ■ Hawaiian Journal of History
Hawaiian Historical Society
560 Kawaiahao St.
Honolulu, HI 96813
Phone: (808)537-6271
Fax: (808)537-6271
Publication E-mail: ipo@hawaiianhistory.org
Journal covering Hawaiian and Pacific history. **Freq:** Annual. **Key Personnel:** Holly McEldowney, Editor. **ISSN:** 0440--5145 (print). **Subscription Rates:** $12 Individuals. **URL:** http://www.hawaiianhistory.org/publications/journal. **Remarks:** Advertising not accepted. **Circ:** Combined ⊕**1800**.

9574 ■ Honolulu Magazine
Pacific Basin Communications
1000 Bishop St., Ste. 405
Honolulu, HI 96813
Phone: (808)534-7520
Publisher's E-mail: letters@honolulumagazine.com
Magazine covering the Pacific Islands. **Freq:** Monthly. **Print Method:** Web offset. **Trim Size:** 8.125 x 10.875. **Cols./Page:** 3. **Col. Width:** 26 nonpareils. **Col. Depth:** 140 agate lines. **Key Personnel:** Michael Keany, Managing Editor; Alyson Helwagen, Publisher; A. Kam Napier, Editor. **Subscription Rates:** $24.99 Individuals 12 issues; $34.99 Individuals 24 issues; $44.99 Individuals 36 issues. **URL:** http://www.honolulumagazine.com. **Remarks:** Accepts advertising. **Circ:** Paid 40000.

9575 ■ Honolulu Star-Bulletin
Midweek Printing Co.
500 Ala Moana Blvd., No. 7-500
Honolulu, HI 96813
Phone: (808)529-4700
Fax: (808)529-4750
Publisher's E-mail: letters@starbulletin.com
General newspaper. **Freq:** Mon.-Sun. **Print Method:** Offset. **Trim Size:** 69 picas x 129 picas. **Cols./Page:** 6. **Col. Width:** 10 picas. **Col. Depth:** 129 picas. **Key Personnel:** Lucy Young-Oda, Assistant Editor, phone: (808)529-4762; Dennis Francis, President, Publisher, phone: (808)529-4702; Frank Bridgewater, Editor, phone: (808)529-4791; Michael Rovner, Managing Editor, phone: (808)529-4758. **USPS:** 249-460. **Subscription Rates:** $180.96 Individuals Mon.-Sun. **URL:** http://www.staradvertiser.com. **Remarks:** Accepts advertising. **Circ:** Mon.-Sun. 66000.

9576 ■ Honolulu Weekly
Honolulu Weekly Inc.
1111 Fort St. Mall
Honolulu, HI 96813
Phone: (808)528-1475
Fax: (808)528-3144
Alternative newsweekly. **Freq:** Weekly (Wed.). **Print Method:** Web offset. **Trim Size:** 10 1/4 x 15. **ISSN:** 1057--414X (print). **URL:** http://honoluluweekly.com. **Ad Rates:** BW $2,875; 4C $3,375. **Remarks:** Accepts advertising. **Circ:** (Not Reported).

9577 ■ Journal of World History
University of Hawaii Press
c/o Fabio Lopez Lazaro, Ed.
Dept. of History
University of Hawaii
2530 Dole St.
Honolulu, HI 96822-2383
Publisher's E-mail: uhpbooks@hawaii.edu
Journal centering on historical analysis from a global point of view. **Freq:** Quarterly March, June, September, December. **Trim Size:** 6 x 9. **Key Personnel:** Cindy Chun, Editor; Jerry H. Bentley, Editor, Founder; Fabio Lopez Lazaro, Editor. **ISSN:** 1045--6007 (print); **EISSN:** 1527--8050 (electronic). **Subscription Rates:** $160 Institutions 1 year; $288 Institutions 2 years; $45 Institutions single issue; Included in membership. **URL:** http://www.uhpress.hawaii.edu/t-journal-of-world-history.aspx; http://www.uhpress.hawaii.edu/p-8517-journal-of-world-history.aspx?journal=1. **Ad Rates:** BW $200. **Remarks:** Accepts advertising. **Circ:** Paid 1282, 1282.

9578 ■ Kapio
Board of Student Publications
Kapiolani Community College
4303 Diamond Head Rd.
Honolulu, HI 96816
Phone: (808)734-9000
Collegiate newspaper. **Freq:** Weekly (Tues.). **Print Method:** Offset. **Trim Size:** 11 x 16. **Cols./Page:** 5. **Col. Width:** 11 picas. **Col. Depth:** 210 agate lines. **Key Personnel:** Paige L. Jinbo, Editor. **URL:** http://kapionews.kapiolani.hawaii.edu. **Remarks:** Accepts advertising. **Circ:** 2,500.

9579 ■ Korean Studies
University of Hawaii Press
1881 E W Rd.
Center for Korean Studies
Honolulu, HI 96822
Publication E-mail: uhpjourn@hawaii.edu
Journal addressing a broad range of topics through interdisciplinary and multicultural articles, book reviews and scholarly essays. **Freq:** Annual 1 issue per year (December). **Trim Size:** 6 x 9. **Key Personnel:** Michael E. MacMillan, Managing Editor; Cindy Chun, Editor; Min-Sun Kim, Editor. **ISSN:** 0145--840X (print); **EISSN:** 1529--1529 (electronic). **Subscription Rates:** $30 Individuals 1 year; $54 Two years; $50 Institutions 1 year; $90 Institutions 2 years; $54 Two years Individual. **URL:** http://www.uhpress.hawaii.edu/t-korean-studies.aspx; http://www.uhpress.hawaii.edu/p-8518-korean-studies.aspx?journal=1. **Ad Rates:** BW $200. **Remarks:** Accepts advertising. **Circ:** Paid 107.

9580 ■ Language Learning and Technology
University of Hawaii National Foreign Language Resource Center
1859 East-West Rd., No. 106
Honolulu, HI 96822-2322
Phone: (808)956-9424
Fax: (808)956-5983
Publisher's E-mail: nflrc@hawaii.edu
Publication covering the use of technology in language teaching and learning. **Freq:** 3/year. **Key Personnel:** Dorothy Chun, Editor-in-Chief; Trude Heift, Associate Editor; Mark Warschauer, Editor-in-Chief. **ISSN:** 1094--3501 (print). **Subscription Rates:** Free. **Online:** Gale. **URL:** http://llt.msu.edu. **Remarks:** Advertising not accepted. **Circ:** Non-paid 3944.

9581 ■ Manoa: A Pacific Journal of International Writing
University of Hawaii Press
Dept. of English
University of Hawaii
Kuykendall 626
Honolulu, HI 96822
Publisher's E-mail: uhpbooks@hawaii.edu
Journal presenting U.S. and international fiction, poetry, essays, book reviews. **Freq:** 2/yr. **Print Method:** Offset. **Trim Size:** 7 x 10. **Key Personnel:** Cindy Chun, Editor; Pat Matsueda, Managing Editor; Frank Stewart, Editor. **ISSN:** 1045--7909 (print); **EISSN:** 1527--943X (electronic). **Subscription Rates:** $50 Institutions print or electronic; $70 Individuals print and electronic. **URL:** http://muse.jhu.edu/journals/man; http://www.uhpress.hawaii.edu/t-manoa.aspx; http://www.jstor.org/journals/10457909.html. **Ad Rates:** BW $200. **Remarks:** Accepts advertising. **Circ:** 1013.

9582 ■ Marine Georesources and Geotechnology
Taylor & Francis Group Journals
c/o John C. Wiltshire, Editor-in-Chief
University of Hawaii
Dept. of Ocean Resources & Engineering
1000 Pope Rd.
Honolulu, HI 96822
Phone: (808)956-6042
Fax: (808)956-2136
Publisher's E-mail: customerservice@taylorandfrancis.com
Journal publishing research on scientific and engineering aspects of sea floor sediments and rocks, and marine minerals exploration. **Freq:** Quarterly. **Print Method:** Offset. **Trim Size:** 7 x 10. **Cols./Page:** 1. **Col. Width:** 51 nonpareils. **Col. Depth:** 96 agate lines. **Key Personnel:** Ronald Chaney, Editor-in-Chief; John C. Wiltshire, Editor-in-Chief. **ISSN:** 1064--119X (print); **EISSN:** 1521--0618 (electronic). **Subscription Rates:** $526 Individuals print only; $869 Institutions online only; $993 Individuals print and online. **URL:** http://www.tandfonline.com/toc/umgt20/current. **Remarks:** Accepts advertising. **Circ:** (Not Reported).

9583 ■ Modern Luxury Hawaii
Modern Luxury Media
2155 Kalakaua Ave., Ste. 701
Honolulu, HI 96815
Phone: (808)924-6622
Fax: (808)924-6623
Magazine covering affluent lifestyle in Hawaii. **Freq:** Quarterly. **Key Personnel:** Meredith Low, Publisher; Emmy Kasten, Editor-in-Chief. **Subscription Rates:** $40 Individuals; $60 Two years. **URL:** http://modernluxury.com/modern-luxury-hawaii. **Remarks:** Accepts advertising. **Circ:** (Not Reported).

9584 ■ Oceanic Linguistics
University of Hawaii Press
2840 Kolowalu St.
Honolulu, HI 96822-1888
Phone: (808)956-8255
Fax: (808)988-6052
Publication E-mail: oceanic@hawaii.edu
Journal focusing on the study of indigenous languages of the Oceanic area. **Freq:** Semiannual. **Trim Size:** 6 x 9. **Key Personnel:** John Lynch, Editor; Cindy Chun, Editor. **ISSN:** 0029--8115 (print); **EISSN:** 1527--9421 (electronic). **Subscription Rates:** $40 Individuals 1 year; $72 Two years; $25 Single issue individual; $120 Institutions 1 year; $216 Institutions 2 years; $65 Single issue institution. **URL:** http://www.uhpress.hawaii.edu/t-oceanic-linguistics.aspx; http://www.uhpress.hawaii.edu/p-8521-oceanic-linguistics.aspx?journal=1; http://www.jstor.org/journals/00298115.html. **Ad Rates:** BW $200. **Remarks:** Accepts advertising. **Circ:** Paid 283.

9585 ■ Oriental Insects: A Journal of Taxonomy & Zoogeography of Old World
Associated Publishers
c/o Neal L. Evenhuis, Editorial Board
Dept. of Natural Sciences
Bernice P. Bishop Museum
1525 Bernice St.
Honolulu, HI 96817-0916
Publisher's E-mail: assopubl@yahoo.com
Professional journal covering insects of the Tropics. **Freq:** Annual. **Print Method:** Offset. **Trim Size:** 7 x 11. **Cols./Page:** 1. **Col. Width:** 5 2/10 inches. **Key Personnel:** Neal L. Evenhuis, Board Member; K.-G. Heller, Board Member; Ai-Ping Liang, Board Member; Zhi-Qiang Zhang, Board Member; V.V. Ramamurthy, Editor, Publisher; Girish Chandra, Business Manager; Ian J. Kitching, Board Member; Virendra K. Gupta, Editor, Publisher. **ISSN:** 0030--5316 (print). **Subscription Rates:** $75 Individuals. **URL:** http://www.mapress.com/AP/oi.html. **Remarks:** Accepts advertising. **Circ:** (Not Reported).

9586 ■ Pacific Business News
American City Business Journals Inc.
1833 Kalakaua Ave., 7th Fl.
Honolulu, HI 96815
Phone: (808)955-8100
Fax: (808)955-8078
Publication E-mail: pacific@bizjournals.com
Business tabloid. **Freq:** Weekly. **Print Method:** Offset. **Trim Size:** 11 1/2 x 16. **Cols./Page:** 6. **Col. Width:** 19 nonpareils. **Col. Depth:** 207 agate lines. **Key Personnel:** Mary Beth Lohman, Publisher; James George, Managing Editor; Kevin Bumgarner, Editor; Bob Charlet, Publisher, phone: (808)955-8052. **USPS:** 417-340. **Subscription Rates:** $92 Individuals print & digital; $4.99 Single issue. **URL:** http://www.bizjournals.com/pacific/news. **Ad Rates:** BW $6200; 4C $6800; BW $6640. **Remarks:** Accepts advertising. **Circ:** (Not Reported).

9587 ■ Pacific Magazine with Islands Business
PacificBasin Communications
1000 Bishop St., Ste. 405
Honolulu, HI 96813
Phone: (808)537-9500
Fax: (808)537-6455
Publication E-mail: pacmag@ntamar.com info@pacificmagazine.net
Magazine covering business in Hawaii. **Freq:** Monthly. **Key Personnel:** Giff Johnson, Editor; Floyd K. Takeuchi, Publisher, phone: (808)534-7519. **Subscription Rates:** $15 Individuals; $55 Other countries airmail; $25 Two years. **URL:** http://www.pacificmagazine.net/. **Remarks:** Accepts advertising. **Circ:** (Not Reported).

9588 ■ Pacific Science: A Quarterly Devoted to the Biological and Physical Sciences of the Pacific Region
University of Hawaii Press
c/o Curtis C. Daehler, Editor
University of Hawaii at Manoa, Dept. of Botany
St. John 413A
Honolulu, HI 96822
Publisher's E-mail: uhpbooks@hawaii.edu
Journal Focusing on the Biological and Physical Sciences of the Pacific Region. **Freq:** Quarterly January, April, July, October. **Print Method:** Offset. **Trim Size:** 7 x 10. **Cols./Page:** 2. **Col. Width:** 16 picas. **Col. Depth:** 46.5 picas. **Key Personnel:** Julie H. Bailey-Brock, Board Member; Allen Allison, Board Member; Robert H. Cowie, Board Member; Curtis C. Daehler, Editor; Curt Daehler, Editor. **ISSN:** 0030--8870 (print); **EISSN:** 1534--6188 (electronic). **Subscription Rates:** $50 Individuals /year; $18 Individuals single issue; $100 Institutions /year; $180 Institutions two years; $30 Institutions single issue; $90 Two years; Included in membership. **URL:** http://www.uhpress.hawaii.edu/t-pacific-science.aspx; http://www.pacificscience.org/pacscijournal.html. **Ad Rates:** BW $200. **Remarks:** Accepts advertising. **Circ:** Paid ‡525.

9589 ■ Philosophy East & West: A Quarterly of Comparative Philosophy
University of Hawaii Press
c/o Roger T. Ames, Editor
University of Hawaii
Sakamaki B-302
Honolulu, HI 96822-2383
Publisher's E-mail: uhpbooks@hawaii.edu
Journal on comparative philosophy. **Freq:** Quarterly. **Print Method:** Offset. **Trim Size:** 7 x 10. **Cols./Page:** 1. **Col. Width:** 26.5 picas. **Col. Depth:** 46.5 picas. **Key Personnel:** Roger T. Ames, Editor; Arindam Chakrabarti, Associate Editor. **ISSN:** 0031--8221 (print); **EISSN:** 1527--943X (electronic). **Subscription Rates:** $50 Individuals /year; $90 Individuals two years; $18 Individuals single issue; $160 Institutions /year; $288 Institutions two years; $45 Institutions single issue. **URL:** http://www.uhpress.hawaii.edu/t3-philosophy-east-and-west.aspx. **Ad Rates:** BW $200. **Remarks:** Accepts advertising. **Circ:** Paid ‡775.

9590 ■ The Review of Disability Studies
Center on Disability Studies
University of Hawaii at Manoa
1776 University Ave., No. UA4-6
Honolulu, HI 96822
Phone: (808)956-5688
Publisher's E-mail: rdsj@hawaii.edu
Peer-reviewed journal that publishes research articles, essays, and bibliographies relating to people with disabilities. **Freq:** Quarterly. **Key Personnel:** Robert A. Stodden, PhD, Editor-in-Chief. **ISSN:** 1553--3697 (print); **EISSN:** 1552--9215 (electronic). **Subscription Rates:** $50 Individuals individuals (online); $100 Institutions libraries and institutions (online); $25 Students students (online). **URL:** http://www.rds.hawaii.edu. **Remarks:** Accepts advertising. **Circ:** (Not Reported).

9591 ■ Spotlight Big Island Gold
Honolulu Publishing Company Ltd.
707 Richards St., No. 525
Honolulu, HI 96813
Phone: (808)524-7400
Fax: (808)531-2306
Free: 800-272-5245
Magazine serving as a visitor's guide to the island of Hawaii, the "Big Island". **Freq:** Quarterly. **Print Method:** Offset. **Trim Size:** 4 x 10 3/4. **Cols./Page:** 1. **Col. Width:** 3 1/2 inches. **Col. Depth:** 10 inches. **Key Personnel:** Gina Jacobs, Administrative Assistant; Ruben Ablog, Director, Production; Sandra Kinsella, Publisher; Ron Ihori, Editor. **Subscription Rates:** $4 Individuals; $5 Canada; $5.50 Individuals in Mexico; $8.50 Other countries. **URL:** http://www.spotlighthawaii.com. **Ad Rates:** BW $1,275; 4C $1,695. **Remarks:** Accepts advertising. **Circ:** Non-paid 50000.

9592 ■ Spotlight Kauai
Spotlight Hawaii Publishing
532 Cummins St.
Honolulu, HI 96814
Phone: (808)593-9404
Fax: (808)593-9494
Magazine serving as a visitor's guide to Kauai. **Freq:** Quarterly. **Print Method:** Offset. **Trim Size:** 4 x 10 3/4. **Cols./Page:** 1. **Col. Width:** 3 1/2 inches. **Col. Depth:** 10 inches. **Key Personnel:** Ron Ihori, Editor; Sandra Kinsella, Publisher; Ruben Ablog, Director, Production. **URL:** http://www.spotlighthawaii.com/Kauai/2015-12SLK. **Ad Rates:** BW $1300; 4C $1720. **Remarks:** Accepts advertising. **Circ:** Non-paid 42000.

9593 ■ Spotlight Oahu
Spotlight Hawaii Publishing
532 Cummins St.
Honolulu, HI 96814
Phone: (808)593-9404
Fax: (808)593-9494
Magazine serving as a visitor's guide to Oahu, Kauai, Maui and Big Island. **Freq:** Bimonthly. **Print Method:** Web Offset. **Trim Size:** 4 x 10 3/4. **Cols./Page:** 1. **Col. Width:** 3 1/2 inches. **Col. Depth:** 10 inches. **Key Personnel:** Larry W. King, Vice President; Ruben Ablog, Director, Production; Sandra Kinsella, Publisher; William R. Schoen, President; Ron Ihori, Editor. **ISSN:** 0273--8422 (print). **URL:** http://www.spotlighthawaii.com/Oahu/2015-10SLO/files/22.html. **Ad Rates:** BW $710; 4C $855. **Remarks:** Accepts advertising. **Circ:** Non-paid 35000.

9594 ■ This Week Big Island
This Week Publications
130 Iolana Pl.
Honolulu, HI 96819-2234
Phone: (808)834-5813
Free: 877-255-8532
Visitor magazine with maps, coupons, and tourist information for Big Island visitors. **Freq:** Quarterly. **Print Method:** Offset. **Trim Size:** 4 x 10.75. **Cols./Page:** 2. **Col. Width:** 22 nonpareils. **Key Personnel:** Sarah Yamanaka, Editor; Stan Mulkey, Chief Operating Officer, Publisher. **URL:** http://www.thisweekhawaii.com/big-island. **Remarks:** Accepts advertising. **Circ:** 68000.

9595 ■ This Week Kauai
This Week Publications
130 Iolana Pl.
Honolulu, HI 96819-2234
Phone: (808)834-5813
Free: 877-255-8532
Visitor magazine with maps, coupons, and tourist information for Kauai. **Freq:** Quarterly. **Print Method:** Offset. **Trim Size:** 4 x 10.75. **Cols./Page:** 2. **Col. Width:** 22 nonpareils. **Col. Depth:** 140 agate lines. **Key Personnel:** Sarah Yamanaka, Editor; Stan Mulkey, Chief Operating Officer, Publisher. **URL:** http://www.thisweekhawaii.com/kauai. **Remarks:** Accepts advertising. **Circ:** 40000.

9596 ■ This Week Maui
This Week Publications
130 Iolana Pl.
Honolulu, HI 96819-2234
Phone: (808)834-5813
Free: 877-255-8532
Visitor magazine with maps, coupons, and visitor information. **Freq:** Bimonthly. **Print Method:** Offset. **Trim Size:** 4 x 10.75. **Cols./Page:** 2. **Col. Width:** 22 nonpareils. **Col. Depth:** 140 agate lines. **Key Personnel:** Sarah Yamanaka, Editor; Stan Mulkey, Publisher. **Subscription Rates:** Free. **URL:** http://www.thisweekhawaii.com/maui. **Ad Rates:** BW $642; 4C $760; PCI $32.10. **Remarks:** Accepts advertising. **Circ:** 72000.

9597 ■ This Week Oahu
This Week Publications
130 Iolana Pl.
Honolulu, HI 96819-2234
Phone: (808)834-5813
Free: 877-255-8532
Magazine with maps, coupons, and information for visitors to Hawaii. Does not include information for business travel. **Freq:** Monthly. **Print Method:** Offset. **Trim Size:** 4 x 10.75. **Cols./Page:** 2. **Col. Width:** 22 nonpareils. **Col. Depth:** 140 agate lines. **Key Personnel:** Najee Lynne, Editor; Stan Mulkey, Chief Operating Officer, Publisher. **URL:** http://thisweekhawaii.com/oahu. **Remarks:** Accepts advertising. **Circ:** ‡160000.

9598 ■ The Voice of Hawaii
University of Hawaii at Manoa
2500 Campus Rd.
Honolulu, HI 96822
Phone: (808)956-8111
Free: 800-956-8975
Publisher's E-mail: uhmanoa.admissions@hawaii.edu
Collegiate newspaper (tabloid). **Freq:** 5/week. **Print Method:** Offset. **Trim Size:** 11 1/2 x 17. **Cols./Page:** 5. **Col. Width:** 22 nonpareils. **Col. Depth:** 224 agate lines. **Key Personnel:** Will Caron, Editor-in-Chief; Jaimie Kim, Managing Editor; Brandon Panoke, Business Manager. **Subscription Rates:** $80 Individuals daily mailed, first class; $55 Individuals first class. **URL:** http://manoa.hawaii.edu. **Ad Rates:** PCI $11.50. **Remarks:** Accepts advertising. **Circ:** Mon.-Fri. ‡18000.

9599 ■ Waterbirds: The International Journal of Waterbird Biology
Waterbird Society
Pacific Cooperative Studies Unit
Department of Botany
University of Hawaii Manoa
3190 Maile Way
Honolulu, HI 96822
Phone: (808)956-3932
Fax: (808)973-2936
Specializes in the biology, status, ecology, management and conservation of all waterbird species living in marine, estuarine and freshwater habitats. **Freq:** Quarterly. **Print Method:** Offset. **Cols./Page:** 2. **Col. Width:** 24 nonpareils. **Col. Depth:** 119 agate lines. **Key Personnel:** Stephanie L. Jones, Editor. **ISSN:** 1574--4695 (print). **Subscription Rates:** Included in membership. **URL:** http://www.waterbirds.org/journal. **Formerly:** Colonial Waterbirds. **Remarks:** Advertising accepted; rates available upon request. **Circ:** ‡800.

9600 ■ Cable TV Services
841 Bishop St., Ste.2001
Honolulu, HI 96813
Owner: Starstream Communications, 590 Kelly Ave., Half Moon Bay, CA 94019. **Founded:** 1985. **Formerly:** Clearview TV Cable of Hawaii Inc. **Key Personnel:** Robin Hollison, Contact. **Cities Served:** subscribing households 3075. **URL:** http://hbe.ehawaii.gov/documents/business.html?fileNumber=12649G6.

9601 ■ FOCUS-TV - 49
1122 Mapunapuna St.
Honolulu, HI 96819
Phone: (808)834-0007
Fax: (808)836-2546
Email: olelo@olelo.org
Owner: Olelo Community Media, Kahuku High & Intermediate School, 56-490 Kamehameha Hwy. Bldg. Z, Kahuku, HI 96731, Ph: (808)834-0007, Fax: (808)836-2546. **URL:** http://www.focustv.it.

9602 ■ H. Hawaii Media
900 Fort St. Mall, Ste. 450
Honolulu, HI 96813
Phone: (808)538-1180
Fax: (808)538-9548
Format: Hip Hop; Oldies; Eighties; Country; Classic Rock; Alternative/New Music/Progressive. **Founded:** 2000. **Ad Rates:** Advertising accepted; rates available upon request. **URL:** http://www.hhawaiimedia.com.

9603 ■ KAAH-TV - 26
1152 Smith St.
Honolulu, HI 96817
Owner: Trinity Broadcasting Network Inc., PO Box A, Santa Ana, CA 92711, Ph: (714)832-2950, Free: 888-731-1000. **URL:** http://www.tbn.org.

Circulation: ★ = AAM; △ or • = BPA; ♦ = CAC; ❑ = VAC; ⊕ = PO Statement; ‡ = Publisher's Report; Boldface figures = sworn; Light figures = estimated.

9604 ■ KAIM-FM - 95.5
1160 N King St., 2nd Fl.
Honolulu, HI 96817
Phone: (808)533-0065
Fax: (808)524-2104
Format: Contemporary Christian. **Networks:** Fox. **Owner:** Salem Media of Hawaii Inc., 1160 N King St., Honolulu, HI 96817. **Founded:** 1953. **Operating Hours:** Continuous; 100% local. **ADI:** Honolulu, HI. **Wattage:** 100,000 ERP. **Ad Rates:** Noncommercial. **URL:** http://www.thefishhawaii.com.

KANO-FM - See Hilo

9605 ■ Kauai Cablevision
Ste. 1600, Pauahi Twr., 1001 Bishop St.
Honolulu, HI 96813
Owner: InterMedia Partners, at above address. **Founded:** 1980. **Formerly:** Princeville Cablevision. **URL:** http://hbe.ehawaii.gov/documents/business.html?fileNumber=4950L5.

9606 ■ KBFD-TV - 32
1188 Bishop St.
Penthouse 1
Honolulu, HI 96813
Phone: (808)521-8066
Fax: (808)521-5233
Email: news@kbfd.com
Format: Commercial TV. **Networks:** NBC. **Owner:** The Allen Broadcasting Corp., at above address, Honolulu, HI. **Founded:** 1986. **Operating Hours:** 7:00 a.m. - Midnight. **ADI:** Honolulu, HI. **Wattage:** 49,600 ERP. **Ad Rates:** Advertising accepted; rates available upon request. **URL:** http://www.kbfd.com.

9607 ■ KCCN-FM - 100.3
900 Fort St. Mall, Ste. 700
Honolulu, HI 96813
Phone: (808)275-1000
Email: info@hiwedmagazine.com
Owner: Cox Radio Inc., 6205 Peachtree Dunwood Rd., Atlanta, GA 30328-4524, Ph: (678)645-0000, Fax: (678)645-5002. **Founded:** 1990. **ADI:** Honolulu, HI. **Key Personnel:** Wayne Maria, Operations Mgr., wayne.maria@summitmediacorp.com. **Wattage:** 100,000 ERP H; 8,100. **Ad Rates:** Advertising accepted; rates available upon request. $70 for 30 seconds; $84 for 60 seconds. **URL:** http://www.kccnfm100.com.

9608 ■ KDDB-FM - 102.7
765 Amana St., Ste. 200
Honolulu, HI 96814
Phone: (808)947-1500
Format: Hip Hop; News; Sports. **Owner:** Visionary Related Entertainment, PO Box 1730, Rohnert Park, CA 94927. **Founded:** 1988. **Formerly:** KKHN-FM. **Operating Hours:** 5:30 a.m. - Midnight Monday - Friday.10:00 a.m. - 3:00 p.m. Saturday - Sunday. **Wattage:** 61,000 ERP Horizonta. **Ad Rates:** $50-100 for 30 seconds. **URL:** http://1027dabomb.net.

9609 ■ KDNN-FM - 98.5
650 Iwilei Rd., Ste. 400
Honolulu, HI 96817
Phone: (808)550-9200
Fax: (808)550-9288
Format: Hawaiian. **Owner:** iHeartMedia Inc., 200 E Basse Rd., San Antonio, TX 78209, Ph: (210)832-3314. **ADI:** Honolulu, HI. **Key Personnel:** Jamie Hyatt, Dir. of Programs; Jovi Santiago, Sales Mgr. **Wattage:** 51,000. **Ad Rates:** Noncommercial. **URL:** http://www.island985.com.

9610 ■ KFVE-TV - 5
420 Waiakamilo Rd., Ste. 205
Honolulu, HI 96817
Phone: (808)847-9375
Fax: (808)847-9315
Format: Commercial TV. **Networks:** Independent. **Founded:** 1988. **Operating Hours:** Continuous. **ADI:** Honolulu, HI. **Key Personnel:** Mark Holmes, VP; Bryan Holmes, Contact; Andrea Jacobson, Contact; Ron Chung, Contact. **Ad Rates:** Advertising accepted; rates available upon request. **URL:** http://www.k5thehometeam.com/story/4758449/contact.

KGMD-TV - See Hilo

9611 ■ KGMZ-FM - 107.9
1160 N King St., 2nd Fl.
Honolulu, HI 96817
Phone: (808)533-0065
Fax: (808)524-2104
Format: Oldies. **Owner:** Salem Media of Hawaii Inc., 1160 N King St., Honolulu, HI 96817. **Operating Hours:** Continuous. **Ad Rates:** Advertising accepted; rates available upon request. **URL:** http://www.oldies1079honolulu.com.

9612 ■ KGU-AM - 760
1160 N King St.
Honolulu, HI 96817
Phone: (808)533-0065
Email: info@kguradio.com
Format: Talk. **Networks:** Business Radio; ESPN Radio. **Owner:** Salem Media Group Inc., 4880 Santa Rosa Rd., Camarillo, CA 93012, Ph: (805)987-0400, Fax: (805)384-4520. **Founded:** 1922. **Operating Hours:** Continuous. **ADI:** Honolulu, HI. **Key Personnel:** Jack Waters, Dir. of Programs, jwaters@hawaii-radio.net; David Serrone, Sales Mgr., dserrone@hawaii-radio.net. **Wattage:** 10,000. **Ad Rates:** Accepts Advertising. **URL:** http://www.kguradio.com.

9613 ■ KHCM-AM - 690
4880 Santa Rosa Rd.
Camarillo, CA 93012
Phone: (805)987-0400
Format: Country. **URL:** http://www.975countrykhcm.com.

9614 ■ KHCM-FM - 97.5
1160 N King St., 2nd Fl.
Honolulu, HI 96817
Phone: (808)533-0065
Format: Country. **Owner:** Salem Media of Hawaii Inc., 1160 N King St., Honolulu, HI 96817. **Operating Hours:** Continuous. **ADI:** Honolulu, HI. **Key Personnel:** Dita Holifield, Contact. **Wattage:** 80,000 ERP. **URL:** http://www.975countrykhcm.com.

9615 ■ KHET-TV - 11
2350 Dole St.
Honolulu, HI 96822
Phone: (808)973-1000
Fax: (808)973-1090
Free: 800-238-4847
Email: email@pbshawaii.org
Format: Public TV. **Networks:** Public Broadcasting Service (PBS). **Founded:** 1972. **Operating Hours:** Continuous. **ADI:** Honolulu, HI. **Key Personnel:** Karen Yamamoto, Sr. VP of Admin., Sr. VP of Fin. **Ad Rates:** Noncommercial. **Mailing address:** PO Box 11599, Honolulu, HI 96828-0599. **URL:** http://www.pbshawaii.org.

9616 ■ KHNL-TV - 8
420 Waiakamilo Rd., Ste. 205
Honolulu, HI 96817
Phone: (808)847-3246
Fax: (808)845-3616
Email: news@hawaiinewsnow.com
Networks: NBC. **Owner:** Raycom Media Inc., 201 Monroe St., RSA Twr., 20th Fl., Montgomery, AL 36104-3731, Ph: (334)206-1400. **Founded:** July 04, 1962. **URL:** http://www.hawaiinewsnow.com.

9617 ■ KHNR-AM - 690
1160 N King St., 2nd Fl.
Honolulu, HI 96817
Phone: (808)533-0065
Fax: (808)524-2104
Email: info@khnr.com
Format: News; Talk. **Owner:** Salem Media Group Inc., 4880 Santa Rosa Rd., Camarillo, CA 93012, Ph: (805)987-0400, Fax: (805)384-4520. **Ad Rates:** Advertising accepted; rates available upon request. **URL:** http://www.khnr.com.

9618 ■ KHNR-FM - 97.5
1160 N King St., 2nd Fl.
Honolulu, HI 96817
Phone: (808)533-0065
Format: News; Talk. **Owner:** Salem Media Group Inc., 4880 Santa Rosa Rd., Camarillo, CA 93012, Ph: (805)987-0400, Fax: (805)384-4520. **Operating Hours:** Continuous. **Key Personnel:** Rudi Camello, Contact, rudi@hawaii-radio.net. **Ad Rates:** Advertising accepted; rates available upon request. **URL:** http://www.khnr.com.

9619 ■ KHON-TV - 2
88 Piikoi St.
Honolulu, HI 96814
Phone: (808)591-2222
Format: Commercial TV. **Networks:** Fox. **Owner:** New Vision Television, Inc., 11766 Wilshire Blvd., Ste. 405, Los Angeles, CA 90025, Ph: (310)478-3200, Fax: (310)478-3222. **Founded:** 1955. **Operating Hours:** 5 a.m.-2:30 a.m. **ADI:** Honolulu, HI. **Key Personnel:** Ana Jones, Traffic Mgr., ana.jones@khon2.com. **Local Programs:** *Hawaii's Kitchen.* **Wattage:** 100,000. **Ad Rates:** Noncommercial. **URL:** http://www.khon2.com.

9620 ■ KHPR-FM - 88.1
738 Kaheka St.
Honolulu, HI 96814
Phone: (808)955-8821
Fax: (808)946-3863
Format: Public Radio. **Networks:** National Public Radio (NPR); Public Radio International (PRI); AP. **Owner:** Hawaii Public Radio, 738 Kaheka St., Honolulu, HI 96814, Ph: (808)955-8821, Fax: (808)946-3863. **Founded:** 1981. **Operating Hours:** Continuous; 40% network, 60% local. **ADI:** Honolulu, HI. **Key Personnel:** Gene Schiller, Music Dir., gschiller@hawaiipublicradio.org; Judy Neale, Promotions Dir., jneale@hawaiipublicradio.org; Bill Dorman, News Dir., news@hawaiipublicradio.org; Charles Husson, Dir. of Operations; Michael Titterton, Gen. Mgr.; Valerie Yee, Asst. GM. **Wattage:** 27,000. **Ad Rates:** Noncommercial. **URL:** http://www.hawaiipublicradio.org.

9621 ■ KHUI-FM - 99.5
1160 N King St., 2nd Fl.
Honolulu, HI 96817
Phone: (808)954-4350
Fax: (808)524-2104
Free: 800-896-1669
Format: Adult Contemporary. **Owner:** Salem Media Group Inc., 4880 Santa Rosa Rd., Camarillo, CA 93012, Ph: (805)987-0400, Fax: (805)384-4520. **Key Personnel:** Ed Kanoi, Prog. Dir., edkanoi@salemhawaii.com. **Wattage:** 100,000. **Ad Rates:** Advertising accepted; rates available upon request. **URL:** http://khui-fm.fimc.net.

9622 ■ KHVH-AM - 830
650 Iwilei Rd., Ste. 400
Honolulu, HI 96817
Phone: (808)550-9200
Fax: (808)550-9288
Free: 888-565-8388
Format: Talk. **Founded:** 1957. **Ad Rates:** Noncommercial. **URL:** http://www.khvhradio.iheart.com.

9623 ■ KIKI-AM - 990; 990
650 Iwilei Rd., Ste. 400
Honolulu, HI 96817
Phone: (808)550-9200
Fax: (808)550-9510
Format: News; News; Talk; Sports. **Networks:** Fox. **Owner:** iHeartMedia Inc., 200 E Basse Rd., San Antonio, TX 78209, Ph: (210)832-3314. **Founded:** 1948. **Formerly:** KHBZ-AM. **Operating Hours:** Continuous. **ADI:** Honolulu, HI. **Key Personnel:** Kevin Jones, Promotions Dir., kevinjones@iheartmedia.com; Rob Welsh, Gen. Mgr., robertwelsh@iheartmedia.com. **Wattage:** 5,000. **Ad Rates:** Advertising accepted; rates available upon request. **URL:** http://foxsports990.iheart.com/.

9624 ■ KIKU-TV - 20
737 Bishop St., Ste. 1430
Honolulu, HI 96813
Phone: (808)847-2021
Fax: (808)841-3326
Email: info@kikutv.com
Format: Commercial TV. **Networks:** Independent. **Founded:** 1983. **Operating Hours:** Continuous. **ADI:** Honolulu, HI. **Key Personnel:** Phyllis Kihara, Gen. Mgr., pkihara@kikutv.com. **Ad Rates:** Noncommercial. **URL:** http://www.kikutv.com/Default.asp.

9625 ■ KINE-FM - 105.1
900 Fort St., Ste. 700
Honolulu, HI 96813
Email: tj.malievsky@summitmediacorp.com
Format: Adult Contemporary; Hawaiian. **Owner:** Cox Radio Inc., 6205 Peachtree Dunwood Rd., Atlanta, GA 30328-4524, Ph: (678)645-0000, Fax: (678)645-5002. **Founded:** 1988. **Formerly:** KHFX-FM. **Operating**

Hours: Continuous. **Key Personnel:** Wayne Maria, Operations Mgr. **Wattage**: 100,000. **Ad Rates:** Noncommercial. **URL:** http://www.hawaiian105.com.

9626 ■ KIPO-FM - 89.3
738 Kaheka St.
Honolulu, HI 96814
Phone: (808)955-8821
Fax: (808)946-3863
Free: 800-955-8821
Email: mail@hawaiipublicradio.org
Format: Public Radio. **Networks:** Public Radio International (PRI); National Public Radio (NPR). **Owner:** Hawaii Public Radio, 738 Kaheka St., Honolulu, HI 96814, Ph: (808)955-8821, Fax: (808)946-3863. **Founded:** 1989. **Operating Hours**: Continuous. **ADI**: Honolulu, HI. **Key Personnel:** Gene Schiller, Music Dir., gschiller@hawaiipublicradio.org; Charles Husson, Dir. of Operations, chusson@hawaiipublicradio.org; Bill Dorman, News Dir., bdorman@hawaiipublicradio; Michael Titterton, President, Gen. Mgr. **Wattage**: 3,200. **Ad Rates:** Noncommercial. **URL:** http://www.hawaiipublicradio.org.

9627 ■ KITV-TV - 4
801 S King St.
Honolulu, HI 96813
Phone: (808)535-0400
Networks: ABC. **Owner:** Hearst Television Inc., 300 W 57th St., New York, NY 10019-3741, Ph: (212)887-6800, Fax: (212)887-6855. **Founded:** 1954. **Operating Hours**: Continuous. **ADI**: Honolulu, HI. **Key Personnel:** Bill Gaeth, VP of Sales, gaeth@kitv.com. **Local Programs**: *KITV4 News*, Monday Tuesday Wednesday Thursday Friday Saturday Sunday 5:00 a.m.; 5:00 p.m.; 6:00 p.m.; 10:00 p.m. 6:00 a.m. 5:00 p.m.; 6:00 p.m.; 10:00 p.m. 6:00 a.m.; 5:00 p.m.; 10:00 p.m.; *Merrie Monarch Festival, Mixed Plate*. **Ad Rates:** Advertising accepted; rates available upon request. **URL:** http://www.kitv.com.

9628 ■ KKAI-TV - 50
PO Box 47
Honolulu, HI 96810
Fax: (808)441-0092
Email: info@kkai.tv
URL: http://www.kkai.tv/index.html.

9629 ■ KKEA-AM - 1420
1088 Bishop St., Ste. LL2
Honolulu, HI 96813
Format: Sports; Talk. **Simulcasts:** KPUA, KAOI, KQNG. **Formerly**: Diamond Head Radio Inc.; Cox Radio Inc./KCCN AM. **Operating Hours**: Continuous. **ADI**: Honolulu, HI. **Key Personnel:** Kenny Harrison, Contact. **Wattage**: 5,000. **Ad Rates:** $50-500 for 30 seconds. Combined advertising rates available with Cox Radio Hawaii. **URL:** http://www.sportsradio1420.com/.

9630 ■ KKNE-AM - 940
900 Fort St. Mall, Ste. 700
Honolulu, HI 96813
Owner: Cox Radio Inc., 6205 Peachtree Dunwood Rd., Atlanta, GA 30328-4524, Ph: (678)645-0000, Fax: (678)645-5002. **Wattage**: 10,000. **Ad Rates:** Advertising accepted; rates available upon request.

9631 ■ KKOL-FM - 107.9
1160 N King St., 2nd Fl.
Honolulu, HI 96817
Phone: (808)296-1079
Fax: (808)524-2104
Format: Oldies. **Owner:** Salem Media Group Inc., 4880 Santa Rosa Rd., Camarillo, CA 93012, Ph: (805)987-0400, Fax: (805)384-4520. **Wattage**: 100,000 H;80,000 V. **URL:** http://www.1079koolgold.com.

KKUA-FM - See Wailuku

9632 ■ KLHI-FM - 101.1
900 Fort Street Mall, No. 450
Honolulu, HI 96813
Phone: (808)538-1180
Fax: (808)538-9548
Format: Adult Contemporary; Oldies. **Networks:** Unistar; Westwood One Radio. **Founded:** 1984. **Operating Hours**: 7 pm - 12 pm. **Key Personnel:** Virginia Parsons, Gen. Mgr.; Audrey Dougherty, Office Mgr. **Wattage**: 100,000 ERP H; 8,100. **Ad Rates:** $8-20 for 30 seconds; $10-23 for 60 seconds. **URL:** http://www.korl1011.com.

9633 ■ KNDI-AM - 1270
1734 S King St.
Honolulu, HI 96826
Phone: (808)946-2844
Fax: (808)947-3531
Email: kndiradio@hawaii.rr.com
Format: Religious. **Networks:** Independent. **Owner:** Broadcast House of the Pacific Inc., at above address. **Founded:** 1960. **Operating Hours**: Continuous. **ADI**: Honolulu, HI. **Key Personnel:** Leona Jona, Gen. Mgr., President. **Wattage:** 5,000. **Ad Rates:** $30-35 for 30 seconds; $40-45 for 60 seconds. **URL:** http://www.kndi.com.

9634 ■ KORL-FM - 101.1
900 Fort St. Mall, Ste. 450
Honolulu, HI 96813
Phone: (808)538-1180
Fax: (808)538-9548
Format: Jazz. **Owner:** Hhawaii Media, 900 Fort Street Mall, Ste. 450, Honolulu, HI 96813, Ph: (808)332-7976, Fax: (808)332-7830. **URL:** http://www.hhawaiimedia.com/stations.html.

9635 ■ KPHW-FM - 104.3
900 Fort St. Mall, Ste. 700
Honolulu, HI 96813
Phone: (808)275-1000
Fax: (808)536-2528
Format: Contemporary Hit Radio (CHR); Urban Contemporary. **Owner:** Cox Radio Inc., 6205 Peachtree Dunwood Rd., Atlanta, GA 30328-4524, Ph: (678)645-0000, Fax: (678)645-5002. **Operating Hours**: Continuous. **Ad Rates:** Advertising accepted; rates available upon request. **URL:** http://www.power1043.com.

9636 ■ KPOI-FM - 105.9
1833 Kalakaua Ave., Ste. 500
Honolulu, HI 96815
Phone: (808)591-9369
Fax: (808)591-9349
Format: Alternative/New Music/Progressive; News; Sports. **Owner:** Visionary Related Entertainment, Inc., at above address, Honolulu, HI. **Founded:** 1964. **ADI**: Honolulu, HI. **Wattage**: 100,000 ERP Horizon. **Ad Rates:** $50-100 per unit. **URL:** http://alt1059.com.

9637 ■ KPXO-TV - 66
875 Waimanu St., Ste. 630
Honolulu, HI 96813
Phone: (808)591-1275
Fax: (808)591-1409
Owner: ION Media Networks Inc., 601 Clearwater Park Rd., West Palm Beach, FL 33401-6233, Ph: (561)659-4122, Fax: (561)659-4252. **Key Personnel:** Brandon Burgess, Chairman, CEO. **URL:** http://www.ionmedia.tv.

9638 ■ KQMQ-FM - 93.1
1000 Bishop St.
Honolulu, HI 96813
Phone: (808)947-1500
Format: News; Music of Your Life. **Simulcasts:** KQMQ-AM. **Founded:** 1967. **Operating Hours**: Continuous. **ADI**: Honolulu, HI. **Key Personnel:** Bernie Armstrong, Gen. Mgr.; Diane Ward, Gen. Sales Mgr.; Jamie Hyatt, Dir. of Production; Cary Ebesugawa, Bus. Mgr. **Wattage**: 100,000 ERP. **Ad Rates:** Advertising accepted; rates available upon request. **URL:** http://931dapaina.com.

9639 ■ KRTR-AM - 650
900 Fort St. Mall, Ste. 700
Honolulu, HI 96813
Phone: (808)275-1000
Format: Adult Contemporary. **Owner:** Cox Radio Inc., 6205 Peachtree Dunwood Rd., Atlanta, GA 30328-4524, Ph: (678)645-0000, Fax: (678)645-5002. **Key Personnel:** Michol Klabo, Gen. Sales Mgr., michol@650amhawaii.com; Wayne Maria, Operations Mgr., wayne@650amhawaii.com; Mike Kelly, Gen. Mgr., VP, mike@650amhawaii.com.

9640 ■ KRTR-FM - 96.3
900 Fort St. Mall, Ste. 700
Honolulu, HI 96813
Phone: (808)275-1000
Format: Adult Contemporary. **Owner:** Cox Radio Inc., 6205 Peachtree Dunwood Rd., Atlanta, GA 30328-4524, Ph: (678)645-0000, Fax: (678)645-5002. **Founded:** 1978. **Operating Hours**: Continuous; 100% local. **Key Personnel:** Wade Faildo, Promotions Dir.; Wayne Maria, Operations Mgr., wayne@krater96.com. **Wattage**: 75,000. **Ad Rates:** Noncommercial. Combined advertising rates available with KGMZ-FM, KINE-FM, KCCN-FM, KXME. **URL:** http://www.krater963.com.

9641 ■ KSSK-AM - 590
650 Iwilei Rd., Ste. 400
Honolulu, HI 96817
Phone: (808)550-9200
Fax: (808)550-9288
Format: Adult Contemporary. **Networks:** ABC. **Owner:** iHeartMedia Inc., 200 E Basse Rd., San Antonio, TX 78209, Ph: (210)832-3314. **Founded:** 1929. **Formerly**: KGMB-AM. **Operating Hours**: Continuous. **Key Personnel:** Rob Welsh, Gen. Sales Mgr.; Jamie Hyatt, Dir. of Operations, Dir. of Programs; Chuck Cotton, Gen. Mgr., VP, chuckcotton@clearchannel.com. **Wattage**: 7,500. **Ad Rates:** Noncommercial. $35-$90 for 30 seconds; $40-$105 for 60 seconds. Combined advertising rates available with KSSK-FM. **URL:** http://www.ksskradio.com.

9642 ■ KSSK-FM - 92.3
650 Iwilei Rd., Ste. 400
Honolulu, HI 96817
Phone: (808)550-9200
Fax: (808)550-9288
Email: studio@ksskradio.com
Format: Adult Contemporary. **Owner:** iHeartMedia Inc., 200 E Basse Rd., San Antonio, TX 78209, Ph: (210)832-3314. **Founded:** 1976. **Key Personnel:** Jamie Hyatt, Dir. of Programs, jamiehyatt@clearchannel.com; Chuck Cotton, Gen. Mgr., VP, chuckcotton@clearchannel.com; Rob Welsh, Sales Mgr., robertwelsh@iheartmedia.com. **Wattage**: 100,000 ERP. **Ad Rates:** Advertising accepted; rates available upon request. Combined advertising rates available with KSSK-AM. **URL:** http://www.ksskradio.iheart.com.

9643 ■ KTUH-FM - 90.1
2445 Campus Rd.
Hemenway Hall, No. 203
Honolulu, HI 96822
Phone: (808)956-5288
Email: office@ktuh.org
Format: Hawaiian; Alternative/New Music/Progressive; Educational. **Owner:** University of Hawaii-Manoa, 2500 Campus Rd., Honolulu, HI 96822, Ph: (808)956-8111. **Founded:** 1968. **Operating Hours**: Continuous. **ADI**: Honolulu, HI. **Local Programs**: *The Best of Monday Night Live*, Monday 9:00 a.m. - 12:00 p.m. **Wattage**: 7,000 ERP H. **Ad Rates:** Noncommercial. Underwriting available. **URL:** http://www.ktuh.org.

9644 ■ KUCD-FM - 101.9
650 Iwilei Rd., Ste. 400
Honolulu, HI 96817
Phone: (808)550-9200
Fax: (808)550-9288
Format: Alternative/New Music/Progressive. **Owner:** iHeartMedia Inc., 200 E Basse Rd., San Antonio, TX 78209, Ph: (210)832-3314. **Key Personnel:** Rob Welsh, Sales Mgr., robwelsh@clearchannel.com. **Wattage**: 100,000 H ERP; 81,000 V ERP. **Ad Rates:** Advertising accepted; rates available upon request. **URL:** http://www.star1019.com.

9645 ■ KUMU-AM - 1500
765 Amana St., Ste. 200
Honolulu, HI 96814
Format: Sports. **Key Personnel:** John Aeto, Gen. Mgr., john.aeto@vrehawaii.com; Stuart Chang, Sales Mgr., stuart.chang@vrehawaii.com; David Onoue, Sales Exe., david.onoue@vrehawaii.com. **URL:** http://www.am1500hawaii.com.

9646 ■ KUMU-FM - 94.7
1000 Bishop St., Ste. 200
Honolulu, HI 96813
Phone: (808)947-1500
Format: Full Service. **Founded:** 1963. **Operating Hours**: Continuous. **ADI**: Honolulu, HI. **Wattage**: 100,000 ERP. **Ad Rates:** Advertising accepted; rates available upon request. **URL:** http://www.kumu.com.

9647 ■ KWAI-AM - 1080
100 N Beretania St., Ste. 401
Honolulu, HI 96817

Circulation: ★ = AAM; △ or • = BPA; ♦ = CAC; ❑ = VAC; ⊕ = PO Statement; ‡ = Publisher's Report; Boldface figures = swom; Light figures = estimated.

Phone: (808)523-3868
Fax: (808)531-6532
Format: Talk. **Networks:** Independent. **Owner:** Radio Hawaii, Inc., at above address. **Founded:** 1970. **Formerly**: KZHI-AM. **Operating Hours**: Continuous; 10% network, 90% local. **ADI**: Honolulu, HI. **Key Personnel:** Barry Wagenvoord, Gen. Mgr. **Wattage**: 5,000. **Ad Rates:** $29 for 30 seconds; $48 for 60 seconds. **URL:** http://www.kwai1080am.com.

9648 ■ KWHE-TV - 14
1188 Bishop St., Ste. 502
Honolulu, HI 96813
Phone: (808)538-1414
Fax: (808)526-0326
Free: 800-218-1414
Email: kwhe@lesea.com
Format: Commercial TV; Religious. **Networks:** Independent. **Owner:** Le Sea Broadcasting Corp., The Harvest Show, 61300 Ironwood Rd., South Bend, IN 46614. **Founded:** 1986. **Operating Hours:** Continuous. **Ad Rates:** Advertising accepted; rates available upon request. Barter. **URL:** http://www.kwhe.com.

9649 ■ KXME-FM - 104.3
900 Fort St., Ste. 700
Honolulu, HI 96813
Phone: (808)275-1000
Fax: (808)536-2528
Format: Hip Hop. **Owner:** Cox Radio Inc., 6205 Peachtree Dunwood Rd., Atlanta, GA 30328-4524, Ph: (678)645-0000, Fax: (678)645-5002. **Key Personnel:** Wade Faildo, Director; Mike Kelly, Gen. Mgr., VP, mike@power1043.com; Wayne Maria, Operations Mgr., wayne@power1043.com. **Ad Rates:** Advertising accepted; rates available upon request. **URL:** http://www.power1043.com.

9650 ■ KZOO-AM - 1210
2454 S Beretania St., Ste. 203
Honolulu, HI 96826
Phone: (808)947-5966
Founded: 1963. **ADI:** Honolulu, HI. **Wattage:** 1,000. **Ad Rates:** Noncommercial. **URL:** http://kzoohawaii.com.

9651 ■ 93.9 JAMZ (KHJZ-FM) - 93.9
650 Iwilei Rd., Ste. 400
Honolulu, HI 96817
Format: Contemporary Hit Radio (CHR). **Networks:** Independent. **Founded:** 1978. **Formerly:** KMAI-FM; KIKI-FM. **Operating Hours:** Continuous. **ADI:** Honolulu, HI. **Key Personnel:** Jovi Santiago, Sales Mgr., jovisantiago@iHeartMedia.com; Jamie Hyatt, Dir. of Programs, jamiehyatt@iHeartMedia.com; Kevin Jones, Promotions Dir., KevinJones@iHeartMedia.com. **Wattage:** 100,000. **Ad Rates:** Noncommercial. $90-$100 for 30 seconds; $100-$120 for 60 seconds. Combined advertising rates available with KIKI-AM. **URL:** http://www.939jamz.com.

9652 ■ Oceanic Time Warner Cable
PO Box 30050
Honolulu, HI 96820-0050
Owner: Time Warner Cable Inc. Company L.P., PO Box 30050, Honolulu, HI 96820-0050. **Founded:** 1969. **Cities Served:** Lahaina, West Maui, Hawaii: subscribing households 350,000; 109 channels; 3 community access channels. **URL:** http://www.oceanic.com.

KAHULUI

9653 ■ KAKU-FM - 88.5
333 Dairy Rd., Ste. 104
Kahului, HI 96732
Format: Adult Contemporary; News; Jazz. **Owner:** Akaku Community Television. **Wattage:** 100. **URL:** http://akaku.org/kaku-fm.

9654 ■ KDLX-FM - 94.3
Box 38
Kahului, HI 96732
Phone: (808)244-9145
Format: Country. **Owner:** Visionary Related Entertainment, Inc., at above address, Honolulu, HI. **Founded:** 1980. **Operating Hours:** Continuous. **Wattage:** 6,000.

9655 ■ KJKS-FM - 99.9
311 Ano St.
Kahului, HI 96732-1304
Phone: (808)877-5566
Format: Adult Contemporary. **Owner:** Pacific Radio Group Inc., 311 Ano S, Kahului, HI 96732. **Key Personnel:** Chuck Bergson, CEO, President; Pamela Tsutsui, Gen. Mgr. **URL:** http://www.kissfmmaui.com.

9656 ■ KJMD-FM - 98.3
311 Ano St.
Kahului, HI 96732-1304
Phone: (808)877-5566
Format: Contemporary Hit Radio (CHR). **Owner:** Pacific Radio Group Inc., 311 Ano S, Kahului, HI 96732. **Founded:** 1984. **Operating Hours:** Continuous. **Key Personnel:** Pamela Tsutsui, Gen. Mgr. **Wattage:** 50,000. **Ad Rates:** Advertising accepted; rates available upon request. Combined advertising rates available with KMVI-AM. **URL:** http://www.dajam983.com.

9657 ■ KLHI-FM - 92.5
311 Ano St.
Kahului, HI 96732
Phone: (808)877-5566
Fax: (808)871-0666
Email: info_maui@pacificradiogroup.com
Format: Classic Rock. **Owner:** Pacific Radio Group Inc., 311 Ano S, Kahului, HI 96732. **Founded:** 1994. **Key Personnel:** Pamela Tsutsui, Gen. Mgr.; Sherri Grimes, Promotions Dir. **URL:** http://www.pacificradiogroup.com/johnson.html.

9658 ■ KLUA-FM - 93.9
311 Ano St.
Kahului, HI 96732-1304
Format: Hawaiian; Contemporary Hit Radio (CHR). **Simulcasts:** KPVS-FM. **Owner:** Pacific Radio Group Inc., 311 Ano S, Kahului, HI 96732. **Operating Hours:** 6:00 a.m. - Midnight Monday - Friday, 6:00 a.m. - 7:00 p.m. Saturday - Sunday. **Key Personnel:** Chuck Bergson, CEO. **Wattage:** 7,300. **Ad Rates:** Advertising accepted; rates available upon request. **URL:** http://www.dabeatfm.com.

9659 ■ KMVI-AM - 550
311 Ano St.
Kahului, HI 96732-1304
Phone: (808)877-5566
Fax: (808)877-2888
Email: support@espnmaui.com
Format: Sports. **Networks:** CNN Radio. **Owner:** Pacific Radio Group Inc., 311 Ano S, Kahului, HI 96732. **Founded:** 1947. **Operating Hours:** Continuous. **Wattage:** 5,000. **Ad Rates:** Noncommercial. Combined advertising rates available with KMVI-FM. **URL:** http://www.espn550.com.

9660 ■ KNUI-AM - 900
311 Ano S
Kahului, HI 96732-1304
Phone: (808)877-5566
Fax: (808)871-0666
Owner: Pacific Radio Group Inc., 311 Ano S, Kahului, HI 96732. **Founded:** 1962. **Wattage:** 5,000. **Ad Rates:** $10-25 for 30 seconds; $12-27 for 60 seconds. $10-$25 for 30 seconds; $12-$27 for 60 seconds. Combined advertising rates available with KNUI-FM.

9661 ■ KNUI-FM - 900
311 Ano St.
Kahului, HI 96732-1304
Phone: (808)877-5566
Fax: (808)877-2888
Email: studio@foxnews900.com
Format: Adult Contemporary. **Networks:** ABC. **Owner:** Pacific Radio Group Inc., 311 Ano S, Kahului, HI 96732. **Founded:** 1984. **Formerly:** KHUI-FM. **Operating Hours:** Continuous; 100% local. **Key Personnel:** Pamela Tsutsui, Gen. Mgr.; Sherri Grimes, Promotions Dir.; Debbie Probst, Sales Mgr. **Wattage:** 100,000. **Ad Rates:** $15-25 for 30 seconds; $17-27 for 60 seconds. $10-$25 for 30 seconds; $11-$27 for 60 seconds; Combined advertising rates available with KLHI-FM. **URL:** http://www.espn550.com.

9662 ■ KPOA-FM - 93.5
311 Ano St.
Kahului, HI 96732-1304
Phone: (808)877-5566
Email: studio@kpoa.com
Format: Adult Contemporary. **Owner:** Pacific Radio Group Inc., 311 Ano S, Kahului, HI 96732. **Founded:** 1984. **Operating Hours:** Continuous. **Key Personnel:** Chuck Bergson, President, CEO; Sherri Grimes, Promotions Dir.; Pamela Tsutsui, Gen. Mgr.; Valerie Toro, Music Dir., sistahval@kpoa.com. **Wattage:** 69,000. **Ad Rates:** $20-42 for 30 seconds; $25-55 for 60 seconds. Combined advertising rates available with KLHI-FM, KNUI AM, KJMD FM, KMVI AM, KNUI FM. **URL:** http://www.kpoa.com.

9663 ■ KUAU-AM - 1570
777 Mokulele Hwy.
Kahului, HI 96732
Fax: (808)891-9708
Free: 888-404-7729
Email: info@kingscathedral.com
Format: Talk; Religious. **Owner:** King's Cathedral and Chapels, 777 Mokulele Hwy., Kahului, HI 96732, Free: 888-404-7729. **Key Personnel:** James Marocco, Contact. **URL:** http://www.kingscathedral.com.

KAILUA

NC HI. Honolulu Co. 40 mi. SE of Kaneohe.

9664 ■ The Journal for Spiritual and Consciousness Studies
Academy of Religion and Psychical Research
c/o Michael E. Tymn, Ed.-in-Ch.
641 Keolu Dr.
Kailua, HI 96734
Phone: (808)262-6604
Scholarly journal covering religion and psychical research. **Freq:** Quarterly. **Print Method:** Offset. **Trim Size:** 5 1/2 x 8 1/2. **Cols./Page:** 1. **Col. Width:** 4 1/2 inches. **Col. Depth:** 8 inches. **Key Personnel:** Michael E. Tymn, Editor-in-Chief; Boyce Batey, Managing Editor. **ISSN:** 1731--2148 (print). **Subscription Rates:** Included in membership. **URL:** http://www.ascsi.org/ASCS/Publications/publications.shtml. **Formerly:** The Journal of Spirituality and Paranormal Studies. **Remarks:** Advertising not accepted. **Circ:** (Not Reported).

KAILUA KONA

9665 ■ West Hawaii Today
Stephens Media L.L.C.
75-5580 Kuakini Hwy.
Kailua Kona, HI 96740-1647
Phone: (808)329-9311
Publication E-mail: wht@aloha.net
General newspaper. **Print Method:** Offset. **Cols./Page:** 5. **Col. Width:** 1 1/16 inches. **Col. Depth:** 15 13/16 inches. **Key Personnel:** Tracey Fosso, Publisher, phone: (808)329-2644. **USPS:** 744-459. **URL:** http://www.westhawaiitoday.com; http://stephensmedia.com/west-hawaii-today. **Ad Rates:** BW $975.75; 4C $1,265.75; SAU $13.01; PCI $13.01. **Remarks:** Accepts classified advertising. **Circ:** Mon.-Sat. ♦**11062**, Sun. ♦**13357**.

9666 ■ KAOY-FM - 101.5
74-5615 Luhia St., Ste. A2
Kailua Kona, HI 96740
Phone: (808)323-2400
Fax: (808)323-3186
Networks: ABC. **Owner:** Visionary Related Entertainment, Inc., at above address, Honolulu, HI. **Founded:** 1963. **Formerly**: KOAS, 1992. **Operating Hours**: Continuous. **Wattage:** 7,000. **Ad Rates:** $21 for 30 seconds; $25 for 60 seconds. **URL:** http://www.kwxx.com.

KAMUELA

9667 ■ KWYI-FM - 106.9
PO Box 6540
Kamuela, HI 96743
Phone: (808)885-9866
Fax: (808)885-6480
Format: Adult Contemporary; Oldies. **Key Personnel:** Colin H. Naito, Owner. **Wattage:** 5,500. **Ad Rates:** Advertising accepted; rates available upon request.

KANEOHE

SC HI. Honolulu Co. On Oahu Island, 9 mi. NW of Honolulu. Windward Community College; Hawaii Loa College. Sea Life Park, Ulu Mau Village and fishpond Valley of Temples.

9668 ■ Hawaii Army Weekly
RFD Publications Inc.

45-525 Luluku Rd.
Kaneohe, HI 96744
Military newspaper. **Freq:** Weekly (Fri.). **Print Method:** Offset. **Trim Size:** 11 1/2 x 13 1/2. **Cols./Page:** 6. **Key Personnel:** Molly Hayden, Writer, phone: (808)656-3155. **Subscription Rates:** Free; $117 Out of state shipping and handling fee. **Ad Rates:** GLR $.85; BW $1534; 4C $1980; PCI $11.89. **Remarks:** Accepts advertising. **Circ:** (Not Reported).

9669 ■ Hawaii Bride & Groom
Hawaii Bride & Groom
47-472 Hui Kelu St.
Kaneohe, HI 96744
Phone: (808)428-1596
Publisher's E-mail: info@hawaiibride.com
Bridal magazine. **Freq:** Semiannual. **Key Personnel:** Julie Aragaki, Executive Editor, Director, Advertising and Sales. **URL:** http://hawaiibride.com. **Remarks:** Accepts advertising. **Circ:** (Not Reported).

9670 ■ The Heartland Shopping News
MidWeek Printing Inc.
45-525 Luluku Rd.
Kaneohe, HI 96744
Phone: (808)235-5881
Fax: (808)247-7246
Shopping guide. **Freq:** Weekly (Sun.). **URL:** http://www.themidweek.com/online-papers. **Remarks:** Accepts classified advertising. **Circ:** (Not Reported).

9671 ■ The Midweek
MidWeek Printing Inc.
45-525 Luluku Rd.
Kaneohe, HI 96744
Phone: (808)235-5881
Fax: (808)247-7246
Shopping guide. **Freq:** Weekly (Sun.). **Key Personnel:** Ron Nagasawa, Publisher; Yu Shing Ting, Managing Editor; Don Chapman, Editor-in-Chief. **Subscription Rates:** Free. **URL:** http://www.midweek.com. **Remarks:** Accepts advertising. **Circ:** Paid ♦**71**, Non-paid ♦**266225**.

9672 ■ Midweek Magazine
RFD Publications Inc.
45-525 Luluku Rd.
Kaneohe, HI 96744
Consumer magazine covering local news and entertainment. **Freq:** Weekly (Wed.). **Key Personnel:** Don Chapman, Editor-in-Chief; Ron Nagasawa, Publisher; Yu Shing Ting, Managing Editor. **URL:** http://www.midweek.com. **Remarks:** Advertising accepted; rates available upon request. **Circ:** (Not Reported).

KAPAA

9673 ■ Hinduism Today
Himalayan Academy
107 Kaholalele Rd.
Kapaa, HI 96746-9304
Phone: (808)822-3012
Free: 800-822-4351
Publisher's E-mail: contact@hindu.org
Newspaper reporting on Hindu events and people worldwide. **Freq:** Quarterly. **Print Method:** Web press. **Trim Size:** 11 x 17. **Cols./Page:** 4. **Col. Width:** 2 1/2 inches. **Col. Depth:** 16 inches. **Key Personnel:** Satguru Bodhinatha Veylanswami, Publisher; Paramacharya Palaniswami, Editor-in-Chief; Sannyasin Arumugaswami, Managing Editor. **ISSN:** 0896--0801 (print). **Subscription Rates:** $35 Individuals /year; $65 Two years; $499 Individuals life. **Alt. Formats:** E-book; PDF. **URL:** http://www.hinduismtoday.com. **Formerly:** New Saivite World. **Ad Rates:** BW $570. **Remarks:** Accepts advertising. **Circ:** Paid ‡3200, Controlled ‡6800.

KEALAKEKUA

SE HI. Hawaii Co. 30 mi. S. of Kailua.

9674 ■ KKON-AM - 790
PO Box 845
Kealakekua, HI 96750
Phone: (808)961-0651
Format: Oldies; Ethnic. **Networks:** ABC. **Founded:** 1963. **Operating Hours:** Continuous. **Key Personnel:** Mark Taylor, Gen. Mgr. **Wattage:** 5,000. **Ad Rates:** Advertising accepted; rates available upon request. **URL:** http://www.espnhawaii.com/page.php?page_id=68.

KIHEI

9675 ■ KONI-FM - 104.7
300 Ohukai Rd., Ste. C-318
Kihei, HI 96753
Phone: (808)875-8866
Fax: (808)875-8870
Format: Contemporary Hit Radio (CHR). **URL:** http://hhawaiimedia.com.

LAHAINA

E HI. Maui Co. 15 mi. NE of Lanai.

9676 ■ Lahaina News
Hawaii Publications Inc.
143 Dickenson St., No. 203
Lahaina, HI 96761
Phone: (808)667-7866
Publication E-mail: lahnews@maui.net
Community newspaper (tabloid). **Freq:** Weekly. **Print Method:** Offset. **Cols./Page:** 4. **Col. Width:** 2 3/8 inches. **Col. Depth:** 182 agate lines. **Key Personnel:** Mark Vieth, Editor. **URL:** http://www.lahainanews.com. **Ad Rates:** BW $885; 4C $1350. **Remarks:** Accepts advertising. **Circ:** Paid ‡350, Free ‡8607.

LANAI CITY

9677 ■ Horn Call
International Horn Society
c/o Heidi Vogel, Executive Secretary
PO Box 630158
Lanai City, HI 96763-0158
Phone: (808)565-7273
Fax: (808)565-7273
Publisher's E-mail: exec-director@hornsociety.org
Freq: 3/year October, February and May. **ISSN:** 0046-7928 (print). **Subscription Rates:** Included in membership. **URL:** http://www.hornsociety.org/publications/horn-call. **Ad Rates:** 4C $925; BW $390. **Remarks:** Accepts advertising. **Circ:** 3600.

LIHUE

W HI. Kauai Co. On Kauai Island, 100 mi. NW of Honolulu. Sugar mills; canneries. Resorts. Fisheries. Agriculture. Sugar cane, pineapples.

9678 ■ The Garden Island: Serving the people of Kauai since 1902
Kauai Publishing Co.
3137 Kuhio Hwy.
Lihue, HI 96766
Phone: (808)245-3681
Fax: (808)245-5286
Free: 800-296-2880
Publisher's E-mail: customerservice@thegardenisland.com
General newspaper. **Freq:** Mon.-Sat. (eve.). **Print Method:** Offset. **Cols./Page:** 6. **Col. Width:** 24 nonpareils. **Col. Depth:** 301 agate lines. **Key Personnel:** Randy Kozerski, Publisher; Nathan Eagle, Editor. **URL:** http://thegardenisland.com. **Mailing address:** PO Box 231, Lihue, HI 96766. **Ad Rates:** 4C $254; SAU $9.90. **Remarks:** Accepts advertising. **Circ:** Mon.-Fri. ★**8703**, Sun. ★**9093**, Sat. ★**8366**.

9679 ■ Kauai Magazine
H and S Publishing L.L.C.
4330 Kauai Beach Dr., Ste. G12
Lihue, HI 96766
Phone: (808)212-5333
Fax: (808)245-5233
Magazine featuring the beauty, culture, and people of Kauai, Hawaii. **Freq:** Quarterly. **Print Method:** Offset. **Cols./Page:** 5. **Col. Width:** 13 inches. **Col. Depth:** 224 agate lines. **URL:** http://www.kauaimagazine.com. **Remarks:** Accepts advertising. **Circ:** (Not Reported).

9680 ■ KFMN-FM - 96.9
PO Box 1566
Lihue, HI 96766-5566
Phone: (808)246-1197
Fax: (808)246-9697
Format: Adult Contemporary. **Networks:** AP. **Founded:** 1988. **Operating Hours:** Continuous. **Wattage:** 100,000. **Ad Rates:** $27 for 30 seconds; $32 for 60 seconds.

9681 ■ KHJC-FM - 88.9
PO Box 391
Twin Falls, ID 83303
Fax: (208)736-1958
Free: 800-357-4226
Format: Religious. **Key Personnel:** Ray Gorney, Asst. Dir.; Don Mills, Prog. Dir.; Kelly Carlson, Dir. of Engg. **Wattage:** 2,500. **Ad Rates:** Noncommercial. **URL:** http://www.csnradio.com/stations/studiowaivered/KHJC.php.

9682 ■ KITH-FM - 98.9
4334 Rice St., Ste. 204-B
Lihue, HI 96766
Phone: (808)246-4444
Fax: (808)246-4405
Format: Hawaiian. **Wattage:** 450 ERP. **Ad Rates:** Accepts Advertising. **URL:** http://www.islandradio989.com.

9683 ■ KJMQ-FM - 98.1
4334 Rice St.
Lihue, HI 96766
Format: Hip Hop. **Key Personnel:** Danny Hill, Contact. **Wattage:** 450. **URL:** http://www.jamz981.com.

9684 ■ KQNG-AM - 570
4271 Halenani St.
Lihue, HI 96766
Phone: (808)245-9527
Format: Talk; News; Sports. **Founded:** 1939. **Operating Hours:** Continuous. **Wattage:** 1,000. **Ad Rates:** Noncommercial. Combined advertising rates available with KQNG-AM: $15-$29 for 30 seconds; $18-$34 for 60 seconds.

9685 ■ KQNG-FM - 93.5
4271 Halenani St.
Lihue, HI 96766
Phone: (808)245-9527
Format: Contemporary Hit Radio (CHR). **Networks:** AP. **Owner:** Visionary Related Entertainment, Inc., at above address, Honolulu, HI. **Founded:** 1983. **Operating Hours:** Continuous. **Wattage:** 51,000 H;13,000 V. **Ad Rates:** Combined advertising rates available with KQNG-AM: $18-$34 for 30 seconds; $22-$42 for 60 seconds. **URL:** http://www.kongradio.com.

9686 ■ KTOH-FM - 99.9
4334 Rice St., Ste. 206
Lihue, HI 96766
Phone: (808)246-4444
Fax: (808)246-4405
Format: Adult Contemporary. **Wattage:** 450. **URL:** http://www.hhawaiimedia.com.

9687 ■ Oceanic Time Warner
2956 Aukele St., Ste. 101
Lihue, HI 96766
Founded: 1970. **Formerly:** Garden Isle Telecommunications; Kauai CableVision. **Key Personnel:** Bill Harkins, President; Ron Crown, Engineer. **Cities Served:** Barking Sands Naval Base, Kauai County, Hawaii: subscribing households 20,000; 62 channels; 3 community access channels; 504 hours per week community access programming. **URL:** http://www.oceanic.com/help-and-support/customer-care-centers.

MILILANI

9688 ■ Oceanic Time Warner Cable L.L.C.
200 Akimainui St.
Mililani, HI 96789-3912
Phone: (808)625-2100
Fax: (808)625-5888
Founded: 1969. **Formerly:** Oceanic Cablevision Inc. **Key Personnel:** Don Carroll, President; Kit Beuret, Contact, kbeurret@oceanic.com. **Cities Served:** subscribing households 245,000. **URL:** http://www.oceanic.com.

PRINCEVILLE

Kauai Co.

9689 ■ The Coconut Wireless
Save Our Seas
PO Box 223508
Princeville, HI 96722
Phone: (808)651-3452
Publisher's E-mail: sos@saveourseas.org
Freq: Quarterly. **Subscription Rates:** Included in membership. **Alt. Formats:** PDF. **URL:** http://

Circulation: ★ = AAM; △ or • = BPA; ♦ = CAC; ❑ = VAC; ⊕ = PO Statement; ‡ = Publisher's Report; Boldface figures = sworn; Light figures = estimated.

saveourseas.wordpress.com/news. **Remarks:** Accepts advertising. **Circ:** (Not Reported).

WAILUKU

E HI. Maui Co. On Maui Island, 90 mi. SE of Honolulu. Nearest port is three miles, Kahului. Tourist resort. Sugar factory. Agriculture. Sugar cane, pineapples.

9690 ■ Edible Hawaiian Islands
Edible Communities Inc.
PO Box 849
Wailuku, HI 96793
Phone: (808)463-7494
Publication E-mail: contact@ediblehawaiianislands.com
Magazine covering the local food of the Hawaiian Islands. **Freq:** Quarterly. **Key Personnel:** Gloria Cohen, Founder. **Subscription Rates:** $28 Individuals print; $12 Individuals online. **URL:** http://hawaiianislands.ediblefeast.com; http://ediblehi.com. **Remarks:** Accepts advertising. **Circ:** (Not Reported).

9691 ■ Maui News
Maui Publishing
100 Mahalani St.
Wailuku, HI 96793
Phone: (808)244-3981
Free: 800-827-0347
Publisher's E-mail: letters@mauinews.com
General newspaper. **Freq:** Published weekdays and Sundays. **Print Method:** Offset. **Cols./Page:** 6. **Col. Width:** 25 nonpareils. **Col. Depth:** 301 agate lines. **Key Personnel:** Dawne Miguel, Manager, Advertising; Joe Bradley, General Manager, Publisher; David Hoff, Editor; Chris M. Minford, Manager, Circulation. **Subscription Rates:** $68.26 Individuals 7 day mail subscription; $66.96 Individuals 1 day home delivery; $18 Individuals 7 day home delivery - easy; $48.77 By mail Monday thru Saturday (Hana, Lanai, Molokai); $286.03 By mail Monday thru Saturday (Mainland); $127.44 Individuals Monday thru Saturday (neighbor island). **URL:** http://www.mauinews.com. **Remarks:** Accepts advertising. **Circ:** Mon.-Fri. ★**20,454**, Sat. ★**20,505**, Sun. ★**25,546**.

9692 ■ Oahu Visitor
Aloha Visitor Guides
66 Kuukama St.
Wailuku, HI 96793
Phone: (808)873-9677
Publication E-mail: vm@visitormagazines.com
Magazine covering entertainment, tourism, dining, hotels, and other travel information for Oahu. **Freq:** Monthly. **Subscription Rates:** Free. **URL:** http://www.alohavisitorguides.com/oahu. **Circ:** (Not Reported).

9693 ■ KDLX-FM - 94.3
1900 Main St., Ste. 6
Wailuku, HI 96793
Phone: 244-9145
Email: info@kdlx943.com
Format: Country. **Owner:** Visionary Related Entertainment, Inc., at above address, Honolulu, HI. **Founded:** 1960. **Operating Hours:** Mon.- Fri. 7 a.m. to 1 a.m.; Sat.- Sun. 9 a.m. to 1 a.m. **Wattage:** 3,000. **Ad Rates:** Noncommercial. **URL:** http://www.kdlx943.com/.

9694 ■ KEAO-FM - 91.5
PO Box 1145
Wailuku, HI 96793
Phone: (808)244-2032
Fax: (808)243-9626
Format: Eclectic. **Owner:** Mana'o Radio, PO Box 2203, Wailuku, HI 96793, Ph: (808)242-5666, Fax: (808)242-5668. **URL:** http://manaoradio.com.

9695 ■ KKUA-FM - 90.7
738 Kaheka St.
Honolulu, HI 96814
Phone: (808)955-8821
Fax: (808)946-3863
Free: 877-941-3689
Email: admin@hawaiipublicradio.org
Format: Public Radio. **Networks:** AP; National Public Radio (NPR); Public Radio International (PRI). **Owner:** Hawaii Public Radio, 738 Kaheka St., Honolulu, HI 96814, Ph: (808)955-8821, Fax: (808)946-3863. **Founded:** 1988. **Operating Hours**: Continuous. **ADI**: Honolulu, HI. **Key Personnel:** Michael Titterton, President, Gen. Mgr.; Gene Schiller, Music Dir., gschiller@hawaiipublicradio.org; Charles Husson, Dir. of Operations, chusson@hawaiipublicradio.org; Bill Dorman, News Dir., bdorman@hawaiipublicradio. **Local Programs**: *Morning Concert*, Monday Tuesday Wednesday Thursday Friday 10:05 a.m. - 12:00 p.m.; *Music Through the Night*, Monday Tuesday Wednesday Thursday Friday Saturday Sunday 12:00 a.m. - 5:00 a.m.; 10:00 p.m. - 11:00 p.m. 12:00 a.m. - 5:00 a.m.; 11:00 p.m. 12:00 a.m. - 6:00 a.m.; 11:00 p.m.; *Art Song Contest*. **Wattage:** 7,000. **Ad Rates:** Noncommercial. **URL:** http://www.hawaiipublicradio.org.

9696 ■ KMKK-FM - 102.3
1900 Main St., Ste. 6
Wailuku, HI 96793
Phone: (808)244-9145
Fax: (808)244-8247
Format: Contemporary Country. **Owner:** Visionary Related Entertainment, Inc., at above address, Honolulu, HI. **Mailing address:** PO Box 1437, Wailuku, HI 96793.

9697 ■ KNUQ-FM - 103.9
1900 Main St., Ste. 6
Wailuku, HI 96793
Format: Top 40. **Owner:** Visionary Related Entertainment, Inc., at above address, Honolulu, HI. **Wattage**: 100,000. **Mailing address:** PO Box 1437, Wailuku, HI 96793. **URL:** http://vremaui.com.

9698 ■ KTBH-FM - 102.1
1900 Main St., Ste. 6
Wailuku, HI 96793
Phone: (808)244-9145
Fax: (808)244-8247
Format: Adult Contemporary. **Owner:** Visionary Related Entertainment, Inc., at above address, Honolulu, HI. **Mailing address:** PO Box 1437, Wailuku, HI 96793.

ALBION

9699 ■ K212DR-FM - 90.3
PO Box 391
Twin Falls, ID 83303
Format: Religious; Contemporary Christian. **Owner:** CSN International, PO Box 391, Twin Falls, ID 83303, Ph: (208)736-1958, Fax: (208)736-1958, Free: 800-357-4226. **URL:** http://www.csnradio.com.

ARCO

S. ID. Butte Co. 90 mi. NW of Pocatello. Silver, lead mines. Dairy, stock, grain farms. Hay, potatoes.

9700 ■ The Arco Advertiser
The Arco Advertiser
146 S Front St.
Arco, ID 83213
Phone: (208)527-3038
Publisher's E-mail: arcoadv@aol.com
Community newspaper. **Freq:** Weekly (Thurs.). **Print Method:** Offset. **Trim Size:** 14 x 22 1/2. **Cols./Page:** 6. **Col. Width:** 26 nonpareils. **Col. Depth:** 294 agate lines. **ISSN:** 0890--1511 (print). **USPS:** 029-800. **Subscription Rates:** $27 Individuals in Buttle & Custer Counties; $32 Out of area. **URL:** http://arcoadvertiser.com. **Ad Rates:** GLR $.23; BW $150; 4C $567; PCI $4.50. **Remarks:** Color advertising not accepted. **Circ:** ‡2185.

BLACKFOOT

C. ID. Bingham Co. 23 mi. N. of Pocatello. Farm machinery, sugar beets.

9701 ■ KBLY-AM - 1260
One Mile S Hwy. 91
Blackfoot, ID 83221
Format: News; Talk. **Owner:** Riverband Communications L.L.C., 400 W Sunnyside Rd., Idaho Falls, ID 83402. **Operating Hours:** Continuous. **Key Personnel:** Neal Larson, Contact, neal@eiradio.com. **Ad Rates:** Noncommercial; underwriting available. **URL:** http://www.eastidahonews.com.

9702 ■ KTHK-FM - 105.5
1 Mile S Hwy. 91
Blackfoot, ID 83221
Phone: (208)785-1400
Format: Country. **Operating Hours:** Continuous. **Ad Rates:** Advertising accepted; rates available upon request.

BOISE

SW ID. Ada Co. On the Boise River, 45 mi. E. of the Oregon border. The State Capital. Boise State University. The central city of the intermountain region. Manufacturing trade and service industries.

9703 ■ Alert: The Drug and Alcohol Abuse Prevention Magazine
Golden West Publications
PO Box 4833
Boise, ID 83711
Phone: (208)375-7911
Fax: (208)376-0770
Free: 800-398-0842
Publisher's E-mail: alertmagazine@aol.com
Magazine aiming to reduce drug and alcohol abuse in teens. **Freq:** Semiannual. **Key Personnel:** Steven D. Rix, Managing Editor; Bryan Swain, Editor. **Subscription Rates:** Free to high schools. **URL:** http://www.alertmagazine.org/. **Circ:** (Not Reported).

9704 ■ The Arbiter
Arbiter
1910 University Dr., MS 1340
Boise, ID 83725
Phone: (208)426-6300
Fax: (208)426-3884
Collegiate newspaper. **Print Method:** Offset. **Cols./Page:** 6. **Col. Width:** 20 nonpareils. **Col. Depth:** 420 agate lines. **Subscription Rates:** $1 Individuals. **URL:** http://www.arbiteronline.com. **Ad Rates:** PCI $8.30. **Remarks:** Accepts advertising. **Circ:** Free ‡6000.

9705 ■ Boise Family Magazine
Boise Family Magazine
13191 W Scotfield St.
Boise, ID 83713
Phone: (208)938-2119
Fax: (208)938-2117
Publisher's E-mail: magazine@treasurevalleyfamily.com
Local consumer magazine covering parenting and family issues. **Freq:** Monthly. **Print Method:** Web. **Trim Size:** 8 x 10 3/4. **Cols./Page:** 3. **Col. Width:** 2 1/4 inches. **Col. Depth:** 9 1/2 inches. **Key Personnel:** Liz Buckingham, Editor; Debbie Arstein, General Manager, phone: (208)861-2049. **Subscription Rates:** $15 Individuals. **Ad Rates:** BW $925; 4C $1,150. **Remarks:** Accepts advertising. **Circ:** Controlled 20000.

9706 ■ Genealogical Journal of Jefferson County, New York
NewYorkAncestry.com
PO Box 4311
Boise, ID 83711
Phone: (208)469-0673
Journal of genealogical information. **Freq:** Quarterly. **Key Personnel:** Patricia R. James, Editor. **ISSN:** 1045--8166 (print). **Subscription Rates:** $20 Individuals plus postage. **Remarks:** Advertising not accepted. **Circ:** Paid ‡200.

9707 ■ The Idaho Business Review
Idaho Business Review
855 W Broad St., Ste. 103
Boise, ID 83702
Phone: (208)336-3768
Fax: (208)336-5534
Business newspaper (tabloid). **Founded:** May 1984. **Freq:** Weekly. **Print Method:** Offset. **Trim Size:** 11 1/4 x 17 1/2. **Cols./Page:** 5. **Col. Width:** 12 picas. **Col. Depth:** 210 agate lines. **Key Personnel:** Anne Wallace Allen, Managing Editor; Sean Evans, Publisher, Vice President. **Subscription Rates:** $63 Individuals 6 months; $225.47 Individuals 3 year, print and digital, 156 issues; $187.74 Two years in state of Idaho, print and digital, 104 issues; $121.70 Individuals 1 year, print and digital, 52 issues; $93.40 Individuals digital only. **URL:** http://idahobusinessreview.com. **Mailing address:** PO Box 8866, Boise, ID 83702. **Ad Rates:** BW $720; 4C $876; SAU $14; PCI $14. **Remarks:** Advertising accepted; rates available upon request. **Circ:** Paid 3,100, Free 450.

9708 ■ Idaho Catholic Register
Roman Catholic Diocese of Boise
1501 S Federal Way, Ste. 400
Boise, ID 83705
Phone: (208)342-1311
Fax: (208)342-0224
Free: 800-654-6695
Publisher's E-mail: idcathreg@rcdb.org
Newspaper for the Catholic community. **Freq:** Semimonthly. **Print Method:** Offset. **Trim Size:** 11 x 14 1/2. **Cols./Page:** 5. **Col. Width:** 25 nonpareils. **Col. Depth:** 210 agate lines. **Key Personnel:** Michael Driscoll, Publisher; Michael Brown, Editor; Loretta Gossi, Administrative Assistant; Ann Bixby, Contact. **ISSN:** 0891--5792 (print). **USPS:** 225-940. **URL:** http://www.catholicidaho.org/ICRarchives. **Formerly**: Idaho Register. **Ad Rates:** GLR $.70; BW $750; 4C $1125; PCI $10. **Remarks:** Accepts advertising. **Circ:** (Not Reported).

9709 ■ The Idaho Statesman
Gannett Company Inc.
1200 N Curtis Rd.
Boise, ID 83706
Phone: (208)377-6200
Free: 800-635-8934
General newspaper. **Freq:** Weekly. **Print Method:** Offset. **Cols./Page:** 6. **Col. Width:** 2 inches. **Col. Depth:** 22 inches. **Key Personnel:** Vicki S. Gowler, Editor, Vice President, phone: (208)377-6403; Bill Manny, Reporter, phone: (208)377-6406. **ISSN:** 0093--1179 (print). **USPS:** 256-020. **Subscription Rates:** $4 Individuals in Ada/Canyon County; Monday-Sunday; $2 Individuals in Ada/Canyon County; Sundays & holidays; $2.50 Individuals in Ada/Canyon County; Friday-Sunday & holidays. **URL:** http://www.idahostatesman.com. **Mailing address:** PO Box 40, Boise, ID 83707. **Ad Rates:** PCI $60.20. **Remarks:** Accepts advertising. **Circ:** Mon.-Fri. ★**52444**, Sun. ★**73247**, Sat. ★**53551**.

9710 ■ ie: The Business of International Events
International Festivals & Events Association
2603 W Eastover Ter.
Boise, ID 83706
Phone: (208)433-0950
Fax: (208)433-9812
Freq: Quarterly. **Subscription Rates:** Included in membership; $50 for nonmembers; $25 additional subscription for members. **URL:** http://www.ifea.com/p/resources/iemagazine. **Remarks:** Accepts advertising. **Circ:** (Not Reported).

9711 ■ Journal of Raptor Research
Raptor Research Foundation
c/o Rick Watson, Conservation Committee Co-Chairman
5668 W Flying Hawk Ln.
Boise, ID 83709
Phone: (208)362-8272
Peer-reviewed journal focusing on raptor species. **Freq:**

Circulation: ★ = AAM; △ or • = BPA; ◆ = CAC; ❑ = VAC; ⊕ = PO Statement; ‡ = Publisher's Report; Boldface figures = sworn; Light figures = estimated.

Quarterly. **Key Personnel:** Cheryl Dykstra, Editor-in-Chief. **ISSN:** 0892--1016 (print). **Subscription Rates:** Included in membership. **URL:** http://www.raptorresearchfoundation.org/publications/journal-of-raptor-research. **Remarks:** Advertising not accepted. **Circ:** (Not Reported).

9712 ■ The Line Rider
Idaho Cattle Association
2120 Airport Way
Boise, ID 83715
Phone: (208)343-1615
Fax: (208)344-6695
Publisher's E-mail: info@idahocattle.org
Official magazine of the Idaho cattle industry. **Freq:** Bimonthly. **Mailing address:** PO Box 15397, Boise, ID 83715. **Ad Rates:** BW $355; 4C $455. **Remarks:** Accepts advertising. **Circ:** ‡1100.

9713 ■ KAID-TV - 4
1455 N Orchard St.
Boise, ID 83706
Phone: (208)373-7324
Fax: (208)373-7245
Free: 800-543-6868
Format: Public TV. **Networks:** Public Broadcasting Service (PBS). **Owner:** State of Idaho, at above address, BOISE, ID. **Founded:** 1971. **Operating Hours:** 7 a.m.-11 p.m.; 90% network, 10% local. **ADI:** Boise, ID. **Key Personnel:** Peter Morrill, Gen. Mgr.; Penny Traylor, Director, penny.traylor@idahoptv.org. **Local Programs:** *Truth Soviet-Style*; *Trail*. **Ad Rates:** Noncommercial. **URL:** http://www.idahoptv.org.

9714 ■ KARO-FM - 98.7
PO Box 2118
Omaha, NE 68172-9626
Free: 888-937-2471
Format: Contemporary Christian. **Owner:** Educatiobal Media Foundation, 2351 Sunset Blvd., Ste. 170-218, Rocklin, CA 95765, Free: 800-434-8400. **URL:** http://www.air1.com/.

9715 ■ KAWO-FM - 104.3
827 E Park Blvd., Ste. 201
Boise, ID 83712-7782
Phone: (208)344-6363
Format: Country. **Owner:** iHeartMedia and Entertainment Inc. , 200 E Basse Rd., San Antonio, TX 78209, Ph: (210)822-2828. **Founded:** 1979. **Formerly:** KLTB-FM. **ADI:** Boise, ID. **Wattage:** 52,000. **Ad Rates:** Advertising accepted; rates available upon request. $11-30 per unit.

9716 ■ KBOI-AM - 670
1419 W Bannock St.
Boise, ID 83702
Phone: (208)336-3670
Free: 800-529-5264
Format: News; Talk. **Networks:** CNN Radio. **Owner:** Citadel Broadcasting Corp., 7201 W Lake Mead Blvd., Ste. 400, Las Vegas, NV 89128-8366, Ph: (702)804-5200, Fax: (702)804-8250. **Founded:** 1947. **Operating Hours:** Continuous. **ADI:** Boise, ID. **Key Personnel:** Ken Weaver, Contact; David Allen, Contact, david.allen@citcomm.com; Matt Nielsen, Contact. **Local Programs:** *Zamzow's Garden Show*, Saturday 11:00 a.m. - 12:00 p.m.; *Dining Out Idaho*, Saturday 8:00 a.m. - 9:00 a.m. **Wattage:** 50,000. **Ad Rates:** Advertising accepted; rates available upon request. **URL:** http://www.kboi.com.

9717 ■ KBOI-TV - 2
140 N 16th St.
Boise, ID 83702
Phone: (208)472-2222
Fax: (208)472-2212
Email: sales@kboi2.com
Format: Commercial TV. **Networks:** CBS. **Owner:** Fisher Communications Inc., 140 4th Ave. N, Ste. 500, Seattle, WA 98109-4940, Ph: (206)404-7000, Fax: (206)404-6037. **Founded:** 1953. **Operating Hours:** 5:30 a.m.-2 a.m. **ADI:** Boise, ID. **Key Personnel:** Larry Roberts, Gen. Mgr.; Eric Jordan, Gen. Mgr. **Ad Rates:** $15-400 for 30 seconds; $30-800 for 60 seconds. **URL:** http://www.kboi2.com.

9718 ■ KBSJ-FM - 91.3
1910 University Dr.
Boise, ID 83725-1915
Phone: (208)426-3663
Email: boisestatepublicradio@boisestate.edu
Format: Public Radio. **Owner:** Boise State Public Radio, 1910 University Dr. , Boise, ID 83725, Ph: (208)426-3663. **Key Personnel:** John Hess, Gen. Mgr., johnhess@boisestate.edu. **URL:** http://www.boisestatepublicradio.org.

9719 ■ KBSK-FM - 89.9
1910 University Dr.
Boise, ID 83725
Phone: (208)426-3663
Format: Jazz. **Owner:** Boise State Public Radio, 1910 University Dr. , Boise, ID 83725, Ph: (208)426-3663. **Operating Hours:** Continuous. **Wattage:** 220.

9720 ■ KBSM-FM - 91.7
1910 University Dr.
Boise, ID 83725
Phone: (208)426-3663
Fax: (208)344-6631
Email: boisestatepublicradio@boisestate.edu
Format: Public Radio; Classical. **Simulcasts:** KBSU-FM. **Networks:** National Public Radio (NPR); Public Radio International (PRI). **Owner:** BSU Radio Network, 1910 University Dr.,, Boise, ID 83725-1916. **Operating Hours:** Continuous; 70% network, 30% local. **ADI:** Boise, ID. **Key Personnel:** Eric Jones, Mgr.; John Hess, Gen. Mgr. **Wattage:** 220. **Ad Rates:** Noncommercial. **URL:** http://www.boisestatepublicradio.org.

9721 ■ KBSQ-FM - 90.7
1910 University Dr.
Boise, ID 83725
Phone: (208)426-3663
Fax: (208)344-6631
Email: boisestatepublicradio@boisestate.edu
Format: News; Talk. **Owner:** Boise State Public Radio, 1910 University Dr. , Boise, ID 83725, Ph: (208)426-3663. **Key Personnel:** John Hess, Gen. Mgr., johnhess@boisestate.edu. **Ad Rates:** Noncommercial. **URL:** http://www.boisestatepublicradio.org.

9722 ■ KBSU-FM - 90.3
1910 University Dr.
Boise, ID 83725
Phone: (208)426-3663
Fax: (208)344-6631
Format: Public Radio; Classical; News. **Networks:** National Public Radio (NPR); Public Radio International (PRI). **Owner:** BSU Radio Network, 1910 University Dr.,, Boise, ID 83725-1916. **Founded:** 1977. **Operating Hours:** Continuous; 70% network, 30% local. **ADI:** Boise, ID. **Key Personnel:** John Hess, Gen. Mgr. **Wattage:** 19,000. **Ad Rates:** Noncommercial. **URL:** http://boisestatepublicradio.org.

9723 ■ KBSX-FM - 91.5
1910 University Dr.
Boise, ID 83725
Phone: (208)426-3663
Email: kbsxnewsroom@boisestate.edu
Format: Public Radio. **Owner:** Boise State Public Radio, 1910 University Dr. , Boise, ID 83725, Ph: (208)426-3663. **Key Personnel:** John Hess, Gen. Mgr., johnhess@boisestate.edu. **Ad Rates:** Noncommercial. **URL:** http://www.boisestatepublicradio.org.

9724 ■ KBSY-FM - 91
1910 University Dr.
Boise, ID 83725-1915
Phone: (208)426-3663
Fax: (208)344-6631
Email: boisestatepublicradio@boisestate.edu
Format: News; Information. **Networks:** National Public Radio (NPR). **Owner:** Idaho State Board of Education, 650 W State St., 3rd Fl., Boise, ID 83702, Ph: (208)334-2270, Fax: (208)334-2632. **Founded:** Oct. 1998. **Operating Hours:** Continuous. **Key Personnel:** Eric Jones, Mgr., Member Svcs., ejones@boisestate.edu; John Hess, Gen. Mgr., johnhess@boisestate.edu; Tom Taylor, Dir. of Engg., Dir. of Operations, ttaylor@boisestate.edu. **Ad Rates:** Noncommercial. **URL:** http://www.boisestatepublicradio.org.

9725 ■ KBXL-FM - 94.1
1440 S Weideman Ave.
Boise, ID 83709-1450
Phone: (208)377-3790
Fax: (208)377-3792
Email: info@myfamilyradio.com
Format: Religious. **Networks:** USA Radio. **Owner:** KBXL-FM, at above address, Ph: (208)377-3790, Fax: (208)377-3792. **Founded:** 1970. **Operating Hours:** Continuous; 50% local, 50% network. **ADI:** Boise, ID. **Key Personnel:** Beth Schafer, Gen. Mgr., Owner, President; David Schafer, Station Mgr., david@myfamilyradio.com. **Wattage:** 40,000. **Ad Rates:** Noncommercial. Combined advertising rates available with KSPD-AM. **URL:** http://www.myfamilyradio.com.

9726 ■ KCID-FM - 107.1
5601 Cassia
Boise, ID 83705
Phone: (208)344-3511
Fax: (208)336-3264
Simulcasts: KCID-AM. **Owner:** Journal Broadcast Group, 5257 Fairview Ave., No. 260, Boise, ID 83706. **Founded:** 1983. **Operating Hours:** Continuous. **ADI:** Boise, ID. **Key Personnel:** Bob Rosenthal, Gen. Mgr., VP, rosenthal@journalbroadcastgroup.com; Larry Doss, Dir. of Programs, doss@journalbroadcastgroup.com. **Wattage:** 3,000.

9727 ■ KCIX-FM - 105.9
827 E Park Blvd., No. 201
Boise, ID 83712
Phone: (208)344-6363
Format: Adult Contemporary. **Networks:** Independent. **Owner:** Peak Broadcasting, at above address. **Founded:** 1985. **Operating Hours:** Continuous; 100% local. **ADI:** Boise, ID. **Wattage:** 50,000. **Ad Rates:** $40 for 30 seconds; $60 for 60 seconds. Combined advertising rates available with KIDO, KKLT, KSAS, KLTB, KFXD. **URL:** http://www.mix106radio.com/pages/main.

9728 ■ KEZJ-AM - 1450
1910 University Dr.
Boise, ID 83725
Phone: (208)426-3663
Format: Jazz. **Networks:** CBS; NBC. **Founded:** 1946. **Operating Hours:** 5 a.m.-midnight; 29% network, 71% local. **ADI:** Twin Falls, ID. **Key Personnel:** John Hess, Gen. Mgr., johnhess@boisestate.edu; Elizabeth Duncan, News Dir., elizabethduncan@boisestate.edu; Betsy Micone, Bus. Mgr., bmicone@boisestate.edu. **Wattage:** 1,000. **Ad Rates:** Noncommercial.

9729 ■ KFXD-AM - 630
827 Park Blvd., No. 201
Boise, ID 83712
Phone: (208)344-6363
Fax: (208)372-8800
Format: Country. **Networks:** Fox. **Founded:** 1920. **ADI:** Boise, ID. **Key Personnel:** Mike Sutton, Contact. **Wattage:** 5,000 Day;5,000 Nigh. **Ad Rates:** Advertising accepted; rates available upon request. **URL:** http://www.kfxd.com.

9730 ■ KGEM-AM - 1140
5601 Cassia
Boise, ID 83705
Format: News; Talk. **Founded:** 1945. **Operating Hours:** Continuous. **ADI:** Boise, ID. **Wattage:** 10,000. **Ad Rates:** Noncommercial. Underwriting available. **URL:** http://www.saltandlightradio.com/.

9731 ■ KHEZ-FM - 103.3
Lakeharbor, Ste. 120
Boise, ID 83703-0063
Phone: (208)384-1033
Fax: (208)343-2103
Format: Easy Listening. **Founded:** 1987. **Operating Hours:** Continuous. **Key Personnel:** Gregory Williamson, Gen. Mgr. **Wattage:** 100,000 ERP. **Ad Rates:** $8-40 per unit.

9732 ■ KIDO-AM - 580
827 E Park Blvd., No. 100
Boise, ID 83712
Phone: (208)344-6363
Free: 888-580-5436
Format: Talk; News; Sports. **Networks:** NBC; ABC. **Founded:** 1928. **Operating Hours:** Continuous; 60% network, 40% local. **ADI:** Boise, ID. **Key Personnel:** Kevin Godwin, Gen. Mgr., Sr. VP, kevin.godwin@peakbroadcasting.com. **Local Programs:** *Weekend Idaho*, Saturday Sunday 5:00 a.m. - 8:00 a.m. **Wattage:** 5,000. **Ad Rates:** Advertising accepted; rates available upon request. Combined advertising rates available with KLIX, KCIX, KSAS, KFXD, KXLT. **URL:** http://www.580kido.com.

9733 ■ KJOT-FM - 105.1
5257 Fairview Ave., Ste. 260
Boise, ID 83706
Phone: (208)344-3511
Format: Classic Rock. **Owner:** Journal Broadcast Corp., 333 W State St., Milwaukee, WI 53203, Ph: (414)332-9611, Fax: (414)967-5400. **Founded:** 1979. **Operating Hours**: Continuous. **ADI**: Boise, ID. **Wattage**: 43,000. **Ad Rates:** Advertising accepted; rates available upon request. **URL:** http://www.varietyrocks.com.

9734 ■ KKGL-FM - 96.9
1419 W Bannock St.
Boise, ID 83702
Phone: (208)336-3670
Format: Classic Rock. **Owner:** Citadel Broadcasting Corp., 7201 W Lake Mead Blvd., Ste. 400, Las Vegas, NV 89128-8366, Ph: (702)804-5200, Fax: (702)804-8250. **Founded:** Sept. 16, 2006. **Operating Hours:** Continuous. **Key Personnel:** Forrest Smithkors, Contact, forrest.smithkors@kkgl.com. **Wattage**: 48,000 ERP. **Ad Rates:** Advertising accepted; rates available upon request. **URL:** http://www.96-9theeagle.com.

9735 ■ KQFC-FM - 97.9
1419 W Bannock St.
Boise, ID 83702
Phone: (208)336-3298
Format: Country. **Networks:** Independent. **Owner:** Citadel Broadcasting Corp., 7201 W Lake Mead Blvd., Ste. 400, Las Vegas, NV 89128-8366, Ph: (702)804-5200, Fax: (702)804-8250. **Founded:** 1960. **Formerly**: KBOI-FM. **Operating Hours**: Continuous; local. **Key Personnel:** Tom Newman, Sales Mgr., tom.newman@citcomm.com. **Wattage**: 48,000. **Ad Rates:** Advertising accepted; rates available upon request. Combined advertising rates available with KBOI, KKGL-FM, KIZN, KZMG. **URL:** http://www.nashfm979.com.

9736 ■ KQXR-FM - 100.3
5257 Fairview Ave., Ste. 240
Boise, ID 83706
Email: comments@xrock.com
Format: Alternative/New Music/Progressive. **URL:** http://www.xrock.com.

9737 ■ KRTK-AM - 1490
1440 S Weideman Ave.
Boise, ID 83709
Phone: (208)237-9500
Email: krtk@calvarychapel.com
Format: Religious. **Founded:** Sept. 13, 2006. **Ad Rates:** Noncommercial.

9738 ■ KRVB-FM - 94.9
5257 Fairview Ave., Ste. 240
Boise, ID 83706
Phone: (208)344-3511
Fax: (208)947-6765
Format: Adult Album Alternative. **Operating Hours:** Continuous. **Wattage**: 49,000. **Ad Rates:** Noncommercial. **URL:** http://www.riverinteractive.com.

9739 ■ KSAS-FM - 103.3
827 E Park Blvd., No. 100
Boise, ID 83712
Phone: (208)344-6363
Format: Contemporary Hit Radio (CHR). **ADI**: Boise, ID. **Wattage:** 54,000. **Ad Rates:** Noncommercial.

9740 ■ KSPD-AM - 790
1440 S Weideman Ave.
Boise, ID 83709-1450
Phone: (208)377-3790
Fax: (208)377-3792
Email: info@myfamilyradio.com
Format: Religious; Talk. **Networks:** Moody Broadcasting; USA Radio; International Broadcasting; Ambassador Inspirational Radio. **Owner:** Inspirational Family Radio, at above address. **Operating Hours**: Continuous. **ADI**: Boise, ID. **Key Personnel:** David Schafer, Contact, david@myfamilyradio.com; David Schafer, Contact, david@myfamilyradio.com. **Wattage**: 1,000. **Ad Rates:** Advertising accepted; rates available upon request. KBXL-FM Combined advertising rates available with. **URL:** http://www.790kspd.com.

9741 ■ KTHI-FM - 107.1
5257 Fairview Ave., Ste. 260
Boise, ID 83706
Phone: (208)344-3511
Format: Classical; Oldies. **Wattage:** 52,000. **Ad Rates:** Noncommercial. **URL:** http://www.khits.fm.

9742 ■ KTIK-AM - 1350
1419 W Bannock St.
Boise, ID 83702
Phone: (208)336-3670
Format: Sports. **Owner:** Cumulus Media Inc., 3280 Peachtree Rd. NW, Ste. 2300, Atlanta, GA 30305-2455, Ph: (404)949-0700, Fax: (404)949-0740. **Founded:** 1962. **Formerly**: KANR-AM. **Operating Hours**: Continuous; 100% local. **ADI**: Boise, ID. **Key Personnel:** John Cunningham, Dir. of Operations; John Patrick, Contact; Jeff Caves, Contact, jeff.caves@cumulus.com; John Patrick, Contact; Tom Scott, Contact. **Local Programs**: *Idaho Sports Talk*, Monday Tuesday Wednesday Thursday Friday 3:00 p.m. - 6:00 p.m. **Wattage**: 1,000. **Ad Rates:** $15 per unit. **URL:** http://www.ktik.com.

9743 ■ KTVB-TV - 7
PO Box 7
Boise, ID 83707
Fax: (208)375-7277
Format: Commercial TV. **Networks:** NBC. **Owner:** Belo Corp., 400 S Record St., Dallas, TX 75202-4841, Ph: (214)977-6606, Fax: (214)977-6603. **Founded:** 1953. **Formerly**: KIDO-TV. **Operating Hours**: Continuous. **ADI**: Boise, ID. **Key Personnel:** Doug Armstrong, Gen. Mgr., President; Kristi Edmunds, Dir. of Sales & Mktg. **Ad Rates:** Advertising accepted; rates available upon request. **URL:** http://www.ktvb.com.

9744 ■ K294AE-FM
PO Box 391
Twin Falls, ID 83303
Fax: (208)736-1958
Free: 800-357-4226
Owner: CSN International, PO Box 391, Twin Falls, ID 83303, Ph: (208)736-1958, Fax: (208)736-1958, Free: 800-357-4226. **Key Personnel:** Mike Kestler, President; Don Mills, Music Dir., Prog. Dir.; Daniel Davidson, Dir. of Operations. **URL:** http://www.csnradio.com.

9745 ■ KWEI-AM - 1450
1156 N Orchard St.
Boise, ID 83706
Phone: (208)367-1859
Fax: (208)383-9170
Format: Hispanic. **Networks:** CNN Radio; Univision. **Owner:** Treasure Valley Broadcasting Inc., 1156 N Orchard, Boise, ID 83706, Ph: (208)367-1269. **Founded:** 1947. **Operating Hours**: Continuous; 6 a.m. to sunset. **ADI**: Boise, ID. **Key Personnel:** Debra Patterson, Sales Mgr., dp@kweiradio.com; Belia Paz, Station Mgr., bp@kweiradio.com. **Wattage**: 10,000. **Ad Rates:** $22.50 for 60 seconds. Combined advertising rates available with KWEI-FM.

9746 ■ KWEI-FM - 99.5
1156 N Orchard St.
Boise, ID 83706
Phone: (208)367-1859
Fax: (208)383-9170
Format: Hispanic. **Owner:** Treasure Valley Broadcasting Inc., 1156 N Orchard, Boise, ID 83706, Ph: (208)367-1269. **Founded:** 1978. **Operating Hours**: Continuous. **ADI**: Boise, ID. **Key Personnel:** Debra Patterson, Sales Mgr., dp@kweiradio.com. **Wattage**: 50,000. **Ad Rates:** $16.50-24.50 for 60 seconds. Combined advertising rates available with KWEI-AM.

9747 ■ KXLT-FM - 107.9
827 E Park Blvd., Ste. 100
Boise, ID 83712
Phone: (208)344-6363
Format: Adult Contemporary. **Owner:** Peak Broadcasting, at above address. **Founded:** Aug. 12, 1994. **Wattage**: 45,000. **Ad Rates:** Noncommercial. **URL:** http://www.liteonline.com.

9748 ■ KZMG-FM - 93.1
1419 W Bannock St.
Boise, ID 83702
Phone: (208)424-9300
Fax: (208)336-3734
Email: kissin92@kizn.com
Format: Top 40; Country. **Networks:** Westwood One Radio; CBS. **Owner:** Citadel Broadcasting Corp., 7201 W Lake Mead Blvd., Ste. 400, Las Vegas, NV 89128-8366, Ph: (702)804-5200, Fax: (702)804-8250. **Founded:** 1982. **Formerly**: KBBK-FM. **Operating Hours**: Continuous. **Key Personnel:** Bob Rosenthal, Sales Mgr., bob.rosenthal@cumulus.com; Rich Summers, Operations Mgr., Prog. Dir., rich.summers@cumulus.com; Brenda Mee, News Dir., brenda.mee@cumulusm.com; Ben Bieri, Promotions Dir., ben.bieri@cumulus.com. **Local Programs:** *Kevin & Brenda Mee.* **Wattage**: 50,000. **Ad Rates:** $30 for 30 seconds; $50 for 30 seconds; $40 for 30 seconds; $30-75 for 60 seconds; $50 for 60 seconds; $65 for 60 seconds.

BONNERS FERRY

C. ID. Boundary Co. 75 mi. NNE of Coeur d'Alene. Sawmills, farming, and mining.

9749 ■ Bonners Ferry Herald
Bonners Ferry Herald
7183 Main St.
Bonners Ferry, ID 83805
Phone: (208)267-5521
Fax: (208)267-5523
Publisher's E-mail: bfherald@cdapress.com
Community newspaper. **Freq:** Semiweekly (Wed. and Fri.). **Cols./Page:** 6. **Col. Width:** 2 1/8 inches. **Col. Depth:** 21 1/2 inches. **Key Personnel:** David Keyes, Publisher; Linda Johnson, Office Manager. **Subscription Rates:** $29.50 Out of area; $31.50 Out of state; $27.50 Individuals senior rate. **URL:** http://www.bonnersferryherald.com. **Ad Rates:** BW $600; 4C $900; SAU $8; PCI $7. **Remarks:** Accepts advertising. **Circ:** ‡3200.

9750 ■ KBFI-AM
305 1st St.
Bonners Ferry, ID 83805
Phone: (208)267-5234
Fax: (208)267-5594
Format: Country. **Networks:** ABC. **Owner:** Radio Bonners Ferry, at above address. **Founded:** 1978. **Key Personnel:** Mike Brown, News Dir., mikeb@953kpnd.com. **Wattage**: 1,000. **Ad Rates:** $3-6.50 for 30 seconds; $3.75-8.13 for 60 seconds. **Mailing address:** PO Box X, Bonners Ferry, ID 83805.

9751 ■ KIBX-FM - 92.1
2319 N Monroe St.
Spokane, WA 99205
Phone: (509)328-5729
Fax: (509)328-5764
Free: 800-328-5729
Email: kpbx@kpbx.org
Format: Public Radio. **Owner:** Spokane Public Radio, 2319 N. Monroe Street, Spokane, WA 99205, Ph: (509)328.5729, Fax: (509)328.5764, Free: 800-328.5729. **Key Personnel:** Verne Windham, Dir. of Programs, vwindham@kpbx.org. **Ad Rates:** Noncommercial. **URL:** http://www.spokanepublicradio.org.

CALDWELL

SW ID. Canyon Co. 30 mi. W. of Boise.

9752 ■ KBGN-AM - 1060
3303 E Chicago St.
Caldwell, ID 83605
Phone: (208)459-3635
Email: kbgn@kbgnradio.com
Format: Contemporary Christian. **Networks:** USA Radio. **Owner:** Nelson M. Wilson or Karen E. Wilson. **Founded:** 1960. **Operating Hours**: 6 a.m.-two hours past sunset; 10% network, 90% local. **ADI**: Boise, ID. **Key Personnel:** Nelson M. Wilson, Gen. Mgr.; Marnie Fillmore, Dir. of Operations. **Local Programs**: *Answers With Ken Ham*, Monday Tuesday Wednesday Thursday Friday 11:58 a.m. **Wattage**: 10,000. **Ad Rates:** Advertising accepted; rates available upon request. **URL:** http://www.kbgnradio.com.

9753 ■ KCID-AM
PO Box 968
Caldwell, ID 83606-0968
Phone: (208)459-3608
Fax: (208)454-1490
Format: Adult Contemporary; Sports; Hispanic. **Networks:** AP. **Owner:** TDS Broadcasting, PO Box 968. **Founded:** 1947. **Key Personnel:** Sam Bass, News Dir; Cheryl Wolf, Contact. **Wattage**: 1,000. **Ad Rates:** $10-15 for 30 seconds; $13-18 for 60 seconds.

Circulation: ★ = AAM; △ or • = BPA; ♦ = CAC; ❑ = VAC; ⊕ = PO Statement; ‡ = Publisher's Report; Boldface figures = sworn; Light figures = estimated.

9754 ■ KDJQ-AM - 890
1014 N 3rd Ave.
Caldwell, ID 83605
Phone: (208)283-1441
Format: Oldies.

9755 ■ KTSY-FM - 89.5
16115 S Montana Ave.
Caldwell, ID 83607
Format: Contemporary Christian. **Wattage:** 8,300. **Ad Rates:** Noncommercial. **URL:** http://www.895ktsy.org.

CASCADE

9756 ■ K238AG-FM
PO Box 391
Twin Falls, ID 83303
Free: 800-357-4226
Owner: CSN International, PO Box 391, Twin Falls, ID 83303, Ph: (208)736-1958, Fax: (208)736-1958, Free: 800-357-4226.

CHALLIS

C. ID. Custer Co. 50 mi. SE of Salmon. Residential.

9757 ■ The Challis Messenger
Custer Publishing Inc.
PO Box 405
Challis, ID 83226
Phone: (208)879-4445
Publisher's E-mail: info@challismessenger.com
Community newspaper. **Freq:** Weekly (Thurs.). **Print Method:** Offset. **Trim Size:** 11 1/2 x 17 1/2. **Cols./Page:** 5. **Col. Width:** 11.5 picas. **Col. Depth:** 16 inches. **Key Personnel:** Margaret Wimborne, Editor. **USPS:** 099-660. **Subscription Rates:** $28.50 Individuals local, 1 year; $35 Out of area 1 year; $24 Individuals online only, 1 year; $14.25 Individuals local, 6 months; $17.50 Individuals non-local, 6 months; $12 Individuals online only, 6 months. **URL:** http://www.challismessenger.com. **Ad Rates:** GLR $5.25; BW $5.25; 4C $6.18; PCI $4.25. **Remarks:** Accepts advertising. **Circ:** Paid ‡1825.

CHUBBUCK

9758 ■ KPIF-TV - 476 - 482
5023 Rainbow Ln.
Chubbuck, ID 83202
Phone: (208)237-5743
Fax: (208)237-5768
Owner: KM Communications, Inc., 3654 W Jarvis Ave., Skokie, IL 60076. **ADI:** Idaho Falls-Pocatello, ID. **Wattage:** 239,000.

COEUR D ALENE

9759 ■ Coeur d'Alene Press
Coeur d'Alene Press
215 N Second St.
Coeur d Alene, ID 83814
Phone: (208)664-8176
Publisher's E-mail: sports@cdapress.com
General newspaper. **Freq:** Mon.-Sat. (morn.). **Print Method:** Offset. **Cols./Page:** 6. **Col. Width:** 25 nonpareils. **Col. Depth:** 294 agate lines. **Key Personnel:** Jim Thompson, Publisher; Mike Patrick, Managing Editor, phone: (208)664-0227; Paul Burke, Director, Advertising. **Subscription Rates:** $100 Individuals online. **URL:** http://www.cdapress.com. **Ad Rates:** GLR $.75; BW $1450.59; 4C $1780.54. **Remarks:** Accepts advertising. **Circ:** Mon.-Sat. ‡24000, Sun. ‡31000.

9760 ■ Hungry Horse News
Hagadone Hospitality
111 S First St.
Coeur d Alene, ID 83814
Phone: (208)667-3431
Fax: (208)664-7206
Publication E-mail: info@hungryhorsenews.com
Community newspaper. **Freq:** Weekly (Wed.). **Print Method:** Offset. Uses mats. **Cols./Page:** 6. **Col. Width:** 26 nonpareils. **Col. Depth:** 294 agate lines. **Key Personnel:** Rick Weaver, Publisher; David Reese, Editor. **USPS:** 254-320. **Subscription Rates:** $38 Individuals; $35 Out of area; $28 Out of state; $23.50 Individuals e-edition. **URL:** http://www.flatheadnewsgroup.com/hungryhorsenews. **Remarks:** Accepts advertising. **Circ:** ‡4,200.

9761 ■ KVNI-AM - 1080
504 E Sherman
Coeur d Alene, ID 83814-2731
Format: News; Sports. **Founded:** 1946. **Key Personnel:** Dick Haugen, News Dir. **Wattage:** 10,000 Daytime; 100. **Ad Rates:** $20-35 per unit. Combined advertising rates available with KHTQ-FM. **URL:** http://kootenaifm.com/.

COEUR D'ALENE

N. ID. Kootenai Co. On Coeur d'Alene Lake and Spokane River, 33 mi. E. of Spokane, WA. Boat connections. Ski Resorts. Vacation Area. Manufactures lumber, shingles, railroad ties, boats, electronic equipment, box shooks, flour, dairy products. Timber. Agriculture.

9762 ■ Nickel's Worth
Nickel's Worth
107 N Fifth St.
Coeur d'Alene, ID 83816
Publisher's E-mail: ads@nickelsworth.com
Shopping guide. **Freq:** Weekly (Thurs.). **Key Personnel:** Tim Rostkoski, Director, Distribution, Publisher. **URL:** http://www.nickelsworth.com. **Mailing address:** PO Box 2048, Coeur d'Alene, ID 83816. **Remarks:** Accepts advertising. **Circ:** (Not Reported).

COTTONWOOD

C. ID. Idaho Co. 56 mi. S. of Lewiston. Logging; grain elevators. Pine timber. Grain, dairy, stock, poultry farms. Wheat, hogs.

9763 ■ Cottonwood Chronicle
Cottonwood Chronicle
503 King St.
Cottonwood, ID 83522-0157
Phone: (208)962-3851
Fax: (208)962-7131
Community newspaper. **Freq:** Weekly (Thurs.). **Print Method:** Offset. **Cols./Page:** 5. **Col. Width:** 26 nonpareils. **Col. Depth:** 182 agate lines. **Subscription Rates:** $32 Individuals 1 year; $20 Individuals 6 months; $38 Out of area 1 year ; $23 Out of area 6 months; $23 Students 9 months. **URL:** http://www.cottonwoodchronicle.com. **Mailing address:** PO Box 157, Cottonwood, ID 83522-0157. **Ad Rates:** GLR $4.50. **Remarks:** Accepts advertising. **Circ:** ‡1050.

DRIGGS

E. ID. Teton Co. 50 mi. NE of Idaho Falls. Ski Resort. Diversified farming. Wheat, barley, hay, seed potatoes.

9764 ■ Teton Valley News
Teton Valley News
75 N Main St.
Driggs, ID 83422
Phone: (208)354-8101
Fax: (208)354-8621
Local newspaper. **Freq:** Weekly (Thurs.). **Print Method:** Offset. **Trim Size:** 11 3/8 x 17. **Cols./Page:** 6. **Col. Width:** 20 nonpareils. **Col. Depth:** 224 agate lines. **Key Personnel:** Meg Heinen, Contact; Scott Anderson, Publisher; Lisa Nyren, Managing Editor. **ISSN:** 0889--9851 (print). **Subscription Rates:** $40 Individuals; $44 Out of area. **URL:** http://www.tetonvalleynews.net. **Ad Rates:** BW $384; 4C $518.40; SAU $5.50; PCI $6. **Remarks:** Color advertising not accepted. **Circ:** ‡2300.

9765 ■ KCHQ-FM - 102.1
PO Box 54
Driggs, ID 83422
Phone: (208)354-4103
Fax: (208)354-4104
Format: Country. **Key Personnel:** Dave Plourde, News Dir., dave@q102fm.net.

EMMETT

W. ID. Gem Co. 20 mi. NE of Caldwell. Residential.

9766 ■ Messenger Index
Messenger Index
PO Box 577
Emmett, ID 83617
Phone: (208)365-6066
Fax: (208)365-6068
Publisher's E-mail: customerservice@messenger-index.com
Newspaper. **Freq:** Weekly. **Print Method:** Offset. **Cols./Page:** 6. **Col. Width:** 25 nonpareils. **Col. Depth:** 297 agate lines. **Key Personnel:** Tonja Hyder, General Manager; Diana Baird, Managing Editor. **URL:** http://www.messenger-index.com. **Ad Rates:** GLR $.43; BW $909.45; 4C $1159.45; SAU $7.05. **Remarks:** Accepts advertising. **Circ:** 7000.

HAGERMAN

9767 ■ Aquaculture Research
Wiley-Blackwell
c/o Dr. Ronald W. Hardy, Ed.
Aquaculture Research Institute, University of Idaho
Hagerman Fish Culture Sta.
3059F National Fish Hatchery Rd.
Hagerman, ID 83332
Phone: (208)837-9096
Publisher's E-mail: customerservice@oxon.blackwellpublishing.com
Journal focusing on research and reference needs of all working and studying within the many varied areas of aquaculture. **Freq:** 16/yr. **Key Personnel:** Dr. Ronald W. Hardy, Editor. **ISSN:** 1355-557X (print). **Subscription Rates:** $377 Members print & online; £229 Members print & online; $5365 Institutions print & online; £2527 Institutions print or online; $4664 Institutions print or online; €342 Members print & online; £2906 Institutions print & online. **URL:** http://as.wiley.com/WileyCDA/WileyTitle/productCd-ARE.html. **Remarks:** Accepts advertising. **Circ:** (Not Reported).

HAILEY

S. ID. Blaine Co. 75 mi. W. of Twin Falls. Recreation. Mining. Agriculture.

9768 ■ KECH-FM - 95.3
201 S Main St.
Hailey, ID 83333
Phone: (208)726-5324
Fax: (208)726-5459
Format: Classic Rock. **Founded:** 1988. **Key Personnel:** Scott Parker, Gen. Mgr. **Wattage:** 2,500 ERP. **Ad Rates:** $17-20 per unit. **URL:** http://kech95fm.com.

9769 ■ KSKI-FM - 94.5
201 S Main St.
Hailey, ID 83333
Phone: (208)788-7118
Fax: (208)788-7119
Format: Alternative/New Music/Progressive. **Owner:** Chaparral Broadcasting, 645 South Cache, Jackson, WY. **Founded:** 1966. **Operating Hours:** Continuous. **Key Personnel:** Sandie Fulks, Gen. Mgr., sandie@richbroadcasting.com. **Wattage:** 2,500. **Ad Rates:** KECH, KWYS, KYZK, KEZQ. **Mailing address:** PO Box 2750, Hailey, ID 83333. **URL:** http://945kski.com.

HAYDEN

9770 ■ KHTQ-FM - 94.5
500 W Boone Ave.
Spokane, WA 99201
Phone: (509)324-4200
Format: Classic Rock. **Owner:** Queenb Radio, Inc., at above address, Spokane, WA. **Key Personnel:** Brian Paul, VP. **Ad Rates:** Advertising accepted; rates available upon request. **URL:** http://www.rock945.com.

9771 ■ KHTQ-FM - 94.5
15047 N Government Way
Hayden, ID 83835
Format: Alternative/New Music/Progressive. **URL:** http://rock945.com/auto-credit-sales-etw-rock-hard-at-the-park-tickets/.

IDAHO FALLS

E. ID. Bonneville Co. 50 mi. NE of Pocatello. Potato, flour, dairy factories; bottling works; foundry; planing mill. Ships agriculture products. Agriculture. Potatoes, wheat, seed peas, dairy, sheep, cattle.

9772 ■ Boating Sportsman
Harris Publishing Inc.
360 B St.
Idaho Falls, ID 83402
Phone: (208)524-7000
Fax: (208)522-5241
Free: 800-638-0135

Publisher's E-mail: customerservice@harrispublishing.com
Magazine covering various aspects of jet boat manufacturing. Also covers information on destinations for jet-boating adventure and other related topics. **Freq:** Bimonthly. **Print Method:** Offset. **Trim Size:** 8 x 10 3/4. **Cols./Page:** 3. **Col. Width:** 27 nonpareils. **Col. Depth:** 140 agate lines. **Key Personnel:** Brad Anderson, Contact; Greg Larsen, Publisher. **Subscription Rates:** $9.95 Individuals online. **Remarks:** Advertising not accepted. **Circ:** (Not Reported).

9773 ■ Houseboat Magazine: The Family Magazine for American Houseboaters
Harris Publishing Inc.
360 B St.
Idaho Falls, ID 83402
Phone: (208)524-7000
Fax: (208)522-5241
Free: 800-638-0135
Publisher's E-mail: customerservice@harrispublishing.com
Magazine for houseboating in America. **Freq:** Monthly. **Trim Size:** 8 x 10-3/4. **Cols./Page:** 3. **Col. Width:** 13.5 picas. **Col. Depth:** 59 picas. **Key Personnel:** Chris Searle, Account Executive, fax: (208)542-2252; Brady L. Kay, Executive Editor; Greg Larsen, Director, Advertising and Sales, Publisher, fax: (208)542-2216. **Subscription Rates:** $19.95 U.S. /year (print and online); $6.99 Individuals /year (online); $39.95 Other countries /year (print and online). **URL:** http://www.houseboatmagazine.com. **Ad Rates:** 4C $3976. **Remarks:** Accepts advertising. **Circ:** Paid 25000.

9774 ■ Mountainwest Golf
Harris Publishing Inc.
360 B St.
Idaho Falls, ID 83402
Phone: (208)524-7000
Fax: (208)522-5241
Free: 800-638-0135
Publisher's E-mail: customerservice@harrispublishing.com
Magazine covering local golfing. **Freq:** Quarterly. **Print Method:** Offset. **Trim Size:** 8 3/8 x 10 7/8. **Key Personnel:** Magdalene Mercado, Secretary, phone: (208)542-2217; Jason Harris, Publisher, phone: (208)542-2222; Dave Alexander, Director, Advertising, phone: (208)542-2213; Steve Smeed, Editor, phone: (208)542-2254. **Subscription Rates:** $8.95 Individuals; $15.95 Two years; $21.95 Individuals 3 years; $28.95 Other countries; $55.95 Other countries 2 years; $81.95 Other countries 3 years; $23.95 Canada; $45.95 Canada 2 years; $66.95 Canada 3 years. **URL:** http://mountainwestgolf.com. **Formerly**: Idaho Golf. **Remarks:** Advertising accepted; rates available upon request. **Circ:** Combined 25000.

9775 ■ PDB Magazine
Harris Publishing Inc.
360 B St.
Idaho Falls, ID 83402
Phone: (208)524-7000
Fax: (208)522-5241
Free: 800-638-0135
Publisher's E-mail: customerservice@harrispublishing.com
Magazine for pontoon and deck boat owners. **Freq:** 11/year. **Key Personnel:** Greg Larsen, Director, Advertising, phone: (208)542-2216; Brady L. Kay, Editor, phone: (208)542-2251; Brandon Barrus, Assistant Editor. **Subscription Rates:** $19.97 Individuals 1 year; $33.97 Two years; $39.97 Other countries 1 year; $73.97 Other countries 2 years. **URL:** http://www.pontoon.net; http://www.pdbmagazine.com. **Formerly**: Pontoon & Deck Boat Magazine. **Ad Rates:** BW $6,331; 4C $9,258. **Remarks:** Advertising accepted; rates available upon request. **Circ:** Combined 82000.

9776 ■ The Post-Register
The Post-Register
333 Northgate Mile
Idaho Falls, ID 83401
Phone: (208)522-1800
Fax: (208)529-3142
General newspaper. **Freq:** Mon.-Sun. **Print Method:** Offset. **Cols./Page:** 6. **Col. Width:** 25 nonpareils. **Col. Depth:** 301 agate lines. **Key Personnel:** Ivy Berry, Officer, Finance, phone: (208)542-6710; Dean Miller, Division Manager; Roger Plothow, Editor, Publisher; Bill Bradshaw, Managing Editor. **Subscription Rates:** $180 Individuals daily; $150 Individuals Wednesday, Friday and Sunday; $276 Individuals 5 Sunday and 1 daily; $90 Individuals 6 months; $75 Individuals 6 months; Wednesday, Friday and Sunday; $138 Individuals 6 months; 5 Sunday and 1 daily. **Mailing address:** PO Box 1800, Idaho Falls, ID 83401. **Remarks:** Accepts advertising. **Circ:** ‡19500, ‡22000.

9777 ■ Potato Grower
Harris Publishing Inc.
360 B St.
Idaho Falls, ID 83402
Phone: (208)524-7000
Fax: (208)522-5241
Free: 800-638-0135
Publisher's E-mail: customerservice@harrispublishing.com
Magazine serving the potato growing, shipping, and processing industries. **Freq:** Monthly. **Print Method:** Offset. **Trim Size:** 8 x 10.75. **Cols./Page:** 3. **Col. Width:** 27 nonpareils. **Col. Depth:** 140 agate lines. **Key Personnel:** Dave Alexander, Director, Advertising, phone: (208)542-2213; Rob Erickson, Account Executive, phone: (208)542-2218; Tyler Baum, Editor, phone: (208)542-2259; Jason Harris, Publisher, phone: (208)542-2222. **Subscription Rates:** $24 U.S.; $43 Two years; $120 Other countries; $180 Other countries 2 years. **URL:** http://www.potatogrower.com; http://www.potatogrower.com/past-issues. **Remarks:** Accepts advertising. **Circ:** ‡9700.

9778 ■ SnoWest
Harris Publishing Inc.
360 B St.
Idaho Falls, ID 83402
Phone: (208)524-7000
Fax: (208)522-5241
Free: 800-638-0135
Publisher's E-mail: customerservice@harrispublishing.com
Magazine for snowmobilers. **Freq:** 10/year. **Print Method:** Offset. **Trim Size:** 8 x 10 3/4. **Cols./Page:** 3. **Col. Width:** 2 1/4 nonpareils. **Col. Depth:** 10 agate lines. **Key Personnel:** Steve Janes, Publisher; Gregg Manwaring, Manager, Advertising; Lane Lindstrom, Editor. **Subscription Rates:** $19.95 Individuals print and digital; $34.95 Two years print and digital; $34.95 Other countries; $64.95 Other countries two years. **URL:** http://www.snowest.com. **Remarks:** Accepts advertising. **Circ:** (Not Reported).

9779 ■ The Sugar Producer
Harris Publishing Inc.
360 B St.
Idaho Falls, ID 83402
Phone: (208)524-7000
Fax: (208)522-5241
Free: 800-638-0135
Publisher's E-mail: customerservice@harrispublishing.com
Magazine for sugar beet growers. **Freq:** Monthly. **Print Method:** Offset. **Trim Size:** 8 3/8 x 10 7/8. **Cols./Page:** 3. **Col. Width:** 28 nonpareils. **Col. Depth:** 140 agate lines. **Key Personnel:** Nancy Sanchez, Editor; Jason Harris, Publisher; Dave Alexander, Director, Advertising. **Subscription Rates:** $20 U.S. 1 year; $38 Two years; $90 Other countries 1 year; $180 Other countries 2 years. **URL:** http://www.sugarproducer.com. **Remarks:** Accepts advertising. **Circ:** ‡9800.

9780 ■ CableOne
1525 Sherry Ave.
Idaho Falls, ID 83403
Email: user@cableone.net
Owner: Cable One Inc., 210 E Earll Dr., Phoenix, AZ 85012, Fax: (602)364-6010. **Founded:** 1965. **Key Personnel:** Thomas O. Might, CEO, Chmn. of the Bd. **Cities Served:** Ammon, Basalt, Blackfoot, Firth, Iona, Rexburg, Rigby, Ririe, Ririe, Saint Anthony, Shelly, Sugar City, Idaho: subscribing households 6,90,000; 265 channels. **URL:** http://www.cableone.net.

9781 ■ KBJX-FM - 98.1
1327 E 17th St.
Idaho Falls, ID 83401
Phone: (208)529-6926
Fax: (208)529-6927
Ad Rates: Advertising accepted; rates available upon request.

9782 ■ KBLI-AM - 690
1190 Lincoln Rd.
Idaho Falls, ID 83401
Phone: (208)523-3722
Format: News; Talk. **Operating Hours:** Continuous. **Key Personnel:** Neal Larson, News Dir., neal@eiradio.com. **Ad Rates:** Advertising accepted; rates available upon request. **URL:** http://www.eastidahonews.com.

9783 ■ KBLY-AM - 1260
400 W Sunnyside Rd.
Idaho Falls, ID 83402
Phone: (208)523-3722
Format: News; Talk. **Operating Hours:** Continuous. **Key Personnel:** Neal Larson, Dir. of Programs, news@eiradio.com. **Ad Rates:** Advertising accepted; rates available upon request. **URL:** http://www.eastidahonews.com.

9784 ■ KCVI-FM - 101.5
400 W Sunnyside Rd.
Idaho Falls, ID 83402
Phone: (208)523-3722
Format: Classic Rock. **Owner:** Bonneville International Corp., 55 North 300 West, Salt Lake City, UT 84101-3502, Ph: (801)575-7500. **Founded:** Sept. 15, 2006. **Ad Rates:** Noncommercial. **URL:** http://www.kbear.fm.

9785 ■ KFTZ-FM - 103
1190 Lincoln Rd.
Idaho Falls, ID 83401
Phone: (208)523-3722
Format: Contemporary Hit Radio (CHR). **Networks:** Independent. **Founded:** 1987. **Operating Hours:** Continuous; 100% local. **ADI**: Idaho Falls-Pocatello, ID. **Wattage**: 52,000. **Ad Rates:** $6-20 for 30 seconds; $7-25 for 60 seconds. **URL:** http://www.z103.fm.

KGTM-FM - See Rexburg

9786 ■ KID-AM - 590
1406 Commerce Way
Idaho Falls, ID 83401
Phone: (208)522-5900
Fax: (208)522-9696
Format: News; Talk. **Networks:** CBS; Precision Racing. **Owner:** Gapwest Broadcasting, 4300 N Miller Rd., Ste. 116, Scottsdale, AZ 85251, Ph: (480)970-1360, Fax: (480)423-6966. **Founded:** 1929. **Operating Hours**: Continuous; 65% network, 35% local. **ADI**: Idaho Falls-Pocatello, ID. **Key Personnel:** Lisa Smith, Sales Mgr., lisasmith@gapbrodcasting.com; Jeff Evans, Operations Mgr., Prog. Dir., jevans@gapbroadcasting.com. **Wattage**: 5,000. **Ad Rates:** Advertising accepted; rates available upon request. **URL:** http://www.590kid.com/main.html.

9787 ■ KID-FM - 96.1
1406 Commerce Way
Idaho Falls, ID 83404
Phone: (208)524-5900
Fax: (208)522-9696
Format: Country; News. **Owner:** Clear Channel Radio, Inc., San Antonio, TX. **Founded:** 1965. **Operating Hours**: Continuous. **ADI**: Idaho Falls-Pocatello, ID. **Wattage**: 100,000 ERP. **Ad Rates:** $1-20 per unit. **URL:** http://www.rivercountryfm.com.

9788 ■ KIDK-TV - 3
1915 N Yellowstone Hwy.
Idaho Falls, ID 83401
Phone: (208)528-2145
Fax: (208)529-2443
Format: Commercial TV. **Networks:** CBS. **Owner:** Fisher Communication, Inc., at above address. **Operating Hours:** 8 a.m.-5:30 p.m. **ADI**: Idaho Falls-Pocatello, ID. **Key Personnel:** Mark Danielson, Gen. Mgr., mdanielson@localnews8.com; Monte Young, Gen. Mgr., monte.young@localnews8.com; Curtis Jackson, News Dir., cjackson@localnews8.com. **Ad Rates:** Noncommercial. **URL:** http://www.localnews8.com.

9789 ■ KIFI-TV - 8
1915 N Yellowstone Hwy.
Idaho Falls, ID 83401
Phone: (208)528-2145
Fax: (208)522-1930

Circulation: ★ = AAM; △ or • = BPA; ♦ = CAC; ❑ = VAC; ⊕ = PO Statement; ‡ = Publisher's Report; Boldface figures = sworn; Light figures = estimated.

Email: newsdesk@localnews8.com

Format: News. **Networks:** ABC. **Founded:** 1961. **Operating Hours**: Continuous. **ADI**: Idaho Falls-Pocatello, ID. **Key Personnel:** Mark Danielson, Gen. Mgr., mdanielson@localnews8.com; Monte Young, Gen. Mgr., monte.young@localnews8.com; Curtis Jackson, News Dir., cjackson@localnews8.com. **Ad Rates:** Noncommercial. **URL:** http://www.localnews8.com.

9790 ■ KLLP-FM - 98.5
1406 Commerce Way
Idaho Falls, ID 83401
Phone: (208)524-5900

Format: Soft Rock; Adult Contemporary; News; Country; Classic Rock. **Owner:** Clear Channel Radio, 50 E Rivercenter Blvd., 12th Fl., Covington, KY 41011, Ph: (859)655-2267. **Key Personnel:** Tim Murphy, Gen. Mgr. **URL:** http://star98radio.com/station-information.

9791 ■ KRXK-AM - 1230
1406 Commerce Way
Idaho Falls, ID 83401
Phone: (208)356-3651
Fax: (208)356-0628

Format: Hot Country. **Simulcasts:** KRXX-FM. **Networks:** ABC; InterMountain; Unistar. **Founded:** 1951. **Operating Hours**: Continuous. **Key Personnel:** David Grow, President. **Wattage**: 1,000. **Ad Rates:** $7 for 30 seconds; $10 for 60 seconds.

9792 ■ K206CX-FM - 89.1
PO Box 391
Twin Falls, ID 83303
Free: 800-357-4226

Format: Religious; Contemporary Christian. **Owner:** CSN International, PO Box 391, Twin Falls, ID 83303, Ph: (208)736-1958, Fax: (208)736-1958, Free: 800-357-4226. **Key Personnel:** Don Mills, Prog. Dir., Div. Dir. **URL:** http://www.csnradio.com.

JEROME

S. ID. Jerome Co. 105 mi. E. of Boise. Manufactures cinder block, plows, plastic moldings, business forms. Machine shop. Grain, truck, fruit, poultry farms. Beans, beets, potatoes, alfalfa, clover seed.

9793 ■ KART-AM - 1400
47 North 100 West
Jerome, ID 83338
Phone: (208)324-8181
Email: kentlee@safelink.net

Format: News. **Networks:** CBS; Westwood One Radio. **Founded:** 1964. **ADI**: Twin Falls, ID. **Key Personnel:** Broc Johnson, Prog. Dir. **Wattage**: 1,000 KW. **Ad Rates:** for 30 seconds; for 60 seconds. Combined advertising rates available with KKMV-FM, KZDX-FM. **URL:** http://www.hot100now.com.

9794 ■ KMVX-FM - 103.1
47 North 100 West
Jerome, ID 83338
Phone: (208)324-8181
Fax: (208)324-7124
Email: kentlee@safelink.net

Format: Soft Rock. **Founded:** 1970. **Formerly:** KFMA-FM. **Key Personnel:** Jeff Edwards, Dir. of Programs; Kent Lee, Gen. Mgr. **Wattage**: 71,000 ERP. **Ad Rates:** Advertising accepted; rates available upon request. $5-$14 for 30 seconds; $6-$16 for 60 seconds. Combined advertising rates available with KART-AM. **URL:** http://www.1031theedge.com.

KAMIAH

W. ID. Lewis Co. 50 mi. E. of Lewiston. Nezperce Indian Reservation. Tourist resort. Logging, sawmill. Grain, stock farms.

9795 ■ The Clearwater Progress
The Clearwater Progress Inc.
PO Box 428
Kamiah, ID 83536-0428
Phone: (208)935-0838
Fax: (208)935-0973
Publisher's E-mail: progress@clearwaterprogress.com

Community newspaper. **Freq:** Weekly (Wed.). **Print Method:** Offset. Uses mats. **Cols./Page:** 6. **Col. Width:** 26 nonpareils. **Col. Depth:** 294 agate lines. **Key Personnel:** John Bennett, Publisher; Susan Bennett, Publisher; Ben Jorgensen, Editor. **USPS:** 117-260. **Subscription Rates:** $28.30 Individuals Idaho and Lewis Co.; $32.20 Individuals Idaho; $37 Out of state; $47.70 Two years Idaho and Lewis Co.; $54 Two years Idaho; $59.30 Two years outside Idaho. **Ad Rates:** BW $7.95, display advertising - per column inch local rate; 4C $12, display advertising - per column inch local rate; BW $655.88, full page; BW $6, classified display advertising - per column inch; 4C $9, classified display advertising - per column inch. **Remarks:** Accepts advertising. **Circ:** ‡4325.

KETCHUM

S. ID. Blaine Co. Adjoining Sun Valley, 80 mi. N. of Twin Falls. Summer and winter resort.

9796 ■ Idaho Mountain Express
Express Publishing Inc.
591 1st Ave. N
Ketchum, ID 83340
Phone: (208)726-8060
Fax: (208)726-2329

Community newspaper (tabloid). **Freq:** Biweekly Wednesday and Friday. **Print Method:** Offset. **Cols./Page:** 5. **Col. Width:** 2 inches. **Col. Depth:** 16 inches. **Key Personnel:** Pam Morris, Publisher; David Thouvenel, Manager, Advertising. **USPS:** 720-490. **Subscription Rates:** $46 Individuals in Blaine County; $68 Individuals online; $70 Individuals outside Blaine County; $52 Individuals Wood River Valley. **URL:** http://www.mtexpress.com. **Remarks:** Accepts advertising. **Circ:** ‡9000.

LEWISTON

NW ID. Nez Perce Co. At head of Snake River, 110 mi. S. of Spokane, WA. Boat connections. Flour, lumber, veneer, pulp, paper mills; fruit, vegetable canning and freezing. Manufactures beverages, tents, awnings. White pine timber. Stock, fruit, grain farms.

9797 ■ Lewiston Tribune
Lewiston Morning Tribune
PO Box 957
Lewiston, ID 83501
Phone: (208)743-9411
Free: 800-745-9411
Publisher's E-mail: alajr@lmtribune.com

General newspaper. **Freq:** Daily. **Print Method:** Offset. **Cols./Page:** 6. **Col. Width:** 1 13/16 inches. **Col. Depth:** 21 1/2 inches. **Key Personnel:** Bob Reitz, Director, Advertising, phone: (208)848-2292; Mike McBride, Manager, Circulation, phone: (208)848-2220; Doug Bauer, Managing Editor, phone: (208)848-2269; Nathan Alford, Editor, phone: (208)848-2208. **Subscription Rates:** $16 Individuals /month - online. **URL:** http://lmtribune.com. **Formerly**: Lewiston Morning Tribune. **Ad Rates:** BW $90. **Remarks:** Accepts advertising. **Circ:** Mon.-Sun. ‡26330, Sun. ‡27608.

9798 ■ Moneysaver Lewis-Clark Edition
Eagle Newspapers Inc.
626 Thain Rd.
Lewiston, ID 83501
Phone: (208)746-0483
Free: 888-473-4158

Free shopper. **Freq:** Weekly (Thurs.) morning. **Print Method:** Offset. **Trim Size:** 11 1/4 x 15 1/2. **Cols./Page:** 7. **Col. Width:** 8 picas. **Col. Depth:** 15 1/2 inches. **Subscription Rates:** Free. **URL:** http://www.lcmoneysaver.com. **Remarks:** Accepts advertising. **Circ:** Free ■ **42500**.

9799 ■ Moscow Moneysaver: Palouse Edition
Triad News Publishing Inc.
626 Thain Rd.
Lewiston, ID 83501
Phone: (208)746-0483
Fax: (208)746-8507
Free: 800-473-4158
Publisher's E-mail: ads@lcmoneysaver.com

Community shopping guide. **Freq:** Weekly (Thurs.). **Trim Size:** 6 x 15 1/2. **Col. Width:** 9.5 picas. **Key Personnel:** Diane Johnson, Publisher. **Subscription Rates:** $65 By mail. **Formerly:** ADmart. **Mailing address:** PO Box 682, Lewiston, ID 83501. **Ad Rates:** PCI $8.40. **Remarks:** Accepts advertising. **Circ:** 5622.

9800 ■ KCLK-AM - 1430
403 C St.
Lewiston, ID 83501
Phone: (208)743-6564
Fax: (208)798-0110

Format: Sports; Talk. **Networks:** CNN Radio; ESPN Radio. **Owner:** Pacific Empire Radio, at above address. **Founded:** 1971. **Operating Hours**: Continuous; 90% network, 10% local. **ADI**: Spokane, WA. **Wattage**: 5,000. **Ad Rates:** $11-14 for 30 seconds. Combined advertising rates available with KCLK-FM & KVAB-FM KATW-FM.

9801 ■ KCLK-FM - 94.1
403 C St.
Lewiston, ID 83501
Phone: (509)758-3361
Fax: (509)758-4986

Format: Oldies. **Networks:** Mutual Broadcasting System. **Owner:** Pacific Empire Radio, at above address. **Founded:** 1973. **Operating Hours**: Continuous; 10% network, 90% local. **ADI**: Spokane, WA. **Wattage**: 100,000. **Ad Rates:** $11-14 for 30 seconds; $15-17 for 60 seconds. Combined advertising rates available with KCLK-AM KVAB-FM KATW-FM. **URL:** http://kool94fm.com.

9802 ■ KCLX-AM - 1450
805 Stewart Ave.
Lewiston, ID 83501
Phone: (208)791-2605

Format: Country. **Simulcasts:** KZZL FM 99.5/. **Networks:** ABC; CNN Radio. **Owner:** Inland Northwest Broadcasting, LLC, at above address. **Founded:** 1950. **Operating Hours**: Controlled. **Key Personnel:** Robert G. Hauser, Contact. **Wattage**: 1,000. **Ad Rates:** Noncommercial. Combined advertising rates available with KZZL 99.5FM/KRAO 102.5FM/KMAX 840AM. **URL:** http://www.listentothegame.com.

9803 ■ KLEW-TV - 3
2626 17th St.
Lewiston, ID 83501
Phone: (208)746-2636
Fax: (208)746-4819
Email: info@klewtv.com

Format: Commercial TV. **Networks:** CBS. **Owner:** Fisher Communications Inc., 140 4th Ave. N, Ste. 500, Seattle, WA 98109-4940, Ph: (206)404-7000, Fax: (206)404-6037. **Founded:** 1956. **Operating Hours**: 20 hours; 45% network, 55% local. **ADI**: Spokane, WA. **Key Personnel:** Fred Fickenwirth, Contact, klewfred@klewtv.com; Ann Fickenwirth, News Dir., ann@klewtv.com. **Wattage**: 56,200 video; 12,300 audio. **Ad Rates:** $10-150 per unit. **URL:** http://www.klewtv.com.

9804 ■ KLHS-FM - 88.9
500 8th Ave.
Lewiston, ID 83501-2698
Phone: (208)792-2418

Founded: 1967. **Operating Hours**: Continuous. **Key Personnel:** Cheryl Flory, Gen. Mgr. **Wattage**: 230. **Ad Rates:** Noncommercial. **URL:** http://www.klcz.com.

9805 ■ KMOK-FM - 106.9
805 Stewart Ave.
Lewiston, ID 83501-4709
Phone: (208)743-1551
Fax: (208)743-4440

Owner: Ida-Vend Company Inc., at above address. **Founded:** 1983. **Wattage**: 99,000. **Ad Rates:** $12-18 for 30 seconds; $15-23 for 60 seconds.

9806 ■ KORT-AM - 1230
PO Box 936
Lewiston, ID 83501
Phone: (208)743-2502
Fax: (208)743-1995

Owner: 4-K Radio Inc., at above address. **Ad Rates:** $10 for 30 seconds; $15 for 60 seconds.

9807 ■ KORT-FM - 92.7
PO Box 936
Lewiston, ID 83501
Phone: (208)743-2502
Fax: (208)743-1995

Owner: 4-K Radio Inc., at above address. **Wattage**: 360. **Ad Rates:** $10 for 30 seconds; $15 for 60 seconds.

9808 ■ KOZE-AM - 950
2560 Snake River Ave.
Lewiston, ID 83501
Phone: (208)743-2502

Format: Talk. **Networks:** ABC. **Owner:** 4-K Radio Inc., at above address. **Founded:** 1955. **Operating Hours**:

Continuous. **Key Personnel:** Jason Ford, News Dir., jford@koze.com. **Wattage**: 5,000 Days; 1,000 Nights. **Ad Rates:** Advertising accepted; rates available upon request. $7-$11 for 30 seconds; $10-$14 for 60 seconds. Combined advertising rates available with KOZE-FM. **Mailing address:** PO Box 936, Lewiston, ID 83501. **URL:** http://www.koze950.com.

9809 ■ KOZE-FM - 96.5
2575 Snake River Ave.
Lewiston, ID 83501
Phone: (208)743-2502

Format: Album-Oriented Rock (AOR). **Networks:** ABC. **Owner:** 4-K Radio Inc., at above address. **Founded:** 1961. **Operating Hours**: Continuous. **Key Personnel:** Mike Ripley, Gen. Mgr., President; Lisa Jensen, Sales Mgr.; Jason Ford, News Dir. **Wattage**: 25,000 ERP. **Ad Rates:** $7-11 for 30 seconds; $10-14 for 60 seconds. $7-$11 for 30 seconds; $10-$14 for 60 seconds. Combined advertising rates available with KOZE-AM. **URL:** http://www.koze.com/contact.

9810 ■ KPLL-FM - 94.9
1212 19th St.
Lewiston, ID 83501-3068

Format: Contemporary Christian. **Owner:** Positive Life Radio, 204 S College Ave., College Place, WA 99324. **Key Personnel:** Walter Cox, Chief Engineer. **URL:** http://www.plr.org.

9811 ■ KRAO-FM - 102.5
805 Stewart Ave.
Lewiston, ID 83501
Phone: (208)882-2551
Email: kzzlkrow@colfax.com

Format: Classic Rock. **Networks:** ABC; CNN Radio. **Owner:** Inland Northwest Broadcasting, LLC, at above address. **Founded:** 1994. **Operating Hours**: Continuous. **Wattage**: 25,000. **Ad Rates:** Advertising accepted; rates available upon request. Combined advertising rates available with KZZL-FM; KCCX-AM; KMAX-AM.

9812 ■ KRLC-AM
805 Stewart Ave.
Lewiston, ID 83501-4709
Phone: (208)743-1551
Fax: (208)743-4440

Owner: Ida-Vend Company Inc., at above address. **Founded:** 1935. **Ad Rates:** $14-20 for 30 seconds; $16-25 for 60 seconds.

9813 ■ K207DO-FM
PO Box 391
Twin Falls, ID 83303
Fax: (208)736-1958
Free: 800-357-4226

Owner: CSN International, PO Box 391, Twin Falls, ID 83303, Ph: (208)736-1958, Fax: (208)736-1958, Free: 800-357-4226. **URL:** http://www.csnradio.com.

9814 ■ K228DU-FM - 93.5
PO Box 391
Twin Falls, ID 83303
Fax: (208)736-1958
Free: 800-357-4226

Format: Religious; Contemporary Christian. **Owner:** CSN International, PO Box 391, Twin Falls, ID 83303, Ph: (208)736-1958, Fax: (208)736-1958, Free: 800-357-4226. **Key Personnel:** Mike Kestler, President; Don Mills, Music Dir., Prog. Dir.; Kelly Carlson, Dir. of Engg.; Ray Gorney, Asst. Dir. **URL:** http://www.csnradio.com.

9815 ■ KVTY-FM - 105.1
805 Stewart Ave.
Lewiston, ID 83501
Phone: (208)746-1551
Fax: (208)743-4440

Format: Adult Contemporary. **Networks:** AP. **Owner:** IDAVEND Co., 2108 1st Ave. N, Lewiston, ID 83501. **Founded:** 1998. **Operating Hours**: Continuous. **Key Personnel:** Robert Prasil, Gen. Mgr., rprasil@idavend.com; Melva Prasil, Sales Mgr., mprasil@idavend.com; Ben Bonfield, Sales Mgr. **Wattage**: 500. **Ad Rates:** $14-20 for 30 seconds; $16-25 for 60 seconds. Combined advertising rates available with KMOK-FM, KRLC-AM.

MARSING

9816 ■ Fido Friendly
Fido Friendly
PO Box 160
Marsing, ID 83639
Publisher's E-mail: inquiries@fidofriendly.com

Magazine offers information on traveling with a dog including groomers, kennels, restaurants, and dog friendly parks. **Freq:** Quarterly. **Key Personnel:** Lorraine Chittock, Writer. **Subscription Rates:** $19.95 Individuals print; $26.99 Individuals print and online; $12.99 Individuals online only. **URL:** http://www.fidofriendly.com. **Remarks:** Advertising accepted; rates available upon request. **Circ:** (Not Reported).

9817 ■ KAWS-FM - 89.1
PO Box 391
Twin Falls, ID 83303
Fax: (208)736-1958
Free: 800-357-4226

Format: Religious; Contemporary Christian. **Owner:** CSN International, PO Box 391, Twin Falls, ID 83303, Ph: (208)736-1958, Fax: (208)736-1958, Free: 800-357-4226. **URL:** http://www.csnradio.com.

MCCALL

C. ID. Valley Co. 97 mi. N. of Boise. Tourism. Sawmill; logging. Timber. Agriculture. Stock farms.

9818 ■ The Star-News
Central Idaho Publishing
1000 1st. St.
McCall, ID 83638
Phone: (208)634-2123

Community newspaper. **Founded:** 1915. **Freq:** Weekly (Thurs.). **Print Method:** Offset. **Cols./Page:** 6. **Col. Width:** 24 nonpareils. **Col. Depth:** 294 agate lines. **Key Personnel:** Tomi Grote, Publisher; A.L. Alford, Jr., Publisher. **ISSN:** 0747-248X (print). **Subscription Rates:** $40 Individuals local; print and online; $60 Two years local; print and online; $50 Out of area non-local; print and online; $80 Out of area 2 years; print and online; $40 Individuals online; $60 Two years online. **URL:** http://www.mccallstarnews.com/. **Ad Rates:** BW $1,102.50; PCI $8.75. **Remarks:** Accepts advertising. **Circ:** ‡4500.

9819 ■ KDZY-FM - 98.3
707 N Mission St.
McCall, ID 83638
Phone: (208)634-3781
Fax: (208)634-3799

Format: Country. **Owner:** KSPD, Inc., at above address. **Wattage**: 500. **Mailing address:** PO Box 2114, McCall, ID 83638. **URL:** http://kdzy.tripod.com.

9820 ■ K256AN-FM - 99.1
PO Box 391
Twin Falls, ID 83303
Fax: (208)736-1958
Free: 800-357-4226

Format: Religious; Contemporary Christian. **Owner:** CSN International, PO Box 391, Twin Falls, ID 83303, Ph: (208)736-1958, Fax: (208)736-1958, Free: 800-357-4226. **Key Personnel:** Don Mills, Music Dir., Director; Kelly Carlson, Dir. of Engg. **URL:** http://www.csnradio.com.

MERIDIAN

SW ID. Ada Co. 10 mi. W. of Boise. Feed mills; pre-built home factory; meat packing plant. Manufactures lumber, custom doors, furniture. Fruit, dairy, stock, grain, poultry farms.

9821 ■ The Chemical Educator
The Chemical Educator
2640 South Bear Claw Way
Meridian, ID 83642
Phone: (208)440-1866
Fax: (208)426-4493
Publisher's E-mail: chemeducator@gmail.org

Online journal for chemical educators with a print archive version. **Freq:** Annual. **Key Personnel:** Clifford LeMaster, Editor-in-Chief; Brian P. Coppola, Board Member; Yehudit Judy Dori, Board Member; Hugh Cartwright, Editor; Raymond Chang, Board Member. **ISSN:** 1430--4171 (print). **Subscription Rates:** $29.95 Individuals online; $149.95 Institutions online; $299 U.S. print; $349 Other countries print. **URL:** http://chemeducator.org. **Remarks:** Accepts advertising. **Circ:** (Not Reported).

9822 ■ Horseless Carriage Gazette
Horseless Carriage Club of America
1301 N Manship Pl.
Meridian, ID 83642-5072
Phone: (626)287-4222
Publication E-mail: john@horseless.com

Auto hobby magazine covering automobiles produced prior to 1916. **Freq:** Bimonthly. **Print Method:** Offset. **Trim Size:** 8 1/2 x 11. **Cols./Page:** 3. **Col. Width:** 14 picas. **Col. Depth:** 59 picas. **Key Personnel:** John C. Meyer, III, Editor, phone: (818)703-7421. **ISSN:** 0018--5213 (print). **Subscription Rates:** Included in membership. **URL:** http://www.hcca.org/gazette.html. **Ad Rates:** BW $595. **Remarks:** Accepts advertising. **Circ:** 5000, 5000.

9823 ■ Veterinary Ophthalmology
American College of Veterinary Ophthalmologists
PO Box 1311
Meridian, ID 83680
Phone: (208)466-7624
Fax: (208)895-7872
Publisher's E-mail: office16@acvo.org

Freq: Bimonthly. **Key Personnel:** David A. Wilkie, Editor. **ISSN:** 1463--5216 (print); **EISSN:** 1463--5224 (electronic). **Subscription Rates:** $1157 Institutions; £846 Institutions UK; €1075 Institutions Europe; $1656 Institutions, other countries; $1389 Institutions print and online; £1016 Institutions print and online; €1290 Institutions print and online; $1988 Institutions, other countries print and online; $224 Individuals print and online; £158 Individuals print and online, UK, Europe (non euro zone) and Rest of the world; €226 Individuals print and online, Europe; $217 Individuals print only; £798 Institutions print or online; £153 Individuals print only; €1014 Institutions print or online; €219 Individuals print only; $1562 Institutions, other countries print or online. **Alt. Formats:** PDF. **URL:** http://onlinelibrary.wiley.com/journal/10.1111/(ISSN)1463-5224; http://www.acvo.org/new/public/publications/ophtho_journal.shtml. **Remarks:** Accepts advertising. **Circ:** (Not Reported).

MIDVALE

9824 ■ Midvale Telephone Exchange Inc.
2205 Keithly Creek Rd.
Midvale, ID 83645
Phone: (208)355-2211
Free: 800-462-4523
Email: info@mtecom.net

Founded: 1909. **Cities Served:** United States. **Mailing address:** PO Box 7, Midvale, ID 83645. **URL:** http://www.mtecom.net.

MONTPELIER

C. ID. Bear Lake Co. 70 mi. Se of Pocatello. Manufactures gloves. Stone quarries.

9825 ■ KVSI-AM - 1450
PO Box 340
Montpelier, ID 83254
Phone: (208)847-1450
Fax: (208)847-1451
Email: kvsi@dcdi.net

Format: Country. **Networks:** ABC. **Owner:** Tri-State Broadcasting Company Inc., at above address. **Founded:** 1965. **Operating Hours:** 6 a.m.-7 p.m. **Key Personnel:** Keith Martindale, Owner; Ada Jane Hillier, Dir. of Traffic. **Wattage:** 1,000. **Ad Rates:** Advertising accepted; rates available upon request. **URL:** http://www.kvsi.com.

MOSCOW

NW ID. Latah Co. 85 mi. SE of Spokane, WA. University of Idaho. Manufactures bricks, clay products, flour, pea harvesters, lumber, creamery products. Split pea and seed pea plants. Timber; clay deposits. Dairy and grain farms. Wheat, peas, lentils, dairy products.

9826 ■ Appaloosa Journal
Appaloosa Horse Club
2720 W Pullman Rd.
Moscow, ID 83843
Phone: (208)882-5578

Circulation: ★ = AAM; △ or • = BPA; ♦ = CAC; ❑ = VAC; ⊕ = PO Statement; ‡ = Publisher's Report; Boldface figures = sworn; Light figures = estimated.

Fax: (208)882-8150
Freq: Quarterly. **Key Personnel:** Dana Russell, Editor. **Subscription Rates:** $3 /issue; $29.95 for nonmembers in U.S.; $41.95 for nonmembers in Canada; $56.95 for nonmembers international. **URL:** http://www.appaloosajournal.com. **Remarks:** Accepts advertising. **Circ:** 32000.

9827 ■ Appaloosa Journal: Official Publication of the Appaloosa Horse Club
Appaloosa Horse Club
2720 W Pullman Rd.
Moscow, ID 83843
Phone: (208)882-5578
Fax: (208)882-8150
Magazine about Appaloosa horses and the people making an impact on the industry. **Freq:** Monthly. **Print Method:** Web offset. **Trim Size:** 8.125 x 10.875. **Cols./Page:** 3. **Col. Width:** 13 picas. **Col. Depth:** 58 picas. **Key Personnel:** Dana Russell, Editor. **ISSN:** 0892-385X (print). **Subscription Rates:** $29.95 Individuals; $41.95 Canada; $56.95 Other countries; $25 Members; $54.90 Two years. **URL:** http://www.appaloosajournal.com/. **Formerly:** Appaloosa News. **Ad Rates:** BW $580; 4C $1,025. **Remarks:** Accepts advertising. **Circ:** 30000.

9828 ■ The Argonaut
The Argonaut
Student Media
301 Student Union
Moscow, ID 83844-4271
Publisher's E-mail: arg-news@uidaho.edu
Collegiate newspaper. **Founded:** 1898. **Freq:** Semiweekly. **Print Method:** Offset. **Trim Size:** 11 x 17. **Cols./Page:** 6. **Col. Width:** 2 1/16 inches. **Col. Depth:** 21 1/2 inches. **Key Personnel:** Loren Morris, Manager, Production; Elizabeth Rudd, Editor-in-Chief; Abby Skubitz, Manager, Advertising. **ISSN:** 0896-1409 (print). **URL:** http://www.uiargonaut.com. **Remarks:** Accepts advertising. **Circ:** Paid 250, Free 6,000.

9829 ■ Classis
Association of Classical and Christian Schools
205 E 5th St.
Moscow, ID 83843
Phone: (208)882-6101
Fax: (208)882-9097
Publisher's E-mail: info@accsedu.org
Freq: Quarterly. **Alt. Formats:** PDF. **URL:** http://www.accsedu.org/school-resources/classis-(journal)-and-forum-(newsletter). **Mailing address:** PO Box 9741, Moscow, ID 83843. **Remarks:** Advertising not accepted. **Circ:** (Not Reported).

9830 ■ Credenda/Agenda
Credenda/Agenda
PO Box 8741
Moscow, ID 83843-1241
Phone: (208)882-2034
Fax: (208)892-8724
Publisher's E-mail: contact@credenda.org
Magazine featuring all areas of life from a biblical, classical Protestant perspective. **Freq:** Bimonthly. **Key Personnel:** Douglas Wilson, Editor; Ben Merkle, Managing Editor. **URL:** http://www.credenda.org. **Circ:** (Not Reported).

9831 ■ Daily News
Moscow-Pullman Daily News
220 E 5th St., Ste. 205
Moscow, ID 83843
Phone: (208)882-5561
Fax: (208)883-8205
Free: 800-776-4137
Community newspaper. **Founded:** 1911. **Freq:** Daily weekend edition on Saturday Morning. **Print Method:** Offset. **Cols./Page:** 6. **Col. Width:** 25 nonpareils. **Col. Depth:** 301 agate lines. **Key Personnel:** Nathan Alford, Publisher, Editor; Wayne Hollingshead, General Manager; Lee Rozen, Managing Editor. **Subscription Rates:** $188.88 By mail. **URL:** http://dnews.com. **Remarks:** Accepts advertising. **Circ:** Combined 23000.

9832 ■ Idaho Law Review
University of Idaho College of Law
875 Perimeter Dr., MS 2321
Moscow, ID 83844-2321
Phone: (208)885-4977
Publication E-mail: review@uidaho.edu
Journal of law review. **Freq:** 3/yr. **Key Personnel:** KC Harding, Editor-in-Chief. **ISSN:** 0019--1205 (print). **Subscription Rates:** $33 Individuals print; $15 Single issue; $25 Individuals online; $40 Individuals print and online. **URL:** http://www.uidaho.edu/law/law-review. **Ad Rates:** GLR $350. **Remarks:** Accepts advertising. **Circ:** (Not Reported).

9833 ■ Latah Legacy
Latah County Historical Society
327 E 2nd St.
Moscow, ID 83843
Phone: (208)882-1004
Freq: Annual. **Key Personnel:** Julie Monroe, Editor. **ISSN:** 0759--3282 (print). **Subscription Rates:** Included in membership. **URL:** http://www.latahcountyhistoricalsociety.org/#!blank/c1826. **Remarks:** Advertising not accepted. **Circ:** (Not Reported).

9834 ■ MaryJanesFarm
Belvoir Media Group L.L.C.
PO Box 8691
Moscow, ID 83843
Free: 888-750-6004
Magazine featuring organic farming. **Key Personnel:** John Pagliaro, Publisher. **Subscription Rates:** $19.95 Individuals; C$36 Canada; $36 Other countries. **URL:** http://www.maryjanesfarm.org/magazine.html; http://shop.maryjanesfarm.org/Magazine. **Remarks:** Accepts advertising. **Circ:** (Not Reported).

9835 ■ Native Plants Journal
University of Wisconsin Press
c/o Kasten R. Dumroese, Editor-in-Chief
USDA Forest Service, SRS
1221 S Main St.
Moscow, ID 83843-4211
Publisher's E-mail: uwiscpress@uwpress.wisc.edu
Peer-reviewed journal featuring practical information about planting and growing North American (Canada, Mexico, and US) native plants and includes articles that are both useful and understandable by growers and planters and contribute significantly to the scientific literature. **Freq:** 3/year. **Key Personnel:** R. Kasten Dumroese, Editor-in-Chief; Candace Akins, Managing Editor. **ISSN:** 1522--8339 (print); **EISSN:** 1548--4785 (electronic). **Subscription Rates:** $62 Individuals print and online; $52 Individuals online only; $177 Institutions print and online; $151 Institutions online only. **URL:** http://npj.uwpress.org; http://uwpress.wisc.edu/journals/journals/npj.html. **Ad Rates:** BW 480. **Remarks:** Accepts advertising. **Circ:** (Not Reported).

9836 ■ Women in Natural Resources
University of Idaho
PO Box 44136
Moscow, ID 83844-1136
Phone: (208)885-6754
Publication E-mail: winr@uidaho.edu
Periodical for women in forestry, wildlife, range, fisheries, recreation, and related environmental sciences. **Freq:** Quarterly. **Trim Size:** 8 1/2 x 11. **Key Personnel:** Dr. Sandra Martin, Editor. **URL:** http://www.webpages.uidaho.edu/winr. **Formerly:** Women in Forestry. **Remarks:** Accepts advertising. **Circ:** (Not Reported).

9837 ■ KRFP-FM - 92.5
114 E 3rd St.
Moscow, ID 83843
Email: info@radiofreemoscow.org
Format: Alternative/New Music/Progressive; News. **Operating Hours:** Continuous. **Key Personnel:** Cass Davis, President, lefty@krfp.org. **Ad Rates:** Noncommercial. **URL:** http://radiofreemoscow.org.

9838 ■ KRPL-AM - 1400
1114 N Almon St.
Moscow, ID 83843
Phone: (208)882-2551
Fax: (208)883-3571
Email: benb@ldavend.com
Format: Oldies. **Networks:** ABC. **Owner:** KRPL Inc., at above address. **Founded:** 1947. **Operating Hours:** Continuous. **Key Personnel:** Ben Bonfield, Sales Mgr.; Gary Cummings, Gen. Mgr. **Wattage:** 1,000. **Ad Rates:** Noncommercial.

9839 ■ KUID-TV - 8
875 Perimeter Dr., MS3101
Moscow, ID 83844-3101
Phone: (208)885-1226
Free: 800-424-1226
Owner: Idaho Public Television, at above address, Boise, ID 83706-2239. **URL:** http://www.idahoptv.org/about/kuid.cfm.

9840 ■ KUOI-FM - 89.3
3rd Fl., Student Union Bldg.
CB 444272
Moscow, ID 83844-4272
Phone: (208)885-2218
Email: kuoi@uidaho.edu
Format: Alternative/New Music/Progressive. **Networks:** Pacifica. **Owner:** University of Idaho, 875 Perimeter Dr., Moscow, ID 83844, Ph: (208)885-6111. **Founded:** 1945. **Operating Hours:** Continuous; 4% network, 96% local. **ADI:** Spokane, WA. **Key Personnel:** Anthony Saia, Dir. of Programs, anthony@kuoi.org. **Wattage:** 400. **Ad Rates:** Noncommercial; underwriting available. $5 per unit. **URL:** http://www.kuoi.org.

9841 ■ KZFN-FM - 106.1
PO Box 8849
Moscow, ID 83843
Phone: (208)882-2551
Fax: (208)883-3571
Format: Contemporary Hit Radio (CHR). **Networks:** ABC. **Owner:** KRPL Inc., at above address. **Founded:** 1972. **Operating Hours:** Continuous. **ADI:** Spokane, WA. **Key Personnel:** Gary Cummings, Gen. Mgr. **Wattage:** 62,100 ERP.

MOUNTAIN HOME

SW ID. Elmore Co. 40 mi. SE of Boise. Sawmills; chick hatchery. Silver, gold, copper mines. Pine timber. Stock, sugar beets, potatoes, hay. Lava rock.

9842 ■ Mountain Home News
The Mountain Home News
195 S 3rd E St.
Mountain Home, ID 83647
Phone: (208)587-3331
Fax: (208)587-9205
Publisher's E-mail: advertising@mountainhomenews.com
Community newspaper. **Freq:** Weekly (Wed.). **Print Method:** Offset. Uses mats. **Cols./Page:** 6. **Col. Width:** 28 nonpareils. **Col. Depth:** 294 agate lines. **Key Personnel:** Coleen W. Swenson, Publisher, phone: (208)587-3331; Kelly Everitt, Managing Editor; Brenda Fincher, Business Manager. **Subscription Rates:** $39 Individuals in County; $44 Individuals in state; $50 Out of state. **Mailing address:** PO Box 1330, Mountain Home, ID 83647. **Ad Rates:** PCI $10.55, net. **Remarks:** Accepts advertising. **Circ:** ‡3500.

9843 ■ KMHI-AM - 1240
PO Box 704
Mountain Home, ID 83647
Fax: (208)736-1958
Format: Contemporary Christian. **Simulcasts:** KAWZ. **Owner:** Locally Owned Radio LLC, 21361 Highway 30., Twin Falls, ID 83301, Ph: (208)735-8300. **Founded:** 1992. **Formerly:** KFLI-FM; KJCY-FM. **Operating Hours:** Continuous. **Key Personnel:** Kelly Carlson, Dir. of Engg.; Ray Gorney, Dir. of Engg.; Jack Jensen, Mgr.; Brian Mobley, Production Mgr.; Penni Jensen, Office Mgr. **Wattage:** 1,000 KW. **Ad Rates:** $8 for 30 seconds; $15 for 60 seconds. **URL:** http://www.csnradio.com.

9844 ■ KTPZ-FM - 99.1
Mountain Home, ID
Format: Top 40. **Founded:** 1206. **URL:** http://www.ktpz.com.

9845 ■ K272DV-FM - 102.3
PO Box 391
Twin Falls, ID 83303
Owner: CSN International, PO Box 391, Twin Falls, ID 83303, Ph: (208)736-1958, Fax: (208)736-1958, Free: 800-357-4226. **Key Personnel:** Mike Kestler, President.

MOYIE SPRINGS

9846 ■ NATHHAN News
National Challenged Homeschoolers Associated Network
PO Box 310
Moyie Springs, ID 83845
Phone: (208)267-6246
Free: 800-266-9837
Publisher's E-mail: info@nathhan.org

Magazine containing articles pertaining to raising and homeschooling challenged children, how to adopt special needs children and letters from families with the same experience. **Freq:** Quarterly. **Alt. Formats:** Download; PDF. **URL:** http://www.nathhan.com/downloads2.htm. **Remarks:** Accepts advertising. **Circ:** (Not Reported).

NAMPA

SW ID. Canyon Co. 16 mi. W. of Boise. Northwest Nazarene College. College of Idaho. Manufactures wood mouldings, corrugated cardboard containers, cheese, mobile homes, furniture, computer chips. Wineries. Agriculture. Seeds, fruit, livestock.

9847 ■ Crusader
Northwest Nazarene University
623 S University Blvd.
Nampa, ID 83686
Phone: (208)467-8011
Collegiate newspaper. **Founded:** 1938. **Freq:** Irregular. **Print Method:** Offset. **Cols./Page:** 5. **Col. Width:** 21 nonpareils. **Col. Depth:** 185 agate lines. **URL:** http://www.nnu.edu/. **Circ:** Paid 100, Non-paid 1400.

9848 ■ El Centinela
Pacific Press Publishing Association
PO Box 5353
Nampa, ID 83653-5353
Magazine for the Christian community. **Freq:** Monthly. **Subscription Rates:** $13.44 Individuals; $20.44 Other countries. **URL:** http://www.elcentinela.com. **Circ:** (Not Reported).

9849 ■ Idaho Press-Tribune
Idaho Press Tribune
1618 N Midland Blvd.
Nampa, ID 83651
Phone: (208)467-9251
Fax: (208)467-9562
Publisher's E-mail: newsroom@idahopress.com
General newspaper. **Freq:** Daily (morn.). **Print Method:** Offset. **Cols./Page:** 6. **Col. Width:** 24 nonpareils. **Col. Depth:** 301 agate lines. **Key Personnel:** Brian Doane, Director, Advertising; Vickie Holbrook, Managing Editor. **Subscription Rates:** $16 Members full digital; $22 Individuals Sunday home delivery + digital; $26 Individuals 7 day print home delivery + full digital access. **Mailing address:** PO Box 9399, Nampa, ID 83652. **Remarks:** Accepts advertising. **Circ:** (Not Reported).

9850 ■ Our Little Friend
Pacific Press Publishing Association
1350 N Kings Rd.
Nampa, ID 83687-3193
Phone: (208)465-2500
Fax: (208)465-2531
Magazine containing colored pictures, stories, and memory verses for children ages 1 to 6. **Freq:** Weekly. **Key Personnel:** Aileen Andres Sox, Editor. **ISSN:** 0030--6894 (print). **Subscription Rates:** $28.04 Individuals; $35.04 Other countries. **URL:** http://www.ourlittlefriend.com. **Mailing address:** PO Box 5353, Nampa, ID 83653-5353. **Circ:** (Not Reported).

9851 ■ Primary Treasure
Pacific Press Publishing Association
1350 N Kings Rd.
Nampa, ID 83687-3193
Phone: (208)465-2500
Fax: (208)465-2531
Magazine containing stories about God's love for children ages 7 to 9. **Freq:** Weekly. **Key Personnel:** Aileen Andres Sox, Editor. **ISSN:** 0032--8316 (print). **Subscription Rates:** $36.36 Individuals; $43.36 Other countries. **URL:** http://www.primarytreasure.com. **Mailing address:** PO Box 5353, Nampa, ID 83653-5353. **Circ:** (Not Reported).

9852 ■ Signs of the Times
Pacific Press Publishing Association
PO Box 5398
Nampa, ID 83653-5398
Religious magazine. **Founded:** June 04, 1874. **Freq:** Monthly. **Print Method:** Offset. **Trim Size:** 8 1/8 x 10 5/8. **Cols./Page:** 3. **Col. Width:** 26 nonpareils. **Col. Depth:** 139 agate lines. **ISSN:** 0037-5047 (print). **USPS:** 496-480. **Subscription Rates:** $16.49 U.S.; $23.49 Other countries. **URL:** http://www.signstimes.com. **Remarks:** Advertising not accepted. **Circ:** (Not Reported).

9853 ■ KDBI-FM - 101.9
3307 Caldwell Blvd., Ste. 101
Nampa, ID 83651-6403
Phone: (208)463-2900
Fax: (208)466-8750
Format: Hispanic. **Owner:** Bustos Media, LLC, 3100 Fite Cir., Ste. 101, Sacramento, CA 95827.

9854 ■ KIVI-TV - 6
1866 E Chisholm Dr.
Nampa, ID 83687
Phone: (208)336-0500
Fax: (208)381-6682
Email: news@kivitv.com
Format: Commercial TV. **Networks:** ABC. **Owner:** Journal Broadcast Group, 5257 Fairview Ave., No. 260, Boise, ID 83706. **Founded:** 1974. **Operating Hours:** Continuous Sun.-Thurs., midnight-12:30 a.m. Fri., 6 a.m.-2 a.m. Sat. **ADI:** Boise, ID. **Key Personnel:** Ken Ritchie, Gen. Sales Mgr. **Ad Rates:** Advertising accepted; rates available upon request. **URL:** http://www.kivitv.com.

9855 ■ KJOT-FM - 105.1
1866 E Chisholm Dr.
Nampa, ID 83687
Phone: (208)336-0500
Format: Classic Rock. **URL:** http://www.varietyrocks.com.

9856 ■ KNIN-TV - 9
1866 E Chrisholm
Nampa, ID 83687
Phone: (208)336-0500
Owner: Journal Broadcast Group Inc., 333 W State St., Milwaukee, WI 53203-1305, Ph: (414)332-9611, Fax: (414)967-5400. **Key Personnel:** Ken Ritchie, VP, Gen. Mgr., kritchie@todays6.com. **URL:** http://www.jrn.com.

9857 ■ KSAW-TV - 51
1866 E Chisholm Dr.
Nampa, ID 83687
Fax: (208)381-6682
Email: news@kivitv.com
Owner: Journal Broadcast Group, 5257 Fairview Ave., No. 260, Boise, ID 83706. **Key Personnel:** Ken Ritchie, VP, Gen. Mgr. **URL:** http://www.kivitv.com/twin-falls.

OROFINO

NW ID. Clearwater Co. 44 mi. E. of Lewiston. Dworshak Dam. Hunting, skiing. Steelhead fishing. Boating saw and planing mills; machine shop; logging. White pine timber. Diversified farming. Hay, grain, dairy products, beef.

9858 ■ Clearwater Tribune
Clearwater Tribune
PO Box 71
Orofino, ID 83544
Publisher's E-mail: cleartrib@cebridge.net
Community newspaper. **Founded:** 1910. **Freq:** Weekly (Thurs.). **Print Method:** Offset. **Cols./Page:** 6. **Col. Width:** 25 nonpareils. **Col. Depth:** 294 agate lines. **Key Personnel:** Cloann McNall, Publisher; Marcie Stanton, Publisher; Andrea Dell, Manager, Advertising. **Subscription Rates:** $40 Individuals online; $38 Individuals print; $63 Two years print. **URL:** http://www.clearwatertribune.com. **Ad Rates:** GLR $.35; BW $611.10; 4C $600; PCI $4.25. **Remarks:** Accepts advertising. **Circ:** ‡3000.

9859 ■ SAR Magazine
Idaho Society of the Sons of the American Revolution
283 Skyline Heights Dr.
Orofino, ID 83544
Phone: (208)476-5783
Magazine featuring historical articles and member activities from the Sons of the American Revolution, Idaho Society. **Freq:** Quarterly. **Key Personnel:** Steve Vest, Editor. **ISSN:** 0161-0511 (print). **Subscription Rates:** $10 U.S. and Canada; $25 Other countries. **URL:** http://www.sar.org/SAR-Magazine; http://sar.epubxp.com/read/account_titles/170192. **Ad Rates:** 4C $1,800. **Remarks:** Accepts advertising. **Circ:** (Not Reported).

9860 ■ KLER-AM - 1300
PO Box 32
Orofino, ID 83544-0032
Phone: (208)476-5702
Fax: (208)476-5703
Email: klerorofino@clearwater.net
Format: Country. **Networks:** ABC; Jones Satellite. **Owner:** Central Idaho Broadcasting, Not Available. **Founded:** 1958. **Operating Hours:** Continuous. **Key Personnel:** Jeff Jones, Gen. Mgr. **Wattage:** 5,000 Day; 1,000 Night. **Ad Rates:** $5-6 for 30 seconds; $7.50-9 for 60 seconds. $4.50-$5.50 for 30 seconds; $7.50-$8.50 for 60 seconds. Combined advertising rates available with KLER-FM.

9861 ■ KLER-FM - 95.3
PO Box 32
Orofino, ID 83544
Phone: (208)476-5702
Fax: (208)476-5703
Email: klerorofino@clearwater.net
Format: Adult Contemporary. **Networks:** Jones Satellite; ABC. **Owner:** Central Idaho Broadcasting, Not Available. **Founded:** 1979. **Operating Hours:** Continuous. **Wattage:** 2,300. **Ad Rates:** $5-6 for 30 seconds; $7.50-10 for 60 seconds. Combined advertising rates available with KLER-AM.

OSBURN

NE ID. Shoshone Co. 5 mi. N. of Wallace.

9862 ■ KWAL-AM - 620
PO Box U
Osburn, ID 83849
Phone: (208)752-1141
Fax: (208)753-5111
Email: kwalradio@usamedia.tv
Format: Country. **Networks:** AP. **Founded:** 1938. **Operating Hours:** Continuous. **Wattage:** 1,000. **Ad Rates:** $3.50-4.75 for 15 seconds; $4.80-7.75 for 30 seconds; $7.20-10.50 for 60 seconds.

POCATELLO

SE ID. Power Co. 50 mi. SW of Idaho Falls. Idaho State University. Flour and feed mills; heavy mining equipment, phosphate fertilizer and chemical factories; cement plants. Electronics manufacturing. Diversified farming.

9863 ■ BlueRibbon Magazine
BlueRibbon Coalition
4555 Burley Dr., Ste. A
Pocatello, ID 83202-1945
Phone: (208)237-1008
Fax: (208)237-9424
Publisher's E-mail: brc_admin@sharetrails.org
Consumer magazine covering off-highway recreation and political issues. **Freq:** Monthly. **Key Personnel:** Michael Patty, Editor. **URL:** http://sharetrails.org/publications. **Remarks:** Advertising accepted; rates available upon request. **Circ:** 19000.

9864 ■ Idaho State Journal
Idaho State Journal
305 S Arthur Ave.
Pocatello, ID 83204
Phone: (208)232-4161
Fax: (208)233-1642
Local newspaper. **Freq:** 6/wk. (Tuesday-Sunday). **Print Method:** Offset. **Cols./Page:** 6. **Col. Width:** 25 nonpareils. **Col. Depth:** 301 agate lines. **Key Personnel:** Bill Kunerth, Publisher; Matt Petrie, Director, Advertising; Ian Fennell, Managing Editor. **Subscription Rates:** $4.95 Members /month - full digital; $7.95 Individuals /month - Sunday home delivery + digital; $11.75 Individuals /month - 6 day print home delivery + full digital access. **Remarks:** Accepts advertising. **Circ:** (Not Reported).

9865 ■ KEGE-FM - 92.1
259 E Center St.
Pocatello, ID 83201
Phone: (208)233-1133
Owner: Gapwest Broadcasting, at above address. **Ad Rates:** Advertising accepted; rates available upon request.

9866 ■ KFXP-TV - 31
902 E Sherman St.
Pocatello, ID 83201
Phone: (208)232-3141
Fax: (208)233-6678

Circulation: ★ = AAM; △ or • = BPA; ♦ = CAC; ❑ = VAC; ⊕ = PO Statement; ‡ = Publisher's Report; Boldface figures = sworn; Light figures = estimated.

Key Personnel: Shelly Goings, Gen. Mgr.

9867 ■ KISU-TV - 10
921 S 8th Ave.
Pocatello, ID 83209-8111
Phone: (208)282-2857
Format: Public TV. **Networks:** Public Broadcasting Service (PBS). **Owner:** Idaho State Board of Education, 650 W State St., 3rd Fl., Boise, ID 83702, Ph: (208)334-2270, Fax: (208)334-2632. **Founded:** 1971. **Formerly**: KBGL-TV. **Operating Hours**: 6 a.m.-1 a.m. **ADI**: Idaho Falls-Pocatello, ID. **Local Programs**: *Healthy Minds*, Saturday 6:30 a.m.; *After You've Gone*, Saturday 9:30 p.m.; *American Masters*; *Baking with Julia*, Sunday 11:00 a.m.; *Blue Realm*, Tuesday 2:00 a.m.; *Bob the Builder*, Sunday 9:00 a.m.; *Bridging World History*, Sunday Monday Thursday, 11:01 a.m.; 11:30 a.m. 2:01 p.m.; 2:30 p.m. 3:00 a.m.; 3:30 a.m.; *Closer to Truth*; *Consuelo Mack WealthTrack*, Friday Saturday 7:30 p.m. 8:00 a.m.; *Western Tradition*, Tuesday Thursday, 2:00 a.m. - 3:00 a.m.; 2:00 p.m. - 3:00 p.m.; *Idaho Edens*; *Connect with English*, Tuesday Friday 5:30 a.m.; *Democracy In America*, Monday Tuesday Wednesday Thursday Friday Saturday 4:30 a.m. 2:00 a.m.; 2:30 a.m.; 2:00 p.m.; 2:30 p.m.; *Doctor Who Series*, Saturday 11:00 p.m.; *Donna Dewberry Show*, Monday Friday Sunday 1:00 p.m.; *Design Squad*; *European Journal*, Saturday 5:00 p.m. - 5:30 p.m.; *Economics USA*; *Eyes of Nye*; *Outdoor Idaho*; *Equitrekking*; *Ethics In America II*; *Fetch! With Ruff Ruffman*; *Fitness Show*; *Fokus Deutsch*; *Food Trip with Todd English*; *Autism: We Thought You'd Never Ask*; *Education News Parents Can Use*, Wednesday 1:00 a.m.; *For The Rights of All: Ending Jim Crow In Alaska*. **Ad Rates:** Noncommercial. **URL:** http://www.idahoptv.org.

9868 ■ KLLP-FM - 98.5
259 E Ctr.
Pocatello, ID 83201
Format: Adult Contemporary. **Ad Rates:** Advertising accepted; rates available upon request. **URL:** http://www.star98radio.com.

9869 ■ KMGI-FM - 102.5
544 N Arthur Ave.
Pocatello, ID 83204
Phone: (208)233-2121
Fax: (208)234-7682
Format: Classic Rock; Sports; Talk. **Networks:** Westwood One Radio; Mutual Broadcasting System; ABC; CBS. **Owner:** Pacific Empire Communications, Inc., at above address. **Founded:** 1978. **Formerly**: KSEI-FM; Conway Broadcasting. **Operating Hours**: Continuous. **ADI**: Idaho Falls-Pocatello, ID. **Wattage**: 100,000 ERP. **Ad Rates:** Noncommercial. $10-$16 for 60 seconds. Combined advertising rates available with KSEI-AM. **URL:** http://www.102kmgi.com.

9870 ■ KPKY-FM - 94.9
259 E Ctr.
Pocatello, ID 83201
Phone: (208)524-5900
Format: Classic Rock. **Networks:** ABC. **Owner:** Gapwest Broadcasting, at above address. **Founded:** 1980. **Operating Hours**: Continuous; 1% network, 99% local. **ADI**: Idaho Falls-Pocatello, ID. **Wattage**: 100,000. **Ad Rates:** Advertising accepted; rates available upon request. **URL:** http://www.949therock.com.

9871 ■ KPVI-TV - 6
902 E Sherman
Pocatello, ID 83201
Phone: (208)232-6666
Fax: (208)233-6678
Email: newsroom@kpvi.com
Format: Commercial TV. **Networks:** NBC. **Owner:** Oregon Trail Broadcasting Co., at above address, Pocatello, ID. **Founded:** 1974. **Operating Hours**: Continuous; 69% network, 31% local. **ADI**: Idaho Falls-Pocatello, ID. **Key Personnel:** Robin Estopinal, Chief Engineer, restopinal@kpvi.com; Scott Larkin, Dir. of Creative Svcs., slarkin@kpvi.com. **Ad Rates:** Advertising accepted; rates available upon request. **URL:** http://www.kpvi.com.

9872 ■ K206CY-FM - 89.1
PO Box 391
Twin Falls, ID 83303
Fax: (208)736-1958
Free: 800-357-4226
Format: Religious; Contemporary Christian. **Owner:** CSN International, PO Box 391, Twin Falls, ID 83303, Ph: (208)736-1958, Fax: (208)736-1958, Free: 800-357-4226. **Key Personnel:** Ray Gorney, Dir. of Engg.; Kelly Carlson, Dir. of Engg.; Mike Kestler, Contact; Don Mills, Music Dir. **URL:** http://www.csnradio.com.

9873 ■ KZBQ-AM - 1290
93 7 FM 97
Pocatello, ID 83204
Format: Contemporary Country. **Founded:** 1959. **Operating Hours**: Continuous. **ADI**: Idaho Falls-Pocatello, ID. **Wattage**: 1,000. **Ad Rates:** $5-7 for 30 seconds; $6-9 for 60 seconds. **URL:** http://kzbq.com/contact.php.

9874 ■ KZBQ-FM - 93.7
93 7 FM 97
Pocatello, ID 83204
Format: Contemporary Country. **Owner:** Idaho Wireless Corp., 436 N Main St., Pocatello, ID 83204, Ph: (208)234-1290, Fax: (208)234-9451. **Founded:** 1969. **Operating Hours**: Continuous. **ADI**: Idaho Falls-Pocatello, ID. **Key Personnel:** Paul E. Anderson, Gen. Mgr. **Wattage**: 100,000 ERP. **Ad Rates:** $13-35 for 30 seconds; $15-40 for 60 seconds. **URL:** http://kzbq.com/contact.php.

PRESTON

SE ID. Franklin Co. 28 mi. N. of Logan, UT. Meat packing plant; flour mill. Agriculture. Dairy products, stock, poultry.

9875 ■ Preston Citizen
Preston Citizen
77 S State St.
Preston, ID 83263-1242
Phone: (208)852-0155
Fax: (208)852-0158
Community newspaper. **Freq:** Weekly (Wed.). **Print Method:** Offset. **Cols./Page:** 6. **Col. Width:** 2 1/16 inches. **Col. Depth:** 21 1/2 inches. **Key Personnel:** Ann Rawlings, Contact; Nancy Cale, Contact; Greg Madson, Publisher; Rod Boam, Editor; Robert Merrill, Assistant Editor. **Subscription Rates:** $26 Individuals in Franklin County; $45 Out of area. **URL:** http://www.prestoncitizen.com. **Mailing address:** PO Box 472, Preston, ID 83263-1242. **Ad Rates:** 4C $285; PCI $7.52. **Circ:** 2950.

9876 ■ KACH-AM - 1340
1633 N Radio Station Rd.,
Preston, ID 83263-5318
Phone: (208)852-1340
Fax: (208)852-1342
Email: kach@plmw.com
Format: Adult Contemporary; Full Service; Information. **Owner:** Alan and Nelada White, at above address. **Founded:** 1948. **Local Programs**: *Let's Talk*, Tuesday 9:05 a.m. **Wattage**: 1,000. **Ad Rates:** Accepts Advertising. **URL:** http://www.kachradio.com.

PRIEST RIVER

N. ID. Bonner Co. 45 mi. NE of Spokane, WA. Fishing. Logging, saw, shingle, grain mills. Pine timber. Dairy farms. Hay, alfalfa, potatoes.

9877 ■ The Priest River Times
The Priest River Times
5809 Hwy. 2, Ste. C
Priest River, ID 83856
Phone: (208)448-2431
Publication E-mail: prtimes@cdapress.com
Local newspaper. **Freq:** Weekly (Wed.). **Print Method:** Offset. **Cols./Page:** 6. **Col. Width:** 2 inches. **Col. Depth:** 21 1/2 inches. **Mailing address:** PO Box 10, Priest River, ID 83856. **Ad Rates:** BW $1,109.40; 4C $375; PCI $8.60. **Remarks:** Color advertising accepted; rates available upon request. **Circ:** Free ‡10000.

REXBURG

E. ID. Madison Co. 28 mi. Ne of Idaho Falls. Ricks College. Sugar, cheese, concrete block, dehydrated potato products factories; lumber mill. Agriculture. Sugar beets, wheat, cattle, sheep, potatoes, dairying, poultry.

9878 ■ Rexburg Standard Journal
RexburgStandardJournal.com
PO Box 10
Rexburg, ID 83440
Phone: (208)356-5441
Local newspaper. **Freq:** 3/week. **Print Method:** Offset. **Cols./Page:** 6. **Col. Width:** 26 nonpareils. **Col. Depth:** 301 agate lines. **Key Personnel:** Kristy J. Geisler, Publisher; Matt Eichner, Editor; Jeremy Cooley, Director, Development. **USPS:** 464-460. **Subscription Rates:** $1.98 Members /month - full digital access; $7.80 Individuals /month - home delivery on Tuesday and Friday + full digital access. **Ad Rates:** 4C $1855; PCI $17.70. **Remarks:** Accepts advertising. **Circ:** (Not Reported).

9879 ■ KBYI-FM - 100.5
525 S Center St.
102 RGS
Rexburg, ID 83460-1700
Phone: (208)496-2050
Email: kbyi@byui.edu
Format: Public Radio. **Networks:** National Public Radio (NPR). **Owner:** Brigham Young University - Idaho, 525 S Center St., Rexburg, ID 83460, Ph: (208)496-1411, Free: 866-672-2984. **Founded:** 1984. **Formerly**: KRIC-FM. **Operating Hours**: Continuous. **Key Personnel:** Mark Bailey, Coord., baileym@byui.edu. **Wattage**: 100,000. **Ad Rates:** Noncommercial. **URL:** http://www.byui.edu/kbyi.

9880 ■ KBYR-FM - 91.5
525 S Center St.
Rexburg, ID 83460
Phone: (208)496-2050
Email: kbyr@byui.edu
Format: Full Service. **Ad Rates:** Advertising accepted; rates available upon request. **URL:** http://www.byui.edu.

9881 ■ KGTM-FM - 98.1
1327 E 17th St.
Idaho Falls, ID 83404
Phone: (208)529-6926
Fax: (208)529-6927
Owner: Pacific Empire Radio, at above address. **Wattage**: 100,000. **Ad Rates:** Accepts Advertising.

RUPERT

S. ID. Minidoka Co. 40 mi. E. of Twin Falls. Manufactures cheese. Bean processing warehouses; frozen food plants. Potatoes shipped. Agriculture. Potatoes, beans, sugar beets, alfalfa, wheat, cattle, sheep.

9882 ■ KBAR-AM - 1230
120 South 300 West
Rupert, ID 83350-9667
Phone: (208)436-4757
Format: News. **Founded:** 1945. **Key Personnel:** Broc Johnson, Prog. Dir.; Kim Lee, Gen. Mgr.; Ben Reed, Engineer, Prog. Dir. **Wattage**: 1,000 KW. **Ad Rates:** $9.00-11.00 for 30 seconds; $11.00-15.00 for 60 seconds. **URL:** http://www.hot100now.com.

9883 ■ KKMV-FM - 106.1
120 S 300 W
Rupert, ID 83350
Free: 800-724-5288
Format: Contemporary Country. **Owner:** Tri-Market Radio Broadcasters, Inc., 3219 Laurel Wood Rd., Twin Falls, ID 83301, Ph: (208)733-2974. **Operating Hours**: Continuous. **Key Personnel:** Kim Lee, Spec., Ad./Sales, kimlee@leeradio.net. **Wattage**: 25,000. **Ad Rates:** Noncommercial. **URL:** http://www.kat106.com.

SALMON

C. ID. Lemhi Co. 140 mi. S. of Missoula, MT. Tourism. Steelhead, salmon fishing; boating. Cheese factory. Lumber mills. Mining. Beef. Agriculture.

9884 ■ The Recorder-Herald
The Recorder-Herald
519 Van Dreff St.
Salmon, ID 83467
Phone: (208)756-2221
Fax: (208)756-2222
Community newspaper. **Freq:** Weekly (Thurs.). **Print Method:** Offset. **Trim Size:** 14 x 22 3/4. **Cols./Page:** 6. **Col. Width:** 12 picas. **Col. Depth:** 21 inches. **Key Personnel:** Ricky Hodges, Editor; Sheila Johnson, Sales Executive. **USPS:** 458-060. **Subscription Rates:** $18 Individuals; $10 Individuals 6 months; $22 Out of state; $14 Out of state 6 months. **Mailing address:** PO Box 310, Salmon, ID 83467. **Ad Rates:** BW $718.20; 4C $300; SAU $4.65; PCI $5.95. **Remarks:** Accepts advertising. **Circ:** (Not Reported).

9885 ■ KSRA-FM - 92.7
315 Riverfront Dr.
Salmon, ID 83467
Phone: (208)756-2218
Fax: (208)756-2098
Email: info@ksraradio.com
Format: Country. **Simulcasts:** KSRA-AM. **Networks:** ABC. **Founded:** 1974. **Operating Hours:** 6 a.m.-10 p.m. **Key Personnel:** Rick Sessions, Contact. **Wattage:** 1,700 ERP. **Ad Rates:** $3.25-4.50 for 15 seconds; $4. 50-6.50 for 30 seconds; $5.75-8 for 60 seconds. **URL:** http://www.ksraradio.com.

SANDPOINT

NW ID. Bonner Co. On Lake Pend d'Oreille, 60 mi. NE of Spokane, WA. Lake and ski resort. Lumber, shingle mills. Timber. Agriculture. Dairy products, potatoes, cattle.

9886 ■ The Bonner County Daily Bee
The Bonner County Daily Bee
310 Church St.
Sandpoint, ID 83864
Phone: (208)263-9534
Fax: (208)263-9091
Newspaper with a Democratic orientation. **Freq:** Weekly (Wed.). **Print Method:** Offset. **Cols./Page:** 6. **Col. Width:** 25 nonpareils. **Col. Depth:** 294 agate lines. **Key Personnel:** Caroline Lobsinger, Editor; David Keyes, Publisher. **Subscription Rates:** $7.58 By mail weekend; monthly; $13 By mail 6 days a week; monthly; $29.95 Individuals 12 weeks; $24 By mail 4 weeks; $10 Individuals e-edition. **URL:** http://bookshelf.cdapresshost.com/index_db.php. **Mailing address:** PO Box 159, Sandpoint, ID 83864. **Remarks:** Accepts advertising. **Circ:** (Not Reported).

9887 ■ MultiLingual
Multilingual Computing Inc.
319 N 1st Ave., Ste. 2
Sandpoint, ID 83864-1495
Phone: (208)263-8178
Fax: (208)263-6310
Publication E-mail: info@multilingual.com
Magazine for international business readers especially in the software development fields who need technology to do business, produce and market their products and materials in foreign languages. Features product reviews, announcements and press releases, user guidelines, and technology and innovation updates. **Freq:** 9/year. **Print Method:** Offset. **Trim Size:** 8 1/2 x 10 7/8. **Cols./Page:** 3. **Col. Width:** 2 1/4 inches. **Col. Depth:** 10 inches. **Key Personnel:** Jeff Allen, Contact. **ISSN:** 1523--0309 (print). **Subscription Rates:** $28 Individuals one year digital only; $50 Two years digital only ; $58 U.S. one year digital and print ; $85 Other countries 2 years (digital and print); $100 U.S. 2 years (digital and print); $154 Other countries 2 years (digital and print); $145 U.S. 3 years (digital and print); $226 Other countries 3 years (digital and print). **URL:** http://multilingual.com/current-issue/. **Formerly:** Multilingual Computing; Multilingual Communications & Computing; Multilingual Communications & Technology; MultiLingual Computing & Technology. **Ad Rates:** BW $3,450; 4C $4,400. **Remarks:** Accepts advertising. **Circ:** Combined 7000.

9888 ■ K212EY-FM - 90.3
PO Box 391
Twin Falls, ID 83303
Fax: (208)736-1958
Free: 800-357-4226
Format: Religious; Contemporary Christian. **Owner:** CSN International, PO Box 391, Twin Falls, ID 83303, Ph: (208)736-1958, Fax: (208)736-1958, Free: 800-357-4226. **Key Personnel:** Kelly Carlson, Dir. of Engg.; Ray Gorney, Asst. Dir.; Don Mills, Music Dir., Prog. Dir. **URL:** http://www.csnradio.com.

9889 ■ Northland Communications
509 N 5th Ave., Ste. B
Sandpoint, ID 83864
Phone: (208)263-4070
Fax: (208)263-1713
Founded: 1981. **Formerly:** Northland Cable Television. **Cities Served:** 71 channels. **Mailing address:** PO Box 1488, Sandpoint, ID 83864. **URL:** http://www.northlandcabletv.com/sandpoint.

SHELLEY

SE ID. Bingham Co. 9 mi. S. of Idaho Falls. Recreation. Flour, potato processing. Manufactures potato digging machinery. Stock, grain, dairy, swine production, poultry farms.

9890 ■ The Shelley Pioneer
The Shelley Pioneer
650 N State
Shelley, ID 83274
Phone: (208)357-7661
Fax: (208)357-3435
Publisher's E-mail: info@theshelleypioneer.com
Community newspaper. **Freq:** Weekly (Wed.). **Print Method:** Offset. **Cols./Page:** 5. **Col. Width:** 12 nonpareils. **Col. Depth:** 224 agate lines. **Subscription Rates:** $24 Individuals in county; $32 Out of state; $36 Two years in county; $52 Out of state 2 years; $20 Individuals in county (online only); $32 Two years in county (online only). **Mailing address:** PO Box P, Shelley, ID 83274. **Remarks:** Advertising accepted; rates available upon request. **Circ:** (Not Reported).

SODA SPRINGS

SE ID. Caribou Co. 63 mi. SE of Pocatello. Mineral springs. Pine timber. Phosphate mines and smelters. Agriculture. Stock, grain, poultry.

9891 ■ Caribou County Sun
Caribou County Sun
159 S Main
Soda Springs, ID 83276
Community newspaper. **Freq:** Weekly (Thurs.). **Print Method:** Offset. **Cols./Page:** 6. **Col. Width:** 12 picas. **Col. Depth:** 300 agate lines. **Key Personnel:** Mark Steele, Editor; Shirley Bails, Manager, Advertising. **USPS:** 090-560. **Subscription Rates:** $20 Individuals in county; $25 Individuals out of county. **Ad Rates:** BW $825.60; PCI $6.40. **Remarks:** Accepts advertising. **Circ:** ‡3000.

9892 ■ Independent Cable Systems of Idaho
132 S Main St.
Soda Springs, ID 83276
Phone: (208)909-5000
Fax: (208)909-5001
Founded: 1988. **Formerly:** Premier Cable. **Key Personnel:** Jeff England, CFO. **Cities Served:** Aberdeen, Arco, Ashton, Bancroft, Challis, Downey, Driggs, Georgetown, Georgetown, Grace, Lava Hot Springs, Mackay, Idaho: subscribing households 14,000; Various communities in Idaho, Utah, Montana, California, and Oregon.; 81 channels; 16 community access channels. **URL:** http://www.silverstar.com.

9893 ■ KBRV-AM - 790
PO Box 777
Soda Springs, ID 83276
Phone: (208)547-2400
Fax: (208)547-3775
Format: Talk; Oldies; Country; News; Sports. **Networks:** UPI. **Founded:** 1957. **Operating Hours:** Continuous. **ADI:** Idaho Falls-Pocatello, ID. **Key Personnel:** Doug Mathis, Gen. Mgr., Contact, doug@kbrv790.com; Cindy Mathis, News Dir; Doug Mathis, Contact, doug@kbrv790.com. **Wattage:** 5,000. **Ad Rates:** $8 for 30 seconds; $4.75-6.25 for 30 seconds; $10 for 60 seconds; $6-7.50 for 60 seconds.

TWIN FALLS

SW JID. Twin Falls Co. 140 mi. E. of Boise. Manufactures sugar, dried and canned fruit, flour, creamery and meat products, potato starch, tallow, vinegar, beverages, frozen potatoes, concrete pipe, bags, potato machinery. Extensive shipping of agricultural products. Beans, potatoes, sugar beets, stock.

9894 ■ Times-News
Lee Enterprises Inc.
132 Fairfield St. W
Twin Falls, ID 83301
Phone: (208)733-0931
Publication E-mail: twinad@micron.net
General newspaper. **Founded:** Oct. 28, 1904. **Freq:** Mon.-Sun. (morn.). **Print Method:** Offset. **Trim Size:** 13 3/4 x 22. **Cols./Page:** 6. **Col. Width:** 25 nonpareils. **Col. Depth:** 301 agate lines. **Key Personnel:** Brad Hurd, Publisher; John Pfeifer, Director, Advertising; Tracey Emery, Web Administrator; James Wright, Editor. **Subscription Rates:** $27.60 Individuals 12 weeks; $16.56 Individuals 12 weeks, Saturday/Sunday delivery. **URL:** http://www.magicvalley.com/; http://www.lee.net/publishing/. **Ad Rates:** GLR $1.11; BW $2,193; 4C $2,548; SAU $17. **Remarks:** Advertising accepted; rates available upon request. **Circ:** Mon.-Sat. ★**18603**, Sun. ★**20563**.

9895 ■ Cable One
261 Eastland Dr.
Box 1946
Twin Falls, ID 83301
Phone: (208)733-6230
Owner: AT&T Intellectual Property, 55 Commerce Valley Dr. W, Ste. 700, Thornhill, ON, Canada L3T 7V9, Ph: (905)762-7390, Free: 888-844-4424. **Founded:** 1977. **Formerly:** AT&T Broadband; Continental Cablevision; TCI. **Key Personnel:** Tim Williams, Tech. Mgr.; Russ Young, Mktg. Mgr. **Cities Served:** Burley, Burley, Filer, Gooding, Hansen, Heyburn, Jerome, Kimberly, Oakley, Paul, Rupert, Twin Falls, Wendell, Idaho: subscribing households 18,462; 52 channels. **URL:** http://www.cableone.net/li/pages/twinfalls-id.aspx.

CSN International - See Tooele, UT

KAWS-FM - See Marsing

KAWZ 89.9 FM - See Great Falls, MT

KAWZ-FM - See Tooele, UT

9896 ■ KBAX-TV - 27
4002 N 3300 E
Twin Falls, ID 83301-0354
Owner: Christian Broadcasting of Idaho, 4002 N 3300 E, Twin Falls, ID 83301, Ph: (208)734-6633. **URL:** http://www.cbitv.com.

9897 ■ KBGH-TV - 19
PO Box 1238
Twin Falls, ID 83303
Phone: (208)736-3046
Fax: (208)736-2188
Free: 888-859-5279
Email: akblowther@orion1.csi.cc.id.us
Format: Educational. **Owner:** State of Idaho Board of Education, 650 W State St., Ste. 307, Boise, ID 83720, Ph: (208)332-1595, Fax: (208)334-2632. **Key Personnel:** Ken Campbell, Gen. Mgr.; Tom Lowther, Chief Engineer; Leo Malburg, Operations Mgr.

9898 ■ KBSW-FM - 91.7
315 Falls Ave.
Twin Falls, ID 83301
Phone: (208)736-3046
Fax: (208)736-2188
Free: 888-859-5279
Format: Public Radio; Classical; News. **Simulcasts:** KBSU-FM Boise, ID. **Networks:** National Public Radio (NPR); American Public Radio (APR). **Owner:** BSU Radio Network, 1910 University Dr.,, Boise, ID 83725-1916. **Operating Hours:** Continuous; 70% network, 30% local. **ADI:** Boise, ID. **Wattage:** 1,950. **Ad Rates:** Noncommercial.

9899 ■ KCIR-FM - 90.7
1446 Filer Ave. E
Twin Falls, ID 83301-4121
Phone: (208)734-5777
Format: Contemporary Christian; Religious. **Networks:** SOS Radio; SOS Radio. **Owner:** Faith Communications Corp., 2201 S 6th St., Las Vegas, NV 89104, Ph: (702)731-5452, Free: 800-804-5452. **Founded:** 1982. **Operating Hours:** 3:30 a.m. - 10:00 p.m. Monday - Friday, 3:00 a.m. - 9:00 a.m. Saturday, 3:00 a.m. 7:00 a.m. Sunday. **ADI:** Twin Falls, ID. **Key Personnel:** Jack French, Contact, jack@sosradio.net; Duane Luchsinger, Station Mgr.; Brad Staley, Gen. Mgr.; Chris Staley, Mgr., chris@sosradio.net; Jack French, Contact, jack@sosradio.net. **Wattage:** 44,100 ERP. **Ad Rates:** Accepts Advertising. **URL:** http://www.sosradio.net/.

9900 ■ KCJY-TV - 55
4002 North 3300 E
Twin Falls, ID 83301
Owner: Christian Broadcasting of Idaho, 4002 N 3300 E, Twin Falls, ID 83301, Ph: (208)734-6633. **Mailing address:** PO Box 391, Twin Falls, ID 83303. **URL:** http://www.cbitv.com.

Circulation: ★ = AAM; △ or • = BPA; ♦ = CAC; ❑ = VAC; ⊕ = PO Statement; ‡ = Publisher's Report; Boldface figures = sworn; Light figures = estimated.

9901 ■ KCTF-TV - 45
4002 N 3300 E
Twin Falls, ID 83301
Phone: (208)734-6633
Fax: (208)736-1958
Owner: Christian Broadcasting of Idaho, 4002 N 3300 E, Twin Falls, ID 83301, Ph: (208)734-6633. **Operating Hours**: Continuous. **Key Personnel:** Mike Stocklin, Station Mgr. **Mailing address:** PO Box 391, Twin Falls, ID 83303. **URL:** http://www.cbitv.com.

KDJC-FM - See Baker City, OR

9902 ■ KEFX-FM - 88.9
PO Box 271
Twin Falls, ID 83303
Phone: (208)734-2049
Fax: (208)736-1958
Free: 800-357-4226
Format: Contemporary Christian. **Key Personnel:** Drew Hartney, Music Dir., Prog. Dir. **Ad Rates:** Noncommercial. **URL:** http://www.effectradio.com.

9903 ■ KEZJ-FM - 95.7
415 Park Ave.
Twin Falls, ID 83301
Phone: (208)733-7512
Format: Country. **Networks:** ABC. **Owner:** Townsquare Media Inc., 240 Greenwich Ave., Greenwich, CT 06830-6507, Ph: (203)861-0900. **Founded:** 1976. **Operating Hours**: Continuous; 2% network, 98% local. **ADI**: Twin Falls, ID. **Key Personnel:** Janice Degner, Gen. Mgr., janicedegner@townsquaremedia.com; Brad Weiser, Dir. of Programs, bradweiser@townsquaremedia.com; Chris Mulvaney, Dir. of Sales, chrismulvaney@townsquaremedia.com. **Wattage**: 50,000. **Ad Rates:** Advertising accepted; rates available upon request. **URL:** http://www.kezj.com.

9904 ■ KFTA-AM - 970
3219 Laurelwood Dr.
Twin Falls, ID 83301
Phone: (208)733-2974
Email: supertalk1230@hotmail.com
Format: Public Radio. **Founded:** 1955. **Formerly**: KAYT-AM. **Operating Hours**: Continuous. **Key Personnel:** Kim Lee, Gen. Mgr. **Wattage**: 2,500 Day; 900 Night. **Ad Rates:** $8 for 30 seconds; $10 for 60 seconds. Combined advertising rates available with KKMV-FM, KZDX-FM, KBAR-AM.

KGSF-FM - See Green Forest, AR

KHJC-FM - See Lihue, HI

9905 ■ KIKX-FM - 104.7
21361 Hwy. 30
Twin Falls, ID 83301
Phone: (208)733-5459
Fax: (208)733-4196
Email: ljohnson@kikx.com
Format: Classic Rock. **Owner:** Local Owned Radio, LLC, at above address, Ph: (208)735-8300. **Key Personnel:** Larry Johnson, Gen. Mgr. **Ad Rates:** Noncommercial. **URL:** http://www.1047bobfm.com.

KJCC-FM - See Carnegie, OK

KJCH-FM - See Coos Bay, OR

KJFT-FM - See Missoula, MT

KKJA-FM - See Redmond, OR

9906 ■ KLIX-AM - 1310
415 Park Ave.
Twin Falls, ID 83301
Phone: (208)733-7512
Format: Talk; News. **Networks:** ABC; Westwood One Radio; Canadian Broadcasting Corporation (CBC)/ Societe Radio-Canada (SRC). **Owner:** Townsquare Media Inc., 240 Greenwich Ave., Greenwich, CT 06830-6507, Ph: (203)861-0900. **Founded:** 1946. **Operating Hours**: Continuous; 95% network, 5% local. **ADI**: Twin Falls, ID. **Key Personnel:** Janice Degner, Gen. Mgr., janicedegner@townsquaremedia.com; James Tidmarsh, News Dir., jamestidmarsh@townsquaremedia.com. **Wattage**: 5,000. **Ad Rates:** Advertising accepted; rates available upon request. **URL:** http://www.newsradio1310.com.

9907 ■ KLIX-FM - 96.5
415 Park Ave.
Twin Falls, ID 83301
Phone: (208)733-7512
Fax: (208)733-7525
Format: Oldies. **Networks:** ABC; Satellite Music Network. **Founded:** 1974. **Operating Hours:** Continuous. **ADI**: Twin Falls, ID. **Key Personnel:** Connie Lively, Contact, connielively@townsquaremedia.com; Janice Degner, Gen. Mgr., janicedegner@townsquaremedia.com. **Wattage**: 100,000. **Ad Rates:** Noncommercial. **URL:** http://www.kool965.com.

9908 ■ KMVT-TV - 11
1100 Blue Lake Blvd. N
Twin Falls, ID 83301
Phone: (208)733-1100
Format: Commercial TV. **Networks:** CBS. **Owner:** Neuhoff Communications Inc., 1340 US Hwy. 1, Ste. 135, Jupiter, FL 33469. **Founded:** 1955. **Operating Hours**: 80% network, 20% local. **ADI**: Twin Falls, ID. **Key Personnel:** Chris Pruitt, Gen. Mgr., chrispruitt@neuhoffmedia.com; Deborah Flores, Traffic Mgr.; Tom Frank, Dir. of Creative Svcs.; Paul Johnson, Mktg. Mgr., Promotions Mgr., pjohnson@kmvt.com. **Ad Rates:** $10-500 per unit. **URL:** http://www.kmvt.com.

KNMA-FM - See Tularosa, NM

KPIJ-FM - See Junction City, OR

9909 ■ KSNQ-FM - 98.3
415 Park Ave.
Twin Falls, ID 83303
Format: Classic Rock. **Owner:** Townsquare Media Inc., 240 Greenwich Ave., Greenwich, CT 06830-6507, Ph: (203)861-0900. **Key Personnel:** Amanda Miller, Dir. of Sales, amanda.miller@townsquaremedia.com; Janice Degner, Gen. Mgr.; Kendra Wolfe, Dir. of Programs. **URL:** http://www.983thesnake.com.

KTBJ-FM - See Festus, MO

9910 ■ KTFI-AM
PO Box 5599
Twin Falls, ID 83303-5599
Phone: (208)733-1270
Fax: (208)733-4196
Email: ktfi@impactradio.com
Format: Full Service; Adult Contemporary. **Networks:** ABC; Northern Agricultural. **Owner:** Impact Radio Group, Inc., 5660 Franklin Rd., Ste. 200, Nampa, ID 83687, Ph: (208)465-9966, Fax: (208)465-2922. **Founded:** 1928. **ADI**: Twin Falls, ID. **Key Personnel:** Larry Johnson, Gen. Mgr.; Shannon Rinehart, Sales Mgr., shannonr@impactradio.com; Eula Martinez, Contact. **Wattage**: 5,000 Day; 1,000 Nig. **Ad Rates:** $9-12 for 30 seconds; $11-14 for 60 seconds. **URL:** http://www.saltandlightradio.com/.

9911 ■ KTFY-FM - 88.1
131 Grandview Dr.
Twin Falls, ID 83301
Phone: (208)735-0881
Email: webmaster@ktfy.org
Format: Contemporary Christian. **Key Personnel:** Brian Yeager, Gen. Mgr., brian@ktsy.org; Chris Gilbreth, Director, chris@ktsy.org; Melody Christensen, Dir. of Production, production@ktsy.org.

K200AA-FM - See Sun Valley, NV

K208CG-FM - See Oklahoma City, OK

K208DS-FM - See Cherokee, IA

K218CE-FM - See Marshalltown, IA

K218CF-FM - See New Braunfels, TX

9912 ■ K218CH-FM - 91.9
PO Box 391
Twin Falls, ID 83303
Phone: (208)734-2049
Fax: (208)736-1958
Free: 800-357-4226
Format: Religious. **Owner:** Calvary Chapel of Twin Falls Inc., 4002 N 3300 E, Twin Falls, ID 83301. **Key Personnel:** Brian Harman, Prog. Dir. **Wattage**: 100. **Ad Rates:** Noncommercial. **URL:** http://www.csnradio.com.

K218CP-FM - See Santa Barbara, CA

K218CX-FM - See Yakima, WA

K218DE-FM - See Jonesboro, AR

K218DF-FM - See Ellensburg, WA

K218DN-FM - See Bozeman, MT

K218DU-FM - See Ridgecrest, CA

K218DX-FM - See Box Elder, SD

K208EK-FM - See Parsons, KS

K208FE-FM - See Topeka, KS

K280BK-FM - See Selma, OR

K288BO-FM - See Paso Robles, CA

K288DR-FM - See Desert Hot Springs, CA

K288FT-FM - See Portland, OR

K285EW-FM - See San Luis Obispo, CA

K289AK-FM - See Orting, WA

K289AN-FM - See Bakersfield, CA

K281BB-FM - See Sonoma, CA

K211DC-FM - See Las Vegas, NV

K211DG-FM - See Firebaugh, CA

K211DS-FM - See Paris, TX

K211EI-FM - See Lamar, CO

K211EL-FM - See Tonopah, NV

K211EM-FM - See Durant, OK

K211EN-FM - See Las Cruces, NM

K215CG-FM - See Helena, MT

K215CW-FM - See Glendive, MT

K215DX-FM - See Round Mountain, NV

K215EE-FM - See Fayetteville, AR

K215EG-FM - See Gallup, NM

K258AL-FM - See Groom Creek, AZ

K258AP-FM - See Whitefish, MT

K258AR-FM - See Eugene, OR

K254AR-FM - See Truckee, CA

K259AK-FM - See Carson City, NV

K256AN-FM - See McCall

K252CK-FM - See Salinas, CA

K252DL-FM - See Walton, OR

K205CK-FM - See Grand Junction, CO

K205DF-FM - See Enumclaw, WA

K205DH-FM - See Shelton, WA

K205DM-FM - See Roseburg, OR

K205DT-FM - See Indio, CA

K205ED-FM - See Aberdeen, SD

K205EG-FM - See The Dalles, OR

K247AQ-FM - See Ashland, OR

K246BB-FM - See Klamath Falls, OR

K204CX-FM - See Hamilton, MT

K204DH-FM - See Hanford, WA

K204DN-FM - See Paragould, AR

K204DO-FM - See Pine Bluff, AR

K204DQ-FM - See Wichita, KS

K204DT-FM - See Rogersville, MO

K204DX-FM - See San Antonio, TX

K204EQ-FM - See Woodward, OK

K204ES-FM - See Brainerd, MN

K204EV-FM - See Missoula, MT

K204FR-FM - See Lovelock, NV

K214CM-FM - See Roseburg, OR

K214CT-FM - See Mariposa, CA

K214ED-FM - See Bakersfield, CA

K209CY-FM - See Blythe, CA

K209DC-FM - See Evanston, WY

K209DS-FM - See Grand Rapids, MN

K209EN-FM - See Des Moines, IA

K209EW-FM - See Kerrville, TX

K219CG-FM - See Pinetop, AZ

K219CL-FM - See Cave Junction, OR

K219DW-FM - See Norfolk, NE

K219KL-FM - See Ninnekah, OK

K219KP-FM - See Sequim, WA

K219KQ-FM - See Payson, AZ

K290BK-FM - See Seaside, OR

K298AF-FM - See Redding, CA

K295AJ-FM - See North Las Vegas, NV

K294AE-FM - See Boise
K291BN-FM - See Reno, NV
K296BS-FM - See Medford, OR
K292FF-FM - See San Antonio, TX
K201CW-FM - See Moab, UT
K201DF-FM - See San Luis Obispo, CA
K201DH-FM - See Pendleton, OR
K201DL-FM - See Hutchinson, KS
K201DP-FM - See Saint George, UT
K201DV-FM - See Brookings, OR
K201EM-FM - See Olympia, WA
K201EQ-FM - See Gold Beach, OR
K201EY-FM - See Kalispell, MT
K201FD-FM - See Forks, WA
K201FF-FM - See Winnemucca, NV
K201FG-FM - See Culbertson, MT
K201FJ-FM - See Williston, ND
K201FK-FM - See Burlington, CO
K201FN-FM - See Dickinson, ND
K201FO-FM - See Jennings, LA
K201FP-FM - See Arapaho, OK
K201FQ-FM - See Hilo, HI
K201FT-FM - See Wellsville, UT
K201FW-FM - See Los Gatos, CA
K201HL-FM - See Garberville, CA
K207BT-FM - See Joplin, MO
K207CE-FM - See Cottonwood, CA
K207CS-FM - See Wenatchee, WA
K207CT-FM - See Lakehead, CA
K207CW-FM - See Paris, AR
K207DN-FM - See Byron, CA
K207DO-FM - See Lewiston
K207DP-FM - See Fergus Falls, MN
K207DQ-FM - See Florence, OR
K207DS-FM - See Wister, OK
K207EI-FM - See Emporia, KS
K217CN-FM - See Holbrook, AZ
K217DG-FM - See Rawlins, WY
K217DN-FM - See Ely, NV
K217EA-FM - See Brownsville, CA
K217EL-FM - See Borrego Springs, CA
K217EM-FM - See Billings, MT
K217EQ-FM - See Coalinga, CA
K275AL-FM - See Denham Springs, LA
K279AK-FM - See Granger, WA
K276EF-FM - See Muscoy, CA
K276EO-FM - See Grants Pass, OR
K273AI-FM - See Ariel, WA
K273AW-FM - See Midland, TX
K272CH-FM - See Scotia, CA
K272DV-FM - See Mountain Home
K272DX-FM - See Grass Valley, CA
K206CF-FM - See Austin, TX
K206CH-FM - See Nevada, MO
K206CL-FM - See Chinook, WA
K206CU-FM - See Mount Vernon, WA
K206CX-FM - See Idaho Falls
K206CY-FM - See Pocatello
K206DC-FM - See Odessa, TX
K206DG-FM - See Kenai, AK
K206DH-FM - See Winslow, AZ
K206DL-FM - See Granite Falls, WA
K206DM-FM - See Bremerton, WA
K206DO-FM - See Port Townsend, WA
K216AX-FM - See Laurel, CA
K216CX-FM - See Yucca Valley, CA
K216DF-FM - See Kodiak, AK
K216DG-FM - See Ketchikan, AK
K216EC-FM - See Happy Camp, CA
K216EH-FM - See Colton, OR
K216EW-FM - See Kernville, CA
K216FQ-FM - See Santa Maria, CA
K260BI-FM - See Havilah, CA
K268AQ-FM - See Bentonville, AR
K268AS-FM - See Bozeman, MT
K267AJ-FM - See Mount Shasta, CA
K262AI-FM - See Laramie, WY
K262BR-FM - See Redmond, OR
K210DP-FM - See Coos Bay, OR
K213CF-FM - See Grants Pass, OR
K213CK-FM - See Montrose, CO
K213CQ-FM - See Salt Lake City, UT
K213DC-FM - See Ephraim, UT
K213EA-FM - See Roswell, NM
K213EH-FM - See Chico, CA
K238AG-FM - See Cascade
K238AL-FM - See Reedsport, OR
K238AY-FM - See Sacramento, CA
K235AG-FM - See Dorris, CA
K237EW-FM - See Port Allen, LA
K203CU-FM - See Burney, CA
K203CW-FM - See Burns, OR
K203DB-FM - See Creston, IA
K203DD-FM - See Sterling, CO
K203DY-FM - See Baker City, OR
K203EB-FM - See Farmington, NM
K203EF-FM - See Mount Vernon, IL
K212AK-FM - See Corvallis, OR
K212BD-FM - See Barstow, CA
K212DF-FM - See Red Bluff, CA
K212DG-FM - See Amarillo, TX
K212DR-FM - See Albion
K212EJ-FM - See Scottsbluff, NE
K212EK-FM - See Victorville, CA
K212EP-FM - See Landers, CA
K212EY-FM - See Sandpoint
K228DU-FM - See Lewiston
K220EU-FM - See New Roads, LA
K225AJ-FM - See Redding, CA
K225AV-FM - See Midland, TX
K220FT-FM - See Portales, NM
K220FW-FM - See Seldovia, AK
K220FY-FM - See Sitka, AK
K220GI-FM - See Camp Verde, AZ
K220GL-FM - See Pleasanton, TX

9913 ■ K220HA-FM - 91.9
PO Box 391
Twin Falls, ID 83303
Fax: (208)736-1958
Format: Information. **Key Personnel:** Mike Kestler, President; Don Mills, Prog. Dir.; Ray Gorney, Operator; Kelly Carlson, Engineer. **Ad Rates:** Underwriting available. **URL:** http://www.csnradio.com.

K220HD-FM - See Fall City, WA
K220HE-FM - See Chehalis, WA
K220HG-FM - See Elko, NV
K220HI-FM - See Clarkston, UT
K220HT-FM - See Saint Louis, MO
K220HX-FM - See Franklin, NE
K220II-FM - See Lakeview, OR
K220IJ-FM - See Yuma, CO
K220IK-FM - See Limon, CO
K220IN-FM - See Portland, OR
K220IO-FM - See Clifton, AZ
K220IR-FM - See Redding, CA
K229AF-FM - See Eureka, CA
K223AM-FM - See Wells, NV
K223BC-FM - See Naches, WA
K202CC-FM - See Provo, UT
K202DN-FM - See Lafayette, LA
K202DS-FM - See Port Angeles, WA
K202DU-FM - See San Juan Bautista, CA
KVJC-FM - See Phoenix, AZ
KWCF-FM - See Sheridan, WY
KWRC-FM - See Hermosa, SD
KWYC-FM - See Cheyenne, WY

9914 ■ KZDX-FM - 99.9
953 Blue Lakes Blvd., N
Twin Falls, ID 83301
Phone: (208)735-0999
Free: 866-735-0999
Owner: Eagle Rock Broadcasting Co., Inc., at above address. **Founded:** 1974. **Wattage:** 27,000. **Ad Rates:** $9-11 for 30 seconds; $11-15 for 60 seconds.

WIFF-FM - See Binghamton, NY

9915 ■ WODY-AM - 900
PO Box 391
Twin Falls, ID 83303
Free: 800-357-4226
Format: Talk; News; Gospel; Information. **Owner:** E. Arnold Terry, 206 Woodlawn Rd., Collinsville, VA 24078, Ph: (703)647-8497. **Founded:** 1960. **Operating Hours:** 12:00 a.m.-9:00 p.m. monday-friday; 6:00 a.m.-7:00 p.m. saturday; 5:30 a.m.-8:00 p.m. sunday. **Key Personnel:** Sara Terry, Traffic Mgr.; Jay Scott, Music Dir.; Troy Spencer, Chief Engineer. **Wattage:** 1,100 Day; 180 Night. **Ad Rates:** $5-8.50 for 30 seconds; $7.75-10 for 60 seconds. **URL:** http://www.csnradio.com.

WREQ-FM - See Ridgebury, PA
WSMA-FM - See Braintree, MA
W300AS-FM - See Orange Park, FL

9916 ■ WTOD-AM - 1560
PO Box 391
Twin Falls, ID 83303
Phone: (419)725-5700
Fax: (208)736-1958
Free: 800-357-4226
Format: Eclectic; News. **Networks:** ABC. **Owner:** Cumulus Media Inc., 3280 Peachtree Rd. NW, Ste. 2300, Atlanta, GA 30305-2455, Ph: (404)949-0700, Fax: (404)949-0740. **Founded:** 1947. **Operating Hours:** 10:00 p.m. - 12:00 a.m. Monday - Friday;4:00 a.m. - 10:00 p.m. Saturday;3:30 a.m. - 11:00 p.m. Sunday. **Key Personnel:** Norman Warner, Dir. of Programs, norm.warner@cumulus.com; Nick Gnau, Dir. of Mktg., Mktg. Mgr., nick.gnau@cumulus.com. **Wattage:** 1,500. **Ad Rates:** $5-125 per unit. **URL:** http://www.csnradio.com.

W208BA-FM - See Myrtle Beach, SC
W208BB-FM - See Royal Oak, MI
W218BK-FM - See Brunswick, GA
W218BV-FM - See Waynesboro, MS
W218CB-FM - See Frogmore, SC
W288BG-FM - See Lebanon, TN
W285DE-FM - See Binghamton, NY
W289AJ-FM - See Danville, VA
W283AW-FM - See Tallahassee, FL
W211AY-FM - See Menomonie, WI
W211BV-FM - See Lexington, SC
W215BE-FM - See Biloxi, MS
W215BF-FM - See Manitowoc, WI
W205AS-FM - See Gulf Breeze, FL
W205AT-FM - See Hamler, OH
W205BJ-FM - See Charleston, SC
W205BY-FM - See Lexington, NC
W245AH-FM - See Ridgeland, MS
W244CD-FM - See Greensboro, NC
W246AS-FM - See Columbia, SC
W204AL-FM - See Kingstree, SC

Circulation: ★ = AAM; △ or • = BPA; ♦ = CAC; ❑ = VAC; ⊕ = PO Statement; ‡ = Publisher's Report; Boldface figures = sworn; Light figures = estimated.

W204BH-FM - See Boones Mill, VA
W204BK-FM - See Sherwood, WI
W204BN-FM - See Gainesville, GA
W204CD-FM - See Panama City, FL
W214AR-FM - See Oswego, NY
W214AS-FM - See Waleska, GA
W214AY-FM - See Walker, MI
W214BN-FM - See Fairhope, AL
W214BQ-FM - See Brentwood, TN
W214BR-FM - See Geneva, NY
W209BJ-FM - See Danielsville, GA
W209BL-FM - See Huntsville, AL
W209BM-FM - See De Pere, WI
W219CB-FM - See Bluffton, SC
W219CV-FM - See Raymond, MS
W219CW-FM - See Danbury, NC
W219CX-FM - See Richmond, VA
W290AK-FM - See Martinsville, VA
W291AN-FM - See Eden, NC
W201BJ-FM - See Athens, GA
W201BN-FM - See Milledgeville, GA
W201CC-FM - See Buford, GA
W201CF-FM - See Baldwin, MI
W207BA-FM - See Erie, PA
W207BQ-FM - See Columbia, SC
W207BX-FM - See Caro, MI
W217AQ-FM - See Meridian, MS
W217BA-FM - See Glasgow, KY
W217BC-FM - See Fredericksburg, VA
W217BI-FM - See Cincinnati, OH
W217BL-FM - See Jacksonville, FL
W217BQ-FM - See Elizabeth City, NC
W274AM-FM - See Louisville, KY
W273AJ-FM - See Athens, AL
W206AI-FM - See Lake Villa, IL
W206AR-FM - See Florence, SC
W206AT-FM - See Savannah, GA
W206AY-FM - See Fruitland, MD
W206BO-FM - See Dickson, TN
W216BM-FM - See Okolona, KY
W216BQ-FM - See Thomasville, GA
W216BX-FM - See Benton Harbor, MI
W216CC-FM - See Bowling Green, KY
W213BD-FM - See Greenville, SC
W213BE-FM - See Snellville, GA
W213BI-FM - See Decatur, IL
W236AL-FM - See Summerfield, NC
W203AY-FM - See West Palm Beach, FL
W203AZ-FM - See Chattanooga, TN
W203BA-FM - See Blue Ridge, GA
W203BB-FM - See Norwalk, CT
W203BG-FM - See Conway, SC
W203BH-FM - See Macon, GA
W220BT-FM - See Cape May, NJ
W220BX-FM - See York, PA
W220CC-FM - See Johnsonville, TN
W220CD-FM - See Enka, NC
W220DF-FM - See Key West, FL
W228BE-FM - See Winston-Salem, NC
W224BC-FM - See Burlington, NC
W224BS-FM - See Roanoke, VA
W229AG-FM - See Atlanta, GA
W229AH-FM - See Jacksonville, FL
W202BA-FM - See Warner Robins, GA
WUJC-FM - See Tallahassee, FL

VICTOR

9917 ■ The Avalanche Review
American Avalanche Association
c/o Jaime Musnicki, Executive Director
PO Box 248
Victor, ID 83455
Phone: (307)699-2049
Publisher's E-mail: aaa@avalanche.org
Freq: Quarterly. **Subscription Rates:** $30 /year; Included in membership. **Alt. Formats:** PDF. **URL:** http://www.americanavalancheassociation.org/tar-archives. **Remarks:** Advertising not accepted. **Circ:** (Not Reported).

ALEDO

Mercer Co. Mercer Co. (NW). 30 m S of Rock Island. Feed mill. Stock, dairy, grain farms.

9918 ■ The Times-Record
The Times-Record
219 S College Rd.
Aledo, IL 61231
Phone: (309)582-5112
Free: 800-582-4373
Publication E-mail: timesrecord@mchsi.com
Newspaper with a Republican orientation. **Founded:** 1857. **Freq:** Weekly (Wed.). **Print Method:** Offset. **Cols./Page:** 6. **Col. Width:** 28 nonpareils. **Col. Depth:** 301 agate lines. **Key Personnel:** Melonie McLaughlin, Publisher; Robert Blackford, Editor; Teresa Welch, Director, Advertising. **Subscription Rates:** $45 Individuals. **URL:** http://www.aledotimesrecord.com/. **Ad Rates:** GLR $9.04; PCI $9.04. **Remarks:** Accepts advertising. **Circ:** Paid 3500, Non-paid 8600.

9919 ■ WRMJ-FM - 102.3
2104 SE Third St.
Aledo, IL 61231-0187
Phone: (309)582-5666
Fax: (309)582-5667
Email: contactus@wrmj.com
Format: Country. **Owner:** Hoscheidt Broadcasting, at above address. **Founded:** 1979. **Operating Hours:** Continuous. **Key Personnel:** Jim Taylor, News Dir., Sports Dir; Jim Taylor, Contact. **Local Programs:** *Focus*, Wednesday 9:20 a.m.; *Sportsline*, Saturday 9:05 a.m. **Wattage:** 3,000 ERP. **Mailing address:** PO Box 187, Aledo, IL 61231-0187. **URL:** http://www.wrmj.com.

ALMA

9920 ■ NANPA Expressions
North American Nature Photography Association
6382 Charleston Rd.
Alma, IL 62807-2026
Phone: (618)547-7616
Fax: (618)547-7438
Publisher's E-mail: info@nanpa.org
Freq: Annual. **URL:** http://www.nanpa.org/expressions.php. **Remarks:** Advertising not accepted. **Circ:** 3,000.

9921 ■ NANPA Outdoor Photographer
North American Nature Photography Association
6382 Charleston Rd.
Alma, IL 62807-2026
Phone: (618)547-7616
Fax: (618)547-7438
Publisher's E-mail: info@nanpa.org
Freq: 11/year. **URL:** http://www.outdoorphotographer.com. **Remarks:** Advertising not accepted. **Circ:** (Not Reported).

ALTAMONT

Effingham Co. Effingham Co. (S). 40 m SW of Mattoon. Panelized housing manufactured. Grain elevator. Grain, livestock, dairy, poultry farms.

9922 ■ The Altamont News
Altamont News Banner
7 Do It Dr.
Altamont, IL 62411
Phone: (618)483-6176
Fax: (618)483-5177
Publication E-mail: news@altnewsban.com
Community newspaper. **Freq:** Weekly (Tues.). **Print Method:** Offset. **Key Personnel:** Omer W. Siebert, Editor. **Subscription Rates:** $22 Individuals online only; $32 Individuals in County; $34 Individuals out of County; $36 Out of state. **Alt. Formats:** PDF. **URL:** http://altnewsban.com/online. **Mailing address:** PO Box 315, Altamont, IL 62411. **Remarks:** Accepts advertising. **Circ:** (Not Reported).

ALTON

Madison Co. Madison Co. (SW). On Mississippi River, 25 m N of St Louis. Lewis and Clark Community College, Principia College. Tourism. Boat connections. Coal mines. Limestone quarries. Oil refineries; foundries.

9923 ■ AdVantage News
Today's Advantage
192-A Alton Square Mall Dr.
Alton, IL 62002
Phone: (618)463-0612
Fax: (618)463-0733
Community newspaper (tabloid). **Founded:** 1986. **Freq:** Weekly-Midweek. **Print Method:** Offset. **Cols./Page:** 5. **Col. Depth:** 16 1/2 INS. **Subscription Rates:** Free. **URL:** http://advantagenews.com. **Formerly:** Today's Advantage. **Mailing address:** PO Box 8003, Alton, IL 62002. **Ad Rates:** BW $1,485; 4C $1,770; PCI $18. **Remarks:** Accepts advertising. **Circ:** ‡86025.

9924 ■ All Around Alton Official Visitor's Guide
Alton Regional Convention & Visitors Bureau
200 Piasa St.
Alton, IL 62002-6271
Phone: (618)465-6676
Fax: (618)465-6151
Publisher's E-mail: website@visitalton.com
Magazine containing tourist information about the Alton region. **Freq:** Annual. **Key Personnel:** Sissy McClean, Manager, Sales. **URL:** http://www.visitalton.com/index.cfm. **Remarks:** Accepts advertising. **Circ:** (Not Reported).

9925 ■ The Telegraph
The Telegraph
111 E Broadway
Alton, IL 62002
Phone: (618)463-2500
General newspaper. **Founded:** Jan. 15, 1836. **Freq:** Mon.-Sun. (morn.). **Print Method:** Offset. **Trim Size:** 12 x 21 5/8. **Cols./Page:** 6. **Col. Width:** 1 7/8 inches. **Col. Depth:** 21 5/8 inches. **Key Personnel:** Jim Shrader, Publisher; Dan Brannan, Executive Editor; Johnny Aguirre, Director, Advertising. **Subscription Rates:** $3.78 Individuals per week, home delivery; $6 Other countries per week, mail. **URL:** http://www.thetelegraph.com. **Formerly:** Alton Telegraph. **Ad Rates:** BW $3,250.55; 4C $3,665.55; SAU $26.02. **Remarks:** Accepts advertising. **Circ:** Mon.-Sat. ♦**18460**, Sun. ♦**20397**.

9926 ■ WBGZ-AM - 1570
227 Market St.
Alton, IL 62002
Phone: (618)465-3535
Fax: (618)465-3546
Email: wbgz@wbgzradio.com
Format: Talk; News; Sports. **Owner:** Metroplex Communications Inc., 227 Market St., Alton, IL 62002, Ph: (618)465-3535, Fax: (618)465-3546. **Operating Hours:** Continuous. **Key Personnel:** Mark Ellebracht, News Dir. **Wattage:** 1,000. **Ad Rates:** $16.75-22.65 for 30 seconds; $21-28.70 for 60 seconds. **Mailing address:** PO Box 615, Alton, IL 62002. **URL:** http://www.wbgzradio.com.

AMBOY

Lee Co. Lee Co. (N). 40 m SW of Rockford. Food processing, packaging plant. Dairy, grain farms,

9927 ■ The Amboy News
News Media Corp.
219 E Main St.
Amboy, IL 61310
Phone: (815)857-2311
Fax: (815)857-2517
Publication E-mail: amboyedit@amboynews.com
Community newspaper. **Freq:** Weekly (Thurs.). **Print Method:** Offset. **Trim Size:** 11 1/4 x 17. **Cols./Page:** 4. **Col. Width:** 14 nonpareils. **Col. Depth:** 16 agate lines. **Key Personnel:** Jennifer Campbell, Writer; Bonnie Morris, Editor, phone: (815)539-9396; Nancy Herrald, Director, Advertising, phone: (815)857-2311. **USPS:** 016-820. **Subscription Rates:** $34.25 Individuals /year auto pay; $36.25 Individuals /year manual pay; $38.75 Out of area /year auto pay; $40.75 Out of area /year manual pay. **URL:** http://www.amboynews.com/v2_main_page.php. **Remarks:** Accepts advertising. **Circ:** (Not Reported).

ANNA

Union Co. Union Co. (S). 30 m N of Cairo. Stone quarries. Manufactures shoes, truck trailers, mobile homes. Flour mill; fruit and vegetable packaging, marble and granite works. Agriculture. Fruits, vegetables, grain, soybeans, alfalfa, oats. Nursery stock production.

9928 ■ WIBH-AM - 1440
330 S Main St.
Anna, IL 62906
Phone: (618)833-9424
Fax: (618)833-9091
Email: onair@wibhradio.com
Format: Country. **Networks:** ABC. **Founded:** 1957. **Formerly:** WRAJ-AM. **Operating Hours:** Continuous; 7.5% network, 92.5% local. **Key Personnel:** Ron Ellis, Gen. Mgr., ron@wibhradio.com; Moury Bass, Owner, moury@wibhradio.com. **Wattage:** 500. **Ad Rates:** $5.50 for 30 seconds; $8.25 for 60 seconds. WRAJ-FM. **URL:** http://www.wibhradio.com.

ARCOLA

Douglas Co. Douglas Co. (E). 40 m SE of Decatur. Collegiate caps, gowns and brooms manufactured. Oil production. Grain farms. Broom corn.

Circulation: ★ = AAM; △ or • = BPA; ♦ = CAC; ❑ = VAC; ⊕ = PO Statement; ‡ = Publisher's Report; Boldface figures = sworn; Light figures = estimated.

9929 ■ Arcola Record Herald
Rankin Publishing
204 E Main St.
Arcola, IL 61910-0130
Phone: (217)268-4959
Fax: (217)268-4815
Community newspaper. **Freq:** Weekly (Thurs.). **Cols./Page:** 8. **Col. Width:** 10.5 picas. **Col. Depth:** 21 inches. **Key Personnel:** Jill Broomer, Editor; Don Rankin, Publisher; Linda Rankin, Publisher. **Subscription Rates:** $29 Individuals Douglas, Coles, Moultrie - yearly; $32 Other countries yearly. **URL:** http://www.arcolarecordherald.com. **Mailing address:** PO Box 130, Arcola, IL 61910-0130. **Ad Rates:** BW $500; 4C $840. **Remarks:** Accepts advertising. **Circ:** 2100.

9930 ■ Broom, Brush, & Mop
Rankin Publishing
204 E Main St.
Arcola, IL 61910-0130
Phone: (217)268-4959
Fax: (217)268-4815
Magazine for the broom, mop and brush trade. **Freq:** Monthly. **Print Method:** Offset. **Trim Size:** 8 1/2 x 11. **Cols./Page:** 3. **Col. Width:** 28 nonpareils. **Col. Depth:** 131 agate lines. **Key Personnel:** Harrell Kerkhoff, Editor; Linda Rankin, Publisher; Don Rankin, Publisher. **Subscription Rates:** $25 U.S.; $35 Canada and Mexico; $100 Other countries; $2 Single issue for subscribers; $5 Single issue plus postage for non-subscribers; $10 Individuals /copy for suppliers directory. **Alt. Formats:** PDF. **URL:** http://www.broombrushandmop.com. **Mailing address:** PO Box 130, Arcola, IL 61910-0130. **Ad Rates:** BW $392, net advertising rate; 4C $859, net advertising rate; 4C $995, commissionable advertising rate; BW $444, commissionable advertising rate. **Remarks:** Accepts advertising. **Circ:** (Not Reported).

9931 ■ Busline Magazine
Rankin Publishing
204 E Main St.
Arcola, IL 61910-0130
Phone: (217)268-4959
Fax: (217)268-4815
Publication E-mail: drankin@consolidated.net
Magazine for motorcoach and transit vehicle industries. **Freq:** Bimonthly. **Trim Size:** 8 3/8 x 10 7/8. **Key Personnel:** Don Rankin, Publisher; Linda Rankin, Publisher; Harrell Kerkhoff, Editor. **Subscription Rates:** Free to qualified subscribers. **Alt. Formats:** PDF. **URL:** http://www.buslinemag.com; http://www.rankinpublishing.com. **Mailing address:** PO Box 130, Arcola, IL 61910-0130. **Ad Rates:** BW $1346; 4C $2360. **Remarks:** Accepts advertising. **Circ:** (Not Reported).

9932 ■ Discover Central Illinois
Rankin Publishing
204 E Main St.
Arcola, IL 61910-0130
Phone: (217)268-4959
Fax: (217)268-4815
Publication E-mail: drankin@consolidated.net
Magazine for tourists and visitors of Central Illinois. **Freq:** Annual. **Print Method:** Web offset. **Trim Size:** 8 1/2 x 11. **Key Personnel:** Don Rankin, Publisher; Linda Rankin, Publisher; Harrell Kerkhoff, Editor. **Subscription Rates:** Free to qualified subscribers. **Alt. Formats:** PDF. **URL:** http://www.rankinpublishing.com/discover; http://www.rankinpublishing.com. **Mailing address:** PO Box 130, Arcola, IL 61910-0130. **Ad Rates:** BW $1364; 4C $2500. **Remarks:** Accepts advertising. **Circ:** (Not Reported).

ARLINGTON HEIGHTS

Cook Co. Cook Co. (NE). 23 m NW of Chicago. Residential. Manufactures marking systems, folding doors, kitchen cabinets, machine metal parts, ornamental iron, patterns, minted coins, plateware, playground equipment, concrete products, precision castings, sewer pipe, silos, swim pools, textiles, tools and dies.

9933 ■ Advanced Imaging
Cygnus Business Media
3030 Salt Creek Ln., Ste. 200
Arlington Heights, IL 60005
Publisher's E-mail: info@cygnus.com
Magazine covering the full range of electronic imaging technology and its uses. **Freq:** 11/yr. **Print Method:** Offset. **Trim Size:** 7 7/8 x 10 3/4. **Cols./Page:** 3. **Col. Width:** 2 3/16 inches. **Col. Depth:** 10 inches. **Key Personnel:** Barry Hochfelder, Editor, phone: (847)454-2726; Jack Johnson, Associate Publisher, phone: (847)454-2707; Stacey Meacham, Managing Editor, phone: (920)563-1602. **USPS:** 535-680. **URL:** http://www.advancedimagingpro.com/magazine.jsp. **Remarks:** Accepts advertising. **Circ:** △**44009**.

9934 ■ Biology Blood and Marrow Transplantation
American Society for Blood and Marrow Transplantation
85 W Algonquin Rd., Ste. 550
Arlington Heights, IL 60005-4460
Phone: (847)427-0224
Fax: (847)427-9656
Publisher's E-mail: mail@asbmt.org
Freq: Monthly. **Subscription Rates:** $362 Individuals; $561 Institutions; $181 Students and residents; $455 Other countries; $661 Institutions, other countries; $227 Other countries students and residents; $56 Single issue. **URL:** http://asbmt.org/news-publications/biology-of-blood-marrow-transplantation. **Remarks:** Accepts advertising. **Circ:** (Not Reported).

9935 ■ Biology of Blood and Marrow Transplantation
American Society for Blood and Marrow Transplantation
85 W Algonquin Rd., Ste. 550
Arlington Heights, IL 60005-4460
Phone: (847)427-0224
Fax: (847)427-9656
Publisher's E-mail: mail@asbmt.org
Professional journal covering transplantation issues. **Freq:** Monthly. **Key Personnel:** Robert Korngold, PhD, Editor-in-Chief. **ISSN:** 1083--8791 (print). **Subscription Rates:** $537 Individuals print and online; $264 Students print and online; $637 Individuals print and online - Canada and international; $332 Students print and online - Canada and international. **URL:** http://www.asbmt.org/?page=BBMT; http://www.bbmt.org. **Remarks:** Accepts advertising. **Circ:** (Not Reported).

9936 ■ Building Design & Construction: Inspiring the Building Team
SGC Horizon L.L.C.
3030 W Salt Creek Ln., Ste. 201
Arlington Heights, IL 60005
Phone: (847)391-1000
Fax: (847)390-0408
Magazine on business and technology for the design and construction of commercial, institutional, and industrial buildings. **Freq:** Monthly. **Print Method:** Offset. **Trim Size:** 9 x 10 3/4. **Cols./Page:** 3 and 2. **Col. Width:** 27 and 40 nonpareils. **Col. Depth:** 140 agate lines. **Key Personnel:** Jay W. Schneider, Editor, phone: (847)954-7941; Robert Cassidy, Executive Editor, phone: (847)391-1040. **ISSN:** 0007--3407 (print). **URL:** http://www.bdcnetwork.com. **Remarks:** Açcepts advertising. **Circ:** Non-paid △**60244**.

9937 ■ Chicago Shimpo
Chicago Shimpo
2045 S Arlington Heights Rd., Ste. 108C
Arlington Heights, IL 60005
Japanese language community newspaper. **Freq:** Semiweekly (Wed. and Fri.) Weekly & semiweekly. **Key Personnel:** Yoshiko Urayama, Publisher, phone: (773)478-6170. **Subscription Rates:** $77 Individuals. **URL:** http://chicagoshimpo.com. **Ad Rates:** BW $980. **Remarks:** Accepts advertising. **Circ:** Combined 5000.

9938 ■ Daily Herald
Paddock Publications Inc.
PO Box 280
Arlington Heights, IL 60006-0280
Phone: (847)427-4300
Fax: (847)427-1301
General newspaper. **Founded:** 1872. **Freq:** Mon.-Sun. (morn.). **Print Method:** Offset. **Trim Size:** 13 1/2 x 22. **Cols./Page:** 6. **Col. Width:** 26 nonpareils. **Col. Depth:** 294 agate lines. **Key Personnel:** Teresa Schmedding; Ted Cox; Daniel E. Baumann, Contact; Dave Beery, Director, Editorial; Douglas Ray, Chief Executive Officer, President, Publisher. **Subscription Rates:** $189.80 Individuals 7 days (Mon.-Sun.); $78 Individuals Sunday only. **URL:** http://www.dailyherald.com. **Ad Rates:** GLR $8.86; PCI $71.80. **Remarks:** Advertising accepted; rates available upon request. **Circ:** Mon.-Sat. ★**144107**, Sun. ★**144073**.

9939 ■ The Diapason
Scranton Gillette Communications Inc.
3030 W Salt Creek Ln., Ste. 201
Arlington Heights, IL 60005-5025
Phone: (847)391-1000
Fax: (847)390-0408
Magazine devoted to pipe organ building, organ and church music performance, and repertoire. **Freq:** Monthly. **Print Method:** Offset. **Trim Size:** 10 x 14 1/4. **Cols./Page:** 4. **Col. Width:** 2 1/16 inches. **Col. Depth:** 13 inches. **Key Personnel:** Jerome Butera, Director, Sales, phone: (847)391-1045; Joyce Robinson, Director, Editorial, phone: (847)391-1044. **ISSN:** 0012--2378 (print). **Subscription Rates:** $40 Individuals 1 year, domestic; $50 Other countries 1 year; $20 Students 1 year. **URL:** http://www.thediapason.com. **Ad Rates:** 4C $1230; BW $228, per column inch; 4C $264, per column inch. **Remarks:** Advertising accepted; rates available upon request. **Circ:** (Not Reported).

9940 ■ Die Casting Engineer
North American Die Casting Association
3250 N Arlington Heights Rd., Ste. 101
Arlington Heights, IL 60004
Phone: (847)279-0001
Fax: (847)279-0002
Publication E-mail: dce@diecasting.org
Trade magazine serving the die casting industry. **Freq:** Bimonthly. **Print Method:** Offset. **Trim Size:** 8 1/4 x 11 1/4. **Cols./Page:** 3 and 2. **Col. Width:** 13 and 20 picas. **Col. Depth:** 10 and 10 inches. **Key Personnel:** Andy Ryzner, Managing Editor. **ISSN:** 0012--253X (print). **Subscription Rates:** $80 Individuals /year in North American; $160 Individuals 2 year in North American; $150 Other countries 1 year; $300 Other countries 2 year. **URL:** http://www.diecasting.org/wcm/Communications/Die_Casting_Engineer/wcm/Communications/DCE.aspx?hkey=ba709ce8-0aef-472f-905d-d4cdea5217d8. **Ad Rates:** BW $1,680; 4C $2,730. **Remarks:** Accepts advertising. **Circ:** ‡2500.

9941 ■ Diseases of the Colon and Rectum
American Society of Colon and Rectal Surgeons
85 W Algonquin Rd., Ste. 550
Arlington Heights, IL 60005
Phone: (847)290-9184
Fax: (847)290-9203
Publisher's E-mail: ascrs@fascrs.org
Freq: Monthly. **Key Personnel:** Robert Madoff, MD, Editor-in-Chief. **ISSN:** 0012--3706 (print); **EISSN:** 1530--0358 (electronic). **Subscription Rates:** $624 Individuals; $1501 Institutions; $737 Individuals U.K., Australia and other countries; $1778 Institutions U.K., Australia and other countries; $703 Canada and Mexico; $1744 Institutions, Canada and Mexico. **URL:** http://www.fascrs.org/diseases-colon-rectum; http://journals.lww.com/dcrjournal/pages/default.aspx. **Remarks:** Accepts advertising. **Circ:** (Not Reported).

9942 ■ Greenhouse Product News
Scranton Gillette Communications Inc.
3030 W Salt Creek Ln., Ste. 201
Arlington Heights, IL 60005-5025
Phone: (847)391-1000
Fax: (847)390-0408
Magazine covering commercial grower industry. **Key Personnel:** Tim Hudson, Director, Editorial, phone: (847)391-1019, fax: (847)390-0408; Bob Bellew, Publisher, Vice President, phone: (847)391-1056. **URL:** http://www.gpnmag.com; http://www.scrantongillette.com. **Ad Rates:** 4C $5460. **Remarks:** Advertising accepted; rates available upon request. **Circ:** (Not Reported).

9943 ■ Inmotion
Air Movement and Control Association International, Inc.
30 W University Dr.
Arlington Heights, IL 60004
Phone: (847)394-0150
Fax: (847)253-0088
Publisher's E-mail: communications@amca.org
Magazine keeping professionals abreast of rapidly changing codes, requirements, laws, advancements, and aware of best practices. **Freq:** Annual. **Alt. Formats:** PDF. **URL:** http://www.amca.org/resources/inmotion.php. **Circ:** (Not Reported).

9944 ■ International Journal of Oral & Maxillofacial Implants
Academy of Osseointegration
85 W Algonquin Rd., Ste. 550
Arlington Heights, IL 60005
Phone: (847)439-1919
Fax: (847)427-9656
Free: 800-656-7736
Publisher's E-mail: membership@osseo.org
Freq: Bimonthly. **ISSN:** 0882--2786 (print). **Alt. Formats:** CD-ROM. **URL:** http://www.osseo.org/NEWIJOMI.html. **Remarks:** Accepts advertising. **Circ:** 7200.

9945 ■ Journal of the IEST
Institute of Environmental Sciences and Technology
2340 S Arlington Heights Rd., Ste. 620
Arlington Heights, IL 60005-4510
Phone: (847)981-0100
Fax: (847)981-4130
Publisher's E-mail: information@iest.org
Professional journal. **Founded:** 1958. **Freq:** Annual. **Print Method:** Offset. **Trim Size:** 8 1/4 x 11. **Cols./Page:** 2. **Col. Width:** 42 nonpareils. **Col. Depth:** 140 agate lines. **Key Personnel:** Diana Granitto, Director, Communications; Roberta Burrows, Executive Director, Managing Editor; Linda Gajda, Coordinator, Information; Heather Wooden, Coordinator, Marketing. **ISSN:** 1098-4321 (print). **Subscription Rates:** $185 Institutions prepaid; Included in membership; $150 Nonmembers. **URL:** http://www.iest.org/Journal. **Formerly:** Journal of Environmental Sciences; Journal of the IES; Journal of The Institute of Environmental Sciences and Technology. **Remarks:** Accepts advertising. **Circ:** ‡5000.

9946 ■ Locksmith Ledger International
Cygnus Business Media
c/o Gale Johnson, Ed.-in-Ch.
3030 Salt Creek Ln., Ste. 200
Arlington Heights, IL 60005
Phone: (847)454-2702
Fax: (847)454-2759
Publisher's E-mail: info@cygnus.com
Industry trade magazine delivering information on electronic technology, automotive security, installation and safe servicing, as well as special product focuses. **Freq:** 13/yr. **Key Personnel:** Gale Johnson, Editor-in-Chief, phone: (847)454-2703; Emily Pike, Managing Editor; Nancy Levenson-Brokamp, Publisher, phone: (847)454-2702. **URL:** http://www.locksmithledger.com/magazine/ll/issue/2015/dec. **Ad Rates:** BW $2,820; 4C $1,170. **Remarks:** Accepts advertising. **Circ:** △**11500**.

9947 ■ Northern Hi-Lites
Professional Photographers of America of Northern Illinois
c/o Joseph A. Weber, Executive Secretary
303 S Donald Ave.
Arlington Heights, IL 60004-6850
Publisher's E-mail: info@ppani.org
Magazine containing technical, business articles and association news of Professional Photographers of America of Northern Illinois. **Freq:** Monthly. **URL:** http://www.ppani.org/northern-hi-lites/. **Remarks:** Accepts advertising. **Circ:** (Not Reported).

9948 ■ Osteopathic Family Physician
American College of Osteopathic Family Physicians
330 E Algonquin Rd., Ste. 1
Arlington Heights, IL 60005
Phone: (847)952-5100
Fax: (847)228-9755
Free: 800-323-0794
Publisher's E-mail: membership@acofp.org
Freq: Bimonthly. **Key Personnel:** Belinda Bombei, Managing Editor. **ISSN:** 1877--573X (print). **URL:** http://ofpjournal.com/index.php/ofp. **Ad Rates:** BW $1415, full page; BW $1160, half page. **Remarks:** Accepts advertising. **Circ:** 15,000.

9949 ■ Professional Builder: The Magazine of the Housing and Light Construction Industry
SGC Horizon L.L.C.
3030 W Salt Creek Ln., Ste. 201
Arlington Heights, IL 60005
Phone: (847)391-1000
Fax: (847)390-0408
The integrated engineering magazine of the building construction industry. **Freq:** Monthly. **Print Method:** Offset. **Trim Size:** 7 x 10. **Cols./Page:** 3. **Col. Width:** 39 picas. **Col. Depth:** 140 agate lines. **Key Personnel:** Patrick O'Toole, Director, Editorial, Publisher, phone: (847)954-7919; David Barista, Editor, phone: (847)954-7929. **ISSN:** 0885--8020 (print). **Subscription Rates:** Free. **URL:** http://www.probuilder.com; http://www.scrantongillette.com/market/building-construction. **Remarks:** Accepts advertising. **Circ:** 107226.

9950 ■ Professional Remodeler
SGC Horizon L.L.C.
3030 W Salt Creek Ln., Ste. 201
Arlington Heights, IL 60005
Phone: (847)391-1000
Fax: (847)390-0408
Trade magazine covering information for professional remodelers. **Freq:** Monthly. **Key Personnel:** Timothy J. Gregorski, Editor-in-Chief, phone: (847)954-7941; Patrick O'Toole, Director, Editorial, Publisher, phone: (847)954-7919. **ISSN:** 1521--9135 (print). **Subscription Rates:** Free. **URL:** http://www.proremodeler.com. **Remarks:** Accepts advertising. **Circ:** (Not Reported).

9951 ■ Residential Lighting
Scranton Gillette Communications Inc.
3030 W Salt Creek Ln., Ste. 201
Arlington Heights, IL 60005-5025
Phone: (847)391-1000
Fax: (847)390-0408
Magazine catering to lighting showroom dealers, manufacturers of lighting products, and related electrical distributors. **Freq:** Monthly. **Trim Size:** 8 x 10 3/4. **Key Personnel:** Laura Van Zeyl, Director, Editorial, Publisher. **ISSN:** 1072--1614 (print). **Subscription Rates:** Free. **Alt. Formats:** PDF. **URL:** http://www.residentiallighting.com; http://scrantongillette.com/news/residential-lighting-named-2015-jesse-h-neal-award-finalist. **Ad Rates:** 4C $3,395. **Remarks:** Accepts advertising. **Circ:** ★**10085**.

9952 ■ Roads & Bridges Magazine
Scranton Gillette Communications Inc.
3030 W Salt Creek Ln., Ste. 201
Arlington Heights, IL 60005-5025
Phone: (847)391-1000
Fax: (847)390-0408
Magazine containing information on highway, road, and bridge design, construction, and maintenance for government agencies, contractors, and consulting engineers. **Freq:** Monthly. **Print Method:** Offset. **Cols./Page:** 3. **Col. Width:** 26 nonpareils. **Col. Depth:** 140 agate lines. **Key Personnel:** Allen Zeyher, Managing Editor, phone: (847)391-1052; Ryan Hanson, Publisher, phone: (847)391-1059; Bill Wilson, Director, Editorial, phone: (847)391-1029. **URL:** http://www.roadsbridges.com; http://www.scrantongillette.com/market/infrastructure. **Formerly:** Rural and Urban Roads. **Remarks:** Accepts advertising. **Circ:** Controlled ‡60000.

9953 ■ Water & Wastes Digest
Scranton Gillette Communications Inc.
3030 W Salt Creek Ln., Ste. 201
Arlington Heights, IL 60005-5025
Phone: (847)391-1000
Fax: (847)390-0408
Magazine (tabloid) featuring product news for decision makers in the municipal and industrial water and water pollution control industries. **Freq:** Monthly. **Print Method:** Offset. **Trim Size:** 11 x 16. **Cols./Page:** 3. **Col. Width:** 3 3/8 inches. **Col. Depth:** 15 inches. **Key Personnel:** Neda Simeonova, Director, Editorial, phone: (847)391-1011; Elizabeth Lisican, Managing Editor, phone: (847)391-1012. **URL:** http://www.wwdmag.com; http://www.scrantongillette.com/brand/water-wastes-digest. **Remarks:** Accepts advertising. **Circ:** (Not Reported).

ASHTON

Lee Co. Lee Co. (N) 35 m S of Rockford. Cement vaults; ice cream stabilizers manufactured. Diversified farming.

9954 ■ The Ashton Gazette
News Media Corp.
813 Main St.
Ashton, IL 61006
Phone: (815)453-2551
Fax: (815)453-2422
Community newspaper (tabloid). **Freq:** Weekly (Thurs.). **Print Method:** Offset. **Cols./Page:** 4. **Col. Width:** 14 picas. **Col. Depth:** 16 inches. **Key Personnel:** Monetta Young, Editor; Mike Feltes, General Manager. **Subscription Rates:** $35.65 Individuals /year auto pay; $37.30 Individuals /year manual pay; $37.75 Out of area /year auto pay; $39.55 Out of area /year manual pay. **URL:** http://www.ashtongazette.com/v2_main_page.php. **Remarks:** Accepts advertising. **Circ:** (Not Reported).

ASTORIA

Fulton Co. Fulton Co. (W). 52 m SW of Peoria. Printing plant and welding shop. Feed mill. Diversified farming. Grain, hay, soybeans.

9955 ■ The Astoria South Fulton Argus
K.K. Stevens Publishing Co.
100 N Pearl St.
Astoria, IL 61501
Phone: (309)329-2151
Fax: (309)329-2344
Free: 800-344-0819
Community newspaper for areas of Fulton County, IL. **Freq:** Weekly (Wed.). **Print Method:** Offset. **Cols./Page:** 8. **Col. Width:** 22 nonpareils. **Col. Depth:** 294 agate lines. **Key Personnel:** Judy Beaird, Editor; Jodie Ragle, Manager, Circulation. **ISSN:** 0034--9600 (print). **Subscription Rates:** $24.95 Individuals Fulton County addresses - 12 months; $29.95 Out of area out of county addresses - 12 months; $.75 Single issue /issue. **URL:** http://www.kkspc.com/argus. **Mailing address:** PO Box 590, Astoria, IL 61501-0427. **Ad Rates:** PCI $4, local open (black and white); PCI $3.50, standing ads (black and white); PCI $8, local open (full color); PCI $7, standing ads (full color). **Remarks:** Accepts display and classified advertising. **Circ:** ‡2000.

ATLANTA

9956 ■ WLCN-FM - 96.3
PO Box 505
Atlanta, IL 61723
Phone: (217)648-5510
Email: lincolncountry@yahoo.com
Format: Country. **URL:** http://www.wlcnonline.com.

9957 ■ WMNW-FM - 96.3
PO Box 505
Atlanta, IL 61723
Format: Full Service; Talk; Contemporary Country. **Key Personnel:** Jim Ash, Gen. Mgr. **URL:** http://www.wlcnonline.com.

AUBURN

Sangamon Co. Sangamon Co. (C). 13 m SW of Springfield. Grain, dairy, stock, poultry farms. Corn, wheat, oats, soybeans.

Divernon News - See Divernon, IL

AURORA

Kane Co. Kane Co. (NE). 38 m W of Chicago. Aurora University. Waubonsee. Community College. Illinois Mathematics and Science Academy. Sand, gravel pits. Manufactures rubber, plastics, furniture, paper and paper products, fabricated metal products, clothing, glass, chemicals, transportation equipment, farm and machinery, aluminum products.

9958 ■ Ewing Family Journal
Ewing Family Association
1330 Vaughn Ct.
Aurora, IL 60504
Freq: Semiannual. **Subscription Rates:** Included in membership. **Alt. Formats:** PDF. **URL:** http://ewingfamilyassociation.org/communications/ewing-family-journal. **Formerly:** Journal of Clan Ewing. **Remarks:** Advertising not accepted. **Circ:** (Not Reported).

9959 ■ Jones Intercable, Inc.
8 E Galena
Aurora, IL 60505
Phone: (708)897-2288
Fax: (708)897-8521
Owner: Jones Intercable, Inc., Gerogetown, CO. **Founded:** 1971. **Formerly:** Centel. **Key Personnel:** Paul Vacek, Gen. Mgr. **Cities Served:** Boulder Hill, DuPage County, Kane County, Kendall County, Montgomery, North Aurora, Oswego, Plano, Sandwich, Yorkville, Yorkville, Illinois: subscribing households 38,959; 55

Circulation: ★ = AAM; △ or • = BPA; ♦ = CAC; ❑ = VAC; ⊕ = PO Statement; ‡ = Publisher's Report; Boldface figures = sworn; Light figures = estimated.

channels; 2 community access channels.

9960 ■ KEEN-TV - 17
2880 Vision Ct.
Aurora, IL 60506
Phone: (630)801-3838
Fax: (630)801-3839
Email: mail@tln.com
Owner: Total Living Network, at above address, Plainfield, IL 60585. **URL:** http://www.tln.com/index2.html.

9961 ■ WBIG-AM - 1280
620 Eola Rd.
Aurora, IL 60504
Phone: (630)851-5200
Fax: (630)851-5286
Format: News; Talk; Sports. **Founded:** 1938. **Formerly:** WMRO-AM; WYSY-AM. **Operating Hours:** Continuous. **ADI:** Chicago (LaSalle), IL. **Local Programs:** *Radio Shopping Show*, Saturday Monday Tuesday Thursday Friday Wednesday 8:00 a.m. - 11:00 a.m. 10:00 A.M. - 12:00 P.M.; 4:00 p.m. - 6:00 p.m. 10:00 a.m. - 11:00 a.m.; 4:00 pm. - 6:00 p.m. **Wattage:** 1,000. **Ad Rates:** Advertising accepted; rates available upon request. **URL:** http://www.wbig1280.com.

9962 ■ WERV-FM - 95.9
1884 Plain Ave.
Aurora, IL 60502
Phone: (630)898-1580
Fax: (630)898-2463
Format: News; Classic Rock. **Owner:** NM Licensing, LLC, 6312 S FiddlerSouth Green Cir., Ste. 360E, Englewood, CO 80111-4927. **Founded:** 1960. **Operating Hours:** Continuous. **ADI:** Chicago (LaSalle), IL. **Key Personnel:** Brian Foster, Gen. Mgr., brian.foster@alphamediausa.com. **Wattage:** 2,850 ERP. **Ad Rates:** Advertising accepted; rates available upon request. $50 for 30 seconds; $60 for 60 seconds. $36 for 30 seconds; $39 for 60 seconds. Combined advertising rates available with WKKD-AM. **URL:** http://www.959theriver.com.

9963 ■ WKKD-AM - 1580
1884 Plain Ave.
Aurora, IL 60502
Free: 800-329-1165
Format: News; Sports; Classic Rock. **Networks:** USA Radio. **Owner:** Kovas Communications, at above address. **Founded:** 1961. **Operating Hours:** Continuous. **ADI:** Chicago (LaSalle), IL. **Wattage:** 250. **Ad Rates:** $36 for 30 seconds; $42 for 60 seconds. $36 for 30 seconds; $39 for 60 seconds. Combined advertising rates available with WKKD-FM.

AVA

Jackson Co. Jackson Co. (SW). 5 m S of Campbell Hill.

9964 ■ WXAN-FM - 103.9
9077 Ava Rd.
Ava, IL 62907
Phone: (618)426-3308
Fax: (618)426-3310
Format: Gospel. **Networks:** USA Radio. **Owner:** Harold L. Lawder, Not Available. **Founded:** 1982. **Operating Hours:** Continuous; 30% network, 70% local. **Wattage:** 6,000. **Ad Rates:** $7 for 30 seconds; $10 for 60 seconds.

BARRINGTON

Lake Co. Lake Co. (NE). 12 m NE of Elgin. Sand, gravel pits. Coffee and tea packing; dresses, pressure canners and cookers, castings, machine tools, aircraft cameras and controls, electronic equipment, weather instruments manufactured. Mink, poultry, grain farms.

9965 ■ Commercial Building Products: Serving Architects, Contractors and Owners in Commercial Construction
ConSource L.L.C.
1300 S Grove Ave., Ste. 105
Barrington, IL 60010
Phone: (847)382-8100
Fax: (847)304-8603
Magazine provides comprehensive new product coverage for the professionals who buy and specify for low- and mid-rise commercial and institutional construction market. **Freq:** Bimonthly. **Key Personnel:** Gary L. Parr, Director, Editorial, Publisher; Marga Parr, Assistant Editor. **ISSN:** 1558--8440 (print). **URL:** http://cbpmagazine.com. **Remarks:** Advertising accepted; rates available upon request. **Circ:** △44500.

BARTLETT

Kane Co.

9966 ■ Bartlett/Wayne Examiner
Examiner Publications
4N781 Gerber Rd.
Bartlett, IL 60103
Phone: (630)830-4145
Publisher's E-mail: news@examinerpublications.com
Local newspaper. **Freq:** Weekly (Wed.). **Print Method:** Web offset. **Trim Size:** 11 x 17. **Cols./Page:** 4. **Col. Width:** 14 picas. **Col. Depth:** 15 7/8 inches. **USPS:** 625-680. **Subscription Rates:** $24 Individuals for Cook, Dupage or Kane County; $52 Out of state. **URL:** http://www.examinerpublications.com. **Ad Rates:** 4C $275. **Remarks:** Accepts advertising. **Circ:** Combined ‡10000.

9967 ■ Carol Stream Examiner
Examiner Publications
4N781 Gerber Rd.
Bartlett, IL 60103
Phone: (630)830-4145
Publisher's E-mail: news@examinerpublications.com
Community newspaper. **Freq:** Weekly (Wed.). **Print Method:** Web Offset. **Trim Size:** 11 x 17. **Cols./Page:** 4. **Col. Width:** 14 picas. **Col. Depth:** 15 7/8 inches. **Key Personnel:** Randall Petrik, President, Publisher. **USPS:** 625-680. **Subscription Rates:** $24 Individuals for Cook, Dupage or Kane County; $52 Individuals all other Counties & States; Included in membership. **URL:** http://www.examinerpublications.com; http://www.examinerpublications.com/index.php?m=6&s=2. **Ad Rates:** BW $448, full page; BW $112, quarter page. **Remarks:** Accepts advertising. **Circ:** 7000.

9968 ■ Hanover Park Examiner
Examiner Publications
4N781 Gerber Rd.
Bartlett, IL 60103
Phone: (630)830-4145
Publisher's E-mail: news@examinerpublications.com
Local newspaper. **Freq:** Weekly (Wed.). **Print Method:** Web Offset. **Trim Size:** 11 x 17. **Cols./Page:** 4. **Col. Width:** 14 picas. **Col. Depth:** 15 7/8 inches. **USPS:** 625-680. **URL:** http://www.examinerpublications.com/index.php?m=6&s=3. **Ad Rates:** 4C $275. **Remarks:** Accepts advertising. **Circ:** ‡5,500.

9969 ■ St. Charles Examiner
Examiner Publications
4N781 Gerber Rd.
Bartlett, IL 60103
Phone: (630)830-4145
Publisher's E-mail: news@examinerpublications.com
Community newspaper. **Freq:** Weekly (Wed.). **Print Method:** Web Offset. **Trim Size:** 11 x 17. **Cols./Page:** 4. **Col. Width:** 16 picas. **Col. Depth:** 10 agate lines. **URL:** http://www.examinerpublications.com/index.php?m=6&s=5. **Ad Rates:** BW $672; PCI $25. **Remarks:** Accepts advertising. **Circ:** ‡37800.

9970 ■ Streamwood Examiner
Examiner Publications
4N781 Gerber Rd.
Bartlett, IL 60103
Phone: (630)830-4145
Publisher's E-mail: news@examinerpublications.com
Community newspaper. **Freq:** Weekly (Wed.). **Print Method:** Web Offset. **Trim Size:** 11 x 17. **Cols./Page:** 4. **Col. Width:** 14 picas. **Col. Depth:** 15 7/8 inches. **Key Personnel:** Randall Petrik, President, Publisher. **USPS:** 625-680. **Subscription Rates:** $24 Individuals for Cook, Dupage or Kane County; $52 Individuals all other Counties & states; accessible only to members. **URL:** http://www.examinerpublications.com. **Ad Rates:** BW $448, full page; BW $112, quarter page. **Remarks:** Accepts advertising. **Circ:** ‡7000.

BATAVIA

Kane Co. Kane Co. (NE) 40 m W of Chicago. Manufactures cosmetics, toilet preparations, electric switches, automatic controlles. Accelerator laboratory for atom smasher.

9971 ■ Journal of Psychology and Christianity
Christian Association for Psychological Studies
PO Box 365
Batavia, IL 60510-0365
Phone: (630)639-9478
Fax: (630)454-3799
Publication E-mail: info@caps.net
Freq: Quarterly March, June, September, & December. **ISSN:** 0733- 4273 (print). **Subscription Rates:** Included in membership; $110 Members regular; $60 Individuals associate member; $50 Students; $103 Nonmembers. **URL:** http://caps.net/membership/publications/jpc. **Remarks:** Accepts advertising. **Circ:** 2500.

BEARDSTOWN

Cass Co.

9972 ■ Cass County Star-Gazette
Beardstown Newspapers Inc.
1210 Wall St.
Beardstown, IL 62618
Phone: (217)323-1010
Fax: (217)323-5402
Publisher's E-mail: stargazette@casscomm.com
Community newspaper. **Founded:** 1872. **Freq:** Weekly (Thurs.). **Print Method:** Offset. **Trim Size:** 13 x 21.5. **Cols./Page:** 8. **Col. Width:** 1 1/2 inches. **Col. Depth:** 21 inches. **Key Personnel:** June Conner; Patricia Wellenkamp, Publisher, Manager, Sales. **USPS:** 257-460. **Subscription Rates:** $35 Individuals online; $33 Individuals print and online; $42 Elsewhere print and online; 47 Out of state print and online. **URL:** http://www.beardstownnewspapers.com/. **Formed by the merger of:** Virginia Gazette; Illinoian Star. **Mailing address:** PO Box 79, Beardstown, IL 62618. **Ad Rates:** GLR $7.05; BW $872; 4C $1,172; SAU $6.92. **Remarks:** Accepts advertising. **Circ:** Mon.-Thurs. 3100.

9973 ■ Star Gazette Extra
Beardstown Newspapers Inc.
1210 Wall St.
Beardstown, IL 62618
Phone: (217)323-1010
Fax: (217)323-5402
Publisher's E-mail: stargazette@casscomm.com
Shopper. **Founded:** 1969. **Freq:** Weekly (Mon.). **Print Method:** Offset. **Cols./Page:** 8. **Col. Width:** 1 1/2 inches. **Col. Depth:** 21 inches. **Subscription Rates:** $10 Individuals 3 months; $15 Individuals 6 months; $25 Individuals 12 months. **URL:** http://www.beardstownnewspapers.com. **Formerly:** The Star Shopper. **Mailing address:** PO Box 79, Beardstown, IL 62618. **Ad Rates:** GLR $9.36; BW $1,074; 4C $1,334; PCI $7.75. **Remarks:** Accepts advertising. **Circ:** Free ‡11900.

9974 ■ Tricounty Times
Beardstown Newspapers Inc.
1210 Wall St.
Beardstown, IL 62618
Phone: (217)323-1010
Fax: (217)323-5402
Publication E-mail: news@tctimes.com
Local newspaper. **Founded:** 1889. **Freq:** Semiweekly (Wed. and Sun.). **Print Method:** Offset. **Cols./Page:** 8. **Col. Width:** 16 inches. **Col. Depth:** 294 agate lines. **Key Personnel:** Richard Rockman, Sr., Publisher. **Subscription Rates:** $5 Individuals 1 day access; $10 Individuals 1 week access; $15 Individuals 1 month access; $25 Individuals 3 months access; $40 Individuals 6 months access; $55 Individuals 1 year access. **URL:** http://www.tctimes.com. **Formerly:** Bluffs Times; Triopia Tribune. **Mailing address:** PO Box 79, Beardstown, IL 62618. **Ad Rates:** GLR $.28; BW $168; PCI $3. **Remarks:** Accepts advertising. **Circ:** Non-paid ‡500, Sun. 24,875, Wed. 13,825.

9975 ■ Bley Cable Inc.
PO Box 215
Beardstown, IL 62618
URL: http://www.ilsos.gov/corporatellc/CorporateLlcController.

9976 ■ WVIL-FM - 101.3
108 E Main St.
Beardstown, IL 62618
Phone: (217)323-1790
Fax: (217)323-1705

Format: Sports. **Networks:** Fox; NBC; ESPN Radio. **Founded:** Sept. 07, 2006. **Operating Hours:** Continuous. **Wattage:** 4,000 ERP. **Ad Rates:** Accepts Advertising. **URL:** http://www.wvilfm.com.

BEECHER

Will Co. Will Co. (NE). 20 m S of Chicago Heights.

9977 ■ Beecher Herald
Russell Publications
120 W North St.
Peotone, IL 60468
Phone: (708)258-3473
Fax: (708)258-6295
Community newspaper. **Freq:** Weekly (Wed.). **Cols./Page:** 5. **Col. Width:** 2 inches. **Col. Depth:** 16 inches. **Key Personnel:** Gilbert L. Russell, Publisher. **Subscription Rates:** $35 Individuals residents of Will, Kankakee, or Cook counties; $41 Individuals all other Illinois residents; $45 Out of state; $85 Other countries. **URL:** http://www.russell-publications.com/beecher. **Mailing address:** PO Box 429, Peotone, IL 60468. **Ad Rates:** BW $236; PCI $3.45. **Remarks:** Accepts advertising. **Circ:** 1,700.

BELLEVILLE

St. Clair Co. St Clair Co. (SW). 15 m SE of St Louis. Scott Air Force Base. Manufactures stoves, shoes, dresses, tacks, patterns, and dies, boilers, industrial furnaces, castings, drinking fountains, beer, stencil machines, bricks, concrete blocks, chemicals, shingle and brick tile, cutting and mining machinery, enameled ware, leather products, corrugated paper boxes, batteries, cryogenic equipment. Coal.

9978 ■ Belleville News-Democrat
McClatchy Newspapers Inc.
120 S Illinois St.
Belleville, IL 62220-2130
Phone: (618)234-1000
Free: 800-642-3878
Publisher's E-mail: pensions@mcclatchy.com
General newspaper. **Freq:** Daily. **Print Method:** Offset. **Cols./Page:** 6. **Col. Depth:** 21 1/2 inches. **Key Personnel:** Jeanne Newton, Director, Human Resources, phone: (618)239-2515; John Grove, Manager, Circulation; Randy Atkisson, Vice President, Finance and Operations; Jeffry Couch, Executive Editor, Vice President; Jay Tebbe, President, Publisher. **URL:** http://www.bnd.com; http://www.mcclatchy.com/2012/06/28/2756/belleville-news-democrat.html. **Mailing address:** PO Box 427, Belleville, IL 62220-2130. **Ad Rates:** BW $5676; 4C $6226; SAU $1.75; PCI $44. **Remarks:** Accepts advertising. **Circ:** Mon.-Fri. ‡53053, Sun. ‡56011.

9979 ■ The Gold Rose of Beta Sigma Psi
Beta Sigma Psi
2408 Lebanon Ave.
Belleville, IL 62221-2529
Phone: (618)235-0014
Fax: (618)235-0051
Publisher's E-mail: office@betasigmapsi.org
Freq: Semiannual. **Remarks:** Accepts advertising. **Circ:** 7500.

WIL-AM - See Creve Coeur, MO

9980 ■ WXOZ-AM - 1510
100 W Main St.
Belleville, IL 62220
Phone: (618)235-2160
Format: Talk; Oldies. **Owner:** Insane Broadcasting Company, at above address.

BELVIDERE

Boone Co. Boone Co. (N). 14 m E of Rockford. Manufactures plastic foam, silk screening, tools and dies, men's work clothes, wire products, rubber products, milk and milk products, beauty supplies, chemicals, tools boxes, paper, paper food containers. Automobile assembly. Canned and frozen food plants. Grain elevator. Grain, dairy farms. Hogs.

9981 ■ Belvidere Daily Republican
Belvidere Daily Republican
130 S State St.
Belvidere, IL 61008
General newspaper. **Freq:** Weekly (Sat.). **Print Method:** Offset. **Trim Size:** 14 x 22 3/4. **Cols./Page:** 6. **Col. Width:** 2 1/16 inches. **Col. Depth:** 21 inches. **Key Personnel:** Kristin Rosa, Editor. **URL:** http://rvpnews.com/?cat=7. **Ad Rates:** SAU $8.20. **Remarks:** Advertising accepted; rates available upon request. **Circ:** (Not Reported).

9982 ■ Boone County Shopper, Inc.
Boone County Shopper Inc.
112 Leonard Ct.
Belvidere, IL 61008
Phone: (815)544-2166
Fax: (815)544-5558
Publisher's E-mail: info@boonecountyshopper.com
Shopper. **Freq:** Weekly (Thurs.). **Print Method:** Offset. **Cols./Page:** 6. **Col. Width:** 24 nonpareils. **Col. Depth:** 210 agate lines. **Key Personnel:** Bill Branom, Publisher; Ed Branom, President. **URL:** http://www.boonecountyshopper.com. **Ad Rates:** PCI $9.15. **Remarks:** Accepts advertising. **Circ:** 20000.

BENSENVILLE

Cook and DuPage Counties. NE Illinois. 18 mi WNW of Chicago.

9983 ■ PM
BNP Media
1050 IL Rte. 83, Ste. 200
Bensenville, IL 60106-1096
Phone: (630)694-4006
Publication E-mail: pm@halldata.com
Trade magazine for reaching contractors on the plumbing-piping-hydronic heating side of the plumbing and mechanical market. **Subscription Rates:** Free. **URL:** http://www.pmmag.com/. **Remarks:** Accepts advertising. **Circ:** △**49005**.

9984 ■ Security: For Buyers of Security Products, Systems, and Services
BNP Media
1050 Illinois Rte. 83, Ste. 200
Bensenville, IL 60106
Phone: (630)616-0200
Publisher's E-mail: asm@halldata.com
Magazine presenting news and technology for loss prevention and asset protection. **Freq:** Monthly. **Print Method:** Offset. **Trim Size:** 8 3/8 x 10 7/8. **Cols./Page:** 3. **Col. Width:** 13.4 picas. **Col. Depth:** 66 agate lines. **Key Personnel:** Bill Zalud, Editor, phone: (773)929-6859, fax: (248)502-1018; Erin J. Wolford, Managing Editor, phone: (630)694-4002. **ISSN:** 0890--8826 (print). **Subscription Rates:** Free to qualified subscribers. **URL:** http://www.securitymagazine.com; http://www.bnpmedia.com/Articles/Publications/Safety. **Formerly:** Security World. **Remarks:** Accepts advertising. **Circ:** Combined △**35014**.

BENTON

Franklin Co. Franklin Co. (S). 8 m N of West Frankfort. Coal mine industry. Manufactures boats, boat trailers, rubber, mining equipment, hose, brass.

9985 ■ News
Benton Evening News Co.
111 E Church St.
Benton, IL 62812
Phone: (618)438-5611
Publisher's E-mail: newsroom@bentoneveningnews.com
General newspaper. **Founded:** 1921. **Freq:** Mon.-Sat. (eve.). **Print Method:** Offset. **Cols./Page:** 6. **Col. Width:** 24 nonpareils. **Col. Depth:** 301 agate lines. **Subscription Rates:** $21 Individuals. **URL:** http://www.bentoneveningnews.com/news/. **Ad Rates:** PCI $5.68. **Remarks:** Accepts advertising. **Circ:** (Not Reported).

9986 ■ WNSV-FM - 104.7
186 E Saint Louis St.
Benton, IL 62812
Phone: (618)327-4444
Fax: (618)327-3716
Free: 800-595-7252
Format: Adult Contemporary. **Networks:** Jones Satellite. **Owner:** Dana Communications Inc., 2 E Broad St., Hopewell, NJ 08525-1810, Ph: (609)466-9187, Fax: (609)466-0285. **Founded:** July 01, 1994. **Operating Hours:** Continuous. **Key Personnel:** Brad Meyer, Sales Mgr. **Wattage:** 6,000. **Ad Rates:** $11-20 for 30 seconds; $13-22 for 60 seconds. **URL:** http://www.v1047.com.

9987 ■ WQRL-FM - 106.3
303 N Main St.
Benton, IL 62812
Phone: (618)439-4100
Fax: (618)435-8102
Free: 800-439-1063
Email: info@wqrlradio.com
Format: Oldies. **Operating Hours:** Continuous. **Wattage:** 25,000. **Ad Rates:** $14 for 30 seconds. **Mailing address:** PO Box 818, Benton, IL 62812. **URL:** http://www.wqrlradio.com/index.php.

BERKELEY

9988 ■ WCKG AM 1530 - 1530
5629 Street Charles Rd., Ste. 208
Berkeley, IL 60163
Format: Talk. **Networks:** Standard Broadcast News. **Owner:** Joseph J. Gentile Inc., at above address. **Founded:** Oct. 10, 1974. **Operating Hours:** Sunrise-sunset; 75% network, 25% local. **Wattage:** 760. **Ad Rates:** Noncommercial; Advertising accepted; rates available upon request.

BERWYN

Cook Co. Cook Co. (NE). 10 m SW of Chicago. Residential. Small business retail center.

9989 ■ El Dia Newspaper
El Dia Newspaper
6331 W 26th St.
Berwyn, IL 60402
Phone: (708)652-6397
Fax: (708)956-7285
Publication E-mail: eldia@eldianews.com
Community newspaper (English, Spanish). **Freq:** Weekly (Fri.). **Print Method:** Broadsheet. **Trim Size:** 10.5 x 13.875. **Cols./Page:** 6. **Col. Width:** 2 inches. **Col. Depth:** 21 1/2 inches. **Key Personnel:** Jorge A. Montes de Oca, Publisher. **Subscription Rates:** $52 Individuals; $94 Two years. **URL:** http://www.eldianews.com. **Ad Rates:** BW $2,198.88; 4C $399; SAU $18.20; PCI $19.11. **Remarks:** Advertising accepted; rates available upon request. **Circ:** Fri. 60000.

BLOOMINGDALE

DuPage Co DuPage Co. DuPage County. NE Illinois. 27 mi W. of Chicago.

9990 ■ The Dental Assistant
American Dental Assistants Association
140 N Bloomingdale Rd.
Bloomingdale, IL 60108-1017
Phone: (630)994-4247
Fax: (630)351-8490
Free: 877-874-3785
Freq: Bimonthly. **ISSN:** 1088--3886 (print). **Subscription Rates:** Included in membership; $30 Nonmembers. **URL:** http://www.adaausa.org/Publications/Dental-Assistant-Journal. **Ad Rates:** BW $1,100. **Remarks:** Accepts advertising. **Circ:** ‡37,000.

9991 ■ The Dental Assistant: Journal of the American Dental Assistants Association
American Dental Assistants Association
140 N Bloomingdale Rd.
Bloomingdale, IL 60108-1017
Phone: (630)994-4247
Fax: (630)351-8490
Free: 877-874-3785
Official journal of American Dental Assistants Association. **Freq:** Bimonthly. **Print Method:** Offset. **Trim Size:** 8 3/8 x 10 7/8. **Cols./Page:** 2. **Col. Depth:** 60 picas. **Key Personnel:** Doug McDonough, Editor; Michi Trota, Managing Editor. **ISSN:** 1088--3886 (print). **URL:** http://www.adaausa.org/Publications/Dental-Assistant-Journal. **Ad Rates:** BW $100. **Remarks:** Accepts advertising. **Circ:** Paid ‡14500, 37000.

9992 ■ User Experience
User Experience Professionals Association
140 N Bloomingdale Rd.
Bloomingdale, IL 60108-1017
Phone: (630)980-4997
Publisher's E-mail: office@uxpa.org

Circulation: ★ = AAM; △ or • = BPA; ♦ = CAC; ❑ = VAC; ⊕ = PO Statement; ‡ = Publisher's Report; Boldface figures = sworn; Light figures = estimated.

Freq: Quarterly. **Subscription Rates:** $18 /copy for nonmembers; Included in membership. **URL:** http://www.usabilityprofessionals.org/uxmagazine/land-your-dream-ux-research-rol. **Remarks:** Accepts advertising. **Circ:** 1700.

BLOOMINGTON

McLean Co. McLean Co. (C). 42 m SE of Peoria. Adjoins Normal. Illinois Wesleyan University. Illinois State Univ. Manufactures electric control switches, farm machinery, vacuum cleaners, air conditioning and ventilating equipment, feeds, electronic equipment, insulations, machine parts, candy, paper and dairy products, railroad equipment, institutional furniture, tires. Food processing plant.

9993 ■ New Waves: Educational Research and Development
Chinese American Educational Research and Development Association
PO Box 355
Bloomington, IL 61702-355
Publisher's E-mail: info@caerda.org
Peer-reviewed journal covering literature in educational research and development. **Freq:** Quarterly. **ISSN:** 1526- 8659 (print). **Subscription Rates:** Included in membership. **Alt. Formats:** PDF. **URL:** http://www.viethconsulting.com/members/publication/new_waves_home.php; http://www.caerda.org/journal/index.php/newwaves/index. **Remarks:** Advertising not accepted. **Circ:** (Not Reported).

9994 ■ The Pantagraph
Pantagraph Publishing Co.
301 W Washington St.
Bloomington, IL 61702-2907
Phone: (309)829-9000
Fax: (309)829-7000
Free: 800-747-7323
Publisher's E-mail: newsroom@pantagraph.com
General newspaper. **Founded:** 1837. **Freq:** Daily. **Print Method:** Offset. **Trim Size:** 12 1/2 x 22 5/8. **Cols./Page:** 6. **Col. Width:** 11.1 picas. **Col. Depth:** 21 1/2 inches. **Key Personnel:** Shannon Brinker, Director, Advertising; Richard Johnston, Publisher; Matt Vance, Manager, Accounting; Dan O'Brien, Director, Operations; Barry Winterland, General Manager; Bob Scott, Director. **URL:** http://www.pantagraph.com. **Formerly:** The Intelligencer. **Mailing address:** PO Box 2907, Bloomington, IL 61702-2907. **Ad Rates:** BW $275; 4C $595. **Remarks:** Accepts advertising. **Circ:** Mon.-Fri. ★**46,057**, Sun. ★**50,245**, Sat. ★**50,245**.

9995 ■ WBBE-FM - 97.9
520 N Center St.
Bloomington, IL 61701
Phone: (309)834-1100
Fax: (309)834-4390
Format: Eclectic. **Owner:** Connoisseur Media L.L.C., 180 Post Rd., E, Ste. 201, Westport, CT 06880, Ph: (203)227-1978. **Ad Rates:** Noncommercial. **URL:** http://www.bob979.com.

9996 ■ WBNQ-FM - 101.5
236 Greenwood Ave.
Bloomington, IL 61704
Phone: (309)829-1221
Email: wbnq@wbnq.com
Format: Top 40. **Founded:** 1947. **Operating Hours:** Continuous. **ADI:** Peoria-Bloomington, IL. **Wattage:** 50,000 ERP. **Ad Rates:** Advertising accepted; rates available upon request. **URL:** http://www.wbnq.com.

9997 ■ WBWN-FM - 104.1
PO Box 1665
Bloomington, IL 61702-1665
Phone: (309)663-1041
Fax: (309)662-8598
Free: 800-552-0104
Email: wbwn@wbwn.com
Format: Talk; Country; News. **Owner:** Townsquare Media Inc., 240 Greenwich Ave., Greenwich, CT 06830-6507, Ph: (203)861-0900; Mid America Broadcast Group, Martinsville, IN, Ph: (317)349-1485. **Founded:** 1990. **Formerly:** WMLA-FM; WRXZ-FM. **Operating Hours:** Continuous. **Wattage:** 470,000 ERP. **Ad Rates:** Advertising accepted; rates available upon request. $50-75 per unit. **URL:** http://www.wbwn.com.

9998 ■ WESN-FM - 88.1
PO Box 2900
Bloomington, IL 61702
Phone: (860)676-7100
Fax: (860)676-7199
Free: 800-654-7570
Format: Contemporary Hit Radio (CHR). **Owner:** Illinois Wesleyan University, 1312 Park St., Bloomington, IL 61701, Ph: (309)556-1000. **Operating Hours:** Continuous. **Key Personnel:** Jessica Meyer, Promotions Dir., jmeyer2@iwu.edu. **Wattage:** 100. **Ad Rates:** Noncommercial. **URL:** http://www.wesn.org/881.

9999 ■ WEWT-FM - 103.3
PO Box 1012
Bloomington, IL 61702-1012
Phone: (309)807-0105
Format: Contemporary Christian; Album-Oriented Rock (AOR); Hip Hop; Rap; Religious. **Owner:** Rock In Victory Ministries Inc., at above address. **Founded:** Sept. 21, 2005. **Operating Hours:** Continuous. **Ad Rates:** Noncommercial; underwriting available. **URL:** http://www.truth103.com.

10000 ■ WIHN-FM - 96.7
520 N Center St.
Bloomington, IL 61701
Phone: (309)834-1100
Fax: (309)834-4390
Format: Classic Rock. **Founded:** 1974. **Formerly:** I-97 Rocks Cutting Edge 2000-2002. **Operating Hours:** Continuous. **ADI:** Peoria-Bloomington, IL. **Wattage:** 6,000. **Ad Rates:** $27 for 30 seconds; $30 for 60 seconds. **URL:** http://www.967irock.com.

10001 ■ WJBC-AM - 1230
236 Greenwood Ave.
Bloomington, IL 61704
Phone: (309)829-1221
Email: info@wjbc.com
Format: Talk; News. **Networks:** ABC. **Founded:** 1925. **Wattage:** 1,000. **Ad Rates:** Advertising accepted; rates available upon request. **URL:** http://www.wjbc.com.

10002 ■ WTRX-FM - 93.7
236 Greenwood Ave.
Bloomington, IL 61704
Phone: (309)829-1221
Email: info@wjbc.com
Format: Oldies. **Owner:** Townsquare Media Inc., 2000 Fifth Third Ctr. 511 Walnut St., Cincinnati, OH 45202, Ph: (513)651-1190. **Operating Hours:** Continuous. **Key Personnel:** Ron Ross, Contact; Erin Walsh, Prog. Dir; Ron Ross, Contact. **Wattage:** 25,000. **Ad Rates:** Advertising accepted; rates available upon request. **URL:** http://www.wjbc.com.

BOODY

Macon Co. (C) 10 m S of Decatur. Residential.

10003 ■ Full Cry
Gault Publications Inc.
PO Box 10
Boody, IL 62514
Phone: (217)865-2332
Consumer magazine for trail and tree hound enthusiasts. **Freq:** Monthly. **Print Method:** Offset. **Trim Size:** 8 1/4 x 10 7/8. **Cols./Page:** 3. **Col. Width:** 28 nonpareils. **Col. Depth:** 10 inches. **Key Personnel:** Seth R. Gault, Editor. **ISSN:** 0016--2620 (print). **Subscription Rates:** $32 Individuals 1 year, 12 issues; $59 Two years 24 issues. **URL:** http://www.treehound.com/html/fullcry.html; http://www.huntinghoundsmen.com/subscribe/full-cry-magazine. **Ad Rates:** BW $250; PCI $15. **Remarks:** Color advertising not accepted. **Circ:** (Not Reported).

BOURBONNAIS

Kankakee Co. Kankakee Co. (E). 50 m S.W. of Chicago.

10004 ■ The Herald/Country Market
B and B Publishing Co.
500 Brown Blvd.
Bourbonnais, IL 60914
Phone: (815)933-1131
Fax: (815)933-3785
Publisher's E-mail: news@bbherald.com
Community newspaper. **Freq:** Weekly. **Print Method:** Offset. **Trim Size:** 10 x 16. **Cols./Page:** 5. **Col. Width:** 22 nonpareils. **Col. Depth:** 224 agate lines. **Key Personnel:** Toby Olszewski, Editor; Jami Mc Elroy, Contact; Lynda Marti, Contact. **USPS:** 111-210. **URL:** http://www.bbherald.com. **Ad Rates:** BW $991.20; 4C $350; SAU $11.67; PCI $12.39. **Remarks:** Accepts advertising. **Circ:** Combined ‡38997, Combined ‡40883.

10005 ■ The-A-Ki-Ki
Kankakee Valley Genealogical Society
PO Box 442
Bourbonnais, IL 60914
Publisher's E-mail: webmaster@kvgs.org
Local genealogical journal. **Freq:** Quarterly. **URL:** http://www.kvgs.org/k3socpub.html. **Remarks:** Advertising not accepted. **Circ:** (Not Reported).

10006 ■ WONU-FM - 89.7
1 University Ave.
Bourbonnais, IL 60914
Phone: (815)939-5330
Fax: (815)939-5087
Free: 800-987-9668
Format: Contemporary Christian. **Networks:** CNN Radio. **Owner:** Olivet Nazarene University, at above address, Bourbonnais, IL 60914-2345. **Founded:** 1967. **Formerly:** WKOC-FM. **Operating Hours:** Continuous. **Key Personnel:** Justin Knight, Station Mgr., jknight1@olivet.edu; Jonathan Eltrevoog, Dir. of Programs, jeltrevo@olivet.edu; Seth Hurd, Promotions Dir., shurd@olivet.edu. **Wattage:** 35,000. **Ad Rates:** Underwriting available.

BREESE

Clinton Co. Clinton Co. (SW) 38 m E of St. Louis, Mo. Agricultural center. Storage buildings, industry. Dairy, grain farms.

10007 ■ Breese Journal
Breese Journal
8060 Old Hwy. 50
Breese, IL 62230
Phone: (618)526-7211
Fax: (618)526-2590
Publisher's E-mail: bjpc@breesepub.com
Newspaper. **Freq:** Weekly (Wed.). **Print Method:** Offset. **Trim Size:** 11 1/2 x 21 1/2. **Cols./Page:** 6. **Col. Width:** 11 1/2 INS. **Col. Depth:** 21 1/2 INS. **Key Personnel:** Dave Mahlandt, Publisher; Kelly Ross, Reporter; Mandy Ribbing, Manager, Advertising. **USPS:** 063-780. **URL:** http://www.thebreesejournal.com. **Ad Rates:** GLR $.17; BW $819; 4C $1069; SAU $6.77; PCI $5.9. **Remarks:** Advertising accepted; rates available upon request. **Circ:** Combined ‡6630.

BROOKFIELD

Cook Co Cook Co. Cook Co. (WC). 10 m W of Chicago. Residential.

10008 ■ American Sokol
American Sokol Organization
9126 Ogden Ave.
Brookfield, IL 60513-1943
Phone: (708)255-5397
Publisher's E-mail: aso@american-sokol.org
Magazine featuring the following sections: the Sokol gymnast, four pages of teaching aids and instruction, the Sokol educator and an informative article on Sokol, Czech, Slovak and American history. **Freq:** 9/year January, February, March/April, May, June, July/August, September, October, November/December. **Subscription Rates:** Included in membership; $12 Individuals. **Alt. Formats:** Download; PDF. **URL:** http://american-sokol.org/publication. **Ad Rates:** BW $500, Full page; BW $300, half page. **Remarks:** Accepts advertising. **Circ:** 5200.

10009 ■ IAJRC Journal
International Association of Jazz Record Collectors
c/o Ian Tiele, Treasurer
PO Box 524
Brookfield, IL 60513-0524
Journal containing the etymology, history, feature icons, CD and book reviews, correspondence, and worldwide news about jazz music. **Freq:** Quarterly. **URL:** http://www.iajrc.org/index.php/the-journal. **Remarks:** Accepts advertising. **Circ:** (Not Reported).

10010 ■ Journal of the International Association of Jazz Record Collectors
International Association of Jazz Record Collectors
c/o Ian Tiele, Treasurer

PO Box 524
Brookfield, IL 60513-0524
Magazine for record collectors. **Freq:** Quarterly. **Print Method:** Offset. **Trim Size:** 8 1/2 x 11. **Cols./Page:** 2. **Key Personnel:** Andy Simons, Editor. **ISSN:** 0098--9487 (print). **Subscription Rates:** $35 Members; $40 Individuals rest of world; $45 Libraries; $6 U.S. back issue; $10 Other countries back issue. **URL:** http://iajrc.org/index.php/the-journal/about-the-journal. **Ad Rates:** BW $100, full page; BW $70, 1/2 page; BW $50, 1/3 page; BW $34, 1/4 page. **Remarks:** Accepts advertising. **Circ:** ★**2000**.

BUFFALO GROVE

Lake Co. Lake Co. 25 m NW of Chicago.

10011 ■ Buffalo Grove Countryside
Sun-Times Media L.L.C.
350 N Orleans St., 10th Fl.
Chicago, IL 60654
Phone: (312)321-3000
Free: 888-848-4637
Publisher's E-mail: customerservice@suntimes.com
Newspaper covering Buffalo Grove, Wheeling, and North Arlington Heights in northwest Cook County. **Freq:** Weekly. **Print Method:** Offset. **Cols./Page:** 4. **Col. Width:** 28 nonpareils. **Col. Depth:** 184 agate lines. **Key Personnel:** Jennifer Thomas, Editor, phone: (847)486-7358. **Subscription Rates:** 0.99 Individuals /week - digital only. **URL:** http://www.chicagotribune.com/suburbs/buffalo-grove. **Remarks:** Accepts advertising. **Circ:** (Not Reported).

BURR RIDGE

DuPage Co.

10012 ■ Fishing Facts Magazine: Written by Fisherman, for Fisherman
MidWest Outdoors Ltd.
111 Shore Dr.
Burr Ridge, IL 60527
Phone: (630)887-7722
Publisher's E-mail: info@midwestoutdoors.com
Magazine on freshwater sport fishing. **Freq:** Bimonthly. **Print Method:** Offset. **Trim Size:** 8 1/4 x 10 7/8. **Cols./Page:** 3. **Col. Width:** 26 nonpareils. **Col. Depth:** 140 agate lines. **USPS:** 199-260. **Subscription Rates:** $44.85 3 years. **Ad Rates:** BW $1,438; 4C $2,091; PCI $63. **Remarks:** Accepts advertising. **Circ:** (Not Reported).

10013 ■ The Spine Journal
North American Spine Society
7075 Veterans Blvd.
Burr Ridge, IL 60527
Phone: (630)230-3600
Fax: (630)230-3700
Free: 866-960-6277
Publisher's E-mail: info@spine.org
Freq: Monthly. **Key Personnel:** Eugene J. Carragee, MD, Editor-in-Chief. **ISSN:** 1529-9430 (print). **Subscription Rates:** Included in membership; $230 Individuals print and online; $264 Individuals Other Countries (print and online). **URL:** http://www.thespinejournalonline.com; http://www.elsmediakits.com/search/journal_listview_sp/TmV1cm9zdXJnZXJ5L1NwaW5l. **Ad Rates:** BW $1695. **Remarks:** Accepts advertising. **Circ:** 7,000.

10014 ■ SpineLine
North American Spine Society
7075 Veterans Blvd.
Burr Ridge, IL 60527
Phone: (630)230-3600
Fax: (630)230-3700
Free: 866-960-6277
Publisher's E-mail: info@spine.org
Freq: Bimonthly. **Subscription Rates:** Included in membership; $100 Nonmembers /year. **URL:** http://www.spine.org/Pages/Publications/SpineLine/BrowseIssues.aspx. **Ad Rates:** BW $1,325. **Remarks:** Accepts advertising. **Circ:** 7,700.

BUSHNELL

McDonough Co. McDonough Co. (NE). 29 m S of Galesburg. Agricultural, stockyards, nurseries; manufactures garden tools.

10015 ■ The McDonough Democrat
Spoon River Press
358 E Main St.
Bushnell, IL 61422-0269
Phone: (309)772-2129
Fax: (309)772-3994
Free: 800-686-3116
Community newspaper. **Freq:** Weekly (Wed.). **Print Method:** Web press. **Trim Size:** 16 1/2 x 20. **Cols./Page:** 8. **Col. Width:** 11 picas. **Col. Depth:** 21 inches. **Subscription Rates:** $17 Individuals; $21.75 Out of state. **URL:** http://www.themcdonoughdemocrat.com. **Mailing address:** PO Box 269, Bushnell, IL 61422-0269. **Ad Rates:** GLR $0.40; BW $630; SAU $5; PCI $3.75. **Remarks:** Accepts advertising. **Circ:** ‡2500.

CAIRO

Alexander Co. Alexander Co. (S). 6 m S of Mounds. Residential.

10016 ■ Kane County Herald
Herald
711 Washington Ave.
Cairo, IL 62914-0033
Phone: (618)734-4242
Fax: (618)734-4244
Newspaper with Republican orientation. **Freq:** Weekly (Wed.). **Print Method:** Offset. **Cols./Page:** 6. **Col. Width:** 22 nonpareils. **Col. Depth:** 224 agate lines. **URL:** http://www.dailyherald.com/news/county/kane. **Mailing address:** PO Box 33, Cairo, IL 62914-0033. **Remarks:** Accepts advertising. **Circ:** (Not Reported).

10017 ■ WKRO-AM
Rte. 1, US-51
Box 311
Cairo, IL 62914
Phone: (618)734-0884
Fax: (618)734-0884
Free: 800-800-9576
Format: Country. **Owner:** Benjamin L. Stratemeyer, at above address, Ph: (618)734-1490. **Founded:** 1942. **Wattage:** 1,000. **Ad Rates:** $5.25-9.25 for 30 seconds; $6.50-10.75 for 60 seconds.

CAMBRIDGE

Henry Co. Henry Co. (NW). 30 m N.E. of Galesburg. Agriculture. Hogs, beef cattle.

10018 ■ Cambridge Chronicle
GateHouse Media Inc.
119 W Exchange
Cambridge, IL 61238
Phone: (309)937-3303
Fax: (309)937-3303
Newspaper with a Republican orientation. **Founded:** 1858. **Freq:** Daily and Sun. **Print Method:** Offset. **Cols./Page:** 6. **Col. Width:** 1 3/4 inches. **Col. Depth:** 21 1/2 inches. **URL:** http://www.cambridgechron.com/. **Formerly:** Chronicle. **Ad Rates:** GLR $2.40; BW $8; 4C $150; SAU $14.70; PCI $8.30. **Remarks:** Accepts advertising. **Circ:** Paid ★**12226**.

CANTON

Fulton Co. Fulton Co. (W). 31 m SW of Peoria. Overall and implement factories. Millwork. Coal mines. Clay pits. Diversified farming.

10019 ■ The Daily Ledger
GateHouse Media Inc.
53 W Elm St.
Canton, IL 61520
Phone: (309)647-5100
Fax: (309)647-4665
General newspaper. **Founded:** 1849. **Freq:** Daily (eve.) and Sat. (morn.). **Print Method:** Offset. **Cols./Page:** 8. **Col. Width:** 22 nonpareils. **Col. Depth:** 301 agate lines. **Key Personnel:** Alyse Thompson, Economist, phone: (309)647-5100; Michele Long, Publisher; Linda Woods, Editor. **URL:** http://www.cantondailyledger.com/. **Mailing address:** PO Box 540, Canton, IL 61520. **Ad Rates:** GLR $1.40; BW $817; 4C $1017; SAU $6.36; PCI $4.75. **Remarks:** Accepts advertising. **Circ:** (Not Reported).

10020 ■ WBYS-AM - 1560
1000 E Linn St.
Canton, IL 61520
Phone: (309)647-1560
Fax: (309)647-1563
Format: News; Talk. **Simulcasts:** 6a.m.-10a.m. WBYS-FM. **Networks:** ABC; Tribune Radio; RFD Illinois. **Owner:** Praire Radio Communications, at above address. **Founded:** 1947. **Operating Hours:** Sunrise-sunset. **Key Personnel:** BJ Stone, Gen. Mgr., bj.stone@prairiecommunications.net; Mark Bixler, Contact. **Wattage:** 250. **Ad Rates:** Noncommercial. Combined advertising rates available with WBYS-FM. **URL:** http://www.prairiecommunications.net.

10021 ■ WCDD-FM - 107.9
1000 E Linn St.
Canton, IL 61520
Phone: (309)647-1560
Email: wbysradio@yahoo.com
Format: Classic Rock; Adult Contemporary. **Key Personnel:** B.J. Stone, Bus. Mgr., bj.stone@prairiecommunications.net. **Mailing address:** PO Box 600, Canton, IL 61520.

CARBONDALE

Jackson Co. Jackson Co. (SW). 50 m S of Centraila. Southern Illinois University. Manufactures ladies fashions, tape, wildlife materials. Coal mines. Nursery. Grain, fruit, truck, poultry farms.

10022 ■ Daily Egyptian
Southern Illinois University at Carbondale
1263 Lincoln Dr.
Carbondale, IL 62901-6899
Phone: (618)453-2121
Publisher's E-mail: admissions@siu.edu
Collegiate newspaper (tabloid). **Freq:** Daily Mon. to Fri. **Print Method:** Offset. **Trim Size:** 11 x 17. **Cols./Page:** 5. **Col. Width:** 11.5 picas. **Col. Depth:** 16 inches. **Key Personnel:** Sarah Gardner, Editor-in-Chief; Jack Robinson, Managing Editor. **URL:** http://www.dailyegyptian.com; http://mcma.siu.edu/journalism/about/daily-egyptian.php. **Ad Rates:** PCI $10.60. **Remarks:** Accepts advertising. **Circ:** ‡15000.

10023 ■ Erigenia
Illinois Native Plant Society
PO Box 271
Carbondale, IL 62903
Phone: (708)613-0163
Publisher's E-mail: illinoisplants@gmail.com
Freq: Annual. **Key Personnel:** Andrew West, Editor. **ISSN:** 1094--9607 (print). **Subscription Rates:** Included in membership. **Alt. Formats:** PDF. **URL:** http://www.ill-inps.org/erigenia. **Remarks:** Advertising not accepted. **Circ:** (Not Reported).

10024 ■ Hydrological Science and Technology
American Institute of Hydrology
Southern Illinois University Carbondale
1230 Lincoln Dr.
Carbondale, IL 62901
Phone: (618)453-7809
Fax: (651)484-8357
Publisher's E-mail: aih@engr.siu.edu
Professional journal for hydrologists and hydrogeologists. **Key Personnel:** Helen Klose, Managing Editor. **URL:** http://aih.engr.siu.edu/publications.html. **Circ:** (Not Reported).

10025 ■ International Journal of Computational Intelligence Theory and Practice
Serials Publications Private Ltd.
c/o Shahram Rahimi, Editor-in-Chief
Dept. of Computer Science
Southern Illinois University
Carbondale, IL 62901-4511
Publisher's E-mail: serials@mail.com
Journal covering artificial neural networks, fuzzy systems, evolutionary computation, intelligent agents, hybrid systems and other areas of artificial intelligence. **Freq:** Semiannual. **Key Personnel:** Raheel Ahmad, Editor; Shahram Rahimi, Editor-in-Chief. **ISSN:** 0973--5267 (print). **URL:** http://www.serialsjournals.com/journal-detail.php?journals_id=62. **Circ:** (Not Reported).

10026 ■ Journal of Banking & Finance
RELX Group plc
Department of Finacne, Southern Illinois University
Carbondale, IL 62901-4626
Journal focusing on the scholarly research concerning financial institutions and the money and capital markets.

Circulation: ★ = AAM; △ or • = BPA; ♦ = CAC; ❑ = VAC; ⊕ = PO Statement; ‡ = Publisher's Report; Boldface figures = sworn; Light figures = estimated.

Freq: Monthly. **Key Personnel:** I. Mathur, Editor; Carol Alexander, Editor. **ISSN:** 0378-4266 (print). **Subscription Rates:** $3073.80 Institutions online only; $4098 Institutions print only; $211 Individuals print only. **URL:** http://www.journals.elsevier.com/journal-of-banking-and-finance/. **Circ:** (Not Reported).

10027 ■ Journal of Legal Medicine
Taylor & Francis Group Journals
c/o Ross D. Silverman, Ed.-in-Ch.
South Illinois University
School of Law
Carbondale, IL 62901-6804
Phone: (618)453-8741
Fax: (618)453-3317
Publisher's E-mail: customerservice@taylorandfrancis.com
Scholarly publication that fosters and encourages research in the field of legal medicine. **Freq:** Quarterly. **Print Method:** Offset. **Trim Size:** 7 x 10. **Cols./Page:** 1. **Col. Width:** 5 inches. **Col. Depth:** 7 1/2 inches. **Key Personnel:** Marshall B. Kapp, Editor; Michael G. Getty, Assistant Editor; Paul J. Connors, MD, Board Member; Susan Wirth Balter, Board Member; Ross D. Silverman, Editor-in-Chief; Marvin H. Firestone, MD, Board Member; Arnold J. Rosoff, Editor; Dorothy Rasinski Gregory, MD, Board Member; Alan C. Hoffman, Board Member; Edward E. Hollowell, Board Member; Dale H. Cowan, MD, Board Member; Alicejane Lippner, MD, Board Member; Theodore R. Leblang, Editor. **ISSN:** 0194-7648 (print); **EISSN:** 1521-057X (electronic). **Subscription Rates:** $584 Institutions print and online; $302 Individuals print only; $511 Institutions online only. **URL:** http://www.tandfonline.com/toc/ulgm20/current. **Remarks:** On request. **Circ:** Paid ‡1622.

10028 ■ Journal of Rehabilitation Administration
National Association for Rehabilitation Leadership
c/o William Crimando, Editor
Southern Illinois University
Carbondale, IL 62901-4609
Phone: (618)536-7704
Fax: (618)453-8271
Publisher's E-mail: Email@NARL.us
Journal of the National Rehabilitation Administration Association. **Freq:** Semiannual. **Key Personnel:** William Crimando, Editor. **URL:** http://www.elliottfitzpatrick.com/jra.html. **Remarks:** Advertising accepted; rates available upon request. **Circ:** Paid 2000, ‡500.

10029 ■ North American Journal of Aquaculture
American Fisheries Society
c/o Christopher C. Kohler, Ed.
Fisheries & Illinois Aquaculture Center
Southern Illinois University
Mailcode 6511
Carbondale, IL 62901-6511
Publication E-mail: journals@fisheries.org
Aquaculture journal. **Freq:** Quarterly. **Print Method:** Offset. **Trim Size:** 7 x 10. **Cols./Page:** 2. **Col. Width:** 32 nonpareils. **Col. Depth:** 114 agate lines. **Key Personnel:** Christopher C. Kohler, Editor; Bruce A. Barton, Editor. **ISSN:** 1522--2055 (print); **EISSN:** 1548--8454 (electronic). **Subscription Rates:** $479 Institutions print & online; $419 Institutions online only (credit card). **URL:** http://www.tandfonline.com/toc/unaj20/current. **Formerly**: The Progressive Fish-Culturist. **Remarks:** Accepts advertising. **Circ:** ‡2200.

10030 ■ SIU Law Journal
Southern Illinois University School of Law
1263 Lincoln Dr.
Carbondale, IL 62901-6899
Phone: (618)453-2121
Publisher's E-mail: lawadmit@siu.edu
Journal containing articles on issues in the society. **Freq:** Quarterly. **Key Personnel:** Adam J. Loos, Editor-in-Chief. **URL:** http://www.law.siu.edu/academics/journals/law-journal/index.html. **Circ:** (Not Reported).

10031 ■ Southern Illinoisan
Southern Illinoisan
710 N Illinois Ave.
Carbondale, IL 62902
Phone: (618)529-5454
Free: 800-228-0429
Publisher's E-mail: customerservice@thesouthern.com
General newspaper. **Founded:** 1877. **Freq:** Mon.-Sun. (morn.). **Print Method:** Offset. **Cols./Page:** 6. **Col. Width:** 24 nonpareils. **Col. Depth:** 301 agate lines. **Key Personnel:** John Pfeifer, Publisher, phone: (618)351-5038. **Subscription Rates:** $178 By mail; $110.75 By mail Monday to Saturday; $98.75 By mail Fri., Saturday and Sunday. **URL:** http://thesouthern.com/. **Mailing address:** PO Box 2108, Carbondale, IL 62902. **Ad Rates:** SAU $275. **Remarks:** Accepts advertising. **Circ:** Mon.-Sat. ★27,446, Sun. ★36,491.

10032 ■ WDBX-FM - 91.1
224 N Washington St.
Carbondale, IL 62901
Phone: (618)529-5900
Format: Eclectic. **Owner:** Heterodyne Broadcasting Co., 224 N Washington St., Carbondale, IL 62901, Ph: (618)529-5900. **Founded:** Feb. 06, 1996. **Operating Hours**: Continuous. **Local Programs**: *Back to Bluegrass*, Tuesday 4:00 p.m. - 5:00 p.m.; *Star Child*, Saturday 4:00 p.m. - 6:00 p.m.; *The Random Show*, Wednesday 6:00 p.m. - 7:00 p.m.; *The Jazz Buffet*, Friday 12:00 p.m. - 2:00 p.m.; *Music From Beyond the Lakes*, Sunday 8:00 p.m. - 10:00 p.m. **Wattage**: 3,000. **Ad Rates:** Noncommercial. **URL:** http://www.wdbx.org.

10033 ■ WIDB-FM - 104.3
Student Ctr., 4th Fl.
1255 Lincoln Dr.
Carbondale, IL 62901
Phone: (618)536-2361
Format: Classic Rock; Top 40. **Owner:** Southern Illinois University, 1263 Lincoln Dr., Carbondale, IL 62901. **Founded:** Apr. 12, 1970. **Operating Hours**: Continuous. **Key Personnel:** Kyle Fisher, Dir. of Programs; Eric Hirschi, Gen. Mgr. **Wattage**: 100. **Ad Rates:** Advertising accepted; rates available upon request. **URL:** http://www.widb.net.

10034 ■ WSIU-FM - 91.9
1100 Lincoln Dr., Ste. 1003
Carbondale, IL 62901-4306
Phone: (618)453-4343
Fax: (618)453-6246
Free: 866-498-5561
Format: News; Talk. **Networks:** National Public Radio (NPR); American Public Radio (APR). **Owner:** Southern Illinois University Board of Trustees, at above address, Carbondale, IL 62901, Ph: (618)536-3357. **Founded:** 1958. **Operating Hours**: 5 a.m.- 1 a.m.; 50% network, 50% local. **Key Personnel:** Jeff Williams, Station Mgr. **Wattage**: 50,000. **Ad Rates:** Noncommercial. **Mailing address:** PO Box 6602, Carbondale, IL 62901-4306. **URL:** http://www.wsiu.org.

10035 ■ WSIU-TV - 8
1100 Lincoln Dr., Ste. 1003
Carbondale, IL 62901-4306
Phone: (618)453-4343
Fax: (618)453-6186
Free: 866-498-5561
Format: Public TV. **Networks:** Public Broadcasting Service (PBS). **Owner:** Southern Illinois University, 1263 Lincoln Dr., Carbondale, IL 62901. **Founded:** 1961. **Operating Hours**: Continuous. **ADI**: Paducah,KY-Cape Girardeau,MO-Marion,IL. **URL:** http://www.wsiu.org.

10036 ■ WUSI-FM - 90.3
1100 Lincoln Dr., Ste. 1003
SIU Mailcode 6602
Carbondale, IL 62901-4306
Phone: (618)453-4343
Fax: (618)453-6186
Free: 866-498-5561
Format: News; Talk. **Owner:** Southern Illinois University, 1263 Lincoln Dr., Carbondale, IL 62901. **Operating Hours:** Continuous. **Ad Rates:** Noncommercial; underwriting available. **URL:** http://www.wsiu.org.

10037 ■ WUSI-TV - 16
1100 Lincoln Dr., Ste. 1003
Carbondale, IL 62901-4306
Phone: (618)453-4343
Fax: (618)453-6186
Free: 866-498-5561
Networks: Public Broadcasting Service (PBS). **Owner:** Southern Illinois University, 1263 Lincoln Dr., Carbondale, IL 62901. **Founded:** 1968. **Operating Hours**: 6 a.m.-1 a.m. **ADI**: Terre Haute, IN. **Key Personnel:** Beth Spezia, Contact. **Wattage**: 10,000. **Ad Rates:** $50-100 per unit. **URL:** http://www.wsiu.org.

WVSI-FM - See Mount Vernon

CARLINVILLE

Macoupin Co. Macoupin Co. (SWC). 45 m SW of Springfield. Blackburn College. Truck bodies, tubular steel, butter manufactured. Nursery; Creamery. Diversified farming. Corn, wheat, livestock, milk.

10038 ■ The Enquirer-Democrat
Macoupin County Enquirer Inc.
125 E Main
Carlinville, IL 62626
Phone: (217)854-2534
Publisher's E-mail: printorders@enquirerdemocrat.com
Community newspaper. **Freq:** Weekly (Thurs.). **Print Method:** Offset. **Cols./Page:** 7. **Col. Width:** 2 inches. **Col. Depth:** 21 1/2 inches. **Subscription Rates:** $35 Individuals /year; $40 Out of area /year. **URL:** http://enquirerdemocrat.com. **Formerly**: Macoupin County Enquirer. **Ad Rates:** GLR $.75; 4C $200; PCI $5.50. **Remarks:** Accepts advertising. **Circ:** Combined 5500.

10039 ■ WIBI-FM - 91.1
PO Box 140
Carlinville, IL 62626
Phone: (217)854-4800
Fax: (217)854-4810
Free: 800-707-9191
Format: Contemporary Christian. **Simulcasts:** WSCT & WBMV. **Owner:** Illinois Bible Institute, c/o Lake Williamson Christian Conference Ctr. 17280 Lakeside Dr., Carlinville, IL 62626, Ph: (217)854-4820. **Founded:** 1975. **Operating Hours**: Continuous; 100% local. **ADI**: St. Louis, MO (Mt. Vernon, IL). **Wattage**: 50,000. **Ad Rates:** Noncommercial.

10040 ■ WTSG-FM - 90.1
PO Box 140
Carlinville, IL 62626
Phone: (217)854-4800
Format: Gospel. **Founded:** Sept. 08, 2006. **Wattage**: 5,000.

WVNL-FM - See Vandalia, IL

CARLYLE

Clinton Co. Clinton Co. (SW). 50 m E of East St. Louis. Large Lake attraction. Oil well. Manufactures placemats, infant's shoes, steel fabrication, plastic products. Diversified farming. Dairy production.

10041 ■ WDLJ-FM - 97.5
16808 Old Hwy. 50
Carlyle, IL 62231
Phone: (618)594-2620
Fax: (618)594-2569
Format: Classic Rock. **Operating Hours**: Continuous. **Key Personnel:** Bruce Loyd, Gen. Mgr., bruce@wdlj.com. **Ad Rates:** Advertising accepted; rates available upon request. **Mailing address:** PO Box 2, Carlyle, IL 62231. **URL:** http://www.wdlj.com.

CARMI

White Co White Co. White Co. (SE). 5 m E of Enfield. White Co. (SC). 45 m ESE of Mt. Vernon. Bottling plant, grain elevator.

10042 ■ WROY-AM - 1460
PO Box 400
Carmi, IL 62821
Phone: (618)382-4161
Fax: (618)382-4162
Format: Country. **Simulcasts:** 12 midnight to 5 am. **Networks:** RFD Illinois; ABC. **Founded:** 1948. **Operating Hours:** Continuous; 10% network, 90% local. **ADI**: Evansville, IN (Madisonville, KY). **Wattage**: 1,000. **Ad Rates:** $9.75 for 30 seconds; $13 for 60 seconds. WRUL-FM. **URL:** http://www.wrul.com.

10043 ■ WRUL-FM - 97.3
PO Box 400
Carmi, IL 62821
Phone: (618)382-4161
Fax: (618)382-4162
Format: Country. **Simulcasts:** WROY. **Networks:** ABC; AP. **Founded:** 1951. **Formerly:** WROY-FM. **Operating Hours:** Continuous; 95% network, 5% local. **ADI**: Evansville, IN (Madisonville, KY). **Wattage:** 50,000. **Ad Rates:** $11-14.25 for 30 seconds; $14.25-17.25 for 60

seconds. **URL:** http://pressreleasejet.com.

CAROL STREAM

DuPage Co.

10044 ■ Books & Culture
Christianity Today International
465 Gundersen Dr.
Carol Stream, IL 60188-2415
Phone: (630)260-6200
Fax: (630)260-0114
Free: 877-247-4787
Publication E-mail: bceditor@booksandculture.com
Analysis of the books and ideas that shape society from an evangelical Protestant viewpoint. **Freq:** Bimonthly. **Print Method:** Offset. **Trim Size:** 10 3/4 x 14 5/8. **Key Personnel:** John Wilson, Editor; David Neff, Executive Editor. **ISSN:** 1082--8931 (print). **Subscription Rates:** $29.95 Individuals. **URL:** http://www.booksandculture.com. **Remarks:** Accepts advertising. **Circ:** Non-paid 6009.

10045 ■ Christianity Today: A Magazine of Evangelical Conviction
Christianity Today International
465 Gundersen Dr.
Carol Stream, IL 60188-2415
Phone: (630)260-6200
Fax: (630)260-0114
Free: 877-247-4787
Publication E-mail: letters@christianitytoday.com
Religious magazine. **Freq:** Monthly. **Print Method:** Offset. **Trim Size:** 8 x 10 3/4. **Cols./Page:** 3. **Col. Width:** 2 1/4 inches. **Col. Depth:** 10 inches. **Key Personnel:** Mark Galli, Managing Editor; David Neff, Editor-in-Chief. **ISSN:** 0009--5753 (print). **Subscription Rates:** $24.99 Individuals; $44.99 Two years; $59.99 Individuals 3 years. **URL:** http://www.christianitytoday.com. **Ad Rates:** BW $6673; 4C $7637. **Remarks:** Accepts advertising. **Circ:** ‡140,000.

10046 ■ Constructech
Specialty Publishing Co.
135 E St. Charles Rd., Ste. D
Carol Stream, IL 60188
Phone: (630)933-0844
Fax: (630)933-0845
Magazine covering construction technology for top executives. **Freq:** Annual. **Key Personnel:** Mike Carrozzo, Executive Editor; Peggy Smedley, Director, Editorial, President; Laura Black, Editor, phone: (630)933-0844. **URL:** http://constructech.com. **Remarks:** Accepts advertising. **Circ:** (Not Reported).

10047 ■ Global Cosmetic Industry: The Business Magazine for the Global Beauty Industry
Allured Business Media
336 Gundersen Dr., Ste. A
Carol Stream, IL 60188-2403
Phone: (630)653-2155
Fax: (630)653-2192
Publisher's E-mail: customerservice@allured.com
Trade publication covering the cosmetics industry worldwide. **Freq:** 9/year. **Print Method:** Web offset. **Trim Size:** 8.188 x 10.875. **Key Personnel:** Jeff Falk, Editor-in-Chief, phone: (630)344-6071. **ISSN:** 1523--9470 (print). **URL:** http://www.gcimagazine.com; http://www.allured.com/our-markets/cosmetics-and-personal-care/#market-316. **Ad Rates:** 4C $6,139. **Remarks:** Accepts advertising. **Circ:** △**15017**.

10048 ■ Ignite Your Faith: Ignite/College Guide
Christianity Today International
465 Gundersen Dr.
Carol Stream, IL 60188-2415
Phone: (630)260-6200
Fax: (630)260-0114
Free: 877-247-4787
Publication E-mail: iyf@igniteyourfaith.com
Magazine for high school and early college students espousing Christian-centered values and faith. **Freq:** 10/year. **Print Method:** Offset. **Trim Size:** 8 x 10 3/4. **Cols./Page:** 3. **Col. Width:** 2 1/4 inches. **Col. Depth:** 10 inches. **Key Personnel:** Billy Graham, Founder; Harold B. Smith, Editor-in-Chief. **ISSN:** 0008--2538 (print). **URL:** http://www.christianitytoday.com/iyf. **Formerly:** Campus Life. **Ad Rates:** BW $251; 4C $6647. **Remarks:** Accepts advertising. **Circ:** (Not Reported).

10049 ■ Leadership: A Practical Journal for Church Leaders
Christianity Today International
465 Gundersen Dr.
Carol Stream, IL 60188-2415
Phone: (630)260-6200
Fax: (630)260-0114
Free: 877-247-4787
Publication E-mail: ljeditor@leadershipjournal.net
Christian ministry leadership journal. **Freq:** Quarterly. **Print Method:** Offset. **Trim Size:** 8 1/2 x 11. **Cols./Page:** 3 and 2. **Col. Width:** 27 and 36 nonpareils. **Col. Depth:** 140 agate lines. **Key Personnel:** Marshall Shelley, Editor; Skye Jethani, Managing Editor. **ISSN:** 0199--7661 (print). **Subscription Rates:** $24.99 Individuals; $28 Other countries. **URL:** http://www.christianitytoday.com/le/. **Ad Rates:** BW $2952. **Remarks:** Accepts advertising. **Circ:** Combined 48000.

10050 ■ Men of Integrity: Your Daily Guide to the Bible and Prayer
Christianity Today International
465 Gundersen Dr.
Carol Stream, IL 60188-2415
Phone: (630)260-6200
Fax: (630)260-0114
Free: 877-247-4787
A pocket-size daily devotional guide that applies biblical truth to the specific gritty issues men face. **Freq:** Bimonthly. **Print Method:** Offset. **Trim Size:** 4 x 6 3/8. **Cols./Page:** 2. **Col. Width:** 1 1/2 inches. **Col. Depth:** 5 7/8 inches. **Key Personnel:** Christopher Lutes, Editor. **ISSN:** 1524--1122 (print). **Subscription Rates:** $19.99 Individuals 1 year; $34.99 Two years; $39.99 Individuals 3 years. **URL:** http://www.christianitytoday.com/moi. **Remarks:** Accepts advertising. **Circ:** (Not Reported).

10051 ■ Monthly Prayer Journal
The Evangelical Alliance Mission
400 S Main Pl.
Carol Stream, IL 60188
Phone: (630)653-5300
Fax: (630)653-1826
Free: 800-343-3144
Journal containing collections of people seeking guidance and assistance through prayer support. **Freq:** Monthly latest issue April 2016. **Alt. Formats:** PDF. **URL:** http://team.org/blog/category/prayer-journals. **Remarks:** Advertising not accepted. **Circ:** (Not Reported).

10052 ■ M2M Premier
Specialty Publishing Co.
135 E St. Charles Rd., Ste. D
Carol Stream, IL 60188
Phone: (630)933-0844
Fax: (630)933-0845
Trade publication covering the machine-to-machine communication market, including many types of communication such as machine-to-machine, machine-to-man, man-to-machine, machine-to-mobile, and mobile-to-machine. **Freq:** 7/yr including December sourcebook. **Key Personnel:** Peggy Smedley, Publisher. **URL:** http://connectedworld.com/m2m-premier. **Remarks:** Accepts advertising. **Circ:** (Not Reported).

10053 ■ Produce Blueprints
Blue Book Services Inc.
845 E Geneva Rd.
Carol Stream, IL 60188
Phone: (630)668-3500
Journal covering the fresh produce supply chain. **Freq:** Quarterly. **Subscription Rates:** Free. **URL:** http://www.producebluebook.com. **Remarks:** Accepts advertising. **Circ:** (Not Reported).

10054 ■ TEAM Horizons Magazine
The Evangelical Alliance Mission
400 S Main Pl.
Carol Stream, IL 60188
Phone: (630)653-5300
Fax: (630)653-1826
Free: 800-343-3144
Magazine featuring stories from the field of what God is doing among the nations. **Freq:** Semiannual latest issue Summer 2015. **Alt. Formats:** PDF. **URL:** http://horizons.team.org. **Remarks:** Advertising not accepted. **Circ:** (Not Reported).

10055 ■ Today's Christian Woman
Christianity Today International
465 Gundersen Dr.
Carol Stream, IL 60188-2415
Phone: (630)260-6200
Fax: (630)260-0114
Free: 877-247-4787
Religious magazine for contemporary Christian women. **Freq:** Biweekly. **Print Method:** Offset. **Trim Size:** 8 x 10 3/4. **Cols./Page:** 3. **Col. Width:** 2 1/4 inches. **Col. Depth:** 10 inches. **Key Personnel:** Harold B. Smith, Vice President; Ginger Kolbaba, Editor; Marian Liautaud, Managing Editor; Amy Simpson, Publisher; Ashley Moore, Coordinator; Jane Johnson Struck, Editor; Camerin Courtney, Managing Editor; Harold L. Myra, Publisher; Raelynn Eickhoff, Coordinator. **ISSN:** 0163--1799 (print). **Subscription Rates:** $14.99 Individuals; $24.99 Two years; $29.99 Individuals 3 years. **Alt. Formats:** PDF. **URL:** http://www.todayschristianwoman.com; http://www.kyria.com/. **Ad Rates:** BW $4818.65; 4C $6025.65; PCI $330. **Remarks:** Accepts advertising. **Circ:** Paid ‡256000, Non-paid ‡6892.

CARTERVILLE

Williamson Co. Williamson Co. (SC). 10 m W of Marion.

10056 ■ American Brittany
American Brittany Club, Directors Chapter
c/o Mary Jo Trimble, Secretary
10370 Fleming Rd.
Carterville, IL 62918
Phone: (618)985-2336
Freq: Monthly. **Key Personnel:** Robert Gordon, Managing Editor; Ron Smith, Publisher. **Subscription Rates:** $55 U.S. and Canada first class mail; $4 Single issue; $30 Individuals; $30 /year; $55 U.S. first class postage; C$75 Canada; Included in membership. **URL:** http://clubs.akc.org/brit/Magazine/Rates&Info.htm. **Ad Rates:** BW $120; 4C $260. **Remarks:** Advertising accepted; rates available upon request. **Circ:** 3300.

KPOB-TV - See Poplar Bluff, MO

10057 ■ WCIL-FM - 101.5
1431 Country Aire Dr.
Carterville, IL 62918
Phone: (618)985-4843
Free: 800-341-1015
Format: Contemporary Hit Radio (CHR). **Key Personnel:** Jon Brookmyer, Chief Engineer, jonb@riverradio.net. **Ad Rates:** Noncommercial. **URL:** http://www.cilfm.com.

10058 ■ WJPF-AM - 1340
1431 Country Aire Dr.
Carterville, IL 62918
Phone: (618)985-4843
Fax: (618)985-6529
Format: News. **Owner:** River Radio, Not Available; Max Broadcast Group Holdings, LLC, 230 E High St., Charlottesville, VA 22902, Ph: (434)979-2070, Fax: (434)979-1145. **Founded:** 1940. **Operating Hours:** Continuous. **Key Personnel:** Steve Falat, Sales Mgr., stevef@riverradio.net; Tom Miller, Dir. of Programs, tomm@riverradio.net. **Wattage:** 1,000. **Ad Rates:** $4-6 for 15 seconds; $6-8 for 30 seconds; $12 for 30 seconds; $8-10 for 60 seconds; $19 for 60 seconds. Combined advertising rates available with $16.15-$28.99 for 30 seconds; $19.34-$31.79 for 60 seconds. Combined advertising rates available with WCIL-FM. **URL:** http://www.wjpf.com/.

10059 ■ WOOZ-FM - 100
1431 Country Aire Dr.
Carterville, IL 62918
Phone: (618)985-4843
Free: 800-455-1100
Format: Hot Country. **Networks:** Unistar. **Owner:** Zimmer Communications, PO Box 1749, Cape Girardeau, MO 63702-1749. **Founded:** 1947. **Formerly:** WEBQ-FM. **Operating Hours:** Continuous. **Key Personnel:** Tom Miller, Operations Mgr., tomm@riverradio.net; Steve Falat, Gen. Mgr., stevef@riverradio.net; Tracy McSherry-McKown, Dir. of Programs, tracym@riverradio.net. **Wattage:** 50,000. **Ad Rates:** Advertising accepted; rates available upon request. **URL:** http://www.z100fm.com.

10060 ■ WSIL-TV - 3
1416 Country Aire
Carterville, IL 62918

Circulation: ★ = AAM; △ or • = BPA; ♦ = CAC; ❑ = VAC; ⊕ = PO Statement; ‡ = Publisher's Report; Boldface figures = sworn; Light figures = estimated.

Phone: (618)985-2333
Fax: (618)985-3709
Format: Commercial TV. **Simulcasts:** KPOB-TV. **Networks:** ABC. **Owner:** WSIL, Inc., at above address. **Founded:** 1953. **ADI:** Paducah,KY-Cape Girardeau,MO-Marion,IL. **Key Personnel:** Steve Wheeler, Mgr., swheeler@wsiltv.com; Mike Snuffer, Contact, msnuffer@wsiltv.com; Darren Kinnard, Sports Dir., dkinnard@wsiltv.com; Bonnie Wheeler, Contact, bwheeler@wsiltv.com. **Ad Rates:** Advertising accepted; rates available upon request. **URL:** http://www.wsiltv.com.

10061 ■ WXLT-FM - 103.5
1431 Country Air Dr.
Carterville, IL 62918
Phone: (618)985-4843
Fax: (618)985-6529
Format: Adult Contemporary. **Owner:** Mississippi River Radio-Marion/Carbondale, Not Available. **URL:** http://www.wxlt.com.

CARTHAGE

Hancock Co. Hancock Co. (W). 14 m E of Keokuk, Iowa. Agriculture. Livestock, corn.

10062 ■ Hancock County Journal Pilot
Hancock County Journal Pilot
31 N Washington St.
Carthage, IL 62321
Phone: (217)357-2149
Fax: (217)357-2177
Community newspaper. **Freq:** Weekly. **Print Method:** Offset. **Trim Size:** 13 x 21 1/2. **Cols./Page:** 8. **Col. Width:** 1 1/2 inches. **Col. Depth:** 21 1/2 inches. **Key Personnel:** Mark Smidt, Publisher; Hollis Dean, General Manager, Manager, Sales; Zach Short, Editor. **USPS:** 234-220. **Subscription Rates:** $29 Individuals in County; $41 Out of country; $29 Individuals online. **URL:** http://www.journalpilot.com. **Mailing address:** PO Box 478, Carthage, IL 62321. **Ad Rates:** GLR $0.60; BW $946; 4C $150; SAU $8.80; PCI $5.50. **Remarks:** Accepts advertising. **Circ:** Paid ‡4000.

10063 ■ KMDY-FM - 90.9
521 Main St.
Carthage, IL 62321
Fax: (217)357-3001
Free: 888-357-5639
Email: kmdy@adams.net
Format: Religious. **Owner:** Moody Broadcasting Network, 820 N La Salle Blvd., Chicago, IL 60610, Ph: (312)329-4300, Fax: (312)329-4339, Free: 800-356-6639. **Wattage**: 7,700. **URL:** http://www.kmdy.org.

10064 ■ WCAZ-AM - 990
PO Box 498
Carthage, IL 62321
Phone: (217)357-3128
Fax: (217)357-2014
Free: 888-990-2225
Format: Talk. **Networks:** UPI; RFD Illinois. **Owner:** Ralla Broadcasting, Inc., at above address. **Founded:** 1918. **Operating Hours**: Continuous; 25% network, 75% local. **Key Personnel:** Keith Yex, Contact; Rob Dunham, Contact; Keith Yex, Contact; Rob Dunham, Contact. **Wattage**: 1,000. **Ad Rates:** Noncommercial. **URL:** http://www.wcazam990.com.

CENTRALIA

Marion Co. Marion Co. (S). 65 m E of St. Louis, Mo. Manufactures plastics, fiberglass Laminates, pipe, casting, armatures, potato chips, candy, dresses. Meat packing. Fruit, dairy, poultry, grain farms.

10065 ■ WIBV-FM - 102.1
PO Box 1626
Centralia, IL 62801
Phone: (618)249-6025
Format: Country. **Owner:** Stratemeyer Media, 6120 Waldo Church Rd., Metropolis, IL 62960, Ph: (618)564-9836, Fax: (618)564-3202. **Operating Hours**: Continuous. **Wattage**: 25,000. **Ad Rates:** Advertising accepted; rates available upon request. **URL:** http://www.wibv102.com.

CHAMPAIGN

Champaign Co. Champaign Co. (E). 125 m SW of Chicago. University of Illinois is situated equally in Urbana and Champaign. Manufactures computer software, castings, drop forgings, paper cup products, road machinery, concrete culverts, butter, vegetable shortening, athletic equipment, railroad registers. Soybean oil processing. Agriculture. Corn.

10066 ■ The Advisor
National Association of Advisors for the Health Professions, Inc.
108 Hessel Blvd., Ste. 101
Champaign, IL 61820-6574
Phone: (217)355-0063
Fax: (217)355-1287
Publisher's E-mail: naahp.membership@naahp.org
Journal publishing articles on health professions advising. **Freq:** Quarterly. **URL:** http://www.naahp.org/Publications/TheAdvisorOnline.aspx. **Remarks:** Advertising not accepted. **Circ:** (Not Reported).

10067 ■ American Journal of Theology & Philosophy
University of Illinois Press
1325 S Oak St., MC-566
Champaign, IL 61820-6903
Phone: (217)333-0950
Fax: (217)244-8082
Publisher's E-mail: uipress@uillinois.edu
Peer-reviewed journal focusing on topics related to theology and philosophy. **Freq:** 3/year. **Key Personnel:** Michael S. Hogue, Editor. **ISSN:** 0194--3448 (print); **EISSN:** 2156--4795 (electronic). **Subscription Rates:** $45 Individuals print + online; $125 Institutions print + online; $109 Institutions print or online; $33 Single issue. **URL:** http://www.press.uillinois.edu/journals/ajtp.html. **Ad Rates:** BW $200. **Remarks:** Accepts advertising. **Circ:** (Not Reported).

10068 ■ Arboriculture & Urban Forestry
International Society of Arboriculture
2101 W Park Ct.
Champaign, IL 61821
Phone: (217)355-9411
Fax: (217)355-9516
Free: 888-472-8733
Publisher's E-mail: isa@isa-arbor.com
Peer-reviewed journal focusing on dissemination of knowledge in the science and art of planting and caring for trees in the urban environmenton tree care research. **Freq:** Bimonthly. **Trim Size:** 7 1/4 x 9 3/4. **Cols./Page:** 2. **Key Personnel:** Aaron Bynum, Managing Editor. **ISSN:** 0278--5226 (print). **Subscription Rates:** $160 Individuals 1 year. **URL:** http://www.isa-arbor.com/education/publications/auf.aspx. **Formerly**: Journal of Arboriculture. **Mailing address:** PO Box 3129, Champaign, IL 61826-3129. **Remarks:** Advertising not accepted. **Circ:** Controlled 11500.

10069 ■ Arborist News
International Society of Arboriculture
2101 W Park Ct.
Champaign, IL 61821
Phone: (217)355-9411
Fax: (217)355-9516
Free: 888-472-8733
Publisher's E-mail: isa@isa-arbor.com
Freq: Bimonthly. **URL:** http://www.isa-arbor.com/education/publications/arboristnews.aspx. **Mailing address:** PO Box 3129, Champaign, IL 61826-3129. **Remarks:** Accepts advertising. **Circ:** 22,000.

10070 ■ Arborist News Magazine
International Society of Arboriculture
2101 W Park Ct.
Champaign, IL 61821
Phone: (217)355-9411
Fax: (217)355-9516
Free: 888-472-8733
Publication E-mail: editor@isa-arbor.com
Trade magazine covering tree care. **Freq:** Bimonthly. **Print Method:** Sheetfed offset. **Trim Size:** 8 1/4 x 10 7/8. **Cols./Page:** 3. **Key Personnel:** Kathy Ashmore, Coordinator, phone: (217)355-9411. **ISSN:** 1542--2399 (print). **Subscription Rates:** $7 Nonmembers single issue. **URL:** http://www.isa-arbor.com/education/publications/arboristNews.aspx. **Mailing address:** PO Box 3129, Champaign, IL 61826-3129. **Ad Rates:** BW $2,275; 4C $3,075. **Remarks:** Accepts advertising. **Circ:** 22000.

10071 ■ The Bulletin of the Center for Children's Books
Graduate School of Library and Information Sciences
501 E Daniel St., Rm. 112
Champaign, IL 61820-6211
Phone: (217)333-3280
Fax: (217)244-3302
Publication E-mail: bccb@illinois.edu
Journal containing concise summaries and critical evaluations of books for children. **Freq:** 11/year except August. **Print Method:** Offset. **Trim Size:** 6 x 9. **Cols./Page:** 1. **Col. Width:** 70 nonpareils. **Col. Depth:** 110 agate lines. **Key Personnel:** Deborah Stevenson, Editor; Betsy Hearne, Professor. **ISSN:** 0008--9036 (print); **EISSN:** 1558--6766 (electronic). **Subscription Rates:** $55 Individuals print; $99 Individuals /2 years (print); $108 Institutions print; $216 Institutions /2 years (print); $62 Individuals electronic; $111.60 Individuals /2 years (electronic). **URL:** http://bccb.lis.illinois.edu; http://www.lis.illinois.edu/newsroom/publications/bulletin; http://www.press.jhu.edu/journals/bulletin_of_the_center_for_childrens_books. **Ad Rates:** BW $325. **Remarks:** Accepts advertising. **Circ:** Combined ‡1876.

10072 ■ Bulletin of the Council for Research in Music Education
Bulletin of the Council for Research in Music Education
University of Illinois Press
325 S Oak St.
Champaign, IL 61820
Phone: (217)244-0626
Fax: (217)244-9910
Free: 866-244-0626
Publisher's E-mail: journals@uillinois.edu
Music education journal. **Founded:** 1963. **Freq:** Quarterly. **Print Method:** Offset. **Trim Size:** 6 x 9. **Cols./Page:** 1. **Col. Width:** 72 nonpareils. **Col. Depth:** 126 agate lines. **Key Personnel:** Janet R. Barrett, Editor; Eve Harwood, Editor; Tina Happ, Business Manager. **ISSN:** 0010-9894 (print); **EISSN:** 2162-7223 (electronic). **Subscription Rates:** $48 Individuals print only; electronic only; $70 Individuals print and electronic; $80 Institutions print only; electronic only; $122 Institutions print and electronic; $11 Canada and Mexico; $35 Other countries; $25 back issues. **URL:** http://bcrme.press.illinois.edu/about.html. **Ad Rates:** BW $200. **Remarks:** Advertising not accepted. **Circ:** Paid ‡1000, Non-paid ‡100, ‡600.

10073 ■ Comparative Labor Law & Policy Journal
University of Illinois College of Law
116 Law Bldg.
Champaign, IL 61820
Scholarly journal covering international comparison issues in labor law and employment policies. **Freq:** Quarterly. **Print Method:** Offset litho. **Trim Size:** 6 3/4 x 10. **Cols./Page:** 1. **Col. Width:** 28 picas. **Col. Depth:** 48 picas. **Key Personnel:** Stacey Ballmes, Managing Editor, phone: (217)333-9852; Prof. Matthew W. Finkin, Editor; Sanford Jacoby, Editor. **ISSN:** 1095--6654 (print). **Subscription Rates:** $40 U.S.; $50 Other countries; $25 Individuals online only; $28 Members. **URL:** http://www.law.illinois.edu/publications/cllpj/board.html. **Formerly**: Comparative Labor Law Journal. **Remarks:** Accepts advertising. **Circ:** Combined 650.

10074 ■ Comparative Labor Law and Policy Journal
University of Illinois College of Law
504 E Pennsylvania Ave.
Champaign, IL 61820
Phone: (217)333-0931
Fax: (217)244-1478
Journal containing articles on issues in labor law, employment policy and social security. **Key Personnel:** Prof. Matthew W. Finkin, Editor. **Subscription Rates:** $40 U.S.; $50 Other countries. **URL:** http://www.law.illinois.edu/publications/cllpj. **Circ:** (Not Reported).

10075 ■ The Daily Illini
Illini Media Co.
512 E Green St.
Champaign, IL 61820
Phone: (217)337-8300
Fax: (217)337-8303
Publication E-mail: news@dailyillini.com
Collegiate newspaper. **Freq:** Daily (morn.). **Print Method:** Offset. **Cols./Page:** 5. **Col. Width:** 24

nonpareils. **Col. Depth:** 224 agate lines. **Key Personnel:** Lilyan Levant, Publisher, phone: (217)337-8310; Kit Donahue, Director, Production, phone: (217)337-8323; Johnathan Hettinger, Editor-in-Chief. **Subscription Rates:** $50 Individuals. **URL:** http://www.dailyillini.com. **Mailing address:** PO Box 497, Champaign, IL 61820. **Ad Rates:** PCI $12.90. **Remarks:** Advertising accepted; rates available upon request. **Circ:** Combined ‡27000.

10076 ■ Elder Law Journal
University of Illinois College of Law
504 E Pennsylvania Ave.
Champaign, IL 61820
Phone: (217)333-0931
Fax: (217)244-1478
Journal containing articles on legal laws pertinent to the elderly. **Freq:** Semiannual spring and fall. **Key Personnel:** Ashley Dus, Editor-in-Chief. **Subscription Rates:** $25 U.S.; $35 Other countries. **URL:** http://publish.illinois.edu/elderlawjournal. **Circ:** (Not Reported).

10077 ■ Feminist Teacher
University of Illinois Press
1325 S Oak St., MC-566
Champaign, IL 61820-6903
Phone: (217)333-0950
Fax: (217)244-8082
Publisher's E-mail: uipress@uillinois.edu
Journal covering feminism-related topics. **Freq:** 3/year. **Key Personnel:** Gail E. Cohee, Editor; Theresa D. Kemp, Editor; Monica Barron, Editor. **ISSN:** 0882--4843 (print); **EISSN:** 1934--6034 (electronic). **Subscription Rates:** $45 Individuals print or online; $50 Individuals print + online; $127 Institutions print or online; $139 Institutions print + online; $15 Single issue; $20 Students online only. **URL:** http://www.press.uillinois.edu/journals/ft.html. **Ad Rates:** BW $200. **Remarks:** Accepts advertising. **Circ:** 350.

10078 ■ Illinois Business Law Journal
University of Illinois College of Law
504 E Pennsylvania Ave.
Champaign, IL 61820
Phone: (217)333-0931
Fax: (217)244-1478
Journal containing information on recent developments affecting business law. **Key Personnel:** Keith M. St. Aubin, Editor-in-Chief. **URL:** http://www.law.illinois.edu/bljournal. **Circ:** (Not Reported).

10079 ■ Illinois Classical Studies
Stipes Publishing L.L.C.
204 W University Ave.
Champaign, IL 61820
Phone: (217)356-8391
Fax: (217)356-5753
Publisher's E-mail: stipes01@sbcglobal.net
Scholarly journal covering classical studies. **Freq:** Annual. **Print Method:** Offset. **Trim Size:** 6 x 9. **Cols./Page:** 1. **Col. Width:** 4 1/4 inches. **Col. Depth:** 7 inches. **Key Personnel:** Danuta Shanzer, Editor. **ISSN:** 0353--1923 (print); **EISSN:** 2328--5265 (electronic). **Subscription Rates:** $55 Individuals print only; $65 Individuals online only; $91 Individuals print + online; $88 Institutions print only; $104 Institutions online only; $134 Institutions print + online. **URL:** http://www.press.uillinois.edu/journals/ics.html. **Mailing address:** PO Box 526, Champaign, IL 61820. **Remarks:** Advertising not accepted. **Circ:** (Not Reported).

10080 ■ Illinois Technograph
Illini Media Co.
512 E Green St.
Champaign, IL 61820
Phone: (217)337-8300
Fax: (217)337-8303
Publisher's E-mail: sales@illinimedia.com
Magazine for students, faculty and affiliates of the College of Engineering at the University of Illinois. **Freq:** Quarterly during the academic year. **Print Method:** Offset. **Trim Size:** 8 1/2 x 11. **Cols./Page:** 3. **Col. Width:** 27 nonpareils. **Col. Depth:** 140 agate lines. **Key Personnel:** Darshan Patel, Editor-in-Chief; David Ng, Editor; Nabeel Ahmed, Executive Editor; Mary Cory, Publisher; Jon Huff, Designer; Erik Wotring, Writer; Rahim Sultanally, Writer; Nikhil Prashar, Managing Editor. **USPS:** 258-760. **URL:** http://www.readtechnograph.com; http://technograph.illinimedia.com. **Mailing address:** PO Box 497, Champaign, IL 61820. **Ad Rates:** BW $550; 4C $1025; PCI $13.15. **Remarks:** Accepts advertising. **Circ:** Paid ‡800, Non-paid ‡4,000.

10081 ■ The International Journal of Accounting
Elsevier Inc.
c/o Prof. A. Rashad Abdel-Khalik, Ed.
University of Illinois
320 Commerce W
1206 S 6th St.
Champaign, IL 61820
Publisher's E-mail: healthpermissions@elsevier.com
Scholarly journal covering global accounting issues. **Freq:** Quarterly. **Trim Size:** 7 x 10. **Cols./Page:** 1. **Col. Width:** 5 inches. **Col. Depth:** 8 inches. **Key Personnel:** Prof. A. Rashad Abdel-Khalik, Editor; I. Haw, Editor; E. Feroz, Editor; A. Charitou, Editor. **ISSN:** 0020-7063 (print). **Subscription Rates:** $152 Individuals print; $613 Institutions print; $612 Institutions online. **URL:** http://www.journals.elsevier.com/the-international-journal-of-accounting. **Circ:** (Not Reported).

10082 ■ International Journal of Aquatic Research and Education
Human Kinetics Inc.
1607 N Market St.
Champaign, IL 61820
Phone: (217)351-5076
Fax: (217)351-1549
Free: 800-747-4457
Publisher's E-mail: info@hkusa.com
Peer-reviewed journal dedicated to advancing the knowledge and practices of aquatic professionals. **Freq:** Quarterly. **Key Personnel:** Kathryn Azevedo, Board Member; Michael Beach, Board Member; Bruce Erhart Becker, Board Member; Ellen Broach, Board Member; Mary E. Sanders, Board Member; Jonathan B. Smith, Board Member; Stephen J. Langendorfer, Editor. **ISSN:** 1932--9997 (print); **EISSN:** 1932--9253 (electronic). **Subscription Rates:** $89 Individuals online and print; $519 Institutions online and print; $72 Students online and print; $69 Individuals online; $52 Students online; $419 Institutions online. **URL:** http://journals.humankinetics.com/IJARE. **Mailing address:** PO Box 5076, Champaign, IL 61825-5076. **Ad Rates:** BW $399; 4C $599. **Remarks:** Accepts advertising. **Circ:** (Not Reported).

10083 ■ International Journal of Sport Nutrition & Exercise Metabolism
Human Kinetics Inc.
1607 N Market St.
Champaign, IL 61820
Phone: (217)351-5076
Fax: (217)351-1549
Free: 800-747-4457
Publisher's E-mail: info@hkusa.com
Journal advancing the understanding of nutritional aspects of human physical and athletic performance. **Freq:** Bimonthly February, April, June, August, October, December. **Print Method:** Offset. **Trim Size:** 6 x 9. **Key Personnel:** Ronald Maughan, PhD, Editor, phone: (44)150 9226329, fax: (44)150 9226301; Emily M. Haymes, Editor; Elizabeth Broad, Associate Editor. **ISSN:** 1526-484X (print); **EISSN:** 1543-2742 (electronic). **Subscription Rates:** $129 Individuals print and online; $780 Institutions print and online; $104 Students print and online; $99 Individuals online; $619 Institutions online; $74 Students online. **URL:** http://journals.humankinetics.com/IJSNEM. **Mailing address:** PO Box 5076, Champaign, IL 61825-5076. **Ad Rates:** BW $300. **Remarks:** Accepts advertising. **Circ:** (Not Reported).

10084 ■ International Journal of Sports Physiology and Performance
Human Kinetics Inc.
1607 N Market St.
Champaign, IL 61820
Phone: (217)351-5076
Fax: (217)351-1549
Free: 800-747-4457
Publisher's E-mail: info@hkusa.com
Journal dedicated to sport and exercise physiologists, sports-performance researchers, and other sports scientists. **Freq:** Bimonthly January, March, May, July, September and November. **Print Method:** Offset. **Trim Size:** 6 x 9. **Cols./Page:** 6. **Col. Width:** 26 nonpareils. **Col. Depth:** 294 agate lines. **Key Personnel:** Jonathon Fowles, Board Member; Carl Foster, Editor; David Pyne, PhD, Editor; Inigo Mujika, Associate Editor; Andrew Jones, Board Member; Will Hopkins, Board Member; Inigo Mujika, PhD, Associate Editor. **ISSN:** 1555--0265 (print); **EISSN:** 1555--0273 (electronic). **Subscription Rates:** $149 Individuals print + online; $119 Students print + online; $899 Institutions print + online; $119 Individuals electronic only; $739 Institutions electronic only; $89 Students electronic only. **URL:** http://journals.humankinetics.com/IJSPP. **Mailing address:** PO Box 5076, Champaign, IL 61825-5076. **Circ:** (Not Reported).

10085 ■ Journal of Aging and Physical Activity
International Coalition for Aging and Physical Activity
1607 N Market St.
Champaign, IL 61820-2220
Publisher's E-mail: aacc@hkusa.com
Journal examining the relationship between physical activity and the aging process. **Freq:** Quarterly Bimonthly January, April, July, October. **Print Method:** Offset. **Trim Size:** 6 x 9. **Cols./Page:** 1. **Col. Width:** 65 nonpareils. **Col. Depth:** 108 agate lines. **Key Personnel:** Diane E. Whaley, Editor; Philip D. Chilibeck, Editor. **ISSN:** 1063--8652 (print); **EISSN:** 1543-267X (electronic). **Subscription Rates:** $101 Individuals online and print; $81 Students online and print; $609 Institutions online and print; $81 Individuals online only; $61 Students online only; $499 Institutions online only; $91 Individuals online and print subscription 1 yr; $68 Students online and print subscription 1 yr; $173 Individuals online and print subscription 2 yrs; $130 Students online and print subscription 2 yrs; $246 Individuals online and print subscription 3 yrs; $184 Students online and print subscription 3 yrs. **URL:** http://journals.humankinetics.com/JAPA; http://journals.humankinetics.com/journal/japa. **Mailing address:** PO Box 5076, Champaign, IL 61825-5076. **Ad Rates:** BW $300. **Remarks:** Accepts advertising. **Circ:** (Not Reported).

10086 ■ Journal of Aging and Physical Activity
Human Kinetics Inc.
1607 N Market St.
Champaign, IL 61820
Phone: (217)351-5076
Fax: (217)351-1549
Free: 800-747-4457
Publisher's E-mail: aacc@hkusa.com
Journal examining the relationship between physical activity and the aging process. **Freq:** Quarterly Bimonthly January, April, July, October. **Print Method:** Offset. **Trim Size:** 6 x 9. **Cols./Page:** 1. **Col. Width:** 65 nonpareils. **Col. Depth:** 108 agate lines. **Key Personnel:** Diane E. Whaley, Editor; Philip D. Chilibeck, Editor. **ISSN:** 1063--8652 (print); **EISSN:** 1543-267X (electronic). **Subscription Rates:** $101 Individuals online and print; $81 Students online and print; $609 Institutions online and print; $81 Individuals online only; $61 Students online only; $499 Institutions online only; $91 Individuals online and print subscription 1 yr; $68 Students online and print subscription 1 yr; $173 Individuals online and print subscription 2 yrs; $130 Students online and print subscription 2 yrs; $246 Individuals online and print subscription 3 yrs; $184 Students online and print subscription 3 yrs. **URL:** http://journals.humankinetics.com/JAPA; http://journals.humankinetics.com/journal/japa. **Mailing address:** PO Box 5076, Champaign, IL 61825-5076. **Ad Rates:** BW $300. **Remarks:** Accepts advertising. **Circ:** (Not Reported).

10087 ■ Journal of American Folklore: Journal of the American Folklore Society
University of Illinois Press
1325 S Oak St., MC-566
Champaign, IL 61820-6903
Phone: (217)333-0950
Fax: (217)244-8082
Publisher's E-mail: uipress@uillinois.edu
Quarterly Journal deals with articles reflecting current attitudes and issues in folklore and related disciplines. **Freq:** Quarterly. **Print Method:** Offset. **Trim Size:** 6 3/4 x 10. **Cols./Page:** 1. **Col. Width:** 52 nonpareils. **Col. Depth:** 108 agate lines. **Key Personnel:** Ann K. Ferrell, Editor-in-Chief. **ISSN:** 0021--8715 (print); **EISSN:** 1535--1882 (electronic). **Subscription Rates:** $149 Institutions print or electronic; $187 Institutions print & electronic. **URL:** http://www.press.uillinois.edu/journals/jaf.html. **Ad Rates:** BW $330. **Remarks:** Accepts advertising. **Circ:** 1600.

Circulation: ★ = AAM; △ or • = BPA; ♦ = CAC; ❑ = VAC; ⊕ = PO Statement; ‡ = Publisher's Report; Boldface figures = sworn; Light figures = estimated.

10088 ■ Journal of Animal Science
American Society of Animal Science
c/o Greg S. Lewis, Editor-in-Chief
PO Box 7410
Champaign, IL 61826
Publisher's E-mail: asas@asas.org
Professional journal covering animal science. **Freq:** Monthly. **Print Method:** Offset. **Trim Size:** 8 1/2 x 11. **Key Personnel:** Greg S. Lewis, Editor-in-Chief. **ISSN:** 0021--8812 (print); **EISSN:** 1525--3163 (electronic). **Subscription Rates:** $400 Individuals online. **Alt. Formats:** CD-ROM. **URL:** http://www.journalofanimalscience.org. **Remarks:** Advertising not accepted. **Circ:** (Not Reported).

10089 ■ Journal of Applied Poultry Research
Poultry Science Association
1800 S Oak St., Ste. 100
Champaign, IL 61820-6974
Phone: (217)356-5285
Fax: (217)398-4119
Publisher's E-mail: psa@assochq.org
Journal covering original research reports, field reports, and reviews on breeding, hatching, health and disease, layer management, meat bird processing and products, meat bird management, microbiology, food safety, nutrition, environment, sanitation, welfare and economics. **Freq:** Quarterly. **ISSN:** 1537- 0437 (print); **EISSN:** 1056-6171 (electronic). **Subscription Rates:** $300 U.S. /year, print + online; $335 Elsewhere /year, print + online; $162 Individuals online; $37.50 Single issue. **URL:** http://www.poultryscience.org/journal_access.asp?autotry=true&ULnotkn=true. **Remarks:** Advertising not accepted. **Circ:** (Not Reported).

10090 ■ Journal of Dairy Science
American Dairy Science Association
1880 S Oak St., Ste. 100
Champaign, IL 61820-6974
Phone: (217)356-5146
Fax: (217)398-4119
Publisher's E-mail: adsa@assochq.org
Journal devoted to dairy science research. **Freq:** Monthly. **Print Method:** Offset. **Trim Size:** 8 1/2 x 11. **Cols./Page:** 2. **Key Personnel:** Roger D. Shanks, Editor-in-Chief; D. Bannerman, Board Member. **ISSN:** 0022--0302 (print); **EISSN:** 1525--3198 (electronic). **Subscription Rates:** $1150 Institutions print; $850.67 Institutions, other countries ejournal; Included in membership online access. **URL:** http://www.journalofdairyscience.org; http://www.journals.elsevier.com/journal-of-dairy-science. **Remarks:** Advertising not accepted. **Circ:** ‡5062.

10091 ■ Journal of Law, Technology & Policy
University of Illinois College of Law
504 E Pennsylvania Ave.
Champaign, IL 61820
Phone: (217)333-0931
Fax: (217)244-1478
Publication E-mail: law-jltp@illinois.edu
Peer-reviewed journal featuring topics on the intersection between law, technology, and policy. **Freq:** Semiannual. **Key Personnel:** Emily Elizabeth Dory, Editor-in-Chief. **Subscription Rates:** $30 Individuals print; $40 Other countries print. **URL:** http://illinoisjltp.com/journal/. **Circ:** (Not Reported).

10092 ■ Journal of Law, Technology and Policy
University of Illinois College of Law
504 E Pennsylvania Ave.
Champaign, IL 61820
Phone: (217)333-0931
Fax: (217)244-1478
Journal containing articles on legal issues at the intersection of law and technology. **Freq:** Semiannual. **Key Personnel:** Emily Elizabeth Dory, Editor-in-Chief. **Subscription Rates:** $30 Individuals domestic (print); $40 Individuals foreign (print). **URL:** http://illinoisjltp.com/journal. **Circ:** (Not Reported).

10093 ■ Journal of Leisure Research
National Recreation and Park Association
c/o Kimberly J. Shinew, Ed.
Department of Recreation, Sport & Tourism
University of Illinois
104 Huff Hall, 1206 S 4th St.
Champaign, IL 61820
Publisher's E-mail: customerservice@nrpa.org
Key Personnel: Kimberly J. Shinew, Editor. **ISSN:** 0022--2216 (print); **EISSN:** 2159--6417 (electronic). **URL:** http://www.nrpa.org/jlr. **Remarks:** Accepts advertising. **Circ:** (Not Reported).

10094 ■ Journal of Mammalogy
American Society of Mammalogists
Illinois Natural History Survey
1816 S Oak St.
Champaign, IL 61820
Phone: (217)265-7301
Fax: (217)244-0802
Publisher's E-mail: asm@allenpress.com
Magazine covering original research on terrestrial and marine mammals. Official publication of the American Society of Mammalogists. **Freq:** Bimonthly. **Print Method:** Offset. **Key Personnel:** Joseph F. Merritt, Editor; Barbara H. Blake, Editor, phone: (336)334-4965, fax: (336)334-5839; Jane Cigard, Managing Editor. **ISSN:** 0022-2372 (print); **EISSN:** 1545-1542 (electronic). **Subscription Rates:** $294 Institutions online and print; $370 Institutions, other countries online and print. **URL:** http://www.mammalsociety.org/journal-mammalogy; http://www.asmjournals.org/page/information. **Ad Rates:** BW $500. **Remarks:** Advertising accepted; rates available upon request. **Circ:** (Not Reported).

10095 ■ Journal of Park and Recreation Administration: American Academy for Park and Recreation Administration
Sagamore Publishing LLC
804 N Neil St.
Champaign, IL 61820
Publisher's E-mail: books@sagamorepub.com
Scholarly online journal that provides a forum for the analysis of management and organization of the delivery of park, recreation, and leisure services. **Freq:** Quarterly. **Trim Size:** 6 X 9. **Key Personnel:** Dr. Robert Burns, Editor; Denise Anderson, Associate Editor. **ISSN:** 0735--1968 (print). **Subscription Rates:** $80 Individuals online; $100 Individuals print and online; $120 Other countries print and online; $330 Institutions online; $380 Institutions print and online; $410 Institutions, other countries print and online. **URL:** http://www.sagamorejournals.com/jpra. **Remarks:** Advertising not accepted. **Circ:** (Not Reported).

10096 ■ Journal of Seventeenth-Century Music
University of Illinois Press
1325 S Oak St., MC-566
Champaign, IL 61820-6903
Phone: (217)333-0950
Fax: (217)244-8082
Peer-reviewed journal providing a refereed forum for scholarly studies of the musical cultures of the seventeenth century. **Freq:** Annual. **Key Personnel:** Kelley Harness, Editor-in-Chief; Richard Charteris, Board Member. **ISSN:** 1089--747X (print). **URL:** http://sscm-jscm.org. **Remarks:** Advertising not accepted. **Circ:** (Not Reported).

10097 ■ Journal of Sport Management
Human Kinetics Inc.
1607 N Market St.
Champaign, IL 61820
Phone: (217)351-5076
Fax: (217)351-1549
Free: 800-747-4457
Publisher's E-mail: info@hkusa.com
Journal focusing on the theory and application of management to sport, exercise, dance, and play. **Freq:** Bimonthly January, March, May, July, September and November. **Print Method:** Offset. **Trim Size:** 6 x 9. **Cols./Page:** 1. **Col. Width:** 65 nonpareils. **Col. Depth:** 108 agate lines. **Key Personnel:** David Shilbury, Editor-in-Chief. **ISSN:** 0888-4773 (print); **EISSN:** 1543--270X (electronic). **Subscription Rates:** $135 Individuals online and print; $101 Students online and print; $105 Individuals online only; $76 Students online only. **URL:** http://journals.humankinetics.com/jsm. **Mailing address:** PO Box 5076, Champaign, IL 61825-5076. **Ad Rates:** BW $300. **Remarks:** Accepts advertising. **Circ:** Paid 1250.

10098 ■ National Association of Advisors for the Health Professions--The Advisor
National Association of Advisors for the Health Professions, Inc.
108 Hessel Blvd., Ste. 101
Champaign, IL 61820-6574
Phone: (217)355-0063
Fax: (217)355-1287
Publisher's E-mail: naahp.membership@naahp.org
Freq: Quarterly. **ISSN:** 0736- 0436 (print). **Subscription Rates:** Included in membership. **URL:** http://www.naahp.org/Publications/TheAdvisorOnline.aspx. **Remarks:** Advertising not accepted. **Circ:** 1,200.

10099 ■ Perspectives on Work
University of Illinois Press
1325 S Oak St., MC-566
Champaign, IL 61820-6903
Phone: (217)333-0950
Fax: (217)244-8082
Publisher's E-mail: uipress@uillinois.edu
Journal covering industrial relations and human resources. Official publication of the Industrial Relations Research Association. **Freq:** Semiannual June and December. **Key Personnel:** Susan Cass, Editor. **ISSN:** 1534-2976 (print). **Subscription Rates:** $195 Individuals regular member; $25 Individuals additional family member; $95 Individuals emeritus member; $300 Individuals contributing member; $250 Institutions and library member; $25 Students online only; $12 Single issue. **URL:** http://www.press.uillinois.edu/journals/pow.html; http://leraweb.org/publications/perspectives-work. **Ad Rates:** BW $600. **Remarks:** Accepts advertising. **Circ:** 1700.

10100 ■ The Pluralist
University of Illinois Press
1325 S Oak St., MC-566
Champaign, IL 61820-6903
Phone: (217)333-0950
Fax: (217)244-8082
Publisher's E-mail: uipress@uillinois.edu
Peer-reviewed journal focusing on the ends of philosophical thought and dialogue in all widely used philosophical methodologies. **Freq:** 3/yr. **Key Personnel:** Roger Ward, Editor. **ISSN:** 1930-7365 (print); **EISSN:** 1944-6489 (electronic). **Subscription Rates:** $45 Individuals print only; $50 Individuals print + online; $111 Institutions print only; $123 Institutions print + online; $30 Single issue. **URL:** http://www.press.uillinois.edu/journals/plur.html. **Remarks:** Accepts advertising. **Circ:** (Not Reported).

10101 ■ Policy Futures in Education
wwwords Ltd.
c/o Prof. Michael A. Peters, Ed.
University of Illinois at Urbana-Champaign
360 Education Bldg.
1310 S Sixth St.
Champaign, IL 61820
Peer-reviewed journal focusing on innovative thinking in education policy. **Freq:** 8/year. **Key Personnel:** Prof. Michael A. Peters, Editor; Julie Allan, Board Member; Michael Apple, Board Member. **ISSN:** 1478--2103 (print). **Subscription Rates:** $1020 Libraries; $60 Individuals. **URL:** http://www.wwwords.co.uk/pfie/index.html; http://www.symposium-journals.co.uk/prices.html. **Circ:** (Not Reported).

10102 ■ Radical Teacher: A Socialist, Feminist and Anti-Racist Journal on the Theory and Practice of Teaching
University of Illinois Press
1325 S Oak St., MC-566
Champaign, IL 61820-6903
Phone: (217)333-0950
Fax: (217)244-8082
Publication E-mail: info@radicalteacher.org
Periodical containing articles, photos, interviews, and book reviews on radical feminist theory and practice in education. **Freq:** 3/year. **Key Personnel:** Leonard Vogt, Managing Editor. **ISSN:** 0191--4847 (print); **EISSN:** 1941--0832 (electronic). **URL:** http://www.press.uillinois.edu/journals/rt.html. **Remarks:** Advertising accepted; rates available upon request. **Circ:** (Not Reported).

10103 ■ Reclamation Matters
American Society of Mining and Reclamation
1305 Weathervane
Champaign, IL 61821
Phone: (217)333-9489
Magazine covering reclamation and rehabilitation of distressed land and waterways. **Freq:** Semiannual. **Subscription Rates:** Free to active member; $10 Nonmembers. **URL:** http://www.asmr.us/Publications/ReclamationMatters/ReclamationMatters.htm. **Ad**

Rates: BW $1259.50; 4C $550. **Remarks:** Accepts advertising. **Circ:** 5,000.

10104 ■ Recreational Sports Journal
Human Kinetics Inc.
1607 N Market St.
Champaign, IL 61820
Phone: (217)351-5076
Fax: (217)351-1549
Free: 800-747-4457
Publisher's E-mail: info@hkusa.com
Journal covering source of empirical, theoretical in the field of recreational sports. **Freq:** Semiannual April and October. **Print Method:** Offset. **Trim Size:** 6 x 9. **Key Personnel:** Dr. Paul R. Milton, Editor, phone: (419)207-6165, fax: (419)289-5460. **ISSN:** 1558-8661 (print); **EISSN:** 1558-867X (electronic). **Subscription Rates:** $72 Individuals print + online; $438 Institutions print + online; $56 Students print + online. **URL:** http://journals.humankinetics.com/RSJ. **Mailing address:** PO Box 5076, Champaign, IL 61825-5076. **Circ:** (Not Reported).

10105 ■ Sport History Review
Human Kinetics Inc.
1607 N Market St.
Champaign, IL 61820
Phone: (217)351-5076
Fax: (217)351-1549
Free: 800-747-4457
Publisher's E-mail: info@hkusa.com
Journal on the history of sports. **Freq:** Semiannual May, November. **Print Method:** Offset. **Trim Size:** 6 x 9. **Cols./Page:** 1. **Col. Width:** 65 nonpareils. **Col. Depth:** 108 agate lines. **Key Personnel:** Carly Adams, PhD, Editor-in-Chief; Don Morrow, PhD, Editor, phone: (519)661-4128. **ISSN:** 1087-1659 (print); **EISSN:** 1543--2947 (electronic). **Subscription Rates:** $65 Individuals online only; $79 Individuals online and print; $49 Students online only; $59 Students online and print. **URL:** http://journals.humankinetics.com/action/showJournal?journalCode=shr. **Mailing address:** PO Box 5076, Champaign, IL 61825-5076. **Ad Rates:** BW $300. **Remarks:** Accepts advertising. **Circ:** (Not Reported).

10106 ■ The Sport Psychologist
Human Kinetics Inc.
1607 N Market St.
Champaign, IL 61820
Phone: (217)351-5076
Fax: (217)351-1549
Free: 800-747-4457
Publisher's E-mail: info@hkusa.com
Journal designed for educational and clinical sport psychologists. **Freq:** Quarterly March, June, September, December. **Key Personnel:** Dave Smith, Associate Editor; Sheldon Hanton, Editor. **ISSN:** 0888-4781 (print); **EISSN:** 1543-2793 (electronic). **Subscription Rates:** $101 Individuals online and print; $81 Students online and print; $587 Institutions online and print; $81 Individuals online only; $61 Students online only; $479 Institutions online only. **URL:** http://journals.humankinetics.com/TSP. **Mailing address:** PO Box 5076, Champaign, IL 61825-5076. **Ad Rates:** BW $300. **Remarks:** Accepts advertising. **Circ:** (Not Reported).

10107 ■ Transactions on Ultrasonics, Ferroelectrics, and Frequency Control
IEEE - Ultrasonics, Ferroelectrics, and Frequency Control Society
1800 S Oak St., Ste 100
Champaign, IL 61820
Phone: (217)356-3182
Publisher's E-mail: uffcsociety@assochq.org
Journal featuring organizational events in the field of ultrasonics, ferroelectrics, and frequency control. **Freq:** Bimonthly. **Key Personnel:** Steven Freear, Editor-in-Chief. **ISSN:** 0885--3010 (print). **Subscription Rates:** Included in membership. **URL:** http://www.ieee-uffc.org/publications/tr. **Remarks:** Advertising not accepted. **Circ:** (Not Reported).

10108 ■ Visual Arts Research
University of Illinois Press
1325 S Oak St., MC-566
Champaign, IL 61820-6903
Phone: (217)333-0950
Fax: (217)244-8082
Professional journal covering art education. **Freq:** Semiannual. **Trim Size:** 6 x 9. **Cols./Page:** 2. **Key Personnel:** Tyler Denmead, Editor. **ISSN:** 0736--0770 (print); **EISSN:** 2151--8009 (electronic). **Subscription Rates:** $50 Individuals print or online; $60 Institutions print or online; $60 Individuals print + electronic; $75 Institutions print + electronic; $20 Single issue. **URL:** http://www.press.uillinois.edu/journals/var.html. **Remarks:** Advertising not accepted. **Circ:** Paid 500.

10109 ■ World History Connected
University of Illinois Press
1325 S Oak St., MC-566
Champaign, IL 61820-6903
Phone: (217)333-0950
Fax: (217)244-8082
Publication E-mail: worldhistoryconnected@wsu.edu
Journal covering a variety of global history topics for teachers and students. **Freq:** 3/year first week in October, February and June. **Key Personnel:** Marc Jason Gilbert, Editor; Tom Laichas, Associate Editor; Heidi Roupp, Managing Editor. **ISSN:** 1931--8642 (print). **URL:** http://worldhistoryconnected.press.illinois.edu. **Circ:** (Not Reported).

WBCP-AM - See Urbana

10110 ■ WBGL-FM - 91.7
4101 Fieldstone Rd.
Champaign, IL 61822
Phone: (217)359-8232
Fax: (217)359-7374
Free: 800-475-9245
Email: joeb@wbgl.org
Format: Religious. **Networks:** USA Radio. **Founded:** 1982. **Operating Hours:** Continuous; 25% network, 75% local. **ADI:** Terre Haute, IN. **Key Personnel:** Jennifer Briski, Mgr.; Joe Buchanan, Music Dir., joeb@wbgl.org; Ryan Springer, Dir. of Programs, ryan@wbgl.org; Jeff Scott, Station Mgr., jeff@wbgl.org; Steve Thompson, Div. Dir. **Wattage:** 20,000. **Ad Rates:** Noncommercial. **URL:** http://www.wbgl.org.

10111 ■ WCCU-TV - 27
250 S Country Fair Dr.
Champaign, IL 61821
Fax: (217)403-1007
Networks: Fox. **Founded:** Aug. 10, 1987. **Operating Hours:** Continuous. **ADI:** Springfield-Decatur-Champaign, IL. **Wattage:** 003. **Ad Rates:** $15-1600 per unit. Combined advertising rates available with WRSP-TV. **URL:** http://www.foxillinois.com.

10112 ■ WCFF-FM - 92.5
2603 W Bradley Ave.
Champaign, IL 61821
Phone: (217)352-4141
Fax: (217)352-1256
Format: Adult Contemporary. **Owner:** Saga Communications Inc., 73 Kercheval Ave., Ste. 201, Grosse Pointe Farms, MI 48236, Ph: (313)886-7070, Fax: (313)886-7150. **Key Personnel:** Jonathan Drake, Operations Mgr., jdrake@mix945.com; Alan Beck, Gen. Mgr., abeck@illiniradio.com. **Ad Rates:** Advertising accepted; rates available upon request. **URL:** http://www.sagacommunications.com.

WCFN-TV - See Springfield

10113 ■ WCIA-TV - 3
509 S Neil St.
Champaign, IL 61820
Phone: (217)356-8333
Networks: CBS. **Founded:** 1953. **Operating Hours:** Continuous. **ADI:** Springfield-Decatur-Champaign, IL. **Ad Rates:** $100-800 for 30 seconds. **URL:** http://illinoishomepage.net.

10114 ■ WDWS-AM - 1400
2301 S Neil
Champaign, IL 61820
Phone: (217)351-5300
Format: Talk; News; Sports. **Networks:** CBS. **Owner:** DWS Inc., 7401 Morton Ave., Ste. E, Newark, CA 94560, Ph: (510)797-4584, Fax: (510)797-0189, Free: 800-934-1581. **Founded:** 1937. **Operating Hours:** Continuous; 3% network, 97% local. **Key Personnel:** Dave Burns, Mgr. **Wattage:** 1,000. **Ad Rates:** Noncommercial. Combined advertising rates available with WHMS-FM. **Mailing address:** PO Box 3939, Champaign, IL 61826-3939. **URL:** http://www.wdws.com.

10115 ■ WGKC-FM - 105.9
4112C Fieldstone Rd.
Champaign, IL 61822
Phone: (217)367-1195
Fax: (217)367-3291
Format: Classic Rock. **Operating Hours:** Continuous. **Key Personnel:** Ken Cunningham, Dir. of Programs, ken.cunningham@sjbroadcasting.com; Josh Laskowski, Promotions Dir., josh.laskowski@sjbroadcasting.com. **Ad Rates:** Advertising accepted; rates available upon request. **URL:** http://www.wgkc.net.

10116 ■ WHMS-FM - 97.5
2301 S Neil
Champaign, IL 61820
Phone: (217)351-5300
Format: Adult Contemporary. **Owner:** DWS Inc., 7401 Morton Ave., Ste. E, Newark, CA 94560, Ph: (510)797-4584, Fax: (510)797-0189, Free: 800-934-1581. **Founded:** 1949. **Formerly:** WDWS-FM. **Operating Hours:** 100% Local. **Wattage:** 50,000. **Ad Rates:** Advertising accepted; rates available upon request. Combined advertising rates available with WDWS-AM. **Mailing address:** Po Box 3939, Champaign, IL 61826-3939. **URL:** http://www.whms.com.

10117 ■ WICD-TV - 15
250 S Country Fair Dr.
Champaign, IL 61821
Phone: (217)351-8500
Email: news@wicd15.com
Format: Commercial TV. **Simulcasts:** WICS-TV. **Networks:** ABC. **Owner:** Sinclair Broadcast Group Inc., 10706 Beaver Dam Rd., Hunt Valley, MD 21030, Ph: (410)568-1500, Fax: (410)568-1533. **Founded:** 1958. **Operating Hours:** 5:30 a.m.-1:30 a.m. **ADI:** Springfield-Decatur-Champaign, IL. **Key Personnel:** Steve Breitwieser, Sports Dir. **Wattage:** 358 visual; 035 aural. **Ad Rates:** Advertising accepted; rates available upon request. Combined advertising rates available with WICS-TV. **URL:** http://wicd15.com.

10118 ■ WIXY-FM - 100.3
2603 W Bradley Ave.
Champaign, IL 61821
Phone: (217)352-4141
Fax: (217)352-1256
Format: Country. **Key Personnel:** Jonathan Drake, Operations Mgr., jdrake@mix945.com. **Ad Rates:** Noncommercial. **URL:** http://www.wixy.com.

10119 ■ WKIO-FM
PO Box 3939
Champaign, IL 61826
Phone: (217)352-1040
Fax: (217)356-3330
Format: Oldies. **Networks:** CNN Radio. **Owner:** Saga Communications Inc., at above address. **Founded:** 1967. **Ad Rates:** Noncommercial. $120 for 60 seconds.

10120 ■ WLFH-FM - 95.3
4112 Fieldstone Rd.
Champaign, IL 61822-8801
Phone: (217)367-1195
Fax: (217)367-3291
Format: Country. **Simulcasts:** WEBX-FM. **Owner:** Radiostar, Inc, at above address. **Founded:** 1995. **Formerly:** WBNB-FM; WEVX-FM. **Operating Hours:** Continuous. **ADI:** Springfield-Decatur-Champaign, IL. **Key Personnel:** Ken Cunningham, Dir. of Programs; Steve Miller, Gen. Sales Mgr.; Josh Laskowski, Promotions Dir., promo@cu-radio.com. **Wattage:** 3,000. **Ad Rates:** Advertising accepted; rates available upon request.

10121 ■ WLRW-FM - 94.5
2603 W Bradley Ave.
Champaign, IL 61821
Phone: (217)352-4141
Fax: (217)352-1256
Format: Adult Contemporary. **Owner:** Saga Communications of Illinois, LLC, at above address, Grosse Pointe, MI. **Founded:** 1942. **Operating Hours:** Continuous. **ADI:** Springfield-Decatur-Champaign, IL. **Key Personnel:** Jonathan Drake, Dir. of Programs, jdrake@mix945.com; Karen Cochrane, Sales Mgr.; Sheila Wetherell, Bus. Mgr., swetherell@illiniradio.com; Mark Spalding, Chief Engineer, mark@illiniradio.com; Ryan Leskis, Promotions Dir., ryan@illiniradio.com.

Circulation: ★ = AAM; △ or • = BPA; ♦ = CAC; ❑ = VAC; ⊕ = PO Statement; ‡ = Publisher's Report; Boldface figures = sworn; Light figures = estimated.

Wattage: 50,000. **Ad Rates:** Advertising accepted; rates available upon request. **URL:** http://www.mix945.com.

10122 ■ WPCD-FM - 88.7
2400 W Bradley Ave.
Champaign, IL 61821
Phone: (217)373-3790

Format: Alternative/New Music/Progressive. **Networks:** AP. **Owner:** Parkland College, 2400 W Bradley Ave., Champaign, IL 61821, Ph: (217)351-2200, Free: 888-467-6065. **Founded:** 1978. **Operating Hours:** Continuous; 5% network, 95% local. **ADI:** Springfield-Decatur-Champaign, IL. **Wattage:** 10,500. **Ad Rates:** Noncommercial. **URL:** http://wpcd.parkland.edu.

10123 ■ WPGU-FM - 107.1
512 E Green St.
Champaign, IL 61820-5720
Phone: (217)531-1456

Format: Alternative/New Music/Progressive. **Networks:** ABC. **Owner:** Illini Media Co., 512 E Green St., Champaign, IL 61820, Ph: (217)337-8300, Fax: (217)337-8303. **Founded:** 1967. **Operating Hours:** Continuous; 100% local. **ADI:** Springfield-Decatur-Champaign, IL. **Key Personnel:** Courtney Yuen, Prog. Dir., yuen7@illinimedia.com; Erik Hasenberg, Dir. of Programs, hasenbe1@illinimedia.com. **Wattage:** 3,000. **Ad Rates:** $2-39 per unit. **URL:** http://wpgu.com/contest-rules.

10124 ■ WXTT-FM
2603 W Bradley
Champaign, IL 61821
Phone: (217)352-4141
Fax: (217)352-1256

Key Personnel: Zack Hunter, Contact, zack@extra991.com; Lon Ray, Contact, lon@extra991.com. **Ad Rates:** Advertising accepted; rates available upon request.

CHARLESTON

Coles Co. Coles Co. (E). 50 m S. of Champaign-Urbana. Eastern Illinois University. Manufactures, truck trailers, urethane foam insulation, business forms, plastic packaging, pre fab modular home, agricultural and commercial building, gray castings, paper coating. Agriculture. Corn, soybeans, wheat, broom corn.

10125 ■ Daily Eastern News
Eastern Illinois University
600 Lincoln Ave.
Charleston, IL 61920-3099
Phone: (217)581-5000
Publisher's E-mail: webmaster@eiu.edu

Collegiate newspaper. **Freq:** Daily (morn.) during the academic year. **Print Method:** Offset. **Trim Size:** 11 x 17. **Cols./Page:** 5. **Col. Width:** 11.5 picas. **Col. Depth:** 16 inches. **Key Personnel:** Kayleigh Zyskowski, Editor; Emily Steele, Managing Editor. **ISSN:** 0894--1599 (print). **URL:** http://www.dailyeasternnews.com. **Ad Rates:** GLR $10.25; 4C $360; PCI $7. **Remarks:** Accepts advertising. **Circ:** ‡9000.

10126 ■ Karamu
Eastern Illinois University
600 Lincoln Ave.
Charleston, IL 61920-3099
Phone: (217)581-5000
Publisher's E-mail: webmaster@eiu.edu

Literary journal. **Freq:** Annual. **Print Method:** Perfect bound. **Trim Size:** 5 x 8. **Key Personnel:** Olga Abella, PhD, Editor, phone: (217)581-6297. **ISSN:** 0022--8990 (print). **Subscription Rates:** $8 Individuals. **URL:** http://www.eiu.edu. **Remarks:** Advertising not accepted. **Circ:** Combined 600.

10127 ■ WEIU-FM - 88.9
1521 Buzzard Hall
Charleston, IL 61920
Phone: (217)581-6116
Fax: (217)581-6650
Free: 877-727-9348

Format: Public Radio. **Owner:** Eastern Illinois University, 600 Lincoln Ave., Charleston, IL 61920-3099, Ph: (217)581-5000. **Founded:** 1985. **Operating Hours:** 8 a.m.-midnight. **ADI:** Springfield-Decatur-Champaign, IL. **Key Personnel:** Lori Casey, Contact. **Wattage:** 2,836. **Ad Rates:** Noncommercial. **URL:** http://www.weiu.net/index.php/weiu-radio/fm-program-page.

10128 ■ WEIU-TV - 51
1521 Buzzard Hall
600 Lincoln Ave.
Charleston, IL 61920
Phone: (217)581-5956
Fax: (217)581-6650
Free: 877-727-9348
Email: weiu@weiu.net

Format: Public TV. **Networks:** Public Broadcasting Service (PBS). **Owner:** Eastern Illinois University, 600 Lincoln Ave., Charleston, IL 61920-3099, Ph: (217)581-5000. **Founded:** 1986. **Operating Hours:** Continuous. **Key Personnel:** Kelly Runyon, News Dir. **Local Programs:** *News Watch*; *Sports Talk*; *Heartland Highways*, Friday 7:30 p.m. **Wattage:** 255,000 ERP H. **Ad Rates:** Noncommercial. Underwriting available. **URL:** http://www.weiu.net.

CHESTER

10129 ■ KSGM-AM - 980
600 State St., Ste. 301
Chester, IL 62233

Format: Country; Talk. **Owner:** Donze Communications Inc., 122D Perry Plz., Perryville, MO 63775-4203, Ph: (573)547-8005. **Founded:** July 05, 1947. **Wattage:** 1,000. **URL:** http://ksgm980.com.

CHICAGO

DuPage Co. Cook Co. (NE). On Lake Michigan and Chicago River. Two hundred twenty six colleges and universities; many medical, law, theological, music, art, commercial, technical, dental colleges and preparatory schools. Nations convention center. One of the great commercial centers of the United States. The livestock and grain market of the world and the largest mail order distributing center. Leads the United States in the production of telephone equipment, musical instruments, machinery, steel, diesel engines, office machines, radio and TV sets, auto accessories.

10130 ■ AAII Journal
American Association of Individual Investors
625 N Michigan Ave.
Chicago, IL 60611
Phone: (312)280-0170
Fax: (312)280-9883
Free: 800-428-2244
Publication E-mail: journal@aaii.com

Journal containing practical information on personal finance and investment. **Freq:** Monthly. **Trim Size:** 8 1/2 x 11. **Cols./Page:** 2. **Key Personnel:** Charles Rotblut, Editor. **ISSN:** 0192-3315 (print). **URL:** http://www.aaii.com/journal/. **Remarks:** Advertising not accepted. **Circ:** ‡150000.

10131 ■ AALL Spectrum
American Association of Law Libraries
105 W Adams St., Ste. 3300
Chicago, IL 60603
Phone: (312)939-4764
Fax: (312)431-1097

Professional magazine covering issues of interest to law libraries and other legal information professionals, and association news. **Freq:** Bimonthly. **Trim Size:** 8.375 x 10.875. **Key Personnel:** Catherine Lemmer, Director, Editorial. **ISSN:** 1089--8689 (print). **Subscription Rates:** $75 Nonmembers. **URL:** http://www.aallnet.org/mm/Publications/spectrum. **Ad Rates:** GLR $30; BW $1,310; 4C $735. **Remarks:** Accepts advertising. **Circ:** 5000.

10132 ■ ABA Journal
American Bar Association
321 N Clark St.
Chicago, IL 60654
Phone: (312)988-5000
Free: 800-285-2221

Legal publication. **Freq:** Weekly. **Print Method:** Offset. **Trim Size:** 8 3/16 x 10 3/4. **Cols./Page:** 3. **Col. Width:** 27 nonpareils. **Col. Depth:** 140 agate lines. **Key Personnel:** Reginald Davis, Assistant Managing Editor; James Podgers, Assistant Managing Editor; Richard Brust, Assistant Managing Editor; Molly McDonough, Managing Editor; Mark Hansen, Writer; Terry Carter, Writer; Debra Cassens Weiss, Writer; Allen Pusey, Editor, Publisher. **ISSN:** 0747--0088 (print). **Subscription Rates:** $75 Individuals domestic; $120 Institutions; $99 Other countries; $144 Institutions, other countries. **URL:** http://www.abajournal.com. **Remarks:** Accepts advertising. **Circ:** ‡356508.

10133 ■ ACHE Journal of Healthcare Management
American College of Healthcare Executives
1 N Franklin St., Ste. 1700
Chicago, IL 60606-3529
Phone: (312)424-2800
Fax: (312)424-0023
Publisher's E-mail: contact@ache.org

Freq: Bimonthly. **ISSN:** 1096--9012 (print). **Subscription Rates:** $135 Other countries /year; $135 U.S. /year; $35 Individuals /issue. **URL:** http://ache.org/pubs/jhm/jhm_index.cfm; http://www.ache.org/pubs/jhm/jhm_index.cfm. **Remarks:** Accepts advertising. **Circ:** (Not Reported).

10134 ■ ADA News
American Dental Association
211 E Chicago Ave.
Chicago, IL 60611-2678
Phone: (312)440-2500
Fax: (312)440-3542
Free: 800-947-4746

Dental newspaper (tabloid). **Freq:** Biweekly (with single insurance in July & Dec.). **Print Method:** Offset. **Trim Size:** 11 x 14 3/4. **Cols./Page:** 4. **Col. Width:** 2 1/2 inches. **Col. Depth:** 13 1/4 inches. **Key Personnel:** Peter Solarz, Art Director; Duane Billek, Manager, Advertising and Sales; Michelle Boyd, Manager; Judy Jakush, Editor; Anita M. Mark, Coordinator; Laura A. Kosden, Publisher; James H. Berry, Associate Publisher; Beth Cox, Director, Production; Gabriela Radulescu, Associate Publisher; Lisbeth R. Maxwell, Director, Editorial; Janice Snider, Editor. **ISSN:** 0895-2930 (print). **Subscription Rates:** $121 Individuals U.S. possessions and mexico; $231 Individuals international; $139 Individuals Canada; $167 Institutions U.S. possessions and mexico w/ airmail; $279 Institutions international; $186 Institutions Canada; Free to members. **URL:** http://www.ada.org/news/news.aspx; http://www.ada.org/en/publications/ada-news/. **Ad Rates:** 4C $6,505. **Remarks:** Accepts advertising. **Circ:** ‡180699.

10135 ■ ADA News
ADA Publishing
211 E Chicago Ave.
Chicago, IL 60611
Phone: (312)440-2500

Dental newspaper (tabloid). **Freq:** Biweekly (with single insurance in July & Dec.). **Print Method:** Offset. **Trim Size:** 11 x 14 3/4. **Cols./Page:** 4. **Col. Width:** 2 1/2 inches. **Col. Depth:** 13 1/4 inches. **Key Personnel:** Peter Solarz, Art Director; Duane Billek, Manager, Advertising and Sales; Michelle Boyd, Manager; Judy Jakush, Editor; Anita M. Mark, Coordinator; Laura A. Kosden, Publisher; James H. Berry, Associate Publisher; Beth Cox, Director, Production; Gabriela Radulescu, Associate Publisher; Lisbeth R. Maxwell, Director, Editorial; Janice Snider, Editor. **ISSN:** 0895-2930 (print). **Subscription Rates:** $121 Individuals U.S. possessions and mexico; $231 Individuals international; $139 Individuals Canada; $167 Institutions U.S. possessions and mexico w/ airmail; $279 Institutions international; $186 Institutions Canada; Free to members. **URL:** http://www.ada.org/news/news.aspx; http://www.ada.org/en/publications/ada-news/. **Ad Rates:** 4C $6,505. **Remarks:** Accepts advertising. **Circ:** ‡180699.

10136 ■ Advances in Neonatal Care
National Association of Neonatal Nurses
8735 W Higgins Rd., Ste. 300
Chicago, IL 60631
Phone: (847)375-3660
Fax: (866)927-5321

Peer-reviewed journal reporting on improvements in the care of infants and their families. **Freq:** Bimonthly. **Key Personnel:** Debra Brandon, PhD, Editor-in-Chief; Jacqueline M. McGrath, Editor-in-Chief. **ISSN:** 1536--0903 (print). **Subscription Rates:** $131 Individuals print; $367 Institutions; $150 Individuals Canada/Mexico; $381 Institutions Canada/Mexico; $223 Individuals UK/Australia; $475 Institutions UK/Australia. **URL:** http://journals.lww.com/advancesinneonatalcare/pages/default.aspx; http://www.lww.com/product/?1536-0903. **Ad Rates:** BW $2,355; 4C $1,700. **Remarks:** Advertising not accepted. **Circ:** ‡8497.

10137 ■ Advancing Philanthropy: Journal of the National Society of Fund Raising Executives
Association of Fundraising Professionals
303 E Wacker Dr., Ste. 1030
Chicago, IL 60601
Phone: (312)946-1900
Fax: (312)946-1922
Publication E-mail: nsfre@nsfre.org
Professional journal covering philanthropy. **Freq:** Quarterly. **Key Personnel:** Jackie Boice, Editor-in-Chief, Publisher; Andrew Watt, Chief Executive Officer, President. **ISSN:** 1056--2443 (print). **Subscription Rates:** $80 Members /year; $100 Nonmembers U.S - 4 issues; $125 Nonmembers international - 4 issues; $165 Nonmembers 2 years - 8 issues; $215 Nonmembers 2 years; international - 8 issues. **Alt. Formats:** PDF. **URL:** http://www.afpnet.org/Publications/IssueDetail.cfm?ItemNumber=32212; http://www.afpnet.org/Publications/?&navItemNumber=506. **Circ:** (Not Reported).

10138 ■ Adweek/Midwest
VNU Business Publications Inc.
200 W Jackson Blvd., Ste. 2700
Chicago, IL 60606-6910
Publisher's E-mail: info@adweek.com
Periodical covering advertising, marketing, sales promotion. **Freq:** Weekly. **Print Method:** Offset. **Trim Size:** 8 3/8 x 10 7/8. **Cols./Page:** 3. **Col. Width:** 2 3/8 inches. **Col. Depth:** 10 inches. **Key Personnel:** Brian Braiker, Assistant; James Cooper, Executive Editor; Tim Nudd, Senior Editor; Erica Bartman, Publisher; Lisa Granatstein, Managing Editor. **Subscription Rates:** $69 Individuals print and online; $49 Individuals iPad access. **URL:** http://www.adweek.com. **Ad Rates:** 4C $39200. **Remarks:** Accepts advertising. **Circ:** ‡45084, ‡45651.

10139 ■ AGD Impact Newsletter
Academy of General Dentistry
560 W Lake St., 6th Fl.
Chicago, IL 60661-6600
Free: 888-243-DENT
Publisher's E-mail: membership@agd.org
Dental newsmagazine. Covers the issues and trends that impact on general dentists and the profession. **Freq:** Monthly. **Print Method:** Web offset. **Trim Size:** 8 3/8 x 10 7/8. **Cols./Page:** 2 and 3. **Key Personnel:** Chris Zayner, Managing Editor; Cathy McNamara Fitzgerald, Director, Communications; Beth Garcia, Managing Editor. **ISSN:** 0194--729X (print). **Subscription Rates:** $65 Institutions print; $70 Institutions, Canada print; $55 Nonmembers Canada (print); $80 Institutions, other countries print; $65 Nonmembers other countries (print); $85 Institutions, other countries only. **URL:** http://www.agd.org/publications-media/publications/agd-impact.aspx. **Formerly**: (1977) National News; (1978) AGD News. **Ad Rates:** BW $4570; 4C $5910. **Remarks:** Advertising accepted; rates available upon request. **Circ:** ‡50012.

10140 ■ Agnieszka's Dowry: For the Nonlinear and Color-Filled Experience
A Small Garlic Press
5445 Sheridan Rd., Ste. 3003
Chicago, IL 60640-7477
Magazine that features poetry, arts, letters, and essays. **Freq:** Periodic. **Print Method:** Direct digital - Docutech DT 135. **Trim Size:** 5 1/2 x 8. **Key Personnel:** Katrina Grace Craig, Editor; Marek Lugowski, Editor. **ISSN:** 1088--4300 (print). **URL:** http://asgp.org/agnieszka.html. **Remarks:** Advertising not accepted. **Circ:** (Not Reported).

10141 ■ AHA News: American Hospital Association News
Health Forum L.L.C.
155 N Wacker Dr., Ste. 400
Chicago, IL 60606
Phone: (312)893-6800
Fax: (312)422-4500
Free: 800-821-2039
Tabloid for healthcare industry professionals covering related business issues, legislative policies, and hospital management issues. **Freq:** Biweekly. **Print Method:** Web Offset. **Trim Size:** 11 3/8 x 14 1/2. **Cols./Page:** 4. **Col. Width:** 14 picas. **Col. Depth:** 14 1/2 inches. **Key Personnel:** Jerry Stoeckigt, Director, Advertising, phone: (312)893-6839; Eric Podewell, Manager, Circulation, phone: (312)893-6835; Alicia Mitchell, Executive Editor, phone: (202)626-2339; Gary Luggiero, Managing Editor, phone: (202)626-2317. **ISSN:** 0891-6608 (print). **Subscription Rates:** $75 Members 2 years; 2nd class mail; $125 Members 2 years; 1st class mail; $195 Members 2 years; other countries (prepaid); $375 Members 2 years; international air (prepaid); $160 Nonmembers 2 years; 2nd class mail; $210 Nonmembers 2 years; 1st class mail; $280 Nonmembers 2 years; other countries (prepaid); $460 Nonmembers international air (prepaid). **URL:** http://www.ahanews.com. **Ad Rates:** BW $8,130; PCI $275. **Remarks:** Accepts advertising. **Circ:** ‡28489.

10142 ■ AIDS Book Review Journal
University of Illinois at Chicago Library
PO Box 8198
Chicago, IL 60680-8198
Phone: (312)996-2716
Fax: (312)413-0424
Publication E-mail: aidsbkrv@uicvm
Professional journal reviewing books and videos that cover AIDS and sexually transmitted diseases. **Freq:** Quarterly. **Print Method:** electronic only. **Key Personnel:** Robert H. Malinowsky, Editor. **ISSN:** 1068-4174 (print). **Subscription Rates:** Free. **URL:** http://www.uic.edu/depts/lib/aidsbkrv. **Remarks:** Advertising not accepted. **Circ:** Non-paid 5000.

10143 ■ ALARM
ALARM Press
900 N Franklin, Ste. 300
Chicago, IL 60610
Phone: (312)341-1290
Publisher's E-mail: info@alarmpress.com
Magazine featuring up and coming independent musicians and artists. **Freq:** Quarterly. **Key Personnel:** Chris Force, Publisher. **Subscription Rates:** $50 Individuals; $70 Two years. **URL:** http://alarmpress.com/; http://alarm-magazine.com. **Remarks:** Accepts advertising. **Circ:** (Not Reported).

10144 ■ Alzheimer's and Dementia: The Journal of the Alzheimer's Association
Alzheimer's Association
225 N Michigan Ave., 17th Fl.
Chicago, IL 60601-7633
Phone: (312)335-8700
Free: 866-699-1246
Publisher's E-mail: info@alz.org
Freq: Bimonthly. **Key Personnel:** Zaven Khachaturian, PhD, Editor-in-Chief. **ISSN:** 1552- 5260 (print). **Subscription Rates:** $194 Individuals print and online - US; $127 Students print and online - US; $204 Individuals print and online - Canada, Mexico and other Countries; $135 Students print and online - Canada, Mexico and other Countries. **URL:** http://www.alzheimersanddementia.org/; http://www.alz.org/research/stay_current/alzheimers_and_dementia_journal.asp. **Ad Rates:** BW $2,285. **Remarks:** Accepts advertising. **Circ:** △**1,850**.

10145 ■ AMA Alliance Today
American Medical Association
AMA Plaza
330 N Wabash Ave.
Chicago, IL 60611
Phone: (312)464-4430
Fax: (312)464-5226
Free: 800-621-8335
Publisher's E-mail: admin@amaalliance.org
Magazine for the families of physicians. **Freq:** Bimonthly three times a year. **Print Method:** Offset. **Trim Size:** 8 3/8 x 10 7/8. **Cols./Page:** 3. **Col. Width:** 27 nonpareils. **Col. Depth:** 140 agate lines. **Key Personnel:** Rosetta Gervasi, Editor; Jo Posselt, Executive Director. **ISSN:** 0163--0512 (print). **Subscription Rates:** $7 Individuals; Included in membership. **Alt. Formats:** PDF. **Formerly**: MD's Wife; Facets. **Remarks:** Accepts advertising. **Circ:** (Not Reported).

10146 ■ The American Archivist
Society of American Archivists
17 N State St., Ste. 1425
Chicago, IL 60602-4061
Phone: (312)606-0722
Fax: (312)606-0728
Free: 866-722-7858
Publisher's E-mail: servicecenter@archivists.org
Peer-reviewed journal for the North American archival profession discussing trends in archival theory and practice and also featuring book reviews. **Freq:** Semiannual. **Print Method:** Offset. Uses mats. **Trim Size:** 6 3/4 x 10. **Cols./Page:** 1. **Col. Width:** 58 nonpareils. **Col. Depth:** 90 agate lines. **Key Personnel:** Mary Jo Pugh, Editor; Nancy Beaumont, Executive Director. **ISSN:** 0360--9081 (print). **Subscription Rates:** $229 Individuals print or online; $279 Individuals print and online. **URL:** http://www2.archivists.org/american-archivist. **Ad Rates:** BW $489. **Remarks:** Accepts advertising. **Circ:** 5300, 4600.

10147 ■ American Art
The University of Chicago Press
1427 E 60th St.
Chicago, IL 60637
Phone: (773)702-7700
Fax: (773)702-7212
Publisher's E-mail: custserv@press.uchicago.edu
Scholarly journal covering the history of U.S. art, architecture, landscape design, photography, film, video, and other visual media. **Founded:** 1987. **Freq:** 3/yr. **Trim Size:** 9 x 11. **Key Personnel:** Douglas Nickel, Board Member. **ISSN:** 1073-9300 (print). **Subscription Rates:** $49 Individuals print and electronic; $39 Members SAAM/NPG, print and electronic; $39 Members CAA, print and electronic; $88 Two years print and electronic; $70 Members CAA, Two years; $125 Individuals print and electronic, three years. **URL:** http://www.jstor.org/page/journal/americanart/about.html. **Formerly**: Smithsonian Studies in American Art. **Ad Rates:** BW $551; 4C $1,985. **Remarks:** Accepts advertising. **Circ:** 974.

10148 ■ American Coin-Op
Crain Associated Enterprises Inc. - American Trade Magazines
360 N Michigan Ave.
Chicago, IL 60601-3806
Phone: (312)649-5200
Trade magazine on coin-operated laundries and drycleaners. **Freq:** Monthly. **Print Method:** Web Offset. **Trim Size:** 8 1/8 x 10 7/8. **Cols./Page:** 3. **Col. Width:** 25 nonpareils. **Col. Depth:** 140 agate lines. **Key Personnel:** Paul Partyka, Editor, phone: (312)397-5507; Charlie Thompson, President, Publisher, phone: (312)361-1680. **USPS:** 964-740. **URL:** http://americancoinop.com. **Ad Rates:** BW $3055; 4C $4505. **Remarks:** Advertising accepted; rates available upon request. **Circ:** (Not Reported).

10149 ■ American Dental Hygienists' Association Access
American Dental Hygienists' Association
444 N Michigan Ave., Ste. 3400
Chicago, IL 60611
Phone: (312)440-8900
Magazine covering current dental hygiene topics, regulatory and legislative developments, and association news. **Freq:** 10/year. **Trim Size:** 8-3/8 x 10-7/8. **Key Personnel:** Christine A. Hovliaras-Delozier, Editor-in-Chief. **URL:** http://www.adha.org/access-magazine. **Remarks:** Accepts advertising. **Circ:** (Not Reported).

10150 ■ American Drycleaner: The Industry's Number One Magazine
Crain Associated Enterprises Inc. - American Trade Magazines
360 N Michigan Ave.
Chicago, IL 60601-3806
Phone: (312)649-5200
Magazine on drycleaning. **Freq:** Monthly. **Print Method:** Web Offset. **Trim Size:** 5 1/4 x 7 1/2. **Cols./Page:** 2. **Col. Width:** 26 nonpareils. **Col. Depth:** 90 agate lines. **Key Personnel:** Bruce Beggs, Director, Editorial, phone: (312)361-1683. **ISSN:** 0002--8258 (print). **URL:** http://americandrycleaner.com. **Ad Rates:** BW $2760; 4C $4210. **Remarks:** Advertising accepted; rates available upon request. **Circ:** Controlled ‡23600.

10151 ■ American Field
American Field
542 S Dearborn St., Ste. 650
Chicago, IL 60605
Phone: (312)663-9797
Fax: (312)663-5557
Publication E-mail: amfieldpub@att.net

Circulation: ★ = AAM; △ or • = BPA; ♦ = CAC; ❏ = VAC; ⊕ = PO Statement; ‡ = Publisher's Report; Boldface figures = sworn; Light figures = estimated.

Journal featuring pure-bred sporting dogs. **Freq:** Weekly. **Print Method:** Offset. **Trim Size:** 10 3/4 x 13 3/4. **Cols./Page:** 4. **Col. Width:** 13.5 picas. **Col. Depth:** 72 picas. **ISSN:** 0002--8452 (print). **Subscription Rates:** $58 Individuals print; $60 Individuals online. **URL:** http://americanfield.villagesoup.com/p/the-american-field-magazine/150538. **Ad Rates:** BW $800; 4C $965; PCI $26. **Remarks:** Accepts advertising. **Circ:** (Not Reported).

10152 ■ American Journal of Chinese Medicine
Tang Center for Herbal Medicine Research
Pritzker School of Medicine
University of Chicago
5841 S Maryland Ave., MC 4028
Chicago, IL 60637
Phone: (773)834-2399
Fax: (773)834-0601
Publisher's E-mail: TangCenter@dacc.uchicago.edu
Medical journal covering traditional ethnomedicine of all cultures, including scientific and clinical research, plants, and traditional medical theories. **Founded:** 1973. **Freq:** Annual Bimonthly. **Trim Size:** 7 x 10. **Key Personnel:** Chun-Su Yuan, Editor-in-Chief; Xiaoyu Wang, Managing Editor. **ISSN:** 0192-415X (print). **Subscription Rates:** $693 Institutions electronic and print; $630 Institutions electronic only. **URL:** http://www.worldscientific.com/worldscinet/ajcm; http://tangcenter.uchicago.edu/research/journal.shtml. **Remarks:** Advertising not accepted. **Circ:** (Not Reported).

10153 ■ American Journal of Cosmetic Surgery
American Academy of Cosmetic Surgery
225 W Wacker Dr., Ste. 650
Chicago, IL 60606
Phone: (312)981-6760
Fax: (312)265-2908
Journal for professionals in cosmetic surgery. **Freq:** Quarterly. **Trim Size:** 8 1/2 x 11. **Key Personnel:** Jane A. Petro, MD, FACS. **ISSN:** 0748--8068 (print); **EISSN:** 2374--7722 (electronic). **Subscription Rates:** $250 Individuals print only; $255 Individuals print and online; $283 Institutions online only; $308 Institutions print only; $314 Institutions print and online. **URL:** http://acs.sagepub.com. **Ad Rates:** BW $1167.90; 4C $1004.70. **Remarks:** Accepts advertising. **Circ:** ‡3000, ‡2957.

10154 ■ American Journal of Sociology
The University of Chicago Press
1155 E, 60th St.
Chicago, IL 60637
Phone: (773)702-8580
Fax: (773)702-6207
Publication E-mail: ajs@press.uchicago.edu
Journal presenting work on theory, methods, practice, and history of sociology. **Freq:** Bimonthly. **Print Method:** Offset. **Trim Size:** 6 x 9. **Cols./Page:** 1. **Col. Width:** 52 nonpareils. **Col. Depth:** 110 agate lines. **Key Personnel:** Andrew Abbott, Editor; Susan Allan, Managing Editor; Steve Raudenbush, Associate Editor. **ISSN:** 0002--9602 (print). **Subscription Rates:** $68 Individuals print and electronic; $62 Individuals electronic only; $63 Individuals print only; $48 Members print & electronic; $34 Students electronic only. **URL:** http://www.journals.uchicago.edu/toc/ajs/current. **Ad Rates:** BW $730. **Remarks:** Accepts advertising. **Circ:** 3490, 1975.

10155 ■ American Laundry News: The Newspaper of Record for Institutional Launderers
Crain Associated Enterprises Inc. - American Trade Magazines
360 N Michigan Ave.
Chicago, IL 60601-3806
Phone: (312)649-5200
Institutional laundry magazine. **Freq:** Monthly. **Print Method:** Web offset. **Trim Size:** 11 1/4 x 14 3/4. **Cols./Page:** 4. **Col. Width:** 28 nonpareils. **Col. Depth:** 195 agate lines. **Key Personnel:** Bruce Beggs, Editor, phone: (312)397-5509. **ISSN:** 0164--5765 (print). **URL:** http://americanlaundrynews.com. **Formerly:** Laundry News. **Ad Rates:** BW $3010; 4C $3720. **Remarks:** Accepts advertising. **Circ:** (Not Reported).

10156 ■ The American Naturalist: Devoted to the Conceptual Unification of the Biological Sciences
The University of Chicago Press
1427 E 60th St.
Chicago, IL 60637
Phone: (773)702-7700
Fax: (773)702-7212
Publication E-mail: amnat@press.uchicago.edu
Peer-reviewed journal focusing on ecology, evolution, and population and integrative biology research. **Freq:** Monthly. **Print Method:** Offset. **Trim Size:** 81/4 x 10 7/8. **Cols./Page:** 1. **Col. Width:** 54 nonpareils. **Col. Depth:** 102 agate lines. **Key Personnel:** Patricia Morse, Managing Editor; Mark A. McPeek, Editor; Judith L. Bronstein, Editor-in-Chief. **ISSN:** 0003--0147 (print); **EISSN:** 1537--5323 (electronic). **Subscription Rates:** $40 Members print; $80 Members print and online. **URL:** http://www.jstor.org/journal/amernatu; http://www.press.uchicago.edu/ucp/journals/journal/an.html. **Ad Rates:** BW $730. **Remarks:** Accepts advertising. **Circ:** ‡543.

10157 ■ American Political Thought
The University of Chicago Press
1427 E 60th St.
Chicago, IL 60637
Phone: (773)702-7700
Fax: (773)702-7212
Publisher's E-mail: custserv@press.uchicago.edu
Journal containing articles on political concepts such as democracy, constitutionalism, equality, liberty, citizenship, political identity, and the role of the state. **Freq:** Quarterly. **ISSN:** 2161--1580 (print); **EISSN:** 2161--1599 (electronic). **Subscription Rates:** $32 Individuals print and electronic; $29 Individuals print only; $26 Individuals electronic; $24 Students print and electronic. **URL:** http://www.press.uchicago.edu/ucp/journals/journal/apt.html. **Circ:** (Not Reported).

10158 ■ Anesthesia and Analgesia
Society of Cardiovascular Anesthesiologists
8735 W Higgins Rd., Ste. 300
Chicago, IL 60631
Fax: (847)375-6323
Free: 855-658-2828
Publisher's E-mail: ronna.ekhouse@wolterskluwer.com
Medical journal. **Freq:** Monthly. **Print Method:** Offset. **Trim Size:** 8 1/4 x 11. **Cols./Page:** 2. **Col. Width:** 3 1/4 inches. **Col. Depth:** 10 inches. **Key Personnel:** Steven L. Shafer, MD, Editor-in-Chief; Nancy Lynly, Managing Editor; Steven L. Shafer, Editor-in-Chief. **ISSN:** 0003-2999 (print). **Subscription Rates:** included in membership dues; $1371 Institutions /year for nonmember; $1653 Institutions, other countries; $1607 Institutions, Canada and Mexico. **URL:** http://www.iars.org/publications/about_aa/; http://www.anesthesia-analgesia.org/; http://www.iars.org/publications/; http://www.stahq.org/resources/aanda-magazine/; http://www.lww.com/Product/0003-2999; http://journals.lww.com/anesthesia-analgesia/pages/default.aspx. **Mailing address:** PO Box 908, Philadelphia, PA 19106-3621. **Remarks:** Accepts advertising. **Circ:** 30000, 21000, 16868.

10159 ■ Anesthesia Progress
American Dental Society of Anesthesiology
211 E Chicago Ave.
Chicago, IL 60611
Phone: (312)664-8270
Fax: (312)224-8624
Publisher's E-mail: adsahome@mac.com
Journal containing review articles, reports on clinical techniques, case reports, conference summaries, and articles of opinion pertinent to the control of pain and anxiety in dentistry. **Freq:** Quarterly. **ISSN:** 0003--3006 (print). **Subscription Rates:** $175 Individuals print and online; $250 Other countries print and online; $151 Individuals online only; $338 Institutions online only; $386 Institutions print and online; $448 Institutions, other countries print and online. **URL:** http://www.anesthesiaprogress.org; http://www.adsahome.org/ap.html. **Ad Rates:** BW $887; 4C $1,886. **Remarks:** Accepts advertising. **Circ:** (Not Reported).

10160 ■ Anglican Advance: Official Publication of the Episcopal Diocese of Chicago
Diocese of Chicago
65 E Huron St.
Chicago, IL 60611
Phone: (312)751-4200
Fax: (312)787-4534
Episcopal newspaper. **Freq:** Monthly 8/yr Jan., Feb., April, May, June, Sept., Oct., Dec. **Print Method:** Offset. **Trim Size:** 11 x 17. **Cols./Page:** 4. **Col. Width:** 14 picas. **Col. Depth:** 11 picas. **Key Personnel:** David Skidmore, Editor. **ISSN:** 1059--6763 (print). **URL:** http://www.episcopalchicago.org. **Ad Rates:** BW $1000. **Remarks:** Accepts advertising. **Circ:** 16000.

10161 ■ Annals of Thoracic Surgery
Southern Thoracic Surgical Association
633 N St. Clair St., 23rd Fl.
Chicago, IL 60611-3658
Phone: (312)202-5892
Fax: (773)289-0871
Free: 800-685-7872
Journal reporting on advances in chest and cardiovascular surgery. **Freq:** Monthly. **Key Personnel:** Henry L. Edmunds, Jr., Editor; G Alexander Patterson, MD, Editor. **ISSN:** 0003--4975 (print). **Subscription Rates:** $574 Individuals international and Canada; $489 Individuals U.S. **URL:** http://www.annalsthoracicsurgery.org; http://www.journals.elsevier.com/the-annals-of-thoracic-surgery/#description. **Remarks:** Advertising not accepted. **Circ:** (Not Reported).

10162 ■ Another Chicago Magazine
Left Field Press
3709 N Kenmore
Chicago, IL 60613
Literary journal covering poetry and fiction. **Freq:** Semiannual. **Trim Size:** 5.5 x 8.5. **Key Personnel:** Sara Skolnik, Senior Editor; Barry Silesky, Publisher, Editor; Sharon Solwitz, Editor; Lauren Reno, Managing Editor; Jacob Knabb, Editor. **ISSN:** 0272--4359 (print). **Subscription Rates:** $14.95 Individuals 1 year (2 issues); $24.95 Two years four issues; $8 Single issue. **URL:** http://www.webdelsol.com/ACM. **Remarks:** Accepts advertising. **Circ:** 2000.

10163 ■ Antique Toy World
Antique Toy World
PO Box 34509
Chicago, IL 60634
Phone: (773)725-0633
Fax: (773)725-3449
Free: 866-404-9800
Magazine featuring antique toys. **Freq:** Monthly. **Key Personnel:** Dale Kelley, Editor. **Subscription Rates:** $44.95 Individuals /year; $80 Individuals /year (first class); $80 Canada /year; $90 Other countries /year. **URL:** http://www.antiquetoyworld.com. **Remarks:** Accepts advertising. **Circ:** (Not Reported).

10164 ■ APICS magazine
APICS
8430 W Bryn Mawr Ave., Ste. 1000
Chicago, IL 60631
Phone: (773)867-1777
Fax: (773)639-3000
Free: 800-444-2742
Publisher's E-mail: service@apics.org
Subscription Rates: Included in membership; Free (U.S members); $65 Nonmembers U.S; $77 Canada and Mexico nonmembers; $93 Other countries nonmembers; $8 Single issue; $12 Other countries single copy. **URL:** http://www.apics.org/industry-content-research/publications/apics-magazine-home/about-apics-magazine; http://www.apics.org/industry-content-research/publications/apics-magazine-home. **Circ:** (Not Reported).

10165 ■ The Appraisal Journal
Appraisal Institute
200 W Madison St., Ste. 1500
Chicago, IL 60606
Phone: (312)335-4401
Fax: (312)335-4415
Free: 888-756-4624
Publisher's E-mail: aiservice@appraisalinstitute.org
Real estate appraisal journal. **Freq:** Quarterly. **Print Method:** Offset. **Cols./Page:** 2. **Col. Width:** 16 picas. **Col. Depth:** 57 picas. **ISSN:** 0003--7087 (print). **Subscription Rates:** $48 Individuals 1 year; $95 Other countries; $20 Students; $65 Other countries students; $100 Libraries; $145 Libraries international. **URL:** http://www.myappraisalinstitute.org/taj. **Remarks:** Advertising not accepted. **Circ:** (Not Reported).

10166 ■ Armed Forces & Society
Inter-University Seminar on Armed Forces and Society
Dept. of Political Science
Loyola University Chicago
1032 W Sheridan Rd.
Chicago, IL 60660
Phone: (773)508-2930
Fax: (773)508-2929
Publisher's E-mail: sales@pfp.sagepub.com
Peer-reviewed journal on the military and civil-military relations. Official journal of the Inter-University Seminar on Armed Forces and Society. **Freq:** Quarterly January , April , July , October. **Cols./Page:** 1. **Col. Width:** 4.25 inches. **Col. Depth:** 7.25 inches. **Key Personnel:** Douglas Bland, Associate Editor; Deborah Avant, Associate Editor; Anthony King, Board Member, Editor; Patricia M. Shields, Editor. **ISSN:** 0095-327X (print); **EISSN:** 1556-0848 (electronic). **Subscription Rates:** £27 Single issue print; £84 Individuals print only; £105 Institutions single print issue; £352 Institutions e-access; £383 Institutions print only; £391 Institutions print and e-access; £430 Institutions current volume print and all online content; £720 Institutions e- access (content through 1998); $443 Institutions for print and online; $399 Institutions e-access; $434 Institutions print only; $110 Individuals print only; $119 Institutions single print; $36 Individuals single print; $487 Institutions current volume print and all online content; $814 Institutions online content thru 1999. **URL:** http://afs.sagepub.com; http://www.sagepub.com/journalsProdDesc.nav?prodId=Journal201730; http://uk.sagepub.com/en-gb/asi/armed-forces-society/journal201730; http://www.iusafs.org/about/journal.asp. **Ad Rates:** BW $725. **Remarks:** Accepts advertising. **Circ:** Paid ‡1700, 5000.

10167 ■ ASDA News
American Student Dental Association
211 E Chicago Ave., Ste. 700
Chicago, IL 60611-2663
Phone: (312)440-2795
Fax: (312)440-2820
Free: 800-621-8099
Publication E-mail: editors@asdanet.org
Newspaper (tabloid) for predoctoral dental students who are members of the ASDA. **Freq:** Monthly. **Print Method:** Offset. **Trim Size:** 10.875 x 16.875. **Cols./Page:** 4. **Col. Width:** 2 9/16 inches. **Col. Depth:** 14 inches. **Key Personnel:** Nancy Honeycutt, C.A.E., Executive Director. **ISSN:** 0277--3627 (print). **URL:** http://www.asdanet.org/asdanews.aspx. **Remarks:** Accepts advertising. **Circ:** (Not Reported).

10168 ■ Asian Perspectives: The Journal of Archaeology for Asia and the Pacific
University of Hawaii Press
University of Illinois at Chicago
Dept. of Anthropology M/C 027
1007 W Harrison St.
Chicago, IL 60607-7139
Fax: (312)413-3573
Publication E-mail: asianperspectiveseditor@gmail.com
Peer-reviewed journal publishing articles on the archaeology and prehistory of Asia and the Pacific. **Freq:** Semiannual March & September. **Trim Size:** 7 x 10. **Cols./Page:** 1. **Key Personnel:** Fang Hui, Board Member; Gina L. Barnes, Board Member; Ian Glover, Board Member; Peter Bellwood, Board Member; Laura Junker, Editor; Anne Underhill, Board Member; Deborah Bekken, Board Member. **ISSN:** 0066--4835 (print); **EISSN:** 1535--8283 (electronic). **Subscription Rates:** $40 Individuals 1 year; $72 Two years; $25 Single issue; $120 Institutions 1 year; $216 Institutions 2 years; $55 Single issue institution. **URL:** http://www.uhpress.hawaii.edu/t-asian-perspectives.aspx; http://www.uhpress.hawaii.edu/p-8510-asian-perspectives.aspx?journal=1. **Ad Rates:** BW $200. **Remarks:** Accepts advertising. **Circ:** Paid 313.

10169 ■ Automation World
Summit Publishing Co.
330 N Wabash Ave., Ste. 2401
Chicago, IL 60611
Phone: (312)222-1010
Fax: (312)222-1310
Publisher's E-mail: sales@packworld.com
Magazine covering automation strategies and applications for business managers. **Freq:** Monthly. **Key Personnel:** Gary Mintchell, Editor; Jim Powers, Regional Manager; Jim Chrzan, Publisher, Vice President; Renee Robbins Bassett, Managing Editor. **ISSN:** 1553--1244 (print). **Subscription Rates:** $200 Individuals; $285 Canada and Mexico; $475 Individuals Europe; $715 Other countries. **URL:** http://www.packworld.com. **Ad Rates:** BW $7830; 4C $9840. **Remarks:** Accepts advertising. **Circ:** (Not Reported).

10170 ■ AWMA Magazine
American Working Malinois Association
c/o Angie Stark, Membership Chair
PO Box 9183
Chicago, IL 60609
Phone: (708)359-4113
Publisher's E-mail: awmamembership@gmail.com
Magazine containing articles and editorials essential for dog management and handling. Features dog competitions and shows. **Freq:** Quarterly. **Remarks:** Advertising not accepted. **Circ:** (Not Reported).

10171 ■ Baby & Kids
Talcott Communication Corp.
233 N Michigan Ave., Ste. 1780
Chicago, IL 60601
Phone: (312)849-2220
Fax: (312)849-2174
Free: 800-229-1967
Publisher's E-mail: bmowrey@talcott.com
Magazine featuring new products for baby and youth market. **Freq:** 6/year. **Key Personnel:** Daniel von Rabenau, President, Publisher. **Subscription Rates:** $20 Individuals /year (4 issues). **URL:** http://babyandkidsmagazine.com. **Ad Rates:** 4C $3750. **Remarks:** Accepts advertising. **Circ:** (Not Reported).

10172 ■ Baking Management
Penton Media, Inc.
330 N Wabash Ave., Ste. 2300
Chicago, IL 60611
Phone: (312)595-1080
Fax: (312)595-0295
Professional magazine covering the baking industry. **Freq:** Monthly. **Trim Size:** 7.75 x 10.875. **Key Personnel:** Matt Reynolds, Managing Editor. **Subscription Rates:** Free. **Ad Rates:** BW $3500. **Remarks:** Accepts advertising. **Circ:** Non-paid △**10825**.

10173 ■ Banking Strategies: Management Insights in Financial Services
Bank Administration Institute
115 S La Salle St., Ste. 3300
Chicago, IL 60603-3801
Fax: (312)683-2373
Free: 800-224-9889
Publisher's E-mail: info@bai.org
Freq: Bimonthly Monthly. **Print Method:** Web Offset. **Trim Size:** 8 x 10 1/2. **ISSN:** 1091-6350 (print). **Subscription Rates:** $66.50 Individuals; $101.50 Out of country; $14.50 Single issue; $59 /year in U.S.; $89 /year outside U.S. **URL:** http://www.bai.org/bankingstrategies/Home.aspx. **Formerly**: Banking Strategies; Bank Management. **Ad Rates:** BW $7,800; 4C $9,780. **Remarks:** Accepts advertising. **Circ:** Paid △**32000**.

10174 ■ Bar Leader
American Bar Association
321 N Clark St.
Chicago, IL 60654
Phone: (312)988-5000
Free: 800-285-2221
A news magazine covering important issues and trends that affect bar association leaders at the state and local levels. **Freq:** Bimonthly. **Key Personnel:** Marilyn Cavicchia, Editor. **ISSN:** 0099--1031 (print). **URL:** http://www.americanbar.org/publications/bar_leader/2015-16/november-december.html. **Remarks:** Advertising not accepted. **Circ:** (Not Reported).

10175 ■ Barrington Courier-Review
Sun-Times Media L.L.C.
350 N Orleans St., 10th Fl.
Chicago, IL 60654
Phone: (312)321-3000
Free: 888-848-4637
Publisher's E-mail: customerservice@suntimes.com
Community newspaper (tabloid). **Freq:** Weekly. **Print Method:** Offset. **Cols./Page:** 5. **Col. Width:** 11 picas. **Col. Depth:** 196 agate lines. **Key Personnel:** Ed Rooney, Director, Advertising, phone: (847)797-5125; Mike Martinez, Managing Editor; Rich Martin, Senior Editor, phone: (847)797-5106. **URL:** http://www.chicagotribune.com/suburbs/barrington. **Remarks:** Accepts advertising. **Circ:** (Not Reported).

10176 ■ The Beacon-News
Sun-Times Media L.L.C.
350 N Orleans St., 10th Fl.
Chicago, IL 60654
Phone: (312)321-3000
Free: 888-848-4637
Publication E-mail: beaconviewpoint@scn1.com
General newspaper. **Freq:** Mon.-Sun. (morn.). **Key Personnel:** John Russell, Associate Editor, phone: (630)978-8394. **USPS:** 037-800. **Subscription Rates:** $0.99 Individuals digital - 4 weeks only. **URL:** http://www.chicagotribune.com/suburbs/aurora-beacon-news. **Formerly**: The Aurora Beacon-News. **Remarks:** Advertising accepted; rates available upon request. **Circ:** (Not Reported).

10177 ■ Beverage World
Beverage World
200 E Randolph St., 7th Fl.
Chicago, IL 60601
Publisher's E-mail: info@beverageworld.com
Trade magazine for corporate, marketing, distribution, production, and purchasing top and middle management in the multi-product beverage industry. **Freq:** Monthly. **Print Method:** Offset. **Trim Size:** 8.375 x 10.75. **Cols./Page:** 3 and 2. **Col. Width:** 26 and 40 nonpareils. **Col. Depth:** 140 agate lines. **Key Personnel:** Andrew Kaplan, Managing Editor, phone: (646)708-7301; Kevin Francella, Publisher, phone: (646)708-7327; Jeff Cioletti, Editor-in-Chief, phone: (646)708-7303. **ISSN:** 0098-2318 (print). **Subscription Rates:** $99 Individuals. **Ad Rates:** 4C $10,190. **Remarks:** Accepts advertising. **Circ:** Non-paid ‡34000.

10178 ■ Beverage World en Espanol
Beverage World
200 E Randolph St., 7th Fl.
Chicago, IL 60601
Publisher's E-mail: info@beverageworld.com
Magazine covering the state of beer in Latin America. **Key Personnel:** Jeff Cioletti, Editor-in-Chief. **URL:** http://www.beverageworld.com. **Remarks:** Accepts advertising. **Circ:** Combined ‡11100.

10179 ■ Beverage World International
Beverage World
200 E Randolph St., 7th Fl.
Chicago, IL 60601
Publisher's E-mail: info@beverageworld.com
Magazine for beverage company owners, executives, and managers in Europe, Asia, Africa, Latin America and the Middle East. **Freq:** Monthly. **Print Method:** Offset. **Trim Size:** 8 1/8 x 11 1/8. **Cols./Page:** 3. **Col. Width:** 28 nonpareils. **Col. Depth:** 140 agate lines. **Key Personnel:** Jeff Cioletti, Editor-in-Chief; Kevin Francella, Publisher. **Remarks:** Accepts advertising. **Circ:** ‡14000.

10180 ■ The Beverly Review
TR Communications Inc.
10546 S Western Ave.
Chicago, IL 60643
Phone: (773)238-3366
Fax: (773)238-1492
Publication E-mail: beverlyreview@earthlink.net
Community newspaper. **Freq:** Weekly (Wed.). **Print Method:** Offset. **Trim Size:** 11 x 16. **Cols./Page:** 5. **Col. Width:** 23 nonpareils. **Col. Depth:** 224 agate lines. **Key Personnel:** Susan Olszewski, Business Manager; Patrick Thomas, Writer. **USPS:** 054-080. **Subscription Rates:** $26 Individuals; $50 Two years; $72 Individuals 3 years. **URL:** http://www.beverlyreview.net . **Remarks:** Accepts advertising. **Circ:** (Not Reported).

10181 ■ Billiards Digest
Luby Publishing Inc.
55 E Jackson Blvd., Ste. 401
Chicago, IL 60604
Phone: (312)341-1110
Fax: (312)341-1469
Billiards industry magazine. **Freq:** Monthly. **Print Method:** Offset. **Trim Size:** 8 1/2 x 11. **Cols./Page:** 2 and 3. **Col. Width:** 36 and 28 nonpareils. **Col. Depth:** 140 agate lines. **Key Personnel:** Gianmarc Manzione,

Circulation: ★ = AAM; △ or • = BPA; ♦ = CAC; ❑ = VAC; ⊕ = PO Statement; ‡ = Publisher's Report; Boldface figures = sworn; Light figures = estimated.

Editor. **Subscription Rates:** $28 Individuals; $53 Other countries. **URL:** http://www.billiardsdigest.com; http://www.lubypublishing.com/billiards-digest. **Remarks:** Advertising accepted; rates available upon request. **Circ:** (Not Reported).

10182 ■ Bioelectromagnetics
Bioelectromagnetics Society
c/o James C. Lin. Editor-in-Chief
University of Illinois
851 S Morgan St.
Chicago, IL 60607-7053
Fax: (312)413-0024
Journal covering original data on biological effects and applications of electromagnetic fields that ranges in frequency from zero hertz (static fields) to the terahertz undulations of visible light. **Freq:** 8/year. **ISSN:** 0197-8462 (print); **EISSN:** 1521-186X (electronic). **Subscription Rates:** $2114 Institutions USA, Canada and Mexico, ROW (online); £1083 Institutions UK, online; €1366 Institutions Europe, online; $2537 Institutions USA, online and print; £1403 Institutions UK, print and online; €1769 Institutions Europe, print and online; $2705 Institutions ROW, print and online; $2144 Institutions USA, print; $2226 Institutions Canada and Mexico, print ; £1169 Institutions UK, print ; €1474 Institutions Europe, print ; $2282 Institutions ROW, print. **URL:** http://www.bems.org/journal; http://onlinelibrary.wiley.com/journal/10.1002/(ISSN)1521-186X. **Remarks:** Accepts advertising. **Circ:** (Not Reported).

10183 ■ Bioelectromagnetics: Journal of the Bioelectromagnetics Society and the Society for Physical Regulation in Biology and Medicine
John Wiley & Sons Inc.
c/o James C. Lin, Ed.-in.-Ch.
University of Illinois
851 S Morgan St.
Chicago, IL 60607-7053
Fax: (312)996-6465
Publisher's E-mail: info@wiley.com
Bioelectromagnetics journal. **Freq:** 8/year. **Print Method:** Offset. **Trim Size:** 7 1/4 x 10 1/4. **Cols./Page:** 1. **Col. Width:** 119 nonpareils. **Col. Depth:** 138 agate lines. **Key Personnel:** Ben Greenebaum, Board Member; Andrei Pakhomov, Associate Editor, fax: (757)314-2397; Raphael C. Lee, Board Member; Dariusz Leszczynski, Board Member; James C. Lin, Editor-in-Chief; Marvin C. Ziskin, Board Member; Maila Hietanen, Board Member. **ISSN:** 0197--8462 (print); **EISSN:** 1521--186X (electronic). **Subscription Rates:** $2648 Institutions print and online; $2788 Institutions, Canada and Mexico print and online; £1464 Institutions print and online; €1847 Institutions print and online; $2382 Institutions, other countries print and online. **URL:** http://onlinelibrary.wiley.com/journal/10.1002/(ISSN)1521-186X. **Ad Rates:** BW $757; 4C $1,009. **Remarks:** Accepts advertising. **Circ:** Paid 5950.

10184 ■ Black MBA
National Black MBA Association
1 E Wacker Dr., Ste. 3500
Chicago, IL 60601
Publisher's E-mail: help@nbmbaa.org
Magazine featuring information for business professionals of the African American community. **Freq:** Semiannual. **Key Personnel:** Elaine Richardson, Managing Editor, phone: (850)668-7400. **Subscription Rates:** Included in membership. **URL:** http://www.nbmbaa.org/digitalMedia/blackMBAConnect.aspx. **Remarks:** Accepts advertising. **Circ:** (Not Reported).

10185 ■ Book Links: Connecting Books, Libraries and Classrooms
Library and Information Technology Association
50 E Huron St.
Chicago, IL 60611-2795
Phone: (312)944-6780
Fax: (312)280-3257
Free: 800-545-2433
Publisher's E-mail: lita@ala.org
Magazine featuring themed bibliographies of children's books to support literature-based curriculum. **Freq:** Quarterly. **Trim Size:** 8 3/8 x 10 7/8. **Key Personnel:** Laura Tillotson, Editor; Bill Ott, Publisher; Kristen Mckulski, Associate Editor. **ISSN:** 1055--4742 (print). **Subscription Rates:** $147.50 Individuals; $170 Other countries; $225 Two years; $295 Other countries two years; $147.50 Canada; $255 Canada two years. **URL:** http://www.ala.org/offices/publishing/booklist/booklinks. **Ad Rates:** BW $5,200; 4C $8,685. **Remarks:** Accepts advertising. **Circ:** Combined 14000.

10186 ■ Booklist
Library and Information Technology Association
50 E Huron St.
Chicago, IL 60611-2795
Phone: (312)944-6780
Fax: (312)280-3257
Free: 800-545-2433
Publication E-mail: info@booklistonline.com
Reviews library materials for school and public libraries. Provides a guide to current print and non-print materials worthy of consideration for purchase by libraries and schools. Includes more than 8,000 reviews annually, and more than 160,000 reviews and features in the online archive. **Freq:** 22/yr. **Key Personnel:** Keir Graff, Editor; Joanne Wilkinson, Editor; Bill Ott, Editor, Publisher. **ISSN:** 0006--7385 (print). **Subscription Rates:** $159.50 U.S. and Canada 1 year; $275 U.S. and Canada 2 years; $184 Other countries 1 year; $320 Other countries 2 years; $380 U.S. and Canada 3 years; $445 Other countries 3 years. **URL:** http://www.booklistonline.com; http://www.ala.org/offices/publishing/booklist. **Ad Rates:** BW $6545; 4C $2500. **Remarks:** Accepts advertising. **Circ:** ‡13200.

10187 ■ Booklist
American Library Association
50 E Huron St.
Chicago, IL 60611-2795
Phone: (312)944-6780
Fax: (312)440-9374
Free: 800-545-2433
Publication E-mail: info@booklistonline.com
Reviews library materials for school and public libraries. Provides a guide to current print and non-print materials worthy of consideration for purchase by libraries and schools. Includes more than 8,000 reviews annually, and more than 160,000 reviews and features in the online archive. **Freq:** 22/yr. **Key Personnel:** Keir Graff, Editor; Joanne Wilkinson, Editor; Bill Ott, Editor, Publisher. **ISSN:** 0006--7385 (print). **Subscription Rates:** $159.50 U.S. and Canada 1 year; $275 U.S. and Canada 2 years; $184 Other countries 1 year; $320 Other countries 2 years; $380 U.S. and Canada 3 years; $445 Other countries 3 years. **URL:** http://www.booklistonline.com; http://www.ala.org/offices/publishing/booklist. **Ad Rates:** BW $6545; 4C $2500. **Remarks:** Accepts advertising. **Circ:** ‡13200.

10188 ■ Bowlers Journal International
Luby Publishing Inc.
55 E Jackson Blvd., Ste. 401
Chicago, IL 60604
Phone: (312)341-1110
Fax: (312)341-1469
Sports magazine - bowling's premier magazine. **Freq:** Monthly. **Print Method:** Offset. **Trim Size:** 8 1/4 x 10 7/8. **Cols./Page:** 3. **Col. Width:** 26 nonpareils. **Col. Depth:** 140 agate lines. **Key Personnel:** Barbara Peltz, Director, Sales; Keith Hamilton, President. **Subscription Rates:** $32 Individuals; $48 Two years; $62 Individuals 3 years; $57 Other countries; $98 Other countries 2 years; $137 Other countries 3 years. **URL:** http://www.bowlersjournal.com; http://www.lubypublishing.com/bowlers-journal-international. **Remarks:** Advertising accepted; rates available upon request. **Circ:** Paid ⊕**17000.**

10189 ■ Bridgeport News
Bridgeport News
3506 S Halsted St.
Chicago, IL 60609
Phone: (773)927-0025
Fax: (773)337-6995
Community newspaper. **Founded:** 1938. **Freq:** Weekly (Wed.). **Print Method:** Offset. **Cols./Page:** 9. **Col. Width:** 19 nonpareils. **Col. Depth:** 301 agate lines. **Key Personnel:** Joe Feldman, Publisher. **URL:** http://www.bridgeportnews.net. **Ad Rates:** GLR $1.65; BW $4347; 4C $4947; PCI $23. **Remarks:** Advertising accepted; rates available upon request. **Circ:** (Not Reported).

10190 ■ Brighton Park-McKinley Park Life
Brighton Park/McKinley Park LIFE
2949 W Pope John Paul II Dr.
Chicago, IL 60632-2554
Phone: (773)523-3663
Fax: (773)523-3983
Publisher's E-mail: brightonparklife@aol.com
Community newspaper. **Freq:** Weekly (Thurs.). **Print Method:** Offset. **Cols./Page:** 8. **Col. Width:** 9 picas. **Col. Depth:** 301 agate lines. **Key Personnel:** Albert H. Silinski, Editor. **Alt. Formats:** PDF. **URL:** http://www.brightonparklife.com. **Remarks:** Advertising accepted; rates available upon request. **Circ:** (Not Reported).

10191 ■ Broward Jewish Journal
The Tribune Media Co.
435 N Michigan Ave.
Chicago, IL 60611-4066
Phone: (312)222-9100
Fax: (312)222-4206
Free: 800-874-2863
Publisher's E-mail: sales@atlanticsyndication.com
Jewish interest newspaper (tabloid). **Freq:** Weekly (Thurs.). **Print Method:** web. **Trim Size:** 11 1/4 x 13 1/2. **Cols./Page:** 6. **Col. Width:** 2 1/16 inches. **Col. Depth:** 13 inches. **Key Personnel:** Andrew Polin, Editor; Rabbi Bruce Warshal, Publisher, phone: (954)574-5332, fax: (954)421-9003. **Subscription Rates:** Free. **URL:** http://www.sun-sentinel.com/florida-jewish-journal. **Ad Rates:** BW $2,830; 4C $3,130; PCI $53.20. **Remarks:** Accepts advertising. **Circ:** Free 72000.

10192 ■ BtoB Magazine: The Magazine for Marketing Strategists
Crain Communications Inc.
150 N Michigan Ave.
Chicago, IL 60601-7553
Phone: (312)649-5200
Fax: (312)280-3150
Free: 888-446-1422
Publisher's E-mail: info@crain.com
Trade magazine on business-to-business marketing news, strategy, and tactics. **Freq:** Monthly. **Print Method:** Web. **Trim Size:** 11 x 14 1/2. **Cols./Page:** 5. **Col. Width:** 2 3/16 inches. **Col. Depth:** 14 inches. **Key Personnel:** David Bernstein, Associate Publisher; John Obrecht, Editor; Bob Felsenthal, Publisher, Vice President. **ISSN:** 0745--5933 (print). **Subscription Rates:** $59 Individuals; $69 Canada; $89 Other countries. **URL:** http://www.btobonline.com; http://adage.com/section/btob/976?=btob=1; http://www.businessinsurance.com/section/crain-brands. **Formerly:** Industrial Marketing; Business Marketing. **Remarks:** Advertising accepted; rates available upon request. **Circ:** Controlled 45000.

Buffalo Grove Countryside - See Buffalo Grove

10193 ■ Bulletin of the Atomic Scientists
Bulletin of the Atomic Scientists
1155 E 60th St.
Chicago, IL 60637
Phone: (707)481-9372
Publisher's E-mail: admin@thebulletin.org
Magazine informing the public about the threats to survival and development of humanity from nuclear weapons, climate change and emerging technologies. **Freq:** Bimonthly. **Print Method:** Offset. **Trim Size:** 8 1/4 x 10 7/8. **Cols./Page:** 3. **Col. Width:** 13 picas. **Col. Depth:** 57 picas. **Key Personnel:** Rachel Bronson, Executive Director, Publisher. **ISSN:** 0096--3402 (print); **EISSN:** 1938--3282 (electronic). **Subscription Rates:** $58 Individuals online only; $302 Institutions online only. **URL:** http://thebulletin.org. **Remarks:** Accepts advertising. **Circ:** (Not Reported).

10194 ■ Business & Commercial Law Journal
DePaul University College of Law
25 E Jackson Blvd.
Chicago, IL 60604
Phone: (312)362-8701
Fax: (312)362-6918
Free: 800-428-7453
Publisher's E-mail: lawinfo@depaul.edu
Journal covering legal issues about business and commercial law. **Freq:** Quarterly. **ISSN:** 1542--2763 (print). **Subscription Rates:** $85 Individuals /year; $95 Individuals /year - foreign; $25 Single issue. **URL:** http://law.depaul.edu/student-resources/student-activities/journals/business-commercial-law/Pages/default.aspx. **Circ:** (Not Reported).

10195 ■ The Business Lawyer
American Bar Association Business Law Section

321 N Clark St.
Chicago, IL 60654
Phone: (312)988-5588
Fax: (312)988-5578
Publisher's E-mail: businesslaw@americanbar.org
Freq: Quarterly. **Print Method:** Offset. **Trim Size:** 6 x 9. **Cols./Page:** 1. **Col. Width:** 54 nonpareils. **Col. Depth:** 104 agate lines. **Key Personnel:** William D. Johnston, Board Member; Gregory M. Duhl, Editor-in-Chief. **ISSN:** 0007--6899 (print). **Subscription Rates:** $65 U.S.; $75 Other countries; $20 Single issue; Included in membership. **URL:** http://www.americanbar.org/publications/the_business_lawyer.html. **Remarks:** Accepts advertising. **Circ:** (Not Reported).

10196 ■ The Canadian Journal of Occupational Therapy
Association Canadienne des Ergothérapeutes
c/o Dr. Marcia Finlayson, Ed.
Department of Occupational Therapy
University of Illinois
1919 W Taylor St.
Chicago, IL 60612-7250
Publisher's E-mail: communications@caot.ca
Peer-reviewed journal covering practice, theory, research, and education in occupational therapy. **Freq:** 5/year February, April, June, October, December. **Print Method:** Sheetfed. **Trim Size:** 8.5 x 11. **Cols./Page:** 2. **Col. Width:** 27 nonpareils. **Col. Depth:** 138 agate lines. **Key Personnel:** Dr. Marcia Finlayson, Editor. **ISSN:** 0008--4174 (print); **EISSN:** 1911--9828 (electronic). **Subscription Rates:** $34 Individuals single print issue; $59 Institutions single print issue; $130 Individuals print and e-access; $248 Institutions e-access; $270 Institutions print only; $275 Institutions print and e-access; $276 Institutions e-access; all online content; $303 Institutions current print volume and all online content; $1368 Institutions e-access (content through 1998). **URL:** http://www.caot.ca/default.asp?pageid=6; http://www.caot.ca/default.asp?ChangeID=25&pageID=6; http://us.sagepub.com/en-us/nam/canadian-journal-of-occupational-therapy/journal202151. **Also known as:** Revue Canadienne d' Ergotherapie. **Remarks:** Accepts advertising. **Circ:** (Not Reported).

10197 ■ The Catholic Journalist
Catholic Press Association
205 W Monroe St., Ste. 470
Chicago, IL 60606
Phone: (312)380-6789
Fax: (312)361-0256
Newspaper containing news and features of interest to Catholic journalists. **Freq:** Monthly. **Print Method:** Offset. **Cols./Page:** 4. **Col. Width:** 14 picas. **Col. Depth:** 14 inches. **Key Personnel:** Bob Zyskowski. **ISSN:** 0008--8129 (print). **Subscription Rates:** $18 Individuals; $12 U.S.; $15 Canada; $20 Other countries. **Alt. Formats:** PDF. **URL:** http://www.catholicpress.org/?page=JournalistArchives. **Ad Rates:** BW $515; PCI $20. **Remarks:** Accepts advertising. **Circ:** 1000, 2700.

10198 ■ Catholic Library World
Catholic Library Association
205 W Monroe St., Ste. 314
Chicago, IL 60606-5061
Phone: (312)739-1776
Fax: (312)739-1778
Free: 855-739-1776
Publisher's E-mail: sbaron@regent.edu
Freq: Quarterly. **ISSN:** 0008-820X (print). **Subscription Rates:** Included in membership; $60 Nonmembers. **URL:** http://www.cathla.org/catholic-library-world. **Remarks:** Accepts advertising. **Circ:** 3000.

10199 ■ Catholic Library World: The Official Journal of the Catholic Library Association
Catholic Library Association
205 W Monroe St., Ste. 314
Chicago, IL 60606-5061
Phone: (312)739-1776
Fax: (312)739-1778
Free: 855-739-1776
Publisher's E-mail: sbaron@regent.edu
Professional, referred journal covering libraries. **Freq:** Quarterly September, December, March and June. **Print Method:** Offset. **Trim Size:** 8 1/2 x 11. **Cols./Page:** 3. **Col. Width:** 26 nonpareils. **Col. Depth:** 140 agate lines. **Key Personnel:** Jean Bostley, Executive Director; Sigrid Kelsey, Editor; Bland O'Connor, Executive Chairman of the Board. **ISSN:** 0008-820X (print). **Subscription Rates:** $100 Nonmembers; $25 Single issue back issues; Included in membership. **URL:** http://www.cathla.org/catholic-library-world. **Ad Rates:** BW $425; SAU $390. **Remarks:** Color advertising accepted; rates available upon request. **Circ:** ‡3000.

10200 ■ The Catholic New World
New World Publications
835 N Rush St.
Chicago, IL 60611
Phone: (312)534-7777
Fax: (312)534-7310
Publication E-mail: editorial@catholicnewworld.com
Catholic newspaper (tabloid). **Freq:** Semimonthly. **Print Method:** Offset. **Trim Size:** 11 1/8 x 14 1/2. **Cols./Page:** 5. **Col. Width:** 10 inches. **Col. Depth:** 13 1/2 inches. **Key Personnel:** Dawn Vidmar, General Manager, phone: (312)534-7110; Michelle Martin, Writer, phone: (312)534-7261; Joyce Duriga, Editor. **ISSN:** 1527--4757 (print). **Subscription Rates:** $25 Individuals; $40 Two years; $50 Other countries surface mail; $150 Other countries air mail. **URL:** http://www.catholicnewworld.com . **Formerly:** The New World. **Ad Rates:** BW $108. **Remarks:** Accepts advertising. **Circ:** ‡46000.

10201 ■ CDS Review
Chicago Dental Society
401 N Michigan Ave., Ste. 200
Chicago, IL 60611-5585
Phone: (312)836-7300
Fax: (312)836-7337
Dental journal. **Founded:** 1921. **Freq:** 7/yr. **Print Method:** Sheetfed Offset. **Trim Size:** 8 1/2 x 10 5/8. **Cols./Page:** 3. **Col. Width:** 14.5 picas. **Col. Depth:** 126 agate lines. **Subscription Rates:** $25 Individuals; $30 Institutions and schools in USA & Canada; $45 Other countries; $5 Single issue domestic; $8 Single issue foreign. **URL:** http://www.cds.org/cds_review/. **Ad Rates:** BW $2090; 4C $3465. **Remarks:** Accepts advertising. **Circ:** 8,000.

10202 ■ Chef Educator Today
Talcott Communication Corp.
233 N Michigan Ave., Ste. 1780
Chicago, IL 60601
Phone: (312)849-2220
Fax: (312)849-2174
Free: 800-229-1967
Publisher's E-mail: bmowrey@talcott.com
Magazine featuring information for foodservice educators. **Freq:** 6/year. **Key Personnel:** Daniel von Rabenau, President, Publisher; Lacey Griebeler, Managing Editor. **Subscription Rates:** $32 Individuals. **Ad Rates:** 4C $8,000. **Remarks:** Accepts advertising. **Circ:** 12196.

10203 ■ Chef: The Food Magazine for Professionals
Talcott Communication Corp.
233 N Michigan Ave., Ste. 1780
Chicago, IL 60601
Phone: (312)849-2220
Fax: (312)849-2174
Free: 800-229-1967
Publisher's E-mail: bmowrey@talcott.com
Food information for chefs. **Freq:** 11/year. **Print Method:** Offset. **Trim Size:** 8 1/8 x 10 7/8. **Cols./Page:** 3. **Col. Width:** 24 nonpareils. **Col. Depth:** 140 agate lines. **Key Personnel:** Daniel Von Rabenau, President, Publisher. **ISSN:** 1087--061X (print). **Subscription Rates:** $32 Individuals /year; $47 Two years; $96 Other countries /year. **URL:** http://www.chefmagazine.com. **Formerly:** Chef Institutional. **Ad Rates:** 4C $8000. **Remarks:** Accepts advertising. **Circ:** (Not Reported).

10204 ■ Chicago Bride
R.E.N. Publishing Co.
3500 W Peterson Ave., No. 403
Chicago, IL 60659
Phone: (773)866-9900
Fax: (773)866-9881
Publisher's E-mail: rencpublishing@earthlink.net
Magazine featuring all the information and services about wedding in Chicago. **Key Personnel:** Cathy Demetropoulos, Editor. **Subscription Rates:** $4.95 Individuals current issue. **URL:** http://www.chicagobridemagazine.com/default.html. **Remarks:** Accepts advertising. **Circ:** (Not Reported).

10205 ■ Chicago Catolico
Echo Media
900 Circle 75 Pky., Ste. 1600
Atlanta, GA 30339
Phone: (770)955-3535
Fax: (770)955-3599
Publisher's E-mail: salesinfo@echo-media.com
Hispanic publication, published by the Archdiocese of Chicago. **Freq:** Weekly (Sun.). **URL:** http://echomedia.com/medias/details/5032. **Remarks:** Accepts advertising. **Circ:** Sun. 28500.

10206 ■ Chicago Crusader
Crusader Newspapers
6429 S King Dr.
Chicago, IL 60637
Phone: (773)752-2500
Fax: (773)752-2817
Publication E-mail: news@chicagocrusader.com
Black community newspaper (tabloid). **Freq:** Weekly. **Print Method:** Offset. **Trim Size:** 10 x 14. **Cols./Page:** 5. **Col. Width:** 2 inches. **Col. Depth:** 14 inches. **Key Personnel:** Dorothy R. Leavell, Editor. **USPS:** 596-080. **Alt. Formats:** PDF. **Remarks:** Accepts advertising. **Circ:** 500000.

10207 ■ Chicago Daily Law Bulletin
Law Bulletin Publishing Co.
415 N State St.
Chicago, IL 60654
Phone: (312)644-7800
Publisher's E-mail: circulation@lbpc.com
Legal and business newspaper. **Freq:** Daily except weekends and holidays. **Print Method:** Offset. **Trim Size:** 16 1/2 x 22 3/4. **Cols./Page:** 7. **Col. Width:** 25 nonpareils. **Col. Depth:** 294 agate lines. **Key Personnel:** Michael B. Kramer, Publisher; Olivia Clarke, Editor. **ISSN:** 0362--6148 (print). **Subscription Rates:** $299 Individuals; $499 Two years; $699 Individuals 3 years. **URL:** http://www.lawbulletin.com/legal/newspapers-and-magazines/chicago-daily-law-bulletin. **Remarks:** Accepts advertising. **Circ:** (Not Reported).

10208 ■ Chicago Defender
Echo Media
4445 S Dr. Martin Luther King Jr. Dr.
Chicago, IL 60653-3310
Phone: (312)225-2400
Fax: (312)225-9231
Publisher's E-mail: salesinfo@echo-media.com
African-American newspaper serving the Chicago area. **Freq:** Weekly (Wed.). **Key Personnel:** Roland Martin, Writer. **URL:** http://chicagodefender.com. **Remarks:** Accepts advertising. **Circ:** (Not Reported).

10209 ■ Chicago Dental Society News
Chicago Dental Society
401 N Michigan Ave., Ste. 200
Chicago, IL 60611-5585
Phone: (312)836-7300
Fax: (312)836-7337
Trade magazine covering dentistry in Chicago. **Freq:** 7/year. **Trim Size:** 8 3/8 x 10 7/8. **Cols./Page:** 3. **Col. Width:** 2 1/8 inches. **Col. Depth:** 9 inches. **Key Personnel:** Randall B. Grove, Executive Director; Barry Ranallo, Associate Director; Lennoree Cleary, Office Manager; Tom Long, Coordinator, Graphic Designer; Dr. Michael Stablein, President; Keri Kramer, Director, Communications; Joanne Girardi, Director, Exhibits; Dr. Ian Elliott, President. **USPS:** 573-520. **Subscription Rates:** $5 U.S. single issue - CD; $8 Canada and Mexico single issue - CD. **URL:** http://www.cds.org/. **Formerly:** Fortnightly Review. **Ad Rates:** BW $1,450; 4C $1,100; SAU $600. **Remarks:** Accepts advertising. **Circ:** Non-paid 8000.

10210 ■ Chicago Home and Garden
Chicago Home & Garden
435 N Michigan Ave., Ste. 1100
Chicago, IL 60611
Phone: (312)222-8999
Publisher's E-mail: chicagohome@chicagomag.com
Magazine covering home and garden style in the Chicago, IL, area. **Freq:** Quarterly. **Key Personnel:** Jan Parr, Editor; Vickie Bales, Director, Production. **ISSN:** 1085--4363 (print). **Subscription Rates:** $12 Individuals print. **URL:** http://www.chicagomag.com/Chicago-

Circulation: ★ = AAM; △ or • = BPA; ♦ = CAC; ❑ = VAC; ⊕ = PO Statement; ‡ = Publisher's Report; Boldface figures = sworn; Light figures = estimated.

Home/. **Remarks:** Accepts advertising. **Circ:** (Not Reported).

10211 ■ Chicago Journal of International Law
William S. Hein and Company Inc.
The University of Chicago Law School
1111 E 60th St.
Chicago, IL 60637-2786
Phone: (773)834-4464
Fax: (773)702-0730
Publication E-mail: cjil@law.uchicago.edu
Journal covering law worldwide. **Freq:** Semiannual. **Key Personnel:** Lindsay Short, Editor-in-Chief; Jeffrey Levine, Executive Editor. **ISSN:** 1529--0816 (print). **Subscription Rates:** $40 Individuals; $45 Other countries. **Alt. Formats:** Microform. **URL:** http://cjil.uchicago.edu; http://www.wshein.com/catalog/1940. **Remarks:** Advertising not accepted. **Circ:** (Not Reported).

10212 ■ Chicago Journal of International Law
University of Chicago Law School
1111 E 60th St.
Chicago, IL 60637
Phone: (773)702-9494
Fax: (773)834-0942
Journal containing articles on international law and policy issues. **Freq:** Semiannual. **Key Personnel:** Elise Meyer, Editor-in-Chief. **ISSN:** 1529--0816 (print). **Subscription Rates:** $40 Individuals 1 year; $45 Individuals mailed to U.S address. **URL:** http://cjil.uchicago.edu. **Circ:** (Not Reported).

10213 ■ Chicago Journal of Theoretical Computer Science
The University of Chicago Press
1427 E 60th St.
Chicago, IL 60637
Phone: (773)702-7700
Fax: (773)702-7212
Publisher's E-mail: custserv@press.uchicago.edu
Peer-reviewed journal dealing with theoretical computer science. **Key Personnel:** Eric Allender, Associate Editor, phone: (732)445-2001, fax: (732)445-0537; Janos Simon, Editor-in-Chief, phone: (773)702-3488, fax: (773)702-8487; Martin Abadi, Board Member. **ISSN:** 1073--0486 (print). **URL:** http://www.journals.uchicago.edu. **Circ:** (Not Reported).

10214 ■ Chicago Lawyer
Law Bulletin Publishing Co.
415 N State St.
Chicago, IL 60654
Phone: (312)644-7800
Publisher's E-mail: circulation@lbpc.com
Legal magazine (Tabloid). **Freq:** Monthly. **Print Method:** Offset. **Trim Size:** 10 5/8 x 15 5/16. **Cols./Page:** 4. **Col. Width:** 30 nonpareils. **Col. Depth:** 182 agate lines. **Key Personnel:** Michael Kramer, Publisher. **ISSN:** 0199--8374 (print). **Subscription Rates:** $60 Individuals; $96 Two years; $120 Individuals 3 years. **URL:** http://www.lawbulletin.com/legal/newspapers-and-magazines/chicago-lawyer. **Remarks:** Accepts advertising. **Circ:** (Not Reported).

10215 ■ Chicago Life
Chicago Life
PO Box 11311
Chicago, IL 60611-0311
Publisher's E-mail: info@chicagolife.net
Lifestyle magazine for Metropolitan Chicago residents. **Freq:** Bimonthly. **Print Method:** Offset. **Trim Size:** 8 3/8 x 10 7/8. **Cols./Page:** 3. **Col. Width:** 2 1/2 inches. **Col. Depth:** 9 5/8 inches. **Key Personnel:** Pam Berns, Editor. **URL:** http://www.chicagolife.net . **Ad Rates:** 4C $14820. **Remarks:** Accepts advertising. **Circ:** ‡102000.

10216 ■ Chicago Magazine
Chicago Tribune Co.
435 N Michigan Ave.
Chicago, IL 60611
Phone: (312)222-3232
Fax: (312)222-4674
Free: 800-874-2863
Publisher's E-mail: corp.info@tribune.com
Metropolitan magazine for the Chicago area. **Founded:** 1975. **Freq:** Monthly. **Print Method:** Offset. **Trim Size:** 8 x 10.5. **Cols./Page:** 3. **Col. Width:** 27 nonpareils. **Col. Depth:** 140 agate lines. **Key Personnel:** Tom Conradi, Director, Development, Director, Sales. **ISSN:** 0362-4595 (print). **Subscription Rates:** $12 Individuals; $9.99 online. **URL:** http://www.chicagomag.com. **Feature Editors:** David Bernstein, dbernstein@chicagomag.com. **Remarks:** Advertising accepted; rates available upon request. **Circ:** ★160,092.

10217 ■ The Chicago Maroon
The Chicago Maroon
1212 E 59th St.
Lower Level
Chicago, IL 60637
Phone: (773)702-1403
Fax: (773)702-3032
Publisher's E-mail: editor@chicagomaroon.com
Community newspaper. **Freq:** Semiweekly. **Print Method:** Offset. Uses mats. **Trim Size:** 10 x 16. **Cols./Page:** 4. **Col. Width:** 29 nonpareils. **Col. Depth:** 210 agate lines. **Key Personnel:** Jordan Larson, Editor-in-Chief; Sharan Shetty, Editor-in-Chief; Colin Bradley, Managing Editor. **URL:** http://chicagomaroon.com. **Remarks:** Advertising accepted; rates available upon request. **Circ:** (Not Reported).

10218 ■ Chicago Medicine
Chicago Medical Society
515 N Dearborn St.
Chicago, IL 60654
Phone: (312)670-2550
Fax: (312)670-3646
Publisher's E-mail: cms@cmsdocs.org
Magazine for members of the Chicago Medical Society. Including features on practice management and medical and legal information. **Freq:** Annual. **Print Method:** Letterpress and offset. **Trim Size:** 8 x 10 7/8. **Cols./Page:** 2 and 3. **Key Personnel:** Theodore Kanellakes, Executive Director; Elizabeth Sidney, Editor; Scott Warner, Editor. **ISSN:** 0009--3637 (print). **Subscription Rates:** Included in membership. **Alt. Formats:** Download; PDF. **URL:** http://www.cmsdocs.org/news-publications/chicago-medicine-magazine. **Ad Rates:** 4C $1900. **Remarks:** Accepts advertising. **Circ:** (Not Reported).

10219 ■ Chicago Reader
Chicago Reader Inc.
350 N Orleans St.
Chicago, IL 60654
Phone: (312)222-6920
Publisher's E-mail: mail@chicagoreader.com
Alternative newspaper covering urban issues and politics, arts and entertainment. **Freq:** Weekly. **Print Method:** Offset. **Trim Size:** 11 x 17. **Cols./Page:** 5. **Col. Width:** 11.5 picas. **Col. Depth:** 16 inches. **Key Personnel:** Alison Draper, Publisher; Mary Jo Madden, General Manager; Jake Malooley, Editor. **ISSN:** 1096--6919 (print). **Subscription Rates:** Free. **URL:** http://www.chicagoreader.com . **Remarks:** Accepts advertising. **Circ:** Free ‡90000.

10220 ■ The Chicago Reporter
Community Renewal Society
111 W. Jackson Blvd., Ste. 820
Chicago, IL 60604
Publisher's E-mail: info@communityrenewalsociety.org
Publication focusing on issues of race and poverty in the Chicago Metropolitan area. **Freq:** 3/year. **Print Method:** Standard web. **Trim Size:** 8.5 X 11. **Key Personnel:** Susan Smith Richardson; Rui Kaneya, Editor. **Subscription Rates:** $20 Individuals print only; $30 Two years print only; $15 Individuals online only. **URL:** http://www.chicagoreporter.com. **Mailing address:** 111 W. Jackson Blvd., Ste. 820, Chicago, IL 60604. **Remarks:** Advertising not accepted. **Circ:** Paid 1,500, Non-paid 4,000.

10221 ■ Chicago Review
The University of Chicago Press
1427 E 60th St.
Chicago, IL 60637
Phone: (773)702-7700
Fax: (773)702-7212
Publisher's E-mail: custserv@press.uchicago.edu
Literary magazine presenting original poetry, short fiction, non-fiction, and art. **Freq:** Quarterly. **Print Method:** Offset. **Trim Size:** 6 x 9. **Cols./Page:** 1. **Col. Width:** 25 picas. **Col. Depth:** 44 picas. **Key Personnel:** Andrew Peart, Editor. **ISSN:** 0009--3696 (print). **Subscription Rates:** $25 Individuals; $45 Two years; $35 Canada and Mexico; $55 Other countries. **URL:** http://chicagoreview.org. **Ad Rates:** BW $350. **Remarks:** Accepts advertising. **Circ:** (Not Reported).

10222 ■ Chicago Social Brides
Modern Luxury Media
200 W Hubbard
Chicago, IL 60654
Phone: (312)274-2500
Fax: (312)274-2501
Magazine featuring the latest trends in wedding arrangements. **Freq:** Semiannual. **Key Personnel:** Amy Allen, Publisher; Elise Hofer, Editor-in-Chief. **Subscription Rates:** $20 Individuals; $35 Two years. **URL:** http://www.modernluxury.com/brides-chicago. **Remarks:** Accepts advertising. **Circ:** (Not Reported).

10223 ■ Chicago Sun-Times
Sun-Times Media L.L.C.
350 N Orleans St., 10th Fl.
Chicago, IL 60654
Phone: (312)321-3000
Free: 888-848-4637
Publisher's E-mail: customerservice@suntimes.com
General newspaper. **Freq:** Mon.-Sun. (morn.). **Print Method:** Letterpress. **Trim Size:** 10 9/16 x 13 7/8. **Cols./Page:** 5. **Col. Width:** 26 nonpareils. **Col. Depth:** 196 agate lines. **Key Personnel:** Ted Knight, Chief Executive Officer; Jim Kirk, Publisher, Editor-in-Chief, phone: (312)321-2577. **Subscription Rates:** $11.99 Out of state Wednesday, Thursday, Friday and Sunday; $3.99 online only; $18.99 per month (Monday - Sunday); print and online.; 5.99 per month (Sunday); print and online. **Online:** LexisNexis; Sun-Times Media L.L.C. Sun-Times Media L.L.C.; NewsBank Inc. **URL:** http://www.suntimes.com. **Ad Rates:** GLR $15.18; BW $10305; 4C $13205; PCI $212.45. **Remarks:** Accepts advertising. **Circ:** Mon.-Fri. 486,936, Sat. 287,863, Sun. 378,371.

10224 ■ Chicago's Northwest Side Press
NADIG Newspapers Inc.
4937 N Milwaukee Ave.
Chicago, IL 60630
Phone: (773)286-6100
Publisher's E-mail: news@nadignewspapers.com
Community newspaper. **Freq:** Weekly (Wed.). **Print Method:** Offset. **Cols./Page:** 8. **Col. Width:** 9.5 picas. **Col. Depth:** 294 agate lines. **URL:** http://nadignewspapers.com/publication. **Circ:** (Not Reported).

10225 ■ Chief Learning Officer
MediaTec Publishing
111 E Wacker, Ste. 1290
Chicago, IL 60601
Phone: (312)676-9900
Fax: (312)676-9910
Magazine that focuses on solutions for enterprise productivity in the enterprise learning market. **Freq:** Monthly. **Key Personnel:** Norm Kamikow, Editor-in-Chief, President. **Subscription Rates:** Free U.S. (print, digital, print and digital); Free Canada and other countries (digital); $195 Canada print and digital; $228 Other countries print and digital; $29.99 Single issue print; $9.99 Single issue PDF. **Alt. Formats:** PDF. **URL:** http://www.clomedia.com. **Remarks:** Accepts advertising. **Circ:** (Not Reported).

10226 ■ Children and Libraries: The Journal of The Association for Library Service to Children
Association for Library Service to Children
50 E Huron St.
Chicago, IL 60611-2795
Fax: (312)280-5271
Free: 800-545-2433
Publisher's E-mail: alsc@ala.org
Freq: 3/year. **Print Method:** Offset. **Trim Size:** 7.375 x 70.875. **Key Personnel:** Sharon Korbeck Verbeten, Editor. **ISSN:** 1542- 9806 (print). **Subscription Rates:** Included in membership; $50 Nonmembers U.S.; $60 Nonmembers Canada, Mexico and all Other Countries. **URL:** http://www.ala.org/alsc/compubs/childrenlib. **Ad Rates:** BW $625; 4C $1,450. **Remarks:** Accepts display advertising. **Circ:** 4538.

10227 ■ The Christian Century: Thinking Critically. Living Faithfully
The Christian Century
104 S Michigan Ave., Ste. 1100
Chicago, IL 60603
Phone: (312)263-7510
Fax: (312)263-7540
Free: 800-208-4097
Publisher's E-mail: main@christiancentury.org

Religious magazine. **Freq:** Biweekly. **Print Method:** Web offset. **Trim Size:** 8 1/4 x 10 7/8. **Cols./Page:** 3 and 2. **Col. Width:** 27 and 43 nonpareils. **Col. Depth:** 140 agate lines. **Key Personnel:** Rev. John M. Buchanan, Editor, Publisher; Heidi Baumgaertner, Manager, Advertising; David Heim, Executive Editor; Debra Bendis, Senior Editor. **ISSN:** 0009--5281 (print). **Subscription Rates:** $65 Individuals print and online; $117 Two years print and online. **URL:** http://www.christiancentury.org . **Remarks:** Accepts advertising. **Circ:** (Not Reported).

10228 ■ civil + structural ENGINEER
Mercor Media
330 N Wabash, Ste. 3201
Chicago, IL 60611
Trade magazine serving civil engineers and land surveyors engaged in land development, highways, bridges, structural, environmental, geotechnical, water resources, and industrial engineering projects including surveying. **Freq:** Monthly. **Print Method:** Heatset. **Trim Size:** 8 1/8 x 10 7/8. **Cols./Page:** 3. **Col. Width:** 2 3/16 inches. **Col. Depth:** 9 3/4 inches. **Key Personnel:** Bob Drake, Editor-in-Chief. **ISSN:** 1051-9629 (print). **Subscription Rates:** $30 Individuals print and online; $60 Two years print and online. **URL:** http://www.cenews.com. **Formerly**: CE News; Civil Engineering News. **Ad Rates:** BW $9,130; 4C $9,990. **Remarks:** Accepts advertising. **Circ:** (Not Reported).

10229 ■ Classical Philology
The University of Chicago Press
University of Chicago
1010 E 59th St.
Chicago, IL 60637
Phone: (773)702-2564
Publisher's E-mail: custserv@press.uchicago.edu
Philological magazine. **Freq:** Quarterly. **Print Method:** Offset. **Trim Size:** 6 x 9. **Cols./Page:** 1. **Col. Width:** 52 nonpareils. **Col. Depth:** 100 agate lines. **Key Personnel:** Mark Payne, Associate Editor. **ISSN:** 0009--837X (print); **EISSN:** 1546--072X (electronic). **Subscription Rates:** $66 Individuals print and electronic; $60 Individuals electronic only; $61 Individuals print only; $132 Two years print and electronic; $120 Two years electronic only; $122 Two years print only; $33 Students electronic only; $66 Students 2 years (electronic only). **URL:** http://www.jstor.org/action/showPublication?journalCode=clasphil&; http://www.press.uchicago.edu/ucp/journals/journal/cp.html. **Ad Rates:** BW $690. **Remarks:** Accepts advertising. **Circ:** ‡453.

10230 ■ Clinical Infectious Diseases
The University of Chicago Press
1427 E 60th St.
Chicago, IL 60637
Phone: (773)702-7700
Fax: (773)702-7212
Publisher's E-mail: custserv@press.uchicago.edu
Journal presenting comprehensive articles in clinical infectious disease research. **Freq:** Semimonthly. **Print Method:** Offset. **Trim Size:** 8 1/4 x 10. **Cols./Page:** 2. **Col. Width:** 36 nonpareils. **Col. Depth:** 116 agate lines. **Key Personnel:** Jerome O. Klein, Associate Editor; Neil R. Blacklow, Associate Editor; Donald A. Goldmann, Associate Editor; John R. Graybill, Associate Editor; Robert T. Schooley, Associate Editor; Sherwood L. Gorbach, Editor. **ISSN:** 1058--4838 (print). **URL:** http://www.jstor.org. **Ad Rates:** BW $1100; 4C $2000. **Remarks:** Accepts advertising. **Circ:** 11136.

10231 ■ Clinical Leadership & Management Review
Clinical Laboratory Management Association
330 N Wabash Ave., Ste. 2000
Chicago, IL 60611
Phone: (312)321-5111
Publisher's E-mail: info@clma.org
Freq: Quarterly. **ISSN:** 1527- 3954 (print). **Subscription Rates:** Included in membership; $150 Nonmembers /year. **URL:** http://www.clma.org/p/cm/ld/fid=44. **Remarks:** Accepts advertising. **Circ:** 5500.

10232 ■ Clinical Leadership and Management Review: CLMR
Clinical Laboratory Management Association
330 N Wabash Ave., Ste. 2000
Chicago, IL 60611
Phone: (312)321-5111
Publisher's E-mail: info@clma.org
Business magazine for clinical laboratory managers. **Freq:** Bimonthly. **Print Method:** Web Offset. **Trim Size:** 8 3/8 x 10 7/8. **Key Personnel:** Tony Kurec, Editor. **ISSN:** 0888--7950 (print). **URL:** http://www.clma.org/p/cm/ld/fid=44. **Formerly**: Clinical Laboratory Management Review. **Remarks:** Accepts advertising. **Circ:** ‡2000.

10233 ■ The CMA Today
American Association of Medical Assistants
20 N Wacker Dr., Ste. 1575
Chicago, IL 60606
Phone: (312)899-1500
Fax: (312)899-1259
Free: 800-228-2262
Publication E-mail: cmatoday@aama-ntl.org
Freq: Bimonthly. **Print Method:** Offset. **Trim Size:** 8 1/4 x 10 7/8. **Cols./Page:** 2 and 3. **Col. Width:** 40 and 26 nonpareils. **Col. Depth:** 134 agate lines. **Key Personnel:** Jean M. Lynch, Contact. **ISSN:** 0033-0140 (print). **Subscription Rates:** Included in membership; $60 Nonmembers. **Alt. Formats:** PDF. **URL:** http://www.aama-ntl.org/cmatoday/about.aspx; http://www.aama-ntl.org/cma-today. **Formerly**: Professional Medical Assistant; The PMA. **Ad Rates:** BW $1,000, No additional charge for four-color ads. **Remarks:** Accepts advertising. **Circ:** 28000.

10234 ■ College & Research Libraries
Association of College and Research Libraries
50 E Huron St.
Chicago, IL 60611-2729
Phone: (312)280-2523
Fax: (312)280-2520
Free: 800-545-2433
Publisher's E-mail: acrl@ala.org
Freq: Bimonthly. **ISSN:** 0010-0870 (print); **EISSN:** 2150-6701 (electronic). **Subscription Rates:** Included in membership; $15 Single issue. **URL:** http://crl.acrl.org/; http://www.ala.org/acrl/publications. **Remarks:** Accepts advertising. **Circ:** (Not Reported).

10235 ■ Commercial Investment Real Estate
CCIM Institute
430 N Michigan Ave., Ste. 800
Chicago, IL 60611
Phone: (312)321-4460
Fax: (312)321-4530
Free: 800-621-7027
Publisher's E-mail: info@cciminstitute.com
Professional development magazine for commercial investment professionals and allied fields. **Freq:** Bimonthly. **Print Method:** Web offset. **Trim Size:** 8 1/2 x 10 3/4. **Key Personnel:** Sara Drummond, Executive Editor, phone: (312)321-4469; Rich Rosfelder, Editor, phone: (312)321-4507. **ISSN:** 1524--3249 (print). **Subscription Rates:** $45 Nonmembers; $55 Other countries. **Alt. Formats:** E-book. **URL:** http://www.ccim.com/cire-magazine/issues/novdec15 . **Remarks:** Accepts advertising. **Circ:** (Not Reported).

10236 ■ Commercial Investment Real Estate Magazine
CCIM Institute
430 N Michigan Ave., Ste. 800
Chicago, IL 60611
Phone: (312)321-4460
Fax: (312)321-4530
Free: 800-621-7027
Publisher's E-mail: info@cciminstitute.com
Freq: Bimonthly. **ISSN:** 0744--6446 (print). **Subscription Rates:** Free for members; $45 Nonmembers /year. **URL:** http://www.ccim.com/cire-magazine. **Remarks:** Accepts advertising. **Circ:** 18000.

10237 ■ Comparative Education Review
The University of Chicago Press
1427 E 60th St.
Chicago, IL 60637
Phone: (773)702-7700
Fax: (773)702-7212
Publication E-mail: cer@psu.edu
Comparative education studies journal. **Freq:** Quarterly 3/year. **Print Method:** Offset. **Trim Size:** 6 3/4 X 10. **Cols./Page:** 1. **Col. Width:** 59 nonpareils. **Col. Depth:** 107 agate lines. **Key Personnel:** Bjom H. Nordtveit, Editor; David Post, Editor. **ISSN:** 0010--4086 (print); **EISSN:** 1545--701X (electronic). **Subscription Rates:** $78 Members print and electronic; $39 Students print and electronic. **URL:** http://www.press.uchicago.edu/ucp/journals/journal/cer.html; http://www.cies.us/?page=CERJournal; http://www.jstor.org/journal/compeducrevi. **Ad Rates:** BW $690. **Remarks:** Accepts advertising. **Circ:** ‡2532.

10238 ■ Complete Woman: For All the Women You Are
Associated Publications Inc.
875 N Michigan Ave., Ste. 3434
Chicago, IL 60611
Phone: (312)266-8680
Publication E-mail: letters@associatedpub.com
Women's general interest. **Freq:** Bimonthly. **Print Method:** Offset. **Cols./Page:** 3. **Col. Width:** 27 nonpareils. **Col. Depth:** 142 agate lines. **Key Personnel:** Bonnie L. Krueger, Editor-in-Chief; Lora Wintz, Executive Editor. **Subscription Rates:** $19.25 Individuals 4 issues; $38 Individuals 8 issues. **URL:** http://www.associatedpub.com/our-titles/complete-woman. **Ad Rates:** BW $2,475; 4C $3,218. **Remarks:** Accepts advertising. **Circ:** Paid 350000, Non-paid 5000.

10239 ■ Comprehensive Reviews in Food Science and Food Safety
Institute of Food Technologists
525 W Van Buren St., Ste. 1000
Chicago, IL 60607
Phone: (312)782-8424
Fax: (312)782-8348
Free: 800-438-3663
Publisher's E-mail: info@ift.org
Peer-reviewed journal providing comprehensive, critical reviews on topics of current issues in food science, technology and safety. Coverage includes topics in chemical, physical, engineering, physiological, psychological, microbiological, nutritional, sensory, risk analysis (assessment, management, communication), genetic engineering, analytical, cost, or standardization issues in foods, food ingredients, food packaging, food processing /storage, or food safety. **Freq:** Bimonthly. **Key Personnel:** Mary Ellen Camire, Board Member. **EISSN:** 1541--4337 (electronic). **URL:** http://onlinelibrary.wiley.com/journal/10.1111/%28ISSN%291541-4337. **Remarks:** Accepts advertising. **Circ:** (Not Reported).

10240 ■ Computerized Investing
American Association of Individual Investors
625 N Michigan Ave.
Chicago, IL 60611
Phone: (312)280-0170
Fax: (312)280-9883
Free: 800-428-2244
Magazine covering the use of computers for investment analysis. **Freq:** Bimonthly. **Cols./Page:** 3. **Key Personnel:** John Bajkowski, Managing Editor. **ISSN:** 0734--4597 (print). **Subscription Rates:** $20 Members annual; $40 Nonmembers annual; $40 Nonmembers domestic U.S.; $45 Nonmembers other countries, international. **URL:** http://www.aaii.com/computerized-investing. **Remarks:** Advertising not accepted. **Circ:** Paid ‡42000.

10241 ■ The Concrete Producer
Hanley Wood Media Inc.
8725 W Higgins Rd., Ste. 600
Chicago, IL 60631
Phone: (773)824-2400
Publication E-mail: tcp@omeda.com
Magazine for ready-mix and precast producers. **Freq:** Monthly. **Key Personnel:** Rick Yelton, Editor-in-Chief; Tom Bagsarian, Managing Editor; Jeane S. Mundy, Director, Production. **URL:** http://www.theconcreteproducer.com. **Ad Rates:** 4C $5,835. **Remarks:** Accepts advertising. **Circ:** Combined 20002.

10242 ■ Contemporary Clinical Trials
Mosby Inc.
211 E Chicago Ave., Ste. 1600
Chicago, IL 60611
Phone: (312)475-3633
Fax: (312)475-2692
Journal publishing design, methods, and operational aspects of clinical trials. **Freq:** Quarterly. **Key Personnel:** Kathleen Drennan, Associate Editor; Denise Faustman, Associate Editor; Joseph Collins, Associate Editor; Christine Armbruster, Associate Editor; Rochelle Tractenberg, Associate Editor; Su Zheng, Editor-in-Chief. **ISSN:** 1551--7144 (print). **Subscription Rates:** $363

Circulation: ★ = AAM; △ or • = BPA; ♦ = CAC; ❑ = VAC; ⊕ = PO Statement; ‡ = Publisher's Report; Boldface figures = sworn; Light figures = estimated.

Other countries. **URL:** http://contemporaryclinicaltrials.com. **Formerly**: Controlled Clinical Trials. **Circ:** (Not Reported).

10243 ■ Contract Packaging
Summit Publishing Co.
330 N Wabash Ave., Ste. 2401
Chicago, IL 60611
Phone: (312)222-1010
Fax: (312)222-1310
Publisher's E-mail: sales@packworld.com
Magazine focusing on contract publishing issues and news. Official publication of the Contract Packaging Association. **Freq:** Bimonthly. **Trim Size:** 8 3/8 x 11 1/8. **Key Personnel:** Patrick Reynolds, Editor, Vice President; Joseph Angel, Publisher; Iris Zavala, Managing Editor; Eric F. Greenberg, Editor. **URL:** http://www.packworld.com/contract-packaging-magazine. **Ad Rates:** BW $3940. **Remarks:** Accepts advertising. **Circ:** Combined ‡25000.

10244 ■ Contractor Magazine: The News Magazine of Mechanical Contracting
Penton Media, Inc.
330 N Wabash Ave., Ste. 2300
Chicago, IL 60611
Phone: (312)595-1080
Fax: (312)595-0295
Industry news and management how-to magazine for heating, plumbing, piping, fire sprinkler, and other mechanical specialties contracting firms. **Freq:** Monthly. **Print Method:** Web Offset. **Trim Size:** 9 3/4 x 13 1/2. **Cols./Page:** 4. **Col. Width:** 24 nonpareils. **Col. Depth:** 196 agate lines. **Key Personnel:** Steve Spaulding, Senior Editor, phone: (312)840-8492; Dan Ashenden, Publisher, phone: (312)840-8402; Robert P. Mader, Editor-in-Chief, phone: (312)840-8404, fax: (312)755-1128. **ISSN:** 0897--7135 (print). **URL:** http://contractormag.com. **Ad Rates:** 4C $13611, tabloid page; 4C $11055, standard page; BW $276, classified. **Remarks:** Accepts advertising. **Circ:** (Not Reported).

10245 ■ Contrary
The University of Chicago Press
1427 E 60th St.
Chicago, IL 60637
Phone: (773)702-7700
Fax: (773)702-7212
Publication E-mail: chicago@contrarymagazine.com
Literary magazine featuring commentary, poetry, and fiction. **Freq:** Quarterly. **Key Personnel:** Jeff McMahon, Editor; Shevi Berlinger, Associate Editor. **ISSN:** 1549--7038 (print). **URL:** http://contrarymagazine.com. **Circ:** (Not Reported).

10246 ■ Convene
Professional Convention Management Association
35 E Wacker Dr., Ste. 500
Chicago, IL 60601-2105
Phone: (312)423-7262
Fax: (312)423-7222
Free: 877-827-7262
Publisher's E-mail: deborah.sexton@pcma.org
Magazine for suppliers of association meetings and conventions and association meeting managers and CEOs. **Founded:** Mar. 1986. **Freq:** Monthly. **Print Method:** Web offset. **Trim Size:** 8 1/8 x 10 7/8. **Cols./Page:** 3. **Col. Width:** 2 1/8 inches. **Col. Depth:** 9 inches. **Key Personnel:** Michelle Russell, Editor-in-Chief; Chris Durso, Executive Editor. **Subscription Rates:** $50 Individuals; $99 Other countries. **URL:** http://www.pcma.org/convene-content/november-2014. **Ad Rates:** BW $9,230, full page; BW $7,090, half page. **Remarks:** Accepts advertising. **Circ:** Combined △**32700**.

10247 ■ CorrectCare
National Commission on Correctional Health Care
1145 W Diversey Pky.
Chicago, IL 60614
Phone: (773)880-1460
Fax: (773)880-2424
Publisher's E-mail: info@ncchc.org
Freq: Quarterly. **Alt. Formats:** PDF. **URL:** http://www.ncchc.org/correctcare. **Remarks:** Accepts advertising. **Circ:** (Not Reported).

10248 ■ The Covenant Companion
Covenant Publications
8303 W Higgins Rd.
Chicago, IL 60631
Phone: (773)907-3305
Fax: (773)784-4366
Free: 800-621-1290
Religious magazine. **Freq:** Bimonthly. **Print Method:** Offset. **Trim Size:** 8 x 10 7/8. **Cols./Page:** 3. **Col. Width:** 134 nonpareils. **Col. Depth:** 133 agate lines. **Key Personnel:** Jane Swanson-Nystrom, Managing Editor. **ISSN:** 0011--0671 (print). **Subscription Rates:** $19.95 Individuals; $31.95 Other countries; $5 Single issue. **URL:** http://covenantcompanion.com. **Ad Rates:** GLR $4; BW $1000; PCI $38. **Remarks:** Advertising accepted; rates available upon request. **Circ:** (Not Reported).

10249 ■ Crain's Chicago Business
Crain Communications Inc.
150 N Michigan Ave., 16th Fl.
Chicago, IL 60601
Phone: (312)649-5200
Fax: (312)280-3150
Publication E-mail: editor@chicagobusiness.com
Newspaper covering news stories about various aspects of business and labor activity in the Chicago market. **Freq:** Weekly. **Print Method:** Offset. **Trim Size:** 11 x 14 3/4. **Cols./Page:** 5. **Col. Width:** 22 nonpareils. **Col. Depth:** 196 agate lines. **Key Personnel:** David Snyder, Publisher, phone: (312)649-5410. **ISSN:** 0149--6956 (print). **Subscription Rates:** $99 Individuals print & online; $59.99 Individuals online. **Online:** Crain Communications Inc.; LexisNexis. **URL:** http://www.chicagobusiness.com. **Ad Rates:** BW $19110; 4C $23841. **Remarks:** Accepts advertising. **Circ:** (Not Reported).

10250 ■ Criminal Justice Magazine
American Bar Association
321 N Clark St.
Chicago, IL 60654
Phone: (312)988-5000
Free: 800-285-2221
Magazine providing practical treatment of aspects of criminal law. **Freq:** Quarterly. **Print Method:** Web offset. **Trim Size:** 8 1/2 x 11. **Cols./Page:** 2. **Col. Width:** 3 inches. **Col. Depth:** 9 1/2 inches. **Key Personnel:** John O'Hearn, Manager, Advertising, phone: (312)988-6114, fax: (312)988-6030; MaryAnn Dadisman, Editor. **ISSN:** 0887--7785 (print). **Subscription Rates:** $48 Individuals non-member U.S.; $57 Individuals non-member outside U.S.; $15.95 Individuals shipping and handling included; Free members of the ABA Criminal Justice Section. **URL:** http://www.americanbar.org/publications/criminal_justice_magazine_home.html. **Ad Rates:** BW $890; 4C $1,690. **Remarks:** Accepts advertising. **Circ:** Paid 9000, Non-paid 1252.

10251 ■ Critical Historical Studies
The University of Chicago Press, Journals Div.
1427 E 60th St.
Chicago, IL 60637
Phone: (773)702-7700
Free: 877-705-1878
Publisher's E-mail: subscriptions@press.uchicago.edu
Journal featuring research on the implications of socio-economic transformations for cultural, political, and social change. **ISSN:** 2326--4462 (print); **EISSN:** 2326--4470 (electronic). **Subscription Rates:** $27 Individuals electronic only; $30 Individuals print and electronic; $14 Students electronic only; $15 Students print and electronic. **URL:** http://www.press.uchicago.edu/ucp/journals/journal/chs.html. **Circ:** (Not Reported).

10252 ■ Critical Inquiry
The University of Chicago Press
University of Chicago
Wieboldt Hall 202
1050 E 59th St.
Chicago, IL 60637
Phone: (773)702-8477
Fax: (773)702-3397
Publisher's E-mail: custserv@press.uchicago.edu
Journal containing multidisciplinary articles by critics, scholars, and artists on literature, music, visual arts, film, history, and culture, with emphasis on principles and theories of criticism. **Freq:** Quarterly. **Print Method:** Offset. **Trim Size:** 6 x 9. **Cols./Page:** 1. **Col. Width:** 54 nonpareils. **Col. Depth:** 103 agate lines. **Key Personnel:** W.J.T. Mitchell, Editor; Arnold I. Davidson, Editor. **ISSN:** 0093--1896 (print); **EISSN:** 1539--7858 (electronic). **Subscription Rates:** $58 Individuals print and electronic; $50 Individuals electronic only; $51 Individuals print only; $116 Two years print and electronic; $100 Two years electronic only; $102 Two years print only; $29 Students electronic only; $58 Students 2 years (electronic only). **URL:** http://www.press.uchicago.edu/ucp/journals/journal/ci.html; http://www.jstor.org/journal/criticalinquiry. **Ad Rates:** BW $730. **Remarks:** Accepts advertising. **Circ:** ‡1166.

10253 ■ CS
Modern Luxury Media
200 W Hubbard
Chicago, IL 60654
Phone: (312)274-2500
Fax: (312)274-2501
Magazine featuring affluent lifestyle in Chicago. **Freq:** Monthly. **Trim Size:** 10 x 12. **Key Personnel:** Korey Karnes Huyler, Editor-in-Chief. **Subscription Rates:** $40 Individuals; $60 Two years. **URL:** http://www.modernluxury.com/cs. **Also known as**: Chicago Social. **Remarks:** Accepts advertising. **Circ:** (Not Reported).

10254 ■ CS Interiors
Modern Luxury Media
200 W Hubbard
Chicago, IL 60654
Phone: (312)274-2500
Fax: (312)274-2501
Magazine covering current trends in interior design. **Freq:** Quarterly. **Key Personnel:** Jennifer Polachek, Publisher; Meghan McEwen, Editor-in-Chief. **Subscription Rates:** $20 Individuals; $35 Two years. **URL:** http://www.modernluxury.com/interiors-chicago. **Remarks:** Accepts advertising. **Circ:** (Not Reported).

10255 ■ CTBUH Review
Council on Tall Buildings and Urban Habitat
c/o Patti Thurmond, Manager of Operations
SR Crown Hall
Illinois Institute of Technology
3360 S State St.
Chicago, IL 60616
Phone: (312)567-3487
Fax: (312)567-3820
Publisher's E-mail: info@ctbuh.org
Freq: Quarterly. **Subscription Rates:** Included in membership; $150 Nonmembers. **URL:** http://www.ctbuh.org/Publications/Journal/Reviews/tabid/1091/language/en-GB/Default.aspx. **Remarks:** Accepts advertising. **Circ:** 1500.

10256 ■ The Daily Press
The Tribune Media Co.
435 N Michigan Ave.
Chicago, IL 60611-4066
Phone: (312)222-9100
Fax: (312)222-4206
Free: 800-874-2863
Publication E-mail: letters@dailypress.com
General newspaper. **Founded:** 1896. **Freq:** Daily (morn.). **Print Method:** Offset. **Trim Size:** 13 7/8 x 22. **Cols./Page:** 6. **Col. Width:** 26 nonpareils. **Col. Depth:** 294 agate lines. **Key Personnel:** Robin McCormick, Managing Editor, phone: (757)247-4735; Tracey Cooper, Manager, Production, phone: (757)247-4521; Ernest C. Gates, Editor, Vice President, phone: (757)247-4628; Digby A. Solomon, President, Publisher, phone: (757)247-4612. **USPS:** 144-900. **Subscription Rates:** $3.81 Individuals home delivery; $99 Individuals /year; digitalPlus. **URL:** http://www.dailypress.com/. **Feature Editors:** Karen Morgan, phone: (757)247-4757, kmorgan@dailypress.com. **Ad Rates:** SAU $53. **Remarks:** Accepts advertising. **Circ:** Mon.-Sat. ★**88570**, Sun. ★**110229**.

Deerfield Review: With News of Lincolnshire, Riverwoods, and Bannockburn - See Deerfield

10257 ■ Defined Contribution Insights
Plan Sponsor Council of America
200 S Wacker Dr., Ste. 3164
Chicago, IL 60606
Phone: (312)419-1863
Fax: (312)419-1864
Publisher's E-mail: psca@psca.org
Magazine featuring articles exclusively on employer-sponsored retirement plans. **Freq:** Quarterly. **Subscrip-**

tion Rates: Included in membership. **URL:** http://www.psca.org/insights-magazines. **Remarks:** Accepts advertising. **Circ:** 2500.

10258 ■ Desert Cities Magazine: The Magazine for Rancho Mirage, Palm Desert, Indian Wells and La Quinta
R.E.N. Publishing Co.
3500 W Peterson Ave., No. 403
Chicago, IL 60659
Phone: (773)866-9900
Fax: (773)866-9881
Publisher's E-mail: rencpublishing@earthlink.net
Magazine covering the places and the people investing, living, and working within Rancho Mirage, Palm Desert, La Quinta and Indian Wells. **Subscription Rates:** Free first issue. **URL:** http://www.desertcitiesmagazine.com. **Remarks:** Accepts advertising. **Circ:** (Not Reported).

10259 ■ The Diabetes Educator: The Journal of the American Association of Diabetes Educators
American Association of Diabetes Educators
200 W Madison St., Ste. 800
Chicago, IL 60606
Fax: (312)424-2427
Free: 800-338-3633
Publisher's E-mail: membership@aadenet.org
Journal featuring original literature from all disciplines regarding diabetes and diabetes patient education. **Freq:** Bimonthly. **Print Method:** Offset. **Trim Size:** 8 3/8 x 10 7/8. **Cols./Page:** 3 and 2. **Col. Width:** 27 and 40 nonpareils. **Col. Depth:** 140 agate lines. **Key Personnel:** James A. Fain, PhD, Editor-in-Chief. **ISSN:** 0145--7217 (print); **EISSN:** 1554--6063 (electronic). **Subscription Rates:** $122 Individuals print only; $237 Institutions e-access; $258 Institutions print; $263 Institutions all online content; print and online; $289 Institutions current volume print & all online content; $484 Institutions content through 1998; $26 Individuals single issue; $47 Institutions single issue. **URL:** http://www.diabeteseducator.org/news-publications/the-diabetes-educator-journal; http://tde.sagepub.com. **Ad Rates:** BW $1485; 4C $1855. **Remarks:** Advertising accepted; rates available upon request. **Circ:** Paid ‡13320.

10260 ■ Dispute Resolution
American Bar Association
321 N Clark St.
Chicago, IL 60654
Phone: (312)988-5000
Free: 800-285-2221
Magazine for lawyers and legal professionals providing information regarding the latest developments, news and trends in the field of dispute resolution. **Freq:** Quarterly. **Key Personnel:** Joseph B. Stulberg, Co-Chairman of the Board; Nancy A. Welsh, Board Member; Gina Viola Brown, Editor. **Subscription Rates:** $55 Nonmembers /year; Included in membership. **URL:** http://www.americanbar.org/publications/dispute_resolution_magazine.html. **Remarks:** Accepts advertising. **Circ:** (Not Reported).

10261 ■ The DO
American Osteopathic Association
142 E Ontario St.
Chicago, IL 60611-2864
Phone: (312)202-8000
Fax: (312)202-8200
Free: 800-621-1773
Publisher's E-mail: info@osteopathic.org
Freq: Monthly. **Print Method:** Offset. **Trim Size:** 7 7/8 x 10 7/8. **Cols./Page:** 3. **Col. Width:** 26 nonpareils. **Col. Depth:** 127 agate lines. **Key Personnel:** Robert Orenstein, Editor-in-Chief. **ISSN:** 0011--5088 (print). **URL:** http://thedo.osteopathic.org. **Ad Rates:** BW $2459; 4C $1909. **Remarks:** Accepts advertising. **Circ:** (Not Reported).

10262 ■ The Doings Clarendon Hills
Sun-Times Media L.L.C.
350 N Orleans St., 10th Fl.
Chicago, IL 60654
Phone: (312)321-3000
Free: 888-848-4637
Publication E-mail: doingsnews@pioneerlocal.com
Community newspaper. **Freq:** Weekly. **Key Personnel:** Brett Johnson, Editor, phone: (630)320-5417. **URL:** http://clarendonhills.chicagotribune.com. **Remarks:** Accepts advertising. **Circ:** (Not Reported).

10263 ■ The Doings Oak Brook
Sun-Times Media L.L.C.
350 N Orleans St., 10th Fl.
Chicago, IL 60654
Phone: (312)321-3000
Free: 888-848-4637
Publication E-mail: doingsnews@pioneerlocal.com
Community newspaper. **Freq:** Weekly. **Key Personnel:** Brett Johnson, Editor. **Subscription Rates:** $2.99 Individuals weekly (print and unlimited digital access); $2.25 Individuals weekly (digital access only). **URL:** http://oakbrook.chicagotribune.com. **Remarks:** Accepts advertising. **Circ:** (Not Reported).

10264 ■ The Doings Weekly
Sun-Times Media L.L.C.
350 N Orleans St., 10th Fl.
Chicago, IL 60654
Phone: (312)321-3000
Free: 888-848-4637
Publication E-mail: doingsnews@pioneerlocal.com
Community newspaper. **Freq:** Weekly. **Print Method:** offset. **Key Personnel:** Brett Johnson, Editor. **Subscription Rates:** $20 Individuals; $84 Out of state. **URL:** http://burrridge.chicagotribune.com. **Remarks:** Accepts advertising. **Circ:** (Not Reported).

10265 ■ The Doings Western Springs
Sun-Times Media L.L.C.
350 N Orleans St., 10th Fl.
Chicago, IL 60654
Phone: (312)321-3000
Free: 888-848-4637
Publication E-mail: doingsnews@pioneerlocal.com
Local newspaper. **Freq:** Weekly. **Key Personnel:** Brett Johnson, Editor, phone: (630)320-5417. **Subscription Rates:** $28 Individuals; $84 Out of state. **URL:** http://westernsprings.chicagotribune.com. **Remarks:** Accepts advertising. **Circ:** (Not Reported).

10266 ■ Dystonia Dialogue
Dystonia Medical Research Foundation
1 E Wacker Dr., Ste. 2810
Chicago, IL 60601-1905
Phone: (312)755-0198
Fax: (312)803-0138
Free: 800-377-3978
Publisher's E-mail: dystonia@dystonia-foundation.org
Freq: 3/year in spring, summer and winter. **Subscription Rates:** $40 Individuals donation. **Alt. Formats:** PDF. **URL:** http://www.dystonia-foundation.org/dialogue. **Remarks:** Advertising not accepted. **Circ:** 46000.

10267 ■ Ebony
Johnson Publishing Company L.L.C.
200 S Michigan Avenue, 21st Floor,
Chicago, IL 60604
Phone: (312)322-9200
Fax: (312)322-1082
General editorial magazine geared toward African-Americans. **Freq:** Monthly. **Print Method:** Offset. **Cols./Page:** 3. **Col. Width:** 30 nonpareils. **Col. Depth:** 140 agate lines. **Key Personnel:** John H. Johnson, Chairman, Publisher; Linda Johnson Rice, Chief Executive Officer, President; Mitzi Miller, Editor-in-Chief. **Subscription Rates:** $11.97 Individuals 12 issues; $17.97 Individuals 24 issues. **URL:** http://www.ebony.com; http://www.johnsonpublishing.com/index.php/press-release/ebony-magazine-appoints-aliya-s-king-as-entertainment-editor. **Ad Rates:** BW $81167; 4C $60083. **Remarks:** Accepts advertising. **Circ:** Paid **★1280000**.

10268 ■ Economic Perspectives
Federal Reserve Bank of Chicago
230 S LaSalle St.
Chicago, IL 60604
Phone: (312)322-5322
Free: 888-372-2457
Publication covering the field of economics. **Freq:** Quarterly. **Key Personnel:** Helen Koshy, Editor, phone: (312)322-5830. **ISSN:** 0164-0682 (print). **URL:** http://www.chicagofed.org/webpages/publications/economic_perspectives/index.cfm. **Mailing address:** PO Box 834, Chicago, IL 60604-1427. **Circ:** (Not Reported).

10269 ■ El Heraldo Newspaper: El Heraldo Nuevo, Ltd
Displays Publishing
70 E Lake St., Ste. 520
Chicago, IL 60601
Phone: (312)201-8488
Fax: (312)201-8444
Community newspaper (Spanish). **Freq:** Weekly. **Print Method:** Offset. **Trim Size:** 11 1/2 x 17. **Cols./Page:** 5. **Col. Width:** 2 1/16 inches. **Col. Depth:** 15 inches. **Key Personnel:** Marta Foster, Publisher. **Subscription Rates:** $45 IND. **Formerly:** El Heraldo de Chicago. **Ad Rates:** BW $1,200; 4C $1,625; SAU $18.46; PCI $15.38. **Remarks:** Accepts advertising. **Circ:** (Not Reported).

10270 ■ Electrical Apparatus: The Magazine of Electromechanical & Electronic Application & Maintenance
Barks Publications Inc.
500 N Michigan Ave., Ste. 901
Chicago, IL 60611
Phone: (312)321-9440
Fax: (312)321-1288
Free: 800-288-7493
Publication E-mail: eamagazine@barks.com
Professional magazine focusing on the application and maintenance of electromechanical apparatus. **Freq:** Monthly. **Print Method:** Web offset. **Trim Size:** 8 x 10 3/4. **Cols./Page:** 2 and 3. **Col. Width:** 13 and 20 picas. **Col. Depth:** 10 inches. **Key Personnel:** Kevin N. Jones, Senior Editor; Horace B. Barks, Editor; Kathleen Shannon, Manager, Circulation; Elsie Dickson, Publisher; Elizabeth Van Ness, Associate Publisher; Joseph S. Hoff, Associate Editor; Richard L. Nailen, Editor; William H. Wiersema, Editor. **ISSN:** 0190--1370 (print). **Subscription Rates:** $50 Individuals; $85 Two years; $100 Other countries US Airmail; $185 Two years US Airmail. **URL:** http://barks.com/for-readers/about-electrical-apparatus-magazine. **Formerly:** Electrical Apparatus Service magazine. **Remarks:** Advertising accepted; rates available upon request. **Circ:** (Not Reported).

10271 ■ Electromagnetics
Taylor & Francis Group Journals
c/o David H.Y. Yang, Ed.-in-Ch.
Dept. of Electrical Engineering & Computer Science
University of Illinois
Chicago, IL 60607-7053
Publisher's E-mail: customerservice@taylorandfrancis.com
Journal publishing refereed papers spanning the field of electromagnetics. **Freq:** 8/year. **Print Method:** Offset. **Trim Size:** 7 x 10. **Cols./Page:** 1. **Col. Width:** 63 nonpareils. **Col. Depth:** 115 agate lines. **Key Personnel:** Franco De Flaviis, Board Member; Yehuda Leviatan, Board Member; Jianming Jin, Board Member; Hisamatsu Nakano, Board Member; Aklesh Lakhtakia, Board Member; Daniel Du Zutter, Board Member; David H.Y. Yang, Editor-in-Chief; Roberto D. Graglia, Board Member. **ISSN:** 0272--6343 (print); **EISSN:** 1532-527X (electronic). **Subscription Rates:** $1769 Institutions print & online; $1548 Institutions online only; $1206 Individuals print only. **URL:** http://www.tandfonline.com/toc/uemg20/current#.VGM3TzQwrlc. **Remarks:** Accepts advertising. **Circ:** (Not Reported).

10272 ■ The Elementary School Journal
The University of Chicago Press
1427 E 60th St.
Chicago, IL 60637
Phone: (773)702-7700
Fax: (773)702-7212
Publisher's E-mail: custserv@press.uchicago.edu
Journal relating social science research in elementary education theory and the classroom. **Freq:** 4/yr. **Print Method:** Offset. **Trim Size:** 6 3/4 x 10. **Cols./Page:** 2. **Col. Width:** 32 nonpareils. **Col. Depth:** 113 agate lines. **Key Personnel:** Russell Gersten, Editor-in-Chief; Greg Scherban, Managing Editor; Addison Stone, Editor. **ISSN:** 0013--5984 (print); **EISSN:** 1554--8279 (electronic). **Subscription Rates:** $56 Individuals print and electronic; $49 Individuals electronic only; $50 Individuals print only; $40 Members NAESP, print and electronic; $28 Students electronic only; $101 Two years print and electronic; $72 Two years NAESP member, print and electronic; $50 Two years student, electronic only; $143 Individuals three years, print and electronic; $71 Students three years, electronic only. **URL:** http://

Circulation: ★ = AAM; △ or • = BPA; ♦ = CAC; ❑ = VAC; ⊕ = PO Statement; ‡ = Publisher's Report; Boldface figures = sworn; Light figures = estimated.

www.journals.uchicago.edu/toc/esj/current. **Ad Rates:** BW $690. **Remarks:** Accepts advertising. **Circ:** ‡868.

10273 ■ The Elks Magazine
Benevolent and Protective Order of Elks
2750 N Lakeview Ave.
Chicago, IL 60614-1889
Phone: (773)755-4700
Fax: (773)755-4790
Publisher's E-mail: grandlodge@elks.org
Fraternal magazine. **Freq:** 10/year. **Print Method:** Offset. **Trim Size:** 8 x 10 13/16. **Cols./Page:** 3. **Col. Width:** 27 nonpareils. **Col. Depth:** 140 agate lines. **Key Personnel:** Anna L. Idol, Editor, Publisher, phone: (773)755-4740, fax: (773)755-4792; Phil Claiborne, Manager, Circulation. **ISSN:** 0013--6263 (print). **Alt. Formats:** PDF. **URL:** http://www.elks.org/ElksMag. **Ad Rates:** GLR $25; BW $19800; 4C $24000; PCI $364. **Remarks:** Accepts advertising. **Circ:** (Not Reported).

10274 ■ Employee Rights and Employment Policy Journal
Illinois Institute of Technology Chicago-Kent College of Law
565 W Adams St.
Chicago, IL 60661-3691
Phone: (312)906-5000
Fax: (312)906-5280
Journal discussing legal law on employee rights in the work place. **Freq:** Semiannual. **Subscription Rates:** $60 Individuals /volume; $30 Single issue; Free online. **URL:** http://www.kentlaw.iit.edu/institutes-centers/institute-for-law-and-the-workplace/publications/employee-rights-employment-policy-journal. **Circ:** (Not Reported).

10275 ■ Engineering Journal
American Institute of Steel Construction
1 E Wacker Dr., Ste. 700
Chicago, IL 60601-1802
Phone: (312)670-2400
Fax: (312)670-5403
Publisher's E-mail: solutions@aisc.org
Magazine devoted exclusively to the design of steel structures featuring papers of practical design value. Provides the latest information on steel design, research, and construction to structural engineers, architects, and educators. **Freq:** Quarterly. **Print Method:** Offset. **Cols./Page:** 2. **Col. Width:** 20 nonpareils. **Col. Depth:** 127 agate lines. **Key Personnel:** Stephen E. Porter, Treasurer; Lawrence A. Cox, Director; Rex I. Lewis, Chairman; Scott L. Melnick, Vice President, Communications, phone: (312)670-8314; Louis H. Gurthet, President; Cynthia J. Duncan, Editor; Keith A. Grubb, Managing Editor, phone: (312)670-8318. **ISSN:** 0013--8029 (print). **Subscription Rates:** $40 Members /year US (print); $160 Nonmembers /year US (print); $80 Members /year Canada/Mexico (print); $160 Nonmembers /year Canada/Mexico (print). **URL:** http://www.aisc.org/content.aspx?id=31270. **Remarks:** Advertising not accepted. **Circ:** ‡6500.

10276 ■ Event World
International Special Events Society
330 N Wabash Ave., Ste. 2000
Chicago, IL 60611
Phone: (312)321-6853
Fax: (312)673-6953
Free: 800-688-4737
Publisher's E-mail: info@ises.com
Magazine containing stories, photos, happenings and highlights of previous ISES Eventworld. **Freq:** Monthly. **URL:** http://www.ises.com/event-world-2012. **Remarks:** Accepts advertising. **Circ:** 25000.

10277 ■ Experience
American Bar Association
321 N Clark St.
Chicago, IL 60654
Phone: (312)988-5000
Free: 800-285-2221
Magazine for lawyers and legal professionals dealing with issues facing senior lawyers. **Freq:** Quarterly. **Trim Size:** 8 1/2 x 11. **Key Personnel:** Hon. Francis J. Larkin, Co-Chairman of the Board; Lisa Comforty, Managing Editor, phone: (312)988-6121. **ISSN:** 1054-3473 (print). **Subscription Rates:** $45 Individuals regular. **URL:** http://www.abanet.org/abastore/index.cfm?section=main&fm=Product.AddToCart& pid=5460100; http://www.americanbar.org/groups/senior_lawyers/publications.html. **Remarks:** Accepts advertising. **Circ:** (Not Reported).

10278 ■ Extension
Catholic Church Extension Society
150 S Wacker Dr., Ste. 2000
Chicago, IL 60606
Phone: (800)842-7804
Fax: (312)236-5276
Publisher's E-mail: info@catholicextension.org
Magazine reporting on activities and issues of American Catholic missions. **Freq:** Quarterly. **Print Method:** Offset. **Trim Size:** 8 x 10 7/8. **Cols./Page:** 3. **Col. Width:** 13 picas. **Col. Depth:** 57 picas. **Key Personnel:** Jack Wall, President. **ISSN:** 0884-7533 (print). **Subscription Rates:** Free. **Alt. Formats:** PDF. **URL:** http://www.catholicextension.org/news-media/extension-magazine. **Remarks:** Advertising not accepted. **Circ:** Controlled ‡85000.

10279 ■ EXTRA
EXTRA Publications Inc.
3906 W North Ave.
Chicago, IL 60647
Phone: (773)252-3534
Fax: (773)252-6031
Publisher's E-mail: editor@extranews.net
Community newspaper. **Founded:** 1981. **Freq:** Weekly (Thurs.). **Key Personnel:** Mila Tellez, Publisher; Sylvana Tabares, Managing Editor; Abel Arciniega, Manager, Production. **URL:** http://extranews.net. **Formerly**: Southwest EXTRA. **Remarks:** Accepts advertising. **Circ:** ‡4926.

10280 ■ Fancy Food & Culinary Products
Talcott Communication Corp.
233 N Michigan Ave., Ste. 1780
Chicago, IL 60601
Phone: (312)849-2220
Fax: (312)849-2174
Free: 800-229-1967
Publication E-mail: fancyfood@talcott.com
Trade magazine for specialty food retailers. **Freq:** Bimonthly. **Print Method:** Offset. **Trim Size:** 10 7/8 x 14 5/8. **Cols./Page:** 4. **Col. Width:** 13 picas. **Key Personnel:** Joanne Fallon, Contact; Naurice Olivera, Manager, Circulation, phone: (800)229-1967; Claire Johnson, Managing Editor; Daniel von Rabenau, President, Publisher. **Subscription Rates:** $26 U.S.; $37 U.S. Two years; $47 U.S. Three years; $32 Canada; $60 Other countries. **URL:** http://www.fancyfoodmagazine.com; http://www.talcott.com/contact.htm. **Formerly**: Fancy Food. **Ad Rates:** BW $4200; 4C $5900. **Remarks:** Accepts advertising. **Circ:** △**63,700**.

10281 ■ FF Journal
Trend Publishing Inc.
625 N Michigan Ave., Ste. 1100
Chicago, IL 60611-3110
Phone: (312)654-2300
Publisher's E-mail: jdalexander@trendpublishing.com
Trade publication covering fabricating and forming technology. **Freq:** 9/year. **Print Method:** Web Offset. **Trim Size:** 7 x 10. **Key Personnel:** Michael D'Alexander, Publisher, Vice President; Lynn Stanley, Senior Editor. **URL:** http://www.ffjournal.net. **Ad Rates:** BW $5,690; 4C $6,630. **Remarks:** Accepts advertising. **Circ:** △**45111**.

10282 ■ Fin de Semana Chicago
Tribune Publishing
435 N Michigan Ave.
Chicago, IL 60611
Phone: (312)222-9100
Publisher's E-mail: gweitman@tribune.com
Newspaper covering news and events relevant to the Hispanic community within Cook County and nearby areas. **Freq:** Weekly (Sun.). **Key Personnel:** Fernando Diaz, Director, Editorial, phone: (312)527-8445; John Trainor, General Manager, phone: (312)527-8429. **URL:** http://www.vivelohoy.com/findesemana/chicago. **Remarks:** Accepts advertising. **Circ:** Non-paid ♦**297959**.

10283 ■ The Final Call
FCN Publishing
734 W 79th St.
Chicago, IL 60620
Phone: (773)602-1230
Newspaper serving the black community. **Freq:** Weekly. **Print Method:** Web offset. **Trim Size:** 11 3/8 x 13 3/4. **Cols./Page:** 5. **Col. Width:** 11.5 picas. **Col. Depth:** 12 1/2 inches. **Key Personnel:** Dora Muhammed, Managing Editor; Barnar C. Muhammad, Director, Editor; Duane Muhammed, General Manager. **Subscription Rates:** $23 Individuals 25 Issues; $50 Individuals 50 Issues. **URL:** http://finalcall.com. **Remarks:** Accepts advertising. **Circ:** 900000.

10284 ■ Finest Hour: Journal of the Churchill Centre
Churchill Centre
c/o Lee Pollock, Executive Director
131 S Dearborn St., Ste. 1700
Chicago, IL 60603
Phone: (312)263-5637
Journal covering Winston Churchill. **Freq:** Quarterly. **Key Personnel:** Richard Langworth, Chairman. **ISSN:** 0882--3715 (print). **Subscription Rates:** Included in membership. **URL:** http://www.winstonchurchill.org/publications/finest-hour. **Formerly**: Journal of Winston Churchill. **Remarks:** Accepts advertising. **Circ:** (Not Reported).

10285 ■ Firewatch!
National Association of Fire Equipment Distributors
180 N Wabash Ave., Ste. 401
Chicago, IL 60603
Phone: (312)461-9600
Fax: (312)461-0777
Magazine publishing articles on fire protection equipment companies, personnel and products. **Freq:** Quarterly. **Subscription Rates:** Included in membership. **URL:** http://www.nafed.org/firewatch. **Remarks:** Accepts advertising. **Circ:** 2,500.

10286 ■ The Flutist Quarterly
National Flute Association
70 E Lake St., No. 200
Chicago, IL 60601
Phone: (312)332-6682
Fax: (312)332-6684
Freq: Quarterly. **Print Method:** Offset. **Trim Size:** 8 1/2 x 11. **Cols./Page:** 2. **Col. Width:** 3 3/8 inches. **Col. Depth:** 9 3/8 inches. **Key Personnel:** Glennis M. Stout, Editor; Victoria Jicha, Manager, Advertising. **ISSN:** 8756--8667 (print). **Alt. Formats:** Download. **URL:** http://www.nfaonline.org/Publications/The-Flutist-Quarterly. **Formerly**: Newsletter of the National Flute Association. **Ad Rates:** BW $520; 4C $820. **Remarks:** Accepts advertising. **Circ:** ‡5000.

10287 ■ Food Industry News
Foodservice Publishing Co.
2702 W Touhy
Chicago, IL 60645
Phone: (312)743-4200
Fax: (312)743-4559
Restaurant industry. **Freq:** Monthly. **Print Method:** Offset. **Cols./Page:** 3. **Col. Width:** 26 nonpareils. **Col. Depth:** 140 agate lines. **Key Personnel:** Terry Minnich, Editor. **Subscription Rates:** $20 Individuals 1 year; $38 Two years; $49.95 Individuals 3 years. **URL:** http://www.foodindustrynews.com. **Ad Rates:** BW $4128; 4C $5993. **Remarks:** Advertising accepted; rates available upon request. **Circ:** Combined ‡23170.

10288 ■ Food Technology: The Voice of food science and technology
Institute of Food Technologists
525 W Van Buren St., Ste. 1000
Chicago, IL 60607
Phone: (312)782-8424
Fax: (312)782-8348
Free: 800-438-3663
Publisher's E-mail: info@ift.org
Food technology and science magazine. **Freq:** Monthly. **Print Method:** Offset. **Trim Size:** 8 1/8 x 10 7/8. **Cols./Page:** 3 and 2. **Col. Width:** 26 and 40 nonpareils. **Col. Depth:** 140 agate lines. **Key Personnel:** Karen Nachay, Editor-in-Chief; Bob Swientek, Director, Publications, Editor-in-Chief. **ISSN:** 0015--6639 (print). **Subscription Rates:** $190 Individuals; $199.50 Canada GST included; $190 Individuals in Mexico; $190 Other countries; Included in membership. **URL:** http://www.ift.org/food-technology.aspx. **Ad Rates:** BW $3780; 4C $1400. **Remarks:** Accepts advertising. **Circ:** Combined ⋆**17431**.

10289 ■ Forest Leaves
Sun-Times Media L.L.C.
350 N Orleans St., 10th Fl.
Chicago, IL 60654
Phone: (312)321-3000
Free: 888-848-4637
Publisher's E-mail: customerservice@suntimes.com
Community newspaper (tabloid). **Founded:** 1907. **Freq:** Weekly. **Print Method:** Offset. **Cols./Page:** 5. **Col. Width:** 10 inches. **Col. Depth:** 14 inches. **Key Personnel:** Jennifer Clark, Managing Editor, phone: (703)524-4412; Rick Hibbert, Editor, phone: (847)486-7526. **Subscription Rates:** $20 Individuals; $84 Out of state. **URL:** http://riverforest.suntimes.com. **Circ:** (Not Reported).

10290 ■ Frame Building News
National Frame Builders Association
8735 W Higgins Rd., Ste. 300
Chicago, IL 60631
Fax: (847)375-6495
Free: 800-557-6957
Publisher's E-mail: info@nfba.org
Magazine focusing on the building system techniques and ways of the post-frame construction for the benefit of post-frame building contractors, general contractors, and building component manufacturers and distributors. **Freq:** 5/year. **Key Personnel:** Kyler Pope, Contact. **Subscription Rates:** Free. **URL:** http://www.nfba.org/Resources/content/framenews.html; http://www.constructionmagnet.com/frame-building-news. **Remarks:** Accepts advertising. **Circ:** 32000.

10291 ■ Franchise Law Journal
American Bar Association
321 N Clark St.
Chicago, IL 60654
Phone: (312)988-5000
Free: 800-285-2221
Journal for lawyers, franchisors and franchisees dealing with issues relating to franchise law. **Freq:** Quarterly. **Key Personnel:** Wendy J. Smith, Editor; Christopher P. Bussert, Editor-in-Chief. **ISSN:** 8756--7962 (print). **Subscription Rates:** Included in membership; $31 Individuals /year for non-lawyers; $50 Individuals. **Alt. Formats:** PDF. **URL:** http://www.americanbar.org/publications/franchising_law_journal_home.html. **Remarks:** Advertising not accepted. **Circ:** (Not Reported).

Franklin Park Herald-Journal - See Franklin Park

10292 ■ Freshwater Science
The University of Chicago Press, Journals Div.
1427 E 60th St.
Chicago, IL 60637
Phone: (773)702-7700
Free: 877-705-1878
Publisher's E-mail: subscriptions@press.uchicago.edu
Journal containing topics regarding all types of inland aquatic ecosystems (lakes, rivers, streams, reservoirs, subterranean, and estuaries) and ecosystems at the interface between aquatic and terrestrial habitats (wetlands, riparian areas, and floodplains). **ISSN:** 2161--9549 (print); **EISSN:** 2161--9565 (electronic). **URL:** http://www.press.uchicago.edu/ucp/journals/journal/fws.html. **Circ:** (Not Reported).

10293 ■ The Friend: Draugas
Lithuanian Catholic Press Society
4545 W 63rd St.
Chicago, IL 60629-5532
Phone: (773)585-9500
Fax: (773)585-8284
Publisher's E-mail: redakcija@draugas.org
Lithuanian Catholic daily newspaper. **Freq:** 3/week Tue.-Thu.-Sat. **Print Method:** Offset. **Cols./Page:** 7. **Col. Width:** 25 nonpareils. **Col. Depth:** 280 agate lines. **Key Personnel:** Dalia Cidzikaite, Editor-in-Chief. **USPS:** 161-000. **Subscription Rates:** $150 Individuals print; $115 Individuals online. **URL:** http://www.draugas.org/about.html. **Also known as**: Draugas. **Ad Rates:** BW $840.60; PCI $6. **Remarks:** Accepts advertising. **Circ:** ‡6200.

10294 ■ Front Desk Chicago
Modern Luxury Media
200 W Hubbard
Chicago, IL 60654
Phone: (312)274-2500
Fax: (312)274-2501
Magazine covering the best social hotspots and gift buys in Chicago. **Freq:** Monthly. **Key Personnel:** Marissa Conrad, Editor-in-Chief. **Subscription Rates:** $20 Individuals; $35 Two years. **URL:** http://media.modernluxury.com/digital.php?e=FDCH; http://modernluxury.com/front-desk-chicago/digital-edition. **Remarks:** Accepts advertising. **Circ:** (Not Reported).

10295 ■ Frontiers of Health Services Management
Health Administration Press
1 N Franklin St., Ste. 1700
Chicago, IL 60606-3529
Phone: (312)424-2800
Fax: (312)424-0023
Publisher's E-mail: geninfo@ache.org
Freq: Quarterly Latest Edition: 2015. **Print Method:** Offset. **Trim Size:** 8 1/2 x 11. **Cols./Page:** 1 and 2. **Col. Width:** 29 INS19 INS. **Col. Depth:** 51 INS51 INS. **Key Personnel:** Margaret F. Schulte, Editor. **ISSN:** 0748--8157 (print). **Subscription Rates:** $135 Individuals U.S; $145 Individuals Canada and all other countries; $35 Single issue. **URL:** http://ache.org/pubs/Frontiers/frontiers_index.cfm; http://www.ache.org/pubs/Frontiers/frontiers_index.cfm. **Remarks:** Advertising not accepted. **Circ:** ‡2500, 800.

10296 ■ Frontiers of Health Services Management
American College of Healthcare Executives
1 N Franklin St., Ste. 1700
Chicago, IL 60606-3529
Phone: (312)424-2800
Fax: (312)424-0023
Publisher's E-mail: geninfo@ache.org
Freq: Quarterly Latest Edition: 2015. **Print Method:** Offset. **Trim Size:** 8 1/2 x 11. **Cols./Page:** 1 and 2. **Col. Width:** 29 INS19 INS. **Col. Depth:** 51 INS51 INS. **Key Personnel:** Margaret F. Schulte, Editor. **ISSN:** 0748--8157 (print). **Subscription Rates:** $135 Individuals U.S; $145 Individuals Canada and all other countries; $35 Single issue. **URL:** http://ache.org/pubs/Frontiers/frontiers_index.cfm; http://www.ache.org/pubs/Frontiers/frontiers_index.cfm. **Remarks:** Advertising not accepted. **Circ:** ‡2500, 800.

10297 ■ Futures
The Alpha Pages
217 N Jefferson Ste. 601
Chicago, IL 60661
Phone: (312)846-4600
Periodical covering social science and international business. **Freq:** Monthly. **Key Personnel:** James T. Holter, Editor; Daniel Collins, Editor-in-Chief. **ISSN:** 0016-3287 (print). **Subscription Rates:** $85 U.S. print and online; $195 Other countries print and online; $99 Canada print and online; $55 Individuals digital. **URL:** http://www.futuresmag.com/. **Remarks:** Accepts advertising. **Circ:** (Not Reported).

10298 ■ The Futurist: A Journal of Forecasts, Trends, and Ideas About the Future
World Future Society
333 N Lasalle St.
Chicago, IL 60654
Free: 800-989-8274
Publication E-mail: info@wfs.org
Magazine exploring social and technological changes. **Founded:** Feb. 1967. **Freq:** Bimonthly. **Trim Size:** 10 3/4 x 8 1/4. **Key Personnel:** Cynthia G. Wagner, Editor; Edward S. Cornish, Editor. **ISSN:** 0016-3317 (print). **Subscription Rates:** $79 Individuals; $89 Libraries. **URL:** http://www.wfs.org/futurist.htm. **Ad Rates:** BW $1250; 4C $1880. **Remarks:** Accepts advertising. **Circ:** ‡15,955, Combined ‡9,807.

10299 ■ Gazette Chicago
The Near West Gazette
1335 W Harrison St.
Chicago, IL 60612-3248
Phone: (312)243-4288
Fax: (312)243-4270
Publisher's E-mail: info@gazettechicago.com
Local newspaper. **Freq:** Monthly. **Print Method:** Offset. **Trim Size:** 8.75 x 12.5. **Cols./Page:** 4. **Col. Width:** 12 picas. **Col. Depth:** 140 agate lines. **Key Personnel:** Mark J. Valentino, Editor, Publisher; William Bike, Associate Editor; Carmen P. Valentino, Manager, Advertising. **ISSN:** 1068--8213 (print). **Formerly:** The Near West Gazette. **Remarks:** Accepts advertising. **Circ:** (Not Reported).

10300 ■ The German-American Journal
German-American National Congress
4740 N Western Ave., Ste. 206
Chicago, IL 60625-2013
Phone: (773)275-1100
Fax: (773)275-4010
Free: 888-872-3265
Publisher's E-mail: office@dank.org
Freq: Bimonthly. **ISSN:** 0273- 5261 (print). **Subscription Rates:** $15 Nonmembers /year (6 issues); $2.50 Individuals. **URL:** http://www.dank.org/journal; http://www.dank.org/journal/about. **Remarks:** Accepts advertising. **Circ:** (Not Reported).

10301 ■ Getty Research Journal
The University of Chicago Press, Journals Div.
1427 E 60th St.
Chicago, IL 60637
Phone: (773)702-7700
Free: 877-705-1878
Publisher's E-mail: subscriptions@press.uchicago.edu
Journal containing research related to the Getty's collections, initiatives, and research projects. **Freq:** Annual. **ISSN:** 1944--8740 (print); **EISSN:** 2329--1249 (electronic). **Subscription Rates:** $45 Individuals electronic only; $65 Individuals print and electronic; $55 Individuals print only. **URL:** http://www.press.uchicago.edu/ucp/journals/journal/grj.html. **Circ:** (Not Reported).

10302 ■ Giftware News
Talcott Communication Corp.
233 N Michigan Ave., Ste. 1780
Chicago, IL 60601
Phone: (312)849-2220
Fax: (312)849-2174
Free: 800-229-1967
Publisher's E-mail: bmowrey@talcott.com
Magazine serving professionals in the gift, stationery, collectibles, tabletop, and home accessories industries. **Freq:** 10/year. **Print Method:** Offset. **Trim Size:** 7.5 x 10.75. **Cols./Page:** 4. **Col. Width:** 27 nonpareils. **Col. Depth:** 196 agate lines. **Key Personnel:** Daniel Von Rabenau, Publisher; Barbara Wujcik, Associate Editor. **Subscription Rates:** $43 Individuals; $59 Two years; $82 Individuals 3 years; $55 Canada; $196 Other countries. **URL:** http://www.giftwarenews.com. **Remarks:** Accepts advertising. **Circ:** 21000.

10303 ■ Glencoe News
Sun-Times Media L.L.C.
350 N Orleans St., 10th Fl.
Chicago, IL 60654
Phone: (312)321-3000
Free: 888-848-4637
Publisher's E-mail: customerservice@suntimes.com
Community newspaper (tabloid). **Freq:** Weekly. **Print Method:** Offset. **Trim Size:** 11 x 14. **Cols./Page:** 5. **Col. Width:** 9 3/4 inches. **Col. Depth:** 12 3/4 inches. **Key Personnel:** Jeff Wisser, Editor-in-Chief, phone: (847)486-6848. **USPS:** 219-700. **URL:** http://glencoe.suntimes.com. **Remarks:** Accepts advertising. **Circ:** (Not Reported).

10304 ■ Glenview Announcements
Sun-Times Media L.L.C.
350 N Orleans St., 10th Fl.
Chicago, IL 60654
Phone: (312)321-3000
Free: 888-848-4637
Publisher's E-mail: customerservice@suntimes.com
Community newspaper (tabloid). **Freq:** Weekly. **Print Method:** Offset. **Trim Size:** 11 x 14. **Cols./Page:** 5. **Col. Width:** 9 3/4 inches. **Col. Depth:** 12 3/4 inches. **URL:** http://glenview.suntimes.com. **Remarks:** Accepts advertising. **Circ:** (Not Reported).

10305 ■ Global Strategy Journal
Strategic Management Society
Rice Bldg., Ste. 215
815 W Van Burren St.
Chicago, IL 60607-3567
Phone: (312)492-6224
Fax: (312)492-6223
Publisher's E-mail: sms@strategicmanagement.net
Journal containing managerially-oriented global strategy research. **Freq:** Quarterly. **Key Personnel:** Stephen Tallman, Editor. **ISSN:** 2042--5791 (print); **EISSN:** 2042--5805 (electronic). **Subscription Rates:** $565 Institutions print or online (large); $678 Institutions print and

Circulation: ⋆ = AAM; △ or • = BPA; ♦ = CAC; ❑ = VAC; ⊕ = PO Statement; ‡ = Publisher's Report; Boldface figures = sworn; Light figures = estimated.

online (large); $434 Institutions print or online (medium); $521 Institutions print and online (medium); $305 Institutions print and online (small); $366 Institutions print and online (small). **URL:** http://gsj.strategicmanagement.net. **Circ:** (Not Reported).

10306 ■ Globalizations
Global Studies Association North America
1250 N Wood St.
Chicago, IL 60622
Publisher's E-mail: book.orders@tandf.co.uk
Peer-reviewed journal covering articles on globalization. **Freq:** 6/year. **Key Personnel:** Barry Gills, PhD, Editor, Founder; Benjamin Barber, Board Member; Saskia Sassen, Board Member; Spike V. Peterson, Board Member; Rebecca Harris, Assistant Editor; Isidro Morales, Board Member; Mark Amen, Editor; Barry Gills, Editor-in-Chief. **ISSN:** 1474--7731 (print); **EISSN:** 1474--774X (electronic). **Subscription Rates:** $217 Individuals print only; $185 Individuals online only; $2017 Individuals print only; $882 Institutions online only; $1008 Institutions print and online. **URL:** http://www.tandfonline.com/toc/rglo20/current. **Remarks:** Advertising accepted; rates available upon request. **Circ:** (Not Reported).

10307 ■ Government Finance Review
Government Finance Officers Association of United States and Canada
203 N LaSalle St., Ste. 2700
Chicago, IL 60601-1210
Phone: (312)977-9700
Fax: (312)977-4806
Membership magazine covering finance and financial management for state and local governments. **Founded:** Apr. 1985. **Freq:** Bimonthly. **Print Method:** Offset. **Trim Size:** 8 1/2 x 11. **Cols./Page:** 3. **Col. Width:** 14 picas. **Col. Depth:** 116 agate lines. **Key Personnel:** Marcy Boggs, Managing Editor; Jeffrey Esser, Chief Executive Officer, Executive Director; Rebecca Russum, Senior Editor; Krisztina Dommer, Manager. **USPS:** 368-120. **Subscription Rates:** $35 Individuals; Included in membership. **URL:** http://www.gfoa.org/GFR. **Ad Rates:** BW $1505; 4C $3390. **Remarks:** Advertising accepted; rates available upon request. **Circ:** ‡18,100.

10308 ■ Government Health IT
101communications LLC
230 E Ohio St., Ste. 500
Chicago, IL 60611-3270
Phone: (312)664-4467
Fax: (312)664-6143
Magazine that covers public policy and the health care services community for government and civilian leaders in the health IT industry. **Freq:** Bimonthly. **Trim Size:** 8 x 10 3/4. **Key Personnel:** Mary Mosquera, Senior Editor; Paul McCloskey, Editor-in-Chief; Matt Schlossberg, Senior Editor; H. Stephen Lieber, Chief Executive Officer, President. **Subscription Rates:** Free to qualified subscribers. **URL:** http://www.govhealthit.com. **Ad Rates:** 4C $7,956. **Remarks:** Accepts advertising. **Circ:** 59999.

10309 ■ Gynecologic Oncology
Society of Gynecologic Oncology
230 W Monroe St., Ste. 710
Chicago, IL 60606-4703
Phone: (312)235-4060
Fax: (312)235-4059
Publisher's E-mail: sgo@sgo.org
Journal containing clinical and investigative articles that concern tumors of the female reproductive tract. **ISSN:** 0090--8258 (print). **URL:** http://www.sgo.org/gynecologic-oncology. **Circ:** (Not Reported).

10310 ■ Harlem-Irving Times
Sun-Times Media L.L.C.
350 N Orleans St., 10th Fl.
Chicago, IL 60654
Phone: (312)321-3000
Free: 888-848-4637
Publisher's E-mail: customerservice@suntimes.com
Community newspaper, now defunct. **Freq:** Semiweekly (Mon. and Thurs.). **Print Method:** Offset. **Trim Size:** 13 x 21 1/4. **Cols./Page:** 6. **Col. Width:** 25 nonpareils. **Col. Depth:** 297 agate lines. **Ad Rates:** BW $1995; 4C $2470; SAU $54.90. **Circ:** Paid 2715.

10311 ■ Health Care Management Review
Lippincott Williams and Wilkins
c/o L. Michelle Issel, PhD, Ed.-in-Ch.
University of Illinois
1603 W Taylor St., MC 923
Chicago, IL 60612
Publisher's E-mail: ronna.ekhouse@wolterskluwer.com
Peer-reviewed journal devoted to management issues in health care and administration. **Freq:** Quarterly. **Trim Size:** 8 1/2 x 11. **Cols./Page:** 2. **Col. Width:** 20 picas. **Col. Depth:** 50 picas. **Key Personnel:** Ingrid Nembhard, Associate Editor, Board Member; Natalie McGroarty, Publisher; L. Michele Issel, Editor-in-Chief. **ISSN:** 0361--6274 (print); **EISSN:** 1550--5030 (electronic). **Subscription Rates:** $137 U.S.; $144 Canada and Mexico; $282 UK/Australia; $264 Other countries; $571 Institutions; $597 Institutions, Canada and Mexico; $810 Institutions UK/Australia; $791 Institutions, other countries. **URL:** http://journals.lww.com/hcmrjournal/pages/default.aspx; http://www.lww.com/product/?0361-6274. **Ad Rates:** BW $975; 4C $2405. **Remarks:** Accepts advertising. **Circ:** ‡417.

10312 ■ Health Care's Most Wired Magazine
Health Forum L.L.C.
155 N Wacker Dr., Ste. 400
Chicago, IL 60606
Phone: (312)893-6800
Fax: (312)422-4500
Free: 800-821-2039
Publication E-mail: mostwired@healthforum.com
Magazine that aims to use case studies to identify how actual information technology practices help solve strategic problems in health care. **Freq:** Quarterly. **ISSN:** 1549--6104 (print). **URL:** http://www.hhnmostwired.com. **Ad Rates:** BW $6,750; 4C $8,450. **Remarks:** Accepts advertising. **Circ:** (Not Reported).

10313 ■ Health Facilities Management
Health Forum L.L.C.
155 N Wacker Dr., Ste. 400
Chicago, IL 60606
Phone: (312)893-6800
Fax: (312)422-4500
Free: 800-821-2039
Magazine covering health care. **Founded:** 1988. **Freq:** Monthly. **Print Method:** Web offset. **Trim Size:** 8 1/8 x 10 7/8. **Cols./Page:** 3. **Key Personnel:** Bob Kehoe, Associate Publisher; Mary Grayson, Director, Editorial; Mike Hrickiewicz, Editor. **ISSN:** 0899-6210 (print). **Subscription Rates:** Free. **URL:** http://www.hfmmagazine.com. **Ad Rates:** BW $6,680; 4C $8,230. **Remarks:** Accepts advertising. **Circ:** ‡63000.

10314 ■ Health Facilities Management Magazine
American Society for Healthcare Engineering
155 N Wacker Dr., Ste. 400
Chicago, IL 60606-1719
Phone: (312)422-3800
Fax: (312)422-4571
Publisher's E-mail: ashe@aha.org
Freq: Monthly. **URL:** http://www.hfmmagazine.com. **Remarks:** Accepts advertising. **Circ:** Combined △**33361**.

10315 ■ Healthcare Executive
American College of Healthcare Executives
1 N Franklin St., Ste. 1700
Chicago, IL 60606-3529
Phone: (312)424-2800
Fax: (312)424-0023
Publisher's E-mail: contact@ache.org
Health care management magazine examining trends, issues, and innovations. **Freq:** Bimonthly. **Print Method:** Offset. **Trim Size:** 8 1/8 x 10 7/8. **Cols./Page:** 3. **Col. Width:** 13 picas. **Col. Depth:** 60 picas. **ISSN:** 0883--5381 (print). **Subscription Rates:** $110 Individuals in the U.S.; Included in membership online. **URL:** http://www.ache.org/HEOnline/digital/heonline_index.cfm. **Ad Rates:** BW $7,220; 4C $9,485. **Remarks:** Advertising accepted; rates available upon request. **Circ:** Combined △**41331**.

10316 ■ Healthcare Packaging
Summit Publishing Co.
330 N Wabash Ave., Ste. 2401
Chicago, IL 60611
Phone: (312)222-1010
Fax: (312)222-1310
Publisher's E-mail: sales@packworld.com
Online magazine covering packaging for health care products. **Freq:** Monthly. **Key Personnel:** Jim Butschi, Editor-in-Chief; Jim Chrzan, Publisher. **Subscription Rates:** Free. **URL:** http://www.healthcarepackaging.com. **Remarks:** Accepts advertising. **Circ:** Combined △**19500**.

Highland Park News - See Highland

10317 ■ History of Religions
The University of Chicago Press
University of Chicago
Swift Hall 005
1025 E 58th St.
Chicago, IL 60637
Phone: (773)702-8216
Publisher's E-mail: custserv@press.uchicago.edu
Journal presenting multidisciplinary research and inquiry into religious phenomena within particular traditions and across cultural boundaries from prehistory to modern times. **Freq:** Quarterly. **Print Method:** Offset. **Trim Size:** 6 x 9. **Cols./Page:** 1. **Col. Width:** 54 nonpareils. **Col. Depth:** 102 agate lines. **Key Personnel:** Matthew Kapstein, Editor; Wendy Doniger, Editor; Christian Wedemeyer, Editor. **ISSN:** 0018--2710 (print); **EISSN:** 1545--6935 (electronic). **Subscription Rates:** $60 Individuals print and electronic; $50 Individuals electronic only; $51 Individuals print only; $42 Individuals alumni, print and electronic; $30 Students electronic only; $108 Two years print and electronic; $76 Two years alumni, print and electronic; $54 Students two years, electronic only. **URL:** http://www.journals.uchicago.edu/toc/hr/current. **Ad Rates:** BW $724. **Remarks:** Accepts advertising. **Circ:** 1114, 628, 514.

10318 ■ Horizon: Journal of the National Religious Vocation Conference
National Religious Vocation Conference
5401 S Cornell Ave., Ste. 207
Chicago, IL 60615
Phone: (773)363-5454
Fax: (773)363-5530
Publisher's E-mail: nrvc@nrvc.net
Catholic publication on vocation ministry. **Freq:** Quarterly. **Print Method:** Offset. **Trim Size:** 8 1/2 x 11. **Cols./Page:** 2. **Col. Width:** 3 1/4 INS. **Key Personnel:** Paul Bednarczyk, Executive Director; Carol Schuck Scheiber, Editor. **ISSN:** 1042--8461 (print). **Subscription Rates:** $95 Nonmembers; $40 Members. **URL:** http://nrvc.net/signup_horizon. **Formerly:** Call to Growth/Ministry. **Remarks:** Advertising not accepted. **Circ:** (Not Reported).

10319 ■ Hospitals & Health Networks
American Hospital Association
155 N Wacker Dr.
Chicago, IL 60606
Phone: (312)422-3000
Print Method: Web Offset. **Trim Size:** 8 x 10 3/4. **Key Personnel:** Matthew Weinstock, Assistant Managing Editor; Bill Santamour, Managing Editor; Mary A. Grayson, Director, Editorial. **Subscription Rates:** Free to qualified subscribers. **URL:** http://www.hhnmag.com. **Ad Rates:** BW $14,165, full page; 4C $16,450, full page; 4C $10,550, half page; BW $9,310, half page. **Remarks:** Accepts advertising. **Circ:** Paid ‡70000.

10320 ■ Hospitals & Health Networks
Health Forum L.L.C.
155 N Wacker Dr., Ste. 400
Chicago, IL 60606
Phone: (312)893-6800
Fax: (312)422-4500
Free: 800-821-2039
Print Method: Web Offset. **Trim Size:** 8 x 10 3/4. **Key Personnel:** Matthew Weinstock, Assistant Managing Editor; Bill Santamour, Managing Editor; Mary A. Grayson, Director, Editorial. **Subscription Rates:** Free to qualified subscribers. **URL:** http://www.hhnmag.com. **Ad Rates:** BW $14,165, full page; 4C $16,450, full page; 4C $10,550, half page; BW $9,310, half page. **Remarks:** Accepts advertising. **Circ:** Paid ‡70000.

10321 ■ Hotel Amerika
Hotel Amerika
600 Sh Michigan Ave.
Columbia College
600 S Michigan Ave.
Chicago, IL 60605-1996
Phone: (312)369-8175
Poetry magazine. **Freq:** Semiannual. **Key Personnel:** David Lazar, Editor; Lisa Wagner, Managing Editor. **Subscription Rates:** $16 Single issue; $25 Two years. **Ad**

Rates: BW $150. **Remarks:** Accepts advertising. **Circ:** (Not Reported).

10322 ■ HOTELS: The Magazine of the Worldwide Hotel Industry
Marketing & Technology Group Inc.
1415 N Dayton St.
Chicago, IL 60622
Phone: (312)266-3311
Fax: (312)266-3363
Magazine covering management and operations as well as foodservice and design in the hospitality industry. **Freq:** Monthly. **Print Method:** Offset. **Trim Size:** 8 3/8 x 10 7/8. **Cols./Page:** 4 and 3. **Col. Width:** 9.6 and 13 picas. **Key Personnel:** Laurie Hachmeister, Director, Production, phone: (312)274-2203; Mark Lefens, President, phone: (312)274-2202; Jeff Weinstein, Editor-in-Chief, phone: (312)274-2226; Dan Hogan, Publisher, Vice President, phone: (312)274-2221. **ISSN:** 1047-2975 (print). **Subscription Rates:** Free to qualified subscribers. **URL:** http://www.hotelsmag.com/. **Ad Rates:** BW $11,760; 4C $14,660. **Remarks:** Accepts advertising. **Circ:** Free ‡59228.

10323 ■ Hoy, Chicago
The Tribune Media Co.
435 N Michigan Ave.
Chicago, IL 60611-4066
Phone: (312)222-9100
Fax: (312)222-4206
Free: 800-874-2863
Publisher's E-mail: sales@atlanticsyndication.com
Newspaper for the Hispanic households in Chicago. **Remarks:** Accepts advertising. **Circ:** (Not Reported).

10324 ■ HR Pulse
American Society for Healthcare Human Resources Administration
155 N Wacker Dr., Ste. 400
Chicago, IL 60606
Phone: (312)422-3720
Fax: (312)422-4577
Publisher's E-mail: ashhra@aha.org
Freq: Quarterly. **Subscription Rates:** Included in membership; $39 Nonmembers. **URL:** http://www.ashhra.org/publications/hr_pulse_public.shtml. **Remarks:** Advertising not accepted. **Circ:** (Not Reported).

10325 ■ HSR: Impacting Health Practice and policy through state-of-the-art Research and Thinking
Health Research and Educational Trust
155 N Wacker, Ste. 400
Chicago, IL 60606
Phone: (312)422-2600
Fax: (312)422-4568
Professional journal covering healthcare administration. **Freq:** Bimonthly. **Key Personnel:** Jose Escarce, PhD, Editor-in-Chief; Laurence Baker, PhD, Associate Editor. **ISSN:** 0017--9124 (print); **EISSN:** 1475--6773 (electronic). **Subscription Rates:** $1286 Institutions print and online; $1071 Institutions print or online; $126 Members print and online; $164 Individuals print and online. **URL:** http://www.hsr.org. **Remarks:** Advertising accepted; rates available upon request. **Circ:** 7139.

10326 ■ Human Rights
American Bar Association
321 N Clark St.
Chicago, IL 60654
Phone: (312)988-5000
Free: 800-285-2221
Magazine for lawyers, legal professionals and others involved with human and civil rights. **Freq:** Quarterly. **Key Personnel:** Stephen Wermiel, Board Member, Chairperson. **ISSN:** 0046-8185 (print). **Subscription Rates:** $18 Nonmembers; Free section members. **URL:** http://www.americanbar.org/publications/human_rights_magazine_home.html. **Remarks:** Accepts advertising. **Circ:** (Not Reported).

10327 ■ Hyde Park Herald
Herald Newspaper Inc.
1435 E Hyde Park Blvd.
Chicago, IL 60615
Phone: (773)643-8533
Fax: (773)643-8542
Publisher's E-mail: hpherald@aol.com
Newspaper. **Freq:** Weekly (Wed.). **Print Method:** Offset. **Cols./Page:** 6. **Col. Width:** 22 nonpareils. **Col. Depth:** 182 agate lines. **Key Personnel:** Gabriel Piemonte, Editor; Susan J. Walker, General Manager, Vice President; Bruce Sagan, Publisher. **Subscription Rates:** $20 Individuals 1 year; $31 Individuals 2 years; $43 Individuals 3 years. **URL:** http://www.hpherald.com. **Ad Rates:** GLR $4.87; BW $2838.69; 4C $3288.69; PCI $35.34. **Remarks:** Accepts classified advertising. **Circ:** Paid ‡9000, Free ‡17600.

10328 ■ IAUG Insights
International Avaya Users Group
330 N Wabash Ave.
Chicago, IL 60611
Phone: (312)321-5126
Publisher's E-mail: info@iaug.org
Freq: Quarterly. **Subscription Rates:** Included in membership. **URL:** http://iaug.org/p/cm/ld/fid=124. **Remarks:** Accepts advertising. **Circ:** (Not Reported).

10329 ■ IDUG Solutions Journal
International DB2 Users Group
330 N Wabash, Ste. 2000
Chicago, IL 60611-4267
Phone: (312)321-6881
Fax: (312)673-6688
Publisher's E-mail: support@idug.org
Freq: 3/year. **Subscription Rates:** Included in membership. **Alt. Formats:** PDF. **URL:** http://idug.org/p/cm/ld/fid=79. **Remarks:** Advertising not accepted. **Circ:** (Not Reported).

10330 ■ IFT Food Technology
Institute of Food Technologists
525 W Van Buren St., Ste. 1000
Chicago, IL 60607
Phone: (312)782-8424
Fax: (312)782-8348
Free: 800-438-3663
Publisher's E-mail: info@ift.org
Freq: Annual. **Key Personnel:** Bob Swientek, Editor-in-Chief. **ISSN:** 0015- 6639 (print). **Subscription Rates:** Included in membership; $190 U.S. and other countries non-members; $199.50 Canada non-members; $30 U.S. single issue; $35 Canada and Mexico single issue; $40 Other countries. **URL:** http://www.ift.org/food-technology.aspx. **Ad Rates:** 4C $5,180. **Remarks:** Accepts advertising. **Circ:** 27000.

10331 ■ Illinois Entertainer
Illinois Entertainer
657 W Lake St., Ste. A
Chicago, IL 60661
Phone: (312)930-9333
Fax: (312)930-9341
Publisher's E-mail: service@illinoisentertainer.com
Music entertainment magazine. **Freq:** Monthly. **Print Method:** Offset. **Trim Size:** 10 7/8 x 12. **Cols./Page:** 6. **Col. Width:** 21 nonpareils. **Col. Depth:** 189 agate lines. **Subscription Rates:** Free. **URL:** http://illinoisentertainer.com; http://illinoisentertainer.com/current-issue. **Circ:** Combined 74606.

10332 ■ In These Times
Institute for Public Affairs
2040 N Milwaukee Ave.
Chicago, IL 60647-4002
Phone: (773)772-0100
Fax: (773)772-4180
National political newsmagazine. **Freq:** Monthly. **Print Method:** Offset. **Trim Size:** 8 1/8 x 10 5/8. **Key Personnel:** Joel Bleifuss, Editor, Publisher; Terry J. Allen, Senior Editor. **ISSN:** 0160--5992 (print). **Subscription Rates:** $19.95 U.S. /year (print); $34.95 U.S. two years (print); $34.95 Canada (print); $40.95 Other countries (print); $9.95 Individuals /year (online); $14.95 Individuals two years (online). **URL:** http://inthesetimes.com. **Ad Rates:** BW $900; 4C $1000. **Remarks:** Accepts advertising. **Circ:** ‡17000.

10333 ■ India Tribune
India Tribune Publications
3302 W Peterson Ave.
Chicago, IL 60659-3510
Phone: (773)588-5077
Fax: (773)588-7011
Special interest newspaper (tabloid) featuring news of India for the Indian community in Chicago. **Freq:** Weekly (Sat.). **Trim Size:** 11 1/2 x 17. **Cols./Page:** 5. **Key Personnel:** Prashant Shah, Editor. **USPS:** 380-230. **Subscription Rates:** $40 Individuals; $25 Individuals 26 issues; $351 Individuals life. **URL:** http://www.indiatribune.com/. **Remarks:** Accepts advertising. **Circ:** (Not Reported).

10334 ■ Information Technology and Libraries
Library and Information Technology Association
50 E Huron St.
Chicago, IL 60611-2795
Phone: (312)944-6780
Fax: (312)280-3257
Free: 800-545-2433
Publisher's E-mail: lita@ala.org
Freq: Quarterly. **Print Method:** Offset. **Trim Size:** 8 1/8 x 10 7/8. **Cols./Page:** 2 and 1. **Col. Width:** 42 and 20 picas. **Col. Depth:** 54 INS. **Key Personnel:** Marc Truitt, Contact; Mark Dehmlow, Board Member. **ISSN:** 2163--5226 (print). **Alt. Formats:** PDF. **URL:** http://ejournals.bc.edu/ojs/index.php/ital/index; http://www.ala.org/lita/publications. **Formerly:** Journal of Library Automation. **Ad Rates:** BW $675; 4C $1400. **Remarks:** Accepts advertising. **Circ:** Paid ‡4770, 7500.

10335 ■ Inland Architect: The Midwestern Building Arts Magazine
Real Estate News Corp.
3525 W Peterson Ave.
Chicago, IL 60659
Phone: (773)866-9900
Fax: (773)866-9881
Freq: Quarterly. **Print Method:** Offset. **Trim Size:** 8 3/4 x 11 1/2. **Cols./Page:** 3. **Col. Width:** 25 nonpareils. **Col. Depth:** 140 agate lines. **Key Personnel:** Richard Solomon, Editor; Timothy Hill, Administrator; Barbara Hower, Senior Editor. **ISSN:** 0020--1472 (print). **Subscription Rates:** $49.95 Single issue plus shipping and handling ($14.95). **URL:** http://www.inlandarchitectmag.com/default.html; http://www.renpublishing.com. **Ad Rates:** BW $1500; 4C $1950. **Remarks:** Accepts advertising. **Circ:** Paid ‡6000, Non-paid ‡500.

10336 ■ Inside
Inside Publications
6221 N Clark St.
Chicago, IL 60660
Phone: (773)465-9700
Fax: (773)465-9800
Publication E-mail: inside@britsys.net
Community newspaper covering Chicago's North Side neighborhoods. **Founded:** Dec. 01, 1968. **Freq:** Weekly (Wed.). **Print Method:** Web offset. **Cols./Page:** 5. **Col. Width:** 2 inches. **Col. Depth:** 13 1/2 inches. **Subscription Rates:** Free. **URL:** http://www.insideonline.com/. **Ad Rates:** GLR $3.50; BW $1,650; 4C $2,250; PCI $21.48. **Remarks:** 3.50. **Circ:** Free ‡49500.

10337 ■ Insight
Illinois CPA Society
550 W Jackson Blvd., Ste. 900
Chicago, IL 60661-5742
Phone: (312)993-0407
Fax: (312)993-9954
Free: 800-993-0407
Publisher's E-mail: illinoiscpasociety@icpas.org
Professional journal for Certified Public Accountants in Chicago, IL. **Founded:** 1920. **Freq:** Quarterly. **Print Method:** Sheetfed Web. **Trim Size:** 8 3/8 x 10 7/8. **Cols./Page:** 2. **ISSN:** 1053-8542 (print). **Subscription Rates:** $30 U.S.; $40 Canada; $42 Canada and Mexico. **URL:** http://www.icpas.org/insight.htm. **Ad Rates:** BW $1,095; 4C $1,645. **Remarks:** Accepts advertising. **Circ:** Controlled ⊕**27000**.

10338 ■ The International Doula
DONA International
35 E Wacker Dr., Ste. 850
Chicago, IL 60601-2106
Phone: (312)224-2595
Fax: (312)644-8557
Free: 888-788-3662
Publisher's E-mail: dona@dona.org
Magazine featuring articles, columns, and literary posts of experts and doulas about the trends, education, training opportunities, and new researches about motherhood. Includes organizational news, conferences, events, member news and benefits. **Freq:** Quarterly. **Subscription Rates:** Free to qualified subscribers. **URL:** http://www.dona.org/publications/id.php. **Remarks:** Accepts advertising. **Circ:** (Not Reported).

Circulation: ★ = AAM; △ or • = BPA; ♦ = CAC; ❑ = VAC; ⊕ = PO Statement; ‡ = Publisher's Report; Boldface figures = sworn; Light figures = estimated.

10339 ■ International Journal of Heat and Mass Transfer
RELX Group P.L.C.
c/o W.J. Minkowycz, Editor-in-Chief
Mechanical Engineering (M/C 251)
The University of Illinois at Chicago
842 W Taylor St., 2049 ERF
Chicago, IL 60607-7022
Publisher's E-mail: amsterdam@relx.com
Journal focusing on analytical and experimental research in the field of heat and mass transfer. **Freq:** Monthly. **Key Personnel:** W.J. Minkowycz, Editor-in-Chief. **ISSN:** 0017--9310 (print). **Subscription Rates:** $726 Individuals print; $10050 Institutions print; $10049.60 Institutions e-journal. **URL:** http://www.journals.elsevier.com/international-journal-of-heat-and-mass-transfer. **Remarks:** Accepts advertising. **Circ:** (Not Reported).

10340 ■ International Journal of Plant Sciences
The University of Chicago Press
University of Chicago
1101 E 57th St.
Chicago, IL 60637
Phone: (773)702-8292
Fax: (773)702-9740
Publication E-mail: ijps@press.uchicago.edu
Peer-reviewed journal presenting research in all areas of plant biology. **Freq:** 9/year. **Print Method:** Offset. **Trim Size:** 8 1/2 x 11. **Cols./Page:** 2. **Col. Width:** 52 nonpareils. **Col. Depth:** 97 agate lines. **Key Personnel:** Elena Kramer, Editor; Richard Ree, Editor; M. Ruddat, Editor; James Ellis, Managing Editor. **ISSN:** 1058--5893 (print); **EISSN:** 1537--5315 (electronic). **Subscription Rates:** $102 Individuals print and electronic; $184 Two years print and electronic; $95 Individuals electronic only; $171 Two years electronic only; $51 Students electronic only; $92 Students electronic only. **URL:** http://www.press.uchicago.edu/ucp/journals/journal/ijps.html; http://www.jstor.org/journal/intejplanscie. **Ad Rates:** BW $650. **Remarks:** Advertising accepted; rates available upon request. **Circ:** ‡290.

10341 ■ International Surgery
International College of Surgeons
1516 N Lakeshore Dr.
Chicago, IL 60610
Phone: (312)642-3555
Fax: (312)787-1624
Publisher's E-mail: info@icsglobal.org
Freq: Bimonthly. **ISSN:** 0020--8868 (print). **Subscription Rates:** $600 Institutions /year ; $450 Nonmembers /year for individual. **URL:** http://www.internationalsurgery.org. **Remarks:** Accepts advertising. **Circ:** 3000.

10342 ■ International UFO Reporter
J. Allen Hynek Center for UFO Studies
PO Box 31335
Chicago, IL 60631
Phone: (773)271-3611
Publisher's E-mail: infocenter@cufos.org
Freq: Quarterly. **ISSN:** 0720-174X (print). **Subscription Rates:** Included in membership. **Alt. Formats:** PDF. **URL:** http://www.cufos.org/pubs.html. **Remarks:** Accepts advertising. **Circ:** 800.

10343 ■ ISEH Experimental Hematology
International Society for Experimental Hematology
330 N Wabash Ave., Ste. 2000
Chicago, IL 60611
Phone: (312)321-5114
Fax: (312)673-6923
Publisher's E-mail: info@iseh.org
Freq: Monthly. **ISSN:** 0301- 472X (print). **Subscription Rates:** $299 U.S. personal, non-members; online and print. **URL:** http://www.iseh.org/?page=EH; http://secure.jbs.elsevierhealth.com/action/ecommerce?code=exphem-site. **Remarks:** Accepts advertising. **Circ:** (Not Reported).

10344 ■ ISIS: An International Review Devoted to the History of Science and its Cultural Influences
The University of Chicago Press
1427 E 60th St.
Chicago, IL 60637
Phone: (773)702-7700
Fax: (773)702-7212
Publisher's E-mail: custserv@press.uchicago.edu
Journal on the history of science. **Freq:** Quarterly. **Print Method:** Offset. **Trim Size:** 6 3/4 x 10. **Cols./Page:** 2. **Col. Width:** 30 nonpareils. **Col. Depth:** 113 agate lines. **Key Personnel:** H. Floris Cohen, Editor. **ISSN:** 0021--1753 (print). **Subscription Rates:** $562 Institutions print only. **URL:** http://www.journals.uchicago.edu/toc/isis/current. **Remarks:** Advertising accepted; rates available upon request. **Circ:** (Not Reported).

10345 ■ Ivy Leaf
Alpha Kappa Alpha
5656 S Stony Island Ave.
Chicago, IL 60637
Phone: (773)684-1282
Publisher's E-mail: exec@aka1908.com
Freq: Quarterly. **Print Method:** Offset. **Trim Size:** 8 1/2 x 11. **Cols./Page:** 3. **Col. Width:** 14 picas. **Col. Depth:** 140 agate lines. **Key Personnel:** Nicole H. Barett, Deputy Director; Patricia A. Watkins, Director, Member Services; Deborah L. Dangerfield, Executive Director. **ISSN:** 0021--3276 (print). **URL:** http://www.aka1908.com. **Remarks:** Accepts advertising. **Circ:** 40000.

10346 ■ JAMA Dermatology
American Medical Association
132 E Delaware Pl., No. 5806
Chicago, IL 60611
Publisher's E-mail: amalibrary@ama-assn.org
Peer-reviewed educational/clinical journal for dermatologists. **Freq:** Monthly and published online weekly every Wednesday. **Print Method:** Offset. **Trim Size:** 8 x 10 3/4. **Cols./Page:** 2. **Col. Width:** 41 nonpareils. **Col. Depth:** 140 agate lines. **Key Personnel:** June K. Robinson, MD, Editor; Jeffrey P. Callen, MD, Associate Editor. **ISSN:** 2168--6068 (print); **EISSN:** 2168--6084 (electronic). **Subscription Rates:** $267 Members physician (print and online); $445 Nonmembers physician and other profession (print and online); $114 Students medical (print and online); $1159 Institutions print only. **URL:** http://archderm.jamanetwork.com/journal.aspx; http://www.ama-assn.org. **Formerly:** Archives of Dermatology. **Remarks:** Accepts advertising. **Circ:** (Not Reported).

10347 ■ JAMA Internal Medicine
American Medical Association
AMA Plaza
330 N Wabash Ave.
Chicago, IL 60611
Phone: (312)464-4430
Fax: (312)464-5226
Free: 800-621-8335
Publisher's E-mail: amalibrary@ama-assn.org
Peer-reviewed educational/clinical journal for internists, cardiologists, gastroenterologists, and other internal medicine subspecialists. **Freq:** Monthly and weekly for online publishing. **Print Method:** Offset. **Trim Size:** 8 x 10 3/4. **Cols./Page:** 2. **Col. Width:** 41 nonpareils. **Col. Depth:** 140 agate lines. **Key Personnel:** Charles L. Bennett, MD, Board Member; Rita F. Redberg, MD, Editor. **ISSN:** 2168--6106 (print); **EISSN:** 2168--6114 (electronic). **Subscription Rates:** $167 Members physician (print and online); $279 Nonmembers physician and other profession (print and online); $114 Students medical (print and online); $985 Institutions print only. **Online:** American Medical Association American Medical Association. **URL:** http://archinte.jamanetwork.com/journal.aspx. **Formerly:** Archives of Internal Medicine. **Remarks:** Advertising accepted; rates available upon request. **Circ:** (Not Reported).

10348 ■ JAMA Otolaryngology--Head & Neck Surgery
American Medical Association
AMA Plaza
330 N Wabash Ave.
Chicago, IL 60611
Phone: (312)464-4430
Fax: (312)464-5226
Free: 800-621-8335
Publisher's E-mail: amalibrary@ama-assn.org
Educational/clinical journal for otolaryngologists. **Freq:** 12/yr. **Print Method:** Offset. **Trim Size:** 8 x 10 3/4. **Cols./Page:** 2. **Col. Width:** 41 nonpareils. **Col. Depth:** 140 agate lines. **ISSN:** 0886- 4470 (print). **Subscription Rates:** $193 Members print and online.; $322 Nonmembers print and online.; $114 Students Medical students; print and online.; $322 Individuals Other profession; print and online.; $921 Institutions print only. **URL:** http://archotol.jamanetwork.com/journal.aspx. **Formerly:** Archives of Otolaryngology--Head and Neck Surgery. **Ad Rates:** BW $1,328; 4C $2,759. **Remarks:** Accepts advertising. **Circ:** 12,000, Combined ‡12,086.

10349 ■ JAMA Psychiatry
American Medical Association
AMA Plaza
330 N Wabash Ave.
Chicago, IL 60611
Phone: (312)464-4430
Fax: (312)464-5226
Free: 800-621-8335
Publisher's E-mail: amalibrary@ama-assn.org
Educational/clinical journal for psychiatrists. **Freq:** Monthly and published online weekly every Wednesday. **Print Method:** Offset. **Trim Size:** 8 x 10 3/4. **Cols./Page:** 2. **Col. Width:** 41 nonpareils. **Col. Depth:** 140 agate lines. **Key Personnel:** Stephan Heckers, MD, Editor. **ISSN:** 2168--622X (print); **EISSN:** 2168--6238 (electronic). **Subscription Rates:** $200 Members physician (print and online); $334 Nonmembers physician and other profession (print and online); $114 Single issue medical (print and online); $1238 Institutions print only. **URL:** http://archpsyc.jamanetwork.com/journal.aspx. **Formerly:** Archives of General Psychiatry. **Remarks:** Accepts advertising. **Circ:** (Not Reported).

10350 ■ JAMA Surgery
American Medical Association
AMA Plaza
330 N Wabash Ave.
Chicago, IL 60611
Phone: (312)464-4430
Fax: (312)464-5226
Free: 800-621-8335
Publication E-mail: archsurg@jamanetwork.org
Peer-reviewed educational/clinical journal for general surgeons and surgical specialists. **Freq:** Monthly and published online weekly every Wednesday. **Print Method:** Offset. **Trim Size:** 8 x 10 3/4. **Cols./Page:** 2. **Col. Width:** 41 nonpareils. **Col. Depth:** 140 agate lines. **Key Personnel:** Melina R. Kibbe, MD, Editor. **ISSN:** 2168--6254 (print); **EISSN:** 2168--6262 (electronic). **Subscription Rates:** $219 Members physician (print and online); $365 Nonmembers physician and other profession (print and online); $114 Students medical (print and online); $985 Institutions print only. **URL:** http://archsurg.jamanetwork.com/journal.aspx. **Formerly:** Archives of Surgery. **Remarks:** Advertising accepted; rates available upon request. **Circ:** (Not Reported).

10351 ■ Jetrader
International Society of Transport Aircraft Trading
330 N Wabash Ave., Ste. 2000
Chicago, IL 60611
Phone: (312)321-5169
Fax: (312)673-6579
Publisher's E-mail: istat@istat.org
Magazine publishing news, case studies and feature articles in the field of aviation. **Freq:** Quarterly. **Subscription Rates:** Included in membership. **URL:** http://www.istat.org/media. **Remarks:** Accepts advertising. **Circ:** 1,200.

10352 ■ The John Marshall Journal of Information Technology & Privacy Law
John Marshall Law School Center for Intellectual Property, Information and Privacy Law
315 S Plymouth Ct.
Chicago, IL 60604
Phone: (312)386-2818
Fax: (312)427-5280
Journal providing current, relevant legal analysis regarding international information technology and privacy law. **Freq:** Quarterly. **Key Personnel:** Adam Florek, Editor-in-Chief. **ISSN:** 1078--4128 (print). **Subscription Rates:** $97.20 Individuals; $110 Other countries. **URL:** http://jitpl.jmls.edu. **Formerly:** The John Marshall Journal of Computer and Information Law. **Circ:** (Not Reported).

10353 ■ Journal of the Academy of Nutrition and Dietetics
Academy of Nutrition and Dietetics
120 S Riverside Plz, Ste. 2000
Chicago, IL 60606-6995
Phone: (312)899-0040
Free: 800-877-1600

Journal publishing articles authored by dieticians. **Freq:** Monthly. **Print Method:** Web offset. **Trim Size:** 8 x 10 1/2. **Key Personnel:** Linda G. Snetselaar, PhD, Editor-in-Chief; Jason T. Switt, Editor; Sandra G. Affenito, PhD, Board Member. **ISSN:** 2212--2672 (print). **Subscription Rates:** $370 U.S. print and online; $454 Canada print and online; $441 Other countries print and online; $370 Students print and online; $454 Students, Canada print and online; $441 Students, other countries print and online. **URL:** http://www.journals.elsevier.com/journal-of-the-academy-of-nutrition-and-dietetics; http://www.andjrnl.org. **Formerly:** Journal of the American Dietetic Association. **Ad Rates:** BW $6,250; 4C $2,255. **Remarks:** Accepts advertising. **Circ:** Paid △**65365**, 65000.

10354 ■ Journal of Affordable Housing and Community Development Law
American Bar Association
321 N Clark St.
Chicago, IL 60654
Phone: (312)988-5000
Free: 800-285-2221
Journal for lawyers, legal professionals and concerned laypersons dealing with issues related to affordable housing and community development. **Freq:** Quarterly. **Key Personnel:** Cynthia E. Geerdes, Editor-in-Chief; Wendy J. Smith, Editor. **ISSN:** 1061--4354 (print). **URL:** http://www.americanbar.org/publications/journal_of_affordable_housing_home.html. **Remarks:** Advertising not accepted. **Circ:** (Not Reported).

10355 ■ Journal of AHIMA
American Health Information Management Association
233 N Michigan Ave., 21st Fl.
Chicago, IL 60601-5809
Phone: (312)233-1100
Fax: (312)233-1090
Free: 800-335-5535
A professional development tool for health information managers. Disseminates new knowledge, best practices, and industry news. **Freq:** 11/year. **Print Method:** Offset. **Trim Size:** 8 1/2 x 11. **Key Personnel:** Kevin Heubusch, Editor-in-Chief; Meg Featheringham, Assistant Editor, Manager, Advertising; Sue Bowman, Editor. **ISSN:** 1060--5487 (print). **Subscription Rates:** $100 Individuals domestic; $110 Canada; $120 Other countries; Included in membership. **URL:** http://journal.ahima.org; http://www.ahima.org/about/communications. **Formerly:** Journal of AMRA. **Ad Rates:** BW $2073; 4C $3384. **Remarks:** Advertising accepted; rates available upon request. **Circ:** Paid 59485.

10356 ■ Journal of the American Academy of Matrimonial Lawyers
American Academy of Matrimonial Lawyers
150 N Michigan Ave., Ste. 1420
Chicago, IL 60601
Phone: (312)263-6477
Fax: (312)263-7682
Publisher's E-mail: office@aaml.org
Journal featuring articles on a selected family-law theme. **Freq:** Semiannual. **Subscription Rates:** $100 Individuals. **URL:** http://law.umkc.edu/academics/journals/journal-of-the-american-academy-of-matrimonial-lawyers; http://www.aaml.org/library/journal-of-the-american-academy-of-matrimonial-lawyers. **Circ:** (Not Reported).

10357 ■ Journal of the American College of Surgeons
American College of Surgeons
633 N St. Clair St.
Chicago, IL 60611-3211
Phone: (312)202-5000
Fax: (312)202-5001
Free: 800-621-4111
Publisher's E-mail: postmaster@facs.org
Journal publishing peer-reviewed contributions in all aspects of surgery. **Freq:** Monthly. **Print Method:** Web offset. **Trim Size:** 8 x 10 3/4. **Cols./Page:** 2. **Col. Width:** 3 1/2 inches. **Col. Depth:** 10 inches. **Key Personnel:** Timothy J. Eberlein, Editor-in-Chief; Timothy Buchman, Editor; Kathryn D. Anderson, Senior Editor; Nancy L. Ascher, Editor; Barbara L. Bass, Editor; Timothy R. Billiar, Editor; Stanley W. Ashley, Editor; Timothy J. Eberlein, MD, Editor-in-Chief; Joan S. Chmiel, PhD, Statistician. **ISSN:** 1072--7515 (print). **Subscription Rates:** $318 U.S. and Canada print and online; $494 Other countries print and online; $117 Students print and online; $328 Students, Canada print and online; $304 Students, other countries print and online; $337 Individuals print and online. **URL:** http://www.journalacs.org; http://www.facs.org/publications/jacs; http://www.journals.elsevier.com/journal-of-the-american-college-of-surgeons. **Formerly:** Surgery, Gynecology & Obstetrics. **Ad Rates:** BW $4,265; 4C $2,045. **Remarks:** Accepts advertising. **Circ:** △**55510**, Paid ‡13176, Controlled ‡6832.

10358 ■ Journal of the American Dental Association
American Dental Association
211 E Chicago Ave.
Chicago, IL 60611-2678
Phone: (312)440-2500
Fax: (312)440-3542
Free: 800-947-4746
Trade journal for the dental profession. **Freq:** Monthly. **Print Method:** Web. **Trim Size:** 2 1/8 x 10 7/8. **Cols./Page:** 3. **Col. Width:** 13 picas. **Col. Depth:** 10 INS. **Key Personnel:** James H. Berry, Associate Publisher; Gilbert X. Munoz, Director, Production; Jill Philbin, Manager, Marketing; Lisbeth R. Maxwell, Director, Editorial; Dr. Michael Glick, Editor. **ISSN:** 0002-8177 (print). **Subscription Rates:** $179 Individuals online plus print; $226 Institutions print. **Alt. Formats:** PDF. **URL:** http://jada.ada.org. **Ad Rates:** BW $9,580; 4C $10,980. **Remarks:** Advertising accepted; rates available upon request. **Circ:** Paid 100000.

10359 ■ Journal of the American Dental Association
ADA Publishing
211 E Chicago Ave.
Chicago, IL 60611
Phone: (312)440-2500
Trade journal for the dental profession. **Freq:** Monthly. **Print Method:** Web. **Trim Size:** 2 1/8 x 10 7/8. **Cols./Page:** 3. **Col. Width:** 13 picas. **Col. Depth:** 10 INS. **Key Personnel:** James H. Berry, Associate Publisher; Gilbert X. Munoz, Director, Production; Jill Philbin, Manager, Marketing; Lisbeth R. Maxwell, Director, Editorial; Dr. Michael Glick, Editor. **ISSN:** 0002-8177 (print). **Subscription Rates:** $179 Individuals online plus print; $226 Institutions print. **Alt. Formats:** PDF. **URL:** http://jada.ada.org. **Ad Rates:** BW $9,580; 4C $10,980. **Remarks:** Advertising accepted; rates available upon request. **Circ:** Paid 100000.

10360 ■ Journal of the American Osteopathic Association
American Osteopathic Association
142 E Ontario St.
Chicago, IL 60611-2864
Phone: (312)202-8000
Fax: (312)202-8200
Free: 800-621-1773
Publisher's E-mail: info@osteopathic.org
Osteopathic clinical journal. **Freq:** Monthly. **Print Method:** Offset. **Trim Size:** 8 x 10 7/8. **Cols./Page:** 3. **Key Personnel:** Jane Reiling, Manager, Production, phone: (312)202-8177; Michael Fitzgerald, Publisher, Associate Editor. **ISSN:** 0098--6151 (print); **EISSN:** 1945--1997 (electronic). **Subscription Rates:** $180 Individuals domestic (print and online); $300 Individuals international (print and online); $500 Institutions print and online; $60 Individuals domestic (online); $60 Individuals international (online); $450 Institutions online; $25 Single issue domestic; $40 Single issue international. **URL:** http://jaoa.org; http://www.osteopathic.org/inside-aoa/news-and-publications/Pages/default.aspx. **Ad Rates:** BW $2459; 4C $1909. **Remarks:** Accepts advertising. **Circ:** (Not Reported).

10361 ■ Journal of the American Planning Association
American Planning Association
205 N Michigan Ave., Ste. 1200
Chicago, IL 60601
Phone: (312)431-9100
Fax: (312)786-6700
Publication E-mail: japa@utah.edu
Professional journal covering city planning. **Freq:** Quarterly. **Print Method:** Sheetfed offset. **Trim Size:** 8 1/2 X 11. **Key Personnel:** Randall Crane, Editor; Amy Helling, PhD, Managing Editor; Thom Sanchez, Editor; David Sawicki, PhD, Editor. **ISSN:** 0194--4363 (print). **Subscription Rates:** $48 Individuals. **URL:** http://www.planning.org/japa. **Ad Rates:** BW $1,150. **Remarks:** Accepts advertising. **Circ:** Paid ⊕**11400**, 12,800.

10362 ■ Journal of Art, Technology, & Intellectual Property Law
DePaul University College of Law
25 E Jackson Blvd.
Chicago, IL 60604
Phone: (312)362-8701
Fax: (312)362-6918
Free: 800-428-7453
Publisher's E-mail: lawinfo@depaul.edu
Journal containing legal issues and policy in arts, technology and intellectual property law. **Freq:** Semiannual. **URL:** http://law.depaul.edu/student-resources/student-activities/journals/art-technology-intellectual-property-law/Pages/default.aspx. **Circ:** (Not Reported).

10363 ■ Journal of the Association for Consumer Research
The University of Chicago Press, Journals Div.
1427 E 60th St.
Chicago, IL 60637
Phone: (773)702-7700
Free: 877-705-1878
Publisher's E-mail: subscriptions@press.uchicago.edu
Journal containing thematic explorations from the Association for Consumer Research. **Freq:** Quarterly. **ISSN:** 2378--1815 (print); **EISSN:** 2378--1823 (electronic). **Subscription Rates:** $35 Individuals electronic only; $45 Individuals print and electronic. **URL:** http://www.press.uchicago.edu/ucp/journals/journal/jacr.html. **Circ:** (Not Reported).

10364 ■ Journal of the Association of Environmental and Resource Economists
The University of Chicago Press, Journals Div.
1427 E 60th St.
Chicago, IL 60637
Phone: (773)702-7700
Free: 877-705-1878
Publisher's E-mail: subscriptions@press.uchicago.edu
Journal containing articles on environmental and natural resource issues. **Freq:** Quarterly. **ISSN:** 2333--5955 (print); **EISSN:** 2333--5963 (electronic). **Subscription Rates:** $75 Individuals electronic only; $89 Individuals print and electronic. **URL:** http://www.press.uchicago.edu/ucp/journals/journal/jaere.html. **Circ:** (Not Reported).

10365 ■ Journal of British Studies
The University of Chicago Press
1427 E 60th St.
Chicago, IL 60637
Phone: (773)702-7700
Fax: (773)702-7212
Publisher's E-mail: custserv@press.uchicago.edu
British history journal, from antiquity to the present, and geographically from British Isles and Commonwealth to Britain's former colonies in America. **Freq:** Quarterly. **Print Method:** Offset. **Trim Size:** 6 3/4 x 10. **Cols./Page:** 1. **Col. Width:** 52 nonpareils. **Col. Depth:** 98 agate lines. **Key Personnel:** Elizabeth Elbourne, Editor; Brian Cowan, Editor; Jeffrey Collins, Associate Editor; Nancy Partner, Associate Editor. **ISSN:** 0021--9371 (print). **Ad Rates:** BW $578. **Remarks:** Accepts advertising. **Circ:** 1826.

10366 ■ Journal of Broadcasting & Electronic Media
Taylor & Francis Online
c/o Zizi Papacharissi, Editor
University of Illinois at Chicago
Dept. of Communications
1007 W Harrison St., BSB 1140
Chicago, IL 60607-7137
Phone: (312)996-3188
Publisher's E-mail: support@tandfonline.com
Scholarly journal on broadcasting and the electronic media. **Freq:** Quarterly. **Print Method:** Offset. **Trim Size:** 6 x 9. **Cols./Page:** 1. **Col. Width:** 54 nonpareils. **Col. Depth:** 102 agate lines. **Key Personnel:** Zizi Papacharissi, Editor, phone: (312)996-3188. **ISSN:** 0883--8151 (print); **EISSN:** 1550--6878 (electronic). **Subscription Rates:** Included in membership; $258 Institutions online only; $295 Institutions print and online; $79

Circulation: ★ = AAM; △ or • = BPA; ♦ = CAC; ❑ = VAC; ⊕ = PO Statement; ‡ = Publisher's Report; Boldface figures = sworn; Light figures = estimated.

Individuals print and online. **URL:** http://www.beaweb.org/wp/?page_id=118; http://www.tandfonline.com/loi/hbem20#.V4gkgNKrQdW. **Formerly:** Journal of Broadcasting. **Remarks:** Accepts advertising. **Circ:** (Not Reported).

10367 ■ Journal of Cardiopulmonary Rehabilitation and Prevention
American Association of Cardiovascular and Pulmonary Rehabilitation
330 N Wabash Ave., Ste. 200
Chicago, IL 60611
Phone: (312)321-5146
Fax: (312)673-6924
Publisher's E-mail: aacvpr@aacvpr.org
Freq: 6/year. **ISSN:** 1932--7501 (print). **URL:** http://www.aacvpr.org/Events-Education/Publications. **Formerly:** Journal of Cardiopulmonary Rehabilitation. **Remarks:** Accepts advertising. **Circ:** (Not Reported).

10368 ■ Journal of Clinical Neurophysiology
Lippincott Williams & Wilkins
c/o John S. Ebersole, Ed.-in-Ch.
University of Chicago
Dept. of Neurology
5841 S Maryland Ave., MC 2030
Chicago, IL 60637
Phone: (773)834-4702
Fax: (773)834-4800
Peer-reviewed journal reviewing topics in electroencephalography and potentials, clinical neurology, neurosurgery, psychiatry, and experimental research of the central nervous system. **Freq:** Bimonthly February, April, June, August, October, December. **Print Method:** Offset, Sheetfed. **Trim Size:** 8 1/4 x 11. **Key Personnel:** Aatif M. Husain, M.D., Editor-in-Chief. **ISSN:** 0736--0258 (print); **EISSN:** 1537--1603 (electronic). **Subscription Rates:** $577 Individuals; $661 Canada and Mexico; $675 Other countries; $1633 Institutions; $1744 Institutions, Canada and Mexico; $1758 Institutions, other countries; $236 Individuals in-training; $250 Other countries in-training. **URL:** http://journals.lww.com/clinicalneurophys/pages/default.aspx. **Remarks:** Accepts advertising. **Circ:** (Not Reported).

10369 ■ Journal of College Reading and Learning
College Reading and Learning Association
Columbia College
618 S Michigan Ave.
Chicago, IL 60605
Phone: (315)369-8827
Fax: (312)369-8429
Publication E-mail: jcrl@crla.net
Forum for the theory, research and policy related to reading improvement and learning assistance at the two-and four-year college level. **Freq:** Semiannual. **Key Personnel:** Nita Meola, Editor. **ISSN:** 1079--0195 (print); **EISSN:** 2332--7413 (electronic). **Subscription Rates:** $90 Institutions online only; $103 Institutions print and online. **URL:** http://www.crla.net/index.php/publications/jcrl-journal-of-college-reading-and-learning; http://www.tandfonline.com/loi/ucrl20#.VfKhN9Kqqko. **Circ:** (Not Reported).

10370 ■ Journal of Consumer Research: An Interdisciplinary Quarterly
The University of Chicago Press
1427 E 60th St.
Chicago, IL 60637
Phone: (773)702-7700
Fax: (773)702-7212
Publication E-mail: jcr@bus.wisc.edu
Journal publishing scholarly research on consumer behavior. **Freq:** Bimonthly. **Print Method:** Offset. **Trim Size:** 8 1/2 x 11. **Cols./Page:** 2. **Col. Width:** 36 nonpareils. **Col. Depth:** 116 agate lines. **Key Personnel:** Mary Frances Luce, Editor; Mary-Ann Twist, Managing Editor; Darren Dahl, Editor-in-Chief. **ISSN:** 0093--5301 (print); **EISSN:** 1537--5277 (electronic). **Subscription Rates:** $345 Institutions FTEs under 6,000 - online-only access; $414 Institutions FTEs 6,000 to 16,999 - online-only access; $483 Institutions FTEs 17,000 to 35,999 - online-only access; $518 Institutions FTEs 36,000 and above - online-only access; $401 Institutions FTEs under 6,000 - print and online; $482 Institutions FTEs 6,000 to 16,999 - print and online; $562 Institutions FTEs 17,000 to 35,999 - print and online; $603 Institutions FTEs 36,000 and above - print and online; $369 Institutions Print; $155 Individuals Online-only access; $177 Individuals Print; $25 Students Online-only access; $25 Students Print. **URL:** http://www.ejcr.org. **Ad Rates:** BW $740. **Remarks:** Accepts advertising. **Circ:** 2774.

10371 ■ The Journal of Criminal Law & Criminology
Northwestern University School of Law
357 E Chicago Ave.
Chicago, IL 60611-3069
Phone: (312)503-3100
Journal encouraging a dialogue on the criminal law and criminology issues and their reforms. **Founded:** 1910. **Freq:** Quarterly. **Key Personnel:** Stephen Laudone, Editor-in-Chief. **Subscription Rates:** $50 Individuals; $85 Other countries; $15 Single issue; $18 Other countries single issue. **Alt. Formats:** PDF. **URL:** http://scholarlycommons.law.northwestern.edu/jclc. **Circ:** (Not Reported).

10372 ■ Journal of Dental Hygiene
American Dental Hygienists' Association
444 N Michigan Ave., Ste. 3400
Chicago, IL 60611
Phone: (312)440-8900
Publication E-mail: communications@adha.net
Professional journal on dental hygiene. **Founded:** 1923. **Freq:** Quarterly. **Print Method:** Offset. **Trim Size:** 8 1/8 x 10 7/8. **Cols./Page:** 2. **Col. Width:** 19.5 picas. **Col. Depth:** 59.5 picas. **Key Personnel:** Rebecca Wilder, Editor-in-Chief; Celeste M. Abraham, Board Member; Tricia S. Moore, Board Member; Josh Snyder, Editor; Laura J. Howerton, Board Member. **ISSN:** 1043-254X (print). **Subscription Rates:** $60 Individuals. **URL:** http://www.adha.org/jdh..**Ad Rates:** GLR $15; BW $2,534; 4C $3,734; PCI $120. **Remarks:** Accepts advertising. **Circ:** Paid ‡36000, Non-paid ‡2000.

10373 ■ The Journal of Dentistry for Children
American Academy of Pediatric Dentistry
211 E Chicago Ave., Ste. 1600
Chicago, IL 60611-2637
Phone: (312)337-2169
Fax: (312)337-6329
Freq: 3/year. **ISSN:** 0022- 0353 (print). **Subscription Rates:** $110 Individuals; $163 Institutions for 5 IP address; $580 Institutions for over 5 IP address. **URL:** http://www.aapd.org/publications/. **Remarks:** Accepts advertising. **Circ:** (Not Reported).

10374 ■ Journal of Environmental and Energy Law
Illinois Institute of Technology Chicago-Kent College of Law
565 W Adams St.
Chicago, IL 60661-3691
Phone: (312)906-5000
Fax: (312)906-5280
Journal containing legal issues on environmental law and policy. **Freq:** Annual. **URL:** http://studentorgs.kentlaw.iit.edu/ckjeel/. **Circ:** (Not Reported).

10375 ■ Journal of Food Science Education
Institute of Food Technologists
525 W Van Buren St., Ste. 1000
Chicago, IL 60607
Phone: (312)782-8424
Fax: (312)782-8348
Free: 800-438-3663
Publisher's E-mail: info@ift.org
Freq: Quarterly Latest Edition: Volume 13, Issue 2 (April 2014). **Subscription Rates:** $1080 Institutions print and online, The America's; £586 Institutions print and online, UK; €741 Institutions print and online, Euro and non Euro zone; $1140 Institutions print and online, ROW; $900 Institutions online, The America's; £488 Institutions online, UK; €617 Institutions online, Euro and non Euro zone; $950 Institutions online, ROW. **URL:** http://www.ift.org/knowledge-center/read-ift-publications/journal-of-food-science-education.aspx; http://onlinelibrary.wiley.com/journal/10.1111/%28ISSN%291541-4329. **Remarks:** Advertising not accepted. **Circ:** (Not Reported).

10376 ■ The Journal of Geology
The University of Chicago Press
1427 E 60th St.
Chicago, IL 60637
Phone: (773)702-7700
Fax: (773)702-7212
Publisher's E-mail: custserv@press.uchicago.edu
Journal presenting original contributions on all aspects of earth sciences from geochemistry and geophysics to paleontology and related space sciences. **Freq:** 6/year. **Print Method:** Offset. **Trim Size:** 8 1/2 x 11. **Cols./Page:** 2. **Col. Width:** 30 nonpareils. **Col. Depth:** 103 agate lines. **Key Personnel:** David Rowley, Editor; Barbara J. Sivertsen, Managing Editor. **ISSN:** 0022--1376 (print); **EISSN:** 1537--5269 (electronic). **Subscription Rates:** $66 Individuals print and electronic; $56 Individuals electronic only; $57 Individuals print only; $33 Students electronic only; $132 Two years print and electronic; $112 Two years electronic; $114 Two years print; $66 Two years student; electronic. **URL:** http://www.journals.uchicago.edu/toc/jg/current. **Ad Rates:** BW $690. **Remarks:** Accepts advertising. **Circ:** 1231, 589.

10377 ■ The Journal of Hand Surgery
American Society for Surgery of the Hand
822 W Washington Blvd.
Chicago, IL 60607
Phone: (312)880-1900
Fax: (847)384-1435
Publisher's E-mail: info@assh.org
Journal publishing original, peer-reviewed articles related to the diagnosis, treatment, and pathophysiology of diseases and conditions of the upper extremity; these include both clinical and basic science studies, along with case reports. **Freq:** Bimonthly. **ISSN:** 0363-5023 (print). **Subscription Rates:** $449 Individuals print and online, US; $594 Individuals print and online, international; $205 Students print and online, US; $307 Students print and online, international; Included in membership. **URL:** http://www.jhandsurg.org; http://www.assh.org/Member-Resources/Journal-of-Hand-Surgery. **Remarks:** Advertising not accepted. **Circ:** (Not Reported).

10378 ■ Journal of Health Care Law
DePaul University College of Law
25 E Jackson Blvd.
Chicago, IL 60604
Phone: (312)362-8701
Fax: (312)362-6918
Free: 800-428-7453
Publisher's E-mail: lawinfo@depaul.edu
Journal covering issues regarding the development in health law field. **Freq:** Quarterly. **Key Personnel:** Sydney Mayer, Editor-in-Chief. **ISSN:** 1551--8426 (print). **Subscription Rates:** $50 Individuals; $25 Single issue. **URL:** http://via.library.depaul.edu/jhcl/. **Circ:** (Not Reported).

10379 ■ Journal of Health Politics, Policy and Law
Duke University Press
School of Social Service Administration
University of Chicago
969 E 60th St.
Chicago, IL 60637
Phone: (773)702-5966
Fax: (773)702-7222
Publication E-mail: jhppl@ssa.uchicago.edu
Journal on the initiation, formulation, and implementation of health policy. **Freq:** Bimonthly. **Trim Size:** 4 1/4 x 7 1/8. **Key Personnel:** Colleen M. Grogan, Editor. **ISSN:** 0361--6878 (print); **EISSN:** 1527--1927 (electronic). **Subscription Rates:** $60 Individuals; $35 Students. **URL:** http://www.dukeupress.edu/Journal-of-Health-Politics-Policy-and-Law; http://jhppl.dukejournals.org. **Ad Rates:** BW $450, full page. **Remarks:** Accepts advertising. **Circ:** (Not Reported).

10380 ■ Journal of Healthcare Information Management
Healthcare Information and Management Systems Society
33 W Monroe St., Ste. 1700
Chicago, IL 60603-5616
Phone: (312)664-4467
Fax: (312)664-6143
Publisher's E-mail: himss@himss.org
Freq: Quarterly. **URL:** http://www.himss.org/jhim; http://www.himss.org/health-it-publications. **Remarks:** Advertising not accepted. **Circ:** (Not Reported).

10381 ■ Journal of Healthcare Management
Health Administration Press

1 N Franklin St., Ste. 1700
Chicago, IL 60606-3529
Phone: (312)424-2800
Fax: (312)424-0023
Publisher's E-mail: geninfo@ache.org
Professional journal focusing on healthcare management.Offers timely healthcare management articles that inform and guide executives, managers, educators, and researchers,. **Freq:** Bimonthly. **Print Method:** Offset. **Trim Size:** 7 x 10. **Cols./Page:** 1. **Col. Width:** 32 picas. **Col. Depth:** 47 picas. **Key Personnel:** Bita A. Kash, PhD, Editor. **ISSN:** 1096--9012 (print). **Subscription Rates:** $130 Individuals /year; softbound; $135 Other countries /year; softbound; $35 Single issue. **URL:** http://www.ache.org/Publications/SubscriptionPurchase.aspx#jhm. **Remarks:** Advertising not accepted. **Circ:** Paid ‡1500, Controlled ‡27000.

10382 ■ Journal for Healthcare Quality: The Official Journal of the National Association for Healthcare Quality
National Association for Healthcare Quality
8735 W Higgins Rd., Ste. 300
Chicago, IL 60631
Phone: (847)375-4720
Fax: (847)375-6320
Free: 800-966-9392
Publication E-mail: jhq@nahq.org
Professional publication that explores safe, cost-effective, quality healthcare. **Freq:** Bimonthly. **Print Method:** Sheetfed offset. **Trim Size:** 8 1/2 x 11. **Cols./Page:** 2. **Col. Width:** 2 5/16 inches. **Col. Depth:** 8 5/8 inches. **Key Personnel:** Maria R. Shirey, PhD, Editor-in-Chief; Diane Brown, PhD, Board Member; Maulik Joshi, PhD, Editor-in-Chief. **ISSN:** 1062--2551 (print); **EISSN:** 1945--1474 (electronic). **Subscription Rates:** $215 Individuals print; $330 Institutions print; Members free; $15 Nonmembers. **URL:** http://journals.lww.com/jhqonline/pages/default.aspx; http://www.nahq.org/Quality-Community/journal/jhq.html. **Formerly**: Journal of Quality Assurance. **Remarks:** Advertising accepted; rates available upon request. **Circ:** Paid 6000, Controlled 500.

10383 ■ Journal of Healthcare Risk Management
American Society for Healthcare Risk Management
155 N Wacker Dr., Ste. 400
Chicago, IL 60606
Phone: (312)422-3980
Fax: (312)422-4580
Publisher's E-mail: ashrm@aha.org
Freq: Quarterly. **Trim Size:** 8 1/2" x 11". **Subscription Rates:** Included in membership; $208 Individuals print and online. **URL:** http://staging.ashrm.org/pubs/journal.dhtml; http://www.ashrm.org/pubs/journal.dhtml. **Ad Rates:** BW $1,575; 4C $1,960. **Remarks:** Accepts advertising. **Circ:** 6000.

10384 ■ Journal of Human Capital
The University of Chicago Press
1427 E 60th St.
Chicago, IL 60637
Phone: (773)702-7700
Fax: (773)702-7212
Publication E-mail: journalofhumancapital@press.uchicago.edu
Peer-reviewed journal covering human capital and its expanding economic and social roles in the knowledge economy. **Freq:** Quarterly. **Key Personnel:** Isaac Ehrlich, Editor-in-Chief; Tim Besley, Associate Editor. **ISSN:** 1932-8575 (print); **EISSN:** 1932-8664 (electronic). **Subscription Rates:** $62 Individuals print and online; $55 Individuals online only; $31 Students online only; $157 Institutions museum, library. **URL:** http://www.jstor.org/action/showPublication?journalCode=jhumancapital. **Remarks:** Accepts advertising. **Circ:** (Not Reported).

10385 ■ Journal of Intellectual Property
Illinois Institute of Technology Chicago-Kent College of Law
565 W Adams St.
Chicago, IL 60661-3691
Phone: (312)906-5000
Fax: (312)906-5280
Journal containing articles on intellectual property rights. **Freq:** Annual. **Key Personnel:** Micah Hensley, Editor-in-Chief. **URL:** http://studentorgs.kentlaw.iit.edu/ckjip. **Circ:** (Not Reported).

10386 ■ Journal of the International Association of Physicians in AIDS Care
Journal of the International Association of Physicians in AIDS Care
123 Madison St., Ste. 1704
Chicago, IL 60602
Phone: (312)795-4930
Fax: (312)795-4938
Publication E-mail: editor@iapac.org
Magazine featuring topics affecting the care of HIV-positive people. **Founded:** Feb. 1995. **Freq:** Bimonthly. **Print Method:** 4-color press. **Trim Size:** 8 1/8 x 11 1/8. **Cols./Page:** 3. **Key Personnel:** John G. Bartlett, MD, Editor; Peter Mugyeni, MD, Editor; Jose Zuniga, Editor-in-Chief; Jose M. Zuniga, Chief Executive Officer, President. **ISSN:** 1545-1097 (print); **EISSN:** 2325-9582 (electronic). **Subscription Rates:** $444 Institutions print & e-access; $400 Institutions e-access; $435 Institutions print; $102 Individuals print; $80 Institutions single print; $22 Individuals single print; $105 Individuals print only; $23 Individuals single print issue. **URL:** http://www.sagepub.com/journalsProdDesc.nav?prodId=Journal201760; http://www.sagepub.com/journalsProdDesc.nav?ct_p=&prodId=Journal201760; http://jia.sagepub.com. **Ad Rates:** BW $3,295; 4C $5,795; 4C $2,550. **Remarks:** Accepts advertising. **Circ:** Paid 5575, Non-paid 2900.

10387 ■ Journal of International Human Rights
Northwestern University School of Law
357 E Chicago Ave.
Chicago, IL 60611-3069
Phone: (312)503-3100
Publisher's E-mail: law-web@law.northwestern.edu
Journal dealing with issues related to human rights, and also covers law based on international human rights. **Freq:** Annual. **Key Personnel:** Stephanie Le, Editor-in-Chief. **ISSN:** 1549--828X (print). **URL:** http://www.law.northwestern.edu/research-faculty/journals; http://scholarlycommons.law.northwestern.edu/njihr. **Circ:** (Not Reported).

10388 ■ Journal of International Law and Business
Northwestern University School of Law
357 E Chicago Ave.
Chicago, IL 60611-3069
Phone: (312)503-3100
Journal covering analysis of transnational and international law and its effects on private entities. **Freq:** 3/year. **Key Personnel:** Kara Cooper, Editor-in-Chief. **Subscription Rates:** $40 domestic; $15 Single issue domestic; $18 Single issue foreign. **URL:** http://scholarlycommons.law.northwestern.edu/njilb. **Circ:** (Not Reported).

10389 ■ Journal of Knot Theory and Its Ramifications
World Scientific Publishing Company Inc.
c/o L.H. Kauffman, Ed.-in-Ch.
University of Illinois at Chicago
851 S Morgan St.
Chicago, IL 60607-7045
Publisher's E-mail: wspc@wspc.com
Journal covering developments in knot theory and ramifications in math and other sciences. **Freq:** 14/yr. **Trim Size:** 6 1/2 x 9 3/4. **Cols./Page:** 1. **Col. Width:** 5 inches. **Col. Depth:** 8 inches. **Key Personnel:** R. Benedetti, Academic Director; J.E. Andersen, Academic Director; C. Blanchet, Academic Director; F. Bonahon, Academic Director; M. Boileau, Academic Director; J.S. Carter, Managing Editor; V.G. Turaev, Academic Director; L.H. Kauffman, Editor-in-Chief. **ISSN:** 0218--2165 (print); **EISSN:** 1793--6527 (electronic). **Subscription Rates:** $2664 Institutions print + electronic; $2377 Institutions electronic only; £1838 Institutions print + electronic; £1640 Institutions electronic only; S$4245 Institutions print + electronic; S$3787 Institutions electronic only; $78 Institutions for postage; £55 Institutions for postage; S$104 Institutions for postage. **URL:** http://www.worldscientific.com/worldscinet/jktr. **Remarks:** Advertising not accepted. **Circ:** (Not Reported).

10390 ■ Journal of Labor Economics
The University of Chicago Press
1155 E 60th St., Rm. 252
Chicago, IL 60637
Phone: (773)256-6232
Fax: (773)256-6132
Publisher's E-mail: custserv@press.uchicago.edu
Journal presenting both theoretical and applied papers in labor economics. **Freq:** Quarterly. **Print Method:** Offset. **Trim Size:** 6 x 9. **Cols./Page:** 1. **Col. Width:** 54 nonpareils. **Col. Depth:** 97 agate lines. **Key Personnel:** Paul Oyer, Editor-in-Chief; Dan Black, Board Member; Maggie Newman, Managing Editor. **ISSN:** 0734--306X (print); **EISSN:** 1537--5307 (electronic). **Subscription Rates:** $82 Individuals print and electronic or electronic only; $60 Students print and electronic or electronic only; $164 Two years print and electronic or electronic only; $120 Two years print and electronic or electronic only; $246 Individuals print and electronic or electronic only; $180 Students print and electronic or electronic only. **URL:** http://www.journals.uchicago.edu/toc/jole/current. **Ad Rates:** BW $690. **Remarks:** Accepts advertising. **Circ:** 880.

10391 ■ Journal of Law and Courts
The University of Chicago Press, Journals Div.
1427 E 60th St.
Chicago, IL 60637
Phone: (773)702-7700
Free: 877-705-1878
Publisher's E-mail: subscriptions@press.uchicago.edu
Journal containing topics regarding law and courts intellectual community. **ISSN:** 2164--6570 (print); **EISSN:** 2164--6589 (electronic). **Subscription Rates:** $32 Individuals print and electronic. **URL:** http://www.press.uchicago.edu/ucp/journals/journal/jlc.html. **Circ:** (Not Reported).

10392 ■ The Journal of Law and Economics
The University of Chicago Press
c/o Maureen Callahan, Mng. Ed.
The University of Chicago Law School
1111 E 60th St.
Chicago, IL 60637
Phone: (773)702-9603
Fax: (773)834-3729
Publisher's E-mail: custserv@press.uchicago.edu
Journal exploring the relationships between law and economics, focusing on the influence of regulation and legal institutions on the operation of economic systems. **Freq:** Quarterly. **Print Method:** Offset. **Trim Size:** 6 x 9. **Cols./Page:** 1. **Key Personnel:** Dennis W. Carlton, Editor; Maureen Callahan, Managing Editor; John Gould, Editor; Sam Peltzman, Editor. **ISSN:** 0022--2186 (print); **EISSN:** 1537--5285 (electronic). **Subscription Rates:** $33 Individuals; $39 Individuals electronic and print; $70 Individuals electronic and print, 2 years; $99 Individuals print and electronic, 3 years. **URL:** http://www.press.uchicago.edu/ucp/journals/journal/jle.html. **Ad Rates:** BW $690. **Remarks:** Accepts advertising. **Circ:** Paid 1345.

10393 ■ Journal of Law & Economics
University of Chicago Law School
1111 E 60th St.
Chicago, IL 60637
Phone: (773)702-9494
Fax: (773)834-0942
Journal containing analysis of current public policy issues. **Freq:** Quarterly. **ISSN:** 0022--2186 (print); **EISSN:** 1537--5285 (electronic). **Subscription Rates:** $33 Individuals online or print; $39 Individuals print and online; $70 Two years print and online; $20 Students online; $43 Members print and online. **URL:** http://www.press.uchicago.edu/ucp/journals/journal/jle.html. **Circ:** (Not Reported).

10394 ■ Journal of Law and Social Policy
Northwestern University School of Law
357 E Chicago Ave.
Chicago, IL 60611-3069
Phone: (312)503-3100
Journal discussing the impact of law in different aspects of society. **Key Personnel:** Shirin Savliwala, Editor-in-Chief. **ISSN:** 1557--2447 (print). **URL:** http://scholarlycommons.law.northwestern.edu/njlsp. **Circ:** (Not Reported).

Circulation: ★ = AAM; △ or • = BPA; ♦ = CAC; ❑ = VAC; ⊕ = PO Statement; ‡ = Publisher's Report; Boldface figures = sworn; Light figures = estimated.

10395 ■ Journal of Legal Nurse Consulting
American Association of Legal Nurse Consultants
330 N Wabash Ste. 2000
Chicago, IL 60611-4267
Fax: (312)673-6655
Free: 877-402-2562
Publication E-mail: jlnc@aalnc.org
Journal featuring up-to-date information on a broad spectrum of medical-legal topics; timely articles on subjects such as medical and products liability issues, managed care, life care planning, use of experts, and forensics; and valuable business advice and networking tips. **Freq:** Semiannual. **Subscription Rates:** free for members; $165.00 Nonmembers. **URL:** http://www.aalnc.org/page/the-journal-of-legal-nurse-consulting. **Remarks:** Accepts advertising. **Circ:** (Not Reported).

10396 ■ The Journal of Legal Studies
The University of Chicago Press
c/o Maureen Callahan, Mng. Ed.
The University of Chicago Law School
1111 E 60th St.
Chicago, IL 60637
Phone: (773)702-9603
Fax: (773)834-3729
Publisher's E-mail: custserv@press.uchicago.edu
Interdisciplinary journal of theoretical and empirical research on law and legal institutions. **Freq:** Semiannual. **Print Method:** Offset. **Trim Size:** 6 x 9. **Cols./Page:** 1. **Key Personnel:** Omri Ben-Shahar, Editor; Maureen Callahan, Managing Editor. **ISSN:** 0047-2530 (print); **EISSN:** 1537-5366 (electronic). **Subscription Rates:** $29 Individuals 1 year; $34 Individuals 1 year, electronic and print; $61 Individuals 2 years, electronic and print; $87 Individuals 3 years, print and electronic. **URL:** http://www.press.uchicago.edu/ucp/journals/journal/jls.html. **Ad Rates:** BW $690. **Remarks:** Accepts advertising. **Circ:** Paid 792.

10397 ■ Journal of Legal Studies
University of Chicago Law School
1111 E 60th St.
Chicago, IL 60637
Phone: (773)702-9494
Fax: (773)834-0942
Journal containing articles on social and political issues. **Freq:** Semiannual. **ISSN:** 0047--2530 (print); **EISSN:** 1537--5366 (electronic). **Subscription Rates:** $29 Individuals online or print; $34 Individuals print and online; $61 Two years print and online; $17 Students online; $43 Members print and online. **URL:** http://www.press.uchicago.edu/ucp/journals/journal/jls.html. **Circ:** (Not Reported).

10398 ■ Journal of Liberal Religion
Meadville Lombard Theological School
610 S Michigan Ave.
Chicago, IL 60637-1901
Phone: (773)256-3000
Fax: (312)327-7002
Publisher's E-mail: dbieber@meadville.edu
Journal focusing on liberal religion studies. **Freq:** Semiannual. **Key Personnel:** Bill Murry, Editor. **ISSN:** 1527--9324 (print). **URL:** http://www.meadville.edu/page.php?page=71. **Circ:** (Not Reported).

10399 ■ Journal of Marketing
American Marketing Association
311 S Wacker Dr., Ste. 5800
Chicago, IL 60606
Phone: (312)542-9000
Fax: (312)542-9001
Free: 800-AMA-1150
Freq: Bimonthly. **Key Personnel:** Christopher Bartone, Director, Publications, phone: (312)542-9029, fax: (312)922-3763; Gary L. Frazier, Editor, phone: (213)740-5032. **ISSN:** 0022-2429 (print). **Subscription Rates:** $175 U.S. and Canada print and online; $205 Other countries print and online; $145 U.S. and Canada print only; $460 Institutions print and online; $485 Institutions, other countries print and online; $415 Institutions, other countries print only; $385 Institutions U.S, Canada and other Countries; online only; $490 Institutions, other countries print + online; $455 Institutions print + online. **URL:** http://www.ama.org/publications/JournalOfMarketing/Pages/Current-Issue.aspx; http://www.ama.org/publications/JournalOfMarketing/Pages/About.aspx. **Ad Rates:** BW $1,500. **Remarks:** Accepts advertising. **Circ:** Paid ‡6600, 9000.

10400 ■ Journal of Marketing Research
American Marketing Association
311 S Wacker Dr., Ste. 5800
Chicago, IL 60606
Phone: (312)542-9000
Fax: (312)542-9001
Free: 800-AMA-1150
Peer-reviewed journal concentrates on marketing research. **Freq:** Bimonthly. **Print Method:** Offset. **Trim Size:** 8 1/2 x 11. **Cols./Page:** 2. **Col. Width:** 40 nonpareils. **Col. Depth:** 140 agate lines. **Key Personnel:** Robert Meyer, Editor; Christopher Bartone, Director, Publications; Andy Seagram, Managing Editor. **ISSN:** 0022--2437 (print); **EISSN:** 1547--7193 (electronic). **Subscription Rates:** $385 Institutions US and Canada (print only); $415 Institutions, other countries print only; $385 Institutions online only; $460 Institutions US and Canada (print and online); $480 Institutions, other countries print and online. **URL:** http://www.ama.org/publications/JournalOfMarketingResearch/Pages/About.aspx. **Ad Rates:** BW $1020. **Remarks:** Accepts advertising. **Circ:** Paid ‡3100, 6000.

10401 ■ Journal of the Medical Library Association
Medical Library Association
65 E Wacker Pl., Ste. 1900
Chicago, IL 60601-7246
Phone: (312)419-9094
Fax: (312)419-8950
Publisher's E-mail: websupport@mail.mlahq.org
MLA's peer-reviewed, scholarly journal is the definitive source of information about the latest technologies and innovations in the health information field. Health information professionals depend on this valuable forum for current research and information about biomedical library management, technology, and administration. Regular features include symposia, book and software reviews, and comment and opinion. **Freq:** Quarterly. **Print Method:** Letterpress and offset. **Trim Size:** 8 1/2 x 11. **Cols./Page:** 2 and 3. **Col. Width:** 3 1/4 and 2 1/8 inches. **Col. Depth:** 8 5/8 and 8 1/4 inches. **Key Personnel:** Susan Talmage, Editor. **ISSN:** 1536--5050 (print). **Subscription Rates:** $190 U.S., Canada, and Mexico 2nd class mail; $205 U.S., Canada, and Mexico 1st class mail; $215 Other countries; $15 Single issue back issue; Included in membership. **URL:** http://www.mlanet.org/p/cm/ld/fid=62. **Formerly:** Bulletin of the Medical Library Association. **Ad Rates:** BW $2150; 4C $3025. **Remarks:** Accepts advertising. **Circ:** (Not Reported).

10402 ■ The Journal of Medical Practice Management
Lippincott Williams and Wilkins
C/o Marcel Frenkel, M.D., Editor
University of Chicago
Vision Sciences Center
939 E. 57th St.
Chicago, IL 60637
Phone: (312)236-7277
Fax: (312)236-7276
Publication E-mail: miranda@nfdc.com
Journal covering legislation, litigation, office management and other issues affecting medical practices. Features a host of proven strategies for dealing with fiscal management, marketing, information technology, benefits and compensation, legal and tax issues, office operations, coding, and human resources that practice administrators, practice managers and physicians face on a daily basis. **Freq:** Bimonthly. **Print Method:** Offset. **Trim Size:** 8 1/8 x 10 7/8. **Cols./Page:** 2. **Col. Width:** 32 nonpareils. **Col. Depth:** 119 agate lines. **Key Personnel:** Marcel Frenkel, M.D., Editor; Nancy Collins, Publisher, phone: (410)329-9788; Marjory Spraycar, Managing Editor, phone: (410)337-3794; Jennifer LaGreca, Manager, Advertising and Sales, phone: (410)327-3170, fax: (775)599-2570. **ISSN:** 1055-8675 (print). **Subscription Rates:** $284 Individuals 6 issues in U.S.; $386 Institutions U.S; $47 Single issue U.S; $332 Out of country; $399 Out of country institution; $55 Out of country single issue; $159 Out of country in-training. **Available online. URL:** http://www.greenbranch.com/store/index.cfm/product/4_31/the-journal-of-medical-practice-management.cfm. **Remarks:** Accepts advertising. **Circ:** Paid ‡2430, Non-paid ‡110.

10403 ■ Journal of the Midwest Modern Language Association
Midwest Modern Language Association
Dept. of English
1032 W Sheridan Rd.
Chicago, IL 60660
Phone: (773)508-6083
Fax: (773)508-6062
Publication E-mail: mmla@uiowa.edu
Scholarly journal covering book reviews and other academic writing. **Freq:** Semiannual. **Print Method:** Offset. **Trim Size:** 6 x 9. **Key Personnel:** David Posner, Editor, Executive Director. **ISSN:** 0742--5562 (print). **Subscription Rates:** $30 Institutions; $35 Institutions, Canada and Mexico; $40 Institutions, other countries. **URL:** http://www.luc.edu/mmla/journal. **Formerly:** Bulletin of the Midwest Modern Language Association. **Ad Rates:** BW $250. **Remarks:** Accepts advertising. **Circ:** Paid 1200.

10404 ■ The Journal of Modern History
The University of Chicago Press
Social Science Research Bldg., Box 122
1126 E 59th St.
Chicago, IL 60637
Phone: (773)702-7227
Fax: (773)702-8830
Publication E-mail: jmh@uchicago.edu
Journal exploring the political, diplomatic, military, social, and intellectual events and movements that have shaped the European continent. **Freq:** Quarterly. **Print Method:** Offset. **Trim Size:** 6 x 9. **Cols./Page:** 1. **Col. Width:** 52 nonpareils. **Col. Depth:** 102 agate lines. **Key Personnel:** Jan E. Goldstein, Editor; Mary Van Steenbergh, Managing Editor; John W. Boyer, Editor. **ISSN:** 0022--2801 (print); **EISSN:** 1537--5358 (electronic). **Subscription Rates:** $268 Institutions print and electronic (with basic access); $262 Institutions electronic only (with unlimited access); $304 Institutions print and electronic (with unlimited access); $231 Individuals electronic only (with basic access); $49 Individuals print only; $58 Individuals print and electronic; $48 Individuals electronic only. **URL:** http://www.journals.uchicago.edu/toc/jmh/current. **Ad Rates:** BW $730. **Remarks:** Accepts advertising. **Circ:** 2337, 1392.

10405 ■ Journal of Near Eastern Studies
The University of Chicago Press
c/o The Oriental Institute
University of Chicago
1155 E 58th St.
Chicago, IL 60637
Phone: (773)702-9592
Publication E-mail: jnes@uchicago.edu
Journal devoted to examination of ancient and medieval civilizations of the Near East, including Old Testament and Islamic studies. **Freq:** Quarterly. **Print Method:** Offset. **Trim Size:** 6 5/8 x 9 1/2. **Cols./Page:** 2. **Col. Width:** 62 nonpareils. **Col. Depth:** 107 agate lines. **Key Personnel:** Seth Richardson, Managing Editor; Christopher Woods, Editor. **ISSN:** 0022--2968 (print); **EISSN:** 1545--6978 (electronic). **Subscription Rates:** $428 Institutions print and electronic; $372 Institutions electronic only; $273 Institutions print only; $164 Institutions single copy; $68 Individuals print and electronic; $60 Individuals electronic only; $61 Individuals print only; $54 Members print and electronic; $34 Students electronic only. **URL:** http://www.journals.uchicago.edu/toc/jnes/current. **Ad Rates:** BW $690. **Remarks:** Accepts advertising. **Circ:** 655.

10406 ■ Journal of Neurological and Orthopaedic Medicine and Surgery
American Academy of Neurological and Orthopaedic Surgeons
1516 N Lakeshore Dr.
Chicago, IL 60610
Phone: (312)787-1608
Fax: (312)787-9289
Publisher's E-mail: aanos@aanos.org
Contains articles on medical and surgical neurology and orthopedics. **Key Personnel:** Charles F. Xeller, M.D., Editor-in-Chief. **URL:** http://aanos.org/publications. **Remarks:** Advertising not accepted. **Circ:** (Not Reported).

10407 ■ Journal of Pain
American Pain Society
8735 W Higgins Rd., Ste. 300
Chicago, IL 60631-2738

Phone: (847)375-4715
Publisher's E-mail: info@americanpainsociety.org
Freq: Monthly. **Trim Size:** 8 1/4 x 11. **Key Personnel:** Mark P. Jensen, Editor-in-Chief; G.F. Gebhart, Editor, Founder; Mark P. Jensen, PhD, Editor-in-Chief. **ISSN:** 1526--5900 (print). **Subscription Rates:** $489 Individuals USA (print and online); $653 Individuals Canada (print and online); $634 Individuals other countries (print and online); $210 Students USA (print and online); $321 Students, Canada print and online; $312 Students, other countries print and online. **URL:** http://www.jpain.org. **Remarks:** Accepts advertising. **Circ:** (Not Reported).

10408 ■ Journal of Pediatric Hematology/ Oncology
American Society of Pediatric Hematology/Oncology
8735 W Higgins Rd., Ste. 300
Chicago, IL 60631-2738
Phone: (847)375-4716
Fax: (847)375-6483
Publication E-mail: jpho@ymail.com
Freq: 8/year 9/year. **Print Method:** Sheetfed Offset. **Trim Size:** 8 1/4 x 11. **Key Personnel:** Bruce M. Camitta, Editor-in-Chief; David Myers, Coordinator; Amy Newman, Coordinator; Barton A. Kamen, MD, Editor. **ISSN:** 1077-4114 (print); **EISSN:** 1536-3678 (electronic). **Subscription Rates:** $677 Individuals; $2167 Institutions; $237 Individuals in-training; $823 Other countries; $1997 Institutions, other countries; $256 Other countries in-training. **URL:** http://journals.lww.com/jpho-online/pages/default.aspx; http://www.lww.com/product/?1077-4114. **Ad Rates:** BW $1,405; 4C $1,525. **Remarks:** Accepts advertising. **Circ:** 277.

10409 ■ Journal of Pediatric Psychology
Kluwer Academic/Plenum Publishing Corp.
c/o Grayson N. Holmbeck, Editor
Dept. of Psychology
Loyola University Chicago
1032 W Sheridan Rd.
Chicago, IL 60660
Phone: (773)508-2967
Fax: (773)508-8713
Publisher's E-mail: kluwer@wkap.com
Pediatric Psychology journal. **Freq:** 10/year. **Print Method:** Offset. **Trim Size:** 6 x 9. **Cols./Page:** 1. **Col. Width:** 54 nonpareils. **Col. Depth:** 103 agate lines. **Key Personnel:** Ron Brown, PhD, Board Member; Michael C. Roberts, Board Member; Rayson N. Holmbeck, PhD, Editor. **ISSN:** 0146--8693 (print); **EISSN:** 1465--735X (electronic). **Subscription Rates:** $1328 Institutions print and online; $1063 Institutions online; $1222 Institutions print; $293 Individuals print; $105 Students print. **URL:** http://www.apadivisions.org/division-54/publications/journals/pediatric-psychology/index.aspx; http://jpepsy.oxfordjournals.org. **Remarks:** Advertising accepted; rates available upon request. **Circ:** 1700.

10410 ■ Journal of Periodontology
American Academy of Periodontology
737 N Michigan Ave., Ste. 800
Chicago, IL 60611-6660
Phone: (312)787-5518
Scholarly journal covering periodontology. **Freq:** Monthly. **Print Method:** Web. **Trim Size:** 8 1/8 x 10 7/8. **Key Personnel:** Kenneth S. Kornman, PhD, Editor-in-Chief; Julie Daw, Managing Editor, phone: (312)573-3224, fax: (312)573-3225. **ISSN:** 0022--3492 (print). **Subscription Rates:** $268 Individuals; $24 Single issue back issue; $319 Other countries; $30 Single issue back issue; international. **URL:** http://www.joponline.org; http://www.perio.org/journal/journal.html. **Ad Rates:** BW $2,699. **Remarks:** Accepts advertising. **Circ:** Combined 9000.

10411 ■ Journal of Political Economy
The University of Chicago Press
University of Chicago
1126 E 59th St.
Chicago, IL 60637
Phone: (773)702-8421
Fax: (773)702-8490
Publication E-mail: jpe@press.uchicago.edu
Journal presenting analytical, interpretive, and empirical studies in economics, history of economic thought, and social economics. **Freq:** Bimonthly. **Print Method:** Offset. **Trim Size:** 6 x 9. **Cols./Page:** 1. **Col. Width:** 54 nonpareils. **Col. Depth:** 102 agate lines. **Key Personnel:** Harald Uhlig, Editor; James J. Heckman, Editor; Vicky M. Longawa, Editor; Connie Fritsche, Managing Editor. **ISSN:** 0022--3808 (print); **EISSN:** 1537--534X (electronic). **Subscription Rates:** $76 Individuals print and electronic; $66 Individuals electronic only; $67 Individuals print only; $38 Students electronic only; $152 Two years print and electronic; $132 Two years electronic only; $134 Two years print only; $76 Two years student. **URL:** http://www.jstor.org/journal/jpoliecon; http://www.press.uchicago.edu/ucp/journals/journal/jpe.html; http://www.journals.uchicago.edu/toc/jpe/current. **Ad Rates:** BW $730. **Remarks:** Accepts advertising. **Circ:** 3758, 2099.

10412 ■ Journal of the Precast/Prestressed Concrete Institute
Precast/Prestressed Concrete Institute
200 W Adams St., No. 2100
Chicago, IL 60606
Phone: (312)786-0300
Freq: Bimonthly. **Subscription Rates:** $80 U.S. 1 year - print and digital; $200 U.S. 3 years - print and digital; $170 Other countries 1 year - print and digital; $470 Other countries 3 years - print and digital; $80 Individuals 1 year - digital only; $15 Single issue. **URL:** http://www.pci.org/Publications/PCI_Journal. **Remarks:** Accepts advertising. **Circ:** (Not Reported).

10413 ■ Journal of Prevention & Intervention in the Community
Routledge Journals Taylor & Francis Group
c/o Joseph R. Ferrari, PhD, Editor-in-Chief
DePaul University
2219 N Kenmore Ave.
Chicago, IL 60614
Journal devoted to the application of prevention in and effective interventions community based facility. Representative of community psychology. **Freq:** Quarterly. **Trim Size:** 6 x 8 3/8. **Cols./Page:** 1. **Col. Width:** 4 3/8 inches. **Col. Depth:** 7 1/8 inches. **Key Personnel:** Joseph R. Ferrari, PhD, Editor-in-Chief; Joseph Ferrari, Editor-in-Chief. **ISSN:** 1085--2352 (print); **EISSN:** 1540--7330 (electronic). **Subscription Rates:** $1328 Institutions online only; $329 Individuals online only; $1518 Institutions print and online; $364 Individuals print and online. **URL:** http://www.tandfonline.com/toc/wpic20/current#.VePvmSWqqko. **Formerly:** Prevention in Human Services. **Ad Rates:** BW $315; 4C $550. **Remarks:** Accepts advertising. **Circ:** (Not Reported).

10414 ■ Journal of Property Management
Institute of Real Estate Management
430 N Michigan Ave.
Chicago, IL 60611
Fax: (800)338-4736
Free: 800-837-0706
Publication E-mail: jpmsub@irem.org
Magazine serving real estate managers. **Freq:** Bimonthly. **Print Method:** Offset. **Trim Size:** 8 1/8 x 10 7/8. **Cols./Page:** 3. **Col. Width:** 26 nonpareils. **Col. Depth:** 138 agate lines. **Key Personnel:** Ronald Goss, President. **ISSN:** 0022--3905 (print). **Subscription Rates:** $62.95 U.S. /year; print and online; $72.95 Canada /year; print and online; $110.95 Other countries /year; print and online; $62.95 Other countries /year; online only. **URL:** http://www.irem.org/resources/jpm. **Ad Rates:** 4C $5365; BW $4085. **Remarks:** Accepts advertising. **Circ:** ‡19000.

10415 ■ The Journal of Prosthetic Dentistry
American Equilibration Society
207 E Ohio St., Ste. 399
Chicago, IL 60611
Phone: (847)965-2888
Fax: (609)573-5064
Peer-reviewed journal emphasizing new techniques, evaluation of dental materials, pertinent basic science concepts, and patient psychology in restorative dentistry. **Freq:** Monthly. **Print Method:** Offset. **Trim Size:** 8 1/8 x 10 7/8. **Cols./Page:** 2. **Col. Width:** 39 nonpareils. **Col. Depth:** 140 agate lines. **Key Personnel:** Stephen F. Rosenstiel, Editor. **ISSN:** 0022--3913 (print). **Subscription Rates:** $350 Individuals print + online; $454 Canada print + online; $433 Other countries print + online; $173 Students print + online; $231 Students, other countries print + online; $292 Individuals online; $324 Individuals print and online; $160 Students print and online. **Alt. Formats:** PDF. **URL:** http://www.thejpd.org. **Ad Rates:** BW $2,205; 4C $1,525. **Remarks:** Accepts advertising. **Circ:** 2300.

10416 ■ Journal of Prosthodontics
American College of Prosthodontists
211 E Chicago Ave., Ste. 1000
Chicago, IL 60611
Phone: (312)573-1260
Professional journal covering dentistry. **Freq:** 8/year. **Print Method:** Sheetfed Offset. **Trim Size:** 8 1/4 x 10 7/8. **Key Personnel:** David Felton, Editor-in-Chief. **ISSN:** 1059--941X (print); **EISSN:** 1532--849X (electronic). **Subscription Rates:** $246 Individuals print and online; $777 Institutions print and online; €825 Institutions print and online; £652 Institutions print and online; $647 Institutions online or print; €687 Institutions online or print; Included in membership. **URL:** http://as.wiley.com/WileyCDA/WileyTitle/productCd-JOPR.html; http://onlinelibrary.wiley.com/journal/10.1111/(ISSN)1532-849X. **Ad Rates:** BW $1,490; 4C $1,395. **Remarks:** Accepts advertising. **Circ:** Paid ‡3184.

10417 ■ Journal of Prosthodontics--Clinical Journal
American College of Prosthodontists
211 E Chicago Ave., Ste. 1000
Chicago, IL 60611
Phone: (312)573-1260
Publisher's E-mail: info@wiley.com
Journal promoting the advanced study and practice of prosthodontics, implant, esthetic, and reconstructive dentistry. **Freq:** 8/year. **ISSN:** 1059--941X (print); **EISSN:** 1532--849X (electronic). **Subscription Rates:** $246 Individuals print and online; $777 Institutions print and online. **URL:** http://onlinelibrary.wiley.com/journal/10.1111/(ISSN)1532-849X. **Ad Rates:** BW $1597, full page. **Remarks:** Accepts advertising. **Circ:** (Not Reported).

10418 ■ Journal of Public Policy & Marketing
American Marketing Association
311 S Wacker Dr., Ste. 5800
Chicago, IL 60606
Phone: (312)542-9000
Fax: (312)542-9001
Free: 800-AMA-1150
Peer-reviewed journal of marketing. **Freq:** Semiannual. **Print Method:** Offset. **Trim Size:** 8 1/2 x 11. **Cols./Page:** 2. **Key Personnel:** David W. Stewart, Editor-in-Chief; Christopher Bartone, Director, Publications. **ISSN:** 0743--9156 (print); **EISSN:** 1547--7207 (electronic). **Subscription Rates:** $140 Institutions print only and online; $170 Institutions print + online; $195 Institutions, other countries print + online; $105 Individuals print + online; $120 Other countries print + online. **URL:** http://www.ama.org/publications/JournalOfPublicPolicyAndMarketing/Pages/About.aspx. **Remarks:** Advertising accepted; rates available upon request. **Circ:** (Not Reported).

10419 ■ The Journal of Religion
The University of Chicago Press
University of Chicago
Swift Hall 005
1025 E 58th St.
Chicago, IL 60637
Phone: (773)702-8216
Publisher's E-mail: custserv@press.uchicago.edu
Journal focusing on theology and religion. **Freq:** Quarterly. **Print Method:** Offset. **Trim Size:** 6 x 9. **Cols./Page:** 1. **Col. Width:** 54 nonpareils. **Col. Depth:** 101 agate lines. **Key Personnel:** David Brakke, Board Member; Matthew Creighton, Assistant Editor; Richard A. Rosengarten, Editor; James T. Robinson, Editor. **ISSN:** 0022--4189 (print); **EISSN:** 1549--6538 (electronic). **Subscription Rates:** $48 Individuals print and electronic; $41 Individuals electronic only; $42 Individuals print only; $34 Individuals alumni, print and electronic; $24 Students electronic only; $86 Two years print and electronic; individuals; $61 Two years print and electronic; alumni; $43 Two years print and electronic; students. **URL:** http://www.journals.uchicago.edu/toc/jr/current. **Ad Rates:** BW $690. **Remarks:** Accepts advertising. **Circ:** ‡628.

10420 ■ Journal of Second Language Writing
RELX Group P.L.C.
c/o C.M. Tardy, Ed.
Department of Writing, Rhetoric & Discourse

Circulation: ★ = AAM; △ or • = BPA; ♦ = CAC; ❑ = VAC; ⊕ = PO Statement; ‡ = Publisher's Report; Boldface figures = sworn; Light figures = estimated.

DePaul University
802 W Belden Ave.
Chicago, IL 60614
Publisher's E-mail: amsterdam@relx.com
Journal covering reports or research relating to second and foreign language writing and writing instruction. **Freq:** 4/yr. **Key Personnel:** C.M. Tardy, Editor; R.M. Manchon, Board Member. **ISSN:** 1060--3743 (print). **Subscription Rates:** $97 Individuals print; $663 Institutions print; $552 Institutions ejournal. **URL:** http://www.journals.elsevier.com/journal-of-second-language-writing. **Circ:** (Not Reported).

10421 ■ Journal for Social Justice
DePaul University College of Law
25 E Jackson Blvd.
Chicago, IL 60604
Phone: (312)362-8701
Fax: (312)362-6918
Free: 800-428-7453
Publisher's E-mail: lawinfo@depaul.edu
Journal containing articles on social justice policy issues. **Key Personnel:** Katherine Davis, Editor-in-Chief. **URL:** http://law.depaul.edu/student-resources/student-activities/journals/journal-for-social-justice/Pages/default.aspx. **Circ:** (Not Reported).

10422 ■ Journal of the Society of Architectural Historians
Society of Architectural Historians
1365 N Astor St.
Chicago, IL 60610-2144
Phone: (312)573-1365
Publisher's E-mail: info@sah.org
Professional magazine devoted to architectural history. **Freq:** Quarterly. **Print Method:** offset Lithography. **Trim Size:** 8 1/2 x 11. **Cols./Page:** 3. **Col. Width:** 2 1/4 inches. **Col. Depth:** 9 1/2 inches. **Key Personnel:** Patricia Morton, Editor. **ISSN:** 0037--9808 (print). **Subscription Rates:** Included in membership. **URL:** http://www.sah.org/publications-and-research/jsah. **Remarks:** Accepts advertising. **Circ:** (Not Reported).

10423 ■ Journal of the Society for Social Work and Research
The University of Chicago Press, Journals Div.
1427 E 60th St.
Chicago, IL 60637
Phone: (773)702-7700
Free: 877-705-1878
Publisher's E-mail: subscriptions@press.uchicago.edu
Peer-reviewed journal containing original research on social problems, intervention programs, and policies. **Freq:** Quarterly. **ISSN:** 2334--2315 (print); **EISSN:** 1948--822X (electronic). **URL:** http://www.press.uchicago.edu/ucp/journals/journal/jsswr.html. **Circ:** (Not Reported).

10424 ■ Journal of Trauma and Acute Care Surgery
American Association for the Surgery of Trauma
633 N St. Clair St., Ste. 2600
Chicago, IL 60611
Fax: (312)202-5064
Free: 800-789-4006
Publisher's E-mail: ronna.ekhouse@wolterskluwer.com
Surgery journal. **Freq:** Monthly. **Print Method:** Offset. **Trim Size:** 8 1/8 x 10 7/8. **Cols./Page:** 2. **Col. Width:** 32 nonpareils. **Col. Depth:** 119 agate lines. **Key Personnel:** Jo Fields, Assistant Editor; Ernest E. Moore, M.D., Editor; Jennifer Crebs, Managing Editor, phone: (303)602-1816. **ISSN:** 0022--5282 (print); **EISSN:** 2163--0763 (electronic). **Subscription Rates:** $646 Individuals /year; $794 Canada and Mexico; $816 Other countries; $1271 Institutions; $1547 Canada and Mexico; $1569 Other countries. **URL:** http://journals.lww.com/jtrauma/pages/default.aspx; http://www.lww.com/Product/2163-0755. **Formerly**: Journal of Trauma: Injury, Infection, and Critical Care. **Mailing address:** PO Box 908, Philadelphia, PA 19106-3621. **Ad Rates:** BW $1,195; 4C $2,850. **Remarks:** Accepts advertising. **Circ:** 2706, Non-paid ‡278.

10425 ■ Journal of UFO Studies
J. Allen Hynek Center for UFO Studies
PO Box 31335
Chicago, IL 60631
Phone: (773)271-3611
Publisher's E-mail: infocenter@cufos.org
Freq: Periodic. **URL:** http://www.cufos.org/pubs3.html. **Remarks:** Advertising not accepted. **Circ:** (Not Reported).

10426 ■ Journal of the Ukrainian Medical Association of North America
Ukrainian Medical Association of North America
2247 W Chicago Ave.
Chicago, IL 60622-8957
Phone: (773)278-6262
Fax: (773)278-6962
Publisher's E-mail: umana@umana.org
Freq: Quarterly. **Subscription Rates:** By mail free for members; $25 each, for back issues. **Alt. Formats:** PDF. **URL:** http://www.umana.org/about.php; http://www.umana.org/library.php. **Remarks:** Advertising not accepted. **Circ:** 1000.

10427 ■ Journal of Vascular Surgery
Society for Vascular Surgery
633 N St. Clair St., 22nd Fl.
Chicago, IL 60611-5098
Phone: (312)334-2300
Fax: (312)334-2320
Free: 800-258-7188
Publisher's E-mail: vascular@vascularsociety.org
Freq: Monthly. **Subscription Rates:** $518 U.S. and Canada print and online; $643 Other countries print and online; $273 Students print and online; $331 Students, other countries print and online. **URL:** http://www.vascularweb.org/educationandmeetings/Pages/journal-of-vascular-surgery.aspx. **Remarks:** Advertising not accepted. **Circ:** (Not Reported).

10428 ■ Journal of Vascular Surgery: Official Journal of the Society for Vascular Surgery
Elsevier, Health Sciences Division
633 N St. Clair, 22nd Fl.
Chicago, IL 60611
Fax: (312)334-2320
Publisher's E-mail: h.licensing@elsevier.com
Journal providing a forum for the advances in knowledge of the peripheral vascular system. Publishes peer-reviewed original articles on all aspects of disease and injury to the arterial and venous systems. **Freq:** Monthly. **Print Method:** Offset. **Trim Size:** 8 1/8 x 10 7/8. **Cols./Page:** 2. **Col. Width:** 39 nonpareils. **Col. Depth:** 140 agate lines. **Key Personnel:** Anton N. Sidawy, Editor; Bruce A. Perler, Editor. **ISSN:** 0741--5214 (print). **Subscription Rates:** $534 Individuals print and online; $662 Other countries print and online; $281 Students print and online; $341 Students, other countries print and online. **URL:** http://www.jvascsurg.org. **Remarks:** Accepts advertising. **Circ:** (Not Reported).

10429 ■ Journal of Women, Gender & Law
DePaul University College of Law
25 E Jackson Blvd.
Chicago, IL 60604
Phone: (312)362-8701
Fax: (312)362-6918
Free: 800-428-7453
Publisher's E-mail: lawinfo@depaul.edu
Journal containing articles on legal rights of woman. **Freq:** Annual latest edition; spring 2016. **Key Personnel:** Abigail R. Durkin, Editor-in-Chief. **URL:** http://via.library.depaul.edu/jwgl. **Circ:** (Not Reported).

10430 ■ The Judges' Journal
American Bar Association
321 N Clark St.
Chicago, IL 60654
Phone: (312)988-5000
Free: 800-285-2221
Magazine for judges, lawyers and others dealing with courts and how they operate. **Freq:** Quarterly. **Key Personnel:** Melissa Ladwig, Editor. **ISSN:** 0047--2972 (print). **Subscription Rates:** Included in membership; $23 /year for non-lawyers; $25 Individuals; $6.50 Single issue. **Alt. Formats:** PDF. **URL:** http://www.americanbar.org/publications/judges_journal/2014/spring.html. **Remarks:** Advertising not accepted. **Circ:** 4500.

10431 ■ JUF News
Jewish United Fund / Jewish Federation of Metropolitan Chicago
Ben Gurion Way
30 S Wells St.
Chicago, IL 60606-5054
Phone: (312)346-6700
Publication E-mail: jufnews@juf.org
Jewish magazine. **Founded:** 1960. **Freq:** Monthly. **Print Method:** Offset. **Trim Size:** 11" x 12". **Cols./Page:** 5. **Col. Width:** 29 agate lines. **Col. Depth:** 181 agate lines. **URL:** http://www.juf.org/news/default.aspx. **Ad Rates:** BW $3457; 4C $3857. **Remarks:** Accepts advertising. **Circ:** 40,200.

10432 ■ Kerala Express
Kerala Express
2050 W Devon Ave.
Chicago, IL 60659
Phone: (773)465-5359
Fax: (773)304-1917
Malayalam newspaper for people from Kerala, India. **Freq:** Weekly. **Print Method:** Offset. **Trim Size:** 10.25 x 15.5. **Cols./Page:** 5. **Col. Width:** 22 nonpareils. **Col. Depth:** 98 agate lines. **Subscription Rates:** $49 Individuals; $90 Two years; $375 Individuals lifetime. **URL:** http://www.keralaexpress.com. **Ad Rates:** GLR $1.60; BW $450; 4C $500. **Remarks:** Accepts advertising. **Circ:** Paid ‡120, Free ‡2000.

10433 ■ Key Magazine This Week in Chicago
Key Magazines Inc.
226 E Ontario St., Ste. 300
Chicago, IL 60611
Phone: (312)943-0838
Fax: (312)664-6113
Publisher's E-mail: info@keymilwaukee.com
Visitors' guide covering Chicago, Illinois. **Freq:** Weekly. **Key Personnel:** Walter West, Publisher; Ruthie Kott, Editor. **URL:** http://www.keymagazine.com; http://www.keymagazinechicago.com. **Remarks:** Accepts advertising. **Circ:** (Not Reported).

10434 ■ Kidney Cancer Journal
Kidney Cancer Association
PO Box 803338, No. 38269
Chicago, IL 60680-3338
Phone: (847)332-1051
Free: 800-850-9132
Publisher's E-mail: office@kidneycancer.org
Peer-reviewed journal publishing information on the diagnosis and treatment of renal cell carcinoma and all of its tumor types. **Freq:** Quarterly. **URL:** http://kidney-cancer-journal.com/. **Remarks:** Advertising not accepted. **Circ:** (Not Reported).

10435 ■ Knowledge Quest
American Association of School Librarians
50 E Huron St.
Chicago, IL 60611-2729
Phone: (312)280-4382
Fax: (312)280-5276
Free: 800-545-2433
Publisher's E-mail: aasl@ala.org
Freq: Bimonthly. **ISSN:** 1094-9046 (print). **Subscription Rates:** $50 Nonmembers; $60 Other countries; $12 Single issue. **URL:** http://www.ala.org/aasl/kq. **Remarks:** Advertising not accepted. **Circ:** (Not Reported).

10436 ■ Lab Medicine
American Society for Clinical Pathology
33 W Monroe St., Ste. 1600
Chicago, IL 60603
Phone: (312)541-4999
Fax: (312)541-4998
Publisher's E-mail: info@ascp.org
Freq: Quarterly. **Key Personnel:** Roger L. Bertholf, PhD, Editor. **Subscription Rates:** £89 Institutions online only; $139 Institutions online only; €127 Institutions online only; £112 Institutions print and online; $174 Institutions print and online; €159 Institutions print and online; £75 Individuals online only; $116 Individuals online only; €106 Individuals online only; £93 Individuals print only; $145 Individuals print only; €132 Individuals print only. **URL:** http://labmed.oxfordjournals.org. **Remarks:** Accepts advertising. **Circ:** (Not Reported).

10437 ■ Labor: Studies in Working-Class History of the Americas
Duke University Press
Dept. of History, MC 198
University of Illinois at Chicago
913 University Hall
601 S Morgan St.
Chicago, IL 60607
Phone: (312)413-9358
Fax: (312)996-6377
Publication E-mail: labor@uic.edu

Periodical for the study of the history of working-class people, their communities, and their organizations in the United States. **Freq:** Quarterly. **Key Personnel:** Jim Daniels, Associate Editor; John French, Associate Editor; Julie Greene, Member; Joan Sangster, Associate Editor; Cindy Hahamovitch, Editor; James R. Barrett, Editor; Leon Fink, Editor. **ISSN:** 1547--6715 (print); **EISSN:** 1558--1454 (electronic). **Subscription Rates:** $50 Individuals includes membership in LAWCHA; $25 Students valid student ID required. **URL:** http://www.dukeupress.edu/Labor. **Ad Rates:** BW $400. **Remarks:** Accepts advertising. **Circ:** (Not Reported).

10438 ■ Laboratory Medicine: An Official Publication of the American Society for Clinical Pathology
American Society for Clinical Pathology
33 W Monroe St., Ste. 1600
Chicago, IL 60603
Phone: (312)541-4999
Fax: (312)541-4998
Publication E-mail: labmed@ascp.org
Professional journal covering medical technology and pathology. **Freq:** Quarterly. **Print Method:** Offset. **Trim Size:** 8 1/8 x 10 7/8. **Cols./Page:** 3. **Col. Width:** 26 nonpareils. **Col. Depth:** 140 agate lines. **Key Personnel:** Kevin Land, MD, Associate Editor; Roger L. Bertholf, PhD, Editor-in-Chief. **ISSN:** 0007--5027 (print); **EISSN:** 1943--7730 (electronic). **Subscription Rates:** £93 Individuals print; $145 Individuals print; €132 Individuals print; £112 Institutions print and online; $174 Institutions print and online; €159 Institutions print and online; £75 Individuals online only access; $116 Individuals online only access; €106 Individuals online only access; £89 Institutions online only access; $139 Institutions online only access; €127 Institutions online only access. **URL:** http://labmed.oxfordjournals.org. **Formerly**: American Society of Clinical Pathologists. **Remarks:** Accepts advertising. **Circ:** (Not Reported).

10439 ■ Lake County News-Sun
Sun-Times Media L.L.C.
350 N Orleans, 10 S
Chicago, IL 60654
Publisher's E-mail: customerservice@suntimes.com
Community newspaper. **Freq:** Mon.-Sat. **Key Personnel:** Jeff Bonato, Editor, phone: (847)249-7231. **URL:** http://newssun.chicagotribune.com. **Remarks:** Accepts advertising. **Circ:** Mon.-Fri. 21048, Sat. 22362, Fri. 21975, Tues. 22967.

10440 ■ Lake Forester: Serving Lake Bluff
Sun-Times Media L.L.C.
350 N Orleans St., 10th Fl.
Chicago, IL 60654
Phone: (312)321-3000
Free: 888-848-4637
Publisher's E-mail: customerservice@suntimes.com
Community newspaper (tabloid). **Freq:** Weekly. **Print Method:** Offset. **Trim Size:** 11 x 14. **Cols./Page:** 5. **Col. Width:** 9 3/4 inches. **Col. Depth:** 12 3/4 inches. **Key Personnel:** David Sweet, Managing Editor, phone: (847)599-6944; Elisabeth Mistretta, Editor, phone: (312)321-2328. **ISSN:** 0774-7973 (print). **Subscription Rates:** $20 Individuals; $84 Out of area. **URL:** http://lakeforest.suntimes.com. **Remarks:** Accepts advertising. **Circ:** (Not Reported).

10441 ■ Lake Zurich Courier
Sun-Times Media L.L.C.
350 N Orleans St., 10th Fl.
Chicago, IL 60654
Phone: (312)321-3000
Free: 888-848-4637
Publisher's E-mail: customerservice@suntimes.com
Community newspaper for Lake Co., IL. **Freq:** Weekly. **Print Method:** Offset. **Cols./Page:** 4. **Col. Width:** 11 picas. **Col. Depth:** 184 agate lines. **Key Personnel:** Rich Martin, Senior Editor, phone: (847)486-7481; Peter Kendall, Managing Editor. **Subscription Rates:** $0.99 Individuals /week - digital only. **URL:** http://www.chicagotribune.com/suburbs/lake-zurich. **Remarks:** Accepts advertising. **Circ:** (Not Reported).

10442 ■ Landslide
American Bar Association
321 N Clark St.
Chicago, IL 60654
Phone: (312)988-5000
Free: 800-285-2221
Magazine discussing intellectual property issues. **Freq:** Bimonthly. **Key Personnel:** Marisia L. Campbel, Editor-in-Chief. **ISSN:** 1942--7239 (print). **Subscription Rates:** $295 Individuals; $350 Other countries; $35 Members. **URL:** http://shop.americanbar.org/eBus/Store/ProductDetails.aspx?productId=215148; http://www.americanbar.org/publications/landslide/2015-16/january-february.html. **Circ:** **24824**.

10443 ■ Law Library Journal
American Association of Law Libraries
105 W Adams St., Ste. 3300
Chicago, IL 60603
Phone: (312)939-4764
Fax: (312)431-1097
Freq: Quarterly. **Subscription Rates:** $110 Nonmembers. **URL:** http://www.aallnet.org/main-menu/Publications/llj. **Remarks:** Accepts advertising. **Circ:** 5500.

10444 ■ Law Practice Management
American Bar Association
321 N Clark St.
Chicago, IL 60654
Phone: (312)988-5000
Free: 800-285-2221
Magazine covering the marketing, management, technology and finance of law practice. **Freq:** Bimonthly. **Print Method:** Web Offset. **Trim Size:** 8 3/8 x 10 7/8. **Cols./Page:** 3. **Col. Width:** 28 nonpareils. **Col. Depth:** 138 agate lines. **Key Personnel:** Daniel E. Pinnington, Board Member. **ISSN:** 0360--1439 (print). **Subscription Rates:** Included in membership; $64 Nonmembers. **URL:** http://www.americanbar.org/publications/law_practice_magazine/2016/sept-oct.html; http://www.lawpracticemagazine.com. **Formerly**: Legal Economics. **Remarks:** Advertising accepted; rates available upon request. **Circ:** (Not Reported).

10445 ■ Law & Social Inquiry: Journal of the American Bar Foundation
American Bar Foundation
750 N Lake Shore Dr.
Chicago, IL 60611-4403
Phone: (312)988-6500
Fax: (312)988-6579
Multidisciplinary journal on the sociolegal processes. **Freq:** Quarterly. **Print Method:** Offset. **Trim Size:** 6 3/4 x 10. **Cols./Page:** 1. **Col. Width:** 59 nonpareils. **Col. Depth:** 112 agate lines. **Key Personnel:** Christopher Schmidt, Editor; Christopher W. Schmidt. **ISSN:** 0897--6546 (print); **EISSN:** 1747--4469 (electronic). **Subscription Rates:** $278 Institutions online only - The Americas; £176 Institutions online only - UK; €223 Institutions online only - Europe; $343 Institutions online only - rest of the world; $354 Institutions print and online - The Americas; £212 Institutions print and online - UK; €268 Institutions print and online - Europe; $412 Institutions print and online - rest of the world; $58 Individuals print and online - The Americas; £36 Individuals print and online - UK, Europe (non-Euro zone) and rest of the world; €56 Individuals print and online - Europe; $44 Students print and online - The Americas; £29 Students print and online - UK, Europe (non-Euro zone) and rest of the world; €47 Students print and online - Europe. **Online:** Wiley Online Library Wiley Online Library. **URL:** http://onlinelibrary.wiley.com/journal/10.1111/(ISSN)1747-4469. **Ad Rates:** BW $375. **Remarks:** Accepts advertising. **Circ:** 12000, 5100.

10446 ■ Leaven
La Leche League International
35 E Wacker Dr., Ste. 850
Chicago, IL 60601
Phone: (312)646-6260
Fax: (312)644-8557
Free: 800-525-3243
Publisher's E-mail: info@llli.org
Magazine for volunteer lactation specialists who help mothers breastfeed their infants. **Founded:** 1965. **Freq:** Quarterly. **Print Method:** Offset. **Trim Size:** 8.5 x 10.875. **Cols./Page:** 3. **Col. Width:** 2 1/4 inches. **Col. Depth:** 10 inches. **Key Personnel:** Dena Smith-Givens, Manager, Advertising; Carol Wrede, Managing Editor; Judy Torgus, Executive Editor. **ISSN:** 8750-2011 (print). **Subscription Rates:** $30 Members box of back issues; $35 Individuals box of back issues; online; $35 Individuals box of back issues. **URL:** http://www.llli.org/llleaderweb/lv/index.html; http://www.llli.org/lvdate. **Ad Rates:** BW $1,105; 4C $800. **Remarks:** Accepts advertising. **Circ:** Paid ⊕**6849**, Controlled ⊕**225**.

10447 ■ Legal Management: The Magazine of the Association of Legal Administrators
Association of Legal Administrators
Presidents Plz.
8700 W Bryn Mawr Ave., Ste. 110S
Chicago, IL 60631-3512
Phone: (847)267-1252
Fax: (847)267-1329
Publisher's E-mail: membership@alanet.org
Magazine covering aspects of law office management, including systems and technology, human resource management, finance, planning, and marketing. **Freq:** 10/year. **Print Method:** Offset. **Trim Size:** 8 1/8 x 10 7/8. **Cols./Page:** 3. **Col. Width:** 24 1/4 inches. **Col. Depth:** 10 inches. **Key Personnel:** Rich Murowski, Manager, Advertising, phone: (630)980-6570, fax: (630)980-6583; John Delavan, Editor-in-Chief, phone: (847)267-1392. **ISSN:** 0745--0532 (print). **Subscription Rates:** Included in membership; $195 Nonmembers. **URL:** http://www.alanet.org/legalmgmt/default.aspx. **Formerly**: Legal Administrator. **Remarks:** Accepts advertising. **Circ:** (Not Reported).

10448 ■ Libertyville Review
Sun-Times Media L.L.C.
350 N Orleans St., 10th Fl.
Chicago, IL 60654
Phone: (312)321-3000
Free: 888-848-4637
Publisher's E-mail: customerservice@suntimes.com
Community newspaper (tabloid). **Freq:** Weekly. **Print Method:** Offset. **Cols./Page:** 5. **Col. Width:** 10 inches. **Col. Depth:** 14 inches. **Key Personnel:** David Sweet, Managing Editor, phone: (847)599-6944; Kevin Reiterman, Editor, phone: (847)486-7480. **Subscription Rates:** $84 Out of area; $20 Individuals. **URL:** http://libertyville.chicagotribune.com. **Remarks:** Accepts advertising. **Circ:** (Not Reported).

10449 ■ Library Resources & Technical Services: The Official Journal of the Association of Library Collections & Technical Services
Library and Information Technology Association
50 E Huron St.
Chicago, IL 60611-2795
Phone: (312)944-6780
Fax: (312)280-3257
Free: 800-545-2433
Publisher's E-mail: lita@ala.org
Magazine focusing on library cataloging, classification, acquisitions, and technical services operations, including the preservation and reproduction of library materials. **Freq:** Quarterly. **Print Method:** Offset. **Trim Size:** 8 3/8 x 10 7/8. **Cols./Page:** 2. **Col. Width:** 3 3/8 inches. **Col. Depth:** 8 3/4 inches. **Key Personnel:** Mary Beth Weber, Editor. **ISSN:** 0024--2527 (print); **EISSN:** 2159--9610 (electronic). **Subscription Rates:** Included in membership. **URL:** http://www.ala.org/alcts/resources/lrts. **Remarks:** Advertising accepted; rates available upon request. **Circ:** (Not Reported).

10450 ■ Library Technology Reports
Library and Information Technology Association
50 E Huron St.
Chicago, IL 60611-2795
Phone: (312)944-6780
Fax: (312)280-3257
Free: 800-545-2433
Publisher's E-mail: lita@ala.org
Publication covering library and information science. **Freq:** 8/year. **ISSN:** 0024--2586 (print). **Subscription Rates:** $325 Individuals print and online; $370 Out of country; $43 Single issue. **URL:** http://www.alatechsource.org/ltr/index. **Ad Rates:** 4C $1,850. **Remarks:** Accepts advertising. **Circ:** (Not Reported).

10451 ■ Light: The Quarterly of Light Verse
Foundation for Light Verse Inc.
PO Box 7500
Chicago, IL 60680
Publication E-mail: lightquarterly@cs.com
Journal featuring light verse. **Freq:** 2/year. **Print Method:** Offset. **Trim Size:** 5.25 x 8.5. **Cols./Page:** 2. **Key Personnel:** John Mella, Editor, Founder. **ISSN:**

Circulation: ★ = AAM; △ or • = BPA; ♦ = CAC; ❑ = VAC; ⊕ = PO Statement; ‡ = Publisher's Report; Boldface figures = sworn; Light figures = estimated.

1064--8186 (print). **URL:** http://lightpoetrymagazine.com/revamp/about. **Ad Rates:** BW $60. **Remarks:** Advertising accepted; rates available upon request. **Circ:** Combined ‡923.

10452 ■ Lincolnshire Review
Sun-Times Media L.L.C.
350 N Orleans St., 10th Fl.
Chicago, IL 60654
Phone: (312)321-3000
Free: 888-848-4637
Publisher's E-mail: customerservice@suntimes.com
Community newspaper. **Freq:** Weekly. **Print Method:** offset. **Key Personnel:** Charles Berman, Editor. **URL:** http://lincolnshire.chicagotribune.com. **Remarks:** Accepts advertising. **Circ:** (Not Reported).

10453 ■ Lithanus: Lithuanian Quarterly Journal of Arts and Sciences
Lituanus Foundation, Inc.
47 W Polk St., Ste. 100-300
Chicago, IL 60605
Phone: (312)341-9396
Publisher's E-mail: admin@lituanus.org
Journal publishing research articles in English as well as literature and art. **Freq:** Quarterly in March, June, September and December. **ISSN:** 0024- 5089 (print). **Subscription Rates:** $30 Individuals print; $20 Individuals electronic. **Formerly:** Lithuanian Quarterly Journal of Arts and Sciences. **Remarks:** Advertising not accepted. **Circ:** 2000.

10454 ■ Lithuanian Museum Review
Balzekas Museum of Lithuanian Culture
6500 S Pulaski Rd.
Chicago, IL 60629-5136
Phone: (773)582-6500
Fax: (773)582-5133
Publisher's E-mail: info@balzekasmuseum.org
Magazine containing information on Lithuania and Lithuanians. **Freq:** Quarterly. **Print Method:** Offset. **Cols./Page:** 3. **Col. Width:** 30 nonpareils. **Col. Depth:** 140 agate lines. **Subscription Rates:** Included in membership. **Remarks:** Advertising not accepted. **Circ:** (Not Reported).

10455 ■ Lituanus
Lituanus Foundation, Inc.
47 W Polk St., Ste. 100-300
Chicago, IL 60605
Phone: (312)341-9396
Publication E-mail: editor@lituanus.org
Peer-reviewed journal on the arts and sciences of Lithuania and the Baltic Topics of History, Linguistics, Art, Music, Political Science, Economics. **Freq:** Quarterly published in March, June, September and December. **Print Method:** Offset. **Trim Size:** 5 1/2 x 8 1/2. **Cols./Page:** 1. **Col. Width:** 47 nonpareils. **Col. Depth:** 95 agate lines. **Key Personnel:** Arvydas Tamulis, Director. **ISSN:** 0024--5089 (print). **Subscription Rates:** $30 Individuals print; $20 Individuals senior/student (print); $30 Other countries senior/student (print); $40 Institutions print; $20 Individuals online; $30 Institutions online. **URL:** http://www.lituanus.org/main.php?id=home. **Remarks:** Advertising not accepted. **Circ:** (Not Reported).

10456 ■ Loyola Magazine
Loyola University Chicago
1032 W Sheridan Rd.
Chicago, IL 60660
Phone: (773)274-3000
Publication E-mail: magazine@loyola.edu
Collegiate magazine. **Freq:** Semiannual. **Print Method:** Offset. **Trim Size:** 11 x 12. **Cols./Page:** 3. **Col. Width:** 26 nonpareils. **Col. Depth:** 140 agate lines. **Key Personnel:** Rita Buettner, Editor. **ISSN:** 1054--7614 (print). **Subscription Rates:** Free. **URL:** http://magazine.loyola.edu. **Circ:** (Not Reported).

10457 ■ Loyola Phoenix
Loyola Phoenix Loyola University of Chicago
1032 N Sheridan Rd.
Chicago, IL 60626
Phone: (773)274-3000
Publication E-mail: phoenix@luc.edu
Collegiate newspaper. **Freq:** Weekly except during school vacations or examinations. **Print Method:** Offset. **Trim Size:** 11 x 17. **Cols./Page:** 4. **Col. Width:** 2 5/16 inches. **Col. Depth:** 16 inches. **Key Personnel:** Esther Castillejo, Editor-in-Chief. **Subscription Rates:** Free. **URL:** http://www.loyolaphoenix.com. **Remarks:** Accepts advertising. **Circ:** (Not Reported).

10458 ■ Loyola University Chicago Law Journal
Loyola University Chicago School of Law
Philip H. Corboy Law Center
25 E Pearson St.
Chicago, IL 60611
Phone: (312)915-7170
Fax: (312)915-7906
Publication E-mail: law-journal@luc.edu
Law Review. **Freq:** Quarterly. **Key Personnel:** Benjamin J. Barnett, Editor-in-Chief. **ISSN:** 0024-7081 (print). **Subscription Rates:** $25 Individuals; $9 Single issue. **URL:** http://www.luc.edu/law/student/publications/llj/index.html. **Formerly:** Loyola University of Chicago Law Journal. **Ad Rates:** BW $100. **Remarks:** Accepts advertising. **Circ:** Controlled ‡650.

10459 ■ Loyola University Chicago Law Journal
Loyola University Chicago School of Law
Philip H. Corboy Law Center
25 E Pearson St.
Chicago, IL 60611
Phone: (312)915-7170
Fax: (312)915-7906
Publication E-mail: law-journal@luc.edu
Journal containing articles on legal issues and problems and to the development of the law. **Freq:** Quarterly. **Key Personnel:** Benjamin J. Barnett, Editor-in-Chief. **Subscription Rates:** $25 Individuals; $9 Single issue. **URL:** http://www.luc.edu/law/student/publications/llj/index.html. **Circ:** (Not Reported).

10460 ■ Lumpen
Lumpen Media Group
960 W 31st St.
Chicago, IL 60608
Phone: (312)829-0022
Publication E-mail: ed@lumpen.com
Magazine investigating mainstream media, exposing and resisting the degradation of our mental and physical environments. **Freq:** Monthly. **Print Method:** Web press. **Trim Size:** 8 1/4 x 11. **Cols./Page:** 3. **Col. Width:** 2 3/8 inches. **Col. Depth:** 9 7/8 inches. **Key Personnel:** Ed Marczewski, Editor. **ISSN:** 1092-3667 (print). **Subscription Rates:** $30 Individuals; $39 Canada; $60 Other countries. **Alt. Formats:** Download. **URL:** http://www.lumpen.com. **Formerly:** The Lumpen Times. **Ad Rates:** BW $725; 4C $1055. **Remarks:** Accepts advertising. **Circ:** Paid 30,000.

10461 ■ The Lutheran
Augsburg Fortress Publishers
8765 W Higgins Rd., 5th Fl.
Chicago, IL 60631-4183
Fax: (773)380-2409
Free: 800-638-3522
Publication E-mail: lutheran@thelutheran.org
Magazine of the Evangelical Lutheran Church in America. **Freq:** Monthly. **Key Personnel:** Daniel J. Lehmann, Editor. **ISSN:** 0024-743X (print). **Subscription Rates:** $19.95 Individuals print; one year; $31.95 Individuals print; two years; $41.95 Individuals print; three years; $11.95 Individuals online. **URL:** http://www.thelutheran.org; http://www.augsburgfortress.org. **Ad Rates:** BW $5,650; 4C $5,650; PCI $425. **Remarks:** Accepts advertising. **Circ:** ‡192000.

10462 ■ Magicol
Magic Collectors' Association
PO Box 13153
Chicago, IL 60613
Publisher's E-mail: info@magicana.com
Magazine covering magic and magicians, including personality sketches, articles on collections, and unusual facts. **Freq:** Quarterly. **Subscription Rates:** $60 Individuals; $75 Other countries. **URL:** http://magicol.magicana.com/magicol. **Remarks:** Advertising not accepted. **Circ:** 500.

10463 ■ Marketing Health Services
American Marketing Association
311 S Wacker Dr., Ste. 5800
Chicago, IL 60606
Phone: (312)542-9000
Fax: (312)542-9001
Free: 800-AMA-1150
Periodical that provides practitioners and academics with the latest research on techniques and applications. **Freq:** Quarterly. **Print Method:** Web offset. **Trim Size:** 8 1/2 x 11. **Cols./Page:** 2. **Col. Width:** 21 picas. **Col. Depth:** 141.75 agate lines. **Key Personnel:** Mary M. Flory, Editor; Melody Udell, Managing Editor; Sally Schmitz, Manager, Production. **ISSN:** 1094--1304 (print). **Subscription Rates:** $140 Individuals print only; $140 Institutions print only; $110.25 Canada print only; $147 Institutions, Canada print only; $175 Institutions, other countries print only; $140 Nonmembers. **URL:** http://www.ama.org/publications/MarketingHealthServices/Pages/About.aspx. **Formerly:** Journal of Health Care Marketing. **Ad Rates:** BW $840; 4C $1050. **Remarks:** Accepts advertising. **Circ:** Paid ‡1500.

10464 ■ Marketing Insights
American Marketing Association
311 S Wacker Dr., Ste. 5800
Chicago, IL 60606
Phone: (312)542-9000
Fax: (312)542-9001
Free: 800-AMA-1150
For the professional whose primary interest is in marketing research. **Founded:** 1989. **Freq:** Quarterly. **Key Personnel:** Sally Schmitz, Manager, Production; Melody Udell, Managing Editor; Mary M. Flory, Managing Editor. **ISSN:** 1040-8460 (print). **Subscription Rates:** $110.25 Canada; $140 Other countries; $147 Institutions, Canada; $175 Institutions, other countries. **URL:** http://www.ama.org/publications/MarketingInsights/Pages/About.aspx. **Formerly:** Marketing Research: A Magazine of Management and Applications. **Ad Rates:** BW $1,490; 4C $1,880. **Remarks:** Accepts advertising. **Circ:** Paid ‡3100.

10465 ■ Marketing News: Reporting on the Marketing Profession
American Marketing Association
311 S Wacker Dr., Ste. 5800
Chicago, IL 60606
Phone: (312)542-9000
Fax: (312)542-9001
Free: 800-AMA-1150
Business magazine focusing on current marketing trends. **Freq:** Monthly. **Print Method:** Web offset. **Trim Size:** 11 x 15. **Cols./Page:** 5. **Col. Width:** 20 picas. **Col. Depth:** 14 inches. **Key Personnel:** Sally Schmitz, Manager, Production; Richard Ballschmiede, Director, Advertising and Sales; Elisabeth Sullivan, Editor-in-Chief. **ISSN:** 0025--3790 (print). **Subscription Rates:** $110 Institutions US/Canada (print only); $140 Institutions other countries (print only); $80 Individuals US/Canada (print only); $110 Individuals other countries (print only). **URL:** http://www.ama.org/publications/MarketingNews/Pages/Current-Issue.aspx. **Remarks:** Accepts advertising. **Circ:** (Not Reported).

10466 ■ Meatingplace
Marketing & Technology Group Inc.
1415 N Dayton St.
Chicago, IL 60622
Phone: (312)266-3311
Fax: (312)266-3363
Magazine focusing on red meat industry. **Freq:** Monthly latest edition March 2016. **Key Personnel:** Tom Johnston, Managing Editor; Lisa Keefe, Editor. **Subscription Rates:** $120 Other countries by mail. **URL:** http://www.meatingplace.com/Archives/Archives. **Circ:** (Not Reported).

10467 ■ The Men's Book Chicago
Modern Luxury Media
33 W Monroe, Ste. 2100
Chicago, IL 60603-5410
Phone: (312)274-2500
Fax: (312)274-2501
Magazine featuring men's lifestyle and fashion. **Freq:** Semiannual. **Key Personnel:** Matt Lee, Editor-in-Chief; Amy Wimer, Publisher. **Subscription Rates:** $20 Individuals; $35 Two years. **URL:** http://modernluxury.com/mens-book-chicago. **Remarks:** Accepts advertising. **Circ:** (Not Reported).

10468 ■ Mergers and Acquisitions
Association for Corporate Growth
125 S Wacker Dr., Ste. 3100
Chicago, IL 60606
Free: 877-358-2220

Journal providing coverage and analysis of key deals and influential developments in mergers and acquisitions. **Freq:** Monthly. **Key Personnel:** Matt Switzer, Editor. **ISSN:** 0026- 0010 (print). **Subscription Rates:** Free. **URL:** http://www.acg.org/global/library/mergersandacquisitionsjournal.aspx. **Remarks:** Advertising not accepted. **Circ:** (Not Reported).

10469 ■ Metro Chicago Real Estate
Law Bulletin Publishing Co.
415 N State St.
Chicago, IL 60654
Phone: (312)644-7800
Publication E-mail: circulation@lbpc.com
Trade publication covering real estate development, investments, leasing, and mortgage lending activities. **Freq:** Bimonthly. **Print Method:** Offset. **Trim Size:** 8 1/2 x 11. **Cols./Page:** 3. **Col. Width:** 26 picas. **Col. Depth:** 140 agate lines. **Key Personnel:** Mark Menzies, Publisher. **ISSN:** 0893--0775 (print). **Subscription Rates:** $29 Individuals; $49 Two years. **URL:** http://www.lawbulletin.com/real-estate/real-estate-publishing-group/metro-chicago-real-estate-magazine; http://www.lawbulletin.com/real-estate/real-estate-publishing-group/metroch%20icago-real-estate-magazine; http://www.rejournals.com/publications/illinois-real-estate-journal. **Formerly**: Real Estate Magazine; Chicagoland's Real Estate Advertiser. **Remarks:** Accepts advertising. **Circ:** (Not Reported).

10470 ■ The Microscope
McCrone Research Institute
2820 S Michigan Ave.
Chicago, IL 60616-3230
Phone: (312)842-7100
Fax: (312)842-1078
Publication E-mail: themicroscope@mcri.org
Peer-reviewed scientific journal on light microscopy, instruments, and techniques.Dedicated to the advancement of all forms of microscopy for the biologist, mineralogist, metallographer or chemist. **Founded:** 1937. **Freq:** Quarterly. **Print Method:** Offset. **Trim Size:** 8 x 11. **Cols./Page:** 2. **Col. Width:** 54 nonpareils. **Col. Depth:** 154 agate lines. **Key Personnel:** Dr. Gary J. Laughlin, Editor. **ISSN:** 0026-282X (print). **Subscription Rates:** $75 Institutions; $67.50 Libraries; $56.25 Individuals; $99 Institutions, other countries; $91.50 Libraries international; 80.25 Individuals international. **URL:** http://mcri.org/home/section/71-72/the-microscope-journal. **Ad Rates:** BW $250; 4C $900. **Remarks:** Accepts advertising. **Circ:** Paid ‡900, Controlled ‡50.

10471 ■ Modern Baking
Penton Media, Inc.
330 N Wabash, Ste. 2300
Chicago, IL 60611
Magazine on news, products, and trends of the baking industry. **Freq:** Monthly. **Print Method:** Offset. **Trim Size:** 8 x 10 7/8. **Key Personnel:** Bill Dooley, Director, Advertising, phone: (508)771-3500; Katie Martin, Executive Editor. **ISSN:** 0897--6201 (print). **URL:** http://modern-baking.com. **Ad Rates:** BW $5,400; 4C $2,150. **Remarks:** Advertising accepted; rates available upon request. **Circ:** Controlled ‡12000.

10472 ■ Modern Healthcare: The Weekly Healthcare Business News Magazine
Crain Communications Inc.
150 N Michigan Ave.
Chicago, IL 60601-7553
Phone: (312)649-5200
Fax: (312)280-3150
Free: 888-446-1422
Publication E-mail: subs@crain.com
Weekly business news magazine for healthcare management. **Freq:** Weekly. **Print Method:** Offset. **Trim Size:** 8 1/8 x 10 7/8. **Cols./Page:** 3. **Col. Width:** 2 3/16 inches. **Key Personnel:** Harris Meyer, Managing Editor, phone: (312)649-5343; Merrill Goozner, Editor, phone: (312)649-5439. **ISSN:** 0160--7480 (print). **Subscription Rates:** $169 Individuals print only; $199 Individuals classic; $399 Individuals premium. **URL:** http://www.modernhealthcare.com. **Remarks:** Accepts advertising. **Circ:** ‡70295.

10473 ■ Modern Metals
Trend Publishing Inc.
625 N Michigan Ave., Ste. 1100
Chicago, IL 60611-3110
Phone: (312)654-2300
Publisher's E-mail: jdalexander@trendpublishing.com
Metals fabrication magazine. **Founded:** 1945. **Freq:** Monthly. **Print Method:** Web offset. **Trim Size:** 7 1/8 x 10 3/4. **Cols./Page:** 3. **Col. Width:** 27 nonpareils. **Col. Depth:** 140 agate lines. **Key Personnel:** Jim D'Alexander, Chief Operating Officer, Vice President; Lauren Duensing, Editor-in-Chief; Mike D'Alexander, Publisher, Vice President, phone: (803)407-7545. **USPS:** 357-640. **Subscription Rates:** $180 Individuals; $270 Two years; $260 Individuals airmail; $430 Two years airmail. **URL:** http://www.modernmetals.com. **Ad Rates:** BW $5,690; 4C $6,630. **Remarks:** Accepts advertising. **Circ:** △**34008**.

10474 ■ Modern Philology
University of Chicago Press Journals Division
University of Chicago
1050 E 59th St.
Chicago, IL 60637
Phone: (773)702-8497
Publisher's E-mail: marketing@press.uchicago.edu
Scholarly journal devoted to research in medieval and modern literature. **Freq:** Quarterly. **Print Method:** Offset. **Trim Size:** 6 x 9. **Cols./Page:** 1. **Col. Width:** 54 nonpareils. **Col. Depth:** 96 agate lines. **Key Personnel:** Richard Strier, Editor, phone: (773)702-8497; Jessica K. Printz, Managing Editor. **ISSN:** 0026--8232 (print); **EISSN:** 1545--6951 (electronic). **Subscription Rates:** $54 Individuals print and electronic; $49 Individuals print only; $48 Individuals electronic only; $97 Two years print and electronic; $27 Students electronic only; $49 Students 2 years (electronic only); $38 Members print and electronic; $68 Members 2 years (electronic only). **URL:** http://www.journals.uchicago.edu/toc/mp/current. **Ad Rates:** BW $724. **Remarks:** Accepts advertising. **Circ:** ‡352.

10475 ■ Modern Physician
Crain Communications Inc.
150 N Michigan Ave.
Chicago, IL 60601-7553
Phone: (312)649-5200
Fax: (312)280-3150
Free: 888-446-1422
Publisher's E-mail: info@crain.com
Professional publication covering issues for physicians. **Freq:** Quarterly. **Key Personnel:** Merrill Goozner, Editor, phone: (312)649-5439; Harris Meyer, Managing Editor, phone: (312)649-5343. **ISSN:** 1098--1845 (print). **Subscription Rates:** $164 Individuals print; $255 Canada print; $218 Other countries print. **URL:** http://www.modernhealthcare.com/section/articles?tagID=42. **Ad Rates:** GLR $4,020. **Remarks:** Accepts advertising. **Circ:** 71400, Combined 10000.

10476 ■ Modern Steel Construction
American Institute of Steel Construction
1 E Wacker Dr., Ste. 700
Chicago, IL 60601-1802
Phone: (312)670-2400
Fax: (312)670-5403
Publisher's E-mail: solutions@aisc.org
Magazine covering fabricated structural steel design, application, and costs. For construction industry professionals including architects, engineers, and fabricators. **Freq:** Monthly. **Print Method:** Offset. **Trim Size:** 8 3/8 x 11 1/8. **Cols./Page:** 3. **Col. Width:** 28 nonpareils. **Col. Depth:** 114 agate lines. **Key Personnel:** Scott L. Melnick, Editor, Publisher, phone: (312)670-8314. **ISSN:** 0026--8445 (print). **Subscription Rates:** Free to qualified subscribers members in USA, Canada and Mexico. **URL:** http://msc.aisc.org/modernsteel. **Ad Rates:** BW $5580; 4C $6570. **Remarks:** Accepts advertising. **Circ:** Combined ‡49270.

10477 ■ Modern Trader
Futures Magazine Inc.
250 S Wacker Dr., Ste. 1150
Chicago, IL 60606
Phone: (312)846-4600
Fax: (312)846-4638
Free: 800-972-9316
Publisher's E-mail: gszala@futuresmag.com
Magazine covering news, analysis and strategies for futures, options and derivatives traders. **Freq:** Monthly. **Print Method:** Web offset. **Trim Size:** 7 7/8 x 10 7/8. **Cols./Page:** 3 and 3. **Col. Width:** 27 nonpareils. **Col. Depth:** 138 agate lines. **Key Personnel:** Steve Zwick, Editor; Ginger Szala, Director, Editorial, Publisher; Daniel P. Collins, Managing Editor. **ISSN:** 0746--2468 (print). **Subscription Rates:** $89 U.S. print and online; $55 Individuals online only; $199 Other countries print and online; $99 Canada print and online. **URL:** http://www.futuresmag.com/ModernTraderMag. **Formerly**: Futures Magazine. **Remarks:** Accepts advertising. **Circ:** △**60000**.

10478 ■ The Monist: An International Quarterly Journal of General Philosophical Inquiry
The Hegeler Institute
c/o George Reisch, Mng. Ed.
70 E Lake St., Ste. 800
Chicago, IL 60601
Publication E-mail: managingeditor@themonist.org
An international quarterly of general philosophy and inquiry. Each issue is devoted to a single topic announced in advance. **Freq:** Quarterly. **Print Method:** Offset. **Trim Size:** 6 x 9. **Cols./Page:** 1. **Col. Width:** 54 nonpareils. **Col. Depth:** 98 agate lines. **Key Personnel:** Barry Smith, Editor; George Reisch, Managing Editor. **ISSN:** 0026--9662 (print). **Subscription Rates:** $77 Institutions Print; $100 Institutions Online-only access; $125 Institutions Print and online; $75 Individuals Print. **URL:** http://themonist.org. **Remarks:** Accepts advertising. **Circ:** Paid ‡1500, Non-paid ‡200.

10479 ■ Morton Grove Champion Review
Sun-Times Media L.L.C.
350 N Orleans St., 10th Fl.
Chicago, IL 60654
Phone: (312)321-3000
Free: 888-848-4637
Publisher's E-mail: customerservice@suntimes.com
Community newspaper (tabloid). **Freq:** Weekly (Thurs.). **Print Method:** Offset. **Cols./Page:** 5. **Col. Width:** 10 inches. **Col. Depth:** 14 inches. **Key Personnel:** Rich Martin, Editor, phone: (312)321-2587; John Puterbaugh, Editor, phone: (312)321-2485. **Subscription Rates:** $4.99 Individuals /month. **URL:** http://mortongrove.suntimes.com/index.html. **Remarks:** Accepts advertising. **Circ:** (Not Reported).

10480 ■ Mouth
American Student Dental Association
211 E Chicago Ave., Ste. 700
Chicago, IL 60611-2663
Phone: (312)440-2795
Fax: (312)440-2820
Free: 800-621-8099
Publisher's E-mail: membership@asdanet.org
Freq: Quarterly. **Subscription Rates:** Included in membership; $10 Nonmembers. **URL:** http://www.asdanet.org/asdamouth.aspx. **Remarks:** Advertising not accepted. **Circ:** (Not Reported).

10481 ■ Mouth: Journal of the American Student Dental Association
Alliance of the American Dental Association
211 E Chicago Ave., Ste. 730
Chicago, IL 60611-2616
Fax: (312)440-2587
Free: 800-621-8099
Publisher's E-mail: Alliance@allianceada.org
Magazine for dental students and new dentists. **Founded:** Dec. 1981. **Freq:** Quarterly in fall, winter, spring and summer. **Print Method:** Offset. **Trim Size:** 8 3/8 x 10 7/8. **Cols./Page:** 3. **Col. Width:** 28 nonpareils. **Col. Depth:** 127 agate lines. **Key Personnel:** Nancy Honeycutt, Executive Director. **ISSN:** 1529-5044 (print). **Subscription Rates:** Free to qualified subscribers. **URL:** http://www.asdanet.org/ASDAMouth.aspx?id=218&token=. **Formerly**: Dentistry. **Ad Rates:** BW $2370. **Remarks:** Accepts advertising. **Circ:** 20,000.

10482 ■ Mundelein Review
Sun-Times Media L.L.C.
350 N Orleans St., 10th Fl.
Chicago, IL 60654
Phone: (312)321-3000
Free: 888-848-4637
Publisher's E-mail: customerservice@suntimes.com
Community newspaper (tabloid). **Freq:** Weekly. **Print Method:** Offset. **Cols./Page:** 5. **Col. Width:** 10 inches. **Col. Depth:** 14 inches. **Key Personnel:** Peter Kendall,

Circulation: ★ = AAM; △ or • = BPA; ♦ = CAC; ❑ = VAC; ⊕ = PO Statement; ‡ = Publisher's Report; Boldface figures = sworn; Light figures = estimated.

Managing Editor. **Subscription Rates:** $20 Individuals; $84 Out of state. **URL:** http://mundelein.suntimes.com. **Remarks:** Accepts advertising. **Circ:** (Not Reported).

10483 ■ Mushroom the Journal: The Journal of Wild Mushrooming
Mushroom the Journal
1511 E 54th St.
Chicago, IL 60615
Publisher's E-mail: leon@mushroomthejournal.com
Magazine featuring articles about wild mushroom hunting and the cultivation of exotic mushrooms. **Freq:** Quarterly. **Print Method:** Offset. **Trim Size:** 8 1/2 x 11. **Cols./Page:** 3. **Col. Width:** 13.5 picas. **Col. Depth:** 9 1/2 inches. **ISSN:** 0740--8161 (print). **Subscription Rates:** $32 U.S. and Canada; $57 Other countries. **URL:** http://www.mushroomthejournal.com. **Remarks:** Accepts advertising. **Circ:** ‡2000.

10484 ■ Music Theory Spectrum
Society for Music Theory
Dept. of Music
University of Chicago
1010 E 59th St.
Chicago, IL 60637
Phone: (773)834-3821
Publisher's E-mail: president@societymusictheory.org
Official print journal of the Society for Music Theory featuring topics relating to music theory and analysis. **Freq:** Semiannual. **Key Personnel:** Michael Cherlin, Editor; Mark Spicer, Associate Editor. **ISSN:** 0195--6167 (print); **EISSN:** 1533--8339 (electronic). **Subscription Rates:** £110 Institutions print and online ; $208 Institutions print and online; €164 Institutions print and online; £101 Institutions print only ; $192 Institutions print only; €152 Institutions print only; £86 Institutions online only; $163 Institutions online only; €129 Institutions online only; £136 Institutions print and online - corporate; $260 Institutions print and online - corporate; €205 Institutions print and online - corporate; £107 Institutions online - corporate ; $204 Institutions online - corporate; €161 Institutions online - corporate; £126 Institutions print - corporate ; $240 Institutions print - corporate; €189 Institutions print - corporate. **URL:** http://mts.oxfordjournals.org; http://societymusictheory.org/music-theory-spectrum. **Remarks:** Accepts advertising. **Circ:** 1250.

10485 ■ The Naperville Sun
Sun-Times Media L.L.C.
350 N Orleans, 9th Fl.
Chicago, IL 60654
Phone: (630)978-8880
Publisher's E-mail: customerservice@suntimes.com
Community newspaper. **Freq:** 3/week. **Print Method:** Offset. Uses mats. **Cols./Page:** 5. **Col. Width:** 2 1/16 inches. **Col. Depth:** 224 agate lines. **Key Personnel:** R.J. Gerber, Editor; John Russell, Editor; Heather Pfundstein, Editor, phone: (312)321-2942. **URL:** http://www.chicagotribune.com/suburbs/naperville-sun. **Remarks:** Accepts advertising. **Circ:** ★**20000**.

10486 ■ NAPFA Advisor
National Association of Personal Financial Advisors
8700 W Bryn Mawr Ave., Ste. 700N
Chicago, IL 60630
Phone: (847)483-5400
Fax: (847)483-5415
Free: 888-333-6659
Publisher's E-mail: info@napfa.org
Magazine providing vital information that helps build practices, serve clients, and achieve greater efficiencies. Covering NAPFA activities as well as industry-wide issues that change the way advisors and clients interact. **Freq:** Monthly. **Subscription Rates:** Included in membership; $85 Nonmembers. **URL:** http://napfa.org/market/NAPFAAdvisorAdvertising.asp. **Ad Rates:** BW $3430, full page; BW $2215, half page. **Remarks:** Accepts advertising. **Circ:** 7500.

10487 ■ NAR Commercial Real Estate Outlook
National Association of Realtors
430 N Michigan Ave.
Chicago, IL 60611-4087
Free: 800-874-6500
Publisher's E-mail: infocentral@realtors.org
Magazine offering overall projections for four major commercial sectors and analyzing quarterly data in the office, industrial, retail and multifamily markets. **Freq:** Monthly. **Subscription Rates:** $95 Members; $200 Nonmembers /year. **Alt. Formats:** Download. **URL:** http://www.realtor.org/reports/commercial-real-estate-outlook. **Remarks:** Advertising not accepted. **Circ:** (Not Reported).

10488 ■ Narod Polish
Polish Roman Catholic Union of America
984 N Milwaukee Ave.
Chicago, IL 60642-4101
Phone: (773)782-2600
Fax: (773)278-4595
Free: 800-772-8632
Publication E-mail: narod@prcua.org
Catholic and Polish American newspaper (tabloid; English and Polish). **Freq:** Monthly. **Print Method:** Offset. **Trim Size:** 11 x 14 1/2. **Cols./Page:** 3. **Key Personnel:** Kathryn Rosypal, Executive Editor. **ISSN:** 0027--7894 (print). **URL:** http://www.prcua.org/narodpolski/Default.htm. **Also known as**: Polish Nation. **Remarks:** Advertising not accepted. **Circ:** Non-paid ‡25000.

10489 ■ Natural Resources & Environment
American Bar Association
321 N Clark St.
Chicago, IL 60654
Phone: (312)988-5000
Free: 800-285-2221
Magazine for the legal professional dealing with legal issues involving environmental, resource and energy policy. **Freq:** Quarterly. **Key Personnel:** Christine LeBel, Executive Editor; Lindsay Cummings, Editor. **ISSN:** 0822--3812 (print). **URL:** http://www.americanbar.org/publications/natural_resources_environment_home.html. **Remarks:** Advertising not accepted. **Circ:** (Not Reported).

10490 ■ N'DIGO
N'DIGO
1006 S Michigan Ave., Ste. 200
Chicago, IL 60605
Phone: (312)822-0202
Fax: (312)822-0288
Newspaper covering lifestyle, entertainment, and other issues for an upscale, middle-class, African-American audience. **Freq:** Weekly (Thurs.). **Trim Size:** 10.125 x 11.5. **Cols./Page:** 5. **Col. Width:** 2 inches. **Key Personnel:** Hermene D. Hartman, Editor-in-Chief, Publisher; David Smallwood, Editor. **Ad Rates:** GLR $57.80; BW $4866; 4C $1408; PCI $82.11. **Remarks:** Accepts advertising. **Circ:** Thurs. ■ **79884**, Sun. ■ **10000**.

10491 ■ New Accountant
Real Estate News Corp.
3525 W Peterson Ave.
Chicago, IL 60659
Phone: (773)866-9900
Fax: (773)866-9881
Publication E-mail: editor@newaccountantusa.com
Magazine for business-oriented accountants of all ages. Includes practical articles, features, and columns on careers. **Freq:** 8/year. **Print Method:** Offset. **Trim Size:** 8 x 10 3/4. **Cols./Page:** 2 and 3. **Col. Width:** 26 and 40 nonpareils. **Col. Depth:** 126 agate lines. **Key Personnel:** Steven Polydoris, Editor, Publisher. **Subscription Rates:** $38 Individuals graduates; $35 Students faculty, new accounting grads, seniors; $50 Libraries; $85 Individuals professional. **Alt. Formats:** PDF. **URL:** http://www.newaccountantusa.com. **Ad Rates:** BW $4,045; 4C $5,195. **Remarks:** Accepts advertising. **Circ:** (Not Reported).

10492 ■ New Beginnings
La Leche League International
35 E Wacker Dr., Ste. 850
Chicago, IL 60601
Phone: (312)646-6260
Fax: (312)644-8557
Free: 800-525-3243
Publisher's E-mail: info@llli.org
Magazine offering education, information, and support to women who wish to breastfeed their infants. **Founded:** 1958. **Freq:** Bimonthly. **Print Method:** Offset. **Trim Size:** 8 x 10 3/4. **Cols./Page:** 3. **Col. Width:** 2 1/4 inches. **Col. Depth:** 9 3/8 inches. **Key Personnel:** Barbara Higham, Managing Editor. **ISSN:** 8756-9981 (print). **URL:** http://www.llli.org/nbdate.html. **Ad Rates:** BW $2,280; 4C $2,736. **Remarks:** Accepts advertising. **Circ:** Paid ⊕**29463**, Controlled ⊕**300**.

10493 ■ News & Letters
News & Letters Committees
228 S Wabash Ave., Ste. 230
Chicago, IL 60604-2383
Phone: (312)431-8242
Fax: (312)431-8252
Publication E-mail: arise@newsandletters.org
Marxist-Humanist newspaper. **Founded:** 1955. **Freq:** Bimonthly. **Print Method:** Letterpress and offset. Uses mats. **Cols./Page:** 3. **Col. Width:** 39 nonpareils. **Col. Depth:** 196 agate lines. **Key Personnel:** Raya Dunayevskaya, Chairperson; Terry Moon, Managing Editor; Charles Denby, Editor; Felix Martin, Editor. **ISSN:** 0028-8969 (print). **Subscription Rates:** $5 Individuals; $10 Individuals domestic first class; $17 Other countries foreign airmail. **URL:** http://www.newsandletters.org. **Circ:** ‡7000.

Norridge Harwood Heights News - See Harwood Heights

10494 ■ Northbrook Star
Sun-Times Media L.L.C.
350 N Orleans St., 10th Fl.
Chicago, IL 60654
Phone: (312)321-3000
Free: 888-848-4637
Publisher's E-mail: customerservice@suntimes.com
Community newspaper (tabloid). **Freq:** Weekly. **Print Method:** Offset. **Trim Size:** 10 x 14. **Cols./Page:** 5. **Col. Width:** 10 inches. **Col. Depth:** 14 inches. **Key Personnel:** Rich Martin, Editor, phone: (847)486-7481; Ryan Nilsson, Managing Editor, phone: (312)321-2694. **ISSN:** 0774-9550 (print). **Subscription Rates:** $84 Out of state; $40 Individuals; $76 Two years. **URL:** http://northbrook.chicagotribune.com. **Remarks:** Accepts advertising. **Circ:** (Not Reported).

10495 ■ Northwestern Journal of Technology and Intellectual Property
Northwestern University School of Law
357 E Chicago Ave.
Chicago, IL 60611-3069
Phone: (312)503-3100
Publisher's E-mail: law-web@law.northwestern.edu
Journal covering areas pertaining to law, including law and biotechnology, copyrights, the Internet, media, patents, telecommunications, and trademarks. **Freq:** 3/year. **Key Personnel:** Heath Ingram, Editor-in-Chief; Hugh McLaughlin, Editor-in-Chief. **Alt. Formats:** PDF. **URL:** http://scholarlycommons.law.northwestern.edu/njtip. **Circ:** (Not Reported).

10496 ■ Northwestern University Law Review
University of Illinois Press
357 E Chicago Ave.
Chicago, IL 60611
Phone: (312)503-9230
Publisher's E-mail: uipress@uillinois.edu
Law journal. **Freq:** Quarterly. **Print Method:** Offset. **Key Personnel:** Beau C. Tremitiere, Editor-in-Chief; Meghan Claire Hammond, Editor-in-Chief. **ISSN:** 0029--3571 (print). **Subscription Rates:** $50 U.S.; $15 Single issue domestic; $18 Single issue foreign. **URL:** http://www.northwesternlawreview.org; http://northwesternlawreview.org. **Remarks:** Advertising not accepted. **Circ:** (Not Reported).

10497 ■ Numerical Heat Transfer: An International Journal of Computation and Methodology
Taylor & Francis Group Journals
c/o W.J. Minkowycz, Ed.-in-Ch.
The University of Illinois
Department of Mechanical Engineering (MC 251)
842 W Taylor St., Rm. 2049
Chicago, IL 60607-7022
Phone: (312)996-3467
Fax: (312)413-0447
Publication E-mail: wjm@uic.edu
Journal containing information on all aspects of the methodology for the numerical solution of problems in heat and mass transfer as well as fluid flow. **Freq:** Monthly. **Trim Size:** 7 x 10. **Key Personnel:** W.J. Minkowycz, Editor-in-Chief; B.R. Baliga, Advisor; P. Cheng, Advisor; N.K. Anand, Advisor; R.M. Szandra, Associate Editor; E.M. Sparrow, Chairman, Advisor; A.J. Baker, Advisor; G. De Vahl Davis, Advisor; M. Peric, Advisor; G.E. Schneider, Advisor. **ISSN:** 1040--7790 (print); **EISSN:** 1521--0626 (electronic). **Subscription**

Rates: $1276 Individuals print only; $2711 Institutions online only; $3098 Institutions print & online. **URL:** http://www.tandfonline.com/toc/unhb20/current#.UvtPZ2lyldU. **Remarks:** Accepts advertising. **Circ:** (Not Reported).

10498 ■ Numerical Heat Transfer, Part A: Applications: An International Journal of Computation and Methodology
Taylor & Francis Group Journals
c/o W.J. Minkowycz, Editor-in-Chief
Dept. of Mechanical & Industrial Engineering
University of Illinois at Chicago
842 W Taylor St., Rm. 2049
Chicago, IL 60607-7022
Phone: (312)996-3467
Fax: (312)413-0447
Publisher's E-mail: customerservice@taylorandfrancis.com
Journal publishing research in the field of heat and mass transfer, and fluid flow. **Freq:** 24/yr. **Print Method:** Offset. Uses mats. **Trim Size:** 7 x 10. **Key Personnel:** W.J. Minkowycz, Editor-in-Chief. **ISSN:** 1040-7782 (print); **EISSN:** 1521-0634 (electronic). **Subscription Rates:** $10066 Institutions print and online; $3837 Individuals print; $8808 Institutions online only. **URL:** http://www.tandfonline.com/pricing/journal/unht20#.VdGeTe-BkpQ. **Remarks:** Accepts advertising. **Circ:** ‡586.

10499 ■ O, the Oprah Magazine
Harpo Productions Inc.
110 N Carpenter St.
Chicago, IL 60607-2146
Phone: (312)633-1000
Consumer magazine covering lifestyle and issues for women. **Freq:** Monthly. **Key Personnel:** Jill Seelig, Publisher, Vice President. **Subscription Rates:** $19 Individuals print and online; $18 Individuals print or online; $4.50 Single issue. **URL:** http://www.oprah.com/app/o-magazine.html. **Remarks:** Accepts advertising. **Circ:** (Not Reported).

10500 ■ Official Journal of the American Association of Occupational Health Nurses
American Association of Occupational Health Nurses
330 N Wabash Ave., Ste. 2000
Chicago, IL 60611
Phone: (312)321-5173
Fax: (312)673-6719
Publisher's E-mail: info@aaohn.org
Freq: Monthly. **URL:** http://www.aaohn.org/component/jnews/mailing/view/mailingid-57.html. **Remarks:** Accepts advertising. **Circ:** (Not Reported).

10501 ■ The Onion
Onion Inc.
730 N Franklin, 7th Fl.
Chicago, IL 60654
Phone: (312)751-0503
Fax: (312)751-4137
Publisher's E-mail: chicago@theonion.com
Humor, satire, entertainment newspaper, and website. **Freq:** Weekly (Thurs.). **Key Personnel:** Cole Bolton, Editor-in-Chief. **URL:** http://www.theonion.com. **Remarks:** Advertising accepted; rates available upon request. **Circ:** Free ‡293144.

10502 ■ Orthopaedic Nursing
National Association of Orthopaedic Nurses
c/o Mary F. Rodts, Ed.-in-Ch.
Rush University College of Nursing
600 S Paulina, Rm. 1072A
Chicago, IL 60612
Publisher's E-mail: naon@orthonurse.org
Freq: 6/year. **Print Method:** Offset/Sheetfed. **Trim Size:** 7 7/8 x 10 7/8. **Key Personnel:** Mary Faut Rodts, Editor; Eugene Berg, MD, Board Member; Brenda Luther, PhD, Board Member. **ISSN:** 0744--6020 (print); **EISSN:** 1542--538X (electronic). **Subscription Rates:** $95 Individuals print; $395 Institutions print; $109 Canada and Mexico print; $424 Institutions, Canada and Mexico print; $132 Individuals print - UK/ Australia; $477 Institutions print - UK/ Australia; $194 Other countries print; $557 Institutions, other countries print. **URL:** http://journals.lww.com/orthopaedicnursing/pages/default.aspx; http://www.orthonurse.org/p/cm/ld/fid=49. **Ad Rates:** BW $2,295; 4C $1,675. **Remarks:** Accepts advertising. **Circ:** 6598.

10503 ■ Out! Resource Guide: Guide to Gay and Lesbian Supportive Businesses and Organizations
Lambda Publications Inc.
1115 W Belmont Ave., Ste. 2-D
Chicago, IL 60657
Phone: (773)871-7610
Fax: (773)871-7609
Publication E-mail: outlines@suba.com
A business resource guide geared toward the gay and lesbian community. **Freq:** Semiannual. **Trim Size:** 4 x 9. **Cols./Page:** 1. **Col. Width:** 3 1/2 inches. **Col. Depth:** 8 1/2 inches. **Key Personnel:** Tracy Baim, Publisher. **Subscription Rates:** Free. **URL:** http://www.windycitymediagroup.com. **Ad Rates:** BW $345. **Remarks:** Accepts advertising. **Circ:** Non-paid 25000.

10504 ■ The Owl of Minerva: The Journal of the Hegel Society of America
Philosophy Documentation Center
c/o Ardis B. Collins, Ed.
Department of Philosophy
Loyola University
6525 N Sheridan Rd.
Chicago, IL 60626
Publication E-mail: order@pdcnet.org
Journal of the Hegel Society of America covering issues pertaining to Hegel and a Hegelian approach to philosophical issues. **Freq:** Semiannual. **Key Personnel:** Ardis B. Collins, Editor; Michael Baur, Associate Editor. **ISSN:** 0030--7580 (print); **EISSN:** 2153--3385 (electronic). **Subscription Rates:** $48 Institutions double issues; $35 Individuals double issues; $24 Institutions single/back issues; $18 Individuals single/back issues; $48 Institutions print; $173 Institutions print and online; $144 Institutions online only. **URL:** http://www.pdcnet.org/pdc/bvdb.nsf/journal?openform&journal=pdc_owl. **Circ:** (Not Reported).

10505 ■ Packaging World
Summit Publishing Co.
330 N Wabash Ave., Ste. 2401
Chicago, IL 60611
Phone: (312)222-1010
Fax: (312)222-1310
Publication E-mail: info@packworld.com
Packaging trade magazine. **Freq:** Monthly. **Print Method:** Web offset. **Trim Size:** 11 x 15 3/4. **Key Personnel:** Joseph L. Angel, Publisher, President; Iris Zavala, Managing Editor; Patrick Reynolds, Editor, Vice President. **ISSN:** 1073--7367 (print). **Subscription Rates:** Free. **URL:** http://www.packworld.com/magazine. **Remarks:** Accepts advertising. **Circ:** (Not Reported).

10506 ■ Pain Medicine
American Academy of Pain Medicine
8735 W Higgins Rd., Ste. 3000
Chicago, IL 60631-2738
Phone: (847)375-4731
Fax: (847)375-6477
Publisher's E-mail: info@painmed.org
Freq: Monthly. **ISSN:** 1526--2375 (print); **EISSN:** 1526--4637 (electronic). **Subscription Rates:** $1309 Institutions print and online; $1204 Institutions print only; $394 Individuals print only; $951 Individuals print or online; $1047 Individuals online; $1204 Individuals print; €980 Individuals online; €1127 Individuals print. **URL:** http://www.painmed.org/library/pain-medicine-journal; http://painmedicine.oxfordjournals.org. **Remarks:** Accepts advertising. **Circ:** 5271.

10507 ■ Palm Beach Jewish Journal South
The Tribune Media Co.
435 N Michigan Ave.
Chicago, IL 60611-4066
Phone: (312)222-9100
Fax: (312)222-4206
Free: 800-874-2863
Publisher's E-mail: sales@atlanticsyndication.com
Jewish community newspaper (tabloid). **Freq:** Weekly (Tues.). **Print Method:** Web. **Trim Size:** 11 1/4 x 13 1/2. **Cols./Page:** 5. **Col. Width:** 2 1/16 inches. **Col. Depth:** 13 inches. **Subscription Rates:** Free. **URL:** http://www.afcp.org. **Formerly:** Palm Beach Jewish Journal. **Ad Rates:** BW $750; 4C $1,050; SAU $9.10; PCI $23.10. **Remarks:** Accepts advertising. **Circ:** (Not Reported).

10508 ■ Pastoral Liturgy
Liturgy Training Publications
3949 S Racine Ave.
Chicago, IL 60609-2523
Phone: (773)579-4900
Fax: (773)579-4929
Free: 800-933-1800
Journal following the course of the liturgical year to provide guidance for liturgical preparation. **Founded:** 1963. **Freq:** Bimonthly. **Print Method:** Sheetfed. **Trim Size:** 8 1/2 x 11. **Cols./Page:** 2. **ISSN:** 1046-9990 (print). **Subscription Rates:** $25 Individuals; $40 Two years; $13 U.S. group; $34 Other countries; $55 Other countries 2 years. **URL:** http://www.pastoralliturgy.org; http://www.ltp.org/c-75-pastoral-liturgy.aspx. **Formerly:** Liturgy 70; Liturgy 80; Liturgy 90; RITE. **Remarks:** Accepts advertising. **Circ:** Paid ‡4800, Non-paid ‡2000.

10509 ■ Pediatric Dentistry
American Academy of Pediatric Dentistry
211 E Chicago Ave., Ste. 1600
Chicago, IL 60611-2637
Phone: (312)337-2169
Fax: (312)337-6329
Freq: Bimonthly. **ISSN:** 0164- 1263 (print); **EISSN:** 1942-5473 (electronic). **Subscription Rates:** $250 Institutions domestic, print and online; $300 Institutions foreign, print and online; $167 Individuals domestic, print and online; $250 Institutions foreign; $50 Individuals issues, print and online; $633 Institutions unlimited access over 5 IP address, print and online; $165 Individuals online only; $244 Institutions limited access 5 IP address, online only; $615 Institutions unlimited access over 5 IP address, online only. **URL:** http://www.aapd.org/publications/. **Remarks:** Accepts advertising. **Circ:** 4,900.

10510 ■ People's World/Mundo Popular
Long View Publishing
3339 S Halsted St.
Chicago, IL 60608
Phone: (773)446-9920
Fax: (773)446-9928
Publication E-mail: pww@pww.org
Newspaper of the Communist Party USA. **Freq:** Weekly (Sat.). **Print Method:** Offset. Uses mats. **Trim Size:** 11 x 17. **Cols./Page:** 5. **Col. Width:** 24 nonpareils. **Col. Depth:** 224 agate lines. **Key Personnel:** Barbara Russum, Manager, Production; Teresa Albano, Associate Editor. **ISSN:** 1076--0091 (print). **Subscription Rates:** $30 Individuals U.S./Puerto Rico; $75 Institutions U.S./Puerto Rico; $95 Canada and Mexico; $160 Individuals outside Canada & Mexico. **URL:** http://www.peoplesworld.org. **Formerly:** People's Daily World; Daily Worker; People's Weekly World: Nuestro Mundo - Spanish language section. **Remarks:** Accepts advertising. **Circ:** Paid ‡40000, Non-paid ‡1500.

10511 ■ Perspectives in Genetic Counseling
National Society of Genetic Counselors
330 N Wabash Ave., Ste. 2000
Chicago, IL 60611
Phone: (312)321-6834
Fax: (312)673-6972
Publisher's E-mail: nsgc@nsgc.org
Magazine featuring in-depth articles about issues, news, trends, best practices and other highly topical content that directly relates to medical genetics and genetic counselors. **Freq:** Quarterly. **Key Personnel:** kirsty McWalter, MS, CGC, Executive Editor. **Subscription Rates:** Included in membership. **URL:** http://nsgc.org/p/cm/ld/fid=41. **Remarks:** Advertising not accepted. **Circ:** (Not Reported).

10512 ■ Philosophy Today
DePaul University
DePaul University
2352 N Clifton Ave.
Chicago, IL 60614
Phone: (773)325-7267
Fax: (773)325-7268
Publication E-mail: philosophytoday@depaul.edu
Magazine on contemporary philosophy and philosophers. **Freq:** Quarterly. **Print Method:** Offset. **Trim Size:** 7 x 10. **Cols./Page:** 2. **Col. Width:** 40 nonpareils. **Col. Depth:** 108 agate lines. **Key Personnel:** Peg Birmingham, Editor. **ISSN:** 0031--8256 (print); **EISSN:** 2329--8596 (electronic). **Subscription Rates:** $45 Individuals print or online; $58 Individuals print and online; $65 Institutions print; $150 Institutions online;

Circulation: ★ = AAM; △ or • = BPA; ♦ = CAC; ❑ = VAC; ⊕ = PO Statement; ‡ = Publisher's Report; Boldface figures = sworn; Light figures = estimated.

$180 Institutions print and online. **URL:** http://www.pdcnet.org/philtoda. **Remarks:** Accepts advertising. **Circ:** (Not Reported).

10513 ■ The Pineville Sun: Bell Co.'s Oldest Established Newspaper
Associated Publications Inc.
875 N Michigan Ave., Ste. 3434
Chicago, IL 60611
Phone: (312)266-8680
Publisher's E-mail: info@associatedpub.com
Community newspaper. **Founded:** May 1908. **Freq:** Weekly (Thurs.). **Print Method:** Offset. **Trim Size:** 7 x 21 1/2. **Cols./Page:** 8. **Col. Width:** 9 picas. **Col. Depth:** 21 inches. **Key Personnel:** Sam Gambrell, Editor; Gary Ferguson, General Manager; Rhonda Broughton, Manager, Advertising. **Subscription Rates:** $8.50 Individuals; $9.50 Out of area; $10.50 Out of state. **URL:** http://www.thesuncourier.com/. **Formerly**: Cumberland Courier. **Ad Rates:** BW $378; 4C $653; SAU $2.75. **Remarks:** Accepts advertising. **Circ:** 2062.

10514 ■ Plate
Marketing & Technology Group Inc.
1415 N Dayton St.
Chicago, IL 60622
Phone: (312)266-3311
Fax: (312)266-3363
Magazine that aims to inform food service professionals and owners food and focuses on how menu items are come up with. **Freq:** Bimonthly. **URL:** http://www.plateonline.com. **Ad Rates:** BW $8,510; 4C $9,960. **Remarks:** Accepts advertising. **Circ:** △**35200**.

10515 ■ Poetry
The Poetry Foundation
61 W Superior St.
Chicago, IL 60654
Phone: (312)787-7070
Fax: (312)787-6650
Publisher's E-mail: mail@poetryfoundation.org
Contemporary poetry magazine. **Founded:** Oct. 1912. **Freq:** 11/year. **Print Method:** Offset. **Trim Size:** 5 1/2 x 9. **Cols./Page:** 1. **Col. Width:** 45 nonpareils. **Col. Depth:** 98 agate lines. **Key Personnel:** Don Share, Contact; Sarah Dodson, Managing Editor, phone: (312)787-7070, fax: (312)787-6650. **ISSN:** 0032-2032 (print). **Subscription Rates:** $35 Individuals 11 issues; $47 Canada 11 issues; $47 Other countries 11 issues; $63 Individuals 22 issues; $86 Canada 22 issues; $86 Other countries 22 issues; Free online (back issues). **URL:** http://www.poetryfoundation.org/poetrymagazine. **Ad Rates:** BW $800. **Remarks:** Accepts advertising. **Circ:** (Not Reported).

10516 ■ Polish Daily News
Alliance Printers and Publishers Inc.
5711 N Milwaukee
Chicago, IL 60646-6215
Phone: (773)763-3343
Publisher's E-mail: info@dziennikzwiazkowy.com
Polish newspaper (English and Polish). **Freq:** Daily (morn.). **Print Method:** Offset. **Trim Size:** 10 x 13. **Cols./Page:** 4. **Col. Width:** 2 5/16 inches. **Col. Depth:** 182 agate lines. **Key Personnel:** Emily Leszczynski, General Manager. **ISSN:** 0742--6615 (print). **USPS:** 163-400. **URL:** http://dziennikzwiazkowy.com. **Also known as**: Dziennik Zwiazkowy. **Ad Rates:** GLR $.80; 4C $600; PCI $9. **Remarks:** Advertising accepted; rates available upon request. **Circ:** Paid ‡10847, Free ‡203.

10517 ■ Post-Tribune
Sun-Times Media L.L.C.
350 N Orleans St., 10th Fl.
Chicago, IL 60654
Phone: (312)321-3000
Free: 888-848-4637
Publisher's E-mail: customerservice@suntimes.com
General newspaper. **Freq:** Daily. **Key Personnel:** John O'Neill, Managing Editor; Lisa Tatina, Publisher. **Subscription Rates:** $109.20 Individuals; $61.36 Individuals Thur. & Sun. only. **URL:** http://www.post-trib.com. **Remarks:** Advertising accepted; rates available upon request. **Circ:** Mon.-Fri. ★**68102**, Sun. ★**65269**, Sat. ★**65041**.

10518 ■ Print Solutions: Award-Winning Coverage of the Printing Industry
Print Services and Distribution Association
330 N Wabash Ave., Ste. 2000
Chicago, IL 60611
Fax: (312)673-6880
Free: 800-230-0175
Publisher's E-mail: psda@psda.org
Trade magazine on business forms and other printed products, document management, electronic data interchange, and electronic forms. **Founded:** 1962. **Freq:** 10/year. **Print Method:** Offset. **Trim Size:** 8 1/8 x 10 7/8. **Cols./Page:** 3. **Col. Width:** 12 3/5 picas. **Col. Depth:** 140 agate lines. **Key Personnel:** John Delavan, Editor. **ISSN:** 0532-1700 (print). **Subscription Rates:** Free to members; $199 Nonmembers. **URL:** http://www.printsolutionsmag.com. **Formerly:** FORM Magazine. **Ad Rates:** BW $4,100; 4C $2,300. **Remarks:** Accepts advertising. **Circ:** Paid ‡13000.

10519 ■ Probate and Property
American Bar Association
321 N Clark St.
Chicago, IL 60654
Phone: (312)988-5000
Free: 800-285-2221
Legal publication on real estate, wills, trusts, and financial planning. **Freq:** Bimonthly. **Print Method:** Offset. **Trim Size:** 8 3/8 x 10 7/8. **Cols./Page:** 3. **Col. Width:** 2 1/4 inches. **Col. Depth:** 9 11/16 inches. **Key Personnel:** Edward T. Brading, Editor. **ISSN:** 0164--0372 (print). **Subscription Rates:** Included in membership; $60 Individuals. **URL:** http://shop.americanbar.org/eBus/Store/ProductDetails.aspx?productId=215270. **Ad Rates:** BW $2,470; 4C $3,570. **Remarks:** Accepts advertising. **Circ:** Paid 30000, Controlled 1391.

10520 ■ The Professional Lawyer
American Bar Association
321 N Clark St.
Chicago, IL 60654
Phone: (312)988-5000
Free: 800-285-2221
Magazine providing a forum for the exchange of views and ideas on professionalism and ethics issues for bar leaders, lawyers, law school educators, and others. **Freq:** Quarterly. **Trim Size:** 8 1/2 x 11. **Cols./Page:** 3. **Col. Width:** 2 1/4 inches. **Col. Depth:** 9 1/2 inches. **Key Personnel:** Art Garwin, Contact, phone: (312)988-5294. **ISSN:** 1042--5675 (print). **Subscription Rates:** $60 Nonmembers; $20 Single issue current issue; Included in membership. **Alt. Formats:** Print. **URL:** http://www.americanbar.org/publications/professional_lawyer_home.html. **Remarks:** Advertising not accepted. **Circ:** (Not Reported).

10521 ■ Progress in Transplantation
International Transplant Nurses Society
8735 W Higgins Rd., Ste. 300
Chicago, IL 60631
Phone: (847)375-6340
Fax: (847)375-6341
Publisher's E-mail: info@itns.org
Freq: Quarterly. **ISSN:** 1526- 9248 (print). **Subscription Rates:** $55 for nonmembers; included in membership dues; included in membership dues; $65 /year for nonmembers in U.S.; $99 /year for nonmembers outside U.S. **Remarks:** Advertising not accepted. **Circ:** 3000.

10522 ■ Public Contract Law Journal
American Bar Association
321 N Clark St.
Chicago, IL 60654
Phone: (312)988-5000
Free: 800-285-2221
Journal presenting scholarly analyses and insight into issues affecting the broad scope of public contract and grant law. **Freq:** Quarterly. **Key Personnel:** Amy Novak Fuentes, Editor-in-Chief. **Subscription Rates:** $90 Individuals; $100 Other countries. **URL:** http://pclj.org. **Circ:** (Not Reported).

10523 ■ The Public Lawyer
American Bar Association
321 N Clark St.
Chicago, IL 60654
Phone: (312)988-5000
Free: 800-285-2221
Magazine for public lawyers. **Freq:** Semiannual. **Key Personnel:** John Jay Douglass, Editor-in-Chief; Katherine Mikkelson, Editor, phone: (312)988-5809; Joseph W. Downey, Board Member; Michael D. Crain, Board Member. **URL:** http://www.americanbar.org/publications/government_public_sector_periodicals/public_lawyer_index.html. **Remarks:** Advertising not accepted. **Circ:** (Not Reported).

10524 ■ Public Libraries
Library and Information Technology Association
50 E Huron St.
Chicago, IL 60611-2795
Phone: (312)944-6780
Fax: (312)280-3257
Free: 800-545-2433
Publisher's E-mail: lita@ala.org
Professional journal covering librarianship. **Freq:** Bimonthly. **Trim Size:** 8 3/8 x 10 7/8. **Key Personnel:** Kathleen M. Hughes, Editor. **ISSN:** 0163--5506 (print). **Subscription Rates:** $65 Nonmembers; $75 Other countries nonmember; Included in membership; $10 back issues. **URL:** http://www.ala.org/offices/library/alaperiodicals#p; http://publiclibrariesonline.org. **Ad Rates:** BW $830; 4C $1620. **Remarks:** Accepts advertising. **Circ:** Combined ‡11670.

10525 ■ Pulmonary Circulation
The University of Chicago Press, Journals Div.
1427 E 60th St.
Chicago, IL 60637
Phone: (773)702-7700
Free: 877-705-1878
Publisher's E-mail: subscriptions@press.uchicago.edu
Peer-reviewed journal containing research in the fields of pulmonary circulation and pulmonary vascular disease. **Freq:** Quarterly. **ISSN:** 2045--8932 (print); **EISSN:** 2045--8940 (electronic). **Subscription Rates:** $48 Individuals e-book only. **URL:** http://www.press.uchicago.edu/ucp/journals/journal/pc.html. **Circ:** (Not Reported).

10526 ■ La Raza
ImpreMedia L.L.C.
225 W Ohio St.
Chicago, IL 60654
Community newspaper (tabloid) (Spanish). **Freq:** Weekly (Sun.). **Print Method:** Offset. **Cols./Page:** 5. **Col. Width:** 18 nonpareils. **Col. Depth:** 196 agate lines. **URL:** http://www.laraza.com. **Remarks:** Accepts advertising. **Circ:** (Not Reported).

10527 ■ RBM: A Journal of Rare Books, Manuscripts and Cultural Heritage
Association of College and Research Libraries
50 E Huron St.
Chicago, IL 60611-2729
Phone: (312)280-2523
Fax: (312)280-2520
Free: 800-545-2433
Publisher's E-mail: acrl@ala.org
Journal containing issues pertaining to the world inhabited by special collections libraries and cultural heritage institutions. **Freq:** Semiannual. **ISSN:** 0884-450X (print). **Subscription Rates:** $48 Individuals /year; $59 Individuals /year outside U.S. and Canada; $64 Other countries /year; $26 Single issue. **URL:** http://rbm.acrl.org; http://www.ala.org/acrl/publications. **Ad Rates:** BW $600. **Remarks:** Accepts advertising. **Circ:** (Not Reported).

10528 ■ Real Estate Business Magazine
Real Estate Business Institute
430 N Michigan Ave.
Chicago, IL 60611
Phone: (312)321-4414
Fax: (312)329-8882
Free: 800-621-8738
Publisher's E-mail: info@rebinstitute.com
Magazine covering timely topics of concern to the real estate industry's most dynamic brokers, owners, managers and sales associates. **Freq:** Bimonthly. **ISSN:** 0744--642X (print). **URL:** http://www.crb.com/newsandevents/publications/reb/default.aspx. **Ad Rates:** BW $1,500. **Remarks:** Accepts advertising. **Circ:** 7500.

10529 ■ Real Estate Issues
Counselors of Real Estate
430 N Michigan Ave.
Chicago, IL 60611-4089
Phone: (312)329-8427
Publication E-mail: rei@cre.org

Trade publication covering the real estate industry. **Freq:** 3/year. **Key Personnel:** Carol Scherf, Manager, Communications. **ISSN:** 0146--0595 (print). **Subscription Rates:** $60 Individuals; $25 Single issue; $48 Nonmembers. **Alt. Formats:** PDF. **URL:** http://www.cre.org/publications/rei.cfm. **Remarks:** Accepts advertising. **Circ:** 1800.

10530 ■ Real Property, Trust and Estate Law Journal
American Bar Association
321 N Clark St.
Chicago, IL 60654
Phone: (312)988-5000
Free: 800-285-2221
Journal focusing on real estate. **Freq:** 3/year. **Key Personnel:** Brian M. Lysell, Editor-in-Chief. **ISSN:** 1540-8469 (print). **URL:** http://www.americanbar.org/publications/real_property_trust_and_estate_law_journal_home.html; http://law.sc.edu/rptelj/. **Formerly:** Real Property, Probate and Trust Journal. **Remarks:** Advertising not accepted. **Circ:** (Not Reported).

10531 ■ Real Property, Trust, and Estate Law Journal
American Bar Association
321 N Clark St.
Chicago, IL 60654
Phone: (312)988-5000
Free: 800-285-2221
Publisher's E-mail: lawweb@law.sc.edu
Journal covering topics of interest for practitioners and academicians in the areas of real property, probate, estate planning, and trust law. **Freq:** 3/year. **Alt. Formats:** PDF. **URL:** http://www.americanbar.org/publications/real_property_trust_and_estate_law_journal_home.html. **Circ:** (Not Reported).

10532 ■ Realtor Magazine: The Business tool for Real Estate Professionals
National Association of Realtors
430 N Michigan Ave.
Chicago, IL 60611-4087
Free: 800-874-6500
Publisher's E-mail: infocentral@realtors.org
Real estate magazine. **Freq:** Bimonthly. **Print Method:** Offset. **Trim Size:** 8 x 10 1/2. **Cols./Page:** 3. **Col. Width:** 7 inches. **Col. Depth:** 9 1/2 inches. **Key Personnel:** Stacey Moncrieff, Publisher, phone: (312)329-8496; Wendy Cole, Managing Director, Managing Editor. **ISSN:** 1522--0842 (print). **Subscription Rates:** $56 Nonmembers; $83 Nonmembers Canada; $103 Nonmembers International. **URL:** http://realtormag.realtor.org. **Remarks:** Accepts advertising. **Circ:** (Not Reported).

10533 ■ REALTORS Land Institute
National Association of Realtors
430 N Michigan Ave.
Chicago, IL 60611-4087
Free: 800-874-6500
Publisher's E-mail: infocentral@realtors.org
Newsletter and journal. **Freq:** 6/year. **Print Method:** Offset. **Cols./Page:** 3. **Col. Width:** 28 nonpareils. **Col. Depth:** 140 agate lines. **ISSN:** 0888--5427 (print). **URL:** http://www.rliland.com; http://www.realtor.org/topics/realtors-land-institute. **Remarks:** Accepts advertising. **Circ:** (Not Reported).

10534 ■ Recognition Review
Awards and Personalization Association
8735 W Higgins Rd., Ste. 300
Chicago, IL 60631
Phone: (847)375-4800
Fax: (847)375-6480
Publisher's E-mail: info@awardspersonalization.org
Freq: Monthly. **Key Personnel:** Joseph Agnew, Editor. **Subscription Rates:** Included in membership; $55 Individuals Europe; standard mail; $83 Individuals Africa, Asia, Australia and Pacific Rim countries; standard mail; $42 Nonmembers. **URL:** http://www.ara.org/recognition_review; http://www.ara.org/recognition_review/index.cfm. **Ad Rates:** 4C $2,709. **Remarks:** Accepts advertising. **Circ:** 9000.

10535 ■ Reference and User Services Quarterly
Reference and User Services Association of the American Library Association
50 E Huron St.
Chicago, IL 60611
Phone: (312)280-4395
Fax: (312)280-5273
Free: 800-545-2433
Publisher's E-mail: rusa@ala.org
Freq: Quarterly. **ISSN:** 1094- 9054 (print). **Subscription Rates:** Included in membership; $65 Nonmembers /year. **URL:** http://rusa.metapress.com/home/main.mpx; http://rusa.metapress.com/content/g8qk566w7636/. **Remarks:** Accepts advertising. **Circ:** (Not Reported).

10536 ■ Reference and User Services Quarterly: The Official Journal of the Reference and User Services Association of the American Library Association
Library and Information Technology Association
50 E Huron St.
Chicago, IL 60611-2795
Phone: (312)944-6780
Fax: (312)280-3257
Free: 800-545-2433
Publisher's E-mail: lita@ala.org
Scholarly journal focusing on library reference and adult services. **Freq:** Annual. **Trim Size:** 8 3/8 x 10 7/8. **Key Personnel:** Diane Zabel, Editor-in-Chief. **ISSN:** 0033--7072 (print). **Subscription Rates:** Included in membership; $65 Nonmembers. **URL:** http://journals.ala.org/rusq; http://www.ala.org/rusa/communications/rusqinfo. **Formerly:** RQ. **Remarks:** Accepts advertising. **Circ:** ‡3240.

10537 ■ Renaissance Drama
The University of Chicago Press, Journals Div.
1427 E 60th St.
Chicago, IL 60637
Phone: (773)702-7700
Free: 877-705-1878
Publisher's E-mail: subscriptions@press.uchicago.edu
Journal containing topics on theatrical and performance traditions and practices in early modern Europe and intersecting cultures. **Freq:** Semiannual. **ISSN:** 0486--3739 (print); **EISSN:** 2164--3415 (electronic). **Subscription Rates:** $55 Individuals print and electronic; $35 Students print and electronic. **URL:** http://www.journals.uchicago.edu/toc/rd/current. **Circ:** (Not Reported).

10538 ■ Reporter/Journal
NADIG Newspapers Inc.
4937 N Milwaukee Ave.
Chicago, IL 60630
Phone: (773)286-6100
Publisher's E-mail: news@nadignewspapers.com
Community newspaper. **Freq:** Saturday. **Print Method:** Offset. **Trim Size:** 11 1/2 x 17. **Cols./Page:** 6. **Col. Width:** 9.5 picas. **Col. Depth:** 16 inches. **Key Personnel:** Randy Erickson, Editor. **Subscription Rates:** $115 Individuals print; $25 Individuals online. **URL:** http://nadignewspapers.com/. **Ad Rates:** BW $744; PCI $7.75. **Remarks:** Advertising accepted; rates available upon request. **Circ:** Free ‡1000.

10539 ■ Representor
Electronics Representatives Association
309 W Washington St., Ste. 500
Chicago, IL 60606
Phone: (312)419-1432
Fax: (312)419-1660
Publisher's E-mail: info@era.org
Freq: Quarterly. **Subscription Rates:** Included in membership; $24 Nonmembers /year; $6 Nonmembers /issue; $40 /year for nonmembers, international. **Alt. Formats:** Download; PDF. **URL:** http://era.org/?p=1871. **Remarks:** Accepts advertising. **Circ:** 5000.

10540 ■ The Residential Specialist
Council of Residential Specialists
430 N Michigan Ave., 3rd Fl.
Chicago, IL 60611
Phone: (312)321-4400
Fax: (312)329-8551
Free: 800-462-8841
Trade magazine for residential sales agents. **Freq:** Bimonthly. **Print Method:** Offset. **Trim Size:** 8 x 10 3/4. **Cols./Page:** 3. **Col. Width:** 2 3/16 inches. **Col. Depth:** 8 inches. **Key Personnel:** Michael Fenner, Editor; Michael J. Mrvica, Manager, Advertising. **ISSN:** 0744--642X (print). **Subscription Rates:** Included in membership. **URL:** http://trsmag.com; http://crs.com/magazine; http://www.crs.com/magazine. **Formerly:** Real Estate Business. **Ad Rates:** 4C $5340. **Remarks:** Accepts advertising. **Circ:** (Not Reported).

10541 ■ Review of Accounting & Finance
Emerald Group Publishing Limited
College of Business Administration
University of Illinois at Chicago
601 S Morgan m/c 006
Chicago, IL 60607-7183
Publisher's E-mail: emerald@emeraldinsight.com
Peer-reviewed journal publishing innovative empirical, behavioural, theoretical and historical articles on accounting and finance issues, including the role of accounting internal and external communications on capital market valuation, papers related to microstructure, asset pricing and corporate financial decision making, users' and preparers' behaviour and public policy. **Freq:** Quarterly. **Key Personnel:** Dr. Ahmed Riahi-Belkaoui, Editor, Founder; Andrew Smith, Publisher; Laura Wilson, Managing Editor. **ISSN:** 1475--7702 (print). **URL:** http://www.emeraldinsight.com/loi/raf. **Circ:** (Not Reported).

10542 ■ Review of Intellectual Property Law
John Marshall Law School
315 S Plymouth Ct.
Chicago, IL 60604-3907
Phone: (312)427-2737
Publication E-mail: ripl@jmls.edu
Journal covering patent, trademark, copyright and trade secret law in the field of intellectual property. **Freq:** Quarterly. **Key Personnel:** Benjamin Lee, Editor-in-Chief. **ISSN:** 1930--8140 (print); **EISSN:** 2154--9893 (electronic). **Subscription Rates:** Free to qualified subscribers. **URL:** http://www.jmripl.com; http://ripl.jmls.edu. **Circ:** (Not Reported).

10543 ■ Review of Intellectual Property Law
John Marshall Law School, Chicago
315 S Plymouth Ct.
Chicago, IL 60604
Phone: (312)987-1406
Fax: (312)427-5136
Free: 800-537-4280
Publication E-mail: ripl@jmls.edu
Journal covering patent, trademark, copyright and trade secret law in the field of intellectual property. **Freq:** Quarterly. **Key Personnel:** Benjamin Lee, Editor-in-Chief. **ISSN:** 1930--8140 (print); **EISSN:** 2154--9893 (electronic). **Subscription Rates:** Free to qualified subscribers. **URL:** http://www.jmripl.com; http://ripl.jmls.edu. **Circ:** (Not Reported).

10544 ■ Revolution: Voice of the Revolutionary Communist Party, USA
RCP Publications Inc.
Merchandise Mart
Chicago, IL 60654-0486
Phone: (773)227-4066
Fax: (773)227-4497
Political newspaper (English and Spanish). **Freq:** Weekly. **Print Method:** Offset. **Trim Size:** 11 x 17. **Cols./Page:** 3. **Col. Width:** 26 nonpareils. **Col. Depth:** 140 agate lines. **URL:** http://www.revcom.us. **Formerly:** The Revolutionary Worker. **Mailing address:** PO Box 3486, Chicago, IL 60654-0486. **Circ:** (Not Reported).

10545 ■ Roctober
Roctober Magazine
1507 E 53rd St., No. 617
Chicago, IL 60615
Publication E-mail: editor@roctober.com
Consumer magazine covering rock and other types of music, pop culture, and comics. **Freq:** Triennial. **Key Personnel:** Jake Austen, Editor-in-Chief; Benjamin Edmonds, Editor; John Battles, Assistant Editor. **Subscription Rates:** $4 Individuals; $8 Canada and Mexico; $11 Other countries. **URL:** http://www.roctober.com/roctober. **Remarks:** Accepts advertising. **Circ:** (Not Reported).

10546 ■ Salt of the Earth
Claretian Publications
205 W Monroe St.
Chicago, IL 60606
Phone: (312)236-7782
Fax: (312)236-8207
Magazine reviewing Catholic social teaching and parish-based organizing for social justice. **Freq:** Monthly. **URL:** http://salt.claretianpubs.org/index.html. **Circ:** (Not Reported).

Circulation: ★ = AAM; △ or • = BPA; ♦ = CAC; ❑ = VAC; ⊕ = PO Statement; ‡ = Publisher's Report; Boldface figures = sworn; Light figures = estimated.

10547 ■ Salvo
Fellowship of Saint James
PO Box 410788
Chicago, IL 60641
Phone: (773)481-1090
Publisher's E-mail: webmaster@fsj.org
Freq: Quarterly. **Subscription Rates:** $25.99 U.S. 1 year print only; $45.99 U.S. 2 years print only; $63.99 U.S. 3 years print only; $32.99 Canada 1 year print only; $59.99 Canada 2 years print only; $84.99 Canada 3 years print only; $37.99 Other countries 1 year print only; $67.99 Other countries 2 years print only; $99.99 Other countries 3 years print only; $15.99 Individuals digital. **URL:** http://www.salvomag.com/new/mag.php; http://fsj.org/new/subscribe.php. **Remarks:** Accepts advertising. **Circ:** 2500.

10548 ■ School Library Research
American Association of School Librarians
50 E Huron St.
Chicago, IL 60611-2729
Phone: (312)280-4382
Fax: (312)280-5276
Free: 800-545-2433
Promotes and publishes high quality research concerning management, implementation and evaluation of school library media programs. **Founded:** 1998. **Key Personnel:** Ruth V. Small, Ph.D, Editor. **ISSN:** 1523-4320 (print). **Subscription Rates:** Free online only. **URL:** http://www.ala.org/aasl/slr. **Formerly**: School Library Media Quarterly Online; School Library Media Research. **Ad Rates:** BW $630; 4C $1,500. **Remarks:** Accepts advertising. **Circ:** (Not Reported).

10549 ■ The SciTech Lawyer
American Bar Association
321 N Clark St.
Chicago, IL 60654
Phone: (312)988-5000
Free: 800-285-2221
Law magazine for lawyers and legal professionals dealing with law and legal issues in science, medicine and technology. **Freq:** Quarterly. **Trim Size:** 8 1/2 x 11. **Key Personnel:** Julie A. Fleming, Editor-in-Chief; Lois Mermelstein, Editor. **Subscription Rates:** $55 Nonmembers /year; $65 Nonmembers /year (other countries). **URL:** http://www.americanbar.org/publications/scitech_lawyer/2015/fall.html. **Remarks:** Accepts advertising. **Circ:** (Not Reported).

10550 ■ Screen Magazine
Screen Enterprises Inc.
676 N LaSalle Blvd., Ste. 501
Chicago, IL 60654
Phone: (312)640-0800
Fax: (312)640-1928
Publication E-mail: screen@screenmag.com
Trade magazine presenting news of Midwest-originated motion picture, video, and audiovisual, multimedia production, and national news. **Freq:** Biweekly. **Print Method:** Sheet fed. **Trim Size:** 8 1/2 x 11. **Cols./Page:** 3. **Col. Width:** 13 picas. **Col. Depth:** 59 picas. **Key Personnel:** Andrew Schneider, Jr., Editor, Publisher. **ISSN:** 0276--153X (print). **Subscription Rates:** $60 Individuals; $110 Two years; $130 Other countries. **URL:** http://www.screenmag.tv. **Mailing address:** PO Box 1613, Chicago, IL 60654. **Ad Rates:** BW $1,500. **Remarks:** Accepts advertising. **Circ:** ‡15000.

10551 ■ Serif
Serif
Dept. W-1
2038 N Clark St.
Chicago, IL 60614
Phone: (312)953-3679
Fax: (312)602-1014
Free: 877-634-1811
Publication E-mail: serif@quixote.com
Trade magazine covering the typographic arts. **Freq:** Quarterly. **Subscription Rates:** $28 Individuals; $32 Canada and Mexico; $36 Elsewhere; $50 Two years; $58 Two years Canada and Mexico; $66 Two years elsewhere; $7.95 Single issue. **URL:** http://www.serifmagazine.com. **Mailing address:** PO Box 377, Chicago, IL 60614. **Ad Rates:** BW $456. **Remarks:** Advertising accepted; rates available upon request. **Circ:** (Not Reported).

10552 ■ Services: The Magazine for the Building Service Contracting Industry
Building Service Contractors Association International
330 N Wabash Ave., Ste. 2000
Chicago, IL 60611
Phone: (312)321-5167
Fax: (312)673-6735
Free: 800-368-3414
Publisher's E-mail: info@bscai.org
Trade journal for maintenance and cleaning contractors and facility management companies. **Freq:** Bimonthly. **Print Method:** Offset. **Trim Size:** 8 1/8 x 10 7/8. **Cols./Page:** 3. **Col. Width:** 2 1/4 inches. **Col. Depth:** 10 inches. **Key Personnel:** Jennifer Siorek, Account Executive, phone: (877)234-1863. **ISSN:** 0279--0548 (print). **URL:** http://www.servicesmag.org. **Remarks:** Accepts advertising. **Circ:** (Not Reported).

10553 ■ ShelfImpact!: Strategies for successful package design and marketing
Summit Publishing Co.
330 N Wabash Ave., Ste. 2401
Chicago, IL 60611
Phone: (312)222-1010
Fax: (312)222-1310
Publisher's E-mail: sales@packworld.com
Online magazine covering package design, marketing, and in-store displays. **Freq:** Monthly. **Key Personnel:** Anne Marie Mohan, Managing Editor; Iris Zavala. **Subscription Rates:** Free. **URL:** http://www.packworld.com/design. **Remarks:** Accepts advertising. **Circ:** (Not Reported).

10554 ■ Signs
The University of Chicago Press, Journals Div.
1427 E 60th St.
Chicago, IL 60637
Phone: (773)702-7700
Free: 877-705-1878
Publisher's E-mail: subscriptions@press.uchicago.edu
Journal containing articles on gender, race, culture, class, nation, and sexuality. **Freq:** Quarterly. **ISSN:** 0097--9740 (print); **EISSN:** 1545--6943 (electronic). **Subscription Rates:** $54 Individuals electronic only; $60 Individuals print and electronic; $56 Individuals print only; $30 Students electronic only. **URL:** http://www.journals.uchicago.edu/toc/signs/current. **Circ:** (Not Reported).

10555 ■ Signs and Society
The University of Chicago Press, Journals Div.
1427 E 60th St.
Chicago, IL 60637
Phone: (773)702-7700
Free: 877-705-1878
Publisher's E-mail: subscriptions@press.uchicago.edu
Journal containing articles on humanities and social sciences focusing on the study of sign process (or semiosis) in the realms of social action, cognition, and cultural form. **Freq:** Semiannual. **ISSN:** 2326--4489 (print); **EISSN:** 2326--4497 (electronic). **Subscription Rates:** $57 Individuals print only. **URL:** http://www.journals.uchicago.edu/toc/sas/current. **Circ:** (Not Reported).

10556 ■ Social Service Review
The University of Chicago Press
School of Social Service Administration
University of Chicago
969 E 60th St.
Chicago, IL 60637
Phone: (773)702-1165
Fax: (773)702-0874
Publisher's E-mail: custserv@press.uchicago.edu
Journal presenting objective studies of social welfare policies, and its practices. **Freq:** Quarterly. **Print Method:** Offset. **Trim Size:** 6 x 9. **Cols./Page:** 1. **Col. Width:** 52 nonpareils. **Col. Depth:** 103 agate lines. **Key Personnel:** Susan Lambert, Editor. **ISSN:** 0037--7961 (print); **EISSN:** 1537--5404 (electronic). **Subscription Rates:** $18 Individuals online only. **URL:** http://www.jstor.org/journal/sociservrevi. **Ad Rates:** BW $690. **Remarks:** Accepts advertising. **Circ:** ‡579.

10557 ■ The Sondheim Review
The Sondheim Review
PO Box 11213
Chicago, IL 60611-0213
Phone: (773)275-4254
Free: 800-584-1020
Publication E-mail: editor@sondheimreview.com
Consumer magazine covering the works of composer and lyricist, Stephen Sondheim. **Freq:** Quarterly. **Key Personnel:** Ray Birks, Publisher; Rick Pender, Editor. **ISSN:** 1076--450X (print). **Subscription Rates:** $19.95 Individuals; $24.95 Canada and Mexico; $29.95 Elsewhere; $8 Single issue. **Ad Rates:** BW $500; 4C $1,000. **Remarks:** Accepts advertising. **Circ:** Controlled 3700.

10558 ■ Sophisticate's Black Hairstyles and Care Guide
Associated Publications Inc.
875 N Michigan Ave., Ste. 3434
Chicago, IL 60611
Phone: (312)266-8680
Publisher's E-mail: info@associatedpub.com
Black hairstyle magazine. **Freq:** Bimonthly. **Print Method:** Web Offset. **Key Personnel:** Bonnie L. Krueger, Director, Publications. **Subscription Rates:** $51.50 Individuals 8 issues; $81.25 Other countries 8 issues; $103 Individuals 16 issues; $162.50 Other countries 16 issues. **URL:** http://www.sophisticatesblackhairstyles.com. **Ad Rates:** BW $4,709. **Remarks:** Accepts advertising. **Circ:** Paid ★166016.

10559 ■ Special Care in Dentistry
Special Care Dentistry Association
330 N Wabash Ave., Ste. 2000
Chicago, IL 60611
Phone: (312)527-6764
Fax: (312)673-6663
Publisher's E-mail: scda@scdaonline.org
Dental journal. **Freq:** Bimonthly. **Print Method:** Offset. **Cols./Page:** 3 and 2. **Col. Width:** 26 and 40 nonpareils. **Col. Depth:** 133 agate lines. **Key Personnel:** Marc B. Ackerman, Editor. **ISSN:** 0275--1879 (print); **EISSN:** 1754--4505 (electronic). **URL:** http://www.scdaonline.org/?page=SCDAJournal. **Ad Rates:** BW $683. **Remarks:** Accepts advertising. **Circ:** (Not Reported).

10560 ■ SPN Journal of Pediatric Nursing
Society of Pediatric Nurses
330 N Wabash Ave., Ste. 2000
Chicago, IL 60611-7621
Phone: (312)321-5154
Fax: (312)673-6754
Publisher's E-mail: info@pedsnurses.org
Peer-reviewed journal publishing up-to-date information and practices in the field of pediatric nursing. **Freq:** Bimonthly. **Subscription Rates:** $140 Individuals online and print; $294 Other countries online and print. **URL:** http://www.pediatricnursing.org. **Ad Rates:** BW $1385. **Remarks:** Accepts advertising. **Circ:** 4117.

10561 ■ The State and Local Tax Lawyer
American Bar Association
321 N Clark St.
Chicago, IL 60654
Phone: (312)988-5000
Free: 800-285-2221
Law journal for lawyers, tax managers and accountants dealing with state and local taxation. **Freq:** Annual. **Key Personnel:** Jeffrey C. Glickman, Editor-in-Chief; Michael W. McLoughlin, Editor-in-Chief; John M. Allan; Brandee Tilman, Editor; Don S. Kovacic; Kendall L. Houghton; Debra S. Herman, Editor-in-Chief; Garry G. Fujita. **Subscription Rates:** $95 Nonmembers; $75 Members. **URL:** http://www.americanbar.org/publications/state_and_local_tax_lawyer_home.html. **Remarks:** Advertising not accepted. **Circ:** (Not Reported).

10562 ■ Strategize Magazine: tomorrow's ideas for today's business
Avenir Publishing Inc.
65 E Wacker Pl., Ste. 400
Chicago, IL 60601
Phone: (312)577-7200
Fax: (312)263-0952
Publisher's E-mail: contact@avenirpublishing.com
Magazine for business improvement and innovation. **Freq:** Quarterly. **Key Personnel:** James R.H. Potter, Editor-in-Chief; Christopher Broadbent, Director, Advertising. **URL:** http://www.strategizemagazine.com. **Remarks:** Advertising accepted; rates available upon request. **Circ:** (Not Reported).

10563 ■ StreetWise: Empowering People to Self-Sufficiency Through Employment
StreetWise
4554 N Broadway St.
Chicago, IL 60640

Phone: (773)334-6600
Fax: (773)334-6604
Alternative street newspaper. **Freq:** Weekly (Wed.). **Key Personnel:** Suzanne Hanney, Editor-in-Chief; Ron Madere, Contact. **Subscription Rates:** $100 Individuals. **URL:** http://streetwise.org. **Ad Rates:** BW $1,695; 4C $2,470. **Remarks:** Accepts advertising. **Circ:** 13000.

10564 ■ Student Doctor
Student Osteopathic Medical Association
142 E Ontario St.
Chicago, IL 60611-2864
Phone: (312)202-8193
Fax: (312)202-8200
Free: 800-621-1773
Publisher's E-mail: administration@studentdo.com
Magazine containing scholarship information, medical updates, and links to related organizations. **Freq:** Semiannual. **Subscription Rates:** Included in membership. **Alt. Formats:** PDF. **Remarks:** Advertising not accepted. **Circ:** (Not Reported).

10565 ■ Supreme Court Economic Review
The University of Chicago Press
1427 E 60th St.
Chicago, IL 60637
Phone: (773)702-7700
Fax: (773)702-7212
Publication E-mail: scer@gmu.edu
Professional publication covering law. **Freq:** Annual. **Key Personnel:** Michelle Crawford Rickert, Managing Editor; Douglas H. Ginsburg, Editor. **ISSN:** 0736--9921 (print); **EISSN:** 2156--6208 (electronic). **Subscription Rates:** $63 Individuals print and online; $41 Individuals online only; $21 Students online only; $126 Two years print and online; $82 Two years online only; $42 Students online only - 2 years. **URL:** http://www.journals.uchicago.edu/toc/scer/current; http://www.jstor.org/journal/suprcoureconrevi. **Circ:** (Not Reported).

10566 ■ Supreme Court Review
University of Chicago Law School
1111 E 60th St.
Chicago, IL 60637
Phone: (773)702-9494
Fax: (773)834-0942
Publisher's E-mail: custserv@press.uchicago.edu
Professional publication covering law. **Freq:** Annual every Spring. **Key Personnel:** David A. Strauss, Editor, phone: (773)702-9601; Dennis J. Hutchinson, Editor; Geoffrey R. Stone, Editor, phone: (773)702-4907. **ISSN:** 0081--9557 (print); **EISSN:** 2158--2459 (electronic). **Subscription Rates:** $83 Individuals print and online; $62 Individuals online only; $31 Students online only; $166 Two years print and online; $124 Two years online only; $62 Students online only - 2 years; $249 Individuals print and online - 3 years; $186 Individuals online only - 3 years; $93 Students online only - 3 years. **URL:** http://www.press.uchicago.edu/ucp/journals/journal/scr.html; http://www.journals.uchicago.edu/toc/scr/current. **Circ:** (Not Reported).

10567 ■ Supreme Court Review
The University of Chicago Press
1427 E 60th St.
Chicago, IL 60637
Phone: (773)702-7700
Fax: (773)702-7212
Publisher's E-mail: custserv@press.uchicago.edu
Professional publication covering law. **Freq:** Annual every Spring. **Key Personnel:** David A. Strauss, Editor, phone: (773)702-9601; Dennis J. Hutchinson, Editor; Geoffrey R. Stone, Editor, phone: (773)702-4907. **ISSN:** 0081--9557 (print); **EISSN:** 2158--2459 (electronic). **Subscription Rates:** $83 Individuals print and online; $62 Individuals online only; $31 Students online only; $166 Two years print and online; $124 Two years online only; $62 Students online only - 2 years; $249 Individuals print and online - 3 years; $186 Individuals online only - 3 years; $93 Students online only - 3 years. **URL:** http://www.press.uchicago.edu/ucp/journals/journal/scr.html; http://www.journals.uchicago.edu/toc/scr/current. **Circ:** (Not Reported).

10568 ■ Surge
American Academy of Cosmetic Surgery
225 W Wacker Dr., Ste. 650
Chicago, IL 60606
Phone: (312)981-6760
Fax: (312)265-2908
Publisher's E-mail: info@cosmeticsurgery.org
Freq: Quarterly latest issues, 2015. **Subscription Rates:** Accessible only to members. **URL:** http://www.cosmeticsurgery.org/?page=Surge; http://cosmeticsurgery.site-ym.com/?page=Surge. **Remarks:** Advertising not accepted. **Circ:** (Not Reported).

10569 ■ Surgery News
American College of Surgeons
633 N St. Clair St.
Chicago, IL 60611-3211
Phone: (312)202-5000
Fax: (312)202-5001
Free: 800-621-4111
Publisher's E-mail: postmaster@facs.org
Newspaper that provides coverage of clinical, regulatory, legislative, and financial aspects of surgery and medicine. **Freq:** Monthly. **Key Personnel:** Alan Imhoff, President, Publisher, phone: (973)290-8216; Mary Jo Dales, Executive Director, phone: (240)221-2470; Mark Branca, Director, phone: (973)290-8246, fax: (973)290-8250. **ISSN:** 1553--6785 (print). **Subscription Rates:** $199 Individuals; $230 Individuals. **URL:** http://www.esng-meded.com; http://www.acssurgerynews.com; http://www.esng-meded.com/surgerynews/index.php. **Remarks:** Accepts advertising. **Circ:** △**36000**.

10570 ■ SWE, Magazine of the Society of Women Engineers
Society of Women Engineers
203 N La Salle St., Ste. 1675
Chicago, IL 60601
Free: 877-793-4636
Publisher's E-mail: hq@swe.org
Magazine for engineering students and for women and men working in the engineering and technology fields. Covers career guidance, continuing development and topical issues. **Freq:** Quarterly. **Trim Size:** 8 1/2 x 11. **Cols./Page:** 2 and 3. **Key Personnel:** Anne M. Perusek, Editor; John Goodrich, Manager, Advertising. **ISSN:** 1070--6232 (print). **Subscription Rates:** $30 Individuals; $47.50 Other countries; $7.50 Individuals single issue. **URL:** http://societyofwomenengineers.swe.org/swe-magazine-new. **Formerly**: SWE Newsletter. **Remarks:** Accepts advertising. **Circ:** ‡27000.

10571 ■ Swedish-American Historical Quarterly
Swedish-American Historical Society
3225 W Foster Ave.
Chicago, IL 60625
Phone: (773)583-5722
Publisher's E-mail: info@swedishamericanhist.org
Journal devoted to Swedish-American contributions to the history and growth of the United States. **Freq:** Quarterly. **Trim Size:** 6 1/4 x 9 1/4. **Key Personnel:** Paul A. Varg, Editor; Franklin D. Scott, Editor; Arnold Barton, Editor; Raymond Jarvi, Editor; Byron Nordstrom, Editor. **ISSN:** 0730--028X (print). **URL:** http://www.swedishamericanhist.org/publications/index.html; http://collections.carli.illinois.edu/cdm/landingpage/collection/npu_sahq. **Formerly**: Swedish Pioneer Historical Quarterly. **Mailing address:** PO Box 48, Chicago, IL 60625. **Remarks:** Accepts advertising. **Circ:** (Not Reported).

10572 ■ Talent Management Magazine: The Business of Talent Management
MediaTec Publishing
111 E Wacker, Ste. 1290
Chicago, IL 60601
Phone: (312)676-9900
Fax: (312)676-9910
Magazine covering workplace performance and effectiveness. **Freq:** Monthly. **Subscription Rates:** Free U.S. (print, digital, print and digital); Free Canada and other countries (digital); $195 Canada print and digital; $228 Other countries print and digital; $29.99 Single issue print; $9.99 Single issue PDF. **Alt. Formats:** PDF. **URL:** http://www.talentmgt.com. **Formerly**: Workforce Performance Solutions. **Remarks:** Accepts advertising. **Circ:** (Not Reported).

10573 ■ Taste of Home
Reiman Media Group
233 N Michigan Ave., Ste. 1740
Chicago, IL 60601
Publisher's E-mail: rpsubscustomercare@custhelp.com
Consumer magazine covering food and cooking. **Freq:** 6/year. **Print Method:** Web. **Trim Size:** 7.75 x 10.50. **Key Personnel:** Lora Gier, Publisher, Vice President, phone: (312)540-4816, fax: (312)540-0028. **ISSN:** 1071--5878 (print). **Subscription Rates:** $10 U.S. one year; $19.98 Canada one year; $25.98 Other countries one year. **Remarks:** Accepts advertising. **Circ:** Paid ★**3200000**.

10574 ■ Theory of Computing
The University of Chicago Press
1427 E 60th St.
Chicago, IL 60637
Phone: (773)702-7700
Fax: (773)702-7212
Publisher's E-mail: custserv@press.uchicago.edu
Journal covering high quality research papers in the field of Theoretical Computer Science. **Key Personnel:** Laszlo Babai, Editor-in-Chief; Satya V. Lokam, Managing Editor; Oded Regev, Associate Editor. **ISSN:** 1557--2862 (print). **Subscription Rates:** Free. **URL:** http://theoryofcomputing.org. **Remarks:** Advertising not accepted. **Circ:** (Not Reported).

10575 ■ Time Out Chicago
Time Out Chicago Partners L.L.L.P.
247 S State St., 17th Fl.
Chicago, IL 60604
Entertainment magazine. **Trim Size:** 8 x 10.5. **Key Personnel:** Frank Senneth, Editor-in-Chief, President; Amy Carr, Executive Editor; David Garland, Publisher. **URL:** http://www.timeout.com/chicago. **Circ:** (Not Reported).

10576 ■ Tort Trial & Insurance Practice Law Journal
American Bar Association
321 N Clark St.
Chicago, IL 60654
Phone: (312)988-5000
Free: 800-285-2221
Scholarly journal on current or emerging issues of national scope in the fields of tort and insurance law. **Freq:** Quarterly. **Trim Size:** 6 x 9. **Cols./Page:** 1. **ISSN:** 0015-8356 (print). **Subscription Rates:** $50 Individuals; $65 Other countries; Included in membership. **URL:** http://www.abanet.org/tips/lawjournal.html; http://www.americanbar.org/publications/tort_insurance_law_journal_home.html. **Formerly**: The Forum; Tort & Insurance Law Journal. **Remarks:** Advertising not accepted. **Circ:** (Not Reported).

10577 ■ Touchstone: A Journal of Mere Christianity
Fellowship of Saint James
PO Box 410788
Chicago, IL 60641
Phone: (773)481-1090
Publisher's E-mail: webmaster@fsj.org
Freq: Bimonthly. **ISSN:** 0897--327X (print). **Subscription Rates:** $29.95 U.S. print edition; $54.95 U.S. 2 years print edition; $36.95 Canada 1 year print edition; $68.95 Canada 2 years print edition; $41.95 Other countries 1 year print edition; $78.95 Other countries 2 years print edition; $19.95 Individuals 1 year digital edition; $35.90 Individuals 2 year digital edition. **URL:** http://fsj.org/new/subscribe.php. **Remarks:** Accepts advertising. **Circ:** 10000.

10578 ■ Transportation Journal
American Society of Transportation and Logistics
8430 W Bryn Mawr Ave., Ste. 1000
Chicago, IL 60631
Phone: (773)355-4900
Fax: (773)355-4888
Publisher's E-mail: info@astl.org
Freq: Quarterly. **ISSN:** 0041- 1612 (print). **Subscription Rates:** $132 Individuals print or online; $271 Institutions print or online; $264 Two years print or online; individuals.; $542 Two years print or online; institutions. **URL:** http://www.astl.org/i4a/pages/index.cfm?pageid=3288. **Remarks:** Advertising not accepted. **Circ:** (Not Reported).

10579 ■ Trauma Surgery & Acute Care Open
American Association for the Surgery of Trauma
633 N St. Clair St., Ste. 2600
Chicago, IL 60611
Fax: (312)202-5064

Circulation: ★ = AAM; △ or • = BPA; ♦ = CAC; ❑ = VAC; ⊕ = PO Statement; ‡ = Publisher's Report; Boldface figures = sworn; Light figures = estimated.

Free: 800-789-4006
Publisher's E-mail: aast@aast.org
Open access journal containing international research on trauma and acute care. **Freq:** Continuous. **EISSN:** 2397--5776 (electronic). **Subscription Rates:** Free. **URL:** http://tsaco.bmj.com. **Circ:** (Not Reported).

10580 ■ Trustee: The Magazine for Hospital Governing Boards
Health Forum L.L.C.
155 N Wacker Dr., Ste. 400
Chicago, IL 60606
Phone: (312)893-6800
Fax: (312)422-4500
Free: 800-821-2039
Magazine for hospital and health care system governing board members containing information about events and issues affecting the health care industry. **Freq:** Monthly. **Print Method:** Offset. **Trim Size:** 8 x 10 3/4. **Cols./Page:** 3. **Col. Width:** 32 nonpareils. **Col. Depth:** 115 agate lines. **Key Personnel:** Alden Solovy, Associate Publisher; Jane Jeffries, Editor; Lisa Schulte, Contact, phone: (800)453-9706, fax: (636)227-8892; M.J. Mrvica, Contact, phone: (856)768-9360, fax: (856)753-0064. **ISSN:** 0041--3674 (print). **Subscription Rates:** $59 Individuals; $125 Other countries. **URL:** http://www.trusteemag.com. **Remarks:** Accepts advertising. **Circ:** ‡145000.

10581 ■ TYA Today
Theatre for Young Audiences USA
c/o Theatre School at DePaul University
2350 N Racine Ave.
Chicago, IL 60614
Phone: (773)325-7981
Fax: (773)325-7920
Publisher's E-mail: info@tyausa.org
Freq: Semiannual. **Subscription Rates:** Included in membership. **URL:** http://assitej-usa.org/?page_id=84. **Ad Rates:** BW $800; 4C $950. **Remarks:** Accepts advertising. **Circ:** (Not Reported).

10582 ■ U.S. Catholic
Claretian Publications
205 W Monroe St.
Chicago, IL 60606
Phone: (312)236-7782
Fax: (312)236-8207
Catholic magazine. **Founded:** 1935. **Freq:** Monthly. **Print Method:** Offset. **Cols./Page:** 3. **Col. Width:** 27 nonpareils. **Col. Depth:** 140 agate lines. **Key Personnel:** John Molyneux, Editor; Bryan Cones, Managing Editor; Meinrad Scherer-Emunds, Executive Editor. **Subscription Rates:** $29 Individuals; $50 Two years; $70 Individuals 3 years; $10 Other countries 2 years. **URL:** http://www.uscatholic.org. **Ad Rates:** BW $1575; 4C $1775. **Remarks:** Accepts advertising. **Circ:** 30,000.

10583 ■ University of Chicago Magazine
University of Chicago Magazine
5235 S Harper Ct.
Chicago, IL 60615
Phone: (773)702-2163
Fax: (773)702-2166
Publisher's E-mail: uchicago-magazine@uchicago.edu
University alumni magazine. **Freq:** Bimonthly. **Print Method:** Offset. **Trim Size:** 8 1/8 x 10 7/8. **Cols./Page:** 3. **Col. Width:** 14.5 picas. **Col. Depth:** 58.25 picas. **Key Personnel:** Mary Ruth Yoe, Executive Editor; Amy M. Braverman Puma, Editor; Lydialyle Gibson, Associate Editor. **ISSN:** 0041--9508 (print). **Ad Rates:** BW $7305; 4C 10745. **Remarks:** Accepts advertising. **Circ:** (Not Reported).

10584 ■ UnRated Magazine
UnRated Magazine
5425 S Richmond
Chicago, IL 60632
Phone: (773)737-0209
Fax: (702)554-4928
Publication E-mail: info@unratedmagazine.com
Magazine featuring artists and celebrities. **Key Personnel:** Bill Schupp, Editor-in-Chief. **URL:** http://www.unratedmagazine.com. **Circ:** (Not Reported).

10585 ■ The Urban Lawyer: The National Quarterly on State and Local Government Law
American Bar Association
321 N Clark St.
Chicago, IL 60654
Phone: (312)988-5000
Free: 800-285-2221
Articles on various areas of urban, state, and local government law. **Freq:** Quarterly. **Print Method:** Offset. **Trim Size:** 6 x 9. **Cols./Page:** 1. **Key Personnel:** Stephanie L. Hill, Managing Editor; Thomas E. Roberts, Advisor, Board Member; Rebecca M. Abeln, Editor; Robert H. Freilich, Editor; Dan Emersonr, Editor; Christin E. Keele, Editor; Erin M. Dedrickson, Editor-in-Chief; Julie M. Cheslik, Editor; Richard W. Bright, Editor. **ISSN:** 0042--0905 (print). **Subscription Rates:** $69 Individuals; $74 Other countries. **Alt. Formats:** PDF. **URL:** http://www.americanbar.org/publications/urban_lawyer_home.html. **Remarks:** Advertising not accepted. **Circ:** Paid 5250, Non-paid 150.

10586 ■ Urgent Communications: Technical Information for Paging, Trunking and Private Wireless Networks
Penton Media, Inc.
330 N Wabash Ave., Ste. 2300
Chicago, IL 60611
Phone: (312)595-1080
Fax: (312)595-0295
Technical magazine for the mobile communications industry. **Freq:** Monthly. **Print Method:** Web Offset. **Trim Size:** 7 7/8 x 10 3/4. **Cols./Page:** 3. **Col. Width:** 2 1/4 inches. **Col. Depth:** 10 inches. **Key Personnel:** Dennis Hegg, Sales Representative, phone: (707)526-4377; Greg Herring, Vice President; Donny Jackson, Editor, phone: (414)529-4514; Glenn Bischoff, Publisher, phone: (312)840-8467. **ISSN:** 0745-7626 (print). **URL:** http://urgentcomm.com/. **Formerly**: Mobile Radio Technology. **Remarks:** Accepts advertising. **Circ:** △**31410.**

10587 ■ Valuation
Appraisal Institute
200 W Madison St., Ste. 1500
Chicago, IL 60606
Phone: (312)335-4401
Fax: (312)335-4415
Free: 888-756-4624
Publisher's E-mail: aiservice@appraisalinstitute.org
Trade magazine covering news and trends in the real estate appraisal field. **Founded:** 1996. **Freq:** Quarterly. **Trim Size:** 8 1/2 x 11. **Key Personnel:** Adam Webster, Managing Editor, phone: (312)335-4459. **ISSN:** 1087-0148 (print). **Subscription Rates:** $90 Individuals; $135 Other countries; $260 Libraries; $120 Libraries other countries. **URL:** http://www.appraisalinstitute.org/publications/valuation-magazine/. **Ad Rates:** 4C $2650. **Remarks:** Advertising accepted; rates available upon request. **Circ:** Combined 82000.

10588 ■ Velocity
Strategic Account Management Association
10 N Dearborn St., 2nd Fl.
Chicago, IL 60602
Phone: (312)251-3131
Fax: (312)251-3132
Covers account management issues in the U.S. and worldwide. **Freq:** Quarterly. **Trim Size:** 8 1/2 x 11. **Cols./Page:** 8. **Subscription Rates:** $65 Individuals; $25 Single issue; $10 Individuals article; Included in membership. **URL:** http://www.strategicaccounts.org/Resource/Velocity. **Formerly**: N.A.M.A. Journal. **Remarks:** Accepts advertising. **Circ:** Controlled 2500, 4000, 5000.

10589 ■ Vernon Hills Review
Sun-Times Media L.L.C.
350 N Orleans St., 10th Fl.
Chicago, IL 60654
Phone: (312)321-3000
Free: 888-848-4637
Publisher's E-mail: customerservice@suntimes.com
Community newspaper (tabloid). **Freq:** Weekly (Thurs.). **Print Method:** Offset. **Cols./Page:** 5. **Col. Width:** 10 inches. **Col. Depth:** 14 inches. **Key Personnel:** Kevin Reiterman, Editor, phone: (847)486-7480; David Sweet, Managing Editor, phone: (847)599-6944. **Subscription Rates:** $4.99 Individuals /month. **URL:** http://vernonhills.suntimes.com. **Remarks:** Accepts advertising. **Circ:** (Not Reported).

10590 ■ Via Times Newsmagazine
Via Times Newsmagazine
3108 W Belmont Ave., Apt. 2
Chicago, IL 60618
Phone: (773)866-0811
Publisher's E-mail: viatimes@sbcglobal.net
Consumer magazine for Filipino-Americans in English and some Tagalog. **Freq:** Monthly. **Key Personnel:** Veronica Leighton, Editor, Publisher. **URL:** http://www.viatimes.com. **Ad Rates:** BW $600. **Remarks:** Accepts advertising. **Circ:** ‡25000.

10591 ■ Victims & Offenders
Routledge
c/o Arthur J. Lurigio, PhD, Senior Editor
Loyola University Chicago
College of Arts & Sciences
6525 N Sheridan Rd.
Chicago, IL 60626
Phone: (773)508-3503
Publisher's E-mail: book.orders@tandf.co.uk
Peer-reviewed journal covering articles on victims and offender theories, research, and practices. **Freq:** Quarterly. **Key Personnel:** James M. Byrne, PhD, Editor-in-Chief; Donald Hummer, PhD, Associate Editor; David P. Farrington, PhD, Editor; Jay Albanese, PhD, Board Member; James Austin, PhD, Board Member; Jodi Lane, PhD, Board Member; Todd Clear, PhD, Board Member; Arthur J. Lurigio, PhD, Senior Editor; Francis T. Cullen, PhD, Board Member. **ISSN:** 1556--4886 (print); **EISSN:** 1556--4991 (electronic). **Subscription Rates:** $206 Individuals print only; $703 Institutions online; $803 Institutions print and online. **URL:** http://www.tandfonline.com/toc/uvao20/current; http://www.tandfonline.com/loi/uvao20#.VzWYLtR96mU. **Circ:** (Not Reported).

10592 ■ Visible Language
University of Cincinnati College of Design, Architecture, Art, and Planning
c/o Prof. Sharon Helmer Poggenpohl, Editor/Publisher
IIT Institute of Design
350 N LaSalle St.
Chicago, IL 60610
Scholarly journal about written language. **Freq:** 3/yr. **Print Method:** Offset. **Trim Size:** 6 x 9. **Cols./Page:** 1. **Col. Width:** 51 nonpareils. **Col. Depth:** 94 agate lines. **ISSN:** 0022-2224 (print). **Subscription Rates:** $35 Individuals United States; $44 Individuals Canada; $56 Individuals foreign; C$65 Institutions United States; $74 Institutions Canada; $86 Institutions foreign. **URL:** http://www.risd.edu; http://visiblelanguagejournal.com. **Formerly**: The Journal of Typographic Research. **Remarks:** Advertising not accepted. **Circ:** ‡1,300.

10593 ■ Vision Magazine: Alumni Report
University of Illinois at Chicago College of Pharmacy Institute for Tuberculosis Research
833 S Wood St.
College of Pharmacy, Rm. 412
Chicago, IL 60612-7231
Phone: (312)355-4132
Fax: (312)355-2693
News for and about dentistry alumni. **Founded:** 1985. **Freq:** Semiannual. **Print Method:** Offset. **Trim Size:** 8 1/2 x 11. **Cols./Page:** 3. **Key Personnel:** William S. Bike, Director; Irwin Robinson, Executive Editor. **ISSN:** 1088-9108 (print). **Subscription Rates:** $6 Individuals; $3 Single issue. **URL:** http://dentistry.uic.edu/alumni/alumni_association. **Formerly**: Alumni Report. **Remarks:** Accepts advertising. **Circ:** Non-paid 5500.

10594 ■ Visions
Easter Seal Society Publications
233 S Wacker Dr., Ste. 2400
Chicago, IL 60606
Free: 800-221-6827
Magazine promoting beauty salon services and products. **Freq:** Quarterly. **Subscription Rates:** Free. **Ad Rates:** BW $7,245. **Remarks:** Accepts advertising. **Circ:** Non-paid 1100069.

10595 ■ Visions: PDMA Practitioner Magazine
Product Development and Management Association
330 N Wabash Ave., Ste. 2000
Chicago, IL 60611
Phone: (312)321-5145
Fax: (312)673-6885
Free: 800-232-5241
Publisher's E-mail: pdma@pdma.org
Freq: Quarterly. **Subscription Rates:** Included in membership; $25 Nonmembers. **URL:** http://www.pdma.org/visions. **Remarks:** Accepts advertising. **Circ:** 2900.

10596 ■ West 86th: A Journal of Decorative Arts, Design History, and Material Culture
The University of Chicago Press
1427 E 60th St.
Chicago, IL 60637
Phone: (773)702-7700
Fax: (773)702-7212
Publisher's E-mail: custserv@press.uchicago.edu
Journal focusing on scholarship in material culture, design history and decorative arts. **Freq:** Semiannual. **ISSN:** 2153--5531 (print); **EISSN:** 2153--5558 (electronic). **Subscription Rates:** $35 Individuals /year (print and online). **URL:** http://www.journals.uchicago.edu/toc/wes/current. **Circ:** (Not Reported).

10597 ■ Windy City Times
Windy City Times
5315 N Clark St., No. 192
Chicago, IL 60640
Phone: (773)871-7610
Publication E-mail: editor@windycitymediagroup.com
Gay and lesbian community newspaper. **Freq:** Weekly. **Print Method:** Web. **Trim Size:** 11 x 17. **Cols./Page:** 4. **Col. Width:** 2 7/16 inches. **Col. Depth:** 10 inches. **Key Personnel:** Tracy Baim, Editor, Publisher; Andrew Davis, Managing Editor; Jean Albright, Manager, Circulation. **URL:** http://www.windycitymediagroup.com/windycitytimes.php. **Ad Rates:** BW $1540; 4C $2190. **Remarks:** Accepts advertising. **Circ:** ‡15,000.

10598 ■ World Future Review: A Journal of Strategic Foresight
World Future Society
333 N Lasalle St.
Chicago, IL 60654
Free: 800-989-8274
Publication E-mail: info@wfs.org
Peer-reviewed journal focusing on future studies methodology. **Freq:** Quarterly. **Key Personnel:** Wendell Bell, Board Member; Timothy Mack, Editor; Clement Bezold, Board Member. **ISSN:** 1946--7567 (print); **EISSN:** 2169--2793 (electronic). **Subscription Rates:** $386 Institutions print and online; $347 Institutions online online; $378 Institutions print only; $109 Individuals print only; $104 Institutions single print issue; $35 Individuals single print issue. **URL:** http://www.wfs.org/wfr. **Formed by the merger of:** Futures Research Quarterly; Future Survey. **Remarks:** Advertising not accepted. **Circ:** ‡1500.

10599 ■ Young Adult Library Services
American Library Association Young Adult Library Services Association
50 E Huron St.
Chicago, IL 60611
Phone: (312)280-4390
Fax: (312)280-5276
Free: 800-545-2433
Publisher's E-mail: yalsa@ala.org
Freq: Quarterly. **Key Personnel:** Beth Yoke, Executive Director. **ISSN:** 1541--4302 (print). **Subscription Rates:** Included in membership. **URL:** http://www.yalsa.ala.org/yals; http://www.ala.org/yalsa/products%26publications. **Remarks:** Advertising accepted; rates available upon request. **Circ:** (Not Reported).

10600 ■ Zgoda
Polish National Alliance of the United States of North America
6100 N Cicero Ave.
Chicago, IL 60646
Phone: (773)286-0500
Free: 800-621-3723
Publisher's E-mail: info@pna-znp.org
Freq: Semimonthly. **Alt. Formats:** Download; PDF. **URL:** http://www.pna-znp.org/zgoda-magazine.html. **Remarks:** Advertising not accepted. **Circ:** (Not Reported).

10601 ■ Zygon: Journal of Religion & Science
Institute on Religion in an Age of Science
c/o Dan Solomon, Membership Coordinator
6434 N Mozart St.
Chicago, IL 60645
Journal covering philosophy and religion. **Freq:** Quarterly. **Key Personnel:** Willem B. Drees, Editor; Philip Hefner, Advisor. **ISSN:** 0591--2385 (print); **EISSN:** 1467--9744 (electronic). **Subscription Rates:** $94 Individuals print and online; €94 Individuals print and online; £83 Individuals print and online; $77 Members print and online; €77 Members print and online; £64 Members print and online; $414 Institutions print and online; £345 Institutions print and online; €435 Institutions print and online; $633 Other countries print and online; $345 Institutions America (online only); $59 Students America (print + online); £287 Institutions UK (online only); £287 Institutions UK (print only); £53 Students UK and Europe - non Euro zone (print + online); €362 Institutions Europe (online only); €362 Institutions Europe (print only); €59 Students Europe - Euro zone (print + online). **Online:** Gale. **URL:** http://onlinelibrary.wiley.com/journal/10.1111/(ISSN)1467-9744; http://www.iras.org/zygon.html. **Remarks:** Accepts advertising. **Circ:** (Not Reported).

10602 ■ KCJM-FM - 107.9
c/o Gray Research
Chicago, IL 60611-8468
Free: 800-556-9774
Email: info@jamcentral.com
Format: Blues; Hip Hop. **Ad Rates:** Advertising accepted; rates available upon request. **Mailing address:** PO Box 118468, Chicago, IL 60611-8468.

10603 ■ Tribune Radio Networks
435 N Michigan Ave.
Chicago, IL 60611
Phone: (312)222-3342
Fax: (312)222-4876
Broadcasting firm provides multiple radio and television stations. **Key Personnel:** Peter E. Murphy, Founder. **URL:** http://www.tribunemedia.com.

10604 ■ WBBM-AM - 780
2 Prudential Plz., Ste. 1100
Chicago, IL 60601
Free: 800-784-6397
Format: News. **Networks:** CBS. **Owner:** CBS Radio Inc., 1271 Avenue of the Americas, 44th Fl., New York, NY 10020-1401, Ph: (212)649-9600. **Founded:** 1923. **Operating Hours:** Continuous. **ADI:** Chicago (LaSalle), IL. **Wattage:** 50,000. **Ad Rates:** Advertising accepted; rates available upon request. **URL:** http://www.chicago.cbslocal.com.

10605 ■ WBBM-FM - 96.3
180 N Stetson, Ste. 963
Chicago, IL 60601
Phone: (312)591-9696
Email: info@b96.com
Format: Contemporary Hit Radio (CHR). **Networks:** CBS. **Owner:** CBS Radio Inc., 40 W 57th St., New York, NY 10019, Ph: (212)846-3939, Fax: (212)315-2162. **Founded:** 1941. **Operating Hours:** Continuous. **ADI:** Chicago (LaSalle), IL. **Wattage:** 5,000. **Ad Rates:** Noncommercial. **URL:** http://b96.cbslocal.com.

10606 ■ WBBM-TV - 2
22 W Washington St.
Chicago, IL 60602
Phone: (312)899-2222
Fax: (312)849-7200
Format: Commercial TV. **Networks:** CBS. **Owner:** CBS Corp., 51 W 52nd St., New York, NY 10019-6188, Ph: (212)975-4321, Fax: (212)975-4516, Free: 877-227-0787. **Operating Hours:** Continuous. **ADI:** Chicago (LaSalle), IL. **Ad Rates:** Advertising accepted; rates available upon request. **URL:** http://chicago.cbslocal.com.

10607 ■ WBEQ-FM - 90.7
848 E Grand Ave., Navy Pier
Chicago, IL 60611
Phone: (312)948-4600
Format: Public Radio. **Owner:** WBEZ 91.5, 848 E Grand Ave., Navy Pier, Chicago, IL 60611, Ph: (312)948-4600. **Key Personnel:** Torey Malatia, CEO; Alison Scholly, COO. **Ad Rates:** Noncommercial; underwriting available. **URL:** http://www.wbez.org.

10608 ■ WBEZ-FM - 91.5
848 E Grand Ave.
Chicago, IL 60611
Phone: (312)948-4600
Format: Public Radio; Talk; News; Eclectic. **Networks:** National Public Radio (NPR); BBC World Service; Canadian Broadcasting Corporation (CBC)/Societe Radio-Canada (SRC). **Owner:** WBEZ 91.5, 848 E Grand Ave., Navy Pier, Chicago, IL 60611, Ph: (312)948-4600. **Founded:** 1943. **Operating Hours:** Continuous. **ADI:** Chicago (LaSalle), IL. **Local Programs:** *Here and Now,* Monday Tuesday Wednesday Thursday 1:00 p.m.; *Eight Forty-Eight,* Monday Tuesday Wednesday Thursday Friday 9:00 a.m.; *Worldview,* Monday Tuesday Wednesday Thursday Friday 12:00 p.m. - 1:00 p.m. **Wattage:** 8,300. **Ad Rates:** Noncommercial. **URL:** http://www.wbez.org.

10609 ■ WBGX-AM - 1570
5956 S Michigan Ave.
Chicago, IL 60637
Phone: (773)752-1570
Fax: (773)752-2242
Free: 866-305-1570
Format: Gospel. **Networks:** Independent. **Founded:** 1955. **Formerly:** WBEE-AM. **Operating Hours:** Continuous. **ADI:** Chicago (LaSalle), IL. **Key Personnel:** Tim Gallagher, Owner, President. **Wattage:** 5,000. **Ad Rates:** $20-45 for 30 seconds; $45-95 for 60 seconds. **URL:** http://www.gospel1570.com.

WCEV-AM - See Cicero

10610 ■ WCFS-FM - 105.9
Two Prudential Plz., Ste. 1059
Chicago, IL 60601
Phone: (312)240-7900
Email: fresh1059@cbsradio.com
Format: Adult Contemporary. **Networks:** Independent. **Owner:** CBS Radio Inc., 1271 Avenue of the Americas, 44th Fl., New York, NY 10020-1401, Ph: (212)649-9600. **Formerly:** WCKG-FM. **Operating Hours:** Continuous. **ADI:** Chicago (LaSalle), IL. **Key Personnel:** Mike LeBaron, Contact; Dell Schwartz, Contact. **Wattage:** 4,200. **Ad Rates:** Noncommercial.

10611 ■ WCIU-TV - 26
26 N Halsted St.
Chicago, IL 60661
Phone: (312)705-2600
Format: Commercial TV. **Networks:** Independent. **Owner:** Weigel Broadcasting, 26 N Halsted, Chicago, IL 60661, Ph: (312)705.2600. **Founded:** 1964. **Operating Hours:** Continuous. **ADI:** Chicago (LaSalle), IL. **URL:** http://www.wciu.com.

10612 ■ WCPQ-FM - 99.9
6012 S Pulaski Rd.
Chicago, IL 60629
Phone: (773)767-1000
Fax: (773)767-1100
Format: Talk; Alternative/New Music/Progressive. **Owner:** Newsweb Radio Co., 5475 N Milwaukee Ave., Chicago, IL 60630. **Founded:** 1962. **Formerly:** WBYG-FM; WBUS-FM; WRZA-FM. **Operating Hours:** Continuous. **ADI:** Chicago (LaSalle), IL. **Wattage:** 50,000. **Ad Rates:** Noncommercial. WZCH-FM. **URL:** http://www.chicagoprogressivetalk.com.

10613 ■ WCPT-AM - 820
6012 S Pulaski Rd.
Chicago, IL 60629
Format: Talk. **Operating Hours:** Sunrise-sunset. **Key Personnel:** Jeff Chardell, Dir. of Sales, jchardell@newswebradio.net. **Ad Rates:** Advertising accepted; rates available upon request. **URL:** http://www.chicagoprogressivetalk.com.

10614 ■ WCPY-FM - 92.7
6020 W Higgins Ave.
Chicago, IL 60630
Phone: (773)888-5152
Email: info@polski.fm
Format: Talk; Alternative/New Music/Progressive; Sports; Contemporary Hit Radio (CHR). **Owner:** Newsweb Corp., 1645 W Fullerton Ave., Chicago, IL 60614, Ph: (773)975-0400, Fax: (773)975-6975. **Founded:** 1960. **Formerly:** WCBR-FM; WKIE-FM; WCPT-FM. **Operating Hours:** Continuous. **Key Personnel:** Charles Fernandez, CEO, President; Rich Marston, Gen. Mgr. **Wattage:** 3,000. **URL:** http://polski.fm.

10615 ■ WCRX-FM - 88.1
33 E Congress Pky.
Chicago, IL 60605
Phone: (312)369-8256
Email: clientservices@colum.edu
Format: Alternative/New Music/Progressive. **Owner:** Columbia College Chicago, 600 S Michigan Ave., Chicago, IL 60605, Ph: (312)369-8300, Fax: (312)369-8036. **Founded:** 1996. **ADI:** Chicago (LaSalle), IL. **Ad Rates:** Noncommercial. **URL:** http://www.colum.edu.

Circulation: ★ = AAM; △ or • = BPA; ♦ = CAC; ❑ = VAC; ⊕ = PO Statement; ‡ = Publisher's Report; Boldface figures = sworn; Light figures = estimated.

10616 ■ WDKT-AM - 730
PO Box 067607
Chicago, IL 60661
Format: Urban Contemporary. **Networks:** Independent. **Founded:** 1983. **Operating Hours:** Continuous. **Key Personnel:** Watson McMillan, Gen. Mgr. **Wattage:** 1,000.

10617 ■ WDRV-FM - 97.1
875 N Michigan Ave., Ste. 1510
Chicago, IL 60611
Phone: (312)274-9710
Fax: (312)274-1304
Format: Classic Rock. **Founded:** Sept. 12, 2006. **Key Personnel:** Greg Solk, Sr. VP. **URL:** http://www.wdrv.com.

10618 ■ WFLD-TV - 32
205 N Michigan Ave.
Chicago, IL 60601
Phone: (312)565-5532
Email: news@foxchicago.com
Format: Commercial TV. **Networks:** Fox. **Owner:** Fox Television Stations Inc., 1999 S Bundy Dr., Los Angeles, CA 90025-5235, Ph: (310)584-2000. **Operating Hours:** Continuous. **ADI:** Chicago (LaSalle), IL. **Ad Rates:** Noncommercial. **URL:** http://www.myfoxchicago.com.

10619 ■ WFMT-FM - 98.7
5400 N St. Louis Ave.
Chicago, IL 60625-4698
Phone: (773)279-2000
Format: Classical. **Networks:** Independent. **Owner:** Window to the World Communications, Inc., at above address. **Founded:** 1951. **Operating Hours:** Continuous. **ADI:** Chicago (LaSalle), IL. **Key Personnel:** Reese P. Marcusson, CFO, Exec. VP; Daniel J. Schmidt, CEO, President; Steve Robinson, Exec. VP. **Local Programs:** *Chicago Symphony Orchestra*, Sunday 1:00 p.m.; *The Tuesday Night Opera*, Tuesday 8:00 p.m.; *Best of Studs Terkel*, Friday 11:05 p.m. **Wattage:** 133,000. **Ad Rates:** Advertising accepted; rates available upon request. **URL:** http://www.wfmt.com.

10620 ■ WGBO-TV - 66
541 N Fairbanks Ct., 11th Fl.
Chicago, IL 60611
Phone: (312)494-6492
Networks: Univision. **Owner:** WGBO License Partnership, G.P., at above address. **Founded:** 1981. **Formerly:** WFBN-TV. **Operating Hours:** Continuous. **ADI:** Chicago (LaSalle), IL. **Key Personnel:** Vincent Cordero, Gen. Mgr., VP, vcordero@univision.net; Andrew Wallace, Gen. Sales Mgr., awallace@univision.net. **Wattage:** 5,000,000. **Ad Rates:** for 30 seconds; for 60 seconds.

10621 ■ WGCI-FM - 107.5
233 N Michigan Ave., Ste. 2800
Chicago, IL 60601
Phone: (312)540-2000
Format: Urban Contemporary. **Networks:** Independent. **Owner:** iHeartMedia Inc., 200 E Basse Rd., San Antonio, TX 78209, Ph: (210)832-3314. **Founded:** 1958. **Operating Hours:** Continuous. **ADI:** Chicago (LaSalle), IL. **Key Personnel:** Earl Jones, President; Darlene Park, Gen. Sales Mgr., darlenepark@clearchannel.com; Craig Morton, Sales Mgr., craigmorton@clearchannel.com. **Wattage:** 33,000. **Ad Rates:** Advertising accepted; rates available upon request. **URL:** http://www.wgci.com/main.html.

10622 ■ WGN-AM - 720
435 N Michigan Ave., Ste. 720
Chicago, IL 60611
Phone: (312)222-4700
Email: asktroy@wgnradio.com
Format: News; Information; Sports. **Networks:** ABC; NBC. **Owner:** Tribune Broadcasting, 7700 Westpark Dr., Houston, TX 77063. **Founded:** 1922. **Operating Hours:** Continuous. **ADI:** Chicago (LaSalle), IL. **Key Personnel:** Tom Langmyer, Gen. Mgr., VP; Dave Eanet, Sports Dir. **Local Programs:** *Steve and Johnnie*; *John Williams Show*, Saturday 1:00 p.m. - 3:00 p.m. **Wattage:** 50,000 ERP. **Ad Rates:** Advertising accepted; rates available upon request. **URL:** http://wgnradio.com/on-air.

10623 ■ WGN-TV - 9
2501 W Bradley Pl.
Chicago, IL 60618-4718
Phone: (773)528-2311
Format: Commercial TV. **Networks:** Warner Brothers Studios. **Owner:** The Tribune Media Co., 435 N Michigan Ave., Chicago, IL 60611-4066, Ph: (312)222-9100, Fax: (312)222-4206, Free: 800-874-2863. **Founded:** Apr. 1948. **Operating Hours:** Continuous. **ADI:** Chicago (LaSalle), IL. **Key Personnel:** Greg Caputo, News Dir.; Diana Dionisio, Reg. Dir. **Local Programs:** *Illinois Lottery*; *Live with Regis and Kelly*; *Mega Millions*; *The Vampire Diaries*, Thursday 8:00 p.m.; *Family Guy*, Monday Tuesday Wednesday Thursday Friday Saturday 1:00 a.m. - 1:30 a.m.; *Chicago Cubs/Chicago White Sox/ Chicago Bulls*; *Adelante Chicago*, Saturday 5:30 a.m. **Wattage:** 110 KW. **Ad Rates:** Noncommercial. **URL:** http://www.wgntv.com.

10624 ■ WGRB-AM - 1390
233 N Michigan Ave., 28th Fl.
Chicago, IL 60601
Phone: (312)540-2000
Fax: (312)938-4399
Format: Gospel. **Operating Hours:** Continuous. **ADI:** Chicago (LaSalle), IL. **Wattage:** 5,000 ERP. **Ad Rates:** Noncommercial. **URL:** http://www.inspiration1390.com.

10625 ■ WHPK-FM - 88.5
Reynolds Club
5706 S University Ave.
Chicago, IL 60637
Phone: (773)702-8289
Fax: (773)702-7718
Email: contact@whpk.org
Format: Eclectic. **Owner:** University of Chicago, 5801 S Ellis Ave., Chicago, IL 60637, Ph: (773)702-1234, Fax: (773)834-1095. **Founded:** 1945. **Operating Hours:** Continuous. **Wattage:** 100. **Ad Rates:** Noncommercial. **URL:** http://www.whpk.org.

10626 ■ WIIT-FM - 88.9
3201 S State St.
Chicago, IL 60616
Phone: (312)567-3088
Email: wiit@iit.edu
Format: Alternative/New Music/Progressive; Urban Contemporary; Album-Oriented Rock (AOR). **Networks:** Independent. **Owner:** Illinois Institute of Technology, 3300 S Federal St., Chicago, IL 60616, Ph: (312)567-3000. **Founded:** 1974. **Operating Hours:** 12 p.m-3 a.m.; 100% local. **Wattage:** 100. **Ad Rates:** Noncommercial. **URL:** http://www.radio.iit.edu.

10627 ■ WILV-FM - 91.1
1 Prudential Plz.
130 E Randolph St., Ste. 2780
Chicago, IL 60601
Format: Adult Contemporary. **Founded:** 1947. **Operating Hours:** Continuous. **Wattage:** 7,000. **Ad Rates:** Advertising accepted; rates available upon request.

10628 ■ WJMK-FM - 104.3
180 N Stetson, Ste. 900
Chicago, IL 60601
Phone: (312)870-6400
Format: Oldies. **Networks:** Unistar. **Founded:** 1961. **Operating Hours:** Continuous. **Wattage:** 4,100 ERP. **Ad Rates:** Noncommercial. **URL:** http://www.khitschicago.cbslocal.com.

10629 ■ WKKC-FM - 89.3
6301 S Halsted St.
Chicago, IL 60621
Phone: (773)602-5000
Format: Full Service. **Networks:** Independent. **Owner:** City Colleges of Chicago Kennedy-King College, 6301 S Halsted St., Chicago, IL 60621-2709, Ph: (773)602-5000. **Founded:** 1972. **Operating Hours:** 8 a.m.-midnight; 100% local. **ADI:** Chicago (LaSalle), IL. **Wattage:** 250. **Ad Rates:** $7.50 for 30 seconds; $15 for 60 seconds. **URL:** http://www.ccc.edu/colleges/kennedy.

10630 ■ WKQX-FM - 101.1
222 Merchandise Mart Plz., Ste. 230
Chicago, IL 60654
Phone: (312)527-8348
Fax: (312)527-3620
Format: Alternative/New Music/Progressive. **Networks:** Independent. **Founded:** 1948. **Operating Hours:** Continuous. **Key Personnel:** Ryan Lieberman, Contact, rlieberman@emmischicago.com; Corinna Schroeder, Contact, cschroeder@emmischicago.com. **Wattage:** 8,100. **Ad Rates:** Advertising accepted; rates available upon request. **URL:** http://www.101wkqx.com.

10631 ■ WKSC-FM
233 N Michigan Ave.
Chicago, IL 60601
Phone: (312)540-2000
Format: Contemporary Hit Radio (CHR). **Wattage:** 4,300 ERP. **URL:** http://1035kissfm.iheart.com/.

10632 ■ WLEY-FM - 107.9
150 N Michigan Ave., Ste. 1040
Chicago, IL 60601-7524
Phone: (312)920-9500
Fax: (312)920-9515
Email: info@laley1079.com
Format: Hispanic; Adult Contemporary. **Simulcasts:** WLEY-AM 1080. **Operating Hours:** Continuous. **Wattage:** 21,000. **URL:** http://www.laley1079.com.

10633 ■ WLIT-FM - 93.9
233 N Michigan Ave., No. 2800
Chicago, IL 60601
Phone: (312)540-2000
Email: wlitpromotions@clearchannel.com
Format: Adult Contemporary. **Networks:** Independent. **Founded:** 1956. **Formerly:** WLAK-FM. **Operating Hours:** Continuous; 100% local. **ADI:** Chicago (LaSalle), IL. **Key Personnel:** Melissa Forman, Contact, melissaforman@clearchannel.com; Rick Zurick, Contact, rickzurick@clearchannel.com. **Wattage:** 4,600. **Ad Rates:** $300-800 for 60 seconds. Combined advertising rates available with WGCI-AM & FM; WNUA, WKSC, WVAZ. **URL:** http://www.939myfm.com.

10634 ■ WLS-AM - 890
190 N State St.
Chicago, IL 60601
Phone: (312)984-0890
Email: support@marketron.com
Format: News; Talk. **Networks:** ABC. **Founded:** 1924. **Operating Hours:** Continuous. **ADI:** Chicago (LaSalle), IL. **Key Personnel:** Rush Limbaugh, Contact. **Wattage:** 50,000. **Ad Rates:** Advertising accepted; rates available upon request. WXCD-FM. **URL:** http://www.wlsam.com.

10635 ■ WLS-FM - 94.7
190 N State St.
Chicago, IL 60601
Phone: (312)984-9923
Fax: (312)263-1241
Format: Classic Rock. **Networks:** ABC. **Owner:** Cumulus Media Inc., 3280 Peachtree Rd. NW, Ste. 2300, Atlanta, GA 30305-2455, Ph: (404)949-0700, Fax: (404)949-0740. **Founded:** May 01, 1997. **Formerly:** WKXK-FM; WZZN-FM. **Operating Hours:** Continuous. **ADI:** Chicago (LaSalle), IL. **Key Personnel:** Brian Thomas, Dir. of Operations. **Wattage:** 4,400. **Ad Rates:** Advertising accepted; rates available upon request. **URL:** http://www.947wls.com/.

10636 ■ WLS-TV - 7
190 N State St.
Chicago, IL 60601
Phone: (312)750-7777
Networks: ABC. **Owner:** Disney/ABC Television Group, 77 W 66th St., New York, NY 10023, Ph: (212)456-7777. **Founded:** 1939. **Formerly:** WBKB-TV. **Operating Hours:** Continuous. **ADI:** Chicago (LaSalle), IL. **Wattage:** 55,000 visual; 11,200 audio. **Ad Rates:** Advertising accepted; rates available upon request. **URL:** http://www.abc7chicago.com.

10637 ■ WLUP-FM - 97.9
222 Merchandise Mart Plz., Ste. 230
Chicago, IL 60654
Phone: (312)245-1200
Fax: (312)527-3620
Format: Classic Rock. **Operating Hours:** Continuous. **ADI:** Chicago (LaSalle), IL. **Key Personnel:** Cristina Wilson, Contact. **Wattage:** 4,000 ERP. **Ad Rates:** Advertising accepted; rates available upon request. **URL:** http://www.wlup.com.

10638 ■ WLUW-FM - 88.7
c/o Music Department, 820 N Michigan Ave.
Chicago, IL 60626
Phone: (773)508-8080
Fax: (773)508-8082
Format: Alternative/New Music/Progressive; Reggae; News. **Networks:** ABC; Pacifica. **Owner:** Loyola University Chicago, 1032 W Sheridan Rd., Chicago, IL 60660, Ph: (773)274-3000. **Founded:** 1978. **Operating Hours:** Continuous. **Wattage:** 100. **Ad Rates:** Advertising ac-

cepted; rates available upon request. **URL:** http://wluw.org.

10639 ■ WMAQ-TV - 5
NBC Tower
454 N Columbus Dr.
Chicago, IL 60611-5555
Phone: (312)836-5555
Format: Commercial TV. **Networks:** NBC. **Owner:** National Broadcasting Co. **Operating Hours:** Continuous. **ADI:** Chicago (LaSalle), IL. **Key Personnel:** Larry Wert, Gen. Mgr., President, larry.wert@nbcuni.com; Dianne Hannes, VP of Creative Dev., diane.hannes@nbcuni.com; Camille Edwards, News Dir., camille.edwards@nbcuni.com. **Ad Rates:** Advertising accepted; rates available upon request. **URL:** http://www.nbcchicago.com.

10640 ■ WMBI-AM - 1110
820 N LaSalle Dr.
Chicago, IL 60610
Phone: (312)329-4300
Fax: (312)329-4468
Email: wmbi@moody.edu
Format: Religious. **Networks:** Moody Broadcasting. **Owner:** Moody Bible Institute, 820 N LaSalle Blvd., Chicago, IL 60610, Free: 800-356-6639. **Founded:** 1926. **Operating Hours:** Sunrise-sunset. **ADI:** Chicago (LaSalle), IL. **Key Personnel:** Bruce Everhart, Contact. **Wattage:** 5,000. **Ad Rates:** Noncommercial. **URL:** http://www.moodyradiochicago.fm.

10641 ■ WMBI-FM - 90.1
820 N LaSalle Blvd.
Chicago, IL 60610
Phone: (312)329-4300
Fax: (312)329-4468
Email: wmbi@moody.edu
Format: Religious. **Networks:** Sun Radio; AP. **Owner:** Moody Bible Institute, 820 N LaSalle Blvd., Chicago, IL 60610, Free: 800-356-6639. **Founded:** 1926. **Operating Hours:** Continuous. **Key Personnel:** Sam Beiruti, Contact; John Hayden, Contact. **Wattage:** 100,000. **Ad Rates:** Noncommercial. **URL:** http://www.moodyradiochicago.fm.

10642 ■ WMEU-TV - 48
26 N Halsted St.
Chicago, IL 60661
Phone: (312)705-2600
Owner: Weigel Broadcasting, 26 N Halsted, Chicago, IL 60661, Ph: (312)705.2600. **ADI:** Chicago (LaSalle), IL. **Ad Rates:** Advertising accepted; rates available upon request. **URL:** http://metvnetwork.com.

10643 ■ WNTD-AM - 950
541 N Fairbanks Ct.
Chicago, IL 60611
Format: Hispanic. **Owner:** Multicultural Radio Broadcasting Inc., 27 William St., 11th Fl., New York, NY 10005, Ph: (212)966-1059, Fax: (212)966-9580.

10644 ■ WNUA-FM - 95.5
233 N Michigan Ave., Ste. 2800
Chicago, IL 60601
Phone: (312)540-2000
Format: Hispanic. **Networks:** Independent. **Founded:** 1959. **Formerly:** WDHF-FM; WRXR-FM; WMET-FM. **Operating Hours:** Continuous; 100% local. **ADI:** Chicago (LaSalle), IL. **Wattage:** 8,300. **Ad Rates:** Noncommercial. **URL:** http://www.big955chicago.com.

10645 ■ WNVR-AM - 1030
3656 W Belmont Ave.
Chicago, IL 60618
Format: Ethnic. **Owner:** Polnet Communications, Ltd., at above address. **Founded:** 1988. **Operating Hours:** Continuous. **Wattage:** 5,400. **Ad Rates:** Noncommercial. International Network. **URL:** http://www.polskieradio.com/ludzik.aspx?id=15.

10646 ■ WOJO-FM - 105.1
625 N Michigan Ave., Ste. 300
Chicago, IL 60611-3110
Phone: (312)981-1800
Fax: (312)981-1820
Format: Hispanic. **Networks:** Independent. **Owner:** Univision Radio Inc., 3102 Oak Lawn Ave., Ste. 215, Dallas, TX 75219-4259, Ph: (214)525-7700, Fax: (214)525-7750. **Founded:** 1946. **Operating Hours:** Continuous. **ADI:** Chicago (LaSalle), IL. **Key Personnel:** Joe Uva, CEO; Ray Rodriguez, COO, President; Andrew W. Hobson, CFO, Sr. Exec. VP; Douglas C. Kranwinkle, Exec. VP, Gen. Counsel. **Wattage:** 6,000. **Ad Rates:** $78-114 for 30 seconds; $97-142 for 60 seconds.

10647 ■ WOW!
825 E 99th St.
Chicago, IL 60628
Free: 866-496-9669
Key Personnel: Colleen Abdoulah, Chmn. of the Bd.; Steven Cochran, CEO, President. **Cities Served:** Chicagoland; 128 channels. **URL:** http://www.wowway.com.

10648 ■ WPPN-FM - 106.7
625 N Michigan, Ste. 300
Chicago, IL 60611
Phone: (312)981-1800
Format: Hispanic. **Owner:** Univision Radio Inc., 3102 Oak Lawn Ave., Ste. 215, Dallas, TX 75219-4259, Ph: (214)525-7700, Fax: (214)525-7750. **Operating Hours:** Continuous. **Key Personnel:** Joe Uva, CEO, President. **Wattage:** 50,000. **Ad Rates:** Advertising accepted; rates available upon request.

10649 ■ WRKL-AM - 910
3656 W Belmont Ave.
Chicago, IL 60618
Phone: (773)588-6300
Fax: (773)267-4913
Email: radiomarketing@polskieradio.com
Format: Talk; Full Service; News. **Owner:** Polnet Communications Ltd., 3656 W Blemont Ave., Chicago, IL 60618, Ph: (773)588-6300, Fax: (773)267-4913. **Founded:** 1964. **Formerly:** Polskie Radio New York 910 am. **Operating Hours:** Continuous. **ADI:** New York, NY. **Key Personnel:** Marcin Filipowski, Mktg. Mgr. **Wattage:** 1,000. **Ad Rates:** Advertising accepted; rates available upon request. **URL:** http://www.polskieradio.com.

10650 ■ WRTE-FM
848 E Grand Ave.
Chicago, IL 60611-3248
Email: info@radioarte.org
Format: Talk. **Wattage:** 006 ERP.

10651 ■ WSBC-AM - 1240
5625 N Milwaukee Ave.
Chicago, IL 60646
Phone: (773)792-1121
Fax: (773)792-2904
Format: Religious; Ethnic; News; Talk. **Simulcasts:** WCFJ 1470am Chicago Heights. **Owner:** Newsweb Radio Co., 5475 N Milwaukee Ave., Chicago, IL 60630. **Founded:** 1925. **Formerly:** WCRW 1926-1996/WEDC 1926-1997. **ADI:** Chicago (LaSalle), IL. **Key Personnel:** Roy J. Bellavia, Contact. **Wattage:** 1,000 KW. **Ad Rates:** Noncommercial. $12.80 for 30 seconds; $26 for 60 seconds. **URL:** http://accessradiochicago.com.

10652 ■ WSCR-AM - 670
180 N Stetson Ave., Ste. 1250
Chicago, IL 60601
Phone: (312)644-6767
Email: comments@670thescore.com
Format: Sports; News. **Networks:** CBS; CNN Radio. **Owner:** CBS Radio Inc., 1271 Avenue of the Americas, 44th Fl., New York, NY 10020-1401, Ph: (212)649-9600. **Founded:** 1992. **Formerly:** WMAQ-AM. **Operating Hours:** Continuous. **ADI:** Chicago (LaSalle), IL. **Key Personnel:** Rick Starr, Contact. **Wattage:** 50,000. **Ad Rates:** Advertising accepted; rates available upon request. **URL:** http://chicago.cbslocal.com.

10653 ■ WSNS-TV - 44
454 N Columbus Dr.
Chicago, IL 60611
Phone: (312)836-3110
Format: Commercial TV. **Networks:** Telemundo. **Founded:** 1970. **Operating Hours:** 8 a.m.-1 a.m. **ADI:** Chicago (LaSalle), IL. **URL:** http://www.telemundochicago.com.

10654 ■ WTAQ-AM - 1300
3656 W Belmont Ave.
Chicago, IL 60618
Phone: (773)588-8881
Format: News; Talk; Contemporary Christian. **Simulcasts:** WNVR-AM. **Founded:** 1985. **Operating Hours:** Continuous. **ADI:** Chicago (LaSalle), IL. **Key Personnel:** Mary McEvilly-Hernandez, Gen. Mgr.; Leon Martinez, News Dir.; Jose Alanis, Dir. of Programs; Maria Colunga, Promotions Mgr.; Nora Dominguez, Traffic Mgr. **Wattage:** 4,500. **Ad Rates:** $78 for 30 seconds; $92 for 60 seconds. **URL:** http://www.polskieradio.com.

10655 ■ WTMX-FM - 101.9
1 Prudential Plz.
130 E Randolph St., Ste. 2700
Chicago, IL 60601
Phone: (312)946-1019
Fax: (312)946-0202
Format: Adult Contemporary. **Networks:** Independent. **Owner:** Bonneville International Corp., 55 North 300 West, Salt Lake City, UT 84101-3502, Ph: (801)575-7500. **Founded:** 1960. **Formerly:** WCLR-FM. **Operating Hours:** Continuous; 100% local. **ADI:** Chicago (LaSalle), IL. **Key Personnel:** Nikki Chuminatto, Prog. Dir., nchuminatto@wtmx.com; Mary Ellen Kachinske, Dir. of Mktg., mek@wtmx.com; Craig Volpe, VP of Fin., cvolpe@hubbardradio.com; Sara McMurray, Gen. Mgr., smcmurray@wtmx.com; Kent Lewin, Gen. Mgr., klewin@hubbardradio.com. **Wattage:** 4,200 ERP. **Ad Rates:** Noncommercial. **URL:** http://www.wtmx.com.

10656 ■ WTTW-TV - 11
5400 N St. Louis Ave.
Chicago, IL 60625-4698
Phone: (773)583-5000
Fax: (773)509-5303
Email: wttwadsales@wttw.com
Format: Public TV. **Networks:** Public Broadcasting Service (PBS); CBS. **Owner:** Window to the World Communications, Inc., at above address. **Operating Hours:** Continuous. **ADI:** Chicago (LaSalle), IL. **Key Personnel:** Daniel J. Schmidt, CEO, President. **Wattage:** 300,000 ERP H. **Ad Rates:** Advertising accepted; rates available upon request. **URL:** http://www.wttw.com.

10657 ■ WUSN-FM - 99.5
Two Prudential Plz., Ste. 1000
Chicago, IL 60601
Phone: (312)649-0099
Format: Country. **Networks:** Independent. **Owner:** CBS Radio Inc., 40 W 57th St., New York, NY 10019, Ph: (212)846-3939, Fax: (212)315-2162. **Founded:** 1940. **Operating Hours:** Continuous. **ADI:** Chicago (LaSalle), IL. **Key Personnel:** Lisa Dent, Contact; Lisa Dent, Contact. **Wattage:** 8,300. **Ad Rates:** Advertising accepted; rates available upon request. **URL:** http://www.us995.cbslocal.com.

10658 ■ WVAZ-FM - 102.7
233 N Michigan Ave., Ste. 2700
Chicago, IL 60601
Phone: (312)540-2000
Format: Blues; Urban Contemporary. **Networks:** ABC. **Owner:** iHeartMedia Inc., 200 E Basse Rd., San Antonio, TX 78209, Ph: (210)832-3314. **Founded:** 1950. **Formerly:** WBMX-FM. **Operating Hours:** Continuous. **ADI:** Chicago (LaSalle), IL. **Key Personnel:** Earl Jones, Mktg. Mgr., President; Derrick Brown, Dir. of Programs, derrick@v103.com; Echo Robinson, Promotions Dir., echorobinson@clearchannel.com. **Wattage:** 6,000 ERP. **Ad Rates:** Noncommercial. **URL:** http://www.v103.com.

10659 ■ WVIV-FM - 103.1
625 N Michigan Ave., Ste. 300
Chicago, IL 60611
Phone: (312)981-1800
Format: News; Sports. **Simulcasts:** 93.5. **Owner:** Univision Radio Inc., 3102 Oak Lawn Ave., Ste. 215, Dallas, TX 75219-4259, Ph: (214)525-7700, Fax: (214)525-7750. **Wattage:** 6,000. **Ad Rates:** Advertising accepted; rates available upon request.

10660 ■ WVIX-FM - 93.5
625 N Michigan Ave., Ste. 300
Chicago, IL 60611
Phone: (312)981-1800
Format: Hispanic. **Owner:** Univision Radio Inc., 3102 Oak Lawn Ave., Ste. 215, Dallas, TX 75219-4259, Ph: (214)525-7700, Fax: (214)525-7750. **Key Personnel:** Jerry Ryan, Gen. Mgr.

10661 ■ WVON-AM - 1690
1000 E 87th St.
Chicago, IL 60619-6397
Free: 877-591-1690
Format: Talk; Oldies; Blues. **Networks:** Mutual Broadcasting System; American Urban Radio; ABC. **Owner:** Midway Broadcasting Corp., 1000 E 87th St., Chicago,

Circulation: ★ = AAM; △ or • = BPA; ♦ = CAC; ❑ = VAC; ⊕ = PO Statement; ‡ = Publisher's Report; Boldface figures = sworn; Light figures = estimated.

IL 60619, Ph: (773)721-2271. **Founded:** 1979. **Formerly**: WXOL-AM. **Operating Hours**: 10 p.m.-1 p.m. **ADI**: Chicago (LaSalle), IL. **Key Personnel:** Pervis Spann, Contact. **Local Programs**: *The Al Sharpton Show*, Monday Tuesday Wednesday Thursday Friday 12:00 p.m. - 3:00 p.m. **Wattage**: 1,000. **Ad Rates:** Advertising accepted; rates available upon request; Noncommercial. **URL:** http://www.wvon.com.

10662 ■ WWDV-FM - 96.9
875 N Michigan Ave., Ste. 1510
Chicago, IL 60611
Phone: (312)274-9710
Fax: (312)274-1304
Format: Classic Rock. **Owner:** Bonneville International Corp., 55 North 300 West, Salt Lake City, UT 84101-3502, Ph: (801)575-7500. **Operating Hours**: Continuous. **Key Personnel:** Jerry Schnacke, Gen. Mgr., VP; Greg Solk, VP of Operations, gsolk@wdrv.com; Patty Martin, Dir. of Programs, pmartin@wdrv.com; Drew Medland, Sales Mgr. **Ad Rates:** Advertising accepted; rates available upon request. **URL:** http://www.wdrv.com/home.php.

10663 ■ WWME-TV - 23
26 N Halsted St.
Chicago, IL 60661
Phone: (312)705-2600
Email: feedback-metv@metvnetwork.com
Owner: Weigel Broadcasting, 26 N Halsted, Chicago, IL 60661, Ph: (312)705.2600. **ADI**: Chicago (LaSalle), IL. **Ad Rates:** Advertising accepted; rates available upon request. **URL:** http://metvnetwork.com.

10664 ■ WXAV-FM - 88.3
3700 W 103rd St.
Chicago, IL 60655
Phone: (773)298-3376
Fax: (773)298-3381
Email: wxavnews@gmail.com
Format: Classic Rock. **Owner:** St. Xavier University, 3700 W 103rd St., Chicago, IL 60655, Ph: (773)298-3000, Free: 844-GOTO-SXU. **Founded:** Oct. 1991. **Operating Hours**: 10 a.m.-10 p.m. **Key Personnel:** Peter Kreten, Div. Dir., pkreten@sxu.edu; Sean Anderson, Music Dir. **Wattage**: 150. **Ad Rates:** Noncommercial. **URL:** http://www.wxav.com.

10665 ■ WXEX-FM - 107.9
150 N Michigan Ave., No. 1040
Chicago, IL 60601
Phone: (312)920-9500
Fax: (312)920-9515
Format: Public Radio. **Networks:** Independent. **Owner:** Spanish Broadcasting System Inc., Pablo Raul Alarcon Media Ctr., 7007 NW 77th Ave., Miami, FL 33166, Ph: (305)441-6901, Fax: (305)883-3375. **Founded:** July 04, 1997. **Formerly**: WYSY. **Operating Hours**: Continuous; 100% local. **ADI**: Chicago (LaSalle), IL. **Key Personnel:** Mario Paez, Gen. Mgr., mpaez@sbschicago.com; Margarita Vazquez, Dir. of Programs. **Wattage**: 50,000 ERP. **Ad Rates:** $250-500 for 60 seconds. **URL:** http://www.laley1079.com.

10666 ■ WXRT-FM - 93.1
455 N CityFront Plz., 6th Fl.
Chicago, IL 60611
Phone: (312)240-9978
Fax: (312)240-7973
Email: xrtcomments@wxrt.com
Format: Adult Album Alternative. **Networks:** CBS. **Owner:** CBS Radio Inc., 1271 Avenue of the Americas, 44th Fl., New York, NY 10020-1401, Ph: (212)649-9600. **Founded:** 1959. **Operating Hours**: Continuous. **Key Personnel:** Norm Winer, Prog. Dir. **Wattage**: 50,000. **Ad Rates:** Advertising accepted; rates available upon request. **URL:** http://wxrt.cbslocal.com.

10667 ■ WYCC-TV - 20
6258 S Union Ave.
Chicago, IL 60621
Phone: (773)905-1519
Fax: (773)783-2906
Free: 888-993-9922
Email: info@wycc.org
Format: Public TV. **Networks:** Public Broadcasting Service (PBS). **Owner:** City Colleges of Chicago, 226 W Jackson, Chicago, IL 60606, Ph: (312)553-2500. **Founded:** 1983. **Operating Hours**: 6 a.m.-midnight. **ADI**: Chicago (LaSalle), IL. **Key Personnel:** Paul Buckner, Station Mgr. **Local Programs**: *Tavis Smiley*; *RT News*, Sunday Monday Tuesday Wednesday Thursday Friday Saturday 4:00 p.m. - 4:30 p.m. **URL:** http://www.wycc.org.

10668 ■ WZRD-FM - 88.3
5500 N St. Louis Ave.
Chicago, IL 60625
Phone: (773)442-4578
Fax: (773)442-4586
Email: info@wzrdchicago.org
Format: Eclectic. **Networks:** Pacifica. **Owner:** Northeastern Illinois University, 5500 N St. Louis Ave., Chicago, IL 60625-4699, Ph: (773)583-4050. **Founded:** 1972. **Operating Hours**: Variable. **Wattage**: 100. **Ad Rates:** Noncommercial. **URL:** http://www.wzrdchicago.org.

CHICAGO HEIGHTS

Cook Co. Cook Co. (NE). 28 m S of Chicago. Manufactures steel, glass containers, railroad equipment, textiles, boxes, castings, school and steel furniture, tile accessories, asphalt products, road materials, chemicals, fertilizer; food processing plant; foundries. Truck farms.

10669 ■ Prairie State College Student Review
Prairie State College
202 S Halsted St.
Chicago Heights, IL 60411
Phone: (708)709-3500
Collegiate newspaper. **Freq:** Monthly. **Print Method:** Offset. **Cols./Page:** 4. **Col. Width:** 28 nonpareils. **Col. Depth:** 196 agate lines. **Key Personnel:** Annaliese Avery, Editor-in-Chief. **URL:** http://prairiestate.edu/student-life/student-clubs/the-student-review/index.aspx. **Ad Rates:** BW $175. **Remarks:** Accepts advertising. **Circ:** (Not Reported).

CHILLICOTHE

Peoria Co. Peoria Co. (NC). 5 m M of Rome.

10670 ■ Chillicothe Times-Bulletin
GateHouse Media Inc.
300 W Pine, Ste. 4
Chillicothe, IL 61523
Phone: (309)274-2185
Fax: (309)686-3101
Publication E-mail: ctb@timestoday.com
Community newspaper. **Freq:** Weekly (Wed.). **Print Method:** Offset. **Trim Size:** 12 1/2 x 21 1/2. **Cols./Page:** 6. **Col. Width:** 11 picas. **Col. Depth:** 21 1/2 inches. **Key Personnel:** Jeanette Kendall, Executive Editor; Marianne Gillespie, Editor. **URL:** http://www.chillicothetimesbulletin.com; http://www.gatehousemedia.com/section/publications. **Ad Rates:** BW $2,515.50; 4C $2,751.50; PCI $19.50. **Remarks:** Accepts advertising. **Circ:** Paid 1871.

CICERO

Cook Co Cook Co. Cook Co. (EC). Suburb of Chicago. Copper products, Industry, Rubber. Cook Co.

10671 ■ Lawndale News
Lawndale News
5533 W 25th St.
Cicero, IL 60804
Phone: (708)656-6400
Fax: (708)656-2433
Publisher's E-mail: subscribe@lawndalenews.com
Newspaper. **Freq:** Semiweekly Thursday and Sunday. **Print Method:** Offset. Uses mats. **Trim Size:** 11 x 14. **Cols./Page:** 6. **Col. Width:** 19 nonpareils. **Col. Depth:** 210 agate lines. **Key Personnel:** Lynda Nardini, Publisher; Gary Miller, Manager, Sales. **Remarks:** Accepts advertising. **Circ:** (Not Reported).

10672 ■ Tele Guia de Chicago
Tele Guia Publications
3116 S Austin Blvd.
Cicero, IL 60804
Phone: (708)656-6666
Publisher's E-mail: info@teleguia.us
Community newspaper (Spanish). **Freq:** Weekly (Thurs.). **Print Method:** Web offset. **Trim Size:** 8 1/2 x 11. **Cols./Page:** 5. **Col. Width:** 1 1/2 inches. **Col. Depth:** 10 inches. **Key Personnel:** Rose Montes, Publisher, Vice President; Zeke Montes, President; Martha Saldana, Editor; Lilia Calderon, Office Manager. **Alt. Formats:** PDF. **Ad Rates:** BW $11100; 4C $1400. **Remarks:** Accepts advertising. **Circ:** ‡29,796.

10673 ■ WCEV-AM - 1450
5356 W Belmont Ave.
Chicago, IL 60641-4192
Phone: (773)282-6700
Email: wcev@wcev1450.com
Format: Gospel. **Owner:** Migala Communications Corp., 5356 W Belmont Ave., Chicago, IL 60641-4192. **Founded:** 1979. **Operating Hours**: 1:00 p.m. - 10:00 p.m. Monday - Friday; 1:00 p.m. - 8:30 p.m. Saturday; 5:00 a.m. - 10:00 p.m. Sunday. **Key Personnel:** Lucyna Migala, Prog. Dir.; George Migala, Gen. Mgr.; Barbara Holtzinger, Bus. Mgr. **Local Programs**: *Chet Schafer Show*, Sunday 1:00 p.m. - 1:55 p.m.; *Voice of American Czestochowa*, Wednesday 8:00 p.m. - 8:15 p.m.; *Mosaic*, Monday Friday Sunday 8:00 p.m. - 8:25 p.m. 5:35 p.m. - 6:00 p.m.; *Senior Notes*, Saturday Sunday 3:00 p.m. - 3:05 p.m. 9:00 p.m. - 9:05 p.m. **Wattage**: 1,000. **Ad Rates:** Advertising accepted; rates available upon request. **URL:** http://www.wcev1450.com.

WKAM-AM - See Goshen, IN

CISSNA PARK

Iroquois Co. Iroquois Co. (E). 40 m S of Kankakee. Silo, drain tile, building block factories; light industry. Grain, stock, dairy farms.

10674 ■ Park TV & Electronics Inc.
205 E Fire Ln.
Cissna Park, IL 60924
Phone: (815)457-2659
Free: 800-825-3882
URL: http://www.parktvcable.com.

CLINTON

De Witt Co. De Witt Co. (C). 22 m N of Decatur. Nuclear power plant. Manufactures copper tubing, copper kitchen utensils, boxes, business forms, gasoline storage tanks, ceramic, lamps, metal buildings. Grain farms.

10675 ■ Clinton Daily Journal
Clinton Daily Journal
111 S Monroe
Clinton, IL 61727
Phone: (217)935-3171
Fax: (217)935-6086
General newspaper. **Freq:** Daily (eve.). **Print Method:** Offset. **Cols./Page:** 8. **Col. Width:** 9 picas. **Col. Depth:** 300 agate lines. **Key Personnel:** Gordon Woods, Editor, phone: (217)935-3171. **Subscription Rates:** $60.95 annual value plan, in area, auto pay; $63.85 annual value plan, in area, manual pay; $81.85 Out of area annual value plan, auto pay; $85.70 Out of area annual value plan, manual pay. **URL:** http://www.clintondailyjournal.com/v2_main_page.php. **Remarks:** Accepts advertising. **Circ:** (Not Reported).

10676 ■ WHOW-AM - 1520
2980 US Hwy. 51
Clinton, IL 61727
Phone: (217)935-9590
Fax: (217)935-9909
Email: whownews@randyradio.com
Format: Talk; News. **Simulcasts:** WHOW-FM. **Founded:** 1947. **Operating Hours**: Sunrise-sunset; 1% network, 99% local. **Wattage**: 5,000. **Ad Rates:** $10-12 for 30 seconds; $15-16.40 for 60 seconds. $12 for 30 seconds; $16.40 for 60 seconds; Combined advertising rates available with WHOW-FM. **Mailing address:** PO Box 497, Clinton, IL 61727-0497. **URL:** http://www.dewittdailynews.com.

10677 ■ WHOW-FM - 95.9
2980 US Hwy. 51
Clinton, IL 61727-0497
Phone: (217)935-9590
Fax: (217)935-9909
Email: whow@randyradio.com
Format: Adult Contemporary. **Simulcasts:** WHOW-AM. **Founded:** 1947. **Operating Hours**: 6 a.m.-midnight; 1% network, 99% local. **Wattage**: 3,000. **Ad Rates:** $10-12 for 30 seconds; $15-16.40 for 60 seconds. $12 for 30 seconds; $16.40 for 60 seconds; Combined advertising rates available with WHOW-AM. **Mailing address:** PO Box 497, Clinton, IL 61727-0497. **URL:** http://www.dewittdailynews.com.

COAL CITY

Grundy Co. Grundy Co. (NE). 26 m SW of Joliet. Manufactures clothing, aerosol canned and chemical products, furniture. Coal mine and clay pits. Grain farms.

10678 ■ The Braidwood Journal
The Free Press Newspapers
271 S Broadway
Coal City, IL 60416
Newspaper. **Freq:** Weekly (Wed.). **Print Method:** Offset. **Cols./Page:** 8. **Col. Width:** 21 nonpareils. **Col. Depth:** 294 agate lines. **USPS:** 550-940. **Subscription Rates:** $39 Individuals; $46 Out of area; $51 Out of state; $37 Individuals senior citizen. **URL:** http://freepressnewspapers.com/main.asp?SectionID=13. **Ad Rates:** BW $487.20; SAU $3.30; PCI $2.90. **Remarks:** Accepts advertising. **Circ:** 1,300.

COLLINSVILLE

St. Clair Co. Madison Co. (SW). 12 m NE of St. Louis, Mo. Race track, tourism. Cahokia mounds world heritage site. Manufactures food products, dresses and aprons. Agriculture.

10679 ■ Filtration News
Eagle Publications Inc.
2 Eastport Plaza Dr.
Collinsville, IL 62234-6109
Phone: (618)345-5400
Fax: (618)345-5474
Publisher's E-mail: info@hometownphonebook.com
Magazine focusing on industrial particulate removal. **Freq:** Bimonthly. **Print Method:** Web offset. **Trim Size:** 8 1/2 x 11. **Cols./Page:** 2 and 3. **Col. Width:** 38 and 25 nonpareils. **Col. Depth:** 98 agate lines. **Key Personnel:** Ken Norberg, Editor-in-Chief. **ISSN:** 1078--4136 (print). **USPS:** 025-412. **Subscription Rates:** $65 U.S., Canada, and Mexico; $125 Other countries. **URL:** http://www.filtnews.com. **Ad Rates:** BW $2805; 4C $3850. **Remarks:** Accepts advertising. **Circ:** Controlled ‡12000.

COUNTRY CLUB HILLS

Cook Co. Cook Co. (NE). 3 m S of Oak Forest. Residential.

10680 ■ International Journal of Choice Theory and Reality Therapy
William Glasser Institute
4053 W 183rd St., No. 2666
Country Club Hills, IL 60478
Phone: (708)957-6048
Freq: Semiannual. **ISSN:** 2168--4782 (print); **EISSN:** 1099--7717 (electronic). **Subscription Rates:** Included in membership. **URL:** http://www.mwsu.edu/academics/education/journalreality/index. **Formerly**: International Journal of Reality Therapy. **Remarks:** Advertising not accepted. **Circ:** (Not Reported).

CREST HILL

10681 ■ WCCQ-FM - 98.3
2410-B Caton Farm Rd.
Crest Hill, IL 60435
Phone: (815)556-0100
Fax: (815)577-9231
Free: 888-254-9830
Email: email@wccq.com
Format: Country; Contemporary Country. **Networks:** Satellite Music Network. **Owner:** Three Eagles Communications, 3800 Cornhusker Hwy., Lincoln, NE 68504, Ph: (402)466-1234, Fax: (402)467-4095. **Founded:** 1976. **Operating Hours:** Continuous; 60% network, 40% local. **Key Personnel:** Doug Boyd, Sales Mgr.; Brian Foster, Gen. Mgr.; Roy Gregory, Dir. of Programs, roygregory@nextmediachicago.com; Dan Waddick, Promotions Dir., dwaddick@nextmediachicago.com; Mike Dinger, Engineer. **Wattage:** 3,000. **Ad Rates:** Advertising accepted; rates available upon request. **URL:** http://www.wccq.com.

10682 ■ WJOL-AM - 1340
2410-B Caton Farm Rd.
Crest Hill, IL 60403
Phone: (815)556-0100
Fax: (815)577-9231
Format: News; Information; Talk; Sports. **Networks:** ABC. **Owner:** NextMedia, 6312 S Fiddlers Green Cir., Ste. 205 E, Greenwood Village, CO 80111, Ph: (303)694-9118, Fax: (303)694-4940. **Founded:** 1924. **Operating Hours:** Sunrise - Sunset. **Key Personnel:** Dan Waddick, Promotions Dir., dan.waddick@alphamediausa.com; Doug Boyd, Sales Mgr. **Local Programs:** *The Outsiders Sports Show*, Saturday 9:00 a.m. - 12:00 p.m. **Wattage:** 1,000 Day. **Ad Rates:** Advertising accepted; rates available upon request. Combined advertising rates available with WJTW-FM. **URL:** http://www.wjol.com.

10683 ■ WRXQ-FM - 100.7
2410-B Caton Farm Rd.
Crest Hill, IL 60435
Phone: (815)556-0100
Fax: (815)577-9231
Format: Classic Rock. **Owner:** NextMedia, 6312 S Fiddlers Green Cir., Ste. 205 E, Greenwood Village, CO 80111, Ph: (303)694-9118, Fax: (303)694-4940. **Operating Hours:** Continuous. **Key Personnel:** Dan Waddick, Promotions Dir.; Mark Zander, Contact; Doug Boyd, Gen. Sales Mgr.; Brian Foster, Gen. Mgr. **Ad Rates:** Advertising accepted; rates available upon request. **URL:** http://www.wrxq.com.

10684 ■ WSSR-FM - 96.7
2410-B Caton Farm Rd.
Crest Hill, IL 60435
Phone: (815)556-0100
Fax: (815)577-9231
Format: Adult Contemporary. **Owner:** NextMedia, 6312 S Fiddlers Green Cir., Ste. 205 E, Greenwood Village, CO 80111, Ph: (303)694-9118, Fax: (303)694-4940. **Operating Hours:** Continuous. **Key Personnel:** Doug Boyd, Gen. Sales Mgr.; Dan Waddick, Promotions Dir., dwaddick@nextmediachicago.com; Carol McGowan, Comm. Aff. Dir.; Scott Childers, Div. Dir. **Ad Rates:** Advertising accepted; rates available upon request. **URL:** http://www.star967.net.

CRESTWOOD

10685 ■ Journal of Electrology
American Electrology Association
c/o Pearl G. Warner, President
4711 Midlothian Tpke. 13
Crestwood, IL 60445
Phone: (708)293-1400
Fax: (708)293-1405
Freq: Semiannual. **Subscription Rates:** $40 Nonmembers; Included in membership. **URL:** http://professionals.electrology.com/continuing-education/home-study-programs.html. **Remarks:** Accepts advertising. **Circ:** (Not Reported).

CREVE COEUR

Tazewell Co. Tazewell Co. (NW).

10686 ■ WHOI-TV - 19
500 N Stewart St.
Creve Coeur, IL 61610
Phone: (309)698-1919
Fax: (309)698-1910
Free: 800-348-9282
Format: Commercial TV. **Networks:** ABC. **Owner:** Sinclair Broadcast Group Inc., 10706 Beaver Dam Rd., Hunt Valley, MD 21030, Ph: (410)568-1500, Fax: (410)568-1533. **Founded:** 1953. **Formerly**: WRAU-TV. **Operating Hours**: 5 a.m.-2 a.m. **ADI**: Peoria-Bloomington, IL. **Key Personnel:** Leo Henning, Gen. Mgr., Regional VP, lhenning@whoitv.com; Tom Stemmler, Operations Mgr., tstemmler@whoitv.com; Jolie Alois, News Dir., jalois@whoitv.com; Valerie Bricka, Sales Mgr., vbricka@whoitv.com. **Ad Rates:** Noncommercial. **URL:** http://www.cinewsnow.com.

CRYSTAL LAKE

McHenry Co. McHenry Co. (NE). 16 m N of Elgin. Manufactures twist drills, industrial laundry dryers, ceramic kelm, tools, concrete, switches, metal products, auto parts. Tool and dies; steel treating; engraving.

10687 ■ WAIT-AM - 850
8800 Rte. 14
Crystal Lake, IL 60012
Phone: (815)459-7000
Fax: (815)459-7027
Free: 888-755-9248
Owner: Newsweb Corp., at above address. **Founded:** 1965. **Wattage**: 2,500 Daytime. **Ad Rates:** Accepts Advertising. **URL:** http://www.relevantradio.com/netcommunity.

10688 ■ WWYW-FM - 103.9
8800 US Hwy. 14
Crystal Lake, IL 60012
Phone: (972)458-9300
Format: Oldies. **Operating Hours**: Continuous. **Key Personnel:** Shawn Powers, Contact; Jeff Davis, Contact; Stew Cohen, News Dir; Jim Shea, Contact; Shawn Powers, Contact; Jeff James, Contact; Jeff Davis, Contact; Molly Summy, Contact; Libby Collins, Contact. **Ad Rates:** Advertising accepted; rates available upon request. **URL:** http://www.rockthefox.com.

10689 ■ WZSR-FM - 105.5
8800 US Highway 14
Crystal Lake, IL 60012
Phone: (815)459-7000
Fax: (815)459-7027
Free: 800-861-1055
Format: Adult Contemporary. **Networks:** Westwood One Radio. **Founded:** 1974. **Formerly**: WAIT-FM. **Operating Hours**: Continuous. **Key Personnel:** Stew Cohen, News Dir., stew@star105.com; Steve Cherry, Contact, stevecherry@star105.com. **Wattage**: 3,000. **Ad Rates:** Advertising accepted; rates available upon request. **URL:** http://www.star105.com.

CUBA

Fulton Co. Fulton Co. (W). 38 m SW of Peoria. Coal mines. Stock and grain farms.

10690 ■ Banner Sheep Magazine
Banner Publications Inc.
PO Box 500
Cuba, IL 61427-0500
Phone: (309)785-5058
Fax: (309)785-5050
Publication E-mail: banner@sybertech.net
Magazine covering sheep breeding programs. **Freq:** 9/year. **Trim Size:** 8 1/2 x 11. **Cols./Page:** 3. **Col. Width:** 14 picas. **Col. Depth:** 10 inches. **Key Personnel:** Greg Deakin, Publisher, Editor. **ISSN:** 0194--7230 (print). **Subscription Rates:** $25 Individuals; $45 Two years; $60 Canada and Mexico. **URL:** http://www.bannersheepmagazine.com. **Ad Rates:** BW $495; 4C $860; PCI $23. **Remarks:** Accepts advertising. **Circ:** ‡3500.

DANVILLE

Vermilion Co. Vermilion Co. (E). 125 m S of Chicago. Manufactures artificial decorations, awnings, boxes, cartons, candy, canvas goods, casket hardware, castings, concrete blocks, fertilizer, fireworks, machine shop supplies, safety wearing apparel, uniforms, lift trucks, core binders, jackets, contract fillers, aerosol cans, cellulose casings, air conditioning equipment, diesel engine crank shaft forgings.

10691 ■ Commercial-News
Gannett Company Inc.
17 W North St.
Danville, IL 61832
Phone: (217)446-1000
Dedicated to property management. **Freq:** Daily (eve.), Sat. and Sun. (morn.). **Print Method:** Offset. **Trim Size:** 13 1/2 x 22 3/4. **Cols./Page:** 6. **Col. Width:** 22 nonpareils. **Col. Depth:** 301 agate lines. **Key Personnel:** Garry Swaney, Director, Production; Chris Voccio, Publisher; Larry Smith, Editor; Paula Campbell, Business Manager; Kathy Robinson, Manager, Circulation. **USPS:** 048-680. **URL:** http://www.commercial-news.com. **Remarks:** Advertising accepted; rates available upon request. **Circ:** (Not Reported).

10692 ■ Heritage of Vermilion County
Vermilion County Museum Society
116 N Gilbert St.
Danville, IL 61832
Phone: (217)442-2922
Fax: (217)442-2001
Freq: Quarterly. **Print Method:** Offset. **Trim Size:** 8 1/2 x 11. **Key Personnel:** Donald G. Richter, Contact, phone: (217)354-4367; Susan E. Richter, Contact, phone: (217)354-4367. **ISSN:** 0018--0718 (print). **Sub-**

Circulation: ★ = AAM; △ or • = BPA; ♦ = CAC; ❑ = VAC; ⊕ = PO Statement; ‡ = Publisher's Report; Boldface figures = sworn; Light figures = estimated.

scription Rates: $20 Individuals; $2.50 Single issue; Included in membership. **URL:** http://www.vermilioncountymuseum.org/heritage.htm. **Remarks:** Advertising not accepted. **Circ:** Controlled ⊕**1500.**

10693 ■ Insight Communications
806 1/2 E Main St., Ste A
Danville, IL 61832
Phone: (217)443-2941
Formerly: Warner Cable of Danville. **Cities Served:** subscribing households 16,000. **URL:** http://www.insight.com.

10694 ■ WDAN-AM - 1490
1501 N Washington
Danville, IL 61832
Phone: (217)442-1700
Fax: (217)431-1489
Format: Talk; News; Sports. **Networks:** CBS. **Owner:** Neuhoff Broadcasting, at above address. **Founded:** 1938. **Operating Hours**: Continuous; 70% network, 30% local. **ADI**: Springfield-Decatur-Champaign, IL. **Key Personnel:** Michael Hulvey, Prog. Dir., Station Mgr., michaelhulvey@neuhoffmedia.com; Bill Pickett, News Dir.; Michelle Campbell, Asst. Mgr., Sales Mgr. **Wattage**: 1,000. **Ad Rates:** $15 for 30 seconds; $25 for 60 seconds. Combined advertising rates available with WDNL-FM, WRHK-FM. **URL:** http://b96.cbslocal.com.

10695 ■ WDNL-FM - 102.1
1501 N Washington
Danville, IL 61832
Phone: (217)442-1700
Format: Adult Contemporary. **Simulcasts:** WDAN-AM. **Networks:** Unistar; Westwood One Radio. **Founded:** 1967. **Operating Hours**: Continuous; 5% Network, 95% Local. **Wattage**: 50,000. **Ad Rates:** $12-20 for 30 seconds; $16-25 for 60 seconds. Combined advertising rates available with WDAN-AM, WRHK-FM. **URL:** http://www.wdnlfm.com.

10696 ■ WITY-AM - 980
PO Box 142
Danville, IL 61834
Phone: (217)446-1312
Fax: (217)446-1314
Format: Adult Contemporary; News. **Networks:** ABC. **Founded:** 1953. **Operating Hours**: Continuous. **Key Personnel:** David Brown, Gen. Mgr.; Bob Iverson, News Dir.; Linda Murphy, Sales Mgr. **Wattage**: 1,000. **Ad Rates:** Advertising accepted; rates available upon request. $8-12.50 per unit. **URL:** http://wityradio.com/.

10697 ■ WRHK-FM
1501 N Washington Ave.
Danville, IL 61832
Phone: (217)442-1700
Fax: (217)431-1489
Format: Classic Rock. **Wattage**: 6,000 ERP. **Ad Rates:** Noncommercial. **URL:** http://www.vermilioncountyfirst.com.

10698 ■ WSKL-FM - 92.9
PO Box 67
Danville, IL 61834-0067
Phone: (217)443-4004
Fax: (765)793-4644
Format: Oldies. **Ad Rates:** Advertising accepted; rates available upon request. **URL:** http://www.kooloIdies.net.

DARIEN

DuPage Co.

10699 ■ The Carmelite Review
The Carmelites
8501 Bailey Rd.
Darien, IL 60561-8418
Phone: (630)971-0724
Fax: (630)971-0817
Publisher's E-mail: review@carmelnet.org
Newspaper providing a forum for the exchange of news, information, and opinions for Catholic membership. **Freq:** Quarterly. **Print Method:** Offset. **Trim Size:** 8 1/2 x 11. **Cols./Page:** 4. **Col. Width:** 2 1/4 inches. **Col. Depth:** 10 inches. **Key Personnel:** John Welch, Publisher; Sal Lema, Editor-in-Chief; Gregory Houck, Editor. **URL:** http://www.carmelites.net/cr. **Remarks:** Advertising not accepted. **Circ:** Controlled ‡25.

10700 ■ Journal of Clinical Sleep Medicine
American Academy of Sleep Medicine
2510 N Frontage Rd.
Darien, IL 60561
Phone: (630)737-9700
Fax: (630)737-9790
Publisher's E-mail: inquiries@aasmnet.org
Subscription Rates: $140 Institutions; $75 Individuals. **URL:** http://www.aasmnet.org/jcsm. **Remarks:** Accepts advertising. **Circ:** (Not Reported).

10701 ■ Sleep
Associated Professional Sleep Societies
2510 N Frontage Rd.
Darien, IL 60561
Phone: (630)737-9700
Fax: (630)737-9789
Publisher's E-mail: sleepmeeting@apss.org
Peer-reviewed journal covering findings on sleep and circadian rhythms. **Founded:** 1978. **Freq:** Monthly. **Print Method:** Offset, sheet-fed. **Trim Size:** 8 1/2 x 11. **Cols./Page:** 2. **Col. Width:** 3 5/8 inches. **Col. Depth:** 9 1/8 inches. **Key Personnel:** David Dinges, PhD, Editor-in-Chief; Andrew Miller, Managing Editor; Jerome A. Barrett, Executive Director. **ISSN:** 0161-8105 (print). **Subscription Rates:** $425 Nonmembers institution - online only; Free member - online only; $225 Members individual - online only. **URL:** http://www.journalsleep.org/. **Ad Rates:** BW $875; 4C $2,100. **Remarks:** Accepts advertising. **Circ:** Paid 11000.

DECATUR

Macon Co. Macon Co. (C). On Lake Decatur, 38 m E of Springfield. Millikin University. Richland Community College. Manufactures earth moving tractors, tires, electronic equipment, plastics, carburetors, water and gas distribution systems, brass goods, steel tanks, rotary pumps, pressure valves, castings, women's garments. Corn, and soybean processing. Meat packing. Gasohol production.

10702 ■ Herald & Review
Herald & Review Newspapers
601 E William St.
Decatur, IL 62523-1142
Phone: (217)429-5151
Fax: (217)421-6913
General newspaper. **Founded:** 1880. **Freq:** Mon.-Sun. (morn.). **Print Method:** Letterpress. **Cols./Page:** 6. **Col. Width:** 26 nonpareils. **Col. Depth:** 301 agate lines. **Key Personnel:** David Dawson, Managing Editor, phone: (217)421-7980; Gary Sawyer, Editor, phone: (217)421-6975; Tim Cain, Editor, phone: (217)421-6908. **URL:** http://herald-review.com. **Remarks:** Accepts advertising. **Circ:** Mon.-Sat. ★**29,638**, Sun. ★**44,044**.

10703 ■ WAND-TV - 17
904 S Slide Dr.
Decatur, IL 62521
Phone: (217)424-2500
Format: Public TV. **Networks:** ABC. **Founded:** 1953. **Operating Hours**: 5 a.m.- 3 a.m. **ADI**: Springfield-Decatur-Champaign, IL. **Key Personnel:** Ron Pulera, Gen. Mgr., ron.pulera@wandtv.com; Elaine Voelker, Mgr., elaine.voelker@wandtv.com. **Ad Rates:** Advertising accepted; rates available upon request. **URL:** http://www.wandtv.com.

10704 ■ WDZ-AM - 1050
250 N Water St., Ste. 100
Decatur, IL 62523
Phone: (217)423-9744
Format: News; Talk; Sports. **Networks:** ESPN Radio. **Founded:** 1921. **Operating Hours**: Continuous. **ADI**: Springfield-Decatur-Champaign, IL. **Wattage**: 1,000 Day; 250 Night. **Ad Rates:** Noncommercial. $13 for 30 seconds; $15 for 60 seconds.

10705 ■ WDZQ-FM - 95.1
250 N Water St., Ste. 100
Decatur, IL 62523
Phone: (217)429-9595
Fax: (217)423-9764
Format: Contemporary Country. **Owner:** Next Media Group L.L.C., at above address. **Founded:** 1976. **Operating Hours**: Continuous. **ADI**: Springfield-Decatur-Champaign, IL. **Key Personnel:** Kimmy Kay, Contact, kimmy@95q.com. **Wattage**: 50,000. **Ad Rates:** for 30 seconds; for 60 seconds. **URL:** http://www.95q.com.

10706 ■ WEJT-FM - 105.1
410 N Water St., Ste. B
Decatur, IL 62523
Phone: (217)428-4487
Fax: (217)428-4501
Format: Oldies. **Owner:** The Cromwell Group, Inc., 1824 Murfreesboro Rd., Nashville, TN 37217, Ph: (615)361-7560, Fax: (615)366-4313. **Operating Hours**: Continuous. **Key Personnel:** Chris Bullock, Gen. Mgr.; Tara Nickerson, Operations Mgr. **Wattage**: 13,000. **Ad Rates:** Advertising accepted; rates available upon request. **URL:** http://www.decaturradio.com.

10707 ■ WJMU-FM - 89.5
1184 W Main St.
Decatur, IL 62522
Free: 800-373-7733
Format: Alternative/New Music/Progressive. **Owner:** Millikin University, 1184 W Main St., Decatur, IL 62522. **Founded:** 1971. **Operating Hours**: 12:00 p.m. - 1:00 a.m. **Key Personnel:** Jill Johnson, Office Mgr. **Wattage**: 1,000. **Ad Rates:** Noncommercial. **URL:** http://www.millikin.edu.

10708 ■ WSOY-AM - 1340
250 N Water St., Ste. 100
Decatur, IL 62523
Phone: (217)423-9744
Fax: (217)423-9764
Free: 800-500-WSOY
Email: news@wsoyam.com
Format: Talk; News. **Networks:** CBS. **Founded:** 1925. **Operating Hours**: Continuous; 90% local. **ADI**: Springfield-Decatur-Champaign, IL. **Key Personnel:** Shelby Larrick, News Dir., shelbylarrick@neuhoffmedia.com; Jeff Daly, Dir. of Programs, jeffdaly@neuhoffmedia.com. **Wattage**: 1,000. **URL:** http://www.wsoyam.com.

10709 ■ WSOY-FM - 102.9
250 N Water St.
Decatur, IL 62523
Phone: (217)877-5371
Format: Adult Contemporary. **Networks:** CBS; ABC. **Owner:** Neuhoff Communication, Not Available. **Founded:** 1948. **Operating Hours**: Continuous. **ADI**: Springfield-Decatur-Champaign, IL. **Wattage**: 54,000. **Ad Rates:** Noncommercial. Combined advertising rates available with WSOY-AM, WDZQ-FM, WDZ-AM, WCZQ-FM. **URL:** http://www.y103.com.

10710 ■ W213BI-FM - 90.5
PO Box 391
Twin Falls, ID 83303
Fax: (208)736-1958
Free: 800-357-4226
Format: Religious; Contemporary Christian. **Owner:** CSN International, PO Box 391, Twin Falls, ID 83303, Ph: (208)736-1958, Fax: (208)736-1958, Free: 800-357-4226. **Key Personnel:** Kelly Carlson, Dir. of Engg.; Ray Gorney, Asst. Dir. **URL:** http://www.csnradio.com.

10711 ■ WYDS-FM - 93.1
410 N Water St., Ste. B
Decatur, IL 62523
Phone: (217)421-1293
Email: tnickerson@cromwellradio.com
Format: Top 40. **URL:** http://www.partydecatur.com.

10712 ■ WZNX-FM
410 N Water St., Ste. B
Decatur, IL 62523
Phone: (217)428-4487
Fax: (217)428-4501
Owner: The Cromwell Group, Inc., 1824 Murfreesboro Rd., Nashville, TN 37217, Ph: (615)361-7560, Fax: (615)366-4313. **Ad Rates:** Advertising accepted; rates available upon request.

10713 ■ WZUS-FM - 100.9
410 N Water St., Ste. C
Decatur, IL 62523
Phone: (217)428-4487
Fax: (217)428-4501
Format: Talk. **Owner:** The Cromwell Group, Inc., 1824 Murfreesboro Rd., Nashville, TN 37217, Ph: (615)361-7560, Fax: (615)366-4313. **Founded:** 1977. **Formerly:** WXKO-FM; WKXK-FM; WEGY-FM. **Operating Hours**: Continuous; 10% network, 90% local. **Wattage**: 4,200. **Ad Rates:** Noncommercial.

DEERFIELD

Lake Co. Lake Co. (NE). 25 m N of Chicago. Manufactures machinery, fabricated wire products, marking devices, metal doors, sash, semiconductor devices, dies, tools, musical instruments. Frozen food.

10714 ■ Consumers Digest
Consumers Digest Inc.
520 Lake Cook Rd., Ste. 500
Deerfield, IL 60015
Publisher's E-mail: postmaster@consumersdigest.com
Magazine featuring product and service evaluation, information, and advice. **Freq:** Bimonthly. **Print Method:** Offset. **Trim Size:** 8 x 10 7/8. **Cols./Page:** 3. **Col. Width:** 13.5 nonpareils. **Col. Depth:** 140 agate lines. **Key Personnel:** Randy Weber, Publisher. **ISSN:** 0010--7182 (print). **Subscription Rates:** $19 Individuals /year; $5 Individuals /month. **URL:** http://www.consumersdigest.com . **Remarks:** Accepts advertising. **Circ:** (Not Reported).

10715 ■ Deerfield Review: With News of Lincolnshire, Riverwoods, and Bannockburn
Sun-Times Media L.L.C.
350 N Orleans St., 10th Fl.
Chicago, IL 60654
Phone: (312)321-3000
Free: 888-848-4637
Publisher's E-mail: customerservice@suntimes.com
Community newspaper (tabloid). **Freq:** Weekly. **Print Method:** Offset. **Trim Size:** 11 x 14. **Cols./Page:** 5. **Col. Width:** 9 3/4 inches. **Col. Depth:** 12 3/4 inches. **Key Personnel:** Jeff Wisser, Editor, Designer, phone: (847)486-6848; John Puterbaugh, Editor. **USPS:** 151-300. **URL:** http://www.chicagotribune.com/suburbs/deerfield. **Remarks:** Accepts advertising. **Circ:** (Not Reported).

10716 ■ Food & Beverage Packaging: The Information Source for Food and Drug Packagers
BNP Media
155 Pfingsten Rd., Ste. 205
Deerfield, IL 60015
Phone: (847)405-4000
Fax: (847)405-4100
Publisher's E-mail: asm@halldata.com
Trade magazine for packaging professionals in food and pharmaceutical industries. **Founded:** Jan. 01, 1959. **Freq:** Monthly. **Print Method:** Web Offset. **Trim Size:** 8 x 10 3/4. **Cols./Page:** 3. **Key Personnel:** Elisabeth Cuneo, Editor-in-Chief; Vince Miconi, Manager, Production, phone: (248)244-6254. **ISSN:** 1085-2077 (print). **URL:** http://www.foodandbeveragepackaging.com. **Formerly**: The New Food & Drug Packaging; Food & Drug Packaging. **Ad Rates:** BW $6,580; 4C $8,530; SAU $940; PCI $100. **Remarks:** Accepts advertising. **Circ:** Combined △**45000**.

10717 ■ Industria Alimenticia
BNP Media
155 Pfingsten Rd., Ste. 205
Deerfield, IL 60015
Phone: (847)405-4000
Fax: (847)405-4100
Publisher's E-mail: asm@halldata.com
Trade magazine for the Latin American food and beverage industry. **Freq:** 11/year. **Print Method:** Offset. **Trim Size:** 8 x 10 3/4. **Cols./Page:** 3. **Key Personnel:** Pam Mazurka, Manager, Sales, Publisher, phone: (847)247-0018. **Subscription Rates:** Free to qualified subscribers. **URL:** http://www.industriaalimenticia.com; http://www.industriaalimenticia.com/publications/3. **Ad Rates:** BW $4,330. **Remarks:** Accepts advertising. **Circ:** ■ **18608**.

10718 ■ Law and Order: The Magazine for Police Management
Hendon Publishing Co.
130 Waukegan Rd.
Deerfield, IL 60015-5652
Phone: (847)444-3300
Fax: (847)444-3333
Free: 800-843-9764
Publication E-mail: law&ordermag@halldata.com
Law enforcement trade magazine. **Freq:** Monthly. **Print Method:** Offset. **Trim Size:** 8 1/8 x 10 7/8. **Cols./Page:** 3. **Col. Width:** 26 nonpareils. **Col. Depth:** 140 agate lines. **Key Personnel:** Henry Kingwill, Publisher; Yesenia Salcedo, Managing Editor; Ed Sanow, Director, Editorial. **USPS:** 079-430. **Subscription Rates:** $24.95 Individuals print; 1 year; $39.95 Individuals print; 2 years; $55 Individuals print; 3 years. **URL:** http://www.hendonpub.com/law_and_order. **Ad Rates:** BW $2,400; 4C $3,100. **Remarks:** Advertising accepted; rates available upon request. **Circ:** (Not Reported).

10719 ■ The National Provisioner
BNP Media
155 Pfingsten Rd., Ste. 205
Deerfield, IL 60015
Phone: (847)405-4000
Fax: (847)405-4100
Publisher's E-mail: asm@halldata.com
Magazine covering information and technical editorials on the meat, poultry and seafood industry. **Freq:** Monthly. **Trim Size:** 8 X 10-3/4. **Key Personnel:** Rick Parsons, Associate Publisher; Andy Hanacek, Editor-in-Chief, phone: (847)405-4011. **URL:** http://www.provisioneronline.com. **Ad Rates:** BW $4,140; 4C $1,530; PCI $145. **Remarks:** Accepts advertising. **Circ:** (Not Reported).

10720 ■ PM Engineer
BNP Media
155 N Pfingsten Rd., No. 205
Deerfield, IL 60015
Phone: (847)405-4007
Publication E-mail: pme@halldata.com
Trade publication for plumbing specifying engineers on the 'wet' side of the industry. **Freq:** Monthly. **Key Personnel:** Mike Miazga, Manager; Bob Miodonski, Editor, Publisher. **ISSN:** 1080--353X (print). **URL:** http://www.pmengineer.com. **Remarks:** Accepts advertising. **Circ:** Non-paid △**25000**.

10721 ■ Police Fleet Manager
Hendon Publishing Co.
130 Waukegan Rd.
Deerfield, IL 60015-5652
Phone: (847)444-3300
Fax: (847)444-3333
Free: 800-843-9764
Publication E-mail: pfmmag@gmail.com
Police car trade magazine. **Print Method:** Web Offset. **Trim Size:** 8 1/8 x 10 7/8. **Key Personnel:** Ed Sanow, Director, Editorial; Peter Kingwill, Publisher. **URL:** http://www.hendonpub.com/police_fleet_manager. **Remarks:** Accepts advertising. **Circ:** (Not Reported).

10722 ■ Prepared Foods
BNP Media
155 Pfingsten Rd., Ste. 205
Deerfield, IL 60015
Phone: (630)694-4344
Fax: (630)227-0527
Publication E-mail: preparedfoods@bnpmedia.com
Product development magazine focusing on new product and technology challenges for R&D and Marketing customers. **Key Personnel:** David Feder, Managing Editor, phone: (847)405-4081; Bob Garrison, Executive Editor, fax: (248)502-9035; Michael Leonard, Publisher. **Subscription Rates:** Free. **URL:** http://www.preparedfoods.com/. **Remarks:** Accepts advertising. **Circ:** Combined △**40000**.

10723 ■ Process Cooling
BNP Media
Process Cooling & Equipment
155 Pfingsten Rd., Ste. 205
Deerfield, IL 60015
Phone: (847)405-4000
Publisher's E-mail: asm@halldata.com
Trade publication covering the engineering and manufacturing industries. **Freq:** Bimonthly. **Key Personnel:** Linda Becker, Editor, phone: (847)405-4020; Beth McClelland, Manager, Production, phone: (412)306-4354, fax: (248)502-1077; Anne Armel, Publisher, phone: (847)405-4043. **ISSN:** 1525--9498 (print). **Subscription Rates:** Free to qualified subscribers. **URL:** http://www.process-cooling.com; http://www.process-cooling.com/publications/3. **Formerly:** Process Cooling and Equipment: A Supplement to Process Heating Magazine. **Ad Rates:** BW $3,790; 4C $5,085. **Remarks:** Accepts advertising. **Circ:** Combined ‡16625.

10724 ■ Process Heating: For Manufacturing Engineers Who Use Heat Processing Equipment and Supplies
BNP Media
155 Pfingsten Rd., Ste. 205
Deerfield, IL 60015
Phone: (847)405-4000
Publication E-mail: pheditors@bnpmedia.com
Trade magazine covering industrial heat processing to 1000 degrees Fahrenheit. **Freq:** Monthly. **Print Method:** Web offset. **Trim Size:** 8 x 10 3/4. **Cols./Page:** 3. **Col. Width:** 2 1/8 inches. **Key Personnel:** Linda Becker, Associate Publisher, Editor, phone: (630)694-4332; Beth McClelland, Manager, Production, phone: (412)306-4354, fax: (248)502-1076; Anne Armel, Publisher, phone: (847)405-4043, fax: (248)786-1441. **ISSN:** 1077-5870 (print). **URL:** http://www.process-heating.com. **Ad Rates:** BW $4985; 4C $6280; PCI $100. **Remarks:** Accepts advertising. **Circ:** Controlled △**18,143**.

10725 ■ Public Safety IT
Hendon Publishing Co.
130 Waukegan Rd.
Deerfield, IL 60015-5652
Phone: (847)444-3300
Fax: (847)444-3333
Free: 800-843-9764
Publication E-mail: publicsafetyitmag@halldata.com
Magazine focusing on public safety in information systems technologies. **Key Personnel:** Jennifer Gavigan, Editor; Henry Kingwill, Publisher; Yesenia Salcedo, Managing Editor. **URL:** http://www.hendonpub.com/publications/publicsafetyit. **Remarks:** Accepts advertising. **Circ:** (Not Reported).

10726 ■ Quality
BNP Media
155 Pfingston Rd., Ste. 205
Deerfield, IL 60015
Phone: (847)405-4000
Fax: (847)405-4100
Publisher's E-mail: asm@halldata.com
Magazine for manufacturing professionals. Providing information that can be use to initiate, implement, manage and reinforce quality on the shop floor and company wide. Reports, documents and supports advances in quality-related technology and techniques. Also providing industry information such as manufacturers and users of test inspection and measurement equipment, publishers and users of associated software, and providers and users of services such as training and standards. **Freq:** Monthly. **Subscription Rates:** Free. **URL:** http://www.qualitymag.com/. **Remarks:** Accepts advertising. **Circ:** △**51008**.

10727 ■ Refrigerated and Frozen Foods
BNP Media
155 Pfingsten Rd., Ste. 205
Deerfield, IL 60015
Phone: (847)405-4000
Fax: (847)405-4100
Publisher's E-mail: asm@halldata.com
Trade publication covering the frozen food industry. **Freq:** Monthly. **Print Method:** Offset. **Trim Size:** 8 x 10 3/4. **Key Personnel:** Paul Kelly, District Manager; Wayne Wiggins, Jr., District Manager; Marina Mayer, Editor-in-Chief; Patrick Young, Publisher, District Manager, phone: (610)436-4220, fax: (248)502-2123. **ISSN:** 1061--6152 (print). **Subscription Rates:** Free to qualified subscribers. **URL:** http://www.refrigeratedfrozenfood.com; http://www.refrigeratedfrozenfood.com/publications/3. **Ad Rates:** BW $5,050. **Remarks:** Accepts advertising. **Circ:** (Not Reported).

10728 ■ Successful Dealer
Kona Communications Inc.
707 Lake Cook Rd.
Deerfield, IL 60015
Phone: (847)498-3180
Fax: (847)498-3197
Trade magazine for dealers of heavy-duty trucks and trailers. **Founded:** 1978. **Freq:** Bimonthly. **Print Method:** Offset. **Trim Size:** 8 1/4 x 11. **Cols./Page:** 3. **Col. Width:** 13 picas. **Col. Depth:** 59 picas. **Key Personnel:** Doug Early, Associate Publisher, phone: (770)354-1558; Denise L. Rondini, Editor, phone: (800)767-5662. **ISSN:** 0161-6080 (print). **URL:** http://

Circulation: ★ = AAM; △ or • = BPA; ♦ = CAC; ❑ = VAC; ⊕ = PO Statement; ‡ = Publisher's Report; Boldface figures = sworn; Light figures = estimated.

www.successfuldealer.com. **Ad Rates:** BW $8655; 4C $11590; PCI $150. **Remarks:** Accepts advertising. **Circ:** ‡23,100.

10729 ■ Tactical Response
Hendon Publishing Co.
130 Waukegan Rd.
Deerfield, IL 60015-5652
Phone: (847)444-3300
Fax: (847)444-3333
Free: 800-843-9764
Publication E-mail: tacticalresponsemag@gmail.com
Tactical trade magazine. **Print Method:** Web Offset. **Trim Size:** 8 1/8 x 10 7/8. **Key Personnel:** Ed Sanow, Director, Editorial; Jennifer Gavigan, Editor. **URL:** http://www.hendonpub.com/tactical_response. **Remarks:** Accepts advertising. **Circ:** (Not Reported).

DEKALB

DeKalb Co. De Kalb Co. (N). 58 m W of Chicago. Northern Illinois University. Manufactures wire and wire products, pianos, bed springs, mattresses, women's cloth and fur trimmed coats, truck bodies, electric motors, road building equipment, canned food, tools, stoves. Hatchery. Dairy, stock, poultry, hybrid seed corn farms.

10730 ■ African Conflict and Peacebuilding Review
Indiana University Press
c/o Abu Bakarr Bah, Editor-in-Chief
Dept. of Sociology
Northern Illinois University
DeKalb, IL 60115
Peer-reviewed journal publishing articles on studies of conflict and peace in Africa. **Freq:** Semiannual. **Key Personnel:** Abu Bakarr Bah, Founder, Editor, phone: (815)753-6427. **ISSN:** 2156--695X (print); **EISSN:** 2156--7263 (electronic). **Subscription Rates:** $35.07 Individuals in Africa; print + online. **URL:** http://www.iupress.indiana.edu/pages.php?pID=20&CDpath=4. **Circ:** (Not Reported).

10731 ■ Communication Studies
Central States Communication Association
c/o Jimmie Manning, Executive Director
Northern Illinois University
Dept. of Communication
305 Watson Hall
DeKalb, IL 60115
Phone: (815)753-1563
Fax: (614)392-1559
Publication E-mail: commstudies@luther.edu
Publication covering communication, language and linguistics. **Freq:** 5/year. **Key Personnel:** Robert Littlefield. **ISSN:** 0008--9575 (print); **EISSN:** 1745--1035 (electronic). **Subscription Rates:** $185 Individuals; $176 Individuals online only. **URL:** http://associationdatabase.com/aws/CSCA/pt/sp/journal. **Circ:** (Not Reported).

10732 ■ Daily Chronicle
Daily Chronicle
1586 Barber Greene Rd.
DeKalb, IL 60115
Phone: (815)756-4841
Free: 877-688-4841
Publisher's E-mail: news@daily-chronicle.com
General newspaper. **Founded:** 1870. **Freq:** Daily (eve.). **Print Method:** Offset. **Cols./Page:** 6. **Col. Width:** 21 nonpareils. **Col. Depth:** 294 agate lines. **Key Personnel:** Don Bricker, Publisher, phone: (815)756-4841; Jason Schaumburg, Editor. **Subscription Rates:** $114.35 Individuals in town; $127.35 Individuals motor route; $179.40 By mail USA. **URL:** http://www.daily-chronicle.com/. **Ad Rates:** SAU $8.25. **Remarks:** Accepts advertising. **Circ:** Paid ‡14215, Controlled 2092.

10733 ■ The MidWeek
The Midweek Inc.
1586 Barber Greene Rd.
DeKalb, IL 60115
Phone: (815)756-4841
Fax: (815)758-5059
Publisher's E-mail: readit@midweeknews.com
Community newspaper. **Founded:** Apr. 05, 1967. **Freq:** Weekly. **Print Method:** Offset. **Cols./Page:** 6. **Col. Width:** 9.5 picas. **Col. Depth:** 224 agate lines. **Key Personnel:** Bill Braksick, Managing Editor. **Subscription Rates:** Free. **URL:** http://www.midweeknews.com. **Ad Rates:** GLR $.65; BW $1546; 4C $1738; SAU $15; PCI $1.15. **Remarks:** Accepts advertising. **Circ:** Free ‡31,000.

10734 ■ The Midweek
The Midweek Inc.
1586 Barber Greene Rd.
DeKalb, IL 60115
Phone: (815)756-4841
Fax: (815)758-5059
Publisher's E-mail: readit@midweeknews.com
Shopper. **Founded:** 1970. **Freq:** Weekly. **Print Method:** Offset. **Trim Size:** 16 1/2 x 11. **Cols./Page:** 6. **Col. Width:** 20 nonpareils. **Col. Depth:** 210 agate lines. **Key Personnel:** Karen Huber, Editor. **URL:** http://www.westfargopioneer.com/index.cfm?&forumcomm_check_return; http://www.forumcomm.com/newspaper/?page=westfargopioneer. **Ad Rates:** GLR $9; BW $1,286; 4C $1,714; PCI $10. **Remarks:** Accepts advertising. **Circ:** Free ‡52750.

10735 ■ The Northern Star
Northern Illinois University
1425 W Lincoln Hwy.
DeKalb, IL 60115-2828
Phone: (815)753-1000
Fax: (815)753-2000
Publisher's E-mail: univinfo@niu.edu
Collegiate newspaper. **Founded:** 1899. **Freq:** Daily (morn.) (during the academic year). **Print Method:** Offset. **Trim Size:** 11 3/8 x 17. **Cols./Page:** 5. **Col. Width:** 2 inches. **Col. Depth:** 16 inches. **Key Personnel:** Jim Killam, Advisor, phone: (815)753-4239; Dave Thomas, Editor-in-Chief, phone: (815)753-0105. **URL:** http://northernstar.info. **Ad Rates:** GLR $.40; BW $892; 4C $1242; PCI $10.90. **Remarks:** Advertising accepted; rates available upon request. **Circ:** Mon.-Thurs. ‡16,000, Fri. 13,000, ‡12,500.

10736 ■ The Sigma Tau Delta Rectangle
Sigma Tau Delta
711 N 1st St.
DeKalb, IL 60115
Phone: (815)981-9974
Publisher's E-mail: sigmatd@niu.edu
Freq: Annual. **Key Personnel:** Karlyn Crowley, Editor. **Subscription Rates:** Free. **Alt. Formats:** PDF. **URL:** http://english.org/sigmatd/publications/index.shtml. **Remarks:** Advertising not accepted. **Circ:** (Not Reported).

10737 ■ The Sigma Tau Delta Review
Sigma Tau Delta
711 N 1st St.
DeKalb, IL 60115
Phone: (815)981-9974
Publisher's E-mail: sigmatd@niu.edu
Freq: Annual. **Key Personnel:** Karlyn Crowley, Editor. **Alt. Formats:** PDF. **URL:** http://www.english.org/sigmatd/publications/index.shtml. **Remarks:** Advertising not accepted. **Circ:** (Not Reported).

10738 ■ Thresholds in Education
Thresholds in Education Foundation
Northern Illinois University
1425 W Lincoln Hwy.
DeKalb, IL 60115-2828
Phone: (815)753-0446
Journal covering future trends in education. **Freq:** Quarterly. **Print Method:** Offset. **Trim Size:** 8 1/2 x 11. **Cols./Page:** 2. **Key Personnel:** Charles Howell, Executive Editor; Marilyn Justus, Managing Editor. **ISSN:** 0196--9641 (print). **URL:** http://www.cedu.niu.edu. **Remarks:** Accepts advertising. **Circ:** (Not Reported).

10739 ■ WDEK-FM - 92.5
711 N 1st St.
DeKalb, IL 60115
Phone: (815)758-8686
Fax: (815)756-9723
Format: Contemporary Hit Radio (CHR); Top 40. **Networks:** Superadio. **Founded:** 1961. **Operating Hours**: Continuous. **Key Personnel:** Dianne Leifheit, Gen. Mgr.; Keith Bansemer, Prog. Dir., Operations Mgr., Contact; Keith Bansemer, Contact. **Wattage**: 20,000. **Ad Rates:** $35 for 60 seconds.

10740 ■ WLBK-AM - 1360
2410 Sycamore Rd., Ste. C
DeKalb, IL 60115
Phone: (815)748-1000
Fax: (815)787-9300
Email: wlbk-news@nelsonmultimedia.net
Format: Information; News. **Networks:** AP; Illinois Farm Bureau. **Founded:** 1947. **Operating Hours**: 12 a.m.-7 p.m. **Key Personnel:** Terry Ryan, Dir. of Programs, terryr@nelsonmultimedia.net; Scott Zak, News Dir., scottz@nelsonmultimedia.net. **Wattage:** 1,000. **Ad Rates:** $15-30 for 30 seconds; $20-45 for 60 seconds. **URL:** http://www.wlbkradio.com.

WNIE-FM - See Freeport

10741 ■ WNIJ-FM - 89.5
NIU Broadcast Ctr.
801 N 1st St.
DeKalb, IL 60115
Phone: (815)753-9000
Fax: (815)753-9938
Format: Public Radio. **Networks:** National Public Radio (NPR). **Owner:** Northern Illinois University, 1425 W Lincoln Hwy., Dekalb, IL 60115. **Founded:** 1991. **Operating Hours**: Continuous; 50% network; 50% local. **ADI:** Rockford, IL. **Key Personnel:** Bill Drake, Dir. of Programs, wdrake@niu.edu; Jeff Glass, Chief Engineer, jglass@niu.edu. **Wattage;** 50,000. **Ad Rates:** Noncommercial. **URL:** http://www.northernpublicradio.org.

WNIQ-FM - See Sterling

10742 ■ WNIU-FM - 90.5
801 N 1st St.
DeKalb, IL 60115
Phone: (815)753-9000
Fax: (815)753-9938
Email: dklefstad@niu.edu
Format: Public Radio. **Networks:** National Public Radio (NPR). **Owner:** Northern Illinois University, 1425 W Lincoln Hwy., Dekalb, IL 60115. **Founded:** 1954. **Operating Hours**: Continuous; 25% network; 75% local. **ADI:** Rockford, IL. **Key Personnel:** Jeff Glass, Chief Engineer, jglass@niu.edu; Bill Drake, Dir. of Programs, wdrake@niu.edu; Eric Hradecky, Div. Dir., ehradecky@charter.net. **Wattage:** 50,000. **Ad Rates:** Noncommercial. **URL:** http://www.northernpublicradio.org.

WNIW-FM - See LaSalle

DENNISON

10743 ■ WKZI-AM - 800
18889 N 2350 St.
Dennison, IL 62423
Phone: (217)826-9673
Free: 877-939-1480
Email: wkzi@rr1.net
Format: Contemporary Christian. **Networks:** Moody Broadcasting. **Owner:** Word Power, Inc., 3775 West Dugger Ave., West Terre Haute, IN 47885-9794. **Founded:** 1963. **Operating Hours**: Continuous. **Wattage**: 250. **Ad Rates:** Noncommercial. **URL:** http://www.wordpower.us.

WPFR-AM - See Terre Haute, IN

10744 ■ WPFR-FM - 93.9
18889 N 2350 St.
Dennison, IL 62423
Phone: (217)826-9673
Free: 877-939-1480
Email: wpfr@joink.com
Format: Religious; Talk. **Networks:** Moody Broadcasting. **Owner:** Word Power, Inc., 3775 West Dugger Ave., West Terre Haute, IN 47885-9794. **Founded:** June 06, 2000. **Operating Hours**: Continuous. **Wattage**: 2,350. **Ad Rates:** Noncommercial. Combined advertising rates available with WPFR-AM, WKZI. **URL:** http://www.wordpower.us.

DES PLAINES

Cook Co. Cook Co. (NE). 17 m NW of Chicago. Residential. Manufactures machine tools, steel strapping, fuses, cosmetics, electronics, photo copiers, chemicals, laundry equipment, cement blocks, nuclear instruments. Research Laboratories.

10745 ■ Academic Emergency Medicine
Society for Academic Emergency Medicine
2340 S River Rd., Ste. 208
Des Plaines, IL 60018
Phone: (847)813-9823
Fax: (847)813-5450

Publisher's E-mail: saem@saem.org
Subscription Rates: $346 Institutions online only; $416 Institutions print and online; $196 Individuals print and online; $107 Members print and online. **URL:** http://www.saem.org/publications/aem-journal. **Circ:** (Not Reported).

10746 ■ ASHI Reporter
American Society of Home Inspectors
932 Lee St., Ste. 101
Des Plaines, IL 60016
Phone: (847)759-2820
Fax: (847)759-1620
Freq: Monthly. **Print Method:** Sheet-fed. **Trim Size:** 8.5 x 11. **Subscription Rates:** $44.95 Individuals Annual Subscription.; $79.90 Individuals 2 years Subscription. **URL:** http://www.homeinspector.org/ASHI-Reporter-magazine. **Remarks:** Accepts advertising. **Circ:** 6,300.

10747 ■ Consumer Magazine Advertising Source
Kantar Media SRDS
1700 Higgins Rd., 5th Fl.
Des Plaines, IL 60018-5610
Free: 800-851-7737
Publisher's E-mail: contact@srds.com
Reference guide to current advertising rates and media information in consumer and agricultural magazines. **Founded:** 1919. **Freq:** Quarterly. **Print Method:** Offset. **Trim Size:** 10 5/16 x 11. **Cols./Page:** 4. **ISSN:** 1086-8208 (print). **USPS:** 130-040. **Subscription Rates:** $890 Individuals shipping & taxes extra. **URL:** http://www.srds.com/portal/main?action=LinkHit&frameset=yes&link=ips. **Formerly**: SRDS Consumer Magazine and Agri-Media Rates and Data; Consumer Magazine and Agri-Media Source. **Ad Rates:** BW $5,429; 4C $5,874. **Remarks:** Accepts advertising. **Circ:** Paid 1978.

10748 ■ GasLine
Gas Technology Institute
1700 S Mount Prospect Rd.
Des Plaines, IL 60018-1804
Phone: (847)768-0500
Fax: (847)768-0501
Free: 866-484-5227
Publication E-mail: publications@gastechnology.org
Gas technology database reviewing U.S. and foreign journals and papers proceedings and conferences. **Founded:** 1945. **URL:** http://www.gastechnology.org. **Formerly**: Gas Abstracts. **Remarks:** Advertising not accepted. **Circ:** (Not Reported).

10749 ■ GTI Journal
Gas Technology Institute
1700 S Mount Prospect Rd.
Des Plaines, IL 60018-1804
Phone: (847)768-0500
Fax: (847)768-0501
Free: 866-484-5227
Publisher's E-mail: publicrelations@gastechnology.org
Freq: Semiannual. **Subscription Rates:** $100 /year. **Remarks:** Advertising not accepted. **Circ:** (Not Reported).

10750 ■ The Inlander
Inland Press Association
701 Lee St., Ste. 925
Des Plaines, IL 60016
Phone: (847)795-0380
Fax: (847)795-0385
Publisher's E-mail: inland@inlandpress.org
Newspaper featuring operational advice for the newspaper industry. **Freq:** Monthly. **Subscription Rates:** included in membership dues. **URL:** http://www.inlandpress.org. **Remarks:** Accepts advertising. **Circ:** Paid ⊕**4,700**.

10751 ■ The Inspector
American Society of Home Inspectors
932 Lee St., Ste. 101
Des Plaines, IL 60016
Phone: (847)759-2820
Fax: (847)759-1620
Magazine publishing articles related to home inspectors. **Freq:** Monthly. **Subscription Rates:** Included in membership. **URL:** http://www.nachi.org/bbsystem/viewtopic.php?t=4242&PHPSESSID=5093079eb32b966f5ed272940ebb8972. **Remarks:** Accepts advertising. **Circ:** Free ‡50000, 200.

10752 ■ Journal of Emergency Nursing
Emergency Nurses Association
915 Lee St.
Des Plaines, IL 60016-6569
Phone: (847)460-4123
Free: 800-900-9659
Publisher's E-mail: education@ena.org
Journal comprising of peer-reviewed articles, original research and updates in the field emergency nursing and trauma departments. **Freq:** Bimonthly. **ISSN:** 0099-1767 (print). **Subscription Rates:** $106 Individuals online only; $118 Individuals print and online; $149 Other countries print and online; $118 Students print and online; $149 Students print and online. **URL:** http://www.ena.org/publications/jen/Pages/Default.aspx; http://www.jenonline.org. **Remarks:** Accepts advertising. **Circ:** (Not Reported).

10753 ■ OCCurrence
Oakton Community College
1600 E Golf Rd.
Des Plaines, IL 60016
Phone: (847)635-1600
Publication E-mail: occurrence@oakton.edu
Collegiate newspaper. **Freq:** Bimonthly. **Print Method:** Offset. **Cols./Page:** 5. **Col. Width:** 26 nonpareils. **Key Personnel:** Sue Fox, Advisor, phone: (847)635-1678. **URL:** http://www.oakton.edu/studentlife/student_activities/student_newspaper/index.php; http://issuu.com/oaktonoccurrence/docs. **Ad Rates:** BW $375; PCI $8. **Remarks:** Accepts advertising. **Circ:** Free ‡3750.

10754 ■ SPCP 10-Year Journal
Society of Permanent Cosmetic Professionals
69 N Broadway St.
Des Plaines, IL 60016
Phone: (847)635-1330
Fax: (847)635-1326
Publisher's E-mail: admin@spcp.org
Subscription Rates: $99 /set; $79 /set (for trainers only). **Remarks:** Advertising not accepted. **Circ:** (Not Reported).

DIVERNON

Sangamon Co. Sangamon Co. (C). 18 m S of Springfield. Agriculture. Wheat, corn, oats and soybeans.

10755 ■ Divernon News
South County Publications
110 N Fifth St.
Auburn, IL 62615
Phone: (217)438-6155
Fax: (217)438-6156
Publisher's E-mail: southco@royell.org
Community newspaper. **Freq:** Weekly (Thurs.). **Print Method:** Offset. **Cols./Page:** 7. **Col. Width:** 23 nonpareils. **Col. Depth:** 301 agate lines. **Key Personnel:** Connie Michelich, Manager, Advertising; Joseph Michelich, Jr., Publisher; Joseph M. Michelich, Managing Editor; Joe Pritchett, Editor. **Subscription Rates:** $30 Individuals in Sangamon County; $32 Individuals in Illinois; $37 Out of state; $27 Individuals seniors (65 or older), in Sangamon County; $29 Individuals seniors (65 or older), in Illinois; $34 Out of state seniors (65 or older). **URL:** http://www.southcountypublications.com/DivernonNews/DivyArchives.html. **Ad Rates:** SAU $3.50; PCI $2.75. **Circ:** ‡500.

DIXON

Lee Co. Lee Co. (N). 100 m W of Chicago. Manufactures cement, paper bags, automotive parts, plastic products, shoes, electronic parts, metal specialties, dairy products, cereals, stock feed, candy, cheese, condensed milk, garage doors. Sand, gravel pits. Hatcheries. Stock, poultry, grain farms.

10756 ■ Ledger-Sentinel
Shaw Media
444 Pine Hill Dr.
Dixon, IL 61021
Phone: (815)284-4000
Publisher's E-mail: info@shawmedia.com
Community newspaper serving Oswego, Boulder Hill, and Montgomery. **Freq:** Weekly (Thurs.). **Print Method:** Offset. **Cols./Page:** 6. **Col. Width:** 19 nonpareils. **Col. Depth:** 224 agate lines. **Key Personnel:** Jeff Farren, Editor. **Subscription Rates:** $26 Individuals; $34 Elsewhere; $45 Other countries. **URL:** http://www.ledgersentinel.com/. **Ad Rates:** GLR $.29; BW $384; SAU $5.20. **Remarks:** Accepts advertising. **Circ:** ‡3100.

10757 ■ WIXN-AM - 1460
1460 S College Ave.
Dixon, IL 61021
Phone: (815)288-3341
Fax: (815)284-1017
Format: Adult Contemporary. **Simulcasts:** WSEY 0600-0825 Mon. Thru Sat. **Networks:** ABC. **Owner:** NRG Media, 2875 Mount Vernon Rd. SE, Cedar Rapids, IA 52403, Ph: (319)862-0300, Fax: (319)286-9383. **Founded:** 1961. **Operating Hours**: Continuous. **Key Personnel:** Al Knickrehm, Gen. Mgr., aknickrehm@nrgmedia.com; Mary Quass, President, mquass@nrgmedia.com. **Wattage**: 1,000. **Ad Rates:** Noncommercial. WIXN/FM; WSEY/FM. **URL:** http://www.myrockriverradio.com.

10758 ■ WRCV-FM - 101.7
1460 S College Ave.
Dixon, IL 61021
Phone: (815)288-3341
Fax: (815)284-1017
Format: Country. **Owner:** NRG Media, 2875 Mount Vernon Rd. SE, Cedar Rapids, IA 52403, Ph: (319)862-0300, Fax: (319)286-9383.

DOWNERS GROVE

DuPage Co. Du Page Co. (NE). 21 m SW of Chicago. Residential. Manufactures spiral bevel gears, fabricated metal products, plastic molds and coils, condensers, bearings, chain conveyors, construction equipment, boiler feed systems. Nurseries. Dairy, poultry, truck farms.

10759 ■ Bensenville Press
Shaw Media
1101 W 31st St.
Downers Grove, IL 60515-5581
Phone: (630)368-1100
Publisher's E-mail: info@shawmedia.com
Community newspaper. **Freq:** Weekly. **Print Method:** Offset. **Key Personnel:** J. Tom Shaw, Publisher. **URL:** http://www.mysuburbanlife.com/bensenville. **Remarks:** Advertising accepted; rates available upon request. **Circ:** (Not Reported).

10760 ■ Bolingbrook/Romeoville Reporter
GateHouse Media Inc.
1101 W 31st St.
Downers Grove, IL 60515-5581
Phone: (630)368-1100
Community newspaper. **Freq:** Weekly (Thurs.). **Print Method:** Offset. **Key Personnel:** Mark Colosimo, Editor, phone: (630)368-8914. **Subscription Rates:** $40 Individuals. **URL:** http://www.mysuburbanlife.com/romeoville; http://www.mysuburbanlife.com/bolingbrook. **Remarks:** Advertising accepted; rates available upon request. **Circ:** Combined 9200.

10761 ■ Downers Grove Reporter
Shaw Media
1101 W 31st St.
Downers Grove, IL 60515
Phone: (630)368-1100
Publisher's E-mail: info@shawmedia.com
Community newspaper. **Freq:** Weekly (Wed.). **Print Method:** Offset. **Trim Size:** 11 1/2 x 17. **Cols./Page:** 5. **Col. Width:** 11 picas. **Col. Depth:** 16 inches. **Key Personnel:** J. Tom Shaw, Publisher. **Subscription Rates:** $40 Individuals; $33 Individuals. **URL:** http://www.mysuburbanlife.com/downersgrove. **Remarks:** Advertising accepted; rates available upon request. **Circ:** Combined ♦**14227**, Paid ♦**555**, Non-paid ♦**16240**.

10762 ■ eMatrimony
Worldwide Marriage Encounter
3943 W End Rd.
Downers Grove, IL 60515
Magazine containing articles of encouragement for couples as well as messages on relationships, spirituality, and family. **Freq:** Quarterly. **Key Personnel:** Larry Eck, Editor; Mary Sue Eck, Manager, Advertising; Rev. Don Skerry, SVD, Editor. **Alt. Formats:** PDF. **URL:** http://www.ematrimony.org/index.htm. **Circ:** (Not Reported).

Circulation: ★ = AAM; △ or • = BPA; ♦ = CAC; ❑ = VAC; ⊕ = PO Statement; ‡ = Publisher's Report; Boldface figures = sworn; Light figures = estimated.

10763 ■ Geneva Republican
Liberty Suburban Chicago Newspapers
1101 W 31st St.
Downers Grove, IL 60515-5581
Phone: (630)368-1100
Publisher's E-mail: mjames@libertysuburban.com
Community newspaper. **Freq:** Weekly (Thurs.). **Print Method:** Offset. **Cols./Page:** 5. **URL:** http://www.mysuburbanlife.com/geneva. **Remarks:** Advertising accepted; rates available upon request. **Circ:** Combined ♦**8684**.

10764 ■ Glen Ellyn News
GateHouse Media Inc.
1101 W 31st St.
Downers Grove, IL 60515-5581
Phone: (630)368-1100
Community newspaper. **Freq:** Weekly (Thurs.). **Print Method:** Offset. **Cols./Page:** 5. **Key Personnel:** Jonathan Schuler, Executive Editor, phone: (630)368-8939; Mark Colosimo, Editor, phone: (630)368-8914. **URL:** http://www.mysuburbanlife.com/glenellyn/. **Remarks:** Accepts advertising. **Circ:** Combined ‡9211.

10765 ■ Glen Ellyn Press
Liberty Surburban Chicago Newspapers Press Publications
1101 W 31st St., Ste. 100
Downers Grove, IL 60515
Phone: (630)368-1100
Community newspaper. **Freq:** Weekly (Thurs.). **Print Method:** Offset. **Cols./Page:** 5. **Col. Width:** 24 nonpareils. **Col. Depth:** 224 agate lines. **Key Personnel:** Mark Colosimo, Publisher, phone: (630)368-8914; Don Stamper, Director, Operations, phone: (630)368-1100; Jonathan Schuler, Managing Editor, phone: (630)368-8939. **Subscription Rates:** $17 Individuals. **URL:** http://www.mysuburbanlife.com/glenellyn. **Ad Rates:** SAU $8.94. **Remarks:** Accepts advertising. **Circ:** Paid ‡219, Free ‡4252.

10766 ■ Hinsdale/Clarendon Hills/Oak Brook Suburban Life
GateHouse Media Inc.
1101 W 31st St.
Downers Grove, IL 60515
Phone: (630)368-1100
Community newspaper. **Key Personnel:** J. Tom Shaw, Publisher, phone: (630)427-6210; David Lemery, Managing Editor, phone: (630)427-6250. **Subscription Rates:** $24 Individuals. **URL:** http://www.mysuburbanlife.com/hinsdale; http://www.mysuburbanlife.com/clarendonhills; http://www.mysuburbanlife.com/oakbrook. **Remarks:** Accepts advertising. **Circ:** (Not Reported).

10767 ■ Itasca Press: Serving Bartlett/Hanover Park/Steamwood Press
Shaw Media
1101 W 31st St.
Downers Grove, IL 60515-5581
Phone: (630)368-1100
Publisher's E-mail: info@shawmedia.com
Community newspaper. **Freq:** Weekly (Thurs.). **Print Method:** Offset. **Key Personnel:** J. Tom Shaw, Publisher. **Subscription Rates:** $30 Individuals. **URL:** http://www.mysuburbanlife.com/itasca. **Remarks:** Advertising accepted; rates available upon request. **Circ:** (Not Reported).

10768 ■ Lemont Reporter/Metropolitan
Shaw Media
1101 W 31st St.
Downers Grove, IL 60515
Phone: (630)368-1100
Publisher's E-mail: info@shawmedia.com
Community newspaper. **Freq:** Weekly. **Key Personnel:** David Lemery, Editor. **Subscription Rates:** $40 Individuals. **URL:** http://www.mysuburbanlife.com/lemont. **Formed by the merger of:** Lemont Reporter; Lemont Metropolitan. **Remarks:** Advertising accepted; rates available upon request. **Circ:** Combined ‡4300.

10769 ■ Lombard Suburban Life
Shaw Media
1101 W 31st St.
Downers Grove, IL 60515
Phone: (630)368-1100
Publication E-mail: dgood@shawmedia.com
Community newspaper. **Freq:** Weekly (Thurs.) Biweekly. **Print Method:** Offset. **Key Personnel:** Jonathan Schuler, Executive Editor, phone: (630)368-8939; Mark Colosimo, Editor, phone: (630)368-8914. **URL:** http://www.mysuburbanlife.com/lombard. **Formerly:** Lombard Spectator. **Remarks:** Advertising accepted; rates available upon request. **Circ:** Combined ‡8377.

10770 ■ Mid-America Standardbred & Harness News
Resource Development Press Ltd.
2235 Durand Dr.
Downers Grove, IL 60515
Phone: (630)963-0398
Fax: (630)963-2625
Racing news (standardbreds). **Freq:** Monthly. **Print Method:** Uses mats. Offset. **Trim Size:** 8 3/8 x 10 7/8. **Cols./Page:** 3. **Col. Width:** 27 nonpareils. **Col. Depth:** 140 agate lines. **Key Personnel:** Sam Lilly, Editor, Publisher. **Subscription Rates:** $29 Individuals 1 year; $55 Individuals 2 years; $79 Individuals 3 years. **URL:** http://www.trotandpace.com/ad_info.htm. **Formerly:** Illinois Standardbred and Sulky News; Illinois Standardbred & Mid-America Harness News. **Mailing address:** PO Box 399, Downers Grove, IL 60515. **Ad Rates:** BW $457; 4C $627; PCI $25. **Remarks:** Accepts advertising. **Circ:** 1540.

10771 ■ Nuclear Plant Journal: An International Publication Published in the United States
Nuclear Plant Journal
1400 Opus Pl., Ste. 904
Downers Grove, IL 60515
Phone: (630)858-6161
Fax: (630)852-8787
Publication E-mail: npj@goinfo.com
Magazine focusing on nuclear power plants. **Freq:** Bimonthly. **Print Method:** Web offset. **Trim Size:** 8 1/4 x 10 7/8. **Cols./Page:** 3. **Col. Width:** 27 nonpareils. **Col. Depth:** 98 agate lines. **Key Personnel:** Anu Agnihotri, Publisher, Manager, Sales; Michelle Gaylord, Contact. **ISSN:** 0892--2055 (print). **Subscription Rates:** Free to industry professionals. **URL:** http://www.nuclearplantjournal.com. **Ad Rates:** BW $4720. **Remarks:** Accepts advertising. **Circ:** △**12000**.

10772 ■ OAG Air Cargo Guide
Official Airline Guides
3025 Highland Pkwy., Ste. 200
Downers Grove, IL 60515-5561
Phone: (630)515-5300
Fax: (630)515-5301
Free: 800-342-5624
Publisher's E-mail: contactus@oag.com
Guide to shipping freight by air containing current domestic, international and combination passenger cargo flight schedules. **Freq:** Monthly. **Print Method:** Web Offset. **Trim Size:** 8 1/4 x 11 11/16. **Cols./Page:** 3. **Col. Width:** 27 nonpareils. **Col. Depth:** 140 agate lines. **ISSN:** 0191--152X (print). **URL:** http://www2.oag.com/tt/catalog/freight.html. **Ad Rates:** BW $1,488; 4C $3,396. **Remarks:** Accepts advertising. **Circ:** ‡10.

10773 ■ OAG Flight-Finder Asia Pacific Plus
Official Airline Guides
3025 Highland Pkwy., Ste. 200
Downers Grove, IL 60515-5561
Phone: (630)515-5300
Fax: (630)515-5301
Free: 800-342-5624
Publisher's E-mail: contactus@oag.com
Guide containing quick reference airline schedules within and between all countries of the Pacific geographic area; plus all schedules between the area and North America, Europe, the Middle East, Africa, and Central/South America. **Freq:** Monthly. **Print Method:** Offset. **Trim Size:** 4 3/16 x 8 3/8. **Cols./Page:** 2. **USPS:** 952-620. **Subscription Rates:** $208 Individuals. **URL:** http://www.oag.com/oag-store. **Ad Rates:** BW $2,000. **Remarks:** Accepts advertising. **Circ:** (Not Reported).

10774 ■ Oak Brook Suburban Life
Shaw Media
1101 W 31st St.
Downers Grove, IL 60515-5581
Publisher's E-mail: info@shawmedia.com
Community newspaper. **Freq:** Weekly. **Key Personnel:** Mark Colosimo, Editor, phone: (630)368-8914. **URL:** http://www.mysuburbanlife.com/oakbrook. **Formerly:** Suburban LIFE Citizen. **Ad Rates:** SAU $22.75. **Remarks:** Accepts advertising. **Circ:** Paid 24119.

10775 ■ Roselle Press
Shaw Media
1101 W 31st
Downers Grove, IL 60515-5581
Phone: (630)368-1100
Publisher's E-mail: info@shawmedia.com
Community newspaper. **Freq:** Weekly. **Print Method:** Offset. **Key Personnel:** J. Tom Shaw, Publisher. **URL:** http://www.mysuburbanlife.com/roselle. **Remarks:** Advertising accepted; rates available upon request. **Circ:** (Not Reported).

10776 ■ St. Charles Republican
GateHouse Media Inc.
1101 W 31st St.
Downers Grove, IL 60515-5581
Phone: (630)368-1100
Community newspaper. **Freq:** Weekly (Thurs.). **Print Method:** Offset. **Cols./Page:** 5. **Key Personnel:** Mark Colosimo, Editor, phone: (630)368-8914. **Subscription Rates:** $40 Individuals. **URL:** http://www.mysuburbanlife.com/stcharles. **Remarks:** Advertising accepted; rates available upon request. **Circ:** Combined ♦**12147**.

10777 ■ Warrenville Press
GateHouse Media Inc.
1101 W 31st St.
Downers Grove, IL 60515-5581
Phone: (630)368-1100
Community newspaper. **Freq:** Weekly. **Key Personnel:** Mark Colosimo, Editor, phone: (630)368-8914. **URL:** http://www.mysuburbanlife.com/warrenville. **Remarks:** Advertising accepted; rates available upon request. **Circ:** Paid ‡337.

10778 ■ Western Springs Suburban Life
GateHouse Media Inc.
1101 W 31st St.
Downers Grove, IL 60515-5581
Phone: (630)368-1100
Community newspaper. **Freq:** Semiweekly (Wed. and Sun.) Wed. & Sun. **Print Method:** Offset. **Cols./Page:** 5. **Key Personnel:** Mark Colosimo, Publisher, phone: (630)368-8914; Lesley Valadez, Assistant Managing Editor, phone: (630)368-8897; Jonathan K. Schuler, Executive Editor, phone: (630)368-8939. **Subscription Rates:** $24 Individuals /year. **URL:** http://www.mysuburbanlife.com/westernsprings; http://www.mysuburbanlife.com/magazine. **Remarks:** Advertising accepted; rates available upon request. **Circ:** Paid 20850.

10779 ■ Wheaton Leader
GateHouse Media Inc.
1101 W 31st St.
Downers Grove, IL 60515-5581
Phone: (630)368-1100
Community newspaper. **Freq:** Weekly (Thurs.). **Print Method:** Offset. **Cols./Page:** 5. **Col. Width:** 2 inches. **Col. Depth:** 14 inches. **Key Personnel:** Mark Colosimo, Editor, phone: (630)368-8914; Jonathan Schuler, Executive Editor, phone: (630)368-8939. **URL:** http://www.mysuburbanlife.com/wheaton. **Remarks:** Advertising accepted; rates available upon request. **Circ:** Combined ‡10168.

10780 ■ Winfield Press
GateHouse Media Inc.
1101 W 31st St.
Downers Grove, IL 60515-5581
Phone: (630)368-1100
Community newspaper. **Freq:** Weekly. **Print Method:** Offset. **Key Personnel:** Mark Colosimo, Editor, phone: (630)368-8914. **Subscription Rates:** $40 Individuals. **URL:** http://www.mysuburbanlife.com/winfield. **Remarks:** Advertising accepted; rates available upon request. **Circ:** Combined ‡3909.

10781 ■ WDGC-FM
6301 Springside Ave
Downers Grove, IL 60516-2488
Email: wdgcfm@hotmail.com
Format: Full Service. **Founded:** 1965. **Key Personnel:** John Waite, Gen. Mgr. **Ad Rates:** Noncommercial.

DU QUOIN

10782 ■ Du Quoin Evening Call
GateHouse Media Inc.
9 N Division St.
Du Quoin, IL 62832
Phone: (618)542-2133

Fax: (618)542-2726
Community newspaper covering local news. **Freq:** Daily. **Key Personnel:** John H. Croessman, Publisher; Doug Daniels, Editor; Patty Malinee, Manager, Circulation. **URL:** http://www.duquoin.com/. **Circ:** (Not Reported).

10783 ■ WDQN-AM - 1580
PO Box 190
Du Quoin, IL 62832
Format: Country. **Networks:** ABC. **Owner:** Duquoin Broadcasting Co., 2327 US Rte. 51, Du Quoin, IL 62832, Ph: (618)542-3894. **Founded:** 1951. **Operating Hours:** Continuous. **Wattage:** 250.

EAST DUNDEE

10784 ■ Lawn Institute Turf News
The Lawn Institute
2 E Main St.
East Dundee, IL 60118
Phone: (847)649-5555
Fax: (847)649-5678
Free: 800-405-8873
Publisher's E-mail: info@thelawninstitue.org
Freq: Annual. **Subscription Rates:** free. **Alt. Formats:** CD-ROM. **Remarks:** Accepts advertising. **Circ:** 1500.

10785 ■ Official Club Binder
Anheuser-Busch Collectors Club
1070 Dundee Ave., Ste. A
East Dundee, IL 60118
Phone: (847)428-3150
Fax: (847)428-3170
Free: 800-498-3215
Publisher's E-mail: steinland@aol.com
Subscription Rates: included in membership dues. **Remarks:** Advertising not accepted. **Circ:** (Not Reported).

10786 ■ Turf News
Turfgrass Producers International
2 E Main St.
East Dundee, IL 60118
Phone: (847)649-5555
Fax: (847)649-5678
Free: 800-405-8873
Publisher's E-mail: info@turfgrasssod.org
Focuses on the business of turfgrass by targeting farm owners and managers. **Freq:** Bimonthly. **Print Method:** Offset. **Trim Size:** 8 1/8 x 10 7/8. **Cols./Page:** 3. **Col. Width:** 2 3/4 inches. **Key Personnel:** Den Gardner, Editor; Lynn Grooms, Managing Editor. **ISSN:** 0899--417X (print). **Subscription Rates:** Included in membership. **URL:** http://www.turfgrasssod.org/pages/resources/turf-news/?professional-resources; http://www.turfgrasssod.org/pages/resources/turf-news/?advertising. **Ad Rates:** BW $1,790; 4C $2,240; PCI $150. **Remarks:** Accepts advertising. **Circ:** ‡2050.

EAST MOLINE

10787 ■ WDLM-AM - 960
PO Box 149
East Moline, IL 61244
Phone: (309)234-5111
Fax: (309)234-5114
Free: 800-221-9356
Email: wdlm@moody.edu
Format: Religious. **Networks:** Moody Broadcasting. **Owner:** The Moody Bible Institute of Chicago, 820 N Lasalle St., Chicago, IL 60610, Ph: (312)329-4000, Free: 800-356-6639. **Founded:** 1960. **Operating Hours:** 12 a.m.-10:25 p.m. Mon.-Fri.; 12 a.m.-11 p.m. Saturday and Sunday. **ADI:** Daveport,IA-Rock Island, Moline,IL. **Wattage:** 1,000 Day; 102 Night. **Ad Rates:** Noncommercial. **URL:** http://www.moodyradioqc.fm.

10788 ■ WDLM-FM - 89.3
PO Box 149
East Moline, IL 61244
Phone: (309)234-5111
Fax: (309)234-5114
Free: 800-221-9356
Email: wdlm@moody.edu
Format: Religious. **Networks:** Moody Broadcasting. **Owner:** The Moody Bible Institute of Chicago, 820 N Lasalle St., Chicago, IL 60610, Ph: (312)329-4000, Free: 800-356-6639. **Founded:** 1980. **Operating Hours:** Continuous. **ADI:** Daveport,IA-Rock Island, Moline,IL. **Wattage:** 100,000. **Ad Rates:** Noncommercial. **URL:** http://www.moodyradioqc.fm.

EAST PEORIA

Tazewell Co. Tazewell Co. (NC). 5 m E of Peoria.

10789 ■ WAOE-TV - 59
2907 Springfield Rd.
East Peoria, IL 61611
Phone: (309)674-5900
Fax: (309)674-5959
Key Personnel: Sara Horn, Station Mgr. **Ad Rates:** Advertising accepted; rates available upon request. **URL:** http://www.my59.tv.

10790 ■ WBQD-TV - 26
2907 Springfield Rd.
East Peoria, IL 61611
Phone: (309)674-5900
Fax: (309)674-5959
Key Personnel: Sara Horn, Contact; Trent A. Poindexter, Gen. Sales Mgr., VP, trent.poindexter@wqad.com; Sara Horn, Contact. **Ad Rates:** Advertising accepted; rates available upon request. **URL:** http://www.abc57.com.

10791 ■ WEEK-TV - 25
2907 Springfield Rd.
East Peoria, IL 61611
Phone: (309)698-2525
Format: Commercial TV. **Networks:** NBC. **Owner:** Granite Broadcasting Corp., 767 3rd Ave., 34th Fl., New York, NY 10017-2083, Ph: (212)826-2530, Fax: (212)826-2858. **Founded:** 1953. **Operating Hours:** Continuous; 60% network, 40% local. **ADI:** Peoria-Bloomington, IL. **Wattage:** 1,410,000 ERP. **Ad Rates:** Advertising accepted; rates available upon request. **URL:** http://www.cinewsnow.com.

EDWARDSVILLE

Madison Co. Madison Co. (SW). 21 m NE of St. Louis, Mo. Southern Illinois University, Edwardsville Campus. Brick plant. Nursery. Hatcheries. Diversified farming.

10792 ■ Edwardsville Intelligencer
Edwardsville Publishing Company Inc.
117 N Second St.
Edwardsville, IL 62025
Phone: (618)656-4700
Fax: (618)656-7618
Local newspaper. **Freq:** Daily (eve.) and Sat. (morn.). **Print Method:** Offset. **Trim Size:** 13 3/4 x 22 3/4. **Cols./Page:** 6. **Col. Width:** 24 nonpareils. **Col. Depth:** 301 agate lines. **Key Personnel:** Carl Green, Managing Editor; Bill Roseberry, Editor. **Subscription Rates:** $45.25 Individuals 12 Weeks; $78 Individuals 24 Weeks; $129.50 Individuals 48 Weeks. **URL:** http://www.theintelligencer.com. **Ad Rates:** GLR $1.18; BW $1362; 4C $1737; SAU $10.56. **Remarks:** Accepts advertising. **Circ:** Mon.-Sat. ★**4990**.

10793 ■ Edwardsville Journal of Sociology: A scholarly journal for the students and faculty of Southern Illinois University Edwardsville
Southern Illinois University at Edwardsville
Dept. of Sociology
Edwardsville, IL 62026
Phone: (618)650-2000
Free: 800-447-SIUE
Publisher's E-mail: help@siue.edu
Online scholarly journal for students and faculty at the Department of Sociology and Criminal Justice Studies at Southern Illinois University Edwardsville. **Freq:** Annual. **Subscription Rates:** Free online. **URL:** http://www.siue.edu/artsandsciences/sociology/ejs/index_new.shtml. **Circ:** (Not Reported).

10794 ■ Papers on Language & Literature: A Journal for Scholars and Critics of Language and Literature
Papers on Language & Literature
S Illinois University
Edwardsville, IL 62026-1434
Phone: (618)650-2000
Free: 800-447-7483
Publication E-mail: pll@siue.edu
Literary history, theory, and interpretation. **Freq:** Quarterly. **Print Method:** Offset. Uses mats. **Trim Size:** 6 x 9. **Cols./Page:** 1. **Col. Width:** 54 nonpareils. **Col. Depth:** 110 agate lines. **Key Personnel:** Jack G. Voller, Editor; Melanie Ethridge, Managing Editor; Brian Abel Ragen, Associate Editor. **ISSN:** 0031--1294 (print). **Subscription Rates:** $120 Institutions; $40 Individuals. **Online:** EBSCO; Gale; H.W. Wilson. **Alt. Formats:** Microform. **URL:** http://www.siue.edu/pll/about_journal.shtml. **Ad Rates:** BW $60. **Remarks:** Advertising accepted; rates available upon request. **Circ:** (Not Reported).

10795 ■ Postmedieval: A journal of medieval cultural studies
Palgrave Macmillan
c/o Eileen A. Joy, Ed.
Peck Hall, Rm. 3206
Southern Illinois University Edwardsville
Edwardsville, IL 62026-1431
Publication E-mail: postmedieval@palgrave.com
Peer-reviewed journal focusing on medieval culture. **Freq:** Quarterly. **Key Personnel:** Eileen Joy, Editor; Myra Seaman, Editor. **ISSN:** 2040--5960 (print); **EISSN:** 2040--5979 (electronic). **Subscription Rates:** $108 Individuals; £66 Individuals Europe and rest of the world; $797 Institutions U.S.A.; £470 Institutions Europe and rest of the world. **URL:** http://www.palgrave-journals.com/pmed/index.html. **Circ:** (Not Reported).

10796 ■ WSIE-FM - 88.7
Southern Illinois University Edwardsville
S Illinois University
Edwardsville, IL 62026-1773
Phone: (618)650-2228
Fax: (888)325-8870
Free: 888-325-8870
Email: wsie887@siue.edu
Format: Religious. **Networks:** National Public Radio (NPR); Public Radio International (PRI). **Owner:** Southern Illinois University, 1263 Lincoln Dr., Carbondale, IL 62901. **Founded:** 1970. **Operating Hours:** Continuous; 10% network, 90% local. **ADI:** St. Louis, MO (Mt. Vernon, IL). **Wattage:** 50,000. **Ad Rates:** Noncommercial. **Mailing address:** PO Box 1773, Edwardsville, IL 62026-1773. **URL:** http://www.wsieradio.com.

EFFINGHAM

Effingham Co. Effingham Co. (S). 60 m SE of Decatur. Manufactures clutch plates, air conditioning, feed, insecticides, printing ink, electrographics, hardwood lumber, gloves, wood blocks, laminated furniture components, oil, prefabricated homes. Milling.

10797 ■ Effingham Daily News
Community Newspaper Holdings Inc.
201 N Banker St.
Effingham, IL 62401
Phone: (217)347-7151
Fax: (217)342-9315
Free: 800-526-7205
Publication E-mail: edn@effinghamdailynews.com
Newspaper serving Effingham County, Illinois and the counties of Clay, Cumberland, Fayette, Jasper and Shelby. **Freq:** Daily. **Key Personnel:** Donna Riley-Gordon, Managing Editor; Cathy Thoele-Griffith, Reporter; Steve Raymond, Publisher. **Subscription Rates:** $132 Individuals motor route; $129 Individuals carrier; $138 By mail; $177 Out of state mail. **URL:** http://www.effinghamdailynews.com. **Mailing address:** PO Box 370, Effingham, IL 62401. **Remarks:** Accepts advertising. **Circ:** Mon.-Sat. ★**10774**.

10798 ■ WCRA-AM - 1090
405 S Banker St., Ste. 201
Effingham, IL 62401
Phone: (217)342-4141
Fax: (217)342-4143
Format: Talk; News. **Networks:** Independent. **Owner:** The Cromwell Group, Inc., 1824 Murfreesboro Rd., Nashville, TN 37217, Ph: (615)361-7560, Fax: (615)366-4313. **Founded:** 1947. **Operating Hours:** 12 hours Daily; 100% local. **Wattage:** 1,000. **Ad Rates:** $10-25 per unit. **URL:** http://www.cromwellradio.com.

10799 ■ WCRC-FM - 95.7
405 S Banker St., No. 201
Effingham, IL 62401
Phone: (217)342-4141
Fax: (217)342-4143
Format: Country. **Networks:** Independent. **Owner:** The Cromwell Group, Inc., 1824 Murfreesboro Rd., Nashville,

Circulation: ★ = AAM; △ or • = BPA; ♦ = CAC; ❑ = VAC; ⊕ = PO Statement; ‡ = Publisher's Report; Boldface figures = sworn; Light figures = estimated.

TN 37217, Ph: (615)361-7560, Fax: (615)366-4313. **Founded:** 1963. **Operating Hours:** Continuous. **Key Personnel:** Marv Phillips, Gen. Mgr. **Wattage:** 50,000. **Ad Rates:** $10-25 per unit. **URL:** http://www.effinghamradio.com.

10800 ■ WEFI-FM - 89.5
PO Drawer 2440
Tupelo, MS 38803
Free: 800-326-4543
Format: Religious. **Owner:** American Family Association, at above address. **URL:** http://www.afa.net.

10801 ■ WKJT-FM - 102.3
206 S Willow St.
Effingham, IL 62401
Phone: (217)347-5518
Fax: (217)347-5519
Format: Country. **Ad Rates:** Noncommercial. **URL:** http://www.kjcountry.com.

10802 ■ WXEF-FM - 97.9
206 S Willow St.
Effingham, IL 62401
Phone: (217)347-5518
Fax: (217)347-5519
Email: info@thexradio.com
Format: Hot Country. **Founded:** Sept. 08, 2006. **Key Personnel:** Tonya Siner, VP of Operations, tonya@thexradio.com; Greg Sapp, Station Mgr., greg@thexradio.com; Teresa Klingler, Office Mgr., teresa@thexradio.com. **Ad Rates:** Noncommercial. **URL:** http://www.thexradio.com.

ELBURN

Kane Co. Kane Co. (NE). 45 m W of Chicago. Light manufacturing. Dairy, stock, poultry, grain farms.

10803 ■ The Elburn Herald
Kaneland Publications Inc.
123 N Main St.
Elburn, IL 60119
Phone: (630)365-6446
Fax: (630)365-2251
Publisher's E-mail: info@elburnherald.com
Community newspaper. **Freq:** Weekly (Thurs.). **Print Method:** Offset. **Trim Size:** 22 3/4 x 17. **Cols./Page:** 4. **Col. Width:** 2 1/2 inches. **Col. Depth:** 16 inches. **Key Personnel:** Carly Shaw, Business Manager, phone: (630)365-6446; Keith G. Beebe, Editor, phone: (630)365-6446; Ryan Wells, Publisher, phone: (630)365-6446. **USPS:** 171-180. **Subscription Rates:** $25 Individuals /year; $50 Individuals 2 years; $7.50 Individuals 6 months. **URL:** http://kanelandpublications.com/category/local-news/elburn. **Ad Rates:** GLR $1.25; BW $640; 4C $865; PCI $10. **Remarks:** Accepts advertising. **Circ:** ‡3300.

ELDORADO

Saline Co. Saline Co. (S). 45 m SW of Evansville, Ind. Hatcheries. Coal mines, oil wells. Mirrors manufactured. Grain farms. Corn, soybeans, popcorn.

10804 ■ WEBQ-FM - 102.3
701 S Commercial
Harrisburg, IL 62946
Phone: (618)253-7812
Fax: (618)252-2366
Email: webq@yourclearwave.com
Format: Adult Contemporary. **Networks:** ABC. **Owner:** Withers Broadcasting Companies, 1822 N Court St., Marion, IL 62959, Ph: (303)242-5000. **Founded:** 1971. **Formerly:** WKSI-FM. **Operating Hours:** Continuous. **Wattage:** 3,000. **Ad Rates:** $2.25-8.50 for 30 seconds; $3.25-10 for 60 seconds. Combined advertising rates available with Withers Broadcasting & Dana Communication stations. **URL:** http://www.webqradio.com/.

ELGIN

Kane Co. Kane Co (NE). On Fox River, 38 m NW of Chicago. Judson College. Manufactures food products, metal fasteners, street sweepers, steel kitchens, switchboards, electric appliances, paper boxes, novelties, filling machinery, oil seals, steel tube containers, diamond cutting tools and abrasives, flexible metal hose, furniture, paint, steel, iron, pottery, plastic cloth. Woodworking.

10805 ■ Disability
American Academy of Disability Evaluating Physicians
2575 Northwest Pky.
Elgin, IL 60124
Phone: (312)663-1171
Fax: (312)663-1175
Free: 800-456-6095
Publisher's E-mail: aadep@aadep.org
Freq: Quarterly. **Remarks:** Accepts advertising. **Circ:** (Not Reported).

10806 ■ FEDA News and Views
Foodservice Equipment Distributors Association
2250 Point Blvd., Ste. 200
Elgin, IL 60123
Phone: (224)293-6500
Fax: (224)293-6505
Publisher's E-mail: feda@feda.com
Magazine reporting association and industry news. **Freq:** Bimonthly. **Key Personnel:** Jim Hanson, President, phone: (614)488-2378, fax: (614)488-4732; Raymond W. Herrick, Editor; Stacy Ward, Managing Editor. **ISSN:** 0746- 9675 (print). **Subscription Rates:** $175 Individuals /year. **URL:** http://www.feda.com/magazine. **Ad Rates:** BW $1,970, full page; BW $1350, 1/2 page island; BW $1230, 1/2 page horizontal or vertical; BW $1000, 1/3 page horizontal or vertical; BW $650, 1/4 page; 4C $5500, 4-color full page spread; 4C $5460, 1/2 page horizontal 4-color spread. **Remarks:** Accepts advertising. **Circ:** Controlled 1300, 1600.

10807 ■ Messenger
Church of the Brethren General Board
1451 Dundee Ave.
Elgin, IL 60120
Phone: (847)742-5100
Fax: (847)742-6103
Free: 800-323-8039
Publisher's E-mail: cobweb@brethren.org
Religious magazine. **Founded:** Apr. 1851. **Freq:** 10/year. **Print Method:** Letterpress and offset. **Trim Size:** 8 1/2 x 11. **Cols./Page:** 2 and 3. **Col. Width:** 42 and 28 nonpareils. **Col. Depth:** 140 agate lines. **Key Personnel:** Randy Miller, Editor; Diane Stroyeck, Contact. **ISSN:** 0026-0355 (print). **Subscription Rates:** $17.50 Individuals print + online; $14.50 Members church club; print + online; $32 Two years print + online; $1.25 Students /month; print + online; $25 Other countries Western Hemisphere; $30 Other countries Europe; $35 Other countries Africa/Asia/Pacific. **URL:** http://www.brethren.org/messenger/. **Ad Rates:** BW $1,200; 4C $1,300; PCI $110. **Remarks:** Advertising accepted; rates available upon request. **Circ:** ‡12000.

10808 ■ WEPS-FM - 88.9
355 E Chicago St.
Elgin, IL 60120
Phone: (847)888-5000
Email: info@u-46.org
Format: Public Radio; Educational. **Owner:** School District U-46, 355 E Chicago St., Elgin, IL 60120-6543, Ph: (847)888-5000. **Founded:** 1950. **Operating Hours:** Continuous. **Key Personnel:** Jeff King, COO, jeffking@u-46.org. **Wattage:** 740. **Ad Rates:** Noncommercial. **URL:** http://www.u-46.org/npps/section.cfm?sid=9.

10809 ■ WRMN-AM - 1410
14 Douglas Ave.
Elgin, IL 60120
Phone: (847)741-7700
Format: Talk; News. **Owner:** Elgin Broadcasting Company Inc., at above address. **Founded:** 1949. **Operating Hours:** Continuous; 20% network, 80% local. **Key Personnel:** Rick Jakle, CEO, President, rickjakle@jakle.com. **Local Programs:** *People to People*, Tuesday 8:00 a.m. - 9:00 a.m.; *The Morning Wakeup Call*, Monday Tuesday Wednesday Thursday Friday 6:00 a.m. - 8:00 a.m.; *Your Turn*, Monday 8:00 a.m. - 9:00 a.m. **Wattage:** 1,000 Day; 500 Night. **Ad Rates:** $22.50-37.50 per unit. **URL:** http://www.wrmn1410.com.

ELK GROVE VILLAGE

DuPage Co DuPage Co. Cook Co. (NW). NW suburb of Chicago. Cook Co. (NW). NW of Chicago. Residential.

10810 ■ AAP Grand Rounds
American Academy of Pediatrics
141 NW Point Blvd.
Elk Grove Village, IL 60007-1098
Phone: (847)434-4000
Fax: (847)434-8000
Free: 800-433-9016
Publisher's E-mail: president@aap.org
The journal is meant for pediatricians by providing synopses and critiques to current insights in pediatrics. Online version of the journal provides for CME activities. **Freq:** Monthly. **Key Personnel:** Leslie Barton, Editor-in-Chief; Joe Puskarz, Managing Editor. **Subscription Rates:** $145 Nonmembers print and online; $116 Members print and online; $110 Nonmembers online only; $88 Members online only. **URL:** http://shop.aap.org/2016-AAP-Grand-Rounds. **Remarks:** Advertising not accepted. **Circ:** (Not Reported).

10811 ■ Adolescent Medicine: State of the Art Reviews (AM:STARs)
Pediatric Research in Office Settings
American Academy of Pediatrics
141 NW Point Blvd.
Elk Grove Village, IL 60007
Fax: (847)434-8910
Free: 800-433-9016
Journal publishing a series of clinical reviews that detail advances in the diagnosis and management of a wide range of health problems affecting adolescents. **Freq:** 3/year. **Key Personnel:** Donald E. Greydanus, MD, Editor; Victor C. Strasburger, MD, Editor. **ISSN:** 1547-3368 (print). **Subscription Rates:** $114.95 Members; $124.95 Nonmembers; $63 Students; $174.95 Institutions. **URL:** http://www2.aap.org/sections/adolescenthealth/AMSTARs.cfm. **Formerly:** Adolescent Medicine Clinics: Official Journal of the Section on Adolescent Health of the American Academy of Pediatrics. **Circ:** (Not Reported).

10812 ■ Gear Technology: The Journal of Gear Manufacturing
Randall Publishing Inc.
1425 Lunt Ave.
Elk Grove Village, IL 60007
Phone: (847)437-6604
Fax: (847)437-6618
Publication E-mail: publisher@geartechnology.com
Magazine featuring design, testing, processing, and new technology for gears and gear manufacturing products, and equipment. **Founded:** 1984. **Freq:** Bimonthly. **Print Method:** Web offset. **Trim Size:** 8 x 10 3/4. **Cols./Page:** 2 and 3. **Col. Width:** 20 and 13 nonpareils. **Col. Depth:** 150 agate lines. **Key Personnel:** Michael Goldstein, Editor-in-Chief, President, Publisher; Matt Jaster, Associate Editor; William R. Stott, Managing Editor. **ISSN:** 0743-6858 (print). **Subscription Rates:** $70 Other countries; Free to qualified subscribers. **URL:** http://www.geartechnology.com/. **Ad Rates:** 4C $5,215. **Remarks:** Accepts advertising. **Circ:** Paid △**13000**.

10813 ■ Healthy Children
American Academy of Pediatrics
141 NW Point Blvd.
Elk Grove Village, IL 60007-1098
Phone: (847)434-4000
Fax: (847)434-8000
Free: 800-433-9016
Publisher's E-mail: president@aap.org
Magazine featuring in-depth articles on important health topics such as immunization guidelines, common childhood illnesses and conditions, developmental and behavioral issues, and nutrition and fitness recommendations. **Freq:** Quarterly. **URL:** http://www.healthychildren.org/English/Pages/default.aspx. **Circ:** (Not Reported).

10814 ■ Journal of Occupational and Environmental Medicine
American College of Occupational and Environmental Medicine
25 NW Point Blvd., Ste. 700
Elk Grove Village, IL 60007-1030
Phone: (847)818-1800
Fax: (847)818-9266
Publisher's E-mail: memberinfo@acoem.org
Occupational and environmental medicine journal. **Freq:** Monthly. **Trim Size:** 8 1/8 x 10 7/8. **Key Personnel:** Paul W. Brandt-Rauf, MD, Editor; Marjory Spraycar, Managing Editor, phone: (410)321-5031, fax: (410)321-1456. **ISSN:** 1076--2752 (print); **EISSN:** 1536--5948 (electronic). **USPS:** 153-6 5948. **Subscription Rates:** $550 Individuals / year; $759 Individuals Canada/

Mexico; $792 Individuals UK/Australia and rest of the world; $1189 Institutions U.S.; $1491 Institutions Canada/Mexico; $1524 Institutions UK/Australia and rest of the world. **URL:** http://www.lww.com/Product/1076-2752; http://journals.lww.com/joem/pages/default.aspx. **Formerly**: Journal of Occupational Medicine. **Ad Rates:** GLR $1,915; BW $2,030; 4C $3,900. **Remarks:** Accepts display and classified advertising. **Circ:** Combined ‡4854, 7000.

10815 ■ The National Dipper: The Magazine for Frozen Dessert Retailers
The National Dipper
1028 W Devon Ave.
Elk Grove Village, IL 60007
Phone: (847)301-8400
Fax: (847)301-8402
Magazine catering to ice cream retail stores. **Freq:** 6/year. **Trim Size:** 8 1/2 x 10 7/8. **Key Personnel:** Lynda Utterback, Editor. **ISSN:** 0895--9722 (print). **Alt. Formats:** PDF. **URL:** http://www.nationaldipper.com. **Ad Rates:** BW $2,790, full page; BW $1,670, half page; 4C $240, 2/3 page; 4C $200, half page. **Remarks:** Accepts advertising. **Circ:** Non-paid 17000.

10816 ■ Pediatric Asthma Virtual Journal
American Academy of Pediatrics
141 NW Point Blvd.
Elk Grove Village, IL 60007-1098
Phone: (847)434-4000
Fax: (847)434-8000
Free: 800-433-9016
Publisher's E-mail: president@aap.org
Journal covering aetiology, diagnosis, treatment, and management of asthma and related conditions. **Key Personnel:** Renee R. Jenkins, MD, President; David T. Tayloe, Jr., President; Errol R. Alden, MD, Executive Director. **URL:** http://www2.aap.org/sections/allergy/online.cfm. **Remarks:** Advertising not accepted. **Circ:** (Not Reported).

10817 ■ Pediatrics
American Academy of Pediatrics
141 NW Point Blvd.
Elk Grove Village, IL 60007-1098
Phone: (847)434-4000
Fax: (847)434-8000
Free: 800-433-9016
Publication E-mail: journals@aap.org
Medical journal reporting on pediatrics. **Freq:** Monthly. **Print Method:** Web offset. **Trim Size:** 8 1/8 x 10 7/8. **Cols./Page:** 2. **Key Personnel:** Lewis R. First, Editor; Phyllis A. Dennery, Associate Editor; Joe Puskarz, Managing Editor. **ISSN:** 0031--4005 (print); **EISSN:** 1098--4275 (electronic). **Subscription Rates:** $199 Individuals. **Online:** American Academy of Pediatrics American Academy of Pediatrics; Ovid Technologies Inc. **URL:** http://pediatrics.aappublications.org/content/137/1?current-issue=y. **Remarks:** Accepts advertising. **Circ:** (Not Reported).

10818 ■ Pediatrics in Review
American Academy of Pediatrics
141 NW Point Blvd.
Elk Grove Village, IL 60007-1098
Phone: (847)434-4000
Fax: (847)434-8000
Free: 800-433-9016
Publisher's E-mail: president@aap.org
Journal covering general pediatricians. **Freq:** Monthly. **Key Personnel:** Lawrence F. Nazarian, MD, Editor. **ISSN:** 0191--9601 (print); **EISSN:** 1526--3347 (electronic). **Subscription Rates:** $198 Nonmembers online; $156 Members online. **URL:** http://pedsinreview.aappublications.org/content/37/3?current-issue=y; http://www.aap.org/en-us/continuing-medical-education/continuing-medical-education-publications/pages/continuing-medical-education-publications.aspx. **Remarks:** Advertising not accepted. **Circ:** (Not Reported).

10819 ■ WIND-AM - 560
25 NW Pt., Ste. 400
Elk Grove Village, IL 60007
Phone: (847)437-5200
Format: Hispanic; Talk; News. **Owner:** Salem Media Group Inc., 4880 Santa Rosa Rd., Camarillo, CA 93012, Ph: (805)987-0400, Fax: (805)384-4520. **Founded:** 1927. **Operating Hours**: Continuous. **ADI**: Chicago (La-Salle), IL. **Key Personnel:** Jeff Reisman, Gen. Mgr., jreisman@salemradiochicago.com; Marcus Brown, Dir. of Programs, mbrown@salemradiochicago.com. **Wattage:** 5,000. **Ad Rates:** Noncommercial. **URL:** http://www.560wind.com.

ELMHURST

DuPage Co. Du Page Co. (NE). 16 m W of Chicago. Elmhurst College. Residential.

10820 ■ Down Beat: Jazz, Blues & Beyond
Maher Publications Inc.
102 N Haven Rd.
Elmhurst, IL 60126
Phone: (630)941-2030
Fax: (630)941-3210
Free: 800-554-7470
Publisher's E-mail: editor@downbeat.com
Magazine edited for the learning musician. **Freq:** Monthly. **Print Method:** Offset. **Trim Size:** 8 1/8 x 10 7/8. **Cols./Page:** 3. **Col. Width:** 2 1/4 inches. **Col. Depth:** 9 7/8 inches. **Key Personnel:** Kevin Maher, Publisher. **ISSN:** 0012--5768 (print). **Subscription Rates:** $27.99 U.S. /year (print and online); $39.99 Canada /year (print and online); $51.99 Other countries /year (print and online); $19.99 Individuals /year (online). **URL:** http://www.downbeat.com. **Mailing address:** PO Box 11688, Saint Paul, MN 55111-0688. **Ad Rates:** BW $4315; 4C $5215; PCI $230. **Remarks:** Accepts advertising. **Circ:** ‡93797.

10821 ■ Journal of Technology, Management, and Applied Engineering
Association of Technology, Management and Applied Engineering
275 N York St., Ste. 401
Elmhurst, IL 60126
Phone: (630)433-4514
Freq: Quarterly January, April, July and October. **Key Personnel:** Dr. Nir Keren, Editor-in-Chief. **Subscription Rates:** Free. **URL:** http://www.atmae.org/?page=JTMAE. **Formerly**: Journal of Industrial Technology. **Remarks:** Accepts advertising. **Circ:** (Not Reported).

10822 ■ Music Inc.: For Progresive Music Retailers
Maher Publications Inc.
102 N Haven Rd.
Elmhurst, IL 60126
Phone: (630)941-2030
Fax: (630)941-3210
Free: 800-554-7470
Publication E-mail: editor@musicincmag.com
Magazine serving retailers of music and sound products. **Freq:** 11/year. **Print Method:** Offset. **Trim Size:** 8 1/4 x 10 7/8. **Cols./Page:** 3. **Col. Width:** 27 nonpareils. **Col. Depth:** 140 agate lines. **Key Personnel:** Kevin Maher, Publisher; Frank Alkyer, Director, Editorial. **URL:** http://www.musicincmag.com/magazine.html. **Mailing address:** PO Box 11688, Saint Paul, MN 55111-0688. **Ad Rates:** BW $1,470; 4C $2,095. **Remarks:** Accepts advertising. **Circ:** Paid ‡8300.

10823 ■ Prospect
Elmhurst College
190 Prospect Ave.
Elmhurst, IL 60126-3296
Phone: (630)617-3500
Publisher's E-mail: admit@elmhurst.edu
Collegiate magazine. **Founded:** 1967. **Freq:** Semiannual. **Print Method:** Sheetfed Offset. **Trim Size:** 9.5 x 11.5. **Key Personnel:** James W. Winters, Contact; Jim Winters, Editor; Judith Crown, Managing Editor. **URL:** http://issuu.com/elmhurstcollege/docs/elmhurst_prospect_summer_2010/15?e=0; http://public.elmhurst.edu/alumni/122682844.html. **Formerly**: Elmhurst College Magazine. **Remarks:** Advertising not accepted. **Circ:** Controlled ‡35000.

10824 ■ WRSE-FM - 88.7
190 Prospect Ave.
Elmhurst, IL 60126
Format: Public Radio. **Networks:** Independent. **Owner:** Elmhurst College, 190 Prospect Ave., Elmhurst, IL 60126-3296, Ph: (630)617-3500. **Founded:** 1947. **Operating Hours:** 4 p.m.-1 a.m. Sun.-Fri. **Wattage:** 100. **Ad Rates:** Underwriting available.

10825 ■ WRXX-FM - 95.3
205 E Butterfield Rd., Ste. 426
Elmhurst, IL 60126
Wattage: 5,500. **URL:** http://www.billbeecher.com.

EUREKA

Woodford Co. Woodford Co. (NC). 17 m E of Peoria. Eureka College. Manufactures automatic livestock feeding systems, road building machinery. Grain, stock farms.

10826 ■ Journal of the Lepidopterists' Society
Allen Press Inc.
c/o Michael Tolliver, Sec.
Department of Biology, Eureka College
300 E College
Eureka, IL 61530-1500
Publisher's E-mail: sales@allenpress.com
Professional journal covering the study of insects (butterflies and moths). **Freq:** Quarterly. **Key Personnel:** Keith Summerville, Editor. **ISSN:** 0024-0966 (print). **URL:** http://www.lepsoc.org/journal.php. **Remarks:** Accepts advertising. **Circ:** (Not Reported).

10827 ■ The News Bulletin
Legal Record Corp.
PO Box 203
Eureka, IL 61530
Free: 888-568-7488
Publication E-mail: customerservice@legalrecord.net
Newspaper (tabloid) publishing court and commercial news. **Founded:** Mar. 1924. **Freq:** Weekly (Wed.). **Print Method:** Letterpress. **Trim Size:** 11 x 17. **Cols./Page:** 5. **Col. Width:** 12 picas. **Col. Depth:** 15 inches. **USPS:** 427-720. **URL:** http://www.legalrecord.net. **Formerly**: Peoria Daily Record; The Daily Record. **Remarks:** Accepts advertising. **Circ:** Paid 2000, Free 3800.

10828 ■ WQEZ-FM - 94.3
108 N Main St., Ste. J
Eureka, IL 61530
Free: 877-620-7362
Format: Adult Contemporary; Soft Rock. **Networks:** Satellite Music Network. **Founded:** 1977. **Formerly**: WTXR-FM; WBZM-FM; WKZW-FM. **Operating Hours**: Continuous. **ADI**: Peoria-Bloomington, IL. **Key Personnel:** Bill Bro, President. **Wattage:** 6,000 ERP. **Ad Rates:** $60 for 30 seconds; $70 for 60 seconds. **URL:** http://wpmjradio.com.

EVANSTON

Cook Co. Cook Co. (NE). On Lake Michigan, adjacent to Chicago. Primarily suburban residential. Northwestern University and two famed hospitals. Manufactures auto and truck accessories, baking and packaging machinery, candy, cosmetics, electronic equipment, fancy food products, film projection equipment, hospital supplies, household chemicals, laundry and dry cleaning equipment, paints, pharmaceuticals, photocopy equipment, pumps, margarine, rust preventer, sashes and screens, steel products, toys, containers, postal scales. Headquarters for more than forty national firms.

10829 ■ Alpha Phi Quarterly
Alpha Phi International Fraternity
1930 Sherman Ave.
Evanston, IL 60201
Phone: (847)475-0663
Fax: (847)475-6820
Publication E-mail: quarterly@alphaphi.org
College sorority magazine. **Freq:** Quarterly. **Key Personnel:** Christine Spiegel, Editor-in-Chief. **Subscription Rates:** $25 Nonmembers; Included in membership. **URL:** http://www.alphaphi.org/quarterly. **Remarks:** Advertising accepted; rates available upon request. **Circ:** 135000.

10830 ■ Baseball Digest
Century Publishing Co.
990 Grove St., Ste. 400
Evanston, IL 60201-6510
Phone: (847)491-6440
Fax: (847)491-0459
Magazine featuring major league baseball. **Freq:** Bimonthly. **Print Method:** Web offset. **Trim Size:** 4 7/8 x 7. **Cols./Page:** 2. **Col. Width:** 24 nonpareils. **Col. Depth:** 91 agate lines. **Key Personnel:** Irene Froehlich, Contact, phone: (269)637-5790, fax: (269)637-6372;

Circulation: ★ = AAM; △ or • = BPA; ♦ = CAC; ❑ = VAC; ⊕ = PO Statement; ‡ = Publisher's Report; Boldface figures = sworn; Light figures = estimated.

John Kuenster, Editor. **ISSN:** 0005--609X (print). **USPS:** 492-630. **Subscription Rates:** $38.95 U.S. /year; $48.95 Canada /year; $53.95 Other countries /year. **URL:** http://baseballdigest.com. **Ad Rates:** BW $4550; 4C $6500. **Remarks:** Advertising accepted; rates available upon request. **Circ:** Paid ‡225000.

10831 ■ Brilliant Star
National Spiritual Assembly of the Baha'is of the U.S.
1233 Central St.
Evanston, IL 60201
Phone: (847)733-3400
Magazine containing stories, activities, puzzles, interviews, comics, music, and colorful art that help tweens aged 8 - 12 develop as global citizens. **Subscription Rates:** $18 Individuals 1 year 6 issues; $32 Individuals 2 years 12 issues; $28 Canada and Mexico 1 year 6 issues; $48 Canada and Mexico 2 years 12 issues; $38 Other countries 1 year 6 issues; $68 Other countries 2 years 12 issues. **URL:** http://www.brilliantstarmagazine.org. **Remarks:** Advertising not accepted. **Circ:** (Not Reported).

10832 ■ Cruise Travel Magazine: The Number One Worldwide Cruise Vacation Magazine
World Publishing Co.
990 Grove St.
Evanston, IL 60201
Phone: (847)491-6440
Fax: (847)491-0459
Publisher's E-mail: cs@cruisetravelmag.com
Magazine covering consumer-oriented cruise-ship vacations. **Freq:** Bimonthly. **Print Method:** Offset. **Trim Size:** 8 x 10 1/2. **Cols./Page:** 3. **Col. Width:** 13.5 picas. **Col. Depth:** 134 agate lines. **Key Personnel:** Charles Doherty, Editor; Dale Jacobs, Manager, Production. **ISSN:** 0199--5111 (print). **Subscription Rates:** $38.95 U.S. /year; $48.95 Canada /year; $53.95 Other countries /year. **URL:** http://www.cruisetravelmag.com. **Remarks:** Advertising accepted; rates available upon request. **Circ:** Paid ⋆**158802**.

10833 ■ The Daily Northwestern
Northwestern University Students Publishing Co.
1999 Campus Dr.
1999 Campus Dr.
Evanston, IL 60201
Phone: (847)491-7206
Fax: (847)491-9905
Free: 888-649-7784
Collegiate. **Freq:** Daily Monday through Friday during the school year. **Print Method:** Offset. **Trim Size:** 10 3/8 x 15 7/8. **Cols./Page:** 4. **Col. Width:** 2 1/2 inches. **Col. Depth:** 2 1/2 inches. **Key Personnel:** Ciara McCarthy, Editor-in-Chief. **USPS:** 852-520. **Subscription Rates:** $160 Students. **URL:** http://www.dailynorthwestern.com. **Ad Rates:** BW $552; 4C $1,052; SAU $19.50; PCI $23. **Remarks:** Accepts advertising. **Circ:** (Not Reported).

10834 ■ The Georgist Journal
Council of Georgist Organizations
c/o Sue Walton, Administrator
PO Box 57
Evanston, IL 60204
Phone: (847)209-0047
Publisher's E-mail: webmaster@cgocouncil.org
Journal covering news of conferences, movement events, Land Value Tax - implementation progress and topics focusing on Georgist political economy. **Freq:** Quarterly. **Subscription Rates:** Included in membership. **URL:** http://www.georgistjournal.org/. **Remarks:** Advertising not accepted. **Circ:** (Not Reported).

10835 ■ International Journal for Numerical Methods in Engineering: Published in Parallel with Communications in Numerical Methods
John Wiley & Sons Inc.
c/o Prof. Charbel Farhat, Ed.-in-Ch.
Dept. of Mechanical Engineering
Northwestern University
Evanston, IL 60208
Publication E-mail: ijnme-us@northwestern.edu
Journal focusing on significant developments in numerical techniques engineering problems in various areas, including heat transfer, fluid mechanics, and network theory. **Freq:** Weekly. **Key Personnel:** Prof. Roland W. Lewis, Editor; Prof. Charbel Farhat, Editor-in-Chief. **ISSN:** 0029--5981 (print); **EISSN:** 1097--0207 (electronic). **Subscription Rates:** $17712 Institutions online or print - USA/Canada & Mexico/ROW; $21255 Institutions print & online - USA/Canada & Mexico/ROW; £9041 Institutions online or print - UK; £10850 Institutions print & online - UK; €11430 Institutions online or print - Europe; €13716 Institutions print & online - Europe. **URL:** http://onlinelibrary.wiley.com/journal/10.1002/(ISSN)1097-0207. **Remarks:** Accepts advertising. **Circ:** (Not Reported).

10836 ■ Journal of Economics and Management Strategy
Blackwell Publishing Inc.
c/o Daniel F. Spulber, Ed.
Kellogg GSM, Leverone Hall
Northwestern University
Evanston, IL 60208-2013
Phone: (847)467-1776
Fax: (847)467-1777
Publisher's E-mail: journaladsusa@bos.blackwellpublishing.com
Journal providing a forum for research and discussion on competitive strategies of managers and the organizational structure of firms. **Founded:** 1992. **Freq:** Quarterly. **Trim Size:** 6 x 9. **Key Personnel:** Daniel F. Spulber, Editor; Jeffrey L. Coles, Editor; Zhiqi Chen, Editor; Luis M.B. Cabral, Editor; Esther Gal-Or, Editor. **ISSN:** 1058-6407 (print). **Subscription Rates:** $66 Individuals print & online; €97 Individuals print & online; £65 Other countries print & online, individuals; $63 Individuals online; €93 Individuals online; £61 Other countries online, individuals; $527 Institutions print & online; €527 Institutions print & online; $811 Institutions, other countries print & online. **URL:** http://www.wiley.com/WileyCDA/WileyTitle/productCd-JEMS.html; http://onlinelibrary.wiley.com/journal/10.1111/(ISSN)1530-9134. **Ad Rates:** BW $350. **Remarks:** Accepts advertising. **Circ:** 1000.

10837 ■ Journal of International Human Rights
Northwestern University School of Law Office of Legal Publications
633 Clark St.
Evanston, IL 60208
Phone: (847)491-3741
Publisher's E-mail: law-web@law.northwestern.edu
Journal dealing with issues related to human rights, and also covers law based on international human rights. **Freq:** Annual. **Key Personnel:** Stephanie Le, Editor-in-Chief. **ISSN:** 1549--828X (print). **URL:** http://www.law.northwestern.edu/research-faculty/journals; http://scholarlycommons.law.northwestern.edu/njihr. **Circ:** (Not Reported).

10838 ■ The Magazine of Sigma Chi
Sigma Chi Fraternity
1714 Hinman Ave.
Evanston, IL 60201
Phone: (847)869-3655
Fax: (847)869-4906
College fraternity publication. **Freq:** Quarterly. **Print Method:** Web offset. **Cols./Page:** 3. **Col. Width:** 26 nonpareils. **Col. Depth:** 134 agate lines. **Key Personnel:** Susan Lorimor, Editor, phone: (847)869-3655. **URL:** http://sigmachi.org/the-magazine-of-sigma-chi. **Ad Rates:** BW $1008; 4C $1428. **Remarks:** Advertising accepted; rates available upon request. **Circ:** ‡56000, 56000.

10839 ■ Massage Therapy Journal
American Massage Therapy Association
500 Davis St., Ste. 900
Evanston, IL 60201-4695
Free: 877-905-0577
Publisher's E-mail: info@amtamassage.org
Magazine focusing on professional massage therapy benefits, techniques, research, news, and practitioners. **Freq:** Quarterly. **Key Personnel:** Christina Rompon, Contact; Michael Schwanz, Editor. **ISSN:** 0895- 0814 (print). **Subscription Rates:** $25 Individuals /year. **URL:** http://www.amtamassage.org/articles/3/mtj/index.html?src=navdropdown. **Ad Rates:** $2555-2975, for full page; $1680-1955, for 1/2 page; $990-1165, for 1/4 page; $4025-4685, for spread; $2395-3150, for inside covers; $3460-3675, for back cover. 4C $, for full page4C $, for 1/2 page4C $, for 1/4 page4C $, for spread4C $, for inside covers4C $, for back coverBW $2,036; 4C $2,975. **Remarks:** Accepts advertising. **Circ:** 64,000, 68561.

10840 ■ Northwestern
Northwestern University
633 Clark St.
Evanston, IL 60208
Phone: (847)491-3741
Publisher's E-mail: ug-admission@northwestern.edu
Alumni magazine for Northwestern University. **Freq:** Quarterly. **Subscription Rates:** Free to qualified subscribers. **URL:** http://www.northwestern.edu/magazine. **Remarks:** Accepts advertising. **Circ:** Free 227,000.

10841 ■ Northwestern Journal of International Law & Business
Northwestern University School of Law Office of Legal Publications
633 Clark St.
Evanston, IL 60208
Phone: (847)491-3741
Publisher's E-mail: law-web@law.northwestern.edu
Journal covering business law issues worldwide. **Freq:** 3/year. **Print Method:** Offset. **Trim Size:** 6 3/4 x 10. **Cols./Page:** 1. **Col. Width:** 28 picas. **Col. Depth:** 50 picas. **Key Personnel:** Alexandra Anderson, Editor-in-Chief; Alan Iverson, Managing Editor. **ISSN:** 0196--3228 (print). **Subscription Rates:** $40 Individuals; $15 Single issue; $18 Single issue international; $65 Other countries. **URL:** http://scholarlycommons.law.northwestern.edu/njilb. **Remarks:** Advertising not accepted. **Circ:** Combined 598.

10842 ■ Northwestern Journal of Technology and Intellectual Property
Northwestern University School of Law Office of Legal Publications
633 Clark St.
Evanston, IL 60208
Phone: (847)491-3741
Publisher's E-mail: law-web@law.northwestern.edu
Journal covering areas pertaining to law, including law and biotechnology, copyrights, the Internet, media, patents, telecommunications, and trademarks. **Freq:** 3/year. **Key Personnel:** Heath Ingram, Editor-in-Chief; Hugh McLaughlin, Editor-in-Chief. **Alt. Formats:** PDF. **URL:** http://scholarlycommons.law.northwestern.edu/njtip. **Circ:** (Not Reported).

10843 ■ Quodlibet Online Journal of Christian Theology and Philosophy
Quodlibet Journal
530 Sheridan Rd. 3A
Evanston, IL 60202
Journal focusing on theological and philosophical issues of Christian faith. **Freq:** Quarterly. **EISSN:** 1526--6575 (electronic). **Subscription Rates:** Free. **URL:** http://www.quodlibet.net. **Remarks:** Advertising not accepted. **Circ:** (Not Reported).

10844 ■ RHINO Poetry
The Poetry Forum Inc.
PO Box 591
Evanston, IL 60204
Journal featuring poetry, short stories and translations. **Freq:** Annual. **Key Personnel:** Ralph Hamilton, Editor-in-Chief. **ISSN:** 1521--8414 (print). **Subscription Rates:** $14 Individuals; $31.50 Two years. **URL:** http://rhinopoetry.org. **Circ:** (Not Reported).

10845 ■ The Rotarian
Rotary International
1 Rotary Ctr.
1560 Sherman Ave.
Evanston, IL 60201-3698
Free: 866-976-8279
Publisher's E-mail: registration@rotary.org
General interest magazine on community service and international understanding. **Freq:** Monthly. **Print Method:** Offset. **Trim Size:** 8 x 10 1/2. **Cols./Page:** 3. **Col. Width:** 2 1/4 inches. **Col. Depth:** 140 agate lines. **Key Personnel:** Marla Donato, Managing Editor; Marjoleine Tel, Editor. **ISSN:** 0035--838X (print). **URL:** http://www.rotary.org/myrotary/en/news-media/magazines; http://www.rotary.nl. **Ad Rates:** GLR $30; BW $10000; 4C $14000; PCI $420. **Remarks:** Accepts advertising. **Circ:** Paid ⋆**500000**, Combined 872000.

10846 ■ TriQuarterly
Northwestern University Press
629 Noyes St.
Evanston, IL 60208-4210
Phone: (847)491-7420
Fax: (847)491-8150
Free: 800-621-2736

Publication E-mail: triquarterly@northwestern.edu
Scholarly journal covering writing, art, and culture. **Freq:** Semiannual. **Key Personnel:** Susan Hahn, Editor; Kirstie Felland, Business Manager. **ISSN:** 0041--3097 (print). **URL:** http://www.triquarterly.org. **Remarks:** Advertising accepted; rates available upon request. **Circ:** (Not Reported).

10847 ■ The Vintage Microcar Club Microcar News
Microcar and Minicar Club
PO Box 6136
Evanston, IL 60204-6136
Phone: (630)642-7622
Publisher's E-mail: hello@microcar.org
Magazine covering microcar news. **Freq:** Quarterly. **Subscription Rates:** Included in membership. **URL:** http://www.microcar.org/current-issue.html. **Remarks:** Accepts display advertising. **Circ:** (Not Reported).

10848 ■ World Order
National Spiritual Assembly of the Baha'is of the U.S.
1233 Central St.
Evanston, IL 60201
Phone: (847)733-3400
Religious magazine. **Freq:** Quarterly. **Print Method:** Offset. **Trim Size:** 7 x 10. **Cols./Page:** 3. **Col. Width:** 27 nonpareils. **Col. Depth:** 140 agate lines. **Key Personnel:** Dr. Betty J. Fisher, Managing Editor. **ISSN:** 0043--8804 (print). **Subscription Rates:** $19 Individuals; $4.75 Single issue; $19 /year. **URL:** http://www.bahai.us/2006/07/07/bahai-journal-wins-design-award-2. **Remarks:** Advertising not accepted. **Circ:** ‡1500.

10849 ■ Zoobooks
Wildlife Education Ltd.
2418 Noyes St.
Evanston, IL 60201
Phone: (847)733-7830
Free: 800-992-5034
Publisher's E-mail: helpdesk@zoobooks.com
Magazine devoted to covering photography of animals including illustrations, diagrams, and descriptions. **Freq:** 10/year. **Print Method:** Offset. Uses mats. **Cols./Page:** 7. **Col. Width:** 15/16 inches. **Col. Depth:** 11 1/2 inches. **Key Personnel:** Kurt Von Hertsenberg, Manager, Sales. **Subscription Rates:** $19.95 Individuals digital only. **URL:** http://zoobooks.com. **Circ:** (Not Reported).

10850 ■ Zootles
Wildlife Education Ltd.
2418 Noyes St.
Evanston, IL 60201
Phone: (847)733-7830
Free: 800-992-5034
Publisher's E-mail: helpdesk@zoobooks.com
Magazine promoting knowledge of animals for young children, pre-readers and beginning readers. **Freq:** Bimonthly. **Print Method:** Offset. **Trim Size:** 7.75 x 10.5. **Cols./Page:** 3. **Col. Width:** 27 nonpareils. **Col. Depth:** 137 agate lines. **ISSN:** 0746--4223 (print). **Subscription Rates:** $19.95 Individuals digital only. **Circ:** (Not Reported).

10851 ■ WCGO-AM - 1590
2100 Lee St.
Evanston, IL 60202
Phone: (847)475-1590
Email: info@1590wcgo.com
Format: Hispanic; Ethnic. **Networks:** Independent. **Founded:** 1947. **Formerly:** WNMP-AM; WLTD-AM; WONX-AM. **Operating Hours:** Continuous. **Wattage:** 7,000 day; 2,500 night. **URL:** http://1590wcgo.com.

10852 ■ WKTA-AM - 1330
4320 Dundee Rd.
Northbrook, IL 60062
Phone: (847)498-3350
Fax: (847)498-5743
Email: pclradio@techinter.com
Format: Contemporary Christian; News. **Owner:** Polnet Communications Ltd., 3656 W Blemont Ave., Chicago, IL 60618, Ph: (773)588-6300, Fax: (773)267-4913. **Founded:** 1953. **Formerly:** WSSY-AM. **Operating Hours:** Continuous. **Key Personnel:** Scott Davidson, Contact; Walter Kotaba, Contact. **Wattage:** 5,000 Day; 017 Night. **Ad Rates:** Advertising accepted; rates available upon request. $40 for 30 seconds; $80 for 60 seconds. International Network. **URL:** http://www.pclradio.com.

FAIRFIELD

Wayne Co. Wayne Co. (S). 32 m N.E. of Mt Vernon. Manufactures auto parts, doors, windows, children wear and uniforms, component parts. Oil wells Grain, dairy, poultry farms. Corn, soybeans.

10853 ■ WFIW-AM - 1390
Hwy. 15 E
Fairfield, IL 62837
Phone: (618)842-2159
Fax: (618)847-5907
Email: wfiw@originalcompany.com
Format: News; Talk. **Networks:** ABC. **Owner:** Wayne County Broadcasting Company Inc., at above address. **Founded:** 1953. **Operating Hours:** Continuous. **ADI:** Evansville, IN (Madisonville, KY). **Key Personnel:** Thomas S. Land, Founder; Len Wells, News Dir.; Vicky Strange, Office Mgr. **Wattage:** 1,000. **Ad Rates:** $12.40 for 30 seconds; $17 for 60 seconds. Combined advertising rates available with WFIW-FM, WOKZ-FM. **Mailing address:** PO Box 310, Fairfield, IL 62837. **URL:** http://www.wfiwradio.com.

10854 ■ WFIW-FM - 104.9
Hwy. 15 E
Fairfield, IL 62837
Phone: (618)842-2159
Fax: (618)847-5907
Email: wfiwwokz@fairfieldwireless.net
Format: Contemporary Hit Radio (CHR). **Networks:** ABC; Jones Satellite. **Owner:** Wayne County Broadcasting Company Inc., at above address. **Founded:** 1965. **Operating Hours:** Continuous. **ADI:** Evansville, IN (Madisonville, KY). **Key Personnel:** David H. Land, Gen. Mgr., President; Len Wells, News Dir.; Vicky Strange, Office Mgr. **Wattage:** 6,000. **Ad Rates:** $12.40 for 30 seconds; $17 for 60 seconds. Combined advertising rates available with WFIW-AM & WOKZ-FM. **Mailing address:** PO Box 310, Fairfield, IL 62837. **URL:** http://www.wfiwradio.com.

10855 ■ WOKZ-FM - 105.9
Hwy. 15 E
Fairfield, IL 62837
Phone: (618)842-2159
Fax: (618)847-5907
Format: Country. **Owner:** Wayne County Broadcasting Company Inc., at above address. **Founded:** 1996. **Operating Hours:** Continuous. **ADI:** Evansville, IN (Madisonville, KY). **Key Personnel:** Len Wells, News Dir. **Wattage:** 6,000. **Ad Rates:** $12.40 for 30 seconds; $17 for 60 seconds. Combined advertising rates available with WFIW-AM & WFIW-FM. **Mailing address:** PO Box 310, Fairfield, IL 62837. **URL:** http://www.wfiwradio.com.

FAIRVIEW

10856 ■ Mid Century Telephone Cooperative
285 MidCentury Ln.
Fairview, IL 61432
Phone: (309)778-8611
Fax: (309)783-3297
Free: 877-643-2368
Founded: Aug. 14, 1950. **Cities Served:** 90 channels. **Mailing address:** PO Box 380, Fairview, IL 61432. **URL:** http://www.midcentury.com.

FARMER CITY

De Witt Co. De Witt Co. (C). 18 m NE of Clinton.

10857 ■ WWHP-FM - 98.3
407 N Main St.
Farmer City, IL 61842
Phone: (309)928-9876
Fax: (309)928-3708
Format: Bluegrass; Alternative/New Music/Progressive; Country; Religious; Album-Oriented Rock (AOR); Blues. **Networks:** Satellite Music Network; Motor Racing; Brownfield. **Owner:** WMSI INC., at above address, New York, NY. **Founded:** 1983. **Operating Hours:** Continuous. **Wattage:** 3,000. **Ad Rates:** Noncommercial. **URL:** http://www.wwhp.com.

FISHER

Champaign Co. Champaign Co. (E). On Sangamon River, 40 m E of Bloomington. Agriculture. Corn, soybeans, oats.

10858 ■ WGNJ-FM - 89.3
PO Box 550
Fisher, IL 61843
Phone: (217)367-7777
Email: staff@greatnewsradio.org
Format: Religious. **Key Personnel:** Karen Harrison, Office Mgr.; Stephen McClarey, Director; Herb Ketchum, Contact; Max Norman, Contact. **Ad Rates:** Noncommercial. **URL:** http://www.greatnewsradio.org.

10859 ■ WGNN-FM - 102.5
PO Box 550
Fisher, IL 61843
Phone: (217)367-7777
Email: staff@greatnewsradio.org
Format: Religious. **Key Personnel:** Karen Harrison, Office Mgr.; Stephen McClarey, Director; Max Norman, Contact. **Ad Rates:** Noncommercial. **URL:** http://www.greatnewsradio.org.

FLORA

Clay Co. Clay Co. (SE). 100 m E of St. Louis, Mo. Manufactures shoes, wood stains, steel products, marine parts, rayon garments, automotive parts. Oil producers. Argiculture. Clover seed, soybeans, peas.

10860 ■ Daily Clay County Advocate-Press
Clay County Advocate Press Inc.
105 W North Ave.
Flora, IL 62839
Phone: (618)662-2108
Fax: (618)662-2939
General newspaper. **Freq:** Daily (eve.). **Print Method:** Offset. **Trim Size:** 14 x 23. **Cols./Page:** 6. **Col. Width:** 12 picas. **Col. Depth:** 21.5 inches. **Key Personnel:** Natalie Berry, Editor; Nancy Bible, Manager, Advertising; Jennifer Lewis, Manager, Circulation. **USPS:** 116-560. **URL:** http://www.advocatepress.com/?refresh=true. **Remarks:** Accepts advertising. **Circ:** (Not Reported).

10861 ■ WNOI-FM - 103.9
1001 N Olive Rd.
Flora, IL 62839
Phone: (618)662-8331
Email: info@wnoi.com
Format: News; Information. **Networks:** Jones Satellite; RFD Illinois. **Owner:** HandR Communications Inc., at above address. **Founded:** 1971. **Operating Hours:** Continuous; 9% network, 91% local. **ADI:** Terre Haute, IN. **Wattage:** 3,300. **Ad Rates:** $6.90 for 30 seconds; $9.90 for 60 seconds. **Mailing address:** PO Box 368, Flora, IL 62839. **URL:** http://www.wnoi.com.

FLOSSMOOR

Cook Co.

10862 ■ Homewood Flossmoor High School District 233 - 88.5
999 Kedzie Ave.
Flossmoor, IL 60422
Phone: (708)799-3000
Format: News; Eclectic; Talk; Classic Rock. **Founded:** 1959. **Wattage:** 1,500 ERP. **URL:** http://www.hfhighschool.org.

10863 ■ WHFH-FM - 88.5
999 Kedzie Ave.
Flossmoor, IL 60422
Phone: (708)799-3000
Format: Educational. **Networks:** Independent. **Owner:** Homewood Flossmoor High School District 233, 999 Kedzie Ave., Flossmoor, IL 60422, Ph: (708)799-3000. **Founded:** 1965. **Operating Hours:** 8:00 a.m.-9 p.m. every school day. **ADI:** Chicago (LaSalle), IL. **Key Personnel:** Kevin Thomas, Chairman; Thomas Wagner, Dir. of Operations. **Wattage:** 1,500. **Ad Rates:** Noncommercial. **URL:** http://www.hfhighschool.org.

FORD HEIGHTS

Cook Co. Cook Co.

10864 ■ WCFJ-AM - 1470
1000 Lincoln Hwy.
Ford Heights, IL 60411-2946

Circulation: ★ = AAM; △ or • = BPA; ♦ = CAC; ❑ = VAC; ⊕ = PO Statement; ‡ = Publisher's Report; Boldface figures = sworn; Light figures = estimated.

Phone: (708)758-8600
Fax: (708)737-7124
Format: Gospel; Contemporary Christian; Religious. **Networks:** Independent. **Founded:** 1963. **Formerly:** WMPP-AM. **Operating Hours**: Continuous. **Key Personnel:** Darryl Chavers, Gen. Mgr. **Wattage**: 1,000. **Ad Rates:** $10 for 30 seconds; $20 for 60 seconds.

FOREST PARK

Cook Co. Cook Co. (NE). 3 m S of Elmwood Park. Residential.

10865 ■ S Gaugian
Heimburger House Publishing Co.
7236 W Madison St.
Forest Park, IL 60130
Phone: (708)366-1973
Fax: (708)366-1973
Publisher's E-mail: info@heimburgerhouse.com
Magazine focusing on "S" scale (1:64 scale) model railroading news, feature articles, photos and plans. **Freq:** Bimonthly. **Print Method:** Offset. **Trim Size:** 8 1/2 x 11. **Cols./Page:** 3. **Col. Width:** 2 1/4 inches. **Col. Depth:** 9 3/4 inches. **ISSN:** 0273--6241 (print). **Subscription Rates:** $39 Individuals; $73 Canada; $86 Elsewhere. **URL:** http://www.heimburgerhouse.com/s_gaugian.php. **Ad Rates:** BW $278; 4C $435. **Remarks:** Advertising accepted; rates available upon request. **Circ:** ‡4500.

10866 ■ Sn3 Modeler
Heimburger House Publishing Co.
7236 W Madison St.
Forest Park, IL 60130
Phone: (708)366-1973
Fax: (708)366-1973
Publisher's E-mail: info@heimburgerhouse.com
Consumer magazine with news and features, photos and plans covering 1:64 scale narrow gauge model railroading. **Freq:** Semiannual. **Print Method:** Offset. **Trim Size:** 8 1/2 x 11. **Subscription Rates:** $18 Individuals; $34 Elsewhere; $30 Canada; $11.50 Single issue sample copy. **URL:** http://heimburgerhouse.com/sn3_modeler.php. **Ad Rates:** BW $198. **Remarks:** Accepts advertising. **Circ:** Paid 2000.

FOX RIVER GROVE

10867 ■ The Journal of Diving History
Historical Diving Society U.S.A.
c/o Greg Platt, Treasurer
PO Box 453
Fox River Grove, IL 60021-0453
Phone: (805)934-1660
Publisher's E-mail: hdscanada@nuytco.com
Freq: Quarterly. **Key Personnel:** Steve Kushner, President; Ed Cassano, Director; Drew Richardson, Director. **Subscription Rates:** Included in membership. **URL:** http://www.hds.org/the-journal. **Formerly**: Historical Diver. **Remarks:** Advertising not accepted. **Circ:** (Not Reported).

FRANKLIN

Morgan Co. Morgan Co. (WC). 12 m SE of Jacksonville. Agriculture.

10868 ■ The Franklin Times
Franklin Times Publishing
208 Main St.
Franklin, IL 62638
Phone: (217)675-2461
Fax: (217)675-2470
Newspaper. **Founded:** 1867. **Freq:** Weekly (Thurs.). **Print Method:** Offset. **Trim Size:** 10 1/4 x 16. **Cols./Page:** 5. **Col. Width:** 24 nonpareils. **Col. Depth:** 218 agate lines. **Key Personnel:** Ira Lionts, Publisher. **USPS:** 208-520. **Subscription Rates:** $14 Individuals; $10 Students; $20 Out of area; $.40 Single issue. **Alt. Formats:** PDF. **URL:** http://franklinillinois.net/franklintimes.htm. **Ad Rates:** GLR $5; BW $180; CNU $.30; PCI $2.75. **Remarks:** Accepts advertising. **Circ:** ‡600.

FRANKLIN GROVE

10869 ■ The Lincoln Highway Forum
Lincoln Highway Association
136 N Elm St.
Franklin Grove, IL 61031
Phone: (815)456-3030
Publisher's E-mail: hq@lincolnhighwayassoc.org
Freq: Quarterly. **Subscription Rates:** Included in membership. **Alt. Formats:** PDF. **URL:** http://www.lincolnhighwayassoc.org/forum. **Mailing address:** PO Box 308, Franklin Grove, IL 61031. **Remarks:** Advertising accepted; rates available upon request. **Circ:** 1200.

FRANKLIN PARK

Cook Co.

10870 ■ AIM Liturgy Resources
J.S. Paluch Company Inc.
3708 River Rd., Ste. 400
Franklin Park, IL 60131-2158
Phone: (847)678-9300
Fax: (847)233-2940
Free: 800-621-5197
Publisher's E-mail: customercare@jspaluch.com
Magazine on liturgy, pastoral planning, parish ministry, and church music. **Freq:** Quarterly. **Print Method:** Web Offset. **Trim Size:** 8 1/4 x 10 1/4. **Key Personnel:** Mary Prete, Vice President; Alan J. Hommerding, Editor; Mary Beth Kunde-Anderson, Director. **ISSN:** 1079--459X (print). **Subscription Rates:** $18 Individuals 1 to 4 subscriptions; $25 Other countries; $11 Individuals 5 or more subscriptions; $13 Individuals single subscription. **URL:** http://www.wlp.jspaluch.com/8062.htm. **Formerly**: AIM: Aids in Ministry. **Circ:** Paid 20000.

10871 ■ Franklin Park Herald-Journal
Sun-Times Media L.L.C.
350 N Orleans St., 10th Fl.
Chicago, IL 60654
Phone: (312)321-3000
Free: 888-848-4637
Publisher's E-mail: customerservice@suntimes.com
Community newspaper (tabloid). **Freq:** Daily. **Print Method:** Offset. **Cols./Page:** 5. **Col. Width:** 10 inches. **Col. Depth:** 14 inches. **Subscription Rates:** $18.99 Individuals /month, daily delivery (Monday - Sunday) plus online; $11.99 Individuals /month, Wednesday, Thursday, Friday and Sunday delivery plus online ; $5.99 Individuals /month, Sunday only plus online; $3.99 Individuals /month, online only. **URL:** http://www.chicagotribune.com/suburbs/franklin-park. **Remarks:** Accepts advertising. **Circ:** (Not Reported).

FREEBURG

St. Clair Co. St Clair Co. (SW). 7 m SE of Belleville. Manufactures brass and aluminum castings, electrical supplies, fire engines. Flour mills. Coal mines. White oak timber. Dairy, stock, truck, grain farms.

10872 ■ The Freeburg Tribune
The Freeburg Tribune
820 S State
Freeburg, IL 62243
Phone: (618)539-3320
Fax: (618)539-3346
Publication E-mail: newsroom@freeburgtribune.com
Weekly. **Freq:** Weekly (Thurs.). **Print Method:** Offset. **Cols./Page:** 6. **Col. Width:** 2 1/4 inches. **Col. Depth:** 301 agate lines. **Subscription Rates:** $20 Individuals In St. Clair County; $26 Individuals In Monroe or Randolph; $30 Elsewhere. **Remarks:** Accepts advertising. **Circ:** (Not Reported).

FREEPORT

Stephenson Co. Stephenson Co. (N). 116 m NW of Chicago. Manufactures water coolers, batteries, patent medicines, dental processing, hardware, farm and woodworking machinery, plastics, precision screw products, construction vehicle components, metal plating, ultrasonic equipment barbecue grills, spices, cosmetics, brooms, boxes, potato chips, curtain rods, tires, plaques, switches, concrete vaults, Foundries. Grain, dairy farms. Corn, oats, soybeans. feed pellets.

10873 ■ Freeport Journal-Standard
The Journal-Standard
27 S State Ave.
Freeport, IL 61032
Phone: (815)232-1171
General newspaper. **Freq:** Daily (morn.). **Print Method:** Offset. **Cols./Page:** 6. **Col. Width:** 26 nonpareils. **Col. Depth:** 300 agate lines. **Key Personnel:** Paul Gaier, Publisher. **Remarks:** Accepts advertising. **Circ:** (Not Reported).

10874 ■ WFPS-FM - 92.1
PO Box 807
Freeport, IL 61032
Phone: (815)235-7191
Fax: (815)235-4318
Format: Country. **Owner:** Big Radio, Not Available. **Founded:** Nov. 01, 1970. **Operating Hours**: Continuous. **ADI:** Rockford, IL. **Wattage:** 6,000. **Ad Rates:** $10-30 for 30 seconds. Combined advertising rates available with WFRL-AM. **URL:** http://www.wekz.com.

10875 ■ WFRL-AM - 1570
834 N Tower Rd.
Freeport, IL 61032-0747
Phone: (815)235-7191
Fax: (815)235-4318
Format: News; Sports. **Owner:** RadioWorks, Inc., at above address. **Founded:** Oct. 28, 1947. **Operating Hours**: Sunrise to Sunset. **Wattage:** 5,000. **Ad Rates:** Advertising accepted; rates available upon request. $12-35 for 60 seconds. Combined advertising rates available with WFPS-FM. **Mailing address:** PO Box 747, Freeport, IL 61032-0747. **URL:** http://www.bigradio.fm.

10876 ■ WNIE-FM - 89.1
801 N First St.
DeKalb, IL 60115
Phone: (815)753-9000
Fax: (815)753-9938
Email: npr@niu.edu
Format: Public Radio. **Owner:** Northern Illinois University, 1425 W Lincoln Hwy., Dekalb, IL 60115. **Key Personnel:** Bill Drake, Dir. of Programs, wdrake@niu.edu; Jeff Glass, Chief Engineer, jglass@niu.edu. **URL:** http://www.northernpublicradio.org.

10877 ■ WQLF-FM - 102.1
834 N Tower Rd.
Freeport, IL 61032
Phone: (815)235-7191
Fax: (815)235-4318
Format: Classic Rock. **Operating Hours**: Continuous. **Key Personnel:** Scott Thompson, Contact; Scott Thompson, Contact; Ben Thompson, Contact; Don Wertz, Contact; Dan Blum, Contact. **Wattage:** 6,000. **Ad Rates:** Advertising accepted; rates available upon request. **Mailing address:** PO Box 807, Freeport, IL 61032. **URL:** http://www.wekz.com.

GALENA

Jo Daviess Co. Jo Daviess Co. (NW). On Galena River, 20 m SE of Dubuque, Ia. Foundries. Manufactures stoves, lubricating oil, mining machinery, neon signs, dairy products, batteries. Dairy farms.

10878 ■ Galena Gazette and Advertiser
Galena Gazette Publications Inc.
716 S Bench St.
Galena, IL 61036
Phone: (815)777-0019
Community newspaper. **Freq:** Weekly (Wed.). **Print Method:** Offset. **Trim Size:** 10.5 x 16. **Cols./Page:** 4. **Col. Width:** 15 picas. **Col. Depth:** 16 inches. **Key Personnel:** Jay Dickerson, Manager, Advertising; Carter Newton, Publisher. **USPS:** 574-400. **Subscription Rates:** Free to qualified subscribers online only; $3.99 Individuals one-month subscription ; $33 Individuals one-year subscription. **URL:** http://galenagazette.com. **Ad Rates:** BW $912; PCI $14.25. **Remarks:** Accepts advertising. **Circ:** ‡5200.

GALESBURG

Knox Co. Knox Co. (NWC). 53 m NW of Peoria. Knox College. Coal mines. Manufactures foundry products, refrigerators, steel stampings and enameling products, sanitary supplies, uniforms, marine accessories, prefabricated metal buildings, industrial hose, tanks, gates, ladders, garage doors, auto parts, paint, railway equipment, air conditioners, power mowers, bricks, overalls, dairy products.

10879 ■ Knox Student
Knox College
2 E South St.
Galesburg, IL 61401-4999
Phone: (309)341-7000
Collegiate newspaper. **Freq:** Weekly. **Print Method:** Letterpress and offset. **Trim Size:** 11 x 17. **Cols./Page:** 5. **Col. Width:** 4 nonpareils. **Col. Depth:** 224 agate lines. **Key Personnel:** Megan Scott, Editor. **Subscription Rates:** Free. **URL:** http://www.knox.edu/campus-life/clubs-and-organizations/the-knox-student. **Ad Rates:** PCI $5. **Remarks:** Accepts advertising. **Circ:** ‡1000.

10880 ■ The Register-Mail
The Register-Mail
140 S Prairie St.
Galesburg, IL 61401
Phone: (309)343-7181
Publisher's E-mail: news@register-mail.com
General newspaper. **Freq:** Daily (eve.) and Sat. (morn.). **Print Method:** Offset. **Cols./Page:** 6. **Col. Width:** 25 nonpareils. **Col. Depth:** 301 agate lines. **Key Personnel:** Tom Martin, Editor. **USPS:** 213-060. **Subscription Rates:** $5.75 Individuals /week, print and online + home delivery ; $299 Individuals all access. **URL:** http://www.galesburg.com. **Ad Rates:** GLR $1.04; BW $2174.94; 4C $2384.94; SAU $16.86; PCI $14.56. **Remarks:** Accepts advertising. **Circ:** Mon.-Sat. ★**14743**, Sun. ★**14359**.

10881 ■ The Zephyr
Norm Winick
PO Box 1
Galesburg, IL 61402
Phone: (309)342-2010
Fax: (309)342-2728
Publication E-mail: editor@thezephyr.com
Community newspaper. **Founded:** 1989. **Freq:** Weekly (Thurs.). **Print Method:** Offset. **Trim Size:** 11 x 17. **Cols./Page:** 6. **Col. Width:** 1 5/8 inches. **Key Personnel:** Norm Winick, Editor. **USPS:** 004-515. **Subscription Rates:** $20 Individuals per year, residents of Knox County, Illinois; $25 Individuals per year, Knox County Snowbirds; $30 Out of state per year; $.50 Individuals per copy, places around Galesburg; $2.50 By mail per copy, places around Galesburg. **URL:** http://www.thezephyr.com. **Ad Rates:** SAU $4; PCI $4. **Remarks:** Accepts advertising. **Circ:** Paid 2000.

10882 ■ Nova Cablevision Inc.
677 W Main St.
Galesburg, IL 61402
Phone: (309)342-9681
Fax: (309)342-4408
Email: novariocable@hotmail.com
Founded: 1988. **Key Personnel:** Rob Fisher, Technician; Robert G. Fisher, Contact. **Cities Served:** subscribing households 698. **Mailing address:** PO Box 1412, Galesburg, IL 61402. **URL:** http://nova1net.com/.

10883 ■ WAAG-FM - 94.9
154 E Simmons St.
Galesburg, IL 61401
Phone: (309)342-5131
Fax: (309)342-0619
Email: fm95@fm95online.com
Format: Country. **Owner:** Galesburg Broadcasting Co., at above address. **Founded:** 1966. **Operating Hours:** Continuous; 100% local. **Wattage:** 50,000. **Ad Rates:** $18-36 for 30 seconds; $20-40 for 60 seconds. Combined advertising rates available with WGIL, WLSR, and WKAY. **URL:** http://www.fm95online.com.

10884 ■ WGIL-AM - 1400
154 E Simmons St.
Galesburg, IL 61401
Phone: (309)342-5131
Fax: (309)342-0840
Email: news@wgil.com
Format: Sports; News; Talk. **Owner:** Galesburg Broadcasting Co., at above address. **Founded:** 1938. **Operating Hours:** Continuous. **Key Personnel:** Roger Lundeen, Gen. Mgr., rogerl@galesburgradio.com; Brian Prescott, Operations Mgr., brianp@fm95online.com; Chris Postin, Team Ldr., chrisp@galesburgradio.com; John Pritchard, Owner. **Wattage:** 740. **Ad Rates:** Combined advertising rates available with WAAG, WLSR, and WKAY. **URL:** http://www.wgil.com.

10885 ■ WKAY-FM - 105.3
154 E Simmons St.
Galesburg, IL 61401
Phone: (309)342-5131
Fax: (309)342-0619
Email: kfm@1053kfm.com
Format: Soft Rock; Album-Oriented Rock (AOR). **Key Personnel:** Chris McIntyre, Contact, chrism@1053kfm.com. **Wattage:** 3,700. **Ad Rates:** Advertising accepted; rates available upon request. **URL:** http://1053kfm.Com.

10886 ■ WLSR-FM - 92.7
154 E Simmons St.
Galesburg, IL 61401
Phone: (309)342-5131
Fax: (309)342-0619
Format: Album-Oriented Rock (AOR). **Networks:** ABC. **Owner:** Galesburg Broadcasting Co., at above address. **Founded:** 1978. **Formerly**: WGBQ-FM. **Operating Hours**: Continuous; 1% network, 99% local. **Wattage**: 3,000. **Ad Rates:** $5.25-11 for 30 seconds; $7.25-13 for 60 seconds. **URL:** http://www.thelaseronline.com.

GENESEO

Henry Co. Henry Co. (NW). 25 m E of Moline. Grain, stock, poultry farms. Hybrid seed corn. Cattle and hogs.

10887 ■ WAXR-FM
PO Box 2440
Tupelo, MS 38801-2440
Format: Contemporary Christian. **Owner:** American Family Association, at above address. **Founded:** Sept. 14, 2006. **Ad Rates:** Noncommercial.

GENEVA

Kane Co. Kane Co. (NE). On Fox River, 10 m N of Aurora. Manufactures interval timers and time switches, metal filings, farm machinery, wire-cable products, electronics components, foundry products, auto parts, batteries. Greenhouses. Grain, dairy farms.

10888 ■ Dermatologic Surgery
International Society of Hair Restoration Surgery
303 W State St.
Geneva, IL 60134
Phone: (630)262-5399
Fax: (630)262-1520
Free: 800-444-2737
Publisher's E-mail: info@ishrs.org
Journal containing articles, commentaries, and researches in the field of dermatology (the hair, nails, skin and its diseases) in both medical and surgical aspects for health and cosmetic purposes. **Freq:** Monthly. **Subscription Rates:** Included in membership. **Remarks:** Advertising not accepted. **Circ:** (Not Reported).

GIBSON CITY

10889 ■ WGCY-FM - 106.3
PO Box 192
Gibson City, IL 60936
Phone: (217)784-8661
Fax: (217)784-8677
Free: 888-784-9429
Format: Easy Listening. **Key Personnel:** Gary McCullough, Owner, wgcyproduction@hotmail.com; Frank McCullough, Sports Dir., frankmccullough@hotmail.com; Jim Cotter, Contact, cott83@yahoo.com. **Ad Rates:** Noncommercial. **URL:** http://www.wgcyradio.com.

GLEN ELLYN

DuPage Co. Du Page Co. (NE). 6 m N. of Woodridge. College of Dupage. Residential. Historical sites. Antique and specialty shops.

10890 ■ Courier
College of DuPage
425 Fawell Blvd.
Glen Ellyn, IL 60137
Phone: (630)858-2800
Publisher's E-mail: contactus@cod.edu
Collegiate newspaper. **Founded:** 1969. **Freq:** Weekly (Fri.). **Print Method:** Offset. **Cols./Page:** 4. **Col. Width:** 28 nonpareils. **Col. Depth:** 224 agate lines. **Subscription Rates:** Free. **URL:** http://www.cod.edu/courier/. **Ad Rates:** BW $512. **Remarks:** off campus. **Circ:** Free ‡5000.

10891 ■ Law Enforcement Legal Review
Law Enforcement Legal Publications
421 Ridgewood Ave., Ste. 100
Glen Ellyn, IL 60137-4900
Phone: (630)858-6092
Publisher's E-mail: lelp@xnet.com
Journal for the public and private safety sectors who have an interest in civil litigation and criminal law involving state, county, and municipal public safety agencies and private security. **Freq:** Bimonthly. **Print Method:** Offset. **Trim Size:** 8 x 10. **Cols./Page:** 2. **Key Personnel:** James P. Manak, Publisher. **ISSN:** 1070--9967 (print). **Subscription Rates:** $98 Individuals. **URL:** http://home.xnet.com/~lelp/lelr/index.htm. **Remarks:** Advertising not accepted. **Circ:** Paid 1000.

10892 ■ WDCB-FM - 90.9
College of DuPage
425 Fawell Blvd.
Glen Ellyn, IL 60137
Phone: (630)942-4200
Fax: (630)942-2788
Email: info@wdcb.org
Format: Public Radio; Jazz; News. **Owner:** College of DuPage, 425 Fawell Blvd., Glen Ellyn, IL 60137, Ph: (630)858-2800. **Founded:** 1977. **Operating Hours**: Continuous. **Key Personnel:** Brian O'Keefe, Dir. Pub. Aff.; Ken Scott, Dir. of Mktg., scottk@cod.edu; Paul Abella, Music Dir., abella@cod.edu. **Wattage:** 5,000. **Ad Rates:** Noncommercial; underwriting available. $48-100 per unit. **URL:** http://www.wdcb.org.

GLENVIEW

Cook Co. Cook Co. (NE). 16 m N of Chicago. Residential. Grove (national historic preserve). Commercial, industrial and manufacturing.

10893 ■ CHEST Journal
American College of Chest Physicians
2595 Patriot Blvd.
Glenview, IL 60026
Phone: (224)521-9800
Fax: (224)521-9801
Free: 800-343-2227
Publication E-mail: chestcustomersupport@chestnet.org
Freq: Monthly. **Print Method:** Web. **Trim Size:** 8 x 10 3/4. **Cols./Page:** 2. **Col. Width:** 45 nonpareils. **Col. Depth:** 130 agate lines. **Key Personnel:** Richard S. Irwin, MD, Editor-in-Chief; John E. Heffner, MD, Editor; Cynthia T. French, Assistant Editor; Paul A. Markowski, Executive Vice President, Chief Executive Officer; Stephen J. Welch, Publisher; Jean Rice, Manager, Operations. **ISSN:** 0012--3692 (print); **EISSN:** 1931--3543 (electronic). **USPS:** 157-860. **Subscription Rates:** $396 U.S. and Canada print & online (Institution); $25 Single issue; Included in membership; $444 Other countries print & online (Institution); $300 Institutions worldwide. **URL:** http://journal.publications.chestnet.org; http://www.chestnet.org/Publications/CHEST-Publications/CHEST-Journal. **Formerly**: Chest: The Cardiopulmonary and Critical Care Journal. **Ad Rates:** BW $2,320; 4C $4,080; SAU $685. **Remarks:** Accepts advertising. **Circ:** 23000.

10894 ■ Chest Meeting Abstracts
American College of Chest Physicians
2595 Patriot Blvd.
Glenview, IL 60026
Phone: (224)521-9800
Fax: (224)521-9801
Free: 800-343-2227
Journal featuring clinical investigations in the multidisciplinary specialties of chest medicine, including pulmonology, cardiology, thoracic surgery, transplantation, sleep and breathing, and airways diseases. **Freq:** Annual. **Print Method:** Offset. **Cols./Page:** 6. **Col. Width:** 25 nonpareils. **Col. Depth:** 301 agate lines. **Key Personnel:** Richard S. Irwin, MD, Editor-in-Chief; Peter J. Barnes, Associate Editor; Christopher E. Brightling, Associate Editor; Nancy A. Collop, Associate Editor. **URL:** http://journal.publications.chestnet.org/ss/meetingabstracts.aspx. **Remarks:** Accepts advertising. **Circ:** (Not Reported).

Circulation: ★ = AAM; △ or • = BPA; ♦ = CAC; ❑ = VAC; ⊕ = PO Statement; ‡ = Publisher's Report; Boldface figures = sworn; Light figures = estimated.

10895 ■ Evanston Review
Sun-Times Media L.L.C.
3701 W Lake Ave.
Glenview, IL 60026
Phone: (847)486-9200
Publisher's E-mail: customerservice@suntimes.com
Community newspaper (tabloid). **Freq:** Weekly. **Print Method:** Offset. **Trim Size:** 11 x 14. **Cols./Page:** 5. **Col. Width:** 9 3/4 inches. **Col. Depth:** 123/4 inches. **Key Personnel:** John Puterbaugh, Editor, phone: (312)321-2485; Rich Martin, Editor, phone: (847)486-7481; Ryan Nilsson, Managing Editor, phone: (312)321-2694. **ISSN:** 1044--7733 (print). **URL:** http://www.chicagotribune.com/suburbs/evanston. **Remarks:** Accepts advertising. **Circ:** (Not Reported).

10896 ■ International Journal of Laboratory Hematology
International Society for Laboratory Hematology
2111 Chestnut Ave., Ste. 145
Glenview, IL 60025
Phone: (847)737-1584
Fax: (312)896-5614
Publisher's E-mail: journaladsusa@bos.blackwellpublishing.com
Journal focusing on new developments, research topics and the practice of clinical and laboratory haematology. **Freq:** Bimonthly. **Key Personnel:** Dr. Steve Kitchen, Associate Editor; Szu-Hee Lee, Editor-in-Chief. **ISSN:** 1751--5521 (print); **EISSN:** 1751--553X (electronic). **Subscription Rates:** $2255 Institutions print or online; £1219 Institutions print or online; €1549 Institutions print or online; $2630 Institutions, other countries print or online; $2706 Institutions print and online; £1463 Institutions print and online; €1859 Institutions print and online; $3156 Institutions, other countries print and online. **URL:** http://onlinelibrary.wiley.com/journal/10.1111/(ISSN)1751-553X. **Formerly**: Clinical and Laboratory Haematology. **Remarks:** Accepts advertising. **Circ:** (Not Reported).

10897 ■ Lincolnwood Review
Sun-Times Media L.L.C.
3701 W Lake Ave.
Glenview, IL 60026
Phone: (847)486-9200
Fax: (847)486-7451
Publisher's E-mail: customerservice@suntimes.com
Community newspaper. **Freq:** Weekly. **Key Personnel:** Ryan Nilsson, Managing Editor. **URL:** http://lincolnwood.suntimes.com/index.html. **Remarks:** Accepts advertising. **Circ:** (Not Reported).

Niles Herald-Spectator - See Niles

10898 ■ Park Ridge Herald--Advocate
Sun-Times Media L.L.C.
3701 W Lake Ave.
Glenview, IL 60026
Phone: (847)486-9200
Publisher's E-mail: customerservice@suntimes.com
Community newspaper (tabloid). **Freq:** Weekly. **Print Method:** Offset. **Cols./Page:** 5. **Col. Width:** 10 inches. **Col. Depth:** 14 inches. **Key Personnel:** Rich Martin, Director, Sports, phone: (847)486-7481. **Subscription Rates:** $20 Individuals; $84 Out of state. **URL:** http://parkridge.chicagotribune.com. **Remarks:** Accepts advertising. **Circ:** (Not Reported).

10899 ■ Rehabilitation Nursing: The Official Journal of the Association of Rehabilitation Nurses
Association of Rehabilitation Nurses
4700 W Lake Ave.
Glenview, IL 60025
Phone: (847)375-4710
Fax: (847)375-6481
Free: 800-229-7530
Publisher's E-mail: info@rehabnurse.org
Magazine focusing on rehabilitation nursing involving clinical practice, research, education, and administration. **Freq:** Bimonthly. **Print Method:** Offset. **Trim Size:** 8 1/2 x 11. **Cols./Page:** 2 and 3. **Col. Width:** 20.6 and 13.6 picas. **Col. Depth:** 52 picas. **Key Personnel:** Elaine Tilka Miller, Editor. **ISSN:** 0278--4807 (print). **Subscription Rates:** $165 Individuals print + online; The Americas; $264 Individuals print + online; USA, Canada & Mexico, and rest of the world; £169 Individuals print + online; UK; €199 Individuals print + online; Europe; $290 Institutions print only or online only; The Americas, USA, Canada & Mexico, and rest of the world; £183 Institutions print only or online only; UK; €208 Institutions print only or online only; Europe; $348 Institutions print + online; The Americas, USA, Canada & Mexico, and rest of the world; £220 Institutions print + online; UK; €250 Institutions print + online; Europe; Included in membership. **Ad Rates:** BW $1,805; 4C $2,700. **Remarks:** Accepts advertising. **Circ:** ‡8700.

10900 ■ Rehabilitation Professional
International Association of Rehabilitation Professionals
1926 Waukegan Rd., Ste. 1
Glenview, IL 60025-1770
Phone: (847)657-6964
Fax: (847)657-6963
Free: 888-427-7722
Journal containing research and reports on industry developments. **Freq:** Quarterly. **Subscription Rates:** $25 Members 4 printed editions; $25 Members single issue; $85 Nonmembers 4 printed editions; $35 Nonmembers single issue. **URL:** http://www.rehabpro.org/publications. **Remarks:** Accepts advertising. **Circ:** (Not Reported).

10901 ■ River Forest Leaves
Pioneer Press Newspapers
3701 W Lake Ave.
Glenview, IL 60026
Phone: (847)486-9200
Fax: (847)486-7451
Community newspaper. **Freq:** Weekly. **URL:** http://www.chicagotribune.com/suburbs/river-forest/news. **Remarks:** Accepts advertising. **Circ:** (Not Reported).

Skokie Review - See Skokie

10902 ■ Wilmette Life: With News of Kenilworth
Sun-Times Media L.L.C.
3701 W Lake Ave.
Glenview, IL 60026
Phone: (847)486-9200
Fax: (847)486-7451
Publisher's E-mail: customerservice@suntimes.com
Community newspaper (tabloid). **Freq:** Weekly. **Print Method:** Offset. **Trim Size:** 11 x 14. **Cols./Page:** 5. **Col. Width:** 9 3/4 inches. **Col. Depth:** 12 3/4 inches. **Key Personnel:** Jeff Wisser, Editor-in-Chief, phone: (847)486-6848; Gary Taylor, Managing Editor, phone: (847)486-6850; Rich Martin, Editor, phone: (847)486-7481. **ISSN:** 0745-0044 (print). **Subscription Rates:** $84 Out of state; $40 Individuals. **URL:** http://wilmette.suntimes.com. **Remarks:** Accepts advertising. **Circ:** (Not Reported).

Winnetka Talk - See Winnetka

GODFREY

Madison Co. Madison Co.

10903 ■ WLCA-FM - 89.9
5800 Godfrey Rd.
Godfrey, IL 62035
Phone: (618)468-4940
Fax: (618)466-7458
Email: wlca@lc.edu
Format: Alternative/New Music/Progressive; Eclectic. **Networks:** USA Radio. **Owner:** Lewis and Clark Community College, at above address. **Founded:** 1974. **Operating Hours**: 8:00 p.m. - Midnight Monday; 9:00 p.m. - Midnight Tuesday - Thursday,Saturday; 3:00 p.m. - Midnight Friday; 6:00 p.m. - Midnight Sunday. **Key Personnel:** Michael Lemons, Station Mgr., mlemons@lc.edu. **Wattage**: 1,500 ERP. **Ad Rates:** $5 for 30 seconds; $8 for 60 seconds. **URL:** http://www.wlcafm.com.

GOLDEN

Adams Co. Adams Co. (W). 30 m NE of Quincy. Grist mill. Grain, stock farms. Corn, wheat, beans.

10904 ■ Adams Telcom Inc.
405 Emminga Rd.
Golden, IL 62339
Phone: (217)696-4611
Fax: (217)696-8411
Free: 800-892-0123
Email: info@adams.net
Founded: July 11, 1952. **Cities Served:** subscribing households 2,065. **Mailing address:** PO Box 217, Golden, IL 62339. **URL:** http://www.adams.net.

GRANITE CITY

Madison Co. Madison Co. (SW). 5 m E of St. Louis, Mo. Manufactures railway equipment, steel and steel castings, oxygen and nitrogen products, lubricants, corn syrup, earth pigment, chemicals, magnesium, coke, tar and creosoted products, fire brick, fertilizer, auto frames, soft drinks, roofing material, plastics. Meat packing.

10905 ■ Granite City Press Record
Suburban Journals
1815 Delmar Ave.
Granite City, IL 62040
Phone: (618)877-7700
Community newspaper. **Freq:** Weekly (Thurs.). **Print Method:** Offset. **Cols./Page:** 6. **Col. Width:** 156 nonpareils. **Col. Depth:** 301 agate lines. **Key Personnel:** Douglas L. Garbs, Manager, Advertising; Dennis Grubaugh, Editor; Rick Jarvis, Publisher. **URL:** http://www.stltoday.com. **Ad Rates:** BW $1511.40; 4C $2151; SAU $11.45. **Remarks:** Accepts advertising. **Circ:** ‡19762.

GRANT PARK

10906 ■ Grant Park Gazette
Russell Publications
120 W North St.
Peotone, IL 60468
Phone: (708)258-3473
Fax: (708)258-6295
Community newspaper. **Freq:** Weekly (Thurs.). **Cols./Page:** 5. **Col. Width:** 2 inches. **Col. Depth:** 16 inches. **Key Personnel:** Gilbert L. Russell, Publisher. **Subscription Rates:** $35 Individuals residents of Will, Kankakee, or Cook counties; $41 Individuals all other Illinois residents; $45 Out of state; $85 Other countries. **URL:** http://www.russell-publications.com/grantpark. **Mailing address:** PO Box 429, Peotone, IL 60468. **Ad Rates:** PCI $3.45. **Remarks:** Accepts advertising. **Circ:** 880.

GREENVILLE

Bond Co. Bond Co. (S). 44 m NE of St. Louis, Mo. Greenville College. Manufactures condensed milk, food flavoring, uniforms, steel products, rubber roofing, ball pitching machine, springs, electric scoreboards. Agriculture. Dairy products, grain, alfalfa.

10907 ■ Papyrus: The Greenville College Student Newspaper
Greenville College
315 E College Ave.
Greenville, IL 62246-1145
Phone: (618)664-2800
Free: 800-345-4400
Collegiate Free-Methodist newspaper. **Freq:** Weekly. **Print Method:** Offset. **Cols./Page:** 5. **Col. Width:** 1 1/2 inches. **Col. Depth:** 160 agate lines. **Key Personnel:** Kaylee Summers, Editor-in-Chief. **URL:** http://papyrus.greenville.edu. **Ad Rates:** PCI $3. **Remarks:** Accepts advertising. **Circ:** 1000.

10908 ■ WGEL-FM - 101.7
309 W Main
Greenville, IL 62246
Phone: (618)664-3300
Format: Contemporary Country. **Networks:** USA Radio. **Owner:** Bond Broadcasting, Inc., at above address. **Founded:** 1984. **Operating Hours:** Continuous. **Wattage:** 3,000. **Ad Rates:** $16 for 30 seconds; $20 for 60 seconds. **URL:** http://www.wgel.com.

10909 ■ WGRN-FM - 89.5
315 E College Ave.
Greenville, IL 62246
Phone: (618)664-2800
Free: 800-345-4440
Format: Religious; Contemporary Christian. **Networks:** USA Radio. **Owner:** Greenville College Educational Broadcasting Foundation, 315 E College Ave., Greenville, IL 62246-1145. **Founded:** 1953. **Operating Hours**: Continuous. **Key Personnel:** Jessica Goodman, Station Mgr., wgrnstationmanager@greenville.edu; Gregg Wandsneider, Dir. of Programs, wgrnprogramdirector@greenville.edu; Ashlee Schenke, Music Dir., wgrnmusicdirector@greenville.edu. **Wattage**: 300. **Ad Rates:** $8 per unit.

GURNEE

Lake Co. Lake Co. (NE). 5 m W of Waukegan. Suburban area. Marriott's Great America Theme Park. Manufactures plastic glass and lumber products, electronic commponents. Horse, grain.

10910 ■ Children, Churches & Daddies: the unreligious, non-family-oriented literary & art magazine
Scars Publications and Design
829 Brian Ct.
Gurnee, IL 60031-3155
Publication E-mail: editor@scars.tv
Magazine containing poetry, short stories, art, news, and philosophy. **Freq:** Monthly. **Print Method:** Perfect bound, saddle-stitched, electronic. **Key Personnel:** Janet Kuypers, Publisher. **ISSN:** 1068--5154 (print); **EISSN:** 1555--1555 (electronic). **Subscription Rates:** $5 Single issue plus 1 shipping and handling in U.S. **URL:** http://scars.tv/perl/ccd.htm. **Remarks:** Advertising accepted; rates available upon request. **Circ:** 125.

HAMILTON

Hancock Co. Hancock Co. (W). On Mississippi River, opposite Keokuk, Ia. with bridge connections. Stone quarry. Beekeepers' suppliers factory. Grain, stock farms. Corn, wheat, soybeans.

10911 ■ American Bee Journal
Dadant and Sons Inc.
51 S Second St.
Hamilton, IL 62341
Phone: (217)847-3324
Fax: (217)847-3660
Free: 888-922-1293
Publication E-mail: info@americanbeejournal.com
Magazine for hobbyist and professional beekeepers. Covers hive management, honey handling, disease control, honey markets, foreign beekeeping, beekeeping history, bee laws, honey plants, marketing, and government beekeeping research. **Freq:** Monthly. **Print Method:** Offset. **Trim Size:** 8 x 10 3/4. **Cols./Page:** 3. **Col. Width:** 26 nonpareils. **Col. Depth:** 136 agate lines. **Key Personnel:** Marta Menn, Manager, Advertising; Joe Graham, Editor. **ISSN:** 0002-7626 (print). **Subscription Rates:** $28 Individuals; $53 Two years; $43 Canada; $82 Canada 2 years; $52 Other countries; $99 Other countries 2 years; $63 Canada airmail; $123 Other countries airmail. **URL:** http://www.americanbeejournal.com. **Ad Rates:** BW $957.43; 4C $1052.10; CNU $839; PCI $51.50. **Remarks:** Accepts advertising. **Circ:** Paid ‡11,000.

HANOVER PARK

DuPage Co. Cook & Du Page Co. (NE). 35 m W of Evanston. Residential.

10912 ■ The International Journal of Oral & Maxillofacial Implants: Official Journal of the Academy of Osseointegration
Quintessence Publishing Company Inc.
4350 Chandler Dr.
Hanover Park, IL 60133
Phone: (630)736-3600
Fax: (630)736-3633
Free: 800-621-0387
Publisher's E-mail: contact@quintbook.com
Dentistry journal covering implant modalities. **Freq:** Bimonthly. **Print Method:** Sheetfed offset. **Trim Size:** 8 1/8 x 10 7/8. **Cols./Page:** 2. **Col. Width:** 18 1/2 picas. **Col. Depth:** 55 picas. **Key Personnel:** William R. Laney, DMD, Editor; Steven E. Eckert, Editor-in-Chief. **ISSN:** 0882--2786 (print). **Subscription Rates:** $195 Individuals; $585 Institutions; $100 Students; $235 Out of country; $625 Institutions outside North America; 140 Students outside North America; $40 Single issue. **URL:** http://www.quintpub.com/journals/omi/#.VHXCntIW2qZ. **Ad Rates:** BW $2,620; 4C $1,850. **Remarks:** Accepts advertising. **Circ:** ‡9500.

10913 ■ The International Journal of Periodontics & Restorative Dentistry
Quintessence Publishing Company Inc.
4350 Chandler Dr.
Hanover Park, IL 60133
Phone: (630)736-3600
Fax: (630)736-3633
Free: 800-621-0387
Publisher's E-mail: contact@quintbook.com
Journal for periodontists and general practitioners. **Freq:** Bimonthly. **Print Method:** Sheetfed offset. **Trim Size:** 8 1/4 x 11. **Cols./Page:** 3. **Col. Width:** 13 picas. **Col. Depth:** 50 picas. **Key Personnel:** Marc L. Nevins, Editor; Myron Nevins, DDS, Editor. **ISSN:** 0198--7569 (print); **EISSN:** 1945--3388 (electronic). **Subscription Rates:** $250 Individuals; $750 Institutions; $195 Students. **URL:** http://www.quintpub.com/journals/prd/aboutjournal.php?journal_name=PRD; http://quintpub.com/journals/prd/index.php#.Vm4-XNJ962w. **Ad Rates:** BW $2,400; 4C $1,650. **Remarks:** Accepts advertising. **Circ:** ‡5000.

10914 ■ The International Journal of Prosthodontics: Official Journal of the International College of Prosthodontists and the International Society for Maxillofacial Rehabilitation
Quintessence Publishing Company Inc.
4350 Chandler Dr.
Hanover Park, IL 60133
Phone: (630)736-3600
Fax: (630)736-3633
Free: 800-621-0387
Publisher's E-mail: contact@quintbook.com
Journal covering current information on all areas of prosthodontics. **Freq:** Bimonthly. **Print Method:** Sheetfed offset. **Trim Size:** 8 1/8 x 10 7/8. **Cols./Page:** 2. **Col. Width:** 18.5 picas. **Col. Depth:** 55 picas. **Key Personnel:** George A. Zarb, Editor-in-Chief. **ISSN:** 0893-2174 (print). **Subscription Rates:** $185 Individuals; $555 Institutions; $95 Students; $225 Out of country surface mail; $595 Institutions, other countries surface mail; $135 Students, other countries surface mail; $265 Individuals air mail - outside North America; $635 Individuals air mail - outside North America; $175 Students air mail - outside North America. **URL:** http://www.quintpub.com/journals/ijp/gp.php?journal_name=ijp. **Ad Rates:** BW $1,790; 4C $1,850. **Remarks:** Accepts advertising. **Circ:** ‡2300.

10915 ■ Journal of Oral & Facial Pain and Headache
Quintessence Publishing Company Inc.
4350 Chandler Dr.
Hanover Park, IL 60133
Phone: (630)736-3600
Fax: (630)736-3633
Free: 800-621-0387
Publisher's E-mail: contact@quintbook.com
Professional publications covering facial pain, headaches, and occlusion for the dental industry. **Freq:** Quarterly. **Print Method:** Sheetfed offset. **Trim Size:** 8 1/8 x 10 7/8. **Key Personnel:** Alain Woda, PhD, Associate Editor; Dr. Barry J. Sessle, Editor-in-Chief. **ISSN:** 2333--0384 (print); **EISSN:** 2333--0376 (electronic). **Subscription Rates:** $138 Individuals. **Alt. Formats:** PDF. **URL:** http://www.quintpub.com/journals/ofph/gp.php?journal_name=OFPH&name_abbr=OFPH. **Formerly:** Journal of Orofacial Pain. **Ad Rates:** BW $650; 4C $1950. **Remarks:** Accepts advertising. **Circ:** 2000.

10916 ■ Little Circus Wagon
Circus Model Builders International
c/o Armando Ortiz, Membership Secretary
1649 Park Ave.
Hanover Park, IL 60133-3610
Freq: 6/year. **Subscription Rates:** Included in membership. **URL:** http://www.circusmodelbuilders.club/#!magazine/cee5. **Remarks:** Accepts advertising. **Circ:** (Not Reported).

10917 ■ Oral & Craniofacial Tissue Engineering
Quintessence Publishing Company Inc.
4350 Chandler Dr.
Hanover Park, IL 60133
Phone: (630)736-3600
Fax: (630)736-3633
Free: 800-621-0387
Publisher's E-mail: contact@quintbook.com
Journal covering multiple disciplinary lines involving specialties of both dentistry and medicine. **Freq:** Quarterly. **Key Personnel:** Ole T. Jensen, Editor-in-Chief. **ISSN:** 2158--3722 (print); **EISSN:** 2158--3706 (electronic). **Subscription Rates:** $40 Single issue; $138 Individuals /yr. **URL:** http://www.quintpub.com/journals/octe/gp.php?journal_name=OCTE. **Ad Rates:** BW $1,490. **Remarks:** Accepts advertising. **Circ:** 3000.

10918 ■ QDT
Quintessence Publishing Company Inc.
4350 Chandler Dr.
Hanover Park, IL 60133
Phone: (630)736-3600
Fax: (630)736-3633
Free: 800-621-0387
Publisher's E-mail: contact@quintbook.com
Professional magazine covering dental laboratory practice. **Freq:** Annual. **Print Method:** Sheetfed offset. **Trim Size:** 8 1/8 x 10 7/8. **Key Personnel:** Dr. Avishai Sadan, Editor. **ISSN:** 0896--6532 (print). **Subscription Rates:** $9.99 Individuals. **URL:** http://www.quintpub.com/display_detail.php3?psku=J0619#.VsLLuLR96ig. **Ad Rates:** BW $1,545; 4C $2,595. **Remarks:** Accepts advertising. **Circ:** 3000.

10919 ■ Quintessence International: The Journal of Practical Dentistry
Quintessence Publishing Company Inc.
4350 Chandler Dr.
Hanover Park, IL 60133
Phone: (630)736-3600
Fax: (630)736-3633
Free: 800-621-0387
Publisher's E-mail: contact@quintbook.com
Publication featuring information on clinical and research advances in all forms of dentistry. **Freq:** 10/year. **Print Method:** Sheet-fed Offset. **Trim Size:** 8 1/8 x 10 7/8. **Key Personnel:** Matthias Karl, Associate Editor; Eli Eliav, PhD, Editor-in-Chief. **ISSN:** 0033--6572 (print). **Subscription Rates:** $198 Individuals; $465 Individuals; $98 Students. **URL:** http://www.quintpub.com/journals/qi/aboutjournal.php?journal_name=QI. **Ad Rates:** BW $2,940; 4C $1,450. **Remarks:** Accepts advertising. **Circ:** 16000.

HARRISBURG

Saline Co. Saline Co. (S). 68 m NE of Cairo. Manufactures wood cabinets. Coal mines; timber. Diversified farming. Fruit, wheat, corn.

10920 ■ The Daily Register
American Publishing
35 S Vine St.
Harrisburg, IL 62946-1725
Phone: (618)253-7146
Fax: (618)252-0863
Publication E-mail: editor@yourclearwave.com
General newspaper. **Founded:** 1869. **Freq:** Mon.-Sat. (morn.). **Print Method:** Offset. **Cols./Page:** 6. **Col. Width:** 25 nonpareils. **Col. Depth:** 308 agate lines. **Key Personnel:** Scott Carr, Publisher. **Subscription Rates:** $133 By mail in Saline, Gallatin, Pope, Hardin counties; $145.90 Out of area; $158.70 Out of state. **URL:** http://www.dailyregister.com. **Ad Rates:** SAU $7. **Remarks:** Accepts classified advertising. **Circ:** (Not Reported).

10921 ■ WEBQ-AM - 1240
PO Box 1508
Mount Vernon, IL 62864-1508
Phone: (618)242-3500
Format: Country; Agricultural. **Networks:** ABC; RFD Illinois; Brownfield. **Owner:** Withers Broadcasting Companies, 1822 N Court St., Marion, IL 62959, Ph: (303)242-5000. **Founded:** 1923. **Operating Hours:** Continuous; 20% network, 80% local. **ADI:** Paducah,KY-Cape Girardeau,MO-Marion,IL. **Wattage:** 1,000. **Ad Rates:** $2.25-8.50 for 30 seconds; $3.25-10 for 60 seconds.

WEBQ-FM - See Eldorado, IL

HARWOOD HEIGHTS

Cook Co.

10922 ■ Norridge Harwood Heights News
Sun-Times Media L.L.C.
350 N Orleans St., 10th Fl.
Chicago, IL 60654
Phone: (312)321-3000
Free: 888-848-4637
Publisher's E-mail: customerservice@suntimes.com
Community newspaper (tabloid). **Freq:** Weekly. **Print Method:** Offset. **Cols./Page:** 5. **Col. Width:** 11 picas. **Col. Depth:** 14 inches. **Key Personnel:** Rick Hibbert, Editor, phone: (847)486-7256; Mike Martinez, Managing

Circulation: ★ = AAM; △ or • = BPA; ♦ = CAC; ❑ = VAC; ⊕ = PO Statement; ‡ = Publisher's Report; Boldface figures = sworn; Light figures = estimated.

Editor, phone: (708)524-4410. **Subscription Rates:** $84 Out of state; $28 Individuals. **URL:** http://www.chicagotribune.com/suburbs/norridge. **Remarks:** Accepts advertising. **Circ:** (Not Reported).

HAVANA

Mason Co. Mason Co. (W). 38 m SW of Peoria. Flour, farm implements, and gasoline engines.

10923 ■ Mason County Democrat
Martin Publishing Inc.
219 W Market St.
Havana, IL 62644
Phone: (309)543-3311
Fax: (309)543-6844
Publisher's E-mail: mcdemo@havanaprint.com
Local newspaper. **Freq:** Weekly. **Print Method:** Offset. **Trim Size:** 14 x 22 3/4. **Cols./Page:** 6. **Col. Width:** 12 picas. **Col. Depth:** 21.5 inches. **Key Personnel:** Wendy Martin, Editor. **ISSN:** 0000--7451 (print). **Subscription Rates:** $42 Individuals in county (print, includes free online access); $73 Two years out of county (print, includes free online access); $59 Out of country print, includes free online access; $99 Out of country two years (print, includes free online access); $32 Individuals online. **URL:** http://www.masoncountydemocrat.com. **Formerly**: Havana Mason County Democrat. **Ad Rates:** SAU $7. **Remarks:** Accepts advertising. **Circ:** Combined 6300.

HENRY

Marshall Co. Marshall Co. (NC). On Illinois River, 35 m NE of Peoria. Boat connections. Hunting, fishing resort. Oak timber. Nurseries. Hatcheries. Grain elevators. Creamery. Manufactures chemicals, farm equipment, hunting goods. Stock, poultry, fruit, grain farms.

10924 ■ Henry News-Republican
Henry News-Republican Inc.
709 3rd St.
Henry, IL 61537
Phone: (309)364-3250
Newspaper with a Republican orientation. **Freq:** Weekly (Wed.). **Print Method:** Offset. **Trim Size:** 16 x 23 1/2. **Cols./Page:** 7. **Col. Width:** 24 nonpareils. **Col. Depth:** 294 agate lines. **Key Personnel:** Doug Ziegler, Contact. **Ad Rates:** GLR $.31; BW $624; 4C $815.08; SAU $3.90. **Remarks:** Advertising accepted; rates available upon request. **Circ:** 2,850.

HIGHLAND

Madison Co. Madison Co. (SW). 32 m E of St. Louis, Mo. Manufactures pipe organs, cellophane products, tools and dies, transformers, electronic equipment, feed, paint, boxboard, machine and screw products. Dairy, poultry, grain farms. Livestock. Wheat corn.

10925 ■ Highland News Leader
Highland News Leader
PO Box 218
Highland, IL 62249
Phone: (618)654-2366
Publication E-mail: hnlnews@bnd.com
Newspaper with a Republican orientation. **Freq:** Weekly (Thurs.). **Print Method:** Offset. **Cols./Page:** 9. **Col. Width:** 22 nonpareils. **Col. Depth:** 294 agate lines. **Key Personnel:** Gay Bentlage, Manager, Advertising. **URL:** http://www.highlandillinois.com/media.asp. **Ad Rates:** SAU $12.85. **Remarks:** Accepts advertising. **Circ:** Paid 6500, Free ‡8500, ‡6000.

10926 ■ Highland Park News
Sun-Times Media L.L.C.
350 N Orleans St., 10th Fl.
Chicago, IL 60654
Phone: (312)321-3000
Free: 888-848-4637
Publisher's E-mail: customerservice@suntimes.com
Community newspaper. **Founded:** 1971. **Freq:** Weekly. **Print Method:** Offset. **Cols./Page:** 4. **Col. Width:** 24 nonpareils. **Col. Depth:** 196 agate lines. **Key Personnel:** Jeff Wisser, Editor-in-Chief, phone: (847)486-6848. **Subscription Rates:** $40 Individuals; $84 Out of state. **URL:** http://highlandpark.suntimes.com. **Remarks:** Accepts advertising. **Circ:** (Not Reported).

WIJR-AM - See Saint Louis, MO

HIGHLAND PARK

Lake Co. Lake Co. (NE). On Lake Michigan, 23 m N of Chicago. Residential suburb of Chicago.

10927 ■ Made to Measure: The Uniform Magazine
Halper Publishing Co.
210 Skokie Valley Rd., Ste. 4
Highland Park, IL 60035
Publication E-mail: news@uniformmarket.com
Trade magazine for the uniform, career apparel, and allied trades. **Freq:** Semiannual. **Trim Size:** 6.75 x 9.75. **Subscription Rates:** $5 Single issue; $20 Single issue international. **URL:** http://www.madetomeasuremag.com. **Ad Rates:** BW $2,320; 4C $4,840. **Remarks:** Accepts advertising. **Circ:** Controlled ⊕**25000**.

HILLSBORO

Montgomery Co. Montgomery Co. (SC). 50 m SE of Springfield. Glass beverage bottles manufactured. Coal mines. Agriculture. Zinc smelters. Electrical generating. Dairy and grain farms. Corn, wheat, hay, soybeans.

10928 ■ WAOX-FM - 105.3
6308 IL Route 16
Hillsboro, IL 62049
Phone: (618)635-6000
Fax: (217)532-2431
Email: waox@waoxradio.com
Format: Adult Contemporary. **Networks:** ABC. **Owner:** Talley Broadcasting Corp., 1610 Oakbrook Dr., Hillsboro, IL 62049-2277. **Founded:** 1999. **Operating Hours:** Continuous. **ADI:** St. Louis, MO (Mt. Vernon, IL). **Key Personnel:** Brian Talley, Operations Mgr., brian@waoxradio.com; Mike Niehaus, Sales Mgr., mike@waoxradio.com; Terry Todt, Sports Dir., terry@waoxradio.com. **Wattage:** 6,000. **Ad Rates:** Advertising accepted; rates available upon request. **Mailing address:** PO Box 10, Hillsboro, IL 62049. **URL:** http://www.waox.com.

HILLSIDE

10929 ■ Catholic Cemetery
Catholic Cemetery Conference
Bldg. No. 3
1400 S Wolf Rd.
Hillside, IL 60162-2197
Phone: (708)202-1242
Fax: (708)202-1255
Free: 888-850-8131
Publisher's E-mail: info@catholiccemeteryconference.org
Magazine on cemetery administration, maintenance, and equipment. **Freq:** Monthly. **Print Method:** Offset. **Trim Size:** 8 1/2 x 11. **Cols./Page:** 3 and 2. **Col. Width:** 26 and 40 nonpareils. **Col. Depth:** 133 agate lines. **Key Personnel:** Christine Kohut, Managing Editor. **USPS:** 093-600. **URL:** http://catholiccemeteryconference.org/magazine. **Ad Rates:** BW $895; 4C $1695. **Remarks:** Accepts advertising. **Circ:** (Not Reported).

10930 ■ Life Safety Digest
Firestop Contractors International Association
4415 W Harrison St., Ste. 436
Hillside, IL 60162-1906
Phone: (708)202-1108
Fax: (708)449-0837
Publisher's E-mail: info@fcia.org
Magazine containing information about fire and life safety systems including effective compartmentation, fire resistance, and smoke resistant systems. **Freq:** Quarterly. **URL:** http://www.fcia.org/magazine.htm. **Ad Rates:** BW $1535, full page - nonmember; BW $955, half page - nonmember; BW $1155, full page - member; BW $715, half page - member. **Remarks:** Accepts advertising. **Circ:** (Not Reported).

HINSDALE

DuPage Co. Du Page Co. (NE). 17 m SW of Chicago. Residential. Commercial office center.

10931 ■ WHSD-FM - 88.5
55th & Grant Sts.
Hinsdale, IL 60521
Phone: (630)655-6100
Fax: (630)325-9153
Format: Public Radio. **Owner:** Hinsdale Central High School, 5500 S Grant St., Hinsdale, IL 60521, Ph: (630)570-8000, Fax: (630)887-1362. **Founded:** 1970. **Operating Hours**: 6:30 a.m.-7:45 a.m. and 3 p.m.-10 p.m.; 100% local. **Wattage**: 125. **Ad Rates:** Noncommercial. **URL:** http://hinsdale86.org.

HOFFMAN ESTATES

Kane Co. Cook Co. (NE). 6 m W of Evanston. Residential.

10932 ■ Danish Pioneer: Den Danske Pioneer
Bertelsen Publishing Co.
1582 Glen Lake Rd.
Hoffman Estates, IL 60169-4023
Phone: (847)882-2552
Fax: (847)882-7082
Publication E-mail: dpioneer@aol.com
Danish interest newspaper. **Freq:** Biweekly. **Print Method:** Offset. **Trim Size:** 10 x 13. **Cols./Page:** 5. **Col. Width:** 24 nonpareils. **Col. Depth:** 210 agate lines. **Key Personnel:** Linda Steffense, Editor. **ISSN:** 0747--3869 (print). **Subscription Rates:** $40 Individuals; $58 By mail first class; $60 Canada by mail; $70 Other countries by mail. **URL:** http://www.thedanishpioneer.com. **Also known as:** Den Danske Pioneer. **Ad Rates:** BW $450; PCI $7. **Remarks:** Accepts advertising. **Circ:** Paid ‡3000, Non-paid ‡250.

10933 ■ Nurse.com--Florida Edition
Gannett Healthcare Group
2353 Hassell Rd., No. 110
Hoffman Estates, IL 60169
Free: 800-770-0866
Publisher's E-mail: editor@nurse.com
Trade publication for the nursing profession. **Freq:** Biweekly. **Trim Size:** 10.875 x 12.75. **Key Personnel:** Cynthia Saver, RN, Director, Production. **Formerly**: Nursing Spectrum--Florida Edition. **Ad Rates:** GLR $59.9; BW $44900. **Remarks:** 59.90. **Circ:** 57000.

10934 ■ Nurse.com--Greater Chicago/Tri-State Edition
Gannett Healthcare Group
2353 Hassell Rd., No. 110
Hoffman Estates, IL 60169
Free: 800-770-0866
Publisher's E-mail: editor@nurse.com
Trade publication for the nursing profession. **Freq:** Biweekly. **Key Personnel:** Janet Boivin, RN, Director, Editorial; Mike Milinac, Director, Production. **URL:** http://www.nurse.com. **Formerly:** Nursing Spectrum--Greater Chicago/Tri-State Edition. **Remarks:** Accepts advertising. **Circ:** (Not Reported).

10935 ■ Nurse.com--New York & New Jersey Edition
Gannett Healthcare Group
2353 Hassell Rd., No. 110
Hoffman Estates, IL 60169
Free: 800-770-0866
Publisher's E-mail: editor@nurse.com
Trade publication for the nursing profession. **Freq:** Biweekly. **Trim Size:** 10.875 x 12.75. **Key Personnel:** Melyni Serpa, Executive Vice President, Operations. **URL:** http://news.nurse.com/category/regional/new-yorknew-jersey-metro. **Formerly**: Nursing Spectrum--New York & New Jersey Edition. **Ad Rates:** GLR $59.9; BW $44900. **Remarks:** 59.90. **Circ:** 120175.

10936 ■ Nurse.com--Philadelphia/Tri-State Edition
Gannett Healthcare Group
2353 Hassell Rd., No. 110
Hoffman Estates, IL 60169
Free: 800-770-0866
Publisher's E-mail: editor@nurse.com
Trade publication for the nursing profession. **Freq:** Biweekly. **Trim Size:** 10.875 x 12.75. **URL:** http://news.nurse.com/category/regional/philadelphiatri-state. **Formerly**: Nursing Spectrum--Philadelphia/Tri-State Edition. **Ad Rates:** GLR $59.9; BW $44,900. **Remarks:** 59.90. **Circ:** 54000.

HOMEWOOD

Cook Co. Cook Co. (NE). 22 m S of Chicago. Residential.

10937 ■ Muslim Journal
Muslim Journal Enterprises Inc.

1141 W 175st St.
Homewood, IL 60430
Phone: (708)647-9600
Fax: (708)647-0754
Free: 800-837-8402
Publisher's E-mail: info@muslimjournal.net
International Islamic newspaper. **Freq:** Weekly (Fri.). **Print Method:** Offset. **Cols./Page:** 5. **Col. Width:** 22 nonpareils. **Col. Depth:** 208 agate lines. **Key Personnel:** Ayesha K. Mustafaa, Editor; Ngina Muhammad, Director, Advertising. **ISSN:** 0883--816X (print). **Subscription Rates:** $70 Individuals 1 year (print or online); $43 Individuals 6 months (print or online); $12 Individuals 1 month (print or online). **URL:** http://muslimjournal.net. **Ad Rates:** BW $975; 4C $1170; PCI $15. **Remarks:** Advertising accepted; rates available upon request. **Circ:** (Not Reported).

HOOPESTON

Vermilion Co. Vermilion Co. (E). 25 m N of Danville. Manufactures battery charges, tin cans, canning machinery, canned vegetables, malleable castings. Agriculture.

10938 ■ WHPO-FM - 100.9
912 S Dixie Hwy.
Hoopeston, IL 60942
Phone: (217)283-7744
Fax: (217)283-6090
Free: 800-245-4101
Email: whpo@whporadio.com
Format: Country. **Networks:** Jones Satellite. **Owner:** Hoopeston Radio Inc., Not Available. **Founded:** 1979. **Operating Hours:** Continuous; 70% network, 30% local. **Key Personnel:** Larry Baughn, Contact, larry@whporadio.com. **Wattage:** 3,000. **Ad Rates:** $10-12 for 30 seconds; $12-15 for 60 seconds. **URL:** http://www.whporadio.com.

ILLIOPOLIS

Sangamon Co. Sangamon Co. (C). 18 m W of Decatur. Grain elevator; chemical factory. Diversified farming. Corn, wheat, oats, poultry.

10939 ■ Illiopolis Sentinel
Wilson Publications
PO Box 300
Illiopolis, IL 62539
Phone: (217)486-6496
Community newspaper. **Freq:** Weekly. **Print Method:** Offset. **Cols./Page:** 5. **Col. Depth:** 280 agate lines. **Key Personnel:** Cindy Wilson, Editor, Publisher. **URL:** http://www.illiopolis.com/pages/members/illiopolis_sentinel.htm. **Ad Rates:** GLR $.40; BW $150; PCI $2.60. **Remarks:** Accepts advertising. **Circ:** Paid ‡675, Free ‡50.

ITASCA

DuPage Co. DuPage Co. (NE). 6 m N of Glen Ellyn. Residential

10940 ■ Chemical Processing
Putman Media Inc.
555 W Pierce Rd., Ste. 301
Itasca, IL 60143-2649
Phone: (630)467-1301
Fax: (630)467-1120
Magazine for the chemical process industry. **Founded:** 1938. **Freq:** Monthly. **Print Method:** Offset. **Trim Size:** 8 x 10 3/4. **Cols./Page:** 3. **Col. Width:** 26 nonpareils. **Col. Depth:** 140 agate lines. **Key Personnel:** Mark Rosenzweig, Editor-in-Chief; Traci Purdum, Senior Editor; Amanda Joshi, Managing Editor. **ISSN:** 0009-2630 (print). **URL:** http://www.chemicalprocessing.com. **Ad Rates:** BW $8680; 4C $7800. **Remarks:** Accepts advertising. **Circ:** △**48,000**.

10941 ■ Control
Putman Media Inc.
555 W Pierce Rd., Ste. 301
Itasca, IL 60143-2649
Phone: (630)467-1301
Fax: (630)467-1120
Magazine targeting instrumentation and control systems professionals in the process industries. **Founded:** Oct. 1988. **Freq:** Monthly. **Print Method:** Offset. **Trim Size:** 8 x 10 3/4. **Cols./Page:** 3. **Col. Width:** 7 inches. **Col. Depth:** 10 inches. **ISSN:** 1049-5541 (print). **Subscription Rates:** Free. **URL:** http://www.controlglobal.com. **Ad Rates:** BW $9,015; 4C $1,745. **Remarks:** Accepts advertising. **Circ:** △**60121**.

10942 ■ Control Design
Putman Media Inc.
555 W Pierce Rd., Ste. 301
Itasca, IL 60143-2649
Phone: (630)467-1301
Fax: (630)467-1120
Magazine for OEM professionals responsible for optimization of industrial manufacturing applications. **Freq:** 8/yr. **Key Personnel:** Joe Feeley, Editor-in-Chief; Mike Bacidore, Managing Editor; Jim Montague, Executive Editor. **ISSN:** 1094--3366 (print). **Subscription Rates:** Free digital; Free to qualified subscribers print. **URL:** http://www.controldesign.com. **Ad Rates:** BW $7,400. **Remarks:** Accepts advertising. **Circ:** 40020.

10943 ■ Food Processing
Putman Media Inc.
555 W Pierce Rd., Ste. 301
Itasca, IL 60143-2649
Phone: (630)467-1301
Fax: (630)467-1120
Print and online magazine devoted to coverage of the food processing industry, from new product development through manufacturing and packaging. **Founded:** 1940. **Freq:** Monthly. **Print Method:** Web offset. **Trim Size:** 8 1/4 x 11. **Key Personnel:** Dave Fusaro, Editor-in-Chief, phone: (630)467-1300; Larry Bagan, Publisher; Jerry Clark, Vice President; Diane Toops, Editor. **ISSN:** 0015-6523 (print). **Subscription Rates:** Free to qualified subscribers. **URL:** http://www.foodprocessing.com. **Ad Rates:** BW $7230. **Remarks:** Accepts advertising. **Circ:** △**62,532**.

10944 ■ Industrial Networking
Putman Media Inc.
555 W Pierce Rd., Ste. 301
Itasca, IL 60143-2649
Phone: (630)467-1301
Fax: (630)467-1120
Magazine covering the design and implementation of networked systems in industrial environments. **Freq:** Quarterly. **Key Personnel:** Joe Feeley, Editor-in-Chief; Mike Bacidore, Editor; Jim Montague, Executive Editor. **URL:** http://www.putmanmedia.com/momentum/market-5. **Remarks:** Accepts advertising. **Circ:** ‡70000.

10945 ■ Pharmaceutical Manufacturing
Putman Media Inc.
555 W Pierce Rd., Ste. 301
Itasca, IL 60143-2649
Phone: (630)467-1301
Fax: (630)467-1120
Magazine for professionals in the pharmaceutical manufacturing industry. **Freq:** Monthly. **Key Personnel:** Tonia Becker, Publisher. **ISSN:** 1550-6509 (print). **URL:** http://www.pharmamanufacturing.com. **Ad Rates:** 4C $5,900; PCI $265. **Remarks:** Accepts advertising. **Circ:** Combined △**25020**.

10946 ■ Plant Services
Putman Media Inc.
555 W Pierce Rd., Ste. 301
Itasca, IL 60143-2649
Phone: (630)467-1301
Fax: (630)467-1120
Magazine on plant maintenance professionals. **Founded:** 1980. **Freq:** Monthly. **Print Method:** Web Offset. **Trim Size:** 8 1/8 x 10 3/4. **Cols./Page:** 2 and 3. **Key Personnel:** Mike Brenner, Publisher. **ISSN:** 0199-8013 (print). **Subscription Rates:** Free online; Free to qualified subscribers print. **URL:** http://www.plantservices.com. **Ad Rates:** BW $13,155; 4C $14,155. **Remarks:** Accepts advertising. **Circ:** ‡35000.

10947 ■ Safety and Health
National Safety Council
1121 Spring Lake Dr.
Itasca, IL 60143-3201
Phone: (630)285-1121
Free: 800-621-7615
Publisher's E-mail: customerservice@nsc.org
Magazine featuring articles on all aspects of occupational safety. **Freq:** Monthly. **Subscription Rates:** Free. **URL:** http://www.safetyandhealthmagazine.com. **Remarks:** Accepts advertising. **Circ:** (Not Reported).

10948 ■ Sketches
Walt Disney Collectors Society
PO Box 249
Itasca, IL 60143-0249
Freq: Quarterly. **Remarks:** Advertising not accepted. **Circ:** (Not Reported).

10949 ■ Today's Supervisor
National Safety Council
1121 Spring Lake Dr.
Itasca, IL 60143-3201
Phone: (630)285-1121
Free: 800-621-7615
Publisher's E-mail: customerservice@nsc.org
Contains articles, news and information related to safety and health. **Freq:** Monthly. **Print Method:** Offset. **Trim Size:** 5 1/2 x 8 1/2. **Cols./Page:** 2. **Col. Width:** 26 nonpareils. **Col. Depth:** 104 agate lines. **ISSN:** 0734--3302 (print). **Alt. Formats:** PDF. **Remarks:** Advertising not accepted. **Circ:** (Not Reported).

10950 ■ Wellness Foods
Putman Media Inc.
555 W Pierce Rd., Ste. 301
Itasca, IL 60143-2649
Phone: (630)467-1301
Fax: (630)467-1120
Magazine covering the healthy foods and beverages market. **Freq:** 6/year. **Key Personnel:** Dave Fusaro, Editor-in-Chief; Anetta Gauthier, Manager, Production; Larry Bagan, Publisher. **ISSN:** 1545--6366 (print). **Subscription Rates:** Free to qualified subscribers. **URL:** http://www.putmanmedia.com/uncategorized/wellness-foods/mission-10. **Remarks:** Accepts advertising. **Circ:** 62532.

JACKSONVILLE

Morgan Co. Morgan Co. (WC). 35 m SW of Springfield. Illinois College, MacMurray College. Manufactures and processors.

10951 ■ WEAI-FM - 107.1
2161 Old State Rd.
Jacksonville, IL 62650
Phone: (217)245-7171
Fax: (217)245-6711
Format: Oldies; News; Sports. **Networks:** NBC; Interstate Radio. **Founded:** 1989. **Operating Hours:** 5:30 a.m.-midnight. **Key Personnel:** Mark Whalen, Sales Mgr., mwhalen@wlds.com. **Wattage:** 6,000. **Ad Rates:** Noncommercial. Combined advertising rates available with WLDS-AM. **Mailing address:** PO Box 1180, Jacksonville, IL 62650. **URL:** http://www.weai.com.

10952 ■ WJIL-AM - 1550
1251 E Morton Rd.
Jacksonville, IL 62651
Phone: (217)245-5119
Format: News; Information. **Owner:** Morgan County Broadcasting Co., Inc., at above address. **Founded:** 1961. **Operating Hours:** Continuous. **ADI:** Jacksonville (Brunswick), FL. **Key Personnel:** Sarah Hautala, Gen. Mgr. **Wattage:** 1,000 KW. **Ad Rates:** Advertising accepted; rates available upon request. $14-17 for 30 seconds; $18-22 for 60 seconds. **Mailing address:** PO Box 1055, Jacksonville, IL 62651. **URL:** http://wjvofm.com/.

10953 ■ WLDS-AM - 1180
2161 E Old State Rd.
Jacksonville, IL 62650
Phone: (217)245-7171
Fax: (217)245-6711
Email: wlds@wlds.com
Format: Talk; Adult Contemporary; Full Service; Agricultural. **Networks:** CBS. **Founded:** 1941. **Operating Hours:** Sunrise-sunset; 10% network, 90% local. **Key Personnel:** Bob Thomas, Contact, bthomas@wlds.com; Bob Thomas, Contact, bthomas@wlds.com. **Wattage:** 1,000. **Ad Rates:** $22-30 for 30 seconds; $30-40 for 60 seconds. Combined advertising rates available with WEAI-FM. **Mailing address:** PO Box 1180, Jacksonville, IL 62650. **URL:** http://www.wlds.com.

JERSEYVILLE

Jersey Co. Jersey Co. (SW). 17 NW of Alton. Manufactures railroad utility machines, specialty vehicles, pedestal cranes, truck cranes and rail gear, spreading

Circulation: ★ = AAM; △ or • = BPA; ♦ = CAC; ❑ = VAC; ⊕ = PO Statement; ‡ = Publisher's Report; Boldface figures = sworn; Light figures = estimated.

equipment, seed cleaners, concrete products, beverage. Ships apples fruit, poultry, stock farms.

10954 ■ WJBM-AM - 1480
1010 Shipman Rd.
Jerseyville, IL 62052
Phone: (618)498-8255
Fax: (618)498-8265
Format: News; Talk; Sports. **Networks:** ABC; Brownfield. **Owner:** D.J. Two Rivers Radio, at above address. **Operating Hours**: 12 a.m.-12 a.m; 25% network, 75% local. **ADI**: St. Louis, MO (Mt. Vernon, IL). **Wattage**: 500. **Ad Rates:** $9 for 30 seconds; $14 for 60 seconds. **URL:** http://wjbmradio.com.

JOLIET

Will Co. Will Co. (NE). On Des Plaines River, with barge terminal on Lakes to Gulf Waterway, 37 m SW of Chicago. College of St. Francis, Lewis University, Joliet Junior College. Limestone quarries. Oil refineries. Manufactures wallpaper, wire, roofing, chemicals, fire brick, tanks, cartons, earth moving equipment, bakery machinery, packaging machines, barrels, dairy products, clothing.

10955 ■ The Blazer
Joliet Junior College
1215 Houbolt Rd.
Joliet, IL 60431-8938
Phone: (815)729-9020
Publication E-mail: blazermail@jjc.edu
Collegiate newspaper. **Freq:** Semimonthly. **Print Method:** Offset. **Cols./Page:** 4. **Col. Width:** 28 nonpareils. **Col. Depth:** 192 agate lines. **Key Personnel:** Richard Maska, Editor-in-Chief; Alex Forgue, Editor-in-Chief; Brittney Andersen, Manager, Production; Sarah Lake, Manager, Advertising. **Subscription Rates:** Free to qualified subscribers. **Alt. Formats:** PDF. **URL:** http://www.jjc.edu/blazer. **Ad Rates:** BW $180; SAU $3; PCI $4. **Remarks:** Accepts advertising. **Circ:** Free ‡3000.

10956 ■ Dawn: Zarja - The Dawn
Slovenian Union of America
431 N Chicago St.
Joliet, IL 60432-1703
Phone: (815)727-1926
Publication E-mail: wprokup@aol.com
Ethnic magazine. Reports on membership branches located in 14 states. **Freq:** Bimonthly. **Print Method:** Offset. **Trim Size:** 8 x 11. **Cols./Page:** 3. **Col. Width:** 13 picas. **Col. Depth:** 60 picas. **Key Personnel:** Bonnie Pohar Prokup, Director, Programs. **ISSN:** 0044--1848 (print). **Subscription Rates:** $15 Nonmembers; $3.99 Single issue; Included in membership. **URL:** http://slovenianunion.org/zarja. **Also known as**: Karja. **Ad Rates:** 4C $1,500. **Remarks:** Color advertising not accepted. **Circ:** Paid ‡4800, Controlled ‡25.

10957 ■ The Encounter
University of St. Francis
500 Wilcox St.
Joliet, IL 60435
Free: 800-735-7500
Collegiate newspaper (tabloid). **Founded:** 1976. **Freq:** Periodic during the academic year. **Print Method:** Offset. **Trim Size:** 11 1/2 x 17. **Cols./Page:** 5. **Col. Width:** 22 nonpareils. **Col. Depth:** 224 agate lines. **Key Personnel:** Jackie Oliver, Editor-in-Chief. **URL:** http://www.stfrancis.edu/content/lib/newWebsite/onlinecoll.html. **Ad Rates:** GLR $.34; BW $320; PCI $5. **Remarks:** Accepts advertising. **Circ:** Free ‡1000.

10958 ■ Glasilo KSKJ Americanski Slovenec
American Slovenian Catholic Union
2439 Glenwood Ave.
Joliet, IL 60435
Phone: (815)741-2001
Fax: (815)741-2002
Free: 800-843-5755
Publication E-mail: kskj@kskjlife.com
Religious newspaper (Slovenian). **Freq:** Biweekly. **Subscription Rates:** $7.50 Individuals. **URL:** http://www.kskjlife.com. **Circ:** (Not Reported).

10959 ■ The Joliet Herald News
Sun Publications
300 Caterpillar Dr.
Joliet, IL 60436
General newspaper. **Freq:** Daily. **Key Personnel:** Julie Todd, Executive Editor, phone: (815)729-6012; Dave Monoghan, Managing Editor, phone: (815)729-6124; Larry Randa, Publisher, phone: (815)729-6069; Steve Vanisko, Director, Advertising, phone: (815)729-6120; Brian Garrigan, Manager, Advertising, phone: (815)729-6140. **Subscription Rates:** $1.50 Individuals per week; $39 Individuals 26 weeks - 6 day delivery; $26 Individuals 26 weeks - Sunday only. **URL:** http://www.suburbanchicagonews.com/heraldnews; http://www.theherald-news.com; http://www.suntimes.com/advertising/mediakit/heraldnews.html. **Feature Editors:** Sue Baker, phone: (815)729-6047. **Circ:** Mon.-Fri. **★40408**, Sun. **★43527**, Sat. **★38572**.

10960 ■ Network Marketing Business Journal
Network Marketing Business Journal
16525 W 159th, Ste. 311
Joliet, IL 60433
Phone: (815)726-5555
Fax: (708)301-9307
Publisher's E-mail: editors@nmbj.com
Trade journal covering business for the network marketing and direct sales industries. **Freq:** Monthly. **Trim Size:** 6.75 x 10. **Key Personnel:** Keith B. Laggos, PhD, Publisher. **ISSN:** 1050--5852 (print). **Subscription Rates:** $28 U.S. 12 months; $47 Canada 27.95(each)+19.05(Shipping and handling); $69 Other countries 27.95(each)+41.05(Shipping and handling). **URL:** http://www.nmbj.net. **Formerly**: Money Maker's Monthly. **Remarks:** Advertising accepted; rates available upon request. **Circ:** (Not Reported).

10961 ■ ZARJA - The Dawn
Slovenian Union of America
431 N Chicago St.
Joliet, IL 60432-1703
Phone: (815)727-1926
Publisher's E-mail: sua@slovenianunion.org
Freq: Bimonthly. **ISSN:** 0044--1848 (print). **Subscription Rates:** Included in membership. **URL:** http://slovenianunion.org/zarja. **Remarks:** Accepts advertising. **Circ:** (Not Reported).

10962 ■ WCSF-FM - 88.7
500 Wilcox St.
Joliet, IL 60435
Free: 800-735-7500
Email: solutions@stfrancis.edu
Format: Eclectic. **Owner:** University of St. Francis, 500 Wilcox St., Joliet, IL 60435, Free: 800-735-7500. **Operating Hours**: Continuous. **Key Personnel:** Scot Stewart, Contact; Dan Okrzesik, Contact. **Wattage**: 100 ERP. **URL:** http://www.wcsf.fm.

10963 ■ WWHN-AM
714 S Joliet St.
Joliet, IL 60436-2714
Format: Oldies; Urban Contemporary. **Founded:** 1964. **Formerly**: WJRC-AM. **Wattage**: 1,000 Day; 600 CH.

KANKAKEE

Kankakee Co. Kankakee Co. (E). On Kankakee River, 57 m SW of Chicago. Kankakee Community College, Olivet Nazarene College. Manufactures furniture, stoves, work clothing, brick, tile, paint, asphalt products, iron castings, glass containers, concrete products, hydraulic tools, agricultural implements, water heaters, industrial batteries, chemicals, pharmaceuticals; steel fabricating; foundry; magnesium refinery; soybean and corn processing plants. Stone quarries.

10964 ■ The Daily Journal
Small Newspaper Group
8 Dearborn Sq.
Kankakee, IL 60901
Newspaper. **Founded:** 1884. **Freq:** Mon.-Sat. **Print Method:** Offset. **Cols./Page:** 6. **Col. Width:** 25 nonpareils. **Col. Depth:** 301 agate lines. **Key Personnel:** Neil Shannon, Director, Advertising; Susy Schultz, Managing Editor; Len R. Small, Publisher, Editor. **USPS:** 289-780. **Subscription Rates:** $15.60 Individuals /month (daily subscription); $10.20 Individuals /month (Wednesday and weekend); $7.25 Individuals /month (weekend only). **URL:** http://www.daily-journal.com. **Ad Rates:** GLR $1.09; BW $1,786.65; 4C $2,081.65; SAU $13.85. **Remarks:** Accepts advertising. **Circ:** Combined ‡22000, Combined ‡28000.

10965 ■ WKAN-AM - 1320
70 Meadowview Ctr.
Kankakee, IL 60901
Phone: (815)935-9555
Fax: (815)935-9593
Format: Talk; News; Agricultural; Sports. **Owner:** Staradio Corp., 1300 Central Ave., West Great Falls, MT 59404, Ph: (406)761-2800. **Operating Hours**: Continuous. **Key Personnel:** Dave Becker, Contact. **Wattage**: 1,000. **Ad Rates:** $12-33 for 30 seconds; $12-39 for 60 seconds. **URL:** http://www.wkan.com.

10966 ■ WKAN-FM - 1320
70 Meadowview Ctr.
Kankakee, IL 60901
Format: Talk. **Networks:** Independent. **Owner:** Star Radio, 3 W 35th St., New York, NY 10001, Ph: (212)564-2520. **Founded:** 1986. **Operating Hours**: Continuous; 100% local. **ADI**: Chicago (LaSalle), IL. **Wattage**: 3,000. **Ad Rates:** $12-33 for 30 seconds; $12-39 for 60 seconds. **URL:** http://www.wkan.com.

10967 ■ WXNU-FM - 106.5
70 Meadowview Ctr.
Kankakee, IL 60901
Phone: (815)935-9555
Free: 877-777-1065
Format: Country.

10968 ■ WYKT-FM - 105.5
70 Meadowview Ctr.
Kankakee, IL 60901
Phone: (815)935-9555
Format: Adult Contemporary. **Networks:** Independent. **Owner:** Staradio Corp., 1300 Central Ave., West Great Falls, MT 59404, Ph: (406)761-2800. **Founded:** 1980. **Formerly**: WDND-FM. **Operating Hours**: Continuous. **Key Personnel:** Mike Tomano, Gen. Mgr., mtomano@staradio.com; Steve Touhy, Operations Mgr., steve.touhy@radio.com. **Wattage**: 1,300. **Ad Rates:** $10-20 for 30 seconds; $12-25 for 60 seconds.

KEMPTON

10969 ■ World Explorer
World Explorer Club
One Adventure Place
Kempton, IL 60946-0074
Phone: (815)253-9000
Fax: (815)253-6300
Magazine for people who love adventures and mysteries. **Key Personnel:** David Hatcher Childress, Founder. **Subscription Rates:** $30 Individuals; $55 Other countries. **URL:** http://www.wexclub.com/wexclub_magazine.html. **Circ:** (Not Reported).

KEWANEE

Henry Co. Henry Co. (NW). 50 m SE of Rock Island. Manufactures boilers, window and door frames, leather goods, farm equipment, window guards, heavy construction equipment, truck and farm trailers. Agriculture.

10970 ■ Star-Courier
GateHouse Media Inc.
105 E Central Blvd.
Kewanee, IL 61443
Phone: (309)852-2181
Community newspaper. **Founded:** 1876. **Freq:** Mon.-Sat. (morn.). **Print Method:** Offset. **Trim Size:** 13 3/4 x 23. **Cols./Page:** 6. **Col. Width:** 26 nonpareils. **Col. Depth:** 301 agate lines. **Key Personnel:** Dee Evans, Publisher; Mike Landis, Editor; Mike Berry, Associate Editor. **Subscription Rates:** $6.99 Individuals online, monthly; $2 Individuals online + home delivery,weekly. **URL:** http://www.starcourier.com. **Remarks:** Accepts classified advertising. **Circ:** (Not Reported).

10971 ■ WGEN-AM - 1500
133 E Division St.
Kewanee, IL 61443-0266
Phone: (309)944-1500
Fax: (309)853-4474
Email: regionalradionews@wkei.com
Format: News; Talk. **Simulcasts:** WHHK-FM. **Networks:** Brownfield; Tribune Radio; RFD Illinois; ABC. **Founded:** 1963. **Operating Hours**: 16.5 hours Daily; 75% network, 25% local. **ADI**: Daveport,IA-Rock Island, Moline,IL. **Wattage**: 250. **Ad Rates:** $8.50-15 for 30 seconds; $12.50-20 for 60 seconds. Combined advertising rates available with WHHK-FM. **Mailing address:** PO Box 266, Kewanee, IL 61443-0266.

10972 ■ WJRE-FM - 102.5
133 E Division St.
Kewanee, IL 61443
Phone: (309)853-4471
Free: 800-346-4473
Format: Country. **Owner:** Miller Media Group, 918 E Park St., Taylorville, IL 62568-0169, Ph: (217)824-3395, Fax: (217)824-3301. **Founded:** Oct. 01, 1966. **Operating Hours:** Continuous. **Wattage:** 6,000. **Ad Rates:** Noncommercial. **Mailing address:** PO Box 266, Kewanee, IL 61443. **URL:** http://www.regionaldailynews.com/pages.

10973 ■ WKEI-AM - 1450
133 E Division St.
Kewanee, IL 61443-0266
Phone: (309)853-4471
Free: 800-346-4473
Format: Talk; News; Sports. **Networks:** CBS. **Founded:** 1952. **Operating Hours:** Continuous. **Wattage:** 500 Day; 1,000 Night. **Ad Rates:** Noncommercial. **Mailing address:** PO Box 266, Kewanee, IL 61443-0266. **URL:** http://www.regionaldailynews.com/pages/index.cfm?id=67.

10974 ■ WYEC-FM - 93.9
133 E Division St.
Kewanee, IL 61443
Phone: (309)853-4471
Email: news@regionaldailynews.com
Format: Adult Contemporary. **Ad Rates:** Advertising accepted; rates available upon request. **Mailing address:** PO Box 266, Kewanee, IL 61443. **URL:** http://www.regionaldailynews.com.

KINGSTON MINES

10975 ■ Family Reformation
Family Reformation L.L.C.
PO Box 19
Kingston Mines, IL 61539
Phone: (281)492-6050
Magazine offers information on Christian lifestyle, family, and worship. **Freq:** Quarterly. **Key Personnel:** James McDonald, Publisher; Stacy McDonald, Editor-in-Chief. **Subscription Rates:** Free. **URL:** http://familyreformation.org. **Remarks:** Accepts advertising. **Circ:** (Not Reported).

LA GRANGE

Cook Co. Cook Co. (NE). Adjoins Brookfield. Residential. Limestone quarries. Manufactures diesel locomotives, aluminum utensils.

10976 ■ The Plastics Distributor & Fabricator Magazine
Plastics Distributor and Fabricator Magazine
PO Box 669
La Grange, IL 60525-0669
Phone: (708)588-1845
Fax: (708)588-1846
Publisher's E-mail: pdfm@plasticsmag.com
Magazine containing news for distributors and fabricators in the plastics industry. **Freq:** Bimonthly. **Print Method:** Offset. **Trim Size:** 8 1/8 x 10 13/16. **Cols./Page:** 2. **Col. Width:** 3 1/2 inches. **Col. Depth:** 10 inches. **Key Personnel:** David Whelan, Editor; Lynette Zeitler, Art Director; Riia O'Donnell, Associate Editor. **Subscription Rates:** $50 Other countries; Free to qualified subscribers U.S. and Canada. **Ad Rates:** BW $4194. **Remarks:** Accepts advertising. **Circ:** Non-paid ‡23256.

10977 ■ WLTL-FM - 88.1
100 S Brainard Ave.
La Grange, IL 60525
Phone: (708)482-9585
Format: Album-Oriented Rock (AOR); Alternative/New Music/Progressive; Sports; Urban Contemporary; Talk. **Operating Hours:** Continuous. **Wattage:** 180. **Ad Rates:** Advertising accepted; rates available upon request. **URL:** http://www.wltl.net.

LA GRANGE PARK

13,359 13,359. Cook Co Cook Co. Cook County. NE Illinois. West suburb of Chicago. Cook County. NE Illinois. West suburb of Chicago.

10978 ■ Fusion Science and Technology
American Nuclear Society
555 N Kensington Ave.
La Grange Park, IL 60526
Phone: (708)352-6611
Fax: (708)352-0499
Free: 800-323-3044
Publication E-mail: fst@ans.org
Fusion energy research and technical engineering. **Freq:** 8/year. **Print Method:** Offset. **Trim Size:** 8 1/2 x 11. **Cols./Page:** 2. **Col. Width:** 39 nonpareils. **Col. Depth:** 126 agate lines. **Key Personnel:** Dr. Nermin A. Uckan, Editor. **Subscription Rates:** $2295 Individuals print; $2325 Individuals online; $2525 Individuals print and online; $79 Members online ; $165 Members print and online ; $165 Members print. **URL:** http://www.ans.org/pubs/journals/fst. **Formerly:** Fusion Technology. **Remarks:** Advertising not accepted. **Circ:** (Not Reported).

10979 ■ Nuclear News
American Nuclear Society
555 N Kensington Ave.
La Grange Park, IL 60526
Phone: (708)352-6611
Fax: (708)352-0499
Free: 800-323-3044
Publisher's E-mail: nuclear@ans.org
Magazine focusing on applications of nuclear energy. **Freq:** Monthly. **Key Personnel:** Sarah Ross, Editor. **ISSN:** 0029--5574 (print). **Subscription Rates:** $580 Individuals print; $580 Individuals print and online; $510 Individuals online only. **URL:** http://www.new.ans.org/pubs/magazines/nn. **Ad Rates:** BW $3,120; 4C $900. **Remarks:** Accepts advertising. **Circ:** ★**11548**.

10980 ■ Nuclear Science and Engineering
American Nuclear Society
555 N Kensington Ave.
La Grange Park, IL 60526
Phone: (708)352-6611
Fax: (708)352-0499
Free: 800-323-3044
Publication E-mail: nse@ans.org
Scientific research journal. **Founded:** 1956. **Freq:** 9/year. **Print Method:** Offset. **Trim Size:** 8 1/2 x 11. **Cols./Page:** 2. **Col. Width:** 40 nonpareils. **Col. Depth:** 126 agate lines. **Key Personnel:** Prof. Dan G. Cacuci, Editor. **ISSN:** 0029-5639 (print). **Subscription Rates:** $1931 Individuals print only; $2007 Individuals online only; 2210. **URL:** http://www.ans.org/pubs/journals/nse. **Remarks:** Advertising not accepted. **Circ:** 1200.

10981 ■ Nuclear Technology
American Nuclear Society
555 N Kensington Ave.
La Grange Park, IL 60526
Phone: (708)352-6611
Fax: (708)352-0499
Free: 800-323-3044
Publisher's E-mail: nuclear@ans.org
Nuclear power; science and engineering. **Freq:** Monthly. **Key Personnel:** Dr. Nicholas Tsoulfanidis, Editor, phone: (708)579-8281, fax: (708)352-6464. **ISSN:** 0029--5450 (print). **Subscription Rates:** $2260 Individuals print only; $2337 Individuals online only; $2490 Individuals print and online. **URL:** http://www.ans.org/pubs/journals/nt. **Remarks:** Advertising not accepted. **Circ:** 1300.

10982 ■ Radwaste Solutions
American Nuclear Society
555 N Kensington Ave.
La Grange Park, IL 60526
Phone: (708)352-6611
Fax: (708)352-0499
Free: 800-323-3044
Publisher's E-mail: nuclear@ans.org
Magazine promoting awareness and understanding of the application of nuclear science and technology. **Freq:** Semiannual Spring (March) and Fall (September). **Print Method:** Offset. **Cols./Page:** 6. **Col. Width:** 24 nonpareils. **Col. Depth:** 301 agate lines. **ISSN:** 1529--4900 (print). **Subscription Rates:** $435 Individuals print; $400 Individuals print and online; $400 Individuals online. **URL:** http://www.ans.org/pubs/magazines/rs; http://www.ans.org/pubs. **Ad Rates:** BW $1,950. **Remarks:** Accepts advertising. **Circ:** (Not Reported).

LA SALLE

La Salle Co. LaSalle Co. (N). On Illinois River 90 m W of Chicago. Chemicals, electronic components, cement, aluminum, zinc. Manufactures automotive transmissions. Agriculture.

10983 ■ Illinois Agri-News
Agri-News Publications
420 2nd St.
La Salle, IL 61301
Fax: (815)223-5997
Free: 800-426-9438
Publisher's E-mail: aginfo@agrinews-pubs.com
Farm and rural community magazine. **Freq:** Weekly. **Print Method:** Offset. **Trim Size:** 12 1/2 x 22 3/4. **Cols./Page:** 6. **Col. Width:** 1.833 inches. **Col. Depth:** 301 agate lines. **Key Personnel:** Lynn Barker, Publisher; James Henry, Executive Editor. **Subscription Rates:** $25 Individuals; $40 Two years; $50 Individuals 3 years. **URL:** http://www.agrinews-pubs.com; http://www.agrinewsonline.com/default.asp. **Ad Rates:** BW $5,430; 4C $6,031; PCI $42.10. **Remarks:** Accepts advertising. **Circ:** Paid ‡34000.

10984 ■ News-Tribune
News-Tribune Publication
426 2nd St.
La Salle, IL 61301
Phone: (815)223-3200
Publication E-mail: newsitib@ivnet.com
Local newspaper. **Founded:** 1891. **Freq:** Mon.-Sat. (eve.). **Print Method:** Offset. **Cols./Page:** 6. **Col. Width:** 25 nonpareils. **Col. Depth:** 301 agate lines. **Key Personnel:** Craig Sterrett, Editor; D.J. Bice, Editor. **Subscription Rates:** $144 Individuals /year. **URL:** http://newstrib.com/index.asp. **Ad Rates:** GLR $2.25; BW $2818.65; 4C $3118.65; SAU $12; PCI $21.85. **Remarks:** Accepts advertising. **Circ:** Mon.-Sat. ♦**15873**.

LAKE BLUFF

Lake Co. Lake Co. (NE). 3m N of Lake Forest. Residential.

10985 ■ American Journal of Therapeutics
Lippincott Williams & Wilkins
c/o John C. Somberg, MD, Editor-in-Chief
21 N Skokie Hwy., Ste. G-3
Lake Bluff, IL 60044
Phone: (847)735-1170
Fax: (847)735-1173
Peer-reviewed journal prescribing physicians who want to access pharmacological developments in cardiology, infectious disease, oncology, anesthesiology, nephrology and other fields. **Freq:** Bimonthly. **Key Personnel:** John C. Somberg, MD, Editor-in-Chief. **ISSN:** 1075--2765 (print); **EISSN:** 1536--3686 (electronic). **Subscription Rates:** $446 Individuals online. **URL:** http://journals.lww.com/americantherapeutics/pages/default.aspx. **Remarks:** Accepts advertising. **Circ:** ‡163.

LAKE FOREST

Lake Co. Lake Co. (NE). On Lake Michigan, 8 m S of Waukegan. Barat College of the Sacred Heart (Cath. women); Lake Forest College. Suburban residential town.

10986 ■ WMXM-FM - 88.9
555 N Sheridan Rd.
Lake Forest, IL 60045
Phone: (847)735-5220
Email: booking@wmxm.org
Format: News. **Networks:** Independent. **Owner:** Lake Forest College, 555 N Sheridan Rd., Lake Forest, IL 60045. **Founded:** 1970. **Operating Hours:** Continuous. **Key Personnel:** Reid Wilson, Gen. Mgr. **Wattage:** 295 ERP. **Ad Rates:** Noncommercial. **URL:** http://www.wmxm.org.

LAKE VILLA

Lake Co. Lake Co. (NE). 15 m W of Waukegan. Suburban residental area. Resort. Chain O'Lakes Area. Manufactures plastics. Tool and die works. Diversified farming.

10987 ■ W206AI-FM - 89.1
PO Box 391
Twin Falls, ID 83303

Circulation: ★ = AAM; △ or • = BPA; ♦ = CAC; ❑ = VAC; ⊕ = PO Statement; ‡ = Publisher's Report; Boldface figures = sworn; Light figures = estimated.

Fax: (208)736-1958
Free: 800-357-4226
Format: Religious; Contemporary Christian. **Owner:** CSN International, PO Box 391, Twin Falls, ID 83303, Ph: (208)736-1958, Fax: (208)736-1958, Free: 800-357-4226. **URL:** http://www.csnradio.com.

LASALLE

10988 ■ WNIW-FM - 91.3
801 N First St.
DeKalb, IL 60115
Phone: (815)753-9000
Fax: (815)753-9938
Email: npr@niu.edu
Format: Public Radio. **Owner:** Northern Illinois University, 1425 W Lincoln Hwy., Dekalb, IL 60115. **Founded:** 1998. **Key Personnel:** Bill Drake, Dir. of Programs; Jeff Glass, Chief Engineer. **URL:** http://www.northernpublicradio.org.

LAWRENCEVILLE

Lawrence Co. Lawrence Co. (SE). 9 m W of Vincennes, Ind. Manufactures telephone and oil well equipment, asphalt products, chemicals. Oil and gas wells. Stock, grains farms.

10989 ■ Daily Record
Daily Record
1209 State St.
Lawrenceville, IL 62439
Phone: (618)943-2331
Fax: (618)943-3976
Publisher's E-mail: lawnews@lawdailyrecord.com
General newspaper. **Founded:** 1847. **Freq:** Daily Monday-Friday. **Print Method:** Offset. **Cols./Page:** 6. **Col. Width:** 25 nonpareils. **Col. Depth:** 294 agate lines. **Subscription Rates:** $76 Individuals city carrier delivery; $62 Individuals mail delivery; $86 Out of area by mail; $36 Elsewhere. **URL:** http://www.lawdailyrecord.com/. **Ad Rates:** BW $611.10; SAU $4.85. **Remarks:** Accepts advertising. **Circ:** (Not Reported).

10990 ■ WAKO-AM - 910
PO Box 210
Lawrenceville, IL 62439
Phone: (618)943-3354
Fax: (618)943-4173
Free: 800-939-4806
Format: Adult Contemporary. **Simulcasts:** WAKO-FM. **Networks:** CNN Radio. **Founded:** 1959. **Operating Hours:** 19 hours Daily; 9% network, 91% local. **Key Personnel:** Steve Anderson, News Dir; Kent Lankford, Contact. **Wattage:** 500. **Ad Rates:** $7.50-14 for 30 seconds; $9.50-16 for 60 seconds. **URL:** http://www.wakoradio.com.

10991 ■ WAKO-FM - 103.1
PO Box 210
Lawrenceville, IL 62439
Phone: (618)943-3354
Fax: (618)943-4173
Format: Adult Contemporary. **Simulcasts:** WAKO-AM. **Networks:** CNN Radio. **Founded:** 1959. **Operating Hours:** 19 hours Daily; 9% network, 91% local. **Key Personnel:** Kent Lankford, Contact. **Wattage:** 6,000. **Ad Rates:** Noncommercial. **URL:** http://www.wakoradio.com.

LEBANON

St. Clair Co. St Clair Co. (SW). 12 m NE of Belleville. Mckendree College. Grain farms. Corn, wheat.

10992 ■ Scholars: The McKendree College Journal of Undergraduate Research
McKendree University
701 College Rd.
Lebanon, IL 62254
Phone: (618)537-4481
Free: 800-BEA-RCAT
Journal featuring undergraduate research and scholarly writing. **Key Personnel:** Dr. Brian Frederking, Contact. **URL:** http://www.mckendree.edu/academics/scholars. **Circ:** (Not Reported).

LEMONT

10993 ■ Applied Physics Letters
American Institute of Physics
c/o Nghi Q. Lam, Ed.
Argonne National Laboratory, Bldg. 203, Rm. R-127
9700 S Cass Ave.
Lemont, IL 60439-4843
Phone: (630)252-4200
Fax: (630)252-4973
Publication E-mail: apl@anl.gov
Journal focusing on research in applied physics and applications for industry. **Freq:** Weekly. **Print Method:** Offset. **Trim Size:** 8 1/4 x 11 1/4. **Cols./Page:** 2. **Col. Width:** 41 nonpareils. **Col. Depth:** 136 agate lines. **Key Personnel:** Lynn E. Rehn, Associate Editor; Samuel D. Bader, Associate Editor; David Long Price, Associate Editor; Paul R. Okamoto, Associate Editor; Linda Young, Associate Editor; Orlando Auciello, Associate Editor; Nghi Q. Lam, Editor. **ISSN:** 0003--6951 (print); **EISSN:** 1077-3118 (electronic). **Subscription Rates:** $652 Members print and online; $1112 Members foreign, print and online; $3500 Institutions print and online; $145 /year for members of AIP and its affiliates; $1900 /year for nonmembers. **Online:** American Institute of Physics American Institute of Physics. **URL:** http://scitation.aip.org/content/aip/journal/apl. **Ad Rates:** BW $1,120; 4C $1,150. **Remarks:** Accepts advertising. **Circ:** 4600.

10994 ■ Chicago District Golfer
Chicago District Golf Association
Midwest Golf House
11855 Archer Ave.
Lemont, IL 60439
Phone: (630)257-2005
Fax: (630)257-2088
Magazine for members of the Chicago District Golf Association. **Freq:** Quarterly Bimonthly April, June, July, August, September and November. **Key Personnel:** William Daniels, Editor. **ISSN:** 1087-6502 (print). **Subscription Rates:** Included in membership; $15 Nonmembers. **URL:** http://www.cdga.org/detail.asp?id=99. **Remarks:** Advertising accepted; rates available upon request. **Circ:** Controlled 85000.

10995 ■ Journal of Applied Physics
American Institute of Physics
Argonne National Laboratory
Bldg. 203, Rm. R-127
9700 S Cass Ave.
Lemont, IL 60439-4801
Phone: (630)252-8700
Fax: (630)252-8711
Publication E-mail: jap@aip.org
Journal focusing on research in applied physics with applications for industry. **Freq:** Daily 48/yr. **Key Personnel:** James P. Viccaro, Editor; Roy Benedek, Associate Editor; Robert C. Birtcher, Associate Editor. **ISSN:** 0021--8979 (print); **EISSN:** 1089--7550 (electronic). **Subscription Rates:** $5745 Institutions domestic, print & online; $6105 Institutions surface freight, print & online; $6160 Institutions air freight, print & online; $4255 Institutions domestic, online only; $201 Members; $220 /year for members of AIP and its affiliates; $2185 /year for nonmembers. **URL:** http://scitation.aip.org/content/aip/journal/jap. **Remarks:** Accepts advertising. **Circ:** (Not Reported).

10996 ■ Journal of Magnetism and Magnetic Materials
RELX Group P.L.C.
c/o S.D. Bader, Ed.-in-Ch.
Division of Materials Science, 223 Rm. S-201
Argonne National Laboratory
Lemont, IL 60439-4845
Publisher's E-mail: amsterdam@relx.com
Journal covering topics on basic magnetism, technology and applications of magnetic materials and magnetic recording. **Freq:** 24/yr. **Key Personnel:** S.D. Bader, Editor-in-Chief; R.W. Chantrell, Board Member; D. Givord, Board Member. **ISSN:** 0304--8853 (print). **Subscription Rates:** $10155 Institutions print; $7996 Institutions ejournal. **URL:** http://www.journals.elsevier.com/journal-of-magnetism-and-magnetic-materials. **Circ:** (Not Reported).

10997 ■ Physica C: Superconductivity and Its Applications
RELX Group P.L.C.
c/o W.K. Kwok, Ed.
Argonne National Laboratory
Bldg. 223, Rm. S-231
9700 S Cass Ave.
Lemont, IL 60439
Publisher's E-mail: amsterdam@relx.com
Journal devoted to superconductivity including physical properties of superconducting materials as well as the phenomena occurring in the vortex state of type-II superconductors. Applications including power and high magnetic fields. **Freq:** Monthly. **Key Personnel:** W.K. Kwok, Editor; V.A. Maroni, Advisor. **ISSN:** 0921--4534 (print). **Subscription Rates:** $4391.33 Institutions online; $7310 print. **URL:** http://www.journals.elsevier.com/physica-c-superconductivity-and-its-applications. **Circ:** (Not Reported).

LEWISTOWN

Fulton Co. Fulton Co. (W). 15 m SW of Canton. Coal mines. Grain, stock farms.

10998 ■ Fulton Democrat
Fulton Democrat
165 W Lincoln Ave.
Lewistown, IL 61542
Phone: (309)547-3055
Fax: (309)547-3056
Publisher's E-mail: fultondemocrat@att.net
Community newspaper. **Freq:** Weekly (Wed.). **Key Personnel:** Robert Martin, Publisher. **Subscription Rates:** $42 Individuals print; $73 Two years print; $59 Out of country print; $99 Two years out of county - print; $32 Individuals online. **URL:** http://www.democratnewspapers.com/95030/2409/1/home. **Mailing address:** PO Box 191, Lewistown, IL 61542. **Circ:** Free 4,800.

LIBERTY

Adams Co. Adams Co. (W). 10 m S of Clayton. Residential.

10999 ■ Liberty Bee-Times
Elliott Publishing Inc.
103 E Hannibal St.
Liberty, IL 62347
Phone: (217)645-3033
Fax: (217)645-3083
Publication E-mail: libertyb@adams.net
Community newspaper. **Freq:** Weekly. **Print Method:** Offset. Uses mats. **Trim Size:** 10 1/4 x 16. **Cols./Page:** 5. **Col. Width:** 11.5 picas. **Col. Depth:** 16 inches. **Key Personnel:** Marcia Elliot, General Manager. **USPS:** 311-640. **Subscription Rates:** $24 Individuals; $26 Out of state; $28 Out of area. **URL:** http://www.elliott-publishing.com/newspapers.html. **Mailing address:** PO Box 198, Liberty, IL 62347. **Ad Rates:** GLR $2.50; BW $200; 4C $365; SAU $4.25; PCI $2. **Remarks:** Accepts advertising. **Circ:** Wed. 1500.

Mendon Dispatch-Times - See Mendon

LINCOLN

Logan Co. Logan Co. (C). 31 m NE of Springfield. Manufactures glass bottles, plate glass, store fixtures, paper boxes, cosmetics, electric controls. Dairy, stock, grain, poultry farms. Sand and gravel pits.

11000 ■ WLLM-AM - 1370
800 S Postville Dr.
Lincoln, IL 62656
Fax: (217)735-9736
Email: wllmam@juno.com
Format: Contemporary Christian. **Key Personnel:** Beverly Tibbs, Operations Mgr. **URL:** http://www.wllmradio.com.

LINCOLNSHIRE

Lake Co Lake Co Lake Co. Lake County. NE Illinois. 25 mi. NW of Chicago. Lake County. NE Illinois. 25 mi. NW of Chicago.

11001 ■ Closets
Vance Publishing Corp.
400 Knightsbridge Pkwy.
Lincolnshire, IL 60069-3613
Phone: (847)634-2600
Fax: (847)634-4342
Free: 800-255-5113
Magazine devoted to closets and closet design. **Freq:** Bimonthly. **Key Personnel:** Laurel Didier, Publisher, Vice President; Karen M. Koenig, Editor-in-Chief. **ISSN:** 1550--8536 (print). **Subscription Rates:** Free to qualified subscribers. **URL:** http://www.woodworkingnetwork.

com/home-storage-solutions. **Mailing address:** PO Box 1400, Lincolnshire, IL 60069-1400. **Remarks:** Accepts advertising. **Circ:** Combined △**20010**.

11002 ■ CWB Custom Woodworking Business: Environmental Studies
Vance Publishing Corp.
400 Knightsbridge Pkwy.
Lincolnshire, IL 60069-3613
Phone: (847)634-2600
Fax: (847)634-4342
Free: 800-255-5113
Magazine for professional custom woodworkers. **Freq:** Monthly. **Print Method:** Web Offset. **Trim Size:** 8 x 10 3/4. **Key Personnel:** Bill Esler, Associate Publisher, Editor-in-Chief; Karen Koenig, Editor; Laurel Didier, Publisher. **URL:** http://www.woodworkingnetwork.com/magazine. **Mailing address:** PO Box 1400, Lincolnshire, IL 60069-1400. **Ad Rates:** BW $4830; 4C $6880. **Remarks:** Accepts advertising. **Circ:** Controlled ‡60000.

11003 ■ The Grower: Profitable Business Strategies for Fruit and Vegetable Growers
Vance Publishing Corp.
400 Knightsbridge Pkwy.
Lincolnshire, IL 60069-3613
Phone: (847)634-2600
Fax: (847)634-4342
Free: 800-255-5113
Magazine providing management information for the commercial fruit and vegetable producer with emphasis on management, industry trends, effective marketing, chemicals, and legislative and regulatory environments. **Freq:** Monthly. **Print Method:** Web Offset. **Trim Size:** 7 7/8 x 10 3/4. **Cols./Page:** 3. **Col. Width:** 13 picas. **Col. Depth:** 60 picas. **Key Personnel:** Vicky Boyd, Editor. **ISSN:** 0745--1784 (print). **URL:** http://www.thepacker.com/thegrower. **Mailing address:** PO Box 1400, Lincolnshire, IL 60069-1400. **Ad Rates:** GLR $1.05; BW $3636; 4C $1975; PCI $135. **Remarks:** Accepts advertising. **Circ:** △**22048**.

11004 ■ Modern Salon
Vance Publishing Corp.
400 Knightsbridge Pkwy.
Lincolnshire, IL 60069-3613
Phone: (847)634-2600
Fax: (847)634-4342
Free: 800-255-5113
Magazine focusing on hairstyling salons for men and women. **Freq:** Monthly. **Print Method:** Web Offset. **Trim Size:** 8 7/8 x 10 3/4. **Cols./Page:** 3 and 2. **Col. Width:** 26 and 40 nonpareils. **Col. Depth:** 140 agate lines. **Key Personnel:** Michele Musgrove, Associate Publisher, Director, Editorial; Steve Reiss, Director, Publications. **ISSN:** 0148--4001 (print). **Subscription Rates:** $28 U.S. 1 year; $37 Canada and Mexico 1 year; $98 Other countries 1 year; $40 U.S. 2 year; $57 Canada and Mexico 2 year; $50 U.S. 3 year; $73 Canada and Mexico 3 year. **URL:** http://www.modernsalon.com. **Mailing address:** PO Box 1400, Lincolnshire, IL 60069-1400. **Ad Rates:** BW $12,540; 4C $14,615. **Remarks:** Accepts advertising. **Circ:** Paid △**19002**, Non-paid △**85133**.

11005 ■ PorkNetwork
Vance Publishing Corp.
400 Knightsbridge Pkwy.
Lincolnshire, IL 60069-3613
Phone: (847)634-2600
Fax: (847)634-4342
Free: 800-255-5113
Magazine on pork production and marketing. **Freq:** Monthly. **Print Method:** Offset. **Trim Size:** 7 7/8 x 10 3/4. **Cols./Page:** 3. **Col. Width:** 26 nonpareils. **Col. Depth:** 140 agate lines. **Key Personnel:** Rick Jordahl, Associate Editor; Marlys Miller, Editor. **ISSN:** 0745--3787 (print). **URL:** http://legacy.www.porknetwork.com. **Formerly**: Pork: The Business Magazine for Professional Pork Producers. **Mailing address:** PO Box 1400, Lincolnshire, IL 60069-1400. **Remarks:** Accepts advertising. **Circ:** △**16236**.

11006 ■ PORKNetwork
Vance Publishing Corp.
400 Knightsbridge Pkwy.
Lincolnshire, IL 60069-3613
Phone: (847)634-2600
Fax: (847)634-4342
Free: 800-255-5113
Publisher's E-mail: customerservice@farmjournal.com
Professional magazine providing information on improving business and service opportunities for vets serving pork producers. **Freq:** 8/year. **Print Method:** Web Offset. **Trim Size:** 7 7/8 x 10 3/4. **Cols./Page:** 3. **Col. Width:** 13 nonpareils. **Col. Depth:** 140 agate lines. **ISSN:** 0745-3787 (print). **URL:** http://www.porknetwork.com. **Formerly**: Swine Practitioner. **Ad Rates:** BW $3,143; 4C $4,243. **Remarks:** Accepts advertising. **Circ:** △**3340**.

11007 ■ Produce Retailer: The Industry's Only Magazine for Producer Retailers
Vance Publishing Corp.
400 Knightsbridge Pkwy.
Lincolnshire, IL 60069-3613
Phone: (847)634-2600
Fax: (847)634-4342
Free: 800-255-5113
Magazine covering the retail produce industry. **Freq:** Monthly. **Print Method:** Offset. **Trim Size:** 7 7/8 x 10 3/4. **Cols./Page:** 3. **Col. Width:** 13 picas. **Col. Depth:** 8 inches. **Key Personnel:** Pamela Riemenschneider, Editor; Tony Reyes, Art Director; Shannon Shuman, Publisher. **URL:** http://www.produceretailer.com. **Formerly**: Produce Merchandising. **Mailing address:** PO Box 1400, Lincolnshire, IL 60069-1400. **Ad Rates:** BW $5,088; 4C $1,975. **Remarks:** Accepts advertising. **Circ:** △**12003**.

11008 ■ Salon Today Magazine
Vance Publishing Corp.
400 Knightsbridge Pkwy.
Lincolnshire, IL 60069-3613
Phone: (847)634-2600
Fax: (847)634-4342
Free: 800-255-5113
Management guide for beauty salon owners and managers. **Freq:** Monthly. **Print Method:** Web Offset. **Trim Size:** 7 7/8 x 10 3/4. **Cols./Page:** 3. **Col. Width:** 13.5 picas. **Col. Depth:** 8 1/2 inches. **Key Personnel:** Stacey Soble, Editor-in-Chief. **ISSN:** 0743--6394 (print). **Subscription Rates:** $45 Individuals; $63 Other countries; $75 Two years; $111 Two years other countries. **URL:** http://www.vancepublishing.com/salon/salontoday. **Mailing address:** PO Box 1400, Lincolnshire, IL 60069-1400. **Ad Rates:** BW $3500; 4C $4455. **Remarks:** Accepts advertising. **Circ:** ‡30000.

11009 ■ Wood Products
Vance Publishing Corp.
400 Knightsbridge Pkwy.
Lincolnshire, IL 60069-3613
Phone: (847)634-2600
Fax: (847)634-4342
Free: 800-255-5113
Magazine for furniture, cabinet, and woodworking industry. **Freq:** Monthly. **Print Method:** Web Offset. **Trim Size:** 8 x 10 3/4. **Cols./Page:** 3. **Col. Width:** 26 nonpareils. **Col. Depth:** 140 agate lines. **Key Personnel:** Rich Christianson, Associate Publisher, Editor; Bill Esler, Associate Publisher, Editor-in-Chief; Karen Koenig, Editor-in-Chief. **Formerly**: Wood & Wood Products. **Mailing address:** PO Box 1400, Lincolnshire, IL 60069-1400. **Ad Rates:** BW $3,990; 4C $5,590. **Remarks:** Accepts advertising. **Circ:** (Not Reported).

11010 ■ WAES-FM - 88.1
1 Stevenson Dr.
Lincolnshire, IL 60069
Phone: (847)415-4000
Fax: (847)634-7309
Format: Educational. **Owner:** Adlai E. Stevenson High School, 1 Stevenson Dr., Lincolnshire, IL 60069, Ph: (847)415-4000. **URL:** http://www.d125.org/sbn/waes-live.

LINCOLNWOOD

Cook Co. Cook Co (NE). 6 m SW of Evanston.

11011 ■ Diabetic Cooking
Publications International Ltd.
7373 N Cicero Ave.
Lincolnwood, IL 60646
Phone: (847)676-3470
Fax: (847)676-3671
Magazine focusing on dietary cooking for people with diabetes. **Subscription Rates:** $14.95 Individuals; $24.95 Two years. **URL:** http://pilbooks.com/product/3-books-in-1-all-new-diabetic-cooking-appetizers-entrees-sweet-treats. **Circ:** (Not Reported).

11012 ■ Metal Architecture
Modern Trade Communications Inc.
7250 Cicero Ave., Ste. 100
Lincolnwood, IL 60712
Trade journal serving architectural, engineering, and construction firms. **Freq:** Monthly. **Print Method:** Web Offset. **Trim Size:** 10.375 x 13. **Cols./Page:** 4. **Col. Width:** 14 picas. **Key Personnel:** Paul Deffenbaugh, Director, Editorial; Marcy Marro, Editor. **ISSN:** 0885--5781 (print). **Subscription Rates:** $75 Canada and Mexico; $150 Other countries; $45 Individuals. **URL:** http://www.metalarchitecture.com. **Remarks:** Advertising accepted; rates available upon request. **Circ:** △**30557**.

LISLE

DuPage Co. Du Page Co. (NE). 28 m W of Chicago. Benedictine College.(Co-ed.) Suburban area. Light manufacturing.

11013 ■ ABNF Journal
Tucker Publications Inc.
PO Box 580
Lisle, IL 60532
Phone: (630)969-0221
Fax: (630)969-3895
Publisher's E-mail: info@tuckerpub.com
Professional journal covering health care related to minority clients, students, and faculty members. **Freq:** Quarterly. **Print Method:** Offset. **Trim Size:** 7 x 10. **Cols./Page:** 2. **Key Personnel:** Beatrice Adderley-Kelly, PhD, Board Member; Marsha Atkins, Board Member; Geraldine Brown, PhD, Board Member; Wilma J. Calvert, PhD, Board Member; Dr. Sallie Tucker-Allen, Editor; Margaret T. Beard, PhD, Board Member; Dr. Gloria J. McNeal, Editor. **ISSN:** 1046-7041 (print). **Subscription Rates:** $303 Institutions annual; $168 Individuals annual; $400 Other countries annual; $30 reprint - back issues. **URL:** http://www.tuckerpub.com/abnf.htm; http://iibp.chadwyck.com/infopage/publ/abn.htm. **Ad Rates:** GLR $30; BW $2,275; 4C $2,825. **Remarks:** Accepts advertising. **Circ:** Combined 562.

11014 ■ BoTales
Original Hobo Nickel Society
c/o Becky Jirka, Secretary
5111 Illinois Ave.
Lisle, IL 60532-2015
Magazine specializing in hobo nickels but also has interesting stories such as Britt, The National Hobo Convention, and the book by Gypsy Moon, Done and Been, plus many more interesting hobo related stories. **Freq:** Quarterly. **Subscription Rates:** Included in membership. **URL:** http://www.hobonickels.org/threes_a_match2.html. **Remarks:** Advertising not accepted. **Circ:** (Not Reported).

11015 ■ Fifth Wednesday Journal
Fifth Wednesday Books
PO Box 4033
Lisle, IL 60532-9033
Publisher's E-mail: editors@fifthwednesdayjournal.org
Magazine featuring poetry, fiction, essays, and photography. **Freq:** Semiannual. **Key Personnel:** Vern Miller, Editor; Rachel Hamsmith, Managing Editor. **Subscription Rates:** $20 Individuals; $37 Two years; $36 Other countries; $65 Other countries 2 years. **URL:** http://www.fifthwednesdayjournal.com. **Circ:** (Not Reported).

11016 ■ Journal of Cultural Diversity: An Interdisciplinary Journal
Tucker Publications Inc.
PO Box 580
Lisle, IL 60532
Phone: (630)969-0221
Fax: (630)969-3895
Publication E-mail: jcd@tuckerpub.com
Scholarly journal covering cultural diversity for educators, researchers, and practitioners. **Freq:** Quarterly. **Print Method:** offset. **Trim Size:** 7 x 10. **Key Personnel:** Dr. Kay Edwards, Editor; Dr. Barbara A. Broome, Editor; Dr. Carol Patsdaughter, Editor. **ISSN:** 1071--5568 (print). **Subscription Rates:** $374 Institutions /year; $220.50 Individuals /year; $425 Other countries /year;

Circulation: ★ = AAM; △ or • = BPA; ♦ = CAC; ❑ = VAC; ⊕ = PO Statement; ‡ = Publisher's Report; Boldface figures = sworn; Light figures = estimated.

$30 Single issue /article - reprints. **URL:** http://www.tuckerpub.com/jcd.htm. **Ad Rates:** GLR $25; BW $1,600; 4C $2,250. **Remarks:** Accepts advertising. **Circ:** Combined 1000.

11017 ■ Journal of Theory Construction Testing
Tucker Publications Inc.
PO Box 580
Lisle, IL 60532
Phone: (630)969-0221
Fax: (630)969-3895
Publisher's E-mail: info@tuckerpub.com
Peer-reviewed journal focusing on advancement and development of the scientific basis of nursing as a practice discipline. **Freq:** Semiannual April and October. **Print Method:** Offset. **Trim Size:** 7 x 10. **Cols./Page:** 2. **Key Personnel:** Dr. Charles Walker, PhD, Editor. **ISSN:** 1086--4431 (print). **Subscription Rates:** $140 Institutions; $92.40 Individuals; $225 Other countries. **URL:** http://www.tuckerpub.com/jtct.htm. **Ad Rates:** GLR $25; BW $1,600; 4C $2,250. **Remarks:** Accepts advertising. **Circ:** Combined 570.

11018 ■ Midwest Engineer: News Magazine of the Western Society of Engineers
Western Society of Engineers
1111 Burlington Ave., Ste. 108
Lisle, IL 60532-1290
Phone: (630)724-9770
Fax: (630)241-0142
Publisher's E-mail: wse@wsechicago.org
Magazine containing information on industries. **Freq:** 3/year. **Print Method:** Offset. **Trim Size:** 8 3/4 x 10 7/8. **Cols./Page:** 3 and 2. **Col. Width:** 32 and 42 nonpareils. **Col. Depth:** 135 agate lines. **Key Personnel:** Tim Seeden, Executive Director, phone: (630)724-9770, fax: (630)241-0142. **ISSN:** 0026--3370 (print). **Alt. Formats:** PDF. **Remarks:** Advertising accepted; rates available upon request. **Circ:** (Not Reported).

11019 ■ Voices Magazine: News From Benedictine University
Benedictine University
5700 College Rd.
Lisle, IL 60532-0900
Phone: (630)829-6000
Alumni magazine/collegiate magazine. **Freq:** 3/year. **Print Method:** Offset. **Trim Size:** 8 1/2 x 11. **Cols./Page:** 3. **Col. Width:** 13 picas. **Col. Depth:** 60 picas. **Key Personnel:** Mercy Robb, Director, Public Relations, phone: (630)829-6095; Linda Hale, Editor, phone: (630)829-6092. **Subscription Rates:** Free. **URL:** http://www.ben.edu/marcom/voices/index.cfm. **Formerly:** Illinois Benedictine College. **Remarks:** Advertising not accepted. **Circ:** Non-paid ‡25000.

LITCHFIELD

Montgomery Co. Montgomery Co. (SC). 44 m S of Springfield. Manufactures shoes, milk, plastic products and plastic pipe paper and aluminum products, brake parts, soft drinks, steel specialties, farm equipment attachments, dresses, athletic equipment. Dairy farms. Corn, wheat, soybeans.

11020 ■ WSMI-AM - 1540
PO Box 10
Litchfield, IL 62056
Phone: (217)324-5921
Fax: (217)532-2431
Email: wsmi@wsmiradio.com
Format: Country. **Owner:** Talley Broadcasting Corp., 1610 Oakbrook Dr., Hillsboro, IL 62049-2277. **Founded:** Nov. 02, 1950. **Operating Hours:** Continuous. **Key Personnel:** Hayward L. Talley, Gen. Mgr., President, hayward@wsmiradio.com; Brian C. Talley, President, Gen. Mgr., brian@wsmiradio.com; Terry Todt, Director, terry@wsmiradio.com; Mike Niehaus, Sales Mgr., mike@wsmiradio.com. **Wattage:** 50,000. **Ad Rates:** Advertising accepted; rates available upon request. **URL:** http://www.wsmiradio.com.

11021 ■ WSMI-FM - 106.1
PO Box 10
Litchfield, IL 62056
Phone: (217)324-5921
Fax: (217)532-2431
Email: wsmi@wsmiradio.com
Format: Country. **Networks:** CNN Radio. **Owner:** Talley Broadcasting Corp., 1610 Oakbrook Dr., Hillsboro, IL 62049-2277. **Founded:** 1950. **Operating Hours:** 20.5 hours Daily. **Key Personnel:** Terry Todt, Sports Dir., terry@wsmiradio.com. **Wattage:** 50,000. **Ad Rates:** Advertising accepted; rates available upon request. Combined advertising rates available with WSMI & WAOX. **URL:** http://www.wsmiradio.com.

LOMBARD

DuPage Co. Du Page Co. (NE). 22 m NW of Chicago. Chiropractic College. Engineering College. Printing. Manufactures boxes, packaging materials.

11022 ■ Journal of Business Logistics
Council of Supply Chain Management Professionals
333 E Butterfield Rd., Ste. 140
Lombard, IL 60148
Phone: (630)574-0985
Fax: (630)574-0989
Publisher's E-mail: onlinelibrarysales@wiley.com
Freq: Quarterly. **Key Personnel:** Mathew A. Waller, Editor. **ISSN:** 0735--3766 (print); **EISSN:** 2158--1592 (electronic). **Subscription Rates:** $311 U.S., Canada, and Mexico Instituitons - Online only; £222 Institutions U.K - Online only; €255 Institutions Europe - Online only; $311 Institutions, other countries Online only; $87 U.S., Canada, and Mexico Personal - Online only; £62 Individuals U.K - Online only; €71 Individuals Europe - Online only; $87 Other countries Online only. **URL:** http://cscmp.org/member-benefits/journal-business-logistics; http://onlinelibrary.wiley.com/journal/10.1002/%28ISSN%292158-1592. **Remarks:** Advertising not accepted. **Circ:** (Not Reported).

11023 ■ The Journal of IMA
Islamic Medical Association of North America
101 W 22nd St., Ste. 104
Lombard, IL 60148
Phone: (630)932-0000
Fax: (630)932-0005
Publisher's E-mail: hq@imana.org
Freq: 3/year latest issue 2012. **URL:** http://jima.imana.org. **Remarks:** Accepts advertising. **Circ:** (Not Reported).

11024 ■ Lombardian
Lombardian
116 S Main St.
Lombard, IL 60148
Phone: (630)627-7010
Fax: (630)627-7027
Publication E-mail: lombardian@sbcglobal.net
Newspaper with a Republican orientation. **Freq:** Weekly. **Print Method:** Offset. **Cols./Page:** 5. **Col. Width:** 22 nonpareils. **Col. Depth:** 224 agate lines. **Key Personnel:** Bonnie Lee MacKay, Publisher. **Subscription Rates:** $45 Individuals; $50 Out of area. **URL:** http://www.lombardian.info. **Ad Rates:** GLR $.44; BW $624; 4C $100; PCI $7.80. **Remarks:** Accepts advertising. **Circ:** ‡21500.

11025 ■ Villa Park Review/Lombardian
Lombardian
116 S Main St.
Lombard, IL 60148
Phone: (630)627-7010
Fax: (630)627-7027
Publication E-mail: lombardian@sbcglobal.net
Newspaper with a Republican orientation. **Freq:** Weekly. **Print Method:** Offset. Uses mats. **Cols./Page:** 5. **Col. Width:** 22 nonpareils. **Col. Depth:** 224 agate lines. **Key Personnel:** Bonnie MacKay, Publisher; Scott Lee MacKay, Contact. **Subscription Rates:** $45 Individuals; $50 Out of area. **URL:** http://www.lombardian.info. **Ad Rates:** GLR $.50; BW $664; 4C $100; PCI $8.30. **Remarks:** Accepts advertising. **Circ:** ‡21500, 13500.

LONG GROVE

Lake Co. Lake Co. (NE). 17 m S of Fox Lake. Residential.

11026 ■ The Proceedings
Conference of Consulting Actuaries
3880 Salem Lake Dr., Ste. H
Long Grove, IL 60047-5292
Phone: (847)719-6500
Publisher's E-mail: conference@ccactuaries.org
Freq: Annual. **Subscription Rates:** $35 Individuals. **URL:** http://www.ccactuaries.org/publications/proceedings.cfm. **Remarks:** Advertising not accepted. **Circ:** (Not Reported).

LOVES PARK

Winnebago Co. Winnebago Co. (EC). NE of Rockford.

11027 ■ WILV-FM - 91.1
5375 Pebble Creek Trl.
Loves Park, IL 61111
Owner: Christian Life Center School, 1780 Lincoln Ave. SE, Port Orchard, WA 98366, Ph: (360)876-5595. **Founded:** 1988. **Wattage:** 7,000. **Ad Rates:** Noncommercial; underwriting available.

11028 ■ WQFL-FM - 100.9
5375 Pebble Creek Tr.
Loves Park, IL 61111
Phone: (815)654-1200
Fax: (815)282-7779
Format: Contemporary Christian. **Networks:** Independent. **Founded:** 1974. **Operating Hours:** Continuous. **ADI:** Rockford, IL. **Key Personnel:** Jeremy DeWeerdt, Contact; Nick Guzzardo, Contact. **Wattage:** 6,000. **Ad Rates:** $12-22.50 for 30 seconds; $16-30 for 60 seconds. Combined advertising rates available with WGSL-FM.

LOVINGTON

Moultrie Co. Moultrie Co. (SC). 20 m N of Sullivan.

11029 ■ Moultrie Telecommunications, Inc.
111 State & Broadway
Lovington, IL 61937
Founded: 1981. **Cities Served:** Lovington, Illinois: subscribing households 444; 43 channels; 1 community access channel; 168 hours per week community access programming. **URL:** http://www.moultriemulticorp.com/about.htm.

LYNWOOD

11030 ■ Journal of Community Practice
Association for Community Organization and Social Administration
20560 Bensley Ave.
Lynwood, IL 60411
Phone: (708)757-4187
Fax: (708)757-4234
Journal designed to provide a forum for community practice, including community organizing, planning, social administration, organizational development, community development, and social change. **Freq:** Quarterly. **Key Personnel:** Alice K. Johnson Butterfield, PhD, Editor; Lorraine M. Gutierrez, PhD, Board Member; Darlyne Bailey, Board Member; Marie O. Weil, PhD, Editor, Founder; Ana H. Santiago, Editor. **ISSN:** 1070--5422 (print); **EISSN:** 1543--3706 (electronic). **Subscription Rates:** $536 Institutions online only; $155 Individuals online; $613 Institutions online and print; $177 Individuals print + online. **URL:** http://www.tandfonline.com/toc/wcom20/current; http://www.acosa.org/joomla/journalinfo. **Ad Rates:** BW $315; 4C $550. **Remarks:** Accepts advertising. **Circ:** (Not Reported).

MACHESNEY PARK

11031 ■ News Gazette
Rock Valley Publishing
11512 N Second St.
Machesney Park, IL 61115
Phone: (815)877-4044
Fax: (815)654-4857
Community newspaper. **Founded:** 1858. **Freq:** Weekly (Wed.). **Print Method:** Offset. **Trim Size:** 10 1/8 x16. **Cols./Page:** 4. **Col. Width:** 22 nonpareils. **Col. Depth:** 224 agate lines. **Key Personnel:** John Foreman, Editor; Sandy Pistole, Director, Advertising; Jackie Martin, Manager, Advertising. **Subscription Rates:** $14.33 Individuals per month; $17.78 Individuals ng vip member; $7.99 Individuals digital only; $3.99 Individuals Illini HQ only. **URL:** http://www.news-gazette.com. **Ad Rates:** GLR $.45; PCI $5.23. **Remarks:** Accepts advertising. **Circ:** ‡7400.

MACOMB

McDonough Co. McDonough Co. (W). 40 m SW of Galesburg. Western Illinois University.Spoon River College. Museum. State Park. Manufactures pottery, porcelain insulators, clay and steel products, metal furniture, industrial bearings, chicken incubators, agriculture equipment. Coal mines. Clay deposits. Agriculture. Corn, soybeans, hogs, cattle.

11032 ■ Avon Sentinel
Eagle Publications
210 S Randolph
Macomb, IL 61455
Phone: (309)837-4428
Fax: (309)462-3221
Free: 800-500-1961
Community newspaper. **Freq:** Weekly (Thurs.). **Print Method:** Offset. **Cols./Page:** 6. **Col. Width:** 20 nonpareils. **Col. Depth:** 224 agate lines. **Key Personnel:** Deb Fowlks, Managing Editor; Tom Hutson, Publisher; Joyce Cannon, Contact. **Subscription Rates:** $30 Individuals in county; $35 Other countries; $40 Out of state. **URL:** http://eaglepublications.com/avon.html; http://www.eaglepublications.com/avon.html. **Ad Rates:** GLR $2.10; BW $201.60; 4C $541.60; SAU $3.10; CNU $4; PCI $2. **Remarks:** Accepts advertising. **Circ:** Paid ‡650, Free ‡100.

11033 ■ Eagle Scribe
Eagle Publications
210 S Randolph
Macomb, IL 61455
Phone: (309)837-4428
Fax: (309)462-3221
Free: 800-500-1961
Publication E-mail: eaglepub@macomb.com
Community newspaper. **Freq:** Weekly. **Print Method:** Offset. **Cols./Page:** 6. **Col. Width:** 11 nonpareils. **Col. Depth:** 19 inches. **Key Personnel:** Lea A. Flack, Editor; John T. Flack, Editor. **USPS:** 639-380. **Subscription Rates:** $30 Individuals in County; $35 Out of country; $40 Out of state. **URL:** http://www.eaglepublications.com/current.php?paper=Augusta&type=News. **Ad Rates:** BW $153.60; SAU $1.60; PCI $1.60. **Remarks:** Accepts advertising. **Circ:** ‡552.

11034 ■ Elsevier: Industrial Crops and Products
Association for the Advancement of Industrial Crops
c/o Winthrop Phippen, Treasurer
Western Illinois University
1 University Cir.
Macomb, IL 61455
Publisher's E-mail: aaic@wiu.edu
Freq: Monthly. **ISSN:** 0926--6690 (print). **Subscription Rates:** $2176 Individuals (print); $2178.40 Institutions (online); $247 Individuals personal. **URL:** http://www.journals.elsevier.com/industrial-crops-and-products. **Remarks:** Advertising not accepted. **Circ:** (Not Reported).

11035 ■ Lhasa Bulletin
American Lhasa Apso Club
c/o Joyce Johanson, Membership Chair
126 W Kurlene Dr.
Macomb, IL 61455-1008
Phone: (309)837-1665
Magazine containing information on Lhasa Apso dog breeding, latest dog shows, and events of the American Lhasa Apso Club. **Freq:** 3/year Spring, Fall, and Winter. **Subscription Rates:** Included in membership. **URL:** http://www.lhasaapso.org/bulletin.html. **Remarks:** Advertising not accepted. **Circ:** (Not Reported).

11036 ■ Palaestra: Forum of Sport, Physical Education & Recreation for Those with Disabilities
Challenge Publications Ltd.
PO Box 508
Macomb, IL 61455
Phone: (309)833-1902
Publisher's E-mail: challpub@macomb.com
Journal focusing on sports, physical education, and recreation for persons with disabilities.Feature articles focus on the activities of various disability sports organizations (DSOs), including special events and national/international championships, photo essays, historical features, personality studies, and all aspects of human anatomy, kinesiology, psychology, and sociology that can be applied to the development of practical physical education, training and skill techniques for the recreational, as well as the competitive individual. **Freq:** Quarterly. **Print Method:** Sheet-fed offset. **Key Personnel:** David P. Beaver, Editor-in-Chief; Phyllis Gould Beaver, Managing Editor; Julian U. Stein, Associate Editor. **ISSN:** 8756--5811 (print). **Subscription Rates:** $60 Individuals print and online; $80 Other countries print and online; $240 Institutions print and online; $300 Institutions, other countries print and online. **URL:** http://www.palaestra.com/issues. **Ad Rates:** 4C $4284, 2-page spread; 4C $2289, full page; 4C $1145, 1/2 page; 4C $763, 1/3 page; 4C $573, 1/4 page; 4C $382, 1/6 page. **Remarks:** Accepts advertising. **Circ:** Combined ‡5000.

11037 ■ Rural Realities
Rural Sociological Society
Western Illinois University
1 University Cir.
Macomb, IL 61455-1367
Phone: (309)298-3518
Publisher's E-mail: rssiira@wiu.edu
Alt. Formats: PDF. **URL:** http://www.ruralsociology.org/?page_id=825. **Remarks:** Advertising not accepted. **Circ:** (Not Reported).

11038 ■ The Rural Sociologist
Rural Sociological Society
Western Illinois University
1 University Cir.
Macomb, IL 61455-1367
Phone: (309)298-3518
Publisher's E-mail: rssiira@wiu.edu
Freq: Quarterly. **ISSN:** 2154--7599 (print). **Alt. Formats:** PDF. **URL:** http://www.ruralsociology.org/?page_id=112. **Remarks:** Accepts advertising. **Circ:** (Not Reported).

11039 ■ Rural Sociology
Rural Sociological Society
Western Illinois University
1 University Cir.
Macomb, IL 61455-1367
Phone: (309)298-3518
Publisher's E-mail: rssiira@wiu.edu
Scholarly journal for social scientists, policy makers, and agency professionals concerned with rural people, places and problems. **Freq:** Quarterly. **Print Method:** Offset. **Trim Size:** 6 x 9. **Cols./Page:** 1. **Col. Width:** 52 nonpareils. **Col. Depth:** 98 agate lines. **Key Personnel:** Stephen Sapp, Dr., Editor; Alessandro Bonanno, Editor. **ISSN:** 0036--0112 (print); **EISSN:** 1549--0831 (electronic). **Subscription Rates:** $423 Institutions, Canada and Mexico print or online; U.S., Canada and Mexico; $508 Institutions, Canada and Mexico print & online; U.S., Canada and Mexico; £261 Institutions print or online; UK; £314 Institutions print & online; UK; €306 Institutions print or online; Europe; €368 Institutions print & online; Europe; $476 Institutions, other countries print or online; $572 Institutions, other countries print & online. **URL:** http://www.ruralsociology.org; http://www.ruralsociology.org/?page_id=106; http://onlinelibrary.wiley.com/journal/10.1111/(ISSN)1549-0831. **Remarks:** Accepts advertising. **Circ:** (Not Reported).

11040 ■ Rural Studies Series
Rural Sociological Society
Western Illinois University
1 University Cir.
Macomb, IL 61455-1367
Phone: (309)298-3518
Publisher's E-mail: rssiira@wiu.edu
Journal promoting the generation application and dissemination of sociological knowledge and also featuring books on a wide range of topics related to rural societies. **URL:** http://wvupressonline.com/series/rural_studies; http://www.ruralsociology.org/?page_id=108. **Remarks:** Advertising not accepted. **Circ:** (Not Reported).

11041 ■ Symbolic Interaction
Society for the Study of Symbolic Interaction
c/o Patrick McGinty, Vice President
Morgan Hall 404
1 University Cir.
Macomb, IL 61455
Freq: Quarterly. **ISSN:** 0195-6086 (print); **EISSN:** 1533-8665 (electronic). **Subscription Rates:** $477 Institutions U.S., Canada and Mexico - online only; $573 Institutions U.S., Canada and Mexico - print + online; £308 Institutions online only; £370 Institutions print + online; €361 Institutions online only; €494 Institutions print + online; $477 Institutions, other countries online only; $573 Institutions, other countries print + online. **URL:** http://sites.google.com/site/sssinteraction/home/journal-symbolic-interaction; http://onlinelibrary.wiley.com/journal/10.1002/%28ISSN%291533-8665/homepage/ForAuthors.html. **Remarks:** Accepts advertising. **Circ:** (Not Reported).

11042 ■ Western Courier
Macomb Area Economic Development Corporation
510 N Pearl St., Ste. 300
Macomb, IL 61455
Phone: (309)837-4684
Publication E-mail: westerncourier@gmail.com
Collegiate newspaper. **Freq:** 3/week. **Print Method:** Offset. **Trim Size:** 10 3/4 x 16. **Cols./Page:** 5. **Col. Width:** 11.8 picas. **Col. Depth:** 1 inches. **Key Personnel:** Erika Ward, Editor-in-Chief. **URL:** http://www.westerncourier.com/. **Ad Rates:** BW $549.50; 4C $849.50; SAU $7; PCI $7.50. **Remarks:** Accepts advertising. **Circ:** 6500.

11043 ■ WIUM-FM - 91.3
One University Cir.
Macomb, IL 61455-1390
Phone: (309)298-1873
Fax: (309)298-2133
Free: 800-895-2912
Email: publicradio@wiu.edu
Format: Public Radio. **Networks:** Public Radio International (PRI); National Public Radio (NPR); Illinois Public Radio. **Owner:** Tri-States Public Radio, One University Cir., Macomb, IL 61455, Ph: (309)298-1873, Fax: (309)298-2133, Free: 800-895-2912. **Founded:** 1956. **Operating Hours:** Continuous; 80% network, 20% local. **Key Personnel:** Dorie Vallillo, Gen. Mgr., d-vallillo@wiu.edu; Rich Egger, News Dir., rg-egger@wiu.edu; Ken Thermon, Operations Mgr., kw-thermon@wiu.edu; Ken Zahnle, Music Dir., ks-zahnle@wiu.edu; Jonathan Ahl, Gen. Mgr., j-ahl@wiu.edu. **Wattage:** 50,000. **Ad Rates:** Noncommercial. **URL:** http://tspr.org.

11044 ■ WIUS-FM - 88.3
One University Cir.
1 University Cir.
Macomb, IL 61455
Email: info@wiu.edu
Format: Urban Contemporary; Adult Album Alternative. **Owner:** Western Illinois University, 1 University Cir., Macomb, IL 61455, Ph: (309)298-1414. **Founded:** Jan. 1982. **Operating Hours:** 8 a.m.-1 a.m. Mon.-Fri.; 12 p.m.-2 a.m. Sat.-Sun. **Wattage:** 120 ERP. **Ad Rates:** Noncommercial; underwriting available. **URL:** http://www.wiu.edu/cofac/wiusfm.

11045 ■ WIUW-FM - 89.5
One University Cir.
Macomb, IL 61455
Phone: (309)298-1873
Fax: (309)298-2133
Free: 800-895-2912
Email: publicradio@wiu.edu
Format: Public Radio. **Founded:** 1970. **Key Personnel:** Dorie Vallillo, Gen. Mgr., d-vallillo@wiu.edu; Ken Thermon, Operations Mgr., kw-thermon@wiu.edu; Sharon Faust, Dir. of Dev., sk-faust@wiu.edu; Rich Egger, News Dir., rg-egger@wiu.edu; Ken Zahnle, Music Dir., ks-zahnle@wiu.edu; Jonathan Ahl, Gen. Mgr., j-ahl@wiu.edu. **Wattage:** 10,000. **Ad Rates:** Noncommercial. Combined advertising rates available with WIUM-FM. **URL:** http://www.tristatesradio.com.

11046 ■ WJEQ-FM - 102.7
31 E Side Sq.
Macomb, IL 61455
Phone: (309)833-2121
Fax: (309)836-3291
Format: Classic Rock; News; Sports. **Key Personnel:** Mike Gillett, Dir. of Programs, mikegillett@prestigeradio.com; Kim Williams, Dir. of Production, kimwilliams@prestigeradio.com. **Ad Rates:** Noncommercial. **URL:** http://wjeqfm.com.

11047 ■ WKAI-FM - 100.1
31 E Side Sq.
Macomb, IL 61455
Phone: (309)833-2121
Format: Adult Contemporary. **Owner:** Prestige Communications, LLP, at above address, Fayetteville, GA. **Ad Rates:** Advertising accepted; rates available upon request. **URL:** http://www.wkaifm.com.

Circulation: ★ = AAM; △ or • = BPA; ♦ = CAC; ❑ = VAC; ⊕ = PO Statement; ‡ = Publisher's Report; Boldface figures = sworn; Light figures = estimated.

11048 ■ WLMD-FM - 104.7
31 E Side Sq.
Macomb, IL 61455
Phone: (309)833-2121
Fax: (309)836-3291
Format: Country. **Ad Rates:** Noncommercial. **URL:** http://www.wlmdfm.com.

11049 ■ WLRB-AM - 1510
1034 W Jackson
Macomb, IL 61455
Phone: (309)833-2121
Fax: (309)836-3291
Email: radio@prestigeradio.com
Format: News; Agricultural. **Networks:** ABC; Jones Satellite. **Founded:** 1947. **Formerly:** WKAI-AM. **Operating Hours:** 7 a.m.-5:00 p.m.; 90% network, 10% local. **Wattage:** 1,000. **Ad Rates:** $5-12 for 30 seconds; $7.50-18 for 60 seconds. Combined advertising rates available with WKAI-FM, WLMD-FM. **URL:** http://www.wlrbam.com.

11050 ■ WMQZ-FM - 104.1
31 E Side Sq.
Macomb, IL 61455
Phone: (309)833-2121
Fax: (309)836-3291
Format: Oldies. **Owner:** Prestige Communications, Inc., at above address. **Operating Hours:** Continuous. **Key Personnel:** Kim Williams, Dir. of Production. **Wattage:** 6,000 ERP. **URL:** http://wmqzfm.com.

11051 ■ WNLF-FM - 95.9
31 E Side Sq.
Macomb, IL 61455
Phone: (309)833-2121
Fax: (309)836-3291
Format: Album-Oriented Rock (AOR). **Ad Rates:** Noncommercial. **URL:** http://www.wnlffm.com.

MANHATTAN

11052 ■ Kraus Electronics Systems Inc.
305 State St.
Manhattan, IL 60442
Phone: (815)478-4000
Free: 800-442-2253
Founded: Sept. 05, 2006. **Cities Served:** 98 channels. **URL:** http://www.krausonline.com.

11053 ■ Manhattan Cable TV Co.
305 State St.
Manhattan, IL 60442
Phone: (815)478-4000
Founded: 1980. **Cities Served:** Manhattan, Illinois; 42 channels.

MANSFIELD

11054 ■ International Flying Farmer
International Flying Farmers
PO Box 309
Mansfield, IL 61854
Phone: (217)489-9300
Fax: (217)489-9280
Publication E-mail: flyingfarmersmagazine@hotmail.com
Association magazine covering the activities of people with agricultural and/or aviation interests. **Freq:** Bimonthly. **Trim Size:** 8 1/4 x 11. **Cols./Page:** 3. **Col. Width:** 14 picas. **Col. Depth:** 10 inches. **Key Personnel:** Patricia L. Amdor, Editor, Office Manager. **ISSN:** 0020--675X (print). **Subscription Rates:** Included in membership. **URL:** http://www.internationalflyingfarmers.org/magazine-archives. **Remarks:** Accepts advertising. **Circ:** (Not Reported).

MARION

Williamson Co. Williamson Co. (S). 55 m S of Centralia. Manufactures explosives, fiberglass boats. Coal mines. Fruit, grain and livestock farms.

11055 ■ Marion Daily Republican
Liberty Group
502 W Jackson St.
Marion, IL 62959-0490
Phone: (618)993-2626
General newspaper. **Founded:** 1908. **Freq:** Mon.-Sun. **Print Method:** Offset. **Cols./Page:** 6. **Col. Width:** 24 nonpareils. **Col. Depth:** 300 agate lines. **Key Personnel:** Tim Petrowich, Publisher; Bill Swinford, Editor; Larry Henry, Manager, Advertising. **Subscription Rates:** $56.50 Individuals print (by mail); $39.99 Individuals digital (all access). **URL:** http://www.dailyrepublicannews.com. **Mailing address:** PO Box 490, Marion, IL 62959-0490. **Ad Rates:** BW $1,025.55; 4C $1,250.55; PCI $7.95. **Remarks:** Accepts advertising. **Circ:** (Not Reported).

11056 ■ Portsmouth Daily Times
APMS
606 N Van Buren
Marion, IL 62959
General newspaper. **Freq:** Daily excluding Mondays. **Print Method:** Offset. **Cols./Page:** 6. **Key Personnel:** John S. Clark, Publisher; LouAnn Blair, Manager, Circulation; Jon Noel, Manager, Advertising. **Ad Rates:** GLR $.97; BW $1179; 4C $1429; PCI $13.60. **Remarks:** Accepts advertising. **Circ:** Mon.-Sat. ★**12,840**, Sun. ★**12,118**.

11057 ■ WAQP-TV - 49
11717 Rte. 37 N
Marion, IL 62959
Phone: (618)997-4700
Fax: (618)997-8936
Format: Commercial TV; Religious. **Networks:** Independent. **Owner:** TCT, 11717 Rte. 37, Marion, IL 62959, Ph: (618)997-4700, Fax: (618)993-9778, Free: 800-232-9855. **Founded:** 1985. **Operating Hours:** Continuous; 60% network, 40% local. **ADI:** Flint-Saginaw-Bay City, MI. **Wattage:** 1,000,000. **Ad Rates:** Noncommercial. **Mailing address:** PO Box 1010, Marion, IL 62959.

11058 ■ WAWJ-FM - 90.1
PO Box 2440
Tupelo, MS 38803
Phone: (662)844-8888
Format: Religious. **Owner:** American Family Association, at above address.

11059 ■ WBVN-FM - 104.5
PO Box 1126
Marion, IL 62959
Phone: (618)997-1500
Format: Contemporary Christian; Religious. **Owner:** Ken Anderson, Not Available. **Founded:** 1990. **Operating Hours:** Continuous; 50% local; 50% network. **Key Personnel:** Ken Anderson, Station Mgr. **Wattage:** 6,000. **Ad Rates:** Noncommercial. **URL:** http://www.wbvn.org.

11060 ■ WDDD-AM - 810
1822 N Ct.
Marion, IL 62959
Phone: (618)997-8123
Fax: (618)993-2319
Format: News; Sports; Talk. **Simulcasts:** WDDD-FM. **Founded:** 1979. **Operating Hours:** Continuous. **ADI:** Paducah,KY-Cape Girardeau,MO-Marion,IL. **Wattage:** 250. **Ad Rates:** Advertising accepted; rates available upon request.

11061 ■ WDDD-FM - 107.3
1822 North Ct.
Marion, IL 62959
Phone: (618)997-8123
Fax: (618)993-2319
Format: Country; Top 40. **Networks:** CBS. **Founded:** 1970. **ADI:** Paducah,KY-Cape Girardeau,MO-Marion,IL. **Wattage:** 50,000 ERP. **Ad Rates:** Accepts Advertising. **URL:** http://www.w3dcountry.com.

11062 ■ WFRX-AM - 1300
1822 N Court St.
Marion, IL 62959
Phone: (618)997-8123
Fax: (618)993-2319
Format: Middle-of-the-Road (MOR). **Operating Hours:** Continuous. **ADI:** Rockford, IL. **Wattage:** 1,000 ERP. **Ad Rates:** Noncommercial. **URL:** http://www.mywithersradio.com.

11063 ■ WGGH-AM - 1150
1801 E Main St.
Marion, IL 62959
Phone: (618)993-8102
Format: Talk. **Owner:** Vine Broadcasting, Inc., at above address. **Founded:** 1949. **Operating Hours:** Continuous. **ADI:** Paducah,KY-Cape Girardeau,MO-Marion,IL. **Wattage:** 5,000. **Ad Rates:** Noncommercial. **Mailing address:** PO Box 340, Marion, IL 62959. **URL:** http://www.wggh.net.

WLXI-TV - See Greensboro, NC

11064 ■ WNYB-TV - 26
11717 Rt. 37 N
Marion, IL 62959
Phone: (618)997-4700
Fax: (618)993-9778
Free: 800-232-9855
Email: ask@tct.tv
Format: Religious. **Owner:** Tri-State Christian Television Inc., PO Box 1010, Marion, IL 62959, Ph: (618)997-4700, Fax: (618)993-9778. **Founded:** 1990. **Operating Hours:** Continuous. **ADI:** Buffalo (Jamestown), NY. **Wattage:** 5,000,000 ERP. **Ad Rates:** Advertising accepted; rates available upon request. **Mailing address:** PO Box 1010, Marion, IL 62959. **URL:** http://www.tct.tv.

11065 ■ WTAO-FM - 105.1
1822 North Ct.
Marion, IL 62959
Phone: (618)997-8123
Format: Soft Rock. **Operating Hours:** Continuous. **Ad Rates:** Advertising accepted; rates available upon request. **URL:** http://www.105tao.com.

11066 ■ WTCT-TV - 27
11717 Rt. 37 N
Marion, IL 62959
Phone: (618)997-4700
Fax: (618)993-9778
Format: Contemporary Christian. **Owner:** Tri-State Christian TV, at above address. **Founded:** 1981. **Operating Hours:** Continuous (except midnight-6 a.m. Mon.). **Wattage:** 3,000,000. **Ad Rates:** $40 for 30 seconds; $60 for 60 seconds. **Mailing address:** PO Box 1010, Marion, IL 62959. **URL:** http://www.tct.tv.

11067 ■ WTLJ-TV - 54
11717 Rt. 37 N
Marion, IL 62959
Phone: (618)997-4700
Fax: (618)993-9778
Format: Religious. **Owner:** TCT, 11717 Rte. 37, Marion, IL 62959, Ph: (618)997-4700, Fax: (618)993-9778, Free: 800-232-9855. **Founded:** 1986. **Operating Hours:** Continuous. **ADI:** Grand Rapids-Kalamazoo-Battle Creek, MI. **Wattage:** 4,400,000. **Ad Rates:** Noncommercial. **Mailing address:** PO Box 1010, Marion, IL 62959. **URL:** http://www.tct.tv.

11068 ■ WVZA-FM - 92.7
1822 North Ct.
Marion, IL 62959
Free: 800-345-2804
Format: Top 40. **Mailing address:** PO Box 127, Marion, IL 62959. **URL:** http://kissfm927.com.

MARSHALL

Clark Co. Clark Co. (E). 16 m SW of Terre Haute, Ind. Camping. Curio shops. plastic and rock crushing plants. Electronics. Farming.

11069 ■ WMMC-FM - 105.9
PO Box 158
Marshall, IL 62441
Phone: (217)826-8017
Fax: (217)826-8519
Free: 800-832-0208
Format: Full Service. **Networks:** Satellite Music Network. **Founded:** 1963. **Operating Hours:** 5 a.m.-1 a.m.; 70% network, 30% local. **ADI:** Terre Haute, IN. **Wattage:** 3,300 ERP. **Ad Rates:** Noncommercial. **URL:** http://www.clarkcountyil.org/Marketplace/wmmc.htm.

11070 ■ WYDO-TV - 14
13865 E Elliot Dr.
Marshall, IL 62441
Phone: (252)756-0814
Format: Commercial TV. **Networks:** Fox. **Owner:** Piedmont Television, LLC, at above address. **Ad Rates:** Noncommercial.

MASCOUTAH

St. Clair Co. St Clair Co. (SW). 10 m SE of Belleville. Manufactures cooking ranges, foundry products, carpets. Coal mines. Grain, stock, farms.

11071 ■ Herald Scott Flyer
Herald Publications
314 East Church St.

Drawer C
Mascoutah, IL 62258
Phone: (618)566-8282
Fax: (618)566-8282
Publisher's E-mail: ccn@cbnstl.com
Community newspaper. **Freq:** Weekly (Thurs.). **Subscription Rates:** $5 Individuals. **URL:** http://heraldpubs.com. **Mailing address:** PO Box C, Mascoutah, IL 62258. **Remarks:** Accepts advertising. **Circ:** (Not Reported).

11072 ■ Mascoutah Herald
Herald Publications
314 East Church St.
Drawer C
Mascoutah, IL 62258
Phone: (618)566-8282
Fax: (618)566-8282
Publisher's E-mail: ccn@cbnstl.com
Community newspaper. **Freq:** Weekly. **Subscription Rates:** $32 Individuals In country - 1 year subscription to print and online newspaper; $37 Out of area 1 year subscription to print and online newspaper; $29.50 Individuals seniors - 1 year subscription to print and online newspaper. **URL:** http://heraldpubs.com. **Mailing address:** PO Box C, Mascoutah, IL 62258. **Remarks:** Advertising accepted; rates available upon request. **Circ:** (Not Reported).

11073 ■ The Tribune
Herald Publications
314 East Church St.
Drawer C
Mascoutah, IL 62258
Phone: (618)566-8282
Fax: (618)566-8282
Publication E-mail: tribune@mmcable.com
Community newspaper. **Founded:** 1965. **Freq:** Weekly (Thurs.). **Print Method:** Offset. **Trim Size:** 10 1/4 x 16. **Cols./Page:** 5 and 6. **Col. Width:** 22 nonpareils and 2 1/8 inches. **Col. Depth:** 219 agate lines and 21 inches. **Key Personnel:** Gloria Quaid, Editor; Cynthia Carpenter, Director, Advertising; Greg Hoskins, Publisher; Les Hostetler, Editor; Kera Andersen, Editor; Patti Olson, Contact. **USPS:** 418-960. **Subscription Rates:** $19.50 Individuals; $17 Individuals; $18 Individuals; $21 Out of area; $26 Out of state; $14 senior citizens. **Formerly:** Tribune-Review. **Mailing address:** PO Box 488, Monument, CO 80132-0488. **Ad Rates:** GLR $.47; BW $528; 4C $85; PCI $7.85; BW $245; SAU $4.50; PCI $7. **Remarks:** Advertising accepted; rates available upon request. **Circ:** Paid ‡4444, Free ‡145, ‡1800, 3500.

MATTOON

Coles Co. Coles Co. (E). 178 m S of Chicago. Manufactures heavy road machinery, radiators, quartz lighting, pet food, paper products, roofing, frozen food products, commercial printing, metal hose. Grain, stock, fruit, broom corn.

11074 ■ JG-TC
Mid-Illinois Newspapers Inc.
700 Broadway Ave. E, Ste. 9A
Mattoon, IL 61938
Phone: (217)235-5656
Local newspaper. **Founded:** 1874. **Freq:** Mon.-Sat. (morn.). **Print Method:** Offset. **Cols./Page:** 6. **Col. Width:** 25 nonpareils. **Col. Depth:** 301 agate lines. **Key Personnel:** Carl Walworth, Editor, Publisher, phone: (217)238-6822. **Subscription Rates:** $12 Individuals /month; digital-only access; $20 Individuals /month; full access (print + digital). **URL:** http://www.jg-tc.com/. **Formerly:** Journal-Gazette. **Ad Rates:** BW $1,470.60; 4C $1,695.60; SAU $11.40. **Circ:** Mon.-Fri. ★**8303**, Sat. ★**8151**.

11075 ■ Times-Courier
Lee Enterprises Inc.
700 Broadway Ave., E Ste. 9A
Mattoon, IL 61938
Phone: (217)235-5656
General newspaper. **Founded:** 1840. **Freq:** Mon.-Sat. (morn.). **Print Method:** Offset. **Cols./Page:** 6. **Col. Width:** 25 nonpareils. **Col. Depth:** 301 agate lines. **Key Personnel:** Carl Walworth, President, Publisher, phone: (217)238-6822; Bob Craig, Specialist, Circulation, phone: (217)238-6844. **Subscription Rates:** $179.40 Individuals carrier home delivery; $12 Individuals digital access per month; $20 Individuals full access per month. **URL:** http://jg-tc.com/. **Ad Rates:** SAU $8.85. **Remarks:** Accepts advertising. **Circ:** Mon.-Sat. ★**5174**.

11076 ■ WCBH-FM - 104.3
209 Lakeland Blvd.
Mattoon, IL 61938
Phone: (217)235-5624
Format: Adult Contemporary. **Networks:** The Source. **Owner:** The Cromwell Group, Inc., 1824 Murfreesboro Rd., Nashville, TN 37217, Ph: (615)361-7560, Fax: (615)366-4313. **Founded:** 1988. **Operating Hours:** Continuous. **ADI:** Terre Haute, IN. **Wattage:** 25,000 ERP. **Ad Rates:** $12.50-19 for 30 seconds; $15-21 for 60 seconds. Combined advertising rates available with WCRC/WCRA. **URL:** http://www.myradiolink.com.

11077 ■ WLBH-FM
PO Box 1848
Mattoon, IL 61938
Phone: (217)234-6464
Fax: (217)234-6019
Email: livesay@wlbh.com
Format: Adult Contemporary. **Networks:** ABC. **Owner:** Mattoon Broadcasting Co., at above address. **Founded:** 1949. **Wattage:** 50,000 ERP. **Ad Rates:** Noncommercial.

11078 ■ WLKL-FM - 89.9
5001 Lake Land Blvd.
Mattoon, IL 61938
Phone: (217)234-5253
Fax: (217)234-5506
Free: 800-252-4121
Format: Alternative/New Music/Progressive; Hip Hop; Top 40. **Owner:** Lake Land College Board of Trustees, 5001 Lake Land Blvd., Mattoon, IL 61938. **Founded:** Jan. 20, 1975. **Operating Hours:** Continuous. **ADI:** Springfield-Decatur-Champaign, IL. **Key Personnel:** Kenneth Beno, Station Mgr., Contact, kbeno@lakeland.cc.il.us; Greg Powers, Station Mgr; Kenneth Beno, Contact. **Wattage:** 1,300 ERP. **Ad Rates:** Noncommercial; Underwriting available. **URL:** http://www.899themax.com.

11079 ■ WMCI-FM - 101.3
209 Lakeland Blvd.
Mattoon, IL 61938
Phone: (217)235-5624
Format: Country. **URL:** http://www.myradiolink.com.

11080 ■ WWGO-FM - 92.1
209 Lakeland Blvd.
Mattoon, IL 61938
Phone: (217)235-5624
Format: Classic Rock. **URL:** http://www.myradiolink.com.

MAYWOOD

Cook Co.

11081 ■ Journal of Burn Care & Research
Lippincott Williams & Wilkins
c/o Richard L. Gamelli, MD, Editor-in-Chief
Loyola University Medical Ctr.
2160 S First Ave.
Maywood, IL 60153
Phone: (708)216-9222
Freq: Bimonthly. **Print Method:** Offset. **Trim Size:** 8 1/8 x 10 7/8. **Cols./Page:** 2. **Col. Width:** 39.5 picas. **Col. Depth:** 53 picas. **Key Personnel:** Richard L. Gamelli, MD, Editor-in-Chief; John Ewers, Publisher. **ISSN:** 1559--047X (print); **EISSN:** 1559--0488 (electronic). **Subscription Rates:** $251 Individuals U.S.; $496 Institutions U.S.; $144 Individuals in-training; $323 Other countries individual; $560 Institutions, other countries; $205 Other countries in-training; Included in membership. **URL:** http://journals.lww.com/burncareresearch/pages/default.aspx; http://www.ameriburn.org/resources_publications.php. **Formerly:** Journal of Burn Care & Rehabilitation. **Ad Rates:** BW $2075; 4C $1475. **Remarks:** Accepts advertising. **Circ:** 3006, 5,000.

MCHENRY

McHenry Co. McHenry Co. (NE). On Fox River, 24 m N of Elgin. Manufactures boats, radios, dresses, piston rings, auto brake systems, springs. Dairy, grain, poultry farms. Alfalfa.

11082 ■ Lynn--Linn Lineage Quarterly
Phyllis J. Bauer, Editor and Publisher
5747 Fieldstone Trl.
McHenry, IL 60050-2283
Publisher's E-mail: pjbauer@mc.net
Trade publication covering genealogy. **Freq:** Quarterly. **Print Method:** photocopy. **Trim Size:** 8 x 11. **Cols./Page:** 1. **Key Personnel:** Pyhllis J. Bauer, Editor. **ISSN:** 0892--418X (print). **Subscription Rates:** $22 Individuals. **Circ:** Combined 150.

MCLEANSBORO

11083 ■ The Northern Light
McLeansboro Times-Leader
200 S Washington St.
Mcleansboro, IL 62864
Phone: (618)643-2387
Fax: (618)643-3426
Newspaper. **Founded:** 1913. **Freq:** Weekly (Wed.). **Print Method:** Offset. **Trim Size:** 13 x 21 1/2. **Cols./Page:** 6. **Col. Width:** 28 nonpareils. **Col. Depth:** 301 agate lines. **Key Personnel:** Patrick J. Grubb, Managing Editor, Publisher; Louise H. Mugar, Associate Publisher, Manager, Advertising; Carissa Wright, Office Manager. **URL:** http://www.thenorthernlight.com. **Ad Rates:** GLR $1. **Remarks:** Accepts advertising. **Circ:** (Not Reported).

11084 ■ Princeton Times
McLeansboro Times-Leader
200 S Washington St.
Mcleansboro, IL 62864
Phone: (618)643-2387
Fax: (618)643-3426
Publication E-mail: production@bdtonline.com
Community newspaper. **Freq:** Weekly (Thurs.). **Print Method:** Offset. **Cols./Page:** 6. **Col. Width:** 24 nonpareils. **Col. Depth:** 301 agate lines. **Key Personnel:** Tammie Toler, Editor, General Manager. **URL:** http://www.ptonline.net. **Remarks:** Accepts classified advertising. **Circ:** (Not Reported).

MCLEANSBORO

Hamilton Co. Hamilton Co. (S). 30 m NE of Johnston City. Residential.

11085 ■ WMCL-AM - 1060
RR 1, PO Box 46A
McLeansboro, IL 62859
Phone: (618)435-8100
Fax: (618)435-8102
Email: wmcl@midwest.net
Format: Talk; Sports; News. **Simulcasts:** WISH-FM. **Owner:** Dana Communications, 303 N Main, Benton, IL 62812. **Founded:** 1968. **Key Personnel:** Dana Withers, Gen. Mgr., Owner; Dean Cramer, News Dir; Edna Rosenberger, Contact. **Wattage:** 2,500 Daytime; 002 Nig. **Ad Rates:** $19 for 30 seconds; $22 for 60 seconds. WQRL FM/ WISH FM. **URL:** http://www.wqrlradio.com.

MELROSE PARK

Cook Co. Cook Co. (NE). 12 m NW of Chicago. Manufactures plastic, cosmetic type products, screw machine, steel and rubber products, tractors, T.V. picture tubes, railroad supplies, paint, hydraulic presses, tools, dies, cement blocks.

11086 ■ Northlake Star-Sentinel
Shannon Publications Inc.
1440 W North Ave., Ste. 210
Melrose Park, IL 60160
Community newspaper. **Freq:** Weekly (Wed.). **Print Method:** Offset. **Trim Size:** 11 x 14. **Cols./Page:** 6. **Col. Width:** 20 nonpareils. **Col. Depth:** 170 agate lines. **URL:** http://www.newspaper-classifieds.com/directory/newsaddress/nbc/nbc_65.htm. **Ad Rates:** GLR $.45; BW $475; 4C $775; SAU $4.75. **Remarks:** Accepts advertising. **Circ:** Mon.-Sat. 2200.

MENDON

Adams Co. Adams Co. (NC). 11 m NNE of Quincy. Agriculture.

11087 ■ Mendon Dispatch-Times
Elliott Publishing Inc.

Circulation: ★ = AAM; △ or • = BPA; ♦ = CAC; ❑ = VAC; ⊕ = PO Statement; ‡ = Publisher's Report; Boldface figures = sworn; Light figures = estimated.

103 E Hannibal St.
Liberty, IL 62347
Phone: (217)645-3033
Fax: (217)645-3083
Local newspaper. **Freq:** Weekly. **Print Method:** Offset web. **Trim Size:** 11 1/4 x 17 1/2. **Cols./Page:** 5. **Col. Width:** 2 inches. **Col. Depth:** 16 inches. **Key Personnel:** Jim Elliott, President; Marcia Elliott, General Manager. **Subscription Rates:** $28 Out of state; $26 Out of area; $24 Individuals in Adams County. **URL:** http://www.elliott-publishing.com/. **Mailing address:** PO Box 198, Liberty, IL 62347. **Ad Rates:** GLR $2.75; BW $378; SAU $4. **Remarks:** Accepts advertising. **Circ:** Combined 3600.

MENDOTA

La Salle Co. La Salle Co. (N). 16 m N of La Salle. Manufactures woodworking machinery, farm implements, feed, concrete and building products, cranes, furnaces. Vegetable cannery. Grain, stock farms. Corn, hogs, cattle.

11088 ■ Mendota Reporter
News Media Corp.
703 Illinois Ave.
Mendota, IL 61342
Phone: (815)539-9396
Fax: (815)539-7862
Local newspaper. **Freq:** Weekly (Wed.). **Print Method:** Offset. **Trim Size:** 13 3/4 x 22 1/2. **Cols./Page:** 6. **Col. Width:** 12.5 picas. **Col. Depth:** 301 agate lines. **Key Personnel:** Mark Elston, General Manager; Kip Cheek, Publisher; Bonnie Morris, Editor. **USPS:** 339-100. **Subscription Rates:** $52 Individuals print + online (in area); $72.35 Individuals print + online (out of area). **URL:** http://www.mendotareporter.com. **Remarks:** Advertising accepted; rates available upon request. **Circ:** Paid ‡4400, Free ‡8000.

METAMORA

Woodford Co. Woodford Co. (NC). 18 m NE of Peoria. Furniture factory. Machine shop. Agriculture.

11089 ■ Tel-Star Cablevision Inc.
1295 Lourdes Rd.
Metamora, IL 61548
Fax: (309)383-2657
Free: 888-842-0258
Founded: 1989. **Cities Served:** 82 channels. **URL:** http://www.telstar-online.net.

METROPOLIS

Massac Co. Massac Co. (S). On Ohio River, 12 m NW of Paducah, Ky. Chemicals, coat hangers, gloves, railroad ties, hardwood lumber, pearl buttons, implement woodwork manufactured. Timber. Diversified farming. Corn, hay, soybeans. Cattle, hogs.

11090 ■ Metropolis Planet
Metropolis Planet
111 E 5th St.
Box 820
Metropolis, IL 62960
Phone: (618)524-2141
Fax: (618)524-4727
Publisher's E-mail: news@metropolisplanet.com
Local newspaper. **Freq:** Weekly (Wed.). **Print Method:** Offset. **Cols./Page:** 6. **Col. Width:** 1 7/8 inches. **Col. Depth:** 21 1/4 inches. **Key Personnel:** Linda Kennedy, Editor; Areia Hathcock, General Manager. **USPS:** 776-360. **Subscription Rates:** $26 Individuals 6 months; $29 Students 9 months; $39 Individuals; $66 Two years; $38 Elsewhere 6 months; $42 Students elsewhere; 9 months; $50.50 Elsewhere; $88 Elsewhere 2 years; $35 Individuals online; $9 Individuals print. **URL:** http://www.metropolisplanet.com. **Mailing address:** PO Box 820, Metropolis, IL 62960. **Ad Rates:** GLR $8.25; BW $4,660; 4C $26.60; PCI $7.30. **Remarks:** Accepts advertising. **Circ:** ‡4100.

KZMA-FM - See Poplar Bluff, MO

11091 ■ Rock 98.3 WJLI FM - 98.3
6120 Waldo Church Rd.
Metropolis, IL 62960
Phone: (618)564-9836
Format: Adult Contemporary. **Networks:** AP; ABC. **Owner:** Sun Media, Inc., at above address. **Formerly:** WRAJ-FM; WRIK-FM. **Operating Hours:** Continuous. **ADI:** Paducah,KY-Cape Girardeau,MO-Marion,IL. **Wattage:** 100,000. **Ad Rates:** $10 for 30 seconds; for 30 seconds; $15 for 60 seconds; $15 for 60 seconds. WRAJ-FM. **URL:** http://www.wrik.fm.

11092 ■ WGKY-FM - 95.9
339 Fairgrounds Rd.
Metropolis, IL 62960
Phone: (270)538-5251
Fax: (270)415-0599
Free: 866-711-0959
Format: Oldies. **Networks:** Jones Satellite. **Owner:** Withers Broadcasting Companies, 1822 N Court St., Marion, IL 62959, Ph: (303)242-5000. **Founded:** 1986. **Formerly:** WYMC-FM. **Operating Hours:** Continuous; 80% network, 20% local. **ADI:** Paducah,KY-Cape Girardeau,MO-Marion,IL. **Key Personnel:** Christie Bell, Contact, cbell@withersradio.net. **Wattage:** 3,000. **Ad Rates:** $8-12 for 30 seconds; $12-18 for 60 seconds. **URL:** http://www.959wgky.com.

11093 ■ WMOK-AM - 920
339 Fairgrounds Rd.
Metropolis, IL 62960
Phone: (618)524-4400
Fax: (618)524-3133
Free: 800-926-5590
Email: wmok920@frontier.com
Format: Country. **Networks:** CBS. **Owner:** Withers Broadcasting Co., 19 S Kingshighway, Cape Girardeau, MO 63703, Ph: (573)339-7000, Fax: (573)339-1550. **Founded:** 1951. **Operating Hours:** Continuous; 8% network; 92% local. **ADI:** Paducah,KY-Cape Girardeau,MO-Marion,IL. **Key Personnel:** Evan Spencer, Prog. Dir., evan.wmok@frontier.com; Rick Lambert, Gen. Mgr., rlambert@withersradio.net. **Wattage:** 5,000. **Ad Rates:** Noncommercial. **URL:** http://www.920wmok.com.

MIDLOTHIAN

Cook Co. Cook Co. (NE). 5 m S of Blue Island. Residential.

11094 ■ Burbank Stickney Independent
Southwest Messenger Press Inc.
3840 W 147th St.
Midlothian, IL 60445
Phone: (708)388-2425
Fax: (708)385-7811
Publisher's E-mail: spressnews@aol.com
Community newspaper. **Freq:** Weekly (Thurs.). **Print Method:** Offset. **Cols./Page:** 6. **Col. Width:** 1 3/4 inches. **Col. Depth:** 16 inches. **Subscription Rates:** $15 Individuals; $18 Out of area; $24 out of state. **URL:** http://www.moreenergy.com/illinois.html. **Ad Rates:** GLR $.66; BW $887.04; 4C $300; SAU $11.08; PCI $9.24. **Circ:** ‡5900.

MILFORD

Iroquois Co. Iroquois Co. (NE). 40 m N of Danville. Manufactures nuts, bolts, screws, electronic components and motors. Canning factory. Diversified farming. Hybrid seed corn, popcorn and bird seeds.

11095 ■ WJCZ-FM - 91.3
150 W Lincolnway, Ste. 2001
Valparaiso, IN 46383
Phone: (219)548-5800
Fax: (219)548-5808
Email: info@calvaryradionetwork.com
Format: Religious. **Owner:** Calvary Radio Network Inc., 150 West Lincolnway Ste. 2001, Valparaiso, IN 46383, Ph: (219)548-5800, Fax: (219)548-5808. **Key Personnel:** Jim Motshagen, Operations Mgr. **URL:** http://www.calvaryradionetwork.com.

MOKENA

Will Co.

11096 ■ Radiant Heating Report
Radiant Professionals Alliance
18927 Hickory Creek Dr., Ste. 220
Mokena, IL 60448
Fax: (708)479-6023
Free: 877-427-6601
Publisher's E-mail: RPA@radiantprofessionalsalliance.org
Magazine showcasing newest technology, products and training for radiant heating/cooling professionals. **Freq:** Annual. **Subscription Rates:** Included in membership. **URL:** http://www.pmmag.com/topics/2751-radiant-heating-report. **Remarks:** Advertising not accepted. **Circ:** (Not Reported).

MOLINE

Rock Island Co. Rock Island Co. (NW). On Mississippi River, opposite Davenport, Iowa., 168 m SW of Chicago. Blackhawk Community College. Manufactures agricultural implements, traffic signals, heating and ventilating equipment, paint, tools and dies, electric welding apparatus, candy; fabricated steel; forgings; elevators and escalators; iron foundry.

11097 ■ ADextra
Moline Dispatch Publishing Co.
1720 5th Ave.
Moline, IL 61265
Phone: (309)764-4344
Fax: (309)764-8868
Publisher's E-mail: press@qconline.com
Shopping guide. **Freq:** Weekly (Fri.). **Key Personnel:** Jerry Taylor, Editor, phone: (309)757-4924; Val Yazbec, Director, Advertising, phone: (309)757-4958. **URL:** http://www.qconline.com/. **Circ:** Non-paid ♦**23570**.

11098 ■ ARA Rental Management
American Rental Association
1900 19th St.
Moline, IL 61265-4179
Phone: (309)764-2475
Fax: (309)764-1533
Free: 800-334-2177
Magazine covering all market segments such as light construction & DIY, construction & industrial and party, event & wedding rental. **Freq:** Monthly. **URL:** http://www.rentalmanagementmag.com; http://www.ararental.org/Publications/RM-Group/Rental-Management-Magazine. **Ad Rates:** BW $3580; 4C $4760. **Remarks:** Accepts advertising. **Circ:** (Not Reported).

11099 ■ The Chieftain
Black Hawk College
6600 34th ave
Moline, IL 61265
Phone: (309)796-5000
Free: 800-334-1311
Publisher's E-mail: info@bhc.edu
Collegiate newspaper. **Founded:** 1970. **Freq:** Weekly. **Print Method:** Offset. **Trim Size:** 13 1/2 x 21. **Cols./Page:** 5. **Col. Width:** 24 nonpareils. **Col. Depth:** 224 agate lines. **Key Personnel:** Gayle Grundstrom, Editor-in-Chief. **Alt. Formats:** PDF. **URL:** http://www.bhc.edu. **Ad Rates:** PCI $5. **Remarks:** Accepts advertising. **Circ:** Free ‡2000.

11100 ■ The Dispatch
Moline Dispatch Publishing Co.
1720 5th Ave.
Moline, IL 61265
Phone: (309)764-4344
Fax: (309)764-8868
Publication E-mail: sysop@qconline.com press@qconline.com
Newspaper with a Republican orientation. **Founded:** 1868. **Freq:** Daily and Sat. (morn.). **Print Method:** Offset. **Cols./Page:** 6. **Col. Width:** 25 nonpareils. **Col. Depth:** 21 1/2 nonpareils. **Key Personnel:** Jerry Taylor, Editor, phone: (309)757-4924; Val Yazbec, Director, Advertising, phone: (309)757-4958. **Subscription Rates:** $4.85 Individuals /week (home delivery/carrier collect/office pay); $5.10 Individuals /week (motor route). **URL:** http://qconline.com. **Remarks:** Accepts advertising. **Circ:** Mon. ♦**24798**, Tues. ♦**24694**, Wed. ♦**24893**, Sat. ♦**25201**, Sun. ♦**28379**.

11101 ■ The Gold Book
Moline Dispatch Publishing Co.
1720 5th Ave.
Moline, IL 61265
Phone: (309)764-4344
Fax: (309)764-8868
Publisher's E-mail: press@qconline.com
Magazine covering the Quad-cities. **Founded:** 1985. **Freq:** Monthly. **Print Method:** Offset. **Trim Size:** 6 x 9. **Cols./Page:** 4. **URL:** http://www.qconline.com/mdpc/webgold.html. **Remarks:** Advertising accepted; rates available upon request. **Circ:** (Not Reported).

11102 ■ Rental Management: Official Magazine of the American Rental Association
American Rental Association
1900 19th St.
Moline, IL 61265-4179
Phone: (309)764-2475
Fax: (309)764-1533
Free: 800-334-2177
Magazine for business owners who rent equipment to consumers, industries, institutions and commercial firms. **Freq:** Monthly. **Print Method:** Web offset. **Trim Size:** 8 1/4 x 10 7/8. **Cols./Page:** 3. **Col. Width:** 2 1/4 inches. **Col. Depth:** 10 inches. **Key Personnel:** Ken Hughes, Publisher; Wayne Walley, Editor; Erin Jorgensen, Managing Editor. **ISSN:** 0098--8529 (print). **Subscription Rates:** Included in membership. **URL:** http://www.rentalmanagementmag.com. **Ad Rates:** BW $3,510; 4C $4,665. **Remarks:** Accepts advertising. **Circ:** Non-paid △**10454**, Paid △**9666**.

11103 ■ Rock Island Argus
Moline Dispatch Publishing Co.
1720 5th Ave.
Moline, IL 61265-7907
Publisher's E-mail: press@qconline.com
General newspaper. **Freq:** Daily. **Print Method:** Offset. **Trim Size:** 13 x 21 1/2. **Cols./Page:** 6. **Col. Width:** 1 7/8 inches. **Col. Depth:** 21 1/2 inches. **Key Personnel:** Jerry Taylor, Editor, Publisher. **Subscription Rates:** $25 Individuals 12 weeks. **URL:** http://www.qconline.com. **Remarks:** Accepts advertising. **Circ:** Paid ♦**10563**, Paid ♦**11163**.

11104 ■ WQAD-TV - 8
3003 Park 16th St.
Moline, IL 61265
Phone: (309)764-8888
Email: news@wqad.com
Format: News. **Networks:** ABC. **Owner:** Local TV L.L. C., at above address. **Founded:** 1963. **Operating Hours:** Continuous. **ADI:** Daveport,IA-Rock Island, Moline,IL. **Key Personnel:** Alan Baker, News Dir. **Wattage:** 1,000,000 ERP H. **Ad Rates:** Advertising accepted; rates available upon request. **URL:** http://www.wqad.com.

11105 ■ WQPT-TV - 24
3300 River Dr.
Moline, IL 61265
Phone: (309)764-2400
Fax: (309)764-2410
Format: Educational. **Networks:** Public Broadcasting Service (PBS). **Owner:** Black Hawk College, 6600 34th ave, Moline, IL 61265, Ph: (309)796-5000, Free: 800-334-1311. **Founded:** 1983. **Operating Hours:** Continuous. **ADI:** Daveport,IA-Rock Island, Moline,IL. **Key Personnel:** Rick Best, Gen. Mgr., bestr@bhc.edu; Jerry Myers, Program Mgr., myersj@bhc.edu; Lora Adams, Dir. of Mktg., adamsl@bhc.edu. **Wattage:** 30,000. **URL:** http://www.wqpt.org.

MOMENCE

Kankakee Co. Kankakee Co. (E). 14 m E of Kankakee. Stone quarries. Manufactures textiles, health and dog foods, venetian blinds, steel products, pharmaceuticals, truck bodies. Diversified farming. Milk condensery.

11106 ■ Momence Progress-Reporter
The Momence Progress-Reporter
110 W River St.
Momence, IL 60954
Phone: (815)472-2000
Fax: (815)472-3877
Publisher's E-mail: m.reporter@mchsi.com
Newspaper with a Republican orientation. **Freq:** Weekly (Wed.). **Print Method:** Offset. **Cols./Page:** 5. **Col. Width:** 22 nonpareils. **Col. Depth:** 224 agate lines. **Subscription Rates:** $35 Individuals print and online; $28 Individuals print (in county); $30 Out of country print ; $33 Individuals print ; $25 Individuals online. **URL:** http://momenceprogressreporter.com. **Ad Rates:** GLR $.400; BW $204; SAU $2.90; PCI $2.75. **Remarks:** Accepts advertising. **Circ:** ‡2150.

MONMOUTH

Warren Co. Warren Co. (W). 16 m W of Galesburg. Monmouth College. Warren Achievement School and Center for Handicapped. Manufactures pottery, farm implements, boats, toys, feed. Diversified farming. Beef cattle, hogs, corn, soybeans.

11107 ■ Classical Journal
Classical Association of the Middle West and South
Dept. of Classics
Monmouth College
700 E Broadway
Monmouth, IL 61462
Phone: (309)457-2284
Fax: (815)346-2565
Publisher's E-mail: camws@camws.org
Classical language and literature journal. **Freq:** Quarterly October-November, December-January, February-March, April-May. **Print Method:** Letterpress. **Trim Size:** 6 x 9. **Cols./Page:** 2. **Col. Width:** 25 nonpareils. **Col. Depth:** 105 agate lines. **Key Personnel:** Laurel Fulkerson, Editor; Jeane Neumann, Editor. **ISSN:** 0009--8353 (print). **Subscription Rates:** $123 U.S. and Canada libraries, print only; $143 Other countries libraries; $55 Individuals print only; Included in membership. **Alt. Formats:** PDF. **URL:** http://cj.camws.org. **Ad Rates:** BW $250. **Remarks:** Accepts advertising. **Circ:** ‡3000.

11108 ■ The Courier
Monmouth College
700 E Broadway
Monmouth, IL 61462
Phone: (309)457-2190
Free: 800-747-2687
Publication E-mail: courier@monm.edu
Collegiate newspaper. **Founded:** 1867. **Freq:** Irregular. **Print Method:** Offset. **Trim Size:** 10.25 x 16. **Cols./Page:** 5. **Col. Width:** 11 picas. **Col. Depth:** 180 agate lines. **URL:** http://www.monmouthcollegecourier.com/. **Formerly**: The Monmouth Oracle; The Oracle. **Ad Rates:** GLR $.393; BW $396; 4C $516; PCI $6. **Remarks:** Advertising accepted; rates available upon request. **Circ:** Free 1350.

11109 ■ Daily Review Atlas
GateHouse Media Inc.
400 S Main St.
Monmouth, IL 61462
Phone: (309)734-3176
Local newspaper. **Founded:** 1846. **Freq:** Mon.-Sat. (eve.). **Print Method:** Offset. **Cols./Page:** 6. **Col. Width:** 1.76 inches. **Col. Depth:** 21 inches. **Key Personnel:** Tony Scott, Publisher. **Subscription Rates:** $5.99 Individuals /month; online; $2 Individuals /week; print + online. **URL:** http://www.reviewatlas.com/. **Ad Rates:** BW $948; 4C $1,128; SAU $7.95; PCI $7.35. **Remarks:** Accepts advertising. **Circ:** ‡4,000.

11110 ■ WAIK-AM - 1590
55 Public Sq.
Monmouth, IL 61462
Phone: (309)734-9452
Fax: (390)734-3276
Format: News; Talk; Sports. **Networks:** ABC. **Founded:** 1957. **Formerly**: WQUB-AM. **Operating Hours**: Continuous. **Key Personnel:** Vanessa Wetterling, Gen. Mgr., vanessa.wetterling@prairiecommunications.net. **Wattage:** 5,000. **Ad Rates:** Noncommercial. Combined advertising rates available with WBYS-AM/FM. **URL:** http://prcmonmouth.wix.com.

11111 ■ WMOI-FM - 97.7
55 Public Sq.
Monmouth, IL 61462
Phone: (309)734-9452
Fax: (309)734-3276
Format: Adult Contemporary. **Founded:** 1977. **Formerly**: WDRL-FM. **Operating Hours:** Continuous; 100% local. **Key Personnel:** Vanessa Wetterling, Gen. Mgr., vanessa.wetterling@prairiecommunications.net. **Wattage:** 6,000. **Ad Rates:** $11.15-16.50 for 30 seconds; $14.45-35 for 60 seconds. **URL:** http://prcmonmouth.wix.com.

11112 ■ WRAM-AM - 1330
55 Public Sq.
Monmouth, IL 61462
Phone: (309)734-9452
Fax: (309)734-3276
Format: Country. **Founded:** 1957. **Operating Hours**: Continuous; 90% local. **Key Personnel:** Vanessa Wetterling, Gen. Mgr., vanessa.wetterling@prairiecommunications.net. **Local Programs**: *The Fresh Grocer, Successful Farming.* **Wattage:** 1,000. **Ad Rates:** $10.15-16.50 for 30 seconds; $12.45-20.75 for 60 seconds. **URL:** http://prcmonmouth.wix.com.

MONTICELLO

Piatt Co. Piatt Co. (C). 25 m NE of Decatur. Agriculture.

11113 ■ WCZQ-FM - 105.5
PO Box 105
Monticello, IL 61856
Phone: (217)762-2588
Free: 800-962-5590
Email: wczq@piatt.com
Format: Hip Hop. **Owner:** NextMedia, 6312 S Fiddlers Green Cir., Ste. 205 E, Greenwood Village, CO 80111, Ph: (303)694-9118, Fax: (303)694-4940. **Founded:** 1972. **Formerly**: WVLJ-FM. **Operating Hours:** Continuous; 100% local. **ADI:** Springfield-Decatur-Champaign, IL. **Wattage**: 3,000. **Ad Rates:** $17-4 for 30 seconds; $7-24 for 60 seconds. **URL:** http://www.wczq.piatt.com.

MOOSEHEART

Kane Co. (NE). 5 m N of Aurora. Residential.

11114 ■ Moose Magazine
Moose International
155 S International Dr.
Mooseheart, IL 60539-1169
Phone: (630)906-3658
Publisher's E-mail: helpdesk@mooseintl.org
Freq: 6/year. **Print Method:** Offset/Gravure. **Trim Size:** 8 x 10.75. **Cols./Page:** 3. **Col. Width:** 13.5 picas. **Col. Depth:** 10 inches. **Key Personnel:** Brenda Buschbacher, Executive Editor; Kurt N. Wehrmeister, Director, Publications; William B. Airey, Contact. **ISSN:** 1063--6226 (print). **Subscription Rates:** Included in membership. **URL:** http://www.mooseintl.org/index.php/moose-magazine. **Remarks:** Accepts advertising. **Circ:** Controlled ‡950000, 1300000.

MORRIS

Grundy Co. Grundy Co. (NE). On Illinois River and Lakes to Gulf Waterway, 23 m SW of Joliet. Synthetic natural gas. Manufactures aluminum sheet, rubber products, vending machines, fire bricks, explosives, industrial resins, paper board. Stock farms.

11115 ■ Morris Daily Herald
Shaw Media
1804 N Division St.
Morris, IL 60450
Phone: (815)942-3221
Fax: (815)942-0988
Publication E-mail: news@morrisdailyherald.com
General newspaper. **Freq:** Daily Tuesday-Saturday. **Print Method:** Offset. **Trim Size:** 22 3/4 x 27 1/2. **Cols./Page:** 6. **Col. Width:** 2 1/16 inches. **Col. Depth:** 21 1/2 inches. **Key Personnel:** Rich Ponulak, Director, Advertising; Kate Schott, Editor; Steve Vanisko, Director, Advertising, phone: (815)280-4103; Patrick Graziano, Managing Editor. **USPS:** 363-560. **Subscription Rates:** $1.50 Individuals /week; mail delivery; 5 days a week; $39 Individuals 26 weeks (Sunday through Friday); $26 Individuals 26 weeks (Saturday only); $1 Individuals /week; mail delivery; Saturday only. **URL:** http://www.morrisdailyherald.com; http://www.shawmedia.com. **Ad Rates:** BW $1,096.50; 4C $1,246.50; PCI $9.20. **Remarks:** Accepts advertising. **Circ:** Paid ♦**4944**.

11116 ■ Comcast Cable
1150 E Washington St.
Morris, IL 60450
Founded: 1963. **Key Personnel:** Brian L. Roberts, Chairman; Neil Smit, President, CEO. **Cities Served:** 142 channels. **URL:** http://www.comcast.com.

11117 ■ WCFL-FM - 104.7
852 School St.
Morris, IL 60450
Phone: (815)942-4400
Fax: (815)942-4401
Free: 800-520-9235
Owner: Illinois Bible Institute, c/o Lake Williamson Christian Conference Ctr. 17280 Lakeside Dr., Carlinville, IL 62626, Ph: (217)854-4820. **Founded:** 1994. **Formerly**: WLLZ-FM. **Wattage:** 50,000 ERP. **Mailing address:** PO Box 111, Morris, IL 60450. **URL:** http://www.wcfl.com.

Circulation: ★ = AAM; △ or • = BPA; ♦ = CAC; ❑ = VAC; ⊕ = PO Statement; ‡ = Publisher's Report; Boldface figures = sworn; Light figures = estimated.

11118 ■ WCSJ-AM - 1550
219 W Washington St.
Morris, IL 60450
Phone: (815)941-1000
Fax: (815)941-9300
Format: News; Sports. **Simulcasts:** WCSJ-FM. **Owner:** DMR Media, at above address. **Founded:** 1964. **Operating Hours**: 5:00 a.m. - 7:30 p.m. Monday - Friday; 6:00 a.m. - 10:15 a.m. Saturday; 9:05 a.m. - Noon Sunday. **Key Personnel:** Dick Steele, Sports Dir., Prog. Dir.; Lorn Brown, Dir. of Production; Dean Tambling, News Dir.; Ann Jones, Dir. of Traffic; Mike Williams, Sports Dir., mike.williams@nelsonmultimedia.com. **Wattage**: 250 day; 006 night. **Ad Rates:** Advertising accepted; rates available upon request. **URL:** http://www.wcsjfm.com.

MORRISON

Whiteside Co. Whiteside Co. NW. 15 m W of Sterling. Automatic control devices, furniture, oils manufactured. Limestone quarries. Grain, dairy, stock farms. Hay.

11119 ■ WZZT-FM - 102.7
PO Box 1508
Mount Vernon, IL 62864-1508
Phone: (618)242-3500
Format: Oldies. **Owner:** Withers Broadcasting Co. of Rock River, LLC, at above address. **Founded:** 1992. **Operating Hours**: Continuous. **Key Personnel:** Sherry Smith, Bus. Mgr.; Brian Zschiesche, Gen. Mgr. **Wattage**: 6,000. **Ad Rates:** $15 per unit.

MORTON GROVE

Cook Co.

11120 ■ Agency Sales Magazine
Manufacturers' Agents National Association
6321 W Dempster St., Ste. 110
Morton Grove, IL 60053
Phone: (949)859-4040
Fax: (949)855-2973
Free: 877-626-2776
Publisher's E-mail: mana@manaonline.org
Magazine for manufacturers' agents and manufacturers. Includes tax developments and tips, management aids for manufacturers and agents, legal bulletins, trend-identifying market data, classified ads. **Freq:** Monthly. **Print Method:** Offset. **Trim Size:** 8 3/8 x 10 7/8. **Cols./Page:** 3. **Col. Width:** 28 nonpareils. **Col. Depth:** 137 agate lines. **Key Personnel:** Bert Holtje, Editor; Jack Foster, Editor; Jane Holm, Director, Advertising. **ISSN:** 0749--2332 (print). **Subscription Rates:** $109 Individuals; $149 Other countries. **Alt. Formats:** CD-ROM. **URL:** http://www.manaonline.org/agency-sales-magazine. **Ad Rates:** GLR $15; BW $1,166; 4C $1,714; PCI $96; BW $2074; 4C $3171. **Remarks:** Accepts advertising. **Circ:** ‡9000.

MOUNT CARMEL

Wabash Co. Wabash Co. (SE). On Wabash River, 25 m SW of Vincennes, Ind. Manufactures radio coils, tools, electronic components, women's dresses, flintkote roofing. Coal mines. Oil well. Agriculture. Corn, wheat, soybeans.

11121 ■ Daily Republican Register
Daily Republican Register
115 E 4th St.
Mount Carmel, IL 62863-0550
Phone: (618)262-5144
Fax: (618)263-4437
Free: 877-598-7604
Publisher's E-mail: news@mtcarmelregister.com
General newspaper. **Freq:** Daily except Wed., Sat., and Sun. **Print Method:** Offset. **Trim Size:** 11 1/2 x 12 1/2. **Cols./Page:** 6. **Col. Width:** 1.833 inches. **Col. Depth:** 294 agate lines. **Key Personnel:** Phil Summers, Publisher; Andrea Howe, Editor. **USPS:** 145-780. **Subscription Rates:** $94.25 Individuals carrier; $106.25 Individuals motor route; $90.25 By mail in Wabash County; $115.25 By mail surrounding counties; $168 By mail out or area. **URL:** http://tristate-media.com/drr/news/local_news. **Mailing address:** PO Box 550, Mount Carmel, IL 62863-0550. **Ad Rates:** BW $1,312.92; 4C $1,472.92; PCI $10.42. **Remarks:** Accepts classified advertising. **Circ:** (Not Reported).

11122 ■ WSJD-FM - 100.5
328 Market St.
Mount Carmel, IL 62863
Phone: (618)262-4102
Fax: (618)262-4103
Format: Oldies. **Founded:** 1960. **Formerly**: WYER-FM; WRBT-FM. **Operating Hours**: Continuous. **Key Personnel:** Scott Allen, Dir. of Programs. **Wattage**: 6,000. **Ad Rates:** Noncommercial. $10-15 for 30 seconds. Combined advertising rates available with WVMC-AM.

11123 ■ WVJC-FM - 89.1
2200 College Dr.
Mount Carmel, IL 62863
Phone: (618)262-8641
Format: Alternative/New Music/Progressive. **Networks:** AP. **Owner:** Illinois Eastern Community College District 529, 233 E Chestnut, Olney, IL 62450, Ph: (618)393-2982, Fax: (618)392-4816, Free: 866-529-4322. **Founded:** 1973. **Operating Hours**: Continuous; 100% local. **ADI:** Evansville, IN (Madisonville, KY). **Key Personnel:** Kyle Peach, Contact, peachk@iecc.edu. **Wattage**: 50,000. **Ad Rates:** Noncommercial. **URL:** http://myweb.iecc.edu/wvjc/.

11124 ■ WVMC-AM
606 Market St.
Mount Carmel, IL 62863
Phone: (618)262-4102
Fax: (618)262-4103
Email: wsjd@midwest.net
Owner: Southern Wabash Communications Corp., at above address. **Founded:** 1949. **Formerly**: WYER-AM. **Ad Rates:** Accepts Advertising. **URL:** http://www.wvmc.com.

11125 ■ WYNG-FM - 94.9
127 W Third St.
Mount Carmel, IL 62863
Phone: (618)263-3500
Fax: (618)263-3520
Format: Adult Contemporary. **Networks:** CBS. **Founded:** 1964. **Operating Hours**: Continuous; 5% network, 95% local. **Key Personnel:** Sally Voigt, Account Exec. **Wattage**: 50,000. **Ad Rates:** $50-90 for 30 seconds. WGBF-AM, WGBF-FM, WDKS-FM, WKRI-FM. **URL:** http://www.wyngfm.com.

MOUNT PROSPECT

Cook Co. Cook Co. (NE). 24 m NW of Chicago. Industrial Park. Central business district. Shopping centers. Manufactures copying equipment, pharmaceutical products.

11126 ■ Critical Care Medicine
Society of Critical Care Medicine
500 Midway Dr.
Mount Prospect, IL 60056
Phone: (847)827-6869
Fax: (847)827-6886
Publisher's E-mail: info@sccm.org
Interdisciplinary journal for ICU and CCU specialists. **Freq:** Monthly. **Print Method:** Offset. **Trim Size:** 8 1/8 x 10 7/8. **Cols./Page:** 2. **Col. Width:** 32 nonpareils. **Col. Depth:** 119 agate lines. **Key Personnel:** Timothy G. Buchman, PhD, Editor-in-Chief; Joseph E. Parrillo, MD, Editor; Sophie Tosta, Managing Editor. **ISSN:** 009-0-3493 (print); **EISSN:** 153-0-0293 (electronic). **Subscription Rates:** $532 Individuals; $1107 Institutions; $672 Individuals; $1296 Institutions; $695 Other countries; $1319 Institutions, other countries. **URL:** http://journals.lww.com/ccmjournal/pages/default.aspx. **Ad Rates:** BW $2440; 4C $4335. **Remarks:** Accepts classified advertising. **Circ:** Paid ‡18500, 15000.

11127 ■ National Catholic Forester
National Catholic Society of Foresters
320 S School St.
Mount Prospect, IL 60056
Phone: (847)342-4500
Fax: (847)342-4556
Free: 800-344-6273
Magazine informing membership of new products and activities. **Freq:** Quarterly. **Subscription Rates:** Free. **URL:** http://www.ncsf.com/; http://www.ncsf.com/magazine_archives.html. **Remarks:** Advertising not accepted. **Circ:** 32400.

11128 ■ NSGA Now Magazine
National Sporting Goods Association
1601 Feehanville Dr., Ste. 300
Mount Prospect, IL 60056
Phone: (847)296-6742
Fax: (847)391-9827
Free: 800-815-5422
Publisher's E-mail: info@nsga.org
Membership magazine focusing on sporting goods retailing. **Freq:** Bimonthly. **Print Method:** Offset. **Trim Size:** 8 1/2 x 11. **Key Personnel:** Paul M. Prince, Vice President. **ISSN:** 1045--2087 (print). **Subscription Rates:** Free; $50 Nonmembers. **URL:** http://nsga.org/news/publications; http://nsga.org/news/publications/NSGA_Now. **Formerly**: NSGA Retail Focus. **Ad Rates:** BW $1,264; 4C $2,205. **Remarks:** Accepts advertising. **Circ:** Paid ‡2300.

11129 ■ Pediatric Critical Care Medicine
Society of Critical Care Medicine
c/o Society of Critical Care Medicine
500 Midway Dr.
Mount Prospect, IL 60056
Phone: (847)827-6869
Fax: (847)827-6886
Publication E-mail: journals@sccm.org
Peer-reviewed journal covering pediatric critical care medicine and critical care neonatology for pediatricians, neonatologists and others worldwide. **Freq:** 9/year. **Key Personnel:** Patrick M. Kochanek, MD, MCCM, Editor; John Ewers, Publisher; Patrick M. Kochanek, MD, Editor; Sophie M. Tosta, Managing Editor. **ISSN:** 1529--7535 (print); **EISSN:** 1947--3893 (electronic). **Subscription Rates:** $383 Individuals; $766 Two years; $743 Institutions; $1486 Two years; $201 Members; $402 Two years; $186 Individuals in-training; $372 Two years in-training; $477 Other countries individual; $815 Other countries institution. **URL:** http://journals.lww.com/pccmjournal/pages/default.aspx; http://www.sccm.org/Member-Center/Journals/Pages/Pediatric-Critical-Care-Medicine.aspx; http://www.lww.com/Product/1529-7535. **Ad Rates:** BW $965; 4C $1,455. **Remarks:** Accepts advertising. **Circ:** 2480.

MOUNT PULASKI

Logan Co. Logan Co. (C). 11 m SE of Lincoln. Manufactures corn cob products, molasses, feed. Diversified farming. Corn, wheat, soybeans, hay.

11130 ■ Mt. Pulaski Weekly News
Times
c/o Michael Lakin, Publisher
311 S Washington St.
Mount Pulaski, IL 62548
Phone: (217)792-5557
Publisher's E-mail: times@frontiernet.net
Community newspaper. **Founded:** 1884. **Freq:** Monthly. **Print Method:** Offset. **Cols./Page:** 5. **Key Personnel:** Michael Lakin, Editor. **USPS:** 441-400. **Subscription Rates:** Free. **URL:** http://www.mtpulaskiil.com. **Formerly**: Weekly News. **Mailing address:** PO Box 114, Mount Pulaski, IL 62548. **Ad Rates:** GLR $6; SAU $6; PCI $6. **Remarks:** Accepts advertising. **Circ:** 3300.

MOUNT VERNON

Jefferson Co. Jefferson Co. (S). 20 m SE of Centralia. Manufactures radial tires, auto radiators, power cores, transformers, dryers and evaporators, feed. Diversified farming. Fruits, poultry, corn, soybeans.

11131 ■ Register-News
Register-News
911 Broadway St.
Mount Vernon, IL 62864
Phone: (618)242-0113
Fax: (618)242-8286
General newspaper. **Founded:** 1871. **Freq:** except Mon, Sat. **Print Method:** Offset. **Cols./Page:** 6. **Col. Width:** 24 nonpareils. **Col. Depth:** 294 agate lines. **Key Personnel:** Bonnie Pratt, Publisher. **Subscription Rates:** $95 Individuals; $95 By mail. **URL:** http://www.register-news.com. **Ad Rates:** BW $1,464.15; 4C $1,674.15; SAU $11.35. **Remarks:** Accepts advertising. **Circ:** (Not Reported).

11132 ■ Charter Communications
5111 Lake Ter. N
Mount Vernon, IL 62864
Free: 888-438-2427
Key Personnel: Neil Smit, CEO, President; Marwan

Fawaz, Chief Tech. Ofc., Exec. VP. **Cities Served:** 95 channels. **URL:** http://www.charter.com.

11133 ■ K203EF-FM - 88.5
PO Box 391
Twin Falls, ID 83303
Fax: (208)736-1958
Free: 800-357-4226
Format: Religious; Contemporary Christian. **Owner:** CSN International, PO Box 391, Twin Falls, ID 83303, Ph: (208)736-1958, Fax: (208)736-1958, Free: 800-357-4226. **Key Personnel:** Ray Gorney, Dir. of Engg.; Kelly Carlson, Dir. of Engg.; Mike Kestler, Contact; Don Mills, Music Dir. **URL:** http://www.csnradio.com.

11134 ■ WAPO-FM - 90.5
PO Box 3206
Tupelo, MS 38803
Format: Religious. **Owner:** American Family Radio, at above address. **Founded:** 1977. **URL:** http://www.afr.net.

11135 ■ WDML-FM - 106.9
PO Box 1591
Mount Vernon, IL 62864-0031
Phone: (618)242-3333
Fax: (618)242-2490
Free: 800-491-2980
Format: Classic Rock; Alternative/New Music/Progressive. **Operating Hours:** Continuous. **Wattage:** 3,000. **URL:** http://www.wdml.com.

WEBQ-AM - See Harrisburg

11136 ■ WMIX-AM
PO Box 1508
Mount Vernon, IL 62864-1508
Phone: (618)242-3500
Fax: (618)242-4444
Format: Adult Contemporary. **Networks:** Mutual Broadcasting System. **Owner:** Withers Broadcasting Co. of Illinois, PO Box 1508, Mount Vernon, IL 62864. **Founded:** 1946. **Wattage:** 5,000 Day; 1,500 Nig. **Ad Rates:** $15-26 for 30 seconds; $21-32 for 60 seconds.

WSDR-AM - See Sterling, IL

WSSQ-FM - See Sterling, IL

11137 ■ WVSI-FM - 88.9
1100 Lincoln Dr., Ste. 1003
SIU Mailcode 6602
Carbondale, IL 62901-4306
Phone: (618)453-4343
Fax: (618)453-6186
Free: 866-498-5561
Email: info@wsiu.org
Format: Public Radio. **Owner:** Southern Illinois University, 1263 Lincoln Dr., Carbondale, IL 62901. **Operating Hours:** Continuous. **Key Personnel:** Jeff Williams, News Dir., Div. Dir. **Wattage:** 6,000. **Ad Rates:** Advertising accepted; rates available upon request. **URL:** http://www.wsiu.org.

WZZT-FM - See Morrison, IL

MUNDELEIN

Lake Co.

11138 ■ The Classical Bulletin
Bolchazy-Carducci Publishers Inc.
1570 Baskin Rd.
Mundelein, IL 60060
Phone: (847)526-4344
Fax: (847)526-2867
Free: 800-392-6453
Publisher's E-mail: info@bolchazy.com
Scholarly Journal on classical languages, history, and literature. **Freq:** Semiannual. **Print Method:** Offset. **Trim Size:** 6 x 9. **Cols./Page:** 1. **Key Personnel:** Shannon N. Byrne, Editor; Edmund P. Cueva, Editor. **ISSN:** 0009-+8337 (print). **Circ:** (Not Reported).

MURPHYSBORO

Jackson Co.

11139 ■ Murphysboro American
GateHouse Media Inc.
1400 Walnut St.
Murphysboro, IL 62966
Community newspaper. **Freq:** Weekly. **Trim Size:** 6 x 12. **Cols./Page:** 6. **Col. Width:** 12 picas. **Col. Depth:** 21 1/2 inches. **Key Personnel:** Tom Tiernan, Publisher. **Mailing address:** PO Box 550, Murphysboro, IL 62966. **Remarks:** Accepts advertising. **Circ:** (Not Reported).

11140 ■ WINI-AM - 1420
10519 Hwy. 149, Ste. A
Murphysboro, IL 62966
Phone: (618)684-2128
Fax: (618)687-4318
Free: 800-861-6800
Format: News; Oldies; Sports. **Simulcasts:** WINI. **Networks:** People's Network. **Founded:** 1954. **Operating Hours:** Week Days 5 am- 5 am ; Saturday 7 am - Midnight;. **Key Personnel:** Nancy Engel, Operations Mgr. **Wattage:** 420 day; 500 night. **Ad Rates:** $10.50 for 30 seconds; $12.50 for 60 seconds. **URL:** http://www.southernillinoisiscool.com.

NAPERVILLE

Will Co. Du Page Co. (SW). 29 m W of Chicago. North Central College. Manufactures carbon, concrete products, machine tools, cotton and burlap bags, chewing gum, dietetic foods, cereal. Research and development center. Boiler works.

11141 ■ Business Ledger
Ledger Publishing Co.
1260 Iroquois Ave., Ste. 200
Naperville, IL 60563
Phone: (630)428-8788
Publication E-mail: blnews@dailyherald.com
Regional business newspaper covering DuPage, Northwest Cook County and the Fox Valley. **Founded:** Apr. 1993. **Freq:** 26/yr. **Key Personnel:** James E. Elsener, Manager; Kim Mikus, Editor. **ISSN:** 1082-8397 (print). **Subscription Rates:** $45 Individuals; $70 Two years. **URL:** http://dhbusinessledger.com. **Formerly:** Northwest Business Ledger; DuPage Business Ledger. **Ad Rates:** BW $1,450; 4C $1,845. **Remarks:** Advertising accepted; rates available upon request. **Circ:** 10000.

11142 ■ Catholic Forester Magazine
Catholic Order of Foresters
355 Shuman Blvd.
Naperville, IL 60563
Phone: (630)983-4900
Free: 800-552-0145
Publication E-mail: magazine@catholicforester.com
Fraternal and general interest magazine. **Freq:** Quarterly. **Print Method:** Offset. **Trim Size:** 8 1/4 x 10 3/4. **Cols./Page:** 2 and 3. **Col. Width:** 40 and 26 nonpareils. **Col. Depth:** 137 agate lines. **Key Personnel:** Danielle Marsh, Contact. **ISSN:** 0008--8048 (print). **Subscription Rates:** Included in membership. **URL:** http://www.catholicforester.org/membership. **Mailing address:** PO Box 3012, Naperville, IL 60566-7012. **Remarks:** Advertising not accepted. **Circ:** Free ‡140000.

11143 ■ Journal of Urgent Care Medicine
Urgent Care Association of America
387 Shuman Blvd., Ste. 235W
Naperville, IL 60563
Phone: (331)472-3739
Fax: (331)457-5439
Free: 877-698-2262
Publisher's E-mail: info@ucaoa.org
Freq: 11/year. **Subscription Rates:** Free to qualified subscribers online; Included in membership print; $50 Nonmembers. **URL:** http://www.ucaoa.org/general/custom.asp?page=ePublications. **Ad Rates:** PCI $180. **Remarks:** Accepts advertising. **Circ:** (Not Reported).

11144 ■ WONC-FM - 89.1
30 N Brainard St.
Naperville, IL 60566
Phone: (630)637-8989
Fax: (630)637-5900
Format: Album-Oriented Rock (AOR). **Networks:** Independent. **Owner:** North Central College, 30 N Brainard St., Naperville, IL 60540, Ph: (630)637-5100, Fax: (630)637-5989. **Founded:** 1968. **Operating Hours:** Continuous; 100% local. **Key Personnel:** John Madormo, Gen. Mgr., jvmadormo@noctrl.edu; Paige Spangler, Dir. of Programs. **Local Programs:** *From the Upper Deck*, Sunday 6:00 p.m. - 8:00 p.m.; *Mission Rock*. **Wattage:** 1,500. **Ad Rates:** Noncommercial; underwriting available. **Mailing address:** PO Box 3063, Naperville, IL 60540. **URL:** http://wonc.org.

NEWTON

Jasper Co. Jasper Co. (SE). 50 m SW of Terre Haute, Ind. Manufactures academic caps and gowns, choir and clergy robes, girls gym suits, brooms, handles, battery cables, automotive wiring hardness, beverages. Oil fields. Agriculture. Soybeans, corn, livestock, poultry.

11145 ■ Newton Press-Mentor
Newton Press-Mentor
700 W Washington
Newton, IL 62448
Phone: (618)783-2324
Community newspaper. **Freq:** Semiweekly (Mon. and Thurs.). **Print Method:** Offset. **Trim Size:** 22 3/4. **Cols./Page:** 6. **Col. Width:** 24 nonpareils. **Col. Depth:** 294 agate lines. **Key Personnel:** Ray McGrew, Publisher; Vanette King, Editor, phone: (618)783-2324. **Subscription Rates:** $26 Individuals. **URL:** http://www.pressmentor.com. **Ad Rates:** GLR $.23; BW $588; PCI $5.60. **Remarks:** Accepts advertising. **Circ:** ‡4000.

NILES

Cook Co. Cook Co. (NE). 14 m NW of Chicago. Manufactures tools and dies, office machines, stationary supplies, video games, dental products, bus parts, gloves soft drinks, testing products, heating controls.

11146 ■ Journal of Analytical Toxicology
Preston Publications Inc.
6600 W Touhy Ave.
Niles, IL 60714
Publication E-mail: bruce-goldberger@ufl.edu
Peer-reviewed journal for clinical and forensic toxicologists. **Founded:** 1977. **Freq:** 9/year. **Print Method:** Offset. **Trim Size:** 8 1/4 x 11. **Cols./Page:** 2. **Col. Width:** 3 1/4 inches. **Col. Depth:** 9 5/5 inches. **Key Personnel:** Bruce A. Goldberger, Editor; Yale H. Caplan, Associate Editor; Tinsley S. Preston, Publisher; Julie Weber-Roark, Managing Editor. **ISSN:** 0146-4760 (print); **EISSN:** 1945-2403 (electronic). **Subscription Rates:** $963 Institutions print and online; $886 Institutions print; $778 Institutions online. **URL:** http://jat.oxfordjournals.org. **Mailing address:** PO Box 48312, Niles, IL 60714. **Remarks:** Accepts advertising. **Circ:** Paid ‡1250, Non-paid ‡64.

11147 ■ Journal of Chromatographic Science
Preston Publications Inc.
6600 W Touhy Ave.
Niles, IL 60714
Magazine focusing on chemical analysis. **Freq:** 10/year. **Print Method:** Offset. **Trim Size:** 8 1/4 x 11. **Cols./Page:** 3. **Col. Width:** 2 1/8 inches. **Col. Depth:** 10 inches. **Key Personnel:** Huba Kalasz, Editor; Tinsley Preston, Publisher; Michael Graves, Managing Editor; Neil Danielson, Editor. **ISSN:** 0021--9665 (print); **EISSN:** 1945--239X (electronic). **Subscription Rates:** $817 Institutions print and online; $751 Institutions print; $666 Institutions online; $93 Single issue. **URL:** http://chromsci.oxfordjournals.org. **Mailing address:** PO Box 48312, Niles, IL 60714. **Ad Rates:** BW $1,100; 4C $1,800. **Remarks:** Accepts advertising. **Circ:** Paid ‡1581, Non-paid ‡63.

11148 ■ Marina/Dock Age
Preston Publications Inc.
6600 W Touhy Ave.
Niles, IL 60714
Magazine for marina and boat yard owners and managers. **Freq:** 8/year. **Print Method:** Web offset. **Trim Size:** 8 1/8 x 10 7/8. **Cols./Page:** 2. **Col. Width:** 20 picas. **Col. Depth:** 10 inches. **Key Personnel:** Anna Townshend, Editor; Barbara McLester, Manager, Sales. **ISSN:** 1079--1930 (print). **Subscription Rates:** Free For professionals in the marina industry, individual dock owners, and owners/managers of other recreational waterfront facilities within the U.S. **URL:** http://www.marinadockage.com. **Mailing address:** PO Box 48312, Niles, IL 60714. **Remarks:** Accepts advertising. **Circ:** (Not Reported).

11149 ■ Niles Herald-Spectator
Sun-Times Media L.L.C.
3701 W Lake Ave.
Glenview, IL 60026
Phone: (847)486-9200
Fax: (847)486-7300
Publisher's E-mail: customerservice@suntimes.com

Circulation: ★ = AAM; △ or • = BPA; ♦ = CAC; ❑ = VAC; ⊕ = PO Statement; ‡ = Publisher's Report; Boldface figures = sworn; Light figures = estimated.

Community newspaper (tabloid). **Freq:** Weekly. **Print Method:** Offset. **Cols./Page:** 5. **Col. Width:** 10 inches. **Col. Depth:** 14 inches. **Key Personnel:** Ryan Nilsson, Managing Editor. **Subscription Rates:** $20 Individuals; $84 Out of state. **URL:** http://niles.chicagotribune.com. **Remarks:** Accepts advertising. **Circ:** (Not Reported).

NOKOMIS

Montgomery Co. Montgomery Co. (SC). 42 m SW of Decatur. Concrete block. Manufactures electronics, novelty stuffed toys. Rock quarries.

11150 ■ Free Press-Progress
Free Press Inc.
112 W State St.
Nokomis, IL 62075-0130
Phone: (217)563-2115
Fax: (217)563-7464
Publication E-mail: freepress@consolidated.net
Community newspaper. **Freq:** Weekly (Wed.). **Print Method:** Offset. **Cols./Page:** 8. **Col. Width:** 22 nonpareils. **Col. Depth:** 301 agate lines. **Key Personnel:** Thomas J. Phillips, Jr., Publisher; Thomas Latonis, Managing Editor; Brenda L. Compton, General Manager. **Subscription Rates:** $38 Individuals Montgomery and Christian counties; $43 Individuals other areas in Illinois; $47 Out of state. **URL:** http://www.nokomisonline.com/fp-p.html. **Ad Rates:** GLR $.40; BW $438.60; PCI $2.65. **Remarks:** Advertising accepted; rates available upon request. **Circ:** 2300.

NORMAL

McLean Co. McLean Co. (C). Adjoins Bloomington. Illinois State University. Residential. Canning factories; nurseries. Dairy, stock farms. Corn, wheat, oats.

11151 ■ JAC: A Journal of Rhetoric, Culture & Politics
Illinois State University English Department
CB 4240
Stevenson Hall, Rm. 409
Normal, IL 61790-4240
Phone: (309)438-3667
Fax: (309)438-5414
Publication E-mail: jac@ilstu.edu
Journal focusing on rhetoric, writing, multiple literacies, and the politics of education. **Freq:** Quarterly. **Key Personnel:** Lynn Worsham, Editor; Julie Jung, Senior Editor; David Bleich, Board Member; Lynn Z. Bloom, Board Member; Patricia Bizzell, Board Member; Kyle Jensen, Editor; Chris Mays, Assistant Editor. **ISSN:** 0731--6755 (print). **Subscription Rates:** $32 Individuals; $55 Institutions; $62 Two years; $12 Single issue. **URL:** http://www.jaconlinejournal.com. **Remarks:** Accepts advertising. **Circ:** (Not Reported).

11152 ■ Journal of the Gilded Age and Progressive Era
Journal of the Gilded Age and Progressive Era
Department Of Economics, Illinois State University, Campus
Dept. of History
Illinois State University, Box 4420
Normal, IL 61790-4200
Peer-reviewed journal that publishes original essays and reviews scholarly books on all aspects of U.S. history for the period from 1865 through 1920. **Freq:** Quarterly. **Key Personnel:** Alan Lessoff, Editor; John F. McClymer, Editor; Nancy C. Unger, Editor. **ISSN:** 1537--7814 (print); **EISSN:** 1943--3557 (electronic). **Subscription Rates:** $137 Institutions online only; £86 Institutions online only; $175 Institutions online and print; £114 Institutions online and print. **URL:** http://www.cambridge.org/core/journals/journal-of-the-gilded-age-and-progressive-era. **Mailing address:** PO Box 4200, Normal, IL 61790-4200. **Circ:** (Not Reported).

11153 ■ The Normalite
Normalite
1702 W College Ave., Ste. G
Normal, IL 61761
Phone: (309)454-5476
Fax: (309)454-5476
Local newspaper. **Freq:** Weekly. **Print Method:** Offset. **Trim Size:** 10 3/4 x 16. **Cols./Page:** 5. **Col. Width:** 11.5 picas. **Key Personnel:** Edward Pyne, Editor. **USPS:** 391-720. **Subscription Rates:** $24.95 Individuals; $27.95 Out of state. **URL:** http://www.normalite.com. **Formerly:** Normal Normalite. **Mailing address:** PO Box 67, Normal, IL 61761. **Ad Rates:** GLR $.30; BW $240; 4C $500; SAU $4.20. **Remarks:** Accepts advertising. **Circ:** Combined ‡4900.

11154 ■ Spoon River Poetry Review
Spoon River Poetry Review
Illinois State University
CB 4241
Normal, IL 61790-4241
Publication E-mail: contact@srpr.org
Literary magazine covering poetry. **Freq:** Semiannual. **Print Method:** Laser. **Trim Size:** 5 1/2 x 8 1/2. **Key Personnel:** Kirstin Hotelling Zona, Editor; Tara Reeser, Director, Publications. **ISSN:** 0738--8993 (print). **Subscription Rates:** $18 Individuals; $10 Individuals single copy for individual or 1 year subscription for students; $20 Institutions; $30 Two years. **URL:** http://www.srpr.org; http://www.srpr.org/archive.php. **Formerly:** Spoon River Quarterly. **Ad Rates:** BW $200. **Remarks:** Accepts advertising. **Circ:** Combined 1400.

11155 ■ WDQZ-FM - 99.5
108 Boeykens Pl.
Normal, IL 61761
Phone: (309)888-4496
Fax: (309)452-9677
Format: Oldies. **Ad Rates:** Noncommercial.

11156 ■ WGLT-FM - 89.1
Illinois State University
CB 8910
Normal, IL 61790-8910
Phone: (309)438-2255
Fax: (309)438-7870
Email: wglt@ilstu.edu
Format: Jazz; Blues; News. **Networks:** National Public Radio (NPR); AP. **Owner:** Illinois State University, Campus Box 4000, Normal, IL 61790-4000, Ph: (309)438-2111, Free: 800-366-2478. **Founded:** 1966. **Operating Hours:** Continuous; 20% network, 80% local. **Key Personnel:** Bruce Bergethon, Gen. Mgr., blberge@ilstu.edu; Mike McCurdy, Prog. Dir., mike@wglt.org; Jon Norton, Music Dir., j.norton@ilstu.edu. **Wattage:** 25,000. **Ad Rates:** Noncommercial. **URL:** http://wglt.org/music/blues/blues-playlist.php.

11157 ■ WRPW-FM
108 Boeykens Pl.
Normal, IL 61761
Phone: (309)888-4496
Format: Top 40. **Wattage:** 6,000 ERP. **Ad Rates:** Advertising accepted; rates available upon request. **URL:** http://www.cities929.com.

11158 ■ WZND-FM
CB 8910
Normal, IL 61790-8000
Phone: (309)438-5491
Fax: (309)438-3048
Email: wznd@hotmail.com
Format: Alternative/New Music/Progressive; Blues; News; Sports. **Owner:** Illinois State University, Campus Box 4000, Normal, IL 61790-4000, Ph: (309)438-2111, Free: 800-366-2478. **Wattage:** 011 ERP.

NORTH AURORA

11159 ■ The VW Autoist
Volkswagen Club of America
PO Box 154
North Aurora, IL 60542
Freq: Bimonthly. **Subscription Rates:** Included in membership. **Remarks:** Accepts advertising. **Circ:** 2500.

NORTH RIVERSIDE

11160 ■ Oakbrook Terrace Argus
Liberty Suburban Chicago Newspapers
7222 W Cermak Rd., Ste. 505
North Riverside, IL 60546
Phone: (708)447-9810
Fax: (708)447-9871
Publisher's E-mail: mjames@libertysuburban.com
Community newspaper. **Freq:** Weekly (Fri.). **Print Method:** Offset. **Subscription Rates:** $42 Individuals. **URL:** http://www.mysuburbanlife.com/oakbrookterrace. **Remarks:** Advertising accepted; rates available upon request. **Circ:** Combined ‡962.

NORTHBROOK

Cook Co. Cook Co. (NE). 6 m NW of Winnetka. Residential.

11161 ■ Cutting Tool Engineering
CTE Publications Inc.
40 Skokie Blvd., Ste. 450
Northbrook, IL 60062
Phone: (847)498-9100
Fax: (847)559-4444
Publisher's E-mail: info@ctemag.com
Metal working and tooling news. **Freq:** Monthly. **Print Method:** Offset. **Trim Size:** 8 1/8 x 10 7/8. **Cols./Page:** 3 and 2. **Col. Width:** 26 and 40 nonpareils. **Col. Depth:** 140 agate lines. **Key Personnel:** John William Roberts, Publisher. **ISSN:** 0011--4189 (print). **Subscription Rates:** $75 U.S. One year subscription (free to qualified subscribers within the U.S.); $125 Canada One year subscription; $125 Other countries One year subscription; $195 Individuals one year - airmail. **Alt. Formats:** PDF. **URL:** http://www.ctemag.com/magazine. **Ad Rates:** GLR $.105; BW $2985; 4C $4065; PCI $105. **Remarks:** Accepts advertising. **Circ:** Non-paid 41851.

11162 ■ ISSA Today
International Sanitary Supply Association
3300 Dundee Rd.
Northbrook, IL 60062
Phone: (847)982-0800
Fax: (847)982-1012
Free: 800-225-4772
Publisher's E-mail: info@issa.com
Freq: Bimonthly. **Subscription Rates:** $20; C$30; €25. **URL:** http://www.issa.com/publications/issa-today/#.VOaNJeYwrlc; http://issatoday.issa.com/?issueID=32&pageID=1. **Ad Rates:** BW $3,100. **Remarks:** Accepts advertising. **Circ:** (Not Reported).

11163 ■ Oil & Gas Financial Journal
PennWell Corp., Advanced Technology Div.
PO Box 3264
Northbrook, IL 60065-3264
Phone: (847)763-9540
Fax: (847)763-9607
Periodical for petroleum industry managers, analysts and investors covering financial developments in the oil and gas business. **Freq:** Monthly. **Key Personnel:** Don Stowers, Editor. **Subscription Rates:** $ Free to qualified subscribers; $149 Other countries. **URL:** http://www.ogfj.com/index.html. **Remarks:** Accepts advertising. **Circ:** (Not Reported).

11164 ■ Plumbing Engineer
TMB Publishing Inc.
1838 Techny Ct.
Northbrook, IL 60062
Phone: (847)564-1127
Publisher's E-mail: info@solarlogicllc.com
Trade journal for consulting engineering, mechanical engineering, architecture, and contracting professionals. **Freq:** Monthly. **Print Method:** Offset. **Trim Size:** 8 1/4 x 11. **Cols./Page:** 3. **Key Personnel:** Jim Schneider, Director, Editorial; Ashlei Williams, Assistant Editor; Cate Brown, Manager, Production. **ISSN:** 0192--1711 (print). **URL:** http://www.plumbingengineer.com. **Ad Rates:** BW $3,985. **Remarks:** Accepts advertising. **Circ:** △**25646**.

11165 ■ Teutopolis Press and Dieterich Special Gazette
Liberty Group Publishing
3000 Dundee Rd., Ste. 202
Northbrook, IL 60062
Phone: (847)272-2244
Fax: (847)272-6244
Publication E-mail: news@teutopolispress.com
Community newspaper. **Freq:** Weekly (Wed.). **Print Method:** Offset. **Cols./Page:** 5. **Key Personnel:** Nancy Bence, Office Manager; Lynne Campbell, President, Publisher, phone: (618)932-2146. **URL:** http://www.teutopolispress.com. **Ad Rates:** GLR $.18; PCI $4.60. **Remarks:** Accepts advertising. **Circ:** (Not Reported).

11166 ■ Water & Wastewater International
PennWell Corp.
PO Box 3264
Northbrook, IL 60065
Phone: (847)763-9540
Fax: (847)763-9607
Publication E-mail: wwwi@omeda.com wwi@halldata.com
Trade journal covering the water industry for managers, engineers, operators, consultants and others in the field worldwide. **Founded:** 1896. **Freq:** Bimonthly. **Key Personnel:** James Laughlin, Editor; Tom Freyberg,

Editor-in-Chief. **Subscription Rates:** $271 Individuals; $152 Individuals digital. **URL:** http://www.waterworld.com/world-regions.html. **Ad Rates:** BW $9,590; PCI $100. **Remarks:** Accepts advertising. **Circ: 25378**.

11167 ■ WEEF-AM - 1430
4320 Dundee Rd.
Northbrook, IL 60062
Phone: (847)498-3350
Format: Contemporary Christian. **Owner:** Polnet Communications Ltd., 3656 W Blemont Ave., Chicago, IL 60618, Ph: (773)588-6300, Fax: (773)267-4913. **Founded:** 1963. **Operating Hours**: Sunrise-sunset. **Key Personnel:** Chris Bagat, Station Mgr; Maria Alesi, Contact. **Wattage:** 1,000. **Ad Rates:** $21.50-39.00 for 30 seconds; $34.50-47.00 for 60 seconds. **URL:** http://www.pclradio.com/1430_weef/index.html.

WKTA-AM - See Evanston, IL

NORTHFIELD

Cook Co. Cook Co. (NE). 17 m N of Chicago. Residential.

11168 ■ CAP Today
College of American Pathologists
325 Waukegan Rd.
Northfield, IL 60093-2750
Phone: (847)832-7000
Fax: (847)832-8000
Free: 800-323-4040
Magazine covering advances in pathology tests and equipment, clinical lab management and operations trends, and related regulatory and legislative changes. **Freq:** Monthly. **Print Method:** Offset. **Trim Size:** 10 7/8 x 15 3/4. **Cols./Page:** 4. **Col. Width:** 26 nonpareils. **Col. Depth:** 296 agate lines. **ISSN:** 0891--1525 (print). **Subscription Rates:** $100 U.S. 1 year; $125 Canada 1 year; $225 Other countries 1 year; Included in membership; $20 U.S. single copy; $25 Canada single copy; $35 Other countries single copy. **URL:** http://www.cap.org/apps/cap.portal?_nfpb=true&cntvwrPtlt_actionOverride=/portlets/contentViewer/show&_windowLabel=cntvwrPtlt&cntvwrPtlt=cap_today/cap_today_index.html&_state=maximized&_pageLabel=cntvwr; http://www.cap.org/web/home/resources/cap-today?_afrLoop=22114566321066 6#!%40%40%3F_afrLoop%3D221145663210666%26_adf.ctrl-state%3D10khjkv7pc_4. **Remarks:** Accepts display and classified advertising. **Circ:** (Not Reported).

11169 ■ Dental Lab Products
MEDEC Dental Communications
2 Northfield Plz., Ste. 300
Northfield, IL 60093-1219
Phone: (847)441-3700
Fax: (847)441-3702
Free: 800-323-3337
Professional tabloid for dental laboratory owners and managers. Covering new products, training seminars, conferences, and techniques. **Freq:** Bimonthly. **Print Method:** Offset. **Trim Size:** 10 7/16 x 133 3/4. **Cols./Page:** 3 and 4. **Col. Width:** 39 and 28 nonpareils. **Col. Depth:** 189 agate lines. **Key Personnel:** Stan Goff, Executive Editor. **ISSN:** 0146-9738 (print). **Subscription Rates:** Free. **URL:** http://www.dentalproductsreport.com/lab. **Remarks:** Accepts advertising. **Circ:** Non-paid 18827.

11170 ■ Dental Lab Products
UBM Medica LLC
535 Connecticut Ave., Ste. 300
Norwalk, CT 06854
Professional tabloid for dental laboratory owners and managers. Covering new products, training seminars, conferences, and techniques. **Freq:** Bimonthly. **Print Method:** Offset. **Trim Size:** 10 7/16 x 133 3/4. **Cols./Page:** 3 and 4. **Col. Width:** 39 and 28 nonpareils. **Col. Depth:** 189 agate lines. **Key Personnel:** Stan Goff, Executive Editor. **ISSN:** 0146-9738 (print). **Subscription Rates:** Free. **URL:** http://www.dentalproductsreport.com/lab. **Remarks:** Accepts advertising. **Circ:** Non-paid 18827.

11171 ■ The Financial Manager
Broadcast Cable Credit Association
550 W Frontage Rd., Ste. 3600
Northfield, IL 60093
Phone: (847)881-8757
Fax: (847)784-8059
Publisher's E-mail: info@bccacredit.com
Magazine focusing on credit and collections and other financial topics of interest to the media industry. **Freq:** Bimonthly. **Subscription Rates:** $60 Individuals /year. **Remarks:** Accepts advertising. **Circ:** (Not Reported).

11172 ■ The Instrumentalist
Instrumentalist Co.
200 Northfield Rd.
Northfield, IL 60093
Phone: (847)446-5000
Fax: (847)446-6263
Free: 888-446-6888
Publisher's E-mail: advertising@theinstrumentalist.com
Magazine for school band and orchestra directors, professional instrumentalists, and students. **Freq:** Monthly. **Print Method:** Offset. **Trim Size:** 8 1/4 x 10 7/8. **Cols./Page:** 3. **Col. Width:** 26 nonpareils. **Col. Depth:** 140 agate lines. **Key Personnel:** James Rohner, Publisher. **ISSN:** 0020--4331 (print). **Subscription Rates:** $11 Students; $21 Individuals; $32 Two years; $42 Individuals 3 years; $40 Out of country. **URL:** http://www.theinstrumentalist.com/index.php. **Ad Rates:** BW $1,895; 4C $2,095; PCI $75. **Remarks:** Accepts advertising. **Circ:** Paid ‡16594.

11173 ■ McKnight's Long-Term Care News
McKnight's Long-Term Care News
One Northfield Plz., Ste. 521
Northfield, IL 60093-1216
Phone: (847)784-8706
Free: 800-558-1703
Publication E-mail: ltcn-webmaster@mltcn.com
Professional magazine. **Freq:** 16/yr. **Print Method:** Offset. **Trim Size:** 10 7/8 x 14. **Cols./Page:** 4. **Col. Width:** 28 nonpareils. **Col. Depth:** 140 agate lines. **Key Personnel:** Jim Berklan, Editor; Karmen Maurer, Publisher; John O'Connor, Associate Publisher, Director, Editorial; Paul Silver, Manager, Circulation; Elizabeth Newman, Senior Editor. **ISSN:** 1084--3314 (print). **Subscription Rates:** $60 Individuals; $108 Two years; $75 Canada; $135 Canada two years; $75 Other countries; $135 Other countries two years. **URL:** http://www.mcknights.com. **Formerly**: Today's Nursing Home. **Ad Rates:** BW $5,950; 4C $1,650; PCI $120. **Remarks:** Accepts advertising. **Circ:** Paid ‡850, Controlled ‡50025.

11174 ■ Piano Explorer
Instrumentalist Co.
200 Northfield Rd.
Northfield, IL 60093
Phone: (847)446-5000
Fax: (847)446-6263
Free: 888-446-6888
Publisher's E-mail: advertising@theinstrumentalist.com
Magazine covering piano lessons. **Freq:** 10/year. **Print Method:** Offset. **Trim Size:** 8 1/4 X 10 7/8. **Cols./Page:** 6. **Col. Width:** 1 7/8 inches. **Col. Depth:** 21 inches. **Subscription Rates:** $12 Individuals. **URL:** http://www.instrumentalistmagazine.com/Current%20Issue.php. **Ad Rates:** BW $1,156; 4C $1,156; PCI $76. **Remarks:** Accepts advertising. **Circ:** (Not Reported).

OAK BROOK

DuPage Co. DuPage Co. (NE). 17 m SW of Chicago. Residential.

11175 ■ American Journal of Neuroradiology
American Society of Neuroradiology
800 Enterprise Dr., Ste. 205
Oak Brook, IL 60523
Phone: (630)574-0220
Fax: (630)574-0661
Publication E-mail: ajnrinfo@asnr.org
Freq: Monthly. **Key Personnel:** Jeffrey S. Ross, Dr., Editor-in-Chief; Mauricio Castillo, MD, Editor-in-Chief; Karen Halm, Managing Editor. **ISSN:** 0195--6108 (print); **EISSN:** 1936--959X (electronic). **Subscription Rates:** $380 Individuals print and online; $305 Individuals online only; $450 Other countries print and online; $440 Institutions print and online - basic; $365 Institutions online only - basic; $510 Institutions, other countries print and online; $875 Institutions print and online - extended; $790 Institutions online only - extended; $940 Institutions, other countries print and online - extended. **URL:** http://www.ajnr.org. **Remarks:** Advertising accepted; rates available upon request. **Circ:** (Not Reported).

11176 ■ American Journal of Neuroradiology
American Society of Pediatric Neuroradiology
c/o Kristine Kulpaka, Coordinator
800 Enterprise Dr., Ste. 205
Oak Brook, IL 60523-4216
Phone: (630)574-0220
Publication E-mail: ajnrinfo@asnr.org
Freq: Monthly. **Key Personnel:** Jeffrey S. Ross, Dr., Editor-in-Chief; Mauricio Castillo, MD, Editor-in-Chief; Karen Halm, Managing Editor. **ISSN:** 0195--6108 (print); **EISSN:** 1936--959X (electronic). **Subscription Rates:** $380 Individuals print and online; $305 Individuals online only; $450 Other countries print and online; $440 Institutions print and online - basic; $365 Institutions online only - basic; $510 Institutions, other countries print and online; $875 Institutions print and online - extended; $790 Institutions online only - extended; $940 Institutions, other countries print and online - extended. **URL:** http://www.ajnr.org. **Remarks:** Advertising accepted; rates available upon request. **Circ:** (Not Reported).

11177 ■ Children's Literature Association Quarterly
Children's Literature Association
1301 W 22nd St., Ste. 202
Oak Brook, IL 60523
Phone: (630)571-4520
Fax: (708)876-5598
Publication E-mail: chlaquarterly@tamu.edu.
Journal publishing children's scholarly literature. **Freq:** Quarterly. **Print Method:** Offset. **Cols./Page:** 2. **Col. Width:** 42 nonpareils. **Col. Depth:** 135 agate lines. **Key Personnel:** Katharine Capshaw Smith, Editor. **ISSN:** 0885--0429 (print). **Subscription Rates:** $145 Individuals; $160 Institutions U.S. base; $175 Individuals those outside the U.S. or Canada; $10 Individuals specify issues; Included in membership. **URL:** http://www.childlitassn.org/index.php?page=about&family=publications; http://childlitassn.org/chla-quarterly. **Remarks:** Advertising not accepted. **Circ:** ‡1000, 850.

11178 ■ Construction Equipment Distribution
Associated Equipment Distributors
600 22nd St., Ste. 220
Oak Brook, IL 60523
Phone: (630)574-0650
Freq: Monthly. **Print Method:** Offset. **Trim Size:** 8.25 x 10.875. **Cols./Page:** 3 and 2. **Col. Width:** 27 and 40 nonpareils. **Col. Depth:** 140 agate lines. **Key Personnel:** Kim Phelan, Director, Editorial, Editor, Program Director, fax: (630)574-0132; Al Ramirez, Manager, Advertising and Sales, fax: (630)574-0132. **ISSN:** 0010--6755 (print). **Subscription Rates:** $79 U.S. and Canada nonmembers; $39 U.S. and Canada members; $109 Members overseas; $179 Nonmembers overseas. **URL:** http://www.cedmag.com; http://netforum.avectra.com/eweb/shopping/shopping.aspx?site=aed&webcode=shopping&prd_key=78e7c4bc-114c-49fc-9363-7a4fb94d37ab. **Ad Rates:** BW $2,320; 4C $2,970. **Remarks:** Accepts advertising. **Circ:** ‡4000, 5000.

11179 ■ Consulting-Specifying Engineer
CFE Media L.L.C.
1111 W 22nd St., Ste. 250
Oak Brook, IL 60523
Phone: (630)571-4070
Fax: (630)214-4504
Publisher's E-mail: customerservice@cfemedia.com
The integrated engineering magazine of the building construction industry. **Freq:** 13/yr. **Print Method:** Offset. **Trim Size:** 7 7/8 x 10 1/2. **Cols./Page:** 2. **Key Personnel:** Amara Rozgus, Editor-in-Chief, Manager; Jim Langhenry, President, Publisher; Steve Rourke, President. **ISSN:** 0892--5046 (print). **Subscription Rates:** Free United States only. **URL:** http://www.csemag.com. **Ad Rates:** BW $11000, gross; BW $9350, net. **Remarks:** Accepts advertising. **Circ:** (Not Reported).

11180 ■ Control Engineering: Covering Control, Instrumentation, and Automation Systems Worldwide
CFE Media L.L.C.
1111 W 22nd St., Ste. 250
Oak Brook, IL 60523
Phone: (630)571-4070

Circulation: ★ = AAM; △ or • = BPA; ♦ = CAC; ❑ = VAC; ⊕ = PO Statement; ‡ = Publisher's Report; Boldface figures = sworn; Light figures = estimated.

Fax: (630)214-4504
Publication E-mail: controleng@cfemedia.com
Magazine covering control and instrumentation systems. **Freq:** Monthly. **Print Method:** Offset. **Trim Size:** 8 x 10 3/4. **Cols./Page:** 3. **Col. Width:** 27 nonpareils. **Col. Depth:** 140 agate lines. **Key Personnel:** David Greenfield, Director, Editorial, phone: (678)654-1692; Renee Robbins, Senior Editor, phone: (630)288-8013; Mark T. Hoske, Editor-in-Chief, phone: (630)288-8570. **ISSN:** 0010--8049 (print). **Subscription Rates:** Free to qualified subscribers. **URL:** http://www.controleng.com; http://www.controleng.com/index.php?id=7989. **Ad Rates:** 4C $10200. **Remarks:** Accepts advertising. **Circ:** Combined ‡81590.

11181 ■ Interior Construction
Ceilings and Interior Systems Construction Association
1010 Jorie Blvd., Ste. 30
Oak Brook, IL 60523
Phone: (630)584-1919
Fax: (866)560-8537
Publisher's E-mail: cisca@cisca.org
Magazine covering interior system construction. **Freq:** Quarterly. **Print Method:** Offset. **Trim Size:** 8 x 10 7/8. **Cols./Page:** 3 and 2. **Col. Width:** 26 and 40 nonpareils. **Col. Depth:** 126 agate lines. **ISSN:** 0888--0387 (print). **Subscription Rates:** $75 Nonmembers; $40 Members. **URL:** http://www.cisca.org/i4a/pages/index.cfm?pageid=3281. **Ad Rates:** BW $1300; 4C $2000. **Remarks:** Accepts advertising. **Circ:** (Not Reported).

11182 ■ The Landscape Contractor: Landscape Contracting
Illinois Landscape Contractors Association
2625 Butterfield Rd., Ste. 104S
Oak Brook, IL 60523-1234
Phone: (630)472-2851
Fax: (630)472-3150
Publisher's E-mail: information@ilca.net
Magazine for the landscape trade. **Freq:** Monthly. **Print Method:** WEB. **Trim Size:** 8 1/2 x 11. **Cols./Page:** 3 and 2. **Col. Width:** 26 and 40 nonpareils. **Col. Depth:** 140 agate lines. **Key Personnel:** Rick Reuland, Publisher, Editor. **ISSN:** 0194--7257 (print). **Subscription Rates:** $75 Individuals. **URL:** http://www.ilca.net/publications. **Ad Rates:** BW $750; 4C $1355. **Remarks:** Accepts advertising. **Circ:** Combined ‡2500, Combined 2000.

11183 ■ The Lion Magazine
Lions Clubs International
300 W 22nd St.
Oak Brook, IL 60523-8842
Phone: (630)571-5466
Publication E-mail: magazine@lionsclubs.org
Magazine containing club news for service minded men and women. **Freq:** 10/year. **Print Method:** Offset. **Trim Size:** 8 x 10 1/2. **Cols./Page:** 3. **Col. Width:** 2 1/8 INS. **Col. Depth:** 140 agate lines. **ISSN:** 0024--4163 (print). **Subscription Rates:** $6 Individuals /year, for those living in North America; $12 Individuals /year, if mailed outside North America; $1 Single issue. **Alt. Formats:** Download. **URL:** http://www.lionsclubs.org/EN/news-and-events/lion-magazine/index.php. **Ad Rates:** $5420-6660, offset,for 1 page; $3685-4520, offset,for 2/3 page; $2790-3425, offset,for 1/2 page; $1870-2300, offset,for 1/3 page; $1025-1250, offset,for 1/6 page. BW $4,845; 4C $5,950; BW $, offset,for 1 pageBW $, offset,for 2/3 pageBW $, offset,for 1/2 pageBW $, offset,for 1/3 pageBW $, offset,for 1/6 page. **Remarks:** Accepts advertising. **Circ:** Paid ★**385705**, 365587.

11184 ■ Metal Center News
Metal Center News
1100 Jorie Blvd., Ste. 207
Oak Brook, IL 60523
Phone: (630)571-1067
Publication E-mail: info@metalcenternews.com
Magazine for the metal distributing industry. **Founded:** 1962. **Freq:** 13/year. **Print Method:** Offset. **Trim Size:** 8 1/4 x 11. **Cols./Page:** 3 and 2. **Col. Width:** 26 and 40 nonpareils. **Col. Depth:** 140 agate lines. **Key Personnel:** Patrick Bernardo, Publisher; Tim Triplett, Editor-in-Chief. **Subscription Rates:** $85 Single issue; $109 U.S.; $125 Canada and Mexico; $179 Other countries. **URL:** http://www.metalcenternews.com/. **Ad Rates:** BW $4,283. **Remarks:** Accepts advertising. **Circ:** Controlled 13042.

11185 ■ Plant Engineering
CFE Media L.L.C.
1111 W 22nd St., Ste. 250
Oak Brook, IL 60523
Phone: (630)571-4070
Fax: (630)214-4504
Publisher's E-mail: customerservice@cfemedia.com
Magazine focusing on engineering support and maintenance in industry. **Founded:** 1947. **Freq:** Monthly. **Key Personnel:** Bob Vavra, Manager; Jim Langhenry, Founder, Publisher; Paul Brouch, Web Administrator. **ISSN:** 0032-082X (print). **Subscription Rates:** Free. **URL:** http://www.plantengineering.com/. **Ad Rates:** BW $10,000; 4C $1,000. **Remarks:** Accepts advertising. **Circ:** (Not Reported).

11186 ■ RadioGraphics
Radiological Society of North America
820 Jorie Blvd.
Oak Brook, IL 60523-2251
Phone: (630)571-2670
Fax: (630)571-7837
Free: 800-381-6660
Publication E-mail: rarnold@rsna.org
Freq: Bimonthly with 7th out-of-frequency issue. **Print Method:** Offset. **Trim Size:** 8 1/4 x 10 7/8. **Cols./Page:** 2. **Col. Width:** 19 picas. **Col. Depth:** 55 picas. **Key Personnel:** William W. Olmsted, MD, Editor. **ISSN:** 0271--5333 (print). **Subscription Rates:** $169 Individuals; $131 U.S., Canada, and Mexico print; $179 Other countries print; $35 U.S., Canada, and Mexico single issue; $50 Other countries single issue; Tiered pricing for institutions ranges from $363 to $1297. **Alt. Formats:** Handheld. **URL:** http://pubs.rsna.org/journal/radiographics; http://www.rsna.org/Journals.aspx; http://pubs.rsna.org/toc/radiographics/current; http://pubs.rsna.org/journal/radiology. **Ad Rates:** $550-1500. BW $3,480; 4C $4,980; 4C $. **Remarks:** Accepts advertising. **Circ:** 28000, 26000.

11187 ■ Radiology
Radiological Society of North America
820 Jorie Blvd.
Oak Brook, IL 60523-2251
Phone: (630)571-2670
Fax: (630)571-7837
Free: 800-381-6660
Publisher's E-mail: mwatson@rsna.org
Freq: Monthly. **Print Method:** Offset. **Trim Size:** 8 1/4 x 11 1/4. **Cols./Page:** 3. **Col. Width:** 2 1/4 inches. **Col. Depth:** 10 inches. **Key Personnel:** Herbert Y. Kressel, MD, Editor. **ISSN:** 0033--8419 (print); **EISSN:** 1527--1315 (electronic). **Subscription Rates:** $230 U.S., Canada, and Mexico; $305 Other countries; $35 U.S., Canada, and Mexico single issue; $50 Other countries single issue. **Alt. Formats:** Handheld. **URL:** http://pubs.rsna.org/journal/radiology; http://www.rsna.org/Journals.aspx; http://pubs.rsna.org/toc/radiology/current. **Ad Rates:** $550-1500. BW $3,480; 4C $3,475; 4C $. **Remarks:** Advertising accepted; rates available upon request. **Circ:** ‡36500, 36000.

11188 ■ RSNA News
Radiological Society of North America
820 Jorie Blvd.
Oak Brook, IL 60523-2251
Phone: (630)571-2670
Fax: (630)571-7837
Free: 800-381-6660
Publisher's E-mail: mwatson@rsna.org
Freq: Monthly. **Key Personnel:** David M. Hovsepian, MD, Editor. **Alt. Formats:** PDF. **URL:** http://www.rsna.org/News. **Remarks:** Accepts advertising. **Circ:** (Not Reported).

11189 ■ Springs: The International Magazine of Spring Manufacture
Spring Manufacturers Institute
2001 Midwest Rd., Ste. 106
Oak Brook, IL 60523-1335
Phone: (630)495-8588
Fax: (630)495-8595
Publisher's E-mail: info@smihq.org
Freq: Quarterly. **ISSN:** 0584- 9667 (print). **Subscription Rates:** free; $50 Other countries. **URL:** http://www.smihq.org/public/publications/springsmagazine.html. **Remarks:** Accepts advertising. **Circ:** 8000.

11190 ■ We Need Not Walk Alone
Compassionate Friends
1000 Jorie Blvd., Ste. 140
Oak Brook, IL 60523-4494
Phone: (630)990-0010
Fax: (630)990-0246
Free: 877-969-0010
Publisher's E-mail: nationaloffice@compassionatefriends.org
Magazine containing bereavement support for families during the death of a family member. **Freq:** 3/year. **Subscription Rates:** $20 Individuals; $23 Canada; $30 Other countries. **URL:** http://www.compassionatefriends.org/we_need_not_walk_alone.aspx. **Mailing address:** PO Box 3696, Oak Brook, IL 60522-3696. **Circ:** (Not Reported).

11191 ■ The Zontian
Zonta International
1211 W 22nd St., Ste. 900
Oak Brook, IL 60523-3384
Phone: (630)928-1400
Fax: (630)928-1559
Publisher's E-mail: zontaintl@zonta.org
Service club organization magazine of interest to executives and professionals concerned with the status of women. **Freq:** Biennial. **Print Method:** Web press. **Trim Size:** 8 1/4 x 10 7/8. **Cols./Page:** 3. **Col. Width:** 26 nonpareils. **Col. Depth:** 115 agate lines. **ISSN:** 0279--3229 (print). **Alt. Formats:** Download; PDF. **URL:** http://www.zonta.org/Media-News/Zontian-Magazine. **Remarks:** Advertising not accepted. **Circ:** (Not Reported).

11192 ■ Comcast Cable
2001 York Rd.
Oak Brook, IL 60523
Phone: (630)879-9430
Founded: 1963. **Key Personnel:** Ralph J. Roberts, Chairman; Brian L. Roberts, Chairman, CEO; Stephen B. Burke, Chairman, CEO; Mark A. coblitz, Sr. VP of Strategic Bus. Operations. **Cities Served:** 69 channels. **URL:** http://www.comcast.com.

11193 ■ WUBR-AM
701 Harger Rd.
Oak Brook, IL 60523
Format: Music of Your Life. **Networks:** Jones Satellite; AP. **Owner:** Noordyk Broadcasting, Inc., Chicago, IL. **Founded:** 1981. **Formerly**: WPBK-AM; WEFG-AM. **ADI**: Baton Rouge, LA. **Key Personnel:** Bob Bolton, Gen. Mgr. **Wattage**: 1,200 Day; 051 Night. **Ad Rates:** $22-26 for 60 seconds.

OAK BROOK TERRACE

11194 ■ Journal of Nuclear Materials Management
Institute of Nuclear Materials Management
1 Parkview Plz., Ste. 800
Oak Brook Terrace, IL 60181
Phone: (847)686-2236
Fax: (847)686-2253
Scholarly/technical journal for professionals involved in nuclear materials management and safeguards. **Freq:** Quarterly. **Print Method:** Sheetfed offset. **Trim Size:** 8 1/8 x 10 7/8. **Key Personnel:** Patricia Sullivan, Managing Editor; Jill Hronek, Director, Advertising. **ISSN:** 0893--6188 (print). **Subscription Rates:** $200 Individuals; $500 Institutions. **URL:** http://www.inmm.org/Journal_of_Nuclear_Materials_Management/4239.htm. **Formerly**: Nuclear Materials Management. **Ad Rates:** BW $1200, full page; BW $1005, 2/3 page; BW $700, 1/2 page; BW $500, 1/3 page. **Remarks:** Accepts advertising. **Circ:** Paid ‡8000.

OAK PARK

Cook Co. Cook Co. (NE). Adjoins Chicago on the west. Residential suburb. Manufactures food products, veneer machinery, tools and dies, transformers, candy.

11195 ■ American Lift & Handlers
KHL Group
c/o Lindsey Anderson, Ed.
127 N Marion St., Ste. 8
Oak Park, IL 60302
Phone: (312)795-5611
Fax: (312)223-1492
Publisher's E-mail: info@khl.com
Magazine for telehandler and aerial work platform industry in North America. **Freq:** 7/year. **Key Personnel:** Lindsey Anderson, Editor. **URL:** http://khl.com/

magazines/access-lift-and-handlers. **Ad Rates:** 4C $1,280. **Remarks:** Accepts display advertising. **Circ:** 12992.

11196 ■ Chicago Parent Magazine: Connecting with Families
Wednesday Journal Inc.
141 S Oak Park Ave.
Oak Park, IL 60302
Phone: (708)524-8300
Fax: (708)524-0447
Publication E-mail: chiparent@chicagoparent.com
Parenting news magazine featuring child-related issue articles and comprehensive calendar of events, programs, and activities for the greater Chicago area. **Freq:** Monthly. **Print Method:** Offset. **Trim Size:** 10 1/4 x 12 1/2. **Cols./Page:** 4. **Col. Width:** 2 1/4 inches. **Col. Depth:** 11 3/8 inches. **Key Personnel:** Tamara O'Shaughnessy, Editor. **URL:** http://www.chicagoparent.com. **Remarks:** Accepts advertising. **Circ:** ‡100000.

11197 ■ Cold Facts
Cryogenic Society of America
c/o Laurie Huget, Executive Director
218 Lake St.
Oak Park, IL 60302-2609
Phone: (708)383-6220
Fax: (708)383-9337
Publisher's E-mail: csa@cryogenicsociety.org
Magazine covering the study of science and technology of very low temperatures. **Freq:** 6/year. **ISSN:** 1085--5262 (print). **Subscription Rates:** Included in membership; Free first six issues. **URL:** http://www.cryogenicsociety.org/cold_facts. **Ad Rates:** 4C $2524; BW $1693. **Remarks:** Accepts advertising. **Circ:** 4,500.

11198 ■ Current Bioinformatics
Bentham Science Publishers Ltd.
PO Box 446
Oak Park, IL 60303
Journal covering biomedicine, genomics, computational proteomics, systems biology and metabolic pathway engineering. **Freq:** 5/year. **Print Method:** Offset. **Cols./Page:** 4. **Col. Width:** 28 nonpareils. **Col. Depth:** 182 agate lines. **Key Personnel:** I. Ghosh, Board Member; J. Fang, Board Member; I.J. Del-Favero, Board Member; J. Dickerson, Board Member. **ISSN:** 1574--8936 (print); **EISSN:** 2212--392X (electronic). **USPS:** 159-560. **Subscription Rates:** $1450 Institutions corporate; print or online; $890 Institutions academic; print or online; $280 Individuals print; $1740 Institutions corporate; print and online; $980 Institutions academic; print and online. **URL:** http://benthamscience.com/journal/index.php?journalID=cbio. **Remarks:** Advertising accepted; rates available upon request. **Circ:** (Not Reported).

11199 ■ Current Metabolomics
Bentham Science Publishers Ltd.
PO Box 446
Oak Park, IL 60303
Journal covering articles latest advancements and applications of metabolomics. **Freq:** Quarterly. **Key Personnel:** Robert Powers, Editor-in-Chief. **ISSN:** 2213--235X (print); **EISSN:** 2213--2368 (electronic). **Subscription Rates:** $720 Institutions print and online, corporate rates; $600 Institutions print or online, corporate rates; $410 Institutions print and online, academic rates; $370 Institutions print or online, academic rates; $120 Individuals print. **URL:** http://benthamscience.com/journals/current-metabolomics/#top. **Ad Rates:** BW $600; 4C $800. **Remarks:** Accepts advertising. **Circ:** (Not Reported).

11200 ■ Current Microwave Chemistry
Bentham Science Publishers Ltd.
PO Box 446
Oak Park, IL 60303
Journal featuring advances in the use of the microwave in the fields of chemistry, biology, medicine, biomedical science and engineering. **Freq:** Semiannual. **Key Personnel:** Bimal K. Banik, Editor-in-Chief. **ISSN:** 2213--3356 (print); **EISSN:** 2213--3364 (electronic). **Subscription Rates:** $1080 Institutions print and online, corporate rates; $900 Institutions print or online, corporate rates; $620 Institutions print and online, academic rates; $560 Institutions print or online, academic rates; $180 Individuals print only. **URL:** http://benthamscience.com/journal/index.php?journalID=cmic. **Ad Rates:** BW $700; 4C $900. **Remarks:** Accepts advertising. **Circ:** (Not Reported).

11201 ■ Current Organocatalysis
Bentham Science Publishers Ltd.
PO Box 446
Oak Park, IL 60303
Journal featuring significant topics in all areas of organocatalysis. **Freq:** Semiannual. **Key Personnel:** Bimal K. Banik, Editor-in-Chief. **ISSN:** 2213--3372 (print); **EISSN:** 2213--3380 (electronic). **Subscription Rates:** $1080 Institutions print and online, corporate rates; $900 Institutions print or online, corporate rates; $620 Institutions print and online, academic rates; $560 Institutions print or online, academic rates; $180 Individuals print only. **URL:** http://benthamscience.com/journal/index.php?journalID=cocat. **Remarks:** Accepts advertising. **Circ:** (Not Reported).

11202 ■ Current Pharmaceutical Design
Bentham Science Publishers Ltd.
PO Box 446
Oak Park, IL 60303
Journal covering all subject areas of major importance to modern drug design, including medicinal chemistry, pharmacology, drug targets, and disease mechanism. **Freq:** 38/yr. **Key Personnel:** William A. Banks, Editor-in-Chief. **ISSN:** 1381-6128 (print); **EISSN:** 1873-4286 (electronic). **Subscription Rates:** $20830 Institutions corporate; print and online; $17360 Institutions corporate; print or online; $9660 Institutions academic; print and online; $8780 Institutions academic; print or online; $1720 Individuals print. **URL:** http://benthamscience.com/journals/current-pharmaceutical-design. **Circ:** (Not Reported).

11203 ■ Edible Chicago
Edible Communities Inc.
159 N Marion St. No. 306
Oak Park, IL 60301
Phone: (708)386-6781
Fax: (708)221-6756
Publisher's E-mail: info@ediblecommunities.com
Magazine featuring the local food industry of Chicago. **Freq:** Quarterly. **Key Personnel:** Ann Flood, Founder, Managing Editor, Publisher. **Subscription Rates:** $28 Individuals. **URL:** http://www.ediblechicago.com. **Ad Rates:** 4C $2500. **Remarks:** Accepts advertising. **Circ:** (Not Reported).

11204 ■ Forest Park Review
Wednesday Journal Inc.
141 S Oak Park Ave.
Oak Park, IL 60302
Phone: (708)524-8300
Fax: (708)524-0447
Publisher's E-mail: circulation@wjinc.com
Community newspaper. **Freq:** Weekly (Wed.). **Print Method:** Offset. **Trim Size:** Tabloid. **Cols./Page:** 4. **Col. Width:** 14.5 picas. **Col. Depth:** 12 3/4 inches. **Key Personnel:** Dan Haley, Publisher. **Subscription Rates:** $20 Individuals 1 year; $36 Two years; $52 Individuals 3 years; $28 Individuals 1 year; $44 Individuals 2 years. **URL:** http://www.forestparkreview.com. **Remarks:** Accepts advertising. **Circ:** (Not Reported).

11205 ■ Irish American News
Irish American News
7115 W North Ave., Ste. 327
Oak Park, IL 60302
Phone: (708)445-0700
Fax: (708)445-2003
Tabloid for Irish-Americans. **Freq:** Monthly. **Print Method:** Offset. **Trim Size:** 11 x 13. **Cols./Page:** 5. **Col. Width:** 2 inches. **Col. Depth:** 12 5/8 inches. **Key Personnel:** Cliff Carlson, Editor; Sean O'Ceallachain, Editor. **USPS:** 013-454. **Subscription Rates:** $30 Individuals standard; $40 Individuals first class; $55 Two years standard; $70 Two years first class; $100 Individuals 3 years ; first class; $3 Single issue. **URL:** http://www.irishamericannews.com. **Mailing address:** PO Box 7, Zion, IL 60099. **Ad Rates:** BW $900; 4C $1695; PCI $25. **Remarks:** Accepts advertising. **Circ:** Paid ‡15013.

11206 ■ Oak Leaves
Sun-Times Media L.L.C.
1010 Lake St.
Oak Park, IL 60301
Phone: (708)383-3200
Fax: (708)383-3678
Publisher's E-mail: customerservice@suntimes.com
Community newspaper (tabloid). **Freq:** Weekly. **Print Method:** Offset. **Cols./Page:** 5. **Col. Width:** 10 inches. **Col. Depth:** 14 inches. **Key Personnel:** Rich Martin, Editor. **Subscription Rates:** $20 Individuals; $84 Out of state. **URL:** http://oakpark.chicagotribune.com. **Remarks:** Advertising accepted; rates available upon request. **Circ:** (Not Reported).

11207 ■ Technology Transfer and Entrepreneurship
Bentham Science Publishers Ltd.
PO Box 446
Oak Park, IL 60303
Journal featuring articles related to the business of biomedical and research. Discussing topics connected to the translation of basic scientific discoveries into commercial opportunities. **Freq:** Semiannual. **Key Personnel:** Chad E. Beyer, Editor. **ISSN:** 2213--8099 (print); **EISSN:** 2213--8102 (electronic). **Subscription Rates:** $740 Institutions print and online, corporate rates; $620 Institutions print or online, corporate rates; $430 Institutions print and online, academic rates; $390 Institutions print or online, academic rates; $130 Individuals print only. **URL:** http://benthamscience.com/journal/index.php?journalID=tte. **Remarks:** Accepts advertising. **Circ:** (Not Reported).

11208 ■ Wednesday Journal of Oak Park & River Forest
Wednesday Journal Inc.
141 S Oak Park Ave.
Oak Park, IL 60302
Phone: (708)524-8300
Fax: (708)524-0447
Publisher's E-mail: circulation@wjinc.com
Community newspaper. **Freq:** Weekly (Wed.). **Print Method:** Offset. **Trim Size:** Tabloid. **Cols./Page:** 4. **Col. Width:** 14.5 picas. **Col. Depth:** 12 3/4 inches. **Key Personnel:** Dan Haley, Editor, phone: (708)613-3301; Terry Dean, Editor. **Subscription Rates:** $32 Individuals; $57 Two years two years; $40 Out of country; $65 Out of country 2 years. **URL:** http://www.oakpark.com. **Remarks:** Accepts advertising. **Circ:** (Not Reported).

11209 ■ WPNA-AM - 1490
408 S Oak Park Ave.
Oak Park, IL 60302
Phone: (708)848-8980
Fax: (708)848-9220
Format: Ethnic. **Networks:** Independent. **Founded:** 1987. **Formerly**: WOPA-AM. **Operating Hours**: Continuous; 100% local. **Key Personnel:** Alan Kearns, Operations Mgr. **Wattage**: 1,000. **Ad Rates:** $25-28 for 30 seconds; $32-40 for 60 seconds. **URL:** http://www.wpna1490am.com.

OAKBROOK TERRACE

DuPage Co DuPage Co. Cook Co. 16 m W of Chicago.

11210 ■ APSA Journal of Pediatric Surgery
American Pediatric Surgical Association
1 Parkview Plz., Ste. 800
Oakbrook Terrace, IL 60181
Phone: (847)686-2237
Fax: (847)686-2253
Publisher's E-mail: eapsa@eapsa.org
Freq: Monthly. **ISSN:** 0022--3468 (print). **Subscription Rates:** $948 Other countries 1 year; $1890 Institutions, other countries 1 year; $679 U.S. 1 year; $1623 Institutions U.S - 1 year. **URL:** http://www.eapsa.org/research/publications. **Remarks:** Advertising not accepted. **Circ:** (Not Reported).

11211 ■ The Joint Commission Journal on Quality and Patient Safety
The Joint Commission Journal on Quality Improvement
1 Renaissance Blvd.
Oakbrook Terrace, IL 60181
Phone: (630)792-5453
Fax: (630)792-4453
Publisher's E-mail: support@jcrinc.com
Magazine directed to health care providers and administrators quality assurance/improvement managers and researchers concerned with the quality of health care; specifically quality improvement, CQI/TQM, and risk management. **Freq:** Monthly. **Key Personnel:** Steven Berman, Executive Editor. **ISSN:** 1553--7250 (print). **Subscription Rates:** $995 Institutions 1 year (site

Circulation: ★ = AAM; △ or • = BPA; ♦ = CAC; ❑ = VAC; ⊕ = PO Statement; ‡ = Publisher's Report; Boldface figures = sworn; Light figures = estimated.

license); $299 Individuals online only - single user; $319 Individuals print and online; $1750 Institutions 2 years (site license); $448 Individuals 2 years (online only - single user); $538 Individuals 2 years (print and online). **URL:** http://www.jcrinc.com/the-joint-commission-journal-on-quality-and-patient-safety. **Formerly**: The Joint Commission Journal on Quality Improvement; Quality Review Bulletin. **Remarks:** Advertising accepted; rates available upon request. **Circ:** (Not Reported).

11212 ■ Journal of Interior Design
Interior Design Educators Council
1 Parkview Plz., Ste. 800
Oakbrook Terrace, IL 60181
Phone: (630)544-5057
Publisher's E-mail: info@idec.org
Freq: 3/year. **Key Personnel:** John Turpin, Editor-in-Chief. **ISSN:** 1071--7641 (print); **EISSN:** 1939--1668 (electronic). **Subscription Rates:** $629 Institutions print and online; £306 Institutions print and online; €464 Institutions print and online; $714 Institutions, other countries print and online; $79 Individuals print and online; £42 Individuals print and online; €62 Individuals print and online; £42 Other countries print and online; $30 Students print and online; £17 Students print and online; €23 Students print and online; £21 Students, other countries print and online. **URL:** http://onlinelibrary.wiley.com/journal/10.1111/(ISSN)1939-1668. **Remarks:** Advertising not accepted. **Circ:** (Not Reported).

11213 ■ Journal of Traumatic Stress
International Society for Traumatic Stress Studies
1 Parkview Plz., Ste. 800
Oakbrook Terrace, IL 60181
Phone: (847)686-2234
Fax: (847)686-2251
Publisher's E-mail: info@wiley.com
Freq: Bimonthly. **Trim Size:** 7 x 10. **Key Personnel:** Daniel S. Weiss, PhD, Editor. **ISSN:** 0894--9867 (print); **EISSN:** 1573--6598 (electronic). **Subscription Rates:** $1281 Institutions online Only; $1538 Institutions print + online; $1281 Institutions print only; $110 Individuals online only; $212 Individuals print + online; $110 Individuals print only. **URL:** http://onlinelibrary.wiley.com/journal/10.1002/(ISSN)1573-6598. **Remarks:** Accepts advertising. **Circ:** (Not Reported).

11214 ■ Omega -- Journal of Death and Dying
Association for Death Education and Counseling
1 Parkview Plz., Ste. 800
Oakbrook Terrace, IL 60181
Phone: (847)686-2240
Fax: (847)686-2251
Publisher's E-mail: adec@adec.org
Freq: 8/year. **Key Personnel:** Kenneth J. Doka, Editor-in-Chief. **ISSN:** 0030--2228 (print); **EISSN:** 1541--3764 (electronic). **Subscription Rates:** £480 Institutions print & e-access; £432 Institutions e-access; £470 Institutions print only; £122 Individuals print & e-access. **URL:** http://www.sagepub.com/journals/Journal202394. **Remarks:** Advertising not accepted. **Circ:** (Not Reported).

11215 ■ PlanetLaundry
Coin Laundry Association
1 S 660 Midwest Rd., Ste. 205
Oakbrook Terrace, IL 60181
Fax: (630)953-7925
Free: 800-570-5629
Publisher's E-mail: info@coinlaundry.org
Magazine containing news and information related to the coin laundry industry. **Freq:** Monthly. **URL:** http://www.planetlaundry.com/home; http://www.coinlaundry.org/publications/planetlaundry. **Formerly**: The Journal of the Coin Laundry Industry. **Ad Rates:** 4C $5452, full page, national manufacturer. **Remarks:** Accepts advertising. **Circ:** ‡20500.

OGLESBY

La Salle Co. La Salle Co. (NC). 7 m SW of Ottawa.

11216 ■ WAJK-FM - 99.3
One Broadcast Ln.
Oglesby, IL 61348
Phone: (815)223-3100
Fax: (815)223-3095
Format: Adult Contemporary. **Networks:** Independent. **Owner:** La Salle County Broadcasting Corp., One Broadcast Ln., Oglesby, IL 61348, Ph: (815)223-3100, Fax: (815)366-1267. **Founded:** Dec. 04, 1964. **Formerly**: WLPO-FM. **Operating Hours**: Continuous; 100% local. **ADI**: Chicago (LaSalle), IL. **Key Personnel:** Mark Lippert, VP of Sales & Mktg; Tricia Salata, Contact, traffic@993wajk.com. **Wattage**: 11,000. **Ad Rates:** $5-13 for 15 seconds; $7-17 for 30 seconds; $9-22 for 60 seconds. Combined advertising rates available with WLPO-AM. **URL:** http://www.wajk.com.

11217 ■ WKOT-FM - 96.5
1 Broadcast Ln.
Oglesby, IL 61348
Phone: (815)223-3100
Format: Oldies. **Founded:** Nov. 16, 1947. **Key Personnel:** John Spencer, Dir. of Programs, programdirector@965wkot.com.

11218 ■ WLPO-AM - 1220
1 Broadcast Lane
Oglesby, IL 61348
Phone: (815)223-3100
Fax: (815)223-3095
Format: Talk; News. **Networks:** NBC. **Founded:** Nov. 16, 1947. **Operating Hours**: Continuous; 25% network, 75% local. **ADI:** Chicago (LaSalle), IL. **Key Personnel:** Joyce McCullough, Gen. Mgr.; Mark Lippert, Sales Mgr., VP of Sales & Mktg.; John Spencer, Dir. of Programs, VP of Operations. **Wattage**: 1,000 Day 500 Night. **Ad Rates:** $7-15 for 15 seconds; $10-20 for 30 seconds; $12-25 for 60 seconds. Combined advertising rates available with WAJK-FM. **URL:** http://www.wlpo.net.

OLNEY

Richland Co. Richland Co. (SE). 60 m NW of Evansville, Ind. Manufactures toys, vinegar, chain link fence and fence fittings, bicycle accessary, tire repairing equipment. Oil production. Oak, walnut timber. Machine shop. Diversified farming.

11219 ■ Carmi Times
Liberty Group
206 Whittle Ave.
Olney, IL 62450
Phone: (618)393-2931
Fax: (618)392-2953
General newspaper. **Founded:** 1950. **Freq:** Daily (eve.) and Sat. (morn.). **Print Method:** Offset. **Cols./Page:** 6. **Col. Width:** 2 inches. **Col. Depth:** 21 1/2 inches. **Key Personnel:** Braden Willis; Lynne Campbell, President, Publisher, phone: (618)932-2146. **Subscription Rates:** $75 Individuals. **URL:** http://www.carmitimes.com. **Mailing address:** PO Box 340, Olney, IL 62450. **Ad Rates:** GLR $1.35; BW $496.65; 4C $796.65; SAU $4.95. **Remarks:** Accepts advertising. **Circ:** 3350.

11220 ■ Olney Daily Mail: The Olney Daily Mail
GateHouse Media Inc.
206 S Whittle Ave.
Olney, IL 62450
Publication E-mail: news@olneydailymail.com
General newspaper. **Freq:** Daily (eve.) and Sat. (morn.). **Print Method:** Offset. **Cols./Page:** 6. **Col. Width:** 25 nonpareils. **Col. Depth:** 301 agate lines. **Key Personnel:** Ray McGrew, Publisher, phone: (618)302-1743; Mark Allen, Editor; Justin Hatten, Editor. **Subscription Rates:** $4.99 Individuals /month (online); $1.91 Individuals /week (print and online). **URL:** http://www.olneydailymail.com. **Ad Rates:** SAU $6.50. **Remarks:** Accepts advertising. **Circ:** (Not Reported).

11221 ■ WIKK-FM - 103.5
4667 E Radio Tower Ln.
Olney, IL 62450
Phone: (618)393-2156
Format: Classic Rock. **Networks:** CNN Radio. **Owner:** Forcht Broadcasting, 2216 Young Dr., Lexington, KY 40505, Ph: (859)335-0365, Fax: (859)335-0453. **Founded:** 1992. **Operating Hours**: Continuous. **ADI:** Terre Haute, IN. **Key Personnel:** Mike Shipman, Gen. Mgr., mishipman@forchtbroadcasting.com. **Wattage:** 25,000. **Ad Rates:** Advertising accepted; rates available upon request. Combined advertising rates available with WVLN and WSEI.

11222 ■ WVLN-AM - 740
4667 E Radio Tower Ln.
Olney, IL 62450
Phone: (618)393-2156
Format: Talk; Sports; News. **Networks:** RFD Illinois; ESPN Radio; Brownfield. **Founded:** 1947. **Operating Hours:** Continuous; 5% network; 17% local; 78% other. **ADI:** Terre Haute, IN. **Wattage:** 250. **Ad Rates:** $8 for 30 seconds; $10 for 60 seconds. **URL:** http://wvlnam.com.

OREGON

Ogle Co. Ogle Co. (N). On Rock River, 100 m W of Chicago. Manufactures piano plates, tanks, street sprinklers, agricultural cutters; silica plant.; yard spinning. Agriculture. Corn, oats, hay.

11223 ■ Mt. Morris Times
Ogle County Newspapers
121 A S 4th St.
Oregon, IL 61061
Phone: (815)732-6166
Fax: (815)732-4238
Free: 800-798-4085
Publisher's E-mail: news@oglecountynews.com
Local newspaper. **Freq:** Weekly (Thurs.). **Print Method:** Offset. Uses mats. **Key Personnel:** Vinde Wells, Editor, phone: (815)732-6166; Earleen Hinton, General Manager, phone: (815)732-6166. **Subscription Rates:** $39 Individuals in Ogle county (52 weeks); $52 Out of area; $1 Single issue. **URL:** http://www.oglecountynews.com/public-notices/mount-morris. **Remarks:** Advertising accepted; rates available upon request. **Circ:** ‡7200.

11224 ■ Ogle County Life
Ogle County Life
311 W Washington
Oregon, IL 61061
Phone: (815)732-2156
Fax: (815)732-6154
Publication E-mail: tonja@oglecountylife.com
Newspaper. **Freq:** Weekly (Mon.). **Print Method:** Offset. **Trim Size:** 11 3/8 x 15 1/4. **Cols./Page:** 6. **Col. Width:** 1 5/8 inches. **Col. Depth:** 14 inches. **Key Personnel:** Gerianne Rorbeck, Office Manager; Tina Ketter, Editor, phone: (815)732-2156; Lesley Divers, Contact, phone: (815)561-2154. **Subscription Rates:** Free to all homes in our designated service area. **URL:** http://www.oglecountylife.com/v2_main_page.php. **Ad Rates:** GLR $.51; BW $331; SAU $5.39; PCI $3.95. **Remarks:** Accepts advertising. **Circ:** Paid ‡1324, Free ‡11535.

11225 ■ Oregon Republican-Reporter
Ogle County Newspapers
121 A S 4th St.
Oregon, IL 61061
Phone: (815)732-6166
Fax: (815)732-4238
Free: 800-798-4085
Publication E-mail: ocnads@shawnnews.com
Local newspaper. **Freq:** Weekly (Thurs.). **Print Method:** Offset. **Cols./Page:** 8. **Col. Width:** 24 nonpareils. **Col. Depth:** 315 agate lines. **Key Personnel:** Jennifer Baratta, Director, Advertising; Trevis Mayfield, Publisher. **Subscription Rates:** $39 Individuals in Ogle county; $52 Out of area; $1 Single issue. **URL:** http://www.oglecountynews.com/contact_us. **Ad Rates:** BW $445.05; 4C $610.05; SAU $3.45. **Remarks:** Accepts advertising. **Circ:** Paid 1300, Free 2000.

ORLAND PARK

Cook Co. Cook Co. (NE). 5 m S W of Blue Island.

11226 ■ The Frankfort Station
22nd Century Media
11516 W 183rd St.
Unit SW, Office Condo No. 3
Orland Park, IL 60467
Phone: (708)326-9170
Fax: (708)326-9179
Publisher's E-mail: support@22ndcenturymedia.com
Community newspaper. **Freq:** Weekly (Thurs.). **Key Personnel:** Rebecca Susmarski, Editor. **Subscription Rates:** Free. **URL:** http://www.frankfortstation.com; http://www.22ndcenturymedia.com/publication/frankfort-station. **Remarks:** Accepts advertising. **Circ:** Non-paid ♦10323.

11227 ■ The Homer Horizon
22nd Century Media
11516 W 183rd St.
Unit SW, Office Condo No. 3
Orland Park, IL 60467
Phone: (708)326-9170
Fax: (708)326-9179

Publisher's E-mail: support@22ndcenturymedia.com
Community newspaper. **Freq:** Weekly (Thurs.). **Key Personnel:** Thomas Czaja, Editor. **Subscription Rates:** Free. **URL:** http://www.homerhorizon.com; http://www.22ndcenturymedia.com/publication/homer-horizon. **Remarks:** Accepts advertising. **Circ:** Non-paid ♦**13384**.

11228 ■ The Mokena Messenger
22nd Century Media
11516 W 183rd St.
Unit SW, Office Condo No. 3
Orland Park, IL 60467
Phone: (708)326-9170
Fax: (708)326-9179
Publisher's E-mail: support@22ndcenturymedia.com
Community newspaper. **Freq:** Weekly (Thurs.). **Key Personnel:** Danny Ciamprone, Editor. **Subscription Rates:** Free. **URL:** http://www.mokenamessenger.com; http://www.22ndcenturymedia.com/publication/mokena-messenger. **Remarks:** Accepts advertising. **Circ:** Non-paid ♦**7798**.

11229 ■ The New Lenox Patriot
22nd Century Media
11516 W 183rd St.
Unit SW, Office Condo No. 3
Orland Park, IL 60467
Phone: (708)326-9170
Fax: (708)326-9179
Publisher's E-mail: support@22ndcenturymedia.com
Community newspaper. **Freq:** Weekly (Thurs.). **Key Personnel:** Meredith Dobes, Editor. **Subscription Rates:** Free. **URL:** http://www.newlenoxpatriot.com; http://www.22ndcenturymedia.com/publication/new-lenox-patriot. **Remarks:** Accepts advertising. **Circ:** Non-paid ♦**12185**.

11230 ■ The Orland Park Prairie
22nd Century Media
11516 W 183rd St.
Unit SW, Office Condo No. 3
Orland Park, IL 60467
Phone: (708)326-9170
Fax: (708)326-9179
Publisher's E-mail: support@22ndcenturymedia.com
Community newspaper. **Freq:** Weekly (Thurs.). **Key Personnel:** Amanda Jarzynski, Assistant Editor; Bill Jones, Editor. **Subscription Rates:** Free. **URL:** http://www.opprairie.com; http://www.22ndcenturymedia.com/publication/orland-park-prairie. **Remarks:** Accepts advertising. **Circ:** Non-paid ♦**25601**.

11231 ■ Penny Bank Post
Still Bank Collectors Club of America
13239 Bundoran Ct.
Orland Park, IL 60462
Freq: 3/year. **Subscription Rates:** Included in membership. **Alt. Formats:** Download. **URL:** http://www.stillbankclub.com/Penny%20Bank%20Post/default.html. **Remarks:** Advertising not accepted. **Circ:** 525.

11232 ■ The Tinley Junction
22nd Century Media
11516 W 183rd St.
Unit SW, Office Condo No. 3
Orland Park, IL 60467
Phone: (708)326-9170
Fax: (708)326-9179
Publisher's E-mail: support@22ndcenturymedia.com
Community newspaper. **Freq:** Weekly (Thurs.). **Key Personnel:** Amanda Jarzynski, Assistant Editor; Michael Gilbert, Editor. **Subscription Rates:** Free. **URL:** http://www.tinleyjunction.com; http://www.22ndcenturymedia.com/publication/tinley-junction. **Remarks:** Accepts advertising. **Circ:** Non-paid ♦**23732**.

OTTAWA

La Salle Co. La Salle Co. (N). On Illinois and Fox Rivers and Lakes to Gulf Waterway, 16 m E of La Salle. Manufactures plates and safety glass, glass marbles, plastics, raw material and finished products, asphalt, indicating devices, dredge pumps, tools, auto parts. Silica sand pits. Diversified farming.

11233 ■ The Times
Small Publishing Group Inc.
110 W Jefferson St.
Ottawa, IL 61350
Phone: (815)433-2000
Fax: (815)433-1626
Publication E-mail: thetimes@theramp.net
Newspaper with Republican orientation. **Founded:** 1844. **Freq:** Mon.-Sat. (eve.). **Print Method:** Offset. **Cols./Page:** 6. **Col. Width:** 24 nonpareils. **Col. Depth:** 301 agate lines. **USPS:** 565-800. **Subscription Rates:** $166.40 Individuals. **URL:** http://mywebtimes.com/contacts.php. **Formerly:** The Daily Times; The Times-Press. **Remarks:** Accepts advertising. **Circ:** Mon.-Sat. ♦**14315**, Wed. ♦**20593**.

11234 ■ WCMY-AM - 1430
216 W Layafette St.
Ottawa, IL 61350
Phone: (815)434-6050
Fax: (815)434-5311
Email: info@ottawaradio.net
Format: Adult Contemporary. **Key Personnel:** John Harris, Gen. Mgr.; Rick Koshko, News Dir; Phil Ahearn, Contact. **URL:** http://www.ottawaradio.net.

11235 ■ WRKX-FM - 95.3
216 W Lafayette St.
Ottawa, IL 61350
Phone: (815)434-6050
Fax: (815)434-5311
Email: info@ottawaradio.net
Format: Adult Contemporary. **Founded:** 1964. **Operating Hours:** Continuous. **Key Personnel:** John Harris, Gen. Mgr. **Wattage:** 4,300 ERP. **Ad Rates:** Noncommercial. **URL:** http://www.ottawaradio.net.

11236 ■ WWTO-TV - 35
420 E Stevenson Rd.
Ottawa, IL 61350
Phone: (815)434-2700
Fax: (815)434-2458
Format: Religious; News; Commercial TV; Contemporary Christian. **Owner:** Trinity Broadcasting Network, PO Box A, Industrysanta Ana, CA 92711. **Founded:** 1986. **Operating Hours:** Continuous. **Key Personnel:** Marlene Zepeda, Station Mgr. **Wattage:** 80,000 Horizontal. E. **Ad Rates:** Advertising accepted; rates available upon request. **URL:** http://www.tbn.org.

PALATINE

Cook Co. Cook Co. (NW). 28 m N.W. of Chicago. Residential. Commercial Manufactures safety glass and equipment, plastic molds, fuses, bulletin boards, signs, adhesives and coatings, electronic testing equipment, electrical equipment, bar BQ grills.

11237 ■ The Chamber Guide
Palatine Area Chamber of Commerce
579 First Bank Dr., Ste. 205
Palatine, IL 60067
Phone: (847)359-7200
Fax: (847)359-7246
Publisher's E-mail: info@palatinechamber.com
Magazine of the Palatine, IL area chamber of commerce. **Freq:** Annual. **URL:** http://www.palatinechamber.com/pages/ChamberBenefits. **Circ:** (Not Reported).

PALOS HEIGHTS

Cook Co. Cook Co. (NE). 18 m SW of Chicago.

11238 ■ Illinois Music Educator
Illinois Music Education Association
7270 W College Dr., Ste. 201
Palos Heights, IL 60463
Phone: (708)479-4000
Fax: (708)361-5638
Scholarly journal of the Illinois Music Educators Association covering music and music research. **Freq:** 3/year fall, winter and spring. **Trim Size:** 8 1/2 x 11. **Cols./Page:** 3. **Col. Width:** 2 1/4 inches. **Col. Depth:** 10 inches. **Key Personnel:** William Froom, Editor. **URL:** http://www.ilmea.org/publications. **Ad Rates:** BW $350; 4C $805. **Remarks:** Accepts advertising. **Circ:** (Not Reported).

11239 ■ Regional News
Regional Publishing Corp.
12243 S Harlem Ave.
Palos Heights, IL 60463-1431
Phone: (708)448-4000
Community newspaper. **Founded:** Oct. 07, 1941. **Freq:** Weekly (Thurs.). **Print Method:** Offset. **Trim Size:** 12.5 x 22.75. **Cols./Page:** 6. **Col. Width:** 1.8 inches. **Col. Depth:** 21 1/4 inches. **Key Personnel:** Amy Richards, Publisher. **USPS:** 419-260. **Subscription Rates:** $42 Individuals print only. **URL:** http://regionalpublishing.com/?page_id=251. **Formerly:** Palos Regional. **Ad Rates:** GLR $1.35; BW $2,000; 4C $2,400; PCI $18.94. **Remarks:** Accepts advertising. **Circ:** (Not Reported).

11240 ■ The Reporter: Published Every Thursday
Regional Publishing Corp.
12247 S Harlem Ave.
Palos Heights, IL 60463-1431
Phone: (708)448-6161
Paid Community newspaper. **Freq:** Weekly. **Print Method:** Offset. **Trim Size:** 12.5 x 22.75. **Cols./Page:** 6. **Col. Width:** 1.8 inches. **Col. Depth:** 21.25 inches. **Key Personnel:** Amy Richards, Publisher, phone: (708)448-6161. **USPS:** 118-690. **URL:** http://regionalpublishing.com/?page_id=254. **Formerly:** Worth-Palos Reporter; Palos Hills-Hickory Hills; Worth-Ridge Reporter. **Ad Rates:** GLR $1.28; BW $2000; 4C $2250; PCI $18.94. **Circ:** Paid ‡18000.

11241 ■ Teaching Music
Illinois Music Education Association
7270 W College Dr., Ste. 201
Palos Heights, IL 60463
Phone: (708)479-4000
Fax: (708)361-5638
Publisher's E-mail: memberservices@nafme2.org
Freq: Quarterly. **Print Method:** Offset. **Trim Size:** 8 1/4 x 10 3/4. **Cols./Page:** 3. **Col. Width:** 26 nonpareils. **Col. Depth:** 140 agate lines. **Key Personnel:** Linda Brown, Editor. **ISSN:** 1069--7446 (print). **Subscription Rates:** Included in membership. **URL:** http://nafme.org; http://www.nafme.org/my-classroom/journals-magazines. **Ad Rates:** BW $2704; 4C $3402. **Remarks:** Advertising accepted; rates available upon request. **Circ:** Paid 80000.

PALOS PARK

Cook Co.

11242 ■ Bandworld
Women Band Directors International
c/o Carol Nendza, Treasurer
10611 Ridgewood Dr.
Palos Park, IL 60464
Magazine containing articles regarding Women Band Directors International Association, its members and other relevant ideas. **Subscription Rates:** Included in membership; $15 online. **URL:** http://www.womenbanddirectors.org/publications.html. **Remarks:** Advertising not accepted. **Circ:** (Not Reported).

11243 ■ Woman Conductor
Women Band Directors International
c/o Carol Nendza, Treasurer
10611 Ridgewood Dr.
Palos Park, IL 60464
Magazine featuring articles and information about Women Band Directors International. **Freq:** 3/year published February, May and October. **Subscription Rates:** Included in membership. **URL:** http://www.womenbanddirectors.org/publications.html. **Remarks:** Advertising not accepted. **Circ:** 500.

PARIS

Edgar Co. Edgar Co. (E). 39 m S Danville. Grain milling. Manufacturing industrial machinery, truck bodies, wood furniture, wood milling, porcelain, steel fabrication, steel sinks, metal products, pet foods, farm seeds. Farming.

11244 ■ Paris Beacon-News
Beacon News Publishing
218 N Main St.
Paris, IL 61944
Phone: (217)465-6424
Publisher's E-mail: news@parisbeacon.com
Newspaper with a Republican orientation. **Freq:** Mon.-Sat. (eve.). **Print Method:** Offset. **Cols./Page:** 6. **Col. Width:** 25 nonpareils. **Col. Depth:** 294 agate lines. **Key Personnel:** Shawn Storie, Manager, phone: (765)361-1684; Tay Smith, Publisher. **Subscription Rates:** $9.99 Individuals 30 days; $33 Individuals 90 days; $64 Individuals 180 days; $92 Individuals 270 days; $112 Individuals 365 days. **URL:** http://www.parisbeacon.com/news. **Mailing address:** PO Box 100, Paris, IL 61944.

Circulation: ★ = AAM; △ or • = BPA; ♦ = CAC; ❑ = VAC; ⊕ = PO Statement; ‡ = Publisher's Report; Boldface figures = sworn; Light figures = estimated.

Ad Rates: BW $819; 4C $1,069; PCI $6.50. **Remarks:** Advertising accepted; rates available upon request. **Circ:** (Not Reported).

11245 ■ Skytower Communications Group L.L.C. - 98.5
12861 Illinois Hwy. 133
Paris, IL 61944
Phone: (217)465-6336
Email: wacfcountry@hotmail.com
Format: Country. **Networks:** NBC; ABC; Westwood One Radio. **Founded:** 1952. **Operating Hours:** Continuous; 10% network, 90% local. **ADI:** Terre Haute, IN. **Key Personnel:** Phil Johnson, Gen. Mgr. **Wattage:** 50,000. **Ad Rates:** $12-17 for 60 seconds. **Mailing address:** PO Box 277, Paris, IL 61944.

PARK RIDGE

Cook Co. Cook Co. (NE). 13 m NW of Chicago. Residential.

11246 ■ AANA Journal
American Association of Nurse Anesthetists
222 S Prospect Ave.
Park Ridge, IL 60068-4001
Phone: (847)692-7050
Fax: (847)692-6968
Free: 855-526-2262
Publisher's E-mail: info@aana.com
Nursing and anesthesia journal. **Freq:** Bimonthly Semiannual Feb., Apr., June, Aug., Oct., and Dec. **Print Method:** Web offset. **Trim Size:** 8 1/8 x 10 7/8. **Cols./Page:** 2. **Col. Width:** 19.6 picas. **Col. Depth:** 40.6 picas. **Key Personnel:** Chuck Biddle, Editor-in-Chief; Sally Aquino, Managing Editor. **ISSN:** 0094--6354 (print). **USPS:** 283-260. **Subscription Rates:** Included in membership; $24 Nonmembers. **URL:** http://www.aana.com/newsandjournal/pages/aanajournalonline.aspx; http://www.aane.org/asperger_resources/aane_journal.html. **Ad Rates:** BW $3,775; 4C $2,265. **Remarks:** Accepts advertising. **Circ:** ⊕**36459**.

11247 ■ AANA Journal
AANA Publishing Inc.
222 S Prospect Ave.
Park Ridge, IL 60068-4001
Phone: (847)692-7050
Fax: (847)692-6968
Publisher's E-mail: info@aana.com
Nursing and anesthesia journal. **Freq:** Bimonthly Semiannual Feb., Apr., June, Aug., Oct., and Dec. **Print Method:** Web offset. **Trim Size:** 8 1/8 x 10 7/8. **Cols./Page:** 2. **Col. Width:** 19.6 picas. **Col. Depth:** 40.6 picas. **Key Personnel:** Chuck Biddle, Editor-in-Chief; Sally Aquino, Managing Editor. **ISSN:** 0094--6354 (print). **USPS:** 283-260. **Subscription Rates:** Included in membership; $24 Nonmembers. **URL:** http://www.aana.com/newsandjournal/pages/aanajournalonline.aspx; http://www.aane.org/asperger_resources/aane_journal.html. **Ad Rates:** BW $3,775; 4C $2,265. **Remarks:** Accepts advertising. **Circ:** ⊕**36459**.

11248 ■ Beef Today: The Magazine of American Beef Producers
Farm Journal Media Inc.
1550 NW Hwy., Ste. 403
Park Ridge, IL 60068
Free: 800-320-7992
Publisher's E-mail: customerservice@farmjournal.com
Magazine for farmers and ranchers raising beef cows, feeders, and backgrounder cattle. **Freq:** 10/year. **Print Method:** Offset. **Trim Size:** 8 x 10 1/2. **Cols./Page:** 3. **Col. Width:** 2 1/4 inches. **Col. Depth:** 140 agate lines. **Key Personnel:** Kim Watson, Editor; Sara Brown, Editor. **ISSN:** 1056-1390 (print). **URL:** http://www.agweb.com/livestock/beef. **Formerly:** Beef Extra. **Ad Rates:** BW $7,800; 4C $9,300. **Remarks:** Accepts advertising. **Circ:** (Not Reported).

11249 ■ Clinical Orthopaedics and Related Research
The Association of Bone and Joint Surgeons
300 S Northwest Hwy., Ste. 203
Park Ridge, IL 60068
Phone: (847)720-4186
Fax: (847)720-4013
Publisher's E-mail: service-ny@springer.com
Contains original articles on general orthopedics and specialty topics covering advances in current research and practice. **Freq:** Monthly. **Trim Size:** 8 1/4 x 11. **Key Personnel:** Seth S. Leopold, Editor-in-Chief. **ISSN:** 0009--921X (print); **EISSN:** 1528--1132 (electronic). **Subscription Rates:** $954 Institutions print incl. free access or e-only. **URL:** http://www.springer.com/medicine/orthopedics/journal/11999; http://www.abjs.org/clinical-orthopaedics-and-related-research-2. **Ad Rates:** BW $1,825; 4C $1,300. **Remarks:** Accepts advertising. **Circ:** Paid 2200.

11250 ■ Dairy Today: The Magazine of American Dairy Producers
Farm Journal Media Inc.
1550 NW Hwy., Ste. 403
Park Ridge, IL 60068
Free: 800-320-7992
Publisher's E-mail: customerservice@farmjournal.com
Agricultural magazine for dairy managers and producers. **Freq:** Annual. **Print Method:** Offset. **Trim Size:** 8 x 10 1/2. **Cols./Page:** 3. **Col. Width:** 2 1/4 inches. **Col. Depth:** 140 agate lines. **Key Personnel:** Jim Dickrell, Editor; Bill Newham, Publisher, phone: (816)889-9400, fax: (816)889-9404. **ISSN:** 1056-1382 (print). **URL:** http://www.farmjournalmedia.com/dairy-today-magazine. **Formerly:** Dairy Extra. **Ad Rates:** 4C $7000. **Remarks:** Accepts advertising. **Circ:** (Not Reported).

11251 ■ Farm Journal: The Magazine of American Agriculture
Farm Journal Media Inc.
1550 NW Hwy., Ste. 403
Park Ridge, IL 60068
Free: 800-320-7992
Publisher's E-mail: feedback@farmjournal.com
Agricultural news magazine for people who own or operate farms or ranches. **Freq:** Monthly. **Print Method:** Offset. **Trim Size:** 8 x 10 1/2. **Cols./Page:** 3. **Col. Width:** 2 1/4 inches. **Col. Depth:** 140 agate lines. **Key Personnel:** Charlene Finck, Editor, phone: (573)581-9642; Katie Humphreys, Managing Editor; Steve Custer, Publisher. **ISSN:** 0014-8008 (print). **URL:** http://www.agweb.com/farmjournal/issues. **Ad Rates:** BW $32,650; 4C $43,000. **Remarks:** Accepts advertising. **Circ:** Combined ★**404417**.

11252 ■ Implement & Tractor
Farm Journal Media Inc.
1550 NW Hwy., Ste. 403
Park Ridge, IL 60068
Free: 800-320-7992
Publisher's E-mail: customerservice@farmjournal.com
Magazine about agricultural equipment and machinery. **Freq:** Bimonthly. **Print Method:** sheet. **Trim Size:** 8 1/8 x 10 7/8. **Cols./Page:** 3. **Col. Width:** 2 1/8 INS. **Col. Depth:** 10 INS. **Key Personnel:** Margy Fischer, Editor. **ISSN:** 0019--2953 (print). **URL:** http://www.farmjournalmedia.com/implement-and-tractor; http://www.farm-equipment.com. **Remarks:** Advertising accepted; rates available upon request. **Circ:** (Not Reported).

11253 ■ Journal of Safety, Health and Environmental Research
American Society of Safety Engineers
520 N Northwest Hwy.
Park Ridge, IL 60068
Phone: (847)699-2929
Fax: (847)768-3434
Publisher's E-mail: customerservice@asse.org
Journal focused on concepts and terminology related to chemical spills. **Key Personnel:** Anthony Veltri, EdD, Editor-in-Chief. **Alt. Formats:** PDF. **URL:** http://www.asse.org/academicsjournal. **Formerly:** Journal of SH and E Research. **Remarks:** Advertising not accepted. **Circ:** (Not Reported).

11254 ■ PORKNetwork
Farm Journal Media Inc.
1550 NW Hwy., Ste. 403
Park Ridge, IL 60068
Free: 800-320-7992
Publisher's E-mail: customerservice@farmjournal.com
Professional magazine providing information on improving business and service opportunities for vets serving pork producers. **Freq:** 8/year. **Print Method:** Web Offset. **Trim Size:** 7 7/8 x 10 3/4. **Cols./Page:** 3. **Col. Width:** 13 nonpareils. **Col. Depth:** 140 agate lines. **ISSN:** 0745-3787 (print). **URL:** http://www.porknetwork.com. **Formerly:** Swine Practitioner. **Ad Rates:** BW $3,143; 4C $4,243. **Remarks:** Accepts advertising. **Circ:** △**3340**.

11255 ■ Professional Safety: Journal of the American Society of Safety Engineers
American Society of Safety Engineers
520 N Northwest Hwy.
Park Ridge, IL 60068
Phone: (847)699-2929
Fax: (847)768-3434
Publisher's E-mail: customerservice@asse.org
Peer-reviewed journal focusing on professional safety, risk management, and loss prevention. **Freq:** Monthly. **Print Method:** Offset. Uses mats. **Trim Size:** 8 1/8 x 10 7/8. **Cols./Page:** 3. **Col. Width:** 26 nonpareils. **Col. Depth:** 140 agate lines. **Key Personnel:** Cathy Baker, Assistant Editor; Sue Trebswether, Editor; Tina Angley, Associate Editor. **ISSN:** 0099--0027 (print). **Subscription Rates:** $60 U.S., Canada, and Mexico; $70 Other countries; $51 Institutions libraries; $60 Libraries foreign; $45 Individuals online. **URL:** http://www.asse.org/professional-safety. **Ad Rates:** BW $3150; 4C $5180; PCI $80. **Remarks:** Accepts advertising. **Circ:** Paid 32123.

11256 ■ Round the Table
Million Dollar Round Table
325 W Touhy Ave.
Park Ridge, IL 60068-4265
Phone: (847)692-6378
Fax: (847)518-8921
Publisher's E-mail: info@mdrt.org
Freq: Bimonthly. **Print Method:** Web Press. **Trim Size:** 8 1/2 x 11. **ISSN:** 0161--7125 (print). **Subscription Rates:** $20 Individuals; $36 Two years; $30 Other countries; $50 Other countries 2 years; $4 Single issue. **Alt. Formats:** PDF. **URL:** http://www.mdrtstore.org/c/267/round-the-table-magazine. **Remarks:** Advertising not accepted. **Circ:** 32000.

11257 ■ STLE Tribology Transactions
Society of Tribologists and Lubrication Engineers
840 Busse Hwy.
Park Ridge, IL 60068-2302
Phone: (847)825-5536
Freq: Quarterly. **ISSN:** 0569- 8197 (print). **Subscription Rates:** $111 Individuals online. **URL:** http://www.stle.org/research/transactions/. **Remarks:** Advertising not accepted. **Circ:** (Not Reported).

11258 ■ Tribology & Lubrication Technology
Society of Tribologists and Lubrication Engineers
840 Busse Hwy.
Park Ridge, IL 60068-2302
Phone: (847)825-5536
Magazine sent to STLE members focusing on lubrication related research, theory, and practice. **Freq:** Monthly. **Print Method:** Offset. **Trim Size:** 8 1/2 x 11 1/4. **Cols./Page:** 3 and 2. **Col. Width:** 26 and 40 nonpareils. **Col. Depth:** 140 agate lines. **Key Personnel:** Thomas T. Astrene, Editor-in-Chief, Publisher; Karl M. Phipps, Associate Manager. **ISSN:** 0024--7154 (print). **Subscription Rates:** $216 U.S.; $281 Other countries; $352 Two years; $471 Other countries 2 years. **URL:** http://www.stle.org/files/Publications/TLT_Magazine.aspx. **Formerly:** Lubrication Engineering. **Ad Rates:** BW $2,510; 4C $3,460. **Remarks:** Accepts advertising. **Circ:** 7000.

11259 ■ WMTH-FM - 90.5
2601 W Dempster St.
Park Ridge, IL 60068
Phone: (847)825-8484
Format: Public Radio. **Owner:** Maine East High School, 2601 Dempster St., Park Ridge, IL 60068, Ph: (847)825-4484. **Founded:** 1957. **Operating Hours:** Various; 100% local. **Key Personnel:** Jim Francois, Contact; Barb Rieger, Contact. **Wattage:** 016. **Ad Rates:** Noncommercial.

PAXTON

Ford Co. Ford Co. (E). 25 m N of Champaign. Manufacturers brooms, electronic components, industrial air conditioners, air coils; corn processing. Agriculture. Corn, soybeans.

11260 ■ Green Diamond
Illinois Central Railroad Historical Society
PO Box 288
Paxton, IL 60957

Publisher's E-mail: contactus@icrrhistorical.org

Magazine containing articles and historical stories about the Illinois Central Railroad. **Freq:** 4/yr. **Subscription Rates:** $6.50 Nonmembers. **URL:** http://www.icrrhistorical.org/Publications.html. **Remarks:** Advertising not accepted. **Circ:** (Not Reported).

11261 ■ WPXN-FM - 104.9
361 N Railroad Ave.
Paxton, IL 60957
Phone: (217)379-9796

Format: Oldies; News; Information. **Owner:** Paxton Broadcasting Co., 361 Railroad Ave., Paxton, IL 60957, Ph: (217)379-9796. **Founded:** 1984. **Wattage:** 3,000 ERP. **Ad Rates:** Advertising accepted; rates available upon request. **URL:** http://www.wpxnradio.com.

PEKIN

Tazewell Co. Tazewell Co. (NC). On Illinois River, 10 m S of Peoria. Marine grain elevator on Illinois Waterways. Manufactures health products, corn products, liquors, alcohol, malt, cereal, wire and concrete products, burial vaults, chip board, tractor, automotive parts. Brass, copper, iron, aluminum castings. Non-ferrous metal processing. Coal mines. Agriculture.

11262 ■ Pekin Daily Times
Howard Publications
20 S Fourth St.
Pekin, IL 61554
Phone: (309)346-1111
Free: 800-888-6397

General newspaper. **Founded:** 1853. **Freq:** Daily (eve.) and Sat. (morn.). **Print Method:** Offset. **Cols./Page:** 6. **Col. Width:** 2 1/16 inches. **Col. Depth:** 21 inches. **Key Personnel:** Michelle Teheux, Editor. **Subscription Rates:** $78 Individuals; $90 Out of state. **URL:** http://www.pekintimes.com. **Mailing address:** PO Box 430, Pekin, IL 61554. **Ad Rates:** GLR $8.35; BW $1,562.40; 4C $1,862.40; SAU $10; PCI $12.40. **Remarks:** Accepts advertising. **Circ:** Mon.-Sat. 12610.

11263 ■ WBNH-FM - 88.5
1919 Mayflower Dr.
Pekin, IL 61554
Phone: (309)636-8850
Fax: (877)631-8850
Email: wbnh@wbnh.org

Format: Religious. **Networks:** Moody Broadcasting. **Owner:** Central Illinois Radio Fellowship Inc., 20186 Sterling Rd., Bloomington, IL 61705-5328. **Operating Hours:** Continuous. **Key Personnel:** Jim Huber, Station Mgr., jim@wbnh.org; Keith Lang, Operations Mgr., keith@wbnh.org; Nancy Theobald, Office Mgr., nancy@wbnh.org; Daniel Cushman, Production Mgr., daniel@wbnh.org. **Wattage:** 48,000 ERP. **Ad Rates:** Advertising accepted; rates available upon request. **URL:** http://www.wbnh.org.

PEORIA

Peoria Co. Peoria Co. (NWC). On Illinois River, linked to the Gulf Waterway on the south and the St. Lawrence Seaway to the north. 160 m SW of Chicago. Bradley University. Illinois Central College Boat facilities. Manufactures of tractors, alcohol and solvents, brick, tile, caskets, castings, cordage, cotton goods, fencing and wire products, nails, feed, pharmaceuticals, steel, paper, household products, furnaces, oil burners, road machinery, heavy graders, strawboard, tools, dies, labels. Millwork.

11264 ■ Catholic Post
Catholic Post
PO Box 1722
Peoria, IL 61656
Free: 800-340-5630
Publisher's E-mail: development@cdop.org

Catholic newspaper. **Freq:** Weekly (Fri.). **Print Method:** Offset. **Trim Size:** 14 x 22 3/4. **Cols./Page:** 6. **Col. Width:** 2 inches. **Col. Depth:** 21 1/2 inches. **Key Personnel:** Rev. Daniel R. Jenky, Publisher; Tom Dermody, Editor-in-Chief; Sonia Nelson, Manager, Advertising. **USPS:** 557-000. **Subscription Rates:** $25 Individuals; $26 Out of state. **URL:** http://thecatholicpost.com/post. **Ad Rates:** BW $1083.50; SAU $1312.62; PCI $13.90. **Remarks:** Accepts advertising. **Circ:** 50000.

11265 ■ Journal Star
The Peoria Journal Star Inc.
One News Plz.
Peoria, IL 61614
Phone: (309)686-3000
Publisher's E-mail: mwieland@pjstar.com

General newspaper. **Freq:** Mon.-Sun. (morn.). **Print Method:** Letterpress. **Trim Size:** 13 x 21 1/2. **Cols./Page:** 6. **Col. Width:** 2 1/16 inches. **Col. Depth:** 21 1/2 INS. **Key Personnel:** Ken Mauser, Publisher, phone: (309)686-3005. **Subscription Rates:** $9.99 Individuals online; /month; $2.40 Individuals print and online; /week. **URL:** http://www.pjstar.com. **Circ:** Mon.-Fri. ***65320**, Sat. ***70255**, Sun. ***80394**.

11266 ■ The Labor Paper
The Labor Paper
400 NE Jefferson, No. 400
Peoria, IL 61603
Phone: (309)674-3148
Fax: (309)674-9714

Labor tabloid. **Freq:** Semimonthly. **Print Method:** Offset. **Cols./Page:** 4. **Col. Width:** 28 nonpareils. **Col. Depth:** 182 agate lines. **Key Personnel:** Marty Helfers, Publisher; Sharon K. Williams, Business Manager, Editor. **Subscription Rates:** $15 Individuals 1 year (print); $12 Members; $40 Individuals 3 year (print). **URL:** http://www.westcentralbtc.org/labor%20paper.htm. **Ad Rates:** BW $560; 4C $875; SAU $35. **Circ:** ‡20000.

11267 ■ Morton Times News
GateHouse Media Inc.
PO Box 9426
Peoria, IL 61612
Phone: (309)692-6600

Community newspaper. **Freq:** Weekly (Wed.). **Print Method:** Offset. **Trim Size:** 12 1/2 x 21 1/2. **Cols./Page:** 6. **Col. Width:** 11 picas. **Col. Depth:** 21.5 inches. **Key Personnel:** Jeanette Brickner, Executive Editor. **URL:** http://www.mortontimesnews.com. **Ad Rates:** BW $2,967; 4C $3,267; PCI $23. **Remarks:** Accepts advertising. **Circ:** 2416.

11268 ■ Shooting Times
RentPath Inc.
PO Box 1790
Peoria, IL 61656
Publication E-mail: shootingtimes@emailcustomerservice.com

Magazine focusing on guns and shooting sports. **Freq:** Monthly. **Print Method:** Offset. **Trim Size:** 7 7/8 x 10 1/2. **Cols./Page:** 3. **Col. Width:** 27 nonpareils. **Col. Depth:** 140 agate lines. **Key Personnel:** Matt Johnson, General Manager; Joseph von Benedikt, Editor. **Subscription Rates:** $12 Individuals; $15 Two years; $25 Canada; $41 Canada 2 years; $27 Other countries; $45 Other countries 2 years; $10 Individuals 1 year (12 issues). **URL:** http://www.shootingtimes.com. **Remarks:** Advertising accepted; rates available upon request. **Circ:** Paid ***174684**.

11269 ■ The Short Line
The Short Line
1318 S Johanson Rd.
Peoria, IL 61607-1130
Phone: (309)697-1400
Fax: (309)697-5387
Publisher's E-mail: theshortline@hotmail.com

Journal covering current events and the history of the Shortline railroad. **Freq:** Bimonthly. **Key Personnel:** M. Peterson, Editor. **ISSN:** 0199-4050 (print). **USPS:** 130-330. **Subscription Rates:** $19.95 Individuals U.S. & Mexico; $25.95 Individuals air mail (Europe); $20.95 Individuals Canada; $27.95 Individuals air mail (Far East, Pacific areas). **URL:** http://www.the-short-line.com. **Ad Rates:** BW $650. **Remarks:** Accepts advertising. **Circ:** (Not Reported).

11270 ■ 99.9 WWCT FM - 99.9
4234 N Brandywine Dr., Ste. D
Peoria, IL 61614
Phone: (309)686-0101
Email: community@wwctfm.com

Format: Album-Oriented Rock (AOR); Classic Rock; Alternative/New Music/Progressive; Blues. **Founded:** 1976. **ADI:** Peoria-Bloomington, IL. **Key Personnel:** Bruce Foster, Contact. **Wattage:** 1,500 ERP. **Ad Rates:** Advertising accepted; rates available upon request. **URL:** http://wwctfm.com.

11271 ■ WCBU-FM - 89.9
1501 W Bradley Ave.
Peoria, IL 61625
Phone: (309)677-3690
Fax: (309)677-3462
Email: wcbu@bradley.edu

Format: Public Radio. **Networks:** National Public Radio (NPR). **Owner:** Bradley University, 1501 W Bradley Ave., Peoria, IL 61625, Ph: (309)676-7611, Fax: (309)677-4053. **Key Personnel:** Lisa Polnitz, Office Mgr., lpolnitz@bradley.edu; Nathan Irwin, Dir. of Programs, nirwin@bradley.edu; Cindy Dermody, Mgr., cdermody@bradley.edu; Betty Beard, Mgr., Member Svcs., bbeard@bradley.edu; Tom Hunt, Exec. Dir., thunt@bradley.edu; Bill Porter, Chief Engineer; Daryl Scott, Operations Mgr. **Ad Rates:** Noncommercial. **URL:** http://www.peoriapublicradio.org.

11272 ■ WCIC-FM - 91.5
3902 W Baring Trace
Peoria, IL 61615
Phone: (309)692-9242
Email: wcic@wcicfm.org

Format: Contemporary Christian. **Owner:** Illinois Bible Institute, c/o Lake Williamson Christian Conference Ctr. 17280 Lakeside Dr., Carlinville, IL 62626, Ph: (217)854-4820. **Founded:** 1983. **Operating Hours:** Continuous Monday - Friday; 6:00 a.m. - Midnight Saturday - Sunday. **Key Personnel:** Joe Buchanan, Music Dir., joeb@newlifemedia.org. **Local Programs:** *Doing Life With The Traceys*, Monday Tuesday Wednesday Thursday Friday 5:30 a.m. - 10:00 a.m. **Wattage:** 47,000 ERP. **Ad Rates:** Noncommercial; underwriting available. Underwriting available. **URL:** http://www.wcicfm.org.

11273 ■ WFYR-FM - 97.3
120 Eaton St.
120 Eaton St.
Peoria, IL 61603
Phone: (309)673-0973

Format: Country. **Ad Rates:** Noncommercial. **URL:** http://www.973nashfm.com.

11274 ■ WGLO-FM - 95.5
120 Eaton St.
Peoria, IL 61603
Phone: (309)676-5000
Fax: (309)676-2600
Free: 888-676-9595

Format: Classic Rock. **Founded:** Sept. 12, 2006. **Key Personnel:** Matt Bahan, Operations Mgr., Prog. Dir.; Brad Creek, Sales Mgr. **Ad Rates:** Noncommercial. **URL:** http://www.955glo.com.

11275 ■ WHPI-FM - 101.1
4234 N Brandywine Dr.
Peoria, IL 61614
Phone: (309)691-0101
Free: 866-930-JACK

Format: Oldies. **Networks:** ESPN Radio. **Owner:** Independence Media Group, PO Box 364, Broomall, PA 19008. **Formerly:** WXMP-FM. **Operating Hours:** 9:00 a.m. - 5:00 p.m. Monday - Friday. **Wattage:** 3,300 ERP. **Ad Rates:** Advertising accepted; rates available upon request. **URL:** http://www.myhippie.com/.

11276 ■ WIRL-AM - 1290
331 Fulton, Ste. 1200
Peoria, IL 61602
Phone: (309)637-3700

Format: Country. **Key Personnel:** Kevin Cassulo, Sales Mgr., kevincassulo@jmpradio.com. **URL:** http://www.1290wirl.com.

11277 ■ WMBD-AM - 1470
331 Fulton St., Ste. 1200
Peoria, IL 61602
Phone: (309)685-1470

Format: Talk; News; Sports. **Networks:** CBS; Westwood One Radio. **Founded:** 1927. **Operating Hours:** Continuous. **Key Personnel:** Shaun Newell, News Dir., shaunnewell@1470wmbd.com; Wayne R. Miller, Chief Engineer, wrm@jmpradio.com. **Local Programs:** *The Glenn Beck Show*, Monday Tuesday Wednesday Thursday Friday 9:00 a.m. - 11:00 a.m. **Wattage:** 5,000. **Ad Rates:** Noncommercial. **URL:** http://www.1470wmbd.com.

Circulation: ★ = AAM; △ or • = BPA; ♦ = CAC; ❑ = VAC; ⊕ = PO Statement; ‡ = Publisher's Report; Boldface figures = sworn; Light figures = estimated.

11278 ■ WMBD-TV - 31
3131 N University
Peoria, IL 61604
Phone: (309)688-3131
Networks: CBS. **Owner:** Nexstar Broadcasting Group Inc., 545 E John Carpenter Fwy., Ste. 700, Irving, TX 75062, Ph: (972)373-8800. **Founded:** Jan. 01, 1958. **Operating Hours**: Continuous. **ADI**: Peoria-Bloomington, IL. **Key Personnel:** Coby Cooper, Gen. Mgr., cobyc@wmbd.com; Rick Moll, News Dir., rickm@wmbd.com; Steve Mason, Dir. of Sales, stevem@wmbd.com. **Ad Rates:** Advertising accepted; rates available upon request. **URL:** http://www.centralillinoisproud.com.

11279 ■ WOAM-AM - 1350
PO Box 1017
Peoria, IL 61653
Phone: (309)685-1350
Fax: (309)685-7150
Format: Big Band/Nostalgia; Music of Your Life; Oldies; Middle-of-the-Road (MOR). **Networks:** ABC. **Owner:** Kelly Communications Inc., at above address. **Founded:** 1980. **Operating Hours**: Continuous. **ADI**: Peoria-Bloomington, IL. **Key Personnel:** Bob Kelly, Owner; Joyce Powell, Sales Mgr., jpowell@1350woam.com; Lee Malcolm, Dir. of Production, lmalcolm@1350woam.com; Dave Murphy, Sports Dir., dmurphy@1350woam.com. **Wattage**: 1,000. **Ad Rates:** $5 for 15 seconds; $10 for 30 seconds; $20 for 60 seconds. WPMJ-FM 94.3.

11280 ■ WPBG-FM - 93.3
331 Fulton St., 12th Fl.
Peoria, IL 61602
Phone: (309)637-3700
Fax: (309)686-8659
Format: Adult Contemporary. **Networks:** Independent. **Owner:** JMP Radio Group. **Founded:** 1947. **Formerly**: WKZW-AM; WMXP-FM. **Operating Hours**: Continuous. **ADI**: Peoria-Bloomington, IL. **Key Personnel:** Kevin Cassulo, Contact, kevincassulo@jmpradio.com; Rick Hirschmann, Prog. Dir., rick.hirschmann@alphamediausa.com; Kevin Cassulo, Contact, kevincassulo@jmpradio.com; Rick Hirschmann, Contact, rickhirschmann@jmpradio.com. **Wattage**: 41,000. **Ad Rates:** Advertising accepted; rates available upon request. **URL:** http://www.933thedrive.com.

11281 ■ WPEO-AM - 1020
PO Box 1
Peoria, IL 61650
Phone: (309)698-9736
Fax: (309)698-9740
Free: 800-728-1020
Format: Contemporary Christian. **Owner:** Pinebrook Foundation Inc., 1708 Highview Rd., East Peoria, IL 61611. **Founded:** 1946. **Operating Hours**: 6 a.m. to 8:15 p.m. Mon.-Sat.; 6 a.m. to 8 p.m. Sun. **Key Personnel:** Robert Ulrich, Gen. Mgr.; Nelson Hostetler, Dir. of Production. **Wattage**: 1,000. **Ad Rates:** Noncommercial. **URL:** http://citylinktv.com.

11282 ■ WPIA-FM - 98.5
4232 N Brandywine Dr., Ste. G
Peoria, IL 61614
Phone: (309)686-0101
Format: Contemporary Hit Radio (CHR). **Operating Hours**: Continuous. **Ad Rates:** Advertising accepted; rates available upon request. **URL:** http://www.kisspeoria.com.

11283 ■ WPMJ-FM - 94.3
3641 Meadowbrook Rd.
Peoria, IL 61604
Phone: (309)685-0977
Fax: (309)685-7150
Format: Oldies. **Key Personnel:** Joyce Powell, Contact, jpowell@trueoldies943.com. **URL:** http://www.wpmjradio.com.

11284 ■ WSWT-FM - 107
331 Fulton St., 12th Fl.
Peoria, IL 61602
Phone: (309)637-3700
Fax: (309)673-9538
Free: 800-597-1069
Format: Soft Rock. **Owner:** JMP Media L.L.C., at above address, Peoria, IL 61602-1475. **Founded:** 1968. **Operating Hours**: Continuous. **Wattage**: 50,000. **Ad Rates:** Advertising accepted; rates available upon request. **URL:** http://www.literock107.com.

11285 ■ WTAZ-FM - 102.3
PO Box 6255
Peoria, IL 61601-6255
Phone: (309)263-2915
Free: 800-948-0102
Email: talk@wtaz.com
Format: Talk. **Networks:** ABC; NBC; EFM; Westwood One Radio; CBS. **Owner:** Morton-Washington Broadcasting Co., Peoria, IL. **Founded:** 1976. **Operating Hours**: Continuous; 90% network, 10% local. **ADI**: Peoria-Bloomington, IL. **Key Personnel:** Jerry Scott, Station Mgr.; John Malone, Operations Mgr. **Wattage**: 6,000. **Ad Rates:** $28 for 30 seconds; $35 for 60 seconds.

11286 ■ WTVP-TV - 47
101 State St.
Peoria, IL 61602-1547
Phone: (309)677-4747
Email: development@wtvp.org
Format: Public TV. **Networks:** Public Broadcasting Service (PBS). **Owner:** Illinois Valley Public Telecommunications Corp., at above address. **Founded:** 1971. **Operating Hours**: Continuous. **ADI**: Peoria-Bloomington, IL. **Key Personnel:** Linda Miller, VP, Comm., linda.miller@wtvp.org; William Baker, Exec. Producer, william.baker@wtvp.org. **Local Programs**: *Illinois Adventure*, Thursday Sunday 8:00 p.m. 4:00 p.m. **Wattage**: 190,000 ERP. **Ad Rates:** Accepts Advertising. **URL:** http://www.wtvp.org.

11287 ■ WVEL-AM - 1140
120 Eaton St.
Peoria, IL 61603
Phone: (309)673-1140
Format: Contemporary Christian. **Founded:** 1948. **Operating Hours**: Continuous. **Key Personnel:** Robert Butch Caruth, Prog. Dir., robert.caruth@townsquaremedia.com. **Wattage**: 5,000. **Ad Rates:** Advertising accepted; rates available upon request. $15 for 30 seconds; $20 for 60 seconds. Combined advertising rates available with WGLO-FM, WFRY-FM, WIXO-FM. **URL:** http://www.wvel.com.

11288 ■ WXCL-FM - 104.9
331 Fulton St., 12th Fl.
Peoria, IL 61602
Phone: (309)637-3700
Format: Country. **Networks:** Independent. **Founded:** 1973. **Formerly**: WKQA-FM. **Operating Hours**: Continuous. **ADI**: Peoria-Bloomington, IL. **Key Personnel:** Wayne Miller, Contact, wrm@jmpradio.com; Kevin Cassulo, Contact, kevincassulo@jmpradio.com. **Wattage**: 3,000. **Ad Rates:** $4-40 for 15 seconds; $5-50 for 30 seconds; $10-60 for 60 seconds. **URL:** http://www.1049thewolf.com.

11289 ■ WYZZ-TV - 43
3131 N University
Peoria, IL 61604
Phone: (309)688-3131
Format: Commercial TV. **Networks:** Fox; Independent. **Owner:** Nexstar Broadcasting Group Inc., 545 E John Carpenter Fwy., Ste. 700, Irving, TX 75062, Ph: (972)373-8800. **Founded:** 1982. **ADI**: Peoria-Bloomington, IL. **Key Personnel:** Nancy Linebaugh, Sales Mgr., nancyl@wmbd.com; Steve Mason, Dir. of Sales, stevem@wmbd.com; David Tomlianovich, Dir. of Creative Svcs., davidt@wmbd.com. **Ad Rates:** Advertising accepted; rates available upon request. **URL:** http://centralillinoisproud.com.

11290 ■ WZPN-FM - 96.5
4234 N Brandywine Dr.
Peoria, IL 61614
Phone: (309)686-0101
Email: studio@965espn.com
Format: Sports. **URL:** http://www.lro7.com.

11291 ■ WZPW-FM - 92.3
120 Eaton St.
Peoria, IL 61603
Phone: (309)676-5000
Free: 866-686-9292
Format: Urban Contemporary. **Owner:** Townsquare Media Inc., 2000 Fifth Third Ctr. 511 Walnut St., Cincinnati, OH 45202, Ph: (513)651-1190. **Founded:** Sept. 07, 2006. **Operating Hours**: Continuous. **Wattage**: 25,000. **Ad Rates:** Advertising accepted; rates available upon request. **URL:** http://www.powerpeoria.com.

PEOTONE

Beecher Herald - See Beecher

11292 ■ Crete-Monee Record-Monitor
Russell Publications
120 W North St.
Peotone, IL 60468
Phone: (708)258-3473
Fax: (708)258-6295
Community newspaper. **Freq:** Weekly (Thurs.). **Cols./Page:** 5. **Col. Width:** 2 inches. **Col. Depth:** 16 inches. **Key Personnel:** Chris Russell, Editor. **Subscription Rates:** $29.50 Individuals for residents of Will, Kankakee, or Cook counties; $35 Individuals for all other Illinois residents; $39 Out of state; $79 Other countries; $25 Students. **URL:** http://www.russell-publications.com/cretemonee. **Formerly**: Crete Record. **Mailing address:** PO Box 429, Peotone, IL 60468. **Ad Rates:** BW $236; PCI $2.95. **Remarks:** Accepts advertising. **Circ:** 2,100.

Grant Park Gazette - See Grant Park

11293 ■ Manhattan American
Russell Publications
120 W North St.
Peotone, IL 60468
Phone: (708)258-3473
Fax: (708)258-6295
Community newspaper. **Freq:** Weekly (Wed.). **Cols./Page:** 5. **Col. Width:** 11 1/2 picas. **Col. Depth:** 16 inches. **Key Personnel:** Gilbert L. Russell, Publisher. **Subscription Rates:** $35 Individuals residents of Will, Kankakee, or Cook counties; $41 Individuals all other Illinois residents; $45 Out of state; $82 Other countries. **URL:** http://www.russell-publications.com/manhattan. **Mailing address:** PO Box 429, Peotone, IL 60468. **Ad Rates:** PCI $3.45. **Remarks:** Advertising accepted; rates available upon request. **Circ:** 1,350.

11294 ■ Peotone Vedette
Russell Publications
120 W North St.
Peotone, IL 60468
Phone: (708)258-3473
Fax: (708)258-6295
Community newspaper. **Freq:** Weekly (Wed.). **Cols./Page:** 5. **Col. Width:** 11 1/2 picas. **Col. Depth:** 16 inches. **Key Personnel:** Gilbert L. Russell, Publisher. **Subscription Rates:** $35 Individuals residents of Will, Kankakee, or Cook counties; $41 Individuals all other Illinois residents; $45 Out of state; $85 Other countries. **URL:** http://www.russell-publications.com/peotone. **Mailing address:** PO Box 429, Peotone, IL 60468. **Ad Rates:** BW $236; PCI $3.45. **Remarks:** Accepts advertising. **Circ:** 2,600.

PERU

La Salle Co. LaSalle Co. (WC). 15 m W of Ottawa.

11295 ■ Lion Roars
Lionel Collectors Club of America
PO Box 529
Peru, IL 61354-0529
Fax: (815)223-0791
Publisher's E-mail: office@lionelcollectors.org
Freq: 5/year February, April, June, October, December. **ISSN:** 1079--0993 (print). **Subscription Rates:** Included in membership. **Alt. Formats:** PDF. **URL:** http://www.lionelcollectors.org/lcca-newsstand/publications.aspx; http://www.lionelcollectors.org/lcca-newsstand/publications/thelionroars.aspx. **Remarks:** Advertising not accepted. **Circ:** (Not Reported).

11296 ■ WALS-FM - 102.1
3905 Progress Blvd.
Peru, IL 61354
Phone: (815)224-2100
Format: Country. **Owner:** The Radio Group, at above address. **Founded:** Jan. 29, 1993. **Key Personnel:** Cole Studstill, Contact, cole@theradiogroup.net; Lee Studstill, Contact, lstudstill@theradiogroup.net; Cole Studstill, Contact, cole@theradiogroup.net. **Wattage**: 6,000. **Ad Rates:** Advertising accepted; rates available upon request. **URL:** http://www.walls102.com.

11297 ■ WBZG-FM - 100.9
3905 Progress Blvd.
Peru, IL 61354
Phone: (815)224-2100

Format: Classic Rock. **Simulcasts:** WSPL-AM. **Owner:** Mendota Broadcasting Inc., at above address. **Operating Hours**: Continuous Monday - Friday. **Wattage**: 3,000 ERP. **Ad Rates:** Advertising accepted; rates available upon request. Combined advertising rates available with WGLC-FM, WALS-FM, WIVQ-FM; WSPL; WSTQ-FM; WYYS-FM. **URL:** http://www.wbzg.net.

11298 ■ WGLC-FM - 100.1
3905 Progress Blvd
Peru, IL 61354
Phone: (815)539-6751
Email: wglc@softfarm.com
Format: Country. **Simulcasts:** WGLC, WALS. **Networks:** ABC; Jones Satellite. **Owner:** Mendota Broadcasting Inc., at above address. **Founded:** 1965. **Operating Hours**: Continuous. **Wattage**: 6,000. **Ad Rates:** Advertising accepted; rates available upon request.

11299 ■ WIVQ-FM - 103.3
3905 Progress Blvd.
Peru, IL 61354
Phone: (815)224-2100
Format: Top 40. **Simulcasts:** WSTQ-FM. **Founded:** 1995. **Operating Hours**: Continuous. **Key Personnel:** Cole Studstill, Contact, cole@theradiogroup.net; Cole Studstill, Contact, cole@theradiogroup.net; Lee Studstill, Contact, lstudsti@theradiogroup.net; David Kuharski, Contact, david@theradiogroup.net. **Wattage**: 6,000. **Ad Rates:** Noncommercial. Combined advertising rates available with WGLC-FM, WBZG-FM, WALS-FM, WSTQ-FM, WYYS-FM, WSPL. **URL:** http://www.qhitmusic.com.

PETERSBURG

Menard Co. Menard Co. (C). 23 m NW of Springfield. New Salem State Park (historical). Manufactures electrical connectors. Bottling works. Grain, stock farms.

11300 ■ The Petersburg Observer
Petersburg Observer
235 E Sangamon Ave.
Petersburg, IL 62675-1245
Phone: (217)632-2236
Publication E-mail: info@petersburgil.com
Community newspaper (broadsheet). **Freq:** Weekly (Wed.). **Print Method:** Offset. **Cols./Page:** 8. **Col. Width:** 11.5 picas. **Col. Depth:** 21 inches. **Key Personnel:** Jane Shaw Cutright, Editor; Doug Willis, Manager, Production; Dennis Boeker, Office Manager. **USPS:** 429-140. **Subscription Rates:** $21 Individuals in state; $24 Out of state. **URL:** http://petersburgil.com. **Ad Rates:** PCI $4.90. **Remarks:** Accepts advertising. **Circ:** ‡3150.

PITTSFIELD

Pike Co. Pike Co. (W). 40 m SE of Quincy. Feed mills. Cheese and garment factories; dried milk processing; meat packing. Agriculture. Corn, wheat, soybeans, livestock.

11301 ■ Pike Press
Pike County Publishing Co.
115 W Jefferson
Box 70
Pittsfield, IL 62363
Phone: (217)285-2345
Fax: (217)285-5222
Publication E-mail: ppnews@campbellpublications.net
Community newspaper. **Freq:** Weekly (Wed.). **Print Method:** Offset. **Trim Size:** 14 x 22 3/4. **Cols./Page:** 6. **Col. Width:** 2 1/16 inches. **Col. Depth:** 21 1/2 inches. **Key Personnel:** Julie Boren, Publisher. **USPS:** 602-540. **Subscription Rates:** $19 Individuals military (online trade area); $60 Out of area print, outside trade area; $30 Individuals print and online; $87 Out of country outside US; $30 Individuals online. **URL:** http://pikepress.com/index1.htm. **Ad Rates:** SAU $11.37. **Remarks:** Advertising accepted; rates available upon request. **Circ:** ‡7900.

11302 ■ WBBA-FM
PO Box 312
Pittsfield, IL 62363
Phone: (217)285-9750
Fax: (217)285-4006
Format: Contemporary Country. **Networks:** Jones Satellite; Illinois Farm Bureau; Brownfield. **Owner:** Brown Radio Group, Inc., at above address. **Founded:** 1965. **Key Personnel:** David Fuhler, Contact. **Wattage**: 10,000 ERP. **Ad Rates:** $10 for 30 seconds; $13 for 60 seconds.

PLAINFIELD

Will Co. Will Co. (NE). 9 m NW of Joliet. Lake Renwick Bird Sanctuary. Small business. Industrial. Grain farms.

11303 ■ The Enterprise
Voyager Media Publications
Publication E-mail: enterprisenewspaper@comcast.net
Community newspaper. **Founded:** Aug. 1887. **Freq:** Weekly (Thurs.). **Print Method:** Offset. **Cols./Page:** 5 and 6. **Col. Width:** 22 nonpareils and 9.5 picas. **Col. Depth:** 224 agate lines and 14 inches. **Key Personnel:** Michael Jameson, General Manager; Pat Ryan, Manager, Advertising. **Subscription Rates:** $20.09 Individuals Will country; $30 Out of area in state; $50 Out of state; $10; $11 out of county; $13 Out of state; $0.25 Single issue. **Formerly**: Benld Enterprise and Gillespie Newsleader. **Ad Rates:** 4C $175; PCI $9,50; BW $120; PCI $1.50. **Remarks:** Accepts advertising. **Circ:** 11100, 2600.

11304 ■ Herald News
Sun-Times Media L.L.C.
43 S Rte. 30
Plainfield, IL 60544
Publication E-mail: heraldnews@scn1.com
Community newspaper. **Founded:** 1894. **Freq:** Daily and Sun. **Print Method:** Offset. **Cols./Page:** 6. **Col. Width:** 24 nonpareils. **Col. Depth:** 294 agate lines. **Key Personnel:** Joe Biesk, Managing Editor, phone: (815)439-5302; Matt Cappellini, Associate Editor, phone: (815)439-5304; Michelle Holmes, Editor. **USPS:** 168-300. **Subscription Rates:** $39 By mail 26 weeks (Sunday through Friday); $26 By mail 26 weeks (Sunday only). **URL:** http://www.theherald-news.com. **Ad Rates:** GLR $.28; BW $327.60; SAU $4.40; PCI $4.40. **Remarks:** Accepts advertising. **Circ:** Paid 3167.

11305 ■ The Niles Bugle
Bugle Publications
23856 Andrew Rd.
Plainfield, IL 60585
Phone: (847)588-1900
Fax: (815)436-2592
Local community newspaper (tabloid). **Founded:** June 1957. **Freq:** Weekly (Thurs.). **Print Method:** Offset. **Trim Size:** 10 x 13. **Cols./Page:** 5. **Col. Width:** 1 7/8 inches. **Col. Depth:** 13 inches. **Subscription Rates:** $25 Individuals; $30 Out of state; $50 Out of area. **URL:** http://www.buglenewspapers.com/niles. **Formerly:** The Bugle. **Ad Rates:** GLR $4; BW $1,250; 4C $1,500; PCI $35. **Remarks:** Accepts advertising. **Circ:** Free ‡20000.

PLANO

Kendall Co. Kendall Co. (NE). 18 m S.W. of Aurora. Birthplace of the harvesters.

11306 ■ WSPY-FM
1 Broadcast Ctr.
Plano, IL 60545
Phone: (708)552-1000
Fax: (708)552-9300
Format: Talk; Adult Contemporary; News. **Networks:** ABC. **Founded:** 1974. **Key Personnel:** Larry W. Nelson, President. **Wattage**: 3,100 ERP. **Ad Rates:** $28 for 60 seconds.

POLO

Ogle Co. Ogle Co. (N). 12 m N of Dixon. Creamery; hatchery. Manufactures cheese, pre-fabricated buildings, refrigeration units, lawn tools, hair dryers. Livestock, dairy, poultry farms.

11307 ■ National Bus Trader: The Magazine of Bus Equipment for the United States and Canada
National Bus Trader Inc.
9698 W Judson Rd.
Polo, IL 61064
Phone: (815)946-2341
Fax: (815)946-2347
Publication E-mail: nbt@busmag.com
Magazine for bus tour planners. **Freq:** Quarterly. **Print Method:** Offset. **Trim Size:** 8 1/2 x 11. **Cols./Page:** 3. **Col. Width:** 14 picas. **Col. Depth:** 60 picas. **Key Personnel:** Larry Plachno, Editor. **ISSN:** 0194-939X (print). **Subscription Rates:** $25 Individuals; $30 Other countries. **URL:** http://www.busmag.com. **Ad Rates:** BW $1,300; 4C $1,900. **Remarks:** Accepts advertising. **Circ:** Paid 4500.

PONTIAC

Livingston Co. Livingston Co. (NEC). 35 m NE of Bloomington. Publishing houses. Manufactures chairs, pallet racks, molded concrete products, gloves, hybrid seed, engineered products for metal industries, flexible conduit, lawn mowing equipment, diesel engine parts.

11308 ■ Pontiac Daily Leader
GateHouse Media Inc.
318 N Main St.
Pontiac, IL 61764
Phone: (815)842-1153
Daily newspaper. **Freq:** Daily (eve.) and Sat. (morn.). **Print Method:** Offset. **Cols./Page:** 6. **Col. Width:** 25 nonpareils. **Col. Depth:** 301 agate lines. **Key Personnel:** Lois Westermeyer, Managing Editor; Linda J. Stiles, Business Manager; Erich Murphy, Editor. **Subscription Rates:** $6.99 Individuals digital access/month; $2 Individuals digital + home delivery/week (Tuesday-Saturday). **URL:** http://www.pontiacdailyleader.com. **Ad Rates:** SAU $7.26; PCI $8.75. **Remarks:** Advertising accepted; rates available upon request. **Circ:** (Not Reported).

11309 ■ WJEZ-FM - 98.9
315 N Mill St.
Pontiac, IL 61764
Phone: (815)844-6101
Format: Classical. **Networks:** CNN Radio. **Founded:** 1969. **Operating Hours**: Continuous. **Wattage**: 1,300 ERP. **Ad Rates:** Advertising accepted; rates available upon request. **URL:** http://www.wjez.com.

PRINCETON

Bureau Co. Bureau Co. (NW). 22 m W of La Salle. Nursery. Produce packing. Manufactures locks, air compressors, gas jets, sealing wax, fertilizer. Stock, poultry, grain farms. Spots of historical interest.

11310 ■ Bulletin for Biblical Research
Institute for Biblical Research
PO Box 305
Princeton, IL 61356
Publisher's E-mail: ibr.bbr@gmail.com
Freq: Semiannual. **ISSN:** 1065- 223X (print). **Subscription Rates:** $12.50 Individuals; $17.50 Institutions. **URL:** http://www.ibr-bbr.org/bulletin-biblical-research. **Remarks:** Advertising not accepted. **Circ:** 1000.

11311 ■ Bureau County Republican
Bureau County Republican
316 S Main
Princeton, IL 61356
Phone: (815)875-4461
Fax: (815)875-1235
Free: 800-639-7237
Publication E-mail: news@bcrnews.com
Community newspaper. **Freq:** 3/week. **Print Method:** Offset. **Trim Size:** 13 x 21 1/2. **Cols./Page:** 6. **Col. Width:** 21 nonpareils. **Col. Depth:** 301 agate lines. **Key Personnel:** Sam Fisher, Publisher; Terri Simon, Editor. **ISSN:** 0894--1181 (print). **Subscription Rates:** $90 Individuals carrier rates and motor route; $174 By mail out of area; $90 By mail; $90 Individuals internet edition (1year). **URL:** http://www.bcrnews.com/contact_us/#subrates. **Ad Rates:** GLR $.50; BW $945; 4C $1,145; SAU $7.90; PCI $5.75. **Remarks:** Accepts advertising. **Circ:** ‡6900.

11312 ■ WRVY-FM - 100.5
2209 S Main St.
Princeton, IL 61356
Phone: (815)875-8014
Fax: (815)872-0308
Format: Classic Rock. **Ad Rates:** Noncommercial. **Mailing address:** PO Box 69, Princeton, IL 61356. **URL:** http://www.wzoe.com.

11313 ■ WZOE-AM - 1490
2209 S Main
Princeton, IL 61356
Phone: (815)875-8014

Circulation: ★ = AAM; △ or • = BPA; ♦ = CAC; ❑ = VAC; ⊕ = PO Statement; ‡ = Publisher's Report; Boldface figures = sworn; Light figures = estimated.

Format: News; Sports; Information. **Networks:** CBS. **Founded:** 1961. **Operating Hours:** Continuous. **Key Personnel:** Steve Samet, Gen. Mgr. **Wattage:** 1,000. **Ad Rates:** Advertising accepted; rates available upon request. **URL:** http://wzoe.com/.

11314 ■ WZOE-FM - 98.1
Broadcast Ctr.
2209 S Main St.
Princeton, IL 61356
Phone: (815)875-8014
Fax: (309)364-4411
Format: Oldies. **Founded:** 1980. **Operating Hours:** Continuous; 100% local. **Key Personnel:** Steve Samet, Gen. Mgr. **Wattage:** 6,000. **Ad Rates:** Advertising accepted; rates available upon request. Combined advertising rates available with WZOE-AM and WRVY-FM. **Mailing address:** PO Box 69, Princeton, IL 61356. **URL:** http://www.wzoe.com.

QUAD CITIES

11315 ■ WLKU-FM - 98.9
PO Box 2098
Omaha, NE 68103
Free: 800-525-5683
Email: info@klove.com
Format: Contemporary Christian. **Owner:** Educational Media Foundation, 5700 W Oaks Blvd., CA 95765, Free: 800-800434-8400. **URL:** http://www.klove.com.

QUINCY

Adams Co. Adams Co. (W). On Mississippi River, 110 m N of St. Louis, Mo. Bridge to West Quincy, Mo. Quincy College. Manufactures pumps, elevators, stoves, store fixtures, poultry supplies, radio and television receivers and transmitters, broadcasting equipment, truck bodies, farms wagons, women's wear, shirts, overalls, air compressors, wallboard, stock food, air conditioning and heating units, stereo phonographs, limestone and fertilizer spreaders, industrial trailers, rock drills, electric signs, metal wheels, steel fabrication, paper board specialties, paper bags.

11316 ■ The Quincy Herald Whig
The Quincy Herald-Whig
130 S Fifth St.
Quincy, IL 62301
Phone: (217)223-5100
Fax: (217)221-3395
Free: 800-373-9444
Publisher's E-mail: digital@whig.com
General newspaper. **Freq:** Daily (eve.), Sat. and Sun. (morn.). **Print Method:** Offset. **Cols./Page:** 6. **Col. Width:** 26 nonpareils. **Col. Depth:** 294 agate lines. **Key Personnel:** Don Crim, Managing Editor, phone: (217)221-3361. **Subscription Rates:** $13.95 Individuals monthly (print and online); $9.95 Individuals all digital. **URL:** http://www.whig.com. **Mailing address:** PO Box 909, Quincy, IL 62306-0909. **Remarks:** Accepts advertising. **Circ:** Mon.-Fri. ★**21763**, Sun. ★**26030**.

11317 ■ KGRC-FM - 92.9
329 Maine
Quincy, IL 62301
Format: Full Service. **Owner:** Staradio Corp., 1300 Central Ave., West Great Falls, MT 59404, Ph: (406)761-2800. **Founded:** 1968. **Operating Hours:** Continuous; 5% network, 95% local. **ADI:** Quincy, IL-Hannibal, MO. **Wattage:** 100,000. **Ad Rates:** $19-37 for 30 seconds; $23-42 for 60 seconds.

11318 ■ KHQA-TV - 7
301 S 36th St.
Quincy, IL 62301
Phone: (217)222-6200
Fax: (217)228-3164
Free: 800-929-3518
Format: Commercial TV. **Networks:** CBS. **Owner:** Barrington Broadcasting Group, LLC, 2500 W Higgins Rd., Ste. 155, Hoffman Estates, IL 60169. **Founded:** Sept. 1953. **Operating Hours:** Continuous. **ADI:** Quincy, IL-Hannibal, MO. **Key Personnel:** Nora Baldner, Managing Ed., nbaldner@khqa.com. **Local Programs:** *Tri State This Morning*. **Ad Rates:** Advertising accepted; rates available upon request. **URL:** http://www.connecttristates.com.

11319 ■ KICK-FM - 97.9
408 N 24th St.
Quincy, IL 62301
Phone: (217)223-5292
Format: Country. **Key Personnel:** Ed Foxall, Gen. Mgr., efoxall@hqradio.com. **URL:** http://www.979kickfm.com.

11320 ■ KIKF-FM
329 Maine St.
Quincy, IL 62301
Format: Country. **Founded:** July 17, 2001. **Wattage:** 94,000 ERP. **Ad Rates:** Noncommercial.

11321 ■ KJIR-FM - 91.7
220 N 6th St.
Quincy, IL 62301
Phone: (217)221-9410
Format: Southern Gospel. **Key Personnel:** Beverly Geisendorfer, Music Dir. **Ad Rates:** Noncommercial. **Mailing address:** PO Box 1189, Quincy, IL 62306. **URL:** http://www.kjir.org.

11322 ■ KQDI-AM
329 Maine St.
Quincy, IL 62301
Phone: (217)224-4102
Format: News; Talk. **Networks:** Westwood One Radio; EFM. **Owner:** Sunbrook Communications, at above address. **Formerly:** KMSL-AM. **ADI:** Great Falls, MT. **Wattage:** 720. **Ad Rates:** $3.50 per unit.

11323 ■ KRRY-FM - 100.9
408 N 24th St.
Quincy, IL 62301
Phone: (217)223-5292
Format: Top 40. **Key Personnel:** Dennis Oliver, Contact, doliver@hqradio.com. **Wattage:** 28,000. **Ad Rates:** Noncommercial. **URL:** http://www.y101radio.com.

11324 ■ KWBZ-FM - 107.5
1645 Hwy. 104, Ste. G
Quincy Regional Airport - Baldwin Field
Quincy, IL 62305
Phone: (217)224-4653
Fax: (217)885-3233
Email: radio@wpwqfm.com
Format: Oldies. **Key Personnel:** Larry Bostwick, Owner, Gen. Mgr., larry.bostwick@gmail.com. **Wattage:** 10,000. **Ad Rates:** Noncommercial. **URL:** http://www.wpwqfm.com.

11325 ■ KZZK-FM - 105.9
329 Maine St.
Quincy, IL 62301
Phone: (217)224-4102
Fax: (217)224-4133
Free: 800-900-1059
Format: Album-Oriented Rock (AOR). **Owner:** Staradio Corp., 1300 Central Ave., West Great Falls, MT 59404, Ph: (406)761-2800. **Key Personnel:** Mike Moyers, Gen. Mgr., VP; Phil Reilly, Chief Engineer; Brenda Park, Gen. Sales Mgr. **Wattage:** 25,000. **Ad Rates:** Noncommercial. **URL:** http://www.kzzk.com.

11326 ■ WCOY-FM - 99.5
329 Maine St.
Quincy, IL 62301
Format: Country. **Ad Rates:** Noncommercial. **URL:** http://www.wcoy.com.

11327 ■ WGCA-FM - 88.5
535 Maine, Ste. 10
Quincy, IL 62301
Phone: (217)224-9422
Email: themix@wgca.org
Format: Religious. **Simulcasts:** K257DR , W209AL. **Networks:** USA Radio. **Founded:** 1987. **Operating Hours:** Continuous. **Key Personnel:** Bruce Rice, Exec. Dir., br@wgca.org; Maxine Rice, Assoc. Dir., mixmax@wgca.org. **Wattage:** 40,000. **Ad Rates:** Noncommercial; underwriting available. **URL:** http://www.wgca.org.

11328 ■ WGEM-AM - 1440
PO Box 80
Quincy, IL 62306
Phone: (217)228-6600
Fax: (217)228-6670
Format: Sports. **Networks:** ABC. **Founded:** 1948. **Operating Hours:** Continuous. **Key Personnel:** Greg Haubrich, Operations Mgr., ghaubrich@wgem.com; Carlos Fernandez, Gen. Mgr., VP, cfernandez@wgem.com. **Wattage:** 5,000-Day; 1,000-Night. **Ad Rates:** $6-31 for 30 seconds; $8.25-85 for 60 seconds. **URL:** http://www.wgem.com.

11329 ■ WGEM-FM - 105.1
513 Hampshire St.
Quincy, IL 62301
Phone: (217)228-6600
Fax: (217)228-6670
Free: 800-728-6600
Format: News; Talk. **Networks:** ABC. **Owner:** Quincy Newspapers, Inc., at above address. **Founded:** 1947. **Formerly:** WQNI-FM; WQDI. **Operating Hours:** Continuous. **Key Personnel:** Greg Haubrich, Operations Mgr., ghaubrich@wgem.com; Carlos Fernandez, Gen. Mgr., VP, cfernandez@wgem.com. **Wattage:** 27,500. **Ad Rates:** $8.25-47 for 30 seconds; $11.75-85 for 60 seconds. Combined advertising rates available with WGEM-AM. **URL:** http://www.wgem.com.

11330 ■ WGEM-TV - 10
513 Hampshire St.
Quincy, IL 62301
Phone: (217)228-6600
Fax: (217)228-6670
Email: sendit@wgem.com
Networks: NBC. **Owner:** Quincy Broadcasting Co., at above address. **Founded:** Sept. 03, 1953. **Operating Hours:** Continuous. **ADI:** Quincy, IL-Hannibal, MO. **Key Personnel:** Greg Haubrich, Operations Mgr.; Jim Lawrence, Dir. of Engg., jlawrence@wgem.com. **Wattage:** 316,000. **Ad Rates:** Noncommercial. **URL:** http://www.wgem.com.

11331 ■ WPWQ-FM - 106.7
1645 Hwy. 104, Ste. G, Quincy Regional Airport
Quincy Regional Airport - Baldwin Field
Quincy, IL 62305
Phone: (217)224-4653
Fax: (217)885-3233
Free: 877-453-1067
Email: sales@wpwqfm.com
Format: Oldies. **Key Personnel:** Larry Bostwick, Gen. Mgr. **URL:** http://www.wpwqfm.com.

11332 ■ WQCY-FM - 103.9
329 Maine St.
Quincy, IL 62301
Phone: (217)224-4102
Fax: (217)228-1031
Free: 888-569-9729
Email: wqcy@bcl.net
Format: Classic Rock; Adult Contemporary. **Networks:** ABC; Unistar. **Owner:** Tele-Media Broadcasting, 4414 Lafayette Blvd., Ste. 100, Fredericksburg, VA 22408, Ph: (540)891-9959, Free: 888-760-1045. **Founded:** 1948. **Operating Hours:** Continuous. **ADI:** Quincy, IL-Hannibal, MO. **Wattage:** 50,000 ERP. **URL:** http://www.q104wqcy.com.

11333 ■ WQIN-FM - 102.9
PO Box 3812
Quincy, IL 62305
Phone: (217)224-7399
Email: info@wqinfm.com
Format: Religious; Contemporary Christian. **Operating Hours:** Continuous. **Wattage:** 100. **Ad Rates:** Noncommercial; underwriting available. **URL:** http://www.wqinfm.com.

11334 ■ WQUB-FM - 90.3
1800 College Ave.
Quincy, IL 62301-2699
Phone: (217)228-5410
Format: Public Radio. **Networks:** National Public Radio (NPR); Public Radio International (PRI). **Owner:** Quincy University, 1800 College Ave., Quincy, IL 62301, Ph: (217)222-8020. **Founded:** 1974. **Formerly:** WWQC-FM. **Operating Hours:** 18 hours Daily; 60% network, 40% local. **Key Personnel:** Maureen Hill, Mgr., Member Svcs., hillma@quincy.edu. **Wattage:** 28,000. **Ad Rates:** Noncommercial.

11335 ■ WTAD-AM - 930
329 Maine St.
Quincy, IL 62301
Phone: (217)224-4102
Fax: (217)224-4133
Free: 800-228-9823
Format: News; Talk. **Networks:** CBS; Mutual Broadcasting System. **Owner:** Staradio Corp., 1300 Central Ave., West Great Falls, MT 59404, Ph: (406)761-2800.

Founded: 1926. **Operating Hours:** Continuous. **ADI:** Quincy, IL-Hannibal, MO. **Key Personnel:** Mary Griffith, Contact. **Wattage:** 5,000 Day; 1,000 Night. **Ad Rates:** Noncommercial. **URL:** http://www.wtad.com.

11336 ■ WTJR-TV - 16
222 N Sixth St.
Quincy, IL 62301
Phone: (217)228-1616
Format: News; Country; Religious. **Networks:** Fox; CBS; Public Broadcasting Service (PBS); NBC; ABC. **Owner:** Christian Television Network Inc., 6922 142nd Ave, Largo, FL 33771, Ph: (727)535-5622, Fax: (727)531-2497. **Operating Hours:** Continuous. **ADI:** Quincy, IL-Hannibal, MO. **Key Personnel:** A. Donette Douglas, Prog. Dir., Station Mgr. **Wattage:** 100,000 ERP H. **Ad Rates:** Accepts Advertising. **URL:** http://www.wtjr.org.

RANTOUL

Champaign Co. Champaign Co. (E). 15 m N of Champaign. Technical Air Force training center. Light industry. Stock farms. Corn, oats, beans.

11337 ■ Rantoul Press
East Central Communications Inc.
1332 Harmon Dr. E
Rantoul, IL 61866-3310
Phone: (217)892-9613
Fax: (217)892-9451
Publication E-mail: news@rantoulpress.com
Community newspaper. **Freq:** Weekly (Wed.). **Print Method:** Offset. **Trim Size:** 12 1/2 x 22 3/4. **Cols./Page:** 6. **Col. Width:** 1 13/16 picas. **Col. Depth:** 21.5 inches. **Key Personnel:** Melinda Carpenter, Manager, Circulation, phone: (217)892-9613, fax: (217)892-9451; Tim Evan, General Manager; Bob Shelton, Manager, Production. **Subscription Rates:** $38 Individuals; $30 Individuals for 9 months; $20.65 Individuals for 6 months; $23 Students for 9 months. **URL:** http://www.rantoulpress.com. **Mailing address:** PO Box 5110, Rantoul, IL 61866-3310. **Ad Rates:** GLR $.90; BW $1,637.01; 4C $2,042.01; SAU $11.97; CNU $12.69; PCI $15.82. **Remarks:** Accepts advertising. **Circ:** Combined ‡9227.

RIVER FOREST

Cook Co. Cook Co. (NE) 25 m W. of Chicago. Residential.

11338 ■ Lutheran Education
Lutheran Education Association
7400 Augusta St.
River Forest, IL 60305
Phone: (708)209-3343
Fax: (708)209-3458
Publisher's E-mail: lea@lea.org
Journal covering information on Lutheran education. **Freq:** Quarterly. **Key Personnel:** John F. Johnson, Publisher. **ISSN:** 0024--7488 (print). **Subscription Rates:** Included in membership; $10 Nonmembers. **URL:** http://lej.cuchicago.edu. **Remarks:** Advertising not accepted. **Circ:** (Not Reported).

11339 ■ Shaping the Future
Lutheran Education Association
7400 Augusta St.
River Forest, IL 60305
Phone: (708)209-3343
Fax: (708)209-3458
Publisher's E-mail: lea@lea.org
Freq: 3/year spring/summer, fall and winter. **Subscription Rates:** Included in membership. **URL:** http://www.lea.org/Resources/ShapingtheFuture.aspx. **Remarks:** Advertising not accepted. **Circ:** (Not Reported).

11340 ■ World Libraries: An International Journal Focusing on Libraries and Socio-Economic
Dominican University Graduate School of Library and Information Science
7900 W Division St.
River Forest, IL 60305
Phone: (708)524-6845
Fax: (708)524-6657
Publisher's E-mail: gslis@dom.edu
Peer-reviewed professional journal covering library and information science. **Freq:** Semiannual. **Trim Size:** 6 x 9. **Key Personnel:** Debra Mitts-Smith, Editor-in-Chief; Melanie Wilson, Managing Editor. **ISSN:** 1092--7441 (print). **URL:** http://www.worlib.org. **Formerly:** Third World Libraries. **Remarks:** Advertising not accepted. **Circ:** (Not Reported).

RIVER GROVE

Cook Co. Cook Co. (NE). 3 m N of Maywood. Residential.

11341 ■ Amici Journal
Amici Journal Inc.
PO Box 595
River Grove, IL 60171
Phone: (773)836-1595
Fax: (773)622-2766
Publisher's E-mail: amitalia@sbcglobal.net
Lifestyle magazine focusing on Italian-American art and cultural history. **Freq:** Quarterly. **Trim Size:** 8 1/2 x 11. **Subscription Rates:** $24.95 Individuals; $32.95 Two years. **URL:** http://www.amiciorgit.net/. **Ad Rates:** BW $1,200. **Remarks:** Accepts advertising. **Circ:** 32600.

11342 ■ WRRG-FM - 88.9
2000 Fifth Ave.
River Grove, IL 60171
Phone: (708)583-3110
Format: Educational; Public Radio. **Networks:** Independent. **Owner:** Triton College Radio, 2000 Fifth Ave., River Grove, IL 60171, Ph: (708)456-0300. **Founded:** 1975. **Operating Hours:** 8:30 a.m - 12 a.m; 100% Local. **ADI:** Chicago (LaSalle), IL. **Wattage:** 100. **Ad Rates:** Noncommercial. **URL:** http://www.wrrg.org.

RIVERSIDE

11343 ■ Riverside Review
Worral Publishing Inc.
27 Riverside Rd.
Riverside, IL 60546
Phone: (708)447-2700
Publication E-mail: review@buffnet.net
Local newspaper. **Freq:** Bimonthly. **Print Method:** Offset. **Trim Size:** 11 1/2 x 17. **Cols./Page:** 6. **Col. Width:** 1 5/8 inches. **Col. Depth:** 16 inches. **Key Personnel:** Kevin Wachtel, Director. **Subscription Rates:** Free. **URL:** http://www.riverside.il.us. **Remarks:** Accepts advertising. **Circ:** (Not Reported).

RIVERTON

Sangamon Co. Sangamon Co. (NC).

11344 ■ WQLZ-FM - 97.7
1510 N Third St.
Riverton, IL 62561
Phone: (217)629-7077
Fax: (217)629-7952
Email: alice@alice.fm
Format: Adult Contemporary; Alternative/New Music/Progressive. **Owner:** Mid-West Family Broadcasting Group, 730 Rayovac Dr., Madison, WI 53711, Ph: (608)273-1000. **Formerly:** WYVR-FM; WLCE-FM. **Key Personnel:** Kevan Kavanaugh, Gen. Mgr., President, kevank@alice.fm. **URL:** http://www.alice.fm.

RIVERWOODS

Lake Co.

11345 ■ Automobile Law Reports Insurance Cases
DTI
2700 Lake Cook Rd.
Riverwoods, IL 60015
Free: 888-224-7377
Publisher's E-mail: cust_serv@cch.com
Insurance publication. **Freq:** Biweekly. **Print Method:** Offset. **Trim Size:** 6 x 9. **Cols./Page:** 2. **Col. Width:** 40 nonpareils. **Col. Depth:** 133 agate lines. **Key Personnel:** Daniel Newquist, Editor. **ISSN:** 0162--1785 (print). **Subscription Rates:** $980 Individuals. **Mailing address:** PO Box 4307, Carol Stream, IL 60197-4307. **Circ:** ‡500.

11346 ■ The Chamber Music Journal
Cobbett Association for Chamber Music Research
601 Timber Trail
Riverwoods, IL 60015-3846
Phone: (847)374-1800
Publisher's E-mail: cobbettassociation@gmail.com
Journal containing informative articles on chamber music, evaluation of recommended works and record reviews. **Freq:** Quarterly. **ISSN:** 1535--1726 (print). **Subscription Rates:** Included in membership. **URL:** http://chambermusicjournal.org/chamber-music-journal.htm. **Remarks:** Advertising not accepted. **Circ:** (Not Reported).

11347 ■ Commercial Lending Review
DTI
CCH Inc.
2700 Lake Cook Rd.
Riverwoods, IL 60015
Phone: (847)267-7000
Fax: (978)371-2961
Publisher's E-mail: cust_serv@cch.com
Journal covering all aspects of lending for commercial banks, community and regional banks and other financial institutions. **Freq:** Bimonthly Quarterly. **Key Personnel:** Claire Green, Editor, phone: (978)369-6285. **ISSN:** 0886-8204 (print). **Subscription Rates:** $445 Individuals. **Online:** Gale. **Remarks:** Accepts advertising. **Circ:** Paid 1000.

11348 ■ Copyright Law Reports
DTI
2700 Lake Cook Rd.
Riverwoods, IL 60015
Free: 888-224-7377
Publisher's E-mail: cust_serv@cch.com
Copyright law publication. **Freq:** Monthly. **Print Method:** Offset. Uses mats. **Trim Size:** 6 x 9. **Cols./Page:** 2. **Col. Width:** 40 nonpareils. **Col. Depth:** 133 agate lines. **Key Personnel:** Janette Spencer-Davis, Editor. **USPS:** 006-843. **Mailing address:** PO Box 4307, Carol Stream, IL 60197-4307. **Remarks:** Advertising not accepted. **Circ:** (Not Reported).

11349 ■ Financial and Estate Planning
DTI
2700 Lake Cook Rd.
Riverwoods, IL 60015
Free: 888-224-7377
Publisher's E-mail: cust_serv@cch.com
Monthly plus the monthly Estate Planning Review; financial planning to build and preserve wealth; forms and planning aids; will and trust forms and clauses; investment plans; insurance and annuity forms; tax planning and administration for estates and trusts; in-depth articles offering new planning ideas; analysis of court decisions; new rulings and legislative developments; year begins first of any month. **Freq:** Monthly. **Key Personnel:** Sidney Kess, Editor. **ISSN:** 0273-7302 (print). **USPS:** 562-590. **Subscription Rates:** $1479 Individuals CD-ROM; $1465 Individuals print. **URL:** http://tax.cchgroup.com/FEP/default. **Mailing address:** PO Box 4307, Carol Stream, IL 60197-4307. **Remarks:** Advertising not accepted. **Circ:** (Not Reported).

11350 ■ Journal of Tax Practice Management
DTI
2700 Lake Cook Rd.
Riverwoods, IL 60015
Free: 888-224-7377
Publisher's E-mail: cust_serv@cch.com
Journal that publishes papers on current issues and trends in the representation of taxpayers before the IRS. **Freq:** Bimonthly. **Key Personnel:** Neil Allen, Contact, phone: (847)267-2179; Leslie Bonacum, Contact, phone: (847)267-7153; Jeffrey S. Pawlow, Editor-in-Chief. **ISSN:** 1541--9169 (print). **Mailing address:** PO Box 4307, Carol Stream, IL 60197-4307. **Circ:** (Not Reported).

11351 ■ Labor Law Journal
DTI
2700 Lake Cook Rd.
Riverwoods, IL 60015
Free: 888-224-7377
Publisher's E-mail: cust_serv@cch.com
Legal journal. **Freq:** Quarterly. **Print Method:** Offset. **Trim Size:** 8 1/2 x 11. **Cols./Page:** 2. **Col. Width:** 20 picas. **Key Personnel:** Matthew A. Pavich, Managing Editor. **USPS:** 300-460. **Subscription Rates:** $503 Individuals. **URL:** http://hr.cch.com/labor-law-journal-submissions. **Mailing address:** PO Box 4307, Carol Stream, IL 60197-4307. **Remarks:** Advertising not accepted. **Circ:** (Not Reported).

Circulation: ★ = AAM; △ or • = BPA; ♦ = CAC; ❑ = VAC; ⊕ = PO Statement; ‡ = Publisher's Report; Boldface figures = sworn; Light figures = estimated.

11352 ■ Pension Plan Guide
DTI
2700 Lake Cook Rd.
Riverwoods, IL 60015
Free: 888-224-7377
Publisher's E-mail: cust_serv@cch.com
Loose leaf series on pension plans. **Freq:** Weekly. **Print Method:** Offset. **Trim Size:** 6 x 9. **Cols./Page:** 2. **Col. Width:** 40 nonpareils. **Col. Depth:** 133 agate lines. **Alt. Formats:** CD-ROM. **URL:** http://www.cchgroup.com/roles/accounting-firms/accounting-and-audit/research/pension-plan-guide. **Mailing address:** PO Box 4307, Carol Stream, IL 60197-4307. **Remarks:** Advertising not accepted. **Circ:** (Not Reported).

11353 ■ Taxes--The Tax Magazine
DTI
2700 Lake Cook Rd.
Riverwoods, IL 60015
Free: 888-224-7377
Publisher's E-mail: cust_serv@cch.com
Magazine on tax laws and regulations. **Founded:** 1920. **Freq:** Monthly. **Trim Size:** 8 1/2 x 11. **Key Personnel:** Shannon Jett Fischer, Editor. **ISSN:** 0040-0181 (print). **Subscription Rates:** $460 Individuals. **URL:** http://www.cchgroup.com/store/products/taxes-tax-magazine-19551000/journal-internet-19551000-journal-internet-19551000#. **Mailing address:** PO Box 4307, Carol Stream, IL 60197-4307. **Remarks:** Advertising not accepted. **Circ:** Paid ‡10,745, Non-paid ‡500.

ROANOKE

Woodford Co. Woodford Co. (NC). 28 m NE of Peoria. Manufactures concrete blocks, slats, and pumps; incinerators. Grain farms. Corn, oats, wheat.

11354 ■ Woodford County Journal-Roanoke Edition
Woodford County Journal
105 E Broad
Roanoke, IL 61561
Phone: (309)923-5841
Community newspaper. **Freq:** Weekly. **Print Method:** Offset. **Cols./Page:** 6. **Col. Width:** 1 3/4 inches. **Col. Depth:** 21 1/2 inches. **Key Personnel:** Cheryl Wolfe, Editor; Mark Barra, Director. **USPS:** 690-440. **Subscription Rates:** $52 Individuals 1 year; $56 Out of area 1 year; $70 Out of state 1 year. **URL:** http://www.pantagraph.com/wcj. **Formerly:** Roanoke Review. **Mailing address:** PO Box 200, Roanoke, IL 61561. **Ad Rates:** GLR $7; BW $1,087.47; 4C $1,237.47; PCI $6. **Remarks:** Accepts advertising. **Circ:** (Not Reported).

ROBINSON

Crawford Co. Crawford Co. (SE). 5 m W of Palestine.

11355 ■ Robinson Daily News
Robinson Daily News
302 S Cross St.
Robinson, IL 62454
Phone: (618)544-2101
General newspaper. **Freq:** Daily. **Print Method:** Offset. **Key Personnel:** Greg Bilbrey, Managing Editor; Winnie Piper, Manager, Advertising. **Subscription Rates:** $99 Individuals carrier delivery; $84 By mail Crawford and adjoining counties; $99 Elsewhere by mail; $52 Individuals 6 months; carrier delivery; $47 By mail 6 months; Crawford and adjoining counties; $52 Elsewhere 6 months; by mail. **URL:** http://www.robdailynews.com. **Remarks:** Accepts advertising. **Circ:** Paid ⊕**6825**.

ROCHELLE

Ogle Co. Ogle Co. (N). 25 m S of Rockford. Manufactures canned vegetables, worsted yarn, sweaters, hauling machinery, furtilizers, plastics naphtha filters, prestressed concrete beans, electrical controls, milk. Meat packing plant. Cold storage warehouse. Agriculture.

11356 ■ Bridger Valley Pioneer
News Media Corp.
211 Hwy. 38
Rochelle, IL 61068
Phone: (815)562-4171
Community newspaper. **Freq:** Weekly. **Print Method:** Offset. **Cols./Page:** 6. **Col. Width:** 12.5 picas. **Col. Depth:** 21 inches. **Key Personnel:** Virginia Giorgis, Editor, phone: (307)787-3229; Mark Tesoro, Publisher. **USPS:** 373-430. **Subscription Rates:** $31 Individuals MAI (in County); $18 Individuals MAI (in County, for six months); $36 Individuals OOA (by mail); $22.50 Individuals OOA (by mail, for six months). **URL:** http://www.bridgervalleypioneer.com/v2_main_page.php. **Ad Rates:** BW $857; 4C $1107. **Remarks:** Accepts advertising. **Circ:** Paid ‡1800, Free ‡123.

11357 ■ Business Farmer
News Media Corp.
211 Hwy. 38
Rochelle, IL 61068
Phone: (815)562-4171
Trade newspaper covering farm news. **Freq:** Monthly. **Print Method:** Web Offset. **Cols./Page:** 6. **Col. Width:** 9 picas. **Col. Depth:** 13 picas. **Key Personnel:** Jeff Robertson, Publisher, phone: (307)532-2184; Craig Allen, Director, Advertising, phone: (308)635-3110; Andrew Cummins, Editor, phone: (308)635-3110; Jean Good, Office Manager, phone: (307)532-2184. **Subscription Rates:** $10.50 Individuals 10-weeks manual pay; $7.50 Individuals 10-weeks auto pay; $37.95 Individuals 1 year manual pay; $34.95 Individuals 1 year auto pay; $10.95 Out of country 10-weeks manual pay; $9.95 Out of country 10-weeks auto pay; $44.95 Out of country 1 year auto pay; $48.95 Out of country 1 year manual pay. **URL:** http://www.thebusinessfarmer.com/v2_main_page.php. **Ad Rates:** GLR $7; BW $7; PCI $7.25. **Remarks:** Accepts advertising. **Circ:** Paid 2750.

11358 ■ Gonzales Tribune
News Media Corp.
211 Hwy. 38
Rochelle, IL 61068
Phone: (815)562-4171
Community newspaper. **Freq:** Weekly (Wed.). **Print Method:** Offset. **Trim Size:** 14 x 22 3/4. **Cols./Page:** 6. **Col. Width:** 26 nonpareils. **Col. Depth:** 294 agate lines. **Key Personnel:** Sheryl Bailey, Manager, Advertising; Sean Roney, Editor. **USPS:** 849-760. **Subscription Rates:** $47.50 Individuals auto pay (in area) ; $49.70 Individuals manual pay (in area); $12.75 Individuals 10 weeks/manual pay (in area) ; $12 Individuals 10 weeks/auto pay (in area) ; $13.85 Out of area 10 weeks (manual pay) ; $13 Out of area 10 weeks (auto pay) ; $50.55 Out of area 1 year (auto pay) ; $52.95 Out of area 1 year (manual pay). **Alt. Formats:** Electronic publishing; PDF. **URL:** http://www.gonzalestribune.com/v2_main_page.php. **Ad Rates:** SAU $8.45. **Remarks:** Accepts advertising. **Circ:** ‡705.

11359 ■ Lake Powell Chronicle
News Media Corp.
PO Box 1716
Page, AZ 86040
Phone: (928)645-8888
Fax: (928)645-2209
Community newspaper. **Freq:** Weekly (Wed.). **Print Method:** Offset. **Cols./Page:** 6. **Col. Width:** 12 picas. **Col. Depth:** 21 inches. **Key Personnel:** Tonja Greenfield, Publisher. **Subscription Rates:** $12.95 Individuals 10 weeks manual pay (In Area); $12.20 Individuals 10 weeks auto pay (In Area); $51 Individuals 1 year auto pay (In Area); $53.15 Individuals 1 year manual pay (In Area); $18.55 Out of area 10 weeks manual pay; $17.60 Out of area 10 weeks auto pay; $73 Out of area 1 year auto pay; $76.30 Out of area 1 year manual pay. **Mailing address:** PO Box 1716, Page, AZ 86040. **Ad Rates:** GLR $.30; BW $437.22; 4C $722.22; SAU $6. **Remarks:** Accepts advertising. **Circ:** ‡3100.

11360 ■ News-Leader
News-Leader
211 Hwy. 38 E
Rochelle, IL 61068
Phone: (815)562-4171
Fax: (815)562-2161
Community newspaper. **Founded:** 1921. **Freq:** 3/week (Sun., Tues., and Thurs.). **Print Method:** Offset. **Cols./Page:** 8. **Col. Width:** 21 nonpareils. **Col. Depth:** 301 agate lines. **URL:** http://www.rochellenews-leader.com/v2_main_page.php. **Formed by the merger of:** News; Leader. **Ad Rates:** GLR $9.95; SAU $8.27; PCI $6.95. **Remarks:** Accepts advertising. **Circ:** Paid ‡4850, Non-paid ‡150.

11361 ■ Uinta County Herald
News Media Corp.
211 Hwy. 38
Rochelle, IL 61068
Phone: (815)562-4171
Newspaper. **Freq:** Biweekly (Tues. and Fri.). **Print Method:** Offset. **Cols./Page:** 6. **Col. Width:** 12 picas. **Col. Depth:** 21 1/2 inches. **Key Personnel:** Mark Tesoro, Publisher. **URL:** http://www.uintacountyherald.com. **Remarks:** Accepts advertising. **Circ:** ‡4700.

11362 ■ WRHL-AM - 1060
400 May Mart Dr.
Rochelle, IL 61068
Phone: (815)562-7001
Fax: (815)562-7002
Format: News; Talk. **Networks:** CBS. **Owner:** Rochelle Broadcasting Company Inc., 315 N Lagrange Rd., Apt. 522, Rochelle, IL 61068. **Operating Hours:** Continuous. **Key Personnel:** Jay Burlison, Production Mgr., jay@wrhl.net; Becky Leininger, Asst. GM, becky@wrhl.net; Rick Green, Asst. GM, rjg@wrhl.net. **Wattage:** 250 Day; 050 Night. **Ad Rates:** Advertising accepted; rates available upon request. **Mailing address:** PO Box 177, Rochelle, IL 61068. **URL:** http://www.wrhl.net.

11363 ■ WRHL-FM - 102.3
400 May Mart Dr.
Rochelle, IL 61068
Format: Contemporary Hit Radio (CHR). **Owner:** Rochelle Broadcasting Company Inc., 315 N Lagrange Rd., Apt. 522, Rochelle, IL 61068. **Operating Hours:** Continuous. **Key Personnel:** Becky Leininger, Asst. GM, becky@wrhl.net; Jay Burlison, Production Mgr., jay@wrhl.net. **Wattage:** 6,000 ERP. **Ad Rates:** Advertising accepted; rates available upon request. **Mailing address:** PO Box 177, Rochelle, IL 61068. **URL:** http://www.wrhl.net.

ROCK ISLAND

Rock Island Co. Rock Island Co. (NE). On Mississippi River, opposite Davenport, Ia., 168 m SW of Chicago. Augustana College. Manufactures agricultural implements, government supplies and munitions, rubber footwear, clothing, oil burners, furnaces, machine tools, electrical appliances, paper containers. Foundries.

11364 ■ Augustana College Magazine
Augustana College
639 38th St.
Rock Island, IL 61201-2296
Phone: (309)794-7000
Free: 800-798-8100
Publication E-mail: acmks@augustana.edu
College alumni magazine. **Freq:** Semiannual. **Print Method:** Offset. **Trim Size:** 8 x 11 1/2. **Cols./Page:** 3. **Col. Width:** 2 1/2 inches. **Col. Depth:** 9 1/4 inches. **Key Personnel:** Kai Swanson, Editor, phone: (309)794-7473, fax: (309)794-3461; Debbie Blaylock, Contact. **URL:** http://www.augustana.edu/alumni/augustana-magazine-archive. **Remarks:** Advertising not accepted. **Circ:** Controlled ‡26500.

11365 ■ Chiropractic History: The Archives and Journal of the Association of the History of Chiropractic
Association for the History of Chiropractic
4430 8th St.
Rock Island, IL 61201-6608
Phone: (309)788-0799
Freq: Semiannual. **ISSN:** 0736- 4377 (print). **URL:** http://www.historyofchiropractic.org/the-journal. **Remarks:** Advertising not accepted. **Circ:** (Not Reported).

11366 ■ Chiropractic History: The Archives and Journal of the Association for the History of Chiropractic
Association for the History of Chiropractic
4430 8th St.
Rock Island, IL 61201-6608
Phone: (309)788-0799
Journal.Contains topics related to the history of chiropractic profession. **Freq:** Semiannual. **Key Personnel:** John Wolfe, Editor. **ISSN:** 0736--4377 (print). **Subscription Rates:** $30 Individuals single issue. **Alt. Formats:** PDF. **URL:** http://www.historyofchiropractic.org/the-journal. **Ad Rates:** BW $150. **Remarks:** Accepts advertising. **Circ:** Paid ‡523, Non-paid ‡250.

11367 ■ The Modern Woodmen
Modern Woodmen of America
1701 1st Ave.
Rock Island, IL 61201-8724
Fax: (309)793-5547

Free: 800-447-9811
Freq: Quarterly. **Print Method:** Webb Offset. **Trim Size:** 8 3/8 x 10 1/2. **Cols./Page:** 3. **Key Personnel:** Sharon Snawerdt, Contact, phone: (309)793-5630. **ISSN:** 0279--8670 (print). **Subscription Rates:** Included in membership. **URL:** http://www.modernwoodmen.org/being-a-member/member-benefits. **Mailing address:** PO Box 2005, Rock Island, IL 61204-2005. **Remarks:** Advertising not accepted. **Circ:** ‡400000.

11368 ■ The Royal Neighbor
Royal Neighbors of America
230 16th St.
Rock Island, IL 61201-8645
Free: 800-627-4762
Publisher's E-mail: contact@royalneighbors.org
Print Method: Offset. **Trim Size:** 8 1/2 x 11. **Cols./Page:** 3. **Col. Width:** 27 nonpareils. **Col. Depth:** 140 agate lines. **Key Personnel:** Rita Toalson, Managing Editor. **ISSN:** 0035--905X (print). **Subscription Rates:** Included in membership. **URL:** http://www.royalneighbors.org/membership-benefits/the-royal-neighbor-magazine. **Remarks:** Advertising not accepted. **Circ:** ‡190000.

11369 ■ Swedish American Genealogist
Augustana College Swenson Swedish Immigration Research Center
639 38th St.
Rock Island, IL 61201-2296
Phone: (309)794-7000
Fax: (309)794-7443
Free: 800-798-8100
Publication E-mail: sag@etgenealogy.se
Professional journal covering Swedish American genealogy, biography, and personal history. **Founded:** Mar. 1981. **Freq:** Quarterly. **Trim Size:** 6 x 9. **Cols./Page:** 1. **Key Personnel:** Elisabeth Thorsell, Editor. **ISSN:** 0275-9314 (print). **Subscription Rates:** $30 Individuals; $15 Members. **URL:** http://www.augustana.edu/x13918.xml. **Remarks:** Advertising not accepted. **Circ:** Controlled 1100.

11370 ■ WHBF-TV - 66 - 72
231 18th St.
Rock Island, IL 61201
Format: Full Service. **Networks:** CBS. **ADI:** Daveport,IA-Rock Island, Moline,IL. **Wattage:** 33,700. **Ad Rates:** Advertising accepted; rates available upon request.

11371 ■ WVIK-FM - 90.3
639 38th St.
Rock Island, IL 61201
Phone: (309)794-7500
Fax: (309)794-1236
Email: info@wvik.org
Format: Public Radio. **Networks:** National Public Radio (NPR). **Owner:** Augustana College, 639 38th St., Rock Island, IL 61201-2296, Ph: (309)794-7000, Free: 800-798-8100. **Founded:** 1980. **Operating Hours:** Continuous. **ADI:** Daveport,IA-Rock Island, Moline,IL. **Key Personnel:** Kai Swanson, Contact, kaiswanson@augustana.edu; Dave Garner, Operations Mgr., davidgarner@wvik.org; Mindy Heusel, Music Dir., mindyheusel@wvik.org; Colleen Sibthorp, Bus. Mgr., colleensibthorp@wvik.org; Herb Trix, News Dir., herbtrix@wvik.org. **Wattage:** 31,000 ERP. **Ad Rates:** Noncommercial. **URL:** http://www.wvik.org.

ROCKFORD

Winnebago Co. Winnebago Co. (N). On Rock River, 90 m NW of Chicago. Rockford College. Manufactures airplane and auto parts, air conditioning and heating equipment, castings, chewing gum, furniture, gears, governors, hardware, leather goods, machine tools, packaging equipment, paint, pet food, plastics, pumps, tin containers, farm machinery, wire goods, motors, scales, sports equipment, screw products and fasteners.

11372 ■ Canadian Industrial Machinery: Canada's Metalworking & Fabricating Technology Magazine
Canadian Industrial Publishing Inc.
833 Featherstone Rd.
Rockford, IL 61107
Phone: (815)399-8700
Fax: (815)484-7700
Publisher's E-mail: info@cimindustry.com
Trade magazine covering the metal manufacturing industry in Canada. **Freq:** Monthly. **Key Personnel:** Joe Thompson, Editor, phone: (289)337-3290. **Subscription Rates:** Free. **URL:** http://www.cimindustry.com/publication/cim. **Remarks:** Accepts advertising. **Circ:** Combined 23812.

11373 ■ Chronicles: A Magazine of American Culture
The Rockford Institute
928 N Main St.
Rockford, IL 61103
Phone: (815)964-5053
Publisher's E-mail: polemics@chroniclesmagazine.org
Magazine containing book reviews, cultural criticism, and opinion. **Founded:** Sept. 1977. **Freq:** Monthly. **Print Method:** Web offset. **Trim Size:** 8 1/2 x 11. **Cols./Page:** 2 and 3. **Key Personnel:** Scott P. Richert, Executive Editor; Aaron D. Wolf, Associate Editor; Thomas J. Fleming, Editor. **ISSN:** 0887-5731 (print). **Subscription Rates:** $44.99 Individuals; $79.99 Two years; $104.99 Individuals 3 years. **URL:** http://www.chroniclesmagazine.org. **Formerly:** Chronicles of Culture. **Remarks:** Advertising accepted; rates available upon request. **Circ:** (Not Reported).

11374 ■ The Fabricator
Fabricators and Manufacturers Association, International
833 Featherstone Rd.
Rockford, IL 61107
Phone: (815)399-8700
Free: 888-394-4362
Publication E-mail: press_releases@thefabricator.com
Freq: Monthly. **Print Method:** Offset. Heat-set Web. **Trim Size:** 10 1/2 x 13 5/8. **Cols./Page:** 4. **Col. Width:** 14 picas. **Col. Depth:** 11 picas. **Key Personnel:** Tim Heston, Senior Editor; Michael Lacny, Advertising Representative; Dan Davis, Editor-in-Chief. **ISSN:** 0192--8066 (print). **Subscription Rates:** Free to qualified subscribers; $95 Canada and Mexico /year ; $140 Other countries /year. **URL:** http://www.thefabricator.com; http://www.thefabricator.com/publication/fab. **Ad Rates:** BW $8,845; 4C $10,280; PCI $55. **Remarks:** Accepts advertising. **Circ:** Controlled 55000.

11375 ■ Industria Avicola
Watt Publishing Co.
303 N Main St., Ste. 500
Rockford, IL 61101-1049
Phone: (815)966-5400
Fax: (815)966-6416
Magazine for all phases of the Latin American poultry industry. Printed in Spanish. **Freq:** Monthly. **Print Method:** Web Offset. **Trim Size:** 8 x 10 3/4. **Cols./Page:** 2. **Col. Width:** 3 3/8 inches. **Col. Depth:** 10 inches. **Key Personnel:** Benjamin Ruiz, Editor-in-Chief. **ISSN:** 0019--7467 (print). **Subscription Rates:** Free online. **URL:** http://www.industriaavicola-digital.com/#&pageSet=0&contentItem=0. **Ad Rates:** 4C $6040. **Remarks:** Accepts advertising. **Circ:** ‡14003.

11376 ■ Meat Processing Global
Watt Publishing Co.
303 N Main St., Ste. 500
Rockford, IL 61101-1049
Phone: (815)966-5400
Fax: (815)966-6416
Publication covering meat processing. **Freq:** Bimonthly. **Key Personnel:** Jeff Cummings, Contact. **URL:** http://www.iian.ibeam.com/events/watt001/21540/. **Formerly:** Meat Processing International. **Remarks:** Advertising accepted; rates available upon request. **Circ:** (Not Reported).

11377 ■ The Observer
Catholic Diocese of Rockford
PO Box 7044
Rockford, IL 61125-7044
Phone: (815)399-4300
Publication E-mail: observer@rockforddiocese.org
Catholic tabloid. **Founded:** 1935. **Freq:** Weekly (Fri.). **Print Method:** Offset. **Trim Size:** 10 1/4 x 14. **Cols./Page:** 6. **Col. Width:** 19 nonpareils. **Col. Depth:** 210 agate lines. **ISSN:** 0029-7739 (print). **Subscription Rates:** $28 Individuals. **URL:** http://observer.rockforddiocese.org/. **Ad Rates:** GLR $.79; BW $990; 4C $1,800; PCI $13. **Remarks:** Accepts advertising. **Circ:** Paid ‡38000, Non-paid ‡309.

11378 ■ Petfood Industry
Watt Publishing Co.
303 N Main St., Ste. 500
Rockford, IL 61101-1049
Phone: (815)966-5400
Fax: (815)966-6416
Magazine for pet food manufacturers. **Founded:** 1959. **Freq:** Monthly. **Print Method:** Web Offset. **Trim Size:** 8 x 10 3/4. **Cols./Page:** 2 and 3. **Col. Width:** 3 3/8 and 2 1/8 inches. **Col. Depth:** 140 and 140 agate lines. **Key Personnel:** Debbie Phillips-Donaldson, Editor-in-Chief; Jessica Taylor, Managing Editor; Steve Akins, Publisher. **ISSN:** 0031-6245 (print). **Subscription Rates:** $14 Single issue. **URL:** http://www.petfoodindustry.com; http://www.petfoodindustry-digital.com/petfoodindustry/201109#pg1. **Ad Rates:** BW $3,145; 4C $5,565; PCI $135. **Remarks:** Accepts advertising. **Circ:** Free 11030.

11379 ■ Pig International
Watt Publishing Co.
303 N Main St., Ste. 500
Rockford, IL 61101-1049
Phone: (815)966-5400
Fax: (815)966-6416
Magazine focusing on pig production and marketing. **Freq:** Bimonthly. **Print Method:** Web Offset. **Trim Size:** 8 x 10 3/4. **Cols./Page:** 2 and 2. **Col. Width:** 3 3/8 and 2 1/8 inches. **Col. Depth:** 140 and 140 agate lines. **Key Personnel:** Roger Abbott, Editor; Bill Spranger, Director, Production; Peter Best, Editor; Steve Akins, Publisher. **ISSN:** 0191--8834 (print). **URL:** http://www.piginternational-digital.com/#&pageSet=0&contentItem=0; http://www.wattagnet.com. **Ad Rates:** BW $4,910; 4C $7,375. **Remarks:** Accepts advertising. **Circ:** ‡17825.

11380 ■ Poultry International
Watt Publishing Co.
303 N Main St., Ste. 500
Rockford, IL 61101-1049
Phone: (815)966-5400
Fax: (815)966-6416
Magazine serving the poultry industry in Europe, Middle East/Africa, and Asia/Pacific. **Freq:** Monthly. **Print Method:** Web offset. **Trim Size:** 8 x 10 3/4. **Cols./Page:** 2 and 3. **Col. Width:** 2 3/8 and 2 inches. **Col. Depth:** 10 inches. **Key Personnel:** Mark Clements, Editor; Jim Riedl, Manager, Production. **ISSN:** 0032--5767 (print). **URL:** http://www.poultryinternational-digital.com/#&pageSet=0&contentItem=0; http://www.wattglobalmedia.com/publications/poultry-international. **Ad Rates:** BW $4,975; 4C $7,725. **Remarks:** Accepts advertising. **Circ:** ‡20046.

11381 ■ Practical Welding Today
Fabricators and Manufacturers Association, International
833 Featherstone Rd.
Rockford, IL 61107
Phone: (815)399-8700
Free: 888-394-4362
Publication E-mail: press_releases@thefabricator.com
Freq: Bimonthly. **Trim Size:** 8 1/4 x 10 3/4. **Cols./Page:** 3. **Col. Width:** 14 picas. **Key Personnel:** Sean Smith, Advertising Representative, phone: (815)227-8265; Michael Lacny, Advertising Representative, phone: (815)227-8264; Dave Brambert, Publisher, phone: (815)227-8250; Amanda Carlson, Associate Editor; Dan Davis, Editor-in-Chief. **ISSN:** 1092--3942 (print). **Subscription Rates:** Free to qualified subscribers. **Alt. Formats:** PDF. **URL:** http://fma-communications.com/pwt. **Ad Rates:** BW $4,355; 4C $5,555. **Remarks:** Accepts advertising. **Circ:** Controlled 40000, 40000.

11382 ■ The Rock River Times: The Voice of the Community
The Rock River Times
128 N Church St.
Rockford, IL 61107
Phone: (815)964-9767
Fax: (815)964-9825
Publisher's E-mail: contact@rockrivertimes.com
Free Newspaper. **Freq:** Weekly. **Key Personnel:** Jody Marshall, Manager, Sales; Frank Schier, Editor, Publisher. **URL:** http://rockrivertimes.com. **Remarks:** Advertising accepted; rates available upon request. **Circ:** Non-paid 22000.

Circulation: ★ = AAM; △ or • = BPA; ♦ = CAC; ❑ = VAC; ⊕ = PO Statement; ‡ = Publisher's Report; Boldface figures = sworn; Light figures = estimated.

11383 ■ Sales and Marketing Management: The Nations's Comprehensive News Source for Successful Sales & Marketing Strategies
Hughes Communications Inc.
211 W State St.
Rockford, IL 61105-0197
Phone: (815)963-4000
Fax: (815)963-7773
Free: 800-435-2937
Publication E-mail: info@salesandmarketingmag.com
Magazine on sales and marketing. **Freq:** Bimonthly. **Print Method:** Web heatset. **Trim Size:** 8 x 10 3/4. **Key Personnel:** Mike Murrell, President, Publisher, phone: (952)401-1283. **ISSN:** 1066--5463 (print). **Subscription Rates:** $48 Individuals in U.S.; $67 Individuals in Canada; $146 Other countries. **URL:** http://www.salesandmarketing.com. **Mailing address:** PO Box 197, Rockford, IL 61105-0197. **Ad Rates:** BW $11,930; 4C $16,750. **Remarks:** Accepts advertising. **Circ:** (Not Reported).

11384 ■ Stamping Journal
Fabricators and Manufacturers Association, International
833 Featherstone Rd.
Rockford, IL 61107
Phone: (815)399-8700
Free: 888-394-4362
Publisher's E-mail: info@thefabricator.com
Freq: Monthly. **Subscription Rates:** Free to qualified subscribers; $65 U.S.; $75 Canada and Mexico; $95 Other countries. **Remarks:** Accepts advertising. **Circ:** 34000.

11385 ■ TPJ - The Tube and Pipe Journal
Tube and Pipe Association, International
833 Featherstone Rd.
Rockford, IL 61107-6301
Phone: (815)399-8700
Free: 888-394-4362
Publisher's E-mail: info@fmanet.org
Magazine featuring useful articles regarding tube and pipe technology. **Freq:** 8/year. **Key Personnel:** Eric Lundin, Editor. **Subscription Rates:** Free to qualified subscribers. **URL:** http://www.fma-communications.com/tpj/. **Remarks:** Accepts advertising. **Circ:** 25000.

11386 ■ TPJ--The Tube & Pipe Journal
Fabricators and Manufacturers Association, International
833 Featherstone Rd.
Rockford, IL 61107
Phone: (815)399-8700
Free: 888-394-4362
Publication E-mail: press_releases@thefabricator.com
Trade magazine covering metal tube and pipe production and metal tube and pipe fabricating. **Founded:** 1990. **Freq:** 8/year. **Trim Size:** 8 1/4 x 10 3/4. **Cols./Page:** 3. **Col. Width:** 14 picas. **Key Personnel:** Dan Davis, Editor-in-Chief; Eric Lundin, Editor. **ISSN:** 1091-2460 (print). **Subscription Rates:** Free. **URL:** http://www.fma-communications.com/tpj/. **Formerly**: TPQ--The Tube & Pipe Quarterly. **Remarks:** Advertising accepted; rates available upon request. **Circ:** Controlled ‡30000.

11387 ■ VietNow National Magazine
VietNow National
1835 Broadway
Rockford, IL 61104
Phone: (815)227-5100
Free: 800-837-8669
Publisher's E-mail: nationalhq@vietnow.com
Freq: Quarterly. **Key Personnel:** Christian Nelson, Editor. **Subscription Rates:** Included in membership. **URL:** http://www.vietnow.com/vietnow-national-magazine. **Remarks:** Advertising not accepted. **Circ:** (Not Reported).

11388 ■ The Voice
Rockford Chamber of Commerce
308 W State St.
Rockford, IL 61101
Phone: (815)987-8100
Fax: (815)987-8122
Publication E-mail: editor@rockfordchamber.com
Newspaper containing information regarding the region of Rockford. **Freq:** Monthly. **Trim Size:** 8.25 x 11. **URL:** http://www.rockfordchamber.com/publications/voice.asp. **Ad Rates:** BW $1,335; 4C $1,995. **Remarks:** Accepts advertising. **Circ:** Combined 9000.

11389 ■ WATT Poultry USA
Watt Publishing Co.
303 N Main St., Ste. 500
Rockford, IL 61101-1049
Phone: (815)966-5400
Fax: (815)966-6416
Magazine focusing on production, processing, and marketing in the U.S. poultry meat industry. **Founded:** 1938. **Freq:** Monthly. **Print Method:** Offset. **Trim Size:** 8 x 10 3/4. **Cols./Page:** 3. **Col. Width:** 27 nonpareils. **Col. Depth:** 140 agate lines. **Key Personnel:** Terrence O'Keefe, Editor; Gary Thornton, Director; Kayla Kling, Associate Editor. **ISSN:** 1529-1677 (print). **Subscription Rates:** Free online. **URL:** http://www.wattagnet.com; http://www.wattpoultryusa-digital.com. **Formed by the merger of**: Broiler Industry; Turkey World. **Ad Rates:** BW $3,800; 4C $5,940. **Remarks:** Accepts advertising. **Circ:** ‡15,067.

11390 ■ NTA-FM - 100.5
2830 Sandy Hollow Rd.
Rockford, IL 61109
Phone: (815)874-7861
Fax: (815)874-2202
Format: News; Talk. **Owner:** Airplay Broadcasting Corp., 11591 Inverway, Belvidere, IL 61008-1724. **Founded:** 1953. **Formerly**: WXTA-AM; WYBR-AM; WKKN-AM. **ADI**: Rockford, IL. **Key Personnel:** Ken DeCoster, Contact; Mark Mayhew, Contact. **Ad Rates:** Advertising accepted; rates available upon request. $11-33 for 30 seconds; $15-37 for 60 seconds. **Mailing address:** PO Box 7180, Rockford, IL 61114.

11391 ■ WFEN-FM - 88.3
4721 S Main St.
Rockford, IL 61102
Phone: (815)964-9336
Fax: (815)964-0550
Email: info@wfen.org
Format: Religious. **Ad Rates:** Noncommercial. **URL:** http://www.wfen.org.

11392 ■ WGFB-FM - 103.1
2830 Sandy Hollow Rd.
Rockford, IL 61109
Phone: (815)874-2103
Free: 866-800-2103
Format: Adult Contemporary. **Owner:** Maverick Media, at above address. **Founded:** 1961. **Formerly**: WRWC-FM. **Operating Hours**: Continuous. **Key Personnel:** Gail Lewis, Contact. **Wattage**: 1,200. **Ad Rates:** Advertising accepted; rates available upon request. Combined advertising rates available with WXRX-FM, WYHY-FM, WNTA-AM. **URL:** http://www.b103fm.com.

11393 ■ WIFR-TV - 23
2523 North Meridian Road
Rockford, IL 61101
Phone: (815)987-5300
Fax: (815)987-0981
Email: talkto23@wifr.com
Format: Commercial TV. **Networks:** CBS. **Owner:** Gray Television Inc., 4370 Peachtree Rd. NE, No. 400, Atlanta, GA 30319-3054, Ph: (404)266-8333. **Founded:** 1965. **Operating Hours**: Continuous (Sun.-Thurs.). **ADI**: Rockford, IL. **Key Personnel:** Pat Gostele, Sports Dir., patrick.gostele@wifr.com; Dave Smith, News Dir., dave.smith@wifr.com. **Ad Rates:** Advertising accepted; rates available upon request. **URL:** http://www.wifr.com/station/bios.

11394 ■ WKGL-FM - 96.7
3901 Brenwood Rd.
Rockford, IL 61107
Phone: (815)399-2233
Format: Classic Rock. **Owner:** Cumulus Media Inc., 3280 Peachtree Rd. NW, Ste. 2300, Atlanta, GA 30305-2455, Ph: (404)949-0700, Fax: (404)949-0740. **Founded:** 1964. **Formerly**: WLUV-FM; WZMX-FM; WSHK. **Operating Hours**: Continuous. **Key Personnel:** Richard Denning, Gen. Counsel, VP; Becky Riojas, Gen. Mgr. **Wattage**: 2,200 ERP. **Ad Rates:** Advertising accepted; rates available upon request. **URL:** http://967theeagle.net.

11395 ■ WLUV-AM
2272 Elmwood Rd.
Rockford, IL 61103
Phone: (815)877-9588
Fax: (815)877-9649
Format: Country; Sports. **Networks:** CBS. **Owner:** Angelo Joseph Salvi, at above address. **Founded:** 1962. **Key Personnel:** Angelo Joseph Salvi, Gen. Mgr. **Wattage**: 500 Day; 013 Night. **Ad Rates:** $7.50-12.50 for 10 seconds; $12.50-17.50 for 30 seconds; $15-20 for 60 seconds.

11396 ■ WREX-TV - 13
10322 Auburn Rd.
Rockford, IL 61103
Phone: (815)335-2213
Fax: (815)335-2055
Email: news@wrex.com
Format: Commercial TV. **Networks:** NBC. **Founded:** 1953. **Operating Hours**: Continuous. **Key Personnel:** John Chadwick, Gen. Mgr., VP, jchadwick@wrex.com; Dan Whealy, Chief Engineer, dwhealy@wrex.com; Kim Carney, Sales Mgr., kcarney@wrex.com; Maggie Hradecky, News Dir., mhradecky@wrex.com; Joe Viglietta, Sales Mgr., jviglietta@wrex.com. **Ad Rates:** Noncommercial. **URL:** http://www.wrex.com.

11397 ■ WROK-AM - 1440
3901 Brendenwood Rd.
Rockford, IL 61107
Phone: (815)399-2233
Fax: (815)484-2432
Format: News; Talk. **Networks:** ABC. **Owner:** Cumulus Media Inc., 3280 Peachtree Rd. NW, Ste. 2300, Atlanta, GA 30305-2455, Ph: (404)949-0700, Fax: (404)949-0740. **Founded:** 1923. **Operating Hours**: Continuous. **ADI**: Rockford, IL. **Key Personnel:** Scot Bertram, Dir. of Programs, scot.bertram@1440wrok.com; Scott Maenner, Sales Mgr., scott.maenner@cumulus.com. **Local Programs**: *Twilight Zone Radio Dramas*, Sunday 7:00 p.m. - 9:00 p.m. **Wattage**: 5,000. **Ad Rates:** $21-45 for 30 seconds; $29-52 for 60 seconds. $12-$60 for 30 seconds; $15-$74 for 60 seconds. Combined advertising rates available with WZOK-FM. **URL:** http://www.1440wrok.com.

WRTB-FM - See Winnebago

11398 ■ WTCL-AM - 1580
7749 N Rockton
Rockford, IL 61103
Format: Urban Contemporary. **Networks:** USA Radio. **Founded:** 1963. **Formerly**: WENO-AM. **Operating Hours**: Daytime. **Key Personnel:** John Blessinger, Gen. Mgr. **Wattage**: 10,000. **Ad Rates:** $4.68-6.17 for 30 seconds; $5.86-7.75 for 60 seconds.

11399 ■ WTVO-TV - 17
1917 N Meridian Rd.
Rockford, IL 61101
Phone: (815)963-5413
Fax: (815)963-0029
Format: Commercial TV. **Networks:** NBC; Fox; CBS; ABC. **Owner:** Young Broadcasting Inc., 599 Lexington Ave., New York, NY 10022-6030, Ph: (212)754-7070, Fax: (212)758-1229. **Founded:** 1953. **Operating Hours**: Continuous. **ADI**: Rockford, IL. **Key Personnel:** Michael Khouri, Gen. Mgr.; Paul Freifeld, News Dir; Wilma Hollis, Contact; Terry Kowalski, Contact. **Wattage**: 196,000 ERP H. **Mailing address:** PO Box 470, Rockford, IL 61105. **URL:** http://www.mystateline.com.

11400 ■ WXRX-FM - 104.9
2830 Sandy Hollow Rd.
Rockford, IL 61108
Phone: (815)874-7861
Email: dad@wxrx.com
Format: Album-Oriented Rock (AOR). **Owner:** Maverick Media, at above address. **Founded:** 1971. **Key Personnel:** Michelle Marcomb, Contact, michellemarcomb@maverick-media.ws. **Wattage**: 4,000 ERP. **Ad Rates:** Advertising accepted; rates available upon request. Combined advertising rates available with WYHY-FM, WGFB-FM, WNTA-AM. **URL:** http://www.wxrx.com.

11401 ■ WXXQ-FM - 98.5
3901 Brendenwood Rd.
Rockford, IL 61107
Phone: (815)229-0985
Format: Country. **Networks:** Tribune Radio; CBS. **Owner:** Cumulus Media Inc., 3280 Peachtree Rd. NW, Ste. 2300, Atlanta, GA 30305-2455, Ph: (404)949-0700, Fax: (404)949-0740. **Founded:** 1997. **Operating Hours**: Continuous; 100% local. **Key Personnel:** Scott Maenner, Managing Ed., Scott.Maenner@

townsquaremedia.com; Steve Summers, Dir. of Programs, steve@q985online.com; Becky Riojas, Gen. Mgr. **Wattage**: 50,000. **Ad Rates:** $15-30 for 60 seconds. **URL:** http://www.q985online.com.

11402 ■ WYHY-FM - 95.3
2830 Sandy Hollow Rd.
Rockford, IL 61109
Format: News; Adult Album Alternative. **Simulcasts:** WXRX. **Networks:** ABC. **Owner:** RadioWorks, Inc., PO Box 6159, Portsmouth, VA 23703, Ph: (757)484-0140, Free: 800-280-8327. **Founded:** 1970. **Formerly**: WKMQ - Oldies. **ADI**: Rockford, IL. **Wattage**: 1,250 ERP. **Ad Rates:** Advertising accepted; rates available upon request. **URL:** http://www.953thebull.com.

11403 ■ WZOK-FM - 97.5
3901 Brendenwood Rd.
Rockford, IL 61107
Phone: (815)399-2233
Format: Contemporary Hit Radio (CHR). **Owner:** Cumulus Media Inc., 3280 Peachtree Rd. NW, Ste. 2300, Atlanta, GA 30305-2455, Ph: (404)949-0700, Fax: (404)949-0740. **Founded:** 1949. **Operating Hours:** Continuous. **ADI**: Rockford, IL. **Key Personnel:** Andrea Bogdonas, Promotions Dir., andrea.bogdonas@cumulus.com; Scott Maenner, Sales Mgr., scott.maenner@cumulus.com. **Wattage**: 50,000. **Ad Rates:** $27-65 for 30 seconds; $38-78 for 60 seconds. **URL:** http://www.97zokonline.com.

ROCKTON

Winnebago Co.

11404 ■ The Herald
Rock Valley Publishing
1107 N Blackhawk
Rockton, IL 61072
Phone: (815)624-6211
Fax: (815)624-8018
Community newspaper for Rockford, Illinois, suburbs. **Founded:** 1875. **Freq:** Weekly. **Print Method:** Web Offset. **Trim Size:** 11 1/2 x 17. **Cols./Page:** 5. **Col. Width:** 2 1/2 inches. **Col. Depth:** 16 inches. **Subscription Rates:** Free. **URL:** http://www.rvpublishing.com. **Formerly**: Rockton-Roscoe Herald; North Suburban Herald. **Ad Rates:** BW $692; 4C $360; SAU $8.65; PCI $8.65. **Remarks:** Accepts advertising. **Circ:** (Not Reported).

ROLLING MEADOWS

Cook Co. Cook Co. (NE). 4 m NW of Mt. Prospect. Residential. Commercial. Industrial.

11405 ■ AANS Neurosurgeon
American Association of Neurological Surgeons
5550 Meadowbrook Dr.
Rolling Meadows, IL 60008-3852
Phone: (847)378-0500
Fax: (847)378-0600
Free: 888-566-2267
Publisher's E-mail: info@aans.org
Professional magazine covering neurosurgery. **Freq:** Quarterly. **Key Personnel:** Michael Schulder, MD, Editor. **Subscription Rates:** Included in membership. **URL:** http://www.aansneurosurgeon.org. **Formerly**: American Association of Neurological Surgeons Bulletin. **Remarks:** Accepts advertising. **Circ:** (Not Reported).

11406 ■ Dermatologic Surgery Journal
American Society for Dermatologic Surgery
5550 Meadowbrook Dr., Ste. 120
Rolling Meadows, IL 60008
Phone: (847)956-0900
Fax: (847)956-0999
Journal providing expansive and in-depth reviews of advances in cosmetic and reconstructive cutaneous surgery. **Freq:** Monthly. **Subscription Rates:** Included in membership. **URL:** http://www.asds.net/_DoctorResources.aspx?id=5804. **Remarks:** Accepts advertising. **Circ:** (Not Reported).

11407 ■ ISACA Journal
Information Systems Audit and Control Association
3701 Algonquin Rd., Ste. 1010
Rolling Meadows, IL 60008
Phone: (847)253-1545
Fax: (847)253-1443
Freq: 6/year. **ISSN:** 1076--4100 (print). **Subscription Rates:** Accessible only for members.; $80 U.S. 1 year; $95 Other countries 1 year; $147 U.S. 2 years; $175 Other countries 2 years; $219 U.S. 3 years; $261 Other countries 3 years. **URL:** http://www.isaca.org/journal/archives/pages/default.aspx. **Ad Rates:** 4C $4530. **Remarks:** Accepts advertising. **Circ:** 31000.

11408 ■ Journal of Neurosurgery: Pediatrics
American Association of Neurological Surgeons
5550 Meadowbrook Dr.
Rolling Meadows, IL 60008-3852
Phone: (847)378-0500
Fax: (847)378-0600
Free: 888-566-2267
Publisher's E-mail: info@aans.org
Journals containing recent articles that address the fetal and postnatal morphological development of the brain sulci, transcardiac cerebral angiography in a pediatric case and hospital care of childhood traumatic head injury in the United States. **Freq:** Monthly. **Subscription Rates:** Included in membership. **Alt. Formats:** PDF. **URL:** http://thejns.org/action/showCoverGallery?journalCode=ped; http://www.aans.org/AANS%20and%20JNSPG%20Publications/Publications/Journal%20of%20Neurosurgery.aspx. **Ad Rates:** BW $2,575. **Remarks:** Accepts advertising. **Circ:** (Not Reported).

11409 ■ Journal of Neurosurgery: Spine
American Association of Neurological Surgeons
5550 Meadowbrook Dr.
Rolling Meadows, IL 60008-3852
Phone: (847)378-0500
Fax: (847)378-0600
Free: 888-566-2267
Publisher's E-mail: info@aans.org
Freq: Monthly. **Subscription Rates:** Included in membership. **URL:** http://thejns.org/toc/spi/current; http://www.aans.org/AANS%20and%20JNSPG%20Publications/Publications/Journal%20of%20Neurosurgery.aspx. **Ad Rates:** BW $2,575. **Remarks:** Accepts advertising. **Circ:** (Not Reported).

ROMEOVILLE

Will Co.

11410 ■ Catholic Explorer
Catholic Explorer
St. Charles Borromeo Pastoral Ctr.
402 S Independence Blvd.
Romeoville, IL 60446-2264
Phone: (815)838-6475
Fax: (815)834-4068
Official Catholic newspaper for the Diocese of Joliet. **Freq:** 46/yr. **Print Method:** Offset. **Trim Size:** 13 x 21. **Cols./Page:** 6 and 4. **Col. Width:** 12.5 and 14.6 picas. **Col. Depth:** 21 and 13 inches. **ISSN:** 1044--8322 (print). **Subscription Rates:** $20 Individuals home or office. **URL:** http://www.catholicexplorer.com. **Formerly**: New Catholic Explorer. **Remarks:** Advertising accepted; rates available upon request. **Circ:** ‡22500.

11411 ■ WLRA-FM - 88.1
One University Pkwy.
Romeoville, IL 60446
Phone: (815)836-5000
Format: Eclectic. **Owner:** Lewis University, One University Pky., Romeoville, IL 60446-2200, Ph: (815)838-0500, Free: 800-897-9000. **Founded:** 1974. **Operating Hours**: Continuous. **Wattage**: 140. **Ad Rates:** Noncommercial. **URL:** http://www.wlraradio.com.

ROSEMONT

Cook Co. Cook Co. (NE). 14 m N.W. of Chicago.

11412 ■ The American Journal of Sports Medicine
American Orthopaedic Society for Sports Medicine
9400 W Higgins Rd., Ste. 300
Rosemont, IL 60018
Phone: (847)292-4900
Fax: (847)292-4905
Free: 877-321-3500
Publisher's E-mail: info@aossm.org
Medical journal. **Freq:** Monthly. **Print Method:** Web press. **Trim Size:** 8 1/8 x 10 7/8. **Cols./Page:** 2. **Col. Width:** 32 nonpareils. **Col. Depth:** 119 agate lines. **Key Personnel:** Bruce Reider, MD, Editor; Allen Anderson, Associate Editor; Jack Hughston, Founder. **ISSN:** 0363--5465 (print); **EISSN:** 1552--3365 (electronic). **Subscription Rates:** £131 Institutions print and online; £14 Individuals single print issue; £57 Institutions single print issue. **URL:** http://ajs.sagepub.com. **Ad Rates:** BW $1450; 4C $1505. **Remarks:** Accepts advertising. **Circ:** Paid ‡8540, 11000.

11413 ■ AMT Events
American Medical Technologists
10700 W Higgins Rd., Ste. 150
Rosemont, IL 60018
Phone: (847)823-5169
Fax: (847)823-0458
Free: 800-275-1268
Publisher's E-mail: membership@amt1.com
Professional journal of the American Medical Technologists. **Freq:** Quarterly. **Key Personnel:** Diane Powell, Director, Publications. **ISSN:** 0746-9217 (print). **Subscription Rates:** $50 Nonmembers; $60 Nonmembers out of country. **Alt. Formats:** Download; PDF. **URL:** http://www.americanmedtech.org/BeInvolved/OurPublications/AMTPublicationPreviewPage.aspx. **Ad Rates:** GLR $10; BW $975; 4C $1,675. **Remarks:** Accepts advertising. **Circ:** Controlled **40000.**

11414 ■ AMT Events and Continuing Education Supplement
American Medical Technologists
10700 W Higgins Rd., Ste. 150
Rosemont, IL 60018
Phone: (847)823-5169
Fax: (847)823-0458
Free: 800-275-1268
Publisher's E-mail: membership@amt1.com
Freq: 3/year March, June and September. **ISSN:** 0746--9217 (print). **Subscription Rates:** Included in membership; $50 Nonmembers /year; $60 Nonmembers /year - outside U.S. **URL:** http://www.americanmedtech.org/BeInvolved.aspx#177433-publications. **Ad Rates:** BW $975, full page; BW $550, half page. **Remarks:** Accepts advertising. **Circ:** 60,000.

11415 ■ Archives of Physical Medicine and Rehabilitation
American Academy of Physical Medicine and Rehabilitation
9700 W Bryn Mawr Ave., Ste. 200
Rosemont, IL 60018-5706
Phone: (847)737-6000
Fax: (847)737-6001
Free: 877-227-6799
Publication E-mail: archivesmail@aapmr.org
Online journal concerning physical medicine and rehabilitation. **Freq:** Monthly. **Trim Size:** 8 1/2 x 11. **Key Personnel:** Martin D. Hoffman, MD, Board Member; Jeffrey R. Basford, MD, Editor-in-Chief; Allen W. Heinemann, PhD, Editor; Karen K. Parks, Assistant Editor; Kenneth M. Jaffe, MD, Board Member; Leighton Chan, MD, Editor; Patrick K. Murray, MD, Board Member. **ISSN:** 0003--9993 (print). **Subscription Rates:** $438 U.S.; $809 Institutions; $572 Other countries; $1004 Institutions, other countries. **Online:** ScienceDirect; Elsevier Inc. Health Sciences Division Saunders. **URL:** http://www.journals.elsevier.com/archives-of-physical-medicine-and-rehabilitation; http://www.us.elsevierhealth.com/product.jsp?isbn=00039993. **Ad Rates:** BW $1065; 4C $955. **Remarks:** Accepts advertising. **Circ:** ‡3,030.

11416 ■ Arthroscopy: The Journal of Arthroscopic and Related Surgery
Arthroscopy Association of North America
9400 W Higgins Rd., Ste. 200
Rosemont, IL 60018
Phone: (847)292-2262
Fax: (847)292-2268
Publisher's E-mail: info@aana.org
Peer-reviewed journal discussing the advantages and disadvantages of arthroscopic techniques. **Freq:** Quarterly. **Key Personnel:** G.G. Poehling, MD, Board Member; Dr. J.H. Lubowitz, Editor-in-Chief. **ISSN:** 0749--8063 (print). **Subscription Rates:** $629 U.S. for personal, online + print; $305 U.S. for student, online + print; $817 Canada for personal, online + print; $597 Canada for student, online + print; $817 Other countries

Circulation: ★ = AAM; △ or • = BPA; ♦ = CAC; ❑ = VAC; ⊕ = PO Statement; ‡ = Publisher's Report; Boldface figures = sworn; Light figures = estimated.

for personal, online + print; $597 Other countries for student, online + print. **URL:** http://www.arthroscopyjournal.org. **Ad Rates:** BW $1745, full page; 4C $1495, full page. **Remarks:** Accepts advertising. **Circ:** ‡9200.

11417 ■ Foot & Ankle International
American Orthopedic Foot and Ankle Society
9400 W Higgins Rd., Ste. 220
Rosemont, IL 60018-3315
Phone: (847)698-4654
Fax: (847)692-3315
Free: 800-235-4855
Publisher's E-mail: info@datatrace.com
Peer-reviewed journal featuring surgical and medical management as well as basic clinical research related to foot and ankle problems. **Freq:** Monthly. **Key Personnel:** David B. Thordarson, MD, Editor-in-Chief. **ISSN:** 1071--1007 (print); **EISSN:** 1944--7876 (electronic). **Subscription Rates:** $99 Individuals in-training; $259 Individuals; $370 Institutions; $159 Other countries in-training; $319 Other countries; $430 Institutions, other countries; £506 Institutions print & e-access; £557 Institutions current volume print & all online content; £455 Institutions e-access; £506 Institutions all online content; £736 Institutions e-access (Content through 1998); £496 Individuals print only; £306 Individuals print & e-access; £275 Individuals e-access; £300 Individuals print only; £45 Institutions single print; £33 Individuals single print. **URL:** http://datatrace.com/medical/FAI_print_body.htm; http://www.aofas.org/publications/pages/foot-and-ankle-international.aspx; http://fai.sagepub.com/. **Mailing address:** PO Box 1239, Brooklandville, MD 21022. **Ad Rates:** BW $995; 4C $2,385. **Remarks:** Accepts advertising. **Circ:** (Not Reported).

11418 ■ Journal of the American Academy of Orthopaedic Surgeons: A Comprehensive Review
American Academy of Orthopaedic Surgeons
9400 W Higgins Rd.
Rosemont, IL 60018-4262
Phone: (847)823-7186
Fax: (847)823-8125
Free: 800-346-2267
Publisher's E-mail: customerservice@aaos.org
Journal covering current topics of interest to Orthopaedic Surgeons. **Freq:** Monthly. **Print Method:** Web offset. **Trim Size:** 8 1/4 x 10 7/8. **Cols./Page:** 3. **Col. Width:** 13 picas. **Col. Depth:** 53 picas. **Key Personnel:** Jeffrey S. Fischgrund, MD, Editor-in-Chief; John W. Frymoyer, MD, Editor. **ISSN:** 1067--151X (print); **EISSN:** 1940--5480 (electronic). **Subscription Rates:** $311 Individuals; $344 Other countries; $1299 Institutions; $1299 Institutions, other countries; $124 Individuals residents; $194 Other countries residents. **Alt. Formats:** CD-ROM. **URL:** http://journals.lww.com/jaaos/pages/default.aspx. **Ad Rates:** BW $3570; 4C $5790. **Remarks:** Accepts classified advertising. **Circ:** Paid ‡27398.

11419 ■ Journal of Continuing Education Topics & Issues
American Medical Technologists
10700 W Higgins Rd., Ste. 150
Rosemont, IL 60018
Phone: (847)823-5169
Fax: (847)823-0458
Free: 800-275-1268
Publisher's E-mail: membership@amt1.com
Freq: 3/year in January, April and August. **Subscription Rates:** $8 Nonmembers for back issue; Free for members. **URL:** http://www.americanmedtech.org/BeInvolved.aspx#177433-publications. **Ad Rates:** BW $975, full page; BW $550, half page. **Remarks:** Accepts advertising. **Circ:** 60,000.

11420 ■ Journal of Orthopaedic Research
Orthopaedic Research Society
9400 W Higgins Rd., Ste. 225
Rosemont, IL 60018-4976
Phone: (847)823-5770
Fax: (847)823-5772
Publisher's E-mail: ors@ors.org
Journal containing articles on the experimental, theoretical, and clinical aspects of orthopaedics. **Freq:** Monthly. **Print Method:** Offset, sheet-fed. **Trim Size:** 8 1/4 x 11. **Cols./Page:** 2. **Key Personnel:** Linda J. Sandell, Ph.D., Editor-in-Chief. **ISSN:** 0736--0266 (print); **EISSN:** 1554--527X (electronic). **Subscription Rates:** $930 Institutions print or online - USA online only - Canada & Mexico/ROW; $1116 Institutions print + online; $381 Individuals print only; $1330 Institutions, Canada and Mexico print + online; $930 Institutions, Canada and Mexico print only; £476 Institutions online only UK; £736 Institutions print + online UK; £613 Institutions print only UK. **URL:** http://www.ors.org/journal-of-orthopaedic-research; http://onlinelibrary.wiley.com/journal/10.1002/(ISSN)1554-527X. **Remarks:** Accepts advertising. **Circ:** (Not Reported).

11421 ■ Professional Roofing
National Roofing Contractors Association
10255 W Higgins Rd., Ste. 600
Rosemont, IL 60018-5607
Phone: (847)299-9070
Fax: (847)299-1183
Roofing industry magazine. **Freq:** Monthly. **Print Method:** Offset. **Trim Size:** 8 1/4 x 10 7/8. **Cols./Page:** 3. **Col. Width:** 13.5 picas. **Col. Depth:** 58.5 picas. **Key Personnel:** Carl Good, Publisher; Ambika Puniani Bailey, Editor; Chrystine Hanus, Associate Editor. **ISSN:** 0896--5552 (print). **Subscription Rates:** Free. **URL:** http://www.professionalroofing.net. **Formerly**: Roofing Spec. **Ad Rates:** BW $4960. **Remarks:** Accepts advertising. **Circ:** (Not Reported).

ROUND LAKE

Lake Co. Lake Co. (NE). 14 m W of Waukegan. Suburban. Manufactures industrial ovens, electronic equipment machine tools, medicial equipment, commercial signs, printed circuits.

11422 ■ WRLR-FM - 98.3
PO Box 98
Round Lake, IL 60073
Phone: (224)338-9757
Email: studio@wrlr.fm
Format: Talk; Heavy Metal; News; Oldies. **Founded:** 2005. **Operating Hours**: Continuous. **Key Personnel:** Bish Krywko, President; George Buchardt, Office Mgr.; Dennis Whiton, Sports Dir. **Wattage**: 096 ERP. **Ad Rates:** Noncommercial. **URL:** http://www.wrlr.fm.

SAINT CHARLES

Kane Co. Kane Co. (NE). On Fox River, 38 m W of Chicago. Manufactures fibre products, steel kitchens, malleable iron, tubular steel furniture, audio radio equipment; sausage processing.

11423 ■ Carolina/Virginia Farmer
Farm Progress Companies Inc.
255 38th Ave., Ste. P
Saint Charles, IL 60174-5410
Phone: (630)690-5600
Fax: (630)462-2869
Free: 800-441-1410
Publisher's E-mail: circhelp@farmprogress.com
Agricultural newspaper. **Freq:** Monthly. **Print Method:** Offset. **Trim Size:** 11 1/2 X 13 3/4. **Cols./Page:** 4. **Col. Width:** 14.25 picas. **Col. Depth:** 180 agate lines. **Key Personnel:** Richard Davis, Editor, phone: (252)237-4422, fax: (252)237-8999. **Subscription Rates:** $26.95 Individuals. **URL:** http://southeastfarmpress.com. **Ad Rates:** BW $1,575; 4C $900. **Remarks:** Accepts advertising. **Circ:** ‡15177.

11424 ■ Country Business: The Magazine for Today's Independent Gift Retailers
Country Sampler Group
707 Kautz Rd.
Saint Charles, IL 60174-5302
Phone: (630)377-8000
Fax: (630)377-8194
Publisher's E-mail: csgsales@countrysampler.com
Trade magazine covering issues for independent gift retailers. **Freq:** Bimonthly. **Remarks:** Advertising accepted; rates available upon request. **Circ:** Combined 30000.

11425 ■ Country Sampler
Country Sampler Group
707 Kautz Rd.
Saint Charles, IL 60174-5302
Phone: (630)377-8000
Fax: (630)377-8194
Publisher's E-mail: csgsales@countrysampler.com
Country arts, crafts, interior design, and lifestyle magazine. **Freq:** Bimonthly. **Print Method:** Web Offset. **Trim Size:** 8 1/8 x 10 3/4. **Key Personnel:** Donna Marcel, Editor; Elizabeth Preston, Associate Editor; Lisa Buchanan, Business Manager. **ISSN:** 1047--3955 (print). **Subscription Rates:** $19.96 U.S. 1 year; $37.96 U.S. and Canada 2 years; $29.96 Canada 1 year; $57.96 Canada 2 years; $35.96 Other countries 1 year; $69.96 Other countries 2 years. **URL:** http://www.countrysampler.com. **Ad Rates:** BW $11475; 4C $13500. **Remarks:** Accepts advertising. **Circ:** Paid ★**280,048**.

11426 ■ Crown Jewels of the Wire
Crown Jewels of the Wire
PO Box 1003
Saint Charles, IL 60174
Phone: (630)513-1544
Magazine of collecting, research, and humor. **Founded:** May 1969. **Freq:** Monthly. **Print Method:** Offset. **Trim Size:** 5 1/2 x 8 1/2. **Cols./Page:** 2. **Col. Width:** 2 inches. **Col. Depth:** 7 inches. **Key Personnel:** Howard Banks, Editor. **ISSN:** 0884-7983 (print). **USPS:** 903-740. **Subscription Rates:** $30.00 Individuals periodicals postage; $38.00 Individuals first class ; $42.00 Canada Air Mail; $60.00 Other countries Air Mail; $7.00 Single issue back issue. **URL:** http://www.cjow.com. **Ad Rates:** BW $40. **Remarks:** Accepts advertising. **Circ:** Paid ⊕**1670**, Non-paid ⊕**15**.

11427 ■ Dietary Manager
Association of Nutrition and Foodservice Professionals
406 Surrey Woods Dr.
Saint Charles, IL 60174
Phone: (630)587-6336
Fax: (630)587-6308
Free: 800-323-1908
Publisher's E-mail: info@anfponline.org
Freq: 10/year. **Subscription Rates:** $40 /year. **Remarks:** Accepts advertising. **Circ:** 17000.

11428 ■ The Farmer
Farm Progress Companies Inc.
255 38th Ave., Ste. P
Saint Charles, IL 60174-5410
Phone: (630)690-5600
Fax: (630)462-2869
Free: 800-441-1410
Publisher's E-mail: circhelp@farmprogress.com
Trade magazine covering local and national farming information, including crop and livestock production, marketing, news, and rural lifestyle information. **Freq:** Monthly. **Key Personnel:** Paula Mohr, Editor, phone: (763)753-4388; Frank Holdmeyer, Executive Editor, phone: (515)278-7782, fax: (515)278-7796. **Subscription Rates:** $26.95 Individuals; $45 Two years; $59.95 Individuals three years. **URL:** http://farmprogress.com/the-farmer/. **Remarks:** Accepts advertising. **Circ:** (Not Reported).

11429 ■ Farmer-Stockman
Farm Progress Companies Inc.
255 38th Ave., Ste. P
Saint Charles, IL 60174-5410
Phone: (630)690-5600
Fax: (630)462-2869
Free: 800-441-1410
Publisher's E-mail: circhelp@farmprogress.com
General agricultural magazine. **Freq:** Monthly. **Print Method:** Offset. **Trim Size:** 8 x 10 7/8. **Cols./Page:** 3. **Col. Width:** 30 nonpareils. **Col. Depth:** 140 agate lines. **Key Personnel:** J.T. Smith, Editor, phone: (325)554-7388, fax: (325)554-7389; Dan Crummett, Executive Editor, phone: (405)372-5521, fax: (405)372-5529. **ISSN:** 0279-165X (print). **Subscription Rates:** $29.95 Individuals 1 year. **URL:** http://www.farmprogress.com/western-farmerstockman/. **Ad Rates:** BW $3,350; 4C $4,690; PCI $135. **Remarks:** Accepts advertising. **Circ:** (Not Reported).

11430 ■ Journal of Biomolecular Screening
Society for Laboratory Automation and Screening
100 Illinois St., Ste. 242
Saint Charles, IL 60174
Phone: (630)256-7527
Fax: (630)741-7527
Free: 877-990-SLAS
Publisher's E-mail: sales@pfp.sagepub.com
Peer-reviewed journal focusing on drug discovery sciences, with an emphasis on screening methods and technologies. **Freq:** 10/year. **Key Personnel:** Robert M. Campbell, PhD, Editor-in-Chief; Steven Kahl, Associate

Editor; Mark Beggs, Associate Editor. **ISSN:** 1087--0571 (print); **EISSN:** 1552--454X (electronic). **Subscription Rates:** £430 Individuals print; £812 Institutions e-access; £884 Institutions print; £902 Institutions print and e-access; £56 Individuals single print issue; £97 Institutions single print issue; Included in membership; $750 Individuals print only; $1454 Institutions online only. **URL:** http://jbx.sagepub.com; http://www.slas.org/publications/scientific-journals. **Ad Rates:** BW $1,630; 4C $2,165. **Remarks:** Accepts advertising. **Circ:** (Not Reported).

11431 ■ Journal of Laboratory Automation
Society for Laboratory Automation and Screening
100 Illinois St., Ste. 242
Saint Charles, IL 60174
Phone: (630)256-7527
Fax: (630)741-7527
Free: 877-990-SLAS
Publisher's E-mail: slas@slas.org
Journal publishing current developments in the field of laboratory robotics. **Freq:** Bimonthly. **Key Personnel:** Dean Ho, PhD, Editor-in-Chief. **ISSN:** 2211--0682 (print); **EISSN:** 1540--2452 (electronic). **Subscription Rates:** £185 Individuals print; £284 Institutions online; £310 Institutions print; £316 Institutions combined - print & E-access; £40 Single issue; £57 Institutions single issue. **URL:** http://jla.sagepub.com; http://www.sagepub.com/journals/Journal202089. **Formerly**: Journal of The Association for Laboratory Automation. **Remarks:** Advertising not accepted. **Circ:** (Not Reported).

11432 ■ Kane County Chronicle
Chronicle Newspapers Inc.
333 N Randall Rd., Ste. 1
Saint Charles, IL 60174
Phone: (630)232-9222
Fax: (630)444-1641
Free: 800-589-9363
Community newspaper serving St. Charles, Geneva, Batavia, and Elburn, IL. **Freq:** Mon.-Sat. **Print Method:** Offset. **Trim Size:** 13 1/2 x 22 3/4. **Cols./Page:** 6. **Col. Width:** 2 1/16 inches. **Col. Depth:** 21 inches. **Key Personnel:** Kara Hansen, Manager, Circulation; Kathy Gresey, Editor. **Subscription Rates:** $1.30 Individuals /week (5 days home delivery); $.75 Individuals /week (Saturday home delivery); $103.48 Individuals /year; $1.25 Individuals /week. **URL:** http://www.kcchronicle.com. **Formerly**: St. Charles Chronicle, Geneva Chronicle, Batavia Chronicle, and Elburn Chronicle. **Ad Rates:** BW $2,719.08; 4C $3,084.08; PCI $22.23. **Remarks:** Accepts advertising. **Circ:** (Not Reported).

11433 ■ Nutrition & Foodservice Edge Magazine
Association of Nutrition and Foodservice Professionals
406 Surrey Woods Dr.
Saint Charles, IL 60174
Phone: (630)587-6336
Fax: (630)587-6308
Free: 800-323-1908
Publisher's E-mail: info@anfponline.org
Professional magazine focusing on nutrition and management issues encountered by dietary managers in non-commercial food service. **Freq:** 10/year. **Key Personnel:** Diane Everett, Editor. **ISSN:** 1062-1121 (print). **Subscription Rates:** $40 Individuals 1 year; Included in membership. **URL:** http://www.anfponline.org/news-resources/nutrition-and-foodservice-magazine. **Formerly**: Dietary Manager Magazine. **Ad Rates:** BW $800; 4C $1,300; PCI $60. **Remarks:** Advertising accepted; rates available upon request. **Circ:** 15000.

11434 ■ Prairie Farmer
Farm Progress Companies Inc.
255 38th Ave., Ste. P
Saint Charles, IL 60174-5410
Phone: (630)690-5600
Fax: (630)462-2869
Free: 800-441-1410
Publisher's E-mail: circhelp@farmprogress.com
Magazine covering commercial farming. **Print Method:** Offset. **Trim Size:** 8 x 10 3/4. **Cols./Page:** 3. **Col. Width:** 2 1/8 inches. **Col. Depth:** 10 inches. **Key Personnel:** Josh Flint, Editor; Holly Spangler, Associate Editor, phone: (309)926-6082, fax: (309)926-6083. **ISSN:** 0162-7104 (print). **Subscription Rates:** $29.95 Individuals; $48.95 Two years; 64.95 Individuals 3 years. **URL:** http://farmprogress.com/prairie-farmer. **Remarks:** Advertising accepted; rates available upon request. **Circ:** (Not Reported).

11435 ■ Wisconsin Agriculturist
Farm Progress Companies Inc.
255 38th Ave., Ste. P
Saint Charles, IL 60174-5410
Phone: (630)690-5600
Fax: (630)462-2869
Free: 800-441-1410
Publisher's E-mail: circhelp@farmprogress.com
Magazine serving commercial farmers in Wisconsin. **Freq:** Monthly. **Print Method:** Offset. **Trim Size:** 8 x 10 3/4. **Cols./Page:** 3. **Col. Width:** 2 1/8 inches. **Col. Depth:** 10 inches. **Key Personnel:** Fran O'Leary, Editor, phone: (920)346-2285. **Subscription Rates:** $29.95 Individuals. **URL:** http://farmprogress.com/wisconsin-agriculturist. **Remarks:** Accepts advertising. **Circ:** (Not Reported).

SALEM

Marion Co. Marion Co. (S). 11 m NE of Centralia. Residential. Industrial.

11436 ■ WJBD-AM - 1350
310 W McMackin
Salem, IL 62881
Phone: (618)548-2000
Fax: (618)548-2079
Format: News; Sports; Information. **Owner:** NewRadio Group L.L.C., 2875 Mt. Vernon Rd. SE, Cedar Rapids, IA 52403, Ph: (319)862-0300, Fax: (319)286-9383. **Founded:** 1956. **ADI**: Daveport,IA-Rock Island, Moline,IL. **Ad Rates:** Advertising accepted; rates available upon request. **Mailing address:** PO Box 70, Salem, IL 62881. **URL:** http://www.wjbdradio.com.

11437 ■ WJBD-FM - 100.1
310 W McMackin
Salem, IL 62881
Phone: (618)548-2000
Fax: (618)548-2079
Email: news@wjbdradio.com
Format: Adult Contemporary. **Networks:** NBC; Illinois Farm Bureau; Illinois News. **Founded:** 1972. **Operating Hours**: Continuous; 10% network; 90% local. **ADI**: St. Louis, MO (Mt. Vernon, IL). **Key Personnel:** Bruce Kropp, Gen. Mgr., News Dir., brucekropp@wjbdradio.com; Toby Gullion, Div. Dir., sports@wjbdradio.com. **Wattage**: 1,600. **Ad Rates:** $10.50-18.75 for 30 seconds; $14-23 for 60 seconds. **Mailing address:** PO Box 70, Salem, IL 62881. **URL:** http://www.wjbdradio.com.

11438 ■ WSLE-FM - 91.3
PO Drawer 2440
Tupelo, MS 38803
Phone: (662)844-8888
Format: Religious. **Owner:** American Family Association, at above address. **URL:** http://www.afa.net.

SAVANNA

Carroll Co. Carroll Co. (NW). On Mississippi River, 20 m NE of Clinton, Iowa. Bridge to Sabula, Iowa Manufactures thermostats, fast food dispensing systems, valves, wooden pallets, wooden boxes. Dairy, stock, grain farms.

11439 ■ WCCI-FM - 100.3
316 Main St.
Savanna, IL 61074
Phone: (815)273-7757
Fax: (815)273-2760
Email: dee@wcciradio.com
Format: Country. **Networks:** Brownfield; Illinois Farm Bureau. **Founded:** 1971. **Operating Hours**: Continuous; 10% network, 90% local. **Key Personnel:** Wayne Larkey, Prog. Dir.; Ann Murphy, Dir. of Traffic, ann@wcciradio.com; Leslie Smith, Music Dir., leslie@wcciradio.com; Brian Reusch, Sales Mgr., brian@wcciradio.com; Dee Miller, News Dir., dee@wcciradio.com; Johnna Richardson, Dir. of Pub. Prog. & Svcs., Dir. of Traffic, johnna@wcciradio.com; Beaver Miller, Station Mgr., beaver@wcciradio.com. **Local Programs**: *In Touch*, Monday Tuesday Wednesday Thursday Friday 11:42 a.m. - 11:55 a.m. **Wattage**: 25,000. **Ad Rates:** Noncommercial. **Mailing address:** PO Box 310, Savanna, IL 61074. **URL:** http://www.wcciradio.com.

SCHAUMBURG

DuPage Co. Cook & Du Page Co. (NE). 19 m W of Evanston. Residential.

11440 ■ American Journal of Veterinary Research
American Veterinary Medical Association
1931 N Meacham Rd., Ste. 100
Schaumburg, IL 60173-4360
Fax: (847)925-1329
Free: 800-248-2862
Veterinary research on nutrition and diseases of domestic, wild, and furbearing animals. **Freq:** Monthly. **Print Method:** Offset. **Trim Size:** 8 1/8 x 10 7/8. **Cols./Page:** 2. **Col. Width:** 45 nonpareils. **Col. Depth:** 60 picas. **Key Personnel:** Bruce G. McLaughlin, Editor; Kurt J. Matushek, Editor-in-Chief; Gussie J. Tessier, PhD, Associate Editor; Craig A. Smith, PhD, Associate Editor; Helen L. Simons, PhD, Assistant Editor. **ISSN:** 0002--9645 (print). **Subscription Rates:** $255 Nonmembers /year for individuals in U.S.; $265 Nonmembers /year for individuals outside U.S.; $40 Nonmembers /copy in U.S.; $45 Nonmembers /copy outside U.S.; $40 Students /year; $60 Members /year combo. **URL:** http://avmajournals.avma.org/loi/ajvr; http://avmajournals.avma.org. **Ad Rates:** BW $2,425; 4C $3,675. **Remarks:** Accepts display advertising. **Circ:** 6500.

11441 ■ Andrology
American Society of Andrology
1100 E Woodfield Rd., Ste. 350
Schaumburg, IL 60173-5125
Phone: (847)619-4909
Fax: (847)517-7229
Publisher's E-mail: info@andrologysociety.org
Journal publishing papers on publishes papers on all aspects of andrology, ranging from basic molecular research to the results of clinical investigations. **Freq:** Bimonthly. **Print Method:** Sheetfed offset. **Trim Size:** 8 1/2 x 11. **Cols./Page:** 2. **Col. Width:** 39 nonpareils. **Col. Depth:** 140 agate lines. **Key Personnel:** Arthur Burnett, Associate Editor; Ewa Rajpert-De Meyts, Editor-in-Chief. **ISSN:** 2047--2919 (print); **EISSN:** 2047--2927 (electronic). **Subscription Rates:** $1634 Institutions print and online; £886 Institutions print and online; €1324 Institutions print and online; $1910 Institutions, other countries print and online; $1361 Institutions print or online; £738 Institutions print or online; €1103 Institutions print or online; $1591 Institutions, other countries print or online. **URL:** http://onlinelibrary.wiley.com/journal/10.1111/(ISSN)2047-2927?globalMessage=0; http://onlinelibrary.wiley.com/journal/10.1111/(ISSN)2047-2927. **Formed by the merger of**: Journal of Andrology; International Journal of Andrology: The Official Journal of the European Academy of Andrology. **Ad Rates:** BW $600; 4C $870. **Remarks:** Accepts advertising. **Circ:** 1120, ‡1200.

11442 ■ Anesthesiology Journal
American Society of Anesthesiologists
1061 American Ln.
Schaumburg, IL 60173-4973
Phone: (847)825-5586
Fax: (847)825-1692
Publication E-mail: editorial-office@anesthesiology.org
Journal covering the fields of anesthesia and critical care medicine. **Key Personnel:** James Eisenach, MD, Editor-in-Chief; Druanne Martin, Associate Editor. **ISSN:** 0003--3022 (print). **Subscription Rates:** $835 Individuals; $1714 Institutions; $335 Individuals in training; $934 Other countries; $1957 Institutions, other countries; $388 Other countries in training. **URL:** http://anesthesiology.pubs.asahq.org/journal.aspx. **Remarks:** Accepts advertising. **Circ:** (Not Reported).

11443 ■ Global Casting Magazine
American Foundry Society
1695 N Penny Ln.
Schaumburg, IL 60173
Phone: (847)824-0181
Fax: (847)824-7848
Free: 800-537-4237
Magazine on metal casting plants and pattern shops. **Freq:** Quarterly. **Print Method:** Offset. **Trim Size:** 8 x 10 7/8. **Cols./Page:** 3. **Col. Width:** 26 nonpareils. **Col. Depth:** 140 agate lines. **Key Personnel:** Alfred Spada, Editor-in-Chief, phone: (847)824-0181, fax: (847)824-7848; Shannon Wetzel, Managing Editor; Denise Kapel,

Circulation: ★ = AAM; △ or • = BPA; ♦ = CAC; ❑ = VAC; ⊕ = PO Statement; ‡ = Publisher's Report; Boldface figures = sworn; Light figures = estimated.

Senior Editor. **ISSN:** 0026--7562 (print). **Subscription Rates:** Free. **URL:** http://www.globalcastingmagazine.com. **Formerly:** Modern Casting Magazine. **Ad Rates:** BW $5080; 4C $940. **Remarks:** Accepts advertising. **Circ:** ‡20000.

11444 ■ Journal of the American Academy of Dermatology
American Academy of Dermatology
930 E Woodfield Rd.
Schaumburg, IL 60173
Phone: (847)240-1280
Fax: (847)240-1859
Free: 866-503-7546
Publisher's E-mail: MRC@aad.org
Journal containing peer-reviewed articles on clinical and investigative studies, treatments, new diagnostic techniques, and other topics related to the prevention, diagnosis and treatment of skin disorders. **Freq:** Monthly. **ISSN:** 0190-9622 (print). **Subscription Rates:** $422 Individuals print and online; $551 Other countries print and online; $111 Students print and online. **URL:** http://www.jaad.org; http://www.aad.org/members/publications. **Mailing address:** PO Box 4014, Schaumburg, IL 60168. **Remarks:** Advertising not accepted. **Circ:** (Not Reported).

11445 ■ Journal of the American Veterinary Medical Association
American Veterinary Medical Association
1931 N Meacham Rd., Ste. 100
Schaumburg, IL 60173-4360
Fax: (847)925-1329
Free: 800-248-2862
Publication E-mail: subscriptions@avma.org
Peer-reviewed, general scientific journal that provides reports of clinical research, feature articles, and regular columns of interest to veterinarians in private and public practice. **Freq:** Bimonthly. **Print Method:** Web Offset. **Trim Size:** 8 1/8 x 10 7/8. **Key Personnel:** Dr. Kurt J. Matushek, Editor-in-Chief; Dr. Craig A. Smith, Associate Editor; Nicholas T. De Luca, Managing Editor; Dr. Helen L. Simons, Associate Editor; Dr. Gussie J. Tessier, Associate Editor. **ISSN:** 0003-1488 (print). **USPS:** 183-840. **Subscription Rates:** $260 Nonmembers per year, print + online; $270 Nonmembers per year outside U.S., print + online; $40 Single issue; $45 Single issue outside U.S.; $40 Students per year, print + online; Included in membership; $60 Members per year, combined subscription to American Journal of Veterinary Research (AJVR). **URL:** http://www.avma.org/news/journals/pages/javma-about.aspx; http://avmajournals.avma.org/loi/javma. **Ad Rates:** BW $8675, 1X frequency; BW $8475, 6X frequency; BW $8185, 12X frequency; BW $7875, 18X frequency; BW $7685, 24X frequency; BW $7475, 36X frequency; BW $7025, 48X frequency; 4C $2200, plus space. **Remarks:** All classified employment ads must be submitted online through the Veterinary Career Center. **Circ:** Paid △**1492**, Non-paid △**76695**.

11446 ■ MEEN Diagnostic and Invasive Technology
Reilly Publishing Co.
16 E Schaumburg Rd.
Schaumburg, IL 60194-3536
Trade magazine serving users and buyers of diagnostic and invasive cardiology technology. **Freq:** 9/year. **Print Method:** Heat-set web offset. **Trim Size:** 10 1/2 x 13 3/4. **Cols./Page:** 4. **Col. Width:** 2 1/4 inches. **Col. Depth:** 12 1/4 inches. **Key Personnel:** E.S. Gillette, Chief Executive Officer, President; Dave Fornell; Sean P. Reilly, President; Helen Kuhl, Director, Editorial. **ISSN:** 0361-4174 (print). **Subscription Rates:** $90 Canada and Mexico; $120 Other countries. **Formerly:** Medical Electronics & Equipment News; MEEN Cardiology/Critical Care Technology. **Ad Rates:** BW $4,685; 4C $1,400. **Remarks:** Accepts advertising. **Circ:** Combined 27872.

11447 ■ MEEN Diagnostic and Invasive Technology
Reilly Communications Group
16 E Schaumburg Rd.
Schaumburg, IL 60194-3551
Trade magazine serving users and buyers of diagnostic and invasive cardiology technology. **Freq:** 9/year. **Print Method:** Heat-set web offset. **Trim Size:** 10 1/2 x 13 3/4. **Cols./Page:** 4. **Col. Width:** 2 1/4 inches. **Col. Depth:** 12 1/4 inches. **Key Personnel:** E.S. Gillette, Chief Executive Officer, President; Dave Fornell; Sean P. Reilly, President; Helen Kuhl, Director, Editorial. **ISSN:** 0361-4174 (print). **Subscription Rates:** $90 Canada and Mexico; $120 Other countries. **Formerly:** Medical Electronics & Equipment News; MEEN Cardiology/Critical Care Technology. **Ad Rates:** BW $4,685; 4C $1,400. **Remarks:** Accepts advertising. **Circ:** Combined 27872.

11448 ■ Neurosurgery
Congress of Neurological Surgeons
10 N Martingale Rd., Ste. 190
Schaumburg, IL 60173
Phone: (847)240-2500
Fax: (847)240-0804
Free: 877-517-1CNS
Publisher's E-mail: info@1cns.org
Journal that brings readers the latest on innovative surgical techniques and advances in instrumentation. **Freq:** Monthly. **ISSN:** 0148--396X (print). **Subscription Rates:** $784 Individuals; $1494 Institutions; $1136 Other countries; $1998 Institutions, other countries. **URL:** http://www.cns.org/education/browse-type/neurosurgery. **Remarks:** Advertising not accepted. **Circ:** (Not Reported).

11449 ■ North American Actuarial Journal
Society of Actuaries
475 N Martingale Rd., Ste. 600
Schaumburg, IL 60173
Phone: (847)706-3500
Fax: (847)706-3599
Publisher's E-mail: book.orders@tandf.co.uk
Scholarly journal covering actuarial science and practice, including life and health insurance, pensions, employee benefits, property and casualty insurance, and finance and investments for professionals and others. **Freq:** Quarterly. **Print Method:** Web offset. **Trim Size:** 8 1/2 x 11. **Cols./Page:** 2. **Col. Width:** 3 1/2 inches. **Col. Depth:** 9 inches. **Key Personnel:** Patrick L. Brockett, PhD, Editor; Mary R. Hardy, PhD, Editor; Sven Sinclair, PhD, Editor. **ISSN:** 1092--0277 (print); **EISSN:** 2325--0453 (electronic). **Subscription Rates:** $143 Individuals online; $211 Institutions online; $241 Institutions print and online. **URL:** http://www.soa.org/news-and-publications/publications/journals/naaj/naaj-detail.aspx; http://www.tandfonline.com/pricing/journal/uaaj20#.U9WjyNIW2qZ. **Formerly:** Transactions. **Remarks:** Advertising not accepted. **Circ:** Non-paid 17000.

11450 ■ Outside Plant Magazine: The Only Full-Time Outside Plant Telecommunications Publication
Practical Communications Inc.
1320 Tower Rd.
Schaumburg, IL 60173
Phone: (773)754-3250
Fax: (773)754-3259
Telecommunications magazine. **Freq:** Monthly. **Print Method:** Offset. **Trim Size:** 8 1/8 x 10 7/8. **Cols./Page:** 3. **Col. Width:** 27 nonpareils. **Col. Depth:** 140 agate lines. **Key Personnel:** Karen Adolphson, Managing Editor, phone: (773)754-3251; Sharon Vollman, Director, Editorial, President, phone: (773)754-3256; Robin Queenan, Publisher, phone: (773)754-3255. **ISSN:** 0747--8763 (print). **Subscription Rates:** Free to qualified subscribers. **URL:** http://www.ospmag.com. **Ad Rates:** BW $8611; 4C $1193. **Remarks:** Accepts advertising. **Circ:** ‡23000.

11451 ■ Refresher Courses in Anesthesiology
American Society of Anesthesiologists
1061 American Ln.
Schaumburg, IL 60173-4973
Phone: (847)825-5586
Fax: (847)825-1692
Publisher's E-mail: communications@asahq.org
Journal containing peer-reviewed lectures on topics of current clinical interest selected from the ASA Refresher Courses presented at each year's annual meeting and regional courses. **Freq:** Annual Latest edition; Volume 42, 2014. **ISSN:** 0363--471X (print); **EISSN:** 1537--1905 (electronic). **URL:** http://journals.lww.com/asa-refresher/pages/default.aspx. **Remarks:** Advertising not accepted. **Circ:** (Not Reported).

11452 ■ Skeletal Radiology
International Skeletal Society
1100 E Woodfield Rd., Ste. 350
Schaumburg, IL 60173
Phone: (847)517-7225
Fax: (847)517-7229
Publisher's E-mail: info@internationalskeletalsociety.com
Journal containing information dealing with disorders of the musculoskeletal system including the spine. **Freq:** Monthly. **ISSN:** 0364--2348 (print); **EISSN:** 1432--2161 (electronic). **Subscription Rates:** €125.21 Individuals online. **Alt. Formats:** PDF. **URL:** http://www.internationalskeletalsociety.com/Journal/Skeletal-Radiology.aspx; http://www.springer.com/medicine/radiology/journal/256. **Remarks:** Advertising not accepted. **Circ:** (Not Reported).

SESSER

Franklin Co. Franklin Co. (S). 35 m S of Centralia. Dairy, stock farms. Coal mining.

11453 ■ American Cooner
C & H Publishing
114 E Franklin Ave.
Sesser, IL 62884-1844
Free: 800-851-7507
Publisher's E-mail: ads@mychoice.net
Hounds and coon hunting magazine. **Freq:** Monthly. **Print Method:** Offset. **Trim Size:** 8.25 x 10.99. **Cols./Page:** 3. **Col. Width:** 28 nonpareils. **Col. Depth:** 139 agate lines. **Subscription Rates:** $55 Two years; $30 Individuals /year. **URL:** http://www.huntinghoundsmen.com/category/mags/american-cooner. **Mailing address:** PO Box 777, Du Quoin, IL 62832. **Ad Rates:** BW $220; 4C $420; PCI $13. **Remarks:** Accepts advertising. **Circ:** Paid 18000.

11454 ■ The Hunter's Horn
Hunter's Horn Inc.
PO Box 777
Sesser, IL 62884
Phone: (618)625-2711
Fax: (618)625-6221
Free: 800-851-7507
Publisher's E-mail: copy@chpub.net
Magazine containing breed and competition information about the foxhound. **Freq:** Monthly. **Trim Size:** 8 1/4 x 11. **Cols./Page:** 3. **Key Personnel:** Terry Walker, Editor. **Subscription Rates:** $32 Individuals /year; $59 Two years. **URL:** http://www.huntinghoundsmen.com/category/mags/hunters-horn. **Ad Rates:** BW $120; PCI $5. **Remarks:** Accepts advertising. **Circ:** ‡8500.

SHELBYVILLE

Shelby Co. Shelby Co. (SC). On Kaskaskia River, 37 m S of Decatur. Coal mines. Manufactures hairpins, hay balers, milk products. Hatcheries. Diversified farming. Soybeans, corn, hay.

11455 ■ Shelbyville Daily Union
Community Newspaper Holdings Inc.
100 W Main St.
Shelbyville, IL 62565
Phone: (217)774-2161
Fax: (217)774-5732
Newspaper serving Shelbyville, Illinois area. **Freq:** Daily. **Key Personnel:** Jodi Large, Manager, Circulation; Cathy Daniel, Office Manager; Frank Mulholland, Managing Editor; Paul Semple, Publisher. **Subscription Rates:** $49.50 Individuals mail delivery; $60 Out of area mail delivery. **URL:** http://www.shelbyvilledailyunion.com. **Remarks:** Accepts advertising. **Circ:** (Not Reported).

11456 ■ WRAN-FM - 98.3
918 East Pk.
Taylorville, IL 62568-0169
Phone: (217)824-3395
Fax: (217)824-3301
Free: 866-500-WRAN
Format: Adult Contemporary. **Networks:** CBS. **Owner:** Kaskaskia Broadcasting, Inc., 918 East Park, Taylorville, IL 62568 0169, Ph: (217)824-3395. **Founded:** Nov. 25, 1997. **Operating Hours:** Continuous. **ADI:** Springfield-Decatur-Champaign, IL. **Key Personnel:** Randal J. Miller, Contact. **Wattage:** 3,700. **Ad Rates:** Advertising accepted; rates available upon request. Combined advertising rates available with WTIM, WMKR, WKEI, WJRE, WYEC, NGEN. **Mailing address:** PO Box 169, Taylorville, IL 62568-0169. **URL:** http://www.taylorvilledailynews.com.

SIDELL

Vermilion Co. Vermillion Co. (E). 18 m SW of Danville. Residential.

11457 ■ Sidell Reporter
Sidell Reporter
116 E Market
Sidell, IL 61876
Phone: (217)288-9365
Publisher's E-mail: editor@thesidellreporter.com
Community newspaper. **Freq:** Weekly (Thurs.). **Print Method:** Offset. **Cols./Page:** 6. **Col. Width:** 27 nonpareils. **Col. Depth:** 294 agate lines. **Key Personnel:** Rinda Maddox, Editor, Owner. **Subscription Rates:** $32 Individuals in Vermilion County (1 year); $37 Out of country 1 year. **URL:** http://www.thesidellreporter.com. **Formerly:** Sidell Journal. **Mailing address:** PO Box 475, Sidell, IL 61876. **Ad Rates:** GLR $5; BW $504; 4C $604; SAU $4.25; PCI $4.75. **Remarks:** Accepts advertising. **Circ:** ‡817.

SKOKIE

Cook Co. Cook Co. (NE). 3 m SW of Evanston. Manufactures steel products, pharmaceuticals, concrete & wood products, gauges, electric appliances, plastic products, toys, iron and aluminum castings, movie cameras, duplicating and sports equipment, chemicals, electronics, temperature controls. Residential.

11458 ■ Expo
EXPO Magazine Inc.
PO Box 2160
Skokie, IL 60076
Trade magazine for those in the exposition industry. **Freq:** Monthly. **ISSN:** 1046--3925 (print). **Subscription Rates:** Free U.S. residents only. **URL:** http://www.expoweb.com. **Ad Rates:** BW $4,305; 4C $5,580. **Remarks:** Accepts advertising. **Circ:** 8439.

11459 ■ Healthcare Informatics
Healthcare Informatics
PO Box 2178
Skokie, IL 60076-7878
Phone: (847)763-9291
Fax: (847)963-9287
Publication E-mail: healthcare_informatics@halldata.com
Trade magazine focusing on information technology in healthcare facilities and organizations. **Freq:** Monthly. **Subscription Rates:** $36 Free to qualified subscribers; $54 Individuals; $75 Canada and Mexico; $75 Other countries. **URL:** http://www.healthcare-informatics.com/ME2/default.asp. **Remarks:** Advertising accepted; rates available upon request. **Circ:** (Not Reported).

11460 ■ Industrial Market Place
Industrial Market Place Inc.
7842 Lincoln Ave., Ste. 100
Skokie, IL 60077
Phone: (847)676-1900
Fax: (847)676-0063
Free: 800-323-1818
Publisher's E-mail: info@industrialmktpl.com
Trade magazine focusing on metal and metalworking machinery, and plant & factory equipment. **Freq:** Biweekly. **Print Method:** Offset. **Trim Size:** 9 x 13. **Cols./Page:** 7. **Col. Width:** 18 nonpareils. **Col. Depth:** 196 agate lines. **Key Personnel:** Joel Wineberg, Publisher. **URL:** http://www.impmagazine.com. **Ad Rates:** BW $1070. **Remarks:** Advertising accepted; rates available upon request. **Circ:** Controlled ‡117824.

11461 ■ INsider Magazine: Careers, Issues and Entertainment for the Next Generation
College Marketing Bureau Inc.
4124 W Oakton St.
Skokie, IL 60076
Phone: (847)673-3703
Fax: (847)329-0358
Publication E-mail: editor@insider-magazine.com
Magazine focusing on entertainment, careers, and issues concerning 18-34 year olds. **Freq:** Bimonthly. **Print Method:** Web offset. **Trim Size:** 8 3/8 x 10 7/8. **Cols./Page:** 3. **Col. Width:** 2 1/4 inches. **Key Personnel:** John Caylor, Chief Executive Officer, Editor. **ISSN:** 1070--6534 (print). **URL:** http://www.insider-magazine.com. **Formerly:** Collegiate Insider; T & B. **Ad Rates:** BW $29,910; 4C $36,910; PCI $479. **Remarks:** Accepts advertising. **Circ:** Paid 1000000.

11462 ■ International Journal of Software Engineering and Knowledge Engineering
World Scientific Publishing Company Inc.
c/o S.K. Chang, Editor-in-Chief
Knowledge Systems Institute
3420 Main St.
Skokie, IL 60076
Publisher's E-mail: wspc@wspc.com
Journal focusing on the interplay between software engineering and knowledge engineering. **Freq:** Bimonthly. **Trim Size:** 9 3/4 x 6 1/2. **Cols./Page:** 1. **Col. Width:** 5 inches. **Col. Depth:** 8 inches. **Key Personnel:** S.K. Chang, Editor-in-Chief. **ISSN:** 0218--1940 (print); **EISSN:** 1793--6403 (electronic). **Subscription Rates:** $1522 Institutions electronic + print; £1206 Institutions electronic + print; S$2428 Institutions electronic + print; $1359 Institutions electronic only; £1077 Institutions electronic only; S$2168 Institutions electronic only. **URL:** http://www.worldscientific.com/worldscinet/ijseke. **Remarks:** Advertising not accepted. **Circ:** (Not Reported).

11463 ■ The Journal of the Assyrian Academic Society
Assyrian Academic Society
8324 Lincoln Ave.
Skokie, IL 60077-2436
Publisher's E-mail: info@aas.net
Freq: Semiannual. **URL:** http://www.aas.net/aas-journal. **Remarks:** Advertising not accepted. **Circ:** (Not Reported).

11464 ■ Landscape Management
Questex L.L.C.
PO Box 2090
Skokie, IL 60076-7990
Publication E-mail: landscapemanagement@halldata.com
Magazine for professionals in landscape, grounds management and lawn care, construction, and maintenance. **Freq:** Annual. **Print Method:** Web offset. **Trim Size:** 7 3/4 x 10 1/2. **Cols./Page:** 3. **Key Personnel:** Marisa Palmieri, Editor-in-Chief; Martin Whitford, Director, Editorial. **ISSN:** 0894-1254 (print). **Subscription Rates:** $55 U.S. 1 year - print; $76 U.S. 2 years - print; $87 Canada and Mexico 1 year - print; $127 Canada and Mexico 2 years - print; $165 Other countries 1 year - print; $246 Other countries 2 years - print. **Alt. Formats:** PDF. **URL:** http://www.landscapemanagement.net/landscape/. **Remarks:** Accepts advertising. **Circ:** Combined ‡60014.

11465 ■ Skokie Review
Sun-Times Media L.L.C.
3701 W Lake Ave.
Glenview, IL 60026
Phone: (847)486-9200
Publisher's E-mail: customerservice@suntimes.com
Community newspaper (tabloid). **Freq:** Weekly (Thurs.). **Print Method:** Letterpress and Offset. **Cols./Page:** 5. **Col. Width:** 10 inches. **Col. Depth:** 14 inches. **Key Personnel:** Ryan Nilsson, Managing Editor. **URL:** http://www.chicagotribune.com/suburbs/skokie. **Remarks:** Accepts advertising. **Circ:** (Not Reported).

11466 ■ Visual Merchandising and Store Design
ST Media Group International Inc.
PO Box 1060
Skokie, IL 60076-9785
Phone: (847)763-4938
Fax: (847)763-9030
Publication E-mail: vmsd@halldata.com
The leading magazine of the retail design industry covering the latest trends in retail design, store planning, and merchandise presentation. **Freq:** Monthly. **Print Method:** Web offset. **Trim Size:** 8 x 10 7/8. **Cols./Page:** 2. **Col. Width:** 40 nonpareils. **Col. Depth:** 140 agate lines. **Key Personnel:** Murray Kasmenn, Publisher; Jennifer Acevedo, Editor-in-Chief. **ISSN:** 0745-4295 (print). **Subscription Rates:** $53 U.S.; $73 Two years; $84 Canada; $132 Two years; $101 Other countries; $183 Other countries. **URL:** http://vmsd.com. **Ad Rates:** BW $6,169; 4C $7,369. **Remarks:** Accepts advertising. **Circ:** Paid 3146, Non-paid 23796.

11467 ■ WMKB-FM
3654 W Jarvis Ave
Skokie, IL 60076
Email: lighthouse@wlnlradio.com
Format: Religious. **Founded:** 1988. **Wattage:** 2,150 ERP. **Ad Rates:** $9-11 for 30 seconds; $10-14 for 60 seconds.

SOUTH BARRINGTON

11468 ■ Leadership Journal
Willow Creek Association
67 E Algonquin Rd.
South Barrington, IL 60010-6132
Free: 800-570-9812
Publisher's E-mail: crc@willowcreek.org
Freq: Quarterly. **Subscription Rates:** $24.99 Individuals. **URL:** http://www.ctlibrary.com/le. **Mailing address:** PO Box 3188, Barrington, IL 60011-3188. **Circ:** (Not Reported).

SOUTH HOLLAND

Cook Co. Cook Co. (NE). 10 m S of Chicago. Manufactures furniture, boxes, concrete products. Diversified farming.

11469 ■ Parish Liturgy
American Catholic Press
16565 S State St.
South Holland, IL 60473
Phone: (708)331-5485
Fax: (708)331-5484
Publisher's E-mail: acp@acpress.org
Magazine for clergy, musicians, and others who plan the liturgy. **Freq:** Quarterly. **Print Method:** Sheetfed offset. **Trim Size:** 9 x 12. **ISSN:** 0164-6443 (print). **Subscription Rates:** $26 Individuals; $44 Two years; $58 Individuals 3 years. **URL:** http://www.americancatholicpress.org/parLit.html. **Remarks:** Advertising not accepted. **Circ:** Non-paid 200.

SPARTA

Randolph Co. Randolph Co. (SW). 38 m SE of Belleville. Manufactures dresses, pipe refurbishing, aluminum castings, post office lock boxes. Coal mines. Publishing house. Timber. Grain, stock, dairy, poultry farms.

11470 ■ WHCO-AM - 1230
Hwy. 154 W
Sparta, IL 62286
Phone: (618)443-2121
Fax: (618)443-2280
Free: 877-443-1230
Format: News; Country; Sports; Agricultural. **Networks:** RFD Illinois; Brownfield; CBS. **Founded:** 1955. **Operating Hours:** Continuous. **Key Personnel:** Mike Arnold, News Dir.; Dan Schnoeker, Sports Dir.; Mike Hoefft, Editor; B.K. Joiner, Contact. **Wattage:** 1,000. **Ad Rates:** Advertising accepted; rates available upon request. **Mailing address:** PO Box 255, Sparta, IL 62286. **URL:** http://realcountry1230.com/.

SPRING VALLEY

Bureau Co. Bureau Co. (NW). 42 m NE of Peoria. Industrial Park. Recreational. Casters, automobile headlights, grain elevators, printing forms manufactured. Sand, gravel pits. Diversified farming.

11471 ■ WSOG-FM - 88.1
PO Box 34
Spring Valley, IL 61362
Phone: (815)220-1929
Format: Religious. **Owner:** EWTN Global Catholic Network, 5817 Old Leeds Rd., Irondale, AL 35210, Ph: (205)271-2900. **Key Personnel:** Jim Perona, Sr., Founder, Gen. Mgr. **URL:** http://www.wsogradio.com.

SPRINGFIELD

Sangamon Co. Sangamon Co. (C). The State Capital, 96 m NE of St. Louis, Mo. and 185 m SW of Chicago. Springfield College, Southern Illinois Univ. School of Medicine, Sangamon State University, Lincoln Land Community College. State Capitol and other state buildings. Manufactures tractors, electric meters, radio parts, flour, cereal products, automatic coffeemakers, mattresses, plastic pipe, farm implements, yeast, power plant boiler installations; printed circuits, steel storage tanks.

Circulation: ★ = AAM; △ or • = BPA; ♦ = CAC; ❑ = VAC; ⊕ = PO Statement; ‡ = Publisher's Report; Boldface figures = sworn; Light figures = estimated.

11472 ■ Focus on Surgical Education
Association for Surgical Education
3085 Stevenson Dr., Ste. 200
Springfield, IL 62703
Phone: (217)529-6503
Publisher's E-mail: membership@surgicaleducation.com
Magazine covering information on surgical education. **Freq:** Quarterly. **Subscription Rates:** Included in membership. **URL:** http://www.surgicaleducation.com. **Remarks:** Advertising not accepted. **Circ:** 700.

11473 ■ Illinois Banker
Illinois Bankers Association
524 S 2nd St., Ste. 600
Springfield, IL 62701
Phone: (217)789-9340
Free: 800-783-2265
Magazine serving the Illinois professional trade association for banking. **Freq:** Monthly. **Print Method:** Offset. **Trim Size:** 9 x 11 7/8. **Cols./Page:** 3. **Col. Width:** 28 nonpareils. **Col. Depth:** 120 agate lines. **Key Personnel:** Sheila Matthews, President, Chief Executive Officer; Debbie Jemison, Contact. **URL:** http://www.ilbanker.com/About/Join-IBA/Associate-Membership.aspx. **Ad Rates:** BW $1210; 4C $1910. **Remarks:** Accepts advertising. **Circ:** 3000.

11474 ■ Illinois Issues
University of Illinois
1 University Plz.
Springfield, IL 62703
Phone: (217)206-6600
Publisher's E-mail: admissions@uis.edu
Magazine focusing on public affairs and state and local government. **Founded:** 1975. **Freq:** 10/year. **Print Method:** Offset. **Trim Size:** 8 3/4 x 11 1/4. **Cols./Page:** 3. **Col. Width:** 14 picas. **Col. Depth:** 56.5 picas. **Key Personnel:** Dana Heupel, Director, Executive Editor; Maureen McKinney, Managing Editor; Toni L. Langdon, Business Manager. **ISSN:** 0738-9663 (print). **Subscription Rates:** $39.95 Individuals. **URL:** http://illinoisissues.uis.edu. **Ad Rates:** BW $1,275; 4C $1,810. **Remarks:** Accepts advertising. **Circ:** Paid ‡6000, Non-paid ‡500.

11475 ■ The Illinois Manufacturer: The Official Magazine of the Illinois Manufacturers' Association
Illinois Manufacturers' Association
220 E Adams St.
Springfield, IL 62701
Phone: (217)522-1240
Fax: (217)522-2367
Free: 800-875-4462
Publisher's E-mail: ima@ima-net.org
Journal focusing on the economic, social, environmental and governmental conditions affecting manufacturing in Illinois. **Freq:** Quarterly. **Trim Size:** 8 3/8 x 10 7/8. **Col. Width:** 7 INS. **Key Personnel:** Stefany Henson, Editor. **URL:** http://www.ima-net.org/the-illinois-manufacturer. **Ad Rates:** BW $2,488; 4C $3,313. **Remarks:** Accepts advertising. **Circ:** Paid 7000.

11476 ■ Illinois Master Plumber
Illinois Plumbing, Heating, Cooling Contractors Association
821 S Grand Ave. W
Springfield, IL 62704
Phone: (217)522-7219
Free: 800-795-7422
Magazine containing news, product, and service information for PHC contractors. **Freq:** Monthly. **Print Method:** Offset. **Trim Size:** 8 1/2 x 11. **Cols./Page:** 3. **Col. Width:** 27 nonpareils. **Col. Depth:** 138 agate lines. **Key Personnel:** Beverly A. Potts, Executive Director. **Subscription Rates:** Included in membership. **Alt. Formats:** PDF. **URL:** http://www.ilphcc.com/illinois-master-plumber. **Ad Rates:** BW $450. **Remarks:** Advertising accepted; rates available upon request. **Circ:** Controlled 2000.

11477 ■ Illinois Parks & Recreation Magazine
Illinois Association of Park Districts
211 E Monroe St.
Springfield, IL 62701-1186
Phone: (217)523-4554
Fax: (217)523-4273
Publication E-mail: iapd@ILparks.org
Publication for park conservation, recreation, and forest preservation agencies. **Freq:** Bimonthly. **Print Method:** Offset. **Trim Size:** 8 1/2 x 11. **Cols./Page:** 2. **Col. Width:** 27 nonpareils. **Col. Depth:** 126 agate lines. **Key Personnel:** Todd Silvey, Editor. **ISSN:** 0019--2155 (print). **Subscription Rates:** $25 Individuals. **URL:** http://www.ilparks.org/?page=ipr_magazine. **Ad Rates:** BW $765; 4C $1,085. **Remarks:** Accepts advertising. **Circ:** 6000.

11478 ■ Illinois Pharmacist
Illinois Pharmacists Association
204 W Cook St.
Springfield, IL 62704-2526
Phone: (217)522-7300
Fax: (217)522-7349
Publisher's E-mail: ipha@ipha.org
Freq: Quarterly. **Print Method:** Offset. **Trim Size:** 8 1/2 x 11. **Cols./Page:** 3. **Col. Width:** 40 nonpareils. **Col. Depth:** 210 agate lines. **Key Personnel:** Stacy Ashbaker, Director, Publications; Michael J. Patton, Executive Director. **ISSN:** 0195--2099 (print). **Alt. Formats:** CD-ROM. **URL:** http://www.ipha.org/illinois-pharmacist. **Ad Rates:** BW $525; 4C $1,500. **Remarks:** Accepts advertising. **Circ:** ‡2610, 5400.

11479 ■ Illinois School Board Journal
Illinois Association of School Boards
2921 Baker Dr.
Springfield, IL 62703-5929
Phone: (217)528-9688
Freq: Bimonthly. **Print Method:** Offset. **Trim Size:** 8 1/4 x 11 1/4. **Cols./Page:** 3. **Col. Width:** 13 picas. **Col. Depth:** 10 inches. **Key Personnel:** Dana Heckrodt, Administrative Assistant; James Russell, Associate Director; Linda Dawson, Director, Editorial. **ISSN:** 0019--221X (print). **Subscription Rates:** $18 Individuals; $21 Other countries; Included in membership. **Ad Rates:** BW $600; 4C $1,250. **Remarks:** Color advertising accepted; rates available upon request. **Circ:** Paid ‡7737, Non-paid ‡690.

11480 ■ Illinois Times
Central Illinois Communications L.L.C.
1320 S State St.
Springfield, IL 62704
Phone: (217)753-2226
Fax: (217)753-2281
Publisher's E-mail: classified@illinoistimes.com
Local newspaper (tabloid). **Freq:** Weekly (Thurs.). **Print Method:** Offset. **Trim Size:** 10 1/4 x 12. **Cols./Page:** 4. **Col. Width:** 2.4 inches. **Col. Depth:** 12 inches. **Key Personnel:** Fletcher Farrar, Editor; Sharon Whalen, Publisher. **Mailing address:** PO Box 5256, Springfield, IL 62704. **Remarks:** Accepts advertising. **Circ:** ‡28000.

11481 ■ ILMDA Advantage
Illinois Lumber and Material Dealers Association
932 S Spring St.
Springfield, IL 62704
Phone: (217)544-5405
Fax: (217)544-4206
Free: 800-252-8641
Magazine for lumber and building material dealers. **Freq:** Quarterly. **Print Method:** Offset. **Trim Size:** 8 1/4 x 11 1/4. **Cols./Page:** 3. **Col. Width:** 26 nonpareils. **Col. Depth:** 140 agate lines. **Key Personnel:** J. Barry Johnson, Executive Director. **Alt. Formats:** PDF. **URL:** http://www.ilmda.com/publications. **Remarks:** Advertising accepted; rates available upon request. **Circ:** (Not Reported).

11482 ■ Journal of the Abraham Lincoln Association
University of Illinois Press
c/o Christian McWhirter, Editor
Abraham Lincoln Presidential Library
112 North Sixth St.
Springfield, IL 62701
Phone: (217)785-9130
Fax: (217)524-6973
Publisher's E-mail: uipress@uillinois.edu
Scholarly journal covering Abraham Lincoln. **Freq:** Semiannual winter and summer. **Key Personnel:** Thomas Schwartz, Board Member. **ISSN:** 0898--4212 (print); **EISSN:** 1945--7987 (electronic). **Subscription Rates:** $32 Individuals print only; $43 Institutions print only; $14 Single issue; $19 Single issue non-U.S. postage. **URL:** http://www.press.uillinois.edu/journals/jala.html. **Ad Rates:** BW $260. **Remarks:** Accepts advertising. **Circ:** 800.

11483 ■ Journal of the Association of Lunar and Planetary Observers
Association of Lunar and Planetary Observers
c/o Matthew L. Will, Secretary
PO Box 13456
Springfield, IL 62791
Freq: Quarterly. **ISSN:** 0039- 2502 (print). **Subscription Rates:** Included in membership. **URL:** http://alpo-astronomy.org. **Remarks:** Accepts advertising. **Circ:** 650.

11484 ■ Journal of the Illinois Optometric Association
Illinois Optometric Association
304 W Washington St.
Springfield, IL 62701
Phone: (217)525-8012
Fax: (217)525-8018
Publisher's E-mail: ioa@ioaweb.org
Professional journal containing clinical material, research reports, practice management articles, and material of interest to practicing optometrists who are members of the association. **Freq:** Quarterly. **Print Method:** Offset. Uses mats. **Trim Size:** 8 1/2 x 11. **Cols./Page:** 2. **Col. Width:** 38 nonpareils. **Col. Depth:** 12 agate lines. **Key Personnel:** Nicole Jensen, Editor. **Subscription Rates:** $9 Members; $18 Nonmembers. **URL:** http://www.ioaweb.org. **Ad Rates:** BW $360; 4C $930; PCI $.30. **Remarks:** Accepts advertising. **Circ:** 1200.

11485 ■ Journal of the Illinois State Historical Society
Illinois State Historical Society
5255 Shepherd Rd.
Springfield, IL 62703
Phone: (217)525-2781
Fax: (217)525-2783
Journal of the Illinois State Historical Society. **Freq:** Quarterly spring, summer, autumn, and winter. **Key Personnel:** Eileen McMahon, Editor; Mary Lou Johnsrud, Office Manager; William Furry, Executive Director. **ISSN:** 1522-1067 (print). **Subscription Rates:** Free to members. **URL:** http://www.historyillinois.org; http://historyillinois.org/files/Publications/Journal/db_journal_index.php. **Circ:** (Not Reported).

11486 ■ Journal of Public Health Dentistry
American Association of Public Health Dentistry
3085 Stevenson Dr., Ste. 200
Springfield, IL 62703
Phone: (217)529-6941
Fax: (217)529-9120
Publisher's E-mail: info@aaphd.org
Magazine for professionals in public health dentistry. **Freq:** Quarterly. **Print Method:** Letterpress. **Trim Size:** 8 1/2 x 11. **Cols./Page:** 3. **Key Personnel:** Robert Weyant, Editor-in-Chief. **ISSN:** 0022--4006 (print); **EISSN:** 1752-7325 (electronic). **Subscription Rates:** $369 Institutions America (online); $443 Institutions America (print and online); $63 Members American Dental Education Association (America; online only); $95 Members American Dental Education Association (America; print and online); £231 Institutions UK (online); £278 Institutions UK (print and online); £32 Members American Dental Education Association (UK and Europe non-Euro zone; online only); £50 Members American Dental Education Association (UK and Europe non-Euro zone; print and online); €291 Institutions Europe (online); €350 Institutions Europe (print and online); €47 Members American Dental Education Association (Europe Euro zone; online); €50 Members American Dental Education Association (Europe Euro zone; print and online). **URL:** http://onlinelibrary.wiley.com/journal/10.1111/(ISSN)1752-7325. **Remarks:** Accepts advertising. **Circ:** Controlled ‡1300, 1500.

11487 ■ Journal of Spinal Cord Medicine
Academy of Spinal Cord Injury Professionals
206 S 6th St.
Springfield, IL 62701
Phone: (718)803-3782
Fax: (718)803-0414
Publisher's E-mail: aps@unitedspinal.org
Professional journal covering spinal injuries and treatment. **Freq:** 5/yr. **Trim Size:** 8 1/8 X 10 7/8. **Key Personnel:** Donald R. Bodner, MD, Associate Editor. **Subscription Rates:** Included in membership. **URL:** http://www.academyscipro.org; http://www.tandfonline.com/toc/yscm20/39/3. **Ad Rates:** BW $830; 4C $1,000.

Remarks: Accepts advertising. **Circ:** Paid 1500.

11488 ■ Keep on Truckin News
Mid-West Truckers Association Inc.
2727 N Dirksen Pky.
Springfield, IL 62702
Phone: (217)525-0310
Publisher's E-mail: info@mid-westtruckers.com
Freq: Monthly. **Subscription Rates:** Included in membership. **URL:** http://www.mid-westtruckers.com/resources.aspx. **Remarks:** Accepts advertising. **Circ:** (Not Reported).

11489 ■ Legislative Synopsis and Digest
Legislative Reference Bureau
112 State House
Springfield, IL 62706
Phone: (217)782-6625
Government publication covering a synopsis of each bill and resolution introduced and the action of those bills and resolutions in Illinois. **Freq:** Weekly. **Key Personnel:** Rebecca A. Hankiewicz, Editor. **Alt. Formats:** PDF. **URL:** http://www.ilga.gov/commission/lrb/lrb_digest_indices.asp. **Remarks:** Advertising not accepted. **Circ:** (Not Reported).

11490 ■ The Living Museum
Illinois State Museum
502 S Spring St.
Springfield, IL 62706-5000
Phone: (217)782-7386
Fax: (217)782-1254
Publication E-mail: subscriptions@museum.state.il.us
Magazine devoted to anthropology, art, natural history, and museum topics. **Freq:** Quarterly. **Print Method:** Offset. **Trim Size:** 8 1/2 x 11. **Cols./Page:** 3. **Col. Width:** 27 nonpareils. **Col. Depth:** 131 agate lines. **ISSN:** 0024--5283 (print). **Subscription Rates:** Free. **URL:** http://www.museum.state.il.us/publications. **Remarks:** Accepts advertising. **Circ:** (Not Reported).

11491 ■ Oral Surgery, Oral Medicine, Oral Pathology, Oral Radiology and Endodontics
American Academy of Oral and Maxillofacial Radiology
3085 Stevenson Dr., Ste. 200
Springfield, IL 62703
Publisher's E-mail: admin@aaomr.org
Journal providing a practical and complete overview of the medical and surgical techniques of dental practice in five areas. Topics covered include such current issues as dental implants, treatment of HIV-infected patients, and evaluation and treatment of TMJ disorders. **Freq:** Monthly. **Subscription Rates:** $55 Individuals; $32 Other countries. **URL:** http://aaomr.site-ym.com/store/ListProducts.aspx?catid=76618. **Remarks:** Advertising not accepted. **Circ:** (Not Reported).

11492 ■ The Post-Abortion Review
Elliot Institute
PO Box 7348
Springfield, IL 62791-7348
Phone: (217)525-8202
Fax: (217)525-8212
Free: 888-412-2676
Publisher's E-mail: elliotinstitute@gmail.com
Professional journal covering the physical and psychological effects of abortion. **Freq:** Quarterly. **Key Personnel:** David Reardon, PhD, Publisher; Amy R. Sobie, Managing Editor. **ISSN:** 1083--9496 (print). **Alt. Formats:** PDF. **URL:** http://afterabortion.org/1999/the-post-abortion-review. **Remarks:** Advertising not accepted. **Circ:** Controlled 1050.

11493 ■ The State Journal-Register
State Journal Register Inc.
1 Copley Plz.
Springfield, IL 62701
Phone: (217)788-1504
General newspaper. **Freq:** Daily and Sun. (morn.). **Print Method:** Offset. **Trim Size:** 13 3/4 x 22 3/4. **Cols./Page:** 6. **Col. Width:** 26 nonpareils. **Col. Depth:** 297 agate lines. **Key Personnel:** Clarissa Williams, Publisher, phone: (217)788-1500; Angie Muhs, Executive Editor, phone: (217)788-1505; Erin Orr, Managing Editor, phone: (217)788-1505; Jason Nevel, Reporter. **USPS:** 614-200. **Subscription Rates:** $29.99 Individuals Monday-Sunday; carrier delivery; 1 month. **URL:** http://www.sj-r.com. **Mailing address:** PO Box 219, Springfield, IL 62705-0219. **Ad Rates:** PCI $29.84. **Remarks:** Accepts advertising. **Circ:** Mon.-Fri. ★**49839**, Sat. ★**49108**, Sun. ★**58272**.

11494 ■ Township Perspective
Township Officials of Illinois
3217 Northfield Dr.
Springfield, IL 62702
Phone: (217)744-2212
Fax: (217)744-7419
Free: 866-897-4688
Publication E-mail: jimtoi@toi.org
Magazine for township officials. **Freq:** 11/year July/August is a combined issue. **Print Method:** Offset. **Cols./Page:** 3. **Col. Width:** 27 nonpareils. **Col. Depth:** 133 agate lines. **Key Personnel:** Jerry B. Crabtree, Associate Director; Erin J. Valentine, Associate Editor; Bryan E. Smith, Executive Director. **Subscription Rates:** $25 Individuals. **URL:** http://www.toi.org/Township-Perspective/Latest-Issues. **Ad Rates:** BW $550; PCI $21. **Remarks:** Accepts advertising. **Circ:** 13000.

11495 ■ Insight Communications
801 Adlai Stevenson Dr.
Springfield, IL 62703
Owner: Insight Communications, 575 Boulder Way, Roswell, GA 30075, Ph: (613)823-2634. **Formerly:** Rock River Cablevision Co. **URL:** http://www.ilsos.gov/corporatellc/CorporateLlcController.

11496 ■ WABZ-FM - 93.9
3501 E Sangamon Ave.
Springfield, IL 62707
Phone: (217)753-5400
Format: Album-Oriented Rock (AOR). **Owner:** Saga Communications of Illinois, LLC, at above address, Grosse Pointe, MI. **Ad Rates:** Advertising accepted; rates available upon request. **URL:** http://www.abefm.com.

11497 ■ WCFN-TV - 49
509 S Neil St.
Champaign, IL 61820
Phone: (217)356-8333
Fax: (217)373-3680
Owner: Nexstar Broadcasting Group Inc., 545 E John Carpenter Fwy., Ste. 700, Irving, TX 75062, Ph: (972)373-8800. **ADI:** Springfield-Decatur-Champaign, IL. **Ad Rates:** Noncommercial.

11498 ■ WDBR-FM - 103.7
3501 E Sangamon Ave.
Springfield, IL 62707
Phone: (217)753-5400
Fax: (217)753-7902
Format: Top 40. **Owner:** Saga Communications of Illinois, LLC, at above address, Grosse Pointe, MI. **Ad Rates:** Noncommercial. **URL:** http://www.wdbr.com.

11499 ■ WFMB-AM - 1450
3055 S 4th St.
Springfield, IL 62703
Phone: (217)528-3033
Fax: (217)528-5348
Email: sportsradio1450@sportsradio1450.com
Format: Sports. **Networks:** ABC; ESPN Radio; Tribune Radio. **Owner:** Neuhoff Communications Inc., 1340 US Hwy. 1, Ste. 135, Jupiter, FL 33469. **Founded:** 1927. **Formerly:** WCVS-AM. **Operating Hours:** Continuous; 5% network, 95% local. **ADI:** Springfield-Decatur-Champaign, IL. **Key Personnel:** Kevin O'Dea, Gen. Mgr., kevino'dea@neuhoffmedia.com; Jeff Hofmann, Contact, jeffhofmann@neuhoffmedia.com. **Wattage:** 1,000. **Ad Rates:** Advertising accepted; rates available upon request. **URL:** http://www.sportsradio1450.com.

11500 ■ WFMB-FM - 104.5
3055 S Fourth St.
Springfield, IL 62703
Phone: (217)528-3033
Fax: (217)528-5348
Format: Country. **ADI:** Springfield-Decatur-Champaign, IL. **Key Personnel:** Kevin O'Dea, Gen. Mgr., kevino'dea@neuhoffmedia.com. **Wattage:** 43,000 ERP. **URL:** http://www.wfmb.com.

11501 ■ WICS-TV - 20
2680 E Cook St.
Springfield, IL 62703
Phone: (217)753-5620
Free: 800-263-9720
Email: news@wics.com
Format: Commercial TV. **Simulcasts:** WICD-TV. **Networks:** ABC. **Owner:** Sinclair Broadcasting Group, 10706 Beaver Dam Rd., Hunt Valley, MD 21030, Ph: (410)568-1500. **Founded:** 1953. **Operating Hours:** Continuous. **ADI:** Springfield-Decatur-Champaign, IL. **Wattage:** 676. **Ad Rates:** Advertising accepted; rates available upon request. **URL:** http://www.wics.com.

11502 ■ WIPA-FM - 89.3
One University Plz.
CBM-130
Springfield, IL 62703-5407
Phone: (217)206-9847
Free: 866-206-9847
Email: wuis@wuis.org
Format: Public Radio. **Founded:** Jan. 03, 1975. **Key Personnel:** Bill Wheelhouse, Gen. Mgr., wwhee2@uis.edu; Bob Meyer, Production Mgr., rmeye1@uis.edu; Karl Scroggin, Music Dir., kscro1@uis.edu; Sean Crawford, News Dir., scraw1@uis.edu; Sandra McGinnis, Dir. of Bus. Dev., smcgi2@uis.edu. **URL:** http://www.wuis.org.

11503 ■ WLUJ-FM - 89.7
600 W Mason St.
Springfield, IL 62702-5025
Phone: (217)528-2300
Free: 800-932-9585
Email: comments@wluj.org
Format: Contemporary Christian. **Networks:** Moody Broadcasting. **Founded:** 1986. **Operating Hours:** Continuous; 85% network, 15% local. **Key Personnel:** Howard Fouks, Production Mgr.; Joey Krol, Chief Engineer; John McBride, Operations Mgr. **Wattage:** 20,000. **Ad Rates:** Noncommercial. **URL:** http://www.wluj.org.

11504 ■ WLWJ-FM - 88.1
600 West Mason St.
Springfield, IL 62702
Free: 800-932-9585
Format: Religious. **Key Personnel:** Howard Fouks, Chief Engineer; Joey Krol, Operations Mgr. **Ad Rates:** Noncommercial. **URL:** http://www.wluj.org.

11505 ■ WMAY-AM - 970
PO Box 460
Springfield, IL 62705
Phone: (217)629-7077
Fax: (217)629-7952
Format: News; Talk. **Networks:** ABC. **Owner:** Mid-West Family Broadcasting Group, 730 Rayovac Dr., Madison, WI 53711, Ph: (608)273-1000. **Founded:** 1950. **Operating Hours:** Continuous. **Key Personnel:** Jim Leach, News Dir., Prog. Dir. **Local Programs:** *Jim Leach*, Monday Tuesday Wednesday Thursday Friday Saturday Sunday 3:00 p.m. - 6:00 p.m. 5:00 a.m. - 5:30 a.m. 5:30 a.m. - 6:00 a.m. **Wattage:** 1,000 Day; 500 Night. **Ad Rates:** $12-33 for 60 seconds. $12-$33 for 60 seconds. Combined advertising rates available with WNNS-FM. **URL:** http://www.wmay.com.

11506 ■ WMEC-TV - 22
PO Box 6248
Springfield, IL 62708
Phone: (217)483-7887
Fax: (217)483-1112
Free: 800-232-3605
Format: Public TV. **Networks:** Public Broadcasting Service (PBS). **Owner:** Network Knowledge, at above address. **Founded:** 1984. **Formerly:** WIUM-TV. **Operating Hours:** 6 a.m.-12 a.m.; 75% network, 25% local. **Key Personnel:** Dr. Jerold Gruebel, CEO, President; Mary Jane Bates, Bus. Mgr.; Stephanie Cole, Dir. of Traffic. **Ad Rates:** Noncommercial. **URL:** http://www.networkknowledge.tv.

11507 ■ WNNS-FM - 98.7
PO Box 460
Springfield, IL 62705
Phone: (217)629-7077
Fax: (217)629-7952
Format: Soft Rock. **Networks:** Independent. **Owner:** Mid-West Family Broadcasting Group, 730 Rayovac Dr., Madison, WI 53711, Ph: (608)273-1000. **Founded:** 1979. **Operating Hours:** Continuous; 100% local. **Key Personnel:** Chris Murphy, Dir. of Programs. **Wattage:** 50,000. **Ad Rates:** $59.50 for 30 seconds; $100 for 60 seconds. $59.50 for 30 seconds; $100 for 60 seconds.

Circulation: ★ = AAM; △ or • = BPA; ♦ = CAC; ❑ = VAC; ⊕ = PO Statement; ‡ = Publisher's Report; Boldface figures = sworn; Light figures = estimated.

Combined advertising rates available with WMAY-AM and WQLZ-FM. **URL:** http://www.wnns.com.

11508 ■ WQLZ-FM - 92.7
PO Box 460
Springfield, IL 62705
Phone: (217)629-7077
Fax: (217)629-7952
Format: Album-Oriented Rock (AOR). **Networks:** Independent. **Owner:** Mid-West Family Broadcasting Group, 730 Rayovac Dr., Madison, WI 53711, Ph: (608)273-1000. **Founded:** Mar. 16, 1993. **Formerly:** WTJY-FM. **Operating Hours:** Continuous. **Wattage:** 11,500. **Ad Rates:** Noncommercial. **URL:** http://www.wqlz.com.

11509 ■ WQNA-FM - 88.3
2201 Toronto Rd.
Springfield, IL 62712
Phone: (217)529-5431
Email: info@wqna.org
Format: Eclectic; Educational. **Simulcasts:** Cable TV. **Owner:** Capital Area Career Center, 611 Hagadorn Rd., Mason, MI 48854. **Founded:** 1979. **Operating Hours:** Continuous. **ADI:** Springfield-Decatur-Champaign, IL. **Key Personnel:** Jim Pemberton, Contact; Jim Pemberton, Contact. **Wattage:** 250. **Ad Rates:** Noncommercial. **URL:** http://www.wqna.org.

11510 ■ WQQL-FM - 101.9
3501 E Sangamon Ave.
Springfield, IL 62707
Phone: (217)753-5400
Fax: (217)753-7902
Format: Oldies. **Key Personnel:** Dave Daniels, Dir. of Programs, ddaniels@capitolradiogroup.com; John Williams, Sales Mgr., jwilliams@capitolradiogroup.com. **Ad Rates:** Noncommercial. **URL:** http://www.cool939.com.

11511 ■ WRLJ-FM
600 W Mason St.
Springfield, IL 62702
Phone: (217)528-2300
Free: 800-932-9585
Format: Religious; Contemporary Christian. **Key Personnel:** Howard Fouks, Contact; John McBride, Contact; Howard Fouks, Contact; Rich Beaman, Contact; John McBride, Contact. **Wattage:** 2,000 ERP. **Ad Rates:** Noncommercial.

11512 ■ WRSP-TV - 55
3003 Old Rochester Rd.
Springfield, IL 62703
Phone: (217)523-8855
Fax: (217)523-4410
Format: Commercial TV. **Simulcasts:** WCCU-TV. **Networks:** Fox; Independent. **Founded:** June 01, 1979. **Operating Hours:** Continuous. **ADI:** Springfield-Decatur-Champaign, IL. **Key Personnel:** Tom Gray, President. **Wattage:** 001. **Ad Rates:** $15-1000 for 30 seconds. **URL:** http://foxillinois.com.

11513 ■ WSEC-TV - 8
PO Box 6248
Springfield, IL 62708
Free: 800-232-3605
Format: Public TV. **Owner:** Network Knowledge, at above address. **Founded:** 1984. **Operating Hours:** 6 a.m.-12 a.m.; 75% network, 25% local. **ADI:** Springfield-Decatur-Champaign, IL. **Key Personnel:** Dr. Jerold Gruebel, CEO, President; Mary Jane Bates, Bus. Mgr.; Stephanie Cole, Dir. of Traffic. **Ad Rates:** Noncommercial. **URL:** http://www.networknowledge.tv.

11514 ■ WTAX-AM - 1240
3501 E Sangamon Ave.
Springfield, IL 62707
Phone: (217)753-5400
Fax: (217)753-7902
Format: News; Talk. **Networks:** CBS. **Owner:** Saga Communications Inc., 73 Kercheval Ave., Ste. 201, Grosse Pointe Farms, MI 48236, Ph: (313)886-7070, Fax: (313)886-7150. **Founded:** 1930. **Operating Hours:** Continuous; 15% network, 85% local. **ADI:** Springfield-Decatur-Champaign, IL. **Key Personnel:** John LaTessa, Tech. Dir., jlatessa@wtax.com. **Wattage:** 1,000. **Ad Rates:** $40 for 30 seconds; $60 for 60 seconds. **URL:** http://www.wtax.com.

11515 ■ WUIS-FM - 91.9
University of Illinois at Springfield
One University Plz.
Springfield, IL 62703-5407
Phone: (217)206-9847
Email: wuis@uis.edu
Format: Public Radio; News; Classical. **Simulcasts:** WIPA-FM. **Networks:** National Public Radio (NPR); Public Radio International (PRI); Illinois Public Radio. **Owner:** University of Illinois at Springfield, 1 University Plz., Springfield, IL 62703-5407, Ph: (217)206-6600, Fax: (217)206-7623, Free: 800-252-8533. **Founded:** 1975. **Formerly:** WSSU-FM; WSSR-FM. **Operating Hours:** Continuous. **ADI:** Springfield-Decatur-Champaign, IL. **Key Personnel:** Sean Crawford, Managing Ed., scraw1@uis.edu; Karl Scroggin, Music Dir., kscro1@uis.edu; Sandra McGinnis, Dir. of Fin., smcg2@uis.edu. **Wattage:** 50,000. **Ad Rates:** Noncommercial. **URL:** http://www.wuis.org.

11516 ■ WXAJ-FM - 99.7
3055 S 4th St.
Springfield, IL 62703
Phone: (217)528-3033
Fax: (217)528-5348
Format: Contemporary Hit Radio (CHR). **Key Personnel:** Kevin O'Dea, Gen. Mgr., kevino'dea@neuhoffmedia.com. **Wattage:** 50,000. **URL:** http://www.997kissfm.com.

11517 ■ WYMG-FM - 100.5
3501 E Sangamon Ave.
Springfield, IL 62707-9777
Phone: (217)753-5400
Fax: (217)753-7902
Format: Classic Rock. **Networks:** Independent. **Owner:** Saga Communications Inc., 73 Kercheval Ave., Ste. 201, Grosse Pointe Farms, MI 48236, Ph: (313)886-7070, Fax: (313)886-7150. **Founded:** 1948. **Formerly:** WEAI-FM. **Operating Hours:** Continuous; 100% local. **ADI:** Springfield-Decatur-Champaign, IL. **Key Personnel:** Jane Cochran, Dir. of Programs, jane@wymg.com; Jeff Hall, Promotions Dir., jhall@capitolradiogroup.com; Liz Willis, Contact, liz@wymg.com. **Wattage:** 50,000. **Ad Rates:** Advertising accepted; rates available upon request. **URL:** http://www.wymg.com.

11518 ■ WY2K-AM - 1690
610 Martin L. King
Springfield, IL 62703
Phone: (217)544-8850
Format: Classical; Blues; Oldies. **Owner:** Billy Washington. **Operating Hours:** Continuous. **Key Personnel:** Billy Washington, Owner, Station Mgr.

STAUNTON

Macoupin Co. Macoupin Co. (SWC). 38 m NE of St Louis, Mo. Residential. Oil wells. Grain, dairy farms.

11519 ■ Staunton Star-Times
Star-Times Publishing Company Inc.
108 West Main St.
Staunton, IL 62088
Phone: (618)635-2000
Fax: (618)635-5281
Publication E-mail: startime@madisontelco.com
Community newspaper. **Freq:** Weekly (Wed.). **Print Method:** Offset. **Cols./Page:** 6. **Col. Width:** 12 picas. **Col. Depth:** 21.5 inches. **Key Personnel:** Walter Haase, Editor, phone: (618)635-2000, fax: (618)635-5281. **USPS:** 520-800. **Subscription Rates:** $22 Individuals /year (in Madison & Macoupin counties); $28 Individuals /year (all other counties). **URL:** http://www.stauntonstartimes.com. **Mailing address:** P O Box 180, Staunton, IL 62088. **Remarks:** Advertising accepted; rates available upon request. **Circ:** (Not Reported).

11520 ■ Madison Communications
21668 Double Arch Rd.
Staunton, IL 62088
Phone: (618)635-3214
Fax: (618)635-7213
Free: 800-422-4848
Email: infomtc@madisontelco.com
Cities Served: 16 channels. **URL:** http://www.gomadison.com.

STERLING

Whiteside Co. Whiteside Co. (NW). 38 m SW of Rockford. Manufactures builders' hardware, industrial fasteners, garage doors, garden tools, wire specialties, electrical appliances. Dairy, stock, truck, grain farms.

11521 ■ WNIQ-FM - 91.5
801 N First St.
DeKalb, IL 60115
Phone: (815)753-9000
Fax: (815)753-9938
Email: npr@niu.edu
Format: Public Radio. **Owner:** Northern Illinois University, 1425 W Lincoln Hwy., Dekalb, IL 60115. **Founded:** 1954. **Key Personnel:** Bill Drake, Dir. of Programs, wdrake@niu.edu; Jeff Glass, Chief Engineer, jglass@niu.edu; John Hill, Director, jhill@niu.edu; Susan Stephens, News Dir., sstephens@niu.edu. **Wattage:** 010. **Ad Rates:** Noncommercial. **URL:** http://www.northernpublicradio.org.

11522 ■ WSDR-AM - 1240
3501 Broadway
Mount Vernon, IL 62864-1508
Phone: (815)625-3400
Fax: (815)625-6940
Format: Talk; News. **Networks:** CBS. **Owner:** Withers Broadcasting Companies, 1822 N Court St., Marion, IL 62959, Ph: (303)242-5000. **Founded:** 1949. **Operating Hours:** Continuous. **ADI:** Daveport,IA-Rock Island, Moline,IL. **Wattage:** 1,000 Day; 500 Night. **Ad Rates:** $35-80 for 30 seconds. Combined advertising rates available with WSSQ-FM, WZZT-FM. **Mailing address:** PO Box 1508, Mount Vernon, IL 62864-1508.

11523 ■ WSSQ-FM - 94.3
3501 Broadway
Mount Vernon, IL 62864-1508
Phone: (815)625-3400
Fax: (815)625-6940
Format: Adult Contemporary. **Networks:** Westwood One Radio. **Owner:** Withers Broadcasting Companies, 1822 N Court St., Marion, IL 62959, Ph: (303)242-5000. **Founded:** 1966. **Formerly:** WJVM-FM. **Operating Hours:** Continuous. **ADI:** Daveport,IA-Rock Island, Moline,IL. **Wattage:** 6,000. **Ad Rates:** $20-28 for 30 seconds; $30-44 per unit. Combined advertising rates available with WSDR-AM. **Mailing address:** PO Box 1508, Mount Vernon, IL 62864-1508.

STREAMWOOD

Cook Co. Cook Co. (NE). 22 m W of Evanston. Residential. Commercial. Industrial.

11524 ■ National Locksmith
National Publishing Company Inc.
1533 Burgundy Pkwy.
Streamwood, IL 60107
Phone: (630)837-2044
Publication E-mail: info@thenationallocksmith.com
Magazine focusing on physical security and locksmithing. **Founded:** 1929. **Freq:** 13/yr. **Print Method:** Web offset. **Trim Size:** 8 1/4 x 11. **Cols./Page:** 3. **Col. Width:** 27 nonpareils. **Col. Depth:** 140 agate lines. **Key Personnel:** Greg Mango, Editor; Marc Goldberg, Publisher. **ISSN:** 0364-3719 (print). **Subscription Rates:** $29.95 Individuals. **URL:** http://www.thenationallocksmith.com/. **Ad Rates:** BW $2,240; 4C $3,290. **Remarks:** Accepts advertising. **Circ:** (Not Reported).

STREATOR

Livingston Co. La Salle Co. (N). 98 m SW of Chicago. Manufactures bricks, sewer cleaning and street sweeping equipment, truck bodies, spreader, snow plows, glass containers, foam packing materials, steel tubing, carbonated beverages, syrups, peanut butter.

11525 ■ WSPL-AM - 1250
PO Box 377
Streator, IL 61364-0377
Phone: (815)673-8000
Founded: 1953. **Formerly:** WIZZ-AM. **Ad Rates:** Advertising accepted; rates available upon request. $7.50-12 for 30 seconds; $10.50-15 for 60 seconds. Combined advertising rates available with WSTQ, WALS, WGLC, WBZG, WIVQ, WYYS. **URL:** http://am1250wspl.com.

STRONGHURST

Henderson Co. Henderson Co. (W). 16 m SE of Burlington Ia. Ships stock. Dairy farms. Corn, cattle, hogs.

11526 ■ Hancock County Quill
Hancock-Henderson Quill Inc.
PO Box 149
Stronghurst, IL 61480-0149
Phone: (309)924-1871
Fax: (309)924-1212
Publication E-mail: quill@hcil.net
Newspaper. **Freq:** Weekly (Wed.). **Print Method:** Offset. **Cols./Page:** 6. **Col. Width:** 22 nonpareils. **Col. Depth:** 231 agate lines. **Key Personnel:** Shirley Linder, Editor; Dessa Rodeffer, Owner, Publisher. **URL:** http://www.quillnewspaper.com. **Ad Rates:** GLR $.45; BW $220; SAU $6; PCI $3.35. **Circ:** ‡1250.

11527 ■ The Henderson County Quill
Hancock-Henderson Quill Inc.
PO Box 149
Stronghurst, IL 61480-0149
Phone: (309)924-1871
Fax: (309)924-1212
Publication E-mail: quill@hcil.net
Community newspaper. **Freq:** Semiweekly. **Print Method:** Offset. **Trim Size:** 11 1/2 x 17 1/2. **Cols./Page:** 6. **Col. Width:** 22 nonpareils. **Col. Depth:** 231 agate lines. **Key Personnel:** Dessa Rodeffer, Owner, Publisher. **URL:** http://quillnewspaper.com. **Remarks:** Accepts advertising. **Circ:** (Not Reported).

SULLIVAN

Moultrie Co. Moultrie Co. (SEC). 16 m NW of Mattoon. Impregrated apparatus for export, candy, steel subassembly, garage doors manufactured. Corn, soybeans, wheat.

11528 ■ News Progress
News Progress
100 W Monroe St.
Sullivan, IL 61951
Phone: (217)728-7381
Fax: (217)728-2020
Community newspaper. **Founded:** 1981. **Freq:** Weekly (Wed.). **Print Method:** Offset. **Cols./Page:** 6. **Col. Width:** 11 picas. **Col. Depth:** 294 agate lines. **Key Personnel:** R.R. Best, Publisher; Keith Stewart, Managing Editor; Barry Morgan, Director, Advertising. **USPS:** 744-141. **Subscription Rates:** $32.50 Individuals out of county; $27.50 Individuals in county. **URL:** http://www.newsprogress.com. **Mailing address:** PO Box 290, Sullivan, IL 61951. **Remarks:** Accepts classified advertising. **Circ:** Paid ‡3800, Free ‡154.

SUMMIT

Cook Co. Cook Co. (NE). 11 m SW of Chicago. Residential.

11529 ■ Des Plaines Valley News
Des Plaines Valley News
7704 W 62nd Pl.
Summit, IL 60501-0348
Phone: (708)594-9340
Fax: (708)594-9494
Publisher's E-mail: editor@desplainesvalleynews.com
Newspaper. **Freq:** Weekly (Thurs.). **Print Method:** Offset. Uses mats. **Trim Size:** 11 1/2 x 15. **Cols./Page:** 6. **Col. Width:** 9.5 picas. **Col. Depth:** 250 agate lines. **Subscription Rates:** $15 Individuals /year; $32 Two years; $13 Individuals senior (65 and older). **URL:** http://desplainesvalleynews.com/index90.htm. **Mailing address:** PO Box 348, Summit, IL 60501-0348. **Remarks:** Accepts advertising. **Circ:** (Not Reported).

11530 ■ Southwest News-Herald
Vondrak Publishing
7676 W 63rd St.
Summit, IL 60501
Publisher's E-mail: vonpub@aol.com
Community newspaper. **Freq:** Semiweekly (Wed. and Fri.). **Print Method:** Offset. **Cols./Page:** 9. **Col. Width:** 21 nonpareils. **Col. Depth:** 301 agate lines. **Key Personnel:** James Vondrak, Publisher; Bob Gusanders, General Manager. **Subscription Rates:** $27.50 52 weeks. **Alt. Formats:** PDF. **URL:** http://swnewsherald.com/home-1.htm. **Remarks:** Accepts advertising. **Circ:** Paid ‡9300.

11531 ■ WARG-FM - 88.9
7329 W 63rd St.
Summit, IL 60501
Phone: (708)467-5589
Fax: (708)467-5864
Email: warg@argohs.net
Format: Eclectic. **Networks:** AP. **Founded:** 1976. **Operating Hours**: 10 a.m. -6:30 p.m. Mon.-Fri. **Wattage**: 500. **Ad Rates:** Noncommercial. **URL:** http://www.warg889.net.

SUMNER

Lawrence Co. Lawrence Co. (SE). 18 m W of Vincennes, Ind. Oil and natural gas wells. Agriculture.

11532 ■ The Sumner Press
The Sumner Press Inc.
PO Box 126
Sumner, IL 62466
Phone: (618)936-2212
Fax: (618)936-2858
Publication E-mail: editor@sumnerpress.com
Community newspaper. **Freq:** Weekly (Thurs.). **Print Method:** Offset. **Cols./Page:** 6. **Col. Width:** 11 picas. **Col. Depth:** 21 inches. **USPS:** 525-820. **Subscription Rates:** $25 Individuals in County; $27.50 Out of area; $35 Other countries. **URL:** http://www.sumnerpress.com. **Ad Rates:** GLR $.30; BW $504; 4C $2,116; SAU $5.20; CNU $5; PCI $5.20. **Remarks:** Accepts advertising. **Circ:** ‡2150.

SWANSEA

11533 ■ Fairview Heights/O'Fallon Journal
Suburban Journal
5050 Old Collinsville Rd.
Swansea, IL 62226-2009
Phone: (618)622-5050
Newspaper, now defunct. **Freq:** Weekly (Wed.). **Print Method:** Offset. **Cols./Page:** 6. **Col. Width:** 252 nonpareils. **Col. Depth:** 308 agate lines. **Ad Rates:** SAU $9.75. **Remarks:** Accepts advertising. **Circ:** (Not Reported).

SYCAMORE

DeKalb Co. De Kalb Co. (N). 4 m N of Dekalb.

11534 ■ WSQR-AM
1851 Coltonville Rd.
Sycamore, IL 60178
Phone: (815)899-0000
Fax: (815)899-9000
Format: Country. **Networks:** CNN Radio. **Owner:** Dekalb County Broadcasters Inc., 1 Broadcast Center, Plano, IL 60545, Ph: (630)552-1000, Fax: (630)552-9300. **Founded:** 1982. **Formerly**: WTIM-AM. **Wattage**: 900 Day; 001 Night. **Ad Rates:** $8-10 for 30 seconds; $10-12 for 60 seconds.

TAYLORVILLE

Christian Co. Christian Co. (C). 28 m SE of Springfield. Coal mines. Manufactures paper, feed, tools, steel products, stationery and greeting cards, dresses, cigars. Hatcheries; grain drying & soybean processing plant. Dairy, stock, poultry farms. Soybeans.

11535 ■ Breeze-Courier
Breeze-Courier
212 S Main St.
Taylorville, IL 62568
Phone: (217)824-2233
Publisher's E-mail: breezenews@breezecourier.com
General newspaper. **Freq:** Mon.-Sat. (eve.) Mon.-Fri. eve., Sun. morn. **Print Method:** Offset. **Cols./Page:** 6. **Col. Width:** 25 nonpareils. **Col. Depth:** 294 agate lines. **Subscription Rates:** $30.28 Individuals for a 13-week carrier; $27.25 Individuals for a 13-week carrier senior; $31.67 Individuals for a 13-week in-county; $28.51 Individuals for a 13-week in-county senior; $58.97 Individuals for a 26-week carrier; $53.07 Individuals for a 26-week in-county senior; $40 Individuals online. **URL:** http://breezecourier.com. **Mailing address:** PO Box 440, Taylorville, IL 62568. **Ad Rates:** BW $693; 4C $973; SAU $7.20; PCI $5.50. **Remarks:** Accepts advertising. **Circ:** Mon.-Fri. ★**5557**, Sun. ★**5676**.

11536 ■ WMKR-FM - 94.3
918 E Park St.
Taylorville, IL 62568-0169
Phone: (217)824-3395
Fax: (217)824-3301
Format: Country; Agricultural; Information. **Owner:** Miller Media Group, 2855 Coolidge Hwy., Ste. 201A, Troy, MI 48084, Ph: (248)528-3600. **Founded:** July 12, 1996. **Operating Hours**: Continuous. **Wattage**: 5,600. **Ad Rates:** Advertising accepted; rates available upon request. Combined advertising rates available with WTIM, WRAN, WKEI, WJRE, WYEC, WGEN. **Mailing address:** PO Box 169, Taylorville, IL 62568-0169. **URL:** http://www.taylorvilledailynews.com.

WRAN-FM - See Shelbyville

11537 ■ WTIM-FM - 97.3
918 E Pk.
Taylorville, IL 62568
Phone: (217)824-3395
Fax: (214)824-3301
Free: 866-500-9726
Format: News; Talk; Sports. **Networks:** Illinois Farm Bureau; CNN Radio. **Owner:** Miller Media Group, 2855 Coolidge Hwy., Ste. 201A, Troy, MI 48084, Ph: (248)528-3600. **Founded:** 1952. **Formerly**: WTIM-AM. **Operating Hours**: Continuous; 5% network, 95% local. **Wattage**: 4,600. **Ad Rates:** Advertising accepted; rates available upon request. Combined advertising rates available with WMKR, WRAN, WKEI, WJRE, WYEC, WSEN. **Mailing address:** P.O. Box 169, Taylorville, IL 62568. **URL:** http://www.taylorvilledailynews.com.

TECHNY

11538 ■ Divine Word Missionaries
Divine Word Missionaries
1835 Waukegan Rd.
Techny, IL 60082
Phone: (847)272-7600
Free: 800-275-0626
Publisher's E-mail: info@svdmissions.org
Magazine reporting on the Society's missionary activities. **Freq:** Quarterly. **Alt. Formats:** PDF. **URL:** http://www.svdmissions.org/news-and-events/magazine.aspx; http://www.svdvocations.org/Missionaries.aspx. **Mailing address:** PO Box 6099, Techny, IL 60082-6099. **Remarks:** Advertising not accepted. **Circ:** Free 210000.

TINLEY PARK

Will Co. Cook Co. (NE). 23 m SW of Chicago.

11539 ■ Daily Southtown
Sun-Times Media L.L.C.
6901 W 159th St.
Tinley Park, IL 60477
Phone: (708)633-4800
Fax: (708)633-5999
Publisher's E-mail: customerservice@suntimes.com
General newspaper. **Freq:** Mon.-Sun. (morn.). **Print Method:** Offset. **Cols./Page:** 6. **Col. Width:** 25 nonpareils. **Col. Depth:** 301 agate lines. **Key Personnel:** Michelle Homes, Editor, phone: (708)633-6751. **URL:** http://www.chicagotribune.com/suburbs/daily-southtown. **Remarks:** Accepts advertising. **Circ:** (Not Reported).

11540 ■ WJYS-TV - 62
18600 S Oak Park Ave.
Tinley Park, IL 60477
Phone: (708)633-0001
Format: Religious. **Networks:** Independent. **Owner:** Jovon Broadcasting Inc., 18600 Oak Park Ave., Tinley Park, IL 60477, Ph: (708)633-0001, Fax: (708)633-0040. **Wattage**: 145,000 ERP. **Ad Rates:** Advertising accepted; rates available upon request. **URL:** http://www.wjys.tv.

TOLONO

Champaign Co. Champaign Co. (E). 10 m S of Urbana. Stock, poultry, grain farms.

11541 ■ Journal of the American Killifish Association
American Killifish Association
c/o Bob Meyer
733 County Road 600 E
Tolono, IL 61880
Phone: (508)643-4603
Publisher's E-mail: membership@aka.org
Journal containing variety of articles about new species of fish and other relevant ideas. **Freq:** Bimonthly. **Sub-**

Circulation: ★ = AAM; △ or • = BPA; ♦ = CAC; ❑ = VAC; ⊕ = PO Statement; ‡ = Publisher's Report; Boldface figures = sworn; Light figures = estimated.

scription Rates: Included in membership. **Alt. Formats:** PDF. **URL:** http://www.aka.org/aka/modules/content/index.php?id=17. **Remarks:** Accepts advertising. **Circ:** (Not Reported).

TRENTON

Clinton Co. Clinton Co. (SW). 20 m NE of Belleville. Grain, stock, dairy, poultry farms.

11542 ■ Sun
Sun Trenton Publishing
PO Box 118
Trenton, IL 62293
Phone: (618)224-9422
Fax: (618)224-2646
Publisher's E-mail: sybil@trentonsun.net
Community newspaper. **Founded:** July 01, 1880. **Freq:** Weekly (Wed.). **Print Method:** Offset. **Trim Size:** 17 3/4 x 23. **Cols./Page:** 8. **Col. Width:** 11 picas. **Col. Depth:** 21 inches. **Key Personnel:** Sybil Conley, Contact. **USPS:** 638-200. **Subscription Rates:** $21 Individuals; $35 Out of area; $40 Out of country. **URL:** http://www.trentonsun.net/. **Ad Rates:** GLR $.50; BW $294; SAU $3; PCI $1.75. **Remarks:** Color advertising not accepted. **Circ:** Paid ‡1750.

UNIVERSITY PARK

11543 ■ The GSU Innovator
Governors State University
1 University Pkwy.
University Park, IL 60484-0975
Phone: (708)534-5000
Collegiate newspaper (tabloid). **Freq:** Biweekly. **Print Method:** Offset. **Cols./Page:** 5. **Col. Width:** 21 nonpareils. **Col. Depth:** 223 agate lines. **ISSN:** 0888--8469 (print). **Subscription Rates:** Free. **URL:** http://opus.govst.edu/innovator/. **Ad Rates:** BW $200; 4C $350; PCI $5.18. **Remarks:** Accepts advertising. **Circ:** Free ‡3000.

URBANA

Champaign Co. Champaign Co. (E). 125 m SW of Chicago. University of Illinois. Manufactures scientific instruments, track and field equipment, paper cups, concrete products. Agriculture.

11544 ■ American Literary History
Oxford University Press
Dept. of English
608 S Wright St.
University of Illinois
Urbana, IL 61801-3668
Publication covering literature and writing. **Freq:** 4/yr. **Print Method:** Offset. **Trim Size:** 8 1/2 x 11. **Cols./Page:** 3. **Col. Width:** 43.5 nonpareils. **Key Personnel:** Prof. Gordon Hutner, Editor; William Cain, Editor; Richard Brodhead, Editor; David Bergman, Board Member; Robert A. Ferguson, Board Member; Lawrence Buell, Board Member; Bruce Burgett, Editor. **ISSN:** 0896--7148 (print); **EISSN:** 1468--4365 (electronic). **Subscription Rates:** £277 Institutions corporate, print and online; $413 Institutions corporate, print and online; €374 Institutions corporate, print and online; £220 Institutions print and online; $330 Institutions print and online; €298 Institutions print and online; £61 Individuals print only; $91 Individuals print only; €84 Individuals print only; £44 Members print only; $65 Members print only; €60 Members print only. **URL:** http://alh.oxfordjournals.org/. **Remarks:** Accepts advertising. **Circ:** (Not Reported).

11545 ■ Analytical Chemistry
American Chemical Society
c/o Jonathan Sweedler, Editor
University of Illinois
Dept. of Chemistry
600 S Mathews Ave., 63-5
Urbana, IL 61801
Phone: (217)244-7866
Fax: (217)265-6290
Publisher's E-mail: help@acs.org
Journal covering measurement science. **Freq:** Semimonthly. **Print Method:** Offset. **Trim Size:** 8 3/16 x 11 1/4. **Cols./Page:** 3 and 2. **Col. Width:** 26 and 40 nonpareils. **Col. Depth:** 140 agate lines. **Key Personnel:** Jonathan V. Sweedler, Editor-in-Chief, phone: (217)244-7866, fax: (217)265-6290. **ISSN:** 0003--2700 (print); **EISSN:** 1520--6882 (electronic). **Online:** American Chemical Society American Chemical Society. **URL:** http://pubs.acs.org/journal/ancham. **Ad Rates:** BW $4520; 4C $5880; PCI $210. **Remarks:** Accepts advertising. **Circ:** ‡12410.

11546 ■ AOCS INFORM
American Oil Chemists' Society
2710 S Boulder Dr.
Urbana, IL 61802-6996
Phone: (217)359-2344
Fax: (217)351-8091
Publisher's E-mail: general@aocs.org
Magazine providing international news on fats, oils, surfactants, detergents and related materials. **Freq:** Monthly. **ISSN:** 0897--8026 (print). **Subscription Rates:** $195 U.S. non member; $230 Out of country non member; $320 Individuals non member airmail for outside US; Free members. **Alt. Formats:** Download. **URL:** http://www.aocs.org/Membership/content.cfm?ItemNumber=956. **Mailing address:** PO Box 17190, Urbana, IL 61803-7190. **Remarks:** Accepts advertising. **Circ:** (Not Reported).

11547 ■ Behavioral & Social Sciences Librarian
Routledge Journals Taylor & Francis Group
c/o Lisa Romero, Ed.
Communication Library
122 Gregory Hall, 810 S Wright St.
Urbana, IL 61801
Peer-reviewed journal focusing on all aspects of library information in the social and behavioral sciences. **Freq:** Quarterly. **Trim Size:** 6 x 8 3/8. **Key Personnel:** Lisa Romero, Editor. **ISSN:** 0163-9269 (print); **EISSN:** 1544-4546 (electronic). **Subscription Rates:** $116 Individuals online only; $133 Individuals print + online; $365 Institutions online only; $417 Institutions print + online. **URL:** http://www.tandfonline.com/loi/wbss20#.Vej2ISWqqko; http://www.tandfonline.com/toc/wbss20/current#.Vej2DiWqqkq. **Ad Rates:** BW $315; 4C $550. **Remarks:** Accepts advertising. **Circ:** 367.

11548 ■ Brain, Behavior, and Immunity
Psychoneuroimmunology Research Society
Laboratory of Immunophysiology
University of Illinois at Urbana-Champaign
227 Edward R. Madigan Laboratory
1201 W Gregory Dr.
Urbana, IL 61801
Publisher's E-mail: pnirs@pnirs.org
Freq: 8/year Bimonthly. **Trim Size:** 6 7/8 x 10. **Key Personnel:** Kelly W. Kelley, Editor-in-Chief; R. Dantzer, Associate Editor; M. Irwin, Board Member. **ISSN:** 0889-1591 (print). **Subscription Rates:** $495 Individuals print; $618.97 Institutions online - access for 5 users and 4 years of archives; $1485 Institutions print; Included in membership. **URL:** http://www.journals.elsevier.com/brain-behavior-and-immunity; http://www.pnirs.org/society/society_journal.cfm. **Remarks:** Accepts advertising. **Circ:** (Not Reported).

11549 ■ Champaign County Genealogical Society Quarterly
Champaign County Genealogical Society of Illinois
c/o Champaign County Historical Archives
210 W Green St.
Urbana, IL 61801-3283
Phone: (217)367-4025
Publisher's E-mail: webmaster@ilccgs.org
Genealogical publication. **Freq:** Quarterly March, June, September and December. **Print Method:** Offset. **Trim Size:** 8 1/2 x 11. **Key Personnel:** Joan Lund, Editor; Gina Gericke, Treasurer. **URL:** http://ilccgs.org/about.php. **Remarks:** Advertising not accepted. **Circ:** (Not Reported).

11550 ■ College Composition and Communication
Conference on College Composition and Communication
1111 W Kenyon Rd.
Urbana, IL 61801-1010
Phone: (217)328-3870
Free: 877-369-6283
Publication E-mail: cccedit@yahoo.com
Magazine providing forum for teachers of writing in two- and four-year colleges. Contributions discuss the theory and practice of teaching composition or communication, and relate them to the teaching of literature and language. **Freq:** Quarterly (September, December, February, and June). **Print Method:** Offset. **Trim Size:** 7 x 9 1/4. **Cols./Page:** 1. **Col. Width:** 56 nonpareils. **Col. Depth:** 102 agate lines. **Key Personnel:** Kathleen Blake Yancey, Editor; Rona Smith, Editor. **ISSN:** 0010--096X (print). **Subscription Rates:** $75 Nonmembers; $25 Members; $12.50 Students; $12.50 Individuals Emeritus; $9 Individuals single issue for nonmembers; $6 Individuals single issue for members. **URL:** http://www.ncte.org/cccc/ccc. **Remarks:** Accepts advertising. **Circ:** 7000, 7000, 10000.

11551 ■ College English
National Council of Teachers of English
1111 W Kenyon Rd.
Urbana, IL 61801-1010
Phone: (217)328-3870
Fax: (217)328-9645
Free: 877-369-6283
Publication E-mail: collengsubs@gmail.com
Magazine containing articles on the working concepts of criticism, the nature of critical and scholarly reasoning, pedagogy and educational theory, and issues of concern to college English teachers. Contemporary poetry, reviews of recent books, Comment and Response section. **Freq:** Bimonthly September, November, January, March, May, and July. **Print Method:** Offset. Uses mats. **Trim Size:** 6 3/4 x 9 1/4. **Cols./Page:** 2 and 1. **Col. Width:** 29 and 60 nonpareils. **Col. Depth:** 106 agate lines. **Key Personnel:** Kelly Ritter, Editor. **ISSN:** 0010--0994 (print); **EISSN:** 2161--8178 (electronic). **Subscription Rates:** $25 Members; $75 Nonmembers; $12.50 Students; $12.50 Individuals Emeritus. **URL:** http://www.ncte.org/journals/ce. **Remarks:** Accepts advertising. **Circ:** 5200.

11552 ■ Combustion Theory & Modelling
Taylor & Francis Group Journals
c/o Prof. Moshe Matalon, Ed.-in-Ch.
Department of Mechanical Science & Engineering,
University of Illinois at Urbana-Champaign
Mechanical Engineering Bldg., 1206 W Green St., MC-244
Urbana, IL 61801-2906
Publisher's E-mail: customerservice@taylorandfrancis.com
Freq: 6/year. **Key Personnel:** Prof. Moshe Matalon, Editor-in-Chief; Prof. Mitchell D. Smooke, Editor-in-Chief; Jyh-Yuan Chen, Board Member; Satoru Ishizuka, Board Member; Ashwani Kapila, Board Member; Gaetano Continillo, Board Member; John Buckmaster, Board Member; Vincent Giovangigli, Board Member. **ISSN:** 1364--7830 (print); **EISSN:** 1741--3559 (electronic). **Subscription Rates:** $387 Individuals print; $891 Institutions online; $1018 Institutions print and online. **URL:** http://www.tandfonline.com/toc/tctm20/current. **Remarks:** Advertising not accepted. **Circ:** (Not Reported).

11553 ■ The Council Chronicle
National Council of Teachers of English
1111 W Kenyon Rd.
Urbana, IL 61801-1010
Phone: (217)328-3870
Fax: (217)328-9645
Free: 877-369-6283
Publication E-mail: chronicle@ncte.org
Magazine for teachers of English or language arts at all levels who are members of the National Council of Teachers of English. **Founded:** 1991. **Freq:** 3/year. **Print Method:** Offset. **Trim Size:** 10 3/8 x 12 3/4. **Cols./Page:** 4. **Col. Width:** 14.5 picas. **Col. Depth:** 78 picas. **ISSN:** 1057-4190 (print). **URL:** http://www.ncte.org/magazine. **Ad Rates:** BW $2,100; 4C $2,700. **Remarks:** Accepts advertising. **Circ:** 35000.

11554 ■ Current Opinion in Solid State & Materials Science
Elsevier
c/o I. Robertson, Editor-in-Chief
University of Illinois at Urbana-Champaign
1304 W Green St.
Urbana, IL 61801
Publisher's E-mail: t.reller@elsevier.com
Journal focused on latest research and advances in materials science. **Freq:** 6/year. **Print Method:** Offset. **Trim Size:** 10 1/4 x 13 3/8. **Cols./Page:** 3 and 5. **Col. Width:** 16 1/2 and 10 picas. **Col. Depth:** 70 picas. **Key Personnel:** I. Robertson, Editor-in-Chief. **ISSN:** 1359--

0286 (print). **Subscription Rates:** $524 Individuals print; $1059.20 Institutions ejournal; $3178 Institutions print. **URL:** http://www.journals.elsevier.com/current-opinion-in-solid-state-and-materials-science. **Circ:** (Not Reported).

11555 ■ Discrete Mathematics
Elsevier B.V.
c/o Douglas B. West, Ed.-in-Ch.
Department of Mathematics
University of Illinois
Urbana, IL 61801-2975
Publisher's E-mail: ensci@elsevier.com
Journal publishing research articles on all areas of combinatorial mathematics and related areas. Covers graph and hypergraph theory, network theory, coding theory, block designs, lattice theory, the theory of partially ordered sets, combinatorial geometrics, matroid theory, extremal set theory, logic and automata, matrices, polyhedra, and discrete probability theory. **Freq:** Monthly. **ISSN:** 0012--365X (print). **Subscription Rates:** $3726.40 Institutions e-journal, access for 5 users and access to 4 years of archives; $3944 Institutions print. **URL:** http://www.journals.elsevier.com/discrete-mathematics. **Remarks:** Accepts advertising. **Circ:** (Not Reported).

11556 ■ English Education: Journal of the Conference on English Education (CEE)
National Council of Teachers of English
1111 W Kenyon Rd.
Urbana, IL 61801-1010
Phone: (217)328-3870
Fax: (217)328-9645
Free: 877-369-6283
Publication E-mail: englisheducationjournal@gmail.com
Magazine containing articles for instructors involved in teacher preparation and in service education. **Freq:** Quarterly Published October, January, April, and July. **Print Method:** Offset. **Trim Size:** 6 x 9. **Cols./Page:** 1. **Col. Width:** 54 nonpareils. **Col. Depth:** 97 agate lines. **Key Personnel:** Leslie S. Rush, Editor; Lisa Scherff, Editor. **ISSN:** 0007--8204 (print). **Subscription Rates:** $75 Nonmembers; $25 Members; $12.50 Students; $12.50 Individuals emeritus. **URL:** http://www.ncte.org/journals/ee. **Ad Rates:** BW $575. **Remarks:** Accepts advertising. **Circ:** 2000, 3200.

11557 ■ English Leadership Quarterly
National Council of Teachers of English
1111 W Kenyon Rd.
Urbana, IL 61801-1010
Phone: (217)328-3870
Fax: (217)328-9645
Free: 877-369-6283
Journal containing short articles on a variety of issues important to decision makers in the English language arts. **Freq:** Quarterly. **Key Personnel:** Susan L. Groenke, Editor. **ISSN:** 0738--1409 (print). **Subscription Rates:** $75 Nonmembers; $25 Members; $12.50 Students emeritus. **URL:** http://www.ncte.org/journals/elq. **Remarks:** Advertising accepted; rates available upon request. **Circ:** (Not Reported).

11558 ■ Illinois Alumni: The University of Illinois Alumni Association Magazine
University of Illinois Alumni Association
Alice Campbell Alumni Ctr.
601 S Lincoln Ave.
Urbana, IL 61801
Phone: (217)333-1471
Fax: (217)244-8527
Free: 800-355-2586
Publisher's E-mail: illinoisalumni@uillinois.edu
Alumni association magazine. **Freq:** Quarterly September, December, March and June. **Print Method:** Offset. **Trim Size:** 8 3/8 x 10 7/8. **Key Personnel:** Vanessa Faurie, Editor; Beatrice Pavia, Managing Editor; Mary Timmins, Associate Editor. **ISSN:** 1096--5866 (print). **URL:** http://illinoisalumni.org/stories. **Formerly:** Illinois Quarterly. **Remarks:** Accepts advertising. **Circ:** (Not Reported).

11559 ■ Illinois Journal of Mathematics
University of Illinois Dept. of Mathematics
1409 W Green St.
Urbana, IL 61801
Phone: (217)333-3350
Fax: (217)333-9576
Publication E-mail: ijm@math.uiuc.edu
Mathematics research journal. **Freq:** Quarterly. **Print Method:** Offset. **Trim Size:** 6 x 9. **Cols./Page:** 1. **Col. Width:** 56 nonpareils. **Col. Depth:** 106 agate lines. **Key Personnel:** Mario Bonk, Board Member; Steven Bradlow, Board Member; Luchezar L. Avramov, Board Member. **ISSN:** 0019--2082 (print). **Subscription Rates:** $350 Individuals print + online; plus 30 postage outside U.S., Canada and Mexico; $310 Individuals online only. **URL:** http://ijm.math.illinois.edu; http://www.math.uiuc.edu/Publications. **Circ:** Paid ‡1200.

11560 ■ International Journal of Number Theory
World Scientific Publishing Company Private Ltd.
c/o Bruce C. Berndt, Mng. Ed.
University of Illinois at Urbana-Champaign
Dept. of Mathematics
1409 W Green St.
Urbana, IL 61801-2975
Phone: (217)333-3970
Fax: (217)333-9576
Publisher's E-mail: wspc@wspc.com.sg
Peer-reviewed journal publishing original research papers and review articles on all areas of Number Theory, including elementary number theory, analytic number theory, algebraic number theory, arithmetic algebraic geometry, geometry of numbers, diophantine equations, diophantine approximation, transcendental number theory, probabilistic number theory, modular forms, multiplicative number theory, additive number theory, partitions and computational number theory. **Freq:** 8/year 8/yr. **Key Personnel:** Bruce C. Berndt, Managing Editor; Umberto Zannier, Managing Editor, phone: (30)050 509262; R. Sujatha, Managing Editor. **ISSN:** 1793--0421 (print); **EISSN:** 1793--7310 (electronic). **Subscription Rates:** $1050 print and online - institution and libraries; £670 print and online - institution and libraries; S$1543 print and online - institution and libraries; $937 online - institution and libraries; £598 online - institution and libraries; S$1377 online - institution and libraries. **URL:** http://www.worldscientific.com/worldscinet/ijnt. **Circ:** (Not Reported).

11561 ■ The Journal of Aesthetic Education
University of Illinois Press
c/o Pradeep A. Dhillon, Editor
University of Illinois
377 Education Bldg.
1310 S 6th St., MC-708
Urbana, IL 61801
Phone: (217)333-5236
Publisher's E-mail: uipress@uillinois.edu
Journal exploring aspects of aesthetic and humanities education. **Freq:** Quarterly. **Print Method:** Offset. **Trim Size:** 6 x 9. **Cols./Page:** 1. **Col. Width:** 52 nonpareils. **Col. Depth:** 107 agate lines. **Key Personnel:** Laurie Matheson, Editor-in-Chief, phone: (217)244-4685. **ISSN:** 0021--8510 (print); **EISSN:** 1543--7809 (electronic). **Subscription Rates:** $50 Individuals print or online; $55 Individuals print and online; $140 Institutions print or online; $152 Institutions print and online; $25 Students online only; $10 Canada and Mexico; $35 Other countries; $25 Institutions single issue; $95 Institutions back issue. **URL:** http://www.press.uillinois.edu/journals/jae.html. **Ad Rates:** BW $225. **Remarks:** Accepts advertising. **Circ:** Paid 250.

11562 ■ Journal of Educational Finance
University of Illinois Press
c/o Kern Alexander, Ed.
406 W Florida Ave.
Urbana, IL 61801
Phone: (217)344-0237
Fax: (217)344-6963
Publisher's E-mail: uipress@uillinois.edu
Journal covering educational funding. **Freq:** Quarterly summer, spring, fall and winter. **Key Personnel:** Kern Alexander, Editor. **ISSN:** 0098--9495 (print); **EISSN:** 1944--6470 (electronic). **Subscription Rates:** $70 Individuals print only; $120 Institutions print or online; $140 Institutions print + online; $40 Students print only; $25 Single issue; $65 Individuals back volumes. **URL:** http://www.press.uillinois.edu/journals/jef.html. **Remarks:** Accepts advertising. **Circ:** (Not Reported).

11563 ■ Journal of English and Germanic Philology: A Medieval Studies Journal
University of Illinois Press
c/o Charles D. Wright, Editor
208 English Bldg.
608 S Wright St., MC-718
Urbana, IL 61801
Publisher's E-mail: uipress@uillinois.edu
Philology journal. **Freq:** Quarterly. **Print Method:** Offset. **Trim Size:** 6 x 9. **Cols./Page:** 1. **Col. Width:** 52 nonpareils. **Col. Depth:** 101 agate lines. **Key Personnel:** Charles D. Wright, Editor; Marianne E. Kalinke, Editor. **ISSN:** 0363--6941 (print); **EISSN:** 1945--662X (electronic). **Subscription Rates:** $56 Individuals print or online; $62 Individuals print + online; $163 Institutions print or online; $186 Institutions print + online; $25 Students online only; $30 Institutions single issue; $115 Institutions back issue. **URL:** http://www.press.uillinois.edu/journals/jegp.html. **Ad Rates:** BW $200. **Remarks:** Advertising accepted; rates available upon request. **Circ:** 350.

11564 ■ Journal of Macromolecular Science, Part B: Physics
Taylor & Francis Group Journals
c/o Phillip H. Geil, Exec. Ed.
Dept. Materials Science & Engineering
University of Illinois
1304 W Green St.
Urbana, IL 61801
Phone: (217)333-0149
Fax: (217)333-2736
Publisher's E-mail: customerservice@taylorandfrancis.com
Journal focusing on the publication of significant fundamental contributions to the physics of macromolecular solids and liquids. **Freq:** Monthly. **Key Personnel:** Phillip H. Geil, Executive Editor; Anthony J. Ryan, Advisor, Board Member. **ISSN:** 0022--2348 (print); **EISSN:** 1525--609X (electronic). **Subscription Rates:** $1340 Individuals print only; $6481 Institutions online only; $7407 Institutions print and online. **URL:** http://www.tandfonline.com/toc/lmsb20/current. **Circ:** (Not Reported).

11565 ■ Journal of Spatial Hydrology
Journal of Spatial Hydrology
c/o Dr. Prasanta K. Kalita, EDC
University of Illinois at Urbana-Champaign
S-209, Greater Kailash-I
1304 W Pennsylvania Ave.
Urbana, IL 61801
Phone: (217)333-0945
Fax: (217)244-0323
Journal that publishes peer-reviewed scientific research the field of Earth Sciences. **Freq:** Semiannual. **Key Personnel:** Dr. Daniel P. Ames, Editor; Ashok Verma, Editor. **ISSN:** 1530--4736 (print). **Alt. Formats:** CD-ROM. **URL:** http://www.spatialhydrology.net/index.php/JOSH. **Remarks:** Accepts advertising. **Circ:** (Not Reported).

11566 ■ Journal of Surfactants and Detergents
American Oil Chemists' Society
2710 S Boulder Dr.
Urbana, IL 61802-6996
Phone: (217)359-2344
Fax: (217)351-8091
Publisher's E-mail: general@aocs.org
Peer-reviewed journal covering practical and theoretical aspects of chemical and petrochemical surfactants, soaps, and detergents. **Freq:** Monthly. **Print Method:** Offset. **Trim Size:** 11.975 x 21 1/2. **Cols./Page:** 6. **Col. Width:** 11 picas. **Col. Depth:** 301 agate lines. **Key Personnel:** Jean-Louis Salager, Editor. **ISSN:** 1097--3958 (print). **USPS:** 398-840. **Subscription Rates:** $185 Members; $828 Individuals; $180 Members. **URL:** http://www.aocs.org/Journals/jsd.cfm. **Mailing address:** PO Box 17190, Urbana, IL 61803-7190. **Remarks:** Accepts advertising. **Circ:** (Not Reported).

11567 ■ Language Arts: Children's Literature in the 21st Century
National Council of Teachers of English
1111 W Kenyon Rd.
Urbana, IL 61801-1010
Phone: (217)328-3870
Fax: (217)328-9645
Free: 877-369-6283

Circulation: ★ = AAM; △ or • = BPA; ♦ = CAC; ❑ = VAC; ⊕ = PO Statement; ‡ = Publisher's Report; Boldface figures = sworn; Light figures = estimated.

Magazine containing practical, classroom-tested ideas for helping children (grades K-8) learn to read, write, and speak more effectively. Covers such topics as language development, ethnic studies, creativity, and uses of varied media. Regular features include new research findings, instructional materials, and current books for children. **Freq:** 6/year Published September, November, January, March, May, and July. **Print Method:** Offset. **Trim Size:** 8 1/2 x 11. **Cols./Page:** 2 and 1. **Col. Width:** 18 picas. **Col. Depth:** 52 picas. **Key Personnel:** Peggy Albers, Editor; Caitlin Dooley, Editor; Amy Seely Flint, Editor; Teri Holbrook, Editor; Laura May, Editor. **ISSN:** 0360--9170 (print). **Subscription Rates:** $75 Nonmembers; $25 Members; $12.50 Students. **URL:** http://www.ncte.org/journals/la. **Ad Rates:** 4C $1,800; BW $1,200. **Remarks:** Accepts advertising. **Circ:** 6000, ‡5000.

11568 ■ Plant Physiology: American Society of Plant Biologists
American Society of Plant Biologists
c/o Donald R. Ort, Ed.-in-Ch.
U.S. Dept. of Agriculture/Agricultural Research Service
University of Illinois, Dept. of Plant Biology
190 ERML, 1201 W Gregory Dr.
Urbana, IL 61801-3838
Phone: (217)333-2093
Fax: (217)244-0656
Publisher's E-mail: info@aspb.org
Journal on plant science. **Freq:** Monthly. **Print Method:** Offset. **Trim Size:** 8 1/8 x 10 7/8. **Cols./Page:** 2. **Col. Width:** 3 5/16 inches. **Col. Depth:** 9 inches. **Key Personnel:** Michael R. Blatt, Editor-in-Chief, phone: 330-2381; Donald R. Ort, Editor-in-Chief; Bonnie Bartel, Associate Editor, phone: (713)348-5602. **ISSN:** 0032--0889 (print); **EISSN:** 1532--2548 (electronic). **Subscription Rates:** $240 Members regular; $475 Nonmembers; $175 Members postdoctoral/student. **URL:** http://www.plantphysiol.org. **Ad Rates:** BW $1106; 4C $1095. **Remarks:** Accepts advertising. **Circ:** ‡1600.

11569 ■ Quarterly Review of Economics and Finance
Elsevier - Mosby Journal Div.
University of Illinois at Urbana-Chanpaign
201 N Goodwin Ave.
Urbana, IL 61801
Phone: (217)333-2681
Fax: (217)333-1398
Publisher's E-mail: info@elsevier.com
Magazine on economics and finance. **Founded:** 1961. **Freq:** Quarterly. **Print Method:** Offset. **Trim Size:** 6 x 9. **Cols./Page:** 1. **Col. Width:** 28 picas. **Col. Depth:** 52 picas. **Key Personnel:** H.S. Esfahani, Editor-in-Chief; R. Aggarwal, Board Member; R.E. Baldwin, Board Member; A. Beller, Board Member. **ISSN:** 1062-9769 (print). **Subscription Rates:** $142 Individuals print; $760 Institutions print or online. **URL:** http://www.journals.elsevier.com/the-quarterly-review-of-economics-and-finance. **Formerly**: Quarterly Review of Economics & Business. **Remarks:** Accepts advertising. **Circ:** (Not Reported).

11570 ■ Research in the Teaching of English
National Council of Teachers of English
1111 W Kenyon Rd.
Urbana, IL 61801-1010
Phone: (217)328-3870
Fax: (217)328-9645
Free: 877-369-6283
Publication E-mail: rte.ncte@gmail.com
Magazine on language teaching and learning. A forum for researchers, and a background source for teachers and curriculum planners at all levels. **Freq:** Quarterly August, November, February, and May. **Print Method:** Offset. **Trim Size:** 6 x 9. **Cols./Page:** 1. **Col. Width:** 56 nonpareils. **Col. Depth:** 102 agate lines. **Key Personnel:** Ellen Cushman, PhD, Editor; Mary Juzwik, Editor; Mark Dressman, Editor; Sarah McCarthey, Editor; Paul Prior, Editor. **ISSN:** 0034--527X (print). **Subscription Rates:** $75 Nonmembers; $25 Members; $12.50 Individuals emeritus; $12.50 Students. **URL:** http://www.ncte.org/journals/rte. **Also known as**: RTE. **Remarks:** Accepts advertising. **Circ:** 3000.

11571 ■ Steward Anthropological Society Journal
University of Illinois Department of Anthropology
109 Davenport Hall
607 S Matthews Ave.
Urbana, IL 61801
Phone: (217)333-3616
Fax: (217)244-3490
Publication E-mail: stewardjournal@uiuc.edu
Scholarly journal of anthropological interest. **Freq:** Annual. **Print Method:** Web offset. **Trim Size:** 5 x 8. **Cols./Page:** 1. **Col. Width:** 4 inches. **Col. Depth:** 7 inches. **Key Personnel:** Kayoko Toshihara. **ISSN:** 0039--1344 (print). **Subscription Rates:** $18 Individuals; $25 Institutions. **Remarks:** Advertising not accepted. **Circ:** Paid 150.

11572 ■ Studies in the Linguistic Sciences
University of Illinois at Urbana-Champaign - Subscriptions Department
4080 Foreign Language Bldg.
707 S Mathews Ave., MC-168
Urbana, IL 61801
Phone: (217)333-3563
Fax: (217)244-8430
Publication E-mail: slsillinois@gmail.com
Academic journal covering linguistics. **Freq:** Semiannual. **Key Personnel:** Daniel Ross, Editor. **ISSN:** 0049--2388 (print). **Alt. Formats:** PDF. **URL:** http://sls.linguistics.illinois.edu. **Remarks:** Advertising not accepted. **Circ:** (Not Reported).

11573 ■ Teaching English in the Two-Year College
National Council of Teachers of English
1111 W Kenyon Rd.
Urbana, IL 61801-1010
Phone: (217)328-3870
Fax: (217)328-9645
Free: 877-369-6283
Journal providing a national forum for English teachers to share and find professional ideas and information. **Freq:** Quarterly (September, December, March, and May). **Print Method:** Offset. **Trim Size:** 6 x 9. **Cols./Page:** 2. **Col. Width:** 13.5 picas. **Col. Depth:** 45 picas. **Key Personnel:** Rona Smith, Editor; Kurt Austin, Division Director; Jeff Sommers, Editor; Shellie Elson, Coordinator. **ISSN:** 0098--6291 (print). **Subscription Rates:** $25 Members; $75 Nonmembers; $12.50 Students; $12.50 Individuals emeritus. **URL:** http://www.ncte.org/journals/tetyc. **Also known as**: TETYC. **Remarks:** Accepts advertising. **Circ:** 3000.

11574 ■ Thin Solid Films
RELX Group P.L.C.
c/o Prof. J.E. Greene, Editor-in-Chief
University of Illinois at Urbana-Champaign
Frederick Seitz Materials Research Laboratory
104 S Goodwin Ave.
Urbana, IL 61801
Publisher's E-mail: amsterdam@relx.com
Journal reporting advances in thin-film production, which is a convergence of materials science, surface science and applied physics. **Freq:** 24/yr. **Key Personnel:** Prof. J.E. Greene, Editor-in-Chief; P. Desjardins, Associate Editor. **ISSN:** 0040--6090 (print). **Subscription Rates:** $19167 Institutions print; $15972.66 Institutions online. **URL:** http://www.journals.elsevier.com/thin-solid-films. **Circ:** (Not Reported).

11575 ■ Voices from the Middle
National Council of Teachers of English
1111 W Kenyon Rd.
Urbana, IL 61801-1010
Phone: (217)328-3870
Fax: (217)328-9645
Free: 877-369-6283
Journal offering articles on research and best practices in middle level reading, writing, speaking, and listening in the visual and language arts. **Freq:** Quarterly September, December, March, and May. **Key Personnel:** Doug Fisher, Editor. **ISSN:** 1074--4762 (print). **Subscription Rates:** $75 Nonmembers; $25 Members; $12.50 Students emeritus. **URL:** http://www.ncte.org/journals/vm. **Ad Rates:** 4C $1800; BW $1340. **Remarks:** Accepts advertising. **Circ:** (Not Reported).

11576 ■ UPTV-TV - 6
400 S Vine St.
Urbana, IL 61801
Phone: (217)384-2452
URL: http://urbanaillinois.us/terms/uptv.

11577 ■ WBCP-AM - 1580
904 N 4th St., Ste. D
Champaign, IL 61820
Phone: (217)359-1580
Fax: (217)359-1583
Email: info@wbcp1580.com
Format: Urban Contemporary; Adult Contemporary. **Networks:** American Urban Radio; ABC. **Founded:** 1948. **Operating Hours**: Continuous. **ADI**: Springfield-Decatur-Champaign, IL. **Wattage**: 250. **Ad Rates:** Noncommercial. **URL:** http://wbcp1580.com.

11578 ■ WEBX-FM - 93.5
2702 Boulder Dr.
Urbana, IL 61802
Phone: (217)367-1195
Format: Album-Oriented Rock (AOR); Sports; Talk. **Owner:** Radiostar, Inc, at above address. **Operating Hours**: Continuous. **Key Personnel:** Corey Berkemann, Gen. Mgr., corey@cu-radio.com; Jon Mayotte, Dir. of Programs, mayo@cu-radio.com; Josh Laskowski, Promotions Dir., promo@cu-radio.com. **Wattage**: 5,000 ERP. **Ad Rates:** Noncommercial; Advertising accepted; rates available upon request. **URL:** http://www.espncu.com.

11579 ■ WILL-AM - 580
Campbell Hall for Public Telecommunication
300 N Goodwin Ave.
Urbana, IL 61801
Phone: (217)333-7300
Fax: (217)244-2656
Format: News; Talk; Agricultural. **Networks:** National Public Radio (NPR); American Public Radio (APR). **Owner:** University of Illinois, 601 E John St., Champaign, IL 61820. **Founded:** 1922. **Formerly**: WRM-AM. **Operating Hours**: Continuous. **Key Personnel:** Jack Brighton, Contact; Jay Pearce, Station Mgr. **Wattage**: 5,000. **Ad Rates:** Noncommercial. **URL:** http://will.illinois.edu/tags/will-am.

11580 ■ WILL-FM - 90.9
300 N Goodwin Ave.
Urbana, IL 61801-2316
Phone: (217)333-7300
Fax: (217)244-2656
Email: willamfm@mx.uillinois.edu
Format: Classical; Jazz; Folk; World Beat; Big Band/Nostalgia. **Key Personnel:** Rick Finnie, Chief Engineer. **Ad Rates:** Noncommercial. **URL:** http://www.will.illinois.edu.

11581 ■ WILL-TV - 12
Campbell Hall for Public Telecommunication
300 N Goodwin Ave.
Urbana, IL 61801
Phone: (217)333-7300
Email: will-tv@uiuc.edu
Networks: Public Broadcasting Service (PBS); National Public Radio (NPR). **Owner:** University of Illinois, 601 E John St., Champaign, IL 61820. **Founded:** 1955. **Operating Hours**: Continuous. **ADI**: Springfield-Decatur-Champaign, IL. **Key Personnel:** Carl Caldwell, Station Mgr.; David Thiel, Dir. of Programs; Rick Finnie, Chief Engineer; Mike Pritchard, Contact, mrp@uiuc.edu. **Local Programs**: *Illinois Gardener*. **URL:** http://www.will.illinois.edu.

11582 ■ WQQB-FM - 96.1
2702 Boulder Dr.
Urbana, IL 61802
Phone: (217)328-9600
Fax: (217)367-3291
Format: Eclectic. **Key Personnel:** Ken Cunningham, Prog. Dir.; Josh Laskowski, Div. Dir. **Ad Rates:** Advertising accepted; rates available upon request. **URL:** http://www.wqqb.com.

11583 ■ WRFU-FM - 104.5
202 S Broadway, No. 112
Urbana, IL 61801
Phone: (217)344-2536
Format: Eclectic; News; Information. **Owner:** Creative Commons, 171 2nd St., Ste. 300, San Francisco, CA 94105-3810, Ph: (415)369-8480, Fax: (415)278-9419. **Operating Hours**: Continuous. **Ad Rates:** Noncommercial; underwriting available.

VANDALIA

Fayette Co. Fayette Co. (S). 68 m NE of St. Louis Mo. Manufactures pencils, draperies, mechanical seals, concrete building products, feed, electric transformers, telephone booths, plastic bottles. Oil wells. Grain, dairy farms. Corn, wheat, beans.

11584 ■ Vandalia Leader Union
Landmark Community Newspapers L.L.C.
229 S Fifth St.
Vandalia, IL 62471
Phone: (618)283-3374
Publisher's E-mail: marketing@lcni.com
Community newspaper. **Freq:** Weekly (Wed.). **Print Method:** Offset. **Cols./Page:** 6. **Col. Width:** 12 picas. **Col. Depth:** 301 agate lines. **Key Personnel:** Rich Bauer, Managing Editor; David Bell, Publisher; Jonathan Stark, Editor. **URL:** http://www.leaderunion.com. **Ad Rates:** BW $942; 4C $1,173; SAU $7. **Remarks:** Accepts advertising. **Circ:** 5300.

11585 ■ WKRV-FM - 107.1
232 S 4th St.
Vandalia, IL 62471-2810
Phone: (618)283-2325
Email: wkrv@sbcglobal.net
Format: Classical. **Key Personnel:** Todd Stapleton, Contact, tstapleton@cromwellradio.com. **URL:** http://www.vandaliaradio.com/pages/14290313.php.

11586 ■ WPMB-AM - 1500
232 S Fourth St.
Vandalia, IL 62471
Phone: (618)283-2325
Fax: (618)283-1503
Format: News; Information. **Simulcasts:** 6-8am, Noon, 5-5:15pm. **Owner:** The Cromwell Group, Inc., 1824 Murfreesboro Rd., Nashville, TN 37217, Ph: (615)361-7560, Fax: (615)366-4313. **Founded:** 1963. **Operating Hours:** 12 hours Daily; 5% network, 95% local. **Key Personnel:** Todd Stapleton, Contact, tstapleton@cromwellradio.com. **Wattage:** 250. **Ad Rates:** $9-15.25 for 30 seconds; $11.25-18.25 for 60 seconds. **URL:** http://www.vandaliaradio.com.

11587 ■ WVNL-FM - 91.7
PO Box 140
Carlinville, IL 62626
Phone: (217)854-4800
Fax: (217)854-4810
Owner: Illinois Bible Institute, c/o Lake Williamson Christian Conference Ctr. 17280 Lakeside Dr., Carlinville, IL 62626, Ph: (217)854-4820. **Wattage:** 100.

VERNON HILLS

Lake Co. Lake Co. (NE) 8 m N of Prairie View. Residential.

11588 ■ Fed Tech Magazine
CDW Corp.
200 N Milwaukee Ave.
Vernon Hills, IL 60061-1577
Phone: (847)465-6000
Fax: (847)465-6800
Free: 800-838-4239
Magazine offers information for IT buyers and implementers in government positions. **Freq:** Quarterly. **Key Personnel:** Jim Garlow, Publisher; Vanessa Roberts, Director, Editorial; Ryan Petersen, Editor-in-Chief. **URL:** http://www.fedtechmagazine.com. **Circ:** (Not Reported).

11589 ■ MHEDA Journal
Material Handling Equipment Distributors Association
201 US Highway 45
Vernon Hills, IL 60061
Phone: (847)680-3500
Fax: (847)362-6989
Publisher's E-mail: connect@mheda.org
Professional magazine covering the materials handling industry. **Freq:** Quarterly. **Key Personnel:** Jill Andreu, Publisher; Gregory Morrison, Contact. **Subscription Rates:** Included in membership. **URL:** http://www.themhedajournal.org. **Ad Rates:** BW $3319.50. **Remarks:** Advertising accepted; rates available upon request. **Circ:** (Not Reported).

VIENNA

Johnson Co. Johnson Co. (S). 34 m NW of Paducah, Ky. Nursery. Timber. Diversified farming. Corn, dairy products, beef cattle.

11590 ■ The Vienna Times
The Vienna Times
PO Box 457
Vienna, IL 62995
Phone: (618)658-4321
Fax: (618)658-4322
Publisher's E-mail: viennatimes@frontier.com
Community newspaper. **Founded:** 1879. **Freq:** Weekly (Thurs.). **Print Method:** Offset. **Cols./Page:** 6. **Col. Width:** 24 nonpareils. **Col. Depth:** 294 agate lines. **Key Personnel:** Lonnie J. Hinton, Publisher. **Subscription Rates:** $34 Individuals /year; $36 Out of state /year; $40 Out of area /year. **URL:** http://www.theviennatimes.com. **Ad Rates:** GLR $.24; BW $526.32; SAU $5.06. **Remarks:** Accepts advertising. **Circ:** ‡2600.

VILLA GROVE

Douglas Co. Douglas Co. (E). 23 m S of Champaign. Manufactures farm implements. Machine shop. Cannery. Grain elevator. Coal mining. Hybrid see growing. Diversified farming.

11591 ■ Villa Grove News
Holmes Publications
PO Box 20
Villa Grove, IL 61956-1522
Community newspaper. **Freq:** Weekly (Thurs.). **Print Method:** Offset. **Cols./Page:** 6. **Col. Width:** 29 nonpareils. **Col. Depth:** 294 agate lines. **Key Personnel:** Jeffrey W. Holmes, Editor. **Subscription Rates:** $25 Individuals; $30 Individuals out of state; $46 Individuals two years. **URL:** http://www.villagrovenews.com. **Remarks:** Accepts advertising. **Circ:** ‡1675.

VIRDEN

Sangamon Co. Macoupin Co. (SWC). 25 m SW of Springfield. Concrete block, tile, plants. Coal mines. Diversified farming. Corn, wheat, soybeans, cattle, hogs.

11592 ■ The Virden Recorder
Gold Nugget Publications Inc.
PO Box 440
Virden, IL 62690-0440
Phone: (217)965-3355
Fax: (217)965-4512
Community newspaper. **Freq:** Weekly (Wed.). **Print Method:** Offset. **Cols./Page:** 7. **Col. Width:** 28 nonpareils. **Col. Depth:** 300 agate lines. **Key Personnel:** Norris E. Jones, Editor; Charles E. Jones, Publisher; Dorothy Jones, Publisher; Nathan E. Jones, Manager, Advertising. **URL:** http://gnnews.net. **Ad Rates:** GLR $.33; BW $500; SAU $4. **Remarks:** Accepts advertising. **Circ:** ‡2400.

VIRGINIA

Cass Co. Cass Co. (WC). 11 m SE of Beardstown. Residential.

11593 ■ Cass Cable TV Inc.
100 Redbud Rd.
Virginia, IL 62691
Phone: (217)452-7725
Fax: (217)452-7797
Free: 800-252-1799
Email: solutions@casscomm.com
Founded: 1990. **Key Personnel:** Mike Reynolds, VP; Linda Hodges, Office Mgr.; Marvin Seward, VP; Donna Troutman, Mktg. Mgr.; Tom Allen, VP. **Cities Served:** Ashland, Ashland, Baylis, Chandlerville, Chatham, Divernon, Easton, Glenarm, Havana, Kampsville, Manito, Milton, Mt. Sterling, Pawnee, Pleasant Plains, Rushville, Tallula, Versailles, Virginia, Illinois; Palmyra, Palmyra, Missouri: subscribing households 16,521; 69 channels; 1 community access channel; 24 hours per week community access programming. **Mailing address:** PO Box 200, Virginia, IL 62691. **URL:** http://www.casscomm.com.

WALNUT

Bureau Co. Bureau Co. (NW). 20 m S of Sterling. Construction of gravel screening equipment & conveyors and cheese plants. Grain, dairy farms. Corn, wheat, oats.

11594 ■ The Walnut Leader
The Walnut Leader
110 Jackson St.
Walnut, IL 61376-0280
Phone: (815)379-9290
Publication E-mail: wleader@mchsi.com
Community newspaper. **Freq:** Weekly (Mon.). **Print Method:** Offset. **Cols./Page:** 6. **Col. Width:** 21 nonpareils. **Col. Depth:** 224 agate lines. **Key Personnel:** Gary Brooks, Contact; Linda Brooks, Editor. **Subscription Rates:** $12 Individuals. **URL:** http://www.walnutillinois.com/#!members/c1yws. **Mailing address:** PO Box 280, Walnut, IL 61376-0280. **Ad Rates:** 4C $130.56; SAU $1.43. **Remarks:** Accepts advertising. **Circ:** ‡2000.

WASHINGTON

Tazewell Co. Tazewell Co. (NC). 12 m E of Peoria. Residential.

11595 ■ Material Handling Network
Material Handling Network Inc.
2407 Washington Rd.
Washington, IL 61571
Phone: (309)699-4431
Fax: (309)698-0801
Free: 800-447-6901
Publisher's E-mail: mhnetwork@wcinet.com
Trade magazine for the materials handling industry. **Freq:** Monthly. **Key Personnel:** Nancy Gudat, Account Executive; Andra Stephens, Associate, Publisher; Bob Behrens, General Manager. **Subscription Rates:** $73 U.S., Canada, and Mexico first class; $33 Individuals third class; $165 Out of country. **URL:** http://www.mhnetwork.com. **Ad Rates:** BW $625; 4C $910. **Remarks:** Accepts advertising. **Circ:** Controlled 32000, Non-paid 13475.

WATERLOO

Monroe Co. Monroe Co. (SW). 24 m S of St Louis, Mo. Suburban. Retail trade center. Feed mill; grain elevators. Diversified farming.

11596 ■ Republic Times
Republic Times L.L.C.
PO Box 147
Waterloo, IL 62298
Phone: (618)939-3814
Fax: (618)939-3815
Publisher's E-mail: rtamber@htc.net
Community newspaper. **Freq:** Weekly (Wed.). **Print Method:** Offset. **Trim Size:** 14 1/2 x 22 3/4. **Cols./Page:** 6. **Col. Width:** 2 1/16 inches. **Col. Depth:** 21 1/2 inches. **Key Personnel:** Kermit Constantine, General Manager; Corey Saathoff, Editor. **USPS:** 669-060. **Subscription Rates:** $25 Individuals in Monroe County (online); $30 Individuals in Monroe County (print); $35 Individuals in Monroe County (print and online); $25 Out of state online only; $35 Out of country print only; $45 Out of state print and online. **URL:** http://www.republictimes.net/category/news. **Ad Rates:** GLR $.6; BW $8.50; 4C $225; PCI $6.6. **Remarks:** Advertising accepted; rates available upon request. **Circ:** ‡5629.

11597 ■ The Shopper
Republic Times L.L.C.
PO Box 147
Waterloo, IL 62298
Phone: (618)939-3814
Fax: (618)939-3815
Shopper. **Founded:** 1981. **Freq:** Weekly (Mon.). **Print Method:** Offset. **Trim Size:** 14 1/2 x 22 3/4. **Cols./Page:** 6. **Col. Width:** 25 9 1/2 nonpareils picas. **Col. Depth:** 297 16 agate lines inches. **Key Personnel:** Angelo G. Palmero, Editor; Bonnie Michaels, Editor; Dan McGinnis, Publisher; Marvin Cortner, Managing Editor; Nancy Self, Manager, Advertising. **Formerly:** Republic Times Shopper; Wolcot-Red Creek Pennysaver. **Mailing address:** PO Box 66, Wolcott, NY 14590. **Ad Rates:** BW $8.50; 4C $225; GLR $.325; BW $187.20; SAU $6; PCI $2.75. **Remarks:** Advertising accepted; rates available upon request. **Circ:** Free ‡7548.

WATSEKA

Iroquois Co. Iroquois Co. (E). 25 m SE of Kankakee. Cheese, butter, radio condensers, business forms, transformers manufactured. Greenhouse. Hatchery. Stock, poultry, grain, dairy farms.

Circulation: ★ = AAM; △ or • = BPA; ♦ = CAC; ❑ = VAC; ⊕ = PO Statement; ‡ = Publisher's Report; Boldface figures = sworn; Light figures = estimated.

11598 ■ Iroquois County's Times-Republic
Twin States Publishing
1492 E Walnut St.
Watseka, IL 60970
Phone: (815)432-5227
Publisher's E-mail: cwaters@intranix.com
Local newspaper. **Freq:** Daily (eve.). **Print Method:** Offset. **Trim Size:** 11 1/4 x 13. **Cols./Page:** 6. **Col. Width:** 9.5 picas. **Col. Depth:** 12.5 inches. **Key Personnel:** Don Hurd, President, Publisher; Carla A. Waters, Managing Editor; Roberta Kempen, Director, Advertising. **ISSN:** 6695--2000 (print). **Subscription Rates:** $45 Individuals print; in County, 3 months; $59 Individuals print; out of County, 3 months; $73 Individuals print; in County, 6 months; $92 Individuals print; out of County, 6 months; $128 Individuals print; in County, 1 year; $150 Individuals print; out of County, 1 year. **URL:** http://www.newsbug.info/iroquois_countys_times-republic. **Mailing address:** PO Box 250, Watseka, IL 60970. **Ad Rates:** GLR $6.07; BW $455.25; PCI $9.27. **Remarks:** Accepts advertising. **Circ:** (Not Reported).

11599 ■ WGFA-AM - 1360
1973 E 1950 N Rd.
Watseka, IL 60970
Phone: (815)432-4955
Fax: (815)432-4957
Email: info@wgfaradio.com
Format: News; Sports. **Simulcasts:** WGFA-FM 94.1. **Networks:** ABC. **Founded:** 1960. **Operating Hours:** 6 a.m.-8 p.m. **Wattage:** 1,000. **Ad Rates:** $19-37 for 30 seconds; $25-46 for 60 seconds. Combined rates with WGFA-FM. **URL:** http://www.wgfaradio.com.

11600 ■ WGFA-FM - 94.1
1973 E 1950 N Rd.
Watseka, IL 60970
Phone: (815)432-4955
Fax: (815)432-4957
Email: info@wgfaradio.com
Format: Adult Contemporary. **Networks:** ABC. **Owner:** Iroquois County Broadcasting Co., at above address. **Founded:** 1961. **Operating Hours:** Continuous. **Wattage:** 50,000. **Ad Rates:** Noncommercial. Combined advertising rates available with WGFA-AM. **URL:** http://www.wgfaradio.com.

WAUCONDA

Lake Co. Lake Co. (NE). 20 m SW of Waukegan. Suburban. Summer resort. Light Industry. Dairy Farms.

11601 ■ Commercial Law World
Commercial Law League of America
1000 N Rand Rd., Ste. 214
Wauconda, IL 60084
Phone: (312)240-1400
Fax: (847)526-3993
Publisher's E-mail: info@clla.org
Magazine featuring best practices on leadership, management, marketing and operations in the industry; including industry profiles and practice aids. **Freq:** Quarterly. **ISSN:** 0888--8000 (print). **URL:** http://clla.org/?page=news_index. **Formerly:** Commercial Law Bulletin; Debt3. **Ad Rates:** BW $975, member; 4C $1090, non-member. **Remarks:** Accepts advertising. **Circ:** (Not Reported).

11602 ■ WLIM-AM - 1580
700 N Main St.
Wauconda, IL 60084
Format: Hispanic; Religious. **Owner:** Polnet Communications, Ltd., at above address. **Founded:** 1981. **Operating Hours:** Continuous. **Key Personnel:** Brad Behnke, Gen. Mgr., brad@radio-formula.com. **Wattage:** 10,000. **Ad Rates:** Noncommercial. **URL:** http://www.polskieradio.com.

WAUKEGAN

Lake Co. Lake Co. (NE). On Lake Michigan, 36 m N of Chicago. Good harbor. Fisheries. Manufactures asbestos and gypsum products, roofing, glass products, electronic components, pharmaceuticals, bakery goods, iron and brass castings, outboard motors, auto accessories, confectionery, envelopes, milling machines, lacquers, tools, dies. mink farms.

11603 ■ WKRS-AM - 1220
3250 Belvidere Rd.
Waukegan, IL 60085
Phone: (847)336-7900
Fax: (847)336-1523
Format: News; Talk. **Networks:** ABC; Illinois News. **Owner:** NextMedia Group Inc., 6312 S Fiddlers Green Cir., Ste. 360 E, Englewood, CO 80111, Ph: (303)694-9118, Fax: (303)694-4940. **Founded:** 1949. **Operating Hours:** 6 a.m.-10 p.m. **ADI:** Chicago (LaSalle), IL. **Key Personnel:** Libby Collins, Contact, lcollins@nextmediachicago.com. **Wattage:** 1,000. **Ad Rates:** Noncommercial. **URL:** http://www.wkrs.com.

11604 ■ WXLC-FM - 102.3
3250 Belvidere Rd.
Waukegan, IL 60085
Phone: (847)336-7900
Fax: (847)336-1523
Format: Adult Contemporary. **Networks:** Independent. **Owner:** NextMedia, 6312 S Fiddlers Green Cir., Ste. 205 E, Greenwood Village, CO 80111, Ph: (303)694-9118, Fax: (303)694-4940. **Operating Hours:** Continuous. **Key Personnel:** Karl Wertzler, Bus. Mgr., kwertzler@nextmediachicago.com; Deb Castile, Bus. Mgr., dcastile@nextmediachicago.com; Haynes Johns, Promotions Dir., hjohns@nextmediachicago.com; Janelle Rominski, Promotions Dir., jrominski@nextmediachicago.com; Chris Williams, VP, Mktg. Mgr. **Wattage:** 3,000. **Ad Rates:** Advertising accepted; rates available upon request. **URL:** http://www.1023xlc.com.

WEST CHICAGO

DuPage Co. Du Page Co. (NE). 14 m NE of Aurora.

11605 ■ FloraCulture International Magazine
Ball Publishing
622 Town Rd.
West Chicago, IL 60186
Phone: (630)231-3675
Fax: (630)231-5254
Free: 888-888-0013
Publisher's E-mail: info@ballpublishing.com
Trade magazine for professional growers of cut flowers and flowering plants worldwide. **Freq:** Bimonthly. **Print Method:** Offset. **Trim Size:** 8 x 10 3/4. **Cols./Page:** 3. **Col. Width:** 27 nonpareils. **Col. Depth:** 140 agate lines. **Key Personnel:** Ron van del Ploeg, Editor; Jaap Kras, Publisher. **ISSN:** 1051--9076 (print). **Subscription Rates:** €142.50 Individuals; €75 Individuals. **URL:** http://www.floracultureinternational.com. **Mailing address:** PO Box 1660, West Chicago, IL 60186. **Ad Rates:** BW $3,675; 4C $3,404. **Remarks:** Accepts advertising. **Circ:** Combined 16986, ‡19495.

11606 ■ Green Profit Magazine
Ball Publishing
622 Town Rd.
West Chicago, IL 60186
Phone: (630)231-3675
Fax: (630)231-5254
Free: 888-888-0013
Publisher's E-mail: info@ballpublishing.com
Trade magazine for flower and plant retailers. **Freq:** 9/year. **Print Method:** Offset. **Trim Size:** 8 1/8 x 10 7/8. **Cols./Page:** 3. **Col. Width:** 27 nonpareils. **Col. Depth:** 140 agate lines. **Key Personnel:** Chris Beytes, Editor. **ISSN:** 1094--0650 (print). **URL:** http://ballpublishing.com/GreenProfit/CoverStory.aspx?articleid=18051. **Mailing address:** PO Box 1660, West Chicago, IL 60186. **Ad Rates:** BW $2,888; 4C $3,939. **Remarks:** Accepts advertising. **Circ:** 28201.

11607 ■ Grower Talks
Ball Publishing
622 Town Rd.
West Chicago, IL 60186
Phone: (630)231-3675
Fax: (630)231-5254
Free: 888-888-0013
Publisher's E-mail: info@ballpublishing.com
Trade magazine covering issues for commercial greenhouse growers with a focus on North American production. **Freq:** Monthly. **Print Method:** Web offset. **Trim Size:** 8 1/8 x 10 7/8. **Key Personnel:** Chris Beytes, Editor; Jennifer Zurko, Associate Editor. **ISSN:** 0276--9433 (print). **Subscription Rates:** $35 U.S. and Canada; $99 Other countries. **URL:** http://www.ballpublishing.com/GrowerTalks/default.aspx. **Mailing address:** PO Box 1660, West Chicago, IL 60186. **Remarks:** Advertising accepted; rates available upon request. **Circ:** Combined 28201.

WEST DUNDEE

11608 ■ Hotel F & B Executive
Hotel Forums L.L.C.
613 Kane St.
West Dundee, IL 60118
Phone: (847)551-9956
Magazine that addresses the needs of the hospitality F&B markets, which include hotels, resorts, cruise lines and conference, and convention & meeting centers. **Freq:** Bimonthly. **Key Personnel:** Larry Walters, Chief Executive Officer, phone: (773)728-4995; Jeanne Bischoff, President, Publisher, phone: (847)551-9956; Jen Bergren, Director, Production. **Subscription Rates:** Free print and online. **URL:** http://www.hotelfandb.com. **Remarks:** Accepts advertising. **Circ:** (Not Reported).

WEST FRANKFORT

Franklin Co. Franklin Co. (S). 115 m SE of St. Louis, Mo. Manufactures dresses, concrete products, boats. Machine shop. Coal Mines.

11609 ■ The Daily American
GateHouse Media Inc.
111 S Emma
West Frankfort, IL 62896
Phone: (618)932-2146
Community newspaper. **Founded:** 1916. **Freq:** Mon.-Sat. (eve.). **Print Method:** Offset. **Cols./Page:** 6. **Col. Width:** 26 nonpareils. **Col. Depth:** 301 agate lines. **Key Personnel:** Heather Little, Manager, Circulation; Jim Murphy, Publisher; Alec Ramsay, Editor. **Subscription Rates:** $158 Individuals per year; in-county mail or carrier; $302 Individuals per year; out-of-county mail; $96 Elsewhere per year; online. **URL:** http://www.dailyamericannews.com/. **Ad Rates:** BW $637; 4C $827; SAU $5.34. **Remarks:** Accepts advertising. **Circ:** (Not Reported).

WHEATON

DuPage Co. Du Page Co. (NE). 25 m W of Chicago. Wheaton College. Residential. Nurseries. Diversified farming.

11610 ■ Evangelical Missions Quarterly
Evangelism and Missions Information Service
PO Box 794
Wheaton, IL 60187
Phone: (630)752-7158
Fax: (630)752-7155
Publication E-mail: emq@wheaton.edu
Freq: Quarterly. **Print Method:** Offset. **Trim Size:** 5 1/2 x 8 1/2. **Cols./Page:** 2. **Col. Width:** 42 nonpareils. **Col. Depth:** 105 agate lines. **ISSN:** 0140--3359 (print). **Subscription Rates:** $24.95 Individuals /year online only; $36.95 Individuals /year, print only; $52.95 Individuals /year, print and online; $29.99 Libraries 1-50 online users; $99.99 Libraries 100 plus online users; $65.95 Individuals /year, print only; $94.95 Individuals print and online, 2 years; $44.95 Individuals /year online, 2 years; $32.95 Libraries /year, print; $59.99 Libraries 51-100 online users. **URL:** http://www.emqonline.com. **Formerly:** Evangelical Missions Quarterly: The Journal for Professional Missionaries. **Ad Rates:** BW $600; 4C $1075. **Remarks:** Advertising accepted; rates available upon request. **Circ:** ‡5500.

11611 ■ Journal of the American Liszt Society
American Liszt Society
c/o Alexander Djordjevic, Membership Secretary
PO Box 1020
Wheaton, IL 60187-6777
Phone: (845)586-4457
Membership journal covering the composer Liszt. **Freq:** Annual. **Key Personnel:** Jonathan Kregor, Editor. **URL:** http://americanlisztsociety.net/journal.php. **Circ:** (Not Reported).

11612 ■ The Quest: A Bimonthly Journal of Philosophy, Science, Religion, and the Arts
Theosophical Society in America
1926 N Main St.
Wheaton, IL 60187
Phone: (630)668-1571
Free: 800-669-9425
Publication E-mail: questeditor@theosophical.org

Journal focusing on a holistic world view of philosophy, religion, science, and the arts. **Freq:** Quarterly. **Print Method:** Web offset. **Key Personnel:** Betty Bland, President. **ISSN:** 1040-533X (print). **Subscription Rates:** $27.97 Individuals; $38.97 Canada; $42.97 Other countries; $52.80 Two years; $72 Canada 2 years; $79.20 Other countries 2 years; $76.80 Individuals 3 years; $105 Canada 3 years; $115.20 Other countries 3 years; $8.95 Single issue back issues; $11 Single issue back issues - foreign. **URL:** http://www.theosophical.org/publications/quest-magazine. **Mailing address:** PO Box 270, Wheaton, IL 60187-0270. **Remarks:** Advertising not accepted. **Circ:** 7,000.

11613 ■ Comcast Cable
218 E Geneva Rd.
Wheaton, IL 60187
Cities Served: 123 channels. **URL:** http://www.comcast.com.

11614 ■ WETN-FM - 88.1
501 College Ave.
Wheaton, IL 60187
Phone: (630)752-5074
Email: wetn@wheaton.edu
Format: Contemporary Christian. **Owner:** Wheaton College Board of Trustees, 501 College Ave., Wheaton, IL 60187- 5501, Ph: (630)752-5000. **Founded:** 1962. **Operating Hours**: Continuous. **Local Programs**: *Hour of Decision*; *Contemporary Christian music.* **Wattage**: 250. **Ad Rates:** Noncommercial. **URL:** http://www.wheaton.edu/wetn.

WHEELING

Lake Co. Cook Co. (NE). 23 m NW of Chicago. Manufactures office and data communications products, paint, paint shakers, insecticides, aluminum foil, tools and dies.

11615 ■ The Cremationist of North America
Cremation Association of North America
499 Northgate Pky.
Wheeling, IL 60090-2646
Phone: (312)245-1077
Fax: (312)321-4098
Publisher's E-mail: info@cremationassociation.org
Trade magazine on cremation. **Freq:** Quarterly. **Print Method:** Offset. **Trim Size:** 7 x 10. **Cols./Page:** 3. **Col. Width:** 26 nonpareils. **Col. Depth:** 140 agate lines. **Key Personnel:** Sara Corkery, Managing Editor. **Subscription Rates:** Included in membership. **URL:** http://www.cremationassociation.org. **Ad Rates:** BW $885; 4C $1,460. **Remarks:** Accepts advertising. **Circ:** (Not Reported).

WILMETTE

Cook Co. Cook Co. (NE). 14 m N of Chicago. Residential.

11616 ■ BWI Journal
Boating Writers International
108 9th St.
Wilmette, IL 60091
Phone: (847)736-4142
Publisher's E-mail: info@bwi.org
Freq: 11/year. **Subscription Rates:** Included in membership. **URL:** http://www.bwi.org/category/bwi-journal/. **Remarks:** Advertising not accepted. **Circ:** 500.

11617 ■ Journal of Solid State Chemistry
RELX Group P.L.C.
c/o M.G. Kanatzidis, Ed.-in-Ch.
Northwestern University
1523 Central Ave.
Wilmette, IL 60091
Publisher's E-mail: amsterdam@relx.com
Journal covering major developments and studies in the field of solid state chemistry. **Freq:** Monthly. **Trim Size:** 8 1/2 x 11. **Key Personnel:** M.G. Kanatzidis, Editor-in-Chief; J. Li, Associate Editor. **ISSN:** 0022--4596 (print). **Subscription Rates:** $2991.33 Institutions online - access for 5 users and 4 years of archives; $7179 Institutions print. **URL:** http://www.journals.elsevier.com/journal-of-solid-state-chemistry. **Remarks:** Accepts advertising. **Circ:** (Not Reported).

WILMINGTON

Greene Co. Will Co. (NE). 16 m S of Joliet. Manufactures tissues, napkins, feminine hygiene products, felts, roofing materials. Agriculture.

11618 ■ The Coal City Courant
The Free Press Newspapers
111 S Water St.
Wilmington, IL 60481
Phone: (815)476-7966
Fax: (815)476-7002
Community newspaper. **Freq:** Weekly (Wed.). **Print Method:** Offset. **Cols./Page:** 6. **Col. Depth:** 21 nonpareils. **Key Personnel:** Pam Monson, Editor. **USPS:** 120-060. **Subscription Rates:** $39 Individuals Will or Grundy County; $46 Out of state other Illinois Counties; $51 Out of state; $37 Individuals Will & Grundy County (senior). **URL:** http://freepressnewspapers.com. **Remarks:** Accepts advertising. **Circ:** (Not Reported).

WINNEBAGO

Winnebago Co.

11619 ■ WRTB-FM - 95.3
2830 Sandy Hollow Rd.
Rockford, IL 61109
Format: Alternative/New Music/Progressive. **Owner:** Maverick Media of Rockford, LLC, at above address. **Ad Rates:** Advertising accepted; rates available upon request.

WINNETKA

Cook Co. Cook Co. (NE). 19 m N of Chicago. Residential.

11620 ■ Winnetka Talk
Sun-Times Media L.L.C.
3701 W Lake Ave.
Glenview, IL 60026
Phone: (847)486-9200
Fax: (847)486-7451
Publisher's E-mail: customerservice@suntimes.com
Community newspaper (tabloid). **Freq:** Weekly. **Print Method:** Offset. **Cols./Page:** 5. **Col. Width:** 10 inches. **Col. Depth:** 14 inches. **Key Personnel:** Rich Martin, Editor, phone: (847)486-7481; Liza Roche, Managing Editor, phone: (847)486-6842. **USPS:** 686-780. **Subscription Rates:** $84 Out of state; $40 Individuals. **URL:** http://winnetka.suntimes.com. **Remarks:** Accepts advertising. **Circ:** (Not Reported).

11621 ■ WNTH-FM - 88.1
385 Winnetka Ave.
Winnetka, IL 60093
Phone: (847)784-2322
Email: wnth@newtrier.k12.il.us
Format: Alternative/New Music/Progressive. **Owner:** New Trier High School, Seven Happ Rd., Northfield, IL 60093, Ph: (847)446-7000, Fax: (847)784-7500. **Founded:** Dec. 10, 1961. **Operating Hours**: 6:30 a.m.-10 p.m. **Local Programs**: *Night Talk*, Thursday 8:30 p.m. - 10:00 p.m. **Wattage**: 100. **Ad Rates:** Noncommercial. **URL:** http://www.newtrier.k12.il.us.

WOODRIDGE

Will Co.

11622 ■ Chinese Music
Chinese Music Society of North America
PO Box 5275
Woodridge, IL 60517
Phone: (630)910-1551
Fax: (630)910-1561
Freq: Quarterly. **ISSN:** 0192--3749 (print). **Subscription Rates:** Individuals included in membership dues; $28 Individuals /year for nonmembers; $53.75 Institutions /year. **Remarks:** Accepts advertising. **Circ:** (Not Reported).

WOODSTOCK

McHenry Co. McHenry Co. (NE). 51 m NW of Chicago. Manufactures electrical components, lamp shades, plastics, microscopes, typewriters, milk products. Machine shops; printers. Hatcheries. Nurseries. Agriculture. Dairying.

11623 ■ The Woodstock Independent
The Woodstock Independent
671 E Calhoun St.
Woodstock, IL 60098
Phone: (815)388-8040
Fax: (815)338-8177
Publisher's E-mail: ads@thewoodstockindependent.com
Community newspaper. **Freq:** Weekly (Wed.). **Key Personnel:** Mike Neumann, Editor; Cheryl Wormley, Publisher; John Trione, General Manager. **Subscription Rates:** $42 Individuals in Snowbird; $50 Elsewhere; $72 Two years in Snowbird; $95 Two years elsewhere; $20 By mail PDF; $35 Students. **Alt. Formats:** PDF. **URL:** http://www.thewoodstockindependent.com. **Ad Rates:** 4C $110; SAU $2.50; PCI $9. **Remarks:** Accepts advertising. **Circ:** Paid ⊕**3500**.

YORKVILLE

Kendall Co. Kendall Co. (NE). On Fox River, 12 m SW of Aurora. Grain elevator. Grain farms. Corn, oats, soybeans, cattle and hogs.

11624 ■ Kendall County Record
Kendall County Record Inc.
222 S Bridge St.
Yorkville, IL 60560-0256
Phone: (630)553-7034
Fax: (630)553-7085
Publication E-mail: circulation@kendallcountynow.com
Community newspaper. **Freq:** Weekly (Thurs.). **Print Method:** Offset. **Cols./Page:** 6. **Col. Width:** 20 nonpareils. **Col. Depth:** 224 agate lines. **Key Personnel:** Kathy Farren, Contact; Jeffery A. Farren, Contact. **Subscription Rates:** $26 Individuals in Kendall County; $34 Individuals in Illinois; $45 Out of state. **URL:** http://www.kendallcountyrecord.com. **Ad Rates:** GLR $.25. **Remarks:** Advertising accepted; rates available upon request. **Circ:** ‡3600.

11625 ■ Ledger-Sentinel
Kendall County Record Inc.
222 S Bridge St.
Yorkville, IL 60560-0256
Phone: (630)553-7034
Fax: (630)553-7085
Publisher's E-mail: info@shawmedia.com
Community newspaper serving Oswego, Boulder Hill, and Montgomery. **Freq:** Weekly (Thurs.). **Print Method:** Offset. **Cols./Page:** 6. **Col. Width:** 19 nonpareils. **Col. Depth:** 224 agate lines. **Key Personnel:** Jeff Farren, Editor. **Subscription Rates:** $26 Individuals; $34 Elsewhere; $45 Other countries. **URL:** http://www.ledgersentinel.com/. **Ad Rates:** GLR $.29; BW $384; SAU $5.20. **Remarks:** Accepts advertising. **Circ:** ‡3100.

ZION

Lake Co. Lake Co. (NE). 6 m N of Waukegan. Manufactures candy, bakery products, curtains, microfilm industrial coatings, carriers. Horse farms.

11626 ■ Zion Benton News
Zion-Benton News
2711 Sheridan Rd.
Zion, IL 60099
Phone: (847)746-9000
Fax: (847)746-9150
Community newspaper. **Freq:** Weekly (Thurs.). **Print Method:** Offset. **Cols./Page:** 5. **Col. Width:** 20 nonpareils. **Col. Depth:** 182 agate lines. **Key Personnel:** Sandy Dickson, Reporter; Frank Misureli, Publisher; Mona Shannon, Editor. **Subscription Rates:** $33.95 Individuals Lake and Kenosha counties; $35.95 Elsewhere. **URL:** http://www.zion-bentonnews.com; http://zion-bentonnews.com/community_news.html. **Ad Rates:** GLR $1; PCI $6. **Remarks:** Accepts advertising. **Circ:** ‡3500.

Circulation: ★ = AAM; △ or • = BPA; ♦ = CAC; ❑ = VAC; ⊕ = PO Statement; ‡ = Publisher's Report; Boldface figures = sworn; Light figures = estimated.

ALEXANDRIA

Madison Co. Madison Co. (E). 10 m N of Anderson. Manufactures insulation, redwood outdoor furniture, cement mixers, gospel music printing and recording, plastics, boilers, tool and die fabrication, wire and metal products. Farming.

11627 ■ Alexandria Times-Tribune
Elwood Publishing Co.
One Harrison Sq.
Alexandria, IN 46001
Phone: (765)724-4469
Fax: (765)724-4460
Publication E-mail: alextribune@elwoodpublishing.com
Community newspaper. **Freq:** Weekly (Wed.). **Print Method:** Offset. **Cols./Page:** 6. **Col. Width:** 1.833 inches. **Col. Depth:** 21 1/2 inches. **Key Personnel:** Robert Nash, Publisher. **ISSN:** 1063--553X (print). **Subscription Rates:** $46 Individuals in state in county, 1 year, print and online; $58 Individuals in state out of county, 1 year, print and online; $64 Individuals out of state, 1 year, print and online; $34 Individuals in state in county, 1 year, print; $46 Individuals in state out of county, 1 year, print; $52 Individuals out of state, 1 year, print; $30 Individuals 6 months, online; $46 Individuals 1 year, online; $79 Two years online. **URL:** http://www.elwoodpublishing.com. **Mailing address:** PO Box 330, Alexandria, IN 46001. **Ad Rates:** 4C $200; SAU $8.50; PCI $8.50. **Remarks:** Advertising accepted; rates available upon request. **Circ:** Paid 2000.

ANDERSON

Madison Co. Madison Co. (EC). 38 m NE of Indianapolis. Anderson College. Manufactures auto electrical equipment, paperboard products, studio couches, pumps, castings, tools, furniture springs, glass, brick, machinery, oil engines, playground equipment; meat packing.

11628 ■ Anderson Herald-Bulletin
Anderson Herald-Bulletin
1133 Jackson St.
Anderson, IN 46016
Phone: (765)622-1212
Free: 800-750-5049
General newspaper. **Freq:** Daily (morn.). **Print Method:** Offset. Broadsheet. **Cols./Page:** 6. **Col. Width:** 26 nonpareils. **Col. Depth:** 21 1/2 inches. **Key Personnel:** Connie Alexander, Contact, phone: (765)640-2312; Henry Bird, Publisher, phone: (765)640-2307. **ISSN:** 0893--908X (print). **Subscription Rates:** $20.99 Individuals print and online; $16.99 Individuals online. **URL:** http://www.heraldbulletin.com. **Ad Rates:** GLR $2.31; BW $4186.05; 4C $4466.05; PCI $32.45. **Remarks:** Accepts advertising. **Circ:** Mon.-Sat. ★**21199**, Sun. ★**22508**.

11629 ■ Signatures: The Alumni Quarterly of Anderson University
Anderson University
1100 E 5th St.
Anderson, IN 46012-3495
Phone: (765)641-4100
Fax: (765)641-3888
Free: 800-428-6414
Publisher's E-mail: alumni@anderson.edu
Magazine for college alumni. **Freq:** Quarterly. **Print Method:** Offset. Uses mats. **Trim Size:** 8 1/2 x 11. **Cols./Page:** 4. **Col. Depth:** 210 agate lines. **Alt. Formats:** PDF. **URL:** http://www.anderson.edu/signatures. **Formerly**: Anderson College News. **Remarks:** Advertising not accepted. **Circ:** Free ‡24000.

11630 ■ WBSB-FM - 89.5
2000 W University Ave.
Muncie, IN 47306
Phone: (765)285-5888
Fax: (765)285-8937
Free: 800-646-1812
Format: Public Radio. **Owner:** Ball State University, 2000 W University Ave., Muncie, IN 47306, Ph: (765)289-1241, Free: 800-382-8540. **Founded:** 1997. **Key Personnel:** Marcus Jackman, Gen. Mgr., mjackman@bsu.edu; Emly Kowalski, Office Mgr., elkowalski@bsu.edu; Terry Heifetz, News Dir., tjheifetz@bsu.edu. **Ad Rates:** Noncommercial. **URL:** http://indianapublicradio.org.

11631 ■ WFOF-FM - 90.3
1920 W 53rd St.
Anderson, IN 46013
Fax: (765)642-4033
Free: 888-877-9467
Format: Religious. **Networks:** Moody Broadcasting. **Owner:** Moody Radio, 820 N La Salle Blvd., Chicago, IL 60610, Ph: (312)329-4000, Free: 800-356-6639. **Founded:** 1984. **Operating Hours:** Continuous. **Key Personnel:** Tom Winn, Dir. of Programs, tom.winn@moody.edu. **Wattage**: 19,000. **Ad Rates:** Noncommercial.

11632 ■ WGNR-AM - 1470
1920 W 53rd St.
Anderson, IN 46013
Fax: (765)642-4033
Free: 888-877-9467
Email: wgnr@moody.edu
Format: Religious. **Owner:** Moody Broadcasting Network, at above address. **Founded:** 1998. **Key Personnel:** Ray Hashley, Mgr., ray.hashley@moody.edu; Tom Winn, Prog. Dir., tom.winn@moody.edu. **Ad Rates:** Noncommercial. **URL:** http://www.moodyradioindiana.fm.

11633 ■ WGNR-FM - 97.9
1920 W 53rd St.
Anderson, IN 46013
Fax: (765)642-4033
Free: 888-877-9467
Format: Religious. **Key Personnel:** Dan Craig, Program Mgr.; Doug Hastings, Gen. Mgr. **URL:** http://www.moodyradio.org.

11634 ■ WIWC-FM
1920 W 53rd St.
Anderson, IN 46013
Format: Religious. **Wattage**: 2,100 ERP. **URL:** http://www.moodyradioindiana.fm/.

11635 ■ WMBL-FM - 88.1
1920 W 53rd St.
Anderson, IN 46013
Format: Religious. **URL:** http://www.moodyradioindiana.fm.

11636 ■ WQME-FM - 98.7
1100 E 5th St.
Anderson, IN 46012
Phone: (765)641-4349
Fax: (765)641-3825
Free: 866-987-9763
Format: Adult Contemporary. **Networks:** CNN Radio. **Owner:** Anderson University, 316 Blvd., Anderson, SC 29621, Ph: (864)231-2000, Free: 800-542-3594. **Founded:** Nov. 30, 1990. **Operating Hours**: 6 a.m. - midnight Sun.- Thur.; 6 a.m. - 2 a.m. Fri.- Sat. **ADI**: Indianapolis (Marion), IN. **Key Personnel:** Matt Rust, Dir. of Programs, mrust@wqme.com; Jill O'Malia, Contact. **Wattage**: 4,500. **Ad Rates:** Noncommercial. **URL:** http://www.wqme.com.

ANGOLA

Steuben Co. Steuben Co. (NE). 42 m NE of Ft. Wayne. Tri-State University. Summer-Resort. Manufactures automobiles and trucks parts, wire, abrasive and honing equipment, gauges, die casting and metal spinning, air control cylinders, airplane parts, business forms. Grain and dairy farms.

11637 ■ WEAX-FM - 88.3
One University Ave.
Angola, IN 46703
Phone: (260)665-4883
Email: weaxradio@trine.edu
Format: Alternative/New Music/Progressive. **Networks:** CNN Radio. **Owner:** Trine University, 1 University Ave., Angola, IN 46703, Ph: (260)665-4100, Free: 800-347-4878. **Founded:** 1979. **Operating Hours**: Continuous. **Wattage:** 1,000. **Ad Rates:** Underwriting available. **URL:** http://www.88xradio.com.

11638 ■ WLKI-FM - 100.3
330 Intertech Pkwy., Ste. 300
Angola, IN 46703
Phone: (260)665-9554
Fax: (260)668-4487
Email: wlki@wlki.com
Format: Adult Contemporary. **Key Personnel:** Jim Measel, Contact. **URL:** http://www.wlki.com.

11639 ■ WMSH-AM - 1230
PO Box 999
Angola, IN 46703
Phone: (219)665-9554
Format: Sports. **Simulcasts:** WMSH-FM. **Networks:** ABC; Jones Satellite. **Owner:** Swick Broadcasting Co. Inc., at above address. **Founded:** 1951. **Formerly**: WSTR-AM. **Operating Hours**: Continuous. **ADI**: Grand Rapids-Kalamazoo-Battle Creek, MI. **Wattage**: 1,000. **Ad Rates:** $6-12 for 30 seconds; $7-15 for 60 seconds. Combined advertising rates available with WTHD-FM, WLKI-FM. **URL:** http://www.foxsportssturgis.com.

ATTICA

Fountain Co. Fountain Co. (W). On Wabash River, 21 m SW of Lafayette. Manufactures steel castings, electronic components, batteries. Grain, stock, dairy, poultry farms.

Circulation: ★ = AAM; △ or • = BPA; ♦ = CAC; ❑ = VAC; ⊕ = PO Statement; ‡ = Publisher's Report; Boldface figures = sworn; Light figures = estimated.

11640 ■ WFWR-FM - 91.5
909 S McDonald St.
Attica, IN 47918
Phone: (765)764-1934
Wattage: 165.

AUBURN

De Kalb Co. DeKalb Co. (NE) 25 m NE of Fort Wayne. Residential. Classic car museum.

11641 ■ WFGA-FM - 106.7
1153 W 15th St.
Auburn, IN 46706
Phone: (260)920-3602
Fax: (260)920-3604
Format: Adult Contemporary; News; Sports. **Key Personnel:** Woodrow Zimmerman, Gen. Mgr., Sales Mgr., woodrow@ilovefroggy.com; Kevin Kreigh, Dir. of Production, kevin@ilovefroggy.com. **Ad Rates:** Advertising accepted; rates available upon request.

11642 ■ WGLL-AM
5446 CR 29
Auburn, IN 46706
Fax: (219)925-1345
Format: Talk. **Networks:** CNN Radio. **Founded:** 1968. **Formerly**: WIFF-AM. **Wattage**: 500 day; 151 night.

AVON

11643 ■ Hendricks County Flyer
The Flyer Group
8109 Kingston Rd., Ste. 500
Avon, IN 46123
Phone: (317)272-5800
Fax: (317)272-5887
Free: 800-359-3747
Community newspaper. **Freq:** Semiweekly (Wed. and Sat.). **Print Method:** Offset. **Cols./Page:** 6. **Col. Width:** 21 1/2 nonpareils. **Col. Depth:** 224 agate lines. **Key Personnel:** Kathy Linton, Editor; Harold Allen, Publisher. **URL:** http://www.flyergroup.com. **Remarks:** Accepts advertising. **Circ:** (Not Reported).

11644 ■ Hendricks County Flyer/Weekend Edition
The Flyer Group
8109 Kingston Rd., Ste. 500
Avon, IN 46123
Phone: (317)272-5800
Fax: (317)272-5887
Free: 800-359-3747
Newspaper with a Democratic orientation. **Freq:** Weekly (Thurs.). **Print Method:** Offset. **Cols./Page:** 6. **Col. Width:** 21 1/2 nonpareils. **Col. Depth:** 297 agate lines. **Key Personnel:** Kathy Linton, Editor; Harold Allen, Publisher. **URL:** http://www.flyergroup.com. **Formerly**: The Weekend Flyer. **Remarks:** Color advertising accepted; rates available upon request. **Circ:** Combined 36500.

11645 ■ Westside Flyer
The Flyer Group
8109 Kingston Rd., Ste. 500
Avon, IN 46123
Phone: (317)272-5800
Fax: (317)272-5887
Free: 800-359-3747
Newspaper with a Republican orientation. **Freq:** Weekly (Mon.). **Print Method:** Offset. **Cols./Page:** 6. **Col. Width:** 21.5 nonpareils. **Col. Depth:** 224 agate lines. **Key Personnel:** Kathy Linton, Editor; Harold Allen, Publisher. **URL:** http://www.flyergroup.com/site/about-us.html. **Remarks:** Advertising accepted; rates available upon request. **Circ:** 15000.

BATESVILLE

Ripley Co. Franklin & Ripley Co. (SE). 49 m NW of Cincinnati, Oh. Manufactures furniture, caskets, hospital and metal equipment. Agriculture.

11646 ■ The Herald-Tribune
Community Newspaper Holdings Inc.
475 N Huntersville Rd.
Batesville, IN 47006
Phone: (812)934-4343
Fax: (812)934-6406
Newspaper with a Democratic orientation. **Founded:** 1891. **Freq:** Semiweekly (Wed. and Sat.). **Print Method:** Offset. **Cols./Page:** 6. **Col. Width:** 22 nonpareils. **Col. Depth:** 294 agate lines. **Key Personnel:** Bryan Helvie, Editor; Sue Gillespie, Manager, Circulation. **Subscription Rates:** $49 Individuals home delivery; $58 By mail. **URL:** http://www.batesvilleheraldtribune.com. **Ad Rates:** GLR $.62. **Remarks:** Advertising accepted; rates available upon request. **Circ:** ‡4,500.

11647 ■ WRBI-FM - 103.9
133 S Main St.
Batesville, IN 47006
Phone: (812)934-5111
Email: news@wrbiradio.com
Format: Country. **Networks:** CNN Radio. **Owner:** White River Broadcasting Co., 3212 Washington St, Columbus, IN 47203, Ph: (812)372-4448. **Founded:** 1977. **Operating Hours:** Continuous; 10% network, 90% local. **Key Personnel:** Ron Green, Gen. Mgr., rongreen@wrbiradio.com. **Wattage:** 3,000. **Ad Rates:** $14-16 for 30 seconds; $17-19 for 60 seconds. **URL:** http://wrbiradio.com/heavy-snow-wreaks-road-havoc-school-closures.

BEDFORD

Lawrence Co. Lawrence Co. (S). 24 m S of Bloomington. Quarrying and fabricating building stone; foundry; saw and excelsior mills. Manufactures stoneworking machinery, saws, work shirts. Diversified farming.

11648 ■ American Trapper
National Trappers Association
2815 Washington Ave.
Bedford, IN 47421
Phone: (812)277-9670
Fax: (812)277-9672
Free: 866-680-8727
Publisher's E-mail: ntaheadquarters@nationaltrappers.com
Fur trade magazine. **Freq:** 5/year. **Print Method:** Offset. **Trim Size:** 8 1/2 x 11. **Cols./Page:** 3. **Col. Width:** 13 picas. **Col. Depth:** 60 picas. **Key Personnel:** Buddy Marsyada, Editor. **ISSN:** 1050-4036 (print). **Subscription Rates:** $3 Single issue back issue add $2 for shipping & handling. **URL:** http://www.nationaltrappers.com/americantrapper.html. **Formerly**: Voice of the Trapper. **Ad Rates:** BW $300; 4C $600; PCI $10. **Remarks:** Accepts advertising. **Circ:** ‡11,500.

11649 ■ Herald-Times
Hoosier-Times Inc.
16th St.
Bedford, IN 47421
Phone: (812)275-3355
Fax: (812)275-4191
Free: 800-782-4405
Publisher's E-mail: tmnews@tmnews.com
Newspaper with a Republican orientation. **Founded:** 1877. **Freq:** Mon.-Sat. (morn.). **Print Method:** Offset. **Cols./Page:** 6. **Col. Width:** 12 picas. **Col. Depth:** 21 inches. **Key Personnel:** Robert S. Zaltsberg, Editor; Mayer E. Maloney, Jr., Publisher, phone: (812)331-4251. **Subscription Rates:** $167 Individuals daily & Sun.; $155 Individuals daily & Sat.; $107 Individuals weekends; $23 By mail daily & Sunday, 1 month; $20 By mail weekdays & Saturday, 1 month; $20 By mail weekdays only, 1 month; $18 By mail weekends only, 1 month; $69 By mail daily & Sunday, 3 months; $60 By mail weekdays & Saturday, 3 months; $60 By mail weekdays only, 3 months. **URL:** http://www.heraldtimesonline.com/. **Remarks:** Accepts advertising. **Circ:** Mon.-Fri. ★**26,713**, Sat. ★**29,732**.

11650 ■ Missionary Herald
Evangelistic Faith Missions
PO Box 609
Bedford, IN 47421
Phone: (812)275-7531
Publisher's E-mail: efm.pres@gmail.com
Freq: Monthly. **Subscription Rates:** $2 Individuals /year. **URL:** http://www.efm-missions.org/Herald/Home. **Remarks:** Advertising not accepted. **Circ:** 20000.

11651 ■ Reporter-Times
Hoosier-Times Inc.
16th St.
Bedford, IN 47421
Phone: (812)275-3355
Fax: (812)275-4191
Free: 800-782-4405
Publisher's E-mail: tmnews@tmnews.com
Community newspaper. **Freq:** Daily. **Print Method:** Offset. **Cols./Page:** 6. **Col. Width:** 13.5 picas. **Col. Depth:** 301 agate lines. **Key Personnel:** Brian Culp, Managing Editor; E. Mayer Maloney, Jr., Publisher. **Subscription Rates:** $6.95 Individuals online only/month; $30 Individuals home delivery for 6 months; $10.95 Individuals daily delivered to your home (includes web access). **URL:** http://www.reporter-times.com. **Formerly**: Martinsville Daily Reporter. **Remarks:** Advertising accepted; rates available upon request. **Circ:** (Not Reported).

11652 ■ The Times-Mail
Times-Mail
16th St.
Bedford, IN 47421
Phone: (812)275-3355
Fax: (812)275-4191
Free: 800-782-4405
Publisher's E-mail: webstaff@schurz.com
Newspaper. **Freq:** Daily. **Print Method:** Offset. **Trim Size:** 11 5/8 x 13 3/4. **Cols./Page:** 8. **Col. Width:** 19 nonpareils. **Col. Depth:** 294 agate lines. **Key Personnel:** Mike Lewis, Managing Editor, phone: (812)277-7258; E. Mayer Maloney, Jr., Publisher, phone: (812)331-4251; Sean Duncan, Editor, phone: (812)277-7283. **Subscription Rates:** $6.95 Individuals online; $11.95 Individuals Monday-Saturday, per month, home delivery; $8.95 Individuals Sunday, per month, home delivery; $13.95 Individuals daily and Sunday, includes web access. **URL:** http://www.tmnews.com. **Mailing address:** PO Box 849, Bedford, IN 47421. **Remarks:** Accepts advertising. **Circ:** Mon.-Sat. ★**13051**.

11653 ■ WBIW-AM - 1340
424 Heltonville Rd.
Bedford, IN 47421
Phone: (812)275-7555
Fax: (812)279-8046
Email: tips@wbiw.com
Format: News; Talk. **Simulcasts:** WQRK, WQRJ (6 to 10:00 a.m.). **Networks:** ABC. **Owner:** Ad-Venture Media Inc., 424 Heltonville Rd., Bedford, IN 47421, Ph: (812)275-7555, Fax: (812)279-8046. **Founded:** 1948. **Operating Hours**: Continuous; 60% network, 40% local. **ADI**: Louisville, KY. **Wattage**: 1,000. **Ad Rates:** Advertising accepted; rates available upon request. Combined advertising rates available with WQRK, WQRJ. **Mailing address:** PO Box 1307, Bedford, IN 47421. **URL:** http://www.wbiw.com.

11654 ■ WPHZ-FM - 102.5
424 Heltonville Rd.
Bedford, IN 47421
Phone: (812)275-7555
Fax: (812)279-8046
Email: comments@wphz.com
Format: Adult Contemporary. **Owner:** Mitchell Broadcasting. **Operating Hours**: Continuous. **Key Personnel:** Andrew Mullen, Consultant. **Ad Rates:** Advertising accepted; rates available upon request. **Mailing address:** PO Box 1307, Bedford, IN 47421. **URL:** http://www.wphz.com.

11655 ■ WQRK-FM - 105.5
PO Box 1307
Bedford, IN 47421
Phone: (812)275-7555
Fax: (812)279-8046
Format: Oldies. **Simulcasts:** WQRK, WQRJ (6:00 am-10 am). **Networks:** ABC. **Owner:** Ad-Venture Media Inc., 424 Heltonville Rd., Bedford, IN 47421, Ph: (812)275-7555, Fax: (812)279-8046. **Founded:** 1975. **Formerly**: WBIF-FM. **Operating Hours**: Continuous. **Wattage:** 3,000. **Ad Rates:** Advertising accepted; rates available upon request. **URL:** http://www.superoldies.net.

BEECH GROVE

Marion Co. Marion Co. (SC). 7 m SE of Indianapolis. Electrical equipment, dairy farms.

11656 ■ The Southside Times
The Southside Times
301 Main St.
Beech Grove, IN 46107
Phone: (317)787-3291
Publication E-mail: rick@ss-times.com

Community newspaper. **Freq:** Weekly (Thurs.). **Print Method:** Offset. **Cols./Page:** 6. **Col. Width:** 1 13/16 inches. **Col. Depth:** 21 1/2 inches. **Key Personnel:** Roger Huntzinger, Publisher; Sherri Coner, Editor. **URL:** http://ss-times.com. **Formerly**: The Perry Township Weekly. **Ad Rates:** BW $1663.20; 4C $1843.20; PCI $15.30. **Remarks:** Accepts advertising. **Circ:** Free ‡21500.

BERNE

Adams Co. Adams Co. (NE). 33 m SE of Fort Wayne. Manufactures furniture, men's clothing, cedar chests, components, tubing, novelty boxes; electronics industry. Hatcheries. Diversified farming.

11657 ■ Berne Tri-Weekly News
Berne Tri-Weekly News
153 S Jefferson St.
Berne, IN 46711
Phone: (260)589-2101
Fax: (260)589-8614
Publication E-mail: news@bernetriweekly.com
Agricultural newspaper with a Republican orientation. **Freq:** Triweekly Mon., Wed., Fri. (except holidays). **Print Method:** Offset. **Cols./Page:** 6. **Col. Width:** 12 picas. **Col. Depth:** 21 inches. **Key Personnel:** Jessica Elzey, Director, Advertising; Clint Anderson, General Manager; Kay Bower, Office Manager. **Subscription Rates:** $56 Individuals Adams County; $62 Individuals Indiana - out of county; $70 Out of state; $350 Other countries; $40 Individuals college. **URL:** http://www.bernetriweekly.com. **Ad Rates:** GLR $.18; BW $5; 4C $295; SAU $5; PCI $6.20. **Remarks:** Accepts advertising. **Circ:** ‡2500.

11658 ■ CardMaker: Paper Crafting, Stamping, Embellishing & More!
Annie's
306 E Parr Rd.
Berne, IN 46711-1138
Phone: (260)589-4000
Fax: (260)589-8093
Publisher's E-mail: mailpreference@annies-publishing.com
Magazine covering sewing, patchwork, knitting, embroidery, crochet, and cross-stitch. **Freq:** Bimonthly. **Trim Size:** 8 x 10 3/4. **Key Personnel:** Tanya Fox, Editor. **ISSN:** 0892--8223 (print). **Subscription Rates:** $21.97 Individuals plus $2.98 delivery; $21.97 Canada plus $9.98 delivery. **URL:** http://www.cardmakermagazine.com. **Formerly:** Quick & Easy Crafts; Creative Crafter; PaperWorks; GiftMaker. **Ad Rates:** BW $3078; 4C $2526. **Remarks:** Accepts advertising. **Circ:** ‡80000, ‡70000.

11659 ■ Crazy for Cross Stitch
Annie's
306 E Parr Rd.
Berne, IN 46711-1138
Phone: (260)589-4000
Fax: (260)589-8093
Publisher's E-mail: mailpreference@annies-publishing.com
Magazine that offers information about cross-stitching for every skill level. **Freq:** Bimonthly. **Trim Size:** 8 x 10 3/4. **Subscription Rates:** $19.97 Individuals. **URL:** http://static.netmagazines.com/crazyforcrossstitch/. **Remarks:** Accepts advertising. **Circ:** (Not Reported).

11660 ■ Crochet!
Annie's
306 E Parr Rd.
Berne, IN 46711-1138
Phone: (260)589-4000
Fax: (260)589-8093
Publication E-mail: customer_care@crochetmagazine.com
Consumer magazine covering crochet techniques, stitches, fiber options and other facts about crochet. **Freq:** Bimonthly. **Print Method:** Offset. **Trim Size:** 8 x 10 3/4. **Key Personnel:** Michelle Thorpe, Director, Advertising; Carol Alexander, Executive Editor. **Subscription Rates:** $21.97 Individuals plus $1.98 postage; $21.97 Canada plus $9.98 postage. **URL:** http://www.crochetmagazine.com. **Ad Rates:** 4C $2,648. **Remarks:** Accepts advertising. **Circ:** Combined 70000.

11661 ■ Crochet World: The Magazine for Crochet Lovers
Annie's
306 E Parr Rd.
Berne, IN 46711-1138
Phone: (260)589-4000
Fax: (260)589-8093
Publisher's E-mail: mailpreference@annies-publishing.com
Magazine containing crochet ideas and patterns, including toys, afghans, dolls, doilies, clothing, and household accessories. **Freq:** Bimonthly. **Print Method:** Offset. **Trim Size:** 8 x 10 3/4. **Cols./Page:** 3. **Col. Width:** 13.5 picas. **Col. Depth:** 58 picas. **Key Personnel:** Carol Alexander, Editor. **ISSN:** 0164--7962 (print). **Subscription Rates:** $21.97 Individuals + 2.98 delivery; $21.97 Canada + 9.98 delivery; $19.97 Individuals online; /year. **URL:** http://drgnetwork.com; http://www.crochet-world.com. **Ad Rates:** BW $1158.55; 4C $1363. **Remarks:** Accepts advertising. **Circ:** ‡125000, ‡115000.

11662 ■ Gold Old Days Specials
Annie's
306 E Parr Rd.
Berne, IN 46711-1138
Phone: (260)589-4000
Fax: (260)589-8093
Publisher's E-mail: mailpreference@annies-publishing.com
Magazine that features true stories and photographs of times gone by. **Freq:** 6/year. **Key Personnel:** John Boggs, Contact. **Subscription Rates:** $15.97 Individuals. **URL:** http://www.goodolddaysmagazine.com. **Ad Rates:** BW $7243; 4C $10130. **Remarks:** Accepts advertising. **Circ:** 225,000, 215,000.

11663 ■ Good Old Days: The Magazine That Remembers the Best
Annie's
306 E Parr Rd.
Berne, IN 46711-1138
Phone: (260)589-4000
Fax: (260)589-8093
Publication E-mail: editor@goodolddaysonline.com
Magazine on the nostalgic past, including authentic photos, drawings, cartoons, memories, features, songs, poems, and advertising. **Freq:** Bimonthly. **Print Method:** Offset. **Trim Size:** 8 x 10 3/4. **Cols./Page:** 3. **Col. Width:** 13.5 picas. **Col. Depth:** 58 picas. **Key Personnel:** Ken Tate, Editor. **ISSN:** 0046--6158 (print). **Subscription Rates:** $15.97 U.S. plus $2.98 delivery; $15.97 Canada plus $9.98 delivery. **URL:** http://www.goodolddaysmagazine.com. **Ad Rates:** BW $7169; 4C $10130. **Remarks:** Accepts advertising. **Circ:** ‡255,000.

11664 ■ Home Cooking
Annie's
306 E Parr Rd.
Berne, IN 46711-1138
Phone: (260)589-4000
Fax: (260)589-8093
Publisher's E-mail: mailpreference@annies-publishing.com
Magazine with approximately 100 recipes for home cooks who wish to make home-style foods with common ingredients. **Founded:** 1973. **Freq:** Monthly. **Key Personnel:** Shelly Vaughan James, Editor; Carl H. Muselman, Editor. **Subscription Rates:** $20 Individuals 6 issues; $25 Canada 6 issues; $2 Individuals postage and processing. **URL:** http://www.drgnetwork.com/drg_news/newsrelease_detail.html?release_id=231. **Remarks:** Accepts advertising. **Circ:** (Not Reported).

11665 ■ Just CrossStitch
Annie's
306 E Parr Rd.
Berne, IN 46711-1138
Phone: (260)589-4000
Fax: (260)589-8093
Publisher's E-mail: mailpreference@annies-publishing.com
Magazine providing information on cross-stitch products of all shapes, sizes, and skill levels. **Freq:** 7/year. **Trim Size:** 7.875 x 10.5. **Key Personnel:** Christy Schmitz, Editor. **Subscription Rates:** $19.97 Individuals digital. **URL:** http://www.just-crossstitch.com. **Remarks:** Accepts advertising. **Circ:** 60000.

11666 ■ Sewing Savvy
Annie's
306 E Parr Rd.
Berne, IN 46711-1138
Phone: (260)589-4000
Fax: (260)589-8093
Publication E-mail: customer_service@whitebirches.com
Consumer magazine covering home decor sewing techniques, patterns and product information for home sewers. **Freq:** Bimonthly. **Print Method:** Offset. **Trim Size:** 8 x 10 3/4. **Key Personnel:** Julie Johnson, Editor. **Subscription Rates:** $19.97 Individuals; $24.97 Canada. **URL:** http://www.anniescatalog.com/sewing_savvy.php. **Ad Rates:** BW $1,092.25; 4C $1,285. **Remarks:** Accepts advertising. **Circ:** Paid 57000.

11667 ■ Wearable Crafts: Wearable Art For Real People
Annie's
306 E Parr Rd.
Berne, IN 46711-1138
Phone: (260)589-4000
Fax: (260)589-8093
Publisher's E-mail: mailpreference@annies-publishing.com
How-to magazine featuring wearable art projects. **Freq:** Bimonthly. **Key Personnel:** Beth Schwartz, Editor; Beth Schwartz Wheeler, Editor. **Formerly**: Wearable Wonders. **Remarks:** Advertising accepted; rates available upon request. **Circ:** Paid 130000.

11668 ■ WZBD-FM - 92.7
PO Box 4050
Berne, IN 46711
Phone: (260)589-9300
Email: wzbd@onlyinternet.net
Format: Adult Contemporary; News; Sports. **Founded:** Sept. 07, 2006. **URL:** http://www.wzbd.com.

BLOOMINGTON

Monroe Co. Monroe Co. (SWC). 50 m S of Indianapolis. Indiana University. Manufactures color TV receivers, refrigerators, capacitors, elevators, specialized medical instruments, semi-conductors, brake linings, paper speciality products, limestone quarrying & limestone products.

11669 ■ Africa Today
Indiana University Press
Indiana University
221 Woodburn Hall
Bloomington, IN 47405
Publication E-mail: afrtoday@indiana.edu
Journal on political, social, and economic conditions in Africa. **Freq:** Quarterly. **Print Method:** Offset. **Trim Size:** 6 x 9. **Cols./Page:** 1. **Col. Width:** 66 nonpareils. **Col. Depth:** 119 agate lines. **Key Personnel:** Eileen Julien, Editor; Maria Grosz-Ngate, Editor; Patrick McNaughton, Editor; Samuel Obeng, Editor; Hassan Wahab, Managing Editor. **ISSN:** 0001--9887 (print); **EISSN:** 1527--1978 (electronic). **Subscription Rates:** $55 Individuals print; $52.50 Individuals electronic; $60.50 Individuals electronic & print; $150 Institutions print; $135 Institutions electronic; $199.50 Institutions electronic & print. **URL:** http://www.indiana.edu/~afrist/about/AfricaToday.shtml. **Remarks:** Accepts advertising. **Circ:** (Not Reported).

11670 ■ Agricultural Water Management
RELX Group P.L.C.
c/o D. Wichelns, Editor
Bloomington, IN 47401
Publisher's E-mail: amsterdam@relx.com
Journal covering various aspects of the management of agricultural water such as irrigation and drainage of cultivated areas, collection and storage of precipitation water in relation to soil properties and vegetation cover. **Freq:** 16/yr. **Key Personnel:** D. Wichelns, Editor; J.D. Oster, Board Member, phone: (909)684-7889; B. Clothier, Editor. **ISSN:** 0378--3774 (print). **Subscription Rates:** $1318 Institutions online; $3162 Included in membership print. **URL:** http://www.journals.elsevier.com/agricultural-water-management. **Remarks:** Accepts advertising. **Circ:** (Not Reported).

11671 ■ Aleph: Historical Studies in Science and Judaism
Indiana University Press
601 N Morton St.
Bloomington, IN 47404-3797
Phone: (812)855-9449
Fax: (812)855-8507
Free: 800-842-6796

Circulation: ★ = AAM; △ or • = BPA; ♦ = CAC; ❑ = VAC; ⊕ = PO Statement; ‡ = Publisher's Report; Boldface figures = sworn; Light figures = estimated.

Peer-reviewed journal exploring the connection between Judaism and science through history. **Freq:** Semiannual. **Key Personnel:** Gad Freudenthal, Editor; Esti Micenmacher, Managing Editor; Tony Travis, Managing Editor. **ISSN:** 1565--1525 (print); **EISSN:** 1565--5423 (electronic). **Subscription Rates:** $52.50 Individuals print and online; $47.50 Individuals print only; $45.50 Individuals online only; $96.50 Institutions print and online; $72.50 Institutions print only; $65.50 Institutions online only. **URL:** http://www.jstor.org/journal/aleph. **Remarks:** Accepts advertising. **Circ:** (Not Reported).

11672 ■ American Journal of Physical Anthropology
National Association of Student Anthropologists
c/o Suzanne Marie Barber, President
Indiana University
107 S Indiana Ave.
Bloomington, IN 47405
Freq: Monthly. **Key Personnel:** Dr. Clark Larsen, Editor-in-Chief. **ISSN:** 0002--9483 (print); **EISSN:** 1096--8644 (electronic). **Subscription Rates:** $3974 U.S., Canada, and Mexico online only; £2029 Individuals online only; €2568 Individuals online only; $3974 Other countries online only. **URL:** http://www.physanth.org/publications. **Remarks:** Accepts advertising. **Circ:** 2000.

11673 ■ Anthropological Linguistics
Anthropological Linguistics
c/o Indiana University
American Indian Studies Research Institute
Dept. of Anthropology
130/170 E Kirkwood Ave.
Bloomington, IN 47405-7100
Phone: (812)855-4123
Fax: (812)855-7529
Publisher's E-mail: anthling@indiana.edu
Journal covering scholarly study of worldwide languages and cultures, with particular focus on natives of America. Also covering research reports addressing cultural, historical, and philological aspects of linguistic study, and studies of linguistic prehistory and genetic classification. **Founded:** 1959. **Freq:** Quarterly. **Trim Size:** 5 x 8. **Key Personnel:** Douglas R. Parks, Editor; John A. Erickson, Managing Editor; Raymond J. DeMallie, Associate Editor; Victor Golla, Associate Editor; Philip S. LeSourd, Associate Editor. **ISSN:** 0003-5483 (print). **Subscription Rates:** $179 Institutions; $209 Institutions, other countries; $57 Individuals; $87 Other countries. **URL:** http://www.indiana.edu/~anthling. **Ad Rates:** BW $250. **Remarks:** Accepts advertising. **Circ:** (Not Reported).

11674 ■ Bloom
Bloom Magazine Inc.
PO Box 1204
Bloomington, IN 47402
Phone: (812)323-8959
Fax: (812)323-8965
Publication E-mail: subscribe@magbloom.com
Culture and lifestyle magazine. **Freq:** Bimonthly. **Key Personnel:** Lynae Sowinski, Associate Editor; Malcolm Abrams, Editor-in-Chief; Erica De Santis, Associate Publisher, Representative, Advertising and Sales. **Subscription Rates:** $23.95 Individuals; $42.95 Two years; $5.95 Single issue. **URL:** http://www.magbloom.com; http://caballero.es/productos/bloom. **Remarks:** Accepts advertising. **Circ:** 15000.

11675 ■ Bluebird
North American Bluebird Society
PO Box 7844
Bloomington, IN 47407
Phone: (812)200-5700
Publication E-mail: info@nabluebirdsociety.org
Journal covering research reports, bibliography, and statistics on wildlife conservation for members. **Freq:** Quarterly. **Key Personnel:** Bernie Daniel, Director; Sherry Linn, President; Scott Gillihan, Managing Editor. **Subscription Rates:** $7.50 Individuals. **Alt. Formats:** PDF. **URL:** http://www.nabluebirdsociety.org/Publications/publications.htm. **Remarks:** Advertising accepted; rates available upon request. **Circ:** (Not Reported).

11676 ■ Bridges: A Jewish Feminist Journal
Indiana University Press
601 N Morton St.
Bloomington, IN 47404-3797
Phone: (812)855-9449
Fax: (812)855-8507
Free: 800-842-6796
Journal devoted to humanities and social sciences. **Freq:** Semiannual. **Print Method:** Offset. **Trim Size:** 11 1/2 x 17 1/2. **Cols./Page:** 5. **Col. Width:** 30 nonpareils. **Col. Depth:** 224 agate lines. **Key Personnel:** Clare Kinberg, Managing Editor; Carolivia Herron, Editor; Jessica Stein, Editor. **ISSN:** 1046--8358 (print); **EISSN:** 1558--9552 (electronic). **Subscription Rates:** $37.40 Individuals print and online; $34 Individuals print only; $30.60 Individuals online only; $78.40 Institutions print and online; $56 Institutions print only; $50.40 Institutions online only. **Circ:** (Not Reported).

11677 ■ Business Horizons
RELX Group P.L.C.
c/o M. J. Dollinger, Ed.
Indiana University
Kelley School of Business
1309 E 10th St.
Bloomington, IN 47405-1701
Phone: (812)856-5063
Publisher's E-mail: amsterdam@relx.com
Business management magazine presenting in non-technical language. **Founded:** 1958. **Freq:** Bimonthly. **Print Method:** Offset. **Trim Size:** 8 1/2 x 11. **Cols./Page:** 2. **Key Personnel:** M. J. Dollinger, Editor; C.G. Brush, Board Member; Lisa F. Miller, Managing Editor. **ISSN:** 0007-6813 (print). **Subscription Rates:** $519 Institutions. **URL:** http://www.journals.elsevier.com/business-horizons. **Circ:** 3300.

11678 ■ Concurrency and Computation: Practice and Experience
John Wiley & Sons Inc.
c/o Prof. Geoffrey C. Fox, Ed.
Community Grid Computing Lab.
Indiana University
501 N Morton St., Ste. 224
Bloomington, IN 47404
Publisher's E-mail: info@wiley.com
Scientific journal focusing on concurrent computers and solutions to problems specific to concurrent computer designers. **Freq:** 18/yr. **Key Personnel:** Prof. Anthony J.G. Hey, Editor; Prof. Geoffrey C. Fox, Editor, phone: (812)856-7977, fax: (812)856-7972. **ISSN:** 1532--0626 (print); **EISSN:** 1532--0634 (electronic). **URL:** http://onlinelibrary.wiley.com/doi/10.1002/cpe.v26.2/issuetoc. **Formerly:** Concurrency; Concurrency: Practice & Experience. **Remarks:** Accepts advertising. **Circ:** (Not Reported).

11679 ■ e-Service Journal
Indiana University Press
Indiana University
Kelley School of Business
Godfrey Graduate & Executive Education Ctr., Rm. 2000S
1275 E Tenth St.
Bloomington, IN 47405
Phone: (812)855-2641
Peer-reviewed journal that publishes research on the design, delivery, and impact of e-services via a variety of computing applications and communication technologies. **Freq:** 3/year. **Key Personnel:** Dr. Ramesh Venkataraman, Editor-in-Chief; Chad Christensen, Managing Editor; Laku Chidambaram, Executive Editor. **ISSN:** 1528--8226 (print); **EISSN:** 1528--8234 (electronic). **Subscription Rates:** $55 Individuals print and online; $50 Individuals print only; $45 Individuals online only; $180 Institutions print and online; $143.75 Institutions print only; $130 Institutions online only. **URL:** http://www.jstor.org/action/showPublication?journalCode=eservicej&; http://www.e-sj.org. **Remarks:** Accepts advertising. **Circ:** (Not Reported).

11680 ■ Educational Horizons
Pi Lambda Theta
320 W 8th St., Ste. 216
Bloomington, IN 47404
Phone: (812)339-1156
Fax: (812)339-0018
Free: 800-766-1156
Publisher's E-mail: plt@pdkintl.org
Journal for professionals in education. **Freq:** Quarterly. **Trim Size:** 8 1/8 x 10 7/8. **Cols./Page:** 3. **Key Personnel:** Juli Knutson, Editor. **ISSN:** 0013--175X (print); **EISSN:** 2162--3163 (electronic). **Subscription Rates:** Included in membership. **URL:** http://pilambda.org/about-plt/publications/educational-horizons. **Mailing address:** PO Box 7888, Bloomington, IN 47407-7888. **Remarks:** Advertising not accepted. **Circ:** (Not Reported).

11681 ■ Evolution & Development
Wiley-Blackwell
Myers Hall 150
Indiana University
915 E Third St.
Bloomington, IN 47405-7107
Journal serving as a voice for the rapidly growing research community at the interface of evolutionary and developmental biology. **Freq:** Bimonthly. **Key Personnel:** Rudolf A. Raff, Editor-in-Chief; Michael I. Coates, Editor; Vivian Irish, Editor; Gregory Wray, Editor; Wallace Arthur, Editor; Sean B. Carroll, Board Member; Ann Campbell Burke, Board Member; Graham E. Budd, Board Member; Paul M. Brakefield, Board Member; Michael Akam, Board Member. **ISSN:** 1520--541X (print); **EISSN:** 1525--142X (electronic). **Subscription Rates:** $771 Institutions print & online; $800 Institutions, Canada and Mexico print & online; €730 Institutions print and online; £579 Institutions print and online; $642 Institutions print or online; $666 Institutions, Canada and Mexico print or online. **URL:** http://onlinelibrary.wiley.com/journal/10.1111/%28ISSN%291525-142X. **Ad Rates:** BW $1575; 4C $1230. **Remarks:** Accepts advertising. **Circ:** ‡107.

11682 ■ Film History: An International Journal
Indiana University Press
Indiana University
800 E. 3rd St.
Bloomington, IN 47405
Publication E-mail: filmhist@indiana.edu
Publication covering motion picture historiography. **Freq:** Quarterly. **Print Method:** Offset. **Key Personnel:** Gregory A. Waller, Editor. **ISSN:** 0892--2160 (print); **EISSN:** 1553--3905 (electronic). **Subscription Rates:** $86.75 Individuals print and online; $78.75 Individuals print only; $71 Individuals online only; $279.50 Institutions print and online; $210 Institutions print only; $189 Institutions online only. **URL:** http://www.jstor.org/journal/filmhistory. **Remarks:** Accepts advertising. **Circ:** (Not Reported).

11683 ■ Indiana Alumni Magazine
Indiana University Alumni Association
Virgil T. DeVault Alumni Ctr.
1000 E 17th St.
Bloomington, IN 47408-1521
Phone: (812)855-4822
Fax: (812)855-8266
Free: 800-824-3044
Publication E-mail: iualumni@indiana.edu
Magazine for college alumni. **Freq:** Quarterly. **Print Method:** Web. **Trim Size:** 8.375 x 10.875. **Cols./Page:** 3. **Col. Width:** 28 nonpareils. **Col. Depth:** 131 agate lines. **Key Personnel:** J.D. Denny, Managing Editor, phone: (812)855-2982; Mike Wright, Editor-in-Chief, fax: (812)855-2981; Amanda Zuicens-Williams, Manager, Advertising, phone: (812)855-6415. **Subscription Rates:** Included in membership. **URL:** http://alumni.indiana.edu/magazine/fall-2014/index.html. **Ad Rates:** BW $3075; 4C $1915. **Remarks:** Advertising accepted; rates available upon request. **Circ:** ‡63954.

11684 ■ Indiana Business Review
Indiana University Kelley School of Business Indiana Business Research Center
100 S College Ave., Ste. 240
Bloomington, IN 47404
Phone: (812)855-5507
Fax: (812)855-7763
Publication E-mail: ibrc@iupui.edu
Magazine on Indiana business. **Founded:** 1926. **Freq:** Quarterly. **Print Method:** Offset. **Trim Size:** 8 1/2 x 11. **Cols./Page:** 2. **Col. Width:** 33 nonpareils. **Col. Depth:** 210 agate lines. **Key Personnel:** Jerry Conover, Director, Publisher; Carol O. Rogers, Chief Information Officer; Rachel M. Justis, Managing Editor. **URL:** http://www.ibrc.indiana.edu/ibr/. **Remarks:** Advertising not accepted. **Circ:** Controlled 2,000.

11685 ■ Indiana Daily Student
Indiana University
107 S Indiana Ave.
Bloomington, IN 47405-7000
Phone: (812)855-4848
Publication E-mail: ids@indiana.edu

Collegiate newspaper. **Freq:** Daily (during academic year). **Print Method:** Offset. **Cols./Page:** 6. **Col. Width:** 24 nonpareils. **Col. Depth:** 294 agate lines. **Key Personnel:** Philip Bantin, Director. **URL:** http://www.idsnews.com. **Ad Rates:** GLR $13.43; BW $1692; 4C $2142; PCI $7.62. **Remarks:** Accepts advertising. **Circ:** ‡17000.

11686 ■ Indiana Journal of Global Legal Studies
Indiana University Maurer School of Law
211 S Indiana Ave.
Bloomington, IN 47405-7001
Phone: (812)855-7995
Fax: (812)855-1967
Publisher's E-mail: lawadmis@indiana.edu
Peer-reviewed journal focusing on global and legal regimes, markets, politics, technologies and cultures. **Freq:** Semiannual. **Key Personnel:** Alexandra Muir, Editor-in-Chief. **ISSN:** 1080-0727 (print). **Subscription Rates:** $40 Individuals electronic only; $38 Individuals print; $60 Individuals print & electronic; $70 Institutions print; $75 Institutions electronic only; $110 Institutions print & electronic. **URL:** http://ijgls.indiana.edu/. **Remarks:** Accepts advertising. **Circ:** (Not Reported).

11687 ■ Indiana Journal of Global Legal Studies
Indiana University Bloomington Michael Maurer School of Law
211 S Indiana Ave.
Bloomington, IN 47405-7001
Phone: (812)855-7995
Peer-reviewed journal containing articles on domestic and global issues. **Freq:** Semiannual winter and summer. **Key Personnel:** Alexandra Muir, Editor-in-Chief. **ISSN:** 1080--0727 (print). **Subscription Rates:** $70 Institutions print; $75 Institutions online; $110 Institutions print and online; $38 Individuals print; $40 Individuals online; $60 Individuals print and online. **URL:** http://ijgls.indiana.edu. **Circ:** (Not Reported).

11688 ■ Indiana Journal of Law and Social Equality
Indiana University Bloomington Michael Maurer School of Law
211 S Indiana Ave.
Bloomington, IN 47405-7001
Phone: (812)855-7995
Journal containing articles on legal and policy issues. **Key Personnel:** Alyson Schwartz, Editor-in-Chief. **URL:** http://www.repository.law.indiana.edu/ijlse. **Circ:** (Not Reported).

11689 ■ Indiana Law Journal
Indiana University Maurer School of Law
211 S Indiana Ave.
Bloomington, IN 47405-7001
Phone: (812)855-7995
Fax: (812)855-1967
Publication E-mail: ilj@indiana.edu
Professional journal covering law. **Freq:** Quarterly. **Key Personnel:** Richard C. Culbert, Editor-in-Chief. **ISSN:** 0019--6665 (print). **Subscription Rates:** $35 U.S. and Canada /year; $40 Other countries /year; $10 Single issue back issue. **URL:** http://ilj.law.indiana.edu. **Ad Rates:** BW $150. **Remarks:** Accepts advertising. **Circ:** Combined 750.

11690 ■ Indiana Law Journal
Indiana University Bloomington Michael Maurer School of Law
211 S Indiana Ave.
Bloomington, IN 47405-7001
Phone: (812)855-7995
Journal containing articles on academic legal issues. **Freq:** Quarterly. **Key Personnel:** Riley H. Floyd, Editor-in-Chief. **ISSN:** 0019--6665 (print). **Subscription Rates:** $35 U.S. and other countries; $40 Single issue. **URL:** http://ilj.law.indiana.edu. **Circ:** (Not Reported).

11691 ■ Indiana Libraries
Association for Indiana Media Educators
c/o Judy Dye
Indiana University
Main Library, Rm. 170
Bloomington, IN 47405
Phone: (812)855-7699
Fax: (812)855-2576
Publication E-mail: ilf@indy.net
Freq: Semiannual Biennial. **Print Method:** Web offset. **Trim Size:** 8 1/8 x 10 3/4. **Key Personnel:** Judy Dye, Editor; Patty Tallman, Manager, Advertising. **Subscription Rates:** $10 Individuals; $5 Single issue. **URL:** http://www.indianalibrariesjournal.org; http://ilfonline.site-ym.com/?page=publications; http://journals.iupui.edu/index.php/IndianaLibraries/index. **Ad Rates:** BW $100; 4C $150. **Remarks:** Accepts advertising. **Circ:** Controlled 3500.

11692 ■ Indiana Magazine of History
Indiana University Press
Indiana University
742 Ballantine Hall
1020 E Kirkwood Ave.
Bloomington, IN 47405
Phone: (812)855-4139
Fax: (812)855-3378
Publication E-mail: imaghist@indiana.edu
Peer-reviewed journal featuring Indiana/and Midwestern history. **Freq:** Quarterly. **Trim Size:** 4.25 x 7.5. **Key Personnel:** Eric Sandweiss, Editor; Dawn E. Bakken, Associate Editor. **ISSN:** 0019--6673 (print). **Subscription Rates:** $24 Individuals; $30 Other countries. **URL:** http://www.indiana.edu/~imaghist. **Ad Rates:** BW $400; PCI $3. **Remarks:** Accepts advertising. **Circ:** 8000.

11693 ■ Indiana Review
Indiana Review
465 Ballantine Hall
1020 E Kirkwood Ave.
Bloomington, IN 47405-7103
Publisher's E-mail: inreview@indiana.edu
Literary magazine covering fiction, poetry, nonfiction, interviews and art. **Freq:** Semiannual. **Print Method:** Offset. **Key Personnel:** Rachel Lyon, Editor; Deborah Kim, Editor. **ISSN:** 0738--386X (print). **Subscription Rates:** $20 Individuals 1 year; $23 Institutions 1 year; $36 Two years; $42 Institutions 2 years. **URL:** http://indianareview.org; http://indianareview.org/the-magazine. **Ad Rates:** BW $300. **Remarks:** Accepts advertising. **Circ:** Combined 3500.

11694 ■ Indiana University Mathematics Journal
Indiana University Mathematics Journal
831 E 3rd St.
Bloomington, IN 47405-7106
Phone: (812)855-4933
Publisher's E-mail: iumj@indiana.edu
Magazine on pure and applied mathematics. **Freq:** Bimonthly. **Print Method:** Offset. **Trim Size:** 7 x 10. **Cols./Page:** 1. **Col. Width:** 58 nonpareils. **Col. Depth:** 101 agate lines. **Key Personnel:** Michael Larsen, Editor, phone: (812)855-1064; Hari Bercovici, Managing Editor, phone: (812)855-1989; Nets Katz, Editor, phone: (812)855-0433; Eric Bedford, Editor, phone: (812)855-6674; Peter Sternberg, Editor, phone: (812)855-6726. **ISSN:** 0022--2518 (print). **Subscription Rates:** $490 Institutions print; $388 Institutions online only; $155 Individuals print; $50 Individuals online only. **URL:** http://www.iumj.indiana.edu. **Remarks:** Advertising not accepted. **Circ:** Paid 600, Non-paid 165.

11695 ■ The Information Society: An International Journal
Routledge
Dept. of Telecommunications
Indiana University
Bloomington, IN 47405-5501
Publisher's E-mail: book.orders@tandf.co.uk
Multidisciplinary journal commenting on the political, social, economic, and cultural implications of the Information Age. **Founded:** 1981. **Freq:** 5/year. **Print Method:** Offset. **Trim Size:** 7 x 10. **Cols./Page:** 1. **Col. Width:** 54 nonpareils. **Col. Depth:** 98 agate lines. **Key Personnel:** Harmeet Sawhney, Editor-in-Chief. **ISSN:** 0197-2243 (print). **Subscription Rates:** $219 Individuals print only; $533 Institutions online only; $609 Institutions print and online. **URL:** http://www.tandfonline.com/toc/utis20/current. **Remarks:** Accepts advertising. **Circ:** ‡417.

11696 ■ Israel Studies
Indiana University Press
601 N Morton St.
Bloomington, IN 47404-3797
Phone: (812)855-9449
Fax: (812)855-8507
Free: 800-842-6796
Publication E-mail: istudies@bgu.ac.il
Scholarly journal covering Israeli history, politics, society and culture. **Freq:** 3/year. **Print Method:** offset. **Trim Size:** 6 x 9. **Key Personnel:** S. Ilan Troen, Editor; Natan Aridan, Editor. **ISSN:** 1084--9513 (print); **EISSN:** 1527--201X (electronic). **Subscription Rates:** $45 Individuals print; $42.75 Individuals online; $49.50 Individuals print and online; $115 Institutions print (standard non-tiered). **URL:** http://www.iupress.indiana.edu/pages.php?pID=82&CDpath=4; http://www.jstor.org/journal/israelstudies. **Ad Rates:** BW $275. **Remarks:** Accepts advertising. **Circ:** 400.

11697 ■ Italica
American Association of Teachers of Italian
c/o Colleen M. Ryan
626 Ballantine Hall
Department of French and Italian
Indiana University
Bloomington, IN 47405
Phone: (815)855-1429
Journal on the study of Italian literature and language (English and Italian) culture, film, and Italian-American studies. **Freq:** Quarterly. **Print Method:** Offset. **Trim Size:** 6 x 9. **Cols./Page:** 1. **Col. Width:** 48 nonpareils. **Col. Depth:** 94 agate lines. **Key Personnel:** Michael Lettieri, Editor. **ISSN:** 0021-3020 (print). **URL:** http://www.utm.utoronto.ca/~aati/italica.html; http://www.aati-online.org. **Remarks:** Accepts advertising. **Circ:** 1500.

11698 ■ Journal of African Language Learning and Teaching
African Language Teachers Association
708 Eigennmann Hall
Indiana University
1900 E 10th St.
Bloomington, IN 47406
Phone: (812)856-4185
Fax: (812)856-4189
Publisher's E-mail: secretariat@altaonweb.org
URL: http://altaonweb.org/resources/publications/jallt. **Remarks:** Advertising not accepted. **Circ:** (Not Reported).

11699 ■ Journal of the African Language Teachers Association
African Language Teachers Association
708 Eigennmann Hall
Indiana University
1900 E 10th St.
Bloomington, IN 47406
Phone: (812)856-4185
Fax: (812)856-4189
Publisher's E-mail: secretariat@altaonweb.org
URL: http://altaonweb.org/resources/publications/jalta. **Remarks:** Advertising not accepted. **Circ:** (Not Reported).

11700 ■ Journal of American Folklore
American Folklore Society
Indiana University
1900 E 10th St.
Bloomington, IN 47406
Phone: (812)856-2379
Fax: (812)856-2483
Publisher's E-mail: americanfolkloresociety@gmail.com
Freq: Quarterly. **Key Personnel:** Ann K. Ferrell, Editor-in-Chief. **ISSN:** 0021- 8715 (print). **Subscription Rates:** $15 Members back issues; $25 Nonmembers back issues. **URL:** http://www.afsnet.org/?page=JAF. **Remarks:** Accepts advertising. **Circ:** 2600.

11701 ■ The Journal of American History
Organization of American Historians
1215 E Atwater Ave.
Bloomington, IN 47401
Phone: (812)855-2816
Fax: (812)855-9939
Publication E-mail: jah@oah.org
History journal. **Freq:** Quarterly March, June, September, December. **Print Method:** offset. **Trim Size:** 6 1/2 x 10. **Cols./Page:** 1. **Col. Width:** 75 nonpareils. **Col. Depth:** 140 agate lines. **Key Personnel:** Edward T. Linenthal, Editor; Nancy J. Croker, Director, Operations. **ISSN:** 0021--8723 (print); **EISSN:** 1945--2314 (electronic). **Subscription Rates:** $402 Institutions online; $374 Institutions print; $354 Institutions print and online; Included in membership. **URL:** http://www.

Circulation: ★ = AAM; △ or • = BPA; ♦ = CAC; ❑ = VAC; ⊕ = PO Statement; ‡ = Publisher's Report; Boldface figures = sworn; Light figures = estimated.

journalofamericanhistory.org. **Ad Rates:** BW $650. **Remarks:** Accepts advertising. **Circ:** 9000.

11702 ■ Journal of the American Society for Information Science and Technology: The Official Journal of the American Society for Information Science
John Wiley & Sons Inc.
c/o Blaise Cronin, Ed.-in-Ch.
Indiana University
1320 E 10th St.
Bloomington, IN 47405-3907
Phone: (812)885-2848
Fax: (812)855-6166
Publisher's E-mail: info@wiley.com
International journal serves as a forum for discussion and experimentation concerning the theory and practice of communicating information. Covers computer technology, operations research, librarianship, communications, management, information storage and retrieval, reprography, and systems design. Also includes Perspectives, a journal within a journal, containing collections of papers analyzing a single topic. **Freq:** Monthly. **Print Method:** Offset. **Trim Size:** 7 1/4 x 10 1/4. **Cols./Page:** 1. **Col. Width:** 102 nonpareils. **Col. Depth:** 154 agate lines. **Key Personnel:** Javed Mostafa, Editor-in-Chief. **ISSN:** 233--01635 (print); **EISSN:** 2330--1643 (electronic). **Subscription Rates:** $3005 Institutions print or online - The Americas; $3302 Institutions, other countries print or online - USA; $3116 Institutions, Canada and Mexico print or online; £1534 Institutions print or online UK; €2131 Institutions print or online Europe; $3674 Institutions print & online - The Americas; $4039 U.S. and other countries print & online - institutions; $3811 Institutions, Canada and Mexico print & online; £1878 Institutions print & online - UK; €2608 Institutions print & online - Europe. **URL:** http://onlinelibrary.wiley.com/journal/10.1002/(ISSN)2330-1643; http://as.wiley.com/WileyCDA/WileyTitle/productCd-ASI.html. **Formerly**: Journal of the American Society for Information Science, American Documentation; Journal of the American Society for Information Science. **Ad Rates:** BW $1241; 4C $1545. **Remarks:** Accepts advertising. **Circ:** 33600.

11703 ■ Journal of Applied Behavior Analysis
Society for the Experimental Analysis of Behavior
Indiana University
Psychological and Brain Sciences
1101 E 10th St.
Bloomington, IN 47405-7007
Phone: (812)336-1257
Fax: (812)855-4691
Journal publishing research articles on applications of the experimental analysis of behavior to problems of social importance. **Freq:** Quarterly. **Key Personnel:** Thomas S. Higbee, Board Member; Dorothea C. Lerman, Board Member; Timothy R. Vollmer, PhD, Editor. **ISSN:** 0021--8855 (print); **EISSN:** 1938--3703 (electronic). **Subscription Rates:** $154 Institutions U.S. and other countries (print + online); £99 Institutions U.K. (print + online); €116 Institutions Europe zone (print + online); $48 Individuals U.S., Canada, and Mexico (print + online); £45 Individuals U.K. (print + online); €54 Individuals Europe (print + online); $68 Other countries (print + online); $29 U.S., Canada, and Mexico student/retiree (print + online); £32 Individuals student/retiree in U.K. (print + online); €41 Individuals student/retiree in Europe (print + online); $50 Other countries student/retiree (print + online). **URL:** http://www.jeabjaba.org/jaba; http://onlinelibrary.wiley.com/journal/10.1002/(ISSN)1938-3703. **Remarks:** Accepts advertising. **Circ:** (Not Reported).

11704 ■ Journal of the Experimental Analysis of Behavior
Society for the Experimental Analysis of Behavior
Indiana University
Psychological and Brain Sciences
1101 E 10th St.
Bloomington, IN 47405-7007
Phone: (812)336-1257
Fax: (812)855-4691
Publication E-mail: jeab@indiana.edu
Journal on experiments relevant to the behavior of individual organisms. **Freq:** Monthly. **Print Method:** Offset. **Trim Size:** 7 x 10. **Cols./Page:** 2. **Col. Width:** 34 nonpareils. **Col. Depth:** 115 agate lines. **Key Personnel:** Gregory J. Madden, Editor; Victor Laties, Executive Editor; Monica Bonner, Business Manager; Jackson Marr, Editor. **ISSN:** 0022--002 (print); **EISSN:** 1938--711 (electronic). **Subscription Rates:** £166 Institutions UK, print and online; €191 Institutions Europe, print and online; $261 Institutions U.S. and other countries, print and online; £138 Institutions UK, online only; €159 Institutions Europe, online only; $217 Institutions U.S. and other countries, online only. **URL:** http://onlinelibrary.wiley.com/journal/10.1002/(ISSN)1938-3711. **Ad Rates:** BW $230. **Remarks:** Accepts advertising. **Circ:** Paid 2000, Non-paid 100.

11705 ■ Journal of Folklore Research: An International Journal of Folklore and Ethnomusicology
Indiana University Press
1320 E 10th St.
Bloomington, IN 47405-3907
Peer-reviewed journal covering anthropology and folklore. **Freq:** 3/year. **Key Personnel:** Michael Dylan Foster, Editor; Chad Edward Buterbaugh, Managing Editor. **ISSN:** 0737--7037 (print); **EISSN:** 1543--0413 (electronic). **Subscription Rates:** $41.50 Individuals print and online; $90.75 Institutions print and online. **URL:** http://www.iupress.indiana.edu/pages.php?pID=85&CDpath=4. **Ad Rates:** BW $275. **Remarks:** Accepts advertising. **Circ:** (Not Reported).

11706 ■ Journal of Slavic Linguistics
Slavica Publishers
Indiana University, 1430 N Willis Dr.
2611 E 10th St.
Bloomington, IN 47404-2146
Phone: (812)856-4186
Fax: (812)856-4187
Free: 877-752-8422
Publisher's E-mail: slavica@indiana.edu
Journal covering issues in the description and analysis of Slavic languages of general interest to linguists. **Freq:** Semiannual. **Key Personnel:** Steven Franks, Editor-in-Chief. **ISSN:** 1068--2090 (print); **EISSN:** 1543--0391 (electronic). **Subscription Rates:** Included in membership; $60 Institutions; $71 Institutions, other countries. **URL:** http://slavica.indiana.edu/journalListings/jsl. **Circ:** (Not Reported).

11707 ■ Kritika: Explorations in Russian & Eurasian History
Slavica Publishers
Indiana University, 1430 N Willis Dr.
2611 E 10th St.
Bloomington, IN 47404-2146
Phone: (812)856-4186
Fax: (812)856-4187
Free: 877-752-8422
Publisher's E-mail: slavica@indiana.edu
Journal covering the history and culture of Russia and Eurasia. **Freq:** Quarterly. **Print Method:** Offset. **Cols./Page:** 6. **Col. Width:** 26 nonpareils. **Col. Depth:** 301 agate lines. **Key Personnel:** Sergei Bogatyrev, Associate Editor; Jan Plamper, Associate Editor; Carolyn Pouncy, Managing Editor. **ISSN:** 1531--023X (print); **EISSN:** 1538--5000 (electronic). **Subscription Rates:** $95 Institutions /year; $50 Individuals /year; $40 Students /year; $40 Individuals online; $30 Students online. **URL:** http://kritika.georgetown.edu. **Remarks:** Accepts advertising. **Circ:** (Not Reported).

11708 ■ Meridians: Feminism, Race, Transnationalism
Indiana University Press
601 N Morton St.
Bloomington, IN 47404-3797
Phone: (812)855-9449
Fax: (812)855-8507
Free: 800-842-6796
Peer-reviewed journal on Afro American women in U.S. and international set up. **Freq:** Semiannual. **Key Personnel:** Paula J. Giddings, Editor. **ISSN:** 1536--6936 (print); **EISSN:** 1547--8424 (electronic). **Subscription Rates:** $40 Individuals print; $38 Individuals online; $90 Institutions online; $100 Institutions print only; $28.50 Students print only; $25.65 Students online. **URL:** http://www.smith.edu/meridians; http://www.iupress.indiana.edu/pages.php?pID=87&CDpath=4; http://www.jstor.org/journal/meridians. **Ad Rates:** BW $250. **Remarks:** Accepts advertising. **Circ:** ‡300.

11709 ■ MIS Quarterly Executive
Indiana University
107 S Indiana Ave.
Bloomington, IN 47405-7000
Phone: (812)855-4848
Journal that aims to encourage practice-based research in the information systems field and to disseminate the results of that research in a manner that makes its relevance and utility readily apparent. **Freq:** Quarterly. **Key Personnel:** Alan Dennis, Editor; Dorothy E. Leidner, Editor-in-Chief. **ISSN:** 1540--1960 (print). **Subscription Rates:** $50 Individuals electronic access; $495 Institutions electronic access; $495 Libraries electronic access. **URL:** http://misqe.org/ojs2/index.php/misqe/index. **Remarks:** Accepts advertising. **Circ:** (Not Reported).

11710 ■ Mongolian Studies
Mongolia Society
703 Eigenmann Hall
1900 E 10th St.
Indiana University
Bloomington, IN 47406-7512
Phone: (812)855-4078
Fax: (812)855-4078
Publisher's E-mail: monsoc@indiana.edu
Freq: Annual. **URL:** http://www.mongoliasociety.org/?q=section/200706225.htm. **Mailing address:** PO Box 2552, Bloomington, IN 47402. **Remarks:** Advertising not accepted. **Circ:** (Not Reported).

11711 ■ Nashim: A Journal of Jewish Women's Studies & Gender Issues
Indiana University Press
601 N Morton St.
Bloomington, IN 47404-3797
Phone: (812)855-9449
Fax: (812)855-8507
Free: 800-842-6796
Publication E-mail: nashim@schechter.ac.il
Peer-reviewed journal dealing with Jewish studies related to women and gender issues. **Freq:** Semiannual. **Key Personnel:** Deborah Greniman, Managing Editor; Renee Levine Melammed, Board Member. **ISSN:** 0793--8934 (print); **EISSN:** 1565--5288 (electronic). **Subscription Rates:** $33 Individuals online only; $35 Individuals print only; $38.50 Individuals print and online; $58.50 Institutions online only; $65 Institutions print only; $86 Institutions print and online. **URL:** http://www.iupress.indiana.edu/pages.php?pID=88&CDpath=4. **Circ:** (Not Reported).

11712 ■ Permaculture Design Magazine
Permaculture Activist Magazine
PO Box 5516
Bloomington, IN 47407
Phone: (812)335-0383
Publisher's E-mail: info@permacultureactivist.net
Journal featuring descriptive information on small-scale technology for self-reliant food production, ecological land use, land restoration, and lifestyle change. **Freq:** Quarterly. **Print Method:** Offset. **Trim Size:** 8 1/2 x 11. **Cols./Page:** 3. **Col. Width:** 27 nonpareils. **Col. Depth:** 137 agate lines. **Key Personnel:** Peter Bane, Editor; John Wages, Publisher, Editor. **ISSN:** 0897--7348 (print). **Subscription Rates:** $25 Individuals; $31 Canada; $38 Individuals in Mexico; $45 Other countries. **URL:** http://permaculturedesignmagazine.com. **Formerly**: The Permaculture Activist: A Quarterly Voice for the Permaculture Movement in North America. **Ad Rates:** BW $370; 4C $540. **Remarks:** Accepts advertising. **Circ:** (Not Reported).

11713 ■ Phi Delta Kappan: Professional Journal for Education
Phi Delta Kappa
320 W 8th St., Ste. 216
Bloomington, IN 47404
Phone: (812)339-1156
Fax: (812)339-0018
Free: 800-766-1156
Magazine for professional educators. **Freq:** 8/year. **Print Method:** Offset. **Trim Size:** 7 7/8 x 10 7/8. **Cols./Page:** 3. **Col. Width:** 13.5 picas. **Col. Depth:** 54 picas. **Key Personnel:** Carol Bucheri, Director; David Ruetschlin, Managing Editor. **ISSN:** 0031--7217 (print); **EISSN:** 1940--6487 (electronic). **Subscription Rates:** Included in membership; $248 Institutions US; $269 Institutions foreign; $58 /year; free for members; $269 institutions in US. **URL:** http://pdk.sagepub.com; http://pdkintl.org/publications/kappan/. **Mailing address:** PO Box 7888,

Bloomington, IN 47407-7888. **Ad Rates:** BW $3885; 4C $4340; 4C $3,045; BW $2,200. **Remarks:** no classified advertising. **Circ:** ‡75000, 25000.

11714 ■ Phi Delta Kappan: Professional Journal for Education
Phi Delta Kappa International
320 W 8th St., Ste. 216
Bloomington, IN 47404
Phone: (812)339-1156
Fax: (812)339-0018
Free: 800-766-1156
Magazine for professional educators. **Freq:** 8/year. **Print Method:** Offset. **Trim Size:** 7 7/8 x 10 7/8. **Cols./Page:** 3. **Col. Width:** 13.5 picas. **Col. Depth:** 54 picas. **Key Personnel:** Carol Bucheri, Director; David Ruetschlin, Managing Editor. **ISSN:** 0031--7217 (print); **EISSN:** 1940--6487 (electronic). **Subscription Rates:** Included in membership; $248 Institutions US; $269 Institutions foreign; $58 /year; free for members; $269 institutions in US. **URL:** http://pdk.sagepub.com; http://pdkintl.org/publications/kappan/. **Mailing address:** PO Box 7888, Bloomington, IN 47407-7888. **Ad Rates:** BW $3885; 4C $4340; 4C $3,045; BW $2,200. **Remarks:** no classified advertising. **Circ:** ‡75000, 25000.

11715 ■ Philosophy of Music Education Review
Indiana University Press
c/o Estelle R. Jorgensen, Ed.
Indiana University School of Music
1201 E Third St.
Bloomington, IN 47405-7006
Phone: (812)855-2051
Fax: (812)855-4936
Journal covering philosophical research in music education for music professionals and scholars. **Freq:** Semiannual. **Key Personnel:** Estelle R. Jorgensen, Editor; Mary Reichling, Editor. **ISSN:** 1063--5734 (print). **Subscription Rates:** $38.50 Individuals print and online; $35 Individuals print only; $33.50 Individuals online only; $93.50 Institutions print and online; $70 Institutions print only; $63 Institutions online only. **URL:** http://music.indiana.edu/departments/academic/music-education/PMER.shtml; http://www.jstor.org/action/showPublication?journalCode=philmusieducrevi. **Ad Rates:** BW $250. **Remarks:** Accepts advertising. **Circ:** Paid 500.

11716 ■ The Proceedings and Membership List of the Thomas Wolfe Society
Thomas Wolfe Society
PO Box 1146
Bloomington, IN 47402-1146
Freq: Annual. **Subscription Rates:** Included in membership. **URL:** http://www.thomaswolfe.org/about-tws/tws-publications. **Remarks:** Advertising not accepted. **Circ:** (Not Reported).

11717 ■ Prooftexts: A Journal of Jewish Literary History
Indiana University Press
601 N Morton St.
Bloomington, IN 47404-3797
Phone: (812)855-9449
Fax: (812)855-8507
Free: 800-842-6796
Publication E-mail: prooftexts@jtsa.edu
Peer-reviewed journal dealing with Jewish literary studies. Seeks to integrate the study of modern Jewish literatures (in Hebrew, Yiddish, and European languages) with the literary study of the Jewish classical tradition. **Freq:** 3/year. **Key Personnel:** Barbara Mann, Editor; Jeremy A. Dauber, Editor. **ISSN:** 0272-9601 (print); **EISSN:** 1086-3311 (electronic). **Subscription Rates:** $49.50 Individuals print and online; $45 Individuals print only; $42.75 Individuals online only; $153 Institutions print and online; $115 Institutions print only; $103.50 Institutions online only. **URL:** http://inscribe.iupress.org/loi/pft; http://www.jstor.org/action/showPublication?journalCode=prooftexts. **Ad Rates:** BW $275. **Remarks:** Accepts advertising. **Circ:** (Not Reported).

11718 ■ Public Budgeting and Finance
American Association for Budget and Program Analysis
School of Public & Environmental Affairs
Indiana University
Bloomington, IN 47405
Phone: (812)855-0732
Fax: (812)877-7802
Publisher's E-mail: aabpa@aabpa.org
Journal exploring theory and practice in financial management and budgeting at all levels of public sector government. **Freq:** Quarterly. **Print Method:** Offset. **Trim Size:** 6 3/4 x 10. **Cols./Page:** 3. **Col. Width:** 25 nonpareils. **Col. Depth:** 140 agate lines. **Key Personnel:** John L. Mikesell, Board Member; Philip G. Joyce, Editor. **ISSN:** 0275-1100 (print); **EISSN:** 1540-5850 (electronic). **Subscription Rates:** $463 Institutions America (print or online); $556 Institutions America (print and online); $99 Individuals America (print); $80 Members American Historical Association/American Political Science Association (America, UK, Europe-nonEuro zoneAmerican---print and online); £366 Institutions UK (print or online); £440 Institutions UK (print and online); £97 Individuals UK and Europe-nonEuro zone (print and online); €463 Institutions Europe (print or online); €556 Institutions Europe (print and online); €148 Individuals Europe-Euro zone (print and online); $148 Members American Historical Association/American Political Science Association (Europe-Euro zone----print and online). **URL:** http://onlinelibrary.wiley.com/journal/10.1111/(ISSN)1540-5850. **Ad Rates:** BW $325. **Remarks:** Accepts advertising. **Circ:** Non-paid ‡2100, Paid ‡900.

11719 ■ Race/Ethnicity: Multidisciplinary Global Context
Indiana University Press
601 N Morton St.
Bloomington, IN 47404-3797
Phone: (812)855-9449
Fax: (812)855-8507
Free: 800-842-6796
Peer-reviewed journal offering a critical intervention into contemporary thinking on race and ethnicity by recognizing and responding to these shared challenges. **Freq:** Semiannual. **Key Personnel:** John A. Powell, Executive Editor; Leslie Birdwell Shortlidge, Managing Editor; Andrew Grant-Thomas. **ISSN:** 1935--8644 (print); **EISSN:** 1935--8562 (electronic). **Subscription Rates:** $62.25 Individuals print and online; $56.50 Individuals print only; $50.95 Individuals online only; $136.50 Institutions print and online; $101.50 Institutions print only; $91.25 Institutions online only. **URL:** http://www.jstor.org/journal/racethmulglocon; http://www.iupress.indiana.edu/em/email_images/JRNLS_Presspage/CAT_IUPJ_SUM11.pdf. **Circ:** (Not Reported).

11720 ■ The Ryder
The Ryder
1316 E Third St.
Bloomington, IN 47401
Phone: (812)339-2002
Publication E-mail: theryder@theryder.com
Magazine featuring arts and entertainment. **Founded:** 1979. **Freq:** Monthly. **Print Method:** Offset. **Trim Size:** 8 x 10 1/2. **Cols./Page:** 3. **Col. Width:** 26 nonpareils. **Col. Depth:** 136 agate lines. **Subscription Rates:** $12 Individuals. **URL:** http://theryder.com/the-ryder-magazine/. **Remarks:** Accepts advertising. **Circ:** Non-paid 19000.

11721 ■ Serbian Studies: Journal of the North American Society for Serbian Studies
Slavica Publishers
Indiana University, 1430 N Willis Dr.
2611 E 10th St.
Bloomington, IN 47404-2146
Phone: (812)856-4186
Fax: (812)856-4187
Free: 877-752-8422
Publisher's E-mail: slavica@indiana.edu
Peer-reviewed journal publishing articles in all aspects of the Serbian cultural heritage, archival documents, and source material related to the Serbian immigration to North America. **Freq:** Semiannual. **Key Personnel:** Bogdan Rakic, Editor. **ISSN:** 0742--3330 (print); **EISSN:** 1941--9511 (electronic). **Subscription Rates:** Included in membership; $60 Institutions; $71 Institutions, other countries. **URL:** http://slavica.indiana.edu/journalListings/serbian. **Circ:** (Not Reported).

11722 ■ TechTrends
Association for Educational Communications and Technology
320 W 8th St., Ste. 101
Bloomington, IN 47404-3745
Phone: (812)335-7675
Free: 877-677-2328
Publisher's E-mail: aect@aect.org
Professional magazine for educators and trainers. **Freq:** 6/year. **Print Method:** Offset. Uses mats. **Trim Size:** 8 1/2 x 11. **Cols./Page:** 3. **Col. Width:** 26 nonpareils. **Col. Depth:** 133 agate lines. **Key Personnel:** Philip Harris, Publisher; Daniel W. Surry, Editor-in-Chief. **ISSN:** 8756--3894 (print); **EISSN:** 1559--7075 (electronic). **Subscription Rates:** Included in membership; €63.02 Individuals online only. **URL:** http://aect.site-ym.com/?page=techtrends; http://springer.com/education+%26+language/learning+%26+instruction/journal/11528. **Ad Rates:** BW $1,700; 4C $3,700. **Remarks:** Accepts advertising. **Circ:** ‡8000.

11723 ■ The Thomas Wolfe Review
Thomas Wolfe Society
PO Box 1146
Bloomington, IN 47402-1146
Freq: Annual. **ISSN:** 0276--5683 (print). **Subscription Rates:** $10 Students; $30 per year. **URL:** http://www.thomaswolfe.org/the-thomas-wolfe-review. **Remarks:** Accepts advertising. **Circ:** 500.

11724 ■ Victorian Studies
Indiana University Press
Indiana University
Ballatine Hall 338
Bloomington, IN 47405
Phone: (812)855-9533
Fax: (812)855-9534
Publication E-mail: victstu@indiana.edu
Scholarly journal covering English culture of the Victorian period. **Freq:** Quarterly. **Print Method:** Offset. **Trim Size:** 8 x 10. **Key Personnel:** Ivan Kreilkamp, Editor; Andrew H. Miller, Editor; Maureen Hattrup, Managing Editor. **ISSN:** 0042--5222 (print); **EISSN:** 1527--2052 (electronic). **Subscription Rates:** $49.50 Individuals online; $52 Individuals print; $57.50 Individuals print and online; $135 Institutions online; $150 Institutions print; $199.50 Institutions print and online. **URL:** http://www.indiana.edu/~victstu/victorianStudies.shtml. **Ad Rates:** BW $400. **Remarks:** Accepts advertising. **Circ:** 2300.

11725 ■ Yearbook of Comparative Literature
University of Toronto Press Journals Division
923 Ballantine Hall
Indiana University
Bloomington, IN 47405
Publication E-mail: yearbook@indiana.edu
Publication focusing on theoretically informed research in literary studies with a comparative, intercultural, or interdisciplinary emphasis. Publishes articles on the comparative study of the arts, film studies with a focus on literature, international literary relations, pedagogy, and the theory and practice of translation, as well as on the study of genres and modes, themes and motifs, periods, and movements. **Freq:** Annual. **Key Personnel:** Ben Garceau, Managing Editor; Eyal Peretz, Editor. **ISSN:** 0084--3695 (print); **EISSN:** 1947--2978 (electronic). **Subscription Rates:** $32 Canada print; $55 Institutions, Canada print; $45 Other countries print; $65 Institutions, other countries print. **URL:** http://www.utpjournals.com/Yearbook-of-Comparative-Literature.html; http://www.indiana.edu/~ycgl/index.html. **Remarks:** Advertising not accepted. **Circ:** (Not Reported).

11726 ■ Minnesota Public Television Association - 95.1
2723 N Walnut St.
Bloomington, IN 47401
Phone: (812)335-9500
Fax: (812)335-8880
Format: Contemporary Christian; Adult Contemporary. **Founded:** Sept. 16, 2006. **Wattage:** 6,000. **Ad Rates:** Advertising accepted; rates available upon request. **URL:** http://www.spirit95fm.com.

11727 ■ WBWB-FM - 96.7
304 S State Road 446
Bloomington, IN 47401
Phone: (812)336-8000
Fax: (812)336-7000
Format: Contemporary Hit Radio (CHR). **Networks:** Independent. **Owner:** Artistic Media Partners Inc., 5520 E 75th St., Indianapolis, IN 46250, Ph: (317)594-0600.

Circulation: ★ = AAM; △ or • = BPA; ♦ = CAC; ❑ = VAC; ⊕ = PO Statement; ‡ = Publisher's Report; Boldface figures = sworn; Light figures = estimated.

Founded: 1978. **Operating Hours:** Continuous. **ADI:** Indianapolis (Marion), IN. **Key Personnel:** Arthur Angotti, III, President; Rick Evans, Prog. Dir. **Wattage:** 3,000. **Ad Rates:** Advertising accepted; rates available upon request. Combined advertising rates available with WGCT-FM. **URL:** http://www.wbwb.com.

11728 ■ WCLS-FM - 97.7
318 E 3rd St.
Bloomington, IN 47401
Phone: (812)339-9700
Format: Oldies; News; Classic Rock; Information. **Networks:** ABC. **Key Personnel:** Tony Kale, Program Mgr., wclsfm@smithville.net. **Wattage:** 6,000 ERP. **Ad Rates:** Advertising accepted; rates available upon request. **URL:** http://www.wclsfm.com/.

11729 ■ WFHB-FM - 91.3
108 W Fourth St.
Bloomington, IN 47404
Phone: (812)323-1200
Fax: (812)323-0320
Email: wfhb@wfhb.org
Format: Talk. **Operating Hours:** Continuous. **ADI:** Peoria-Bloomington, IL. **Key Personnel:** Jim Manion, Music Dir., music@wfhb.org. **Wattage:** 1,600 ERP. **Ad Rates:** Noncommercial. Underwriting available. **URL:** http://www.wfhb.org.

11730 ■ WFIU-FM - 103.7
Radio-TV Ctr., 1229 E Seventh St.
1229 E 7th St.
Bloomington, IN 47405
Phone: (812)855-1357
Fax: (812)855-5600
Free: 800-662-3311
Format: Classical; Public Radio; Jazz; Information; News. **Networks:** National Public Radio (NPR); Public Radio International (PRI). **Founded:** 1950. **Operating Hours:** Continuous. **Key Personnel:** Christina Kuzmych, Station Mgr., ckuzmych@indiana.edu; Stan Jastrzebski, News Dir., stanjast@indiana.edu. **Local Programs:** *Saint Paul Sunday*, Sunday 12:00 p.m. **Wattage:** 34,000. **Ad Rates:** Noncommercial. **URL:** http://www.indianapublicmedia.org.

11731 ■ WGCL-AM - 1370
400 One City Ctr.
Bloomington, IN 47404
Phone: (812)332-3366
Fax: (812)331-4570
Format: News; Talk. **Networks:** ABC; ESPN Radio. **Owner:** Sarkes Tarzian Inc., PO Box 62, Bloomington, IN 47402, Ph: (812)332-7251, Fax: (812)331-4575. **Founded:** 1949. **Operating Hours:** Continuous. **ADI:** Indianapolis (Marion), IN. **Key Personnel:** Brad Holtz, Prog. Dir., brad@wgclradio.com; Geoff Vargo, Gen. Mgr., VP, geoff@wgclradio.com. **Wattage:** 5,000 Day; 500 Night. **Ad Rates:** Noncommercial. **URL:** http://www.wgclradio.com/category/localprograms/inside-outdoors.

11732 ■ WHCC-FM - 105.1
304 State Rd., 446
Bloomington, IN 47401-8837
Phone: (812)335-1051
Fax: (812)336-7000
Email: whcc105@whcc105.com
Format: Country. **Operating Hours:** Continuous. **Key Personnel:** Sheila Stephen, Contact, sheila@whcc105.com. **Wattage:** 1,850 ERP. **Ad Rates:** Advertising accepted; rates available upon request. **URL:** http://www.whcc105.com.

11733 ■ WTIU-TV - 30
1229 E Seventh St.
Bloomington, IN 47405-5501
Phone: (812)855-5900
Fax: (812)855-0729
Email: wtiu@indiana.edu
Format: Public TV. **Networks:** Public Broadcasting Service (PBS). **Owner:** Trustees of Indiana University, 107 S Indiana Ave., Bloomington, IN 47405, Ph: (812)855-4311, Fax: (812)855-3584. **Founded:** 1969. **Operating Hours:** Continuous; 95% network, 5% local. **ADI:** Indianapolis (Marion), IN. **Key Personnel:** Perry S. Metz, Exec. Dir., metz@indiana.edu; Phil Meyer, Station Mgr., pwmeyer@indiana.edu. **Local Programs:** *Take One Step*; *The War That Made America*; *The Woodwright's Shop*; *The Face of Russia*. **Ad Rates:** Noncommercial. **URL:** http://www.indiana.edu.

11734 ■ WTTS-FM - 92.3
400 1 City Ctr.
Bloomington, IN 47404
Phone: (812)332-3366
Fax: (812)331-4570
Format: Classic Rock. **Owner:** Sarkes Tarzian Inc., PO Box 62, Bloomington, IN 47402, Ph: (812)332-7251, Fax: (812)331-4575. **Founded:** 1960. **Operating Hours:** Continuous. **ADI:** Indianapolis (Marion), IN. **Key Personnel:** Geoff Vargo, Gen. Mgr., VP, geoff@wttsfm.com; Daryl McIntire, Dir. of Sales, mac@wttsfm.com; Brad Holtz, Music Dir., brad@wttsfm.com; Laura Duncan, Dir. of Production, laura@wttsfm.com. **Wattage:** 37,000. **Ad Rates:** Noncommercial. **URL:** http://www.wttsfm.com.

BLUFFTON

Wells Co. Wells Co. (NE). On Wabash River, 24 m S of Fort Wayne. Manufactures pumps, animal feeds and supplements, motors, machinery; agriculture feed systems. Limestone quarries. Agriculture.

11735 ■ Bluffton News-Banner
News Banner Publications Inc.
125 N Johnson St.
Bluffton, IN 46714-1907
Phone: (260)824-0224
Fax: (260)824-0700
Publication E-mail: email@news-banner.com
Newspaper. **Freq:** Mon.-Sat. **Print Method:** Web Offset. **Cols./Page:** 6. **Col. Width:** 1 13/16 inches. **Col. Depth:** 21 1/2 inches. **Key Personnel:** Mark F. Miller, General Manager, Publisher; Glen Werling, Managing Editor; Howard Jones, Jr., Manager, Production; Martha Poling, Business Manager. **Subscription Rates:** $90 Individuals online, 1 year; $128 Individuals by foot carrier delivery, print, 1 year; $138 Individuals by motor route delivery, print, 1 year; $199 By mail (in state), print, 1 year; $240 By mail (out of state), print, 1 year. **URL:** http://www.news-banner.com. **Mailing address:** PO Box 436, Bluffton, IN 46714. **Ad Rates:** PCI $10.50. **Remarks:** Advertising accepted; rates available upon request. **Circ:** (Not Reported).

11736 ■ The Ossian Journal
News Banner Publications Inc.
125 N Johnson St.
Bluffton, IN 46714-1907
Phone: (260)824-0224
Fax: (260)824-0700
Publisher's E-mail: email@news-banner.com
Newspaper. **Freq:** Weekly (Thurs.). **Print Method:** Web offset. **Cols./Page:** 6. **Col. Width:** 2 1/16 inches. **Col. Depth:** 21 1/2 inches. **Key Personnel:** Michael Puffer, Chief Executive Officer; Kelly Elarbee, Media Specialist; Alice Haynie, Chief Financial Officer, Chief Operating Officer. **URL:** http://echo-media.com/medias/details/6823. **Mailing address:** PO Box 436, Bluffton, IN 46714. **Ad Rates:** GLR $5.20; BW $516; SAU $4; PCI $4. **Remarks:** Accepts advertising. **Circ:** Paid ‡700.

BOONVILLE

Warrick Co. Warrick Co. (SW) 20 m NE of Evansville. Manufactures aluminum rods and billets, ammunition casing, machine shops, plastic custom molding. Coal mines. Agriculture. Fruit, tomatoes, grain, soybeans.

11737 ■ Boonville Standard
Warrick Publishing Co.
204 W Locust St.
Boonville, IN 47601
Phone: (812)897-2330
Fax: (812)897-3703
Publication E-mail: newsroom@warricknews.com
Newspaper with a Republican orientation. **Freq:** Weekly (Thurs.). **Print Method:** Offset. **Cols./Page:** 6. **Col. Width:** 12.4 picas. **Col. Depth:** 301 agate lines. **Key Personnel:** Debi Neal, Business Manager; Gary Neal, Publisher; Tim Young, Managing Editor. **Subscription Rates:** $30 Individuals Warrick County per year; $19 Individuals Warrick County 6 months ; $40 Individuals elsewhere in Indiana per year; $50 Individuals outside of Indiana per year. **URL:** http://tristate-media.com/warrick/site/about/. **Mailing address:** PO Box 266, Boonville, IN 47601. **Ad Rates:** SAU $9.89; CNU $7.42; PCI $5.76. **Remarks:** Accepts advertising. **Circ:** 4000.

11738 ■ Newburgh Chandler Register
Warrick Publishing Co.
204 W Locust St.
Boonville, IN 47601
Phone: (812)897-2330
Fax: (812)897-3703
Publisher's E-mail: newsroom@warricknews.com
Local newspaper. **Freq:** Weekly (Thurs.). **Print Method:** Offset. **Cols./Page:** 6. **Col. Width:** 12.4 picas. **Col. Depth:** 301 agate lines. **Key Personnel:** Gary Neal, Publisher; Debi Neal, Business Manager; Tim Young, Managing Editor. **Subscription Rates:** $26 Individuals in county; $32 Individuals standard out of county; $50 Individuals standard out of state; $52 Individuals register out of county or out of state; $22 Individuals in county senior citizen. **URL:** http://www.tristate-media.com/warricknews/. **Formed by the merger of:** Newburgh Register; Chandler Post. **Mailing address:** PO Box 266, Boonville, IN 47601. **Ad Rates:** SAU $10.19; PCI $10.19. **Remarks:** Accepts advertising. **Circ:** ‡10000.

11739 ■ WBNL-AM - 1540
PO Box 270
Boonville, IN 47601
Phone: (812)897-2080
Email: rturpen@radio1540.net
Format: Easy Listening. **Networks:** Network Indiana. **Owner:** Turpen Communications L.L.C., Radion Station State Rt 61, Boonville, IN 47601, Ph: (812)897-2080. **Founded:** 1950. **Operating Hours:** Continuous; 15% network, 85% local. **Wattage:** 250. **Ad Rates:** $12-18 for 60 seconds. **URL:** http://www.radio1540.net.

BRAZIL

Clay Co. Clay Co. (W). 16 m NE of Terre Haute. Manufactures clay products, extension cord assembly, jet engine components, mobile homes, semi trailers. Coal mines; clay pets. Agriculture. Corn, wheat, oats and soybeans.

11740 ■ The Brazil Times
The Brazil Times Publishing Corp.
100 N Meridian St.
Brazil, IN 47834
Phone: (812)446-2216
Fax: (812)446-0938
Newspaper with a Republican orientation. **Freq:** Daily (eve.) and Sat. (morn.). **Print Method:** Offset. **Trim Size:** 22 3/4 x 13 3/4. **Cols./Page:** 6. **Col. Width:** 26 nonpareils. **Col. Depth:** 301 agate lines. **Key Personnel:** Randy List, Publisher; Jason Moon, Managing Editor; Lynne Llewellyn, General Manager. **Subscription Rates:** $78.50 Individuals. **URL:** http://www.thebraziltimes.com. **Mailing address:** PO Box 429, Brazil, IN 47834. **Ad Rates:** GLR $.47; BW $788; 4C $988; SAU $6.50; PCI $6.50. **Remarks:** Advertising accepted; rates available upon request. **Circ:** Paid ‡5242.

BREMEN

Marshall Co. Marshall Co. (NC). 15 m NE of Plymouth.

11741 ■ Farm and Home News
The Pilot Company Inc.
PO Box 230
Bremen, IN 46506
Phone: (574)209-0704
Fax: (574)546-5170
Shopper. **Founded:** 1954. **Freq:** Weekly (Wed.). **Print Method:** Offset. **Trim Size:** 18 x 22 1/2. **Cols./Page:** 6. **Col. Width:** 24 nonpareils. **Col. Depth:** 301 agate lines. **Key Personnel:** Barbara Keiser, Editor; Keith Isley, Manager, Advertising. **Subscription Rates:** Free; $5 By mail. **Ad Rates:** BW $554.70; 4C $894.70; SAU $4.84. **Remarks:** Accepts advertising. **Circ:** Free 18500.

11742 ■ Nappanee Advance News: Serving Nappanee and Wakarusa
The Pilot Company Inc.
PO Box 230
Bremen, IN 46506
Phone: (574)209-0704
Fax: (574)546-5170
Publication E-mail: advance@npcc.net
Local newspaper. **Freq:** Weekly (Thurs.). **Print Method:** Offset. **Trim Size:** 18 x 22 1/2. **Cols./Page:** 6. **Col. Width:** 24 nonpareils. **Col. Depth:** 301 agate lines. **Key Personnel:** Rick Kreps, Publisher; Angel Perkins, Editor. **URL:** http://www.thepilotnews.com/category/nappanee-advance-news. **Remarks:** Accepts advertising. **Circ:** (Not Reported).

BROOKVILLE

Franklin Co. Franklin Co. (E). On Whitewater River, 40 m NW of Cincinnati, Ohio. Manufactures roofing, rubber, plastic products, feed, boys garments. Agriculture. Corn, wheat, tobacco.

11743 ■ Liberty Herald
Liberty Herald
531 Main St.
Brookville, IN 47012
Phone: (765)647-4221
Fax: (765)647-4811
Publisher's E-mail: info@whitewaterpub.com
Newspaper with a Republican orientation. **Freq:** Weekly (Thurs.). **Print Method:** Offset. **Trim Size:** 13.75 x 22. 75. **Cols./Page:** 6. **Col. Width:** 12 picas. **Col. Depth:** 21 inches. **USPS:** 311-720. **URL:** http://www.whitewaterpub.com/?page=liberty. **Remarks:** Accepts advertising. **Circ:** (Not Reported).

BROWNSTOWN

Jackson Co. Jackson Co. (S). 10 m w of Seymour. Tourism. State and National Forests. Manufacturers floating radio sub warning devices. Paper flour, bricks, holloware, canned goods. Hatcheries. Agriculture. Melons, corn, wheat, soybeans.

11744 ■ The Jackson County Banner
The Jackson County Banner
116 E Cross St.
Brownstown, IN 47220
Phone: (812)358-2111
Fax: (812)358-5606
Publication E-mail: news@thebanner.com
Community newspaper with Democratic orientation. **Freq:** Tuesday and Thursday. **Print Method:** Offset. **Cols./Page:** 6. **Col. Width:** 27 nonpareils. **Col. Depth:** 301 agate lines. **Key Personnel:** Patricia Robertson, Publisher; Joe Persinger, Editor. **USPS:** 067-920. **Subscription Rates:** $60 Individuals Jackson & Adjoining; $65 Individuals Rest of Indiana; $71 Out of state. **URL:** http://www.thebanner.com. **Mailing address:** PO Box G, Brownstown, IN 47220. **Ad Rates:** GLR $.252; BW $457.95; 4C $757.95; SAU $4.20. **Remarks:** Accepts advertising. **Circ:** Paid 3800, Free 5.

BUTLER

De Kalb Co. De Kalb Co. (NE). 32 m NE of Fort Wayne. Manufactures automobile jacks, bicycle parts, shipping cartons, fertilizer, truck axles, aluminum billets. Dairy, stock, poultry farms. Corn, wheat, oats.

11745 ■ The Butler Bulletin
The Butler Bulletin
PO Box 39
Butler, IN 46721
Phone: (260)868-5501
Fax: (260)925-2625
Newspaper with a Democratic orientation. **Freq:** Weekly (Tues.). **Print Method:** Offset. **Cols./Page:** 8. **Col. Width:** 22 nonpareils. **Col. Depth:** 172 agate lines. **Key Personnel:** Jeff Jones, Editor. **Subscription Rates:** $29 Individuals. **URL:** http://www.kpcnews.com/eedition_new/eedition_butler_bulletin. **Ad Rates:** SAU $8.09; PCI $6. **Remarks:** Accepts advertising. **Circ:** Paid 1000.

11746 ■ WINM-TV - 63
PO Box 159
Butler, IN 46721-0159
Email: winm@tct_net.org
Format: Commercial TV; Religious. **Networks:** Independent. **Owner:** Tri-State Christian Network, Marion, IL. **Founded:** 1988. **Operating Hours:** Continuous. **ADI:** Fort Wayne (Angola), IN. **Key Personnel:** Rev. Joseph E. Robinson, Gen. Mgr., Sales Mgr., jer@tct_net.org. **Wattage:** 001.005 million. **Ad Rates:** $40 for 30 seconds; $60 for 60 seconds.

CAMPBELLSBURG

11747 ■ Harp and Hound
Irish Wolfhound Club of America
c/o Kathy Welling, Secretary
180 W 3rd St.
Campbellsburg, IN 47108
Phone: (317)727-4954
Freq: Semiannual. **Subscription Rates:** Included in membership. **Remarks:** Advertising not accepted. **Circ:** (Not Reported).

CARMEL

Hamilton Co. Hamilton Co. (C). 15 m N of Indianapolis. Manufactures extension cords, seat belts, screw products; high-tech industry. Nurseries. Farming. Corn and soybeans.

11748 ■ Endless Vacation: Your Vacation Guide
Resort Condominiums International L.L.C.
9998 N Michigan Rd.
Carmel, IN 46032
Phone: (317)805-8000
Fax: (317)805-9335
Free: 800-338-7777
Publication E-mail: evletters@rci.com
Travel magazine. **Freq:** Quarterly. **Print Method:** Offset. **Trim Size:** 8 1/8 x 10 7/8. **Cols./Page:** 3. **Col. Width:** 2 1/4 inches. **Col. Depth:** 10 1/4 inches. **Key Personnel:** Barbara Peck, Editor-in-Chief; Eunice Yap, Contact. **ISSN:** 0279--4853 (print). **Subscription Rates:** $84 Individuals. **Alt. Formats:** PDF. **URL:** http://www.endlessvacation.com/; http://www.rci.com/pre-rci-en_SG/vacation-ideas/EV-Mag-index.page?promo=Multi30S2MPOenSGOFRpromoxEVASIANTHUMBNAIL. **Ad Rates:** BW $71,650; PCI $350. **Remarks:** Accepts advertising. **Circ:** Paid ⋆**1750000.**

11749 ■ Journal of Performance Management
Association for Management Information in Financial Services
14247 Saffron Cir.
Carmel, IN 46032
Phone: (317)815-5857
Publisher's E-mail: ami2@amifs.org
Journal covering various areas of management accounting and outstanding presentations from association conferences and workshops. **Freq:** 3/yr. **ISSN:** 1070-941X (print). **URL:** http://www.amifs.org/. **Formerly:** Journal of Bank Cost & Management Accounting. **Remarks:** Advertising not accepted. **Circ:** 650.

11750 ■ PFIA Protector
Police and Firemen's Insurance Association
101 E 116th St.
Carmel, IN 46032
Phone: (317)581-1913
Fax: (317)571-5946
Free: 800-221-7342
Freq: Quarterly. **Subscription Rates:** Included in membership; $10 Nonmembers; $15 Other countries non-members; $5 Single issue; $35 Individuals premium/month; $269 Individuals optimum/month. **URL:** http://issuu.com/pfia. **Remarks:** Advertising not accepted. **Circ:** (Not Reported).

11751 ■ Precast Inc.
National Precast Concrete Association
1320 City Center Dr., Ste. 200
Carmel, IN 46032
Phone: (317)571-0041
Fax: (317)571-0041
Free: 800-366-7731
Trade magazine covering the precast concrete industry in North America. **Freq:** Bimonthly. **Print Method:** web. **Trim Size:** 8.5 x 11. **Key Personnel:** Brenda Ibitz, Contact, phone: (317)582-5109; Ron Hyink, Managing Editor, phone: (317)582-2320. **ISSN:** 1940--9184 (print). **Subscription Rates:** Free. **URL:** http://precast.org/publications/magazines. **Formerly:** MC Magazine. **Remarks:** Accepts classified advertising. **Circ:** (Not Reported).

11752 ■ Bright House Networks
516 E Carmel Dr.
Carmel, IN 46032
Phone: (317)972-9700
Email: customersupport.indiana@mybrighthouse.com
Founded: 1988. **Formerly:** Jones Intercable Corp. **Cities Served:** Carmel, Fortville, Indianapolis, Lizton, Marion, Whitestown, Zionsville, Indiana: subscribing households 15,564; 290 channels; 1 community access channel; 168 hours per week community access programming. **URL:** http://brighthouse.com.

11753 ■ WHJE-FM - 91.3
520 E Main St.
Carmel, IN 46032
Phone: (317)846-7721
Fax: (317)571-4066
Email: whje@whje.com
Format: Alternative/New Music/Progressive. **Networks:** Network Indiana. **Owner:** Carmel-Clay Schools, 5201 E Main St., Carmel, IN 46033, Ph: (317)844-9961, Fax: (317)844-9965. **Founded:** 1963. **Operating Hours:** Continuous; 100% local. **Wattage:** 13,000. **Ad Rates:** Noncommercial. **URL:** http://www.whje.com.

11754 ■ WRDZ-FM - 98.3
630 W Carmel Dr., Ste. 160
Carmel, IN 46032-2521
Phone: (317)574-2000
Format: Contemporary Hit Radio (CHR). **Networks:** ABC. **Owner:** Radio Disney, 500 S Buena Vista St. MC 7663, Burbank, CA 91521-7716. **Founded:** 1982. **Formerly:** WXIR-FM. **Operating Hours:** Continuous. **ADI:** Indianapolis (Marion), IN. **Wattage:** 3,000. **Ad Rates:** $50-75 for 30 seconds.

CENTERVILLE

Wayne Co. Wayne Co. (E). 4 m W of Richmond. Historical Areas. Manufactured automatic tools and caskets.

11755 ■ Vintage Ford
Model T Ford Club of America
119 W Main St.
Centerville, IN 47330
Phone: (765)855-5248
Fax: (765)855-3428
Trade magazine covering antique automobiles, especially Model T Ford. **Founded:** Nov. 1965. **Freq:** Bimonthly. **ISSN:** 0042-6350 (print). **URL:** http://www.mtfca.com/clubpages/magazine.htm. **Mailing address:** PO Box 126, Centerville, IN 47330. **Remarks:** Accepts advertising. **Circ:** Controlled 8500.

CHARLESTOWN

Clark Co. Clark Co. (SE). NE of Jeffersonville. Chemicals.

11756 ■ The Leader
Green Banner Publications Inc.
382 Main Cross St.
Charlestown, IN 47111
Phone: (812)256-3377
Community newspaper. **Founded:** 1956. **Freq:** Weekly (Wed.). **Print Method:** Offset. **Trim Size:** 11 3/8 x 17. **Cols./Page:** 5. **Col. Width:** 25 nonpareils. **Col. Depth:** 224 agate lines. **Key Personnel:** Joe Green, Publisher. **Subscription Rates:** $6 Individuals local; $8 Individuals commissionable. **URL:** http://www.gbpnews.com/index.php?option=com_content&view=category&layout=blog&id=36&Itemid=58. **Ad Rates:** GLR $.38; BW $424; SAU $5.30; PCI $5.30. **Remarks:** Advertising accepted; rates available upon request. **Circ:** (Not Reported).

CHESTERTON

Porter Co. Porter Co. (NC). 5 m S of Lake Michigan. Bronze castings.

11757 ■ WDSO-FM - 88.3
2125 S 11st St.
Chesterton, IN 46304
Phone: (219)983-3777
Fax: (219)983-3773
Format: Educational. **Networks:** Network Indiana. **Owner:** Duneland School Corp., 601 W Morgan Ave., Chesterton, IN 46304, Ph: (219)983-3600, Fax: (219)983-3775. **Founded:** 1976. **Operating Hours:** 6 am-6 pm, Mon, Wed, Fri; 6 am-4 pm Tues.; 6 am-4:30 pm Thur. **Wattage:** 400. **Ad Rates:** Noncommercial. **URL:** http://www.duneland.k12.in.us.

CHURUBUSCO

Whitley Co. Whitley Co. (NE). 15 m NW of Ft Wayne. Manufactures automotive gaskets and rubber products, oil seals, water conditioning equipment.

11758 ■ Churubusco News
Churubusco News and Printing
123 N Main St.
Churubusco, IN 46723

Circulation: ⋆ = AAM; △ or • = BPA; ♦ = CAC; ❑ = VAC; ⊕ = PO Statement; ‡ = Publisher's Report; Boldface figures = sworn; Light figures = estimated.

Phone: (260)693-3949
Fax: (260)693-6545
Publication E-mail: busconews@busconews.com
Community newspaper. **Freq:** Weekly. **Print Method:** Offset. **Trim Size:** 11 x 17. **Cols./Page:** 6. **Col. Width:** 1 1/2 inches. **Col. Depth:** 15 3/4 inches. **Key Personnel:** Robert L. Allman, Publisher; Vivian Sade, Editor. **USPS:** 009-385. **URL:** http://busconews.com. **Remarks:** Accepts advertising. **Circ:** (Not Reported).

CLARKSVILLE

11759 ■ WJYL-TV - 45
PO Box 2605
Clarksville, IN 47131-2605
Phone: (812)949-9595
Email: prayer@wjyl.org
Operating Hours: Continuous. **ADI**: Louisville, KY. **Key Personnel:** John Smith, Founder. **URL:** http://www.wjyl.org.

11760 ■ WNDA-AM - 1570
PO Box 2623
Clarksville, IN 47131
Phone: (812)949-1570
Fax: (812)949-9632
Format: Oldies. **Key Personnel:** Ashley Robinson, News Dir., news@indiana9.com; Corissa Smith, Gen. Sales Mgr., csmith@indiana9.com. **Wattage**: 1,570.

CLINTON

Vermillion Co. Vermillion Co. (W). On Wabash River, 16 m N of Terre Haute. Manufactures antibiotics, fertilizers, overalls, shirts. Meat packing Coal mine; gravel. Aluminum products. Grain farms.

11761 ■ The Daily Clintonian
Clinton Color Crafters
422 S Main St.
Clinton, IN 47842
Newspaper with a Republican orientation. **Freq:** Daily (eve.). **Print Method:** Offset. **Trim Size:** 17 1/2 x 22 3/4. **Cols./Page:** 7. **Col. Width:** 12.5 picas. **Col. Depth:** 294 agate lines. **Key Personnel:** George B. Carey, President, Publisher. **USPS:** 142-300. **URL:** http://www.ccc-clintonian.com/. **Ad Rates:** GLR $.15; BW $1,176; SAU $8; PCI $8. **Remarks:** Accepts advertising. **Circ:** (Not Reported).

CLOVERDALE

Putnam Co. Putnam Co. (WC). 20 m NE of Terre Haute. Residential

11762 ■ The Hoosier Topics
Hoosier Topics
1 N Main St.
Cloverdale, IN 46120
Phone: (765)795-4438
Fax: (765)795-3121
Free: 877-795-4438
Publisher's E-mail: htopics@ccrtc.com
Shopping guide. **Freq:** Weekly (Tues.). **Key Personnel:** John A. Gillaspy, General Manager; Jenny Snyder, Office Manager; Faye Gaddis, Compositor. **URL:** http://www.thehoosiertopics.com. **Mailing address:** PO Box 496, Cloverdale, IN 46120. **Remarks:** Accepts advertising. **Circ:** Combined 20208.

COLUMBIA CITY

Whitley Co. Whitley Co. (NE). 20 m NW of Fort Wayne.

11763 ■ The Post & Mail
Columbia City Publishing Co.
PO Box 128
Columbia City, IN 46725
Phone: (260)248-5112
Fax: (260)244-7598
General newspaper. **Freq:** Mon.-Sat. (eve.). **Print Method:** Offset. **Cols./Page:** 6. **Col. Depth:** 21 1/2 inches. **Key Personnel:** Nicole Ott, Editor; Rick Kreps, Publisher; Phil Smith, Managing Editor; Betsy Didier, Manager, Advertising. **ISSN:** 0746--9950 (print). **Subscription Rates:** $17 Individuals print, 4 weeks mail delivery (outside Whitley County); $15 Individuals print, 4 weeks mail delivery (in Whitley County); $.95 Individuals online, 1 day ; $18 Individuals online, 17 weeks; $36 Individuals online, 6 months; $72 Individuals online, 12 months. **URL:** http://www.thepostandmail.com. **Remarks:** Advertising accepted; rates available upon request. **Circ:** ‡4867.

11764 ■ WJHS-FM - 91.5
600 N Whitley St.
Columbia City, IN 46725
Phone: (260)248-8915
Format: Adult Album Alternative. **Networks:** AP. **Owner:** Columbia City High School, 600 N Whitley St., Columbia City, IN 46725, Ph: (260)244-6136, Fax: (260)244-7326. **Founded:** 1986. **Operating Hours**: 1% network, 99% local. **Wattage**: 2,650. **Ad Rates:** Noncommercial. **URL:** http://www.wjhs915.org.

COLUMBUS

Bartholomew Co. Bartholomew Co. (SE). 45 m S of Indianapolis. Manufactures auto parts, variable transmissions, diesel engines, metal furniture, metal, plastic products specialties, cement products, electric motors. Diversified farming.

11765 ■ The Republic
The Republic
333 Second St.
Columbus, IN 47201
Phone: (812)372-7811
Publisher's E-mail: editorial@therepublic.com
Newspaper with a Republican orientation. **Freq:** Daily (morn.). **Print Method:** Offset. **Cols./Page:** 6. **Col. Width:** 25 nonpareils. **Col. Depth:** 301 agate lines. **Key Personnel:** Chuck Wells, Publisher; Mark Baldwin, Editor; Harry McCawley, Associate Editor. **URL:** http://www.therepublic.com. **Ad Rates:** GLR $.98; BW $1902.75; 4C $2177.75; SAU $14.75; PCI $14.75. **Remarks:** Accepts advertising. **Circ:** Paid ♦**15691**, Non-paid ♦**17946**.

11766 ■ WCSI-AM - 1010
3212 Washington St.
Columbus, IN 47203
Phone: (812)372-4448
Email: wcsi@wcsiradio.com
Format: News; Talk; Sports. **Networks:** Mutual Broadcasting System; ESPN Radio; AP. **Owner:** White River Broadcasting Company Inc., at above address. **Founded:** 1957. **Operating Hours**: Continuous. **Key Personnel:** John Foster, Dir. of Programs, jfoster@wcsiradio.com. **Local Programs**: *Stirring Something Up*, Saturday 8:00 a.m. - 8:30 a.m.; *Kid's Count Show*, Sunday 7:00 a.m. - 7:30 a.m. **Wattage**: 330. **Ad Rates:** $14 for 60 seconds. **URL:** http://www.wcsi.whiterivernews.com.

11767 ■ WINN-FM - 104.9
3212 Washington St.
Columbus, IN 47203
Phone: (812)372-4448
Email: studio@win1049.com
Format: Oldies. **Key Personnel:** Bob Morrison, Sales Mgr.; Mike Sullivan, Mgr.; David Glass, VP, Director. **Ad Rates:** Advertising accepted; rates available upon request. **Mailing address:** PO Box 1789, Columbus, IN 47202. **URL:** http://www.win1049.com.

11768 ■ WKKG-FM - 101.5
3212 Washington St.
Columbus, IN 47203
Phone: (812)372-4448
Free: 877-269-1015
Email: studio@wkkg.com
Format: Contemporary Country. **Networks:** Mutual Broadcasting System. **Owner:** Findlay Publishing Co., 701 W Sandusky St., Findlay, OH 45840, Ph: (419)422-5151. **Founded:** 1958. **Operating Hours**: Continuous. **Key Personnel:** Scott Michaels, Dir. of Programs. **Wattage**: 50,000 ERP. **Ad Rates:** $42 for 60 seconds. **URL:** http://www.wkkg.com.

11769 ■ WRZQ-FM - 107.3
825 Washington St.
Columbus, IN 47201
Phone: (812)379-1077
Email: news@qmix.com
Format: Adult Contemporary. **Owner:** Keith Reising, 1680 Hwy., 62 NE, Corydon, IN 47112-7739. **Founded:** 1968. **Formerly**: WTRE-FM. **Operating Hours**: Continuous. **Key Personnel:** Mike King, Station Mgr., mking@qmix.com; Michelle Hardcastle, Gen. Sales Mgr., mhardcastle@qmix.com. **Wattage**: 25,000 ERP. **Ad Rates:** $21-34 for 60 seconds. Combined advertising rates available with WTRE-AM. **URL:** http://www.qmix.com.

11770 ■ WWWY-FM - 104.9
3212 Washington St.
Columbus, IN 47203
Phone: (812)372-4448
Free: 888-262-1061
Email: rockme@y106.com
Format: Adult Contemporary. **Networks:** Westwood One Radio. **Owner:** White River Broadcasting Co., 3212 Washington St, Columbus, IN 47203, Ph: (812)372-4448. **Founded:** 1975. **Operating Hours**: Continuous. **ADI**: Indianapolis (Marion), IN. **Key Personnel:** Tasha Mann, Gen. Mgr., tasha@y106.com. **Wattage**: 6,000. **Ad Rates:** $10-18 for 30 seconds; $13-22 for 60 seconds. Combined advertising rates available with WJCP-FM, WIKI-FM. **Mailing address:** PO Box 1789, Columbus, IN 47202-1789. **URL:** http://www.y106.com.

11771 ■ WYGB-FM - 102.9
825 Washington St.
Columbus, IN 47201
Phone: (812)379-1077
Format: Contemporary Country. **Operating Hours**: Continuous. **Key Personnel:** Mike King, District Mgr., mking@qmix.com; Michelle Hardcastle, District Mgr. **Ad Rates:** Advertising accepted; rates available upon request. **URL:** http://www.korncountry.com.

11772 ■ WYGS-FM - 91.1
825 Washington St.
Columbus, IN 47202-2626
Phone: (812)373-9947
Free: 800-603-9873
Format: Gospel; Full Service. **Operating Hours**: Continuous. **Key Personnel:** Melissa Burton, Office Mgr.; Matt Bond, Operations Mgr., mbond@wygs.org. **Mailing address:** PO Box 2626, Columbus, IN 47202-2626. **URL:** http://www.wygs.org.

CONNERSVILLE

Fayette Co. Fayette Co. (E). On Whitewater River and canal, 60 m E of Indianapolis. Manufactures auto parts, rotary blowers, dishwashers, flour, metal and enamel products, tools, dies. Diversified farming.

11773 ■ Indiana Audubon Quarterly
Indiana Audubon Society
3499 S Bird Sanctuary Rd.
Connersville, IN 47331
Phone: (765)827-5109
Scientific journal covering birds. **Freq:** Quarterly. **Key Personnel:** Alan Bruner, Contact. **ISSN:** 0019-6525 (print). **Subscription Rates:** Included in membership. **URL:** http://indianaaudubon.org/the-indiana-audubon-quarterly. **Remarks:** Advertising not accepted. **Circ:** Combined 556.

11774 ■ News-Examiner
Connersville News Examiner
406 Central Ave.
Connersville, IN 47331
Phone: (765)825-0581
Fax: (765)825-4599
Publisher's E-mail: newsexaminer@newsexaminer.com
General newspaper. **Founded:** Oct. 19, 1887. **Freq:** Daily. **Print Method:** Web Offset. **Cols./Page:** 6. **Col. Width:** 2 1/16 inches. **Col. Depth:** 21 inches. **Key Personnel:** Rachael Raney, Publisher, phone: (765)825-0581; James Sprague, Editor, phone: (765)825-0588; Bob Hansen, Managing Editor; Kelly Pierce, General Manager. **Subscription Rates:** $300 Individuals mail, per year; $15.50 Individuals print, 1 month. **URL:** http://www.newsexaminer.com. **Mailing address:** PO Box 287, Connersville, IN 47331. **Remarks:** Accepts advertising. **Circ:** Paid ‡5,960, Paid ‡6,002.

11775 ■ Poultry Press
Poultry Press
943 N My Ln.
Connersville, IN 47331
Phone: (765)827-0932
Fax: (765)827-4186
Publisher's E-mail: info@poultrypress.net
Newspaper (tabloid) containing articles and features on poultry and poultry shows. **Freq:** Monthly. **Print Method:** Offset. **Trim Size:** 11 1/2 x 16. **Cols./Page:** 5. **Col. Width:** 1 3/4 inches. **Col. Depth:** 16 inches. **Key Personnel:** William F. Wulff, Editor. **ISSN:** 0032--5783

(print). **Subscription Rates:** $30 Individuals; $59 Two years; $86 Individuals 3 years; $85 Other countries. **URL:** http://www.poultrypress.com. **Mailing address:** PO Box 542, Connersville, IN 47331. **Remarks:** Accepts advertising. **Circ:** ‡5500.

11776 ■ WIFE-FM - 94.3
406 1/2 Central Ave.
Connersville, IN 47331
Phone: (765)825-6411
Fax: (765)825-2411
Free: 866-225-1506
Format: Country; Contemporary Country. **Simulcasts:** WIFE-AM. **Networks:** AgriAmerica; Network Indiana; USA Radio. **Owner:** White Water Broadcasting, 2301 W Main St., Richmond, IN 47374; Rodgers Broadcasting Corp., c/o WCBK, Martinsville, IN 46151, Ph: (317)342-3394. **Founded:** 1949. **Operating Hours:** Continuous. **ADI:** Indianapolis (Marion), IN. **Key Personnel:** Ted Cramer, Contact, ted@wifefm.com; Mike Peacock, Contact. **Local Programs:** *American Christian Music Review,* Sunday 6:00 a.m. - 8:00 a.m. **Wattage:** 36,000. **Ad Rates:** $16 for 30 seconds; $11.50-16 for 30 seconds; $19 for 60 seconds; $13.50-19 for 60 seconds. Combined advertising rates available with WFMG-FM, WKBV-AM, WZZY-FM. **Mailing address:** PO Box 619, Connersville, IN 47331. **URL:** http://www.wifefm.com.

CORYDON

Harrison Co. Harrison Co. (S) 25 m W of Louisville, Ky. Manufactures furniture, glass, cabinets. Battery separating plant. Poultry processing.

11777 ■ The Corydon Democrat
O'Bannon Publishing Company Inc.
301 N Capitol Ave.
Corydon, IN 47112
Phone: (812)738-2211
Fax: (812)738-1909
Publisher's E-mail: clarionnews@seidata.com
Newspaper with a Democratic orientation. **Freq:** Weekly (Wed.). **Print Method:** Letterpress and offset. **Cols./Page:** 6. **Col. Width:** 27 nonpareils. **Col. Depth:** 297 agate lines. **Key Personnel:** Jonathan O'Bannon, President, Publisher; Randy West, Editor. **Subscription Rates:** $39 Individuals local (Indiana zip codes 471 and Kentucky zip codes 400, 401, 402); $44 Elsewhere Indiana and Kentucky; $53 Out of state. **URL:** http://www.corydondemocrat.com. **Remarks:** Advertising accepted; rates available upon request. **Circ:** 8,289.

11778 ■ WOCC-AM - 1550
211 N Capitol Ave.
Corydon, IN 47112
Phone: (812)738-9622
Fax: (812)738-1676
Format: Oldies. **Networks:** USA Radio. **Owner:** WOCC Radio, 211 N Capitol Ave., Corydon, IN 47112, Ph: (812)738-9622. **Founded:** 1964. **Formerly:** WJDW-AM. **Operating Hours:** Sunrise-sunset. **Local Programs:** *Five Minutes Live.* **Wattage:** 250. **Ad Rates:** $8.00 for 30 seconds; $12.00 for 60 seconds. **Mailing address:** PO Box 838, Corydon, IN 47112.

COVINGTON

Fountain Co.

11779 ■ WKZS-FM - 103.1
PO Box 67
Covington, IN 47932-0067
Phone: (765)793-5477
Format: Country. **Networks:** Jones Satellite. **Owner:** Benton-Weatherford Broadcasting, Inc. of IN, 820 Railroad Street, Covington, IN 47932, Ph: (765)793-4823. **Founded:** 1982. **Formerly:** WCDV-FM; WVWV-FM. **Operating Hours:** Continuous; 100% local. **Key Personnel:** Tara Duncan, Contact. **Wattage:** 3,000. **Ad Rates:** $18-34 for 30 seconds; $28-44 for 60 seconds. KOOL 92.9 WSKL. **URL:** http://www.kisscountryradio.com.

CRAWFORDSVILLE

Montgomery Co. Montgomery Co. (W). 45 m NW of Indianapolis. Wabash College.

11780 ■ Journal Review
Montgomery County Newspapers Inc.
119 N Green St.
Crawfordsville, IN 47933
Phone: (765)362-1200
Fax: (765)364-5427
Free: 800-488-4414
Publisher's E-mail: sstorie@jrpress.com
General newspaper. **Freq:** Mon.-Sat. (morn.). **Print Method:** Offset. **Trim Size:** 13 3/4 x 22 3/4. **Cols./Page:** 6. **Col. Width:** 26 nonpareils. **Col. Depth:** 301 agate lines. **Key Personnel:** Shawn Storie, Publisher, Manager, phone: (765)362-1200; Tina McGrady, Managing Editor, phone: (765)362-1200; Amanda Beasley, Manager, Advertising. **Subscription Rates:** $139 Individuals 1 year; $163 Out of area 1 year; 243 Out of country 1 year. **URL:** http://www.journalreview.com. **Remarks:** Advertising accepted; rates available upon request. **Circ:** Paid ♦5386.

11781 ■ WCVL-AM - 1550
PO Box 603
Crawfordsville, IN 47933
Phone: (765)362-8200
Format: Oldies. **Networks:** ABC; Network Indiana. **Founded:** 1964. **Operating Hours:** midnight. **Key Personnel:** Steve Carter, Contact. **Wattage:** 250. **Ad Rates:** $5-23 for 30 seconds; $7-28 for 60 seconds. **URL:** http://wcvlam.com.

11782 ■ WIMC-FM
1800 North Rd. 200
Crawfordsville, IN 47933
Phone: (765)362-8200
Fax: (765)364-1550
Format: Adult Contemporary. **Networks:** Network Indiana. **Owner:** Forcht Broadcasting, 2216 Young Dr., Lexington, KY 40505, Ph: (859)335-0365, Fax: (859)335-0453. **Founded:** 1974. **Formerly:** WLFQ-FM. **Key Personnel:** Rob Lee, News Dir. **Wattage:** 1,350 ERP. **Ad Rates:** $8-23 for 30 seconds; $11-28 for 60 seconds. **Mailing address:** PO Box 603, Crawfordsville, IN 47933.

11783 ■ WNDY-FM - 91.3
301 W Wabash Ave.
Crawfordsville, IN 47933
Phone: (765)361-6240
Email: helpdesk@wabash.edu
Format: News; Alternative/New Music/Progressive. **Owner:** Wabash College Radio, Inc., 301 W Wabash Ave., Crawfordsville, IN 47933. **Founded:** 1964. **Formerly:** WWCR-FM. **Operating Hours:** 6 p.m. - 3 a.m. **Key Personnel:** Greg Adams, Gen. Mgr.; Homer Twigg, Dir. of Programs; Joe Emmick, Sports Dir.; Peter List, News Dir; Mike Inman, Contact. **Wattage:** 3,000. **Ad Rates:** Noncommercial. **URL:** http://www.wabash.edu.

CROTHERSVILLE

11784 ■ Crothersville Times
Crothersville Times
510 Moore St., Ste. 100
Crothersville, IN 47229
Phone: (812)793-2188
Publication E-mail: ctimes@hsonline.net
Community newspaper. **Freq:** Weekly (Wed.). **Print Method:** Offset. **Trim Size:** 10 1/4 x 13. **Cols./Page:** 6. **Col. Width:** 1 5/8 inches. **Col. Depth:** 13 inches. **Key Personnel:** Curt Kovener, Editor. **USPS:** 586-710. **Subscription Rates:** $25 Individuals. **URL:** http://crothersvilletimes.com. **Ad Rates:** BW $156; 4C $309.20; PCI $2.75. **Remarks:** Accepts advertising. **Circ:** ‡2800.

CROWN POINT

Lake Co. Lake Co. (NW). 16 m S of Gary. Manufactures machinery, wagon bodies, pulleys, golf balls, color film processing, cabinets. Agriculture. Corn, wheat, oats, soybeans.

11785 ■ Cedar Lake-Lowell Star
Cedar Lake-Lowell Star
112 W Clark St.
Crown Point, IN 46308-0419
Phone: (219)663-4212
Newspaper with an independent slant. **Freq:** Weekly (Thurs.). **Print Method:** Offset. **Trim Size:** 11 1/2 x 14. **Cols./Page:** 6. **Col. Width:** 9.5 picas. **Col. Depth:** 175 agate lines. **Key Personnel:** Andrew Steele, Managing Editor; Beth Monstwillo, Business Manager; John Schoon, General Manager. **USPS:** 139-120. **Subscription Rates:** $26 Individuals in Indiana; $37 Out of state. **Formerly:** Crown Point Register. **Mailing address:** PO Box 419, Crown Point, IN 46308-0419. **Ad Rates:** GLR $.63; BW $686.40; 4C $836.40; PCI $8.80. **Remarks:** Accepts advertising. **Circ:** (Not Reported).

DALEVILLE

11786 ■ WERK-FM - 104.9
9821 W CR 800 W
Daleville, IN 47334
Phone: (765)288-4403
Fax: (765)378-2090
Format: News. **Owner:** Backyard Broadcasting, at above address. **Founded:** 1986. **Operating Hours:** Continuous; 100% local. **Wattage:** 6,000 ERP. **Ad Rates:** Advertising accepted; rates available upon request. **URL:** http://www.werkradio.com.

11787 ■ WHTI-FM - 96.7
9821 South 800 West
Daleville, IN 47334
Format: Classic Rock. **Simulcasts:** WHTI, WERK, WURN. **Owner:** Backyard Broadcasting, at above address. **Founded:** 1980. **Formerly:** WAXT. **Operating Hours:** Continuous; 100% local. **Key Personnel:** Amy Dillon, Gen. Sales Mgr., amy.dillon@bybradio.com; John Seneff, Sales Mgr., john.seneff@bybradio.com; Bob Willoughby, Prog. Dir. **Wattage:** 2,500. **Ad Rates:** $21 for 30 seconds; $24 for 60 seconds. **URL:** http://www.easy1009.com.

11788 ■ WHTY-FM
9821 S 800 W
Daleville, IN 47334
Phone: (765)378-2094
Fax: (765)378-2090

DECATUR

Adams Co. Adams Co. (NE). 21 m SE of Fort Wayne. Manufactures small motors, soybean oil, modular homes, livestock feed, mobile homes, recreational vehicles, pipes, boats, cartons, boxes, castings, cement products. Ash, elm timber. Grain, dairy cattle farms. Soybeans.

11789 ■ Decatur Daily Democrat
Decatur Publishing Company Inc.
141 S 2nd St.
Decatur, IN 46733
Phone: (260)724-2121
Fax: (260)724-7981
Publisher's E-mail: comp@decaturdailydemocrat.com
General newspaper. **Freq:** Mon.-Sat. (morn.). **Print Method:** Offset. **Trim Size:** 13 3/4 x 22 3/4. **Cols./Page:** 6. **Col. Width:** 2 1/16 inches. **Col. Depth:** 21 1/2 inches. **Key Personnel:** Pam Mohr, Manager, Circulation; Janaya Andrews, Associate Editor; Ron L. Storey, Publisher. **Subscription Rates:** $187 Individuals 12 months, print (outside Adams, Allen, Wells, Jay County) ; $147 Individuals 12 moths, print (in Allen, Wells, Jay County); $120 Individuals 12 moths, print (Adams County); $120 Individuals 12 months, online. **URL:** http://www.decaturdailydemocrat.com. **Remarks:** Advertising accepted; rates available upon request. **Circ:** ‡5939.

ELKHART

Elkhart Co. Elkhart Co. (N). On St Joseph River, 100 m E of Chicago. Manufacturers band instruments, brass, sheet metal and rubber products, ethical and proprietary medicine, railway, telephone, television controls, auto radio equipment, machinery, cardboard containers, castings, furniture, plastics, mobile homes, recreational vehicles and van conversion.

11790 ■ Beyond Ourselves
Mennonite Voluntary Service
3145 Benham Ave., Ste. 3
Elkhart, IN 46517
Phone: (574)523-3000
Fax: (316)283-0454
Free: 866-866-2872
Publisher's E-mail: info@mennonitemission.net
Freq: Quarterly. **URL:** http://www.mennonitemission.net/Stories/BeyondOurselves/OurStories/Pages/Home.aspx. **Mailing address:** PO Box 370, Elkhart, IN 46515-0370.

Circulation: ★ = AAM; △ or • = BPA; ♦ = CAC; ❑ = VAC; ⊕ = PO Statement; ‡ = Publisher's Report; Boldface figures = sworn; Light figures = estimated.

Remarks: Advertising not accepted. **Circ:** (Not Reported).

11791 ■ The Elkhart Truth
Truth Publishing Company Inc.
421 S 2nd St.
Box 487
Elkhart, IN 46516-3227
Phone: (574)294-1661
Fax: (574)294-3895
General newspaper. **Freq:** Daily (eve.) and Sat. (morn.) Sun. (morn.). **Print Method:** Offset. **Cols./Page:** 6. **Col. Width:** 24 nonpareils. **Col. Depth:** 301 agate lines. **Key Personnel:** Marshall King, Managing Editor, phone: (574)296-5805; Brandon Erlacher, Publisher; Greg Halling, Editor; Mary Alexander, Director, Advertising. **URL:** http://www.elkharttruth.com. **Ad Rates:** GLR $1.23; BW $2360.70; 4C $2690.70; SAU $14.01; PCI $18.30. **Remarks:** Accepts advertising. **Circ:** Mon. ‡21985, ‡21965, Wed. ‡22497, Thurs. ‡22899, Fri. ‡24057.

11792 ■ WEID-LP - 18
PO Box A
Santa Ana, CA 92711
Phone: (714)832-2950
Free: 888-731-1000
Owner: Trinity Broadcasting Network Inc., PO Box A, Santa Ana, CA 92711, Ph: (714)832-2950, Free: 888-731-1000. **Formerly**: W18CF. **URL:** http://www.tbn.org.

11793 ■ WFRI-FM - 100.1
PO Box 307
Elkhart, IN 46515
Phone: (574)875-5166
Fax: (574)875-6662
Free: 800-933-0501
Format: Contemporary Christian; Full Service; Talk; Information. **Simulcasts:** WFRN-FM and WFRN-AM. **Operating Hours**: Continuous. **Wattage**: 6,000 ERP. **Ad Rates:** Advertising accepted; rates available upon request. **URL:** http://wfrn.com.

11794 ■ WFRN-AM - 1270
PO Box 307
Elkhart, IN 46515
Phone: (574)875-5166
Fax: (574)875-6662
Free: 800-933-0501
Email: music@wfrn.com
Format: Gospel; Talk. **Networks:** USA Radio. **Owner:** Progressive Broadcasting System Inc., at above address. **Founded:** 1956. **Formerly**: WCMR-AM. **Operating Hours**: Continuous. **ADI**: South Bend-Elkhart, IN. **Wattage**: 5,000 Day; 1,000 Night. **Ad Rates:** $10-16 for 30 seconds; $12-24 for 60 seconds. Combined advertising rates available with WFRN-FM. **URL:** http://www.wfrn.com.

11795 ■ WFRN-FM - 104.7
PO Box 307
Elkhart, IN 46515
Phone: (574)875-5166
Fax: (574)875-6662
Free: 800-933-0501
Email: events@wfrn.com
Format: Contemporary Christian. **Networks:** USA Radio. **Owner:** Progressive Broadcasting System Inc., at above address. **Founded:** 1963. **Formerly**: WXAX. **Operating Hours**: Continuous. **Wattage**: 50,000 ERP. **Ad Rates:** $30 for 30 seconds; $38 for 60 seconds. Combined advertising rates available with WFRN-AM. **URL:** http://www.wfrn.com.

11796 ■ WSJV-TV - 28
58096 County Rd., 7 S
Elkhart, IN 46517
Phone: (574)679-9758
Fax: (574)294-1267
Email: fox28@fox28.com
Format: Commercial TV; News; Sports. **Networks:** Fox. **Owner:** Quincy Newspapers Inc., 130 S 5th St., Quincy, IL 62306, Ph: (217)223-5100. **Founded:** 1954. **Operating Hours**: Continuous. **ADI**: South Bend-Elkhart, IN. **Key Personnel:** Sam Weiss, Sales Mgr; David Gooding, Contact, dgooding@fox28.com. **Wattage**: 5,000,000. **Ad Rates:** Noncommercial. **URL:** http://www.fox28.com.

11797 ■ WTRC-AM - 1340
421 S Second St.
Elkhart, IN 46516
Phone: (574)296-5941
Format: Talk; News. **Networks:** ABC; Westwood One Radio. **Owner:** Federated Media/Pathfinder Communications Corp., 245 Edison Rd., Ste. 250, Mishawaka, IN 46545, Free: 888-333-6133. **Founded:** 1931. **Formerly**: WJAK-AM. **Operating Hours**: Continuous; 70% network, 30% local. **ADI**: South Bend-Elkhart, IN. **Key Personnel:** Kevin Musselman, Contact. **Wattage**: 1,000. **Ad Rates:** $4-47 for 30 seconds; $5-56 for 60 seconds. **URL:** http://www.michiananewschannel.com.

11798 ■ WVPE-FM - 88.1
2424 California Rd.
Elkhart, IN 46514
Phone: (574)674-8895
Fax: (574)262-5700
Free: 888-399-9873
Email: wvpe@wvpe.org
Format: Public Radio; Jazz. **Networks:** National Public Radio (NPR). **Owner:** Elkhart Community School Corp., 2720 California Rd., Elkhart, IN 46514, Ph: (574)262-5500. **Founded:** 1972. **ADI**: South Bend-Elkhart, IN. **Key Personnel:** Anthony Hunt, Station Mgr., ahunt@wvpe.org. **Wattage**: 11,500 ERP. **Ad Rates:** Noncommercial. **URL:** http://www.wvpe.org.

ELWOOD

Tipton Co. Madison Co. (NW). 25 m WNW of Muncie. Industrial center in tomato growing section.

11799 ■ The Call-Leader
Elwood Publishing Co.
317 S Anderson St.
Elwood, IN 46036
Phone: (765)552-3355
Publication E-mail: elpub@elwoodpublishing.com
Local newspaper. **Freq:** Weekly (Wed.). **Print Method:** Offset. **Trim Size:** 12 1/2 x 22 3/4. **Cols./Page:** 6. **Col. Width:** 1.8332 inches. **Col. Depth:** 21 1/2 inches. **Key Personnel:** Robert Nash, Publisher; Sandy Burton, Managing Editor. **USPS:** 174-640. **Subscription Rates:** $152 Individuals print and online; 1 year, in town carrier routes; $174 Individuals print and online; 1 year, motor routes; $207 Individuals print and online; 1 year, in county mail; $232 Out of country print and online; 1 year; $297 Out of state print and online; 1 year; $227 Individuals print and online; 1 year, handmail; $140 Individuals print only; 1 year, in town carrier routes; $162 Individuals print only; 1 year, motor routes; $195 Individuals print only; 1 year, in county mail; $220 Out of country print only; 1 year; $285 Out of state print only; 1 year; $215 Individuals print only; 1 year, handmail. **URL:** http://www.elwoodpublishing.com. **Mailing address:** PO Box 85, Elwood, IN 46036. **Ad Rates:** BW $1000; 4C $135; SAU $7.75; PCI $7.75. **Remarks:** Advertising accepted; rates available upon request. **Circ:** Paid ‡2800.

11800 ■ Tipton Tribune
Elwood Publishing Co.
317 S Anderson St.
Elwood, IN 46036
Phone: (765)552-3355
Publisher's E-mail: elpub@elwoodpublishing.com
General newspaper. **Freq:** Daily (eve.) and Sat. (morn.). **Print Method:** Offset. **Cols./Page:** 6. **Col. Width:** 25 nonpareils. **Col. Depth:** 301 agate lines. **ISSN:** 0746--0619 (print). **Subscription Rates:** $174 Individuals in town motor routes; $152 Individuals in town carrier routes; $207 Individuals in county mail; $232 Individuals out of county mail; $297 Individuals out of state mail; $227 Individuals handmail. **URL:** http://www.elwoodpublishing.com/68097/2328/online-editiontipton-county-tribune. **Mailing address:** PO Box 85, Elwood, IN 46036. **Remarks:** Accepts advertising. **Circ:** Paid 2600.

EVANSVILLE

Vanderburgh Co. Vanderburgh Co (SW). On Ohio River, 164 m S of Indianapolis. Bridges to Henderson, Ky. University of Evansville. University of Southern Indiana. Manufactures refrigerators, flour, beer, farm and garden implements, excavating machinery, aluminum, chemicals, furniture, plastics, mattresses, infant nutritionals, pottery, cigars, textiles. Meat, fruit, vegetable packing plants.

11801 ■ The Message
Catholic Diocese of Evansville
PO Box 4169
Evansville, IN 47724-0169
Phone: (812)424-5536
Free: 800-637-1731
Publication E-mail: message@evansville-diocese.org
Catholic newspaper. **Founded:** Oct. 02, 1970. **Freq:** Weekly (Fri.). **Print Method:** Web. **Trim Size:** 17 1/8 x 11 3/8. **Cols./Page:** 5. **Col. Width:** 22 nonpareils. **Col. Depth:** 224 agate lines. **Key Personnel:** Bishop Charles C. Thompson, Publisher; Tim Lilley, Editor, phone: (812)424-5536; Carol Funke, Coordinator, Marketing. **Subscription Rates:** $24 Individuals 1 year; print; $12 Individuals 1 year; online; $9 Students 1 year; online. **URL:** http://www.themessageonline.org. **Ad Rates:** GLR $.42; BW $400; 4C $300; PCI $8.12. **Remarks:** Accepts advertising. **Circ:** Controlled ‡7,200.

11802 ■ Sinfonian
Phi Mu Alpha Sinfonia Fraternity of America
10600 Old State Rd.
Evansville, IN 47711
Phone: (812)867-2433
Free: 800-473-2649
Publisher's E-mail: nhq@sinfonia.org
Freq: Semiannual. **Subscription Rates:** $5 Members /year. **URL:** http://www.sinfonia.org/communications/publications/sinfonian/. **Remarks:** Advertising not accepted. **Circ:** (Not Reported).

11803 ■ Insight Communications
1900 N Fares Ave.
Evansville, IN 47711
Phone: (812)422-1167
Free: 800-824-4003
Key Personnel: Kevin Dowell, Sr. VP; Michael S. Willner, CEO, V. Ch.; Dinni Jain, COO, President; John Abbot, CFO, Exec. VP; Elliot Brecher, Gen. Counsel, Sr. VP; Gregg Graff, Sr. VP. **Cities Served:** 101 channels.

11804 ■ WABX-FM - 107.5
1162 Mt. Auburn Rd.
Evansville, IN 47720
Phone: (812)424-8284
Fax: (812)426-7928
Format: Classic Rock. **Networks:** ABC. **Owner:** South Central Communications Inc., 45 North 100 West, Escalante, UT 84726, Ph: (435)826-4211, Fax: (435)826-4900, Free: 888-826-4211. **ADI**: Evansville, IN (Madisonville, KY). **Key Personnel:** Rusty James, Mgr., rusty.james@wabx.net. **Wattage**: 2,000 ERP. **Ad Rates:** Noncommercial. **URL:** http://www.wabx.net.

11805 ■ WBGW-FM - 101.5
PO Box 4164
Evansville, IN 47724
Fax: (812)768-5552
Free: 800-264-5550
Format: Religious. **Simulcasts:** WBHW-FM (88.7), WBJW-FM (91.7). **Networks:** Moody Broadcasting. **Owner:** Thy Word Network, PO Box 4164, Evansville, IN 47724. **Founded:** 1990. **Operating Hours**: Continuous; 95% network, 5% local. **Key Personnel:** Floyd Turner, Chief Engineer. **Wattage**: 2,100. **Ad Rates:** Noncommercial. **URL:** http://www.thyword.us.

11806 ■ WBHW-FM - 88.7
PO Box 4164
Evansville, IN 47724
Fax: (812)768-5552
Free: 800-264-5550
Format: Religious. **Owner:** Thy Word Network, PO Box 4164, Evansville, IN 47724. **Key Personnel:** Floyd Turner, Chief Engineer; Don Chagle, Contact. **Ad Rates:** Noncommercial. **URL:** http://www.thyword.us.

WBJW-FM - See Albion, MI

11807 ■ WEHT-TV - 25
PO Box 25
Evansville, IN 47701
Fax: (270)827-0561
Free: 800-879-8549
Format: Commercial TV. **Networks:** ABC. **Owner:** Gilmore Broadcasting Corp., 162 E Michigan Ave., Kalamazoo, MI 49007-3908. **Founded:** 1953. **Operating Hours**: Mon - Fri., Continuous, Saturday & Sunday 6 a.m.-2 a.m. **ADI**: Evansville, IN (Madisonville, KY). **Key Personnel:** Curt Molander, VP, Gen. Mgr. **Wattage**: 1,124,000. **Ad Rates:** Noncommercial. **URL:** http://www.abc25.com.

11808 ■ WEVV-TV - 44
44 Main St.
Evansville, IN 47708
Phone: (812)464-4444
Fax: (812)465-4559
Networks: CBS. **Owner:** Communications Corporation of Indiana, at above address. **Founded:** 1983. **Operating Hours**: 20 hours Daily; 75% network, 25% local. **ADI**: Evansville, IN (Madisonville, KY). **Key Personnel:** Greg Murdach, Contact, greg.murdach@.wevv.com; Jim Baronet, Contact. **Ad Rates:** $10-400 for 30 seconds. Combined advertising rates available with WTSN-TV. **URL:** http://www.wevv.com.

11809 ■ WFIE-TV - 14
PO Box 1414
Evansville, IN 47701
Phone: (812)426-1414
Fax: (812)426-1945
Email: newsdesk@14wfie.com
Format: Commercial TV. **Networks:** NBC. **Owner:** Raycom Media Inc., 201 Monroe St., RSA Twr., 20th Fl., Montgomery, AL 36104-3731, Ph: (334)206-1400. **Founded:** 1953. **Operating Hours**: 6 a.m.-1:30 a.m.; 65% network, 35% local. **ADI**: Evansville, IN (Madisonville, KY). **Key Personnel:** Maria Hillenbrand, Asst. GM, mhillenbrand@14wfie.com; Nick Ulmer, Gen. Mgr., nulmer@14wfie.com; Mike Blake, Sports Dir., mblake@14wfie.com. **Ad Rates:** $30 for 30 seconds. **URL:** http://www.14news.com.

11810 ■ WGAB-AM - 1180
2601 S Boeke Rd.
Evansville, IN 47714
Phone: (812)479-5342
Free: 888-708-8936
Email: info@faithbroadcastingonline.com
Format: Religious. **Networks:** Jones Satellite. **Owner:** Faith Broadcasting International, 2601 S Boeke Rd., Evansville, IN 47714, Ph: (812)479-5342, Fax: (888)708-8936. **Founded:** Mar. 05, 1984. **Operating Hours**: Continuous. **ADI**: Evansville, IN (Madisonville, KY). **Wattage**: 670. **Ad Rates:** Noncommercial. **Mailing address:** PO Box 2463, Evansville, IN 47728. **URL:** http://www.faith1180.com.

11811 ■ WGBF-AM - 1280
117 SE Fifth St.
Evansville, IN 47708
Phone: (812)425-4226
Format: News; Talk; Information. **Networks:** ABC; Westwood One Radio. **Owner:** Townsquare Media Inc., 240 Greenwich Ave., Greenwich, CT 06830-6507, Ph: (203)861-0900. **Founded:** 1923. **Formerly**: WWOK-AM. **Operating Hours**: Continuous; 90% network, 10% local. **ADI**: Evansville, IN (Madisonville, KY). **Key Personnel:** Angie Ross, Dir. of Sales; LeDonne Craig, Gen. Mgr., ladonne.craig@townsquaremedia.com; John Story, Dir. of Programs, john.story@townsquaremedia.com. **Wattage**: 5,000. **Ad Rates:** $10-25 for 30 seconds; $12-30 for 60 seconds. Combined advertising rates available with WGBF-FM; WYNG-FM; WKDQ-FM; WDKS-FM; WJLT-FM. **URL:** http://www.newstalk1280.com.

11812 ■ WGBF-FM - 103.1
117 SE Fifth St.
Evansville, IN 47708
Phone: (812)425-4226
Fax: (812)421-0005
Free: 888-900-WGBF
Format: Album-Oriented Rock (AOR). **Networks:** Westwood One Radio. **Owner:** Townsquare Media Inc., 240 Greenwich Ave., Greenwich, CT 06830-6507, Ph: (203)861-0900. **Founded:** 1971. **Formerly**: WHKC-FM. **Operating Hours**: Continuous; 15% network, 85% local. **ADI**: Evansville, IN (Madisonville, KY). **Key Personnel:** Angie Ross, Managing Ed., angie.ross@townsquaremedia.com; Mike Sanders, Dir. of Sales, mike.sanders@townsquaremedia.com. **Wattage**: 6,000. **Ad Rates:** Noncommercial. **URL:** http://www.103gbfrocks.com.

11813 ■ WIKY-FM - 104.1
1162 Mt. Auburn Rd.
Evansville, IN 47720
Phone: (812)424-8284
Format: Adult Contemporary. **Networks:** Univision. **Owner:** South Central Communications Inc., 45 North 100 West, Escalante, UT 84726, Ph: (435)826-4211, Fax: (435)826-4900, Free: 888-826-4211. **Founded:** 1948. **Operating Hours**: Continuous. **ADI**: Evansville, IN (Madisonville, KY). **Local Programs:** *Evansville in the Morning*, Monday Tuesday Wednesday Thursday Friday 5:30 a.m. **Wattage**: 39,000 ERP. **Ad Rates:** Advertising accepted; rates available upon request. **URL:** http://www.wiky.com.

11814 ■ WJLT-FM - 105.3
117 SE 5th St.
Evansville, IN 47705
Free: 800-431-5928
Format: Oldies. **Owner:** Townsquare Media Inc., 2000 Fifth Third Ctr. 511 Walnut St., Cincinnati, OH 45202, Ph: (513)651-1190. **Operating Hours**: Continuous. **Key Personnel:** LaDonne Craig, Dir. of Sales, ladonne@wbkr.com. **Wattage**: 50,000. **Ad Rates:** Advertising accepted; rates available upon request. **URL:** http://espnevansville.com.

11815 ■ WJPS-AM - 1400
915 Main St., Ste. 001
Evansville, IN 47708
Phone: (812)424-8864
Fax: (812)424-9946
Format: Information; Full Service; Adult Contemporary; Urban Contemporary; Talk; Gospel. **Owner:** South Central Communications Corp., PO Box 3848, Evansville, IN 47736, Ph: (812)463-7950. **Founded:** 1936. **Formerly**: WROZ-AM. **Operating Hours**: Continuous; 100% local. **ADI**: Evansville, IN (Madisonville, KY). **Key Personnel:** Craig Ladonne; Rob Burton, Gen. Mgr.; Randy Wheeler, News Dir. **Wattage**: 1,000. **Ad Rates:** $10-65 for 30 seconds; $13-75 for 60 seconds. **URL:** http://www.weoa985fm.com.

11816 ■ WKDQ-FM - 99.5
117 SE Fifth St.
Evansville, IN 47708
Phone: (812)425-4226
Free: 877-437-5995
Format: Contemporary Country. **Networks:** ABC. **Founded:** 1947. **Operating Hours**: Continuous. **Key Personnel:** Dave Fields, Mgr., dave@wkdq.com; LaDonne Craig, Gen. Mgr., ladonne.craig@townsquaremedia.com. **Wattage**: 98,000 ERP. **Ad Rates:** Advertising accepted; rates available upon request. **URL:** http://www.wkdq.com.

11817 ■ WNIN-FM - 88.3
405 Carpenter St.
Evansville, IN 47708
Phone: (812)423-2973
Fax: (812)428-7548
Email: events@wnin.org
Format: Classical. **Networks:** Public Radio International (PRI); National Public Radio (NPR). **Founded:** 1982. **Operating Hours**: Continuous. **ADI**: Evansville, IN (Madisonville, KY). **Key Personnel:** Tim Black, VP of Dev., tblack@wnin.org; John Gibson, Producer, jgibson@wnin.org; Carlin Beckman, VP of Fin. & Admin., cbeckman@wnin.org; Wayne Aldridge, Director, Producer; Daniel Moore, Prog. Dir., dmoore@wnin.org; Steve Burger, VP, sburger@wnin.org; Tony Voss, Dir. of Operations. **Wattage**: 17,000 ERP. **Ad Rates:** Advertising accepted; rates available upon request. **URL:** http://www.wnin.org/radio/radio-reading-service.

11818 ■ WNIN-TV - 9
405 Carpenter St.
Evansville, IN 47708
Phone: (812)423-2973
Email: events@wnin.org
Key Personnel: David Dial, Gen. Mgr., President; Carlin Beckman, VP of Fin. & Admin. **Ad Rates:** Noncommercial. **URL:** http://www.wnin.org/television/home.

11819 ■ WOW!
6045 Wedeking Ave.
Evansville, IN 47713
Phone: (812)437-0345
Free: 866-496-9669
Key Personnel: Colleen Abdoulah, Chmn. of the Bd.; Steven Cochran, CFO, COO. **Cities Served:** 136 channels. **URL:** http://www1.wowway.com.

11820 ■ WPSR-FM - 90.7
5400 1st Ave.
Evansville, IN 47710
Phone: (812)435-8241
Email: wpsr@evsc.k12.in.us
Format: Music of Your Life; News; Sports. **Owner:** Evansville-Vanderburgh School Corp., 951 Walnut St., Evansville, IN 47713. **Founded:** 1957. **Operating Hours**: Continuous. **ADI**: Evansville, IN (Madisonville, KY). **Wattage**: 14,000 ERP. **Ad Rates:** Noncommercial. Underwriting available. **URL:** http://www.wpsrhd.com.

11821 ■ WSTO-FM - 96.1
1162 Mount Auburn Rd.
Evansville, IN 47720
Phone: (812)421-9696
Fax: (812)421-3273
Format: Top 40; Contemporary Hit Radio (CHR). **Mailing address:** PO Box 3848, Evansville, IN 47736. **URL:** http://www.wsto.com.

11822 ■ WSWI-AM - 820
Radio Ctr.
8600 University Blvd.
Evansville, IN 47712
Phone: (812)465-1665
Owner: University of Southern Indiana, 8600 University Blvd., Evansville, IN 47712, Ph: (812)464-8600, Fax: (812)464-0029. **Founded:** 1947. **ADI**: Evansville, IN (Madisonville, KY). **Key Personnel:** John Morris, Gen. Mgr. **Wattage**: 250 ERP. **Ad Rates:** Accepts Advertising.

11823 ■ WTVW-TV - 7
477 Carpenter St.
Evansville, IN 47708
Phone: (812)424-7777
Email: newstips@wtvw.com
Format: Commercial TV. **Networks:** Fox. **Owner:** Nexstar Broadcasting Group Inc., 545 E John Carpenter Fwy., Ste. 700, Irving, TX 75062, Ph: (972)373-8800. **Founded:** 1956. **Operating Hours**: Continuous; 30% network, 70% local. **ADI**: Evansville, IN (Madisonville, KY). **Key Personnel:** Jeremy Moore, Production Mgr.; Bob Freeman, News Dir.; Jeff Fisher, Gen. Sales Mgr., jfisher@wtvw.com; Mike Smith, Gen. Mgr., msmith@wtvw.com. **Wattage**: 316,000. **Ad Rates:** $20-800 per unit. **URL:** http://www.tristatehomepage.com.

11824 ■ WUEV-FM - 91.5
1800 Lincoln Ave.
Evansville, IN 47722
Phone: (812)488-2022
Free: 800-423-8633
Format: Talk; Sports; Jazz. **Networks:** Network Indiana. **Owner:** Board of Trustees of University of Evansville. **Founded:** 1951. **Formerly**: WEVC-FM. **Operating Hours**: Continuous; 100% local. **Key Personnel:** Tom Benson, Gen. Mgr. **Local Programs**: *The Other Side*, Sunday Monday Tuesday Wednesday 9:00 p.m. - 3:00 a.m.; *Rated G*, Saturday 8:00 a.m. - 11:00 a.m.; *Party Lights*, Thursday Friday Saturday 9:00 p.m. - 3:00 a.m. **Wattage**: 6,100. **Ad Rates:** Noncommercial. **URL:** http://www.evansville.edu.

11825 ■ WVHI-AM - 1330
2207 E Morgan Ave., Ste. J
Evansville, IN 47711
Phone: (812)475-9930
Format: Religious. **Founded:** 1964. **Operating Hours**: Continuous. **ADI**: Evansville, IN (Madisonville, KY). **Key Personnel:** Krista Denton, Contact. **Wattage**: 5,000 Day; 1,000 Nig. **Ad Rates:** $16 for 30 seconds; $20 for 60 seconds. **URL:** http://www.wvhi.com.

FARMERSBURG

Sullivan Co. Sullivan Co. (SW). 16 m S of Terre Haute. Saw, flour mills. Coal mines. Grain, poultry, stock farms. Corn, wheat, hay.

11826 ■ WBAK-TV - 38
10849 N US Highway 41
Farmersburg, IN 47850
Phone: (440)526-2227
Format: Commercial TV. **Networks:** Fox. **Owner:** Bahakel Communications, Ltd., PO Box 32488, Charlotte, NC 28232, Ph: (704)372-4434. **Founded:** 1973. **Formerly**: WIIL-TV. **Operating Hours**: 6 a.m.-1 a.m. **Key Personnel:** Mike Brooks, Gen. Mgr., mbrooks@abcs.com; Carla Peters, Operations Mgr. **Ad Rates:** $25-600 per unit. **Mailing address:** PO Box 9268, Terre Haute, IN 47808. **URL:** http://www.mywabashvalley.com.

Circulation: ★ = AAM; △ or • = BPA; ♦ = CAC; ❑ = VAC; ⊕ = PO Statement; ‡ = Publisher's Report; Boldface figures = sworn; Light figures = estimated.

FERDINAND

Dubois Co. Dubois Co. (SW). 50 m NE of Evansville. Manufactured furniture, kitchen cabinets, aluminum windows and doors. Oak timber. Grain farms. Corn, wheat, oats.

11827 ■ The Ferdinand News
Dubois Spencer Counties Publishing Company Inc.
PO Box 38
Ferdinand, IN 47532
Phone: (812)367-2041
Fax: (812)367-2371
Free: 800-463-9720
Publication E-mail: ferdnews@psci.net
Newspaper with a Democratic orientation. **Freq:** Weekly (Wed.). **Print Method:** Offset. **Cols./Page:** 6. **Col. Width:** 2 inches. **Col. Depth:** 21 1/2 inches. **Key Personnel:** Kathy Tretter, Publisher; Brian Bohne, Editor. **USPS:** 189-860. **Subscription Rates:** $36.50 Individuals print and online; 1 year; Snowbird rate; $29 Individuals print and online; 1 year; in 475 zip; $37.50 Individuals print and online; 1 year; outside 475 in Indiana; $48 Individuals print and online; 1 year; outside Indiana; $15 Individuals online; 1 year. **URL:** http://www.ferdinandnews.com/v2/content.aspx?IsHome=1&MemberID=1995&ID=24232. **Remarks:** Advertising accepted; rates available upon request. **Circ:** Wed. ‡3500.

FISHERS

Hamilton Co.

11828 ■ Wesleyan Life: The Official Publication of The Wesleyan Church
Wesleyan Publishing House
13300 Olio Rd.
Fishers, IN 46037
Phone: (317)774-7900
Fax: (800)788-3535
Free: 800-493-7539
Publisher's E-mail: communications@wesleyan.org
Magazine. **Freq:** Quarterly. **Print Method:** Offset. **Trim Size:** 8 1/2 x 11. **Cols./Page:** 3. **Col. Width:** 27 nonpareils. **Col. Depth:** 133 agate lines. **Key Personnel:** Wayne MacBeth, Executive Editor. **ISSN:** 0043--289X (print). **Subscription Rates:** Included in membership. **URL:** http://www.wesleyan.org/wesleyanlifeonline. **Formerly:** The Wesleyan Advocate. **Mailing address:** PO Box 50434, Fishers, IN 46037. **Remarks:** Accepts advertising. **Circ:** (Not Reported).

11829 ■ WLQI-FM - 97.7
14074 Trade Center Dr., Ste. 141
Fishers, IN 46038
Phone: (317)770-0970
Fax: (317)770-0972
Free: 800-342-6276
Format: Adult Contemporary. **Wattage:** 3,300. **Ad Rates:** Noncommercial. **URL:** http://www.indianabroadcasters.org.

FLORA

Carroll Co. Carroll Co. (NWC) 20 m NE of Lafayette.

11830 ■ Carroll County Comet
Carroll Papers Inc.
PO Box 26
Flora, IN 46929-0026
Phone: (574)967-4135
Fax: (574)967-3384
Publication E-mail: editor@carrollcountycomet.com
Community newspaper. **Freq:** Weekly (Wed.). **Print Method:** Offset. **Trim Size:** 14 x 22 3/4. **Cols./Page:** 6. **Col. Width:** 2 1/16 inches. **Col. Depth:** 21.5 inches. **Key Personnel:** Joseph Moss, Director, Advertising, Publisher; Susan Scholl, Editor, Publisher. **USPS:** 258-840. **Subscription Rates:** $50 Individuals print and online; in county; $57 Individuals print and online; in state; $64 Out of state print and online; $35 Individuals online. **URL:** http://www.carrollcountycomet.com. **Remarks:** Advertising accepted; rates available upon request. **Circ:** Paid ‡4100, Free ‡35.

FORT BRANCH

Gibson Co. Gibson Co. (SW). 20 m N of Evansville. Meat packing. Diversified farming.

11831 ■ South Gibson Star-Times
South Gibson Star-Times
203 S McCreary St.
Fort Branch, IN 47648-1317
Phone: (812)753-3553
Fax: (812)753-4251
Publisher's E-mail: editor@sgstartimes.com
Community newspaper. **Freq:** Weekly. **Print Method:** Offset. **Trim Size:** 12 1/2 x 22 3/4. **Cols./Page:** 6. **Col. Width:** 11 picas. **Col. Depth:** 21 inches. **Key Personnel:** Rachael Heuring, Publisher; Frank Heuring, Publisher, phone: (812)354-8500, fax: (812)753-4251. **USPS:** 205-620. **Subscription Rates:** $29 Individuals print and NetEdition; $24 Individuals print; $30 Individuals NetEdition; $37 Out of area print and NetEdition; $32 Out of area print; $30 Out of area NetEdition. **URL:** http://sgstartimes.com. **Formerly:** Fort Branch Times; The Owensville Star-Echo. **Ad Rates:** BW $598.50; 4C $748.50; SAU $5.60; PCI $5.60. **Remarks:** Accepts advertising. **Circ:** Paid ⊕2700.

FORT WAYNE

Allen Co. Allen Co. (NE). On Maumee, St Joseph and St Mary's Rivers, 105 m NE of Indianapolis. Indiana Institute of Technology, Concordia College (Luth. men), St. Francis College (Cath. co-ed), Fort Wayne Bible College (Missionary and co-ed), Indiana Purdue Fort Wayne Campus. Manufactures electric motors and supplies, trucks, tires, clothing, public speaking systems, television and electronic equipment, radios, valves, radio parts, copper wire, diamond wire dies, tools, trailers, aluminum pistons, gasoline pumps, liquid metering equipment, tanks and compressors, automotive axles, plastic, boats, feed, beer, paint, cranes and dredges, paper boxes, precision gears and counters, mobile homes.

11832 ■ Abbott and Costello
Abbott and Costello International Fan Club
PO Box 5566
Fort Wayne, IN 46895-5566
Publisher's E-mail: ACQtrly@aol.com
Magazine containing articles of researches, charitable programs, children's services, and funding for cancer research in children case studies on the international level, by the fans and admirers of notable people, Bud Abbott and Lou Costello. **Freq:** Quarterly. **URL:** http://www.abbottandcostellofanclub.com/current.html. **Remarks:** Accepts advertising. **Circ:** (Not Reported).

11833 ■ Business People Magazine
Michiana Business Publications Inc.
7729 Westfield Dr.
Fort Wayne, IN 46825
Phone: (219)497-0433
Fax: (219)497-0822
Consumer magazine covering business for Northeast Indiana. **Freq:** Monthly. **Print Method:** Sheetfed offset. **Cols./Page:** 3. **Key Personnel:** Daniel C. Copeland, Publisher; Lynette Fager, Editor. **Subscription Rates:** $19.99 Individuals; $31.99 Two years; $89.99 lifetime. **URL:** http://businesspeople.com/Subscription. **Ad Rates:** BW $1,115; 4C $1,540. **Remarks:** Accepts advertising. **Circ:** 8500.

11834 ■ Concordia Theological Quarterly
Concordia Theological Seminary
6600 N Clinton St.
Fort Wayne, IN 46825
Phone: (260)452-2100
Publication E-mail: gardas@ctsfw.edu
Religion and theology journal. **Freq:** Quarterly Published January, April, July, and October. **Print Method:** Offset. **Trim Size:** 6 x 9. **Cols./Page:** 1. **Col. Width:** 54 nonpareils. **Col. Depth:** 98 agate lines. **Key Personnel:** Lawrence Rast, Jr., Editor; David P. Scaer, Editor, phone: (260)452-2134; Charles Gieschen, Associate Editor. **ISSN:** 0038--8610 (print). **Subscription Rates:** $30 U.S.; $35 Canada and Mexico; $45 Other countries. **URL:** http://www.ctsfw.edu/resources/concordia-theological-quarterly. **Ad Rates:** BW $500. **Remarks:** Accepts advertising. **Circ:** Paid 400, Non-paid 9000.

11835 ■ The Forensic Therapist
National Association of Forensic Counselors
PO Box 8827
Fort Wayne, IN 46898
Phone: (260)426-7234
Fax: (260)426-7431
Publisher's E-mail: nafc@nationalafc.com
Magazine publishing articles in all areas of criminal justice, corrections, mental health and addictions. **Subscription Rates:** Included in membership. **URL:** http://www.forensiccounselor.org/?The_Forensic_Therapist. **Remarks:** Advertising accepted; rates available upon request. **Circ:** (Not Reported).

11836 ■ Fort Wayne Journal-Gazette
Fort Wayne Journal-Gazette
600 W Main St.
Fort Wayne, IN 46801-0088
Phone: (260)461-8383
Fax: (260)461-8648
Publisher's E-mail: advertising@fwn.fortwayne.com
General newspaper. **Freq:** Daily and Sun. **Print Method:** Letterpress. **Cols./Page:** 6. **Key Personnel:** Julie Inskeep, Publisher, phone: (260)461-8490; Craig Klugman, Editor, phone: (260)461-8853; Sherry Skufca, Managing Editor, phone: (260)461-8201. **URL:** http://www.journalgazette.net. **Mailing address:** PO Box 88, Fort Wayne, IN 46801-0088. **Remarks:** Accepts advertising. **Circ:** (Not Reported).

11837 ■ FortWayne.com
Knight-Ridder
c/o Fort Wayne Newspapers
600 W Main St.
Fort Wayne, IN 46802
Fax: (800)444-3303
Publisher's E-mail: rtadmin@hcc.net
Online newspaper that offers news, sports, and classifieds of the Fort Wayne area. **Freq:** Monthly. **Key Personnel:** Michael J. Christman, Publisher, phone: (260)461-8369. **Subscription Rates:** $18 Individuals. **URL:** http://www.fortwayne.com. **Mailing address:** PO Box 100, Fort Wayne, IN 46802. **Remarks:** Accepts advertising. **Circ:** (Not Reported).

11838 ■ Frost Illustrated
Frost Inc.
3121 S Calhoun St.
Fort Wayne, IN 46807
Phone: (260)745-0552
Black community newspaper. **Freq:** Weekly (Wed.). **Print Method:** Offset. **Cols./Page:** 5. **Key Personnel:** Freddie Basnight, Contact, phone: (260)402-2843. **Subscription Rates:** $30 Individuals; $35 Out of area. **URL:** http://www.frostillustrated.com. **Ad Rates:** GLR $.60; BW $832; 4C $1,032; PCI $12.80. **Circ:** Paid ‡1,342, Free ‡32.

11839 ■ Indiana Genealogist
Indiana Genealogical Society
PO Box 10507
Fort Wayne, IN 46852-0507
Publication E-mail: quarterly@indgensoc.org
Freq: Quarterly March, June, September and December. **Key Personnel:** Rachel Popma, Editor. **ISSN:** 1558--0458 (print). **Subscription Rates:** Included in membership. **URL:** http://www.indgensoc.org/publications/quarterly.php. **Remarks:** Advertising not accepted. **Circ:** (Not Reported).

11840 ■ The Journal Gazette
The Journal Gazette Co.
600 W Main St.
Fort Wayne, IN 46802
Phone: (260)461-8773
Fax: (260)461-8648
Free: 800-444-3303
Publication E-mail: jgnews@jg.net
General newspaper. **Founded:** 1863. **Freq:** Daily. **Print Method:** Flexographic letterpress. **Trim Size:** 23 9/16. **Cols./Page:** 6. **Col. Width:** 12 picas. **Col. Depth:** 22 inches. **Key Personnel:** Tom Pellegrene, Jr., Manager, phone: (260)461-8377; Tom Germuska, Assistant Managing Editor, phone: (260)461-8428; Richard Inskeep, President, phone: (260)461-8202; Julie Inskeep, Publisher, phone: (260)461-8490; Jim Touvell, Editor, phone: (260)461-8629; Sherry Skufca, Managing Editor, phone: (260)461-8201; Craig Klugman, Editor, phone: (260)461-8335. **Subscription Rates:** $49.40 Individuals 13 weeks. **URL:** http://www.journalgazette.net. **Feature Editors:** Terri Richardson, phone: (219)461-8304, trich@jg.net. **Mailing address:** PO Box 100, Fort Wayne, IN 46802. **Circ:** Mon.-Fri. ★**67830**, Sun. ★**126988**, Sat. ★**99199**.

11841 ■ Journal of Individual Psychology
North American Society of Adlerian Psychology

429 E Dupont Rd., No. 276
Fort Wayne, IN 46825
Phone: (260)267-8807
Fax: (260)818-2098
Publisher's E-mail: info@alfredadler.org
Journal containing theoretical and research based articles on Adlerian Psychology. **Freq:** Quarterly. **ISSN:** 0277- 7010 (print); **EISSN:** – (electronic). **Subscription Rates:** $58 Individuals U.S; $75 Individuals Canada; $83 Individuals International; $216 Institutions U.S; $233 Institutions, Canada; $241 Institutions International; $23 Individuals U.S, single issue; $35 Individuals Canada, single issue; $41 Individuals International, single issue; $60 Institutions U.S; $72 Institutions Canada, single issue; $78 Institutions International, single issue. **URL:** http://adlerjournals.com; http://utpress.utexas.edu/index.php/journals/journal-of-individual-psychology. **Remarks:** Advertising not accepted. **Circ:** (Not Reported).

11842 ■ Macedonian Tribune
Macedonian Patriotic Organization
124 W Wayne St.
Fort Wayne, IN 46802
Phone: (260)422-5900
Fax: (260)422-1348
Publication E-mail: mtfw@macedonian.org
Ethnic newspaper (English). **Freq:** Monthly. **Print Method:** Offset. **Trim Size:** 11 x 17. **Cols./Page:** 4. **Col. Width:** 2 3/8 inches. **Col. Depth:** 15 inches. **Key Personnel:** Virginia Surso, Editor-in-Chief. **ISSN:** 0024--9009 (print). **URL:** http://www.macedonian.org/Tribune/default.asp. **Also known as:** Makedonska Tribuna. **Remarks:** Advertising accepted; rates available upon request. **Circ:** ‡1600.

11843 ■ Missionary Church Today
Missionary Church, Inc.
3811 Vanguard Dr.
Fort Wayne, IN 46809-3304
Phone: (260)747-2027
Fax: (260)747-5331
Publisher's E-mail: mcdenomusa@mcusa.org
Freq: Quarterly. **Alt. Formats:** PDF. **Remarks:** Advertising not accepted. **Circ:** (Not Reported).

11844 ■ Sheltie Pacesetter
Sheltie Pacesetter
9428 Blue Mound Dr.
Fort Wayne, IN 46804
Phone: (260)434-1566
Fax: (260)434-1566
Publication E-mail: s.pacesetter@sheltie.com
Trade magazine covering Shetland Sheepdogs (Shelties). **Freq:** Quarterly. **Print Method:** Sheetfed offset. **Trim Size:** 8 1/2 x 11. **Key Personnel:** Nancy Lee Cathcart, Editor. **ISSN:** 0774--6608 (print). **URL:** http://www.sheltie.com/Sheltie_Pacesetter/Home.html. **Remarks:** Advertising accepted; rates available upon request. **Circ:** (Not Reported).

11845 ■ Today's Catholic: Newspaper of the Diocese of Fort Wayne-South Bend
Catholic Diocese of Fort Wayne - South Bend
PO Box 11169
Fort Wayne, IN 46856
Phone: (260)456-2824
Newspaper. **Freq:** Weekly. **Print Method:** Offset. **Trim Size:** 11 3/8 x 15 1/2. **Cols./Page:** 5. **Col. Width:** 1.875 inches. **Col. Depth:** 195 agate lines. **Key Personnel:** Tim Johnson, Editor; Kathy Denice, Business Manager. **ISSN:** 0891--1533 (print). **USPS:** 403-630. **Subscription Rates:** Free. **URL:** http://www.todayscatholicnews.org. **Ad Rates:** BW $925; 4C $1079; PCI $10.80. **Remarks:** Accepts advertising. **Circ:** ‡52,000, ‡49,000.

11846 ■ Waynedale News
Waynedale News
2505 Lower Huntington Rd.
Fort Wayne, IN 46809
Publisher's E-mail: news@waynedalenews.com
Community newspaper. **Freq:** Semiweekly. **Print Method:** Offset. **Cols./Page:** 6. **Col. Width:** 20 nonpareils. **Col. Depth:** 196 agate lines. **Key Personnel:** Cynthia Cornwell, Editor; Cindy Cornwell, Executive Editor; Alex Cornwell, Manager, Marketing; Robert L. Stark, Editor. **Subscription Rates:** Free. **URL:** http://thewaynedalenews.com. **Ad Rates:** GLR $20; BW $312; PCI $3.50; 4C $1128.75. **Remarks:** Accepts advertising. **Circ:** Free ‡12,000.

11847 ■ WAJI-FM - 95.1
347 W Berry St., Ste. 600
Fort Wayne, IN 46802
Phone: (260)423-3676
Format: Adult Contemporary. **Networks:** Independent. **Founded:** 1959. **Formerly:** WPTH-FM; WFWQ-FM. **Operating Hours:** Continuous. **ADI:** Fort Wayne (Angola), IN. **Key Personnel:** Marti Taylor, Promotions Dir., Music Dir., martitaylor@waji.com. **Wattage:** 39,000. **Ad Rates:** Advertising accepted; rates available upon request. Combined advertising rates available with WLDE-FM. **URL:** http://www.951bestfm.com.

11848 ■ WANE-TV - 15
2915 W State Blvd.
Fort Wayne, IN 46808
Phone: (260)424-1515
Format: Commercial TV. **Networks:** CBS. **Owner:** LIN TV Corp., One W Exchange St., Ste. 5A, Providence, RI 02903-1064, Ph: (401)454-2880, Fax: (401)454-6990. **Founded:** 1954. **Operating Hours:** 6 a.m.-2:30 a.m. **ADI:** Fort Wayne (Angola), IN. **URL:** http://www.wane.com.

WBCJ-FM - See Spencerville, OH

11849 ■ WBCL-FM - 90.3
1115 W Rudisill Blvd.
Fort Wayne, IN 46807
Phone: (260)745-0576
Fax: (260)745-2001
Format: Contemporary Christian. **Simulcasts:** WBCJ-FM; WBCY-FM. **Networks:** AP. **Owner:** Taylor University Broadcasting Inc., 1115 W Rudisill Blvd., Fort Wayne, IN 46807, Ph: (260)745-0576, Fax: (260)456-2913. **Founded:** 1976. **Operating Hours:** Continuous. **Key Personnel:** Ron Schneemann, Dir. of Production; Craig Albrecht, Operations Mgr.; Larry Bower, News Dir.; Ross McCampbell, Exec. Dir. **Local Programs:** *Mid-Morning*, Monday Tuesday Wednesday Thursday Friday 10:00 a.m. - 11:00 a.m. **Wattage:** 50,000. **Ad Rates:** Noncommercial; underwriting available. **URL:** http://www.wbcl.org.

WBCY-FM - See Archbold, OH

11850 ■ WBNI-FM - 94.1
PO Box 8459
Fort Wayne, IN 46808
Phone: (260)452-1189
Fax: (260)452-1188
Free: 800-471-9264
Format: Public Radio; Classical. **Networks:** National Public Radio (NPR); American Public Radio (APR); AP; Public Radio International (PRI). **Owner:** Northeast Indiana Public Radio Inc., 3204 Clairmont Ct., Fort Wayne, IN 46808, Ph: (260)452-1189, Fax: (260)452-1188. **Founded:** 1978. **Formerly:** WIPU-FM. **Operating Hours:** Continuous; 35% network, 65% local. **ADI:** Fort Wayne (Angola), IN. **Key Personnel:** David Hunter, Dir. of Dev.; Joan Baumgartner Brown, Gen. Mgr., President, jbrown@nipr.fm; Ed Didier, Chief Engineer, edidier@nipr.fm; Jackie Didier, Bus. Mgr., jdidier@nipr.fm. **Wattage:** 34,000. **Ad Rates:** Noncommercial. **URL:** http://wboi.org.

11851 ■ WBOI-FM - 89.1
3204 Clairmont Ct.
Fort Wayne, IN 46808
Phone: (260)452-1189
Fax: (260)452-1188
Free: 800-471-9264
Format: Jazz; News. **Owner:** Northeast Indiana Public Radio Inc., 3204 Clairmont Ct., Fort Wayne, IN 46808, Ph: (260)452-1189, Fax: (260)452-1188. **Key Personnel:** Jackie Didier, Bus. Mgr., jdidier@nipr.fm; Ed Didier, Chief Engineer, edidier@nipr.fm; Lea Denny, Office Mgr., ldenny@nipr.fm; David Hunter, Dir. of Dev. **URL:** http://wboi.org.

11852 ■ WBTU-FM - 93.3
2100 Goshen Rd., Ste. 232
Fort Wayne, IN 46808
Phone: (260)482-9288
Fax: (260)482-8655
Format: Contemporary Country. **Networks:** CNN Radio; ABC. **Owner:** Oasis Radio Group, Ph: (260)482-9288. **Founded:** 1948. **Operating Hours:** Continuous. **Key Personnel:** Dave Steele, Dir. of Programs, dave.steele@oasisradiogroup.com; Phil Becker, Dir. of Programs, VP, phil.becker@oasisradiogroup.com; Roger Diehm, Gen. Mgr., President, pete.desimone@oasisradiogroup.com. **Wattage:** 50,000. **Ad Rates:** $40-90 per unit.

11853 ■ WBYR-FM - 98.9
1005 Production Rd.
Fort Wayne, IN 46808
Phone: (260)471-5100
Format: Album-Oriented Rock (AOR). **Founded:** 1962. **Formerly:** WKSD; WERT-FM. **Operating Hours:** Continuous; 100% local. **Local Programs:** *Perfect 10 at 10*, Monday Tuesday Wednesday Thursday Friday 10:00 a.m. **Wattage:** 50,000. **Ad Rates:** $50-120 per unit. **URL:** http://www.989thebear.com.

11854 ■ WCKZ-FM
8 Martin Luther Dr.
Fort Wayne, IN 46825
Phone: (260)747-1511
Fax: (260)747-3999
Format: Classic Rock. **Wattage:** 2,000 ERP.

11855 ■ WCYT-FM - 91.1
4310 Homestead Rd.
Fort Wayne, IN 46814
Phone: (260)431-2911
Format: Alternative/New Music/Progressive. **Key Personnel:** Adam Schenkel, Station Mgr., adam@wcyt.org. **Ad Rates:** Noncommercial. **URL:** http://www.wcyt.org.

11856 ■ WEXI-FM - 102.9
2541 Goshen Rd.
Fort Wayne, IN 46808-1440
Fax: (219)482-5751
Format: Classic Rock; Album-Oriented Rock (AOR). **ADI:** Fort Wayne (Angola), IN. **Key Personnel:** Angela Smith, Station Mgr.; D. West, Music Dir., Prog. Dir. **Ad Rates:** Advertising accepted; rates available upon request.

11857 ■ WFCV-AM - 1090
3737 Lake Ave.
Fort Wayne, IN 46805
Phone: (260)423-2337
Fax: (260)423-6355
Format: Contemporary Christian. **Networks:** Independent. **Owner:** Bott Radio Network, 10550 Barkley, Overland Park, KS 66212, Ph: (913)642-7770, Fax: (913)642-1319, Free: 800-345-2621. **Founded:** 1980. **Operating Hours:** Sunrise-sunset. **ADI:** Fort Wayne (Angola), IN. **Key Personnel:** Dale Gerke, Mgr.; Kathy McClish, Operations Mgr. **Wattage:** 2,500. **Ad Rates:** $9-15 for 30 seconds; $15-22 for 60 seconds. **URL:** http://www.bottradionetwork.com.

11858 ■ WFFT-TV - 55
3707 Hillegas Rd.
Fort Wayne, IN 46808
Phone: (260)471-5555
Fax: (260)484-4331
Format: Commercial TV. **Networks:** Fox. **Founded:** 1977. **Operating Hours:** Continuous. **ADI:** Fort Wayne (Angola), IN. **Key Personnel:** Bill Ritchhart, Gen. Mgr., britchhart@wfft.com; Fred Brunell, Chief Engineer, fbrunell@wfft.com; John Parker, Dir. of Creative Svcs., jparker@wfft.com. **Ad Rates:** Noncommercial. **URL:** http://www.fortwaynehomepage.net.

11859 ■ WFWA-TV - 39
2501 E Coliseum Blvd.
Fort Wayne, IN 46805-1562
Phone: (260)484-8839
Free: 888-484-8839
Email: info@wfwa.org
Format: Public TV. **Networks:** Public Broadcasting Service (PBS). **Founded:** 1972. **Operating Hours:** Continuous. **ADI:** Fort Wayne (Angola), IN. **Key Personnel:** Joe Martin, Secretary; Bruce Haines, President, Gen. Mgr., brucehaines@wfwa.org; Todd Grimes, Production Mgr. **Local Programs:** *Healthline*, Tuesday 7:30 p.m.; *Matters of the Mind*, Monday 7:30 p.m. **Wattage:** 152,800 H ERP. **Ad Rates:** Noncommercial. Underwriting available. **URL:** http://www.wfwa.org.

11860 ■ WFWI-FM - 92.3
1005 Production Rd.
Fort Wayne, IN 46808
Format: Classic Rock. **Operating Hours:** Continuous. **ADI:** Fort Wayne (Angola), IN. **Key Personnel:** Sharon

Circulation: ★ = AAM; △ or • = BPA; ♦ = CAC; ❑ = VAC; ⊕ = PO Statement; ‡ = Publisher's Report; Boldface figures = sworn; Light figures = estimated.

Ummel, Contact, summel@fwi.com. **Wattage:** 2,200. **Ad Rates:** Advertising accepted; rates available upon request.

11861 ■ WGL-AM - 1250
2000 Lower Huntington Rd.
Fort Wayne, IN 46819
Phone: (260)747-1511
Fax: (260)747-3999
Format: Adult Contemporary. **Simulcasts:** WGLL-AM. **Networks:** CBS; Westwood One Radio. **Owner:** Summit City Radio Group L.L.C., 2000 Lower Huntington Rd., Fort Wayne, IN 46819, Ph: (260)747-5100. **Founded:** 1923. **Operating Hours**: Continuous; 90% network, 10% local. **Key Personnel:** Chris Monk, Gen. Mgr.; Jj Fabini, Dir. of Programs, jj@rock104radio.com; Scott Howard, Sales Mgr., scott@summitcityradio.com. **Wattage**: 2,500 Day; 1,400 Night. **Ad Rates:** Advertising accepted; rates available upon request. **URL:** http://softrock1039.com.

11862 ■ WISE-TV - 33
3401 Butler Rd.
Fort Wayne, IN 46808
Phone: (260)483-0584
Fax: (260)483-2568
Founded: Sept. 07, 2006. **Key Personnel:** Mr. Jerry Giesler, Gen. Mgr. **Ad Rates:** Advertising accepted; rates available upon request. **URL:** http://www.indianasnewscenter.com.

11863 ■ WJFX-FM - 107.9
9604 Coldwater Rd., Ste. 201
Fort Wayne, IN 46825
Phone: (260)482-9288
Fax: (260)482-8655
Format: Hip Hop. **Operating Hours**: Continuous. **Ad Rates:** Advertising accepted; rates available upon request. **URL:** http://www.hot1079online.com.

11864 ■ WJOE-FM - 106.3
2100 Goshen Rd.
Fort Wayne, IN 46808
Phone: (260)482-9288
Fax: (260)482-8655
Format: Adult Contemporary. **Owner:** Oasis Radio Group, Ph: (260)482-9288. **Formerly**: WVBB-FM. **Key Personnel:** Phil Becker, Dir. of Programs, phil.becker@oasisradiogroup.com; Lynn Williams, Promotions Dir., lynn.williams@oasisradiogroup.com; Bart Schacht, Gen. Sales Mgr., bart.schacht@oasisradiogroup.com. **URL:** http://www.1063joefm.com.

11865 ■ WKJG-TV - 33
3401 Butler Rd.
Fort Wayne, IN 46808
Phone: (706)922-5644
Format: Commercial TV. **Networks:** NBC. **Founded:** 1953. **Operating Hours**: Continuous. **Key Personnel:** John Dawson, Gen. Mgr., VP, News Dir., newsmgr@nbc33.com; Tad Frank, Promotions Dir., Contact, weather@nbc33.com; Dave Stevens, Sales Mgr., Gen. Mgr., gm@nbc33.com; Mark Meyer, Dir. of Programs, sports@nbc33.com; Matt Kyle, Dir. of Engg., mkyle@nbc33.com; John Martin, Sales Mgr., jmartin@nbc33.com; Kathy Baugh, News Dir., kbaugh@nbc33.com; Elly Price, Dir. Pub. Aff., eprice@nbc33.com; Ed Shick, Controller, eshick@nbc33.com; Tad Frank, Contact. **URL:** http://www.21alive.com/nbc33.

11866 ■ WLAB-FM - 88.3
6600 N Clinton St.
Fort Wayne, IN 46825
Phone: (260)483-8236
Fax: (260)482-7707
Format: Religious; Contemporary Christian. **Simulcasts:** W209BA , W215BB. **Networks:** USA Radio. **Owner:** The Lutheran Church - Missouri Synod, 1333 S Kirkwood Rd., Saint Louis, MO 63122-7226, Ph: (314)996-9000, Free: 888-843-5267. **Founded:** 1970. **Operating Hours:** Continuous; 5% network, 95% local. **Key Personnel:** Melissa Montana, Gen. Mgr., Music Dir., melissa@star883.com; Don Buettner, Dir. of Programs, don@star883.com; Leesa Huston, Dir. of Admin., leesa@star883.com. **Wattage:** 7,000. **Ad Rates:** Noncommercial. **URL:** http://www.star883.com.

11867 ■ WLDE-FM - 101.7
347 W Berry St., Ste. 600
Fort Wayne, IN 46802
Phone: (260)426-5343
Fax: (260)422-5266
Format: Oldies. **Key Personnel:** Lee Tobin, Contact; Shelly Steckler, Contact; Katrina Newman, Contact. **URL:** http://www.fun1017.com.

11868 ■ WLYV-AM - 1450
4618 E State Blvd.
Fort Wayne, IN 46815
Email: info@redeemerradio.com
Format: Religious. **Networks:** Unistar. **Owner:** Redeemer Radio, 4618 E State Blvd., Ste. 200, Fort Wayne, IN 46815, Ph: (260)436-9598, Fax: (260)432-6179, Free: 888-436-1450. **Founded:** 1948. **Formerly**: WANE-AM. **Operating Hours**: Continuous; 100% local. **Key Personnel:** Dave Stevens, Exec. Dir. **Wattage**: 1,000. **Ad Rates:** Noncommercial. **URL:** http://www.wlyv.com.

11869 ■ WMEE-FM - 97.3
2915 Maples Rd.
Fort Wayne, IN 46816
Phone: (260)447-5511
Fax: (260)447-7546
Format: Contemporary Hit Radio (CHR). **Networks:** Independent. **Owner:** Federated Media, at above address. **Founded:** 1947. **Formerly**: WKJG-FM. **Operating Hours**: Continuous. **ADI**: Fort Wayne (Angola), IN. **Key Personnel:** Jimmy Knight, Operations Mgr. **Wattage:** 47,000 ERP. **Ad Rates:** Advertising accepted; rates available upon request. **URL:** http://www.wmee.com.

11870 ■ WNHT-FM - 96.3
2000 Lower Huntington Rd.
Fort Wayne, IN 46819
Phone: (260)747-1511
Fax: (260)747-3999
Format: Top 40. **Owner:** Summit City Radio Group L.L.C., 2000 Lower Huntington Rd., Fort Wayne, IN 46819, Ph: (260)747-5100. **Operating Hours**: Continuous. **Ad Rates:** Advertising accepted; rates available upon request. **URL:** http://hot1079online.com.

11871 ■ WNUY-FM - 100.1
3737 Lake Ave.
Fort Wayne, IN 46805
Format: Talk. **Networks:** Tribune Radio. **Owner:** Bott Radio Network, 10550 Barkley, Overland Park, KS 66212, Ph: (913)642-7770, Fax: (913)642-1319, Free: 800-345-2621. **Founded:** 1963. **Formerly**: WCRD-FM. **Operating Hours**: midnight. **ADI**: Fort Wayne (Angola), IN. **Key Personnel:** Richard Bott, II, CEO, President, rbott@bottradionetwork.com. **Wattage**: 6,000. **Ad Rates:** Noncommercial. **URL:** http://www.bottradionetwork.com.

11872 ■ WOWO-AM - 1190
2915 Maples Rd.
Fort Wayne, IN 46816
Phone: (260)447-5511
Fax: (260)447-7546
Free: 800-333-1190
Format: News; Talk. **Networks:** ABC; Fox. **Owner:** Federated Media, at above address. **Founded:** 1925. **Operating Hours:** Continuous; 5% network, 95% local. **Key Personnel:** Ben Saurer, Gen. Sales Mgr., bsaurer@wowo.com. **Local Programs**: *Mutual Fund Show*, Saturday 11:00 a.m. - 12:00 p.m.; *Kim Komando Show*, Saturday 12:00 p.m. - 3:00 p.m.; *Dead Doctors Don't Lie*, Sunday 5:00 a.m. - 6:00 a.m.; *Best of Rush Limbaugh*, Saturday 6:00 a.m. - 7:00 a.m.; 3:00 p.m. - 6:00 p.m.; *Beyond the Beltway*, Sunday 7:00 p.m. - 9:00 p.m.; *Fort Wayne's Morning News with Charly Butcher*, Monday Tuesday Wednesday Thursday Friday 5:00 a.m. - 9:00 a.m. **Wattage:** 50,000. **Ad Rates:** Advertising accepted; rates available upon request. **URL:** http://wowo.com.

11873 ■ WPTA-TV - 21
3401 Butler Rd.
Fort Wayne, IN 46808
Phone: (260)483-0584
Fax: (260)483-2568
Email: salesinfo@incnow.tv
Format: Commercial TV. **Networks:** ABC. **Owner:** Granite Broadcasting Corp., 767 3rd Ave., 34th Fl., New York, NY 10017-2083, Ph: (212)826-2530, Fax: (212)826-2858. **Founded:** 1957. **Operating Hours:** Continuous. **ADI**: Fort Wayne (Angola), IN. **Key Personnel:** Ron Ross, Gen. Mgr. **Wattage**: 30,000 transmitter; ERP 490 KW visual; 049 KW aural. **Ad Rates:** Advertising accepted; rates available upon request. **URL:** http://www.indianasnewscenter.com.

11874 ■ WQHK-FM - 105.1
2915 Maples Rd.
Fort Wayne, IN 46816
Phone: (260)447-5511
Format: Country. **Key Personnel:** Dave Michaels, Operations Mgr., dmichaels@k105fm.com. **URL:** http://www.k105fm.com.

11875 ■ WXKE-FM - 103.9
2000 Lower Huntington Rd.
Fort Wayne, IN 46819
Phone: (260)747-1511
Fax: (260)747-3999
Format: Album-Oriented Rock (AOR); Classic Rock; Alternative/New Music/Progressive. **Networks:** Independent. **Owner:** Summit City Radio Group L.L.C., 2000 Lower Huntington Rd., Fort Wayne, IN 46819, Ph: (260)747-5100. **Founded:** 1976. **Operating Hours**: Continuous; 100% local. **ADI**: Fort Wayne (Angola), IN. **Wattage**: 3,000. **Ad Rates:** Noncommercial. **URL:** http://www.rock104radio.com.

11876 ■ WXTW-FM - 102.3
8208 Fawncrest Pl.
Fort Wayne, IN 46835
Phone: (260)471-6055
Format: News. **ADI**: Fort Wayne (Angola), IN. **Wattage**: 6,000 ERP. **Ad Rates:** Advertising accepted; rates available upon request. **URL:** http://www.1023launica.com.

FRANKFORT

Clinton Co. Clinton Co. (NC). 45 m NW of Indianapolis. Park, recreation and historical sites.

11877 ■ Times
Frankfort Times Inc.
251 E Clinton St.
Frankfort, IN 46041-1906
Publication E-mail: news@ftimes.com
General newspaper. **Founded:** 1894. **Freq:** Daily (eve.) and Sat. (morn.). **Print Method:** Offset. **Cols./Page:** 6. **Col. Width:** 1.833 inches. **Col. Depth:** 21 1/2 inches. **USPS:** 208-000. **Subscription Rates:** $261 By mail; $159 Individuals by motor route; $153 Individuals by carrier. **URL:** http://www.ftimes.com. **Mailing address:** PO Box 9, Frankfort, IN 46041-1906. **Ad Rates:** BW $2,423.91; 4C $2,913.91; PCI $18.79. **Remarks:** Advertising accepted; rates available upon request. **Circ:** (Not Reported).

11878 ■ WILO-AM - 1570
PO Box 545
Frankfort, IN 46041
Phone: (765)659-3338
Free: 800-447-4463
Email: rk@kasparradio.com
Format: Country; Agricultural; Sports. **Owner:** Kaspar Broadcasting Co., PO Box 220, Warrenton, MO 63383, Ph: (636)377-2300, Free: 877-259-7373. **Founded:** Sept. 20, 2006. **Operating Hours**: 5:15 a.m.-11 p.m. **Wattage**: 50,000. **Ad Rates:** Advertising accepted; rates available upon request. **Mailing address:** PO Box 545, Frankfort, IN 46041. **URL:** http://www.wilo.us.

11879 ■ WIRE-FM - 100.9
2890 Washington Ave.
Frankfort, IN 46041
Phone: (317)239-9473
Owner: Boone County Broadcasters, Inc., at above address. **Founded:** 1967. **Formerly**: WNON-FM. **ADI**: Indianapolis (Marion), IN. **Key Personnel:** John R. Dotas, Contact. **Wattage**: 3,000. **Ad Rates:** $6-9.50 for 30 seconds; $8-14 for 60 seconds.

11880 ■ WSHW-FM
1401-03 W Barner St.
Frankfort, IN 46041
Free: 800-447-4463
Format: Adult Contemporary; Agricultural. **Networks:** AP. **Owner:** Kaspar Broadcasting Co., PO Box 220, Warrenton, MO 63383, Ph: (636)377-2300, Free: 877-259-7373. **Founded:** 1962. **Key Personnel:** Vern Kaspar, Contact; Jim Riggs, Contact. **Wattage**: 50,000 ERP. **URL:** http://www.shine99.com.

FRANKLIN

Johnson Co. Johnson Co. (SC). 20 m S of Indianapolis. Franklin College.

11881 ■ Daily Journal
Home News Enterprises L.L.C.
30 S Water St., 2nd Fl., Ste. A
Franklin, IN 46131
Phone: (317)736-2777
Free: 888-736-7101
General newspaper. **Founded:** 1963. **Freq:** Daily (eve.). **Print Method:** Offset. **Trim Size:** 13 x 21 1/2. **Cols./Page:** 6. **Key Personnel:** Scarlett Syse, Editor; Tammy Smith, Manager, Administration, phone: (317)736-2751; Michelle Bright, Project Manager, phone: (317)736-2767; Chuck Wells, Publisher. **USPS:** 565-520. **Subscription Rates:** $228 Two years; $118.80 Individuals; $87.60 Individuals 8 months; $41.60 Individuals 4 months; $21.50 Individuals 2 months; $108 Individuals; $72 Individuals 8 months; $36 Individuals 4 months; $11 Individuals /month (online only). **URL:** http://www.dailyjournal.net. **Ad Rates:** BW $240; 4C $313; PCI $14.45. **Circ:** Paid ♦**1,676**, Paid ♦**13,414**.

11882 ■ Indiana Prairie Farmer
Farm Progress Companies Inc.
599N, 100 W Franklin
Franklin, IN 46131
Phone: (317)738-0565
Fax: (317)738-5441
Publisher's E-mail: circhelp@farmprogress.com
Farm production and management magazine for Indiana farmers. **Freq:** Monthly. **Print Method:** Offset. **Trim Size:** 8 x 10. **Cols./Page:** 3. **Col. Width:** 33 nonpareils. **Col. Depth:** 175 agate lines. **Key Personnel:** Frank Holdmeyer, Executive Editor, phone: (515)278-7782, fax: (515)278-7796; John Otte, Editor, phone: (515)278-7785, fax: (515)278-7797; Alan Newport, Editor, phone: (580)362-3483, fax: (580)362-3483; Willie Vogt, Director, Editorial, phone: (651)454-6994, fax: (651)994-0661. **ISSN:** 0162--7104 (print). **Subscription Rates:** $29.95 Individuals; $48.95 Two years; $64.95 Individuals 3 years. **URL:** http://farmprogress.com/indiana-prairie-farmer. **Mailing address:** PO Box 247, Franklin, IN 46131. **Remarks:** Accepts advertising. **Circ:** ‡35000.

11883 ■ WFCI-FM - 89.5
101 Branigin Blvd.
Franklin, IN 46131
Free: 800-852-0232
Format: Top 40; Educational. **Owner:** Franklin College of Indiana, 101 Branigin Blvd., Franklin, IN 46131, Free: 800-852-0232. **Founded:** 1960. **Operating Hours:** 3 a.m.-2 a.m. **ADI:** Indianapolis (Marion), IN. **Key Personnel:** Joel Cramer, Advisor, jcramer@franklincollege.edu. **Wattage:** 1,150. **Ad Rates:** Noncommercial. **URL:** http://www.franklincollege.edu.

WIAU-FM - See Franklin, IN

11884 ■ WIAU-FM - 95.9
645 Industrial Dr.
435 N Michigan Ave.
Franklin, IN 46131
Phone: (317)736-4040
Fax: (317)736-4781
Format: News; Talk; Contemporary Christian; Information. **Simulcasts:** WXLW-AM. **Owner:** Pilgrim Communications Inc., Indianapolis, IN, Ph: (317)655-9999, Fax: (317)655-9995. **Founded:** 1988. **Formerly:** WIJY-FM; WGAQ-FM; WIFN-FM. **Operating Hours:** Continuous. **Wattage:** 34,000 ERP. **Ad Rates:** Advertising accepted; rates available upon request. **URL:** http://www.freedom95.us.

11885 ■ WXLW-AM - 950
645 Industrial Dr.
Franklin, IN 46131
Phone: (317)736-4040
Fax: (317)736-4781
Email: info@freedom95.us
Format: Talk; Sports. **Owner:** Pilgrim Communications, LLC, 645 Industrial Dr., Franklin, IN 46131, Ph: (317)736-4040, Fax: (317)736-4781. **Founded:** 1948. **Operating Hours:** Continuous. **ADI:** Indianapolis (Marion), IN. **Wattage:** 1,000 Day; 013 Night. **Ad Rates:** Advertising accepted; rates available upon request. **URL:** http://www.freedom95.us.

FRENCH LICK

Orange Co. Orange Co. (S). 50 m N of Louisville, Ky. Health resort. Mineral springs. Stone quarry. Timber. Bottling works. Furniture factory. Agriculture. Stock, fruit, poultry.

11886 ■ Springs Valley Herald
Springs Valley Herald
8481 W College St.
French Lick, IN 47432
Phone: (812)936-9630
Fax: (812)723-2592
Free: 888-884-5553
Publisher's E-mail: admin@springsvalleyherald.com
Newspaper with a Democratic orientation. **Freq:** Weekly (Wed.). **Print Method:** Offset. **Cols./Page:** 6. **Col. Width:** 24 nonpareils. **Col. Depth:** 21 inches. **Key Personnel:** Arthur W. Hampton, Publisher, Editor. **Subscription Rates:** $28 Individuals /year; online only; Orange County addresses; $37 Individuals /year; online only; outside Orange County; $18.50 Students. **URL:** http://springsvalleyherald.com. **Ad Rates:** GLR $3; 4C $85; PCI $4.25. **Remarks:** Advertising accepted; rates available upon request. **Circ:** ‡2800.

11887 ■ WFLQ-FM - 100.1
PO Box 100
French Lick, IN 47432
Phone: (812)936-9100
Email: wflqfm@smithville.net
Format: Country. **Networks:** Satellite Music Network; Satellite Network News. **Owner:** Willtronics Broadcasting, Not Available. **Founded:** 1983. **Operating Hours:** 6 a.m.-midnight; 93% network, 7% local. **Key Personnel:** Mike Hole, Account Exec. **Local Programs:** *Tradio*, Monday Wednesday Friday 1:06 p.m.; *Daily Dose*, Monday Tuesday Wednesday Thursday Friday 6:50 a.m.; 4:20 p.m.; *My Utmost For His Highest*, Monday Tuesday Wednesday Thursday Friday 7:02 p.m. **Wattage:** 6,000. **Ad Rates:** $4.50 for 10 seconds; $5.50 for 15 seconds; $6-8.50 for 30 seconds; $7.50-10 for 60 seconds. **URL:** http://wflq.com.

FRIENDSHIP

Ripley Co. (SE). 22 m S of Batesville. Agriculture. Corn, wheat, hay.

11888 ■ Muzzle Blasts
National Muzzle Loading Rifle Association
State Road 62 Maxine Moss Dr.
Friendship, IN 47021
Phone: (812)667-5131
Fax: (812)667-5136
Free: 800-745-1493
Publication E-mail: mblastmag@seidata.com
Freq: Monthly. **Print Method:** Web offset. **Trim Size:** 8 1/4 x 10 5/8. **Cols./Page:** 3. **Col. Width:** 2 1/8 inches. **Col. Depth:** 9 1/2 inches. **Key Personnel:** Morgan Mundell, Managing Director; Lee A. Larkin, Editor. **ISSN:** 0027--5360 (print). **URL:** http://nmlra.org/muzzle-blasts. **Formerly:** Muzzle Blasts: Historical and Modern Muzzle-loading Arms Magazine,. **Mailing address:** PO Box 67, Friendship, IN 47021. **Ad Rates:** BW $768; 4C $1,535; PCI $35. **Remarks:** Advertising accepted; rates available upon request. **Circ:** ‡19000.

GARRETT

De Kalb Co. De Kalb Co. (NE). 20 m N of Fort Wayne. Manufactures wood specialities, hospital furniture, electric motors, plastics, molded rubber products, machine shop. Agriculture. Corn, wheat, oats.

11889 ■ The Garrett Clipper
KPC Media Group, Inc.
PO Box 59
Garrett, IN 46738
Publisher's E-mail: contact@kpcmedia.com
Newspaper. **Freq:** Weekly. **Print Method:** Offset. **Cols./Page:** 6. **Col. Width:** 10.8 picas. **Col. Depth:** 21 inches. **Key Personnel:** Susan Carpenter, Editor. **USPS:** 214-260. **Subscription Rates:** $44 Individuals print; home delivered; $52 Individuals print; mailed (in county); $64 Individuals print; mailed (out of county); $54.95 Individuals online; $99.95 Two years online. **URL:** http://kpcmedia.com/publications/garrett-clipper. **Ad Rates:** GLR $4.95; BW $638.55; 4C $888.55; CNU $452; PCI $6.88. **Remarks:** Accepts advertising. **Circ:** ‡1200.

GARY

Lake Co. Lake Co. (NW). On Lake Michigan 31 m SE of Chicago, Ill. Indiana Dunes State Park and National Park; Campus of Indiana University Northwest; Extensive iron, steel, sheet and tin plate, rail and cement plants. Car wheels, axles, structural shapes, alloys, coke, ammonium sulphate, tar, bridges, steel seamless tubes, steel springs, plastics, auto bodies, auto accessories, screws, jet engines, bolts, rivets, women's men's and children's wear, hosiery, lighting fixtures, bricks manufactured.

11890 ■ The Northwest Phoenix
Indiana University Northwest
3400 Broadway
Gary, IN 46408
Phone: (219)980-6501
Free: 888-968-7486
College newspaper. **Freq:** Semimonthly. **Print Method:** Offset. **Trim Size:** 11 x 14. **Cols./Page:** 8. **Col. Width:** 21 nonpareils. **Col. Depth:** 224 agate lines. **Key Personnel:** Don Sjoerdsma, Editor-in-Chief. **URL:** http://www.iun.edu/~phoenixn/. **Remarks:** Accepts advertising. **Circ:** Free ‡2500.

11891 ■ WGVE-FM - 88.7
620 E 10th Pl.
Gary, IN 46402
Phone: (219)962-9483
Email: sste1963@aol.com
Format: Educational; Talk; Adult Album Alternative. **Simulcasts:** TV-WJPN. **Owner:** Gary Community School Corp., 620 E 10th Pl., Gary, IN 46402, Ph: (219)886-6400. **Founded:** 1954. **Operating Hours:** Continuous. **Wattage:** 2,100. **Ad Rates:** $45-75 for 30 seconds.

11892 ■ WLTH-AM
487 Broadway
Gary, IN 46402
Phone: (219)885-1370
Fax: (219)885-1371
Format: News; Talk. **Networks:** Independent. **Owner:** Michilliana Broadcasting L.L.C., Gary, IN 46403. **Founded:** 1950. **Key Personnel:** Pluria Marshall, Gen. Mgr. **Wattage:** 1,000 Day; 500 Night. **Ad Rates:** $40-85 for 30 seconds. **URL:** http://wlth1370.com.

GOSHEN

Elkhart Co. Elkhart Co. (N). 10 m SE of Elkhart. Goshen College (Menno.). Manufactures rubber goods, furniture, condensed milk, hydraulic presses, ladders, electric controls, batteries, sashes, doors, tanks, steel, glass and aluminum boats, trailers, plastics, lightning rods. Hardwood timber. Farming.

11893 ■ Goshen College Bulletin
Goshen College
1700 S Main St.
Goshen, IN 46526
Phone: (219)535-7000
Free: 800-348-7422
Publisher's E-mail: info@goshen.edu
College alumni magazine. **Freq:** 2-3/yr. **Print Method:** Offset. **Trim Size:** 8 1/2 x 11. **Cols./Page:** 2 and 3. **Col. Width:** 42 and 28 nonpareils. **Col. Depth:** 116 agate lines. **Key Personnel:** Jodi H. Beyeler, Editor. **ISSN:** 0017--2308 (print). **Subscription Rates:** Free to qualified subscribers. **URL:** http://www.goshen.edu/bulletin. **Remarks:** Advertising not accepted. **Circ:** ‡23000.

11894 ■ The Goshen News
Goshen News
114 S Main St.
Goshen, IN 46526
Phone: (574)533-2151
Fax: (574)533-0839
Free: 800-487-2151
Newspaper with a Republican orientation. **Freq:** Mon.-Sun. **Print Method:** Offset. **Cols./Page:** 6. **Col. Width:** 24 nonpareils. **Col. Depth:** 301 agate lines. **Key Personnel:** Michael Wanbaugh, Managing Editor; Stacey Ramsey, Director, Advertising; Ron Smith, Publisher. **Subscription Rates:** $15.99 Individuals print and online; /month; $13.99 Individuals online ; /month. **URL:** http://www.goshennews.com/. **Mailing address:** PO Box 569, Goshen, IN 46527. **Ad Rates:** BW $1,100; 4C $1,250; SAU $10.88. **Remarks:** Accepts advertising. **Circ:** Mon.-Sat. 16517, Sun. 16246.

Circulation: ★ = AAM; △ or • = BPA; ♦ = CAC; ❑ = VAC; ⊕ = PO Statement; ‡ = Publisher's Report; Boldface figures = sworn; Light figures = estimated.

11895 ■ The Mennonite: A magazine to serve Mennonite Church USA by helping readers glorify God, grown in Faith and become agents of healing and hope in the world
The Mennonite
1700 S Main St.
Goshen, IN 46526
Phone: (574)535-6052
Fax: (574)535-6050
Free: 800-790-2498
Publisher's E-mail: editor@themennonite.org
Mennonite magazine. **Freq:** Monthly. **Print Method:** Offset. **Trim Size:** 8 1/2 x 11. **Cols./Page:** 5. **Key Personnel:** Gordon Houser, Associate Editor; Everett J. Thomas, Contact. **ISSN:** 0017--2340 (print). **Subscription Rates:** $46 Individuals; $82 Two years; $54 Canada; $93 Other countries; $24 Students 6 month. **URL:** http://themennonite.org. **Formerly**: The Gospel Herald. **Ad Rates:** 4C $1559; PCI $25. **Remarks:** Accepts advertising. **Circ:** ‡11500.

11896 ■ Mennonite Health Journal
Mennonite Healthcare Fellowship
PO Box 918
Goshen, IN 46527
Free: 888-406-3643
Publisher's E-mail: info@mennohealth.org
Journal featuring articles for healthcare workers, discussions of biomedical ethics, facilitates nurse relationships and reports on Mennonite Nurses Association events. **Freq:** Quarterly. **ISSN:** 1525--6766 (print). **URL:** http://mennohealth.org/communications/journal. **Remarks:** Advertising not accepted. **Circ:** (Not Reported).

11897 ■ The Mennonite Quarterly Review
Mennonite Historical Society
1700 Main St.
Goshen, IN 46526
Phone: (574)535-7433
Publication E-mail: mqr@goshen.edu
Journal covering Anabaptist, Mennonite, Amish, and Hutterite current events, history, and theology. **Freq:** Quarterly. **Print Method:** Offset. **Trim Size:** 6 x 9. **Cols./Page:** 1. **Col. Width:** 54 nonpareils. **Col. Depth:** 105 agate lines. **Key Personnel:** John D. Roth, Editor. **ISSN:** 0025--9373 (print). **Subscription Rates:** $35 U.S. and Canada; $10 Single issue; $45 Other countries; $20 U.S. and Canada student; $30 Students, other countries. **Alt. Formats:** PDF. **URL:** http://www.goshen.edu/mqr. **Remarks:** Advertising not accepted. **Circ:** Paid ‡820, Controlled ‡180.

11898 ■ WGCS-FM - 91.1
1700 S Main St.
Goshen, IN 46526
Phone: (574)535-7488
Fax: (574)535-7293
Format: Eclectic; Full Service. **Networks:** Public Radio International (PRI). **Owner:** Goshen College Broadcasting Corp., 1700 S Main St., Goshen, IN 46526, Ph: (574)535-7000. **Founded:** 1958. **Operating Hours:** Daily. **Key Personnel:** Jason Samuel, Gen. Mgr.; Paul Housholder, Tech. Dir., pauldh@goshen.edu. **Local Programs**: *Patterns in American Music*; *A Women's Circle*; *Could Lead to Dancing*; *A Women's Circle*. **Wattage**: 6,000. **Ad Rates:** Noncommercial.

11899 ■ WKAM-AM - 1460
5713 W Cermak Rd.
Cicero, IL 60804
Phone: (708)780-1428
Format: Adult Contemporary. **Networks:** CNN Radio; Brownfield. **Owner:** I.B. Communication, Ltd., at above address. **Founded:** 1947. **Operating Hours:** Continuous. **Wattage**: 2,500 Day; 500 Night. **Ad Rates:** $10.60-12.95 for 30 seconds; $12.95-15.30 for 60 seconds. Combined advertising rates available with WZOW-FM.

GRABILL

Allen Co. Allen Co. (NE). 15 m NE of Fort Wayne. Manufactures furniture ornamental iron, plastic auto parts, steering wheels, wooden cabinets. Trucking. Grain, dairy, poultry farms.

11900 ■ East Allen Courier
East Allen Courier
PO Box 77
Grabill, IN 46741-0077
Phone: (219)627-2728
Community Newspaper. **Freq:** Weekly. **Print Method:** Offset. **Cols./Page:** 6. **Col. Width:** 9.5 picas. **Col. Depth:** 224 agate lines. **Key Personnel:** Waldo P. Dick, Editor. **Subscription Rates:** Free to qualified subscribers. **URL:** http://www.courierprinting.biz/east-allen-courier. **Ad Rates:** GLR $4/col.; BW $400; 4C $670; PCI $10. **Remarks:** Accepts advertising. **Circ:** Paid ‡450, Free ‡7500.

GRANGER

11901 ■ National Kart News
National Kart News Inc.
51535 Bittersweet Rd.
Granger, IN 46530
Phone: (574)277-0033
Fax: (574)277-4279
Free: 800-942-0033
Publisher's E-mail: fjaworski@nkn.com
Magazine covering news on karting. **Freq:** Monthly. **Trim Size:** 7.5 x 10.125. **Key Personnel:** Curt Paluzzi, Publisher. **Subscription Rates:** $12 Members online. **URL:** http://nkn.com/online. **Ad Rates:** 4C $950. **Remarks:** Accepts advertising. **Circ:** (Not Reported).

GREENCASTLE

Putnam Co. Putnam Co. (WC). 40 m SW of Indianapolis. De Pauw University. Manufactures office products, cement, crushed stone. Lumber mill. Limestone quarries. Timber, stock, dairy farms.

11902 ■ Banner-Graphic
Truth Publishing Co.
100 N Jackson St.
Greencastle, IN 46135-1240
Phone: (317)653-5151
Fax: (317)653-2063
General newspaper. **Freq:** Mon.-Sat. (eve.). **Print Method:** Offset. **Trim Size:** 14 x 23. **Cols./Page:** 6. **Col. Width:** 28 nonpareils. **Col. Depth:** 294 agate lines. **Key Personnel:** Eric Bernsee, Editor; Daryl Taylor, General Manager; Chris Pruett, Publisher. **Subscription Rates:** $17 Individuals Print; 3 months; $8.50 Individuals Print; 1 month; $9.50 Individuals print and online. **URL:** http://www.bannergraphic.com. **Ad Rates:** BW $878.22. **Remarks:** Accepts advertising. **Circ:** 6181.

11903 ■ The DePauw: Indiana's Oldest College Newspaper
De Pauw University Pulliam Center for Contemporary Media
609 S Locust St.
Greencastle, IN 46135
Phone: (765)658-4475
Fax: (765)658-4455
Collegiate newspaper. **Freq:** Semiweekly Tuesday and Friday during the academic year. **Print Method:** Offset. **Trim Size:** Tabloid. **Cols./Page:** 5. **Col. Width:** 22 nonpareils. **Col. Depth:** 179 agate lines. **Key Personnel:** Paige Powers, Business Manager; Becca Stanek, Managing Editor; Abby Margulis, Editor-in-Chief. **USPS:** 150-120. **Subscription Rates:** $75 Individuals one semester; $100 Individuals; Free students, faculty, staff, and administration. **URL:** http://www.thedepauw.com. **Remarks:** Accepts advertising. **Circ:** Paid 400, Free 3000.

11904 ■ DePauw Magazine
DePauw University
PO Box 37
Greencastle, IN 46135-0037
Phone: (765)658-4800
Alumni magazine for DePauw University. **Freq:** 3/year. **Subscription Rates:** Free to qualified subscribers. **URL:** http://www.depauw.edu/news-media/depauw-magazine. **Circ:** (Not Reported).

11905 ■ Science Fiction Studies
SF-TH Inc.
DePauw University
Greencastle, IN 46135-0037
Phone: (765)658-4800
Scholarly journal devoted to the study of science fiction. **Founded:** 1973. **Freq:** 3/yr. **Print Method:** Perfect bound, laminated. **Trim Size:** 4.5 x 7.5. **Key Personnel:** Prof. Arthur B. Evans, Editor. **ISSN:** 0091-7729 (print). **Subscription Rates:** $30 Individuals electronic only; $50 Institutions electronic only; $65 Institutions print + electronic; $40 Individuals print + electronic. **URL:** http://www.depauw.edu/site/sfs. **Ad Rates:** BW $200. **Remarks:** Accepts advertising. **Circ:** Controlled 1150.

11906 ■ WGRE-FM - 91.5
313 S Locust St.
Greencastle, IN 46135
Phone: (765)658-4800
Format: Educational; Eclectic; Full Service. **Networks:** AP. **Owner:** DePauw University, PO Box 37, Greencastle, IN 46135-0037, Ph: (765)658-4800. **Founded:** 1949. **Operating Hours**: Continuous; 5% network, 95% local. **Key Personnel:** Tyler Archer, Station Mgr., tylerarcher_2011@depauw.edu; Katie Logan, Dir. of Programs, katielogan_2012@depauw.edu; Jonathan Saddler, Web Adm., wgre@depauw.edu; John Dwyer, Bd. Member. **Wattage**: 800. **Ad Rates:** Noncommercial. **Mailing address:** PO Box 37, Greencastle, IN 46135. **URL:** http://www.wgre.org.

GREENFIELD

Hancock Co. Hancock Co. (EC). 20 m E of Indianapolis. Manufactures prepainted metals, wire products, tool boxes, drugs, lock washers, knitwear. Farming. Wheat, corn, soybeans.

11907 ■ Daily Reporter
Daily Reporter
22 W New Rd.
Greenfield, IN 46140
Phone: (317)462-5528
Publisher's E-mail: editorial@greenfieldreporter.com
General newspaper. **Founded:** 1908. **Freq:** Daily (eve.). **Print Method:** Offset. **Trim Size:** 13 3/4 x 22 3/4. **Cols./Page:** 6. **Col. Width:** 2 1/16 inches. **Col. Depth:** 21 1/2 inches. **Key Personnel:** Chuck Wells, Publisher. **USPS:** 228-720. **Subscription Rates:** $97 Individuals Hancock County with online; $50 Individuals 6 months, Hancock County with online; $80 Individuals online; $8 Individuals one month, online. **URL:** http://www.greenfieldreporter.com/view/page/DR_Pub_Daily_Reporter. **Mailing address:** PO Box 279, Greenfield, IN 46140. **Ad Rates:** BW $1006; 4C $1156; SAU $7.80. **Remarks:** Accepts advertising. **Circ:** Combined ‡8,942.

11908 ■ WERK-AM - 990
15 Wood St.
Greenfield, IN 46140
Phone: (317)467-1064
Email: wade@netusa1.net
Simulcasts: WERK-FM. **Networks:** Independent. **Owner:** Dream Weaver Broadcasting, Inc., PO Box 17, Elwood, IN 46036, Ph: (765)552-1017, Fax: (765)552-0506, Free: 800-456-5203. **Founded:** 1965. **Operating Hours:** 6 a.m. - 7 p.m. 100% local. **Key Personnel:** Phil Dashler, News Dir.; Mandy Adams, Bus. Mgr; Walter Weaver, Contact. **Ad Rates:** Combined advertising rates available with WLHN.

11909 ■ WJCF-FM - 88.1
PO Box 846
Greenfield, IN 46140
Phone: (317)462-9523
Format: Religious. **Operating Hours**: Continuous. **URL:** http://www.wjcfradio.com.

11910 ■ WRGF-FM
110 W North St.
Greenfield, IN 46140
Format: Alternative/New Music/Progressive. **Founded:** 1206.

GREENSBURG

Decatur Co. Decatur Co. (SE). 30 m NE of Columbus.

11911 ■ Critical Care Nursing Quarterly
Lippincott Williams & Wilkins
c/o Janet M. Barber, Ed.
9383 E County Rd., 500 S
Greensburg, IN 47240-8138
Publication E-mail: journals@ovid.com
Journal providing coverage of advances, procedures, and techniques in the clinical management of the critically ill or injured patient. **Freq:** Quarterly. **Trim Size:** 7 x 10. **Cols./Page:** 2. **Col. Width:** 16 picas. **Col. Depth:** 45 picas. **Key Personnel:** Janet M. Barber, Editor. **ISSN:** 0887--9303 (print); **EISSN:** 1550--5111 (electronic). **Subscription Rates:** $130 Individuals; $137 Canada and Mexico; $244 Other countries; $490 Institutions; $513 Institutions, Canada and Mexico; $713 Institutions, other

countries; $72 Individuals in-training. **URL:** http://journals.lww.com/ccnq/pages/default.aspx. **Formerly:** Critical Care Quarterly. **Ad Rates:** BW $1,070; 4C $1,380. **Remarks:** Accepts advertising. **Circ:** ‡820, ‡712.

11912 ■ The Greensburg Daily News
Community Newspaper Holdings Inc.
135 S Franklin St.
Greensburg, IN 47240
Phone: (812)663-3111
Fax: (812)663-2985
Free: 877-253-7758
General newspaper. **Freq:** Mon.-Sat. (eve.). **Print Method:** Offset. Uses slicks and veloxes. **Cols./Page:** 6. **Col. Width:** 26 nonpareils. **Col. Depth:** 301 agate lines. **Key Personnel:** Adam Huening, Editor. **ISSN:** 2289--8000 (print). **Subscription Rates:** $13.99 Individuals print and online; /month; $11.99 Individuals online; /month. **URL:** http://www.greensburgdailynews.com. **Ad Rates:** GLR $1.85; BW $872; 4C $1,072; SAU $7.95; PCI $7.95. **Remarks:** Accepts advertising. **Circ:** ‡6750.

11913 ■ WTRE-AM - 1330
220 E Main St.,
Greensburg, IN 47240
Phone: (812)663-3000
Format: Country; News; Sports. **Founded:** 1968. **Key Personnel:** Sandy Biddinger, Contact; Gene McCoy, Mgr. **Wattage:** 500. **Ad Rates:** Advertising accepted; rates available upon request. **URL:** http://www.wtrecommunity.com.

GREENWOOD

Johnson Co. Johnson Co. (SC) 11 m S of Indianapolis. Auto accessories, canned goods, stock remedies, mineral feeds manufactured. Dairy, stock, grain farms. Corn, wheat, oats, tomatoes.

11914 ■ Music Clubs Magazine
National Federation of Music Clubs
1646 Smith Valley Rd.
Greenwood, IN 46142
Phone: (317)882-4003
Fax: (317)882-4019
Magazine featuring events, conferences, book reviews, organizations and institutions, music clubs, organizations, and individuals directly or indirectly connected with musical activities. **Freq:** Quarterly. **Subscription Rates:** Included in membership senior members; $7 Nonmembers. **URL:** http://www.nfmc-music.org/index.php?src=gendocs&ref=Periodicals&category=About. **Remarks:** Accepts advertising. **Circ:** (Not Reported).

11915 ■ WCLJ-TV - 42
2528 US 31 Hwy. S
Greenwood, IN 46143
Phone: (714)832-2950
Format: Commercial TV. **Founded:** 1987. **Key Personnel:** Martha Erp, Contact, wclj_pray@hotmail.com. **Wattage:** 850,000 ERP. **Ad Rates:** $75 for 30 seconds; $100 for 60 seconds. **URL:** http://www.tbn.org/.

HAMMOND

Lake Co. Lake Co. (NW). 20 m SE of Chicago, Ill. Oil refineries. Aluminum reprocessing; basic steel and fabrications. Manufactures soap products, oleomargarine, railway steel forgings, chemical products, locomotive superheaters, valves, castings, corn starch, candies, pulp products and plastics.

11916 ■ Dow Theory Forecasts
Horizon Publishing Company L.L.C.
7412 Calumet Ave.
Hammond, IN 46324-2622
Fax: (219)931-6487
Free: 800-233-5922
Publication E-mail: custserv@horizonpublishing.com
Financial magazine. **Freq:** Weekly. **Print Method:** Offset. **Key Personnel:** Richard Moroney, CFA, Editor, Vice President; Bob Sweet, CFA, Managing Editor; Charles Carlson, CFA, Editor. **ISSN:** 0300--7324 (print). **URL:** http://www.dowtheory.com/index.asp. **Remarks:** Advertising not accepted. **Circ:** Paid 16000.

11917 ■ Global Media Journal
Global Media Journal
Purdue University Calumet
Dept. of Communication & Creative Arts
2200 169th St.
Hammond, IN 46323-2094
Phone: (219)989-2880
Fax: (219)989-2008
Electronic journal that seeks to address the interests of media and journalism scholars, researchers, teachers, students, and institutions engaged in international activities, particularly communication. **Freq:** Semiannual. **Key Personnel:** Yahya R. Kamalipour, PhD, Editor-in-Chief. **ISSN:** 1550--7521 (print). **Subscription Rates:** Free. **URL:** http://www.globalmediajournal.com. **Circ:** (Not Reported).

11918 ■ Globalisation for the Common Good
Global Media Journal
Purdue University Calumet
Dept. of Communication & Creative Arts
2200 169th St.
Hammond, IN 46323-2094
Phone: (219)989-2880
Fax: (219)989-2008
Journal offering a critical analysis of global capitalism and globalization. **Freq:** Semiannual. **Print Method:** Offset. **Cols./Page:** 6. **Col. Width:** 25 nonpareils. **Col. Depth:** 301 agate lines. **Key Personnel:** Kamran Mofid, PhD, Director, Founder; Yahya R. Kamalipur, PhD, Editor. **ISSN:** 1931--8138 (print). **Subscription Rates:** Free. **URL:** http://lass.purduecal.edu/cca/jgcg/jgcj-about-us.htm. **Circ:** (Not Reported).

11919 ■ WJOB-AM - 1230
7150 Indianapolis Blvd.
Hammond, IN 46324
Phone: (219)844-1230
Fax: (219)989-8500
Format: Talk. **Networks:** Independent. **Founded:** 1924. **Operating Hours:** Continuous; 100% local. **Key Personnel:** Jim Dedelow, Officer, jed@wjob1230.com; Debbie Wargo, Gen. Mgr., debbie@wjob1230.com; Alexis Vasquez Dedelow, Owner, alexis@heyregion.com. **Wattage:** 1,000. **Ad Rates:** $40-61 for 60 seconds. **URL:** http://www.wjob1230.com/contest.html.

11920 ■ WPWX-FM - 92.3
6336 Calumet Ave.
Hammond, IN 46324
Phone: (219)933-4455
Format: Urban Contemporary. **Ad Rates:** Noncommercial. **URL:** http://www.power92chicago.com.

11921 ■ WYCA-FM - 102.3
6336 Calumet Ave.
Hammond, IN 46324
Phone: (773)734-4455
Email: events@crawfordbroadcasting.com
Format: Contemporary Christian; Gospel. **Owner:** Crawford Broadcasting Co., 2821 S Parker Rd., Ste. 1205, Denver, CO 80014, Ph: (303)433-5500, Fax: (303)433-1555. **Founded:** 1959. **Operating Hours:** Continuous. **ADI:** Chicago (LaSalle), IL. **Key Personnel:** Darryll King, Contact. **Wattage:** 1,000. **Ad Rates:** Advertising accepted; rates available upon request. **URL:** http://www.crawfordbroadcasting.com.

HARTFORD CITY

Blackford Co. Blackford Co. (NE). 18 m N of Muncie. Manufactures paper, plastic - injection molded products, glass, hardware, garage doors. Food packing plants. Agriculture. Corn, wheat, oats.

11922 ■ Hartford City News Times
Community Media Group Inc.
123 S Jefferson St.
Hartford City, IN 47348
Phone: (765)348-0110
Fax: (765)348-0112
General newspaper. **Freq:** Mon.-Sat. (eve.). **Print Method:** Offset. **Cols./Page:** 6. **Col. Width:** 12 picas. **Col. Depth:** 21.5 inches. **Key Personnel:** Danny K Careins, Managing Editor; Tom High, Managing Editor; Cynthia Eschbach Payne, Publisher. **ISSN:** 2362--6000 (print). **Subscription Rates:** $135 Individuals /year; in county; $140 Individuals /year; out of county. **URL:** http://www.hartfordcitynewstimes.com. **Mailing address:** PO Box 690, Hartford City, IN 47348. **Ad Rates:** GLR $5.06; BW $652.74; 4C $752.74; SAU $5.06. **Remarks:** Accepts advertising. **Circ:** ‡2800.

HOPE

Bartholomew Co. Bartholomew Co. (SE). 40 m SE of Indianapolis. Agricultural community. Corn, beans.

11923 ■ Hope Star-Journal
The Hope Star-Journal
645 Harrison St.
Hope, IN 47246
Phone: (812)546-4940
Fax: (812)546-4944
Publication E-mail: hopestar@hsonline.net
Newspaper with a Democratic orientation. **Freq:** Weekly (Thurs.). **Print Method:** Offset. Broad sheet. **Cols./Page:** 6. **Col. Width:** 2 inches. **Col. Depth:** 21 1/2 inches. **Key Personnel:** Larry Simpson, Publisher; Stephanie Shoaf, Manager, Production; Jo Ellen Seright, Office Manager. **USPS:** 519-480. **URL:** http://www.hopestarjournal.com. **Mailing address:** PO Box 65, Hope, IN 47246. **Ad Rates:** 4C $819, standard rate; PCI $6.50, standard rate. **Remarks:** Advertising accepted; rates available upon request. **Circ:** Paid 1312, Free 102.

HOWE

11924 ■ WQKO-FM
3000 W MacArthur Blvd.
Santa Ana, CA 92707
Phone: (714)918-6207
Owner: Calvary Radio Network Inc., 150 West Lincolnway Ste. 2001, Valparaiso, IN 46383, Ph: (219)548-5800, Fax: (219)548-5808. **Founded:** May 14, 1993. **Ad Rates:** Noncommercial.

HUNTINGBURG

11925 ■ WBDC-FM - 100.9
501 Old State Rd.
Huntingburg, IN 47542
Phone: (812)683-4144
Format: Country. **Networks:** Westwood One Radio; CNN Radio; Brownfield. **Owner:** Dubois County Broadcasting Inc., PO Box 1009, Jasper, IN 47547, Ph: (812)634-9232, Fax: (812)482-3696. **Founded:** Dec. 23, 1975. **Operating Hours:** Continuous. **ADI:** Evansville, IN (Madisonville, KY). **Wattage:** 11,000. **Ad Rates:** $13-20 for 30 seconds; $16-23 for 60 seconds. Combined advertising rates available with WAXL-FM & WRZR-FM. **URL:** http://www.dcbroadcasting.com.

HUNTINGTON

Huntington Co. Huntington Co. (NE). 25 m SW of Fort Wayne. Huntington College (U. Brethren).

11926 ■ The Catholic Answer
Our Sunday Visitor
200 Noll Plz.
Huntington, IN 46750
Phone: (260)356-8400
Fax: (260)356-8472
Free: 800-348-2440
Publication E-mail: tcanswer@osv.com
Magazine exploring and explaining Catholic beliefs, traditions, and history. **Freq:** Bimonthly. **Print Method:** Offset. **Trim Size:** 7 x 10. **Cols./Page:** 2. **Col. Width:** 2 1/4 inches. **Col. Depth:** 7 1/4 inches. **Key Personnel:** Therese Calouette, Manager, Advertising; Mathew Bunson, Editor; Greg Erlandson, Publisher. **USPS:** 007-379. **Subscription Rates:** $26.95 Individuals; $46 Two years; $63 Individuals 3 years; $32 Other countries; $55 Two years Canada and International; $76 Other countries 3 years. **URL:** http://www.osv.com/Magazines/TheCatholicAnswer.aspx. **Ad Rates:** BW $2,010; 4C $2,513; PCI $75. **Remarks:** Accepts advertising. **Circ:** Paid 30000.

11927 ■ Catholic Parent Know-How
Our Sunday Visitor
200 Noll Plz.
Huntington, IN 46750
Phone: (260)356-8400
Fax: (260)356-8472
Free: 800-348-2440
Publisher's E-mail: envservice@osv.com
Magazine featuring tips for Catholic parents raising children. **Freq:** Bimonthly. **Key Personnel:** Joseph White, Author; Ana Arista White, Author. **ISSN:** 1875--

Circulation: ★ = AAM; △ or • = BPA; ♦ = CAC; ❑ = VAC; ⊕ = PO Statement; ‡ = Publisher's Report; Boldface figures = sworn; Light figures = estimated.

1956 (print). **Subscription Rates:** $1.95 Individuals. **URL:** http://www.osv.com/Shop/ParishResources/CatholicParentKnowHow.aspx. **Formerly**: Catholic Parent. **Circ:** (Not Reported).

11928 ■ Herald-Press
Huntington Newspapers Inc.
7 N Jefferson St.
Huntington, IN 46750-2839
Phone: (260)356-6700
Publication E-mail: hpnews@h-ponline.com
Community newspaper. **Founded:** 1848. **Freq:** Daily (eve.). **Print Method:** Offset. **Cols./Page:** 6. **Col. Width:** 26 nonpareils. **Col. Depth:** 294 agate lines. **Key Personnel:** Andy Eads, Publisher; Rebecca Sandlin, Editor; Brenda Ross, Manager, Advertising. **USPS:** 254-560. **Subscription Rates:** $88 Individuals 365 days; $8 Individuals 30 days. **URL:** http://www.h-ponline.com; http://www.chronicle-tribune.com/site/services. **Remarks:** Accepts advertising. **Circ:** Mon.-Fri. ‡6500.

11929 ■ My Daily Visitor
Our Sunday Visitor
200 Noll Plz.
Huntington, IN 46750
Phone: (260)356-8400
Fax: (260)356-8472
Free: 800-348-2440
Publication E-mail: mdvisitor@osv.com
Magazine containing meditations and daily readings from scripture. **Freq:** Bimonthly. **Print Method:** Letterpress and offset. **Trim Size:** 4 x 6. **Cols./Page:** 1. **Col. Width:** 34 nonpareils. **Col. Depth:** 64 agate lines. **Key Personnel:** Monica Dodds, Editor; Bill Dodds, Editor; Greg Erlandson, Publisher. **USPS:** 369-360. **Subscription Rates:** $17.95 Individuals 1 year; $28 Individuals 2 years; $38 Individuals 3 years. **URL:** http://www.osv.com/Shop/NewspapersMagazines/MyDailyVisitor.aspx. **Ad Rates:** BW $330. **Remarks:** Accepts advertising. **Circ:** Paid 25000.

11930 ■ Our Sunday Visitor
Our Sunday Visitor
200 Noll Plz.
Huntington, IN 46750
Phone: (260)356-8400
Fax: (260)356-8472
Free: 800-348-2440
Publication E-mail: oursunvis@osv.com
Roman Catholic weekly newspaper. **Freq:** Weekly (Sun.). **Print Method:** Offset. **Trim Size:** 10 1/4 x 13 1/4. **Cols./Page:** 5. **Col. Width:** 24 nonpareils. **Col. Depth:** 185 agate lines. **Key Personnel:** Mgr. Owen F. Campion, Associate Publisher, Editor; Greg Erlandson, President, Publisher. **ISSN:** 0030--6967 (print). **Subscription Rates:** $3.99 Individuals /month (all access plus); $2.99 Individuals /month (casual access). **URL:** http://www.osv.com. **Ad Rates:** BW $3,900; 4C $4,875; PCI $90. **Remarks:** Accepts advertising. **Circ:** Paid 48000.

11931 ■ The Priest
Our Sunday Visitor
200 Noll Plz.
Huntington, IN 46750
Phone: (260)356-8400
Fax: (260)356-8472
Free: 800-348-2440
Publication E-mail: tpriest@osv.com
Magazine for Catholic clergy, seminarians, and permanent deacons. **Freq:** Monthly. **Print Method:** Offset. **Trim Size:** 8 1/4 x 11. **Cols./Page:** 3. **Col. Width:** 13.5 picas. **Col. Depth:** 139 agate lines. **Key Personnel:** Murray W. Hubley, Associate Editor; Mgr. Owen F. Campion, Editor; Greg Erlandson, Publisher. **ISSN:** 0032--8200 (print). **Subscription Rates:** $45.95 U.S. 12 issues; $79 U.S. 24 issues; $111 U.S. 36 issues; $56 Individuals 12 issues (Canada and International); $100 Individuals 24 issues (Canada and International); $142 Individuals 36 issues (Canada and International). **URL:** http://www.osv.com/Shop/NewspapersMagazines/ThePriest.aspx. **Ad Rates:** BW $940; 4C $1,175; PCI $43. **Remarks:** Accepts advertising. **Circ:** Paid 5000.

11932 ■ WQHC-FM - 105.5
2303 College Ave.
Huntington, IN 46750
Phone: (260)356-6000
Format: Contemporary Christian. **Owner:** Huntington College Radio. **Operating Hours**: Continuous. **Key Personnel:** Dr. Lance Clark, Gen. Mgr. **Ad Rates:** Noncommercial.

11933 ■ WVSH-FM - 91.9
1360 Warren Rd.
Huntington, IN 46750
Phone: (219)356-7812
Owner: Huntington County Community School Corporation, at above address, Huntington, IN. **Wattage**: 920.

INDIANAPOLIS

Marion Co. (C). The State Capital. On White River in center of State. Butler University, Indiana University, Purdue University at Indianapolis, University of Indianapolis. Colleges, private schools and many state institutions. Children's Museum (largest in the world), Indianapolis Museum of Art. Site of the "500 Mile Race". Home of the U.S. Clay Courts Sports Center (tennis stadium). Indianapolis Symphony Orchestra. Trucking and insurance center. Major producers of food and automotive products. Electrical equipment, heavy machinery, pharmaceuticals manufactured.

11934 ■ American Legion Auxiliary's National News
American Legion Auxiliary
8945 N Meridian St., Ste. 200
Indianapolis, IN 46260
Phone: (317)569-4500
Fax: (317)569-4502
Publisher's E-mail: alahq@alaforveterans.org
Magazine for Auxiliary members. **Freq:** Bimonthly. **Print Method:** Web offset. **Trim Size:** 7 3/4 x 10 1/2. **Cols./Page:** 3. **Col. Width:** 13.5 picas. **Col. Depth:** 46 picas. **Key Personnel:** Tom Bowman, Manager, Advertising, phone: (317)849-6110, fax: (317)576-5859. **Subscription Rates:** $7 Individuals. **URL:** http://www.alaforveterans.org/Media/News-Releases. **Ad Rates:** BW $15173; 4C $20834; PCI $373. **Remarks:** Accepts advertising. **Circ:** Paid **★700000.**

11935 ■ American Legion Magazine
American Legion
700 N Pennsylvania St.
Indianapolis, IN 46206
Phone: (317)630-1200
Fax: (317)630-1223
Publication E-mail: magazine@legion.org
General interest magazine for veterans. **Freq:** Monthly. **Print Method:** Offset. **Trim Size:** 8 1/8 x 10 7/8. **Cols./Page:** 3. **Col. Width:** 25 nonpareils. **Col. Depth:** 136 agate lines. **Subscription Rates:** $15 Individuals; $21 Other countries; Included in membership. **URL:** http://www.legion.org/magazine. **Mailing address:** PO Box 1055, Indianapolis, IN 46206. **Ad Rates:** BW $36,980; 4C $50,180; PCI $728. **Remarks:** Accepts advertising. **Circ:** Paid **★2531867**, 3100000.

11936 ■ American Trucker--Buckeye Edition: Serving Ohio
Primedia Business
PO Box 603
Indianapolis, IN 46206
Phone: (317)297-5500
Fax: (317)299-1356
Free: 800-827-7468
Publisher's E-mail: atmarketing@primediabusiness.com
Truck trader magazine. **Freq:** Monthly. **Print Method:** Offset. **Trim Size:** 7 1/2 x 10 1/8. **Cols./Page:** 3. **Col. Width:** 2 5/16 inches. **Col. Depth:** 9 3/4 inches. **ISSN:** 1090--9656 (print). **Subscription Rates:** $48 Individuals. **URL:** http://www.trucker.com. **Remarks:** Advertising accepted; rates available upon request. **Circ:** Combined 44008.

11937 ■ American Trucker--Illinois Edition: Serving Eastern Missouri, Illinois
Primedia Business
PO Box 603
Indianapolis, IN 46206
Phone: (317)297-5500
Fax: (317)299-1356
Free: 800-827-7468
Publisher's E-mail: atmarketing@primediabusiness.com
Truck Trader Magazine. **Freq:** Monthly. **Print Method:** Offset. **Trim Size:** 7 1/2 x 10 1/8. **Cols./Page:** 3. **Col. Width:** 2 5/16 inches. **Col. Depth:** 9 3/4 inches. **ISSN:** 1090--9702 (print). **Subscription Rates:** $48 Individuals; Free to qualified subscribers. **URL:** http://www.trucker.com. **Remarks:** Accepts advertising. **Circ:** Combined 48387.

11938 ■ American Trucker--Indiana Edition: Serving Indiana
Primedia Business
PO Box 603
Indianapolis, IN 46206
Phone: (317)297-5500
Fax: (317)299-1356
Free: 800-827-7468
Publisher's E-mail: atmarketing@primediabusiness.com
Truck trader magazine. **Freq:** Monthly. **Print Method:** Offset. **Trim Size:** 7 1/2 x 10 1/8. **Cols./Page:** 3. **Col. Width:** 2 5/16 nonpareils. **Col. Depth:** 9 3/4 agate lines. **ISSN:** 1090--9710 (print). **Subscription Rates:** $48 Individuals; Free to qualified subscribers. **URL:** http://trucker.com/home. **Remarks:** Accepts advertising. **Circ:** Combined 38045.

11939 ■ American Trucker--South Central Edition: Serving Arkansas, Louisiana, Oklahoma, Texas
Primedia Business
PO Box 603
Indianapolis, IN 46206
Phone: (317)297-5500
Fax: (317)299-1356
Free: 800-827-7468
Publisher's E-mail: atmarketing@primediabusiness.com
Truck Trade magazine. **Freq:** Monthly. **Print Method:** Offset. **Trim Size:** 7 1/2 x 10 1/8. **Cols./Page:** 3. **Col. Width:** 2 5/16 inches. **Col. Depth:** 9 3/4 inches. **ISSN:** 1090--980X (print). **Subscription Rates:** Free to qualified subscribers. **URL:** http://www.trucker.com. **Remarks:** Accepts advertising. **Circ:** Combined 79058.

11940 ■ ARNOVA Nonprofit and Voluntary Sector Quarterly
Association for Research on Nonprofit Organizations and Voluntary Action
550 W North St., Ste. 301
Indianapolis, IN 46202
Phone: (317)684-2120
Fax: (317)684-2128
Freq: 6/year Bimonthly February, April, June, August, October, and December. **ISSN:** 0899--7640 (print). **Subscription Rates:** $538 Institutions Print and E-access; $592 Institutions Current Volume Print and All Online Content; $484 Institutions E-access only; $538 Institutions All Online Content; $1111 Institutions E-access content through 1998; $527 Institutions Print Only; $97 Individuals Print Only; $97 Institutions Single Print Issue; $21 Individuals Single Print Issue. **URL:** http://nvs.sagepub.com. **Remarks:** Accepts advertising. **Circ:** (Not Reported).

11941 ■ Branches Magazine
Apple Press Inc.
PO Box 30920
Indianapolis, IN 46230
Phone: (317)255-5594
Publication E-mail: editor@branches.com
Consumer magazine covering spirituality, health care and the environment, focusing on Indiana. **Freq:** Bimonthly. **Key Personnel:** Thomas P. Healy, Manager, Advertising, Publisher; Elsa F. Kramer, Editor. **Subscription Rates:** Free hundreds of locations throughout Indiana. **URL:** http://www.branches.com. **Ad Rates:** BW $950; 4C $1,000. **Remarks:** Accepts advertising. **Circ:** Combined 25000.

11942 ■ California Builder & Engineer
California Builder and Engineer Inc.
1200 Madison Ave., LL20
Indianapolis, IN 46225
Phone: (317)423-7080
Magazine on California, Hawaii, Western Nevada, and Western Arizona building and engineering. **Freq:** Biweekly. **Print Method:** Offset. **Trim Size:** 8 1/8 x 10 7/8. **Cols./Page:** 3. **Col. Width:** 26 nonpareils. **Col. Depth:** 140 agate lines. **USPS:** 975-580. **URL:** http://californiabuilder.acppubs.com. **Ad Rates:** BW $1590; 4C $2085; PCI $35. **Remarks:** Advertising accepted; rates available upon request. **Circ:** (Not Reported).

11943 ■ Christian Outlook
Pentecostal Assemblies of the World
3939 N Meadows Dr.
Indianapolis, IN 46205-3113
Phone: (317)547-9541

Fax: (317)543-0513
Freq: Bimonthly. **Subscription Rates:** $5 Individuals. **URL:** http://estore.pawinc.org/SearchResults.asp?Cat=1842. **Remarks:** Accepts advertising. **Circ:** (Not Reported).

11944 ■ Clinical Nurse Specialist: The Journal for Advanced Nursing Practice
Lippincott Williams and Wilkins
1111 Middle Dr., No. 414
Indianapolis, IN 46202-5107
Phone: (317)274-2421
Fax: (317)278-1856
Publication E-mail: jasfulto@iupui.edu
Nursing journal. **Freq:** Bimonthly. **Print Method:** Offset. **Trim Size:** 7 3/4 x 10 3/4. **Key Personnel:** Janet S. Fulton, PhD, Editor; Kathleen Phelan, Publisher. **ISSN:** 0887--6274 (print); **EISSN:** 1538--9782 (electronic). **Subscription Rates:** $136 U.S. print; $144 Canada and Mexico; $279 Individuals UK/Australia; $274 Other countries; $553 Institutions U.S.; $577 Institutions, Canada and Mexico; $798 Institutions, other countries. **URL:** http://journals.lww.com/cns-journal/pages/default.aspx; http://www.lww.com/product/?0887-6274. **Ad Rates:** BW $1,020; 4C $1,585. **Remarks:** Accepts advertising. **Circ:** 3170.

11945 ■ Court & Commercial Record
Court & Commercial Record
41 E Washington St.
Indianapolis, IN 46204-3560
Phone: (317)636-0200
Fax: (317)263-5259
Free: 800-425-2201
Newspaper of legal record. **Freq:** 3/week Monday, Wednesday and Friday. **Trim Size:** 10 x 16. **Cols./Page:** 4. **Col. Width:** 2 inches. **Key Personnel:** Rebecca Collier, Editor; Karen Aruta, Administrative Assistant; Bill Wright, Manager, Circulation; Jeff Basch, Chief Financial Officer; Lisa Bradley, Director, Advertising; Jane Wilcoxon, Office Manager; Judy Smith, Coordinator; Sherry Robinson, Manager, Finance. **Subscription Rates:** $34 Individuals 156 issues + 6 Bonus - Print and CCR Digital Editions. **URL:** http://www.courtcommercialrecord.com. **Formerly**: The Indianapolis Commercial. **Remarks:** Accepts advertising. **Circ:** Controlled ⊕**1127**.

11946 ■ The Criterion
Archdiocese of Indianapolis
1400 N Meridian St.
Indianapolis, IN 46202
Free: 800-382-9836
Publisher's E-mail: info@archindy.org
Official weekly church newspaper of the Roman Catholic Archdiocese of Indianapolis. **Founded:** 1960. **Freq:** Weekly. **Print Method:** Offset. **Trim Size:** 17 1/2 x 11 1/4. **Cols./Page:** 6. **Col. Width:** 1 5/8 INS. **Col. Depth:** 224 agate lines. **Key Personnel:** Greg A. Otolski, Associate Publisher, phone: (317)236-1579; Rev. Daniel M. Buechlein, Publisher; Michael Krokos, Editor, phone: (317)236-1598. **Subscription Rates:** $22 Individuals. **URL:** http://www.archindy.org/criterion/local/forms2/index.html. **Ad Rates:** GLR $1.07; BW $1,447; 4C $1,747; PCI $28.70. **Remarks:** 1.07. **Circ:** Paid 72000.

11947 ■ Current Alzheimer Research
Bentham Science Publishers Ltd.
Dept. of Psychiatry
Indiana University School of Medicine
Indianapolis, IN 46202
Publisher's E-mail: subscriptions@benthamscience.org
Journal publishing peer-reviewed frontier review and research articles on all areas of Alzheimer's disease. **Freq:** 10/yr. **Key Personnel:** Prof. Debomoy K. Lahiri, Editor-in-Chief. **ISSN:** 1567--2050 (print); **EISSN:** 1875--5828 (electronic). **Subscription Rates:** $380 Individuals print; $1500 print and online - academics; $1360 print or online - academics; $2950 print and online - corporate; $2460 print or online - corporate. **URL:** http://benthamscience.com/journals/current-alzheimer-research. **Ad Rates:** BW $700; 4C $900. **Remarks:** Accepts advertising. **Circ:** ‡1000.

11948 ■ Delta Upsilon Quarterly
Delta Upsilon
8705 Founders Rd.
Indianapolis, IN 46268
Phone: (317)875-8900
Fax: (317)876-1629
Publisher's E-mail: history@deltau.org
Freq: Quarterly. **URL:** http://www.deltau.org/nosecrets/quarterly/historyofthequarterly. **Remarks:** Accepts advertising. **Circ:** 65000.

11949 ■ Diary
Alpha Kappa Psi
7801 E 88th St.
Indianapolis, IN 46256-1233
Phone: (317)872-1553
Fax: (317)872-1567
Publisher's E-mail: mail@akpsi.org
Freq: 3/year. **Subscription Rates:** Included in membership. **URL:** http://www.akpsi.org/page.aspx?pid=394. **Remarks:** Advertising not accepted. **Circ:** 25000.

11950 ■ Educational Forum
Kappa Delta Pi
3707 Woodview Trace
Indianapolis, IN 46268
Phone: (317)871-4900
Fax: (317)704-2323
Free: 800-284-3167
Publisher's E-mail: pubs@kdp.org
Freq: Quarterly. **Subscription Rates:** $25 Members Annually; $45 Members 2 years; $98 Nonmembers Annually; $169 Institutions Online only; $193 Institutions Print and online. **URL:** http://www.kdp.org/publications/theeducationalforum/. **Remarks:** Advertising not accepted. **Circ:** (Not Reported).

11951 ■ Electric Consumer
Indiana Statewide Association Rural Electric Cooperative
PO Box 24517
Indianapolis, IN 46224
Publication E-mail: ec@electricconsumer.org
Rural electric cooperative newspaper. **Freq:** Monthly. **Print Method:** Offset. **Trim Size:** 10 x 12 1/4. **Cols./Page:** 3. **Col. Width:** 16.5 picas. **Col. Depth:** 149 agate lines. **Key Personnel:** Richard G. Biever, Senior Editor; Emily Schilling, Editor. **ISSN:** 0745--4651 (print). **Subscription Rates:** $12 Individuals. **URL:** http://www.electricconsumer.org. **Remarks:** Advertising not accepted. **Circ:** (Not Reported).

11952 ■ Encounter: Creative Theological Scholarship
Christian Theological Seminary
1000 W 42nd St.
Indianapolis, IN 46208
Phone: (317)924-1331
Free: 800-585-0117
Publisher's E-mail: admissions@cts.edu
Religious journal. **Freq:** Quarterly. **Print Method:** Offset. **Trim Size:** 6 3/4 x 10. **Cols./Page:** 1. **Col. Width:** 54 nonpareils. **Col. Depth:** 112 agate lines. **Key Personnel:** Ronald J. Allen, Editor; Rebecca Furnish, Managing Editor. **ISSN:** 0013--7081 (print). **Subscription Rates:** $18 Individuals /year. **URL:** http://www.cts.edu/about-cts/publications.aspx. **Remarks:** Advertising not accepted. **Circ:** Paid ‡218, Non-paid ‡219.

11953 ■ FFA Advisors Making a Difference: The Resource for Agriculture Educators
National FFA Organization
6060 FFA Dr.
Indianapolis, IN 46278-1370
Phone: (317)802-6060
Free: 888-332-2668
Publisher's E-mail: webmaster@ffa.org
Professional journal for agricultural educators. **Founded:** 1992. **Freq:** 8/yr. **Trim Size:** 8 1/4 x 10 3/4. **Cols./Page:** 10. **Key Personnel:** Jeri Mattics Omernik, Managing Editor; Larry Gossen, Team Leader, phone: (317)802-4352. **URL:** http://www.ffa.org/FFAResources/Publications/MakingADifference/Pages/default.aspx. **Formerly**: Between Issues. **Mailing address:** PO Box 68960, Indianapolis, IN 46268-0960. **Remarks:** Advertising not accepted. **Circ:** Combined 13200.

11954 ■ FFA New Horizons Magazine
National FFA Organization
6060 FFA Dr.
Indianapolis, IN 46278-1370
Phone: (317)802-6060
Free: 888-332-2668
Publisher's E-mail: webmaster@ffa.org
Freq: Bimonthly. **ISSN:** 0027--9315 (print). **Subscription Rates:** Included in membership; $5 Nonmembers /year. **Alt. Formats:** Download. **URL:** http://www.ffanewhorizons.org/magazine. **Mailing address:** PO Box 68960, Indianapolis, IN 46268-0960. **Remarks:** Accepts advertising. **Circ:** (Not Reported).

11955 ■ FFA New Horizons: The Magazine of the National FFA Organization
National FFA Organization
6060 FFA Dr.
Indianapolis, IN 46278-1370
Phone: (317)802-6060
Free: 888-332-2668
Publisher's E-mail: webmaster@ffa.org
Youth magazine. **Freq:** Quarterly. **Print Method:** Web Offset. **Trim Size:** 8 1/8 x 10 1/2. **Cols./Page:** 3. **Col. Width:** 27 nonpareils. **Col. Depth:** 143 agate lines. **Key Personnel:** Julie Woodard, Manager. **ISSN:** 0027--9315 (print). **Subscription Rates:** Included in membership. **URL:** http://www.ffanewhorizons.org. **Formerly**: The National Future Farmer. **Mailing address:** PO Box 68960, Indianapolis, IN 46268-0960. **Remarks:** Accepts advertising. **Circ:** (Not Reported).

11956 ■ Hardware Retailing: Serving Hardware, Home Center, Building Material Retailers
North American Retail Hardware Association
136 N Delaware St.
Indianapolis, IN 46204
Phone: (317)275-9400
Fax: (317)275-9403
Free: 800-772-4424
Publisher's E-mail: hwegeng@nrha.org
Trade magazine for hardware retailers selling do-it-yourself products. **Freq:** Monthly. **Print Method:** Offset. **Trim Size:** 8 x 10 3/4. **Cols./Page:** 3. **Col. Width:** 13 picas. **Col. Depth:** 10 inches. **ISSN:** 0889--2989 (print). **Subscription Rates:** $8 Individuals; $2 Single issue. **URL:** http://www.hardwareretailing.com. **Formerly**: Hardware Retailing; Do-It-Yourself Retailing. **Ad Rates:** BW $5375; 4C $7355. **Remarks:** Accepts advertising. **Circ:** 60000.

11957 ■ Heart Rhythm
Mosby Inc.
Div. of Cardiology & the Krannert Inst. of Cardiology
Indiana University School of Medicine
1800 N Capitol Ave.
Indianapolis, IN 46202
Journal covering the study and management of cardiac arrhythmia. **Freq:** Monthly. **Key Personnel:** Douglas P. Zipes, MD, Board Member; Joan Zipes, Executive Editor; Peng-Sheng Chen, Editor-in-Chief. **ISSN:** 1547--5271 (print). **Subscription Rates:** $283 Individuals; $696 Institutions; Included in membership; $283 Individuals Outside United States; $696 Institutions, other countries. **URL:** http://www.journals.elsevier.com/heart-rhythm; http://www.hrsonline.org/Science-Research/HeartRhythm-Journal#axzz3Z9pPRjBN. **Formerly**: PACE: The Journal of Pacing and Clinical Electrophysiology. **Remarks:** Accepts advertising. **Circ:** 6,100.

11958 ■ Hexagon
Alpha Chi Sigma Fraternity, Inc.
6296 Rucker Rd., Ste. B
Indianapolis, IN 46220
Phone: (317)357-5944
Fax: (317)351-9702
Free: 800-252-4369
Publisher's E-mail: national@alphachisigma.org
Freq: Quarterly. **Key Personnel:** Brian P. Coppola. **Subscription Rates:** Accessible only to members. **URL:** http://www.alphachisigma.org/about-us/hexagon-and-news. **Remarks:** Advertising not accepted. **Circ:** (Not Reported).

11959 ■ Hoosier Banker: The magazine of the Indiana Bankers Association
Indiana Bankers Association
6925 Parkdale Pl.
Indianapolis, IN 46254-4673
Phone: (317)387-9380
Fax: (317)387-9374
Magazine for bankers providing in-depth analysis of Indiana banking developments. **Freq:** Monthly. **Print Method:** Offset. **Trim Size:** 8 3/8 x 10 7/8. **Cols./Page:** 3. **Col. Width:** 2 1/4 inches. **Col. Depth:** 11 1/8 inches. **Key Personnel:** Laura Wilson, Contact, phone: (317)387-9380; S. Joe DeHaven, Chief Executive Of-

Circulation: ★ = AAM; △ or • = BPA; ♦ = CAC; ❑ = VAC; ⊕ = PO Statement; ‡ = Publisher's Report; Boldface figures = sworn; Light figures = estimated.

ficer, President. **ISSN:** 0018--473X (print). **Subscription Rates:** $67.75 Nonmembers. **Alt. Formats:** PDF. **URL:** http://indianabankers.org/hoosier-banker. **Ad Rates:** BW $1,000. **Remarks:** Accepts advertising. **Circ:** ‡6500.

11960 ■ The Hoosier Farmer
Indiana Farm Bureau
225 S East St.
Indianapolis, IN 46206
Fax: (317)692-7854
Free: 800-327-6287
Publisher's E-mail: askus@infb.org
Agricultural magazine. **Freq:** Quarterly. **Print Method:** Offset. **Trim Size:** 8 1/4 x 10 7/8. **Cols./Page:** 3. **Key Personnel:** Kathleen Dutro, Managing Editor, phone: (317)692-7824. **ISSN:** 0018--4748 (print). **USPS:** 249-880. **URL:** http://www.infarmbureau.org/thf/thehoosierfarmer. **Mailing address:** PO Box 1290, Indianapolis, IN 46206-1290. **Ad Rates:** BW $3,720; 4C $4,605. **Remarks:** Accepts advertising. **Circ:** ‡270000.

11961 ■ The Hoosier Legionnaire
American Legion Department of Indiana
575 N Pennsylvania St., Rm. 325
Indianapolis, IN 46204
Phone: (317)630-1300
Newspaper (tabloid) for members of the American Legion in Indiana. **Freq:** Quarterly. **Key Personnel:** Hugh Dagley, Publisher. **ISSN:** 0018--4772 (print). **USPS:** 010-445. **Subscription Rates:** Free to members. **Alt. Formats:** PDF. **URL:** http://www.indianalegion.org/the-hoosier-legionnaire.html. **Remarks:** Advertising accepted; rates available upon request. **Circ:** ‡171200.

11962 ■ Human Communication Research
John Wiley and Sons Inc.
10475 Crosspoint Blvd.
Indianapolis, IN 46256
Phone: (317)572-3000
Fax: (317)572-4000
Interpersonal communication journal. **Founded:** 1974. **Freq:** Quarterly 4/yr. **Print Method:** Offset. **Trim Size:** 6 x 9. **Cols./Page:** 1 and 5. **Col. Width:** 50 nonpareils. **Col. Depth:** 100 agate lines and 1 3/4 inches. **Key Personnel:** John A. Courtright, Editor-in-Chief; Prof. Howard Giles, Board Member; James E. Katz, Editor; Tamara Afifi, Board Member; Walid Afifi, Associate Editor; James P. Dillard, Editor. **ISSN:** 0360-3989 (print). **Subscription Rates:** $115 Individuals print and online; $1736 Institutions print and online; $1446 Institutions online only; $84 Individuals print + online; €93 Individuals print + online; £62 Individuals print + online; $61 Individuals; $209 Institutions; $111 Individuals print and online; €119 Individuals print and online; £80 Individuals print and online. **URL:** http://cscc.scu.edu/trends/journals/hcr.html; http://as.wiley.com/WileyCDA/WileyTitle/productCd-HCRE.html; http://hcr.oupjournals.org/; http://onlinelibrary.wiley.com/journal/10.1111/(ISSN)1468-2958. **Ad Rates:** BW $479; BW $445. **Remarks:** Advertising accepted; rates available upon request. **Circ:** Paid ‡6,200.

11963 ■ Humanity and Society
Association for Humanist Sociology
Esch Hall, Rm. 230
University of Indianapolis
1400 E Hanna Ave.
Indianapolis, IN 46227
Phone: (317)788-3365
Freq: Quarterly February, May, August and November. **Key Personnel:** David G. Embrick, Editor-in-Chief. **ISSN:** 0160-5976 (print); **EISSN:** 2372-9708 (electronic). **Subscription Rates:** £231 Institutions E-access; £252 Institutions print only; £257 Institutions print + E-access; £69 Single issue print only. **URL:** http://www.humanist-sociology.org/journal; http://has.sagepub.com. **Remarks:** Advertising not accepted. **Circ:** (Not Reported).

11964 ■ Humpty Dumpty's Magazine
Children's Better Health Institute
1100 Waterway Blvd.
Indianapolis, IN 46202-2156
Phone: (317)634-1100
Publication E-mail: humptydumpty@uskidsmags.com
Health, exercise, nutrition, and safety magazine for children ages four to six. **Freq:** Bimonthly. **Print Method:** Web Offset. **Trim Size:** 7 5/8 x 10 1/8. **Cols./Page:** 1. **ISSN:** 0273-7590 (print). **Subscription Rates:** $14.98 Individuals; $27.98 Two years; $29.94 Other countries. **URL:** http://www.uskidsmags.com/magazines/humpty-dumpty. **Mailing address:** PO Box 567, Indianapolis, IN 46206-0567. **Ad Rates:** BW $5; 4C $5,520. **Remarks:** Accepts advertising. **Circ:** (Not Reported).

11965 ■ IN Magazine
National Association of Mutual Insurance Companies
3601 Vincennes Rd.
Indianapolis, IN 46268
Phone: (317)875-5250
Fax: (317)879-8408
Magazine covering the property/casualty and farm mutual insurance industries. **Freq:** Quarterly. **Subscription Rates:** $40 Individuals. **URL:** http://www.namic.org/in/default.asp. **Remarks:** Accepts advertising. **Circ:** 5,000.

11966 ■ Indiana Agri-News
Agri-News Publications
2575 E 55th Pl., Ste. A
Indianapolis, IN 46220
Phone: (317)726-5391
Fax: (317)726-5390
Free: 800-772-9354
Publisher's E-mail: aginfo@agrinews-pubs.com
Farm and rural community magazine. **Freq:** Weekly. **Print Method:** Offset. **Trim Size:** 14 5/8 x 22 3/4. **Cols./Page:** 9. **Col. Width:** 16 nonpareils. **Col. Depth:** 301 agate lines. **Key Personnel:** Lynn Barker, Publisher; James Henry, Executive Editor. **Subscription Rates:** $25 Individuals; $40 Two years; $50 Individuals 3 years. **URL:** http://www.agrinews-pubs.com; http://agrinewsonline.com. **Remarks:** Accepts advertising. **Circ:** Paid ‡8000, Controlled ‡21000.

11967 ■ Indiana Beef
Indiana Beef Cattle Association
8425 Keystone Crossing, Ste. 240
Indianapolis, IN 46240
Phone: (317)293-2333
Fax: (317)295-8421
Publication E-mail: jbiesecker@indianabeef.org
Freq: Monthly Bimonthly. **Print Method:** Offset. **Trim Size:** 8 1/2 x 11. **Cols./Page:** 3. **Col. Width:** 2 1/4 inches. **Col. Depth:** 9 15/16 inches. **Key Personnel:** Jennifer Biesecker, Editor. **Subscription Rates:** Included in membership. **URL:** http://www.indianabeef.org; http://www.indianabeef.org/assn/about-membership.html. **Ad Rates:** BW $535; 4C $695; 4C $855, full page. **Remarks:** Accepts advertising. **Circ:** 5200.

11968 ■ Indiana Beef
Indiana Beef Council
8425 Keystone Crossing Ste. 240
Indianapolis, IN 46240
Phone: (317)293-2333
Fax: (317)295-8421
Publication E-mail: jbiesecker@indianabeef.org
Freq: Monthly Bimonthly. **Print Method:** Offset. **Trim Size:** 8 1/2 x 11. **Cols./Page:** 3. **Col. Width:** 2 1/4 inches. **Col. Depth:** 9 15/16 inches. **Key Personnel:** Jennifer Biesecker, Editor. **Subscription Rates:** Included in membership. **URL:** http://www.indianabeef.org; http://www.indianabeef.org/assn/about-membership.html. **Ad Rates:** BW $535; 4C $695; 4C $855, full page. **Remarks:** Accepts advertising. **Circ:** 5200.

11969 ■ The Indiana Jewish Post and Opinion
The National Jewish Post and Opinion
1427 W 86th St., No. 228
Indianapolis, IN 46260
Publication E-mail: jpostopinion@gmail.com
National Jewish newspaper. **Freq:** Biweekly. **Print Method:** Web offset. **Trim Size:** 11 1/2 x 15. **Cols./Page:** 5. **Col. Width:** 11.5 picas. **Col. Depth:** 14 inches. **Key Personnel:** Jennie Cohen, Publisher, Editor. **USPS:** 275-580. **Subscription Rates:** $36 Individuals; $24 Students senior; $24 Individuals Senior. **URL:** http://www.jewishpostopinion.com. **Ad Rates:** BW $1,120; PCI $16.80. **Remarks:** Color advertising not accepted. **Circ:** (Not Reported).

11970 ■ Indiana Law Review
Indiana University, Indianapolis Robert H. McKinney School of Law
530 W New York St.
Indianapolis, IN 46202-3225
Phone: (317)274-8523
Fax: (317)274-3955
Publication E-mail: cpaynter@iupui.edu
Student-run law review. **Freq:** Quarterly. **Key Personnel:** Chris Paynter, Contact. **ISSN:** 0090--4198 (print). **Subscription Rates:** $30 Individuals; $35 Other countries; $10 Single issue; $20 Single issue survey issue; $15 Individuals single symposium issue. **URL:** http://indylaw.indiana.edu/ilr/. **Formerly:** Indianapolis School of Law. **Ad Rates:** BW $100. **Remarks:** Accepts advertising. **Circ:** Combined 850.

11971 ■ Indiana Pharmacist
Indiana Pharmacists Alliance
729 N Pennsylvania St.
Indianapolis, IN 46204-1128
Phone: (317)634-4968
Fax: (317)632-1219
Publisher's E-mail: inpharm@indianapharmacists.org
Magazine for pharmacists. **Freq:** Quarterly. **Print Method:** Offset. **Trim Size:** 8 1/2 x 11. **Cols./Page:** 2. **Col. Width:** 27 nonpareils. **Col. Depth:** 140 agate lines. **Key Personnel:** Lawrence J. Sage, Executive Vice President. **Subscription Rates:** $15 Individuals. **URL:** http://www.indianapharmacists.org/store_product.asp?prodid=37. **Ad Rates:** BW $450; 4C $950. **Remarks:** Accepts advertising. **Circ:** ‡1500.

11972 ■ The Indianapolis Recorder
George P. Stewart Printing Company Inc.
2901 N Tacoma Ave.
Indianapolis, IN 46218
Phone: (317)924-5143
Publication E-mail: newsroom@indyrecorder.com
Black community newspaper. **Freq:** Weekly. **Print Method:** Offset. **Cols./Page:** 6. **Col. Width:** 13 picas. **Col. Depth:** 298 agate lines. **Key Personnel:** William G. Mays, Publisher, Owner. **USPS:** 262-660. **Subscription Rates:** $15 Individuals; $25 Two years. **URL:** http://www.indianapolisrecorder.com. **Ad Rates:** PCI $14.01. **Remarks:** Accepts advertising. **Circ:** 13300.

11973 ■ The Indianapolis Star
Gannett Company Inc.
PO Box 145
Indianapolis, IN 46206-0145
Phone: (317)444-4000
Free: 800-669-7827
General newspaper. **Founded:** 1903. **Freq:** Mon.-Sun. **Print Method:** Letterpress. **Cols./Page:** 6. **Col. Width:** 2 1/16 inches. **Col. Depth:** 22 inches. **Key Personnel:** Karen Crotchfelt, President, Publisher; Steve Swails, Director, Distribution. **Subscription Rates:** $18.05 Individuals month; 7 days; $13.70 Individuals month; 4-day; $9.35 Individuals Sundays. **URL:** http://www.indystar.com. **Remarks:** Accepts advertising. **Circ:** Mon.-Fri. ★**193525**, Sun. ★**289017**, Sat. ★**171632**.

11974 ■ Indianapolis Visitor Guide
Visit Indy
200 S Capitol Ave., Ste. 300
Indianapolis, IN 46225-1063
Phone: (317)262-3000
Free: 800-323-INDY
Publisher's E-mail: info@visitindy.com
Hotel inroom Indianapolis visitors guide. **Freq:** Semiannual. **Print Method:** Web offset. **Trim Size:** 8 3/8 x 10 7/8. **Cols./Page:** 3. **Col. Width:** 2 1/4 inches. **Col. Depth:** 10 inches. **Key Personnel:** Mary K. Huggard, Vice President. **Subscription Rates:** Free. **URL:** http://www.visitindy.com/indianapolis-guides-maps. **Formerly:** This is Indianapolis. **Ad Rates:** BW $10,800; 4C $13,600. **Remarks:** Accepts advertising. **Circ:** Controlled 300000.

11975 ■ Indy's Child: Indiana's Number 1 Magazine for Parents
Indy's Child Inc.
921 E 86th St., Ste. 130
Indianapolis, IN 46240
Phone: (317)722-8500
Fax: (317)722-8510
Magazine covering parenting news. **Freq:** Monthly. **Print Method:** Web press. **Trim Size:** 11 x 13 1/2. **Cols./Page:** 4. **Col. Width:** 2 3/8 inches. **Col. Depth:** 12 1/2 inches. **Key Personnel:** Mary Wynne-Cox, Publisher, phone: (317)722-8500; Karen Ring, Coordinator, Advertising. **Subscription Rates:** $36 Individuals. **URL:** http://www.indyschild.com. **Remarks:** Advertising accepted; rates available upon request. **Circ:** (Not Reported).

11976 ■ Interscholastic Athletic Administration
National Interscholastic Athletic Administrators Association
9100 Keystone Xing, Ste. 650
Indianapolis, IN 46240
Phone: (317)587-1450
Fax: (317)587-1451
Magazine covering articles on a wide spectrum of topics which are beneficial to the school athletic or activities director. **Freq:** Quarterly. **Subscription Rates:** $15 Individuals; Included in membership. **URL:** http://www.niaaa.org/resources/publications-products. **Remarks:** Accepts advertising. **Circ:** 10000.

11977 ■ Interscholastic Athletic Administration
National Federation of State High School Associations
PO Box 690
Indianapolis, IN 46206-0690
Phone: (317)972-6900
Fax: (317)822-5700
Magazine covering articles on a wide spectrum of topics which are beneficial to the school athletic or activities director. **Freq:** Quarterly. **Subscription Rates:** $15 Individuals; Included in membership. **URL:** http://www.niaaa.org/resources/publications-products. **Remarks:** Accepts advertising. **Circ:** 10000.

11978 ■ Jack and Jill
Children's Better Health Institute
1100 Waterway Blvd.
Indianapolis, IN 46202-2156
Phone: (317)634-1100
Publication E-mail: jackandjill@uskidsmags.com
General magazine for children ages 7-10. **Freq:** Bimonthly. **Print Method:** Offset. **Trim Size:** 7 5/8 x 10 1/8. **ISSN:** 0021-3829 (print). **Subscription Rates:** $14.98 Individuals; $27.98 Two years. **URL:** http://www.uskidsmags.com/magazines/jack-and-jill. **Mailing address:** PO Box 567, Indianapolis, IN 46206-0567. **Ad Rates:** BW $4,788; 4C $6,300. **Remarks:** Accepts advertising. **Circ:** (Not Reported).

11979 ■ Journal of the American Society of Hypertension
Elsevier - Mosby Journal Div.
c/o Myron H. Weinberger, MD, Ed.-in-Ch.
Hypertension Research Ctr.
Indiana University School of Medicine
541 Clinical Dr., Rm. 423
Indianapolis, IN 46202
Phone: (317)274-8153
Fax: (317)278-0673
Publisher's E-mail: info@elsevier.com
Journal featuring articles on the topics of basic, applied, and translational research on blood pressure, hypertension, and related cardiovascular disorders and factors. **Freq:** Bimonthly. **Key Personnel:** Myron H. Weinberger, MD, Editor-in-Chief; Daniel Levy, Editor-in-Chief. **ISSN:** 1933-1711 (print). **Subscription Rates:** $183 Individuals; $142 Students. **URL:** http://www.ashjournal.com/home. **Circ:** (Not Reported).

11980 ■ Journal of Applied Sport Psychology
Association for Applied Sport Psychology
8365 Keystone Crossing, Ste. 107
Indianapolis, IN 46240
Phone: (317)205-9225
Fax: (317)205-9481
Publisher's E-mail: info@appliedsportpsych.org
Journal containing refereed articles, research, and reviews on applied aspects of sport and exercise psychology. **Freq:** Quarterly. **ISSN:** 1041- 3200 (print); **EISSN:** 1533- 1571 (electronic). **Subscription Rates:** $191 Individuals print; $511 Institutions print + online; $447 Institutions online. **URL:** http://www.appliedsportpsych.org/publications/journal-of-applied-sport-psychology; http://www.tandfonline.com/pricing/journal/uasp20#.VpY2Ve82u2w. **Remarks:** Advertising not accepted. **Circ:** (Not Reported).

11981 ■ The Journal of Gift Planning
Partnership for Philanthropic Planning
233 McCrea St., Ste. 300
Indianapolis, IN 46225
Phone: (317)269-6274
Fax: (317)269-6268
Publisher's E-mail: info@pppnet.org
Journal covering topics related to charitable gift and estate planning. **Freq:** Quarterly. **Key Personnel:** Barbara Yeager. **ISSN:** 1096--5297 (print). **Subscription Rates:** Included in membership; $22.50 /year for nonmembers. **URL:** http://pppnet.org/competence. **Remarks:** Accepts advertising. **Circ:** (Not Reported).

11982 ■ Journal of Labelled Compounds and Radiopharmaceuticals
John Wiley & Sons Inc.
c/o W.J. Wheeler, Ed.
12030 Emerald Buff
Indianapolis, IN 46236
Publisher's E-mail: info@wiley.com
Freq: 14/yr. **Trim Size:** 9 3/4 x 6 1/2. **Key Personnel:** B. Langstrom, Editor; W.J. Wheeler, Editor; T. Moenius, Editor. **ISSN:** 0362-4803 (print); **EISSN:** 1099- 1344 (electronic). **Subscription Rates:** $6839 U.S., Canada, and Mexico online only; £3490 Institutions online only; €4414 Institutions online only ; $3235 Members online only (USA, Canada and Mexico, UK, Europe). **URL:** http://onlinelibrary.wiley.com/journal/10.1002/(ISSN)1099-1344; http://www.intl-isotope-soc.org/wiley/. **Remarks:** Accepts advertising. **Circ:** Paid 4900.

11983 ■ Journal of Nursing Scholarship
Sigma Theta Tau International
550 W North St.
Indianapolis, IN 46202
Phone: (317)634-8171
Free: 888-634-7575
Peer-reviewed journal covering nursing. **Freq:** Quarterly. **Trim Size:** 8 1/2 x 11. **Key Personnel:** Susan Gennaro, Editor; Sabina De Geest, PhD, Associate Editor. **ISSN:** 1527--6546 (print); **EISSN:** 1547--5069 (electronic). **Subscription Rates:** $368 Institutions print and online; £267 Institutions print and online; €341 Institutions print and online; $522 Institutions, other countries print and online; $79 Individuals print and online; £60 Individuals print and online - UK, Europe (non euro zone) and rest of the world; €89 Individuals print and online; Included in membership; $82 Individuals print and online; $325 Institutions online only. **URL:** http://onlinelibrary.wiley.com/journal/10.1111/(ISSN)1547-5069; http://www.nursingsociety.org/learn-grow/publications/journal-of-nursing-scholarship. **Ad Rates:** BW $2,785. **Remarks:** Accepts advertising. **Circ:** 130000.

11984 ■ Journal of the OCA 1948-1958
The Osteopathic Cranial Academy
3535 E 96th St., Ste. 101
Indianapolis, IN 46240
Phone: (317)581-0411
Fax: (317)580-9299
Publisher's E-mail: info@cranialacademy.org
Trim Size: 8 1/2 x 11. **Key Personnel:** Mark Rosen, Editor. **Subscription Rates:** $50 Individuals. **URL:** http://cranialacademy.org/product/journal-of-the-oca-1948-1958. **Formerly:** Journal of OCA 1948, 49, 54, 57, & 58. **Remarks:** Advertising not accepted. **Circ:** (Not Reported).

11985 ■ Journal of Phi Rho Sigma
Phi Rho Sigma Medical Society
PO Box 90264
Indianapolis, IN 46290
Publication E-mail: journal_editor@phirhosigma.org
Journal covering medicine. **Freq:** Continuous Annual. **ISSN:** 0022--3581 (print). **Alt. Formats:** PDF. **URL:** http://www.phirhosigma.org/archived_journals.html. **Remarks:** Advertising not accepted. **Circ:** (Not Reported).

11986 ■ Journal of Prosthodontics--Clinical Journal
John Wiley and Sons Inc.
10475 Crosspoint Blvd.
Indianapolis, IN 46256
Phone: (317)572-3000
Fax: (317)572-4000
Publisher's E-mail: info@wiley.com
Journal promoting the advanced study and practice of prosthodontics, implant, esthetic, and reconstructive dentistry. **Freq:** 8/year. **ISSN:** 1059--941X (print); **EISSN:** 1532--849X (electronic). **Subscription Rates:** $246 Individuals print and online; $777 Institutions print and online. **URL:** http://onlinelibrary.wiley.com/journal/10.1111/(ISSN)1532-849X. **Ad Rates:** BW $1597, full page. **Remarks:** Accepts advertising. **Circ:** (Not Reported).

11987 ■ Journal for the Scientific Study of Religion
Society for the Scientific Study of Religion
Indiana University - Purdue University Indianapolis
Cavanaugh Hall 417
425 University Blvd.
Indianapolis, IN 46202-5148
Phone: (317)278-6491
Publisher's E-mail: sssr@iupui.edu
Freq: Quarterly. **ISSN:** 0021--8294 (print); **EISSN:** 1468--5906 (electronic). **Subscription Rates:** $231 U.S. online or online; $278 U.S. print and online; £176 Institutions print or online; £212 Institutions print and online; €223 Institutions print or online; €268 Institutions print and online; $343 Institutions, other countries; $412 Institutions, other countries. **URL:** http://onlinelibrary.wiley.com/journal/10.1111/(ISSN)1468-5906. **Circ:** (Not Reported).

11988 ■ Kappa Delta Pi Record
Kappa Delta Pi
3707 Woodview Trace
Indianapolis, IN 46268
Phone: (317)871-4900
Fax: (317)704-2323
Free: 800-284-3167
Publisher's E-mail: pubs@kdp.org
Trade magazine covering education for teachers. **Freq:** Quarterly. **Print Method:** Web offset. **Trim Size:** 8 1/4 x 10 3/4. **Cols./Page:** 3. **Key Personnel:** Kathie-Jo Arnoff, Editor. **ISSN:** 0022--8958 (print); **EISSN:** 2163--1611 (electronic). **USPS:** 216-31611. **Subscription Rates:** $103 Institutions online only; $118 Institutions print and online; $39 Individuals print and online. **URL:** http://www.tandfonline.com/toc/ukdr20/current. **Remarks:** Advertising not accepted. **Circ:** Paid 25,000.

11989 ■ Kiwanis Magazine: Serving the Children of the World
Kiwanis International
3636 Woodview Trace
Indianapolis, IN 46268-3196
Phone: (317)875-8755
Fax: (317)879-0204
Free: 800-549-2647
Publication E-mail: magazine@kiwanis.org
Magazine covering business, professional, and topics of general interest to Kiwanis. **Freq:** Bimonthly. **Print Method:** Offset. **Trim Size:** 8 x 10 7/8. **Cols./Page:** 3. **Col. Width:** 2 1/8 inches. **Col. Depth:** 10 inches. **Key Personnel:** Jack Brockley, Managing Editor; Stan D. Soderstrom, Contact. **ISSN:** 0162--5276 (print). **Alt. Formats:** Download. **URL:** http://www.kiwanis.org/kiwanis/stories/kiwanis-magazine. **Ad Rates:** GLR $20; BW $6,100; 4C $6,100; PCI $250. **Remarks:** Accepts advertising. **Circ:** 171000.

11990 ■ Light and Life
Free Methodist Church of North America
770 N High School Rd.
Indianapolis, IN 46214
Phone: (317)244-3660
Free: 800-342-5531
Church magazine. **Freq:** Bimonthly. **Print Method:** Offset web. **Trim Size:** 8 3/8 x 10 7/8. **Cols./Page:** 3. **Col. Width:** 27 nonpareils. **Col. Depth:** 120 agate lines. **Key Personnel:** Jeff Finley, Managing Editor, phone: (317)616-4776; Erin Newton, Contact. **ISSN:** 0024--3299 (print). **URL:** http://fmcusa.org/lightandlifemag. **Ad Rates:** BW $850; 4C $950. **Remarks:** Advertising accepted; rates available upon request. **Circ:** Paid ‡55000.

11991 ■ The Lion
Alpha Epsilon Pi
8815 Wesleyan Rd.
Indianapolis, IN 46268-1185
Phone: (317)876-1913
Fax: (317)876-1057
Publisher's E-mail: office@aepi.org
Freq: Quarterly. **ISSN:** 1041- 6935 (print). **Remarks:** Accepts advertising. **Circ:** 25000.

11992 ■ The Lion of Alpha Epsilon Pi
Alpha Epsilon Pi
8815 Wesleyan Rd.
Indianapolis, IN 46268-1185
Phone: (317)876-1913
Fax: (317)876-1057
Publisher's E-mail: office@aepi.org

Circulation: ★ = AAM; △ or • = BPA; ♦ = CAC; ❑ = VAC; ⊕ = PO Statement; ‡ = Publisher's Report; Boldface figures = sworn; Light figures = estimated.

Fraternity magazine. **Freq:** Quarterly. **Print Method:** Web offset. **Trim Size:** 8 1/2 x 11. **Cols./Page:** 3 and 2. **Col. Width:** 26 and 48 nonpareils. **Col. Depth:** 130 agate lines. **Key Personnel:** Adam Matsil, Editor. **ISSN:** 1041--6935 (print). **Subscription Rates:** $10 Individuals. **URL:** http://www.aepi.org/thelion. **Ad Rates:** GLR $20; BW $1,000. **Remarks:** Accepts advertising. **Circ:** 30000.

11993 ■ Medicine and Science in Sports and Exercise
American College of Sports Medicine
c/o Kenneth O. Wilson, Mng. Ed.
401 W Michigan St.
Indianapolis, IN 46202-3233
Phone: (317)634-8932
Fax: (317)634-8927
Publisher's E-mail: publicinfo@acsm.org
Medical journal. **Freq:** Monthly. **Print Method:** Web offset. **Trim Size:** 8 1/8 x 10 7/8. **Cols./Page:** 2. **Col. Width:** 32 nonpareils. **Col. Depth:** 119 agate lines. **Key Personnel:** Andrew J. Young, PhD, Editor-in-Chief, phone: (508)233-5141, fax: (508)233-4869; Kenneth O. Wilson, Managing Editor. **ISSN:** 0195--9131 (print); **EISSN:** 1530--0315 (electronic). **Subscription Rates:** $665 Individuals /year; $753 Other countries; $1515 Institutions; $1734 Institutions, other countries. **URL:** http://journals.lww.com/acsm-msse/pages/default.aspx. **Ad Rates:** BW $1,845; 4C $3,725; SAU $650. **Remarks:** Accepts advertising. **Circ:** Paid ‡12244.

11994 ■ Mid-Stream: An Ecumenical Journal
Disciples Ecumenical Consultative Council
c/o Council on Christian Unity
PO Box 1986
Indianapolis, IN 46206
Phone: (317)713-2585
Publication E-mail: midstreamthf@aol.com
Journal covering Christian issues. **Freq:** Bimonthly. **Key Personnel:** Leo Haber, Editor; Sam E. Bloch, Business Manager; Fraidy Burstein, Manager, Production. **Subscription Rates:** $18 Individuals; $32 Two years; $45 Individuals 3 years. **Circ:** (Not Reported).

11995 ■ Mine & Quarry Trader
Mine & Quarry Trader
7355 Woodland Dr.
Indianapolis, IN 46278-1737
Free: 800-827-7468
Trade magazine featuring mining and aggregate equipment, supplies, and services. **Freq:** Monthly. **Print Method:** Web. **Trim Size:** 7 1/2 x 10 1/8. **Cols./Page:** 2 and 3. **Col. Width:** 3 5/16 and 2 1/8 inches. **Col. Depth:** 120 agate lines. **Key Personnel:** Scott Bieda, Publisher; Christin Doran, Sales Representative; Gina Kelly, Sales Representative. **ISSN:** 1049--1805 (print). **Subscription Rates:** Free; $60 Other countries. **URL:** http://www.miningmarketplace.com. **Ad Rates:** BW $1,050; 4C $1,605; PCI $75. **Remarks:** Accepts advertising. **Circ:** (Not Reported).

11996 ■ NFHS Music Association Journal
NFHS Music Association
c/o National Federation of State High School Associations
PO Box 690
Indianapolis, IN 46206-0690
Phone: (317)972-6900
Fax: (317)822-5700
Journal publishing articles and analyses of current styles and techniques in music. **Freq:** Semiannual. **Remarks:** Advertising not accepted. **Circ:** 900.

11997 ■ Nursing Outlook
Mosby Inc.
c/o Marion E. Broome, Editor
Prof. & University Dean
School of Nursing, Indiana University
1111 Middle Dr., NU 132
Indianapolis, IN 46202-5107
Official journal of the American Academy of Nursing, reporting on trends and issues in nursing. **Freq:** Bimonthly. **Print Method:** Offset. **Trim Size:** 8 1/8 x 10 7/8. **Cols./Page:** 3. **Col. Width:** 2 1/4 inches. **Col. Depth:** 10 inches. **Key Personnel:** Marion E. Broome, PhD, Editor. **ISSN:** 0029--6554 (print). **Subscription Rates:** $114 Individuals USA (print and online); $176 Individuals Canada (print and online); $168 Individuals other countries (print and online); $97 Individuals online only. **URL:** http://www.nursingoutlook.org. **Ad Rates:** BW $2030; 4C $1530. **Remarks:** Accepts display advertising; Advertising accepted; rates available upon request. **Circ:** Paid ‡4881, ‡3209.

11998 ■ Operative Dentistry
Indiana University School of Dentistry
1121 W Michigan St., Rm. S411
Indianapolis, IN 46202
Phone: (317)274-7957
Fax: (317)274-2419
Publication E-mail: editor@jopdent.org
Scholarly journal for practicing dentists. **Founded:** 1976. **Freq:** Bimonthly. **Key Personnel:** Jeffrey Platt, Editor; Timothy J. Carlson, Managing Editor; Joan Matis, Office Manager. **ISSN:** 0361-7734 (print). **Subscription Rates:** $135 Individuals online and 1 paper copy; $150 Other countries online and 1 paper copy; $290 Institutions online and 1 paper copy; $340 Institutions, other countries online and 1 paper copy; $75 Individuals online only; $85 Other countries online only; $200 Institutions online only; $250 Institutions, other countries online only; $115 Individuals print only; $135 Other countries print only; $245 Institutions print only; $285 Institutions, other countries print only; $55 Students with enrollment verification from school official or professor on letterhead. **URL:** http://www.jopdent.org. **Remarks:** Advertising not accepted. **Circ:** (Not Reported).

11999 ■ Percussive Notes
Percussive Arts Society
110 W Washington St., Ste. A
Indianapolis, IN 46204
Phone: (317)974-4488
Fax: (317)974-4499
Publisher's E-mail: percarts@pas.org
Freq: Bimonthly January, March, May, July, September and November. **ISSN:** 0553- 6502 (print). **Subscription Rates:** Included in membership; $85 Individuals /year for professionals; $55 Students; $90 Libraries. **URL:** http://www.pas.org/publications/latest-issues/percussivenotes.aspx. **Remarks:** Accepts advertising. **Circ:** 6500.

12000 ■ Physical Educator
Phi Epsilon Kappa Fraternity
901 W New York St.
Indianapolis, IN 46202
Trade publication covering issues in physical education. **Freq:** Quarterly. **ISSN:** 0031--8981 (print). **Subscription Rates:** $60 Individuals; $85 Other countries; $299 Institutions online. **Online:** Gale. **URL:** http://www.phiepsilonkappa.org/public.html. **Circ:** (Not Reported).

12001 ■ POA: Pony of the Americas
Pony of the Americas Club
3828 S Emerson Ave.
Indianapolis, IN 46203
Phone: (317)788-0107
Fax: (317)788-8974
Trade magazine. **Freq:** Monthly. **Print Method:** Offset. **Trim Size:** 8 1/2 x 11. **Cols./Page:** 3. **Col. Width:** 14 picas. **Col. Depth:** 135 agate lines. **ISSN:** 0882--9624 (print). **URL:** http://www.poac.org/poac-magazine.htm. **Ad Rates:** BW $150; 4C $1,200. **Remarks:** Accepts advertising. **Circ:** ‡1600.

12002 ■ Previews: News and Events for Museum Members
Indianapolis Museum of Art
4000 Michigan Rd.
Indianapolis, IN 46208-4196
Phone: (317)923-1331
Fax: (317)931-1978
Publisher's E-mail: ima@imamuseum.org
Publication covering exhibitions and programming. **Freq:** Quarterly. **Print Method:** Offset. **Trim Size:** 8 1/2 x 11. **Cols./Page:** 4. **Col. Width:** 1.725 inches. **Col. Depth:** 127 agate lines. **URL:** http://www.imamuseum.org. **Formerly**: IMA Calendar/Previews. **Remarks:** Advertising not accepted. **Circ:** Controlled ‡12000.

12003 ■ The Public Historian
National Council on Public History
127 Cavanaugh Hall
425 University Blvd.
Indianapolis, IN 46202
Phone: (317)274-2716
Publisher's E-mail: ncph@iupui.edu
Journal covering public history and policy. **Freq:** Quarterly February, May, August, November. **Print Method:** Offset. **Trim Size:** 6 x 9. **Key Personnel:** Randolph Bergstrom, Editor; Shelley Bookspan, Senior Editor; Lindsey Reed, Senior Editor. **ISSN:** 0272-3433 (print); **EISSN:** 1533-8576 (electronic). **Subscription Rates:** $218 Institutions 1 year - online only; $76 Single issue institution; $20 Single issue; $273 Institutions 1 year - print and online. **URL:** http://tph.ucpress.edu. **Ad Rates:** BW $325. **Remarks:** Advertising accepted; rates available upon request. **Circ:** 1600, 1500.

12004 ■ Quill
Society of Professional Journalists
Eugene Pulliam National Journalism Ctr.
3909 N Meridian St.
Indianapolis, IN 46208
Phone: (317)927-8000
Fax: (317)920-4789
Publisher's E-mail: spj@spj.org
Magazine for professional journalists and students of journalism. **Founded:** 1912. **Freq:** 9/yr. **Print Method:** Web Offset. **Trim Size:** 8 1/4 x 10 3/4. **Cols./Page:** 3. **Col. Width:** 2 1/4 inches. **Col. Depth:** 10 inches. **Key Personnel:** Scott Leadingham, Editor; Joe Skeel, Publisher. **ISSN:** 0033-6475 (print). **Subscription Rates:** $72 Individuals; $10 Individuals back issues. **URL:** http://www.spj.org/quill.asp. **Ad Rates:** BW $2970, full page; BW $2425, 2/3 page vertical; BW $1890, 1/2 page vertical or horizontal; BW $1455, 1/3 page square or vertical; BW $910, 1/6 vertical or horizontal. **Remarks:** 2. **Circ:** ‡13500.

12005 ■ Radical Philosophy Review: A Journal for Progressive Thought
Philosophy Documentation Center
c/o Harry van der Linden, Editor
Department of Philosophy & Religion
Butler University
4600 Sunset Ave.
Indianapolis, IN 46208
Phone: (317)940-9974
Fax: (317)940-8815
Publisher's E-mail: order@pdcnet.org
Peer-reviewed journal covering philosophy. **Freq:** Semiannual. **Trim Size:** 6 x 9. **Cols./Page:** 1. **Key Personnel:** Harry van der Linden, Editor. **ISSN:** 1388--4441 (print); **EISSN:** 1569--1659 (electronic). **Subscription Rates:** $249 Institutions print & online(IP authentication); $69 Institutions print; $207 Institutions online only(IP authentication); $24 Individuals single issue; $35 Institutions single issue. **URL:** http://www.pdcnet.org/radphilrev/Radical-Philosophy-Review. **Formerly**: Radical Philosophy Review of Books. **Ad Rates:** BW $150. **Remarks:** Accepts advertising. **Circ:** (Not Reported).

12006 ■ Reflections on Nursing Leadership
Sigma Theta Tau International
550 W North St.
Indianapolis, IN 46202
Phone: (317)634-8171
Free: 888-634-7575
Publisher's E-mail: memserv@stti.org
Freq: Quarterly. **Key Personnel:** James E. Mattson, Editor. **ISSN:** 0885--8144 (print). **URL:** http://www.reflectionsonnursingleadership.org. **Remarks:** Accepts advertising. **Circ:** (Not Reported).

12007 ■ Religion and American Culture: A Journal of Interpretation
University of California Press - Journals and Digital Publishing Division
c/o Thomas Davis, Mng. Ed.
Indiana University-Purdue University at Indianapolis
Ctr. for the Study of Religion & American Culture
425 University Blvd., CA 417
Indianapolis, IN 46202-5140
Publication E-mail: iock100@iupui.edu
Scholarly journal covering religion in American culture. **Founded:** 1989. **Freq:** Semiannual January, July. **Trim Size:** 6 x 9. **Key Personnel:** Philip Goff, Editor; Peter J. Thuesen, Editor; Stephen J. Stein, Editor; Thomas J. Davis, Editor; Rachel Wheeler, Editor. **ISSN:** 1052-1151 (print); **EISSN:** 1533-8568 (electronic). **Subscription Rates:** $49 Individuals; $27 Students and retired; $27 Single issue; $98 Institutions single issue. **URL:** http://www.ucpressjournals.com/journal.asp?j=rac. **Ad Rates:** BW $325. **Remarks:** Accepts advertising. **Circ:** 575.

12008 ■ The Saturday Evening Post
Saturday Evening Post Society
1100 Waterway Blvd.
Indianapolis, IN 46202

Phone: (317)634-1100
Free: 800-829-5576
Publication E-mail: editor@saturdayeveningpost.com
General interest magazine. **Freq:** Bimonthly. **Print Method:** Offset. **Trim Size:** 8 1/8 x 10 13/16. **Cols./Page:** 3. **Col. Width:** 27 nonpareils. **Col. Depth:** 140 agate lines. **Key Personnel:** Joan SerVaas, Chief Executive Officer, President; Dwight Lamb, Manager, Production. **Subscription Rates:** $14.98 Individuals; $25.98 Two years; $35.98 Individuals three years. **URL:** http://www.saturdayeveningpost.com. **Ad Rates:** BW $15,000; 4C $19,500. **Circ:** Paid ★**350000**.

12009 ■ Seminars in Pediatric Surgery
Elsevier Inc.
c/o Jay L. Grosfeld, MD, Ed.
JW Riley Hospital for Children
Dept. of Surgery
702 Barnhill Dr., Ste. 2500
Indianapolis, IN 46202
Publication E-mail: elspcs@elsevier.com
Scholarly journal covering reviews of subjects concerning the surgical care of young patients. **Freq:** Quarterly. **Print Method:** Sheetfed. **Trim Size:** 8 1/4 x 11. **Key Personnel:** Jay L. Grosfeld, MD, Editor. **ISSN:** 1055-8586 (print). **Subscription Rates:** $378 Individuals print and online; $312 Institutions online only; $190 Students print and online; $156 Students online only. **URL:** http://www.sempedsurg.org; http://www.journals.elsevier.com/seminars-in-pediatric-surgery. **Ad Rates:** BW $985; 4C $1,240. **Remarks:** Accepts advertising. **Circ:** Combined ‡645.

12010 ■ Traces of Indiana and Midwestern History
Indiana Historical Society Press
450 W Ohio St.
Indianapolis, IN 46202-3269
Phone: (317)232-1882
Fax: (317)234-0076
Free: 800-447-1830
Publisher's E-mail: ijrhs@indianahistory.org
Illustrated history magazine. **Freq:** Quarterly. **Print Method:** Offset. **Trim Size:** 8 1/2 x 11. **Key Personnel:** Ray E. Boomhower, Managing Editor; John Herbst, Chief Executive Officer, President. **ISSN:** 1040-788X (print). **Subscription Rates:** $40 Individuals; $7 Single issue. **URL:** http://www.indianahistory.org/our-services/books-publications/magazines/em-traces-em. **Remarks:** Advertising not accepted. **Circ:** 11000.

12011 ■ TRIAD
Acacia Fraternity
8777 Purdue Rd., Ste. 225
Indianapolis, IN 46268
Phone: (317)872-8210
Fax: (317)872-8213
Publisher's E-mail: communications@acacia.org
Freq: Semiannual. **Key Personnel:** Patrick W. McGovern, Editor. **Alt. Formats:** PDF. **Remarks:** Advertising not accepted. **Circ:** (Not Reported).

12012 ■ Turtle Magazine for Preschool Kids
Children's Better Health Institute
1100 Waterway Blvd.
Indianapolis, IN 46202-2156
Phone: (317)634-1100
Publisher's E-mail: editor@saturdayeveningpost.com
Magazine for children (ages 2-5 years) with an emphasis on health, fitness and exercise. **Freq:** 8/yr. **Print Method:** Web Offset. **Trim Size:** 7 5/8 x 10 1/8. **Key Personnel:** Rebecca Ray, Art Director; Greg Joray, Publisher; Cory SerVaas, MD, Director, Editorial; Terry Harshman, Editor. **ISSN:** 0191-3654 (print). **Subscription Rates:** $14.98 Individuals; $27.98 Two years. **Formerly**: Turtle. **Mailing address:** PO Box 567, Indianapolis, IN 46206-0567. **Ad Rates:** BW $5,320; 4C $7,000. **Remarks:** Accepts advertising. **Circ:** (Not Reported).

12013 ■ U.S.A. Gymnastics
USA Gymnastics
132 E Washington St., Ste. 700
Indianapolis, IN 46204-3674
Phone: (317)237-5050
Free: 800-345-4719
Publisher's E-mail: membership@usagym.org
Magazine covering major gymnastics competitions; promotes health, fitness, and safety. **Freq:** Quarterly. **Print Method:** Web offset. **Trim Size:** 8 1/2 x 11. **Key Personnel:** Karen Saladyaga, Communications Specialist, phone: (317)829-5679. **ISSN:** 0748-6006 (print). **USPS:** 005-666. **Subscription Rates:** $19.95 U.S.; $32 Canada; $45 Other countries. **URL:** http://usagym.org/pages/index.html; http://usagym.org/pages/magazines/index.html. **Remarks:** Advertising accepted; rates available upon request. **Circ:** (Not Reported).

12014 ■ Vintage Times
Association of Retired Americans
6505 E 82nd St., No. 130
Indianapolis, IN 46250
Fax: (317)915-2510
Free: 800-806-6160
Magazine containing updates on ARA member services, changes to Medicare and other insurance and other articles of interest to active Americans. **Freq:** Periodic. **Subscription Rates:** Included in membership. **URL:** http://www.aracares.com/VintageTimes.aspx. **Remarks:** Accepts advertising. **Circ:** (Not Reported).

12015 ■ The Word
Word Publications
110 E Washington St., Ste. 1402
Indianapolis, IN 46204
Phone: (317)632-8840
Publication E-mail: ted@midwestword.com
Gay and lesbian community newspaper. **Founded:** June 1991. **Freq:** Monthly. **Print Method:** Offset. **Trim Size:** 10 1/4 x 11 1/4. **Cols./Page:** 4. **Col. Width:** 2 1/2 inches. **Key Personnel:** Ted Fleischaker, Publisher. **Subscription Rates:** Free. **URL:** http://www.the-word-online.com. **Ad Rates:** BW $889; 4C $1,149. **Remarks:** Accepts advertising. **Circ:** (Not Reported).

12016 ■ Word Ways: The Journal of Recreational Linguistics
Word Ways
9144 Aintree Dr.
Indianapolis, IN 46250
Journal covers recreational linguistics. **Freq:** Quarterly. **Print Method:** Offset. **Trim Size:** 7 x 10. **Cols./Page:** 1. **Col. Width:** 72 nonpareils. **Col. Depth:** 119 agate lines. **ISSN:** 0043-7980 (print). **Subscription Rates:** $33 U.S.; $35 Canada and Mexico; $45 Other countries Europe; $60 Elsewhere; $20 Individuals online. **Ad Rates:** BW $75. **Remarks:** Accepts advertising. **Circ:** ‡500.

12017 ■ Bright House Networks
3030 Roosevelt Ave.
Indianapolis, IN 46218
Founded: 2002. **Formerly**: Time Warner Cable. **Cities Served:** subscribing households 118,000. **URL:** http://indiana.mybrighthouse.com.

12018 ■ Omega Communications Inc.
41 E Washington St., Ste. 110
Indianapolis, IN 46204-3517
Fax: (317)264-4020
Email: service@omegac.com
Founded: 1971. **Cities Served:** subscribing households 2,00,000. **Mailing address:** PO Box 1766 , Indianapolis, IN 46206-1766. **URL:** http://www.omegac.com.

12019 ■ WBDG-FM
1200 N Girls School Rd.
Indianapolis, IN 46214-3403
Phone: (317)227-4122
Fax: (317)243-5506
Format: Contemporary Hit Radio (CHR). **Owner:** Metropolitan School District of Wayne Township, 1220 S High School Rd., IN 46241. **Founded:** 1965. **Formerly**: Radio Spectrum B91; Giant 90.1. **Key Personnel:** Jon Easter, Station Mgr.; Shelby Reynolds, Music Dir.; Tramaine Jones, News Dir. **Wattage**: 400 ERP. **Ad Rates:** Noncommercial.

12020 ■ WBRI-AM - 1500
4802 E 62nd St.
Indianapolis, IN 46220-5236
Phone: (317)255-5484
Email: info@wilkinsradio.com
Format: Contemporary Christian. **Networks:** Independent. **Owner:** Wilkins Communications Network Inc., 292 S Pine St., Spartanburg, SC 29302, Ph: (864)585-1885, Fax: (864)597-0687, Free: 888-989-2299. **Founded:** 1964. **Operating Hours**: Daytime. **ADI**: Indianapolis (Marion), IN. **Key Personnel:** Keith Smiley, Station Mgr. **Wattage**: 5,000. **Ad Rates:** $30-45 for 30 seconds. **URL:** http://www.wilkinsradio.com/article.asp?id=2126272.

12021 ■ WCBW-FM - 104.9
8203 Indy Ct.
Indianapolis, IN 46214-2300
Phone: (317)487-1006
Fax: (317)487-4148
Free: 800-878-9229
Format: Religious; Contemporary Christian. **Networks:** Independent. **Owner:** Continental Broadcast Group, Inc., 8203 Indy Court, Indianapolis, IN 46214. **Founded:** 1964. **Operating Hours**: Continuous; 100% local. **ADI**: St. Louis, MO (Mt. Vernon, IL). **Key Personnel:** Marvin Kosofsky, Owner; Greg Lhamon, Gen. Mgr.; Greg Cassidy, Dir. of Programs; Sandi Brown, Operations Mgr.; Phil Lewis, Gen. Sales Mgr. **Wattage**: 7,800.

12022 ■ WDNI-TV - 19
21 E St. Joseph St.
Indianapolis, IN 46204
Phone: (317)266-9600
Fax: (317)261-4664
Owner: Radio One Inc., 1010 Wayne Ave., 14th Fl., Silver Spring, MD 20910, Ph: (301)306-1111, Fax: (302)636-5454. **Operating Hours**: Continuous. **ADI**: Indianapolis (Marion), IN.

12023 ■ WEDJ-FM - 107.1
1800 N Meridian St., Ste. 603
Indianapolis, IN 46202
Phone: (317)924-1071
Fax: (317)924-7766
Format: Hispanic. **Simulcasts:** WSYW-AM. **Wattage**: 1,800 ERP. **Ad Rates:** Advertising accepted; rates available upon request. **URL:** http://www.wedjfm.com.

12024 ■ WEDM-FM - 91.1
9651 E 21st St.
Indianapolis, IN 46229
Phone: (317)532-6301
Fax: (317)532-6199
Format: Contemporary Hit Radio (CHR). **Networks:** Network Indiana. **Owner:** Metropolitan School District of Warren Township, 975 N Post Rd, INDIANAPOLIS, IN 46219, Ph: (317)869-4300, Fax: (317)869-4399. **Founded:** 1970. **Operating Hours**: Continuous; 1% network, 99% local. **ADI**: Indianapolis (Marion), IN. **Key Personnel:** Daniel J. Henn, Station Mgr. **Wattage**: 180. **Ad Rates:** Noncommercial.

12025 ■ WENS-FM - 97.1
40 Monument Cir.
40 Monument Plaza, Ste. 600
Indianapolis, IN 46204
Format: Country. **Owner:** Emmis Broadcasting, 40 Monument Cir., Ste. 700, IN 46204. **Founded:** 1986. **Formerly**: WSUL-FM. **ADI**: Indianapolis (Marion), IN. **Key Personnel:** Christine Woodward-Duncan, Gen. Mgr.; J. Chapman, Sales Mgr.; Patty England, Sales Mgr.; Donna Dwyer-Pitz, Sales Mgr.; Kim Moore, Promotions Mgr.; Shelly Grimes, Traffic Mgr.; Jessie Schwer, Bus. Mgr.; Greg Dunkin, Program Mgr. **Wattage**: 23,000 ERP. **Ad Rates:** $40-165 per unit. **URL:** http://www.hankfm.com.

12026 ■ WFBQ-FM - 94.7
6161 Fall Creek Rd.
Indianapolis, IN 46220-5097
Phone: (317)257-7565
Format: Album-Oriented Rock (AOR). **Owner:** iHeartMedia Inc., 200 E Basse Rd., San Antonio, TX 78209, Ph: (210)832-3314. **ADI**: Indianapolis (Marion), IN. **Wattage**: 58,000 ERP. **Ad Rates:** Advertising accepted; rates available upon request. **URL:** http://www.q95.com.

12027 ■ WFMS-FM - 95.5
6810 N Shadeland Ave.
Indianapolis, IN 46220
Phone: (317)255-WFMS
Fax: (317)921-1996
Email: info@wfms.com
Format: Country. **Networks:** Independent. **Owner:** Cumulus Media Partners Indiana. **Founded:** 1957. **Operating Hours**: Continuous. **Key Personnel:** Karyn Sullyvan, Contact. **Wattage**: 13,000 ERP. **Ad Rates:** Advertising accepted; rates available upon request. **URL:** http://www.wfms.com.

Circulation: ★ = AAM; △ or • = BPA; ♦ = CAC; ❑ = VAC; ⊕ = PO Statement; ‡ = Publisher's Report; Boldface figures = sworn; Light figures = estimated.

12028 ■ WFYI-FM - 90.1
1630 N Meridian St.
Indianapolis, IN 46202-1429
Phone: (317)636-2020
Fax: (317)283-6645
Format: Public Radio; Talk; Classical; News. **Networks:** National Public Radio (NPR); Public Radio International (PRI). **Owner:** Metropolitan Indianapolis Public Broadcasting Inc., at above address. **Founded:** 1954. **Formerly:** WIAN-FM. **Operating Hours:** Continuous; 50% network, 50% local. **ADI:** Indianapolis (Marion), IN. **Key Personnel:** Jeanelle Adamak, Exec. VP; Lloyd Wright, President. **Local Programs:** *Indianapolis Chamber Orchestra*, Monday Sunday 10:00 p.m. 9:00 p.m.; *Film Soceyology*, Saturday Monday Sunday 10:00 a.m. 2:00 p.m.; *Stolen Moments*, Sunday Tuesday 6:00 p.m. 9:00 p.m.; *The Blues House Party*, Saturday 8:00 p.m.; *Sound Medicine*, Tuesday Sunday 9:00 p.m. 2:00 p.m.; *Indiana Lawmakers*, Thursday Friday 6:30 p.m. 11:00 p.m.; *Indiana Week in Review*, Friday 6:00 p.m.; *Inside Indiana Business*, Tuesday 5:00 p.m. - 6:00 p.m.; *Indianapolis Symphony Orchestra*; *Art Of The Matter*, Tuesday Saturday 7:30 p.m. 6:30 p.m.; *The Indianapolis Symphony Orchestra*, Sunday Tuesday. **Wattage:** 10,000. **Ad Rates:** Noncommercial. Combined advertising rates available with WFYI-TV. **URL:** http://www.wfyi.org.

12029 ■ WFYI-TV - 20
1630 N Meridian St.
Indianapolis, IN 46202
Phone: (317)636-2020
Fax: (317)283-6645
Format: Public TV. **Networks:** Public Broadcasting Service (PBS). **Owner:** Metropolitan Indianapolis Public Broadcasting Inc., at above address. **Founded:** 1970. **Operating Hours:** Continuous. **Key Personnel:** Lloyd Wright, President; Norman G. Tabler, Jr., Chairman; Barbara E. Branic, V. Ch. **Wattage:** 060 KW. **Ad Rates:** Noncommercial. **URL:** http://www.wfyi.org.

12030 ■ WHHH-FM
21 E St. Joseph St.
Indianapolis, IN 46204-1025
Phone: (317)266-9600
Fax: (317)328-3870
Format: Contemporary Hit Radio (CHR). **Founded:** 1991. **Key Personnel:** Bill Shirk, Gen. Mgr.; Scott Wheeler, Dir. of Programs. **Wattage:** 3,300 ERP. **Ad Rates:** $10-100. **URL:** http://hot963.com.

12031 ■ WIBC-FM - 1070
40 Monument Cir., Ste. 400
Indianapolis, IN 46204
Phone: (317)266-9422
Fax: (317)684-2021
Free: 800-571-9422
Email: news@wibc.com
Format: Talk; News. **Networks:** ABC. **Owner:** Emmis Communications Corp., One Emmis Plz., 40 Monument Cir., Ste. 700, Indianapolis, IN 46204-3011, Ph: (317)266-0100. **Founded:** 1938. **Formerly:** WIBC-AM. **Operating Hours:** Continuous. **ADI:** Indianapolis (Marion), IN. **Key Personnel:** John Long, Sales Mgr.; Alan Furst, Dir. of Programs, alan@wibc.com; Eric Wunnenberg, Gen. Sales Mgr., ewunnenberg@indy.emmis.com; Sean Matthews, Dir. of Production, smatthews@wibc.emmis.com; Mike Wilson, News Dir. **Local Programs:** *Spotlight Indianapolis*, Sunday 5:30 a.m. - 6:00 a.m.; *Crime Beat*. **Wattage:** 50,000. **Ad Rates:** Noncommercial. **URL:** http://www.wibc.com.

12032 ■ WICR-FM - 88.7
1400 E Hanna Ave.
Indianapolis, IN 46227-3697
Phone: (317)788-3280
Fax: (317)788-3490
Format: Classical; Jazz. **Networks:** Public Radio International (PRI); BBC World Service. **Owner:** University of Indianapolis, 1400 E Hanna Ave., Indianapolis, IN 46227, Ph: (317)788-3368, Free: 800-232-8634. **Founded:** 1962. **Operating Hours:** Continuous. **ADI:** Indianapolis (Marion), IN. **Key Personnel:** Doug Housemeyer, Dev. Dir. **Local Programs:** *Choral Colors*, Sunday 8:00 a.m.; *Sounds of Jazz*, Sunday 1:00 p.m. - 4:00 p.m. **Wattage:** 30,000. **Ad Rates:** Noncommercial. **URL:** http://www.wicronline.org.

12033 ■ WISG-FM - 93.9
6810 N Shadeland Ave.
Indianapolis, IN 46220
Phone: (404)949-0700
Fax: (317)921-1996
Email: wisg@indyradio.com
Format: Contemporary Christian. **Owner:** Cumulus Broadcasting Inc., 3280 Peachtree Rd. NW, Ste. 2300, Atlanta, GA 30305-2447, Ph: (404)949-0700, Fax: (404)949-0740. **Operating Hours:** Continuous. **Ad Rates:** Advertising accepted; rates available upon request. **URL:** http://www.939thebeat.com.

12034 ■ WISH-TV - 8
1950 N Meridian St.
Indianapolis, IN 46202
Phone: (317)923-8888
Fax: (317)926-1144
Email: newsdesk@wishtv.com
Format: Commercial TV. **Networks:** CBS. **Owner:** LIN TV Corp., One W Exchange St., Ste. 5A, Providence, RI 02903-1064, Ph: (401)454-2880, Fax: (401)454-6990. **Operating Hours:** Continuous. **ADI:** Indianapolis (Marion), IN. **Ad Rates:** Noncommercial. **URL:** http://www.wishtv.com.

12035 ■ WJEL-FM - 89.3
1901 E 86th St.
Indianapolis, IN 46240
Phone: (317)259-5265
Format: Top 40. **Founded:** Sept. 03, 1975. **Key Personnel:** Rob Hendrix, Dir. of Programs, rhendrix@msdwt.k12.in.us; Tyler Hindman, Dir. Pub. Aff., thindman@msdwt.k12.in.us. **Wattage:** 1,000. **Ad Rates:** Noncommercial. **URL:** http://www.jelcc.com.

12036 ■ WJJK-FM - 104.5
6810 N Shadeland Ave.
Indianapolis, IN 46220
Phone: (317)842-9550
Fax: (317)921-1996
Format: News; Adult Contemporary. **Networks:** CNN Radio. **Owner:** Cumulus Broadcasting Inc., 3280 Peachtree Rd. NW, Ste. 2300, Atlanta, GA 30305-2447, Ph: (404)949-0700, Fax: (404)949-0740. **Operating Hours:** 8:30 a.m. - 5:30 p.m. Monday - Friday. **ADI:** Indianapolis (Marion), IN. **Key Personnel:** Michele Kiefer, Contact, michele.kiefer@cumulus.com. **Wattage:** 50,000. **Ad Rates:** Advertising accepted; rates available upon request. **URL:** http://www.1045wjjk.com.

12037 ■ WLHK-FM - 97.1
40 Monument Cir., Ste. 600
Indianapolis, IN 46204
Phone: (317)266-9700
Format: Country. **Operating Hours:** Continuous. **Key Personnel:** Sharon Caruana, Receivables Contact, scaruana@indy.emmis.com. **Ad Rates:** Advertising accepted; rates available upon request. **URL:** http://www.hankfm.com.

12038 ■ WNDE-AM - 1260
6161 Fall Creek Rd.
Indianapolis, IN 46220
Phone: (317)257-7565
Fax: (317)253-6501
Format: Sports; News. **Networks:** ESPN Radio. **Owner:** iHeartMedia Inc., 200 E Basse Rd., San Antonio, TX 78209, Ph: (210)832-3314. **Founded:** 1924. **Operating Hours:** Continuous. **ADI:** Indianapolis (Marion), IN. **Key Personnel:** Buzz Casey, Contact, buzzcasey@clearchannel.com. **Wattage:** 5,000. **Ad Rates:** Advertising accepted; rates available upon request. Combined advertising rates available with WFBQ, WRZY. **URL:** http://www.wnde.com.

12039 ■ WNDU-AM - 1490
5520 E 75th St.
Indianapolis, IN 46250
Phone: (317)594-0600
Fax: (317)594-9567
Owner: Michiana Telecasting Corp., 54516 Business US 31 North, South Bend, IN 46637. **Founded:** 1944. **ADI:** South Bend-Elkhart, IN. **Key Personnel:** Bill Mitchell, Contact; Lou Pierce, Promotions Dir.; Debra Miles, News Dir; Bill Mitchell, Contact; Bill Mitchell, Contact. **Wattage:** 1,000 KW. **Ad Rates:** $5-43 for 30 seconds; $5-50 for 60 seconds. $14 $25 for 30 seconds; $5-$30 for 60 seconds. Combined advertising rates available with WNDU-FM. **URL:** http://artisticradio.com.

12040 ■ WNDY-TV - 23
1950 N Meridian St.
Indianapolis, IN 46202
Phone: (317)923-8888
Fax: (317)926-1144
Email: newsdesk@wishtv.com
Format: Commercial TV; Talk. **Networks:** United Paramount Network. **Owner:** LIN TV Corp., One W Exchange St., Ste. 5A, Providence, RI 02903-1064, Ph: (401)454-2880, Fax: (401)454-6990. **Founded:** 1987. **Operating Hours:** Continuous. **ADI:** Indianapolis (Marion), IN. **Local Programs:** *I Love Lucy*; *The Wendy Williams Show*, Monday 2:00 p.m. - 3:00 p.m. **Wattage:** 5,000. **Ad Rates:** Advertising accepted; rates available upon request. **URL:** http://www.myndytv.com.

12041 ■ WNOU-FM - 100.9
21 E St. Joseph St.
Indianapolis, IN 46204
Email: inquiry@radio-one.com
Format: Contemporary Hit Radio (CHR). **Networks:** AP. **Owner:** Radio One Inc., 1010 Wayne Ave., 14th Fl., Silver Spring, MD 20910, Ph: (301)306-1111, Fax: (302)636-5454. **Founded:** 1968. **Formerly:** WKLR-FM; WNAP-FM. **Operating Hours:** Continuous. **Key Personnel:** Chuck Williams, Gen. Mgr. **Wattage:** 12,500. **Ad Rates:** $150 for 60 seconds. $150 for 60 seconds. **URL:** http://www.radio-one.com.

12042 ■ WNTR-FM - 107.9
9245 N Meridian St., Ste. 300
Indianapolis, IN 46260
Phone: (317)228-1079
Fax: (317)816-4035
Format: Adult Contemporary. **Key Personnel:** Jeff Kuhn, Mktg. Mgr., Promotions Dir.; Ben Hoffman, Dir. of Sales. **Ad Rates:** Advertising accepted; rates available upon request. **URL:** http://www.indysmix.com.

12043 ■ WNTS-AM - 1590
3547 W Washington St.
Indianapolis, IN 46241
Phone: (317)472-7137
Fax: (317)472-7138
Format: Hispanic. **Networks:** USA Radio. **Owner:** Davidson Media Group, 1945 JN Pease Pl., Ste. 101, Charlotte, NC 28262, Ph: (704)987-3585. **Founded:** 1974. **Operating Hours:** Continuous. **ADI:** Indianapolis (Marion), IN. **Key Personnel:** Rocio Correa, Contact, rociocorrea@ley1590am.com; Manuel Castro, Contact, manuelcastro@laley1590.net. **Wattage:** 5,000 Day; 500 Night.

12044 ■ WQRA-FM
5700 W Oaks Blvd.
Rocklin, CA 95765
Free: 888-937-2471
Format: Contemporary Christian. **Owner:** Educational Media Foundation, 2351 Sunset Blvd., Ste. 170-218, Rocklin, CA 95677, Ph: (800)434-8400. **Wattage:** 6,000 ERP. **URL:** http://www.air1.com.

12045 ■ WRFT-FM - 91.5
6215 S Franklin Rd.
Indianapolis, IN 46259
Phone: (317)862-6649
Format: Eclectic. **Owner:** Franklin Twp. Comm. School Corp., at above address. **Founded:** 1978. **ADI:** Indianapolis (Marion), IN. **Wattage:** 130 ERP. **Ad Rates:** Noncommercial. **URL:** http://www.wrft.itgo.com.

12046 ■ WRTV-TV - 6
1330 N Meridian St.
Indianapolis, IN 46202-2364
Phone: (317)635-9788
Fax: (317)269-1400
Format: News. **Networks:** ABC. **Owner:** The E. W. Scripps Co., 312 Walnut St., Cincinnati, OH 45202, Ph: (513)977-3000. **Founded:** 1949. **Formerly:** WFBM-TV. **Operating Hours:** 5:30 a.m.- 2:30 a.m. **Key Personnel:** Don Lundy, Gen. Mgr., VP. **Ad Rates:** Noncommercial. **URL:** http://www.theindychannel.com.

12047 ■ WRWM-FM - 93.9
6810 N Shadeland Ave.
Indianapolis, IN 46220
Phone: (317)842-9550
Fax: (317)921-1996
Format: Hip Hop; Sports; News. **Networks:** CNN Radio. **Owner:** Cumulus Broadcasting Inc., 3280 Peachtree Rd. NW, Ste. 2300, Atlanta, GA 30305-2447, Ph:

(404)949-0700, Fax: (404)949-0740. **Formerly**: WWFT-FM. **Operating Hours**: Continuous. **Key Personnel:** Michele Kiefer, Contact. **Wattage**: 8,400 ERP. **Ad Rates:** Advertising accepted; rates available upon request. **URL:** http://www.i94hits.com/.

12048 ■ WRZX-FM - 103.3
6161 Fall Creek Rd.
Indianapolis, IN 46220
Phone: (317)257-7565
Fax: (317)254-9619
Email: xfiles@x103.com
Format: Alternative/New Music/Progressive; Album-Oriented Rock (AOR). **Owner:** Broadcast Alchemy L.P., at above address. **Founded:** 1964. **Formerly**: WMJC-FM; WFXF-FM. **Operating Hours**: Continuous. **Wattage**: 18,000 ERP. **Ad Rates:** $75-500 for 60 seconds. Combined advertising rates available with DUSTER. **URL:** http://www.alt1033.com//main.html.

12049 ■ WSPM-FM - 89.1
3500 DePauw Blvd., Ste. 2085
Indianapolis, IN 46268
Phone: (317)870-8400
Fax: (317)870-8404
Email: jim@catholicradioindy.org
Format: Religious. **Owner:** Hoosier Broadcasting Corporation, at above address. **Operating Hours**: Continuous. **Key Personnel:** Jim Ganley, Gen. Mgr. **Ad Rates:** Noncommercial; underwriting available. **URL:** http://www.catholicradioindy.org.

12050 ■ WSYW-AM - 810
1800 N Meridian St., Ste. 603
Indianapolis, IN 46202
Phone: (317)924-7767
Fax: (317)924-7766
Format: Hispanic. **Networks:** UPI; ABC. **Owner:** Continental Broadcast Group, LLC, at above address. **Founded:** 1963. **Formerly**: WATI-AM; WGRT-AM. **Operating Hours**: Daytime. **ADI**: Indianapolis (Marion), IN. **Wattage**: 250. **Ad Rates:** $12.50-25 per unit. **URL:** http://www.pescador810.com.

12051 ■ WSYW-FM - 107.1
1800 N Meridian St., Ste. 201
Indianapolis, IN 46202
Phone: (317)924-1071
Fax: (317)924-7766
Format: Classical. **Networks:** ABC. **Owner:** Continental Broadcast Group, LLC, at above address. **Founded:** 1975. **Formerly**: WGRT-FM. **Operating Hours**: Continuous. **ADI**: Indianapolis (Marion), IN. **Key Personnel:** Martha Miller, Gen. Mgr., Gen. Mgr.; Marcia York, Sales Mgr. **Wattage**: 1,800 ERP. **Ad Rates:** $25-40 for 30 seconds; $25-50 for 60 seconds. **URL:** http://www.wedjfm.com.

12052 ■ WTHR-TV - 13
1000 N Meridian St.
Indianapolis, IN 46204
Phone: (317)636-1313
Format: News. **Networks:** NBC. **Owner:** The Dispatch Broadcast Co., 770 Twin Rivers Dr., Columbus, OH 43215, Ph: (614)460-3700. **Founded:** 1957. **Formerly**: WLWI-TV. **Operating Hours**: Continuous Sun.- Thurs.; 6am - 3am Fri.- Sat. **Key Personnel:** Jim Tellus, Gen. Mgr., VP; Steve Click, Sales Mgr., sclick@wthr.com. **Local Programs**: *Eyewitness News 11 p.m.*, Monday Tuesday Wednesday Thursday Friday 11:00 p.m.; *Eyewitness News 6 p.m.*, Monday Tuesday Wednesday Thursday Friday 6:00 p.m.; *Eyewitness News Sunrise*, Monday Tuesday Wednesday Thursday Friday 5:00 a.m. - 6:00 a.m. **Wattage**: 316,000 visual 69,500 aural. **Ad Rates:** Advertising accepted; rates available upon request. ## Sky Trak Weather. **URL:** http://www.wthr.com.

12053 ■ WTLC-AM - 1310
2255 Hawthorne Ln.
Indianapolis, IN 46218
Phone: (317)351-1310
Fax: (317)351-1307
Format: Adult Contemporary; Urban Contemporary. **Networks:** CBS. **Founded:** 1941. **Formerly**: WMLF-AM; WIFE-AM; WTUX-AM. **Operating Hours**: Continuous; 10% network, 90% local. **Wattage**: 5,000.

12054 ■ WTLC-FM - 106.7
21 E St. Joseph's St.
Indianapolis, IN 46204
Phone: (317)266-9600
Fax: (317)328-3870
Format: Urban Contemporary. **Networks:** CBS. **Owner:** Radio One Inc., 1010 Wayne Ave., 14th Fl., Silver Spring, MD 20910, Ph: (301)306-1111, Fax: (302)636-5454. **Founded:** 1968. **Operating Hours**: Continuous. **ADI**: Indianapolis (Marion), IN. **Key Personnel:** Brian Wallace, Contact; Brian Harrington, Contact. **Wattage**: 50,000. **Ad Rates:** Advertising accepted; rates available upon request. Combined advertising rates available with WTLC-AM. **URL:** http://tlcnaptown.hellobeautiful.com.

WTTK-TV - See Kokomo

12055 ■ WTTV-TV - 4
6910 Network Pl.
Indianapolis, IN 46278
Phone: (317)632-5900
Fax: (317)715-6251
Format: Commercial TV. **Founded:** 1949. **Operating Hours**: Continuous. **ADI**: Indianapolis (Marion), IN. **Wattage**: 055 KW ERP. **Ad Rates:** Advertising accepted; rates available upon request. **URL:** http://cbs4indy.com.

12056 ■ WXIN-TV - 59
6910 Network Pl.
Indianapolis, IN 46278
Phone: (317)632-5900
Format: Commercial TV. **Networks:** Fox. **Owner:** Tribune Broadcasting, 7700 Westpark Dr., Houston, TX 77063. **Founded:** 1984. **Formerly**: WPDS-TV. **Operating Hours**: Continuous. **ADI**: Indianapolis (Marion), IN. **Key Personnel:** Larry Delia, Gen. Mgr., VP; Lee Rosenthal, News Dir. **Local Programs**: *Fox 59 Morning News*; *TMZ*; *Fox 59 News*. **Wattage**: 5,000,000. **Ad Rates:** Noncommercial. **URL:** http://www.fox59.com.

12057 ■ WXNT-AM - 1430
9245 N Meridian St., Ste. 300
Indianapolis, IN 46260
Phone: (317)228-1430
Fax: (317)816-4035
Free: 866-440-1430
Format: News; Talk. **Owner:** Entercom Communications Corp., 401 City Ave., Ste. 809, Bala Cynwyd, PA 19004-1130, Ph: (610)660-5610, Fax: (610)660-5620. **Key Personnel:** Scotts Roddy, Dir. of Programs, sroddy@entercom.com; Toni Moore, Promotions Dir., tmoore@entercom.com; Erika Estridge, Gen. Sales Mgr., eestridge@entercom.com. **URL:** http://www.cbssports1430.com.

12058 ■ WXXP-FM - 97.9
36 S Pennsylvania St., Ste. 200
Indianapolis, IN 46204-3627
Fax: (765)644-1775
Free: 800-452-9997
Email: wxxp@aol.com
Format: Adult Contemporary. **Owner:** Anderson Radio, G.P., at above address. **Founded:** 1973. **Formerly**: WLHN-FM. **Operating Hours**: Continuous;. **ADI**: Indianapolis (Marion), IN. **Key Personnel:** Kevin Spencer, Music Dir., Program Mgr.; Robin Chester, Sales Mgr.; Steve Brown, Gen. Mgr; Stephen D. Brown, Contact. **Wattage**: 50,000. **Ad Rates:** $37 for 60 seconds.

12059 ■ WYJZ-FM - 100.9
21 E St. Joseph St.
Indianapolis, IN 46204
Format: Jazz; Music of Your Life; News. **Operating Hours**: Continuous. **ADI**: Indianapolis (Marion), IN. **Key Personnel:** Nikki Wills, Contact, nwills@radio-one.com; Nikki Wills, Contact, nwills@radio-one.com. **Wattage**: 6,000 ERP. **Ad Rates:** Advertising accepted; rates available upon request. **URL:** http://radionowindy.com.

12060 ■ WYXB-FM - 105.7
40 Monument Cir., Ste. 500
Indianapolis, IN 46204
Phone: (317)684-1057
Fax: (317)684-2021
Format: Soft Rock. **Ad Rates:** Noncommercial.

12061 ■ WZPL-FM - 99.5
9245 N Meridian St., Ste. 300
Indianapolis, IN 46260
Phone: (317)816-4000
Format: Contemporary Hit Radio (CHR). **Owner:** Entercom Indianapolis, LLC, at above address. **Founded:** 1962. **Operating Hours**: Continuous. **Key Personnel:** Jeff Kuhn, Dir. of Mktg., jkuhn@entercom.com. **Wattage**: 50,000 ERP. **Ad Rates:** $90-160 per unit. **URL:** http://www.wzpl.com.

JASPER

Dubois Co. Dubois Co. (SW). 50 m N of Evansville.

12062 ■ The Herald
The Herald
PO Box 31
Jasper, IN 47547-0031
Phone: (812)482-2424
Publication E-mail: news@dcherald.com
Newspaper with a Democratic orientation. **Founded:** 1895. **Freq:** Mon.-Sat. (eve.). **Print Method:** Offset. **Cols./Page:** 5. **Col. Width:** 24 nonpareils. **Col. Depth:** 224 agate lines. **Subscription Rates:** $15 Individuals print & online. **URL:** http://www.dcherald.com. **Ad Rates:** BW $720; PCI $9. **Remarks:** Accepts advertising. **Circ:** Paid ‡12600.

12063 ■ Insight Communications
2856 Cathy Ln.
Jasper, IN 47546-9400
Phone: (812)482-4588
Cities Served: 122 channels.

12064 ■ WAXL-FM - 103.3
PO Box 1009
Jasper, IN 47547
Phone: (812)634-9232
Fax: (812)482-3696
Email: mailbox@waxl.us
Format: Hot Country; Contemporary Hit Radio (CHR); Adult Contemporary. **Owner:** DCBroadcasting Inc., at above address. **URL:** http://www.dcbroadcasting.com.

12065 ■ WITZ-AM - 990
PO Box 167
Jasper, IN 47546
Email: contest@witzamfm.com
Format: Full Service; Information. **Networks:** Fox. **Owner:** Jasper On the Air, Inc., 1978 S Witz Road, Jasper, IN 47546, Ph: (812)482-2131. **Founded:** 1948. **ADI**: Evansville, IN (Madisonville, KY). **Key Personnel:** Walt Ferber, Dir. of Programs; Gene Kuntz, Operations Mgr., Sales Mgr., Gen. Mgr. **Wattage**: 1,000 Day time; 006 Ni. **Ad Rates:** Advertising accepted; rates available upon request. **URL:** http://www.witzamfm.com.

12066 ■ WJTS-TV - 18
511 Newton St., Ste. 204
Jasper, IN 47546
Phone: (812)482-2727
Owner: DCBroadcasting Inc., at above address. **Founded:** 1993. **Mailing address:** PO Box 1009, Jasper, IN 47546. **URL:** http://www.wjts.tv.

12067 ■ WQKZ-FM - 98.5
PO Box 167
Jasper, IN 47546
Phone: (812)482-2131
Fax: (812)482-9609
Format: Hot Country. **Networks:** Jones Satellite. **Owner:** Gem Communications, 5857 Randolph Blvd., San Antonio, TX 78233, Ph: (210)590-4800, Fax: (210)590-8789. **Founded:** Nov. 01, 1991. **Operating Hours**: Continuous. **ADI**: Evansville, IN (Madisonville, KY). **Key Personnel:** Gene Kuntz, Operations Mgr. **Wattage**: 3,600. **Ad Rates:** Advertising accepted; rates available upon request. **URL:** http://www.witzamfm.com.

12068 ■ WRZR-FM - 94.5
PO Box 1009
Jasper, IN 47547
Phone: (812)634-9232
Fax: (812)482-3696
Format: Classic Rock. **Founded:** 1975. **Key Personnel:** Ron Spaulding, Gen. Sales Mgr. **Ad Rates:** Noncommercial. **URL:** http://www.dcbroadcasting.com.

JEFFERSONVILLE

Clark Co. Clark Co. (SE). On Ohio River, opposite Louisville, Ky.

12069 ■ The Evening News
The Evening News

Circulation: ★ = AAM; △ or • = BPA; ♦ = CAC; ❑ = VAC; ⊕ = PO Statement; ‡ = Publisher's Report; Boldface figures = sworn; Light figures = estimated.

221 Spring St.
Jeffersonville, IN 47130
Phone: (812)206-6397
Fax: (812)206-4598
Publisher's E-mail: info@newsandtribune.com
Newspaper with a Democratic orientation. **Founded:** 1872. **Freq:** Daily. **Print Method:** Offset. **Cols./Page:** 6. **Col. Width:** 25 nonpareils. **Col. Depth:** 297 agate lines. **Key Personnel:** Jim Grahn, Publisher; Nina Fulda-Portman, Business Manager. **URL:** http://www.newsandtribune.com/. **Remarks:** Accepts advertising. **Circ:** Paid 10500.

12070 ■ Insight Communications
3408 Industrial Pky.
Jeffersonville, IN 47130
Free: 800-273-0144
Owner: Insight Communications Company L.P. **Founded:** 1986. **Cities Served:** Jeffersonville, Indiana: subscribing households 28,000; Oldham County, KY. **Postal Areas Served:** 47130.

12071 ■ WAVG-AM - 1450
213 Magnolia St.
Jeffersonville, IN 47130
Phone: (502)419-4744
Format: News; Sports. **Networks:** Jones Satellite. **Owner:** Susquehanna Radio Corp., 221 W Philadelphia St., York, PA 17404, Ph: (717)852-2132, Fax: (717)771-1436. **Founded:** 1961. **Formerly:** WXVW-AM. **Operating Hours:** Continuous. **ADI:** Louisville, KY. **Key Personnel:** Kelly Trask, Gen. Mgr., Promotions Mgr., kelly@wavg1450.com; Connie Aynes, Bus. Mgr., Coord., Public Svcs., connie@wavg1450.com; Douglas Wolverton, Operations Mgr., douglas@wavg1450.com; Lisa Thomasson, Dir. of Traffic, lisa@wavg1450.com. **Wattage:** 1,000. **Ad Rates:** $25 per unit. **URL:** http://1450thesportsbuzz.com.

12072 ■ WQMF-FM
Jeffersonville, IN
Format: Classic Rock. **Wattage:** 28,500 ERP. **Ad Rates:** Noncommercial. **URL:** http://www.wqmf.com.

KENDALLVILLE

Noble Co. Noble Co. (NE). 26 m N of Fort Wayne.

12073 ■ Advance Leader
KPC Media Group, Inc.
102 N Main St.
Kendallville, IN 46755
Phone: (260)347-0400
Publisher's E-mail: contact@kpcmedia.com
Newspaper. **Freq:** Weekly (Thurs.). **Print Method:** Offset. **Cols./Page:** 6. **Col. Width:** 12.5 picas. **Col. Depth:** 21 1/2 inches. **Key Personnel:** Bob Buttgen, Editor; Octavia Yoder, Editor. **URL:** http://kpcnews.com/news/latest/advanceleader. **Remarks:** Accepts advertising. **Circ:** ‡1000.

12074 ■ News-Sun
KPC Media Group, Inc.
102 N Main St.
Kendallville, IN 46755
Phone: (260)347-0400
Publisher's E-mail: contact@kpcmedia.com
General newspaper. **Founded:** 1911. **Freq:** Daily. **Print Method:** Offset. **Trim Size:** 11 1/2 x 14. **Cols./Page:** 6. **Col. Width:** 12.5 picas. **Col. Depth:** 21 1/4 inches. **Key Personnel:** Dave Kurtz, Executive Editor; James Tew, Editor; Terry Housholder, Chief Executive Officer, President. **Subscription Rates:** $169 Individuals home delivered; $216 By mail; $54.95 Individuals online; $99.95 Two years online. **URL:** http://www.kpcnews.com/. **Remarks:** Accepts advertising. **Circ:** Mon.-Sat. ★8637, Sun. ★8419.

12075 ■ WAWK-AM - 1140
931 East Ave.
Kendallville, IN 46755
Phone: (219)347-2400
Fax: (219)347-2524
Email: wawk@locl.net
Format: Classic Rock; Full Service; Oldies; Agricultural. **Owner:** Don Moore-Wawk, at above address. **Founded:** 1957. **Operating Hours:** 5:00 a.m. - 7:00 p.m. Monday - Friday; 6:00 a.m. - Midnight. Saturday; 4:30 a.m. - Midnight. Sunday. **Key Personnel:** Don Moore, Sales Mgr; Mike Shultz, Contact. **Wattage:** 250 Daytime. **Ad Rates:** Advertising accepted; rates available upon request. $10-15 for 30 seconds; $12.50-18.75 for 60 seconds. **URL:** http://www.wawk.com.

KENTLAND

Newton Co. Newton Co. (NW). 35 m W of Monticello. Residential.

12076 ■ Newton County Enterprise
Twin States Publishing
305 E Graham St.
Kentland, IN 47951
Phone: (219)474-5532
Fax: (219)474-5354
Publisher's E-mail: nceeditor@centurylink.net
Newspaper with a Republican orientation. **Freq:** Weekly (Wed.). **Print Method:** Offset. **Cols./Page:** 6. **Col. Width:** 9.5 picas. **Col. Depth:** 14 inches. **Key Personnel:** Betty Long, Officer, Administration; Cheri Glancy, Managing Editor. **USPS:** 390-060. **Subscription Rates:** $34 Individuals 6 months; $51 Out of country 6 months; $52 Individuals /year; 73 Out of country. **URL:** http://www.newsbug.info/newton_county_enterprise/. **Mailing address:** PO Box 107, Kentland, IN 47951. **Ad Rates:** BW $264.60; SAU $5.76; PCI $3.15. **Remarks:** Accepts advertising. **Circ:** (Not Reported).

KNIGHTSTOWN

Henry Co. Henry Co. (E). 17 m SW of New Castle. Manufactures furniture, funeral car bodies, caskets and accessories. Stock, grain farms. Corn, wheat, hogs.

12077 ■ AntiqueWeek Eastern Edition
MidCountry Media, Inc.
27 N Jefferson St.
Knightstown, IN 46148
Phone: (765)345-5133
Fax: (765)345-3398
Free: 800-876-5133
Publisher's E-mail: mthoe@midcountrymedia.com
Periodical covering antiques auctions and shows in Connecticut, Delaware, Washington, D.C., Maryland, New Jersey, New York, North Carolina, eastern Pennsylvania, Rhode Island, South Carolina, Virginia, and West Virginia. **Freq:** Weekly. **Cols./Page:** 4. **Col. Width:** 15 picas. **Col. Depth:** 16 inches. **Key Personnel:** Tony Gregory, Publisher. **Subscription Rates:** $41 Individuals; $75 Two years; $102 Individuals 3 years; $20.50 Individuals 6 months; $30 Individuals /year; online only. **URL:** http://www.antiqueweek.com. **Mailing address:** PO Box 90, Knightstown, IN 46148. **Remarks:** Advertising accepted; rates available upon request. **Circ:** (Not Reported).

12078 ■ Farm World
MidCountry Media, Inc.
27 N Jefferson St.
Knightstown, IN 46148
Phone: (765)345-5133
Fax: (765)345-3398
Free: 800-876-5133
Publisher's E-mail: mthoe@midcountrymedia.com
Newspaper covering agriculture in Indiana, Ohio, and Kentucky. **Founded:** Feb. 1955. **Freq:** Weekly (Wed.). **Print Method:** Letterpress. **Trim Size:** 11 1/2 x 7. **Cols./Page:** 4. **Col. Width:** 29 nonpareils. **Col. Depth:** 224 agate lines. **Key Personnel:** Tony Gregory, Publisher; Toni Hodson, Manager, Advertising; Dave Blower, Jr., Editor. **Subscription Rates:** $41 Individuals AntiqueWeek Central edition; $41 Individuals AntiqueWeek Eastern edition; $35 Individuals Farm World (in area); $47.25 Out of area Farm World; $65 Individuals combo (AWC + IA); $69.30 Individuals combo (AWC + AWE); $30 Individuals Farm World Online Only; $20 Individuals AntiqueWest. **URL:** http://www.farmworldonline.com. **Formerly:** Farmweek. **Mailing address:** PO Box 90, Knightstown, IN 46148. **Ad Rates:** GLR $1.10; BW $960; PCI $15. **Remarks:** Accepts classified advertising. **Circ:** (Not Reported).

12079 ■ Knightstown Banner
Eric M. Cox
PO Box 116
Knightstown, IN 46148
Community newspaper. **Freq:** Weekly (Wed.). **Print Method:** Offset. **Key Personnel:** Eric Cox, Editor, Publisher; Stacy Cox, General Manager. **Subscription Rates:** $13 Individuals online; $40 Individuals print; $45 Out of state print. **URL:** http://www.thebanneronline.com. **Formerly:** Tri-County Banner. **Ad Rates:** GLR $6; BW $480; 4C $200; PCI $6.96. **Remarks:** Accepts advertising. **Circ:** ‡5000.

12080 ■ WKPW-FM - 90.7
8149 W US 40
Knightstown, IN 46148
Phone: (765)345-9070
Fax: (765)345-7977
Email: wkpw@wkpwfm.com
Format: Adult Contemporary. **Founded:** Sept. 1993. **Operating Hours:** Continuous. **Key Personnel:** Robert Hobbs, Prog. Dir. **Wattage:** 4,400. **Ad Rates:** Noncommercial. **URL:** http://web01.cabeard.k12.in.us.

KNOX

Starke Co. Starke Co. (NW). 45 m SW of South Bend. Manufactures electrical appliances, pickles, hydraulic cylinders, aluminum containers, cabinets. Poultry, truck, grain farms.

12081 ■ WKVI-AM - 1520
400 W Culver Rd.
Knox, IN 46534
Phone: (574)772-6241
Format: Eclectic; News. **Owner:** Kanakee Valley Broadcasting Co., 400 W Culver Rd., Knox, IN 46534, Ph: (574)772-6241, Fax: (574)772-5920. **Founded:** 1969. **Key Personnel:** Jim Conner, Mgr.; Ted Hayes, News Dir.; Harold Welter, Sports Dir; Ed Hasnerl, Contact. **Wattage:** 250. **Ad Rates:** Advertising accepted; rates available upon request. **URL:** http://www.wkvi.com.

12082 ■ WKVI-FM - 99.3
400 W Culver Rd.
Knox, IN 46534
Phone: (574)772-6241
Format: News. **Operating Hours:** Continuous. **Key Personnel:** Jim Conner, Mgr. **Ad Rates:** Noncommercial. **URL:** http://www.wkvi.com.

KOKOMO

Howard Co. Howard Co. (NC). 54 m N of Indianapolis. Manufactures aluminum products, alarm systems, hydraulic equipment, glass products, asphalt paving material, gloves, breakfast bars, dairy products, steel, wire, fencing, nails, abrasive and corrosive alloys, radio, auto transmission, plumbing supplies, tools, auto parts, castings, stamped metal, springs, electric signs, pottery; meat packing plant; canning factory.

12083 ■ The Gourd
American Gourd Society
PO Box 2186
Kokomo, IN 46904-2186
Publisher's E-mail: agsmembership@comcast.net
Freq: Quarterly. **ISSN:** 0888--5672 (print). **Subscription Rates:** Included in membership 4 issues; $7.50 Single issue back issue. **URL:** http://www.americangourdsociety.org/magazine/toc.html. **Ad Rates:** BW $100; 4C $150. **Remarks:** Accepts advertising. **Circ:** (Not Reported).

12084 ■ Kokomo Perspective
Kokomo Perspective
209 N Main St.
Kokomo, IN 46901
Phone: (765)452-0055
Fax: (765)457-7209
Community newspaper. **Freq:** Weekly. **Key Personnel:** Don Wilson; Patrick Munsey, Editor; Bill Eldridge, Contact. **Subscription Rates:** $39 Individuals 6 months; $49 Individuals; $22 Individuals 3 months. **URL:** http://kokomoperspective.com. **Ad Rates:** BW $1,670.55; 4C $2,065.55; PCI $14.95. **Remarks:** Advertising accepted; rates available upon request. **Circ:** Paid ‡32000.

12085 ■ Kokomo Tribune
Kokomo Tribune
PO Box 9014
Kokomo, IN 46904
Phone: (765)459-3121
General newspaper. **Founded:** 1850. **Freq:** Daily (eve.), Sat. and Sun. (morn.). **Print Method:** Offset. **Trim Size:** 13 7/8 x 22 5/8. **Cols./Page:** 6. **Col. Width:** 25 nonpareils. **Col. Depth:** 300 agate lines. **Key Personnel:** Patrick Ethridge, Editor, Managing Editor; Robyn McCloskey, Publisher; Jeff Kovaleski, Managing Editor. **Subscription Rates:** $169.20 Individuals carrier delivery; $88 Individuals 6 months (carrier delivery); $45.50

Individuals 3 months (carrier delivery); $132 Individuals weekend delivery; $66 Individuals 6 months (weekend delivery); $33 Individuals 3 months (weekend delivery). **URL:** http://www.kokomotribune.com. **Ad Rates:** BW $23.05; SAU $16.17; PCI $23.05. **Remarks:** Accepts advertising. **Circ:** Mon.-Sat. ★**20587**, Sun. ★**20570**.

12086 ■ WIOU-AM - 1350
PO Box 2208
Kokomo, IN 46904
Phone: (765)453-1212
Fax: (765)455-3882
Format: Sports; News; Talk. **Networks:** CBS. **Owner:** Mid-America Radio Group, Inc., 60 N Wayne St., Martinsville, IN 46151, Ph: (765)349-1485. **Founded:** 1948. **Operating Hours:** Controlled. **ADI:** Indianapolis (Marion), IN. **Key Personnel:** Steven La Mar, Gen. Mgr., svlamar76@aol.com; Carolyn Monroe, Contact. **Wattage:** 5,000. **Ad Rates:** Noncommercial.

12087 ■ WMYK-FM - 98.5
671 East 400 South
Kokomo, IN 46902-2208
Phone: (765)455-9850
Fax: (765)455-3882
Format: Classic Rock. **Owner:** Mid America Radio Group, 1639 Burton Ln., Martinsville, IN 46151. **Founded:** Mar. 15, 1999. **Operating Hours:** 10:00 a.m. - 1:00 a.m. Monday – Friday. **Key Personnel:** Lora Lacy, Sales Mgr.; Allan James, Operations Mgr. **Wattage:** 6,000. **Ad Rates:** Noncommercial. **URL:** http://www.rock985.com.

12088 ■ WTTK-TV - 29
c/o WTTV-TV
3490 Bluff Rd.
Indianapolis, IN 46217
Phone: (317)782-4444
Fax: (317)780-5464
Format: News; Sports. **Owner:** Sinclair Broadcast Group, 2000 W. 41st St., Baltimore, MD 21211, Ph: (410)662-1449, Fax: (410)662-1450. **Wattage:** 550,000 ERP. **URL:** http://cbs4indy.com.

12089 ■ WWKI-FM - 100.5
519 N Main St.
Kokomo, IN 46901
Phone: (765)459-4191
Fax: (765)456-1111
Free: 800-444-WWKI
Format: Country; News. **Owner:** Cumulus Media Inc., 3280 Peachtree Rd. NW, Ste. 2300, Atlanta, GA 30305-2455, Ph: (404)949-0700, Fax: (404)949-0740. **Founded:** 1962. **Key Personnel:** Dave Broman, Contact, dave.broman@howardcountymuseum.org. **Wattage:** 50,000 ERP. **Ad Rates:** Advertising accepted; rates available upon request. **URL:** http://www.wwki.com.

12090 ■ WZWZ-FM - 92.5
671 E 400 S
Kokomo, IN 46902
Phone: (765)453-1212
Format: Adult Contemporary. **Founded:** 1964. **Operating Hours:** Continuous. **ADI:** Indianapolis (Marion), IN. **Wattage:** 6,000 ERP. **Ad Rates:** $34 for 30 seconds; $38 for 60 seconds. Combined advertising rates available with WIOU-AM: $45 for 30 seconds; $52 for 60 seconds. **URL:** http://www.z925fm.com.

LA PORTE

La Porte Co. La Porte Co. (NW). 65 m SE of Chicago, Ill. Lake resort.

12091 ■ LaPorte Herald-Argus
LaPorte Herald-Argus
701 State St.
La Porte, IN 46350
Phone: (219)362-2161
Fax: (219)362-2166
Free: 866-362-2167
Publisher's E-mail: circulation@heraldargus.com
General newspaper. **Founded:** 1880. **Freq:** Daily. **Print Method:** Press-Single wide offset. **Trim Size:** 12 1/2 x 27 3/4. **Key Personnel:** Julie McKiel, Manager, Circulation, phone: (219)326-3886; Brad Reisig, Director, Advertising, phone: (219)326-3881; Adam Parkhouse, Editor, phone: (219)326-3869. **Subscription Rates:** $159.25 Individuals city route; $170.34 Individuals motor route; $318.75 Individuals mail. **URL:** http://www.heraldargus.com. **Ad Rates:** PCI $12.50. **Remarks:** Accepts advertising. **Circ:** Paid 11251.

12092 ■ WCOE-FM - 96.7
1700 Lincolnway Pl., Ste. 8
La Porte, IN 46350
Phone: (219)362-5290
Format: Contemporary Country. **Networks:** ABC. **Owner:** La Porte County Broadcasting Company Inc., 1700 Lincolnway Pl. Suite 8 , La Porte, IN 46350, Ph: (219)362-6144, Fax: (219)324-7418. **Founded:** 1964. **Operating Hours:** Continuous. **Key Personnel:** Dennis Siddall, Contact, denny@wcoefm.com; Norma Sabie, Sales Mgr., normas@wcoefm.com. **Wattage:** 3,000 ERP. **Ad Rates:** $22.50 for 30 seconds; $23.50-23.50 for 60 seconds. **URL:** http://wcoefm.com.

12093 ■ WLOI-AM - 1540
1700 Lincolnway Pl., Ste. 8
La Porte, IN 46350-3194
Phone: (219)362-6144
Fax: (219)324-7418
Format: Adult Contemporary. **Networks:** Westwood One Radio; Satellite Music Network. **Owner:** La Porte County Broadcasting Company Inc., 1700 Lincolnway Pl. Suite 8 , La Porte, IN 46350, Ph: (219)362-6144, Fax: (219)324-7418. **Founded:** 1948. **Operating Hours:** Sunrise-sunset; 8% network, 92% local. **Wattage:** 250. **Ad Rates:** Noncommercial.

LAFAYETTE

Tippecanoe Co. Tippecanoe Co. (NWC). On Wabash River, 63 m NW of Indianapolis. Purdue University. Computer software, toys.

12094 ■ The Catholic Moment: Newspaper of the Diocese of Lafayette-in-Indiana
The Catholic Moment
PO Box 1603
Lafayette, IN 47902
Phone: (765)742-2050
Fax: (765)742-7513
Publication E-mail: moment@dol-in.org
Official newspaper (tabloid) of the Catholic Diocese of Lafayette, IN. **Freq:** (47 times a year) except for the second and fourth weeks of July and August and the last week of December. **Key Personnel:** Rev. Timothy L. Doherty, Publisher; Kevin Cullen, Editor; Laurie Cullen, Assistant Editor. **ISSN:** 1087--2604 (print). **USPS:** 403-610. **Subscription Rates:** $25 Individuals; $20 Individuals through the parish. **Formerly:** The Sunday Visitor; Lafayette Sunday Visitor. **Ad Rates:** BW $845; 4C $995; PCI $13. **Remarks:** Accepts advertising. **Circ:** ‡27000.

12095 ■ Journal and Courier
Federated Publications Inc.
217 N 6th St.
Lafayette, IN 47901
Free: 800-456-3223
General newspaper. **Freq:** Daily. **Print Method:** Letterpress. **Cols./Page:** 6. **Col. Width:** 25 nonpareils. **Col. Depth:** 298 agate lines. **Key Personnel:** Gary M. Suisman, President, Publisher, phone: (765)420-5314; Julie Doll, Executive Editor, phone: (765)420-5242; Jim Holm, Director, Advertising, phone: (765)420-5272. **Subscription Rates:** $9.99 Individuals Sunday Only; 3 months (print); $14.99 Individuals Thursday - Sunday; 3 months (print); $19.99 Individuals Monday - Sunday; 3 months (print); $4.31 Individuals 1 month (online). **URL:** http://www.jconline.com. **Remarks:** Accepts advertising. **Circ:** Mon.-Fri. ★**34666**, Sun. ★**40694**, Sat. ★**35037**.

12096 ■ Protein Science
John Wiley & Sons Inc.
Dept. of Biochemistry
Purdue University Biochemistry Bldg. W
Lafayette, IN 47907
Phone: (765)496-3460
Fax: (765)496-3460
Publisher's E-mail: info@wiley.com
Journal focusing on the exploration of proteins. **Freq:** Monthly. **Key Personnel:** Brian W. Matthews, Editor-in-Chief. **ISSN:** 0961--8368 (print); **EISSN:** 1469--896X (electronic). **Subscription Rates:** $2398 Institutions online, United States, Canada & Mexico, and rest of the world; $2330 Institutions online, The Americas; £1224 Institutions online only - UK; €1548 Institutions online only - Europe. **URL:** http://onlinelibrary.wiley.com/journal/10.1002/(ISSN)1469-896X. **Ad Rates:** BW $700. **Remarks:** Accepts advertising. **Circ:** 50000.

12097 ■ WASK-AM - 1450
3575 McCarty Ln.
Lafayette, IN 47905
Phone: (765)447-2186
Fax: (765)448-4452
Format: Sports. **Networks:** AP; NBC. **Owner:** Schurz Communications Inc., 1301 E Douglas Rd., Mishawaka, IN 46545, Ph: (574)247-7237. **Founded:** 1942. **Operating Hours:** Continuous; Mon. 5:30 a.m.-Sun. midnight. **Wattage:** 1,000. **Ad Rates:** $12-31.20 for 30 seconds; $15-39 for 60 seconds. **URL:** http://www.wask.com.

12098 ■ WASK-FM - 98.7
3575 McCarty Ln.
Lafayette, IN 47905
Phone: (765)447-2186
Fax: (765)448-4452
Format: Oldies; Country; News. **Networks:** ABC. **Owner:** Schurz Communications Inc., 1301 E Douglas Rd., Mishawaka, IN 46545, Ph: (574)247-7237. **Founded:** 1964. **Operating Hours:** Continuous. **ADI:** Lafayette, IN. **Wattage:** 4,400. **Ad Rates:** Noncommercial. $12-31.20 for 30 seconds; $15-39 for 60 seconds. **URL:** http://www.wask.com.

12099 ■ WAZY-AM
3824 s 18th St.
Lafayette, IN 47909
Phone: (765)474-1410
Fax: (765)474-3442
Email: andrewazy@hotmail.com
Owner: Artistic Media Partners Inc., 5520 E 75th St., Indianapolis, IN 46250, Ph: (317)594-0600. **Founded:** 1984. **Formerly:** WFTE-AM; WCFY-AM. **Key Personnel:** Arthur Angotti, Gen. Mgr. **Ad Rates:** $10 per unit. for Theater spot run 24 times per week. **URL:** http://www.wazy.com/contact/contact-info.

12100 ■ WAZY-FM - 96.5
3824 S 18th St.
Lafayette, IN 47909-9102
Phone: (765)474-1410
Fax: (765)474-3442
Format: Contemporary Hit Radio (CHR). **Owner:** Artistic Media Partners Inc., 5520 E 75th St., Indianapolis, IN 46250, Ph: (317)594-0600. **Founded:** 1964. **ADI:** Lafayette, IN. **Key Personnel:** Arthur A. Angotti, III, President; Judy Perkins, Bus. Mgr. **Wattage:** 50,000 ERP. **Ad Rates:** Advertising accepted; rates available upon request. **URL:** http://www.wazy.com.

12101 ■ WJEF-FM - 91.9
1801 S 18th St.
Lafayette, IN 47905
Phone: (765)772-4700
Format: Oldies. **Networks:** Independent. **Owner:** Lafayette School Corp., 2300 Cason St., Lafayette, IN 47904, Ph: (765)771-6000, Fax: (765)771-6000. **Founded:** 1972. **Formerly:** WJJE-FM. **Operating Hours:** Continuous. **ADI:** Lafayette, IN. **Key Personnel:** Randy Brist, Contact. **Wattage:** 250. **Ad Rates:** Noncommercial. **URL:** http://jeff92.org/home_page/Home.html.

12102 ■ WKHY-FM - 93.5
3575 McCarty Ln.
Lafayette, IN 47905
Format: Classic Rock; Album-Oriented Rock (AOR). **Networks:** AP; Fox; Westwood One Radio. **Owner:** Wask Inc., 3575 McCarty Lane , Lafayette, IN 47905, Ph: (765)447-2186 , Fax: (765)448-4452. **Founded:** 1970. **ADI:** Lafayette, IN. **Key Personnel:** Jeff Strange, Contact. **Wattage:** 6,000. **Ad Rates:** Noncommercial. WXXB-FM. **URL:** http://www.wkhy.com.

12103 ■ WQSG-FM - 90.7
PO Box 2440
Tupelo, MS 38803
Phone: (662)844-8888
Format: Religious. **Owner:** American Family Radio, at above address. **URL:** http://www.afa.net.

12104 ■ WTGO-FM - 97.7
724 Wabash Ave.
Lafayette, IN 47905
Phone: (765)429-1113

Circulation: ★ = AAM; △ or • = BPA; ♦ = CAC; ❏ = VAC; ⊕ = PO Statement; ‡ = Publisher's Report; Boldface figures = sworn; Light figures = estimated.

Format: Religious; Contemporary Christian. **Founded:** 2004. **Operating Hours:** Continuous. **Key Personnel:** Brett W. Estes, Station Mgr. **Ad Rates:** Noncommercial. **URL:** http://www.wtgoradio.com.

12105 ■ WXXB-FM - 102.9
3575 McCarty Ln.
Lafayette, IN 47905
Phone: (765)447-2186
Fax: (765)448-4452
Format: Contemporary Hit Radio (CHR); Alternative/New Music/Progressive. **Networks:** AP. **Owner:** Wask Inc., 3575 McCarty Lane , Lafayette, IN 47905, Ph: (765)447-2186 , Fax: (765)448-4452. **Founded:** 1984. **Formerly:** WNJY-FM. **Operating Hours:** Continuous. **ADI:** Lafayette, IN. **Wattage:** 6,000. **Ad Rates:** 93.5 WKHY. **URL:** http://www.b1029.com.

12106 ■ WYCM-FM - 95.7
3824 S 18th St.
Lafayette, IN 47909
Format: Classic Rock. **Founded:** Sept. 07, 2006. **Wattage:** 3,100. **Ad Rates:** Advertising accepted; rates available upon request.

LAGRANGE

12107 ■ LaGrange Standard
LaGrange Publishing Co.
PO Box 148
LaGrange, IN 46761
Phone: (260)463-2166
Fax: (260)463-2734
Free: 800-552-2404
Publisher's E-mail: lagpubco@kuntrynet.com
Community newspaper. **Freq:** Weekly. **Print Method:** Offset. Broadsheet. **Trim Size:** 16 1/2 x 23. **Cols./Page:** 7. **Col. Width:** 12.75 picas. **Col. Depth:** 301 agate lines. **Subscription Rates:** $20 Individuals; $35 Individuals in India & St. Joseph and Branch counties in Michigan; $60 Out of country. **URL:** http://www.lagrangepublishing.com/openpublish. **Ad Rates:** GLR $.59; SAU $8.26; PCI $7.70. **Remarks:** Color advertising not accepted. **Circ:** ‡5706.

12108 ■ WTHD-FM - 105.5
206 S High St.
LaGrange, IN 46761
Phone: (260)463-8500
Fax: (260)463-8580
Email: wthd@wthd.net
Format: Country. **Networks:** ABC; Jones Satellite. **Owner:** Lake Cities Broadcasting Corp., at above address. **Operating Hours:** Continuous. **Key Personnel:** Tim Murray, News Dir., tmurray@wthd.net. **Ad Rates:** Advertising accepted; rates available upon request. **URL:** http://radio-locator.com.

LAWRENCEBURG

Dearborn Co. Dearborn Co. (SE). On Ohio River, 25 m W of Cincinnati, Ohio. Manufactures feed, veneer, caskets, lumber, grain aerating machinery. Glass Bottles, rock crushing. Distilleries. Agriculture. Stock, dairy, grain farms.

12109 ■ Dearborn County Register
Register Publications
126 W High St.
Lawrenceburg, IN 47025
Phone: (812)537-0063
Fax: (812)537-5576
Newspaper with a Democratic orientation. **Freq:** Weekly (Thurs.). **Print Method:** Offset. **Trim Size:** 14 1/2 x 22 3/4. **Cols./Page:** 6. **Col. Width:** 13 millimeters. **Col. Depth:** 21 inches. **Key Personnel:** Erika Schmidt Russell, Editor. **USPS:** 150-580. **Subscription Rates:** $5 Individuals Dearborn County Register (daily) ; $41.50 Individuals digital Only (Includes Journal Press); $41.55 Individuals print & Digital (In Dearborn/Ohio County and Harrison. Includes Journal Press); $63.10 Out of country print & Digital (Includes Journal Press); $91.90 Out of state print & Digital (Includes Journal Press). **URL:** http://www.thedcregister.com. **Remarks:** Accepts display and classified advertising. **Circ:** (Not Reported).

12110 ■ The Journal Press
Register Publications
126 W High St.
Lawrenceburg, IN 47025
Phone: (812)537-0063
Fax: (812)537-5576
Newspaper with a Republican orientation. **Founded:** 1858. **Freq:** Weekly (Tues.). **Print Method:** Offset. **Trim Size:** 14 1/2 x 22 3/4. **Cols./Page:** 6. **Col. Width:** 13 millimeters. **Col. Depth:** 21 inches. **Key Personnel:** Tom Brooker, Publisher, phone: (812)537-0063; Loretta Day, Director, Advertising. **ISSN:** 0378-8800 (print). **URL:** http://www.thejournal-press.com. **Ad Rates:** PCI $8. **Remarks:** Accepts classified advertising. **Circ:** ‡6700.

12111 ■ Ohio County News
Register Publications
126 W High St.
Lawrenceburg, IN 47025
Phone: (812)537-0063
Fax: (812)537-5576
Community newspaper. **Freq:** Weekly (Thurs.). **Print Method:** Offset. **Trim Size:** 14 1/2 x 24 1/2. **Cols./Page:** 6. **Col. Width:** 12 picas. **Col. Depth:** 194 agate lines. **Key Personnel:** Joe Awad, Editor; Tom Brooker, Publisher. **ISSN:** 4044--0000 (print). **Subscription Rates:** $21 Individuals online only ; $21 Individuals print and online; $26.25 Individuals in state or Harrison, Ohio (print and online); $38.75 Out of state. **URL:** http://www.theohiocountynews.com. **Remarks:** Accepts advertising. **Circ:** (Not Reported).

12112 ■ Rising Sun Recorder
Register Publications
126 W High St.
Lawrenceburg, IN 47025
Phone: (812)537-0063
Fax: (812)537-5576
Community newspaper. **Freq:** Weekly (Thurs.). **Print Method:** Offset. **Trim Size:** 14 1/2 x 24 1/2. **Cols./Page:** 6. **Col. Width:** 12 6/10 picas. **Col. Depth:** 294 agate lines. **Key Personnel:** Tim Hillman, Editor. **ISSN:** 4665--2000 (print). **Subscription Rates:** $26 Individuals in state or Harrison, Ohio (print and online); $38.75 Out of state print and online; $21 Individuals online only ; $21 Individuals in Ohio County (print and online). **URL:** http://www.theohiocountynews.com. **Remarks:** Accepts advertising. **Circ:** (Not Reported).

12113 ■ WSCH-FM - 99.3
20 E High St.
Lawrenceburg, IN 47025
Phone: (812)537-0944
Fax: (812)537-5735
Email: info@eaglecountryonline.com
Format: Contemporary Country. **Networks:** CNN Radio. **Owner:** Wagon Wheel Broadcasting, 20 E High St., Lawrenceburg, IN 47025, Ph: (812)537-5735, Free: 888-537-9724. **Founded:** 1970. **Operating Hours:** 6 a.m.-10 p.m. **Wattage:** 3,000. **Ad Rates:** Advertising accepted; rates available upon request. **URL:** http://eaglecountryonline.com.

LEBANON

Boone Co. Boone Co. (C). 24 m NW of Indianapolis.

12114 ■ The Lebanon Reporter
The Lebanon Reporter
117 E Washington St.
Lebanon, IN 46052
Phone: (765)482-4650
Newspaper with a Republican orientation. **Freq:** Mon.-Sat. (eve.). **Print Method:** Offset. **Trim Size:** 14 x 22 3/4. **Cols./Page:** 6. **Col. Width:** 11 picas. **Col. Depth:** 294 agate lines. **Key Personnel:** Rod Rose, Assistant Managing Editor; Greta Sanderson, Publisher; Andrea Badger, Editor. **URL:** http://www.reporter.net. **Remarks:** Accepts advertising. **Circ:** (Not Reported).

LINTON

Greene Co. Greene Co. (SW). 10 m S of Worthington.

12115 ■ WYTJ 89.3 FM - 89.3
12970 W 500 N
Linton, IN 47441
Phone: (812)847-7442
Format: Religious. **URL:** http://www.wytj893fm.org.

LOGANSPORT

Cass Co. Cass Co. (NC). On Wabash and Eel Rivers, 70 m NW of Indianapolis.

12116 ■ Pharos-Tribune
Community Newspaper Holdings Inc.
517 E Broadway
Logansport, IN 46947
Phone: (574)722-5000
Fax: (574)732-5070
Newspaper serving the Logansport, Indiana area. **Freq:** Mon.-Sun. **Key Personnel:** Kim Dillon, General Manager; Kelly Hawes, Managing Editor; Judy Kercheval, Director, Advertising; Robyn McCloskey, Publisher. **Subscription Rates:** $155 Individuals carrier delivery. **URL:** http://www.pharostribune.com. **Mailing address:** PO Box 210, Logansport, IN 46947. **Remarks:** Accepts advertising. **Circ:** Mon.-Fri. ★**9722**, Sun. ★**9818**, Sat. ★**9113**.

12117 ■ WHZR-FM - 103.7
425 2nd St.
Logansport, IN 46947
Phone: (574)732-1037
Fax: (574)739-1037
Wattage: 6,000. **Mailing address:** PO Box 719, Logansport, IN 46947.

12118 ■ WLHM-FM - 102.3
425 2nd St.
Logansport, IN 46947
Phone: (574)722-4000
Owner: Logansport Radio Corp. **Founded:** 1965. **Formerly:** WSAL-FM. **Wattage:** 3,000 ERP. **Ad Rates:** Noncommercial. **Mailing address:** PO Box 719, Logansport, IN 46947.

12119 ■ WSAL-AM - 1230
425 2nd St.
Logansport, IN 46947
Phone: (574)739-1230
Fax: (574)722-4010
Format: Full Service. **Networks:** ABC. **Owner:** Logansport Radio Corp. **Founded:** 1949. **Operating Hours:** Continuous. **ADI:** Indianapolis (Marion), IN. **Key Personnel:** Dan Keister, Gen. Mgr., dan@midamericaradio.net; Lisa Keister, Traffic Mgr., lisa.keister@gmail.com; Lisa Downham, Account Exec., sales@midamericaradio.net. **Local Programs:** *Talk of the Town*, Monday Tuesday Wednesday Thursday Friday 8:00 a.m. - 9:00 a.m. **Wattage:** 1,000. **Ad Rates:** Noncommercial. Combined advertising rates available with WLHM-FM. **URL:** http://www.indianasbestradio.com/index-wsal.php.

LOOGOOTEE

Martin Co. Martin Co. (SW). 10 m NW of Shoals.

12120 ■ Loogootee Tribune
Loogootee Tribune
PO Box 277
Loogootee, IN 47553
Phone: (812)295-2500
Fax: (812)295-5221
Publisher's E-mail: advertising@loogooteetribune.com
Community newspaper. **Freq:** Weekly (Thurs.). **Cols./Page:** 6. **Col. Width:** 12 3/10 picas. **Col. Depth:** 21 inches. **Key Personnel:** Charlotte Winkler, Editor; Larry Hembree, Publisher. **Subscription Rates:** $26 Individuals Daviess Martin and Dubois counties; $52 Two years Daviess Martin and Dubois counties; $29 Out of area; $58 Out of area 2 years; $32 Out of state; $64 Out of state 2 years. **URL:** http://loogooteetribune.com. **Ad Rates:** GLR $2; PCI $2.50. **Remarks:** Advertising accepted; rates available upon request. **Circ:** 2,504.

LOWELL

Lake Co. Lake Co. (NW). 45 m SE of Chicago, Il. Manufactures asphalt felts and coatings, concrete blocks, septic tanks, electronic components. Sand and gravel pits. Hatchery; nursery. Agriculture. Dairy products.

12121 ■ The Lowell Tribune
Pilcher Publishing Company Inc.
116 Clark St.
Lowell, IN 46356
Newspaper with a Republican orientation. **Freq:** Weekly (Tues.). **Print Method:** Offset. **Cols./Page:** 8. **Col. Width:** 10 1/2 picas. **Col. Depth:** 21 inches. **Key Personnel:** Matt Pilcher, Publisher; Gary Pilcher, Director, Advertising. **URL:** http://www.thelowelltribune.com/29842/2044/1/the-lowell-tribunepdf. **Mailing address:** PO Box 248, Lowell, IN 46356. **Ad Rates:** BW $1,058.

40; PCI $6.30. **Remarks:** Accepts advertising. **Circ:** ‡4650.

12122 ■ WTMK-FM - 88.5
150 W Lincolnway, Ste. 150
Valparaiso, IN 46383
Phone: (219)548-5800
Fax: (219)548-5808
Email: info@calvaryradionetwork.com
Format: Religious. **Owner:** Calvary Radio Network Inc., 150 West Lincolnway Ste. 2001, Valparaiso, IN 46383, Ph: (219)548-5800, Fax: (219)548-5808. **Wattage:** 3,400. **URL:** http://calvaryradionetwork.com.

LYNNVILLE

12123 ■ Bonsai Journal
American Bonsai Society
PO Box 6
Lynnville, IN 47619
Phone: (812)922-5451
Trade journal covering bonsai. **Freq:** Quarterly. **Trim Size:** 8 x 11. **URL:** http://absbonsai.org. **Remarks:** Accepts advertising. **Circ:** (Not Reported).

MADISON

Jefferson Co. Jefferson Co. (SE). On Ohio River, 50 m NE of Louisville, Ky.

12124 ■ The Madison Courier
The Madison Courier
310 Courier Sq.
Madison, IN 47250
Phone: (812)265-3641
Fax: (812)273-6903
Free: 800-333-2885
Newspaper. **Freq:** Daily (eve.) and Sat. (morn.). **Print Method:** Offset. **Trim Size:** 13 3/4 x 22 3/4. **Cols./Page:** 6. **Col. Width:** 2 1/16 inches. **Col. Depth:** 21 1/2 inches. **ISSN:** 3250--0000 (print). **Subscription Rates:** $102.03 Individuals eCourier Only Subscribers 12 months; $52.62 Individuals eCourier Only Subscribers 6 months; $26.85 Individuals eCourier Only Subscribers 3 months; $8.95 Individuals eCourier Only Subscribers 1 month; $102.03 Individuals NEW Madison Courier Home Delivery 12 Months Print w/ eCourier(FREE); $52.62 Individuals NEW Madison Courier Home Delivery 6 Months Print; $26.85 Individuals NEW Madison Courier Home Delivery 3 Months Print; $8.95 Individuals NEW Madison Courier Home Delivery 1 Month Print; $12.95 Individuals NEW Madison Courier Mail Local 1 Month Print (Jeff & Switzerland, IN, Caroll & Trimble, KY); $31.95 Individuals NEW Madison Courier Mail Local 3 Months Print (Jeff & Switzerland, IN, Caroll & Trimble, KY); $59.95 Individuals NEW Madison Courier Mail Local 6 Months Print (Jeff & Switzerland, IN, Caroll & Trimble, KY); $110.95 Individuals NEW Madison Courier Mail Local 12 Months Print (Jeff & Switzerland, IN, Caroll & Trimble, KY); $110.95 Individuals NEW Madison Courier Mail Local 12 Months Print w/ eCourier(free) Jeff & Switzerland, IN, Caroll & Trimble, KY ; $12.95 Individuals NEW Mail Non Local 1 Month Print; $39.95 Individuals NEW Mail Non Local 3 Months Print; $71.95 Individuals NEW Mail Non Local 6 Months Print; $143.95 Individuals NEW Mail Non Local 12 Months Print w/ eCourier(FREE); $94.95 Students Student Mail per school year. **URL:** http://www.madisoncourier.com. **Remarks:** Accepts advertising. **Circ:** (Not Reported).

12125 ■ The Weekly Herald
The Madison Courier
310 Courier Sq.
Madison, IN 47250
Phone: (812)265-3641
Fax: (812)273-6903
Free: 800-333-2885
Community newspaper. **Founded:** 1837. **Freq:** Weekly (Fri.). **Print Method:** Offset. **Trim Size:** 13 3/4 x 22 3/4. **Cols./Page:** 6. **Col. Width:** 2 1/16 inches. **Col. Depth:** 21 1/2 inches. **Subscription Rates:** $17.28 Individuals; $21.84 Out of state; $33.48 Other countries. **URL:** http://www.madisoncourier.com. **Remarks:** Advertising not accepted. **Circ:** ‡386.

12126 ■ WORX-FM - 96.7
PO Box 95
Madison, IN 47250
Phone: (812)265-3322
Fax: (812)273-5509
Email: thebestmusic@worxradio.com
Format: Eclectic; Full Service. **Networks:** Independent; USA Radio; AP. **Owner:** Dubois County Broadcasting Inc., PO Box 1009, Jasper, IN 47547, Ph: (812)634-9232, Fax: (812)482-3696. **Founded:** 1950. **Operating Hours:** Continuous; 100% local. **Key Personnel:** Jesi Brooks, Account Exec., jbrooks@worxradio.com; Tim Torrance, Operations Mgr., timmyt@worxradio.com. **Local Programs:** *Morning Livestock Report*, Monday Tuesday Wednesday Thursday Friday 6:02 a.m.; *Indiana Report*, Monday Tuesday Wednesday Thursday Friday 6:05 a.m. - 6:08 a.m.; *Dairy Update*, Monday Tuesday Wednesday Thursday Friday 6:08 a.m. - 6:20 a.m.; *Local News & Weather Check*, Monday Tuesday Wednesday Thursday Friday 6:30 a.m. - 6:40 a.m.; *Commodity Report*, Monday Tuesday Wednesday Thursday Friday 6:40 a.m. - 6:50 a.m.; *American Countryside Report*, Monday Tuesday Wednesday Thursday Friday 8:05 a.m. 8:15 a.m.; *Rural Issues Forum...Farmbreak*, Monday Tuesday Wednesday Thursday Friday 12:02 p.m. - 12:30 p.m.; *Lunch Menu's...Carroll Co. & Trimble Co.*, Monday Tuesday Wednesday Thursday Friday 6:20 a.m. - 6:30 a.m.; *Retro All Request Lunch...Hits from the 60's & 70's*, Monday Tuesday Wednesday Thursday Friday 11:30 a.m. - 12:02 p.m. **Wattage:** 3,000. **Ad Rates:** $8. 25-16 for 30 seconds; $11.25-19 for 60 seconds. Combined advertising rates available with WXGO-AM. **URL:** http://www.worxradio.com.

12127 ■ WXGO-AM - 1270
PO Box 95
Madison, IN 47250
Phone: (812)265-3322
Fax: (812)273-5509
Email: thebestmusic@worxradio.com
Format: Oldies; Full Service. **Networks:** Independent; USA Radio; AP. **Owner:** Dubois County Broadcasting Inc., PO Box 1009, Jasper, IN 47547, Ph: (812)634-9232, Fax: (812)482-3696. **Founded:** 1956. **Formerly:** WORX-AM. **Operating Hours:** Continuous; 100% local. **Wattage:** 1,000. **Ad Rates:** $5.25-13 for 30 seconds; $7.25-15 for 60 seconds. Combined advertising rates available with WORX-FM. **URL:** http://www.worxradio.com.

MARION

Grant Co. Grant Co. (NEC). 60 m NE of Indianapolis. Marion College (Wes. Meth.); Taylor University.

12128 ■ Chronicle-Tribune
Gannett Company Inc.
610 S Adams St.
Marion, IN 46953
Phone: (765)664-5111
Free: 800-955-7888
General newspaper. **Founded:** 1867. **Freq:** Mon.-Sun. (morn.). **Print Method:** Offset. **Cols./Page:** 6. **Col. Width:** 25 nonpareils. **Col. Depth:** 300 agate lines. **Key Personnel:** David Penticuff, Editor, phone: (765)671-2250; Linda Kelsay, President, Publisher; Stan Howard, Director, Advertising. **Subscription Rates:** $10 Individuals monthly, online subscription; $110 Individuals /yr, online subscription; $2 daily, online subscription. **URL:** http://www.chronicle-tribune.com. **Ad Rates:** GLR $4. 38; BW $2,237; 4C $408; PCI $17.34; GLR $4.85; BW $2,396; 4C $408. **Remarks:** Accepts display and classified advertising. **Circ:** Mon.-Sat. ★**12043**, Sun. ★**14468**.

12129 ■ Bomar Broadcasting Company-Marion
820 S Pennsylvania St.
Marion, IN 46953
Phone: (765)664-7396
Owner: Mid America Broadcasting, at above address. **Founded:** 1948. **Ad Rates:** Noncommercial. **URL:** http://860espn.com.

12130 ■ Bright House Networks
2923 S Western Ave.
Marion, IN 46953
Phone: (317)972-9700
Email: customersupport.indiana@mybrighthouse.com
Cities Served: Gas City, Jonesboro, Indiana: subscribing households 16,100; 65 channels; 1 community access channel; 30 hours per week community access programming. **URL:** http://www.brighthouse.com.

12131 ■ WBAT-AM - 1400
820 South Pennsylvania St.
Marion, IN 46953
Phone: (765)664-6239
Fax: (765)662-0730
Format: Oldies; Sports; News. **Networks:** CBS; ESPN Radio. **Owner:** Hoosier AM/FM, at above address. **Founded:** 1947. **Operating Hours:** Continuous. **ADI:** Indianapolis (Marion), IN. **Wattage:** 1,000. **Ad Rates:** Advertising accepted; rates available upon request. Combined advertising rates available with WCJC-FM. **URL:** http://www.wbat.com.

12132 ■ WBSW-FM - 90.1
Ball State University
2000 W University Ave.
Muncie, IN 47306
Phone: (765)289-1241
Free: 800-382-8540
Format: Public Radio. **Ad Rates:** Noncommercial. **URL:** http://www.cms.bsu.edu.

12133 ■ WCJC-FM - 99.3
820 S Pennsylvania St.
Marion, IN 46953
Phone: (765)664-6239
Fax: (765)662-0730
Format: Country. **Networks:** ABC. **Founded:** 1989. **ADI:** Indianapolis (Marion), IN. **Key Personnel:** Jim Brunner, Contact, jimmyb@wbat.com; Patti Sevier, Contact, pdsvr@wcjc.com. **Wattage:** 3,000 ERP. **Ad Rates:** Advertising accepted; rates available upon request. Combined advertising rates available with WBAT. **URL:** http://www.wcjc.com.

12134 ■ WIWU-FM - 94.3
4201 S Washington St.
Marion, IN 46953
Phone: (765)468-6498
Email: 94.3@indwes.edu
Format: Contemporary Christian; Religious. **Owner:** Indiana Wesleyan University, 4201 S Washington St., Marion, IN 46953, Ph: (866)468-6498. **URL:** http://wiwu.fm.

12135 ■ WIWU-TV - 51
4201 S Washington St.
Marion, IN 46953
Phone: (765)677-2775
Format: News; Sports; Religious. **Owner:** Indiana Wesleyan University, 4201 S Washington St., Marion, IN 46953, Ph: (866)468-6498. **Operating Hours:** Continuous. **ADI:** Indianapolis (Marion), IN. **Wattage:** 1,450 ERP. **URL:** http://www.wiwutv51.com.

12136 ■ WMRI-AM - 860
820 S Pennsylvania Ave.
Marion, IN 46952
Free: 800-765-1069
Format: Talk; News; Sports. **Networks:** Network Indiana. **Founded:** 1955. **Formerly:** WGOM-AM. **Operating Hours:** Continuous; 75% network, 25% local. **ADI:** Indianapolis (Marion), IN. **Wattage:** 1,000. **Ad Rates:** Noncommercial. Combined advertising rates available with WMRI-FM. **URL:** http://www.wmri.com.

12137 ■ WSOT-TV - 27
2172 W Chapel Pke.
Marion, IN 46952
Phone: (765)664-3047
Owner: Sunnycrest Baptist Church, 2172 W Chapel Pk., Marion, IN 46952, Ph: (765)664-3047 , Fax: (765)671-2151. **ADI:** Indianapolis (Marion), IN. **Key Personnel:** Angela Stepp, Sales Mgr., sales@wsot-tv.com; Jason Stepp, Operations Mgr., operations@wsot-tv.com; Floyd Broegman, Dir. of Programs, traffic@wsot-tv.com. **URL:** http://sunnycrest.weebly.com/wsot-tv.html.

MARTINSVILLE

Morgan Co. Morgan Co. (C). 30 m SW of Indianapolis. Manufactures, electronic equipment, industrial gratings, motorcycle farings, formed packaging, aircraft components; goldfish hatcheries; timber. Grain farms. Wheat, corn, oats, soybeans.

12138 ■ Camping Magazine
American Camp Association
5000 State Road 67 N
Martinsville, IN 46151-7902
Phone: (765)342-8456

Circulation: ★ = AAM; △ or • = BPA; ♦ = CAC; ❑ = VAC; ⊕ = PO Statement; ‡ = Publisher's Report; Boldface figures = sworn; Light figures = estimated.

Fax: (765)342-2065
Free: 800-428-2267
Publication E-mail: magazine@aca-camps.org
Magazine on organized camp management. **Founded:** Feb. 1926. **Freq:** Bimonthly. **Print Method:** Offset. **Trim Size:** 8 1/2 x 11. **Cols./Page:** 3. **Col. Width:** 13 picas. **Col. Depth:** 9 1/4 inches. **USPS:** 074-041. **Subscription Rates:** $29.95 Individuals U.S. mainland; $56 Two years U.S. mainland; $48 Individuals Alaska, Hawaii, Puerto Rico; Canada & Mexico; $92 Two years Alaska, Hawaii, Puerto Rico; Canada & Mexico; $54 Other countries; $104 Other countries 2 years; Included in membership. **URL:** http://www.acacamps.org/camping-magazine. **Ad Rates:** 4C $2,673. **Remarks:** Advertising accepted; rates available upon request. **Circ:** Combined 7000.

12139 ■ The Times
Reporter-Times Inc.
PO Box 1636
Martinsville, IN 46151
Phone: (765)342-3311
Fax: (765)342-1446
Free: 800-804-8420
Community newspaper. **Freq:** Semiweekly (Wed. and Sat.). **Print Method:** Offset. **Trim Size:** 13 x 21. **Cols./Page:** 6. **Col. Width:** 27 nonpareils. **Col. Depth:** 301 agate lines. **USPS:** 362-360. **Subscription Rates:** $208.80 Individuals mail delivery; $112.80 Individuals home delivery. **URL:** http://www.reporter-times.com. **Remarks:** Accepts advertising. **Circ:** (Not Reported).

12140 ■ WCBK-FM - 102.3
1639 Burton Ln.
Martinsville, IN 46151
Phone: (765)342-3394
Fax: (765)342-5020
Format: Country. **Simulcasts:** WMCB-AM. **Networks:** USA Radio. **Owner:** Mid America Radio Group, 1639 Burton Ln., Martinsville, IN 46151. **Founded:** 1968. **Operating Hours:** Continuous. **Key Personnel:** Steve Vail, News Dir., stevevail@wcbk.com; John Taylor, Dir. of Operations, john@wcbk.com. **Wattage:** 6,000. **Ad Rates:** $12-20 for 30 seconds; $17-25 for 60 seconds. **URL:** http://wcbk.com.

12141 ■ WMCB-AM - 1540
1639 Burton Ln.
Martinsville, IN 46151
Format: Country. **Simulcasts:** WCBK-FM. **Networks:** USA Radio. **Owner:** Rodgers Broadcasting Corp., 2301 W Main St., Richmond, IN 47374, Ph: (765)962-6533. **Founded:** 1967. **Operating Hours:** Sunrise-sunset. **Key Personnel:** David Rodgers, Gen. Mgr. **Wattage:** 500.

MENTONE

12142 ■ Rotorcraft
Popular Rotorcraft Association
12296 West 600 South
Mentone, IN 46539
Phone: (574)353-7227
Fax: (574)353-7021
Publisher's E-mail: prahq@medt.com
Magazine focusing on private rotorcraft flying. **Freq:** 9/year. **Print Method:** Offset. **Trim Size:** 8 1/2 x 11. **Cols./Page:** 3. **Col. Width:** 2 5/16 INS. **Col. Depth:** 7 1/4 INS. **Key Personnel:** Paul Bergen Abbott, Editor. **ISSN:** 0032--4620 (print). **Subscription Rates:** Included in membership; $49.95 U.S. print - annual; $74 Other countries print - annual. **Alt. Formats:** PDF. **URL:** http://www.pra.org/default.aspx?p=EZinePage&i=5. **Formerly:** Popular Rotorcraft Flying. **Ad Rates:** BW $960; PCI $32. **Remarks:** Accepts advertising. **Circ:** ‡4600, 4000.

MERRILLVILLE

Lake Co. Lake Co. (NW). 10 m S of Gary. Residential.

12143 ■ Northwest Indiana Catholic
Northwest Indiana Catholic
9292 Broadway
Merrillville, IN 46410-7047
Phone: (219)769-9292
Fax: (219)738-9034
Publication E-mail: nwic@dcgary.org
Official newspaper of the Diocese of Gary. **Freq:** Weekly. **Print Method:** Offset. **Cols./Page:** 6. **Col. Width:** 1 1/2 inches. **Col. Depth:** 224 agate lines. **Key Personnel:** Steve Euvino, General Manager, Managing Editor; Carol Macinga, Manager, Circulation. **USPS:** 403-670. **Subscription Rates:** $26 Individuals parish and non-parish affiliated; $13 Students partial subscription only. **Ad Rates:** BW $58; 4C $125; PCI $10.14. **Remarks:** Accepts advertising. **Circ:** Paid ‡40000.

12144 ■ WYIN-TV - 56
8625 Indiana Pl.
Merrillville, IN 46410
Phone: (219)756-5656
Fax: (219)755-4312
Email: info@lakeshorepublicmedia.org
Format: Public TV. **Networks:** Public Broadcasting Service (PBS). **Owner:** Northwest Indiana Public Television Inc., at above address. **Founded:** 1987. **Operating Hours:** 6:00 a.m.-12 a.m. **ADI:** Chicago (LaSalle), IL. **Key Personnel:** Joe Arredondo, Sports Dir.; Matt Franklin, Production Mgr. **Wattage:** 1,350,000. **Ad Rates:** Noncommercial. **URL:** http://www.lakeshorepublicmedia.org.

12145 ■ WZVN-FM - 107.1
8105 Georgia St.
Merrillville, IN 46410-6224
Phone: (219)738-1071
Fax: (219)736-6411
Owner: M&M Broadcasting, 6405 Olcott, Hammond, IN 46323. **Founded:** 1972. **Formerly:** WLCL-FM. **Wattage:** 2,650 ERP. **Ad Rates:** $30-35 for 30 seconds; $38-43 for 60 seconds. **URL:** http://www.calunet.com/biz/wzvw.

MICHIGAN CITY

La Porte Co. La Porte Co. (NW). On Lake Michigan, 50 m SE of Chicago, Ill. Beach resort. Fisheries. Indiana State Prison. Lake commerce.

12146 ■ The Beacher
The Beacher
911 Franklin St.
Michigan City, IN 46360
Phone: (219)879-0088
Fax: (219)879-8070
Publisher's E-mail: beacher@thebeacher.com
Newspaper covering news and events in southwestern Michigan and northern Indiana. **Freq:** Weekly (Wed.). **Subscription Rates:** Free. **Alt. Formats:** PDF. **URL:** http://www.thebeacher.com. **Ad Rates:** BW $235. **Remarks:** Accepts advertising. **Circ:** 4000.

12147 ■ The News-Dispatch
Nixon Newspapers Inc.
121 W Michigan Blvd.
Michigan City, IN 46360
Phone: (219)874-7211
Free: 800-489-9292
Publication E-mail: news@thenewsdispatch.com
General newspaper. **Freq:** Daily (eve.). **Print Method:** Offset. **Trim Size:** 13 7/8 x 21 3/4. **Cols./Page:** 6. **Col. Width:** 25 nonpareils. **Col. Depth:** 300 agate lines. **Key Personnel:** Adam Parkhouse, Managing Editor, phone: (219)214-4171; Chris Schable, Executive Editor. **URL:** http://www.thenewsdispatch.com. **Remarks:** Accepts advertising. **Circ:** (Not Reported).

12148 ■ WEFM-FM - 95.9
1903 Springland Ave.
Michigan City, IN 46360
Phone: (219)879-8201
Fax: (219)879-8202
Email: wefmr@yahoo.com
Format: Adult Contemporary; Oldies. **Networks:** Network Indiana. **Owner:** Michigan City FM Broadcasting Inc., 1903 Springland Ave., Michigan City, IN 46360-2644, Ph: (219)879-8201. **Founded:** 1966. **Formerly:** WMCB-FM. **Operating Hours:** Continuous; 2% network, 98% local. **Wattage:** 3,000. **Ad Rates:** Noncommercial.

12149 ■ WIMS-AM - 1420
685 E 1675 N
Michigan City, IN 46360
Phone: (219)879-9810
Fax: (219)879-9813
Format: Talk; News. **Networks:** CNN Radio; Westwood One Radio. **Owner:** Vazquez Development L.L.C., 6405 Olcott St., Hammond, IN 46320, Ph: (219)844-1416. **Founded:** 1947. **Operating Hours:** Continuous. **ADI:** South Bend-Elkhart, IN. **Key Personnel:** Ric Federighi, Gen. Mgr., ric@wimsradio.com; Johnny Rush, Dir. of Programs, rush@wimsradio.com. **Local Programs:** *Mornings with Ric Federighi*, Monday Tuesday Wednesday Thursday Friday 6:00 a.m. - 9:00 a.m.; *Live and Local*, Sunday Monday Tuesday Wednesday Thursday Friday Saturday; *Into the Outdoors*, Thursday 7:00 p.m.; *Steve Dale's Pet World*, Sunday 8:00 a.m. - 9:00 a.m.; *Free Talk Live*, Monday Tuesday Wednesday Thursday Friday Saturday 12:00 a.m. - 3:00 a.m.; *Meet the Press*, Sunday; *The Wall St. Journal*, Monday Tuesday Wednesday Thursday Friday Saturday 4:00 a.m. - 6:00 a.m.; *Into the 70's with John Landecker*, Saturday 8:00 p.m. - 11:00 p.m.; *View-points/Radio Health Journal*, Sunday 5:00 a.m. - 6:00 a.m.; *Randy Jackson's Hit List*, Saturday 5:00 p.m. - 9:00 p.m. **Wattage:** 5,000. **Ad Rates:** Advertising accepted; rates available upon request. WJOB Hammond, IN. **URL:** http://www.wimsradio.com.

MIDDLEBURY

Elkhart Co. Elkhart Co. (N). 12 m E of Elkart.

12150 ■ Middlebury Independent
Largrange Publishing Company Inc.
100 S State Rd. 9
Middlebury, IN 46540-0068
Phone: (260)463-2166
Fax: (260)463-2734
Free: 800-552-2404
Publisher's E-mail: website@lagrangepublishing.com
Newspaper with a Democratic orientation. **Freq:** Weekly (Wed.). **Print Method:** Offset. **Cols./Page:** 6. **Col. Width:** 19 nonpareils. **Col. Depth:** 203 agate lines. **Subscription Rates:** $20 Individuals. **URL:** http://www.lagrangepublishing.com. **Mailing address:** PO Box 148, Middlebury, IN 46540-0068. **Ad Rates:** GLR $.20; SAU $2.35; PCI $2.25. **Remarks:** Advertising accepted; rates available upon request. **Circ:** 780.

MILFORD

Kosciusko Co. Kosciusko Co. (N). 13 m S of Goshen. Lake resort.--Manufactures trailers, feedbins, poultry equipment. Diversified farming. Corn, wheat, oats.

12151 ■ The Mail-Journal
The Papers Inc.
206 S Main St.
Milford, IN 46542-3004
Phone: (574)658-4111
Free: 800-733-4111
Community newspaper with a Democratic orientation. **Freq:** Weekly (Wed.). **Print Method:** Offset. **Trim Size:** 15 x 22 3/4. **Cols./Page:** 7. **Col. Width:** 11 picas. **Col. Depth:** 21 1/2 inches. **Key Personnel:** Jeri Seely, Editor-in-Chief. **USPS:** 325-840. **Subscription Rates:** $1 Single issue; $40 Individuals in Kosciusko; $51 Out of area; $60 Out of state out of country (USA); $30 Individuals online only. **URL:** http://www.the-papers.com/publication.aspx?pub=mailjournal. **Mailing address:** PO Box 188, Milford, IN 46542-0188. **Remarks:** Advertising accepted; rates available upon request. **Circ:** 2350, 2700.

12152 ■ The Paper Elkhart County Edition
The Papers Inc.
206 S Main St.
Milford, IN 46542-3004
Phone: (574)658-4111
Free: 800-733-4111
Newspaper. **Freq:** Weekly (Tues.). **Print Method:** Offset. **Trim Size:** 11 3/8 x 16 3/4. **Cols./Page:** 5. **Col. Width:** 11 picas. **Col. Depth:** 16 inches. **Key Personnel:** Jeri Seely, Editor-in-Chief. **Subscription Rates:** Free. **URL:** http://www.the-papers.com/publication.aspx?pub=thepaper. **Mailing address:** PO Box 188, Milford, IN 46542-0188. **Ad Rates:** BW $680; 4C $730; PCI $10.25. **Remarks:** Accepts advertising. **Circ:** ♦29100.

12153 ■ The Paper Kosciusko County Edition
The Papers Inc.
206 S Main St.
Milford, IN 46542
Phone: (574)658-4111
Free: 800-733-4111
Free newspaper. **Freq:** Weekly (Tues.). **Print Method:** Offset. **Trim Size:** 11 3/8 x 16 3/4. **Cols./Page:** 5. **Col. Width:** 22 nonpareils. **Col. Depth:** 224 agate lines. **Key Personnel:** Jeri Seely, Editor; Ron Baumgartner, General Manager; Kip Schumm, Publisher. **Subscription Rates:** Free. **URL:** http://www.the-papers.com/

publication.aspx?pub=thepaper. **Ad Rates:** BW $496; 4C $744; PCI $7.85. **Remarks:** Advertising accepted; rates available upon request. **Circ:** 22350.

12154 ■ Senior Life Allen County Edition
The Papers Inc.
206 S Main St.
Milford, IN 46542-3004
Phone: (574)658-4111
Free: 800-733-4111
News magazine serving adults 50 and older in Fort Wayne and surrounding communities. **Freq:** Monthly. **Print Method:** Web. **Trim Size:** 11 3/8 x 16 3/4. **Cols./Page:** 5. **Col. Width:** 11 picas. **Col. Depth:** 16 inches. **Key Personnel:** Lauren Zeugner, Associate Editor; Deb Patterson, Associate Editor; Vicky Howell, Director, Publications. **Subscription Rates:** $30 Individuals; $54 Two years. **URL:** http://www.the-papers.com/publication.aspx?pub=seniorlife. **Mailing address:** PO Box 188, Milford, IN 46542-0188. **Ad Rates:** BW $1,256; 4C $1,401; PCI $15.70. **Remarks:** Accepts advertising. **Circ:** ♦**24500.**

12155 ■ Senior Life St. Joseph Edition
The Papers Inc.
206 S Main St.
Milford, IN 46542-3004
Phone: (574)658-4111
Free: 800-733-4111
News magazine serving adults 50 and older in St. Joseph county and surrounding communities. **Freq:** Monthly. **Print Method:** Web. **Trim Size:** 11 3/8 x 16 3/4. **Cols./Page:** 5. **Col. Width:** 11 picas. **Col. Depth:** 16 inches. **Key Personnel:** Vicky Howell, Director, Publications. **Subscription Rates:** $30 Individuals; $54 Two years. **URL:** http://seniorlifenewspapers.com. **Mailing address:** PO Box 188, Milford, IN 46542-0188. **Ad Rates:** BW $1,184; 4C $1,380; PCI $14.80. **Remarks:** Accepts advertising. **Circ:** 149950.

MISHAWAKA

St. Joseph Co. St. Joseph Co. (N). On St. Joseph River, at head of navigation adjacent to South Bend. Manufactures guided missiles, rubberized canvas, woolen and leather footwear, foam rubber cushions and mattresses, raincoats, foundry supplies, military vehicles, and equipment, concrete sewer and drain pipes.

12156 ■ The Interior Journal
Schurz Communications Inc.
1301 E Douglas Rd.
Mishawaka, IN 46545
Phone: (574)247-7237
Publisher's E-mail: info@schurz.com
Community newspaper. **Freq:** Weekly (Thurs.). **Print Method:** Offset. **Cols./Page:** 6. **Col. Width:** 24 nonpareils. **Col. Depth:** 294 agate lines. **Key Personnel:** Gina Cooper, Office Manager. **USPS:** 929-840. **Subscription Rates:** Included in membership. **URL:** http://www.centralkynews.com/theinteriorjournal. **Ad Rates:** BW $535.50; 4C $785; SAU $4.25; PCI $3.85. **Remarks:** Accepts advertising. **Circ:** 3416.

12157 ■ South Bend Tribune
Schurz Communications Inc.
1301 E Douglas Rd.
Mishawaka, IN 46545
Phone: (574)247-7237
Publisher's E-mail: subscriberservices@sbtinfo.com
General newspaper. **Freq:** Daily. **Print Method:** Offset. **Trim Size:** 13 1/2 x 22. **Cols./Page:** 6. **Col. Width:** 2 1/16 inches. **Col. Depth:** 294 agate lines. **USPS:** 501-980. **Subscription Rates:** $13 Individuals daily (print); $13 Individuals daily (online); $7.80 Individuals Weekend all access; $6.50 Individuals Sunday all access. **URL:** http://www.southbendtribune.com. **Ad Rates:** BW $8,568; 4C $9,668; PCI $68. **Remarks:** Accepts advertising. **Circ:** ***62000**, ***80000**.

12158 ■ AT & T Broadband
6501 N Grape Rd., Ste. 564b
Mishawaka, IN 46545
Fax: (574)243-8069
Owner: AT & T Communications Inc., 5098 S Federal Blvd., Englewood, CO 80110, Ph: (303)267-5500, Fax: (303)779-1228. **Founded:** 1968. **Formerly:** Valley Cable; Indiana Cablevision; Heritage Cablevision. **Cities Served:** Elkhart, Goshen, Mishawaka, Osceola, Plymouth, Rochester, South Bend, Indiana; Edwardsburg, Edwardsburg, Michigan: subscribing households 80,000; 42 channels; 1 community access channel; 39 hours per week community access programming. **URL:** http://www.att.com.

12159 ■ WAOR-FM - 95.3
245 W Edison Rd., Ste. 250
Mishawaka, IN 46545
Phone: (574)258-5483
Fax: (574)258-0930
Format: Classic Rock. **Founded:** 1957. **Operating Hours:** Continuous. **ADI:** South Bend-Elkhart, IN. **Wattage:** 3,300. **Ad Rates:** Noncommercial. $45-70 per unit. Combined advertising rates available with WNIL-AM. **URL:** http://www.waor.com.

12160 ■ WBND-TV - 57
3665 Park Pl. W
Mishawaka, IN 46545
Phone: (574)243-4316
Fax: (574)243-4326
URL: http://www.abc57.com.

12161 ■ WBYT-FM - 100.7
237 Edison Rd.
Mishawaka, IN 46545
Phone: (574)258-5483
Fax: (574)258-0930
Free: 888-817-2100
Format: Country. **Networks:** ABC. **Owner:** Pathfinders Communication Corp. **Founded:** 1947. **Formerly:** WYEZ-FM; WLTA-FM. **Operating Hours:** Continuous. **ADI:** South Bend-Elkhart, IN. **Key Personnel:** Jesse Garcia, Dir. of Programs, jesse@b100.com. **Wattage:** 50,000 ERP. **Ad Rates:** $85-120 for 30 seconds; $85-120 for 60 seconds. **URL:** http://www.b100.com.

12162 ■ WCWW-TV - 25
3665 Park Pl. W
Mishawaka, IN 46545
Phone: (574)243-4321
Fax: (574)243-4326

12163 ■ WMYS-TV - 69
3665 Park Pl. W
Mishawaka, IN 46545
Phone: (574)243-4316
Fax: (574)243-4326
Founded: 1962. **Key Personnel:** Jeff Guy, Gen. Mgr.; Josh Bramer, Sales Mgr. **URL:** http://www.mymichianatv.com.

12164 ■ WNIL-AM - 1290
237 W Edison Rd.
Mishawaka, IN 46545
Phone: (574)258-5483
Fax: (574)258-0930
Format: News; Talk. **Networks:** Mutual Broadcasting System; Jones Satellite. **Owner:** Federated Media, at above address. **Founded:** 1956. **Operating Hours:** 6 a.m.-6 p.m., winter; Sunrise-sunset, summer; 80% network, 20% local. **ADI:** South Bend-Elkhart, IN. **Key Personnel:** Brad Williams, Gen. Mgr., bwilliams@federatedmedia.com; Stephanie Michel, Contact, smichel@federatedmedia.com; Stephanie Michel, Contact, smichel@federatedmedia.com. **Wattage:** 500. **Ad Rates:** $10-20 for 60 seconds. WAOR-FM.

12165 ■ WNSN-FM - 101.5
1301 E Douglas Rd.
Mishawaka, IN 46545
Email: info@schurz.com
Format: Adult Contemporary. **Networks:** Independent. **Owner:** Schurz Communications Inc., 1301 E Douglas Rd., Mishawaka, IN 46545, Ph: (574)247-7237. **Founded:** 1962. **Operating Hours:** Continuous. **ADI:** South Bend-Elkhart, IN. **Key Personnel:** Chief Jim Roberts, Contact, roberts@sunny1015.com; Jim Roberts, Contact, roberts@sunny1015.com. **Wattage:** 13,000. **Ad Rates:** Noncommercial. Combined advertising rates available with WSBT, WZOC, WHFB. **URL:** http://www.schurz.com.

12166 ■ WRBR-FM - 103.9
237 W Edison Rd.
Mishawaka, IN 46545
Phone: (574)258-5483
Fax: (574)258-0930
Format: Classic Rock; Album-Oriented Rock (AOR). **Networks:** Independent. **Owner:** WRBR Radio, 237 W Edison Rd., Mishawaka, IN 46545, Ph: (574)258-5483, Fax: (317)258-0930. **Founded:** 1964. **Operating Hours:** Continuous; 100% local. **Key Personnel:** Clint Marsh, Gen. Mgr., cmarsh@federatedmedia.com; Francine Whiteford, Gen. Sales Mgr., fwhiteford@wrbr.com; Brad Williams, Gen. Mgr., bwilliams@federatedmedia.com. **Wattage:** 3,000. **Ad Rates:** $40-52 per unit. **URL:** http://www.wrbr.com.

12167 ■ WSBT-AM - 960
1301 E Douglas Rd.
Mishawaka, IN 46545
Phone: (574)233-3141
Fax: (574)239-4231
Email: sales@wsbt.com
Format: News. **Networks:** CBS. **Owner:** Schurz Communications Inc., 1301 E Douglas Rd., Mishawaka, IN 46545, Ph: (574)247-7237. **Founded:** Apr. 1922. **Operating Hours:** Continuous. **ADI:** South Bend-Elkhart, IN. **Key Personnel:** Bill Gamble, Operations Mgr., bgamble@wsbt.com; Bob Montgomery, News Dir., Program Mgr., montgom@wsbt.com. **Local Programs:** *Week Day Sports Beat,* Monday Tuesday Wednesday Thursday Friday 6:00 a.m. - 8:00 a.m. **Wattage:** 5,000. **Ad Rates:** Noncommercial. WNSN, WZOC, WHFB. **URL:** http://www.wsbt.com.

12168 ■ WSBT-TV - 22
1301 E Douglas Rd.
Mishawaka, IN 46545
Phone: (574)233-3141
Fax: (574)288-6630
Email: wsbtnews@wsbt.com
Format: Commercial TV. **Networks:** CBS. **Owner:** Schurz Communications Inc., 1301 E Douglas Rd., Mishawaka, IN 46545, Ph: (574)247-7237. **Founded:** 1952. **Operating Hours:** Continuous; 60% network, 40% local. **ADI:** South Bend-Elkhart, IN. **Key Personnel:** Bob Johnson, Dir. of Operations, Prog. Dir., johnson@wsbt.com. **Wattage:** 4,790 KW. **Ad Rates:** Advertising accepted; rates available upon request. **URL:** http://www.wsbt.com.

MONTICELLO

White Co. White Co. (EC). 25 m NNE of Lafayette. Resort.

12169 ■ Monticello Herald Journal
Monticello Herald Journal
114 S Main St.
Monticello, IN 47960
Phone: (574)583-5121
Fax: (574)583-4241
Free: 800-541-7906
Publication E-mail: editor@thehj.com
Local newspaper. **Freq:** Mon.-Sat. (morn.). **Print Method:** Offset. **Trim Size:** 13 x 21 1/2. **Cols./Page:** 6. **Col. Width:** 2 1/16 inches. **Col. Depth:** 21 1/2 inches. **Key Personnel:** Karen Franscoviak, General Manager; Trent Wright, Editor. **Subscription Rates:** $120 Individuals /year in county; $145 Individuals /year out of county. **URL:** http://www.newsbug.info/monticello_herald_journal. **Remarks:** Accepts advertising. **Circ:** (Not Reported).

12170 ■ WMRS-FM - 107.7
132 N Main St.
Monticello, IN 47960
Phone: (574)583-8933
Fax: (574)583-8933
Email: brandi@wmrsradio.com
Format: Adult Contemporary. **Founded:** 1989. **Ad Rates:** Noncommercial. **URL:** http://www.wmrsradio.com.

MOUNT VERNON

Posey Co. Posey Co. (SW). On Ohio River, 20 m W of Evansville. Manufactures polycarbonates, hospital & industrial gases, roofing products, handles, flour, machinery, corn products, petroleum terminal and refinery. Agriculture. wheat, corn, hay.

12171 ■ Mount Vernon Democrat
Landmark Community Newspapers L.L.C.
231 A Main St.
Mount Vernon, IN 47620-0767
Phone: (812)838-4811
Publisher's E-mail: marketing@lcni.com

Circulation: * = AAM; △ or • = BPA; ♦ = CAC; ❑ = VAC; ⊕ = PO Statement; ‡ = Publisher's Report; Boldface figures = sworn; Light figures = estimated.

Newspaper with a Democratic orientation. **Freq:** Weekly (Wed.). **Print Method:** Offset. **Cols./Page:** 6. **Col. Width:** 24 nonpareils. **Col. Depth:** 287 agate lines. **URL:** http://www.lcni.com/properties/indiana/mt_vernon.htm. **Mailing address:** PO Box 767, Mount Vernon, IN 47620-0767. **Remarks:** Accepts advertising. **Circ:** (Not Reported).

12172 ■ WRCY-AM1590 - 1590
7109 Upton Rd.
Mount Vernon, IN 47620
Phone: (812)838-4484
Fax: (812)882-7770
Format: Country. **Owner:** The Original Co., Vincennes, IN 47591. **Key Personnel:** Mark Lange, President. **Mailing address:** PO Box 242, Vincennes, IN 47591. **URL:** http://www.originalcompany.com.

MUNCIE

Delaware Co. Delaware Co. (NE). On White River, 54 m NE of Indianapolis. Ball State University. Manufactures auto parts and accessories, fencing, bottles, malleable castings, auto batteries, wire structural steel, electrical goods, lawn mowers, metal furniture, screw machine, industrial transformer products, auto transmissions, jet engine parts.

12173 ■ American Journal of Business
Ball State University
2000 W University Ave.
Muncie, IN 47306
Phone: (765)289-1241
Free: 800-382-8540
Publisher's E-mail: askus@bsu.edu
Journal informing business professionals about recent research developments and their practical implications. **Freq:** Semiannual September and March. **Trim Size:** 8 1/2 x 11. **Cols./Page:** 2. **Col. Width:** 3 3/8 INS. **Col. Depth:** 9 1/8 INS. **Key Personnel:** Ashok Gupta, PhD, Editor-in-Chief. **ISSN:** 1935--5181 (print). **URL:** http://www.emeraldinsight.com/journal/ajb; http://cms.bsu.edu/academics/collegesanddepartments/mcob/rankingsandrecognitions/ajb. **Formerly:** Mid-American Journal of Business. **Circ:** (Not Reported).

12174 ■ American Journal of Business
Ball State University Bureau of Business Research
Whitinger Business Bldg., Rm. 149
2000 W University Ave.
Muncie, IN 47306
Phone: (765)285-5926
Fax: (765)285-8024
Publisher's E-mail: askus@bsu.edu
Journal informing business professionals about recent research developments and their practical implications. **Freq:** Semiannual September and March. **Trim Size:** 8 1/2 x 11. **Cols./Page:** 2. **Col. Width:** 3 3/8 INS. **Col. Depth:** 9 1/8 INS. **Key Personnel:** Ashok Gupta, PhD, Editor-in-Chief. **ISSN:** 1935--5181 (print). **URL:** http://www.emeraldinsight.com/journal/ajb; http://cms.bsu.edu/academics/collegesanddepartments/mcob/rankingsandrecognitions/ajb. **Formerly:** Mid-American Journal of Business. **Circ:** (Not Reported).

12175 ■ Ball State Daily News
Ball State University Daily News
Art and Journalism Bldg. 278
Muncie, IN 47306
Phone: (765)285-8255
Publication E-mail: advertisings@bsudailynew.com
Collegiate newspaper. **Founded:** Mar. 30, 1922. **Freq:** Daily (morn.). **Print Method:** Offset. **Trim Size:** 11.625 x 21 1/2. **Cols./Page:** 6. **Col. Width:** 1.833 inches. **Col. Depth:** 20.5 inches. **Key Personnel:** Benjamin Dashley, Editor-in-Chief. **USPS:** 144-360. **Subscription Rates:** $50 Individuals; $8 Individuals summer only; $24 Individuals semester. **URL:** http://www.bsudailynews.com. **Formerly:** DNA. **Ad Rates:** GLR $9.95; BW $1,223.85; SAU $9.95; PCI $335. **Remarks:** Accepts advertising. **Circ:** 14000.

12176 ■ Feedback
Broadcast Education Association
c/o Joe Misiewicz, Editor
Department of Telecommunications
Ball State University
Muncie, IN 47306
Publisher's E-mail: help@beaweb.org
Journal focusing on radio and TV broadcasting. **Founded:** 1959. **Freq:** Quarterly. **Print Method:** Offset. **Trim Size:** 6 X 9. **Cols./Page:** 1. **Col. Width:** 130 millimeters. **Col. Depth:** 182 millimeters. **Key Personnel:** Joe Misiewicz, Editor. **Alt. Formats:** PDF. **URL:** http://www.beaweb.org/feedback.html. **Ad Rates:** BW $50. **Remarks:** Accepts advertising. **Circ:** Paid ‡1,600, Non-paid ‡100.

12177 ■ LIT Journal
Lambda Iota Tau
Ball State University
Dept. of English
2000 W University Ave.
Muncie, IN 47306-0460
Phone: (765)285-8370
Fax: (765)285-3765
Publisher's E-mail: mcupchurch@bsu.edu
Freq: Annual. **Subscription Rates:** Included in membership. **Remarks:** Accepts advertising. **Circ:** 1100.

12178 ■ Model Aviation
Academy of Model Aeronautics
5161 E Memorial Dr.
Muncie, IN 47302
Fax: (765)289-4248
Free: 800-435-9262
Freq: Monthly. **URL:** http://www.modelaircraft.org/publications/ma.aspx. **Remarks:** Advertising not accepted. **Circ:** (Not Reported).

12179 ■ Psychology in the Schools
John Wiley & Sons Inc.
c/o David E. McIntosh, PhD, Editor
Department of Special Education
Ball State University
Teachers College Rm. 722
Muncie, IN 47306-1099
Phone: (765)285-5701
Fax: (765)285-4280
Publisher's E-mail: info@wiley.com
Peer-reviewed journal focusing on the use of psychology in schools. **Freq:** 10/year. **Print Method:** Offset. **Trim Size:** 7 1/4 x 10 1/4. **Cols./Page:** 1. **Col. Width:** 61 nonpareils. **Col. Depth:** 111 agate lines. **Key Personnel:** LeAdelle Phelps, PhD, Editor; David E. McIntosh, PhD, Editor. **ISSN:** 0033--3085 (print); **EISSN:** 1520--6807 (electronic). **Subscription Rates:** $136 Individuals online; $1060 Institutions print only; $1272 Institutions print with online; $105 Individuals print. **URL:** http://onlinelibrary.wiley.com/journal/10.1002/(ISSN)1520-6807. **Ad Rates:** BW $1241; 4C $1576. **Remarks:** Accepts advertising. **Circ:** (Not Reported).

12180 ■ The Star Press
Muncie Newspapers
345 S High
Muncie, IN 47305
Phone: (765)747-5754
Free: 800-783-7827
General newspaper. **Founded:** 1899. **Freq:** Mon.-Sun. (morn.). **Print Method:** Letterpress. **Cols./Page:** 6. **Col. Width:** 2 1/16 inches. **Col. Depth:** 22 inches. **Key Personnel:** Lisa Nellesen-Lara, Executive Editor, phone: (765)213-5840; Cheryl Lindus, Director, Advertising, phone: (765)213-5701. **Subscription Rates:** $21 Individuals daily; $14 Individuals Fri./Sun.; $12 Individuals Sundays only. **URL:** http://www.thestarpress.com. **Formerly:** The Muncie Star; The Muncie Evening Press. **Remarks:** Accepts advertising. **Circ:** Mon.-Sat. ***32049**, Sun. ***34091**.

12181 ■ Technology Interface: The electronic journal for engineering technology
Ball State University
2000 W University Ave.
Muncie, IN 47306
Phone: (765)289-1241
Free: 800-382-8540
Publisher's E-mail: askus@bsu.edu
Journal for the engineering technology profession serving education and industry. **Freq:** latest issue: 2009. **Key Personnel:** Philip David Weinsier, Editor; Michael Morrell, Associate Editor; Farrokh Attarzadeh, Associate Editor. **ISSN:** 1523--9926 (print). **Circ:** (Not Reported).

WBSB-FM - See Anderson

12182 ■ WBSH-FM - 91.1
2000 W University Ave.
Muncie, IN 47306
Phone: (765)285-5888
Fax: (765)285-8937
Free: 800-646-1812
Format: Public Radio. **Owner:** Ball State University, 2000 W University Ave., Muncie, IN 47306, Ph: (765)289-1241, Free: 800-382-8540. **Founded:** 1997. **Ad Rates:** Noncommercial. **URL:** http://indianapublicradio.org.

WBSJ-FM - See Portland

12183 ■ WBST-FM - 92.1
Ball State University
2000 W University Ave.
Muncie, IN 47306
Phone: (765)285-5888
Fax: (765)285-5548
Free: 800-382-8540
Format: Public Radio; Classical. **Networks:** National Public Radio (NPR). **Owner:** Ball State University, 2000 W University Ave., Muncie, IN 47306, Ph: (765)289-1241, Free: 800-382-8540. **Founded:** 1960. **Operating Hours:** Continuous; 60% network, 90% local. **Key Personnel:** Brian Beaver, Producer, Reporter, bmbeaver@bsu.edu; Brian Eckstein, Production Mgr., beckstein@bsu.edu; Marcus Jackman, Gen. Mgr., mjackman@bsu.edu; Terry Heifetz, News Dir., tjheifetz@bsu.edu; Angie Rapp, Mktg. Mgr., arapp@bsu.edu. **Wattage:** 3,000. **Ad Rates:** Noncommercial. WBSB, WBSJ, WBSH, WBSW. **URL:** http://www.bsu.edu/ipr.

WBSW-FM - See Marion

12184 ■ WHBU-AM - 1240
800 E 29th St.
Muncie, IN 47302
Phone: (765)288-4403
Fax: (765)288-0429
Format: Talk; News; Music of Your Life. **Simulcasts:** WHBU-FM. **Networks:** CBS; NBC. **Owner:** Backyard Broadcasting, 4237 Salisbury Rd., Ste. 225, Jacksonville, FL 32216, Ph: (904)674-0260, Fax: (904)854-4596. **Founded:** 1923. **Operating Hours:** Continuous; 5% network, 95% local. **Local Programs:** *Rush Limbaugh*, Monday Tuesday Wednesday Thursday Friday 12:00 p.m. - 3:00 p.m. **Wattage:** 700 Day; 700 Night. **Ad Rates:** Advertising accepted; rates available upon request. **URL:** http://www.1240whbu.com.

12185 ■ WIPB-TV - 49
2000 W University Ave.
Muncie, IN 47306
Phone: (765)285-1249
Fax: (765)285-5548
Free: 800-252-9472
Format: Public TV. **Networks:** Public Broadcasting Service (PBS). **Owner:** Ball State University, 2000 W University Ave., Muncie, IN 47306, Ph: (765)289-1241, Free: 800-382-8540. **Founded:** 1971. **Operating Hours:** Continuous. **ADI:** Indianapolis (Marion), IN. **Local Programs:** *Back to the Floor*, Friday 10:00 p.m.; *Aging Out*; *America at a Crossroads*; *Becoming American*; *Beyond the Border*; *Brothermen*; *Body & Soul*, Monday Tuesday Wednesday Thursday Friday 7:00 p.m. - 8:30 p.m.; *Flashpoints USA*; *Dragonfly TV*; *PBS Preview*; *Wild TV*, Thursday 8:00 p.m.; *Weekend Explorer*; *Walking the Bible*; *Wide Angle*; *Soundstage*; *Earth On Edge*; *At Close Range with National Geographic*, Monday; *California and the American Dream*, Thursday; *New Scandinavian Cooking With Andreas Viestad*, Friday Tuesday Monday Friday Saturday 7:00 p.m.; 1:00 p.m. 1:00 a.m. 7:00 a.m.; 1:00 p.m. 1:00 a.m.; 6:30 a.m.; 7:30 a.m.; 9:00 a.m.; 6:30 p.m. **Wattage:** 678 KW. **Ad Rates:** Noncommercial. **URL:** http://www.bsu.edu.

12186 ■ WLBC-FM - 104.1
800 E 29th St.
Muncie, IN 47302
Phone: (765)288-4403
Fax: (765)288-0429
Format: Country. **Founded:** 1947. **ADI:** Dayton, OH (Richmond, IN). **Key Personnel:** Steve Lindell, Dir. of Operations, VP, steve.lindell@bybradio.com. **Wattage:** 41,000 ERP. **Ad Rates:** Advertising accepted; rates available upon request. $21 for 30 seconds; $26 for 60 seconds. **URL:** http://www.wlbc.com.

12187 ■ WWHI-FM - 91.3
2000 W University Ave.
LB 200
Muncie, IN 47306
Phone: (765)285-1467

Fax: (765)285-9278
Format: Full Service. **Owner:** Ball State University, 2000 W University Ave., Muncie, IN 47306, Ph: (765)289-1241, Free: 800-382-8540. **Key Personnel:** Alberto Pimienta, Dir. of Programs, wcrdprogramming@gmail.com. **URL:** http://cms.bsu.edu.

12188 ■ WWWO-FM - 93.5
800 E 29th St.
Muncie, IN 47302
Phone: (765)288-4403
Format: Classic Rock; News. **Owner:** Viking Communications Inc., 1421 S 62nd St., Milwaukee, WI 53214. **Founded:** 1965. **Formerly**: WWHC-FM. **Key Personnel:** Judy Kvale, Gen. Mgr., President, Contact; Sean Mattlingly, Operations Mgr.; Rick Stephens, Sales Mgr; Judy Kvale, Contact. **Wattage:** 3,000 ERP. **Ad Rates:** $13-34 for 30 seconds; $17-40 for 60 seconds. **URL:** http://www.maxrocks.net.

12189 ■ WXFN-AM - 1340
800 E 29th St.
Muncie, IN 47302
Phone: (765)289-9522
Fax: (765)288-0429
Format: Sports. **Networks:** ABC. **Owner:** Backyard Broadcasting, at above address. **Founded:** 1926. **Operating Hours**: Continuous. **ADI**: Indianapolis (Marion), IN. **Key Personnel:** Bill Hatheway, Mktg. Mgr., VP, william.hatheway@bybradio.com; Steve Lindell, Dir. of Operations, VP, steve.lindell@bybradio.com; Amy Dillon, Gen. Sales Mgr., amy.dillon@bybradio.com. **Wattage:** 1,000. **Ad Rates:** $16 for 30 seconds; $21 for 60 seconds. **URL:** http://www.wlbc.com.

MUNSTER

12190 ■ Nikon Journal
Nikon Historical Society
RJR Publishing Inc.
PO Box 3213
Munster, IN 46321
Freq: Quarterly. **URL:** http://www.nikonhistoricalsociety.com. **Remarks:** Accepts advertising. **Circ:** (Not Reported).

12191 ■ The Times
Howard Publications
601 W 45th Ave.
Munster, IN 46321
Phone: (219)933-3200
Fax: (219)933-3325
Free: 866-301-3223
General newspaper. **Freq:** Daily (eve.), Sat. and Sun. (morn.). **Print Method:** Offset. **Cols./Page:** 9. **Col. Width:** 13 nonpareils. **Col. Depth:** 294 agate lines. **URL:** http://nwitimes.com. **Ad Rates:** PCI $62.29. **Remarks:** Accepts classified advertising. **Circ:** (Not Reported).

NASHVILLE

Brown Co. Brown Co. (SC). 40 m S of Indianapolis. Tourist center. Hardwood timber. Diversified farming. Apples, peaches, stock.

12192 ■ Brown County Democrat
Home News Enterprizes
PO Box 277
Nashville, IN 47448
Phone: (812)988-2221
Fax: (812)988-6502
Free: 877-988-2221
Publisher's E-mail: ads@bcdemocrat.com
Community newspaper. **Freq:** Weekly (Wed.). **Print Method:** Offset. **Trim Size:** 13 x 21. **Cols./Page:** 6. **Col. Width:** 2 1/16 inches. **Col. Depth:** 21 inches. **USPS:** 067-640. **Subscription Rates:** $50 Individuals /year, in Brown county; $60 Out of area /year; $30 Individuals 6 months; $38 Out of country 6 months. **URL:** http://www.bcdemocrat.com. **Remarks:** Accepts advertising. **Circ:** (Not Reported).

NEW ALBANY

Floyd Co. Floyd Co. (S). On Ohio River, 7 m NW of downtown Louisville, Ky., connected by bridge. Cultural centers. Manufactures apparel, food, lumber and plywood, veneer, chemicals, leather goods, electronic components, concrete products and award plaques.

12193 ■ The New Albany Tribune
CNHI
303 Scribner Dr.
New Albany, IN 47150
Phone: (812)206-6397
Fax: (812)206-4598
Publication E-mail: newsroom@newsandtribune.com
General newspaper. **Freq:** Weekly (Sun.). **Print Method:** Offset. **Cols./Page:** 6. **Col. Width:** 25 nonpareils. **Col. Depth:** 294 agate lines. **Key Personnel:** Shea VanHoy, Editor; Bill Hanson, Publisher. **Subscription Rates:** $14.99 Individuals print and online/month; $12.99 Individuals online/month. **URL:** http://www.newsandtribune.com. **Mailing address:** PO Box 997, New Albany, IN 47150. **Remarks:** Accepts advertising. **Circ:** (Not Reported).

12194 ■ Insight Communications
1608 Vance Ave.
New Albany, IN 47150
Phone: (502)357-4400
Free: 800-273-0144
Founded: 1985. **Key Personnel:** Michael S. Willner, CEO, V. Ch.; Dinni Jain, COO, President; John Abbot, CFO, Exec. VP; Hamid Heidary, Exec. VP of Operations; Christopher Slattery, Exec. VP of Operations; Gregg Graff, Sr. VP; Elliot Brecher, Gen. Counsel, Sr. VP; Sandra D. Colony, Sr. VP of Corp. Comm. **Cities Served:** 79 channels.

WAY-FM - See Louisville, KY

12195 ■ WNAS-FM - 88.1
1020 Vincennes St.
New Albany, IN 47150
Fax: 949-6926
Format: Eighties; News. **Owner:** New Albany/Floyd County School Corp., 802 E Market, New Albany, IN 47150, Ph: (812)949-4200. **Founded:** 1949. **Operating Hours:** 2:30 p.m. - 9:00 p.m. Monday, 7:00 a.m. 2:30 p.m. Tuesday, 2:30 p.m. - 8:30 p.m. Wednesday, 7:00 a.m. - 2:30 p.m. Thursday. **Key Personnel:** Lee Kelly, Gen. Mgr. **Wattage**: 2,850 ERP. **Ad Rates:** per unit. **URL:** http://wnas.org/.

12196 ■ WWSZ-AM - 1570
410 Mt. Tabor Rd.
New Albany, IN 47150
Format: Sports. **Operating Hours**: Continuous. **Key Personnel:** Zach McCrite, Dir. of Programs. **Wattage:** 1,500. **Ad Rates:** Advertising accepted; rates available upon request.

NEW CASTLE

Henry Co. Henry Co. (E). 18 m S of Muncie. Manufactures auto parts, folding partitions, heavy castings, structural steel, rolled steel products. Greenhouses. Stock, poultry farms. Corn, wheat, tomatoes.

12197 ■ Courier-Times
Courier-Times
201 S 14th St.
New Castle, IN 47362
Phone: (765)529-1111
Publisher's E-mail: information@thecouriertimes.com
General newspaper. **Founded:** 1841. **Freq:** Mon.-Sat. (eve.). **Print Method:** Offset press. **Cols./Page:** 6. **Col. Width:** 28 nonpareils. **Col. Depth:** 301 agate lines. **Key Personnel:** Kelly Miller, Publisher; Scott Hart, Manager, Advertising. **Subscription Rates:** $210 Individuals mail; $194 Individuals online; $342 By mail postal. **URL:** http://thecouriertimes.com/main.asp?SectionID=39&TM=65597.98. **Ad Rates:** GLR $.30. **Remarks:** Accepts advertising. **Circ:** 12000.

12198 ■ WMDH-AM
PO Box 690
New Castle, IN 47362
Phone: (765)529-2600
Owner: Citadel Broadcasting Corp., 7201 W Lake Mead Blvd., Ste. 400, Las Vegas, NV 89128-8366, Ph: (702)804-5200, Fax: (702)804-8250. **Founded:** 1960. **Formerly**: WCTW-AM. **Ad Rates:** Advertising accepted; rates available upon request. **URL:** http://www.nashfm1025.com.

12199 ■ WMDH-FM - 102.5
PO Box 690
New Castle, IN 47362
Phone: (765)529-2600
Fax: (765)529-1688
Format: Country. **Networks:** NBC. **Owner:** Cumulus Media Inc., 3280 Peachtree Rd. NW, Ste. 2300, Atlanta, GA 30305-2455, Ph: (404)949-0700, Fax: (404)949-0740. **Founded:** 1947. **Operating Hours**: Continuous; 100% local. **ADI**: Indianapolis (Marion), IN. **Local Programs:** *Saturday Morning Memories*, Saturday 5:00 a.m. - 9:00 a.m. **Wattage:** 50,000. **Ad Rates:** Advertising accepted; rates available upon request. **URL:** http://www.nashfm1025.com.

NEW HARMONY

Posey Co. Posey Co. (SW). 22 m NW of Evansville. Residential. Tourism. Art gallery. Oil. Chemicals. Agriculture. Agriculture.

12200 ■ Posey County News: Weekly Newspaper
Posey County News
641 S Third St.
New Harmony, IN 47631
Phone: (812)682-3950
Fax: (812)682-3944
Publisher's E-mail: news1@poseycountynews.com
Newspaper with a Republican orientation. **Freq:** Weekly (Tues.). **Print Method:** Offset. **Cols./Page:** 6. **Col. Width:** 26 nonpareils. **Col. Depth:** 294 agate lines. **Key Personnel:** Dave Pearce, General Manager; Michelle Gibson, Office Manager. **USPS:** 439-500. **Subscription Rates:** $39 Individuals in County; $48 Out of state. **URL:** http://poseycountynews.com. **Formerly**: Poseyville News; New Harmony Times. **Feature Editors:** Pam Robinson, pamelawrite@sbcglobal.net. **Mailing address:** PO Box 397, New Harmony, IN 47631. **Remarks:** Accepts advertising. **Circ:** 3700.

NEW PARIS

Elkhart Co. (N). 6 m S of Goshen. Boats, campers, cabinets, dairy and feed grain products manufactured. Agriculture. Corn, wheat, soybeans, dairy, livestock.

12201 ■ Farmer's Exchange
Exchange Publishing Corp.
19401 Industrial Dr.
New Paris, IN 46553
Phone: (574)831-2138
Fax: (574)831-2131
Agricultural newspaper. **Founded:** 1926. **Freq:** Weekly (Fri.). **Print Method:** Offset. **Cols./Page:** 6. **Col. Width:** 19 nonpareils. **Col. Depth:** 224 agate lines. **Key Personnel:** Jerry Goshert, Editor; Steve Yeater, Publisher. **USPS:** 187-560. **Subscription Rates:** $35 Individuals /year; $62 Two years; $90 three years. **URL:** http://www.farmers-exchange.net. **Mailing address:** PO Box 45, New Paris, IN 46553. **Ad Rates:** GLR $.49; BW $630; 4C $790; PCI $6.90. **Circ:** Paid ‡13800, Free ‡800.

NEW YORK

12202 ■ Insight Communications
810 7th Ave., 41st Fl.
New York, IN 10019
Phone: (917)286-2300
Founded: 1985. **Cities Served:** 107 channels.

NOBLESVILLE

Hamilton Co. Hamilton Co. (C). 24 m N of Indianapolis. Manufactures industrial rubber products, truck bodies, electronic components, furniture, castings. Stock grain farms. Wheat, corn, oats.

12203 ■ Noblesville Daily Ledger
PO Box 1478
Noblesville, IN 46060
Phone: (317)773-1210
Fax: (317)773-3872
Local newspaper with a Republican orientation. **Freq:** Mon.-Sat. (eve.). **Print Method:** Offset. **Trim Size:** 14 x 22 3/4. **Cols./Page:** 6. **Col. Width:** 25 nonpareils. **Col. Depth:** 301 agate lines. **Key Personnel:** David Lewis, Publisher; Tom Jekel, Editor. **USPS:** 391-120. **Subscription Rates:** $86 Individuals. **Ad Rates:** BW $1,238.40; 4C $1,463.40; PCI $9.60. **Circ:** Paid 9383, Non-paid 6.

12204 ■ The Times
The Times

Circulation: ★ = AAM; △ or • = BPA; ♦ = CAC; ❑ = VAC; ⊕ = PO Statement; ‡ = Publisher's Report; Boldface figures = sworn; Light figures = estimated.

641 Westfield Rd.
Noblesville, IN 46062
Phone: (317)770-7777
Fax: (317)773-9960
Publisher's E-mail: news@thetimes24-7.com
Community newspaper serving Noblesville and Hamilton County. **Freq:** Weekly (Thurs.). **Cols./Page:** 5. **Col. Width:** 11 picas. **Col. Depth:** 16 inches. **URL:** http://www.thetimes24-7.com/. **Formerly**: Noblesville Times. **Circ:** 350.

NORTH MANCHESTER

Wabash Co. Wabash Co. (NE). 15 m N of Wabash. Residential.

12205 ■ The News Journal
North Manchester News-Journal Inc.
PO Box 368
North Manchester, IN 46962-1844
Newspaper with an independent orientation. **Founded:** 1873. **Freq:** Semiweekly Tuesday, Friday. **Print Method:** Offset. **Cols./Page:** 5. **Col. Width:** 1 15/16 inches. **Col. Depth:** 15 1/2 inches. **USPS:** 396-760. **Subscription Rates:** $35 Individuals; $40 Out of area. **URL:** http://www.nmpaper.com. **Ad Rates:** GLR $2.50; BW $520; 4C $600; SAU $7.70; PCI $6.50. **Remarks:** Accepts advertising. **Circ:** Paid ‡2000.

12206 ■ WBKE-FM - 89.5
Manchester College
Box 19
North Manchester, IN 46962
Fax: (219)982-5043
Format: Educational. **Networks:** Network Indiana; UPI. **Owner:** Manchester University, 604 E College Ave., North Manchester, IN 46962, Ph: (219)982-5000, Free: 800-852-3648. **Founded:** 1968. **Operating Hours**: Continuous. **Key Personnel:** Matt Baker, Dir. of Programs; Chris Lake, Sports Dir.; Aaron Gardner, Promotions Dir. **Wattage**: 3,000. **URL:** http://www.wbke.manchester.edu/.

NORTH VERNON

Jennings Co. Jennings Co. (SE). 60 m S of Indianapolis. Manufactures plastics, gas filter tubes, injection molds, area rugs, plastic injection products, sausage. Hot and cold forgings. Metal work.

12207 ■ North Vernon Plain Dealer
North Vernon Plain Dealer and Sun
528 E O&M Ave.
North Vernon, IN 47265
Phone: (812)346-3973
Fax: (812)346-8368
Community newspapers. **Freq:** Weekly (Thurs.). **Print Method:** Offset. **Cols./Page:** 6. **Col. Width:** 24 nonpareils. **Col. Depth:** 294 agate lines. **Key Personnel:** Sharon Hamilton, Editor; Josh Taylor, Manager, Advertising; Barbara King, Publisher; Mike Walters, Advertising Representative; Bryce Mayer, Editor. **Subscription Rates:** $40 Individuals in county (print and online); $49 Individuals out of county (print and online); $54 Out of area print and online; $40 Individuals online only. **URL:** http://plaindealer-sun.com. **Mailing address:** PO Box 988, North Vernon, IN 47265. **Remarks:** Advertising accepted; rates available upon request. **Circ:** (Not Reported).

12208 ■ North Vernon Sun
North Vernon Plain Dealer and Sun
528 E O&M Ave.
North Vernon, IN 47265
Phone: (812)346-3973
Fax: (812)346-8368
Local newspaper with a democratic orientation. **Freq:** Weekly (Tues.). **Print Method:** Offset. **Cols./Page:** 6. **Col. Width:** 24 nonpareils. **Col. Depth:** 294 agate lines. **Key Personnel:** Bryce Mayer, Editor; Josh Taylor, Manager, Advertising; Sharon Hamilton, Editor; Mike Walters, Advertising Representative; Barbara King, Publisher. **USPS:** 395-080. **Subscription Rates:** $40 Individuals local (print and online) ; $49 Individuals rest of Indiana (print and online); $54 Individuals rest of the U.S. (print and online); $40 Individuals online only. **URL:** http://plaindealer-sun.com. **Mailing address:** PO Box 988, North Vernon, IN 47265. **Remarks:** Accepts advertising. **Circ:** (Not Reported).

12209 ■ WIKI-FM - 95.3
2470 N State Hwy. 7
North Vernon, IN 47265-7184
Format: Contemporary Country. **Networks:** CNN Radio. **Founded:** 1968. **Formerly**: WVCM-FM. **Operating Hours**: Continuous. **Key Personnel:** Larry Duke, Sports Dir., News Dir. **Wattage:** 1,800 ERP. **Ad Rates:** Advertising accepted; rates available upon request. $7.50-18.25 for 30 seconds; $9.50-21.75 for 60 seconds. **URL:** http://953wiki.com/.

NOTRE DAME

St. Joseph Co. (N). 3 m N of South Bend. University of Notre Dame. St Mary's College (Cath. Women).

12210 ■ American Journal of Jurisprudence
University of Notre Dame Law School
PO Box 780
Notre Dame, IN 46556
Phone: (574)631-6627
Fax: (574)631-3980
Publisher's E-mail: ndlaw@nd.edu
Journal containing articles on legal and current historical issues and philosophy of law. **Freq:** Semiannual. **Subscription Rates:** £114 Institutions; $173 Institutions; €134 Institutions; £143 Institutions corporate; $216 Institutions corporate; €168 Institutions corporate; £28 Individuals; $42 Individuals; €32 Individuals. **URL:** http://scholarship.law.nd.edu/ajj; http://oxfordjournals.org/our_journals/ajj/about.html. **Circ:** (Not Reported).

12211 ■ Current Drug Targets
Bentham Science Publishers Ltd.
230 Raclin-Carmichael Hall
University of Notre Dame
Notre Dame, IN 46556
Publisher's E-mail: subscriptions@benthamscience.org
Journal covering all the latest and outstanding developments on the medicinal chemistry and pharmacology of molecular drug targets, e.g. disease specific proteins, receptors, enzymes, genes. **Freq:** 14/yr. **Key Personnel:** Francis J. Castellino, Editor-in-Chief. **ISSN:** 1389--4501 (print); **EISSN:** 1873--5592 (electronic). **Subscription Rates:** $810 Individuals print; $3970 print and online - academic; $3610 print or online - academic; $7700 print and online - corporate; $6420 print or online - corporate. **URL:** http://benthamscience.com/journals/current-drug-targets. **Ad Rates:** BW $700; 4C $900. **Remarks:** Accepts advertising. **Circ:** ‡1000.

12212 ■ German Quarterly
American Association of Teachers of German
University of Notre Dame
Department of German and Russian Languages and Literatures
318 O Shaughnessy Hall
Notre Dame, IN 46556
Publisher's E-mail: info@aatg.org
Journal covering cultural and literary studies. **Freq:** Quarterly. **Trim Size:** 6 x 9. **Key Personnel:** Carl Niekerk, Editor. **ISSN:** 0016--8831 (print); **EISSN:** 1756--1183 (electronic). **Subscription Rates:** $212 U.S. and other countries online; £109 online (Institutional Community College); €80 online (Institutional Community College); $130 U.S. and other countries print and online (Institutional Community College); £82 print and online (Institutional Community College); €96 print and online (Institutional Community College); $212 U.S. and other countries online; £133 Institutions online; €155 Institutions online; $255 U.S. and other countries print and online; £160 Institutions print and online; €186 Institutions print and online. **URL:** http://germanquarterly.aatg.org; http://www.aatg.org/?page=Publications; http://onlinelibrary.wiley.com/journal/10.1111/(ISSN)1756-1183/homepage/Advertise.html. **Ad Rates:** BW $335. **Remarks:** Accepts advertising. **Circ:** Combined 4500.

12213 ■ Isis
History of Science Society
University of Notre Dame
440 Geddes Hall
Notre Dame, IN 46556
Phone: (574)631-1194
Fax: (574)631-1533
Publisher's E-mail: info@hssonline.org
Freq: Quarterly. **ISSN:** 0021-1753 (print); **EISSN:** 1545-6994 (electronic). **Subscription Rates:** included in membership dues; $528 print ; $158 Institutions single copy. **URL:** http://hssonline.org/resources/publications/isis-osiris/. **Remarks:** Accepts advertising. **Circ:** 4,500.

12214 ■ Journal of College and University Law
University of Notre Dame Law School
PO Box 780
Notre Dame, IN 46556
Phone: (574)631-6627
Fax: (574)631-3980
Publisher's E-mail: nacua@nacua.org
Legal journal covering law and education. **Freq:** 3/year. **Trim Size:** 6 3/4 x 10. **Cols./Page:** 1. **Col. Width:** 4 5/8 inches. **Col. Depth:** 8 inches. **Key Personnel:** John H. Robinson, Contact. **ISSN:** 0093--8688 (print). **Subscription Rates:** $75 Nonmembers /year; $37.50 Members /year; Free online subscription for members; $29.50 Single issue; $85 Individuals international. **URL:** http://www.nacua.org; http://www3.nd.edu/~jcul; http://www3.nd.edu/~jcul/subscriptions_online.html. **Remarks:** Advertising not accepted. **Circ:** Paid 248.

12215 ■ Journal of Hindu Christian Studies
Society for Hindu-Christian Studies
232 Malloy Hall
University of Notre Dame
Notre Dame, IN 46556
Phone: (574)631-7128
Publisher's E-mail: infol@hcstudies.org
Freq: Annual. **ISSN:** 2164--6279 (print). **Subscription Rates:** Free individuals located in India; $15 Individuals digital and print subscription; $10 Out of area digital subscription ; $20 Out of area digital and print subscription for individuals outside of India; $20 Institutions digital and print subscription ; $25 Out of area digital subscription; $35 Out of area digital and print subscription. **Alt. Formats:** Download. **URL:** http://www.hcstudies.org/jrnl.html. **Remarks:** Advertising not accepted. **Circ:** (Not Reported).

12216 ■ Journal of Legislation
University of Notre Dame Law School
PO Box 780
Notre Dame, IN 46556
Phone: (574)631-6627
Fax: (574)631-3980
Publication E-mail: ndlaw@nd.edu
Professional legal journal covering legislation and public policy issues. **Freq:** Semiannual. **Key Personnel:** Veronica N. Meffe, Editor-in-Chief. **ISSN:** 0146--9584 (print). **URL:** http://scholarship.law.nd.edu/jleg. **Formerly**: New Dimensions in Legislation. **Remarks:** Advertising accepted; rates available upon request. **Circ:** (Not Reported).

12217 ■ Journal of Philosophical Research
Philosophy Documentation Center
c/o Michael DePaul, Editor
University of Notre Dame
Department of Philosophy
100 Malloy Hall
Notre Dame, IN 46556-4619
Publication E-mail: order@pdcnet.org
Peer-reviewed scholarly journal covering philosophy. Publishes papers in any branch of philosophy and from any philosophical orientation. **Freq:** Annual. **Trim Size:** 6 x 9. **Key Personnel:** Michael DePaul, Editor. **ISSN:** 1053--8364 (print); **EISSN:** 2153--7984 (electronic). **Subscription Rates:** $35 Individuals print or online; $55 Individuals print and online; $77 Institutions print; $231 Institutions online; $277 Institutions print and online. **URL:** http://pdcnet.org/pdc/bvdb.nsf/journal?openform&journal=pdc_jpr; http://pdcnet.org/jpr/Journal-of-Philosophical-Research. **Remarks:** Accepts advertising. **Circ:** Paid 300.

12218 ■ The Journal of Symbolic Logic
Association for Symbolic Logic
c/o Peter Cholak, Coord. Ed.
Dept. of Mathematics
University of Notre Dame
255 Hurley
Notre Dame, IN 46556-4618
Publisher's E-mail: asl@vassar.edu
Scientific journal containing research on symbolic logic. Subscription price includes The Bulletin of Symbolic Logic. **Founded:** 1936. **Freq:** Quarterly. **Print Method:** offset. **Trim Size:** 7 x 10. **Key Personnel:** Noam Greenberg; Bradd Hart, Editor. **ISSN:** 0022-4812 (print). **Subscription Rates:** $690 Nonmembers print; Individuals included in membership dues; Institutions included in membership dues. **Alt. Formats:** Microfiche; Microfilm.

URL: http://www.aslonline.org/journals-journal.html. **Remarks:** Advertising not accepted. **Circ:** ‡2500.

12219 ■ Notre Dame Journal of International and Comparative Law
University of Notre Dame Law School
PO Box 780
Notre Dame, IN 46556
Phone: (574)631-6627
Fax: (574)631-3980
Publisher's E-mail: ndlaw@nd.edu
Journal containing articles on human rights and other legal issues. **Freq:** Annual. **Key Personnel:** Michael Mercurio, Editor-in-Chief. **ISSN:** 2325--2235 (print). **URL:** http://scholarship.law.nd.edu/ndjicl. **Circ:** (Not Reported).

12220 ■ Notre Dame Journal of Law, Ethics & Public Policy
University of Notre Dame Law School
PO Box 780
Notre Dame, IN 46556
Phone: (574)631-6627
Fax: (574)631-3980
Publication E-mail: ndjlepp@nd.edu
Journal covering ethics of federal, state and local government policy. **Freq:** Semiannual. **Cols./Page:** 1. **Col. Width:** 6 inches. **Col. Depth:** 8 inches. **Key Personnel:** Nathan S. Catanese, Editor-in-Chief; Michael J. Mogavero, Executive Editor; Maureen L. McCluskey, Managing Editor. **ISSN:** 0883--3648 (print). **Subscription Rates:** $35 Individuals /year; $40 Canada /year; $45 Other countries /year. **URL:** http://scholarship.law.nd.edu/ndjlepp. **Ad Rates:** BW $100. **Remarks:** Accepts advertising. **Circ:** Controlled 490.

12221 ■ Notre Dame Magazine
University of Notre Dame
Notre Dame, IN 46556
Phone: (574)631-5000
Fax: (574)631-8212
Publication E-mail: ndmag@nd.edu
Magazine for university alumni and friends. **Freq:** Quarterly. **Print Method:** Offset. **Trim Size:** 9 x 12. **Cols./Page:** 3. **Col. Width:** 30 nonpareils. **Col. Depth:** 150 agate lines. **Key Personnel:** Julie Ettl, Business Manager; Kerry Temple, Editor; Carol Schaal, Managing Editor, Web Administrator. **ISSN:** 0161--987X (print). **Subscription Rates:** $30 Individuals /year; $45 Two years. **URL:** http://magazine.nd.edu. **Remarks:** Advertising not accepted. **Circ:** (Not Reported).

12222 ■ Notre Dame Technical Review
Notre Dame Technical Review
917 Flanner Hall
University of Notre Dame
Notre Dame, IN 46556
Phone: (574)631-5000
Publisher's E-mail: techrev@nd.edu
Magazine for engineering students. **Freq:** Quarterly. **Key Personnel:** Alfredo Arvide, Editor-in-Chief; Katherine May, Associate Director. **ISSN:** 0029-4543 (print). **Alt. Formats:** PDF. **URL:** http://www.nd.edu/~techrev/index.html. **Ad Rates:** BW $1,000, back cover; BW $900, inside back cover; BW $650, full page; BW $350, 1/2 page; BW $200, 1/4 page. **Remarks:** Accepts advertising. **Circ:** 1700.

12223 ■ The Observer: The Independent Newspaper Serving Notre Dame and Saint Mary's
University of Notre Dame
Notre Dame, IN 46556
Phone: (574)631-5000
Fax: (574)631-8212
Publisher's E-mail: admissions@nd.edu
Newspaper. **Freq:** Monday-Friday. **Print Method:** Offset. **Trim Size:** 10 x 16. **Cols./Page:** 5. **Col. Width:** 22 nonpareils. **Col. Depth:** 224 agate lines. **Key Personnel:** Ann Marie Jakubowski, Editor-in-Chief, phone: (574)631-4542. **ISSN:** 5992--4000 (print). **URL:** http://ndsmcobserver.com. **Remarks:** Accepts advertising. **Circ:** Combined 6000.

12224 ■ Religion and Literature
University of Notre Dame Department of English
University of Notre Dame
B009F McKenna Hall
Notre Dame, IN 46556
Publisher's E-mail: english@nd.edu
Scholarly journal covering the intersection between literature and religious belief. **Freq:** 3/year. **ISSN:** 0029--4500 (print). **URL:** http://english.nd.edu/events/2015/11/02/37593-2015-religion-literature-lecture-shira-wolosky. **Formerly:** NDEJ: A Journal of Religion in Literature. **Ad Rates:** BW $100. **Remarks:** Accepts advertising. **Circ:** Paid 450.

12225 ■ The Review of Politics
Review of Politics
547 Flanner Hall
University of Notre Dame
Notre Dame, IN 46556-0762
Phone: (574)631-6623
Fax: (574)631-3103
Publication E-mail: rop.editor.1@nd.edu
Journal covering political science, philosophy, and foreign affairs. **Freq:** Quarterly February, May, August, and November. **Print Method:** Letterpress and offset. **Trim Size:** 6 x 9. **Cols./Page:** 1. **Col. Width:** 48 nonpareils. **Col. Depth:** 128 agate lines. **Key Personnel:** Catherine H. Zuckert, Editor-in-Chief, phone: (574)631-6620; Dennis William Moran, Managing Editor. **ISSN:** 0034--6705 (print); **EISSN:** 1748--6858 (electronic). **Subscription Rates:** $207 Institutions print and online; $171 Institutions online only; $197 Institutions print only; $48 Individuals print only; £27 Individuals print only; £120 Institutions print and online; £104 Institutions online only; £119 Institutions print only. **URL:** http://reviewofpolitics.nd.edu. **Remarks:** Advertising accepted; rates available upon request. **Circ:** (Not Reported).

12226 ■ WSND-FM - 88.9
Student Ctr.
315 LaFortune
Notre Dame, IN 46556
Phone: (574)631-7342
Email: wsnd@nd.edu
Format: Classical. **Owner:** University of Notre Dame, Notre Dame, IN 46556, Ph: (574)631-5000, Fax: (574)631-8212. **Founded:** 1962. **Operating Hours:** 7 a.m.-2 a.m. Mon.-Fri.; 9 a.m.-2 a.m. Sat. and Sun. **Key Personnel:** Laurie McFadden, Contact, laurie.e.mcfadden.20@nd.edu. **Wattage:** 3,430. **Ad Rates:** Noncommercial. **URL:** http://www.nd.edu.

12227 ■ WVFI-AM - 640
University of Notre Dame
200 LaFortune Hall
Notre Dame, IN 46556
Phone: (574)631-6888
Email: wvfi@nd.edu
Format: Album-Oriented Rock (AOR). **Owner:** University of Notre Dame, Notre Dame, IN 46556, Ph: (574)631-5000, Fax: (574)631-8212. **Key Personnel:** Nicolle Walkling, Station Mgr., nwalklin@nd.edu. **Ad Rates:** Noncommercial. **URL:** http://www.nd.edu.

PAOLI

Orange Co. Orange Co. (S). 24 m S of Bedford. Manufactures wood dimension parts, shoes, handles, furniture, chairs, electronics; lumber kilm drying; hardwood timber. Agriculture. Corn, wheat, hay.

12228 ■ News
Orange County Publishing Company Inc.
PO Box 190
Paoli, IN 47454
Phone: (812)723-2572
Fax: (812)723-2592
Publication E-mail: cdupuis@kiva.net
Community newspaper. **Founded:** 1958. **Freq:** Weekly (Thurs.). **Print Method:** Offset. **Cols./Page:** 6 and 8. **Col. Width:** 30 and 21 nonpareils. **Col. Depth:** 294 and 301 agate lines. **USPS:** 695-160. **Subscription Rates:** $9.50 Individuals; $27 Individuals; $12 Individuals; $13; $15.50 Individuals; $18.50 Out of area; $21.50 Out of state; $11.50. **Formerly:** Yale Record. **Ad Rates:** GLR $.264; GLR $.19; PCI $3.50; GLR $.17; GLR $.35; SAU $4.82; BW $348.30; 4C $903.15; SAU $3.00; PCI $2.70; GLR $.311; SAU $4.35. **Circ:** ‡1100, 3200, 1650, ‡3250, Paid ‡1472, Free ‡52, 2000.

12229 ■ Republican
Orange County Publishing Company Inc.
PO Box 190
Paoli, IN 47454
Phone: (812)723-2572
Fax: (812)723-2592
Publication E-mail: newsroom@therepublicannews.com
Newspaper with a Republican orientation. **Founded:** 1875. **Freq:** Weekly (Tues.). **Print Method:** Offset. **Cols./Page:** 6. **Col. Width:** 25 nonpareils. **Col. Depth:** 294 agate lines. **Subscription Rates:** $42 Individuals print and online; $35 Individuals print or online. **URL:** http://www.therepublicannews.com. **Ad Rates:** GLR $.19; SAU $3; PCI $3.50; 4C $225. **Remarks:** Accepts advertising. **Circ:** 3,200, 8,200.

12230 ■ WUME-FM - 95.3
PO Box 26
Paoli, IN 47454
Phone: (812)723-4484
Format: Adult Contemporary. **Networks:** ABC. **Owner:** Diamond Shores Broadcasting L.L.C., at above address. **Founded:** 1972. **Operating Hours:** Continuous. **Wattage:** 3,000. **Ad Rates:** Advertising accepted; rates available upon request. Combined advertising rates available with WSEZ-AM. **URL:** http://www.wume953.com.

PEKIN

(corporate name New Pekin); Washington Co. (S). 25 m NW of New Albany. Poultry processing plant. Ships berries. Diversified farming. Berries, poultry and dairy products.

12231 ■ The Banner-Gazette
Green Banner Publications Inc.
490 E State Road 60
Pekin, IN 47165
Phone: (812)967-3176
Fax: (812)967-3194
Community newspaper. **Freq:** Weekly (Wed.). **Print Method:** Offset. **Trim Size:** 11 3/8 x 17. **Cols./Page:** 5. **Col. Width:** 25 nonpareils. **Col. Depth:** 224 agate lines. **Key Personnel:** Joe Green, Publisher. **URL:** http://www.gbpnews.com/index.php?option=com_content&view=category&layout=blog&id=3&Itemid=56. **Mailing address:** PO Box 38, Pekin, IN 47165. **Ad Rates:** GLR $.69; BW $771; SAU $9.64; PCI $9.64. **Remarks:** Advertising accepted; rates available upon request. **Circ:** Combined 18200.

PENDLETON

Madison Co. Madison Co. (EC). 30 m NE of Indianapolis. Residential.

12232 ■ WEEM-FM - 91.7
One Arabian Dr.
Pendleton, IN 46064
Phone: (765)778-2161
Fax: (765)778-0605
Format: Contemporary Hit Radio (CHR). **Owner:** South Madison Community School Corp., 203 S Heritage Way, Pendleton, IN 46064, Ph: (765)778-2152, Fax: (765)778-8207. **Founded:** 1971. **Operating Hours:** 6:30am-5:00pm Mon-Fri; 8 am-5 pm Sat; 5% network; 95%. **Key Personnel:** Alex Anderson, Dir. of Programs. **Wattage:** 1,200. **Ad Rates:** Noncommercial. **URL:** http://917weem.org.

PERU

Miami Co. Miami Co. (NC). On Wabash River, 65 m N of Indianapolis. Manufacturing. Meat packing plants. Grain farms.

12233 ■ Peru Daily Tribune
Nixon Newspapers Inc.
26 W 3rd St.
Peru, IN 46970-2155
General newspaper. **Freq:** Daily (eve.) and Sat. (morn.). **Print Method:** Offset. **Cols./Page:** 6. **Col. Width:** 26 nonpareils. **Col. Depth:** 301 agate lines. **Key Personnel:** Laurie Kiefaber, Editor; Aaron Turner, Managing Editor. **Subscription Rates:** $105 Individuals /year; $10 Individuals /month; $2 Individuals /day. **URL:** http://www.chronicle-tribune.com. **Remarks:** Accepts advertising. **Circ:** (Not Reported).

12234 ■ WADM-AM - 1540
133 W Main St.
Peru, IN 46970
Phone: (765)472-2077
Format: Country. **Ad Rates:** Noncommercial. **URL:** http://www.wjzi.com.

Circulation: ★ = AAM; △ or • = BPA; ♦ = CAC; ❑ = VAC; ⊕ = PO Statement; ‡ = Publisher's Report; Boldface figures = sworn; Light figures = estimated.

12235 ■ WARU-AM - 1600
PO Box 1010
Peru, IN 46970
Phone: (765)473-4448
Fax: (765)473-4449
Free: 866-259-1019
Format: Eighties. **Simulcasts:** WARU-FM. **Networks:** ABC; Network Indiana. **Owner:** Miami County B-Casting, Not Available. **Founded:** 1954. **Operating Hours:** Continuous. **Key Personnel:** Wade Weaver, Gen. Mgr., Owner, wade@mitunes1019.com. **Wattage:** 900. **Ad Rates:** $15 for 60 seconds. Combined advertising rates available with WARU-FM. **URL:** http://www.mitunes1019.com.

12236 ■ WARU-FM - 101.9
1711 E Wabash Rd.
Peru, IN 46970
Phone: (765)473-4448
Fax: (765)473-4449
Free: 866-259-1019
Format: Sports. **Networks:** AP; Network Indiana. **Owner:** Mid America Broadcasting, at above address. **Founded:** 1954. **Key Personnel:** Mark Ramsey, Sports Dir., News Dir., sports@realcountry1019.com; Wade Weaver, Gen. Mgr., wade@1059thebash.com; Tammy Johnson, Office Mgr., waru@sbcglobal.net; Randy Latta, Contact, randy@realcountry1019.com. **Wattage:** 3,600 ERP. **Ad Rates:** $15-40 for 60 seconds. Combined advertising rates available with WARU-AM. **URL:** http://www.mitunes1019.com.

PETERSBURG

Pike Co. Pike Co. (SW). 20 m SE of Vincennes. Wood tools and structural steel manufactured. Generating plants. Coal mines. Oil wells. Diversified farming.

12237 ■ The Press-Dispatch
The Press-Dispatch
PO Box 68
Petersburg, IN 47567
Phone: (812)354-8500
Fax: (812)354-2014
Publisher's E-mail: contact@pressdispatch.net
Community newspaper. **Founded:** 1885. **Freq:** Weekly (Thurs.). **Print Method:** Offset. **Cols./Page:** 6. **Col. Width:** 2 1/2 inches. **Col. Depth:** 21 inches. **Key Personnel:** Andy Heuring, Managing Editor. **USPS:** 604-340. **Subscription Rates:** $32 Individuals. **URL:** http://www.pressdispatch.net/. **Formerly:** The Pike County Dispatch; The Petersburg Press. **Ad Rates:** GLR $.25; BW $390.60; 4C $635.60; PCI $3.95. **Circ:** (Not Reported).

PLAINFIELD

Hendricks Co. Hendricks Co. (C). 14 m SW of Indianapolis. Residential. Agriculture. Corn, wheat, oats, soybeans.

12238 ■ Stunt News
Precision Aerobatics Model Pilots Association
PO Box 320
Plainfield, IN 46168-0320
Magazine containing information relevant to the various aspects of participating in the aerobatics. **Freq:** Bimonthly. **Subscription Rates:** Included in membership. **Alt. Formats:** Download. **URL:** http://www.pampacl.org. **Remarks:** Accepts advertising. **Circ:** 2000.

12239 ■ Sweeping: The Journal of Chimney and Venting Technology
National Chimney Sweep Guild
2155 Commercial Dr.
Plainfield, IN 46168
Phone: (317)837-1500
Fax: (317)837-5365
Trade magazine covering technical information for chimney sweeps and venting technologists, including information on tools, products, industry trends, and safety measures. **Freq:** Monthly. **Print Method:** Sheetfed offset. **Key Personnel:** Darcy Marlett, Director, Marketing, Director, Communications; Malisa Minetree, Contact, phone: (317)815-4688, fax: (317)582-0607. **ISSN:** 1041--6692 (print). **Subscription Rates:** Included in membership. **URL:** http://www.ncsg.org/About_NCSG/sweeping_magazine.aspx. **Ad Rates:** BW $678; 4C $992. **Remarks:** Accepts advertising. **Circ:** (Not Reported).

PLYMOUTH

Marshall Co. Marshall Co. (N). 10 m NW of Bourbon. Industrial area.

12240 ■ Bremen Enquirer
The Pilot Co.
PO Box 220
Plymouth, IN 46563
Phone: (574)936-3101
Fax: (574)936-7491
Free: 800-933-0356
Publication E-mail: enquirer@fourway.net
Community newspaper. **Freq:** Weekly (Wed.). **Print Method:** Offset. **Cols./Page:** 6. **Col. Width:** 2 inches. **Col. Depth:** 21 1/2 inches. **Key Personnel:** Rick Kreps, Publisher; Jerry Bingle, General Manager; Maggie Nixon, Managing Editor. **Subscription Rates:** $23 Individuals carrier delivery; $28 Individuals mail delivery in Indiana; $35 Individuals mail delivery outside Indiana. **URL:** http://www.thepilotnews.com/subscriptions; http://www.thepilotnews.com/content/contact. **Ad Rates:** PCI $4.72. **Remarks:** Accepts advertising. **Circ:** ‡1,900.

12241 ■ WIKV-FM - 89.3
PO Box 2098
Omaha, NE 68103
Free: 800-525-5683
Format: Contemporary Christian. **Owner:** Educational Media Foundation, 5700 W Oaks Blvd., CA 95765, Free: 800-800434-8400. **URL:** http://www.klove.com.

12242 ■ WTCA-AM - 1050
112 W Washington St.
Plymouth, IN 46563
Phone: (574)936-4096
Fax: (574)936-6776
Email: info@am1050.com
Format: Oldies. **Networks:** Independent; CNN Radio. **Owner:** Plymouth Broadcasting Inc., at above address. **Founded:** 1964. **Operating Hours:** 6 a.m.-5:07 p.m.; 8:06 a.m.-12 p.m. Sun. **Key Personnel:** Kathy Bottorf, Station Mgr.; Jim Bottorf, Sales Mgr. **Wattage:** 250. **Ad Rates:** $5.00-10.97 for 15 seconds; $8.15-16.45 for 30 seconds; $10.86-21.93 for 60 seconds. **URL:** http://www.am1050.com.

12243 ■ WZOC-FM - 94.3
1301 East Douglas Rd.
Plymouth, IN 46563
Phone: (574)936-4096
Fax: (574)936-6776
Free: 888-943-6539
Format: Oldies. **Key Personnel:** Chief Jim Roberts, Contact, jroberts@wsbt.com; Buddy King, Contact, buddy@buddyking.net; Tony Ross, Contact, theboss@hoosierisp.com; Jim Roberts, Contact, jroberts@wsbt.com. **URL:** http://www.z943radio.com.

PORTAGE

12244 ■ The Hegewisch News
The Hegewisch News
3017 Wood St.
Portage, IN 46368-4336
Community newspaper. **Freq:** Weekly (Thurs.). **Print Method:** Offset. **Cols./Page:** 5. **Col. Width:** 24 nonpareils. **Subscription Rates:** $10 Individuals. **Ad Rates:** BW $144; PCI $4. **Remarks:** Accepts advertising. **Circ:** ‡1900.

12245 ■ WNDZ-AM
2576 Portage Mall
Portage, IN 46368-3006
Phone: (219)763-2750
Fax: (219)762-0539
Format: Ethnic; Religious; News. **Founded:** 1987. **Key Personnel:** Steve Bertok, Contact. **Wattage:** 15,000 Day. **Ad Rates:** Advertising accepted; rates available upon request.

PORTLAND

Jay Co. Jay Co. (NE). 27 m NE of Muncie. Manufacturing. Meat packing plant, molded & extruded plastic products. Agriculture. Corn, wheat, oats, soybeans.

12246 ■ The Commercial Review
The Commercial Review
309 W Main St.
Portland, IN 47371
Phone: (260)726-8141
Fax: (260)726-8143
Publication E-mail: cr.news@comcast.net cr.ads@comcast.net
Newspaper with a Republican orientation. **Founded:** 1871. **Freq:** Daily (eve.) and Sat. (morn.). **Print Method:** Offset. **Cols./Page:** 6. **Col. Width:** 21 nonpareils. **Col. Depth:** 294 agate lines. **USPS:** 125-820. **Subscription Rates:** $87 Individuals. **URL:** http://thecr.com/index.asp. **Mailing address:** PO Box 1049, Portland, IN 47371. **Ad Rates:** PCI $9. **Remarks:** Accepts advertising. **Circ:** 5000.

12247 ■ WBSJ-FM - 91.7
Ball State University
2000 W University Ave.
Muncie, IN 47306
Phone: (765)289-1241
Free: 800-382-8540
Format: Public Radio. **Ad Rates:** Noncommercial. **URL:** http://www.cms.bsu.edu.

12248 ■ WPGW-AM - 1440
1891 Indiana 67
Portland, IN 47371-8394
Phone: (260)726-8780
Format: Adult Contemporary. **Networks:** Westwood One Radio; Brownfield; AgriAmerica. **Owner:** WPGW Inc., 1891 W State Rd. 67, Portland, IN 47371. **Founded:** 1951. **Operating Hours:** 6 a.m.-10 p.m. **Key Personnel:** Robert A. Weaver, Owner, President. **Wattage:** 500 Day; 045 Night. **Ad Rates:** Noncommercial. $7.15-$8.90 for 30 seconds; $11.00-$12.85 for 60 seconds. Combined advertising rates available with WPGW-FM. **URL:** http://www.wpgwradio.com.

12249 ■ WPGW-FM - 100.9
1891 W State Road 67
Portland, IN 47371
Phone: (260)726-8729
Fax: (260)726-4311
Format: Country. **Networks:** Brownfield; Westwood One Radio. **Owner:** WPGW Inc., 1891 W State Rd. 67, Portland, IN 47371. **Founded:** 1975. **Operating Hours:** Continuous. **Key Personnel:** Rob Weaver, Gen. Mgr., President. **Wattage:** 4,600. **Ad Rates:** Noncommercial. $7.15-$8.90 for 30 seconds; $11.50-$12.85 for 60 seconds. Combined advertising rates available with WPGW-AM. **URL:** http://www.wpgwradio.com.

12250 ■ WPGW Inc.
1891 W State Rd. 67
Portland, IN 47371
Email: wpgw@jayco.net
Format: Adult Contemporary; Country. **Ad Rates:** Advertising accepted; rates available upon request. **URL:** http://www.wpgwradio.com.

PRINCETON

Gibson Co. Gibson Co. (SW). 28 m N of Evansville. Electric clocks, relays, oil well supplies manufactured. Hatcheries. Coal mines; gas and oil wells. Farming. Wheat, corn, melons, soybeans, livestock.

12251 ■ Gibson County Today
Princeton Publishing Inc.
100 N Gibson St.
Princeton, IN 47670
Phone: (812)385-2525
Fax: (812)386-6199
Free: 800-467-5130
Publisher's E-mail: news@pdclarion.com
Shopper with features. **Freq:** Weekly (Mon.). **Print Method:** Offset. **Cols./Page:** 6. **Col. Width:** 21 nonpareils. **Col. Depth:** 194 agate lines. **Key Personnel:** Gary Blackburn, Publisher; Lori Martin, Manager, Advertising. **Subscription Rates:** Free. **URL:** http://www.tristate-media.com/site/publications/gibson_county_today. **Formerly:** Gibson Dollar Saver. **Remarks:** Advertising accepted; rates available upon request. **Circ:** (Not Reported).

12252 ■ Princeton Daily Clarion
Princeton Publishing Inc.
100 N Gibson St.
Princeton, IN 47670
Phone: (812)385-2525
Fax: (812)386-6199
Free: 800-467-5130
Publisher's E-mail: news@pdclarion.com

General newspaper. **Freq:** Daily (morn.) except Saturday, Sunday and holidays. **Print Method:** Offset. **Cols./Page:** 6. **Col. Width:** 1.833 inches. **Col. Depth:** 21 inches. **Key Personnel:** Marietta Nelson, Business Manager; Andrea Howe, Editor; Maggie Armstrong, Manager, Advertising. **USPS:** 444-920. **URL:** http://www.pdclarion.com. **Remarks:** Accepts classified advertising. **Circ:** (Not Reported).

12253 ■ WRAY-AM - 1250
1900 W Broadway
Princeton, IN 47670
Phone: (812)386-1250
Fax: (812)386-6249
Format: News; Information; Talk. **Simulcasts:** WRAY-FM. **Networks:** AP. **Owner:** Princeton Broadcasting Company Inc., at above address, Princeton, IN 47670. **Founded:** 1950. **Operating Hours:** Continuous; 5% network, 95% local. **ADI:** Evansville, IN (Madisonville, KY). **Key Personnel:** Jeff Lankford, Contact. **Wattage:** 1,000. **Ad Rates:** $20-25 for 30 seconds; $25-30 for 60 seconds. **Mailing address:** PO Box 8, Princeton, IN 47670. **URL:** http://www.wrayradio.com.

12254 ■ WRAY-FM - 98.1
1900 W Broadway
Princeton, IN 47670
Phone: (812)386-1250
Fax: (812)386-6249
Email: wray@wrayradio.com
Format: Hot Country; Country. **Simulcasts:** WRAY-AM. **Networks:** AP. **Founded:** 1960. **Operating Hours:** Continuous; 5% network, 95% local. **ADI:** Evansville, IN (Madisonville, KY). **Key Personnel:** Lynn Roach, Contact; Charlene Garrison, Contact. **Wattage:** 50,000. **Ad Rates:** $20-25 for 30 seconds; $25-30 for 60 seconds. **Mailing address:** PO Box 8, Princeton, IN 47670. **URL:** http://www.wrayradio.com.

RENSSELAER

Jasper Co. Jasper Co. (NW). 40 m N of Lafayette. Manufactures cushion springs, trailers, fertilizer, toy trains. Grain and beef farms. Corn, oats, wheat.

12255 ■ WPUM-FM - 93.3
US Hwy., Rte. 231
Rensselaer, IN 47978
Phone: (219)866-6000
Format: Eclectic. **Networks:** Independent. **Founded:** 1970. **Formerly:** WOWI-FM. **Operating Hours:** Continuous. **Key Personnel:** Sally Berger, Fac. Adv., sallyn@saintjoe.edu. **Wattage:** 010. **Ad Rates:** Noncommercial. **Mailing address:** PO Box 870, Rensselaer, IN 47978. **URL:** http://www.saintjoe.edu.

12256 ■ WRIN-AM - 1560
PO Box D
Rensselaer, IN 47978
Phone: (219)866-5105
Fax: (219)866-5106
Format: Oldies. **Networks:** ABC; AgriAmerica; Brownfield. **Owner:** Brothers Broadcasting Corp., PO Box D, Rensselaer, IN 47978. **Founded:** 1963. **Operating Hours:** Sunrise-sunset. **Key Personnel:** Dan McKay, Dir. of Operations; Jerry Stifle, Asst. Dir. **Wattage:** 1,000 day; 500 night. **Ad Rates:** Noncommercial.

RICHMOND

Wayne Co. Wayne Co. (E). 68 m E of Indianapolis. Earlham College. Rose growing. Manufacturing.

12257 ■ Palladium-Item
Palladium Publishing
1175 N A St.
Richmond, IN 47374
Phone: (765)962-1575
Publication E-mail: palitem@richmond.gannett.com
General newspaper. **Founded:** 1831. **Freq:** Daily (eve.), Sat. and Sun. (morn.). **Print Method:** Offset. **Cols./Page:** 6. **Col. Width:** 2 1/16 inches. **Col. Depth:** 21 inches. **Subscription Rates:** $20 Individuals /month; $10 Individuals online only /month. **URL:** http://www.palitem.com. **Ad Rates:** PCI $13.91. **Remarks:** Accepts advertising. **Circ:** Mon.-Sat. ★**15453**, Sun. ★**19289**.

12258 ■ Quaker Life: Informing and Equipping Friends
Friends United Meeting
101 Quaker Hill Dr.
Richmond, IN 47374-1926
Phone: (765)962-7573
Publisher's E-mail: info@fum.org
Religious magazine. **Freq:** 6/year. **Print Method:** Offset. **Trim Size:** 8 1/2 x 11. **Cols./Page:** 3. **Col. Width:** 26 nonpareils. **Col. Depth:** 134 agate lines. **Key Personnel:** Katie Terrell, Editor. **ISSN:** 0033--5061 (print). **Subscription Rates:** $40 U.S. and Canada /year; $50 Other countries /year. **URL:** http://ycfb2.5acto.servertrust.com/category_s/4.htm. **Remarks:** Advertising accepted; rates available upon request. **Circ:** (Not Reported).

12259 ■ WFMG-FM - 101.3
2301 W Main St.
Richmond, IN 47374
Phone: (765)962-6533
Fax: (765)966-1499
Free: 877-939-1013
Format: Adult Contemporary. **Founded:** 1926. **Formerly:** WKBV-FM. **Operating Hours:** Continuous. **ADI:** Dayton, OH (Richmond, IN). **Key Personnel:** Steve Frey, Contact, steve@g1013.com; John Rose, Contact, johnrose@g1013.com; Steve Frey, Contact, steve@g1013.com. **Wattage:** 50,000. **Ad Rates:** Advertising accepted; rates available upon request. Combined advertising rates available with WKBV-AM. **URL:** http://www.g1013.com.

12260 ■ WHON-AM - 930
2626 Tingler Rd.
Richmond, IN 47374
Phone: (765)962-1595
Fax: (765)966-4824
Free: 800-395-9807
Format: News; Talk; Sports. **Networks:** Mutual Broadcasting System. **Owner:** Brewer Broadcasting Corp., 1305 Carter St., Chattanooga, TN 37402, Ph: (423)265-9494, Fax: (423)266-2335. **Operating Hours:** Continuous. **ADI:** Dayton, OH (Richmond, IN). **Key Personnel:** Dave Strycker, Gen. Mgr.; Lindsey Bell, Office Mgr., lindseyb@kicks96.com; Jeff Lane, News Dir., jeffl@kicks96.com. **Wattage:** 500. **Ad Rates:** $10 for 30 seconds; $16 for 60 seconds. **URL:** http://www.1017thepoint.com.

12261 ■ WKBV-AM - 1490
2301 W Main St.
Richmond, IN 47374
Phone: (765)962-6533
Fax: (765)966-1499
Owner: Rodgers Broadcasting Corp., 2301 W Main St., Richmond, IN 47374, Ph: (765)962-6533. **Founded:** 1926. **ADI:** Dayton, OH (Richmond, IN). **Wattage:** 1,000. **Ad Rates:** $15 for 60 seconds.

12262 ■ WKOI-TV - 43
PO Box 1057
Richmond, IN 47375
Phone: (765)935-2390
Fax: (765)935-5367
Format: Commercial TV; Religious. **Owner:** Trinity Broadcasting Network, 2442 Michelle Dr., Tustin, CA 92780, Ph: (714)665-3619. **Founded:** 1982. **Wattage:** 600,000 ERP.

12263 ■ WQLK-FM - 96.1
2626 Tingler Rd.
Richmond, IN 47374
Phone: (765)962-1595
Fax: (765)966-4824
Free: 800-395-9807
Format: Country. **Owner:** Brewer Broadcasting Corp., 1305 Carter St., Chattanooga, TN 37402, Ph: (423)265-9494, Fax: (423)266-2335. **Formerly:** WGLM-FM. **Operating Hours:** Continuous; 2% network, 98% local. **ADI:** Dayton, OH (Richmond, IN). **Key Personnel:** Dave Strycker, Gen. Mgr., daves@kicks96.com; Lindsey Bell, Office Mgr. **Wattage:** 50,000. **Ad Rates:** $20 for 30 seconds; $25 for 60 seconds. **URL:** http://www.kicks96.com.

12264 ■ WVXR-FM - 89.3
PO Box 1018
Laguna Beach, CA 92652
Fax: (469)241-6795
Free: 800-639-5433
Format: Religious. **Owner:** New Life Ministries, 330 Wellington Ave., Rochester, NY 14619. **Key Personnel:** Stephen Arterburn, Chairman, Founder. **URL:** http://www.newlife.com/Radio/findradio.asp?id=IN&t=Indiana.

12265 ■ WZZY-FM - 98.3
PO Box 1646
Richmond, IN 47375
Free: 877-983-9833
Format: Adult Contemporary. **Networks:** ABC. **Owner:** Whitewater Broadcasting, 2301 W Main St., Richmond, IN 47374. **Founded:** 1970. **Operating Hours:** Continuous. **Wattage:** 3,000. **Ad Rates:** Noncommercial. **URL:** http://www.todaysmusicmix.com.

ROCHESTER

Fulton Co. Fulton Co. (N). 44 m S of South Bend. Manufacturing. Summer resort. Dairy, stock, grain farms.

12266 ■ The Rochester Sentinel
Rochester Sentinel
118 E Eigth St.
Rochester, IN 46975
Phone: (574)223-2111
Fax: (574)223-5782
Free: 800-686-2112
Publisher's E-mail: news@rochsent.com
General newspaper. **Freq:** Daily except Sun. **Key Personnel:** Christina M. Seiler, Editor, fax: (574)224-5327; Karen Vojtasek, Director, Advertising, phone: (574)224-5323; Sarah O. Wilson, Publisher, phone: (574)224-5331. **Subscription Rates:** $159 By mail same-day; $195 Out of area. **URL:** http://www.rochsent.com. **Mailing address:** PO Box 260, Rochester, IN 46975. **Remarks:** Accepts advertising. **Circ:** Paid 3900, Sat. 4100.

12267 ■ Shopping Guide News
Shopping Guide News
617 Main St.
Rochester, IN 46975
Phone: (574)223-5417
Fax: (574)223-8330
Publication E-mail: shoppingguide@rtcol.com
Shopping guide. **Freq:** Weekly (Wed.). **Print Method:** Web offset. **Trim Size:** 10 1/4 x 15. **Cols./Page:** 6. **Col. Width:** 9.5 picas. **Col. Depth:** 15 inches. **Subscription Rates:** $30 Individuals. **URL:** http://www.rtcol.com/~shoppingguide. **Mailing address:** PO Box 229, Rochester, IN 46975. **Ad Rates:** GLR $6.20; BW $432; SAU $5.95; PCI $6.20. **Remarks:** Accepts advertising. **Circ:** ‡9550.

12268 ■ WQKV-FM - 88.5
PO Box 2098
Omaha, NE 68103
Free: 800-525-5683
Format: Contemporary Christian. **Owner:** Educational Media Foundation, 5700 W Oaks Blvd., CA 95765, Free: 800-800434-8400. **Key Personnel:** Alan Mason, COO; Mike Novak, President, CEO. **URL:** http://www.klove.com.

12269 ■ WROI-FM - 92.1
110 E 8th St.
Rochester, IN 46975
Phone: (574)223-6059
Fax: (574)223-2238
Format: Oldies. **Networks:** Brownfield; ABC. **Owner:** Bair Communications Inc., at above address. **Founded:** 1971. **Operating Hours:** 24. **Key Personnel:** Tom Bair, Gen. Mgr.; Sue Bair, Gen. Sales Mgr., sue@rtcol.com. **Wattage:** 4,300. **Ad Rates:** Advertising accepted; rates available upon request. **URL:** http://www.wroifm.com.

ROCKPORT

Spencer Co. Spencer Co. (SW). On Ohio River, 32 m E of Evansville. Parks. Tourism. National trucking terminal operation. Manufacturing. Diversified farming. Wheat, corn, soybeans tobacco. Cattle, pigs.

12270 ■ The Spencer County Journal-Democrat
Landmark Community Newspapers L.L.C.
541 Main St.
Rockport, IN 47635
Phone: (812)649-9196
Publisher's E-mail: marketing@lcni.com
Community newspaper. **Freq:** Weekly (Thurs.). **Print Method:** Offset. **Cols./Page:** 6. **Col. Width:** 12 picas. **Col. Depth:** 21 1/2 inches. **URL:** http://www.

Circulation: ★ = AAM; △ or • = BPA; ♦ = CAC; ❑ = VAC; ⊕ = PO Statement; ‡ = Publisher's Report; Boldface figures = sworn; Light figures = estimated.

spencercountyjournal.com. **Mailing address:** PO Box 6, Rockport, IN 47635. **Remarks:** Accepts advertising. **Circ:** (Not Reported).

ROCKVILLE

Parke Co. Parke Co. (W). 25 m NE of Terre Haute. State Parks. Historical area. Feed mill. Coal mines. Appliance industries. Timber Agriculture. Livestock.

12271 ■ Parke County Sentinel
Torch Newspapers
125 W High St.
Rockville, IN 47872
Phone: (317)569-2033
Newspaper. **Freq:** Weekly (Wed.). **Print Method:** Offset. **Cols./Page:** 7. **Col. Width:** 20 nonpareils. **Col. Depth:** 294 agate lines. **Key Personnel:** Larry Bemis, Editor; Kimberly White, Business Manager; Mary Jo Harney, Publisher. **ISSN:** 1044--7822 (print). **Subscription Rates:** $60 Individuals 12 months - in state (print and online); $65 Out of state (print and online); $37 Individuals 12 months - print only - in state; $47 Out of area 12 months - print only - out of state; 42 Individuals 12 months - online only. **URL:** http://www.parkecountysentinel.com. **Mailing address:** PO Box 187, Rockville, IN 47872. **Remarks:** Accepts advertising. **Circ:** (Not Reported).

RUSHVILLE

Rush Co. Rush Co. (SEC). 39 m SE of Indianapolis. Manufacturing. Meat packing; vibration eliminators for heavy equipment; bottling works. Stone quarry. Agriculture. Cattle, hogs.

12272 ■ Rushville Republican
Rushville Newspapers Inc.
126 S Main St.
Rushville, IN 46173
Phone: (765)932-2222
Fax: (765)932-4358
Newspaper with a Republican orientation. **Founded:** 1840. **Freq:** Daily (eve.). **Print Method:** Offset. **Cols./Page:** 6. **Col. Width:** 25 nonpareils. **Col. Depth:** 301 agate lines. **Key Personnel:** Laura Welborn, Publisher, phone: (812)663-3111. **Subscription Rates:** $110 Individuals carrier delivery. **URL:** http://www.rushvillerepublican.com. **Mailing address:** PO Box 189, Rushville, IN 46173-0189. **Ad Rates:** SAU $5.88. **Remarks:** Accepts advertising. **Circ:** ‡3983.

SALEM

Washington Co. Washington Co. (S). 35 m NW of New Albany. Manufacturing. Hardwood timber. Rock quarries. Largest cattle producing county in the state. Diversified farming. Corn, wheat, oats.

12273 ■ The Salem Democrat
Leader Publishing Company of Salem Inc.
117-119 E Walnut St.
Salem, IN 47167
Phone: (812)883-3281
Fax: (812)883-4446
Publisher's E-mail: office@salemleader.com
Newspaper with a Democratic orientation. **Freq:** Weekly (Thurs.). **Print Method:** Offset. **Cols./Page:** 6. **Col. Width:** 2 1/32 inches. **Col. Depth:** 21.5 picas. **Key Personnel:** Stephanie Taylor Ferriell, Editor; Nancy Grossman, Publisher; Dennis Miller, Manager, Production. **USPS:** 477-560. **Subscription Rates:** $30 Individuals Washington County ; $45 Individuals Orange, Jackson, Clark, Scott, Floyd, Lawrence, Crawford and Harrison counties; $55 Individuals elsewhere in the State of Indiana ; $65 Individuals outside the State of Indiana. **URL:** http://www.salemleader.com. **Mailing address:** PO Box 506, Salem, IN 47167. **Remarks:** Accepts advertising. **Circ:** (Not Reported).

12274 ■ The Salem Leader
Leader Publishing Company of Salem Inc.
117-119 E Walnut St.
Salem, IN 47167
Phone: (812)883-3281
Fax: (812)883-4446
Publisher's E-mail: office@salemleader.com
Newspaper with a Republican orientation. **Freq:** Weekly (Tues.). **Print Method:** Offset. **Cols./Page:** 6. **Col. Width:** 2 1/32 inches. **Col. Depth:** 21.5 picas. **Key Personnel:** Stephanie Taylor Ferriell, Editor; Nancy Grossman, Publisher; Dennis Miller, Manager, Production. **USPS:** 008-980. **Subscription Rates:** $30 Individuals Washington County; $45 Individuals Orange, Jackson, Clark, Scott, Floyd, Lawrence, Crawford and Harrison counties; $55 Individuals elsewhere in the State of Indiana; $65 Individuals outside the State of Indiana. **URL:** http://www.salemleader.com. **Mailing address:** PO Box 506, Salem, IN 47167. **Circ:** (Not Reported).

12275 ■ The Washington County Edition
Green Banner Publications Inc.
105 E Walnut St.
Salem, IN 47167
Phone: (812)883-5555
Community newspaper. **Freq:** Weekly (Wed.). **Print Method:** Offset. **Trim Size:** 11 3/8 x 17. **Cols./Page:** 5. **Col. Width:** 25 nonpareils. **Col. Depth:** 224 agate lines. **Key Personnel:** Joe Green, Publisher. **URL:** http://www.gbpnews.com/index.php?option=com_content&view=category&layout=blog&id=37&Itemid=59. **Remarks:** Accepts advertising. **Circ:** (Not Reported).

12276 ■ WSLM-AM - 1220
1308 Higway 56-E
Salem, IN 47167
Email: wslm@blueriver.net
Format: Full Service. **Simulcasts:** WSLM-FM. **Owner:** Don H. Martin Inc., at above address. **Founded:** 1953. **Operating Hours**: Continuous. **ADI**: Greensboro-Winston Salem-High Point, NC. **Wattage**: '5,000 Day 082 Night. **Ad Rates:** Advertising accepted; rates available upon request. $15-20 for 30 seconds; $20-25 for 60 seconds. **Mailing address:** PO Box 385, Salem, IN 47167.

12277 ■ WSLM-FM - 97.9
1308 Higway 56-E
Salem, IN 47167
Email: wslm@blueriver.net
Format: Full Service. **Simulcasts:** WSIM-AM 1220. **Owner:** Don H. Martin Inc., at above address. **Founded:** 1962. **Wattage**: 3,000. **Ad Rates:** Advertising accepted; rates available upon request. $15-20 for 30 seconds; $20-25 for 60 seconds. **Mailing address:** PO Box 385, Salem, IN 47167.

SCOTTSBURG

Scott Co. Scott Co. (SE). 31 m N of Louisville, Ky. Unfinished furniture, canning factories. Limestone quarries; hardwood timber. Agriculture. Tomatoes, corn, wheat.

12278 ■ The Giveaway: Online News
Green Banner Publications Inc.
183 E McClain St.
Scottsburg, IN 47170
Phone: (812)752-3171
Community newspaper. **Freq:** Weekly (Wed.). **Print Method:** Offset. **Trim Size:** 11 3/8 x 17. **Cols./Page:** 5. **Col. Width:** 25 nonpareils. **Col. Depth:** 224 agate lines. **Key Personnel:** Mark Grigsby, Editor; Joe Green, Publisher. **URL:** http://www.gbpnews.com/index.php?option=com_content&view=category&layout=blog&id=35&Itemid=57. **Remarks:** Accepts advertising. **Circ:** (Not Reported).

12279 ■ WMPI-FM - 105.3
22 E McClain Ave.
Scottsburg, IN 47170
Phone: (812)752-3688
Free: 800-441-1053
Format: Contemporary Country. **Networks:** ABC. **Owner:** D.R Rice Broadcasting Inc., 22 E McClain Ave., Scottsburg, IN 47170, Free: 800-441-1053. **Founded:** 1956. **Operating Hours**: Continuous; 5% network, 95% local. **ADI**: Louisville, KY. **Key Personnel:** John Ross, Contact, jross@i1053.com; Sharon Love, Contact, slove@i1053.com; John Ross, Contact, jross@i1053.com. **Wattage**: 6,000. **Ad Rates:** $10.35-44 for 60 seconds. **URL:** http://www.i1053country.com.

SELLERSBURG

12280 ■ WLCL-FM - 93.9
3280 Peachtree Rd. NW, Ste. 2300
Atlanta, GA 30305
Phone: (404)949-0700
Fax: (404)949-0740
Format: Classic Rock. **Networks:** Jones Satellite. **Owner:** S.C.I. Broadcasting Inc., Not Available. **Founded:** 1960. **Operating Hours**: Continuous. **Key Personnel:** Paul Agase, VP of Sales; Peter Bolger, Operations Mgr.; Steve Shaw, President. **Wattage**: 2,650. **Ad Rates:** $11-24 for 30 seconds; $14-30 for 60 seconds. WZZB AM/WAVG AM. **URL:** http://www.cumulus.com.

12281 ■ WSEZ-AM - 1560
322 Hunter Station Rd.
Sellersburg, IN 47172
Phone: (812)248-9800
Email: wume@blueriver.net
Format: Oldies. **Networks:** Independent. **Owner:** Diamond Shores Broadcasting L.L.C., at above address. **Founded:** 1963. **Formerly**: WVAK-AM. **Operating Hours**: 6 a.m.-6 p.m.; 100% local. **Wattage**: 250. **Ad Rates:** $6-12 for 30 seconds; $8-14 for 60 seconds. Combined advertising rates available with WUME-FM.

SEYMOUR

Jackson Co. Jackson Co. (S). 59 m S of Indianapolis. Manufacturing. Hardwood timber. Diversified farming.

12282 ■ Seymour Daily Tribune
The Tribune
100 St. Louis Ave.
Seymour, IN 47274
Phone: (812)522-4871
Fax: (812)522-7691
Free: 800-800-8212
Publisher's E-mail: tribune@freedom.com
General newspaper. **Founded:** 1879. **Freq:** Mon.-Sat. **Print Method:** Offset. **Cols./Page:** 6. **Col. Width:** 12.2 picas. **Col. Depth:** 301 agate lines. **Subscription Rates:** $132 Individuals; $234 By mail local; $174.48 By mail in state; $190.20 Out of state mail. **URL:** http://www.tribtown.com. **Formerly**: The Tribune. **Mailing address:** PO Box 447, Seymour, IN 47274. **Remarks:** Accepts advertising. **Circ:** (Not Reported).

12283 ■ WJAA-FM - 96.3
1531 W Tipton St.
Seymour, IN 47274
Phone: (812)523-3343
Fax: (812)523-5116
Format: Adult Album Alternative. **Ad Rates:** Noncommercial. **URL:** http://www.wjaa.net.

12284 ■ WJLR-FM - 91.5
PO Box 2098
Omaha, NE 68103
Free: 800-525-5683
Format: Contemporary Christian. **Owner:** Educational Media Foundation, 5700 W Oaks Blvd., CA 95765, Free: 800-800434-8400. **Key Personnel:** Larry Moody, President, CEO. **URL:** http://www.klove.com.

12285 ■ WZZB-AM - 1390
PO Box 806
Seymour, IN 47274
Phone: (812)522-1390
Fax: (812)522-9541
Format: News; Adult Contemporary; Oldies. **Networks:** Jones Satellite. **Owner:** Midnight Hour Broadcasting L.L.C., at above address. **Founded:** 1949. **Formerly**: WJCD-AM. **Operating Hours**: Continuous. **Key Personnel:** Blair Trask, President. **Wattage**: 1,000. **Ad Rates:** $9-20 for 30 seconds; $12-26 for 60 seconds. WQKC FM/WAVG AM.

SHELBYVILLE

Shelby Co. Shelby Co. (SEC). 28 m SE of Indianapolis. Manufactures magnetic wire, precision aluminum die castings, molded rubber products, phonograph records, custom steel fabrication, business forms. Grain, stock, dairy farms.

12286 ■ The Shelbyville News
Shelbyville Newspapers Inc.
123 E Washington St.
Shelbyville, IN 46176
Phone: (317)398-6631
Fax: (317)398-0194
Publication E-mail: shelbynews@shelbynews.com
General newspaper. **Freq:** Monthly. **Print Method:** Offset. **Trim Size:** 13 3/4 x 22 3/4. **Cols./Page:** 6. **Col. Width:** 2 1/16 inches. **Col. Depth:** 301 agate lines. **Key Personnel:** Rhonda Schwegman, Manager, Advertising and Sales; Rachael Raney, Publisher. **Subscription Rates:** $12.99 Individuals online; $16.50 Individuals 4

Weeks (print); $52.80 Individuals 13 Weeks (print); $100.10 Individuals 26 Weeks (print); $192.50 Individuals 52 Weeks (print). **URL:** http://www.shelbynews.com. **Mailing address:** PO Box 750, Shelbyville, IN 46176. **Ad Rates:** GLR $12.33; BW $1,590.57; 4C $1,880.57; PCI $9.75. **Remarks:** Accepts advertising. **Circ:** Mon.-Sat. ★**8655**.

SHOALS

Martin Co. Martin Co. (SW). 42 m E of Vincennes. Gypsum mines; gypsum wallboard plants. Saw mill. Agriculture.

12287 ■ The Shoals News
The Shoals News
311 High St.
Shoals, IN 47581
Phone: (812)247-2828
Fax: (812)247-2243
Newspaper with a Democratic orientation. **Freq:** Weekly (Wed.). **Print Method:** Offset. **Cols./Page:** 6. **Col. Width:** 24 nonpareils. **Col. Depth:** 294 agate lines. **USPS:** 494-560. **Subscription Rates:** $22 Individuals Martin and adjoining counties; $24 Elsewhere Indiana; $27 Out of state. **URL:** http://www.theshoalsnews.com/our_newspaper/contact_us. **Mailing address:** PO Box 240, Shoals, IN 47581. **Ad Rates:** GLR $.16; SAU $2.40. **Remarks:** Accepts advertising. **Circ:** ‡2700.

SOUTH BEND

St. Joseph Co. St. Joseph Co. (N). On St. Joseph River, adjacent to Mishawaka and 96 m SE of Chicago, Ill. University of Notre Dame, Indiana University at South Bend. St. Mary's College.

12288 ■ Blue & Gold Illustrated--Notre Dame Football
Blue and Gold Illustrated
54377 30th St.
South Bend, IN 46635
Phone: (574)968-1104
Magazine covering Notre Dame Fighting Irish football. **Freq:** 20/yr. **Key Personnel:** Dave Searcy, Director, Advertising; Gail Evans, Manager, Circulation; Stu Coman, Publisher. **Subscription Rates:** $52.95 Individuals print and online; $49.99 Individuals online only. **URL:** http://bluegoldonline.com/store/#!/~/category/id=4564056&offset=0&sort=normal. **Ad Rates:** BW $2,040; 4C $2,520. **Remarks:** Accepts advertising. **Circ:** Paid 55000.

12289 ■ Culture Wars
Ultramontane Associates Inc.
206 Marquette Ave.
South Bend, IN 46617
Phone: (574)289-9786
Fax: (574)289-1461
Magazine exploring social and family issues from the point of view of the Catholic Church. **Freq:** Monthly. **Key Personnel:** Michael E. Jones, PhD, Editor. **Subscription Rates:** $35 online; $49 print. **Alt. Formats:** PDF. **URL:** http://www.culturewars.com. **Formerly:** Fidelity Magazine. **Ad Rates:** BW $400. **Remarks:** Accepts advertising. **Circ:** Paid ‡10000.

12290 ■ The Sign of Peace
Catholic Peace Fellowship
PO Box 4232
South Bend, IN 46634
Phone: (574)232-2811
Publisher's E-mail: staff@catholicpeacefellowship.org
Freq: Periodic. **ISSN:** 0008- 8277 (print). **Subscription Rates:** $5 Single issue. **URL:** http://www.catholicpeacefellowship.org/nextpage.asp?m=1003. **Remarks:** Advertising not accepted. **Circ:** 2000.

12291 ■ South Bend Tribune
South Bend Tribune
225 W Colfax Ave.
South Bend, IN 46626
Phone: (574)235-6161
Fax: (574)236-1765
Publisher's E-mail: subscriberservices@sbtinfo.com
General newspaper. **Freq:** Daily. **Print Method:** Offset. **Trim Size:** 13 1/2 x 22. **Cols./Page:** 6. **Col. Width:** 2 1/16 inches. **Col. Depth:** 294 agate lines. **USPS:** 501-980. **Subscription Rates:** $13 Individuals daily (print); $13 Individuals daily (online); $7.80 Individuals Weekend all access; $6.50 Individuals Sunday all access. **URL:** http://www.southbendtribune.com. **Ad Rates:** BW $8,568; 4C $9,668; PCI $68. **Remarks:** Accepts advertising. **Circ:** ★**62000**, ★**80000**.

12292 ■ WDND-AM - 1620
3371 Cleveland Rd., Ste. 300
South Bend, IN 46628
Format: Sports. **Owner:** Artistic Media Partners Inc., 5520 E 75th St., Indianapolis, IN 46250, Ph: (317)594-0600. **Operating Hours:** Continuous. **Key Personnel:** Rick Evans, Operations Mgr. **Ad Rates:** Advertising accepted; rates available upon request. **URL:** http://www.artisticradio.com.

12293 ■ WETL-FM - 91.7
215 S St. Joseph St.
South Bend, IN 46601
Phone: (574)283-8076
Format: Talk; Information; Eclectic. **Networks:** Longhorn Radio. **Owner:** South Bend Community School Corp., at above address, South Bend, IN 46601. **Founded:** 1958. **Operating Hours:** 8 hours Daily; 10% network, 90% local. **ADI:** South Bend-Elkhart, IN. **Key Personnel:** John Overmyer, Contact. **Wattage:** 3,000. **Ad Rates:** Noncommercial.

12294 ■ WHLY-AM
PO Box 4399
South Bend, IN 46634
Phone: (574)273-9300
Fax: (574)273-9090
Format: Oldies. **Networks:** ABC. **Owner:** Artistic Media Partners Inc., 5520 E 75th St., Indianapolis, IN 46250, Ph: (317)594-0600. **Founded:** Oct. 01, 1999. **Formerly:** WAMJ-AM; WJVA-AM. **Key Personnel:** Bob Henning, Chief Engineer; Arthur Angotti, COO. **Wattage:** 1,000 Day; 500 Night. **Ad Rates:** $12.50 for 30 seconds; $15 for 60 seconds.

12295 ■ WHME-FM - 103.1
61300 S Ironwood Rd.
South Bend, IN 46614
Phone: (574)291-8200
Format: Religious; Contemporary Christian. **Networks:** Independent. **Owner:** LeSEA Broadcasting Network, 61300 Ironwood Rd., South Bend, IN 46614, Free: 800-685-3732. **Founded:** 1968. **Operating Hours:** Continuous. **ADI:** South Bend-Elkhart, IN. **Wattage:** 3,000. **Ad Rates:** Noncommercial. **URL:** http://www.lesea.com.

12296 ■ WHME-TV - 46
61300 S Ironwood Rd.
South Bend, IN 46614
Wattage: 300,000 ERP. **Ad Rates:** Advertising accepted; rates available upon request.

12297 ■ WHPD-FM
61300 Ironwood Rd.
South Bend, IN 46614
Phone: (574)291-8200
Email: pulse@lesea.com
Format: Contemporary Christian. **Owner:** LeSea Broadcasting Corp., at above address. **Founded:** 1960. **Formerly:** WDOW-FM; WVHQ-FM. **Key Personnel:** Anna Riblet, Sales Mgr., ariblet@lesea.com. **Wattage:** 3,300 ERP. **Ad Rates:** Advertising accepted; rates available upon request. $15 per unit.

12298 ■ WHPZ-FM - 96.9
61300 Ironwood Rd.
South Bend, IN 46614
Phone: (574)291-8200
Free: 888-807-8573
Email: pulse@lesea.com
Format: Contemporary Christian. **Founded:** Dec. 1996. **Key Personnel:** Anna Riblet, Sales Mgr., ariblet@lesea.com. **URL:** http://www.pulsefm.com.

12299 ■ WNDU-TV - 16
PO Box 1616
South Bend, IN 46634
Phone: (574)284-3016
Fax: (574)284-3009
Email: tvsales@wndu.com
Format: News. **Networks:** NBC. **Owner:** Gray Television Inc., 4370 Peachtree Rd. NE, No. 400, Atlanta, GA 30319-3054, Ph: (404)266-8333. **Founded:** 1955. **Operating Hours:** Continuous. **ADI:** South Bend-Elkhart, IN. **Key Personnel:** Jim Behling, President. **Local Programs:** *NewsCenter 16*, Monday Tuesday Wednesday Thursday Friday Saturday Sunday 12:00 p.m. - 12:30 p.m.; 5:00 p.m. - 6:30 p.m.; 11:00 p.m. - 11:30 p.m. 6:00 p.m. - 6:30 p.m.; 11:00 p.m. - 11:30 p.m. **Ad Rates:** $45-2000 per unit. **URL:** http://www.wndu.com.

12300 ■ WNDV-FM - 92.9
3371 Cleveland Rd., Ste. 300
South Bend, IN 46628
Phone: (574)273-9300
Fax: (574)273-9090
Format: Top 40. **Ad Rates:** Advertising accepted; rates available upon request. **URL:** http://www.u93.com.

12301 ■ WNIT-TV - 34
300 W Jefferson Blvd.
South Bend, IN 46601
Phone: (574)675-9648
Fax: (574)289-3441
Email: wnit@wnit.org
Format: Public TV. **Networks:** Public Broadcasting Service (PBS). **Owner:** Michiana Public Broadcasting Corp., 300 W Jefferson Blvd., South Bend, IN 46601, Ph: (574)675-9648, Fax: (574)289-3441. **Founded:** 1968. **Operating Hours:** 6 a.m.-12:00 a.m.; 98% network, 2% local. **ADI:** South Bend-Elkhart, IN. **Key Personnel:** Mary Pruess, Gen. Mgr., President, skofeldt@wnit.org; Brian Hoover, Director, bhoover@wnit.org. **Wattage:** 1,300,000. **Ad Rates:** Noncommercial. **URL:** http://www.wnit.org.

12302 ■ WOZW-FM - 103.9
3371 Cleveland Rd., Ste. 300
South Bend, IN 46628
Phone: (574)273-9300
Fax: (574)273-9090
Format: Classic Rock. **Operating Hours:** Continuous. **ADI:** Knoxville (Crossville), TN. **Wattage:** 100. **Ad Rates:** Advertising accepted; rates available upon request. **URL:** http://wzow.com.

12303 ■ WUBS-FM - 89.7
702 Lincolnway W
South Bend, IN 46616
Phone: (574)287-4700
Free: 866-797-1794
Format: Religious. **Owner:** Interfaith Christian Union, Inc., at above address, South Bend, IN. **Wattage:** 1,500. **Ad Rates:** Advertising accepted; rates available upon request. **URL:** http://wubs.org.

12304 ■ WUBU-FM - 106.3
401 E Colfax Ave., Ste. 300
South Bend, IN 46617
Phone: (574)233-3505
Fax: (574)233-0580
Format: Adult Contemporary. **Operating Hours:** Continuous. **Key Personnel:** Amy Mejer, Div. Mgr., emorse@wubufm.com; Tonya Reed, Mktg. Mgr., reed@wubufm.com. **Ad Rates:** Advertising accepted; rates available upon request. **URL:** http://www.wubufm.com.

12305 ■ WYPW-FM - 95.7
54195 Ironwood Rd.
South Bend, IN 46635
Phone: (574)855-1587
Fax: (574)318-4921
Format: Hip Hop. **Owner:** Talking Stick Communications L.L.C., 216 W Market St., Warsaw, IN 46580. **Key Personnel:** Emily Wideman, Sales Mgr. **Ad Rates:** Advertising accepted; rates available upon request. **URL:** http://www.redeemerradio.com.

12306 ■ WZOW-FM - 97.7
3371 Cleveland Rd., Ste. 300
South Bend, IN 46628
Format: Oldies. **Owner:** Artistic Media Partners Inc., 5520 E 75th St., Indianapolis, IN 46250, Ph: (317)594-0600. **Founded:** 1976. **Operating Hours:** Continuous. **ADI:** South Bend-Elkhart, IN. **Key Personnel:** Karen Right, Operations Mgr.; Rita Kinzie, Bus. Mgr.; Pam Homan, Sales Mgr. **Wattage:** 6,000. **Ad Rates:** Noncommercial. Combined advertising rates available with WKAM-AM. **URL:** http://www.wzow.com.

SPENCER

Owen Co. Owen Co. (SWC). 53 m SW of Indianapolis. Manufacturing. Printing. Coal mines; limestone quarries. Agriculture. Corn, livestock, soybeans, apples.

Circulation: ★ = AAM; △ or • = BPA; ♦ = CAC; ❑ = VAC; ⊕ = PO Statement; ‡ = Publisher's Report; Boldface figures = sworn; Light figures = estimated.

12307 ■ Spencer Owen Leader
Spencer Owen Leader
114 E Franklin St.
Spencer, IN 47460-1877
Phone: (812)829-2255
Fax: (812)829-4666
Publisher's E-mail: editor@spencereveningworld.com
Community newspaper. **Freq:** Weekly (Thurs.). **Print Method:** Offset. **Cols./Page:** 7. **Col. Width:** 12.5 picas. **Col. Depth:** 21 inches. **Key Personnel:** Travis Curry, Editor. **USPS:** 416-240. **Subscription Rates:** $52 Individuals Owen County and surrounding counties - print and online; $67 Elsewhere in Indiana - print and online; $77 Out of state print and online; $45 Individuals online only - 1 year. **URL:** http://www.spencereveningworld.com. **Mailing address:** PO Box 226, Spencer, IN 47460. **Ad Rates:** GLR $2; PCI $2.75. **Remarks:** Accepts advertising. **Circ:** (Not Reported).

SULLIVAN

Sullivan Co. Sullivan Co. (SW). 27 m S of Terre Haute. Machine shops. Coal mines; oil and natural gas wells; timber. Dairy, poultry, grain farms.

12308 ■ Daily Times
Daily News
115 W Jackson St.
Sullivan, IN 47882
Phone: (812)268-6356
Fax: (812)268-3110
Free: 800-264-6356
Publisher's E-mail: management.sdt@gmail.com
Newspaper with a Democratic orientation. **Founded:** 1897. **Freq:** Daily. **Print Method:** Offset. **Cols./Page:** 6. **Col. Width:** 2 1/16 inches. **Col. Depth:** 21 inches. **Key Personnel:** Nancy P. Gettinger, Publisher; Tom P. Gettinger, Managing Editor. **Subscription Rates:** $85 Individuals. **URL:** http://www.sullivan-times.com. **Mailing address:** PO Box 130, Sullivan, IN 47882. **Ad Rates:** BW $409.50; SAU $4.10; PCI $3.50. **Remarks:** Accepts advertising. **Circ:** ‡4700.

SUNMAN

12309 ■ Enhanced Telecommunications Corp.
123 Nieman St.
Sunman, IN 47041
Phone: (812)623-2122
Fax: (812)623-4159
Free: 866-382-4968
Formerly: Sunman Telecommunications Corp. **Key Personnel:** Julie Seale, HR Mgr., jseale@etc1.net; Matt Anderson, Div. Mgr., manderson@etc1.net; Chad Miles, CEO, President, cmiles@etc1.net; Dave Smith, Contact, dsmith@etc1.net. **Cities Served:** Napolean, New Point, Saint Leon, Sunman, Indiana: subscribing households 625; United States; 33 channels. **Mailing address:** PO Box 145, Sunman, IN 47041. **URL:** http://www.etczone.com.

TELL CITY

Perry Co. Perry Co. (S). On Ohio River, 45 m E of Evansville. Boat connections. Manufactures furniture, petrochemical filters, electric motors, boats, barges; foundry; flour, planing mills; bottling works; oil refinery; meat packing plants. Coal mines; hardwood timber. Dairy, stock, poultry farms.

12310 ■ The Perry County News
News Publishing Co.
537 Main St.
Tell City, IN 47586
Phone: (812)547-3424
Publisher's E-mail: circulation@perrycountynews.com
Community newspaper. **Freq:** Semiweekly. **Print Method:** Offset. **Cols./Page:** 6. **Col. Width:** 24 nonpareils. **Col. Depth:** 301 agate lines. **Key Personnel:** Vince Luecke, Editor. **URL:** http://www.perrycountynews.com. **Ad Rates:** GLR $5.77; BW $1,039.74; 4C $1,304.55; SAU $8.06; PCI $8.06. **Remarks:** Advertising accepted; rates available upon request. **Circ:** **7490.**

12311 ■ WTCJ-AM - 1230
645 Main St.
Tell City, IN 47586
Owner: The Cromwell Group, Inc., 1824 Murfreesboro Rd., Nashville, TN 37217, Ph: (615)361-7560, Fax: (615)366-4313. **Founded:** 1948. **Wattage:** 850. **Ad Rates:** $6 for 30 seconds; $8.10 for 60 seconds.

TERRE HAUTE

Vigo Co. Vigo Co. (W). On Wabash River, 72 m SW of Indianapolis. Indiana State University, Rose Hulman Institute of Technology. Coal mines; shale and clay deposits; oil field. Manufacturing.

12312 ■ Echoes
Rose-Hulman Institute of Technology John A. Logan Library
5500 Wabash Ave.
Terre Haute, IN 47803
Phone: (812)877-1511
Free: 800-248-7448
Publisher's E-mail: webmaster@rose-hulman.edu
Magazine for college alumni, parents, and friends. **Founded:** 1874. **Freq:** Quarterly (during the academic year). **Print Method:** Offset. **Trim Size:** 8 4/8 x 11. **URL:** http://www.rose-hulman.edu/offices-and-services/publications/echoes.aspx. **Remarks:** Advertising not accepted. **Circ:** Free 22000.

12313 ■ The Indiana Statesman
Indiana State University
200 N 7th St.
Terre Haute, IN 47809-1902
Free: 800-468-6478
Collegiate newspaper. **Freq:** 3/week. **Print Method:** Offset. **Cols./Page:** 6. **Col. Width:** 11 picas. **Col. Depth:** 21 1/2 inches. **Key Personnel:** Carey Ford, Editor-in-Chief. **URL:** http://www.isustudentmedia.com/indiana_statesman. **Ad Rates:** BW 800, campus; BW $850, local; BW $900, non local. **Remarks:** Accepts advertising. **Circ:** Free ‡6500.

12314 ■ The Industrial Geographer
Indiana State University
200 N 7th St.
Terre Haute, IN 47809-1902
Free: 800-468-6478
Journal that publishes articles and research notes that focus on a broad range of economic issues across all economic sectors and explore issues at all scales from the firm to the globe. **Freq:** Semiannual Issue 1 (January-June) and Issue 2 (July-December). **Key Personnel:** F. Calzonetti, Board Member; K. Oshiro, Board Member; J. Bodenman, Board Member; C. Pavlik, Board Member; S. Bagchi-Sen, Board Member; Neil Reid, Editor, Founder; Murray D. Rice, Board Member; Chuck Yeagar, Editor. **ISSN:** 1540--1669 (print). **Subscription Rates:** Free. **URL:** http://igeographer.lib.indstate.edu. **Remarks:** Advertising not accepted. **Circ:** (Not Reported).

12315 ■ The Rose Thorn
Rose-Hulman Institute of Technology John A. Logan Library
5500 Wabash Ave.
Terre Haute, IN 47803
Phone: (812)877-1511
Free: 800-248-7448
Publisher's E-mail: webmaster@rose-hulman.edu
Collegiate newspaper covering local and national issues of interest to the Rose-Hulman Community. **Freq:** Weekly. **Print Method:** Offset. **Cols./Page:** 5. **Col. Width:** 22 nonpareils. **Col. Depth:** 224 agate lines. **Key Personnel:** Bethany Martin, Editor-in-Chief. **Subscription Rates:** Free. **URL:** http://scholar.rose-hulman.edu/rosethorn. **Ad Rates:** BW $500; PCI $6.50. **Remarks:** Color advertising not accepted. **Circ:** Combined ‡3500.

12316 ■ STATE
Indiana State University Alumni Association
30 N 5th St.
Terre Haute, IN 47807
Phone: (812)514-8400
Fax: (812)237-8157
Free: 800-258-6478
Publisher's E-mail: alumni@indstatefoundation.org
Magazine featuring frequent stories, pictures, recaps and highlights of Indiana State University and Alumni Association. **Freq:** Semiannual spring and fall. **Subscription Rates:** Free. **URL:** http://statemagazine.com; http://www.indstate.edu/alumni/stayconnected/index.php. **Formerly**: Indiana State University Magazine. **Remarks:** Advertising not accepted. **Circ:** 72000.

12317 ■ Clinton Cable TV Co. Inc.
PO Box 665
Terre Haute, IN 47808
Phone: (812)235-8174
Fax: (812)235-8174
Owner: Nichols Family, at above address. **Founded:** 1965. **Key Personnel:** John E. Nichols, President; William F. George, Gen. Mgr., Secretary, Treasurer. **Cities Served:** Clinton, Fairview, Parke, Rosedale, Universal, Vermillion, Vigo, Indiana: subscribing households 4,150; 44 channels.

12318 ■ WAXI-FM - 104.9
1301 Ohio St.
Terre Haute, IN 47807
Phone: (812)234-9770
Fax: (812)238-1576
Format: Album-Oriented Rock (AOR). **Networks:** ABC. **Owner:** Crossroads Communications Inc., 50 Desert Sands Ln., Yarmouth Port, MA 02675, Fax: (508)375-9446. **Founded:** 1978. **Operating Hours:** Continuous; 85% network, 15% local. **Wattage:** 1,200. **Ad Rates:** Noncommercial. Combined advertising rates available with WSDM-FM, WSDX-AM, WSJX-AM, WLEZ-FM. **URL:** http://www.trueoldieswaxi.com.

12319 ■ WBOW-AM - 1300
1301 Ohio St.
Terre Haute, IN 47807
Phone: (812)234-9770
Fax: (812)238-1576
Format: Sports; Talk. **Simulcasts:** WSOX-AM. **Networks:** ESPN Radio. **Owner:** Crossroads Communications Inc., 50 Desert Sands Ln., Yarmouth Port, MA 02675, Fax: (508)375-9446. **Founded:** 1958. **Formerly**: WAAC; WMFT; WJSH. **Operating Hours**: Continuous. **ADI**: Terre Haute, IN. **Key Personnel:** John Sherman, Dir. of Programs; Bill Cook, Owner. **Wattage:** 500. **Ad Rates:** $4-16 per unit. Combined advertising rates available with WSDM-FM, WAXI-FM, WBOW-FM.

12320 ■ WBOW-FM - 102.7
1301 Ohio St.
Terre Haute, IN 47807
Phone: (812)234-9770
Fax: (812)238-1576
Format: Adult Contemporary. **Key Personnel:** Kensey Kunkel, Gen. Sales Mgr., kensey@radioworksforme.com; Kandee Cook, Sales Mgr., kandee@radioworksforme.com.

12321 ■ W43BV-TV - 43
PO Box A
Santa Ana, CA 92711
Phone: (714)832-2950
Free: 888-731-1000
Email: comments@tbn.org
Owner: Trinity Broadcasting Network Inc., PO Box A, Santa Ana, CA 92711, Ph: (714)832-2950, Free: 888-731-1000. **URL:** http://www.tbn.org.

12322 ■ WINH-FM - 98.5
824 S 3rd St.
Terre Haute, IN 47807
Format: Music of Your Life; Classic Rock; News. **Owner:** Midwest Communications Inc., 904 Grand Ave., Wausau, WI 54403, Ph: (715)842-1437, Fax: (715)842-7061. **Key Personnel:** Steve Hall, Contact; Danny Wayne, Contact; Charli McKenzie, Contact; Steve Hall, Contact. **URL:** http://985wbow.com.

12323 ■ WISU-FM - 89.7
217 Dreiser Hall
Terre Haute, IN 47809-9989
Phone: (812)237-3241
Format: Album-Oriented Rock (AOR); Urban Contemporary. **Networks:** AP. **Owner:** Indiana State University, 200 N 7th St., Terre Haute, IN 47809-1902, Free: 800-468-6478. **Founded:** Apr. 01, 1964. **Operating Hours:** midnight. **ADI:** Terre Haute, IN. **Wattage:** 13,500. **Ad Rates:** Noncommercial. **URL:** http://www.isustudentmedia.com.

12324 ■ WMGI-FM - 100.7
824 S Third St.
Terre Haute, IN 47807
Phone: (812)232-4161
Fax: (812)234-9999
Format: Contemporary Hit Radio (CHR). **Owner:** Midwest Communications Inc., 904 Grand Ave., Wausau, WI 54403, Ph: (715)842-1437, Fax: (715)842-7061.

Founded: 1960. Operating Hours: Continuous. ADI: Terre Haute, IN. Wattage: 50,000 ERP. Ad Rates: $40-50 for 60 seconds. URL: http://www.mymixfm.com.

12325 ■ WPFR-AM - 1480
18889 N 2350 St.
Dennison, IL 62423
Phone: (217)826-9673
Free: 877-939-1480
Email: wpfr@joink.com
Format: Religious. **Founded:** Sept. 07, 2006. **Ad Rates:** Noncommercial. **URL:** http://www.wordpower.us.

12326 ■ WPRS-AM - 1440
824 S Third St.
Terre Haute, IN 47807
Phone: (812)232-4161
Fax: (812)234-9999
Format: Country. **Networks:** NBC; Business Radio; Global Satellite. **Owner:** Midwest Communications Inc., 904 Grand Ave., Wausau, WI 54403, Ph: (715)842-1437, Fax: (715)842-7061. **Founded:** 1951. **Operating Hours:** 19 hours Daily; 10% network, 90% local. **ADI:** Terre Haute, IN. **Key Personnel:** Peter Tanz, Sr. VP; Duke Wright, CEO, President; Michael Wright, COO. **Wattage:** 1,000 Day; 250 Night. **Ad Rates:** $12.20-17.15 for 60 seconds. **URL:** http://mwcradio.com.

12327 ■ WSDM-FM - 92.7
1301 Ohio St.
Terre Haute, IN 47807
Phone: (812)234-9770
Fax: (812)238-1576
Format: Sports. **Networks:** ABC. **Owner:** Crossroads Communications Inc., 50 Desert Sands Ln., Yarmouth Port, MA 02675, Fax: (508)375-9446. **Founded:** 1972. **Operating Hours:** Continuous. **ADI:** Terre Haute, IN. **Wattage:** 6,000. **Ad Rates:** $16-24 per unit. Combined rates with WBOW/WSDX-AM, WAXI-FM, WBOW-FM.

12328 ■ WSDX-AM - 1130
1301 Ohio St.
Terre Haute, IN 47807
Phone: (812)234-9770
Format: Sports. **Simulcasts:** WBOW. **Networks:** ESPN Radio. **Owner:** Crossroads Communications Inc., 50 Desert Sands Ln., Yarmouth Port, MA 02675, Fax: (508)375-9446. **Founded:** 1959. **Formerly:** WITE-AM; WBZL-AM. **Operating Hours:** Continuous. **ADI:** Terre Haute, IN. **Wattage:** 500. **Ad Rates:** $4-16 per unit. Combined advertising rates available with WSDM-FM, WAXI-FM, WBOW-FM.

12329 ■ WTHI-FM - 99.9
918 Ohio St.
Terre Haute, IN 47807
Phone: (812)232-9481
Fax: (812)234-0089
Free: 800-686-9844
Format: Contemporary Country. **Networks:** ABC. **Owner:** Emmis Communications Corp., One Emmis Plz., 40 Monument Cir., Ste. 700, Indianapolis, IN 46204-3011, Ph: (317)266-0100. **Founded:** 1948. **Operating Hours:** Continuous. **ADI:** Terre Haute, IN. **Wattage:** 50,000 ERP. **Ad Rates:** Advertising accepted; rates available upon request. WWVR-FM, 105.5 The River. **URL:** http://www.hi99.com.

12330 ■ WTHI-TV - 10
918 Ohio St.
Terre Haute, IN 47808
Phone: (812)232-9481
Fax: (812)232-8953
Email: news10@wthitv.com
Format: Commercial TV. **Networks:** CBS. **Owner:** LIN TV Corp., 701 Brazos St., Ste. 800, Austin, TX 78701. **Founded:** 1954. **Formerly:** Wabash Valley Broadcasting Corp. **Operating Hours:** Continuous. **ADI:** Terre Haute, IN. **Key Personnel:** Susan Dinkel, News Dir., sdinkel@wthitv.com; Todd Weber, Gen. Mgr., tweber@wthitv.com; Rod Garvin, Operations Mgr., rgarvin@wthitv.com; Nick Telezyn, Gen. Sales Mgr., ntelezyn@wthitv.com; Scott Arnold, Director. **Ad Rates:** $20-500 for 30 seconds. **URL:** http://www.wthitv.com.

12331 ■ WTWO-TV - 2
PO Box 9268
Terre Haute, IN 47808
Phone: (812)696-2121
Email: mywabashvalley@wtwo.com
Format: Commercial TV. **Networks:** NBC. **Owner:** Nexstar Broadcasting Group Inc., 545 E John Carpenter Fwy., Ste. 700, Irving, TX 75062, Ph: (972)373-8800. **Founded:** Sept. 1965. **Operating Hours:** Continuous. **ADI:** Terre Haute, IN. **Key Personnel:** Tom McClanahan, Mgr.; Bruce Yowell, Chief Engineer, byowell@wtwo.com. **Ad Rates:** Advertising accepted; rates available upon request. **URL:** http://www.mywabashvalley.com.

12332 ■ WWSY-FM - 95.9
824 S 3rd St.
Terre Haute, IN 47807
Phone: (812)232-4161
Fax: (812)234-9999
Format: Adult Contemporary. **Owner:** Midwest Communications Inc., 904 Grand Ave., Wausau, WI 54403, Ph: (715)842-1437, Fax: (715)842-7061. **Founded:** Sept. 07, 2006. **Ad Rates:** Advertising accepted; rates available upon request.

12333 ■ WWVR-FM - 105.5
918 Ohio St.
Terre Haute, IN 47807
Phone: (812)235-1055
Fax: (812)234-0089
Format: Classic Rock; Alternative/New Music/Progressive. **Networks:** USA Radio. **Owner:** Emmis Radio License Corp., 3500 W Olive Ave., Ste. 300, Burbank, CA 91505-4647, Ph: (818)973-2722. **Founded:** 1966. **Operating Hours:** 6 a.m.-1 a.m.; 75% network, 25% local. **Key Personnel:** James Conner, Gen. Mgr., jconner@1055theriver.com. **Wattage:** 3,300. **Ad Rates:** $1 for 30 seconds; $2 for 60 seconds. **URL:** http://www.1055theriver.com.

12334 ■ WZIS-FM - 90.7
5500 Wabash Ave.
Terre Haute, IN 47803-3999
Email: manager@wmhdradio.org
Format: Eclectic. **Owner:** Rose-Hulman Institute of Technology, 5500 Wabash Ave., Terre Haute, IN 47803, Ph: (812)877-1511. **Operating Hours:** 11 HRS Daily. **Wattage:** 160. **Ad Rates:** Noncommercial. **URL:** http://www.wmhdradio.org.

UPLAND

12335 ■ WTUR-FM - 89.7
236 W Reade Ave.
Upland, IN 46989
Free: 800-882-3456
Format: Educational. **Owner:** Taylor University, 236 W Reade Ave., Upland, IN 46989-1001, Ph: (765)998-5134, Free: 800-882-3456. **URL:** http://www.taylor.edu.

VALPARAISO

Porter Co. Porter Co. (NW). 30 m SE of Chicago, Ill. Valparaiso University; Valparaiso Technical School. Residential. Lakes. Summer and Winter outside sports. Manufacturing.

12336 ■ Indiana Musicator
Indiana Music Educators Association
1402 Carriage Dr.
Valparaiso, IN 46383
Phone: (219)464-5087
Publisher's E-mail: office@imeamusic.org
Freq: Quarterly 4/yr (September, November, March, and May). **Print Method:** Offset. **Trim Size:** 8 1/2 x 11. **Cols./Page:** 3. **Col. Width:** 2 1/4 inches. **Col. Depth:** 10 inches. **Key Personnel:** Jeff Doebler, Editor; JoDee Marshall, Business Manager. **ISSN:** 0273--9933 (print). **Subscription Rates:** $20 Nonmembers; Included in membership. **Alt. Formats:** CD-ROM. **URL:** http://old.imeamusic.org/musicator/index.php. **Remarks:** Accepts advertising. **Circ:** (Not Reported).

12337 ■ WAKE-AM - 1500
2755 Sager Rd.
Valparaiso, IN 46383
Format: Full Service. **Owner:** Radio One Communications, at above address, Ph: (219)462-6111, Fax: (219)462-4880. **Founded:** 1964. **Key Personnel:** Scott Rosenberg, Contact; Laura Waluszko, Contact. **Wattage:** '1,000 Day 025 Night. **Ad Rates:** Advertising accepted; rates available upon request. $23 for 30 seconds; $27 for 60 seconds.

12338 ■ WGL-FM - 102.9
150 W Lincolnway, Ste. 2001
Valparaiso, IN 46383
Phone: (260)747-1511
Fax: (260)747-3999
Format: Adult Contemporary. **Owner:** Summit City Radio, at above address. **Founded:** 1997. **Operating Hours:** Continuous. **ADI:** Fort Wayne (Angola), IN. **Key Personnel:** JJ Fabini, Dir. of Programs, jj@rock104radio.com; Scott Howard, Sales Mgr., scott@summitcityradio.com; Rod Tanner, Contact, rodtanner@summitcityradio.com. **Wattage:** 6,000. **Ad Rates:** Noncommercial. **URL:** http://calvaryradionetwork.com.

12339 ■ WHLP-FM - 89.9
150 W Lincolnway, Ste. 2001
Valparaiso, IN 46383
Phone: (219)548-5800
Fax: (219)548-5808
Free: 866-303-9457
Email: info@calvaryradionetwork.com
Format: Religious. **Owner:** Calvary Radio Network Inc., 150 West Lincolnway Ste. 2001, Valparaiso, IN 46383, Ph: (219)548-5800, Fax: (219)548-5808. **URL:** http://www.calvaryradionetwork.com.

WJCZ-FM - See Milford, IL

12340 ■ WLJE-FM - 105.5
2755 Sager Rd.
Valparaiso, IN 46383
Phone: (219)462-6111
Fax: (219)462-4880
Format: Country. **Networks:** ABC. **Owner:** Radio One Communications, at above address, Ph: (219)462-6111, Fax: (219)462-4880. **Founded:** 1967. **Operating Hours:** Continuous; 1% network, 99% local. **Key Personnel:** Scott Rosenberg, Contact. **Wattage:** 3,000. **Ad Rates:** Advertising accepted; rates available upon request. **URL:** http://www.indiana105.com.

12341 ■ WMJC-FM - 91.9
150 W Lincolnway, Ste. 2001
Valparaiso, IN 46383
Phone: (219)548-5800
Fax: (219)548-5808
Email: info@calvaryradionetwork.com
Format: Contemporary Christian. **Networks:** Westwood One Radio. **Owner:** Calvary Radio Network Inc., 150 West Lincolnway Ste. 2001, Valparaiso, IN 46383, Ph: (219)548-5800, Fax: (219)548-5808. **Founded:** 1970. **Formerly:** WCTO-FM. **Operating Hours:** Continuous; 100% local. **Key Personnel:** Jim Motshagen, Operations Mgr. **Wattage:** 3,000. **Ad Rates:** Advertising accepted; rates available upon request. **URL:** http://www.calvaryradionetwork.com.

WTMK-FM - See Lowell, IN

12342 ■ WVUR-FM - 95.1
1809 Chapel Dr.
Valparaiso, IN 46383
Phone: (219)464-5383
Format: Alternative/New Music/Progressive; Sports; News. **Operating Hours:** Continuous. **Key Personnel:** Nick Schroeder, Chief Engineer. **Wattage:** 036. **Ad Rates:** Noncommercial. **URL:** http://www.thesource95.com.

VERSAILLES

Ripley Co. Ripley Co. (SE). 50 m W of Cincinnati, Ohio. Manufactures shoes, metal fasteners, furniture, veneer. Poultry processing plant. Limestone quarries. Dairy, poultry farms. Livestock, grain.

12343 ■ Chamber Page in the Versailles Republican
Ripley County Chamber of Commerce
102 N Main St.
Versailles, IN 47042-8027
Phone: (812)689-6654
Publisher's E-mail: ripleycc@ripleycountychamber.org
Newspaper featuring information about Ripley County Versailles, IN. **Freq:** Quarterly every 1st Thursday of the new quarter. **Subscription Rates:** Included in membership. **URL:** http://www.ripleycountychamber.org/services.asp. **Circ:** (Not Reported).

12344 ■ Osgood Journal
Ripley Publishing Company Inc.

Circulation: ★ = AAM; △ or • = BPA; ♦ = CAC; ❑ = VAC; ⊕ = PO Statement; ‡ = Publisher's Report; Boldface figures = sworn; Light figures = estimated.

115 S Washington St.
Versailles, IN 47042
Phone: (812)689-6364
Fax: (812)689-6508
Publication E-mail: publication@ripleynews.com
Community newspaper. **Freq:** Weekly (Tues.). **Print Method:** Offset. **Cols./Page:** 6. **Col. Width:** 24 nonpareils. **Col. Depth:** 294 agate lines. **URL:** http://www.ripleynews.com/ojhome.html. **Mailing address:** PO Box 158, Versailles, IN 47042. **Ad Rates:** SAU $6.25; PCI $6.25. **Remarks:** Accepts advertising. **Circ:** Paid 4000.

12345 ■ The Versailles Republican
Ripley Publishing Company Inc.
115 S Washington St.
Versailles, IN 47042
Phone: (812)689-6364
Fax: (812)689-6508
Publisher's E-mail: publication@ripleynews.com
Community newspaper. **Freq:** Weekly (Thurs.). **Print Method:** Offset. **Cols./Page:** 6. **Col. Width:** 24 nonpareils. **Col. Depth:** 294 agate lines. **Key Personnel:** Gene Demaree, President; Cindy Roberts, Office Manager; Linda Chandler, Publisher. **URL:** http://www.ripleynews.com/vrhome.html. **Mailing address:** PO Box 158, Versailles, IN 47042. **Ad Rates:** SAU $6.25; PCI $5.25. **Remarks:** Accepts advertising. **Circ:** Paid ‡4000.

VEVAY

Switzerland Co. Switzerland Co. (SE). On Ohio River, 40 m SW of Cincinnati, Ohio. Boats to river ports. Tourism. Flour mills; shoe factory. Diversified farming. Corn, wheat, tobacco and soybeans.

12346 ■ The Switzerland Democrat
Vevay Newspapers Inc.
111 W Market St.
Vevay, IN 47043
Phone: (812)427-2311
Fax: (812)427-2793
Newspaper. **Freq:** Weekly (Thurs.). **Print Method:** Offset. **Cols./Page:** 6. **Col. Width:** 26 nonpareils. **Col. Depth:** 301 agate lines. **Key Personnel:** Don R. Wallis, Publisher. **USPS:** 531-060. **Subscription Rates:** $30 Individuals Switzerland and surrounding counties; $35 Institutions Indiana, Ohio, Kentucky; $40 Canada and Mexico rest of continental United States. **Mailing address:** PO Box 157, Vevay, IN 47043. **Remarks:** Accepts advertising. **Circ:** ‡600.

12347 ■ Vevay Reveille-Enterprise
Vevay Newspapers Inc.
111 W Market St.
Vevay, IN 47043
Phone: (812)427-2311
Fax: (812)427-2793
Newspaper. **Freq:** Weekly (Thurs.). **Print Method:** Offset. **Trim Size:** 13 1/2 x 22 3/4. **Cols./Page:** 6. **Col. Width:** 26 nonpareils. **Col. Depth:** 301 agate lines. **USPS:** 658-620. **Subscription Rates:** $30 Individuals Switzerland and surrounding counties; $35 Individuals Indiana, Ohio, Kentucky; $40 Individuals rest of continental United States. **Mailing address:** PO Box 157, Vevay, IN 47043. **Ad Rates:** BW $667.50; 4C $987.58; PCI $7.66. **Remarks:** Accepts advertising. **Circ:** ‡2842.

12348 ■ WKID-FM - 95.9
118 W Main St.
Vevay, IN 47043
Phone: (812)427-9590
Fax: (812)427-2492
Format: Country. **Key Personnel:** Ken Trimble, Contact, ken@k959froggy.com. **Ad Rates:** Noncommercial.

VINCENNES

Knox Co. Knox Co. (SW). On Wabash River, 50 m N of Evansville. Vincennes University. George Rogers Clark National Historical Park, Fort Knox II, Sonotabac Prehistoric Indian Mound.

12349 ■ Vincennes Sun-Commercial
Vincennes Sun-Commercial
702 Main St.
Vincennes, IN 47591
Phone: (812)886-9955
Free: 800-876-9955
Publication E-mail: vscnews@suncommercial.com
Daily newspaper. **Freq:** Daily and Sun. (eve.). **Print Method:** Offset. **Trim Size:** 12 1/2 x 22 3/4. **Cols./Page:** 6. **Col. Width:** 24 nonpareils. **Col. Depth:** 294 agate lines. **Ad Rates:** GLR $1.62; BW $1,718.64; 4C $1978.64; PCI $13.64. **Remarks:** Accepts advertising. **Circ:** Mon.-Fri. ★**12583**, Sun. ★**14861**.

12350 ■ WAOV-AM - 1450
PO Box 242
Vincennes, IN 47591-0242
Phone: (812)882-6060
Fax: (812)882-7770
Free: 800-876-0173
Format: News; Talk. **Owner:** The Original Co., Vincennes, IN 47591. **Founded:** 1940. **Operating Hours:** Continuous; 5% network, 95% local. **Key Personnel:** Mark Lange, Contact, marklange@waovam.com; Mark Lange, Contact, marklange@waovam.com; Ed Ballinger, Contact, edballinger@waovam.com. **Wattage:** 1,000. **Ad Rates:** Noncommercial. **URL:** http://www.newsknoxcounty.com.

12351 ■ WATI-FM - 89.9
PO Box 3206
Tupelo, MS 38803
Format: Religious. **Owner:** American Family Radio, at above address. **Ad Rates:** Noncommercial.

12352 ■ WBTO-FM - 102.3
522 Busseron St.
Vincennes, IN 47591
Phone: (812)882-6060
Format: Classic Rock. **Owner:** The Original Co., Vincennes, IN 47591. **Operating Hours:** Continuous. **ADI:** Evansville, IN (Madisonville, KY). **Wattage:** 003 KW. **Ad Rates:** Advertising accepted; rates available upon request. **URL:** http://www.wbtofm.com.

12353 ■ WFML-FM - 96.7
1002 N First St.
Vincennes, IN 47591
Phone: (812)886-9696
Format: Country. **Owner:** Vincennes University, 1002 N 1st St., Vincennes, IN 47591, Ph: (812)888-8888, Fax: (812)888-4586, Free: 800-742-9198. **Key Personnel:** Brad Deetz, Contact, braddeetz@wfml.net. **URL:** http://www.967jackfm.com.

12354 ■ WVUB-FM - 91.1
Vincennes University
Vincennes, IN 47591
Phone: (812)888-4347
Fax: (812)882-2237
Email: wvub@vinu.edu
Format: Adult Contemporary. **Owner:** Vincennes University, 1002 N 1st St., Vincennes, IN 47591, Ph: (812)888-8888, Fax: (812)888-4586, Free: 800-742-9198. **Key Personnel:** Phil Smith, Gen. Mgr., psmith@vinu.edu. **URL:** http://www.blazer911wvub.com.

12355 ■ WVUT-TV - 22
1200 N 2nd St.
Vincennes, IN 47591
Phone: (812)888-4345
Format: News; Sports. **Networks:** Public Broadcasting Service (PBS). **Owner:** Vincennes University, Vincennes, IN. **Founded:** 1968. **Operating Hours:** Continuous. **Key Personnel:** Al Rerko, Gen. Mgr.; Sharon Kiefer, Dir. of Programs. **Wattage:** 57,000 ERP Horizonta. **URL:** http://wvut.org/.

12356 ■ WYFX-FM - 106.7
PO Box 242
Vincennes, IN 47591-0242
Phone: (812)882-6060
Free: 800-876-0173
Format: Sports. **Networks:** ABC; Sun Radio. **Owner:** The Original Co., Vincennes, IN 47591. **Founded:** 1955. **Operating Hours:** Continuous; 55% network, 45% local. **ADI:** Evansville, IN (Madisonville, KY). **Key Personnel:** Mark Lange, President, marklange@originalcompany.com; Steve Pierson, Contact, stevepierson@wwbl.com. **Wattage:** 500. **Ad Rates:** Noncommercial. **URL:** http://www.originalcompany.com/pages/7817272.php.

12357 ■ WZDM-FM - 92.1
PO Box 242
Vincennes, IN 47591
Phone: (812)885-2610
Fax: (260)882-7770
Free: 800-876-0173
Format: Adult Contemporary. **Owner:** The Original Co., Vincennes, IN 47591. **Founded:** 1988. **Operating Hours:** Continuous. **ADI:** Terre Haute, IN. **Key Personnel:** Mark Lange, Contact, marklange@wzdm.com. **Wattage:** 4,100. **Ad Rates:** Advertising accepted; rates available upon request. **URL:** http://www.wzdm.com.

WABASH

Wabash Co. Wabash Co. (NEC). On Wabash River, 20 m N of Marion. Manufacturing. Agriculture. Corn, soybeans. Dairy. Hogs, cattle. Duck, squab, veal.

12358 ■ The Paper
The Paper
PO Box 603
Wabash, IN 46992
Phone: (260)563-8326
Fax: (260)563-2863
Publisher's E-mail: ads@thepaperofwabash.com
Community newspaper. **Founded:** 1977. **Freq:** Weekly (Tues.). **Print Method:** Offset. **Cols./Page:** 7. **Col. Width:** 16 nonpareils. **Col. Depth:** 224 agate lines. **Key Personnel:** Wayne W. Rees, Publisher; Julie Frieden, Sales Representative; Mike Rees, General Manager. **Subscription Rates:** $40 Out of area. **URL:** http://www.thepaperofwabash.com. **Ad Rates:** GLR $.40; BW $649.60; 4C $799.60; SAU $10.30; PCI $6.45. **Remarks:** Advertising accepted; rates available upon request. **Circ:** 16561.

12359 ■ Plain Dealer
Paxton Media Group
PO Box 379
Wabash, IN 46992
Phone: (260)563-2131
Fax: (260)563-0816
Publication E-mail: news@wabashplaindealer.com
General newspaper. **Founded:** 1859. **Freq:** Daily (eve.) six days a week. **Print Method:** Offset. **Trim Size:** 13 1/2x22 3/4. **Cols./Page:** 6. **Col. Width:** 12 picas. **Col. Depth:** 21 1/2 inches. **Key Personnel:** Eric Seamans, Managing Editor. **USPS:** 663-940. **Subscription Rates:** $195 Individuals home delivery; $82 Individuals home delivery; Saturday only; $390 By mail. **URL:** http://www.chronicle-tribune.com/wabashplaindealer. **Ad Rates:** GLR $4.90; BW $1,296; 4C $1,521; SAU $10.05. **Remarks:** 4.90. **Circ:** (Not Reported).

12360 ■ WJOT-AM
1350 S Wabash St.
Wabash, IN 46992
Phone: (260)563-1161
Free: 866-563-1161
Email: wjot@verizon.net
Format: Oldies. **Networks:** ABC. **Owner:** Mid-America Radio Group Inc., 60 N Wayne St., IN 46151. **Founded:** 1998. **Formerly:** WAYT-FM. **Wattage:** 250 Day. **Ad Rates:** $8.05-9.78 for 30 seconds.

12361 ■ WKUZ-FM - 95.9
PO Box 342
Wabash, IN 46992
Phone: (260)563-4111
Fax: (260)563-4425
Format: Oldies; Contemporary Hit Radio (CHR). **Networks:** USA Radio; Brownfield; Jones Satellite. **Owner:** Upper Wabash Broadcasting Corp., 1864 A S Wabash St., Wabash, IN 46992. **Founded:** 1966. **Operating Hours:** Continuous. **Key Personnel:** Dan McKay, Contact; John Balvich, Contact. **Wattage:** 4,200. **Ad Rates:** Noncommercial.

WAKARUSA

Elkhart Co. Elkhart Co. (N). 15 m SW of Goshen. Residential.

12362 ■ WYFQ-AM - 930
PO Box 7300
Charlotte, NC 28241-7300
Free: 800-888-7077
Email: bbn@bbnmedia.org
Format: Religious; Contemporary Christian. **Owner:** Bible Broadcasting Network Inc., 11530 Carmel Commons Blvd., Charlotte, NC 28226, Ph: (704)523-5555, Free: 800-888-7077. **Founded:** 1992. **Formerly:** WSOC-AM. **Operating Hours:** Continuous. **ADI:** Charlotte (Hickory), NC. **Wattage:** 5,000 Day; 1,000 Night. **Ad Rates:** Noncommercial. **URL:** http://www.bbnradio.org.

WARREN

Huntington Co. Huntington Co. (NE). 5 m S of Plum Tree.

12363 ■ Warren Cable
426 N Wayne
Warren, IN 46792
Phone: (260)375-2111
Email: info@citznet.com
Owner: Citizens Telephone Corp., at above address. **Founded:** 1985. **Cities Served:** Warren, Indiana: subscribing households 728; 35 channels. **Mailing address:** PO Box 330, Warren, IN 46792. **URL:** http://www.citznet.com.

WARSAW

Kosciusko Co. Kosciusko Co. (N). 45 m NW of Fort Wayne. Manufacturing. Lake resort. Farming.

12364 ■ Times-Union
Reub Williams and Sons Inc.
PO Box 1448
Warsaw, IN 46581-1448
Phone: (219)267-3111
Fax: (219)267-7784
Publication E-mail: news@timesuniononline.com
General newspaper. **Founded:** 1856. **Freq:** Mon.-Sat. **Print Method:** Offset. **Trim Size:** 13 3/4 x 22 1/2. **Cols./Page:** 6. **Col. Width:** 2 1/16 inches. **Col. Depth:** 21 inches. **USPS:** 666-680. **Subscription Rates:** $50 Individuals; $15 Individuals 3 months. **URL:** http://www.timesuniononline.com/index.asp. **Ad Rates:** PCI $9.25. **Remarks:** Accepts advertising. **Circ:** Mon.-Fri. ♦**9445**, Sat. ♦**10220**.

12365 ■ WAWC-FM - 103.5
216 W Market St.
Warsaw, IN 46580
Phone: (574)372-3064
Fax: (574)267-2230
Free: 888-990-1035
Format: Country. **Networks:** Network Indiana; Fox. **Owner:** Talking Stick Communications L.L.C., 216 W Market St., Warsaw, IN 46580. **Founded:** May 31, 1991. **Formerly**: Wawasee 103, 1991-2001. **Operating Hours**: Continuous. **ADI**: South Bend-Elkhart, IN. **Key Personnel:** Clint Marsh, Gen. Mgr., cmarsh@federatedmedia.com; Roger Grossman, News Dir. **Wattage**: 3,000. **Ad Rates:** $1.50-6 for 10 seconds; $3-12 for 30 seconds; $5-18.50 for 60 seconds. **URL:** http://www.willie1035.com.

12366 ■ WIOE-FM - 98.3
722 E Center St.
Warsaw, IN 46580
Phone: (574)268-9830
Format: Oldies. **Owner:** Blessed Beginnings Broadcasting Inc., at above address. **Operating Hours**: Continuous. **Wattage**: 100. **Ad Rates:** Noncommercial. **URL:** http://www.wioe.com.

12367 ■ WLEG-FM - 102.7
216 W Market St.
Warsaw, IN 46580
Phone: (574)372-3064
Fax: (574)267-2230
Format: Country. **Ad Rates:** Advertising accepted; rates available upon request. **URL:** http://thefanindiana.com.

12368 ■ WLZQ-FM - 101.1
PO Box 2020
Warsaw, IN 46580-2020
Phone: (574)268-2500
Free: 800-398-5788
Format: Adult Contemporary. **Founded:** Sept. 08, 2006. **Key Personnel:** Chris Larko, Gen. Mgr., chrislarko@myq101.com; Ron Gregory, Contact, morningshow@myq101.com; Ron Gregory, Contact, morningshow@myq101.com.

12369 ■ WRSW-AM - 1480
216 W Market St.
Warsaw, IN 46580
Phone: (574)372-3064
Fax: (574)267-2230
Format: Sports. **Simulcasts:** WRSW-FM. **Networks:** CNN Radio; Westwood One Radio. **Owner:** Talking Stick Communications L.L.C., 216 W Market St., Warsaw, IN 46580. **Founded:** 1951. **Operating Hours**: Continuous. **ADI**: South Bend-Elkhart, IN. **Key Personnel:** Roger Grossman, Gen. Mgr. **Wattage**: 1,000 Day; 500 Night. **Ad Rates:** Noncommercial. Combined advertising rates available with WRSW-FM. **URL:** http://thefanindiana.com.

12370 ■ WRSW-FM - 107.3
216 W Market St.
Warsaw, IN 46580
Phone: (574)372-3064
Format: Classic Rock; News; Sports. **Key Personnel:** Dan Daggett, Sales Mgr., ddaggett@lakecitymediagroup.com. **Wattage**: 50,000 ERP. **Ad Rates:** Advertising accepted; rates available upon request. **URL:** http://www.wrsw.net.

WASHINGTON

Daviess Co. Daviess Co. (SW). 20 m W of Vincennes. Manufacturing. Processed turkey products. Petroleum measuring and flexible packaging systems. Coal mines; oil and gas wells. Diversified farming. Corn, wheat, apples.

12371 ■ Washington Times-Herald
Community Newspaper Holdings Inc.
102 E Van Trees St.
Washington, IN 47501
Phone: (812)254-0480
Fax: (812)254-7517
General newspaper. **Freq:** Daily. **Print Method:** Offset. **Cols./Page:** 6. **Col. Width:** 26 nonpareils. **Col. Depth:** 301 agate lines. **Key Personnel:** Kelly Overton, Photographer; Todd Lancaster, Editor; Ellen Pride, Business Manager; Melody Brunson, Editor. **Subscription Rates:** $105 Individuals mail delivery. **URL:** http://www.washtimesherald.com. **Remarks:** Accepts classified advertising. **Circ:** (Not Reported).

12372 ■ WAMW-AM - 1580
800 W National Hwy.
Washington, IN 47501
Phone: (812)254-6761
Fax: (812)254-3940
Free: 877-254-9269
Format: Adult Contemporary. **Networks:** ABC; Brownfield. **Founded:** 1955. **Operating Hours**: Sunrise-sunset. **Wattage**: 500. **Ad Rates:** Advertising accepted; rates available upon request. Combined advertising rates available with WAMW-FM. **URL:** http://www.wamwamfm.com.

12373 ■ WAMW-FM - 107.9
800 W National Hwy.
Washington, IN 47501
Phone: (812)254-6761
Fax: (812)254-3940
Format: Classical; Oldies. **Networks:** ABC; Brownfield. **Owner:** DLC Media, Inc., at above address, Elnora, IN. **Founded:** 1989. **Operating Hours**: Continuous. **Key Personnel:** Dave Foster, News Dir.; Andy Morrison, Operations Mgr.; Dave Crooks, President, CEO; Lisa Gray, Div. Dir. **Wattage**: 3,000. **Ad Rates:** Advertising accepted; rates available upon request. Combined advertising rates available with WAMW-AM. **URL:** http://www.memories1079.com.

12374 ■ WQTY-FM - 93.3
PO Box 616
Washington, IN 47501
Phone: (812)254-4300
Free: 800-427-9023
Format: Oldies. **Owner:** The Original Co., Vincennes, IN 47591. **URL:** http://www.originalcompany.com/pages/7816409.php?.

12375 ■ WWBL-FM - 106.5
PO Box 616
Washington, IN 47501-0616
Phone: (812)254-4300
Free: 800-427-9023
Email: wwbl@wwbl.com
Format: Country. **Owner:** The Original Co., Vincennes, IN 47591. **Founded:** 1948. **Formerly**: WRTB-FM. **Operating Hours**: Continuous. **ADI**: Terre Haute, IN. **Key Personnel:** Mark Lange, Contact, President, markbrochin@wwbl.colm; Mark Brochin, Contact, markbrochin@wwbl.colm. **Wattage**: 50,000. **Ad Rates:** Advertising accepted; rates available upon request. Combined advertising rates available with WZDM, WUZR, WAOV, WBTO-FM, WQTY, WREB, WYFX, WRCY. **URL:** http://www.originalcompany.com/pages/7733555.php?.

WEST LAFAYETTE

Tippecanoe Co. Tippecanoe Co. (NW). 5 m W of Lafayette. Residential.

12376 ■ American Journal of Psychology
University of Illinois Press
c/o Robert W. Proctor, Editor
Purdue University
Dept. of Psychological Sciences
703 3rd St.
West Lafayette, IN 47907-2081
Publication E-mail: ajp@psych.purdue.edu
Journal dealing with experimental psychology and basic principles of psychology. **Freq:** Quarterly. **Print Method:** Offset. **Trim Size:** 6 x 9. **Cols./Page:** 1. **Col. Width:** 26 picas. **Col. Depth:** 43 picas. **Key Personnel:** Dominic W. Massaro, Editor, phone: (831)459-2330; Robert W. Proctor, Editor; Alfred H. Fuchs, Editor. **ISSN:** 0002--9556 (print); **EISSN:** 1939--8298 (electronic). **Subscription Rates:** $74 Individuals print or online; $81 Individuals print + online; $295 Institutions print or online; $325 Institutions print + online; $30 Students online only; $60 Institutions single issue. **URL:** http://www.press.uillinois.edu/journals/ajp.html. **Ad Rates:** BW $300. **Remarks:** Advertising accepted; rates available upon request. **Circ:** 1750.

12377 ■ Breeder's Digest
American Berkshire Association
2637 Yeager Rd.
West Lafayette, IN 47906
Phone: (765)497-3618
Fax: (765)497-2959
Publisher's E-mail: berkshire@nationalswine.com
Magazine containing information regarding ABA and its members. **Freq:** 6/year. **Subscription Rates:** $10 Individuals /year; $25 Other countries; $25 Individuals 3 years; Included in membership. **URL:** http://americanberkshire.com/breeders-digest/. **Remarks:** Accepts advertising. **Circ:** (Not Reported).

12378 ■ Geophysical Research Letters
American Geophysical Union
c/o Eric Calais, Ed.-in-Ch.
Purdue University
300 Forest Hill
West Lafayette, IN 47906
Phone: (765)496-2915
Publisher's E-mail: service@agu.org
Journal covering geophysical research letters. **Freq:** 24/yr. **Key Personnel:** Eric Calais, Editor-in-Chief; Noah Diffenbaugh, Editor. **ISSN:** 0094--8276 (print); **EISSN:** 1944--8007 (electronic). **Subscription Rates:** $2829 Institutions online (small); $4394 Institutions online (medium); $6570 Institutions online (large). **URL:** http://agupubs.onlinelibrary.wiley.com/agu/journal/10.1002/(ISSN)1944-8007. **Remarks:** Accepts advertising. **Circ:** (Not Reported).

12379 ■ Journal of the Astronautical Sciences
American Astronautical Society
Purdue University
3233 Armstrong Hall
West Lafayette, IN 47907
Publisher's E-mail: aas@astronautical.org
Archival journal on the sciences and technology of astronautics. **Freq:** Quarterly. **Print Method:** Offset. **Trim Size:** 6 3/4 x 9 1/2. **Cols./Page:** 1. **Key Personnel:** Dr. Nathan Harl, Managing Editor; Dr. Kathleen Howell, Editor-in-Chief. **ISSN:** 0021--9142 (print). **USPS:** 283-960. **Subscription Rates:** $189 Institutions. **URL:** http://astronautical.org/publications/journal. **Remarks:** Accepts advertising. **Circ:** (Not Reported).

12380 ■ Journal of Controlled Release
Controlled Release Society
c/o K. Park, Ed.-in-Ch.
Purdue University
College of Pharmacy
575 Stadium Mall Dr.
West Lafayette, IN 47907-2091
Publication E-mail: jcr-americas@akinainc.com
Journal focusing on current advances pertaining to sustained release and delivery of drugs and other biologically active agents. Topics of interest including

Circulation: ★ = AAM; △ or • = BPA; ♦ = CAC; ❑ = VAC; ⊕ = PO Statement; ‡ = Publisher's Report; Boldface figures = sworn; Light figures = estimated.

gene delivery, tissue engineering and diagnostic agents and mechanisms of release such as diffusion, chemical and enzymatic reactions, dissolution, osmosis, targeting, as well as the utilization and manipulation of biological processes. **Freq:** 24/yr. **Key Personnel:** K. Park, Editor-in-Chief. **ISSN:** 0168--3659 (print). **Subscription Rates:** $5951 Institutions print; $4960 Institutions ejournal; $740 Individuals print. **URL:** http://www.journals.elsevier.com/journal-of-controlled-release/; http://www.controlledreleasesociety.org/publications/Pages/JCR.aspx; http://www.sciencedirect.com/science/journal/01683659. **Remarks:** Accepts advertising. **Circ:** (Not Reported).

12381 ■ Journal of Human Resources in Hospitality & Tourism
Routledge Journals Taylor & Francis Group
c/o Howard Adler, PhD, Editor-in-Chief
Department of Hospitality & Tourism Management
Purdue University
152 Stone Hall
West Lafayette, IN 47906
Scholarly journal covering human resources in hospitality and tourism for researchers and educators. **Freq:** Quarterly. **Trim Size:** 6 x 8 3/8. **Key Personnel:** Susan, PhD, Gordon, Assistant Editor; Howard Adler, PhD, Editor-in-Chief. **ISSN:** 1533--2845 (print); **EISSN:** 1533--2853 (electronic). **Subscription Rates:** $228 Individuals online only; $261 Individuals print and online; $867 Institutions online only; $991 Institutions print and online. **URL:** http://www.tandfonline.com/toc/whrh20/current. **Ad Rates:** BW $315; 4C $550. **Remarks:** Accepts advertising. **Circ:** (Not Reported).

12382 ■ Modern Fiction Studies
Purdue University Dept. of English
500 Oval Dr.
West Lafayette, IN 47907-2038
Phone: (765)494-3740
Fax: (765)494-3780
Publication E-mail: mfs@purdue.edu
Literary journal devoted to criticism and scholarship of 20th century fiction. **Freq:** Quarterly. **Print Method:** Offset Uses mats. **Trim Size:** 6 x 9. **Cols./Page:** 1. **Col. Width:** 51 nonpareils. **Col. Depth:** 104 agate lines. **Key Personnel:** Paul Armstrong, Advisor; Robert P. Marzec, Associate Editor; Lauren Berlant, Advisor; Chris Bongie, Advisor; John N. Duvall, Editor. **ISSN:** 0026--7724 (print); **EISSN:** 1080--658X (electronic). **Subscription Rates:** $45 Individuals print only; $55 Individuals online only; $175 Institutions print only. **URL:** http://www.cla.purdue.edu/english/mfs. **Also known as:** MFS. **Ad Rates:** BW $400. **Remarks:** Accepts advertising. **Circ:** Paid ‡1532.

12383 ■ Philip Roth Studies
Purdue University Press
504 W State St.
West Lafayette, IN 47907-2058
Fax: (419)281-6883
Free: 800-247-6553
Journal devoted to the literary exploration of contemporary novelist Philip Roth. **Freq:** Semiannual. **Key Personnel:** Derek Parker Royal, Board Member; Jessica G. Rabin, Board Member. **ISSN:** 1547--3929 (print); **EISSN:** 1940--5278 (electronic). **URL:** http://www.philiprothsociety.org/#!philip-roth-studies/c1dse. **Remarks:** Advertising not accepted. **Circ:** (Not Reported).

12384 ■ Purdue Alumnus
Purdue Alumni Association
Dick and Sandy Dauch Alumni Ctr.
403 W Wood St.
West Lafayette, IN 47907
Phone: (765)494-5175
Fax: (765)494-9179
Free: 800-414-1541
Publication E-mail: alumnus@purdue.edu
University alumni magazine. **Freq:** Bimonthly. **Print Method:** Offset. Uses mats. **Trim Size:** 8 1/8 x 10 13/16. **Cols./Page:** 3. **Col. Width:** 13 picas. **Col. Depth:** 57 picas. **Subscription Rates:** Included in membership. **URL:** http://purdue.imodules.com/s/1461/alumnus/index.aspx?sid=1461&gid=1001&pgid=1068. **Ad Rates:** BW $2200. **Remarks:** Accepts advertising. **Circ:** 55000.

12385 ■ The Rural Educator: Journal for Rural and Small Schools
National Rural Education Association
100 N University St.
West Lafayette, IN 47907-2098
Phone: (765)494-0086
Fax: (765)496-1228
Publication E-mail: ruraledu@uwyo.edu
Peer-reviewed journal receiving manuscripts related to rural schools and to specific rural populations. **Freq:** 3/year spring, fall, and winter. **Print Method:** Offset-Web. **Trim Size:** 8 1/2 x 11. **Key Personnel:** Heather E. Duncan, Editor. **ISSN:** 0273--446X (print). **Subscription Rates:** Included in membership. **Alt. Formats:** PDF. **URL:** http://www.ruraleducator.net; http://www.nrea.net/index.cfm?pID=7925. **Remarks:** Accepts advertising. **Circ:** (Not Reported).

12386 ■ Seedstock Edge
United Duroc Swine Registry
2639 Yeager Rd.
West Lafayette, IN 47996-2417
Phone: (765)463-3594
Publisher's E-mail: nsr@nationalswine.com
Magazine containing general swine information. **Founded:** 1994. **Freq:** 9/year. **Print Method:** Offset. **Trim Size:** 7 7/8 x 10 3/4. **Cols./Page:** 3. **Col. Width:** 27 nonpareils. **Col. Depth:** 140 agate lines. **Key Personnel:** Christy Couch Lee, Director, Communications. **ISSN:** 1079-7963 (print). **Subscription Rates:** $25 Individuals; $60 Individuals first class; $150 Canada and foreign, first class; $60 Individuals 3 years. **URL:** http://nationalswine.com/seedstockEDGE/. **Formerly:** Hampshire Herdsman; Duroc News; Yorkshire Journal. **Ad Rates:** BW $375; 4C $650; PCI $10. **Remarks:** Accepts advertising. **Circ:** Paid 4500, Non-paid 250.

12387 ■ Strategic Management Journal
John Wiley & Sons Inc.
c/o Lois Gast, Mng. Ed.
Krannert Graduate School of Management
Purdue University
West Lafayette, IN 47907
Publisher's E-mail: info@wiley.com
Journal containing information on all aspects of strategic management including its development and improvement of theory and practice. **Freq:** 13/yr. **Trim Size:** 7 7/8 x 10 1/4. **Key Personnel:** Will Mitchell, Editor; Dan Schendel, Editor, Founder; Richard A. Bettis, Editor; Lois Gast, Managing Editor. **ISSN:** 0143-2095 (print). **Subscription Rates:** $2822 Institutions print; $2822 Institutions, Canada and Mexico print only; $2822 Institutions, other countries print only; €1823 Institutions print only; £1443 Institutions print only. **URL:** http://onlinelibrary.wiley.com/journal/10.1002/(ISSN)1097-0266. **Remarks:** Advertising accepted; rates available upon request. **Circ:** Paid 28000.

12388 ■ Sycamore Review
Purdue University Dept. of English
500 Oval Dr.
West Lafayette, IN 47907-2038
Phone: (765)494-3740
Fax: (765)494-3780
Publication E-mail: sycamore@purdue.edu
Literary journal. **Freq:** Semiannual January and June. **Key Personnel:** Kara Krewer, Editor-in-Chief. **ISSN:** 1043--1497 (print). **URL:** http://www.cla.purdue.edu/english/gradfields/creativewriting/sycamore.html. **Remarks:** Accepts advertising. **Circ:** (Not Reported).

12389 ■ Tribology Transactions
Taylor & Francis Group Journals
c/o Dr. Farshid Sadeghi, Ed.-in-Ch.
Purdue University
School of Mechanical Engineering
585 Purdue Mall
West Lafayette, IN 47907
Phone: (765)494-5719
Publisher's E-mail: customerservice@taylorandfrancis.com
Journal covering articles on society of tribologists and lubrication engineers. **Freq:** 6/yr. **Print Method:** Offset. **Trim Size:** 11 1/2 x 10. **Cols./Page:** 6. **Col. Width:** 9 1/5 picas. **Col. Depth:** 158 agate lines. **Key Personnel:** Christopher DellaCorte, Dr., Editor-in-Chief. **ISSN:** 1040-2004 (print); **EISSN:** 1547-397X (electronic). **Subscription Rates:** $573 Institutions print and online; $501 Institutions online only. **URL:** http://www.tandfonline.com/toc/utrb20/current. **Circ:** (Not Reported).

12390 ■ WBAA-AM - 920
712 Third St.
West Lafayette, IN 47907
Email: ask@wbaa.org
Format: Classical; News. **Networks:** National Public Radio (NPR). **Owner:** Purdue University, 610 Purdue Mall, West Lafayette, IN 47907, Ph: (765)494-4600. **Founded:** Apr. 02, 1993. **Operating Hours:** Continuous. **Key Personnel:** Greg Kostraba, Exec. Dir. **Wattage:** 5,000 Day; 1,000 Nig. **Ad Rates:** Noncommercial. **URL:** http://www.wbaa.org.

12391 ■ WBAA-FM - 101.3
712 Third St.
West Lafayette, IN 47907-2005
Phone: (765)494-5920
Fax: (765)496-1542
Email: wbaa@wbaa.org
Format: Classical; News. **Simulcasts:** WBAA-AM. **Networks:** National Public Radio (NPR); Public Radio International (PRI); Fox; CNN Radio; CBS; BBC World Service; NBC; ESPN Radio; ABC. **Owner:** Purdue University, 610 Purdue Mall, West Lafayette, IN 47907, Ph: (765)494-4600. **Founded:** Feb. 01, 1993. **Operating Hours:** Continuous. **ADI:** Lafayette, IN. **Key Personnel:** Stan Jastrzebski, Gen. Mgr., News Dir.; Greg Kostraba, Exec. Dir., kostraba@purdue.edu. **Wattage:** 14,000 ERP. **Ad Rates:** Noncommercial. Underwriting available. **URL:** http://www.wbaa.org.

12392 ■ WGLM-FM - 106.7
2700 Kent Ave., Ste. A-100
West Lafayette, IN 47906
Phone: (765)497-9456
Fax: (765)497-3299
Free: 800-595-7525
Format: Adult Contemporary. **Key Personnel:** Kelly Busch, Owner. **Ad Rates:** Noncommercial. **URL:** http://www.themix1067.net.

12393 ■ WLFI-TV - 18
2605 Yeager Rd.
West Lafayette, IN 47906
Phone: (765)463-1800
Fax: (765)463-7979
Format: News. **Networks:** CBS. **Owner:** LIN TV Corp., One W Exchange St., Ste. 5A, Providence, RI 02903-1064, Ph: (401)454-2880, Fax: (401)454-6990. **Founded:** 1953. **Operating Hours:** 10 p.m.-12:30 a.m. Sat.-Fri. **Key Personnel:** Tom Combs, Station Mgr., tcombs@wlfi.com; Mark Brooks, Chief Engineer. **Ad Rates:** Advertising accepted; rates available upon request. **URL:** http://wlfi.com.

WEST TERRE HAUTE

Vigo Co. Vigo Co. (SW). 5 m W of Terre Haute.

12394 ■ WTHI-AM - 1480
3775 W Dugger Ave.
West Terre Haute, IN 47885-9794
Phone: (812)535-1937
Format: Religious. **Networks:** Moody Broadcasting. **Owner:** Emmis Communications Corp., One Emmis Plz., 40 Monument Cir., Ste. 700, Indianapolis, IN 46204-3011, Ph: (317)266-0100. **Founded:** 1948. **Operating Hours:** Continuous. **ADI:** Terre Haute, IN. **Key Personnel:** James Conner, Station Mgr., jconner@wthi.emmis.com; Chris Perrott, Promotions Dir., cperrott@wthi.emmis.com. **Wattage:** 5,000 Day; 1,000 Night. **Ad Rates:** Advertising accepted; rates available upon request. **URL:** http://www.wordpower.us.

WILLIAMSPORT

Warren Co. Warren Co. (NW). On Wabash River, 25 m SW of La Fayette. Diversified farming. Grain.

12395 ■ Cable TV Services
222 Oakwood Dr.
Williamsport, IN 47993-1024
Founded: 1967. **Key Personnel:** Steven Mailloux, Gen. Mgr; Scott Mailloux, Contact. **Cities Served:** Sheldon, Illinois; Boswell, Brook, Goodland, Kentland, Indiana: subscribing households 2,100; 44 channels. **URL:** http://bsd.sos.in.gov/PublicBusinessSearch/BusinessInformation?businessId=255543.

WINAMAC

Pulaski Co. Pulaski Co. (NW). 24 m NW of Logansport. Manufacturing. Grain elevators; sawmill; hatcheries.

Dairy, stock, grain farms. Alfalfa, corn, soybeans.

12396 ■ Pulaski County Journal
Pulaski County Journal
114 W Main St.
Winamac, IN 46996
Phone: (574)946-6628
Fax: (574)946-7471
Community newspaper (tabloid). **Freq:** Weekly (Wed.). **Print Method:** Offset. **Cols./Page:** 6. **Col. Width:** 19 nonpareils. **Col. Depth:** 224 agate lines. **Key Personnel:** John Haley, Executive Editor, Publisher. **USPS:** 450-160. **Subscription Rates:** $50 Individuals in County; $60 Out of country; $70 Out of state; $40 Individuals online. **Mailing address:** PO Box 19, Winamac, IN 46996. **Ad Rates:** GLR $.24; BW $268.80; 4C $650; PCI $4.35. **Remarks:** Accepts advertising. **Circ:** 3000.

WORTHINGTON

12397 ■ Worthington Times: Greene County's Oldest Newspaper - Established in 1853
Worthington Times
12 S Lessie St.
Worthington, IN 47471-1513
Phone: (812)875-1504
Publication E-mail: worthingtontimes@reallyfast.info
Community newspaper. **Print Method:** Offset. **Cols./Page:** 5. **Col. Width:** 12.5 picas. **Col. Depth:** 13 inches. **Key Personnel:** Anna Rochelle, Editor, Contact. **USPS:** 693-220. **URL:** http://www.worthingtontimes.com. **Ad Rates:** BW $162.50; SAU $2.50; PCI $3. **Remarks:** Accepts advertising. **Circ:** ‡1000.

ZIONSVILLE

Boone Co. Boone Co. (C). 15 m NW of Indianapolis. Residential. Restored colonial village. Refinery. Manufactures drugs. Dairy, stock farms.

12398 ■ The Baker Street Journal: An Irregular Quarterly of Sherlockiana
The Baker Street Journal
9 Calumet Ct.
Zionsville, IN 46077
Publisher's E-mail: email@bakerstreetjournal.com
Literary journal containing articles about Sherlock Holmes. **Freq:** Quarterly. **Print Method:** Offset. **Trim Size:** 6 x 9. **Cols./Page:** 1. **Col. Width:** 59 nonpareils. **Col. Depth:** 105 agate lines. **ISSN:** 0005--4070 (print). **Subscription Rates:** $41.95 U.S. includes shipping; $55 Other countries includes shipping. **URL:** http://www.bakerstreetjournal.com/home.html. **Mailing address:** PO Box 583, Zionsville, IN 46077. **Ad Rates:** BW $225. **Remarks:** Accepts advertising. **Circ:** Paid ‡1000.

12399 ■ Zionsville Times Sentinel
Zionsville Times Sentinel
250 S Elm St.
Zionsville, IN 46077
Phone: (317)873-6397
Fax: (317)873-6259
Newspaper with a Republican orientation. **Founded:** 1860. **Freq:** Weekly (Wed.). **Print Method:** Offset. **Cols./Page:** 6. **Col. Width:** 25 nonpareils. **Col. Depth:** 301 agate lines. **Key Personnel:** Greta Sanderson; Andrea McCann, Managing Editor. **Subscription Rates:** $30 Individuals; $54 Two years; $38 Out of area; $65 Out of area 2 years; $50 Out of state; $90 Out of state 2 years. **URL:** http://timessentinel.com. **Ad Rates:** GLR $8.90. **Remarks:** Accepts advertising. **Circ:** ‡4000.

Circulation: ★ = AAM; △ or • = BPA; ♦ = CAC; ❑ = VAC; ⊕ = PO Statement; ‡ = Publisher's Report; Boldface figures = sworn; Light figures = estimated.

ACKLEY

SE IA. Hardin Co. 38 mi. W. of Waterloo.

12400 ■ World Journal
Ackley World Journal
736 Main St.
Ackley, IA 50601
Phone: (641)648-2521
Community newspaper. **Founded:** 1895. **Freq:** Weekly. **Print Method:** Offset. **Cols./Page:** 5. **Col. Width:** 6 picas. **Key Personnel:** Becky Schipper, Editor. **USPS:** 004-100. **URL:** http://www.timescitizen.com. **Ad Rates:** BW $302.40; SAU $4.90. **Remarks:** Accepts advertising. **Circ:** Paid 2570, Free 1800.

ADEL

SW IA. Dallas Co. 15 mi. W. of Urbandale. Residential. Manufactures brick and tile.

12401 ■ Dallas County News
Dallas County News Inc.
813 Main St.
Adel, IA 50003
Phone: (515)993-4233
Fax: (515)993-4235
Newspaper with a community orientation. **Freq:** Weekly (Thurs.). **Print Method:** Offset. **Cols./Page:** 6. **Col. Width:** 12 picas. **Col. Depth:** 21.5 inches. **Key Personnel:** Amber Williams, Editor. **Ad Rates:** GLR $5.80; BW $774; 4C $1,024; SAU $6.75; PCI $6. **Remarks:** Accepts advertising. **Circ:** 3100.

ALBIA

S IA. Monroe Co. 68 mi. SE of Des Moines. Coal mines; timber. Diversified farming.

12402 ■ Monroe County News
Albia Newspapers Inc.
109 Benton Ave. E
Albia, IA 52531
Phone: (641)932-7121
Fax: (641)932-2822
Newspaper with a Democratic orientation. **Freq:** Weekly (Tues.). **Print Method:** Offset. **Cols./Page:** 5. **Col. Width:** 12 picas. **Col. Depth:** 13 1/2 inches. **Key Personnel:** Dave Paxton, Publisher; Marilyn Teno, Manager, Advertising; Theresa Christofferson, Office Manager. **URL:** http://www.albianews.com. **Mailing address:** PO Box 338, Albia, IA 52531. **Ad Rates:** PCI $3.65. **Remarks:** Advertising accepted; rates available upon request. **Circ:** Paid 3500, Free 300.

12403 ■ Union Republican
Albia Newspapers Inc.
109 Benton Ave. E
Albia, IA 52531
Phone: (641)932-7121
Fax: (641)932-2822
Newspaper with a Republican orientation. **Freq:** Weekly (Thurs.). **Print Method:** Offset. **Cols./Page:** 6. **Col. Width:** 12 picas. **Col. Depth:** 21 1/2 inches. **Key Personnel:** David A. Paxton, Editor. **Mailing address:** PO Box 338, Albia, IA 52531. **Ad Rates:** PCI $3.65. **Remarks:** Accepts advertising. **Circ:** Paid 3500, Free 300.

ALGONA

N IA. Kossuth Co. On Des Moines River, 42 mi. N. of Fort Dodge. Creameries; hatcheries; fertilizer, motor and aviation testing equipment, motor rebuilding, machine tools, bottled gas, feed manufactured. Seed corn processing plant. Grain farms. Corn, oats, hay, cattle and hogs.

12404 ■ The Algona Upper Des Moines
Algona Publishing Co.
14 E Nebraska St.
Algona, IA 50511
Phone: (515)295-3535
Fax: (515)295-7217
Free: 800-444-1957
Publisher's E-mail: algona@algona.com
Newspaper. **Freq:** Weekly (Thurs.). **Print Method:** Offset. **Cols./Page:** 6. **Col. Width:** 12 picas. **Col. Depth:** 21 1/2 inches. **Key Personnel:** Kurt Dahl, Publisher; Heidi Larson, Office Manager; Mindy Baker, Editor. **USPS:** 013-220. **Subscription Rates:** $55 Individuals in county; $74 Out of area; $65 Out of country. **Ad Rates:** BW $654; 4C $864; SAU $5.07; PCI $5.37. **Remarks:** Accepts advertising. **Circ:** ‡4950.

12405 ■ KLGA-AM - 1600
PO Box 160
Algona, IA 50511
Phone: (515)295-2475
Fax: (515)295-3851
Format: Country. **Networks:** ABC; Radio Iowa. **Owner:** NRG Media, 2875 Mount Vernon Rd. SE, Cedar Rapids, IA 52403, Ph: (319)862-0300, Fax: (319)286-9383. **Founded:** 1956. **Operating Hours:** Continuous. **Key Personnel:** Bob Ketchum, Gen. Mgr., bketchum@nrgmedia.com. **Wattage:** 1,000 Day; 500 Night. **Ad Rates:** for 60 seconds. Combined advertising rates available with KLGA-FM. **URL:** http://www.algonaradio.com.

12406 ■ KLGA-FM - 92.7
2102 80th Ave.
Algona, IA 50511
Phone: (515)295-2475
Fax: (515)295-3851
Format: Adult Contemporary. **Networks:** ABC; Radio Iowa. **Owner:** NRG Media, 2875 Mount Vernon Rd. SE, Cedar Rapids, IA 52403, Ph: (319)862-0300, Fax: (319)286-9383. **Founded:** Sept. 19, 2006. **Operating Hours:** Continuous. **Key Personnel:** Bob Ketchum, Gen. Mgr., bketchum@nrgmedia.com. **Wattage:** 800. **Ad Rates:** Noncommercial. Combined advertising rates available with KLGA-AM.

ALTOONA

C IA. Polk Co. 4 mi. E. of Des Moines. Grain, stock farms.

12407 ■ Altoona Herald-Mitchellville Index
Altoona Herald-Mitchellville Index
100 8th St. SE, Ste. H
Altoona, IA 50009
Phone: (515)699-7000
Fax: (515)699-7098
Publication E-mail: newsubs@dmreg.com
Community newspaper. **Freq:** Weekly (Thurs.). **Print Method:** Offset. **Trim Size:** 12 picas. **Cols./Page:** 6. **Col. Width:** 1.53 inches. **Col. Depth:** 21 inches. **Key Personnel:** Amy Duncan, Publisher, phone: (515)699-7026; Adam Wilson, Editor, phone: (515)699-7028; Becky VanderBerg, Manager, Advertising, phone: (515)699-7027. **Subscription Rates:** $25 Individuals by carrier; $30 Individuals by mail; $33 Out of area. **Mailing address:** PO Box 427, Altoona, IA 50009. **Ad Rates:** GLR $5.25; BW $840; 4C $1055; SAU $4.71; PCI $4. **Remarks:** Accepts advertising. **Circ:** 6000.

AMANA

12408 ■ Communal Societies
Communal Studies Association
PO Box 122
Amana, IA 52203
Phone: (319)622-6446
Publisher's E-mail: info@communalstudies.org
Freq: Semiannual. **ISSN:** 0739- 1250 (print). **Subscription Rates:** $30 U.S. and Canada for nonmembers; $40 Other countries for nonmembers; Included in membership. **URL:** http://www.communalstudies.org/journal. **Remarks:** Advertising not accepted. **Circ:** 380.

AMES

C IA. Story Co. 32 mi. N. of Des Moines. Iowa State University of Science and Technology. Agriculture Experiment Station.Manufactures stock and poultry feeds, jackets, hydrostatic transmission, milk-products, toys, electronic equipment, abrasives, water filters, drawing instruments. Agriculture. Corn, hogs, cattle.

12409 ■ Advances in Strawberry Research
North American Strawberry Growers Association
c/o Dr. Gail R. Nonnecke, Ed.
Dept. of Horticulture
Iowa State University
Ames, IA 50011
Phone: (515)294-0037
Fax: (515)294-0730
Publisher's E-mail: info@nasga.org
Journal describing strawberry research. **Key Personnel:** Dr. Gail R. Nonnecke, Editor. **Circ:** (Not Reported).

12410 ■ Aeon: A Journal of Myth, Science, and Ancient History
Aeon: A Journal of Myth and Science
PO Box 1092
Ames, IA 50014
Fax: (515)292-2603
Publication E-mail: ev@aeonJournal.com
Journal exploring archaeo-astronomical traditions and analysis of common patterns in ancient myths from around the world. **Freq:** 3/year. **Trim Size:** 8 x 11. **Cols./Page:** 2. **Key Personnel:** Dwardu Cardona, Editor; Ev

Circulation: ★ = AAM; △ or • = BPA; ♦ = CAC; ❑ = VAC; ⊕ = PO Statement; ‡ = Publisher's Report; Boldface figures = sworn; Light figures = estimated.

Cochrane, Publisher. **ISSN:** 1066--5145 (print). **Subscription Rates:** $40 U.S. and Canada; $55 Elsewhere. **URL:** http://www.aeonjournal.com. **Ad Rates:** BW $80. **Remarks:** Accepts advertising. **Circ:** Paid 500, Non-paid 100.

12411 ■ Cultural Logic: An Electronic Journal of Marxist Theory and Practice
The EServer
203 Ross Hall
Iowa State University
Ames, IA 50011-1201
Phone: (515)441-1461
Fax: (515)294-6444
Journal dealing with essays, interviews, poetry, reviews within Marxist tradition. **Key Personnel:** David Siar, Editor. **ISSN:** 1097--3087 (print). **Subscription Rates:** Free. **URL:** http://clogic.eserver.org. **Circ:** (Not Reported).

12412 ■ Earth-Science Reviews: The International Geological Journal Bridging the Gap Between Research Articles and Textbooks
RELX Group P.L.C.
c/o E.S. Takle, Mng. Ed.
Iowa State University
International Institute of Theoretical & Applied Science
3010 Agronomy Bldg.
Ames, IA 50011
Publisher's E-mail: amsterdam@relx.com
Journal containing reviews of all aspects of earth sciences or treatises on an expanding Earth Sciences subject. **Freq:** 12/yr. **Key Personnel:** I. Candy, Managing Editor. **ISSN:** 0012--8252 (print). **Subscription Rates:** $2940 Institutions print; $2448.67 online; $222 Individuals print. **URL:** http://www.journals.elsevier.com/earth-science-reviews/. **Circ:** (Not Reported).

12413 ■ Electronic Journal of Linear Algebra
International Linear Algebra Society
c/o Leslie Hogben, Secretary-Treasurer
Carver Hall
Dept. of Mathematics
Iowa State University
Ames, IA 50011
Fax: (515)294-5454
Peer-reviewed journal featuring mathematical articles of high standards that contribute new information and insights to matrix analysis and the various aspects of linear algebra and its applications. **Freq:** Annual 2 volumes. **ISSN:** 1081-3810 (print). **Subscription Rates:** $16 Members plus shipping and handling (vol. 1-4); $20 Members plus shipping and handling (vol. 5-7); $20 Nonmembers plus shipping and handling (vol. 1-4); $25 Nonmembers plus shipping and handling (vol. 5-7). **URL:** http://www.math.technion.ac.il/iic/journal/. **Remarks:** Advertising not accepted. **Circ:** (Not Reported).

12414 ■ Iowa State Daily
Iowa State Daily Publication Board
Iowa State University
108 Hamilton Hall
Ames, IA 50011
Phone: (515)294-4120
Fax: (515)294-4119
Publisher's E-mail: admin@iowastatedaily.com
Collegiate newspaper. **Freq:** Daily (morn.) (during the academic year). **Print Method:** Offset. **Trim Size:** 14 x 22 3/4. **Cols./Page:** 6. **Col. Width:** 2 1/16 inches. **Col. Depth:** 21 inches. **Key Personnel:** Allison Suesse, Editor; Sarah Haas, Editor; Zach Thompson, Editor-in-Chief. **Ad Rates:** BW $10; 4C $260. **Remarks:** Accepts advertising. **Circ:** 10000.

12415 ■ Journal of Food Quality
Wiley-Blackwell
c/o Terri D. Boylston, Ed.-in-Ch.
Iowa State University
2547 Food Sciences Bldg.
Ames, IA 50011-1061
Publisher's E-mail: info@wiley.com
Scientific journal explicitly devoted to issues of food quality covering methodology for monitoring food quality, methodology for monitoring nutritional quality, shelf life testing and validation of rapid shelf life studies, environmental factors affecting food quality, impact of present and proposed regulations on the quality of the food supply, statistical interpretation of quality control data and original techniques for measuring various quality attributes. **Freq:** Bimonthly. **Key Personnel:** Terri D. Boylston, PhD, Editor. **EISSN:** 1745--4557 (electronic). **Subscription Rates:** $576 Institutions online; £393 Institutions online; €497 Institutions online - euro and non euro zone; $767 Institutions online - rest of the world. **URL:** http://onlinelibrary.wiley.com/journal/10.1111/(ISSN)1745-4557. **Remarks:** Advertising accepted; rates available upon request. **Circ:** (Not Reported).

12416 ■ McIlvainea: Journal of America Amateur Mycology
North American Mycological Association
2019 Ashmore Dr.
Ames, IA 50014
Journal covering research reports in the field of mycology. **Freq:** Annual. **Key Personnel:** Michael W. Beug, Editor. **ISSN:** 0099--8400 (print). **URL:** http://www.namyco.org/mcilvainea.php. **Remarks:** Advertising not accepted. **Circ:** (Not Reported).

12417 ■ NDT & E International: Independent Nondestructive Testing and Evaluation
RELX Group P.L.C.
c/o E.D. Chimenti, Editor-in-Chief
Dept. of Aeropspace Engineering
Iowa State University
1200 Howe Hall
Ames, IA 50011-2271
Fax: (515)294-3262
Publisher's E-mail: amsterdam@relx.com
Peer-reviewed journal focusing on results of original research and development in all categories of the fields of nondestructive testing and evaluation including ultrasonics, electromagnetics, radiography, optical and thermal methods. **Freq:** 8/year. **Key Personnel:** E.D. Chimenti, Editor-in-Chief. **ISSN:** 0963--8695 (print). **Subscription Rates:** $278 Individuals print; $1294 Institutions online; $1553 Institutions print. **URL:** http://www.journals.elsevier.com/ndt-and-e-international. **Circ:** (Not Reported).

12418 ■ Needlework Retailer
Yarn Tree Design Inc.
117 Alexander Ave.
Ames, IA 50010
Phone: (515)232-3121
Fax: (515)232-0789
Free: 800-247-3952
Publication E-mail: info@needleworkretailer.com
Trade magazine for the needlework industry, especially small, independent needlework retailers. **Freq:** Bimonthly. **Trim Size:** 8 1/8 x 10 7/8. **URL:** http://yarntree.com; http://needleworkretailer.com. **Mailing address:** PO Box 724, Ames, IA 50010. **Ad Rates:** BW $1,135; 4C $1,585. **Remarks:** Accepts advertising. **Circ:** (Not Reported).

12419 ■ New Directions for Student Services
Jossey-Bass Publishers
c/o John H. Schuh, Assoc Ed.
Professional Studies in Education
N 243 Lagomarcino Hall
Iowa State University
Ames, IA 50011
Publisher's E-mail: info@wiley.com
Monograph series for student services professionals offering guidelines and programs for aiding student intellectual, emotional, social, and physical development, and management of student affairs programs. **Freq:** Quarterly. **Print Method:** Sheetfed Offset. **Trim Size:** 6 x 9. **Cols./Page:** 1. **Col. Width:** 27 picas. **Col. Depth:** 45 picas. **Key Personnel:** John H. Schuh, Associate Editor; Elizabeth Whitt, Editor-in-Chief. **ISSN:** 0164-7970 (print). **Subscription Rates:** $89 U.S., Canada, and Mexico print or online only; $98 U.S., Canada, and Mexico print & online; $113 Other countries print; $335 Institutions online only; $402 Institutions print and online; $335 Institutions print; $375 Institutions, Canada and Mexico; $409 Institutions, other countries. **URL:** http://onlinelibrary.wiley.com/journal/10.1002/(ISSN)1536-0695. **Remarks:** Accepts advertising. **Circ:** (Not Reported).

12420 ■ Our Iowa
Our Iowa Magazine
1510 Buckeye Ave
Ames, IA 50010
Phone: (515)232-0075
Publication E-mail: editors@ouriowamagazine.com
Magazine featuring about living in Iowa. **Freq:** Bimonthly. **Trim Size:** 8 1/2 x 10 7/8. **Subscription Rates:** $18.98 Individuals; $32.98 Two years. **URL:** http://www.ouriowamagazine.com. **Ad Rates:** BW $2898. **Remarks:** Accepts advertising. **Circ:** (Not Reported).

12421 ■ Plant Disease: An International Journal of Applied Plant Pathology
American Phytopathological Society
c/o Mark L. Gleason, Editor-in-Chief
Iowa State University
Ames, IA 50011
Phone: (515)294-0579
Publisher's E-mail: aps@scisoc.org
Journal focusing on research on the applied or practical aspects of diagnosing and treating plant diseases. **Freq:** Monthly. **Print Method:** Sheet-fed offset. **Trim Size:** 8 1/2 x 11. **Cols./Page:** 3. **Col. Width:** 28 nonpareils. **Col. Depth:** 140 agate lines. **Key Personnel:** Mark L. Gleason, Editor-in-Chief; Kendra Baumgartner, Senior Editor; Ronald H. Brlansky, Senior Editor; R. Michael Davis. **ISSN:** 0191-2917 (print). **Subscription Rates:** $895 Institutions and libraries; print, U.S.; $1009 Institutions, other countries and libraries; print. **URL:** http://apsjournals.apsnet.org/loi/pdis. **Ad Rates:** BW $1040; 4C $800; PCI $75. **Remarks:** Accepts advertising. **Circ:** 2,500, 1,100.

12422 ■ Review of Modern Logic: International Journal for the History of Mathematical Logic, Set Theory, and Foundation of Mathematics
Modern Logic Publishing
2408 1/2 W Lincoln Way (Upper Level)
Ames, IA 50014-7217
Publication E-mail: corresponding.editor@modernlogic.org
Journal covering historical studies of 19th- and 20th-century mathematical logic. **Freq:** Quarterly. **Print Method:** Offset. **Trim Size:** 6 x 9. **Cols./Page:** 1. **Key Personnel:** Irving H. Anellis, Editor; John C. Simms, Editor; Mark E. Fuller, Managing Editor. **ISSN:** 1943--7404 (print). **Subscription Rates:** $110. **URL:** http://projecteuclid.org/euclid.rml. **Formerly**: Modern Logic. **Ad Rates:** BW $200. **Remarks:** Accepts advertising. **Circ:** Paid 125, Non-paid 20.

12423 ■ KURE-FM - 88.5
1199 Friley Hall
Ames, IA 50012
Phone: (515)294-4332
Format: Full Service; Classical; Classic Rock. **Owner:** Iowa State University, at above address. **Founded:** 1949. **Wattage:** 250. **Ad Rates:** Noncommercial. KUSR, KPGY. **URL:** http://www.kure.stuorg.iastate.edu.

12424 ■ WOI-AM - 640
2022 Communications Bldg.
Ames, IA 50011-3241
Phone: (515)294-2025
Fax: (515)294-1544
Free: 800-861-8000
Email: woimember@iastate.edu
Format: Public Radio; News. **Simulcasts:** KTPR-FM 91.1 Fort Dodge. **Networks:** National Public Radio (NPR); Public Radio International (PRI). **Owner:** Iowa State University of Science and Technology, at above address. **Founded:** 1921. **Operating Hours:** Continuous; 85% network, 15% local. **ADI:** Des Moines, IA. **Key Personnel:** Karen Bryan, Producer, kbryan@iastate.edu. **Local Programs**: *Talk of Iowa*, Monday Tuesday Wednesday Thursday Friday 10:00 a.m. **Wattage**: 5,000. **Ad Rates:** Noncommercial.

12425 ■ WOI-FM - 90.1
Iowa State University
2022 Communication Bldg.
Ames, IA 50011-3241
Phone: (515)294-2025
Fax: (515)294-1544
Free: 800-861-8000
Format: Public Radio; Classical. **Networks:** National Public Radio (NPR); Public Radio International (PRI). **Owner:** Iowa Radio Group, at above address. **Founded:** 1949. **Operating Hours:** Continuous; 50% network, 50% local. **ADI:** Des Moines, IA. **Key Personnel:** Todd Behrends, Mgr., Member Svcs., behrends@iastate.edu; Dave Knippel, Engineer, dknippel@iastate.edu. **Wattage**: 100,000. **Ad Rates:** Noncommercial. **URL:** http://www.public.iastate.edu.

ANAMOSA

E IA. Jones Co. 20 mi. NE of Cedar Rapids. Iowa State reformatory. Manufactures electric motors, banking equipment, lumber products. Limestone quarries. Grain, stock farms. Seed corn, hogs, cattle.

12426 ■ Wapsipinicon Almanac
Route 3 Press
19948 Shooting Star Rd.
Anamosa, IA 52205
Phone: (319)462-4623
Magazine containing regional essays, fiction, and reviews. **Freq:** Annual. **Print Method:** Letterpress. **Trim Size:** 6 5/8 x 9 3/4. **Cols./Page:** 2. **Col. Width:** 15 picas. **Col. Depth:** 50 picas. **Key Personnel:** Timothy Fay, Editor. **Subscription Rates:** $7 Single issue. **URL:** http://www.wapsialmanac.com/. **Ad Rates:** BW $125. **Remarks:** Accepts advertising. **Circ:** Non-paid 2000.

ANITA

SW IA. Cass Co. 68 mi. W. of Des Moines. Stock, grain, poultry, dairy farms. Cattle, hogs, corn.

12427 ■ Tradition Magazine: The Voice of Traditional Acoustic Music in America
National Traditional Country Music Association
650 Main St.
Anita, IA 50020
Phone: (712)762-4363
Publisher's E-mail: ruralcountrymusic@gmail.com
Magazine promoting the preservation of all forms of acoustic traditional music. **Freq:** Bimonthly (during academic year; periodic during winter months). **Print Method:** News Print. **Trim Size:** 14 1/2 x 10 1/4. **Col. Depth:** 86 agate lines. **Key Personnel:** Bob Everhart, President. **ISSN:** 1071--1864 (print). **Subscription Rates:** Included in membership. **URL:** http://www.ntcma.net. **Mailing address:** PO Box 492, Anita, IA 50020. **Ad Rates:** BW $350. **Remarks:** Accepts advertising. **Circ:** 3500, 3500.

ANKENY

C IA. Polk Co. 6 mi. N. of Des Moines. Manufactures transmissions, farm equipment, prepared feeds, generator sets, fabricated parts, machines. Grain, stock, dairy farms.

12428 ■ Journal of Soil and Water Conservation
Soil and Water Conservation Society
945 SW Ankeny Rd.
Ankeny, IA 50023-9723
Phone: (515)289-2331
Fax: (515)289-1227
Free: 800-843-7645
Publication E-mail: swcs@swcs.org
Journal featuring land and water conservation research, including general interest features, applied research reports, viewpoints, and current events. **Freq:** Bimonthly. **Print Method:** Offset. **Trim Size:** 8 1/2 x 11. **Cols./Page:** 3. **Col. Width:** 28 nonpareils. **Col. Depth:** 140 agate lines. **Key Personnel:** Annie Binder, Editor, Director, Publications. **ISSN:** 0022--4561 (print); **EISSN:** 1941--3300 (electronic). **Subscription Rates:** $115 U.S. print and online; $145 Out of state print; $115 Out of state online; $185 Out of state print and online; $115 Institutions print - inside U.S; $540 Institutions online - inside and outside U.S; $580 Institutions print and online - inside U.S; $145 Institutions print - outside U.S; $610 Institutions print and online - outside U.S. **URL:** http://www.jswconline.org. **Ad Rates:** BW $1500; 4C $625. **Remarks:** Accepts advertising. **Circ:** 9358.

12429 ■ KCWI-TV - 23
2701 SE Convenience Blvd., Ste. 1
Ankeny, IA 50021
Key Personnel: Dave Presler, Gen. Sales Mgr.; Tony Hoffman, Sales Mgr. **URL:** http://www.kcwi23.com.

ANTHON

12430 ■ Sioux Valley News
Southeast Missourian Plus
PO Box 6
Correctionville, IA 51016
Publisher's E-mail: cwu@semissourian.com
Community newspaper. **Freq:** Weekly (Wed.). **Print Method:** Offset. **Trim Size:** 15 x 30. **Cols./Page:** 6. **Col. Width:** 11 picas. **Col. Depth:** 20 inches. **Key Personnel:** Barbara Trimble, Publisher. **USPS:** 026-860. **Subscription Rates:** $18.75; $22.50 Out of area; $27.50 Individuals; $30 Individuals In State; $35 Out of state. **Formerly:** Anthon Herald; Correctionville News. **Ad Rates:** PCI $6.50. **Remarks:** Accepts advertising. **Circ:** ‡1300, ‡1300.

ATLANTIC

SW IA. Cass Co. 45 mi. E. of Council Bluffs. Livestock feed, lamps and lampshades, hatcheries; elevators; steel buildings. Manufactures diesel & automotive bearings, steel boxes, soft drinks. Agriculture. Corn, soybeans. Hogs, cattle.

12431 ■ Atlantic News-Telegraph
Atlantic News-Telegraph
PO Box 230
Atlantic, IA 50022-0230
Phone: (712)243-2624
Fax: (712)243-4988
Free: 800-926-6397
Publisher's E-mail: ccollins@ant-news.com
Newspaper with a Republican orientation. **Freq:** Daily (eve.) and Sat. (morn.). **Print Method:** Offset. **Cols./Page:** 6. **Col. Width:** 25 nonpareils. **Col. Depth:** 294 agate lines. **Key Personnel:** Jeff Lundquist, Managing Editor, Publisher; Drew Herron, Editor. **Subscription Rates:** $151 Individuals mail; $160 Individuals motor route. **URL:** http://www.swiowanewssource.com/atlantic. **Ad Rates:** GLR $.15; BW $711; 4C $820; SAU $6.75; PCI $5.65. **Remarks:** Accepts classified advertising. **Circ:** Paid 6154, Free 18800.

12432 ■ KJAN-AM - 1220
PO Box 389
Atlantic, IA 50022
Phone: (712)243-3920
Free: 800-283-5526
Format: News; Middle-of-the-Road (MOR). **Networks:** ABC; Radio Iowa. **Owner:** Wireless Communications Corp., 315 Kitty Hawk Dr., Morrisville, NC 27560, Ph: (919)786-0891. **Founded:** Sept. 1950. **Operating Hours**: Continuous. **Key Personnel:** Chris Parks, Prog. Dir., kjanprgm@metc.net; Ric Hanson, News Dir., kjannews@metc.net; Stacie Linfor, Dir. of Traffic, kjandesk@metc.net; Lavon Eblen, Contact. **Wattage:** 250 Day; 089 Night. **Ad Rates:** $7.50-17 for 30 seconds; $9-22 for 60 seconds. **URL:** http://www.kjan.com.

12433 ■ KSOM-FM - 96.5
413 Chestnut St.
Atlantic, IA 50022-1247
Phone: (712)243-6885
Free: 800-222-0965
Format: Full Service. **Founded:** Sept. 07, 2006. **Key Personnel:** Tom Robinson, Sports Dir., News Dir. **Wattage:** 100,000 ERP. **Ad Rates:** Advertising accepted; rates available upon request. **URL:** http://www.965ksom.com.

12434 ■ KSWI-FM - 95.7
413 Chestnut St.
Atlantic, IA 50022-1247
Phone: (712)243-6885
Fax: (712)243-1691
Format: Adult Contemporary. **Owner:** Meredith Communications L.C., 413 Chestnut St., Atlantic, IA 50022, Ph: (712)243-6885, Fax: (712)243-1691. **Key Personnel:** Tom Robinson, News Dir. **URL:** http://www.ks957.

AUDUBON

SWC IA. Audubon Co. 75 mi. W. of Des Moines. Farm equipment, feed, fertilizer, chemicals; alfalfa mill; nursery; produce packing house. Agriculture. Corn, hogs, cattle.

12435 ■ Audubon County Advocate Journal
Audubon County Newspapers
514 Leroy Street
Audubon, IA 50025
Phone: (712)563-2661
Fax: (712)563-3118
Free: 800-798-2635
Publication E-mail: news@auduboncountynews.com
Community newspaper. **Freq:** Weekly (Fri.). **Print Method:** Offset. **Cols./Page:** 6. **Col. Width:** 10.5 picas. **Col. Depth:** 21 1/2 inches. **Key Personnel:** Connie Collins, Associate Publisher. **USPS:** 037-060. **Subscription Rates:** $30 Individuals in county; 6 months; $51 Individuals in county; 1 year; $36 Individuals out of county; 6 months; $61 Individuals out of county; 1 year. **URL:** http://www.swiowanewssource.com/audubon. **Formerly**: Audubon News Advocate. **Mailing address:** PO Box 247, Audubon, IA 50025-1101. **Ad Rates:** GLR $6.50; BW $550; 4C $130; PCI $4. **Remarks:** Accepts advertising. **Circ:** Paid 2,425.

12436 ■ Nishna Valley Tribune
Audubon County Newspapers
514 Leroy Street
Audubon, IA 50025
Phone: (712)563-2661
Fax: (712)563-3118
Free: 800-798-2635
Newspaper with a Republican orientation. **Freq:** Weekly (Tues.). **Print Method:** Offset. **Cols./Page:** 8. **Col. Width:** 10 1/2 picas. **Col. Depth:** 21 1/2 inches. **Mailing address:** PO Box 247, Audubon, IA 50025-1101. **Ad Rates:** SAU $5.90; PCI $7. **Remarks:** Accepts advertising. **Circ:** Free 6725.

AYRSHIRE

12437 ■ ATC Cablevision
1405 Silver Lake Ave.
Ayrshire, IA 50515
Phone: (712)426-2800
Fax: (712)426-2008
Free: 888-795-2800
Email: info@ayrshireia.com
Founded: Sept. 06, 2006. **Key Personnel:** Don Miller, Gen. Mgr.; William Myers, VP. **Cities Served:** 87 channels. **Mailing address:** PO Box 248, Ayrshire, IA 50515. **URL:** http://www.ayrshireia.com.

BELMOND

NC IA. Wright Co. On Iowa River, 32 mi. SW of Mason City. Hybrid seed corn, soybean processing, fertilizer and grain drying plants; horse, stock, grain trailers, engine valves, elevators. Farm machinery factory. Agrichemicals. Gravel pits. Stock, grain farms. Corn, hogs, cattle.

12438 ■ Belmond Independent
Belmond Independent
215 E Main St.
Belmond, IA 50421
Phone: (641)444-3333
Fax: (641)444-7777
Community newspaper. **Freq:** Weekly (Thurs.). **Print Method:** Offset. **Cols./Page:** 8. **Col. Width:** 22 nonpareils. **Col. Depth:** 294 agate lines. **Key Personnel:** Dirk Van Der Linden, Publisher; Lee Van Der Linden, Publisher. **USPS:** 049-660. **Subscription Rates:** $38 Individuals local area; $42 Individuals rest of Iowa; $46 Out of state. **Ad Rates:** BW $445; SAU $5.44. **Remarks:** Advertising accepted; rates available upon request. **Circ:** ‡2000.

BETTENDORF

EC IA. Scott Co. 5 mi. E. of Davenport.

12439 ■ WKBF-AM - 1270
1035 Lincoln Rd., Ste. 205
Bettendorf, IA 52722
Phone: (563)355-7973
Format: Hispanic. **Networks:** Westwood One Radio. **Founded:** 1925. **Formerly**: WHBF-AM. **Operating Hours**: Continuous; 95% network, 5% local. **ADI**: Daveport,IA-Rock Island, Moline,IL. **Wattage:** 5,000; 5,400. **Ad Rates:** $12 for 30 seconds; $15 for 60 seconds. **URL:** http://www.lajefa1270.com.

BLAIRSTOWN

12440 ■ Coon Creek Telephone & Cablevision
312 Locust St.
Blairstown, IA 52209-0150
Phone: (319)454-6234
Free: 888-823-6234
Email: cooncrek@netins.net
Key Personnel: Kami Thenhaus, Office Mgr. **Cities Served:** 24 channels. **Mailing address:** PO Box 150, Blairstown, IA 52209-0150. **URL:** http://cooncreektelephone.com.

BLOOMFIELD

SE IA. Davis Co. 20 mi. S. of Ottumwa. Manufactures steel, metal, plastics, truck equipment, feed. Agriculture.

Circulation: ★ = AAM; △ or • = BPA; ♦ = CAC; ❑ = VAC; ⊕ = PO Statement; ‡ = Publisher's Report; Boldface figures = sworn; Light figures = estimated.

Sheep, cattle, hogs, corn, soybeans.

12441 ■ The Bloomfield Democrat
Bloomfield Democrat
207-209 S Madison
Bloomfield, IA 52537
Phone: (641)664-2334
Fax: (641)664-2316
Publication E-mail: bdemo@netins.net
Community newspaper serving Bloomfield and Davis counties in Iowa. **Freq:** Daily. **Subscription Rates:** $49 Individuals; $62 Out of area; $30 Individuals e-edition. **URL:** http://www.bdemo.com. **Mailing address:** PO Box 19, Bloomfield, IA 52537. **Remarks:** Accepts advertising. **Circ:** (Not Reported).

BOONE

C IA. Boone Co. 14 mi. W. of Ames. Manufactures wire, iron and dairy products, refrigerators, cookies, envelopes, hydraulic and automotive equipment. Nurseries; machine shops; meat processing plant. Agriculture. Corn, soybeans, livestock.

12442 ■ Boone County Shopping News
Partnership Press Inc.
2136 E Mamie Eisenhower
Boone, IA 50036
Phone: (515)432-6694
Fax: (515)432-7811
Free: 888-270-0090
Newspaper. **Freq:** Weekly (Wed.). **Cols./Page:** 9. **Col. Width:** 9 picas. **Col. Depth:** 13 inches. **Subscription Rates:** Free. **Mailing address:** PO Box 100, Boone, IA 50036. **Remarks:** Accepts advertising. **Circ:** 25760.

12443 ■ Boone News-Republican
Boone Publishing Inc.
2136 E Mamie Eisenhower
Boone, IA 50036
Phone: (515)432-6694
Fax: (515)432-7811
Free: 888-270-0090
Publisher's E-mail: news@amestrib.com
General newspaper. **Freq:** Published Tuesday, Thursday and Saturday except for holiday. **Print Method:** Offset. **Trim Size:** 14 x 22 3/4. **Cols./Page:** 6. **Col. Width:** 2 1/16 inches. **Col. Depth:** 21 1/2 inches. **Key Personnel:** Gwen Taylor, Sales Representative; Claudia Lovin, Publisher; Greg Eckstrom, Editor. **USPS:** 060-800. **URL:** http://newsrepublican.com. **Mailing address:** PO Box 100, Boone, IA 50036. **Ad Rates:** BW $973.95; 4C $1163.95; SAU $7.55. **Remarks:** Accepts advertising. **Circ:** ‡3149.

12444 ■ Star Magazine
American Media Inc.
PO Box 37095
Boone, IA 50037-0095
Free: 877-566-5831
Publisher's E-mail: strenk@amilink.com
Magazine with celebrity gossip, news and photos. **Freq:** Weekly. **Trim Size:** 7 3/4 x 10 1/2. **Key Personnel:** David Jackson, Publisher, phone: (212)743-6669, fax: (212)743-6515. **URL:** http://americanmediainc.com/brands/star. **Ad Rates:** BW $120,240; 4C $133,590. **Remarks:** Accepts advertising. **Circ:** (Not Reported).

12445 ■ KWBG-AM - 1590
724 Story St., Ste. 201
Boone, IA 50036
Email: kwbg@kwbg.com
Format: News; Sports. **Networks:** Fox; ESPN Radio. **Owner:** NRG Media, 2875 Mount Vernon Rd. SE, Cedar Rapids, IA 52403, Ph: (319)862-0300, Fax: (319)286-9383. **Founded:** 1950. **Operating Hours:** Continuous. **Key Personnel:** Jim Turbes, News Dir.; Ryan Wendt, Sports Dir. **Wattage:** 1,000 Day ; 500 Nigh. **Ad Rates:** Advertising accepted; rates available upon request. **URL:** http://www.kwbg.com.

BREDA

12446 ■ Tele-Services Ltd.
112 E Main St.
Breda, IA 51436-8703
Phone: (712)673-2311
Free: 888-508-2946
Founded: 1905. **Key Personnel:** Chuck Deisbeck, HR Mgr.; Jane Morlok, Account Mgr.; Megan Badding, Cust. Srv. Mgr.; Mike Ludwig, Dept. Mgr.; Kevin Skinner, Dir. of Mktg.; Diane Miller, Dept. Mgr. **URL:** http://www.win-4-u.com.

BROOKLYN

SEC IA. Poweshiek Co. 12 mi. SE of Grinnell. Residential.

12447 ■ Inter-County Cable Co.
129 Jackson St.
Brooklyn, IA 52211-0513
Phone: (641)522-9211
Fax: (641)522-5001
Free: 877-610-0330
Founded: 1992. **Key Personnel:** Tim Atkinson, Gen. Mgr. **Cities Served:** 95 channels. **Mailing address:** PO Box 513, Brooklyn, IA 52211-0513. **URL:** http://brooklyntelco.com.

12448 ■ KSKB-FM - 99.1
104 E 2nd Ave
Brooklyn, IA 52211
Phone: (641)522-7202
Fax: (641)522-7239
Format: Religious. **Owner:** Florida Public Radio Inc., at above address. **Founded:** 1988. **Wattage:** 3,000. **URL:** http://kskb.net/.

BURLINGTON

SE IA. Des Moines Co. On Mississippi River, 60 mi. S. of Davenport. Barge connections. Limestone quarries. Manufactures soap, furniture, desks, mattresses, farm equipment, turbines, plastics, T.V. antennas, statellite dishes, electrical equipment, radio parts, fertilizers, insecticides, germicides, commercial chemicals, safety paper, bread, biscuits, paint, monuments, baskets, cartons, spark plugs. Ordnance works; electric switchgear, storage tanks, storage batteries.

12449 ■ Hawk Eye
Harris Enterprises
800 S Main St.
Burlington, IA 52601
Phone: (319)754-8461
Fax: (319)754-6824
Free: 800-397-1708
Publication E-mail: webmaster@thehawkeye.com
General newspaper. **Founded:** 1837. **Freq:** Daily (morn.). **Print Method:** Offset. **Cols./Page:** 6. **Col. Width:** 24 nonpareils. **Col. Depth:** 301 agate lines. **Key Personnel:** Steve Delaney, Editor; Janet Stottmeister, Manager, Advertising; Dale Alison, Managing Editor, phone: (319)758-8163. **Subscription Rates:** $147 Individuals. **URL:** http://www.thehawkeye.com. **Mailing address:** PO Box 10, Burlington, IA 52601. **Ad Rates:** PCI $9.55. **Remarks:** Accepts display and classified advertising. **Circ:** Mon.-Sat. ■ **17,700**, Sun. ■ **19,224**.

12450 ■ KBKB-AM - 1360
610 N Fourth St.
Burlington, IA 52601
Phone: (319)752-5402
Format: Country. **Networks:** ABC. **Owner:** Pritchard Broadcasting Corp., 610 N Fourth St., Burlington, IA 52601. **Operating Hours:** 5 a.m.-midnight; 10% network, 90% local. **Key Personnel:** John Pritchard, Gen. Mgr., johnp@burlingtonradio.com; Joe Bates, Music Dir., joeb@bigcountry1031.com. **Wattage:** 1,000. **Ad Rates:** Noncommercial. **URL:** http://www.bigcountry1031.com.

12451 ■ KBKB-FM - 101.7
610 N Fourth St., Ste. 310
Burlington, IA 52601
Phone: (319)752-2701
Format: Country. **Networks:** ABC. **Owner:** Titan Broadcasting L.L.C., 610 N Fourth St., Burlington, IA 52601, Ph: (319)752-2701, Fax: (319)752-5287. **Founded:** 1973. **Formerly:** KXGI-FM. **Operating Hours:** Continuous; 10% network, 90% local. **Key Personnel:** Drew Kirby, Dir. of Programs, drew@1017thebull.com. **Wattage:** 50,000. **Ad Rates:** $5.70-10 for 30 seconds. **URL:** http://www.1017thebull.com.

12452 ■ KBUR-AM - 1490
610 N 4th St., Ste. 300
Burlington, IA 52601
Phone: (319)752-5402
Fax: (319)752-4715
Email: info@kbur.com
Format: Talk; News. **Networks:** ABC. **Owner:** Pritchard Broadcasting Corp., 610 N Fourth St., Burlington, IA 52601. **Founded:** 1941. **Operating Hours:** Continuous; 5% network, 95% local. **ADI:** Daveport,IA-Rock Island, Moline,IL. **Key Personnel:** John Pritchard, Gen. Mgr.; Mark Morris, News Dir. **Wattage:** 1,000. **Ad Rates:** $18-39 for 30 seconds; $22-50 for 60 seconds. Combined advertising rates available with KGRS-FM. **URL:** http://www.kbur.com.

12453 ■ KCDM-FM - 98.3
PO Box 28
Burlington, IA 52601
Phone: (319)752-9560
Email: pilgrimages@ewtn.com
Format: Religious. **Owner:** EWTN Global Catholic Network, 5817 Old Leeds Rd., Irondale, AL 35210, Ph: (205)271-2900. **URL:** http://www.kcdmradio.org.

12454 ■ KDMG-FM - 103.1
610 N 4th St., Ste. 300
Burlington, IA 52601
Phone: (319)754-1103
Fax: (319)752-4715
Email: bigcountry1031@bigcountry1031.com
Format: Country. **Owner:** Pritchard Broadcasting Corp., 610 N Fourth St., Burlington, IA 52601. **Founded:** 1993. **Operating Hours:** Continuous. **Key Personnel:** John Pritchard, Gen. Mgr., johnp@burlingtonradio.com; Joe Bates, Music Dir., joeb@bigcountry1031.com. **Wattage:** 12,000. **Ad Rates:** $21 for 30 seconds; $25 for 60 seconds. Combined advertising rates available with KKMI-FM. **URL:** http://www.bigcountry1031.com.

12455 ■ KGRS-FM - 107.3
610 N Fourth St., Ste. 310
Burlington, IA 52601
Phone: (319)752-2701
Fax: (319)752-5287
Email: cosmo@thenewmix.com
Format: Adult Contemporary. **Networks:** ABC. **Owner:** Titan Broadcasting L.L.C., 610 N Fourth St., Burlington, IA 52601, Ph: (319)752-2701, Fax: (319)752-5287. **Founded:** 1946. **Formerly:** KBUR-FM. **Operating Hours:** Continuous; 1% network, 99% local. **ADI:** Daveport,IA-Rock Island, Moline,IL. **Key Personnel:** Tim Brown, Contact, timbrown@thenewmix.com. **Wattage:** 100,000. **Ad Rates:** $18-25 for 30 seconds; $22-31 for 60 seconds. Combined advertising rates available with KBUR-AM. **URL:** http://www.thenewmix.com.

12456 ■ KHDK-FM - 97.3
610 N 4th St., Ste. 300
Burlington, IA 52601
Phone: (319)752-5402
Fax: (319)752-4715
Email: hot973@hot973online.com
Format: Top 40. **Owner:** Pritchard Broadcasting Corp., 610 N Fourth St., Burlington, IA 52601. **URL:** http://www.hot973online.com.

12457 ■ KKMI-FM - 93.5
610 N Fourth St., Ste. 300
Burlington, IA 52601
Phone: (319)752-5402
Fax: (319)752-4715
Email: requests@935kkmi.com
Format: Country; Oldies. **Networks:** Fox; NBC. **Owner:** Pritchard Broadcasting Corp., 610 N Fourth St., Burlington, IA 52601. **Wattage:** 6,000 ERP. **Ad Rates:** Advertising accepted; rates available upon request. $10 for 30 seconds; $12 for 60 seconds. Combined advertising rates available with KDMG-FM. **URL:** http://www.935kkmi.com.

12458 ■ WQKQ-FM - 92.1
610 N 4th St.
Burlington, IA 52601
Phone: (319)754-9208
Fax: (319)752-4715
Format: Classic Rock. **Owner:** Pritchard Broadcasting Corp., 610 N Fourth St., Burlington, IA 52601. **Operating Hours:** Continuous. **Ad Rates:** Advertising accepted; rates available upon request. **URL:** http://www.kq92rocks.com.

CALMAR

12459 ■ Calmar Courier
Calmar Courier
109 N Maryville
Calmar, IA 52132
Phone: (563)562-3488

Publication E-mail: calmarnews@midamericapub.com
Community newspaper. **Freq:** Weekly (Wed.). **Print Method:** Offset. **Cols./Page:** 4. **Col. Width:** 12.5 picas. **Col. Depth:** 15 inches. **Key Personnel:** Tina Hageman, Editor. **Subscription Rates:** $33 Individuals print - local; $33 Individuals print - non local; $33 Individuals online - local and non-local; $65 Two years print - local; $73 Two years print - non local; $65 Two years online - local and non-local. **URL:** http://www.calmarcourier.com. **Mailing address:** PO Box 507, Calmar, IA 52132-8521. **Ad Rates:** GLR $.24; BW $150; 4C $230; PCI $5. **Remarks:** Accepts advertising. **Circ:** 2,000.

CARROLL

WC IA. Carroll Co. 100 mi. NW of Des Moines. Cattle, hogs, poultry, grain farms. Corn, oats, beans.

12460 ■ Iowa Public Radio
2111 Grand Ave., Ste. 100
Des Moines, IA 50312-5393
Phone: (515)725-1700
Free: 800-861-8000
Format: News; Classical. **Networks:** National Public Radio (NPR); Public Radio International (PRI). **Operating Hours:** Continuous. **Key Personnel:** Mary Kramer, Chmn. of the Bd. **URL:** http://iowapublicradio.org.

12461 ■ KCIM-AM
1119 E Plaza Dr.
Carroll, IA 51401
Phone: (712)792-4321
Fax: (712)792-6667
Format: Country; Agricultural; Full Service. **Networks:** CBS. **Owner:** Carroll Broadcasting Co., PO Box 886, Carroll, IA 51401-0886, Ph: (712)792-4321. **Founded:** 1950. **Wattage:** 1,000.

12462 ■ KKRL-FM - 93.7
PO Box 886
Carroll, IA 51401
Format: Adult Contemporary. **Owner:** Carroll Broadcasting Co., PO Box 886, Carroll, IA 51401-0886, Ph: (712)792-4321. **Operating Hours:** Continuous. **Wattage:** 100,000. **Ad Rates:** Advertising accepted; rates available upon request. Combined advertising rates available with KCIM-AM; KIKD-FM. **URL:** http://www.937kkrl.com.

CASCADE

E IA. Jones Co. 24 mi. SW of Dubuque. Concrete block, recreational vehicles, metal products, tool and die companies. Agriculture. Corn, hay, oats.

12463 ■ Cascade Communications Co.
106 Taylor St.
Cascade, IA 52033
Phone: (563)852-3710
Fax: (563)852-9935
Free: 800-890-8434
Email: info@cascadecomm.com
Founded: 1954. **Key Personnel:** David Gibson, Mgr. **Cities Served:** United States; 60 channels. **Mailing address:** PO Box 250, Cascade, IA 52033-0250. **URL:** http://www.cascadecomm.com.

CEDAR FALLS

NEC IA. Black Hawk Co. On Cedar River, 5 mi. NW of Waterloo. University of Northern Iowa. Manufactures rotary pumps, farm equipment, golf equipment, corrugated boxes, steel products, garbage trucks, lightweight paving equipment, hoists, truck loading equipment, tools and dies; nurseries. Diversified farming.

12464 ■ The North American Review
University of Northern Iowa
1222 W 27th St.
Cedar Falls, IA 50614
Phone: (319)273-6455
Publication E-mail: nar@uni.edu
Literary journal including fiction, poetry, nonfiction, and fine illustration. **Freq:** 4/yr. **Print Method:** Offset. **Trim Size:** 8 1/8 x 10 7/8. **Cols./Page:** 3. **Col. Width:** 27 nonpareils. **Col. Depth:** 140 agate lines. **Key Personnel:** Margaret Morganroth Gullette, Editor; Ron Sandvik, Managing Editor; Yusef Komunyakaa, Editor; Barry Sanders, Editor; Susan Bergman, Editor. **ISSN:** 0029--2397 (print). **Subscription Rates:** $22 U.S.; $29 Canada; $32 Other countries; $40 U.S. two years. **URL:** http://northamericanreview.org. **Ad Rates:** BW $500; PCI $25. **Remarks:** Accepts advertising. **Circ:** ‡3400.

12465 ■ Northern Iowan
University of Northern Iowa
1227 W 27th St.
Cedar Falls, IA 50614
Phone: (319)273-2311
Publication E-mail: northern-iowan@uni.edu
Collegiate newspaper (tabloid). **Freq:** Biweekly Tuesday and Friday; during the academic year. **Print Method:** Online. **Trim Size:** 11 1/2 x 17. **Cols./Page:** 5. **Col. Width:** 22 nonpareils. **Col. Depth:** 210 agate lines. **Key Personnel:** Linh Ta, Executive Editor; Michele Smith, Manager; Allie Koolbeck, Editor. **ISSN:** 1217--2000 (print). **Subscription Rates:** Free. **URL:** http://www.northerniowan.com. **Ad Rates:** 4C $120; PCI $6.55. **Remarks:** Accepts advertising. **Circ:** ‡9000.

12466 ■ Trucking Times & Sport Utility News
WiesnerMedia L.L.C.
307 Maryhill Dr.
Cedar Falls, IA 50613
Phone: (319)230-2050
Publication E-mail: ads@truckingtimes.com
Trade magazine for light truck accessory retailers and industry professionals. **Freq:** Bimonthly. **Trim Size:** 8 1/4 x 10 7/8. **Key Personnel:** Dave Herrmeyer, Founder, Publisher; Bart Taylor, Publisher, phone: (303)662-5379. **Subscription Rates:** $16 Canada and Mexico shipping charge; $40 Other countries shipping charge. **URL:** http://www.truckingtimes.com. **Ad Rates:** BW $3,750. **Remarks:** Advertising accepted; rates available upon request. **Circ:** 11,168.

12467 ■ University of Northern Iowa Today
University of Northern Iowa
1227 W 27th St.
Cedar Falls, IA 50614
Phone: (319)273-2311
Publication for Alumni, friends of UNI. **Freq:** 3/year. **Print Method:** Web press. **Trim Size:** 8 1/2 x 11. **Key Personnel:** Denton Ketels, Editor; C.J. Hines, Editor. **Subscription Rates:** Free. **URL:** http://www.unialum.org/unitoday/issues/index.shtml. **Remarks:** Advertising not accepted. **Circ:** ‡91000.

12468 ■ Cedar Falls Municipal Communications Utility
PO Box 769
Cedar Falls, IA 50613
Phone: (319)266-1761
Email: cfu@cfunet.net
Founded: Sept. 06, 2006. **Cities Served:** 106 channels. **URL:** http://www.cfu.net.

12469 ■ KCNZ-AM - 1650
721 Shirley St.
Cedar Falls, IA 50613
Phone: (319)277-1918
Fax: (319)277-5202
Free: 800-913-9479
Format: Talk; Sports. **Simulcasts:** KDNZ-AM. **Networks:** CBS; Westwood One Radio. **Owner:** Fife Communications Co. L.C., 721 Shirley St,, Cedar Falls, IA. **Founded:** 1995. **Formerly:** KCFI-AM. **Operating Hours:** Continuous. **ADI:** Cedar Rapids-Waterloo-Dubuque, IA. **Key Personnel:** Jim Coloff, Contact; Jim Coloff, Contact; Scott Fenzloff, Contact. **Local Programs:** *Diamond Gems*, Saturday 6:00 p.m. - 7:00 p.m.; *The Dan Patrick Show*, Monday Tuesday Wednesday Thursday Friday 8:00 a.m. - 11:00 a.m.; *The Jim Rome Show*, Monday Tuesday Wednesday Thursday Friday 11:00 a.m. - 2:00 p.m.; *First Light with Evan Haning*, Monday Tuesday Wednesday Thursday Friday 5:00 a.m. - 6:00 a.m.; *The Final Lap with Kerry Murphy*, Monday Tuesday Wednesday Thursday Friday 7:40 a.m.; *The Money Pit Home Improvement Radio Show*, Saturday 7:00 a.m. - 9:00 a.m.; *J.T. The Brick with Tomm Looney*, Monday Tuesday Wednesday Thursday Friday 5:00 p.m. - 9:00 p.m.; *The Drive with Chris Meyers*, Monday Tuesday Wednesday Thursday Friday 2:00 p.m. - 6:00 p.m.; *The Money Pit Home Improvement Show*, Saturday 7:00 a.m. - 9:00 a.m.; *The Fan Morning Show with Doug Peterson*, Monday Tuesday Wednesday Thursday Friday 6:00 a.m. - 8:00 a.m. **Wattage:** 10,000. **Ad Rates:** Advertising accepted; rates available upon request. Combined advertising rates available with KCVM-FM, KDNZ-AM. **Mailing address:** PO Box 248, Cedar Falls, IA 50613. **URL:** http://www.kcnzam.com.

12470 ■ KCVM-FM - 96.1
721 Shirley St.
Cedar Falls, IA 50613
Phone: (319)277-1918
Fax: (319)277-5202
Free: 800-913-9479
Email: themix@mix96.net
Format: Adult Contemporary. **Key Personnel:** Bob Foster, News Dir.; Jim Coloff, Gen. Mgr., Owner; Janelle Rench, Office Mgr.; Mary Williams, Station Mgr. **Ad Rates:** Advertising accepted; rates available upon request. **URL:** http://935themix.com.

KRNI-AM - See Mason City

12471 ■ KSMA-FM
3407 Apollo St.
Cedar Falls, IA 50613
Format: Top 40. **Founded:** Sept. 07, 2006. **Wattage:** 25,000 ERP.

12472 ■ KUNI-AM - 1010
322 Communication Arts Ctr.
University of Northern Iowa
Cedar Falls, IA 50614-0359
Free: 800-861-8000
Email: kuni@uni.edu
Format: Adult Contemporary; Classic Rock; Talk; Blues; Reggae. **Operating Hours:** Continuous. **Ad Rates:** Advertising accepted; rates available upon request. **URL:** http://iowapublicradio.org.

12473 ■ KUNI-FM
324 Communication Arts
University of Northern Iowa
Cedar Falls, IA 50614-0359
Phone: (319)273-6400
Fax: (319)273-2682
Free: 800-772-2440
Email: kuni@uni.edu
Format: Adult Contemporary; Classic Rock; Talk; Blues; Reggae. **Wattage:** 94,000 ERP. **Ad Rates:** Underwriting available.

CEDAR RAPIDS

E IA. Linn Co. On Cedar River, 110 mi. NE of Des Moines. Coe College, Mt. Mercy College, Kirkwood College. Manufactures cereal, meat products, electronic equipment, mining machinery, syrup, sugar, automotive tools and machinery, oil burners, furniture, pumps, gravel crushers, cranes, snow plows, trailer parts, candy, office and drainage equipment, rubber goods, plastic bags, medical and chemical products, plumbing supplies, furnaces, livestock feed, structural steel, compressed gas. Meat packing; foundries; rendering plant; building supplies.

12474 ■ Biophilately
American Topical Association Biology Unit
c/o Christopher Dahle
1401 Linmar Dr. NE
Cedar Rapids, IA 52402
Phone: (319)364-4999
Publisher's E-mail: chris-dahle@biophilately.org
Journal covering philately. **Freq:** Quarterly. **Key Personnel:** Christopher Dahle, Associate Editor. **Subscription Rates:** $20 Individuals; $25 Other countries. **URL:** http://www.biophilately.org; http://www.biophilately.org/archive.html. **Circ:** (Not Reported).

12475 ■ Buildings: For Facilities Decision-Makers
Stamats Communications Inc.
615 Fifth St. SE
Cedar Rapids, IA 52406-1888
Phone: (319)364-6167
Fax: (319)365-5421
Free: 800-553-8878
Publisher's E-mail: info@stamats.com
The facilities construction and management magazine covering news, concepts and technologies related to commercial building ownership and facilities management. **Freq:** Monthly. **Print Method:** Offset. **Trim Size:** 7 7/8 x 10 7/8. **Cols./Page:** 3. **Col. Width:** 26 nonpareils. **Col. Depth:** 140 agate lines. **Key Personnel:** Chris Olson; Tony Dellamaria, Publisher, Vice President; Janelle Penny, Associate Editor. **ISSN:** 0007--3725 (print). **Subscription Rates:** $125 Other countries

Circulation: ★ = AAM; △ or • = BPA; ♦ = CAC; ❑ = VAC; ⊕ = PO Statement; ‡ = Publisher's Report; Boldface figures = sworn; Light figures = estimated.

surface mail; $150 Other countries air mail; Members free. **URL:** http://www.buildings.com. **Mailing address:** PO Box 1888, Cedar Rapids, IA 52406-1888. **Remarks:** Advertising accepted; rates available upon request. **Circ:** Non-paid ★**57009**.

12476 ■ Coe Review
Coe College
1220 1st Ave. NE
Cedar Rapids, IA 52402
Phone: (319)399-8500
Free: 877-CAL-LCOE
Literary magazine covering poetry and fiction. **Freq:** Monthly. **URL:** http://coereview.org. **Remarks:** Advertising not accepted. **Circ:** Controlled 1500.

12477 ■ Fraternal Herald
Western Fraternal Life Association
1900 1st Ave. NE
Cedar Rapids, IA 52402-5321
Phone: (319)363-2653
Fax: (319)363-8806
Free: 877-935-2467
Publisher's E-mail: wflains@wflains.org
Fraternal insurance benefit society magazine. **Freq:** Monthly. **Print Method:** Offset. **Trim Size:** 8 1/2 x 11. **Cols./Page:** 2 and 3. **Col. Width:** 21 3/5 and 14 picas. **Col. Depth:** 680 nonpareils. **ISSN:** 0006--9256 (print). **Subscription Rates:** Included in membership. **Alt. Formats:** PDF. **URL:** http://www.wflains.org/member-benefits/fraternal-herald. **Also known as:** Bratrsky Vestnik. **Remarks:** Advertising not accepted. **Circ:** Non-paid ‡24400.

12478 ■ Fraternal Herald: Bratrske Vestnik
Western Fraternal Life Association
1900 1st Ave. NE
Cedar Rapids, IA 52402-5321
Phone: (319)363-2653
Fax: (319)363-8806
Free: 877-935-2467
Publication E-mail: wflains@wflains.org
Freq: Monthly. **ISSN:** 0006- 9256 (print). **Subscription Rates:** Included in membership; $10 Nonmembers /year. **Alt. Formats:** Download; PDF. **URL:** http://www.wflains.org/member-benefits/fraternal-herald; http://www.wflains.org/member-benefits/fraternal-herald/archived-fraternal-heralds. **Remarks:** Advertising not accepted. **Circ:** (Not Reported).

12479 ■ Interiors & Sources: Excellence in Commercial Design
Stamats Business Media
615 5th St. SE
Cedar Rapids, IA 52406-1888
Fax: (319)364-4278
Free: 800-553-8878
Publisher's E-mail: info@stamatsbusinessmedia.com
Magazine focusing on the latest in commercial interior design. **Key Personnel:** Robert Nieminen, Editor, phone: (319)861-5190; Adam Moore, Managing Editor, phone: (319)861-5189; Mike Stanley, Publisher, phone: (800)553-8878. **URL:** http://www.interiorsandsources.com. **Mailing address:** PO Box 1888, Cedar Rapids, IA 52406-1888. **Remarks:** Advertising accepted; rates available upon request. **Circ:** (Not Reported).

12480 ■ Iowa Farmer Today
Iowa Farmer Today
1065 Sierra Ct. NE, Ste. B
Cedar Rapids, IA 52402-6585
Free: 800-475-6655
Publisher's E-mail: news@iowafarmertoday.com
Agricultural newspaper containing production and agribusiness information, serving farmers in the state of Iowa. **Freq:** Weekly. **Key Personnel:** Steve DeWitt, Publisher; Kevin Blind, Managing Editor; Terry Reilly, Associate Publisher. **USPS:** 002-141. **URL:** http://www.iowafarmertoday.com. **Ad Rates:** PCI $79.65. **Remarks:** Advertising accepted; rates available upon request. **Circ:** 66310.

12481 ■ Penny Saver
500 3rd Ave., SE
Cedar Rapids, IA 52401
Shopping guide. **Founded:** 1967. **Freq:** Weekly (Wed.). **Print Method:** Offset. **Trim Size:** 10 3/4 x 12 1/2. **Cols./Page:** 7. **Col. Width:** 1 1/4 inches. **Col. Depth:** 11.5 inches. **Key Personnel:** Ron Bode, Manager, Advertising. **URL:** http://pennysaverguide.com/; http://thegazette.com/section/pennysaver. **Ad Rates:** BW $2,233.88; 4C $2,563.88; PCI $27.75. **Remarks:** Accepts advertising. **Circ:** 89000.

12482 ■ Rural Heritage
Rural Heritage
PO Box 2067
Cedar Rapids, IA 52406-2067
Phone: (319)362-3027
Fax: (319)362-3046
Publisher's E-mail: info@ruralheritage.com
Journal on farming and logging with draft animals (horses, mules and oxen). **Freq:** Bimonthly. **Print Method:** Offset. **Trim Size:** 8 1/2 x 11. **Cols./Page:** 2. **Col. Width:** 2 5/16 inches. **Col. Depth:** 9 inches. **ISSN:** 0889--2970 (print). **Subscription Rates:** $34.95 U.S.; $66 Two years; $96 Individuals 3 years. **URL:** http://www.ruralheritage.com. **Formerly:** The Evener. **Ad Rates:** BW $300; 4C $460. **Remarks:** Accepts advertising. **Circ:** ‡6000.

12483 ■ Russell's Official National Motor Coach Guide: The Official Bus Guide
Russells Guides Inc.
1660 42 St. NE, Ste. R
Cedar Rapids, IA 52402
Phone: (319)364-6138
Magazine containing national bus schedules. **Freq:** Monthly. **Print Method:** Offset. **Trim Size:** 8 1/2 x 9 1/2. **Cols./Page:** 2. **Col. Width:** 45 nonpareils. **Col. Depth:** 123 agate lines. **Key Personnel:** Charlotte Bonar, Editor; Karen Flint, Manager, Circulation, Contact. **ISSN:** 0036--0171 (print). **Subscription Rates:** $178 Individuals /year for U.S.; $27 Single issue U.S.; $231 Canada /year; $34 Single issue Canada. **URL:** http://www.russellsprinting.com/National-Motor-Coach-Guide-Subscription-USA-NMCG-SUB-USA.htm. **Mailing address:** PO Box 11276, Cedar Rapids, IA 52402. **Remarks:** Advertising accepted; rates available upon request. **Circ:** ‡14100.

12484 ■ KCCK-FM - 88.3
6301 Kirkwood Blvd. SW
Cedar Rapids, IA 52404
Format: Jazz. **Owner:** Kirkwood Community College, 6301 Kirkwood Blvd. SW, Cedar Rapids, IA 52404, Ph: (319)398-5517, Fax: (319)398-5566, Free: 800-363-2220. **Founded:** 1972. **Operating Hours:** Continuous. **ADI:** Cedar Rapids-Waterloo-Dubuque, IA. **Local Programs:** *Da Blues*, Saturday 6:00 p.m.; *Back Stage Blues*, Friday 10:00 p.m.; *Beale Street Caravan*, Saturday 1:00 p.m.; *Big Band Memories*, Sunday 1:00 p.m. - 5:00 p.m.; *Brazilian Hour*, Tuesday Sunday 2:00 a.m.; *Cafe Jazz*, Sunday Saturday 6:00 p.m. 5:00 a.m.; *The Crawfish Circuit*, Saturday 10:00 p.m.; *KCCK's Culture Crawl*, Thursday Friday 10:20 a.m.; *Da Friday Night Blues*, Friday 6:00 p.m. - 10:00 p.m.; *Earthsongs*, Monday 1:00 a.m.; *Smooth Brunch*, Wednesday 8:30 p.m. - 11:00 p.m.; *Echoes*, Sunday 9:00 p.m.; *Funk at Five*, Monday Tuesday Wednesday Thursday Friday 5:00 p.m.; *Gentle Jazz*, Sunday 9:00 a.m. - 1:00 p.m.; *Jazz Corner of The World*, Monday Saturday 7:00 p.m - 11:00 p.m. 12:00 p.m. - 1:30 p.m.; *Jazz at Lincoln Center*; *Jazz Masters*, Monday Tuesday Wednesday Thursday Friday 10:00 a.m. - 2:00 p.m.; *Jazz Profiles*, Monday 6:00 p.m. - 7:00 p.m.; *Jazz Rhythm*, Thursday Saturday 4:00 a.m. - 4:30 a.m. 3:00 a.m. - 4:00 a.m. **Wattage:** 10,000 ERP. **Ad Rates:** Noncommercial. Underwriting available. **URL:** http://www.kcck.org.

12485 ■ KCRG-TV - 9
501 2nd Ave. SE
Cedar Rapids, IA 52401
Phone: (319)398-8422
Fax: (319)368-8505
Free: 800-332-5443
Email: online@kcrg.com
Format: News. **Networks:** ABC. **Owner:** Cedar Rapids Television Co., 501 2nd Ave. SE, Cedar Rapids, IA 52401, Ph: (319)398-8422, Fax: (319)368-8505, Free: 800-332-5443. **Founded:** 1954. **Operating Hours:** Continuous. **ADI:** Cedar Rapids-Waterloo-Dubuque, IA. **Key Personnel:** Kirk Schroeder, Chief Engineer, kirk.schroeder@kcrg.com. **Ad Rates:** Noncommercial. **URL:** http://www.kcrg.com.

12486 ■ KDAT-FM - 104.5
425 Second St. SE, 4th Fl.
Cedar Rapids, IA 52401
Phone: (319)365-9431
Email: kdat@kdat.com
Format: Soft Rock. **Owner:** Cumulus Media Inc., 3280 Peachtree Rd. NW, Ste. 2300, Atlanta, GA 30305-2455, Ph: (404)949-0700, Fax: (404)949-0740. **Founded:** Sept. 15, 2006. **ADI:** Cedar Rapids-Waterloo-Dubuque, IA. **Wattage:** 100,000. **URL:** http://www.kdat.com.

12487 ■ KGAN Licensee L.L.C. - 2
600 Old Marion Rd. NE
Cedar Rapids, IA 52402
Phone: (319)395-9060
Fax: (319)395-0987
Free: 800-642-6140
Email: news@cbs2iowa.com
Format: News; Sports. **Networks:** CBS. **Founded:** 1953. **Formerly:** WMT-TV. **Operating Hours:** Continuous. **ADI:** Cedar Rapids-Waterloo-Dubuque, IA. **Key Personnel:** Melissa Hubbard, Dir. of Programs. **Wattage:** 100,000. **Ad Rates:** Noncommercial. **URL:** http://www.kgan.com.

12488 ■ KGYM-AM - 1600
1110 26th Ave. S
Cedar Rapids, IA 52404-3430
Phone: (319)363-2061
Fax: (319)363-2948
Email: info@1600espn.com
Format: Sports. **Networks:** ABC; AP; Fox. **Founded:** 1947. **Formerly:** KCRG-AM. **Operating Hours:** Continuous. **Key Personnel:** Scott Unash, Sports Dir., Prog. Dir., scott.unash@1600espn.com. **Wattage:** 5,000 Daytime;5,000. **Ad Rates:** $10-27 for 30 seconds; $12-32 for 60 seconds. **URL:** http://www.1600espn.com/.

12489 ■ KHAK-FM - 98.1
425 Second St. SE, 4th Fl.
Cedar Rapids, IA 52401
Phone: (319)365-9431
Fax: (319)363-8062
Email: khak@khak.com
Format: Country. **Owner:** Cumulus Media Inc., 3280 Peachtree Rd. NW, Ste. 2300, Atlanta, GA 30305-2455, Ph: (404)949-0700, Fax: (404)949-0740. **Founded:** 1961. **Operating Hours:** Continuous; 5% network, 95% local. **ADI:** Cedar Rapids-Waterloo-Dubuque, IA. **Key Personnel:** Terry Peters, Mgr., terry.peters@townsquaremedia.com. **Wattage:** 100,000. **Ad Rates:** Advertising accepted; rates available upon request. **URL:** http://www.khak.com.

12490 ■ KKSY-FM - 95.7
600 Old Marion Rd.
Cedar Rapids, IA 52402
Phone: (319)395-0530
Fax: (319)393-9600
Format: Contemporary Country. **Simulcasts:** KAPZ-AM. **Networks:** ABC; Arkansas Radio. **Owner:** Clear Channel Communication, Inc., 200 E Basse Rd., San Antonio, TX 78209, Ph: (210)822-2828, Fax: (210)822-2828. **Founded:** 1984. **Operating Hours:** 5 a.m.-midnight; 15% network, 85% local. **Key Personnel:** John Laton, Gen. Mgr., johnlaton@clearchannel.com. **Wattage:** 3,000. **Ad Rates:** $5-8 for 30 seconds; $7-12 for 60 seconds. **URL:** http://www.965kisscountry.com//main.html.

12491 ■ KMJM-AM - 1360
600 Old Marion Rd. NE
Cedar Rapids, IA 52402
Phone: (319)395-0530
Free: 800-933-7767
Format: Sports. **Owner:** iHeartMedia Inc., 200 E Basse Rd., San Antonio, TX 78209, Ph: (210)832-3314. **Operating Hours:** Midnight - 6:00 p.m. **ADI:** Cedar Rapids-Waterloo-Dubuque, IA. **Key Personnel:** Jeanne Kerr, Sr. VP of Sales, jeannekerr@iheartmedia.com; Joel McCrea, Div. Pres., joelmccrea@iheartmedia.com; Brian Thomas, Dir. of Production, brianthomas@iheartmedia.com. **Wattage:** 1,000 Day ; 124 Nigh. **Ad Rates:** Advertising accepted; rates available upon request. **URL:** http://www.1360kmjm.iheart.com.

12492 ■ KPXR-TV - 48
1957 Blairs Ferry Rd. NE
Cedar Rapids, IA 52402
Phone: (319)378-1260
Fax: (319)378-0076
Free: 888-467-2988

Key Personnel: Brandon Burgess, Chairman, CEO. **Ad Rates:** Noncommercial. **URL:** http://www.ionmedia.tv.

12493 ■ KQCR-FM - 102.9
1110 26th Ave. SW
Cedar Rapids, IA 52404
Phone: (319)363-2061

Format: Music of Your Life. **Networks:** Independent. **Owner:** Cedar Rapids/KQCR Ltd., 101 First St. S, Cedar Rapids, IA. **Founded:** 1975. **ADI:** Cedar Rapids-Waterloo-Dubuque, IA. **Key Personnel:** Bill Clymer, Gen. Mgr.; Tom Thomas, Dir. of Programs. **Wattage:** 100,000 ERP. **Ad Rates:** $19 for 30 seconds; $46 for 60 seconds. **URL:** http://www.kzia.com.

12494 ■ KRNA-FM - 94.1
425 2nd St. SE, 4th Fl.
Cedar Rapids, IA 52401
Phone: (319)365-9431
Fax: (319)363-8062

Format: Album-Oriented Rock (AOR); Information. **Networks:** Independent. **Owner:** Cumulus Media Inc., 3280 Peachtree Rd. NW, Ste. 2300, Atlanta, GA 30305-2455, Ph: (404)949-0700, Fax: (404)949-0740. **Founded:** 1974. **Operating Hours:** Continuous; 100% local. **ADI:** Cedar Rapids-Waterloo-Dubuque, IA. **Wattage:** 100,000. **Ad Rates:** $36-60 for 30 seconds; $40-70 for 60 seconds. Combined advertising rates available with KXMX-FM.

12495 ■ KRQN-FM - 107.1
425 Second St. SE, 4th Fl.
Cedar Rapids, IA 52401
Phone: (319)365-9431

Format: Classic Rock. **Wattage:** 4,700. **URL:** http://i1071.com.

12496 ■ K17ET - 17
PO Box A
Santa Ana, CA 92711
Phone: (714)832-2950
Free: 888-731-1000

Owner: Trinity Broadcasting Network Inc., PO Box A, Santa Ana, CA 92711, Ph: (714)832-2950, Free: 888-731-1000.

12497 ■ KZIA-FM - 102.9
1110 26th Ave. SW
Cedar Rapids, IA 52404-3430
Phone: (319)363-2061
Fax: (319)363-2948
Email: info@kzia.com

Format: Top 40. **Owner:** KZIA Inc., 1110 26th Ave. SW, Cedar Rapids, IA 52404-3430, Ph: (319)363-2061. **Founded:** Apr. 1994. **ADI:** Cedar Rapids-Waterloo-Dubuque, IA. **Key Personnel:** Rob Norton, Station Mgr., rob@kzia.com; Kellie Lala, Gen. Sales Mgr., kellie@kzia.com; Greg Runyon, Dir. of Programs, greg@kzia.com; Julie Hein, Dir. of Sales, julie@kzia.com. **Wattage:** 100,000. **Ad Rates:** Noncommercial. **URL:** http://kzia.com.

12498 ■ KZIA Inc.
1110 26th Ave. SW
Cedar Rapids, IA 52404-3430
Phone: (319)363-2061
Email: info@kzia.com
URL: http://www.kzia.com.

12499 ■ Mediacom Communications Corp.
300 Council St. NE, Ste. 1
Cedar Rapids, IA 52402
Phone: (319)395-9674

Founded: 1979. **Formerly:** TCI of Iowa. **Cities Served:** subscribing households 48,000. **URL:** http://www.mediacomcable.com.

12500 ■ WIXN-AM - 1460
2875 Mt. Vernon Rd. SE
Cedar Rapids, IA 52403
Phone: (319)862-0300

Format: News; Sports. **Founded:** 1961. **Key Personnel:** Al Knickrehm, Gen. Mgr.; Mark Baker, Chief Engineer; Sam Ramirez, Sports Dir.; Steve Marco, Dir. of Programs. **Ad Rates:** Advertising accepted; rates available upon request. **URL:** http://www.am1460wixn.com.

12501 ■ WMT-AM - 600
600 Old Marion Rd.
Cedar Rapids, IA 52402

Format: News; Talk. **Networks:** Fox. **Owner:** Clear Channel Communications Inc., at above address, Ph: (210)822-2828, Fax: (210)822-2299. **Founded:** 1922. **Operating Hours:** Continuous. **ADI:** Cedar Rapids-Waterloo-Dubuque, IA. **Key Personnel:** John Laton, Gen. Mgr., johnlaton@clearchannel.com; Ursula Fellows, Bus. Mgr., ursulafellows@clearchannel.com; Brian Thomas, Dir. of Production, brianthomas@clearchannel.com; Jeanne Kerr, President, jeannekerr@iheartmedia.com; Joel Mccrea, Div. Pres., joelmccrea@iheartmedia.com; Randy Lee, Sr. VP, randylee@iheartmedia.com. **Wattage:** 5,000. **Ad Rates:** Advertising accepted; rates available upon request. WMT-FM, KKRQ-FM, KMJM-AM, KXIC-AM, 211 Clear Channel Station. **URL:** http://600.wmtradio.com.

12502 ■ WMT-FM - 96.5
600 Old Marion Rd.
Cedar Rapids, IA 52402
Phone: (319)395-0530
Free: 800-332-5401

Format: News; Adult Contemporary. **Owner:** iHeartMedia Inc., 200 E Basse Rd., San Antonio, TX 78209, Ph: (210)832-3314. **Founded:** 1963. **Operating Hours:** Continuous; 5% network, 95% local. **Key Personnel:** Jeanne Kerr, President, JeanneKerr@iHeartMedia.com. **Wattage:** 100,000 ERP. **Ad Rates:** Noncommercial. Combined advertising rates available with WMT-AM, KKRQ, KMJM, KXIC. **URL:** http://www.965kisscountry.com//main.html.

CENTER POINT

12503 ■ KXGM-AM - 850
PO Box 911
Center Point, IA 52213

Format: Contemporary Christian. **Simulcasts:** KWOF-FM. **Formerly:** KLEU-AM; KWOF-AM. **Operating Hours:** Sunrise-sunset. **Wattage:** 500. **Ad Rates:** $10 per unit. **URL:** http://www.extremegracemedia.org.

CENTERVILLE

S IA. Appanoose Co. 45 mi. SW of Ottumwa. Rathbun Fish Hatchery. Manufactures plastic bags, aluminum castings, heavy duty radiators, metal fabrication, heat transfer products, canvas and nylon products, ready mix concrete, Coal mines; rock quarry; timber. Agriculture. Corn, soybeans, alfalfa. Livestock.

12504 ■ Ad-Express
Ad Express
201 N 13th St.
Centerville, IA 52544
Phone: (641)856-6336
Fax: (641)856-8118
Publisher's E-mail: iowegianpeople@mchsi.com

Shopper. **Founded:** 1864. **Freq:** Weekly (Wed.). **Print Method:** Offset. **Cols./Page:** 8. **Col. Width:** 21 nonpareils. **Col. Depth:** 294 agate lines. **Key Personnel:** Jason McGrann, Managing Editor; Becky Maxwell, Publisher; Patsy Cincotta, Editor. **URL:** http://dailyiowegian.com. **Ad Rates:** BW $735.30; SAU $5.70. **Remarks:** Accepts advertising. **Circ:** Wed. 14000.

12505 ■ Daily Iowegian
Community Newspaper Holdings Inc.
201 N 13th St.
Centerville, IA 52544
Phone: (641)856-6336
Publication E-mail: iowegianeditor@mchsi.com

Newspaper serving Appanoose, Wayne and Putnam counties including the city of Centerville and surrounding communities of Iowa. **Founded:** 1864. **Freq:** Daily Monday, Tuesday, Thursday and Friday. **Key Personnel:** Becky Maxwell, Publisher. **Subscription Rates:** $75 Individuals mail delivery; $85 Out of area. **URL:** http://www.dailyiowegian.com. **Remarks:** Accepts advertising. **Circ:** Combined 3100.

12506 ■ KCOG-AM - 1400
402 N 12th St.
Centerville, IA 52544
Free: 800-373-4930

Format: Adult Contemporary. **Networks:** USA Radio; Brownfield. **Owner:** KCOG Inc., 402 N 12th St., Centerville, IA 52544-1718. **Founded:** 1949. **Operating Hours:** Continuous. **Key Personnel:** Carolyn Jenkins, Sales Mgr., carolyn@kmgo.com. **Wattage:** 500 Day; 1,000 Night. **URL:** http://www.kmgo.com.

12507 ■ KELR-FM - 105.3
402 N 12th St.
Centerville, IA 52544
Phone: (641)437-4242
Free: 800-373-4930
Email: kelr@lisco.com

Owner: FMC Broadcasting, Inc., at above address, Ottumwa, IA. **Founded:** 1985. **Formerly:** KYRS-FM. **Operating Hours:** Continuous; 3% network, 97% local. **Key Personnel:** Nick Hoffman, Gen. Mgr. **Wattage:** 34,000 ERP. **Ad Rates:** $3-4 for 15 seconds; $6-8 for 30 seconds; $10-12 for 60 seconds. **URL:** http://kedbradio.com.

12508 ■ KMGO-FM - 98.7
402 N 12th St.
Centerville, IA 52544
Phone: (641)437-4242

Format: Country. **Networks:** USA Radio. **Founded:** 1974. **Operating Hours:** Continuous. **Key Personnel:** Carolyn Jenkins, Sales Mgr., carolyn@kmgo.com. **Wattage:** 100,000. **Ad Rates:** Noncommercial. **URL:** http://www.kmgo.com.

CHARITON

S IA. Lucas Co. 52 mi. SE of Des Moines. Clothing, cable layers, steel fabricating manufactured. Agriculture. Corn, hogs, cattle.

12509 ■ The Chariton Leader
Chariton Newspapers
815 Braden Ave.
Chariton, IA 50049
Phone: (641)774-2137
Publication E-mail: charnews@charitonleader.com

Community newspaper. **Freq:** Weekly (Tues.). **Print Method:** Offset. **Cols./Page:** 6. **Col. Width:** 2 1/16 inches. **Col. Depth:** 21 1/2 inches. **Key Personnel:** Bill Howes, Associate Editor; Susan Smith, Manager, Advertising. **USPS:** 100-420. **URL:** http://www.charitonleader.com. **Mailing address:** PO Box 651, Chariton, IA 50049. **Ad Rates:** PCI $6.50. **Remarks:** Accepts advertising. **Circ:** ‡3000.

12510 ■ Herald-Patriot
Chariton Newspapers
815 Braden Ave.
Chariton, IA 50049
Phone: (641)774-2137
Publication E-mail: charnews@charitonleader.com

Community newspaper. **Freq:** Weekly (Thurs.). **Print Method:** Offset. **Cols./Page:** 6. **Col. Width:** 2 1/16 inches. **Col. Depth:** 21 1/2 inches. **Key Personnel:** Susan Smith, Advertising Representative; Christy Metzger, Compositor. **USPS:** 100-440. **URL:** http://www.charitonleader.com. **Mailing address:** PO Box 651, Chariton, IA 50049. **Ad Rates:** PCI $6.50. **Remarks:** Accepts advertising. **Circ:** ‡3650.

CHARLES CITY

N IA. Floyd Co. On Cedar River, 30 mi. E. of Mason City. Manufactures fertilizer feed, farm equipment, poultry remedies. Machine shops. Poultry processing. Stock, dairy, poultry farms.

12511 ■ Charles City Press
Charles City Press
801 Riverside Dr.
Charles City, IA 50616
Phone: (641)228-3211
Fax: (641)228-2641
Publication E-mail: editor@charlescitypress.com

General newspaper. **Founded:** 1896. **Freq:** Daily Monday through Friday. **Print Method:** Offset. **Trim Size:** 14 x 21 5/8. **Cols./Page:** 6. **Col. Width:** 12 picas. **Col. Depth:** 21.5 inches. **Key Personnel:** Chris Baldus, Managing Editor; Joel Gray, General Manager, Manager, Advertising; Gene A. Hall, Publisher; Chris Rimrod, Advertising Representative. **USPS:** 100-480. **Subscription Rates:** $125 Individuals in Floyd County; $131 Out of area; $158 Out of state. **URL:** http://www.charlescitypress.com. **Remarks:** Accepts advertising. **Circ:** (Not Reported).

12512 ■ KCHA-AM - 1580
207 N Main St.
Charles City, IA 50616

Circulation: • = AAM; △ or • = BPA; ♦ = CAC; ❑ = VAC; ⊕ = PO Statement; ‡ = Publisher's Report; Boldface figures = sworn; Light figures = estimated.

Phone: (641)228-1000
Fax: (641)228-1200
Format: Adult Contemporary; News; Oldies; Country. **Founded:** 1948. **Operating Hours:** Continuous. **Key Personnel:** Jim Coloff, Gen. Mgr., Owner, jimcoloff@northiowabroadcasting.com. **Wattage:** 500 Day; 010 Night. **Ad Rates:** Advertising accepted; rates available upon request. **URL:** http://www.kchanews.com.

12513 ■ KCHA-FM - 95.9
207 N Main St.
Charles City, IA 50616
Phone: (641)228-1000
Fax: (641)228-1200
Email: kcha@kchanews.com
Format: Adult Contemporary. **Founded:** 1971. **Operating Hours:** Continuous. **ADI:** Rochester, NY. **Wattage:** 3,000. **Ad Rates:** $15 for 30 seconds; $19 for 60 seconds. **URL:** http://www.kchanews.com.

12514 ■ KCZE-FM - 95.1
207 N Main St.
Charles City, IA 50616
Phone: (641)228-1000
Fax: (641)228-1200
Format: Adult Contemporary. **Networks:** NBC. **Owner:** Mega Media Ltd., at above address. **Founded:** 1993. **Operating Hours:** 18 hours Daily. **Wattage:** 5,500. **URL:** http://951thebull.com/.

CHEROKEE

NW IA. Cherokee Co. 50 mi. NE of Sioux City. Manufactures farm equipment, picnic tables, truck bodies, concrete blocks, feeds. Food chain warehouse. Meat packing and processing. Diversified farming.

12515 ■ KCHE-AM - 1440
201 S Fifth St.
Cherokee, IA 51012
Phone: (712)225-2511
Format: Full Service; Information. **Owner:** Jeff Fuller, at above address. **Key Personnel:** Billy Bezoni, Prog. Dir.; Jeff Fuller, Gen. Mgr. **Wattage:** 390 Day time; 029 Nig. **Ad Rates:** Advertising accepted; rates available upon request. **Mailing address:** PO Box 141, Cherokee, IA 51012. **URL:** http://kcheradio.com.

12516 ■ KCHE-FM - 92.1
201 S Fifth St.
Cherokee, IA 51012
Phone: (712)225-2511
Fax: (712)225-2513
Format: Classic Rock; Full Service; Information. **Networks:** ABC. **Owner:** J and J Radio Corp., Not Available. **Operating Hours:** 7:00 a.m. - 5:32 p.m. Monday - Friday. **Key Personnel:** Jeff Fuller, Gen. Mgr.; Billy Bezoni, Dir. of Programs; Curt Carlson, Sales Mgr. **Wattage:** 6,000 ERP. **URL:** http://kcheradio.com.

12517 ■ K208DS-FM - 89.5
PO Box 391
Twin Falls, ID 83303
Fax: (208)736-1958
Free: 800-357-4226
Format: Religious; Contemporary Christian. **Owner:** CSN International, PO Box 391, Twin Falls, ID 83303, Ph: (208)736-1958, Fax: (208)736-1958, Free: 800-357-4226. **Key Personnel:** Kelly Carlson, Dir. of Engg.; Ray Gorney, Asst. Dir.; Don Mills, Music Dir., Prog. Dir. **URL:** http://www.csnradio.com.

CLARENCE

12518 ■ Clarence Telephone Company Inc.
608 Lombard St.
Clarence, IA 52216-7704
Phone: (563)452-3852
Fax: (563)452-3883
Free: 800-695-3896
Email: clarence@netins.net
Founded: 1951. **Cities Served:** United States. **URL:** http://www.clarencetelinc.com.

CLARINDA

SW IA. Page Co. 70 mi. SE of Council Bluffs. Manufactures neon signs, concrete, ball bearings, meat products, automotive tools. Sawmill. Seed houses. Agriculture.

12519 ■ Clarinda Herald-Journal
Southwest Iowa Newsgroup
114 W Main St., Ste. B
Clarinda, IA 51632
Phone: (712)542-2181
Fax: (712)542-5424
Publication E-mail: news@clarindaherald.com
Newspaper. **Freq:** Weekly (Wed.). **Print Method:** Offset. **Trim Size:** 8 1/2 x 11. **Cols./Page:** 6. **Col. Width:** 11 picas. **Col. Depth:** 21.5 inches. **Key Personnel:** John VanNostrand, Publisher. **URL:** http://www.clarindaherald.com. **Mailing address:** PO Box 278, Clarinda, IA 51632. **Ad Rates:** GLR $.27; BW $638.12; SAU $5.64; PCI $4.50. **Remarks:** Accepts advertising. **Circ:** Paid ‡3900, Free ‡250.

CLARION

NC IA. Wright Co. 30 mi. NE of Fort Dodge. Machine shops; hybrid seed corn plants; hatcheries. Ships cattle. Stock, grain, poultry farms. Corn, cattle, oats.

12520 ■ Wright County Monitor
Wright County Monitor
107 2nd Ave. NE
Clarion, IA 50525
Phone: (515)532-2871
Fax: (515)532-2872
Publication E-mail: cmonitor@mchsi.com
Newspaper. **Freq:** Weekly (Thurs.). **Print Method:** Offset. **Cols./Page:** 8. **Col. Width:** 22 nonpareils. **Col. Depth:** 301 agate lines. **Key Personnel:** Jennifer Roberts, Office Manager; Barbara Mussman, Editor. **Subscription Rates:** $42 Individuals /year (print and online); $83 Two years /year (print and online). **URL:** http://www.clarionnewsonline.com. **Mailing address:** PO Box 153, Clarion, IA 50525. **Ad Rates:** GLR $.29; SAU $4.26; PCI $2.75. **Remarks:** Advertising accepted; rates available upon request. **Circ:** ⊕**2000.**

CLARKSVILLE

NC IA. Butler Co. 35 mi. NW of Waterloo. Light industry. Agriculture. Corn, oats, soybeans.

12521 ■ Butler County Tribune Journal
Clarksville Star
101 N Main St.
Clarksville, IA 50619
Phone: (319)278-4641
Publisher's E-mail: clarksvillestar@butler-bremer.com
Newspaper. **Freq:** Weekly (Thurs.). **Print Method:** Offset. **Cols./Page:** 5. **Col. Width:** 24 nonpareils. **Col. Depth:** 238 agate lines. **Key Personnel:** Mira Schmitt-Cash, Editor. **Subscription Rates:** $37 Individuals print and online. **Mailing address:** PO Box 788, Clarksville, IA 50619. **Ad Rates:** GLR $.29. **Remarks:** Accepts advertising. **Circ:** ‡1545.

12522 ■ Clarksville Star
Clarksville Star
101 N Main St.
Clarksville, IA 50619
Phone: (319)278-4641
Publisher's E-mail: clarksvillestar@butler-bremer.com
Newspaper with a Republican orientation. **Freq:** Weekly (Thurs.). **Print Method:** Letterpress and offset. **Cols./Page:** 5. **Col. Width:** 24 nonpareils. **Col. Depth:** 238 agate lines. **Key Personnel:** Paula Barnett, Contact. **Subscription Rates:** $37 Individuals /year (print and online); $73 Two years /year (print and online). **URL:** http://www.butlercountytribune.com. **Mailing address:** PO Box 788, Clarksville, IA 50619. **Remarks:** Accepts advertising. **Circ:** ‡3108.

CLEAR LAKE

NC IA. Cerro Gordo Co. 10 mi. W. of Mason City. Tourism. Residential.

12523 ■ Clear Lake Mirror Reporter
Clear Lake Mirror
12 N 4th St.
Clear Lake, IA 50428
Phone: (641)357-2131
Fax: (641)357-2133
Community newspaper. **Freq:** Weekly (Wed.). **Key Personnel:** Michael J. Finnegan, Owner, Publisher; Marianne Morf, Editor. **Subscription Rates:** $59 Individuals /year (e-edition). **Alt. Formats:** Electronic publishing. **Ad Rates:** BW $1024; PCI $4.06. **Remarks:** Accepts advertising. **Circ:** (Not Reported).

12524 ■ Northland Communications Inc.
Clear Lake Telephone Company
107 N 4th St.
Clear Lake, IA 50428
Phone: (641)357-2111
Fax: (641)357-8800
Cities Served: 24 channels. **Mailing address:** PO Box 66, Clear Lake, IA 50428. **URL:** http://cltel.com.

CLINTON

E IA. Clinton Co. On the Mississippi River, 30 mi. NE of Davenport. Bridges to Fulton and East Clinton, IL. Trade/industrial center. Manufactures corn syrup, sugars, salad oils, house dresses, culvert pipes, dog and cat food, paper cartons, ironworks.

12525 ■ Clinton Herald
Community Newspaper Holdings Inc.
221 6th Ave.
Clinton, IA 52732
Phone: (563)242-7101
Free: 800-729-7101
General newspaper. **Founded:** 1856. **Freq:** Daily. **Print Method:** Offset. **Trim Size:** 13 3/4 x 22 3/4. **Cols./Page:** 6. **Col. Width:** 24 nonpareils. **Col. Depth:** 301 agate lines. **Key Personnel:** Charlene Bielema, Editor; Don Richlen, Publisher; Wayne Larkey, Director, Advertising. **USPS:** 111-680. **Subscription Rates:** $11.99 Individuals /month; $10.99 Individuals digital access /month. **URL:** http://www.clintonherald.com/. **Ad Rates:** GLR $.90; BW $1625; 4C $1840; SAU $12.60. **Remarks:** Accepts advertising. **Circ:** Mon.-Sat. ★**10,623.**

12526 ■ KCLN-AM - 1390
1853 442nd Ave.
Clinton, IA 52732
Phone: (563)243-1390
Format: Music of Your Life. **Networks:** ABC. **Owner:** WPW Broadcasting Inc., at above address. **Founded:** 1956. **Formerly:** KLNT-AM. **Operating Hours:** Continuous. **Key Personnel:** Chris Streets, Gen. Mgr., cstreets@kcln.com. **Wattage:** 100,000. **Ad Rates:** $9-15 for 30 seconds; $14-23 for 60 seconds. $7-$15 for 30 seconds; $11-$19 for 60 seconds. Combined advertising rates available with KZEG-FM.

12527 ■ KMCN-FM - 94.7
1853 442nd Ave.
Clinton, IA 52732
Phone: (563)243-1390
Fax: (563)242-4567
Format: Country. **Networks:** ABC. **Owner:** Prairie Communications Inc., at above address. **Formerly:** KLNT-FM; KZEG-FM. **Operating Hours:** Continuous. **Key Personnel:** Chris Streets, Gen. Mgr., chris.streets@prairiecommunications.net. **Wattage:** 3,000. **Ad Rates:** Noncommercial. $7-$15 for 30 seconds; $11-$19 for 60 seconds. Combined advertising rates available with KCLN-AM. **URL:** http://mac947.wix.com/mac947fm.

12528 ■ KROS-AM - 1340
870 13th Ave. N
Clinton, IA 52732-5116
Phone: (563)242-1252
Fax: (563)242-4825
Format: News. **Networks:** NBC. **Owner:** KROS Broadcasting Inc., 870 13th Ave. N, Clinton, IA 52733-0518, Ph: (563)242-1252, Fax: (563)242-4825. **Founded:** 1941. **Operating Hours:** Continuous. **Key Personnel:** Dave Vickers, Gen. Mgr., dave@krosradio.com; Paul Clark, Prog. Dir., paul@krosradio.com. **Local Programs:** *KWQC Local Weather*; *Weather Summary*; *Something You Should Know*, Monday Tuesday Wednesday Thursday Friday 6:50 a.m.; *Wheel-N-Deal Show*, Monday Tuesday Wednesday Thursday Friday Saturday 9:30 a.m. - 10:00 a.m.; *River City Sports Review with Gary Determan*, Wednesday 7:00 p.m.; *News with Dave Vickers and Radio Iowa.* **Wattage:** 1,000. **Ad Rates:** Advertising accepted; rates available upon request. **URL:** http://krosradio.com.

12529 ■ KROS Broadcasting Inc.
870 13th Ave. N
Clinton, IA 52733-0518
Phone: (563)242-1252
Fax: (563)242-4825
Email: contactus@krosradio.com
Format: Sports; News; Information. **Networks:** CBS. **Key Personnel:** Dave Vickers, Gen. Mgr., Exec. Dir.,

dave@krosradio.com; Paul Clark, Prog. Dir., paul@krosradio.com; Gary Determan, Sports Dir., Dir. of Sales. **Ad Rates:** Advertising accepted; rates available upon request. **Mailing address:** PO Box 0518, Clinton, IA 52733-0518. **URL:** http://www.krosradio.com.

12530 ■ KXJX-FM - 92.5
1496 Bellevue St., Ste. 202
Green Bay, WI 54311
Free: 877-291-0123
Email: info@relevantradio.com
Format: Religious. **Owner:** Relevant Radio, 1496 Bellevue St., Ste. 202, Green Bay, WI 54311, Free: 888-577-5443. **Founded:** 2000. **Key Personnel:** Bob Benes, Chief Sales Ofc. **Ad Rates:** Advertising accepted; rates available upon request. **URL:** http://www.relevantradio.com.

CLIVE

12531 ■ Iowa Pork Producer: The official publication of the Iowa Pork Producers Association
Iowa Pork Producers Association
1636 NW 114th St.
Clive, IA 50325
Phone: (515)225-7675
Fax: (515)225-0563
Free: 800-372-7675
Publisher's E-mail: info@iowapork.org
Livestock magazine/Association newsmagazine (monthly). **Freq:** Monthly. **Print Method:** Offset (Web). **Trim Size:** 8 x 10 3/4. **Cols./Page:** 3. **Col. Width:** 13 picas. **Col. Depth:** 9 3/4 inches. **Key Personnel:** John Weber, President. **Alt. Formats:** PDF. **URL:** http://www.iowapork.org/News/870/magazine.aspx. **Mailing address:** PO Box 71009, Clive, IA 50325. **Ad Rates:** BW $1,400; 4C $2,150. **Remarks:** Accepts advertising. **Circ:** (Not Reported).

COLFAX

12532 ■ Jasper County Tribune
Jasper County Tribune
1 W Howard St.
Colfax, IA 50054
Community newspaper. **Freq:** Weekly (Thurs.). **Cols./Page:** 6. **Col. Width:** 12 picas. **Col. Depth:** 21 inches. **Subscription Rates:** $24 Individuals in Iowa; $27 Out of area. **URL:** http://www.jaspercountytribune.com. **Formerly:** Colfax Tribune. **Ad Rates:** SAU $3.25. **Remarks:** Accepts advertising. **Circ:** 2000.

COLO

12533 ■ Colo Telephone Co.
303 Main St.
Colo, IA 50056
Phone: (641)377-2202
Fax: (641)377-2209
Email: colo@netins.net
Founded: 1906. **Cities Served:** United States; 40 channels. **Mailing address:** PO Box 315, Colo, IA 50056. **URL:** http://www.colotel.org.

COON RAPIDS

WC IA. Carroll Co. 5 mi. S. of Dedham.

12534 ■ Coon Rapids Enterprise
Coon Rapids Enterprise
PO Box 226
Coon Rapids, IA 50058
Phone: (712)999-6397
Fax: (712)999-2821
Publisher's E-mail: crdg@crmu.net
Community newspaper. **Freq:** Weekly (Thurs.). **Cols./Page:** 5. **Col. Width:** 11 1/2 picas. **Col. Depth:** 15 inches. **Key Personnel:** Charles Nixon, Editor. **Subscription Rates:** $30 Individuals print only - resident of Carroll, Greene, Guthrie or Audubon Counties; $40 Elsewhere print only; $25 Individuals /yr. - online. **URL:** http://www.coonrapidsenterprise.com. **Circ:** 1,500.

12535 ■ Coon Rapids Municipal Cable
123 3rd Ave.
Coon Rapids, IA 50058
Phone: (712)999-2225
Fax: (712)999-5148
Founded: 1982. **Key Personnel:** Bradley A. Honold, Gen. Mgr. **Cities Served:** Coon Rapids, Iowa: subscribing households 454; 24 channels; 2 community access channels; 1 hour per week community access programming. **Mailing address:** PO Box 96, Van Horne, IA 52346. **URL:** http://crmu.net/index-4.html.

CORALVILLE

E IA. Johnson Co. 3 mi. NW of Iowa City. Residential.

12536 ■ Mediacom Communications Corp.
1150 Fifth St., Ste. 255
Coralville, IA 52241
Phone: (319)887-2225
Founded: 1980. **Cities Served:** subscribing households 24,000. **URL:** http://mediacomcable.com.

CORRECTIONVILLE

Sioux Valley News - See Anthon

CORYDON

S IA. Wayne Co. 61 mi. SE of Des Moines. Automobile batteries, zipper and plastic bags, soap, road machinery, concrete, bug deflectors manufactured. Hatchery. Dairy, stock, poultry farms.

12537 ■ Times-Republican
Times-Republican
205 W Jackson St.
Corydon, IA 50060-0258
Phone: (641)872-1234
Fax: (641)872-1965
Newspaper. **Founded:** 1870. **Freq:** Weekly (Tues.). **Print Method:** Offset. **Cols./Page:** 6. **Col. Width:** 24 nonpareils. **Col. Depth:** 294 agate lines. **Key Personnel:** Jason W. Selby, Editor; Rhonda Bennett, Publisher; Kathy Schick, Manager, Advertising. **Subscription Rates:** $33 Individuals in county; $40 Out of state; $28 Students. **URL:** http://www.corydontimes.com. **Mailing address:** PO Box 258, Corydon, IA 50060-0258. **Ad Rates:** GLR $4; BW $516; SAU $2; PCI $4. **Remarks:** Accepts advertising. **Circ:** ‡3320.

COUNCIL BLUFFS

SW IA. Pottawattamie Co. On Missouri River, E. of Omaha, NE. Four bridges to Omaha, NE. Iowa School for Deaf. Iowa Western Community College. Manufactures radio crystals and holders, cereals, powdered eggs, canned chickens, bee supplies, freight and passenger elevators, animal foods, remedies and serums, meat packing, foam plastic, oils and greases, steel pipes, plastics, farm machinery, playground equipment and pipe pushers, truck bodies, furniture. Roundhouses. Many grain elevators.

12538 ■ Daily Devotions for the Deaf
Deaf Missions
21199 Greenview Rd.
Council Bluffs, IA 51503-4125
Phone: (712)322-5493
Fax: (712)322-7792
Publisher's E-mail: king@deafmissions.com
Religious publication for the deaf. **Freq:** 3/year. **Print Method:** Offset. **Key Personnel:** Jo Krueger, Editor; Duane King, Founder; Mavis Brink, Business Manager. **ISSN:** 0744--9100 (print). **Subscription Rates:** Free. **URL:** http://www.deafmissions.com. **Remarks:** Advertising not accepted. **Circ:** Non-paid 22000.

12539 ■ The Daily Nonpareil
The Daily Nonpareil
535 West Broadway, No. 300
Council Bluffs, IA 51503
Phone: (712)328-1811
Free: 800-283-1882
General newspaper. **Founded:** 1857. **Freq:** Daily (eve.), Sat. and Sun. (morn.). **Print Method:** Offset. **Cols./Page:** 6. **Col. Width:** 26 nonpareils. **Col. Depth:** 301 agate lines. **Key Personnel:** Shon Barenklau, General Manager; Thomas Schmitt, Publisher, phone: (712)325-5660; Jon Leu, Managing Editor, phone: (712)325-5728. **ISSN:** 1046-1833 (print). **Subscription Rates:** $144 Individuals /year, online; $13.50 Individuals /month. **URL:** http://www.nonpareilonline.com/#openCorner. **Ad Rates:** GLR $1.03; BW $1,860.18; 4C $2,235.18; PCI $14.42. **Remarks:** Accepts advertising. **Circ:** Paid **♦11347**, Paid **♦12368**.

12540 ■ KIWR-FM - 89.7
2700 College Rd.
Council Bluffs, IA 51503
Phone: (712)325-3254
Format: Public Radio; Album-Oriented Rock (AOR). **Owner:** Iowa Western Community College, 2700 College Rd., Council Bluffs, IA 51503, Ph: (712)325-3200, Free: 800-432-5852. **Founded:** 1981. **Operating Hours:** Continuous; 100% local. **ADI:** Omaha, NE. **Key Personnel:** Sophia John, Dir. of Programs, sophiajohn@897theriver.com; Stephanie Doty, Promotions Dir., stephaniedoty@897theriver.com. **Local Programs:** *PS Blues*, Sunday 9:00 a.m. - 12:00 p.m.; *Skratch 'N Sniff*, Friday 10:00 p.m. - 12:00 a.m.; *Subterranean*, Friday 12:00 a.m.; *Grateful Dead Hour*, Sunday 11:00 p.m. - 12:00 a.m.; *New Day Rising*, Sunday 2:00 a.m. - 5:00 a.m.; *The Morning Fiasco*, Monday Tuesday Wednesday Thursday Friday 6:00 a.m. - 10:00 a.m.; *Planet O*, Sunday 6:00 p.m. - 8:00 p.m. **Wattage:** 100,000. **Ad Rates:** Noncommercial; underwriting available. $23-45 per unit. **URL:** http://www.897theriver.com.

12541 ■ KLNG-AM - 1560
120 S 35th St., Ste. 2
Council Bluffs, IA 51501
Phone: (712)323-0100
Email: info@wilkinsradio.com
Format: Religious; Talk. **Owner:** Wilkins Communications Network Inc., 292 S Pine St., Spartanburg, SC 29302, Ph: (864)585-1885, Fax: (864)597-0687, Free: 888-989-2299. **Founded:** 1989. **Operating Hours:** 6 a.m.-9 p.m. **Key Personnel:** Greg Garrett, CFO, Dir. of Operations, Julie@wilkinsradio.com; Bob Wilkins, CEO, bob@wilkinsradio.com; Mitchell Mathis, COO, President, mitchell@wilkinsradio.com; Chuck Yates, Station Mgr., klng@wilkinsradio.com. **Wattage:** 10,000. **Ad Rates:** $15 for 30 seconds; $20 for 60 seconds. **URL:** http://www.wilkinsradio.com.

CRESCO

NE IA. Howard Co. 65 mi. S. of Rochester, MN. Manufactures automobile parts, steel, aluminum horse and livestock trailers, cement blocks, drainage tile, fuel, industrial airfilter. Tool and die shops; creameries; nursery. Dairy, stock, poultry farms.

12542 ■ Times-Plain Dealer
Liberty Group Publishing
214 N Elm St.
Cresco, IA 52136
Weekly newspaper. **Freq:** Weekly (Wed.). **Print Method:** Offset. **Trim Size:** 14 3/4 x 21 1/2. **Cols./Page:** 6. **Col. Width:** 12.5 picas. **Col. Depth:** 294 agate lines. **Key Personnel:** Daniel Evans, Publisher; Ellen Murphy, Office Manager. **USPS:** 617-800. **Subscription Rates:** $34.95 Individuals in Howard county and adjoining counties; $43 Elsewhere in Iowa, Minnesota or Wisconsin; $56 Out of state; $43.95 Individuals snowbird in Howard county and adjoining counties. **URL:** http://www.crescotimes.com. **Mailing address:** PO Box 350, Cresco, IA 52136. **Ad Rates:** GLR $.43; BW $749; 4C $912.78; SAU $7.99; PCI $7.99. **Remarks:** Accepts advertising. **Circ:** Paid ‡3450, Free ‡7650.

12543 ■ KCZQ-FM - 102.3
116 1st Ave. W
Cresco, IA 52136-1514
Phone: (319)547-1000
Fax: (319)547-2200
Format: Adult Contemporary; Oldies. **Networks:** Radio Iowa. **Owner:** Mega Media Ltd., at above address. **Founded:** 1991. **Operating Hours:** 18 HRS Daily. **ADI:** Rochester, MN-Mason City, IA-Austin, MN. **Key Personnel:** James Hebel, Gen. Mgr., President; Debra Lowe, Traffic Mgr. **Wattage:** 3,000 ERP.

CRESTON

S IA. Union Co. 73 mi. SW of Des Moines. Southwestern Community College. Manufactures lubricating devices, coffee makers. Plastic tile, planing mill; aluminum and magnesium foundry castings; food processing; stock yards, anhydrous ammonia plants. Ships livestock, grain. Gravel pits. Agriculture. Hogs, cattle, corn, soybeans.

12544 ■ Creston News Advertiser
Creston Publishing Co.

Circulation: ★ = AAM; △ or • = BPA; ♦ = CAC; ❑ = VAC; ⊕ = PO Statement; ‡ = Publisher's Report; Boldface figures = sworn; Light figures = estimated.

503 W Adams St.
Creston, IA 50801
Phone: (641)782-2141
Fax: (641)782-6628
Publication E-mail: editor@crestonnews.com
General newspaper. **Freq:** Daily (eve.) Monday-Friday. **Print Method:** Web. **Trim Size:** 13 3/4 x 25. **Cols./Page:** 6. **Col. Width:** 12.5 picas. **Col. Depth:** 21.5 inches. **Key Personnel:** Kyle Wilson, Managing Editor; Rich Paulsen, Publisher; Craig Mittag, Manager, Advertising; Larry Peterson, Assistant Managing Editor. **USPS:** 137-820. **Subscription Rates:** $120 Individuals carrier; $120 Individuals online; $190 Individuals motor route; $150 By mail in area; $204 By mail out of area. **URL:** http://www.crestonnews.com. **Remarks:** Advertising accepted; rates available upon request. **Circ:** 4500.

12545 ■ KSIB-AM - 1520
1409 Hwy. 34 W
Creston, IA 50801
Phone: (641)782-2155
Fax: (641)782-6963
Email: ksib@ksibradio.com
Format: Country. **Networks:** ABC. **Owner:** G.O. Radio, Inc., at above address. **Founded:** 1947. **Operating Hours:** 6 a.m.-11 p.m.; 10% network, 45% local; 45% other. **Key Personnel:** Chad Rieck, Gen. Mgr., chad@ksibradio.com; Ben Walter, Dir. of Programs, sales@ksibradio.com; Gary Bucklin, Sports Dir., news@ksibradio.com. **Wattage:** 1,000. **Ad Rates:** $5-8 for 30 seconds; $5.50-10.50 for 60 seconds. **Mailing address:** PO Box 426, Creston, IA 50801. **URL:** http://www.ksibradio.com.

12546 ■ KSIB-FM - 101.3
1409 Hwy. 34 W
Creston, IA 50801
Phone: (641)782-2155
Fax: (641)782-6963
Email: mailbag@ksibradio.com
Format: Country; Big Band/Nostalgia. **Networks:** ABC. **Founded:** 1975. **Formerly:** KITR-FM. **Operating Hours:** 6 a.m.-11 p.m.; 10% network, 50% local, 40% other. **Key Personnel:** Chad Rieck, Gen. Mgr., chad@ksibradio.com; Ben Walter, Dir. of Programs, sales@ksibradio.com; Melinda Mackey, Traffic Mgr., ksib@ksibradio.com. **Wattage:** 25,000. **Ad Rates:** Noncommercial. **Mailing address:** PO Box 426, Creston, IA 50801. **URL:** http://www.ksibradio.com.

12547 ■ K203DB-FM - 89.1
PO Box 391
Twin Falls, ID 83303
Phone: (208)733-3133
Format: Religious; Contemporary Christian. **Owner:** CSN International, PO Box 391, Twin Falls, ID 83303, Ph: (208)736-1958, Fax: (208)736-1958, Free: 800-357-4226. **Key Personnel:** Mike Kestler, President; Don Mills, Music Dir., Prog. Dir.; Daniel Davidson, Dir. of Operations. **URL:** http://www.csnradio.com.

DAVENPORT

E IA. Scott Co. On Mississippi River, 182 mi. W. of Chicago and opposite Rock Island, IL. Bridges to Rock Island and Moline, IL. St. Ambrose College, Marycrest College, and Palmer College of Chiropractic Medicine. Manufactures sheet aluminum, agricultural implements, construction machinery tractors, military equipment, cement and foundry products, cookies, crackers, meat products. Ships grain, limestone and cement.

12548 ■ Burt County Plaindealer
Lee Enterprises Inc.
201 N Harrison St.
Davenport, IA 52801-1932
Phone: (406)443-2842
Fax: (406)443-5480
Free: 888-406-6450
Local newspaper. **Freq:** Weekly (Wed.). **Print Method:** Offset. **Cols./Page:** 6. **Col. Width:** 26 nonpareils. **Col. Depth:** 301 agate lines. **Key Personnel:** Mark Jackson, Reporter; Joe Zink, General Manager; Perky Weatherly, Manager, Production. **USPS:** 080-160. **Subscription Rates:** $32 Individuals in county and Herman, print; $40 Out of country print; $27.89 Students 9-month print; $24 Individuals online only; $17.50 Students 9-month print. **URL:** http://www.midwestmessenger.com/burt_county. **Ad Rates:** BW $677; 4C $782; SAU $6.75; PCI $6.20. **Remarks:** Accepts advertising. **Circ:** (Not Reported).

12549 ■ The Catholic Messenger
Catholic Diocese of Davenport
780 W Central Park Ave.
Davenport, IA 52804
Phone: (563)323-9959
Fax: (563)888-4382
Free: 866-843-9959
Publication E-mail: messenger@davenportdiocese.org
Newspaper covering local, national, and international Catholic news. **Freq:** Weekly (Thurs.) except 1st week of July and last week of December. **Print Method:** Offset. **Trim Size:** 15 x 21. **Cols./Page:** 6. **Col. Width:** 24 nonpareils. **Col. Depth:** 301 agate lines. **Key Personnel:** Barb Arland-Fye, Editor, phone: (563)323-9959; Kathy Weiss, Manager, Advertising, Manager, Marketing, phone: (563)323-9959. **ISSN:** 0008--8234 (print). **Subscription Rates:** $29 Individuals in the Davenport Diocese, print, online; $31 Out of area print, 1 year. **URL:** http://www.catholicmessenger.net. **Ad Rates:** GLR $.50; BW $744.66; SAU $7.30; PCI $7.03. **Remarks:** Accepts advertising. **Circ:** 18300.

12550 ■ Chiropractic Journal of Australia
Chiropractors' Association of Australia
c/o Dr. Dana Lawrence, Editor
2551 E Columbia Ave.
Davenport, IA 52803
Publication E-mail: journal@caa.asn.au
Peer-reviewed journal covering chiropractic science, principles, and practice in Australia. **Freq:** Quarterly. **Key Personnel:** Dana Lawrence, Editor. **ISSN:** 1036--0913 (print). **URL:** http://www.chiropractors.asn.au/component/k2/item/326. **Ad Rates:** BW $715. **Remarks:** Accepts advertising. **Circ:** 1900, 2450.

12551 ■ The Daily Journal
Lee Enterprises Inc.
201 N Harrison St.
Davenport, IA 52801-1932
Phone: (406)443-2842
Fax: (406)443-5480
Free: 888-406-6450
General newspaper. **Founded:** 1930. **Freq:** Daily. **Print Method:** Offset. **Cols./Page:** 6. **Col. Width:** 1.850 inches. **Col. Depth:** 301 agate lines. **Key Personnel:** Doug Smith; Gary Berblinger, Publisher. **Subscription Rates:** $75 Individuals home delivery. **URL:** http://www.dailyjournalonline.com/. **Remarks:** Accepts classified advertising. **Circ:** Mon.-Fri. ★**8156**, Sun. ★**8397**, Sat. ★**7516**.

12552 ■ Elko Daily Free Press
Lee Enterprises Inc.
201 N Harrison St.
Davenport, IA 52801-1932
Phone: (406)443-2842
Fax: (406)443-5480
Free: 888-406-6450
General newspaper. **Freq:** Daily (eve.) and Sat. (morn.). **Print Method:** Offset. **Cols./Page:** 6. **Col. Width:** 11 nonpareils. **Col. Depth:** 301 agate lines. **Key Personnel:** Travis Quast, Editor; Jeffry Mullins, Editor. **Subscription Rates:** $6 Individuals /month (print and online). **URL:** http://elkodaily.com. **Ad Rates:** GLR $9.96; PCI $8. **Remarks:** Accepts advertising. **Circ:** (Not Reported).

12553 ■ Farmington Press
Lee Enterprises Inc.
201 N Harrison St.
Davenport, IA 52801-1932
Phone: (406)443-2842
Fax: (406)443-5480
Free: 888-406-6450
Community newspaper. **Founded:** 1928. **Freq:** Weekly (Thurs.). **Print Method:** Letterpress and offset. Uses Adnet. **Cols./Page:** 6. **Col. Width:** 27 nonpareils. **Col. Depth:** 294 agate lines. **Key Personnel:** Shawnna Robinson, Managing Editor, Editor. **Subscription Rates:** $75 Individuals. **URL:** http://dailyjournalonline.com/farmington-press/. **Formerly:** Daily Press Leader. **Remarks:** Advertising accepted; rates available upon request. **Circ:** Combined ‡4600.

12554 ■ The Hanford Sentinel
Lee Enterprises Inc.
201 N Harrison St.
Davenport, IA 52801-1932
Phone: (406)443-2842
Fax: (406)443-5480
Free: 888-406-6450
Community newspaper. **Freq:** Daily. **Print Method:** Offset. **Cols./Page:** 6. **Col. Width:** 26 nonpareils. **Col. Depth:** 301 agate lines. **Key Personnel:** Jackie Kaczmarek, Executive Editor, phone: (559)583-2403; Greg Barkley, Manager, Circulation, phone: (559)883-2404. **URL:** http://www.hanfordsentinel.com. **Ad Rates:** GLR $2.44; PCI $19.50. **Remarks:** Accepts advertising. **Circ:** Mon.-Sat. ★**9582**.

12555 ■ The Ledger-Independent
Lee Enterprises Inc.
201 N Harrison St.
Davenport, IA 52801-1932
Phone: (406)443-2842
Fax: (406)443-5480
Free: 888-406-6450
Newspaper. **Freq:** Mon.-Sat. (morn.). **Print Method:** Offset. **Cols./Page:** 6. **Col. Width:** 26 nonpareils. **Col. Depth:** 301 agate lines. **Key Personnel:** Bob Hendrickson, Publisher; Mary Ann Kearns, Managing Editor. **Subscription Rates:** $8.80 Individuals per month; online only; $16.50 Individuals print for 5 Days (Mon and Wed through Sat) with online access. **URL:** http://www.maysville-online.com. **Remarks:** Accepts advertising. **Circ:** Mon.-Sat. ★**6999**.

12556 ■ Midwest Messenger
Lee Enterprises Inc.
201 N Harrison St.
Davenport, IA 52801-1932
Phone: (406)443-2842
Fax: (406)443-5480
Free: 888-406-6450
Farm trade shopper. **Freq:** 26/yr. **Print Method:** Web Offset. **Trim Size:** 10 3/8 x 16. **Cols./Page:** 6. **Col. Width:** 10 picas. **Col. Depth:** 16 inches. **Key Personnel:** Perky Weatherly, Manager, Production; Joe Zink, General Manager; Susan McAllister, Manager, Operations. **Subscription Rates:** $35 Individuals north, south and west edition; $35 Individuals iowa edition; $33 Individuals iowa edition-non Nebraska residents; $33 Individuals north, south and west edition-non Nebraska resident. **URL:** http://www.midwestmessenger.com. **Ad Rates:** BW $5328; 4C $6228; SAU $11; PCI $55.50. **Remarks:** Accepts advertising. **Circ:** Combined ‡95,207.

12557 ■ Montana Land Magazine
Lee Enterprises Inc.
201 N Harrison St.
Davenport, IA 52801-1932
Phone: (406)443-2842
Fax: (406)443-5480
Free: 888-406-6450
Real estate magazine. **Freq:** 5/yr. **Print Method:** Offset. **Trim Size:** 8 x 10 1/2. **Cols./Page:** 2. **Col. Width:** 36 nonpareils. **Col. Depth:** 130 agate lines. **ISSN:** 1052--469X (print). **Subscription Rates:** Free in rack locations throughout Montana, Wyoming, Idaho, North Dakota and South Dakota. **URL:** http://homes.montanalandmagazine.com. **Remarks:** Accepts advertising. **Circ:** (Not Reported).

12558 ■ Montana Standard
Lee Enterprises Inc.
201 N Harrison St.
Davenport, IA 52801-1932
Phone: (406)443-2842
Fax: (406)443-5480
Free: 888-406-6450
General newspaper. **Freq:** Mon.-Sun. (morn.). **Print Method:** Offset. **Cols./Page:** 6. **Col. Width:** 24 nonpareils. **Col. Depth:** 301 agate lines. **Key Personnel:** Tyler Miller, Publisher, phone: (406)447-4002. **Subscription Rates:** $11 Individuals full & digital access. **URL:** http://mtstandard.com. **Remarks:** Accepts advertising. **Circ:** (Not Reported).

12559 ■ Operations Research/Management Science
Executive Sciences Institute
1005 Mississippi Ave.
Davenport, IA 52803
Phone: (319)324-4463
Fax: (319)324-3725
Operations research and management science journal. **Freq:** Bimonthly. **Print Method:** Offset. **Trim Size:** 6 x

9. **Cols./Page:** 1. **Key Personnel:** Peter Horner, Editor; John Llewellyn, President. **ISSN:** 0030-3658 (print). **Subscription Rates:** $62 Institutions U.S., 1 year; $79 Institutions, Canada and Mexico 1 year; $85 Institutions, other countries 1 year. **URL:** http://esipublications.com/articles/volumes/journal:OR. **Ad Rates:** BW $1702. **Remarks:** Accepts advertising. **Circ:** (Not Reported).

12560 ■ Plattsmouth Journal
Lee Enterprises Inc.
201 N Harrison St.
Davenport, IA 52801-1932
Phone: (406)443-2842
Fax: (406)443-5480
Free: 888-406-6450
Community newspaper. **Freq:** Semiweekly (Mon. and Thurs.). **Print Method:** Offset. **Cols./Page:** 6. **Col. Width:** 24 nonpareils. **Col. Depth:** 301 agate lines. **Key Personnel:** Jim Ristow, Publisher; Patti Jo Peterson, Editor. **URL:** http://fremonttribune.com/cass-news. **Ad Rates:** GLR $.39; BW $704.34; SAU $5.43. **Remarks:** Advertising accepted; rates available upon request. **Circ:** ‡5234.

12561 ■ Quad-City Times
Lee Enterprises Inc.
201 N Harrison St.
Davenport, IA 52801-1932
Phone: (406)443-2842
Fax: (406)443-5480
Free: 888-406-6450
General newspaper. **Founded:** 1855. **Freq:** Mon.-Sun. **Print Method:** Offset. **Cols./Page:** 6. **Col. Width:** 24 nonpareils. **Col. Depth:** 255 agate lines. **Key Personnel:** Steve Thomas, Editor, phone: (319)383-2334. **Subscription Rates:** $10 Individuals monthly. **URL:** http://qctimes.com. **Remarks:** Accepts advertising. **Circ:** Mon.-Fri. ★**51008**, Sat. ★**58050**, Sun. ★**69003**.

12562 ■ ESPN 1170 AM - 1170
1229 Brady St.
Davenport, IA 52803
Phone: (563)326-2541
Fax: (563)326-1819
Format: Oldies. **Networks:** ESPN Radio; CBS. **Owner:** Cumulus Broadcasting Inc., 3280 Peachtree Rd. NW, Ste. 2300, Atlanta, GA 30305-2447, Ph: (404)949-0700, Fax: (404)949-0740. **Founded:** 1946. **Formerly:** KSTT-AM; KKZX-AM; KJOC-AM. **Operating Hours:** Continuous; 75% network, 50% local. **ADI:** Daveport,IA-Rock Island, Moline,IL. **Wattage:** 1,000. **Ad Rates:** Noncommercial. **URL:** http://1170kbob.com.

12563 ■ KAIP-FM - 88.9
PO Box 2118
Omaha, NE 68103-2118
Free: 888-937-2471
Format: Contemporary Christian. **Owner:** Educational Media Foundation, 2351 Sunset Blvd., Ste. 170-218, Rocklin, CA 95677, Ph: (800)434-8400. **ADI:** Ottumwa, IA-Kirksville, MO (Wapello, IA). **Key Personnel:** Mike Novak, President, CEO. **Wattage:** 001 H;13,500 V. **URL:** http://www.air1.com.

12564 ■ KALA-FM - 88.5
518 W Locust St.
Davenport, IA 52803
Phone: (563)333-6000
Fax: (563)333-6218
Email: kala@sau.edu
Format: Full Service; Contemporary Hit Radio (CHR). **Networks:** Longhorn Radio. **Owner:** St. Ambrose University, 518 W Locust St., Davenport, IA 52803, Ph: (563)333-6000. **Founded:** 1967. **Operating Hours:** Continuous. **Key Personnel:** David Baker, Operations Mgr. **Local Programs:** *Jazz Images*, Monday Friday Sunday 7:00 p.m. 8:00 p.m. 6:00 p.m.; *Rhythm Sweet & Hot*, Monday 8:00 p.m.; *The Tavis Smiley Show*, Monday 8:00 a.m. - 9:00 a.m.; *Mississippi Valley Blues Society*, Tuesday Thursday Wednesday 6:00 p.m. 9:00 p.m. **Wattage:** 10,000. **Ad Rates:** Noncommercial. **URL:** http://www.web.sau.edu.

12565 ■ KBEA-FM - 99.7
1229 Brady St.
Davenport, IA 52803
Phone: (563)326-2541
Format: Top 40. **Owner:** Cumulus Broadcasting of the Quad Cities, 1229 Brady St., Davenport, IA 52803. **Founded:** Sept. 15, 2006. **Key Personnel:** Darren Pitra, Contact, darren.pitra@cumulus.com; Julie Derrer, Contact, julie.derrer@cumulus.com; Darren Pitra, Contact, darren.pitra@cumulus.com. **Wattage:** 100,000. **Ad Rates:** Noncommercial. **URL:** http://www.b100quadcities.com.

12566 ■ KBOB-FM - 104.9
1229 Brady St.
Davenport, IA 52803
Phone: (563)326-2541
Fax: (563)326-1819
Format: Country. **Owner:** Cumulus Media Inc., 3280 Peachtree Rd. NW, Ste. 2300, Atlanta, GA 30305-2455, Ph: (404)949-0700, Fax: (404)949-0740. **Founded:** 1949. **Operating Hours:** Continuous. **ADI:** Daveport,IA-Rock Island, Moline,IL. **Wattage:** 100,000 ERP. **Ad Rates:** Noncommercial. **URL:** http://www.1049thehawk.com.

12567 ■ KCQQ-FM - 106.5
3535 E Kimberly Rd.
Davenport, IA 52807
Phone: (563)344-7054
Fax: (563)359-8524
Format: Classic Rock. **ADI:** Daveport,IA-Rock Island, Moline,IL. **Key Personnel:** John Laton, Gen. Mgr. **Wattage:** 100,000.

12568 ■ KLJB-TV - 18
937 E 53rd St.
Davenport, IA 52807
Phone: (563)386-1818
Fax: (563)386-8543
Email: qandc@kljb.com
Format: Commercial TV. **Networks:** Fox. **Owner:** Grant Broadcasting Systems, at above address. **Founded:** 1985. **Operating Hours:** Continuous. **ADI:** Daveport,IA-Rock Island, Moline,IL. **Key Personnel:** Marshall Porter, Gen. Mgr., mporter@whbf.com. **Local Programs:** *Fox 18 News at Nine*, Monday Tuesday Wednesday Thursday Friday 9:00 p.m. **Ad Rates:** Advertising accepted; rates available upon request. **URL:** http://www.kljb.com.

12569 ■ KMXG-FM - 96.1
3535 E Kimberly Rd.
Davenport, IA 52807
Phone: (563)344-7000
Format: Adult Contemporary. **Owner:** iHeartMedia Inc., 200 E Basse Rd., San Antonio, TX 78209, Ph: (210)832-3314. **Founded:** 1986. **Formerly:** KSAY-FM; KMJC-FM; KLIO-FM. **Operating Hours:** Continuous; 100% local. **ADI:** Daveport,IA-Rock Island, Moline,IL. **Key Personnel:** Jim O'Hara, Dir. of Programs, jimohara@clearchannel.com; Ron Evans, Music Dir., ronevans@clearchannel.com; Kelly Meyer, Sales Mgr. **Wattage:** 100,000. **Ad Rates:** $25-40 for 30 seconds; $45-50 for 60 seconds. **URL:** http://www.mix96online.com.

12570 ■ KRVR-FM - 106.5
3535 E Kimberly Rd.
Davenport, IA 52807
Phone: (563)344-7000
Format: Classic Rock. **Founded:** 1966. **Operating Hours:** Continuous. **Key Personnel:** Sandy McKay, Dir. of Programs. **Wattage:** 100,000 ERP. **Ad Rates:** $3-40 for 30 seconds; $3-50 for 60 seconds. **URL:** http://q106online.iheart.com.

12571 ■ KUUL-FM - 101.3
3535 E Kimberly Rd.
Davenport, IA 52807
Phone: (563)344-7000
Fax: (563)359-8524
Format: Oldies. **Networks:** Unistar; CBS. **Owner:** iHeartMedia Inc., 200 E Basse Rd., San Antonio, TX 78209, Ph: (210)832-3314. **Founded:** 1948. **Formerly:** WOC-FM. **Operating Hours:** Continuous. **ADI:** Daveport,IA-Rock Island, Moline,IL. **Wattage:** 50,000. **Ad Rates:** Advertising accepted; rates available upon request. **URL:** http://www.1013kissfm.com.

12572 ■ KWQC-TV - 6
805 Brady St.
Davenport, IA 52803
Phone: (563)383-7000
Fax: (563)383-7131
Email: news@kwqc.com
Format: Commercial TV. **Networks:** NBC. **Owner:** Young Broadcasting of Davenport Inc., 805 Brady St., Davenport, IA 52803, Ph: (563)383-7000, Fax: (563)383-7129. **Founded:** 1949. **Formerly:** WOC-TV. **Operating Hours:** Continuous. **ADI:** Daveport,IA-Rock Island, Moline,IL. **Key Personnel:** Ken Freedman, Gen. Mgr., kfreedman@kwqc.com. **Wattage:** 1,000,000 H ERP. **Ad Rates:** Advertising accepted; rates available upon request. **URL:** http://www.kwqc.com.

12573 ■ WFXN-AM - 1230
3535 E Kimberly Rd.
Davenport, IA 52807
Phone: (563)344-7000
Format: Sports. **Operating Hours:** Continuous. **ADI:** Daveport,IA-Rock Island, Moline,IL. **Key Personnel:** John Laton, Gen. Mgr. **Wattage:** 1,000 ERP. **Ad Rates:** Noncommercial. **URL:** http://www.foxsportsradio1230.com.

12574 ■ WLLR-AM - 1230
3535 E Kimberly Rd.
Davenport, IA 52807
Phone: (563)344-7000
Fax: (563)359-8524
Format: Country; Sports; Talk. **Simulcasts:** WLLR-FM. **Networks:** Independent. **Founded:** 1946. **Formerly:** WQUA-AM. **Operating Hours:** Continuous; 80% network, 20% local. **ADI:** Daveport,IA-Rock Island, Moline,IL. **Wattage:** 1,000. **Ad Rates:** $30-73 for 30 seconds; $39-90 for 60 seconds. **URL:** http://1037wllr.iheart.com/articles/wllr-contacts-224277/get-in-touch-with-wllr-13089659/.

12575 ■ WLLR-FM - 103.7
3535 E Kimberly Rd.
Davenport, IA 52807
Phone: (563)344-7000
Format: Contemporary Country. **Networks:** Independent. **Founded:** 1975. **Formerly:** WZZC-FM; WEMO-FM. **Operating Hours:** Continuous; 100% local. **ADI:** Daveport,IA-Rock Island, Moline,IL. **Key Personnel:** Ron Evans, Music Dir., ronevans@clearchannel.com. **Local Programs:** *American Country Countdown with Kix Brooks*, Friday 9:00 p.m. - 12:00 a.m. **Wattage:** 50,000. **Ad Rates:** $30-73 for 30 seconds; $39-90 for 60 seconds. **URL:** http://www.wllr.com.

12576 ■ WOC-AM - 1420
3535 E Kimberly Rd.
Davenport, IA 52807
Phone: (563)344-7000
Format: Talk. **Networks:** NBC; CNN Radio; Mutual Broadcasting System; Radio Iowa; Illinois News; ABC. **Owner:** iHeartMedia Inc., 200 E Basse Rd., San Antonio, TX 78209, Ph: (210)832-3314. **Founded:** 1926. **Operating Hours:** Continuous; 45% network, 55% local. **ADI:** Daveport,IA-Rock Island, Moline,IL. **Key Personnel:** John Laton, Gen. Mgr. **Wattage:** 5,000. **Ad Rates:** $12-36 for 30 seconds; $15-42 for 60 seconds.

12577 ■ WXLP-FM - 96.9
1229 Brady St.
Davenport, IA 52803
Phone: (563)326-2541
Format: Classic Rock. **Networks:** Westwood One Radio. **Owner:** Cumulus Media Inc., 3280 Peachtree Rd. NW, Ste. 2300, Atlanta, GA 30305-2455, Ph: (404)949-0700, Fax: (404)949-0740. **Founded:** 1978. **Operating Hours:** Continuous. **ADI:** Daveport,IA-Rock Island, Moline,IL. **Key Personnel:** Rolf Pepple, Mgr., Rolf.Pepple@townsquaremedia.com. **Wattage:** 50,000. **Ad Rates:** Advertising accepted; rates available upon request. **URL:** http://www.97x.com.

DAYTON

NWC IA. Webster Co. 23 mi. SE of Fort Dodge. Camps. Concrete, farm equipment factories. Grain elevator. Stock, poultry, grain farms. Corn, oats, soybeans.

12578 ■ Dayton Review
Dayton Feright
25 S Main St.
Dayton, IA 50530
Phone: (515)547-2811
Fax: (515)547-2337
Publisher's E-mail: daytonreview@lvcta.com
Agricultural newspaper. **Freq:** Weekly (Wed.). **Print Method:** Offset. **Trim Size:** 11 1/2 x 17. **Cols./Page:** 6. **Col. Width:** 25 nonpareils. **Col. Depth:** 224 agate lines. **Key Personnel:** Marybeth Owenson, Contact; Glenn

Circulation: ★ = AAM; △ or • = BPA; ♦ = CAC; ❑ = VAC; ⊕ = PO Statement; ‡ = Publisher's Report; Boldface figures = sworn; Light figures = estimated.

Schreiber, Editor; Amanda Schwering, Office Manager. **USPS:** 149-740. **Mailing address:** PO Box 6, Dayton, IA 50530. **Ad Rates:** GLR $.25; BW $210; SAU $5.24; PCI $4.25. **Remarks:** Accepts advertising. **Circ:** ‡845.

12579 ■ The Gowrie News
Gowrie News
PO Box 6
Dayton, IA 50530-0006
Community newspaper. **Freq:** Weekly (Wed.). **Print Method:** Offset. **Cols./Page:** 7. **Col. Width:** 22 nonpareils. **Col. Depth:** 294 agate lines. **Subscription Rates:** $30 Individuals print + online; $19 Individuals e-edition. **Remarks:** Accepts advertising. **Circ:** (Not Reported).

DECORAH

NE IA. Winneshiek Co. 65 mi. SW of La Crosse, WI. Luther College. Tourism. Creamery; automotive and computer parts, zinc casting, meat packing plants; feed mill; bottling works; machine shops. Grain, dairy, poultry farms. Corn, alfalfa, barley.

12580 ■ Archive for Reformation History
Society for Reformation Research
c/o Victoria and Robert Christman, Treasurer and Membership Secretary
Dept. of History
Luther College
700 College Dr.
Decorah, IA 52101-1045
Journal published in cooperation with the German Verein fur Reformationsgeschichte in English and German. **Freq:** Annual. **Key Personnel:** Susan C. Karant-Nunn, Member. **ISSN:** 0003--9381 (print). **Subscription Rates:** Included in membership. **URL:** http://arg.nd.edu; http://www.reformationresearch.org/Journ.htm. **Remarks:** Advertising not accepted. **Circ:** (Not Reported).

12581 ■ Journal
Decorah Newspapers
107 E Water St.
Decorah, IA 52101
Phone: (563)382-4221
Fax: (563)382-5949
Publisher's E-mail: subscribe@decorahnewspapers.com
Community newspaper. **Founded:** 1864. **Freq:** Weekly (Thurs.). **Print Method:** Offset. **Cols./Page:** 6. **Col. Width:** 30 nonpareils. **Col. Depth:** 301 agate lines. **Key Personnel:** Sarah Strandberg, Editor; Julie Ude, Manager, Advertising; Stephanie Langreck, Manager, Production; Lissa Blake, Reporter; Rick Fromm, Managing Editor; Tanya O'Connor, Advertising Representative; John Anundsen, Publisher. **Subscription Rates:** $35 Individuals; $40 Out of area in Iowa; $45 Out of state. **URL:** http://www.decorahnewspapers.com. **Mailing address:** PO Box 350, Decorah, IA 52101. **Ad Rates:** SAU $4.65; PCI $7. **Remarks:** Accepts advertising. **Circ:** 6000.

12582 ■ Public Opinion
Decorah Newspapers
107 E Water St.
Decorah, IA 52101
Phone: (563)382-4221
Fax: (563)382-5949
Publisher's E-mail: subscribe@decorahnewspapers.com
Community newspaper. **Founded:** 1895. **Freq:** Weekly (Tues.). **Print Method:** Offset. **Cols./Page:** 6. **Col. Width:** 30 nonpareils. **Col. Depth:** 301 agate lines. **Key Personnel:** Julie Ude, Manager, Advertising; Rick Fromm, Managing Editor; Sarah Strandberg, Editor; John Anundsen, Publisher; Jennifer Bissell, Editor. **URL:** http://www.decorahnewspapers.com. **Mailing address:** PO Box 350, Decorah, IA 52101. **Ad Rates:** PCI $7. **Remarks:** Accepts advertising. **Circ:** Paid ‡6000.

12583 ■ KDEC-AM - 1240
110 Highland Dr.
Decorah, IA 52101
Phone: (563)382-4251
Fax: (563)382-9540
Email: kdec@kdecradio.com
Format: News; Sports. **Networks:** ABC; Westwood One Radio. **Owner:** Decorah Broadcasting Inc., at above address. **Founded:** 1948. **Operating Hours:** 17 hours Daily; 50% network, 50% local. **ADI:** Cedar Rapids-Waterloo-Dubuque, IA. **Wattage:** 1,000. **Ad Rates:** $6-10 for 30 seconds; $8-13.23 for 60 seconds. KDEC-FM; Continuous, 30,000 watts. **Mailing address:** PO Box 27, Decorah, IA 52101. **URL:** http://www.kdecradio.net.

12584 ■ KDEC-FM - 100.5
110 Highland Dr.
Decorah, IA 52101
Phone: (563)382-4251
Fax: (563)382-1005
Email: kdec@kdecradio.com
Format: Adult Contemporary. **Networks:** ABC. **Owner:** Decorah Broadcasting Inc., at above address. **Founded:** 1986. **Formerly:** KRDI-FM. **Operating Hours:** Continuous; 6% network, 94% local. **ADI:** Cedar Rapids-Waterloo-Dubuque, IA. **Key Personnel:** Colleen Holtan, Contact; Bob Holtan, Gen. Mgr; Colleen Holtan, Contact. **Wattage:** 30,000. **Ad Rates:** $12-20 for 30 seconds; $16-26.46 for 60 seconds. Combined advertising rates available with KDEC-AM. **Mailing address:** PO Box 27, Decorah, IA 52101. **URL:** http://www.kdecradio.net.

12585 ■ KVIK-FM - 104.7
501 W Water St.
Decorah, IA 52101
Phone: (563)382-5845
Fax: (563)382-5581
Free: 866-881-5845
Email: kvik@kvikradio.com
Format: Classical. **Networks:** Fox. **Founded:** Sept. 07, 2006. **Operating Hours:** Continuous. **Wattage:** 1,950 ERP. **Ad Rates:** Advertising accepted; rates available upon request. **URL:** http://www.kvikradio.com.

DENISON

W IA. Crawford Co. 65 mi. NE of Council Bluffs. Stock waterer manufacturers. Seed houses; machine shops; meat processing plants. Dairy, stock, grain farms. Corn, soybeans, oats, wheat, hogs, poultry, beef.

12586 ■ Review
The Denison Bulletin/Review
1410 Broadway
Denison, IA 51442-0550
Phone: (712)263-2122
Fax: (712)263-8484
Community newspaper with a Republican orientation. **Founded:** 1886. **Freq:** Weekly (Fri.). **Print Method:** Offset. **Trim Size:** 12 1/2 x 23. **Cols./Page:** 6. **Col. Width:** 11 picas. **Col. Depth:** 21 1/2 inches. **Key Personnel:** Greg Wehle, Publisher; Todd Danner, Editor; Gordon Wolf, Editor; Christy Welch, Editor; Jacki Gallagher, Manager, Circulation; Cathy Jacoby, Office Manager. **Subscription Rates:** $55 Individuals cash or check; $62 Out of state; $31 Individuals 6 months; $31 Students 9 months. **URL:** http://www.southwestiowanews.com. **Formerly:** Denison Newspapers, Inc. **Ad Rates:** BW $645; 4C $780; SAU $9; CNU $7; PCI $9. **Remarks:** Accepts advertising. **Circ:** 4,100.

12587 ■ KDSN-AM - 1530
1530 Ridge Rd.
Denison, IA 51442
Phone: (712)263-3141
Fax: (712)263-2088
Email: info@kdsnradio.com
Format: Country. **Networks:** ABC. **Owner:** M & J Radio Corp., 1530 Ridge Rd., Denison, IA 51442, Ph: (712)263-3141, Fax: (712)263-2088. **Founded:** 1956. **Operating Hours:** 6 a.m.-10 p.m.; 2% network, 98% local. **ADI:** Omaha, NE. **Key Personnel:** Michael J. Dudding, Sales Mgr., Owner; Randy Grossman, Account Exec., Sports Dir.; Tom Hamilton, Music Dir., Program Mgr.; Kathy Dudding, Bus. Mgr. **Local Programs:** *Market Settlement Report*, Saturday 8:15 a.m.; *ISU Extension Report*; *Price Discovery Report*, Monday Tuesday Wednesday Thursday Friday 7:45 a.m.; 11:35 a.m.; 1:40 p.m.; *Radio Iowa News*, Monday Tuesday Wednesday Thursday Friday Saturday 5:57 a.m.; 7:57 a.m.; 11:30 a.m.; 3:57 p.m.; 4:57 p.m. 7:57 a.m.; *Odebolt News*, Thursday 8:18 a.m.; *Lannie Miller Report*, Friday 11:45 a.m.; *AM Sign On*, Saturday 6:00 a.m. - 8:15 a.m.; *MF Global Watch*, Monday Tuesday Wednesday Thursday Friday 10:30 a.m.; *Market Flash*, Monday Tuesday Wednesday Thursday Friday 10:59 a.m.; 12:59 p.m.; *Woodbine Coaches Corner*, Saturday 8:30 a.m.; *Radio Iowa & Local Sports*, Monday Tuesday Wednesday Thursday Friday 5:20 p.m.; *Edward Jones Report*, Monday Tuesday Wednesday Thursday Friday 5:25 p.m.; *Saturday Morning Farm Report*, Saturday 8:15 a.m.; *Polka Party*, Saturday Monday Tuesday Wednesday Thursday Friday 10:06 a.m. 1:06 p.m.; *Opening Chicago Board of Trade*, Monday Tuesday Wednesday Thursday Friday 9:35 a.m.; *Bill Miller Variety Show 6-10am*, Sunday 6:04 a.m.; 7:06 a.m.; 8:06 a.m.; 9:06 a.m. **Wattage:** 500. **Ad Rates:** $7.50-14 for 15 seconds; $9.50-16 for 30 seconds; $11-20 for 60 seconds. Combined advertising rates available with KDSN-FM. **Mailing address:** PO Box 670, Denison, IA 51442. **URL:** http://www.kdsnradio.com.

12588 ■ KDSN-FM - 107.1
1530 Ridge Rd.
Denison, IA 51442
Phone: (712)263-3141
Fax: (712)263-2088
Format: Adult Contemporary. **Networks:** ABC. **Owner:** M & J Radio Corp., 1530 Ridge Rd., Denison, IA 51442, Ph: (712)263-3141, Fax: (712)263-2088. **Founded:** 1968. **Operating Hours:** Continuous. **ADI:** Omaha, NE. **Key Personnel:** Michael J. Dudding, Sales Mgr., Owner; Randy Grossman, Sports Dir.; Tom Hamilton, Music Dir., Prog. Dir.; Kathy Dudding, Bus. Mgr.; Mike Earl, News Dir. **Local Programs:** *Flashback*, Sunday 1:00 p.m. - 3:00 p.m.; *Birthday & Anniversary Show*, Monday Tuesday Wednesday Thursday Friday Saturday 8:30 a.m. 8:25 a.m.; *Thy Strong Word*, Monday Tuesday Wednesday Thursday Friday Saturday 6:25 a.m. **Wattage:** 6,000. **Ad Rates:** $7-14 for 15 seconds; $8-17 for 30 seconds; $11-20 for 60 seconds. Combined advertising rates available with KDSN-AM. **Mailing address:** PO Box 670, Denison, IA 51442. **URL:** http://www.kdsnradio.com.

DES MOINES

C IA. Polk Co. On Des Moines and Raccoon Rivers, 340 mi. W. of Chicago. The State Capital. Grand View College; College of Osteopathic Medicine and Surgery; Drake University; College of Law; Pharmacy; Publishing and Trade Centers. Manufactures flour, cosmetics, furnaces, stove and furnace parts, agricultural implements, automotive and creamery equipment, leather products, medicine, brick, tires, clothing, refrigerators, dairy products, cement, crackers, biscuits, vegetable oils, paint, electric switches and elevators. Meat packing plants.

12589 ■ The Bulletin
Polk County Medical Society
1520 High St.
Des Moines, IA 50309
Phone: (515)288-0172
Fax: (515)288-0173
Publisher's E-mail: pcms@pcms.org
Journal containing articles on medical topics and current medical news; also featuring Polk County Medical Society news and member updates. **Founded:** 1851. **Freq:** Bimonthly. **Key Personnel:** Kathie J. Lyman, Managing Editor; Steven R. Eckstat, DO, Editor. **URL:** http://www.pcms.org/Bulletin.html. **Remarks:** Accepts advertising. **Circ:** (Not Reported).

12590 ■ The Catholic Mirror
Diocese of Des Moines
601 Grand Ave.
Des Moines, IA 50309
Phone: (515)237-5046
Fax: (515)237-5070
Publication E-mail: kcollins@dmdiocese.org
Official newspaper of the Diocese of Des Moines. **Freq:** Monthly. **Print Method:** Offset. **Cols./Page:** 5. **Col. Width:** 11 picas. **Col. Depth:** 15 3/4 inches. **Key Personnel:** Rev. Joseph Charron, President; Rev. Richard E. Pates, Publisher; Anne Marie Cox, Editor. **ISSN:** 0896--6869 (print). **Subscription Rates:** $16 Individuals. **Ad Rates:** SAU $13.50. **Remarks:** Accepts advertising. **Circ:** ‡35000.

12591 ■ Central Vac Professional
Vacuum and Sewing Dealers Trade Association
2724 2nd Ave.
Des Moines, IA 50313-4933
Phone: (515)282-9101
Fax: (515)282-4483
Free: 800-367-5651
Publisher's E-mail: mail@vdta.com
Publishing information dedicated to keeping the indepen-

dent floor care/cleaning retailer and central vacuum dealer updated with current industry news, business tips and new product development. **Freq:** Monthly. **Key Personnel:** Beth Vitiritto, Managing Editor. **URL:** http://www.vdta.com/magazines.html. **Also known as:** Floor Care and Central Vac Professional. **Remarks:** Advertising not accepted. **Circ:** (Not Reported).

12592 ■ Cuisine at Home
August Home Publishing Co.
2200 Grand Ave.
Des Moines, IA 50312
Phone: (515)875-7000
Free: 800-311-5441
Publisher's E-mail: woodnet@augusthome.com
Consumer magazine covering cooking. **Freq:** Bimonthly. **Key Personnel:** Don Peschke, Publisher. **Subscription Rates:** $28 Two years. **URL:** http://www.cuisineathome.com; http://www.augusthome.com/brands/cuisineathome. **Formerly:** Cuisine. **Remarks:** Advertising not accepted. **Circ:** (Not Reported).

12593 ■ Des Moines Business Record
Business Publications Corp.
The Depot at 4th, 100 4th St.
Des Moines, IA 50309
Phone: (515)288-3336
Fax: (515)288-0309
Publisher's E-mail: advertising@bpcdm.com
Newspaper covering local business news. **Founded:** 1983. **Freq:** Weekly. **Print Method:** Offset. **Trim Size:** 11 5/8 x 14 5/8. **Cols./Page:** 4. **Col. Width:** 14 picas. **Col. Depth:** 75 picas. **Key Personnel:** Connie Wimer, Chairman; Chris Conetzkey, Editor; Janette Larkin, Publisher. **USPS:** 154-740. **Subscription Rates:** $69.95 Individuals; $43.95 Individuals e-edition. **URL:** http://www.businessrecord.com. **Formerly:** Business Record. **Ad Rates:** BW $3365; 4C $4071. **Remarks:** Accepts classified advertising. **Circ:** (Not Reported).

12594 ■ The Des Moines Register
Gannett Company Inc.
PO Box 957
Des Moines, IA 50306
Phone: (515)284-8000
Free: 800-247-5346
General newspaper. **Freq:** Mon.-Sun. (morn.). **Print Method:** DiLitho. **Cols./Page:** 7. **Col. Width:** 24. nonpareils. **Col. Depth:** 313 agate lines. **Key Personnel:** Rick Green, President, Publisher, phone: (515)284-8502. **Subscription Rates:** $14 Individuals digital only, Sunday Only; $28 Individuals month; Monday- Sunday; $18 Individuals month; Thursday - Sunday. **URL:** http://www.desmoinesregister.com. **Remarks:** Advertising accepted; rates available upon request. **Circ:** Mon.-Fri. ***113,597**, Sun. ***206,138**, Sat. ***119,414**.

12595 ■ Drake Blue: Alumni News of Drake University
Drake University Office of Marketing and Communications
1229 25th St.
Des Moines, IA 50311-4505
Phone: (515)271-2169
Fax: (515)271-3798
Free: 800-44-DRAKE
Publisher's E-mail: marketing@drake.edu
Alumni magazine. **Freq:** Semiannual. **Key Personnel:** Beth Wilson. **URL:** http://www.drake.edu/magazine. **Formerly:** Drake Update. **Remarks:** Advertising not accepted. **Circ:** Controlled 52000.

12596 ■ Drake Journal of Agricultural Law
Drake University Law School
2621 Carpenter Ave.
Des Moines, IA 50311
Phone: (515)271-2824
Free: 800-443-7253
Publisher's E-mail: lawadmit@drake.edu
Journal containing articles on legal issues affecting agricultural industry. **Freq:** 3/year fall, summer and spring. **Key Personnel:** Caitlin Andersen, Editor-in-Chief. **Subscription Rates:** $20 Members; $40 Individuals domestic; $45 Other countries. **URL:** http://students.law.drake.edu/agLawJournal. **Circ:** (Not Reported).

12597 ■ Drake Law Review
Drake University Law School
2621 Carpenter Ave.
Des Moines, IA 50311
Phone: (515)271-2824
Free: 800-443-7253
Publisher's E-mail: lawadmit@drake.edu
Law review journal. **Freq:** Quarterly. **Key Personnel:** Tyler S. Smith, Editor-in-Chief; Torey Robinson, Editor-in-Chief. **ISSN:** 0012--5983 (print). **Subscription Rates:** $33 Individuals Annual subscriptions (4 issues) ; $10 Single issue. **URL:** http://students.law.drake.edu/lawReview; http://drakelawreview.org. **Remarks:** Accepts advertising. **Circ:** (Not Reported).

12598 ■ The Exponent
Iowa Engineering Society
100 Court Ave., Ste. 203
Des Moines, IA 50309
Phone: (515)284-7055
Fax: (515)284-7301
Publisher's E-mail: info@iaengr.org
Magazine containing interesting news to members of the Iowa Engineering Society. **Freq:** Quarterly. **ISSN:** 0089-0572 (print). **URL:** http://iaengr.org. **Remarks:** Accepts advertising. **Circ:** (Not Reported).

12599 ■ Food Protection Trends
International Association for Food Protection
6200 Aurora Ave., Ste. 200W
Des Moines, IA 50322-2864
Phone: (515)276-3344
Fax: (515)276-8655
Free: 800-369-6337
Publisher's E-mail: info@foodprotection.org
Peer-reviewed journal publishing articles on applied research, applications of current technology and general interest subjects for food safety professionals. **Freq:** Bimonthly. **ISSN:** 1541--9576 (print). **Subscription Rates:** $1065 Institutions print and online; $1085 Institutions, Canada and Mexico print and online; $1115 Institutions, other countries print and online; $465 Institutions print only; $485 Institutions, Canada and Mexico print only; $515 Institutions, other countries print only; $600 Institutions online only. **URL:** http://www.foodprotection.org/publications/food-protection-trends. **Remarks:** Accepts advertising. **Circ:** 9000.

12600 ■ Garden Gate
August Home Publishing Co.
PO Box 842
Des Moines, IA 50304-9961
Free: 800-341-4769
Publication E-mail: gardengate@gardengatemag.com
Consumer magazine covering gardening. **Freq:** Bimonthly. **Key Personnel:** Kristin Beane-Sullivan, Managing Editor; Don Peschke, Publisher. **Subscription Rates:** $20 Individuals; $30 Two years; C$35 Canada; $34 Other countries. **URL:** http://www.gardengatemagazine.com; http://www.augusthome.com/brands/gardengate. **Remarks:** Advertising not accepted. **Circ:** (Not Reported).

12601 ■ The Iowa Lawyer
Iowa State Bar Association
625 E Court Ave.
Des Moines, IA 50309
Phone: (515)243-3179
Fax: (515)243-2511
Publisher's E-mail: isba@iowabar.org
Professional magazine covering law. **Freq:** Monthly. **Print Method:** Web offset. **Trim Size:** 8 1/2 x 11. **Cols./Page:** 3. **Subscription Rates:** Included in membership; $40 Individuals. **URL:** http://www.iowabar.org/?page=IowaLawyer. **Remarks:** Advertising accepted; rates available upon request. **Circ:** Controlled 8000.

12602 ■ Iowa Natural Heritage
Iowa Natural Heritage Foundation
505 5th Ave., Ste. 444
Des Moines, IA 50309-2321
Phone: (515)288-1846
Fax: (515)288-0137
Free: 800-475-1846
Publisher's E-mail: info@inhf.org
Freq: Quarterly. **Key Personnel:** Joe McGovern, President; Diane Graves, Contact. **Subscription Rates:** Included in membership. **URL:** http://www.inhf.org/resources/publications. **Remarks:** Advertising not accepted. **Circ:** (Not Reported).

12603 ■ The Iowan
Pioneer Communications Inc.
The Plaza, Ste. 6
300 Walnut St.
Des Moines, IA 50309
Phone: (515)246-0402
Publication E-mail: subscribe@pioneermagazines.com
Regional general interest magazine with an emphasis on in-state travel. **Freq:** Bimonthly. **Print Method:** Offset. **Trim Size:** 9 x 10 7/8. **Cols./Page:** 3 and 2. **Col. Width:** 28 and 43 nonpareils. **Col. Depth:** 144 agate lines. **Key Personnel:** Polly Clark, Publisher; Dan Weeks, Editor. **ISSN:** 0021--0722 (print). **Subscription Rates:** $24 Individuals; $38 Two years. **URL:** http://www.iowan.com. **Ad Rates:** 4C $1,995. **Remarks:** Advertising accepted; rates available upon request. **Circ:** (Not Reported).

12604 ■ The Journal
Iowa Pharmacy Association
8515 Douglas Ave., Ste. 16
Des Moines, IA 50322
Phone: (515)270-0713
Fax: (515)270-2979
Publisher's E-mail: ipa@iarx.org
Pharmacy journal. **Founded:** 1946. **Freq:** Quarterly. **Print Method:** Offset. **Trim Size:** 8 1/2 x 11. **Cols./Page:** 3. **Col. Width:** 26 nonpareils. **Col. Depth:** 140 agate lines. **Key Personnel:** Nicole Schultz, Contact. **ISSN:** 0889-7735 (print). **Subscription Rates:** $120 Nonmembers; $20 Nonmembers outside North America; $20 Single issue. **URL:** http://www.iarx.org/Resources/Publications/TheJournal.aspx. **Ad Rates:** BW $450; 4C $1,050. **Remarks:** Accepts advertising. **Circ:** Paid 1300, Non-paid 50.

12605 ■ Journal of Food Protection
International Association for Food Protection
6200 Aurora Ave., Ste. 200W
Des Moines, IA 50322-2864
Phone: (515)276-3344
Fax: (515)276-8655
Free: 800-369-6337
Publisher's E-mail: info@foodprotection.org
Peer-reviewed scientific journal reporting research in food microbiology for food safety. **Freq:** Monthly. **Print Method:** Offset. **Trim Size:** 8 1/2 x 11. **Cols./Page:** 2. **Col. Width:** 40 nonpareils. **Col. Depth:** 129 agate lines. **Key Personnel:** Lisa Hovey, Managing Editor. **ISSN:** 0362--028X (print). **Subscription Rates:** $465 U.S. print version; $485 Canada and Mexico print version; $515 Other countries print version; $600 U.S. and other countries online; $1065 U.S. print and online; $1085 Canada and Mexico print and online; $1115 Other countries print and online. **URL:** http://www.foodprotection.org/publications/journal-of-food-protection. **Formerly:** Journal of Milk Technology; Journal of Food and Milk Technology. **Ad Rates:** $671-814, back cover, ad placed in one publication; $652-791, inside front and back cover, ad placed in one publication; $583-708, full page, ad placed in one publication; $333-429, 1/2 page, ad placed in one publication; $1008-1219, back cover, ad placed in both publication; $983-1190, inside front and back cover, ad placed in both publication; $876-1061, full page, ad placed in both publication; $567-710, 1/2 page, ad placed in both publication. BW $, back cover, ad placed in one publicationBW $, inside front and back cover, ad placed in one publicationBW $, full page, ad placed in one publicationBW $, 1/2 page, ad placed in both one publicationBW $, back cover, ad placed in both publicationBW $, inside front and back cover, ad placed in both publicationBW $, full page, ad placed in both publicationBW $, 1/2 page, ad placed in both publication4C $800, additional/placement. **Remarks:** Accepts advertising. **Circ:** 3400.

12606 ■ Living with Energy in Iowa
Iowa Association of Electric Cooperatives
8525 Douglas, Ste. 48
Des Moines, IA 50322-2992
Phone: (515)276-5350
Fax: (515)276-7946
Publisher's E-mail: info@iowarec.org
Magazine for members of rural electric cooperatives. **Freq:** Monthly. **Print Method:** Offset. **Trim Size:** 8 1/8 x 10 7/8. **Cols./Page:** 3. **Col. Width:** 14 picas. **Col.**

Circulation: ★ = AAM; △ or • = BPA; ♦ = CAC; ❑ = VAC; ⊕ = PO Statement; ‡ = Publisher's Report; Boldface figures = sworn; Light figures = estimated.

Depth: 133 agate lines. **Key Personnel:** Ann Foster, Director, Communications; Robert Dickelman, Editor. **ISSN:** 0162--2412 (print). **URL:** http://www.livingwithenergyiniowa.com; http://www.iowarec.org/publications/living-with-energy-in-iowa. **Formerly:** Iowa Rural Electric News; Iowa Rural Electric Cooperative News. **Ad Rates:** GLR $.60; BW $967; 4C $1,761; PCI $62. **Remarks:** insurance and alcoholic beverages. **Circ:** Combined ‡80000.

12607 ■ Lupus Now
Lupus Foundation of America Iowa Chapter
3839 Merle Hay Rd., Ste. 222
Des Moines, IA 50310
Phone: (515)279-3048
Free: 888-279-3048
Publisher's E-mail: info@lupusia.org
Magazine containing information about lupus, research, monthly Lupus Foundation of America, Iowa Chapter support group meetings, case histories, and advocacy. **Freq:** 3/year. **Print Method:** Sheetfed offset. **Trim Size:** 8 3/8 x 10 7/8. **ISSN:** 1547-1780 (print). **Subscription Rates:** $25 Individuals; $35 Other countries; $45 Two years; $65 Other countries two years. **URL:** http://www.lupus.org/magazine. **Mailing address:** PO Box 13174, Des Moines, IA 50310. **Circ:** 100000.

12608 ■ My Home My Style
August Home Publishing Co.
2200 Grand Ave.
Des Moines, IA 50312
Phone: (515)875-7000
Free: 800-311-5441
Publisher's E-mail: woodnet@augusthome.com
Magazine covering home design options and style. **Freq:** Bimonthly. **Print Method:** Offset. **Trim Size:** 7 7/8 x 10 3/4. **Cols./Page:** 3. **Col. Width:** 11.9 picas. **Col. Depth:** 57 picas. **Key Personnel:** Kim Downing, Art Director; Don Peschke, Publisher; Dave Stone, Managing Editor. **ISSN:** 0043--8057 (print). **Subscription Rates:** $20 Individuals; C$34 Canada; $34 Other countries. **URL:** http://www.myhomemystyle.com; http://www.augusthome.com/brands/myhomemystyle. **Formerly:** Workbench. **Remarks:** Advertising accepted; rates available upon request. **Circ:** Paid ★353333.

12609 ■ National Pork Report
Pork Publications Inc.
1776 Northwest 114th St.
Des Moines, IA 50306
Phone: (515)223-2600
Fax: (515)223-2646
Publisher's E-mail: info@porkboard.org
Official magazine of the National Pork Producers Council, presenting industry news. **Freq:** 9/year. **Print Method:** Offset. **Trim Size:** 8 1/2 x 10 15/16. **Cols./Page:** 3 and 4. **Key Personnel:** Jan Jorgensen, Editor, phone: (515)223-2644. **URL:** http://www.porkboard.org. **Mailing address:** PO Box 9114, Des Moines, IA 50306. **Ad Rates:** BW $3,895; 4C $4,995; PCI $90. **Remarks:** Accepts advertising. **Circ:** Non-paid ‡109350.

12610 ■ The Saxophone Symposium
North American Saxophone Alliance
Dept. of Music
Drake University
2507 University Ave.
Des Moines, IA 50311-4505
Phone: (515)271-3104
Publisher's E-mail: membership@saxophonealliance.org
Freq: Annual. **Subscription Rates:** $10 Single issue included in membership dues. **URL:** http://www.saxophonealliance.org/publications.asp. **Remarks:** Accepts advertising. **Circ:** (Not Reported).

12611 ■ Sewing Quilting and Embroidery Professional
Vacuum and Sewing Dealers Trade Association
2724 2nd Ave.
Des Moines, IA 50313-4933
Phone: (515)282-9101
Fax: (515)282-4483
Free: 800-367-5651
Publisher's E-mail: mail@vdta.com
Freq: Monthly. **Subscription Rates:** Included in membership. **URL:** http://www.vdta.com/magazines.html. **Formerly:** Sewing and Embroidery Professional. **Remarks:** Advertising not accepted. **Circ:** (Not Reported).

12612 ■ ShopNotes
August Home Publishing Co.
2200 Grand Ave.
Des Moines, IA 50312
Phone: (515)875-7000
Free: 800-311-5441
Publisher's E-mail: woodnet@augusthome.com
Trade magazine covering woodworking. **Freq:** Bimonthly. **Key Personnel:** Bryan Nelson, Editor; Don Peschke, Publisher. **Alt. Formats:** CD-ROM; DVD. **URL:** http://www.shopnotes.com. **Circ:** (Not Reported).

12613 ■ Successful Farming: For Families That Make Farming and Ranching Their Business
Meredith Corp.
1716 Locust St.
Des Moines, IA 50309-3038
Phone: (515)284-3000
Publisher's E-mail: countryhome@meredith.com
Agricultural magazine. **Freq:** Monthly two issues Feb./Mar./Dec., no issue Jun. or Jul. **Print Method:** Offset. **Trim Size:** 8 x 10 1/2. **Cols./Page:** 3. **Col. Width:** 2.5 picas. **Col. Depth:** 140 agate lines. **Key Personnel:** Loren Kruse, Editor-in-Chief; John Walter, Editor. **ISSN:** 0039--4432 (print). **Subscription Rates:** $15.95 U.S. print; $7.95 Individuals online; Free to qualified subscribers. **URL:** http://www.agriculture.com/successful-farming. **Remarks:** Accepts advertising. **Circ:** Paid ‡250,000.

12614 ■ The Times-Delphic
Drake University - Board of Student Communications
2507 University Ave.
Des Moines, IA 50311-4505
Phone: (515)271-2011
Fax: (515)271-2798
Free: 800-443-7253
Collegiate newspaper. **Freq:** Semiweekly (Tues. and Fri.; during the academic year). **Print Method:** Offset. **Trim Size:** 11 x 17. **Cols./Page:** 4. **Col. Width:** 27 nonpareils. **Col. Depth:** 205 agate lines. **Key Personnel:** Jill Van Wyke, Advisor. **URL:** http://www.timesdelphic.com. **Ad Rates:** PCI $7.50. **Remarks:** Advertising accepted; rates available upon request. **Circ:** Free 2700.

12615 ■ Traditional Home
Meredith Corp.
1716 Locust St.
Des Moines, IA 50309-3038
Phone: (515)284-3000
Publication E-mail: traditionalhome@meredith.com
Magazine containing ideas and information on building and decorating homes in the traditional style. **Freq:** 8/year. **Print Method:** Offset. **Trim Size:** 8 x 10 7/8. **Subscription Rates:** $24 Individuals 8 issues. **URL:** http://www.traditionalhome.com; http://www.traditionalhome.com/in-the-magazine. **Ad Rates:** BW $80714; 4C $109316. **Remarks:** Advertising accepted; rates available upon request. **Circ:** Paid ★117,117.

12616 ■ WOOD Magazine
Meredith Corp.
1716 Locust St., LS221
Des Moines, IA 50309-3023
Publisher's E-mail: countryhome@meredith.com
Magazine for people who enjoy woodworking. **Freq:** 7/year. **Print Method:** Web Offset. **Trim Size:** 8 3/8 x 10 7/8. **Key Personnel:** Tom Davis, Publisher, phone: (515)284-2818; Gary Dennis, Advertising Representative, phone: (678)507-0110, fax: (678)507-0118; Lisa Greenwood, Advertising Representative, phone: (312)853-1225. **Subscription Rates:** $29.99 Individuals. **URL:** http://www.woodmagazine.com. **Ad Rates:** BW $49720. **Remarks:** Accepts advertising. **Circ:** ‡463103.

12617 ■ Woodsmith
August Home Publishing Co.
2200 Grand Ave.
Des Moines, IA 50312
Phone: (515)875-7000
Free: 800-311-5441
Publisher's E-mail: woodnet@augusthome.com
Magazine for woodworking hobbyists. **Freq:** Bimonthly. **Print Method:** Web Offset. **Trim Size:** 10 7/8 x 8 3/8. **Key Personnel:** Bryan Nelson, Editor; Donald Peschke, Publisher; Vince Ancona, Managing Editor. **ISSN:** 0164--4114 (print). **Subscription Rates:** $29 U.S.; C$46 Canada; $43 Other countries. **URL:** http://www.woodsmith.com/magazine; http://www.augusthome.com/brands/woodsmith. **Remarks:** Advertising not accepted. **Circ:** Paid 375,000.

Iowa Public Radio - See Carroll

12618 ■ KASI-AM - 1430
2141 Grand Ave.
Des Moines, IA 50312
Format: Talk; News. **Networks:** Fox. **Founded:** 1948. **Operating Hours:** 5:00 a.m. - Midnight Monday - Friday; 6:00 a.m. - Midnight Saturday - Sunday. **Wattage:** 1,000 day; 032 night. **Ad Rates:** Advertising accepted; rates available upon request. Combined advertising rates available with KCCQ-FM. **URL:** http://www.1430kasi.iheart.com.

12619 ■ KAZR-FM - 103.3
1416 Locust St.
Des Moines, IA 50309
Phone: (515)280-1350
Format: Classic Rock. **Ad Rates:** Noncommercial. **URL:** http://www.lazer1033.com.

12620 ■ KCCI-TV - 8
888 9th St.
Des Moines, IA 50309
Phone: (515)247-8888
Format: Commercial TV. **Networks:** CBS. **Owner:** Heartst-Argyle Television Inc., 300 W 57th St., New York, NY 10019-3789, Ph: (212)887-6800, Fax: (212)887-6855. **Founded:** 1955. **Formerly:** KRNT-TV. **Operating Hours:** Continuous. **Key Personnel:** Paul Frederickson, Gen. Mgr.; Dave Busiek, News Dir.; Andy Garman, Sports Dir. **Ad Rates:** Noncommercial. **URL:** http://www.kcci.com.

12621 ■ KCCQ-FM - 105.9
2141 Grand Ave.
Des Moines, IA 50312
Phone: (515)245-8900
Fax: (515)232-1439
Founded: 1968. **Ad Rates:** Noncommercial.

12622 ■ KDFR-FM - 91.3
1350 S Loop Rd., Ste. 130
Alameda, CA 94502
Free: 800-543-1495
Email: info@familyradio.org
Format: Religious. **Owner:** Family Stations Inc., 290 Hegenberger Rd., Oakland, CA 94621, Free: 800-543-1495. **Founded:** 1988. **Operating Hours:** Continuous; 98% network, 2% local. **ADI:** Des Moines, IA. **Wattage:** 32,000. **Ad Rates:** Noncommercial. **URL:** http://www.familyradio.org/iowa.

12623 ■ KDIN-TV - 11
6450 Corporate Dr.
Johnston, IA 50131
Phone: (515)242-3100
Free: 800-532-1290
Email: programming@iptv.org
Format: Public TV. **Networks:** Public Broadcasting Service (PBS). **Owner:** Iowa Public Broadcasting Board, at above address. **Founded:** 1969. **Operating Hours:** 6:30 a.m.-midnight Sat.-Sun.; Continuous Mon.-Fri. **ADI:** Des Moines, IA. **Key Personnel:** Daniel K. Miller, Exec. Dir., Gen. Mgr., dkm@iptv.org; William T. Hayes, Dir. of Engg., hayes@iptv.org. **Mailing address:** PO Box 6450, Johnston, IA 50131. **URL:** http://www.iptv.org.

12624 ■ KDPS-FM - 88.1
1200 Grandview Ave.
Des Moines, IA 50309
Phone: (515)263-2800
Free: 800-444-6083
Format: Eclectic. **Networks:** Independent. **Owner:** Grand View University, 1200 Grandview Ave., Des Moines, IA 50316. **Founded:** 1956. **Operating Hours:** 17 hours Daily. **ADI:** Des Moines, IA. **Wattage:** 5,200 ERP. **Ad Rates:** Noncommercial. **URL:** http://www.grandview.edu.

12625 ■ KDSM-TV - 17
4023 Fleur Dr.
Des Moines, IA 50321
Phone: (515)287-1717
Fax: (515)287-0064
Email: sales@kdsm17.com
Format: Commercial TV. **Networks:** Fox. **Owner:** Sinclair Broadcast Group Inc., 10706 Beaver Dam Rd., Hunt Valley, MD 21030, Ph: (410)568-1500, Fax: (410)568-1533. **Founded:** 1983. **Operating Hours:**

Continuous; 25% network, 75% local. **ADI**: Des Moines, IA. **Key Personnel**: Carolyn Lawrence, Gen. Sales Mgr. **Local Programs**: *Fox 17 Kids Club*, Monday Tuesday Wednesday Thursday Friday. **Ad Rates**: Noncommercial. **URL**: http://www.kdsm17.com.

KDUB-FM - See Dubuque

KDWI-FM - See Ottumwa

KFMG-FM - See Pella

12626 ■ KGVC-LP - 94.1
Grand View University
1200 Grand View Ave.
Des Moines, IA 50316
Phone: (515)263-2810
Fax: (515)263-2974
Format: Eclectic; Eighties; Oldies. **Founded**: 1999. **Operating Hours**: 4 a.m.-4 p.m. weekdays and Sundays. **Key Personnel**: Geoff Conn, Contact, gconn@grandview.edu. **Wattage**: 100. **URL**: http://www.grandview.edu.

12627 ■ KIOA-FM - 93.3
1416 Locust St.
Des Moines, IA 50309
Phone: (515)280-1350
Fax: (515)280-3011
Format: Oldies. **Owner**: Saga Communications of Iowa L.L.C., at above address. **Founded**: 1972. **Formerly**: KMGK-FM. **Operating Hours**: Continuous. **ADI**: Des Moines, IA. **Key Personnel**: Pam Washington, Dir. of Sales. **Wattage**: 100,000. **Ad Rates**: Advertising accepted; rates available upon request. **URL**: http://www.kioa.com.

12628 ■ KJMC-FM - 89.3
1169 25th St.
Des Moines, IA 50311
Phone: (515)279-1811
Email: info@kjmcfm.org
Format: Blues; Gospel; Jazz; Hip Hop. **Owner**: Minority Communications Inc., at above address. **ADI**: Des Moines, IA. **Wattage**: 7,100. **URL**: http://www.kjmcfm.org.

12629 ■ KKDM-FM - 107.5
2141 Grand Ave.
Des Moines, IA 50312
Phone: (515)245-8900
Fax: (515)245-8902
Format: Contemporary Hit Radio (CHR). **Founded**: 1995. **ADI**: Des Moines, IA. **Key Personnel**: Joel Mccrea, Gen. Mgr. **Wattage**: 100,000. **Ad Rates**: Noncommercial. **URL**: http://www.kkdm.com.

12630 ■ KLYF-FM - 106.3
2141 Grand Ave.
Des Moines, IA 50308
Phone: (515)242-3500
Fax: (515)245-8902
Format: Religious; Adult Contemporary. **Networks**: AP. **Founded**: 1948. **Formerly**: KMXD-FM. **Operating Hours**: Continuous. **Wattage**: 100. **Ad Rates**: Advertising accepted; rates available upon request. Combined advertising rates available with WHO-AM, KLYF-FM, KKDM-FM, KXNO-AM. **URL**: http://alt1063.iheart.com/articles/alt-1063-contact-us-468446/contact-info-859142.

12631 ■ KPSZ-AM - 940
1416 Locust St.
Des Moines, IA 50309
Phone: (515)280-1350
Format: Contemporary Christian; Sports. **Owner**: Saga Communications of Iowa, 73 Kercheval Ave., Ste. 201, Grosse Pointe Farms, MI 48236, Ph: (313)886-7070. **Founded**: 1945. **Operating Hours**: Continuous. **Key Personnel**: Geneva Walker, Bus. Mgr.; Jeff Delvaux, Gen. Mgr., jdelvaux@desmoinesradiogroup.com; Pam Washington, Sales Mgr., pwashington@desmoinesradiogroup.com. **URL**: http://www.praise940.com.

12632 ■ KPTL-FM - 106.3
2141 Grand Ave.
Des Moines, IA 50312
Phone: (515)245-8900
Format: Adult Album Alternative. **URL**: http://www.now1051.com.

12633 ■ KRNT-AM - 1350
1416 Locust St.
Des Moines, IA 50309
Phone: (515)280-1350
Format: Adult Contemporary. **Networks**: CBS; Mutual Broadcasting System; Unistar. **Founded**: 1935. **Operating Hours**: Continuous. **ADI**: Des Moines, IA. **Key Personnel**: Jeff Delvaux, Gen. Mgr. **Wattage**: 5,000. **Ad Rates**: Advertising accepted; rates available upon request. **URL**: http://www.sagacom.com.

12634 ■ KSTZ-FM - 102.5
1416 Locust St.
Des Moines, IA 50309
Phone: (515)280-1350
Fax: (515)280-3011
Format: Adult Contemporary. **Owner**: Saga Communications Inc., at above address. **Founded**: 1970. **Formerly**: KRNQ-FM/Q-102. **Operating Hours**: Continuous. **Key Personnel**: Pam Washington, Dir. of Sales; Geneva Walker, Bus. Mgr.; Jeff Delvaux, Gen. Mgr.; Scott Allen, Operations Mgr. **Wattage**: 100,000. **Ad Rates**: Noncommercial. Combined advertising rates available with KIOA; KSTZ; KRNT; KLTI; KAZR. **URL**: http://www.star1025.com.

KSUI-FM - See Iowa City

12635 ■ KTPR-FM - 91.1
2111 Grand Ave., Ste. 100
Des Moines, IA 50312
Phone: (515)725-1700
Free: 800-861-8000
Email: ktpr@duke.iccc.cc.ia.us
Format: Classical; News. **Owner**: Iowa State University, at above address. **Founded**: 1980. **Operating Hours**: Continuous. **Key Personnel**: Katherine Perkins, Dir. of Programs, perkins-k@duke.iccc.cc.ia.us; Bob Wood, Director, wood@duke.iccc.cc.ja.us; John Pemble, Operations Mgr., pemble@duke.iccc.cc.ia.us. **Wattage**: 100,000. **Ad Rates**: Noncommercial. **URL**: http://iowapublicradio.org.

12636 ■ K209EN-FM - 89.7
PO Box 391
Twin Falls, ID 83303
Fax: (208)736-1958
Free: 800-357-4226
Format: Religious; Contemporary Christian. **Owner**: CSN International, PO Box 391, Twin Falls, ID 83303, Ph: (208)736-1958, Fax: (208)736-1958, Free: 800-357-4226. **Key Personnel**: Mike Kestler, Contact; Don Mills, Music Dir., Prog. Dir. **URL**: http://www.csnradio.com.

12637 ■ KUNI-FM - 90.9
2111 Grand Ave., Ste. 100
Des Moines, IA 50312-5393
Format: Public Radio; Eclectic; Ethnic. **Networks**: Public Radio International (PRI); National Public Radio (NPR). **Owner**: University of Northern Iowa, 1227 W 27th St., Cedar Falls, IA 50614, Ph: (319)273-2311. **Founded**: 1960. **Operating Hours**: Continuous; 46% network, 54% local. **Local Programs**: *Under Currents*, Monday Tuesday Wednesday Thursday Friday 12:00 a.m.; *Whad'Ya Know?*, Saturday 12:00 p.m.; *The Splendid Table*, Saturday Sunday 2:00 p.m.; *The Folk Tree*, Sunday 1:00 p.m.; *This American Life*, Saturday Sunday 11:00 a.m. 8:00 p.m.; *Java Blend*, Saturday 2:00 p.m. **Wattage**: 94,000. **Ad Rates**: Noncommercial. **URL**: http://www2.iowapublicradio.org.

12638 ■ KUNY-FM - 91.5
2111 Grand Ave., Ste. 100
Des Moines, IA 50312
Phone: (515)725-1700
Free: 800-772-2440
Email: info@iowapublicradio.org
Format: Public Radio; Eclectic. **Simulcasts**: KUNI-FM. **Networks**: National Public Radio (NPR); Public Radio International (PRI). **Owner**: University of Northern Iowa, 1227 W 27th St., Cedar Falls, IA 50614, Ph: (319)273-2311. **Founded**: 1987. **Operating Hours**: Continuous. **ADI**: Rochester, MN-Mason City, IA-Austin, MN. **Key Personnel**: Al Schares, Music Dir., musicdirector@iowapublicradio.org; Jonathan Ahl, News Dir., jahl@iowapublicradio.org. **Wattage**: 8,000. **Ad Rates**: Noncommercial. **URL**: http://www.iowapublicradio.org.

KUNZ-FM - See Ottumwa

12639 ■ KWKY-AM - 1150
PO Box 838
Des Moines, IA 50304
Format: Talk; Religious. **Networks**: USA Radio. **Founded**: 1948. **Operating Hours**: Continuous. **ADI**: Des Moines, IA. **Wattage**: 1,000. **Ad Rates**: $7.50-15.50 for 30 seconds; $11.50-20 for 60 seconds. **URL**: http://www.iowacatholicradio.com.

12640 ■ KXNO-AM - 1460
2141 Grand Ave.
Des Moines, IA 50312
Phone: (515)245-8900
Fax: (515)245-8902
Format: Sports. **Networks**: Fox. **Founded**: 1961. **Operating Hours**: Continuous. **Key Personnel**: Joel McCrea, Gen. Mgr. **Wattage**: 5,000. **Ad Rates**: Noncommercial. **URL**: http://www.kxno.com//main.html.

12641 ■ Mediacom
2205 Ingersoll Ave.
Des Moines, IA 50312
Founded: 1974. **Formerly**: TCI. **Cities Served**: Polk and Warren Counties. **URL**: http://mediacomcable.com.

12642 ■ Radio Iowa
2700 Grand Ave., Ste. 103
Des Moines, IA 50312
Phone: (515)282-1984
Fax: (515)282-1879
Email: info@radioiowa.com
Radio station that broadcast business and economy news, music, sports and entertainment shows. **Format**: Sports. **Owner**: Learfield Communications Inc., 505 Hobbs Rd., Jefferson City, MO 65109-5788, Ph: (573)893-7200, Fax: (573)893-2321. **Founded**: 1984. **Key Personnel**: Steve Mays, Contact. **Ad Rates**: Advertising accepted; rates available upon request. **URL**: http://www.radioiowa.com.

12643 ■ TCI of Council Bluffs
500 E Court Ave.
Des Moines, IA 50309
Phone: (712)328-7207
Fax: (712)323-0754
Founded: 1975. **Formerly**: American Heritage Cablevision. **Key Personnel**: Steven K. Johnson, Contact; Lynette Langer Keagle, Contact. **Cities Served**: 1 community access channel. **URL**: http://sos.iowa.gov/search/business/(S(x1c5du55ku0540ykgxuyi3z5))/summary.aspx?c=iw7-4brz5ILaKn8UOs6el8wNQkUA9JEcU6oYkfuYhKo1.

12644 ■ WSUI-AM - 910
2111 Grand Ave., Ste. 100
Des Moines, IA 50312
Phone: (515)725-1700
Free: 800-861-8000
Email: info@iowapublicradio.org
Format: Public Radio; Information; News. **Networks**: National Public Radio (NPR). **Owner**: University of Iowa, Iowa City, IA 52242, Ph: (319)335-3500, Fax: (319)335-2535. **Founded**: 1919. **Operating Hours**: Continuous; 70% network, 30% local. **Key Personnel**: Al Schares, Music Dir.; Jonathan Ahl, News Dir. **Wattage**: 5,000. **Ad Rates**: Noncommercial. **URL**: http://www.iowapublicradio.org.

DUBUQUE

E IA. Dubuque Co. On Mississippi River, 183 mi. NW of Chicago, IL. Bridges to East Dubuque, IL, and Wisconsin. University of Dubuque, Clarke College, Loras College, Wartburg Seminary (Lutheran), Univ. of Dubuque Seminary. Lead and zinc mines. Manufactures sashes and doors, pumps, farm implements, kitchen cabinets, metal products, processed meats, clothing, beer, furniture, batteries, snow plows, pipes, boilers, caskets, disinfectants, biscuits, plumbing, magnetic stirrers, plastics. Boat yards; packing plants; foundries. Boilers.

12645 ■ Clarke Courier
Clarke College
1550 Clarke Dr.
Dubuque, IA 52001-3198
Phone: (563)588-6300
Free: 888-825-2753
Collegiate newspaper. **Freq**: Weekly (Fri.). **Print**

Circulation: ★ = AAM; △ or • = BPA; ♦ = CAC; ❑ = VAC; ⊕ = PO Statement; ‡ = Publisher's Report; Boldface figures = sworn; Light figures = estimated.

Method: Offset. **Trim Size:** 11 x 17. **Cols./Page:** 4. **Col. Width:** 28 nonpareils. **Col. Depth:** 216 agate lines. **Key Personnel:** Tyler Oehmen, Editor; Brenden West, Editor; Molli Finn, Manager, Advertising, Manager, Public Relations. **Subscription Rates:** Free. **Alt. Formats:** PDF. **URL:** http://clarke.edu/page.aspx?id=1976. **Ad Rates:** GLR $5. **Remarks:** Accepts advertising. **Circ:** Free 1,000.

12646 ■ The Dubuque Advertiser
The Dubuque Advertiser Inc.
2966 John F. Kennedy Rd.
Dubuque, IA 52002
Phone: (563)588-0162
Fax: (563)582-0335
Publication E-mail: dbqadvertiser@dbqadvertiser.com
Community shopping guide (tabloid). **Freq:** Weekly. **Print Method:** Offset. **Trim Size:** 8 1/2 x 11 1/2. **Cols./Page:** 6. **Col. Width:** 10 picas. **Col. Depth:** 16 inches. **Key Personnel:** Greg Birkett, General Manager; Randy Aird, Owner, Publisher; Lisa Aird, Owner, Publisher. **Subscription Rates:** Free. **Ad Rates:** BW $768; 4C $270; PCI $12.25. **Remarks:** Accepts advertising. **Circ:** 36000.

12647 ■ The Dubuque Area Magazine
Julien's Journal
700 Locust, Ste. 850
Dubuque, IA 52004-0801
Phone: (563)557-1914
Publisher's E-mail: juliensjournal@juliensjournal.com
Community and regional monthly thematic feature magazine. **Freq:** Monthly. **Mailing address:** PO Box 801, Dubuque, IA 52004-0801. **Remarks:** Advertising accepted; rates available upon request. **Circ:** Combined ‡40000.

12648 ■ Great Dane Shopping News
Woodward Communications Inc.
801 Bluff St.
Dubuque, IA 52001-4661
Fax: (563)588-5739
Free: 800-553-4801
Suburban community shopper (tabloid). **Freq:** Weekly (Mon.). **Print Method:** Offset. **Trim Size:** 11 1/2 x 17.5. **Cols./Page:** 6. **Col. Width:** 1.5 picas. **Col. Depth:** 16 inches. **Key Personnel:** Lee Borkowski, General Manager. **URL:** http://www.wcinet.com/wci-products/community-media. **Mailing address:** PO Box 688, Dubuque, IA 52004-0688. **Ad Rates:** BW $615; SAU $8.80. **Remarks:** Accepts advertising. **Circ:** Free ♦28050.

12649 ■ Stovall Journal
Stovall Family Association
c/o Tom Stovall, Treasurer
3345 Tibey Ct.
Dubuque, IA 52002-2849
Phone: (563)581-7220
Journal containing association news and materials of genealogical, historical and biographical interest concerning Stovall's and descendants. **Freq:** Quarterly February, May, August and November. **Subscription Rates:** Included in membership. **URL:** http://stovall.org/?page_id=20. **Circ:** (Not Reported).

12650 ■ Telegraph Herald
Woodward Communications Inc.
801 Bluff St.
Dubuque, IA 52001-4661
Fax: (563)588-5739
Free: 800-553-4801
Publication E-mail: thonline@wcinet.com
General newspaper. **Founded:** 1836. **Freq:** Daily (morn.). **Print Method:** Offset. **Trim Size:** 14 1/2 x 22 1/4. **Cols./Page:** 6. **Col. Width:** 12 3/10 picas. **Col. Depth:** 21 3/4 inches. **Key Personnel:** Cresco Shopper, General Manager, phone: (563)588-5754; Brian Cooper, Executive Editor, phone: (563)588-5662; Amy Gilligan, Managing Editor, phone: (563)588-3823. **Subscription Rates:** $19.99 Individuals per month, daily motor route delivery; $10 Individuals online /month; $18.99 Individuals per month, daily carrier delivery; $8.99 Individuals per month, Sunday only daily carrier delivery. **URL:** http://www.thonline.com. **Mailing address:** PO Box 688, Dubuque, IA 52004-0688. **Ad Rates:** GLR $3.80; BW $3,933; 4C $4,408; PCI $30.14. **Remarks:** Accepts advertising. **Circ:** (Not Reported).

12651 ■ The Witness: Archdiocese of Dubuque
Witness Publishing Co.
PO Box 917
Dubuque, IA 52004-0917
Phone: (563)588-0556
Fax: (536)588-0557
Publisher's E-mail: dbqcwo@arch.pvt.k12.ia.us
Catholic newspaper. **Freq:** Weekly (Sun.) 48/yr. **Print Method:** Offset. **Trim Size:** 21 1/2 x 13 1/16. **Cols./Page:** 8. **Col. Width:** 20 nonpareils. **Col. Depth:** 301 agate lines. **Key Personnel:** Sr. Carol Hoverman, Editor; Arch. Jerome Hanus, Publisher. **ISSN:** 0745--0427 (print). **Subscription Rates:** $25 Individuals; $27 Out of area. **URL:** http://www.dbqarch.org/offices/witness. **Remarks:** Advertising accepted; rates available upon request. **Circ:** Paid ‡18,880, Free 100.

12652 ■ KATF-FM - 92.9
346 8th St.
Dubuque, IA 52001
Format: Alternative/New Music/Progressive. **Owner:** Radio Dubuque, Inc., at above address, New York, NY. **Operating Hours**: Continuous. **ADI**: Cedar Rapids-Waterloo-Dubuque, IA. **Key Personnel:** Mike Callaghan, Contact. **Wattage**: 89,700. **Ad Rates:** Advertising accepted; rates available upon request. **Mailing address:** PO Box 659, Dubuque, IA 52004. **URL:** http://www.katfm.com.

12653 ■ KATW-FM - 92.9
346 8th St.
Dubuque, IA 52001
Phone: (208)743-6564
Format: Adult Contemporary. **Networks:** AP. **Founded:** 1985. **Operating Hours**: Continuous; 10% network, 90% local. **ADI**: Spokane, WA. **Wattage**: 100,000. **Ad Rates:** $20-25 per unit. KCLK-FM, KCLK-AM, KVAB-FM.

12654 ■ KDTH-AM - 1370
346 W 8th St.
Dubuque, IA 52004-0659
Phone: (563)690-0800
Fax: (563)690-0858
Email: kdth@kdth.com
Format: Talk; News; Sports. **Networks:** CBS. **Owner:** Radio Dubuque, Inc., at above address, New York, NY. **Founded:** May 04, 1941. **Operating Hours:** Continuous; 100% local. **ADI:** Cedar Rapids-Waterloo-Dubuque, IA. **Key Personnel:** Michael Kaye, Dir. of Programs. **Wattage**: 5,000. **Ad Rates:** Advertising accepted; rates available upon request. **Mailing address:** PO Box 659, Dubuque, IA 52004-0659. **URL:** http://www.kdth.radiodubuque.com.

12655 ■ KDUB-FM - 89.7
2111 Grand Ave., Ste. 100
Des Moines, IA 50312
Free: 800-861-8000
Email: info@iowapublicradio.org
Format: Public Radio. **Owner:** Iowa Public Radio, 2111 Grand Ave., Ste. 100, Des Moines, IA 50312-5393, Ph: (515)725-1700, Free: 800-861-8000. **Key Personnel:** Al Schares, Music Dir., aschares@iowapublicradio.org; Katherine Perkins, Dir. of Programs, kperkins@iowapublicradio.org; Dave Knippel, Chief Engineer, dknippel@iowapublicradio.org. **URL:** http://iowapublicradio.org.

12656 ■ KGRR-FM
1055 University Ave.
Dubuque, IA 52001
Format: Classic Rock. **Wattage**: 25,000 ERP. **Ad Rates:** Advertising accepted; rates available upon request.

12657 ■ KIAD-FM - 88.5
PO Box 3206
Tupelo, MS 38803
Owner: American Family Radio, at above address. **Wattage**: 750 ERP. **URL:** http://www.afr.net/newafr/default.asp.

12658 ■ KLYV-FM - 105.3
5490 Saratoga Rd.
Dubuque, IA 52002
Phone: (563)557-1040
Format: Contemporary Hit Radio (CHR). **Networks:** ABC. **Owner:** Cumulus Media Inc., 3280 Peachtree Rd. NW, Ste. 2300, Atlanta, GA 30305-2455, Ph: (404)949-0700, Fax: (404)949-0740. **Founded:** 1997. **Operating Hours**: Continuous. **ADI**: Cedar Rapids-Waterloo-Dubuque, IA. **Key Personnel:** Chris Farber, Contact; Jeff Robb, Contact. **Wattage**: 50,000. **Ad Rates:** Noncommercial. **URL:** http://www.y105music.com.

12659 ■ KXGE-FM - 102.3
301 Bell Street Dubuque
Dubuque, IA 52002
Phone: (563)557-1040
Fax: (563)583-4535
Format: Classic Rock. **Owner:** Cumulus Broadcasting Inc., 3280 Peachtree Rd. NW, Ste. 2300, Atlanta, GA 30305-2447, Ph: (404)949-0700, Fax: (404)949-0740. **ADI:** Cedar Rapids-Waterloo-Dubuque, IA. **Ad Rates:** Advertising accepted; rates available upon request. **URL:** http://www.eagle102rocks.com.

12660 ■ WDBQ-AM - 1490
5490 Saratoga Rd.
Dubuque, IA 52002-2593
Phone: (563)557-1040
Format: News; Talk. **Networks:** ABC. **Owner:** Cumulus Media Inc., 3280 Peachtree Rd. NW, Ste. 2300, Atlanta, GA 30305-2455, Ph: (404)949-0700, Fax: (404)949-0740. **Founded:** 1997. **Operating Hours**: Continuous. **ADI**: Cedar Rapids-Waterloo-Dubuque, IA. **Wattage**: 1,000. **Ad Rates:** Noncommercial. **URL:** http://wdbqam.com/shows.

12661 ■ WDBQ-FM - 107.5
5490 Saratoga Rd.
Dubuque, IA 52002
Format: Oldies. **Owner:** Cumulus Broadcasting Inc., 3280 Peachtree Rd. NW, Ste. 2300, Atlanta, GA 30305-2447, Ph: (404)949-0700, Fax: (404)949-0740. **Founded:** 1998. **ADI:** Cedar Rapids-Waterloo-Dubuque, IA. **Wattage**: 6,000 ERP. **Ad Rates:** $15-25 for 60 seconds.

DUMONT

12662 ■ Dumont Telephone Co.
506 Pine St.
Dumont, IA 50625-0349
Phone: (641)857-3211
Fax: (641)857-3300
Free: 800-328-6543
Email: dumontel@netins.net
Founded: 1902. **Cities Served:** Allison, Bristow, Geneva, Iowa: subscribing households 425; United States; 33 channels; 1 community access channel. **Mailing address:** PO Box 349, Dumont, IA 50625-0349. **URL:** http://www.dumonttelephone.com.

DUNLAP

W IA. Harrison Co. 18 mi. NE of Logan. Residential.

12663 ■ The Dunlap Reporter
Dunlap Reporter
114 Iowa Ave.
Dunlap, IA 51529
Phone: (712)643-5380
Fax: (712)643-2173
Newspaper. **Freq:** Weekly (Thurs.). **Print Method:** Offset. **Trim Size:** 16 x 22. **Cols./Page:** 8. **Col. Width:** 20 nonpareils. **Col. Depth:** 294 agate lines. **Key Personnel:** Charles Walker, Editor; Agnes Morris, Manager, Advertising; Dianne Walker, Manager, Publisher. **Subscription Rates:** $32 Individuals Print & Online - 12 months; $39.50 Out of area Print & Online - 12 months; $42.50 Out of country Print & Online - 12 months ; $29.25 Individuals online - 12 months. **URL:** http://www.dunlapiowa.com. **Ad Rates:** SAU $2.95; PCI $3.65. **Remarks:** Advertising accepted; rates available upon request. **Circ:** ‡1,400.

DYERSVILLE

E IA. Dubuque Co. 26 mi. W. of Dubuque. Manufactures scale model farm toys, folding doors and partitions, modular homes. Ships livestock, corn, oats, dairy products.

12664 ■ Dyersville Commercial
Woodward Communications Inc.
223 1st Ave. E,
Dyersville, IA 52040-0350
Phone: (563)875-7131
Fax: (563)875-2279
Free: 800-658-3406
Community newspaper. **Freq:** Weekly (Wed.). **Print Method:** Offset. **Trim Size:** 21 1/2. **Cols./Page:** 6. **Col.**

Width: 13 picas. **Col. Depth:** 21 inches. **Key Personnel:** Mary Ungs-Sogaard, Publisher. **USPS:** 163-300. **URL:** http://dyersvillecommercial.com. **Mailing address:** P.O Box 350, Dyersville, IA 52040. **Ad Rates:** PCI $5. 75. **Remarks:** Accepts advertising. **Circ:** Combined 4,300.

12665 ■ Eastern Iowa Shopping News
Woodward Communications Inc.
223 1st Ave. E
Dyersville, IA 52040
Phone: (563)875-7131
Fax: (563)875-2279
Free: 800-658-3406
Publication E-mail: blutgen@wcinet.com
Shopping guide. **Freq:** Weekly (Tues.). **Print Method:** Offset. **Trim Size:** 16 3/4. **Key Personnel:** Mary Ungs-Sogaard, General Manager; Denise Brady, Sales Representative. **Subscription Rates:** Free. **URL:** http://www.easterniowashoppingnews.com; http://www.wcinet.com/wci-products/community-media. **Mailing address:** PO Box 350, Dyersville, IA 52040. **Ad Rates:** PCI $9. **Remarks:** Accepts advertising. **Circ:** 19500.

12666 ■ KDST-FM - 99.3
1931 20th Ave. SE
Dyersville, IA 52040
Phone: (319)875-8193
Email: news@kdstradio.com
Format: Country. **Networks:** Satellite Music Network; ABC. **Owner:** Design Homes of Chippewa Falls, 2054 125th St., Chippewa Falls, WI 54729, Ph: (715)726-9619. **Founded:** 1988. **Formerly:** KDMC-FM. **Operating Hours:** Continuous. **Key Personnel:** Doug Langston, Operations Mgr. **Wattage:** 3,000. **Ad Rates:** $11.50-15 for 30 seconds; $15.50-19 for 60 seconds. Combined advertising rates available with KCTN-FM, KADR-AM. **URL:** http://www.kdstradio.com/index.html.

DYSART

EC IA. Tama Co. 24 mi. So. of Waterloo. City Park. Fairgrounds. Agriculture. Corn, soybeans. Hogs, cattle, sheep.

12667 ■ The Dysart Reporter
The Dysart Reporter
317 Main St.
Dysart, IA 52224
Phone: (319)476-3550
Fax: (319)478-2813
Community newspaper. **Freq:** Weekly (Thurs.). **Print Method:** Offset. **Cols./Page:** 6. **Col. Width:** 2 inches. **Col. Depth:** 301 agate lines. **Key Personnel:** Jason Staker, Editor; Amy Jantzen, Managing Editor. **USPS:** 633-40. **Subscription Rates:** $11.25 Individuals Mail delivery ; $12 Out of area Mail delivery ; $12.50 Out of state Mail delivery. **URL:** http://dysartreporter.com. **Mailing address:** PO Box 70, Dysart, IA 52224. **Ad Rates:** BW $378.40; 4C $498.40; SAU $7.14; PCI $3.60. **Remarks:** Accepts advertising. **Circ:** ‡900.

EAGLE GROVE

NC IA. Wright Co. 28 mi. NE of Fort Dodge. Maufactures textiles, soybean oil, meal, fertilizer; poultry and livestock remedies. Trucking. Ships hogs. Stock, dairy, poultry, grain farms.

12668 ■ Eagle Grove Eagle
Eagle Grove Eagle
314 W Broadway
Eagle Grove, IA 50533-1712
Phone: (515)448-4745
Fax: (515)448-3182
Publisher's E-mail: egeagle@goldfieldaccess.net
Community newspaper. **Freq:** Weekly (Wed.). **Print Method:** Offset. **Cols./Page:** 6. **Col. Width:** 26 nonpareils. **Col. Depth:** 301 agate lines. **Key Personnel:** Kim Demory, Editor, Manager; Leigh Banwell, Manager, Advertising, Publisher. **Subscription Rates:** $47 Individuals /year, print and online; $93 Two years print and online. **URL:** http://theeaglegroveeagle.com. **Mailing address:** PO Box 6, Eagle Grove, IA 50533-1712. **Ad Rates:** GLR $.44; BW $743; SAU $5.90. **Remarks:** Accepts advertising. **Circ:** ‡2500.

12669 ■ KJYL-FM - 100.7
PO Box 325
Eagle Grove, IA 50533
Phone: (515)448-4588
Fax: (515)448-5267
Free: 800-450-7729
Email: kjyl@kjyl.org
Format: Religious; Contemporary Christian. **Operating Hours:** Continuous. **Key Personnel:** Matt Dorfner, Exec. Dir., matt@newmail.kinshipradio.org; Jay Rudolph, News Dir. **Ad Rates:** Noncommercial. **URL:** http://www.kjyl.org.

EDDYVILLE

12670 ■ KKSI-FM - 101.5
416 E Main
Ottumwa, IA 52501
Phone: (641)684-5563
Fax: (641)684-5832
Free: 800-794-6869
Email: info@ottumwaradio.com
Format: Classic Rock. **Networks:** Jones Satellite. **Owner:** O-Town Communications Inc., 416 E Main St., Ottumwa, IA 52501. **Founded:** 1990. **Operating Hours:** Continuous. **Key Personnel:** Greg H. List, President. **Wattage:** 49,000. **Ad Rates:** $18 for 30 seconds; $27 for 60 seconds. Combined advertising rates available with KRKN-FM. **URL:** http://www.kissclassicrock.com.

ELDRIDGE

E IA. Scott Co. 10 mi. N. of Davenport. Suburban. Agricultural.

12671 ■ The North Scott Press
The North Scott Press
214 N Second St.
Eldridge, IA 52748
Phone: (563)285-8111
Community newspaper. **Freq:** Weekly (Wed.). **Print Method:** Offset. **Cols./Page:** 4. **Col. Width:** 15 picas. **Col. Depth:** 16 inches. **USPS:** 598-420. **Subscription Rates:** $52 Individuals. **Mailing address:** PO Box 200, Eldridge, IA 52748. **Remarks:** Accepts display and classified advertising. **Circ:** (Not Reported).

ELGIN

NE IA. Fayette Co. 60 mi. NE of Waterloo. Medical clinic, ethyl alcohol plant. Veterinarian clinic. Feed mill. Agriculture. Hogs, cattle, poultry.

12672 ■ Fayette Leader
Fayette Leader
227 Center St.
Elgin, IA 52141-9335
Community newspaper. **Freq:** Weekly (Wed.). **Print Method:** Offset. **Cols./Page:** 4. **Col. Width:** 14 picas. **Col. Depth:** 15 inches. **Key Personnel:** LeAnn Larson, Publisher. **URL:** http://www.thefayettecountyunion.com/content/fayette-leader-0. **Ad Rates:** PCI $3.09. **Remarks:** Accepts advertising. **Circ:** ‡2000.

ELK HORN

W IA. Shelby Co. 48 mi. NE of Council Bluffs. Agriculture. Corn, oats, alfalfa.

12673 ■ Marne & Elk Horn Telephone Co.
4242 Main St.
Elk Horn, IA 51531
Phone: (712)764-6161
Fax: (712)764-2773
Free: 888-764-6141
Email: metc@metc.net
Founded: 1903. **Key Personnel:** Janell J. Hansen, Gen. Mgr.; Jill Madsen, Office Mgr., jill@metc.net; Janice Greve, Contact, janice@mets.net. **Cities Served:** Atlantic, Audubon, Brayton, Exira, Kimballton, Marne, Iowa; United States; 60 channels. **Mailing address:** PO Box 120, Elk Horn, IA 51531. **URL:** http://www.metc.net.

ELKADER

NE IA. Clayton Co. 45 mi. NW of Dubuque. Cabinet, wire display, sash and door factories; saw and feed mills. Ships livestock. Agriculture. Dairy, hogs, cattle.

12674 ■ The Clayton County Register
Griffith Press Inc.
PO Box 130
Elkader, IA 52043
Phone: (563)245-1311
Newspaper with a Republican orientation. **Freq:** Weekly (Wed.). **Print Method:** Offset. **Trim Size:** 11 1/4 x 16. **Cols./Page:** 4. **Col. Width:** 30 nonpareils. **Col. Depth:** 210 agate lines. **Key Personnel:** Duane Winn, Editor; Pam Reinig, Manager, Advertising; Dana Richard, Office Manager. **Subscription Rates:** $35 Individuals e-edition - 1 year; $38 Individuals print - 1 year in area; $50 Individuals print - 1 year out of area; $21.50 Individuals print - 6 months in area; $27 Individuals print - 6 months out of area. **Remarks:** Accepts advertising. **Circ:** (Not Reported).

12675 ■ Alpine Communications L.C.
923 Humphrey St.
Elkader, IA 52043
Phone: (563)245-4000
Free: 800-635-1059
Key Personnel: Chris Hopp, Gen. Mgr.; Sara Hertrampf, Mktg. & Sales Mgr.; Margaret Corlett, Mgr. of Fin.; Lori Keppler, Cust. Srv. Mgr.; Dirk Buckman, Operations Mgr. **Cities Served:** 30 channels. **URL:** http://www.alpinecom.net.

12676 ■ KADR-AM - 1400
PO Box 239
Prairie du Chien, WI 53821
Phone: (563)245-1400
Format: Adult Contemporary. **Networks:** Satellite Music Network. **Founded:** 1983. **Operating Hours:** 12 hours Daily; 80% network, 20% local. **Wattage:** 1,000. **Ad Rates:** Noncommercial.

12677 ■ KCTN-FM - 100.1
PO Box 990
Elkader, IA 52043
Phone: (563)245-1400
Fax: (563)245-1402
Free: 888-245-KCTN
Email: kctn@alpinecom.net
Format: Country. **Networks:** Satellite Music Network. **Operating Hours:** Continuous; 95% network, 5% local. **Wattage:** 6,000. **Ad Rates:** $9-14 for 30 seconds; $13-18 for 60 seconds. **URL:** http://kctn.com.

EMMETSBURG

NW IA. Palo Alto Co. On Five Island Lake, 50 mi. NW of Fort Dodge. Iowa Lakes Community College. Lake resort. Manufactures dura-lifts, transmitters. Printing and publishing; Feed mill; rendering works. Seed house. Mill-working.

12678 ■ Emmetsburg Democrat
Emmetsburg Publishing Co.
PO Box 73
Emmetsburg, IA 50536-0073
Phone: (712)852-2323
Community newspaper. **Freq:** Weekly (Thurs.). **Print Method:** Offset web. **Trim Size:** 7 x 11 1/2. **Cols./Page:** 6. **Col. Width:** 12 1/2 picas. **Col. Depth:** 21 1/2 inches. **Key Personnel:** Jane Whitmore, Editor; Dan McCain, General Manager. **Subscription Rates:** $19 By mail inside Palo Alto County; $21 By mail outside Palo Alto County. **Remarks:** Advertising accepted; rates available upon request. **Circ:** (Not Reported).

12679 ■ Emmetsburg Reporter
Emmetsburg Publishing Co.
PO Box 73
Emmetsburg, IA 50536-0073
Phone: (712)852-2323
Community newspaper. **Freq:** Weekly (Tues.). **Print Method:** Offset. **Cols./Page:** 6. **Col. Width:** 12 1/2 picas. **Col. Depth:** 21 1/2 inches. **Key Personnel:** Jane Whitmore, Editor; Dan McCain, General Manager; Linda Hill, Contact. **Subscription Rates:** $19 By mail inside Palo Alto County; $21 By mail outside Palo Alto County. **Remarks:** Advertising accepted; rates available upon request. **Circ:** (Not Reported).

ESTHERVILLE

12680 ■ KILR-AM - 1070
PO Box 453
Estherville, IA 51334
Phone: (712)362-2644
Fax: (712)362-5951
Format: News; Talk. **Networks:** ABC. **Owner:** Jacobson Broadcasting Co., Inc., at above address. **Founded:** 1967. **Operating Hours:** Continuous; 80% network,

Circulation: • = AAM; △ or • = BPA; ♦ = CAC; ❑ = VAC; ⊕ = PO Statement; ‡ = Publisher's Report; Boldface figures = sworn; Light figures = estimated.

20% local. **Key Personnel:** Roger Jacobson, Station Mgr.; Ed Funston, News Dir. **Ad Rates:** Noncommercial. Combined advertising rates available with KILR-FM.

12681 ■ KILR-FM - 95.9
PO Box 453
Estherville, IA 51334
Phone: (712)362-2644
Fax: (712)362-5951
Format: Country. **Networks:** ABC. **Owner:** Jacobson Broadcasting Co., Inc., at above address. **Founded:** 1969. **Operating Hours:** Continuous. **Wattage:** 25,000. **Ad Rates:** $12.50-18.50 for 30 seconds; $14.50-28.50 for 60 seconds. Combined advertising rates available with KILR-AM. **URL:** http://www.kilrradio.com.

EVERLY

NW IA. Clay Co. 9 mi. W. of Spencer. Feed milling.

12682 ■ United Farmers Telephone Co.
216 N Main St.
Everly, IA 51338
Phone: (712)834-2211
Fax: (712)834-2214
Free: 800-864-6043
Founded: 1905. **Cities Served:** United States; 40 channels. **Mailing address:** PO Box 270, Everly, IA 51338. **URL:** http://www.evertek.net.

FAIRFIELD

SE IA. Jefferson Co. 23 mi. E. of Ottumwa. Maharishi International University. Manufactures cranes, washing machines, gloves, aluminum castings, textile, plastic, concrete, automotive, dairy products, feed. Foundries.

12683 ■ The Fairfield Ledger
The Fairfield Ledger
12 E Broadway
Box 171
Fairfield, IA 52556
Phone: (641)472-4129
Local newspaper. **Freq:** Daily (eve.). **Print Method:** Offset. **Trim Size:** 14 x 22 3/4. **Cols./Page:** 6. **Col. Width:** 2 inches. **Col. Depth:** 21.5 inches. **Key Personnel:** Jeff Wilson, Publisher; Gene Luedtke, Manager, Advertising; Vickie Tillis, Editor. **USPS:** 184-200. **Subscription Rates:** $141.25 Individuals carrier; $124.25 Individuals in county; $167.50 Individuals in-state mail delivery; $197.25 Individuals out-of-state mail delivery. **Mailing address:** PO Box 171, Fairfield, IA 52556. **Remarks:** Accepts advertising. **Circ:** (Not Reported).

12684 ■ iPhone Life
Thaddeus Computing Inc.
110 N Court St.
Fairfield, IA 52556
Phone: (641)472-6330
Fax: (641)472-1879
Publisher's E-mail: info@smartphonemag.com
Magazine for iPhone and iPod touch users. **Freq:** Quarterly. **Key Personnel:** Rich Hall, Managing Editor; Hal Goldstein, Editor, Publisher; David Averbach, Chief Executive Officer; Marge Enright, Contact. **Subscription Rates:** $15.97 Individuals print + digital; $24.97 print + digital. **URL:** http://www.iphonelife.com. **Circ:** 40000.

12685 ■ KHOE-FM - 90.5
1000 N 4TH St.
Fairfield, IA 52557
Format: World Beat; Classical; Educational. **Owner:** Fairfield Educational Radio Station, MUM Box 1017, Fairfield, IA 52557, Ph: (641)469-5463. **Founded:** 1994. **Operating Hours:** Continuous. **Wattage:** 100. **Ad Rates:** $5 per unit. **Mailing address:** PO Box 1017, fairfield, IA 52557. **URL:** http://www.khoe.org/supportus.html.

12686 ■ KMCD-AM - 1570
57 S Court St.
Fairfield, IA 52556-3213
Phone: (641)472-4191
Fax: (641)472-2071
Format: News; Talk. **Networks:** ABC. **Founded:** 1958. **Operating Hours:** Continuous. **Key Personnel:** Steven Smith, Contact, ssmith@fairfieldiowaradio.com. **Local Programs:** *Spotlight*, Monday Tuesday Wednesday Thursday Friday 8:35 a.m. **Wattage:** 250 Day; 109 Night. **Ad Rates:** $6.25-8 for 30 seconds; $8.25-10 for 60 seconds. $6.25-$8 for 30 seconds; $8.25-$10 for 60 seconds. Combined advertising rates available with KIIK-FM. **Mailing address:** PO Box 648, Fairfield, IA 52556-3213. **URL:** http://www.exploreseiowa.com.

FAYETTE

NE IA. Fayette Co. 35 mi. NE of Waterloo. Upper Iowa College. Creamery; feed mill; hatchery. Dairy, poultry farms.

12687 ■ Collegian
Upper Iowa University
605 Washington St.
Fayette, IA 52142
Phone: (563)425-5200
Free: 800-553-4150
Publisher's E-mail: info@uiu.edu
Collegiate newspaper. **Founded:** 1883. **Freq:** Weekly. **Print Method:** Offset. **Cols./Page:** 4. **Col. Width:** 24 nonpareils. **Col. Depth:** 210 agate lines. **Subscription Rates:** $10 Individuals. **URL:** http://www.uiu.edu/. **Mailing address:** PO Box 1857, Fayette, IA 52142. **Ad Rates:** GLR $2; PCI $5. **Remarks:** Accepts advertising. **Circ:** 750.

FONTANELLE

SW IA. Adair Co. 50 mi. SW of Des Moines. Residential.

12688 ■ Fontanelle Observer
Fontanelle Observer
313 5th St.
Fontanelle, IA 50846
Phone: (641)745-3161
Fax: (641)745-1201
Publication E-mail: observer1@iowatelecom.net
Community newspaper. **Freq:** Weekly (Wed.). **Print Method:** Offset. **Cols./Page:** 7. **Key Personnel:** Terry Holub, Editor, Manager, Advertising, Publisher. **Mailing address:** PO Box 248, Fontanelle, IA 50846-0248. **Remarks:** Accepts advertising. **Circ:** (Not Reported).

FOREST CITY

N IA. Winnebago Co. 34 mi. NW of Mason City. Manufactures recreational vehicles, motor homes, travel trailers, concrete, pesticides, sporting goods, upholstery filling, fertilizer. Agriculture. Dairying, livestock.

12689 ■ The Britt News-Tribune
Forest City Publishing Co.
105 S Clark St.
Forest City, IA 50436
Phone: (641)585-2112
Fax: (641)585-4442
Publisher's E-mail: email@newsletter.globegazette.com
Local newspaper. **Freq:** Weekly (Wed.). **Print Method:** Offset. **Cols./Page:** 6. **Col. Width:** 2 1/8 inches. **Col. Depth:** 294 agate lines. **Key Personnel:** Dave Stanley, Publisher; Angie Johannsen, Editor. **URL:** http://globegazette.com/brittnewstribune. **Ad Rates:** PCI $3.60. **Remarks:** Accepts advertising. **Circ:** ‡2000.

12690 ■ Forest City Summit
Forest City Publishing Co.
105 S Clark St.
Forest City, IA 50436
Phone: (641)585-2112
Fax: (641)585-4442
Publisher's E-mail: email@newsletter.globegazette.com
Community newspaper. **Freq:** Weekly (Wed.). **Print Method:** Offset. **Trim Size:** 14 x 22 3/4. **Cols./Page:** 6. **Col. Width:** 2 1/16 inches. **Col. Depth:** 21 1/2 inches. **Remarks:** Accepts advertising. **Circ:** (Not Reported).

12691 ■ KIOW-FM - 107.3
18643 360th St.
Forest City, IA 50436
Phone: (641)585-1073
Fax: (641)585-2990
Free: 877-606-5870
Email: kiow@kiow.com
Format: Contemporary Hit Radio (CHR); Sports; News. **Networks:** CNN Radio. **Owner:** Pilot Knob Broadcasting, Inc., at above address. **Founded:** 1978. **Operating Hours:** Continuous; 2% network, 98% local. **ADI:** Rochester, MN-Mason City, IA-Austin, MN. **Wattage:** 25,000. **Ad Rates:** $9-12.53 for 30 seconds; $12.76-17.12 for 60 seconds. **Mailing address:** PO Box 308, Forest City, IA 50436. **URL:** http://www.kiow.com.

12692 ■ KZOW-FM - 91.9
106 S Sixth St.
Forest City, IA 50436
Email: kzowfm@gmail.com
Format: Country. **Owner:** Waldorf College, 106 S 6th St., Forest City, IA 50436. **Operating Hours:** Continuous. **Wattage:** 100 ERP V. **Ad Rates:** Accepts Advertising. **URL:** http://www.kzowfm.com.

FORT DODGE

NWC IA. Webster Co. On Des Moines River, 90 mi. NW of Des Moines. Coal, gypsum mines. Manufactures gypsum and lime products, animal serum, sewer pipes, bricks, tile, building material, electronic components, culverts, plaster, chemicals, farm machinery. Farm feeds; meat packing plants; soybean processing mill; clay works.

12693 ■ American Cattlemen
Heartland Communications Group Inc.
1003 Central Ave., Ste. 1052
Fort Dodge, IA 50501
Phone: (515)955-1600
Publisher's E-mail: info@hlipublishing.com
Magazine focusing on raising cattles. **Freq:** Monthly. **Trim Size:** 8 x 10.875. **Key Personnel:** Rick Thomas, Publisher, Editor. **Subscription Rates:** $9.95 Individuals. **URL:** http://www.americancattlemen.com; http://www.hlipublishing.com/store/agriculture-magazines/american-cattlemen. **Mailing address:** PO Box 1052, Fort Dodge, IA 50501. **Remarks:** Accepts advertising. **Circ:** (Not Reported).

12694 ■ Aviators Hot Line: The Exclusive Source for Piston Aircraft, Parts & Services
Heartland Communications Group Inc.
1003 Central Ave., Ste. 1052
Fort Dodge, IA 50501
Phone: (515)955-1600
Publisher's E-mail: info@hlipublishing.com
Aviators Hot Line is a source to find new and used Airplanes for Sale, repairs and maintenance. **Freq:** Monthly. **Print Method:** Offset. **Trim Size:** 7 5/8 x 10 3/4. **Cols./Page:** 4. **Col. Width:** 1 5/8 inches. **Key Personnel:** Jacob Peed, Director, Publisher. **ISSN:** 0195--0347 (print). **Subscription Rates:** $14.95 Individuals. **URL:** http://www.aviatorshotline.com. **Mailing address:** PO Box 1052, Fort Dodge, IA 50501. **Remarks:** Accepts advertising. **Circ:** (Not Reported).

12695 ■ Business Air Today: The Premiere Source for Corporate Aviation Acquisitions
Heartland Communications Group Inc.
1003 Central Ave., Ste. 1052
Fort Dodge, IA 50501
Phone: (515)955-1600
Publication E-mail: flying@businessair.com
Source for corporate aircraft and services. **Freq:** Monthly. **Print Method:** Offset. **Trim Size:** 8 x 10 3/4. **Key Personnel:** Roxanne Sweazey, Account Executive. **Subscription Rates:** $19.95 Individuals. **URL:** http://www.businessair.com. **Mailing address:** PO Box 1052, Fort Dodge, IA 50501. **Remarks:** Accepts advertising. **Circ:** (Not Reported).

12696 ■ Contractors Hot Line Monthly: The One-of-A-Kind Locating and Pricing Guide for Construction Equipment
Heartland Communications Group Inc.
1003 Central Ave., Ste. 1052
Fort Dodge, IA 50501
Phone: (515)955-1600
Publisher's E-mail: info@hlipublishing.com
Buy, sell, trade publication for the heavy construction industry. **Freq:** Monthly. **Print Method:** Offset. **Trim Size:** 7 7/8 x 10 3/4. **Cols./Page:** 4. **Col. Width:** 1 5/8 inches. **Col. Depth:** 10 inches. **Subscription Rates:** $15.95 Single issue. **URL:** http://www.hlipublishing.com/store/construction-magazines/contractors-hot-line-monthly. **Mailing address:** PO Box 1052, Fort Dodge, IA 50501. **Remarks:** Advertising accepted; rates available upon request. **Circ:** (Not Reported).

12697 ■ Contractors Hot Line Weekly
Heartland Communications Group Inc.
1003 Central Ave., Ste. 1052
Fort Dodge, IA 50501
Phone: (515)955-1600
Publisher's E-mail: info@hlipublishing.com
Buy-sell-trade catalog serving the heavy construction

market. **Freq:** Weekly. **Print Method:** Offset. **Trim Size:** 7 5/8 x 10 3/4. **Cols./Page:** 4. **Col. Depth:** 10 inches. **Key Personnel:** Shannon Bushman, Publisher. **ISSN:** 0192--6330 (print). **Subscription Rates:** $49.95 Individuals print. **Mailing address:** PO Box 1052, Fort Dodge, IA 50501. **Remarks:** Accepts advertising. **Circ:** (Not Reported).

12698 ■ Crane & Rigging Hot Line: The Total source for Crane Buyers, Sellers, Owners and Operators
Maximum Capacity Media L.L.C.
1003 Central Ave.
Fort Dodge, IA 50501
Phone: (515)574-2312
Fax: (515)574-2361
Free: 800-231-8953
Publisher's E-mail: info@maxcapmedia.com
Magazine focusing on crane industry. **Freq:** Monthly. **Key Personnel:** Guy Ramsey, Publisher, phone: (602)368-8552; Barbara Benton, Vice President, Operations. **Subscription Rates:** $14.95 Individuals third class. **URL:** http://www.cranehotline.com. **Formerly**: Crane Hot Line: The Total source for Crane Buyers, Sellers, Owners and Operators. **Mailing address:** PO Box 1052, Fort Dodge, IA 50501. **Remarks:** Accepts advertising. **Circ:** (Not Reported).

12699 ■ Family Fish & Game
Twin Rivers Media L.L.C.
1597 3rd Ave NW,
Fort Dodge, IA 50501
Fax: (515)574-2364
Free: 877-424-4594
Publication E-mail: info@familyfishandgame.com
Magazine featuring information about where to and how to of upland hunting and fishing. **Freq:** Monthly. **Key Personnel:** Jennifer Pudenz, Editor. **Subscription Rates:** $11.95 Individuals. **URL:** http://www.iowasportsman.com; http://www.twinriversmedia.com. **Remarks:** Accepts advertising. **Circ:** (Not Reported).

12700 ■ Farm Equipment Guide
Heartland Communications Group Inc.
1003 Central Ave., Ste. 1052
Fort Dodge, IA 50501
Phone: (515)955-1600
Publication E-mail: subs@hotlineguides.com
Publication with farm machinery prices and locating information. **Freq:** Monthly. **Print Method:** Web. **Trim Size:** 7 3/4 x 10 3/4. **Cols./Page:** 4. **Col. Width:** 39.6 picas. **Col. Depth:** 59 picas. **ISSN:** 1047--725X (print). **Subscription Rates:** $65 Individuals print and online; $45 Individuals print or online. **URL:** http://www.hotlineguides.com. **Mailing address:** PO Box 1052, Fort Dodge, IA 50501. **Remarks:** Accepts advertising. **Circ:** (Not Reported).

12701 ■ Farmers Hot Line: Your Guide to the Newest and Latest Farm Products
Heartland Communications Group Inc.
1003 Central Ave., Ste. 1052
Fort Dodge, IA 50501
Phone: (515)955-1600
Publisher's E-mail: info@hlipublishing.com
Trade magazine. **Freq:** 44/yr. **Print Method:** Offset. **Trim Size:** 7 3/4 x 10 3/4. **Cols./Page:** 4. **Col. Width:** 42 picas. **Col. Depth:** 59 picas. **Key Personnel:** Katherine Dornath-Cook, Editor-in-Chief; Sandy Simonson, Publisher. **ISSN:** 0192--6322 (print). **Subscription Rates:** $29.95 Individuals. **URL:** http://www.farmershotline.com. **Mailing address:** PO Box 1052, Fort Dodge, IA 50501. **Remarks:** Accepts advertising. **Circ:** (Not Reported).

12702 ■ Industrial Machine Trader: The Only Weekly Nationwide Publication that Links Active Buyers and Sellers of New and Used Industrial Machinery
Heartland Communications Group Inc.
1003 Central Ave., Ste. 1052
Fort Dodge, IA 50501
Phone: (515)955-1600
Publisher's E-mail: info@hlipublishing.com
Magazine reporting supply and demand of equipment in machine tool industry. **Freq:** Weekly. **Print Method:** Offset. **Trim Size:** 7 5/8 x 10 3/4. **Cols./Page:** 4. **Col. Width:** 1 5/8 inches. **Key Personnel:** Katherine Dornath-Cook, Editor-in-Chief; Sandra Simonson, Director; Virginia Rodriguez, Publisher. **ISSN:** 1047-4374 (print). **Subscription Rates:** $49 Individuals. **URL:** http://www.industrialmachinetrader.com/publications/imt_weekly/index.cfm. **Mailing address:** PO Box 1052, Fort Dodge, IA 50501. **Ad Rates:** BW $616; 4C $853. **Remarks:** Accepts advertising. **Circ:** Combined ‡12000.

12703 ■ Iowa Sportsman
Twin Rivers Media L.L.C.
1597 3rd Ave NW,
Fort Dodge, IA 50501
Fax: (515)574-2364
Free: 877-424-4594
Publisher's E-mail: info@twinriversmedia.com
Magazine promoting Iowa outdoors to Iowa hunters and anglers. **Freq:** Monthly. **Key Personnel:** Patrick McKinney, Publisher; Amanda Nelson, Manager, Sales; Thomas Allen, Executive Editor. **Subscription Rates:** $14.95 Individuals print and digital; $24.95 Two years print and digital. **URL:** http://www.iowasportsman.com. **Circ:** (Not Reported).

12704 ■ Land & Water
Land and Water
320 A St.
Fort Dodge, IA 50501
Phone: (515)576-3191
Fax: (515)576-2606
Publisher's E-mail: landandwater@frontiernet.net
Magazine on natural resource management and restoration. **Freq:** Bimonthly. **Print Method:** Offset. **Trim Size:** 8 1/4 x 10 7/8. **Cols./Page:** 3. **Col. Width:** 28 nonpareils. **Col. Depth:** 140 agate lines. **Key Personnel:** Shanna Egli, Account Executive; Martha Steinkamp, Manager, Circulation; Amy Dencklau, Publisher. **ISSN:** 0192-9453 (print). **Subscription Rates:** $20 Individuals; $28 Canada and Mexico; $40 Other countries. **Remarks:** Accepts advertising. **Circ:** (Not Reported).

12705 ■ The Messenger
Ogden Newspapers Inc.
713 Central Ave.
Fort Dodge, IA 50501
Phone: (515)573-2141
Fax: (515)573-2148
Free: 800-622-6613
Publication E-mail: messenger@dodgenet.com
Newspaper with Republican orientation. **Founded:** 1856. **Freq:** Mon.-Sun. (morn.). **Print Method:** Letterpress. **Cols./Page:** 6. **Col. Width:** 25 nonpareils. **Col. Depth:** 301 agate lines. **Key Personnel:** Larry Bushman, Publisher. **Subscription Rates:** $51.35 Individuals 7 days home delivery; $16.35 Individuals 7 days home delivery - easy pay; $18.20 Individuals 7 days in-state mail - Easy Pay; $56.55 By mail 7 days home delivery; $19.65 Out of state 7 days mail delivery - easy pay. **URL:** http://www.messengernews.net. **Remarks:** Accepts advertising. **Circ:** Mon.-Sat. ★**16981**, Sun. ★**19207**.

12706 ■ Packaging and Converting Hotline: The Nation's Marketplace Serving Buyers and Sellers of Packaging and Converting Equipment, Materials, Services, and Supplies
IMS L.L.C.
809 Central Ave., 2nd Fl.
Fort Dodge, IA 50501
Phone: (515)574-2248
Free: 888-247-2007
Contains packaging and converting equipment for sale, materials, business, and employment opportunities. **Freq:** Monthly. **Print Method:** Offset. **Trim Size:** 7 5/8 x 10 3/4. **Cols./Page:** 4. **Col. Width:** 1 5/8 inches. **Key Personnel:** Steve Scanlan, President; Theresa McClintock, Publisher. **Subscription Rates:** $39 Individuals first class; $29 Individuals third class; $49 Canada; $59 Mexico; $89 Other countries. **URL:** http://www.packaginghotline.com; http://www.convertinghotline.com. **Formerly**: Packaging Hotline. **Ad Rates:** BW $618; 4C $870. **Remarks:** Accepts advertising. **Circ:** Combined 10000.

12707 ■ Plastics Hot Line: The Nation's Marketplace for Plastics Processing Equipment & Materials, Business and Employment Opportunities
IMS L.L.C.
809 Central Ave., 2nd Fl.
Fort Dodge, IA 50501
Phone: (515)574-2248
Free: 888-247-2007
Trade magazine. **Freq:** Monthly. **Print Method:** Offset. **Trim Size:** 7 5/8 x 10 3/4. **Cols./Page:** 4. **Col. Width:** 1 5/8 inches. **Col. Depth:** 1 inches. **URL:** http://www.plasticshotline.com. **Remarks:** Accepts advertising. **Circ:** (Not Reported).

12708 ■ Printers Hot Line
Heartland Communications Group Inc.
1003 Central Ave., Ste. 1052
Fort Dodge, IA 50501
Phone: (515)955-1600
Publisher's E-mail: info@hlipublishing.com
Trade periodical reporting information on new and used printing equipment. **Freq:** Weekly. **Print Method:** Web offset. **Trim Size:** 7 5/8 x 10 3/4. **Cols./Page:** 4. **Col. Width:** 1 5/8 inches. **Col. Depth:** 9 3/4 inches. **Key Personnel:** Patrick Van Arnam, Chief Executive Officer, President; Joseph W. Peed, Chairman. **URL:** http://www.hlipublishing.com/company_history.htm. **Mailing address:** PO Box 1052, Fort Dodge, IA 50501. **Ad Rates:** BW $688; 4C $850; PCI $20. **Remarks:** Accepts advertising. **Circ:** Paid ‡4000, Non-paid ‡110000.

12709 ■ KEGR Radio - 89.5
PO Box 103
Concord, CA 94522
Phone: (925)680-5347
Free: 800-543-1495
Format: Religious. **Owner:** Family Stations Inc., 290 Hegenberger Rd., Oakland, CA 94621, Free: 800-543-1495. **URL:** http://kegr.org.

12710 ■ KIAQ-FM - 96.9
3800 Cornhusker Hwy.
Lincoln, NE 68504
Phone: (402)466-1234
Fax: (402)467-4095
Format: Country. **Networks:** Iowa Radio. **Owner:** Three Eagles Communications, 3800 Cornhusker Hwy., Lincoln, NE 68504, Ph: (402)466-1234, Fax: (402)467-4095. **Founded:** 1964. **Formerly**: KRIT-FM. **ADI**: Des Moines, IA. **Ad Rates:** Noncommercial.

12711 ■ KICB-FM - 88.1
1 Triton Cir.
Fort Dodge, IA 50501
Phone: (515)574-1215
Format: Educational. **Owner:** Iowa Central Community College, 1 Triton Cir., Fort Dodge, IA 50501, Ph: (515)576-7201, Free: 800-362-2793. **Founded:** 1971. **Operating Hours**: 15.5 hours. Daily; 100% local. **Wattage**: 200. **Ad Rates:** Noncommercial. **URL:** http://www.iccc.cc.ia.us/kicb.

12712 ■ KKEZ-FM - 94.5
3800 Cornhusker Hwy.
Lincoln, NE 68504
Format: Album-Oriented Rock (AOR). **Networks:** Independent. **Owner:** Three Eagles Communications, 3800 Cornhusker Hwy., Lincoln, NE 68504, Ph: (402)466-1234, Fax: (402)467-4095. **Operating Hours:** Continuous; 100% local. **Wattage:** 100,000. **Ad Rates:** $28 for 30 seconds; $43 for 60 seconds. **URL:** http://www.kkez.com.

12713 ■ KTIN-TV - 21
6450 Corporate Dr.
Johnston, IA 50131
Phone: (515)242-3100
Free: 800-532-1290
Format: Public TV. **Simulcasts:** KDIN-TV Des Moines, IA. **Networks:** Public Broadcasting Service (PBS). **Owner:** Iowa Public Television, PO Box 6450, Johnston, IA 50131-6450, Ph: (515)242-3100, Free: 800-532-1290. **Founded:** 1977. **ADI:** Des Moines, IA. **Key Personnel:** Kristine K. Houston, Dir. of Fin.; William T. Hayes, Dir. of Engg., hayes@iptv.org; Daniel K. Miller, Exec. Dir., Gen. Mgr., dkm@iptv.org; Terry Rinehart, Director, terry.rinehart@iptv.org; Molly M. Phillips, Exec. Dir., Gen. Mgr., molly@iptv.org. **Ad Rates:** Noncommercial. **Mailing address:** PO Box 6450, Johnston, IA 50131. **URL:** http://www.iptv.org.

12714 ■ KTLB-FM - 105.9
200 N 10th St.
Fort Dodge, IA 50501
Phone: (515)955-5656
Fax: (515)955-5844

Circulation: ★ = AAM; △ or • = BPA; ♦ = CAC; ❑ = VAC; ⊕ = PO Statement; ‡ = Publisher's Report; Boldface figures = sworn; Light figures = estimated.

Format: News; Information; Sports; Country; Adult Contemporary. **Networks:** ABC; Radio Iowa; Brownfield. **Owner:** Twin Lakes Broadcasting, Inc., 269 North Twin Lakes Rd., Rockwell City, IA 50579, Ph: (712)297-7586. **Founded:** 1975. **Operating Hours:** 5:30 a.m.-11 p.m.; 20% network, 80% local. **Key Personnel:** Pat Palmer, Contact. **Wattage:** 25,000. **Ad Rates:** $6-8 for 30 seconds; $8-12 for 60 seconds. **URL:** http://www.yourfortdodge.com.

12715 ■ KTLB-FM - 105.9
3800 Cornhusker Hwy.
Lincoln, NE 68504
Phone: (402)466-1234
Format: News; Sports. **Wattage:** 25,000. **Ad Rates:** Noncommercial; Advertising accepted; rates available upon request.

12716 ■ KUEL-FM - 92.1
200 N 10th St.
Fort Dodge, IA 50501
Phone: (503)517-6200
Email: purerock@921theblaze.com
Format: Full Service. **Owner:** Three Eagles Communications, 3800 Cornhusker Hwy., Lincoln, NE 68504, Ph: (402)466-1234, Fax: (402)467-4095. **Founded:** 1975. **Formerly:** KSMX-FM; KFTX-FM; KFDC-FM. **Key Personnel:** Bill Wells, Gen. Mgr. **Wattage:** 6,000 ERP. **Ad Rates:** $12-24 per unit. **URL:** http://www.yourfortdodge.com.

12717 ■ KVFD-AM - 1400
300 Cornhusker Hwy.
Lincoln, NE 68504
Phone: (402)466-1234
Format: Middle-of-the-Road (MOR); Full Service; Adult Contemporary; Oldies. **Networks:** CBS. **Owner:** Three Eagles Communications, 3800 Cornhusker Hwy., Lincoln, NE 68504, Ph: (402)466-1234, Fax: (402)467-4095. **Operating Hours:** Continuous; 5% network, 95% local. **Wattage:** 1,000. **Ad Rates:** Noncommercial. **URL:** http://www.threeeagles.com.

12718 ■ KWMT-AM - 540
300 Cornhusker Hwy.
Lincoln, NE 68504
Phone: (402)466-1234
Format: Country; Information; News. **Networks:** ABC. **Owner:** Three Eagles Communications, 3800 Cornhusker Hwy., Lincoln, NE 68504, Ph: (402)466-1234, Fax: (402)467-4095. **Operating Hours:** Continuous; 5% network, 95% local. **ADI:** Des Moines, IA. **Wattage:** 5,000. **Ad Rates:** Noncommercial. Combined advertising rates available with KKEZ-FM. **URL:** http://www.threeeagles.com/.

GARNER

NC IA. Hancock Co. 12 mi. SE of Forest City. Residential.

12719 ■ Garner Leader and Signal
Garner Leader and Signal
365 State St.
Garner, IA 50438
Phone: (641)923-2684
Fax: (641)923-2685
Community newspaper. **Freq:** Weekly (Wed.). **Print Method:** Offset. **Cols./Page:** 7. **Col. Width:** 12 picas. **Col. Depth:** 21 inches. **Key Personnel:** Ryan Harvey, Publisher. **Subscription Rates:** $47 Individuals print and online; $93 Two years print and online. **Remarks:** Accepts advertising. **Circ:** (Not Reported).

12720 ■ The Kanawha Reporter: Legal Newspaper for Kanawha & Klemme and West Hancock School District
The Kanawha Reporter
365 State St.
Garner, IA 50438
Phone: (641)762-3994
Fax: (641)762-3994
Publisher's E-mail: kanawhareporter@gmail.com
Community newspaper. **Freq:** Weekly (Thurs.). **Print Method:** Offset. **Trim Size:** 12 1/2 x 21. **Cols./Page:** 6. **Col. Width:** 2 inches. **Col. Depth:** 21 inches. **Key Personnel:** Rodger Tveiten, Editor, Manager, Advertising. **USPS:** 289-620. **Mailing address:** PO Box 190, Kanawha, IA 50447. **Remarks:** Accepts advertising. **Circ:** (Not Reported).

GEORGE

NW IA. Lyon Co. 45 mi. SE of Sioux Falls, SD. Manufactures feed boxes, tank heaters, washers, farm equipment and machinery, cement blocks. Grain elevator. Stock, grain farms. Corn, oats, soybeans.

12721 ■ Siebring Cable
301 S Main St.
George, IA 51237
Phone: (712)475-3747
Founded: 1981. **Cities Served:** George, Iowa: subscribing households 400; 39 channels; 1 community access channel; 10 hours per week community access programming.

GLADBROOK

EC IA. Tama Co. 20 mi. NE of Marshalltown. Brick, tile, blast meter, mustard factories; soybean processing mill; hatchery. Agriculture. Corn, oats, hogs.

12722 ■ Northern Sun Print
Northern Sun Print
423 Second St.
Gladbrook, IA 50635-0340
Phone: (641)473-2102
Community newspaper. **Freq:** Weekly (Fri.). **Print Method:** Offset. **Cols./Page:** 5. **Col. Width:** 11 1/2 picas. **Col. Depth:** 14 1/2 inches. **Subscription Rates:** $11.25 Individuals in town ; $12 Individuals in Iowa; $12.50 Out of state. **Mailing address:** PO Box 340, Gladbrook, IA 50635-0340. **Remarks:** Accepts advertising. **Circ:** 1350.

GLENWOOD

WC IA. Mills Co. 18 mi. SSE of Council Bluffs. Grain farms.

12723 ■ Glenwood Opinion Tribune
The Glenwood Opinion Tribune
116 S Walnut St.
Glenwood, IA 51534
Phone: (712)527-3191
Fax: (712)527-3193
Publisher's E-mail: news@opinion-tribune.com
Rural newspaper covering Mills County. **Freq:** Weekly. **Print Method:** Offset. **Trim Size:** 11 5/8 x 21 1/2. **Cols./Page:** 6. **Col. Width:** 1 7/8 inches. **Col. Depth:** 21.5 inches. **Key Personnel:** Joel Stevens, Associate Editor; Joe Foreman, Editor; Melissa Lorang, Manager, Advertising and Sales; Karen Herzberg, Manager, Circulation; Liz Felos, Office Manager. **Mailing address:** PO Box 191, Glenwood, IA 51534. **Remarks:** Accepts advertising. **Circ:** (Not Reported).

12724 ■ Science Educator
National Science Education Leadership Association
55466 Forrester Valley Ln.
Glenwood, IA 51534
Phone: (919)561-3612
Fax: (801)659-3351
Publisher's E-mail: membership@nsela.org
Journal containing topics and issues of interest to professionals involved in science education leadership across a variety of roles, institutions and agencies. **Freq:** Semiannual. **URL:** http://www.nsela.org/publications/science-educator-journal. **Remarks:** Accepts advertising. **Circ:** (Not Reported).

GLIDDEN

WC IA. Carroll Co. 75 mi. NW of Des Moines. Egg processing plant; feed mill; grain elevator. Agriculture. Corn, oats, soybeans, hogs, cattle.

12725 ■ Glidden Graphic
Glidden Graphic
111 Idaho St.
Glidden, IA 51443-0607
Phone: (712)659-3144
Fax: (712)659-3143
Publication E-mail: news@gliddengraphic.com
Newspaper with Republican orientation. **Freq:** Weekly (Tues.). **Print Method:** Offset. **Cols./Page:** 7. **Col. Width:** 12.5 picas. **Col. Depth:** 126 picas. **Key Personnel:** Bill Brown, Publisher; Doug Rieder, Editor, General Manager. **Subscription Rates:** $17 Individuals; $24 Out of state. **Ad Rates:** BW $441; PCI $2.50. **Remarks:** Accepts advertising. **Circ:** 588.

GOWRIE

NWC IA. Webster Co. 22 mi. S. of Fort Dodge. Diversified farming. Corn, oats, soybeans, hay.

12726 ■ Gowrie Cablevision
PO Box 415
Gowrie, IA 50543
Free: 800-292-8989
Email: gowrie@wccta.net
Founded: 1997. **Key Personnel:** Paul Johnson, President. **Cities Served:** 40 channels.

GRAETTINGER

NC IA. Palo Alto Co. 10 mi. NNW of Emmetsburg.

12727 ■ The Graettinger Times
The Graettinger Times
102 E Robbins Ave.
Graettinger, IA 51342
Phone: (712)859-3780
Fax: (712)859-3039
Publication E-mail: grtimes@rvtc.net
Community newspaper. **Freq:** Weekly (Wed.). **Cols./Page:** 5. **Col. Width:** 2 inches. **Col. Depth:** 15 inches. **Key Personnel:** Penny Tonderum, Editor, Manager, Publisher; Scott Tonderum, Publisher. **USPS:** 225-140. **Ad Rates:** GLR $3.50; BW $250; SAU $3.50. **Remarks:** Accepts advertising. **Circ:** 628.

GRAND MOUND

12728 ■ Grand Mound Cooperative Telephone Association
705 Clinton St.
Grand Mound, IA 52751-7707
Phone: (563)847-3000
Fax: (563)847-3001
Founded: 1947. **Key Personnel:** Terri Bumann, Office Mgr. **Cities Served:** 27 channels. **Mailing address:** PO Box 316, Grand Mound, IA 52751-0316. **URL:** http://www.gmtel.net.

GRINNELL

SE IA. Poweshiek Co. 50 mi. NE of Des Moines. Grinnell College. Manufactures playground equipment, feed, farm equipment, gloves, jackets, aluminum, fiberglass, mufflers, windows, polyvinyl, chloride, pipe, stadium seating. Hybrid seed corn, alfalfa dehydrating plants. Agriculture. Grain, livestock.

12729 ■ Journal of Linguistic Anthropology
Society for Linguistic Anthropology
c/o Prof. Brigittine M. French, Editor
Dept. of Anthropology
Grinnell College
306 Goodnow Hall
1118 Park St.
Grinnell, IA 50112
Publisher's E-mail: soclinganth@gmail.com
Trade journal covering linguistics and anthropology. **Freq:** 3/year May, August and December. **Trim Size:** 6 X 9. **Key Personnel:** Alexandra Jaffe, Editor-in-Chief; Paul Manning, Editor; Samy H. Alim, Board Member; Bernard Bate, Board Member. **ISSN:** 1055-1360 (print); **EISSN:** 1548-1395 (electronic). **Subscription Rates:** $35 Individuals online; $30 Other countries online; $250 Institutions print & online; $4000 lifetime; $51 Nonmembers; Included in membership. **URL:** http://linguisticanthropology.org/journal/; http://onlinelibrary.wiley.com/journal/10.1111/(ISSN)1548-1395. **Ad Rates:** BW $295. **Remarks:** Accepts advertising. **Circ:** Paid 900, 500.

12730 ■ KDIC-FM - 88.5
1115 8th Ave.
Grinnell, IA 50112
Phone: (641)269-3328
Email: kdicfm@grinnell.edu
Format: Full Service. **Networks:** Independent. **Owner:** Grinell College Board of Trustees, 1121 Park St., Grinnell, IA 50112, Ph: (641)269-4000. **Founded:** 1968. **Key Personnel:** Kramer McLuckie, Music Dir., mcluckie@grinnell.edu; Hannah Kapp-Klote, Dir. of Programs, kappklot@grinnell.edu; Matt Zmudka, News Dir., zmudkama@grinnell.edu. **Wattage:** 130. **Ad Rates:** Noncommercial. **URL:** http://kdic.grinnell.edu.

12731 ■ KGRN-AM - 1410
909 1/2 Main St.
Grinnell, IA 50112
Phone: (641)236-1410
Fax: (641)236-8896
Format: Adult Contemporary. **Networks:** ABC; Brownfield; Radio Iowa. **Operating Hours:** 6 a.m.-10 p.m. **ADI:** Des Moines, IA. **Key Personnel:** Tim Dill, Contact, timkgrn@iowatelecom.net. **Wattage:** 500. **Ad Rates:** $14.25-18.20 for 30 seconds. **URL:** http://www.myiowainfo.com.

GRISWOLD

12732 ■ Griswold American
Griswold American
519 Main St.
Griswold, IA 51535-8050
Phone: (712)778-4337
Fax: (712)778-4350
Publication E-mail: grisamer@netins.net
Community newspaper. **Freq:** Weekly (Wed.). **Cols./Page:** 6. **Col. Width:** 12 1/2 inches. **Col. Depth:** 21 1/2 inches. **Key Personnel:** Janet Reed, Editor; Donna Forsyth, Manager, Advertising. **Subscription Rates:** $30 Individuals in Iowa; $50 Two years in Iowa; $35 Out of state; $55 Out of state 2 years; $22.50 Students in state; $25.50 Students in state 2 years; $19.50 Individuals six months; $23.50 Out of state six months. **URL:** http://www.griswoldamerican.com. **Remarks:** Accepts advertising. **Circ:** ‡1,110.

12733 ■ Griswold Cable TV
607 Main St.
Griswold, IA 51535
Phone: (712)778-2121
Email: gctc@netins.net
Cities Served: 29 channels. **URL:** http://www.griswoldtelco.com.

GRUNDY CENTER

NEC IA. Grundy Co. 30 mi. SW of Waterloo. Manufactures plastic molded parts, wood veneer, chillers, salad dressing. Diversified farming. Corn, oats, soybeans.

12734 ■ The Grundy Register
Register Printing Co.
601 G Ave.
Grundy Center, IA 50638-0245
Phone: (319)824-6958
Fax: (319)824-6288
Publisher's E-mail: registerads@gcmuni.net
Community newspaper. **Freq:** Weekly (Thurs.). **Print Method:** Offset. **Trim Size:** 15 1/2 x 22. **Cols./Page:** 6. **Col. Width:** 14 picas. **Col. Depth:** 21.5 inches. **Key Personnel:** Clinton A. Poock, Publisher. **Subscription Rates:** $47 Individuals print and online. **URL:** http://www.thegrundyregister.com. **Mailing address:** PO Box 245, Grundy Center, IA 50638-0245. **Remarks:** Accepts advertising. **Circ:** (Not Reported).

12735 ■ Treasures: Antique to Modern Collecting
Pioneer Communications Inc.
PO Box 306
Grundy Center, IA 50638
Phone: (319)824-6981
Fax: (319)824-3414
Free: 800-352-8039
Publication E-mail: collectors@collectors-news.com
Magazine covering antiques and collecting for pleasure and profit. **Freq:** Monthly. **Print Method:** Offset. **Trim Size:** 8.5 x 11. **Cols./Page:** 4. **Col. Width:** 1 5/8 inches. **Col. Depth:** 10 inches. **Key Personnel:** Linda Kruger, Managing Editor; Ronda Jans, Manager, Advertising. **ISSN:** 0162--1033 (print). **Subscription Rates:** $34 Individuals; $58 Two years. **URL:** http://www.treasuresmagazine.com. **Formerly:** Collectors News: Serving Coolectors for 50 Years; Collectors News & the Antique Reporter. **Remarks:** Accepts advertising. **Circ:** (Not Reported).

12736 ■ Two-Cylinder Magazine
Two-Cylinder Club
506 2nd St.
Grundy Center, IA 50638
Phone: (319)824-6060
Fax: (319)824-2662
Free: 888-782-2582
Publisher's E-mail: two-cylinder@two-cylinder.com
Magazine covering information about John Deere Tractors and Implements. **Freq:** Bimonthly. **Key Personnel:** Brenda Hamilton, Manager; Jack Cherry, Director, Editorial. **ISSN:** 0899--2258 (print). **Subscription Rates:** $34.95 U.S.; $58.95 U.S. priority mail; $43.95 Canada; $61.95 Canada air mail; $54.95 Other countries; $86.95 Other countries air mail. **Alt. Formats:** CD-ROM. **URL:** http://www.two-cylinder.com/about.htm. **Mailing address:** PO Box 430, Grundy Center, IA 50638-0430. **Ad Rates:** BW $800. **Remarks:** Accepts advertising. **Circ:** (Not Reported).

12737 ■ Two-Cylinder Magazine
Two-Cylinder Ltd.
618 G Ave.
Grundy Center, IA 50638
Fax: (131)824-2662
Publisher's E-mail: two-cylinder@two-cylinder.com
Magazine covering information about John Deere Tractors and Implements. **Freq:** Bimonthly. **Key Personnel:** Brenda Hamilton, Manager; Jack Cherry, Director, Editorial. **ISSN:** 0899--2258 (print). **Subscription Rates:** $34.95 U.S.; $58.95 U.S. priority mail; $43.95 Canada; $61.95 Canada air mail; $54.95 Other countries; $86.95 Other countries air mail. **Alt. Formats:** CD-ROM. **URL:** http://www.two-cylinder.com/about.htm. **Mailing address:** PO Box 430, Grundy Center, IA 50638-0430. **Ad Rates:** BW $800. **Remarks:** Accepts advertising. **Circ:** (Not Reported).

GUTHRIE CENTER

SWC IA. Guthrie Co. 50 mi. W. of Des Moines. Lake resort. Manufactures doors, windows, flour, dairy products. Agriculture. Cattle, hogs, corn.

12738 ■ Guthrie Center Times
Guthrie Center Times
205 State St.
Guthrie Center, IA 50115
Local newspaper. **Freq:** Weekly (Wed.). **Print Method:** Offset. **Trim Size:** 8 1/2 x 11. **Cols./Page:** 8. **Col. Width:** 10 1/2 inches. **Col. Depth:** 21 1/2 inches. **Key Personnel:** Ann Wilson, Publisher. **USPS:** 232-280. **Subscription Rates:** $30 Individuals in Iowa; $35 Out of state. **URL:** http://www.guthriecountynewspapers.com. **Remarks:** Accepts advertising. **Circ:** (Not Reported).

GUTTENBERG

NE IA. Clayton Co. On Mississippi River, 40 mi. NW of Dubuque. Tourism. Tool, toys, electronic assembly, extruded plastic components. Timber. Agriculture. Corn, hogs, beef.

12739 ■ The Guttenberg Press
Guttenberg Publishing
PO Box 937
Guttenberg, IA 52052
Phone: (563)252-2421
Fax: (563)252-1275
Community newspaper. **Freq:** Weekly. **Print Method:** Offset. **Cols./Page:** 4. **Col. Width:** 15 picas. **Col. Depth:** 16 inches. **Key Personnel:** Gary Howe, Owner, Publisher; Jane Thein, Director, Advertising, General Manager, Manager, Production, Manager, Sales; Shelia Tomkins, Office Manager. **Subscription Rates:** $35 Individuals e-edition; $35 Individuals print; $42 Out of area print; $28 Students 9 months; print; in area; $33 Students 9 months; print; out of area. **URL:** http://www.guttenbergpress.com. **Remarks:** Advertising accepted; rates available upon request. **Circ:** (Not Reported).

HAMPTON

NC IA. Franklin Co. 28 mi. S. of Mason City. Beedslake State Park. Manufactures hydraulic cylinders, truck trailers, steel tools, concrete culverts and tile, recreational vehicles, fiberglass, medical supplies. Nursery; cannery. Stock, poultry, grain farms. Corn, hogs.

12740 ■ Conservative Chronicle
Hampton Publishing Co.
PO Box 29
Hampton, IA 50441
Free: 800-888-3039
Publisher's E-mail: conserve@iowaconnect.com
Tabloid reprinting newspaper columns of leading U.S. conservative commentators. **Freq:** Weekly. **Print Method:** Offset. **Trim Size:** 7 1/2 x 11 1/4. **Cols./Page:** 4. **Col. Width:** 12 picas. **Col. Depth:** 10 inches. **ISSN:** 0888-1359 (print). **Subscription Rates:** $23 Individuals print and online or online - 13 weeks; $41 Individuals print and online or online - 26 weeks; $75 Individuals print and online or online - 52 weeks; $149 Two years print and online or online - 104 weeks; $23 Individuals online only - 13 weeks; $41 Individuals online only - 26 weeks; $75 Individuals online only - 52 weeks; $149 Individuals online only - 2 years. **URL:** http://conservativechronicle.com/. **Remarks:** Advertising not accepted. **Circ:** Paid ⊕**57960**, Free 30.

12741 ■ Hampton Chronicle
Hampton Publishing Co.
9 Second St. NW
Hampton, IA 50441
Publisher's E-mail: conserve@iowaconnect.com
General newspaper. **Freq:** Weekly (Wed.). **Print Method:** Offset. **Trim Size:** 15 x 22 3/4. **Cols./Page:** 8. **Col. Width:** 1 3/4 inches. **Col. Depth:** 21 inches. **Key Personnel:** Dan Rodemeyer, Coordinator; Deb Chaney, Manager, Circulation; Ryan Harvey, Publisher, President, Chief Executive Officer. **Subscription Rates:** $52 Individuals print and online; $103 Two years print and online. **URL:** http://hamptonchronicle.com. **Remarks:** Advertising accepted; rates available upon request. **Circ:** (Not Reported).

12742 ■ KLMJ-FM - 104.9
PO Box 495
Hampton, IA 50441
Phone: (641)456-5656
Fax: (641)456-5655
Email: klmj@klmj.com
Format: Contemporary Country. **Networks:** ABC; Brownfield; Radio Iowa. **Owner:** C.D. Broadcasting, Inc., at above address, Hampton, IA. **Founded:** 1983. **Formerly:** KWGG-FM. **Operating Hours:** Continuous; 10% network, 90% local. **Key Personnel:** Craig Donnelly, Gen. Mgr., donnelly@klmj.com; Kathy Donnelly, Office Mgr., kdonnelly@klmj.com; Duane Carstens, Sales Mgr. **Wattage:** 6,000. **Ad Rates:** $9-17 for 30 seconds; $12-20 for 60 seconds. Combined advertising rates available with KQCR-FM. **URL:** http://www.klmj.com.

HARLAN

W IA. Shelby Co. 40 mi. NE of Council Bluffs. Manufactures feeds, cement, farm implements, mill grinders. Agriculture. Corn, cattle, hogs.

12743 ■ Angels on Earth
Guideposts
PO Box 5814
Harlan, IA 51593
Free: 800-932-2145
Publication E-mail: angelseditors@guideposts.org
Religious magazine. **Key Personnel:** Dr. Norman Vincent Peale, Contact. **Subscription Rates:** $19.95 Individuals 6 issues; $35.95 Individuals 12 issues; $21.95 Canada 6 issues; $25.95 Other countries 6 issues; $39.95 Canada 12 issues; $39.95 Other countries 12 issues; $47.95 Other countries two years. **URL:** http://www.guideposts.org/brand/angels-on-earth-magazine. **Circ:** (Not Reported).

12744 ■ Arthur Frommer's Budget Travel: Vacations For Real People
Budget Travel L.L.C.
PO Box 5609
Harlan, IA 51593-1109
Free: 800-829-9121
Publisher's E-mail: letters@budgettravel.com
Consumer magazine covering leisure travel on a budget. **Freq:** 6/year. **Print Method:** Web offset. **Trim Size:** 8 1/4 x 10 7/8. **Cols./Page:** 3. **Col. Width:** 2 1/4 inches. **Col. Depth:** 9 1/4 inches. **Key Personnel:** Nina Willdorf, Editor-in-Chief; Nancy Telliho, Publisher, phone: (646)695-6730, fax: (646)695-6704; Erik Torkells, Editor, phone: (646)695-6700, fax: (646)695-6707. **URL:** http://www.budgettravel.com/magazine. **Remarks:** Accepts advertising. **Circ:** (Not Reported).

Circulation: ★ = AAM; △ or • = BPA; ♦ = CAC; ❑ = VAC; ⊕ = PO Statement; ‡ = Publisher's Report; Boldface figures = sworn; Light figures = estimated.

12745 ■ Guideposts Magazine: A Pratical Guide to Successful Living
Guideposts
PO Box 5814
Harlan, IA 51593
Free: 800-932-2145
Inspirational interfaith magazine. **Freq:** Monthly. **Print Method:** Grauvre. **Trim Size:** 5 1/4 x 7 1/4. **Cols./Page:** 2. **Col. Width:** 24 nonpareils. **Col. Depth:** 91 agate lines. **Key Personnel:** Edward Grinnan, Editor; Richard V. Hopple, Chief Executive Officer, President. **ISSN:** 0017--5331 (print). **Subscription Rates:** C$16.97 Canada. **URL:** http://www.guideposts.org/brand/guideposts-magazine. **Remarks:** Accepts advertising. **Circ:** (Not Reported).

12746 ■ Farmers Mutual Cooperative Telephone Co.
801 19th St.
Harlan, IA 51537
Phone: (712)744-3131
Fax: (712)744-3100
Free: 800-469-3511
Email: support@fmctc.com
Founded: 1904. **Key Personnel:** Kevin Cabbage, Gen. Mgr.; Dennis Crawford, Asst. Mgr.; Scott Boatman, Office Mgr.; Brad Sunderman, Plant Mgr.; Frank Sefrit, Mgr.; Jacque Bates, Acct. Mgr.; Wayne Sederburg, Secretary, Treasurer; Dan Lundgren, Director; Thomas Conry, Gen. Mgr. **Cities Served:** United States; 21 channels. **Mailing address:** PO Box 311, Harlan, IA 51537. **URL:** http://www.fmctc.com.

12747 ■ KNOD-FM - 105.3
902 Chatburn Ave.
Harlan, IA 51537-0723
Phone: (712)755-3883
Fax: (712)755-7511
Free: 800-876-5663
Email: knodnews@harlannet.com
Format: Oldies. **Networks:** ABC; Brownfield; Jones Satellite. **Owner:** Wireless Communications, 1908 E 7th St., Atlantic, IA 50022, Ph: (712)243-4592. **Operating Hours:** Continuous. **Local Programs:** *Iowa Farm Report*; *Sports Wrap*, Saturday 8:30 a.m.; *Successful Farming Radio Magazine*. **Wattage:** 25,000. **Ad Rates:** Noncommercial. KJAN-Atlantic. **URL:** http://www.knodfm.com.

HAVELOCK

12748 ■ Northwest Communications Inc.
844 Wood St.
Havelock, IA 50546
Phone: (712)776-2612
Fax: (712)776-4444
Free: 800-249-5251
Email: nis@ncn.net
Founded: 1963. **Formerly:** Northwest One Inc. **Key Personnel:** Don Miller, CEO. **Cities Served:** United States; 42 channels. **Mailing address:** PO Box 186, Havelock, IA 50546. **URL:** http://www.ncn.net.

HOLSTEIN

12749 ■ The Danbury Review
Danbury Review
PO Box 550
Holstein, IA 51025-0550
Phone: (712)368-4368
Community newspaper. **Freq:** Weekly (Wed.). **Print Method:** Offset. **Cols./Page:** 4. **Col. Width:** 14.5 picas. **Col. Depth:** 14 inches. **Key Personnel:** Jerry Clark, Editor. **URL:** http://www.danbury-ia.com/review. **Remarks:** Accepts advertising. **Circ:** (Not Reported).

12750 ■ The Fenton Press
Advance Publications Inc.
101 S Main
Holstein, IA 51025
Phone: (712)368-4368
Fax: (712)368-4369
Publication E-mail: editor@fentonpress.com
Newspaper serving the Genesee County, Michigan communities of Fenton, Linden, Fenton Township and Argentine Township, in the 48418, 48451, 48430, 48442 and 48462 ZIP codes. **Freq:** Sunday. **URL:** http://www.mlive.com/fenton. **Remarks:** Accepts advertising. **Circ:** (Not Reported).

HOSPERS

EC IA. Sioux Co. 9 mi. SSW of Sheldon. Livestock.

12751 ■ HTC Cablecom
107 2nd Ave. S
Hospers, IA 51238
Phone: (712)752-8100
Free: 800-813-2023
Email: htc@hosperstel.com
Cities Served: 10 channels. **Mailing address:** PO Box 142, Hospers, IA 51238-0142. **URL:** http://www.hosperstel.com.

HUDSON

NEC IA. Black Hawk Co. 9 mi. SW of Waterloo. Manufactures conveyor equipment; hybrid seed processing. Dairy, stock, grain farms.

12752 ■ Hudson Herald
Hudson Herald
411 Jefferson St.
Hudson, IA 50643
Publication E-mail: hudherald@gmail.com
Community newspaper. **Freq:** Weekly (Thurs.). **Print Method:** Offset. **Cols./Page:** 6. **Col. Width:** 13.5 picas. **Col. Depth:** 21.5 inches. **Key Personnel:** Dianna Darold, Owner, Editor. **URL:** http://www.hudherald.com. **Remarks:** Accepts advertising. **Circ:** (Not Reported).

HULL

NW IA. Sioux Co. 55 mi. N. of Sioux City. Elevators. Dairy, stock, poultry farms.

12753 ■ Sioux County Index-Reporter
Lyon County Reporter
1013 1st St.
Hull, IA 51239-0420
Phone: (712)439-1075
Fax: (712)439-2001
Publisher's E-mail: hulleditor@ncppub.com
Tabloid. **Freq:** Weekly (Wed.). **Print Method:** Offset. **Cols./Page:** 7. **Col. Width:** 2 inches. **Col. Depth:** 21 1/2 inches. **Key Personnel:** Lois Kuehl, Advertising Representative. **USPS:** 497-320. **URL:** http://www.ncppub.com/pages/?page_id=2. **Mailing address:** PO Box 420, Hull, IA 51239. **Remarks:** Accepts advertising. **Circ:** (Not Reported).

HUMBOLDT

NWC IA. Humboldt Co. On Des Moines River, 16 mi. N. of Fort Dodge. Manufactures concrete products, high pressure cleaning equipment, truck cover, aluminum awnings, fertilizer, church furniture, farm equipment, hydraulic parts, trailers, motor homes, conveyors, plastic products, truck parts, sporting goods, flashing mobile signs. Hatcheries. Limestone quarries. Agriculture.

12754 ■ Humboldt Independent: Official Newspaper of Humboldt County
Gargano Communications Inc.
PO Box 157
Humboldt, IA 50548
Phone: (515)332-2514
Fax: (515)332-1505
Publisher's E-mail: independent@humboldtnews.com
Community newspaper. **Freq:** Weekly. **Print Method:** Offset. **Trim Size:** 13 x 21. **Cols./Page:** 6. **Col. Width:** 10 INS. **Col. Depth:** 21 inches. **Key Personnel:** Jim Gargano, Publisher. **Remarks:** Accepts advertising. **Circ:** (Not Reported).

12755 ■ KHBT-FM - 97.7
2196 Montana Ave.
Humboldt, IA 50548
Phone: (515)332-4100
Fax: (515)332-2723
Format: Adult Contemporary. **Networks:** AP; Fox. **Owner:** NRG Media, 2875 Mount Vernon Rd. SE, Cedar Rapids, IA 52403, Ph: (319)862-0300, Fax: (319)286-9383. **Founded:** Sept. 19, 2006. **Operating Hours:** Continuous. **ADI:** Cedar Rapids-Waterloo-Dubuque, IA. **Key Personnel:** Mary Quass, CEO, President, mquass@nrgmedia.com. **Wattage:** 5,800. **Ad Rates:** Noncommercial. **URL:** http://www.nrgmedia.com.

IDA GROVE

W IA. Ida Co. 50 mi. SE of Sioux City. Manufactures bolster, marine lines and boat hoists, farm equipment, paving finishing machines, feed, neon signs. Agriculture. Corn, beans, hogs, cattle.

12756 ■ Ida County Courier-Reminder
Ida County Courier-Reminder Inc.
210 Second St.
Ida Grove, IA 51445
Phone: (712)364-3131
Fax: (712)364-3010
Publisher's E-mail: idacourier@frontiernet.net
Newspaper. **Freq:** Weekly (Tues.). **Print Method:** Offset. **Cols./Page:** 6. **Col. Width:** 26 nonpareils and 11 picas. **Col. Depth:** 301 agate lines and 21 inches. **Subscription Rates:** $72 Individuals print and online. **URL:** http://www.idacountycourier.com/?q=content/subscribe-or-renew. **Mailing address:** PO Box 249, Ida Grove, IA 51445. **Remarks:** Accepts advertising. **Circ:** (Not Reported).

INDEPENDENCE

12757 ■ KQMG-AM - 1220
1812 3rd Ave. SE
Independence, IA 50644
Phone: (319)334-3300
Fax: (319)334-6158
Format: Adult Contemporary. **Simulcasts:** KQMG-FM 95.3. **Networks:** ABC. **Owner:** KM Communications, Inc., 3654 W Jarvis Ave., Skokie, IL 60076. **Founded:** 1959. **Formerly:** KOUR-AM. **Operating Hours:** 8 a.m.-5 p.m. Mon.-Fri. **Wattage:** 250 Day; 134 Night. **Ad Rates:** $10.60-16 for 30 seconds. Combined advertising rates available with KQMG-FM.

12758 ■ KQMG-FM - 95.3
1812 3rd Ave. SE
Independence, IA 50644
Phone: (319)332-1812
Fax: (319)332-1300
Format: Adult Contemporary. **Simulcasts:** KQMG-AM 1220. **Networks:** ABC. **Owner:** KM Radio Of Independence, at above address, Independence, IA. **Founded:** 1972. **Formerly:** KOUR-FM. **Key Personnel:** Jeff Carrino, Station Mgr., jeffc@kqmg.com; Ruth McNitt, Traffic Mgr., Office Mgr. **Wattage:** 6,000. **Ad Rates:** Advertising accepted; rates available upon request. Combined advertising rates available with KQMG-AM. **Mailing address:** PO Box 221, Independence, IA 50644.

INDIANOLA

SC IA. Warren Co. 16 mi. S. of Des Moines. Simpson College (Meth.). Balloon museum. Grain elevators. Agriculture. Corn, oats, wheat.

12759 ■ Record-Herald and Indianola Tribune
Register Media
Community newspaper. **Freq:** Weekly Tuesday/Wednesday. **Print Method:** Offset. **Cols./Page:** 6. **Col. Width:** 24 nonpareils. **Col. Depth:** 21 inches. **Key Personnel:** Amy Duncan, Publisher; David Chivers, President. **URL:** http://www.desmoinesregister.com/communities/indianola. **Remarks:** Accepts advertising. **Circ:** ‡17561.

12760 ■ The Simpsonian
Simpson College
701 N C St.
Indianola, IA 50125-1264
Phone: (515)961-6251
Free: 800-362-2454
Publication E-mail: thesimp@simpson.edu
Collegiate newspaper (tabloid). **Freq:** Weekly (Thurs.). **Print Method:** Letterpress and offset. **Trim Size:** 11 1/4 x 13 3/4. **Cols./Page:** 4. **Col. Width:** 2 3/8 inches. **Col. Depth:** 12 1/4 INS. **Key Personnel:** Steffi Lee, Editor-in-Chief. **URL:** http://www.thesimpsonian.com. **Ad Rates:** BW $325; PCI $5. **Remarks:** Accepts advertising. **Circ:** ‡3000.

INWOOD

NW IA. Lyon Co. 32 mi. SE of Sioux Falls, SD. Meat processing plant; hatchery. Agriculture. Stock, grain and mink farms.

12761 ■ West Lyon Herald
Lyon County Reporter
211 S Main St.
Inwood, IA 51240-7807
Phone: (712)753-2258

Fax: (712)753-4864
Community newspaper. **Freq:** Weekly (Wed.). **Print Method:** Offset. **Trim Size:** 11 1/2 x 16. **Cols./Page:** 5. **Col. Width:** 12.2 nonpareils. **Col. Depth:** 210 agate lines. **Key Personnel:** Verdona Kelly, Associate Editor. **Mailing address:** PO Box 340, Inwood, IA 51240-0340. **Remarks:** Accepts advertising. **Circ:** (Not Reported).

IOWA CITY

E IA. Johnson Co. On Iowa River, 28 mi. S. of Cedar Rapids. University of Iowa. Manufactures adhesive paper, tooth brushes, toothpaste tubes, toiletries, foam rubber, feed, iron and sheet metal products, gravel and rock products. Bottling works; hatcheries; alfalfa drying. Stone quarries. Diversified farming, cattle feeding. Corn, oats, hay.

12762 ■ Annals of Iowa
State Historical Society of Iowa
402 Iowa Ave.
Iowa City, IA 52240
Phone: (319)335-3916
Fax: (319)335-3935
State historical journal. **Freq:** Quarterly. **Print Method:** Offset. **Trim Size:** 6 x 9. **Cols./Page:** 1. **Col. Width:** 50 nonpareils. **Col. Depth:** 98 agate lines. **Key Personnel:** Marvin Bergman, Editor, phone: (319)335-3931. **ISSN:** 0003--4827 (print). **Subscription Rates:** $24.95 Individuals; $44.95 Two years; $64.95 Individuals 3 years. **URL:** http://iowaculture.gov/history/research/collections/publications/annals-iowa. **Remarks:** Advertising accepted; rates available upon request. **Circ:** (Not Reported).

12763 ■ Current Research in Social Psychology: An electronic journal
Center for the Study of Group Processes
c/o Alison Bianchi, Director
W28D Seashore Hall
Dept. of Sociology
University of Iowa
Iowa City, IA 52242-1401
Phone: (319)335-2495
Journal dealing with social psychology. **Key Personnel:** Michael Lovaglia, Editor; Shane Soboroff, Managing Editor. **ISSN:** 1088--7423 (print). **Subscription Rates:** Free. **URL:** http://www.uiowa.edu/crisp. **Circ:** (Not Reported).

12764 ■ The Daily Iowan
Student Publications Inc.
E131 Adler Journalism Bldg.
Iowa City, IA 52242
Phone: (319)335-6063
Fax: (319)335-6297
Publication E-mail: daily-iowan@uiowa.edu
General newspaper. **Freq:** Daily. **Print Method:** Offset. **Trim Size:** 11 5/8 x 20. **Cols./Page:** 6. **Col. Width:** 1 7/8 inches. **Col. Depth:** 20 inches. **Key Personnel:** Stacey Murray, Editor-in-Chief; Debra Plath, Business Manager; William B. Casey, Publisher; Cathy Witt, Advertising Representative; Juli Krause, Manager, Circulation. **Subscription Rates:** $50 Individuals in Iowa City and Coralville delivery; $100 Out of area. **URL:** http://daily-iowan.com. **Remarks:** Accepts advertising. **Circ:** (Not Reported).

12765 ■ Early Keyboard Journal
Historical Keyboard Society of North America
c/o David C. Kelzenberg, Secretary
2801 Highway 6 E, Ste. 344
Iowa City, IA 52240
Peer-reviewed journal focusing on músic, performance practices, and organology of keyboard instruments. **Freq:** Annual. **Key Personnel:** John Koster, Editor. **ISSN:** 8998--132X (print). **Subscription Rates:** Included in membership. **URL:** http://historicalkeyboardsociety.org/resources/early-keyboard-journal. **Ad Rates:** BW $145. **Remarks:** Accepts advertising. **Circ:** (Not Reported).

12766 ■ Edible Iowa River Valley
Edible Communities Inc.
22 Riverview Dr. NE
Iowa City, IA 52240-7973
Phone: (319)321-7935
Publication E-mail: info@edibleiowarivervalley.com
Magazine featuring the local food in Iowa. **Freq:** Quarterly. **Key Personnel:** Chief Kurt Michael Friese, Publisher; Kim McWane Friese, Publisher. **Subscription Rates:** $28 Individuals one year; $50 Two years; $65 Individuals three years. **URL:** http://edibleiowa.com. **Remarks:** Advertising accepted; rates available upon request. **Circ:** (Not Reported).

12767 ■ Electronic Journal of Africana Bibliography
The University of Iowa Libraries
100 Main Library
125 W Washington St.
Iowa City, IA 52242-1420
Phone: (319)335-5299
Peer-reviewed journal of bibliographies, including aspects of Africa, its people, their homes, cities, towns, districts, states, countries, regions, including social, economic sustainable development, creative literature, and the arts. **Key Personnel:** Edward A. Miner, Board Member; Dr. Afeworki Paulos, Board Member; Dr. Yuusuf Caruso, Managing Editor. **ISSN:** 1092--9576 (print). **URL:** http://ir.uiowa.edu/ejab/. **Circ:** (Not Reported).

12768 ■ Iowa Alumni Magazine
University of Iowa Alumni Association
PO Box 1970
Iowa City, IA 52244-1970
Phone: (319)335-3294
Fax: (319)335-1079
Free: 800-469-2586
Publisher's E-mail: alumni@uiowa.edu
Magazine featuring stories, news, programs, activities, events and accomplishments of IOWA Alumni. **Freq:** Bimonthly. **Subscription Rates:** Included in membership. **URL:** http://www.iowalum.com/magazine/. **Ad Rates:** BW $1,400; 4C $2,050. **Remarks:** Accepts advertising. **Circ:** 45000.

12769 ■ The Iowa City Press-Citizen
Gannett Company Inc.
PO Box 2480
Iowa City, IA 52244-2480
Phone: (319)337-3181
Fax: (319)339-7342
General newspaper. **Freq:** Daily (eve.) and Sat. (morn.). **Print Method:** Offset. **Trim Size:** 13 1/2 x 22 3/4. **Cols./Page:** 6. **Col. Width:** 2 inches. **Col. Depth:** 21.25 inches. **Key Personnel:** Jim Lewers, Managing Editor; Dale Larson, General Manager. **URL:** http://www.press-citizen.com. **Remarks:** Advertising accepted; rates available upon request. **Circ:** (Not Reported).

12770 ■ Iowa Heritage Illustrated
State Historical Society of Iowa
402 Iowa Ave.
Iowa City, IA 52240
Phone: (319)335-3916
Fax: (319)335-3935
Freq: Quarterly. **Print Method:** Offset. **Trim Size:** 8 1/2 x 11. **Cols./Page:** 2 and 3. **Col. Width:** 36 nonpareils. **Col. Depth:** 102 agate lines. **Key Personnel:** Ginalie Swaim, Editor, phone: (319)335-3932. **ISSN:** 1088--5943 (print). **Formerly**: The Palimpsest, Palimpsest. **Remarks:** Advertising not accepted. **Circ:** (Not Reported).

12771 ■ Iowa Law Review
University of Iowa College of Law
290 Boyd Law Bldg.
Iowa City, IA 52242-1113
Phone: (319)335-9095
Fax: (319)335-9646
Free: 800-553-IOWA
Publisher's E-mail: law-admissions@uiowa.edu
Law journal. **Freq:** 5/year. **Print Method:** Letterpress. **Cols./Page:** 1. **Col. Width:** 56 nonpareils. **Col. Depth:** 112 agate lines. **Key Personnel:** John A. Richter, Editor-in-Chief. **ISSN:** 0021--0552 (print). **URL:** http://ilr.law.uiowa.edu. **Remarks:** Advertising accepted; rates available upon request. **Circ:** 1500.

12772 ■ The Iowa Review
University of Iowa
Iowa City, IA 52242
Phone: (319)335-3500
Fax: (319)335-2535
Publisher's E-mail: english@uiowa.edu
Literary journal. **Freq:** Triennial. **Print Method:** Offset. **Trim Size:** 5 1/2 x 8 1/2. **Key Personnel:** Russell Scott Valentino, Editor-in-Chief; Lynne Nugent, Managing Editor. **ISSN:** 0021--065X (print). **Subscription Rates:** $20 Individuals 1 year; $35 Two years; $50 Individuals 3 years; $8.95 Single issue current issue; $7 Single issue back issue. **URL:** http://www.iowareview.org. **Remarks:** Accepts advertising. **Circ:** (Not Reported).

12773 ■ Journal of Corporation Law
University of Iowa College of Law
University of Iowa
College of Law
188 Boyd Law Bldg.
Iowa City, IA 52242-1113
Publication E-mail: jcl@uiowa.edu
Law journal. **Freq:** Quarterly. **Key Personnel:** Matt Enriquez, Editor-in-Chief; Stephen Spiegel, Contact. **ISSN:** 0360-795X (print). **Subscription Rates:** $48 U.S. and Canada; $56 Other countries. **Online:** Westlaw.Lexis-Nexix. **URL:** http://jcl.law.uiowa.edu. **Ad Rates:** BW $50. **Remarks:** Accepts advertising. **Circ:** Paid 800, Non-paid 200.

12774 ■ Journal of Corporation Law
University of Iowa College of Law
290 Boyd Law Bldg.
Iowa City, IA 52242-1113
Phone: (319)335-9095
Fax: (319)335-9646
Free: 800-553-IOWA
Publisher's E-mail: law-admissions@uiowa.edu
Journal containing legal periodical specializing in corporate law. **Freq:** Quarterly Fall, Winter, Spring, and Summer. **Key Personnel:** Lucas Carney, Editor-in-Chief. **ISSN:** 0360--795X (print). **Subscription Rates:** $48 U.S. and Canada 1 year; $56 Other countries 1 year. **URL:** http://jcl.law.uiowa.edu. **Circ:** (Not Reported).

12775 ■ Journal of Gender, Race, and Justice
University of Iowa College of Law
290 Boyd Law Bldg.
Iowa City, IA 52242-1113
Phone: (319)335-9095
Fax: (319)335-9646
Free: 800-553-IOWA
Publisher's E-mail: law-admissions@uiowa.edu
Journal discussing legal rights and boundaries of justice. **Freq:** 3/year. **Key Personnel:** Devan Rittler, Editor-in-Chief. **Subscription Rates:** $45 Individuals /volume; domestic; $55 Other countries /volume; $25 Individuals /volume; online. **URL:** http://jgrj.law.uiowa.edu. **Circ:** (Not Reported).

12776 ■ Journal of Loss and Trauma: International Perspectives on Stress & Coping
Routledge
c/o John H. Harvey, Ed.-in-Ch.
Dept. of Psychology
University of Iowa
11 Seashore Hall E
Iowa City, IA 52242-1407
Publisher's E-mail: book.orders@tandf.co.uk
Journal devoted to specific policies and techniques related to stress, trauma, and crisis. **Freq:** Bimonthly. **Print Method:** Offset. **Trim Size:** 6 1/3 x 9 1/4. **Cols./Page:** 1. **Col. Width:** 51 nonpareils. **Col. Depth:** 108 agate lines. **Key Personnel:** John H. Harvey, Editor. **ISSN:** 1532--5024 (print); **EISSN:** 1532--5032 (electronic). **Subscription Rates:** $260 Individuals print only; $739 Institutions online only; $845 Institutions print + online; $260 Individuals print + online. **URL:** http://www.tandfonline.com/toc/upil20/current. **Formerly**: Stress, Trauma and Crisis. **Remarks:** Advertising not accepted. **Circ:** (Not Reported).

12777 ■ Journal of Management Accounting Research
American Accounting Association
c/o Prof. Ramji Balakrishnan, Ed.
The University of Iowa
Tippie Scholarship of Business
W262A Pappajohn Business Bldg.
Iowa City, IA 52242
Phone: (319)335-0958
Fax: (319)335-1956
Publisher's E-mail: info@aaahq.org
Academic journal covering the theory and practice of management accounting by promoting applied and theoretical research. **Freq:** 3/year. **Trim Size:** 7 x 10. **Cols./Page:** 1. **Col. Width:** 30 picas. **Col. Depth:** 49 picas. **Key Personnel:** Ranjani Krishnan, Editor. **ISSN:**

Circulation: ★ = AAM; △ or • = BPA; ♦ = CAC; ❑ = VAC; ⊕ = PO Statement; ‡ = Publisher's Report; Boldface figures = sworn; Light figures = estimated.

1049--2127 (print); **EISSN:** 1558--8033 (electronic). **URL:** http://aaajournals.org/loi/jmar. **Ad Rates:** BW $400. **Remarks:** Accepts advertising. **Circ:** Paid 2000.

12778 ■ Journal of Neurogenetics
Informa Healthcare
c/o Chun-Fang Wu, Ed.-in-Ch.
University of Iowa
Iowa City, IA 52242
Publisher's E-mail: healthcare.enquiries@informa.com
Journal publishing papers involving genetic and molecular neurobiology. **Freq:** Quarterly. **Key Personnel:** Chun-Fang Wu, Editor-in-Chief; Jeffrey C. Hall, Editor. **ISSN:** 0167-7063 (print); **EISSN:** 1563-5260 (electronic). **Subscription Rates:** £1533 Institutions; €1683 Institutions; €2105 Institutions. **URL:** http://informahealthcare.com/neg. **Circ:** (Not Reported).

12779 ■ Legislative Studies Quarterly
Comparative Legislative Research Center
University of Iowa
334 Schaeffer Hall
Iowa City, IA 52242
Phone: (319)335-2361
Fax: (319)335-3211
Political science journal. **Freq:** Quarterly. **Print Method:** Offset. **Trim Size:** 6 x 9. **Cols./Page:** 1. **Col. Width:** 51 nonpareils. **Col. Depth:** 98 agate lines. **Key Personnel:** Michelle L. Wiegand, Managing Editor; David T. Canon, Board Member. **ISSN:** 0362--9805 (print); **EISSN:** 1939--9162 (electronic). **Subscription Rates:** $544 Institutions U.S., Canada and Mexico; £406 Institutions U.K.; €470 Institutions Europe; $575 Institutions, other countries; $24 Individuals U.S., Canada, Mexico and other countries; £18 Individuals U.K.; €21 Individuals Europe. **URL:** http://onlinelibrary.wiley.com/journal/10.1002/(ISSN)1939-9162. **Ad Rates:** BW $225. **Remarks:** Accepts advertising. **Circ:** Paid ‡1400, Non-paid ‡40.

12780 ■ Philological Quarterly
University of Iowa Conduit
308 English-Philosophy Bldg.
Department of English
University of Iowa
Iowa City, IA 52242
Publication E-mail: p-q@uiowa.edu
Publication covering literature, language and linguistics. **Freq:** Quarterly. **Key Personnel:** Alvin Snider, Editor. **ISSN:** 0031--7977 (print). **Subscription Rates:** $30 Individuals 1 year; $70 Institutions 1 year; $10 Single issue /copy. **URL:** http://english.uiowa.edu/philological-quarterly. **Circ:** (Not Reported).

12781 ■ Poroi: An Interdisciplinary Journal of Rhetorical Analysis and Invention
University of Iowa Conduit
230 N Clinton
100 Bowman House
Iowa City, IA 52242
Phone: (319)335-2752
Fax: (319)335-1745
Publication E-mail: poroi@uiowa.edu
An open access, peer-reviewed journal for scholarship attuned to rhetoric in inquiry and culture. **Freq:** Semiannual. **Key Personnel:** John S. Nelson, Editor, Founder; Andre Brock, Editor. **ISSN:** 2151--2957 (print). **Subscription Rates:** Free online. **URL:** http://ir.uiowa.edu/poroi. **Remarks:** Advertising not accepted. **Circ:** (Not Reported).

12782 ■ The Sociological Quarterly
Midwest Sociological Society
1613 College Court Pl.
Iowa City, IA 52245
Phone: (319)338-5247
Journal publishing research and theory in all areas of sociological inquiry, focusing on publishing sociological research and writing. **Freq:** Quarterly. **Key Personnel:** Betty A. Dobratz, Editor; Lisa K. Waldner, Editor; Peter Kivisto, Editor, Advisor; Patricia Adler, Editor, Advisor. **ISSN:** 0038--0253 (print); **EISSN:** 1533--8525 (electronic). **Subscription Rates:** $670 Institutions print + online; $558 Institutions print or online; £405 Institutions print + online; £337 Institutions print or online; €512 Institutions print + online; €426 Institutions print or online; $785 Institutions, other countries print and online; $654 Institutions, other countries print or online; free online access for members. **URL:** http://onlinelibrary.wiley.com/journal/10.1111/(ISSN)1533-8525. **Remarks:** Accepts display advertising. **Circ:** 2,000.

12783 ■ KCJJ-AM - 1630
PO Box 2118
Iowa City, IA 52244
Phone: (319)354-1242
Fax: (319)354-1921
Format: Talk. **Networks:** ABC; CNN Radio. **Owner:** River City Radio, Inc., at above address. **Founded:** 1977. **Operating Hours:** Continuous; 100% local. **Key Personnel:** Tom Suter, Gen. Mgr.; Kurt Means, Account Exec., kurtkcjj@aol.com. **Wattage:** 10,000 Day ; 1,000 Night. **Ad Rates:** $14-25 for 30 seconds; $17-28 for 60 seconds. **URL:** http://www.1630kcjj.com.

12784 ■ KIIN-TV - 12
6450 Corporate Dr.
Johnston, IA 50131
Phone: (515)242-3100
Free: 800-532-1290
Format: Public TV. **Simulcasts:** KDIN-TV Des Moines, IA. **Networks:** Public Broadcasting Service (PBS). **Owner:** Iowa Public Television, PO Box 6450, Johnston, IA 50131-6450, Ph: (515)242-3100, Free: 800-532-1290. **Founded:** 1970. **ADI:** Cedar Rapids-Waterloo-Dubuque, IA. **Key Personnel:** Daniel K. Miller, Exec. Dir., Gen. Mgr., dkm@iptv.org; Jeff Horn, Art Dir. **Ad Rates:** Noncommercial. **Mailing address:** PO Box 6450, Johnston, IA 50131. **URL:** http://www.iptv.org.

12785 ■ KRUI-FM - 89.7
University of Iowa
379 Iowa Memorial Union
Iowa City, IA 52242
Phone: (319)335-9525
Email: krui@uiowa.edu
Format: Educational; Full Service; Alternative/New Music/Progressive. **Networks:** AP. **Owner:** Student Broadcasters Inc., at above address. **Founded:** 1984. **Operating Hours:** Continuous; 100% local. **Key Personnel:** Dolan Murphy, Gen. Mgr.; Jake Stanbro, Dir. of Operations; Max Johnson, Music Dir. **Wattage:** 100. **Ad Rates:** Noncommercial. **URL:** http://krui.fm.

12786 ■ KSUI-FM - 91.7
2111 Grand Ave., Ste. 100
Des Moines, IA 50312
Phone: (515)725-1700
Free: 800-861-8000
Email: info@iowapublicradio.org
Format: Public Radio; Classical. **Networks:** National Public Radio (NPR). **Owner:** Iowa Public Radio, 2111 Grand Ave., Ste. 100, Des Moines, IA 50312-5393, Ph: (515)725-1700, Free: 800-861-8000. **Founded:** 1948. **Operating Hours:** Continuous. **Key Personnel:** Mary Grace Herrington, Exec. Dir.; Jonathan Ahl, News Dir., newsdirector@iowapublicradio.org; Al Schares, Music Dir., musicdirector@iowapublicradio.org. **Wattage:** 100,000. **Ad Rates:** Noncommercial. **URL:** http://www.iowapublicradio.org.

12787 ■ KXIC-AM - 800
2401 Scott Blvd.
Iowa City, IA 52240
Phone: (319)354-9500
Format: News; Information; Sports. **Networks:** CNN Radio. **Owner:** iHeartMedia Inc., 200 E Basse Rd., San Antonio, TX 78209, Ph: (210)832-3314. **Founded:** 1948. **Operating Hours:** Continuous; 90% network, 10% local. **Key Personnel:** Ursula Fellows, Contact, ursulafellows@clearchannel.com; Ursula Fellows, Contact, ursulafellows@clearchannel.com. **Wattage:** 5,000. **Ad Rates:** $8-24 for 30 seconds. **URL:** http://www.kxic.com.

12788 ■ PEC Cable
1700 S 1st Ave., Ste. 1
1700 1st Ave., No. 1
Iowa City, IA 52240
Phone: (319)351-2297
Owner: Professional Engineering Consultants, Inc., at above address. **Founded:** 1989. **Key Personnel:** Joe Peterson, VP, joepeter@aol.com. **Cities Served:** subscribing households 95.

IOWA FALLS

C IA. Hardin Co. On Iowa River, 50 mi. W. of Waterloo. Manufactures luggage, pre-stressed concrete beams, plastic injection molded containers, portable grain aerators, steel mandrels. Agriculture. Dairy, stock, grain farms. Corn, soybeans, oats, rye.

12789 ■ Times-Citizen
Times-Citizen Communications Inc.
406 Stevens St.
Iowa Falls, IA 50126-2214
Phone: (641)648-2521
Fax: (641)648-4765
Free: 800-798-2691
Publisher's E-mail: tcc@iafalls.com
Community newspaper. **Freq:** Semiweekly (Wed. and Sat.). **Print Method:** Offset. **Trim Size:** 15 x 22 1/2. **Cols./Page:** 6. **Col. Width:** 12.5 picas. **Col. Depth:** 21 inches. **ISSN:** 2351--8000 (print). **Subscription Rates:** $50 Individuals online. **Formerly:** Hardin County Times; Iowa Falls Citizen. **Mailing address:** PO Box 640, Iowa Falls, IA 50126-0640. **Remarks:** Advertising accepted; rates available upon request. **Circ:** (Not Reported).

12790 ■ KIFG-AM - 1510
406 Stevens St.
Iowa Falls, IA 50126
Phone: (641)648-4281
Fax: (641)648-4765
Email: kifg@iafalls.com
Format: Oldies. **Simulcasts:** KIFG-FM. **Networks:** CNN Radio; Westwood One Radio. **Owner:** Times Citizen Communications Inc., 406 Stevens St., Iowa Falls, IA 50126, Ph: (641)648-2521, Free: 800-798-2691. **Founded:** 1962. **Formerly:** KIFG. **Operating Hours:** Continuous; 7 hours local. **Key Personnel:** Jessica Peters, Gen. Mgr.; John Goossen, Div. Dir.; Becky Schipper, Editor. **Wattage:** 6,000 FM. **Ad Rates:** $5-8 for 30 seconds; $6-10 for 60 seconds. **URL:** http://www.timescitizen.com.

12791 ■ KIFG-FM - 95.3
406 Stevens St.
Iowa Falls, IA 50126
Phone: (641)648-2521
Fax: (641)648-4765
Email: kifg@iafalls.com
Format: Contemporary Hit Radio (CHR). **Simulcasts:** KIFG-AM. **Networks:** Independent. **Owner:** Times Citizen Communications Inc., 406 Stevens St., Iowa Falls, IA 50126, Ph: (641)648-2521, Free: 800-798-2691. **Founded:** 1964. **Operating Hours:** Continuous; 7 hours local. **Key Personnel:** Jessica Peters, Circulation Mgr., ites@iafalls.com; John Goossen, Gen. Mgr., jgoossen@iafalls.com. **Wattage:** 6,000. **Ad Rates:** $5-8 for 30 seconds; $7-10 for 60 seconds. **URL:** http://www.timescitizen.com.

JESUP

NEC IA. Buchanan Co. 9 mi. W. of Independence. Residential.

12792 ■ Citizen Herald
Citizen Herald
930 6th St.
Jesup, IA 50648
Phone: (319)827-1128
Fax: (319)827-1125
Local newspaper. **Freq:** Weekly (Wed.). **Print Method:** Offset. **Trim Size:** 7 1/4 x 11 1/4. **Cols./Page:** 6. **Col. Width:** 12.5 picas. **Col. Depth:** 21.5 inches. **USPS:** 113-980. **Mailing address:** PO Box 545, Jesup, IA 50648-0545. **Remarks:** Advertising accepted; rates available upon request. **Circ:** (Not Reported).

JEWELL

C IA. Hamilton Co. 14 mi. SE of Webster City. Residential.

12793 ■ South Hamilton Record News
South Hamilton Record News
602 Main St.
Jewell, IA 50130-2012
Phone: (515)827-5931
Fax: (515)827-5760
Publication E-mail: shrecnew@netins.net
Local and agriculture business newspaper. **Freq:** Weekly (Wed.). **Print Method:** Offset. **Cols./Page:** 6. **Col. Width:** 24 nonpareils. **Col. Depth:** 301 agate lines. **Key Personnel:** Scott Ervin, Editor, Manager, Circulation, Manager, Advertising, General Manager, Publisher. **Remarks:** Accepts advertising. **Circ:** (Not Reported).

JOHNSTON

C IA. Polk Co. 5 mi. N. of Des Moines. Near Saylorville Lake. Residential.

IPTV-TV - See Sioux City

KDIN-TV - See Des Moines

KHIN-TV - See Red Oak

KIIN-TV - See Iowa City

KRIN-TV - See Waterloo

KSIN-TV - See Sioux City

KTIN-TV - See Fort Dodge

KYIN-TV - See Mason City

KALONA

SE IA. Washington Co. 18 mi. SW of Iowa City. Creamery; elevator. Grain farms. Corn, oats, wheat.

12794 ■ The Kalona News
The Kalona News
PO Box 430
Kalona, IA 52247-0430
Phone: (319)656-2273
Fax: (319)656-2299
Community newspaper. **Freq:** Weekly (Thurs.). **Print Method:** Offset. **Cols./Page:** 6. **Col. Width:** 12 picas. **Col. Depth:** 21.5 inches. **Key Personnel:** Ronald C. Slechta, Editor, Publisher; Helen Slechta, Business Manager. **USPS:** 289-560. **Subscription Rates:** $41 Individuals in Washington, Johnson, Keokuk & Iowa counties; $43 Individuals in state; $50 Out of state. **Remarks:** Accepts advertising. **Circ:** (Not Reported).

KANAWHA

N IA. Hancock Co. 40 mi. NE of Fort Dodge. Northern Iowa Research Station for Iowa State University. Manufactures horse trailers, sportswear. Grain elevators. Agriculture. Corn, soybeans.

12795 ■ Communication 1 Cablevision Inc.
105 S Main
Kanawha, IA 50447
Phone: (641)762-3772
Owner: Communications 1 Network Inc., 105 S Main St., Kanawha, IA 50447, Ph: (641)762-3772, Fax: (641)762-8201, Free: 800-469-3772. **Founded:** 1983. **Cities Served:** Corwith, Kanawha, Klemme, Wesley, Iowa: subscribing households 622; 39 channels; 2 community access channels; 168 hours per week community access programming. **Mailing address:** PO Box 20, Kanawha, IA 50447.

KEOKUK

SE IA. Lee Co. On Mississippi River at mouth of Des Moines River, 18 mi. S. of Fort Madison. Bridge to Hamilton, IL. Boat connections. Hydro-electric power plant. Sawmill. Manufactures starch, corn, dairy products, ferro-alloys, shipping cases, cereals, canned goods, fibre boxes, calcium-carbide, rubber products, steel and aluminum die castings, railroad wheels. Limestone quarries. Diversified farming.

12796 ■ Daily Gate City
Brehm Communications Inc.
1016 Main St.
Keokuk, IA 52632
Phone: (391)524-8300
General newspaper. **Freq:** Daily (eve.). **Print Method:** Offset. **Cols./Page:** 8. **Col. Width:** 18 nonpareils. **Col. Depth:** 301 agate lines. **Key Personnel:** Tom Kirk, Publisher. **Subscription Rates:** $77 Individuals home delivery; $95 By mail in Lee County; $133 Out of area mail delivery; $78 Individuals e-edition; $86 Individuals motor delivery. **URL:** http://www.dailygate.com. **Remarks:** Accepts advertising. **Circ:** (Not Reported).

12797 ■ KOKX-AM - 1310
108 Washington St.
Keokuk, IA 52632-0427
Phone: (319)524-5410
Format: News; Talk; Information. **Networks:** ABC. **Owner:** W. Russell Withers, Jr., PO Box 1591, Mount Vernon, IL 62864, Ph: (618)242-3500. **Founded:** 1947. **Key Personnel:** Jim Worrell, News Dir. **Wattage:** 1,000 KW. **Ad Rates:** $19-27 for 30 seconds; $22-30 for 60 seconds. Combined advertising rates available with KOKX-FM. **Mailing address:** PO Box 427, Keokuk, IA 52632-0427. **URL:** http://radiokeokuk.com/.

12798 ■ KOKX-FM - 95.3
108 Washington St.
Keokuk, IA 52632
Phone: (319)524-5410
Fax: (319)524-7275
Format: Oldies. **Networks:** ABC. **Owner:** Withers Broadcasting of Iowa, 108 Washington St., Keokuk, IA 52632, Ph: (319)524-5410, Fax: (319)524-7275. **Founded:** 1973. **Operating Hours:** Continuous. **Key Personnel:** Gary Folluo, Gen. Mgr., gary@keokukradio.com; Matt Frisbee, Operations Mgr., Prog. Dir., matt@keokukradio.com; Tara Whitnah, Office Mgr. **Wattage:** 100,000. **Ad Rates:** $19-27 for 30 seconds; $22-30 for 60 seconds. Combined advertising rates available with KOKX-AM. **URL:** http://www.keokukradio.com/our-stations/kokx-fm.

12799 ■ KRNQ-FM - 96.3
108 Washington St.
Keokuk, IA 52632
Phone: (319)524-5410
Fax: (319)524-7275
Format: Classic Rock. **Owner:** Withers Broadcasting Companies, 1822 N Court St., Marion, IL 62959, Ph: (303)242-5000.

12800 ■ WCEZ-FM - 93.9
108 Washington St.
Keokuk, IA 52632
Phone: (319)524-5410
Fax: (319)524-7275
Format: Full Service; Easy Listening. **Owner:** Keokuk Radio, 108 Washington St, Keokuk, IA 52632, Ph: (319)524-5410. **Key Personnel:** Gary Folluo, Gen. Mgr., gary@keokukradio.com. **Wattage:** 6,000. **URL:** http://www.keokukradio.com.

KEOTA

SE IA. Keokuk Co. 35 mi. SW of Iowa City. Farm equipment, egg producing factories. Dairy, stock, grain farms. Corn, hogs, cattle.

12801 ■ The Keota Eagle
The Keota Eagle
310 E Broadway Ave.
Keota, IA 52248
Phone: (641)636-2309
Fax: (641)456-2587
Publisher's E-mail: keotaeagle@cloudburst9.net
Newspaper. **Freq:** Weekly (Wed.). **Print Method:** Offset. **Trim Size:** 7 x 11 1/2. **Cols./Page:** 6. **Col. Width:** 11.6 picas. **Col. Depth:** 21. inches. **Key Personnel:** Hailey Brown, Editor. **USPS:** 293-620. **Subscription Rates:** $37 Individuals print and online; $37 Individuals local and non-local (online). **Mailing address:** PO Box 18, Keota, IA 52248. **Remarks:** Accepts advertising. **Circ:** (Not Reported).

KNOXVILLE

SC IA. Marion Co. 38 mi. SE of Des Moines. Ships coal, livestock. Coal mines. Stock, poultry, dairy farms.

12802 ■ Journal-Express
Journal/Express Inc.
122 E Robinson
Knoxville, IA 50138
Phone: (641)842-2155
Fax: (641)842-2929
Community newspaper. **Founded:** 1855. **Freq:** Weekly. **Print Method:** Offset. **Cols./Page:** 6. **Col. Width:** 39 nonpareils. **Col. Depth:** 6 x 21 1 inches. **Key Personnel:** Maureen Miller, Publisher; Steve Woodhouse, Editor. **USPS:** 297-440. **Subscription Rates:** $32 Individuals delivered in Marion County; $37 Out of area. **URL:** http://www.journalexpress.net/. **Mailing address:** PO Box 458, Knoxville, IA 50138-0458. **Ad Rates:** BW $743; 4C $1,049; SAU $6.40. **Remarks:** Accepts classified advertising. **Circ:** 1700.

12803 ■ Knoxville Journal Express
Community Newspaper Holdings Inc.
122 E Robinson St.
Knoxville, IA 50138
Phone: (641)842-2155
Fax: (641)842-2929
Publication E-mail: jenews@iowatelecom.net
Newspaper serving Knoxville and Marion County, Iowa. **Key Personnel:** Maureen Miller, Publisher; Steve Woodhouse, Editor. **Subscription Rates:** $32 By mail in County; $37 Out of area mail delivery. **URL:** http://www.journalexpress.net. **Mailing address:** PO Box 458, Knoxville, IA 50138. **Remarks:** Accepts advertising. **Circ:** (Not Reported).

12804 ■ KNIA-AM - 1320
PO Box 31
Knoxville, IA 50138
Phone: (641)842-3161
Fax: (641)842-5606
Email: kniakrls@kniakrls.com
Format: Oldies; News. **Networks:** USA Radio. **Owner:** M & H Broadcasting Inc., Not Available. **Founded:** 1983. **Operating Hours:** 5 a.m.-11 p.m.; 2% network, 98% local. **Wattage:** 500 Day; 250 Night. **Ad Rates:** for 30 seconds; for 60 seconds. Combined advertising rates available with KRLS-FM. **URL:** http://www.kniakrls.com.

12805 ■ KRLS-FM - 92.1
PO Box 31
Knoxville, IA 50138
Phone: (641)842-3161
Fax: (641)842-5606
Email: kniakrls@kniakrls.com
Format: Adult Contemporary. **Founded:** Sept. 07, 2006. **Key Personnel:** Jim Butler, Gen. Mgr., jimbutler@kniakrls.com. **Ad Rates:** Noncommercial. **URL:** http://www.kniakrls.com.

LA PORTE CITY

NEC IA. Black Hawk Co. 15 mi. SE of Waterloo. Feed mill. Agriculture. Corn, oats, soy beans.

12806 ■ Progress Review
Progress Review
313 Main St.
La Porte City, IA 50651-1333
Phone: (319)342-2429
Publication E-mail: news@theprogressreview.co
Newspaper. **Freq:** Weekly (Wed.) delivered via snail mail, digital edition delivered via e-mail on Mondays. **Print Method:** Offset. **Trim Size:** 8 1/2 x 11. **Cols./Page:** 6. **Col. Width:** 10 inches. **Col. Depth:** 16 inches. **Key Personnel:** Mike Whittlesey, Editor; Jane Whittlesey, Publisher. **Subscription Rates:** $38 Individuals In Iowa (print); $54 Out of state print; $44 Individuals Snowbirds (print); $32 Individuals digital. **Remarks:** Accepts advertising. **Circ:** (Not Reported).

LAKE CITY

12807 ■ The Graphic-Advocate
Remma Inc.
121 North Center St.
Lake City, IA 51449
Community newspaper. **Founded:** 1878. **Freq:** Weekly (Wed.). **Print Method:** Offset. **Cols./Page:** 8. **Col. Width:** 21 nonpareils. **Col. Depth:** 301 agate lines. **USPS:** 468-840. **Subscription Rates:** $36 Individuals print and online or online only; $72 Two years print and online or online only. **URL:** http://thegraphic-advocate.com/. **Formed by the merger of:** Calhoun County Advocate; Lake City Graphic. **Ad Rates:** GLR $.42; SAU $3.60; PCI $3.25. **Remarks:** Accepts advertising. **Circ:** ‡2187.

LAKE MILLS

N IA. Winnebago Co. 25 mi. NW of Mason City. Manufactures plastics, doors, windows, auto filters; creamery. Dairy, grain, stock farms.

12808 ■ Lake Mills Graphic
Lake Mills Graphic
204 N Mill St.
Lake Mills, IA 50450-1316
Phone: (641)592-4222
Fax: (641)592-6397
Publication E-mail: graphic@wctatel.net
Newspaper with a Republican orientation. **Founded:** 1872. **Freq:** Weekly (Wed.). **Print Method:** Offset. **Cols./Page:** 6. **Col. Width:** 28 nonpareils. **Col. Depth:** 301 agate lines. **Key Personnel:** Terry Gasper, Editor, Manager, Publisher. **USPS:** 302-440. **Subscription Rates:** $36 Individuals print or online; $38 Out of state print; $40 Individuals print and online. **URL:** http://www.

Circulation: ★ = AAM; △ or • = BPA; ♦ = CAC; ❑ = VAC; ⊕ = PO Statement; ‡ = Publisher's Report; Boldface figures = sworn; Light figures = estimated.

lmgraphic.com/home/. **Formerly**: Graphic. **Mailing address:** PO Box 127, Lake Mills, IA 50450-1316. **Ad Rates:** GLR $.16; BW $4.50; 4C $125; SAU $6.55. **Remarks:** Accepts advertising. **Circ:** (Not Reported).

12809 ■ Winnebago Co-op Cablevision
704 E Main St.
Lake Mills, IA 50450
Phone: (641)592-6105
Free: 800-592-6105
Owner: Winnebago Cooperative Telecom Association, 704 E Main St., Lake Mills, IA 50450, Ph: (641)592-6105, Free: 800-592-6105. **Founded:** 1980. **Key Personnel:** Terry Wegener, Gen. Mgr. **Cities Served:** Buffalo Center, Forest City, Lake Mills, Thompson, Iowa: subscribing households 2,360; 37 channels; 1 community access channel; 168 hours per week community access programming. **URL:** http://www.wctatel.net.

LE MARS

NW IA. Plymouth Co. 25 mi. NE of Sioux City. Westmar College. Foundry. Manufactures jeans and outerwear; cleaning chemicals processing. District utility headquarters, fertilizer, feed mills; meat processing, beef packing, dairy plants. Ships grain, livestock. Agriculture.

12810 ■ Daily Sentinel
Le Mars Daily Sentinel
41 First Ave. NE
Le Mars, IA 51031
Phone: (712)546-7031
Fax: (712)546-7035
Free: 800-728-0066
Publisher's E-mail: sentinel@lemarscomm.net
General newspaper. **Freq:** Daily. **Key Personnel:** Randy List, Publisher; Monte Jost, Senior General Manager; Shannon Jost, Director; Judy Barnable, Business Manager. **URL:** http://www.lemarssentinel.com. **Remarks:** Accepts advertising. **Circ:** 3061.

12811 ■ KLEM-AM - 1410
37 2nd Ave. NW
Le Mars, IA 51031
Phone: (712)546-4121
Fax: (712)546-9672
Email: klem@lemarscomm.net
Format: Adult Contemporary. **Networks:** AP. **Owner:** Powell Broadcasting, at above address. **Founded:** Oct. 12, 1954. **Operating Hours:** 10% network, 90% local. **ADI:** Sioux City, IA. **Key Personnel:** Denny Callahan, Sports Dir.; Joanne Glamm, News Dir. **Local Programs**: *Mid-Day News*; *Noon Hour Sports*; *Evening News*; *What Now Show*, Monday Tuesday Wednesday Thursday Friday Saturday Sunday. **Wattage:** 1,000. **Ad Rates:** $12 for 30 seconds; $16 for 60 seconds. Combined advertising rates available with KKMA-FM, KSUX-FM, KSCJ-AM. **URL:** http://www.klem1410.com.

LEHIGH

12812 ■ Lehigh Services Inc.
9090 Taylor Rd.
Lehigh, IA 50551
Phone: (515)359-2211
Fax: (515)359-2424
Email: info@lvcta.net
Founded: 2011. **Key Personnel:** Kenneth Sanders, President; Brian Lambert, VP; James Suchan, Mgr. **Cities Served:** 53 channels. **Mailing address:** PO Box 137, Lehigh, IA 50551. **URL:** http://www.lvcta.net.

LENOX

SW IA. Taylor Co. 30 mi. SE of Red Oak. Residential.

12813 ■ Lenox Municipal Cablevision
205 S Main St.
Lenox, IA 50851-0096
Phone: (515)333-2550
Key Personnel: David Ferris, Gen. Mgr. **Cities Served:** subscribing households 540. **URL:** http://www.lenoxutilities.com.

LIME SPRINGS

NE IA. Howard Co. 44 mi. SW of Rochester, MN. Home of restored Lidtke Mill. State conservation area. Food locker. Egg packing plant. Grain elevators. Beef, dairy, grain farms.

12814 ■ Lime Springs Herald
Lime Springs Herald
PO Box 187
Lime Springs, IA 52155
Phone: (563)566-2687
Fax: (563)566-2687
Publication E-mail: evans@frontiernet.net
Newspaper with a Republican orientation. **Freq:** Weekly (Thurs.). **Print Method:** Offset. **Cols./Page:** 6. **Col. Width:** 2 1/4 inches. **Col. Depth:** 21 1/2 inches. **USPS:** 313-300. **Remarks:** Accepts advertising. **Circ:** (Not Reported).

MANCHESTER

E IA. Delaware Co. 43 mi. W. of Dubuque. State trout hatchery. Manufactures gates, batteries, polyethylene film packaging, playground equipment, aluminum and brass castings, feed truck bodies, molded fiberglass containers. Corn, oats, livestock, hogs, poultry, dairy farms.

12815 ■ KMCH-FM - 94.7
PO Box 497
Manchester, IA 52057
Phone: (563)927-6249
Fax: (563)927-4372
Free: 877-927-6249
Email: mix947@kmch.com
Format: Country; Adult Contemporary. **Networks:** CBS; Radio Iowa. **Founded:** Dec. 05, 1991. **Operating Hours:** Continuous. **Key Personnel:** Jackie Coates, Mgr.; Mike Johnson, Prog. Dir.; Jim Coloff, Gen. Mgr., Owner; Rob Edwards, Dir. of Production; Rhonda Mensen, Office Mgr. **Wattage**: 6,000. **Ad Rates:** Noncommercial. **URL:** http://www.kmch.com.

MANILLA

W IA. Crawford Co. 25 mi. SW of Carroll. Residential.

12816 ■ The Manilla Times
Manilla Printing Co.
443 Main St.
Manilla, IA 51454
Phone: (712)654-2632
Fax: (712)654-9182
Local newspaper. **Founded:** 1899. **Freq:** Weekly. **Print Method:** Offset. **Cols./Page:** 6. **Col. Width:** 18 nonpareils. **Col. Depth:** 210 agate lines. **Key Personnel:** Joleen R. Sievertsen, Office Manager. **Subscription Rates:** $30 Individuals local; $35 Out of area; $40 Out of state. **URL:** http://manillaia.com/. **Ad Rates:** SAU $4. **Remarks:** Advertising accepted; rates available upon request. **Circ:** ‡1200.

MANSON

NWC IA. Calhoun Co. 18 mi. W. of Fort Dodge. Manufactures calendars, golf and tote bags, fertilizer. Agriculture. Corn, oats, barley, soybeans, turkeys.

12817 ■ Journal Herald
Dudley Printing
931 Main St.
Manson, IA 50563
Phone: (712)469-3381
Fax: (712)469-2648
Newspaper. **Founded:** 1888. **Freq:** Weekly. **Print Method:** Offset. **Cols./Page:** 7. **Col. Width:** 22 nonpareils. **Col. Depth:** 301 agate lines. **Subscription Rates:** $29 Out of area; $26 Individuals in Calhoun, Webster & Pocahontas County. **URL:** http://www.journalherald.com/. **Formerly**: Herald. **Mailing address:** PO Box 40, Manson, IA 50563. **Ad Rates:** GLR $.12. **Remarks:** Accepts advertising. **Circ:** 1400.

MAQUOKETA

NE IA E IA. Jackson Co Jackson Co. 10 mi. E. of Baldwin 32 mi. S. of Dubuque. Manufactures woven wood shades, oil filters, steel paving reinforcements, tractor cooling systems, dairy products, boat trailers. Ships livestock. Limestone quarries. Agriculture. Corn, alfalfa, dairy products.

12818 ■ Maquoketa Sentinel-Press
Maquoketa Sentinel-Press
108 W Quarry
Maquoketa, IA 52060
Phone: (563)652-2441
Fax: (563)652-6094
Free: 800-747-7377
Publication E-mail: mspress@mpress.net
Local newspaper. **Freq:** Semiweekly (Wed. and Sat.). **Print Method:** Offset. **Cols./Page:** 9. **Col. Width:** 10 picas. **Col. Depth:** 301 agate lines. **Key Personnel:** Douglas Melvold, Editor, Publisher; Rosie Morehead, Manager, Advertising. **USPS:** 589-540. **URL:** http://www.maqnews.com. **Remarks:** Advertising accepted; rates available upon request. **Circ:** Paid ‡3500.

12819 ■ KMAQ-AM - 1320
129 N Main St.
Maquoketa, IA 52060
Phone: (563)652-2426
Free: 800-747-0057
Format: Country. **Owner:** Maquoketa Broadcasting Co., 129 North Main St., Maquoketa, IA 52060, Ph: (563)652-2426, Fax: (563)652-6210, Free: 800-747-0057. **Founded:** 1958. **Wattage**: 500 Day; 135 Night. **Ad Rates:** KMAQ-FM. **Mailing address:** PO Box 940, Maquoketa, IA 52060. **URL:** http://www.kmaq.com.

12820 ■ KMAQ-FM - 95.1
129 N Main St.
Maquoketa, IA 52060
Format: Adult Contemporary. **Owner:** Maquoketa Broadcasting Co., 129 North Main St., Maquoketa, IA 52060, Ph: (563)652-2426, Fax: (563)652-6210, Free: 800-747-0057. **Founded:** 1958. **Operating Hours:** 6:00 a.m. - 10:00 p.m. Monday - Saturday; Sunrise - Sunset Sunday. **Wattage:** 6,000 ERP. **Ad Rates:** KMAQ-AM. **Mailing address:** PO Box 940, Maquoketa, IA 52060. **URL:** http://www.kmaq.com.

MARENGO

SEC IA. Iowa Co. On Iowa River, 32 mi. SW of Cedar Rapids. Manufactures stock feeds, seed corn, modular homes, wood by-products. Dairy, stock, grain, truck, poultry farms.

12821 ■ Pioneer Republican: Newspapers of Iowa County
Pioneer Republican
PO Box 208
Marengo, IA 52301
Phone: (319)642-5506
Fax: (319)642-5509
Free: 800-414-5506
Publisher's E-mail: publish@netins.net
Community newspaper. **Freq:** Weekly (Thurs.). **Print Method:** Offset. **Trim Size:** 15 x 22 3/4. **Cols./Page:** 9. **Col. Width:** 10 nonpareils. **Col. Depth:** 21 1/2 inches. **Key Personnel:** Dan Adix, Editor; Michael T. Simmons, Publisher; Paul D. Thompson, General Manager. **URL:** http://archive.yourweeklypaper.com/blog/category/pioneer-republican. **Ad Rates:** GLR $.54; BW $1,064.25; 4C $1,199.25; SAU $8.25; PCI $5. **Remarks:** Accepts advertising. **Circ:** ‡2675.

12822 ■ Star Press Union
MPC Publishing Co.
100 W Main St.
Marengo, IA 52301
Phone: (319)642-5506
Fax: (319)642-5509
Free: 800-414-5506
Publication E-mail: bpunion@netins.net
Newspaper. **Freq:** Weekly (Wed.). **Print Method:** Offset. **Cols./Page:** 9. **Col. Width:** 18 nonpareils. **Col. Depth:** 301 agate lines. **Key Personnel:** Don E. Magdefrau, Publisher; Jim Magdefrau, Editor. **Subscription Rates:** $28 Individuals; $35 Out of state. **URL:** http://showcase.netins.net/web/bpunion/BentonCounty/Starpresssunion.html. **Formerly**: The Belle Plaine Union. **Mailing address:** PO Box 208, Marengo, IA 52301. **Ad Rates:** GLR $.54; BW $967.50; 4C $1104.13; SAU $7.50; PCI $5. **Remarks:** Accepts advertising. **Circ:** 3465.

MARION

E IA. Linn Co. 5 mi. NE of Cedar Rapids. Manufactures engine and brake reconditioning equipment, specialty packaging, baking equipment, printed circuit board.

12823 ■ Premiere Guitar
Gearhead Communications L.L.C.
Three Research Ctr.
Marion, IA 52302
Phone: (319)447-5550

Free: 877-704-4327
Consumer magazine covering equipment, services, and supplies for professional, performing musicians. **Freq:** Monthly. **Print Method:** Web offset. **Trim Size:** 8 x 10.75. **Cols./Page:** 4. **Col. Width:** 1 5/8 inches. **Col. Depth:** 1 7/8 inches. **Key Personnel:** Adam Moore, Senior Editor; Shawn Hammond, Editor-in-Chief; Gary Ciocci, Managing Editor; Jon Levy, Managing Editor. **Subscription Rates:** $24.95 Individuals; $39.95 Two years; $39.95 Canada; $79.90 Canada 2 years. **URL:** http://www.premierguitar.com. **Formerly:** Midwest Musicians Hotline; Musicians Hotline. **Ad Rates:** BW $970; 4C $1,460; PCI $7. **Remarks:** Accepts advertising. **Circ:** 33011, ‡30249.

12824 ■ Sport Rocketry: America's Complete Sport Rocketry Magazine
National Association of Rocketry
PO Box 407
Marion, IA 52302-0407
Fax: (319)373-8910
Free: 800-262-4872
Publisher's E-mail: nar-hq@nar.org
Freq: Bimonthly. **ISSN:** 0883- 0991 (print). **Subscription Rates:** Included in membership. **Alt. Formats:** PDF. **URL:** http://www.nar.org/sport-rocketry-magazine/. **Remarks:** Accepts advertising. **Circ:** 6000.

MARSHALLTOWN

C IA. Marshall Co. 50 mi. NE of Des Moines. Manufactures furnaces, air conditioners, warm air registers; steam specialties, trowels, pressure gauges, farm machinery, auto accessories, surgical dressings, paper boxes. Iron, brass, aluminum foundries. Stone quarries. Agriculture.

12825 ■ Pennysaver
Pennysaver
135 W Main St.
Marshalltown, IA 50158
Phone: (641)752-6630
Publisher's E-mail: ps@marshalltownpennysaver.com
Shopper. **Founded:** 1973. **Freq:** Semiweekly (Wed. and Sat.). **Print Method:** Offset. **Cols./Page:** 7. **Col. Width:** 16 nonpareils. **Col. Depth:** 224 agate lines. **URL:** http://www.marshalltownpennysaver.com. **Mailing address:** PO Box 246, Marshalltown, IA 50158. **Ad Rates:** BW $812; 4C $957; PCI $8.40. **Remarks:** Accepts advertising. **Circ:** 16,500.

12826 ■ KDAO-AM - 1190
1930 N Center St.
Marshalltown, IA 50158
Phone: (641)752-4122
Email: kdao@kdao.com
Format: Oldies. **Owner:** MTN Broadcasting, Inc., at above address. **Founded:** 1978. **Wattage:** 250 KW. **Ad Rates:** Accepts Advertising. **Mailing address:** PO Box 538, Marshalltown, IA 50158. **URL:** http://www.kdao.com/.

12827 ■ KFJB-AM - 1230
123 W Main St.
Marshalltown, IA 50158
Phone: (641)753-3361
Fax: (641)752-7201
Email: office@marshalltownbroadcasting.com
Format: News; Talk; Information; Sports. **Networks:** ABC. **Owner:** Marshalltown Broadcasting, Inc., at above address. **Founded:** 1923. **Operating Hours:** Continuous. **ADI:** Des Moines, IA. **Key Personnel:** Lance Renaud, News Dir., news@marshalltownbroadcasting.com; Kyle Martin, Operations Mgr., kyle@marshalltownbroadcasting.com; Mike Lindell, Asst. Dir., sports@marshalltownbroadcasting.com. **Wattage:** 1,000. **Ad Rates:** $9-11 for 30 seconds; $14-17 for 60 seconds. $7-$16 for 30 seconds; $11-$24 for 60 seconds. Combined advertising rates available with KXIA-FM. **URL:** http://www.1230kfjb.com.

12828 ■ K218CE-FM - 91.5
PO Box 391
Twin Falls, ID 83303
Fax: (208)736-1958
Free: 800-357-4226
Format: Religious; Contemporary Christian. **Owner:** CSN International, PO Box 391, Twin Falls, ID 83303, Ph: (208)736-1958, Fax: (208)736-1958, Free: 800-357-4226. **Key Personnel:** Don Mills, Prog. Dir., Div. Dir. **URL:** http://www.csnradio.com.

12829 ■ KXIA-FM - 101.1
123 W Main St.
Marshalltown, IA 50158
Phone: (641)753-3361
Fax: (641)752-7201
Email: kixstart@marshalltownbroadcasting.com
Format: Contemporary Country; Full Service. **Networks:** ABC. **Owner:** Marshalltown Broadcasting, Inc., at above address. **Founded:** 1968. **Operating Hours:** Continuous. **ADI:** Des Moines, IA. **Key Personnel:** Todd Collins, Contact, todd@marshalltownbroadcasting.com; Travis Kelly, Contact, travis@marshalltownbroadcasting.com. **Wattage:** 100,000. **Ad Rates:** $14-25 for 30 seconds; $21-38 for 60 seconds. **Mailing address:** PO Box 698, Marshalltown, IA 50158. **URL:** http://www.kixweb.com.

MASHALLTOWN

12830 ■ Times-Republican
135 West Main St.
Mashalltown, IA 50158
Phone: (641)753-6611
Independent newspaper. **Founded:** 1856. **Freq:** Mon.-Sun. **Print Method:** Offset. **Trim Size:** 13 1/2 x 22 3/4. **Cols./Page:** 6. **Col. Width:** 12.5 picas. **Col. Depth:** 21.5 inches. **Key Personnel:** Denise Kemp, Director, Advertising, Director, Marketing; Randy Cutright, Manager, Circulation; Abigail Pelzer, Managing Editor; Mike Schelesinger, Publisher. **USPS:** 331-060. **Subscription Rates:** $14.10 Individuals 7 days home delivery (in-town) - Easy Pay; $15.80 Individuals 7 days home delivery by carrier; $16.45 Individuals 7 days home delivery by motor route; $15.20 Individuals 7 days home delivery by motor route - Easy Pay; $10 Individuals Sunday home delivery by carrier; $7 Individuals Sunday home delivery by carrier or motor route - Easy Pay; $26 Individuals Sunday home delivery by motor route. **URL:** http://www.timesrepublican.com. **Mailing address:** PO Box 1300, Mashalltown, IA 50158. **Remarks:** Advertising accepted; rates available upon request. **Circ:** Mon.-Sat. ★**10019**, Sun. ★**10386**.

MASON CITY

N IA. Cerro Gordo Co. 85 mi. NW of Waterloo. Manufactures ice machines, envelopes, computers, leather goods, cement, foundry products, feed, fertilizer, sand and gravel, wire, metal window and door frames. Meat packing plant. Dairy, stock farms.

12831 ■ Globe-Gazette
Howard Query
300 N Washington Ave.
Mason City, IA 50401
Phone: (641)421-0500
Fax: (641)421-0516
Free: 800-421-0546
General newspaper. **Founded:** 1861. **Freq:** Mon.-Sun. (morn.). **Print Method:** Flexographic. **Cols./Page:** 6. **Col. Width:** 24 nonpareils. **Col. Depth:** 301 agate lines. **Key Personnel:** Jeff Binstock, Manager, Circulation; Howard Query, Publisher, Editor. **Subscription Rates:** $24 Individuals /month; $9 Individuals online /month. **URL:** http://globegazette.com/. **Mailing address:** PO Box 271, Mason City, IA 50401-3222. **Ad Rates:** SAU $13.48. **Remarks:** Accepts advertising. **Circ:** Mon.-Sat. ★**18743**, Sun. ★**23174**.

12832 ■ Logos
North Iowa Area Community College
North Iowa Area Community College
Activity Center 210
Mason City, IA 50401
Collegiate newspaper. **Founded:** 1968. **Freq:** Semiweekly during the academic year. **Print Method:** Offset. **Trim Size:** 10 1/4 x 13. **Cols./Page:** 5. **Col. Width:** 20 nonpareils. **Col. Depth:** 187 agate lines. **Key Personnel:** John Schnackenberg, Editor; Christine Harms, Manager, Advertising. **URL:** http://staff.niacc.edu/logos/vol33/issue4/index.html. **Ad Rates:** BW $225. **Remarks:** Accepts advertising. **Circ:** Non-paid 3000.

12833 ■ The Mason City Shopper
Lee Enterprises Inc.
300 N Washington
Mason City, IA 50401
Phone: (641)421-0500
Fax: (641)421-0592
Free: 800-832-2274
Publication E-mail: classads@globegazette.com
Shopper (tabloid) with community editorial. **Founded:** 1969. **Freq:** Weekly (Tues.). **Print Method:** Offset. **Trim Size:** 10 1/4 x 12. **Cols./Page:** 5. **Key Personnel:** Linda Hawk, General Manager, phone: (641)424-3044, fax: (641)424-6786. **Subscription Rates:** Free. **URL:** http://globegazette.com/ads/; http://www.masoncityshopper.com/. **Ad Rates:** GLR $10; BW $700; 4C $915; PCI $14.90. **Remarks:** Accepts classified advertising. **Circ:** Free 28000.

12834 ■ KBDC-FM - 88.5
PO Box 3206
Tupelo, MS 38803
Format: Contemporary Christian. **Owner:** American Family Radio, at above address. **ADI:** Rochester, MN-Mason City, IA-Austin, MN. **Wattage:** 68,000. **URL:** http://www.afr.net/newafr.

12835 ■ KCMR-FM - 97.9
600 First St. NW, Ste. 101
Mason City, IA 50401
Phone: (641)424-9300
Format: Contemporary Christian. **Networks:** Independent. **Owner:** TLC Broadcasting Corp., 600 1st St., NW, Mason City, IA 50401-3212. **Operating Hours:** Continuous. **ADI:** Rochester, MN-Mason City, IA-Austin, MN. **Wattage:** 6,000. **Ad Rates:** Noncommercial. **URL:** http://www.kcmrfm.com.

12836 ■ KGLO-AM - 1300
341 Yorktown Pke.
Mason City, IA 50401
Phone: (641)423-1300
Format: Agricultural; News; Sports. **Networks:** CBS. **Owner:** Three Eagles Communication, 3800 Cornhusker Hwy., Lincoln, NE 68504, Ph: (402)466-1234, Fax: (402)467-4095. **Founded:** 1938. **Operating Hours:** Continuous; 30% network, 70% local. **Key Personnel:** Dalena Barz, Gen. Mgr., dabarz@masoncity.threeeagles.com; Tim Fleming, Dir. of Programs, tfleming@masoncity.threeeagles.com. **Local Programs:** *Rush Limbaugh*, Monday Tuesday Wednesday Thursday Friday 1:00 p.m. - 4:00 p.m.; *Tim Fleming Morning Show*, Monday Tuesday Wednesday Thursday Friday 5:00 a.m. - 10:00 a.m.; *The KGLO Evening News*, Monday Tuesday Wednesday Thursday Friday Saturday Sunday 5:00 p.m.; *Ask The Mayor Show*, Wednesday; *The Swapfest Show*; *Mark Dorenkamp Mid-Day Show*; *Your Health, Wealth and Spice of Life*, Monday. **Wattage:** 5,000. **Ad Rates:** $20-40 for 60 seconds.

12837 ■ KIAI-FM - 93.9
341 Yorktown Pke.
Mason City, IA
Phone: (641)423-1300
Format: Country. **ADI:** Rochester, MN-Mason City, IA-Austin, MN. **Key Personnel:** Phil O'Reilly, Prog. Dir., oreillyshow@yahoo.com. **Wattage:** 100,000. **Ad Rates:** Noncommercial.

12838 ■ KIMT-TV - 3
112 N Pennsylvania Ave.
Mason City, IA 50401
Phone: (641)423-2540
Fax: (641)423-9309
Email: news@kimt.com
Format: News. **Networks:** CBS. **Owner:** New Vision Television, Inc., 11766 Wilshire Blvd., Ste. 405, Los Angeles, CA 90025, Ph: (310)478-3200, Fax: (310)478-3222. **Founded:** 1954. **Formerly:** KGLO-TV. **Operating Hours:** Continuous. **ADI:** Rochester, MN-Mason City, IA-Austin, MN. **Key Personnel:** Steve Martinson, Gen. Mgr., President; Jaime Copley, News Dir.; Jerome Risting, Dir. of Programs, Promotions Dir.; Mike Fitzgerald, Sales Mgr. **Wattage:** 100. **Ad Rates:** $20-5000 for 30 seconds. **URL:** http://www.kimt.com.

12839 ■ KJCY-FM - 95.5
PO Box 1069
Mason City, IA 50401
Phone: (641)424-5529
Fax: (641)424-5597
Email: kjcy@newmail.kinshipradio.org

Circulation: ★ = AAM; △ or • = BPA; ♦ = CAC; ☐ = VAC; ⊕ = PO Statement; ‡ = Publisher's Report; Boldface figures = sworn; Light figures = estimated.

Format: Religious. **Key Personnel:** Matt Dorfner, Exec. Dir. **Wattage:** 6,000. **Ad Rates:** Noncommercial. **URL:** http://www.kjcy.com.

12840 ■ KLKK-FM - 103.7
201 N Federal Ave.
Mason City, IA 50401
Phone: (641)421-7744
Email: klkk@klkkfm.com
Format: Classic Rock. **Networks:** Independent. **Owner:** North Iowa Broadcasting, at above address. **Founded:** 1979. **Formerly**: KZEV-FM. **Operating Hours**: Continuous; 100% local. **ADI**: Rochester, MN-Mason City, IA-Austin, MN. **Key Personnel:** Jim Coloff, Gen. Mgr., jimcoloff@northiowabroadcasting.com; James Shaman, Dir. of Programs, jamesshaman@northiowabroadcasting.com. **Wattage**: 6,000. **Ad Rates:** Advertising accepted; rates available upon request. **URL:** http://www.klkkfm.com.

12841 ■ KLSS-FM - 106.1
341 S Yorktown Pke.
Mason City, IA 50401
Phone: (641)423-1300
Format: Contemporary Hit Radio (CHR). **Key Personnel:** Dalena Barz, Dir. of Programs, Gen. Mgr., jallen@masoncity.threeeagles.com. **Ad Rates:** Noncommercial. **URL:** http://www.mystar106.com.

12842 ■ KRIB-AM - 1490
341 S Yorktown Pke.
Mason City, IA 50401
Format: News. **ADI**: Rochester, MN-Mason City, IA-Austin, MN. **Wattage**: 1,000(Unlimited).

12843 ■ KRNI-AM - 1010
3rd Fl., Communication Arts Ctr.
Cedar Falls, IA 50614-0359
Free: 800-772-2440
Format: Public Radio; Eclectic. **Simulcasts:** KUNI-FM. **Networks:** National Public Radio (NPR); Public Radio International (PRI). **Owner:** University of Northern Iowa, 1227 W 27th St., Cedar Falls, IA 50614, Ph: (319)273-2311. **Founded:** 1948. **Formerly**: KLSS-AM. **Operating Hours**: 5:30 a.m.-midnight. **ADI**: Rochester, MN-Mason City, IA-Austin, MN. **Wattage**: 1,000. **Ad Rates:** Noncommercial. **URL:** http://www.iowapublicradio.org.

12844 ■ KYIN-TV - 24
6450 Corporate Dr.
Johnston, IA 50131
Phone: (515)242-3100
Free: 800-532-1290
Format: Public TV. **Simulcasts:** KDIN-TV Des Moines, IA. **Networks:** Public Broadcasting Service (PBS). **Owner:** Iowa Public Television, PO Box 6450, Johnston, IA 50131-6450, Ph: (515)242-3100, Free: 800-532-1290. **Founded:** 1977. **ADI**: Rochester, MN-Mason City, IA-Austin, MN. **Key Personnel:** Jeff Horn, Contact; William T. Hayes, Dir. of Engg., hayes@iptv.org; Daniel K. Miller, Exec. Dir., Gen. Mgr., dkm@iptv.org; Terry Rinehart, Dir. Ed., terry.rinehart@iptv.org; Kristine K. Houston, Div. Dir.; Molly M. Phillips, Exec. Dir., Gen. Mgr., molly@iptv.org. **Ad Rates:** Noncommercial. **Mailing address:** PO Box 6450, Johnston, IA 50131. **URL:** http://www.iptv.org.

12845 ■ KYTC-FM - 102.7
341 S Yorktown Pke.
Mason City, IA 50401
Phone: (641)423-1300
Format: Classic Rock. **Owner:** Three Eagles Communications, 3800 Cornhusker Hwy., Lincoln, NE 68504, Ph: (402)466-1234, Fax: (402)467-4095. **Operating Hours**: Continuous. **Key Personnel:** Bob Fisher, Gen. Mgr., News Dir., dabarz@digity.me; Jared Allen, Gen. Mgr., News Dir., Music Dir., dabarz@digity.me. **Wattage**: 25,000. **Ad Rates:** Advertising accepted; rates available upon request. **URL:** http://www.discovernorthiowa.com.

MECHANICSVILLE

E IA. Cedar Co. 22 mi. SE of Cedar Rapids. Residential.

12846 ■ Mechanicsville Telephone Co.
107 N John St.
Mechanicsville, IA 52306
Phone: (563)432-7221
Free: 800-205-1110
Founded: 1901. **Cities Served:** subscribing households 393. **Mailing address:** PO Box 159, Mechanicsville, IA 52306. **URL:** http://www.mechanicsvilletel.net.

MEDIAPOLIS

SE IA. Des Moines Co. 13 mi. N. of Burlington. Industry. Concrete products, grain belt equipment, metal works, fiberglass. Diversified farming. Corn, beans, wheat, oats.

12847 ■ Mediapolis News
Mediapolis Publishing Inc.
521 Main St.
Mediapolis, IA 52637
Phone: (319)394-3174
Fax: (319)394-3134
Free: 800-949-3175
Publisher's E-mail: meponews@mepotelco.net
Community newspaper. **Freq:** Weekly (Thurs.). **Print Method:** Offset. **Cols./Page:** 6. **Col. Width:** 11 nonpareils. **Col. Depth:** 294 agate lines. **ISSN:** 0747--3591 (print). **Subscription Rates:** $38 Individuals In County; $45 Out of area. **URL:** http://mediapolisnews.com/. **Mailing address:** PO Box 548, Mediapolis, IA 52637. **Ad Rates:** BW $609.84; SAU $4.84; PCI $4.84. **Remarks:** Accepts advertising. **Circ:** 1600.

12848 ■ Mediapolis Cablevision Co.
652 Main St.
Mediapolis, IA 52637
Phone: (319)394-3456
Fax: (319)394-9155
Free: 800-762-1527
Email: office@mepotelco.net
Owner: MTC Technologies, at above address. **Founded:** 1983. **Key Personnel:** Bill Malcom, Gen. Mgr., bmalcom@mtctech.net; Angie Rupe, Office Mgr., arupe@mtctech.net. **Cities Served:** subscribing households 450. **Mailing address:** PO Box 398, Mediapolis, IA 52637. **URL:** http://www.mtctech.net.

MILFORD

NW IA. Dickinson Co. 9 mi. S. of Spirit Lake. Residential.

12849 ■ Milford Communications
906 Okoboji Ave.
Milford, IA 51351
Phone: (712)338-4967
Fax: (712)338-4719
Free: 888-404-2525
Founded: Sept. 05, 2006. **Cities Served:** 77 channels. **URL:** http://milfordcomm.net.

MISSOURI VALLEY

W IA. Harrison Co. 22 mi. N. of Council Bluffs. Manufactures sewage treatment parts. Agriculture. Wheat, corn, soybeans, apples, livestock.

12850 ■ Missouri Valley Times News
Missouri Valley Times News
501 E Erie St.
Missouri Valley, IA 51555
Phone: (712)642-2791
Publisher's E-mail: news@missourivalleytimes.com
Community newspaper. **Freq:** Semiweekly (Wed. and Fri.). **Print Method:** Offset. **Cols./Page:** 6. **Col. Width:** 24 nonpareils. **Col. Depth:** 294 agate lines. **Key Personnel:** Brad Swenson, Publisher; Pete Graham, Contact. **USPS:** 355-840. **Subscription Rates:** $49 Individuals Harrison County & Zip Codes 51542 and 51558; $62 Out of area; $71 Out of country. **URL:** http://www.enterprisepub.com/movalley. **Mailing address:** PO Box 159, Missouri Valley, IA 51555. **Ad Rates:** GLR $.39; BW $915.90; 4C $1,110.90; PCI $7.10. **Remarks:** Accepts advertising. **Circ:** 2229.

MONONA

NE IA. Clayton Co. 10 mi. W. of Marquette.

12851 ■ Northeast Iowa Telephone Co./CATV
800 S Main St.
Monona, IA 52159
Owner: Northeast Iowa Telephone Co., 800 S Main St., Monona, IA 52159, Ph: (563)539-2122, Free: 888-740-4824. **Cities Served:** Decorah, Farmersburg, Luana, Monona, Saint Olaf, Iowa: subscribing households 850; 67 channels; 1 community access channel; 168 hours per week community access programming. **URL:** http://www.neitel.com.

MONROE

C IA. Jasper Co. 30 mi. SE of Des Moines. Plastic bottles, earth anchors, fencing, chemicals, fertilizers, printing. Agriculture. Corn, small grains.

12852 ■ Monroe Legacy
Monroe Mirror Inc.
PO Box 340
Monroe, IA 50170
Phone: (641)259-2708
Publication E-mail: mmml@iowatelecom.net
monroemirror@msn.com
Newspaper. **Freq:** Weekly (Thurs.). **Print Method:** Offset. **Trim Size:** 11 1/2 x 18. **Cols./Page:** 5. **Col. Width:** 11 nonpareils. **Col. Depth:** 224 agate lines. **Key Personnel:** Kathleen Darrach, Editor. **USPS:** 359-560. **Subscription Rates:** Free. **URL:** http://www.pcm-news.com. **Formerly:** Monroe Mirror. **Ad Rates:** GLR $.26; BW $208; PCI $2.80. **Remarks:** Accepts advertising. **Circ:** 902.

MONTICELLO

E IA. Jones Co. 35 mi. SW of Dubuque. Manufactures steel building, plastic products, hydraulic motors, pumps, garden tools, road graders, corrugated containers, utility baskets, barn, dairy equipment, livestock feeds, metal castings. Agriculture. Corn, beef cattle, hogs.

12853 ■ The Monticello Express
The Monticello Express
111 E Grand St.
Monticello, IA 52310
Phone: (319)465-3555
Fax: (319)465-4611
Free: 800-841-7172
Publication E-mail: mexpress@n-connect.net
Community newspaper. **Freq:** Weekly (Wed.). **Print Method:** Offset. **Trim Size:** 11 x 17. **Cols./Page:** 6. **Col. Width:** 1 1/2 inches. **Col. Depth:** 16 inches. **Key Personnel:** Mark Spensley, Manager, Advertising, Publisher; Pete Temple, Editor; Kim Brooks, Editor; Dan Goodyear, Manager, Publisher. **USPS:** 361-580. **Subscription Rates:** $40 Individuals; $43 Out of area; $48 Out of state. **URL:** http://monticelloexpress.com. **Mailing address:** PO Box 191, Monticello, IA 52310. **Ad Rates:** BW $365; 4C $440; SAU $6; PCI $9. **Remarks:** Accepts advertising. **Circ:** ‡3400.

MOUNT PLEASANT

SE IA. Henry Co. 28 mi. SE of Cedar Rapids. Iowa Wesleyan College. Manufactures bus bodies, metal fabrication, electronic controls, pennants and badges. Agriculture. Corn, beans, oats.

12854 ■ Mt. Pleasant News
Mount Pleasant News
215 W Monroe St.
Mount Pleasant, IA 52641
Publication E-mail: news@mpnews.net
General newspaper. **Freq:** Daily (eve.). **Print Method:** Offset. **Cols./Page:** 6. **Col. Width:** 25 nonpareils. **Col. Depth:** 301 agate lines. **Key Personnel:** Bill Gray, Editor; Jeff Hunt, Editor; Nathan Leete, Editor. **USPS:** 144-340. **Subscription Rates:** $119.25 Individuals carrier delivery /yr.; $124.25 By mail in county; $197.25 Out of state. **URL:** http://mt-pleasant-ia.villagesoup.com/index.seam. **Ad Rates:** BW $1,158.42; 4C $1,413.42; SAU $8.98; PCI $8.98. **Remarks:** Accepts advertising. **Circ:** Paid ‡2731.

12855 ■ KILJ-AM - 1130
2411 Radio Rd.
Mount Pleasant, IA 52641
Phone: (319)385-8728
Fax: (319)385-4517
Email: kiljradio@kilj.com
Format: Country. **Networks:** ABC. **Founded:** 1974. **Operating Hours**: Sunrise-sunset. **Key Personnel:** John Kuhens, Gen. Mgr., Sports Dir.; Theresa Rose, Div. Dir. **Wattage**: 250. **Ad Rates:** Noncommercial. **URL:** http://www.kilj.com.

12856 ■ KILJ-FM - 105.5
2411 Radio Rd.
Mount Pleasant, IA 52641
Phone: (319)385-8728
Fax: (319)385-4517
Email: kilj@iowatelecom.net
Format: Country. **Key Personnel:** Theresa Rose, News Dir., news.kilj@iowatelecom.net. **Ad Rates:** Advertising accepted; rates available upon request. **URL:** http://www.kilj.com.

MOUNT VERNON

E IA. Linn Co. 17 mi. SE of Cedar Rapids. Cornell College. Manufactures metal name plates, concrete. Produce packed. Stock, grain farms.

12857 ■ The Cornellian
Cornell College
600 1st St. SW
Mount Vernon, IA 52314
Phone: (319)895-4324
Fax: (319)895-5237
Publication E-mail: cornellian@cornellcollege.edu
Collegiate newspaper. **Freq:** Weekly. **Print Method:** Offset. Uses mats. **Cols./Page:** 5. **Col. Width:** 32 nonpareils. **Col. Depth:** 210 agate lines. **Key Personnel:** David Miller, Editor-in-Chief; Tom Kirk, Manager, Advertising. **USPS:** 132-900. **URL:** http://www.thecornellian.com. **Ad Rates:** BW $240; PCI $4. **Remarks:** Accepts advertising. **Circ:** Paid 200, Free 1100.

12858 ■ The Hillsboro Star-Journal
Mt. Vernon-Lisbon Sun
108 First St. SW
Mount Vernon, IA 52314
Phone: (319)895-6216
Fax: (319)895-6217
Publisher's E-mail: news@mtvernonlisbonsun.com
Community newspaper. **Freq:** Weekly (Wed.). **Print Method:** Offset. **Trim Size:** 13 3/4 x 22 3/4. **Cols./Page:** 6. **Col. Width:** 2 1/16 inches. **Col. Depth:** 21 1/2 inches. **Key Personnel:** Donna Bernhardt, Secretary, Treasurer; Melvin Honeyfield, Director, Production. **URL:** http://starj.com. **Ad Rates:** SAU $5. **Remarks:** Accepts advertising. **Circ:** Paid ‡2757, Free ‡150.

12859 ■ The Sun
Mt. Vernon-Lisbon Sun
108 First St. SW
Mount Vernon, IA 52314
Phone: (319)895-6216
Fax: (319)895-6217
Publisher's E-mail: news@mtvernonlisbonsun.com
Community newspaper. **Founded:** Jan. 29, 1869. **Freq:** Weekly (Thurs.). **Print Method:** Offset. **Trim Size:** 12 1/2 x 21 1/2. **Cols./Page:** 6. **Col. Width:** 2 1/16 inches. **Col. Depth:** 21 inches. **Key Personnel:** Margaret Stevens, Associate Editor; Jake Krob, Publisher, Editor; Rich Eskelsen, Manager, Advertising. **USPS:** 367-520. **Subscription Rates:** $29 Individuals; $37 Out of area; $43 Out of state; $24 Students; $31 Out of area students; $35 Out of state students. **URL:** http://www.mvlsun.com. **Formerly:** Mount Vernon Hawkeye. **Ad Rates:** PCI $6.75. **Remarks:** Accepts classified advertising. **Circ:** ‡2203.

12860 ■ KRNL-FM - 89.7
810 Commons Cir.
Mount Vernon, IA 52314
Phone: (319)895-4431
Format: Alternative/New Music/Progressive. **Owner:** Cornell College, 600 1st St. SW, Mount Vernon, IA 52314, Ph: (319)895-4324, Fax: (319)895-5237. **Founded:** 1948. **Operating Hours:** 5 p.m.-1 a.m. weekdays , 12 p.m.-1 a.m. Weekend. **Wattage:** 045. **Ad Rates:** Noncommercial. **URL:** http://orgs.cornellcollege.edu/krnl.

MOVILLE

NC IA. Woodbury Co. 17 mi. E. of Sioux City.

12861 ■ Moville Record
Moville Record
PO Box 546
Moville, IA 51039
Phone: (712)873-3141
Fax: (712)873-3142
Publication E-mail: record@wiatel.net
Community newspaper. **Freq:** Weekly (Thurs.). **Print Method:** Offset. **Trim Size:** 12 1/2 x 22 1/2. **Cols./Page:** 6. **Col. Width:** 11.1 picas. **Col. Depth:** 21.5 inches. **USPS:** 366-960. **Subscription Rates:** $30 Individuals in county; print & online; $30 Individuals in county; print; $35 Out of area print; $30 Individuals online. **URL:** http://movillerecord.com/22162/1989/1/this-weeks-issuepdf. **Ad Rates:** GLR $4.75; BW $300; 4C $400; SAU $3.94; PCI $3.25. **Remarks:** Accepts advertising. **Circ:** ‡1330.

MUSCATINE

SE IA. Muscatine Co. On Mississippi River, 30 mi. SW of Davenport. Boat connections. Manufactures fertilizers, buttons, ladders, machinery, herbicides, sand & gravel, cement blocks. Steel dies, plastics, food processing, concrete culverts. Centrifugal pumps. Commercial fishing, soybean, feed and grain mills. Agriculture. Melons, sweet potatoes, corn, truck crops.

12862 ■ Classic Images
Muscatine Journal
301 E 3rd St.
Muscatine, IA 52761
Phone: (563)263-2331
Fax: (563)262-8042
Free: 800-383-3198
Publication E-mail: classicimages@classicimages.com
Magazine (tabloid) covering classic motion pictures for movie buffs and collectors; including film and video tape reviews, biographies, historical articles, obituaries, classified advertising, and coverage of conventions and festivals. **Founded:** June 1962. **Freq:** Monthly. **Print Method:** Offset. **Trim Size:** 11 x 14. **Cols./Page:** 6. **Col. Width:** 18 nonpareils. **Col. Depth:** 182 agate lines. **Key Personnel:** Bob King, Editor, General Manager. **ISSN:** 0275-8423 (print). **Subscription Rates:** $36 Individuals second class; $52 Individuals first class; $108 Canada and Mexico; $216 Two years airmail. **URL:** http://www.classicimages.com. **Ad Rates:** BW $256; 4C $240. **Remarks:** Accepts advertising. **Circ:** (Not Reported).

12863 ■ Journal of the American Art Pottery Association
American Art Pottery Association
c/o Marie Latta, Trustee
2115 W Fulliam Ave.
Muscatine, IA 52761
Publisher's E-mail: zona@netwtc.net
Membership journal covering pottery art. **Freq:** Bimonthly. **Key Personnel:** Linda Carrigan, Managing Director. **Subscription Rates:** Included in membership; $10 Single issue back issue. **URL:** http://aapa.info/about-the-journal. **Remarks:** Accepts advertising. **Circ:** (Not Reported).

12864 ■ K42HI - 42
PO Box A
Santa Ana, CA 92711
Phone: (714)832-2950
Free: 888-731-1000
Owner: Trinity Broadcasting Network Inc., PO Box A, Santa Ana, CA 92711, Ph: (714)832-2950, Free: 888-731-1000.

12865 ■ KMCS-FM - 93.1
3218 Mulberry Ave.
Muscatine, IA 52761
Format: Adult Contemporary. **Networks:** AP. **Owner:** Prairie Radio Communication. **Formerly:** KWCC-FM. **Operating Hours:** Continuous. **Wattage:** 4,400. **Ad Rates:** $17 for 30 seconds; $20.50 for 60 seconds. Combined advertising rates available with KWPC-AM. **URL:** http://www.vintagesound931.com.

12866 ■ KWPC-AM - 860
3218 Mulberry Ave.
Muscatine, IA 52761
Phone: (563)263-2442
Fax: (563)263-9206
Email: mail@voiceofmuscatine.com
Format: Talk; News; Oldies; Soft Rock. **Networks:** USA Radio; AP. **Owner:** Prairie Radio Communications, at above address, Dekalb, IL 60115. **Founded:** 1947. **Operating Hours:** Continuous. **Key Personnel:** Chuck Morgan, Gen. Mgr., chuck.morgan@prairiecommunications.net. **Wattage:** 250. **Ad Rates:** $13-17 for 30 seconds; $16.50-20.50 for 60 seconds. Combined advertising rates available with KMCS-FM. **URL:** http://prcmuscatineradio.wix.com.

12867 ■ MPW Cable
3205 Cedar St.
Muscatine, IA 52761
Phone: (563)263-2631
Fax: (563)262-3373
Cities Served: 120 channels. **URL:** http://www.mpw.org.

NASHUA

N IA. Chickasaw Co. 8 mi. SE of Ionia. Residential.

12868 ■ Nashua Reporter and Weekly Post
Nashua Reporter and Weekly Post
216 Main St.
Nashua, IA 50658
Phone: (641)394-2111
Fax: (641)394-2113
Publisher's E-mail: nashuareporter@gmail.com
Community newspaper. **Freq:** Weekly (Wed.). **Print Method:** Offset. **Trim Size:** 13 x 21. **Cols./Page:** 6. **Col. Width:** 2 inches. **Col. Depth:** 21.5 picas. **Key Personnel:** Wanda Orric, Contact; Carmen Conklin, Contact. **Subscription Rates:** $10 Individuals 6 months - online; $5 Individuals 1 month - online; $2 Individuals 7 days - online; $1 Individuals 1 day - online. **URL:** http://www.nhtrib.com. **Ad Rates:** GLR $3.50; BW $441; PCI $3.50. **Remarks:** Accepts advertising. **Circ:** Paid ‡1100, Free ‡20.

NEVADA

C IA. Story Co. 9 mi. E. of Ames. Manufactures brick, tile, poultry feeds, fertilizer. Poultry packing, hybrid corn processing plants. Ships livestock. Agriculture. Corn, oats, wheat.

12869 ■ Life Date
Lutherans For Life
1101 5th St.
Nevada, IA 50201-1816
Phone: (515)382-2077
Fax: (515)382-3020
Free: 888-364-LIFE
Publisher's E-mail: info@lutheransforlife.org
Freq: Quarterly. **Subscription Rates:** Included in membership. **URL:** http://www.lutheransforlife.org/media/lifedate. **Mailing address:** PO Box 76, Garden City, IA 50102-0076. **Remarks:** Advertising not accepted. **Circ:** (Not Reported).

12870 ■ Nevada Journal
Nevada Journal
922 Lincoln Hwy.
Nevada, IA 50201
Phone: (515)382-2161
Community newspaper. **Founded:** 1895. **Freq:** Weekly (Thurs.). **Print Method:** Offset. **Cols./Page:** 6. **Col. Width:** 25 nonpareils. **Col. Depth:** 294 agate lines. **Subscription Rates:** $4 Individuals print or online /mo. **URL:** http://nevadaiowajournal.com/. **Mailing address:** PO Box 89, Nevada, IA 50201. **Ad Rates:** SAU $5.60; PCI $5.60. **Remarks:** Accepts advertising. **Circ:** ‡2855.

NEW HAMPTON

NE IA. Chickasaw Co. 40 mi. N. of Waterloo. Food, egg, and feed processing plant; tool manufactured; hatchery. Agriculture. Corn, oats, hogs.

12871 ■ New Hampton Tribune
New Hampton Publishing Co.
10 N Chestnut
New Hampton, IA 50659
Phone: (641)394-2111
Fax: (641)394-2113
Community newspaper. **Freq:** Semiweekly Tuesday and Friday. **Print Method:** Offset. **Cols./Page:** 9. **Col. Width:** 9.5 picas. **Col. Depth:** 21 1/2 inches. **Key Personnel:** Amannda Pemble, Manager, Advertising; Dorothy Huber, Editor; Matt Bryant, Publisher, phone: (641)330-4870; Ruth Walden, Manager, Circulation. **Subscription Rates:** $48 Individuals Chickasaw County and Adjoining Counties - 1 year; $25 Out of state Chickasaw County and Adjoining Counties - 6 months; $55 Out of state. **URL:** http://www.nhtrib.com. **Formerly:** New Hampton Economist. **Mailing address:** PO Box 380, New Hampton, IA 50659. **Ad Rates:** BW $1074; 4C $1200. **Remarks:** Advertising accepted; rates available upon request. **Circ:** Paid 3,400.

NEWTON

SC IA. Jasper Co. 33 mi. E. of Des Moines. Manufactures washing machines, potato diggers, metal stampings, electric units, advertising specialties, dairy products. Foundry. Diversified farming.

12872 ■ The Christian News
Christian Church in the Upper Midwest
5064 Lincoln St.
Newton, IA 50208

Circulation: ⋆ = AAM; △ or • = BPA; ♦ = CAC; ❑ = VAC; ⊕ = PO Statement; ‡ = Publisher's Report; Boldface figures = sworn; Light figures = estimated.

Phone: (515)255-3168
Fax: (641)791-3009
Publisher's E-mail: bsdumw@gmail.com
Newspaper for members of the Christian Church (Disciples of Christ) in Iowa, Minnesota, North and South Dakota. **Freq:** Quarterly. **Print Method:** Letterpress and offset. **Cols./Page:** 4. **Col. Width:** 27 nonpareils. **Col. Depth:** 182 agate lines. **Subscription Rates:** Free. **Remarks:** Advertising not accepted. **Circ:** ‡18000.

12873 ■ The Newton Daily News
Newton Printing Co.
200 1st Ave. E
Newton, IA 50208
Phone: (641)792-3121
Fax: (641)791-7104
Publisher's E-mail: newsroom@newtondailynews.com
Newspaper. **Freq:** Daily Monday through Friday. **Print Method:** offset. **Cols./Page:** 6. **Col. Width:** 11 picas. **Col. Depth:** 21.5 inches. **Key Personnel:** Jeff Holschuh, Manager, Advertising, Manager, Marketing; Dan Goetz, Publisher. **Subscription Rates:** $152.80 Individuals town carrier; $191.20 Individuals motor route; $208 By mail in County; $229 By mail out of County. **URL:** http://www.newtondailynews.com. **Mailing address:** PO Box 967, Newton, IA 50208. **Ad Rates:** BW $1,380.30; SAU $10.70. **Remarks:** Accepts advertising. **Circ:** 5500.

12874 ■ KCOB-AM - 1280
PO Box 66
Newton, IA 50208
Phone: (641)792-5262
Format: Country; Full Service. **Simulcasts:** KCOB-FM. **Networks:** CNN Radio. **Owner:** Central Iowa Broadcasting Inc., Not Available. **Operating Hours:** Continuous Daily; 1% network, 99% local. **ADI:** Des Moines, IA. **Wattage:** 1,000. **Ad Rates:** $10-27 for 30 seconds; $13-32 for 60 seconds. Combined advertising rates available with KRTI-FM. **URL:** http://www.kcobradio.com/program.html.

12875 ■ KKLG-FM - 88.3
PO Box 779002
Rocklin, CA 95677-9972
Fax: (916)251-1901
Free: 800-525-5683
Format: Contemporary Christian. **Owner:** Educational Media Foundation, PO Box 2098, Omaha, NE 68103-2098, Free: 800-434-8400. **Key Personnel:** Mike Novak, President, CEO; Alan Mason, COO. **Wattage:** 400. **URL:** http://www.klove.com.

12876 ■ KRTI-FM - 106.7
1801 N 13th Ave. E
Newton, IA 50208
Phone: (641)792-5262
Free: 800-570-5784
Format: Contemporary Hit Radio (CHR). **Owner:** Central Iowa Broadcasting Inc., Not Available. **Wattage:** 50,000. **Ad Rates:** Advertising accepted; rates available upon request. **URL:** http://energy1067.com.

NORA SPRINGS

NW IA. Floyd Co. 10 mi. E. of Mason City.

12877 ■ Farmers Mutual Telephone Co.
608 E Congress St.
Nora Springs, IA 50458
Phone: (641)749-2531
Fax: (641)749-9510
Free: 877-666-4835
Email: question@omnitel.biz
Founded: 1904. **Cities Served:** United States; 175 channels. **Mailing address:** PO Box 518, Nora Springs, IA 50458-8634. **URL:** http://www.omnitel.biz.

NORWALK

SC IA. Warren Co. 5 mi. N. of Sommerset.

12878 ■ Hobby Greenhouse
Hobby Greenhouse Association
922 Norwood Dr.
Norwalk, IA 50211-1329
Phone: (724)744-7082
Publisher's E-mail: HGAmembershipdirector@hotmail.com
Freq: Quarterly. **Subscription Rates:** included in membership dues. **URL:** http://www.hobbygreenhouse.org/magazine-preview-1. **Remarks:** Accepts advertising. **Circ:** 1400.

ODEBOLT

12879 ■ Sac Co.unty Mutual Telco
108 S Maple
Odebolt, IA 51458
Phone: (712)668-2200
Email: odebolt@netins.net
Founded: 1877. **Cities Served:** 37 channels. **Mailing address:** PO Box 488, Odebolt, IA 51458. **URL:** http://www.odebolt.net.

OELWEIN

NE IA. Fayette Co. 40 mi. NE of Waterloo. Corn cribs, chemicals, sprayers, sausage, mineral feed manufactured; planing mill; nursery. Ships livestock. Stock, dairy, grain, poultry farms.

12880 ■ KOEL-AM - 950
2505 S Frederick Ave.
Oelwein, IA 50662
Phone: (319)283-1234
Fax: (319)283-3790
Format: News; Country; Talk. **Networks:** ABC. **Owner:** Cumulus Broadcasting Inc., 3280 Peachtree Rd. NW, Ste. 2300, Atlanta, GA 30305-2447, Ph: (404)949-0700, Fax: (404)949-0740. **Founded:** 1950. **Operating Hours:** Continuous; 10% network, 90% local. **ADI:** Cedar Rapids-Waterloo-Dubuque, IA. **Key Personnel:** Roger King, News Dir., roger.king@cumulus.com. **Wattage:** 5,000. **Ad Rates:** $11-52 for 30 seconds; $14-57 for 60 seconds. **URL:** http://koel.com.

OGDEN

12881 ■ Ogden Reporter
Mid-America Publishing Corp.
222 W Walnut St.
Ogden, IA 50212-2004
Community newspaper. **Freq:** Weekly (Wed.). **Key Personnel:** Kathy Pierce, Office Manager. **Subscription Rates:** $35 Individuals print & online/year; $35 Individuals online/year; $69 Two years print or online. **URL:** http://www.ogdenreporter.com. **Circ:** (Not Reported).

OKOBOJI

12882 ■ KJIA-FM - 88.9
PO Box 738
Okoboji, IA 51355
Phone: (712)332-2428
Fax: (712)332-2428
Free: 800-450-7729
Email: kjia@newmail.kinshipradio.org
Format: Contemporary Christian; Religious. **Operating Hours:** Continuous. **Key Personnel:** Matt Dorfner, Exec. Dir.; Steve Ware, Dir. of Programs. **Wattage:** 50,000. **URL:** http://www.kjiaradio.com.

ONAWA

W IA. Monona Co. 37 mi. SE of Sioux City. Manufactures machinery, steel culverts. Stock, grain farms.

12883 ■ Onawa Democrat
Wonder and Son Publishing
720 Iowa Ave.
Onawa, IA 51040-0418
Publication E-mail: democrat@longlines.com
Community newspaper. **Freq:** Weekly (Wed.). **Print Method:** Offset. **Cols./Page:** 6. **Col. Width:** 2 inches. **Col. Depth:** 129 inches. **Key Personnel:** William Wonder, Publisher; Freddie Wonder, Publisher. **ISSN:** 0899--6520 (print). **Subscription Rates:** $25 Individuals; $0.50 Single issue. **Alt. Formats:** CD-ROM. **Mailing address:** PO Box 418, Onawa, IA 51040-0418. **Ad Rates:** BW $504; 4C $729; SAU $4; PCI $4. **Remarks:** Accepts advertising. **Circ:** Paid ‡2934.

ORANGE CITY

NW IA. Sioux Co. 45 mi. NE of Sioux City. Steel fabrication, ready mix concrete, sport caps, paint, aircraft, bullets, steel arrowheads, farm equipment manufactured. Dairy, stock, poultry farms.

12884 ■ Ad-Visor
Pluim Publishing Inc.
113 Central Ave. SE
Orange City, IA 51041-1738
Phone: (712)737-4266
Shopper. **Founded:** Mar. 1955. **Freq:** Weekly (Tues.). **Print Method:** Web press. **Cols./Page:** 8. **Col. Width:** 1 1/2 inches. **Col. Depth:** 21 1/2 inches. **Key Personnel:** Bob Hulstein, Publisher; Dennis Den Hartog, Manager, Advertising and Sales. **Subscription Rates:** Free. **URL:** http://www.siouxcountynews.com/advisor.php. **Ad Rates:** PCI $7.25. **Remarks:** Advertising accepted; rates available upon request. **Circ:** Free 8800.

12885 ■ Sioux County Capital-Democrat
Pluim Publishing Inc.
113 Central Ave. SE
Orange City, IA 51041-1738
Phone: (712)737-4266
Newspaper. **Freq:** Weekly (Wed.). **Print Method:** Offset. Uses mats. **Trim Size:** 14 1/2 x 22 3/4. **Cols./Page:** 8. **Col. Width:** 9 1/2 picas. **Col. Depth:** 21 1/2 inches. **Key Personnel:** Doug Calsbeek, Editor; Dale Pluim, Publisher; Dennis Den Hartog, Manager, Advertising. **URL:** http://www.siouxcountynews.com/capdemo.php. **Remarks:** Advertising accepted; rates available upon request. **Circ:** Paid ‡1800, Free ‡50.

OSAGE

N IA. Mitchell Co. 30 mi. NE of Mason City. Commercial drying of farming products. Manufactuers windows, socks, gloves, mittens, feed, business forms. Limestone quarries. Agriculture. Corn, hogs, cattle.

12886 ■ Mitchell County Press-News
Mitchell County Press-News
112 N 6th St.
Osage, IA 50461
Phone: (641)732-3721
Fax: (641)732-5689
Publisher's E-mail: mcpress@mcpress.com
Community newspaper. **Freq:** Weekly (Wed.). **Print Method:** Offset. **Trim Size:** 15 x 21 3/4. **Cols./Page:** 6. **Col. Width:** 2.25 inches. **Col. Depth:** 21.5 inches. **Key Personnel:** Howard Query, Publisher. **Subscription Rates:** $25 Individuals /month. **URL:** http://www.globegazette.com/mcpress. **Mailing address:** PO Box 60, Osage, IA 50461. **Ad Rates:** SAU $5.89; PCI $5.89. **Remarks:** Accepts advertising. **Circ:** (Not Reported).

12887 ■ KLEH-AM - 1290
521 S 7th S
Osage, IA 50461
Phone: (319)462-4384
Format: Contemporary Country. **Networks:** Satellite Music Network. **Owner:** Missouri Valley Productions, Inc., at above address. **Founded:** 1979. **Operating Hours:** 6 a.m.-10 p.m.; 75% network, 25% local. **ADI:** Cedar Rapids-Waterloo-Dubuque, IA. **Key Personnel:** Lanier Korsmeyer, Contact; Janet Blair, Contact; Carla Jesse, Contact. **Wattage:** 500. **URL:** http://sos.iowa.gov/search/business/(S(dsyx04jxsvsgpgfmpp5pnenf))/summary.aspx?c=8-AjWBP6L5T4rW9QKda1JXV95Tbit-xdNqQ9odGo_mc1.

OSCEOLA

S IA. Clarke Co. 45 mi. S. of Des Moines. Manufactures luggage, lingerie. Surge milking products, pressure & electrical switches, steel castings, recreational vehicles, pork sausage products, machine works. Ships hogs. Limestone quarries. Diversified farming. Corn, wheat, hogs, soybeans, alfalfa.

12888 ■ Osceola Sentinel-Tribune
Clarke County Publishing Inc.
111 E Washington St.
Osceola, IA 50213
Phone: (641)342-2131
Fax: (641)342-2060
Publisher's E-mail: ccpnews@osceolaiowa.com
Community newspaper. **Founded:** 1847. **Freq:** Weekly (Thurs.). **Print Method:** Web offset. **Trim Size:** 16 1/2 x 22 1/2. **Key Personnel:** Rich Paulsen, Publisher; Matt Pfiffner, Editor. **Subscription Rates:** $29.50 Individuals office pick-up; $37 By mail In Area; $43.50 Out of area mail; $50 Out of state mail. **URL:** http://www.osceolaiowa.com. **Ad Rates:** PCI $5.25. **Remarks:** Color advertising not accepted. **Circ:** 6900.

12889 ■ KIIC-FM - 97.9
118 W Jefferson St.
Osceola, IA 50213
Phone: (641)342-6536
Fax: (641)342-9966
Email: kiic@iowatelecom.net
Format: Country. **Operating Hours**: Continuous.

OSKALOOSA

SEC IA. Mahaska Co. 55 mi. SE of Des Moines. Residential.

12890 ■ The Oskaloosa Herald
Community Newspaper Holdings Inc.
PO Box 530
Oskaloosa, IA 52577
Phone: (641)672-2581
Fax: (641)672-2294
Free: 888-672-2581
Newspaper serving Oskaloosa, Iowa area. Promotes a unique identity and culture for Oskaloosa and surrounding counties. Advances the business community in this area. **Freq:** Daily. **Key Personnel:** Tim Kurtz, Publisher; Deb Van Engelenhoven, Advertising Representative; Connie Davis, Manager, Circulation; Duane Nollen, Editor. **Subscription Rates:** $10.99 Individuals print and online; $9.99 Individuals online only. **URL:** http://www.oskaloosa.com. **Remarks:** Accepts advertising. **Circ:** Mon.-Fri. ★**3381**.

12891 ■ Oskaloosa Shopper
Oskaloosa Shopper
1901 A Ave. W
Oskaloosa, IA 52577
Phone: (641)672-2581
Free: 888-672-2581
Shopping guide. **Freq:** Weekly (Wed.). **Print Method:** Offset. **Cols./Page:** 6. **Col. Width:** 26 nonpareils. **Col. Depth:** 301 agate lines. **Key Personnel:** Deb Van Englenhoven, Publisher; Connie Davis, Manager, Circulation; Duane Nollen, Editor. **Alt. Formats:** PDF. **URL:** http://www.oskaloosa.com/shopper. **Mailing address:** PO Box 530, Oskaloosa, IA 52577. **Ad Rates:** GLR $.39; BW $664.35; 4C $1,024.35; SAU $5.35. **Remarks:** Accepts advertising. **Circ:** Free 17000.

12892 ■ KBOE-AM - 740
PO Box 380
Oskaloosa, IA 52577-0380
Phone: (641)673-3493
Fax: (641)673-3495
Email: contact@kboeradio.com
Format: Contemporary Country. **Simulcasts:** KBOE-FM. **Networks:** ABC. **Owner:** Jomast Corp. **Founded:** 1950. **Operating Hours**: Continuous. **ADI**: Des Moines, IA. **Key Personnel:** Glenda Lind-Booy, Gen. Mgr., glenda@kboeradio.com; Gary Wilson, Chief Engineer. **Wattage**: 250. **Ad Rates:** $7.30-12.20 for 30 seconds; $10.95-18.30 for 60 seconds. Combined advertising rates available with KBOE-FM. **URL:** http://www.kboeradio.com.

12893 ■ KBOE-FM - 104.9
PO Box 380
Oskaloosa, IA 52577-0380
Phone: (641)673-3493
Fax: (641)673-3495
Email: contact@kboeradio.com
Format: Country. **Networks:** ABC; Radio Iowa; Brownfield. **Owner:** Jomast Corp., 2172 230th St., Oskaloosa, IA 52577. **Founded:** 1964. **Operating Hours**: Continuous. **Key Personnel:** Glenda Lind-Booy, Gen. Mgr., glenda@kboeradio.com; Gary Wilson, Chief Engineer, Tech. Dir. **Wattage**: 50,000. **URL:** http://www.kboeradio.com.

12894 ■ KIGC-FM - 88.7
201 Trueblood Ave.
Oskaloosa, IA 52577
Fax: (641)673-1396
Free: 800-779-7366
Format: Rap; Country; Oldies. **Networks:** Independent. **Owner:** William Penn University, at above address, Oskaloosa, IA 52577. **Founded:** 1965. **Formerly:** KFHL-AM. **Operating Hours**: midnight. **Wattage**: 250. **Ad Rates:** Noncommercial.

OSSIAN

NE IA. Winneshiek Co. 75 mi. E. of Mason City. Fertilizer, feed mixing plants. Grain elevator. Agriculture. Corn, oats, hay, livestock.

12895 ■ The Ossian Bee
Ossain Bee
107 W Main
Ossian, IA 52161-0096
Fax: (319)532-9081
Newspaper with a Democratic orientation. **Freq:** Weekly (Thurs.). **Print Method:** Offset. **Cols./Page:** 6. **Col. Width:** 28 nonpareils. **Col. Depth:** 301 agate lines. **Key Personnel:** Dirk Amundsen, Editor. **Subscription Rates:** $49 Individuals in area; $56 Out of area. **URL:** http://www.westunionfayettecountyunion.com. **Mailing address:** PO Box 96, Ossian, IA 52161-0096. **Ad Rates:** GLR $.28; BW $335.16; 4C $343.06; SAU $2.49; PCI $2.66. **Remarks:** Accepts advertising. **Circ:** ‡1230.

OTTUMWA

SE IA. Wapello Co. 90 mi. SE of Des Moines. Indian Hills Community College. Manufactures agricultural machinery, automobile parts, tile, brick, fiberglass bathtubs and shower stalls. Poultry, food processing. Photo finishing. Meat packing. Agriculture. Livestock, feed.

12896 ■ The Ottumwa Courier
Community Newspaper Holdings Inc.
213 E 2nd St.
Ottumwa, IA 52501-2902
Phone: (641)684-4611
General newspaper. **Freq:** Mon.-Sat. (morn.). **Print Method:** Offset. **Cols./Page:** 6. **Col. Width:** 12.5 picas. **Col. Depth:** 21 3/4 inches. **Key Personnel:** Dan Canny, Director, Advertising; Judy Krieger, Editor; Doug Techel, Manager, Circulation, phone: (641)683-5371; Jeff Hutton, Managing Editor, phone: (641)683-5365; Laura Garrett, Business Manager. **Subscription Rates:** $13.99 Individuals monthly (print and online); $11.99 Individuals in Iowa, 26 weeksmonthly (online). **URL:** http://www.ottumwacourier.com. **Formerly**: News Editor. **Ad Rates:** GLR $9.25; BW $1,305; 4C $1,530; SAU $16.29; PCI $11.90. **Remarks:** Accepts advertising. **Circ:** Mon.-Sat. ★**11596**, Mon.-Fri. ★**12668**.

12897 ■ KBIZ-AM - 1240
416 E Main St.
Ottumwa, IA 52501
Phone: (641)684-5563
Format: News; Information. **Networks:** CBS. **Founded:** 1941. **Operating Hours**: Continuous; 10% network, 90% local. **ADI**: Ottumwa, IA-Kirksville, MO (Wapello, IA). **Key Personnel:** Greg List, Gen. Mgr., President; Jeff Downing, Dir. of Operations, Dir. of Programs, Sports Dir.; Tracy Songer, Dir. of Traffic. **Wattage**: 1,000. **Ad Rates:** $7-9 for 30 seconds; $10.50-13.50 for 60 seconds. KTWA-FM. **URL:** http://www.kbizam.com.

12898 ■ KDWI-FM - 89.1
2111 Grand Ave.
Des Moines, IA 50312
Free: 800-861-8000
Email: info@iowapublicradio.org
Format: Public Radio. **Owner:** Iowa Public Radio, 2111 Grand Ave., Ste. 100, Des Moines, IA 50312-5393, Ph: (515)725-1700, Free: 800-861-8000. **Key Personnel:** Mary Grace Herrington, CEO. **URL:** http://iowapublicradio.org.

12899 ■ K42AM - 42
PO Box A
Santa Ana, CA 92711
Phone: (714)832-2950
Free: 888-731-1000
Owner: Trinity Broadcasting Network Inc., PO Box A, Santa Ana, CA 92711, Ph: (714)832-2950, Free: 888-731-1000. **URL:** http://www.tbn.org.

KKSI-FM - See Eddyville

12900 ■ KLEE-AM - 1480
601 W 2nd St.
Ottumwa, IA 52501
Phone: (641)682-8711
Fax: (641)682-8482
Format: Oldies. **Networks:** CNN Radio; Mutual Broadcasting System; Westwood One Radio; Brownfield; Talknet. **Owner:** FMC Broadcasting, Inc., at above address, Ottumwa, IA. **Founded:** 1954. **Operating Hours**: Continuous; 40% network, 60% local. **ADI**: Ottumwa, IA-Kirksville, MO (Wapello, IA). **Key Personnel:** Richard Palen, Gen. Mgr. **Wattage**: 250 daytime; 017 nights. **Ad Rates:** $9.24 for 30 seconds; $14.12 for 60 seconds. **URL:** http://www.kotm.com.

12901 ■ KOTM-FM
601 W 2nd St.
Ottumwa, IA 52501
Phone: (641)682-8711
Fax: (641)682-8482
Email: kleeam@lisco.net
Format: Contemporary Hit Radio (CHR). **Owner:** FMC Broadcasting, Inc., at above address, Ottumwa, IA. **Founded:** 1976. **Formerly:** KLEE-FM. **Key Personnel:** Fred Jenkins, Chief Engineer. **Wattage:** 19,000 ERP. **Ad Rates:** $9.24 for 30 seconds; $14.12 for 60 seconds.

12902 ■ KRKN-FM - 104.3
416 E Main St.
Ottumwa, IA 52501
Phone: (641)684-5563
Free: 800-794-6869
Format: Contemporary Country. **Networks:** Jones Satellite. **Owner:** O-Town Communications Inc., 416 E Main St., Ottumwa, IA 52501. **Founded:** Aug. 1996. **Operating Hours**: Continuous. **Wattage**: 23,500. **Ad Rates:** Advertising accepted; rates available upon request. Combined advertising rates available with KKSI. **URL:** http://www.krknnewcountry.com.

12903 ■ KTWA-FM - 92.7
416 E Main St.
Ottumwa, IA 52501
Phone: (641)684-5563
Free: 800-794-6869
Format: Adult Contemporary. **Networks:** Satellite Music Network. **Owner:** O-Town Communications Inc., 416 E Main St., Ottumwa, IA 52501. **Founded:** 1985. **Operating Hours**: Continuous; 90% network, 10% local. **ADI**: Ottumwa, IA-Kirksville, MO (Wapello, IA). **Key Personnel:** Greg List, Gen. Mgr., President; Margie Stansberry, Contact. **Wattage**: 50,000. **Ad Rates:** Noncommercial. KBIZ-AM. **URL:** http://www.ktwafm.com.

12904 ■ KUNZ-FM - 91.1
2111 Grand Ave.
Des Moines, IA 50312
Free: 800-861-8000
Email: info@iowapublicradio.org
Format: Public Radio. **Owner:** Iowa Public Radio, 2111 Grand Ave., Ste. 100, Des Moines, IA 50312-5393, Ph: (515)725-1700, Free: 800-861-8000. **Key Personnel:** Al Schares, Music Dir., aschares@iowapublicradio.org; Katherine Perkins, Dir. of Programs, kperkins@iowapublicradio.org. **URL:** http://iowapublicradio.org.

12905 ■ KYOU-TV - 15
820 W 2nd St.
Ottumwa, IA 52501
Email: wyoutv@lisco.com
Format: News; Sports. **Networks:** Fox; Independent; United Paramount Network. **Owner:** Waitt Broadcasting, Inc., at above address, Free: 877-943-6915. **Founded:** 1987. **Formerly**: KOIA-TV. **Operating Hours**: Continuous; 98% network; 2% local. **ADI**: Ottumwa, IA-Kirksville, MO (Wapello, IA). **Key Personnel:** Dianne Little, Promotions Dir., Gen. Sales Mgr., dlittle@kyoutv.com. **Wattage**: 360,000 ERP. **Ad Rates:** Advertising accepted; rates available upon request. **URL:** http://www.kyoutv.com/.

PALMER

12906 ■ Palmer Mutual Telephone Co.
306 Main St.
Palmer, IA 50571
Phone: (712)359-2411
Fax: (712)359-2200
Free: 800-685-7417
Email: palmerone@palmerone.com
Founded: 1904. **Key Personnel:** Steve Trimble, Gen. Mgr; Deb Lenz, Contact. **Cities Served:** United States; 73 channels. **Mailing address:** PO Box 155, Palmer, IA 50571. **URL:** http://www.palmerone.com.

Circulation: ★ = AAM; △ or • = BPA; ♦ = CAC; ❑ = VAC; ⊕ = PO Statement; ‡ = Publisher's Report; Boldface figures = sworn; Light figures = estimated.

PANORA

12907 ■ Guthrie County Vedette
Guthrie County Vedette
111 E Main St.
Panora, IA 50216
Phone: (641)755-2115
Community newspaper. **Freq:** Weekly (Thurs.). **Cols./Page:** 8. **Col. Width:** 10.5 picas. **Col. Depth:** 21 1/2 inches. **Key Personnel:** Ann Wilson, Publisher. **Subscription Rates:** $30 Individuals print or online; $35 Out of state print. **URL:** http://www.guthriecountynewspapers.com/guthrie-county-vedette. **Mailing address:** PO Box 38, Panora, IA 50216. **Remarks:** Accepts advertising. **Circ:** (Not Reported).

12908 ■ Panora Cooperative Cablevision Assocciaion Inc.
114 E Main St.
Panora, IA 50216
Phone: (641)755-2424
Free: 800-205-1110
Email: panora@netins.net
Owner: Panora Communication Cooperative, at above address, Panora, IA. **Founded:** 1981. **Key Personnel:** Bill Dorsett, Plant Mgr., dorsett@netins.net; Andy Randol, Gen. Mgr.; Cheryl Castile, Office Mgr., ccastile@netins.net. **Cities Served:** subscribing households 1,948. **Mailing address:** PO Box 189, Panora, IA 50216. **URL:** http://panoratelco.com.

PELLA

SC IA. Marion Co. 40 mi. SE of Des Moines. Residential.

12909 ■ The Pella Chronicle
Community Newspaper Holdings Inc.
812 Main St.
Pella, IA 50219
Phone: (641)628-3882
Community newspaper. **Freq:** Weekly (Thurs.). **Print Method:** Offset. **Trim Size:** 13 x 21 1/2. **Cols./Page:** 6. **Col. Width:** 12 picas. **Col. Depth:** 21.25 inches. **Key Personnel:** Maureen Miller, Publisher; Clint Brown, Editor; Susan Martin, Office Manager. **Subscription Rates:** $32 By mail; $37 Out of country. **URL:** http://www.pellachronicle.com. **Mailing address:** PO Box 126, Pella, IA 50219. **Ad Rates:** PCI $5. **Remarks:** Accepts advertising. **Circ:** ‡3350.

12910 ■ KCUI-FM - 89.1
812 University
Pella, IA 50219
Phone: (641)628-5262
Format: Alternative/New Music/Progressive. **Owner:** Central University of Iowa, at above address. **Founded:** Feb. 27, 1961. **Operating Hours:** 11 a.m.-1 a.m. **Key Personnel:** Bonnie Dahlke, Gen. Mgr., dahlkeb@central.edu. **Wattage:** 010. **Ad Rates:** Noncommercial. **URL:** http://kcui.tripod.com.

12911 ■ KCWN-FM - 99.9
304 Oskaloosa St.
Pella, IA 50219
Phone: (641)628-9999
Fax: (641)628-9229
Free: 888-506-4562
Email: kcwn@kcwnfm.org
Format: Contemporary Christian. **Ad Rates:** Noncommercial. **URL:** http://wherehopeshines.org.

12912 ■ KFMG-FM - 103.3
PO Box 41143
Des Moines, IA 50311
Phone: (515)244-4146
Format: Album-Oriented Rock (AOR). **Founded:** 1976. **Formerly:** KFMD-FM; KXJX-FM; KDMG-FM. **Operating Hours:** Continuous. **ADI:** Des Moines, IA. **Wattage:** 100,000 ERP. **URL:** http://kfmg.org/contact.

PERRY

SWC IA. Dallas Co. 28 mi. SW of Boone. Manufactures ice cream mix, cultivator shovels, plow welding products, fertilizer. Meat, poultry packing, hybrid seed corn plants; granite works; nursery. Agriculture. Corn, oats, hay, cattle. Hogs, soybeans.

12913 ■ KDLS-AM - 1310
2260 141st St.
Perry, IA 50220
Phone: (515)465-5357
Fax: (515)465-3952
Email: kdls@prairieinet.net
Format: News; Information; Sports; Talk. **Simulcasts:** KDLS-FM. **Owner:** Tom Quinlan, at above address. **Founded:** 1961. **Key Personnel:** Marcia Murphy, Station Mgr. **Wattage:** 500 KW. **Ad Rates:** $8-12 for 30 seconds; $10-15 for 60 seconds. Combined advertising rates available with KDLS-FM. **URL:** http://raccoonvalleyradio.com/.

12914 ■ KKRF-FM - 107.9
2260 141st Dr.
Perry, IA 50220
Phone: (515)523-1107
Fax: (515)465-3952
Email: kkrf@aol.com
Format: Country. **Owner:** Coon Valley Communication Inc., at above address. **Key Personnel:** John France, Promotions Dir.; Pat Delaney, Owner, radiotekpd@aol.com. **Wattage:** 25,000. **Ad Rates:** Advertising accepted; rates available upon request.

PLAINFIELD

12915 ■ Butler-Bremer Communications
715 Main St.
Plainfield, IA 50666
Phone: (319)276-4458
Fax: (319)276-7530
Free: 800-830-1146
Email: comments@butler-bremer.com
Founded: 1905. **Formerly:** Butler-Bremer Mutual Telephone Co. **Cities Served:** United States; 39 channels. **Mailing address:** PO Box 99, Plainfield, IA 50666. **URL:** http://www.butler-bremer.com.

POSTVILLE

NE IA. Clayton Co. 60 mi. NE of Waterloo. Meat and turkey processing plants; laminated plastics, seed house; feed mill. Grain, stock, dairy, poultry farms.

12916 ■ KPVL-FM - 89.1
PO Box 875
Postville, IA 52162
Phone: (563)864-7945
Fax: (563)864-7940
Email: kpvlradio@kpvlradio.com
Format: Educational. **Key Personnel:** Jeff Abbas, Operations Mgr.; Dean Ohloff, Sports Dir. **URL:** http://kpvlradio.com.

PRIMGHAR

NW IA. O'Brien Co. 65 mi. NE of Sioux City. Burial vault factory; hatchery. Grain elevator. Stock, poultry farms. Corn, soybeans, oats, barley.

12917 ■ Community Cable Television Agency of O'Brien County
PO Box 616
Primghar, IA 51245
Phone: (712)957-1313
Fax: (712)957-3015
Founded: 2000. **Formerly:** The Community Agency. **Cities Served:** 56 channels. **URL:** http://www.obriencounty.com/utilities.htm.

READLYN

12918 ■ Readlyn Telephone Co.
121 Main St.
Readlyn, IA 50668
Phone: (319)279-3375
Free: 800-590-7747
Email: readlyn@netins.net
Founded: 1906. **Key Personnel:** Sharon Huck, Gen. Mgr. **Cities Served:** subscribing households 282. **Mailing address:** PO Box 159, Readlyn, IA 50668. **URL:** http://www.readlyntelco.com.

RED OAK

SW IA. Montgomery Co. 50 mi. E. of Council Bluffs. Manufactures art calendars, batteries, automotive seat frames, advertising specialties, hydraulic hoses, machine shops, livestock equipment. Agriculture. Corn, livestock feed, soybeans.

12919 ■ Cooking with Paula Deen
Hoffman Media L.L.C.
PO Box 8459
Red Oak, IA 51591
Free: 877-933-5736
Publication E-mail: pdccustserv@cds-global.com
Magazine that offers cooking recipes and tips featuring Paula Deen. **Freq:** 6/year. **Trim Size:** 8 x 10.875. **Key Personnel:** Paula Deen, Editor-in-Chief. **Subscription Rates:** $22.98 Individuals. **URL:** http://www.pauladeenmagazine.com. **Ad Rates:** BW $45,490; 4C $47,190. **Remarks:** Accepts advertising. **Circ:** (Not Reported).

12920 ■ Giant
Giant Magazine L.L.C.
PO Box 8392
Red Oak, IA 51591-1392
Phone: (212)431-4477
Fax: (212)505-3478
Magazine covers topics of interest to men, including fashion, entertainment, music and sex. **Freq:** Bimonthly. **Trim Size:** 8 x 10 7/8. **Key Personnel:** Reggie Hudson, Manager, Advertising. **Subscription Rates:** $10 Individuals; $16 Two years. **URL:** http://giantmag.com/category/the-magazine. **Ad Rates:** BW $24750; 4C $27500. **Remarks:** Accepts advertising. **Circ:** (Not Reported).

12921 ■ The Red Oak Express
The Red Oak Express
20012 Commerce Dr.
Red Oak, IA 51566
Phone: (712)623-2566
Fax: (712)623-2568
Community newspaper. **Freq:** Weekly (Tues.). **Print Method:** Offset. **Cols./Page:** 6. **Col. Width:** 12.5 picas. **Col. Depth:** 21 1/2 inches. **Key Personnel:** Angie Quick, Manager, Circulation; Liz Felos, Office Manager, Bookkeeper; Gregory Orear, Editor, General Manager. **ISSN:** 0747--3281 (print). **Subscription Rates:** $31 Individuals print and online - annual; $18.50 Individuals print and online - semi-annual ; $10.25 Individuals print and online - quarterly. **URL:** http://redoakexpress.com. **Mailing address:** PO Box 377, Red Oak, IA 51566. **Ad Rates:** GLR $6.70; SAU $5.53; PCI $4.90. **Remarks:** Advertising accepted; rates available upon request. **Circ:** 4950.

12922 ■ Taste of the South
Hoffman Media L.L.C.
PO Box 8459
Red Oak, IA 51591
Free: 877-817-4410
Magazine that offers cooking recipes and tips about southern cooking. **Freq:** 7/year. **Trim Size:** 8 x 10 7/8. **Key Personnel:** Brookr M. Bell, Editor. **Subscription Rates:** $21 Individuals. **URL:** http://www.tasteofthesouthmagazine.com. **Ad Rates:** 4C $5,830. **Remarks:** Accepts advertising. **Circ:** Paid ‡100000.

12923 ■ Woodworker's Journal: The Voice of the Woodworking Community
Rockler Press
PO Box 8572
Red Oak, IA 51591-1572
Free: 800-279-4441
Publication E-mail: letters@woodworkersjournal.com
editor@woodworkersjournal.com
Magazine featuring projects, tips and techniques for novice and experienced woodworking hobbyists. Sister publication: Woodworker's Journal E-zine. Online magazine. **Freq:** Bimonthly. **Key Personnel:** Larry N. Stoiaken, Editor-in-Chief; Rob Johnstone, Editor-in-Chief. **ISSN:** 0199-1892 (print). **Subscription Rates:** $10 U.S. print; plus $2.00 postage; C$25.95 Other countries print; $9.95 Individuals online /year. **URL:** http://www.woodworkersjournal.com. **Formerly:** Today's Woodworker. **Remarks:** Accepts advertising. **Circ:** Paid ★200301.

12924 ■ KCSI-FM - 95.3
PO Box 465
Red Oak, IA 51566
Phone: (712)623-2584
Email: kcsifm@yahoo.com
Format: Contemporary Country; News; Sports; Agricultural; Religious. **Owner:** Hawkeye Communications, Inc., 1991 Ironwood Ave., Red Oak, IA 51566, Ph: (712)623-2584. **Founded:** 1979. **Formerly:** KOAK-FM. **Operating Hours:** Continuous. **Key Personnel:** Jerry

V. Dietz, Mgr., Owner. **Wattage**: 50,000 ERP. **URL:** http://www.kcsifm.com.

12925 ■ KHIN-TV - 36
6450 Corporate Dr.
Johnston, IA 50131
Phone: (515)725-9700
Free: 800-532-1290
Format: Public TV. **Simulcasts:** KDIN-TV Des Moines, IA. **Networks:** Public Broadcasting Service (PBS). **Owner:** Iowa Public Television, PO Box 6450, Johnston, IA 50131-6450, Ph: (515)242-3100, Free: 800-532-1290. **Founded:** 1975. **ADI**: Omaha, NE. **Key Personnel:** Terry Rinehart, Dir. Ed., terry.rinehart@iptv.org; Molly M. Phillips, Exec. Dir., Gen. Mgr., molly@iptv.org; Daniel K. Miller, Exec. Dir., dkm@iptv.org; Kristine K. Houston, Dir. of Admin.; William T. Hayes, Dir. of Engg., hayes@iptv.org. **Ad Rates:** Noncommercial. **Mailing address:** PO Box 6450, Johnston, IA 50131. **URL:** http://www.iptv.org.

12926 ■ KOAK-AM - 1080
1991 Ironwood Ave
Red Oak, IA 51566
Phone: (712)623-2584
Email: kcsifm@yahoo.com
Format: News; Sports; Contemporary Country; Full Service. **Simulcasts:** KCSI-FM. **Networks:** ABC; Radio Iowa; Brownfield. **Owner:** Hawkeye Communications, Inc., 1991 Ironwood Ave., Red Oak, IA 51566, Ph: (712)623-2584. **Founded:** 1968. **Operating Hours**: Continuous. **Wattage**: 250. **Mailing address:** PO Box 465, Red Oak, IA 51566. **URL:** http://www.kcsifm.com/main/_main/default.asp.

REINBECK

NEC IA. Grundy Co. 20 mi. SW of Waterloo. Fertilizer lab, highway construction, landfill services. Poultry and produce packing plant. Agriculture. Corn, hogs, cattle.

12927 ■ Reinbeck Courier
Courier
414 Main St.
Reinbeck, IA 50669
Phone: (319)345-2031
Publisher's E-mail: editor@reinbeckcourier.com
Newspaper with a Republican orientation. **Freq:** Weekly (Thurs.). **Print Method:** Offset. **Cols./Page:** 6. **Col. Width:** 26 nonpareils. **Col. Depth:** 301 agate lines. **Key Personnel:** Mike Schlesinger, Publisher, phone: (641)753-6611; Jessica Larsen, Editor, phone: (319)345-2031; Laura Beard, Bookkeeper, phone: (319)345-2031. **USPS:** 460-120. **Subscription Rates:** $11.25 By mail in country ; $12 By mail in Iowa; $12.50 By mail outside Iowa. **URL:** http://www.reinbeckcourier.com. **Ad Rates:** GLR $0.33; BW $429; 4C $534; SAU $4.72; PCI $4.50. **Remarks:** Accepts advertising. **Circ:** Paid ‡1750.

REMSEN

NW IA. Plymouth Co. 35 mi. NE of Sioux City. Stock, grain farms. Corn, oats, soybeans.

12928 ■ Remsen Bell-Enterprise
Remsen Bell-Enterprise
246 S Washington St.
Remsen, IA 51050
Publication E-mail: remsenbell@midlands.net
Local newspaper. **Freq:** Weekly (Thurs.). **Print Method:** Offset. **Trim Size:** 6 1/4 x 11 1/2. **Cols./Page:** 6. **Col. Width:** 11 picas. **Col. Depth:** 21 inches. **Key Personnel:** Diane Stangl, Office Manager. **USPS:** 048-760. **Subscription Rates:** $16 Individuals; $18 Out of state. **URL:** http://www.remseniowa.net/government.html. **Ad Rates:** GLR $.13; BW $226.80; SAU $2.57; PCI $3.50. **Remarks:** Accepts advertising. **Circ:** ‡1200.

12929 ■ WesTel Systems
012 E 3rd St.
Remsen, IA 51050
Phone: (712)786-1181
Free: 800-352-0006
Email: acctinfo@westelsystems.com
Founded: 1926. **Formerly**: Hooper Telephone Co. **Key Personnel:** Mike Nelson, CFO. **Cities Served:** United States; 84 channels. **Mailing address:** PO Box 330, Remsen, IA 51050. **URL:** http://www.westelsystems.com.

ROCK RAPIDS

NW IA. Lyon Co. On Rock River, 35 mi. E. of Sioux Falls, SD. Manufactures caps and jackets, farm implements, sheet metal. Feed mill. Grain, stock, poultry farms. Corn, cattle, hogs.

12930 ■ Lyon County Reporter
Lyon-Sioux Newspaper Publishing
310 1st Ave. W
Rock Rapids, IA 51246
Publication E-mail: jhoog@ncppub.com
Community newspaper. **Freq:** Weekly (Wed.). **Key Personnel:** Jessica Jensen, Editor. **USPS:** 323-300. **URL:** http://www.lyoncountyreporter.com. **Remarks:** Accepts advertising. **Circ:** Paid ‡2542, Free ‡50.

ROCK VALLEY

NW IA. Sioux Co. 14 mi. W. of Boyden. Residential.

12931 ■ The Rock Valley Bee
The Rock Valley Bee
PO Box 157
Rock Valley, IA 51247-0157
Phone: (712)476-2795
Fax: (712)476-2796
Publication E-mail: rvbee@mtcnet.net
Newspaper with a Republican orientation. **Freq:** Weekly (Tues.). **Print Method:** Offset. **Cols./Page:** 6. **Col. Width:** 18 nonpareils. **Col. Depth:** 224 agate lines. **Key Personnel:** Chris Godfredsen, Editor. **URL:** http://cityofrockvalley.com/site/communications.html. **Ad Rates:** GLR $5.80; BW $556.80. **Remarks:** Accepts advertising. **Circ:** Paid ‡1600, Free ‡4750.

ROCKWELL CITY

NWC IA. Calhoun Co. 25 mi. SW of Fort Dodge. Hatchery; grain elevator. Agriculture. Corn, beans, grain.

12932 ■ Calhoun County Reminder
Dudley Printing Inc.
515 Fourth St.
Rockwell City, IA 50579-0106
Phone: (712)297-8931
Free: 888-712-8931
Publication E-mail: ads@calhouncountyreminder.com
Shopper. **Freq:** Weekly (Wed.). **Print Method:** Offset. **Cols./Page:** 6. **Col. Width:** 19 nonpareils. **Col. Depth:** 224 agate lines. **Key Personnel:** Gary D. Dudley, Publisher. **Subscription Rates:** Free. **URL:** http://www.calhouncountyreminder.com. **Ad Rates:** PCI $5.50. **Remarks:** Accepts advertising. **Circ:** Free ‡6340.

ROYAL

12933 ■ Royal Telephone Co.
307 Main St.
Royal, IA 51357
Phone: (712)933-2615
Fax: (712)933-0015
Email: info@royaltelco.com
Founded: 1911. **Key Personnel:** Sherry Toft, Office Mgr. **Cities Served:** United States. **Mailing address:** PO Box 80, Royal, IA 51357. **URL:** http://www.royaltelco.com.

SCHALLER

12934 ■ Schaller Herald
Schaller Herald
203 S Main
Schaller, IA 51053-7732
Phone: (712)275-4229
Community newspaper. **Freq:** Weekly (Wed.). **Cols./Page:** 8. **Col. Width:** 10 picas. **Col. Depth:** 21 1/2 inches. **Key Personnel:** Betty Bailey, Editor. **Subscription Rates:** $15 Individuals; $18 Out of area; $20 Out of state. **Mailing address:** PO Box 129, Schaller, IA 51053-7732. **Ad Rates:** SAU $4.50. **Remarks:** Accepts advertising. **Circ:** 850.

12935 ■ Comserv Ltd.
111 W Second St.
Schaller, IA 51053
Phone: (712)275-4215
Fax: (712)275-4121
Free: 800-469-9099
Cities Served: Cushing, Galva, Kiron, Odebolt, Schaller, Iowa; 61 channels. **Mailing address:** PO Box 310, Schaller, IA 51053. **URL:** http://www.schallertel.net/comserv/index.htm.

SERGEANT BLUFF

12936 ■ Long Lines Ltd.
501 4th St.
Sergeant Bluff, IA 51054-8509
Phone: (712)271-4000
Free: 866-901-5664
Email: info@longlines.biz
Founded: 1941. **Key Personnel:** Paul Bergmann, CFO; Douglas Maine, Contact; Jeffrey D. Meskin, Contact; Michael H. Salsbury, Contact; John C. Walsh, Contact; Dirk J. Jon Winkel, Contact. **Cities Served:** 23 channels. **URL:** http://www.longlines.com.

SHELDON

NW IA. Sioux Co. 60 mi. N. of Sioux City. Medical equipment, tool and die, truck box fabrication, fiberglass tanks, rendering equipment, working clothes, feed manufactured. Soybean processing mill. Agriculture. Corn, oats, soybeans, livestock.

12937 ■ KIWA-AM - 1550
411 9th St.
Sheldon, IA 51201
Phone: (712)324-2597
Email: newstips@kiwaradio.com
Format: Country; Talk. **Simulcasts:** KIWA-FM. **Networks:** ABC. **Owner:** Sheldon Broadcasting Co., Inc., at above address, SHELDON, IA. **Founded:** 1961. **Operating Hours**: 5:30 a.m.-midnight; 20% network, 80% local. **ADI**: Sioux City, IA. **Key Personnel:** Walt Pruiksma, Gen. Mgr., walt@kiwaradio.com; Scott Van Aartsen, News Dir., scottv@kiwaradio.com; Wayne Barahona, COO, wayne@kiwaradio.com. **Wattage**: 500. **Ad Rates:** Advertising accepted; rates available upon request. **URL:** http://kiwaradio.com.

12938 ■ KIWA-FM - 105.3
411 Ninth St.
Sheldon, IA 51201
Phone: (712)324-2597
Email: newstips@kiwaradio.com
Format: Classic Rock. **Simulcasts:** KIWA-AM. **Networks:** ABC. **Owner:** Sheldon Broadcasting Co., Inc., at above address, SHELDON, IA. **Founded:** 1971. **Operating Hours**: 5:30 a.m.-midnight; 20% network, 80% local. **ADI**: Sioux City, IA. **Key Personnel:** Scott Van Aartsen, News Dir., scottv@kiwaradio.com; Walt Pruiksma, Station Mgr.; Wayne Barahona, Prog. Dir., wayne@kiwaradio.com. **Wattage**: 50,000. **Ad Rates:** Advertising accepted; rates available upon request. **URL:** http://www.kiwaradio.com.

SHELLSBURG

EC IA. Benton Co. 10 mi. SE of Vinton.

12939 ■ Shellsburg Cablevision Corp.
124 Main St.
Shellsburg, IA 52332
Phone: (319)436-2224
Fax: (319)436-2228
Founded: 1984. **Cities Served:** subscribing households 2,546. **Mailing address:** PO Box 390, Shellsburg, IA 52332.

SHENANDOAH

SW IA. Page Co. 52 mi. SE of Omaha, NE. Manufactures aluminum gates, beverages, food flavoring extracts, truck transmissions. Nurseries; seed houses. Poultry and grain farms.

12940 ■ KECR-AM
112 N Elm St.
Shenandoah, IA 51601
Format: Religious. **Wattage**: 5,000.

12941 ■ KFNO-FM
112 N Elm St.
Shenandoah, IA 51601
Format: Religious. **Wattage**: 2,200 ERP. **Ad Rates:** Noncommercial.

12942 ■ KFRB-FM
112 N Elm St.
Shenandoah, IA 51601
Format: Religious. **ADI**: Bakersfield, CA. **Ad Rates:**

Circulation: ★ = AAM; △ or • = BPA; ♦ = CAC; ❑ = VAC; ⊕ = PO Statement; ‡ = Publisher's Report; Boldface figures = sworn; Light figures = estimated.

Advertising accepted; rates available upon request.

12943 ■ KHAP-FM
112 N Elm St.
Shenandoah, IA 51601
Format: Religious. **Wattage:** 12,000 ERP. **Ad Rates:** Advertising accepted; rates available upon request.

12944 ■ KMA-AM - 960
209 North Elm St.
Shenandoah, IA 51601
Phone: (712)246-5270
Fax: (712)246-5275
Free: 800-234-5622
Email: kmaradio@kmaland.com
Format: Contemporary Country; Agricultural; News. **Networks:** ABC; Radio Iowa. **Owner:** May Broadcasting Co., at above address, Ph: (712)246-5270. **Founded:** 1925. **Operating Hours:** 5 a.m.-12 midnight M-Sat; 6 a.m.-12 midnight Sunday. **Key Personnel:** Don Hansen, Station Mgr., dhansen@kmaland.com; Mark Eno, Gen. Mgr., meno@kmaland.com; Sandy Hansen, Contact, shansen@kmaland.com. **Wattage:** 5,000. **Ad Rates:** Advertising accepted; rates available upon request. **URL:** http://www.kmaland.com.

12945 ■ KPFR-FM
112 N Elm St.
Shenandoah, IA 51601
Format: Religious.

12946 ■ KQKD-AM
112 N Elm St.
Shenandoah, IA 51601
Phone: (605)472-1380
Fax: (605)472-1382
Free: 800-529-1300
Email: kqkd@nbc.net
Format: Country. **Networks:** NBC. **Owner:** Robert Ingstead, at above address. **Founded:** 1962. **Formerly:** KFCB-AM. **Wattage:** 500 Day; 142 Night. **Ad Rates:** $7.45-9.45 for 30 seconds.

12947 ■ KYFR-AM - 920
290 Hegenberger Rd.
Oakland, CA 94621
Free: 800-543-1495
Email: info@familyradio.org
Format: Religious. **Owner:** Family Stations Inc., 290 Hegenberger Rd., Oakland, CA 94621, Free: 800-543-1495. **Founded:** 1977. **Formerly:** KFNF-AM. **Operating Hours:** Continuous. **Wattage:** 5,000. **Ad Rates:** Noncommercial. **URL:** http://www.familyradio.org.

12948 ■ WMFL-FM - 88.5
112 N Elm St.
Shenandoah, IA 51601
Format: Religious. **Ad Rates:** Noncommercial.

12949 ■ WMWK-FM
112 N Elm St.
Shenandoah, IA 51601
Format: Religious. **Wattage:** 1,100 ERP. **Ad Rates:** Noncommercial.

SIDNEY

SW IA. Fremont Co. 40 mi. SE of Omaha, NE. Continuous outdoor rodeo. Stock, grain farms. Corn, wheat, soybeans, hay.

12950 ■ The Sidney Argus-Herald: Fremont County's Leading Newspaper
The Sidney Argus-Herald
614 Main St.
Sidney, IA 51652
Phone: (712)374-2251
Publication E-mail: argusherald@iowatelecom.net
Local newspaper. **Freq:** Weekly. **Print Method:** Offset. **Trim Size:** 7 x 11. **Cols./Page:** 6. **Col. Width:** 11 picas. **Col. Depth:** 21 inches. **Key Personnel:** Dennis Bateman, Editor; Ellen West Longman, Publisher. **USPS:** 496-700. **Subscription Rates:** $28 Individuals in Fremont County; $20 Individuals 6 months in Fremont County; $40 Elsewhere 12 months; $30 Elsewhere 6 months. **URL:** http://www.sidneyia.net/news.php. **Mailing address:** PO Box 190, Sidney, IA 51652. **Ad Rates:** GLR $.30; BW $497.70; 4C $607.70; SAU $3.95; PCI $14. **Remarks:** Accepts advertising. **Circ:** Paid ‡1200.

SIGOURNEY

SE IA. Keokuk Co. 30 mi. NE of Ottumwa. Manufactures turkey products. Feed mills. Corn, soybean, hog, cattle farming.

12951 ■ Sigourney News-Review
Sigourney News-Review
114 E Washington St.
Sigourney, IA 52591
Phone: (641)622-3110
Fax: (641)622-2766
Publisher's E-mail: signred@lisco.com
Community newspaper. **Freq:** Weekly (Wed.). **Print Method:** Offset. **Trim Size:** 11 1/2 x 14 1/4. **Cols./Page:** 7. **Col. Width:** 11.5 picas. **Col. Depth:** 21 picas. **Key Personnel:** Ken Chaney, Publisher, Manager, Advertising and Sales. **USPS:** 009-140. **Subscription Rates:** $42 Individuals print and online or online only; $83 Elsewhere print and online or online only. **URL:** http://www.sigourneynewsreview.com. **Ad Rates:** GLR $.75; BW $6.10; PCI $6. **Remarks:** Accepts advertising. **Circ:** Paid ‡2800, Free ‡48.

SIOUX CENTER

NW IA. Sioux Co. 45 mi. N. of Sioux City. Dordt College. Manufactures electric motor components, truck frames. Egg processing; hog processing. Ships hogs. Grain, cattle, stock, dairy farms.

12952 ■ Diamond
Dordt College
498 4th Ave. NE
Sioux Center, IA 51250
Phone: (712)722-6000
Free: 800-343-6738
Collegiate newspaper. **Freq:** Biweekly (during the academic yr.). **Print Method:** Offset. **Cols./Page:** 5. **Col. Width:** 24 nonpareils. **Col. Depth:** 226 agate lines. **URL:** http://www.dordt.edu/campus_life/student_handbook/general_information.shtml. **Remarks:** Advertising accepted; rates available upon request. **Circ:** (Not Reported).

12953 ■ Pro Rege
Dordt College
498 4th Ave. NE
Sioux Center, IA 51250
Phone: (712)722-6000
Free: 800-343-6738
Publication E-mail: prorege@dordt.edu
Christian magazine in the Reformed tradition by the faculty at Dordt College. **Freq:** Quarterly. **Print Method:** Offset. **Trim Size:** 7 1/4 x 10 1/4. **Cols./Page:** 2. **Col. Width:** 2 3/4 inches. **Col. Depth:** 8 inches. **Key Personnel:** Mary Dengler, Editor; Sally Jongsma, Editor. **ISSN:** 0276--4830 (print). **Subscription Rates:** Free. **Alt. Formats:** PDF. **URL:** http://www.dordt.edu/publications/pro_rege. **Remarks:** Advertising not accepted. **Circ:** Non-paid ‡3100.

12954 ■ The Sioux Center News
The Sioux Center News
PO Box 198
Sioux Center, IA 51250
Phone: (712)722-0741
CNP. **Freq:** Weekly (Wed.). **Print Method:** Offset. **Trim Size:** 15 x 21.5. **Cols./Page:** 9. **Col. Width:** 1 5/8 inches. **Col. Depth:** 21.5 inches. **Key Personnel:** Scott Beernink, Publisher. **USPS:** 497-220. **Subscription Rates:** $24 Individuals; $28.50 Out of area. **URL:** http://www.siouxcenter.com/Index.cfm?Page=GeneralInfo.htm. **Ad Rates:** GLR $.35; BW $948.15; 4C $1,047.13; SAU $5.81; PCI $4.90. **Circ:** 2700.

12955 ■ Sioux Center Shopper
Sioux Center Shopper
303 N Main Ave.
Sioux Center, IA 51250
Phone: (712)722-3457
Fax: (712)722-3465
Publisher's E-mail: barbdh@siouxcenterchamber.com
Shopper. **Freq:** Weekly (Wed.). **Print Method:** Offset. **Trim Size:** 11 x 17. **Cols./Page:** 6. **Col. Width:** 24 nonpareils. **Col. Depth:** 226 agate lines. **Key Personnel:** Scott Beernink, Editor. **URL:** http://www.siouxcenter.com/Index.cfm?Page=GeneralInfo.htm. **Ad Rates:** GLR $0.27; BW $436.80; 4C $800; PCI $4.55. **Remarks:** Accepts advertising. **Circ:** Free ‡12000.

12956 ■ KDCR-FM - 88.5
498 4th Ave. NE
Sioux Center, IA 51250
Phone: (712)722-0885
Email: kdcr@dordt.edu
Format: News; Contemporary Christian; Sports. **Networks:** USA Radio. **Owner:** Dordt College, 498 4th Ave. NE, Sioux Center, IA 51250, Ph: (712)722-6000, Free: 800-343-6738. **Founded:** Aug. 16, 1968. **Operating Hours:** Continuous. **Wattage:** 100,000. **Ad Rates:** Noncommercial. **URL:** http://www.kdcr.dordt.edu.

12957 ■ KIHK-FM - 106.9
PO Box 298
Sioux Center, IA 51250
Phone: (712)722-1090
Fax: (712)722-1102
Format: Country. **Founded:** Sept. 07, 2006. **Operating Hours:** Continuous. **Key Personnel:** Craig Aukes, Gen. Mgr., caukes@siouxcountyradio.com; Dan Bonnema, Sales Mgr., dbroek@siouxcountyradio.com; Doug Broek, Sports Dir., News Dir., dbroek@siouxcountyradio.com. **Ad Rates:** Advertising accepted; rates available upon request. **URL:** http://www.ksoufm.com.

12958 ■ KSOU-AM
128 20th St. S
Sioux Center, IA 51250-0298
Phone: (712)722-1090
Fax: (712)722-1102
Email: ksou@mtcnet.net
Format: Contemporary Christian. **Networks:** ABC. **Owner:** Waitt Media, Sioux Falls, SD, Ph: (605)334-1117. **Founded:** 1969. **Formerly:** KVDB-AM. **Wattage:** 500 Day. **Ad Rates:** $8.50-14 for 30 seconds; $10.00-16.00 for 60 seconds. **Mailing address:** PO Box 298, Sioux Center, IA 51250-0298. **URL:** http://www.siouxcountyradio.com/.

12959 ■ KSOU-FM - 93.9
PO Box 298
Sioux Center, IA 51250
Phone: (712)722-1090
Fax: (712)722-1102
Format: Adult Contemporary. **Networks:** ABC. **Founded:** 1974. **Operating Hours:** Continuous. **ADI:** Sioux City, IA. **Key Personnel:** Craig Aukes, Traffic Mgr., caukes@siouxcountyradio.com; Dan Bonnema, Sales Mgr., dbonnema@siouxcountyradio.com; Doug Broek, Sports Dir., News Dir., dbroek@siouxcountyradio.com. **Wattage:** 50,000. **Ad Rates:** Noncommercial. Combined advertising rates available with KIHK-FM & KSOU-AM. **URL:** http://www.ksoufm.com.

12960 ■ Premier Communications Inc.
339 1st Ave. NE
Sioux Center, IA 51250
Phone: (712)722-3451
Fax: (712)722-1113
Free: 800-741-8351
Cities Served: United StatesMelvin, Merrill, Orange City, Ocheyedan, Rock Valley; 125 channels. **Mailing address:** PO Box 200, Sioux Center, IA 51250. **URL:** http://www.mypremieronline.com.

SIOUX CITY

W IA. Woodbury Co. On Missouri River, 100 mi. NW of Council Bluffs. Morningside College, Briar Cliff College. Livestock market and meat packing center. Manufactures auto accessories, fishing tackle, tools, truck bodies and trailers, farm implements, popcorn, dairy, lumber, food products, chemical fertilizers, structural steel, stock feeds, radios, fork lifts, hydraulic cylinders, paper boxes, metal awnings, doors, windows, culverts. Produce packing; foundries; machine shops.

12961 ■ Collegian Reporter
Collegian Reporter
Morningside College
1501 Morningside Ave.
Sioux City, IA 51106
Phone: (712)274-5000
Fax: (712)274-5101
Collegiate newspaper. **Freq:** Weekly (during the academic year). **Print Method:** Offset. **Trim Size:** 11 1/4 x 17. **Cols./Page:** 5. **Col. Width:** 11 picas. **Col. Depth:** 205 agate lines. **Key Personnel:** Adriane Dougherty, Editor; Ross Fuglsang, Advisor, phone: (712)274-5129; Jessie Pick, Contact. **URL:** http://webs.morningside.

edu/masscomm/thecr.html. **Formerly**: Collegian Chief. **Remarks:** Advertising accepted; rates available upon request. **Circ:** Free ‡1000.

12962 ■ Sioux City Journal
Lee Enterprises Inc.
515 Pavonia St.
Sioux City, IA 51102
Phone: (712)293-4250
Free: 800-397-3530
Publication E-mail: Larry.Myhre@lee.net
General newspaper. **Freq:** Daily and Sun. **Print Method:** Offset. **Cols./Page:** 6. **Col. Width:** 26 nonpareils. **Col. Depth:** 301 agate lines. **Key Personnel:** Mitch Pugh, Editor, phone: (712)293-4201; Ron Peterson, Publisher, phone: (712)293-4244; Angie Dye, Manager, Marketing, phone: (712)293-4274; Nicole Schweitzberger, Director, Creative Services, phone: (712)293-4322; Tom LaPlant, Manager, Circulation, phone: (712)293-4278. **URL:** http://siouxcityjournal.com. **Remarks:** Accepts advertising. **Circ:** Mon.-Sat. ★**35335**, Sun. ★**37822**.

12963 ■ Cable One
900 Steuben St.
Sioux City, IA 51101
Phone: (712)233-2000
Email: user@cableone.net
Owner: Cable One Inc., 210 E Earll Dr., Phoenix, AZ 85012, Fax: (602)364-6010. **Founded:** 1979. **Key Personnel:** Thomas O. Might, CEO. **Cities Served:** subscribing households 6,90,000. **URL:** http://www.cableone.net.

12964 ■ IPTV-TV - 27
6450 Corporate Dr.
Johnston, IA 50131
Free: 800-532-1290
Owner: Iowa Public Television, PO Box 6450, Johnston, IA 50131-6450, Ph: (515)242-3100, Free: 800-532-1290. **Key Personnel:** William T. Hayes, Dir. of Engg., hayes@iptv.org; Molly M. Phillips, Exec. Dir., Gen. Mgr.; Daniel K. Miller, Exec. Dir., Gen. Mgr.; Kristine K. Houston, Dir. of Admin.; Terry Rinehart, Div. Dir., terry.rinehart@iptv.org. **Mailing address:** PO Box 6450, Johnston, IA 50131-6450. **URL:** http://www.iptv.org.

12965 ■ KCAU-TV - 9
625 Douglas St.
Sioux City, IA 51101
Phone: (712)277-2345
Fax: (712)277-3733
Email: news@kcautv.com
Founded: 1953. **Key Personnel:** Daniele Feenstra, Promotions Mgr. **Ad Rates:** Noncommercial. **URL:** http://www.kcautv.com.

12966 ■ KILV-FM - 107.5
PO Box 2098
Omaha, NE 68103
Free: 800-525-5683
Format: Contemporary Christian. **Owner:** Educational Media Foundation, 5700 W Oaks Blvd., CA 95765, Free: 800-800434-8400. **Key Personnel:** Mike Novak, President, CEO; Alan Mason, COO. **Wattage**: 25,000. **URL:** http://www.klove.com.

12967 ■ KKMA-FM - 99.5
2000 Indian Hills Dr.
Sioux City, IA 51104
Phone: (712)239-2100
Format: Classic Rock. **Simulcasts:** Combined advertising rates available with KSUX-FM, KSCJ-AM, KLEM-AM. **Owner:** Powell Broadcasting, at above address. **Operating Hours**: 6 a.m.-12 a.m. Mon.-Thurs.; 6 a.m.-11 p.m. Fri.-Sat. **Key Personnel:** Steve Arthur, Contact; Brian Ross, Contact. **Wattage**: 100,000. **Ad Rates:** $14 for 30 seconds; $20 for 60 seconds. **URL:** http://classicrock995.com/.

12968 ■ KKYY-FM - 101.3
2000 Indian Hills Dr.
Sioux City, IA 51104
Phone: (712)239-2100
Format: Country. **Key Personnel:** Dennis Bullock, Gen. Mgr.; Dave Grosenheider, Dir. of Sales, dgrosenh@powelliowa.com.

12969 ■ KMNS-AM - 620
1113 Nebraska St.
Sioux City, IA 51105
Phone: (712)258-5595
Format: Sports; News; Talk. **Networks:** ABC. **Founded:** 1949. **Operating Hours**: Continuous. **Key Personnel:** Laura Schiltz, Gen. Mgr. **Wattage**: 1,000. **Ad Rates:** $20-50 for 30 seconds; $25-55 for 60 seconds. **URL:** http://www.620kmns.com.

12970 ■ KMSC-FM - 92.9
1501 Morningside Ave.
Sioux City, IA 51106
Format: Full Service; Alternative/New Music/Progressive. **Networks:** Independent. **Owner:** Morningside College, 1501 Morning Side Ave., Sioux City, IA 51106, Ph: (712)274-5000, Fax: (712)274-5101, Free: 800-831-0806. **Founded:** 1978. **Operating Hours:** Continuous. **ADI**: Sioux City, IA. **Key Personnel:** Tennessee Bryant, Dir. of Production, kmscproduction@morningside.edu; Nick Burth, Station Mgr.; Sean Roberts, Music Dir. **Wattage**: 012. **Ad Rates:** Noncommercial. **URL:** http://www.webs.morningside.edu.

12971 ■ KOJI-FM - 90.7
4647 Stone Ave.
Sioux City, IA 51106
Phone: (712)274-6406
Fax: (712)274-6411
Free: 800-251-3690
Format: Public Radio; Classical; Jazz. **Key Personnel:** Gretchen Gondek, Gen. Mgr., gretchen.gondek@witcc.edu. **Wattage**: 100,000. **URL:** http://www.kwit.org.

12972 ■ KSCJ-AM - 1360
2000 Indian Hills Dr.
Sioux City, IA 51104
Email: jb@kscj.com
Format: Talk; News; Sports. **Networks:** CBS. **Owner:** Powell Broadcasting, at above address. **Founded:** 1927. **Operating Hours**: Continuous. **ADI**: Sioux City, IA. **Key Personnel:** Tom Beightol, Contact, tbeightol@powelliowa.com; Josie Cooper, Contact, josiecooper@powelliowa.com. **Local Programs**: *Open Line*, Monday Tuesday Wednesday Thursday Friday 8:00 a.m. - 11:00 a.m.; *The Sean Hannity Show*, Monday Tuesday Wednesday Thursday Friday 2:00 p.m. - 5:00 p.m.; *Grow Siouxland*, Saturday 8:10 a.m. - 8:30 a.m.; *Nostalgia Theater*, Saturday 9:00 a.m. - 11:00 a.m.; *The Good Shepherd*, Sunday 8:00 a.m. - 8:30 a.m.; *The Lutheran Hour*, Sunday 8:30 a.m. - 9:00 a.m.; *The Internet Business Hour*, Saturday 2:00 p.m.; *Morningside Lutheran Church*, Sunday 11:00 a.m. - 12:00 p.m.; *Doug Stephan's Talk Countdown*, Sunday 2:00 a.m. - 4:00 a.m.; *Ask Earl May w/ John Kluver*, Saturday 8:30 a.m. - 9:00 a.m.; *The Kim Komando Computer Show*, Saturday 11:00 a.m. - 2:00 p.m.; *Saturday Morning Wake Up Show*, Saturday 6:00 a.m. - 7:00 a.m.; *Mass from Blessed Sacrament Church*, Sunday 9:00 a.m. - 10:00 a.m. **Wattage**: 5,000. **Ad Rates:** Advertising accepted; rates available upon request. Combined advertising rates available with KSUX-FM, KKMA-FM, KLEM-AM. **URL:** http://www.kscj.com.

12973 ■ KSEZ-FM - 97.9
1113 Nebraska St.
Sioux City, IA 51105
Phone: (712)258-5595
Format: Album-Oriented Rock (AOR). **Networks:** ABC; NBC. **Owner:** iHeartMedia Inc., 200 E Basse Rd., San Antonio, TX 78209, Ph: (210)832-3314. **Founded:** 1960. **Operating Hours**: Continuous. **ADI**: Sioux City, IA. **Key Personnel:** Scott Miller, Dir. of Programs, millerscott@clearchannel.com. **Wattage**: 100,000 ERP. **Ad Rates:** Noncommercial. **URL:** http://www.z98rocks.com//main.html.

12974 ■ KSFT-FM - 107.1
1113 Nebraska St.
Sioux City, IA 51104
Phone: (712)258-5595
Fax: (712)252-2430
Format: Adult Contemporary. **Key Personnel:** Rick Schorg, Gen. Mgr. **Wattage**: 2,300. **Ad Rates:** Noncommercial. **URL:** http://1071kissfm.iheart.com.

12975 ■ KSIN-TV - 27
6450 Corporate Dr.
Johnston, IA 50131
Phone: (515)242-3100
Free: 800-532-1290
Email: public_information@iptv.org
Format: Public TV. **Simulcasts:** KDIN-TV Des Moines, IA. **Networks:** Public Broadcasting Service (PBS). **Owner:** Iowa Public Television, PO Box 6450, Johnston, IA 50131-6450, Ph: (515)242-3100, Free: 800-532-1290. **Founded:** 1975. **Operating Hours**: Continuous. **ADI**: Sioux City, IA. **Key Personnel:** Daniel K. Miller, Exec. Dir., Gen. Mgr., dkm@iptv.org; Kristine K. Houston, Dir. of Admin., kris@iptv.org; William T. Hayes, Dir. of Engg., hayes@iptv.org; Terry Rinehart, Director, terry.rinehart@iptv.org; Molly M. Phillips, Exec. Dir., Gen. Mgr., molly@iptv.org. **Mailing address:** PO Box 6450, Johnston, IA 50131. **URL:** http://www.iptv.org.

12976 ■ KSUX-FM - 105.7
2000 Indian Hills Dr.
Sioux City, IA 51104
Phone: (712)274-1057
Fax: (712)252-2430
Format: Country; Contemporary Hit Radio (CHR). **Networks:** ABC. **Owner:** Powell Broadcasting, at above address; iHeartMedia Inc., 200 E Basse Rd., San Antonio, TX 78209, Ph: (210)832-3314. **Founded:** 1991. **Formerly**: KBCM-FM. **Operating Hours**: Continuous. **ADI**: Sioux City, IA. **Key Personnel:** Tony Michaels, Promotions Dir. **Wattage**: 50,000. **Ad Rates:** Advertising accepted; rates available upon request; Noncommercial. Combined advertising rates available with KSCJ-AM; KKMA-FM. **URL:** http://ksux.com.

12977 ■ KTIV-TV - 4
3135 Floyd Blvd.
Sioux City, IA 51108
Phone: (712)239-4100
Fax: (712)239-2621
Email: ktivnews@ktiv.com
Format: News. **Networks:** NBC; ABC. **Owner:** New Jersey Herald Inc., subsidiary of Quincy Newspapers, 2 Spring St., Newton, NJ 07860, Ph: (973)383-1500, Fax: (973)383-8477. **Founded:** 1954. **Operating Hours**: Continuous; 90% network & syndicated, 10% local. **Key Personnel:** Dave Madsen, Station Mgr.; Adrian Wisner, Gen. Sales Mgr., awisner@ktiv.com; Richard Herr, Chief Engineer, rherr@ktiv.com. **Ad Rates:** Advertising accepted; rates available upon request. **URL:** http://www.ktiv.com.

12978 ■ KWSL-AM - 1470
4700 S Lewis Blvd.
Sioux City, IA 51106
Phone: (712)255-1470
Fax: (712)252-2430
Format: Oldies. **Networks:** CNN Radio; Precision Racing; International Broadcasting; Sunstar. **Founded:** 1938. **Operating Hours**: Continuous. **ADI**: Sioux City, IA. **Key Personnel:** Laura Schiltz, Gen. Mgr. **Wattage**: 5,000. **Ad Rates:** Noncommercial. **URL:** http://www.1470kwsl.com.

SOLON

E IA. Johnson Co. 10 mi. N. of Iowa City. Feed, flour mills. Agriculture. Corn, oats, hay.

12979 ■ Solon Economist
Solon Economist
102 N Market st.
Solon, IA 52333
Phone: (319)624-2233
Fax: (319)624-1356
Publisher's E-mail: hybrid@southslope.net
Newspaper. **Freq:** Weekly (Wed.). **Print Method:** Offset. **Cols./Page:** 6. **Col. Width:** 20 nonpareils. **Col. Depth:** 196 agate lines. **Key Personnel:** Doug Lindner, Publisher; Kelly Meyer, Manager, Advertising and Sales, phone: (319)530-7056; Lori Lindner, Editor, phone: (319)936-0981. **Subscription Rates:** $30 Individuals in county; $33 Individuals in state; $36 Out of state; $58 Two years in county; $64 Two years in state; $70 Out of state two years. **URL:** http://www.soloneconomist.com . **Mailing address:** PO Box 249, Solon, IA 52333. **Remarks:** Accepts advertising. **Circ:** (Not Reported).

SPENCER

NW IA. Clay Co. 80 mi. NE of Sioux City. Manufactures hydrostatic transmissions, lifts, garments, machinery, cement blocks, lubricating equipment, rendering works; grain elevator; meat packing. Stock. Agriculture. Livestock, grain farms. Corn, oats, barley.

Circulation: ★ = AAM; △ or • = BPA; ♦ = CAC; ❑ = VAC; ⊕ = PO Statement; ‡ = Publisher's Report; Boldface figures = sworn; Light figures = estimated.

12980 ■ KDWD-FM - 100.1
2303 W 18th St.
Spencer, IA 51301
Phone: (712)264-1074
Fax: (712)264-1077
Format: Information; News; Talk; Sports; Top 40. **Owner:** Jim Dandy Broadcasting, at above address. **Founded:** 1977. **Formerly:** KEMB-FM. **Key Personnel:** Danielle Hitchings, News Dir. **Wattage:** 16,000 ERP. **Ad Rates:** $12 for 30 seconds; $16 for 60 seconds. **URL:** http://www.y100-fm.com.

12981 ■ KICD-AM - 1240
2600 N Highway Blvd.
Spencer, IA 51301
Phone: (712)262-1240
Fax: (712)262-5821
Email: news@kicdam.com
Format: News; Talk; Sports. **Owner:** Saga Communications Inc., at above address. **Operating Hours:** Continuous. **Key Personnel:** Mark Magnuson, Sports Dir., mmagnuson@spencerradiogroup.com; Ryan Long, News Dir., rlong@spencerradiogroup.com. **Local Programs:** *Dow Jones Money Report*, Monday Tuesday Wednesday Thursday Friday 9:25 a.m. **Wattage:** 1,000. **Ad Rates:** Noncommercial; Advertising accepted; rates available upon request. **URL:** http://www.kicdam.com.

12982 ■ KICD-FM - 107.7
2600 Hwy. Blvd.
Spencer, IA 51301
Phone: (712)262-1240
Fax: (712)262-5821
Format: Country. **Networks:** CBS. **Owner:** Saga Communications Inc., at above address. **Founded:** 1965. **Operating Hours:** Continuous Mon. - Sun. **ADI:** Sioux City, IA. **Key Personnel:** Kevin Tlam, Operations Mgr.; Linda Maske, Office Mgr.; Dan Skelton, Director; David Putnam, Gen. Mgr.; Rhonda Wedeking, Dir. of Programs; Ryan Long, News Dir.; Mark Magnuson, Sports Dir. **Local Programs:** *Rhonda Wedeking Show.* **Wattage:** 100,000 ERP. **Ad Rates:** Advertising accepted; rates available upon request. KICD-AM; KLLT-FM. **Mailing address:** PO Box 260, Spencer, IA 51301. **URL:** http://www.cd1077fm.com.

12983 ■ KLLT-FM - 104.9
PO Box 260
Spencer, IA 51301
Phone: (712)262-1240
Fax: (712)262-2076
Format: Adult Contemporary; Easy Listening. **Networks:** NBC. **Owner:** Saga Communications of Iowa L.L.C., at above address. **Founded:** Feb. 1979. **Formerly:** KJJG-FM/KIGL. **Operating Hours:** Continuous. **Key Personnel:** Kevin Tlam, Operations Mgr., ktlam@spencerradiogroup.com; David Putnam, Gen. Mgr., dputnam@spencerradiogroup.com; Linda Maske, Office Mgr., lmaske@spencerradiogroup.com. **Wattage:** 25,000. **Ad Rates:** Noncommercial. **URL:** http://www.more1049.com.

12984 ■ KUYY-FM - 100.1
2303 W 18th St.
Spencer, IA 51301
Phone: (712)264-1074
Fax: (712)264-1077
Format: Sports. **Owner:** NRG Media, 2875 Mount Vernon Rd. SE, Cedar Rapids, IA 52403, Ph: (319)862-0300, Fax: (319)286-9383. **Key Personnel:** Marty Spies, Gen. Mgr., mspies@nrgmedia.com. **Wattage:** 16,000 ERP. **URL:** http://www.y100-fm.com.

SPIRIT LAKE

NW IA. Dickinson Co. 100 mi. E. of Sioux Falls, SD. Lake resort. Industrial wire, air condition equipment, boats, fishing equipment, fiberglass products manufactured. Bottling works. Diversified farming. Corn, hay.

12985 ■ News
News
PO Box AE
Spirit Lake, IA 51360
Local newspaper. **Founded:** 1890. **Freq:** Weekly. **Print Method:** Offset. **Cols./Page:** 6. **Col. Width:** 2 1/16 24 inches nonpareils. **Col. Depth:** 294 agate lines. **Subscription Rates:** $16 Individuals. **Ad Rates:** PCI $5.75; BW $322.50; SAU $2.50; PCI $2.94. **Remarks:** Accepts advertising. **Circ:** 660.

12986 ■ KUOO-FM - 103.9
3200 18th St.
Spirit Lake, IA 51360
Phone: (712)336-5800
Fax: (712)336-1634
Format: Adult Contemporary. **Networks:** ABC. **Owner:** Waitt Radio, Inc., at above address. **Founded:** 1985. **Operating Hours:** Continuous. **ADI:** Sioux City, IA. **Key Personnel:** Marty Spies, Gen. Mgr., mspies@exploreokoboji.com. **Wattage:** 50,000. **Ad Rates:** $7-9.50 for 15 seconds; $10-12.50 for 30 seconds; $14-16.50 for 60 seconds. **Mailing address:** PO Box 528, Spirit Lake, IA 51360. **URL:** http://www.kuooradio.com.

12987 ■ KUQQ-FM - 102.1
3200 18th St.
Spirit Lake, IA 51360
Phone: (712)336-5800
Fax: (712)336-1634
Format: Classic Rock. **Key Personnel:** Marty Spies, Gen. Mgr. **Ad Rates:** Advertising accepted; rates available upon request. **Mailing address:** PO Box 528, Spirit Lake, IA 51360. **URL:** http://www.kuqqfm.com.

STORM LAKE

NW IA. Buena Vista Co. 60 mi. W. of Fort Dodge. Buena Vista College. Manufactures jeans, valve hydrants. Pork and turkey packing plants; hog and poultry houses. Seed corn plants. Agriculture. Livestock, corn, oats, soybeans.

12988 ■ Buena Vista Today: A Buena Vista University Publication
Buena Vista University
610 W Fourth St.
Storm Lake, IA 50588
Fax: (712)749-2037
Free: 800-383-2821
Publication E-mail: bvunews@bvu.edu
Collegiate alumni magazine. **Freq:** Semiannual. **Print Method:** Web Press. **Trim Size:** 8 1/2 x 11. **Cols./Page:** 3. **Col. Width:** 24 nonpareils. **Col. Depth:** 136 agate lines. **Key Personnel:** Frederick V. Moore, President; Shelli Smith, Designer; Ryan Harder, Editor; Jennifer Felton, Art Director; Keith Betts, Vice President, Student Services; Steve Herron, Editor; Kelly Van De Walle, Editor. **USPS:** 069-260. **Remarks:** Advertising not accepted. **Circ:** Controlled ‡18000.

12989 ■ The Pilot-Tribune
Pilot-Tribune
527 Cayuga St.
Storm Lake, IA 50588
Phone: (712)732-3130
Fax: (712)732-3152
Community newspaper. **Founded:** 1870. **Key Personnel:** Dana Larsen, Editor; Paula Buenger, Publisher. **Subscription Rates:** $4.50 Individuals /month; online; $10 Individuals for first three months, then $5 per month. **URL:** http://www.stormlakepilottribune.com/. **Ad Rates:** BW $862.40; 4C $957.40; SAU $7.35. **Remarks:** Accepts advertising. **Circ:** ‡3200.

12990 ■ Storm Lake Times
Storm Lake Times
220 West Rail Road
Storm Lake, IA 50588-0487
Phone: (712)732-4991
Fax: (712)732-4331
Free: 800-732-4992
Publication E-mail: times@stormlake.com
Community newspaper. **Freq:** 22/year. **Print Method:** Web offset. **Cols./Page:** 6. **Key Personnel:** John Cullen, Publisher; Art Cullen, Editor; Michael Diereks, Manager, Sales. **Subscription Rates:** $59.95 Individuals online only; $35.95 Individuals online only - 6 months; $71.95 Elsewhere in Iowa; $41.95 Elsewhere in Iowa - 6 months; $76.95 Out of area; $45.95 Out of area. **URL:** http://www.Stormlake.com. **Mailing address:** PO Box 487, Storm Lake, IA 50588-0487. **Ad Rates:** PCI $6.95, local; PCI $8.20, national. **Remarks:** Accepts advertising. **Circ:** Paid 3,386.

12991 ■ The Tack
Buena Vista University
Buena Vista University
Box 2021
Storm Lake, IA 50588
Publication E-mail: ucbvu@bvu.edu
Collegiate newspaper. **Freq:** Weekly During the school yr. **Print Method:** Offset. **Cols./Page:** 4. **Col. Width:** 28 nonpareils. **Col. Depth:** 203 agate lines. **Key Personnel:** Erika Garcia, Editor-in-Chief; Shauna McKnight, Editor-in-Chief. **URL:** http://www.bvtack.com. **Remarks:** Accepts advertising. **Circ:** (Not Reported).

12992 ■ KAYL-FM - 101.7
910 Flindt Dr.
Storm Lake, IA 50588
Phone: (712)732-3520
Fax: (712)732-1746
Format: Adult Contemporary. **Networks:** ABC. **Owner:** NRG Media, 2875 Mount Vernon Rd. SE, Cedar Rapids, IA 52403, Ph: (319)862-0300, Fax: (319)286-9383. **Founded:** 1949. **Operating Hours:** Continuous. **Key Personnel:** Chris Boeckman, Sports Dir.; Buzz Paterson, Gen. Mgr.; Matt Fisher, Music Dir., Prog. Dir. **Wattage:** 50,000. **Ad Rates:** Noncommercial. **URL:** http://www.stormlakeradio.com.

12993 ■ KBVU-FM - 97.5
610 W Fourth St.
Storm Lake, IA 50588
Phone: (712)749-1234
Email: kbvu@bvu.edu
Format: Alternative/New Music/Progressive. **Owner:** Buena Vista University, 610 W Fourth St., Storm Lake, IA 50588, Fax: (712)749-2037, Free: 800-383-2821. **Founded:** Nov. 17, 1997. **Operating Hours:** Continuous. **Key Personnel:** Miranda Klingeberg, Gen. Mgr.; Peyton Burch, Music Dir. **Wattage:** 6,000. **Ad Rates:** Noncommercial. **URL:** http://www.bvu.edu.

12994 ■ KKIA-FM - 92.9
PO Box 108
Storm Lake, IA 50588
Phone: (712)732-3220
Fax: (712)732-1746
Email: themoose@pionet.net
Format: Hot Country. **Networks:** AP; Jones Satellite. **Founded:** 1999. **Formerly:** KIDA-FM. **Operating Hours:** Continuous. **ADI:** Sioux City, IA. **Wattage:** 25,000. **URL:** http://www.stormlakeradio.com/newsite/?stat=kkia.

STORY CITY

C IA. Story Co. 12 mi. N. of Ames. Residential. Light Industry.

12995 ■ The Story City Herald
The Story City Herald
511 Broad St.
Story City, IA 50248-1133
Phone: (515)663-9890
Fax: (515)733-4319
Free: 800-234-8742
Publisher's E-mail: news@storycityherald.com
Newspapers. **Freq:** Weekly (Wed.). **Print Method:** Offset. **Cols./Page:** 6. **Col. Width:** 11 picas. **Col. Depth:** 21 1/2 inches. **Key Personnel:** Todd Thorson, Editor; Carolyn Honeycutt, Writer. **USPS:** 522-720. **Subscription Rates:** $4 Individuals monthly (print and online or online only). **URL:** http://www.storycityherald.com . **Remarks:** Advertising accepted; rates available upon request. **Circ:** (Not Reported).

STRATFORD

12996 ■ Complete Communications Service
1001 Tennyson Ave.
Stratford, IA 50249
Phone: (515)838-2390
Free: 866-881-2251
Email: info@globalccs.net
Cities Served: 38 channels. **Mailing address:** PO Box 438, Stratford, IA 50249. **URL:** http://www.stratfordtelephone.com.

STRAWBERRY POINT

NE IA. Clayton Co. 18 mi. N. of Manchester. Residential.

12997 ■ Press Journal
Press Journal
PO Box 70
Strawberry Point, IA 52076-0070
Phone: (563)933-4370
Fax: (563)933-4370

Publisher's E-mail: pressj@iowatelecom.net
Newspaper with a Democratic orientation. **Founded:** 1876. **Freq:** Weekly (Wed.). **Print Method:** Offset. **Cols./Page:** 6. **Col. Width:** 19 nonpareils. **Col. Depth:** 196 agate lines. **Key Personnel:** Harry Nolda, Publisher; Kay Falck, Editor. **Subscription Rates:** $15 Individuals. **URL:** http://www.inanews.com/apps/displaypapers.php?county=Clayton&mod=About&acti on=County. **Ad Rates:** SAU $2.10. **Remarks:** Accepts advertising. **Circ:** 1438.

TAMA

EC IA. Tama Co. 48 mi. W. of Cedar Rapids. Manufactures egg case fillers, paper box board, asphalt products; beef processing plant. Ships hogs, eggs. Diversified farming.

12998 ■ The Tama News-Herald
Tama County Publishing Inc.
220 W 3rd St.
Tama, IA 52339
Phone: (641)484-2841
Community newspaper. **Freq:** Weekly (Thurs.). **Print Method:** Offset. **Cols./Page:** 6. **Col. Width:** 11.2 picas. **Col. Depth:** 21 inches. **Key Personnel:** Nancy Sund, Director, Advertising, Manager; John Speer, Editor; Wendy Witt, Advertising Representative. **Subscription Rates:** $11.25 Individuals mail delivery; inside county; $12 Out of state mail delivery; $12.50 Out of country mail delivery. **URL:** http://www.tamatoledonews.com . **Remarks:** Advertising accepted; rates available upon request. **Circ:** (Not Reported).

12999 ■ Toledo Chronicle
Tama County Publishing Inc.
220 W 3rd St.
Tama, IA 52339
Phone: (641)484-2841
Community newspaper. **Freq:** Weekly (Tues.). **Print Method:** Offset. **Cols./Page:** 6. **Col. Width:** 11.2 picas. **Col. Depth:** 21 inches. **Key Personnel:** John Speer, Editor; Nancy Sund, Director, Advertising, Manager; Wendy Witt, Advertising Representative; Deb Kouba, Bookkeeper, Receptionist; Kathy Zars, Reporter. **Subscription Rates:** $47 Individuals 1 year, home delivery in Iowa; $36 Individuals 9 months, home delivery in Iowa; $24 Individuals 6 months, home delivery in Iowa; $12 Individuals 3 months, home delivery in Iowa; $45 Individuals 1 year, home delivery inside county; $33.75 Individuals 9 months, home delivery inside county; $22.50 Individuals 6 months, home delivery inside county; $11.25 Individuals 3 months, home delivery inside county; $49 Individuals 1 year, home delivery outside of Iowa; $37 Individuals 9 months, home delivery outside of Iowa; $25 Individuals 6 months, home delivery outside of Iowa; $12.50 Individuals 3 months, home delivery outside of Iowa. **URL:** http://www.tamatoledonews.com. **Ad Rates:** BW $703; 4C $823; SAU $11.41; PCI $9.78. **Remarks:** Accepts advertising. **Circ:** ‡3200.

TEMPLETON

13000 ■ Templeton Telephone Co.
115 N Main St.
Templeton, IA 51463
Phone: (712)669-3311
Fax: (712)669-3312
Free: 888-669-3311
Email: citytemp@netins.net
Founded: 1884. **Cities Served:** subscribing households 214. **Mailing address:** PO Box 77, Templeton, IA 51463. **URL:** http://www.templetoniowa.com.

TIPTON

E IA. Cedar Co. 30 mi. E. of Iowa City. Manufactures electronics, small parts; feed processing. Grain, livestock.

13001 ■ The Tipton Conservative and Advertiser: Rural Newspaper
Conservative Publishing Co.
124 W Fifth St.
Tipton, IA 52772-0271
Phone: (563)886-2131
Fax: (563)886-6466
Community newspaper. **Freq:** Weekly (Wed.). **Print Method:** Offset. **Cols./Page:** 9. **Col. Width:** 20 nonpareils. **Col. Depth:** 300 agate lines. **Key Personnel:** Stuart Clark, Editor, Publisher; Pat Kroemer, Manager, Advertising; Ryan Stonebraker, Editor. **USPS:** 631-520. **Subscription Rates:** $37 Individuals in Cedar and adjoining counties (print or online); $45 Elsewhere in US (print or online); $46 Other countries online (print or online); $28 Students college; 9 months (print or online). **URL:** http://www.tiptonconservative.com . **Remarks:** Accepts advertising. **Circ:** (Not Reported).

TITONKA

N IA. Kossuth Co. 50 mi. W. of Mason City. Grain elevator. Agriculture. Corn, oats, beans, stock.

13002 ■ Titonka Topic
Titonka Topic
247 Main St. N
Titonka, IA 50480-0321
Phone: (515)928-2110
Fax: (515)928-2897
Free: 800-753-2016
Publication E-mail: titonkatopic@netins.net
Community newspaper. **Freq:** Weekly (Thurs.) except one week in July. **Print Method:** Offset. **Cols./Page:** 6. **Col. Width:** 25 nonpareils. **Col. Depth:** 294 agate lines. **Key Personnel:** Mary Ullmann, Managing Editor. **Subscription Rates:** $26 Individuals; $29 Elsewhere; $22 Students. **URL:** http://www.titonka.com/content/titonka-topic-1. **Mailing address:** PO Box 321, Titonka, IA 50480-0321. **Remarks:** Accepts advertising. **Circ:** (Not Reported).

TRAER

EC IA. Tama Co. 24 mi. S. of Waterloo. Manufactures caskets, metal stampings. Seed corn processing plant. Grain, stock farms. Corn, oats, soybeans, hay.

13003 ■ Star-Clipper
Ogden Publishing
625 Second St.
Traer, IA 50675
Phone: (319)478-2323
Publication E-mail: editor@traerstarclipper.com
Newspaper. **Freq:** Weekly (Thurs.). **Print Method:** Offset. **Cols./Page:** 6. **Col. Width:** 21 1/2 ems. **Col. Depth:** 301 agate lines. **Key Personnel:** Tracey Peters, Editor, phone: (319)478-2323; Ross Bercik, Managing Editor. **Subscription Rates:** $11.25 Individuals mail delivery in country; $12 Individuals mail delivery in Iowa; $12.50 Individuals mail delivery out of Iowa. **Mailing address:** PO Box 156, Traer, IA 50675. **Remarks:** Advertising accepted; rates available upon request. **Circ:** (Not Reported).

TRURO

13004 ■ Interstate Communications
105 N West St.
Truro, IA 50257
Phone: (641)765-4201
Fax: (641)765-4204
Free: 800-765-3738
Email: customerservice@interstatecom.com
Founded: 1965. **Formerly:** Interstate 35 Telephone Co. **Cities Served:** United States; 140 channels. **Mailing address:** PO Box 229, Truro, IA 50257. **URL:** http://www.interstatecom.com.

URBANDALE

SC IA. Polk Co. 10 mi. NW of Des Moines. Living history farms. U.S. Bulk Mail Center.

13005 ■ Iowa Grocer
Iowa Grocery Industry Association
2540 106th St., Ste. 102
Urbandale, IA 50322
Phone: (515)270-2628
Fax: (515)270-0316
Free: 800-383-3663
Publisher's E-mail: info@iowagrocers.com
Freq: Quarterly. **Print Method:** Offset. **Trim Size:** 8 1/2 x 11. **Cols./Page:** 3 and 2. **Col. Width:** 26 and 42 nonpareils. **Col. Depth:** 140 agate lines. **Key Personnel:** Jerry Fleagle, President. **Subscription Rates:** Included in membership. **Alt. Formats:** PDF. **URL:** http://www.iowagrocers.com/publications.cfm. **Formerly:** Iowa Food Dealer. **Ad Rates:** BW $1995; 4C $1225. **Remarks:** Accepts advertising. **Circ:** ‡2500, 1800.

13006 ■ Wallaces Farmer
Farm Progress Companies Inc.
6200 Aurora Ave., Ste. 609E
Urbandale, IA 50322-2838
Phone: (515)278-6693
Fax: (515)278-7796
Publisher's E-mail: circhelp@farmprogress.com
Magazine on commercial farming. **Freq:** Monthly. **Print Method:** Offset. **Trim Size:** 8 x 10 3/4. **Cols./Page:** 3. **Col. Width:** 2 1/8 inches. **Col. Depth:** 10 inches. **Key Personnel:** Rod Swoboda, Editor, phone: (515)278-6693, fax: (515)278-7796; Frank Holdmeyer, Executive Editor, phone: (515)278-7782, fax: (515)278-7796; Willie Vogt, Director, Editorial, phone: (651)454-6994, fax: (651)994-0661; Alan Newport, Editor, phone: (580)362-3483, fax: (580)362-3483; John Otte, Editor, phone: (515)278-7785, fax: (515)278-7796. **ISSN:** 1048--5783 (print). **Subscription Rates:** $29.95 Individuals; $48.95 Two years; $64.95 Individuals 3 years. **URL:** http://farmprogress.com/wallaces-farmer. **Remarks:** Accepts advertising. **Circ:** (Not Reported).

13007 ■ KBGG-AM - 1700
4143 109th St.
Urbandale, IA 50322
Phone: (515)331-9200
Format: Sports; Talk; News. **Networks:** CBS. **Owner:** Cumulus Media Inc., 3280 Peachtree Rd. NW, Ste. 2300, Atlanta, GA 30305-2455, Ph: (404)949-0700, Fax: (404)949-0740. **Founded:** 1947. **Operating Hours:** Continuous. **ADI:** Des Moines, IA. **Key Personnel:** Craig Hodgson, Mktg. Mgr. **Wattage:** 10,000 Day time; 010. **Ad Rates:** Advertising accepted; rates available upon request. **URL:** http://www.1700thechamp.com.

13008 ■ KFPX-TV - 39
4570 114th St.
Urbandale, IA 50322
Phone: (515)331-3939
Fax: (515)331-1312
Founded: Sept. 07, 2006. **Key Personnel:** Brandon Burgess, CEO. **Ad Rates:** Advertising accepted; rates available upon request. **URL:** http://www.iontelevision.com.

13009 ■ KGGO-FM - 94.9
4143 109th St.
Urbandale, IA 50322
Email: feedback@scorestream.com
Format: Classic Rock. **Owner:** Citadel Broadcasting Corp., 7201 W Lake Mead Blvd., Ste. 400, Las Vegas, NV 89128-8366, Ph: (702)804-5200, Fax: (702)804-8250. **Founded:** 1921. **Operating Hours:** Continuous. **ADI:** Des Moines, IA. **Wattage:** 100,000 ERP. **Ad Rates:** Advertising accepted; rates available upon request. **URL:** http://www.kggo.com.

13010 ■ KHKI-FM - 97.3
4143 109th St.
Urbandale, IA 50322
Phone: (515)331-9200
Fax: (515)331-9292
Format: Country. **Owner:** Citadel Broadcasting Corp., 7201 W Lake Mead Blvd., Ste. 400, Las Vegas, NV 89128-8366, Ph: (702)804-5200, Fax: (702)804-8250. **Key Personnel:** Terry Peters, Contact, terry.peters@citcomm.com; Doug Wood, Dir. of Sales; Terry Peters, Contact, terry.peters@citcomm.com. **Ad Rates:** Advertising accepted; rates available upon request. **URL:** http://www.NashFM973.com.

13011 ■ KJJY-FM - 92.5
4143 109th St.
Urbandale, IA 50322
Phone: (515)331-9200
Fax: (515)331-9292
Format: Country. **Networks:** Independent. **Owner:** Citadel Broadcasting Corp., 7201 W Lake Mead Blvd., Ste. 400, Las Vegas, NV 89128-8366, Ph: (702)804-5200, Fax: (702)804-8250. **Founded:** 1947. **Operating Hours:** Continuous. **Key Personnel:** Shannon Quinn, Contact, shannon.quinn@citcomm.com. **Wattage:** 50,000. **Ad Rates:** Advertising accepted; rates available upon request. **URL:** http://www.925nashicon.com.

Circulation: ★ = AAM; △ or • = BPA; ♦ = CAC; ❑ = VAC; ⊕ = PO Statement; ‡ = Publisher's Report; Boldface figures = sworn; Light figures = estimated.

13012 ■ KRKQ-FM - 98.3
4143 109th St.
Urbandale, IA 50322
Phone: (515)331-9200
Free: 866-908-8255
Email: 98rock@dwx.com
Founded: 1973. **Formerly:** KZBA-FM; KWBG-FM; KRUU-FM; Radio Ingstad Iowa; KIAB-FM. **Operating Hours:** Continuous. **Key Personnel:** Kim Jones, President; Jack O'Brien, VP of Operations; Kim Tierney, Dir. of Sales; Mike Reeper, Sales Mgr. **Wattage:** 41,000 ERP. **Ad Rates:** for 60 seconds. **URL:** http://www.983vibe.com.

13013 ■ KWQW-FM - 98.3
4143 109th St.
Urbandale, IA 50322
Phone: (515)331-9200
Fax: (515)331-9292
Free: 866-908-8255
Format: Talk; News. **Key Personnel:** Terry Peters, Gen. Mgr., terry.peters@citcomm.com. **URL:** http://www.983thetorch.com.

VAN HORNE

EC IA. Benton Co. 30 mi. S. of Vinton.

13014 ■ Van Horne Cablevision and Television
204 Main St.
Box 96
Van Horne, IA 52346
Phone: (319)228-8791
Fax: (319)228-8784
Owner: Van Horne Cooperative Telephone Co., 204 Main St., Van Horne, IA 52346, Ph: (319)228-8791, Fax: (319)228-8784. **Founded:** 1983. **Formerly:** Van Horne Cablevision. **Key Personnel:** Donald Whipple, Gen. Mgr. **Cities Served:** Van Horne, Iowa: subscribing households 248; 36 channels; 1 community access channel; 168 hours per week community access programming. **URL:** http://www.vanhornetelephone.com/.

VINTON

EC IA. Benton Co. 32 mi. NW of Cedar Rapids. Concrete vault auto hubs, farm implements, fertilizer spreader, saline feeders. Ships farm products. Agriculture, poultry.

13015 ■ Barr's Post Card News
Barr's Post Card News
1800 W D St.
Vinton, IA 52349-0601
Phone: (319)472-4713
Fax: (319)472-3117
Free: 800-397-0145
Newspaper (tabloid) promoting the collecting of picture post cards. **Freq:** Semimonthly. **Print Method:** Offset. **Trim Size:** 7 1/2 x 10. **Cols./Page:** 3. **Col. Width:** 2 3/8 inches. **Col. Depth:** 10 inches. **Key Personnel:** John Perrotto, Publisher; Connie L. Gewecke, Editor; Shelly Haefner, Business Manager, Manager, Circulation; Janet Lovell, Contact. **ISSN:** 0744--4540 (print). **Subscription Rates:** $55 Individuals; $105 Two years; $95 Canada; $160 Other countries; $20 Individuals online only. **URL:** http://barrspcn.com. **Mailing address:** PO Box 720, Vinton, IA 52349-0601. **Remarks:** Accepts classified advertising. **Circ:** Paid ‡5500, Non-paid ‡550.

WAPELLO

SE IA. Louisa Co. On Iowa River, 21 mi. S. of Muscatine. Wood pallets, furniture, feed, rubber cement dispensers manufactured. Stock, grain, poultry farms.

13016 ■ The Wapello Republican
Louisa Publishing Company Ltd.
301 James L Hodges Ave. S
Wapello, IA 52653
Publication E-mail: lpc@louisacomm.net
Newspaper with a Republican orientation. **Freq:** Weekly (Thurs.). **Print Method:** Offset. **Cols./Page:** 8. **Col. Width:** 21 nonpareils. **Col. Depth:** 294 agate lines. **Key Personnel:** Michael A. Hodges, Manager, Advertising, Publisher; Connie Street, Editor. **Subscription Rates:** $20 in county; $26 Out of area; $30 Out of state. **Mailing address:** PO Box 306, Wapello, IA 52653. **Ad Rates:** SAU $5.03; PCI $4.27. **Remarks:** Accepts advertising. **Circ:** ‡2312.

WASHINGTON

SE IA. Washington Co. 34 mi. S. of Iowa City. Manufactures industrial wire products, valves, concrete, calendars, steel tanks, farm implement, beverages. Soybean, poultry processing plants. Agriculture. Corn, oats, hogs, poultry, soybeans. Cattle feeding.

13017 ■ The Washington Evening Journal
The Washington Evening Journal
111 N Marion Ave.
Washington, IA 52353
Phone: (319)653-2191
Fax: (319)653-7524
Free: 800-369-0341
Publisher's E-mail: sales@villagesoup.com
General newspaper. **Freq:** Daily (eve.) Mon. thru Fri. **Print Method:** Offset. **Trim Size:** 14 x 22 3/4. **Cols./Page:** 6. **Col. Width:** 2 1/16 inches. **Col. Depth:** 21 1/2 inches. **Key Personnel:** Darwin K. Sherman, President, Publisher. **Subscription Rates:** $119.25 Individuals carrier; $124.25 Individuals in-county mail delivery; $167.50 U.S. in-state mail delivery; $197.25 Elsewhere out of state mail delivery. **Remarks:** Accepts advertising. **Circ:** (Not Reported).

13018 ■ KCII-AM - 1380
PO Box 524
Washington, IA 52353
Phone: (319)653-2113
Fax: (319)653-3500
Email: kcii@kciiradio.com
Format: Full Service; Adult Contemporary. **Simulcasts:** KCII-FM. **Networks:** ABC. **Owner:** Home Broadcasting Inc., PO Box 31, Knoxville, IA 50138. **Founded:** 1961. **Operating Hours:** 5:30 a.m.-11 p.m.; 10% network, 90% local. **ADI:** Cedar Rapids-Waterloo-Dubuque, IA. **Key Personnel:** Joe Nichols, Gen. Mgr., joe@kciiradio.com. **Wattage:** 500. **Ad Rates:** Noncommercial. **URL:** http://www.kciiradio.com.

13019 ■ KCII-FM - 106.1
PO Box 524
Washington, IA 52353
Phone: (319)653-2113
Fax: (319)653-3500
Email: kcii@kciiradio.com
Format: Full Service; Adult Contemporary. **Simulcasts:** KCII-AM. **Networks:** Brownfield; AP. **Owner:** Home Broadcasting, Inc., at above address. **Founded:** 1971. **Operating Hours:** 5:00 a.m.-11 p.m.; 10% network, 90% local. **ADI:** Cedar Rapids-Waterloo-Dubuque, IA. **Key Personnel:** Joe Nichols, Gen. Mgr., joe@kciiradio.com. **Wattage:** 3,000. **Ad Rates:** Noncommercial. **URL:** http://kciiradio.com.

WATERLOO

NEC IA. Black Hawk Co. On Cedar River, 93 mi. NE of Des Moines. Manufactures farm tractors, refrigerator shelves, truck mixers, livestock equipment, iron castings, printing systems, athletic uniforms, spreaders, overhead doors, corrugated boxes, feed, sulkies, tool and dies, fertilizers, silos.

13020 ■ Waterloo-Cedar Falls Courier
Howard Publications
501 Commercial St.
Waterloo, IA 50701
Phone: (319)291-1400
Fax: (319)291-2069
Free: 800-798-1717
Publication E-mail: newsroom@wcfcourier.com
General newspaper. **Freq:** Daily and Sun. (eve.). **Print Method:** Offset. **Cols./Page:** 6. **Col. Width:** 25 nonpareils. **Col. Depth:** 315 agate lines. **Key Personnel:** Nancy Newhoff, Editor, phone: (319)291-1445; Pat Kinney, Editor, phone: (319)291-1426. **ISSN:** 8750-0868 (print). **Subscription Rates:** $246.87 Individuals Sunday through Friday Home Delivery (52 weeks); $117 Individuals Sunday Home Delivery with Monday through Friday E-edition (52 weeks). **URL:** http://wcfcourier.com/. **Feature Editors:** Meta Hemanway-Forbes, phone: (319)291-1483, meta.hemenway-forbes@wcfcourier.com; Kelsey Holm, phone: (319)291-1481; Doug Newhoff, phone: (319)291-1462. **Mailing address:** PO Box 540, Waterloo, IA 50701. **Ad Rates:** SAU $26.88; PCI $39.12. **Remarks:** Accepts advertising. **Circ:** Mon.-Fri. ★**41142**, Sun. ★**50322**, Sat. ★**36967**.

13021 ■ KBBG-FM - 88.1
918 Newell St.
Waterloo, IA 50703
Phone: (319)235-1515
Fax: (319)234-6182
Email: realmanagement@kbbg.org
Format: Public Radio; Educational. **Owner:** Afro-American Community Broadcasting Inc., 918 Newell St., Waterloo, IA 50703. **Founded:** 1977. **Operating Hours:** 12 a.m. - 10:30 Monday - Thursday; 2 a.m. - 10:30 p.m. Friday. **ADI:** Cedar Rapids-Waterloo-Dubuque, IA. **Local Programs:** *Isla Earth*, Monday Wednesday Thursday Friday 9:00 a.m.; *SBN News*, Monday Tuesday Wednesday Thursday Friday Saturday Sunday; *A.M. Jazz*; *Keynotes*; *Medical Edge*, Monday Tuesday Wednesday Thursday Friday 8:00 a.m.; 2:00 p.m.; 6:00 p.m.; *Drive Time w/ Lady D*, Monday Tuesday Wednesday Thursday Friday 4:00 p.m.; *Black Health Now*, Monday 5:00 p.m.; *Overnite Show*, Tuesday 12:00 a.m.; *Power Minute with Ed Gray*, Monday Tuesday Wednesday Thursday Friday 10:00 p.m.; *Nite Flyte*, Tuesday Wednesday Friday 9:00 p.m.; *Allen Care*, Thursday 10:00 a.m.; 7:00 p.m.; *Drive Time*, Monday Tuesday Thursday Friday Wednesday 4:00 p.m. - 7:00 p.m. 3:30 p.m. - 7:00 p.m.; *Mayor's Update*, Wednesday 10:30 a.m. - 11:00 a.m.; *White House Report*, Monday Wednesday Thursday Friday 8:50 a.m.; *Bobby Jones Gospel Countdown*, Saturday 6:00 a.m. - 8:00 a.m.; *Parents Love Your Children*, Wednesday Saturday 3:00 p.m. - 3:30 p.m. 11:30 a.m. - 12:00 p.m.; *The Talking Drum*, Saturday 3:00 p.m. - 4:00 p.m.; *Community Rhythms*, Wednesday Saturday 2:00 p.m. - 3:00 p.m. 4:00 p.m. - 5:00 p.m.; *Tell Me More w/ Michel Martin*, Monday Tuesday Wednesday Thursday Friday 11:00 a.m.; 3:00 p.m.; 8:00 p.m.; *Moments To Remember w/ Henry Louis Gates, Jr.*; *Accents in Poetry with Rev. Don Carver*, Monday Tuesday Wednesday Thursday Friday 11:00 p.m. **Wattage:** 10,000. **Ad Rates:** Noncommercial. **URL:** http://www.kbbgfm.org.

13022 ■ KCRR-FM - 97.7
501 Sycamore St., Ste. 300
Waterloo, IA 50703
Phone: (319)833-4800
Fax: (319)233-9770
Free: 800-323-0098
Email: kcrr@kcrr.com
Format: Classic Rock. **Owner:** Cumulus Media Inc., 3280 Peachtree Rd. NW, Ste. 2300, Atlanta, GA 30305-2455, Ph: (404)949-0700, Fax: (404)949-0740. **Founded:** 1983. **Operating Hours:** Continuous. **Wattage:** 25,000. **Ad Rates:** Noncommercial. Combined advertising rates available with KKCV-FM, KOEL-AM, KOEL-FM. **URL:** http://www.kcrr.com.

13023 ■ KFMW-FM - 107.9
514 Jefferson St.
Waterloo, IA 50701
Phone: (319)234-2200
Format: Album-Oriented Rock (AOR); Classic Rock; Contemporary Hit Radio (CHR). **Networks:** CNN Radio. **Owner:** Bahakel Communications Ltd., at above address. **Founded:** 1968. **Formerly:** KWWL-FM. **Operating Hours:** Continuous. **ADI:** Cedar Rapids-Waterloo-Dubuque, IA. **Key Personnel:** Michael Cross, Prog. Dir., cross@rock108.com. **Local Programs:** *Iowa's Pure Rock*, Sunday 12:00 a.m. - 6:00 a.m. **Wattage:** 100,000. **Ad Rates:** Noncommercial. **URL:** http://www.rock108.com/Other/ROCK108TWIZZLERS2015FSIContestRR%24250.pdf.

13024 ■ KNWS-AM - 1090
4880 Texas St.
Waterloo, IA 50702
Phone: (319)296-1975
Fax: (319)296-1977
Format: Contemporary Christian. **Networks:** UPI. **Owner:** University of Northwestern - St. Paul, 3003 N Snelling Ave., Saint Paul, MN 55113-1598, Ph: (651)631-5100, Free: 800-692-4020. **Founded:** 1953. **Operating Hours:** Sunrise-sunset; 15% network, 85% local. **ADI:** Cedar Rapids-Waterloo-Dubuque, IA. **Key Personnel:** Doug Smith, Station Mgr., drsmith@nwc.edu; Dan Raymond, Dir. of Programs. **Wattage:** 1,000. **Ad Rates:** Noncommercial.

13025 ■ KNWS-FM - 101.9
4880 Texas St.
Waterloo, IA 50702

Phone: (319)296-1975
Fax: (319)296-1977
Format: Contemporary Christian. **Networks:** UPI; AP. **Owner:** University of Northwestern - St. Paul, 3003 N Snelling Ave., Saint Paul, MN 55113-1598, Ph: (651)631-5100, Free: 800-692-4020. **Founded:** 1965. **Operating Hours**: 12 a.m.-10 p.m. Mon.-Fri.; 12 a.m.-6 p.m. Sun. **ADI**: Cedar Rapids-Waterloo-Dubuque, IA. **Wattage**: 100,000. **Ad Rates:** Noncommercial. **URL:** http://life1019.com.

13026 ■ KOEL-FM - 98.5
501 Sycamore St., Ste. 300
Waterloo, IA 50703
Phone: (319)833-4800
Fax: (319)833-4866
Email: answers@k985.com
Format: Country. **Networks:** AP. **Owner:** Cumulus Media Inc., 3280 Peachtree Rd. NW, Ste. 2300, Atlanta, GA 30305-2455, Ph: (404)949-0700, Fax: (404)949-0740. **Founded:** 1971. **Operating Hours**: Continuous. **Wattage**: 15,000. **Ad Rates:** Noncommercial. Combined advertising rates available with KKCV-FM, KCRR-FM, KOEL-AM. **URL:** http://www.k985.com.

13027 ■ KOKZ-FM - 105.7
514 Jefferson St.
Waterloo, IA 50701-5422
Phone: (319)234-2200
Format: Oldies; Classic Rock. **Owner:** KXEL Broadcasting Company Inc., at above address. **Founded:** 1962. **Operating Hours**: Continuous. **ADI**: Cedar Rapids-Waterloo-Dubuque, IA. **Wattage**: 100,000 ERP. **Ad Rates:** Noncommercial. **URL:** http://1057kokz.com.

13028 ■ KRIN-TV - 32
6450 Corporate Dr.
Johnston, IA 50131
Phone: (515)242-3100
Format: Public TV. **Simulcasts:** KDIN-TV Des Moines, IA. **Networks:** Public Broadcasting Service (PBS). **Owner:** Iowa Public Television, PO Box 6450, Johnston, IA 50131-6450, Ph: (515)242-3100, Free: 800-532-1290. **Founded:** 1974. **Operating Hours**: Continuous. **ADI**: Cedar Rapids-Waterloo-Dubuque, IA. **Key Personnel:** Daniel K. Miller, Exec. Dir., Gen. Mgr., dkm@iptv.org; Terry Rinehart, Dir. Ed., terry.rinehart@iptv.org. **Ad Rates:** Noncommercial. **Mailing address:** PO Box 6450, Johnston, IA 50131. **URL:** http://www.iptv.org.

13029 ■ KWLO-AM - 1330
514 Jefferson St.
Waterloo, IA 50701
Phone: (319)234-2200
Format: Big Band/Nostalgia. **Networks:** NBC. **Formerly**: KWWL-AM. **Operating Hours**: Continuous; 20% network, 80% local. **ADI**: Cedar Rapids-Waterloo-Dubuque, IA. **Wattage**: 5,000. **Ad Rates:** Noncommercial. **URL:** http://www.1330espnradio.com.

13030 ■ KWWL-TV - 7
500 E Fourth St.
Waterloo, IA 50703-5798
Phone: (319)291-1200
Fax: (319)291-1240
Email: syoungblut@kwwl.com
Format: Commercial TV. **Networks:** NBC; CNN Radio. **Founded:** Nov. 1953. **Operating Hours**: Continuous. **ADI**: Cedar Rapids-Waterloo-Dubuque, IA. **Key Personnel:** John Huff, Gen. Sales Mgr., jhuff@kwwl.com; Kim Leer, Station Mgr., kleer@kwwl.com; Jim McKernan, VP, Gen. Mgr. **Ad Rates**: Advertising accepted; rates available upon request. **URL:** http://www.kwwl.com.

13031 ■ KXEL-AM - 1540
514 Jefferson St.
Waterloo, IA 50701
Phone: (319)234-2200
Format: News; Talk. **Networks:** ABC. **Owner:** KXEL Broadcasting Company Inc., at above address. **Founded:** 1942. **Operating Hours**: Continuous. **ADI**: Cedar Rapids-Waterloo-Dubuque, IA. **Wattage**: 50,000. **Ad Rates:** Advertising accepted; rates available upon request. **URL:** http://www.kxel.com.

13032 ■ KXGM-FM - 92.5
3232 Osage Rd.
Waterloo, IA 50703
Format: Religious; Contemporary Christian. **Simulcasts:** KWOF. **Owner:** Friendship Communications, Not Available. **Formerly**: KTOF-FM KWOF-FM. **Operating Hours**: Continuous. **Wattage**: 57,000 H;56,000 V. **Ad Rates:** Noncommercial. **URL:** http://kwof.com.

13033 ■ Mediacom Communications Corp.
4010 Alexandra Dr.
Waterloo, IA 50702
Free: 800-332-0245
Founded: Sept. 05, 2006. **Cities Served:** 99 channels. **URL:** http://mediacomcable.com.

WAUKEE

13034 ■ KZZQ-FM - 99.5
33365 335th St.
Waukee, IA 50263
Phone: (515)987-9995
Fax: (515)987-9808
Format: Contemporary Christian. **Key Personnel:** Eric Boatwright, Gen. Mgr., eric@pulse995.com; Travis McDaniel, Ad. Rep., travis@pulse995.com; Michelle Hamilton, Contact, michelle@pulse995.com. **Ad Rates:** Noncommercial. **URL:** http://www.kzzq.com.

WAUKON

NE IA. Allamakee Co. 90 mi. NW of Dubuque. Museums. Recreational. Creamery; truck body factory. Ships livestock, lumber. Agriculture. Cattle, hogs, corn, oats.

13035 ■ KNEI-AM - 1140
14 W Main St.
Waukon, IA 52172
Phone: (563)568-3476
Fax: (563)568-3391
Free: 866-946-1035
Email: knei@kneiradio.com
Format: Contemporary Country. **Networks:** CBS; ABC. **Owner:** Wennes Communications Stations Inc., 501 W Water St., Decorah, IA 52101. **Founded:** 1967. **Operating Hours**: 18 hours Daily; 80% local. **Key Personnel:** Josh Blake, Contact, josh@kneiradio.com; Greg Wennes, Owner, greg@kvikradio.com; Les Askelson, Contact, les@kvikradio.com. **Wattage**: 1,000. **Ad Rates:** $8 for 15 seconds; $10 for 30 seconds; $12.50 for 60 seconds. **URL:** http://www.kneiradio.com.

13036 ■ KNEI-FM - 103.5
14 W Main St.
Waukon, IA 52172
Format: Country. **Networks:** Jones Satellite; CBS; Radio Iowa. **Owner:** David H. Hogendorn, at above address, Ph: (319)568-3476, Fax: (319)568-3391. **Founded:** 1968. **Operating Hours**: Continuous. **Key Personnel:** David H. Hogendorn, Contact. **Wattage**: 009.025Kw. **Ad Rates:** $7.50-8. **URL:** http://www.kneiradio.com/contact-us.html.

WAVERLY

NE IA. Bremer Co. On Cedar River, 22 mi. NW of Waterloo. Wartburg College. Instant dairy products processed. Manufactures cranes and excavator machines, remote control equipment, snow plows, fixtures, gauges. Soybeans, corn. Cattle. Pork. Dairying.

13037 ■ The Draft Horse Journal
The Draft Horse Journal
PO Box 670
Waverly, IA 50677
Phone: (319)352-4046
Fax: (319)352-2232
Publication E-mail: editorial@drafthorsejournal.com
Magazine on the heavy horse and mule trade. **Freq:** Quarterly. **Print Method:** Offset. **Trim Size:** 8 x 10 3/4. **Cols./Page:** 3. **Col. Width:** 14 picas. **Col. Depth:** 57 picas. **Key Personnel:** Lynn Telleen, Editor. **ISSN:** 0012--5865 (print). **Subscription Rates:** $55 U.S. print and online; $65 Canada print and online; $68 Other countries print and online. **URL:** http://www.drafthorsejournal.com . **Ad Rates:** BW $575; 4C $975. **Remarks:** Accepts advertising. **Circ:** (Not Reported).

13038 ■ Wartburg Trumpet
Wartburg College
100 Wartburg Blvd.
Waverly, IA 50677
Free: 800-772-2085
Collegiate newspaper. **Freq:** Weekly (Mon.). **Print Method:** Offset. **Cols./Page:** 5. **Col. Width:** 22 nonpareils. **Col. Depth:** 224 agate lines. **Key Personnel:** Jessica Grant, Editor-in-Chief. **ISSN:** 6667--4000 (print). **URL:** http://www.wartburgcircuit.org. **Remarks:** Accepts advertising. **Circ:** (Not Reported).

13039 ■ Waverly Democrat
Waverly Newspapers
311 W Bremer Ave.
Waverly, IA 50677
Phone: (319)352-3334
Fax: (319)352-5135
Free: 800-369-2226
Publisher's E-mail: circ@waverlynewspapers.com
Local newspaper. **Freq:** Weekly (Thurs.). **Print Method:** Offset. **Cols./Page:** 8. **Col. Width:** 9.5 picas. **Col. Depth:** 22 inches. **Key Personnel:** Deb Weigel, Publisher; Anelia Dimitrova, Editor. **Subscription Rates:** $75 Individuals print; $86 Out of area print; $85 Individuals print and online; $95 Out of area print and online; $50 Individuals online. **URL:** http://www.communitynewspapergroup.com/waverly_newspapers. **Remarks:** Accepts advertising. **Circ:** (Not Reported).

13040 ■ KWAR-FM - 89.9
100 Wartburg Blvd.
Waverly, IA 50677
Free: 800-772-2085
Format: Alternative/New Music/Progressive. **Owner:** Wartburg College, 100 Wartburg Blvd., Waverly, IA 50677, Free: 800-772-2085. **Founded:** 1951. **Operating Hours**: 7 a.m.-2 a.m. weekdays, 9-midnight Sat.-Sun. **Key Personnel:** Drew Shradel, Sports Dir., drew.shradel@wartburg.edu; Jack Stout, Web Adm., jonathan.stout@wartburg.edu. **Wattage**: 100. **Ad Rates:** Noncommercial. **URL:** http://www.wartburg.edu.

13041 ■ KWAY-AM - 99.3
110 29th Ave. SW
Waverly, IA 50677
Phone: (319)352-3550
Fax: (319)352-3601
Email: sales@kwayradio.com
Format: Adult Contemporary; Alternative/New Music/Progressive. **Networks:** AP. **Owner:** Ael Suhr Enterprises Inc., at above address. **Operating Hours**: 5:00 a.m. until 12:00 midnight. **Wattage**: 1,000 Day; 061 Night. **Ad Rates:** $6-8 for 30 seconds. **Mailing address:** PO Box 307, Waverly, IA 50677-0307. **URL:** http://www.kwayradio.com.

13042 ■ KWAY-FM - 99.3
110 29th Ave. SW
Waverly, IA 50677
Phone: (319)352-3550
Format: Adult Contemporary; News; Sports. **Owner:** Ael Suhr Enterprises Inc., at above address. **Operating Hours**: Continuous. **Wattage**: 4,600 ERP. **Ad Rates:** $8-9 for 30 seconds; $23-27 for 60 seconds. **Mailing address:** PO Box 307, Waverly, IA 50677. **URL:** http://www.kwayradio.com.

13043 ■ KWVI-FM - 88.9
PO Box 3206
Tupelo, MS 38803
Format: Religious. **Owner:** American Family Radio, at above address. **Wattage**: 20,000. **URL:** http://www.afr.net/newafr.

WEBSTER CITY

C IA. Hamilton Co. 20 mi. E. of Fort Dodge. Manufactures washing machines, aluminum castings, boats, scooters, concrete products, tile spades, hog feeders and waterers, electric scoreboards, metal grain bins, feed. Hatcheries. Ships hogs, cattle. Grain, stock, poultry farms.

13044 ■ KQWC-AM - 1570
1020 E 2nd St.
Webster City, IA 50595
Phone: (515)832-1570
Fax: (515)832-2079
Format: Talk; Agricultural; News; Sports; Classical. **Simulcasts:** KQWC-FM. **Networks:** ABC. **Owner:** NRG Media, 2875 Mount Vernon Rd. SE, Cedar Rapids, IA 52403, Ph: (319)862-0300, Fax: (319)286-9383. **Founded:** Feb. 09, 1950. **Operating Hours**: Continuous. **ADI**: Des Moines, IA. **Key Personnel:** Pat Powers, Dir. of Traffic; Chris Lockwood, Dir. of Programs, dhelton@nrgmedia.com; Mary Harris, Bus. Mgr., mharris@nrgmedia.com. **Wattage**: 250. **Ad Rates:** $10.

Circulation: ★ = AAM; △ or • = BPA; ♦ = CAC; ❑ = VAC; ⊕ = PO Statement; ‡ = Publisher's Report; Boldface figures = sworn; Light figures = estimated.

50-15.50 for 30 seconds; $14-21.50 for 60 seconds. $10.50-$15.50 for 30 seconds; $14-$21.50 for 60 seconds. Combined advertising rates available with KQWC-FM. **Mailing address:** PO Box 550, Webster City, IA 50595. **URL:** http://www.kqradio.com.

13045 ■ KQWC-FM - 95.7
1020 E 2nd St.
Webster City, IA 50595
Phone: (515)832-1570
Fax: (515)832-2079
Format: Talk; Full Service; Adult Contemporary; Information. **Networks:** Mutual Broadcasting System. **Owner:** NRG Media, 2875 Mount Vernon Rd. SE, Cedar Rapids, IA 52403, Ph: (319)862-0300, Fax: (319)286-9383. **Founded:** 1950. **Operating Hours**: Continuous. **ADI**: Des Moines, IA. **Key Personnel:** Pat Powers, News Dir., ppowers@nrgmedia.com; Chris Lockwood, Dir. of Programs; Mary Harris, Gen. Mgr., mharris@nrgmedia.com. **Wattage:** 25,000. **Ad Rates:** $10.50-15.50 for 30 seconds; $14-21.50 for 60 seconds. $10.50-$15.50 for 30 seconds; $14-$21.50 for 60 seconds. Combined advertising rates available with KQWC-AM. **Mailing address:** PO Box 550, Webster City, IA 50595. **URL:** http://www.kqradio.com.

WELLMAN

13046 ■ Riverside Current
Riverside Current
230 8th Ave.
Wellman, IA 52356-4707
Phone: (319)646-2712
Fax: (319)646-5904
Publisher's E-mail: wellnews@netins.net
Community newspaper. **Freq:** Weekly (Fri.). **Cols./Page:** 5. **Col. Width:** 10.5 picas. **Col. Depth:** 13 inches. **Subscription Rates:** $25 Individuals online only; $30 Individuals in county; $40 Out of state; $35 Elsewhere in Iowa. **URL:** http://theriversidecurrent.com. **Mailing address:** PO Box 1, Wellman, IA 52356-4707. **Ad Rates:** GLR $.375; BW $275; SAU $3.75; PCI $3.75. **Remarks:** Accepts advertising. **Circ:** ‡620.

WEST BRANCH

E IA. Cedar Co. 10 mi. E. of Iowa City. Herbert Hoover birthplace. Presidential library. Alfalfa dehydrating plant; feed mill. Printing plant. Foam manufacturing plant. Agriculture. Corn, hogs, cattle.

13047 ■ West Branch Times
West Branch Times
124 W Main St.
West Branch, IA 52358
Phone: (319)643-2131
Community newspaper. **Freq:** Weekly (Wed.). **Print Method:** Offset. **Cols./Page:** 4. **Col. Width:** 14 picas. **Col. Depth:** 16 inches. **Key Personnel:** Stuart Clark, Publisher; Gregory Norfleet, Editor. **USPS:** 630-140. **Subscription Rates:** $29 Individuals e-edition and in Cedar and surrounding counties; $32 Elsewhere in Iowa; $37 Out of state. **URL:** http://www.westbranchtimes.com/about/contact.php . **Mailing address:** PO Box 368, West Branch, IA 52358. **Remarks:** Accepts advertising. **Circ:** (Not Reported).

13048 ■ KWKB-TV - 20
1547 Baker Ave.
West Branch, IA 52358
Owner: KM Communications, Inc., 3654 W Jarvis Ave., Skokie, IL 60076. **Operating Hours**: Continuous. **Wattage**: 5,000,000. **URL:** http://www.kwkb.com/.

WEST BURLINGTON

SE IA. Des Moines Co. 5 mi. NW of Burlington. Manufactures fertilizer, industrial switchgear, antenna, mat or truck line terminals.

13049 ■ KCPS-AM - 1150
205 S Gear Ave.
West Burlington, IA 52655-1003
Phone: (319)754-6698
Email: kcps@aol.com
Format: News; Talk; Sports. **Networks:** CBS; Westwood One Radio; ESPN Radio. **Founded:** 1965. **Formerly**: KYED-AM. **Operating Hours**: Continuous; 50% network, 50% local. **Wattage:** 500. **Ad Rates:** $8.50 for 30 seconds. **Mailing address:** PO Box 100, West Burlington, IA 52655. **URL:** http://kcpsradio.com.

WEST DES MOINES

C IA. Polk Co. 5 mi. W. of Des Moines. Manufactures silos, electric supplies, cement products. Foundry. Stone quarries. Data-processing. Industrial. Agriculture. Corn, wheat, hay.

13050 ■ F.B.I Quarterly
Iowa Restaurant Association
1501 42nd St., Ste. 294
West Des Moines, IA 50266
Phone: (515)276-1454
Fax: (515)276-3660
Publication E-mail: cjordan@restaurantiowa.com
Industry magazine on restaurants, beverages, and volume-feeding. **Founded:** 1932. **Freq:** 4/yr. **Print Method:** Offset. **Trim Size:** 8 1/2 x 11. **Cols./Page:** 3. **Col. Width:** 26 nonpareils. **Col. Depth:** 133 agate lines. **Key Personnel:** Jessica Dunker, Contact. **USPS:** 545-600. **Subscription Rates:** $20 Members. **Alt. Formats:** PDF. **URL:** http://www.restaurantiowa.com/index.cfm?nodeID=32237&audienceID=1. **Formerly**: The Iowa Appetizer; Entree. **Remarks:** Accepts advertising. **Circ:** Non-paid ‡650.

13051 ■ Spokesman
Iowa Farm Bureau Federation
5400 University Ave.
West Des Moines, IA 50266-5950
Phone: (515)225-5400
Fax: (515)225-5419
Free: 800-226-6383
Agricultural newspaper. **Founded:** 1934. **Freq:** Weekly. **Print Method:** Offset. **Trim Size:** 11 1/4 x 17. **Cols./Page:** 5. **Col. Width:** 2 inches. **Col. Depth:** 15 1/2 inches. **Subscription Rates:** $16 Individuals; Included in membership. **URL:** http://www.iowafarmbureau.com. **Ad Rates:** BW $6,710.73; 4C $7,260.73; PCI $86.59. **Remarks:** Accepts advertising. **Circ:** (Not Reported).

13052 ■ KNWI-FM - 107.1
3737 Woodland Ave., Ste. 111
West Des Moines, IA 50266
Email: knwi@desmoines.fm
Format: Contemporary Christian. **Owner:** University of Northwestern - St. Paul, 3003 N Snelling Ave., Saint Paul, MN 55113-1598, Ph: (651)631-5100, Free: 800-692-4020. **Key Personnel:** Dave St. John, Dir. of Programs, dave@desmoines.fm; Dick Whitworth, Station Mgr., dick@desmoines.fm; Paul Gurthie, Contact, paul@desmoines.fm; Meridith Foster, Contact, meridith@desmoines.fm; Jerry Chiarmonte, Contact, jachiaramonte@nwc.edu. **Wattage**: 30,000 ERP. **Ad Rates:** Accepts Advertising. **URL:** http://knwi.nwc.edu/page.php.

13053 ■ KWDM-FM - 88.7
1140 Valley West Dr.
West Des Moines, IA 50266
Phone: (515)633-4103
Format: Classic Rock. **Owner:** West Des Moines Community School District, 3550 Mills Civic Pky., West Des Moines, IA 50265, Ph: (515)633-5000. **Founded:** 1975. **Operating Hours**: 17 hours Sun. - Fri. **ADI:** Des Moines, IA. **Wattage**: 100. **Ad Rates:** Noncommercial.

13054 ■ WOI-TV - 5
3903 Westown Pkwy.
West Des Moines, IA 50266
Phone: (515)457-9645
Fax: (515)457-1025
Free: 800-858-5555
Format: Commercial TV. **Networks:** ABC. **Owner:** Citadel Communications, 190 Sandburg Dr., Sacramento, CA 95819, Ph: (916)456-6000, Fax: (916)732-2070. **Founded:** 1950. **Operating Hours**: Continuous. **ADI**: Des Moines, IA. **Ad Rates:** Advertising accepted; rates available upon request. **URL:** http://www.woitv.com.

WEST LIBERTY

E IA. Muscatine Co. 35 mi. W. of Davenport. Residential.

13055 ■ West Liberty Index
West Liberty Index
PO Box 96
West Liberty, IA 52776-0096
Phone: (319)627-2814
Fax: (319)627-2110
Local newspaper. **Freq:** Weekly. **Print Method:** Offset. **Trim Size:** 12 x 18. **Cols./Page:** 5. **Col. Width:** 11.5 picas. **Col. Depth:** 16 inches. **Key Personnel:** Jake Krob, Publisher; Lindsay Hoeppner, Editor; Tom Burger, Advertising Executive. **USPS:** 675-520. **Subscription Rates:** $30 Individuals in Muscatine and surrounding counties; $32 Individuals elsewhere in Iowa; $34 Individuals other U.S. states. **URL:** http://www.westlibertyindex.com. **Ad Rates:** GLR $5.50; BW $400; 4C $550; PCI $4.75. **Remarks:** 5.50. **Circ:** ‡2000.

WEST UNION

NE IA. Fayette Co. 45 mi. NE of Waterloo. Manufactures pharmaceuticals, luggage, auto parts. Egg and meat processing plants; feed mill. Agriculture. Corn, hogs, dairy products.

13056 ■ Fayette County Union
Fayette County Union Inc.
119 S Vine St.
West Union, IA 52175
Phone: (563)422-3888
Fax: (563)422-3488
Publisher's E-mail: theunion@alpinecom.net
Newspaper. **Freq:** Weekly (Thurs.). **Print Method:** Offset. **Cols./Page:** 6. **Col. Width:** 28 nonpareils. **Col. Depth:** 301 agate lines. **Key Personnel:** Gerald Blue, Senior Vice President; Mike Van Sickle, Editor; Jerry Wadian, Editor. **Subscription Rates:** $49 Individuals print; $112 Out of area print; $56 Individuals online. **URL:** http://www.westunionfayettecountyunion.com . **Mailing address:** PO Box 153, West Union, IA 52175. **Remarks:** Accepts advertising. **Circ:** (Not Reported).

WESTSIDE

13057 ■ The Observer
Kock Publishing Inc.
PO Box 156
Westside, IA 51467-0156
Phone: (712)663-4362
Fax: (712)663-4363
Publisher's E-mail: observer@win-4-u.net
Community newspaper. **Founded:** 1878. **Freq:** Weekly (Thurs.). **Print Method:** Web. **Cols./Page:** 5. **Col. Width:** 12 picas. **Col. Depth:** 15 inches. **Subscription Rates:** $36 Individuals 514 zip codes, print and online; $46 Individuals rest of Iowa, print and online; $48 Out of state print and online; $28 Individuals 514 zip codes, print; $33 Individuals rest of Iowa, print; $35 Out of state print. **URL:** http://www.inanews.com/apps/displaypapers.php?county=Crawford&mod=About&act ion=County; http://www.westsideobserveronline.com/v2/content.aspx?ID=8051&MemberID=1666. **Ad Rates:** BW $200; SAU $3.15; PCI $2.75. **Remarks:** Accepts advertising. **Circ:** ‡1179.

WHAT CHEER

SE IA. Keokuk Co. 60 mi. SE of Des Moines. Residential.

13058 ■ What Cheer Paper: Patriot-Chronicle
What Cheer
410 N Barnes St.
What Cheer, IA 50268
Phone: (641)634-2092
Community newspaper. **Freq:** Weekly (Thurs.). **Print Method:** Offset. **Cols./Page:** 6. **Col. Width:** 13 picas. **Col. Depth:** 20.5 inches. **USPS:** 681-440. **Subscription Rates:** $32 Individuals Keokuk and surrounding counties; $64 Two years Keokuk and surrounding counties; $37 Elsewhere; $74 Elsewhere 2 years. **Formerly**: Patriot-Chronicle. **Mailing address:** PO Box 414, What Cheer, IA 50268. **Ad Rates:** GLR $.25; BW $430; SAU $3.50; PCI $3.50. **Remarks:** Accepts classified advertising. **Circ:** (Not Reported).

WHEATLAND

13059 ■ F and B Cablevision
103 Main St. N
Wheatland, IA 52777-0309
Phone: (563)374-1236
Fax: (563)374-1930
Free: 888-832-4322
Email: info@fbc-tele.com
Key Personnel: Ken Laursen, Gen. Mgr., ken@fbc-tele.com; Julie Steines, Office Mgr., julie@fbc-tele.com. **Cities Served:** 53 channels. **Mailing address:** PO Box 309, Wheatland, IA 52777-0309. **URL:** http://www.fbc.bz.

WINTHROP

NEC IA. Buchanan Co. 10 mi. E. of Aurora. Residential.

13060 ■ The Winthrop News
The Winthrop News
225 W Madison St.
Winthrop, IA 50682
Phone: (319)935-3027
Fax: (319)935-3082
Publication E-mail: news@thewinthropnews.com
Local newspaper. **Freq:** Weekly (Thurs.). **Print Method:** Offset. **Cols./Page:** 6. **Col. Width:** 9.5 picas. **Col. Depth:** 14 inches. **Key Personnel:** Mary Beth Smith, Publisher; Steven C. Smith, Publisher. **Mailing address:** PO Box 9, Winthrop, IA 50682. **Remarks:** Accepts advertising. **Circ:** (Not Reported).

13061 ■ East Buchanan Cable TV
214 3rd St. N
Winthrop, IA 50682-0100
Phone: (319)935-3011
Fax: (319)935-3010
Email: christy.wolfe@eastbuchanan.com
Owner: East Buchanan Telephone Cooperative, at above address. **Founded:** 1963. **Key Personnel:** Butch Rorabaugh, Gen. Mgr.; Roger Olsen, Plant Mgr.; Christy Wolfe, Office Mgr. **Cities Served:** Winthrop, Iowa; 70 channels. **Mailing address:** PO Box 100, Winthrop, IA 50682-0100. **URL:** http://www.eastbuchanan.com.

Circulation: ⋆ = AAM; △ or • = BPA; ♦ = CAC; ❑ = VAC; ⊕ = PO Statement; ‡ = Publisher's Report; Boldface figures = sworn; Light figures = estimated.

ABILENE

NEC KS. Dickinson Co. On the Smoky Hill River, 83 mi. SW of Topeka. Warehousing and distribution center for cattle, grain, and dairy products.

13062 ■ Abilene Reflector Chronicle
Reflector Chronicle Publishing Corp.
303 Broadway
Abilene, KS 67410
Phone: (785)263-1000
Publication E-mail: news@abilene-rc.com
Community Newspaper. **Freq:** Daily (eve.) and Sat. (morn.). **Print Method:** Offset Uses mats. **Cols./Page:** 6. **Col. Width:** 26 nonpareils. **Col. Depth:** 301 agate lines. **Key Personnel:** Janelle J. Gantenbein, Associate Publisher. **Subscription Rates:** $87 Individuals Abilene, Chapman, Enterprise, Hope or Solomon; $93 By mail Dickinson County; $110 Out of area motor route delivery; $120 Individuals by mail outside Kansas. **URL:** http://www.abilene-rc.com. **Mailing address:** PO Box 8, Abilene, KS 67410. **Ad Rates:** GLR $.51; PCI $7.14. **Remarks:** Accepts advertising. **Circ:** Paid 5000, Free 175.

13063 ■ The Greyhound Review
National Greyhound Association
PO Box 543
Abilene, KS 67410-0543
Phone: (785)263-7272
Publisher's E-mail: nga@ngagreyhounds.com
Magazine about Greyhound dog racing. **Freq:** Monthly. **Print Method:** Letterpress and offset. **Cols./Page:** 3. **Col. Width:** 26 nonpareils. **Col. Depth:** 133 agate lines. **Key Personnel:** Gary Guccione, Editor. **Subscription Rates:** $30 Individuals. **Ad Rates:** BW $320; 4C $455. **Remarks:** Accepts advertising. **Circ:** ‡4200.

ALMA

NE KS. Wabaunsee Co. 30 mi. SW of Topeka. Grain, stock, poultry farms.

13064 ■ Wabaunsee County Signal-Enterprise
The Signal-Enterprise
26401 Fairfield Rd.
Alma, KS 66401
Phone: (785)765-3327
Fax: (785)765-3384
Publisher's E-mail: info@wabaunsee.com
Newspaper. **Freq:** Weekly (Thurs.). **Print Method:** Offset. **Cols./Page:** 5. **Col. Width:** 24 nonpareils. **Col. Depth:** 224 agate lines. **Key Personnel:** Ervan D. Stuewe, Owner; Pamela K. Stuewe, Owner. **USPS:** 496-340. **Subscription Rates:** $37 Individuals; $69 Two years; $40 Out of country; $75 Out of country 2 years; $1 Single issue. **URL:** http://signal-enterprise.com. **Mailing address:** PO Box 158, Alma, KS 66401. **Remarks:** Advertising accepted; rates available upon request. **Circ:** (Not Reported).

ARKANSAS CITY

SE KS. Cowley Co. Located at juncture of Arkansas and Walnut rivers, 47 mi. SE of Wichita. Cowley County Community College. Oil refineries; flour mills; meat packing plants. Dairy and grain farms.

13065 ■ The Press: The Cowley Press
Cowley County Community College
125 S 2nd St.
Arkansas City, KS 67005
Phone: (620)442-0430
Fax: (620)441-5350
Free: 800-593-2222
Publisher's E-mail: admissions@cowley.edu
Collegiate newspaper. **Founded:** 1922. **Freq:** Biweekly. **Print Method:** Offset. **Trim Size:** 11 x 17. **Cols./Page:** 4. **Col. Width:** 14 picas. **Col. Depth:** 165 agate lines. **Key Personnel:** Alecia Henson, Manager, Advertising; Tori Addis, Editor-in-Chief. **Subscription Rates:** $7.50 Individuals payments of a semester; online; $12 Individuals online. **URL:** http://www.cowleypress.com. **Formerly:** The Cycle. **Mailing address:** PO Box 1147, Arkansas City, KS 67005. **Ad Rates:** BW $645. **Remarks:** Advertising accepted; rates available upon request. **Circ:** Free 1200, Free ‡1200.

13066 ■ KACY-FM - 102.5
106 N Summit St.
Arkansas City, KS 67005
Phone: (620)442-1102
Fax: (620)442-8102
Format: Classic Rock. **Founded:** 2005. **Ad Rates:** Noncommercial.

13067 ■ KAXR-FM - 91.3
PO Box 3206
Tupelo, MS 38803
Format: Religious. **Owner:** American Family Radio, at above address. **Wattage:** 13,500. **Ad Rates:** Noncommercial. **URL:** http://www.afr.net.

13068 ■ KSOK-AM - 1280
334 E Radio Ln.
Arkansas City, KS 67005
Phone: (620)442-5400
Email: ksok@ksokradio.com
Format: Sports. **Networks:** Broadcast News. **Key Personnel:** Pam Miller, Owner, pam@ksokradio.com. **Wattage:** 1,000 Day; 100 Night. **Ad Rates:** Accepts Advertising. **Mailing address:** PO Box 1014, Arkansas City, KS 67005. **URL:** http://www.ksokfm.com.

13069 ■ KSOK-FM - 95.9
334 E Radio Ln.
Arkansas City, KS 67005
Phone: (620)442-5400
Fax: (620)442-5401
Email: ksok@ksokradio.com
Format: Full Service. **Operating Hours:** Continuous Monday - Friday; 9:00 a.m. - 6:00 p.m. Saturday; 8:00 a.m. - 2:00 p.m. Sunday. **Wattage:** 15,200 ERP. **Ad Rates:** Accepts Advertising. **Mailing address:** PO Box 1014, Arkansas City, KS 67005. **URL:** http://www.ksokfm.com.

ATCHISON

NE KS. Atchison Co. On Missouri river, 20 mi. N. of Leavenworth. St. Benedict's College; Mount St. Scholastica College. Limestone quarry; foundry. Manufactures locomotive parts, leather goods, industrial alcohol, flour. Diversified farming.

13070 ■ Atchison Daily Globe
Atchison Daily Globe
308 Commercial St.
Atchison, KS 66002
Phone: (913)367-0583
Fax: (913)367-7531
Free: 800-748-7615
General newspaper. **Freq:** Daily (eve.) and Sat. (morn.). **Print Method:** Offset. **Cols./Page:** 6. **Col. Width:** 24 nonpareils. **Col. Depth:** 301 agate lines. **Key Personnel:** Christy McKibben, Manager, Advertising; Joe Warren, Editor, Publisher; Marilyn Andre, Business Manager, Manager, Circulation. **Subscription Rates:** $91.04 Individuals in Kansas and in Missouri (print and online); $72.84 Individuals in Atchison County (print and online); $121.40 Out of state print and online. **URL:** http://www.atchisonglobenow.com . **Mailing address:** PO Box 247, Atchison, KS 66002. **Ad Rates:** PCI $14.21. **Remarks:** Accepts advertising. **Circ:** (Not Reported).

13071 ■ KAIR-FM - 93.7
PO Box G
Atchison, KS 66002
Phone: (913)367-1470
Fax: (913)367-7021
Free: 888-367-9370
Email: thewakeupcrew@hotmail.com
Format: Country; Information. **Simulcasts:** KAIR-AM. **Owner:** Mark V Media Group, Inc., 12605 West 130th St., Shawnee Mission, KS 66213, Ph: (913)897-0220. **Founded:** 1995. **Formerly:** KARE. **Operating Hours:** Continuous. **Wattage:** 25,000. **Ad Rates:** Advertising accepted; rates available upon request. $8.50-12 for 30 seconds; $12.50-18 for 60 seconds. Combined advertising rates available with KAIR-AM. **URL:** http://www.kairfm.com.

ATWOOD

NW KS. Rawlins Co. 150 mi. NW of Great Bend. Oil wells; cheese factory; alfalfa pelleting mill. Dairy and grain farms.

13072 ■ The Rawlins County Square Deal
The Rawlins County Square Deal
114 S Fourth St.
Atwood, KS 67730
Phone: (785)626-3600
Fax: (785)626-9299
Publication E-mail: squarddeal@atwoodkansas.com
Community newspaper. **Freq:** Weekly. **Key Personnel:** Rosalie Ross, Contact; Sarah Benda, Contact. **Subscription Rates:** $39 Individuals Rawlins, Decatur, Thomas, Cheyenne, Sherman, Dundy (NE), Hitchcock (NE) and Red Willow (NE); $45 Elsewhere; $49 Out of state; $34 Individuals online only; $25 Students. **URL:** http://www.squaredealnews.com. **Mailing address:** PO Box 371, Atwood, KS 67730. **Ad Rates:** PCI $6. **Circ:** Paid ‡1800.

13073 ■ Atwood Cable Systems Inc.
423 State St.
Atwood, KS 67730
Phone: (785)626-3261
Fax: (785)626-9005

Circulation: ★ = AAM; △ or • = BPA; ♦ = CAC; ❑ = VAC; ⊕ = PO Statement; ‡ = Publisher's Report; Boldface figures = sworn; Light figures = estimated.

Email: cableinfo@atwoodtv.net
Owner: Harold J. Dunker. **Founded:** 1981. **Key Personnel:** Robert J. Dunker, Gen. Mgr.; Teather A. Leitner, Office Mgr. **Cities Served:** 61 channels. **URL:** http://www.atwoodcable.com.

AUGUSTA

SE KS. Butler Co. 20 mi. E. of Wichita. Oil wells. Grain, stock, poultry, and dairy farms.

13074 ■ Augusta Daily Gazette
Augusta Daily Gazette
204 E Fifth St.
Augusta, KS 67010
Phone: (316)775-2218
General newspaper. **Founded:** 1892. **Freq:** Daily (eve.). **Print Method:** Offset. **Trim Size:** 14 x 22 3/4. **Cols./Page:** 6. **Col. Width:** 12 3/5 picas. **Col. Depth:** 21.5 inches. **Key Personnel:** Cristina Janney, Publisher. **USPS:** 037-420. **Subscription Rates:** $72.45 Individuals; $122.26 Out of area. **URL:** http://www.augustagazette.com. **Mailing address:** PO Box 9, Augusta, KS 67010. **Ad Rates:** GLR $.60; BW $1,092; 4C $1,302; SAU $8.47. **Remarks:** Advertising accepted; rates available upon request. **Circ:** ‡2972.

BALDWIN CITY

E KS. Douglas Co. Baker University. Historical sites. Small oil and gas wells. Diversified farming.

13075 ■ The Baldwin City Signal
WorldWest L.L.C.
703 High St.
Baldwin City, KS 66006
Phone: (785)594-7080
Free: 800-578-8748
Community newspaper. **Freq:** Weekly. **Subscription Rates:** $37 Individuals plus tax. **URL:** http://signal.baldwincity.com. **Mailing address:** PO Box 970, Baldwin City, KS 66006. **Remarks:** Accepts advertising. **Circ:** ★41500.

13076 ■ KNBU-FM - 89.7
618 8th St.
Baldwin City, KS 66006-0065
Phone: (785)594-6451
Fax: (785)594-4025
Format: Full Service. **Owner:** Baker University, 618 8th St., Baldwin City, KS 66006, Ph: (785)594-6451. **Founded:** 1965. **Operating Hours:** Continuous. **Key Personnel:** Richard Bayha, Contact. **Wattage:** 100. **Ad Rates:** Noncommercial. **Mailing address:** PO Box 65, Baldwin City, KS 66006-0065. **URL:** http://www.bakeru.edu/mass-media/student-media.

BAXTER SPRINGS

13077 ■ City of Baxter Springs
1004 Military Ave.
Baxter Springs, KS 66713
Founded: 1980. **Cities Served:** Baxter Springs, Kansas: subscribing households 1,682; 35 channels; 1 community access channel; 168 hours per week community access programming. **Mailing address:** PO Box 2, Cawker City, KS 67430. **URL:** http://www.baxterspringschamber.com/Contact_Us.html.

BELLE PLAINE

S KS. Sumner Co. 23 mi. S. of Wichita. Aircraft manufacturer; feed processing; oil wells. Diversified farming.

13078 ■ KANR-FM - 92.7
3436 Edgemont St.
Wichita, KS 67208
Format: Alternative/New Music/Progressive. **Owner:** Daniel D. Smith, 16540 E Pecos Rd, Gilbert, AZ.

BELLEVILLE

NC KS. Republic Co. 68 mi. N. of Salina. Pawnee Indian Village. Manufactures hospital supplies, sand, gravel, and concrete. Diversified agriculture.

13079 ■ Belleville Cable TV
1312 19th St.
Belleville, KS 66935
Cities Served: Hebron, Nebraska. **URL:** http://www.kansas.gov/bess/flow/main;jsessionid=99826D5A9A1B2D50BE1038AD5781DC8D.aptcs03-inst2?execution=e1s14.

13080 ■ KREP-FM - 92.1
2307 US Hwy. 81
Belleville, KS 66935
Phone: (913)527-2266
Fax: (913)527-5919
Format: Country. **Networks:** ABC; Mid-America Ag; Jones Satellite. **Owner:** First Republic Broadcasting Corp., 2307 W Frontage Rd., Belleville, KS 66935. **Founded:** 1984. **Operating Hours:** Continuous; 10% network, 90% local. **Wattage:** 14,500. **Ad Rates:** $12 for 30 seconds; $17 for 60 seconds. **URL:** http://www.kr92country.com.

BELOIT

NC KS. Mitchell Co. On Solomon river, 51 mi. NW of Salina. Agricultural and trade center.

13081 ■ KVSV-AM - 1190
3185 US 24 Hwy.
Beloit, KS 67420
Format: Eclectic. **Ad Rates:** Advertising accepted; rates available upon request. **URL:** http://www.kvsvradio.com/?page=content&id=6.

13082 ■ KVSV-FM - 105.5
3185 US 24 Hwy.
Beloit, KS 67420
Phone: (785)738-2206
Format: Easy Listening. **Operating Hours:** 18 hours Daily. **Key Personnel:** John Swanson, Gen. Mgr. **Wattage:** 50,000. **URL:** http://www.kvsvradio.com/?page=content&id=7.

BIRD CITY

13083 ■ Bird City Times
Bird City Times
PO Box 220
Bird City, KS 67731-0167
Phone: (785)734-7031
Fax: (785)332-3001
Newspaper. **Freq:** Weekly (Thurs.). **Print Method:** Offset. **Col. Width:** 12 picas. **Col. Depth:** 21 inches. **Key Personnel:** Norma Martinez, Editor; Allen Edgington, Manager, Advertising; Karen Krien, Publisher. **Subscription Rates:** $36 Individuals 1 year (online); $36 Individuals 1 year (local, print and online); $39 Individuals 1 year (non-local in Kansas, print and online); $43 Individuals 1 year (out of state, print and online). **URL:** http://www.nwkansas.com/bcwebpages/bcmain.html. **Ad Rates:** BW $384; PCI $4.99. **Remarks:** Accepts advertising. **Circ:** 628.

BONNER SPRINGS

NE KS. Wyandotte Co. 12 mi. SW of Kansas City. Agricultural Hall of Fame. Diversified farming.

13084 ■ Chieftain
Chieftan
128 Oak
Bonner Springs, KS 66012
Phone: (913)422-4048
Free: 800-578-8748
Publication E-mail: publisher@bonnersprings.com
Newspaper with a Republican orientation. **Founded:** 1896. **Freq:** Weekly (Thurs.). **Print Method:** Offset. **Cols./Page:** 6. **Col. Width:** 25 nonpareils. **Col. Depth:** 301 agate lines. **Key Personnel:** Michelle Tevis, Assistant Managing Editor. **Subscription Rates:** $37 Individuals for residents of Wyandotte, Leavenworth, Johnson and Douglas counties; $55 Elsewhere in Kansas; $60 Out of state. **URL:** http://www.bonnersprings.com. **Mailing address:** PO Box 256, Bonner Springs, KS 66012. **Ad Rates:** SAU $4.50. **Remarks:** Accepts advertising. **Circ:** Paid ‡5200, Non-paid ‡7800.

13085 ■ Chieftain Shopper
Chieftan
128 Oak
Bonner Springs, KS 66012
Phone: (913)422-4048
Free: 800-578-8748
Shopper. **Freq:** Weekly. **Print Method:** Offset. **Cols./Page:** 6. **Col. Width:** 25 nonpareils. **Col. Depth:** 301 agate lines. **Key Personnel:** Michelle Tevis, Assistant Managing Editor. **Mailing address:** PO Box 256, Bonner Springs, KS 66012. **Remarks:** Accepts advertising. **Circ:** (Not Reported).

13086 ■ Sentinel
Chieftan
128 Oak
Bonner Springs, KS 66012
Phone: (913)422-4048
Free: 800-578-8748
Newspaper. **Founded:** 1969. **Freq:** Weekly (Thurs.). **Print Method:** Offset. **Cols./Page:** 6. **Col. Width:** 25 nonpareils. **Col. Depth:** 301 agate lines. **Key Personnel:** Teresa M. Thompson, Contact. **Subscription Rates:** $25 Individuals; $40 Individuals other Kansas residents; $45 Out of state. **URL:** http://www.bonnersprings.com. **Mailing address:** PO Box 256, Bonner Springs, KS 66012. **Remarks:** Accepts advertising. **Circ:** Paid ‡5200, Non-paid ‡7800.

BREWSTER

13087 ■ KGCR-FM - 107.7
3410 Rd. 66
Brewster, KS 67732-0009
Phone: (785)694-2877
Fax: (785)694-2875
Email: kgcr@kgcr.org
Format: Religious. **Networks:** Moody Broadcasting; USA Radio; Ambassador Inspirational Radio. **Owner:** The Praise Network, Inc., PO Box 8, Aurora, NE 68818-0008, Ph: (308)946-2656. **Founded:** 1988. **Operating Hours:** Continuous; 15% network, 85% local. **Wattage:** 100,000. **Ad Rates:** $2.50-5 for 30 seconds; $4-6.50 for 60 seconds. **Mailing address:** PO Box 9, Brewster, KS 67732-0009. **URL:** http://wordpress.kgcr.org.

13088 ■ S & T Cable
320 Kansas Ave.
Brewster, KS 67732
Phone: (785)694-2256
Fax: (785)694-2750
Free: 800-432-8294
Founded: Sept. 07, 2006. **Cities Served:** 108 channels. **URL:** http://www.sttelcom.com.

BRONSON

13089 ■ KBJQ-FM - 88.3
PO Box 3206
Tupelo, MS 38803
Format: Religious. **Owner:** American Family Radio, at above address. **Founded:** 1977. **Ad Rates:** Noncommercial.

BUNKER HILL

C. KS. Russell Co. 5 mi. N. of Russell.

13090 ■ KOOD-TV - 33
604 Elm St.
Bunker Hill, KS 67626
Phone: (785)483-6990
Fax: (785)483-4605
Email: shptv@shptv.org
Format: Public TV. **Networks:** Public Broadcasting Service (PBS). **Owner:** Smoky Hills Public Television, 604 Elm St., Bunker Hill, KS 67626, Ph: (785)483-6990, Fax: (785)483-4605. **Founded:** 1978. **Operating Hours:** Continuous. **Key Personnel:** Terry Cutler, Dir. of Engg., tcutler@shptv.org; Glenna Letsch, Dir. of Traffic, gletsch@shptv.org. **Local Programs:** *Spain...on the Road Again*; *Martha Speaks*, Sunday 8:00 a.m.; *New Yankee Workshop*; *For Your Home*; *Ask This Old House*, Wednesday Sunday Monday Thursday 9:00 a.m.; 5:00 p.m.; 9:00 p.m. 3:00 a.m.; *Doctors On Call*, Sunday Tuesday 3:30 p.m. 7:00 p.m.; *Earth On Edge*; *Scoreboard Show*, Friday 11:00 p.m.; *Nick Stellino Cooking With Friends*. **Wattage:** 320,000 ERP Horizont. **Ad Rates:** Accepts Advertising. **Mailing address:** PO Box 9, Bunker Hill, KS 67626. **URL:** http://www.pbs.org/shptv.

KSWK-TV - See Lakin

BURLINGTON

SE KS. Coffey Co. 65 mi. S. of Topeka. Diversified farming. Timber.

13091 ■ Coffey County Republican
Faimon Publications L.L.C.
324 Hudson
Burlington, KS 66839-0218
Phone: (620)364-5325

Publication E-mail: news@coffeycountyonline.com
County newspaper with Republican orientation. **Founded:** 1856. **Freq:** Semiweekly Tue. & Fri. except for some national holidays. **Print Method:** Offset. **Trim Size:** 14 x 22. **Cols./Page:** 6. **Col. Width:** 12.5 picas. **Col. Depth:** 21 inches. **Key Personnel:** Catherine Faimon, Publisher; Mark Petterson, Managing Editor; Chris Faimon, Publisher. **USPS:** 145-700. **Subscription Rates:** $30 Individuals Internet; $46 Individuals carrier delivery, Burlington & New Strawn; $46 Individuals Westphalia, Melvern, Hartford & Neosho Rapids; $50 By mail Elsewhere in Kansas; $60 Out of state. **URL:** http://www.coffeycountyonline.com. **Formed by the merger of:** Coffey County Today; This Week. **Mailing address:** PO Box A, Burlington, KS 66839-0218. **Ad Rates:** PCI $8.55. **Remarks:** Accepts classified advertising. **Circ:** 3000.

13092 ■ KSNP-FM - 97.7
PO Box 233
Burlington, KS 66839
Phone: (620)364-8807
Format: Classic Rock. **Networks:** Independent. **Owner:** My Town Media Inc., 412 North Locust St., Pittsburg, KS 66762, Ph: (620)232-5993. **Founded:** June 1990. **Operating Hours:** 6 a.m.-12 p.m. **Wattage:** 18,000. **Ad Rates:** Noncommercial. **URL:** http://www.977thedawg.com.

CANEY

SE KS. Montgomery Co. 19 mi. W. of Coffeyville. Oil, and gas wells. Corn, wheat, oats.

13093 ■ Good News
Kirk Clinkscales Sr.
124 N State
Caney, KS 67333
Fax: (620)879-2264
Free: 800-942-6397
Publisher's E-mail: editor@goodnewspress.com
Free community newspaper. **Founded:** July 01, 1978. **Freq:** Weekly (Wed.). **Print Method:** Offset. **Trim Size:** 11 1/2 x 15. **Cols./Page:** 6. **Col. Width:** 20 nonpareils. **Col. Depth:** 84 picas. **Key Personnel:** Kirk Clinkscales, Sr., Publisher; June Freisberg, Editor; Donna Clinkscales, Office Manager. **Subscription Rates:** Free. **URL:** http://www.goodnewspress.com/. **Ad Rates:** GLR $1.14; BW $1,149.12; PCI $15.96. **Remarks:** Accepts advertising. **Circ:** Free ‡42000.

13094 ■ Montgomery County Chronicle
Montgomery County Chronicle
202 W 4th St.
Caney, KS 67333
Phone: (620)879-2156
Fax: (620)879-2855
Publication E-mail: chronicle@taylornews.org
Newspaper with a Republican orientation. **Freq:** Weekly (Wed.). **Print Method:** Offset. **Trim Size:** 12 x 18. **Cols./Page:** 5. **Col. Width:** 11.5 picas. **Col. Depth:** 336 agate lines. **Key Personnel:** Rudy M. Taylor, Publisher; Andy Taylor, Editor. **USPS:** 088-340. **Subscription Rates:** $30 Individuals e-edition; $42 Individuals print; $48 Out of country print; $48.50 Out of state print. **URL:** http://www.taylornews.org . **Formerly:** Caney Chronicle. **Mailing address:** PO Box 186, Caney, KS 67333. **Remarks:** Accepts advertising. **Circ:** (Not Reported).

CHANUTE

SE KS. Neosho Co. 45 mi. WSW of Fort Scott. Neosho County Community College. Oil and gas wells; cement works. Diversified farming.

13095 ■ The Chanute Tribune
Chanute Publishing Co.
PO Box 559
Chanute, KS 66720
Phone: (620)431-4100
Fax: (620)431-2635
Publisher's E-mail: news@chanute.com
General newspaper. **Freq:** Mon.-Sat. (eve.). **Print Method:** Offset. **Cols./Page:** 6. **Col. Width:** 25 nonpareils. **Col. Depth:** 301 agate lines. **Key Personnel:** Shanna Guiot, Business Manager, Publisher; Stu Butcher, Executive Editor. **USPS:** 100-140. **Subscription Rates:** $90.53 Individuals carrier - print only; $125 By mail in Kansas - print or online. **Remarks:** Accepts advertising. **Circ:** (Not Reported).

13096 ■ KINZ-FM - 95.3
702 N Plummer
Chanute, KS 66720
Phone: (620)431-3700
Format: Adult Contemporary. **Wattage:** 24,000. **Ad Rates:** Advertising accepted; rates available upon request. **URL:** http://www.kinz.biz.

13097 ■ KKOY-AM - 1460
702 N Plummer
Chanute, KS 66720
Format: Talk; News. **Networks:** ABC; CNN Radio. **Operating Hours:** Continuous. **Wattage:** 1,000 Day; 057 Night. **Ad Rates:** Noncommercial. Combined advertising rates available with KKOY-FM, KSNP-FM, KWXO-FM, KHST-FM. **URL:** http://tallgrassnation.com.

13098 ■ KKOY-FM - 105.5
702 N Plummer Ave.
Chanute, KS 66720
Phone: (620)431-3700
Format: Adult Contemporary. **Networks:** ABC. **Owner:** Tallgrass Broadcasting, LLC, at above address. **Founded:** 1971. **Operating Hours:** Continuous. **Wattage:** 8,000. **Ad Rates:** Combined advertising rates available with KKOY-AM, KSNP-FM, KWXD-FM, DHST-FM. **URL:** http://www.hot1055.net/site.

CLAY CENTER

NEC KS. Clay Co. On Republican river, 82 mi. NW of Topeka. Diversified farming. Manufactures feed and farm equipment.

13099 ■ KCLY-FM - 100.9
1815 Meadowlark Rd.
Clay Center, KS 67432
Phone: (785)632-5661
Format: Full Service; Oldies. **Networks:** AP. **Owner:** Kyle Bauer and Kent Lips. **Founded:** 1978. **Operating Hours:** Continuous. **Key Personnel:** Kyle Bauer, Gen. Mgr., kbauer@kfrm.com; Michelle Tessaro, News Dir., news@kclyradio.com; Rocky Downing, Sports Dir., rocky@kclyradio.com; Duane Toews, Div. Dir., duanet@kfrm.com; Phil Kasper, Div. Dir., phil@kfrm.com; Angie Komar, Production Mgr., angiek@kfrm.com. **Wattage:** 25,000. **Ad Rates:** $9 for 30 seconds; $12 for 60 seconds. Combined advertising rates available with KFRM-AM. **URL:** http://www.kclyradio.com.

13100 ■ KFRM-AM - 550
1815 Meadowlark Rd.
Clay Center, KS 67432
Phone: (785)632-5661
Fax: (785)632-5662
Email: webmaster@kfrm.com
Format: Country; Agricultural; Information. **Owner:** Taylor Communications Inc., at above address. **Founded:** 1947. **Formerly:** KNNN-AM, KICT-AM. **Operating Hours:** Continuous. **Key Personnel:** Kyle Bauer, Gen. Mgr., kbauer@kfrm.com; Rocky Downing, Station Mgr., rocky@kclyradio.com; Rod Keen, Operations Mgr.; Phil Kasper, Div. Dir.; Duane Toews, Div. Dir. **Wattage:** 5,000 Day; 110 Night. **Ad Rates:** Noncommercial. **URL:** http://www.kfrm.com.

CLEARWATER

SC KS. Sedgwick Co. 20 mi. SW of Wichita. Grain and stock farms.

13101 ■ SKT
128 N Gorin St.
Clearwater, KS 67026
Phone: (620)584-2255
Free: 888-568-3509
Email: customerservice@sktc.net
Founded: 1940. **Cities Served:** 73 channels. **URL:** http://www.sktmainstreet.com.

COFFEYVILLE

SE KS. Montgomery Co. 69 mi. W. of Joplin, MO. Coffeyville Community College. Manufactures chemicals, structural steel. Oil refineries.

13102 ■ KGGF-AM - 690
PO Box 457
Coffeyville, KS 67337
Phone: (620)251-3800
Format: News; Talk. **Owner:** Radio Results Group, at above address. **URL:** http://www.radioresultsgroup.com.

13103 ■ KGGF-FM - 104.1
PO Box 1087
Coffeyville, KS 67337
Phone: (620)251-3800
Format: Oldies; Sports. **Owner:** Radio Results Group, at above address. **Wattage:** 7,300. **URL:** http://www.radioresultsgroup.com.

13104 ■ KUSN-FM - 98.1
PO Box 1087
Coffeyville, KS 67337
Phone: (620)251-3800
Format: Country. **Owner:** Radio Results Group, at above address. **URL:** http://www.radioresultsgroup.com.

COLBY

NW KS. Thomas Co. 200 mi. NW of Salina. Colby Community Junior College. Diversified farming.

13105 ■ Colby Free Press
Colby Free Press
155 W Fifth St.
Colby, KS 67701-2312
Phone: (785)462-3963
Fax: (785)462-7749
General newspaper. **Freq:** Mon.-Thurs. eve., Sat. (morn.). **Print Method:** Offset. **Cols./Page:** 6. **Col. Width:** 26 nonpareils. **Col. Depth:** 301 agate lines. **Key Personnel:** Sharon Friedlander, Publisher; Kathryn Ballard, Advertising Representative. **USPS:** 120-920. **Subscription Rates:** $89 Individuals print and online or online only; $99 Out of area print and online. **Alt. Formats:** PDF. **URL:** http://www.nwkansas.com/cfpwebpages/cfpmain.html. **Ad Rates:** GLR $.30; BW $552.12; SAU $4.28. **Remarks:** Accepts advertising. **Circ:** 3300.

13106 ■ KTCC-FM - 91.9
1255 S Range Ave.
Colby, KS 67701
Phone: (785)462-3984
Free: 888-634-9350
Email: support@colbycc.edu
Format: Alternative/New Music/Progressive. **Owner:** Colby Community College, 1255 South Range, Colby, KS 67701, Ph: (785)462-3984, Fax: (888)634-9350, Free: 888-634-9350. **Founded:** 1969. **Operating Hours:** Continuous; 10% network, 90% local. **Wattage:** 3,500. **URL:** http://www.colbycc.edu/?m=8&s=229.

13107 ■ KXXX-AM - 790
1065 S Range Ave.
Colby, KS 67701
Phone: (785)462-3305
Fax: (785)462-3307
Format: Contemporary Country; Agricultural; News. **Networks:** Westwood One Radio. **Owner:** Rocking M Radio Inc., 4806 Vue du Lac Pl., Ste. B, Manhattan, KS 66503, Ph: (785)565-0406, Fax: (785)565-0437. **Founded:** 1947. **Operating Hours:** Continuous. **ADI:** Wichita-Hutchinson, KS. **Wattage:** 5,000. **Ad Rates:** Advertising accepted; rates available upon request. Combined advertising rates available with KQLS-FM. **URL:** http://www.rockingmradio.todayinkansas.com.

13108 ■ S & T Cable
755 Davis Ave.
Colby, KS 67701
Phone: (785)460-7300
Free: 866-790-0241
Founded: 1952. **Cities Served:** 99 channels. **Mailing address:** PO Box 345, Colby, KS 67701. **URL:** http://www.sttelcom.com.

13109 ■ Time Warner Cable
PO Box 345
Colby, KS 67701-0345
Owner: Time Warner Cable, PO Box 6929, Englewood, CO 80155-6929, Ph: (303)799-9599, Fax: (303)649-8090, Free: 800-727-1855. **Founded:** 1967. **Formerly:** Cablevision Industries Inc.; Cablevision Industries. **Key Personnel:** Kim Heilman, Clerk. **Cities Served:** Colby, Kansas; Trenton, Nebraska: subscribing households 2,092; 35 channels; 1 community access channel; 168 hours per week community access programming.

Circulation: ★ = AAM; △ or • = BPA; ♦ = CAC; ❑ = VAC; ⊕ = PO Statement; ‡ = Publisher's Report; Boldface figures = sworn; Light figures = estimated.

CONCORDIA

NC KS. Cloud Co. On Republican River, 50 mi. N. of Salina. Manufactures plastic and bricks. Grain, poultry, dairy, and stock farms.

13110 ■ KNCK-AM - 1390
PO Box 629
Concordia, KS 66901
Phone: (785)243-1414
Fax: (785)243-1391
Format: Oldies. **Networks:** Satellite Music Network. **Founded:** 1954. **Operating Hours:** Continuous. **Wattage:** 500.

13111 ■ KVCO-FM - 88.3
2221 Campus Dr.
Concordia, KS 66901
Phone: (785)243-1435
Free: 800-729-5101
Format: Full Service; Information; Adult Contemporary. **Owner:** Cloud County Community College, 2221 Campus Dr., Concordia, KS 66901-1002, Ph: (785)243-1435, Fax: (785)243-1043, Free: 800-729-5101. **Key Personnel:** Deb Taylor, Office Mgr. **Wattage:** 125. **Ad Rates:** Noncommercial. **Mailing address:** PO Box 1002, Concordia, KS 66901. **URL:** http://www.cloud.edu/Students/clubsorganizations/kvco.

COTTONWOOD FALLS

EC KS. Chase Co. 20 mi. SW of Emporia.

13112 ■ Chase County Leader-News
Chase County Leader-News
306 Broadway
Cottonwood Falls, KS 66845
Phone: (620)273-6391
Fax: (620)273-8674
Community newspaper. **Freq:** Weekly (Thurs.). **Print Method:** Offset. **Cols./Page:** 6. **Col. Width:** 12 INS. **Col. Depth:** 21 inches. **Key Personnel:** Jerry Schwilling, Editor. **ISSN:** 1079--8188 (print). **USPS:** 100-980. **URL:** http://www.angelfire.com/ct3/ccln/reportsanddeaths.html. **Ad Rates:** GLR $.40; BW $354.38; 4C $754.38; SAU $3.75; PCI $3.75. **Remarks:** Accepts advertising. **Circ:** 1700.

COUNCIL GROVE

EC KS. Morris Co. 24 mi. NW of Emporia. Manufactures plastic and metal products, cleaning equipment, and butter. Dairy, grain, poultry, and stock farms.

13113 ■ Council Grove Republican
Council Grove Republican
207 W Main St.
Council Grove, KS 66846
Phone: (620)767-5413
Free: 800-732-9211
Newspaper with a small town, rural orientation. **Freq:** Daily Monday-Friday. **Print Method:** Offset. **Trim Size:** 13 1/2 x 22 3/4. **Cols./Page:** 6. **Col. Width:** 12 picas. **Col. Depth:** 21.5 inches. **Key Personnel:** Don A. McNeal, Contact; Craig A. McNeal, Editor. **USPS:** 134-340. **Alt. Formats:** Microfilm. **Ad Rates:** BW $568.89; 4C $733.89; PCI $4.41. **Remarks:** Accepts advertising. **Circ:** (Not Reported).

DERBY

13114 ■ The American Oil and Gas Reporter
PO Box 343
Derby, KS 67037-0343
Phone: (316)788-6271
Fax: (316)788-7568
Publication E-mail: reporter@aogr.com
Magazine for the independent oil and gas exploration and production industry. **Freq:** Monthly. **Print Method:** Offset. **Trim Size:** 8 1/4 x 10 3/4. **Cols./Page:** 3. **Col. Width:** 27 nonpareils. **Col. Depth:** 140 agate lines. **Key Personnel:** Nicole Guiliano, Manager, Production; Charlie Cookson, Publisher; Bill Campbell, Managing Editor. **Subscription Rates:** $80 U.S. Bundled Print and Online; $300 Canada and Mexico Bundled Print and Online; $500 Other countries Bundled Print and Online; $25 Single issue; $200 Individuals 3 years; $500 Canada and Mexico 3 years, Bundled Print and Online; $1250 Out of country 3 years, Bundled Print and Online; $50 Single issue if more than three months old. **URL:** http://www.aogr.com. **Ad Rates:** BW $2,370; 4C $3,350. **Remarks:** Accepts advertising. **Circ:** ‡13540.

DIGHTON

WC KS. Lane Co. 143 mi. NW of Hutchinson. Oil wells. Stock, poultry, and grain farms.

13115 ■ Feed-Lot
Feed-Lot Magazine
116 E Long
Dighton, KS 67839
Phone: (800)798-9515
Fax: (620)397-2839
Publisher's E-mail: feedlot@st-tel.net
Trade magazine covering feedlot and cattle feeder information. **Freq:** Bimonthly. **Print Method:** Offset web. **Trim Size:** 7 x 10. **Key Personnel:** Robert Strong, Editor, President, Publisher, fax: (620)397-2839. **ISSN:** 1083-5385 (print). **URL:** http://feedlotmagazine.epubxp.com/t/23441-feed-lot. **Mailing address:** PO Box 850, Dighton, KS 67839. **Ad Rates:** BW $2,819; 4C $3,403; PCI $156. **Remarks:** Accepts advertising. **Circ:** △**8906**.

DODGE CITY

SW KS. Ford Co. On Arkansas River, 120 mi. SW of Hutchinson. Flour and grain products mills; beef processing plants.

13116 ■ Dodge City Daily Globe
Morris Communications Inc.
705 2nd Ave.
Dodge City, KS 67801
Phone: (620)408-9918
Publisher's E-mail: darrel.adams@dodgeglobe.com
General newspaper. **Freq:** Mon.-Sat. (morn.). **Print Method:** Offset. **Cols./Page:** 6. **Col. Width:** 2 inches. **Col. Depth:** 21 1/2 inches. **Key Personnel:** Darrel Adams, Editor, Publisher; Ed Oneal, Manager, Circulation. **URL:** http://www.dodgeglobe.com. **Ad Rates:** BW $870.75; 4C $1,017.75; PCI $6.75. **Remarks:** Accepts advertising. **Circ:** ‡9185.

13117 ■ High Plains Journal
High Plains Publishers Inc.
1500 E Wyatt Earp Blvd.
Dodge City, KS 67801
Fax: (620)227-7173
Free: 800-452-7171
Publication E-mail: journal@hpj.com
Agricultural magazine. **Freq:** Weekly. **Print Method:** Offset. **Trim Size:** 11 x 15. **Cols./Page:** 5. **Col. Width:** 11.5 picas. **Col. Depth:** 196 agate lines. **Key Personnel:** John Seatvet, Manager, Sales; Tom Taylor, Publisher, Chief Executive Officer; Holly Martin, Editor; Jeff Keeten, Manager, Circulation. **ISSN:** 0018--1471 (print). **Subscription Rates:** $58 Individuals print or online; $108 Two years print or online; $68 Individuals print and online; $128 Two years print and online. **URL:** http://www.hpj.com. **Mailing address:** PO Box 760, Dodge City, KS 67801. **Ad Rates:** GLR $11.11; BW $10,892; 4C $12,542; PCI $155.60. **Remarks:** Accepts advertising. **Circ:** (Not Reported).

13118 ■ KAHE-FM - 95.5
2601 Central Village Plz., Ste. C
Dodge City, KS 67801
Phone: (620)225-8080
Fax: (620)225-6655
Format: Adult Contemporary. **Owner:** Rocking M Radio Inc., 4806 Vue du Lac Pl., Ste. B, Manhattan, KS 66503, Ph: (785)565-0406, Fax: (785)565-0437. **Wattage:** 100,000. **URL:** http://www.rockingmradio.com.

13119 ■ KBSD-TV - 6
PO Box 157
Dodge City, KS 67801
Phone: (316)838-1212
Format: Commercial TV. **Networks:** CBS; Kansas Broadcasting System. **Owner:** Spartan Communications, Inc., Spartanburg, SC, Ph: (864)576-7777. **Founded:** 1957. **Formerly:** KTVC-TV. **Operating Hours:** Continuous except Friday 5 a.m. - 2 a.m.; 95% network, 5% local. **ADI:** Wichita-Hutchinson, KS. **Key Personnel:** Kerri Baker, Gen. Mgr. **Ad Rates:** $9-60 for 10 seconds; $10.50-70 for 15 seconds; $15-150 for 30 seconds. **URL:** http://www.kwch.com/.

13120 ■ K43HN - 43
PO Box A
Santa Ana, CA 92711
Phone: (714)832-2950
Free: 888-731-1000
Owner: Trinity Broadcasting Network Inc., PO Box A, Santa Ana, CA 92711, Ph: (714)832-2950, Free: 888-731-1000. **URL:** http://www.tbn.org.

13121 ■ KGNO-AM - 1370
2601 Central
Village Plz., Ste. C
Dodge City, KS 67801
Format: Full Service. **Owner:** Goodstar Broadcasting L.L.C., 1660 N Tyler, Wichita, KS 67212, Ph: (316)729-8011, Fax: (316)729-9914. **Founded:** 1930. **Operating Hours:** Continuous. **Wattage:** 5,000 KW. **Ad Rates:** Advertising accepted; rates available upon request. **URL:** http://www.rockingmradio.com/kgno.htm.

13122 ■ KONQ-FM - 91.9
Dodge City Community College
3004 N 14th Ave.
Dodge City, KS 67801
Fax: (316)225-0918
Format: Contemporary Hit Radio (CHR); Religious; Oldies; Blues; Alternative/New Music/Progressive. **Networks:** Independent. **Owner:** Dodge City Community College, 2501 N 14th Ave., KS 67801, Ph: (316)227-9306. **Founded:** 1976. **Formerly:** KINF-FM. **Operating Hours:** 9 a.m.-11 p.m.; 100% local. **Key Personnel:** John Ewy, Operations Mgr.; John Mulhern, Engineer. **Wattage:** 860. **Ad Rates:** Noncommercial.

EL DORADO

SE KS. Butler Co. 28 mi. NE of Wichita. Butler County Community Junior College. Oil refineries. Diversified farming.

13123 ■ KAHS-AM - 1360
1948 SE Hwy. 54
El Dorado, KS 67042
Phone: (316)320-1360
Email: kahs@kahs.kscoxmail.com
Format: Gospel. **Owner:** Reunion Broadcasting, LLC, PO Box 702588, Tulsa, OK 74170, Free: 866-496-7700. **Founded:** Sept. 14, 2005. **Ad Rates:** Noncommercial. **URL:** http://www.kahs1360.com/home.php.

13124 ■ KBTL-FM - 88.1
901 S Haverhill Rd.
El Dorado, KS 67042
Phone: (316)733-3194
Format: Full Service. **Owner:** Butler Community College, 901 S Haverhill Rd., El Dorado, KS 67042, Ph: (316)733-3255. **Key Personnel:** Keith West, Contact. **Wattage:** 400. **URL:** http://www.butlercc.edu/info/200149/mass-communications/112/student-media-outlets/4.

ELKHART

SW KS. Morton Co.

13125 ■ Epic Touch Company Inc.
610 S Cosmos
Elkhart, KS 67950
Phone: (620)697-2233
Free: 800-554-4250
Founded: 1956. **Formerly:** Epic Touch Co.; Elkhart Telephone Company Inc.; Elkhart TV Cable Co. **Cities Served:** Rolla, Kansas; Keyes, Oklahoma: subscribing households 1,062; United States; 94 channels. **URL:** http://www.epictouch.com.

ELLINWOOD

C KS. Barton Co. On Arkansas River, 42 mi. NW of Hutchinson. Oil wells and related equipment. Grain farms.

13126 ■ The Ellinwood Leader
The Leader
PO Box 487
Ellinwood, KS 67526
Phone: (620)564-3116
Fax: (620)564-2550
Publication E-mail: theellinwoodleadernews@yahoo.com
Community newspaper. **Freq:** Weekly (Thurs.). **Print Method:** Offset. **Cols./Page:** 6. **Col. Width:** 28

nonpareils. **Col. Depth:** 294 agate lines. **Key Personnel:** Mary Jo Cunningham, Editor. **Subscription Rates:** $23.97 Individuals; $26.64 Out of area; $26.64 Out of state; $25 Other countries; $18.65 Out of area online. **URL:** http://www.midksnews.com. **Ad Rates:** GLR $.20; BW $504; SAU $2.45; PCI $4.25. **Remarks:** Accepts advertising. **Circ:** ‡1400.

ELLSWORTH

C KS. Ellsworth Co. On Smoky Hill River, 34 mi. SW of Salina. Oil and oil products. Grain.

13127 ■ The Ellsworth Reporter
The Ellsworth Reporter
304 N Douglas Ave.
Ellsworth, KS 67439
Phone: (785)472-5085
Community newspaper. **Freq:** Weekly (Thurs.). **Print Method:** Offset. **Cols./Page:** 6. **Col. Width:** 28 nonpareils. **Col. Depth:** 294 agate lines. **Key Personnel:** Mark McCoy, Editor; Kendra Reid, Advertising Representative; Juanita Kepka, Business Manager; Bill Beckmeyer, Graphic Designer; Alan Rusch, Editor; Linda Mowery Denning, Editor. **Subscription Rates:** $30 Individuals online; $30.45 Individuals print and online; $33.50 Out of state print and online. **URL:** http://www.ellsworthinderep.com. **Remarks:** Advertising accepted; rates available upon request. **Circ:** ‡3050.

EMPORIA

EC KS. Lyon Co. On Neosho and Cottonwood Rivers, 50 mi. SW of Topeka. Way College of Emporia; Emporia State University. Manufactures printing equipment, cheese, flour. Meat packing plant; soybean processing plant.

13128 ■ The Emporia Gazette
Emporia Gazette
517 Merchant St.
Emporia, KS 66801
Phone: (620)342-4800
Fax: (620)342-8108
Publisher's E-mail: newsroom@emporiagazette.com
Newspaper. **Freq:** Mon.-Sat. (eve.) except Sundays and holidays. **Print Method:** Offset. **Cols./Page:** 6. **Col. Width:** 12 picas. **Col. Depth:** 21 inches. **Key Personnel:** Christopher White Walker, Editor. **USPS:** 175-800. **Subscription Rates:** $91.66 Individuals twelve months; $47.34 Individuals six months; $24.43 Individuals three months; $8.40 Individuals one month. **URL:** http://www.emporiagazette.com. **Remarks:** Accepts advertising. **Circ:** Mon.-Sat. ★**6902**.

13129 ■ KANH-FM - 89.7
1120 W 11th St.
University of Kansas
Lawrence, KS 66044
Phone: (785)864-4530
Fax: (785)864-5278
Free: 888-577-5268
Format: Public Radio. **Owner:** Kansas Public Radio, 1120 W 11th St., Lawrence, KS 66044, Ph: (785)864-4530, Fax: (785)864-5278, Free: 888-577-5268. **Key Personnel:** Janet Campbell, Gen. Mgr., jcampbell@ku.edu; Nicci Banman, Bus. Mgr., nbanman@ku.edu; Jason Slote, Production Mgr., jslote@ku.edu. **Ad Rates:** Noncommercial. **URL:** http://kansaspublicradio.org.

13130 ■ KANS-FM - 96
PO Box 893
Emporia, KS 66801
Phone: (620)343-9393
Fax: (620)342-7617
Free: 800-374-5888
Email: thewave@ksradio.com
Format: Contemporary Hit Radio (CHR); Adult Contemporary. **Networks:** Jones Satellite; USA Radio. **Owner:** Kansas Radio, Inc., at above address. **Founded:** May 01, 1998. **Operating Hours:** Continuous. **Key Personnel:** Ken Hanson, Contact; Brook Reed, Traffic Mgr., Office Mgr; Ken Hanson, Contact. **Wattage:** 6,000. **Ad Rates:** $2.35-11.76 for 15 seconds; $3.52-17.64 for 30 seconds; $5.88-23.53 for 60 seconds. KRWV-FM. **URL:** http://www.ksradio.com.

13131 ■ KFFX-FM
PO Box 968
Emporia, KS 66801
Phone: (316)342-1400
Fax: (316)342-0804
Format: Contemporary Hit Radio (CHR). **Owner:** Valu-Broadcasting, Inc., at above address. **Founded:** 1966. **Wattage:** 3,000 ERP.

13132 ■ KPOR-FM - 90.7
1350 S Loop Rd., Ste. 130
Alameda, CA 94502
Free: 800-543-1495
Email: info@familyradio.org
Format: Religious. **Owner:** Family Stations Inc., 290 Hegenberger Rd., Oakland, CA 94621, Free: 800-543-1495. **Wattage:** 2,000. **URL:** http://www.familyradio.org/california.

13133 ■ K207EI-FM - 89.3
PO Box 391
Twin Falls, ID 83303
Fax: (208)736-1958
Free: 800-357-4226
Format: Religious; Contemporary Christian. **Owner:** CSN International, PO Box 391, Twin Falls, ID 83303, Ph: (208)736-1958, Fax: (208)736-1958, Free: 800-357-4226. **Key Personnel:** Kelly Carlson, Dir. of Engg.; Ray Gorney, Asst. Dir.; Don Mills, Music Dir., Prog. Dir. **URL:** http://www.csnradio.com.

13134 ■ KVOE-AM - 1400
PO Box 968
Box 968
Emporia, KS 66801
Phone: (620)342-5863
Fax: (620)342-0804
Format: News; Sports; Talk. **Owner:** Valu-Broadcasting, Inc., at above address. **Founded:** 1939. **Operating Hours:** Continuous. **Wattage:** 1,000 KW. **Ad Rates:** Accepts Advertising. **URL:** http://www.kvoe.com.

13135 ■ KVOE-FM - 101.7
PO Box 968
Emporia, KS 66801
Phone: (620)342-1400
Fax: (620)342-0804
Email: kvoe@kvoe.com
Format: Full Service; Country. **Simulcasts:** KVOE-AM. **Networks:** ABC. **Owner:** Emporia's Radio Stations Inc., at above address. **Founded:** 1985. **Operating Hours:** Continuous. **Key Personnel:** Tim Miller, Div. Dir; Jeff O'Dell, Contact. **Wattage:** 3,000. **Ad Rates:** Advertising accepted; rates available upon request. **URL:** http://www.kvoe.com.

ESKRIDGE

13136 ■ Flint Hills Independent
Flint Hills Independent
121 S Main St.
Eskridge, KS 66423
Phone: (913)449-7272
Fax: (913)449-2411
Publication E-mail: indy96@gulftel.com
Community newspaper. **Founded:** 1900. **Freq:** Weekly (Thurs.). **Print Method:** Web offset. **Trim Size:** 13 x 20. **Cols./Page:** 5 and 6. **Col. Width:** 11 picas and 26 nonpareils. **Col. Depth:** 15 and 294 21 1/2 inches. **Subscription Rates:** $21.50; $25 Out of state; $18 Individuals county; $22 Out of area state of WA; $24 Out of state; $23 Individuals; $13.50 senior citizens. **Formerly:** The Independent. **Mailing address:** PO Box 27, Eskridge, KS 66423. **Ad Rates:** GLR $8; BW $375; 4C $575; BW $529.20; PCI $4.20; GLR $1,064.25; BW $741.75; 4C $1,121.75; SAU $8.25; CNU $7.25; PCI $1,444.25. **Remarks:** Color advertising not accepted. **Circ:** 3100, ‡2350, 4500.

EUREKA

13137 ■ Eureka Herald
Greenwood County Publishing Co.
106 W 2nd St.
Eureka, KS 67045
Phone: (620)583-5721
Fax: (620)583-5922
Publication E-mail: news@eurekaherald.com
Community newspaper. **Freq:** Weekly (Thurs.). **Cols./Page:** 7. **Col. Width:** 2 inches. **Col. Depth:** 21 inches. **Key Personnel:** Robin A. Wunderlich, Editor. **Subscription Rates:** $32 Individuals non mailed; $38 By mail in Greenwood, Woodson & Elk Counties; $45 Elsewhere by mail; $50 By mail outside Kansas. **URL:** http://www.eurekaherald.com. **Mailing address:** PO Box 590, Eureka, KS 67045. **Circ:** 3600.

13138 ■ KOTE-FM - 93.9
PO Box 350
Eureka, KS 67045
Phone: (620)583-7414
Format: Country; Classic Rock. **Networks:** Jones Satellite. **Owner:** Niemeyer Communications L.L.C., at above address. **Operating Hours:** 5:00 a.m.-12:00 a.m. **Wattage:** 3,000. **Ad Rates:** $4-10 for 30 seconds; $6-15 for 60 seconds. **URL:** http://www.kotefm.com.

EVEREST

NE KS. Brown Co. 15 mi. SE of Hiawatha. Sawmills. Dairy, poultry, and grain farms.

13139 ■ Rainbow Communications
608 Main St.
Everest, KS 66424
Free: 800-892-0163
Email: bev@rainbowtel.com
Founded: 1952. **Formerly:** Carson Communications L.L.C. **Key Personnel:** Jason Smith, Asst. GM. **Cities Served:** United States; 27 channels. **Mailing address:** PO Box 147, Everest, KS 66424. **URL:** http://www.rainbowtel.net.

FAIRWAY

13140 ■ KCTV-TV - 5
4500 Shawnee Mission Pkwy.
Fairway, KS 66205
Phone: (913)677-5555
Email: kctv5@kctv5.com
Format: Commercial TV; Sports. **Networks:** CBS. **Owner:** Meredith Corp., 1716 Locust St., Des Moines, IA 50309-3038, Ph: (515)284-3000. **Founded:** 1953. **Formerly:** KCMO-TV. **Operating Hours:** Continuous; 63% network, 37% local. **ADI:** Kansas City, MO (Lawrence, KS). **Key Personnel:** Mike Sulzman, Dir. of Engg. **Wattage:** 100,000. **Ad Rates:** Noncommercial. **URL:** http://www.kctv5.com.

KPXE-TV - See Kansas City, MO

13141 ■ KSMO-TV - 62
4500 Shawnee Mission Pky.
Fairway, KS 66205
Phone: (913)677-5555
Fax: (913)677-7243
Email: ksmo@myksmotv.com
Format: Commercial TV. **Networks:** Christian Broadcasting (CBN); Warner Brothers Studios. **Owner:** Meredith Broadcasting Group, 1716 Locust St.,, Des Moines, IA 50309, Ph: (515)284-3000. **Founded:** Sept. 12, 1983. **Formerly:** KEKR-TV; KZKC-TV. **Operating Hours:** Continuous. **ADI:** Kansas City, MO (Lawrence, KS). **Key Personnel:** Erin Mahoney, Contact, erin.mahoney@meredith.com. **Ad Rates:** Noncommercial. **URL:** http://www.kctv5.com.

FALUN

13142 ■ Smokejumper
National Smokejumper Association
c/o John McDaniel, Membership Coordinator
PO Box 105
Falun, KS 67442-0105
Magazine featuring information about aerial fire management. **Freq:** Quarterly. **Subscription Rates:** Included in membership. **Alt. Formats:** PDF. **URL:** http://smokejumpers.com/index.php/smokejumpermagazine/getall. **Remarks:** Advertising not accepted. **Circ:** (Not Reported).

FORT LEAVENWORTH

NE KS. Leavenworth Co. 22 mi. NW of Kansas City. Military outpost; state penitentiary.

13143 ■ Fort Leavenworth Lamp
Chronicle Shopper
Rm. 112, 600 Thomas Ave.
Fort Leavenworth, KS 66027
Phone: (913)684-5267
Fax: (913)684-3624
Publication E-mail: editor@ftleavenworthlamp.com

Circulation: ★ = AAM; △ or • = BPA; ♦ = CAC; ❑ = VAC; ⊕ = PO Statement; ‡ = Publisher's Report; Boldface figures = sworn; Light figures = estimated.

Community newspaper. **Freq:** Weekly (Thurs.). **Print Method:** Offset. **Trim Size:** 10 x 16. **Cols./Page:** 5. **Key Personnel:** Donna Nolan; Tim Larson, Publisher; Sandy Hattock, Director, Advertising and Sales; Bob Kerr, Editor. **URL:** http://www.ftleavenworthlamp.com. **Ad Rates:** BW $580; 4C $795; CNU $8.75; PCI $8.75. **Remarks:** Accepts advertising. **Circ:** Non-paid **7500**, 8000.

13144 ■ Military Review
USACGSC
Military Review Truesdell Hall
290 Stimson Ave., Unit 2
Fort Leavenworth, KS 66027
Phone: (913)684-9327
Fax: (913)684-9328
Publication E-mail: milrevweb@leavenworth.army.mil
Professional military journal (English, Spanish and Portuguese). **Freq:** Bimonthly for English & Spanish; quarterly for Portuguese. **Print Method:** Film. **Trim Size:** 8 x 10 5/8. **Cols./Page:** 2. **Col. Width:** 35 nonpareils. **Col. Depth:** 92 agate lines. **Key Personnel:** John Garabedian, Associate Editor; Marlys Cook, Managing Editor. **ISSN:** 1067--0653 (print). **Subscription Rates:** $42 Individuals domestic; $58.50 Other countries; Free to qualified subscribers. **URL:** http://usacac.leavenworth.army.mil/cac/milreview/. **Remarks:** Advertising not accepted. **Circ:** ‡12000.

FORT SCOTT

SE KS. Bourbon Co. 143 mi. ENE of Wichita. Fort Scott Community College.

13145 ■ KMDO-AM
2 N National
Fort Scott, KS 66701
Fax: (316)223-5662
Email: kumb@terraworld.net
Format: Full Service. **Networks:** CNN Radio. **Owner:** Timothy James McKenney, Rte. 5, Box A-1, Fort Scott, KS 66701, Ph: (316)223-3405. **Founded:** 1954. **Key Personnel:** Tim J. McKenney, Contact. **Wattage:** 770 Day; 035 Night. **Ad Rates:** $8.95 for 30 seconds; $10.95 for 60 seconds.

13146 ■ KOMB-FM - 103.9
Two N National Ave.
Fort Scott, KS 66701
Format: Contemporary Hit Radio (CHR). **Simulcasts:** KMDO-AM. **Founded:** 1981. **Operating Hours:** 6:00 a.m. - Midnight. **Wattage:** 25,000 ERP. **Ad Rates:** Advertising accepted; rates available upon request. $8.95 for 30 seconds; $10.95 for 60 seconds. KMDO-AM. **URL:** http://www.kombfm.com.

13147 ■ KVCY-FM - 104.7
3434 W Kilbourn Ave.
Milwaukee, WI 53208
Phone: (414)935-3000
Free: 800-729-9829
Email: vcy@vcyamerica.org
Format: Religious. **Networks:** Voice of Christian Youth America. **Owner:** VCY America Inc., 3434 W Kilbourn Ave., Milwaukee, WI 53208, Free: 800-729-9829. **Operating Hours:** Continuous. **Wattage:** 3,000. **Ad Rates:** Noncommercial. **URL:** http://www.vcyamerica.org.

GALENA

13148 ■ Galena Sentinel-Times
The Sentinel-Times
511 Main St.
Galena, KS 66739
Phone: (620)783-5034
Fax: (620)783-1388
Publication E-mail: gstimes@kans.com
Community newspaper. **Freq:** Weekly (Wed.). **Cols./Page:** 6. **Col. Width:** 1 7/8 inches. **Col. Depth:** 21 inches. **Key Personnel:** David F. Nelson, Publisher; Machell Smith, Managing Editor. **USPS:** 213-000. **Subscription Rates:** $33 Individuals Cherokee County; $42 Individuals outside Cherokee County. **URL:** http://www.sentineltimes.com. **Ad Rates:** GLR $3.50. **Remarks:** Accepts advertising. **Circ:** 1350.

GARDEN CITY

SW KS. Finney Co. On Arkansas River, 50 mi. NW of Dodge City. Garden City Community Junior College. Manufactures cattle feeding equipment, alfalfa meal. Diversified farming.

13149 ■ KANZ-FM - 91.1
210 N 7th St.
Garden City, KS 67846
Phone: (620)275-7444
Free: 800-678-7444
Format: Public Radio. **Networks:** National Public Radio (NPR); Public Radio International (PRI). **Owner:** Kanza Society, Inc., at above address, Garden City, KS. **Founded:** Oct. 04, 1979. **Operating Hours:** Continuous. **Key Personnel:** Cindee Talley, Dir. of Programs, ctalley@hppr.org; Mike Fuller, Music Dir., mfuller@hppr.org; Dale Bolton, Dir. of Operations, dbolton@hppr.org. **Wattage:** 100,000. **Ad Rates:** Noncommercial; underwriting available. **URL:** http://www.hppr.org.

13150 ■ KBUF-AM - 1030
1402 E Kansas Ave.
Garden City, KS 67846
Phone: (620)276-2366
Fax: (620)276-3568
Format: Country; Agricultural; Talk. **Networks:** ABC; Kansas Agriculture. **Owner:** KBUF Partnership, at above address. **Founded:** 1948. **Operating Hours:** Continuous. **ADI:** Wichita-Hutchinson, KS. **Key Personnel:** Gil Wohle, Gen. Mgr., gilwohler@wksradio.com; Bob Dale, Station Mgr., bobdale@wksradio.com. **Wattage:** 1,000 Day; 1,000 Night. **Ad Rates:** $12-18 for 30 seconds; $18-27 for 60 seconds. **URL:** http://westernkansasnews.com.

13151 ■ KIUL-AM - 1240
308 N 7th St.
Garden City, KS 67846-0759
Phone: (316)276-3251
Fax: (316)276-3649
Format: Full Service; Middle-of-the-Road (MOR). **Networks:** CBS; Kansas Information; Kansas Agriculture. **Owner:** Threjay, Inc., at above address. **Founded:** 1935. **Operating Hours:** 5:00 a.m.-1 a.m. **Key Personnel:** Bob Dale, Dir. of Programs; Rick Everett, News Dir.; Andrew Mahoney, News Dir., newsdirector@wksradio.com. **Wattage:** 1,000. **Ad Rates:** $6-20 for 30 seconds; $9-21 for 60 seconds. Combined advertising rates available with KWKR-FM: $6-$20 for 30 seconds; $9-$21 for 60 seconds. **Mailing address:** PO Box 759, Garden City, KS 67846-0759. **URL:** http://www.kgso.com/kiul-news-radio.

13152 ■ KKJQ-FM - 97.3
1402 E Kansas Ave.
Garden City, KS 67846
Phone: (620)276-2366
Format: Country; Adult Contemporary. **Networks:** ABC. **Owner:** Western Kansas Broadcast Center, 1402 E Kansas Ave., Garden City, KS 67846. **Founded:** 1962. **Operating Hours:** Continuous. **Wattage:** 100,000. **Ad Rates:** Noncommercial. **URL:** http://www.westernkansasnews.com/q97.

13153 ■ KSKL-FM - 94.5
1402 Kansas Ave.
Garden City, KS 67846
Phone: (620)276-2366
Format: News; Agricultural; Sports; Information. **Key Personnel:** James Janda, Dir. of Programs. **Wattage:** 100,000 ERP. **Ad Rates:** Advertising accepted; rates available upon request. **URL:** http://www.westernkansasnews.com.

13154 ■ K39FW - 39
PO Box A
Santa Ana, CA 92711
Phone: (714)832-2950
Free: 888-731-1000
Owner: Trinity Broadcasting Network Inc., PO Box A, Santa Ana, CA 92711, Ph: (714)832-2950, Free: 888-731-1000.

13155 ■ KTOT-FM - 89.5
210 N 7th St.
Garden City, KS 67846
Phone: (620)275-7444
Fax: (620)275-7496
Free: 800-678-7444
Format: Public Radio. **Owner:** High Plains Public Radio, 210 N 7th St., Garden City, KS 67846, Ph: (620)275-7444, Free: 800-678-7444. **Key Personnel:** Chuck Springer, Chief Engineer, engineer@hppr.org. **Ad Rates:** Noncommercial; underwriting available. **URL:** http://www.hppr.org.

13156 ■ KUPK-TV - 13
2900 E Schulman Ave.
Garden City, KS 67846-9064
Phone: (620)275-1560
Fax: (620)275-1572
Email: kupk@gcnet.com
Ad Rates: Advertising accepted; rates available upon request. **URL:** http://www.kake.com.

13157 ■ KWKR-FM - 99.9
1402 E Kansas Ave.
Garden City, KS 67846
Phone: (620)276-2366
Format: Talk; News; Sports. **Founded:** 1983. **Operating Hours:** 7:30 a.m. - 6:00 p.m. Monday - Friday 7:30 a.m. - 6:00 p.m. Saturday - 1:00 p.m. - 5:00 p.m. Sunday. **Key Personnel:** Gil Wohler, Gen. Mgr., gilwohler@wksradio.com; James Janda, Program Mgr., jamesjanda@wksradio.com. **Wattage:** 99,000 ERP. **Ad Rates:** Advertising accepted; rates available upon request. $6-27 for 30 seconds; $9-40.50 for 60 seconds. Combined advertising rates available with KIUL-AM. **Mailing address:** PO Box 878, Garden City, KS 67846. **URL:** http://westernkansasnews.com.

GARDNER

13158 ■ Gardner News
Tri-County Newspapers
PO Box 303
Gardner, KS 66030-0303
Phone: (913)856-7615
Publisher's E-mail: submissions@gardnernews.com
Community newspaper. **Founded:** 1940. **Freq:** Weekly (Wed.). **Cols./Page:** 6. **Col. Width:** 12.5 picas. **Col. Depth:** 21 inches. **Key Personnel:** Mark Taylor, Editor. **Subscription Rates:** $36 Individuals. **URL:** http://www.gardnernews.com. **Ad Rates:** BW $620; PCI $9. **Remarks:** Accepts advertising. **Circ:** 2000.

GARNETT

EC KS. Anderson Co. 50 mi. SE of Emporia. Oil wells. Grain, poultry, stock, and dairy farms.

13159 ■ Review
Garnett Publishing Inc.
PO Box 409
Garnett, KS 66032
Phone: (785)448-3121
Fax: (785)448-6253
Newspaper. **Founded:** 1865. **Freq:** Weekly (Tues.). **Print Method:** Offset. **Cols./Page:** 6. **Col. Width:** 24 nonpareils. **Col. Depth:** 294 agate lines. **Subscription Rates:** $41.68 Individuals; $50.69 Out of country. **URL:** http://www.garnett-ks.com. **Ad Rates:** GLR $.195. **Remarks:** Accepts advertising. **Circ:** 4074.

GIRARD

C. KS. Crawford Co. 10 mi. NW of Pittsburg. Grain farms.

13160 ■ Craw-Kan Telephone Cooperative Inc.
300 N Ozark St.
Girard, KS 66743-1323
Phone: (620)724-8235
Free: 800-362-0316
Founded: 1952. **Cities Served:** United States; 83 channels. **Mailing address:** PO Box 100, Girard, KS 66743. **URL:** http://web.ckt.net.

GOODLAND

NW KS. Sherman Co. 200 mi. E. of Denver, CO. Grain and livestock farms.

13161 ■ Country Advocate
NorWest Newspapers
1205 Main Ave.
Goodland, KS 67735
Phone: (785)899-2338
Fax: (785)899-6186
Publisher's E-mail: star-news@nwkansas.com
Shopping guide. **Founded:** 1986. **Freq:** Weekly (Wed.). **Print Method:** Offset. **Trim Size:** 13 x 23. **Cols./Page:** 6. **Col. Width:** 2 inches. **Col. Depth:** 21 1/2 inches. **Key Personnel:** Tom Betz, Editor; Steve Haynes, President; Richard Westfahl, General Manager. **URL:** http://www.nwkansas.com. **Ad Rates:** GLR $12.15; BW $1,567; 4C $1,666; SAU $12.15; PCI $12.15. **Remarks:**

Advertising accepted; rates available upon request. **Circ:** (Not Reported).

13162 ■ The Goodland Star-News
NorWest Newspapers
1205 Main Ave.
Goodland, KS 67735
Phone: (785)899-2338
Fax: (785)899-6186
Publisher's E-mail: star-news@nwkansas.com
General newspaper. **Freq:** Biweekly. **Print Method:** Offset. **Trim Size:** 12 x 21.5. **Cols./Page:** 6. **Col. Depth:** 21 1/2 inches. **Key Personnel:** Sheila Smith, Manager, Circulation; Pat Schiefen, Editor; Steve Haynes, President; Tom Betz, Editor. **ISSN:** 0893--0502 (print). **USPS:** 222-460. **URL:** http://www.nwkansas.com/gldwebpages/gsnmain.html. **Formerly**: The Goodland Daily News. **Ad Rates:** GLR $7.15; BW $922; 4C $1,021; SAU $7.15; PCI $7.15. **Remarks:** 6.25. **Circ:** (Not Reported).

13163 ■ KBSL-TV - 10
3023 W 31st
Goodland, KS 67735
Phone: (785)899-2321
Fax: (785)899-3138
Email: kbsl@nwkansas.com
Format: Commercial TV. **Networks:** CBS. **Owner:** Media General Inc., 333 E Franklin St., Richmond, VA 23219, Ph: (804)649-6000, Fax: (502)259-5537. **Founded:** 1960. **Formerly**: KLOE-TV. **Key Personnel:** Don McKenzie, Mgr., Access Svcs. **Wattage**: 84,200 ERP. **Ad Rates:** $10-65 for 30 seconds. **Mailing address:** PO Box 629, Goodland, KS 67735.

13164 ■ KKCI-FM - 102.5
3023 W 31st
Goodland, KS 67735
Phone: (785)899-2309
Fax: (785)899-3062
Format: Adult Contemporary. **Networks:** Satellite Music Network; Westwood One Radio. **Owner:** Melia Communications, at above address, Goodland, KS. **Founded:** 1990. **Operating Hours**: Continuous. **Local Programs**: *Good Neighbor Hour*, Monday Tuesday Wednesday Thursday Friday 6:00 a.m. - 7:00 a.m.; *Evenings with Chelsea K*, Monday Tuesday Wednesday Thursday Friday 4:00 p.m. - 8:00 p.m. **Wattage**: 100,000. **Ad Rates:** Noncommercial. Combined advertising rates available with KLOE-AM.

13165 ■ KLOE-AM - 730
3023 W 31st St.
Goodland, KS 67735
Phone: (785)899-2309
Fax: (785)899-3062
Format: Full Service. **Networks:** ESPN Radio; CBS; Kansas Agriculture. **Owner:** Melia Communications, at above address, Goodland, KS. **Founded:** 1947. **Operating Hours**: 5:30 a.m.-9 p.m. **Local Programs**: *Marketplace Program*, Monday Tuesday Wednesday Thursday Friday 8:00 a.m. - 8:30 a.m. **Wattage**: 1,000 day; 020 night. **Ad Rates:** Advertising accepted; rates available upon request. Combined advertising rates available with KKCI-FM and KWGB-FM. **Mailing address:** PO Box 569, Goodland, KS 67735.

13166 ■ KWGB-FM - 97.9
3023 W 31st St.
Goodland, KS 67735
Phone: (785)899-2309
Fax: (785)899-3062
Format: Country. **Ad Rates:** Noncommercial. **Mailing address:** PO Box 569, Goodland, KS 67735.

GREAT BEND

C KS. Barton Co. On Arkansas River, 50 mi. WNW of Hutchinson. Barton County Community College. Oil and gas wells. Grain farms.

13167 ■ Great Bend Tribune
Great Bend Tribune
2012 Forest Ave.
Great Bend, KS 67530
Phone: (620)792-1211
Fax: (620)792-3441
Free: 800-950-8742
Publisher's E-mail: email@gbtribune.com
General newspaper. **Freq:** Daily and Sun. (eve.). **Print Method:** Offset. **Cols./Page:** 6. **Col. Width:** 24 nonpareils. **Col. Depth:** 301 agate lines. **Key Personnel:** Chuck Smith, Editor; Dale Hogg, Managing Editor; Mary Hoisington, Publisher. **USPS:** 227-260. **Subscription Rates:** $75 Individuals online /year; $132.64 Individuals print and online, motor delivery; $151.88 By mail print and online; $126.61 Individuals by carrier. **URL:** http://www.gbtribune.com/index.php. **Mailing address:** PO Box 228, Great Bend, KS 67530. **Ad Rates:** GLR $0.57; BW $1,185.85; 4C $1,195.85; PCI $8.65. **Remarks:** Advertising accepted; rates available upon request. **Circ:** Tues.-Fri. ★**6219**, Sun. ★**6121**.

13168 ■ KBDA-FM - 89.7
PO Box 3206
Tupelo, MS 38803
Format: Religious. **Owner:** American Family Radio, at above address. **Ad Rates:** Noncommercial.

13169 ■ KBGL-FM - 106.9
1200 Baker
Great Bend, KS 67530
Phone: (620)792-3647
Fax: (620)792-3649
Format: Oldies. **Owner:** Hull Broadcasting Inc., at above address. **Founded:** Apr. 09, 2001. **Key Personnel:** Phil Grossardt, Station Mgr.; Randy Goering, Dir. of Sales, randy.goering@eagleradio.net; JJ McKay, Contact. **Wattage**: 100,000 Watts. **Ad Rates:** Noncommercial.

13170 ■ KHOK-FM - 100.7
1200 Baker St.
Great Bend, KS 67530
Phone: (620)792-3647
Fax: (620)792-3649
Format: Country. **Networks:** ABC. **Owner:** Eagle Radio of Great Bend, 1200 Baker Ave, Great Bend, KS 67530, Ph: (620)792-3647, Fax: (620)792-3649. **Founded:** 1979. **Operating Hours**: Continuous; 2% network, 98% local. **ADI**: Wichita-Hutchinson, KS. **Wattage**: 100,000. **Ad Rates:** for 30 seconds; for 60 seconds. KVGB-AM, KVBG-FM.

13171 ■ KNNS-AM - 1510
5501 W 10th St.
Great Bend, KS 67530
Phone: (620)792-7108
Fax: (620)792-7051
Email: gsnews@greatbend.net
Format: Middle-of-the-Road (MOR). **Networks:** Satellite Network News; ESPN Radio. **Founded:** 1963. **Formerly**: KANS-AM. **Operating Hours**: Continuous. **ADI**: Wichita-Hutchinson, KS. **Key Personnel:** Christopher Miller, President, cmiller@rockingmradio.com. **Wattage**: 1,000. **Ad Rates:** Noncommercial. **URL:** http://rockingmradio.com/contact-us.

13172 ■ KSNC-TV - 2
RR 5, PO Box 262
Great Bend, KS 67530
Phone: (316)265-3333
Fax: (316)292-1195
Format: Commercial TV; News; Sports; Information. **Networks:** NBC. **Founded:** 1954. **Wattage**: 500,000 ERP Horizon. **Ad Rates:** $15-120 for 30 seconds. **URL:** http://www.ksn.com/.

13173 ■ KVGB-AM - 1590
1200 Baker St.
Great Bend, KS 67530
Phone: (620)792-3647
Fax: (620)792-3649
Format: Talk; News; Information. **Networks:** ABC. **Owner:** Eagle Radio, PO Box 550, Baraga, MI 49908, Ph: (906)353-9287, Free: 888-377-9287. **Founded:** Mar. 01, 1937. **Operating Hours**: Continuous. **Key Personnel:** Steve Davis, Dir. of Sales, steve.divis@eagleradio.net. **Wattage**: 5,000. **Ad Rates:** Advertising accepted; rates available upon request. KVGB-FM, KHOK-FM. **Mailing address:** PO Box 609, Great Bend, KS 67530. **URL:** http://www.greatbendpost.com.

13174 ■ KVGB-FM - 104.3
PO Box 609
Great Bend, KS 67530
Phone: (620)792-3647
Fax: (620)792-3649
Format: Classic Rock. **Simulcasts:** KVGB-AM 1590. **Networks:** ABC. **Owner:** Eagle Communication, Inc., 2703 Hall St., Ste. 15, Hays, KS 67601, Ph: (785)625-4000, Fax: (785)625-8030. **Founded:** 1997. **Operating Hours**: Continuous. **Wattage**: 100,000. **Ad Rates:** $7-12 for 30 seconds. KHOK-FM, KVGB-AM. **URL:** http://www.greatbendpost.com.

GREENSBURG

SC KS. Kiowa Co. 80 mi. SW of Hutchinson. Livestock and grain farms.

13175 ■ Kiowa County Signal
Tribune Newspaper Co.
101 S Main St., Ste. 207
Greensburg, KS 67054
Community newspaper. **Freq:** Weekly (Wed.). **Print Method:** Offset. **Trim Size:** 13 x 21 1/2. **Cols./Page:** 6. **Col. Width:** 26 nonpareils. **Col. Depth:** 301 agate lines. **Key Personnel:** Randy Mitchell, Publisher; Patrick Clement, Editor. **USPS:** 295-960. **URL:** http://www.kiowacountysignal.com. **Ad Rates:** GLR $0.20; BW $4; PCI $3.90. **Remarks:** Advertising accepted; rates available upon request. **Circ:** Paid 1600, Free 50.

HALSTEAD

SWC KS. Harvey Co. 23 mi. NNW of Wichita. Wheat.

13176 ■ U.S. Water News
U.S. Water News Inc.
230 Main St.
Halstead, KS 67056-1913
Phone: (316)835-2222
Fax: (316)835-2223
Free: 800-251-0046
Publication E-mail: editor@uswaternews.com
Water industry magazine (tabloid) covering water supply, water quality, government policy, legislation, litigation and water rights, conservation, finances, and markets. **Freq:** Monthly. **Print Method:** Offset. **Trim Size:** 11 x 14. **Cols./Page:** 4. **Col. Width:** 2 1/4 inches. **Col. Depth:** 13 inches. **Key Personnel:** Thomas C. Bell, President, Publisher. **ISSN:** 0749--1980 (print). **URL:** http://www.uswaternews.com. **Ad Rates:** BW $2,150; 4C $2,300. **Remarks:** Accepts advertising. **Circ:** Paid ‡1700, Controlled ‡18300.

HAYS

WC KS. Ellis Co. 100 mi. W. of Salina. Fort Hays State University. Oil well; large dryland farming experiment station.

13177 ■ The Hays Daily News
News Publishing Co.
507 Main St.
Hays, KS 67601
Phone: (785)628-1081
Fax: (785)628-8186
Free: 800-657-6017
General newspaper. **Founded:** Nov. 11, 1929. **Freq:** Daily Sunday through Friday. **Print Method:** Offset. **Trim Size:** 13 3/4 x 22 3/4. **Cols./Page:** 6. **Col. Width:** 2 1/16 inches. **Col. Depth:** 21 1/2 inches. **Key Personnel:** Mary Karst, Director, Advertising; Patrick E. Lowry, Editor; Ron Fields, Managing Editor. **Subscription Rates:** $13.50 Individuals online. **URL:** http://www.hdnews.net/. **Formerly**: The Ellis County News. **Remarks:** Accepts advertising. **Circ:** (Not Reported).

13178 ■ Journal of Academic Leadership
Academic Leadership
600 Park St.
Rarick Hall 219
Hays, KS 67601-4099
Journal focusing on the leadership issues in the academic world. **Key Personnel:** Dr. Jerald W. Spotswood, Editor; Anne L. Jefferson, Associate Editor. **ISSN:** 1533--7812 (print). **Circ:** (Not Reported).

13179 ■ Kansas Music Review
Kansas Music Educators Association
Hays High School
3512 Hillcrest
Hays, KS 67601
Phone: (785)623-2600
Publication E-mail: editor@ksmea.org
Trade magazine covering music. **Freq:** Quarterly. **Trim Size:** 8 1/2 x 11. **Key Personnel:** Robert E. Lee, Manager, Advertising, phone: (620)669-1301; Harold Popp, Editor, phone: (316)729-7450, fax: (316)729-6785; Jean Ney, Vice President, phone: (913)627-6850,

Circulation: ★ = AAM; △ or • = BPA; ♦ = CAC; ❑ = VAC; ⊕ = PO Statement; ‡ = Publisher's Report; Boldface figures = sworn; Light figures = estimated.

fax: (913)627-6884. **Subscription Rates:** $3 Single issue; $3. **Alt. Formats:** CD-ROM; PDF. **URL:** http://kmr.ksmea.org. **Ad Rates:** BW $330; ;. **Remarks:** Accepts advertising. **Circ:** 2500, 2,500.

13180 ■ The University Leader
Fort Hays State University
600 Park St.
Hays, KS 67601
Phone: (785)628-3478
Free: 800-628-FHSU
Publisher's E-mail: tigerinfo@fhsu.edu
Collegiate newspaper. **Freq:** Weekly published each Thursday,. **Print Method:** Offset. **Trim Size:** Broadsheet. **Cols./Page:** 6. **Col. Width:** 11 picas. **Col. Depth:** 21.5 inches. **URL:** http://tmn.fhsu.edu/u-leader. **Remarks:** Advertising accepted; rates available upon request. **Circ:** Free ‡3700.

13181 ■ KAYS-AM - 1400
2300 Hall St.
Hays, KS 67601
Phone: (785)625-2578
Fax: (785)625-3632
Email: admin@hayspost.com
Format: Full Service; Oldies. **Networks:** ABC; ESPN Radio. **Owner:** Eagle Radio, PO Box 550, Baraga, MI 49908, Ph: (906)353-9287, Free: 888-377-9287. **Founded:** 1948. **Operating Hours:** 5:00 a.m.-midnight. **Wattage:** 1,000. **Ad Rates:** Noncommercial. **Mailing address:** PO Box 6, Hays, KS 67601. **URL:** http://www.hayspost.com.

13182 ■ KBSH-TV - 7
2300 Hall St.
Hays, KS 67601
Phone: (785)625-5277
Fax: (785)625-1161
Format: Commercial TV. **Networks:** CBS. **Owner:** Spartan Communications, Inc., Spartanburg, SC, Ph: (864)576-7777. **Founded:** 1958. **Formerly:** KAYS-TV. **Key Personnel:** Wayne Roberts, Station Mgr. **Wattage:** 38,800 ERP. **Ad Rates:** $10-90 for 30 seconds.

13183 ■ KFHS-FM - 98.3
Heather Hall Fort Hays State University
600 Park St.
Hays, KS 67601-4099
Phone: (785)628-4664
Free: 800-628-3478
Format: Country; Classic Rock. **Owner:** KFHS Broadcast Council. **Founded:** 1950. **Operating Hours:** Continuous. **Ad Rates:** Noncommercial; underwriting available. **URL:** http://www.fhsu.edu.

13184 ■ KFIX-FM - 96.9
2300 Hall St.
Hays, KS 67601
Format: Classic Rock. **Key Personnel:** Dwayne Detter, Contact. **Wattage:** 10,500. **Ad Rates:** Advertising accepted; rates available upon request. **URL:** http://www.kfix.com.

13185 ■ KHAZ-FM - 99.5
2300 Hall St.
Hays, KS 67601
Phone: (785)625-2578
Fax: (785)625-3632
Format: Country. **Networks:** ABC. **Operating Hours:** Continuous. **Wattage:** 100,000. **Ad Rates:** Noncommercial. **Mailing address:** PO Box 6, Hays, KS 67601. **URL:** http://www.eagleradioauction.com.

13186 ■ KJLS-FM - 103.3
2300 Hall St.
Hays, KS 67601
Phone: (785)625-2578
Fax: (785)625-3632
Email: admin@hayspost.com
Format: Adult Contemporary; Alternative/New Music/Progressive. **Networks:** ABC. **Owner:** Eagle Radio, PO Box 550, Baraga, MI 49908, Ph: (906)353-9287, Free: 888-377-9287. **Founded:** 1974. **Operating Hours:** Continuous. **Key Personnel:** Todd Lynd, Gen. Mgr., t.lynd@eagleradio.net. **Wattage:** 100,000. **Ad Rates:** Advertising accepted; rates available upon request. KKQY-FM. **Mailing address:** PO Box 6, Hays, KS 67601. **URL:** http://www.hayspost.com.

13187 ■ KKQY-FM - 101.9
2300 Hall St.
Hays, KS 67601
Phone: (785)625-2578
Fax: (785)625-3632
Format: Country. **Owner:** Eagle Communications, Inc., at above address. **Key Personnel:** Dwayne Detter, Contact, dwayne.detter@eagleradio.net. **Ad Rates:** Advertising accepted; rates available upon request. **Mailing address:** PO Box 6, Hays, KS 67601. **URL:** http://www.hayspost.com.

13188 ■ KPRD-FM - 88.9
205 E 7th St., Ste. 218
Hays, KS 67601
Phone: (785)628-6300
Fax: (785)628-6389
Email: kprd@kprd.org
Format: Religious. **Networks:** Moody Broadcasting; SkyLight Satellite; Ambassador Inspirational Radio. **Owner:** The Praise Network, Inc., PO Box 8, Aurora, NE 68818-0008, Ph: (308)946-2656. **Founded:** Aug. 15, 1994. **Operating Hours:** Continuous. **Wattage:** 83,000. **Ad Rates:** Noncommercial. **URL:** http://www.kprdradio.com.

13189 ■ KSFT-AM - 1550
2703 Hall, Ste. 15
Hays, KS 67601
Phone: (816)233-8881
Fax: (816)279-8280
Format: Sports. **Networks:** AP. **Owner:** Eagle Radio, PO Box 550, Baraga, MI 49908, Ph: (906)353-9287, Free: 888-377-9287. **Formerly:** KKJO-AM. **ADI:** St. Joseph, MO. **Key Personnel:** Gary Exline, Gen. Sales Mgr.; Barry Birr, News Dir., barry.birr@eagleradio.net; Kevin Wagner, Dir. of Operations, kevin.wagner@eagleradio.net; Teresa Hetz, Promotions Dir., teresa.hetz@eagleradio.net. **Wattage:** 2,500. **Ad Rates:** $8-18 for 30 seconds; $9-18 for 60 seconds; $12-20 per unit. **URL:** http://www.1550espn.com.

HERINGTON

NEC KS. Morris Co. 30 mi. SE of Abilene. Oil wells. Grain farms.

13190 ■ The Herington Times
The Herington Times
7 N Broadway
Herington, KS 67449
Phone: (785)258-2211
Publisher's E-mail: jr@heringtontimes.com
Community newspaper. **Freq:** Weekly (Thurs.). **Print Method:** Offset. **Cols./Page:** 6. **Col. Width:** 25 nonpareils. **Col. Depth:** 294 agate lines. **USPS:** 242-100. **Subscription Rates:** $40 Individuals; $42 Out of area; $46 Out of state. **URL:** http://www.heringtontimes.com/. **Ad Rates:** GLR $.33; BW $667.80; 4C $847.80; SAU $6.75; PCI $6.75. **Remarks:** Accepts advertising. **Circ:** (Not Reported).

13191 ■ KJRL-FM - 105.7
PO Box 150
Herington, KS 67449
Fax: (785)263-3876
Free: 877-813-5366
Email: kjrl@kjrl.org
Format: Country. **Networks:** USA Radio; Kansas Information; Kansas Agriculture. **Formerly:** KDMM-FM. **Operating Hours:** Continuous. **Key Personnel:** Mark Hinca, Station Mgr., markh@kjil.com. **Wattage:** 12,500. **Ad Rates:** Advertising accepted; rates available upon request. **URL:** http://kjil1057.com/.

HESSTON

SC KS. Harvey Co. 30 mi. NNW of Wichita. Hesston College. Manufactures commercial turf and mowing equipment. Diversified farming.

13192 ■ The Hesston Record
The Hesston Record
347 B Old Hwy. 81
Hesston, KS 67062-0340
Fax: (620)327-4830
Newspaper. **Freq:** Weekly (Thurs.). **Print Method:** Offset. **Trim Size:** 11 1/2 x 14. **Cols./Page:** 5. **Col. Width:** 24 nonpareils. **Col. Depth:** 182 agate lines. **Key Personnel:** Robb Reeves, Publisher; Bob Latta, Editor; Jackie Nelson, Editor. **Subscription Rates:** $37 Individuals in Harvey County; $40 Out of country; $46 Out of state; $70 Two years in Harvey County. **URL:** http://www.hesstonrecord.com. **Ad Rates:** GLR $0.28; BW $237.25; PCI $3.85. **Remarks:** Accepts advertising. **Circ:** Paid ‡1150.

HIAWATHA

NE KS. Brown Co. 54 mi. NNE of Topeka. Diversified farming.

13193 ■ KNZA-FM - 103.9
1828 South Hwy. 73
Hiawatha, KS 66434
Format: Country; Sports; News; Information. **Owner:** KNZA 103.9 FM, 1828 S Hwy. 73, Hiawatha, KS 66434, Ph: (785)547-3461, Fax: (785)547-9900. **Founded:** 1977. **Wattage:** 50,000 ERP. **Ad Rates:** Advertising accepted; rates available upon request. $6-14 for 30 seconds; $10-24 for 60 seconds. **Mailing address:** PO Box 104, Hiawatha, KS 66434-0104. **URL:** http://www.knzafm.com.

13194 ■ KNZA 103.9 FM - 103.9
1828 S Hwy. 73
Hiawatha, KS 66434
Phone: (785)547-3461
Fax: (785)547-9900
Format: News; Sports; Top 40; Information. **Wattage:** 50,000 ERP. **Ad Rates:** Advertising accepted; rates available upon request. **URL:** http://www.knzafm.com.

KTNC-AM - See Falls City, NE

HOLTON

NE KS. Jackson Co. 30 mi. N. of Topeka. Manufactures farm machinery. Diversified farming.

13195 ■ The Holton Recorder
The Holton Recorder
109 West 4th St.
Holton, KS 66436
Phone: (785)364-3141
Fax: (785)364-3422
Publisher's E-mail: holtonrecorder@embarqmail.com
Community newspaper. **Freq:** Semiweekly (Mon. and Thurs.). **Print Method:** Offset. **Trim Size:** 13 3/4 x 22 7/8. **Cols./Page:** 6. **Col. Width:** 25 nonpareils. **Col. Depth:** 294 agate lines. **Key Personnel:** Connie Powls, Editor; David M. Powls, Editor, Publisher; Allen Bowser, Manager, Production. **Subscription Rates:** $40.50 Individuals in Jackson County (print and online); $47.42 Individuals adjoining counties (print and online); $53.41 Elsewhere print and online. **URL:** http://holtonrecorder.net. **Mailing address:** PO Box 311, Holton, KS 66436. **Ad Rates:** PCI $5; PCI $6.50. **Remarks:** Accepts advertising. **Circ:** ‡5000, ‡7600.

HUTCHINSON

C KS. Reno Co. On Arkansas River, 45 mi. NW of Wichita. Hutchinson Community College. Wheat storage; flour mills; salt and oil refineries; meat packing plants.

13196 ■ The Garden City Telegram
Harris Enterprise Inc.
1 N Main St.
Hutchinson, KS 67501
General newspaper. **Freq:** Mon.-Sat. **Print Method:** Offset. **Cols./Page:** 6. **Col. Width:** 24 nonpareils. **Col. Depth:** 301 agate lines. **Key Personnel:** Dena Sattler, Editor. **USPS:** 213-600. **Subscription Rates:** $7.95 Individuals /month. **URL:** http://www.gctelegram.com. **Ad Rates:** GLR $1.14; BW $1,171.32; 4C $1,421.32; PCI $9.08. **Remarks:** Accepts advertising. **Circ:** Mon.-Sat. ■ **6657**.

13197 ■ Hutchinson Collegian
Hutchinson Community College
1300 N Plum
Hutchinson, KS 67501
Phone: (620)665-3500
Free: 888-464-8824
Publisher's E-mail: admissions@hutchcc.edu
Collegiate newspaper. **Freq:** Weekly (Thurs.). **Key Personnel:** Alan Montgomery, Faculty Advisor; Daron Hendrickson, Manager, Advertising. **Subscription Rates:** Free. **Ad Rates:** PCI $4.50. **Remarks:** Advertising accepted; rates available upon request. **Circ:** Free ‡1200.

13198 ■ The Hutchinson News
Hutchinson Publishing Co.
300 W 2nd Ave.

Hutchinson, KS 67504-0190
Phone: (620)694-5700
Fax: (620)662-4186
Free: 800-766-3311
Publisher's E-mail: askhutch@hutchnews.com
General newspaper. **Freq:** Mon.-Sun. (morn.). **Print Method:** Offset. **Trim Size:** 11 3/4 x 21 1/2. **Cols./Page:** 6. **Col. Width:** 11 picas. **Col. Depth:** 301 agate lines. **Key Personnel:** Mary Rintoul, Managing Editor; John D. Montgomery, Editor; Jason Probst, Editor. **Subscription Rates:** $16.30 Individuals print and online /month; $7.95 Individuals online only /month; $9.95 Individuals weekend only plus online. **URL:** http://hutchnews.com. **Mailing address:** PO Box 190, Hutchinson, KS 67504-0190. **Ad Rates:** GLR $1.23; BW $2,554.20; 4C $3,021.70; PCI $19.80. **Remarks:** Accepts advertising. **Circ:** Mon.-Sat. ■ **27628**, Sun. ■ **30892**.

13199 ■ KGGG-FM - 94.7
106 N Main St.
Hutchinson, KS 67501
Phone: (620)665-5758
Fax: (620)665-5758
Format: Oldies. **Networks:** ABC. **Owner:** Ad Astra per Aspera Broadcasting, Inc., 10 E 5th Ave., Hutchinson, KS 67501. **Founded:** 1995. **Operating Hours**: Continuous; 100% local. **ADI**: Wichita-Hutchinson, KS. **Wattage**: 20,000. **Ad Rates:** Noncommercial. Combined advertising rates available with KSKU and KXKU. **URL:** http://www.adastraradio.com/.

13200 ■ KHCC-FM - 90.1
815 N Walnut, Ste. 300
Hutchinson, KS 67501
Phone: (620)662-6646
Email: engineers@radiokansas.org
Format: Public Radio. **Networks:** National Public Radio (NPR). **Owner:** Hutchinson Community College, 1300 N Plum, Hutchinson, KS 67501, Ph: (620)665-3500, Free: 888-464-8824. **Founded:** July 01, 1979. **Operating Hours**: Continuous. **Key Personnel:** Ken Baker, Gen. Mgr., kbaker@radiokansas.org; Sharon Webb, Contact, swebb@radiokansas.org; Mark Simmons, Music Dir., msimmons@radiokansas.org; Ric Jung, Dir. of Engg., rjung@radiokansas.org. **Wattage**: 100,000. **Ad Rates:** Noncommercial; underwriting available. **URL:** http://www.radiokansas.org.

13201 ■ KHCD-FM - 89.5
815 N Walnut St., Ste. 300
Hutchinson, KS 67501-6217
Phone: (620)662-6646
Format: Public Radio. **Networks:** National Public Radio (NPR). **Owner:** Hutchinson Community College, 1300 N Plum, Hutchinson, KS 67501, Ph: (620)665-3500, Free: 888-464-8824. **Founded:** 1988. **Operating Hours:** Continuous. **Key Personnel:** Ken Baker, Gen. Mgr., kbaker@radiokansas.org. **Wattage**: 100,000. **Ad Rates:** Noncommercial; underwriting available. **URL:** http://www.radiokansas.org.

13202 ■ KHCT-FM - 90.9
815 N Walnut, Ste. 300
Hutchinson, KS 67501-6389
Format: Public Radio. **Ad Rates:** Advertising accepted; rates available upon request. **URL:** http://www.radiokansas.org/.

13203 ■ KHMY-FM - 93.1
825 N Main St.
Hutchinson, KS 67501
Phone: (620)662-4486
Fax: (620)662-5357
Email: khmy@cox.net
Format: Adult Contemporary. **Owner:** Goodstar Broadcasting L.L.C., 1660 N Tyler, Wichita, KS 67212, Ph: (316)729-8011, Fax: (316)729-9914. **Founded:** 1965. **Operating Hours**: Continuous. **ADI**: Wichita-Hutchinson, KS. **Key Personnel:** Casey Osburn, Music Dir.; Terry Drouhard, Sales Mgr. **Wattage**: 100,000. **Ad Rates:** $8-20 for 30 seconds; $10-30 for 60 seconds. **URL:** http://khmyfm.com.

13204 ■ KHUT-FM - 102.9
825 N Main
Hutchinson, KS 67501
Phone: (620)662-4486
Email: customercare@eaglecom.net
Format: Country. **Owner:** Eagle Communications Inc., 2703 Hall St., Ste. 15, Hays, KS 67601, Ph: (785)625-4000, Fax: (785)625-8030. **Founded:** 1972. **Operating Hours**: Continuous. **ADI**: Wichita-Hutchinson, KS. **Wattage**: 100,000 ERP. **Ad Rates:** Advertising accepted; rates available upon request. **URL:** http://www.eaglecom.net.

13205 ■ K201DL-FM - 88.1
PO Box 391
Twin Falls, ID 83303
Fax: (208)736-1958
Free: 800-357-4226
Format: Religious; Contemporary Christian. **Owner:** CSN International, PO Box 391, Twin Falls, ID 83303, Ph: (208)736-1958, Fax: (208)736-1958, Free: 800-357-4226. **Key Personnel:** Mike Kestler, Contact; Don Mills, Music Dir., Prog. Dir. **URL:** http://www.csnradio.com.

13206 ■ KWBW-AM - 1450
825 N Main
Hutchinson, KS 67501
Phone: (620)662-4486
Fax: (620)662-5357
Email: info@bwradio.biz
Format: Talk; News; Sports. **Networks:** ABC. **Owner:** Eagle Communications Inc., 2703 Hall St., Ste. 15, Hays, KS 67601, Ph: (785)625-4000, Fax: (785)625-8030. **Founded:** 1935. **Formerly**: KWBG-AM. **Operating Hours**: 4 a.m.-1 a.m.; 70% network, 30% local. **ADI**: Wichita-Hutchinson, KS. **Wattage**: 1,000. **Ad Rates:** Noncommercial. **URL:** http://www.bwradio.biz.

13207 ■ KWHK-FM - 95.9
10 E 5th Ave.
Hutchinson, KS 67501
Phone: (620)665-5758
Fax: (620)665-6655
Format: Oldies. **Owner:** Ad Astra per Aspera Broadcasting, Inc., 10 E 5th Ave., Hutchinson, KS 67501. **Wattage**: 5,500. **URL:** http://www.adastraradio.com/kwhk-95.9.html.

13208 ■ KXKU-FM - 97.1
10 E 5th Ave.
Hutchinson, KS 67501
Phone: (620)665-5758
Fax: (620)665-5758
Format: Country. **Networks:** Independent. **Owner:** Ad Astra per Aspera Broadcasting, Inc., 10 E 5th Ave., Hutchinson, KS 67501. **Founded:** 1972. **Formerly**: KSKU-FM. **Operating Hours**: Continuous; 100% local. **ADI**: Wichita-Hutchinson, KS. **Key Personnel:** Lucky Kidd, News Dir.; Mike Hill, Sales Mgr.; Michelle Ray, Production Mgr. **Wattage**: 100,000. **Ad Rates:** $32 for 30 seconds; $36 for 60 seconds. Combined advertising rates available with KGGG-FM. **URL:** http://www.adastraradio.com.

INDEPENDENCE

SE KS. Montgomery Co. 86 mi. SE of Wichita. Independence Community College. Manufactures cement, corn, wheat. Oil and gas wells.

13209 ■ Independence Daily Reporter
Independence Daily Reporter
320 N 6th St.
Independence, KS 67301
Phone: (620)331-3550
General newspaper. **Freq:** Daily and Sun. (eve.). **Print Method:** Offset. **Trim Size:** 14 x 21 3/4. **Cols./Page:** 6. **Col. Width:** 2 1/16 inches. **Col. Depth:** 21 inches. **Key Personnel:** H.A. Meyer, III, Editor; Steve McBride, Manager, Advertising. **Subscription Rates:** $111.95 Individuals home delivery by carrier; $125.95 Individuals by mail; $177.95 Out of area by mail. **URL:** http://www.indydailyreporter.com. **Ad Rates:** GLR $4.50; BW $873.18; 4C $1,068.18; PCI $6.93. **Remarks:** Accepts advertising. **Circ:** Mon.-Fri. 7992, Sun. 8547.

13210 ■ KBQC-FM - 88.5
PO Box 3206
Tupelo, MS 38803
Format: Religious. **Owner:** American Family Association, at above address. **Wattage**: 20,000. **URL:** http://www.afa.net.

13211 ■ K50JG - 50
PO Box A
Santa Ana, CA 92711
Phone: (714)832-2950
Free: 888-731-1000
Owner: Trinity Broadcasting Network Inc., PO Box A, Santa Ana, CA 92711, Ph: (714)832-2950, Free: 888-731-1000. **URL:** http://www.tbn.org.

13212 ■ KIND-AM
122 W Myrtle St.
Independence, KS 67301-3317
Phone: (620)331-3000
Fax: (620)331-8008
Format: Adult Contemporary. **Networks:** Westwood One Radio; CNN Radio. **Owner:** CBI Holdings, Inc. **Founded:** 1947. **Wattage**: 250 Day; 032 Night. **Ad Rates:** $8-18 for 30 seconds; $10-21 for 60 seconds.

IOLA

SE KS. Allen Co. 100 mi. S. of Kansas City. Allen County Community College. Cement works.

13213 ■ The Iola Register
The Iola Register Inc.
302 S Washington Ave.
Iola, KS 66749
Phone: (620)365-2111
Fax: (620)365-6289
Publication E-mail: register@midusa.net
General newspaper. **Freq:** Daily (eve.). **Print Method:** Offset. **Cols./Page:** 6. **Col. Width:** 24 nonpareils. **Col. Depth:** 301 agate lines. **Key Personnel:** Mark Hastings, Manager, Advertising; Susan Lynn, Editor, Publisher. **Subscription Rates:** $110.89 Individuals by carrier /year; $133.29 Individuals motor in trade /year; $135.54 By mail Kansas /year; $145.59 Out of state by mail /year; $105 Individuals online only /year. **URL:** http://www.iolaregister.com. **Mailing address:** PO Box 767, Iola, KS 66749. **Remarks:** Advertising accepted; rates available upon request. **Circ:** Paid 4200, Free 85.

13214 ■ KIKS-FM - 101.5
2221 S State St.
Iola, KS 66749
Phone: (620)365-3151
Fax: (620)365-5431
Email: radiostation@iolaradio.com
Format: Country. **Networks:** Satellite Network News. **Founded:** 1977. **Operating Hours**: 6 a.m.-12 midnight. **Wattage**: 11,500. **Ad Rates:** Advertising accepted; rates available upon request. Combined advertising rates available with $4 for 15 seconds; $6 for 30 seconds; $9 for 60 seconds. Combined advertising rates available with KALN-AM. **Mailing address:** PO Box 710, Iola, KS 66749. **URL:** http://www.iolaradio.com.

JUNCTION CITY

EC KS. Geary Co. On Kansas River, 62 mi. W. of Topeka. Fort Riley (military post). Feed mills; foundry. Grain, stock, and dairy farms.

13215 ■ Daily Union Extra
PO Box 129
Junction City, KS 66441
Shopper. **Freq:** Weekly (Wed.). **Print Method:** Offset. **Cols./Page:** 6. **Col. Width:** 26 nonpareils. **Col. Depth:** 301 agate lines. **Key Personnel:** John G. Montgomery, Publisher; Mike Heronemus, Managing Editor; Penny Nelson, Office Manager; Brian Elliott, Manager, Circulation; Tom Throne, Editor, General Manager. **Subscription Rates:** $100 Individuals walking routes; $106 Individuals motor routes; $116 Individuals outside motor routes; $140 Individuals local mail; $188 Institutions other mail. **URL:** http://www.dailyu.com. **Ad Rates:** BW $813; 4C $1,233; SAU $6.30; PCI $6.30. **Remarks:** Advertising accepted; rates available upon request. **Circ:** (Not Reported).

13216 ■ KANV-FM - 91.3
1120 W 11th St.
Lawrence, KS 66044
Phone: (785)864-4530
Fax: (785)864-5278
Free: 888-577-5268
Format: Public Radio. **Owner:** Kansas Public Radio, 1120 W 11th St., Lawrence, KS 66044, Ph: (785)864-4530, Fax: (785)864-5278, Free: 888-577-5268. **Key Personnel:** Jeff Watson, Contact; Janet Campbell, Gen. Mgr., jcampbell@ku.edu; Bruce Mensie, Chief Engineer; Jason Slote, Production Mgr.; Nicci Banman, Bus. Mgr.

Circulation: ★ = AAM; △ or • = BPA; ♦ = CAC; ❑ = VAC; ⊕ = PO Statement; ‡ = Publisher's Report; Boldface figures = sworn; Light figures = estimated.

URL: http://kansaspublicradio.org.

13217 ■ KJCK-AM - 1420
PO Box 789
Junction City, KS 66441
Phone: (785)762-5525
Email: platinum@kjck.com
Format: News; Talk. **Networks:** ABC. **Owner:** Platinum Broadcasting Inc., 1030 Southwind Dr., Junction City, KS 66441. **Founded:** 1949. **Operating Hours**: Continuous; 50% network, 50% local. **ADI**: Topeka, KS. **Wattage**: 1,000. **Ad Rates:** $9-19.99 for 30 seconds; $12-24 for 60 seconds. KJCK-FM, KQLA-FM. **URL:** http://www.kjck.com.

13218 ■ KJCK-FM - 97.5
1030 S Wind
Junction City, KS 66441
Phone: (785)762-5525
Format: Contemporary Hit Radio (CHR). **Owner:** Platinum Broadcasting Inc., 1030 Southwind Dr., Junction City, KS 66441. **Founded:** 1965. **Operating Hours**: Continuous; 10% network, 90% local. **ADI**: Topeka, KS. **Wattage**: 100,000. **Ad Rates:** $11.88 for 15 seconds; $10-22 for 30 seconds; $12-24 for 60 seconds. Combined advertising rates available with KJCK-AM, KQLA-FM. **URL:** http://www.powerhits975.com.

13219 ■ KQLA-FM - 103.5
1417 N US Hwy. 77
Junction City, KS 66441
Phone: (785)762-5525
Format: Adult Contemporary. **Networks:** ABC. **Owner:** Platinum Broadcasting Inc., 1030 Southwind Dr., Junction City, KS 66441. **Founded:** 1986. **Operating Hours**: Continuous; 95% network, 5% local. **ADI**: Topeka, KS. **Wattage**: 50,000. **Ad Rates:** Noncommercial. KJCK-AM, KJCK-FM. **URL:** http://www.qcountry1035.com.

13220 ■ K25DS - 25
PO Box A
Santa Ana, CA 92711
Phone: (714)832-2950
Free: 888-731-1000
Owner: Trinity Broadcasting Network Inc., PO Box A, Santa Ana, CA 92711, Ph: (714)832-2950, Free: 888-731-1000.

KANSAS CITY

NW KS. Wyandotte Co. At junction of Missouri and Kansas Rivers, adjacent to Kansas City, MO. Central Baptist Theological Seminary; School of Medicine of University of Kansas. Manufactures fiberglass, cement, paper products, chemicals, brick, tile. Auto assembly plant; oil refining; canning; flour and grain milling. Livestock markets and meat packing plants. Ships corn, wheat, sorghum, and oats.

13221 ■ The Advocate
Kansas City Kansas Community College
7250 State Ave.
Kansas City, KS 66112
Phone: (913)334-1100
Publisher's E-mail: admiss@kckcc.edu
Collegiate newspaper (tabloid). **Founded:** 1969. **Freq:** Semimonthly. **Print Method:** Offset. **Trim Size:** 11 x 13. **Cols./Page:** 4. **Col. Width:** 2 5/16 inches. **Col. Depth:** 16 inches. **Key Personnel:** Bryan Whitehead, Contact. **Subscription Rates:** Free. **URL:** http://www.kckcc.edu/campus-life/student-activities-II/clubs-and-organizations. **Ad Rates:** GLR $.30; BW $135; PCI $5. **Remarks:** Color advertising not accepted. **Circ:** Free ‡2000.

13222 ■ Boilermaker Reporter
International Brotherhood of Boilermakers
753 State Ave., Ste. 570
Kansas City, KS 66101
Phone: (913)371-2640
Fax: (913)281-8104
Newspaper covering trade and union membership news. **Freq:** Quarterly. **Print Method:** Web Offset. **Trim Size:** 10.5 x 16. **Cols./Page:** 4. **Col. Width:** 14 picas. **Col. Depth:** 84 picas. **Key Personnel:** Donald Caswell, Managing Editor; Newton B. Jones, Editor-in-Chief; Carey Allen, Director. **ISSN:** 1078--4101 (print). **Subscription Rates:** $10 Individuals; Included in membership; free for members.; $10 Nonmembers 3 year subscription. **Alt. Formats:** PDF. **URL:** http://www.boilermakers.org/resources/reporter; http://www.boilermakers.org/news/reporter. **Remarks:** Advertising not accepted. **Circ:** Non-paid 85000, 75000.

13223 ■ Dos Mundos Bilingual Newspaper: Dos Mundos Two Worlds
Dos Mondos Bilingual Newspaper
1701 S 55 St.
Kansas City, KS 66106
Phone: (816)221-4747
Fax: (913)287-5881
Publication E-mail: mreyes@dosmundos.com
Community Bilingual Newspaper (Spanish & English). **Freq:** 50/yr. **Cols./Page:** 8. **Col. Width:** 1 1/2 inches. **Col. Depth:** 1 inches. **Key Personnel:** Clara Reyes, Editor; Manuel Reyes, Publisher; Diana Raymer, Director, Advertising. **Subscription Rates:** $45 Individuals /year. **URL:** http://dosmundos.com/webpress. **Formerly**: Dos Mundos Newspaper. **Ad Rates:** BW $2352; SAU $9; PCI $14. **Remarks:** Accepts advertising. **Circ:** (Not Reported).

13224 ■ International Journal of Neuroscience
Informa Healthcare
c/o Kelly E. Lyons PhD, Co-Editor-in-Chief
University of Kansas Medical Center
Parkinson's Disease & Movement Disorder Center
3599 Rainbow Blvd., Mailstop 2012
Kansas City, KS 66160
Phone: (913)588-7159
Fax: (913)588-6920
Publisher's E-mail: healthcare.enquiries@informa.com
Journal focusing on problems of nervous tissue, the nervous system, and behavior. **Freq:** Monthly. **Key Personnel:** Kelly E. Lyons, PhD, Editor-in-Chief; Rajesh Pahwa, MD, Editor-in-Chief. **ISSN:** 0020--7454 (print); **EISSN:** 1543--5245 (electronic). **Subscription Rates:** $10038 Institutions online only; $10566 Institutions print and online. **URL:** http://informahealthcare.com/journal/nes; http://informahealthcare.com/nes. **Remarks:** Accepts advertising. **Circ:** ‡150.

13225 ■ Journal of the Grant Professionals Association
Grant Professionals Association
1333 Meadowlark Ln., Ste. 105
Kansas City, KS 66102-1200
Phone: (913)788-3000
Fax: (913)788-3398
Publisher's E-mail: staff@grantprofessionals.org
Freq: Annual. **URL:** http://www.grantprofessionals.org/journal. **Remarks:** Advertising not accepted. **Circ:** (Not Reported).

13226 ■ Kansas City Kansan
Kansas City Kansan
7815 State Ave.
Kansas City, KS 66112
General newspaper. **Founded:** 1921. **Freq:** Daily Tues.-Fri. (eve.); Sun. (morn.). **Print Method:** Offset. **Cols./Page:** 6. **Col. Width:** 24 nonpareils. **Col. Depth:** 301 agate lines. **Key Personnel:** Nick Sloan, Publisher. **USPS:** 290-160. **Subscription Rates:** $23.55 Individuals Wyandotte County, 3 months; $44.75 Individuals Wyandotte County, 6 months; $84.79 Individuals Wyandotte County; $20.72 Individuals senior (60 yrs. above), 3 months; $39.37 Individuals senior (60 yrs. above), 6 months; $74.63 Individuals senior (60 yrs. above); $33.25 Out of country 3 months; $63.40 Out of country 6 months; $107.44 Out of country. **URL:** http://www.kckansan.com/. **Ad Rates:** SAU $11.25. **Remarks:** Accepts advertising. **Circ:** Mon.-Fri. ‡11027, Sun. ‡12100.

13227 ■ Kansas City Wyandotte Echo
Kansas City Wyandotte Echo
PO Box 2305
Kansas City, KS 66110-2305
Phone: (913)573-5000
Community newspaper. **Freq:** Weekly (Thurs.). **Cols./Page:** 5. **Col. Width:** 2 inches. **Col. Depth:** 18 inches. **Key Personnel:** Jon Males, Editor; Roberta Peterson, Publisher. **URL:** http://www.wyandotteecho.com. **Circ:** 1600.

13228 ■ The Leaven: Official newspaper of the Catholic Archidiocese of Kansas City in Kansas
The Leaven
12615 Parallel Pky.
Kansas City, KS 66109
Phone: (913)721-1570
Publisher's E-mail: jennifer@theleaven.com
Catholic newspaper. **Freq:** Weekly every Friday. **Key Personnel:** Joe Bollig, Reporter; Anita McSorley, Associate Editor; Fr. Mark Goldasich, Editor; Todd Habiger, Manager, Production. **ISSN:** 0194--9799 (print). **Subscription Rates:** $21 Individuals. **Formerly**: Eastern Kansas Register. **Ad Rates:** GLR $8; BW $1,280; PCI $17.50. **Remarks:** Accepts advertising. **Circ:** Paid ‡52800.

13229 ■ Piano Technicians Journal
Piano Technicians Guild
4444 Forest Ave.
Kansas City, KS 66106-3750
Phone: (913)432-9975
Fax: (913)432-9986
Publication E-mail: ptg@ptg.org
Magazine for piano technicians. **Freq:** Monthly. **Print Method:** Offset. **Trim Size:** 8 1/2 x 11. **Cols./Page:** 3. **Col. Width:** 28 nonpareils. **Col. Depth:** 140 agate lines. **Key Personnel:** Steve Brady, Editor. **ISSN:** 0031--9562 (print). **Subscription Rates:** $150 Individuals; $150 /year; $10 Single issue. **Alt. Formats:** CD-ROM; PDF. **URL:** http://www.ptg.org/scripts/4disapi.dll/4DCGI/cms/review.html?Action=CMS_Document&DocID=16&MenuKey=Menu4. **Ad Rates:** GLR $.40; BW $688. **Remarks:** Advertising accepted; rates available upon request. **Circ:** 4000, 4200.

13230 ■ The Piper Press
Wyandotte West Communications Inc.
7735 Washington Ave.
Kansas City, KS 66112
Community newspaper. **Freq:** Weekly (Thurs.). **Print Method:** Offset. **Trim Size:** 11 x 17. **Cols./Page:** 4. **Col. Width:** 13.6 picas. **Col. Depth:** 16 inches. **Key Personnel:** Joe Keefhaver, Editor, General Manager; Jamie Ralston, Manager, Marketing and Sales. **USPS:** 020-388. **Subscription Rates:** $24.25 Individuals; $47.10 Two years. **URL:** http://wyandottewest.blogspot.com/. **Mailing address:** PO Box 12003, Kansas City, KS 66112. **Ad Rates:** GLR $.79; BW $717; 4C $858; SAU $11.20; CNU $11.20; PCI $13.23. **Remarks:** Accepts advertising. **Circ:** (Not Reported).

13231 ■ The Record
The Record Publications
3414 Strong Ave.
Kansas City, KS 66106
Phone: (913)362-1988
Publication E-mail: news@recordnews.com
Newspaper (tabloid). **Founded:** 1887. **Freq:** Weekly (Wed.). **Print Method:** Web offset. Uses mats. **Trim Size:** 11 x 17. **Cols./Page:** 5. **Col. Width:** 22 nonpareils. **Col. Depth:** 224 agate lines. **Subscription Rates:** $10.55 By mail. **URL:** http://www.recordnews.com/html/newscenter/centennial_book_coin.html. **Mailing address:** PO Box 6197, Kansas City, KS 66106. **Ad Rates:** SAU $6.50. **Remarks:** Accepts advertising. **Circ:** ‡1000.

13232 ■ Sacred Ground
Unbound
1 Elmwood Ave.
Kansas City, KS 66103-2118
Phone: (913)384-6500
Fax: (913)384-2211
Free: 800-875-6564
Publisher's E-mail: mail@unbound.org
Freq: Semiannual. **Mailing address:** PO Box 219114, Kansas City, MO 64121-9114. **Remarks:** Advertising not accepted. **Circ:** (Not Reported).

13233 ■ The Wyandotte West
Wyandotte West Communications Inc.
7735 Washington Ave.
Kansas City, KS 66112
Publication E-mail: wywest@toto.net
Community newspaper. **Freq:** Weekly (Thurs.). **Print Method:** Offset. **Trim Size:** 11 x 17. **Cols./Page:** 4. **Col. Width:** 13.6 picas. **Col. Depth:** 16 inches. **Key Personnel:** Marcy Manion, General Manager; Richard Ward, Publisher; Meghan Saint, Manager, Production. **USPS:** 693-720. **Subscription Rates:** $25 Individuals; $48 Two years. **URL:** http://wyandottewest.blogspot.com. **Mailing address:** PO Box 12003, Kansas City, KS 66112. **Ad Rates:** GLR $.79; BW $717; 4C $858; SAU $11.20; CNU $11.20; PCI $11.20. **Remarks:** Advertising accepted; rates available upon request. **Circ:** (Not Reported).

13234 ■ KCNW-AM - 1380
4535 Metropolitan Ave.
Kansas City, KS 66106
Phone: (913)384-1380
Email: info@wilkinsradio.com
Format: Contemporary Christian; Talk. **Owner:** Wilkins Communications Network Inc., 292 S Pine St., Spartanburg, SC 29302, Ph: (864)585-1885, Fax: (864)597-0687, Free: 888-989-2299. **Operating Hours:** Continuous. **Key Personnel:** Kevin Fears, Station Mgr. **Wattage:** 2,500. **Ad Rates:** Noncommercial. **URL:** http://www.wilkinsradio.com.

13235 ■ KDTD-AM - 1340
PO Box 6368
Kansas City, KS 66106
Format: Hispanic. **Networks:** NBC. **ADI:** Kansas City, MO (Lawrence, KS). **URL:** http://perezmediagroup.com/.

13236 ■ KKHK-AM - 1250
813 S 7th St.
Kansas City, KS 66105
Phone: (913)788-1255
Fax: (913)788-1254
Email: sales@lasuperx1250.com
Format: Hispanic. **Founded:** Sept. 13, 2006. **Ad Rates:** Noncommercial.

KIOWA

S KS. Barber Co. 90 mi. SW of Wichita. Manufactures farm implements. Grain, stock, and poultry farms.

13237 ■ News
Kiowa News
614 Main St.
Kiowa, KS 67070
Phone: (620)825-4431
Publication E-mail: cdupuis@kiva.net
Community newspaper. **Founded:** 1958. **Freq:** Weekly (Thurs.). **Print Method:** Offset. **Cols./Page:** 6 and 8. **Col. Width:** 30 and 21 nonpareils. **Col. Depth:** 294 and 301 agate lines. **USPS:** 695-160. **Subscription Rates:** $9.50 Individuals; $27 Individuals; $12 Individuals; $13; $15.50 Individuals; $18.50 Out of area; $21.50 Out of state; $11.50. **Formerly**: Yale Record. **Ad Rates:** GLR $.264; GLR $.19; PCI $3.50; GLR $.17; GLR $.35; SAU $4.82; BW $348.30; 4C $903.15; SAU $3.00; PCI $2.70; GLR $.311; SAU $4.35. **Circ:** ‡1100, 3200, 1650, ‡3250, Paid ‡1472, Free ‡52, 2000.

LA CROSSE

WC KS. Rush Co. 90 mi. NW of Hutchinson. Oil and gas wells. Diversified agriculture.

13238 ■ The Rush County News
The Rush County News
112 W 8th
La Crosse, KS 67548
Phone: (785)222-2555
Publisher's E-mail: rcn@gbta.net
Weekly newspaper. **Freq:** Weekly (Thurs.). **Print Method:** Offset. Uses slicks. **Trim Size:** 13 3/4 x 22 3/4. **Cols./Page:** 6. **Col. Width:** 12.5 picas. **Col. Depth:** 21.5 inches. **Key Personnel:** Mary Engel, Publisher; Tim Engel, Managing Editor. **URL:** http://therushcountynews.com. **Ad Rates:** GLR $.24; BW $535.35; 4C $835.35; SAU $3.95; PCI $3.95. **Remarks:** Accepts advertising. **Circ:** Paid ‡2100, Free ‡200.

LAKIN

SW KS. Kearny Co. On Arkansas River, 70 mi. NW of Dodge City. Gas and oil wells.

13239 ■ KSWK-TV - 3
604 Elm St.
Bunker Hill, KS 67626
Phone: (785)483-6990
Fax: (785)483-4605
Format: Public TV. **Networks:** Public Broadcasting Service (PBS). **Owner:** Smoky Hills Public Television, 604 Elm St., Bunker Hill, KS 67626, Ph: (785)483-6990, Fax: (785)483-4605. **Founded:** 1989. **Operating Hours:** 20 HRS Daily; 77% network, 1% local, 22% other. **ADI:** Wichita-Hutchinson, KS. **Key Personnel:** Glenna Letsch, Dir. of Traffic, gletsch@shptv.org. **Wattage:** 100,000. **Ad Rates:** Noncommercial. **Mailing address:** PO Box 9, Bunker Hill, KS 67626. **URL:** http://www.shptv.org.

LAWRENCE

E KS. Douglas Co. On Kansas River, 26 mi. SE of Topeka. University of Kansas; Haskell Institute (Indian). Manufactures railroad and truck air brakes, paper shipping cartons, fertilizers, chemicals, explosives, precision instruments, mobile homes, electronics equipment. Pharmaceutical research. Diversified farming.

13240 ■ American Journal of Cosmetic Surgery
Allen Marketing and Management
PO Box 1897
Lawrence, KS 66044-8897
Journal for professionals in cosmetic surgery. **Freq:** Quarterly. **Trim Size:** 8 1/2 x 11. **Key Personnel:** Jane A. Petro, MD, FACS. **ISSN:** 0748--8068 (print); **EISSN:** 2374--7722 (electronic). **Subscription Rates:** $250 Individuals print only; $255 Individuals print and online; $283 Institutions online only; $308 Institutions print only; $314 Institutions print and online. **URL:** http://acs.sagepub.com. **Ad Rates:** BW $1167.90; 4C $1004.70. **Remarks:** Accepts advertising. **Circ:** ‡3000, ‡2957.

13241 ■ Biodiversity Informatics
Cottonwood Magazine and Press
1301 Jayhawk Blvd., Rm. 400
Lawrence, KS 66045-7593
Phone: (785)864-2516
Publisher's E-mail: email@ku.edu
Open access, online academic journal that focuses on the emerging field of biodiversity informatics. **Freq:** Continuous. **Key Personnel:** Townsend A. Peterson, Editor; Jorge Soberon, Editor; Robert P. Guralnick, Editor. **ISSN:** 1546--9735 (print). **Subscription Rates:** Free to qualified subscribers online. **URL:** http://journals.ku.edu/index.php/jbi. **Circ:** (Not Reported).

13242 ■ The Bryologist
Allen Press Inc.
810 E Tenth St.
Lawrence, KS 66044
Phone: (785)843-1234
Free: 800-627-0326
Publisher's E-mail: sales@allenpress.com
Journal on the study of bryophytes and lichens. **Freq:** Quarterly. **Print Method:** Offset. **Cols./Page:** 2. **Col. Width:** 30 nonpareils. **Col. Depth:** 112 agate lines. **Key Personnel:** Bernard Goffinet, Editor-in-Chief; Robin Kimmerer, Associate Editor; Bruce McCune, Associate Editor; Scott LaGreca, Editor; Steven K. Rice, Editor; Andrew J. Wood, Associate Editor. **ISSN:** 0007--2745 (print). **URL:** http://psfebus.allenpress.com/abls/JOURNALS/THEBRYOLOGISTATBIOONEJSTOR.aspx. **Mailing address:** PO Box 368, Lawrence, KS 66044-0368. **Circ:** Paid ‡900.

13243 ■ Chelonian Conservation and Biology: International Journal of Turtle and Tortoise Research
Allen Press Inc.
810 E Tenth St.
Lawrence, KS 66044
Phone: (785)843-1234
Free: 800-627-0326
Publisher's E-mail: sales@allenpress.com
Peer-reviewed scientific journal covering turtle and tortoise research. **Freq:** Semiannual. **Key Personnel:** Anders G.J. Rhodin, Editor. **ISSN:** 1071--8443 (print). **Subscription Rates:** $90 Individuals print and online; $115 Other countries print and online; $300 Institutions print and online; $340 Institutions, other countries print and online; $80 Individuals online; $265 Institutions online. **URL:** http://www.chelonianjournals.org; http://www.chelonian.org/ccb. **Mailing address:** PO Box 368, Lawrence, KS 66044-0368. **Circ:** (Not Reported).

13244 ■ Combinatorial Chemistry & High Throughput Screening
Bentham Science Publishers Ltd.
c/o Rathnam Chaguturu, Ed.-in-Ch.
University of Kansas
2034 Becker Dr.
Lawrence, KS 66047
Publisher's E-mail: subscriptions@benthamscience.org
Journal covering articles on robotics and informatics. **Freq:** 10/year. **Key Personnel:** Rathnam Chaguturu, Editor-in-Chief. **ISSN:** 1386--2073 (print); **EISSN:** 1875--5402 (electronic). **URL:** http://benthamscience.com/journals/combinatorial-chemistry-and-high-throughput-screening. **Remarks:** Accepts advertising. **Circ:** (Not Reported).

13245 ■ Copeia
American Society of Ichthyologists and Herpetologists
PO Box 1897
Lawrence, KS 66044-8897
Phone: (785)843-1235
Fax: (785)843-1274
Free: 800-627-0326
Publication E-mail: asih@allenpress.com
Scientific journal covering original research of members on fish, amphibians, and reptiles as study organisms. **Freq:** Quarterly February, May, August and December. **ISSN:** 0045--8511 (print). **Subscription Rates:** $160 Institutions and library, e-journal; $200 Institutions and library, paper and e-journal; Included in membership. **URL:** http://www.asih.org/publications/copeia. **Remarks:** Advertising not accepted. **Circ:** 3700.

13246 ■ Current Research in Earth Sciences
Kansas Geological Survey
1930 Constant Ave.
Lawrence, KS 66047-3726
Phone: (785)864-3965
Fax: (785)864-5317
Peer-reviewed journal dealing with the midcontinental earth-science research. **Freq:** Annual. **Key Personnel:** Rex C. Buchanan, Associate Director. **URL:** http://www.kgs.ku.edu/Current. **Formerly**: Current Research on Kansas Geology. **Circ:** (Not Reported).

13247 ■ Herpetological Monographs
Allen Press Inc.
810 E Tenth St.
Lawrence, KS 66044
Phone: (785)843-1234
Free: 800-627-0326
Publisher's E-mail: sales@allenpress.com
Journal covering amphibians and reptiles research. **Freq:** Annual. **ISSN:** 0733--1347 (print). **Subscription Rates:** $499 Institutions print and online; $425 Institutions online only; $540 Institutions, other countries print and online; Included in membership. **URL:** http://hljournals.org. **Mailing address:** PO Box 368, Lawrence, KS 66044-0368. **Circ:** (Not Reported).

13248 ■ Journal of Avian Medicine and Surgery
Allen Press Inc.
810 E Tenth St.
Lawrence, KS 66044
Phone: (785)843-1234
Free: 800-627-0326
Publisher's E-mail: sales@allenpress.com
Medical journal for veterinarians treating birds, students and technicians with an interest in the field. **Freq:** Quarterly. **Key Personnel:** Kristen Anderson, Managing Editor; James W. Carpenter, Editor-in-Chief. **ISSN:** 1082-6742 (print). **Subscription Rates:** $240 U.S. and Canada; $260 Other countries. **URL:** http://www.aav.org/?page=jamshome. **Mailing address:** PO Box 368, Lawrence, KS 66044-0368. **Ad Rates:** 4C $1,045, full page; 4C $650, half page - vertical or horizontal; BW $770, full page; BW $450, half page - vertical or horizontal. **Remarks:** Accepts advertising. **Circ:** (Not Reported).

13249 ■ Journal of Coastal Research
Allen Press Inc.
810 E Tenth St.
Lawrence, KS 66044
Phone: (785)843-1234
Free: 800-627-0326
Publisher's E-mail: sales@allenpress.com
Journal covering coastal research. **Freq:** Bimonthly. **Key Personnel:** Barbara Russell, Assistant Editor; Dr. Charles W. Finkl, Editor-in-Chief; Tracy Candelaria, Managing Editor. **ISSN:** 0749--0208 (print); **EISSN:** 1551--5036 (electronic). **Subscription Rates:** $173 Individuals print and online; $194 Other countries print and online; $475 Institutions print and online; $499 Institutions, other countries print and online; $116 Individuals online only; $420 Institutions online only. **URL:** http://www.jcronline.org. **Mailing address:** PO Box 368, Lawrence, KS 66044-0368. **Circ:** (Not Reported).

Circulation: ∗ = AAM; △ or • = BPA; ♦ = CAC; ❑ = VAC; ⊕ = PO Statement; ‡ = Publisher's Report; Boldface figures = sworn; Light figures = estimated.

13250 ■ Journal of Endovascular Therapy
Allen Press Inc.
810 E Tenth St.
Lawrence, KS 66044
Phone: (785)843-1234
Free: 800-627-0326
Publisher's E-mail: sales@allenpress.com
Peer-reviewed journal covering endovascular therapy. **Freq:** Bimonthly. **Key Personnel:** Edward B. Diethrich, Editor-in-Chief; Thomas J. Fogarty, Editor-in-Chief. **ISSN:** 1526--6028 (print); **EISSN:** 1545--1550 (electronic). **Subscription Rates:** $303 Individuals print & e-access; $616 Institutions e-access; $615 Institutions e-access (Content through 1998); $670 Institutions print only; $684 Institutions all online content; $752 Institutions current volume print & all online content; $66 Individuals single print; $123 Institutions single print. **URL:** http://jet.sagepub.com. **Mailing address:** PO Box 368, Lawrence, KS 66044-0368. **Ad Rates:** BW $1625; 4C $1775. **Remarks:** Accepts advertising. **Circ:** Paid ‡1340.

13251 ■ Journal of Herpetological Medicine and Surgery
Association of Reptilian and Amphibian Veterinarians
810 E 10th St.
Lawrence, KS 66044
Phone: (480)703-4941
Publisher's E-mail: info@arav.org
Journal covering issues for reptile and amphibian veterinarians. **Freq:** Quarterly. **Key Personnel:** Thomas H. Boyer, Editor; Wilbur B. Amand, Managing Editor; Mark A. Mitchell, Editor-in-Chief. **ISSN:** 1529--9651 (print). **Subscription Rates:** Included in membership. **URL:** http://arav.org/publication; http://jherpmedsurg.com. **Mailing address:** PO Box 1897 , Lawrence, KS 66044. **Remarks:** Advertising accepted; rates available upon request. **Circ:** 1200.

13252 ■ Journal of the Kansas Entomological Society
Allen Press Inc.
c/o Larry R. Kipp, Ed.
University of Kansas
Snow Hall
1460 Jayhawk Blvd.
Lawrence, KS 66045-7523
Publisher's E-mail: sales@allenpress.com
Entomology journal. **Freq:** Quarterly. **Print Method:** Letterpress and offset. **Cols./Page:** 1. **Col. Width:** 48 nonpareils. **Col. Depth:** 98 agate lines. **Key Personnel:** Larry R. Kipp, Editor. **ISSN:** 0022--8567 (print). **URL:** http://www.jstor.org/journals/00228567.html. **Circ:** 950.

13253 ■ Journal of Pharmaceutical Sciences
APhA Academy of Pharmacy Practice and Management
c/o Dr. Ronald T. Borchardt, Ed.-in-Ch.
Dept. of Pharmaceutical Chemistry
The University of Kansas
2095 Constant Ave., Rm. 121A
Lawrence, KS 66047
Phone: (785)864-5919
Fax: (785)864-5875
Publisher's E-mail: infocenter@aphanet.org
Freq: Monthly. **Print Method:** Offset. **Trim Size:** 8 1/4 x 11. **Cols./Page:** 2. **Col. Width:** 3 1/2 inches. **Col. Depth:** 9 1/2 inches. **Key Personnel:** Dr. Ronald T. Borchardt, Editor-in-Chief; Bradley D. Anderson, Editor; Harry Brittain, Editor. **ISSN:** 0022--3549 (print); **EISSN:** 1520--6017 (electronic). **Subscription Rates:** $2217 Institutions online only; $408 Individuals online only; included in membership dues; $396 Nonmembers online only; $2097 Institutions in US, Canada and Mexico (online only); £1166 Institutions online only; €1475 Institutions online only. **URL:** http://onlinelibrary.wiley.com/journal/10.1002/(ISSN)1520-6017; http://www.pharmacist.com/journal-pharmaceutical-sciences; http://www.fip.org/pharmaceutical_sciences; http://onlinelibrary.wiley.com/journal/10.1002/%28ISSN%291520-6017. **Ad Rates:** $795-320. BW $795; 4C $1,040; BW $. **Remarks:** Accepts advertising. **Circ:** Paid ‡5000, Non-paid ‡120, Combined ‡2196, 6,000.

13254 ■ Journal of Wildlife Diseases
Wildlife Disease Association
PO Box 7065
Lawrence, KS 66044-7065
Phone: (785)865-9403
Fax: (785)843-6153
Free: 800-627-0326
Publisher's E-mail: wda@allenpress.com
Journal dealing with all kinds of diseases of wildlife. **Freq:** Quarterly. **Key Personnel:** James N. Mills, Editor. **ISSN:** 0090--3558 (print). **URL:** http://www.jwildlifedis.org. **Circ:** (Not Reported).

13255 ■ Journal-World
Journal-World
609 New Hampshire St.
Lawrence, KS 66044
Phone: (785)843-1000
Fax: (785)843-4512
Free: 800-578-8748
Publication E-mail: webmaster@ljworld.com news@ljworld.com
General newspaper. **Freq:** Mon.-Sun. (morn.). **Print Method:** Offset. **Trim Size:** 13 3/8 x 22. **Cols./Page:** 6. **Col. Width:** 26 nonpareils. **Col. Depth:** 301 agate lines. **Key Personnel:** Dennis Anderson, Managing Editor. **Subscription Rates:** $18.25 Individuals /month. **URL:** http://www2.ljworld.com/. **Mailing address:** PO Box 888, Lawrence, KS 66044. **Remarks:** Accepts advertising. **Circ:** (Not Reported).

13256 ■ Kansas Alumni
University of Kansas Alumni Association
1266 Oread Ave.
Lawrence, KS 66045
Phone: (785)864-4760
Fax: (785)864-5397
Free: 800-584-2957
Publisher's E-mail: kualumni@kualumni.org
University alumni magazine (tabloid). **Freq:** 8/yr (during the academic year). **Print Method:** Offset. **Trim Size:** 11 1/2 x 16. **Cols./Page:** 4. **Col. Width:** 28 nonpareils. **Col. Depth:** 171 agate lines. **Key Personnel:** Jennifer Jackson Sanner, Editor; Steven Hill, Associate Editor. **ISSN:** 0745--3345 (print). **Subscription Rates:** Included in membership. **URL:** http://www.kualumni.org/kansas-alumni-magazine/. **Remarks:** Accepts advertising. **Circ:** Paid ‡30000, Non-paid ‡1500.

13257 ■ Kansas Journal of Law and Public Policy
University of Kansas School of Law
Green Hall
1535 W 15th St.
Lawrence, KS 66045
Phone: (785)864-4550
Publisher's E-mail: admitlaw@ku.edu
Journal containing articles on legal issues in the society. **Freq:** 3/year. **Key Personnel:** Lauren Thomas, Editor-in-Chief. **URL:** http://law.ku.edu/lawjournal. **Circ:** (Not Reported).

13258 ■ Latin American Theatre Review
University of Kansas - College of Liberal Arts and Sciences - International and Interdisciplinary Studies Division Center for Latin American and Caribbean Studies
Bailey Hall, Rm. 320
1440 Jayhawk Blvd.
Lawrence, KS 66045-7574
Phone: (785)864-4213
Publisher's E-mail: latamst@ku.edu
Journal covering Spanish and Portuguese theatre in the U.S. **Founded:** 1967. **Freq:** Semiannual. **Key Personnel:** Dr. Stuart Day, Editor; Jacquelyn E. Bixler, Associate Editor. **ISSN:** 0023-8813 (print). **Subscription Rates:** $25 Individuals print; $65 Institutions print. **URL:** http://latamst.ku.edu/latin-american-theatre-review; http://journals.ku.edu/index.php/latr. **Remarks:** Advertising not accepted. **Circ:** Paid 1100.

13259 ■ Lawrence Journal-World
The Lawrence Journal-World W.C. Simons
609 New Hampshire
Lawrence, KS 66044
Phone: (785)832-1000
Fax: (785)843-4512
Free: 800-578-8748
General newspaper. **Freq:** Mon.-Sun. **Key Personnel:** Dennis Anderson, Managing Editor, phone: (785)832-7194. **Subscription Rates:** $18.25 Individuals /month. **URL:** http://www2.ljworld.com. **Mailing address:** PO Box 888, Lawrence, KS 66044. **Remarks:** Advertising accepted; rates available upon request. **Circ:** Mon.-Sat. ★18840, Sun. ★18840.

13260 ■ Macroeconomic Dynamics
Cambridge University Press
c/o William A. Barnett, Ed.
University of Kansas
Dept. of Economics, Snow Hall, Rm. 356
1460 Jayhawk Blvd.
Lawrence, KS 66045-7585
Publisher's E-mail: newyork@cambridge.org
Journal covering theoretical, empirical, and quantitative research in macroeconomics. **Founded:** 1982. **Freq:** 8/year. **Print Method:** Offset. **Trim Size:** 8 1/8 x 10 3/4. **Cols./Page:** 3. **Col. Width:** 120 picas. **Col. Depth:** 58.5 picas. **Key Personnel:** Michele Boldrin, Editor; Prof. Gregory D. Hess, Editor; William A. Barnett, Editor. **ISSN:** 1365-1005 (print); **EISSN:** 1469-8056 (electronic). **Subscription Rates:** $743 Institutions online; $1018 Institutions online & print; $236 Individuals online and print; £454 Institutions online; £614 Institutions online and print; £134 Individuals online and print; $45 Single issue; £30 Single issue. **URL:** http://journals.cambridge.org/action/displayJournal?jid=MDY. **Ad Rates:** BW $845. **Remarks:** Accepts advertising. **Circ:** 500.

13261 ■ Model for Process in the Soil
Catena Verlag
PO Box 1897
Lawrence, KS 66044-8897
Phone: (913)843-1221
Fax: (913)843-1274
Journal concerning the modelling of the micro- and macroscale processes in the systems of the geo-biosphere. **Freq:** Quarterly. **Key Personnel:** Y. Mualem, Editor. **ISSN:** 0938--9563 (print). **Subscription Rates:** $132. **Formerly:** Modelling of Geo-Biosphere Processes. **Circ:** (Not Reported).

13262 ■ Mycologia
Mycological Society of America
PO Box 1897
Lawrence, KS 66044-8897
Fax: (785)843-6153
Free: 800-627-0326
Publisher's E-mail: msa@allenpress.com
Official journal of the Mycological Society of America. Features primary research and review articles on fungi and lichens (English and Latin). **Freq:** Bimonthly. **Print Method:** Offset. **Trim Size:** 8.5 x 11. **Cols./Page:** 21. **Col. Width:** 16 nonpareils. **Col. Depth:** 112 agate lines. **Key Personnel:** Dr. Christopher L. Schardl, Executive Editor. **ISSN:** 0027--5514 (print); **EISSN:** 1557--2536 (electronic). **Subscription Rates:** $402 Institutions print & online; $435 Institutions, other countries print & online; $341 Institutions online only. **URL:** http://www.mycologia.org. **Ad Rates:** BW $600. **Remarks:** Advertising accepted; rates available upon request. **Circ:** ‡2100.

13263 ■ PALAIOS
SEPM Publications
University of Kansas
Paleontological Institute, Department of Geology
1475 Jawyhawk Blvd., Rm. 120
Lawrence, KS 66045-7613
Phone: (785)864-2737
Fax: (785)864-3636
Publication E-mail: palois@ku.edu
Journal providing information on the impact of life on Earth history as recorded in the paleontological and sedimentological records. Covers areas such as biogeochemistry, ichnology, sedimentology, stratigraphy, paleoecology, paleoclimatology, and paleoceanography. **Founded:** 1986. **Freq:** Semimonthly Continuous (print) every Feb, Apr, June, Aug, Oct, and Dec online. **Key Personnel:** Edith L. Taylor, Editor; Thomas Olszewski, Editor. **ISSN:** 0883-1351 (print). **Subscription Rates:** $500 Individuals for U.S.; online version with CD-ROM; $740 Individuals for U.S.; print and online version with CD-ROM; $620 Other countries online version with CD-ROM; $860 Other countries print and online version with CD-ROM; Included in membership. **URL:** http://palaios.ku.edu/; http://palaios.geoscienceworld.org/. **Circ:** (Not Reported).

13264 ■ Rangelands
Allen Press Inc.
810 E Tenth St.
Lawrence, KS 66044
Phone: (785)843-1234
Free: 800-627-0326
Publisher's E-mail: sales@allenpress.com

Journal for the Society for Range Management. **Freq:** Bimonthly. **ISSN:** 0190--0528 (print). **Mailing address:** PO Box 368, Lawrence, KS 66044-0368. **Remarks:** Accepts advertising. **Circ:** (Not Reported).

13265 ■ The Sociological Quarterly: Official Journal of the Midwest Sociological Society
Midwest Sociological Society
Dept. of Sociology
Fraser Hall, 1415 Jayhawk Blvd., Rm. 716
University of Kansas
Lawrence, KS 66045-7556
Phone: (785)864-4442
Publication E-mail: tsq@ku.edu
Journal publishing cutting-edge research and theory in all areas of sociological inquiry. **Freq:** Quarterly. **Print Method:** Offset. **Trim Size:** 6 7/8 x 10. **Key Personnel:** Betty A. Dobratz, Editor. **ISSN:** 0038--0253 (print); **EISSN:** 1533--8525 (electronic). **Subscription Rates:** $670 Institutions Americas (print plus online); £405 Institutions UK (print plus online); €512 Institutions Europe (print plus online); $785 Institutions, other countries rest of the world (print plus online); $558 Institutions Americas (print or online); £337 Institutions UK (print or online); €426 Institutions Europe (print or online); $654 Institutions, other countries rest of the world (print or online). **URL:** http://onlinelibrary.wiley.com/journal/10.1111/(ISSN)1533-8525; http://www.themss.org/TSQ.html. **Ad Rates:** BW $412. **Remarks:** Accepts advertising. **Circ:** (Not Reported).

13266 ■ Sportsturf
Sports Turf Managers Association
805 New Hampshire St., Ste. E
Lawrence, KS 66044
Phone: (785)843-2549
Fax: (785)843-2977
Free: 800-323-3875
Magazine covering sports field management practices, emerging technologies and research. **Freq:** Monthly. **Key Personnel:** Eric Schroder, Editor. **URL:** http://www.stma.org/sportsturf-magazine; http://sportsturfonline.com/. **Ad Rates:** 4C $4,892. **Remarks:** Accepts advertising. **Circ:** 22,000.

13267 ■ Teacher Education and Special Education: Journal of the Teacher Education Division of the Council for Exceptional
Allen Press Inc.
810 E Tenth St.
Lawrence, KS 66044
Phone: (785)843-1234
Free: 800-627-0326
Publisher's E-mail: sales@allenpress.com
Journal covering personnel preparation in special education. **Freq:** Quarterly February , May , August , November. **Print Method:** Offset. **Trim Size:** 7 x 10. **Cols./Page:** 2. **Col. Width:** 16.5 picas. **Col. Depth:** 52 picas. **Key Personnel:** Dr. Fred Spooner, Editor; Dr. Robert Algozzine, Editor. **ISSN:** 0888-4064 (print); **EISSN:** 1944-4931 (electronic). **Subscription Rates:** £188 Institutions Combined (Print & E-access); £207 Institutions Current Volume Print & All Online Content; £169 Institutions E-access; £188 Institutions All Online Content; £303 Institutions E-access (Content through 1998); £184 Institutions Print Only; £44 Individuals Combined (Print & E-access); £51 Institutions Single Print Issue; £14 Individuals Single Print Issue. **URL:** http://tes.sagepub.com. **Mailing address:** PO Box 368, Lawrence, KS 66044-0368. **Remarks:** Advertising not accepted. **Circ:** Paid 3100.

13268 ■ Tire Science and Technology
Tire Society
810 E 10th St.
Lawrence, KS 66044
Phone: (785)865-9403
Fax: (785)843-6153
Free: 800-627-0326
Publisher's E-mail: office@tiresociety.org
Journal publishing information pertaining to science and technology of tires. **Freq:** Quarterly. **ISSN:** 0090- 8657 (print). **Subscription Rates:** $75 Members print copy; $125 Nonmembers print copy; $175 Nonmembers online. **URL:** http://tiresciencetechnology.org. **Remarks:** Advertising not accepted. **Circ:** (Not Reported).

13269 ■ The University Daily Kansan
Cottonwood Magazine and Press
1301 Jayhawk Blvd., Rm. 400
Lawrence, KS 66045-7593
Phone: (785)864-2516
Publisher's E-mail: email@ku.edu
College newspaper. **Freq:** Daily (morn.). **Print Method:** Offset. **Cols./Page:** 6. **Col. Width:** 11.2 picas. **Col. Depth:** 20 1/2 inches. **Key Personnel:** Malcolm Gibson, General Manager; Nick Gerik, Managing Editor; Alex Garrison; David Cawthon, Managing Editor; Joe Garvey, Business Manager. **ISSN:** 0746--4967 (print). **USPS:** 650-640. **URL:** http://www.kansan.com. **Remarks:** Advertising accepted; rates available upon request. **Circ:** (Not Reported).

13270 ■ Weed Science
Weed Science Society of America
810 E 10th St.
Lawrence, KS 66044
Phone: (785)865-9520
Free: 800-627-0326
Publisher's E-mail: sales@allenpress.com
Peer-reviewed scientific journal covering weeds and their control. **Freq:** Quarterly. **ISSN:** 0043-1745 (print); **EISSN:** 1550-2759 (electronic). **Subscription Rates:** $472 Institutions print and online; $502 Institutions, other countries print and online; $378 Institutions online only. **URL:** http://wssajournals.org/loi/wees. **Mailing address:** PO Box 368, Lawrence, KS 66044-0368. **Remarks:** Advertising not accepted. **Circ:** (Not Reported).

13271 ■ Weed Science
Allen Press Inc.
810 E Tenth St.
Lawrence, KS 66044
Phone: (785)843-1234
Free: 800-627-0326
Publisher's E-mail: sales@allenpress.com
Peer-reviewed scientific journal covering weeds and their control. **Freq:** Quarterly. **ISSN:** 0043-1745 (print); **EISSN:** 1550-2759 (electronic). **Subscription Rates:** $472 Institutions print and online; $502 Institutions, other countries print and online; $378 Institutions online only. **URL:** http://wssajournals.org/loi/wees. **Mailing address:** PO Box 368, Lawrence, KS 66044-0368. **Remarks:** Advertising not accepted. **Circ:** (Not Reported).

13272 ■ Weed Technology
Allen Press Inc.
810 E Tenth St.
Lawrence, KS 66044
Phone: (785)843-1234
Free: 800-627-0326
Publisher's E-mail: sales@allenpress.com
Journal covering weed science research and technology, teaching, extension, industry, consulting, and regulation. **Freq:** Quarterly. **Key Personnel:** Joyce Lancaster, Contact, phone: (785)843-1235, fax: (785)843-1274. **ISSN:** 0890--037X (print); **EISSN:** 1550--2740 (electronic). **Subscription Rates:** $422 Institutions print and online; $452 Institutions, other countries print and online; $322 Institutions online only. **Alt. Formats:** PDF. **URL:** http://wssajournals.org/loi/wete. **Mailing address:** PO Box 368, Lawrence, KS 66044-0368. **Circ:** (Not Reported).

13273 ■ The Wildlife Professional
Allen Press Inc.
810 E Tenth St.
Lawrence, KS 66044
Phone: (785)843-1234
Free: 800-627-0326
Publisher's E-mail: sales@allenpress.com
Journal covering wildlife professionals. **Freq:** Quarterly. **ISSN:** 1933--2866 (print). **Subscription Rates:** Included in membership. **URL:** http://wildlife.org/join. **Mailing address:** PO Box 368, Lawrence, KS 66044-0368. **Circ:** (Not Reported).

13274 ■ Wildlife Society Bulletin
Allen Press Inc.
810 E Tenth St.
Lawrence, KS 66044
Phone: (785)843-1234
Free: 800-627-0326
Publisher's E-mail: sales@allenpress.com
Peer-reviewed journal covering wildlife society management. **Freq:** Quarterly. **Key Personnel:** Christine Ribic, Editor. **ISSN:** 0091--7648 (print); **EISSN:** 1938--5463 (electronic). **Subscription Rates:** $361 Institutions small (online only); $468 Institutions medium (online only); $608 Institutions large (online only). **URL:** http://onlinelibrary.wiley.com/journal/10.1002/(ISSN)1938-5463a. **Mailing address:** PO Box 368, Lawrence, KS 66044-0368. **Circ:** (Not Reported).

KANH-FM - See Emporia

13275 ■ KANU-FM - 91.5
1120 W 11th St.
University of Kansas
Lawrence, KS 66044
Phone: (785)864-4530
Free: 888-577-5268
Format: Public Radio; Classical; Jazz. **Simulcasts:** National Public Radio (NPR). **Owner:** University of Kansas, 1450 Jayhawk Blvd., Lawrence, KS 66045, Ph: (785)864-2700. **Founded:** Sept. 15, 1952. **Operating Hours:** Continuous. **ADI:** Kansas City, MO (Lawrence, KS). **Key Personnel:** Robin Johnson, Dir. of Dev., News Dir., robinfrg@ku.edu; Janet Campbell, Gen. Mgr., jcampbell@ku.edu. **Wattage:** 100,000 ERP. **Ad Rates:** Underwriting available. **URL:** http://kansaspublicradio.org.

KANV-FM - See Junction City

13276 ■ KJHK-FM - 90.7
1301 Jayhawk Blvd., Ste. 370
Lawrence, KS 66045
Phone: (785)864-4745
Format: Full Service; Alternative/New Music/Progressive. **Networks:** ABC. **Owner:** University of Kansas, 1450 Jayhawk Blvd., Lawrence, KS 66045, Ph: (785)864-2700. **Founded:** 1975. **Operating Hours:** Continuous; 100% local. **ADI:** Topeka, KS. **Key Personnel:** Alex Tretbar, Station Mgr.; Zach Marsh, Music Dir. **Local Programs:** *Rotation*; *Jam Sandwich*; *Breakfast For Beatlovers*, Monday Tuesday Wednesday Thursday Friday 9:00a.m. - 12:00 p.m.; *Across The Pond*; *As Heard From The Hill*; *Jazz in the Morning*, Monday Tuesday Wednesday Thursday Friday 6:00 a.m. - 9:00 a.m.; *Hip Hop Hype*, Friday 8:00 p.m. - 10:00 p.m.; *Plow the Fields*, Saturday 8:00 p.m. - 10:00 p.m. **Wattage:** 2,900. **Ad Rates:** Noncommercial. **URL:** http://www.kjhk.org.

13277 ■ KLWN-AM - 1320
3125 W Sixth St.
Lawrence, KS 66049
Phone: (785)843-1320
Format: News; Talk; Sports. **Networks:** Fox. **Owner:** Great Plains Media Inc., at above address. **Founded:** 1951. **Operating Hours:** Continuous. **ADI:** Kansas City, MO (Lawrence, KS). **Wattage:** 500 Day; 250 Night. **Ad Rates:** Advertising accepted; rates available upon request. **URL:** http://www.klwn.com.

13278 ■ KLZR-FM - 105.9
3125 W 6th St.
Lawrence, KS 66049
Phone: (785)843-1320
Fax: (785)841-5941
Format: Top 40. **Networks:** Independent. **Owner:** Great Plains Media Inc., at above address. **Founded:** 1963. **Formerly:** KLWN-FM. **Operating Hours:** Continuous. **ADI:** Topeka, KS. **Key Personnel:** Chris Merrill, Operations Mgr. **Wattage:** 100,000. **Ad Rates:** Noncommercial. **URL:** http://www.1059kissfm.com.

13279 ■ KMXN-FM - 92.9
3125 W 6th St.
Lawrence, KS 66049
Phone: (785)843-1320
Fax: (785)841-5924
Format: Classic Rock. **Owner:** Great Plains Media Inc., at above address. **URL:** http://www.bull929.com.

13280 ■ KUJH-TV - 14
1000 Sunnyside Ave., Rm. 2000
Lawrence, KS 66045
Phone: (785)864-4552
Owner: University of Kansas, 1450 Jayhawk Blvd., Lawrence, KS 66045, Ph: (785)864-2700. **URL:** http://tv.ku.edu.

LEAVENWORTH

NE KS. Leavenworth Co. On Missouri River, 33 mi. NW of Kansas City, MO. U.S. Army Command & General Staff College. Saint Mary College. Federal and state

Circulation: ★ = AAM; △ or • = BPA; ♦ = CAC; ❑ = VAC; ⊕ = PO Statement; ‡ = Publisher's Report; Boldface figures = sworn; Light figures = estimated.

institutions. Manufactures mill and milling machinery, bridge and structural steel, furniture, feed products, auto batteries, marine products and equipment. Grain elevators, machine shops, flour mills. Diversified farming.

13281 ■ Leavenworth Times
Leavenworth Times
422 Seneca
Leavenworth, KS 66048
Phone: (913)682-0305
General newspaper. **Founded:** Mar. 07, 1857. **Freq:** Daily and Sat. (morn.). **Print Method:** Offset. **Key Personnel:** Steve Curd, Publisher; Sandy Hattock, Director, Advertising. **USPS:** 308-180. **URL:** http://www.leavenworthtimes.com. **Ad Rates:** GLR $2.11; BW $1,297.80; 4C $1,437.80. **Remarks:** Accepts advertising. **Circ:** (Not Reported).

13282 ■ KKLO-AM - 1410
481 Muncie Rd.
Leavenworth, KS 66048-4947
Phone: (417)276-0555
Fax: (417)831-4026
Format: Religious; Contemporary Christian. **Owner:** Wodlinger Broadcasting, at above address, Saint Louis, MO 63103. **Founded:** 1948. **Formerly**: KCLO-AM. **Operating Hours**: Continuous; 100% local. **Key Personnel:** Tammy Cross, Station Mgr; Todd Chase, Contact; Bee Fender, Contact; Andrew Logue, Contact. **Wattage**: 5,000. **Ad Rates:** $4-18 for 30 seconds; $9-23 for 60 seconds. **URL:** http://1410kklo.com/.

13283 ■ Time Warner Cable
541 McDonald Rd.
Leavenworth, KS 66048
Phone: (913)682-2113
Owner: Time Warner Inc., 1 Time Warner Ctr., New York, NY 10019-8016, Ph: (212)484-8000. **Founded:** 1989. **Formerly**: American Cablevision. **Key Personnel:** Glenn A. Britt, Chairman, CEO. **Cities Served:** Fort Leavenworth, Lansing, Kansas: subscribing households 14,000; 367 channels; 2 community access channels. **URL:** http://www.timewarnercable.com.

LEAWOOD

13284 ■ American Family Physician
American Academy of Family Physicians
11400 Tomahawk Creek Pkwy.
Leawood, KS 66211-2680
Phone: (913)906-6000
Fax: (913)906-6075
Free: 800-274-2237
Publication E-mail: afpedit@aafp.org
Peer-reviewed clinical journal for family physicians and others in primary care. Review articles detail the latest diagnostic and therapeutic techniques in the medical field. Department features in each issue include 'Tips from other Journals,' CME credit opportunities and course calendar. **Freq:** Semimonthly. **Print Method:** Web Offset. **Trim Size:** 7 3/4 x 10 1/2. **Cols./Page:** 2. **Col. Width:** 2 1/8 inches. **Col. Depth:** 10 inches. **Key Personnel:** Linda Doggett, Associate Publisher, Director, Marketing; Jay Siwek, MD, Editor; Stephanie Hanaway, Publisher. **ISSN:** 1532--0650 (print). **Subscription Rates:** $100 Members international, print + digital; $40 Students print + digital; $245 U.S. print + digital - nonmember physician; $340 Canada print + digital - nonmember physician; $420 Other countries print + digital - nonmember physician; $145 U.S. print + digital - Allied Health Care Professional; $240 Canada print + digital - Allied Health Care Professional; $330 Other countries print + digital - Allied Health Care Professional. **Alt. Formats:** CD-ROM. **URL:** http://www.aafp.org/journals/afp. **Mailing address:** PO Box 11210, Shawnee Mission, KS 66207-1210. **Ad Rates:** 4C $2,700. **Remarks:** Accepts advertising. **Circ:** 150000.

13285 ■ Clinical Journal of Sports Medicine
American Medical Society for Sports Medicine
4000 W 114th St., Ste. 100
Leawood, KS 66211-2622
Phone: (913)327-1415
Fax: (913)327-1491
Publisher's E-mail: office@amssm.org
Freq: Bimonthly. **ISSN:** 1050- 642X (print). **Subscription Rates:** Included in membership; $437 Individuals; $868 Institutions. **URL:** http://www.amssm.org/CommitteesDetails.php?IDcom=11. **Remarks:** Accepts advertising. **Circ:** (Not Reported).

13286 ■ Family Medicine: The Official Journal of the Society of Teachers of Family Medicine
Society of Teachers of Family Medicine
11400 Tomahawk Creek Pky., Ste. 240
Leawood, KS 66211
Phone: (913)906-6000
Fax: (913)906-6096
Free: 800-274-7928
Publication E-mail: fmjournal@stfm.org
Forum for family medicine education and research. **Freq:** 10/year. **Print Method:** Offset. **Trim Size:** 8 1/4 x 10 7/8. **Cols./Page:** 3 and 2. **Col. Width:** 26 and 37 nonpareils. **Col. Depth:** 133 agate lines. **Key Personnel:** John Saultz, MD, Editor. **ISSN:** 0742--3225 (print). **Subscription Rates:** $195 Institutions non-member; Included in membership. **URL:** http://www.stfm.org/NewsJournals/FamilyMedicine. **Ad Rates:** BW $1397. **Remarks:** Accepts advertising. **Circ:** Paid ‡5000.

13287 ■ Family Practice Management
American Academy of Family Physicians
11400 Tomahawk Creek Pkwy.
Leawood, KS 66211-2680
Phone: (913)906-6000
Fax: (913)906-6075
Free: 800-274-2237
Publication E-mail: fpmedit@aafp.org
Magazine covering socio-economic and management topics concerning family physicians. **Freq:** 6/year. **Print Method:** Web Offset. **Trim Size:** 7 3/4 x 10 1/2. **Cols./Page:** 3. **Col. Width:** 2 1/8 inches. **Col. Depth:** 10 inches. **Key Personnel:** Brian W. Arbuckle, Business Manager; Craig Doane, Vice President; Robert Edsall, Editor-in-Chief; Dan Gowan, Associate Publisher, Director, Advertising and Sales; Stephanie Hanaway, Publisher. **ISSN:** 1531--1929 (print). **Subscription Rates:** $30 Members 1 year, print + digital - U.S; $42 Members 1 year, print + digital - Canada; $52 Nonmembers 1 year, print + digital - International; $95 Nonmembers 1 year, print + digital - Physician, U.S; $110 Nonmembers 1 year, print + digital - Physician, Canada; $130 Nonmembers 1 year, print + digital - Physician, International; $75 Nonmembers 1 year, digital only - Physician; $75 Individuals 1 year, print + digital - Allied Health Care Professional, U.S; $90 Individuals 1 year, print + digital - Allied Health Care Professional, Canada; $110 Individuals 1 year, print + digital - Allied Health Care Professional, International; $60 Individuals 1 year, digital only - Allied Health Care Professional; $145 Institutions 1 year, print + digital; $165 Institutions, Canada 1 year, print + digital; $185 Institutions, other countries 1 year, print + digital; $125 Institutions 1 year, digital only. **URL:** http://www.aafp.org/journals/fpm.html. **Mailing address:** PO Box 11210, Shawnee Mission, KS 66207-1210. **Ad Rates:** $5200-20800, for 1 issue; $4940-19760, for 2 issues; $4680-18720, for 3 issues; $4420-17680, for 4 issues; $4160-16640, for 5 issues; $3640-14560, for 6 issues. **Remarks:** Accepts display and classified advertising. **Circ:** ‡127,000.

13288 ■ Journal of Rural Health
National Rural Health Association
4501 College Blvd., No. 225
Leawood, KS 66211-1921
Phone: (816)756-3140
Fax: (816)756-3144
Publisher's E-mail: mail@nrharural.org
Freq: Quarterly. **Key Personnel:** Tyrone Borders, PhD. **ISSN:** 0890--765X (print); **EISSN:** 1748--0361 (electronic). **Subscription Rates:** Included in membership; $395 Institutions print and online; $88 Individuals print and online; $59 Students print and online. **URL:** http://www.ruralhealthweb.org/go/left/publications-and-news/the-journal-of-rural-health. **Remarks:** Accepts advertising. **Circ:** (Not Reported).

13289 ■ Orthodontic Products
Anthem Media L.L.C.
4303 W 119th St.
Leawood, KS 66209
Phone: (913)894-6923
Fax: (913)894-6932
Magazine for orthodontists delivering the most up-to-date information about new products and business management solutions for a successful practice. **Freq:** 10/year. **Key Personnel:** Alison Werner, Editor; Christopher Piehler, Editor. **ISSN:** 1097--797X (print). **URL:** http://www.orthodonticproductsonline.com. **Circ:** (Not Reported).

13290 ■ Rural Roads
National Rural Health Association
4501 College Blvd., No. 225
Leawood, KS 66211-1921
Phone: (816)756-3140
Fax: (816)756-3144
Publisher's E-mail: mail@nrharural.org
Freq: Quarterly. **Subscription Rates:** $20 /year. **URL:** http://www.ruralhealthweb.org/go/left/publications-and-news/rural-roads. **Remarks:** Accepts advertising. **Circ:** (Not Reported).

13291 ■ Sleep Review: The Journal for Sleep Specialists
Anthem Media L.L.C.
4303 W 119th St.
Leawood, KS 66209
Phone: (913)894-6923
Fax: (913)894-6932
Publisher's E-mail: info@ascendmedia.com
Magazine covering case reports, innovative research findings, business news, product and service introductions, as well as offering inspiring stories of leading sleep centers and useful ideas for improving sleep laboratory operations. **Freq:** Bimonthly. **Key Personnel:** John Bethune, Director, Editorial; Roy Felts, Publisher. **URL:** http://www.sleepreviewmag.com. **Ad Rates:** 4C $5365. **Remarks:** Accepts advertising. **Circ:** (Not Reported).

13292 ■ WTUV-FM - 105.7
6721 W 121st St.
Leawood, KS 66209
Phone: (913)344-1500
Email: info@lacalienteradio.com
Format: News; Music of Your Life. **URL:** http://www.espnlouisville.com.

LECOMPTON

E KS. Douglas Co. 8 mi. NW of Lawrence.

13293 ■ Christmas Trees: World's Leading Christmas Tree Magazine
Tree Publishers Inc.
PO Box 107
Lecompton, KS 66050-0170
Phone: (785)887-6324
Publication E-mail: ctreesmag@gmail.com
Magazine covering the Christmas tree industry. **Freq:** Quarterly. **Print Method:** Offset. **Trim Size:** 8 1/2 x 11. **Cols./Page:** 3. **Col. Width:** 14 picas. **Col. Depth:** 10 inches. **Key Personnel:** Catherine Wright Howard, Editor, Manager, Circulation; Chuck Wright, Publisher. **ISSN:** 0199--0217 (print). **Subscription Rates:** $25 Individuals print only; $48 Two years print only; $6.25 Single issue; $20 Individuals online only; $38 Two years online only. **URL:** http://christmastreesmagazine.com. **Remarks:** Accepts advertising. **Circ:** Paid ‡4,391, Controlled ‡41.

LENEXA

NE KS. Johnson Co. 5 mi. S. of Prairie Village.

13294 ■ Children's Mission Education Curriculum
Nazarene Missions International
17001 Prairie Star Pkwy.
Lenexa, KS 66220
Phone: (913)577-2970
Fax: (913)577-0861
Publisher's E-mail: nmi@nazarene.org
Alt. Formats: PDF. **URL:** http://nmi.nazarene.org/10176/story.html. **Remarks:** Advertising not accepted. **Circ:** (Not Reported).

13295 ■ Drovers
Vance Publishing Corp.
10901 W 84th Ter.
Lenexa, KS 66214
Phone: (913)438-8700
Publication E-mail: info@cattlenetwork.com
Trade magazine on beef cattle production and marketing. **Freq:** Monthly. **Print Method:** Offset. **Trim Size:** 8 x 10 3/4. **Cols./Page:** 3. **Col. Width:** 13 nonpareils. **Col. Depth:** 140 agate lines. **Key Personnel:** Alan Newport, Editor. **ISSN:** 0012--6454 (print). **URL:** http://www.cattlenetwork.com. **Formerly**: Drovers Journal. **Ad Rates:** BW $7612; 4C $9224. **Remarks:**

Accepts advertising. **Circ:** (Not Reported).

13296 ■ Grower's Citrus and Vegetable Magazine
Vance Publishing Corp.
10901 W 84th Ter.
Lenexa, KS 66214
Magazine serving citrus and vegetable growers, packers, and processors in Florida. **Freq:** 9/yr. **Print Method:** Web Offset. **Trim Size:** 7 7/8 x 10 3/4. **Key Personnel:** Vicky Boyd, Editor; Don Ransdell, Director, Publications. **ISSN:** 0009--7586 (print). **Subscription Rates:** $45 Individuals; $65 Canada and Mexico; $150 Other countries. **URL:** http://www.vancepublishing.com/agriculture/grower-citrus-vegetable. **Ad Rates:** BW $2,473; 4C $1,095. **Remarks:** Accepts advertising. **Circ:** Controlled △**22,050**.

13297 ■ International Mission Education Journal
Nazarene Missions International
17001 Prairie Star Pkwy.
Lenexa, KS 66220
Phone: (913)577-2970
Fax: (913)577-0861
Publisher's E-mail: nmi@nazarene.org
Freq: Annual. **Alt. Formats:** Download. **URL:** http://nmi.nazarene.org/10068/story.html. **Remarks:** Advertising not accepted. **Circ:** (Not Reported).

13298 ■ Journal of the Association of Genetic Technologists
Association of Genetic Technologists
PO Box 19193
Lenexa, KS 66285
Phone: (913)895-4605
Fax: (913)895-4652
Publisher's E-mail: agt-info@goamp.com
Journal covering new techniques and other issues for cytogeneticists. **Freq:** Quarterly. **Key Personnel:** Mark Terry, Editor, phone: (586)805-9407, fax: (248)628-3025. **ISSN:** 1532--7834 (print). **Subscription Rates:** $115 Institutions hard copy; $100 Members hard copy - member; $25 Members single issue. **Alt. Formats:** PDF. **URL:** http://www.agt-info.org/publications/Pages/default.aspx. **Remarks:** Advertising accepted; rates available upon request. **Circ:** (Not Reported).

13299 ■ The Packer: The Business Newspaper of the Produce Industry
Vance Publishing Corp.
10901 W 84th Ter.
Lenexa, KS 66214
Phone: (913)438-0784
Fax: (913)438-0691
Free: 800-255-5113
Newspaper on produce marketing. **Freq:** Weekly. **Print Method:** Offset. **Trim Size:** 11 1/2 x 21 1/2. **Cols./Page:** 6. **Key Personnel:** Shannon Shuman, Publisher; Fred Wilkinson, Managing Editor; Greg Johnson, Editor, phone: (913)438-0784, fax: (913)438-0691. **ISSN:** 0030--9168 (print). **URL:** http://www.thepacker.com. **Ad Rates:** BW $7360; 4C $1975; PCI $50.85. **Remarks:** Advertising accepted; rates available upon request. **Circ:** △**13022**.

13300 ■ Pharmacotherapy: The Journal of Human Pharmacology and Drug Therapy
American College of Clinical Pharmacy
13000 W 87th Street Pky.
Lenexa, KS 66215-4530
Phone: (913)492-3311
Fax: (913)492-0088
Publisher's E-mail: accp@accp.com
Magazine presenting original research articles on all aspects of human pharmacology and reviews of articles on drugs and drug therapy. **Freq:** Monthly. **Print Method:** Offset. **Trim Size:** 8 1/8 x 10 7/8. **Cols./Page:** 2. **Col. Width:** 37 nonpareils. **Col. Depth:** 135 agate lines. **Key Personnel:** C. Lindsay DeVane, Editor-in-Chief; Denise E. Gibson, Managing Editor. **ISSN:** 0277--0008 (print); **EISSN:** 1875--9114 (electronic). **Subscription Rates:** $572 U.S., Canada, and Mexico online only - Institutions; $687 U.S., Canada, and Mexico print and online - institutions; $572 U.S., Canada, and Mexico print only - institutions; $126 U.S., Canada, and Mexico online only - personal; $170 U.S., Canada, and Mexico print and online - personal; $82 U.S., Canada, and Mexico online only - student; $115 U.S., Canada, and Mexico print and online - student; £370 Institutions print or online - UK; £444 Institutions print and online - UK; £84 Individuals online only - UK; £113 Individuals print and online - UK; £54 Students online only - UK; £84 Students print and online - UK; €429 Institutions print or online - Europe; €515 Institutions print and online - Europe; €95 Individuals online only - Europe; €129 Individuals print and online - Europe; €61 Students online only - Europe; €95 Students print and online - Europe. **URL:** http://onlinelibrary.wiley.com/journal/10.1002/(ISSN)1875-9114; http://www.accp.com/bookstore/th_journal.aspx. **Ad Rates:** BW $1,920. **Remarks:** Accepts advertising. **Circ:** 10766.

13301 ■ Susie: Global Sisterhood for Teen Girls
Premier Studios Publishing
10000 Marshall Dr.
Lenexa, KS 66215
Magazine featuring Christian teen girls. **Freq:** 6/year. **Subscription Rates:** $26 Individuals. **Circ:** (Not Reported).

13302 ■ Veterinary Economics: The Business of Client and Patient Care
Advanstar Veterinary Healthcare Communications
8033 Flint St.
Lenexa, KS 66214
Phone: (913)492-4300
Free: 800-255-6864
Trade magazine on veterinary practice management. **Freq:** Monthly. **Print Method:** Offset. **Trim Size:** 8 x 10 3/4. **Cols./Page:** 3. **Col. Width:** 2 1/8 inches. **Col. Depth:** 7.5 picas. **Key Personnel:** Kristi Reimer, Editor; Kerry Hillard Johnson, Managing Editor; Amanda Wolfe, Associate Editor. **URL:** http://veterinarybusiness.dvm360.com/vetec/cathome/catHome6.jsp?categoryId=46739. **Ad Rates:** BW $5,640; 4C $7,470; PCI $129. **Remarks:** Accepts advertising. **Circ:** Paid 59465.

13303 ■ Veterinary Medicine
Advanstar Veterinary Healthcare Communications
8033 Flint St.
Lenexa, KS 66214
Phone: (913)492-4300
Free: 800-255-6864
Clinical veterinary medicine magazine. **Founded:** 1905. **Freq:** Monthly. **Print Method:** Offset. **Trim Size:** 8 x 10 3/4. **Cols./Page:** 3. **Col. Width:** 32 nonpareils. **Col. Depth:** 119 agate lines. **Key Personnel:** Margaret Rampey, Editor; Mindy Valcarcel, Senior Editor. **ISSN:** 8750-7943 (print). **Subscription Rates:** $49 Individuals. **URL:** http://veterinarymedicine.dvm360.com/. **Ad Rates:** BW $2,130; 4C $3,130. **Remarks:** Accepts advertising. **Circ:** △**56352**.

13304 ■ Youth Curriculum
Nazarene Missions International
17001 Prairie Star Pkwy.
Lenexa, KS 66220
Phone: (913)577-2970
Fax: (913)577-0861
Publisher's E-mail: nmi@nazarene.org
Remarks: Advertising not accepted. **Circ:** (Not Reported).

LEOTI

W KS. Wichita Co. 205 mi. W. of Salina.

13305 ■ Leoti Standard
The Leoti
114 S 4th St.
Leoti, KS 67861
Phone: (620)375-2631
Publisher's E-mail: standard@sunflowertelco.com
Community newspaper. **Freq:** Weekly (Wed.). **Print Method:** Offset. **Cols./Page:** 6. **Col. Width:** 2 inches. **Col. Depth:** 21 1/2 inches. **Subscription Rates:** $24.08 Individuals; $25.22 Out of area. **URL:** http://skyways.lib.ks.us/towns/Leoti/index.html. **Mailing address:** PO Box N, Leoti, KS 67861. **Ad Rates:** GLR $.75; BW $419.25; PCI $3.25. **Remarks:** Color advertising not accepted. **Circ:** ‡1650.

LIBERAL

SW KS. Seward Co. 75 mi. SW of Dodge City. Manufactures material handling equipment, truck bodies. Beef packing plant. Grain milling. Oil and gas fields. Ships agricultural products. Grain and livestock farms.

13306 ■ The Crusader
Seward County Community College
1801 N Kansas Ave.
Liberal, KS 67901-2054
Phone: (620)624-1951
Free: 800-373-9951
Collegiate newspaper. **Founded:** 1969. **Freq:** 12/yr (during the academic year August through May). **Print Method:** Offset. **Trim Size:** Broadsheet. **Cols./Page:** 6. **Col. Width:** 1.958 inches. **Col. Depth:** 19.2 inches. **Key Personnel:** Heidy Molina, Editor; Anita Reed, Advisor. **URL:** http://crusadernews.com. **Mailing address:** PO Box 1137, Liberal, KS 67901-2054. **Ad Rates:** PCI $4. **Remarks:** Accepts advertising. **Circ:** Free ‡2000.

13307 ■ KSCB-AM - 1270
1410 N Western Ave.
Liberal, KS 67901
Phone: (620)624-3891
Fax: (620)624-7885
Free: 800-373-3891
Format: News; Talk; Sports. **Networks:** ABC. **Owner:** Seward County Broadcasting Company Inc., at above address, Liberal, KS 67901. **Founded:** 1948. **Operating Hours**: Continuous; 3% network, 97% local. **ADI**: Wichita-Hutchinson, KS. **Key Personnel:** Stuart Melchert, Gen. Mgr.; Tracy Utz, Bus. Mgr.; Cheryl Collins, Sales Mgr. **Wattage**: 1,000. **Ad Rates:** Noncommercial. $6.80-$12 for 30 seconds; $8.20-$13.60 for 60 seconds. Combined advertising rates available with KSCB-FM.

13308 ■ KSCB-FM - 107.5
1410 N West Ave.
Liberal, KS 67901
Phone: (620)624-3891
Fax: (620)624-7885
Format: Adult Contemporary. **Networks:** ABC. **Owner:** Seward County Broadcasting Company Inc., at above address, Liberal, KS 67901. **Founded:** 1978. **Operating Hours**: Continuous. **ADI**: Wichita-Hutchinson, KS. **Wattage**: 100,000. **Ad Rates:** $6.80-12 for 30 seconds; $8.20-13.60 for 60 seconds. $6.80-$12 for 30 seconds; $8.20-$13.60 for 60 seconds. Combined advertising rates available with KSCB-AM. **URL:** http://www.kscbnews.net.

13309 ■ KSMM-AM - 1470
2810 Heartland Valley Rd.
Manhattan, KS 66503
Phone: (952)361-0019
Fax: (952)361-5529
Format: Classic Rock; News; Sports. **Simulcasts:** KAHE-FM. **Owner:** Rocking M Radio Inc., 1707 Thomas Cir., Ste. A, KS 66502. **Founded:** 1963. **Formerly**: KKCM-AM; KLIB-AM; KILS-AM; KYUU-AM. **Key Personnel:** Christopher Miller, VP, cmiller@rockingmradio.com. **Wattage**: 1,000 Daytime; 170 N. **Ad Rates:** $6 for 15 seconds; $13-17 for 30 seconds; $16-22 for 60 seconds. **URL:** http://www.rockingmradio.com/.

13310 ■ KSMM-FM - 101.5
4806 Vue du Lac Pl., Ste. B
Manhattan, KS 66503
Phone: (620)624-8156
Fax: (620)624-4606
Format: Hispanic. **Networks:** ABC; Westwood One Radio. **Owner:** Rocking M Radio Inc., 1707 Thomas Cir., Ste. A, KS 66502. **Founded:** 1978. **Formerly**: KSLS-FM. **Operating Hours**: Continuous. **ADI**: Wichita-Hutchinson, KS. **Key Personnel:** Christopher Miller, President, cmiller@rockingmradio.com. **Wattage**: 100,000. **Ad Rates:** $12 for 30 seconds; $15 for 60 seconds. Combined advertising rates available with KYUU-AM. **URL:** http://www.rockingmradio.com.

LINDSBORG

C KS. McPherson Co. 20 mi. S. of Salina. Bethany College. Light manufacturing. Diversified farming.

13311 ■ Bethany Magazine
College Relations
335 E Swensson St.
Lindsborg, KS 67456
Phone: (785)227-3380
Fax: (785)227-2004

Circulation: ★ = AAM; △ or • = BPA; ♦ = CAC; ❑ = VAC; ⊕ = PO Statement; ‡ = Publisher's Report; Boldface figures = sworn; Light figures = estimated.

College alumni magazine. **Freq:** 3/year fall, spring, summer. **Print Method:** Offset. **Trim Size:** 8 1/2 x 11. **Cols./Page:** 3. **Col. Width:** 30 nonpareils. **Col. Depth:** 137 agate lines. **Key Personnel:** Stephanie McDowell, Editor. **USPS:** 052-440. **URL:** http://www.bethanylb.edu/alumni/bethany-magazine. **Remarks:** Advertising not accepted. **Circ:** (Not Reported).

LOUISBURG

13312 ■ Louisburg Herald
Louisburg Herald
15 S Broadway
Louisburg, KS 66053
Phone: (913)837-4321
Community newspaper. **Freq:** Weekly (Wed.). **Print Method:** Offset. **Cols./Page:** 6. **Col. Width:** 1 13/16 inches. **Col. Depth:** 21 inches. **Key Personnel:** Brian McCauley, Editor, Publisher; Sandy Nelson, Publisher; Teresa Morrow, Director, Advertising; Lori Massey, Manager, Production. **Subscription Rates:** $50.51 Individuals Miami County resident; $54.33 Individuals outside of Miami County, Kansas ; $99.96 Individuals outside of Kansas and Missouri; $79.31 Individuals Cass County, Missouri. **URL:** http://www.herald-online.com. **Ad Rates:** GLR $.30; BW $504; 4C $704; PCI $4. **Remarks:** Accepts advertising. **Circ:** (Not Reported).

MANHATTAN

NEC KS. Riley Co. On Kansas River, 56 mi. NW of Topeka. Kansas State University of Agricultural and Applied Science. Fort Riley (Military Post). Manufactures cut stones, patterns, mobile homes. Poultry packing and seed houses; bottling works. Stock, poultry, and truck farms.

13313 ■ American Institute of Baking Technical Bulletin
AIB International
1213 Bakers Way
Manhattan, KS 66505-3999
Phone: (785)537-4750
Fax: (785)537-1493
Free: 800-633-5137
Publication E-mail: techbulletins@aibonline.org
Freq: Quarterly. **Key Personnel:** Janette Gelroth, Manager. **Subscription Rates:** $20 Individuals email or print plus shipping/handling; $100 U.S.; $125 Other countries; $175 Individuals online; $20 Single issue. **URL:** http://www.aibonline.org/onlinecatalog/products/bulletins/technical/; http://www.aibonline.org/aibOnline_/GenericForm.aspx?strOpen=/www.aibonline.org/onlinecatalog/products/bulletins/technical/index.html. **Mailing address:** PO Box 3999, Manhattan, KS 66505-3999. **Remarks:** Advertising not accepted. **Circ:** 1700.

13314 ■ American Institute of Baking Technical Bulletin
American Institute of Baking
1213 Bakers Way
Manhattan, KS 66505-3999
Phone: (785)537-4750
Fax: (785)537-1493
Free: 800-633-5137
Publication E-mail: techbulletins@aibonline.org
Freq: Quarterly. **Key Personnel:** Janette Gelroth, Manager. **Subscription Rates:** $20 Individuals email or print plus shipping/handling; $100 U.S.; $125 Other countries; $175 Individuals online; $20 Single issue. **URL:** http://www.aibonline.org/onlinecatalog/products/bulletins/technical/; http://www.aibonline.org/aibOnline_/GenericForm.aspx?strOpen=/www.aibonline.org/onlinecatalog/products/bulletins/technical/index.html. **Mailing address:** PO Box 3999, Manhattan, KS 66505-3999. **Remarks:** Advertising not accepted. **Circ:** 1700.

13315 ■ Communication: Journalism Education Today
Journalism Education Association
105 Kedzie Hall
828 Mid-Campus Dr. S
Manhattan, KS 66506-0008
Phone: (785)532-5532
Fax: (785)532-5563
Free: 866-532-5532
Publisher's E-mail: staff@jea.org
Journal publishing articles about journalism teaching and media advising. **Freq:** Quarterly. **Subscription Rates:** Included in membership. **URL:** http://jea.org/home/for-educators/cjet. **Remarks:** Accepts advertising. **Circ:** 2500.

13316 ■ Geomorphology
RELX Group P.L.C.
c/o R.A. Marston, Ed.-in-Ch.
Kansas State University
Department of Geography
118 Seaton Hall
Manhattan, KS 66506-2904
Phone: (785)532-6727
Fax: (785)532-7310
Publisher's E-mail: amsterdam@relx.com
Peer-reviewed journal of fundamental theory and science to applied research of relevance to sustainable management of the environment. **Freq:** 24/yr. **Key Personnel:** R.A. Marston, Editor-in-Chief; T. Oguchi, Editor-in-Chief; A. Plater, Editor-in-Chief. **ISSN:** 0169--555X (print). **Subscription Rates:** $4000 Institutions print; $3334 online. **URL:** http://www.journals.elsevier.com/geomorphology/. **Circ:** (Not Reported).

13317 ■ Grass & Grain
Ag Press Inc.
1531 Yuma St.
Manhattan, KS 66505
Phone: (785)539-7558
Fax: (785)539-2679
Publisher's E-mail: editor@grassandgrain.com
Agricultural tabloid. **Freq:** Weekly (Tues.). **Print Method:** Letterpress and offset. **Trim Size:** 10 1/2 x 16. **Cols./Page:** 6. **Col. Width:** 23 nonpareils. **Col. Depth:** 232 agate lines. **Key Personnel:** Donna Sullivan, Editor. **USPS:** 937-880. **Subscription Rates:** $43 Individuals; $130 Individuals first class mail; $50 Out of state; $130 Out of state first class mail. **URL:** http://www.grassandgrain.com. **Remarks:** Accepts advertising. **Circ:** Paid 12000.

13318 ■ Journal of Sensory Studies
Wiley-Blackwell
c/o Edgar Chamber, IV
Kansas State University
Sensory Analysis Center
Justin Hall
Manhattan, KS 66506
Publisher's E-mail: info@wiley.com
Journal for readers in academia, food and beverage companies, personal care product companies, wineries and ingredient companies, focusing on human reactions to basic tastes on foods, beverages, the environment, medications and other human exposures in every day life, the purpose being to promote technical and practical advancements in sensory science, a multidisciplinary area that includes food science and technology, psychology/psychophysics, statistics, biology of basic taste, consumer science, material science (textiles/fabrics), marketing research and other allied areas. **Freq:** Bimonthly. **Key Personnel:** H. Heymann, Board Member; Edgar Chambers, IV, Editor. **EISSN:** 1745--459X (electronic). **Subscription Rates:** $711 Institutions online; £366 Institutions online; €464 Institutions online - euro and euro zone; $711 Institutions online - rest of the world. **URL:** http://onlinelibrary.wiley.com/journal/10.1111/(ISSN)1745-459X. **Remarks:** Advertising accepted; rates available upon request. **Circ:** (Not Reported).

13319 ■ Journal of Veterinary Pharmacology and Therapeutics
American Academy of Veterinary Pharmacology and Therapeutics
c/o Jim E. Riviere, Ed.
College of Veterinary Medicine
228 Coles Hall
Manhattan, KS 66505-5802
Phone: (785)532-3783
Publisher's E-mail: aavptsec@gmail.com
Journal focusing on veterinary pharmacology and toxicology, in connection with the American Academy of Veterinary Pharmacology and Therapeutics, the American College of Veterinary Clinical Pharmacology, the Association for Veterinary Clinical Pharmacology and Therapeutics (UK), the European Association for Veterinary Pharmacology and Toxicology, and the Chapter of Veterinary Pharmacology of the Australian College of Veterinary Scientists. **Freq:** Bimonthly. **Key Personnel:** Jim E. Riviere, Editor; Johanna Fink-Gremmels, Editor. **ISSN:** 0140--7783 (print); **EISSN:** 1365--2885 (electronic). **Subscription Rates:** $2580 Institutions print and online; £1398 Institutions print and online; €1776 Institutions print and online; A$3014 Institutions, other countries print and online - Australia and New Zealand; $3014 Institutions, other countries print and online. **URL:** http://onlinelibrary.wiley.com/journal/10.1111/(ISSN)1365-2885. **Remarks:** Advertising accepted; rates available upon request. **Circ:** (Not Reported).

13320 ■ Kansas 4-H Journal
Kansas 4-H Foundation
116 Umberger Hall
1612 Claflin Rd.
Manhattan, KS 66506-3417
Phone: (785)532-5881
Fax: (785)532-6963
Agriculture magazine for 4-H club youth. **Freq:** Bimonthly. **Print Method:** Offset. **Trim Size:** 8 1/2 x 11. **Cols./Page:** 3. **Col. Width:** 28 nonpareils. **Col. Depth:** 140 agate lines. **URL:** http://kansas4hfoundation.org. **Remarks:** Advertising accepted; rates available upon request. **Circ:** 9100.

13321 ■ Kansas Living
Kansas Farm Bureau
2627 KFB Plz.
Manhattan, KS 66503-8116
Phone: (785)587-6000
Farm news magazine. **Freq:** Quarterly. **Print Method:** Offset. **Trim Size:** 8 x 10 3/4. **Cols./Page:** 3. **Key Personnel:** Sandi Cowdin, Manager. **ISSN:** 1077--0453 (print). **URL:** http://kansaslivingmagazine.com. **Remarks:** Accepts advertising. **Circ:** (Not Reported).

13322 ■ Kansas State Collegian
Kansas State University Student Publications Inc.
103 Kedzie Hall
Manhattan, KS 66506
Phone: (785)532-6555
Collegiate newspaper. **Freq:** Daily (morn.) during academic year. **Print Method:** Offset. Broadsheet. **Cols./Page:** 6. **Col. Width:** 2 1/16 inches. **Col. Depth:** 21 inches. **Key Personnel:** Jon Parton, Editor-in-Chief. **URL:** http://www.kstatecollegian.com. **Remarks:** Accepts advertising. **Circ:** (Not Reported).

13323 ■ The Lion and the Unicorn
Johns Hopkins University Press
Kansas State University
Dept. of English
108 English/CS Bldg.
Manhattan, KS 66506
Publication E-mail: lionunicorn@ksu.edu
Peer-reviewed journal on literary studies. **Freq:** 3/year. **Print Method:** Offset. **Trim Size:** 6 x 9. **Cols./Page:** 1. **Col. Width:** 26 picas. **Col. Depth:** 7 inches. **Key Personnel:** Naomi J. Wood, Editor; David L. Russell, Editor; Karin E. Westman, Editor. **ISSN:** 0147--2593 (print); **EISSN:** 1080--6563 (electronic). **Subscription Rates:** $40 Individuals print; $64.80 Two years print; $133 Institutions print; $266 Two years print; $50 Individuals online; $90 Two years online. **URL:** http://www.press.jhu.edu/journals/lion_and_the_unicorn. **Ad Rates:** BW $325. **Remarks:** Accepts advertising. **Circ:** ‡457.

13324 ■ Maintenance Engineering Bulletins
American Institute of Baking
1213 Bakers Way
Manhattan, KS 66505-3999
Phone: (785)537-4750
Fax: (785)537-1493
Free: 800-633-5137
Publisher's E-mail: info@aibonline.org
Publication covering issues for maintenance engineers, including amplifiers and logic gates, magnetism, and electrical troubleshooting. **Freq:** Bimonthly. **Alt. Formats:** CD-ROM. **Mailing address:** PO Box 3999, Manhattan, KS 66505-3999. **Circ:** (Not Reported).

13325 ■ NACADA Journal
National Academic Advising Association
Kansas State University
2323 Anderson Ave., Ste. 225
Manhattan, KS 66502-2912
Phone: (785)532-5717
Fax: (785)532-7732
Publisher's E-mail: nacada@ksu.edu
Freq: Semiannual. **ISSN:** 0271--9517 (print). **Subscription Rates:** Included in membership; $150 Institutions

/year. **URL:** http://www.nacada.ksu.edu/Resources/Journal.aspx. **Remarks:** Accepts advertising. **Circ:** (Not Reported).

13326 ■ KACZ-FM - 96.3
2414 Casement Rd.
Manhattan, KS 66502
Format: Top 40. **Owner:** Manhattan Broadcasting Co., 2414 Casement Rd., Manhattan, KS 66502, Ph: (785)776-1350, Fax: (785)539-1000. **URL:** http://www.z963.com.

13327 ■ KHCA-FM - 95.3
103 N 3rd, Ste. A
Manhattan, KS 66502
Phone: (785)537-9595
Fax: (785)537-2955
Email: info@angel95fm.com
Format: Contemporary Christian. **Owner:** KHCA Inc. **Operating Hours**: Continuous. **Wattage**: 6,000. **Ad Rates:** Noncommercial. **URL:** http://www.angel95fm.com.

13328 ■ KMAN-AM - 1350
2414 Casement Rd.
Manhattan, KS 66502
Phone: (785)776-1350
Fax: (785)539-1000
Format: Talk; News; Sports. **Networks:** Mutual Broadcasting System. **Owner:** Manhattan Broadcasting Co., 2414 Casement Rd., Manhattan, KS 66502, Ph: (785)776-1350, Fax: (785)539-1000. **Founded:** 1950. **Operating Hours**: Continuous; 50% local, 50% network. **ADI**: Topeka, KS. **Key Personnel:** Rob Voelker, Contact, robv@1350kman.com; Rich Wartell, Gen. Mgr., rwartell@1350kman.com; Cathy Dawes, News Dir. **Wattage**: 500. **Ad Rates:** $10-16 for 30 seconds; $12-20 for 60 seconds. **URL:** http://www.1350kman.com.

13329 ■ KMKF-FM - 101.5
2414 Casement Rd.
Manhattan, KS 66502-0011
Phone: (785)776-1350
Format: Album-Oriented Rock (AOR). **Networks:** Westwood One Radio. **Owner:** Manhattan Broadcasting Co., 2414 Casement Rd., Manhattan, KS 66502, Ph: (785)776-1350, Fax: (785)539-1000. **Founded:** 1972. **Operating Hours**: Continuous; 1% network, 99% local. **Key Personnel:** Corey Dean, Contact, cdean@purerock.com. **Wattage**: 36,000. **Ad Rates:** $10-22 for 30 seconds; $13-25 for 60 seconds. **URL:** http://www.purerock.com.

13330 ■ KSDB-FM - 91.9
104 Kedzie Hall
Manhattan, KS 66506-1501
Phone: (785)532-0919
Fax: (785)532-5484
Email: manager@ksdbfm.org
Format: Alternative/New Music/Progressive. **Owner:** Kansas State University, 1800 College Ave., Manhattan, KS 66502, Ph: (785)532-6011, Fax: (785)532-7655. **Founded:** Nov. 1950. **Formerly**: WKSU-FM. **Operating Hours**: Continuous. **Wattage**: 1,400. **Ad Rates:** $5-10 for 30 seconds. **URL:** http://ksdbfm.org.

KSMM-AM - See Liberal
KSMM-FM - See Liberal

13331 ■ K31BW - 31
PO Box A
Santa Ana, CA 92711
Phone: (714)832-2950
Free: 888-731-1000
Owner: Trinity Broadcasting Network Inc., PO Box A, Santa Ana, CA 92711, Ph: (714)832-2950, Free: 888-731-1000.

13332 ■ KXBZ-FM - 104.7
2414 Casement Rd.
Manhattan, KS 66502
Phone: (785)539-1047
Format: Country. **Owner:** Manhattan Broadcasting Co., 2414 Casement Rd., Manhattan, KS 66502, Ph: (785)776-1350, Fax: (785)539-1000. **Key Personnel:** Rich Wartell, Gen. Mgr., rwartell@1350kman.com. **URL:** http://www.b1047.com.

MARYSVILLE

NE KS NE KS. Marshall Co Marshall Co. 95 mi. W. of St. Joseph, MO 5 mi. W. of Home. Manufactures farm machinery, aircraft deicers, paper enveopes. Feed grains, wheat, alfalfa, soybeans, dairy, stock farms.

13333 ■ The Marysville Advocate
The Marysville Advocate
107 S 9th St.
Marysville, KS 66508
Phone: (785)562-2317
Fax: (785)562-5589
Free: 800-228-9248
Newspaper. **Freq:** Weekly (Thurs.). **Print Method:** Offset. **Cols./Page:** 6. **Col. Width:** 24 nonpareils. **Col. Depth:** 294 agate lines. **Key Personnel:** Jan Smith, Business Manager, Manager, Circulation; Sarah Kessinger, Editor, Publisher. **USPS:** 332-260. **Subscription Rates:** $52 Individuals print and online; $53 Individuals print or online; $45 Individuals e-edition. **Mailing address:** PO Box 271, Marysville, KS 66508. **Remarks:** Accepts advertising. **Circ:** (Not Reported).

13334 ■ KDNS-FM - 94.1
937 Jayhawk Rd.
Marysville, KS 66508
Format: Country. **Key Personnel:** Bruce Dierking, Chairman; Wade Gerstner, Gen. Mgr. **URL:** http://www.kdcountry94.com.

13335 ■ KNDY-AM - 1570
937 Jayhawk Rd.
Marysville, KS 66508-9803
Phone: (785)562-2361
Format: Country; Full Service. **Networks:** ABC. **Owner:** Dierking Communications Inc., at above address. **Founded:** 1956. **Operating Hours**: Continuous; 5% network, 95% local. **Key Personnel:** Bruce Dierking, Owner. **Wattage**: 250. **Ad Rates:** Advertising accepted; rates available upon request. **URL:** http://www.kndyradio.com.

13336 ■ KNDY-FM - 95.5
937 Jayhawk Rd.
Marysville, KS 66508
Phone: (785)562-2361
Format: Contemporary Country. **Networks:** ABC. **Owner:** Dierking Communications Inc., at above address. **Founded:** 1974. **Operating Hours**: Continuous; 5% network, 95% local. **Wattage**: 25,000. **Ad Rates:** Noncommercial. **URL:** http://www.kndyradio.com.

13337 ■ KZDY-FM - 96.3
937 Jayhawk Rd.
Marysville, KS 66508
Phone: (785)562-2361
Format: Oldies. **Key Personnel:** Bruce Dierking, Chairman; Wade Gerstner, Gen. Mgr. **URL:** http://www.kdcountry94.com.

MCPHERSON

C. KS. McPherson Co. 50 mi. N. of Wichita. McPherson College (Ch. of Breth). Central College. Manufactures drugs, mobile homes and accessories, concrete products, fibre glass and plastic pipes. Flour mill. Refinery. Grain, dairy, poultry.

13338 ■ McPherson Sentinel
GateHouse Media Inc.
301 S Main St.
McPherson, KS 67460
Phone: (620)241-2422
Publication E-mail: sentinel@sbcglobal.net
Newspaper. **Freq:** Daily (eve.) no Sunday. **Print Method:** Offset. **Cols./Page:** 6. **Col. Width:** 10.8 inches. **Col. Depth:** 301 agate lines. **Key Personnel:** Ashley Miller, Manager, Production; Cristina Janney, Managing Editor. **URL:** http://mcphersonsentinel.com. **Remarks:** Accepts advertising. **Circ:** (Not Reported).

13339 ■ KBBE-FM - 96.7
411 E Euclid St.
McPherson, KS 67460
Phone: (620)241-1504
Fax: (620)241-3196
Format: Full Service. **Simulcasts:** KNGL-AM. **Networks:** ABC; Kansas Agriculture; Kansas Information. **Founded:** 1974. **Formerly**: KNEX-FM. **Operating Hours**: 4 a.m.- midnight. **Key Personnel:** Joe Johnston, Gen. Mgr.; Jolene Koerner, Office Mgr. **Wattage**: 6,000. **Ad Rates:** $6-18 per unit. Combined advertising rates available with KNGC-AM. **Mailing address:** PO Box 1069, McPherson, KS 67460. **URL:** http://www.midkansasradio.com.

13340 ■ KNGL-AM - 1540
411 E Euclid St.
McPherson, KS 67460
Phone: (620)241-1504
Format: Full Service. **Simulcasts:** KBBE-FM. **Networks:** AP; Kansas Information; Kansas Agriculture. **Owner:** Davies Communications Inc., 1920 4th St., Cheney, WA 99004, Ph: (509)235-5144, Fax: (509)235-5158. **Founded:** 1949. **Operating Hours**: 6 a.m.-midnight. **Key Personnel:** Joe Johnston, Gen. Mgr. **Wattage**: 250 Day; 002 Night. **Ad Rates:** $5-6.75 for 30 seconds; $7.85-9.25 for 60 seconds. Combined advertising rates available with KBBE-FM. **Mailing address:** PO Box 1069, McPherson, KS 67460. **URL:** http://www.midkansasradio.com.

MEADE

C. KS. Meade Co. 37 mi. SSW of Dodge City. Agriculture and natural gas-related industries, silica mines, livestock.

13341 ■ Meade County News
Meade County News
105 S Fowler St.
Meade, KS 67864
Phone: (620)873-2118
Fax: (620)338-7412
Publisher's E-mail: mcnews@mcnewsonline.com
Community newspaper. **Freq:** Weekly. **Cols./Page:** 6. **Col. Width:** 2 inches. **Col. Depth:** 21 1/2 inches. **Mailing address:** PO Box 310, Meade, KS 67864. **Remarks:** Color advertising not accepted. **Circ:** (Not Reported).

13342 ■ KJIL-FM - 99.1
909 W Carthage
Meade, KS 67864
Phone: (620)873-2991
Fax: (620)873-2755
Free: 866-480-5545
Email: kjil@kjil.com
Format: Contemporary Christian. **Networks:** USA Radio; Ambassador Inspirational Radio. **Owner:** Great Plains Christian Radio, Inc., at above address. **Founded:** Sept. 05, 1992. **Operating Hours**: Continuous. **Key Personnel:** Mike Luskey, Station Mgr. **Wattage**: 100,000. **Ad Rates:** Noncommercial. **Mailing address:** PO Box 991, Meade, KS 67864. **URL:** http://www.kjil991.com.

MEDICINE LODGE

N. KS. Barber Co. 75 mi. SW of Wichita. Scenic gypsum hills. Gypsum cement factory. Oil and gas wells. Gypsum mines. Refinery. Cattle rancher. Grain.

13343 ■ KREJ-FM - 101.7
301 S Main St.
Medicine Lodge, KS 67104
Phone: (620)886-3537
Format: Contemporary Christian; Talk. **Wattage**: 50,000. **URL:** http://www.krejksns.org.

13344 ■ KSNS-FM - 91.5
301 S Main St.
Medicine Lodge, KS 67104
Phone: (620)886-3537
Format: Contemporary Christian. **Wattage**: 96,000. **URL:** http://www.krejksns.org.

MERRIAM

NE KS. Johnson Co. Suburb SSW of Kansas City.

13345 ■ KUKC-TV - 48
5400 Antioch Dr., Ste. 4
Merriam, KS 66202
Phone: (913)642-6200
Fax: (913)642-6201
Owner: Equity Broadcasting Co., at above address. **URL:** http://www.dlatinos.com.

MISSION

13346 ■ Fibromyalgia Alternative News
Fibromyalgia Coalition International
5201 Johnson Dr., Ste. 210
Mission, KS 66205-2920
Phone: (913)384-4673
Fax: (913)384-8998

Circulation: ★ = AAM; △ or • = BPA; ♦ = CAC; ❑ = VAC; ⊕ = PO Statement; ‡ = Publisher's Report; Boldface figures = sworn; Light figures = estimated.

Publisher's E-mail: info@fibrocoalition.org
Magazine containing articles on health-care issues and tips and natural health-care treatments. **Freq:** Quarterly. **Subscription Rates:** Included in membership. **Remarks:** Advertising not accepted. **Circ:** (Not Reported).

13347 ■ KCFX-FM - 101
5800 Foxridge Dr., 6th Fl.
Mission, KS 66202
Phone: (913)514-3000
Format: Classic Rock. **Networks:** Unistar. **Owner:** Susquehanna Radio Corp., 221 W Philadelphia St., York, PA 17404, Ph: (717)852-2132, Fax: (717)771-1436. **Founded:** 1977. **Formerly:** KIEE-FM. **Operating Hours:** Continuous. **Key Personnel:** Brian Goeke, Dir. of Mktg.; Donna Baker, Sales Mgr., VP of Sales, herndon.hasty@cumulus.com. **Wattage:** 97,000. **Ad Rates:** $150 per unit. **URL:** http://www.101thefox.net.

13348 ■ KCHZ-FM - 95.7
5800 Foxridge Dr., Ste. 600
Mission, KS 66202
Format: Top 40; Alternative/New Music/Progressive. **Key Personnel:** Donna Baker, VP, donna.baker@cumulus.com; Jared Robb, Sales Mgr., jared.robb@cumulus.com; Maurice Devoe, Prog. Dir., maurice.devoe@cumulus.com; Brian Goeke, Dir. of Mktg. **Ad Rates:** Noncommercial. **URL:** http://www.957thevibe.com.

13349 ■ KCJK-FM - 105.1
5800 Foxridge Dr., 6th Fl.
Mission, KS 66202
Phone: (913)514-3000
Format: Adult Contemporary. **Owner:** Cumulus Media Inc., 3280 Peachtree Rd. NW, Ste. 2300, Atlanta, GA 30305-2455, Ph: (404)949-0700, Fax: (404)949-0740. **Key Personnel:** Chris Hoffman, Operations Mgr., chris.hoffmann@cumulus.com; Brian Goeke, Dir. of Mktg., brian.goeke@cumulus.com; Jared Robb, Sales Mgr., jared.robb@cumulus.com. **Ad Rates:** Advertising accepted; rates available upon request. **URL:** http://www.1051jackfm.com.

13350 ■ KCMO-AM - 710
5800 Foxridge Dr., 6th Fl.
Mission, KS 66202
Phone: (913)514-3000
Fax: (913)514-3004
Format: Talk; News; Information. **Networks:** Westwood One Radio. **Owner:** Cumulus Broadcasting Inc., 3280 Peachtree Rd. NW, Ste. 2300, Atlanta, GA 30305-2447, Ph: (404)949-0700, Fax: (404)949-0740. **Operating Hours:** Continuous. **ADI:** Kansas City, MO (Lawrence, KS). **Key Personnel:** Brian Goeke, Dir. of Mktg., brian.goeke@cumulus.com; Tom Bamford, Contact, tbamford@710kcmo.com. **Wattage:** 10,000. **Ad Rates:** Advertising accepted; rates available upon request. **URL:** http://www.kcmotalkradio.com.

13351 ■ KCMO-FM - 94.9
5800 Foxridge Dr., 6th Fl.
Mission, KS 66202
Phone: (913)514-3000
Email: morningshow@949kcmo.com
Format: Oldies. **Key Personnel:** Brian Goeke, Dir. of Mktg.; Joe Russo, Prog. Dir. **Wattage:** 100,000 ERP. **Ad Rates:** Advertising accepted; rates available upon request. **URL:** http://www.949kcmo.com.

13352 ■ KMJK-FM - 107.3
5800 Foxridge Dr., 6th Fl.
Mission, KS 66202
Phone: (913)514-3000
Fax: (913)514-3002
Format: Urban Contemporary. **Networks:** ABC. **Owner:** Cumulus Media Inc., 3280 Peachtree Rd. NW, Ste. 2300, Atlanta, GA 30305-2455, Ph: (404)949-0700, Fax: (404)949-0740. **Formerly:** KXXR-FM. **Operating Hours:** Continuous. **Wattage:** 100,000. **Ad Rates:** Noncommercial. **URL:** http://www.magic1073.com/.

13353 ■ KQRC-FM - 98.9
7000 Squibb Rd.
Mission, KS 66202
Phone: (913)744-3600
Free: 866-989-7625
Format: Album-Oriented Rock (AOR). **Owner:** Entercom Kansas City LLC, at above address. **Key Personnel:** Bob Edwards, Dir. of Programs, bedwards@entercom.com; Nic Merenda, Sales Mgr., nmerenda@entercom.com. **Wattage:** 98,500. **Ad Rates:** Advertising accepted; rates available upon request. **URL:** http://www.989therock.com.

13354 ■ KRBZ-FM - 96.5
7000 Squibb Rd.
Mission, KS 66202
Format: Alternative/New Music/Progressive. **Owner:** Entercom Kansas City Broadcasting, at above address. **Key Personnel:** Sammy Jo Behrens, Contact, sbehrens@entercom.com; Chris Knoeppel, Contact, ck@entercom.com. **Wattage:** 100,000. **Ad Rates:** Noncommercial. **URL:** http://www.965thebuzz.com.

13355 ■ KUDL-FM - 98.1
7000 Squibb Rd.
Mission, KS 66202
Phone: (913)576-7981
Format: Adult Contemporary. **Networks:** AP. **Owner:** Entercom Kansas City Broadcasting, 401 City Ave., Ste. 809, Bala Cynwyd, PA 19004. **Founded:** 1959. **Operating Hours:** Continuous. **ADI:** Kansas City, MO (Lawrence, KS). **Wattage:** 100,000. **Ad Rates:** Noncommercial. **URL:** http://www.997thepoint.com.

13356 ■ KXTR-AM
7000 Squibb Rd.
Mission, KS 66202
Phone: (913)744-3600
Owner: Entcroom Kansas City LLC, at above address. **Ad Rates:** Noncommercial.

13357 ■ KYYS-FM - 99.7
7000 Squibb Rd.
Mission, KS 66202
Phone: (913)576-7997
Format: Classic Rock. **Owner:** Entercom Kansas City Broadcasting, at above address. **Operating Hours:** 5:00 a.m. - 12:00 a.m. Monday – Friday, Continious Weekend. **ADI:** Kansas City, MO (Lawrence, KS). **Key Personnel:** Jennifer Morton, Promotions Dir., jmorton@entercom.com; Greg Bergen, Dir. of Programs, gbergen@entercom.com; Kevin Klein, Dir. of Sales, kcklein@entercom.com. **Wattage:** 98,500. **Ad Rates:** Advertising accepted; rates available upon request. **URL:** http://www.997thepoint.com/contact-us.

13358 ■ WDAF-AM - 610
7000 Squibb Rd.
Mission, KS 66202
Phone: (610)660-5610
Format: Country; News; Sports; Talk. **Simulcasts:** KDAF-FM. **Networks:** ABC; Fox; CNN Radio; CBS; NBC; ESPN Radio. **Owner:** Entercom Kansas City Broadcasting, at above address. **Founded:** 1922. **Operating Hours:** Continuous. **ADI:** Kansas City, MO (Lawrence, KS). **Key Personnel:** Thom McGinty, Operations Mgr., tmcginty@entercom.com; Michael Cruise, Dir. of Programs, mcruise@entercom.com; Dan Prendiville, Sales Mgr., dprendiville@entercom.com; Hillary Woods, Promotions Mgr.; Shana Gochenour, Traffic Mgr. **Wattage:** 5,000 KW. **Ad Rates:** Advertising accepted; rates available upon request. **URL:** http://www.610sports.com.

13359 ■ WDAF-FM - 106.5
7000 Squibb Rd.
Mission, KS 66202
Phone: (913)576-7000
Format: Country. **Owner:** Entercom Communications Corp., 401 City Ave., Ste. 809, Bala Cynwyd, PA 19004-1130, Ph: (610)660-5610, Fax: (610)660-5620. **Key Personnel:** Rob Constantinou, Sales Mgr., rconstantinou@entercom.com. **Ad Rates:** Advertising accepted; rates available upon request. **URL:** http://www.1065thewolf.com.

MOUNDRIDGE

C. KS. McPherson Co. 28 mi. NE of Hutchinson. Manufactured cheese, grain drying equipment, riding mowers, farm equipment, roll forming machines. Feed mills. Oil, gas wells. Agriculture. Chicken, turkey hatcheries. Corn, oats, wheat.

13360 ■ Mid-Kansas Cable Services Inc.
109 N Christian Ave.
Moundridge, KS 67107
Phone: (620)345-2832
Fax: (620)345-6106
Founded: 1904. **Key Personnel:** Delonna Barnett, VP; Carl Krehbiel, Contact. **Cities Served:** subscribing households 465. **Mailing address:** PO Box 960, Moundridge, KS 67107.

MULLINVILLE

SC KS. Kiowa Co. 20 mi. W. of Greensburg. Kiowa Co. (SC). 20 m W of Greensburg.

13361 ■ Mullinville Development Association
100 N Main
Mullinville, KS 67109
Owner: Mullinville Development Assn., at above address. **Founded:** 1972. **Key Personnel:** Donna McDonald, Contact. **Cities Served:** Mullinville, Kansas: subscribing households 110; 14 channels; 1 community access channel. **URL:** http://www.kansas.gov/bess/flow/main;jsessionid=99826D5A9A1B2D50BE1038AD5781DC8D.aptcs03-inst2?execution=e1s12.

NEODESHA

SE KS. Wilson Co. 15 mi. N. of Independence. Alfalfa dehydrating plant; plows, boats, steel fabrication, aerosol products, plastics, insecticide, carpenter tools, cabinet products, dairy products manufactured; foundry. Oil wells. Grain, dairy, poultry, stock farms. Wheat, corn, oats.

13362 ■ Neodesha Derrick
Neodesha Derrick
502 Main St.
Neodesha, KS 66757
Phone: (620)325-3000
Community newspaper. **Freq:** Weekly (Thurs.). **Print Method:** Offset. **Cols./Page:** 6. **Col. Width:** 12.5 picas. **Col. Depth:** 301 agate lines. **Key Personnel:** JoAnne Harper, Publisher. **Formerly:** Neodesh Sun-Register. **Ad Rates:** BW $441; SAU $3.50; PCI $3.50. **Remarks:** Accepts advertising. **Circ:** ‡1800.

NESS CITY

WC KS. Ness Co. 56 mi. N. of Dodge City. Oil wells. Grain, dairy, poultry, livestock farms. Wheat, corn, milo, alfalfa.

13363 ■ Ness County News
Ness County News
110 S Kansas
Ness City, KS 67560
Phone: (785)798-2213
Fax: (785)798-2214
Publisher's E-mail: nessnews@gbta.net
Community newspaper. **Freq:** Weekly (Thurs.). **Print Method:** Offset. **Cols./Page:** 6. **Col. Width:** 24 nonpareils. **Col. Depth:** 294 agate lines. **Key Personnel:** Jerry Clarke, Editor. **USPS:** 377-200. **Subscription Rates:** $18.50 Individuals; $22.50 Out of area; $0.40 Single issue. **Ad Rates:** GLR $.16; SAU $2.80; PCI $2.80. **Remarks:** Accepts advertising. **Circ:** ‡2425.

NEWTON

SC KS. Harvey Co. 25 mi. N. of Wichita. Bethel College (Mennon). Mobile homes manufactured Flour mills. Dairy, stock, grain farms.

13364 ■ Mennonite World Review
Mennonite Weekly Review Inc.
129 W Sixth St.
Newton, KS 67114
Phone: (316)283-3670
Fax: (316)283-6502
Free: 800-424-0178
Tabloid newspaper containing news and commentary regarding churches and institutions of the Mennonite denomination. **Freq:** Weekly. **Print Method:** Offset. **Cols./Page:** 5. **Col. Width:** 24 nonpareils. **Col. Depth:** 224 agate lines. **Key Personnel:** Dana Neff, Associate Editor; Paul R. Schrag, Editor. **ISSN:** 0889--2156 (print). **Subscription Rates:** $54 Individuals; $78 Canada; $99 Two years. **URL:** http://mennoworld.org. **Formerly:** Mennonite Weekly Review. **Mailing address:** PO Box 568, Newton, KS 67114. **Ad Rates:** BW $1600; 4C $1920; PCI $20. **Remarks:** Advertising accepted; rates available upon request. **Circ:** Paid ‡9100.

13365 ■ Timbrel
Mennonite Women U.S.A.
718 N Main St.
Newton, KS 67114-1819

Phone: (316)281-4396
Fax: (316)283-0454
Free: 866-866-2872
Publisher's E-mail: office@mwusa.org
Freq: Bimonthly. **Subscription Rates:** $15 Individuals; 28 Dh Two years; $39 Individuals 3 years. **URL:** http://mennonitewomenusa.org/timbrel. **Remarks:** Advertising not accepted. **Circ:** (Not Reported).

13366 ■ KCVW-FM - 94.3
209 N Meridian Rd.
Newton, KS 67114
Phone: (316)283-4592
Fax: (316)283-3177
Email: comments@bottradionetwork.com
Format: Religious. **Networks:** Business Radio; Sun Radio. **Owner:** Bott Radio Network, 10550 Barkley, Overland Park, KS 66212, Ph: (913)642-7770, Fax: (913)642-1319, Free: 800-345-2621. **Founded:** 1998. **Operating Hours**: Continuous. **ADI:** Wichita-Hutchinson, KS. **Wattage**: 50,000. **Ad Rates:** Noncommercial. **URL:** http://www.bottradionetwork.com.

13367 ■ KJRG-AM
209 N Meridian Rd.
Newton, KS 67114-0567
Phone: (316)283-5150
Fax: (316)284-2684
Format: Religious. **Networks:** USA Radio. **Owner:** KJRG, Inc., at above address. **Founded:** 1953. **Wattage**: 500 Day; 147 Night. **Mailing address:** PO Box 567, Newton, KS 67114-0567.

NORTH NEWTON

Harvey Co.

13368 ■ Bethel College Context
Bethel College
300 E 27th St.
North Newton, KS 67117
Phone: (316)283-2500
Free: 800-522-1887
Alumni magazine. **Freq:** Quarterly. **Print Method:** Offset. **Subscription Rates:** Included in membership. **URL:** http://context.bethelks.edu. **Formerly**: Bethel College Bulletin. **Remarks:** Advertising not accepted. **Circ:** (Not Reported).

13369 ■ KBCU-FM - 88.1
300 E 27th St.
North Newton, KS 67117
Phone: (316)283-2500
Free: 800-522-1887
Email: kbcu@bethelks.edu
Format: Eclectic. **Networks:** AP. **Owner:** Bethel College, 1001 Bethel Cir., Mishawaka, IN 46545, Ph: (574)807-7000, Free: 800-422-4101. **Founded:** 1989. **Operating Hours**: Continuous. **Key Personnel:** Dan Anderson, Contact; Christine Crouse-Dick, Contact; Dan Anderson, Contact; Tim Buller, Contact. **Local Programs**: *KBCU Sunday Gospel Show*, Sunday 6:00 a.m. - 11:00 a.m.; *Sounds of the South Wind*, Saturday Sunday 6:00 a.m. 5:00 p.m. 1:00 p.m. - 5:00 p.m.; *Interfaith Voices*, Saturday Sunday 5:00 p.m. - 6:00 p.m.; *KBCU Chill*, Sunday Monday Tuesday Wednesday Thursday Friday Saturday 12:00 a.m. - 6:00 a.m.; *KBCU Jazz Show*, Monday Wednesday Thursday Friday Tuesday 6:00 a.m. - 5:00 p.m. 6:00 a.m. - 3:00 p.m.; *KBCU Contemporary Christian Saturday Night with Rockin' Ron*, Saturday 6:00 p.m. - 12:00 a.m. **Wattage**: 149. **Ad Rates:** Noncommercial. **URL:** http://www.bethelks.edu/kbcu.

NORTON

NW KS. Norton Co. 200 mi. NW of Salina. State Hospital for Mentally Retarded.

13370 ■ Norton Telegram
Nor'West Newspapers
215 S Kansas Ave.
Norton, KS 67654-0320
General newspaper. **Freq:** Semiweekly Tues.-Fri. **Print Method:** Offset. **Cols./Page:** 6. **Col. Width:** 20 nonpareils. **Col. Depth:** 294 agate lines. **Key Personnel:** Tom Dreiling, Publisher. **URL:** http://www.nwkansas.com/NCTwebpages/ntmain.html. **Formerly**: Norton Daily Telegram. **Ad Rates:** GLR $1.25; BW $370; SAU $4.50; PCI $4.50. **Circ:** Free 1400.

13371 ■ KQNK-AM - 106.7
1530 KQNK Rd.
Norton, KS 67654
Phone: (785)877-3378
Fax: (785)877-3379
Format: Adult Contemporary. **Founded:** 1963. **Operating Hours**: Continuous. **Key Personnel:** Bruce Dierking, Owner, President; Marvin Matchett, Gen. Mgr. **Wattage**: 1,000 AM 3,000 WT FM. **Ad Rates:** Noncommercial. **URL:** http://www.kqnk.com.

13372 ■ KQNK-FM - 106.7
1530 KQNK Rd.
Norton, KS 67654
Phone: (785)877-3378
Format: Adult Contemporary. **Key Personnel:** Marvin Matchett, Gen. Mgr.; Deena Wente, News Dir. **URL:** http://www.kqnk.com.

OBERLIN

NW KS. Decatur Co. 170 mi. NW of Salina. Oil wells. Grain, poultry, stock farms. Wheat, corn, alfalfa.

13373 ■ The Oberlin Herald
Nor'West Newspapers
170 S Penn Ave.
Oberlin, KS 67749
Phone: (785)475-2206
Fax: (785)475-2800
Publication E-mail: obherald@nwkansas.com
Community newspaper. **Freq:** Weekly (Wed.). **Print Method:** Offset. **Cols./Page:** 6. **Col. Width:** 2 inches. **Col. Depth:** 21 inches. **Key Personnel:** Pat Cozad, Manager, Circulation; Kimberly Davis, Editor; Cynthia Haynes, Editor; Steve Haynes, Publisher. **USPS:** 401-600. **URL:** http://www.nwkansas.com/obhwebpages/obhmain.html. **Ad Rates:** GLR $6.15; BW $793.35; 4C $892.35. **Remarks:** Accepts advertising. **Circ:** Paid ‡2127.

OLATHE

E. KS. Johnson Co. 20 mi. SW of Kansas City. State School for the Deaf, Mid-America College. Manufactures batteries, radio and electronic parts for airplanes, X-Ray equipment, air-conditioning cooling towers, drilling machinery, grease, oil, cowboy boots, shoes. Stock, dairy farms.

13374 ■ Frozen & Refrigerated Buyer: We Help Your Business Grow
CT Media Partners
11472 S Wilder St.
Olathe, KS 66061
Phone: (603)252-0507
Magazine featuring the latest information and trends, tactics, and strategies relevant to retailers in the frozen food and dairy industry. **Freq:** Monthly. **Key Personnel:** Warren Thayer, Director, Editorial, phone: (603)252-0507; Paul Chapa, Director, Sales, phone: (913)481-5060. **Subscription Rates:** Free; $40 Individuals non-retailer. **URL:** http://www.fdbuyer.com. **Formerly**: Frozen and Dairy Buyer: We Help Your Business Grow. **Ad Rates:** 4C $4,480. **Remarks:** Accepts advertising. **Circ:** (Not Reported).

13375 ■ The Olathe Daily News
Keltatim Publishing Company Inc.
514 S Kansas Ave.
Olathe, KS 66061
Phone: (913)764-2211
General newspaper. **Freq:** Daily. **Print Method:** Offset. **Cols./Page:** 6. **Col. Width:** 26 nonpareils. **Col. Depth:** 21 1/2 inches. **Key Personnel:** Richard Espinoza, Editor; Kevin Wright, Contact. **ISSN:** 0886--9871 (print). **Subscription Rates:** $76.20 Individuals; $86.60 Out of area; $152 Out of state. **URL:** http://www.theolathenews.com. **Ad Rates:** SAU $10.50; PCI $10.50. **Remarks:** Accepts advertising. **Circ:** 25000.

13376 ■ Perspectives: A Magazine for Graduate Enrollment Management Professionals
National Association of Graduate Admissions Professionals
18000 W 105th St.
Olathe, KS 66061-7543
Phone: (913)895-4616
Fax: (913)895-4652
Publisher's E-mail: info@nagap.org
Freq: 3/year. **Subscription Rates:** Included in membership. **URL:** http://www.nagap.org/nagap-news. **Mailing address:** PO Box 14605, Lenexa, KS 66285-4605. **Remarks:** Accepts advertising. **Circ:** (Not Reported).

13377 ■ Railroadiana Express
Railroadiana Collectors Association Incorporated
c/o Mary Ann James, Secretary
17675 W 113th St.
Olathe, KS 66061
Freq: Quarterly. **Subscription Rates:** Included in membership. **Alt. Formats:** PDF. **Remarks:** Advertising not accepted. **Circ:** (Not Reported).

OSAGE CITY

E. KS. Osage Co. 34 mi. NE of Emporia. Resort area. Manufactures paper napkins, cups and plates. Modular homes. Agriculture. Sorghums, hay, cattle, corn, wheat, soybeans, grain.

13378 ■ Osage County Herald-Chronicle
Osage County Chronicle
527 Market St.
Osage City, KS 66523
Phone: (785)528-3511
Fax: (785)528-4811
Newspaper (local news). **Founded:** Sept. 1863. **Freq:** Weekly (Thurs.). **Print Method:** Offset. **Cols./Page:** 6. **Col. Width:** 26 nonpareils. **Col. Depth:** 301 agate lines. **Key Personnel:** Catherine Faimon, Publisher; Jeremy Gaston, Managing Editor. **Subscription Rates:** $32 Individuals in Osage County; $35 Individuals out of county, in Kansas; $45 Individuals out of Kansas. **URL:** http://www.och-c.com/. **Formed by the merger of**: Osage County Chronicle. **Formerly**: Osage City Journal Free-Press; Lyndon News Herald; Burlingame Enterprise-Chronicle; Overbrook Citizen-Times. **Ad Rates:** GLR $.36; BW $657.90; 4C $180; SAU $5.45; PCI $7.95. **Remarks:** Accepts advertising. **Circ:** ⊕**5029**.

OSBORNE

NC KS. Osborne Co. 70 mi. NW of Salina. Residential.

13379 ■ Osborne County Farmer
Osborne Publishing Company Inc.
210 W Main
Osborne, KS 67473-2405
Publication E-mail: ospubco@ruraitel.net
Local newspaper. **Freq:** Weekly (Thurs.). **Print Method:** Offset. **Cols./Page:** 6. **Col. Width:** 26 nonpareils. **Col. Depth:** 287 agate lines. **Key Personnel:** Dale Worley, Publisher. **ISSN:** 1040-9033 (print). **Subscription Rates:** $24.58 Individuals. **Ad Rates:** GLR $.20; SAU $4.25; PCI $5. **Remarks:** Advertising accepted; rates available upon request. **Circ:** ‡2755.

OTTAWA

E. KS. Franklin Co. 26 mi. S. of Lawrence. Ottawa University. Manufactures milk, steel foundry products, TV antennas, cement, mobile homes, rural advertising signs, yard tractors. Mill work. Rock quarries. Diversified farming. Beef. Corn, wheat, alfalfa.

13380 ■ Ottawa Herald
Ottawa Herald
104 S Cedar
Ottawa, KS 66067
Phone: (785)242-4700
Fax: (785)242-9420
Free: 800-467-8383
Publication E-mail: letters@ottawaherald.com
General newspaper. **Freq:** Daily (eve.). **Print Method:** Offset. **Cols./Page:** 6. **Col. Width:** 10.6 picas. **Col. Depth:** 21.5 inches. **Key Personnel:** Gordon Billingsley, Director; Linda Brown, Director, Marketing; Laurie Blanco, Director, Advertising; Jeanny Sharp, Editor. **Subscription Rates:** $9.22 Individuals /month (digital only); $9.22 Individuals /month (print + digital); $1 Individuals each (back issues). **Alt. Formats:** Microfilm. **URL:** http://www.ottawaherald.com. **Ad Rates:** GLR $2.12; BW $1106.82; 4C $1356.82; PCI $10.52. **Remarks:** Accepts advertising. **Circ:** Paid ■ **3984**.

13381 ■ Ottawa Spirit
Ottawa University
1001 S Cedar St.
Ottawa, KS 66067-3341

Circulation: ★ = AAM; △ or • = BPA; ♦ = CAC; ❑ = VAC; ⊕ = PO Statement; ‡ = Publisher's Report; Boldface figures = sworn; Light figures = estimated.

Phone: (785)242-5200
Fax: (785)229-1008
Free: 800-755-5200
Publisher's E-mail: admiss@ottawa.edu
University alumni and friends magazine. **Freq:** Quarterly. **Print Method:** Offset. **Trim Size:** 8 1/2 x 11. **Cols./Page:** 3. **Col. Width:** 14 picas. **Col. Depth:** 59 picas. **URL:** http://www.ottawa.edu/OttawaSpirit/Home. **Formerly**: Tauy Talk. **Remarks:** Advertising not accepted. **Circ:** Controlled ‡14500.

13382 ■ Ottawa Times Shopper
Ottawa Herald
104 S Cedar
Ottawa, KS 66067
Phone: (785)242-4700
Fax: (785)242-9420
Free: 800-467-8383
Weekly community newspaper. **Freq:** Weekly Tuesday and Thursday. **Print Method:** Offset. **Trim Size:** 11 1/4 x 17. **Cols./Page:** 6. **Col. Width:** 10 picas. **Col. Depth:** 16 inches. **USPS:** 413-660. **Subscription Rates:** $117.28 Individuals; $156.07 Out of state. **URL:** http://www.ottawaherald.com/shopper. **Ad Rates:** GLR $.10; BW $696; 4C $975; SAU $5.75; PCI $7.18. **Remarks:** Color advertising accepted; rates available upon request. **Circ:** Free 14475.

13383 ■ KOFO-AM - 1220
320 E Radio Rd.
Ottawa, KS 66067
Phone: (785)242-1220
Email: kofo@kofo.com
Format: Country; News. **Networks:** ABC; Kansas Information. **Founded:** 1949. **Operating Hours:** Continuous. **Wattage**: 250. **Ad Rates:** $10.60-12.50 for 30 seconds; $12.50-14.70 for 60 seconds. **Mailing address:** PO Box 16, Ottawa, KS 66067. **URL:** http://www.kofo.com.

13384 ■ KRBW-FM - 90.5
320 E Radio Rd.
Ottawa, KS 66067
Format: Contemporary Christian. **Owner:** Ottawa Christian Radio, Inc., at above address. **Operating Hours**: Continuous. **Local Programs**: *Sunday Morning Praise - John Adams*, Sunday 8:00 a.m. - 9:00 a.m. **Wattage**: 430. **Ad Rates:** Noncommercial. **Mailing address:** PO Box 22, Ottawa, KS 66067. **URL:** http://www.internet4christ.com.

13385 ■ KTJO-FM - 88.9
1001 S Cedar St.
Ottawa, KS 66067-3399
Fax: (785)229-1008
Free: 800-755-5200
Format: Album-Oriented Rock (AOR). **Owner:** Ottawa University, 9414 N 25th Ave., Phoenix, AZ 85021, Free: 855-774-7713. **Founded:** 1942. **Operating Hours**: 7 a.m.-11 p.m. Mon.-Sat. **Wattage:** 145. **Ad Rates:** Noncommercial. **URL:** http://www.ottawa.edu.

OVERLAND PARK

E. KS. Johnson Co. 12 mi. SW of Kansas City.

13386 ■ American City and County
Penton
9800 Metcalf Ave.
Overland Park, KS 66212
Phone: (913)967-1710
Publisher's E-mail: corporatecustomerservice@penton.com
Municipal and county administration magazine. **Freq:** Monthly. **Print Method:** Offset. **Trim Size:** 7 7/8 x 10 3/4. **Cols./Page:** 3. **Col. Width:** 26 nonpareils. **Col. Depth:** 140 agate lines. **Key Personnel:** Bill Wolpin, Director, Editorial, phone: (770)618-0112; Lindsay Isaacs, Managing Editor, phone: (770)618-0199; Gregg Herring, Publisher, phone: (770)618-0333. **ISSN:** 0149--337X (print). **URL:** http://americancityandcounty.com. **Ad Rates:** BW $10005; 4C $2485; PCI $160. **Remarks:** Accepts advertising. **Circ:** △**65223**.

13387 ■ American School & University: Shaping Facilities & Business Decisions
Penton
9800 Metcalf Ave.
Overland Park, KS 66212
Phone: (913)967-1710
Publisher's E-mail: corporatecustomerservice@penton.com
Trade magazine. **Freq:** Monthly. **Print Method:** Offset. **Trim Size:** 8 1/8 x 10 7/8. **Cols./Page:** 3. **Col. Width:** 28 nonpareils. **Col. Depth:** 140 agate lines. **Key Personnel:** Gregg Herring, Publisher, phone: (770)618-0333; Joe Agron, Editor-in-Chief, phone: (215)752-2787; Susan Lustig, Executive Editor, phone: (913)967-1960, fax: (913)514-6960. **ISSN:** 0003-0945 (print). **USPS:** 023-180. **URL:** http://asumag.com. **Ad Rates:** BW $9,825. **Remarks:** Accepts advertising. **Circ:** 62209.

13388 ■ The Auctioneer
National Auctioneers Association
8880 Ballentine St.
Overland Park, KS 66214
Phone: (913)541-8084
Fax: (913)894-5281
Publisher's E-mail: support@auctioneers.org
Trade magazine for auctioneers. **Trim Size:** 8.5 x 11. **Key Personnel:** Bryan Scribner, Director, Publications, phone: (913)563-5424; Ryan Putnam, Associate Editor; Hannes Combest, Chief Executive Officer. **ISSN:** 1070-0137 (print). **URL:** http://www.auctioneers.org/find-auctioneer/search. **Ad Rates:** BW $870; 4C $1,200. **Remarks:** Accepts advertising. **Circ:** 4000.

13389 ■ Automobile Red Book
Penton
9800 Metcalf Ave.
Overland Park, KS 66212
Phone: (913)967-1710
Publisher's E-mail: corporatecustomerservice@penton.com
Auto and light truck valuation guide. **Print Method:** Offset. **Trim Size:** 4 1/4 x 7 1/2. **ISSN:** 1074-181X (print). **Subscription Rates:** $69.95 Individuals. **URL:** http://www.autoredbook.com. **Formerly**: NMR's Automobile Blue Book. **Remarks:** Advertising not accepted. **Circ:** Paid ‡1540.

13390 ■ Broker World
Insurance Publications Inc.
9404 Reeds Rd.
Overland Park, KS 66207-1010
Phone: (913)383-9191
Fax: (913)383-1247
Free: 800-762-3387
Publisher's E-mail: info@brokerworldmag.com
Trade magazine on life and health insurance brokering. **Freq:** Monthly. **Print Method:** Offset. **Trim Size:** 8 x 10 7/8. **Cols./Page:** 3. **Col. Width:** 14 picas. **Col. Depth:** 140 agate lines. **Key Personnel:** Sharon A. Chace, Editor; Stephen P. Howard, Publisher. **ISSN:** 0273-6551 (print). **Subscription Rates:** $6 Individuals; $11 Two years; $16 Individuals 3 years. **URL:** http://www.brokerworldmag.com/. **Mailing address:** PO Box 1130, Overland Park, KS 66207-1010. **Ad Rates:** BW $2,235.50; 4C $4,700. **Remarks:** Accepts advertising. **Circ:** ‡30535.

13391 ■ Campus Ledger
Johnson Community College
12345 College Blvd.
Overland Park, KS 66210-1299
Phone: (913)469-8500
Publisher's E-mail: helpdesk@jccc.edu
Collegiate newspaper. **Freq:** Semimonthly (during the academic year). **Print Method:** Offset. **Trim Size:** 10 x 10. **Cols./Page:** 5. **Col. Width:** 10 picas. **Key Personnel:** Jennifer Harris, Editor-in-Chief; Rachel Fredman, Manager, Advertising, Manager, Promotions; Ryan Koenig, Manager, Circulation. **Alt. Formats:** Print. **URL:** http://blogs.jccc.edu/campusledger; http://www.jccc.edu/academics/communications/journalism/campus-ledger.html. **Ad Rates:** BW $680; 4C $830; PCI $13. **Remarks:** Accepts advertising. **Circ:** Free 5600.

13392 ■ Club Industry's Fitness Business Pro
Penton
9800 Metcalf Ave.
Overland Park, KS 66212
Phone: (913)967-1710
Publisher's E-mail: corporatecustomerservice@penton.com
Trade magazine covering trends and news for owners and operators of commercial health and fitness facilities. **Founded:** 1984. **Freq:** Monthly. **Key Personnel:** Pam Kufahl, Editor-in-Chief; Stuart Goldman, Managing Editor. **URL:** http://clubindustry.com. **Ad Rates:** BW $5,045; 4C $6,360. **Remarks:** Accepts advertising. **Circ:** Combined △**30000**.

13393 ■ EC&M
Penton
9800 Metcalf Ave.
Overland Park, KS 66212
Phone: (913)967-1710
Publisher's E-mail: corporatecustomerservice@penton.com
Magazine focusing on electrical engineering, construction, and maintenance. **Freq:** Monthly. **Print Method:** Web Offset. **Trim Size:** 8 x 10 3/4. **Cols./Page:** 3 and 2. **Col. Width:** 13 and 20 picas. **Col. Depth:** 10 inches. **Key Personnel:** David Miller, Publisher, phone: (312)840-8487, fax: (312)840-8470; Michael Eby, Editor-in-Chief, phone: (913)967-1782, fax: (913)514-6782; Ellen Parson, Managing Editor, phone: (913)967-1986, fax: (913)514-6569; Beck Ireland, Writer, phone: (913)967-1806, fax: (913)514-6512. **Alt. Formats:** PDF. **URL:** http://ecmweb.com. **Ad Rates:** BW $15,225. **Remarks:** with EC&M Buyer's Guide. **Circ:** (Not Reported).

13394 ■ Electrical Wholesaling
Penton
9800 Metcalf Ave.
Overland Park, KS 66212
Phone: (913)967-1710
Publisher's E-mail: corporatecustomerservice@penton.com
Magazine focusing on electrical wholesaling for distributors of electrical supplies. **Founded:** 1920. **Freq:** Monthly. **Print Method:** Web Offset. **Cols./Page:** 3. **Col. Width:** 27 nonpareils. **Col. Depth:** 136 agate lines. **Key Personnel:** Doug Chandler, Executive Editor, phone: (913)967-1951; David Miller, Publisher, phone: (312)840-8487, fax: (312)840-8470; Jim Lucy, Editor-in-Chief, phone: (913)967-1743, fax: (913)514-7643. **URL:** http://ewweb.com. **Remarks:** Accepts advertising. **Circ:** (Not Reported).

13395 ■ Engineer's Digest
Penton
9800 Metcalf Ave.
Overland Park, KS 66212
Phone: (913)967-1710
Publisher's E-mail: corporatecustomerservice@penton.com
Trade magazine on the plant facilities market. **Freq:** Monthly. **Print Method:** Offset. **Trim Size:** 11 x 15 7/8. **Cols./Page:** 3. **Col. Width:** 36 nonpareils. **Col. Depth:** 210 agate lines. **Key Personnel:** Larry Beck, Editor. **ISSN:** 0199-0101 (print). **Subscription Rates:** Free to qualified readers. **URL:** http://www.penrose-press.com/idd/card.php?INDEX=MAG16013&SUBJECT=SUB10053. **Ad Rates:** BW $7,919; 4C $9,229. **Remarks:** Accepts advertising. **Circ:** (Not Reported).

13396 ■ Fire Chief
Penton
9800 Metcalf Ave.
Overland Park, KS 66212
Phone: (913)967-1710
Publisher's E-mail: corporatecustomerservice@penton.com
Fire protection magazine. **Founded:** Sept. 1957. **Freq:** Monthly. **Print Method:** Offset. **Trim Size:** 7 3/4 x 10 3/4. **Cols./Page:** 3. **Col. Width:** 26 nonpareils. **Col. Depth:** 140 agate lines. **Key Personnel:** Janet Wilmoth, Associate Publisher, phone: (312)840-8410; Lisa Allegretti, Editor, phone: (312)840-8443. **ISSN:** 0015-2552 (print). **URL:** http://firechief.com. **Ad Rates:** BW $5645; 4C $1900. **Remarks:** Accepts advertising. **Circ:** Combined △**50,312**.

13397 ■ Fleet Owner
Penton
9800 Metcalf Ave.
Overland Park, KS 66212
Phone: (913)967-1710
Publisher's E-mail: corporatecustomerservice@penton.com
Magazine for managers of commercial motor fleets. **Founded:** 1928. **Freq:** Monthly. **Print Method:** Offset. **Trim Size:** 7 7/8 x 10 3/4. **Cols./Page:** 2 and 3. **Col. Width:** 40 and 26 nonpareils. **Col. Depth:** 140 agate lines. **Key Personnel:** Sean Kilcarr, Senior Editor, phone: (703)569-1829; David Cullen, Executive Editor, phone: (203)358-4212; Brian Straight, Managing Editor; Wendy Leavitt, Director, Development, Director, Edito-

rial; Thomas W. Duncan, Publisher; Jim Mele, Editor-in-Chief. **ISSN:** 0731-9622 (print). **Alt. Formats:** Handheld. **URL:** http://fleetowner.com. **Formed by the merger of:** Fleet Owner--Big Fleet Edition; Fleet Owner--Small Fleet Owner. **Ad Rates:** BW $14,166; 4C $18,189. **Remarks:** Accepts advertising. **Circ:** Non-paid ‡105000.

13398 ■ HomeCare
Penton
9800 Metcalf Ave.
Overland Park, KS 66212
Phone: (913)967-1710
Magazine for home medical equipment providers, publishing timely legislative, regulatory and business news, in-depth analysis of various market segments, emerging issues and trends, and practical how-to advice on business operations. **Freq:** Monthly. **Key Personnel:** Jane Longshore, Managing Editor; Wally Evans, Publisher, phone: (205)212-9402; Russ Willcutt, Editor. **Subscription Rates:** Free qualified U.S. readers; $48 U.S.; $125 Other countries. **URL:** http://homecaremag.com. **Ad Rates:** BW $4,290; 4C $5,240. **Remarks:** Accepts advertising. **Circ:** △**17091**.

13399 ■ The IAPD Magazine
International Association of Plastics Distribution
6734 W 121st St.
Overland Park, KS 66209
Phone: (913)345-1005
Fax: (913)345-1006
Publisher's E-mail: iapd@iapd.org
Trade association magazine covering plastics distribution. **Freq:** Bimonthly. **Print Method:** Offset. **Trim Size:** 8 1/2 x 11. **Key Personnel:** Liz Novak, Editor-in-Chief. **Subscription Rates:** $90 Nonmembers 1 year. **URL:** http://www.iapd.org/IAPD/Publications/Publications/IAPD/Publications/Publications.aspx#magazine; http://www.iapd.org/IAPD/Education/Plastics_Technical_Resources.aspx. **Formerly:** The NAPD Magazine. **Ad Rates:** BW $3375. **Remarks:** Accepts advertising. **Circ:** Paid 10000.

13400 ■ Imaging Economics
Ascend Integrated Media
7015 College Blvd., Ste. 600
Overland Park, KS 66211
Phone: (913)469-1110
Publisher's E-mail: info@ascendmedia.com
Magazine providing a high-level forum to address the development, diffusion, acquisition, and utilization of imaging technology. **Freq:** Monthly. **Key Personnel:** Marianne Matthews, Editor. **Subscription Rates:** Free to qualified subscribers. **URL:** http://www.imagingeconomics.com; http://www.axisimagingnews.com/buyers-guide/listing/imaging-economics-magazine. **Circ:** (Not Reported).

13401 ■ Information Management
ARMA International
11880 College Blvd., Ste. 450
Overland Park, KS 66210
Fax: (913)341-3742
Free: 800-422-2762
Publisher's E-mail: headquarters@armaintl.org
Professional journal on records and information management. **Founded:** 1967. **Freq:** Bimonthly. **Print Method:** Sheetfed offset. **Trim Size:** 8 1/2 x 11. **Cols./Page:** 3. **Col. Width:** 27 nonpareils. **Col. Depth:** 136 agate lines. **Key Personnel:** Amy Lanter, Managing Editor. **ISSN:** 1535-2897 (print). **Subscription Rates:** $140 Individuals plus shipping, $20 for destinations outside the U.S., Canada, or Puerto Rico. **URL:** http://www.arma.org; http://content.arma.org/IMM/online/InformationManagement.aspx. **Formerly:** Records Management Quarterly; Information Management Journal. **Ad Rates:** BW $1,882; 4C $2,978. **Remarks:** Accepts advertising. **Circ:** 11000.

13402 ■ International Construction
Penton
9800 Metcalf Ave.
Overland Park, KS 66212
Phone: (913)967-1710
Publisher's E-mail: corporatecustomerservice@penton.com
Trade magazine. **Freq:** 10/year. **Print Method:** Web Offset. **Trim Size:** 210 x 297 mm. **Cols./Page:** 2 and 3. **Col. Width:** 42 and 50 millimeters. **Col. Depth:** 242 millimeters. **Key Personnel:** Chris Sleight, Editor; Alister Williams, Manager, Advertising; Ross Dickson, Manager, Production. **ISSN:** 0020--6415 (print). **Subscription Rates:** Free digital format. **URL:** http://www.khl.com/magazines/international-construction. **Remarks:** Accepts advertising. **Circ:** Combined 26168.

13403 ■ Kansas City Jewish Chronicle
Sun Publications Inc.
4370 W 109th St., Ste. 300
Overland Park, KS 66211
Phone: (913)381-1010
Fax: (913)381-9889
Newspaper (tabloid) for Jewish community. **Freq:** Weekly (Fri.). **Print Method:** Offset. **Trim Size:** 8.5 x 14.5. **Cols./Page:** 6. **Col. Width:** 1.5 inches. **Col. Depth:** 13 1/2 inches. **Key Personnel:** David Small, Publisher; Steve Rose, Publisher; Rick Hellman, Editor. **ISSN:** 0022--8524 (print). **Subscription Rates:** $54.95 Individuals one year; $71.95 Out of area one year; $84.95 Two years two years; $138.95 Out of area two years; $104.95 Individuals 3 years; $167.56 Out of area 3 years. **URL:** http://www.kcjc.com. **Ad Rates:** BW $1644; 4C $1,894; PCI $20.30. **Remarks:** Advertising accepted; rates available upon request. **Circ:** (Not Reported).

13404 ■ Kansas City Nursing News
Sun Publications Inc.
4370 W 109th St., Ste. 300
Overland Park, KS 66211
Phone: (913)381-1010
Fax: (913)381-9889
Publication E-mail: sandynelson@miconews.com
Newspaper covering nursing news in Kansas City, Kansas area. **Freq:** Weekly (Mon.). **Key Personnel:** Arley Hoskin, Editor. **Subscription Rates:** $21.23 Individuals /month, daily; $11.33 Individuals /month - Friday, Sunday; $13.10 Individuals /month - online. **URL:** http://www.newspressnow.com/news/business/article_0acc92a5-5cb2-531b-aedd-fce3d26adcf5.html. **Remarks:** Accepts advertising. **Circ:** (Not Reported).

13405 ■ Learning Disability Quarterly
Council for Learning Disabilities
11184 Antioch Rd.
Overland Park, KS 66210
Phone: (913)491-1011
Fax: (913)491-1011
Freq: Quarterly. **Key Personnel:** David Scanlon, Board Member; Bryan Briant, Editor. **ISSN:** 0731--9487 (print); **EISSN:** 2168--376X (electronic). **Subscription Rates:** £41 Individuals print only; £112 Institutions online only; £112 Institutions print only; £124 Institutions print and online; £13 Individuals single print issue; £34 Institutions single print issue. **URL:** http://ldq.sagepub.com. **Remarks:** Advertising not accepted. **Circ:** (Not Reported).

13406 ■ Live Design
Penton
9800 Metcalf Ave.
Overland Park, KS 66212
Phone: (913)967-1710
Publisher's E-mail: corporatecustomerservice@penton.com
Magazine for staging professionals, rental agencies, and meeting/event planners who are producing high-quality, technology-rich staged events for entertainment and business. **Freq:** 9/year. **Trim Size:** 9x10.875. **Key Personnel:** Marian Sandberg, Editor, phone: (212)204-4266; David Johnson, Associate Publisher, Director, Editorial; Kelly Turner, Manager, Sales. **URL:** http://livedesignonline.com/. **Formed by the merger of:** SRO Magazine; Entertainment Design; Lighting Dimensions. **Remarks:** Accepts advertising. **Circ:** 18000.

13407 ■ Live Design: The Art & Technology of Show Business
Penton
9800 Metcalf Ave.
Overland Park, KS 66212
Phone: (913)967-1710
Publisher's E-mail: corporatecustomerservice@penton.com
The business of entertainment technology and design. **Freq:** 12/yr. **Print Method:** Offset. **Trim Size:** 9 x 10.875. **Cols./Page:** 3. **Col. Width:** 13.5 picas. **Col. Depth:** 140 agate lines. **Key Personnel:** Marian Sandberg, Editor, phone: (212)204-4266, fax: (212)204-4291; David Johnson, Publisher, phone: (212)204-4272, fax: (212)204-4291; Kelly Turner, Manager, Sales, phone: (415)455-8305, fax: (913)514-3817. **ISSN:** 1520--5150 (print). **URL:** http://www.penton.com/markets/design-manufacturing/#13. **Formerly:** TCI. **Ad Rates:** BW $4600; 4C $3723. **Remarks:** Accepts advertising. **Circ:** Controlled 18000.

13408 ■ Medical Meetings
Penton
9800 Metcalf Ave.
Overland Park, KS 66212
Phone: (913)967-1710
Publisher's E-mail: corporatecustomerservice@penton.com
Magazine covering regulatory and educational issues in continuing medical education. **Freq:** 7/yr. **Key Personnel:** Betsy Bair, Director, Editorial, phone: (978)448-0582; Sue Pelletier, Editor, phone: (978)448-0377; Barbara Scofidio, Editor, phone: (978)448-8211. **URL:** http://meetingsnet.com/medicalmeetings/. **Remarks:** Accepts advertising. **Circ:** △**12025**.

13409 ■ Multichannel Merchant
Penton
9800 Metcalf Ave.
Overland Park, KS 66212
Phone: (913)967-1710
Publisher's E-mail: corporatecustomerservice@penton.com
Magazine for marketing and advertising professionals that covers print, web, and cross-channel marketing. **Freq:** 13/yr. **Key Personnel:** Tim Parry, Managing Editor, phone: (203)899-8455. **URL:** http://multichannelmerchant.com. **Remarks:** Accepts advertising. **Circ:** ‡30050.

13410 ■ National Real Estate Investor
Penton
9800 Metcalf Ave.
Overland Park, KS 66212
Phone: (913)967-1710
Publisher's E-mail: corporatecustomerservice@penton.com
Magazine on commercial real estate investment, development and management. **Freq:** Quarterly. **Print Method:** Offset. **Trim Size:** 8 1/8 x 10 7/8. **Cols./Page:** 3. **Col. Width:** 26 nonpareils. **Col. Depth:** 140 agate lines. **Key Personnel:** David Bodamer, Executive Director, phone: (212)204-4207. **ISSN:** 0027--9994 (print). **URL:** http://nreionline.com. **Remarks:** Accepts advertising. **Circ:** (Not Reported).

13411 ■ Operations & Fulfillment
Penton
9800 Metcalf Ave.
Overland Park, KS 66212
Phone: (913)967-1710
Publisher's E-mail: corporatecustomerservice@penton.com
Magazine for direct-to-customer operations and fulfillment professionals, covering receiving, warehousing, picking, packing, and shipping. **Freq:** 10/year. **Key Personnel:** Jim Tierney, Writer; Melissa Dowling, Editor-in-Chief, phone: (203)358-4221; Tim Parry, Writer, phone: (203)358-4161. **Alt. Formats:** Download. **URL:** http://multichannelmerchant.com/opsandfulfillment. **Remarks:** Accepts advertising. **Circ:** (Not Reported).

13412 ■ Pharmacy Times: Practical Information for Today's Pharmacist
Ascend Integrated Media
7015 College Blvd., Ste. 600
Overland Park, KS 66211
Phone: (913)469-1110
Publisher's E-mail: info@ascendmedia.com
Journal providing information on health items (including prescription and over-the-counter drugs and surgical supplies) to independent, chain, and hospital pharmacists. **Freq:** Monthly 1 OTC supplement. **Print Method:** Offset. **Trim Size:** 7 7/8 x 10 3/4. **Cols./Page:** 2. **Col. Width:** 36 nonpareils. **Col. Depth:** 140 agate lines. **Key Personnel:** Bea Riemschneider, Director, Editorial; Randi Hernandez, Associate Editor. **ISSN:** 0003-0627 (print). **URL:** http://www.pharmacytimes.com. **Ad Rates:** BW $11,050; 4C $2,860. **Remarks:** Accepts advertising. **Circ:** △**180666**.

13413 ■ Power Electronics Technology
Penton

Circulation: ★ = AAM; △ or • = BPA; ♦ = CAC; ❑ = VAC; ⊕ = PO Statement; ‡ = Publisher's Report; Boldface figures = sworn; Light figures = estimated.

9800 Metcalf Ave.
Overland Park, KS 66212
Phone: (913)967-1710
Publisher's E-mail: corporatecustomerservice@penton.com
Professional magazine for power electronics designers and system integrators. **Freq:** Monthly. **Print Method:** Web Offset. **Trim Size:** 8 x 10 3/4. **Key Personnel:** Sam Davis, Editor-in-Chief, phone: (818)348-3982; Bill Baumann, Publisher, phone: (201)845-2403. **Alt. Formats:** PDF. **URL:** http://powerelectronics.com. **Formerly**: PCIM, Power Conversion International; PCIM Power Electronic Systems. **Ad Rates:** BW $5725. **Remarks:** Accepts advertising. **Circ:** △**30000**.

13414 ■ Resident & Staff Physician
Ascend Integrated Media
7015 College Blvd., Ste. 600
Overland Park, KS 66211
Phone: (913)469-1110
Publisher's E-mail: info@ascendmedia.com
Peer-reviewed medical journal. **Freq:** Monthly except July/August and November/December. **Print Method:** Offset. **Trim Size:** 8 1/8 x 11. **Cols./Page:** 3. **Col. Width:** 26 nonpareils. **Col. Depth:** 140 agate lines. **Key Personnel:** Robert T. Grant, Advisor; Werner Pfistere, Advisor; Charles E. Driscoll, MD, Editor-in-Chief. **ISSN:** 0034--5555 (print). **Ad Rates:** BW $5845; 4C $2000. **Remarks:** Accepts advertising. **Circ:** Controlled △**75539**.

13415 ■ Southwest Farm Press
Penton
9800 Metcalf Ave.
Overland Park, KS 66212
Phone: (913)967-1710
Publisher's E-mail: corporatecustomerservice@penton.com
Magazine covering agriculture of the southwestern states, encompassing production, management, research and legislative/regulatory issues affect grower of key cotton, wheat, grain sorghum, rice, peanuts, pecans, soybeans, corn and vegetable/citrus crops. **Freq:** 23/yr. **Key Personnel:** Greg Frey, Publisher; Ron Smith, Editor; Forrest Laws, Director. **URL:** http://southwestfarmpress.com. **Remarks:** Accepts advertising. **Circ:** △**28171**.

13416 ■ Special Events Magazine
Penton
9800 Metcalf Ave.
Overland Park, KS 66212
Phone: (913)967-1710
Publisher's E-mail: corporatecustomerservice@penton.com
Magazine for event professionals who design and produce special events in hotels, resorts, banquet facilities and other venues. **Freq:** Monthly. **Key Personnel:** Lisa Hurley, Editor, phone: (310)230-7179; Melissa Fromento, Publisher, phone: (212)204-4237. **Subscription Rates:** $84 Individuals /year. **URL:** http://specialevents.com. **Ad Rates:** 4C $6,620. **Remarks:** Accepts advertising. **Circ:** △**21272**.

13417 ■ Surgical Rounds
Ascend Integrated Media
7015 College Blvd., Ste. 600
Overland Park, KS 66211
Phone: (913)469-1110
Publisher's E-mail: info@ascendmedia.com
Peer-reviewed journal featuring clinical articles of interest to office-based and hospital-based surgeons, including residents, full-time staff, and surgical faculty. **Freq:** Monthly. **Print Method:** Offset. **Trim Size:** 7 7/8 x 10 3/4. **Cols./Page:** 2. **Col. Width:** 30 nonpareils. **Col. Depth:** 140 agate lines. **Key Personnel:** Bernard M. Jaffe, MD, Editor-in-Chief; Christina T. Loguidice, Editor, phone: (609)524-9517; C.L. Melton, Managing Editor, phone: (609)524-9535. **ISSN:** 0161--1372 (print). **Ad Rates:** BW $6350; 4C $2100. **Remarks:** Accepts advertising. **Circ:** Controlled ★**43325**.

13418 ■ Trailer/Body Builders
Penton
9800 Metcalf Ave.
Overland Park, KS 66212
Phone: (913)967-1710
Publisher's E-mail: inquiries@prismb2b.com
Trade magazine for truck trailer, truck body, and tank truck builders, and distributors of truck fleet equipment. **Freq:** Monthly. **Print Method:** Offset. **Trim Size:** 8 1/8 x 10 7/8. **Cols./Page:** 2 and 3. **Col. Width:** 21 and 13 picas. **Col. Depth:** 10 inches. **Key Personnel:** Bruce Sauer, Editor; Rick Weber, Associate Editor; Ray Anderson, Publisher. **USPS:** 636-660. **URL:** http://trailer-bodybuilders.com. **Ad Rates:** BW $3,440; 4C $4,050; BW $3,175. **Remarks:** Accepts advertising. **Circ:** 15550, Combined △**15550**.

13419 ■ Transmission and Distribution World
Penton
9800 Metcalf Ave.
Overland Park, KS 66212
Phone: (913)967-1710
Publisher's E-mail: corporatecustomerservice@penton.com
Magazine about powerline construction, transmission, and distribution. **Freq:** Monthly. **Print Method:** Offset. **Trim Size:** 7 7/8 x 10 3/4. **Cols./Page:** 3. **Col. Width:** 2 1/8 inches. **Col. Depth:** 141 agate lines. **Key Personnel:** David Miller, Publisher; Vito Longo, Editor; Rick Stasi, Manager, Marketing; Rick Bush, Director, Editorial; Emily Saarela, Managing Editor. **ISSN:** 0041-1280 (print). **Alt. Formats:** PDF. **URL:** http://www.tdworld.com. **Formed by the merger of:** Transmission and Distribution; Transmission and Distribution International. **Ad Rates:** BW $11,630; 4C $4,205. **Remarks:** Accepts advertising. **Circ:** (Not Reported).

13420 ■ Urgent Communications: Technical Information for Paging, Trunking and Private Wireless Networks
Penton
9800 Metcalf Ave.
Overland Park, KS 66212
Phone: (913)967-1710
Technical magazine for the mobile communications industry. **Freq:** Monthly. **Print Method:** Web Offset. **Trim Size:** 7 7/8 x 10 3/4. **Cols./Page:** 3. **Col. Width:** 2 1/4 inches. **Col. Depth:** 10 inches. **Key Personnel:** Dennis Hegg, Sales Representative, phone: (707)526-4377; Greg Herring, Vice President; Donny Jackson, Editor, phone: (414)529-4514; Glenn Bischoff, Publisher, phone: (312)840-8467. **ISSN:** 0745-7626 (print). **URL:** http://urgentcomm.com/. **Formerly**: Mobile Radio Technology. **Remarks:** Accepts advertising. **Circ:** △**31410**.

13421 ■ Ward's Auto World
Penton
9800 Metcalf Ave.
Overland Park, KS 66212
Phone: (913)967-1710
Publisher's E-mail: corporatecustomerservice@penton.com
Magazine for the automotive OEM industry, covering news, trends and technology. **Freq:** Monthly. **Key Personnel:** Drew Winter, Senior Editor, phone: (248)799-2625; Christie Schweinsberg, Associate Editor, phone: (248)799-2640; Thomas W. Duncan, Publisher, phone: (203)358-4201; David E. Zoia, Director, Editorial; Tom Murphy, Senior Editor, phone: (248)799-2665; James Amend, Associate Editor; Barbara L. McClellan, Editor, phone: (248)799-2637. **Subscription Rates:** Free online. **URL:** http://wardsauto.com. **Remarks:** Accepts advertising. **Circ:** (Not Reported).

13422 ■ WardsAuto Dealer Business
Penton
9800 Metcalf Ave.
Overland Park, KS 66212
Phone: (913)967-1710
Publisher's E-mail: corporatecustomerservice@penton.com
Business magazine for franchised new car dealers and their management. **Freq:** Monthly. **Print Method:** Web offset. **Trim Size:** 8 x 10 3/4. **Cols./Page:** 3. **Col. Width:** 13.5 picas. **Col. Depth:** 10 inches. **Key Personnel:** Steve Finlay, Senior Editor, phone: (248)799-2664; Christie Schweinsberg, Senior Editor, phone: (248)799-2640. **ISSN:** 1086--1629 (print). **URL:** http://wardsauto.com/wardsauto-dealer-business. **Formerly**: Auto Age Dealer Business; Ward's Dealer Business. **Ad Rates:** BW $4800. **Remarks:** Accepts advertising. **Circ:** △**65667**.

13423 ■ Wearables Business
Penton
9800 Metcalf Ave.
Overland Park, KS 66212
Phone: (913)967-1710
Publisher's E-mail: corporatecustomerservice@penton.com
Trade magazine covering the wearable segment of the promotional products industry for distributors. **Freq:** 10/year. **Key Personnel:** C.J. Mittica, Editor; Melinda Ligos, Editor-in-Chief. **Remarks:** Accepts advertising. **Circ:** Combined 15304.

13424 ■ World Waterpark
World Waterpark Association
8826 Santa Fe Dr., Ste. 310
Overland Park, KS 66212
Phone: (913)599-0300
Fax: (913)599-0520
Publisher's E-mail: wwamemberinfo@waterparks.org
Freq: 10/year. **Subscription Rates:** Included in membership. **URL:** http://www.waterparks.org/web/Magazine.aspx. **Remarks:** Advertising not accepted. **Circ:** (Not Reported).

13425 ■ Bott Radio Network
10550 Barkley
Overland Park, KS 66212
Phone: (913)642-7770
Fax: (913)642-1319
Free: 800-345-2621
Email: comments@bottradionetwork.com
Radio station that broadcasts Christian news and other programs. **Format:** Religious; Gospel. **Formerly**: Bott Broadcasting Co. **Operating Hours**: Continuous. **Key Personnel:** Don Boyd, Mgr.; Richard Bott, Sr., President. **Ad Rates:** Advertising accepted; rates available upon request. **URL:** http://www.bottradionetwork.com.

13426 ■ KCCV-AM - 760
10550 Barkley
Overland Park, KS 66212
Phone: (913)642-7600
Fax: (913)642-1319
Email: comments@bottradionetwork.com
Format: Religious; Talk; Information. **Networks:** USA Radio. **Owner:** Bott Radio Network, 10550 Barkley, Overland Park, KS 66212, Ph: (913)642-7770, Fax: (913)642-1319, Free: 800-345-2621. **Founded:** 1962. **Operating Hours**: Continuous. **ADI**: Kansas City, MO (Lawrence, KS). **Key Personnel:** Richard Bott, Sr., President; Pat Rulon, Regional Mgr., prulon@bottradionetwork.com; Rich Bott, CEO, President. **Wattage**: 6,000. **Ad Rates:** Noncommercial. Combined advertising rates available with KCCV-FM, KAYX-FM, KCVT-FM. **URL:** http://www.bottradionetwork.com.

13427 ■ KCCV-FM - 92.3
10550 Barkley
Overland Park, KS 66212
Phone: (913)642-7600
Fax: (913)642-2424
Free: 800-875-1903
Email: comments@bottradionetwork.com
Format: Religious; Talk; Information. **Networks:** USA Radio. **Owner:** Bott Radio Network, 10550 Barkley, Overland Park, KS 66212, Ph: (913)642-7770, Fax: (913)642-1319, Free: 800-345-2621. **Founded:** Dec. 01, 1993. **Operating Hours**: Continuous. **ADI**: Kansas City, MO (Lawrence, KS). **Key Personnel:** Pat Rulon, Regional Mgr., prulon@bottradionetwork.com. **Local Programs**: *The Complete Story*, Sunday Saturday 6:00 a.m.; 3:00 p.m. 7:30 a.m.; 12:30 p.m. **Wattage**: 26,000. **Ad Rates:** Noncommercial. Combined advertising rates available with KCCV-AM, KAXX-FM, KCVT-FM. **URL:** http://www.bottradionetwork.com.

13428 ■ KCGR-FM - 100.5
10550 Barkley St., Ste. 108
Overland Park, KS 66212
Fax: (913)642-1319
Format: Contemporary Hit Radio (CHR); Eighties; Classic Rock. **Networks:** ABC. **Founded:** Mar. 1994. **Operating Hours**: Continuous. **Wattage**: 5,000. **Ad Rates:** $8-12 for 30 seconds; $10-14 for 60 seconds. KNND-AM country.

13429 ■ KCHZ-FM - 95.7
11900 College Blvd., Ste. 320
Overland Park, KS 66210
Phone: (913)696-3700
Format: Contemporary Hit Radio (CHR). **Owner:** Radio 2000, Inc., at above address. **Founded:** Jan. 16, 1997. **Operating Hours**: Continuous. **Key Personnel:** Frank

Copsides, President; Dave Alexander, VP; Janel Thiesen, Gen. Mgr., VP; Brian Goeke, Dir. of Mktg., brian.goeke@cumulus.com; Jared Robb, Sales Mgr.; Donna Baker, Regional VP. **Wattage**: 19,000. **URL:** http://www.channelz95.com.

13430 ■ KCTE-AM - 1510
6721 W 121st St.
Overland Park, KS 66209
Phone: (913)344-1500
Fax: (913)344-1599
Format: Talk. **Networks:** ESPN Radio. **Owner:** Union Broadcasting Inc., 6721 West 121 Terr., Overland Park, KS 66209. **Founded:** 1993. **Operating Hours:** Sunrise-sunset. **ADI:** Kansas City, MO (Lawrence, KS). **Key Personnel:** Chad Boeger, Gen. Mgr.; Sandy Cohen, Dir. of Sales, VP; Dennis Rooney, News Dir., dennisrooney@1510.com. **Wattage**: 10,000. **Ad Rates:** Advertising accepted; rates available upon request.

13431 ■ KCXM-FM - 95.1
Union Broadcasting Bldg., 2nd Fl.
6271 W 121st St.
Overland Park, KS 66202
Owner: Union Broadcasting Inc., 6721 West 121 Terr., Overland Park, KS 66209. **Wattage**: 007. **Ad Rates:** Advertising accepted; rates available upon request.

13432 ■ KJCV-FM - 89.7
10550 Barkley
Overland Park, KS 66212
Phone: (913)642-7770
Fax: (913)642-1319
Free: 800-875-1903
Format: Religious; Talk. **Owner:** Bott Radio Network, 10550 Barkley, Overland Park, KS 66212, Ph: (913)642-7770, Fax: (913)642-1319, Free: 800-345-2621. **Operating Hours**: Continuous. **Key Personnel:** Pat Rulon, Regional Mgr., prulonl@bottradionetwork.com. **Ad Rates:** Noncommercial; underwriting available. **URL:** http://www.bottradionetwork.com.

13433 ■ KSIV-AM - 1320
10550 Barkley, Ste. 100
Overland Park, KS 66212
Phone: (913)642-7770
Format: Talk; Religious. **Networks:** USA Radio. **Owner:** Bott Radio Network, 10550 Barkley, Overland Park, KS 66212, Ph: (913)642-7770, Fax: (913)642-1319, Free: 800-345-2621. **Founded:** 1982. **Formerly**: KADI-AM. **Operating Hours**: Continuous; 10% network, 5% local, 85% other. **ADI**: St. Louis, MO (Mt. Vernon, IL). **Key Personnel:** Richard P. Bott, II, VP. **Wattage**: 5,000. **Ad Rates:** $20 for 30 seconds; $30 for 60 seconds. **URL:** http://www.bottradionetwork.com.

13434 ■ KTAA-FM - 90.7
10550 Barkley St., Ste. 108
Overland Park, KS 66212
Phone: (913)642-7770
Fax: (913)642-1319
Email: comments@bottradionetwork.com
Format: Religious. **Owner:** Bott Radio Network, 10550 Barkley, Overland Park, KS 66212, Ph: (913)642-7770, Fax: (913)642-1319, Free: 800-345-2621. **Operating Hours:** Continuous. **Key Personnel:** Richard P. Bott, II, VP. **Wattage**: 42,000. **Ad Rates:** Noncommercial. **URL:** http://www.bottradionetwork.com.

13435 ■ KTFC-FM - 103.3
10550 Barkley, Ste. 100
Overland Park, KS 66212
Phone: (913)642-7770
Fax: (913)642-1319
Format: Gospel. **Networks:** Satellite Radio. **Owner:** Don Swanson, at above address. **Founded:** 1965. **Operating Hours**: Continuous. **ADI**: Sioux City, IA. **Key Personnel:** Don Swanson, Contact. **Wattage**: 100,000. **Ad Rates:** Advertising accepted; rates available upon request. **URL:** http://www.bottradionetwork.com.

13436 ■ WHB-AM - 810
6721 W 121st St.
Overland Park, KS 66209
Email: info@810whb.com
Format: Sports. **Networks:** AP. **Owner:** Union Broadcasting Inc., 6721 West 121 Terr., Overland Park, KS 66209. **Founded:** 1922. **Operating Hours**: Continuous. **ADI**: Kansas City, MO (Lawrence, KS). **Key Personnel:** Kevin Kietzman, VP; Sandy Cohen, VP. **Wattage**: 50,000. **Ad Rates:** Advertising accepted; rates available upon request. **URL:** http://www.810whb.com.

PARSONS

NE KS. Labette Co. 28 mi. NE of Independence. Manufactures steel tanks, furnace burners, steel building accessories, garments, furniture, wood products, chemicals, paper boxes, ammunition. Diversified farming. Wheat, corn, hay.

13437 ■ Farm Talk
Community Newspaper Holdings Inc.
1801 S 59 Hwy.
Parsons, KS 67357
Phone: (620)421-9450
Fax: (620)421-9473
Free: 800-356-8255
Publication E-mail: farmtalk@terraworld.net
Agricultural newspaper (tabloid) serving the production agriculture and agribusiness community of Southeast Kansas, Southwest Missouri, Northeast Oklahoma, and Northwest Arkansas. Contains in-depth management and market information and entertainment features. **Freq:** Weekly (Wed.). **Print Method:** Offset. **Trim Size:** 10 x 14. **Cols./Page:** 6. **Col. Width:** 18 nonpareils. **Col. Depth:** 196 agate lines. **Subscription Rates:** $45 Individuals print and online; $85 Two years print and online; $60 Out of state print and online; $115 Out of state 2 years (print and online); $25 Individuals /yera (online only); $45 Two years online only. **URL:** http://www.farmtalknewspaper.com; http://www.cnhi.com/locations. **Mailing address:** PO Box 601, Parsons, KS 67357. **Remarks:** Accepts advertising. **Circ:** (Not Reported).

13438 ■ Parsons Sun
Parsons Publishing Co.
220 S 18th St.
Parsons, KS 67357
Phone: (620)421-2000
Fax: (620)421-2217
General newspaper. **Freq:** Daily (eve.) Monday-Friday afternoons & Saturday mornings. **Print Method:** Offset. **Trim Size:** 13 3/4 x 22 3/4. **Cols./Page:** 6. **Col. Width:** 25 nonpareils. **Col. Depth:** 294 agate lines. **Key Personnel:** Amy Jensen, Manager, Circulation; Ray Nolting, Managing Editor; Shanna L. Guiot, Business Manager. **USPS:** 422-480. **Subscription Rates:** $109.52 Individuals /year (print, carrier delivery); $126 Individuals /year (print or online, mail in state). **URL:** http://www.parsonssun.com. **Mailing address:** PO Box 836, Parsons, KS 67357. **Remarks:** Accepts advertising. **Circ:** 7189.

13439 ■ KLKC-AM - 1540
PO Box 853
Parsons, KS 67357
Phone: (620)421-6400
Format: Talk; News. **Networks:** Independent. **Founded:** 1951. **Operating Hours**: Sunrise-sunset; 100% local. **ADI**: Joplin, MO-Pittsburg, KS. **Wattage**: 250. **Ad Rates:** $4.54-10.45 for 30 seconds; $5.64-12.65 for 60 seconds.

13440 ■ KLKC-FM - 93.5
PO Box 853
Parsons, KS 67357-0853
Phone: (620)421-6400
Format: Talk; News. **Networks:** Independent. **Founded:** 1978. **Operating Hours**: Sunrise-sunset; 100% local. **ADI**: Wichita-Hutchinson, KS. **Wattage**: 3,000. **Ad Rates:** $4.54-10.45 for 30 seconds; $5.64-12.65 for 60 seconds.

13441 ■ K208EK-FM - 89.5
PO Box 391
Twin Falls, ID 83303
Fax: (208)736-1958
Free: 800-357-4226
Format: Religious; Contemporary Christian. **Owner:** CSN International, PO Box 391, Twin Falls, ID 83303, Ph: (208)736-1958, Fax: (208)736-1958, Free: 800-357-4226. **Key Personnel:** Mike Kestler, Contact; Don Mills, Music Dir., Prog. Dir. **URL:** http://www.csnradio.com.

PEABODY

13442 ■ Peabody Gazette-Bulletin
Peabody Gazette-Bulletin
118 N Walnut
Peabody, KS 66866
Phone: (316)983-2185
Community newspaper. **Founded:** 1873. **Freq:** Weekly (Thurs.). **Print Method:** Offset. **Trim Size:** 22 3/4 x 14 1/4. **Cols./Page:** 6. **Col. Width:** 13 1/2 picas. **Col. Depth:** 21 inches. **Key Personnel:** Susan Marshall, Editor; Eric Meyer, President, Publisher. **Subscription Rates:** $39 Individuals Marion County area; $44 Elsewhere in Kansas; $49 Out of state; $35 Individuals Online only. **URL:** http://peabodykansas.com/. **Formerly**: Gazette-Herald. **Mailing address:** PO Box 129, Peabody, KS 66866. **Ad Rates:** BW $378; 4C $648; PCI $3.50. **Remarks:** Accepts advertising. **Circ:** 1400.

PHILLIPSBURG

N. KS. Phillips Co. 60 mi. N. of Hays. Pheasant hunting area. Zeolite asphalt roofing manufactured. Long line trucking. Oil refinery. Grain, stock farms. Cattle, hogs, milo, wheat.

13443 ■ Phillips County Review
Phillips County Review
683 3rd St.
Phillipsburg, KS 67661
Phone: (785)543-5242
Fax: (785)543-5243
Publisher's E-mail: news@phillipscountyreview.com
Weekly newspaper. **Freq:** Weekly (Wed.). **Print Method:** Offset. **Cols./Page:** 6. **Col. Width:** 1.59 inches. **Col. Depth:** 15 1/2 inches. **Key Personnel:** Ronda Hueneke, Manager, Advertising and Sales; Kirby Ross, Editor, phone: (785)543-5242, fax: (785)543-5243. **Subscription Rates:** $23 Individuals in state; $29 Out of state. **URL:** http://www.phillipscountyreview.com. **Mailing address:** PO Box 446, Phillipsburg, KS 67661. **Ad Rates:** BW $4; PCI $4. **Remarks:** Advertising accepted; rates available upon request. **Circ:** Paid ‡2000.

13444 ■ KKAN-AM - 1490
205 F St.
Phillipsburg, KS 67661
Phone: (785)543-2151
Fax: (785)543-2152
Email: radio@kkankqma.com
Format: Big Band/Nostalgia. **Networks:** AP; NBC; CNN Radio. **Owner:** S-Y Communications, at above address, Ph: (650)274-5763. **Founded:** 1959. **Operating Hours**: 18 hours Daily; 20% network, 80% local. **ADI**: Lincoln-Hastings-Kearney, NE. **Key Personnel:** Tad Felts, Sports Dir., tadpoll@kkankqma.com; Bob Yates, Gen. Mgr., bobyates@kkankqma.com. **Wattage**: 1,000. **Ad Rates:** $9 for 30 seconds; $15 for 60 seconds. Combined advertising rates available with KQMA-FM. **Mailing address:** PO Box 548, Phillipsburg, KS 67661. **URL:** http://www.kkankqma.com.

13445 ■ KQMA-FM - 92.5
205 F St.
Phillipsburg, KS 67661
Phone: (785)543-2151
Fax: (785)543-2152
Email: radio@kkankqma.com
Format: Eclectic. **Simulcasts:** KKAN-AM. **Networks:** AP; NBC; CNN Radio. **Owner:** S-Y Communications, at above address, Ph: (650)274-5763. **Founded:** 1985. **Operating Hours**: 18 hours Daily; 20% network, 80% local. **ADI**: Lincoln-Hastings-Kearney, NE. **Key Personnel:** Bob Yates, Gen. Mgr., bobyates@kkankqma.com. **Wattage**: 100,000. **Ad Rates:** $9 for 30 seconds; $15 for 60 seconds. Combined advertising rates available with KKAN-AM. **Mailing address:** PO Box 548, Phillipsburg, KS 67661. **URL:** http://www.kkankqma.com.

PITTSBURG

SE KS. Crawford Co. 30 mi. NW of Joplin, MO. State University. Manufactures ice cream products, mining machinery, coal by-products, metal thermal doors, plastic pipe, flexible packaging, cad-cam systems, sportswear, plastic bags, synthetic sports turf, lawn and garden fertilizer, wood cabinets. Limestone and coal mines. Clay, foundry and machine shop. Diversified farming.

Circulation: ★ = AAM; △ or • = BPA; ♦ = CAC; ❑ = VAC; ⊕ = PO Statement; ‡ = Publisher's Report; Boldface figures = sworn; Light figures = estimated.

13446 ■ Collegio
Pittsburg State University
1701 S Broadway St.
Pittsburg, KS 66762
Phone: (620)231-7000
Publication E-mail: psucollegio@gmail.com
Collegiate newspaper. **Freq:** Weekly (Thurs.). **Print Method:** Offset. **Trim Size:** 11.625 x 21 1/2. **Cols./Page:** 6. **Col. Width:** 11 picas. **Key Personnel:** Madison Dennis, Editor-in-Chief, phone: (620)235-4901; Mandy Toepfer, Editor, phone: (620)235-4900. **URL:** http://www.psucollegio.com. **Ad Rates:** GLR $7; BW $700; 4C $150; SAU $6; PCI $6. **Remarks:** Accepts advertising. **Circ:** Free ‡5000.

13447 ■ The Midwest Quarterly: A Journal of Contemporary Thought
Midwest Quarterly
Pittsburg State University
1701 S Broadway
406b Russ Hall
Pittsburg, KS 66762
Phone: (620)235-4369
Publisher's E-mail: midwestq@pittstate.edu
Scholarly journal. **Freq:** Quarterly Jan., Apr., July, and Oct. **Print Method:** Offset. **Trim Size:** 6 x 9. **Cols./Page:** 1. **Col. Width:** 49 nonpareils. **Col. Depth:** 105 agate lines. **Key Personnel:** James B.M. Schick, Editor-in-Chief; Tim Bailey, Editor; Judy Berry-Bravo, Editor; Maeve Cummings, Director, Management Information Systems; John L.S. Daley, Editor; Earl Lee, Editor; Paul McCallum, Editor. **ISSN:** 0026--3451 (print). **Alt. Formats:** Microfilm. **URL:** http://www.pittstate.edu/department/english/midwest-quarterly/the-midwest-quarterly.dot. **Remarks:** Advertising not accepted. **Circ:** Paid ‡800, Non-paid ‡150.

13448 ■ KBZI-FM - 100.7
1162 E Hwy. 126
Pittsburg, KS 66762
Phone: (620)231-8888
Format: Top 40. **Key Personnel:** Paul Lyle, Gen. Mgr., pual@kkowradio.com. **Ad Rates:** Advertising accepted; rates available upon request.

13449 ■ KFJX-TV - 14
2950 NE Hwy. 69
Pittsburg, KS 66762-0659
Phone: (417)782-1414
Fax: (417)624-3115
Owner: Surtsey Media L.L.C., at above address. **Key Personnel:** Darren Dishman, Gen. Mgr., ddishman@fox14tv.com. **Mailing address:** PO Box 659, Pittsburg, KS 66762-0659. **URL:** http://www.fox14tv.com.

13450 ■ KHST-FM - 101.7
412 N Locust St.
Pittsburg, KS 66762
Phone: (620)232-5993
Format: Oldies. **Ad Rates:** Advertising accepted; rates available upon request. **URL:** http://www.mycountry1017.com.

13451 ■ KJML-FM - 107.1
1162 E Hwy. 126
Pittsburg, KS 66762
Phone: (620)231-7200
Fax: (620)231-3321
Format: Album-Oriented Rock (AOR). **Key Personnel:** Jennifer Isom, Bus. Mgr., jennisom@ami-joplin.com. **Wattage:** 6,000. **URL:** http://rock1071.com.

13452 ■ KKOW-AM - 860
1162 E Hwy. 126
Pittsburg, KS 66762
Phone: (620)231-7200
Fax: (620)231-3321
Email: kkow@kkowradio.com
Format: Country. **Networks:** CBS. **Owner:** American Media Investments Inc., 2510 W 20th, Joplin, MO 64804, Ph: (417)781-1313. **Founded:** 1937. **Formerly:** KOAM-AM. **Operating Hours:** Continuous; 10% network, 90% local. **ADI:** Joplin, MO-Pittsburg, KS. **Key Personnel:** George DeMarco, Gen. Mgr., george@ami-pittsburg.com. **Wattage:** 10,000. **Ad Rates:** $70 for 30 seconds; $90 for 60 seconds. Combined advertising rates available with KKOW-FM, KBZI-FM. **URL:** http://www.kkowradio.com.

13453 ■ KKOW-FM - 96.9
1162 East Hwy. 126
Pittsburg, KS 66762
Phone: (620)231-7200
Format: Contemporary Country. **Owner:** American Media Investments Inc., 2510 W 20th, Joplin, MO 64804, Ph: (417)781-1313. **ADI:** Joplin, MO-Pittsburg, KS. **Wattage:** 10,000 Day time; 050. **Ad Rates:** Advertising accepted; rates available upon request. **URL:** http://www.kkowfm.com.

13454 ■ KOAM-TV - 7
2950 NE Hwy. 69
Pittsburg, KS 66762-0659
Phone: (620)231-0400
Email: news@koamtv.com
Format: Commercial TV. **Networks:** CBS. **Owner:** Saga Communications Inc., 73 Kercheval Ave., Ste. 201, Grosse Pointe Farms, MI 48236, Ph: (313)886-7070, Fax: (313)886-7150. **Founded:** 1953. **Operating Hours:** Continuous. **ADI:** Joplin, MO-Pittsburg, KS. **Key Personnel:** Danny Thomas, Gen. Mgr., President, dwthomas@koamtv.com; Steve Holinsworth, Operations Mgr., hworth@koamtv.com; Darren Dishman, Gen. Mgr., ddishman@fox14tv.com. **Ad Rates:** Advertising accepted; rates available upon request. **Mailing address:** PO Box 659, Pittsburg, KS 66762-0659. **URL:** http://www.koamtv.com.

13455 ■ KRPS-FM - 89.9
PO Box 899
Pittsburg, KS 66762
Phone: (620)235-4288
Format: Public Radio. **Key Personnel:** Missi Kelly, Gen. Mgr., mlindsay@pittstate.edu. **Ad Rates:** Noncommercial. **URL:** http://www.krps.org.

13456 ■ K33HZ - 33
PO Box A
Santa Ana, CA 92711
Phone: (714)832-2950
Free: 888-731-1000
Owner: Trinity Broadcasting Network Inc., PO Box A, Santa Ana, CA 92711, Ph: (714)832-2950, Free: 888-731-1000. **URL:** http://www.tbn.org.

13457 ■ KWXD-FM - 103.5
412 N Locust St.
Pittsburg, KS 66762
Phone: (620)232-5993
Format: Classic Rock. **Operating Hours:** Continuous. **Wattage:** 16,000. **Ad Rates:** Advertising accepted; rates available upon request. **URL:** http://www.1035x.net.

PLEASANTON

13458 ■ Linn County News
Linn County News
808 Main St.
Pleasanton, KS 66075
Phone: (913)352-6235
Free: 888-292-6235
Community newspaper. **Founded:** 1977. **Freq:** Weekly (Wed.). **Print Method:** Offset. **Cols./Page:** 6. **Col. Width:** 2 inches. **Col. Depth:** 21 inches. **Key Personnel:** Dermey Smoot; Jackie Taylor, Publisher, Editor, phone: (913)352-6235. **USPS:** 439-950. **Subscription Rates:** $21.70 Linn county; $28.59 outside Linn county; $33.75 outside Kansas. **Mailing address:** PO Box 478, Pleasanton, KS 66075. **Ad Rates:** SAU $4.50; PCI $3.50. **Remarks:** Accepts advertising. **Circ:** 2600.

PRATT

S. KS. Pratt Co. 80 mi. W. of Wichita. Lawn furniture, hydraulic couplings; farm machinery factory; flour, feed mills; hatchery. Agriculture. Wheat, corn, alfalfa.

13459 ■ The Pratt Tribune
The Pratt Tribune
320 S Main
Pratt, KS 67124
Phone: (620)672-5511
Fax: (620)672-5514
General newspaper. **Founded:** 1917. **Freq:** Daily (eve.). **Print Method:** Offset. **Key Personnel:** Conrad Easterday, Editor; Keith Lippoldt, Publisher; Julie Chenoweth, Manager, Advertising; Yolanda Alvarez, Manager, Circulation. **USPS:** 441-500. **Subscription Rates:** $112 Individuals home delivery. **URL:** http://www.pratttribune.com. **Mailing address:** PO Box 909, Pratt, KS 67124. **Ad Rates:** GLR $.45; BW $813; 4C $1,053; PCI $6.30. **Remarks:** Accepts advertising. **Circ:** ‡2500.

13460 ■ St. John News
The Pratt Tribune
320 S Main
Pratt, KS 67124
Phone: (620)672-5511
Fax: (620)672-5514
Community newspaper. **Freq:** Weekly. **Print Method:** Offset. **Trim Size:** 14 3/4 x 21. **Cols./Page:** 6. **Col. Width:** 13 picas. **Col. Depth:** 21 1/2 inches. **USPS:** 476-120. **Alt. Formats:** Print. **URL:** http://www.sjnewsonline.com. **Mailing address:** PO Box 909, Pratt, KS 67124. **Ad Rates:** BW $316; PCI $3.30. **Remarks:** Accepts advertising. **Circ:** ‡1350.

13461 ■ KMMM-AM - 1290
30129 E Hwy. 54
Pratt, KS 67124
Phone: (620)672-5581
Fax: (620)672-5583
Format: Oldies. **Founded:** 1963. **Key Personnel:** Lisa Coss, Station Mgr.; Carl Raida, Dir. of Programs. **Mailing address:** PO Box 486, Pratt, KS 67124. **URL:** http://www.themighty1290am.com.

13462 ■ KWLS-AM - 1290
30129 E Hwy. 54
Pratt, KS 67124
Phone: (620)672-5581
Fax: (620)672-5583
Format: Oldies. **Networks:** Mid-America Ag; Agri-Voice; ABC; Kansas Information. **Owner:** Lisa E. Coss, Not Available. **Founded:** 1962. **Operating Hours:** Continuous; 12% local, 88% network. **Key Personnel:** Carl Raida, Prog. Dir., craida@rockingmradio.com; Lisa Coss, Gen. Mgr., lcoss@rockingmradio.com. **Wattage:** 5,000 Day; 500 Night. **Ad Rates:** $10 for 30 seconds; $12 for 60 seconds. Combined advertising rates available with KZLS, KILS, KOLS, KSLS, KFNF, KQLS, KGTR, KNNS. **Mailing address:** PO Box 486, Pratt, KS 67124. **URL:** http://www.themighty1290am.com.

ROSE HILL

SE KS. Butler Co. 24 mi. SW of El Dorado.

13463 ■ The Rose Hill Reporter
The Rose Hill Reporter
PO Box 16
Rose Hill, KS 67133
Shopper. **Freq:** Weekly (Thurs.). **Print Method:** Offset. **Cols./Page:** 6. **Col. Width:** 13.5 picas. **Col. Depth:** 21 1/2 inches. **Key Personnel:** Michael Robinson, Publisher; Sally Rathburn, Managing Editor, phone: (316)776-0097. **Subscription Rates:** $32 Individuals 1 year; $40 Out of state 1 year. **URL:** http://rosehillchamber.org/rose-hill-reporter. **Ad Rates:** PCI $2.85. **Remarks:** Accepts advertising. **Circ:** (Not Reported).

RUSH CENTER

13464 ■ Golden Belt Telephone Association Inc.
103 Lincoln St.
Rush Center, KS 67575
Phone: (785)372-4236
Free: 800-432-7965
Email: custservice@gbta.net
Founded: Jan. 02, 1953. **Cities Served:** subscribing households 6000. **Mailing address:** PO Box 229, Rush Center, KS 67575-0229. **URL:** http://www.gbta.net.

RUSSELL

NC KS. Russell Co. 76 mi. W. of Salina. Manufactures oil, wire products, mobile homes. Grain, feed.

13465 ■ Eagle Cable
336 E Wichita
Russell, KS 67665
Phone: (785)483-3244
Fax: (785)483-2569
Owner: Eagle Communications Inc., 2703 Hall St., Ste. 15, Hays, KS 67601, Ph: (785)625-4000, Fax: (785)625-8030. **Formerly:** Russell Cable TV Co. **Key Personnel:** Gary Shorman, CEO, President. **Cities Served:** subscribing households 1,800. **URL:** http://www.eaglecom.net.

13466 ■ KRSL-AM - 990
1984 N Main St.
Russell, KS 67665
Phone: (785)483-3121
Fax: (785)483-6511
Free: 866-483-0990
Email: comments@krsl.com
Format: Sports; News; Classical. **Simulcasts:** KCAY-FM. **Networks:** Satellite Music Network; Kansas Information. **Owner:** West Central Radio Inc., at above address. **Founded:** 1956. **Operating Hours:** Continuous. **Key Personnel:** Larry Calvery, Gen. Mgr., larry@krsl.com; Carol McKenna, News Dir., carol@krsl.com; Mike McKenna, Gen. Mgr., mike@krsl.com; Roy Steinle, Contact, roy@krsl.com. **Wattage:** 250 Day; 030 Night. **Ad Rates:** $7.50-9.50 for 30 seconds; $11-13.50 for 60 seconds. Combined advertising rates available with KCAY-FM. **Mailing address:** PO Box 666, Russell, KS 67665. **URL:** http://www.krsl.com.

13467 ■ KRSL-FM - 95.9
1984 N Main St.
Russell, KS 67665
Phone: (785)483-3121
Fax: (785)483-6511
Free: 866-483-0990
Email: comments@krsl.com
Format: Classical. **Formerly:** KCAY-FM. **Key Personnel:** Mike McKenna, Gen. Mgr; Roy Steinle, Contact, roy@krsl.com. **Ad Rates:** Noncommercial. **Mailing address:** PO Box 666, Russell, KS 67665. **URL:** http://www.krsl.com.

SAINT FRANCIS

NW KS. Cheyenne Co. 185 mi. E. of Denver, Colorado. Grain milling. Stock, grain farms. Wheat, corn, hogs, cattle.

13468 ■ St. Francis Herald
St. Francis Herald
310 W Washington
Saint Francis, KS 67756
Phone: (785)332-3162
Newspaper. **Freq:** Weekly (Thurs.). **Print Method:** Offset. **Cols./Page:** 6. **Col. Width:** 28 nonpareils. **Col. Depth:** 294 agate lines. **Key Personnel:** Karen Krien, Editor; Casey McCormick, Manager, Advertising. **USPS:** 475-960. **Subscription Rates:** $40 Individuals 1 year (online); $40 Individuals 1 year (local, print and online); $45 Individuals 1 year (other Kansas areas, print and online); $51 Individuals 1 year (outside of Kansas, print and online). **URL:** http://www.nwkansas.com/SFHwebpages/sfhmain.html. **Ad Rates:** GLR $.22; BW $396.90. **Remarks:** Accepts advertising. **Circ:** ‡2100.

SAINT MARYS

NE KS. Wabaunsee Co. 23 mi. NW of Topeka. Residential.

13469 ■ KSMK-FM - 98.3
200 E Mission St.
Saint Marys, KS 66536
Email: ksmk@smac.edu
Format: Educational. **Founded:** 2002. **Key Personnel:** Fr. Paul Robinson, Chap. **URL:** http://www.ksmk.org.

SALINA

C. KS. Saline Co. 72 mi. NE of Hutchinson. Kansas Wesleyan College; Marymount College. Center of a rich agriculture district. Distributing and trading center. Manufactures truck bodies, aircraft, fluorescent lamps, uniforms, binder canvas, awnings, mattresses, corn sleds, neon signs, butter, braces, playground equipment. Flour mills. Foundry. Car battery, brick and tile plants. Hatcheries Wheat, alfalfa, poultry products, stock.

13470 ■ The Salina Journal
The Salina Journal
333 S 4th St.
Salina, KS 67401
Phone: (785)823-6363
Fax: (785)823-3207
Free: 800-827-6363
Publication E-mail: webmaster@salina.com
General newspaper. **Freq:** Daily. **Print Method:** Offset. **Trim Size:** 12 3/8 x 22 3/4. **Cols./Page:** 6. **Col. Width:** 10 picas. **Col. Depth:** 297.5 agate lines. **Key Personnel:** Jacki Ryba, Director, Human Resources, phone: (785)822-1493; Ben Wearing, Executive Editor, phone: (785)822-1421; Sharon Montague, Editor. **USPS:** 478-060. **Subscription Rates:** .75 Individuals. **Alt. Formats:** Microfilm. **URL:** http://www.salina.com. **Ad Rates:** GLR $1.59; BW $2715.75; 4C $3171.75; SAU $21.30; PCI $21.30. **Remarks:** Advertising accepted; rates available upon request. **Circ:** Mon.-Sat. ■ **24835**, Sun. ■ **25613**.

13471 ■ KAAS-TV - 18
316 NW St.
Wichita, KS 67203
Phone: (316)942-2424
Fax: (316)942-8927
Format: Commercial TV. **Simulcasts:** KSAS-TV. **Networks:** Fox. **Owner:** Newport Television, LLC, 460 Nichols Rd., Ste. 250, Kansas City, MO 64112, Ph: (816)751-0200, Fax: (816)751-0250. **Founded:** 1988. **Operating Hours:** Continuous; 3% network, 97% local. **ADI:** Wichita-Hutchinson, KS. **Key Personnel:** Denice Petty, Chief Engineer; Michelle Cleaton, Dir. of Programs, michellecleaton@foxkansas.com; Chuck Reid, Gen. Mgr.; Ken Whitney, Production Mgr., kenwhitney@foxkansas.com. **Ad Rates:** Noncommercial. **URL:** http://www.foxkansas.com.

13472 ■ KABI-AM - 1560
131 N Santa Fe
Salina, KS 67402
Phone: (785)823-1111
Fax: (785)823-2034
Email: earl.houser@salinamediagroup.com
Format: News; Sports; Talk. **Networks:** ABC. **Owner:** Alpha Media Salina, at above address. **Founded:** 1963. **Operating Hours:** Continuous; 18% network, 82% local. **Key Personnel:** Bob Protzman, Station Mgr., bob.protzman@salinamediagroup.com; Mitch Drees, Sales Mgr. **Wattage:** 250. **Ad Rates:** Noncommercial. **Mailing address:** PO Box 80, Salina, KS 67402. **URL:** http://www.ksal.com.

13473 ■ KAKA-FM - 88.5
PO Box 3206
Tupelo, MS 38803
Format: Religious. **Owner:** American Family Radio, at above address. **Wattage:** 46,000. **Ad Rates:** Noncommercial. **URL:** http://www.afa.net.

13474 ■ KBLS-FM - 102.5
131 N Santa Fe
Salina, KS 67402
Phone: (785)823-1111
Fax: (785)823-2034
Email: bob.protzman@salinamediagroup.com
Format: Adult Contemporary. **Networks:** Jones Satellite. **Owner:** Alpha Media Salina, at above address. **Founded:** Jan. 01, 1993. **Operating Hours:** Continuous. **Key Personnel:** Bob Protzman, Station Mgr., bob.protzman@salinamediagroup.com; Mitch Drees, Sales Mgr., mitch.drees@salinamediagroup.com. **Wattage:** 100,000. **Ad Rates:** Advertising accepted; rates available upon request. **Mailing address:** PO Box 80, Salina, KS 67402. **URL:** http://www.ksal.com.

13475 ■ K15CN - 15
PO Box A
Santa Ana, CA 92711
Phone: (714)832-2950
Free: 888-731-1000
Owner: Trinity Broadcasting Network Inc., PO Box A, Santa Ana, CA 92711, Ph: (714)832-2950, Free: 888-731-1000. **URL:** http://www.tbn.org.

13476 ■ KINA-AM - 910
1825 S Ohio St.
Salina, KS 67401
Phone: (785)825-4631
Format: News; Talk; Information. **Networks:** CNN Radio; Kansas Information. **Owner:** Eagle Communications Inc., 2703 Hall St., Ste. 15, Hays, KS 67601, Ph: (785)625-4000, Fax: (785)625-8030. **Founded:** 1964. **Operating Hours:** 5:30 a.m.-12:30 a.m.; 10% network, 90% local. **Wattage:** 500. **Ad Rates:** $7-12 for 30 seconds; $10-16 for 60 seconds.

13477 ■ KSAL-AM - 1150
131 N Santa Fe
Salina, KS 67402
Phone: (785)823-1111
Fax: (785)823-2034
Free: 800-608-1150
Format: Talk; News; Sports; Information. **Networks:** ABC. **Owner:** Alpha Media Salina, at above address. **Founded:** 1937. **Operating Hours:** Continuous; 60% network, 40% local. **Key Personnel:** Bob Protzman, Station Mgr., bob.protzman@salinamediagroup.com; Clarke Sanders, Promotions Dir., clarke.sanders@morris.com; Ken Jennison, Dir. of Pub. Prog. & Svcs., kenneth.jennison@salinamediagroup.com. **Local Programs:** *The KSAL Morning News*, Monday Tuesday Wednesday Thursday Friday 5:30 a.m. - 9:00 a.m.; *Bloomberg's First Word*, Monday Tuesday Wednesday Thursday Friday 4:00 a.m. - 5:00 a.m.; *The Glenn Beck Program*, Monday Tuesday Wednesday Thursday Friday 9:00 a.m. - 11:00 a.m.; *Friendly Fire with Clarke Sanders & Nancy Hodges*, Monday Tuesday Wednesday Thursday Friday 5:00 p.m. - 6:00 p.m. **Wattage:** 5,000. **Ad Rates:** $18-27 for 60 seconds. Combined advertising rates available with KYEZ, KZBZ, KABI, KSAJ, KBLS. **Mailing address:** PO Box 80, Salina, KS 67402. **URL:** http://www.ksal.com.

13478 ■ KSAL-FM - 104.9
131 N Santa Fe Ave.
Salina, KS 67401
Phone: (785)823-1111
Fax: (785)823-2034
Format: Classic Rock. **Key Personnel:** Bill Ray, Dir. of Programs, billray@y937.com; Bob Protzman, Station Mgr., bob.protzman@salinamediagroup.com; Mitch Drees, Sales Mgr., mitch.drees@salinamediagroup.com. **Ad Rates:** Advertising accepted; rates available upon request. **Mailing address:** PO Box 80, Salina, KS 67401. **URL:** http://www.1049classichits.com.

13479 ■ KSKG-FM - 99.9
1825 S Ohio St.
Salina, KS 67401-6601
Phone: (785)825-4631
Format: Country; News; Information. **Owner:** Eagle Communications, Inc., at above address. **Founded:** 1960. **Operating Hours:** Continuous. **ADI:** Wichita-Hutchinson, KS. **Wattage:** 100,000. **Ad Rates:** Noncommercial. **URL:** http://www.eaglecom.net.

13480 ■ KYEZ-FM - 93.7
131 N Santa Fe
Salina, KS 67401
Phone: (785)823-1111
Format: Contemporary Country. **Owner:** Morris Communication, 725 Broad St., Augusta, GA 30901, Ph: (706)724-0851, Free: 800-622-6358. **Founded:** 1975. **Operating Hours:** Continuous. **ADI:** Wichita-Hutchinson, KS. **Key Personnel:** Mitch Drees, Dir. of Programs, Sales Mgr. **Wattage:** 100,000 ERP. **Ad Rates:** Advertising accepted; rates available upon request. KSAL, KABI, KSAJ, KBLS, KZBZ. **URL:** http://www.y937.com.

SEDAN

SE KS. Chautauqua Co. 40 mi. W. of Coffeyville. Oil wells. Cattle, hogs and grain farms. Wheat, corn, alfalfa, milo.

13481 ■ Prairie Star
Prairie Media L.L.C.
226 E Main St.
Sedan, KS 67361
Phone: (620)725-3176
Newspaper. **Freq:** Weekly (Wed.). **Print Method:** Letterpress and offset. **Trim Size:** Broadsheet. **Cols./Page:** 6. **Col. Width:** 26 nonpareils. **Col. Depth:** 294 agate lines. **Key Personnel:** Rudy Taylor, Publisher, phone: (620)879-2156; Jenny Diveley, Editor. **Subscription Rates:** $30 Individuals online; $48 Individuals in Kansas counties; $48.50 Out of state. **URL:** http://taylornews.org/newsm. **Formerly:** Flint Hills Express; Sedan Times-Star. **Mailing address:** PO Box 417, Sedan, KS 67361. **Remarks:** Advertising accepted; rates available upon request. **Circ:** ‡2000, Paid ‡2725.

SHARON SPRINGS

W. KS. Wallace Co. 210 mi. E. of Denver, Colorado. Dairy, stock, poultry, grain farms. Wheat, sugar beets, beans, watermelons.

13482 ■ Western Times
The Western Times

Circulation: ★ = AAM; △ or • = BPA; ♦ = CAC; ❑ = VAC; ⊕ = PO Statement; ‡ = Publisher's Report; Boldface figures = sworn; Light figures = estimated.

126 N Main St.
Sharon Springs, KS 67758
Phone: (785)852-4900
Publication E-mail: westimes@fairpoint.net
westerntimes@wbsnet.org
Community newspaper. **Founded:** 1874. **Freq:** Weekly (Thurs.). **Print Method:** Offset. **Cols./Page:** 6. **Col. Width:** 12 picas. **Col. Depth:** 21.5 inches. **USPS:** 679-740. **Subscription Rates:** $31 Individuals online; $39 Individuals within Wallace County/bordering counties; $41 Individuals other Kansas Counties + sales tax; $48 Individuals outside of Kansas; $35 Students + sales tax. **URL:** http://www.thewesterntimes.com/. **Mailing address:** PO Box 279, Sharon Springs, KS 67758. **Remarks:** Accepts advertising. **Circ:** 4,947.

SHAWNEE MISSION

E. KS. Johnson Co. 8 mi. S. of Kansas City. Suburban Residential. Light Industry.

13483 ■ Bank News: The Banking Magazine for the Central States
BankNews Publications
5125 Roe Blvd., Ste. 200
Shawnee Mission, KS 66205-2391
Phone: (913)261-7000
Fax: (913)261-7010
Free: 800-336-1120
Publisher's E-mail: senglert@banknews.com
Magazine for the banking industry. **Freq:** Monthly. **Print Method:** Offset. **Trim Size:** 8 3/8 x 10 7/8. **Cols./Page:** 3. **Col. Width:** 26 nonpareils. **Col. Depth:** 140 agate lines. **Key Personnel:** Bill Poquette, Editor-in-Chief; Sharon Smith, Managing Editor, phone: (913)261-7058. **ISSN:** 0005--5123 (print). **Subscription Rates:** Free to qualified subscribers. **URL:** http://www.banknews.com/current-bank-news. **Mailing address:** PO Box 29156, Shawnee Mission, KS 66205-2368. **Ad Rates:** 4C $4570. **Remarks:** Accepts advertising. **Circ:** (Not Reported).

13484 ■ KMBZ-AM - 980
7000 Squibb Rd.
Shawnee Mission, KS 66202
Phone: (913)744-3600
Format: News; Sports; Talk. **Owner:** Entercom Communications Corp., 401 City Ave., Ste. 809, Bala Cynwyd, PA 19004-1130, Ph: (610)660-5610, Fax: (610)660-5620. **Founded:** 1921. **Formerly:** KMBC-AM. **Operating Hours:** Continuous. **Wattage:** 5,000. **Ad Rates:** Noncommercial. **URL:** http://kmbz.com.

SPRING HILL

13485 ■ Watusi
Ankole Watusi International Registry
22484 W 239 St.
Spring Hill, KS 66083-9306
Phone: (913)592-4050
Publisher's E-mail: watusi@aol.com
Magazine featuring and promoting Ankole-Watusi cattle breed. **Freq:** Quarterly published in January, April, July, and October. **Subscription Rates:** included in membership dues. **URL:** http://www.awir.org/Magazine.htm. **Remarks:** Accepts advertising. **Circ:** (Not Reported).

TONGANOXIE

SW KS. Leavenworth Co. 24 mi. W. of Kansas City.

13486 ■ Tonganoxie Mirror
Lawrence Journal-World Co.
520 E 4th St.
Tonganoxie, KS 66086
Phone: (913)845-2222
Fax: (913)845-9451
Publisher's E-mail: subs@ljworld.com
Community newspaper. **Freq:** Weekly (Wed.). **Print Method:** Offset. **Cols./Page:** 6. **Col. Width:** 2 inches. **Col. Depth:** 21 inches. **Key Personnel:** John Taylor, Editor. **Subscription Rates:** $37 Individuals 52 weeks. **URL:** http://www.tonganoxiemirror.com. **Mailing address:** PO Box 920, Tonganoxie, KS 66086. **Remarks:** Accepts advertising. **Circ:** (Not Reported).

TOPEKA

E. KS. Shawnee Co. On Kansas River, 65 mi. W. of Kansas City. The State Capital. , Washburn University, State institutions. Flour mills; printing and publishing; meat, poultry and egg packing plants; foundry and iron works. Manufactures creamery, pet foods, cellulose products, tires, tents, awnings, serum, steel fixtures, culverts, tanks, medicines, steel jetties.

13487 ■ Capper's Farmer
Ogden Publications Inc.
1503 SW 42nd St.
Topeka, KS 66609
Free: 800-678-5779
Publisher's E-mail: customercare@ogdenpubs.com
Human interest magazine (tabloid). **Freq:** Monthly. **Print Method:** Web Offset. **Trim Size:** 10 3/4 x 12. **Cols./Page:** 5. **Col. Width:** 11 picas. **Col. Depth:** 150 agate lines. **Key Personnel:** K.C. Compton, Editor-in-Chief. **ISSN:** 0892--1148 (print). **URL:** http://www.cappers.com. **Formerly**: Capper's; Capper's Weekly. **Remarks:** Accepts advertising. **Circ:** (Not Reported).

13488 ■ The Community Dance Program
Callerlab - International Association of Square Dance Callers
200 SW 30th St., Ste. 104
Topeka, KS 66611
Phone: (785)783-3665
Fax: (785)783-3696
Free: 800-331-2577
Publisher's E-mail: info@callerlab.org
Alt. Formats: Download; PDF. **Remarks:** Advertising not accepted. **Circ:** (Not Reported).

13489 ■ Family Law Quarterly
American Bar Association
c/o Linda D. Elrod, Ed.-in-Ch.
Washburn University School of Law
1700 SW College Ave.
Topeka, KS 66621
Journal including regular coverage of judicial decisions, legislation, taxation, summaries of state and local bar association projects, and book reviews. **Freq:** Quarterly. **Trim Size:** 6 x 9. **Key Personnel:** Deborah Eisel, Managing Editor; Linda D. Elrod, Editor-in-Chief. **ISSN:** 0014-729X (print). **Subscription Rates:** $79.95 Nonmembers; $89.95 Other countries; Included in membership. **URL:** http://www.americanbar.org/publications/family_law_quarterly_home.html. **Remarks:** Advertising not accepted. **Circ:** 10500.

13490 ■ Florists' Review Magazine
Florist's Review Enterprises Inc.
PO Box 4368
Topeka, KS 66604
Phone: (785)266-0888
Fax: (785)266-0333
Free: 800-367-4708
Publisher's E-mail: mail@floristsreview.com
Retail florist and wholesalers trade magazine. **Freq:** Monthly. **Print Method:** Offset. **Trim Size:** 8 1/8 x 10 7/8. **Cols./Page:** 3. **Col. Width:** 26 nonpareils. **Col. Depth:** 140 agate lines. **Key Personnel:** Frances Dudley, President, Publisher; David L. Coake, Director, Editorial. **ISSN:** 0015--4423 (print). **USPS:** 202-580. **Subscription Rates:** $42 Individuals; $72 Two years; $82 Individuals three years; $55 Canada; $85 Canada 2 years; $60 Other countries; $90 Other countries 2 years. **Ad Rates:** BW $3210. **Remarks:** Accepts advertising. **Circ:** 16314.

13491 ■ Journal of Holistic Nursing
American Holistic Nurses Association
2900 SW Plass Ct.
Topeka, KS 66612-1213
Phone: (785)234-1712
Fax: (785)234-1713
Free: 800-278-2462
Publication E-mail: advertising@sagepub.com
Peer-reviewed journal promoting holism. **Freq:** Quarterly. **Trim Size:** 8 1/8 x 10 7/8. **Key Personnel:** Richard W. Cowling, PhD, Editor. **ISSN:** 0898--0101 (print); **EISSN:** 1552--5724 (electronic). **Subscription Rates:** £26 Individuals single print issue; £384 Institutions print only; £106 Institutions single print issue; £353 Institutions e-access; £384 Institutions print only; £392 Institutions print and e-access; £431 Institutions current volume print and all online content; £481 Institutions e-access (content through 1998); £81 Individuals print only. **URL:** http://jhn.sagepub.com; http://uk.sagepub.com/en-gb/asi/journal-of-holistic-nursing/journal200847. **Ad Rates:** BW $875; 4C $1110, in addition to Black & White rate. **Remarks:** Accepts advertising. **Circ:** (Not Reported).

13492 ■ The Journal of the Kansas Bar Association
Kansas Bar Association
1200 SW Harrison St.
Topeka, KS 66612-1806
Phone: (785)234-5696
Fax: (785)234-3813
Publisher's E-mail: info@ksbar.org
Journal containing legal articles, legal news and summaries of recent Kansas Court of Appeals opinions. **Freq:** 10/year. **ISSN:** 0022--8486 (print). **Subscription Rates:** Included in membership. **URL:** http://www.ksbar.org/?journal. **Ad Rates:** BW $1,000, full page; BW $500, half page. **Remarks:** Accepts display advertising. **Circ:** 7000.

13493 ■ Kansas!
Department of Commerce and Housing Division of Travel and Tourism
1000 SW Jackson St., Ste. 100
Topeka, KS 66612-1354
Phone: (785)296-3481
Fax: (785)296-5055
Consumer magazine covering travel in Kansas. **Freq:** Quarterly. **ISSN:** 0022--8435 (print). **Subscription Rates:** $18 Individuals; $30 Two years. **URL:** http://www.kansasmag.com. **Remarks:** Advertising not accepted. **Circ:** 43000.

13494 ■ The Kansas Anthropologist: Journal of the Kansas Anthropological Association
Kansas Anthropological Association
PO Box 750962
Topeka, KS 66675-0962
Phone: (916)651-6654
Professional journal covering archaeology, ethnohistory and ethnology in Kansas. **Freq:** Annual. **Trim Size:** 8 1/2 x 11. **ISSN:** 1069--0379 (print). **URL:** http://www.katp.org/publications.html. **Remarks:** Advertising not accepted. **Circ:** Paid 300.

13495 ■ The Kansas Banker: The Magazine of the Kansas Bankers Association
Kansas Bankers Association
610 SW Corporate View
Topeka, KS 66615
Phone: (785)232-3444
Fax: (785)232-3484
Publisher's E-mail: kbaoffice@ksbankers.com
Kansas banking industry information magazine. **Freq:** 9/year. **Print Method:** Offset. **Trim Size:** 8 1/4 x 11 1/4. **Cols./Page:** 3. **Col. Width:** 2 1/4 inches. **Col. Depth:** 9 1/2 inches. **ISSN:** 0022--8478 (print). **URL:** http://thenewslinkgroup.com/clients/KBA/index.html. **Mailing address:** PO Box 4407, Topeka, KS 66604-0407. **Remarks:** Accepts advertising. **Circ:** ‡850, 875.

13496 ■ Kansas Country Living
Kansas Electric Cooperative Inc.
PO Box 4877
Topeka, KS 66604-0877
Phone: (785)273-7010
Fax: (785)271-4888
Free: 800-659-1152
Magazine for members of Kansas' electric cooperatives that promotes the uses of electrical energy around the farm and home. **Freq:** Monthly. **Print Method:** Offset. **Trim Size:** 7 7/8 x 10 3/4. **Cols./Page:** 3. **Col. Width:** 26 nonpareils. **Col. Depth:** 135 agate lines. **Key Personnel:** Larry Freeze, Editor. **ISSN:** 0091--9586 (print). **Subscription Rates:** $10 Individuals. **URL:** http://www.kec.org/content/kansas-country-living-magazine. **Ad Rates:** BW $2630. **Remarks:** Accepts advertising. **Circ:** ‡127000.

13497 ■ Kansas Government Journal
League of Kansas Municipalities
300 SW 8th Ave., Ste. 100
Topeka, KS 66603
Phone: (785)354-9565
Fax: (785)354-4186
Publisher's E-mail: info@lkm.org
Magazine covering Kansas' state and local government activities. **Freq:** Monthly. **Print Method:** Offset. **Trim Size:** 8 1/2 x 11. **Cols./Page:** 3. **Col. Width:** 27 nonpareils. **Col. Depth:** 140 agate lines. **Key Personnel:** Amanda Schuster, Contact, phone: (785)354-9565. **URL:** http://www.lkm.org/journal/archive. **Remarks:** Ac-

cepts display advertising. **Circ:** 4000.

13498 ■ Kansas History: A Journal of The Central Plains
Kansas Historical Society
6425 SW 6th Ave.
Topeka, KS 66615-1099
Phone: (785)272-8681
Fax: (785)272-8682
Publisher's E-mail: information@kshs.org
History journal. **Freq:** Quarterly. **Print Method:** Offset. **Trim Size:** 8 1/2 x 11. **Cols./Page:** 2 and 3. **Col. Width:** 36 nonpareils. **Col. Depth:** 123 agate lines. **Key Personnel:** Henry J. Fortunato, Editor; Dr. Virgil W. Dean, Editor. **ISSN:** 0149--9114 (print). **Subscription Rates:** Included in membership. **URL:** http://www.kshs.org/p/kansas-history/12443. **Remarks:** Advertising not accepted. **Circ:** (Not Reported).

13499 ■ Kansas Insurance Agent and Broker
Kansas Association of Insurance Agents
815 SW Topeka Blvd.
Topeka, KS 66612
Phone: (785)232-0561
Fax: (785)232-6817
Free: 800-229-7048
Publisher's E-mail: info@kaia.com
Insurance trade magazine. **Freq:** Bimonthly. **Print Method:** Offset. **Trim Size:** 8 1/2 x 11. **Cols./Page:** 3. **Col. Width:** 14 picas. **Col. Depth:** 58 picas. **Key Personnel:** Rebecca Spriggs, Publisher, Director, Communications. **ISSN:** 0194--634X (print). **URL:** http://www.kaia.com/News/Pages/MarketingToOurMembers/default.aspx; http://www.kaia.com/News/Pages/MarketingToOurMembers/Advertising/default.aspx. **Formerly:** Kansas Insurance. **Ad Rates:** 4C $1,600; BW $633; 4C $1,395. **Remarks:** Advertising accepted; rates available upon request. **Circ:** Paid ‡934, Non-paid ‡106.

13500 ■ Kansas Nurse
Kansas State Nurses Association
1109 SW Topeka Blvd.
Topeka, KS 66612-1602
Phone: (785)233-8638
Fax: (785)233-5222
Publisher's E-mail: ksna@knurses.com
Freq: Bimonthly 10/yr. **Subscription Rates:** $50 Nonmembers; $30 /year for nonmembers. **URL:** http://ksnurses.com/?30. **Ad Rates:** BW $315. **Remarks:** Accepts advertising. **Circ:** Paid ‡1700, Non-paid ‡100.

13501 ■ Kansas Stockman
Kansas Livestock Association
6031 SW 37th
Topeka, KS 66614
Phone: (785)273-5115
Fax: (785)273-3399
Magazine for cattle producers and operators of commercial feedlots. **Freq:** 10/year combined May-June & Nov.-Dec. issues. **Print Method:** Offset. **Trim Size:** 8 1/2 x 11. **Cols./Page:** 3. **Col. Width:** 28 nonpareils. **Col. Depth:** 140 agate lines. **Key Personnel:** Tammy Houk, Manager, Advertising; Todd Domer, Editor. **ISSN:** 0022--8826 (print). **Subscription Rates:** Included in membership. **URL:** http://www.kla.org/kansasstockman.aspx. **Remarks:** Accepts advertising. **Circ:** (Not Reported).

13502 ■ Mid-America Commerce and Industry
M.A.C.I. Inc.
2432 SW Pepperwood
Topeka, KS 66614-5293
Phone: (785)272-5280
Fax: (785)272-3729
Publisher's E-mail: maci@maci-mag.com
Magazine on industrial purchasing. **Freq:** Monthly. **Print Method:** Offset. **Trim Size:** 8 1/2 x 11. **Cols./Page:** 3. **Col. Width:** 13 picas. **Col. Depth:** 10 inches. **Key Personnel:** David Lippe, Managing Editor. **Subscription Rates:** $20 Individuals. **Remarks:** Accepts advertising. **Circ:** (Not Reported).

13503 ■ Motorcycle Classics
Ogden Publications Inc.
1503 SW 42nd St.
Topeka, KS 66609
Free: 800-678-5779
Publisher's E-mail: customercare@ogdenpubs.com
Magazine for motorcycle collectors and enthusiasts. **Freq:** Bimonthly. **Print Method:** Web offset. **Trim Size:** 8.125 x 10.875. **Key Personnel:** Richard Backus, Editor-in-Chief. **Subscription Rates:** $24.95 Individuals print or online; $29.95 Other countries print and online. **URL:** http://www.motorcycleclassics.com. **Ad Rates:** BW $3,150; 4C $4,500. **Remarks:** Accepts advertising. **Circ:** Paid ‡37500.

13504 ■ PostPress
Foil and Specialty Effects Association
2150 SW Westport Dr., Ste. 101
Topeka, KS 66614
Phone: (785)271-5816
Fax: (785)271-6404
Magazine containing happenings in the world of foil stamping and embossing. **Freq:** Quarterly. **Key Personnel:** Jeff Peterson, Publisher; Dianna Brodine, Editor. **URL:** http://www.postpressmag.com. **Ad Rates:** 4C $1400, full page - member; 4C $1150, half page - member; BW $1150, full page; BW $900, half page - member; 4C $1600, full page - nonmember; 4C $1350, half page - nonmember; BW $1350, full page - nonmember; BW $1100, half page - nonmember. **Remarks:** Accepts advertising. **Circ:** 15750.

13505 ■ The Topeka Capital-Journal
The Topeka Capital-Journal
616 SE Jefferson
Topeka, KS 66607
Phone: (785)295-1111
Fax: (785)295-1230
Free: 800-777-7171
Publisher's E-mail: news@cjonline.com
General newspaper. **Freq:** Daily. **Print Method:** Offset. **Cols./Page:** 6. **Col. Width:** 26 nonpareils. **Col. Depth:** 22 inches. **Key Personnel:** Tomari Quinn, Director, Editor; Zach Ahrens, Publisher, President. **Subscription Rates:** $17.90 Individuals home delivery /month (print and online); $9.95 Individuals online /month. **Remarks:** Accepts advertising. **Circ:** (Not Reported).

13506 ■ Utne
Ogden Publications Inc.
1503 SW 42nd St.
Topeka, KS 66609
Free: 800-678-5779
Publisher's E-mail: customercare@ogdenpubs.com
Digest of original articles and material reprinted from alternative and independent media. Keeps readers abreast of new ideas and emerging issues. **Freq:** Bimonthly. **Print Method:** Offset. **Trim Size:** 7 5/8 x 10. **Cols./Page:** 3. **Col. Width:** 2 1/8 inches. **Col. Depth:** 9 inches. **Key Personnel:** Christian Williams, Editor-in-Chief. **ISSN:** 8750--0256 (print). **Subscription Rates:** $31 Individuals print and online. **URL:** http://www.utne.com. **Formerly:** Utne Reader. **Ad Rates:** 4C $16080. **Remarks:** Accepts advertising. **Circ:** (Not Reported).

13507 ■ Washburn Law Journal
Washburn University School of Law
1700 SW College Ave.
Topeka, KS 66621
Phone: (785)670-1060
Publisher's E-mail: admissions@washburnlaw.edu
Journal containing articles on legal issues. **Freq:** 3/year. **Key Personnel:** Nathaniel T. Martens, Editor-in-Chief. **Subscription Rates:** $30 U.S.; $35 Out of state; $15 Single issue. **URL:** http://washburnlaw.edu/publications/wlj. **Circ:** (Not Reported).

13508 ■ KCVT-FM - 92.5
534 Kansas Ave., Ste. 930
Topeka, KS 66603
Owner: Bott Radio Network, 10550 Barkley, Overland Park, KS 66212, Ph: (913)642-7770, Fax: (913)642-1319, Free: 800-345-2621. **Operating Hours:** Continuous. **Wattage:** 6,700. **Ad Rates:** Noncommercial.

13509 ■ KDVV-FM - 100.3
825 S Kansas Ave.
Topeka, KS 66612
Phone: (785)272-2122
Fax: (785)272-6219
Free: 866-297-1003
Format: Album-Oriented Rock (AOR); Contemporary Hit Radio (CHR). **Owner:** Cumulus Broadcasting Inc., 3280 Peachtree Rd. NW, Ste. 2300, Atlanta, GA 30305-2447, Ph: (404)949-0700, Fax: (404)949-0740. **Founded:** 1960. **ADI:** Topeka, KS. **Wattage:** 100,000. **Ad Rates:** Advertising accepted; rates available upon request. **URL:** http://www.v100rocks.com.

13510 ■ KJTY-FM - 88.1
PO Box 35300
Tucson, AZ 85740
Free: 800-776-1070
Format: Contemporary Christian. **Networks:** Moody Broadcasting; USA Radio. **Owner:** Family Life Communications, Inc., 7355 N Oracle Rd., Tucson, AZ 85704, Ph: (520)544-5950, Fax: (520)742-6979, Free: 800-776-1070. **Founded:** 1985. **Operating Hours:** Continuous; 20% network, 80% local. **ADI:** Topeka, KS. **Wattage:** 100,000. **Ad Rates:** Noncommercial. **URL:** http://www.myflr.org.

13511 ■ KMAJ-AM - 1440
825 S Kansas Ave., Ste. 100.
Topeka, KS 66612
Phone: (785)272-2122
Fax: (785)272-6219
Format: Talk. **Founded:** 1947. **ADI:** Topeka, KS. **Key Personnel:** Fritz Reynolds, President; Bill Reed, Gen. Mgr.; Dave Waters, Dir. of Programs; Mike Manns, News Dir. **Wattage:** 5,000 day; 1,000 night. **URL:** http://www.kmaj1440.com/station-information/.

13512 ■ KMAJ-FM - 107.7
825 S Kansas Ave., Ste. 100
Topeka, KS 66612
Phone: (785)272-2122
Fax: (785)272-6219
Free: 877-297-1077
Format: Adult Contemporary. **Owner:** Frederick P. Reynolds, Jr., 5315 W 7th.,, Topeka, KS 66606. **Founded:** 1971. **Operating Hours:** Continuous. **ADI:** Topeka, KS. **Key Personnel:** Pam Anderson, Bus. Mgr. **Wattage:** 100,000. **URL:** http://www.kmaj.com/station-information.

13513 ■ KQTP-FM - 102.9
825 S Kansas Ave.
Topeka, KS 66612
Phone: (785)272-2122
Fax: (785)272-6219
Free: 866-929-1029
Format: Country. **Owner:** Cumulus Broadcasting Inc., 3280 Peachtree Rd. NW, Ste. 2300, Atlanta, GA 30305-2447, Ph: (404)949-0700, Fax: (404)949-0740. **Ad Rates:** Advertising accepted; rates available upon request. **URL:** http://www.nashfm1029.com.

13514 ■ KSNT-TV - 27
6835 NW Hwy. 24
Topeka, KS 66618
Phone: (785)582-4000
Fax: (785)582-4783
Email: 27news@ksnt.com
Format: Commercial TV. **Networks:** NBC. **Founded:** 1967. **Formerly:** KTSB-TV. **Operating Hours:** 5 a.m.-2 a.m. weekdays; 7 a.m.-midnight Sat.-Sun. **ADI:** Topeka, KS. **Key Personnel:** Nate Hill, News Dir.; Jean Turnbough, Gen. Mgr. **Ad Rates:** Advertising accepted; rates available upon request. **URL:** http://www.ksnt.com.

13515 ■ K33IC - 33
PO Box A
Santa Ana, CA 92711
Phone: (714)832-2950
Free: 888-731-1000
Owner: Trinity Broadcasting Network Inc., PO Box A, Santa Ana, CA 92711, Ph: (714)832-2950, Free: 888-731-1000. **URL:** http://www.tbn.org.

13516 ■ KTKA-TV - 49
2121 SW Chelsea Dr.
Topeka, KS 66614-1756
Phone: (785)582-4000
Fax: (785)582-4783
Format: Commercial TV. **Networks:** ABC. **Owner:** FREE State Communications, 644 New Hampshire St., Lawrence, KS 66044. **Founded:** June 20, 1983. **Formerly:** KLDH-TV. **Operating Hours:** Continuous. **ADI:** Topeka, KS. **Key Personnel:** Jean Turnbough, Gen. Mgr. **Wattage:** 348. **Ad Rates:** $15-500 for 30 seconds. **URL:** http://www.kansasfirstnews.com.

Circulation: ★ = AAM; △ or • = BPA; ♦ = CAC; ❑ = VAC; ⊕ = PO Statement; ‡ = Publisher's Report; Boldface figures = sworn; Light figures = estimated.

13517 ■ KTMJ-TV - 43
6835 NW Hwy. 24
Topeka, KS 66618
ADI: Topeka, KS. **Key Personnel:** Jean Turnbough, Gen. Mgr., jturnbough@ksnt.com. **Wattage:** 15,000. **URL:** http://www.myfoxtopeka.com/myfox.

13518 ■ KTOP-AM - 1490
825 S Kansas Ave.
Topeka, KS 66612
Phone: (785)272-2122
Fax: (785)272-6219
Format: Sports. **Owner:** Cumulus Broadcasting Inc., 3280 Peachtree Rd. NW, Ste. 2300, Atlanta, GA 30305-2447, Ph: (404)949-0700, Fax: (404)949-0740. **ADI:** Topeka, KS. **Wattage:** 1,000 ERP. **Ad Rates:** Advertising accepted; rates available upon request. **URL:** http://www.ktop1490.com.

13519 ■ KTPK-FM - 106.9
2121 SW Chelsea Dr.
Topeka, KS 66614
Phone: (785)273-1069
Free: 888-291-1069
Format: Country. **Owner:** KTPK Radio, 1210 SW Executive Dr., Topeka, KS 66615, Ph: (785)273-1069, Fax: (785)273-0123, Free: 888-291-1069. **Founded:** 1974. **Operating Hours:** Continuous. **ADI:** Topeka, KS. **Key Personnel:** Jim Allan, Gen. Mgr., Sales Mgr. **Wattage:** 100,000. **Ad Rates:** Noncommercial. Combined advertising rates available with KTKA-TV. **URL:** http://www.ktpk1069.com.

13520 ■ K208FE-FM - 89.5
PO Box 391
Twin Falls, ID 83303
Fax: (208)736-1958
Free: 800-357-4226
Format: Religious; Contemporary Christian. **Owner:** CSN International, PO Box 391, Twin Falls, ID 83303, Ph: (208)736-1958, Fax: (208)736-1958, Free: 800-357-4226. **Key Personnel:** Mike Kestler, Contact; Don Mills, Music Dir., Prog. Dir. **URL:** http://www.csnradio.com.

13521 ■ KTWU-TV - 11
1700 College Ave.
Topeka, KS 66621-1100
Phone: (785)670-1111
Free: 800-866-5898
Email: prodservices@ktwu.org
Format: Public TV. **Networks:** Public Broadcasting Service (PBS). **Owner:** Washburn University, 1700 SW College Ave., Topeka, KS 66621, Ph: (785)670-1010, Free: 800-332-0291. **Founded:** 1965. **Operating Hours:** Continuous. **ADI:** Topeka, KS. **Key Personnel:** Eugene Williams, CEO, Gen. Mgr., eugene.williams@washburn.edu; Val Van Dersluis, Prog. Dir.; Kevin Goodman, Dir. of Mktg., Promotions Dir. **Local Programs:** *Sunflower Journeys*, Thursday Friday Saturday Wednesday 8:00 p.m. 2:30 p.m. 5:30 p.m. 7:30 p.m. **Wattage:** 38,000 ERP H. **Ad Rates:** Noncommercial. Underwriting available. **URL:** http://www.ktwu.org.

13522 ■ WIBW-AM - 580
1210 SW Executive Dr.
Topeka, KS 66615
Phone: (785)272-3456
Fax: (785)228-7282
Format: News; Sports; Talk. **Owner:** Morris Communications Company L.L.C., 725 Broad St., Augusta, GA 30901, Ph: (706)724-0851, Free: 800-622-6358. **Founded:** May 08, 1927. **ADI:** Topeka, KS. **Key Personnel:** Kelly Lenz, Exec. Dir., kelly.lenz@morris.com; Jeremy Lamb, Sales Mgr., jeremy.lamb@morris.com; Bruce Steinbrock, Dir. of Programs, bruce.steinbrock@morris.com; Cheryl Dubois, Contact, cheryl.dubois@morris.com. **Wattage:** 5,000 Day; 5,000 Nig. **Ad Rates:** Accepts Advertising. **URL:** http://www.wibwnewsnow.com.

13523 ■ WIBW-FM - 94.5
1210 SW Executive Dr.
Topeka, KS 66615
Phone: (785)272-3456
Fax: (785)228-7282
Format: Country; Contemporary Country. **Owner:** Stauffer Topeka Radio Trust, at above address. **Founded:** 1961. **Operating Hours:** Continuous. **ADI:** Topeka, KS. **Key Personnel:** Larry Riggins, Gen. Mgr., laryy.riggins@morris.com; Keith Montgomery, Dir. of Programs, keith.montgomery@morris.com. **Wattage:** 100,000 ERP. **Ad Rates:** Noncommercial. **URL:** http://www.94country.com.

13524 ■ WIBW-TV - 13
631 SW Commerce Pl.
Topeka, KS 66615
Phone: (785)272-6397
Email: feedback@wibw.com
Format: Commercial TV. **Networks:** CBS. **Operating Hours:** Continuous. **ADI:** Topeka, KS. **Key Personnel:** Jim Ogle, Gen. Mgr., jim.ogle@wibw.com. **Wattage:** 42,000 ERP H. **Ad Rates:** Advertising accepted; rates available upon request. **URL:** http://www.wibw.com.

TRIBUNE

W. KS. Greeley Co. 105 mi. NW of Dodge City. Grain, stock farms. Wheat, milo maize, sheep, cattle.

13525 ■ Greeley County Republican
Greeley County Republican
507 Broadway
Tribune, KS 67879
Phone: (620)376-4264
Community newspaper. **Freq:** Weekly (Wed.). **Print Method:** Offset. **Cols./Page:** 6. **Col. Width:** 12 picas. **Col. Depth:** 21.5 inches. **Key Personnel:** Dan Epp, Editor. **USPS:** 228-020. **Mailing address:** PO Box 610, Tribune, KS 67879. **Remarks:** Accepts advertising. **Circ:** (Not Reported).

TURON

13526 ■ The Record
Larry Green
PO Box 38
Turon, KS 67583-0038
Phone: (316)497-6448
Publisher's E-mail: record@sctelcom.net
Community newspaper. **Founded:** 1968. **Freq:** Weekly (Thurs.). **Print Method:** Offset. **Cols./Page:** 6 and 5. **Col. Width:** 26 2 1/8 nonpareils inches and 11.5 picas. **Col. Depth:** 301 21 1/2 and 12.5 agate lines inches. **Key Personnel:** Robert Regis Hyle, Editor; Susan Hyle, Editor; Joan Green, Editor; Larry Green, Publisher; Jacqueline Kiefer, Editor; Maureen Olsen, Publisher; Joseph E. Duerr, Editor. **USPS:** 254-840. **Subscription Rates:** $10 Individuals; $9; $12 Individuals; $3 Individuals; $8.50 Out of area; $10.50 Out of state. **Ad Rates:** BW $308.70; PCI $2.45; BW $400; 4C $640; SAU $3.50; BW $1,100; PCI $16; GLR $.18; BW $130; PCI $2.10. **Remarks:** Accepts advertising. **Circ:** 1200, ‡3500, ‡61700, ‡800.

ULYSSES

SW KS. Grant Co. 70 mi. SW of Dodge City. Liquid petroleum products, carbon black, irrigation pipe manufactured. Grain farms. Wheat, corn, sorghum.

13527 ■ KULY-AM
2917 S Colorado
Ulysses, KS 67880
Phone: (620)356-1420
Fax: (620)356-3635
Format: Contemporary Country. **Networks:** ABC; Westwood One Radio. **Owner:** KBUF Partnership, at above address. **Founded:** 1964. **Key Personnel:** Jeffrey Dyer, Gen. Mgr., Station Mgr.; Bob Dale, Operations Mgr. **Wattage:** 1,000 Day; 500 Night. **Ad Rates:** $13-15 for 30 seconds; $20-23 for 60 seconds.

13528 ■ Pioneer Telephone Association Inc.
120 W Kansas Ave.
Ulysses, KS 67880-2036
Phone: (620)356-3211
Free: 800-308-7536
Email: info@pioncomm.net
Founded: 1952. **Cities Served:** 114 channels. **Mailing address:** PO Box 707, Ulysses, KS 67880-0707. **URL:** http://www.pioncomm.net.

VALLEY CENTER

S. KS. Sedgwick Co. 12 mi. N. of Wichita. Oil, gas wells. Elevator. Agriculture. Wheat, alfalfa, hogs.

13529 ■ Ark Valley News
Ark Valley News
PO Box 120
Valley Center, KS 67147
Phone: (316)755-0821
Fax: (316)755-0644
Publisher's E-mail: news@arkvalleynews.com
Community newspaper. **Freq:** Weekly (Thurs.). **Print Method:** Offset. **Cols./Page:** 4. **Col. Width:** 14.5 picas. **Col. Depth:** 16 inches. **Key Personnel:** Lisa Strunk, Contact. **Remarks:** Advertising accepted; rates available upon request. **Circ:** (Not Reported).

VALLEY FALLS

NE KS. Jefferson Co. 31 mi. NE of Topeka. Truck bodies manufactured. Walnut timber. Grain, stock, poultry, dairy farms. Corn, wheat, alfalfa.

13530 ■ The Oskaloosa Independent
Davis Publications Inc.
416 Broadway
Valley Falls, KS 66088
Phone: (785)945-6170
Fax: (785)945-3444
Community newspaper. **Freq:** Weekly (Thurs.). **Print Method:** Offset. **Cols./Page:** 7. **Col. Width:** 12 picas. **Col. Depth:** 21 inches. **Key Personnel:** Dennis Sharkey, Editor; Peggy Collier, Office Manager; Corey Davis, Manager, Production. **Mailing address:** PO Box 187, Valley Falls, KS 66088. **Ad Rates:** PCI $6. **Remarks:** Accepts display and classified advertising. **Circ:** Paid 2281.

13531 ■ Valley Falls Vindicator
Davis Publications Inc.
416 Broadway St.
Valley Falls, KS 66088-1304
Phone: (785)945-3257
Fax: (785)945-3444
Publication E-mail: vindicator@embarqmail.com
Community newspaper. **Freq:** Weekly (Thurs.). **Print Method:** Offset. **Cols./Page:** 7. **Col. Width:** 25 nonpareils. **Col. Depth:** 294 agate lines. **Key Personnel:** Marveta Davis, Editor; Clarke Davis, Editor; Corey Davis, Manager, Production; Carol Meneley, Manager, Circulation. **USPS:** 655-520. **URL:** http://www.jeffcountynews.com/category/valley-falls-vindicator. **Mailing address:** PO Box 187, Valley Falls, KS 66088-0187. **Remarks:** Accepts display and classified advertising. **Circ:** (Not Reported).

WAMEGO

NE KS. Pottawatomie Co. On Kansas River, 37 mi. NW of Topeka. Manufactures snow plows, bull dozers, cheese, fertilizer, feeds. Grain, stock farms. Wheat, corn, alfalfa, soybeans.

13532 ■ Wamego Telecommunications Company Inc.
1009 Lincoln St.
Wamego, KS 66547
Phone: (785)456-1000
Fax: (785)456-9903
Free: 877-492-6835
Email: support@wtcks.com
Founded: 1912. **Cities Served:** 53 channels. **URL:** http://www.wtcks.com.

WELLINGTON

SC KS. Sumner Co. 30 mi. S. of Wichita. Residential.

13533 ■ Wellington Daily News
Wellington Daily News
113 W Harvey Ave.
Wellington, KS 67152
Phone: (620)326-3326
Newspaper with a Republican orientation. **Founded:** 1901. **Freq:** Daily (eve.) five times a week. **Print Method:** Offset. **Cols./Page:** 6. **Col. Width:** 26 nonpareils. **Col. Depth:** 294 agate lines. **Key Personnel:** Nate Jones, Managing Editor. **URL:** http://www.wellingtondailynews.com/. **Ad Rates:** PCI $6.85. **Remarks:** Advertising accepted; rates available upon request. **Circ:** Paid 3800.

13534 ■ KKLE-AM - 1550
338 S Kley Dr.
Wellington, KS 67152
Phone: (620)326-3341
Fax: (620)326-8512
Free: 800-850-3341
Email: kley@sutv.com

Format: News; Sports. **Owner:** Johnson Enterprises, Inc., at above address. **Formerly**: KVFW-AM. **Operating Hours:** Continuous. **Wattage**: 250. **Ad Rates:** $7 for 30 seconds; $10 for 60 seconds. **URL:** http://www.kkle.com.

13535 ■ KLEY-AM - 1130
338 S Kley Dr.
Wellington, KS 67152
Phone: (620)326-3341
Fax: (620)326-8512
Free: 800-850-3341
Email: kley@sutv.com
Format: Talk; Sports. **Owner:** Johnson Enterprises, Inc., at above address. **Operating Hours**: Continuous. **Wattage:** 250. **Ad Rates:** Noncommercial. Combined advertising rates available with KKLE/KWME. **URL:** http://www.kleyam.com.

13536 ■ KWME-FM - 92.7
338 S KLEY Dr.
Wellington, KS 67152
Phone: (620)326-3341
Fax: (620)326-8512
Free: 800-850-3341
Email: kley@sutv.com
Format: Oldies; News; Sports. **Simulcasts:** KLEY, KKLE. **Operating Hours**: Continuous. **Wattage:** 14,000. **Ad Rates:** $10.06 for 30 seconds; $12.08 for 60 seconds. Combined advertising rates available with KLEY, KKLE. **URL:** http://www.kleyam.com.

13537 ■ Sumner Cable TV Inc.
117 W Harvey Ave.
Wellington, KS 67152
Phone: (620)326-8989
Free: 877-773-8989
Email: support@sumnercomm.net
Owner: Sumner Communications Inc., 24 Stony Hill Rd., Bethel 06801, Ph: (203)748-2050, Fax: (203)830-2072. **Founded:** 1978. **Cities Served:** Wellington, Kansas: subscribing households 3,225; 56 channels; 1 community access channel. **URL:** http://www.sutv.com.

WESTMORELAND

NE KS. Pottawatomie Co. 50 mi. NW of Topeka. Agriculture. Milo, wheat, cattle.

13538 ■ Westmoreland Recorder
Westmoreland Recorder
PO Box 128
Westmoreland, KS 66549
Publisher's E-mail: news@westyrecorder.com
Official county newspaper. **Freq:** Weekly (Thurs.). **Print Method:** Offset. Uses mats. **Cols./Page:** 6. **Col. Width:** 25 nonpareils. **Col. Depth:** 301 agate lines. **Key Personnel:** James I. Travis, Editor. **Remarks:** Advertising accepted; rates available upon request. **Circ:** (Not Reported).

WHITE CITY

13539 ■ Prairie Post
Prairie Post
108 E Mackenie
White City, KS 66872-0326
Phone: (785)349-5516
Fax: (785)349-5516
Free: 800-593-5516
Weekly community newspaper. **Founded:** 1993. **Freq:** Weekly (Fri.). **Print Method:** Offset. **Trim Size:** 11 1/2 x 15. **Cols./Page:** 5. **Col. Width:** 12.4 picas. **Col. Depth:** 14 inches. **Key Personnel:** Joann Kahnt, Editor. **USPS:** 763-570. **URL:** http://www.prairiepost.com/onlinepaper/. **Formerly**: White City Reporter; Alta Vista Journal. **Ad Rates:** GLR $.14; BW $140; PCI $2.80. **Remarks:** Accepts advertising. **Circ:** Paid 840, Controlled 21.

WICHITA

S KS. Sedgwick Co. 195 mi. SW of Kansas City. Friends University. The Wichita State University. Kansas Newman College. Recreational lakes. Mid-American All Indian Center. Historic Cowtown. Culture Center. Center of rich oil producting and wheat growing region. Manufactures airplanes, airplane supplies, heating and air conditioning units, agricultural and auto equipment, machinery, dairy products, household appliances. Oil refining. Grain storage. Meat packing. Flour milling. Steel fabrication.

13540 ■ The Active Age
Active Aging Publishing Inc.
125 S W St., Ste. 105
Wichita, KS 67213-2114
Phone: (316)942-5385
Fax: (316)946-9180
Publisher's E-mail: bfunke@activeagingonline.com
Newspaper serving Wichita metro-area residents over age 55. **Freq:** Monthly. **Print Method:** Offset. **Trim Size:** 10 x 16. **Cols./Page:** 4. **Col. Width:** 14 picas. **Col. Depth:** 16 inches. **Key Personnel:** Fran Kentling, Editor. **Subscription Rates:** Included in membership. **URL:** http://theactiveage.com. **Formerly**: Active Aging. **Remarks:** Advertising accepted; rates available upon request. **Circ:** (Not Reported).

13541 ■ The Decorative Painter
Society of Decorative Painters
1220 E 1st st.
Wichita, KS 67203-5968
Phone: (316)269-9300
Fax: (316)269-9191
Publisher's E-mail: sdp@decorativepainters.org
Magazine containing lessons and projects on decorative painting. **Freq:** Quarterly. **Subscription Rates:** Included in membership. **URL:** http://www.decorativepainters.org/thedp.php. **Remarks:** Accepts advertising. **Circ:** (Not Reported).

13542 ■ The Deputy Sheriff Magazine
United States Deputy Sheriffs' Association
319 S Hydraulic St., Ste. B
Wichita, KS 67211-1908
Phone: (316)263-2583
Publisher's E-mail: info@usdeputy.org
Magazine publishing law enforcement news from around the country. **Freq:** Quarterly. **Subscription Rates:** Included in membership. **URL:** http://www.usdeputy.org. **Remarks:** Advertising not accepted. **Circ:** (Not Reported).

13543 ■ El Perico: Bilingual Newspaper
El Perico
7804 E Funston, Ste. 210
Wichita, KS 67207-3107
Phone: (316)651-0372
Fax: (316)651-0436
Community newspaper (Spanish). **Freq:** Monthly. **Cols./Page:** 4. **Col. Width:** 3.25 picas. **Col. Depth:** 13.5 picas. **Key Personnel:** Anthony J. Ramirez, Editor. **Subscription Rates:** $15. **Ad Rates:** PCI $6.38. **Remarks:** Accepts advertising. **Circ:** 3000.

13544 ■ Journal of Legal Aspects of Sport
Sport and Recreation Law Association
c/o Mary Myers
1621 N Melrose Dr.
Wichita, KS 67212
Freq: Semiannual February and August. **ISSN:** 1072--0316 (print); **EISSN:** 2325--2162 (electronic). **Subscription Rates:** $97 Individuals pint and online; $82 Individuals online only; $73 Students pint and online; $62 Students online only. **URL:** http://journals.humankinetics.com/jlas; http://www.srlawebsite.com/publications. **Remarks:** Advertising not accepted. **Circ:** (Not Reported).

13545 ■ Journal of Service Marketing
Emerald Group Publishing Limited
c/o Prof. Charles L Martin, Ed.
Wichita State University
W Frank Barton School of Business
Wichita, KS 67260
Publisher's E-mail: emerald@emeraldinsight.com
Publication covering advertising, marketing and public relations. **Freq:** 7/yr. **Key Personnel:** Raj Arora, Advisor; Charles L. Martin, Editor; Richard Whitfield, Publisher; Dr. Levent Altinay, Advisor; Michael McBride, Advisor; Jay Kandampully, Editor; Glynn W. Mangold, Advisor; Emin Babakus, Advisor. **ISSN:** 0887--6045 (print). **URL:** http://www.emeraldinsight.com/journal/jsm. **Circ:** (Not Reported).

13546 ■ Kansas Beverage News
Kansas Beverage News
2416 E 37th St. N
Wichita, KS 67219
Phone: (316)838-6700
Liquor trade magazine. **Freq:** Monthly. **Print Method:** Offset. **Trim Size:** 8 1/2 x 11. **Cols./Page:** 3. **Col. Width:** 24 nonpareils. **Col. Depth:** 126 agate lines. **Key Personnel:** Kathy Decker, Editor, Publisher. **USPS:** 875-420. **Subscription Rates:** $12 Individuals. **Ad Rates:** BW $600; 4C $1,400. **Remarks:** Advertising accepted; rates available upon request. **Circ:** 2300.

13547 ■ Kansas Farmer
Farm Progress Companies Inc.
c/o P.J. Griekspoor, Editor
6716 E Bainbridge Rd.
Wichita, KS 67226
Phone: (316)681-2100
Fax: (316)681-2102
Publisher's E-mail: circhelp@farmprogress.com
Agricultural magazine. **Freq:** Monthly. **Print Method:** Offset. **Trim Size:** 8 x 10 3/4. **Cols./Page:** 3. **Col. Width:** 25 nonpareils. **Col. Depth:** 140 agate lines. **Key Personnel:** Frank Holdmeyer, Executive Editor, phone: (515)278-7782, fax: (515)278-7796; P.J. Griekspoor, Editor; John Otte, Editor, phone: (515)278-7785, fax: (515)278-7797; Alan Newport, Editor, phone: (580)362-3483, fax: (580)362-3483; Willie Vogt, Director, Editorial, phone: (651)454-6994, fax: (651)994-0661. **ISSN:** 0022--8583 (print). **Subscription Rates:** $29.95 Individuals /year; $48.95 Two years; $64.95 Individuals three years. **URL:** http://farmprogress.com/kansas-farmer. **Remarks:** Accepts advertising. **Circ:** (Not Reported).

13548 ■ Oklahoma Beverage News
Oklahoma Beverage News
2416 E 37th N
Wichita, KS 67219
Phone: (316)838-6700
Publisher's E-mail: contact@beverage-news.com
Liquor trade magazine. **Freq:** Monthly. **Print Method:** Offset. **Trim Size:** 8 1/2 x 11. **Cols./Page:** 3. **Col. Width:** 24 nonpareils. **Col. Depth:** 126 agate lines. **Key Personnel:** Kathy Decker, Editor, Publisher. **USPS:** 875-420. **Subscription Rates:** $24 Individuals. **URL:** http://www.beverage-news.com/okbeveragenews/index.html. **Ad Rates:** BW $600; 4C $1,400. **Remarks:** Accepts advertising. **Circ:** 1325.

13549 ■ The Sunflower
Wichita State University
1845 Fairmount St.
Wichita, KS 67260
Phone: (316)978-3456
Publisher's E-mail: webmaster@wichita.edu
Collegiate newspaper. **Founded:** 1896. **Freq:** Triweekly Mondays, Wednesdays and Thursdays. **Print Method:** Offset. **Cols./Page:** 4. **Col. Width:** 29 nonpareils. **Col. Depth:** 210 agate lines. **Key Personnel:** Robbie Norton, Business Manager, phone: (316)978-6900; Shelby Reynolds, Editor-in-Chief. **USPS:** 053-050. **URL:** http://www.thesunflower.com. **Mailing address:** PO Box 34, Wichita, KS 67260-0034. **Ad Rates:** BW $100; 4C $300. **Remarks:** Advertising accepted; rates available upon request. **Circ:** Mon. 8000, Wed. 8000, Fri. 8000.

13550 ■ Thunderbird Scoop
Vintage Thunderbird Club International
c/o Rod Wake, President
PO Box 75308
Wichita, KS 67275
Phone: (316)722-2028
Freq: Bimonthly. **Remarks:** Advertising not accepted. **Circ:** (Not Reported).

13551 ■ Vantage
Kansas Newman College
3100 McCormick Ave.
Wichita, KS 67213-2097
Phone: (316)942-4291
Fax: (316)942-4483
Free: 877-639-6268
Publication E-mail: vantage@newmanu.edu
Collegiate newspaper. **Founded:** 1961. **Freq:** Weekly (Wed.). **Print Method:** Offset. **Trim Size:** 11 1/2 x 16. **Cols./Page:** 5. **Col. Width:** 11 picas. **Col. Depth:** 82 picas. **Key Personnel:** Audrey Curtis Hane, Associate Professor. **Subscription Rates:** Free. **URL:** http://www.newmanu.edu/studynu/undergraduate/journalism/vantage. **Ad Rates:** BW $150; PCI $3. **Remarks:** Color advertising not accepted. **Circ:** Free ‡1500, Paid 20.

Circulation: ★ = AAM; △ or • = BPA; ♦ = CAC; ❑ = VAC; ⊕ = PO Statement; ‡ = Publisher's Report; Boldface figures = sworn; Light figures = estimated.

13552 ■ Wichita Business Journal
The Business Journals
121 N Mead, Ste. 100
Wichita, KS 67202
Phone: (316)267-6406
Fax: (316)267-8570
Publisher's E-mail: info@bizjournals.com
Business newspaper. **Freq:** Weekly. **Print Method:** Offset. **Trim Size:** 11 3/8 x 14. **Cols./Page:** 4. **Col. Width:** 2 3/8 inches. **Col. Depth:** 13 inches. **Key Personnel:** Bill Roy, Editor, phone: (316)266-6184. **ISSN:** 0894--4032 (print). **Subscription Rates:** $98 Individuals /year, print and online. **URL:** http://www.bizjournals.com/wichita. **Remarks:** Accepts advertising. **Circ:** (Not Reported).

13553 ■ The Wichita Eagle
McClatchy Newspapers Inc.
825 E Douglas
Wichita, KS 67202
Phone: (316)268-6000
Publisher's E-mail: pensions@mcclatchy.com
General newspaper. **Freq:** Daily. **Print Method:** Letterpress. **Trim Size:** 13 1/2 x 23 1/2. **Cols./Page:** 6. **Col. Width:** 26 nonpareils. **Col. Depth:** 311 agate lines. **Key Personnel:** Sherry Chisenhall, Editor, Vice President, phone: (316)268-6405; Michael Roehrman, Deputy, phone: (316)269-6753; Tom Shine, Deputy, phone: (316)268-6268. **ISSN:** 1046--3127 (print). **Online:** LexisNexis; McClatchy Newspapers Inc. McClatchy Newspapers Inc. **URL:** http://www.kansas.com. **Formerly**: The Wichita Eagle-Beacon. **Remarks:** Advertising accepted; rates available upon request. **Circ:** (Not Reported).

13554 ■ World Series Annual
National Baseball Congress
110 S Main, Ste. 600
Wichita, KS 67202
Phone: (316)977-9400
Fax: (316)462-4506
Publisher's E-mail: josh@wichitawingnuts.com
Freq: Annual. **Subscription Rates:** $3. **Remarks:** Accepts advertising. **Circ:** 6000.

KAAS-TV - See Salina

13555 ■ KAKE-TV - 10
1500 N West St.
Wichita, KS 67203-1323
Phone: (316)943-4221
Fax: (316)943-5160
Free: 800-853-6397
Email: news@kake.com
Format: Commercial TV. **Networks:** ABC. **Owner:** Gray Television Inc., 4370 Peachtree Rd. NE, No. 400, Atlanta, GA 30319-3054, Ph: (404)266-8333; Lockwood Broadcast Group, 3914 Wistar Rd., Richmond, VA 23228, Ph: (804)672-6565, Fax: (804)672-6571. **Founded:** 1954. **Operating Hours**: Continuous; 55% network, 45% local. **Local Programs**: *Good Morning Kansas*, Saturday Monday Tuesday Wednesday Thursday Friday 11:00 a.m. **Ad Rates:** Noncommercial. **Mailing address:** PO Box 10, Wichita, KS 67203-1323. **URL:** http://www.kake.com.

KANR-FM - See Belle Plaine, KS

13556 ■ KCTU-TV - 43
2100 E Douglas
Wichita, KS 67214
Phone: (316)267-8855
Fax: (316)269-2555
Email: kctu@kctu.com
Founded: Aug. 12, 1992. **Ad Rates:** Advertising accepted; rates available upon request. **URL:** http://kctu.com.

13557 ■ KDGS-FM - 93.9
9111 E Douglas, Ste. 130
Wichita, KS 67208
Phone: (316)685-2121
Fax: (316)685-3408
Format: Hip Hop; Urban Contemporary; Rap. **Key Personnel:** Jackie Wise, Gen. Mgr., jwise@entercom.com; Mark Yearout, Sales Mgr., myearout@entercom.com. **Ad Rates:** Advertising accepted; rates available upon request. **URL:** http://www.power939.com/pages/14709713.php.

13558 ■ KEYN-FM - 103.7
2120 N Woodlawn, Ste. 352
Wichita, KS 67208
Phone: (316)436-1037
Format: Oldies; Adult Contemporary. **Founded:** 1968. **Operating Hours:** Continuous. **Key Personnel:** Jack Oliver, Prog. Dir., jack@keyn.com; Jackie Wise, Gen. Mgr., jwise@entercom.com; Lisa Crider, Sales Mgr., lcrider@entercom.com; Rick Parrish, Contact; Dave Windsor, Contact. **Wattage:** 100,000. **Ad Rates:** Advertising accepted; rates available upon request. $3-50 per unit. **URL:** http://www.keyn.com.

13559 ■ KFBZ-FM - 105.3
2120 N Woodlawn, Ste. 352
Wichita, KS 67208
Format: Adult Contemporary. **Key Personnel:** Jackie Wise, Gen. Mgr., jwise@entercom.com; Lisa Crider, Sales Mgr., lcrider@entercom.com; Dusty Hayes, Prog. Dir., dusty@1053thebuzz.com. **Ad Rates:** Noncommercial. **URL:** http://www.1053thebuzz.com.

13560 ■ KFDI-AM
6501 W Kellogg
Wichita, KS 67209
Phone: (316)838-9141
Founded: 1988. **Key Personnel:** Bill Endsley, Contact; Larry Waggoner, Contact. **URL:** http://www.kfdi.com/homepage-showcase/strait-to-vegas.

13561 ■ KFDI-FM - 101.3
4200 N Old Lawrence Rd.
Wichita, KS 67219
Phone: (316)838-9141
Format: Country. **Networks:** ABC. **Owner:** Journal Broadcast Corp., 333 W State St., Milwaukee, WI 53203, Ph: (414)332-9611, Fax: (414)967-5400. **Founded:** 1963. **Operating Hours**: Continuous. **ADI**: Wichita-Hutchinson, KS. **Key Personnel:** Eric McCart, Gen. Mgr., VP. **Wattage**: 100,000 ERP. **Ad Rates:** Advertising accepted; rates available upon request. **URL:** http://www.kfdi.com.

13562 ■ KFH-AM - 1240
2120 N Woodlawn, Ste. 352
Wichita, KS 67208
Phone: (316)436-1240
Format: Sports. **Networks:** ABC; Mutual Broadcasting System. **Owner:** Entercom Communications Corp., 401 City Ave., Ste. 809, Bala Cynwyd, PA 19004-1130, Ph: (610)660-5610, Fax: (610)660-5620. **Founded:** 1977. **Operating Hours**: Continuous. **ADI**: Wichita-Hutchinson, KS. **Key Personnel:** Tony Duesing, Dir. of Programs, tony@kfhradio.com. **Wattage**: 5,000 Day; 1,000 Night. **Ad Rates:** Noncommercial. **URL:** http://www.kfhradio.com.

13563 ■ KFH-FM - 98.7
9111 E Douglas
Wichita, KS 67208
Phone: (316)685-2121
Format: Talk; Sports. **Founded:** Sept. 07, 2006. **Key Personnel:** Tony Duesing, Dir. of Programs, tony@kfhradio.com; Mark Yearout, Sales Mgr., myearout@entercom.com. **Ad Rates:** Advertising accepted; rates available upon request. **URL:** http://www.kfhradio.com.

13564 ■ KFTI-AM - 1070
4200 N Old Lawrence Rd.
Wichita, KS 67219
Phone: (316)838-9141
Fax: (316)436-1013
Format: Country. **Ad Rates:** Advertising accepted; rates available upon request. **URL:** http://www.classiccountry1070.com.

13565 ■ KFTI-FM - 92.3
4200 N Old Lawrence Rd.
Wichita, KS 67219
Phone: (316)838-9141
Fax: (316)838-3607
Format: Country. **Owner:** Journal Broadcast Corp., 333 W State St., Milwaukee, WI 53203, Ph: (414)332-9611, Fax: (414)967-5400. **Ad Rates:** Advertising accepted; rates available upon request. **URL:** http://www.classiccountry1070.com.

13566 ■ KFXJ-FM - 104.5
4200 N Old Lawrence Rd.
Wichita, KS 67219
Phone: (316)838-9141
Fax: (316)838-3607
Format: Classic Rock. **Owner:** Journal Broadcast Group Inc., 1533 Amherst Rd., Knoxville, TN 37909. **Key Personnel:** Eric McCart, Gen. Mgr. **Ad Rates:** Noncommercial. **URL:** http://www.1045thefox.com.

13567 ■ KGPT-TV - 49
110 S Main St., Ste. 300
Wichita, KS 67202
Phone: (316)239-3149
Fax: (316)269-0690
Email: info@kkgpt49.com
Owner: Great Plains Television Network L.L.C., 110 S Main Ste 300 , Wichita, KS 67202-3751, Ph: (316)239-3149. **Key Personnel:** Phil Arensman, Operations Mgr. **URL:** http://www.kgpt49.com.

13568 ■ KIBB-FM - 97.1
Two Brittany Pl.
1938 N Woodlawn
Wichita, KS 67208
Phone: (316)558-8800
Fax: (316)558-8802
Format: Eclectic. **Key Personnel:** Ron Allen, Contact; Ron Allen, Contact. **Wattage**: 18,500. **URL:** http://www.bobfmwichita.com.

13569 ■ KICT-FM - 95.1
4200 N Old Lawrence Rd.
Wichita, KS 67219
Phone: (316)838-9141
Fax: (316)838-3607
Format: Album-Oriented Rock (AOR). **Networks:** ABC. **Owner:** Journal Broadcast Group Inc., 1533 Amherst Rd., Knoxville, TN 37909. **Operating Hours**: Continuous. **ADI**: Wichita-Hutchinson, KS. **Wattage**: 100,000. **Ad Rates:** Advertising accepted; rates available upon request. **URL:** http://www.t95.com.

13570 ■ KKRD-FM - 107.3
905 N Main
Wichita, KS 67203
Phone: (316)265-0721
Fax: (316)265-0129
Format: Contemporary Hit Radio (CHR). **Networks:** Independent. **Founded:** 1967. **Operating Hours**: Continuous; 10% network, 90% local. **Key Personnel:** Jack Oliver, Contact; Jack Oliver, Contact. **Wattage**: 100,000.

13571 ■ KLBY-TV - 4
1500 NW St.
1500 N West St.
Wichita, KS 67203-1323
Phone: (316)943-4221
Free: 800-853-6397
Email: programming@kake.com
Format: Commercial TV; Sports; News. **Networks:** ABC. **Owner:** Gray Television Inc., 4370 Peachtree Rd. NE, No. 400, Atlanta, GA 30319-3054, Ph: (404)266-8333. **Founded:** 1984. **Operating Hours**: 6 a.m.-1 a.m. **ADI**: Wichita-Hutchinson, KS. **Key Personnel:** Terry Cole, Gen. Mgr. **Wattage**: 100,000. **Ad Rates:** $15-120 for 30 seconds. Combined advertising rates available with KUPK, KAKE. **URL:** http://www.kake.com.

13572 ■ KMTW-TV - 36
316 N West St.
Wichita, KS 67203
Phone: (316)942-2424
Fax: (316)942-8927
Key Personnel: Chuck Reid, Dir. of Sales, chuckreid@foxkansas.com. **URL:** http://www.mytvwichita.com.

13573 ■ KMUW-FM - 89.1
3317 E 17th St. N
Wichita, KS 67208
Phone: (316)978-6789
Email: info@kmuw.org
Format: Eclectic. **Networks:** National Public Radio (NPR); Public Radio International (PRI). **Owner:** Wichita State University. **Founded:** 1949. **Operating Hours**: Continuous. **ADI**: Wichita-Hutchinson, KS. **Key Personnel:** Mark McCain, Gen. Mgr.; Lu Anne Stephens, Prog. Dir., Dir. of Operations; Carla Eckels, Producer. **Wattage**: 100,000 ERP. **Ad Rates:** Noncommercial. **URL:** http://www.kmuw.us.

13574 ■ KMXW-FM - 92.3
604 N Main, Ste. F
Wichita, KS 67203
Fax: (316)838-3607

Format: Alternative/New Music/Progressive. **Operating Hours**: Continuous. **Wattage**: 100,000. **Ad Rates:** Advertising accepted; rates available upon request. **URL:** http://www.q92wichita.com.

13575 ■ KNSS Radio - 1330
2120 N Woodlawn, Ste. 352
Wichita, KS 67208
Phone: (316)685-2121
Email: news@knssradio.com
Format: News; Talk. **Owner:** Entercom Wichita L.L.C., 2120 N Woodlawn, Ste. 352, Wichita, KS 67208, Ph: (316)685-2121. **Operating Hours**: Continuous. **ADI**: Wichita-Hutchinson, KS. **Wattage**: 5,000. **Ad Rates:** Advertising accepted; rates available upon request. **URL:** http://www.knssradio.com.

13576 ■ KPTS-TV - 8
320 W 21st St. N
Wichita, KS 67203-2499
Phone: (316)838-3090
Fax: (316)838-8586
Free: 800-794-8498
Email: tv8@kpts.org
Format: Public TV. **Networks:** Public Broadcasting Service (PBS). **Owner:** Kansas Public Telecommunications Service Inc., 320 W 21st St., N, Wichita, KS 67203-2499, Ph: (316)838-3090, Fax: (316)838-8586, Free: 800-794-8498. **Founded:** 1970. **Operating Hours**: Continuous. **ADI**: Wichita-Hutchinson, KS. **Key Personnel:** Dave McClintock, Director, dmcclintock@kpts.org; Phil Searle, Producer, psearle@kpts.org; David Brewer, Program Mgr. **Local Programs**: *Kansas Week*; *Lidia's Italy*; *America's Test Kitchen*, Sunday Monday Wednesday Friday Tuesday Thursday Saturday 1:30 a.m.; 7:30 p.m.; 11:00 p.m. 1:30 a.m. 7:30 p.m.; 11:00 p.m. 11:00 p.m.; *Lap Quilting with Georgia Bonesteel*; *America Sews With Sue Hausmann*. **Wattage**: 302 KW. **Ad Rates:** Noncommercial. **URL:** http://www.kpts.org.

13577 ■ KQAM-AM - 1480
5610 E 29th St. N
Wichita, KS 67220
Format: Educational. **Owner:** Radio Disney, 500 S Buena Vista St. MC 7663, Burbank, CA 91521-7716. **ADI**: Wichita-Hutchinson, KS. **URL:** http://kqamradio.com.

13578 ■ KRBB-FM - 97.9
9323 E 37th St. N
Wichita, KS 67226-2000
Phone: (316)494-6600
Fax: (316)494-6730
Email: comments@b98fm.com
Format: Adult Contemporary. **Networks:** Independent. **Founded:** 1989. **Operating Hours**: Continuous. **Key Personnel:** Dave Wilson, Prog. Dir., dave@b98fm.com; Jeff McCausland, President, jeffmccausland@iheartmedia.com. **Wattage**: 100,000. **Ad Rates:** $20-92 per unit. **URL:** http://www.b98fm.com.

13579 ■ KSAS-TV - 24
316 N West St.
Wichita, KS 67203
Phone: (316)942-2424
Fax: (316)942-8927
Email: tgdisis@foxkansas.com
Format: Commercial TV. **Networks:** Fox. **Owner:** Newport Television, LLC, 460 Nichols Rd., Ste. 250, Kansas City, MO 64112, Ph: (816)751-0200, Fax: (816)751-0250. **Founded:** Aug. 24, 1985. **Operating Hours**: Continuous. **ADI**: Wichita-Hutchinson, KS. **Key Personnel:** Michelle Cleaton, Dir. of Programs, michellecleaton@foxkansas.com; Ken Whitney, Production Mgr., kenwhitney@foxkansas.com; Denice Petty, Traffic Mgr., denicepetty@foxkansas.com; Chuck Reid, Gen. Sales Mgr., chuckreid@foxkansas.com. **Wattage**: 029. **Ad Rates:** Advertising accepted; rates available upon request. **URL:** http://www.foxkansas.com.

13580 ■ KSGL-AM - 900
3337 W Central
Wichita, KS 67203
Phone: (316)942-3231
Fax: (316)942-9314
Email: am900@ksgl.com
Format: Religious. **Networks:** Independent. **Founded:** July 1977. **Operating Hours**: Continuous. **ADI**: Wichita-Hutchinson, KS. **Wattage**: 250 directional. **Ad Rates:** Noncommercial. Combined advertising rates available with KMYR-AM. **URL:** http://ksgl.com.

13581 ■ KSNC-TV - 2
833 N Main St.
Wichita, KS 67203
Phone: (316)265-3333
Fax: (316)292-1195
Ad Rates: Noncommercial. **URL:** http://www.ksn.com.

13582 ■ KSNG-TV - 11
833 N Main St.
Wichita, KS 67203
Phone: (316)292-1111
Fax: (316)292-1195
Email: news@ksn.com
Format: Commercial TV. **Networks:** NBC. **Founded:** 1958. **Formerly**: KGLD-TV. **Operating Hours**: 5:45 a.m.-2 a.m. **ADI**: Wichita-Hutchinson, KS. **Ad Rates:** $3-125 per unit. **URL:** http://www.ksn.com.

13583 ■ KSNK-TV - 8
833 N Main St.
Wichita, KS 67203
Phone: (316)265-3333
Fax: (316)292-1195
Format: Commercial TV. **Simulcasts:** KSNW-TV. **Networks:** NBC. **Owner:** New Vision Television, Inc., 11766 Wilshire Blvd., Ste. 405, Los Angeles, CA 90025, Ph: (310)478-3200, Fax: (310)478-3222. **Founded:** 1959. **Formerly**: KOMC-TV. **Operating Hours**: Continuous. **ADI**: Wichita-Hutchinson, KS. **Ad Rates:** $20-100 per unit. **URL:** http://www.ksn.com.

13584 ■ KSNW-TV - 3
833 N Main St.
Wichita, KS 67203
Phone: (316)265-3333
Fax: (316)292-1195
Email: news@ksn.com
Format: Commercial TV. **Simulcasts:** KSNK-TV, KSNG-TV, and KSNC-TV. **Networks:** NBC. **Founded:** 1955. **Formerly**: KARD-TV. **Operating Hours**: Continuous. **ADI**: Wichita-Hutchinson, KS. **Ad Rates:** Advertising accepted; rates available upon request. **URL:** http://www.ksn.com.

13585 ■ KSRX-AM - 1360
744 N Waco
Wichita, KS 67203
Phone: (316)263-5218
Fax: (316)263-1016
Free: 888-588-5218
Format: News; Talk. **Networks:** Kansas Information; Sun Radio. **Owner:** Violet Communications, Academy Sq., 33 Plymouth St., Ste. 301, Montclair, NY. **Founded:** 1953. **Formerly**: KSPG-AM. **Operating Hours**: 6 a.m.-6 p.m. **Key Personnel:** Terry Preston, Contact; Jamie Van Dever, Contact. **Wattage**: 500. **Ad Rates:** $6 for 30 seconds. **URL:** http://ksrx.co/contact.

13586 ■ KTHR-FM - 107.3
9323 E 37th St. N
Wichita, KS 67226-2000
Phone: (316)494-6600
Fax: (316)494-6730
Format: Classic Rock. **Owner:** iHeartMedia Inc., 200 E Basse Rd., San Antonio, TX 78209, Ph: (210)832-3314. **ADI**: Wichita-Hutchinson, KS. **Key Personnel:** Beth Davis, Div. Pres., bethdavis@iheartmedia.com. **Wattage**: 100,000. **Ad Rates:** Advertising accepted; rates available upon request. **URL:** http://www.1073thebrew.com.

13587 ■ KTLI-FM - 99.1
PO Box 779002
Rocklin, CA 95677-9972
Fax: (916)251-1901
Free: 800-525-5683
Format: Contemporary Christian. **Owner:** Educational Media Foundation, PO Box 2098, Omaha, NE 68103-2098, Free: 800-434-8400. **Key Personnel:** Mike Novak, President, CEO; Alan Mason, COO. **Wattage**: 100,000. **URL:** http://www.klove.com.

13588 ■ K28JB - 28
PO Box A
Santa Ana, CA 92711
Phone: (714)832-2950
Free: 888-731-1000
Owner: Trinity Broadcasting Network Inc., PO Box A, Santa Ana, CA 92711, Ph: (714)832-2950, Free: 888-731-1000. **URL:** http://www.tbn.org.

13589 ■ K204DQ-FM - 88.7
PO Box 391
Twin Falls, ID 83303
Fax: (208)736-1958
Free: 800-357-4226
Format: Religious; Contemporary Christian. **Owner:** CSN International, PO Box 391, Twin Falls, ID 83303, Ph: (208)736-1958, Fax: (208)736-1958, Free: 800-357-4226. **Key Personnel:** Don Mills, Music Dir., Prog. Dir.; Kelly Carlson, Dir. of Engg.; Ray Gorney, Asst. Dir. **URL:** http://www.csnradio.com.

13590 ■ KWCH-TV - 12
2815 E 37th St. N
Wichita, KS 67219
Phone: (316)512-6397
Free: 888-838-1212
Format: Commercial TV. **Networks:** CBS. **Owner:** Schurz Communications Inc., 1301 E Douglas Rd., Mishawaka, IN 46545, Ph: (574)247-7237. **Founded:** 1953. **Operating Hours**: Continuous. **ADI**: Wichita-Hutchinson, KS. **Wattage**: 1,000,000 ERP. **Ad Rates:** Advertising accepted; rates available upon request. **URL:** http://www.kwch.com.

13591 ■ KXLK-FM - 105.3
9111 E Douglas, Ste. 130
Wichita, KS 67207
Phone: (316)869-1053
Format: Music of Your Life. **Networks:** Independent. **Founded:** 1985. **Operating Hours**: Continuous. **ADI**: Wichita-Hutchinson, KS. **Key Personnel:** Jeff Couch, Dir. of Programs; Jackie Wise, Sales Mgr. **Wattage**: 98,000 ERP. **Ad Rates:** $20-46 for 30 seconds; $22-50 for 60 seconds. $20-$46 for 30 seconds; $22-$50 for 60 seconds. Combined advertising rates available with KFH-AM. **URL:** http://www.1053thebuzz.com.

13592 ■ KYQQ-FM - 106.5
4200 N Old Lawrence Rd.
Wichita, KS 67219
Phone: (316)436-1065
Fax: (316)838-3607
Format: Hispanic. **Networks:** Independent. **Owner:** Journal Broadcast Corp., 333 W State St., Milwaukee, WI 53203, Ph: (414)332-9611, Fax: (414)967-5400. **Formerly**: KWKL-FM. **Operating Hours**: Continuous; 100% local. **Wattage**: 100,000. **Ad Rates:** $20-50 per unit. **URL:** http://www.radiolobo1065.com.

13593 ■ KYWA-FM - 90.7
110 S Main St., Ste. 1050
Wichita, KS 67202
Format: Contemporary Christian. **Owner:** WAY-FM Media Group Inc., 5540 Tech Center Dr., Ste. 200, Colorado Springs, CO 80919, Ph: (719)533-0300. **ADI**: Wichita-Hutchinson, KS. **Wattage**: 70,000 H;67,500 V. **Mailing address:** PO Box 4211, Wichita, KS 67204. **URL:** http://www.wayfm.com.

13594 ■ KZCH-FM - 96.3
9323 E 37th St. N
Wichita, KS 67226-2000
Phone: (316)494-6600
Fax: (316)494-6730
Format: Contemporary Hit Radio (CHR). **Owner:** iHeartMedia Inc., 200 E Basse Rd., San Antonio, TX 78209, Ph: (210)832-3314. **ADI**: Wichita-Hutchinson, KS. **Wattage**: 50,000. **Ad Rates:** Noncommercial. **URL:** http://www.channel963.com.

13595 ■ KZSN-FM - 102.1
9323 E 37th St. N
Wichita, KS 67226-2000
Phone: (316)494-6600
Fax: (316)494-6730
Format: Country. **Networks:** Independent. **Founded:** 1986. **Formerly**: KSKU-FM. **Operating Hours**: Continuous; 100% local. **ADI**: Wichita-Hutchinson, KS. **Wattage**: 100,000. **Ad Rates:** Noncommercial. **URL:** http://www.1021thebull.com.

13596 ■ Multimedia Cablevision, Inc.
PO Box 3027
Wichita, KS 67201-3027
Phone: (316)262-4270
Owner: Multimedia Cablevision, Inc., PO Box 3027, Wichita, KS 67201-3027, Ph: (316)262-4270; Gannett,

Circulation: ★ = AAM; △ or • = BPA; ♦ = CAC; ❑ = VAC; ⊕ = PO Statement; ‡ = Publisher's Report; Boldface figures = sworn; Light figures = estimated.

1100 Wilson Blvd., Arlington, VA 22234, Ph: (703)284-6000. **Founded:** 1969. **Cities Served:** Arkansas City, Newkirk, Oklahoma, Winfield, Kansas; Cowley County; 28 channels; 2 community access channels; 168 hours per week community access programming. **Mailing address:** PO Box 3027.

WILSON

C. KS. Ellsworth Co. 55 mi. W. of Salina. Lake. Elevators. Grain, stock, poultry farms. Wheat, maize, cattle.

13597 ■ WTCi Cable Services
2504 Ave. D
Wilson, KS 67490
Free: 800-432-7607
Cities Served: 70 channels.

WINFIELD

SE KS. Cowley Co. 40 mi. SE of Wichita. Southwestern College (Methodist). Manufactures crayons, gas burners, plastic. Aircraft assembly, metal products plants. Oil and gas wells.Diversified farming. Kafir corn, wheat, alfalfa.

13598 ■ International Social Science Review
Pi Gamma Mu
1001 Millington St., Ste. B
Winfield, KS 67156
Phone: (620)221-3128
Fax: (620)221-7124
Publisher's E-mail: executivedirector@pigammamu.org
Freq: Semiannual. **Print Method:** Offset. **Trim Size:** 6 x 9. **Cols./Page:** 1. **Col. Width:** 60 nonpareils. **Col. Depth:** 115 agate lines. **Key Personnel:** Sue Watters, Executive Director. **ISSN:** 0278--2308 (print). **Subscription Rates:** Free. **Alt. Formats:** CD-ROM. **URL:** http://www.pigammamu.org/international-social-science-review.html. **Formerly:** Social Sciences. **Ad Rates:** BW $400. **Remarks:** Accepts advertising. **Circ:** Paid ‡7000, Non-paid ‡150.

13599 ■ Winfield Daily Courier
Winfield Daily Courier
201 E 9th Ave.
Winfield, KS 67156
Phone: (620)221-1050
Fax: (620)221-1101
Free: 800-532-1605
Publication E-mail: courier@horizon.hit.net
Newspaper with a Republican orientation. **Founded:** 1873. **Freq:** Daily each morning Tuesday through Saturday. **Print Method:** Offset. **Trim Size:** 13 3/4 x 22 3/4. **Cols./Page:** 6. **Col. Width:** 2 1/16 inches. **Col. Depth:** 21 inches. **Key Personnel:** Marsha Wesseler, Publisher, Director, Advertising. **Subscription Rates:** $106.44 Individuals Retail Mail (Cowley County + Oxford, Douglas, Grenola, CVale); $98.96 Individuals Out-of-Town Mail (City limits of Udall, Rock, Oxford, Douglas Burden, Cambridge, Dexter, Grenola); $141.86 Individuals Out-of-Retail Mail (Kansas); $74.32 Individuals online; $95.82 By mail Counter; $158.76 Out of state. **URL:** http://www.winfieldcourier.com. **Mailing address:** PO Box 543, Winfield, KS 67156. **Remarks:** Accepts advertising. **Circ:** Mon.-Sat. ★**4458**.

13600 ■ KSJM-FM - 107.9
103 E 9th St., Ste. 211
Winfield, KS 67156
Phone: (316)612-1079
Fax: (316)612-1077
Free: 866-436-1079
Email: ksjm@1079jamz.com
Format: Urban Contemporary; News; Eighties; Country; Information. **Founded:** 2000. **Operating Hours:** Continuous. **Key Personnel:** Don Sherman, Gen. Mgr., President, don@1079jamz.com; Hozie Mack, Dir. of Programs, hozie.mack@1079jamz.com; Rod Carter, Station Mgr., VP, rcarter@1079jamz.com. **Wattage:** 50,000 ERP. **Ad Rates:** Noncommercial; Advertising accepted; rates available upon request. **URL:** http://www.kwlsradio.com.

ALBANY

Clinton Co. Clinton Co. (SC). 100 m SW of Lexington. Oil wells; coal mines; timber. Manufactures flour, feed, cheese, boys' shirts. Truck, poultry, dairy farms. cattle.

13601 ■ Clinton County News
Gibson Printing Company Inc.
112 Washington St.
Albany, KY 42602
Phone: (606)387-5144
Community newspaper. **Founded:** 1949. **Freq:** Weekly (Thurs.). **Print Method:** Offset. **Cols./Page:** 6. **Col. Width:** 25 nonpareils. **Col. Depth:** 294 agate lines. **Key Personnel:** Alan Gibson, Publisher, Editor. **ISSN:** 0011-8480 (print). **USPS:** 115-480. **Subscription Rates:** $18 Individuals. **URL:** http://www.clintonnews.com/apps/pbcs.dll/frontpage. **Ad Rates:** GLR $.25; SAU $3.43. **Remarks:** Accepts advertising. **Circ:** ‡3650.

13602 ■ WANY-AM
PO Box 400
Albany, KY 42602
Phone: (606)387-5186
Format: News; Sports; Country; Religious; Agricultural; Bluegrass. **Networks:** ABC; KyNet. **Owner:** Albany Broadcasting Co., Six Johnson rd., Latham, NY 12110, Ph: (518)786-6600. **Founded:** 1958. **Key Personnel:** Robert Huddleston, Chief Engineer; Darrell Speck, Contact; Randy Speck, Contact; Mike Speck, Contact; Phyllis Butler, Contact; Patricia Bowlin, Contact. **Wattage:** 1,000 Day. **Ad Rates:** Advertising accepted; rates available upon request.

13603 ■ WANY-FM
PO Box 400
Albany, KY 42602
Phone: (606)387-5186
Fax: (606)387-6595
Format: News; Sports; Religious; Agricultural; Bluegrass. **Networks:** ABC; KyNet. **Owner:** Albany Broadcasting Co., Six Johnson rd., Latham, NY 12110, Ph: (518)786-6600. **Founded:** 1958. **Key Personnel:** Larry Nelson, Chief Engineer; Sid Scott, Contact; Phyllis Butler, Contact. **Wattage:** 6,000 ERP. **Ad Rates:** Advertising accepted; rates available upon request.

ALEXANDRIA

13604 ■ WRES-AM - 1080
4114 Beiting Dr.
Alexandria, KY 41001
Format: News; Talk. **Simulcasts:** WDJX-FM. **Networks:** CBS. **Owner:** Regent Communications, Annapolis, MD. **Formerly:** WCII-AM; WDJX-AM. **Operating Hours:** Continuous; 100% local. **Key Personnel:** William Wells, Contact. **Wattage:** 10,000 day; 1,000 night. **Ad Rates:** $55-125 for 30 seconds; for 60 seconds. **URL:** http://app.sos.ky.gov/ftshow/(S(eqjkg2n0g00tlrwkvn2x3qip))/default.aspx?path=ftsearch&id=0958046&ct=06&cs=99999.

ALLEN

13605 ■ WMDJ-FM - 100.1
8911 KY Rt. 1428
Allen, KY 41601
Phone: (606)285-8005
Fax: (606)285-1130
Format: Contemporary Country; Oldies. **Networks:** Fox. **Owner:** Dale McKinney, at above address, Ph: (606)876-8005, Fax: (606)876-0057. **Founded:** 1984. **Key Personnel:** Dale McKinney, Owner. **Wattage:** 2,600 ERP. **Ad Rates:** Advertising accepted; rates available upon request. $2.50 for 15 seconds; $5 for 30 seconds; $7.50 for 60 seconds. **URL:** http://www.wmdjfm.com/.

ASHLAND

Boyd Co. Boyd Co. (NE). On Ohio River, 16 m NW of Huntington, W. Va. Manufactures steel, coke, mining equipment, gas, leather, dresses, chemicals. Metal processing. Coal mines. Gas well. Clay pits.

13606 ■ The Daily Independent
Ashland Publishing Co.
224 17th St.
Ashland, KY 41101-7606
Phone: (606)326-2600
Free: 800-955-5860
Publisher's E-mail: rrakes@dailyindependent.com
General newspaper. **Founded:** 1896. **Freq:** Daily and Sun. (eve.). **Print Method:** Offset. **Cols./Page:** 6. **Col. Width:** 24 nonpareils. **Col. Depth:** 294 agate lines. **Key Personnel:** Eddie Blakeley, Publisher, phone: (606)326-2606. **USPS:** 033-780. **Subscription Rates:** $16.99 Individuals print /month; $14.99 Individuals online /month. **URL:** http://www.dailyindependent.com/. **Ad Rates:** BW $1,669.50; 4C $1,899.50; PCI $13.25. **Remarks:** Accepts advertising. **Circ:** 17000.

13607 ■ Cox Communications
225 Russell Rd., US 23 N.
Box 1357
Ashland, KY 41105
Fax: (606)329-9579
Owner: Times Mirror Cable TV, 2381 Morse Ave., Irvine, CA 92614. **Founded:** 1970. **Formerly:** Dimension Cable. **Cities Served:** Ashland and Boyd Counties.

13608 ■ Kindred Communication
555 5th Ave., Ste. K
Huntington, WV 25701
Phone: (304)523-8401
Email: info@kindredcom.net
Key Personnel: Mike Kirtner, CEO. **URL:** http://www.kindredcom.net.

13609 ■ WAMX-FM - 106.3
134 4th Ave.
Huntington, WV 25701
Phone: (304)525-7788
Fax: (304)525-6281
Free: 800-779-8401
Format: Alternative/New Music/Progressive; Country; Oldies. **Networks:** NBC; ABC. **Founded:** 1988. **Formerly:** WRVC-FM; WCMI-FM. **Operating Hours:** Continuous. **ADI:** Charleston-Huntington, WV. **Key Personnel:** Judy Jennings, Gen. Mgr. of Mktg. & Sales, judyjennings@clearchannel.com. **Wattage:** 1,650. **Ad Rates:** Advertising accepted; rates available upon request. $10-50 for 30 seconds; $15-75 for 60 seconds; $10-35 per unit. Combined advertising rates available with WRVC-AM, WRVC-FM, WCMI-AM. **URL:** http://www.1063thebrew.com//main.html.

13610 ■ WKAS-TV - 25
600 Cooper Dr.
Lexington, KY 40502
Free: 800-432-0951
Email: shop@ket.org
Format: Educational. **Networks:** Public Broadcasting Service (PBS); Kentucky Educational Television. **Owner:** Kentucky Authority for Educational TV, 600 Cooper Dr., Lexington, KY 40502, Ph: (606)258-7170, Fax: (606)258-7390. **Founded:** 1968. **Operating Hours:** 7 a.m.-midnight. **ADI:** Charleston-Huntington, WV. **Key Personnel:** Shae Hopkins, Exec. Dir. **Local Programs:** *Comment on Kentucky*, Monday Friday Saturday Sunday 8:00 a.m.; 6:30 p.m. 8:00 a.m. 6:30 a.m.; 7:30 a.m. 8:30 a.m.; 12:30 p.m. **Wattage:** 135. **Ad Rates:** Noncommercial. **URL:** http://www.ket.org.

13611 ■ WLGC-AM
1401 Winchester Ave., 1St. Fl.
Ashland, KY 41101
Free: 800-551-1057
Format: Sports. **Founded:** 1985. **Formerly:** WTCV-AM. **Key Personnel:** Kent Robinson, Sports Dir; Tom Reeder, Contact. **Wattage:** 5,000 Day; 280 CH. **Ad Rates:** $7-11.20 for 60 seconds. **URL:** http://koolhits1057.com/.

13612 ■ WLGC-FM - 105.7
1401 Winchester Ave.
Ashland, KY 41101-7555
Phone: (606)920-9565
Fax: (606)920-9523
Free: 800-551-1057
Format: News; Sports. **Founded:** 1982. **Key Personnel:** Mark Justice, Dir. of Programs. **Local Programs:** *The Breakfast Club*, Monday Tuesday Wednesday Thursday Friday 5:00 a.m. - 10:00 a.m. **Wattage:** 12,500 ERP. **Ad Rates:** Advertising accepted; rates available upon request. **URL:** http://www.koolhits1057.com.

13613 ■ WPCN-FM - 88.1
3027 Lester Ln.
Ashland, KY 41102
Phone: (877)456-9361
Fax: (606)928-1659
Free: 866-821-4726
Email: joyfm881@yahoo.com
Format: Gospel. **Owner:** Positive Alternative Radio, Inc., PO Box 889, Blacksburg, VA 24063, Ph: (540)961-2377. **Founded:** Oct. 21, 2000. **Operating Hours:** Continuous. **Key Personnel:** Claire Beaver, Account Exec.; Randy Parsons, Gen. Mgr.; Karen Wright, Office Mgr. **Wattage:** 3,000. **Ad Rates:** Noncommercial. **URL:** http://www.walkfm.org/business-partners-faq.

13614 ■ WTSF-TV - 61
3100 Bath Ave.
Ashland, KY 41101-3034

Circulation: ★ = AAM; △ or • = BPA; ♦ = CAC; ❑ = VAC; ⊕ = PO Statement; ‡ = Publisher's Report; Boldface figures = sworn; Light figures = estimated.

Phone: (606)329-2700
Fax: (606)324-9256
Format: Religious. **Networks:** Independent. **Owner:** Tri-State Family Broadcasting, Inc., at above address. **Founded:** 1983. **Operating Hours:** Continuous. **Wattage:** 50,000. **Ad Rates:** Noncommercial.

BARBOURVILLE

Knox Co. Knox Co. (SE). On Cumberland River, 30 m NW of Middleboro. Union College (Meth.). Coal mines; hardwood timber. Manufactures corsets, sealants, concrete blocks, electrical fixtures, bricks, door frames. Woodworking plants. Agriculture. Horses, vegetables, strawberries, sorghum.

13615 ■ Barbourville Utility Commission
202 Daniel Boone Dr.
Barbourville, KY 40906
Cities Served: 71 channels. **URL:** http://www.barbourville.com.

13616 ■ WKKQ-FM
222 Daniel Boone Dr.
Barbourville, KY 40906
Phone: (606)546-4128
Fax: (606)546-4138
Email: mix96@barbourville.com
Format: Adult Contemporary. **Networks:** Independent. **Founded:** 1974. **Formerly:** WBVL; WYWY-FM. **Wattage:** 25,000 ERP. **Ad Rates:** $6.50 for 30 seconds; $9.50 for 60 seconds. **URL:** http://www.wkkqfm.com/.

13617 ■ WYWY-AM - 950
222 Daniel Boone Dr.
Barbourville, KY 40906
Phone: (606)546-4128
Fax: (606)546-4138
Format: Country; Gospel. **Simulcasts:** WKKQ-FM. **Networks:** Independent. **Founded:** 1965. **Key Personnel:** Mildred Engle, President. **Wattage:** 1,000 Daytime;052 Nigh. **Ad Rates:** $2.50-3.30 for 30 seconds; $3.50-5.50 for 60 seconds. **URL:** http://www.wywyradio.com/.

BARDSTOWN

Nelson Co. Nelson Co. (WC). 39 m SE of Louisville. Manufactures bourbon, paper & plastic cups, plates, women's dresses, plastic building materials, office products. Dairy, beef, Tobacco farming.

13618 ■ Kentucky Standard
Landmark Community Newspapers L.L.C.
110 W Stephen Foster Ave.
Bardstown, KY 40004
Phone: (502)348-9003
Fax: (502)348-1971
Publisher's E-mail: marketing@lcni.com
Newspaper. **Freq:** Triweekly. **Print Method:** Web Offset. **Cols./Page:** 6. **Col. Width:** 26 nonpareils. **Col. Depth:** 294 agate lines. **Key Personnel:** Carrie Pride, Community Support; Carol Mudd, Manager, Advertising; Jamie Sizemore, Publisher; Brandi Cheatham, Manager, Circulation. **URL:** http://www.kystandard.com. **Remarks:** Accepts advertising. **Circ:** (Not Reported).

13619 ■ PLG-TV
Landmark Community Newspapers L.L.C.
110 W Stephen Foster Ave.
Bardstown, KY 40004
Phone: (502)348-9003
Publisher's E-mail: marketing@lcni.com
Community newspaper. **URL:** http://www.plgtv.com. **Mailing address:** PO Box 639, Bardstown, KY 40004. **Circ:** (Not Reported).

13620 ■ Bardstown Cable TV
220 N 5th St.
Bardstown, KY 40004
Phone: (502)348-5947
Email: support@bardstowncable.net
Cities Served: 72 channels. **URL:** http://www.bardstowncable.net.

13621 ■ WBRT-AM - 1320
106 S 3rd St.
Bardstown, KY 40004
Phone: (502)348-3943
Fax: (502)348-4043
Email: wbrt@cbcradio.net
Format: Country. **Networks:** AP; KyNet. **Owner:** Commonweath Broadcasting, at above address, Ph: (270)659-2002. **Founded:** 1954. **Key Personnel:** Kenny Fogle, Contact. **Wattage:** 1,000 Day; 044 Night. **Ad Rates:** $7-9.40 for 30 seconds; $11-12 for 60 seconds. $4-$9.40 for 30 seconds; $5-$12 for 60 seconds. Combined advertising rates available with WOKH-FM. **URL:** http://www.wbrtcountry.com.

13622 ■ WOKH-FM - 102.7
106 S 3rd St.
Bardstown, KY 40004
Phone: (502)348-1027
Free: 844-348-1027
Format: Adult Contemporary. **Networks:** ABC. **Founded:** 1979. **Key Personnel:** Tom Isaac, Contact. **Wattage:** 4,000 ERP. **Ad Rates:** Advertising accepted; rates available upon request. $4-9.40 for 30 seconds; $5-12 for 60 seconds. $4-$9.40 for 30 seconds; $5-$12 for 60 seconds. Combined advertising rates available with WBRT-AM. **URL:** http://www.wokhfm.com/.

BARDWELL

Carlisle Co. Carlisle Co. (SW). 30 m SW of Paducah. Feed mill; fertilizer factory. Dairy, stock, poultry, grain farms. Tobacco, cotton, apples.

13623 ■ WBCE-AM - 1200
PO Box 491
Bardwell, KY 42023
Phone: (270)335-5171
Format: Religious. **Networks:** Independent. **Owner:** Bibletime Ministries, Inc., Wickliffe, KY. **Founded:** 1982. **Operating Hours:** Sunrise-sunset; 100% local. **Key Personnel:** Shelby Baggett, Mgr; Jim Baggett, Contact. **Wattage:** 1,000. **Ad Rates:** $2.50-4 for 30 seconds; $3-5 for 60 seconds.

BEATTYVILLE

Lee Co. Lee Co. (EC). 5 m W of St. Helens.

13624 ■ WLJC-FM - 102.1
PO Box Y
Beattyville, KY 41311
Phone: (606)464-3600
Email: wljc@wljc.com
Format: Religious. **Founded:** 1965. **Key Personnel:** Margaret Drake, Contact; Allan Mulford, Chief Engineer, allan@wljc.com; Margaret Drake, Contact. **Ad Rates:** Noncommercial. **URL:** http://www.wljc.com/new2/index.php.

13625 ■ WLJC-TV - 65
PO Box Y
Beattyville, KY 41311
Phone: (606)464-3600
Email: wljc@wljc.com
Format: Commercial TV. **Networks:** Independent. **Owner:** Hour of Harvest Inc., 219 WLJC Dr., Beattyville, KY 41311, Ph: (606)464-3600. **Founded:** 1982. **Operating Hours:** Continuous. **ADI:** Lexington, KY. **Key Personnel:** Margaret Drake, President, margaret@wljc.com. **Local Programs:** *Hour of Harvest.* **Ad Rates:** $75-95 for 30 seconds; $125-145 for 60 seconds. **URL:** http://www.wljc.com.

BEDFORD

Trimble Co. Trimble Co. (C).

13626 ■ The News-Democrat
Landmark Community Newspapers L.L.C.
322 Hwy. 42
Bedford, KY 40006
Phone: (502)255-3205
Fax: (502)255-7797
Publisher's E-mail: marketing@lcni.com
Community newspaper. **Founded:** 1868. **Freq:** Weekly (Wed.). **Print Method:** Web Offset. **Cols./Page:** 6 and 8. **Col. Width:** 1.833 inches. **Col. Depth:** 301 agate lines. **Key Personnel:** Phyllis McLaughlin, Editor; Jeff Moore, Publisher. **Subscription Rates:** $23.32 Individuals in County; $32.88 Individuals in Kentucky; $39 Out of state. **URL:** http://www.mycarrollnews.com. **Mailing address:** PO Box 289, Bedford, KY 40006. **Ad Rates:** GLR $7.10; BW $824; 4C $1,049; PCI $6.39. **Remarks:** Accepts advertising. **Circ:** 3370.

13627 ■ The Trimble Banner
Landmark Community Newspapers L.L.C.
PO Box 289
Bedford, KY 40006
Phone: (502)255-3205
Fax: (502)255-7797
Publisher's E-mail: marketing@lcni.com
County newspaper. **Freq:** Weekly (Thurs.). **Print Method:** Web Press. **Cols./Page:** 6. **Col. Width:** 1.833 inches. **Col. Depth:** 21 1/2 inches. **Key Personnel:** Jeff Moore, Publisher. **URL:** http://www.mytrimblenews.com. **Remarks:** Accepts advertising. **Circ:** (Not Reported).

BENTON

Marshall Co. Marshall Co. (SW). 24 m SE of Paducah. Resort Area. Chemicals manufactured. Agriculture.

13628 ■ Tribune Courier
Tribune Courier
PO Box 410
Benton, KY 42025
Phone: (270)527-3162
Fax: (270)527-4567
Publisher's E-mail: emcgill@tribunecourier.com
Newspaper. **Founded:** 1888. **Freq:** Weekly (Wed.). **Print Method:** Offset. **Trim Size:** 13 x 21. **Cols./Page:** 6. **Col. Width:** 24 nonpareils. **Col. Depth:** 301 agate lines. **Key Personnel:** Emily McGill, Office Manager; Venita Fritz, General Manager. **Subscription Rates:** $31 Individuals Marshall and surrounding Counties; $38 Individuals in state; $40 Out of state. **URL:** http://www.tribunecourier.com. **Ad Rates:** GLR $.31; BW $466; 4C $716; SAU $4.85. **Remarks:** Advertising accepted; rates available upon request. **Circ:** (Not Reported).

13629 ■ WCBL-AM - 1290
PO Box 387
Benton, KY 42025
Phone: (270)527-3102
Free: 800-737-3102
Format: Country. **Simulcasts:** WCBL-FM. **Networks:** NBC; CNN Radio. **Owner:** Freeland Broadcasting Co., at above address, Benton, KY. **Founded:** 1954. **Operating Hours:** Sunrise-sunset. **Wattage:** 5,000. **Ad Rates:** Noncommercial. WCBL-FM.

13630 ■ WCBL-FM - 99.1
PO Box 387
Benton, KY 42025
Phone: (270)527-3102
Fax: (270)527-5606
Format: Oldies. **Networks:** NBC; CNN Radio. **Owner:** Freeland Broadcasting Co., at above address, Benton, KY. **Founded:** 1966. **Operating Hours:** Continuous. **ADI:** Paducah,KY-Cape Girardeau,MO-Marion,IL. **Wattage:** 3,000. **Ad Rates:** Noncommercial. **URL:** http://www.thelakecurrent.com.

WCCK-FM - See Calvert City

BEREA

Madison Co. Madison Co. (C). 40 m S of Lexington. Berea College. Handcraft industries; rubber rings, pressure gauges, greeting cards, fork lifts, brakes manufactured. Dairy, stock, poultry farms. Corn, tobacco, hay.

13631 ■ Appalachian Heritage
Berea College
101 Chestnut St.
Berea, KY 40404
Phone: (859)985-3000
Publication E-mail: appalachianheritage@berea.edu
Literary magazine featuring the southern Appalachian culture. **Freq:** Quarterly February, May, August and November. **Print Method:** Offset. **Trim Size:** 6 x 9. **Cols./Page:** 1. **Col. Width:** 28.5 picas. **Col. Depth:** 44 picas. **Key Personnel:** George Brosi, Editor. **ISSN:** 0363--2318 (print). **Subscription Rates:** $30 Individuals; $58 Two years; $62 Other countries; $122 Other countries 2 years; $40 Institutions; $72 Individuals 2 years. **URL:** http://appalachianheritage.net. **Ad Rates:** BW $250; 4C $350. **Remarks:** Accepts advertising. **Circ:** 600.

13632 ■ Berea College Magazine
Berea College
101 Chestnut St.
Berea, KY 40404
Phone: (859)985-3000
Publisher's E-mail: askadmissions@berea.edu
Magazine for college alumni. **Freq:** Quarterly. **Print Method:** Offset. **Trim Size:** 8 1/2 x 11. **Cols./Page:** 3. **Col. Width:** 28 nonpareils. **Col. Depth:** 140 agate lines. **Key Personnel:** J. Morgan, Editor. **ISSN:** 1539--7394

(print). **Alt. Formats:** PDF. **URL:** http://www.berea.edu/magazine. **Formerly**: The Berea Alumnus. **Remarks:** Advertising not accepted. **Circ:** (Not Reported).

13633 ■ Pinnacle
Berea College
101 Chestnut St.
Berea, KY 40404
Phone: (859)985-3000
Publisher's E-mail: askadmissions@berea.edu
Collegiate newspaper. **Founded:** 1953. **Freq:** Monthly. **Print Method:** Offset. **Trim Size:** 13 x 21. **Cols./Page:** 6. **Col. Width:** 12 3/10 picas. **Col. Depth:** 43 3/10 picas. **URL:** http://www.berea.edu/laborprogram/positions/pinnacle.asp. **Ad Rates:** PCI $1.90. **Remarks:** Advertising accepted; rates available upon request. **Circ:** Paid ‡1800, Free ‡50.

13634 ■ Prostaglandins, Leukotrienes and Essential Fatty Acids
Mountain Association for Community Economic Development
433 Chestnut St.
Berea, KY 40403-1510
Phone: (859)986-2373
Fax: (859)986-1299
Publisher's E-mail: info@maced.org
Journal covering all aspects of the roles of lipids in cellular, organ and whole organism function, and places a particular emphasis on human studies. **Freq:** Monthly. **Key Personnel:** Richard P. Bazinet, Editor-in-Chief; I. Morita, Advisor; A. Nicolaou, Associate Editor. **ISSN:** 0952--3278 (print). **Subscription Rates:** $506 Individuals print; $3252.60 Institutions e-jounal; $4366 Institutions print. **URL:** http://www.journals.elsevier.com/prostaglandins-leukotrienes-and-essential-fatty-acids-plefa. **Remarks:** Accepts advertising. **Circ:** (Not Reported).

13635 ■ Radiologic Clinics of North America
Mountain Association for Community Economic Development
433 Chestnut St.
Berea, KY 40403-1510
Phone: (859)986-2373
Fax: (859)986-1299
Publisher's E-mail: info@maced.org
Journal publishing articles written by leading experts, along with high-quality reproductions of radiographs, MR images, CT scans and sonograms. **Freq:** 6/year. **ISSN:** 0033--8389 (print). **Subscription Rates:** $660 Individuals; $1002 Institutions print. **URL:** http://www.elsevier.com/journals/radiologic-clinics-of-north-america/0033-8389. **Circ:** (Not Reported).

13636 ■ Reproductive Health Matters
Mountain Association for Community Economic Development
433 Chestnut St.
Berea, KY 40403-1510
Phone: (859)986-2373
Fax: (859)986-1299
Publisher's E-mail: info@maced.org
Peer-reviewed journal publishing information on laws, policies, research, and services that meet women's reproductive health needs. **Freq:** Semiannual. **Key Personnel:** Marge Berer, Editor. **ISSN:** 0968--8080 (print). **Circ:** (Not Reported).

13637 ■ Research in Veterinary Science
Mountain Association for Community Economic Development
433 Chestnut St.
Berea, KY 40403-1510
Phone: (859)986-2373
Fax: (859)986-1299
Publisher's E-mail: info@maced.org
Journal publishing original articles, reviews and short communications of a high scientific and ethical standard in the veterinary sciences. **Freq:** Bimonthly. **Key Personnel:** A. Livingston, Editor; P. Pasquali, Editor-in-Chief. **ISSN:** 0034--5288 (print). **Subscription Rates:** $423 Individuals; $1153.60 Institutions online; $1114 Institutions print. **URL:** http://www.journals.elsevier.com/research-in-veterinary-science. **Circ:** (Not Reported).

13638 ■ Resuscitation
Mountain Association for Community Economic Development
433 Chestnut St.
Berea, KY 40403-1510
Phone: (859)986-2373
Fax: (859)986-1299
Publisher's E-mail: info@maced.org
Journal publishing information dealing with the etiology, pathophysiology, diagnosis and treatment of acute diseases. **Freq:** Monthly. **Key Personnel:** Jerry Nolan, Editor-in-Chief; Mike Parr, Editor. **ISSN:** 0300--9572 (print). **Subscription Rates:** $359 Individuals print; $974.13 Institutions e-journal; $2941 Institutions print. **URL:** http://www.journals.elsevier.com/resuscitation. **Remarks:** Accepts advertising. **Circ:** (Not Reported).

BOWLING GREEN

Warren Co. Warren Co. (SW). On Barren River, at head of navigation, 65 m NE of Nashville, Tenn. Western Kentucky University. Manufactures electric controls, auto parts, air compressors, space heaters, dry cleaning equipment and chemicals; woodworking and garment industries, flour, and beverage works; meat packing and poultry processing plants. Burley, tobacco market. Tobacco stemmeries.

13639 ■ Bowling Green
Bowling Green Area Chamber of Commerce
710 College St.
Bowling Green, KY 42101
Free: 866-330-2422
Publisher's E-mail: info@bgchamber.com
Magazine of the Bowling Green Area Chamber of Commerce. **Freq:** Annual. **Subscription Rates:** $3 Individuals. **URL:** http://www.bgchamber.com. **Remarks:** Accepts advertising. **Circ:** (Not Reported).

13640 ■ College Heights Herald
Western Kentucky University
1906 College Heights Blvd.
Bowling Green, KY 42101
Phone: (270)745-0111
Publisher's E-mail: wku@wku.edu
College newspaper. **Freq:** Semiweekly Tuesday and Thursday. **Print Method:** Offset. **Cols./Page:** 6. **Col. Width:** 24 nonpareils. **Col. Depth:** 196 agate lines. **Key Personnel:** Kae Holloway, Editor; Brandon Carter, Editor-in-Chief. **URL:** http://wkuherald.com. **Remarks:** Accepts advertising. **Circ:** (Not Reported).

13641 ■ Country Peddler
Country Peddler
730 College St.
Bowling Green, KY 42101
Phone: (270)842-3314
Shopper (tabloid). **Freq:** Weekly (Thurs.). **Print Method:** Offset. **Cols./Page:** 4. **Col. Width:** 2 3/8 inches. **Col. Depth:** 11 7/6 inches. **Remarks:** Accepts display and classified advertising. **Circ:** ‡25502.

13642 ■ Daily News
Daily News
813 College St.
Bowling Green, KY 42102
Phone: (270)781-1700
General newspaper. **Founded:** 1854. **Freq:** Daily. **Print Method:** Offset. **Cols./Page:** 6. **Col. Width:** 1.833 inches. **Col. Depth:** 21 inches. **Key Personnel:** Pipes Gaines, President, Publisher; Eugene Embry, Editor, phone: (270)783-3241. **Subscription Rates:** $168 Individuals print and online /year. **URL:** http://www.bgdailynews.com/. **Mailing address:** PO Box 90012, Bowling Green, KY 42102. **Ad Rates:** GLR $16.05; BW $2,022.30; 4C $575; GLR $18.48; BW $2,328.48; 4C $2,028; PCI $17.41. **Remarks:** Accepts advertising. **Circ:** Mon.-Fri. ★**21240**, Sun. ★**24805**, Sat. ★**21703**.

13643 ■ Daily News Express
Daily News Publishing Inc.
813 College St.
Bowling Green, KY 42102
Phone: (270)781-1700
Publication E-mail: sgaines@bgdailynews.com
Shopper. **Founded:** Apr. 1976. **Freq:** Semiweekly (Wed. and Sun.). **Print Method:** Offset. **Trim Size:** 13 3/4 x 22 1/2. **Cols./Page:** 6. **Col. Width:** 2 1/16 inches. **Col. Depth:** 21 inches. **Key Personnel:** Pipes Gaines, President, Publisher, fax: (270)781-1700; Glenda Spear, Office Manager; Scott Gaines, General Manager, phone: (270)781-1700. **Subscription Rates:** $168 Individuals. **URL:** http://www.bgdailynews.com. **Formerly**: Daily News Shopping Guide. **Mailing address:** PO Box 90012, Bowling Green, KY 42102. **Ad Rates:** BW $511.56; 4C $616.56; SAU $4.06; PCI $4.06. **Remarks:** Accepts advertising. **Circ:** Wed. 11,500, Sun. 20,000.

13644 ■ Earth Interactions
American Geophysical Union
c/o Rezaul Mahmood, Ed.
Western Kentucky University
Dept. of Geography & Geology
Bowling Green, KY 42101
Phone: (270)745-5979
Fax: (270)745-6410
Publication E-mail: earthinteractions@agu.org
Journal covering biological, physical, and human components of the earth system. **Freq:** Irregular. **Print Method:** Offset. **Trim Size:** 5 1/2 x 8 1/2. **Cols./Page:** 1. **Col. Width:** 50 nonpareils. **Col. Depth:** 100 agate lines. **Key Personnel:** Rezaul Mahmood, Editor. **ISSN:** 0898--9591 (print). **Subscription Rates:** Free. **URL:** http://earthinteractions.org; http://www.earthinteractions.org. **Remarks:** Advertising not accepted. **Circ:** (Not Reported).

13645 ■ Kentucky English Bulletin
Kentucky Council of Teachers of English/Language Arts
c/o Liz Jensen, Membership Chairperson
508 Magnolia St.
Bowling Green, KY 42103-1612
Publication E-mail: keb@kcte.org
Freq: Semiannual. **Print Method:** photocopy. **Trim Size:** 8 1/2 x 11. **Key Personnel:** Judith Szerdahelyi, Editor; Dr. David Lenoire, Editor. **ISSN:** 0023--0197 (print). **Subscription Rates:** $60 Individuals 1 year; $120 Other countries 1 year; $240 Other countries 2 years; Included in membership. **URL:** http://kcte.org/publication/kentucky-english-bulletin; http://kcte.org/publication/kentucky-english-bulletin/keb-inquiries-and-information. **Remarks:** Advertising not accepted. **Circ:** (Not Reported).

13646 ■ WAY-FM - 88.1
1945 Scottsville Rd. B2
PMB 363
Bowling Green, KY 42104-5817
Free: 888-339-2936
Format: Contemporary Christian. **URL:** http://www.wayfm.com.

13647 ■ WBGN-AM - 1340
1919 Scottsville Rd.
Bowling Green, KY 42104
Phone: (270)843-3333
Format: Sports. **Networks:** ESPN Radio; ABC. **Owner:** Forever Communications, Inc., 1919 Scottsville Rd., Bowling Green, KY 42104, Ph: (270)843-3333. **Founded:** 1959. **Operating Hours**: Continuous. **ADI:** Bowling Green (Campbellsville), KY. **Key Personnel:** Norm Haney, Dir. of Programs, sportsguys@1340wbgn.com. **Wattage**: 1,000. **Ad Rates:** $7-12 for 30 seconds; $10-14 for 60 seconds. **URL:** http://www.1340wbgn.com.

13648 ■ WBKO-TV - 13
2727 Russellville Rd.
Bowling Green, KY 42101-3976
Phone: (270)781-1313
Fax: (270)781-1814
Email: pphelps@wbko.com
Format: Full Service. **Networks:** ABC. **Owner:** Gray Television Inc., 4370 Peachtree Rd. NE, No. 400, Atlanta, GA 30319-3054, Ph: (404)266-8333. **Founded:** 1962. **Operating Hours**: Continuous. **ADI:** Bowling Green (Campbellsville), KY. **Key Personnel:** Henry Chu, News Dir., henry.chu@wbko.com; Barbara Powell, Dir. of Programs, barbara.powell@wbko.com; Chris Allen, Exec. Dir., chris.allen@wbko.com; Brad Odil, Station Mgr., VP of Sales, bodil@wbko.com; Paula Phelps, Bus. Mgr., pphelps@wbko.com; David Hosay, Production Mgr., david.hosay@wbko.com; Cliff Cothern, Dir. of Mktg., Promotions Dir., cliff.cothern@wbko.com. **Wattage**: 22,000 ERP. **Ad Rates:** Advertising accepted; rates available upon request. **URL:** http://www.wbko.com.

13649 ■ WBVR-FM - 96.7
1919 Scottsville Rd.
Bowling Green, KY 42104
Phone: (502)843-3333
Free: 800-999-9287

Circulation: ★ = AAM; △ or • = BPA; ♦ = CAC; ❑ = VAC; ⊕ = PO Statement; ‡ = Publisher's Report; Boldface figures = sworn; Light figures = estimated.

Format: Country; News. **Owner:** Forever Communications, Inc., 1919 Scottsville Rd., Bowling Green, KY 42104, Ph: (270)843-3333. **Founded:** June 1994. **Key Personnel:** Scooter Davis, Contact, scooterdavis967@yahoo.com; Myla Thomas, Contact, mylathomas@yahoo.com; Shannon Presley, Contact, shannonpresley@beaverfm.com; Alan Austin, Contact, alanaustin967@yahoo.com. **Wattage:** 45,000 ERP. **Ad Rates:** Advertising accepted; rates available upon request. **URL:** http://www.beaverfm.com.

13650 ■ WCVK-FM - 90.7
1407 Scottsville Rd.
Bowling Green, KY 42102
Phone: (270)781-7326
Fax: (270)781-8005
Free: 800-978-5755
Format: Religious. **Networks:** USA Radio. **Owner:** Bowling Green Community Broadcasting Inc., 1407 Scottsville Rd., Bowling Green, KY 42104-2433. **Founded:** 1986. **Operating Hours:** 5 a.m.-midnight. **ADI:** Bowling Green (Campbellsville), KY. **Key Personnel:** Donna Brown, Office Mgr., donna@christianfamilyradio.com; Ken Burns, Operations Mgr., ken@christianfamilyradio.com; Derek Gregory, Promotions Dir., derek@christianfamilyradio.com. **Wattage:** 14,000. **Ad Rates:** Noncommercial. **Mailing address:** PO Box 539, Bowling Green, KY 42102. **URL:** http://www.christianfamilyradio.com.

13651 ■ WDCL-FM - 89.7
1906 College Heights Blvd., Ste. 11035
Bowling Green, KY 42101-1035
Phone: (270)745-5489
Free: 800-599-9598
Email: wkyufm@wku.edu
Format: Public Radio. **Simulcasts:** WKYU-FM. **Networks:** National Public Radio (NPR); American Public Radio (APR); AP. **Owner:** Western Kentucky University, 1906 College Heights Blvd., Bowling Green, KY 42101, Ph: (270)745-0111. **Founded:** 1985. **Operating Hours:** Continuous. **ADI:** Bowling Green (Campbellsville), KY. **Key Personnel:** Joe Corcoran, Producer; Kevin Willis, News Dir.; Dr. Robert Owen, VP, bob.owen@wku.edu; Dan Modlin, News Dir., daniel.modlin@wku.edu; Lee Stott, Music Dir., leland.stott@wku.edu; Peter Bryant, Prog. Dir., Station Mgr., peter.bryant@wku.edu. **Wattage:** 100,000. **Ad Rates:** Noncommercial. **URL:** http://www.wkyufm.org.

13652 ■ WDNS-FM - 93.3
804 College St.
Bowling Green, KY 42101-2133
Phone: (270)781-2121
Fax: (270)842-0232
Free: 888-847-9367
Format: Classic Rock. **Owner:** Daily News Broadcasting, 804 College St., Bowling Green, KY 42101, Ph: (270)781-2121, Free: 888-847-9367. **Founded:** 1973. **Operating Hours:** Continuous. **Key Personnel:** Alan Cooper, Gen. Mgr., alan@wdnsfm.com. **Wattage:** 25,000. **Ad Rates:** $18-30 for 30 seconds; $24-40 for 60 seconds. Combined advertising rates available with WKCT-AM. **URL:** http://wdnsfm.com.

13653 ■ WGGC-FM - 95.1
1727 US 31-W By-Pass
Bowling Green, KY 42101
Phone: (270)783-8730
Fax: (270)783-8665
Free: 800-275-9442
Format: Country. **Owner:** Heritage Communications Inc., at above address. **Founded:** 1961. **Operating Hours:** Continuous. **Wattage:** 100,000 ERP. **Ad Rates:** Advertising accepted; rates available upon request. Combined advertising rates available with WQXE-FM. **URL:** http://www.wggc.com.

13654 ■ WJVK-FM - 91.7
PO Box 539
Bowling Green, KY 42102
Phone: (270)781-7326
Fax: (270)781-8005
Free: 800-978-5755
Format: Contemporary Christian; Religious. **Owner:** Christian Family Radio, 1407 Scottsville Rd., Bowling Green, KY 42104, Ph: (270)781-7326, Fax: (270)781-8005, Free: 800-978-5755. **Founded:** 1990. **Operating Hours:** Continuous. **Key Personnel:** Mike Wilson, Gen. Mgr., mike@christianfamilyradio.com; Ken Burns, Contact, ken@christianfamilyradio.com; Dale McCubbins, Contact, dale@christianfamilyradio.com. **Ad Rates:** Noncommercial; underwriting available. **URL:** http://www.christianfamilyradio.com.

13655 ■ WKCT-AM - 930
804 College St.
Bowling Green, KY 42101
Phone: (270)781-2121
Fax: (270)842-0232
Free: 866-543-9528
Format: News; Talk; Information. **Networks:** CBS. **Founded:** 1947. **Operating Hours:** Continuous; 70% network, 30% local. **Key Personnel:** Alan Cooper, Gen. Mgr., alan@wdnsfm.com; Chad Young, Dir. of Programs, chad@93wkct.com; Al Arbogast, News Dir. **Wattage:** 5,000 Day; 500 Night. **Ad Rates:** $13-24 for 30 seconds; $17-31 for 60 seconds. Combined advertising rates available with WDNS-FM. **URL:** http://www.93wkct.com.

13656 ■ WKGB-TV - 53
600 Cooper Dr.
Lexington, KY 40502
Phone: (859)258-7000
Free: 800-432-0951
Email: shop@ket.org
Format: Educational. **Networks:** Public Broadcasting Service (PBS); Kentucky Educational Television. **Owner:** Kentucky Educational Television, 600 Cooper Dr., Lexington, KY 40502, Ph: (859)258-7000, Free: 800-432-0951. **Founded:** 1968. **Operating Hours:** 6:15 a.m.-midnight. **ADI:** Bowling Green (Campbellsville), KY. **Key Personnel:** Shae Hopkins, Exec. Dir. **Local Programs:** *Kentucky Life*, Saturday Sunday 8:00 a.m.; 7:00 p.m. 4:00 a.m.; 3:00 p.m.; *Independent Lens*, Monday 9:00 p.m.; *Kentucky Health*, Sunday Tuesday 10:30 a.m. 5:00 a.m.; *Kentucky Author Forum Presents*; *Living by Words*; *Looking at Painting*; *Kentucky Tonight*, Monday 8:00 p.m.; *Mixed Media*; *A Native Presence*, Sunday Friday 2:00 p.m. 10:00 a.m.; *Old Music for New Ears*; *Roundabout U*; *Riding in Stride*; *Run That by Me Again*; *Southern Sex*, Saturday Tuesday 3:30 a.m. 10:30 p.m.; *Louisville's Own Ali*, Tuesday Friday 10:00 a.m. 9:00 p.m.; *Tracks: Impressions of America*; *TV411*; *To the Contrary*, Saturday 8:30 a.m.; *The Visionaries*; *Telling Tales*; *My Kentucky Home*; *Growing Kentucky*; *Comment on Kentucky*, Monday Friday Saturday Sunday 8:00 a.m.; 6:30 p.m. 8:00 p.m. 6:30 a.m.; 7:30 a.m. 8:30 a.m.; 12:30 p.m.; *America Past*; *Alone in the Wilderness*; *Art to Heart*, Saturday 5:30 a.m.; *Bataan: The Harrodsburg Tankers*, Sunday 3:00 p.m.; *Bywords*, Monday Tuesday Wednesday Thursday Friday 6:00 a.m.; *Call to War*; *The CommonHealth of Kentucky*; *Kentucky Afield*, Saturday Sunday 8:30 p.m. 4:30 p.m.; *Crossroads Cafe*; *Cover to Cover*; *DanceSense*; *Distinguished Kentuckian*, Friday Wednesday 5:00 p.m. 2:00 p.m.; *Dialogue on Public Issues*, Friday Tuesday 6:30 a.m. 5:00 a.m.; *Exploring an American Original*, Wednesday Thursday 6:30 a.m. 9:30 a.m.; *The Everlasting Stream*, Friday Saturday Monday 4:00 p.m. 1:00 p.m.; 5:00 p.m. 12:00 a.m.; *The Great Kentucky Gospel Shout Out*, Monday, 12:00 p.m. - 1:00 p.m.; 8:00 p.m. - 9:00 p.m.; *Holiday Train Show with David Hartman*; *Headwaters: Real Stories from Rural America*; *A Program About Unusual Buildings and Other Roadside Stuff*; *Rare Visions & Roadside Revelations*; *Third Lives in the First World*, Monday 9:00 a.m.; 3:00 p.m.; *202nd Army Band of Kentucky National Guard in Concert*; *Churchill Downs: From Start to Photo Finish*, Monday Tuesday Friday 4:00 a.m. 11:00 a.m. 1:00 a.m.; *The Great Kentucky Gospel Shout Out*, Saturday Sunday 4:00 p.m. 2:00 p.m.; *The Land Called...Fort Knox*, Saturday Thursday 3:00 a.m. 11:30 p.m.; *Economic Success Through Minority Empowerment*, Wednesday 11:00 a.m. **Wattage:** 676,000. **Ad Rates:** Noncommercial. **URL:** http://www.ket.org.

13657 ■ WKLX-FM - 100.7
1519 Euclid Ave.
Bowling Green, KY 42103
Phone: (270)651-6050
Fax: (270)651-7666
Format: Adult Contemporary; Sports. **Owner:** Charles M. Anderson, Not Available. **Operating Hours:** Continuous. **Key Personnel:** Derron Steenbergen, Gen. Mgr. **Wattage:** 8,000 ERP.

13658 ■ WKPB-FM - 89.5
1906 College Heights Blvd., No. 11035
Bowling Green, KY 42101-1035
Phone: (270)745-5489
Fax: (270)745-6272
Free: 800-599-9598
Email: wkyufm@wku.edu
Format: Public Radio. **Key Personnel:** Kevin Willis, News Dir., kevin.willis@wku.edu. **Ad Rates:** Noncommercial. **URL:** http://www.wkyufm.org.

13659 ■ WKUE-FM - 90.9
1906 College Heights Blvd., No. 11035
Bowling Green, KY 42101-1035
Phone: (270)745-5489
Free: 800-599-9598
Format: Public Radio. **Founded:** 1906. **Key Personnel:** Robert Owen, VP of Info. Systems; Jack Hanes, Dir. of Telecommunications, jack.hanes@wku.edu; Peter Bryant, Prog. Dir., Station Mgr., peter.bryant@wku.edu; John Campbell, Operations Mgr., john.campbell@wku.edu; Joe Corcoran, Host, Producer, joe.corcoran@wku.edu; Dan Modlin, News Dir., daniel.modlin@wku.edu. **Ad Rates:** Advertising accepted; rates available upon request. **URL:** http://www.wkyufm.org.

13660 ■ WKYU-FM - 88.9
1906 College Heights Blvd., Ste. 11035
Bowling Green, KY 42101-1035
Phone: (270)745-5489
Free: 800-599-9598
Email: wkyufm@wku.edu
Format: Public Radio. **Simulcasts:** WDCL-FM. **Networks:** National Public Radio (NPR); Public Radio International (PRI); AP. **Owner:** Western Kentucky University, 1906 College Heights Blvd., Bowling Green, KY 42101, Ph: (270)745-0111. **Founded:** 1980. **Operating Hours:** Continuous. **ADI:** Bowling Green (Campbellsville), KY. **Key Personnel:** Kevin Willis, News Dir., Station Mgr.; Dan Modlin, News Dir., daniel.modlin@wku.edu; Lee Stott, Music Dir., leland.stott@wku.edu; Jack Hanes, Dir. of Telecommunications, jack.hanes@wku.edu; John Campbell, Operations Mgr., john.campbell@wku.edu. **Wattage:** 100,000. **Ad Rates:** Noncommercial. **URL:** http://www.wkyufm.org.

13661 ■ WKYU-TV - 24
1906 College Heights Blvd., Ste. 11034
Bowling Green, KY 42101-1034
Phone: (270)745-2400
Fax: (270)745-2084
Free: 800-599-2424
Email: wkyutv@wku.edu
Format: Public TV. **Networks:** Public Broadcasting Service (PBS). **Owner:** Western Kentucky University, 1906 College Heights Blvd., Bowling Green, KY 42101, Ph: (270)745-0111. **Founded:** 1989. **Operating Hours:** 8:00 a.m.-10:30 p.m. Sun.-Sat. **Key Personnel:** Cheryl Beckley, Director, Producer; Justin Davis, Operations Mgr. **Ad Rates:** Noncommercial. **URL:** http://www.wkyu.lunchbox.pbs.org.

WLCK-AM - See Scottsville

13662 ■ WLSQ-FM - 94.3
1919 Scottsville Radio Rd.
Bowling Green, KY 42104
Phone: (270)843-3333
Format: Contemporary Hit Radio (CHR); Top 40. **Simulcasts:** WLSZ-FM. **Owner:** F. Darrell Boyd, at above address. **Founded:** Feb. 1995. **Operating Hours:** Continuous. **Wattage:** 6,000. **URL:** http://www.943wdye.com.

13663 ■ WNKY-TV - 40
325 Emmett Ave.
Bowling Green, KY 42101
Phone: (270)781-2140
Fax: (270)842-7140
Email: wnky@wnky.net
Networks: NBC; CBS. **Owner:** Max Media of Kentucky, 900 Laskin Rd., Virginia Beach, VA 23451-3905. **ADI:** Bowling Green (Campbellsville), KY. **Key Personnel:** Kathy Werner, Traffic Mgr. **Ad Rates:** Advertising accepted; rates available upon request. **URL:** http://www.wnky.net.

13664 ■ W216CC-FM - 91.1
PO Box 391
Twin Falls, ID 83303
Fax: (208)736-1958

Free: 800-357-4226
Format: Religious; Contemporary Christian. **Owner:** CSN International, PO Box 391, Twin Falls, ID 83303, Ph: (208)736-1958, Fax: (208)736-1958, Free: 800-357-4226. **URL:** http://www.csnradio.com.

13665 ■ WUHU-FM - 107.1
1919 Scottsville Rd.
Bowling Green, KY 42104
Phone: (270)843-3333
Fax: (270)843-0454
Free: 866-984-8107
Format: Adult Contemporary. **Networks:** Independent. **Owner:** Forever Communications, Inc., 1919 Scottsville Rd., Bowling Green, KY 42104, Ph: (270)843-3333. **Founded:** 1986. **Wattage:** 50,000 ERP. **Ad Rates:** Advertising accepted; rates available upon request. Combined advertising rates available with WBGN-AM; WLYE-FM; WBYR-FM. **URL:** http://www.wuhu107.com.

13666 ■ WWHR-FM
1906 College Heights Blvd.
Bowling Green, KY 42101-1035
Email: info@revolution.fm
Format: Full Service; Heavy Metal; Album-Oriented Rock (AOR). **Wattage:** 1,300 ERP.

13667 ■ WYNU-FM - 92.3
1919 Scottsville Radio Rd.
Bowling Green, KY 42104
Phone: (731)427-3316
Free: 866-762-5923
Email: request@rock923.net
Format: Classic Rock. **Owner:** Forever Communications, Inc., 1919 Scottsville Rd., Bowling Green, KY 42104, Ph: (270)843-3333. **Formerly:** WYNJ-FM. **Operating Hours:** Continuous. **ADI:** Jackson, TN. **Wattage:** 100,000. **Ad Rates:** Combined advertising rates available with WTNV-FM, WTJS-AM.

BRANDENBURG

Meade Co. Meade Co. (WC). On Ohio River, 30 m SW of Louisville. Boat connections. Chemical factory. Oak timber. Diversified farming. Wheat, corn, tobacco.

13668 ■ The Meade County Messenger
The Meade County Messenger
138 Broadway, Ste. A
Brandenburg, KY 40108
Phone: (270)422-2155
Fax: (270)422-2110
Publisher's E-mail: mcmsales@bbtel.com
Community newspaper. **Freq:** Weekly (Wed.). **Print Method:** Offset. **Cols./Page:** 6. **Col. Width:** 1.833 inches. **Col. Depth:** 29.5 agate lines. **Key Personnel:** Jim Mansfield, Executive Editor. **ISSN:** 0746--8113 (print). **Subscription Rates:** $32 Individuals /year (print and online; in Meade, Hardin and Breckinridge counties); $38 Out of area /year (print and online); $18.82 Individuals /year (online). **URL:** http://www.meadecountymessenger.com/28963/2035/1/home-page. **Mailing address:** PO Box 678, Brandenburg, KY 40108. **Remarks:** Accepts display and classified advertising. **Circ:** (Not Reported).

13669 ■ WMMG-AM - 1140
1715 By-Pass Rd.
Brandenburg, KY 40108
Phone: (270)422-3961
Fax: (270)422-3464
Free: 800-203-4175
Email: wmmg935@bbtel.com
Format: Country. **Simulcasts:** WMMG-FM. **Networks:** ABC; Satellite Music Network; KyNet. **Owner:** Meade County Communications Inc., at above address. **Founded:** 1959. **Operating Hours:** Sunrise-sunset. **Key Personnel:** Steve Robbins, Prog. Dir. **Local Programs:** *Morning Tradio On The Radio*, Monday Tuesday Wednesday Thursday Friday 10:00 a.m. - 11:00 a.m. **Wattage:** 250. **Ad Rates:** $11 for 30 seconds; $12 for 60 seconds. Combined advertising rates available with WMMG-FM. **Mailing address:** PO Box 505, Brandenburg, KY 40108. **URL:** http://www.wmmgradio.com.

13670 ■ WMMG-FM - 93.5
1715 By-Pass Rd.
Brandenburg, KY 40108-0505
Phone: (270)422-3961
Fax: (270)422-3464
Format: Country. **Simulcasts:** WMMG-AM. **Networks:** ABC; Satellite Music Network; KyNet; UPI. **Owner:** Meade County Communications Inc., at above address. **Founded:** 1972. **Operating Hours:** Continuous. **Key Personnel:** Steve Robbins, Prog. Dir., Gen. Mgr. **Local Programs:** *Tradio*, Saturday; *The Meade County School Lunch Menus*. **Wattage:** 3,400. **Ad Rates:** Noncommercial. **Mailing address:** PO Box 505, Brandenburg, KY 40108-0505. **URL:** http://www.wmmgradio.com.

BROOKSVILLE

Bracken Co. Bracken Co. (NE). 46 m SE of Newport. Flour mill. Grain, dairy farms. Tobacco, corn, wheat.

13671 ■ Bracken County News
Bay Publishing
216 Frankfort St.
Brooksville, KY 41004
Phone: (606)735-2198
Fax: (606)735-2199
Community newspaper. **Freq:** Weekly (Thurs.). **Print Method:** Offset. **Cols./Page:** 6. **Col. Width:** 1.833 inches. **Col. Depth:** 21 inches. **Key Personnel:** Kathy Bay, Owner, Publisher; Lynn Darnell, Editor. **Subscription Rates:** $20 Individuals /year (in county); $25 Out of area /year; $30 Out of state /year. **Mailing address:** PO Box 68, Brooksville, KY 41004. **Remarks:** Color advertising not accepted. **Circ:** (Not Reported).

BUCKNER

13672 ■ Fastline--Bluegrass Truck Edition
Fastline
4900 Fox Run Rd.
Buckner, KY 40010
Phone: (502)222-0146
Fax: (502)222-0615
Free: 800-626-6409
Publication E-mail: submitad@fastline.com
Illustrated buying guide for the trucking industry. **Freq:** 17/yr. **Subscription Rates:** $30 Individuals; $40 Two years; $60 Canada and Mexico; $125 Other countries. **URL:** http://www.fastline.com/v100/trucking-magazines.aspx. **Mailing address:** PO Box 248, Buckner, KY 40010. **Remarks:** Accepts classified advertising. **Circ:** Combined 22000.

13673 ■ Fastline--Dakota Farm Edition: The Premier Equipment Resource For New and Used Tractors, Trucks and Trailers
Fastline
4900 Fox Run Rd.
Buckner, KY 40010
Phone: (502)222-0146
Fax: (502)222-0615
Free: 800-626-6409
Publication E-mail: submitad@fastline.com
Illustrated buying guide for the farming industry in North and South Dakota. **Freq:** 13/yr. **Subscription Rates:** $30 Individuals; $40 Two years; $125 Other countries; $50 Individuals 3 years. **URL:** http://www.fastline.com/v100/index.aspx. **Mailing address:** PO Box 248, Buckner, KY 40010. **Remarks:** Accepts classified advertising. **Circ:** Combined 22000.

13674 ■ Fastline--Dixie Truck Edition
Fastline
4900 Fox Run Rd.
Buckner, KY 40010
Phone: (502)222-0146
Fax: (502)222-0615
Free: 800-626-6409
Publication E-mail: submitad@fastline.com
Illustrated buying guide for the trucking industry. **Freq:** 13/yr. **Subscription Rates:** $50 Individuals 3 years; $40 Two years; $30 Individuals 1 year; $60 Canada and Mexico; $125 Other countries. **URL:** http://www.fastline.com/v100/index.aspx. **Mailing address:** PO Box 248, Buckner, KY 40010. **Remarks:** Accepts classified advertising. **Circ:** Combined 22000, Combined 22000.

13675 ■ Fastline--Far West Farm Edition
Fastline
4900 Fox Run Rd.
Buckner, KY 40010
Phone: (502)222-0146
Fax: (502)222-0615
Free: 800-626-6409
Publisher's E-mail: helpdesk@fastline.com
Illustrated buying guide for the farming industry. **URL:** http://www.fastline.com/digital-editions/farwest-farm/2016/10. **Mailing address:** PO Box 248, Buckner, KY 40010. **Remarks:** Accepts classified advertising. **Circ:** Combined 22000.

13676 ■ Fastline--Florida Truck Edition
Fastline
4900 Fox Run Rd.
Buckner, KY 40010
Phone: (502)222-0146
Fax: (502)222-0615
Free: 800-626-6409
Publication E-mail: submitad@fastline.com
Illustrated buying guide for the trucking industry. **Freq:** 17/yr. **Subscription Rates:** $30 Individuals; $40 Two years; $60 Canada and Mexico; $125 Other countries. **URL:** http://www.fastline.com/v100/trucking-magazines.aspx. **Mailing address:** PO Box 248, Buckner, KY 40010. **Remarks:** Accepts classified advertising. **Circ:** Combined 22000.

13677 ■ Fastline--Georgia Truck Edition
Fastline
4900 Fox Run Rd.
Buckner, KY 40010
Phone: (502)222-0146
Fax: (502)222-0615
Free: 800-626-6409
Publisher's E-mail: helpdesk@fastline.com
Illustrated buying guide for the trucking industry. **Freq:** 13/yr. **Subscription Rates:** $30 Individuals; $60 Canada and Mexico; $125 Other countries. **URL:** http://www.fastline.com/v100/index.aspx. **Mailing address:** PO Box 248, Buckner, KY 40010. **Remarks:** Accepts classified advertising. **Circ:** Combined 22,000.

13678 ■ Fastline--Illinois Farm Edition
Fastline
4900 Fox Run Rd.
Buckner, KY 40010
Phone: (502)222-0146
Fax: (502)222-0615
Free: 800-626-6409
Publication E-mail: submitad@fastline.com
Illustrated buying guide for the farming industry. **Freq:** 13/yr. **Subscription Rates:** $30 Individuals; $40 Two years; $60 Canada and Mexico; $125 Other countries. **URL:** http://www.fastline.com/v100/index.aspx. **Mailing address:** PO Box 248, Buckner, KY 40010. **Remarks:** Accepts classified advertising. **Circ:** Combined 22,000.

13679 ■ Fastline--Indiana Farm Edition
Fastline
4900 Fox Run Rd.
Buckner, KY 40010
Phone: (502)222-0146
Fax: (502)222-0615
Free: 800-626-6409
Publication E-mail: submitad@fastline.com
Illustrated buying guide for the farming industry. **Freq:** 13/yr. **Subscription Rates:** $50 Individuals 3 years; $40 Two years; $30 Individuals; $60 Canada and Mexico; $125 Other countries. **URL:** http://www.fastline.com/v100/index.aspx. **Mailing address:** PO Box 248, Buckner, KY 40010. **Remarks:** Accepts classified advertising. **Circ:** Combined 22,000.

13680 ■ Fastline--Iowa Farm Edition
Fastline
4900 Fox Run Rd.
Buckner, KY 40010
Phone: (502)222-0146
Fax: (502)222-0615
Free: 800-626-6409
Publisher's E-mail: helpdesk@fastline.com
Illustrated buying guide for the farming industry. **Freq:** 13/yr. **Subscription Rates:** $50 Individuals 3 years; $40 Two years; $30 Individuals; $60 Canada and Mexico; $125 Other countries. **URL:** http://www.fastline.com/v100/index.aspx. **Mailing address:** PO Box 248, Buckner, KY 40010. **Remarks:** Accepts classified advertising. **Circ:** Combined 22,000.

Circulation: ★ = AAM; △ or • = BPA; ♦ = CAC; ❑ = VAC; ⊕ = PO Statement; ‡ = Publisher's Report; Boldface figures = sworn; Light figures = estimated.

13681 ■ Fastline--Kansas Farm Edition
Fastline
4900 Fox Run Rd.
Buckner, KY 40010
Phone: (502)222-0146
Fax: (502)222-0615
Free: 800-626-6409
Publication E-mail: submitad@fastline.com
Illustrated buying guide for the farming industry. **Freq:** 13/yr. **Key Personnel:** Heather Baumgardner, Manager, Sales, fax: (502)222-4522. **Subscription Rates:** $30 Individuals; $40 Two years; $60 Canada and Mexico; $125 Other countries; $50 Individuals 3 years. **URL:** http://www.fastline.com/v100/index.aspx. **Mailing address:** PO Box 248, Buckner, KY 40010. **Remarks:** Accepts classified advertising. **Circ:** Combined 22,000.

13682 ■ Fastline--Kentucky Farm Edition
Fastline
4900 Fox Run Rd.
Buckner, KY 40010
Phone: (502)222-0146
Fax: (502)222-0615
Free: 800-626-6409
Publisher's E-mail: helpdesk@fastline.com
Illustrated buying guide for the farming industry. **Freq:** 13/yr. **Subscription Rates:** $30 Individuals; $40 Two years; C$60 Canada and Mexico; $125 Other countries; $50 Individuals 3 years. **URL:** http://www.fastline.com/v100/index.aspx. **Mailing address:** PO Box 248, Buckner, KY 40010. **Remarks:** Accepts classified advertising. **Circ:** Combined 22,000.

13683 ■ Fastline de Mexico
Fastline
4900 Fox Run Rd.
Buckner, KY 40010
Phone: (502)222-0146
Fax: (502)222-0615
Free: 800-626-6409
Publication E-mail: submitad@fastline.com
Guide to new and used farm equipment in Mexico. **Freq:** 13/yr. **Subscription Rates:** Free. **URL:** http://www.fastlinedemexico.com.mx; http://www.fastlinedemexico.com.mx/nuestra-revista. **Mailing address:** PO Box 248, Buckner, KY 40010. **Remarks:** Accepts advertising. **Circ:** (Not Reported).

13684 ■ Fastline--Mid-Atlantic Farm Edition
Fastline
4900 Fox Run Rd.
Buckner, KY 40010
Phone: (502)222-0146
Fax: (502)222-0615
Free: 800-626-6409
Publisher's E-mail: helpdesk@fastline.com
Illustrated buying guide for the farming industry. **Freq:** 13/yr. **Subscription Rates:** $30 Individuals; $60 Canada and Mexico; $125 Other countries. **URL:** http://www.fastline.com/v100/index.aspx. **Mailing address:** PO Box 248, Buckner, KY 40010. **Remarks:** Accepts classified advertising. **Circ:** Combined 22,000.

13685 ■ Fastline--Mid-South Farm Edition
Fastline
4900 Fox Run Rd.
Buckner, KY 40010
Phone: (502)222-0146
Fax: (502)222-0615
Free: 800-626-6409
Publication E-mail: submitad@fastline.com
Illustrated buying guide for the farming industry. **Freq:** 17/yr. **Subscription Rates:** $30 Individuals; $40 Two years; $60 Canada and Mexico; $125 Other countries; $50 Individuals 3 years. **URL:** http://www.fastline.com/v100/view-digital-editions.aspx; http://www.fastline.com/digital-editions/mid-south-farm/2016/13. **Mailing address:** PO Box 248, Buckner, KY 40010. **Remarks:** Accepts classified advertising. **Circ:** Combined 22000.

13686 ■ Fastline--Minnesota Farm Edition
Fastline
4900 Fox Run Rd.
Buckner, KY 40010
Phone: (502)222-0146
Fax: (502)222-0615
Free: 800-626-6409
Publication E-mail: submitad@fastline.com
Illustrated buying guide for the farming industry. **Freq:** 13/yr. **Subscription Rates:** $30 Individuals; $40 Two years; $60 Canada and Mexico; $125 Other countries. **URL:** http://www.fastline.com/v100/index.aspx. **Mailing address:** PO Box 248, Buckner, KY 40010. **Remarks:** Accepts classified advertising. **Circ:** Combined 22,000.

13687 ■ Fastline--Missouri Farm Edition
Fastline
4900 Fox Run Rd.
Buckner, KY 40010
Phone: (502)222-0146
Fax: (502)222-0615
Free: 800-626-6409
Publication E-mail: submitad@fastline.com
Illustrated buying guide for the farming industry. **Freq:** 13/yr. **Subscription Rates:** $30 Individuals; $40 Two years; $60 Canada and Mexico; $125 Other countries. **URL:** http://www.fastline.com/v100/index.aspx. **Mailing address:** PO Box 248, Buckner, KY 40010. **Remarks:** Accepts classified advertising. **Circ:** Combined 22,000.

13688 ■ Fastline--Nebraska Farm Edition
Fastline
4900 Fox Run Rd.
Buckner, KY 40010
Phone: (502)222-0146
Fax: (502)222-0615
Free: 800-626-6409
Publication E-mail: submitad@fastline.com
Illustrated buying guide for the farming industry. **Freq:** 13/yr. **Subscription Rates:** $30 Individuals; $40 Two years; $60 Canada and Mexico; $125 Other countries; $50 Individuals 3 years. **URL:** http://www.fastline.com/v100/index.aspx. **Mailing address:** PO Box 248, Buckner, KY 40010. **Remarks:** Accepts classified advertising. **Circ:** Combined 22,000.

13689 ■ Fastline--Northeast Farm Edition
Fastline
4900 Fox Run Rd.
Buckner, KY 40010
Phone: (502)222-0146
Fax: (502)222-0615
Free: 800-626-6409
Publication E-mail: submitad@fastline.com
Illustrated buying guide for the farming industry. **Freq:** 13/yr. **Subscription Rates:** $50 Individuals 3 years; $40 Two years; $30 Individuals; $60 Canada and Mexico; $125 Other countries. **URL:** http://www.fastline.com/v100/index.aspx. **Mailing address:** PO Box 248, Buckner, KY 40010. **Remarks:** Accepts classified advertising. **Circ:** Combined 22,000.

13690 ■ Fastline--Northwest Farm Edition
Fastline
4900 Fox Run Rd.
Buckner, KY 40010
Phone: (502)222-0146
Fax: (502)222-0615
Free: 800-626-6409
Publisher's E-mail: helpdesk@fastline.com
Illustrated buying guide for the farming industry. **URL:** http://www.fastline.com/digital-editions/northwest-farm/2016/10. **Mailing address:** PO Box 248, Buckner, KY 40010. **Remarks:** Accepts classified advertising. **Circ:** Combined 22000.

13691 ■ Fastline--Ohio Farm Edition
Fastline
4900 Fox Run Rd.
Buckner, KY 40010
Phone: (502)222-0146
Fax: (502)222-0615
Free: 800-626-6409
Publication E-mail: submitad@fastline.com
Illustrated buying guide for the farming industry. **Freq:** 13/yr. **Subscription Rates:** $30 Individuals; $40 Two years; $60 Canada and Mexico; $125 Other countries; $50 Individuals 3 years. **URL:** http://www.fastline.com/v100/index.aspx. **Mailing address:** PO Box 248, Buckner, KY 40010. **Remarks:** Accepts classified advertising. **Circ:** Combined 22,000.

13692 ■ Fastline--Oklahoma Farm Edition
Fastline
4900 Fox Run Rd.
Buckner, KY 40010
Phone: (502)222-0146
Fax: (502)222-0615
Free: 800-626-6409
Publication E-mail: submitad@fastline.com
Illustrated buying guide for the farming industry. **Freq:** 13/yr. **Subscription Rates:** $30 Individuals; $40 Two years; $60 Canada and Mexico; $125 Other countries; $50 Individuals 3 years. **URL:** http://www.fastline.com. **Mailing address:** PO Box 248, Buckner, KY 40010. **Remarks:** Accepts classified advertising. **Circ:** Combined 22,000.

13693 ■ Fastline--Rocky Mountain Farm Edition
Fastline
4900 Fox Run Rd.
Buckner, KY 40010
Phone: (502)222-0146
Fax: (502)222-0615
Free: 800-626-6409
Publisher's E-mail: helpdesk@fastline.com
Illustrated buying guide for the farming industry. **Freq:** 17/yr. **Subscription Rates:** $50 Individuals 3 years; $40 Two years; $30 Individuals; $60 Canada and Mexico; $125 Other countries. **URL:** http://www.fastline.com/v100/view-digital-editions.aspx; http://www.fastline.com/digital-editions/rocky-mtn-farm/2016/11. **Mailing address:** PO Box 248, Buckner, KY 40010. **Remarks:** Accepts classified advertising. **Circ:** Combined 22000.

13694 ■ Fastline--Southeast Farm Edition
Fastline
4900 Fox Run Rd.
Buckner, KY 40010
Phone: (502)222-0146
Fax: (502)222-0615
Free: 800-626-6409
Publisher's E-mail: helpdesk@fastline.com
Illustrated buying guide for the farming industry. **Freq:** 13/yr. **Subscription Rates:** $30 Individuals; $60 Canada and Mexico; $125 Other countries. **URL:** http://www.fastline.com/v100/index.aspx. **Mailing address:** PO Box 248, Buckner, KY 40010. **Remarks:** Accepts classified advertising. **Circ:** Combined 22,000.

13695 ■ Fastline--Tennessee Farm Edition
Fastline
4900 Fox Run Rd.
Buckner, KY 40010
Phone: (502)222-0146
Fax: (502)222-0615
Free: 800-626-6409
Publication E-mail: submitad@fastline.com
Illustrated buying guide for the farming industry. **Freq:** 17/yr. **Subscription Rates:** $50 Individuals 3 years; $40 Two years; $60 Canada and Mexico; $125 Other countries; $30 Individuals. **URL:** http://www.fastline.com/v100/view-digital-editions.aspx; http://www.fastline.com/digital-editions/tennessee-farm/2016/12. **Mailing address:** PO Box 248, Buckner, KY 40010. **Remarks:** Accepts classified advertising. **Circ:** Combined 22000.

13696 ■ Fastline--Tennessee Truck Edition
Fastline
4900 Fox Run Rd.
Buckner, KY 40010
Phone: (502)222-0146
Fax: (502)222-0615
Free: 800-626-6409
Publication E-mail: submitad@fastline.com
Illustrated buying guide for the trucking industry. **Freq:** Monthly. **Subscription Rates:** $30 Individuals; $40 Two years; $60 Canada and Mexico; $125 Other countries; $50 Individuals 3 years. **URL:** http://www.fastline.com/v100/index.aspx. **Mailing address:** PO Box 248, Buckner, KY 40010. **Remarks:** Accepts classified advertising. **Circ:** Combined 22,000.

13697 ■ Fastline--Texas Farm Edition
Fastline
4900 Fox Run Rd.
Buckner, KY 40010
Phone: (502)222-0146
Fax: (502)222-0615
Free: 800-626-6409
Publication E-mail: submitad@fastline.com
Illustrated buying guide for the farming industry. **Freq:** 13/yr. **Subscription Rates:** $30 Individuals; $40 Two years; $60 Canada and Mexico; $125 Other countries. **URL:** http://www.fastline.com/v100/index.aspx. **Mailing address:** PO Box 248, Buckner, KY 40010. **Remarks:** Accepts classified advertising. **Circ:** Combined 22,000.

13698 ■ Fastline--Tri-State Truck Edition
Fastline
4900 Fox Run Rd.
Buckner, KY 40010
Phone: (502)222-0146
Fax: (502)222-0615
Free: 800-626-6409
Publication E-mail: submitad@fastline.com
Illustrated buying guide for the trucking industry. **Freq:** 13/yr. **Subscription Rates:** $30 Individuals; $40 Two years; $60 Canada and Mexico; $125 Other countries. **URL:** http://www.fastline.com/v100/index.aspx. **Mailing address:** PO Box 248, Buckner, KY 40010. **Remarks:** Accepts classified advertising. **Circ:** Combined 22,000.

13699 ■ Fastline--Wisconsin Farm Edition
Fastline
4900 Fox Run Rd.
Buckner, KY 40010
Phone: (502)222-0146
Fax: (502)222-0615
Free: 800-626-6409
Publication E-mail: submitad@fastline.com
Illustrated buying guide for the farming industry. **Freq:** 13/yr. **Subscription Rates:** $50 Individuals 3 years; $40 Two years; $30 Individuals; $60 Canada and Mexico; $125 Other countries. **URL:** http://www.fastline.com/. **Mailing address:** PO Box 248, Buckner, KY 40010. **Remarks:** Accepts classified advertising. **Circ:** Combined 22,000.

BURKESVILLE

Cumberland Co. Cumberland Co. (SC). On Cumberland River, 110 m S of Louisville. Oil wells. Saw mill. Summer resort. Stock, poultry, fruit, grain farms. Corn, hay, tobacco.

13700 ■ Cumberland County News
Cumberland County News
412 Courthouse Sq.
Burkesville, KY 42717
Phone: (270)864-3891
Publisher's E-mail: ccn@burkesville.com
Community newspaper. **Freq:** Weekly (Wed.). **Print Method:** Offset. **Cols./Page:** 6. **Col. Width:** 24 nonpareils. **Col. Depth:** 294 agate lines. **Key Personnel:** Patsy Judd, Owner, Publisher; Cyndi Pritchett, Editor. **Subscription Rates:** $19 Individuals /year (print; in Cumberland and surrounding Kentucky counties); $27 Elsewhere /year (print; in Kentucky); $30 Out of state /year (print). **URL:** http://cumberlandcountynewspaper.com/category/burkesville. **Mailing address:** PO Box 307, Burkesville, KY 42717. **Remarks:** Accepts classified advertising. **Circ:** (Not Reported).

13701 ■ WKYR-FM - 107.9
PO Box 340
Burkesville, KY 42717
Phone: (270)433-7191
Fax: (270)433-7195
Format: Contemporary Country. **Networks:** ABC; Jones Satellite. **Owner:** Cumberland Broadcasting Company Inc., PO Box 1290, Cumberland, MD 21501, Ph: (301)724-5000. **Founded:** 1988. **Operating Hours:** Controlled. **ADI:** Nashville (Cookeville), TN. **Wattage:** 6,000. **Ad Rates:** Advertising accepted; rates available upon request.

BUTLER

13702 ■ WIDS-AM - 570
4942 US Highway 27 N
Butler, KY 41006
Phone: (859)472-1075
Fax: (859)472-2875
Free: 800-295-1075
Email: wiok@fuse.net
Format: Gospel. **Owner:** Hammond Broadcasting Inc., PO Box 50, Falmouth, KY 41040. **Founded:** 1995. **Operating Hours:** Continuous. **Wattage:** 500. **Ad Rates:** Noncommercial. **Mailing address:** PO Box 50, Falmouth, KY 41040. **URL:** http://www.wiok.com.

13703 ■ WYGH-AM - 1440
4942 US Hwy. 27 N
Butler, KY 41006
Phone: (859)472-1075
Fax: (859)472-2875
Format: Gospel; Hispanic. **Owner:** Hammond Broadcasting Inc., PO Box 50, Falmouth, KY 41040. **Founded:** 1994. **Operating Hours:** Continuous. **Key Personnel:** Jamie Porter, Contact. **Wattage:** 1,000. **Ad Rates:** Noncommercial. **URL:** http://www.wiok.com/WYGH%20Home.html.

CADIZ

Trigg Co. Trigg Co. (SW). 20 m W of Hopkinsville. Manufactures fabricated wire products, hosiery, feed, work clothing. Lumber. Timber. Agriculture. Tobacco, wheat, corn.

13704 ■ The Cadiz Record
Jim Ward
PO Box 1670
Cadiz, KY 42211
Phone: (270)522-6605
Fax: (270)522-3001
Publisher's E-mail: news@cadizrecord.com
Local newspaper with a Democratic orientation. **Freq:** Weekly (Wed.). **Print Method:** Offset. **Cols./Page:** 6. **Col. Width:** 26 nonpareils. **Col. Depth:** 301 agate lines. **Key Personnel:** Justin McGill, General Manager; Christine Hazelmyer, Office Manager; Jimmy Hart, Account Executive; Franklin Clark, Reporter. **URL:** http://www.cadizrecord.com. **Ad Rates:** BW $780; 4C $250; SAU $2.25; PCI $2.75. **Remarks:** Accepts advertising. **Circ:** (Not Reported).

13705 ■ WHVO-AM - 1480
19 Wooldridge Ln.
Cadiz, KY 42211
Phone: (270)522-3232
Fax: (270)522-1110
Format: Oldies. **Networks:** AP. **Owner:** Ham Broadcasting Co. Inc., at above address. **Founded:** 1954. **Formerly:** WKOA-AM; WQKS-AM. **Operating Hours:** Continuous; 75% network, 25% local. **Key Personnel:** Beth A. Mann, Gen. Mgr., bmann@wkdzradio.com; Amy Berry, Gen. Sales Mgr., aberry@oldies1480.com; Bill Booth, Dir. of Programs, bbooth@wkdzradio.com. **Local Programs:** *Hoptown This Morning*, Monday Tuesday Wednesday Thursday Friday 6:00 a.m. - 9:00 a.m.; *Local News*, Sunday Monday Tuesday Wednesday Thursday Friday Saturday 6:00 a.m. - 5:00 p.m.; *The News Edge - Live, Local, Committed*, Monday Tuesday Wednesday Thursday Friday 3:00 p.m. - 5:00 p.m. **Wattage:** 1,000. **Ad Rates:** $5-9 for 30 seconds; $7-11 for 60 seconds. WKDZ Real Country 106.5 FM. **URL:** http://www.oldies1480.com.

13706 ■ WKDZ-FM - 106.5
19 D.J. Everett Dr.
Cadiz, KY 42211
Phone: (270)522-3232
Fax: (270)522-1110
Email: wkdz@wkdzradio.com
Format: Country. **Networks:** ABC; Fox. **Founded:** 1972. **Operating Hours:** Continuous. **ADI:** Nashville (Cookeville), TN. **Key Personnel:** Alan Watts, News Dir., awatts@wkdzradio.com. **Local Programs:** *KDZ Country Club*, Monday Tuesday Wednesday Thursday Friday 6:00 a.m. - 9:00 a.m.; *Live Afternoon Drive*, Monday Tuesday Wednesday Thursday Friday 3:00 p.m. - 5:00 p.m.; *WKDZ News*. **Wattage:** 25,000. **Ad Rates:** $17-22 per unit. Combined advertising rates available with WKDZ-AM, WHVO-AM. **Mailing address:** PO Box 1900, Cadiz, KY 42211. **URL:** http://wkdzradio.com.

CALVERT CITY

13707 ■ Lake News
Mid-Florida Publications Inc.
PO Box 498
Calvert City, KY 42029-0498
Phone: (270)395-5858
Fax: (270)395-5858
Publication E-mail: news@thelakenews.net
Shopper. **Founded:** 1957. **Freq:** Weekly (Wed.). **Print Method:** Offset. **Cols./Page:** 6. **Col. Width:** 20 nonpareils. **Col. Depth:** 231 agate lines. **Key Personnel:** Loyd W. Ford, Editor. **URL:** http://www.thelakenews.net/. **Ad Rates:** GLR $.47. **Remarks:** Accepts advertising. **Circ:** (Not Reported).

13708 ■ WCCK-FM - 95.7
PO Box 387
Benton, KY 42025
Phone: (270)527-3102
Free: 800-737-3102
Email: wcbl@bellsouth.net
Format: Country. **Owner:** Freeland Broadcasting Co., at above address, Benton, KY. **Wattage:** 960. **Ad Rates:** Advertising accepted; rates available upon request.

CAMPBELLSVILLE

Taylor Co. Taylor Co. (C). 70 m S of Louisville. Senior College. Parks. Manufacturer casket, underwear, furniture, interior supply. Cabinet shop. Agriculture. Cattle (dairy & beef), hogs, corn, tobacco.

13709 ■ Central Kentucky News-Journal
Landmark Community Newspapers L.L.C.
428 Woodlawn Ave.
Campbellsville, KY 42718
Phone: (270)465-8111
Fax: (270)465-2500
Publication E-mail: cknj@cknj.com
Community newspaper. **Freq:** Semiweekly (Mon. and Thurs.). **Print Method:** Offset. **Trim Size:** 13 x 24. **Cols./Page:** 6. **Col. Width:** 10.5 picas. **Col. Depth:** 21 1/2 inches. **Key Personnel:** Jeff Moreland, Publisher; Bobby Brockman, Editor; Cheryl Magers, Manager, Advertising. **Subscription Rates:** $48.75 Individuals annual - print and online; $27.99 Individuals semi-annual - print and online; $15.75 Individuals quarterly - print and online; $5.85 Individuals monthly - print and online. **URL:** http://www.cknj.com. **Remarks:** Advertising accepted; rates available upon request. **Circ:** Combined 7612.

13710 ■ WAPD-FM - 91.7
PO Box 3206
Tupelo, MS 38803
Format: Contemporary Christian. **Owner:** American Family Radio, at above address. **Key Personnel:** Rick Robertson, Contact. **Ad Rates:** Noncommercial.

13711 ■ WCKQ-FM - 104.1
50 Friendship Pike
Campbellsville, KY 42719
Phone: (270)789-2401
Format: Top 40. **Networks:** Jones Satellite; ABC. **Owner:** Commonwealth Broadcasting Corp., at above address. **Founded:** 1963. **Formerly:** WTCO-FM. **Operating Hours:** Continuous; 95% local, 5% network. **ADI:** Louisville, KY. **Wattage:** 25,000. **Ad Rates:** $10-20 for 30 seconds; $12-25 for 60 seconds. $4-$20 for 30 seconds; $5-$25 for 60 seconds. Combined advertising rates available with WTCO-AM. **Mailing address:** PO Box 1053, Campbellsville, KY 42719. **URL:** http://www.myq104.com.

13712 ■ WLCU-TV - 22
1 University Dr.
Campbellsville, KY 42718
Phone: (270)789-5000
Free: 800-264-6014
Owner: Campbellsville University, One University Dr., Campbellsville, KY 42718, Ph: (270)789-5000, Free: 800-264-6014. **Key Personnel:** Andrew Franklin, VP. **URL:** http://www.campbellsville.edu/wlcutv.

13713 ■ WTCO-AM - 1450
PO Box 1505
Glasgow, KY 42142
Phone: (270)789-2401
Fax: (888)531-6397
Format: Sports. **Networks:** ESPN Radio; ABC. **Owner:** CBC of Marion & Taylor Counties Inc., at above address. **Founded:** 1948. **Operating Hours:** Continuous; 75% network, 25% local. **ADI:** Louisville, KY. **Wattage:** 1,000. **Ad Rates:** $4-8 for 30 seconds; $6-10 for 60 seconds. $3-$8 for 30 seconds; $3.75-$10 for 60 seconds. Combined advertising rates available with WCKQ-FM. **URL:** http://www.wtcosports.com.

13714 ■ WVLC-FM - 99.9
101 E Main St.
Campbellsville, KY 42718
Phone: (270)789-4998
Fax: (270)789-4584
Format: Country. **Key Personnel:** Jan Royse, Gen. Mgr., bigdawg@wvlc.com; Larry Smith, Contact; Chase

Circulation: ★ = AAM; △ or • = BPA; ♦ = CAC; ❑ = VAC; ⊕ = PO Statement; ‡ = Publisher's Report; Boldface figures = sworn; Light figures = estimated.

McBride, Contact, chase@wvlc.com. **Ad Rates:** Advertising accepted; rates available upon request. **Mailing address:** PO Box 4190, Campbellsville, KY 42718. **URL:** http://www.wvlc.com.

CENTRAL CITY

Muhlenberg Co. Muhlenberg Co. (SW). 32 m S of Owensboro. Manufactures wood products, beverages, boxes, explosives. Coal mines. Oil wells. Hardwood timber. Truck, grain farms. Corn, tobacco, hay.

13715 ■ WNES-AM
Highway 62 W
Central City, KY 42330
Phone: (270)754-3000
Fax: (270)754-9484
Format: Easy Listening. **Networks:** CBS; KyNet. **Owner:** Muhlenberg Broadcasting Co., Inc., at above address. **Founded:** 1955. **Key Personnel:** Stan Barnett, Contact. **Wattage:** 1,000 Day; 172 Night. **Ad Rates:** $2.40-4 for 30 seconds; $4.30-6 for 60 seconds. **Mailing address:** PO Box 471, Central City, KY 42330.

COLUMBIA

Adair Co. Adair Co. (SC). 100 m SE of Louisville. Major sewing industry. Manufactures hydrolic pump, cherry furniture. Lumber mills. Sheet metal works. Agriculture. Tobacco, bell peppers, beef cattle, hogs, horses, fruit, corn, wheat, soybeans.

13716 ■ WAIN-AM - 1270
1521 Liberty Rd.
Columbia, KY 42728
Phone: (270)384-2135
Format: News; Talk. **Networks:** ABC; KyNet. **Owner:** Keybroadcasting. **Founded:** 1952. **Operating Hours:** Continuous. **ADI:** Bowling Green (Campbellsville), KY. **Wattage:** 1,000 Day; 068 Night. **Ad Rates:** $6-8 for 30 seconds; $8-10 for 60 seconds.

13717 ■ WAIN-FM - 93.5
1521 Liberty Rd.
Columbia, KY 42728
Phone: (270)384-2135
Email: wain@keybroadcasting.net
Format: Country. **Simulcasts:** WAIN-AM. **Networks:** ABC; KyNet. **Owner:** Keybroadcasting. **Founded:** 1968. **Operating Hours:** Continuous. **ADI:** Bowling Green (Campbellsville), KY. **Key Personnel:** Stephanie Hatfield, Dir. of Programs. **Wattage:** 5,200. **Ad Rates:** $6.50-9 for 30 seconds; $8.50-11 for 60 seconds. Combined advertising rates available with WAIN-AM 1270.

CORBIN

Whitley Co. Whitley Co. (NE). Auto parts, bricks, corn, coal mining.

13718 ■ Times-Tribune
APMS
T201 N Kentucky Ave.
Corbin, KY 40701
Phone: (606)528-2464
Fax: (606)528-9850
Publication E-mail: times@kih.net
General newspaper. **Founded:** 1892. **Freq:** Weekly. **Print Method:** Offset. **Cols./Page:** 6. **Col. Width:** 2 1/16 inches. **Col. Depth:** 21 1/2 inches. **Key Personnel:** Ernie Horn, Manager, Circulation; Bill Hanson, Publisher; Paula Jones, Business Manager; Samantha Swindler, Managing Editor. **USPS:** 132-480. **Subscription Rates:** $9 Individuals 1-month online subscription; $108 Individuals 1-year online subscription; $15 Individuals 1-month print subscription (In-state); $18 Individuals 1-month print subscription (Out-of-state). **Alt. Formats:** PDF. **URL:** http://www.thetimestribune.com. **Formerly:** Corbin Times Tribune. **Mailing address:** PO Box 516, Corbin, KY 40701. **Ad Rates:** GLR $.94; BW $1,388; 4C $1,627; SAU $10.76; PCI $6.28. **Remarks:** Accepts advertising. **Circ:** 8500.

13719 ■ The Whitley Republican News Journal
Whitley Whiz
PO Box 1524
Corbin, KY 40702
Phone: (606)528-9767
Newspaper with a Republican orientation. **Freq:** Weekly (Wed.). **Print Method:** Offset. **Cols./Page:** 6. **Col. Width:** 26 nonpareils. **Col. Depth:** 301 agate lines. **Key Personnel:** Don Estep, Editor; Jennifer Benfield, Manager, Circulation; Jim McAlister, Editor. **USPS:** 683-320. **Subscription Rates:** $33 Individuals online only /year. **URL:** http://thenewsjournal.net. **Formerly:** The Whitley Republican. **Ad Rates:** PCI $7.75. **Remarks:** Color advertising accepted; rates available upon request. **Circ:** 8107.

13720 ■ WCTT-AM - 680
821 Adams Rd.
Corbin, KY 40701
Phone: (606)528-2818
Fax: (606)523-2068
Email: traffic@wctt.com
Format: Religious; Big Band/Nostalgia. **Networks:** NBC. **Founded:** 1947. **Wattage:** 1,000. **Ad Rates:** $5-16 for 30 seconds. **URL:** http://www.wctt.com.

13721 ■ WCTT-FM - 107.3
821 Adams Rd.
Corbin, KY 40701
Phone: (606)528-6617
Format: Adult Contemporary. **Founded:** 1947. **Wattage:** 50,000. **Ad Rates:** $7.50-54 for 30 seconds. **URL:** http://www.t1073.com.

13722 ■ WEKF-FM - 88.5
102 Perkins Bldg.
521 Lancaster Ave.
Richmond, KY 40475-3102
Email: weku@eku.edu
Format: Classical; Public Radio; Talk. **Operating Hours:** Continuous. **Key Personnel:** Michael Carter, Music Dir., michael.carter@eku.edu; Bill Browning, Chief Engineer, bill.browning@eku.edu; Carol Siler, Dir. of Dev., carol.siler@eku.edu; Julie Tennill, Coord., Member Svcs., julie.tennill@eku.edu. **URL:** http://www.weku.fm.

13723 ■ WKDP-AM - 1330
821 Adams Rd.
Corbin, KY 40701
Phone: (606)528-6617
Format: News; Talk. **Networks:** ABC; USA Radio. **Owner:** Eubanks Broadcasting Inc., 701 Main St., CORBIN, KY 40701, Ph: (606)528-6617. **Founded:** 1967. **Formerly:** WYGO-AM. **Operating Hours:** 12 HRS. Daily. **Wattage:** 5,000. **Ad Rates:** $3-8 for 30 seconds; $6-16 for 60 seconds. **URL:** http://www.kdcountry995.com.

13724 ■ WKDP-FM - 99.5
821 Adams Rd.
Corbin, KY 40701-4708
Phone: (606)528-6617
Format: Country. **Networks:** ABC. **Owner:** Eubanks Broadcasting Inc., 701 Main St., CORBIN, KY 40701, Ph: (606)528-6617. **Founded:** 1967. **Operating Hours:** Continuous; 5% network, 95% local. **ADI:** Lexington, KY. **Wattage:** 50,000. **Ad Rates:** $9.80-16 for 30 seconds; $12.80-32 for 60 seconds. **URL:** http://www.kdcountry995.com.

13725 ■ WRHR-FM - 95.3
1901 Snyder St.
Corbin, KY 40701
Phone: (606)528-4067
Format: News; Information; Eighties. **Operating Hours:** Continuous. **Ad Rates:** Noncommercial.

COVINGTON

Kenton Co. Kenton Co. (N). On Ohio River, opposite Cincinnati. Six bridges connect with Cincinnati. Manufactures machine tools, prison equipment, paper, petroleum, sheet metal products, medicine cabinets, steel, men's clothing, electric safety switches and motor controls, freight cars, parking meters, furniture, stamping dies, steel doors, candied fruit,

13726 ■ WCVN-TV - 54
600 Cooper Dr.
Lexington, KY 40502
Phone: (859)258-7000
Free: 800-432-0951
Email: shop@ket.org
Format: Educational. **Networks:** Public Broadcasting Service (PBS); Kentucky Educational Television. **Owner:** Kentucky Educational Television, 600 Cooper Dr., Lexington, KY 40502, Ph: (859)258-7000, Free: 800-432-0951. **Founded:** 1968. **Operating Hours:** Continuous. **ADI:** Columbus (Chillicothe), OH. **Key Personnel:** Shae Hopkins, Exec. Dir. **Local Programs:** *Comment on Kentucky*, Friday 8:00 p.m.; *Kentucky Afield*, Saturday Sunday 8:30 p.m. 4:30 p.m.; *Kentucky Life*; *Kentucky Tonight*, Monday 8:00 p.m.; *Louisville Life*, Saturday 6:00 a.m. **Wattage:** 162. **Ad Rates:** Noncommercial. **URL:** http://www.ket.org.

CUMBERLAND

Harlan Co Harlan Co. Harlan Co. (NE). 21 m SSE of Hazard Mining Center. Harlan Co. (NE). 21 m SSE of Hazard. Mining center.

13727 ■ Tri-City News
Tri-City News
805 E Main St.
Cumberland, KY 40823-1711
Phone: (606)589-2588
Fax: (606)589-2589
Community newspaper. **Founded:** 1929. **Freq:** Weekly. **Print Method:** Offset. **Trim Size:** 13 x 21 1/2. **Cols./Page:** 6. **Col. Depth:** 21.5 inches. **Key Personnel:** Don Layfield, Manager, Sales; Richard Dal Monte, Editor; Nigel Lark, Publisher. **USPS:** 638-820. **Subscription Rates:** $15 Individuals; $20 Out of state. **URL:** http://www.tricitynews.com/. **Ad Rates:** BW $483.75; 4C $803.75; PCI $4.50. **Remarks:** Accepts classified advertising. **Circ:** ‡2200.

13728 ■ WCPM-AM - 1280
101 Keller St.
Cumberland, KY 40823
Phone: (606)589-4623
Email: wcpmradio@windstream.net
Format: Hot Country; Religious. **Owner:** Cumberland City Broadcasting, Inc., at above address. **Founded:** 1951. **Operating Hours:** Continuous. **Key Personnel:** Laura Hollitt, Traffic Mgr.; Susan Burton, Gen. Mgr. **Wattage:** 1,000 Day; 115 Night. **Ad Rates:** Advertising accepted; rates available upon request. **URL:** http://www.wcpmradio.com.

CYNTHIANA

Harrison Co. Harrison Co. (NEC). 28 m N of Lexington. Tobacco warehouses and redrying plant; cheese, butter, aluminum fabricating, clothing, fertilizer factories; distillery; screws, planing mill; meat processing plant. Stock, dairy, poultry farms. Tobacco.

13729 ■ Cynthiana Democrat
Landmark Community Newspapers L.L.C.
412 Webster Ave.
Cynthiana, KY 41031
Phone: (859)234-1035
Publisher's E-mail: marketing@lcni.com
Community newspaper. **Freq:** Weekly (Thurs.). **Subscription Rates:** $32.86 Individuals annual all access; $18.29 Individuals semi-annual all access; $10.07 Individuals quarterly all access. **URL:** http://www.cynthianademocrat.com. **Mailing address:** PO Box 160, Cynthiana, KY 41031. **Remarks:** Accepts advertising. **Circ:** Paid ‡6000.

13730 ■ WCYN-AM - 1400
130 S Main S
Cynthiana, KY 41031
Format: Oldies. **Founded:** 1956. **Operating Hours:** Continuous. **Wattage:** 500 day; 1,000 night. **Ad Rates:** $4.90-7.00 for 30 seconds; $6.16-8.80 for 60 seconds. Combined advertising rates available with WCYN-FM. **URL:** http://wcyn.com/.

13731 ■ WCYN-FM
111 Court St.
Cynthiana, KY 41031-1516
Phone: (859)234-1400
Fax: (859)234-1425
Format: Country. **Founded:** 1970. **Key Personnel:** Ann Anderson, Gen. Mgr. **Wattage:** 3,400 ERP. **Ad Rates:** $4.90-7 for 30 seconds; $6.16-8.80 for 60 seconds. **URL:** http://www.countryboy102.com/.

DANVILLE

Boyle Co. Boyle Co. (C). 36 m SW of Lexington. Centre College (Presb.). Manufactures farm machinery, gas boilers, conveyors, wire components, trash compactors, auto parts, beverages, automatic ice makers, furniture, glass tubing & incandescent blown bulbs, men's clothing, greeting cards; tobacco warehouse. Stock yards. Agriculture. Tobacco, wheat.

13732 ■ Advocate-Messenger
Advocate-Messenger Co.
330 S 4th St.
Danville, KY 40422-2033
Phone: (859)236-2551
Fax: (859)236-9566
General newspaper. **Freq:** Daily (eve.). **Print Method:** Offset. **Cols./Page:** 6. **Col. Width:** 25 nonpareils. **Col. Depth:** 301 agate lines. **Key Personnel:** Scott C. Schurz, Jr., Editor; Renita Cox, Business Manager; Jerry Dunn, Manager, Advertising. **Subscription Rates:** $99 Individuals online - 1 year; $10 Individuals online - monthly. **URL:** http://centralkynews.com/amnews. **Mailing address:** PO Box 149, Danville, KY 40422. **Ad Rates:** SAU $8.77. **Remarks:** Accepts classified advertising. **Circ:** Mon.-Fri. ★**10395**, Sun. ★**11518**.

13733 ■ Centrepiece
Centre College
600 W Walnut St.
Danville, KY 40422
Phone: (859)238-5200
Fax: (859)238-5373
Free: 800-423-6236
Publisher's E-mail: admission@centre.edu
College alumni magazine. **Freq:** 3/yr. **Print Method:** Sheet. **Trim Size:** 8 1/2 11. **Cols./Page:** 4. **Col. Width:** 1 5/8 nonpareils and 3 9/16 inches. **Col. Depth:** 134 agate lines. **Key Personnel:** Clarence R. Wyatt, Officer. **URL:** http://www.centre.edu/alumni/centrepiece. **Remarks:** Advertising not accepted. **Circ:** ‡18000.

13734 ■ Danville Boyle County Images Magazine
Danville-Boyle County Chamber of Commerce
105 E Walnut St.
Danville, KY 40422
Phone: (859)236-2361
Fax: (859)236-3197
Publisher's E-mail: info@danvilleboylechamber.com
Magazine containing a membership directory and community information for the Danville-Boyle County, Kentucky Chamber of Commerce. **Freq:** Annual. **Subscription Rates:** Included in membership. **URL:** http://www.danvilleboylechamber.com/why-join-the-chamber. **Ad Rates:** 4C. **Remarks:** Accepts advertising. **Circ:** (Not Reported).

13735 ■ WDFB-AM - 1170
3596 Alum Springs Rd.
Danville, KY 40422-9607
Phone: (859)236-9333
Fax: (859)236-3348
Email: wdfb@wdfb.org
Format: Religious. **Networks:** USA Radio; Voice of Christian Youth America. **Owner:** Donald Drake. **Founded:** May 20, 1985. **Operating Hours:** Sunrise-sunset; 5% network, 95% local. **ADI:** Lexington, KY. **Key Personnel:** Mildred Drake, Contact, music@searnet.com; Cindy Pike, Contact, cpike@wdfb.com. **Local Programs:** *Bible Trivia*, Sunday 3:00 p.m. - 5:00 p.m.; *James Dobson Family Minute*, Monday Tuesday Wednesday Thursday Friday 8:25 a.m. - 8:30 a.m.; *Creation Moment*, Monday Tuesday Wednesday Thursday Friday 3:52 p.m. - 4:10 p.m.; *Pleasant Run Baptist*, Saturday 10:30 a.m. - 11:30 a.m.; *Think On These Things*, Sunday, 8:50 a.m. - 9:30 a.m.; 6:05 p.m. - 7:00 p.m.; *Sunday Meetin' Time*, Sunday, 10:00 a.m. - 12:10 p.m.; 8:00 p.m. - 9:00 p.m.; *Children's Bible Hour*, Sunday 12:15 p.m. - 12:30 p.m.; *Family Altar*, Monday Tuesday Wednesday Thursday Friday 10:30 a.m. - 11:45 a.m.; *Christian Working Woman*, Monday Tuesday Wednesday Thursday Friday Saturday, 2:15 a.m. - 2:20 a.m.; 4:20 a.m. - 4:30 a.m.; 5:50 a.m. - 6:15 a.m.; 1:15 p.m. 2:15 a.m. - 2:20 a.m.; 4:20 a.m. - 4:30 a.m.; 8:45 a.m. - 10:01 a.m. **Wattage:** 1,000. **Ad Rates:** $4-5.20 for 30 seconds; $5-6.25 for 60 seconds. **URL:** http://www.wdfb.com.

13736 ■ WDFB-FM - 88.1
3596 Alum Springs Rd.
Danville, KY 40422-9607
Phone: (859)236-9333
Fax: (859)236-3348
Email: wdfb@searnet.com
Format: Religious. **Networks:** USA Radio; Voice of Christian Youth America. **Owner:** Alum Springs Educational Corp., 3596 Alum Springs Rd., Danville, KY 40422-9607. **Founded:** Nov. 1991. **Operating Hours:** Continuous. **Key Personnel:** Lois Wilson, Contact, lgordon@wdfb.com; Cindy Pike, Contact, cpike@wdfb.com; Mildred Drake, Contact, music@searnet.com; Lois Wilson, Contact, lgordon@wdfb.com. **Local Programs:** *Family Altar*, Monday Tuesday Wednesday Thursday Friday 10:30 a.m.; *Country Preaching*, Monday Tuesday Wednesday Thursday Friday Saturday 12:00 a.m.; 3:15 a.m.; 5:00 a.m.; 6:15 a.m.; 7:15 a.m.; 11:45 a.m.; 5:15 p.m. 12:00 a.m.; 3:15 a.m.; *Living Well*, Monday Tuesday Wednesday Thursday Friday Saturday 2:30 a.m.; 8:35 a.m. 2:30 a.m.; *Keys For Kids*, Monday Tuesday Wednesday Thursday Friday Saturday Sunday 2:40 a.m.; 8:30 a.m.; 3:32 p.m.; 6:45 p.m. 2:40 a.m.; 10:01 a.m.; 4:35 p.m. 1:40 a.m.; *Home School Heartbeat*, Monday Tuesday Wednesday Thursday Friday 3:40 a.m.; 4:10 p.m.; *Key To Confident Living*, Monday Tuesday Wednesday Thursday Friday 4:10 a.m.; 6:40 a.m.; 6:55 p.m.; *Foundational Truths*, Monday Tuesday Wednesday Thursday Friday 9:45 a.m.; *Bible Trivia/ Request Time*, Sunday 3:06 p.m. **Wattage:** 170. **Ad Rates:** Noncommercial. **URL:** http://www.wdfb.com.

13737 ■ WHBN-AM - 1420
2063 Shakertown Rd.
Danville, KY 40422
Phone: (859)236-2711
Fax: (859)236-1461
Email: hometownradio@hometownlive.net
Format: Country; News; Information; Gospel. **Networks:** AP. **Owner:** Hometown Broadcasting Inc., 2063 Shakertown Rd., Danville, KY 40422, Ph: (859)236-2711, Fax: (859)236-1461. **Founded:** 1955. **Operating Hours:** Continuous. **ADI:** Lexington, KY. **Wattage:** 1,000. **Ad Rates:** Combined advertising rates available with WHIR-AM & FM, WRNZ-FM. **URL:** http://www.hometownlive.net.

13738 ■ WHIR-AM - 1230
2063 Shakertown Rd.
Danville, KY 40422
Phone: (859)236-2711
Fax: (859)236-1461
Email: hometownradio@hometownlive.net
Format: News; Sports; Talk. **Owner:** Hometown Broadcasting of Danville, Inc., at above address. **Founded:** Oct. 1947. **Operating Hours:** Continuous. **ADI:** Lexington, KY. **Wattage:** 1,000. **Ad Rates:** Advertising accepted; rates available upon request. WHIR-FM, WRNZ-FM, WHBN-AM. **URL:** http://www.hometownlive.net.

13739 ■ WMGE-FM - 107.1
Burgin Rd.
Danville, KY 40422
Phone: (606)236-2711
Format: Country. **Networks:** CNN Radio. **Founded:** 1969. **Operating Hours:** Continuous. **Key Personnel:** Brian Teater, Program Mgr. **Wattage:** 3,000. **Ad Rates:** Advertising accepted; rates available upon request.

13740 ■ WXKY-FM - 96.3
PO Box 2098
Omaha, NE 68103
Free: 800-525-5683
Format: Contemporary Christian. **Owner:** Educational Media Foundation, 5700 W Oaks Blvd., CA 95765, Free: 800-800434-8400.

DAWSON SPRINGS

Hopkins Co. Hopkins Co. (SW). 95 m W of Bowling Green. Pennyrile Forest State Resort Park. Coal mines. Manufactures plastics, clothing, wood products. Agriculture. Dairy, fruit, corn, tobacco, hay.

13741 ■ The Dawson Springs Progress
Progress Publishing Company Inc.
131 S Main St.
Dawson Springs, KY 42408
Phone: (502)797-3271
Publisher's E-mail: progress@vci.net
Community newspaper. **Freq:** Weekly (Thurs.). **Print Method:** Offset. **Cols./Page:** 6. **Col. Width:** 11 picas. **Col. Depth:** 294 agate lines. **Subscription Rates:** $23 Individuals Hopkins county; $31 Individuals in Kentucky; $37 Out of state. **URL:** http://www.hopkinscounty.us/progresspublishing. **Mailing address:** PO Box 460, Dawson Springs, KY 42408. **Ad Rates:** SAU $3.60; PCI $3. **Remarks:** Accepts advertising. **Circ:** 2400.

13742 ■ Insight Communications
116 S Main St.
Dawson Springs, KY 42408-1714
Phone: (270)797-5061
Key Personnel: John Abbot, CFO, Exec. VP; Michael S. Willner, CEO, V. Ch.; Dinni Jain, COO, President. **Cities Served:** 44 channels.

DRY RIDGE

13743 ■ Grant County News
Grant County News
129 S Main, Ste. B
Hogan House
Dry Ridge, KY 41035-9406
Phone: (859)824-3343
Fax: (859)824-5888
Community newspaper. **Freq:** Weekly (Thurs.). **Print Method:** Offset. **Cols./Page:** 6. **Col. Width:** 1.833 inches. **Col. Depth:** 21.5 inches. **Key Personnel:** Bryan Marshall, Editor; Jamie Baker-Nantz, Publisher; John Seebold, Advertising Representative. **Subscription Rates:** $33.92 Individuals print and online (annual); $19.35 Individuals print and online (semi-annual); $10.60 Individuals print and online (quarterly). **URL:** http://www.grantky.com. **Ad Rates:** BW $1,176.48; 4C $1,496.48; SAU $9.12; PCI $9.12. **Remarks:** Advertising accepted; rates available upon request. **Circ:** (Not Reported).

EDDYVILLE

Lyon Co. Lyon Co. (SW). On Barkley Lake, 150 m SW of Louisville. Resort area. Tourist. Limestone quarries; hardwood timber. Agriculture.

13744 ■ Herald Ledger
Jim Ward
PO Box 747
Eddyville, KY 42038
Phone: (270)388-2269
Fax: (270)388-5540
Publisher's E-mail: news@cadizrecord.com
Community newspaper. **Founded:** 1902. **Freq:** Weekly (Wed.). **Print Method:** Offset. **Cols./Page:** 6. **Col. Width:** 24 nonpareils. **Col. Depth:** 297 agate lines. **Key Personnel:** Rae Wagoner, General Manager; Becky Murphy, Office Manager; Bobbie Foust, Reporter. **USPS:** 202-380. **Subscription Rates:** $34 Individuals inside Lyon County; $40 Individuals outside Lyon County; $42 Individuals outside Kentucky. **URL:** http://www.heraldledger.com. **Ad Rates:** GLR $2.90; BW $361; 4C $571; SAU $2.80. **Remarks:** Advertising accepted; rates available upon request. **Circ:** ‡3000.

EDMONTON

Metcalfe Co. Metcalfe (SC). 50 m W of Bowling Green. Manufactures men's and boy's work clothing, plastics, mulch. Agriculture. Corn, tobacco, dairying.

13745 ■ WKNK-FM - 99.1
PO Box 457
Glasgow, KY 42142-0457
Phone: (502)432-7600
Fax: (502)432-7601
Format: Country. **Networks:** KyNet. **Owner:** Metcalfe Communications, Inc, at above address. **Founded:** 1990. **Operating Hours:** Continuous. **ADI:** Nashville (Cookeville), TN. **Key Personnel:** Judy Crabtree, Gen. Mgr.; Pam Prewitt, Operations Mgr. **Wattage:** 3,000. **Ad Rates:** $4-8 for 30 seconds; $5-9 for 60 seconds. $4-$8 for 30 seconds; $5-$9 for 60 seconds. Combined advertising rates available with WHHT-FM.

ELIZABETHTOWN

Hardin Co. Hardin Co. (WC). 48 m S of Louisville. Manufacturers men's slacks, cheese, metal products, ready mix concrete, machinery, package chemicals, fertilizer, fuses, tools, dies, magnets, sealants, adhesives, steel fabrication, sockets, nut runners, telephone cable, beverages, plastics. Limestone quarries. Diversified farming. Corn, wheat, tobacco.

13746 ■ Hardin County Independent
Hardin County Independent
PO Box 1117
Elizabethtown, KY 42702
Phone: (270)737-5585

Circulation: ★ = AAM; △ or • = BPA; ♦ = CAC; ❑ = VAC; ⊕ = PO Statement; ‡ = Publisher's Report; Boldface figures = sworn; Light figures = estimated.

Fax: (270)737-6634
Newspaper with a Republican orientation. **Freq:** Weekly (Thurs.). **Print Method:** Offset. **Trim Size:** 12 1/2 x 22 3/4. **Cols./Page:** 6. **Col. Width:** 1 7/8 inches. **Col. Depth:** 21 1/4 inches. **Key Personnel:** Gerald Lush, Editor. **USPS:** 235-140. **Ad Rates:** GLR $.30; BW $318.75; SAU $3.80; PCI $3. **Remarks:** Accepts advertising. **Circ:** Paid ⊕**4002**.

13747 ■ The News-Enterprise
Landmark Community Newspapers L.L.C.
408 W Dixie Ave.
Elizabethtown, KY 42701
Phone: (270)769-1200
Publisher's E-mail: marketing@lcni.com
Community newspaper. **Freq:** 5/week. **Subscription Rates:** $164.67 Individuals online only; $267.59 Individuals print and online. **URL:** http://www.newsenterpriseonline.com/. **Remarks:** Accepts advertising. **Circ:** Mon.-Fri. ★**16539**, Sun. ★**20122**.

13748 ■ WAKY-FM - 103.5
PO Box 2087
Elizabethtown, KY 42702
Free: 888-766-1035
Email: rbell@waky1035.com
Format: Oldies. **Owner:** W & B Broadcasting. **Key Personnel:** Rene Bell, Contact, rbell@waky1035.com. **URL:** http://www.waky1035.com.

13749 ■ WASE-FM - 103.5
PO Box 2087
Elizabethtown, KY 42702
Phone: (270)982-9259
Free: 888-766-1035
Format: Oldies; Full Service. **Networks:** ABC. **Owner:** J. Michael Badwin/Bill Walters/Rene Bell, at above address. **Founded:** 1967. **Formerly**: WSAC-FM. **Operating Hours**: Continuous;100% local. **ADI**: Louisville, KY. **Key Personnel:** Rene Bell, Gen. Mgr., rbell@wase.org; Karen Allenn, Dir. of Programs, kallenn@bigcat1055.com. **Wattage**: 3,500 ERP. **Ad Rates:** $26.50-31 for 60 seconds. **URL:** http://www.waky1035.com.

13750 ■ WIEL-AM - 1400
PO Box 1505
Glasgow, KY 42142
Phone: (270)659-2002
Fax: (270)769-6349
Format: Sports. **Networks:** ESPN Radio. **Owner:** Elizabethtown Cbc Inc., at above address. **Founded:** 1950. **Operating Hours**: Continuous; 75% network, 25% local. **ADI**: Louisville, KY. **Wattage**: 1,000. **Ad Rates:** $10 for 30 seconds; $11 for 60 seconds. Combined advertising rates available with WRZI, WKMO, WTHX-FM.

13751 ■ WKZT-TV - 23
Elizabethtown, KY
Founded: 1968. **Wattage**: 61,000 ERP. **Ad Rates:** Advertising accepted; rates available upon request. **URL:** http://www.ket.org.

13752 ■ WLVK-FM - 105.5
519 N Miles St.
Elizabethtown, KY 42701
Phone: (270)766-1035
Fax: (270)769-1052
Format: Country. **Operating Hours**: Continuous. **Wattage**: 6,000. **Ad Rates:** Advertising accepted; rates available upon request. **URL:** http://www.bigcat1055.com.

13753 ■ WQXE-FM - 98.3
233 W Dixie Ave.
Elizabethtown, KY 42701
Phone: (502)737-8000
Fax: (502)737-7229
Free: 800-905-0983
Email: quicksie@wqxe.com
Format: Adult Contemporary. **Networks:** CNN Radio. **Owner:** Hardin Co. Broadcasting Inc., at above address. **Founded:** 1969. **Operating Hours**: Continuous. **ADI**: Louisville, KY. **Key Personnel:** Suzanne Ahmad, Contact. **Wattage**: 25,000. **Ad Rates:** $22-33 for 30 seconds; $24-35 for 60 seconds. Combined advertising rates available with WGGC-FM. **URL:** http://www.quicksie983.com.

13754 ■ W39CJ - 39
PO Box A
Santa Ana, CA 92711
Phone: (714)832-2950
Free: 888-731-1000
Email: comments@tbn.org
Owner: Trinity Broadcasting Network Inc., PO Box A, Santa Ana, CA 92711, Ph: (714)832-2950, Free: 888-731-1000. **URL:** http://www.tbn.org.

13755 ■ WTHX-FM - 107.3
611 W Poplar St., C-2
Elizabethtown, KY 42701
Phone: (270)763-0800

13756 ■ WTUV-AM - 103.5
PO Box 2087
Elizabethtown, KY 42702
Email: info@lacalienteradio.com
Format: New Age. **URL:** http://www.waky1035.com.

ELKTON

Todd Co. Todd Co. (SW) 20 m E of Hopkinsville. Manufactures men's clothing, die casting, refrigerator doors, concrete products. Meat product plant. Agriculture. Tobacco, grain, fruit. Beef cattle.

13757 ■ Todd County Standard
Todd County Standard
PO Box 308
Elkton, KY 42220
Phone: (270)265-2439
Fax: (270)265-2571
Community newspaper. **Freq:** Weekly (Wed.). **Print Method:** Offset. **Cols./Page:** 6. **Col. Width:** 11 picas. **Col. Depth:** 294 agate lines. **Key Personnel:** Ryan Craig, Editor. **USPS:** 632-580. **Subscription Rates:** $16 Individuals. **Ad Rates:** GLR $.27; BW $516; 4C $737; SAU $4; PCI $4.25. **Remarks:** Color advertising not accepted. **Circ:** 2223.

13758 ■ WEKT-AM
PO Box 577
Elkton, KY 42220
Fax: (502)265-5637
Format: News; Talk; Southern Gospel; Country. **Networks:** USA Radio. **Founded:** 1989. **Formerly**: WOAM-AM; WSRG-AM. **Key Personnel:** Marshall E. Sidebottom, Contact. **Wattage**: 500 Day; 018 Night. **Ad Rates:** $3.25-4 for 30 seconds; $5.25-6 for 60 seconds.

EMINENCE

Henry Co. Henry Co. (NC). 10 m S of New Castle.

13759 ■ Henry County Local & Shopper
Landmark Community Newspapers L.L.C.
18 S Penn Ave.
Eminence, KY 40019
Phone: (502)845-2858
Fax: (502)845-2921
Publication E-mail: editor@hclocal.com
Community newspaper. **Freq:** Weekly. **Print Method:** Web Offset. **Cols./Page:** 6. **Col. Width:** 2 inches. **Col. Depth:** 21 1/2 inches. **Key Personnel:** Tawnja Morris, Manager, Circulation; Phyllis Banta, Office Manager; Jonna Spelbring Priester, Editor, Publisher. **URL:** http://www.hclocal.com. **Remarks:** Accepts advertising. **Circ:** (Not Reported).

FALMOUTH

Pendleton Co. Pendleton Co. (N). On Licking River, 34 m S of Newport. Manufactures auto engines, feed. Dairy, poultry, grain farms. Hay, corn, tobacco.

The Falmouth Outlook - See Pendleton

13760 ■ WIOK-FM - 107.5
PO Box 50
Falmouth, KY 41040
Phone: (859)472-1075
Fax: (859)472-2875
Free: 800-295-1075
Owner: Hammond Broadcasting Inc., PO Box 50, Falmouth, KY 41040. **Founded:** 1991. **Wattage**: 1,350. **Ad Rates:** Noncommercial.

FLEMINGSBURG

Fleming Co. Fleming Co. (NE). 54 m NE of Lexington. Land of covered bridges. Manufactures shoes, kitchen utensils, mobile homes, auto chrome. Agriculture. Cattle, tobacco, corn, chicken hatcheries.

13761 ■ The Fleming Gazette
The Fleming Gazette
151 E Water St.
Flemingsburg, KY 41041
Phone: (606)845-9211
Community newspaper. **Freq:** Weekly (Thurs.). **Print Method:** Offset. **Cols./Page:** 6. **Col. Width:** 26 nonpareils. **Col. Depth:** 280 agate lines. **Key Personnel:** Guy M. Townsend, Editor; Carolyn Schwartz, Editor. **URL:** http://flemingsburggazette.com. **Mailing address:** PO Box 32, Flemingsburg, KY 41041. **Ad Rates:** GLR $3.75; BW $354.75; 4C $489.75; SAU $3.50. **Remarks:** Accepts advertising. **Circ:** 3600.

13762 ■ WFLE-AM
Fleming County Industrial Park
RR 3, No.1 Radio Dr.
Flemingsburg, KY 41041
Phone: (606)849-4433
Fax: (606)845-9353
Format: Country. **Networks:** ABC; KyNet; Motor Sports Racing. **Founded:** 1985. **Wattage**: 500 Day. **Ad Rates:** $2.50 for 30 seconds; $4.50 for 60 seconds.

WFLE-FM - See Lexington

FORT CAMPBELL

13763 ■ Ft. Campbell Courier
Kentucky New Era
Public Affairs Office
2334 19th St.
Fort Campbell, KY 42223
Publisher's E-mail: lnoeth@kentuckynewera.com
Newspaper for the personnel of Ft. Campbell 101st Airborne Division (Air Assault) Military Base. **Freq:** Weekly (Thurs.). **Print Method:** Offset. **Trim Size:** 13 3/4 x 22 3/4. **Cols./Page:** 6. **Col. Width:** 12.2 picas. **Col. Depth:** 301 agate lines. **Key Personnel:** Dave Campbell, Writer; Michele Vowell, Managing Editor; Kimberly Warren, Editor-in-Chief. **Subscription Rates:** $40 Individuals. **URL:** http://fortcampbellcourier.com/site/about/. **Remarks:** Accepts advertising. **Circ:** 23000.

FRANKFORT

Franklin Co. Franklin Co. (NC). The State Capital. On Kentucky River, 26 m W of Lexington. Kentucky State University. Manufactures candy, beef items used in restaurants, whiskey, air brake components, underwear, parts for automotive appliances, bimetallic temperature control devices, thermostats, variety of pumps, valves and transformers, auto parts. Tobacco, dairy, stock farms. Beef, feed.

13764 ■ Driven
Mothers Against Drunk Driving - Kentucky State
1030 Burlington Ln., No. 2
Frankfort, KY 40601
Phone: (502)871-4210
Free: 877-926-5608
Publisher's E-mail: ky.state@madd.org
Magazine containing information on activities, articles on public policy, youth and victim issues, and profiles of MADD volunteers. **Freq:** Semiannual. **URL:** http://www.madd.org. **Circ:** (Not Reported).

13765 ■ KEA News
Kentucky Education Association
401 Capital Ave.
Frankfort, KY 40601
Phone: (502)875-2889
Fax: (502)227-9002
Free: 800-231-4532
Newspaper (tabloid) for members of the Kentucky Education Association. **Freq:** Monthly (Sept.-June.). **Print Method:** Offset. **Trim Size:** 11 3/8 x 15. **Cols./Page:** 4. **Col. Width:** 2 5/16 inches. **Col. Depth:** 14 inches. **Key Personnel:** Mary Ann Blankenship, Executive Director; Charles Main, Editor. **ISSN:** 0165--3959 (print). **URL:** http://www.kea.org; http://www.kea.org/members-publications-kea-news. **Ad Rates:** BW $728; PCI $26.50. **Remarks:** Accepts advertising. **Circ:** Free 39000.

13766 ■ Kentucky Afield
Kentucky Afield Magazine
Ste. 1 Sportman's Ln.
Frankfort, KY 40601
Free: 800-858-1549
Publication E-mail: ky.afield@mail.state.ky.us
Magazine focusing on wildlife and natural resources conservation, hunting, fishing, boating outdoor

recreation. **Freq:** Quarterly. **Print Method:** Web offset. **Trim Size:** 8 1/2 x 11. **Cols./Page:** 3 and 2. **Col. Width:** 26 and 40 nonpareils. **Col. Depth:** 154 agate lines. **Key Personnel:** Dave Baker, Editor, Writer. **ISSN:** 1059--9177 (print). **Subscription Rates:** $10 Individuals; $18 Two years. **URL:** http://fw.ky.gov/Kentucky-Afield/Pages/default.aspx. **Formerly:** Kentucky Afield, The Magazine. **Remarks:** Advertising not accepted. **Circ:** Paid ‡40000, Controlled ‡4000.

13767 ■ Kentucky Ancestors
Kentucky Historical Society
100 W Broadway
Frankfort, KY 40601
Phone: (502)564-1792
Fax: (502)564-4701
Publisher's E-mail: refdesk@ky.gov
Journal featuring Kentucky family history. **Freq:** Quarterly. **Print Method:** Offset. **Trim Size:** 8 x 11 1/2. **Key Personnel:** Don Rightmyer, Editor. **ISSN:** 0023--0103 (print). **URL:** http://history.ky.gov. **Remarks:** Advertising not accepted. **Circ:** (Not Reported).

13768 ■ Kentucky Bench & Bar Magazine
Kentucky Bar Association
514 W Main St.
Frankfort, KY 40601-1812
Phone: (502)564-3795
Fax: (502)564-3225
Kentucky law magazine. **Freq:** Bimonthly. **Print Method:** Offset. **Trim Size:** 8 1/2 x 11. **Cols./Page:** 3 and 2. **Col. Width:** 13 and 20 picas. **Col. Depth:** 60 picas. **Key Personnel:** Shannon H. Roberts, Manager, Advertising. **ISSN:** 1521--6497 (print). **Subscription Rates:** Included in membership. **URL:** http://www.kybar.org/?BB. **Formerly:** Bench & Bar. **Ad Rates:** BW $1,050. **Remarks:** Advertising accepted; rates available upon request. **Circ:** ‡16600.

13769 ■ Kentucky Engineer: The Official Publication of the Kentucky Society of Professional Engineers
Kentucky Society of Professional Engineers
Kentucky Engineering Ctr.
160 Democrat Dr.
Frankfort, KY 40601
Phone: (502)695-5680
Fax: (502)695-0738
Free: 800-455-5573
Publisher's E-mail: kspe@kyengcenter.org
General information for Kentucky engineers. **Freq:** Quarterly. **Print Method:** 2 color press. **Trim Size:** 8 1/2 x 11. **Cols./Page:** 3. **Col. Width:** 13.5 picas. **Col. Depth:** 57 picas. **URL:** http://kyengcenter.org; http://kyengcenter.org/?page=KYEngineerMagazine. **Formerly:** Professional Engineer in Kentucky. **Ad Rates:** BW $460; 4C $1,010. **Remarks:** Accepts advertising. **Circ:** Paid ⊕**5593**.

13770 ■ The Kentucky Pharmacist
Kentucky Pharmacists Association
1228 US Highway 127 S
Frankfort, KY 40601
Phone: (502)227-2303
Fax: (502)227-2258
Publisher's E-mail: info@kphanet.org
Magazine on community and institutional pharmacy news. **Freq:** Monthly. **Print Method:** Offset. **Cols./Page:** 2 and 3. **Col. Width:** 54 and 36 nonpareils. **Col. Depth:** 140 agate lines. **Subscription Rates:** $35 Individuals. **URL:** http://www.kphanet.org/?page=30. **Ad Rates:** BW $370; 4C $700. **Remarks:** Accepts advertising. **Circ:** Paid ‡1800, Non-paid ‡100.

13771 ■ The Kentucky Press
Kentucky Press Association
101 Consumer Ln.
Frankfort, KY 40601
Phone: (502)223-8821
Fax: (502)875-2624
Magazine focusing on the newspaper industry. **Freq:** Monthly. **Print Method:** Offset. **Cols./Page:** 4. **Col. Width:** 14 picas. **Col. Depth:** 182 agate lines. **Key Personnel:** John Whitlock, News Director. **Subscription Rates:** $8 Individuals. **URL:** http://www.kypressonline.com/blog; http://www.kypressonline.com. **Ad Rates:** GLR $6; BW $300; SAU $6. **Remarks:** Accepts advertising. **Circ:** ‡750.

13772 ■ MADDvocate
Mothers Against Drunk Driving - Kentucky State
1030 Burlington Ln., No. 2
Frankfort, KY 40601
Phone: (502)871-4210
Free: 877-926-5608
Magazine featuring information about victims and survivors of drunk driving crashes and those who work with crash victims. **Freq:** Semiannual. **URL:** http://www.madd.org/media-center/publications/maddvocate.html. **Remarks:** Advertising not accepted. **Circ:** (Not Reported).

13773 ■ Register of Kentucky Historical Society
Kentucky Historical Society
100 W Broadway
Frankfort, KY 40601
Phone: (502)564-1792
Fax: (502)564-4701
Publisher's E-mail: refdesk@ky.gov
Historical journal. **Freq:** Quarterly. **Print Method:** Offset. **Trim Size:** 6 x 9. **Cols./Page:** 1. **Col. Width:** 30 nonpareils. **Col. Depth:** 102 agate lines. **Key Personnel:** James Russell Harris, Associate Editor; Elizabeth J. Van Allen, Associate Editor; Nelson L. Dawson, Editor. **ISSN:** 0023--0243 (print). **Subscription Rates:** $40 Individuals; $60 Institutions; $12 Single issue. **URL:** http://history.ky.gov/the-register-of-the-kentucky-historical-society. **Remarks:** Advertising not accepted. **Circ:** Paid ‡2700.

13774 ■ The SAR Magazine
National Society, Sons of the American Revolution
c/o Stephen Vest, Ed.
106-C St. James Ct.
Frankfort, KY 40601
Phone: (502)227-0053
Fax: (502)227-5009
Magazine reporting on Society activities at the national, state, and local levels. Includes sources for genealogical research. **Founded:** 1908. **Freq:** Quarterly. **Print Method:** Offset. **Trim Size:** 8 1/2 x 11. **Cols./Page:** 3. **Col. Width:** 7 inches. **Col. Depth:** 10 inches. **Key Personnel:** Stephen Vest, Editor; Joe E. Harris, Contact. **ISSN:** 0161-0511 (print). **Subscription Rates:** $10 U.S. and Canada non-members; $25 Other countries; Included in membership. **URL:** http://www.sar.org/SAR-Magazine. **Ad Rates:** BW $1,750; 4C $1,800; PCI $90. **Remarks:** Accepts advertising. **Circ:** Paid 30,000.

13775 ■ State Journal
Frankfort Publishing Co.
1216 Wilkinson Blvd.
Frankfort, KY 40601
Phone: (502)227-4556
Fax: (502)227-2831
General newspaper. **Freq:** Daily and Sun. (eve.). **Print Method:** Offset. **Cols./Page:** 6. **Col. Width:** 25 nonpareils. **Col. Depth:** 301 agate lines. **Key Personnel:** Ann Dix Maenza, Publisher; Lloyd Lynch, Director, Advertising. **Subscription Rates:** $132 Individuals print EZ; $280 By mail print; $99.95 Individuals online. **URL:** http://www.state-journal.com. **Ad Rates:** SAU $5.38. **Remarks:** Accepts advertising. **Circ:** 8,102, 9,607.

13776 ■ Workforce Professional
International Association of Workforce Professionals
1801 Louisville Rd.
Frankfort, KY 40601
Phone: (502)223-4459
Free: 888-898-9960
Publisher's E-mail: iawp@iawponline.org
Magazine about workforce training issues and employment. **Founded:** Mar. 1998. **Freq:** Bimonthly. **Key Personnel:** Wanda Watts, Communications Specialist. **ISSN:** 1542-1033 (print). **Subscription Rates:** Free U.S. members. **Formerly:** Workforce; IAPES News; Workforce Journal. **Remarks:** Accepts advertising. **Circ:** Paid ‡16000.

13777 ■ Frankfort Plant Board Cable Service
317 W 2nd St.
Frankfort, KY 40601-2645
Phone: (502)352-4372
Free: 888-312-4372
Founded: 1943. **Cities Served:** 93 channels. **URL:** http://fewpb.com.

13778 ■ WKED-FM - 103.7
115 W Main St.
Frankfort, KY 40601
Phone: (502)875-1130
Fax: (502)875-1225
Format: Adult Contemporary. **Networks:** CNN Radio; Westwood One Radio. **Founded:** 1991. **Operating Hours:** Continuous. **ADI:** Lexington, KY. **Wattage:** 2,500. **Ad Rates:** Advertising accepted; rates available upon request. Combined advertising rates available with WKED-AM, WFKY-AM, WKYW-FM.

13779 ■ WKYW-FM - 104.9
120 Mero St.
Frankfort, KY 40602
Phone: (502)223-8281
Fax: (502)223-0723
Format: Adult Contemporary. **Owner:** Radio Enterprises, at above address. **Founded:** 1967. **Operating Hours:** 5:30 a.m.-midnight. **Key Personnel:** Gary R. White, Gen. Mgr. **Wattage:** 3,000 ERP. **Mailing address:** PO Box 757, Frankfort, KY 40602.

FRANKLIN

Simpson Co. Simpson Co. (SW). 21 m S of Bowling Green. Manufactures catalogs, corrugated boxes, aerosol & plastic containers, automotive parts, lumber, feed, rubber bands, tubing, adhesive tape. Hardwood timber. Agriculture. Tobacco, soybeans, grain, livestock.

13780 ■ WFKN-AM - 1220
103 N High St.
Franklin, KY 42134
Phone: (270)586-4481
Format: Full Service; Country. **Networks:** KyNet; ABC. **Founded:** 1954. **Operating Hours:** Continuous. **Key Personnel:** Charlie Portmann, Editor, cportmann@franklinfavorite.com. **Wattage:** 250. **Ad Rates:** $4-6.90 for 15 seconds; $4.50-8.50 for 30 seconds; $6-11.30 for 60 seconds. **URL:** http://www.franklinfavorite.com.

GEORGETOWN

Scott Co. Scott Co. (NC). 12 m N of Lexington. Georgetown College (Bapt). Seed cleaning, precision tool, electric wire, auto seat spring factories. Foreign motor industry. Agriculture. Tobacco, corn, wheat, cattle, horses.

13781 ■ The Georgetonian: Georgetown College Student Newspaper
Georgetown College
400 E College St.
Georgetown, KY 40324
Phone: (502)863-8000
Free: 800-788-9985
Publication E-mail: georgetonian@georgetowncollege.edu
Collegiate newspaper. **Freq:** Weekly during the academic year for Georgetown College in Georgetown. **Print Method:** Offset. **Cols./Page:** 6. **Col. Width:** 18 nonpareils. **Col. Depth:** 224 agate lines. **Key Personnel:** Hannah Krieger, Editor-in-Chief. **URL:** http://www.georgetowncollege.edu/georgetonian. **Ad Rates:** BW $150; PCI $1.75. **Remarks:** Accepts advertising. **Circ:** Free ‡2000.

13782 ■ The Georgetown-News Graphic
Georgetown Newspapers Inc.
1481 Cherry Blossom Way
Georgetown, KY 40324
Newspaper. **Freq:** Sunday, Tuesday, Wednesday, Thursday, and Friday. **Print Method:** Offset. **Trim Size:** 10.167 x 11.447. **Cols./Page:** 6. **Col. Width:** 2 1/8 inches. **Col. Depth:** 21 1/2 inches. **Key Personnel:** Mike Scogin, President, Publisher; Brad Toy, Manager, Advertising; Peter Mathews, Editor. **ISSN:** 0886--5965 (print). **Subscription Rates:** $70 Individuals 1 year - print or online; $42.50 Individuals 6 months - print or online; $30 Individuals 3 months - print or online; $90 Out of country 1 year - print or online; $60 Out of country 6 months - print or online; $40 Out of country 3 months - print or online. **URL:** http://www.news-graphic.com. **Formerly:** The Georgetown Graphic; The Georgetown News and Times. **Ad Rates:** 4C $175; PCI $9.15. **Remarks:** Accepts advertising. **Circ:** 4500.

Circulation: ★ = AAM; △ or • = BPA; ♦ = CAC; ❑ = VAC; ⊕ = PO Statement; ‡ = Publisher's Report; Boldface figures = sworn; Light figures = estimated.

GLASGOW

Barren Co. Barren Co. (SWC). 72 m SE of Louisville. Manufactures bearings, truck mirrors, axles, concrete products, capacitor, brush handles, computer cable assemblys, screws, ignition parts, mattresses, ink, overalls, garments. Hardwood timber. Agriculture. Tobacco, corn, poultry & dairy products.

13783 ■ Glasgow Daily Times
Community Newspaper Holdings Inc.
PO Box 1179
Glasgow, KY 42142
Phone: (270)678-5171
Fax: (270)678-5052
General newspaper. **Founded:** 1865. **Freq:** Daily. **Print Method:** Letterpress and Offset. **Cols./Page:** 6. **Col. Width:** 256 nonpareils. **Col. Depth:** 301 agate lines. **Key Personnel:** Daniel Pike; Keith Ponder, Publisher, Director, Advertising. **Subscription Rates:** $9.99 Individuals monthly (print); $8.99 Individuals monthly (online). **URL:** http://www.glasgowdailytimes.com. **Remarks:** Accepts classified advertising. **Circ:** Mon.-Fri. ★8627, Sun. ★9339.

13784 ■ WAVJ-FM - 104.9
PO Box 1505
Glasgow, KY 42142
Fax: (502)365-2073
Format: Soft Rock. **Networks:** Jones Satellite; AP. **Founded:** 1950. **Operating Hours:** 24 hrs.; 75% local, 25% area. **ADI:** Paducah,KY-Cape Girardeau,MO-Marion,IL. **Key Personnel:** David Glass, Mgr. **Wattage:** 6,000. **Ad Rates:** $6.75-7.50 per unit.

13785 ■ WCDS-AM
PO Box 1505
Glasgow, KY 42142
Phone: (502)651-3132
Fax: (502)651-8472
Format: News; Contemporary Country. **Networks:** USA Radio. **Owner:** Ward Communications Corp., 2502 Scottsville Rd., Glasgow, KY 42141, Ph: (502)651-5105. **Founded:** 1962. **Key Personnel:** Mark Ward, Gen. Mgr.; Ann Morgan, Sales Mgr. **Wattage:** 750. **Ad Rates:** $6 for 30 seconds; $8 for 60 seconds.

13786 ■ WCLU-AM
PO Box 1628
Glasgow, KY 42142
Format: News; Sports. **Founded:** Sept. 12, 2006. **Key Personnel:** Henry Royse, Gen. Mgr., henryroyse@wcluradio.com; Joe Myers, Sports Dir., News Dir., joemyers@wcluradio.com; Nellie Pickett, Traffic Mgr., nelliepickett@wcluradio.com. **Wattage:** 1,000. **Ad Rates:** Advertising accepted; rates available upon request.

13787 ■ WCLU-FM - 102.3
PO Box 1628
Glasgow, KY 42142
Phone: (270)651-9149
Fax: (270)651-9222
Format: Adult Contemporary. **Key Personnel:** Henry Royse, President, CEO; Nellie Pickett, Dir. of Traffic. **URL:** http://wcluradio.com.

13788 ■ WFKY-FM - 104.9
PO Box 1505
Glasgow, KY 42142
Phone: (502)875-1130
Fax: (502)875-1225
Format: Country. **Owner:** Forever Communication Inc, at above address, Bowling Green, KY 42104. **Operating Hours:** Continuous. **Key Personnel:** Tonya Moore, Sales Mgr., tonya@forevercomm.com. **Wattage:** 3,400 ERP. **Ad Rates:** Advertising accepted; rates available upon request.

WIEL-AM - See Elizabethtown

WKNK-FM - See Edmonton

13789 ■ WPTQ-FM - 103.7
113 W Public Sq., Ste. 400
Glasgow, KY 42141
Phone: (270)651-6060
Fax: (270)651-7666
Format: Classic Rock. **Owner:** Commonwealth Broadcasting Corp., at above address. **Operating Hours:** Continuous. **Key Personnel:** Derron Steenbergen, Gen. Mgr. **Ad Rates:** Advertising accepted; rates available upon request. **URL:** http://www.1037thepoint.net.

13790 ■ WRZI-FM - 101.5
PO Box 1505
Glasgow, KY 42142
Phone: (270)659-2002
Fax: (270)769-6349
Format: Classic Rock. **Owner:** Commonwealth Broadcasting Corp., at above address. **Operating Hours:** Continuous. **Wattage:** 6,000. **Ad Rates:** Advertising accepted; rates available upon request.

13791 ■ WSGP-FM - 88.3
PO Box 1423
Somerset, KY 42502
Free: 800-408-8888
Format: Gospel. **URL:** http://www.kingofkingsradio.com.

WTCO-AM - See Campbellsville, KY

13792 ■ W217BA-FM - 91.3
PO Box 391
Twin Falls, ID 83303
Fax: (208)736-1958
Free: 800-357-4226
Format: Religious; Contemporary Christian. **Owner:** CSN International, PO Box 391, Twin Falls, ID 83303, Ph: (208)736-1958, Fax: (208)736-1958, Free: 800-357-4226. **URL:** http://www.csnradio.com.

13793 ■ WWWQ-FM - 105.3
PO Box 158
Glasgow, KY 42142-0158
Phone: (502)651-8375
Fax: (502)651-8472
Format: Contemporary Hit Radio (CHR). **Networks:** USA Radio. **Owner:** Ward Communications Corp., 2502 Scottsville Rd., Glasgow, KY 42141, Ph: (502)651-5105. **Founded:** 1972. **Formerly:** WOVO-FM. **Operating Hours:** Continuous; 5% network, 95% local. **ADI:** Nashville (Cookeville), TN. **Key Personnel:** Mark Ward, Contact; Ann Morgan, Sales Mgr; Mark Ward, Contact. **Wattage:** 25,000. **Ad Rates:** $10 for 30 seconds; $12 for 60 seconds.

GRAYSON

Carter Co. Carter Co. (NE), 15 m SW of Ashland. Residential.

13794 ■ Grayson Journal Enquirer
Community Newspaper Holdings Inc.
211 S Carol Malone Blvd.
Grayson, KY 41143
Phone: (606)474-5101
Free: 800-247-6142
Newspaper serving Carter, Lawrence, Greenup, Elliot and Lewis counties, Kentucky. **Freq:** Weekly (Wed.). **Key Personnel:** Keith Kappes, Publisher; Leeann Akers, Editor; Dan Duncan, Director, Advertising. **Subscription Rates:** $1.99 Individuals /month - print and online; $1.49 Individuals /month - online only. **URL:** http://www.journal-times.com. **Remarks:** Accepts advertising. **Circ:** Paid ‡5600.

13795 ■ WGOH-AM - 1370
150 Radio Tower Dr.
Grayson, KY 41143
Phone: (606)474-5144
Fax: (606)474-7777
Free: 800-374-5888
Email: mail@wgohwugo.com
Format: Country. **Simulcasts:** WGOH-FM 102.3. **Networks:** CBS. **Owner:** Carter County Broadcasting, Co., at above address. **Founded:** 1959. **Operating Hours:** Continuous. **Key Personnel:** Jeff Roe, Contact; Bill Craig, Contact; Francis Nash, Gen. Mgr.; Jim Phillips, Contact; Jeff Roe, Contact; Bill Craig, Contact. **Wattage:** 5,000 Day; 021 Night. **Ad Rates:** $2.80-4.50 for 15 seconds; $3.80-5.50 for 30 seconds; $4.80-6.50 for 60 seconds. **Mailing address:** PO Box 487, Grayson, KY 41143. **URL:** http://wgohwugo.com.

13796 ■ WUGO-FM - 102.3
150 Radio Tower Dr.
Grayson, KY 41143
Phone: (606)474-5144
Fax: (606)474-7777
Email: mail@wgohwugo.com
Format: Oldies; Soft Rock. **Networks:** CBS. **Owner:** Carter County Broadcasting Co., Inc., at above address, Grayson, KY. **Founded:** 1967. **Operating Hours:** Continuous. **Key Personnel:** Francis Nash, Gen. Mgr.; Jim Phillips, News Dir.; Jeff Roe, Traffic Mgr., Operations Mgr. **Wattage:** 4,800. **Ad Rates:** Noncommercial. **Mailing address:** PO Box 487, Grayson, KY 41143. **URL:** http://www.wgohwugo.com.

GREENSBURG

Green Co. Green Co. (SC). On Green River, 70 m S of Louisville. Cedar timber; sawmills; wood components, stave, wire and cable, rattan furniture, work clothing, novelties factories; tobacco warehouse; gas chemical stripping plant. Church steeples. Tobacco, grain farms.

13797 ■ Record-Herald
Record-Herald
102 W Court St.
Greensburg, KY 42743
Publisher's E-mail: news@record-herald.com
Newspaper. **Founded:** 1895. **Freq:** Weekly (Wed.). **Print Method:** Offset. **Cols./Page:** 6. **Col. Width:** 24 nonpareils. **Col. Depth:** 210 agate lines. **Key Personnel:** Tom Mills, Contact; Walt Gorin, Publisher. **Subscription Rates:** $20 Individuals Green and surrounding counties (print and online); $38 Two years Green and surrounding counties (print and online); $34 Individuals Outside Green and Adjoining Counties (print and online). **URL:** http://www.record-herald.com/33076/2088/1/this-weeks-issue. **Ad Rates:** BW $497.94; SAU $3.86. **Remarks:** Accepts advertising. **Circ:** Paid 4394.

GREENUP

Greenup Co. Greenup Co. (NE). On Ohio River, 14 m W of Ashland. Steel plant; sawmills. Truck, grain farms.

13798 ■ The Greenup News
The Morehead News
PO Box 724
Greenup, KY 41144
Phone: (606)473-9851
Fax: (606)473-7591
Newspaper with a democratic orientation. **Freq:** Weekly (Thurs.). **Print Method:** Offset. **Cols./Page:** 6. **Col. Width:** 12 picas. **Col. Depth:** 21 1/2 inches. **Subscription Rates:** $35 By mail Rowan and surrounding counties; $48 By mail In-State (Kentucky) ; $51 Out of state. **URL:** http://www.themoreheadnews.com. **Ad Rates:** SAU $3.66; PCI $2.87. **Remarks:** Accepts advertising. **Circ:** ‡3768.

13799 ■ WNXT-AM - 1260
PO Box 685
Greenup, KY 41144
Phone: (740)353-1161
Fax: (740)353-3191
Email: wnxtradio@yahoo.com
Format: News; Information; Sports. **Networks:** ABC. **Owner:** Hometown Broadcasting of Portsmouth Inc., at above address. **Founded:** 1951. **Operating Hours:** Continuous; 10% network, 90% local. **Key Personnel:** Rick Mayne, Gen. Mgr.; Steve Hayes, Promotions Dir. **Wattage:** 5,000. **Ad Rates:** Advertising accepted; rates available upon request.

GREENVILLE

Muhlenberg Co. Muhlenberg Co.

13800 ■ WKYA-FM
464 State Route 189 S
Greenville, KY 42345
Phone: (270)338-6655
Fax: (270)338-7388
Format: Country.

HARDIN

13801 ■ Heartland Ministries Radio
219 College St.
Hardin, KY 42048
Phone: (270)437-4095
Free: 800-467-4095
Format: Contemporary Christian; Gospel. **Mailing address:** PO Box 281, Hardin, KY 42048. **URL:** http://www.heartlandministriesradio.com.

13802 ■ WAAJ-FM - 89.7
219 College St.
Hardin, KY 42048
Phone: (270)437-4095
Fax: (270)437-4098
Free: 800-467-4095
Email: info@hmiradio.com

Format: Bluegrass. **Owner:** Heartland Ministries, Inc., at above address. **Founded:** 2006. **Ad Rates:** Noncommercial. **Mailing address:** PO Box 281, Hardin, KY 42048. **URL:** http://www.heartlandministriesradio.com.

13803 ■ WTRT-FM - 88.1
219 College St.
Hardin, KY 42048
Phone: (270)437-4095
Fax: (270)437-4098
Free: 800-467-4095
Email: info@hmiradio.com
Format: Religious; Contemporary Christian. **Owner:** Heartland Ministries Radio, 219 College St., Hardin, KY 42048, Ph: (270)437-4095, Free: 800-467-4095. **Founded:** June 19, 1989. **Key Personnel:** Eddie Sheridan, Gen. Mgr., eddie.sheridan@hmiradio.com. **Wattage:** 600. **Mailing address:** PO Box 281, Hardin, KY 42048. **URL:** http://www.heartlandministriesradio.com.

13804 ■ WVHM-FM - 90.5
PO Box 281
Hardin, KY 42048
Phone: (270)437-4095
Fax: (270)437-4098
Free: 800-467-4095
Email: info@hmiradio.com
Format: Religious; Contemporary Christian. **Owner:** Heartland Ministries, Inc., at above address. **Founded:** 1989. **Operating Hours:** Continuous. **Ad Rates:** Advertising accepted; rates available upon request. **URL:** http://www.heartlandministriesradio.com.

HARLAN

Harlan Co. Harlan Co. (SE). 30 m NE of Middlesboro. Coal mines. Hardwood timber. Manufactures sign and sheet metal fabrication, electrical coils, beverages. Dairy processing plants. Truck farms.

13805 ■ The Harlan Daily Enterprise
The Harlan Daily Enterprise
1548 US Hwy. 421 S
Harlan, KY 40831
Phone: (606)573-4510
Fax: (606)573-0042
General newspaper. **Freq:** Mon.-Sat. (eve.). **Print Method:** Web. **Trim Size:** 11 5/8 x 21 1/4. **Cols./Page:** 6. **Col. Width:** 25 nonpareils. **Col. Depth:** 301 agate lines. **Key Personnel:** Pat Lay, Publisher; Debbie Caldwell, Managing Editor; Wylene Miniard, Sales Representative. **ISSN:** 1041--7109 (print). **URL:** http://www.harlandaily.com. **Mailing address:** PO Box 1155, Harlan, KY 40831. **Ad Rates:** GLR $.50; BW $1,257.75; 4C $1,512.75; SAU $9.15; PCI $13.48. **Remarks:** Advertising accepted; rates available upon request. **Circ:** (Not Reported).

13806 ■ Harlan Community Television Inc.
124 S First St.
Box 592
Harlan, KY 40831
Phone: (606)573-2945
Key Personnel: Charles Hale, Contact. **Cities Served:** subscribing households 3,250. **URL:** http://www.harlanonline.net/contactmain.htm.

13807 ■ WFSR-AM
PO Box 818
Harlan, KY 40831
Phone: (606)573-1470
Fax: (606)573-1473
Format: Gospel. **Networks:** CNN Radio; Unistar. **Owner:** Mark L. Ford, at above address. **Founded:** 1970. **Wattage:** 5,000 Day; 024 Night. **Ad Rates:** $4.12-5.06 for 15 seconds; $5.50-7.75 for 30 seconds; $6.50-9.75 for 60 seconds.

13808 ■ WHLN-AM - 1410
Ste. 1, 100 Eversole St.
Harlan, KY 40831
Phone: (606)573-2540
Fax: (606)573-7557
Format: Oldies. **Networks:** Jones Satellite. **Owner:** Radio Harlan Inc. **Founded:** 1941. **Operating Hours:** Continuous. **ADI:** Knoxville (Crossville), TN. **Wattage:** 5,000. **Ad Rates:** Advertising accepted; rates available upon request.

HAROLD

Floyd Co.

13809 ■ Gearheart Communications Company Inc.
20 Laynesville Rd.
Harold, KY 41635-9076
Phone: (606)478-9401
Free: 800-635-7052
Email: contactgh@gearheart.com
Owner: Inter Mountain Cable, 20 Laynesville Rd., Harold, KY 41635, Ph: (606)478-9406, Free: 800-635-7052. **Founded:** 1965. **Key Personnel:** Rebecca A. Walters, Contact, rwalters@gearheart.com. **Cities Served:** subscribing households 40,000. **Mailing address:** PO Box 160, Harold, KY 41635-0160. **URL:** http://www.gearheart.com.

13810 ■ WIFX-FM - 94.3
98 Church Rd.
Harold, KY 41635
Phone: (606)478-1200
Fax: (606)478-4202
Free: 866-943-9943
Email: wifx@foxy943.com
Format: Adult Contemporary; Top 40. **Networks:** ABC. **Founded:** 1968. **Formerly:** WREM-FM. **Operating Hours:** Continuous; 100% local. **ADI:** Lexington, KY. **Key Personnel:** Adam Gearheart, Gen. Mgr., adam@gearheart.com. **Wattage:** 50,000. **Ad Rates:** $3.50 for 15 seconds; $4.50-6 for 30 seconds; $8.50-10 for 60 seconds. **Mailing address:** PO Box 1094, Harold, KY 41635. **URL:** http://www.foxy943.com.

13811 ■ WXLR-FM - 104.9
PO Box 1049
Harold, KY 41635
Phone: (606)478-9401
Format: Classic Rock. **Networks:** CBS; Westwood One Radio. **Founded:** Jan. 14, 1994. **Operating Hours:** Continuous. **Key Personnel:** Barry Boyd, Gen. Mgr., Sales Mgr. **Wattage:** 3,000. **Ad Rates:** Noncommercial. **URL:** http://www.washingtonpost.com.

HARRODSBURG

Mercer Co. Mercer Co. (C). 30 m SW of Lexington. Manufactures men's coats, cheese, optical glass, bathroomfixtures, air conditioning coils, packaging foam, auto parts, brush and contact manufacture dust arresting equipment. Agriculture. Tobacco, wheat, dairy.

13812 ■ TCI North Central Kentucky
PO Box 218
Harrodsburg, KY 40330
Phone: (606)734-2305
Fax: (606)734-5755
Free: 800-273-8039
Key Personnel: Thomas Johnson, Gen. Mgr; C.B. Roland, Contact. **Cities Served:** subscribing households 15,000.

HARTFORD

Ohio Co. Ohio Co. (WC). On Rough River, 25 m E of Owensboro. Oil wells; coal mines; limestone quarries; manufactures gloves, auto parts, chemicals. Agriculture. Corn, tobacco, hay.

13813 ■ Ohio County Times-News
Andy Anderson Inc.
314 Main St.
Hartford, KY 42347
Phone: (270)298-7100
Publisher's E-mail: ads@octimesnews.com
Community newspaper. **Freq:** Weekly (Thurs.). **Print Method:** Offset. **Cols./Page:** 6. **Col. Width:** 28 nonpareils. **Col. Depth:** 301 agate lines. **Key Personnel:** Dave McBride, Editor; Tom Ewing, Editor. **Subscription Rates:** $27.50 Individuals in Ohio County (online). **URL:** http://www.octimesnews.com. **Ad Rates:** BW $787.50; PCI $6.25. **Remarks:** Accepts advertising. **Circ:** ‡6700.

13814 ■ WSNR-AM - 1600
PO Box 106
Hartford, KY 42347-0106
Fax: (502)298-9326
Format: News; Sports. **Founded:** 1969. **Formerly:** WLLS-AM. **Operating Hours:** 6 a.m.-sunset. **ADI:** Evansville, IN (Madisonville, KY). **Key Personnel:** Lloyd Spivey, Gen. Mgr. **Wattage:** 1,000. **Ad Rates:** $3.30 for 30 seconds; $4.50 for 60 seconds.

13815 ■ WWHK-FM - 105.5
87 Country Club Ln.
Hartford, KY 42347-9708
Format: News; Classic Rock; Religious. **Networks:** KyNet. **Founded:** 1981. **Formerly:** WGKY-FM. **Operating Hours:** 16 hours Daily; 5% network, 95% local. **Key Personnel:** Lonnie Mercer, Traffic Mgr; LLoyd Spivey, Contact. **Wattage:** 3,000. **Ad Rates:** $3.50-6 for 30 seconds; $5.50-8 for 60 seconds.

HAWESVILLE

Hancock Co. Hancock Co. (WC). On Ohio River, 28 m NE of Owensboro. Aluminum product factories. Paper mill. Coal mines. Oil wells. Agriculture. Tobacco, corn, wheat.

13816 ■ Hancock Clarion
Hancock Clarion
230 Main St
Hawesville, KY 42348
Phone: (270)927-6945
Fax: (270)927-6947
Publication E-mail: hancockclarion@gmail.com
Community newspaper. **Freq:** Weekly (Thurs.). **Print Method:** Offset. **Cols./Page:** 6. **Col. Width:** 2.25 picas. **Col. Depth:** 21 inches. **Key Personnel:** Donn K. Wimmer, Editor, Publisher; Ralph Dickerson, Manager, Advertising. **Subscription Rates:** $30 Individuals in County (print and online or online only); $35 Out of area online. **URL:** http://hancockclarion.com/20300/1954/1/this-weeks-issuepdf. **Mailing address:** PO Box 39, Hawesville, KY 42348. **Ad Rates:** BW $661.50; 4C $786.50; PCI $8. **Remarks:** Accepts advertising. **Circ:** ‡3745.

HAZARD

Perry Co. Perry Co. (SE). 117 m SE of Lexington. Buckhorn Lake State Resort Park. Coal, oil & natural gas. Hardwood timber. Bottling works. Steel fabrication.

13817 ■ Hazard Herald
Hazard Herald
439 High St.
Hazard, KY 41702
Publication E-mail: mzardherald@setel.com
Newspaper. **Freq:** Weekly (Wed.). **Print Method:** Offset. **Cols./Page:** 6. **Col. Width:** 12 picas. **Col. Depth:** 21.5 inches. **Key Personnel:** Joshua Byers, Publisher; Chris Ritchie, Editor. **URL:** http://www.hazard-herald.com. **Formerly:** Hazard Herald-Voice. **Ad Rates:** BW $838.50; 4C $1,151.69; SAU $7.61; PCI $7.61. **Remarks:** Accepts advertising. **Circ:** ‡4917.

13818 ■ WEKH-FM - 90.9
c/o WEKU-FM, 102 Perkins Bldg., 521 Lancaster Ave.
102 Perkins Bldg.
521 Lancaster Ave.
Richmond, KY 40475-3102
Free: 800-621-8890
Format: News; Classical; Public Radio. **Networks:** National Public Radio (NPR). **Owner:** Eastern Kentucky University Board of Regents, 521 Lancaster Ave., Richmond, KY 40475. **Founded:** 1985. **Operating Hours:** Continuous; 15% network, 85% local. **Key Personnel:** Roger Duvall, Station Mgr., roger.duvall@eku.edu. **Wattage:** 33,000. **Ad Rates:** Noncommercial. **URL:** http://www.weku.fm.

13819 ■ WJMD-FM - 104.7
PO Box 7001
Hazard, KY 41702
Phone: (606)439-3358
Fax: (606)439-3371
Email: wjmd@hotmail.com
Format: Religious; Gospel. **Owner:** Hazard Broadcasting Services, Inc., at above address. **Founded:** 1989. **Operating Hours:** Continuous. **ADI:** Lexington, KY. **Key Personnel:** Michael Barnett, Gen. Mgr., President. **Wattage:** 6,000. **Ad Rates:** Noncommercial. $5 for 30 seconds; $7 for 60 seconds.

13820 ■ WKHA-TV - 35
600 Cooper Dr.
Lexington, KY 40502
Phone: (859)258-7000

Circulation: ★ = AAM; △ or • = BPA; ♦ = CAC; ❑ = VAC; ⊕ = PO Statement; ‡ = Publisher's Report; Boldface figures = sworn; Light figures = estimated.

Free: 800-432-0951
Email: shop@ket.org
Format: Educational. **Networks:** Public Broadcasting Service (PBS); Kentucky Educational Television. **Owner:** Kentucky Educational Television, 600 Cooper Dr., Lexington, KY 40502, Ph: (859)258-7000, Free: 800-432-0951. **Founded:** 1968. **Operating Hours:** Continuous. **ADI:** Lexington, KY. **Key Personnel:** Shae Hopkins, Exec. Dir. **Wattage:** 053. **Ad Rates:** Noncommercial. **URL:** http://www.ket.org.

13821 ■ WKIC-AM - 1390
PO Box 7428
Hazard, KY 41702
Format: Music of Your Life. **Networks:** ABC; KyNet. **Founded:** 1947. **Operating Hours:** 6 a.m.-sunset. **ADI:** Lexington, KY. **Key Personnel:** Stuart Shane, News Dir; Ernest Sparkman, Contact; Faron Sparkman, Contact. **Wattage:** 5,000. **Ad Rates:** $5 for 30 seconds; $7 for 60 seconds. **URL:** http://www.wsgs.com.

13822 ■ WSGS-FM - 101.1
PO Box 7428
Hazard, KY 41702
Format: Country. **Owner:** Mountain Broadcasting Service, Inc., at above address. **Founded:** 1959. **ADI:** Lexington, KY. **Wattage:** 100,000. **Ad Rates:** Advertising accepted; rates available upon request.

13823 ■ WYMT-TV - 57
199 Black Gold Blvd.
Hazard, KY 41701-2602
Phone: (606)436-5757
Email: newstip@wymtnews.com
Format: Commercial TV. **Networks:** CBS. **Owner:** Gray Television Inc., 4370 Peachtree Rd. NE, No. 400, Atlanta, GA 30319-3054, Ph: (404)266-8333. **Founded:** 1969. **Operating Hours:** Continuous. **Wattage:** 50,000 ERP H. **Ad Rates:** Advertising accepted; rates available upon request. **URL:** http://www.wymt.com.

HENDERSON

Henderson Co. Henderson Co. (WC). On Ohio River, 7 m S of Evansville, Ind, with bridge connections. Manufactures aluminum, truck axles, tire rims, chemicals plastics, ammonia, furniture, castings, composite cans, wood products, brushes. River terminal for agricultural, petroleum and other products. Agricultural. Soybeans, tobacco, cattle.

13824 ■ The Hill
Henderson Community College
2660 S Green St.
Henderson, KY 42420
Phone: (270)827-1867
Free: 800-696-9958
Publication E-mail: thehill@kctcs.edu
Collegiate tabloid. **Founded:** Sept. 1978. **Freq:** Monthly. **Print Method:** Offset. **Cols./Page:** 5. **Col. Width:** 22 nonpareils. **Col. Depth:** 182 agate lines. **Key Personnel:** B.C. Thomas, Editor; Joe Belt, Editor; Tony Strawn, Faculty Advisor. **Subscription Rates:** Free. **Alt. Formats:** Download; PDF. **URL:** http://henderson.kctcs.edu/Student_Life/Organizations/The_Hill.aspx. **Ad Rates:** BW $110; PCI $5. **Remarks:** Advertising accepted; rates available upon request. **Circ:** Non-paid ‡1200.

13825 ■ WKOH-TV - 31
600 Cooper Dr.
Lexington, KY 40502
Phone: (859)258-7000
Free: 800-432-0951
Email: feedback@ket.org
Format: Public TV; Educational. **Networks:** Public Broadcasting Service (PBS); Kentucky Educational Television. **Owner:** Kentucky Educational Television, 600 Cooper Dr., Lexington, KY 40502, Ph: (859)258-7000, Free: 800-432-0951. **Founded:** 1980. **Operating Hours:** Continuous. **ADI:** Evansville, IN (Madisonville, KY). **Key Personnel:** Shae Hopkins, Exec. Dir. **Wattage:** 708,000. **Ad Rates:** Noncommercial. **URL:** http://www.ket.org.

13826 ■ WSON-AM - 860
530 S Jackson St.
Louisville, KY 40202
Phone: (502)589-0060
Format: Classic Rock. **Networks:** ABC. **Owner:** Henson Media Inc., at above address. **Founded:** 1941. **Operating Hours:** Continuous. **Key Personnel:** Bill Stephens, Dir. Pub. Aff.; Mary June Goodley, Contact; Henry G. Lackey, Contact, hglackey@citi-center.com. **Wattage:** 500. **Ad Rates:** $23-25 for 30 seconds; $27-30 for 60 seconds. **URL:** http://wsonradio.com.

HICKMAN

Fulton Co. Fulton Co. (SW). On Mississippi River, 55 m SW of Paducah. Hunting and fishing area. Graphite products, clothing factories. General cargo loading and unloading facilities. Diversified farming. Soybeans, corn, wheat, hay.

13827 ■ The Hickman Courier
The Hickman Courier
PO Box 70
Hickman, KY 42050
Phone: (270)236-3412
Fax: (270)236-2726
Community newspaper with a Democratic orientation, includes sections on agriculture. **Freq:** Weekly (Thurs.). **Print Method:** Offset. **Trim Size:** 7 x 11. **Cols./Page:** 6. **Col. Width:** 11 picas. **Col. Depth:** 294 agate lines. **Key Personnel:** Barbara Atwill, Manager, Advertising; Charlotte Smith, Editor; Dennis Richardson, Publisher. **USPS:** 243-200. **Subscription Rates:** $56 Individuals print and online; $32 Individuals print; $41 Out of state print; $24 Individuals online. **URL:** http://kypress.com/directory/weekly_detail.php?id=56. **Remarks:** Advertising accepted; rates available upon request. **Circ:** ‡705.

HIGHLAND HEIGHTS

13828 ■ WNKU - 104.1
301 Landrum Academix Ctr.
Highland Heights, KY 41099
Phone: (859)572-6500
Email: radio@wnku.org
Format: Country. **Founded:** 1948. **Operating Hours:** Continuous; 100% local. **Wattage:** 100,000. **Ad Rates:** $18 for 30 seconds; $25 for 60 seconds. WPAY-AM. **URL:** http://wnku.org.

13829 ■ WNKU-FM - 89.7
301 Landrum Academic Ctr.
Highland Heights, KY 41099
Phone: (859)572-6500
Fax: (859)572-6604
Free: 855-897-9658
Email: radio@nku.edu
Format: News; Adult Album Alternative. **Networks:** National Public Radio (NPR); Public Radio International (PRI). **Owner:** Northern Kentucky University, Nunn Dr., Newport, KY 41099, Ph: (859)572-7897. **Founded:** 1985. **Operating Hours:** anywhere from 5 a.m.-2 a.m.; 25% network, 75% local. **Key Personnel:** Chuck Miller, Station Mgr.; Michael Grayson, Dir. of Programs, michael@wnku.org; John Patrick, Music Dir.; Aaron Sharpe, Dir. of Dev. **Wattage:** 12,000. **Ad Rates:** Noncommercial. **URL:** http://www.wnku.org.

HINDMAN

Knott Co. Knott Co. (SE). 15 m NE of Hazard. Residential.

13830 ■ Troublesome Creek Times: Voice of Knott County
Knott County Publishing Company Inc.
PO Box 1500
Hindman, KY 41822
Phone: (606)785-5134
Fax: (606)785-0105
Local newspaper. **Freq:** Weekly (Thurs.). **Print Method:** Offset. **Cols./Page:** 6. **Col. Width:** 2 inches. **Col. Depth:** 21 1/2 inches. **Key Personnel:** Sharon K. Hall, General Manager, Publisher; Karen J. Jones, Editor, Publisher; Jim Watkins, Contact. **USPS:** 583-210. **Subscription Rates:** $19 Individuals Knott County; $23 Out of area Kentucky; $27 Out of state. **URL:** http://www.troublesomecreektimes.com. **Ad Rates:** 4C $200; PCI $5.25. **Remarks:** Accepts advertising. **Circ:** 5,000.

13831 ■ WKCB-FM
Rt 550 West
Hindman, KY 41822
Email: killerb@wkcb.com
Format: Sports; Urban Contemporary. **Key Personnel:** Randy Thompson, Station Mgr.; Paul Hoskins, Program Mgr. **Wattage:** 1,550 ERP. **Ad Rates:** Advertising accepted; rates available upon request.

HODGENVILLE

Larue Co. Larue Co. (WC). 60 m S of Louisville. Manufactures uniforms, limestone quarries; gas wells. Grist, sawmills; hatchery. Tobacco, corn, stock farms.

13832 ■ LaRue County Herald News
Landmark Community Newspapers L.L.C.
40 Shawnee Dr.
Hodgenville, KY 42748
Phone: (270)358-3118
Fax: (270)358-4852
Publisher's E-mail: marketing@lcni.com
Community newspaper. **Freq:** Weekly (Wed.). **Print Method:** Offset. **Cols./Page:** 6. **Col. Width:** 12 nonpareils. **Col. Depth:** 301 agate lines. **Key Personnel:** Allison Shepherd, General Manager, Manager, Advertising; Linda Ireland, Editor; Ramona Coffey, Office Manager. **USPS:** 241-220. **Subscription Rates:** $32.86 Individuals print and online; $19.80 Individuals 6 months; print and online; $10.75 Individuals quarterly; print and online. **URL:** http://www.laruecountyherald.com. **Ad Rates:** BW $797.22; 4C $1,045.22; SAU $5.94; PCI $4.71. **Remarks:** Accepts advertising. **Circ:** Paid 4600.

13833 ■ WXAM-AM - 1430
PO Box 177
Hodgenville, KY 42748
Phone: (502)358-4707
Fax: (502)358-4755
Format: News; Sports; Country; Agricultural. **Networks:** ABC. **Owner:** HEKA Broadcasting, Inc., at above address. **Founded:** 1974. **Formerly:** WLCB-AM. **Operating Hours:** Daytime; 5% network, 95% local. **ADI:** Louisville, KY. **Key Personnel:** John Day, Contact; Herbert Day, Contact; John Day, Contact. **Wattage:** 1,000. **Ad Rates:** $3.97-5.95 for 30 seconds; $4.73-7 for 60 seconds.

HOPKINSVILLE

Christian Co. Christian Co. (SW). 50 m W of Bowling Green. University of Kentucky Community College. Manufactures concrete products, automative bumpers, bowling balls, clothing, flour, corn meal, furniture, furniture hardware, precision springs, textiles, magnet wire, industrial fasteners, dairy products, hydraulic pumps, commercial packaging, graphite, agriculture feeds.

13834 ■ Kentucky New Era
Kentucky New Era
1618 E Ninth St.
Hopkinsville, KY 42240
Phone: (270)886-4444
Fax: (270)887-3222
Free: 877-463-9372
Publisher's E-mail: lnoeth@kentuckynewera.com
General newspaper. **Freq:** Mon.-Sat. **Print Method:** Offset. **Trim Size:** 13 3/4 x 22 3/4. **Cols./Page:** 6. **Col. Width:** 25 nonpareils. **Col. Depth:** 301 agate lines. **Key Personnel:** Chuck Henderson, President; Taylor Wood Hayes, Publisher; Ted Jatczah, Manager, Marketing and Sales; Joe Wilson, Editor. **Subscription Rates:** $39.95 Individuals 3 months, online; $75.95 Individuals 6 months, online; $149.95 Individuals 1 year, online. **URL:** http://www.kentuckynewera.com. **Ad Rates:** BW $1,097; 4C $1,272; PCI $7.34; BW $1,206; 4C $1,381. **Remarks:** Accepts advertising. **Circ:** Mon.-Sat. ★**10784**.

13835 ■ WHOP-AM - 1230
PO Box 709
Hopkinsville, KY 42241
Phone: (270)885-5331
Fax: (270)885-2688
Format: Adult Contemporary; Talk; News. **Networks:** CBS. **Owner:** Hopkinsville Broadcasting Co., Inc., at above address. **Founded:** 1940. **Operating Hours:** Continuous; 10% network, 90% local. **ADI:** Nashville (Cookeville), TN. **Key Personnel:** Jim Love, Contact, whopamfm@bellsouth.net; Mike Chadwell, Gen. Mgr., michadwell@1stcorbin.com; Traci Mason, Gen. Sales Mgr., trmason@1stcorbin.com; Jim Love, Contact, whopamfm@bellsouth.net. **Wattage:** 1,000. **Ad Rates:** $11-17 for 30 seconds; $14.50-22.50 for 60 seconds. $11-$17 for 30 seconds; $14.50-$22.50 for 60 seconds. Combined advertising rates available with WHOP-FM.

URL: http://www.whopam.com.

13836 ■ WHOP-FM - 98.7
PO Box 709
Hopkinsville, KY 42241
Founded: 1948. **Key Personnel:** Jim Love, Contact. **Wattage:** 100,000. **Ad Rates:** Noncommercial.

13837 ■ WNKJ-FM - 89.3
PO Box 1029
Hopkinsville, KY 42241
Phone: (270)886-9655
Fax: (270)885-7210
Free: 877-885-9655
Format: Religious. **Networks:** Moody Broadcasting. **Owner:** Pennyrile Christian Community, Inc., at above address. **Founded:** 1981. **Operating Hours**: Continuous; 24% network, 76% local. **Key Personnel:** Richard Nelson, VP; Jim D. Adams, Jr., Gen. Mgr; Joyce Adams, Contact. **Wattage**: 12,000. **Ad Rates:** Noncommercial. **URL:** http://www.wnkj.org.

13838 ■ WPJI-FM
2935 Woodburn Hay Rd.
Hopkinsville, KY 42240
Phone: (618)627-4651
Format: Talk; Information. **Owner:** Three Angels Broadcasting Network, West Frankfort, IL 62896. **Wattage**: 100 ERP. **Ad Rates:** Underwriting available.

13839 ■ WSPP-FM - 93.5
5817 Old Leeds Rd.
Irondale, AL 35210-2164
Phone: (205)271-2900
Email: viewer@ewtn.com
Format: Religious. **Owner:** EWTN Global Catholic Network, 5817 Old Leeds Rd., Irondale, AL 35210, Ph: (205)271-2900. **URL:** http://www.ewtn.com.

13840 ■ W22CH - 22
PO Box A
Santa Ana, CA 92711
Phone: (714)832-2950
Free: 888-731-1000
Owner: Trinity Broadcasting Network Inc., PO Box A, Santa Ana, CA 92711, Ph: (714)832-2950, Free: 888-731-1000. **URL:** http://www.tbn.org.

HORSE CAVE

Hart Co. Hart Co. (SWC). 81 m S of Louisville. Steel, saw, feed mills; cheese factory; tobacco warehouse. Dairy, stock, poultry, grain farms. Tobacco, corn, wheat.

13841 ■ American Caves
American Cave Conservation Association
119 E Main St.
Horse Cave, KY 42749
Phone: (270)786-1466
Publisher's E-mail: acca@cavern.org
Magazine covering national and local cave conservation issues and calendar of events. **Freq:** Periodic. **Subscription Rates:** included in membership dues; $5 for nonmembers. **URL:** http://caveconservation.com. **Remarks:** Advertising accepted; rates available upon request. **Circ:** (Not Reported).

13842 ■ WHSX-FM - 99.1
1130 S Dixie St.
Horse Cave, KY 42749
Phone: (270)786-1000
Email: wloc@scrtc.com
Format: Blues; Sports. **Wattage**: 6,000. **Ad Rates:** Advertising accepted; rates available upon request. **Mailing address:** PO Box 85, Horse Cave, KY 42749. **URL:** http://www.thehoss.com/.

13843 ■ WLOC-AM - 1150
1130 S Dixie St.
Horse Cave, KY 42749
Phone: (270)786-1000
Fax: (270)786-4402
Free: 888-862-4402
Email: wloc@scrtc.com
Format: Country. **Key Personnel:** Dewayne Forbis, Gen. Mgr.; Chris Jessie, Contact. **Ad Rates:** Advertising accepted; rates available upon request. **Mailing address:** PO Box 98, Horse Cave, KY 42749. **URL:** http://www.am1150wloc.com.

HYDEN

Leslie Co. Leslie Co. (SE). 15 m NW of Leatherwood.

13844 ■ The Leslie County News
Thousand Sticks News
PO Box 967
Hyden, KY 41749
Phone: (606)672-2841
Fax: (606)672-7409
Hispanic newspaper. **Freq:** Weekly (Thurs.). **Print Method:** Offset. **Cols./Page:** 6. **Col. Width:** 21 nonpareils. **Col. Depth:** 287 agate lines. **Key Personnel:** Vernon Baker, Publisher; Reba Baker, Editor; Janice Estep, Manager, Advertising. **Subscription Rates:** $18.55 Individuals; $26 Out of area. **Ad Rates:** GLR $5.80; BW $5.80; SAU $8.40; PCI $5.80. **Remarks:** Accepts advertising. **Circ:** 3950.

IRVINE

Estill Co. Estill Co. (EC). 50 m W of Salyersville. Residential.

13845 ■ Citizen Voice & Times
Citizen Voice Inc.
108 Court St.
Irvine, KY 40336
Phone: (606)723-5161
Fax: (606)723-5509
Publisher's E-mail: rhonda@hatfieldnewspapers.com
Weekly newspaper. **Freq:** Weekly (Thurs.). **Print Method:** Offset. **Cols./Page:** 6. **Col. Width:** 21.5 picas. **Col. Depth:** 21.5 inches. **Key Personnel:** Lisa Bicknell, Editor; Rhonda Smyth, Editor; Teresa Hatfield-Barger, Publisher. **USPS:** 270-120. **Subscription Rates:** $15.95 Individuals in Estill County; $23.95 Elsewhere in Kentucky; $32 Out of state. **URL:** http://www.cvt-news.com/news/. **Mailing address:** PO Box 660, Irvine, KY 40336. **Ad Rates:** GLR $.34; BW $398.61; 4C $652.98; SAU $4.20. **Remarks:** Accepts advertising. **Circ:** Paid ‡3968, Free ‡9700.

13846 ■ Irvine Community Television Inc.
251 Broadway St.
Irvine, KY 40336
Phone: (606)723-4240
Cities Served: 74 channels. **Mailing address:** PO Box 186, Irvine, KY 40336. **URL:** http://www.irvine-cable.net.

JACKSON

Breathitt Co. Breathitt Co. (EC). 5 m S of Wolverine.

13847 ■ The Kentucky Explorer
The Kentucky Explorer
PO Box 227
Jackson, KY 41339
Phone: (606)666-5060
Fax: (606)666-7018
Publisher's E-mail: kyex1@mac.com
Consumer magazine covering local history and genealogy. **Freq:** Monthly. **Key Personnel:** Darlene Howard, Office Manager; Charles Hayes, Jr., Editor. **Subscription Rates:** $21 By mail including postage; $30 Individuals 25 back issues. **Alt. Formats:** CD-ROM. **URL:** http://www.kentuckyexplorer.com. **Circ:** (Not Reported).

13848 ■ Mountain Gospel Radio
1036 Hwy. 541
Jackson, KY 41339
Phone: (606)666-5006
Free: 800-337-5006
Format: Gospel. **Founded:** 1948. **Ad Rates:** Advertising accepted; rates available upon request. **URL:** http://www.wp.mountaingospel.org.

13849 ■ WEKG-AM
1024 College Ave
Jackson, KY 41339-1016
Phone: (606)666-7531
Fax: (606)666-4946
Format: Hot Country; Religious; Bluegrass; Oldies. **Networks:** CNN Radio. **Founded:** 1969. **Wattage**: 5,000 Day. **Ad Rates:** $4-7 for 30 seconds; $5-8 for 60 seconds.

13850 ■ WJSN-FM
1501 Hargis Ln.
Jackson, KY 41339
Phone: (606)666-7531
Fax: (606)666-4946
Format: News; Sports. **Founded:** 1979. **Wattage:** 19,000 ERP. **Ad Rates:** $4-7 for 30 seconds; $5-8 for 60 seconds.

13851 ■ WMTC-AM - 730
1036 Hwy. 541
Jackson, KY 41339
Phone: (606)666-5006
Free: 800-337-5006
Format: Gospel. **Networks:** Independent. **Owner:** Kentucky Mountain Holiness Association, Hwy. 541, Vancleve, KY 41385. **Founded:** June 30, 1948. **Operating Hours:** 6 a.m.-sunset; 100% local. **Key Personnel:** Daniel Lorimer, Gen. Mgr.; Seth Stevenson, Dir. of Programs. **Wattage:** 5,000. **Ad Rates:** $2.50 for 30 seconds; $5 for 60 seconds. Combined advertising rates available with WMTC-FM. **URL:** http://www.wp.mountaingospel.org.

13852 ■ WMTC-FM - 99.9
1036 Hwy. 541
Jackson, KY 41339
Phone: (606)666-5006
Free: 800-337-5006
Format: Religious; Southern Gospel. **Networks:** Sun Radio. **Owner:** Mountain Gospel Radio, 1036 Hwy. 541, Jackson, KY 41339, Ph: (606)666-5006, Free: 800-337-5006. **Founded:** 1991. **Operating Hours:** Continuous. **Key Personnel:** Daniel Lorimer, Gen. Mgr. **Local Programs:** *Birthday Club*, Saturday Monday Tuesday Wednesday Thursday Friday Sunday 8:30 a.m. - 8:45 a.m.; 4:05 p.m. - 4:15 p.m. 10:05 a.m. - 10:15 a.m.; 7:30 p.m. - 7:45 p.m. 8:05 a.m. - 8:15 a.m.; *Hour of Holiness*, Saturday 2:05 p.m. - 2:30 p.m.; *Community Shut-In*, Sunday 5:05 p.m. - 5:30 p.m. **Wattage:** 6,000. **Ad Rates:** $3-6 for 60 seconds. Combined advertising rates available with WMTC-AM. **URL:** http://www.mountaingospel.org.

JAMESTOWN

Russell Co. Russell Co. (SC). 95 m S of Lexington. Underwear plant. Diversified farming. Cattle.

13853 ■ Russell County News
Community Newspaper Holdings Inc.
404 Monument Sq.
Jamestown, KY 42629
Phone: (270)343-5700
Newspaper. **Founded:** Feb. 01, 1913. **Freq:** Weekly (Sat.). **Print Method:** Offset. **Cols./Page:** 6. **Col. Width:** 30 nonpareils. **Col. Depth:** 294 agate lines. **Key Personnel:** David Davenport, Publisher; Greg Wells, Managing Editor; Stephanie Smith, Manager, Advertising. **Subscription Rates:** By mail free to every address in Russell County. **Ad Rates:** GLR $.30; BW $695.52; SAU $5.52; PCI $5.52. **Remarks:** Accepts advertising. **Circ:** Paid 44, Free 10456.

13854 ■ Russell County News-Register
Russell Daily News
404 Monument Sq.
Jamestown, KY 42629
Phone: (270)343-5700
Newspaper. **Founded:** 1930. **Freq:** Weekly. **Print Method:** Offset. **Cols./Page:** 8. **Col. Width:** 22 nonpareils. **Col. Depth:** 301 agate lines. **Key Personnel:** Russell T. Townsley, Publisher; Allan D. Evans, Manager, Advertising; Dan Holder, Editor. **Subscription Rates:** $29 Individuals one year print and online subscription (in Russell County); $39 Individuals one year print and online subscription (outside Russell County); $89 Other countries one year print and online subscription. **URL:** http://www.russellcountynewspapers.com. **Formerly**: Russell Daily News; Russell County News. **Circ:** (Not Reported).

13855 ■ WJRS-FM - 104.9
PO Box 1036
Jamestown, KY 42629
Format: Country; Gospel; Bluegrass. **Simulcasts:** WJKY-AM. **Networks:** Jones Satellite. **Founded:** 1966. **Operating Hours**: Continuous. **ADI**: Joplin, MO-Pittsburg, KS. **Wattage**: 3,000. **Ad Rates:** Noncommercial. Combined advertising rates available with WJKY-AM. **URL:** http://lakercountry.com.

JENKINS

Letcher Co. Letcher Co. (NE). 22 m SSW of Pikesville. Coal mines.

Circulation: ★ = AAM; △ or • = BPA; ♦ = CAC; ❑ = VAC; ⊕ = PO Statement; ‡ = Publisher's Report; Boldface figures = sworn; Light figures = estimated.

13856 ■ WKVG-AM - 1000
9382 Hwy. 805, Ste. B
Jenkins, KY 41537
Phone: (606)832-4655
Fax: (606)832-4656
Format: Gospel. **Owner:** Martins & Associates, Inc., at above address, Cincinnati, OH. **Founded:** 1992. **Operating Hours**: 10 1/2 HRS Daily. **Wattage**: 1,000. **Ad Rates:** Noncommercial. **URL:** http://www.wkvgradio.com.

KEAVY

13857 ■ WVCT-FM - 91.5
968 W City Dam Rd.
Keavy, KY 40737
Phone: (606)528-4671
Fax: (606)526-0589
Format: Religious; Southern Gospel. **Owner:** Sivley Communication, at above address. **Founded:** 1984. **Operating Hours:** Continuous. **Key Personnel:** Rev. Charles Sivley, Owner. **Wattage**: 100. **Ad Rates:** Noncommercial. $3-6 for 30 seconds. **URL:** http://www.thegospeleagle.com.

KEVIL

WGCF-FM - See Paducah, KY

LA GRANGE

Oldham Co. Oldham Co. (NW). 27 m NE of Louisville. Manufactures copper wire, chemicals, food products, prefabricated pools. Greenhouse. Agriculture. Dairying, tobacco, beef cattle.

13858 ■ The Oldham Era
Landmark Community Newspapers L.L.C.
202 S 1st St.
La Grange, KY 40031
Phone: (502)222-7183
Fax: (502)222-7194
Publisher's E-mail: marketing@lcni.com
Local newspaper. **Freq:** Weekly (Thurs.). **Print Method:** Letterpress and Offset. **Cols./Page:** 6. **Col. Width:** 12 nonpareils. **Col. Depth:** 301 agate lines. **Key Personnel:** Mary Johnson, Manager, Circulation. **Subscription Rates:** $54.06 Individuals print and online; $54.14 Out of area print and online; $64 Out of state print and online; $37.10 Individuals online. **URL:** http://www.oldhamera.com. **Ad Rates:** BW $592; 4C $817; SAU $4.86. **Remarks:** Accepts advertising. **Circ:** ‡6900.

LAWRENCEBURG

Anderson Co. Anderson Co. (E). 12 m S of Frankfort. Distillery, cheese, diversified agriculture.

13859 ■ The Anderson News
Landmark Community Newspapers L.L.C.
1080 Bypass S
Lawrenceburg, KY 40342
Phone: (502)839-6906
Fax: (502)839-3118
Publisher's E-mail: marketing@lcni.com
Community newspapers. **Freq:** Weekly (Wed.). **Key Personnel:** Ben Carlson, Publisher, Editor. **Subscription Rates:** $54.06 Individuals print and online; $54.14 Out of area print and online; $64 Out of state print and online; $41.34 Individuals online. **URL:** http://www.theandersonnews.com. **Mailing address:** PO Box 410, Lawrenceburg, KY 40342. **Remarks:** Accepts advertising. **Circ:** ‡5755.

LEBANON

Marion Co. Marion Co. (C). 28 m W of Danville. Distillery, meat packing, tobacco.

13860 ■ The Lebanon Enterprise
Landmark Community Newspapers L.L.C.
119 S Proctor Knott Ave.
Lebanon, KY 40033
Phone: (270)692-6026
Fax: (270)692-2118
Publisher's E-mail: marketing@lcni.com
Community newspaper. **Founded:** 1887. **Freq:** Weekly (Wed.). **Cols./Page:** 6. **Col. Depth:** 21.5 inches. **Key Personnel:** Stevie Lowery, Editor, General Manager; Mary Ann Blair, Manager, Advertising; Stephen Lega, Editor. **Subscription Rates:** $36.04 Individuals print and online; $20.67 Individuals 6 months; print and online. **URL:** http://www.lebanonenterprise.com/. **Ad Rates:** BW $505.68; 4C $805.68; SAU $4.13. **Remarks:** Accepts advertising. **Circ:** 6400.

13861 ■ WLBN-AM - 1590
253 W Main
Lebanon, KY 40033
Phone: (270)692-3126
Fax: (270)692-6003
Free: 888-692-1009
Format: Oldies. **Networks:** Jones Satellite; KyNet; NBC. **Owner:** Commonwealth Broadcasting Corp., at above address. **Founded:** 1953. **Operating Hours:** Sunrise-sunset; 80% network, 20% local. **ADI**: Louisville, KY. **Key Personnel:** Lisa Kearnes, Station Mgr., lkearnes@commonwealthbroadcasting.com; Andy Colley, Dir. of Programs, acolley@commonwealthbroadcasting.com; Cherry Gibson, Contact, cgibson@commonwealthbroadcasting.com. **Wattage:** 1,000. **Ad Rates:** $6-10 for 30 seconds; $10-15 for 60 seconds. Combined advertising rates available with WLSK. **URL:** http://www.1590wlbn.com.

13862 ■ WLSK-FM - 100.9
253 W Main St.
Lebanon, KY 40033
Phone: (270)692-3126
Fax: (270)692-6003
Email: wlsk@commonwealthbroadcasting.com
Format: Country. **Networks:** Jones Satellite; ABC; NBC. **Owner:** Commonwealth Broadcasting Corp., at above address. **Founded:** 1974. **Operating Hours**: Continuous; 10% network, 90% local. **ADI**: Louisville, KY. **Key Personnel:** Lisa Kearnes, Sales Mgr., Station Mgr.; Andy Colley, Operations Mgr., Prog. Dir.; Chad Mattingly, News Dir. **Wattage:** 25,000. **Ad Rates:** Noncommercial. Combined advertising rates available with WLBN-AM. **URL:** http://www.lebanonmike.com.

LEITCHFIELD

Grayson Co. Grayson Co. (WC). 72 m SW of Louisville. Manufactures electronic components, paper novelties, power tools, concrete products, cheese, lumber. Dairy, poultry, grain farms. Tobacco, corn, hay.

13863 ■ Grayson County News-Gazette
Park Newspapers of Kentucky Inc.
40 Public Sq.
Leitchfield, KY 42754
Local newspaper. **Freq:** Semiweekly (Mon. and Thurs.). **Print Method:** Offset. **Cols./Page:** 6. **Col. Width:** 12 nonpareils. **Col. Depth:** 301 agate lines. **Key Personnel:** Matt Lasley, Reporter; Don Brown, Reporter; Theresa Armstrong, Manager, Advertising, General Manager. **Subscription Rates:** $26 Individuals e-edition. **URL:** http://www.gcnewsgazette.com. **Ad Rates:** GLR $.31. **Remarks:** Accepts advertising. **Circ:** ‡6220.

13864 ■ WKHG-FM - 105
2160 Brandenburg Rd.
Leitchfield, KY 42754
Phone: (270)259-5692
Fax: (270)259-5693
Email: info@k105.com
Format: Adult Contemporary. **Ad Rates:** Noncommercial.

13865 ■ WMTL-AM - 870
2160 Brandenburg Rd.
Leitchfield, KY 42754
Phone: (270)259-6000
Email: k105@k105.com
Format: Bluegrass. **Networks:** ABC. **Owner:** Heritage Media of Kentucky, Inc., at above address. **Founded:** 1959. **Operating Hours**: 7 a.m.-7 p.m. **ADI**: Louisville, KY. **Key Personnel:** Mark Buckles, Gen. Mgr., manager@k105.com; Steve Meredith, Dir. of Programs, smeredith@k105.com. **Ad Rates:** $5-9 for 30 seconds; $8-12 for 60 seconds. Combined advertising rates available with WKHG-FM. **URL:** http://www.k105.com.

LEXINGTON

Fayette Co. (NC). 80 m E of Louisville. University of Kentucky; Transylvania University; College of the Bible; Lexington Baptist College. Manufactures tobacco, peanut butter, asphalt paving products, insecticides, crop drying equipment, neon signs, television tuners and boosters, men's suits, women's dresses, medicine, caskets, screens, tools, stoves, electric typewriters and stands, electrical control panels, air conditioning, transistors, airbrake equipment, paper cups, glass, parachutes, livestock feed, motor and machine seals, fork lifts, cranes, furniture. Motor bus shops. Meat packing. Principal outlet for eastern and central Kentucky oil, coal, farm and quarry products. Thoroughbred hoses.

13866 ■ ACUTA Journal
Association for College and University Technology Advancement
152 W Zandale Dr., Ste. 200
Lexington, KY 40503
Phone: (859)278-3338
Fax: (859)278-3268
Journal focusing on best business practices, meeting the security challenge, infrastructure and broadband access. **Freq:** Quarterly. **Key Personnel:** Amy Burton, Advertising Representative; Pat Scott, Editor-in-Chief, Director, Communications. **URL:** http://www.acuta.org/ACUTA/Member_Services/Quarterly_ACUTA_Journal/ACUTA/MemberServices/ACUTA_Journal.aspx?hkey=c343bfe0-704b-4564-8c4c-a53de624fe2a. **Ad Rates:** BW $1500. **Remarks:** Accepts advertising. **Circ:** (Not Reported).

13867 ■ The Agricultural Education Magazine
The Agricultural Education Magazine
c/o Dr. Wm. Jay Jackman
300 Garrigus Bldg.
Lexington, KY 40546-0215
Phone: (859)257-2224
Vocational agriculture education magazine. **Freq:** Monthly. **Print Method:** Offset. **Trim Size:** 8 1/2 x 11. **Cols./Page:** 2. **Col. Width:** 3 1/2 inches. **Col. Depth:** 140 agate lines. **Key Personnel:** Dr. Harry N. Boone, Editor; Dr. Wm. Jay Jackman, Business Manager. **ISSN:** 0732--4677 (print). **Subscription Rates:** $15 Individuals; $25 Other countries; $10 Other countries back issues, /copy; $6 Students. **URL:** http://www.naae.org/profdevelopment/magazine. **Remarks:** Advertising not accepted. **Circ:** ‡5000.

13868 ■ Asphalt
Asphalt Institute
2696 Research Park Dr.
Lexington, KY 40511-8480
Phone: (859)288-4960
Fax: (859)288-4999
Publication E-mail: aimagazine@asphaltinstitute.org
Trade magazine for asphalt users, producers, and others concerned with the asphalt industry. **Founded:** 1919. **Freq:** 3/year. **Trim Size:** 8 1/2 x 10 7/8. **Key Personnel:** Tracie W. Schlich, Publisher. **URL:** http://www.asphaltmagazine.com/. **Remarks:** Accepts advertising. **Circ:** 17800.

13869 ■ ATA Quarterly
American Tarot Association
1020 Liberty Rd.
Lexington, KY 40505-4035
Fax: (859)514-9799
Free: 888-211-1572
Publisher's E-mail: ata@ata-tarot.com
Journal containing informative articles regarding tarot cards and other related ideas. **Freq:** Quarterly. **Subscription Rates:** Included in membership. **Remarks:** Accepts advertising. **Circ:** (Not Reported).

13870 ■ The Blood-Horse
Eclipse Press
3101 Beaumont Centre Cir.
Lexington, KY 40513
Phone: (859)278-2361
Fax: (859)276-6868
Free: 800-866-2361
Publisher's E-mail: info@eclipsepress.com
Trade magazine covering thoroughbred racing and breeding. **Freq:** Weekly. **Trim Size:** 8 1/8 x 10 7/8. **Cols./Page:** 3. **Col. Width:** 2 1/4 inches. **Col. Depth:** 10 inches. **Key Personnel:** Tom LaMarra, Editor, phone: (859)276-6795; Eric Mitchell, Editor-in-Chief. **ISSN:** 0006--4998 (print). **Subscription Rates:** $99 Individuals 1 year. **URL:** http://www.bloodhorse.com/horse-racing. **Remarks:** Accepts advertising. **Circ:** (Not Reported).

13871 ■ Bluegrass Music News
Kentucky Music Educators Association
c/o George Boulden, Ed.
University Of Kentucky

33 Fine Arts Bldg.
Lexington, KY 40506
Magazine for school music educators who teach kindergarten through university-level. **Freq:** Quarterly fall, winter, spring, and summer. **Print Method:** Offset. **Trim Size:** 8 1/2 x 11. **Cols./Page:** 3. **Col. Width:** 28 nonpareils. **Col. Depth:** 140 agate lines. **Key Personnel:** George Boulden, Editor. **ISSN:** 0006--5129 (print). **URL:** http://www.kmea.org/bgmn. **Ad Rates:** BW $345; 4C $524. **Remarks:** Advertising accepted; rates available upon request. **Circ:** ‡2100.

13872 ■ Business Lexington
Smiley Pete Publishing
434 Old Vine St.
Lexington, KY 40507
Phone: (859)266-6537
News journal focusing on Central Kentucky business community. **Freq:** Bimonthly. **Key Personnel:** Chuck Creacy, Publisher; Chris Eddie, Publisher; Tom Martin, Editor-in-Chief. **Subscription Rates:** $29.95 Individuals; $57 Two years; $79 Individuals three years. **URL:** http://bizlex.com. **Remarks:** Accepts advertising. **Circ:** 18000.

13873 ■ Carriage Journal
Carriage Association of America
4075 Iron Works Pky.
Lexington, KY 40511
Phone: (859)231-0971
Fax: (859)231-0973
Publisher's E-mail: info@caaonline.com
Journal containing informative articles about a wide range of subjects: carriage and driving history, restoration, preservation, driving, harnessing and news about CAA meetings and events. **Freq:** 5/year. **Subscription Rates:** Included in membership. **URL:** http://www.caaonline.com/caa_content.asp?PageType=Event&Key=14. **Ad Rates:** BW $395; 4C $495. **Remarks:** Accepts advertising. **Circ:** (Not Reported).

13874 ■ Chevy Chaser
Smiley Pete Publishing
434 Old Vine St.
Lexington, KY 40507
Phone: (859)266-6537
Magazine covering general society and culture. **Key Personnel:** Chuck Creacy, Publisher; Chris Eddie, Publisher; Robbie Clark, Editor. **Alt. Formats:** Handheld. **URL:** http://chevychaser.com. **Remarks:** Accepts advertising. **Circ:** Mon.-Fri. 21000.

13875 ■ Coaching Volleyball
American Volleyball Coaches Association
2365 Harrodsburg Rd., Ste. A325
Lexington, KY 40504
Free: 866-544-2822
Publisher's E-mail: members@avca.org
Freq: Bimonthly. **Key Personnel:** Jackson Silvanik, Editor. **ISSN:** 0894--4237 (print). **Subscription Rates:** Included in membership. **URL:** http://www.avca.org/groups/high-school/coaching-education/coaching-volleyball-magazine.html. **Remarks:** Advertising accepted; rates available upon request. **Circ:** Paid 6,600.

13876 ■ Coaching World
International Coach Federation
2365 Harrodsburg Rd., Ste. A325
Lexington, KY 40504
Phone: (859)219-3580
Fax: (859)226-4411
Free: 888-423-3131
Publisher's E-mail: icfheadquarters@coachfederation.org
Freq: Quarterly. **Subscription Rates:** Free. **Alt. Formats:** PDF. **URL:** http://www.coachfederation.org/about/coachingworldlist.cfm. **Remarks:** Advertising not accepted. **Circ:** (Not Reported).

13877 ■ Cow Country News
Kentucky Cattlemen's Association
176 Pasadena Dr.
Lexington, KY 40503
Phone: (859)278-0899
Fax: (859)260-2060
Publisher's E-mail: info@kycattle.org
Newspaper serving beef cattle industry in Kentucky and surrounding areas. **Freq:** Monthly. **Key Personnel:** Dave Maples, Executive Vice President; Carey Brown, Coordinator. **Subscription Rates:** $30 Individuals. **URL:** http://www.kycattle.org/cowcountrynews.html. **Ad Rates:** BW $604; 4C $1,054. **Remarks:** Accepts advertising. **Circ:** (Not Reported).

13878 ■ Electric Power Components and Systems
Taylor & Francis Group Journals
c/o Jim Cathey, Ed.-in-Ch.
ECE Dept., 453C Anderson Hall
University of Kentucky
Lexington, KY 40506-0046
Phone: (859)257-8043
Fax: (859)257-3092
Publisher's E-mail: customerservice@taylorandfrancis.com
Journal publishing original theoretical and applied research in electromechanics, electric machines, and power systems. **Freq:** 20/yr. **Print Method:** Offset Uses mats. **Trim Size:** 7 x 10. **Cols./Page:** 1. **Col. Width:** 63 nonpareils. **Col. Depth:** 119 agate lines. **Key Personnel:** Dr. Ion Boldea, Editor, Board Member; Jim Cathey, Editor-in-Chief; Prof. M.E. El-Hawary, Associate Editor; Dan M. Ionel, Editor-in-Chief. **ISSN:** 1532--5008 (print); **EISSN:** 1532--5016 (electronic). **Subscription Rates:** $1919 Individuals print only; $4019 Institutions online; $4593 Institutions print & online. **URL:** http://www.tandfonline.com/toc/uemp20/current#.VHLhndIW2qZ; http://www.tandf.co.uk/journals/titles/15325008.asp. **Formerly**: Electric Machines and Power Systems. **Remarks:** Accepts advertising. **Circ:** Combined ‡376.

13879 ■ Equestrian: The Official Magazine of the American Equestrian Sport Since 1937
United States Equestrian Federation
4047 Iron Works Pky.
Lexington, KY 40511
Phone: (859)258-2472
Fax: (859)231-6662
Magazine containing horse show information. **Freq:** Quarterly. **Print Method:** Offset. **Trim Size:** 8 1/8 x 10 7/8. **Cols./Page:** 3. **Col. Width:** 28 nonpareils. **Col. Depth:** 140 agate lines. **Key Personnel:** Brian Sosby, Editor, phone: (859)225-6934. **ISSN:** 1095-3264 (print). **URL:** http://www.usef.org/_iframes/newsmedia/equestrianmagazine.aspx. **Formerly**: Horse Show. **Ad Rates:** BW $1,320; 4C $2,220. **Remarks:** Advertising accepted; rates available upon request. **Circ:** Paid 72884.

13880 ■ Hobby Farms: Rural Living for Pleasure and Profit
Bowtie Inc.
PO Box 8237
Lexington, KY 40533
Fax: (859)260-1154
Free: 888-245-3699
Magazine for rural enthusiasts and farmers. **Freq:** Bimonthly. **Print Method:** Offset. **Cols./Page:** 6. **Col. Width:** 26 nonpareils. **Col. Depth:** 301 agate lines. **Key Personnel:** Stephanie Staton, Editor; Lisa Munniksma, Contact. **Subscription Rates:** $15 Individuals; $21 Other countries. **Remarks:** Advertising accepted; rates available upon request. **Circ:** (Not Reported).

13881 ■ Horseman and Fair World
Horseman Publishing Co.
1910 Harrodsburg Rd., Ste. 200
Lexington, KY 40503
Phone: (859)276-4026
Fax: (859)277-8100
Publisher's E-mail: csproduction@harnessracing.com
Harness racing magazine. **Freq:** Weekly (Wed.). **Print Method:** Web offset. **Trim Size:** 8 1/2 x 10 7/8. **Cols./Page:** 3. **Col. Width:** 24 nonpareils. **Col. Depth:** 140 agate lines. **Key Personnel:** Kathy Parker, Editor, General Manager; Lynne Myers, Manager, Advertising. **Subscription Rates:** $58 Individuals. **URL:** http://www.harnessracing.com. **Ad Rates:** BW $620; 4C $635; PCI $32. **Remarks:** Accepts advertising. **Circ:** ‡7500.

13882 ■ In Stride
Active Interest Media
70 Cigar Ln.
Lexington, KY 40511
Fax: (859)258-9033
Publisher's E-mail: admin@aimmedia.com
Magazine publishing articles on hunter/jumper community and tips on horse care, health and training. **Freq:** Bimonthly. **Key Personnel:** Hunter Messineo, Associate Publisher; Tricia Booker, Managing Editor. **URL:** http://www.aimmedia.com/is.html; http://www.ushja.org/content/news/news_media2.aspx. **Circ:** (Not Reported).

13883 ■ International Journal of Coal Preparation and Utilization
Taylor & Francis Group Journals
c/o B.K. Parekh, Editor-in-Chief
FGX SepTech
3765 Kings Glen Pk.
Lexington, KY 40514
Publisher's E-mail: customerservice@taylorandfrancis.com
Journal for individuals involved with coal preparation, including those in operations, engineering, management, education, and scientific research. **Freq:** Bimonthly. **Key Personnel:** B K Parekh, Editor-in-Chief; G.H. Luttrell, Editor; Dr. Mark S. Klima, Associate Editor; Rick Q. Honaker, Board Member; J.S. Laskowski, Editor, Founder; Peter Hand, Board Member; S. Cierpisz, Board Member; Kevin Galvin, Associate Editor; Barbara Arnold, Board Member; D.W. Brown, Board Member. **ISSN:** 1939--2699 (print); **EISSN:** 1939--2702 (electronic). **Subscription Rates:** $1906 Institutions print and online; $1668 Institutions online only; $623 Individuals print only. **URL:** http://www.tandfonline.com/toc/gcop20/current#.Uv2g7tlW2qY. **Formerly**: Coal Preparation. **Circ:** (Not Reported).

13884 ■ Journal of the American Board of Family Medicine
American Board of Family Medicine
1648 McGrathiana Pky., Ste. 550
Lexington, KY 40511-1247
Phone: (859)269-5626
Fax: (859)335-7501
Publication E-mail: jabfm@med.wayne.edu
Peer-reviewed journal publishing information on advancement of family medicine research and clinical practice. **Freq:** Bimonthly. **Trim Size:** 7 7/8 x 10 3/4. **Cols./Page:** 2. **Col. Width:** 3 inches. **Col. Depth:** 9 1/4 INS. **Key Personnel:** James C. Puffer, MD, Executive Editor; Anne Victoria Neale, PhD, Editor; Marjorie Bowman, MD, Editor. **ISSN:** 1557--2625 (print); **EISSN:** 1558--7118 (electronic). **Subscription Rates:** $160 Institutions; $200 Institutions, other countries; $80 Individuals; $120 Other countries; $40 Single issue; $55 Single issue other countries. **URL:** http://www.jabfm.org. **Formerly**: Journal of the American Board of Family Practice. **Remarks:** Accepts classified advertising. **Circ:** 9000.

13885 ■ Journal of Biocommunication
Association of Medical Illustrators
201 E Main St., Ste. 1405
Lexington, KY 40507
Free: 866-393-4264
Publisher's E-mail: hq@ami.org
Journal providing objective and significant information to the biocommunication community. **Freq:** 3/year Quarterly. **Key Personnel:** Gary Lees, Editor. **ISSN:** 0094--2499 (print). **Alt. Formats:** Download. **URL:** http://www.jbiocommunication.org; http://ami.org/journals-books/journals; http://ami.org/journal-of-biocommunication. **Remarks:** Advertising not accepted. **Circ:** (Not Reported).

13886 ■ Journal of Communications Technology in Higher Education
Association for College and University Technology Advancement
152 W Zandale Dr., Ste. 200
Lexington, KY 40503
Phone: (859)278-3338
Fax: (859)278-3268
Journal publishing articles on higher education information communications technology. **Freq:** Quarterly. **Subscription Rates:** Included in membership. **Alt. Formats:** PDF. **Remarks:** Accepts advertising. **Circ:** (Not Reported).

13887 ■ Journal of Dam Safety
Association of State Dam Safety Officials
239 S Limestone
Lexington, KY 40508-2501
Phone: (859)550-2788
Publisher's E-mail: info@damsafety.org
Freq: Quarterly. **ISSN:** 1944- 9836 (print). **Subscription Rates:** free for members. **URL:** http://www.damsafety.

Circulation: ★ = AAM; △ or • = BPA; ♦ = CAC; ❑ = VAC; ⊕ = PO Statement; ‡ = Publisher's Report; Boldface figures = sworn; Light figures = estimated.

org/resources/?p=2cd56bf7-ea3d-4a48-b2e5-75d75f1b0b94. **Remarks:** Accepts advertising. **Circ:** 3000.

13888 ■ Journal of Nutritional Biochemistry
Mosby Inc.
University of Kentucky
Lexington, KY 40506
Journal publishing experimental nutrition research as it relates to: biochemistry, neurochemistry, molecular biology, toxicology, physiology and pharmacology. **Freq:** Monthly. **Key Personnel:** B. Hennig, PhD, Editor-in-Chief; H.C. Bauer, Board Member; G.H. Anderson, Board Member; R. Asmis, Board Member; P.R. Borum, Board Member; N.K. Fukagawa, Board Member; J.R. Richardson, Manager; K. Fritsche, Board Member. **ISSN:** 0955--2863 (print). **Subscription Rates:** $457 U.S. online & print; $522 Other countries online & print; $400 Individuals online; $457 Students print and online; $522 Students, other countries print and online. **URL:** http://www.journals.elsevier.com/the-journal-of-nutritional-biochemistry; http://www.jnutbio.com. **Ad Rates:** BW $1,610; 4C $3,110. **Remarks:** Accepts advertising. **Circ:** (Not Reported).

13889 ■ Journal of Sport Rehabilitation
Human Kinetics Inc.
c/o Carl G. Mattacola, PhD, Ed.
University of Kentucky - Division of Athletic Training
Health Sciences Bldg., Rm. 210e
900 S Limestone
Lexington, KY 40536-0200
Publisher's E-mail: info@hkusa.com
Journal dedicated to research and practical articles concerning the rehabilitation of sport and exercise injuries. **Freq:** Quarterly February, May, August, November. **Print Method:** Offset. **Trim Size:** 6 x 9. **Key Personnel:** Carl G. Mattacola, PhD, Editor; Kellie Bliven, PhD, Associate Editor. **ISSN:** 1056--6716 (print); **EISSN:** 1543--3072 (electronic). **Subscription Rates:** $101 Individuals print + online; $587 Institutions print + online; $81 Students print + online; $81 Individuals online only; $479 Institutions online only; $61 Students online only. **URL:** http://journals.humankinetics.com/JSR. **Ad Rates:** BW $300. **Remarks:** Accepts advertising. **Circ:** (Not Reported).

13890 ■ Journal of Telecommunications in Higher Education
Association for College and University Technology Advancement
152 W Zandale Dr., Ste. 200
Lexington, KY 40503
Phone: (859)278-3338
Fax: (859)278-3268
Professional journal covering telecommunications and higher education. **Freq:** Quarterly. **Alt. Formats:** PDF. **Remarks:** Advertising accepted; rates available upon request. **Circ:** 2500.

13891 ■ Journal of Trauma Nursing
Society of Trauma Nurses
446 E High St., Ste. 10
Lexington, KY 40507
Phone: (859)271-0607
Fax: (859)977-7456
Freq: Quarterly. **Print Method:** Sheet fed. **Trim Size:** 7 7/8 x 10 7/8. **Key Personnel:** Kathleen M. Phelan, Publisher; Kathryn Schroeter, PhD, Editor-in-Chief. **ISSN:** 1078--7496 (print). **Subscription Rates:** $140 Individuals; $465 Institutions; $66 U.S. in-training; $143 Canada and Mexico; $230 Other countries; $486 Institutions, Canada and Mexico; $605 Institutions, other countries. **Online:** Gale. **URL:** http://journals.lww.com/journaloftraumanursing/pages/default.aspx; http://www.traumanurses.org/journal-of-trauma-nursing; http://www.lww.com/product/?1078-7496. **Ad Rates:** BW $810; 4C $1,415; 4C $1750; BW $1040. **Remarks:** Accepts advertising. **Circ:** Paid ‡2000, 1721.

13892 ■ Kentucky Journal of Equine, Agriculture, and Natural Resources Law
University of Kentucky College of Law
209 Law Bldg.
620 S Limestone St.
Lexington, KY 40506-0048
Phone: (859)257-1678
Fax: (859)257-3140
Publisher's E-mail: lawadmissions@email.uky.edu
Journal containing articles on environmental resources. **Freq:** 3/year. **Key Personnel:** Michelle Balaklaw, Editor-in-Chief. **Subscription Rates:** $20 U.S. outside the Commonwealth of Kentucky ; $21.20 U.S. originating within Kentucky. **URL:** http://www.kjeanrl.com. **Circ:** (Not Reported).

13893 ■ Kentucky Kernel
Kernel Press Inc.
026 Grehan Journalism Bldg.
Lexington, KY 40506-0042
Phone: (859)257-1915
Publisher's E-mail: news@kykernel.com
Collegiate newspaper. **Freq:** Semiweekly every Monday and Thursday. **Print Method:** Offset. **Trim Size:** 78.5 pca x 130.5 pca. **Cols./Page:** 6. **Col. Width:** 25 nonpareils. **Col. Depth:** 301 agate lines. **Key Personnel:** Will Wright, Editor-in-Chief, phone: (724)344-6945; Cheyene Miller, Managing Editor. **Subscription Rates:** Free. **URL:** http://kykernel.com. **Ad Rates:** BW $1528. 65; 4C $1777.50; SAU $12.50; PCI $11.85. **Remarks:** Accepts advertising. **Circ:** 8000.

13894 ■ Kentucky Law Journal
University of Kentucky College of Law
209 Law Bldg.
620 S Limestone St.
Lexington, KY 40506-0048
Phone: (859)257-1678
Fax: (859)257-3140
Publisher's E-mail: lawadmissions@email.uky.edu
Journal covering legal issues. **Freq:** Quarterly. **Print Method:** Offset. **Trim Size:** 6 3/4 x 10. **Cols./Page:** 1. **Col. Width:** 27 picas. **Col. Depth:** 48 picas. **Key Personnel:** Sarah Lawson, Editor-in-Chief; Jane L. Robinson, Managing Editor. **ISSN:** 0023-026X (print). **Subscription Rates:** $44 Individuals. **URL:** http://www.kentuckylawjournal.org. **Remarks:** Advertising not accepted. **Circ:** Paid ‡880, Controlled ‡475.

13895 ■ Kentucky Law Journal
University of Kentucky College of Law
209 Law Bldg.
620 S Limestone St.
Lexington, KY 40506-0048
Phone: (859)257-1678
Fax: (859)257-3140
Publisher's E-mail: lawadmissions@email.uky.edu
Journal containing articles on a broad range of legal topics. **Freq:** Quarterly. **Key Personnel:** K.Kirby Stephens, Editor-in-Chief. **Subscription Rates:** $42 Out of area; $44.52 Individuals within the commonwealth of Kentucky; $47 Other countries. **URL:** http://law.uky.edu/klj. **Circ:** (Not Reported).

13896 ■ The Lane Report: Kentucky's Business News Source
Lane Communications Group
201 E Main St., 14th Fl.
Lexington, KY 40507
Phone: (859)244-3500
Statewide magazine focusing on business, economics, and politics in Kentucky. **Freq:** Monthly. **Trim Size:** 8 1/8 x 10 7/8. **Key Personnel:** Ed Lane, Founder, phone: (859)244-3525; Dick Kelly, Publisher, phone: (859)244-3543. **ISSN:** 1063-925X (print). **Subscription Rates:** $29 Individuals; $53 Two years; $72 Individuals three years. **Ad Rates:** BW $3,000; 4C $3,750. **Remarks:** Accepts advertising. **Circ:** Free ■ **13944**, Paid ■ **601**, Combined ■ **14545**.

13897 ■ Lexington Herald-Leader
ProQuest L.L.C.
100 Midland Ave.
Lexington, KY 40508-1943
Phone: (859)231-3100
Free: 800-999-8881
Publisher's E-mail: info@proquest.com
General newspaper. **Freq:** Daily. **Print Method:** Offset. **Trim Size:** 13 x 21 1/2. **Cols./Page:** 6. **Col. Width:** 2 1/16 inches. **Col. Depth:** 21 1/2 inches. **Key Personnel:** Rufus M. Friday, President, Publisher, phone: (859)231-3248; Peter Baniak, Vice President, Editor, phone: (859)231-3446; Vanessa Gallman, Editor, phone: (859)231-1393. **ISSN:** 0745-4260 (print). **Subscription Rates:** 143.88 /yr.; Mon.-Sun.; online only; $2.50 Individuals Print & online (/week); $1.99 Individuals online (/month). **Online:** LexisNexis; McClatchy Newspapers Inc. McClatchy Newspapers Inc. **Alt. Formats:** Handheld. **URL:** http://www.kentucky.com. **Remarks:** Accepts advertising. **Circ:** Mon.-Fri. ⋆**111214**, Sun. ⋆**138986**.

13898 ■ Lexington Theological Quarterly
Lexington Theological Seminary
631 S Limestone St.
Lexington, KY 40508
Phone: (859)252-0361
Fax: (859)281-6042
Free: 866-296-6087
Publication E-mail: jsumney@lextheo.edu
Theological journal. **Freq:** Quarterly. **Print Method:** Letterpress and offset. **Trim Size:** 5 1/2 x 8 1/2. **Cols./Page:** 1. **Col. Width:** 48 nonpareils. **Col. Depth:** 98 agate lines. **Key Personnel:** Jerry Sumney, Contact. **ISSN:** 0024--1628 (print). **Subscription Rates:** By mail to all alumni/ae free of charge. **URL:** http://www.lextheo.edu/category/quarterly. **Formerly:** College of the Bible Quarterly. **Remarks:** Advertising not accepted. **Circ:** Non-paid 2300.

13899 ■ LiveSpa
International Spa Association
2365 Harrodsburg Rd., Ste. A325
Lexington, KY 40504
Phone: (859)226-4326
Fax: (859)226-4445
Free: 888-651-4772
Publisher's E-mail: ispa@ispastaff.com
Magazine featuring articles on how spa can play an integral part of quest for health. **Remarks:** Advertising not accepted. **Circ:** (Not Reported).

13900 ■ Medical Encounter
American Academy on Communication in Healthcare
201 E Main St., Ste. 1405
Lexington, KY 40507-2004
Phone: (859)514-9211
Fax: (859)514-9207
Publisher's E-mail: info@aachonline.org
Freq: Quarterly. **Subscription Rates:** included in membership dues. **URL:** http://www.aachonline.org/dnn/Resources/MedicalEncounter.aspx. **Remarks:** Accepts advertising. **Circ:** (Not Reported).

13901 ■ National Academies of Practice Forum
National Academies of Practice
201 E Main St., Ste. 1405
Lexington, KY 40507
Phone: (859)514-9184
Fax: (859)514-9188
Publisher's E-mail: info@napractice.org
ISSN: 1097- 5357 (print). **Remarks:** Advertising not accepted. **Circ:** (Not Reported).

13902 ■ Paso Fino Horse World
Lionheart Publishing Inc.
c/o Catherine King, Ed.
4047 Iron Works Pky., Ste. 1
Lexington, KY 40511
Phone: (859)825-6006
Publisher's E-mail: lpi@lionhrtpub.com
Magazine featuring Paso Fino equine breed and its owners. **Trim Size:** 8 3/8 x 10 7/8. **Key Personnel:** Catherine King, Editor; Don Vizi, Executive Director. **Subscription Rates:** $30 Individuals; $45 Canada and Mexico; $95 Other countries. **URL:** http://www.pfha.org/pfha-magazine. **Ad Rates:** BW $590; 4C $770. **Remarks:** Accepts advertising. **Circ:** (Not Reported).

13903 ■ The Phi Gamma Delta
Phi Gamma Delta
1201 Red Mile Rd.
Lexington, KY 40544-4599
Phone: (859)255-1848
Publisher's E-mail: phigam@phigam.org
Fraternity magazine. **Freq:** Quarterly. **Print Method:** Offset. **Cols./Page:** 3. **Col. Width:** 27 nonpareils. **Col. Depth:** 136 agate lines. **Key Personnel:** William A. Martin, III, Editor. **Subscription Rates:** Free. **URL:** http://www.phigam.org/magazine. **Mailing address:** PO Box 4599, Lexington, KY 40544. **Remarks:** Advertising not accepted. **Circ:** ‡90000, 26812.

13904 ■ Pony Club News
United States Pony Clubs
4041 Iron Works Pky.
Lexington, KY 40511
Phone: (859)254-7669
Fax: (859)233-4652

Freq: Quarterly. **Subscription Rates:** Included in membership. **URL:** http://www.ponyclub.org/?page=USPCNews; http://digital.olivesoftware.com/Olive/ODE/USPCNews/. **Remarks:** Accepts advertising. **Circ:** (Not Reported).

13905 ■ Pulse
International Spa Association
2365 Harrodsburg Rd., Ste. A325
Lexington, KY 40504
Phone: (859)226-4326
Fax: (859)226-4445
Free: 888-651-4772
Publisher's E-mail: ispa@ispastaff.com
Magazine informing spa industry professionals of the latest trends and practices and promoting the wellness aspects of spa. **Freq:** Bimonthly. **URL:** http://www.experienceispa.com/media/pulse-magazine/; http://experienceispa.com/#pulse. **Ad Rates:** BW $2700, full page; BW $2000, half page. **Remarks:** Accepts advertising. **Circ:** (Not Reported).

13906 ■ Q&A Magazine
Quest International Users Group
2365 Harrodsburg Rd., Ste. A325
Lexington, KY 40504-3366
Phone: (859)425-5081
Free: 800-225-0517
Publisher's E-mail: quest@questdirect.org
Freq: Quarterly. **URL:** http://questdirect.org/content/view/Qamagazine. **Remarks:** Advertising not accepted. **Circ:** (Not Reported).

13907 ■ Small Craft Advisory
National Association of State Boating Law Administrators
1648 McGrathiana Pky., Ste. 360
Lexington, KY 40511-1385
Phone: (859)225-9487
Publisher's E-mail: info@nasbla.org
Freq: Bimonthly. **ISSN:** 1066--2383 (print). **Alt. Formats:** Electronic publishing. **URL:** http://sca.nasbla.org/. **Remarks:** Advertising accepted; rates available upon request. **Circ:** (Not Reported).

13908 ■ USDF Competitor and Member Guide
United States Dressage Federation
4051 Iron Works Pky.
Lexington, KY 40511
Phone: (859)971-2277
Fax: (859)971-7722
Publisher's E-mail: usdressage@usdf.org
Magazine promoting dressage (a competitive equestrian sport) through articles about dressage tests and competitions, guidelines and rules, shows, awards, educational programs, scholarships and certificate earning events, advertisements, couture suggestions and merchandise. **Freq:** Annual. **URL:** http://www.usdf.org/Publications/. **Formerly:** USDF Directory. **Remarks:** Advertising not accepted. **Circ:** (Not Reported).

13909 ■ USDF Connection
United States Dressage Federation
4051 Iron Works Pky.
Lexington, KY 40511
Phone: (859)971-2277
Fax: (859)971-7722
Publisher's E-mail: usdressage@usdf.org
Magazine containing educational articles, dressage-community news, different personalities of dressage in America, links of related footages and interviews of experts, essays and commentaries by some of the most recognized and respected names in the sport. **Freq:** 10/year. **Subscription Rates:** Included in membership. **URL:** http://www.usdf.org/publications/. **Remarks:** Accepts advertising. **Circ:** (Not Reported).

13910 ■ Classic Rock 921 WBVX - 92.1
401 W Main St., Ste. 301
Lexington, KY 40507
Phone: (859)233-1515
Fax: (859)233-1517
Format: Classic Rock; Oldies. **Key Personnel:** Don Trail, Sales Mgr., dtrail@lmcomm.com. **URL:** http://www.classicrock921fm.com.

13911 ■ WBTF-FM - 107.9
401 W Main St., Ste. 301
Lexington, KY 40507
Phone: (859)233-1515
Fax: (859)233-1517
Format: Urban Contemporary. **Founded:** 1984. **Ad Rates:** Noncommercial. **URL:** http://www.1079thebeat.com.

13912 ■ WBUL-FM - 98.1
2601 Nicholasville Rd.
Lexington, KY 40503
Phone: (859)422-1000
Format: Country. **ADI:** Lexington, KY. **Key Personnel:** Bill Gentry, Gen. Mgr. **Wattage:** 100,000. **Ad Rates:** Noncommercial. **URL:** http://www.wbul.com.

13913 ■ WCDA-FM - 106.3
401 W Main St., Ste. 301
Lexington, KY 40507
Phone: (859)233-1515
Fax: (859)233-1517
Email: info@your1063.com
Format: Adult Contemporary. **Owner:** LM Communications Inc., 401 W Main St., Ste. 301, Lexington, KY 40507, Ph: (859)233-1515, Fax: (859)233-1517. **Operating Hours:** Continuous. **Key Personnel:** Don Trail, Sales Mgr., dtrail@lmcomm.com. **Wattage:** 3,700. **URL:** http://www.your1063.com.

WCVN-TV - See Covington

13914 ■ WDKY-TV - 56
836 Euclid Ave., Ste. 201
Lexington, KY 40502
Phone: (859)269-5656
Fax: (859)293-1578
Format: Commercial TV. **Networks:** Independent; Fox. **Owner:** Sinclair Broadcast Group Inc., 10706 Beaver Dam Rd., Hunt Valley, MD 21030, Ph: (410)568-1500, Fax: (410)568-1533. **Founded:** 1985. **Operating Hours:** 8:30 a.m.-5:30 p.m. **ADI:** Lexington, KY. **Ad Rates:** Advertising accepted; rates available upon request. **URL:** http://foxlexington.com.

13915 ■ WFLE-FM
334 Recreation Park Rd.
Flemingsburg, KY 41041
Phone: (606)849-4433
Fax: (606)845-9353
Format: Country. **Networks:** CNN Radio; KyNet; Meadows Racing. **Owner:** Dreamcatcher Communications, Inc., at above address. **Founded:** 1985. **Wattage:** 2,350 ERP. **Ad Rates:** $2.50 for 30 seconds; $4.50 for 60 seconds.

13916 ■ WGKS-FM - 96.9
401 W Main St., Ste. 301
Lexington, KY 40507
Phone: (859)233-1515
Format: Soft Rock. **Networks:** NBC; ABC; Mutual Broadcasting System. **Owner:** LM Communications Inc., 401 W Main St., Ste. 301, Lexington, KY 40507, Ph: (859)233-1515, Fax: (859)233-1517. **Founded:** 1968. **Formerly:** WCOZ-FM. **Operating Hours:** Continuous. **ADI:** Lexington, KY. **Key Personnel:** Skip Eliot, Dir. of Programs, seliot@lmcomm.com; James MacFarlane, Gen. Mgr., jmac@lmcomm.com. **Wattage:** 50,000. **Ad Rates:** Noncommercial. Combined advertising rates available with WCDA-FM WBVX-FM WLXG-FM WBTF-FM WLXO-FM. **URL:** http://www.969kissfm.com.

WKAS-TV - See Ashland

WKGB-TV - See Bowling Green

WKHA-TV - See Hazard

13917 ■ WKLE-TV - 46
600 Cooper Dr.
Lexington, KY 40502
Phone: (859)258-7000
Free: 800-432-0951
Email: shop@ket.org
Format: Educational. **Networks:** Public Broadcasting Service (PBS); Kentucky Educational Television. **Owner:** Kentucky Educational Television, 600 Cooper Dr., Lexington, KY 40502, Ph: (859)258-7000, Free: 800-432-0951. **Founded:** 1968. **Operating Hours:** Continuous. **ADI:** Lexington, KY. **Key Personnel:** Shae Hopkins, Exec. Dir. **Wattage:** 051. **Ad Rates:** Noncommercial. **URL:** http://www.ket.org.

WKMA-TV - See Madisonville

WKMJ-TV - See Louisville

WKMR-TV - See Morehead

WKMU-TV - See Murray

WKOH-TV - See Henderson

WKON-TV - See Owenton

WKPD-TV - See Paducah

WKPI-TV - See Pikeville

13918 ■ WKQQ-FM - 100.1
2601 Nicholasville Rd.
Lexington, KY 40503
Phone: (859)422-1000
Fax: (859)422-1038
Format: Classic Rock. **Networks:** Independent. **Founded:** 1969. **Operating Hours:** Continuous. **ADI:** Lexington, KY. **Key Personnel:** Bill Gentry, Gen. Mgr. **Wattage:** 100,000. **Ad Rates:** Advertising accepted; rates available upon request. **URL:** http://www.clearchannel.com/Radio/StationSearch.aspx?RadioSearch=WKQQ.

WKSO-TV - See Somerset

13919 ■ WKYT-TV - 27
2851 Winchester Rd.
Lexington, KY 40509
Phone: (859)299-0411
Email: comments@wkyt.com
Format: Commercial TV. **Networks:** CBS. **Owner:** Gray Television Inc., 4370 Peachtree Rd. NE, No. 400, Atlanta, GA 30319-3054, Ph: (404)266-8333. **Founded:** 1957. **Operating Hours:** Continuous per day excluding Friday and Saturday. **ADI:** Lexington, KY. **Key Personnel:** Wayne Martin, Gen. Mgr., wayne.martin@wkyt.com; Barbara Howard, Dir. of Programs, barbara.howard@wkyt.com; Mike Kanarek, VP, mike.kanarek@wkyt.com; Chris Martin, Contact, chris.martin@wkyt.com. **Wattage:** 1,520. **Ad Rates:** $25-2500 for 30 seconds. Combined advertising rates available with WYMT-TV. **URL:** http://www.wkyt.com.

13920 ■ WLAP-AM - 630
2601 Nicholasville Rd.
Lexington, KY 40503
Phone: (859)422-1000
Fax: (859)422-1038
Format: Talk; News. **Networks:** ABC; Fox. **Founded:** 1922. **Operating Hours:** Continuous. **ADI:** Lexington, KY. **Key Personnel:** Michael Jordan, Operations Mgr., michaeljordan@clearchannel.com. **Wattage:** 5,000 Day; 1,000 Night. **Ad Rates:** Advertising accepted; rates available upon request. **URL:** http://www.clearchannel.com/Radio/StationSearch.aspx?RadioSearch=WLAP.

13921 ■ WLEX-TV - 18
PO Box 1457
Lexington, KY 40588-1457
Phone: (859)259-1818
Fax: (859)254-2217
Email: news@lex18.com
Format: Commercial TV. **Networks:** NBC. **Owner:** Evening Post Industries Inc., 134 Columbus St., Charleston, SC 29403, Ph: (843)577-7111. **Founded:** 1955. **Operating Hours:** Continuous. **ADI:** Lexington, KY. **Ad Rates:** Advertising accepted; rates available upon request. **URL:** http://www.lex18.com.

13922 ■ WLKT-FM - 104.5
2601 Nicholasville Rd.
Lexington, KY 40503
Phone: (859)422-1000
Format: Adult Contemporary. **Wattage:** 50,000.

13923 ■ WLTO-FM - 102.5
300 W Vine St., 3rd Fl.
Lexington, KY 40507
Phone: (859)253-5900
Format: Contemporary Hit Radio (CHR); Urban Contemporary. **Owner:** Cumulus Broadcasting Inc., 3280 Peachtree Rd. NW, Ste. 2300, Atlanta, GA 30305-2447, Ph: (404)949-0700, Fax: (404)949-0740. **Key Personnel:** Tabatha Levrault, Dir. of Programs; Steve Bearance, Sales Mgr. **URL:** http://www.hot102.net.

13924 ■ WLXG-AM - 1300
401 W Main St., Ste. 301
Lexington, KY 40507
Phone: (859)233-1515

Circulation: ★ = AAM; △ or • = BPA; ♦ = CAC; ❑ = VAC; ⊕ = PO Statement; ‡ = Publisher's Report; Boldface figures = sworn; Light figures = estimated.

Fax: (859)233-1517
Email: info@wlxg.com
Format: Sports. **Networks:** NBC; ABC; Mutual Broadcasting System. **Owner:** LM Communications Inc., 401 W Main St., Ste. 301, Lexington, KY 40507, Ph: (859)233-1515, Fax: (859)233-1517. **Founded:** 1946. **Operating Hours:** Continuous. **ADI:** Lexington, KY. **Key Personnel:** Chris Cross, Dir. of Programs, ccross@lmcomm.com; Don Trail, Dir. of Sales, dtrail@lmcomm.com. **Wattage:** 1,000. **Ad Rates:** Noncommercial. Combined advertising rates available with WGKS-FM WCDA-FM WBVX-FM WBTF-FM WLXO-FM. **URL:** http://www.wlxg.com.

13925 ■ WLXO-FM - 96.1
401 W Main St., Ste. 301
Lexington, KY 40507
Phone: (859)233-1515
Format: Talk. **Ad Rates:** Noncommercial. **URL:** http://www.hank961.com.

13926 ■ WLXX-FM - 92.9
300 W Vine St.
Lexington, KY 40507
Phone: (859)253-5900
Free: 877-777-9299
Format: Country. **Owner:** Cumulus Broadcasting Inc., 3280 Peachtree Rd. NW, Ste. 2300, Atlanta, GA 30305-2447, Ph: (404)949-0700, Fax: (404)949-0740. **Operating Hours:** Continuous. **ADI:** Lexington, KY. **Wattage:** 100,000 ERP. **Ad Rates:** Advertising accepted; rates available upon request. **URL:** http://www.nashfm929.com.

13927 ■ WMJR-AM - 1380
110 Dennis Dr.
Lexington, KY 40503
Phone: (859)278-0894
Email: info@realliferadio.com
Format: Religious; Contemporary Christian. **Networks:** Independent. **Owner:** Realife Radio. **Operating Hours:** Continuous. **Wattage:** 5,000 Day; 038 Night. **Ad Rates:** Advertising accepted; rates available upon request. **URL:** http://www.realliferadio.com.

13928 ■ WMXL-FM - 94.5
2601 Nicholasville Rd.
Lexington, KY 40503
Phone: (859)422-1000
Fax: (859)422-1038
Format: Adult Contemporary. **Networks:** Independent. **Founded:** 1940. **Operating Hours:** Continuous. **Wattage:** 100,000. **Ad Rates:** Advertising accepted; rates available upon request.

13929 ■ WRFL-FM - 88.1
777 University Sta.
Lexington, KY 40506-0025
Phone: (859)257-4636
Email: contact@wrfl.fm
Format: Jazz; Bluegrass; News; Country; Alternative/New Music/Progressive. **Networks:** Independent. **Owner:** University of Kentucky, Lexington, KY 40506, Ph: (859)257-9000. **Founded:** 1988. **Operating Hours:** Continuous; 100% local. **ADI:** Lexington, KY. **Key Personnel:** Matt Gibson, Gen. Mgr. **Wattage:** 7,900. **Ad Rates:** Noncommercial; underwriting available. **URL:** http://www.wrfl.fm.

13930 ■ WTKT-FM - 103.3
2601 Nicholasville Rd.
Lexington, KY 40503-3307
Format: Oldies. **Networks:** Independent. **Founded:** 1973. **Formerly:** WRMA-FM; WAXU-FM; WMGB-FM. **Operating Hours:** Continuous. **ADI:** Lexington, KY. **Key Personnel:** Gil Dunn, Gen. Mgr.; Stan Isert, Dir. of Programs. **Wattage:** 6,000. **Ad Rates:** $34-39 per unit.

13931 ■ WTVQ-TV - 36
6940 Man O War Blvd.
Lexington, KY 40509
Phone: (859)294-3636
Email: news36@wtvq.com
Format: Commercial TV. **Networks:** ABC. **Owner:** Morris Network Inc., 27 Abercorn, Savannah, GA 31401, Ph: (912)233-1281, Fax: (912)232-4639. **Founded:** 1968. **Operating Hours:** Continuous. **ADI:** Lexington, KY. **Wattage:** 635,000 ERP H. **Ad Rates:** Advertising accepted; rates available upon request. **URL:** http://www.wtvq.com.

13932 ■ WUKY-FM - 91.3
340 McVey Hall
Lexington, KY 40506-0045
Phone: (859)257-3221
Email: wuky@wuky.org
Format: News; Adult Album Alternative. **Networks:** National Public Radio (NPR); Public Radio International (PRI). **Owner:** University of Kentucky, Lexington, KY 40506, Ph: (859)257-9000. **Founded:** 1940. **Formerly:** WBKY-FM. **Operating Hours:** Continuous; 70% network, 30% local. **ADI:** Lexington, KY. **Key Personnel:** Gordon Brandenburg, Contact, gwbran0@uky.edu; Alan Lytle, News Dir., aflytle@uky.edu; Tom Godell, Gen. Mgr., tom.godell@uky.edu; Mike Graves, Music Dir., mgrav1@uky.edu. **Local Programs:** *American Routes*, Saturday 3:00 - 5:00 p.m.; *Crossroads Radio*, Friday Saturday 10:00 p.m. - 11:00 p.m. 9:00 p.m. - 10:00 p.m.; *Blues Before Sunrise*, Sunday 1:00 a.m. - 6:00 a.m.; *Fresh Air Weekend*; *Girls Night Out*, Friday 8:00 p.m. - 9:00 p.m.; *Curtains @ 8*, Tuesday Wednesday Thursday 8:00 p.m. - 9:00 p.m.; *Solo Shots*, Friday 9:00 p.m. - 10:00 p.m.; *Putumayo World Music Hour*, Sunday 10:00 p.m. - 11:00 p.m.; *A Prairie Home Companion*, Saturday Sunday 7:00 p.m. - 8:00 p.m. 2:00 p.m. - 3:00 p.m.; *Curtains at Eight*, Tuesday Wednesday Thursday 8:00 p.m. - 9:00 p.m. **Wattage:** 100,000. **Ad Rates:** Noncommercial. **URL:** http://www.wuky.org.

13933 ■ WVLK-AM - 590
300 W Vine St., 3rd Fl.
Lexington, KY 40507-1814
Phone: (859)253-5900
Free: 877-777-0590
Format: News; Talk. **Owner:** Cumulus Broadcasting Inc., 3280 Peachtree Rd. NW, Ste. 2300, Atlanta, GA 30305-2447, Ph: (404)949-0700, Fax: (404)949-0740. **Founded:** 1946. **ADI:** Lexington, KY. **Wattage:** 5,000 Day; 1,000 Nig. **Ad Rates:** Advertising accepted; rates available upon request. **URL:** http://www.wvlkam.com.

13934 ■ WVLK-FM - 101.5
300 W Vine St., 3 Fl.
Lexington, KY 40507
Phone: (859)253-5959
Free: 877-777-0590
Email: news@wvlkam.com
Format: News. **Owner:** Cumulus Broadcasting Inc., 3280 Peachtree Rd. NW, Ste. 2300, Atlanta, GA 30305-2447, Ph: (404)949-0700, Fax: (404)949-0740. **Founded:** 1961. **Operating Hours:** Continuous. **Key Personnel:** Sue Wylie, Contact, suewylie@wvlkam.com. **Wattage:** 9,000 ERP. **Ad Rates:** Advertising accepted; rates available upon request. **URL:** http://www.wvlkam.com.

13935 ■ WWRW-FM - 105.5
2601 Nicholasville Rd.
Lexington, KY 40503
Phone: (859)422-1000
Format: Oldies; Eighties. **Owner:** iHeartMedia Inc., 200 E Basse Rd., San Antonio, TX 78209, Ph: (210)832-3314. **Founded:** 1948. **Formerly:** WMKJ-FM. **Operating Hours:** Continuous; 50% network, 50% local. **ADI:** Atlanta (Athens & Rome), GA. **Key Personnel:** Michael Jordan, Contact, michaeljordan@clearchannel.com. **Wattage:** 3,000. **Ad Rates:** Noncommercial. **URL:** http://www.rewind1055.com.

13936 ■ WXZZ-FM - 103.3
300 W Vine St., 3rd Fl.
Lexington, KY 40507
Free: 877-444-1033
Format: Classic Rock. **Owner:** Cumulus Broadcasting Inc., 3280 Peachtree Rd. NW, Ste. 2300, Atlanta, GA 30305-2447, Ph: (404)949-0700, Fax: (404)949-0740. **URL:** http://www.zrock103.com.

LIBERTY

Casey Co. Casey Co. (C).

13937 ■ The Casey County News
Landmark Community Newspapers L.L.C.
720 Campbellsville St.
Liberty, KY 42539
Phone: (606)787-7171
Fax: (606)787-8306
Publisher's E-mail: marketing@lcni.com
County newspaper. **Freq:** Weekly (Wed.). **Key Personnel:** Larry Rowell, Editor, Contact. **Subscription Rates:** $54.06 Individuals print and online; $54.16 Out of area print and online; $64 Out of state print and online; $38.16 Individuals online. **URL:** http://www.caseynews.net. **Mailing address:** PO Box 40, Liberty, KY 42539. **Remarks:** Accepts advertising. **Circ:** (Not Reported).

13938 ■ WKDO-AM
988 Dryridge Rd.
Liberty, KY 42539
Phone: (606)787-7331
Fax: (606)787-2166
Format: Country. **Networks:** USA Radio. **Owner:** Carlos Wesley, at above address. **Founded:** 1963. **Formerly:** WPHN-AM. **Wattage:** 1,000 Day. **Ad Rates:** $7 for 60 seconds. **Mailing address:** PO Box 990, Liberty, KY 42539.

13939 ■ WKDO-FM - 98.7
PO Box 990
Liberty, KY 42539
Phone: (606)787-7331
Fax: (606)787-2166
Format: Country; Religious. **Networks:** USA Radio. **Owner:** Carlos Wesley, at above address. **Founded:** 1963. **Operating Hours:** 18 HRS Daily. **Key Personnel:** Rick Wesley, Dir. of Programs. **Wattage:** 25,000. **Ad Rates:** $9 for 60 seconds. **URL:** http://wkdofm.com.

LONDON

Laurel Co. Laurel Co. (SEC). 70 m S of Lexington. Manufactures bakery products, fabricated sheet metal, automatic transfer switches, church furniture, non-woven products, business forms, lumber, fertilizer, fluid milk, ice cream. Cattle, pork grain farms.

13940 ■ The Sentinel-Echo
Community Newspaper Holdings Inc.
123 W Fifth St.
London, KY 40741
Phone: (606)878-7400
Fax: (606)878-7404
Newspaper serving Laurel County, Kentucky. Provides emphasis on timely, accurate, and local news about London and Laurel County. **Freq:** 3/week. **Key Personnel:** Willie Sawyers, Publisher; Kathy Jones, Manager, Advertising; Judy McCowan, Business Manager. **Subscription Rates:** $5.49 Individuals /month - print and online; $3.99 Individuals /month - online only. **URL:** http://www.sentinel-echo.com. **Mailing address:** PO Box 830, London, KY 40741. **Remarks:** Advertising accepted; rates available upon request. **Circ:** (Not Reported).

13941 ■ WKFC-FM - 101.9
1106A S Main St.
London, KY 40741
Phone: (606)878-9532
Fax: (606)546-4138
Free: 844-878-9532
Format: News; Classic Rock; Country. **URL:** http://www.wkfcfm.com.

WMAK-AM - See London, KY, USA

13942 ■ WMAK-AM - 980
948 Moriah Church Rd.
London, KY 40741
Phone: (606)878-0980
Format: Adult Contemporary. **Founded:** 1981. **Key Personnel:** Sam Cornette, Gen. Mgr. **Wattage:** 900.

13943 ■ WWEL-FM - 103.9
534 Tobacco Rd.
London, KY 40741
Phone: (606)864-2048
Format: Adult Contemporary. **Networks:** KyNet. **Owner:** F.T.G. Broadcasting Inc., at above address, Ph: (606)528-8787. **Founded:** 1970. **Operating Hours:** Continuous. **ADI:** Lexington, KY. **Key Personnel:** Frances Wilhoit, Contact, frwilhoit@forchtbroadcasting.com. **Wattage:** 6,000. **Ad Rates:** Advertising accepted; rates available upon request. Combined advertising rates available with WFTG-AM.

13944 ■ WWLT-FM - 103.1
PO Box 2098
Omaha, NE 68103
Free: 800-900-1300
Format: Contemporary Christian. **Owner:** Educational Media Foundation, 5700 W Oaks Blvd., CA 95765, Free: 800-800434-8400. **Founded:** 1969. **Operating Hours:**

Continuous. **Wattage:** 2,100. **Ad Rates:** $4.50-6.50 for 30 seconds; $5.50-8.50 for 60 seconds. **URL:** http://www.wwl.com.

13945 ■ WYGE-FM - 92.3
201 E Second St.
London, KY 40741
Phone: (606)877-1326
Free: 800-883-6424
Format: Religious. **Owner:** Ethel Huff Broadcasting L.L.C., 201 E Second St., London, KY 40741, Ph: (606)877-1326, Fax: (606)864-3702, Free: 800-883-6424. **Founded:** 1994. **Operating Hours:** Continuous. **Key Personnel:** Arlene Zawko, Gen. Mgr.; Leland Worley, Div. Mgr. **Wattage:** 23,500. **Ad Rates:** $5.20-7.50 for 30 seconds. **URL:** http://www.wygeradio.com.

LOUISA

Lawrence Co. Lawrence Co. (NE). On Big Sandy River, 30 m S of Ashland. Manufactures boxes, flour, feed, soft drinks. Oil, gas wells. Coal mines. Fire clay. San pit. Timber. Dairy, stock, poultry farms. Corn, feed, sorghum, tocacco.

13946 ■ The Big Sandy News
The Big Sandy News
PO Box 766
Louisa, KY 41230
Phone: (606)638-4581
Fax: (606)638-9949
Publication E-mail: info@bigsandynews.com
Community newspaper. **Freq:** Semiweekly (Wed. and Fri.). **Print Method:** Offset. **Cols./Page:** 6 and 8. **Col. Width:** 12 and 9 picas. **Col. Depth:** 21 and 21 inches. **Key Personnel:** Becky Crum, Contact; Randy Hale, Contact; Stephanie Couch, Contact. **URL:** http://www.bigsandynews.com. **Ad Rates:** GLR $4.75; BW $333.90; 4C $400; SAU $5; PCI $3. **Remarks:** Advertising accepted; rates available upon request. **Circ:** 12000.

13947 ■ Ignite FM - 92.3
PO Box 176
Louisa, KY 41230
Format: Gospel; Religious. **Owner:** Louisa Communications Inc., 28 W Division St, Morning Sun, IA 52640, Ph: (606)638-9203. **Formerly**: WZAQ-FM. **URL:** http://www.wzaqfm.com.

13948 ■ Lycom Communications Inc.
305 E Pike St.
Louisa, KY 41230
Phone: (606)638-3600
Fax: (606)638-4278
Free: 800-489-0640
Email: info@lycomonline.com
Cities Served: 230 channels. **URL:** http://www.lycomonline.com.

LOUISVILLE

Jefferson Co. Jefferson Co. (NW). On Ohio River, 109 m SW of Cincinnati, Ohio. Boat connections. Five bridges to New Albany, Ind. and Jeffersonville, Ind. University of Louisville, law, medical and dental, theology schools. Kentucky Derby and other race courses. Industrial, financial and educational center. Manufactures electrical appliances, whiskey, cigarettes, bathtubs, plumbing and railway supplies, paint, varnish, barrels, boxes, cabinets, bedding, mattresses, textiles, cement, beer, canned vegetables, biscuits, drying machinery, fire brick, caskets, auto bodies, trailers, steel and wood tanks, shirts, synthetic rubber, aluminum boats, farm machinery, plywood, wood plastics, baseball bats. Meat packing; sugar refining; wood working; creosoting, auto assembly plants; machine shops, oil refineries; phosphate, fluorspar, stone quarries.

13949 ■ Competitions
Competition Project Inc.
PO Box 20445
Louisville, KY 40250
Phone: (502)451-3623
Publisher's E-mail: hotline@competitions.org
Magazine covering design competitions in architecture, landscape architecture, and planning. **Freq:** Quarterly. **Key Personnel:** G. Stanley Collyer, Editor; Udo Greinacher, Editor. **ISSN:** 1058--6539 (print). **Subscription Rates:** $45 Individuals e-magazine, email announcements + annual; $35 Individuals e-magazine, email announcements. **URL:** http://www.competitions.org. **Circ:** (Not Reported).

13950 ■ Computer Times
Computer Times
PO Box 91830
Louisville, KY 40291
Phone: (502)807-9339
Publisher's E-mail: comptimes@aol.com
Online trade magazine covering computer trends and other issues for SOHO users, small businesses, and home users. Includes 'editor's choice' product reviews. **Freq:** Monthly. **Key Personnel:** Terry Kibiloski, Editor; Sean Kibiloski, Editor; Angie Kibiloski, Editor. **URL:** http://www.computertimes.com. **Remarks:** Advertising accepted; rates available upon request. **Circ:** Combined 100000.

13951 ■ The Courier-Journal
The Courier-Journal
PO Box 740031
Louisville, KY 40201-7431
Phone: (502)582-4011
Publisher's E-mail: publisher@courier-journal.com
General newspaper. **Founded:** 1868. **Freq:** Daily and Sun. (morn.). **Print Method:** Letterpress. **Cols./Page:** 6. **Col. Width:** 24 nonpareils. **Col. Depth:** 300 agate lines. **Key Personnel:** Arnold Garson, President, Publisher, phone: (502)582-4101; Bennie Ivory, Executive Editor, Vice President, phone: (502)582-4295; Laura Ungar, Writer; Jessie Halladay, Reporter; Jere Downs, Writer; Dan Blake, Editor; Nancy Rodriguez, Reporter. **Subscription Rates:** $17.75 Individuals Monday through Sunday; $13 Individuals Friday, Saturday and Sunday; $9.90 Individuals Sundays/holidays. **Online:** Dow Jones & Company Inc.; The Courier-Journal The Courier-Journal; NewsBank Inc. **URL:** http://www.courier-journal.com. **Ad Rates:** 4C $2,015. **Remarks:** Accepts advertising. **Circ:** Mon.-Sat. ★**215328**, Sun. ★**258778**.

13952 ■ EarthSave
EarthSave - Louisville Chapter
PO Box 4397
Louisville, KY 40204
Phone: (502)299-9520
Publisher's E-mail: louisville@earthsave.org
Magazine containing educating articles on helping the planet and maintaining a healthy, earth-friendly diet; also featuring updates on the activities of EarthSave, Louisville Chapter. **Freq:** Bimonthly. **Subscription Rates:** Free. **URL:** http://louisville.earthsave.org. **Remarks:** Accepts advertising. **Circ:** (Not Reported).

13953 ■ EGA Needle Arts Magazine
Embroiderers' Guild of America
1355 Bardstown Rd., Ste. 157
Louisville, KY 40204-1353
Phone: (502)589-6956
Fax: (502)584-7900
Technical, trade magazine for needle workers. **Freq:** Quarterly. **Print Method:** Web offset. **Trim Size:** 8 1/8 x 10 7/8. **Cols./Page:** 3. **Col. Width:** 13 picas. **Col. Depth:** 9 1/2 inches. **Key Personnel:** Cheryl Christian, Editor. **Subscription Rates:** $40 Individuals; $7.42 Single issue /back issue. **URL:** http://www.egausa.org/index.php/resources/needlearts-magazine. **Remarks:** Accepts advertising. **Circ:** Paid 18000.

13954 ■ The Filson
Filson Historical Society
1310 S 3rd St.
Louisville, KY 40208
Phone: (502)635-5083
Fax: (502)635-5086
Freq: Quarterly. **Key Personnel:** Mark Wetherington, Director; Judy Miller, Director, Public Relations. **Subscription Rates:** $10 Individuals; Included in membership. **Remarks:** Advertising not accepted. **Circ:** 5000.

13955 ■ The Gateway Press
Gateway Press Inc.
4500 Robards Ln.
Louisville, KY 40218-4537
Phone: (502)454-0431
Fax: (502)459-7930
Publisher's E-mail: comments@galleryofguns.com
Community newspaper. **Freq:** Weekly (Wed.). **Print Method:** Offset. **Cols./Page:** 7. **Col. Width:** 8 picas. **Col. Depth:** 13 3/4 inches. **Key Personnel:** Bob Gaetjens, Editor. **Ad Rates:** BW $735; PCI $7.50. **Remarks:** Accepts advertising. **Circ:** Paid ‡5798.

13956 ■ Henry James Review
Johns Hopkins University Press
c/o Susan M. Griffin, Ed.
University of Louisville
Dept. of English
Louisville, KY 40292
Phone: (502)852-4671
Fax: (502)852-4182
Publication E-mail: hjamesr@louisville.edu
Literary journal. **Freq:** 3/year. **Print Method:** Offset. **Trim Size:** 7 x 10. **Cols./Page:** 1. **Col. Width:** 26 picas. **Col. Depth:** 7 inches. **Key Personnel:** Dr. Leland S. Person, Jr., Board Member; Paul B. Armstrong, Board Member; Martha Banta, Board Member; B. Joanne Webb, Managing Editor; Susan M. Griffin, Editor. **ISSN:** 0273--0340 (print); **EISSN:** 1080--6555 (electronic). **Subscription Rates:** $40 Individuals print; $72 Two years print; $125 Institutions print; $250 Two years print; $50 Individuals online; $90 Two years online. **URL:** http://www.press.jhu.edu/journals/henry_james_review. **Ad Rates:** BW $325. **Remarks:** Accepts advertising. **Circ:** ‡343.

13957 ■ Horizons
Presbyterian Women in the Presbyterian Church U.S.A.
100 Witherspoon St.
Louisville, KY 40202-1396
Fax: (502)569-8080
Free: 888-728-7228
Magazine for Presbyterian women and annual Bible study. **Founded:** 1988. **Freq:** Bimonthly. **Key Personnel:** Susan Jackson Dowd, Communications Specialist. **ISSN:** 1040-0087 (print). **Subscription Rates:** $24.95 Individuals print; $44 Two years print; $34.95 Other countries print. **URL:** http://horizons.pcusa.org. **Formerly**: Concern. **Remarks:** Advertising not accepted. **Circ:** Paid 28000, Non-paid 1000.

13958 ■ Internet Journal of Infectious Diseases
Internet Scientific Publications L.L.C.
c/o Stephen B. Kennedy, MD, Ed.-in-Ch.
Pacific Institute for Research & Evaluation (PIRE)
Louisville Center
1300 S 4th St., Ste. 300
Louisville, KY 40208
Publisher's E-mail: support@ispub.com
Online journal covering infectious diseases. **Freq:** Semiannual. **Key Personnel:** Stephen B. Kennedy, MD, Editor-in-Chief; Ata Nevzat Yalcin, MD, Associate Editor. **ISSN:** 1528--8366 (print). **Subscription Rates:** Free. **URL:** http://ispub.com/IJID. **Remarks:** Advertising accepted; rates available upon request. **Circ:** (Not Reported).

13959 ■ Journal of Animal and Environmental Law
University of Louisville Brandeis School of Law
Louis D. Brandeis School of Law
2301 S 3rd.
Louisville, KY 40292
Phone: (502)852-6358
Fax: (502)852-0862
Publisher's E-mail: lawadmissions@louisville.edu
Peer-reviewed journal covering the awareness of legal issues to animal and environmental law. **Freq:** Semiannual. **Key Personnel:** Katie Bonds, Editor-in-Chief. **URL:** http://www.jael-online.org. **Circ:** (Not Reported).

13960 ■ Journal of Cardiothoracic and Vascular Anesthesia
Elsevier Inc.
c/o Joel A. Kaplan, MD, Ed.-in-Ch.
University of Louisville
Abell Administration Center
323 E Chestnut St.
Louisville, KY 40202-3866
Publication E-mail: elspcs@elsevier.com
Scholarly journal covering cardiac, thoracic, and vascular surgical procedures for anesthesiologists. **Freq:** Bimonthly. **Print Method:** Sheetfed. **Trim Size:** 8 1/4 x 11. **Key Personnel:** P. Slinger, MD, Associate Editor; Joel A. Kaplan, MD, Editor-in-Chief; N.G. Kaplan, Managing Editor. **ISSN:** 1053-0770 (print). **Subscription Rates:** $480 Individuals; $924 Institutions; $240 Students. **URL:** http://www.journals.elsevier.com/journal-

Circulation: ★ = AAM; △ or • = BPA; ♦ = CAC; ❑ = VAC; ⊕ = PO Statement; ‡ = Publisher's Report; Boldface figures = sworn; Light figures = estimated.

of-cardiothoracic-and-vascular-anesthesia/. **Ad Rates:** BW $1,435; 4C $1,490. **Remarks:** Accepts advertising. **Circ:** Combined ‡1425.

13961 ■ Journal of Criminal Justice Education
Routledge Journals Taylor & Francis Group
Dept. of Justice Administration
University of Louisville
2301 S Third St.
208 Brigman Hall
Louisville, KY 40292
Phone: (502)852-0331
Fax: (502)852-0065
Publication E-mail: jcje@louisville.edu
Journal providing a forum for the examination, discussion and debate of a broad range of issues concerning post-secondary education in criminal justice, criminology and related areas. **Freq:** Quarterly. **Key Personnel:** George Higgins, Editor; Jennifer Hartman, Deputy, Editor. **ISSN:** 1051--1253 (print); **EISSN:** 1745--9117 (electronic). **Subscription Rates:** $681 Institutions online only; $778 Institutions print & online. **URL:** http://www.tandfonline.com/toc/rcje20/current. **Remarks:** Accepts advertising. **Circ:** (Not Reported).

13962 ■ Journal of the Evangelical Theological Society
Evangelical Theological Society
2825 Lexington Rd.
Louisville, KY 40280-0001
Phone: (502)897-4388
Fax: (502)897-4386
Publisher's E-mail: director@etsjets.org
Journal of religion and theology. **Freq:** Quarterly usually March, June, September, and December. **Print Method:** Offset. **Trim Size:** 9" x 6". **Cols./Page:** 1. **Col. Width:** 54 nonpareils. **Col. Depth:** 108 agate lines. **Key Personnel:** James Borland, Secretary, Treasurer; Andreas J. Kostenberger, Editor. **ISSN:** 0360--8808 (print). **Subscription Rates:** $30 Individuals /year; $60 Individuals 2 years. **URL:** http://www.etsjets.org/JETS. **Ad Rates:** BW $750. **Remarks:** Accepts advertising. **Circ:** (Not Reported).

13963 ■ Journal of the Kentucky Medical Association
Kentucky Medical Association
4965 US Hwy. 42, Ste. 2000
Louisville, KY 40222
Phone: (502)426-6200
Fax: (502)426-6877
Publisher's E-mail: best@kyma.org
Professional medical journal. **Freq:** Monthly. **Print Method:** Offset. **Trim Size:** 8.25 x 10.875. **Cols./Page:** 2. **Col. Width:** 17.5 picas. **Col. Depth:** 49 picas. **Key Personnel:** Sharon Heckel, MD, Managing Editor. **ISSN:** 2155-661X (print). **Alt. Formats:** PDF. **URL:** http://www.kyma.org/content.asp?q_areaprimaryid=9&q_areasecondaryid=28. **Ad Rates:** BW $395; 4C $400. **Remarks:** Accepts advertising. **Circ:** ⊕**6200**.

13964 ■ Journal of Law and Education
University of Louisville Brandeis School of Law
Louis D. Brandeis School of Law
2301 S 3rd.
Louisville, KY 40292
Phone: (502)852-6358
Fax: (502)852-0862
Publisher's E-mail: lawadmissions@louisville.edu
Journal containing articles on civil law related to American education. **Freq:** Quarterly January, April, July and October. **ISSN:** 0275--6072 (print). **Subscription Rates:** $100 Individuals; $113 Other countries /year. **URL:** http://louisville.edu/law/student-services/student-publications/journal-of-law-education; http://www.law.sc.edu/jled; http://law.sc.edu/about/journals.shtml. **Circ:** (Not Reported).

13965 ■ Kentucky Living
Kentucky Association of Electric Cooperatives
4515 Bishop Ln.
Louisville, KY 40218-4507
Phone: (502)451-2430
Fax: (502)459-3209
Free: 800-357-5232
Magazine on people, places, events, and history of Kentucky. **Freq:** Monthly. **Print Method:** Offset. **Trim Size:** 8.125 x 10.875. **Cols./Page:** 3. **Col. Width:** 2 1/4 inches. **Col. Depth:** 10 inches. **Key Personnel:** Paul Wesslund, Editor. **ISSN:** 0036--0066 (print). **Subscription Rates:** $15 Individuals; $25 Individuals 3 years; Included in membership. **URL:** http://www.kentuckyliving.com. **Mailing address:** PO Box 32170, Louisville, KY 40232-2170. **Ad Rates:** BW $13620; 4C $16332; PCI $195. **Circ:** Paid ★**509077**.

13966 ■ Leader Courier
The Courier-Journal
PO Box 740031
Louisville, KY 40201-7431
Phone: (502)582-4011
Publication E-mail: leadercourier@websurf.net
Community newspaper. **Freq:** Weekly (Tues.). **Cols./Page:** 6. **Col. Width:** 14 picas. **Col. Depth:** 21 1/2 inches. **Key Personnel:** Kelly Kruithoff, Editor; Bruce Odson, Publisher. **Subscription Rates:** $37 Individuals Union and Clay counties in South Dakota, Plymouth and Woodbury counties in Iowa; $47 Out of area. **URL:** http://leadercourier-times.com. **Formerly:** Kingman Journal. **Circ:** ‡1450.

13967 ■ The Louisville Cardinal
University of Louisville
University of Louisville
Houchens Bldg., LL07
Louisville, KY 40292
Publisher's E-mail: cmoffice@louisville.edu
Collegiate newspaper (tabloid). **Freq:** Weekly (Thurs.). **Print Method:** Offset. **Trim Size:** 11 x 17. **Cols./Page:** 6. **Col. Width:** 26 nonpareils. **Col. Depth:** 301 agate lines. **Key Personnel:** Simon Isham, Editor-in-Chief. **Subscription Rates:** $8 By mail. **URL:** http://www.louisvillecardinal.com. **Ad Rates:** BW $482.50; PCI $9.25. **Remarks:** Accepts advertising. **Circ:** Free 17000.

13968 ■ Louisville Eccentric Observer
Louisville Eccentric Observer
301 E Main St., Ste. 201
Louisville, KY 40202
Phone: (502)895-9770
Fax: (502)895-9779
Community newspaper. **Freq:** Weekly (Wed.). **Key Personnel:** Aaron Yarmuth, Executive Editor. **Subscription Rates:** Free. **Remarks:** Accepts advertising. **Circ:** (Not Reported).

13969 ■ Louisville Magazine, Inc.
Louisville Magazine Inc.
137 W Muhammad Ali Blvd., Ste. 101
Louisville, KY 40202
Phone: (502)625-0100
Fax: (502)625-0107
City magazine. **Freq:** Monthly. **Print Method:** Offset. **Trim Size:** 8 3/8 x 10 7.8 in. **Cols./Page:** 3. **Col. Width:** 28 nonpareils. **Col. Depth:** 140 agate lines. **Key Personnel:** Jack Welch, Senior Editor, phone: (502)625-0100; Dan Cruthcher, Publisher. **ISSN:** 0024--6948 (print). **Subscription Rates:** $22 Individuals; $36 Two years; $6 Single issue back issue. **URL:** http://www.loumag.com. **Ad Rates:** BW $1725; 4C $2375. **Remarks:** Accepts advertising. **Circ:** Paid 26520.

13970 ■ The Louisville Review
Spalding University
845 S Third St.
Louisville, KY 40203
Phone: (502)585-9911
Free: 800-896-8941
Publication E-mail: louisvillereview@spalding.edu
Magazine featuring poetry and stories. **Freq:** Semiannual Spring and Fall. **Key Personnel:** Sena Jeter Naslund, Editor; Karen J. Mann, Managing Editor; Kathleen Driskell, Associate Editor. **Subscription Rates:** $14 Individuals; $12 Students. **URL:** http://www.louisvillereview.org. **Circ:** (Not Reported).

13971 ■ Merton Seasonal
International Thomas Merton Society
2001 Newburg Rd.
Louisville, KY 40205
Phone: (502)272-8177
Fax: (502)272-8452
Freq: Quarterly. **ISSN:** 0988- 4927 (print). **Subscription Rates:** $25 for regular subscription; $15 for students. **URL:** http://merton.org/ITMS/seasonal.aspx. **Remarks:** Accepts advertising. **Circ:** 1600.

13972 ■ Needle Arts
Embroiderers' Guild of America
1355 Bardstown Rd., Ste. 157
Louisville, KY 40204-1353
Phone: (502)589-6956
Fax: (502)584-7900
Freq: Quarterly. **Subscription Rates:** Included in membership; $7.42 Single issue back issue. **URL:** http://www.egausa.org/index.php/resources/needlearts-magazine. **Remarks:** Accepts advertising. **Circ:** 13000.

13973 ■ Ohio Valley History
Filson Historical Society
1310 S 3rd St.
Louisville, KY 40208
Phone: (502)635-5083
Fax: (502)635-5086
A Journal of the History and Culture of the Ohio Valley and the Upper South. **Freq:** Quarterly. **Key Personnel:** Mark Wetherington, Executive Director; Judy Miller, Director, Public Relations. **ISSN:** 0746-3472 (print). **Subscription Rates:** $15 Free to qualified subscribers; $30 Individuals; $45 Institutions; Included in membership. **URL:** http://filsonhistorical.org; http://filsonhistorical.org/read-watch-listen/. **Formed by the merger of:** Filson Historical Quarterly. **Formerly:** Bulletin of the Cincinnati Historical Society. **Ad Rates:** BW $300. **Remarks:** Accepts advertising. **Circ:** Controlled 2000, 7500.

13974 ■ Ohio Valley History
Cincinnati Museum Center and The Filson Historical Society
1310 S 3rd St.
Louisville, KY 40208
Phone: (502)635-5083
Fax: (502)635-5086
A Journal of the History and Culture of the Ohio Valley and the Upper South. **Freq:** Quarterly. **Key Personnel:** Mark Wetherington, Executive Director; Judy Miller, Director, Public Relations. **ISSN:** 0746-3472 (print). **Subscription Rates:** $15 Free to qualified subscribers; $30 Individuals; $45 Institutions; Included in membership. **URL:** http://filsonhistorical.org; http://filsonhistorical.org/read-watch-listen/. **Formed by the merger of:** Filson Historical Quarterly. **Formerly:** Bulletin of the Cincinnati Historical Society. **Ad Rates:** BW $300. **Remarks:** Accepts advertising. **Circ:** Controlled 2000, 7500.

13975 ■ The Open Letter
The Fellowship Community
8134 New LaGrange Rd., Ste. 227
Louisville, KY 40222
Phone: (502)425-4630
Publisher's E-mail: office@fellowship.community
Publication acting as a renewal and issues resource for Presbyterians. **Freq:** 5/year. **Print Method:** Offset. **Trim Size:** 8 1/2 x 11. **Cols./Page:** 3. **Key Personnel:** Mathew McGowan, Editor. **ISSN:** 0194--7125 (print). **Circ:** Non-paid ‡63000.

13976 ■ Outdoor Journal
American Crappie Association
220 Mohawk Ave.
Louisville, KY 40209
Phone: (502)384-5924
Fax: (502)384-4232
Publisher's E-mail: office@crappieusa.com
Journal containing articles, reports and schedules on crappie and catfish fishing as well as chapter activities. **Freq:** Quarterly. **URL:** http://www.crappieusa.com/outdoor_library.cfm. **Ad Rates:** BW $825. **Remarks:** Accepts advertising. **Circ:** (Not Reported).

13977 ■ Psychotherapy Research
Society for Psychotherapy Research
University of Louisville
401 E Chestnut St., Unit 610
Louisville, KY 40202-5711
Freq: 6/year. **Print Method:** Offset. **Trim Size:** 7 x 10. **ISSN:** 1050--3307 (print); **EISSN:** 1468--4381 (electronic). **Subscription Rates:** $308 Individuals print; $530 Institutions online; £606 Institutions print & online; included in membership dues; $280 /year for individuals, print only; $482 /year for institutions, online only; $551 /year for institutions, print & online. **Available online. URL:** http://www.tandfonline.com/action/journalInformation?journalCode=tpsr20#.VJgZEusJB; http://www.psychotherapyresearch.org/?page=SPRJournal. **Remarks:** Accepts advertising. **Circ:** Combined ‡1350.

13978 ■ Reproductive Toxicology
RELX Group P.L.C.
c/o Dr. Thomas B. Knudsen, Ed.-in-Ch.

University of Louisville
Birth Defects Center, Rm. 301
501 S Preston St.
Louisville, KY 40202
Phone: (919)541-9776
Fax: (919)541-1194
Publication E-mail: rtx@louisville.edu
Journal covering articles on influence of chemical and physical agents on reproduction focusing mainly for obstetricians, pediatricians, embryologists, teratologists, geneticists, toxicologists, andrologists, and others interested in detecting potential reproductive hazards. **Founded:** 1988. **Freq:** 8/year. **Key Personnel:** Dr. Thomas B. Knudsen, Editor-in-Chief; Dr. Aldert Piersma, Associate Editor. **ISSN:** 0890-6238 (print). **Subscription Rates:** $2419.20 online; $2419 Institutions print; $336 Individuals. **URL:** http://www.journals.elsevier.com/reproductive-toxicology/. **Circ:** (Not Reported).

13979 ■ Review and Expositor
Review and Expositor
PO Box 6681
Louisville, KY 40206-0681
Phone: (502)327-8347
Publisher's E-mail: office@rande.org
Magazine on theology. **Freq:** Quarterly. **Print Method:** Letterpress. **Trim Size:** 7 x 10. **Cols./Page:** 1. **Col. Width:** 48 nonpareils. **Col. Depth:** 126 agate lines. **Key Personnel:** Mark E. Biddle, Managing Editor; Joel Drinkard, Business Manager; Gerald Keown, Recording Secretary. **ISSN:** 0034--6373 (print). **Subscription Rates:** $35 Individuals; $50 Other countries; $95 Libraries; $110 Libraries foreign; $20 Single issue foreign, plus postage & handling; $38 Libraries foreign, plus postage & handling. **URL:** http://rae.sagepub.com. **Mailing address:** PO Box 6681, Louisville, KY 40206-0681. **Ad Rates:** BW $120. **Remarks:** Advertising accepted; rates available upon request. **Circ:** (Not Reported).

13980 ■ Southern Seminary Magazine: News About the Southern Baptist Theological Seminary
Review and Expositor
PO Box 6681
Louisville, KY 40206-0681
Phone: (502)327-8347
Publisher's E-mail: office@rande.org
News and information about Southern Seminary. **Freq:** Quarterly. **Print Method:** Offset. **Trim Size:** 8 3/8 x 10 7/8. **Cols./Page:** 3. **Col. Width:** 27 nonpareils. **Col. Depth:** 132 agate lines. **Key Personnel:** Douglas C. Walker, III, Contact. **ISSN:** 0040--7232 (print). **Subscription Rates:** Free. **Alt. Formats:** Download; PDF. **URL:** http://www.sbts.edu/resources/category/magazines. **Formerly**: The Tie. **Mailing address:** PO Box 6681, Louisville, KY 40206-0681. **Remarks:** Advertising not accepted. **Circ:** Controlled 33000.

13981 ■ Theatre Design & Technology: The journal for design, production and technology professionals in the performing arts and entertainment industry
United States Institute for Theatre Technology
c/o David Rodger, Editor
3001 Springcrest Dr.
Louisville, KY 40241-2755
Phone: (502)426-1211
Fax: (502)423-7467
Magazine covering technical and design advances in theatre, including lighting, sound, scene design, and costuming, as well as health and safety issues. **Freq:** Quarterly. **Print Method:** Letterpress. **Trim Size:** 8 1/2 x 11 1/8. **Cols./Page:** 3. **Key Personnel:** David Rodger, Editor. **ISSN:** 1052--6765 (print). **URL:** http://www.usitt.org/tdt. **Formerly**: TD & T. **Ad Rates:** BW $1040; 4C $1640. **Remarks:** Accepts advertising. **Circ:** 5000.

13982 ■ Unique Opportunities: The Physician's Resource
UO Inc.
214 S 8th St., Ste. 502
Louisville, KY 40202
Phone: (502)589-8250
Fax: (502)587-0848
Free: 800-888-2047
Professional magazine covering career development for physicians. **Freq:** Bimonthly. **Print Method:** Web offset. **Trim Size:** 8 1/8 x 10 7/8. **Cols./Page:** 3. **Key Personnel:** Barbara Barry, Publisher; Kathy Kotcamp, Office Manager; Mollie Hudson, Editor; Bobby C. Baker, MD, Founder; Barbara Alden Wilson, Associate Editor. **ISSN:** 1059--6100 (print). **Subscription Rates:** Free for physicians. **Ad Rates:** BW $4655; 4C $5590. **Remarks:** Accepts advertising. **Circ:** Controlled 80,059.

13983 ■ UofL
University of Louisville Alumni Association
University Club and Alumni Ctr.
200 E Brandeis Ave.
Louisville, KY 40208
Phone: (502)852-6186
Fax: (502)852-6920
Free: 800-813-8635
Magazine containing interesting topics about the University of Louisville for alumni, faculty, staff, students and anyone who is a Louisville Cardinals fan. **Freq:** Quarterly. **Key Personnel:** Rebecca Simpson, Editor-in-Chief. **Subscription Rates:** Included in membership. **URL:** http://louisville.epubxp.com/read/account_titles/158014. **Remarks:** Accepts advertising. **Circ:** 126000.

13984 ■ Western Recorder
Western Recorder Inc.
PO Box 43969
Louisville, KY 40253
Newspaper (tabloid) serving Kentucky Baptist Convention. **Freq:** Weekly (Tues.) except the first week in January, the week of Independence Day and the week of Christmas. **Print Method:** Offset. **Trim Size:** 10 x 14. **Cols./Page:** 4. **Col. Width:** 12 picas. **Col. Depth:** 140 agate lines. **Key Personnel:** Todd Deaton, Editor; Tom Townsend, Business Manager, Manager, Marketing. **ISSN:** 0043--4132 (print). **Subscription Rates:** $17 Individuals print and online; $10.60 Individuals electronic. **URL:** http://www.westernrecorder.org. **Ad Rates:** BW $1600; 4C $1120; PCI $30. **Remarks:** Accepts advertising. **Circ:** Paid 18000.

13985 ■ 989 Radio Now - 98.9
4000 Radio Dr., Ste. 1
Louisville, KY 40218
Phone: (502)479-2222
Format: Contemporary Hit Radio (CHR). **Owner:** iHeartMedia Inc., 200 E Basse Rd., San Antonio, TX 78209, Ph: (210)832-3314. **Operating Hours**: Continuous. **Ad Rates:** Advertising accepted; rates available upon request. **URL:** http://www.989radionow.com.

13986 ■ WAMZ-FM - 97.5
4000 Radio Dr., Ste. 1
Louisville, KY 40218
Phone: (502)479-2222
Format: Country. **Networks:** Independent. **Founded:** 1966. **Operating Hours**: Continuous. **ADI**: Louisville, KY. **Wattage**: 100,000. **Ad Rates:** Advertising accepted; rates available upon request. **URL:** http://www.wamz.com.

13987 ■ WAVE-TV - 3
725 S Floyd St.
Louisville, KY 40203
Phone: (502)585-2201
Fax: (502)561-4115
Format: Commercial TV. **Networks:** NBC. **Owner:** Raycom Media Inc., 201 Monroe St., RSA Twr., 20th Fl., Montgomery, AL 36104-3731, Ph: (334)206-1400. **Operating Hours**: 6 a.m.-3 a.m. **ADI**: Louisville, KY. **Ad Rates:** Noncommercial. **URL:** http://www.wave3.com.

13988 ■ WAY-FM - 104.3
3211 Grant Line Rd., Ste. 1
New Albany, IN 47150
Phone: (812)945-0316
Fax: (812)945-0317
Free: 888-929-1059
Email: supportservices@wayfm.com
Format: Contemporary Christian. **Owner:** WAY-FM Media Group Inc., 5540 Tech Center Dr., Ste. 200, Colorado Springs, CO 80919, Ph: (719)533-0300. **Founded:** 1987. **Key Personnel:** Bryans Johns, Dir. of Operations. **Mailing address:** PO Box 1043, New Albany, IN 47151. **URL:** http://www.wayh.wayfm.com.

13989 ■ WBKI-TV - 34
624 W Muhammad Ali Blvd.
Louisville, KY 40205
Phone: (502)809-3400
Fax: (502)589-5559
Email: feedback@wbki.tv
Founded: 1953. **Key Personnel:** Terry Glaser, Gen. Sales Mgr., tglaser@wbki.tv; Craig Hoffman, Dir. of Operations, choffman@wbki.tv; Steve Ballard, CFO. **URL:** http://www.wbki.tv.

13990 ■ WBNA-TV - 21
3701 Fern Valley Rd.
Louisville, KY 40219
Phone: (502)964-2121
Format: Commercial TV; Music of Your Life; Sports. **Networks:** Independent. **Owner:** WORD Broadcasting, Inc., at above address. **Founded:** 1986. **Operating Hours**: Continuous. **ADI**: Louisville, KY. **Wattage**: 27,000 ERP Horizonta. **Ad Rates:** Advertising accepted; rates available upon request. **URL:** http://www.wbna21.com/.

13991 ■ WDJX-FM - 99.7
520 S 4th St., Ste. 200
Louisville, KY 40202
Phone: (502)625-1220
Fax: (502)625-1256
Format: Contemporary Hit Radio (CHR). **Networks:** Independent. **Owner:** Main Line Broadcasting L.L.C., 520 S Fourth St., Louisville, KY 40202. **Founded:** 1952. **Operating Hours**: Continuous; 100% local. **Key Personnel:** Jo Ellen Embry, Contact; Dale Schaefer, Gen. Mgr; Jo Ellen Embry, Contact. **Wattage**: 24,000 ERP. **Ad Rates:** Advertising accepted; rates available upon request. **URL:** http://www.wdjx.com.

13992 ■ WDRB-TV - 41
624 W Muhammad Ali Blvd.
Louisville, KY 40203
Phone: (502)584-6441
Format: Commercial TV. **Networks:** Fox. **Owner:** Block Communications Inc., 405 Madison Ave., Ste. 2100, Toledo, OH 43604-1224, Ph: (419)724-6212, Fax: (419)724-6167. **Founded:** 1971. **Operating Hours**: Continuous. **ADI**: Louisville, KY. **Key Personnel:** Marti Hazel, Dir. of Sales, VP; James Reed, Sales Mgr.; Bill Lamb, Gen. Mgr., President, billlamb@fox41.com; Barry Fulmer, News Dir., bfulmer@fox41.com; Harry Beam, Dir. of Operations, Dir. of Programs, hbeam@fox41.com; Steve Ballard, CFO, sballard@fox41.com; Gary Schroder, Chief Engineer, gschroder@fox41.com. **Wattage**: 5,000. **Ad Rates:** Advertising accepted; rates available upon request. **URL:** http://www.fox41.com.

13993 ■ WFIA-AM - 900
9960 Corporate Campus Dr., Ste. 3600
Louisville, KY 40223
Phone: (502)339-9470
Fax: (502)423-3139
Format: Religious; Contemporary Christian; Talk. **Networks:** USA Radio. **Owner:** Neon Communications, Inc., at above address; Salem Media Group Inc., 4880 Santa Rosa Rd., Camarillo, CA 93012, Ph: (805)987-0400, Fax: (805)384-4520. **Founded:** 1947. **Operating Hours**: Continuous. **ADI**: Louisville, KY. **Key Personnel:** Tom Hoyt, Gen. Mgr., tom.hoyt@salem.cc. **Wattage**: 1,000. **Ad Rates:** Advertising accepted; rates available upon request. $10-14 for 60 seconds. **URL:** http://www.salemradiogroup.com/ministries/great_commandment_radio.

13994 ■ WFIA-FM - 94.7
9960 Corporate Campus Dr., Ste. 3600
Louisville, KY 40223
Phone: (502)339-9470
Fax: (502)423-3139
Email: info@wfiafm.com
Format: Music of Your Life; Contemporary Christian; Talk. **Networks:** ABC. **Owner:** Salem Media Group Inc., 4880 Santa Rosa Rd., Camarillo, CA 93012, Ph: (805)987-0400, Fax: (805)384-4520. **Operating Hours**: Continuous. **Key Personnel:** Patty Copass, Contact, pcopass@salemradiolouisville.com. **Wattage**: 3,300 ERP. **Ad Rates:** Advertising accepted; rates available upon request. **URL:** http://www.wfia-fm.com.

13995 ■ WFPK-FM - 91.9
619 S Fourth St.
Louisville, KY 40202
Phone: (502)814-6500
Email: info@louisvillepublicmedia.org
Format: Public Radio. **Networks:** Public Radio International (PRI). **Owner:** Louisville Public Media, 619 S 4th St., Louisville, KY 40202. **Founded:** 1954. **Operating**

Circulation: ★ = AAM; △ or • = BPA; ♦ = CAC; ❑ = VAC; ⊕ = PO Statement; ‡ = Publisher's Report; Boldface figures = sworn; Light figures = estimated.

Hours: Continuous; 15% network, 85% local. **ADI**: Louisville, KY. **Key Personnel:** Stacy Owen, Prog. Dir., sowen@wfpk.org. **Wattage**: 100,000. **Ad Rates:** Noncommercial. **URL:** http://www.wfpk.org.

13996 ■ WFPL-FM - 89.3
619 S Fourth St.
Louisville, KY 40202
Phone: (502)814-6500
Email: info@louisvillepublicmedia.org
Format: Public Radio; News; Talk. **Networks:** National Public Radio (NPR); Public Radio International (PRI). **Owner:** Louisville Public Media, 619 S 4th St., Louisville, KY 40202. **Founded:** 1950. **Operating Hours**: Continuous; 80% network, 20% local. **ADI**: Louisville, KY. **Key Personnel:** Erica Peterson, Managing Ed. **Local Programs**: *Science Friday*, Friday 3:00 p.m. - 4:00 p.m.; *BBC Newshour*, Monday Tuesday Wednesday Thursday Friday 9:00 a.m. - 10:00 a.m.; *Fresh Air with Terry Gross*, Monday Tuesday Wednesday Thursday Friday 12:00 p.m. - 1:00 p.m.; 8:00 p.m. - 9:00 p.m.; *Weekend Edition*, Saturday Sunday 8:00 a.m. - 10:00 a.m.; *RadioLab*, Saturday 4:00 p.m. - 5:00 p.m. **Wattage**: 100,000. **Ad Rates:** Noncommercial. **URL:** http://www.wfpl.org.

13997 ■ WGTK-AM - 970
9960 Corporate Campus Dr., Ste. 3600
Louisville, KY 40223
Phone: (502)339-9470
Format: News; Talk. **Key Personnel:** Tim Hartlage, Station Mgr., thartlage@salemradiolouisville.com. **Ad Rates:** Noncommercial. **URL:** http://www.970wgtk.com.

13998 ■ WHAS-AM - 840
4000 1 Radio Dr.
Louisville, KY 40218
Phone: (502)479-2222
Fax: (502)479-2308
Free: 800-444-8484
Email: info@whas.com
Format: News; Talk. **Networks:** Fox; CBS. **Owner:** Clear Channel Radio, 200 E Basse Rd., San Antonio, TX 78209, Ph: (210)822-2828, Fax: (210)832-3428. **Founded:** 1922. **Operating Hours**: Continuous. **ADI**: Louisville, KY. **Key Personnel:** Kim Combest, Contact, kimcombest@clearchannel.com. **Local Programs**: *Tony Cruise & Morning Team*, Monday Tuesday Wednesday Thursday Friday 5:00 a.m. - 9:00 a.m.; *Terry Meiners And Company*, Monday Tuesday Wednesday Thursday Friday 3:00 p.m. - 6:00 p.m.; *The Ric Edelman Show*, Saturday 7:00 p.m. - 9:00 p.m.; *SportsTalk 84 with Lachlan McLean*, Monday Tuesday Wednesday Thursday Friday 7:00 p.m. - 9:00 p.m.; *Living Better With Cindi Sullivan*, Saturday; *Religious & Public Affairs Programming*, Sunday 6:00 a.m. - 8:00 a.m.; *The Great Outdoors with Jim Strader*, Sunday 6:00 p.m. - 8:00 p.m. **Wattage**: 50,000. **Ad Rates:** $20-230 for 30 seconds; $25-265 for 60 seconds. **URL:** http://www.whas.com.

13999 ■ WHAS-TV - 11
520 W Chestnut St.
Louisville, KY 40202
Phone: (502)582-7711
Fax: (502)582-7279
Email: assign@whas11.com
Format: Commercial TV. **Networks:** ABC. **Owner:** Belo Corp., 400 S Record St., Dallas, TX 75202-4841, Ph: (214)977-6606, Fax: (214)977-6603. **Founded:** 1950. **Operating Hours**: Continuous. **ADI**: Louisville, KY. **Wattage**: 16,400 ERP. **Ad Rates:** Advertising accepted; rates available upon request. **URL:** http://www.whas11.com.

14000 ■ WHKW-FM - 98.9
1 Radio Dr., Ste. 4000
Louisville, KY 40218
Phone: (502)479-2222
Email: info@whkw.com
Format: Contemporary Country. **Operating Hours**: Continuous. **ADI**: Louisville, KY. **Key Personnel:** Robert Scherer, Dir. of Mktg., Mktg. Mgr.; Mark Thomas, Gen. Mgr.; Gene Guinn, Gen. Sales Mgr.; Dennis Hill, Dir. of Programs. **Wattage**: 50,000. **Ad Rates:** $10-45 per unit. **URL:** http://989radionow.iheart.com.

14001 ■ WJIE-FM - 88.5
5400 Minors Ln.
Louisville, KY 40219-3019
Phone: (502)968-1220
Fax: (502)962-3143
Operating Hours: Continuous. **Key Personnel:** James M. Fraser, Contact, jimfraser@wjie.org. **Wattage**: 24,500 Horizontal ERP; 18,500 Vertical ERP. **Mailing address:** PO Box 197309, Louisville, KY 40259-7309. **URL:** http://www.wjie.org.

14002 ■ WKJK-AM - 1080
4000 No. 1 Radio Dr.
Louisville, KY 40218
Phone: (502)479-2222
Format: Talk; News. **Operating Hours**: Continuous. **Key Personnel:** Jim Fenn, Contact, jimfenn@clearchannel.com. **Wattage**: 10,000. **Ad Rates:** Noncommercial. Combined advertising rates available with WWKY-AM. **URL:** http://www.talkradio1080.com.

14003 ■ WKMJ-TV - 68
600 Cooper Dr.
Lexington, KY 40502
Phone: (859)258-7000
Free: 800-432-0951
Email: shop@ket.org
Format: Public TV. **Networks:** Public Broadcasting Service (PBS); Kentucky Educational Television. **Owner:** Kentucky Educational Television, 600 Cooper Dr., Lexington, KY 40502, Ph: (859)258-7000, Free: 800-432-0951. **Founded:** 1968. **Operating Hours**: Continuous. **ADI**: Louisville, KY. **Key Personnel:** Shae Hopkins, Exec. Dir. **Wattage**: 061. **Ad Rates:** Noncommercial. **URL:** http://www.ket.org.

14004 ■ WKRD-AM - 790
4000, Ste. 1 Radio Dr.
Louisville, KY 40218
Phone: (502)479-2222
Format: Sports. **Networks:** NBC. **Owner:** iHeartMedia Inc., 200 E Basse Rd., San Antonio, TX 78209, Ph: (210)832-3314. **Formerly**: WWKY-AM; WXXA-AM. **Operating Hours**: Continuous. **Key Personnel:** Jim Fenn, Contact, jimfenn@clearchannel.com. **Wattage**: 5,000 Day; 1,000 Night. **Ad Rates:** $25-28 per unit. **URL:** http://www.790krd.com.

14005 ■ WLCR-AM - 1040
3600 Goldsmith Ln.
Louisville, KY 40220
Phone: (502)451-9527
Format: Religious; Contemporary Christian. **Founded:** 1999. **Operating Hours**: Continuous. **Ad Rates:** Noncommercial; underwriting available. **URL:** http://www.wlcr.org.

14006 ■ WLKY-AM - 970
PO Box 1897
Louisville, KY 40201
Phone: (502)587-0970
Free: 800-848-0318
Format: Top 40. **Networks:** Satellite Music Network; ABC. **Founded:** 1933. **Formerly**: WAVE-AM; WAVG-AM. **Operating Hours**: Continuous; 70% network, 30% local. **ADI**: Louisville, KY. **Key Personnel:** Blair Trask, Contact; Charles Jenkins, Gen. Mgr., President; Ron Chilton, Dir. of Programs; Claude Wayne, Dir. of Production; Bob McIntosh, News Dir; Blair Trask, Contact. **Wattage**: 5,000. **Ad Rates:** $44 for 30 seconds; $44 for 60 seconds. Combined advertising rates available with WXVW-AM.

14007 ■ WLKY-TV - 32
1918 Mellwood Ave.
Louisville, KY 40206-1035
Phone: (502)893-7300
Fax: (502)896-0725
Format: Commercial TV. **Networks:** CBS. **Owner:** Hearst Television Inc., 300 W 57th St., New York, NY 10019-3741, Ph: (212)887-6800, Fax: (212)887-6855. **Founded:** 1961. **Operating Hours**: 6 a.m.-2 a.m. **ADI**: Louisville, KY. **Key Personnel:** Allen Douglas, Sales Mgr.; Greg Baird, Sales Mgr. **Ad Rates:** Advertising accepted; rates available upon request. **URL:** http://www.wlky.com.

14008 ■ WLOU-AM
2001 West Broadway
Lyles Mall, Ste.303
Louisville, KY 40203
Phone: (502)778-3535
Fax: (502)778-7394
Format: Urban Contemporary. **Networks:** American Urban Radio. **Owner:** Johnson Communications, 820 S Michigan Ave., Chicago, IL 60605, Ph: (312)322-9400. **Founded:** 1948. **ADI**: Louisville, KY. **Key Personnel:** Charles Mootry, Contact; Vanessa Gentry, Contact. **Wattage**: 2,200 Day; 500 Night.

14009 ■ WLPP-FM - 101.7
c/o Clear Channel Hispanic Radio
125 W 55th St.
New York, NY 10019
Phone: (212)424-6234
Format: Hispanic. **Operating Hours**: Continuous. **Key Personnel:** Alfredo Alonso, Sr. VP, alfredoalonso@clearchannel.com; Jim Lawson, VP. **Wattage**: 6,000. **Ad Rates:** Advertising accepted; rates available upon request. **URL:** http://clearchannelhispanicradio.com/stationlist.php?page=stations2.

14010 ■ WLRS-FM - 105.1
520 S 4th St.
Louisville, KY 40202
Format: Adult Contemporary; Album-Oriented Rock (AOR). **Owner:** Main Line Broadcasting L.L.C., 520 S Fourth St., Louisville, KY 40202. **Founded:** 1964. **Operating Hours**: Continuous. **Wattage**: 3,000. **Ad Rates:** Noncommercial. **URL:** http://1000.intertechmedia.com.

14011 ■ WMSK-AM
455 S 4th St.
Louisville, KY 40202-2508
Phone: (502)589-0060
Owner: Henson Media Inc., at above address. **Founded:** 1960. **Operating Hours**: Continuous. **Wattage**: 250 Day Time. **Ad Rates:** $3.95-5.25 for 30 seconds; $4.75-6.25 for 60 seconds.

14012 ■ WMSK-FM - 101.3
455 S 4th Ave., 427 Starks Bldg.
Louisville, KY 40202
Phone: (270)389-1550
Format: Country. **Owner:** Henson Media Inc., at above address. **Founded:** 1966. **Formerly**: WYGS. **Operating Hours**: Continuous. **Wattage**: 5,400. **Ad Rates:** Advertising accepted; rates available upon request.

14013 ■ WMYO-TV - 58
624 W Muhammad Ali Blvd.
Louisville, KY 40203
Phone: (502)584-6441
Founded: 1994. **URL:** http://www.wmyo.com.

14014 ■ WNAI-AM - 680
PO Box 197309
Louisville, KY 40259-7309
Phone: (502)240-0602
Fax: (502)240-0940
Email: wnairadio@hotmail.com
Format: News; Talk; Sports. **Networks:** CNN Radio; CNN Radio. **Owner:** Gore-Overgaard Broadcasting Inc., at above address. **Founded:** 1993. **Operating Hours**: Continuous. **Key Personnel:** Ed Moore, Station Mgr., edwnaimgr@aol.com; Gary Major, Operations Mgr., gmam680@aol.com. **Wattage**: 1,000. **Ad Rates:** $25 for 30 seconds; $35 for 60 seconds. **URL:** http://www.espnlouisville.com/common/page.php?pt=contact&id=69.

14015 ■ WPTI-FM - 103.9
612 4th Ave., Ste. 100
Louisville, KY 40202
Phone: (502)589-4800
Format: Country. **Key Personnel:** Matt Killion, Dir. of Programs, matt.killion@coxradio.com; Marji Pilato, Promotions Dir., marji.pilato@coxradio.com; Tim Hartlage, Sales Mgr., tim.hartlage@coxradio.com. **URL:** http://www.hawklouisville.com.

14016 ■ WQMF-FM - 95.7
4000 Radio Dr., Ste. 1
Louisville, KY 40218
Phone: (502)479-2222
Format: Classic Rock. **Founded:** Feb. 1981. **Operating Hours**: Continuous. **ADI**: Louisville, KY. **Key Personnel:** Damon Hildreth, Contact, damonhildreth@clearchannel.com. **Wattage**: 50,000. **Ad Rates:** Noncommercial. Combined advertising rates available with WIFX-FM. **URL:** http://www.wqmf.com.

14017 ■ WRKA-FM - 103.1
612 S 4th St.
Louisville, KY 40202
Phone: (502)589-4800
Format: Country. **Owner:** Cox Enterprises Inc., 6205 Peachtree Dunwoody Rd., Atlanta, GA 30328, Ph:

(678)645-0000, Fax: (678)645-1079. **Founded:** 1964. **Operating Hours:** Continuous. **Key Personnel:** Shane Collins, Operations Mgr., shane.collins@summitmediacorp.com; Brian Eichenberger, Dir. of Mktg., brian.eichenberger@coxmg.com. **Wattage:** 6,000. **Ad Rates:** Noncommercial. Combined advertising rates available with WVEZ-FM, WPTI-FM, WSFR-FM. **URL:** http://www.countrylegends1039.com.

14018 ■ WRVI-FM - 105.9
9960 Corporate Campus Dr., Ste. 3600
Louisville, KY 40223
Phone: (502)423-3122
Format: Contemporary Christian. **Owner:** Salem Media Group Inc., 4880 Santa Rosa Rd., Camarillo, CA 93012, Ph: (805)987-0400, Fax: (805)384-4520. **Operating Hours:** Continuous. **Key Personnel:** Patty Copass, HR Mgr. **Wattage:** 3,000. **Ad Rates:** Noncommercial. **URL:** http://wrvi.salemradiogroup.com/.

WSON-AM - See Henderson

14019 ■ WTFX-FM - 100.5
4000 Radio Dr.
Louisville, KY 40218
Phone: (502)479-2222
Format: Album-Oriented Rock (AOR). **Founded:** Sept. 16, 2006. **Operating Hours:** Continuous. **ADI:** Louisville, KY. **Wattage:** 50,000. **Ad Rates:** Noncommercial. **URL:** http://www.foxrocks.com.

14020 ■ WTSZ-AM - 1600
410 Mt. Tabor Rd.
Louisville, KY 40202
Format: Sports. **Founded:** June 23, 1993. **Operating Hours:** Continuous. **Wattage:** 320. **Ad Rates:** Advertising accepted; rates available upon request.

14021 ■ W274AM-FM - 102.7
PO Box 391
Twin Falls, ID 83303
Fax: (208)736-1958
Free: 800-357-4226
Format: Religious; Contemporary Christian. **Owner:** CSN International, PO Box 391, Twin Falls, ID 83303, Ph: (208)736-1958, Fax: (208)736-1958, Free: 800-357-4226. **URL:** http://www.csnradio.com.

14022 ■ WUOL-FM - 90.5
619 S Fourth St.
Louisville, KY 40202
Phone: (502)814-6500
Email: info@wuol.org
Format: Classical. **Networks:** Beethoven Satellite; Public Radio International (PRI). **Owner:** Louisville Public Media, 619 S 4th St., Louisville, KY 40202. **Founded:** 1976. **Operating Hours:** Continuous; 35% network, 65% local. **ADI:** Louisville, KY. **Key Personnel:** Gray Smith, Contact, gsmith@louisvillepublicmedia.org. **Local Programs:** *The Art of Great Singing*; *Deutsche Welle Festival Concerts*, Friday 8:00 p.m.; *An English Pastorale*; *Sunday Baroque*, Sunday 10:00 a.m. - 1:00 p.m.; *From the Top*, Sunday 6:00 p.m. - 7:00 p.m.; *Louisville In Concert*, Sunday 6:00 p.m.; *Harmonia*, Sunday 6:00 a.m. - 7:00 a.m.; *Opera*, Saturday 1:00 p.m. - 5:00 p.m.; *With Heart and Voice*, Sunday 8:00 a.m. - 9:00 a.m.; *Santa Fe Chamber Music Festival*, Sunday 8:00 p.m.; *The New York Philharmonic This Week*, Saturday 9:00 p.m. **Wattage:** 21,000. **Ad Rates:** Noncommercial. **URL:** http://www.wuol.org.

14023 ■ WVEZ-FM - 106.9
612 4th St., Ste. 100
Louisville, KY 40202
Phone: (502)589-4800
Format: Adult Contemporary. **Owner:** Cox Radio Inc., 6205 Peachtree Dunwood Rd., Atlanta, GA 30328-4524, Ph: (678)645-0000, Fax: (678)645-5002. **Operating Hours:** Continuous; 100% local. **ADI:** Louisville, KY. **Key Personnel:** Brian Eichenberger, Promotions Dir., brian.eichenberger@coxmg.com. **Wattage:** 24,500. **Ad Rates:** Advertising accepted; rates available upon request. **URL:** http://www.lite1069.com.

14024 ■ WXBH-FM - 92.7
PO Box 91695
Louisville, KY 40291
Phone: (502)882-0924
Email: wxbh@wxbh.org
Format: Full Service. **Ad Rates:** Underwriting available.

MADISONVILLE

Hopkins Co. Hopkins Co. 45 m S of Evansville. Manufactures mine equipment, heating and air conditioners, jet engine airfoils, commercial laundry equipment, filter paper, explosives, tires, work clothing, beverages, concrete products. Coal mining; oil wells; timber. Dairy, beef cattle, swine & poultry. Corn, tobacco, soybeans.

14025 ■ The Messenger
The Messenger Newspaper
221 S Main St.
Madisonville, KY 42431
Phone: (270)824-3300
Fax: (270)821-6855
Free: 800-726-6397
Publication E-mail: news@the-messenger.com
General newspaper. **Founded:** 1917. **Freq:** Tues.-Sun. (morn.). **Print Method:** Offset. **Cols./Page:** 6. **Col. Width:** 12 picas. **Col. Depth:** 21.5 inches. **Key Personnel:** Debbie Littlepage, Director, Advertising, phone: (270)824-3278; Rick Welch, Publisher, phone: (270)824-3282. **Subscription Rates:** $204.75 Individuals online only /year. **URL:** http://www.the-messenger.com. **Remarks:** Accepts advertising. **Circ:** Tues.-Fri. ★**7552**, Sun. ★**7515**.

14026 ■ WFMW-AM - 730
PO Box 338
Madisonville, KY 42431
Phone: (270)821-1800
Fax: (270)821-5954
Email: wfmw@wfmw.net
Format: Country. **Networks:** CNN Radio; Westwood One Radio. **Owner:** Sound Broadcasters Inc., at above address. **Founded:** 1947. **Operating Hours:** Continuous. **ADI:** Evansville, IN (Madisonville, KY). **Key Personnel:** Danny Koeber, Dir. of Programs, danny@wfmw.net. **Wattage:** 500. **Ad Rates:** $16 for 60 seconds. Combined advertising rates available with WKTG. **URL:** http://www.wfmw.net/pages/11741709.php.

14027 ■ WKMA-TV - 35
600 Cooper Dr.
Lexington, KY 40502
Phone: (859)258-7000
Free: 800-432-0951
Format: Educational. **Networks:** Public Broadcasting Service (PBS); Kentucky Educational Television. **Owner:** Kentucky Educational Television, 600 Cooper Dr., Lexington, KY 40502, Ph: (859)258-7000, Free: 800-432-0951. **Founded:** 1968. **Operating Hours:** Continuous. **ADI:** Evansville, IN (Madisonville, KY). **Key Personnel:** Shae Hopkins, Exec. Dir., CEO. **Wattage:** 617. **Ad Rates:** Noncommercial. **URL:** http://www.ket.org.

14028 ■ WKTG-FM - 93.9
PO Box 338
Madisonville, KY 42431-9278
Phone: (270)821-1156
Fax: (270)821-5954
Email: wktg@wktg.com
Format: Classic Rock. **Owner:** Sound Broadcasters Inc., at above address. **Founded:** 1950. **Operating Hours:** Continuous. **ADI:** Evansville, IN (Madisonville, KY). **Key Personnel:** Bob Kelley, Gen. Mgr., bob@wktg.com; Bill McClane, Contact, bill@wktg.com. **Wattage:** 50,000. **Ad Rates:** $17 for 60 seconds. Combined advertising rates available with WFMW. **URL:** http://www.wktg.com.

14029 ■ WSOF-FM - 89.9
1415 Island Ford Rd.
Madisonville, KY 42431
Phone: (270)825-3004
Free: 866-897-9763
Email: comments@wsof.org
Format: Religious. **Networks:** USA Radio. **Founded:** 1977. **Operating Hours:** 18 hours Daily; 5% network, 95% local. **ADI:** Chicago (LaSalle), IL. **Wattage:** 39,000. **Ad Rates:** Noncommercial. **URL:** http://www.wsof.org/summer-radio-marathon-june-3-5.

MANCHESTER

Clay Co. Clay Co. (SE). 75 m S of Lexington. Furniture, tooling factories. Coal mines. Hardwood timber. Lumber mill. Agriculture. Corn, tabacco, hay.

14030 ■ The Manchester Enterprise
Enterprise
103 Third St.
Manchester, KY 40962
Phone: (606)598-2319
Newspaper. **Founded:** 1890. **Freq:** Weekly (Wed.). **Print Method:** Letterpress and offset. **Cols./Page:** 6. **Col. Width:** 24 nonpareils. **Col. Depth:** 301 agate lines. **Key Personnel:** Mark Hoskins, Contact. **Subscription Rates:** $28 Individuals Clay County delivery; $34 Out of area. **URL:** http://www.themanchesterenterprise.com/. **Formerly:** Enterprise. **Mailing address:** PO Box 449, Manchester, KY 40962. **Ad Rates:** GLR $.192; SAU $6; PCI $7. **Remarks:** Accepts advertising. **Circ:** Thurs. ♦**1059**.

14031 ■ WKLB-AM - 1290
PO Box 448
Manchester, KY 40962
Phone: (606)598-2445
Fax: (606)598-2653
Format: Country. **Networks:** ABC. **Owner:** Barker Broadcasting Co., Inc., at above address. **Founded:** 1981. **Operating Hours:** Continuous. **ADI:** Lexington, KY. **Key Personnel:** Larry Barker, Contact. **Wattage:** 50,000. **Ad Rates:** $5 for 30 seconds; $10.50 for 60 seconds.

14032 ■ WTBK-FM - 105.7
107 Dickenson St.
Manchester, KY 40962
Phone: (606)598-7588
Fax: (606)598-7598
Format: Classic Rock. **Networks:** AP. **Owner:** Manchester Communications Inc., at above address. **Founded:** 1989. **Operating Hours:** Continuous. **Key Personnel:** Earl Owens, Contact, earl@wtbkradio.com. **Wattage:** 25,000. **Ad Rates:** Advertising accepted; rates available upon request. **URL:** http://www.wtbkradio.com.

MARION

Crittenden Co. Crittenden Co. (C). 35 m ENE of Paducah. Fluorspar mines.

14033 ■ The Crittenden Press: Shopper The Early Bird
The Crittenden Press Inc.
PO Box 191
Marion, KY 42064-0191
Phone: (270)965-3191
Fax: (270)965-2516
Community newspaper. **Freq:** Weekly. **Print Method:** Offset. **Trim Size:** 7 x 10 1/2. **Cols./Page:** 6. **Col. Width:** 24 nonpareils. **Col. Depth:** 301 agate lines. **Key Personnel:** Chris Evans, Publisher; Daryl K. Tabor, Managing Editor. **USPS:** 128-260. **Subscription Rates:** $32 Individuals Crittenden and surrounding counties; $40 Elsewhere for Kentucky subscribers; $55 Out of state; $21.95 Individuals online. **Alt. Formats:** PDF. **URL:** http://crittendenpress.blogspot.com. **Ad Rates:** 4C $300; SAU $4.25; PCI $5.35. **Remarks:** Accepts advertising. **Circ:** 3500.

14034 ■ WMJL-AM
PO Box 68
Marion, KY 42064
Phone: (502)965-2271
Fax: (502)965-2515
Format: Country. **Owner:** Joe Myers Productions, Inc., at above address. **Founded:** 1968. **Wattage:** 175 Day. **Ad Rates:** $6 for 30 seconds; $8 for 60 seconds.

14035 ■ WMJL-FM
PO Box 68
Marion, KY 42064
Phone: (270)965-2271
Fax: (270)965-4464
Format: Country. **Owner:** Joseph Myers Productions, Inc., at above address. **Wattage:** 6,000 ERP. **Ad Rates:** $6.00 for 30 seconds; $8.00 for 60 seconds.

MARTIN

14036 ■ WMDJ-FM - 100.1
69 N River St.
Martin, KY 41649
Phone: (606)285-8005

Circulation: ★ = AAM; △ or • = BPA; ♦ = CAC; ❑ = VAC; ⊕ = PO Statement; ‡ = Publisher's Report; Boldface figures = sworn; Light figures = estimated.

Fax: (606)285-1130
Format: Full Service. **Owner:** Floyd County Broadcasting Co., Inc., at above address, Martin, KY 41649. **Founded:** 1982. **Wattage:** 2,600 ERP. **Ad Rates:** Advertising accepted; rates available upon request. $8 for 30 seconds; $14 for 60 seconds. **Mailing address:** PO Box 1530, Martin, KY 41649. **URL:** http://www.wmdjfm.com.

MAYFIELD

Graves Co. Graves Co. (SW). 25 m from each of three rivers, Ohio, Mississippi and Tennessee. Manufactures clothing, tires, lamps, bottles, bricks, furniture, flour, snuff, gasoline, shoes, compressors, Tobacco warehouses. Clay pots. Timber. Diversified farming. Wheat, corn, tobacco, soybeans.

14037 ■ Mayfield Messenger
Messenger Newspapers Inc.
201 N Eighth St.
Mayfield, KY 42066-1825
Phone: (270)247-5223
Fax: (270)247-6336
General newspaper. **Freq:** Monday-Friday. **Print Method:** Offset. **Cols./Page:** 6. **Col. Width:** 25 nonpareils. **Col. Depth:** 301 agate lines. **Key Personnel:** Tom Berry, Editor; Susan Seay, Director, Advertising, Publisher. **Subscription Rates:** $36 Individuals. **URL:** http://www.kypress.com/directory/daily_detail.php?id=38. **Ad Rates:** SAU $10.58. **Remarks:** Accepts advertising. **Circ:** 3715.

14038 ■ WLLE-FM - 102.1
PO Box 679
Mayfield, KY 42066
Phone: (270)554-0093
Fax: (270)444-6397
Free: 877-588-1021
Format: Country. **Owner:** Bristol Broadcasting Company Inc., 901 E Valley Dr., Bristol, VA 24201, Ph: (276)669-8112, Fax: (276)669-0541. **Founded:** 1955. **Operating Hours:** Continuous 100% local. **ADI:** Paducah,KY-Cape Girardeau,MO-Marion,IL. **Key Personnel:** Jamie Futrell, Contact, jamiefutrell@wkyq.com; Joe Jackson, News Dir; Jamie Futrell, Contact, jamiefutrell@wkyq.com. **Wattage:** 50,000. **Ad Rates:** $12 for 30 seconds; $16 for 60 seconds. **URL:** http://www.willieradio.com.

14039 ■ WNGO-AM - 1320
PO Box 690
Mayfield, KY 42066
Phone: (270)247-5122
Fax: (270)554-5468
Free: 866-570-1320
Format: News; Talk; Sports. **Owner:** Bristol Broadcasting Co., 817 Suncrest Pl., South Charleston, WV 25303, Ph: (304)342-3136, Fax: (304)342-3118; WRUS, Inc., at above address. **Founded:** 1947. **Operating Hours:** Continuous. **ADI:** Paducah,KY-Cape Girardeau,MO-Marion,IL. **Key Personnel:** Greg Dunker, Contact; Randy Gardner, Gen. Mgr; Greg Dunker, Contact. **Wattage:** 1,000. **Ad Rates:** Advertising accepted; rates available upon request. **URL:** http://www.wkyx.com.

14040 ■ WYMC-AM - 1430
197 WYMC Rd.
Mayfield, KY 42066-0036
Phone: (270)247-1430
Fax: (270)247-1825
Email: radio@wymcradio.com
Format: Middle-of-the-Road (MOR). **Networks:** ABC; NBC; Westwood One Radio; St. Louis Cardinals. **Owner:** JDM Communications, Inc., 197 Wymc Dr, Mayfield, KY 42066, Ph: (270)247-1430. **Founded:** 1976. **Operating Hours:** Continuous. **ADI:** Paducah,KY-Cape Girardeau,MO-Marion,IL. **Key Personnel:** Jim Moore, Gen. Mgr. **Wattage:** 1,000. **Ad Rates:** $6-12 for 30 seconds; $9-20 for 60 seconds. **Mailing address:** PO Box V, Mayfield, KY 42066-0036.

MAYKING

14041 ■ WTCW-AM - 920
PO Box 288
Mayking, KY 41837
Phone: (606)633-2711
Fax: (606)633-4445
Email: wxkq@yahoo.com
Format: Contemporary Country. **Networks:** CBS; KyNet. **Founded:** 1953. **Operating Hours:** midnight. **Key Personnel:** Kevin Day, Gen. Mgr., Prog. Dir., kday@forchtbroadcasting.com; Bob Scott, Dir. of Production, boscott@forchtbroadcasting.com. **Wattage:** 5,000. **Ad Rates:** $2.50-3.75 for 30 seconds; $3.40-8 for 60 seconds. **URL:** http://www.1039thebulldog.com.

14042 ■ WXKQ-FM - 103.9
PO Box 288
Mayking, KY 41837
Phone: (606)633-2711
Fax: (606)633-4445
Format: Adult Contemporary. **Founded:** 1963. **ADI:** South Bend-Elkhart, IN. **Ad Rates:** Noncommercial. **URL:** http://www.tunein.com.

MAYSVILLE

Mason Co. Mason Co. (NE). On Ohio River, 60 m SE of Cincinnati, Ohio. Tourism. Historic center. Museum. Manufactures condensed milk, gasoline, motor parts, soft drinks, cotton goods, shoes, bricks, pulleys, cigars, bicycles, motorcycles. Tobacco warehouses and curing plant; distilleries; nursery. Agriculture. Livestock, tobacco, wheat, milk.

14043 ■ Limestone Cablevision Inc.
626 Forest Ave.
Maysville, KY 41056
Phone: (606)564-9220
Fax: (606)564-4291
Free: 800-264-3572
Email: limestone@maysvilleky.net
Founded: Sept. 07, 2006. **Cities Served:** 29 channels. **Mailing address:** PO Box 100, Maysville, KY 41056. **URL:** http://www.limestonecable.com.

14044 ■ WFTM-AM - 1240
626 Forest Ave.
Maysville, KY 41056
Phone: (606)564-3361
Fax: (606)564-4291
Email: wftmsales@maysvilleky.net
Format: Music of Your Life. **Founded:** 1948. **Key Personnel:** Scott Barry, Contact; Dave Bogart, Contact. **Wattage:** 1,000 KW. **Ad Rates:** $5-10 for 30 seconds; $6-11 for 60 seconds. **Mailing address:** PO Box 100, Maysville, KY 41056. **URL:** http://www.wftm.net/.

14045 ■ WFTM-FM - 95.9
PO Box 100
Maysville, KY 41056
Phone: (606)564-3361
Fax: (606)564-4291
Email: wftmsales@maysvilleky.net
Format: Adult Contemporary. **Networks:** Jones Satellite; AP. **Founded:** 1965. **Operating Hours:** Continuous; 10% network, 90% local. **ADI:** Cincinnati, OH. **Key Personnel:** Doug McGill, Gen. Mgr. **Wattage:** 3,000. **Ad Rates:** $5-12 for 30 seconds; $7-15 for 60 seconds. **URL:** http://www.wftm.net.

MC KEE

14046 ■ WWAG-FM - 107.9
1731 Highway 1071
Star Rt. Box 16
Tyner, KY 40486
Phone: (606)287-9924
Format: Country. **Networks:** ABC; Knowledge Network. **Founded:** 1990. **Operating Hours:** Continuous. **Wattage:** 6,000. **Ad Rates:** $7-10 for 60 seconds. **URL:** http://www.wwagfm.com/about-us-1.html.

MCDANIELS

14047 ■ WBFI-FM - 91.5
PO Box 2
McDaniels, KY 40152
Phone: (270)257-2689
Fax: (270)257-8344
Format: Contemporary Christian; Religious. **Key Personnel:** Terrell Smith, Gen. Mgr.; Roger Goostree, Operations Mgr.; Daryl Cook, Production Mgr. **Ad Rates:** Noncommercial.

MCKEE

Jackson Co. Jackson Co. (C).

14048 ■ The Jackson County Sun
The Jackson County Sun
PO Box 130
McKee, KY 40447
Phone: (606)287-7197
Fax: (606)287-7196
County newspaper. **Freq:** Weekly (Thurs.). **Print Method:** Web offset. **Trim Size:** 13 x 21 1/2. **Cols./Page:** 6. **Col. Width:** 12 picas. **Col. Depth:** 21.5 inches. **Key Personnel:** Tammy Spurlock, General Manager. **USPS:** 271-940. **Subscription Rates:** $24 Individuals in-County; $34 Elsewhere. **URL:** http://www.thejacksoncountysun.com. **Ad Rates:** GLR $.10; BW $258; 4C $150; SAU $3.50; PCI $4.50. **Remarks:** Accepts advertising. **Circ:** 4300.

MIDDLESBORO

Bell Co. (SE). 110 m SE of Lexington. National and State parks. Wood products, elastic webbing, shirts, plastic pipe manufactured. Meat packing plant. Tannery, bottling works. Coal mines. Foundry. Machine shop.

14049 ■ Country-Wide Broadcasters Inc. - 1490
2118 Cumberland Ave.
Middlesboro, KY 40965-2831
Phone: (606)248-1560
Fax: (606)248-6397
Free: 800-280-1561
Email: wfxy@aol.com
Format: Adult Contemporary; News. **Networks:** ABC; KyNet; Westwood One Radio. **Founded:** 1968. **Formerly:** WAFI-AM. **Operating Hours:** Continuous; 75% network, 25% local. **ADI:** Knoxville (Crossville), TN. **Key Personnel:** Buzz Armstrong, News Dir.; Kevin Ellis, Dir. of Programs; Boen Farmer, Gen. Mgr. **Wattage:** 1,000. **Ad Rates:** $6 for 30 seconds; $9 for 60 seconds. Combined advertising rates available with WANO-AM and WXJB-FM. **Mailing address:** PO Box 999, Middlesboro, KY 40965-0999.

14050 ■ WANO-AM - 1230
1 Cumberland Ave., Ste. 213
Box 1
Middlesboro, KY 40965
Phone: (606)337-2100
Fax: (606)337-5900
Format: News; Information; Sports; Middle-of-the-Road (MOR); Contemporary Country; Religious; Bluegrass. **Simulcasts:** WZKO-FM. **Networks:** Fox. **Founded:** 1954. **Operating Hours:** Continuous. **Wattage:** 1,000. **Ad Rates:** $6 for 30 seconds; $9.50 for 60 seconds. **URL:** http://1230wano.com.

14051 ■ WMIK-AM - 560
PO Box 608
Middlesboro, KY 40965
Phone: (606)248-5842
Fax: (606)248-7660
Format: Southern Gospel. **Owner:** Gateway Broadcasting, Inc., at above address. **Founded:** 1948. **Wattage:** 2,500 Day; 088 Night. **Ad Rates:** $5-6.50 for 60 seconds.

14052 ■ WMIK-FM - 92.7
PO Box 608
Middlesboro, KY 40965
Phone: (606)248-5842
Fax: (606)248-7660
Email: wmikradio@bellsouth.net
Format: Religious. **Networks:** USA Radio; Moody Broadcasting. **Founded:** 1971. **Operating Hours:** Continuous. **ADI:** Knoxville (Crossville), TN. **Wattage:** 5,000. **Ad Rates:** Noncommercial. **URL:** http://wmikradio.publishpath.com.

MONTICELLO

Wayne Co. Wayne Co. (SC). 100 m S of Lexington. Coal mines; oil wells; rock quarry; timber. Manufactures staves, flour, wood products, machinery; oil refinery. Agriculture. Corn, tobacco, wheat.

14053 ■ Wayne County Outlook
Wayne County Newspaper Inc.
45 E Columbia Ave.
Monticello, KY 42633
Phone: (606)348-3338
Fax: (606)348-8848
Publisher's E-mail: news@wcoutlook.com

Community newspaper. **Founded:** 1904. **Freq:** Weekly (Wed.). **Print Method:** Offset. **Cols./Page:** 6. **Col. Width:** 24 nonpareils. **Col. Depth:** 294 agate lines. **Key Personnel:** Melinda Jones, Publisher, Director, Advertising; Melodie Phelps, Editor. **Subscription Rates:** $21 Individuals; $29 Out of area. **URL:** http://www.wcoutlook.com/. **Mailing address:** PO Box 432, Monticello, KY 42633. **Ad Rates:** GLR $.60; BW $561.15; 4C $4.35; PCI $4.35. **Remarks:** Advertising accepted; rates available upon request. **Circ:** 6000.

14054 ■ Enstar Cable
514 N Main
Monticello, KY 42633
Phone: (606)348-8416
Fax: (606)348-6397
Free: 800-388-8416
Key Personnel: Robert Taylor, Gen. Mgr.

14055 ■ WFLW-AM - 1360
150 Worsham Ln.
Monticello, KY 42633-0696
Phone: (606)348-7083
Email: news@wkym.com
Format: Southern Gospel. **Networks:** KyNet. **Owner:** Stephen Staples Jr., Not Available. **Founded:** 1955. **Operating Hours:** 6 a.m.-6 p.m.; 10% network, 90% local. **ADI:** Lexington, KY. **Key Personnel:** Mary Ellis, Contact, mary@wkym.com. **Wattage:** 1,000. **Ad Rates:** $3-6 for 30 seconds; $4-8 for 60 seconds. Combined advertising rates available with WKYM-FM. **URL:** http://www.wkym.com.

14056 ■ WKYM-FM - 101.7
150 Worsham Ln.
Monticello, KY 42633-0696
Phone: (606)348-7083
Free: 866-898-7625
Email: requests@wkym.com
Format: Classic Rock. **Owner:** Stephen Staples Jr., Not Available. **Founded:** 1965. **Key Personnel:** Mary Ellis, Contact, mary@wkym.com. **Wattage:** 1,750 ERP. **Ad Rates:** Advertising accepted; rates available upon request. $3-$8 for 30 seconds; $4-$10 for 60 seconds. Combined advertising rates available with WFLW-AM. **URL:** http://www.wkym.com.

14057 ■ WMKZ-FM - 93.1
183 Old Hwy. 90
Monticello, KY 42633
Phone: (606)348-3393
Fax: (606)348-3330
Format: Country. **Networks:** Jones Satellite. **Owner:** Monticello-Wayne County Media Inc., 183 Old Hwy 90. **Founded:** 1990. **Operating Hours:** Continuous; 80% network, 20% local. **ADI:** Lexington, KY. **Key Personnel:** Joel D. Catron, Gen. Mgr. **Wattage:** 6,000. **Ad Rates:** $3-6 for 30 seconds; $4.50-7.50 for 60 seconds. **URL:** http://www.wmkz.com.

MOREHEAD

Rowan Co. Rowan Co. (NE). 55 m SW of Ashland. State University. Garment, electric components, concrete products factories. Clay pits. Sawmills. Tobacco warehouse. Diversified farming. Tobacco, cattle.

14058 ■ Baseball Youth
Dugout Media Inc.
PO Box 983
Morehead, KY 40351
Fax: (859)201-1107
Free: 866-966-9683
Publisher's E-mail: info@dugoutmedia.com
Magazine covering youth baseball programs including little league, pony league, Babe Ruth league, Dixie youth baseball, Dizzy Dean baseball, T-ball, AAU, CABA, AABC, PAL, USABA, USSSA, NABF, high school baseball, parks & recreation programs, YMCA youth sports, American Legion Baseball, and all other youth baseball organizations, divisions, leagues, and tournaments. **Freq:** Bimonthly. **Subscription Rates:** $23.95 Individuals; $37.95 Two years; $54.95 Individuals 3 years. **URL:** http://www.baseballyouth.com. **Remarks:** Accepts advertising. **Circ:** (Not Reported).

14059 ■ The Morehead News
The Morehead News
722 W First St.
Morehead, KY 40351
Phone: (606)784-4116
Fax: (606)784-7337
Free: 800-247-6142
Community newspaper. **Freq:** Semiweekly. **Print Method:** Offset. **Cols./Page:** 6. **Col. Width:** 12 picas. **Col. Depth:** 21 agate lines. **Key Personnel:** Stephanie Ockerman, Editor; Dan Duncan, Director, Advertising; Keith Kappes, Publisher. **Subscription Rates:** $35 Individuals in county /year; $48 By mail in State /year; $51 Out of state mail /year. **URL:** http://www.themoreheadnews.com. **Ad Rates:** SAU $5.68; PCI $4.98. **Remarks:** Accepts advertising. **Circ:** Paid ⊕**5629**.

14060 ■ Soccer Youth: The Nation's Soccer Magazine for Kids
Dugout Media Inc.
PO Box 983
Morehead, KY 40351
Fax: (859)201-1107
Free: 866-966-9683
Publisher's E-mail: info@dugoutmedia.com
Soccer magazine for kids including stories on every level from youth leagues to profiles on the hottest Major League Soccer stars and teams. **Freq:** 4/yr. **Subscription Rates:** $12.95 Individuals; $21.95 Two years. **Circ:** (Not Reported).

14061 ■ Softball Youth: The Nation's Softball Magazine for Kids
Dugout Media Inc.
PO Box 983
Morehead, KY 40351
Fax: (859)201-1107
Free: 866-966-9683
Publisher's E-mail: info@dugoutmedia.com
Magazine for 7-14 year-old girls who play fastpitch softball. **Freq:** 4/yr. **Key Personnel:** Scott M. Hacker, Owner, President. **Subscription Rates:** $12.95 Individuals; $21.95 Two years. **URL:** http://www.dugoutmedia.com. **Circ:** (Not Reported).

14062 ■ The Trail Blazer
Morehead State University Board of Student Publications
317 Breckenridge Hall
Morehead, KY 40351
Phone: (606)783-2697
Fax: (606)783-9113
Publisher's E-mail: editor@trailblazeronline.net
Collegiate newspaper. **Founded:** 1930. **Freq:** Weekly (Thurs.). **Print Method:** Offset. **Cols./Page:** 6. **Col. Width:** 11 picas. **Col. Depth:** 294 agate lines. **Key Personnel:** Jordan Simonson, Managing Editor; Rachel Adkins, Editor. **Subscription Rates:** $12 Individuals. **URL:** http://www.thetrailblazeronline.net/. **Ad Rates:** BW $882; 4C $375; PCI $7. **Remarks:** Accepts advertising. **Circ:** Paid 523, Free 7200.

14063 ■ Eagle Video Network
150 University Blvd.
Morehead, KY 40351
Phone: (606)783-2221
Free: 800-585-6781
Cities Served: 65 channels. **URL:** http://www.moreheadstate.edu.

14064 ■ WBMK-FM - 88.5
PO Box 3206
Tupelo, MS 38803
Format: Religious. **Owner:** American Family Association, at above address. **URL:** http://www.afa.net.

14065 ■ WKMR-TV - 38
600 Cooper Dr.
Lexington, KY 40502
Phone: (859)258-7000
Free: 800-432-0951
Email: feedback@ket.org
Format: Public TV; Educational. **Networks:** Public Broadcasting Service (PBS); Kentucky Educational Television. **Owner:** Kentucky Educational Television, 600 Cooper Dr., Lexington, KY 40502, Ph: (859)258-7000, Free: 800-432-0951. **Founded:** 1968. **Operating Hours:** 6:30 a.m.-midnight. **ADI:** Louisville, KY. **Key Personnel:** Shae Hopkins, Exec. Dir. **Wattage:** 676,000. **Ad Rates:** Noncommercial. **URL:** http://www.ket.org.

14066 ■ WMKY-FM - 90.3
Morehead State University
132 Breckinridge Hall
Morehead, KY 40351
Phone: (606)783-2001
Fax: (606)783-2335
Free: 800-286-9659
Email: p.hitchc@moreheadstate.edu
Format: Public Radio. **Networks:** National Public Radio (NPR); Public Radio International (PRI); AP; Corporation for Public Broadcasting. **Owner:** Morehead State University, 150 University Blvd., Morehead, KY 40351, Fax: (606)783-5038, Free: 800-585-6781. **Founded:** 1965. **Operating Hours:** Continuous; 58% network, 42% local. **Key Personnel:** Chuck Mraz, News Dir., c.mraz@moreheadstate.edu; Greg Jenkins, Dir. of Operations, g.jenkins@moreheadstate.edu; Paul Hitchcock, Gen. Mgr., p.hitchc@moreheadstate.edu. **Local Programs:** *Inside Appalachia*, Saturday Sunday 6:00 a.m. - 7:00 a.m. 11:00 a.m. - 12:00 p.m.; *Bluegrass Sunday*, Sunday 12:00 p.m. - 3:00 p.m.; *Pickin' Parlor, Thistle and Shamrock*, Saturday 3:00 p.m. - 4:00 p.m.; *A Time For Tales*, Sunday 3:00 p.m. - 4:00 p.m.; *Mountain Edition*, Monday Tuesday Wednesday Thursday Friday 4:30 p.m. - 5:00 p.m.; *Americana Crossroads*, Thursday 7:00 p.m. - 10:00 p.m.; *The Folk Sampler*, Saturday 2:00 p.m. **Wattage:** 50,000. **Ad Rates:** Noncommercial; underwriting available. **Mailing address:** PO Box 903, Morehead, KY 40351. **URL:** http://www.wmky.org.

MORGANFIELD

Union Co. Union Co. (WC). 23 m S of Henderson. Manufactures metal partitions, plastic and rubber parts for automobiles, fiber tubes and rolls, rebuilt automobile parts. Coal mines. Seed cleaning plant. Agriculture. Pork, corn, livestock.

14067 ■ The Union County Advocate
The Cadiz Record
214 W Main
Morganfield, KY 42437
Phone: (270)389-1833
Fax: (270)389-3926
Publication E-mail: news@ucadvocate.com
Community newspaper. **Freq:** Weekly (Wed.). **Print Method:** Offset. **Cols./Page:** 6. **Col. Width:** 2 1/16 inches. **Col. Depth:** 21 1/2 inches. **USPS:** 648-080. **URL:** http://www.ucadvocate.com. **Mailing address:** PO Box 370, Morganfield, KY 42437. **Remarks:** Accepts advertising. **Circ:** Paid 5300, Free 200.

14068 ■ WEUC-FM
218 Jim Veatch Rd.
Stn. 6
Catholic University
Morganfield, KY 42437
Fax: (809)841-1028
Format: Easy Listening; Educational; Hispanic. **Founded:** 1984. **Key Personnel:** Ruben Rodrigues, Contact.

MORGANTOWN

Butler Co. Butler Co. (SW). On Green River, 25 m NE of Bowling Green. Coal mines; oil wells; timber. Lumber, feed mills; men's and boy's clothing, boat machinery factories. Agriculture. Corn, tobacco, soya beans.

14069 ■ The Butler County and Green River Republican Banner
The Butler County and Green River Republican Banner
PO Box 219
Morgantown, KY 42261
Phone: (270)526-4151
Fax: (270)526-3111
Community newspaper. **Freq:** Weekly (Wed.). **Print Method:** Offset. **Cols./Page:** 6. **Col. Width:** 26 nonpareils. **Col. Depth:** 294 agate lines. **Key Personnel:** Sam Terry, Editor; Jeff Jobe, Chief Executive Officer, Publisher. **ISSN:** 0745--7006 (print). **Subscription Rates:** $21.95 Individuals online; $31.95 Individuals print and online; $40.95 Out of area print and online; $55.95 Out of country print and online; $18.95 online access for seniors and military. **URL:** http://www.jpinews.com/43314/1981/subscribe-to-butler-county-bannerrepublican. **Ad Rates:** BW $378; 4C $498; SAU $3; PCI $3. **Remarks:** Accepts advertising. **Circ:** 4117.

Circulation: ★ = AAM; △ or • = BPA; ♦ = CAC; ❑ = VAC; ⊕ = PO Statement; ‡ = Publisher's Report; Boldface figures = sworn; Light figures = estimated.

14070 ■ WLBQ-AM - 1570
PO Box 130
Morgantown, KY 42261
Phone: (270)526-5393
Format: Country. **Operating Hours**: 16 hours Daily. **Wattage**: 1,000. **Ad Rates:** Noncommercial.

MOUNT STERLING

Montgomery Co. Montgomery Co. (E). 33 m E of Lexington. Manufactures electric motors & components, dishwashers, underwear and knit goods, tool & die makers, automotive parts, concrete products, men's work clothing; feed mill; poultry and packing plants. Dairy, cattle, poultry, grain farms. Tobacco, corn, bell peppers, wheat.

14071 ■ Mt. Sterling Advocate
Mt. Sterling Advocate
219 Midland Trl.
Mount Sterling, KY 40353
Phone: (859)498-2222
Fax: (859)498-2228
Community newspaper. **Freq:** Weekly (Thurs.). **Print Method:** Offset. **Cols./Page:** 6. **Col. Width:** 25 nonpareils. **Col. Depth:** 301 agate lines. **Key Personnel:** Sharon Manning, Manager, Advertising; Jamie Vinson-Sturgill, Editor. **Subscription Rates:** $21.61 Individuals; $23.73 Individuals other Kentucky counties; $30 Out of state. **URL:** http://www.msadvocate.com. **Mailing address:** PO Box 406, Mount Sterling, KY 40353. **Ad Rates:** GLR $.27; SAU $5.50; PCI $4.68. **Remarks:** Accepts advertising. **Circ:** 6350.

14072 ■ WAXG-FM - 88.1
PO Box 3206
Tupelo, MS 38803
Format: Religious. **Owner:** American Family Radio, at above address. **Founded:** Feb. 1991. **Key Personnel:** Rick Robertson, Contact; Rick Robertson, Contact. **Ad Rates:** Noncommercial. **URL:** http://www.afr.net.

WKYN-FM - See Owingsville

14073 ■ WMST-AM - 1150
22 W Main
Mount Sterling, KY 40353
Phone: (859)498-1150
Fax: (606)498-7930
Email: wmstradio@bellsouth.net
Format: Sports; News; Information. **Owner:** Gateway Radio Works, Inc., 22 W Main St., Mount Sterling, KY 40353. **Founded:** 1957. **Key Personnel:** Vernice Taylor, Station Mgr.; Dan Manley, Sports Dir.; Jeff Ray, Gen. Mgr. **Local Programs**: *Gateway Regional News*; *Mornings on Main with Dan*, Monday Tuesday Wednesday Thursday Friday 6:00 a.m. - 1:00 p.m.; *Mid-Mornings on Main w/ Tom & Judy*, Monday Tuesday Wednesday Thursday Friday 8:20 a.m. - 10:30 a.m. **Wattage**: 2,500 KW. **Ad Rates:** Accepts Advertising. **URL:** http://www.wmstradio.com/.

14074 ■ WMST-FM - 105.5
22 W Main St.
Mount Sterling, KY 40353
Phone: (606)498-1150
Fax: (606)498-7930
Format: Eclectic. **Networks:** KyNet. **Founded:** 1968. **Operating Hours**: 6:00 a.m.-11:00 p.m. **ADI**: Lexington, KY. **Wattage:** 3,000. **Ad Rates:** $3-5 for 15 seconds; $4-6 for 30 seconds; $5-7 for 60 seconds. **URL:** http://www.wmstradio.com.

MOUNT VERNON

14075 ■ WRVK-AM - 1460
35 Lovell Ln.
Mount Vernon, KY 40456
Phone: (606)256-2146
Email: dj@wrvk1460.com
Format: Bluegrass; Country. **Networks:** Knowledge Network. **Owner:** Saylor Broadcasting Inc., PO Box 7, Renfro Valley, KY 40473. **Founded:** 1957. **Operating Hours**: 6 a.m.-8 p.m.; 10% network, 80% local. **Key Personnel:** Charles Saylor, Station Mgr.; Charlie Napier, Sales Mgr.; Kevin Roberts, Production Mgr. **Wattage**: 1,200. **Ad Rates:** for 30 seconds; $8 for 60 seconds. **URL:** http://www.wrvk1460.com.

MUNFORDVILLE

Hart Co. Hart Co. (SWC). 73 m S of Louisville. Feed, lumber mills. Poultry, dairy, grain farms. Tobacco, corn.

14076 ■ WLOC-AM - 1150
PO Box 307
Munfordville, KY 42765
Phone: (502)524-4111
Format: Eclectic. **Networks:** Unistar; CNN Radio. **Founded:** 1956. **Operating Hours**: 5 a.m.-midnight. **Key Personnel:** Joe Bern, Contact. **Wattage:** 1,000. **Ad Rates:** $2-4.50 for 15 seconds; $3-6 for 30 seconds; $5-8 for 60 seconds.

MURRAY

Calloway Co. Calloway Co. (SW). 42 m SE of Paducah. Murray State University. Manufactures hosiery, lumber, tobacco, dairy products, popcorn processors, chemicals, oil filters, custom springs, asbestos clothing and gloves, toys. Agriculture. Tobacco, popcorn, corn, soybeans, wheat.

14077 ■ Journal of Business and Public Affairs
Murray State University College of Business and Public Affairs
109 Business and Public Affairs Bldg.
Murray, KY 42071
Phone: (270)809-6970
Publisher's E-mail: cob@murraystate.edu
Scholarly business journal. **Freq:** Annual. **Trim Size:** 8.5 x 11. **Key Personnel:** Seid Hassan, Editor. **ISSN:** 1522--8398 (print). **Subscription Rates:** $5 Individuals; $10 Libraries. **URL:** http://www.murraystate.edu/provost/catalogs/050507.html. **Formerly**: B & PA. **Remarks:** Accepts advertising. **Circ:** (Not Reported).

14078 ■ Murray Ledger and Times
Murray Ledger and Times
1001 Whitnell Ave.
Murray, KY 42071
Phone: (270)753-1916
Fax: (270)753-1927
General newspaper. **Freq:** Mon.-Sat. (eve.). **Print Method:** Offset. **Cols./Page:** 6. **Col. Width:** 18 nonpareils. **Col. Depth:** 294 agate lines. **Key Personnel:** Mike Davis, Publisher; John Wright, Editor; Chris Woodall, Manager, Advertising. **Subscription Rates:** $78 Individuals local delivery; $130 By mail. **URL:** http://murrayledger.com. **Mailing address:** PO Box 1040, Murray, KY 42071. **Ad Rates:** BW $1,064.25; 4C $1,289.25; PCI $8.25. **Remarks:** Accepts classified advertising. **Circ:** Paid ‡7500, Free ‡7500.

14079 ■ The Murray State News
Murray State University
Murray State University
2609 University Station
Murray, KY 42071-3301
Publication E-mail: orville.herndon@murraystate.edu
murraystatenews@icloud.com
Collegiate newspaper. **Freq:** Weekly (Fri.) fall and spring semester. **Print Method:** Offset. **Trim Size:** 13 1/4 x 22 1/2. **Cols./Page:** 6. **Col. Width:** 12.2 picas. **Col. Depth:** 21 inches. **Key Personnel:** Mary Bradley, Editor-in-Chief, phone: (270)809-6877. **Subscription Rates:** $20 Individuals. **URL:** http://thenews.org. **Ad Rates:** PCI $7.10. **Remarks:** Accepts advertising. **Circ:** Paid ‡250, Free ‡7000.

14080 ■ WFGE-FM - 103.7
1500 Diuquid Dr.
Murray, KY 42071
Phone: (270)753-2400
Fax: (270)753-9434
Free: 800-879-9256
Format: Country. **Networks:** Unistar; CNN Radio; Westwood One Radio. **Owner:** Kentucky Lake Productions, LLC, at above address. **Founded:** 1967. **Formerly**: WAAW-FM; WBLN-FM. **Operating Hours**: Continuous. **Key Personnel:** Jason Crockett, Dir. of Programs, jcrockett@forevercomm.com. **Wattage:** 100,000. **Ad Rates:** Noncommercial. **URL:** http://www.froggy103.com.

14081 ■ WKMS-FM - 91.3
2018 University Sta.
Murray, KY 42071
Phone: (270)809-4359
Fax: (270)809-4667
Free: 800-599-4737
Email: msu.wkms@murraystate.edu
Format: Public Radio. **Networks:** National Public Radio (NPR); BBC World Service; American Public Radio (APR); Public Radio International (PRI); AP. **Owner:** Murray State University, 102 Curris Ctr., Murray, KY 42071, Ph: (270)762-3011, Free: 800-272-4678. **Founded:** 1970. **Operating Hours**: Continuous. **Key Personnel:** Kate Lochte, Station Mgr., kate.lochte@murraystate.edu; Tracy Ross, Prog. Dir., tracy.ross@murraystate.edu; Chad Lampe, Station Mgr., chad.lampe@murraystate.edu. **Local Programs**: *Jazzman Show*, Sunday 1:00 p.m.; *The Retro Cocktail Hour*, Friday 11:00 p.m.; *Weekend Energy*, Saturday 11:00 p.m. - 1:00 a.m.; *Weekend Edition Sunday*, Sunday 7:00 a.m.; *The Front Page*, Friday; *Beyond The Edge*, Saturday 8:00 p.m. - 11:00 p.m.; *Music From The Front Porch*, Saturday 10:00 a.m. - 1:00 p.m. **Wattage**: 100,000. **Ad Rates:** Noncommercial; underwriting available. $10 per unit. Underwriting available. **URL:** http://www.wkms.org.

14082 ■ WKMU-TV - 21
600 Cooper Dr.
Lexington, KY 40502
Phone: (859)258-7000
Free: 800-432-0951
Format: Educational. **Networks:** Public Broadcasting Service (PBS); Kentucky Educational Television. **Owner:** Kentucky Educational Television, 600 Cooper Dr., Lexington, KY 40502, Ph: (859)258-7000, Free: 800-432-0951. **Founded:** 1968. **Operating Hours**: 6:15 a.m.-midnight. **ADI**: Paducah,KY-Cape Girardeau,MO-Marion,IL. **Key Personnel:** Shae Hopkins, Exec. Dir., CEO. **Local Programs**: *Comment on Kentucky*, Friday Sunday 8:00 p.m. 12:30 p.m.; *Kentucky Afield*, Thursday Friday Saturday Sunday Tuesday Wednesday 7:00 p.m. 11:00 a.m. 7:00 a.m.; 7:30 p.m. 6:00 a.m.; 3:30 p.m. 4:30 p.m. 4:00 p.m.; *Kentucky Life*, Friday Saturday Sunday Monday Tuesday Wednesday Thursday 11:30 a.m.; 4:30 p.m. 7:30 a.m.; 7:00 p.m. 7:00 a.m.; 3:00 p.m. 4:30 p.m.; 6:00 p.m.; 10:30 p.m. 6:30 a.m.; 4:30 p.m. 7:00 a.m.; 4:30 p.m. 4:30 p.m.; *Kentucky Tonight*, Monday 8:00 p.m.; *Local Flavor*. **Wattage**: 692,000. **Ad Rates:** Noncommercial. **URL:** http://www.ket.org.

14083 ■ WNBS-AM - 1340
1500 Diuguid Dr.
Murray, KY 42071
Phone: (270)753-2400
Format: News; Talk; Sports. **Networks:** CBS. **Owner:** Forever Communications, Inc., 1919 Scottsville Rd., Bowling Green, KY 42104, Ph: (270)843-3333. **Founded:** 1948. **Key Personnel:** Neal Bradley, Contact, nealbradley@gmail.com. **Local Programs**: *Breakfast Show*, Monday Tuesday Wednesday Thursday Friday 7:06 a.m. - 9:00 a.m. **Wattage**: 1,000 Day. **URL:** http://www.1340wnbs.com.

NICHOLASVILLE

Jessamine Co. Jessamine Co. (C). 12 m S of Lexington. Manufactures wire products, paperboard food containers, automotive trim parts, plastic, vehicle mufflers, high security lock systems. Machine works. Dairy, stock, poultry, grain, truck farms. Tobacco, corn, wheat.

14084 ■ The Jessamine Journal
The Jessamine Journal
507 N Main St.
Nicholasville, KY 40356
Phone: (859)885-5381
Fax: (859)887-2966
Publisher's E-mail: news@jessaminejournal.com
Newspaper. **Founded:** 1873. **Freq:** Weekly. **Print Method:** Offset. **Cols./Page:** 6. **Col. Width:** 26 nonpareils. **Col. Depth:** 294 agate lines. **Key Personnel:** David Brock, Editor; Larry Hensley, Editor, President, Publisher, phone: (859)885-5381. **Subscription Rates:** $35 Individuals Jassamine & surrounding counties; $41 Out of area; $50 Out of state. **URL:** http://www.centralkynews.com/jessaminejournal/. **Ad Rates:** BW $1,148.10; 4C $1,343.10; SAU $8.90; PCI $8.90. **Remarks:** Accepts advertising. **Circ:** 7400.

OKOLONA

14085 ■ W216BM-FM - 91.1
PO Box 391
Twin Falls, ID 83303
Fax: (208)736-1958
Free: 800-357-4226
Format: Religious; Contemporary Christian. **Owner:**

CSN International, PO Box 391, Twin Falls, ID 83303, Ph: (208)736-1958, Fax: (208)736-1958, Free: 800-357-4226. **Key Personnel:** Kelly Carlson, Dir. of Engg.; Ray Gorney, Asst. Dir. **URL:** http://www.csnradio.com.

OLIVE HILL

Carter Co. Carter Co. (NE). 22 m N of Lewis. Concrete products, men's and boy's work clothing manufactured. Agriculture. Tobacco, livestock, poultry.

14086 ■ Olive Hill Times
Olive Hill Times
Post Office Bldg.
Olive Hill, KY 41164
Phone: (606)286-4201
Publisher's E-mail: feedback@rootsweb.com
Community newspaper. **Freq:** Weekly (Wed.). **Print Method:** Offset. **Cols./Page:** 6. **Col. Width:** 10.4 picas. **Col. Depth:** 21.5 inches. **Subscription Rates:** $15 Individuals. **URL:** http://www.rootsweb.ancestry.com/~kycarter/news/olive_hill_times.html. **Ad Rates:** SAU $4.05; PCI $3.37. **Remarks:** Accepts advertising. **Circ:** ‡2905.

OWENSBORO

Daviess Co. Daviess Co. (WC). On Ohio River, 38 m SE of Evansville, Ind. Kentucky Wesleyan College; Brescia College. Riverport facilites. Manufactures whiskey, electric lamps, radio tubes, chair, cigars, bricks, iron and steel products, furniture, storm and screen windows, concrete, chemicals, tobacco, flour, oil well supplies, sewer pipes, cheese, canned goods, product bakery, building blocks, stock feeds. Tobacco auction warehouses. Meat and poultry packing plants. Soybean mill. Oil, gas wells. Coal mines. Forgings. Timber. Diversified farming.

14087 ■ Messenger-Inquirer
Owensboro Messenger-Inquirer Inc.
1401 Frederica St.
Owensboro, KY 42301-4804
Phone: (270)926-0123
Fax: (270)685-3446
Publisher's E-mail: mfrancis@messenger-inquirer.com
General newspaper. **Freq:** Mon.-Sun. (morn.). **Print Method:** Offset. **Cols./Page:** 6. **Col. Width:** 25 nonpareils. **Col. Depth:** 294 agate lines. **Key Personnel:** Faye D. Murry, Director, Advertising, phone: (270)691-7240; Robert Morris, Publisher; Matt Francis, Executive Editor. **Subscription Rates:** $221.30 Individuals carrier; $250.20 By mail; $258 Out of state. **URL:** http://www.messenger-inquirer.com. **Mailing address:** PO Box 1480, Owensboro, KY 42301-4804. **Ad Rates:** 4C $550; PCI $23. **Remarks:** Accepts advertising. **Circ:** 25185, 27768.

14088 ■ Western Kentucky Catholic
Diocese of Owensboro
600 Locust St.
Owensboro, KY 42301
Phone: (270)683-1545
Fax: (270)683-6883
Official newspaper of the Diocese of Owensboro. **Freq:** 10/year. **Print Method:** Web offset. **Trim Size:** 10 x 13. **Cols./Page:** 4. **Col. Width:** 14 picas. **Col. Depth:** 10 inches. **Key Personnel:** Mel Howard, Director; Most Rev. John J. McRaith, Publisher. **Subscription Rates:** $10 Individuals; $15 Other countries. **Remarks:** Advertising not accepted. **Circ:** Paid ‡19865.

14089 ■ WBIO-FM - 94.7
1115 Tamarack Rd., No. 500
Owensboro, KY 42301
Phone: (270)683-5200
Fax: (270)688-0108
Format: Country. **Key Personnel:** Lee Wilson, Gen. Mgr., lwilson@cromwellradio.com; Jeff Morgan, Operations Mgr., jmorgan@cromwellradio.com. **Ad Rates:** Advertising accepted; rates available upon request. **URL:** http://www.owensbororadio.com.

14090 ■ WBKR-FM - 92.5
3301 Frederica St.
Owensboro, KY 42301-6082
Phone: (270)683-1558
Format: Country. **Owner:** Townsquare Media Inc., 240 Greenwich Ave., Greenwich, CT 06830-6507, Ph: (203)861-0900. **Key Personnel:** Chad Benefield, Div. Mgr., chad@wbkr.com. **Ad Rates:** Advertising accepted; rates available upon request. **URL:** http://www.wbkr.com.

14091 ■ WKCM-AM - 1160
1115 Tamarack Rd., No. 500
Owensboro, KY 42301
Phone: (270)683-5200
Format: Country. **Ad Rates:** Advertising accepted; rates available upon request. **URL:** http://www.owensbororadio.com.

14092 ■ WKWC-FM - 90.3
3000 Frederica St.
Owensboro, KY 42301
Fax: (502)926-3196
Format: Religious; Eclectic. **Networks:** Independent. **Owner:** Kentucky Wesleyan College, 3000 Frederica St., KY 42301. **Founded:** Sept. 07, 2006. **Operating Hours:** 8 a.m.-midnight weekdays; 9 a.m.-midnight Sat.; 7 a.m.-midnight Sun. **Key Personnel:** Pam Gray, Contact. **Wattage:** 5,000. **Ad Rates:** Noncommercial. **URL:** http://www.kwc.edu.

14093 ■ WLME-FM - 102.7
1115 Tamarack Rd., No. 500
Owensboro, KY 42301
Phone: (270)683-5200
Format: Country. **Ad Rates:** Advertising accepted; rates available upon request. **URL:** http://www.owensbororadio.com.

14094 ■ WQXQ-FM
PO Box 22469
Owensboro, KY 42302
Phone: (270)685-1235
Fax: (270)685-1873
Format: Top 40. **Wattage:** 100,000 ERP.

14095 ■ WSTO-FM - 96.1
100 Industrial Dr.
Box 21828
Owensboro, KY 42301
Phone: (502)685-2991
Fax: (502)685-7098
Format: Contemporary Hit Radio (CHR). **Networks:** ABC. **Owner:** Century Communications, 50 Locust Ave., New Canaan, CT 06840-4737, Ph: (203)972-2000, Fax: (203)966-9228. **Founded:** 1948. **Operating Hours:** Continuous. **ADI:** Evansville, IN (Madisonville, KY). **Wattage:** 100,000 ERP. **Ad Rates:** $11-69 for 30 seconds; $15-79 for 60 seconds. **URL:** http://hot96.com.

14096 ■ WVJS-AM - 1420
1115 Tamarack Rd., Ste. 500
Owensboro, KY 42301-6082
Phone: (270)683-5200
Format: News. **Founded:** 1948. **Wattage:** 980 KW. **Ad Rates:** Advertising accepted; rates available upon request. **URL:** http://www.owensbororadio.com/?err=404.

14097 ■ WXCM-FM - 97.1
1115 Tamarack Rd., No. 500
Owensboro, KY 42301
Phone: (270)683-5200
Format: Classic Rock; Album-Oriented Rock (AOR). **Owner:** The Cromwell Group, Inc., 1824 Murfreesboro Rd., Nashville, TN 37217, Ph: (615)361-7560, Fax: (615)366-4313. **Key Personnel:** Lee Wilson, Gen. Mgr., lwilson@cromwellradio.com. **URL:** http://www.owensbororadio.com.

OWENTON

Owen Co. Owen Co. (NC). 30 m N of Frankfort. Agriculture. Tobacco, corn, cattle.

14098 ■ The News-Herald
The News-Herald
152 W Bryan St.
Owenton, KY 40359
Phone: (502)484-3431
Fax: (502)484-3221
Publisher's E-mail: circulation@owentonnewsherald.com
Community newspaper. **Founded:** 1868. **Freq:** Weekly (Wed.). **Print Method:** Offset. **Cols./Page:** 6. **Col. Width:** 24 nonpareils. **Col. Depth:** 294 agate lines. **Key Personnel:** Sherry Lyons, Office Manager; Molly Haines, Writer. **USPS:** 388-180. **Subscription Rates:** $52 Individuals print and online /year; $31.80 Individuals online only /year. **URL:** http://www.owentonnewsherald.com/. **Mailing address:** PO Box 219, Owenton, KY 40359. **Ad Rates:** GLR $5.35; SAU $4.28; PCI $4.95. **Remarks:** Accepts advertising. **Circ:** ‡3749.

14099 ■ WKON-TV - 52
600 Cooper Dr.
Lexington, KY 40502
Phone: (859)258-7000
Free: 800-432-0951
Email: feedback@ket.org
Format: Public TV. **Networks:** Public Broadcasting Service (PBS); Kentucky Educational Television. **Owner:** Kentucky Authority for Educational TV, 600 Cooper Dr., Lexington, KY 40502, Ph: (606)258-7170, Fax: (606)258-7390. **Founded:** 1968. **Operating Hours:** 6:15 a.m.-midnight. **ADI:** Lexington, KY. **Key Personnel:** Shae Hopkins, Exec. Dir. **Local Programs:** *Comment on Kentucky*, Friday Sunday 8:00 p.m.; 7:00 p.m. 12:30 p.m.; 11:30 a.m.; *Kentucky Afield*, Saturday Sunday 8:30 p.m. 4:30 p.m.; *Kentucky Life*, Saturday Sunday 8:00 p.m. 4:00 p.m.; *Kentucky Tonight*, Monday Wednesday 8:00 p.m. 2:00 a.m.; *Kentucky Muse*. **Wattage:** 676,000. **Ad Rates:** Noncommercial. **URL:** http://www.ket.org.

OWINGSVILLE

Bath Co. Bath Co. (NE). 43 m NE of Lexington. Lumber mill. Agriculture. Tobacco, corn, potatoes.

14100 ■ WKYN-FM - 107.7
22 W Main St.
Mount Sterling, KY 40353
Phone: (859)498-7930
Format: Contemporary Country. **Networks:** ABC. **Owner:** Gateway Radio Works, Inc., 22 W Main St., Mount Sterling, KY 40353. **Founded:** 1983. **Formerly:** WKCA-FM. **Operating Hours:** Continuous; 80% network, 20% local. **ADI:** Lexington, KY. **Wattage:** 6,000. **Ad Rates:** $7-10 for 30 seconds; $10-14 for 60 seconds. **URL:** http://wkynradio.com.

PADUCAH

McCracken Co. McCracken Co. (SW). On the Ohio River, 80 m SW of Evansville, Ind. Manufactures industrial belting, concrete products, barges, metallurgical coke, automotive radiators, chemicals, textile machinery, radio components, castings, pottery, ladies' wearing apparel, barge & railroad cars covers. Important burley tobacco market. Atomic energy plant. Clay, fluorite, coal mines.

14101 ■ American Quilter
Collector Books
5801 Kentucky Dam Rd.
Paducah, KY 42003-9323
Phone: (270)898-6211
Fax: (270)898-8890
Free: 800-626-5420
Publisher's E-mail: info@collectorbooks.com
Consumer magazine covering for information for quilters. **Freq:** Bimonthly. **Print Method:** Web. **Trim Size:** 8 1/4 x 10 3/4. **Key Personnel:** Christine N. Brown, Editor-in-Chief. **ISSN:** 8756--6591 (print). **URL:** http://www.americanquilter.com/publications. **Mailing address:** PO Box 3009, Paducah, KY 42003-9323. **Remarks:** Accepts advertising. **Circ:** (Not Reported).

14102 ■ Carlisle County News: Serving as Carlisle County's Newspaper since 1894
Kentucky Publishing Inc.
701 Jefferson St.
Paducah, KY 42001
Phone: (270)442-7389
Fax: (270)442-5220
Community newspaper. **Freq:** Weekly (Wed.). **Print Method:** Offset. **Cols./Page:** 6. **Col. Width:** 10.9 picas. **Col. Depth:** 294 agate lines. **Key Personnel:** Gregory S. Vaught, Manager, Production; Greg Leneave, Publisher. **Subscription Rates:** $35 Individuals /year (print and online); $21.95 Individuals /year (online); $26 Individuals /year (print); $63 Out of area /year (print). **URL:** http://www.ky-news.com/section/the-carlisle-county-news. **Mailing address:** PO Box 1135, Paducah, KY 42001. **Remarks:** Accepts classified advertising. **Circ:** (Not Reported).

Circulation: ★ = AAM; △ or • = BPA; ♦ = CAC; ❑ = VAC; ⊕ = PO Statement; ‡ = Publisher's Report; Boldface figures = sworn; Light figures = estimated.

14103 ■ The Paducah Sun
The Paducah Sun
408 Kentucky Ave.
Paducah, KY 42003
Phone: (270)575-8600
Free: 800-599-1771
Publisher's E-mail: customerservice@paducahsun.com
General newspaper. **Freq:** Daily and Sun. (morn.). **Print Method:** Offset. **Cols./Page:** 6. **Col. Width:** 24 nonpareils. **Col. Depth:** 298 agate lines. **Key Personnel:** Duke Conover, Managing Editor. **URL:** http://www.paducahsun.com. **Ad Rates:** BW $425; PCI $24. **Remarks:** Accepts advertising. **Circ:** Mon.-Fri. ★**24768**, Sun. ★**26833**, Sat. ★**23455**.

14104 ■ Pain Physician
American Society of Interventional Pain Physicians
81 Lakeview Dr.
Paducah, KY 42001
Phone: (270)554-9412
Fax: (270)554-5394
Publication E-mail: editor@painphysicianjournal.com
Freq: 8/year. **Subscription Rates:** $25 Members; $50 Nonmembers. **URL:** http://www.painphysicianjournal.com; http://www.asipp.org/Journal.htm. **Remarks:** Accepts advertising. **Circ:** (Not Reported).

14105 ■ 94.7 The Mix - 94.7
PO Box 2397
Paducah, KY 42002-2397
Phone: (270)554-8255
Free: 877-947-7736
Format: Classic Rock. **Owner:** Bristol Broadcasting Company Inc., 901 E Valley Dr., Bristol, VA 24201, Ph: (276)669-8112, Fax: (276)669-0541. **Formerly:** WQQR-FM. **URL:** http://www.947themix.com/contacts/.

14106 ■ WDDJ-FM - 96.9
6000 Bristol Dr.
Paducah, KY 42003
Phone: (270)534-9690
Fax: (270)554-5468
Format: Top 40. **Networks:** ABC. **Owner:** Bristol Broadcasting Company Inc., 901 E Valley Dr., Bristol, VA 24201, Ph: (276)669-8112, Fax: (276)669-0541. **Founded:** 1946. **Operating Hours:** Continuous. **Wattage:** 100,000 ERP. **Ad Rates:** Noncommercial. **URL:** http://www.electric969.com.

14107 ■ WDXR-AM - 1450
PO Box 2397
Paducah, KY 42003
Phone: (270)554-8255
Fax: (270)554-5468
Format: Talk. **Owner:** Bristol Broadcasting Co., 817 Suncrest Pl., South Charleston, WV 25303, Ph: (304)342-3136, Fax: (304)342-3118. **Founded:** 1957. **Operating Hours:** Continuous; 75% network, 25% local. **ADI:** Paducah,KY-Cape Girardeau,MO-Marion,IL. **Wattage:** 1,000. **Ad Rates:** $6-12 for 30 seconds. **URL:** http://www.bristolbroadcasting.com/paducahmkt.shtml.

14108 ■ WGCF-FM
US Hwy. 60
Kevil, KY 42053
Phone: (270)462-3020
Free: 866-755-7729
Email: info@wgcf.org
Format: Contemporary Christian; Religious. **Owner:** American Family Association, PO Box 2440, Tupelo, MS 38803, Ph: (662)844-5036. **Key Personnel:** Bill Hughes, Contact; John Riley, Contact; Tim Wildmon, Contact. **Wattage:** 12,000 ERP. **URL:** http://wgcf.afr.net.

14109 ■ WKPD-TV - 29
600 Cooper Dr.
Lexington, KY 40502
Phone: (859)258-7000
Free: 800-432-0951
Format: Public TV. **Networks:** Public Broadcasting Service (PBS); Kentucky Educational Television. **Owner:** Kentucky Authority for Educational TV, 600 Cooper Dr., Lexington, KY 40502, Ph: (606)258-7170, Fax: (606)258-7390. **Founded:** 1980. **Operating Hours:** 6 a.m.-midnight. **ADI:** Lexington, KY. **Key Personnel:** Shae Hopkins, Exec. Dir., CEO. **Local Programs:** *Kentucky Life*, Saturday Sunday 8:00 a.m. - 7:00 p.m. 4:00 a.m. - 3:00 p.m. **Wattage:** 123,000. **Ad Rates:** Noncommercial. **URL:** http://www.ket.org.

14110 ■ WKYQ-FM - 93.3
6000 Bristol Dr.
Paducah, KY 42003
Phone: (270)554-0093
Fax: (270)554-5468
Free: 800-942-9336
Format: Contemporary Country; Agricultural; News. **Networks:** ABC. **Owner:** Bristol Broadcasting Co., 817 Suncrest Pl., South Charleston, WV 25303, Ph: (304)342-3136, Fax: (304)342-3118. **Founded:** 1947. **Operating Hours:** Continuous. **ADI:** Paducah,KY-Cape Girardeau,MO-Marion,IL. **Key Personnel:** Donna Groves, News Dir., news@wkyq.com; Bobby Cook, Operations Mgr., bobby@wkyq.com. **Wattage:** 100,000 ERP. **Ad Rates:** $85-110 per unit. **URL:** http://www.wkyq.com.

14111 ■ WKYX-AM - 570
PO Box 2397
Paducah, KY 42002-2397
Phone: (270)554-8255
Fax: (270)554-5468
Free: 866-570-1320
Email: info@wkyx.com
Format: Talk; News. **Owner:** Bristol Broadcasting Company, Inc., at above address. **Founded:** 1971. **Operating Hours:** Continuous; 40% network, 60% local. **ADI:** Paducah,KY-Cape Girardeau,MO-Marion,IL. **Key Personnel:** Greg Dunker, Prog. Dir. **Wattage:** 1,000 Day; 500 Night. **Ad Rates:** Noncommercial. **URL:** http://www.wkyx.com.

14112 ■ WKYX-FM - 94.3
PO Box 2397
Paducah, KY 42002-2397
Phone: (270)554-8255
Fax: (270)554-5468
Free: 866-570-1320
Format: News; Talk. **Owner:** Bristol Broadcasting Company Inc., 901 E Valley Dr., Bristol, VA 24201, Ph: (276)669-8112, Fax: (276)669-0541. **Operating Hours:** Continuous. **Ad Rates:** Advertising accepted; rates available upon request. **URL:** http://www.wkyx.com.

14113 ■ WPAD-AM - 1560
6000 Bristol Dr.
Paducah, KY 42003
Phone: (270)554-8255
Email: wpad@wkynet.com
Format: Talk; Sports. **Networks:** Westwood One Radio; Mutual Broadcasting System. **Owner:** Purchase Broadcasting, at above address. **Founded:** 1936. **Operating Hours:** Continuous. **ADI:** Paducah,KY-Cape Girardeau,MO-Marion,IL. **Wattage:** 10,000. **Ad Rates:** $5-13 for 30 seconds; $8-16 for 60 seconds. **URL:** http://www.995thefanpaducah.com.

14114 ■ WPSD-TV - 6
100 Television Ln.
Paducah, KY 42003
Format: Commercial TV. **Networks:** NBC. **Owner:** WPSD-TV, LLC, at above address. **Founded:** 1957. **Operating Hours:** Continuous. **ADI:** Paducah,KY-Cape Girardeau,MO-Marion,IL. **Ad Rates:** Noncommercial. **URL:** http://www.wpsdlocal6.com.

14115 ■ WREZ-FM - 105.5
1700 North 8th St.
Paducah, KY 42001
Phone: (270)538-5251
Fax: (270)415-0599
Free: 800-718-3411
Format: Contemporary Hit Radio (CHR); Top 40. **Owner:** Withers Broadcasting Companies, 1822 N Court St., Marion, IL 62959, Ph: (303)242-5000. **Key Personnel:** Rick Lambert, Gen. Mgr., rlambert@withersradio.net. **Ad Rates:** Advertising accepted; rates available upon request. **URL:** http://www.1055thecat.com.

14116 ■ WRIK-AM
PO Box 9105
Paducah, KY 42002-9105
Format: Talk; News. **Networks:** Sun Radio. **Owner:** Sun Media, Inc., 105 W 5th St., Metropolis, IL 62960. **Founded:** 1987. **Formerly:** WZOM-AM. **Key Personnel:** Samuel K. Stratemeyer, Contact. **Wattage:** 500 Day. **Ad Rates:** $10 for 30 seconds; $15 for 60 seconds.

14117 ■ WZZL-FM - 106.7
1700 N 8th St.
Paducah, KY 42001
Phone: (270)554-1067
Fax: (270)415-0599
Free: 800-455-1067
Format: Album-Oriented Rock (AOR). **Founded:** Sept. 07, 2006. **Operating Hours:** Continuous. **Key Personnel:** Rick Lambert, Gen. Mgr. **Ad Rates:** Advertising accepted; rates available upon request. **URL:** http://www.wzzl.com.

PAINTSVILLE

Johnson Co. Johnson Co. (EC). On Big Sandy River, 50 m S of Ashland. Manufactures plumbing fixtures, tobacco. Coal mines. Oil wells. Bottling works. Poultry stock. Truck, grain farms. Apples.

14118 ■ The Paintsville Herald
The Paintsville Herald
978 Broadway Plz.
Paintsville, KY 41240
Phone: (606)789-5315
Fax: (606)789-9717
Free: 888-788-5315
Publisher's E-mail: news@paintsvilleherald.com
Newspaper. **Freq:** Semiweekly Wednesday and Friday. **Print Method:** Offset. **Cols./Page:** 6. **Col. Width:** 12 picas. **Col. Depth:** 21.5 inches. **Key Personnel:** Tim Pelphrey, Editor; Paula Halm, Editor, Publisher; Kathy Prater, Associate Editor. **USPS:** 418-440. **Subscription Rates:** $35 Individuals Johnson county; $70 Out of country; $30 Individuals online only /year. **URL:** http://www.paintsvilleherald.com. **Mailing address:** PO Box 1547, Paintsville, KY 41240. **Ad Rates:** GLR $5.75; BW $741.75; 4C $966.75; PCI $5.75. **Remarks:** Accepts advertising. **Circ:** ‡5200.

14119 ■ WKYH-AM
Paintsville, KY
Email: wkyh@charterinternet.com
Format: Talk; News; Sports. **Wattage:** 5,000 Day; 043 Night. **Ad Rates:** Noncommercial. **URL:** http://www.wkyh.com.

14120 ■ WSIP-AM
PO Box 591
Paintsville, KY 41240
Phone: (606)789-5311
Fax: (606)789-7200
Free: 800-858-5491
Format: Gospel. **Networks:** CBS. **Owner:** Key Broadcating Inc., Corbin, KY. **Founded:** 1949. **Key Personnel:** Glenna Adkins, Contact. **Wattage:** 1,000. **Ad Rates:** $5.88 for 30 seconds; $9.41 for 60 seconds.

14121 ■ WSIP-FM - 98.9
127 Main St.
Paintsville, KY 41240
Phone: (606)789-5311
Fax: (606)789-7200
Format: Country. **Networks:** CBS. **Owner:** SIP Broadcasting Inc., 1.9 Miles Southeast, Paintsville, KY. **Founded:** 1975. **Operating Hours:** Continuous. **ADI:** Lexington, KY. **Wattage:** 100,000. **Ad Rates:** Advertising accepted; rates available upon request. **URL:** http://www.wsipfm.com.

PENDLETON

14122 ■ The Falmouth Outlook
Cynthiana Democrat
PO Box 111
Falmouth, KY 41040-0111
Phone: (859)654-3332
Fax: (859)654-4365
Publication E-mail: news@falmouthoutlook.com
Community newspaper. **Freq:** Weekly (Tues.). **Print Method:** Offset. **Cols./Page:** 6. **Col. Width:** 1.833 INS. **Col. Depth:** 21 1/2 inches. **Key Personnel:** Debbie Dennie, Editor. **ISSN:** 0891--8694 (print). **Subscription Rates:** $30 Individuals 1 year; 22 9 months; 15 3 months. **URL:** http://www.falmouthoutlook.com. **Ad Rates:** GLR $7.88; BW $700; 4C $200; SAU $7.88. **Remarks:** Color advertising accepted; rates available upon request. **Circ:** (Not Reported).

PIKEVILLE

Pike Co. Pike Co. (E) 5 m. S of Millard. Residential.

14123 ■ Appalachian News Express: The Conscience of Eastern Kentucky
Lancaster Management
129 Caroline Ave.
Pikeville, KY 41501
Phone: (606)437-4054
Fax: (606)437-4246
Free: 800-539-4054
Publisher's E-mail: editor@news-expressky.com
Community newspaper. **Freq:** 3/week. **Print Method:** Offset. **Cols./Page:** 6. **Col. Width:** 2 inches. **Col. Depth:** 294 agate lines. **Key Personnel:** Jeff Vanderbeck, Publisher; Lisa Moore, Manager, Circulation; Russ Cassady, Editor. **USPS:** 347-510. **Subscription Rates:** $75 Individuals online or print and online in Pike County; $100 Out of area print and online; $80 Individuals print and online in Pike County. **URL:** http://news-expressky.com. **Ad Rates:** GLR $.37; BW $780.45; 4C $980.45; SAU $4.66; PCI $6.05. **Remarks:** Accepts advertising. **Circ:** ‡10800.

14124 ■ Pikeville Review
University of Pikeville Humanities Dept.
147 Sycamore St.
Pikeville, KY 41501
Phone: (606)218-5250
Fax: (606)218-5269
Publisher's E-mail: brigitteanderson@upike.edu
Literary magazine covering poetry, fiction, essays, and reviews. **Freq:** Annual. **Trim Size:** 6 x 8. **Key Personnel:** Sydney England, Editor. **Subscription Rates:** $4 Individuals; $8 Two years. **URL:** http://www.upike.edu/pikevillereview. **Remarks:** Advertising not accepted. **Circ:** Paid 500.

14125 ■ WBTH-AM - 1400
1240 Radio Dr.
Pikeville, KY 41502
Phone: (606)437-4051
Fax: (606)432-2809
Format: Talk. **Networks:** Westwood One Radio. **Owner:** East Kentucky Broadcasting, at above address. **Founded:** 1939. **Operating Hours:** Continuous. **Key Personnel:** Walter E. May, Owner, Founder. **Wattage:** 5,000. **Ad Rates:** $4.75-8.50 for 30 seconds. **Mailing address:** PO Box 2200, Pikeville, KY 41502. **URL:** http://ekbbuzz.com.

14126 ■ WEKB-AM - 1460
1240 Radio Dr.
Pikeville, KY 41502
Phone: (606)437-4051
Fax: (606)432-2809
Format: Oldies. **Networks:** CNN Radio; Westwood One Radio; ABC. **Owner:** East Kentucky Broadcasting Group, PO Box 2200, Pikeville, KY 41501. **Formerly:** WBPA-AM. **Operating Hours:** Sunrise-sunset; 25% network, 75% local. **ADI:** Charleston-Huntington, WV. **Wattage:** 5,000. **Ad Rates:** Noncommercial. **Mailing address:** PO Box 2200, Pikeville, KY 41502. **URL:** http://ekbbuzz.com.

14127 ■ WJSO-FM - 90.1
PO Box 3237
Pikeville, KY 41502
Fax: (606)432-7339
Email: wjso@moody.edu
Format: Religious; Contemporary Christian. **Networks:** Moody Broadcasting. **Owner:** Moody Broadcasting Network, 820 N La Salle Blvd., Chicago, IL 60610, Ph: (312)329-4300, Fax: (312)329-4339, Free: 800-356-6639. **Founded:** 1989. **Operating Hours:** Continuous; 100% network. **Wattage:** 3,800. **Ad Rates:** Noncommercial. **URL:** http://www.moodyradiopikeville.fm.

14128 ■ WKPI-TV - 22
600 Cooper Dr.
Lexington, KY 40502
Phone: (859)258-7000
Free: 800-432-0951
Email: feedback@ket.org
Format: Public TV; Educational. **Networks:** Public Broadcasting Service (PBS); Kentucky Educational Television. **Owner:** Kentucky Educational Television, 600 Cooper Dr., Lexington, KY 40502, Ph: (859)258-7000, Free: 800-432-0951. **Founded:** 1968. **Operating Hours:** 6:30 a.m.-midnight. **ADI:** Lexington, KY. **Key Personnel:** Shae Hopkins, Exec. Dir. **Wattage:** 1,320,000. **Ad Rates:** Noncommercial. **URL:** http://www.ket.org.

14129 ■ WLSI-AM - 900
1240 Radio Dr.
Pikeville, KY 41502
Phone: (606)437-4051
Fax: (606)432-2809
Format: Talk. **Owner:** East Kentucky Broadcasting Group, PO Box 2200, Pikeville, KY 41501. **Founded:** 1949. **Operating Hours:** Continuous; 100% local. **Key Personnel:** Walter E. May, Owner, Founder; John Roberts, Dir. of Sales, johnr@ekbradio.com; Ted Meadows, Sales Mgr., tedmeadows@wpke.com. **Wattage:** 5,000. **Ad Rates:** Noncommercial. **Mailing address:** PO Box 2200, Pikeville, KY 41502. **URL:** http://ekbbuzz.com/900wlsi/radio/welcome.html.

14130 ■ WPKE-AM - 1240
1240 Radio Dr.
Pikeville, KY 41501
Phone: (606)437-4051
Fax: (606)432-2809
Format: Oldies. **Simulcasts:** WPKE-FM; WBPA-AM. **Networks:** ABC; KyNet. **Owner:** East Kentucky Broadcasting, at above address. **Founded:** July 31, 1949. **Operating Hours:** Continuous. **Key Personnel:** Pat Hall, Sales Mgr. **Wattage:** 1,000. **Ad Rates:** $7.00-8.40 for 15 seconds; $8.75-10.50 for 30 seconds; $10.50-12.60 for 60 seconds. **Mailing address:** PO Box 2200, Pikeville, KY 41502. **URL:** http://www.wpke.com.

14131 ■ WPKE-FM - 103.1
1240 Radio Dr.
Pikeville, KY 41501-4779
Format: News. **Networks:** ABC; KyNet. **Owner:** East Kentucky Broadcasting, at above address. **Founded:** 1949. **Operating Hours:** Continuous. **Wattage:** 320. **Ad Rates:** $7-8.40 for 15 seconds; $8.75-10.50 for 30 seconds; $10.50-12.60 for 60 seconds. **URL:** http://www.wpke.com.

14132 ■ WPRT-AM - 960
PO Box 2200
Pikeville, KY 41502-2200
Phone: (606)437-4051
Format: Adult Contemporary. **Networks:** Independent. **Owner:** Ed Walters Broadcasting, at above address. **Founded:** 1955. **Operating Hours:** 18 hrs. Daily 90% network, 10% local. **ADI:** Charleston-Huntington, WV. **Key Personnel:** Paul Marshall, Contact. **Wattage:** 5,000. **Ad Rates:** $5.25-10.90 for 15 seconds; $7-14.52 for 30 seconds; $8.50-17.55 for 60 seconds.

14133 ■ WVKY-AM - 1270
PO Box 2200
Pikeville, KY 41502-2200
Phone: (606)638-9491
Fax: (606)432-2804
Format: Contemporary Country. **Networks:** ABC; KyNet. **Owner:** Lawrence County Broadcasting Corp., at above address. **Founded:** 1970. **Operating Hours:** 15 hours daily; 10% network, 90% local. **Key Personnel:** David Stratton, President; Lavern Boyd, Gen. Mgr.; Mike Webb, Music Dir.; Diana Webb, Sales Mgr. **Wattage:** 1,000. **Ad Rates:** $8.46-14.52 for 30 seconds; $12.54-17.55 for 60 seconds.

14134 ■ WXCC-FM - 96.5
PO Box 2200
Pikeville, KY 41502
Phone: (304)235-3600
Free: 800-321-4965
Email: wxcc@mikrotec.com
Format: Country; News; Sports. **Owner:** East Kentucky Radio Network, at above address, Ph: (606)437-4051. **Founded:** 1978. **Key Personnel:** Dwayne Amburgey, Gen. Mgr., Sales Mgr.; J.J. Fouts, Bus. Mgr.; Vernon Roberts, Sales Mgr.; Joe Kinzer, Sports Dir., News Dir.; Walter May, Owner. **Wattage:** 75,000 ERP. **Ad Rates:** $6.50-10.75 for 30 seconds. **URL:** http://www.wxccfm.com.

14135 ■ WZLK-FM - 107.5
1240 Radio Dr.
Pikeville, KY 41502
Phone: (606)437-4051
Fax: (606)432-2809
Format: Classic Rock; Album-Oriented Rock (AOR). **Owner:** East Kentucky Broadcasting Group, PO Box 2200, Pikeville, KY 41501. **Founded:** 1990. **Operating Hours:** Continuous. **Key Personnel:** Walter May, Contact; Walter May, Contact. **Wattage:** 1,450 ERP. **Mailing address:** PO Box 2200, Pikeville, KY 41502. **URL:** http://www.1075zrock.com.

PIPPA PASSES

Knott Co. Knott Co.

14136 ■ WWJD-FM - 91.7
100 Purpose Rd.
Pippa Passes, KY 41844
Phone: (606)368-6000
Free: 888-280-4252
Email: wwjd@alc.edu
Format: Educational. **Networks:** Independent. **Owner:** Alice Lloyd College, 100 Purpose Rd., Pippa Passes, KY 41844. **Founded:** 1985. **Operating Hours:** Continuous. **Wattage:** 7,300. **URL:** http://www.alc.edu.

PRESTONSBURG

Floyd Co. Floyd Co. (EC). 60 m S of Ashland. Coal mines. Diversified farming. Corn and truck crops.

14137 ■ The Floyd County Times
Floyd County Newspapers Inc.
263 S Central Ave.
Prestonsburg, KY 41653
Phone: (606)886-8506
Fax: (606)886-3603
Community newspaper. **Freq:** Semiweekly (Wed. and Fri.). **Print Method:** Offset. **Cols./Page:** 6. **Col. Width:** 26 nonpareils. **Col. Depth:** 294 agate lines. **Key Personnel:** Joshua Byers, Publisher; Ralph B Davis, III, Managing Editor; Jamie VanHoose, Manager, Advertising. **Subscription Rates:** $132 Individuals. **URL:** http://www.floydcountytimes.com. **Mailing address:** PO Box 390, Prestonsburg, KY 41653. **Ad Rates:** BW $637.50; SAU $5; PCI $5. **Remarks:** Advertising accepted; rates available upon request. **Circ:** 11400.

14138 ■ WDOC-AM - 1310
PO Box 345
Prestonsburg, KY 41653
Phone: (606)886-2338
Owner: WDOC Inc., 95 Jackson St., Prestonsburg, KY 41653, Ph: (606)886-8409, Fax: (606)263-4923. **Founded:** 1957. **Ad Rates:** Noncommercial.

14139 ■ WQHY-FM - 95.5
95 Jacson St.
Prestonsburg, KY 41653
Phone: (606)886-8409
Fax: (606)263-4923
Format: Adult Contemporary; Oldies. **Networks:** ABC. **Owner:** WDOC Inc., 95 Jackson St., Prestonsburg, KY 41653, Ph: (606)886-8409, Fax: (606)263-4923. **Founded:** 1962. **Operating Hours:** Continuous. **Key Personnel:** Carla Hughes, Dir. of Traffic; Chris Slone, Contact. **Wattage:** 100,000 ERP. **Ad Rates:** Noncommercial. $2.75-12.25 for 30 seconds; $4.58-20.42 for 60 seconds. **Mailing address:** PO Box 345, Prestonsburg, KY 41653. **URL:** http://www.q95fm.net.

PRINCETON

Caldwell Co. Caldwell Co. (SW). 60 m S of Owensboro. Fluorspar mines. Manufactures hosiery, shirts, boilers, concrete products, lumber. Diversified farming.

14140 ■ Times Leader
Times Leader
607 W Washington St.
Princeton, KY 42445
Phone: (270)365-5588
Fax: (270)365-7299
Publication E-mail: chiphutcheson@timesleader.net
Community newspaper. **Founded:** 1871. **Freq:** Semiweekly (Wed. and Sat.). **Print Method:** Offset. **Cols./Page:** 6. **Col. Width:** 24 nonpareils. **Col. Depth:** 21 1/2 inches. **Key Personnel:** Kathy Boyd, Director, Advertising; Ellen Franklin, Business Manager; Chip Hutcheson, Publisher; Anita Baker, Editor. **USPS:** 776-660. **Subscription Rates:** $16 Individuals 3 months; $28 Individuals 6 months; $46 Individuals; $18 Elsewhere in Kentucky; $31 Elsewhere in Kentucky, 6 months; $51 Elsewhere in Kentucky; $21 Out of state 3 months; $36 Out of state 6 months; $61 Out of state. **URL:** http://

Circulation: ★ = AAM; △ or • = BPA; ♦ = CAC; ❑ = VAC; ⊕ = PO Statement; ‡ = Publisher's Report; Boldface figures = sworn; Light figures = estimated.

www.timesleader.net. **Formerly**: Princeton Leader; Caldwell County Times. **Mailing address:** PO Box 439, Princeton, KY 42445. **Remarks:** Accepts advertising. **Circ:** ‡5700.

14141 ■ WPKY-AM
618 Marion Rd.
Princeton, KY 42445
Fax: (502)365-2073
Format: Soft Rock. **Networks:** Independent. **Owner:** Commonwealth Broadcasting Corp., at above address. **Founded:** 1950. **Key Personnel:** Teresa Glass, Sales Mgr. **Wattage**: 250 Day; 009 Night.

PROVIDENCE

Webster Co. Webster Co. (WC). 34 m SW of Henderson. Plastic, feed factories; Lumber mills. Coal mines. Oak timber. Agriculture. Tobacco, corn, hay, livestock.

14142 ■ The Journal-Enterprise
The Journal-Enterprise
100 Walnut St
Providence, KY 42450
Phone: (270)667-2068
Community newspaper. **Freq:** Weekly (Thurs.). **Print Method:** Offset. **Cols./Page:** 6. **Col. Width:** 24 nonpareils. **Col. Depth:** 197 agate lines. **Key Personnel:** Matt Hughes, Editor. **Subscription Rates:** $28 Individuals Webster county; $35 Individuals other Kentucky counties; $39 Out of state. **URL:** http://www.journalenterprise.com. **Ad Rates:** GLR $.16; SAU $2.10. **Remarks:** Accepts advertising. **Circ:** ‡4500.

RICHMOND

Madison Co. Madison Co. (C). 26 m SE of Lexington. Eastern Kentucky University. White Hall State Shrine and Fort Boonesborough State Park. Electric bulb, ice cream, cement block, electric cubes, tools factories; bottling works; tobacco warehouses. Diversified farming. Tobacco, corn, livestock.

14143 ■ The Eastern Progress
The Eastern Progress
Combs Bldg. 326
521 Lancaster Ave.
Richmond, KY 40475
Phone: (859)622-1881
Fax: (859)622-2354
Free: 877-358-7232
Publication E-mail: progressads@eku.edu
Collegiate newspaper of the Department of Communication. **Freq:** Weekly (Thurs.). **Print Method:** Offset. Uses mats. **Cols./Page:** 6. **Col. Width:** 25 nonpareils. **Col. Depth:** 301 agate lines. **Key Personnel:** Dedra Brandenburg, Manager, Advertising. **URL:** http://www.easternprogress.com. **Remarks:** Accepts advertising. **Circ:** Free ‡6000.

14144 ■ Richmond Register
Community Newspaper Holdings Inc.
380 Big Hill Ave.
Richmond, KY 40475
Phone: (859)623-1669
Fax: (859)623-2337
Newspaper serving Richmond, Kentucky area. **Founded:** 1917. **Freq:** Mon.-Sun. **Key Personnel:** Lorie Love Hailey, Editor; Nicholas W. Lewis, Publisher; Sherrie Hawn, Regional Manager. **Subscription Rates:** $119 Individuals; $255 Out of area. **URL:** http://www.richmondregister.com. **Remarks:** Accepts advertising. **Circ:** Mon.-Sat. ★5,690, Sun. ★5,610.

14145 ■ WCBR-AM - 1110
509 Leighway Dr.
Richmond, KY 40475
Phone: (859)623-1235
Format: Contemporary Christian; Religious. **Networks:** USA Radio. **Owner:** WCBR Inc., 1564 Moberly Rd., Richmond, KY 40475-9237. **Founded:** 1969. **Operating Hours**: Sunrise-sunset; 75% local, 25% network. **Wattage**: 250. **Ad Rates:** $5 for 30 seconds; $6.50 for 60 seconds.

14146 ■ WCYO-FM - 100.7
128 Bill Hill Ave.
Richmond, KY 40475
Format: Country. **Networks:** ABC. **Owner:** Wallingford Broadcasting Co. Inc., at above address. **Founded:** 1991. **Operating Hours**: Continuous. **ADI**: Lexington, KY. **Key Personnel:** Sean Hamilton, Gen. Mgr.; Trizdon Reynolds, Sales Mgr. **Wattage**: 25,000. **Ad Rates:** $8-10 for 30 seconds; $10-17 for 60 seconds. $6-$9 for 30 seconds; $9-$16 for 60 seconds. Combined advertising rates available with WIRV-AM, WEKY-AM, WKXO-AM. **URL:** http://www.wcyofm.com.

WEKF-FM - See Corbin

WEKH-FM - See Hazard

14147 ■ WEKU-FM - 88.9
102 Perkins Bldg.
521 Lancaster Ave.
Richmond, KY 40475-3102
Free: 800-621-8890
Format: Public Radio. **Networks:** National Public Radio (NPR). **Owner:** Eastern Kentucky University Board of Regents, 521 Lancaster Ave., Richmond, KY 40475. **Founded:** 1968. **Operating Hours**: Continuous; 15% network, 85% local. **Key Personnel:** Michael Carter, Music Dir., michael.carter@eku.edu; Roger Duvall, Station Mgr., roger.duvall@eku.edu; Charles Compton, News Dir., charles.compton@eku.edu. **Wattage**: 50,000. **Ad Rates:** Noncommercial. **URL:** http://www.weku.fm.

14148 ■ WEKY-AM
120 Big Hill Ave.
Richmond, KY 40475
Fax: (606)986-8675
Format: Adult Contemporary; Oldies; Sports; Agricultural. **Networks:** ABC; KyNet. **Founded:** 1953. **Key Personnel:** Roger Redmon, Contact; Rich Middleton, Contact. **Wattage**: 1,000. **Ad Rates:** $3-4 for 15 seconds; $6-10 for 30 seconds; $8-12 for 60 seconds.

14149 ■ WIRV AM 1550 - 1550
128 Big Hill Ave.
Richmond, KY 40475
Phone: (606)723-5138
Fax: (606)723-5180
Format: News; Talk. **Networks:** KyNet; ABC. **Founded:** 1960. **Operating Hours**: Continuous. **ADI**: Lexington, KY. **Wattage**: 1,000. **Ad Rates:** $8-10 for 30 seconds; $10-17 for 60 seconds. $6-$9 for 30 seconds; $9-$16 for 60 seconds. Combined advertising rates available with WCYO-FM, WEKY-AM, WKXO-AM. **URL:** http://www.wirvam.com.

14150 ■ WKXO-AM
107 S 1st St.
Richmond, KY 40475
Phone: (859)623-1386
Format: Contemporary Country; News. **Networks:** ABC; KyNet. **Founded:** 1972. **Key Personnel:** Bob Spradlin, Contact. **Wattage**: 250 Day. **URL:** http://www.wkxoam.com/.

14151 ■ WLFX-FM - 106.7
128 Big Hill Ave.
Richmond, KY 40475
Phone: (859)623-1340
Format: Classic Rock; Talk. **Operating Hours**: Continuous. **Wattage**: 6,000. **Ad Rates:** Advertising accepted; rates available upon request. **URL:** http://www.wlfxfm.com.

RUSSELL SPRINGS

Russell Co. Russell Co. (SC). 5 m N of Jamestown. Residential.

14152 ■ WHVE-FM - 92.7
7995 Russell Springs Rd.
Russell Springs, KY 42642
Phone: (270)384-7979
Fax: (270)384-6244
Format: Adult Contemporary. **Key Personnel:** Jan Royse, Gen. Mgr. **Ad Rates:** Noncommercial. **URL:** http://www.ridingthewave.com.

RUSSELLVILLE

Logan Co. Logan Co. (SW). 30 m W of Bowling Green. Manufactures aluminum die castings, polyurethane foam, work clothes, motors, metal fasteners, wire, poultry equipment, fertilizer, hosiery. Aluminum can stock, Stone quarries. Timber. Dairy, poultry. stock farms. Tobacco, grain.

14153 ■ News-Democrat & Leader
News-Democrat & Leader
120 Public Sq.
Russellville, KY 42276
Phone: (270)726-8394
Fax: (270)726-8398
Publisher's E-mail: ndlcirculation@civitasmedia.com
Community newspaper. **Freq:** Biweekly Tues. & Fri. **Key Personnel:** Chris Cooper, Reporter; O.J. Stapleton, Editor, General Manager. **Alt. Formats:** Electronic publishing. **Mailing address:** PO Box 270, Russellville, KY 42276. **Remarks:** Accepts advertising. **Circ:** Paid ‡6621.

SALYERSVILLE

Magoffin Co. Magoffin Co. (C).

14154 ■ Salyersville Independent
Salyersville Independent
PO Box 29
Salyersville, KY 41465
Phone: (606)349-2915
Community newspaper. **Freq:** Weekly (Thurs.). **Print Method:** Offset. **Trim Size:** 22 3/4 x 14 1/2. **Cols./Page:** 6. **Col. Width:** 25 1/2 nonpareils. **Col. Depth:** 301 agate lines. **Key Personnel:** Heather Oney, Editor. **Subscription Rates:** $24 Individuals; $32 Out of area. **URL:** http://www.salyersvilleindependent.com. **Ad Rates:** GLR $3.40; BW $296.70; PCI $3. **Remarks:** Accepts advertising. **Circ:** 4100.

14155 ■ WRLV-AM - 1140
129 College St.
West Liberty, KY 41472
Phone: (606)349-6125
Format: Southern Gospel. **Networks:** KyNet; ABC. **Founded:** 1979. **Operating Hours**: Sunrise-sunset; 10% network, 90% local. **Key Personnel:** Kathy Puckett, Gen. Mgr.; Brian Scott Russell, Music Dir.; Sam Baca, News Dir. **Wattage**: 1,000. **Ad Rates:** $2.80 for 30 seconds; $4.25 for 60 seconds. Southern Gospel Network.

14156 ■ WRLV-FM - 106.5
PO Box 338
Salyersville, KY 41465
Phone: (606)349-6125
Fax: (606)349-6129
Format: Contemporary Country. **Networks:** KyNet; ABC. **Founded:** 1989. **Operating Hours**: Continuous. **Key Personnel:** Kathy Puckett, Gen. Mgr.; Sam Baca, News Dir.; Bryan Russell, Music Dir. **Wattage**: 25,000. **Ad Rates:** $5-9.75 for 30 seconds; $9.75-13 for 60 seconds.

SCOTTSVILLE

Allen Co. Allen Co. (SW). 25 m SE of Bowling Green. Overalls, tobacco, drapery, hardware factories. Sawmills. Oil wells. Hardwood timber. Dairy, stock, poultry farms. Tobacco, livestock.

14157 ■ The Citizen-Times
The Citizen-Times
611 E Main St.
Scottsville, KY 42164
Phone: (270)237-3441
Fax: (270)237-4943
Publication E-mail: ctimes@nctc.com
Community newspaper. **Freq:** Weekly (Thurs.). **Print Method:** Offset. **Trim Size:** 13 x 21 1/2. **Cols./Page:** 6. **Col. Width:** 24 nonpareils. **Col. Depth:** 294 agate lines. **Key Personnel:** Matt Pedigo, Editor. **Subscription Rates:** $20 Individuals print; $35 Out of country print; $30 Individuals print and online; $45 Out of country print and online; $20 Individuals online. **URL:** http://www.thecitizen-times.com. **Mailing address:** PO Box 310, Scottsville, KY 42164. **Ad Rates:** GLR $5.25; BW $661; 4C $350; SAU $6; PCI $5. **Remarks:** Accepts advertising. **Circ:** ‡5557.

14158 ■ WLCK-AM - 1250
PO Box 70163
Bowling Green, KY 42101
Phone: (270)782-9595
Format: Religious. **Networks:** USA Radio. **Owner:** Skytower Communications Group L.L.C., at above address. **Founded:** 1958. **Operating Hours**: 6 a.m.-9 p.m.; 25% network, 75% local. **ADI**: Nashville (Cookeville), TN. **Wattage**: 1,000.

14159 ■ WVLE-FM
PO Box 158
Scottsville, KY 42164
Phone: (270)237-3148

Fax: (270)237-3533
Format: Soft Rock. **Networks:** ABC. **Owner:** Sky Tower Communication Group, LLC, at above address. **Founded:** 1967. **Formerly:** WLCK-FM. **Wattage:** 6,000 ERP. **URL:** http://www.wvle.net.

SHELBYVILLE

Shelby Co. Shelby Co. (NWC). 31 m E of Louisville. Manufactures chemicals, metal fabricating products, food utensils, air filters, men's suits, flour. Oil refinery. Loose leaf tobacco. Agriculture. Tobacco, livestock, corn. Horse farm.

14160 ■ Sentinel-News
Landmark Community Newspapers L.L.C.
703 Taylorsville Rd.
Shelbyville, KY 40066
Phone: (502)633-2526
Fax: (502)633-2618
Publisher's E-mail: marketing@lcni.com
Community newspaper. **Freq:** Semiweekly every other Friday plus varied special sections monthly. **Print Method:** Offset. **Cols./Page:** 6. **Col. Width:** 21 nonpareils. **Col. Depth:** 301 agate lines. **Key Personnel:** Todd Martin, Editor; Dan Barry, Manager, Advertising; Kerry Johnson, Publisher. **Subscription Rates:** $49 Individuals 1 year; print and online; $27.50 Individuals 6 months; print and online; $16 Individuals 3 months; print and online; $5.88 Individuals 1 month; print and online. **URL:** http://www.sentinelnews.com. **Ad Rates:** GLR $8.96; BW $1,156; 4C $1,322; SAU $8.66; PCI $8.66. **Remarks:** Accepts advertising. **Circ:** 6400.

14161 ■ WCND-AM - 940
21700 Northwestern Hwy., Tower 14, Ste. 1190
Southfield, MI 48075
Phone: (248)557-3500
Fax: (248)557-2950
Email: sima@birach.com
Format: Oldies. **Networks:** Jones Satellite; KyNet. **Owner:** Birach Broadcasting Corp., at above address. **Founded:** 1964. **Operating Hours:** Sunrise-sunset. **ADI:** Louisville, KY. **Key Personnel:** Sima Birach, CEO. **Wattage:** 250. **Ad Rates:** $10-16 for 30 seconds; $12-18 for 60 seconds. **URL:** http://www.birach.com.

14162 ■ WXLN-AM - 1570
670 Southlawn Dr.
Shelbyville, KY 40065
Format: Religious; Talk. **Networks:** USA Radio. **Founded:** 1949. **Formerly:** WZCC-AM. **Operating Hours:** Continuous; 100% local. **ADI:** Louisville, KY. **Wattage:** 1,500. **Ad Rates:** $20-40 for 60 seconds. **URL:** http://www.wxlnradio.com/?page_id=2.

SHEPHERDSVILLE

Bullitt Co. Bullitt Co. (NWC). 20 m S of Louisville. Hardware factory. Sawmills. Distillery. Publishing and printing firm. Diversified farming. Corn, tobacco, dairying.

14163 ■ Pioneer News
Landmark Community Newspapers L.L.C.
455 N Buckman St.
Shepherdsville, KY 40165
Phone: (502)543-2288
Fax: (502)955-9704
Publisher's E-mail: marketing@lcni.com
Community newspaper. **Founded:** 1882. **Freq:** Semiweekly. **Print Method:** Offset. **Cols./Page:** 6. **Col. Width:** 12 picas. **Col. Depth:** 21 1/2 inches. **Key Personnel:** Thomas Barr, Editor; Linda Sue Myers, Manager, Circulation. **USPS:** 433-740. **Subscription Rates:** $42.40 Individuals print and online. **URL:** http://www.pioneernews.net. **Ad Rates:** SAU $6.01; PCI $7.19. **Remarks:** Accepts advertising. **Circ:** Paid 19622, Free 17000.

14164 ■ Pioneer News Extra
Landmark Community Newspapers L.L.C.
455 N Buckman St.
Shepherdsville, KY 40165
Phone: (502)543-2288
Fax: (502)955-9704
Publisher's E-mail: marketing@lcni.com
Community newspaper for Bullitt County. **Freq:** Semiweekly (Mon. and Wed.). **Print Method:** Web Offset. **Cols./Page:** 6. **Col. Width:** 2 1/4 inches. **Col. Depth:** 21 1/2 inches. **Key Personnel:** Nancy Gray, Representative, Advertising and Sales; Laura Felts, Representative, Advertising and Sales; Brenda Roberts, Graphic Designer; Stephanie Storm, Graphic Designer; Thomas Barr, Editor. **USPS:** 433-740. **URL:** http://www.pioneernews.net. **Remarks:** Accepts advertising. **Circ:** (Not Reported).

SOMERSET

Pulaski Co. Pulaski Co. (SC). 79 m S of Lexington. Lake resort area. Manufactures ceramic, glass, charcoal products, fixtures, men's clothing. Flour mills. Hardwood timber. Bottling works. Coal mines. Oil refinery. Creamery. Stock, poultry farms. Corn, tobacco, hay, fruits, vegetables.

14165 ■ Commonwealth-Journal
CNHI
110-112 E Mount Vernon St.
Somerset, KY 42502
Phone: (606)678-8191
Fax: (606)679-9225
General newspaper. **Freq:** Daily and Sun. (eve.). **Print Method:** Offset. **Cols./Page:** 6. **Col. Width:** 25 nonpareils. **Col. Depth:** 301 agate lines. **Key Personnel:** Eric Dishon, Art Director; Chris Harris, Writer; Steve Cornelius, Editor; Ken Shmidheiser, Managing Editor; Jeff Neal, Editor; Rob McCullough, Publisher. **Subscription Rates:** $14.99 Individuals /month; print and online; $12.99 Individuals /month; print and online. **URL:** http://www.somerset-kentucky.com. **Mailing address:** PO Box 859, Somerset, KY 42502. **Ad Rates:** GLR $6.15; BW $1040; 4C $1250; SAU $8.95. **Remarks:** Accepts advertising. **Circ:** 8663, Sun. 8904.

14166 ■ WKEQ-FM - 97.1
PO Box 740
Somerset, KY 42502
Phone: (606)678-5151
Free: 877-672-5151
Format: Classic Rock. **Owner:** iHeartMedia Inc., 200 E Basse Rd., San Antonio, TX 78209, Ph: (210)832-3314. **Key Personnel:** Rod Zimmerman, Mgr.; Greg Wesley, Bus. Mgr., gregwesley@somersetradio.com; Josh McKinney, Div. Dir. **URL:** http://www.q97rock.com.

14167 ■ WKSO-TV - 29
600 Cooper Dr.
Lexington, KY 40502
Phone: (859)258-7000
Free: 800-432-0951
Email: feedback@ket.org
Format: Public TV; Educational. **Networks:** Public Broadcasting Service (PBS); Kentucky Educational Television. **Owner:** Kentucky Educational Television, 600 Cooper Dr., Lexington, KY 40502, Ph: (859)258-7000, Free: 800-432-0951. **Founded:** 1968. **Operating Hours:** Continuous. **ADI:** Lexington, KY. **Key Personnel:** Shae Hopkins, Exec. Dir. **Wattage:** 589,000. **Ad Rates:** Noncommercial. **URL:** http://www.ket.org.

14168 ■ WKVY-FM - 88.1
PO Box 2098
Omaha, NE 68103
Free: 800-525-5683
Format: Contemporary Christian. **Owner:** Educational Media Foundation, 5700 W Oaks Blvd., CA 95765, Free: 800-800434-8400. **URL:** http://www.klove.com.

14169 ■ WSCC-FM - 92.1
808 S Monticello Rd.
Somerset, KY 42501
Phone: (606)679-8501
Owner: Somerset Community College, 808 Monticello St., Somerset, KY 42501, Ph: (606)679-8501, Free: 877-629-9722. **Founded:** 1967. **Key Personnel:** Paul Secrest, Station Mgr; Walt Williams, Contact. **Wattage:** 010. **Ad Rates:** Accepts Advertising. **URL:** http://www.wscfm.com.

14170 ■ WSEK-FM - 93.9
PO Box 740
Somerset, KY 42502
Phone: (606)678-5151
Free: 877-672-5151
Format: Contemporary Country. **Networks:** Mutual Broadcasting System. **Owner:** iHeartMedia Inc., 200 E Basse Rd., San Antonio, TX 78209, Ph: (210)832-3314. **Founded:** 1964. **Operating Hours:** Continuous. **Key Personnel:** Jim Mercer, Chief Engineer, jamesmercer@somersetradio.com; Rod Zimmerman, Dir. of Programs, rodzimmerman@somersetradio.com; Paula Molen, Traffic Mgr., paulamolen@somersetradio.com; Wynona Padgett, Promotions Dir. **Wattage:** 27,500. **URL:** http://www.k93country.com//main.html.

14171 ■ WSFC-AM - 1240
101 First Radio Ln.
Somerset, KY 42503
Phone: (606)678-5151
Fax: (606)678-2026
Format: News; Talk. **Networks:** ABC. **Owner:** iHeartMedia Inc., 200 E Basse Rd., San Antonio, TX 78209, Ph: (210)832-3314. **Founded:** 1947. **Operating Hours:** Continuous. **Key Personnel:** Rod Zimmerman, Div. Mgr., rodzimmerman@somersetradio.com; Paula Molen, Traffic Mgr., paulamolen@somersetradio.com; Mike Murphy, Div. Dir., michaelmurphy2@somersetradio.com; Wynona Padgett, Div. Dir., wynonapadgett@somersetradio.com; Josh McKinney, Sports Dir., joshmckinney@somersetradio.com. **Wattage:** 790. **Ad Rates:** Noncommercial. **URL:** http://www.wsfcam.com.

14172 ■ WSFE-AM - 910
PO Box 740
Somerset, KY 42502
Phone: (606)678-5151
Free: 877-672-5151
Format: Talk. **Key Personnel:** Bruce Welker, Div. Pres., brucewelker@iheartmedia.com; Greg Wesley, Bus. Mgr., gregwesley@iheartmedia.com; Jim Mercer, Chief Engineer, jimmercer@iheartmedia.com; Mike Murphy, Production Mgr., michaelmurphy2@iheartmedia.com; Wynona Padgett, Promotions Dir., wynonapadgett@iheartmedia.com. **URL:** http://www.defense.gov.

WSGP-FM - See Glasgow

14173 ■ WTHL-FM
PO Box 1423
Somerset, KY 42502
Format: Religious. **Wattage:** 50,000 ERP. **Ad Rates:** Noncommercial.

14174 ■ WTLO-AM - 1480
290 WTLO Rd.
Somerset, KY 42502
Phone: (606)678-8151
Fax: (606)678-8152
Format: Oldies. **Networks:** ABC. **Founded:** 1958. **Operating Hours:** 13 hours Daily; 80% network, 20% local. **ADI:** Lexington, KY. **Key Personnel:** Mike Tarter, Gen. Mgr., mitarter@forchtbroadcasting.com. **Wattage:** 1,000. **Ad Rates:** $12 for 30 seconds; $15 for 60 seconds. **URL:** http://www.wtloam.com.

WWOG-FM - See Cookeville, TN

14175 ■ WWZB-FM - 93.9
PO Box 740
Somerset, KY 42502
Phone: (606)679-8594
Fax: (606)678-2026
Format: Adult Contemporary. **Networks:** CNN Radio. **Owner:** First Radio, Inc., at above address, Ph: (606)678-5151. **Founded:** 1984. **Operating Hours:** Continuous; 95% network, 5% local. **Key Personnel:** Nolan Kenner, Gen. Mgr., President; Mike Tarter, Station Mgr., Contact; Mike Tarter, Contact. **Wattage:** 50,000.

SOUTH SHORE

14176 ■ WOKE-FM - 98.3
PO Box 926
South Shore, KY 41175
Phone: (606)932-2223
Fax: (606)932-6132
Format: Gospel. **Operating Hours:** Continuous. **Key Personnel:** Beth Montavon, Office Mgr., beth@wokejoyfm.org; Paul Hunt, Station Mgr., paul@wokejoyfm.org. **Wattage:** 6,000. **Ad Rates:** Noncommercial.

SPRINGFIELD

Washington Co. Washington Co. (C). 50 m SE of Louisville. Manufactures plastics, butter, clothing, flour, feed, barrels. Tobacco markets and warehouses. Stock, dairy, poultry, grain farms. Tobacco, corn, wheat.

14177 ■ The Springfield Sun
Landmark Community Newspapers L.L.C.

Circulation: ★ = AAM; △ or • = BPA; ♦ = CAC; ❑ = VAC; ⊕ = PO Statement; ‡ = Publisher's Report; Boldface figures = sworn; Light figures = estimated.

108 Progress Ave.
Springfield, KY 40069
Phone: (859)336-3716
Publisher's E-mail: marketing@lcni.com
Community newspaper. **Founded:** 1904. **Freq:** Weekly (Wed.). **Print Method:** Offset. **Trim Size:** 13 x 21 1/2. **Cols./Page:** 6. **Col. Width:** 11 picas. **Col. Depth:** 21 1/2 inches. **Key Personnel:** John Overby, Editor; Shorty Lassiter, Manager, Advertising. **USPS:** 512-920. **Subscription Rates:** $32.86 Individuals print and online; $19.08 Individuals 6 months; print and online. **URL:** http://www.thespringfieldsun.com. **Ad Rates:** GLR $6.6; BW $630; 4C $855; PCI $3.53. **Remarks:** Accepts advertising. **Circ:** Paid ‡4350, Free ‡16.

STANFORD

Lincoln Co. Lincoln Co. (C). 40 m SW of Lexington. Walnut timber. Manufactures cheese, butter, wood products, mobile homes. Dairy, stock, grain farms. Tobacco, corn, wheat.

14178 ■ WPBK-FM - 102.9
201-A E Main St.
Stanford, KY 40484
Phone: (606)365-2126
Format: Full Service. **URL:** http://www.wpbkfm.com.

STANTON

Powell Co. Powell Co. (EC). 5 m S of Clay City.

14179 ■ WBFC-AM - 1470
2401 Paint Creek Rd.
Stanton, KY 40380
Phone: (606)663-6631
Fax: (606)663-2267
Email: beverly@wbfcam.com
Format: Gospel. **Networks:** Independent. **Founded:** 1998. **Operating Hours:** Sunrise-sunset; 100% local. **ADI:** Lexington, KY. **Key Personnel:** James Combs, Owner. **Wattage:** 2,500. **Ad Rates:** $3.75-5 for 30 seconds; $3-5.75 for 60 seconds. **Mailing address:** PO Box 577, Stanton, KY 40380. **URL:** http://www.wbfcam.com.

14180 ■ WSKV-FM - 104.9
28 W Halls Rd.
Stanton, KY 40380
Phone: (606)663-2811
Fax: (606)663-2895
Email: wskv@wskvfm.com
Format: Full Service. **Owner:** Moore Country 104 L.L.C., at above address. **Operating Hours:** Continuous. **Key Personnel:** Ethan Moore, Sales Mgr. **Wattage:** 720 ERP. **Ad Rates:** Advertising accepted; rates available upon request. **Mailing address:** PO Box 610, Stanton, KY 40380. **URL:** http://www.wskvfm.com.

TAYLORSVILLE

14181 ■ Spencer Magnet
Landmark Community Newspapers L.L.C.
100 West Main St.
Taylorsville, KY 40071
Phone: (502)477-2239
Publisher's E-mail: marketing@lcni.com
Community newspaper. **Freq:** Weekly. **Subscription Rates:** $32.86 Individuals annual all access; $10.50 Individuals semi-annual all access; $11 Individuals quarterly all access. **URL:** http://www.spencermagnet.com. **Mailing address:** PO Box 219, Taylorsville, KY 40071. **Remarks:** Accepts advertising. **Circ:** (Not Reported).

TOMPKINSVILLE

Monroe Co. Monroe Co. (SC). 60 m SE of Bowling Green. Timber. Manufactures fertilizer, wire, meat products, work clothes, cheese. Sawmills, pallet mills, beldon wire. Agriculture. Corn, wheat, tobacco, livestock.

14182 ■ Tompkinsville News
Monroe County Press Inc.
105 N Main St.
Tompkinsville, KY 42167
Phone: (270)487-5576
Publisher's E-mail: online@tompkinsvillenews.com
Community newspaper. **Freq:** Weekly (Thurs.). **Print Method:** Offset. **Cols./Page:** 6. **Col. Width:** 12 picas. **Col. Depth:** 21 inches. **Key Personnel:** Blanche B. Trimble, Publisher; Ronda Elam, General Manager. **ISSN:** 0063--3260 (print). **Subscription Rates:** $21.20 Individuals print; Monroe County; $26.50 Individuals print; other Kentucky Counties; $29 Out of state print; $31.80 Individuals print and online; Monroe County; $36.50 Individuals print and online; other Kentucky Counties; $39 Out of state print and online; $21.20 Individuals online. **URL:** http://www.tompkinsvillenews.com. **Remarks:** Accepts advertising. **Circ:** Combined ‡4500.

14183 ■ WTKY-FM
341 Radio Station Rd.
Radio Station Rd.
Tompkinsville, KY 42167
Phone: (502)487-6119
Fax: (502)489-8462
Format: Country. **Founded:** 1972. **Wattage:** 5,300 ERP.

TYNER

WWAG-FM - See Mc Kee

UPTON

14184 ■ WJCR-FM - 90.1
PO Box 91
Upton, KY 42784
Phone: (270)369-8614
Format: Gospel. **Founded:** Feb. 1990. **Operating Hours:** Continuous. **Key Personnel:** Gary Richardson, Contact, garywjcr@yahoo.com; Don Powell, Contact, donjrwjcr@yahoo.com. **Wattage:** 100,000. **Ad Rates:** Noncommercial. **URL:** http://www.wjcr.org.

VANCEBURG

Lewis Co. Lewis Co. (NE). On Ohio River, 20 m SW of Portsmouth, Ohio. Manufactures shoes, railroad ties, lumber. Dairy, stock, truck farms.

14185 ■ WKKS-AM
1106 Fairlane Dr.
Vanceburg, KY 41179
Phone: (606)796-3031
Fax: (606)796-6186
Format: Country; Contemporary Country; Bluegrass; Oldies. **Networks:** Satellite Music Network. **Founded:** 1957. **Wattage:** 1,000 Day. **Ad Rates:** $2.75-3.25 for 30 seconds; $3.75-6 for 60 seconds.

14186 ■ WKKS-FM - 104.9
1106 Fairlane Dr.
Vanceburg, KY 41179
Phone: (606)796-3031
Fax: (606)796-6186
Format: Country. **Founded:** 1983. **Operating Hours:** Continuous. **Wattage:** 3,000.

VERSAILLES

Woodford Co. Woodford Co. (C). 12 m W of Lexington. Manufactures work clothing, knit goods, flour, food containers, temperature controls. Dairy, stock, poultry farms. Tobacco, hemp, bluegrass seed.

14187 ■ Equinews
Kentucky Equine Research Inc.
3910 Delaney Ferry Rd.
Versailles, KY 40383
Phone: (859)873-1988
Fax: (859)873-3781
Free: 888-873-1988
Publisher's E-mail: info@ker.com
Equestrian magazine of the Alberta Arabian Racing Association, Competitive Trail Riders of British Columbia and others. **Freq:** Quarterly. **ISSN:** 0828--864X (print). **URL:** http://www.equinews.com. **Ad Rates:** BW $575; 4C $600; PCI $9. **Remarks:** Accepts advertising. **Circ:** Paid ‡17492, Non-paid ‡800.

14188 ■ Woodford Sun
Woodford Sun
PO Box 29
Versailles, KY 40383
Phone: (859)873-4131
Fax: (859)873-0300
Publisher's E-mail: news@woodfordsun.com
Newspaper. **Freq:** Weekly (Thurs.). **Print Method:** Offset. **Trim Size:** 10 3/8 x 21. **Cols./Page:** 6. **Col. Width:** 9 picas. **Col. Depth:** 294 agate lines. **Key Personnel:** Stephen Peterson, Managing Editor; Jennifer Cardwell, Manager, Advertising, phone: (859)873-3211; Whitney Chandler, Publisher. **USPS:** 690-480. **Subscription Rates:** $25 Individuals Woodford County. **URL:** http://www.woodfordsun.com. **Ad Rates:** BW $787; 4C $280; SAU $5.95; PCI $6.25. **Remarks:** Accepts display and classified advertising. **Circ:** 5500, ‡5300.

14189 ■ WCGW-AM - 770
3950 Lexington Rd.
Versailles, KY 40383
Phone: (859)873-8844
Fax: (859)873-1318
Owner: Christian Broadcasting System Ltd., 5201 S Saginaw, Flint, MI 48507, Ph: (810)694-4146. **Founded:** 1986. **Key Personnel:** Benson Gregory, Station Mgr., benson.gregory@cbslradio.com. **Wattage:** 1,000. **URL:** http://wcgwam.com.

14190 ■ WJMM-FM - 99.1
3950 Lexington Rd.
Versailles, KY 40383
Phone: (859)873-8096
Fax: (859)873-1318
Format: Religious. **Owner:** Christian Broadcasting System Ltd., 5201 S Saginaw, Flint, MI 48507, Ph: (810)694-4146. **Founded:** 1969. **Formerly:** WHBN-FM. **Operating Hours:** Continuous. **Wattage:** 4,500. **Ad Rates:** Advertising accepted; rates available upon request. **URL:** http://wjmm.com.

WARSAW

Gallatin Co. Gallatin Co. (N). On Ohio River, 35 m SW of Cincinnati Ohio. Furniture factory. lumber mill. Nurseries. Livestock, corn, tobacco farms.

14191 ■ Gallatin County News
Gallatin County News
211 Third St.
Warsaw, KY 41095
Phone: (859)567-5051
Fax: (859)567-6397
Publisher's E-mail: galnews@zoomtown.com
Newspaper. **Freq:** Weekly (Wed.). **Print Method:** Offset. **Cols./Page:** 6. **Col. Width:** 20 nonpareils. **Col. Depth:** 301 agate lines. **Key Personnel:** Denny K. Warnick, Publisher; Clay Warnick, Director, Advertising; Kelley Warnick, Editor. **USPS:** 213-160. **Subscription Rates:** $26 Individuals; $19 Students; $28 Out of area; $30 Out of state. **URL:** http://www.thegallatincountynews.com/pages/index.php. **Mailing address:** PO Box 435, Warsaw, KY 41095. **Ad Rates:** GLR $3.95; 4C $638.55; SAU $4.95; PCI $3.95. **Remarks:** Accepts advertising. **Circ:** 2950.

WEST LIBERTY

Morgan Co. Morgan Co. (EC). 78 m E of Lexington. Coal mines. Limestone quarry. Timber. Burley tobacco market. Sawmills. Agriculture. Tobacco, corn, poultry.

14192 ■ WLKS-FM - 102.9
129 College St.
West Liberty, KY 41472-1156
Phone: (606)743-1029
Format: Hot Country. **Owner:** Morgan County Industries Inc., 129 College S, West Liberty, KY 41472-1156. **Founded:** 1994. **Operating Hours:** Continuous. **Key Personnel:** Paul Lyons, Dir. of Programs; Jim Forrest, Sales Mgr. **Wattage:** 6,000. **Ad Rates:** $7 for 30 seconds; $9 for 60 seconds.

14193 ■ WMOR-AM - 1330
129 College St.
West Liberty, KY 41472-1156
Phone: (606)743-1029
Format: Country. **Networks:** ABC. **Owner:** Morgan County Industries Inc., 129 College S, West Liberty, KY 41472-1156. **Founded:** 1955. **Operating Hours:** 6 a.m.-local sunset. **Wattage:** 1,000. **Ad Rates:** $3.15 for 30 seconds; $3.75 for 60 seconds.

14194 ■ WQXX-FM
129 College St.
West Liberty, KY 41472-1156
Phone: (606)784-4141
Owner: Morgan County Industries Inc., 129 College S, West Liberty, KY 41472-1156. **Founded:** 1965. **Formerly:** WQXX. **Ad Rates:** Advertising accepted; rates available upon request.

WRLV-AM - See Salyersville

WEST VAN LEAR

14195 ■ Big Sandy TV Cable Inc.
PO Box 586
West Van Lear, KY 41268
Phone: (606)789-3455
Free: 888-789-3455
Email: info@bigsandybb.com
Cities Served: subscribing households 2,750. **URL:** http://www.bigsandybb.com.

WESTPORT

14196 ■ Glass Patterns Quarterly
Glass Patterns Quarterly Inc.
8300 Hidden Valley Rd.
Westport, KY 40077-9797
Phone: (502)222-5631
Fax: (502)222-4527
Free: 800-719-0769
Publisher's E-mail: info@glasspatterns.com
Consumer magazine covering instructional stained glass making for a general and professional audience. Leading international glass magazine featuring patterns and instruction on glass etching, fusing, leading, copper foil, beveling, tiffany-style lamp construction, slumping, painting, beadmaking. Over 100 how-to photographs, steb-by-step instructions. **Freq:** Quarterly. **Print Method:** Web offset. **Trim Size:** 8 1/8 x 10 7/8. **Cols./Page:** 3. **Key Personnel:** Maureen James, Editor-in-Chief; Kathy Gentry, Manager, Circulation; Steven James, Publisher. **ISSN:** 1041--6684 (print). **Subscription Rates:** $24 Individuals print only; $29 Other countries print only; $59 Other countries via air; print only; $43 Two years print only; $53 Other countries 2 years; print only; $118 Other countries 2 years, via air; print only; $61 Individuals 3 years; print only; $76 Other countries 3 years; print only; $170 Other countries 3 years, via air; print only; $20 Individuals online only; per year. **URL:** http://www.glasspatterns.com. **Mailing address:** PO Box 69, Westport, KY 40077-9797. **Remarks:** Accepts advertising. **Circ:** Paid ⊕**37000**.

WHITESBURG

Letcher Co. Letcher Co. (E). 30 m SW of Pikeville.

14197 ■ The Mountain Eagle
The Mountain Eagle
PO Box 808
Whitesburg, KY 41858
Phone: (606)633-2252
Free: 800-333-8874
Publisher's E-mail: mtneagle@bellsouth.net
Community newspaper. **Founded:** 1907. **Freq:** Weekly (Wed.). **Print Method:** Offset. **Cols./Page:** 6. **Col. Width:** 12 picas. **Col. Depth:** 21 inches. **Key Personnel:** Thomas E. Gish, Publisher; Benjamin T. Gish, Editor; Freddy D. Oakes, Director, Advertising. **Subscription Rates:** $33.50 Individuals print or online; $40.50 Elsewhere print; $63 Individuals print and online combo; $29.50 Individuals print or online; $70 Elsewhere print and online combo. **URL:** http://www.themountaineagle.com/. **Remarks:** Accepts advertising. **Circ:** (Not Reported).

14198 ■ WEZC-AM - 1480
Bill Moore Rd.
Whitesburg, KY 41858
Phone: (606)855-7888
Fax: (606)855-7888
Email: jci@kih.com
Format: Contemporary Christian. **Owner:** Jesus Communications, Inc., at above address. **Founded:** 1956. **Operating Hours:** Sunrise-sunset. **Key Personnel:** F.D. Holbrook, Contact. **Wattage:** 5,000. **Ad Rates:** $3.25 for 15 seconds; $2.15-3.60 for 30 seconds; $3.90-4 for 60 seconds.

14199 ■ WMMT-FM - 88.7
91 Madison Ave.
Whitesburg, KY 41858
Phone: (606)633-0108
Fax: (606)633-1009
Free: 888-396-1208
Format: Eclectic. **Owner:** Appalshop Inc., 91 Madison Ave., Whitesburg, KY 41858, Ph: (606)633-0108, Fax: (606)633-1009, Free: 888-396-1208. **Founded:** 1985. **Operating Hours:** Continuous. **Key Personnel:** Jim Webb, Contact, jwebb@appalshop.org; Rich Kirby, Contact, rkirby@appalshop.org. **Wattage:** 15,000. **Ad Rates:** Noncommercial. Underwriting available. **URL:** http://www.wmmt.org.

WHITLEY CITY

McCreary Co. (SEC). 25 m S of Somerset.

14200 ■ McCreary County Record
Community Newspaper Holdings Inc.
PO Box 9
Whitley City, KY 42653
Phone: (606)376-5357
Fax: (606)376-9565
Newspaper serving McCreary County, Kentucky. **Founded:** 1919. **Freq:** Weekly (Tues.). **Print Method:** Offset. **Cols./Page:** 6. **Col. Width:** 26 nonpareils. **Col. Depth:** 301 agate lines. **Key Personnel:** Ken Shmidheiser, Editor; Rob McCullough, Publisher. **Subscription Rates:** $20 Individuals; $18 Individuals senior citizen; $28 Out of area; $30 Out of state; $25 Individuals military. **URL:** http://www.mccrearyrecord.com. **Remarks:** Accepts advertising. **Circ:** (Not Reported).

14201 ■ WHAY-FM - 98.3
PO Box 69
Whitley City, KY 42653
Phone: (606)376-2218
Fax: (606)376-5146
Email: radio@hay98.com
Format: Eclectic; Bluegrass; Classic Rock. **Ad Rates:** Advertising accepted; rates available upon request. **URL:** http://www.hay98.com.

WILLIAMSBURG

Whitley Co. Whitley Co. (SE). On Cumberland River, 30 m NW of Middlesboro. Coal mines; gas wells; hardwood timber. Clothing and outdoor products factories; planing mill; bottling works. Agriculture. Grains, tobacco, livestock.

14202 ■ WEKC-AM - 710
402 Main St.
Williamsburg, KY 40769-1126
Phone: (606)549-3000
Format: Southern Gospel. **Owner:** Gerald Parks, Not Available. **Founded:** Sept. 1981. **Operating Hours:** Daytime; 10% network, 90% local. **Wattage:** 4,200. **Ad Rates:** $5.90 for 30 seconds; $8.90 for 60 seconds.

14203 ■ WEZJ-FM - 104.3
522 Main St.
Williamsburg, KY 40769
Phone: (606)549-2285
Fax: (606)549-5565
Owner: Whitley Broadcasting Co., Inc., at above address. **Founded:** 1959. **ADI:** Lexington, KY. **Wattage:** 6,200. **Ad Rates:** $8 for 30 seconds; $12 for 60 seconds.

WILLIAMSTOWN

Grant Co. Grant Co. (N). 34 m S of Covington. Ships tobacco, hay, livestock. Dairy, stock, poultry farms.

14204 ■ Grant County News and Express
Landmark Community Newspapers L.L.C.
1406 North Main st., Suite 02
Williamstown, KY 41097
Phone: (859)824-3343
Publisher's E-mail: marketing@lcni.com
Community newspaper. **Freq:** Weekly. **Subscription Rates:** $33.92 Individuals annual all access; $19.35 Individuals semi-annual all access; $10.60 Individuals quarterly all access. **URL:** http://www.grantky.com. **Remarks:** Accepts advertising. **Circ:** (Not Reported).

14205 ■ City of Williamstown Cable
400 N Main St.
Williamstown, KY 41097-1026
Phone: (859)824-3633
Free: 888-394-4772
Email: wmtwncable@aol.com
Owner: City of Williamstown KY, 400 N Main St., Williamstown, KY 41097. **Founded:** 1984. **Key Personnel:** Chuck Hudson, Contact; Chuck Hudson, Contact. **Cities Served:** Williamstown, Kentucky: subscribing households 1090; 55 channels; 1 community access channel; 6 hours per week community access programming. **URL:** http://wkybb.net/.

WILMORE

Jessamine Co. Jessamine Co. (C). 20 m S of Lexington.

14206 ■ Good News: The Bi-Monthly Magazine for United Methodists
Forum for Scriptural Christianity Inc.
308 E Main St.
Wilmore, KY 40390-0150
Phone: (859)858-4661
Free: 800-487-7784
Publication E-mail: info@goodnewsmag.org
Religious magazine for evangelical United Methodists. **Freq:** Bimonthly. **Key Personnel:** Steve Beard, Editor; Rev. Rob Renfroe, President, Publisher. **ISSN:** 0436-1563 (print). **Subscription Rates:** $25 Individuals 1 year (6 issues). **URL:** http://www.goodnewsmag.org. **Mailing address:** PO Box 150, Wilmore, KY 40390-0150. **Remarks:** Accepts advertising. **Circ:** 40000.

14207 ■ WLAI-FM - 107.1
PO Box 2118
Omaha, NE 68103-2118
Free: 888-937-2471
Email: info@air1.com
Format: Contemporary Christian. **Owner:** Educational Media Foundation, 2351 Sunset Blvd., Ste. 170-218, Rocklin, CA 95677, Ph: (800)434-8400. **URL:** http://www.air1.com.

WINCHESTER

Clark Co. Clark Co. (NEC). 18 m E of Lexington. Limestone quarries. Manufactures fertilizer, men's shirts and suits, rubber products, truck axles, bed springs, lumber, seed harvesters, bricks, beverages. Bluegrass seed stripper. Hatcheries. Agriculture. Tobacco, bluegrass seed, livestock.

14208 ■ The Winchester Sun
The Winchester Sun
20 Wall St.
Winchester, KY 40391
Phone: (859)744-3123
Fax: (859)744-0638
Newspaper with a Democratic orientation. **Freq:** Daily (eve.). **Print Method:** Offset. **Trim Size:** 14 1/4 x 22 3/4. **Cols./Page:** 6. **Col. Width:** 25 nonpareils. **Col. Depth:** 294 agate lines. **Key Personnel:** Larry Hensley, Editor, President, Publisher, phone: (859)355-1234; David Stone, Editor, phone: (859)355-1218. **Subscription Rates:** $79 Individuals online only. **URL:** http://www.centralkynews.com/winchestersun. **Ad Rates:** GLR $9.75; BW $1,257; 4C $1,507; SAU $8; PCI $8. **Remarks:** Advertising accepted; rates available upon request. **Circ:** ‡5589.

Circulation: ★ = AAM; △ or • = BPA; ♦ = CAC; ❑ = VAC; ⊕ = PO Statement; ‡ = Publisher's Report; Boldface figures = sworn; Light figures = estimated.

ABBEVILLE

S LA. Vermilion Parish. On Vermilion River, 65 mi. SW of Baton Rouge. Oil and gas wells. Rice mills, sugar and syrup mill. Trapping. Crawfish farming. Agriculture. Livestock, rice, sugar cane.

14209 ■ Abbeville Meridional
Abbeville Meridional
318 N Main St.
Abbeville, LA 70510
Phone: (337)893-4223
Fax: (337)898-9022
General newspaper. **Freq:** Tues.-Fri. (morn.); Sun. (morn.). **Print Method:** Offset. **Trim Size:** 13 3/4 x 22 7/8. **Cols./Page:** 6. **Col. Width:** 22 nonpareils. **Col. Depth:** 300 agate lines. **Key Personnel:** Kathy Cormier, General Manager. **Subscription Rates:** $92 Individuals print and online - carrier delivery; $125 By mail print and online; $75 Individuals online only. **URL:** http://www.vermiliontoday.com. **Mailing address:** PO Box 400, Abbeville, LA 70511-0400. **Ad Rates:** GLR $.37; BW $819.15; 4C $1044.15; PCI $7.35. **Remarks:** Advertising accepted; rates available upon request. **Circ:** Mon.-Fri. 5,457, Sun. 5,860.

ALEXANDRIA

C LA. Rapides Parish. On Red River, 200 mi. NW of New Orleans. Manufactures valves and instruments, linerboard, lumber, paper products, hardwood flooring, furniture, fertilizer, sashes and doors, chemicals, insecticides, mattresses, pine products, lubricating oil, stoves, gasoline. Foundry, meat packing, cotton ginning, creosoting plants. Forestry. Agriculture. Cotton, corn, sugarcane.

14210 ■ The Alexandria News Weekly
The Alexandria News Weekly
1746 Mason St.
Alexandria, LA 71301-6242
Phone: (318)443-7664
Fax: (318)487-1827
General newspaper for the black community. **Freq:** Weekly (Thurs.). **Print Method:** Offset. **Cols./Page:** 6. **Col. Width:** 26 nonpareils. **Col. Depth:** 294 agate lines. **Subscription Rates:** $15 Individuals. **URL:** http://www.alexnewsweekly.zoomshare.com. **Ad Rates:** GLR $.52. **Remarks:** Color advertising accepted; rates available upon request. **Circ:** ‡13,750.

14211 ■ Forests & People
Louisiana Forestry Association
2316 S MacArthur Dr.
Alexandria, LA 71301
Phone: (318)443-2558
Fax: (318)443-1713
Magazine for forest products industries, foresters, and forest landowners. **Freq:** Quarterly March, June, September and December. **Print Method:** Sheet-fed offset. **Trim Size:** 8 1/2 x 11. **Cols./Page:** 3. **Col. Width:** 27 nonpareils. **Col. Depth:** 129 agate lines. **Key Personnel:** Janet Tompkins, Editor. **ISSN:** 0015--7589 (print). **USPS:** 456-930. **URL:** http://www.laforestry.com/. **Mailing address:** PO Box 5067, Alexandria, LA 71307. **Ad Rates:** BW $585; 4C $883. **Remarks:** Accepts advertising. **Circ:** (Not Reported).

14212 ■ Louisiana Baptist Message
The Baptist Message
PO Box 311
Alexandria, LA 71309-0311
Phone: (318)442-7728
Fax: (318)445-8328
Free: 800-376-7728
Publication E-mail: editor@baptistmessage.com
Southern Baptist religious newspaper. **Freq:** Biweekly. **Print Method:** Offset. **Trim Size:** 10 1/4 x 13 1/4. **Cols./Page:** 4. **Col. Width:** 14 picas. **Col. Depth:** 13 1/4 inches. **Key Personnel:** Violet Adams, Director, Advertising, Director, Marketing. **URL:** http://www.baptistmessage.com. **Also known as:** LBM. **Remarks:** Advertising accepted; rates available upon request. **Circ:** Paid 45000.

14213 ■ KALB-TV - 5
605 Washington St.
Alexandria, LA 71301
Phone: (318)445-2456
Format: News. **Networks:** NBC; CBS. **Owner:** Hoak Media Corp., 500 Crescent Ct., Ste. 220, Dallas, TX 75201, Ph: (972)960-4848, Fax: (972)960-4899. **Founded:** 1946. **Operating Hours:** Continuous. **ADI:** Alexandria, LA. **Key Personnel:** Michele Godard, Gen. Mgr., mgodard@kalb.com. **Local Programs:** *News Channel 5*, Monday Tuesday Wednesday Thursday Friday Saturday Sunday 5:00 a.m. - 7:00 a.m.; 12:00 p.m.; 5:00 p.m.; 6:00 p.m.; 10:00 p.m. 6:00 p.m.; 10:00 p.m. 10:00 p.m. **Wattage:** 820,000 ERP H. **Ad Rates:** Advertising accepted; rates available upon request. **URL:** http://www.kalb.com.

14214 ■ KAPM-FM
PO Box 2440
Tupelo, MS 38801-2440
Format: Religious. **Owner:** American Family Radio, at above address. **ADI:** Alexandria, LA. **Wattage:** 1,000 ERP. **Ad Rates:** Noncommercial.

KBCE-FM - See Boyce, LA

KBIO-FM - See Natchitoches, LA

14215 ■ KDBS-AM - 1410
1115 Texas Ave.
Alexandria, LA 71301
Phone: (318)445-1234
Fax: (318)445-7231
Format: Sports. **Networks:** ABC; ESPN Radio. **Owner:** Cenla Broadcasting, 1115 Texas Ave., Alexandria, LA 71301, Ph: (318)445-1234, Fax: (318)445-7231. **Founded:** 1954. **Formerly:** KRRV-AM. **Operating Hours:** Continuous. **Key Personnel:** Taylor Thompson, Station Mgr. **Wattage:** 1,000 Day ; 049 Night. **Ad Rates:** Advertising accepted; rates available upon request. Combined advertising rates available with KZMZ - KRRV - KKST. **URL:** http://www.espn1410.com.

14216 ■ KDEI-AM - 1250
601 Washington St.
Alexandria, LA 71301
Fax: (318)449-9954
Free: 888-408-0201
Format: Religious. **Owner:** Radio Maria USA, 601 Washington St., Alexandria, LA 71301, Ph: (318)561-6145, Fax: (318)449-9954, Free: 888-408-0201. **Founded:** 1983. **Ad Rates:** Noncommercial. **URL:** http://www.radiomaria.us.

14217 ■ KEDG-FM - 106.9
6080 Mt. Moriah
Memphis, TN 38115
Phone: (901)375-9324
Fax: (901)375-5889
Email: mail@flinn.com
Format: Album-Oriented Rock (AOR). **Owner:** Flinn Broadcasting Corporation, at above address. **ADI:** Alexandria, LA. **Wattage:** 6,000. **Ad Rates:** Noncommercial. **URL:** http://www.flinn.com.

14218 ■ KEZP-FM
1847 Sterkx Rd.
Alexandria, LA 71301
Phone: (318)449-1999
Fax: (318)487-8173
Email: kezp104@iamerica.net
Format: Oldies. **Owner:** Owensville Communications, LLC, at above address. **Key Personnel:** Mark Jones, Gen. Mgr. **Wattage:** 19,200 ERP. **Ad Rates:** $30-40 per unit.

14219 ■ K45IY - 45
PO Box A
Santa Ana, CA 92711
Phone: (714)832-2950
Free: 888-731-1000
Owner: Trinity Broadcasting Network Inc., PO Box A, Santa Ana, CA 92711, Ph: (714)832-2950, Free: 888-731-1000.

14220 ■ KJMJ-AM - 580
601 Washington St.
Alexandria, LA 71301
Fax: (318)449-9954
Free: 888-408-0201
Format: Religious. **Founded:** 1983. **Ad Rates:** Noncommercial. **URL:** http://www.radiomaria.us.

14221 ■ KKST-FM - 98.7
1115 Texas Ave.
Alexandria, LA 71301
Phone: (318)473-9898
Fax: (318)473-1960
Free: 877-655-8241
Format: Urban Contemporary. **Founded:** 1972. **Formerly:** KICR-FM. **Operating Hours:** Continuous. **ADI:** Alexandria, LA. **Key Personnel:** Jay Stevens, Office Mgr. **Local Programs:** *Da House Party*, Monday Tuesday Wednesday Thursday Friday Saturday 8:00 p.m. - 10:00 p.m. 6:00 p.m. - 08:00 p.m. **Wattage:** 50,000. **Ad Rates:** Advertising accepted; rates available upon request. **URL:** http://www.kiss987.fm.

14222 ■ KLAX-TV - 31
1811 England Dr.
Alexandria, LA 71303
Phone: (318)473-0031
Format: Commercial TV. **Networks:** ABC. **Owner:** Pollack/Belz Communications Co., Inc., Memphis, TN 38119. **Founded:** 1983. **Operating Hours:** Continuous.

Circulation: ★ = AAM; △ or • = BPA; ♦ = CAC; ❑ = VAC; ⊕ = PO Statement; ‡ = Publisher's Report; Boldface figures = sworn; Light figures = estimated.

ADI: Alexandria, LA. **Wattage**: 200,000 ERP H. **Ad Rates:** Advertising accepted; rates available upon request. **URL:** http://www.klax-tv.com.

14223 ■ KLPA-TV - 25
7733 Perkins Rd.
Baton Rouge, LA 70810
Phone: (225)767-5660
Free: 800-272-8161
Format: Public TV. **Simulcasts:** WLPB-TV Baton Rouge, LA. **Networks:** Public Broadcasting Service (PBS); Louisiana Public Broadcasting. **Owner:** Louisiana Public Broadcasting, 7733 Perkins Rd., Baton Rouge, LA 70810, Ph: (225)767-5660, Fax: (225)767-4288. **Founded:** 1983. **ADI**: Alexandria, LA. **Key Personnel:** Bob Neese, Contact, bneese@lpb.org. **Wattage**: 76,000. **Ad Rates:** Noncommercial; underwriting available. **URL:** http://beta.lpb.org.

14224 ■ KLXA-FM - 89.9
PO Box 779002
Rocklin, CA 95677-9972
Free: 800-525-5683
Format: Contemporary Christian. **Owner:** Educational Media Foundation, PO Box 2098, Omaha, NE 68103-2098, Free: 800-434-8400. **URL:** http://www.klove.com.

KOJO-FM - See Lake Charles

14225 ■ KQID-FM - 93.1
1115 Texas Ave.
Alexandria, LA 71301
Phone: (318)445-1234
Fax: (318)473-1960
Format: Top 40; Contemporary Hit Radio (CHR). **Owner:** Cenla Broadcasting, 1115 Texas Ave., Alexandria, LA 71301, Ph: (318)445-1234, Fax: (318)445-7231. **Wattage**: 100,000. **Ad Rates:** Noncommercial. **URL:** http://www.q93fm.com.

14226 ■ KRRV-FM - 100.3
1115 Texas Ave.
Alexandria, LA 71301
Phone: (318)445-1234
Fax: (318)473-1960
Free: 866-499-1003
Format: Country. **Networks:** ABC. **Owner:** Cenla Broadcasting, 1115 Texas Ave., Alexandria, LA 71301, Ph: (318)445-1234, Fax: (318)445-7231. **Founded:** 1969. **Formerly**: KDBS-FM. **Operating Hours**: Continuous. **ADI**: Alexandria, LA. **Key Personnel**: Hollywood Harrison, Contact. **Local Programs**: *The Big Time*, Monday Tuesday Wednesday Thursday Friday Saturday 7:00 p.m. - 12:00 a.m.; *Solid Gold Sunday's*, Sunday 6:00 a.m. - 12:00 p.m.; *Today's Best Country*, Monday Tuesday Wednesday Thursday Friday Sunday Saturday 1:00 a.m. - 6:00 a.m. 12:00 a.m. - 6:00 a.m. 10:00 a.m. - 2:00 p.m.; *The Big Time Saturday Night*, Saturday 7:00 p.m. - 12:00 a.m. **Wattage**: 100,000. **Ad Rates:** Advertising accepted; rates available upon request. **URL:** http://www.krrvonline.com.

14227 ■ KSYL-AM - 970
1115 Texas Ave.
Alexandria, LA 71301
Phone: (318)445-1234
Fax: (318)445-7231
Format: Talk. **Owner:** Cenla Broadcasting, 1115 Texas Ave., Alexandria, LA 71301, Ph: (318)445-1234, Fax: (318)445-7231. **Founded:** 1947. **ADI**: Alexandria, LA. **Wattage**: 1,000. **Ad Rates:** Advertising accepted; rates available upon request. **URL:** http://www.ksyl.com.

14228 ■ KWDF-AM - 840
3735 Rigolette Rd.
Pineville, LA 71360
Phone: (318)640-4373
Free: 888-989-2299
Email: info@wilkinsradio.com
Format: Religious. **Networks:** USA Radio. **Owner:** Wilkins Communication Network Inc., 292 S Pine St., Spartanburg, SC 29302, Ph: (864)585-1885, Fax: (864)597-0687, Free: 888-989-2299. **Founded:** 1987. **Operating Hours**: Sunrise-sunset. **Wattage**: 8,000. **Ad Rates:** $5 for 30 seconds; $6 for 60 seconds. **URL:** http://www.wilkinsradio.com.

14229 ■ KZMZ-FM - 96.9
1115 Texas Ave.
Alexandria, LA 71301
Phone: (318)445-1234
Fax: (318)473-1960
Format: Classic Rock. **Founded:** 1947. **Operating Hours**: Continuous. **ADI**: Alexandria, LA. **Key Personnel:** Pat Cloud, Music Dir., Prog. Dir., pat@cenlabroadcasting.com; Jon Dogma, Sports Dir., dgma32@aol.com. **Wattage**: 100,000. **Ad Rates:** $25-30 for 30 seconds; $28-60 for 60 seconds. **URL:** http://www.969rocks.com.

WHJM-FM - See Anna, OH

14230 ■ WNTZ-TV - 48
4615 Parliament Dr., Ste. 103
Alexandria, LA 71303
Phone: (318)443-4700
Fax: (318)443-4899
Email: community@fox48tv.com
Founded: Sept. 07, 2006. **Key Personnel:** Mona Dauzat, Bus. Mgr., mona@fox48tv.com; Sharon Rachal, Gen. Mgr., sharon@fox48tv.com. **URL:** http://www.fox48tv.com.

ARABI

SE LA. Saint Bernard Parish. On Mississippi River, adjoining New Orleans. Oil refineries, aluminum plants. Diversified farming.

14231 ■ Saint Bernard Voice
Saint Bernard Voice
234 Mehle Ave.
Arabi, LA 70032
Phone: (504)279-7488
Fax: (504)309-5532
Newspaper with a Democratic orientation. **Freq:** Weekly (Fri.). **Print Method:** Offset. **Trim Size:** 7 x 11. **Cols./Page:** 6. **Col. Width:** 2 1/16 nonpareils. **Col. Depth:** 301 agate lines. **Key Personnel:** Terri Sercovich, Editor. **Subscription Rates:** $25 Individuals print and online or online only; $35 Out of state print and online. **URL:** http://thestbernardvoice.com. **Mailing address:** PO Box 88, Arabi, LA 70032-0088. **Ad Rates:** GLR $.312; BW $481; PCI $4.50. **Remarks:** Advertising accepted; rates available upon request. **Circ:** Paid ⊕**2,600.**

BAKER

SEC LA. East Baton Rouge Parish. 10 mi. N. of Baton Rouge. Residential. Chemicals, petro complex, sugarcane, cotton.

14232 ■ WLFT-TV - 30
13567 Plank Rd.
Baker, LA 70714
Phone: (225)774-7780
Fax: (225)774-7785
Email: emailme@wlft.com
Key Personnel: Spencer Beach, Station Mgr., spencer.beach@bethany.com. **URL:** http://www.wlft.com.

BASTROP

N LA. Morehouse Parish. 29 mi. N. of Monroe. Manufactures paper and paper products, printers ink, varnish, chemicals, farm implements, logging equipment, men's pants. Cotton gins. Diversified farming. Pine, hardwood timber. Gas wells. Cotton, soybeans, rice.

14233 ■ Bastrop Daily Enterprise
Bastrop Newspapers Inc.
119 E Hickory
Bastrop, LA 71220
Phone: (318)281-4421
Fax: (318)283-1699
General newspaper. **Founded:** 1901. **Freq:** Daily (morn.). **Print Method:** Offset. **Cols./Page:** 6. **Col. Width:** 24 nonpareils. **Col. Depth:** 294 agate lines. **Key Personnel:** Terry Ward, Publisher; Mark Rainwater, Editor. **Subscription Rates:** $38.50 Individuals. **URL:** http://www.bastropenterprise.com. **Ad Rates:** PCI $4.85. **Remarks:** Accepts advertising. **Circ:** (Not Reported).

14234 ■ KAXV-FM
PO Box 2440
Tupelo, MS 38801-2440
Format: Religious. **Owner:** American Family Radio, at above address. **Wattage**: 12,000 ERP. **Ad Rates:** Noncommercial.

BATON ROUGE

SEC LA. East Baton Rouge Parish. 75 mi. NW of New Orleans, on the Mississippi River. The State Capital. Louisiana State University, Southern University A. and M. College. Major port for ocean and river transportation. Manufactures synthetic rubber, aluminum, tetraethyl lead, sulphuric and hydrofluoric acid, alcohol, salt, soda ash, chlorine, chemicals, sashes and doors, steel tanks, concrete pipes, mattresses, soft drinks. Food packing. Oil refining.

14235 ■ The Catholic Commentator
Diocese of Baton Rouge
1800 S Acadian Thruway,
Baton Rouge, LA 70808-1998
Phone: (225)387-0561
Fax: (225)242-0299
Publisher's E-mail: mbchevalier@cox.net
Religious newspaper. **Freq:** Biweekly. **Print Method:** Offset. **Cols./Page:** 5. **Col. Width:** 21 nonpareils. **Col. Depth:** 196 agate lines. **Key Personnel:** Wanda L. Koch, Manager, Advertising; Laura G. Deavers, Editor, General Manager. **Subscription Rates:** $14 Individuals. **URL:** http://www.thecatholiccommentator.org/pages. **Mailing address:** PO Box 2028, Baton Rouge, LA 70808-2028. **Ad Rates:** GLR $2.08; BW $825; 4C $1305; PCI $30.08. **Remarks:** Accepts advertising. **Circ:** ‡60,376, Combined ‡47,178.

14236 ■ Communications on Stochastic Analysis
Serials Publications Private Ltd.
c/o Hui-Hsiung Kuo, Editor-in-Chief
Dept. of Mathematics
Louisiana State University
Baton Rouge, LA 70803
Phone: (225)578-1610
Fax: (225)578-4276
Publisher's E-mail: serials@mail.com
Journal covering stochastic analysis. **Freq:** Quarterly. **Key Personnel:** C.C. Bernido, Board Member; Hui-Hsiung Kuo, Editor-in-Chief; L. Accardi, Board Member. **ISSN:** 0973--9599 (print). **URL:** http://www.math.lsu.edu/cosa. **Circ:** (Not Reported).

14237 ■ The Evangelist
Jimmy Swaggart Ministries
PO Box 262550
Baton Rouge, LA 70826
Phone: (225)768-7000
Free: 800-288-8350
Publisher's E-mail: info@jsm.org
Religious magazine. **Founded:** 1970. **Freq:** Monthly. **Print Method:** Offset. **Trim Size:** 8 3/8 x 10 7/8. **Cols./Page:** 3. **Col. Width:** 30 nonpareils. **Col. Depth:** 129 agate lines. **Key Personnel:** Donnie Swaggart, Editor. **URL:** http://www.jsm.org/the-evangelist.html. **Remarks:** Advertising not accepted. **Circ:** (Not Reported).

14238 ■ Exquisite Corpse: A Journal of Letters & Life
Exquisite Corpse
PO Box 25051
Baton Rouge, LA 70894
Phone: (504)388-2823
Publication E-mail: corpse@linknet.net
Magazine covering fiction, poetry, cultural criticism, film, music, and art. **Freq:** Bimonthly. **Print Method:** Offset. **Trim Size:** 6 x 16. **Cols./Page:** 2. **Col. Depth:** 2 1/2 inches. **Key Personnel:** Andrei Codrescu, Editor; Laura Rosenthal, Executive Editor; Dan Olson, Associate Editor. **ISSN:** 0740--7815 (print). **Subscription Rates:** $5 Single issue; $30 YEAR; $5 PER ISSUE. **Remarks:** Advertising not accepted. **Circ:** Paid 5000, Controlled 2000.

14239 ■ Greater Baton Rouge Business Report
Louisiana Business Inc.
PO Box 1949
Baton Rouge, LA 70821
Phone: (225)928-1700
Publication E-mail: editors@businessreport.com
Area business magazine. **Freq:** Semimonthly. **Print Method:** Offset. **Trim Size:** 11 x 14 3/4. **Cols./Page:** 4. **Col. Width:** 30 nonpareils. **Col. Depth:** 196 agate lines. **Key Personnel:** Timothy Boone, Contact. **ISSN:** 0747--4652 (print). **USPS:** 721-890. **URL:** http://www.businessreport.com. **Remarks:** Accepts advertising. **Circ:** Paid ‡2,657, Non-paid ‡6,001.

14240 ■ Interdisciplinary Journal of Teaching and Learning
Southern University at Baton Rouge

PO Box 9942
Baton Rouge, LA 70813
Phone: (225)711-4500
Fax: (225)771-4400
Online academic journal that publishes research and scholarly articles in the field of education and learning. **Freq:** 3/year Spring, Summer, and Fall. **Key Personnel:** Vera I. Daniels, Executive Editor. **ISSN:** 2158--592X (print). **URL:** http://www3.subr.edu/coeijtl. **Formerly**: E-Journal of Teaching and Learning in Diverse Settings. **Circ:** (Not Reported).

14241 ■ International Journal of Fruit Science
Taylor & Francis
Dept. of Horticulture
Louisiana State University
137 Julian Miller Hall
Baton Rouge, LA 70803
Publisher's E-mail: bookorders@dekker.com
Journal focusing on new technologies and approaches to the management and marketing of all types of fruits. **Freq:** Quarterly. **Key Personnel:** Paul E. Read, PhD, Editor; Zora Singh, Board Member; Bruce Barritt, Board Member; Don Elfving, Board Member; J.W. Palmer, Board Member; Philip Lieten, Board Member; John Barden, Board Member; David Ferree, Board Member. **ISSN:** 1553--8362 (print); **EISSN:** 1553--8621 (electronic). **Subscription Rates:** $398 Institutions online; $127 Individuals online; $455 Institutions print and online; $145 Individuals print & online. **URL:** http://www.tandfonline.com/toc/wsfr20/current. **Ad Rates:** BW $315; 4C $550. **Remarks:** Accepts advertising. **Circ:** (Not Reported).

14242 ■ International Journal of Quantum Chemistry
International Society for Theoretical Chemical Physics
c/o Dr. K. Rupnik
Dept. of Chemistry
Louisiana State University
Baton Rouge, LA 70803
Journal containing advanced information on quantum mechanics; fundamental concepts, mathematical structure, and application to atoms, molecules, crystals, and molecular biology. **Freq:** Bimonthly 24/yr. **Print Method:** Offset. **Trim Size:** 8 1/2 x 11 1/4. **Cols./Page:** 1. **Col. Width:** 29 picas. **Col. Depth:** 75 picas. **Key Personnel:** Matteo Cavalleri, Editor-in-Chief; Per Olov Lowdin, Editor, Founder; Yngve Ohrn, Editor. **ISSN:** 0020--7608 (print); **EISSN:** 1097--461X (electronic). **Subscription Rates:** $17324 Institutions U.S. and other countries - online only; £8840 Institutions U.K. - online only; €11177 Institutions Europe - online only. **URL:** http://onlinelibrary.wiley.com/journal/10.1002/(ISSN)1097-461X. **Ad Rates:** BW $772; 4C $1009. **Remarks:** Accepts advertising. **Circ:** (Not Reported).

14243 ■ Journal of Cotton Science
The Cotton Foundation
c/o Dr. Gerald O. Myers, Editor-in-Chief
LSU AgCenter
School of Plant, Environmental & Soil Sciences
104 MB Sturgis Hall
Baton Rouge, LA 70803
Publication E-mail: journal@cotton.org
Journal on cotton science. **Freq:** Quarterly. **Key Personnel:** Dr. Gerald O. Myers, Editor-in-Chief. **ISSN:** 1524--3303 (print). **Alt. Formats:** PDF. **URL:** http://www.cotton.org/journal. **Circ:** (Not Reported).

14244 ■ Journal of Energy Law and Resources
Louisiana State University Paul M. Hebert Law Center
1 East Campus Dr.
Baton Rouge, LA 70803-1000
Phone: (225)578-8491
Publisher's E-mail: info@law.lsu.edu
Journal containing topics in the purview of energy law. **Subscription Rates:** $28 Individuals. **URL:** http://jelr.law.lsu.edu. **Circ:** (Not Reported).

14245 ■ Journal of Manual & Manipulative Therapy
American Academy of Orthopaedic Manual Physical Therapists
8550 United Plaza Blvd., Ste. 1001
Baton Rouge, LA 70809
Phone: (225)360-3124
Fax: (225)408-4422
Publisher's E-mail: support@tandfonline.com
Peer-reviewed journal covering manual and manipulative therapy. **Freq:** 5/year. **Key Personnel:** Jean-Michel Brismee, Editor-in-Chief; Chad Cook, Associate Editor; Daniel Vaughn, Associate Editor. **ISSN:** 1066--9817 (print); **EISSN:** 2042--6186 (electronic). **Subscription Rates:** $510 Institutions print and online; $454 Institutions online only; $166 Individuals print and online; $143 Individuals online only. **URL:** http://www.tandfonline.com/loi/yjmt20. **Remarks:** Accepts advertising. **Circ:** (Not Reported).

14246 ■ Journal of the World Aquaculture Society
World Aquaculture Society
Louisiana State University
143 J.M Parker Coliseum
Baton Rouge, LA 70803
Fax: (225)578-3137
Peer-reviewed journal featuring papers on the culture of aquatic plants and animals. **Freq:** Bimonthly. **Key Personnel:** Carl Webster, Editor; Sungchul Bai, Associate Editor; Dominique Bureau, Associate Editor; Carole Engle, Editor. **ISSN:** 0893--8849 (print); **EISSN:** 1749--7345 (electronic). **Subscription Rates:** £378 Institutions UK (print and online); $564 Institutions Americas (print and online); €432 Institutions Europe (print and online); $667 Institutions, other countries print and online; £315 Institutions UK (print or online only); $519 Institutions Americas (print or online only); €398 Institutions Europe (print or online only); $614 Institutions online, ROW; $623 Institutions print and online ; €478 Institutions print and online ; $737 Institutions print and online, ROW. **URL:** http://onlinelibrary.wiley.com/journal/10.1111/(ISSN)1749-7345; http://www.was.org/View/Journal-of-the-World-Aquaculture-Society.aspx. **Remarks:** Advertising not accepted. **Circ:** (Not Reported).

14247 ■ LAE Voice
Louisiana Association of Educators
8322 One Calais Ave.
Baton Rouge, LA 70809-3412
Phone: (225)343-9243
Free: 800-256-4523
Publisher's E-mail: helpdesk@lae.org
Educational tabloid. **Freq:** Monthly. **Print Method:** Offset. **Trim Size:** 11 x 15. **Cols./Page:** 4. **Col. Width:** 30 nonpareils. **Col. Depth:** 214 agate lines. **URL:** http://www.lae.org/news_center/the_lae_voice.aspx. **Formerly**: LAE News. **Ad Rates:** BW $800. **Remarks:** Accepts advertising. **Circ:** ‡21,000.

14248 ■ Louisiana Agriculture Magazine
LSU Agricultural Center
101 Efferson Hall
Baton Rouge, LA 70803
Phone: (225)578-4161
Fax: (225)578-4143
Agricultural/educational magazine. **Freq:** Quarterly. **Print Method:** Offset. **Trim Size:** 8 7/16 x 11. **Cols./Page:** 3. **Col. Width:** 28 nonpareils. **Col. Depth:** 140 agate lines. **Key Personnel:** Dr. Linda Foster Benedict, Editor. **Subscription Rates:** Free. **URL:** http://lsuagcenter.com/en/communications/publications/agmag. **Remarks:** Advertising not accepted. **Circ:** Controlled 5,000.

14249 ■ The Louisiana Boardmember: LSBA Official Journal
Louisiana School Boards Association
7912 Summa Ave.
Baton Rouge, LA 70809
Phone: (225)769-3191
Fax: (225)769-6108
Free: 877-664-5722
Publication E-mail: lsba@eatel.net
Magazine on education. **Founded:** 1947. **Freq:** Quarterly January, April, July, and October. **Print Method:** Offset. **Trim Size:** @eig. **Col. Width:** 50 nonpareils. **Col. Depth:** 84 agate lines. **Key Personnel:** John T. Mandeville, Contact, phone: (225)769-3191, fax: (225)769-8716. **Subscription Rates:** Free. **URL:** http://www.lsba.com/PageDisplay.asp?p1=799. **Formerly**: The Boardman; The Boardmember. **Ad Rates:** BW $560; 4C $923. **Remarks:** liquor and tobacco. **Circ:** (Not Reported).

14250 ■ Louisiana Engineer & Surveyor Journal
Louisiana Engineering Society
9643 Brookline Ave., Ste. 116
Baton Rouge, LA 70809-1488
Phone: (225)924-2021
Fax: (225)924-2049
Publisher's E-mail: les@les-state.org
Magazine covering the field of engineering. **Freq:** Quarterly. **Print Method:** Offset. **Cols./Page:** 3. **Col. Width:** 25 nonpareils. **Col. Depth:** 136 agate lines. **Key Personnel:** Brenda W. Gajan, Executive Director. **ISSN:** 1527--5965 (print). **Alt. Formats:** PDF. **URL:** http://www.les-state.org/Journal.html. **Formerly**: The Louisiana Engineer. **Ad Rates:** BW $960. **Remarks:** Accepts advertising. **Circ:** Paid 30,000.

14251 ■ Louisiana Law Review
Louisiana State University Law Center
Paul M. Hebert Law Ctr.
1 E Campus Dr.
Baton Rouge, LA 70803-1000
Phone: (225)578-5292
Publication E-mail: lawreview@law.lsu.edu
Scholarly journal covering law. **Freq:** Quarterly. **Key Personnel:** Christopher K. Ulfers, Editor-in-Chief. **ISSN:** 0024--6859 (print). **Subscription Rates:** $45 Out of state; $46.80 Individuals in Louisiana; $57 Other countries; $12 Individuals /issue (plus tax). **URL:** http://lawreview.law.lsu.edu. **Remarks:** Advertising not accepted. **Circ:** Paid ⊕**982**.

14252 ■ Louisiana Libraries
Louisiana Library Association
8550 United Plaza Blvd., Ste. 1001
Baton Rouge, LA 70809
Phone: (225)922-4642
Fax: (225)408-4422
Free: 877-550-7890
Publisher's E-mail: office@llaonline.org
Freq: Quarterly summer, fall, winter, spring. **Print Method:** Offset. **Trim Size:** 8.5 X 11. **Cols./Page:** 2. **Col. Width:** 42 nonpareils. **Col. Depth:** 112 agate lines. **Key Personnel:** Vivian Solar, Editor, phone: (225)647-8924. **ISSN:** 1535--2102 (print). **Subscription Rates:** $25 each. **Alt. Formats:** PDF. **URL:** http://www.llaonline.org/fp/bulletin.php; http://llaonline.org/fp/bulletin.php. **Formerly**: LLA Bulletin. **Ad Rates:** BW $250. **Remarks:** Color advertising not accepted. **Circ:** Non-paid 1,200, 1200.

14253 ■ Louisiana Market Bulletin
Louisiana Department of Agriculture and Forestry
5825 Florida Blvd.
Baton Rouge, LA 70806
Phone: (225)922-1234
Free: 866-927-2476
Publication E-mail: marketbulletin@ldaf.state.la.us
Trade newspaper featuring agriculture-related articles, advertisements, and recipes. **Freq:** Semimonthly. **Print Method:** Offset. **Trim Size:** 11 1/2 x 15. **Cols./Page:** 5. **Col. Width:** 10 inches. **Col. Depth:** 13.5 picas. **Key Personnel:** Laura Pursnell-Lindsay, Managing Editor; Sam Irwin, Editor. **Subscription Rates:** $10 Individuals; $20 Two years; $30 Individuals 3 years. **URL:** http://www.ldaf.state.la.us. **Mailing address:** PO Box 631, Baton Rouge, LA 70821. **Remarks:** Accepts advertising. **Circ:** ‡16,800.

14254 ■ The Louisiana Pharmacist: The Voice of Pharmacy in Louisiana
Louisiana Pharmacists Association
450 Laurel St., Ste. 1400
Baton Rouge, LA 70801
Phone: (225)346-6883
Fax: (225)344-1132
Publisher's E-mail: lpa@pperron.com
Professional journal for registered pharmacists. Official publication of the Louisiana Pharmacists Association. **Freq:** Quarterly. **Print Method:** Offset. **Trim Size:** 8 1/2 x 11. **Cols./Page:** 3. **USPS:** 588-400. **Subscription Rates:** $5 Nonmembers; $5 Single issue. **Remarks:** Advertising accepted; rates available upon request. **Circ:** ‡1500.

14255 ■ Louisiana Rural Economist
Agricultural Economics & Agribusiness
110 LSU Union Square
Louisiana State University
Baton Rouge, LA 70803-0106
Phone: (225)578-3282
Fax: (225)578-2716

Circulation: ★ = AAM; △ or • = BPA; ♦ = CAC; ❑ = VAC; ⊕ = PO Statement; ‡ = Publisher's Report; Boldface figures = sworn; Light figures = estimated.

Magazine covering agricultural economics. **Freq:** Annual. **Print Method:** Offset. **Trim Size:** 6 x 9. **Cols./Page:** 2. **Col. Width:** 27 nonpareils. **Col. Depth:** 112 agate lines. **Key Personnel:** Lynn P. Kennedy, Associate Editor; Dr. Gail L. Cramer, Contact. **ISSN:** 8756--6273 (print). **URL:** http://www.lsuagcenter.com. **Remarks:** Advertising not accepted. **Circ:** Controlled ‡1265.

14256 ■ LSU Alumni Magazine
LSU Alumni Association
3838 W Lakeshore Dr.
Baton Rouge, LA 70808
Phone: (225)578-3838
Fax: (225)388-3816
Free: 888-746-4578
Alumni magazine. **Freq:** Quarterly March, June, September, and December. **Print Method:** Sheetfed. **Trim Size:** 8 3/8 x 10 7/8. **Cols./Page:** 3. **Col. Width:** 28 nonpareils. **Col. Depth:** 140 agate lines. **Key Personnel:** Jackie Barktkiewicz, Editor. **Subscription Rates:** Included in membership. **URL:** http://www.lsualumni.org/alumni-magazine. **Formerly**: LSU Alumni News. **Ad Rates:** BW $1205; 4C $1565. **Remarks:** Accepts advertising. **Circ:** ‡24,000.

14257 ■ Manuscripts
Manuscript Society
14003 Rampart Ct.
Baton Rouge, LA 70810-8101
Journal for collectors of manuscripts and special collections librarians. **Freq:** Quarterly. **Print Method:** Offset. **Trim Size:** 5 1/2 x 8 1/2. **Cols./Page:** 1. **Col. Width:** 46 nonpareils. **Col. Depth:** 94 agate lines. **Key Personnel:** David Chestnut, Editor. **ISSN:** 0025--262X (print). **Subscription Rates:** Included in membership. **URL:** http://www.manuscript.org/2009manuscripts.html. **Remarks:** Accepts advertising. **Circ:** ‡1800.

14258 ■ New Delta Review
Louisiana State University College of Humanities and Social Sciences
260 Allen Hall
Baton Rouge, LA 70803
Phone: (225)578-4086
Fax: (225)578-4129
Publication E-mail: new-delta@lsu.edu
Literary journal covering poetry, fiction, nonfiction and book reviews. **Freq:** Semiannual. **Print Method:** Offset. **Trim Size:** 6 x 8. **Key Personnel:** Laura Theobald, Editor. **ISSN:** 1050--415X (print). **URL:** http://www.lsu.edu/newdeltareview/New_Delta_Review/new_delta_review.html. **Remarks:** Accepts advertising. **Circ:** (Not Reported).

14259 ■ Peptides
RELX Group P.L.C.
c/o Abba J. Kastin, Ed.
Pennington Biomedical Research Ctr.
Louisiana State University System
6400 Perkins Rd.
Baton Rouge, LA 70808-4124
Phone: (225)763-0266
Fax: (225)763-0265
Publication E-mail: peptides@pbrc.edu
Journal publishing creative aid on the chemistry, biochemistry, neurochemistry, endocrinology, gastroenterology, physiology, and pharmacology of peptides, with their neurological, psychological and behavioral effects. **Freq:** Monthly. **Key Personnel:** Abba J. Kastin, Editor; W. Pan, Associate Editor. **ISSN:** 0196--9781 (print). **Subscription Rates:** $5642.66 Institutions online; $6770 Individuals print. **URL:** http://www.journals.elsevier.com/peptides. **Circ:** (Not Reported).

14260 ■ Phi Kappa Phi Forum
Phi Kappa Phi
7576 Goodwood Blvd.
Baton Rouge, LA 70806
Phone: (225)388-4917
Fax: (225)388-4900
Free: 800-804-9880
Publisher's E-mail: info@phikappaphi.org
Freq: Quarterly. **Print Method:** Four colon web press. **Key Personnel:** Pete Szatmary, Editor; Peter Szatmary, Editor. **ISSN:** 1538--5914 (print). **Subscription Rates:** $37.50 Individuals; $55 Other countries; $10 Nonmembers back issues; $37.50 U.S. Annually.; $55 Out of state Annually.; $4 Members back issue. **URL:** http://www.phikappaphi.org/publications-resources/phi-kappa-phi-forum#.VfNn8dLt1Hw; http://www.phikappaphi.org/publications-resources/phi-kappa-phi-forum#.VVFfiY6qqko; http://www.phikappaphi.org/error403?ReturnUrl=/publications-resources/phi-kappa-phi-forum/forum-archive#.VVFgqY6qqko. **Formerly**: National Forum. **Ad Rates:** BW $1,000; 4C $1,300. **Remarks:** Accepts advertising. **Circ:** Paid 105000.

14261 ■ World Aquaculture
World Aquaculture Society
Louisiana State University
143 J.M Parker Coliseum
Baton Rouge, LA 70803
Fax: (225)578-3137
Freq: Quarterly. **ISSN:** 1041- 5602 (print). **Subscription Rates:** $50. **URL:** http://www.was.org/magazine/. **Remarks:** Accepts advertising. **Circ:** 4300.

14262 ■ Communications Corporation of Baton Rouge Inc. - 44
10000 Perkins Rd.
Baton Rouge, LA 70810
Fax: (225)768-9293
Email: info@tvbatonrouge.com
Founded: 1991. **Formerly**: Galloway Media Inc. **URL:** http://www.fox44.com.

14263 ■ Cox Communications, Inc.
7401 Florida Blvd.
Baton Rouge, LA 70806
Phone: (225)663-6160
Free: 888-269-5757
Founded: 1978. **Formerly**: UAE. **Key Personnel:** Patrick J. Esser, President. **Cities Served:** Bossier County; East Baton Rouge County and Central and East Baton Rouge Par ishUnited States; 101 channels. **URL:** http://www.cox.com.

14264 ■ KBRH-AM - 1260
2825 Government St.
Baton Rouge, LA 70806
Phone: (225)388-9030
Format: Blues. **Founded:** 1977. **Ad Rates:** Noncommercial. **URL:** http://www.baton-rouge.com/wbrh.

14265 ■ KDJR-FM - 100.1
8919 World Ministry Ave.
Baton Rouge, LA 70810
Phone: (225)768-3288
Free: 800-342-8430
Email: k100@mail.theriver.net
Format: Country. **Networks:** Missouri. **Founded:** 1991. **Operating Hours**: Continuous. **ADI:** St. Louis, MO (Mt. Vernon, IL). **Key Personnel:** Mike Zimmer, Gen. Mgr; A. Michael Zimmer, Contact. **Wattage:** 6,000. **Ad Rates:** $31 for 30 seconds; $37 for 60 seconds. $4.20-$12 for 30 seconds; $5.20-$14.40 for 60 seconds. Combined advertising rates available with KHAD-AM. **Mailing address:** PO Box 262550, Baton Rouge, LA 70826. **URL:** http://www.jsm.org.

14266 ■ KFMV-FM - 105.5
224 Florida St., Ste. 206
Baton Rouge, LA 70801-1729
Phone: (225)344-2882
Format: Oldies. **ADI:** Baton Rouge, LA. **Wattage**: 6,000 ERP. **Ad Rates:** Advertising accepted; rates available upon request. **URL:** http://kddkfm.com.

14267 ■ K48IT - 48
PO Box A
Santa Ana, CA 92711
Phone: (714)832-2950
Free: 888-731-1000
Owner: Trinity Broadcasting Network Inc., PO Box A, Santa Ana, CA 92711, Ph: (714)832-2950, Free: 888-731-1000. **URL:** http://www.tbn.org.

KLPA-TV - See Alexandria

KLPB-TV - See Lafayette

14268 ■ KLSU-FM - 91.1
B-39 Hodges Hall
Louisiana State University
Baton Rouge, LA 70803
Phone: (225)578-5578
Format: Alternative/New Music/Progressive; Public Radio. **Owner:** Louisiana State University, 1 E Campus Dr., Louisiana State University, Baton Rouge, LA 70803-1000, Ph: (225)578-3202, Fax: (225)578-5991. **Founded:** 1923. **Operating Hours**: Continuous; 100% local. **ADI:** Baton Rouge, LA. **Local Programs**: *Spontaneous Combustion*, Sunday 10:00 a.m. - 2:00 p.m.; *Underground Sounds*, Monday 9:00 p.m. - 11:00 p.m.; *The Rusty Cage with The Witchfinder*, Tuesday 11:00 p.m. - 1:00 a.m. **Wattage**: 5,000. **Ad Rates:** Noncommercial. **URL:** http://www.lsureveille.com.

KLTL-TV - See Lake Charles

KLTM-TV - See Monroe

KLTS-TV - See Shreveport

14269 ■ KNXX-FM
929 Government St.
Baton Rouge, LA 70802-6034
Phone: (225)388-9898
Format: Alternative/New Music/Progressive; Album-Oriented Rock (AOR). **Owner:** Guaranty Media, 929 Government St., #B, Baton Rouge, LA 70802. **Key Personnel:** Owen Weber, Gen. Mgr., owen.weber@gbcradio.com; Dave Dunaway, Office Mgr., dave.dunaway@gbcradio.com. **Wattage**: 3,800 ERP. **Ad Rates:** Advertising accepted; rates available upon request.

14270 ■ KPBN-TV - 11
5500 Florida Blvd., Ste. 105
Baton Rouge, LA 70806
Phone: (225)248-0049
Email: kpbn11@gmail.com
Owner: Pelican Broadcasting Network L.L.C., 5500 Florida St., Baton Rouge, LA 70806. **URL:** http://www.pelicansportstv.com/20278_5570.asp.

14271 ■ KPYN-FM - 100.1
8919 World Ministry Ave.
Baton Rouge, LA 70810
Phone: (225)768-8300
Free: 800-342-8430
Email: kpyn@clover.cleaf.com
Format: Religious. **Owner:** Ark-La-Tex Broadcasting Co., at above address. **Founded:** 1978. **Operating Hours**: Continuous. **Key Personnel:** David Wommack, Jr., Gen. Mgr., Contact; David Wommack, Contact. **Wattage**: 50,000 ERP. **Ad Rates:** $10.00-15.00 for 30 seconds; $15.00-20.00 for 60 seconds. **Mailing address:** PO Box 262550, Baton Rouge, LA 70826. **URL:** http://www.jsm.org.

14272 ■ KQXL-FM - 106.5
631 Main St.
Baton Rouge, LA 70806
Phone: (225)926-1106
Format: Urban Contemporary. **Owner:** Citadel Broadcasting Corp., 7201 W Lake Mead Blvd., Ste. 400, Las Vegas, NV 89128-8366, Ph: (702)804-5200, Fax: (702)804-8250. **Key Personnel:** Deontray Alexander, Prog. Dir. **Wattage**: 50,000. **Ad Rates:** Advertising accepted; rates available upon request. **URL:** http://www.q106dot5.com.

14273 ■ KREK-FM - 104.9
PO Box 262550
Baton Rouge, LA 70826
Phone: (918)367-5501
Format: Contemporary Country. **Networks:** ABC. **Owner:** Big Chief Broadcasting Co. of Bristow, Inc., at above address. **Founded:** 1978. **Operating Hours**: Continuous. **Key Personnel:** Dusty Edwards, Sports Dir; Clifford W. Smith, Contact; Deanna Smith, Contact. **Wattage**: 6,000.

14274 ■ KRVE-FM - 96.1
5555 Hilton Ave., Ste. 500
Baton Rouge, LA 70809
Phone: (225)231-1860
Email: information@murphysamandjodi.com
Format: Adult Contemporary. **Founded:** 1989. **Operating Hours**: Continuous. **Key Personnel:** Jodi Murphy, Contact; Sam Murphy, Contact; Jodi Murphy, Contact; Michelle Southern, Contact, michelle@961theriver.com. **Wattage**: 50,000. **Ad Rates:** $2.50-60 for 30 seconds; $5-70 for 60 seconds. **URL:** http://www.961theriver.com/main.html.

14275 ■ KTOC-FM - 104.9
8919 World Ministry Ave.
Baton Rouge, LA 70801
Phone: (225)768-3102
Format: Gospel; Country. **Founded:** 1967. **Wattage**: 3,000.

14276 ■ WAFB-TV - 9
844 Government St.
Baton Rouge, LA 70802
Phone: (225)383-9999
Format: Commercial TV. **Networks:** CBS. **Owner:** Raycom Media Inc., 201 Monroe St., RSA Twr., 20th Fl., Montgomery, AL 36104-3731, Ph: (334)206-1400. **Founded:** 1953. **Operating Hours**: Continuous. **ADI**: Baton Rouge, LA. **Key Personnel:** Robb Hays, News Dir., rhays@wafb.com; Dale Russell, Dir. of Engg., drussell@wafb.com. **Ad Rates:** $10-950 per unit. **URL:** http://www.wafb.com.

14277 ■ WBKL-FM - 92.7
PO Box 2098
Omaha, NE 68103-2098
Free: 800-525-5683
Format: Religious. **Networks:** Independent. **Owner:** Educational Media Foundation, 2351 Sunset Blvd., Ste. 170-218, Rocklin, CA 95677, Ph: (800)434-8400. **Founded:** 1981. **Formerly**: WFEX-FM; WQCK-FM. **Operating Hours**: Continuous. **ADI**: Baton Rouge, LA. **Wattage**: 32,000. **Ad Rates:** $20 for 30 seconds; $25 for 60 seconds. **URL:** http://www.klove.com.

14278 ■ WBRH-FM - 90.3
2825 Government St.
Baton Rouge, LA 70806
Phone: (225)388-9030
Format: Jazz. **Networks:** National Public Radio (NPR); Louisiana. **Owner:** Baton Rouge Magnet High School, 2825 Government St., Baton Rouge, LA 70806. **Founded:** 1977. **Operating Hours**: Continuous; 1% network 99% local. **ADI**: Baton Rouge, LA. **Wattage**: 21,000. **Ad Rates:** Noncommercial. Combined advertising rates available with KBRH-AM. **URL:** http://www.baton-rouge.com/wbrh/aev2wbrh.htm.

14279 ■ WBRZ-TV - 2
1650 Highland Rd.
Baton Rouge, LA 70802
Phone: (225)387-2222
Fax: (225)336-2246
Email: marketing@wbrz.com
Format: Commercial TV. **Networks:** ABC. **Owner:** Louisiana Television Broadcasting, at above address. **Founded:** 1983. **Operating Hours**: Continuous. **ADI**: Baton Rouge, LA. **Key Personnel:** Chuck Bark, News Dir. **Wattage**: 100,000. **Ad Rates:** Noncommercial. **URL:** http://www.wbrz.com.

14280 ■ WCDV-FM - 103.3
650 Wooddale Blvd.
Baton Rouge, LA 70806
Phone: (225)926-1106
Format: Adult Contemporary. **Owner:** Citadel Broadcasting Corp., 7201 W Lake Mead Blvd., Ste. 400, Las Vegas, NV 89128-8366, Ph: (702)804-5200, Fax: (702)804-8250. **Key Personnel:** Christine Assaf, Bus. Mgr., christine.assaf@citcomm.com. **Ad Rates:** Advertising accepted; rates available upon request.

14281 ■ WDGL-FM - 98.1
929 Government St.
Baton Rouge, LA 70802
Phone: (225)388-9898
Format: Classic Rock. **Owner:** Guaranty Broadcasting Company of Baton Rouge L.L.C., at above address, Baton Rouge, LA 70802. **Founded:** 1968. **Formerly**: WAFB-FM; WGGZ-FM. **Operating Hours**: Continuous. **ADI**: Baton Rouge, LA. **Key Personnel:** Gordy Rush, Mktg. Mgr., gordy.rush@gbcradio.com; Dave Dunaway, Contact, dave.dunaway@gbcradio.com; Cindy Manzella, Contact, cindy.manzella@gbcradio.com; Dave Dunaway, Contact, dave.dunaway@gbcradio.com; Cindy Manzella, Contact, cindy.manzella@gbcradio.com. **Wattage**: 100,000. **Ad Rates:** Noncommercial. **URL:** http://www.eagle981.com.

14282 ■ WEMX-FM - 94.1
650 Wooddale Blvd.
Baton Rouge, LA 70806
Phone: (225)926-1106
Format: Hip Hop; Blues. **Owner:** Citadel Broadcasting Corp., 7201 W Lake Mead Blvd., Ste. 400, Las Vegas, NV 89128-8366, Ph: (702)804-5200, Fax: (702)804-8250. **Operating Hours**: Continuous. **Key Personnel:** Christine Assaf, Bus. Mgr., hr.batonrouge@citcomm.com. **Wattage**: 100,000. **Ad Rates:** Noncommercial. **URL:** http://www.max94one.com.

14283 ■ WFMF-FM - 102.5
5555 Hilton Ave., Ste. 500
Baton Rouge, LA 70808
Phone: (225)231-1860
Fax: (504)231-1869
Format: Contemporary Hit Radio (CHR). **Networks:** Independent. **Owner:** WGUL-FM, Inc., at above address. **Founded:** 1941. **Operating Hours**: Continuous. **ADI**: Baton Rouge, LA. **Wattage**: 100,000 ERP. **Ad Rates:** Advertising accepted; rates available upon request. **URL:** http://www.wfmf.com.

14284 ■ WJBO-AM - 1150
5555 Hilton Ave., Ste. 500
Baton Rouge, LA 70808
Phone: (225)499-9526
Format: Talk; News. **Networks:** CBS; EFM; Major Market Radio. **Founded:** 1934. **Operating Hours**: Continuous. **ADI**: Baton Rouge, LA. **Key Personnel:** Kevin Meeks, Contact, kevin@wjbo.com; Clarence Buggs, Contact, clarence@wjbo.com. **Local Programs**: *WJBO Lawn and Garden Show*, Saturday 8:00 a.m. - 9:00 a.m.; *Arts Council of Greater BR/Of Interest to You*, Sunday 7:00 a.m. - 8:00 a.m. **Wattage**: 5,000. **Ad Rates:** Advertising accepted; rates available upon request. **URL:** http://www.wjbo.com.

WJFM-AM - See Bowling Green, OH

WJFM-FM - See Lufkin, TX

14285 ■ WKJN-FM - 103.3
631 Main St.
Baton Rouge, LA 70801
Phone: (404)949-0700
Format: Classic Rock. **Networks:** ABC. **Owner:** Southern Communications Inc., at above address. **Founded:** 1969. **Formerly**: WTGI-FM. **Key Personnel:** Gary Hail, Dir. of Programs; Carla Cowart, Sales Mgr.; Don Nelson, President; Claire Gipson, Bus. Mgr. **Wattage**: 100,000 ERP. **Ad Rates:** Accepts Advertising. **URL:** http://www.classichits1033.com.

14286 ■ WLPB-TV - 27
7733 Perkins Rd.
Baton Rouge, LA 70810
Phone: (225)767-5660
Free: 800-272-8161
Format: Public TV. **Networks:** Public Broadcasting Service (PBS); Louisiana Public Broadcasting. **Owner:** Louisiana Public Broadcasting, 7733 Perkins Rd., Baton Rouge, LA 70810, Ph: (225)767-5660, Fax: (225)767-4288. **Founded:** 1975. **Operating Hours**: Continuous. **ADI**: Baton Rouge, LA. **Key Personnel:** Jason Viso, Dir. of Programs, jviso@lpb.org; Randy Ward, Dir. of Engg., rward@lpb.org; Clay Fourrier, Producer, cfourrier@lpb.org. **Local Programs**: *Louisiana: The State We're In*, Friday Sunday 7:00 p.m. 4:30 p.m. **Wattage**: 200,000. **Ad Rates:** Noncommercial. **URL:** http://beta.lpb.org.

14287 ■ WNXX-FM - 104.5
929B Government St.
Baton Rouge, LA 70802
Format: Alternative/New Music/Progressive; Heavy Metal; Adult Contemporary. **Owner:** Guaranty Media, 929 Government St., #B, Baton Rouge, LA 70802. **Operating Hours**: Continuous. **Key Personnel:** Cindy Manzella, Contact; Dave Dunaway, Office Mgr; Cindy Manzella, Contact. **Ad Rates:** Advertising accepted; rates available upon request. **URL:** http://www.1045espn.com.

14288 ■ WPFC-AM - 1550
6943 Titian Ave.
Baton Rouge, LA 70806
Phone: (225)926-6550
Free: 866-439-8026
Format: Gospel. **ADI**: Baton Rouge, LA. **Key Personnel:** Cassandra Lang, Contact. **Wattage**: 5,000 Day; 042 Night. **Ad Rates:** Advertising accepted; rates available upon request. **URL:** http://www.wpfc1550am.com.

14289 ■ WPYR-AM
5657 Parhaven Dr.
Baton Rouge, LA 70816
Phone: (225)231-1860
Format: Talk. **ADI**: Baton Rouge, LA. **Wattage**: 5,000 Day; 062 Night. **Ad Rates:** Advertising accepted; rates available upon request.

14290 ■ WRKF-FM - 89.3
3050 Valley Creek Dr.
Baton Rouge, LA 70808
Phone: (225)926-3050
Fax: (225)926-3105
Format: Public Radio. **Networks:** National Public Radio (NPR). **Owner:** WRKF, Public Radio Inc., 3050 Valley Creek Dr., Baton Rouge, LA 70808, Ph: (225)926-3050, Fax: (225)926-3105, Free: 855-893-9753. **Founded:** May 01, 1975. **Operating Hours**: Continuous. **Key Personnel:** David Gordon, Gen. Mgr., President, david@wrkf.org. **Wattage**: 28,000. **Ad Rates:** Noncommercial. **URL:** http://www.wrkf.org.

14291 ■ WSKR-AM - 1210
5555 Hilton Ave., Ste. 500
Baton Rouge, LA 70808
Phone: (225)231-1860
Fax: (225)231-1879
Format: Sports. **Networks:** CBS; ESPN Radio; Westwood One Radio. **Founded:** 1960. **Formerly**: WBIU-AM; WLBI-AM. **Operating Hours**: Continuous. **ADI**: Baton Rouge, LA. **Key Personnel:** Michael Hudson, Gen. Mgr. **Wattage**: 10,000 (Day) 1,000 (Night). **Ad Rates:** $6-8 for 30 seconds; $9-12 for 60 seconds. Combined advertising rates available with KRVE-FM; WYNK-FM; WYNK-AM; WFMF-FM; WJBO-AM.

14292 ■ WTGE-FM - 107.3
929-B Government St.
Baton Rouge, LA 70802
Phone: (225)499-1007
Fax: (225)499-9800
Format: Country. **Owner:** Guaranty Media, 929 Government St., #B, Baton Rouge, LA 70802. **Formerly**: WQXY-FM; WXCT-FM. **Operating Hours**: Continuous. **ADI**: Baton Rouge, LA. **Key Personnel:** Dave Dunaway, Contact; Owen Weber, Gen. Mgr.; Gordy Rush, Dir. of Sales; Randy Chase, Dir. of Programs, randy.chase@gbcradio.com; Dave Dunaway, Contact; Don Nelson, Contact. **Wattage**: 100,000. **Ad Rates:** Advertising accepted; rates available upon request. **URL:** http://www.1007thetiger.com.

14293 ■ WVLA-TV - 33
10000 Perkins Rd.
Baton Rouge, LA 70810
Phone: (225)766-3233
Fax: (225)768-9293
Email: news@nbc33tv.com
Format: Commercial TV. **Networks:** NBC. **Owner:** Knight Broadcasting of Baton Rouge, Inc., at above address, OAK HILL, VA. **Founded:** 1971. **Formerly**: WRBT-TV. **Operating Hours**: Continuous. **ADI**: Baton Rouge, LA. **Key Personnel:** David D'Aquin, News Dir. **Ad Rates:** Noncommercial. **URL:** http://www.nbc33tv.com.

14294 ■ WXOK-AM - 1460
631 Main St.
Baton Rouge, LA 70806
Phone: (225)926-1106
Format: Gospel. **Networks:** Independent. **Owner:** Citadel Broadcasting Corp., 7201 W Lake Mead Blvd., Ste. 400, Las Vegas, NV 89128-8366, Ph: (702)804-5200, Fax: (702)804-8250. **Founded:** 1953. **Operating Hours**: Continuous. **ADI**: Baton Rouge, LA. **Key Personnel:** Denise Johnson, Contact, denise.johnson@citcomm.com; Denise Johnson, Contact, denise.johnson@citcomm.com. **Wattage**: 5,000 Day; 1,000 Night. **URL:** http://www.heaven1460.com.

14295 ■ WYNK-FM - 101.5
5555 Hilton Ave., Ste. 500
Baton Rouge, LA 70808
Phone: (225)231-1860
Format: Country. **Founded:** 1968. **Operating Hours**: Continuous. **Ad Rates:** Advertising accepted; rates available upon request. **URL:** http://www.wynkcountry.com.

14296 ■ WYPY-FM - 100.7
929B Government St.
Baton Rouge, LA 70802
Phone: (225)383-0355
Format: Cajun; Country; News; Information. **Operating Hours**: Continuous. **Key Personnel:** Owen Weber, Gen.

Circulation: ★ = AAM; △ or • = BPA; ♦ = CAC; ❑ = VAC; ⊕ = PO Statement; ‡ = Publisher's Report; Boldface figures = sworn; Light figures = estimated.

Mgr., owen.weber@gbcradio.com. **Ad Rates:** Advertising accepted; rates available upon request. **URL:** http://1007thetiger.com.

BELLE CHASSE

SE LA. Plaquemines Parish. 10 mi. S. of New Orleans. Industrial, small business area. Oil and sulpher; commercial fishing. Dairy, fruit - truck farms.

14297 ■ The Plaquemines Gazette
Plaquemines Newspaper Publishing Inc.
PO Box 700
Belle Chasse, LA 70037
Phone: (504)392-1619
Fax: (504)393-9327
Community newspaper. **Freq:** Weekly (Tues.). **Print Method:** Offset. **Trim Size:** 14 3/4 x 21 1/2. **Cols./Page:** 6. **Col. Width:** 14 picas. **Col. Depth:** 21 inches. **Key Personnel:** Norris Babin, Publisher. **Subscription Rates:** $25 Individuals online; $25 Individuals in Parish - print and online; $35 Out of state print and online. **URL:** http://www.plaqueminesgazette.com. **Ad Rates:** GLR $.32; BW $481; SAU $4.42; 4C $581.95. **Remarks:** Accepts advertising. **Circ:** ‡3,000.

14298 ■ KMEZ-FM - 102.9
201 St. Charles Ave., Ste. 201
New Orleans, LA 70170
Phone: (504)581-7002
Fax: (504)566-4857
Format: News. **Networks:** Satellite Radio. **Founded:** 1990. **Formerly:** KNOK-FM. **Operating Hours:** 9:00 a.m. - 9:30 p.m., school days. **ADI:** New Orleans, LA. **Key Personnel:** Rob Moore, Gen. Mgr.; Nick Ferrera, Program Mgr. **Wattage:** 4,700 ERP. **Ad Rates:** $25-135. **URL:** http://www.power1029.com.

BOGALUSA

E LA. Washington Parish. 60 mi. NE of New Orleans. Manufactures lumber, wood and creosoted products, paper, paper boxes and bags, turpentine, tungoil, auto body parts. Yellow pine, hardwood timber. Grain, truck farms. Sugarcane, sweet potatoes, corn, cotton.

14299 ■ SAC Newsmonthly
Wayne Smith
PO Box 159
Bogalusa, LA 70429
Phone: (985)732-5616
Fax: (985)732-3744
Free: 800-825-3722
Publication E-mail: editor@sacnewsmonthly.com
Magazine providing entry information about arts and crafts shows throughout the U.S. **Freq:** Monthly latest edition March 2006. **Print Method:** Offset. Uses mats. **Trim Size:** 10 x 12. **Cols./Page:** 4. **Col. Width:** 2 1/2 inches. **Col. Depth:** 12 inches. **Key Personnel:** Wayne Smith, Publisher. **ISSN:** 0731--2989 (print). **Subscription Rates:** Free sample issue. **URL:** http://www.sacnewsmonthly.com. **Formed by the merger of:** Art & Crafts Catalyst; Southern Arts & Crafts; The National Arts & Crafts Network; The National Calendar of Open Competitive Exhibitions; Lisa's Report. **Formerly:** Southern Art and Crafts News; Art Scene; National Calendar of Indoor/Outdoor Art Fairs; Arts and Crafts Catalyst. **Ad Rates:** GLR $5; BW $325; PCI $3. **Remarks:** Accepts advertising. **Circ:** Paid ‡2000, Non-paid ‡30, 3000.

14300 ■ WIKC-AM - 1490
PO Box 638
Bogalusa, LA 70429
Phone: (985)732-4190
Fax: (985)732-7594
Email: wikcam@huntnet.net
Format: News; Gospel. **Owner:** Timberlands Broadcasting Corp., 607 Rio Grande St., Los Angeles, CA. **Founded:** 1947. **Operating Hours:** Continuous; 90% network, 10% local. **Wattage:** 1,000. **Ad Rates:** $6.75 for 30 seconds; $10.80 for 60 seconds. Combined advertising rates available with Timberlands Advertiser Newspaper.

BOSSIER CITY

NW LA. Bossier Parish. 1/2 mi. E. of Shreveport. Manufactures house trailers, air conditioning ducts, electrical parts, boat accessories, mattress, candy, toys. Tie preserving plant. Acid and sulphur. Agriculture. Corn, soybeans, cotton, alfalfa. Cattle, thoroughbred horses.

14301 ■ Bossier Press Tribune
Bossier Newspapers
4250 Viking Dr.
Bossier City, LA 71111
Phone: (318)747-7900
Community newspaper. **Freq:** Semiweekly (Mon. and Thurs.) Tuesday & Friday. **Print Method:** Offset. **Cols./Page:** 6. **Col. Width:** 12 picas. **Col. Depth:** 21 inches. **Key Personnel:** Jim Knudsen, Publisher; Randy Brown, Manager, Advertising. **Subscription Rates:** $2 Individuals in Parish, monthly; $2.17 Individuals out of Parish, monthly. **URL:** http://www.bossierpress.com. **Ad Rates:** GLR $1; BW $1229; 4C $1479; PCI $6.15. **Remarks:** Accepts advertising. **Circ:** Paid 2,000, Free 300.

14302 ■ KBED-FM - 102.9
270 Plaza Loop
Bossier City, LA 71111
Phone: (404)949-0700
Format: Adult Contemporary; News; Oldies; Talk. **Owner:** Cumulus Broadcast Cente, at above address. **Operating Hours:** Continuous. **ADI:** Shreveport, LA-Texarkana, TX. **Key Personnel:** C.J. Jones, Gen. Mgr. of Mktg. & Sales; Margie Bueche, Dir. of Sales; Gary Robinson, Promotions Dir. **Wattage:** 42,000. **Ad Rates:** Noncommercial; Advertising accepted; rates available upon request. **URL:** http://www.magic1029fm.com.

14303 ■ KMJJ 99.7 FM - 99.7
Horseshoe Riverdome, 711 Horseshoe Blvd.
Bossier City, LA 71111
Format: Urban Contemporary; News. **Networks:** CNN Radio. **Founded:** Sept. 07, 2006. **ADI:** Shreveport, LA-Texarkana, TX. **Wattage:** 23,500 ERP. **Ad Rates:** Advertising accepted; rates available upon request. **URL:** http://997kmjj.com.

14304 ■ KQHN-FM - 97.3
270 Plaza Loop
Bossier City, LA 71111
Phone: (318)549-8500
Format: Contemporary Hit Radio (CHR). **Operating Hours:** Continuous. **Key Personnel:** Gary Robinson, Contact; Gary Robinson, Contact. **Ad Rates:** Advertising accepted; rates available upon request. **URL:** http://www.i973hits.com.

14305 ■ KRMD-AM - 1340
270 Plaza Loop
Louisiana Boardwalk
Bossier City, LA 71111
Phone: (318)549-8500
Format: Talk; News. **Networks:** ABC. **Owner:** Cumulus Media Inc., 3280 Peachtree Rd. NW, Ste. 2300, Atlanta, GA 30305-2455, Ph: (404)949-0700, Fax: (404)949-0740. **Founded:** 1928. **Operating Hours:** Continuous. **ADI:** Shreveport, LA-Texarkana, TX. **Wattage:** 1,000. **Ad Rates:** $95 for 30 seconds; $120 for 60 seconds. **URL:** http://www.krmd.com.

14306 ■ KRMD-FM - 101.1
270 Plaza Loop
Bossier City, LA 71111
Phone: (318)549-8500
Free: 800-869-5673
Email: krmd@cumulus.com
Format: Contemporary Country. **Networks:** ABC. **Founded:** 1948. **Operating Hours:** Continuous. **ADI:** Shreveport, LA-Texarkana, TX. **Wattage:** 100,000. **Ad Rates:** $95 for 30 seconds; $120 for 60 seconds. **URL:** http://www.krmd.com.

BOUTTE

SE LA. Saint Charles Parish. 4 mi. NE of Paradis. Residential.

14307 ■ St. Charles Herald-Guide
St. Charles Herald-Guide
14236 Hwy. 90
Boutte, LA 70039
Phone: (985)758-2795
Fax: (985)758-7000
Publisher's E-mail: editor@heraldguide.com
Newspaper. **Founded:** 1873. **Freq:** Weekly (Thurs.). **Print Method:** Offset. **Cols./Page:** 6. **Col. Width:** 26 nonpareils. **Col. Depth:** 294 agate lines. **Key Personnel:** Desiree Lewis, Manager, Production; Allen Lottinger, Publisher; Ricky Naquin, Manager, Circulation; Colette Lottinger, Publisher; Jonathan Menard, Editor. **USPS:** 475-680. **Subscription Rates:** $29.99 Individuals in parish; $40 Individuals out of parish; $60 Out of state; $49.99 Two years in parish; $19.99 Individuals 6 months in parish. **URL:** http://www.heraldguide.com. **Formerly:** River Parishes Guide - 1993. **Ad Rates:** GLR $.685; BW $1,208.34; 4C $1,408.34; PCI $9.59. **Remarks:** Accepts advertising. **Circ:** ‡4400.

BOYCE

NC LA. Rapides Parish. 5 mi. S. of Flatwoods.

14308 ■ KBCE-FM - 102.3
2826 Lee St., Ste. 6
Alexandria, LA 71301
Phone: (318)445-0800
Fax: (318)445-1445
Owner: Trinity Broadcasting Corp., at above address. **Founded:** 1982. **ADI:** Alexandria, LA. **Wattage:** 21,000 ERP. **Ad Rates:** Accepts Advertising. **URL:** http://www.b102jamz.com.

CARENCRO

14309 ■ KBCA-TV - 41
3501 NW Evangeline Thruway
Carencro, LA 70520-6240
Phone: (337)886-3200
Owner: CW Network L.L.C., 4000 Warner Blvd., Burbank, CA 91522-0001, Ph: (818)977-2500, Fax: (818)954-7667.

14310 ■ KFXZ-FM - 106.3
3501 NW Evangeline Thruway
Carencro, LA 70520
Phone: (337)896-1600
Format: Music of Your Life; Information. **Owner:** Pittman Broadcast Services, LLC, at above address. **Founded:** 1985. **Operating Hours:** 6:00 a.m. - 10:00 p.m. Monday - Friday. **Key Personnel:** Mary Galyean, Gen. Mgr.; Keith Leblanc, Chief Engineer; Sherri Landry, Office Mgr.; Darlene Prejean, News Dir. **Wattage:** 2,100 ERP. **Ad Rates:** $25-56 for 30 seconds; $29-60 for 60 seconds. **URL:** http://1063radiolafayette.com.

14311 ■ KLWB-TV - 50
3501 NW Evangeline Thruway
Carencro, LA 70520-6240
Phone: (337)896-3200
Fax: (337)896-2681
Key Personnel: Dave Pierce, Gen. Sales Mgr., kates@delta-network.com; Marcus Doucet, Promotions Dir., marcusdoucet@delta-network.com.

14312 ■ KOGM-FM - 107.1
3501 NW Evangeline Thruway
Carencro, LA 70520
Format: Oldies. **Networks:** Independent. **Owner:** KSLO Broadcasting Company Inc., at above address. **Operating Hours:** 5 a.m.-11 p.m. **Wattage:** 750. **Ad Rates:** $11.95-16.85 for 30 seconds; $14.85-17.90 for 60 seconds. Combined advertising rates available with KSLO. **URL:** http://www.mustang877.com.

14313 ■ KVOL-AM - 1330
3501 NW Evangeline Thruway
Carencro, LA 70520
Phone: (337)896-1600
Owner: Pittman Broadcast Services, LLC, at above address. **Founded:** 1935. **ADI:** Lafayette, LA. **Wattage:** 5,000 Day 1,000 Night. **Ad Rates:** $25 for 30 seconds; $25 for 60 seconds. **URL:** http://kvol1330.com.

COLLINSTON

14314 ■ NortheastTel
6402 Howell Ave.
Collinston, LA 71229
Phone: (318)874-7011
Fax: (318)874-2041
Free: 888-318-1998
Email: info@ne-tel.com
Founded: 1987. **Cities Served:** 30 channels. **Mailing address:** PO Box 185, Collinston, LA 71229. **URL:** http://northeasttel.com.

COLUMBIA

N LA. Caldwell Parish. 30 mi. S. of Monroe. Residential.

14315 ■ KAPB-FM - 97.7
PO Box 1319
Columbia, LA 71418
Phone: (318)253-5272
Fax: (318)253-5262
Email: kapbfm@yahoo.com
Owner: Three Rivers Radio Co., Not Available. **Founded:** 1971. **Wattage**: 6,000 ERP. **Ad Rates:** $5-9.50 for 30 seconds; $8-12.50 for 60 seconds.

14316 ■ KCTO-AM - 1540
PO Box 1319
Columbia, LA 71418
Format: Gospel. **Networks:** Progressive Farmer; Louisiana. **Founded:** 1968. **Operating Hours:** Sunrise-sunset. **Key Personnel:** Tom Gay, Owner, Station Mgr.; Bill Mann, Operations Mgr. **Wattage**: 1,000. **Ad Rates:** $2.50 for 30 seconds; $5 for 60 seconds.

14317 ■ KCTO-FM - 103.1
The Radio Group Bldg.
No. 1 Radio Rd.
Columbia, LA 71418
Phone: (318)649-2756
Fax: (318)649-7959
Format: Oldies. **Networks:** Unistar. **Owner:** Tom D. Gay, PO Box 1319, Columbia, LA 71418, Ph: (318)649-7959, Fax: (318)649-2756. **Founded:** 1981. **Operating Hours:** Continuous. **ADI**: Monroe, LA-El Dorado, AR. **Key Personnel:** Carla Reitzell, Station Mgr.; Pat Hurley, Chief Engineer; Tom D. Gay, Contact. **Wattage**: 25,000. **Ad Rates:** $10 for 30 seconds; $15 for 60 seconds.

COUSHATTA

NW LA. Red River Parish. On Red River, 45 mi. SE of Shreveport. Appliance and meat pie plants. Oil wells. Timber. Agriculture. Cotton, corn, hay, grain, soybeans. Beef cattle.

14318 ■ KRRP-AM - 950
5710 Westdale
Houston, TX 77087
Free: 800-374-0323
Format: Classical. **Networks:** CBS. **Owner:** Roberto Feliz, Not Available. **Founded:** 1981. **Operating Hours:** Continuous. **ADI:** Shreveport, LA-Texarkana, TX. **Wattage**: 500 Day 209 Night. **Ad Rates:** $10-15 for 30 seconds; $12-18 for 60 seconds.

COVINGTON

SE LA. St. Tammany Parish. 38 mi. N. of New Orleans. Lumber, concrete products manufactured. Nurseries. Timber. Cattle. Thoroughbred horses.

14319 ■ The Bogalusa Daily News
Pontchartrain Newspapers
PO Box 90
Covington, LA 70434
Fax: (520)458-6166
General newspaper. **Freq:** Daily and Sun. **Print Method:** Offset. **Cols./Page:** 6. **Col. Width:** 25 nonpareils. **Col. Depth:** 301 agate lines. **URL:** http://www.gobogalusa.com. **Remarks:** Advertising accepted; rates available upon request. **Circ:** (Not Reported).

14320 ■ Journal of Medical Primatology
Wiley-Blackwell
c/o Preston A. Marx, Ed.-in-Ch.
Tulane National Primate Research Center
18703 Three Rivers Rd.
Covington, LA 70433
Phone: (985)871-6255
Fax: (985)871-6248
Publisher's E-mail: info@wiley.com
Journal studying primate models and applying the results to the study of human diseases, primate veterinary medicine, primate physiology, husbandry, handling, experimental methodology, and management of primate colonies and laboratories; primate wildlife management; and behavior and sociology as related to medical conditions and captive primate care. **Freq:** Bimonthly. **Key Personnel:** Preston A. Marx, Editor-in-Chief. **ISSN:** 0047--2565 (print). **Subscription Rates:** $1504 Institutions online only; £898 Institutions online only; €1141 Institutions online only; $1758 Institutions online only, rest of world. **URL:** http://onlinelibrary.wiley.com/journal/10.1111/(ISSN)1600-0684. **Remarks:** Advertising accepted; rates available upon request. **Circ:** (Not Reported).

14321 ■ WJSH-FM - 104.7
369170 Hwy., 190 Service Rd. S, No. 1
Covington, LA 70433
Phone: (985)345-0060
Fax: (985)542-6483
Format: Oldies. **Ad Rates:** Noncommercial. **URL:** http://www.highway1047.com.

CROWLEY

SW LA. Acadia Parish. 73 mi. SW of Baton Rouge. Manufactures burlap bags, men's slacks, farm machinery, steel - aluminum pipes. Oil, gas wells. Agriculture. Rice, cotton. soybeans. Livestock.

14322 ■ The Crowley Post-Signal
Crowley Post-Signal
602 N Parkerson Ave.
Crowley, LA 70526
Phone: (337)783-3450
Fax: (337)788-0949
Publisher's E-mail: cpsnews@bellsouth.net
General newspaper. **Freq:** Tues.-Fri. and Sun. **Print Method:** offset. **Cols./Page:** 6. **Col. Width:** 11 5/8 inches. **Col. Depth:** 21 1/2 inches. **Key Personnel:** Harold Gonzales, General Manager; Kathy Duncan, Manager, Production. **Subscription Rates:** $75 Individuals online only; $140 Out of area online; $115 Individuals print and online - Full in Parish; $100 Individuals print only; $129 Out of area print only. **URL:** http://www.crowleypostsignal.com. **Mailing address:** PO Box 1589, Crowley, LA 70527. **Ad Rates:** GLR $7.60; BW $948; 4C $1,238.50; SAU $7. **Remarks:** Accepts advertising. **Circ:** Mon.-Fri. 5329, Sun. 5722, Paid ‡5300.

14323 ■ Crowley Cable TV
2010 N Parkerson Ave.
Crowley, LA 70526
Phone: (318)783-5931
Cities Served: subscribing households 6,958. **URL:** http://www.cabletvinternetserviceproviders.com/.

14324 ■ KAJN-FM - 102.9
110 W Third St.
Crowley, LA 70526
Phone: (337)783-1560
Fax: (337)783-1674
Format: Religious; Gospel. **Owner:** Rice Capitol Broadcasting. **Founded:** 1977. **Operating Hours:** Continuous. **Key Personnel:** Janet Thompson, Div. Mgr.; Barry Thompson, Gen. Mgr., President, barryt@kajn.com; Craig Thompson, Div. Dir., craigt@kajn.com; Steve Cook, Div. Dir., stevec@kajn.com. **Wattage:** 100,000. **Ad Rates:** Advertising accepted; rates available upon request. **URL:** http://www.kajn.com.

14325 ■ KSIG-AM
320 N Parkerson Ave.
Crowley, LA 70526
Fax: (318)783-5744
Format: Country. **Founded:** 1947. **Key Personnel:** Tony Evan, Chief Engineer; Julius Meax, Contact. **Wattage**: 1,000.

DENHAM SPRINGS

SE LA. Livingston Parish. 16 mi. E. of Baton Rouge. Manufactures wood products, plywood, metal doors, sashes, frames, sewage treatment units. Timber. Poultry, truck farms. Strawberries, sheep, cattle raising.

14326 ■ K275AL-FM - 102.9
PO Box 391
Twin Falls, ID 83303
Fax: (208)736-1958
Free: 800-357-4226
Format: Religious; Contemporary Christian. **Owner:** CSN International, PO Box 391, Twin Falls, ID 83303, Ph: (208)736-1958, Fax: (208)736-1958, Free: 800-357-4226. **Key Personnel:** Mike Kestler, President; Don Mills, Music Dir., Prog. Dir. **URL:** http://www.csnradio.com.

DEQUINCY

14327 ■ The DeQuincy News
The DeQuincy News
203 E Harrsion St.
Dequincy, LA 70633
Phone: (337)786-8004
Fax: (337)786-8131
Free: 800-256-7323
Publisher's E-mail: dequincynews@centurytel.net
Community newspaper. **Freq:** Weekly (Wed.). **Print Method:** Offset. **Trim Size:** 11 5/8 x 21. **Cols./Page:** 6. **Col. Width:** 11.1 picas. **Col. Depth:** 295 agate lines. **Key Personnel:** Jerry E. Wise, Editor, Owner, Publisher. **USPS:** 105-200. **Subscription Rates:** $27 Individuals Calcasieu & Beauregard Parishes; $35 Out of state. **URL:** http://www.dequincynews.com. **Mailing address:** PO Box 995, Dequincy, LA 70633. **Ad Rates:** GLR $.27; BW $882; SAU $6.50; PCI $9. **Remarks:** Accepts advertising. **Circ:** ‡3,500.

DERIDDER

14328 ■ Beauregard Daily News
News Leader Inc.
903 W 1st St.
DeRidder, LA 70634-3701
Phone: (318)462-0616
Community newspaper. **Founded:** 1945. **Freq:** Daily. **Print Method:** Offset. **Cols./Page:** 6. **Col. Width:** 26 nonpareils. **Col. Depth:** 294 agate lines. **Key Personnel:** Mickel Ponthieux, Editor; Beaux Victor, General Manager, Publisher; Aaron Powers, Managing Editor. **URL:** http://www.beauregarddailynews.net. **Mailing address:** PO Box 698, DeRidder, LA 70634-0698. **Ad Rates:** GLR $.69; BW $1235; 4C $1685; SAU $11.05. **Remarks:** Accepts advertising. **Circ:** Paid ‡8,400, Free ‡5,400.

14329 ■ KBAN-FM
PO Box 2440
Tupelo, MS 38801-2440
Format: Gospel. **Owner:** American Family Radio, at above address. **Founded:** Feb. 1991. **Key Personnel:** Rick Robertson, Contact. **Wattage**: 20,500 ERP. **Ad Rates:** Noncommercial.

DERIDDER

14330 ■ KDLA-AM
1825 Pelican Rd.
Deridder, LA 70634
Phone: (337)460-7657
Email: kdla1010@bellsouth.net
Format: Gospel. **Wattage**: 1,000 Day; 040 Night. **URL:** http://www.kdla1010.com/.

DONALDSONVILLE

SE LA. Ascension Parish. On Mississippi River, 63 mi. NW of New Orleans. Syrup mills, foundry, hatchery. Oil and gas refinery. Sugarcane loader, fertilizer, synthetics, tool, aluminum factories. Diversified farming. Sugarcane.

14331 ■ Chamber Voice
Donaldsonville Area Chamber of Commerce
714 Railroad Ave.
Donaldsonville, LA 70346
Phone: (225)473-4814
Fax: (225)473-4817
Publisher's E-mail: dvillecoc@bellsouth.net
Journal featuring information about the Donaldsonville, LA area; including chamber of commerce member updates, community business profiles, employee's news, stories and headlines of interest to the Donaldsonville market. **Freq:** Bimonthly. **URL:** http://www.donaldsonvillecoc.org/?src=cv. **Circ:** (Not Reported).

14332 ■ Donaldsonville Chief
Donaldsonville Chief
120 Railroad Ave.
Donaldsonville, LA 70346
Phone: (225)473-3101
Fax: (225)473-4060
Community newspaper. **Freq:** Weekly (Thurs.). **Print Method:** Offset. **Cols./Page:** 6. **Col. Width:** 21 nonpareils. **Col. Depth:** 293 agate lines. **Key Personnel:** Glenn Stifflemire, Publisher, phone: (225)647-1829; Allison Hudson, Editor; Tanya Sellier, Manager, Circulation. **URL:** http://www.donaldsonvillechief.com. **Mailing address:** PO Box 309, Donaldsonville, LA 70346. **Ad Rates:** GLR $4.60; PCI $4.60. **Remarks:** Advertising accepted; rates available upon request. **Circ:**

Circulation: ★ = AAM; △ or • = BPA; ♦ = CAC; ❑ = VAC; ⊕ = PO Statement; ‡ = Publisher's Report; Boldface figures = sworn; Light figures = estimated.

Paid ‡3000, Non-paid ‡3000.

14333 ■ KKAY-AM - 1590
706 Railroad Ave.
Donaldsonville, LA 70346-3338
Format: Cajun; Zydeco. **Networks:** Independent. **Founded:** 1976. **Operating Hours**: Continuous. **ADI**: Baton Rouge, LA. **Key Personnel:** Harry Hoyler, Gen. Mgr. **Wattage**: 1,000. **Ad Rates:** $7 for 30 seconds; $10.50 for 60 seconds. **URL:** http://www.globalradiokkay.com.

DRY PRONG

14334 ■ KVDP-FM - 89.1
PO Box 249
Dry Prong, LA 71423
Phone: (318)899-5336
Fax: (318)899-7624
Format: Religious; Educational. **Networks:** Ambassador Inspirational Radio; USA Radio. **Owner:** Dry Prong Educational Broadcasting Foundation, Inc., at above address, Dry Prong, LA. **Founded:** 1985. **Operating Hours**: Continuous. **Key Personnel:** Coy Edwards, President; Leta Edwards, Gen. Mgr; Rick Hicks, Contact. **Wattage**: 4,500.

EUNICE

SC LA. St. Landry Parish. 45 mi. NW of Lafayette. Sports apparel and furniture manufactured. Processing plants. Oil and gas wells. Rice, cattle, soybeans.

14335 ■ KBAZ-FM - 102.1
PO Box 391
Eunice, LA 70535-0391
Format: Country. **Networks:** Satellite Music Network. **Founded:** 1990. **Operating Hours**: Continuous. **Key Personnel:** Jocelyn Bradley, Traffic Mgr; Robert L. Fontenot, Contact; Missy B. Benoit, Contact; Edna Poullard, Contact. **Wattage**: 25,000. **Ad Rates:** $4.30-5.75 for 30 seconds; $6.45-8.60 for 60 seconds.

14336 ■ KBON-FM - 101.1
109 S 2nd St.
Eunice, LA 70535
Phone: (337)546-0007
Fax: (337)546-0097
Format: Eclectic. **Key Personnel:** Paul Marx, Owner. **URL:** http://www.kbon.com.

14337 ■ KEUN-AM - 1490
PO Box 105-5
Eunice, LA 70535
Phone: (337)457-2348
Format: Talk; News. **Networks:** ABC; Louisiana; Jones Satellite. **Founded:** 1952. **Operating Hours**: Continuous. **ADI**: Lafayette, LA. **Key Personnel:** Rick Nesbitt, Contact, rnesbitt@keunworldwide.com. **Wattage**: 1,000. **Ad Rates:** $12 for 30 seconds; $15 for 60 seconds. Combined advertising rates available with KEUN-FM.

14338 ■ KEUN-FM - 105.5
1237 E Ardion St.
Eunice, LA 70535
Format: Country. **Key Personnel:** Rick Nesbitt, Contact, rnesbitt@keunworldwide.com.

FERRIDAY

NE LA. Concordia Parish. 10 mi. NW of Natchez, MS. Timber, corn.

14339 ■ The Concordia Sentinel
The Concordia Sentinel
421 N 1st St.
Ferriday, LA 71334
Phone: (318)757-3646
Fax: (318)757-3001
Community newspaper. **Freq:** Weekly (Wed.). **Print Method:** offset. **Cols./Page:** 6. **Col. Width:** 2 inches. **Col. Depth:** 21 inches. **Key Personnel:** Sam Hanna, Jr., Editor. **Subscription Rates:** $19.95 Individuals online and e-edition access.; $30 Individuals Inside Concordia.; $35 Out of state; $22 Individuals 66y/o & up; Inside Concordia.; $30 Out of state 66y/o & up. **URL:** http://www.hannapub.com/concordiasentinel. **Ad Rates:** SAU $4; PCI $4.50. **Remarks:** Accepts advertising. **Circ:** ‡5500.

14340 ■ KFNV-FM - 107.1
917 S E.E. Wallace Blvd. S
Ferriday, LA 71334
Phone: (318)757-1071
Fax: (318)757-7689
Free: 800-784-1071
Format: Adult Contemporary; Soft Rock. **Networks:** Louisiana; Mississippi. **Owner:** The Riverside Radio Group, at above address. **Founded:** 1971. **Formerly**: KSTH-FM. **Operating Hours**: Continuous. **Key Personnel:** Desiree Smith, Gen. Mgr.; Eddie Ray, Dir. of Programs. **Wattage**: 18,500. **Ad Rates:** $8.50 for 30 seconds; $12 for 60 seconds. **Mailing address:** PO Box 1510, Ferriday, LA 71334. **URL:** http://kfnvfm.com.

FOLSOM

E LA. St. Tammany Parish. 25 mi. SW of Bogalusa. Residential.

14341 ■ Whispering Wind: American Indian: Past and Present
Written Heritage
PO Box 1390
Folsom, LA 70437-1390
Phone: (985)796-5433
Fax: (985)796-9236
Free: 800-301-8009
Publication E-mail: info@whisperingwind.com
Magazine covering historical events, crafts, and material culture of the American Indian. **Freq:** Bimonthly. **Print Method:** Offset. **Trim Size:** 8 1/2 x 11. **Cols./Page:** 2. **Col. Width:** 35 nonpareils. **Col. Depth:** 151 agate lines. **Key Personnel:** Jack B. Heriard, Contact. **ISSN:** 0300--6565 (print). **Subscription Rates:** $25 Individuals; $45 Two years; $65 Individuals 3 years; $43 Other countries 1 year; $81 Other countries 2 years. **URL:** http://www.whisperingwind.com. **Ad Rates:** BW $212, 1/6; 4C $769, full. **Remarks:** Accepts advertising. **Circ:** ‡5000.

FRANKLIN

S LA. St. Mary Parish. On Bayou Teche. Oil wells, timber. Manufactures lumber, sugar. Agriculture. Sugarcane, rice.

14342 ■ St. Mary and Franklin Banner-Tribune
Franklin Banner-Tribune
115 Wilson St.
Franklin, LA 70538
Phone: (337)828-3706
Fax: (337)828-2874
General newspaper. **Freq:** Daily (eve.). **Print Method:** Offset. **Cols./Page:** 6. **Col. Width:** 24 nonpareils. **Col. Depth:** 294 agate lines. **Key Personnel:** Vanessa Pritchett, Managing Editor; Allan R. Von Werder, Publisher; Debbie Von Weder, Manager, Advertising. **USPS:** 516-320. **Subscription Rates:** $75 Individuals digital; $92 Individuals carrier; $150 By mail. **URL:** http://www.stmarynow.com. **Formerly**: Franklin Banner-Tribune. **Ad Rates:** BW $378; 4C $678; PCI $4.20. **Remarks:** Accepts display and classified advertising. **Circ:** Paid 3280, Non-paid 1720.

14343 ■ KFRA-AM - 1390
103 Wilson St.
Franklin, LA 70538
Owner: Castay Media Inc., Morgan City, LA. **Founded:** 1951. **Wattage**: 500 Daytime;244 Nigh. **Ad Rates:** Advertising accepted; rates available upon request. $5.25 for 30 seconds; $7 for 60 seconds. **Mailing address:** PO Box 1111, Franklin, LA 70538. **URL:** http://www.kfra1390am.com//.

GONZALES

SE LA. Ascension Parish. 22 mi. SE of Baton Rouge. Oil wells, timber. Ships vegetables. Truck farms. Sugarcane, strawberries, beans.

14344 ■ Gonzales Weekly
Gonzales Weekly
231 W Cornerview St.
Gonzales, LA 70737
Phone: (225)644-6397
Fax: (225)644-2069
Publisher's E-mail: editor@weeklycitizen.com
Newspaper with a Democratic orientation. **Freq:** Weekly (Fri.). **Print Method:** Offset. **Cols./Page:** 6. **Col. Width:** 2 inches. **Col. Depth:** 21 1/2 inches. **Key Personnel:** Glenn Stifflemire, Publisher; Brad Day, General Manager; Marie Schexnaydre, Manager, Circulation. **USPS:** 221-760. **URL:** http://www.weeklycitizen.com. **Mailing address:** PO Box 38, Gonzales, LA 70737-0038. **Ad Rates:** PCI $7.70. **Remarks:** Advertising accepted; rates available upon request. **Circ:** 10200.

GRAMBLING

14345 ■ Educational Research Quarterly
Educational Research Quarterly
Grambling State University
Adams 105
Grambling, LA 71245
Phone: (318)274-2511
Fax: (318)274-2695
Education journal. **Freq:** Quarterly. **Print Method:** Offset. **Cols./Page:** 1. **Col. Width:** 52 nonpareils. **Col. Depth:** 98 agate lines. **Key Personnel:** Olatunde Ogunyemi, Editor. **URL:** http://erquarterly.org. **Remarks:** Advertising accepted; rates available upon request. **Circ:** 1350.

14346 ■ KGRM-FM - 91.5
403 Main St.
Grambling, LA 71245
Phone: (318)274-6343
Fax: (318)274-3245
Format: Eclectic; Talk. **Owner:** Grambling State University, 403 Main St., Grambling, LA 71245, Ph: (318)247-3811, Free: 800-569-4714. **Founded:** 1974. **Operating Hours**: Continuous. **Key Personnel:** Joyce Evans, Gen. Mgr., Operations Mgr., evans;b@vaxo.gram.edu. **Wattage**: 50,000. **Ad Rates:** Noncommercial. **Mailing address:** PO Box 4254, Grambling, LA 71245. **URL:** http://www.gram.edu.

GRAND COTEAU

14347 ■ Allen's TV Cable Service Inc.
1580 I-49 N Service Rd.
Grand Coteau, LA 70541
Phone: (337)662-5315
Free: 888-793-9800
Email: info@atvci.net
Founded: 1959. **Cities Served:** 35 channels. **URL:** http://atvci.net.

GREENSBURG

E LA. St. Helena Parish. 70 mi. NW of New Orleans. Feed mills. Dairy - truck farms, beef, chicken. Agriculture.

14348 ■ St. Helena Echo
St. Helena Echo
PO Box 190
Greensburg, LA 70441
Phone: (225)222-4541
Fax: (225)748-7104
Community newspaper. **Freq:** Weekly (Wed.). **Print Method:** Offset. **Cols./Page:** 7. **Col. Width:** 26 nonpareils. **Col. Depth:** 301 agate lines. **Key Personnel:** Carol Brooke, Publisher; Fran Snoddy, Customer Service; Karen McDaniel, Manager, Advertising; Trish Adams, Managing Editor. **Subscription Rates:** $21 Individuals e-Edition Only - 6 months ; $11 Individuals e-Edition Only - 3 months; $1 Individuals e-Edition Only - 1 week. **URL:** http://etypeservices.com/St.%20Helena%20EchoID240; http://etypeservices.com/St.%20Helena%20EchoID240/default.aspx. **Ad Rates:** SAU $4.39. **Remarks:** Accepts advertising. **Circ:** ‡1900.

GRETNA

SE LA. Jefferson Parish. 7 mi. SE of New Orleans. Petroleum products. Cottonseed oil. Molasses.

14349 ■ KKNO-AM - 750
16 Westbank Expy., Ste. 204
Gretna, LA 70053
Format: Gospel. **Networks:** Southern Broadcasting. **Owner:** Robert Blakes Enterprises, 40 Verde St., Kenner, LA 70065. **Founded:** 1989. **Operating Hours**: Sunrise-sunset. **Key Personnel:** Linda Bradley, Dir. of Programs. **Wattage**: 250. **Ad Rates:** $30 per unit. **URL:** http://www.kkno750am.com/.

HAMMOND

SE LA. Tangipahoa Parish. 43 mi. E. of Baton Rouge. Southeastern Louisiana University. Manufactures strawberry crates, mobile homes, plywood, boxes, bricks, foam products, candy, beverages, cabinets, women's wear. Steel mill. Pine, hardwood timber. Truck, dairy, poultry farms. Strawberries.

14350 ■ Hammond Daily Star
Daily Star Publishing Co.
PO Box 1149
Hammond, LA 70404
Phone: (985)254-7827
Publisher's E-mail: webmaster@hammondstar.com
General newspaper. **Freq:** Daily and Sun. (eve.). **Print Method:** Offset. **Trim Size:** 13 3/4 x 22 3/4. **Cols./Page:** 6. **Col. Width:** 2 1/32 inches. **Col. Depth:** 21 1/2 inches. **Key Personnel:** Keenan Gingles, Publisher; Lil Mirando, Executive Editor; Joseph Davis, Business Manager. **Subscription Rates:** $1.25 Individuals 1 day - online; $14.25 Individuals 1 month - online; $42.75 Individuals 3 months - online; $85.50 Individuals 6 months - online; $171 Individuals 1 year - online. **URL:** http://www.hammondstar.com. **Remarks:** Accepts display and classified advertising. **Circ:** Mon.-Fri. ★**10509**, Sun. ★**13673**.

14351 ■ WHMD-FM
200 E Thomas St.
Hammond, LA 70403
Phone: (504)345-1070
Fax: (504)542-9377
Format: Country. **Networks:** AP. **Owner:** Airweb, Inc., PO Box 1829, Hammond, LA 70404. **Founded:** 1974. **Wattage**: 6,000 ERP. **Ad Rates:** $15 for 30 seconds; $24 for 60 seconds. **URL:** http://www.kajun107.net.

HARAHAN

14352 ■ Fleur de Lis
Louisiana Credit Union League
824 Elmwood Park Blvd., Ste. 200
Harahan, LA 70123
Phone: (800)452-7221
Fax: (504)736-3677
Publisher's E-mail: requests@lcul.com
Magazine of the Louisiana Credit Union League. **Freq:** Quarterly. **Remarks:** Advertising not accepted. **Circ:** (Not Reported).

HAYNESVILLE

N LA. Claiborne Parish. 50 mi. NE of Shreveport. Manufactures work gloves, protective clothing, plywood. Oil, gas wells, timber. Agriculture.

14353 ■ KLVU-FM - 105.5
1803 N 1st East St.
Haynesville, LA 71038
Phone: (318)624-0105
Format: Easy Listening. **Simulcasts:** KLVU-AM. **Networks:** Southern States. **Owner:** Phillip Robillard, at above address. **Founded:** 1984. **Operating Hours**: Sunrise-sunset. **Key Personnel:** Phillip Robillard, Contact; Elizabeth G. Robillard, Contact. **Wattage**: 3,000. **Ad Rates:** $6 for 30 seconds; $10 for 60 seconds.

HOMER

WC LA. Claiborne Parish. 47 mi. ENE of Shreveport. Trading center of timber section, petroleum deposits.

14354 ■ The Guardian-Journal
The Guardian-Journal
620 N Main St.
Homer, LA 71040
Phone: (318)927-3541
Fax: (318)927-3542
Publication E-mail: guardian-journal@claiborneOne.com
Community newspaper. **Freq:** Weekly. **Print Method:** Offset. **Cols./Page:** 6. **Col. Width:** 12 picas. **Key Personnel:** Geraldine H. Hightower, Publisher; Michelle Bates, Editor. **Subscription Rates:** $35 Individuals Claiborne, Bienville, Lincoln, Webster; $40 Individuals State of Louisiana; $45 Out of state. **URL:** http://www.claiborneparish.org/chamber-of-commerce.php. **Mailing address:** PO Box 119, Homer, LA 71040. **Ad Rates:** BW $403.20; 4C $641.20; SAU $3; PCI $2.20. **Remarks:** Accepts advertising. **Circ:** Paid 2400, Free 1100.

14355 ■ The Haynesville News
The Haynesville News
604 N Main St.
Homer, LA 71040
Phone: (318)927-3721
Fax: (318)624-1212
Publisher's E-mail: thn@claiborneone.org
Community and parish newspaper. **Freq:** Weekly (Thurs.). **Print Method:** Offset. **Trim Size:** 14 x 22 3/4. **Cols./Page:** 6. **Col. Width:** 2 1/16 inches. **Col. Depth:** 21 inches. **USPS:** 238-040. **Subscription Rates:** $25 Individuals inside Claiborne Parish; $35 Out of area. **URL:** http://www.claiborneone.org/thn/thn.html. **Mailing address:** PO Box 117, Homer, LA 71040. **Ad Rates:** BW $403.20; 4C $578.20; SAU $3.5; PCI $2.24. **Remarks:** Accepts advertising. **Circ:** Paid ‡2754, Free ‡35.

HOUMA

S LA. Terrebonne Parish. 53 mi. SW of New Orleans, on the Intracoastal Waterway. Seafood industry; shrimp, oyster, crabs. Commercial fishing. Oil and gas industry. Agriculture. Sugarcane, soybean.

14356 ■ The Courier
The Courier
3030 Barrow St.
Houma, LA 70361
Phone: (985)850-1100
Publisher's E-mail: news@houmatoday.com
General newspaper. **Founded:** 1878. **Freq:** Daily and Sun. (eve.). **Print Method:** Offset. **Cols./Page:** 6. **Col. Width:** 2 1/16 inches. **Col. Depth:** 21 inches. **URL:** http://www.houmatoday.com/. **Formerly**: Houma Daily Courier. **Mailing address:** PO Box 2717, Houma, LA 70361. **Remarks:** Advertising accepted; rates available upon request. **Circ:** Mon.-Sat. 19471, Sun. 21350.

14357 ■ KXOR-FM - 106.3
120 Prevost Dr.
Houma, LA 70364
Phone: (985)851-1020
Fax: (985)872-4403
Email: info@eagle1063.com
Format: Classic Rock; News; Sports. **Owner:** Guaranty Media, 929 Government St., #B, Baton Rouge, LA 70802. **Founded:** 1966. **Wattage**: 25,000 ERP. **Ad Rates:** Advertising accepted; rates available upon request. $35 for 30 seconds; $35 for 60 seconds. **URL:** http://www.eagle1063.com.

JENA

C LA. La Salle Parish. 40 mi. NE of Alexandria. Manufactures wire and cable, particle board, cotton. Sawmills. Oil wells. Pine and hardwood timber. Agriculture. Cattle, corn.

14358 ■ KJNA-FM
PO Box 1340
Jena, LA 71342
Phone: (318)992-4155
Format: Country. **Networks:** Unistar; Louisiana. **Owner:** Tom Gay, PO Box 1319, Columbia, LA 71418, Ph: (318)649-7959. **Founded:** 1969. **Key Personnel:** Larry Evans, Station Mgr.; B. Mitchell, Dir. of Programs. **Wattage**: 6,000 ERP. **Ad Rates:** $10 for 30 seconds; $12 for 60 seconds.

JENNINGS

SW LA. Jefferson Davis Parish. 30 mi. E. of Lake Charles. Rice mills, water well machinery plants. Oil wells. Oak, gum, pine timber. Agriculture. Rice, cotton, truck crops.

14359 ■ KJEF-AM
122 N Market St.
Jennings, LA 70546
Phone: (318)824-2934
Format: Country; Ethnic; French. **Networks:** NBC. **Founded:** 1950. **Key Personnel:** Bill Bailey, Gen. Mgr. **Wattage**: 1,000 Day; 280 Night. **Ad Rates:** $4-11 for 30 seconds; $5-14 for 60 seconds.

14360 ■ K201FO-FM - 88.1
PO Box 391
Twin Falls, ID 83303
Fax: (208)736-1958
Free: 800-357-4226
Format: Religious; Contemporary Christian. **Owner:** CSN International, PO Box 391, Twin Falls, ID 83303, Ph: (208)736-1958, Fax: (208)736-1958, Free: 800-357-4226. **Key Personnel:** Kelly Carlson, Dir. of Engg.; Ray Gorney, Asst. Dir.; Don Mills, Music Dir., Prog. Dir. **URL:** http://www.csnradio.com.

LA PLACE

14361 ■ L'Observateur Vista Inc.
The L'Observateur Vista Inc.
PO Box 1010
La Place, LA 70069
Phone: (985)652-9545
Fax: (985)652-1633
Publication E-mail: lobnews@bellsouth.net
Newspaper. **Freq:** Semiweekly (Wed. and Sat.). **Print Method:** Offset. **Cols./Page:** 6. **Col. Width:** 11.5 inches. **Col. Depth:** 294 agate lines. **Key Personnel:** Sandy Cunningham, Editor. **URL:** http://www.lobservateur.com. **Ad Rates:** 4C $195; PCI $10.50. **Circ:** Paid 5000, 21000.

LAFAYETTE

S LA. Lafayette Parish. On Vermilion Bayou, 152 mi. W. of New Orleans. University of Southwestern Louisiana. Bricks, oil equipment, cheese, aluminum windows and doors manufactured. Coffee roasters; rice milling; food processing plant; bottling works. Dairy, stock, truck farms. Sugarcane, cotton, corn, rice.

14362 ■ Acadiana Profile Magazine: The Magazine of the Cajun Country
Acadiana Profile Magazine
128 Demanade, Ste. 104
Lafayette, LA 70503
Publisher's E-mail: errol@myneworleans.com
Magazine featuring the French-Acadian culture of the region. **Freq:** Bimonthly. **Key Personnel:** Sarah Ravits, Managing Editor. **Subscription Rates:** $10 Individuals /year; $18 Two years. **URL:** http://www.myneworleans.com/Acadiana-Profile. **Remarks:** Advertising accepted; rates available upon request. **Circ:** (Not Reported).

14363 ■ Advances in Skin & Wound Care
American Professional Wound Care Association
3639 Ambassador Caffery Pky., Ste. 605
Lafayette, LA 70503
Phone: (215)942-6095
Fax: (215)993-7922
Publisher's E-mail: ronna.ekhouse@wolterskluwer.com
Freq: Monthly. **Print Method:** Web offset. **Trim Size:** 7 3/4 x 10 1/2. **Cols./Page:** 3. **Col. Width:** 13 picas. **Col. Depth:** 47 picas. **Key Personnel:** Richard Salcido, MD, Editor-in-Chief. **ISSN:** 1527--7941 (print); **EISSN:** 1538--8654 (electronic). **Subscription Rates:** $131 U.S.; $134 Canada and Mexico; $227 Individuals UK/Australia; $239 Other countries; $724 Institutions; $671 Institutions, Canada and Mexico; $875 Institutions; $858 Institutions, other countries; $66 Individuals in-training; $125 Individuals; $661 Institutions; $128 Canada and Mexico; $228 Other countries. **URL:** http://journals.lww.com/aswcjournal/pages/default.aspx; http://www.apwca.org/page-1491350. **Formerly**: Advances in Wound Care. **Mailing address:** PO Box 908, Philadelphia, PA 19106-3621. **Ad Rates:** BW $3,400; 4C $1,820. **Remarks:** Accepts advertising. **Circ:** ‡18611.

14364 ■ American Communication Journal
American Communication Association
104 E University Cir.
Lafayette, LA 70503
Phone: (337)482-1000
Journal dedicated to the study of communication. **Freq:** Monthly. **Print Method:** Offset. **Trim Size:** 7 3/4 x 10 1/2. **Cols./Page:** 3. **Col. Width:** 27 nonpareils. **Col. Depth:** 140 agate lines. **Key Personnel:** Aziz Douai, Editor. **ISSN:** 1532--5865 (print). **URL:** http://www.ac-journal.org. **Circ:** (Not Reported).

14365 ■ Clinical Linguistics and Phonetics
Informa Healthcare
Department of Communicative Disorders
University of Louisiana at Lafayette
Lafayette, LA 70504-3170
Publisher's E-mail: healthcare.enquiries@informa.com
Journal containing information on speech and language disorders. **Founded:** 1987. **Freq:** Monthly. **Key Personnel:** Martin J. Ball, Editor; Thomas W. Powell, Associate Editor. **ISSN:** 0269-9206 (print). **Subscription Rates:** $2354 Institutions; $4584 Institutions Corporate Single Site. **URL:** http://informahealthcare.com/clp. **Remarks:**

Circulation: ★ = AAM; △ or • = BPA; ♦ = CAC; ❑ = VAC; ⊕ = PO Statement; ‡ = Publisher's Report; Boldface figures = sworn; Light figures = estimated.

Accepts advertising. **Circ:** ‡250.

14366 ■ Deviant Behavior: An Interdisciplinary Journal
Routledge
c/o Craig J. Forsyth, Editor-in-Chief
Dept. of Sociology & Anthropology
University of Louisiana
Lafayette, LA 70504-0198
Publisher's E-mail: book.orders@tandf.co.uk
Journal covering behavioral science and theory in the area of deviant social behavior. **Freq:** Monthly. **Print Method:** Offset. **Trim Size:** 6 x 9. **Cols./Page:** 1. **Col. Width:** 52 nonpareils. **Col. Depth:** 99 agate lines. **Key Personnel:** Bruce Arrigo, PhD, Associate Editor; Ronald L. Akers, PhD, Associate Editor; Joel Best, PhD, Associate Editor; Craig J. Forsyth, PhD, Editor-in-Chief; Clifton D. Bryant, PhD, Chairperson, Editor, Founder. **ISSN:** 0163--9625 (print). **Subscription Rates:** $676 Individuals print only; $1602 Institutions online only; $1831 Institutions print & online; $676 Individuals Print & Online. **URL:** http://www.tandfonline.com/toc/udbh20/current#.VHCDVdlW2qY. **Remarks:** Accepts advertising. **Circ:** 600.

14367 ■ Louisiana History
Louisiana Historical Association
PO Box 40831
Lafayette, LA 70504-0831
Phone: (337)482-6027
Publisher's E-mail: lha@louisiana.edu
Peer-reviewed history journal. **Freq:** Quarterly. **Print Method:** Letterpress and offset. **Trim Size:** 6 x 9. **Cols./Page:** 1. **Col. Width:** 51 nonpareils. **Col. Depth:** 98 agate lines. **Key Personnel:** Carl A. Brasseaux, Managing Editor. **ISSN:** 0024--6816 (print). **URL:** http://www.lahistory.org/site17.php. **Ad Rates:** BW $100. **Remarks:** Accepts advertising. **Circ:** ‡1200.

14368 ■ Rayne Acadian Tribune
The Daily Advertiser
PO Box 5310
Lafayette, LA 70502
Phone: (337)289-6300
Newspaper with a Democratic orientation. **Freq:** Weekly (Thurs.). **Print Method:** Offset. **Cols./Page:** 6. **Col. Width:** 26 nonpareils. **Col. Depth:** 301 agate lines. **Key Personnel:** Paul Kedinger, Managing Editor. **Subscription Rates:** $29 Individuals print and online; in Parish, mail delivery; $34 Out of state print and online; $20 Individuals online. **URL:** http://www.raynetoday.com. **Ad Rates:** GLR $7. **Remarks:** Accepts advertising. **Circ:** Paid ‡4900.

14369 ■ The Times of Acadiana
South Louisiana Publishing
1100 Bertrand Dr. St.
Lafayette, LA 70502
Phone: (337)289-6300
Fax: (337)289-6443
Publisher's E-mail: timesedit@timesofacadiana.com
Newspaper covering politics, lifestyle, entertainment, and general news. **Freq:** Weekly (Thurs.). **Print Method:** Offset. **Trim Size:** 10 11/16 x 14 5/8. **Cols./Page:** 4. **Col. Width:** 28 nonpareils. **Col. Depth:** 194 agate lines. **Key Personnel:** Kathie Zimmerman, Contact. **Subscription Rates:** Free. **URL:** http://theadvertiser.com/topic/91888a22-d739-4f28-bc33-1829bcfeeb0e/times-of-acadiana/. **Ad Rates:** BW $1,494; 4C $1,743. **Remarks:** Accepts advertising. **Circ:** (Not Reported).

14370 ■ The Vermilion
University of Louisiana at Lafayette
104 E University Cir.
Lafayette, LA 70504
Phone: (337)482-1000
Publisher's E-mail: webmaster@louisiana.edu
Collegiate newspaper. **Freq:** Weekly (Wed.). **Print Method:** Offset. **Trim Size:** 10 1/2 x 12 1/2. **Cols./Page:** 4. **Col. Width:** 2 5/16 inches. **Col. Depth:** 76 picas. **Key Personnel:** Corrie Gallien, Business Manager. **URL:** http://thevermilion.com. **Ad Rates:** GLR $7.50; BW $360; 4C $125; PCI $7.50. **Remarks:** Accepts advertising. **Circ:** Free ‡10000.

14371 ■ West Carroll Gazette
Louisiana State Newspapers
600 Jefferson St., Ste. 1103
Lafayette, LA 70508
Phone: (337)266-2154
Fax: (337)266-2123
Community newspaper. **Freq:** Weekly (Wed.). **Print Method:** Offset. **Cols./Page:** 6. **Col. Width:** 25 nonpareils. **Col. Depth:** 294 agate lines. **Key Personnel:** Terry Stockton, Publisher; Johney S. Turner, Editor. **Subscription Rates:** $34.65 Individuals online only. **URL:** http://westcarrollgazette.com. **Mailing address:** PO Box 4033-C, Lafayette, LA 70508. **Ad Rates:** BW $516; 4C $5.75; PCI $5.30. **Remarks:** Accepts advertising. **Circ:** ‡2300.

14372 ■ KADN-TV - 15
1500 Eraste Landry Rd.
Lafayette, LA 70506
Phone: (337)237-1500
Fax: (337)237-2237
Format: Commercial TV. **Networks:** Fox. **Owner:** Comcorp of Louisiana Inc., at above address. **Founded:** 1980. **Operating Hours:** Continuous. **ADI:** Lafayette, LA. **Wattage:** 2,300. **Ad Rates:** $15-500 for 30 seconds; $30-1000 for 60 seconds. **URL:** http://www.kadn.com.

14373 ■ KATC-TV - 3
1103 Eraste Landry Dr.
Lafayette, LA 70506
Phone: (337)235-3333
Format: Commercial TV. **Networks:** ABC. **Owner:** Evening Post Industries Inc., 134 Columbus St., Charleston, SC 29403, Ph: (843)577-7111. **Founded:** Sept. 1962. **ADI:** Lafayette, LA. **Key Personnel:** Don Mouton, Chief Engineer. **Wattage:** 1,000,000 ERP H. **Ad Rates:** Advertising accepted; rates available upon request. **URL:** http://www.katc.com.

14374 ■ KBEB-FM - 106.7
PO Box 60571
Lafayette, LA 70596
Format: Classic Rock. **Owner:** Broadcast Partners, Inc, at above address. **Key Personnel:** Phil Lizotte, Gen. Mgr., Owner. **URL:** http://www.purecountry1067.com/sample-page/eeo-report.

14375 ■ KIKL-FM - 90.9
PO Box 2098
Omaha, NE 68103
Free: 800-525-5683
Format: Contemporary Christian. **Owner:** Educational Media Foundation, 5700 W Oaks Blvd., CA 95765, Free: 800-800434-8400. **ADI:** Lafayette, LA. **Key Personnel:** Mike Novak, President, CEO; Alan Mason, COO. **Wattage:** 8,200. **URL:** http://www.klove.com.

14376 ■ KLAF-TV - 17
1500 Eraste Landry Rd.
Lafayette, LA 70506
Phone: (337)237-1500
Fax: (337)237-2237
Email: contactus@kadn.com
Ad Rates: Noncommercial. **URL:** http://www.klaf.com.

14377 ■ KLFY-TV - 10
1808 Eraste Landry Rd.
Lafayette, LA 70506
Phone: (337)981-4823
Fax: (337)984-8323
Email: news@klfy.com
Format: Full Service; News. **Networks:** CBS. **Owner:** Young Broadcasting Inc., 599 Lexington Ave., New York, NY 10022-6030, Ph: (212)754-7070, Fax: (212)758-1229. **Founded:** 1955. **ADI:** Lafayette, LA. **Key Personnel:** Mike Barras, Gen. Mgr. **Wattage:** 20,300 ERP. **Ad Rates:** Advertising accepted; rates available upon request. **URL:** http://klfy.com.

14378 ■ KLPB-TV - 24
7733 Perkins Rd.
Baton Rouge, LA 70810
Phone: (225)767-5660
Free: 800-272-8161
Format: Public TV. **Simulcasts:** WLPB-TV Baton Rouge, LA. **Networks:** Public Broadcasting Service (PBS); Louisiana Public Broadcasting. **Owner:** Louisiana Public Broadcasting, 7733 Perkins Rd., Baton Rouge, LA 70810, Ph: (225)767-5660, Fax: (225)767-4288. **Founded:** 1981. **Operating Hours:** Continuous. **ADI:** Lafayette, LA. **Key Personnel:** Bob Neese, Contact, bneese@lpb.org. **Wattage:** 50,000. **Ad Rates:** Noncommercial. **URL:** http://beta.lpb.org.

14379 ■ KMDL-FM - 97.3
202A Galcert Rd.
Lafayette, LA 70506
Phone: (318)232-2242
Fax: (318)235-4181
Format: Country. **Networks:** AP. **Owner:** Schilling Media, 301 Leonpacher Rd., Lafayette, LA 70508, Ph: (318)232-9124. **Founded:** 1981. **Operating Hours:** Continuous; 2% network, 98% local. **ADI:** Lafayette, LA. **Key Personnel:** Mike Grimsley, Gen. Mgr. **Wattage:** 50,000. **Ad Rates:** $29-35 for 30 seconds; $45-51 for 60 seconds.

14380 ■ KNEK-AM - 1190
202 Galbert Rd.
Lafayette, LA 70506
Phone: (337)232-1311
Fax: (337)233-3779
Email: events@knek.com
Format: Oldies; Contemporary Hit Radio (CHR). **Owner:** Citadel Broadcasting Corp., 7201 W Lake Mead Blvd., Ste. 400, Las Vegas, NV 89128-8366, Ph: (702)804-5200, Fax: (702)804-8250. **Founded:** 1981. **Operating Hours:** Continuous. **ADI:** Lafayette, LA. **Key Personnel:** Lewis W. Dickey, Jr., President. **Wattage:** 250. **Ad Rates:** Advertising accepted; rates available upon request. $6.30-9.50 for 30 seconds; $8.60-13.05 for 60 seconds. **URL:** http://www.knek.com.

14381 ■ KNEK-FM - 104.7
202 Galbert Rd.
Lafayette, LA 70506
Phone: (337)920-5635
Fax: (337)233-3779
Format: Blues; Oldies. **Networks:** Louisiana. **Owner:** Citadel Broadcasting Corp., 7201 W Lake Mead Blvd., Ste. 400, Las Vegas, NV 89128-8366, Ph: (702)804-5200, Fax: (702)804-8250. **Founded:** 1989. **Operating Hours:** Continuous. **Key Personnel:** Lewis W. Dickey, Jr., President. **Wattage:** 25,000. **Ad Rates:** Noncommercial. **URL:** http://www.knek.com.

14382 ■ KPEL-AM - 1420
1749 Bertrand Dr.
Lafayette, LA 70506
Phone: (337)269-1077
Format: Sports; Talk; News. **Networks:** ABC; CBS; NBC. **Owner:** Townsquare Media Inc., 240 Greenwich Ave., Greenwich, CT 06830-6507, Ph: (203)861-0900. **Founded:** 1950. **Operating Hours:** Continuous. **ADI:** Lafayette, LA. **Key Personnel:** Mike Grimsley, Gen. Mgr., mike.grimsley@townsquaremedia.com; Frank Malambri, Dir. of Sales, frank.malambri@townsquaremedia.com. **Wattage:** 25,000. **Ad Rates:** Advertising accepted; rates available upon request. $35 for 30 seconds; $45 for 60 seconds. **URL:** http://www.espn1420.com.

14383 ■ KQIS-FM - 102.1
PO Box 60571
Lafayette, LA 70596
Format: Contemporary Hit Radio (CHR). **Ad Rates:** Advertising accepted; rates available upon request. **URL:** http://kqis.com.

14384 ■ KRDJ-FM - 93.7
202 Galbert Rd.
Lafayette, LA 70506
Phone: (337)232-1311
Format: Classic Rock. **Owner:** Citadel Broadcasting Corp., 7201 W Lake Mead Blvd., Ste. 400, Las Vegas, NV 89128-8366, Ph: (702)804-5200, Fax: (702)804-8250. **ADI:** Lafayette, LA. **Ad Rates:** Advertising accepted; rates available upon request. **URL:** http://www.rock937fm.com.

14385 ■ KRKA-FM - 103.9
444 Cajundome
Lafayette, LA 70506
Phone: (337)233-6000
Format: Hip Hop. **Owner:** Regent Broadcasting of Lafayette, at above address. **Wattage:** 16,500. **Ad Rates:** Advertising accepted; rates available upon request. **URL:** http://www.1079ishot.com.

14386 ■ KRRQ-FM - 95.5
202 Galbert Rd.
Lafayette, LA 70506
Phone: (337)920-5777
Format: Hip Hop. **Owner:** Citadel Broadcasting Corp., 7201 W Lake Mead Blvd., Ste. 400, Las Vegas, NV

89128-8366, Ph: (702)804-5200, Fax: (702)804-8250. **Operating Hours**: Continuous. **ADI**: Lafayette, LA. **Wattage**: 50,000 ERP. **Ad Rates:** Advertising accepted; rates available upon request. **URL:** http://www.krrq.com.

14387 ■ KSMB-FM - 94.5
202 Galbert Rd.
Lafayette, LA 70506
Phone: (337)232-1311
Format: Sports. **Simulcasts:** KNEK-AM, KRRQ-FM, KXKC-FM. **Networks:** ABC; Fox; CNN Radio; CBS; NBC; ESPN Radio. **Owner:** Citadel Broadcasting Corp., 7201 W Lake Mead Blvd., Ste. 400, Las Vegas, NV 89128-8366, Ph: (702)804-5200, Fax: (702)804-8250. **Founded:** 1964. **Operating Hours**: Continuous. **ADI**: Lafayette, LA. **Wattage**: 100,000 ERP. **Ad Rates:** Noncommercial. **URL:** http://www.ksmb.com.

14388 ■ KTDY-FM - 99.9
1749 Bertrand Dr.
Lafayette, LA 70506
Phone: (337)233-6000
Email: secretary@999ktdy.com
Format: Adult Contemporary; Eighties. **Owner:** Townsquare Media Inc., 2000 Fifth Third Ctr. 511 Walnut St., Cincinnati, OH 45202, Ph: (513)651-1190. **Operating Hours**: Continuous. **ADI**: Lafayette, LA. **Key Personnel:** Frank Malambri, Dir. of Sales, frank.malambri@townsquaremedia.com; Mike Grimsley, Gen. Mgr., mike.grimsley@townsquaremedia.com; Steve Wiley, Contact; Debbie Ray, Contact. **Wattage**: 100,000 ERP. **Ad Rates:** Advertising accepted; rates available upon request. **URL:** http://www.999ktdy.com.

14389 ■ K202DN-FM - 88.3
PO Box 391
Twin Falls, ID 83303
Fax: (208)736-1958
Free: 800-357-4226
Format: Religious; Contemporary Christian. **Owner:** CSN International, PO Box 391, Twin Falls, ID 83303, Ph: (208)736-1958, Fax: (208)736-1958, Free: 800-357-4226. **Key Personnel:** Don Mills, Prog. Dir., Div. Dir. **URL:** http://www.csnradio.com.

14390 ■ KXKC-FM - 99.1
202 Galbert Rd.
Lafayette, LA 70506
Phone: (337)232-1311
Fax: (337)233-3779
Format: Contemporary Country. **Networks:** Independent. **Owner:** Citadel Broadcasting Corp., 7201 W Lake Mead Blvd., Ste. 400, Las Vegas, NV 89128-8366, Ph: (702)804-5200, Fax: (702)804-8250. **Founded:** 1969. **Formerly**: KDEA-FM. **Operating Hours**: Continuous. **ADI**: Lafayette, LA. **Wattage**: 100,000. **Ad Rates:** Noncommercial. **URL:** http://www.nashfm991.com.

LAKE CHARLES

SW LA. Calcasieu Parish. On Calcasieu River, 62 mi. E. of Beaumont, TX. McNeese State University. Pine hardwood timber. Petroleum refining; plastic basics gasoline, caustic, soda ash, chemicals, anhydrous ammonia, catalyst, chlorine, aluminum, synthetic rubber, lumber, bricks, beverages, concrete products manufactured. Agriculture. Rice, cotton, sugar.

14391 ■ Applied Spectroscopy Reviews: An International Journal of Principles, Methods, & Applications
Taylor & Francis Group Journals
c/o Joseph Sneddon, Ed.-in-Ch.
Dept. of Chemical
McNeese State University
Lake Charles, LA 70609
Publisher's E-mail: customerservice@taylorandfrancis.com
Scientific journal covering spectroscopy. **Freq:** 10/year. **Print Method:** Offset. **Trim Size:** 8 1/4 x 10 7/8. **Cols./Page:** 1. **Key Personnel:** Joseph Sneddon, Editor-in-Chief; Yong-Ill Lee, Editor. **ISSN:** 0570--4928 (print); **EISSN:** 1520--569X (electronic). **Subscription Rates:** $1063 Individuals print only; $3780 Institutions online only; $4320 Institutions print & online. **URL:** http://www.tandfonline.com/toc/laps20/current#.UvSc-dIW2qY. **Remarks:** Accepts advertising. **Circ:** (Not Reported).

14392 ■ Contraband
McNeese State University
4205 Ryan St.
Lake Charles, LA 70609
Phone: (337)475-5000
Free: 800-622-3352
Collegiate newspaper. **Freq:** Weekly (Wed.). **Print Method:** Offset. **Trim Size:** 13 1/8 x 22. **Cols./Page:** 6. **Col. Width:** 12.5 picas. **Col. Depth:** 306 agate lines. **Key Personnel:** Brandon Scardigli, Editor; Ross Connor, Editor; Robert Teal, Editor-in-Chief, phone: (337)475-5646. **URL:** http://www.mcneese.edu/policy/faculty_and_student_publications. **Ad Rates:** GLR $4.25; BW $378; 4C $600; SAU $6; PCI $3. **Remarks:** Accepts advertising. **Circ:** ‡4500.

14393 ■ International Journal of Scholarly Academic Intellectual Diversity
National Forum Journals
4000 Lock Ln., Ste. 9
Lake Charles, LA 70605
Peer-reviewed electronic journal covering scholarly academics, intellectualism, and diversity in higher education. **Freq:** Annual. **Key Personnel:** William Kritsonis, PhD, Editor-in-Chief. **ISSN:** 1091--3610 (print). **Alt. Formats:** PDF. **URL:** http://www.nationalforum.com/Journals/IJSAID/IJSAID.htm. **Circ:** (Not Reported).

14394 ■ Lake Charles American Press
Lake Charles American Press
4900 Hwy. 90 E
Lake Charles, LA 70615
Phone: (337)433-3000
Fax: (337)494-4008
Publisher's E-mail: circulation@americanpress.com
General newspaper. **Freq:** Daily and Sun. (morn.). **Print Method:** Offset. **Trim Size:** 12 1/2 x 22 3/4. **Cols./Page:** 6. **Col. Width:** 25 nonpareils. **Col. Depth:** 308 agate lines. **Key Personnel:** Ken Stickney, Executive Editor; Bobby Dower, Managing Editor. **ISSN:** 0739--1196 (print). **Subscription Rates:** $162 Individuals Daily and Sundays; $126 Individuals Fridays, Saturdays and Sundays only; $144 Individuals Weekdays only. **URL:** http://www.americanpress.com. **Ad Rates:** GLR $1.74; SAU $24.56; GLR $2.94; SAU $28.24. **Remarks:** Accepts display and classified advertising. **Circ:** Mon.-Fri. **★36270**, Sun. **★39825**, Sat. **★35775**.

14395 ■ McNeese Review
McNeese State University
4205 Ryan St.
Lake Charles, LA 70609
Phone: (337)475-5000
Free: 800-622-3352
Scholarly journal covering articles and essays in the liberal arts. **Freq:** Annual. **Print Method:** Offset. **Key Personnel:** Jacob Blevins, Editor, phone: (337)475-5309. **ISSN:** 0885--467X (print). **Subscription Rates:** $7 Individuals including postage; $9 Canada and Mexico including postage; $12 Other countries including postage. **Remarks:** Advertising not accepted. **Circ:** Combined 200.

14396 ■ Microchemical Journal
RELX Group P.L.C.
c/o J. Sneddon, Ed.
McNeese State University
Lake Charles, LA 70609
Phone: (337)475-5781
Fax: (337)475-5234
Publisher's E-mail: amsterdam@relx.com
Focuses on microscale chemical analysis including clinically significant methods and procedures. **Freq:** 6/yr. **Trim Size:** 6 7/8 x 10. **Key Personnel:** J. Sneddon, Editor. **ISSN:** 0026--265X (print). **Subscription Rates:** $1978 Institutions print; $824 Institutions online. **URL:** http://www.journals.elsevier.com/microchemical-journal. **Remarks:** Accepts advertising. **Circ:** (Not Reported).

14397 ■ National Forum of Applied Educational Research Journal
National Forum Journals
4000 Lock Ln., Ste. 9
Lake Charles, LA 70605
Peer-reviewed scholarly journal for educational theoreticians and school practitioners and professionals. **Freq:** Semiannual Latest Edition:Volume 29, Number 3, 2016. **Trim Size:** 6 x 9. **Key Personnel:** William Kritsonis, PhD, Editor-in-Chief; Mary Alice Kritsonis, Executive Editor. **ISSN:** 0895--3880 (print). **Alt. Formats:** PDF. **URL:** http://www.nationalforum.com/Journals/NFAERJ/NFAERJ.htm. **Ad Rates:** GLR $25. **Remarks:** Accepts advertising. **Circ:** 7500.

14398 ■ National Forum of Education Administration and Supervision Journal
National Forum Journals
4000 Lock Ln., Ste. 9
Lake Charles, LA 70605
Scholarly refereed, peer-reviewed journal covering educational management and leadership. **Freq:** Quarterly. **Trim Size:** 6 x 9. **Key Personnel:** William Allan Kritsonis, PhD, Editor-in-Chief. **ISSN:** 0888--8132 (print). **Alt. Formats:** PDF. **URL:** http://www.nationalforum.com. **Remarks:** Accepts advertising. **Circ:** 7500.

14399 ■ National Forum of Special Education Journal
National Forum Journals
4000 Lock Ln., Ste. 9
Lake Charles, LA 70605
Peer-reviewed scholarly electronic journal covering special education. **Key Personnel:** William Allan Kritsonis, PhD, Editor-in-Chief; Charles E. Sellers, Web Administrator; Mary Alice Kritsonis, EdD, Executive Editor. **ISSN:** 1043--2167 (print). **Alt. Formats:** PDF. **URL:** http://www.nationalforum.com/Journals/NFSEJ/NFSEJ.htm. **Circ:** 7,500.

14400 ■ National Forum of Teacher Education Journal
National Forum Journals
4000 Lock Ln., Ste. 9
Lake Charles, LA 70605
Peer-reviewed scholarly journal covering teacher education with an urban emphasis. **Freq:** Semiannual Latest Edition:Volume 26, Number 3, 2016. **Trim Size:** 6 x 9. **Key Personnel:** William Kritsonis, PhD, Editor-in-Chief. **ISSN:** 1049--2558 (print). **Alt. Formats:** PDF. **URL:** http://www.nationalforum.com/Journals/NFTEJ/NFTEJ.htm. **Ad Rates:** GLR $25. **Remarks:** Accepts display advertising. **Circ:** 7500.

14401 ■ KBIU-FM - 103.3
425 Broad St.
Lake Charles, LA 70601
Phone: (337)439-3300
Free: 866-930-5225
Format: Adult Contemporary. **Key Personnel:** Jim Ray, Mktg. Mgr., VP, jim.ray@cumulus.com; Lisa D. Sonnier, Gen. Sales Mgr., lisa.daniels@cumulus.com. **Ad Rates:** Advertising accepted; rates available upon request. **URL:** http://www.kbiu.com.

14402 ■ KBXG-FM - 99.5
900 N Lakeshore Dr.
Lake Charles, LA 70601
Phone: (337)433-1641
Format: Contemporary Country. **Founded:** Sept. 07, 2006. **Ad Rates:** Noncommercial. **URL:** http://gator995.com.

14403 ■ KELB-FM - 100.5
210 W Sale Rd., Ste. 74
Lake Charles, LA 70605
Phone: (337)477-1747
Email: support@christiannetcast.com
Format: Religious. **Founded:** May 17, 2000. **Key Personnel:** Barry McCall, President. **Ad Rates:** Noncommercial; underwriting available. **URL:** http://www.kelbradio.com.

14404 ■ K51EC - 51
PO Box A
Santa Ana, CA 92711
Free: 888-731-1000
Owner: Trinity Broadcasting Network Inc., PO Box A, Santa Ana, CA 92711, Ph: (714)832-2950, Free: 888-731-1000.

14405 ■ KHLA-FM - 92.9
900 N Lakeshore Dr.
Lake Charles, LA 70601
Phone: (337)433-1641
Fax: (337)433-2999
Format: Adult Contemporary; Oldies. **Owner:** Apex Broadcasting Inc., 2294 Clements Ferry Rd., Charleston, SC 29492. **Founded:** 1965. **Operating Hours**: Continuous. **ADI**: Lake Charles, LA. **Wattage**: 100,000

Circulation: ★ = AAM; △ or • = BPA; ♦ = CAC; ❑ = VAC; ⊕ = PO Statement; ‡ = Publisher's Report; Boldface figures = sworn; Light figures = estimated.

ERP. **Ad Rates:** $30 for 30 seconds; $35 for 60 seconds. KLCL, KRAW.

14406 ■ KJMH-FM - 107.5
900 N Lakeshore Dr.
Lake Charles, LA 70601
Phone: (337)433-1641
Format: Hip Hop; Blues. **Owner:** Townsquare Media Inc., 240 Greenwich Ave., Greenwich, CT 06830-6507, Ph: (203)861-0900. **Founded:** 1998. **Formerly:** KRAW-FM. **Operating Hours:** Continuous. **Key Personnel:** Erik Tee, Dir. of Programs, eriktee@townsquaremedia.com; Sara Cormier, Contact, saracormier@townsquaremedia.com. **Wattage:** 50,000. **Ad Rates:** Advertising accepted; rates available upon request. Combined advertising rates available with KWLA, KLCL. **URL:** http://www.107jamz.com.

14407 ■ KKGB-FM - 101.3
425 Broad St.
Lake Charles, LA 70601
Phone: (337)439-3300
Format: Classic Rock. **Owner:** Cumulus Broadcasting Inc., 3280 Peachtree Rd. NW, Ste. 2300, Atlanta, GA 30305-2447, Ph: (404)949-0700, Fax: (404)949-0740. **Founded:** 1990. **Operating Hours:** 5:00 a.m. - 7:00 p.m. Monday - Friday; 10:00 a.m. - 4:00 p.m. Saturday - Sunday. **Key Personnel:** Jim Ray, Contact, jim.ray@cumulus.com. **Wattage:** 12,000 ERP. **Ad Rates:** Advertising accepted; rates available upon request. **URL:** http://www.kkgb.com.

14408 ■ KLCL-AM
900 N Lakeshore Dr.
Lake Charles, LA 70601-3067
Phone: (337)433-1641
Fax: (337)433-2999
Format: Cajun; Country. **Owner:** Apex Broadcasting Inc., 2294 Clements Ferry Rd., Charleston, SC 29492. **Founded:** 1935. **Formerly:** KPLC-AM. **ADI:** Lake Charles, LA. **Wattage:** 5,000 Day; 500 Night. **Ad Rates:** $14-20 for 30 seconds; $20-28 for 60 seconds. **Mailing address:** PO Box 3067, Lake Charles, LA 70601-3067. **URL:** http://cajunradio.com/.

14409 ■ KLTL-TV - 18
7733 Perkins Rd.
Baton Rouge, LA 70810
Phone: (225)767-5660
Free: 800-272-8161
Format: Public TV. **Simulcasts:** WLPB-TV Baton Rouge, LA. **Networks:** Public Broadcasting Service (PBS); Louisiana Public Broadcasting. **Owner:** Louisiana Public Broadcasting, 7733 Perkins Rd., Baton Rouge, LA 70810, Ph: (225)767-5660, Fax: (225)767-4288. **Founded:** 1981. **Operating Hours:** Continuous. **ADI:** Lake Charles, LA. **Key Personnel:** Bob Neese, Contact, bneese@lpb.org. **Wattage:** 55,000. **URL:** http://beta.lpb.org.

14410 ■ KNGT-FM - 99.5
900 N Lakeshore Dr.
Lake Charles, LA 70601
Phone: (337)433-1641
Format: Country. **Networks:** ABC. **Owner:** Townsquare Media Inc., 240 Greenwich Ave., Greenwich, CT 06830-6507, Ph: (203)861-0900. **Founded:** 1973. **Operating Hours:** Continuous. **Key Personnel:** Erik Tee, Dept. Mgr.; Todd Stone, Music Dir., Prog. Dir., toddstone@gapbroadcasting.com; Sara Cormier, Gen. Mgr., saracormier@gapbroadcasting.com; Lance Knoll, Dir. of Sales; Leslie Guidry, Gen. Mgr. **Wattage:** 230. **Ad Rates:** Advertising accepted; rates available upon request. **URL:** http://www.gator995.com.

14411 ■ KOJO-FM - 91.1
601 Washington St.
Alexandria, LA 71301
Fax: (318)449-9954
Free: 888-408-0201
Format: Religious. **Owner:** Radio Maria USA, 601 Washington St., Alexandria, LA 71301, Ph: (318)561-6145, Fax: (318)449-9954, Free: 888-408-0201. **Founded:** May 25, 2000. **ADI:** Lake Charles, LA. **Wattage:** 4,000 H;14,000 V. **Ad Rates:** Noncommercial. **URL:** http://www.radiomaria.us.

14412 ■ KPLC-TV - 7
320 Division St.
Lake Charles, LA 70601
Phone: (337)439-9071
Fax: (337)437-7600
Format: Commercial TV. **Networks:** NBC. **Owner:** Raycom Media Inc., 201 Monroe St., RSA Twr., 20th Fl., Montgomery, AL 36104-3731, Ph: (334)206-1400. **Founded:** 1954. **Operating Hours:** 6 a.m.-2 a.m.; 75% network, 25% local. **ADI:** Lake Charles, LA. **Key Personnel:** John Ware, Gen. Sales Mgr.; Frank Brucks, Chief Engineer; Timothy Bourgeois, Dir. of Mktg., Dir. of Production; Jim Serra, Gen. Mgr., VP, jserra@kplctv.com. **Ad Rates:** Advertising accepted; rates available upon request. **Mailing address:** PO Box 1490, Lake Charles, LA 70601. **URL:** http://www.kplctv.com.

14413 ■ KRLR-FM - 89.1
PO Box 779002
Rocklin, CA 95677-9972
Fax: (916)251-1901
Format: Contemporary Christian. **Owner:** Educational Media Foundation, PO Box 2098, Omaha, NE 68103-2098, Free: 800-434-8400. **Key Personnel:** Mike Novak, President, CEO; Alan Mason, COO. **Wattage:** 001 H;16,000 V. **URL:** http://www.klove.com.

14414 ■ KTSR-FM - 92.1
900 N Lakeshore Dr.
Lake Charles, LA 70601
Email: radio@ktsr.com
Format: Classic Rock. **Founded:** 1964. **Formerly:** KTAW-FM. **Operating Hours:** Continuous; 100% local. **ADI:** Waco-Temple-Bryan, TX. **Key Personnel:** Jay Socol, News Dir.; Roger Garrett, Dir. of Programs; Sam Jones, Gen. Sales Mgr.; Ben Downs, Gen. Mgr. **Wattage:** 3,000. **Ad Rates:** $10-21 per unit. **URL:** http://kissfm921.com.

14415 ■ KXZZ-AM - 1580
311 Alamo St.
Lake Charles, LA 70601
Phone: (337)439-3300
Format: Urban Contemporary; Sports. **Networks:** CBS. **Owner:** Dixie Broadcasters, Inc., at above address. **Founded:** 1947. **Formerly:** KLOU-AM. **Operating Hours:** Continuous. **ADI:** Lake Charles, LA. **Key Personnel:** Mike Mitchell, Gen. Sales Mgr; Brian Robinson, Contact. **Wattage:** 1,000 KW. **Ad Rates:** Advertising accepted; rates available upon request. $6-17 for 30 seconds; $10-21 for 60 seconds. Combined advertising rates available with KBLU-FM. **URL:** http://www.kxzz1580am.com/.

14416 ■ KYKZ-FM - 96.1
425 Broad St.
Lake Charles, LA 70601
Phone: (337)439-3300
Free: 800-737-3696
Format: Country. **Owner:** Cumulus Broadcasting Inc., 3280 Peachtree Rd. NW, Ste. 2300, Atlanta, GA 30305-2447, Ph: (404)949-0700, Fax: (404)949-0740. **Founded:** 1976. **Operating Hours:** Continuous. **ADI:** Lake Charles, LA. **Wattage:** 100,000 ERP. **Ad Rates:** Advertising accepted; rates available upon request. Combined advertising rates available with KKGB, KBIU, KXZZ. **URL:** http://www.kykz.com.

14417 ■ KYLC-FM - 90.3
1411 Parish Rd.
Lake Charles, LA 70611
Phone: (337)217-0252
Format: Religious. **Ad Rates:** Noncommercial.

14418 ■ KZWA-FM - 104.9
305 Enterprise Blvd.
Lake Charles, LA 70601
Phone: (337)491-9955
Email: info@kzwafm.com
Format: Jazz; Hip Hop; Zydeco; Blues; Gospel; Urban Contemporary; Adult Contemporary. **Networks:** ABC. **Owner:** Faye Brown-Blackwell, at above address. **Founded:** Apr. 1991. **Operating Hours:** 4:00 a.m. - Midnight Monday - Friday; 7:00 a.m. - Midnight Saturday; 6:00 a.m. - Midnight Sunday. **Wattage:** 25,000 ERP. **Ad Rates:** Advertising accepted; rates available upon request. **URL:** http://www.kzwafm.com.

LAROSE

SE LA. Lafourche Parish. 2 mi. N. of Delta.

14419 ■ The Lafourche Gazette
Lafourche Gazette News
PO Box 1450
Larose, LA 70373
Phone: (985)693-7229
Publication E-mail: lafgazette@thelafourchegazette.com
Community newspaper. **Freq:** Semiweekly (Wed. and Sun.). **Print Method:** Offset. **Trim Size:** 13 x 21. **Cols./Page:** 6. **Col. Width:** 2 inches. **Col. Depth:** 301 agate lines. **URL:** http://www.tlgnewspaper.com. **Ad Rates:** BW $871.92; 4C $270; PCI $6.92; BW $871.92; 4C $1,075.14; PCI $6.92. **Remarks:** Accepts advertising. **Circ:** Free ‡14000.

14420 ■ KLEB-AM - 1600
11603 Hwy. 308
Larose, LA 70373
Phone: (985)798-7792
Fax: (985)798-7793
Format: Cajun; Zydeco; Talk; Sports; Oldies. **Simulcasts:** KLRZ-FM. **Owner:** Coastal Broadcasting Systems Inc., 1602 Rte. 47, 2nd Fl., Rio Grande, NJ 08242, Ph: (609)522-1987. **Founded:** 1951. **Operating Hours:** Continuous. **Key Personnel:** Buddy Miller, Production Mgr. **Local Programs:** *Hot Sauce Express*, Monday Tuesday Wednesday Thursday Friday 6:00 a.m. - 10:00 a.m.; *Talk on the Bayou*, Monday Tuesday Wednesday Thursday Friday 10:00 a.m. - 12:00 p.m. **Wattage:** 7,500 Day; 250 Night. **Ad Rates:** $10 for 30 seconds; $13 for 60 seconds. KLRZ-FM. **Mailing address:** PO Box 1350, Larose, LA 70373. **URL:** http://www.klrzfm.com.

14421 ■ KLRZ-FM - 100.3
11603 Hwy. 308
Larose, LA 70373
Phone: (985)798-7792
Fax: (985)798-7793
Email: klrz@viscom.net
Format: Cajun. **Owner:** Coastal Broadcasting of Larose, Inc., at above address. **Ad Rates:** Advertising accepted; rates available upon request. **Mailing address:** PO Box 1350, Larose, LA 70373. **URL:** http://www.klrzfm.com.

LECOMPTE

14422 ■ Neogram
United States Neapolitan Mastiff Club
c/o Mike McDonald, Treasurer
40 Sam Carroll Rd.
Lecompte, LA 71364
Publisher's E-mail: usnmctreasurer@gmail.com
Freq: Annual. **Subscription Rates:** $35 Members; $50 Members family members.; $6 Nonmembers dependent on availability. **URL:** http://neapolitan.org/neogram.html. **Remarks:** Advertising not accepted. **Circ:** (Not Reported).

LEESVILLE

W LA. Vernon Parish. 50 mi. SW of Alexandria. Garment factory. Lumber mills. Pine, hardwood timber. Agriculture. Cotton, corn, sweet potatoes.

14423 ■ Leesville Daily Leader
News Leader Inc.
206 East Texas St.
Leesville, LA 71446
Phone: (337)239-3444
Fax: (337)238-1152
Daily newspaper. **Founded:** 1898. **Freq:** Irregular Tues.-Fri. (morn.); Sun. (morn.). **Print Method:** Offset. **Cols./Page:** 6. **Col. Width:** 2 1/8 inches. **Col. Depth:** 21 inches. **Key Personnel:** Brian Trahan, Publisher, phone: (337)239-3444; Destiney Jefferson, Manager, Circulation; Tammy Sharp, Editor. **Subscription Rates:** $72 Individuals; $125 Out of area. **URL:** http://www.leesvilledailyleader.com/. **Mailing address:** PO Box 619, Leesville, LA 71446. **Ad Rates:** BW $1,392.30; 4C $1,842.30; SAU $11.05. **Remarks:** Advertising accepted; rates available upon request. **Circ:** Paid ‡6460, Free ‡9153.

14424 ■ KJAE-FM - 93.5
101 Lees Ln.
Leesville, LA 71446-3643
Phone: (337)239-3402
Fax: (337)238-9283
Format: Country. **Networks:** ABC. **Owner:** Penny Scogin, at above address. **Founded:** 1979. **Operating Hours:** Continuous. **Key Personnel:** Penny Scogin, Gen. Mgr. **Wattage:** 7,500. **Ad Rates:** $6.70-12.65 for

30 seconds; $9.45-14.95 for 60 seconds. **URL:** http://www.kjae935.com.

14425 ■ KLLA-AM - 1570
101 Lees Ln.
Leesville, LA 71446-3643
Phone: (318)239-3402
Fax: (318)238-9283
Format: Oldies; Classic Rock. **Founded:** 1956. **Operating Hours:** Sunrise-sunset. **Key Personnel:** Ed Marshall, Gen. Mgr. **Wattage:** 630 Day; 006 Night. **Ad Rates:** Noncommercial.

14426 ■ KROK-FM - 95.7
168 KVVP Dr.
Leesville, LA 71446-5817
Phone: (337)537-9292
Fax: (337)537-4152
Format: Adult Album Alternative; Classic Rock. **Networks:** Independent. **Owner:** West Central Broadcasting Company Inc., at above address. **Founded:** 1985. **Operating Hours:** Continuous. **Wattage:** 25,000. **Ad Rates:** $10.53 for 30 seconds; $17.65 for 60 seconds. Combined advertising rates available with KVVP-FM. **URL:** http://www.krok.com.

MANSFIELD

W LA. De Soto Parish. 35 mi. S. of Shreveport. Manufactures lumber, truck trailers, dragline buckets, garments. Pine and hardwood timber. Oil and gas production. Oil refinery. Agriculture. Cotton, soybeans, corn, wheat, dairy and beef cattle.

14427 ■ KJVC-FM - 92.7
805 Polk St.
Mansfield, LA 71052
Phone: (318)871-5582
Fax: (318)871-2927
Email: kjvc@kjvcfm.com
Format: Country. **Owner:** Metropolitan Radio Group Inc., 2010 S Stewart Ave., Springfield, MO 65804, Ph: (417)862-0852, Fax: (417)862-9079, Free: 800-481-7677. **Operating Hours:** Continuous. **Wattage:** 3,000. **Ad Rates:** Noncommercial. **URL:** http://www.kjvcfm.com/new.

MANY

W LA. Sabine Parish. 68 mi. S. of Shreveport. Tourism. Resort. Recreation. Fishing. Scenic gardens. Museum and park. Lumber mills. Pine, hardwood timber. Oil, gas. Agriculture. Cattle. Dairying. Poultry.

14428 ■ KAVK-FM
PO Box 2440
Tupelo, MS 38801-2440
Format: Religious. **Owner:** American Family Radio, at above address. **Wattage:** 12,000 ERP.

14429 ■ KTEZ-FM - 99.9
605 San Antonio Ave.
Many, LA 71449
Phone: (318)352-9696
Fax: (318)357-9595
Free: 866-357-1007
Format: Adult Contemporary. **Owner:** Baldridge Dumas Communications, 605 San Antonio Ave., Many, LA 71449. **Wattage:** 6,000. **Ad Rates:** Advertising accepted; rates available upon request.

KVCL-FM - See Winnfield, LA

14430 ■ KWLA-AM - 1400
605 San Antonio Ave.
Many, LA 71449
Phone: (318)256-5924
Fax: (318)256-0950
Format: Talk. **Owner:** Baldridge Dumas Communications, 605 San Antonio Ave., Many, LA 71449. **Founded:** 1962. **Operating Hours:** Continuous. **Wattage:** 1,000. **Ad Rates:** Noncommercial. Combined advertising rates available with KWLV-FM.

14431 ■ KWLV-FM - 107.1
605 San Antonio Ave.
Many, LA 71449
Phone: (318)256-5924
Fax: (318)256-0950
Free: 877-308-5958
Format: Country. **Networks:** Satellite Music Network. **Owner:** Baldridge Dumas Communications, 605 San Antonio Ave., Many, LA 71449. **Founded:** Nov. 1978. **Operating Hours:** Continuous. **Key Personnel:** Rhonda Benson, Gen. Mgr., rhondabenson256@hotmail.com; Tedd Wayne-Dumas, Contact, twdumas@bellsouth.net. **Wattage:** 25,000 ERP. **Ad Rates:** $7-12 for 30 seconds; $9-18 for 60 seconds. Combined advertising rates available with KWLA-A.

MERMENTAU

14432 ■ K45DI - 45
PO Box A
Santa Ana, CA 92711
Phone: (714)832-2950
Free: 888-731-1000
Owner: Trinity Broadcasting Network Inc., PO Box A, Santa Ana, CA 92711, Ph: (714)832-2950, Free: 888-731-1000. **URL:** http://www.tbn.org.

METAIRIE

SE LA. Jefferson Parish. 5 mi. NW of New Orleans. Manufactures fabricated wire, concrete, wood products, automobile parts and accessories, carbon paper, electronic computers, fabricated structural steel. Agriculture. Sugarcane, cotton.

14433 ■ Daily Journal of Commerce
New Orleans Publishing Group Inc.
111 Veterans Blvd., Ste. 1440
Metairie, LA 70005
Phone: (504)834-9292
Publisher's E-mail: mail@nopg.com
Trade newspaper covering construction news in Louisiana and Mississippi. **Founded:** June 1922. **Freq:** Daily. **Print Method:** Offset. **Trim Size:** 14 1/2 x 23. **Cols./Page:** 6. **Col. Width:** 2 inches. **Col. Depth:** 21 inches. **Key Personnel:** Anne N. Lovas, General Manager, phone: (504)293-9216; Becky Naquin, Assistant Editor, phone: (504)293-9219; Christian Moises, Editor, phone: (504)293-9249; Lisa Blossman, Publisher, Senior Vice President. **USPS:** 381-800. **Subscription Rates:** $559 Individuals online and print; $405 Individuals 6 months; $275 Individuals 3 months. **URL:** http://djcgulfcoast.com; http://www.djcgulfcoast.com. **Ad Rates:** PCI $10. **Remarks:** Color advertising not accepted. **Circ:** (Not Reported).

14434 ■ Louisiana Life Magazine
Louisiana Life Magazine
110 Veterans Blvd., Ste. 123
Metairie, LA 70005
Phone: (504)828-1380
Fax: (504)828-1385
Regional magazine. **Freq:** 6/year. **Print Method:** Offset. **Trim Size:** 8 1/8 x 10 7/8. **Cols./Page:** 3. **Col. Width:** 31 nonpareils. **Col. Depth:** 133 agate lines. **Key Personnel:** Eric Gernhauser, Art Director, phone: (504)830-7269; Errol Laborde, Editor-in-Chief, phone: (504)828-1380; Morgan Packard, Editor, phone: (504)830-7227. **ISSN:** 0899--0093 (print). **Subscription Rates:** $10 Individuals; $18 Two years; $24 Individuals 3 years. **URL:** http://myneworleans.com/My-New-Orleans/Our-Magazines/. **Formerly:** Louisiana Life--Magazine of the Bayou State. **Ad Rates:** BW $3,150; 4C $3,750. **Remarks:** Accepts advertising. **Circ:** ‡40001.

14435 ■ New Orleans CityBusiness
New Orleans CityBusiness
3445 N Causeway Blvd., Ste. 901
Metairie, LA 70002
Phone: (504)834-9292
Fax: (504)832-3550
Publisher's E-mail: mail@nopg.com
Business newspaper (Tabloid). **Freq:** Weekly. **Print Method:** Web press. **Key Personnel:** Lisa Blossman, Publisher, phone: (504)293-9226; Greg LaRose, Editor. **Subscription Rates:** $129 Individuals print and online; $99 Individuals online only. **URL:** http://neworleanscitybusiness.com. **Remarks:** Advertising accepted; rates available upon request. **Circ:** Combined 12800.

14436 ■ New Orleans Magazine
New Orleans Publishing Group Inc.
111 Veterans Blvd., Ste. 1440
Metairie, LA 70005
Phone: (504)834-9292
Publisher's E-mail: mail@nopg.com
New Orleans lifestyle magazine. **Freq:** Monthly. **Print Method:** Offset. **Trim Size:** 8 1/8 x 11. **Cols./Page:** 3. **Col. Width:** 13 picas. **Col. Depth:** 72 picas. **Key Personnel:** Kristi Ferrante, Executive Assistant, Office Manager; Todd Matherne, Chief Executive Officer; Errol Laborde, Editor-in-Chief, phone: (504)830-7235; Morgan Packard, Managing Editor, phone: (504)830-7227. **ISSN:** 0897--8174 (print). **USPS:** 002-015. **Subscription Rates:** $19.95 Individuals print; $33 Two years print; $45 Individuals print, 3 years. **URL:** http://www.myneworleans.com/New-Orleans-Magazine. **Ad Rates:** 4C $4,300. **Remarks:** Accepts advertising. **Circ:** (Not Reported).

14437 ■ The Oxcart
Society for Costa Rica Collectors
c/o Raul Hernandez, President
4204 Haring Rd.
Metairie, LA 70006
Freq: Quarterly. **ISSN:** 0737--0954 (print). **Subscription Rates:** Included in membership; $2 Single issue back issues. **Alt. Formats:** PDF. **URL:** http://www.socorico.org/oxcart.php. **Remarks:** Accepts advertising. **Circ:** (Not Reported).

14438 ■ Thema
THEMA Literary Journal
PO Box 8747
Metairie, LA 70011-8747
Theme-related literary journal. **Key Personnel:** Virginia Howard, Editor; Gail Howard, Editor. **ISSN:** 1041--4851 (print). **Subscription Rates:** $30 Individuals; $40 Other countries; $15 Single issue USA; $25 Other countries single issue. **URL:** http://themaliterarysociety.com. **Remarks:** Advertising not accepted. **Circ:** (Not Reported).

14439 ■ Cox Communications Louisiana
2121 Airline Dr.
Metairie, LA 70001
Phone: (504)304-7345
Owner: Cox Cable Communications, at above address, Ph: (404)843-5000, Fax: (401)828-3835. **Founded:** 1982. **Formerly:** Cox Cable of New Orleans. **Cities Served:** Orleans, Jefferson and St. Charles Parishes, LA.; 8 community access channels. **URL:** http://www.cox.com.

14440 ■ KGLA-AM - 1540
3850 N Causeway Blvd.
Metairie, LA 70002
Phone: (504)799-4242
Email: sales@kgla.tv
Format: Hispanic. **Founded:** 1969. **Operating Hours:** 6 a.m.-10 p.m. **Key Personnel:** Mario Zavala, Mgr. of Admin., Prog. Dir., mario@kgla.tv. **Wattage:** 1,000. **Ad Rates:** $8 for 30 seconds; $18 for 60 seconds. **URL:** http://www.tropical1540.com.

14441 ■ KGLA-TV - 42
3850 N Causeway Blvd., Ste. 442
Metairie, LA 70002
Phone: (504)799-4242
Fax: (504)799-3434
Key Personnel: Ernesto Schweikert, III, Gen. Mgr., ernesto@kgla.tv; Mario Raul Zavala, Mgr. of Admin., Prog. Dir., mario@kgla.tv. **Wattage:** 1,000.

14442 ■ KNOU-FM - 104.5
4539 N I 10 Service Rd. W, Fl. 3
Metairie, LA 70006
Phone: (504)887-9509
Format: Hip Hop.

14443 ■ WASO-AM - 730
3313 Kingman St.
Metairie, LA 70006
Phone: (504)888-8255
Fax: (504)888-8329
Email: info@hottalkradio.com
Format: Talk; News; Sports. **Networks:** NBC; CNN Radio; Mutual Broadcasting System. **Owner:** America First Communication Inc., at above address. **Founded:** 1954. **Formerly:** WARB-AM. **Operating Hours:** 6 a.m.-10 p.m.; 25% network, 75% local. **Wattage:** 250. **Ad Rates:** $13-24 for 15 seconds; $18-35 for 30 seconds; $25-50 for 60 seconds.

14444 ■ WCKW-FM - 92.3
3501 N Causeway Blvd., Ste. 700
Metairie, LA 70002-3624

Circulation: ★ = AAM; △ or • = BPA; ♦ = CAC; ❑ = VAC; ⊕ = PO Statement; ‡ = Publisher's Report; Boldface figures = sworn; Light figures = estimated.

Format: Adult Contemporary. **Owner:** River Parish Radio, LLC, at above address. **Founded:** 1966. **Operating Hours**: Continuous. **Wattage**: 100,000. **Ad Rates:** Noncommercial.

14445 ■ WFNO-AM
3540 S I-10 Service Rd. W
111 Veterans Blvd. 18th Fl.
Metairie, LA 70001
Format: Hispanic. **Wattage**: 5,000 Day; 750 Night.

14446 ■ WGNO-TV - 26
1 Galleria Blvd., Ste. 850
Metairie, LA 70001
Phone: (504)525-3838
Fax: (504)569-0908
Format: Commercial TV. **Networks:** ABC. **Owner:** The Tribune Media Co., 435 N Michigan Ave., Chicago, IL 60611-4066, Ph: (312)222-9100, Fax: (312)222-4206, Free: 800-874-2863. **Founded:** 1967. **ADI**: New Orleans, LA. **Key Personnel:** Linda Anderson, Sales Mgr., lbanderson@wgno.com; Jeff Funk, Div. Dir., jfunk@wgno.com; Gary English, Bus. Dev. Mgr., genglish@wgno.com; John Cruse, Gen. Mgr., jcruse@wgno.com. **Wattage**: 1,000,000 ERP. **Ad Rates:** Advertising accepted; rates available upon request. **URL:** http://wgno.com.

14447 ■ WLAE-TV - 32
3330 N Causeway Blvd., Ste. 345
Metairie, LA 70002
Fax: (504)840-9838
Email: info@wlae.com
Format: Public TV; Educational. **Networks:** Public Broadcasting Service (PBS). **Owner:** Educational Broadcasting Foundation Inc., 3330 N Causeway Blvd., Metairie, LA 70002. **Founded:** 1982. **Operating Hours**: Continuous. **ADI**: New Orleans, LA. **Key Personnel:** Ron Yager, Gen. Mgr., VP. **Wattage**: 2,900,000. **Ad Rates:** Noncommercial. **URL:** http://www.wlae.com.

14448 ■ WMXZ-FM - 95.7
3525 N Causeway Blvd., Ste. 1053
Metairie, LA 70002
Fax: (504)833-8560
Format: Adult Contemporary. **Networks:** Independent. **Founded:** 1957. **Formerly**: WBYU-FM. **Operating Hours**: Continuous; 100% local. **Key Personnel:** Ric Frances, Gen. Mgr.; Ala Strzesniewski, Sales Mgr.; Bruce Bond, Dir. of Programs; Thea Broussard, News Dir; Pamela Sharp-Brown, Contact. **Wattage**: 100,000. **Ad Rates:** $15-100 for 60 seconds.

14449 ■ WNOL-TV - 38
One Galleria Blvd., Ste. 850
Metairie, LA 70001
Phone: (504)525-3838
Email: wnoltv@tribune.com
Format: Commercial TV. **Networks:** Warner Brothers Studios. **Founded:** 1984. **Operating Hours**: Continuous except Mon. 1 a.m.-6 a.m. **ADI**: New Orleans, LA. **Key Personnel:** Jeff Funk, Div. Dir.; Larry Nuss, Sales Mgr.; Linda Anderson, Sales Mgr.; John Cruse, Gen. Mgr., jcruse@wgno.com; Connie Ernst Brown, Sales Mgr., conniebrown@abc26.com. **Ad Rates:** Advertising accepted; rates available upon request. **URL:** http://wgno.com/tag/nola38.

14450 ■ WPXL-TV - 49
3900 Veterans Memorial Blvd., Ste. 202
Metairie, LA 70002
Phone: (504)887-9795
Fax: (504)887-1518
Owner: ION Media Networks Inc., 601 Clearwater Park Rd., West Palm Beach, FL 33401-6233, Ph: (561)659-4122, Fax: (561)659-4252. **URL:** http://www.ionmedia.tv.

14451 ■ WTIX-FM - 94.3
4539 N I-10 Service Rd., 3rd Fl.
Metairie, LA 70006
Phone: (504)454-9000
Fax: (504)454-9002
Format: Oldies. **URL:** http://wtixfm.com.

14452 ■ WVOG-AM - 600
2730 Loumor Ave.
Metairie, LA 70001
Phone: (504)831-6941
Fax: (504)831-2647
Format: Gospel. **Networks:** Interstate Radio; Sun Radio. **Owner:** F.W. Robbert Broadcasting Company Inc., at above address. **Founded:** 1969. **Formerly**: WWOM-AM. **Operating Hours**: 5:30 a.m.-9:00 p.m. **Key Personnel:** Eric Westenberger, Station Mgr.; Eric Martin, Dir. of Sales, Prog. Dir.; Fred P. Westenberger, President. **Wattage**: 1,000. **Ad Rates:** $8.50 for 30 seconds; $10 for 60 seconds. **URL:** http://www.600wvog.com.

14453 ■ WYES-TV - 12
111 Veterans Blvd., Ste. 250
Metairie, LA 70005
Phone: (504)486-5511
Email: info@wyes.org
Format: Public TV. **Networks:** Public Broadcasting Service (PBS). **Owner:** Greater New Orleans Educational Television Foundation, 916 Navarre Ave., New Orleans, LA 70124, Ph: (504)486-5511. **Founded:** 1957. **Operating Hours**: Continuous. **ADI**: New Orleans, LA. **Key Personnel:** Randall Feldman, President. **Local Programs**: *Informed Sources*, Friday 7:00 p.m. **Wattage**: 316,000 (Visual). **Ad Rates:** Noncommercial. **URL:** http://www.wyes.org.

MINDEN

NW LA. Webster Parish. 30 mi. E. of Shreveport. Manufactures processed meat, fishing tackle, portable buildings, rubber roll covers, corrugated containers, air louvers and dampers, electric power, boats, trucks, trailers, generators, logging equipment. Oil wells. Agriculture. Dairying.

14454 ■ Minden Press-Herald
Minden Press-Herald
203 Gleason St.
Minden, LA 71055
Phone: (318)377-1866
Fax: (318)377-1895
Newspaper. **Freq:** Daily (eve.). **Print Method:** Offset. **Cols./Page:** 6. **Col. Width:** 26 nonpareils. **Col. Depth:** 294 agate lines. **Key Personnel:** Gregg Parks, Publisher, phone: (318)377-1866; Bruce Franklin, Managing Editor, phone: (318)377-1866; Dennis Philebar, Director, Production; Telina Rimsky, Manager, Sales. **Subscription Rates:** $95.88 Individuals online access. **URL:** http://press-herald.com. **Mailing address:** PO Box 1339, Minden, LA 71058. **Ad Rates:** BW $686.70; 4C $896.70; SAU $5.45; PCI $8.50. **Remarks:** Accepts classified advertising. **Circ:** Mon.-Fri. 12500.

14455 ■ KASO-AM - 1240
410 Lakeshore Dr.
Minden, LA 71055
Phone: (318)377-1240
Format: Big Band/Nostalgia. **Networks:** Jones Satellite. **Operating Hours**: Continuous. **Wattage**: 1,000. **Ad Rates:** $20 for 60 seconds. **URL:** http://www.kbef.com.

14456 ■ KBEF-FM - 104.5
410 Lakeshore Dr.
Minden, LA 71055
Phone: (318)377-1240
Fax: (318)377-4619
Format: Contemporary Christian. **Networks:** Satellite Music Network. **Founded:** 2001. **Operating Hours**: 5 a.m.-9 p.m. **Key Personnel:** Cindy Wilson, Contact; Doug Griffin, Contact. **Wattage**: 6,000. **Ad Rates:** $25 for 60 seconds. **URL:** http://www.kbef.com.

MONROE

N LA. Ouachita Parish. On Ouachita River, 74 mi. W. of Vicksburg, MS. Northeast Louisiana University. Manufactures auto headlights, slacks, paper products, chemicals, paper, paper containers, store fixtures, furniture, awnings, pumps, bricks, fertilizer, ink, beverages, lumber, foundries. Oil and gas wells. Paper mill and converting equipment.

14457 ■ The News-Star
The News-Star
411 N Fourth St.
Monroe, LA 71201
Phone: (318)322-5161
Publisher's E-mail: news@thenewsstar.com
General newspaper. **Founded:** 1890. **Freq:** Daily. **Print Method:** Letterpress. **Trim Size:** 10 x 20.833. **Cols./Page:** 7. **Col. Width:** 24 nonpareils. **Col. Depth:** 301 agate lines. **Key Personnel:** David B. Petty, Publisher, phone: (318)362-0345; Mark Henderson, Editor, phone: (318)362-0350; Christina Pierce, Director, Advertising. **Subscription Rates:** $10 Individuals digital only; /month; $21 Individuals monday-sunday; /month. **URL:** http://www.thenewsstar.com. **Formed by the merger of:** The Evening News. **Mailing address:** PO Box 1502, Monroe, LA 71210. **Remarks:** Accepts advertising. **Circ:** Mon.-Fri. ⋆**33239**, Sun. ⋆**37003**, Sat. ⋆**31295**.

14458 ■ Century Tel
100 CenturyTel Dr.
Monroe, LA 71203
Phone: (318)388-9000
Free: 800-256-3352
Owner: Purcelltel Inc., 1334 Shepard Dr., Ste. E, Sterling, VA 20164-4426, Ph: (703)406-4300, Fax: (703)406-4305. **Key Personnel:** Karen A. Puckett, COO, Exec. VP; R. Stewart Ewing, Jr., CFO, Exec. VP; Glen F. Post, III, CEO, President. **Cities Served:** Platteville, Wisconsin. **URL:** http://www.centurylink.com.

14459 ■ KAQY-TV - 11
3100 Sterlington Rd.
Monroe, LA 71203
Phone: (318)325-3011
Key Personnel: Joe Currie, Gen. Mgr.; Carolyn Clampit, Sales Mgr.; Doug Ginn, Program Mgr.; Mike Halbrook, Promotions Mgr.

14460 ■ KBMQ-FM - 88.7
PO Box 3265
Monroe, LA 71210
Phone: (318)387-1230
Fax: (318)387-8856
Free: 800-898-1230
Format: Contemporary Christian. **Owner:** Media Ministries, Inc., at above address. **URL:** http://887thecross.com.

14461 ■ KBYO-FM - 92.7
321 N 2nd St.
Monroe, LA 71201
Phone: (318)323-8886
Format: Country; Adult Contemporary; News; Talk. **Owner:** Ness Sound Inc., at above address. **Founded:** 1983. **Operating Hours**: 5 a.m.-midnight. **Wattage**: 3,000 ERP. **Ad Rates:** Advertising accepted; rates available upon request.

14462 ■ KCRJ-FM - 94.9
527 Lakeshore Dr.
Monroe, LA 71203
Phone: (318)343-0782
Email: lonnie@kcrj.org
Format: Contemporary Christian; Religious. **ADI**: Monroe, LA-El Dorado, AR. **Wattage**: 100. **Ad Rates:** Noncommercial. **URL:** http://Kcrj.Org.

14463 ■ KEDM-FM - 90.3
250 Stubbs Hall
401 Bayou Dr.
Monroe, LA 71209-6805
Phone: (318)342-5556
Fax: (318)342-5570
Format: Public Radio. **Networks:** National Public Radio (NPR); Public Radio International (PRI). **Owner:** University of Louisiana at Monroe, 700 University Ave., Monroe, LA 71209, Ph: (318)342-1000, Fax: (318)342-1915, Free: 800-372-5127. **Founded:** 1991. **Operating Hours**: Continuous; 70% network, 30% local. **Key Personnel:** Jay Curtis, Dir. of Programs; Kenneth Sanders, Tech. Dir. **Local Programs**: *Beale Street Caravan*, Saturday 11:00 p.m.; *Midday Classics*, Friday 12:00 p.m. - 1:00 p.m.; *Jazz, Straight No Chaser*, Saturday Tuesday Thursday 12:00 a.m. - 6:00 a.m. 7:00 p.m. - 10:00 p.m. **Wattage**: 87,100. **Ad Rates:** Noncommercial. **URL:** http://www.kedm.org.

14464 ■ K45IM - 45
PO Box A
Santa Ana, CA 92711
Phone: (714)832-2950
Free: 888-731-1000
Owner: Trinity Broadcasting Network Inc., PO Box A, Santa Ana, CA 92711, Ph: (714)832-2950, Free: 888-731-1000. **URL:** http://www.tbn.org.

14465 ■ KJLO-FM - 104.1
1109 Hudson Ln.
Monroe, LA 71201
Phone: (318)388-2323
Fax: (318)388-0569
Free: 800-432-1041
Format: Country. **Networks:** ABC. **Owner:** Holladay Broadcasting Inc., Not Available. **Founded:** 1983. **For-**

merly: KWEZ-FM. **Operating Hours**: Continuous. **ADI**: Monroe, LA-El Dorado, AR. **Wattage**: 100,000. **Ad Rates:** for 30 seconds; for 60 seconds. Combined advertising rates available with KLIP-FM, KRVV-FM, KJMG-FM, KMLB-AM, KRJO-AM. **URL:** http://www.kjlo.com.

14466 ■ KJMG-FM - 97.3
804 N 31st St.
Monroe, LA 71201
Email: info@majic97.com
Format: Urban Contemporary.

14467 ■ KLIC-AM - 1230
130 N Second St.
Monroe, LA 71201-6749
Phone: (318)387-1230
Fax: (318)387-8856
Free: 800-898-1230
Email: rob@887fm.org
Format: Southern Gospel; Talk. **Networks:** Sun Radio. **Owner:** Media Ministries, Inc., at above address. **Founded:** 1992. **Operating Hours:** Continuous. **Key Personnel:** Bob Beyer, Gen. Mgr., gm@887fm.org; Phillip Brooks, Dir. of Programs, phillip@887fm.org; Ernie Sandidge, Chief Engineer, ernie@887fm.org. **Wattage**: 1,000. **Ad Rates:** $8-25 for 30 seconds. Combined advertising rates available with KBMQ-FM.

14468 ■ KLIP-FM - 105.3
1109 Hudson Ln.
Monroe, LA 71201
Phone: (318)388-2323
Email: la105monroeradio@gmail.com
Format: Classic Rock. **Founded:** Sept. 07, 2006. **Operating Hours:** Continuous. **Key Personnel:** Jim Elliott, Dir. of Programs. **Ad Rates:** Noncommercial. **URL:** http://www.la105.com.

14469 ■ KLTM-TV - 13
7733 Perkins Rd.
Baton Rouge, LA 70810
Phone: (225)767-5660
Free: 800-272-8161
Format: Public TV. **Simulcasts:** WLPB-TV Baton Rouge, LA. **Networks:** Public Broadcasting Service (PBS); Louisiana Public Broadcasting. **Owner:** Louisiana Public Broadcasting, 7733 Perkins Rd., Baton Rouge, LA 70810, Ph: (225)767-5660, Fax: (225)767-4288. **Founded:** 1976. **Operating Hours:** Continuous. **ADI**: Monroe, LA-El Dorado, AR. **Key Personnel:** Gary Allen, Producer; Ken Miller, Production Mgr.; Jason Viso, Div. Dir., jviso@lpb.org; Bob Neese, Contact, bneese@lpb.org; Clay Fourrier, Producer, cfourrier@lpb.org; Beth Courtney, President, CEO. **Wattage**: 17,200. **Ad Rates:** Noncommercial. **URL:** http://beta.lpb.org.

14470 ■ KMBQ-FM - 88.7
130 Art Alley, Ste. C
Monroe, LA 71201
Phone: (318)387-1230
Fax: (318)387-8856
Format: Contemporary Christian; Music of Your Life; News. **Founded:** Sept. 07, 2006. **URL:** http://887thecross.com.

14471 ■ KMLB-AM - 540
1109 Hudson Ln.
Monroe, LA 71201
Phone: (318)388-2323
Fax: (318)388-0569
Free: 800-259-1440
Format: News; Talk. **Networks:** ABC; CBS; Mutual Broadcasting System; EFM; ESPN Radio. **Owner:** Holladay Broadcasting of Louisiana L.L.C., at above address. **Founded:** 1930. **Operating Hours**: Continuous. **ADI**: Monroe, LA-El Dorado, AR. **Local Programs**: *Moon Griffon Show*, Monday Tuesday Wednesday Thursday Friday 9:00 a.m. - 11:00 a.m. **Wattage**: 5,000. **Ad Rates:** for 30 seconds; for 60 seconds. Combined advertising rates available with KLIP-FM, KRVV-FM, KJMG-FM, KRJO-AM, KJLO-FM. **URL:** http://www.kmlb.com.

14472 ■ KMYY-FM - 92.3
1200 N 18th St., Ste. D
Monroe, LA 71201
Phone: (318)322-9237
Fax: (318)322-4585
Format: Country. **Wattage**: 11,500. **Ad Rates:** Advertising accepted; rates available upon request. **URL:** http://www.923thewolf.com.

14473 ■ KNAN-FM - 106.1
1200 N 18th St., Ste. D
Monroe, LA 71201
Phone: (318)387-3922
Fax: (318)322-4585
Format: Classic Rock. **Networks:** NBC. **Owner:** Live Oak Broadcasting, at above address. **Founded:** 1965. **ADI**: Monroe, LA-El Dorado, AR. **Key Personnel:** Joe Geoffroy, Gen. Mgr.; Sonny Catley, Sales Mgr.; Mick Lane, Dir. of Programs. **Wattage**: 97,000 ERP. **URL:** http://www.rock106kxrr.com.

14474 ■ KNOE-TV - 8
1400 Oliver Rd.
Monroe, LA 71201
Phone: (318)388-8888
Fax: (318)325-3405
Format: Commercial TV. **Networks:** CBS. **Founded:** 1953. **Operating Hours:** Continuous. **ADI**: Monroe, LA-El Dorado, AR. **Key Personnel:** Marla Gilcrease, News Dir., marla.gilcrease@knoe.com. **Local Programs**: *Mississippi Headlines*; *Knoe Good Morning Arkansas, Louisiana, Mississippi.* **Ad Rates:** Noncommercial. **URL:** http://www.knoe.com.

14475 ■ KOUS-FM - 96.3
PO Box 9425
Monroe, LA 71211-9425
Format: Blues; Gospel; Urban Contemporary. **Operating Hours:** 12 hours Daily. **ADI**: Monroe, LA-El Dorado, AR. **Wattage**: 093. **Ad Rates:** Noncommercial. **URL:** http://www.mykous.com/.

14476 ■ KRJO-AM - 1680
1109 Hudson Ln.
Monroe, LA 71201
Phone: (318)322-1914
Fax: (318)388-0569
Format: Gospel; Religious. **Operating Hours**: Continuous. **Key Personnel:** Bishop Hamilton C. Murray, Station Mgr., sonshine@bayou.com; Eletha B. Hobson, Account Exec., Coord.; Bob Holladay, Gen. Mgr. **Wattage**: 10,000.

14477 ■ KRVV-FM - 100.1
1109 Hudson Ln.
Monroe, LA 71201
Phone: (318)388-2323
Fax: (318)388-0569
Email: sales@thebeat.net
Format: Hip Hop; Blues. **Networks:** ABC; Louisiana. **Owner:** Holladay Broadcasting of LA L.L.C., at above address. **Founded:** 1957. **Operating Hours**: Controlled. **ADI**: Monroe, LA-El Dorado, AR. **Wattage**: 50,000. **Ad Rates:** Combined advertising rates available with KJLO-FM, KLIP-FM, KJMG-FM, KMLB-AM, KRJO-AM. **URL:** http://www.krvv.com.

14478 ■ KTJC-FM - 92.3
1200 N 18th St., Ste. D
Monroe, LA 71201
Phone: (831)658-5281
Format: Religious. **Networks:** USA Radio; Christian Broadcasting (CBN); Louisiana Public Broadcasting. **Owner:** Ken Diebel, 1207 Louisa St. **Founded:** 1984. **Operating Hours**: 6 a.m.-10 p.m. **Wattage**: 26,000. **URL:** http://www.923thewolf.com.

14479 ■ KXRR-FM - 106.1
1200 N 18th St.
Monroe, LA 71201
Phone: (318)387-0106
Format: Classic Rock; Album-Oriented Rock (AOR). **Owner:** Opus Broadcasting, 511 Rossanley Dr., Medford, OR 97501. **Key Personnel:** Chris Zimmerman, Gen. Mgr. **Wattage**: 100,000. **URL:** http://rock106kxrr.com.

14480 ■ KXUL-FM - 91.1
130 Stubbs Hall
410 Bayou Dr.
Monroe, LA 71209-8821
Phone: (318)342-5986
Format: Alternative/New Music/Progressive; Top 40. **Owner:** University of Louisiana at Monroe, 700 University Ave., Monroe, LA 71209, Ph: (318)342-1000, Fax: (318)342-1915, Free: 800-372-5127. **Founded:** 1973. **Formerly:** KNLU. **Operating Hours:** Continuous; 100% local. **Key Personnel:** Joel Willer, Gen. Mgr., Supervisor; Kenneth Sanders, Engineer. **Wattage**: 8,500. **Ad Rates:** Noncommercial; underwriting available. **URL:** http://www.kxul.com.

14481 ■ KYFL-FM - 89.5
11530 Carmel Commons Blvd.
Charlotte, NC 28226
Phone: (704)523-5555
Free: 800-888-7077
Email: bbn@bbnmedia.org
Format: Religious. **Owner:** Bible Broadcasting Network Inc., 11530 Carmel Commons Blvd., Charlotte, NC 28226, Ph: (704)523-5555, Free: 800-888-7077. **Founded:** 1992. **ADI**: Monroe, LA-El Dorado, AR. **Key Personnel:** Lowell Davey, President. **Wattage**: 25,000. **Ad Rates:** Advertising accepted; rates available upon request. **Mailing address:** PO Box 7300, Charlotte, NC 28241-7300. **URL:** http://www.bbnradio.org.

14482 ■ KZRZ-FM - 98.3
1200 N 18th St., Ste. D
Monroe, LA 71201
Phone: (318)387-3922
Fax: (318)322-4585
Format: Soft Rock. **ADI**: Monroe, LA-El Dorado, AR. **Wattage**: 50,000. **Ad Rates:** Advertising accepted; rates available upon request. **URL:** http://www.sunny983.com.

14483 ■ WBBV-FM
1109 Hudson Ln.
Monroe, LA 71211
Format: Country. **Wattage**: 13,000 ERP. **Ad Rates:** Noncommercial.

MOREAUVILLE

C LA. Avoyelles Parish. 20 mi. NW of Simmesport.

14484 ■ KLIL-FM - 92.1
PO Box 365
Moreauville, LA 71355
Phone: (318)985-2929
Fax: (318)985-2995
Format: Adult Contemporary; Oldies. **Networks:** Jones Satellite. **Owner:** Cajun Broadcasting Inc., at above address. **Founded:** 1980. **Operating Hours**: Continuous. **Wattage**: 6,000. **Ad Rates:** $3.50-5.25 for 15 seconds; $4.25-6 for 30 seconds; $5.25-7 for 60 seconds.

MORGAN CITY

S LA. St. Mary Parish. On Atchafalaya River, 70 mi. W. of New Orleans. Oyster shell, lumber, fur industries, shipbuilding. Commercial fisheries. Oil and gas wells. Timbers. Truck farms. Sugarcane, asparagus, cabbage.

14485 ■ The Daily Review
The Daily Review
1014 Front St.
Morgan City, LA 70380
Phone: (985)384-8370
Fax: (985)384-4255
Publisher's E-mail: news@daily-review.com
Community newspaper. **Founded:** 1872. **Freq:** Daily (eve.). **Print Method:** Offset. **Cols./Page:** 6. **Col. Width:** 25 nonpareils. **Col. Depth:** 301 agate lines. **Key Personnel:** Allan Von Werder, Publisher. **Subscription Rates:** $75 Individuals online; $150 Out of area by mail; $80 Individuals by carrier. **URL:** http://www.daily-review.com/. **Mailing address:** PO Box 948, Morgan City, LA 70380. **Ad Rates:** GLR $.57; BW $1,029.42; 4C $1,329.42; PCI $7.98. **Remarks:** Accepts advertising. **Circ:** ‡6374.

14486 ■ Allen's TV Cable Service Inc.
800 Victor II Blvd.
Morgan City, LA 70380
Phone: (985)384-8335
Free: 888-793-9800
Email: info@atvci.net
Owner: Allen's TV Cable Service Inc., 800 Victor II Blvd., Morgan City 70380, Ph: (985)384-8335. **Cities Served:** Arnaudville, Bayou L'Ourse, Berwick, Grand Coteau, Morgan City, Pierre Part, Port Barre, Saint Landry, Saint Landry, Stephensville, Sunset, Louisiana: subscribing households 9,200; 200 channels. **Mailing address:** PO Box 2643, Morgan City, LA 70380. **URL:** http://www.atvc.net.

Circulation: ★ = AAM; △ or • = BPA; ♦ = CAC; ❑ = VAC; ⊕ = PO Statement; ‡ = Publisher's Report; Boldface figures = sworn; Light figures = estimated.

14487 ■ KBZE-FM - 105.9
1320 Victor II Blvd.
Morgan City, LA 70380
Phone: (985)385-6266
Fax: (985)385-6268
Format: Gospel; Sports. **Networks:** ABC. **Owner:** Hubcast Broadcasting Inc., at above address. **Founded:** 1992. **Operating Hours:** Continuous. **Key Personnel:** Howard J. Castay, Jr., Gen. Mgr., President, howard@kbze.com. **Wattage:** 6,000. **Ad Rates:** Advertising accepted; rates available upon request. Combined advertising rates available with KBZE.COM. **Mailing address:** PO Drawer N, Morgan City, LA 70381. **URL:** http://www.kbze.com.

14488 ■ KMRC-AM - 1430
409 Duke St.
Morgan City, LA 70380
Phone: (985)384-1430
Fax: (985)384-2351
Free: 800-332-5249
Email: kmrc@kmrc1430.com
Format: Polka. **Owner:** Spotlight Broadcasting, LLC, at above address. **Founded:** 1966. **Wattage:** 500 KW. **Ad Rates:** $3-6 for 30 seconds; $8-12 for 60 seconds. **Mailing address:** PO Box 1307, Morgan City, LA 70380. **URL:** http://www.kmrc1430.com/.

14489 ■ KQKI-FM - 95.3
128 Pluto St.
Morgan City, LA 70380
Phone: (985)395-2853
Fax: (985)395-5094
Format: Country. **Networks:** Louisiana. **Owner:** Teche Broadcasting Corp., at above address, Morgan City, LA 70380, Ph: (985)395-2853, Fax: (985)395-5094. **Founded:** 1976. **Operating Hours:** Continuous. **Key Personnel:** Julie Boyne, Gen. Mgr., jaboyne@cox.net; Bryan Protich, Div. Mgr., bryan@kqki.com. **Local Programs**: *Trading Post*, Monday Tuesday Wednesday Thursday Friday 9:05 a.m. - 9:55 a.m. **Wattage**: 16,500. **Ad Rates:** $10.50-16 for 30 seconds; $13.50-20 for 60 seconds. **URL:** http://www.kqki.com.

14490 ■ KWBJ-TV - 39
PO Box 2642
Morgan City, LA 70381
Phone: (985)384-6960
Email: info@kwbj.net
Format: Commercial TV. **Networks:** Warner Brothers Studios. **Founded:** 1986. **Formerly**: K39BJ. **Wattage:** 15,000 ERP. **Ad Rates:** Noncommercial.

14491 ■ WABL-AM - 1570
PO Box 803
Morgan City, LA 70381-0803
Phone: (504)384-1430
Email: wabl1570@hotmail.com
Format: Full Service. **Networks:** Louisiana; Mutual Broadcasting System. **Owner:** Spotlight Broadcasting, LLC, at above address. **Founded:** 1956. **Operating Hours**: Continuous. **ADI**: New Orleans, LA. **Wattage**: 500. **Ad Rates:** $4.50 for 15 seconds; $8 for 30 seconds; $14 for 60 seconds.

NATCHITOCHES

NW LA. Natchitoches Parish. 68 mi. SE of Shreveport. Northwestern State University of Louisiana. Tourism. Historic landmark district. Manufactures gas, brick, lumber, plywood, paper, mobile homes, cottonseed, oil, cement products, garments, linerboard and laminated wood. Food processing. Fish hatchery, Agriculture.

14492 ■ Current Sauce
Northwestern State University
175 Sam Sibley Dr.
Natchitoches, LA 71497
Phone: (318)357-6011
Free: 800-327-1903
Collegiate newspaper. **Freq:** Weekly. **Print Method:** Offset. **Cols./Page:** 6. **Col. Width:** 27 nonpareils. **Col. Depth:** 294 agate lines. **URL:** http://currentsaucenews.com. **Remarks:** Advertising accepted; rates available upon request. **Circ:** ‡3500.

14493 ■ Louisiana English Journal
Northwestern State University Department of Language and Communication
318 Kyser Hall
Natchitoches, LA 71497
Phone: (318)357-6272
Fax: (318)357-5942
Publisher's E-mail: languages@nsula.edu
Scholarly journal covering poetry and fiction from Louisiana. **Freq:** Semiannual. **Print Method:** Offset. **Trim Size:** 4 1/2 x 7 1/2. **Cols./Page:** 1. **Ad Rates:** BW $250; 4C $500. **Remarks:** Accepts advertising. **Circ:** Paid ‡399.

14494 ■ North Louisiana History
North Louisiana Historical Association
c/o Mary Linn Wernet, CA, Head Archivist and University Records Officer
Cammie G. Henry Research Center
Watson Library
Northwestern State University of Louisiana
Natchitoches, LA 71458
Phone: (318)357-4585
Publisher's E-mail: president@northlouisianahistory.org
Journal covering local history. **Freq:** Semiannual. **Key Personnel:** Emilia Gay Means, Editor. **ISSN:** 0739--005X (print). **Subscription Rates:** $5 Single issue. **URL:** http://northlouisianahistory.org/page3.html. **Formerly**: North Louisiana Historical Association Journal. **Remarks:** Advertising not accepted. **Circ:** (Not Reported).

14495 ■ Psychology Journal
Psychological Publishing
PO Box 176
Natchitoches, LA 71458
Publication E-mail: psychjournal@aol.com
Journal dedicated to all areas of the science and practice of counseling and clinical psychology. **Freq:** Semiannual. **Key Personnel:** Kathryn E. Kelly, PhD, Editor; Rich Furman, PhD, Editor; Judith L. Johnson, PhD, Editor; George J. Demakis, PhD, Editor; Steven K. Huprich, PhD, Editor; Karin B. Jordan, PhD, Editor; Len Lecci, Editor. **ISSN:** 1931--5694 (print). **Subscription Rates:** $90 Individuals; $175 Institutions; $25 Single issue. **URL:** http://www.psychologicalpublishing.com/. **Formerly**: Counseling and Clinical Psychology Journal. **Remarks:** Advertising not accepted. **Circ:** (Not Reported).

14496 ■ KBIO-FM - 89.7
601 Washington St.
Alexandria, LA 71301
Fax: (318)449-9954
Free: 888-408-0201
Format: Religious. **Owner:** Radio Maria USA, 601 Washington St., Alexandria, LA 71301, Ph: (318)561-6145, Fax: (318)449-9954, Free: 888-408-0201. **Wattage**: 100. **URL:** http://www.radiomaria.us.

14497 ■ KCIJ-FM - 106.5
213 Renee St.
Natchitoches, LA 71457
Phone: (318)354-4000
Format: Classic Rock. **Owner:** North Face Broadcasting, LLC, at above address, Natchitoches, LA. **Founded:** 2002. **Formerly**: KNSN-FM. **Operating Hours**: Continuous. **ADI**: Shreveport, LA-Texarkana, TX. **Wattage**: 25,000. **Ad Rates:** Noncommercial. Combined advertising rates available with KNOC-FM, KSBH-FM.

14498 ■ KDBH-FM - 97.5
400 Jefferson St.
Natchitoches, LA 71457
Phone: (318)352-9696
Fax: (318)357-9595
Format: Contemporary Country; Adult Contemporary. **Networks:** Jones Satellite. **Owner:** Cane River Communications, at above address. **Founded:** Sept. 07, 2006. **Operating Hours**: Continuous. **Key Personnel:** Rick Beck, Gen. Mgr.; John Brewer, Dir. of Operations, Sales Mgr., Contact; John Brewer, Contact. **Wattage**: 25,000. **Ad Rates:** Advertising accepted; rates available upon request. Combined advertising rates available with KNOC-AM. and KSBH-FM. **URL:** http://www.kzblradio.com/.

14499 ■ KNOC-AM - 1450
213 Renee St.
Natchitoches, LA 71457
Phone: (318)354-4000
Fax: (318)352-9598
Format: Talk; News; Sports. **Networks:** ABC. **Owner:** North Face Broadcasting, LLC, at above address, Natchitoches, LA. **Founded:** 1947. **Operating Hours**: Continuous. **Wattage:** 1,000. **Ad Rates:** Advertising accepted; rates available upon request. Combined advertising rates available with, KSBH-FM & KCIJ-FM.

14500 ■ KNWD-FM - 91.7
109 Keyser Hall
Natchitoches, LA 71497
Email: knwdradio@gmail.com
Format: Full Service. **Owner:** Northwestern State University, 175 Sam Sibley Dr., Natchitoches, LA 71497, Ph: (318)357-6011, Free: 800-327-1903. **Founded:** 1974. **Wattage:** 255. **Ad Rates:** Noncommercial. **Mailing address:** PO Box 3038, Natchitoches, LA 71497.

14501 ■ KZBL-FM - 100.7
400 Jefferson St.
Natchitoches, LA 71457
Phone: (318)357-1007
Fax: (318)318-9595
Format: Oldies. **Founded:** 1985. **ADI**: Shreveport, LA-Texarkana, TX. **Wattage**: 25,000. **Ad Rates:** Noncommercial. **URL:** http://www.kzblradio.com.

NEW IBERIA

S LA. Iberia Parish. On Bayou Tech., 20 mi. SE of Lafayette. Manufactures oil exploration equipment, carbon black, spices, condiments. Sugar, rice, syrup, steel plants. Sawmills. Bottling works. Canneries. Commercial fisheries. Fur trapping. Salt mines. Oil wells. Timber. Diversified farming.

14502 ■ Daily Iberian
The Daily Iberian
PO Box 9290
New Iberia, LA 70562-9290
Phone: (337)365-6773
Fax: (337)367-9640
Free: 800-365-6773
Publisher's E-mail: dailyiberian@cox.net
General newspaper. **Freq:** Irregular Monday through Friday afternoons/Sunday mornings. **Print Method:** Offset. **Cols./Page:** 6. **Col. Width:** 24 nonpareils. **Col. Depth:** 301 agate lines. **Key Personnel:** Will Chapman, Publisher; JP Poirier, Manager, Circulation, phone: (337)321-6759. **Subscription Rates:** $126 Individuals 1 year (home delivery); $63 Individuals 6 months (home delivery); $31.50 Individuals 3 months (home delivery). **URL:** http://www.iberianet.com. **Ad Rates:** SAU $10. **Remarks:** Accepts advertising. **Circ:** Mon.-Fri. ■ **12510**, Sun. ■ **13302**.

14503 ■ KANE-AM - 1240
107 West Main St
New Iberia, LA 70560
Phone: (337)365-3434
Fax: (337)365-9117
Email: kane@kane1240.com
Format: Cajun. **Networks:** ABC. **Owner:** Coastal Broadcasting of Larose Inc., 11603 Hwy. 308, Larose, LA 70373, Ph: (985)798-7792, Fax: (985)798-7793. **Founded:** 1946. **Operating Hours**: Continuous; 11% network, 89% local. **Key Personnel:** Jeff Boggs, Sports Dir. **Local Programs**: *The Breakfast Club*, Monday Tuesday Wednesday Thursday Friday 5:30 a.m. - 10:00 a.m.; *Top Rod Fishing Show*; *News Block and Swamp*, Monday Tuesday Wednesday Thursday Friday 6:00 p.m. - 12:00 a.m.; *Teche Matters*, Monday Tuesday Wednesday Thursday Friday 10:00 a.m. - 1:00 p.m.; *Sports Corner*, Saturday 10:00 a.m. - 12:00 p.m. **Wattage**: 1,000. **Ad Rates:** $11-19.50 for 30 seconds; $14.50-26 for 60 seconds. KLRZ-FM -LAROSE KLEB - Golden Meadow. **URL:** http://www.kane1240.com.

14504 ■ K19FR - 19
PO Box A
Santa Ana, CA 92711
Phone: (714)832-2950
Free: 888-731-1000
Owner: Trinity Broadcasting Network Inc., PO Box A, Santa Ana, CA 92711, Ph: (714)832-2950, Free: 888-731-1000.

14505 ■ KNIR-AM - 1360
PO Box 12948
New Iberia, LA 70562-2948
Networks: Westwood One Radio. **Owner:** Radio Maria USA, 601 Washington St., Alexandria, LA 71301, Ph: (318)561-6145, Fax: (318)449-9954, Free: 888-408-0201. **Founded:** 1969. **Operating Hours**: Continuous. **ADI**: Lafayette, LA. **Key Personnel:** Donald Bonin, President; John Reed, Sales Mgr. **Wattage**: 1,000. **Ad**

Rates: $15-25 for 30 seconds; $15-25 for 60 seconds. **URL:** http://radiomaria.us/contact-us/.

NEW ORLEANS

SE LA. Orleans Parish. On Lake Pontchartrain and Mississippi River, about 100 mi. above its mouth. Boat connections. Important port, shipping, financial and oil center. Cotton market. Extensive fisheries. Tulane University. Loyola University. Xavier University. University of New Orleans, Dillard Univ. & Southern Univ. at New Orleans. Private schools. Tourist center. Annual Mardi Gras Celebration. Manufactures acoustic materials, adhesives, aluminum, asbestos, cotton, electronics, petroleum refinery products, brick, burlap, cans, chemicals, cigars, coffee, clothing, disinfectants, fish oil and meal, floor tile, furniture, livestock feed, luggage, lumber, oil field supplies, paint, paper boxes, plumbing ware, roofing, sea food, ship building, soap and detergents, steel barrels, sugar, syrup and molasses.

14506 ■ Ambush Magazine
Ambush Inc.
828-A Bourbon St.
New Orleans, LA 70116-3137
Phone: (504)522-8049
Fax: (504)522-0907
Free: 800-876-1484
Publisher's E-mail: info@ambushmag.com
Local magazine for a gay, lesbian, bisexual and transgender audience. **Freq:** Semimonthly. **Key Personnel:** Rip R. Naquin-Delain, Editor; Marsha M. Naquin-Delain, Director, Production. **Ad Rates:** BW $445. **Remarks:** Accepts advertising. **Circ:** Combined 25000.

14507 ■ Bayou Magazine
University of New Orleans
2000 Lakeshore Dr.
New Orleans, LA 70148
Phone: (504)280-6000
Free: 888-514-4275
Publication E-mail: bayou@uno.edu
Literary magazine featuring short fiction, non-fiction and poetry. **Freq:** Semiannual. **Key Personnel:** Joanna Leake, Editor-in-Chief. **Subscription Rates:** $15 Individuals; $8 Single issue by mail. **URL:** http://bayoumagazine.org. **Circ:** (Not Reported).

14508 ■ The Black Collegian: The Career & Self Development Magazine for African-American Students
Black Collegiate Services Inc.
140 Carondelet St.
New Orleans, LA 70130-2526
Phone: (504)523-0154
Fax: (504)523-0271
Publisher's E-mail: leon@black-collegiate.com
Career opportunity magazine featuring job searching, role models, interviews, entertainment, art, and African-American history. **Freq:** Semiannual February & October. **Print Method:** Offset. **Trim Size:** 7 7/8 x 10 3/4. **Cols./Page:** 3. **Col. Width:** 13.5 picas. **Col. Depth:** 9 inches. **Key Personnel:** Preston J. Edwards, Publisher. **ISSN:** 0192--3757 (print). **URL:** http://imdiversity.com/channels/eon/the-black-collegian-online. **Ad Rates:** BW $6,300; 4C $8,400. **Remarks:** Accepts advertising. **Circ:** (Not Reported).

14509 ■ Clarion Herald
Clarion Herald Publishing Company Inc.
1000 Howard Ave., Ste. 400
New Orleans, LA 70113
Phone: (504)596-3035
Fax: (504)596-3039
Publisher's E-mail: clarionherald@clarionherald.org
Catholic newspaper (tabloid). **Freq:** Biweekly. **Print Method:** Offset. **Trim Size:** 10 3/8 x 14. **Cols./Page:** 4. **Col. Width:** 2 3/8 inches. **Col. Depth:** 14 inches. **Key Personnel:** Florence L. Herman, Managing Editor; Michael C. Comar, Business Manager, phone: (504)596-3041; Beth Donze, Writer, phone: (504)596-3026; Peter Finney, Jr., Executive Editor, General Manager; Christine L. Bordelon, Associate Editor. **Subscription Rates:** $20 Individuals New Orleans Archdiocese area; $35 Two years New Orleans Archdiocese area; $60 Individuals New Orleans Archdiocese area; 3 years; $25 Individuals outside New Orleans Archdiocese area; $45 Two years outside New Orleans Archdiocese area; $75 Individuals outside New Orleans Archdiocese area; 3 years. **URL:** http://www.clarionherald.org. **Remarks:** Advertising accepted; rates available upon request. **Circ:** 63000.

14510 ■ Composites Part B: Engineering: An International Journal
RELX Group P.L.C.
c/o David Hui, Editor-in-Chief
Dept. of Mechanical Engineering
Univ. of New Orleans, Lake Front
New Orleans, LA 70148
Fax: (504)280-5539
Publisher's E-mail: amsterdam@relx.com
Journal covering research in the field of composites focusing on evaluation and modeling of engineering details and concepts. **Freq:** 24/yr. **Key Personnel:** David Hui, Editor-in-Chief. **ISSN:** 1359--8368 (print). **Subscription Rates:** $2806.67 Institutions online; $3369 Institutions print. **URL:** http://www.journals.elsevier.com/composites-part-b-engineering. **Circ:** (Not Reported).

14511 ■ Electronic Notes in Theoretical Computer Science
RELX Group P.L.C.
c/o M.W. Mislove, Mng. Ed.
Tulane University
Department of Mathematics
6823 St. Charles Ave.
New Orleans, LA 70118
Phone: (504)862-3441
Fax: (504)865-5063
Publisher's E-mail: amsterdam@relx.com
Journal publishing such items where quick reach is important such as conference proceedings, lecture notes, monographs etc. **Key Personnel:** M.W. Mislove, Managing Editor; S. Arora, Editor; G. Ausiello, Editor; S. Brookes, Editor; R. Cleaveland, Editor; P. Crescenzi, Editor. **ISSN:** 1571--0661 (print). **URL:** http://www.elsevier.com/journals/electronic-notes-in-theoretical-computer-science/1571-0661. **Remarks:** Advertising accepted; rates available upon request. **Circ:** (Not Reported).

14512 ■ Gambit Weekly
Gambit Communications
3923 Bienville St.
New Orleans, LA 70119
Phone: (504)486-5900
Publication E-mail: sandys@gambitweekly.com
Publication exploring politics, dining, and entertainment in New Orleans. **Founded:** 1980. **Freq:** Weekly. **Cols./Page:** 4. **Col. Width:** 14.5 picas. **Col. Depth:** 77 picas. **Key Personnel:** Dora Sison, Director, Production; Margo DuBos, Chief Executive Officer, President, Publisher; Kandace Power Graves, Managing Editor; Clancy DuBos, Editor; Kevin Allman, Editor. **ISSN:** 1089-3520 (print). **URL:** http://www.bestofneworleans.com. **Formerly:** Gambit. **Remarks:** Accepts advertising. **Circ:** ‡40,000.

14513 ■ The Global Journal of Finance and Economics
Serials Publications Private Ltd.
c/o M. Kabir Hassan, Editor-in-Chief
Department of Economics & Finance
University of New Orleans
New Orleans, LA 70148
Phone: (504)280-6163
Fax: (504)280-6397
Publisher's E-mail: serials@mail.com
Journal covering international finance topics such as exchange rates, balance of payments, financial institutions, risk analysis, international banking and portfolio management, and financial market regulation. **Freq:** Semiannual. **Key Personnel:** M. Kabir Hassan, Editor-in-Chief. **ISSN:** 0972--9496 (print). **Subscription Rates:** Rs 4500 Individuals print and online; $175 Individuals print and online; Rs 3000 Individuals print or online; $125 Individuals print or online. **URL:** http://www.serialsjournals.com/journal-detail.php?journals_id=51. **Circ:** (Not Reported).

14514 ■ The Louisiana Bar Journal
Louisiana State Bar Association
601 St. Charles Ave.
New Orleans, LA 70130-3404
Phone: (504)566-1600
Fax: (504)566-0930
Free: 800-421-5722
Publisher's E-mail: mmollere@lsba.org
Professional journal covering law in Louisiana for judges and lawyers. **Freq:** Bimonthly. **Trim Size:** 8 1/2 x 10 7/8. **Key Personnel:** Krystal Bellanger, Contact, phone: (504)619-0131, fax: (504)566-0930; Darlene Labranche, Communications Specialist, phone: (504)619-0112. **ISSN:** 0459--8881 (print). **Subscription Rates:** Included in membership. **URL:** http://www.lsba.org/NewsAndPublications/BarJournal.aspx. **Ad Rates:** BW $1,085; 4C $1,540. **Remarks:** Accepts advertising. **Circ:** 20000.

14515 ■ Louisiana Data News Weekly
Data Enterprises Inc.
3501 Napolean Ave.
New Orleans, LA 70125
Phone: (504)821-7421
Fax: (504)821-7622
Black community newspaper. **Freq:** Weekly. **Key Personnel:** Terry Jones, Publisher. **ISSN:** 1043--4445 (print). **URL:** http://ladatanews.com. **Formerly:** New Orleans Black Data; Data Newsweekly. **Ad Rates:** BW $5,188.23; 4C $260; PCI $74.12. **Remarks:** Accepts advertising. **Circ:** Combined 60000.

14516 ■ Louisiana Weekly
Louisiana Weekly
2215 Pelopidas St.
New Orleans, LA 70122
Phone: (504)282-3705
Fax: (504)282-3773
Publication E-mail: info@louisianaweekly.com
Black community newspaper. **Freq:** Weekly (Mon.). **Print Method:** Offset. Uses mats. **Cols./Page:** 6. **Col. Width:** 2 1/8 inches. **Col. Depth:** 21 inches. **Key Personnel:** Edmund W. Lewis, Editor. **USPS:** 320-680. **Subscription Rates:** $26 Individuals in-state; $48 Two years in-state; $31 Individuals out-of-state; $53 Two years out-of-state; $58 Individuals 3 years; $63 Individuals out-of-state (3 years). **URL:** http://www.louisianaweekly.com. **Ad Rates:** BW $2,445.66; PCI $19.41. **Remarks:** Accepts advertising. **Circ:** (Not Reported).

14517 ■ Loyola Law Review
Loyola University New Orleans College of Law
Box 901
7214 St. Charles Ave.
New Orleans, LA 70118
Phone: (504)861-5550
Fax: (504)861-5739
Professional legal journal. **Freq:** Quarterly. **Key Personnel:** H. Rick Yelton, Editor-in-Chief; John B. Stanton, Editor-in-Chief. **ISSN:** 0192--9720 (print). **Subscription Rates:** $30 Individuals domestic; $36 Individuals foreign. **URL:** http://law.loyno.edu/loyola-law-review. **Remarks:** Advertising not accepted. **Circ:** Paid 800.

14518 ■ Loyola Maritime Law Journal
Loyola University New Orleans College of Law
Box 901
7214 St. Charles Ave.
New Orleans, LA 70118
Phone: (504)861-5550
Fax: (504)861-5739
Journal containing articles on legal issues in maritime law. **Freq:** Semiannual. **Key Personnel:** Bryan O'Neill, Editor-in-Chief. **Subscription Rates:** $10 Individuals domestic; $16 Individuals foreign; $10 Single issue. **URL:** http://law.loyno.edu/loyola-maritime-law-journal. **Circ:** (Not Reported).

14519 ■ Loyola University New Orleans Journal of Public Interest Law
Loyola University New Orleans College of Law
Box 901
7214 St. Charles Ave.
New Orleans, LA 70118
Phone: (504)861-5550
Fax: (504)861-5739
Journal discussing national and international legal issues. **Freq:** Semiannual. **Key Personnel:** Kaitlin Locascio, Editor-in-Chief. **Subscription Rates:** $10 Individuals domestic; $16 Individuals foreign; $10 Single issue. **URL:** http://law.loyno.edu/loyola-journal-public-interest-law. **Circ:** (Not Reported).

14520 ■ Naval Reservist News: News of the Total Force Navy for the Naval Reserve Community
Commander Naval Reserve Force

Circulation: ★ = AAM; △ or • = BPA; ♦ = CAC; ❑ = VAC; ⊕ = PO Statement; ‡ = Publisher's Report; Boldface figures = sworn; Light figures = estimated.

4400 Dauphine St.
New Orleans, LA 70146
Free: 866-830-6466
Tabloid newspaper for members of the Naval Reserve. **Freq:** Monthly. **Print Method:** Offset(web). **Trim Size:** 11x17. **URL:** http://www.navyreserve.navy.mil. **Remarks:** Advertising not accepted. **Circ:** Controlled ‡100000.

14521 ■ New Orleans Homes & Lifestyles
Echo Media
900 Circle 75 Pky., Ste. 1600
Atlanta, GA 30339
Phone: (770)955-3535
Fax: (770)955-3599
Publisher's E-mail: salesinfo@echo-media.com
Magazine focusing on home remodeling, trendy fashion styles, and garden furnishing. **Freq:** Quarterly. **URL:** http://echomedia.com/medias/details/5712. **Remarks:** Accepts advertising. **Circ:** 20000.

14522 ■ New Orleans Review
Loyola University
6363 St. Charles Ave.
New Orleans, LA 70118
Phone: (504)865-3240
Free: 800-456-9652
Publisher's E-mail: apply@loyno.edu
Literary magazine featuring poetry, fiction, artwork, and literary and film criticism. **Freq:** Annual. **Print Method:** Perfect Bound. **Trim Size:** 6 x 9. **Cols./Page:** 1. **Col. Width:** 4 1/2 inches. **Col. Depth:** 7 inches. **Key Personnel:** Mark Yakich, Editor. **ISSN:** 0028--6400 (print). **Subscription Rates:** $15 Individuals current issue; $30 Other countries current issue; $25 Two years; $5 Individuals back issue. **URL:** http://www.neworleansreview.org. **Remarks:** Advertising accepted; rates available upon request. **Circ:** Paid ‡1000, Non-paid ‡200.

14523 ■ The Ochsner Journal
The Ochsner Journal
1319 Jefferson Hwy.
New Orleans, LA 70121
Phone: (504)842-7398
Fax: (504)842-2013
Publication E-mail: ocjournal@ochsner.org
Peer-reviewed journal covering health care research and information, with a focus on topics of great societal and medical significance, for practicing physicians, healthcare professionals, and physicians in training. **Freq:** Quarterly March, June, September, and December. **Trim Size:** 8 1/2 x 11. **Key Personnel:** David E. Beck, Editor-in-Chief; M.A. Krousel-Wood, MD, Associate Editor; Alan L. Burshell, MD, Chairman; Julia L. Cook, PhD, Editor; Hector O. Ventura, MD, Section Chief; Kathleen McFadden, Managing Editor. **ISSN:** 1524--5012 (print). **Subscription Rates:** Free. **URL:** http://www.ochsnerjournal.org. **Ad Rates:** BW $1,170. **Remarks:** Accepts advertising. **Circ:** 5000.

14524 ■ OffBeat Magazine: New Orleans' and Louisiana's Music Magazine
OffBeat Publications
421 Frenchman St., Ste. 200
New Orleans, LA 70116
Phone: (504)944-4300
Fax: (504)944-4306
Free: 877-944-4300
Publisher's E-mail: offbeat@offbeat.com
Consumer magazine covering music and entertainment in New Orleans and throughout the state of Louisiana. **Freq:** Monthly. **Key Personnel:** Alex Rawls, Editor; Joseph L. Irrera, Business Manager, Managing Editor; Jan V. Ramsey, Editor-in-Chief, Publisher. **ISSN:** 1090--0810 (print). **Subscription Rates:** $150 U.S. enhanced subscription; $40 U.S. /year; $70 U.S. two years; $100 U.S. three years; $600 U.S. lifetime; $46 Canada /year; $90 Canada two years; $130 Canada three years; $800 Canada lifetime; $105 Other countries /year; $185 Other countries two years; $270 Other countries three years; $1000 Other countries lifetime. **URL:** http://www.offbeat.com; http://www.offbeat.com/issues. **Remarks:** Accepts advertising. **Circ:** (Not Reported).

14525 ■ Pine Chemicals Review
Kriedt Enterprises Ltd.
129 S Cortez St.
New Orleans, LA 70119
Publication covering the Global Pine and Pulp Chemical industry. **Freq:** Bimonthly. **Key Personnel:** James M. Turner, Editor. **Subscription Rates:** $110 Individuals; $145 Other countries; $45 Individuals PDF. **Alt. Formats:** PDF. **URL:** http://www.pinechemicalsreview.com. **Formerly**: Forest Chemicals Review. **Ad Rates:** BW $420; 4C $820. **Remarks:** Accepts advertising. **Circ:** (Not Reported).

14526 ■ Play Meter Magazine
Play Meter Magazine
6600 Fleur de Lis Dr.
New Orleans, LA 70124-1430
Phone: (504)488-7003
Fax: (504)488-7083
Free: 888-473-2376
Magazine for the coin-operated entertainment/FEC industry. **Freq:** Monthly. **Print Method:** Offset. **Trim Size:** 8 1/2 x 10 7/8. **Cols./Page:** 4. **Col. Width:** 27 nonpareils. **Col. Depth:** 140 agate lines. **Key Personnel:** Bonnie Theard, Editor; Carol Lally, Publisher. **ISSN:** 1048--8243 (print). **Subscription Rates:** $60 Individuals; $150 Other countries; $110 Two years; $150 Individuals 3 years. **URL:** http://www.playmeter.com. **Mailing address:** PO Box 337, New Orleans, LA 70124-1430. **Remarks:** Advertising accepted; rates available upon request. **Circ:** ‡3000.

14527 ■ Preservation in Print
Preservation Resource Center of New Orleans
923 Tchoupitoulas St.
New Orleans, LA 70130
Phone: (504)581-7032
Publisher's E-mail: prc@prcno.org
Tabloid emphasizing preservation of New Orleans' & Louisiana's historic architecture and neighborhoods. **Freq:** 9/year. **Print Method:** Offset. **Trim Size:** 11 x 14. **Cols./Page:** 3. **Col. Width:** 27 nonpareils. **Col. Depth:** 205 agate lines. **Key Personnel:** Mary Fitzpatrick, Executive Editor, phone: (504)636-3052; Joel Nelson, Chief Executive Officer, phone: (504)636-3064; Jackie Derks, Manager, Advertising, phone: (504)636-3053. **Subscription Rates:** Included in membership. **URL:** http://www.prcno.org; http://www.prcno.org/programs/preservationinprint/index.php. **Ad Rates:** BW $800; 4C $1,200. **Remarks:** Accepts advertising. **Circ:** Paid ‡9000, Non-paid ‡3000.

14528 ■ Social Policy: intellectual exchange among progressive academics and activists
Institute for Social Justice
1024 Elysian Fields Ave.
New Orleans, LA 70177-3924
Phone: (504)302-1238
Publisher's E-mail: info@socialpolicy.org
Journal covering current social policy and progressive political and social movements. **Freq:** Quarterly spring, summer, fall and winter. **Print Method:** Offset. **Trim Size:** 7 x 11. **Cols./Page:** 2. **Col. Width:** 16 picas. **Col. Depth:** 100 agate lines. **Key Personnel:** Noam Chomsky, Advisor; Janice Fine, Advisor; S.M. Miller, Advisor. **ISSN:** 0037--7783 (print). **Subscription Rates:** $25 Individuals silver subscription; $60 Individuals gold subscription (domestic); $110 Individuals 2 years (domestic); $66 Individuals Canada/Mexico; $125 Individuals 2 years (Canada/Mexico); $80 Individuals rest of the world; $140 Individuals 2 years (rest of the world); $265 Institutions platinum subscription (domestic); $290 Institutions Canada/Mexico; $315 Institutions rest of the world. **URL:** http://www.socialpolicy.org. **Mailing address:** PO Box 3924, New Orleans, LA 70177-3924. **Ad Rates:** BW $400. **Remarks:** Accepts advertising. **Circ:** ‡2000.

14529 ■ Sugar Journal
Kriedt Enterprises Ltd.
3803 Cleveland Ave.
New Orleans, LA 70119
Sugar industry magazine covering the production, processing, and refining of sugar cane, beet and corn. **Freq:** Monthly. **Print Method:** Sheet-fed offset. **Trim Size:** 8.5 x 11. **Cols./Page:** 3. **Col. Width:** 13 picas. **Col. Depth:** 10 inches. **Key Personnel:** Scott Walker, Advertising Representative; Charley Richard, Ph.D, Executive Editor; Romney Richard, Publisher, Editor. **USPS:** 364-710. **Subscription Rates:** $50 Individuals print; $85 Other countries print; $40 Individuals online. **Alt. Formats:** PDF. **URL:** http://www.sugarjournal.com. **Ad Rates:** 4C $2,500. **Remarks:** Accepts advertising. **Circ:** ‡3500.

14530 ■ The Times-Picayune
Times-Picayune Publishing Corp.
3800 Howard Ave.
New Orleans, LA 70125
Phone: (504)822-7355
Fax: (504)822-3369
Free: 800-925-0000
Publisher's E-mail: letters@timespicayune.com
General newspaper. **Freq:** Mon.-Sun. **Print Method:** Offset. **Cols./Page:** 6. **Col. Width:** 2 1/16 inches. **Col. Depth:** 21 1/4 inches. **Key Personnel:** Ray Massett, General Manager, Vice President; Ashton Phelps, Jr., Publisher; Peter Kovacs, Managing Editor; Terri Troncale, Editor; Dan Shea, Managing Editor; Lynn Cunningham, Editor; Jim Amoss, Editor; Philip Ehrhardt, Vice President. **Subscription Rates:** $21.58 Individuals Sunday, Wednesday & Friday print delivery + daily digital edition; $12.36 Individuals Wednesday & Sunday print delivery + daily digital edition; $12.36 Individuals Sunday print delivery + daily digital edition; $11.74 Individuals Wednesday & Friday print delivery + daily digital edition. **URL:** http://www.nola.com/t-p. **Formerly**: The Times-Picayune/States-Item. **Remarks:** Advertising accepted; rates available upon request. **Circ:** Mon.-Fri. **★179834**, Sun. **★199647**, Sat. **★176709**.

14531 ■ Tulane
Tulane University Office of Editorial and Creative Services
200 Broadway, Ste. 219
New Orleans, LA 70115
Phone: (504)865-5714
Fax: (504)865-5621
Publication E-mail: @tulane.edu address
Magazine for college alumni. **Freq:** Quarterly. **Print Method:** Offset. **Trim Size:** 8 3/8 x 10 7/8. **Cols./Page:** 4. **Col. Width:** 9.5 picas. **Col. Depth:** 120 agate lines. **Key Personnel:** Fran Simon, Managing Editor. **ISSN:** 0041--4026 (print). **URL:** http://tulane.edu/tulanian/index.cfm. **Formerly**: Tulanian. **Remarks:** Advertising not accepted. **Circ:** Controlled 83000.

14532 ■ Tulane Environmental Law Journal
Tulane University Law School
John Giffen Weinmann Hall
6329 Freret St.
New Orleans, LA 70118-6231
Phone: (504)865-5939
Journal containing articles on environmental issues affecting individuals and communities. **Freq:** Semiannual. **Key Personnel:** E. Carra Smith, Editor-in-Chief. **Subscription Rates:** $20 Individuals domestic; $25 Individuals international. **URL:** http://www.law.tulane.edu/tlsjournals/enviro. **Circ:** (Not Reported).

14533 ■ Tulane Journal of International and Comparative Law
Tulane University Law School
John Giffen Weinmann Hall
6329 Freret St.
New Orleans, LA 70118-6231
Phone: (504)865-5939
Journal containing articles in all facets of international law. **Freq:** Semiannual. **Subscription Rates:** $30 Individuals domestic; $35 Individuals foreign. **URL:** http://www.law.tulane.edu/tlsjournals/tjicl/index.aspx. **Circ:** (Not Reported).

14534 ■ Tulane Journal of Law & Sexuality
Tulane University Law School
John Giffen Weinmann Hall
6329 Freret St.
New Orleans, LA 70118-6231
Phone: (504)865-5939
Journal covering legal issues of interest to the lesbian, gay, bisexual and transgender community. **Freq:** Annual. **Key Personnel:** Tracy Law, Editor-in-Chief. **Subscription Rates:** $12 Students; $18 Individuals; $20 Institutions; $25 Other countries. **URL:** http://www.law.tulane.edu/tlsjournals/tlas. **Circ:** (Not Reported).

14535 ■ Tulane Journal of Technology and Intellectual Property
Tulane University Law School
John Giffen Weinmann Hall
6329 Freret St.
New Orleans, LA 70118-6231
Phone: (504)865-5939
Journal containing articles on legal issues in the society. **Freq:** Annual. **Key Personnel:** Casey Ebner, Editor-in-

Chief. **URL:** http://www.law.tulane.edu/tlsjournals/jtip. **Circ:** (Not Reported).

14536 ■ Xavier Review
Xavier University of Louisiana
1 Drexel Dr.
New Orleans, LA 70125
Phone: (504)486-7411
Fax: (504)520-7901
Literary journal. **Freq:** Semiannual. **Print Method:** Offset. **Trim Size:** 6 x 9. **Key Personnel:** Nicole P. Greene, Executive Editor, phone: (504)520-5246; Katheryn Laborde, Managing Editor, phone: (504)520-5151. **ISSN:** 0887--6681 (print). **URL:** http://www.xula.edu/review/index.php. **Remarks:** Accepts advertising. **Circ:** (Not Reported).

14537 ■ KHOM-FM - 104.1
929 Howard Ave.
New Orleans, LA 70113
Phone: (504)679-7300
Fax: (504)679-7345
Format: Sports; News. **Owner:** Clear Channel Communications Inc., at above address, Ph: (210)822-2828, Fax: (210)822-2299. **Founded:** 1968. **ADI:** New Orleans, LA. **Key Personnel:** Bill Thorman, Dir. of Programs; Kandy Klutch, Asst. Dir., Contact; Tom Naylor, Music Dir.; Greg Benefield, Sales Mgr; Kandy Klutch, Contact. **Wattage:** 20,000 ERP. **Ad Rates:** Accepts Advertising. **URL:** http://voodoo104.iheart.com.

14538 ■ KKND-FM - 102.9
201 St. Charles Ave., Ste. 201
New Orleans, LA 70170
Phone: (504)581-7002
Fax: (504)566-4857
Format: Country. **Networks:** Westwood One Radio. **Owner:** Citadel Broadcasting Corp., 7201 W Lake Mead Blvd., Ste. 400, Las Vegas, NV 89128-8366, Ph: (702)804-5200, Fax: (702)804-8250. **Operating Hours:** Continuous. **Key Personnel:** Dave Smith, Sales Mgr., david.smith@citcomm.com. **Wattage:** 98,000. **Ad Rates:** Noncommercial. **URL:** http://www.power1029.com.

KMEZ-FM - See Belle Chasse

14539 ■ KTLN-FM - 90.5
University of New Orleans, 2000 Lakeshore Dr.
2000 Lakeshore Dr.
New Orleans, LA 70148
Phone: (504)280-7000
Fax: (504)280-6061
Email: info@wwno.org
Format: Classical; Public Radio; News; Jazz. **Simulcasts:** WWNO-FM. **Networks:** National Public Radio (NPR); Public Radio International (PRI). **Founded:** Aug. 1995. **Operating Hours:** Continuous. **Key Personnel:** Ron Curtis, Dir. of Operations, rcurtis@uno.edu; Jenni Lawson, Production Mgr., jlawson@uno.edu; Robert Carroll, Chief Engineer, r.carroll@uno.edu. **Wattage:** 200. **Ad Rates:** Noncommercial. Combined advertising rates available with WWNO-FM. **URL:** http://www.wwno.org.

14540 ■ K28IL - 28
PO Box A
Santa Ana, CA 92711
Phone: (714)832-2950
Free: 888-731-1000
Owner: Trinity Broadcasting Network Inc., PO Box A, Santa Ana, CA 92711, Ph: (714)832-2950, Free: 888-731-1000. **URL:** http://www.tbn.org.

14541 ■ KYRK-FM - 106.5
929 Howard Ave.
New Orleans, LA 70113
Phone: (504)679-7300
Fax: (504)679-7345
Format: Classic Rock. **Owner:** iHeartMedia Inc., 200 E Basse Rd., San Antonio, TX 78209, Ph: (210)832-3314. **Wattage:** 50,000. **Ad Rates:** Advertising accepted; rates available upon request. **URL:** http://www.voodoo104.com//main.html.

14542 ■ WBOK-AM - 1230
1639 Gentilly Blvd.
New Orleans, LA 70119-2100
Phone: (504)942-0106
Format: Religious; Gospel. **Owner:** Willis Broadcasting Corp., at above address. **Founded:** 1951. **Operating Hours:** Continuous. **ADI:** New Orleans, LA. **Key Personnel:** Annette Pete, Gen. Mgr. **Wattage:** 1,000 KW. **URL:** http://www.wbok1230am.com/.

14543 ■ WBSN-FM - 89.1
3939 Gentilly Blvd.
New Orleans, LA 70126
Phone: (504)816-8000
Format: Contemporary Christian. **Simulcasts:** K249DI. **Founded:** 1978. **Operating Hours:** Continuous. **Wattage:** 11,000 ERP. **Ad Rates:** Noncommercial. **URL:** http://www.lifesongs.com.

14544 ■ WBYU-AM - 1450
1515 St. Charles Ave.
New Orleans, LA 70130-4445
Phone: (504)522-1450
Fax: (504)528-9244
Format: Easy Listening. **Founded:** 1950. **Formerly:** WWIW-AM. **Operating Hours:** Continuous. **ADI:** New Orleans, LA. **Key Personnel:** Dave Smith, Sales Mgr. **Wattage:** 1,000. **Ad Rates:** Advertising accepted; rates available upon request.

14545 ■ WDSU-TV - 6
846 Howard Ave.
New Orleans, LA 70113
Phone: (504)679-0600
Free: 800-416-6397
Format: Commercial TV; News. **Networks:** NBC. **Owner:** Hearst Television Inc., 300 W 57th St., New York, NY 10019-3741, Ph: (212)887-6800, Fax: (212)887-6855. **Founded:** 1948. **Operating Hours:** Continuous. **Key Personnel:** Jonathan Shelley, News Dir. **Local Programs:** *Midday*. **Wattage:** 100,000. **Ad Rates:** Noncommercial. **URL:** http://www.wdsu.com.

14546 ■ WDVW-FM - 92.3
201 St. Charles Ave., Ste. 201
New Orleans, LA 70170
Phone: (504)581-7002
Fax: (504)566-4857
Format: Alternative/New Music/Progressive; Information. **Owner:** Cumulus Media Inc., 3280 Peachtree Rd. NW, Ste. 2300, Atlanta, GA 30305-2455, Ph: (404)949-0700, Fax: (404)949-0740. **Operating Hours:** Continuous. **Ad Rates:** Advertising accepted; rates available upon request.

14547 ■ WEZB-FM - 97
400 Poydras St., 8th Fl.
New Orleans, LA 70130
Phone: (504)260-9797
Free: 888-340-9797
Format: Contemporary Hit Radio (CHR). **Networks:** Independent. **Owner:** Entercom Communications Corp., 401 City Ave., Ste. 809, Bala Cynwyd, PA 19004-1130, Ph: (610)660-5610, Fax: (610)660-5620. **Founded:** 1945. **Operating Hours:** Continuous. **ADI:** New Orleans, LA. **Wattage:** 100,000. **Ad Rates:** Advertising accepted; rates available upon request. **URL:** http://www.b97.com.

14548 ■ WHNO-TV - 20
839 St. Charles Ave., Ste. 309
New Orleans, LA 70130
Phone: (504)681-0120
Fax: (504)681-0180
Free: 800-365-3732
Key Personnel: Dean Powery, Gen. Mgr.; Jennifer Nero, Office Mgr.; Bob Lawrence, Chief Engineer. **URL:** http://www.whno.com/AboutUs/History.cfm.

14549 ■ WIST-AM - 690
1218 B Decatur St.
New Orleans, LA 70116
Phone: (504)552-2412
Format: Talk. **Operating Hours:** 5 a.m. to 12 a.m. Mon.-Fri.;8 a.m. to 12 a.m. Sat.-Sun. **Key Personnel:** John Bradley, Sales Rep., jbradley@wistradio.com; Eric Asher, Contact, easher@wistradio.com; Kaare Johnson, Contact, kaare@wistradio.com. **Wattage:** 10,000. **Ad Rates:** Advertising accepted; rates available upon request.

14550 ■ WKBU-FM - 95.7
400 Poydras St., Ste. 800
New Orleans, LA 70130
Phone: (504)260-9595
Format: Classic Rock. **Owner:** Entercom Communications Corp., 401 City Ave., Ste. 809, Bala Cynwyd, PA 19004-1130, Ph: (610)660-5610, Fax: (610)660-5620. **Formerly:** WKB-FM. **Operating Hours:** Continuous. **Key Personnel:** Jackie Henry, Promotions Dir. **Ad Rates:** Advertising accepted; rates available upon request. **URL:** http://www.bayou957.com.

14551 ■ WLMG-FM - 101.9
400 Poydras St., Ste. 800
New Orleans, LA 70113
Phone: (504)593-6376
Format: Soft Rock. **Owner:** Entercom New Orleans License L.L.C., at above address. **Operating Hours:** Continuous. **Key Personnel:** Wendy Duhon, V. Chmn. of the Bd.; Andy Holt, Dir. of Programs. **Wattage:** 99,000. **Ad Rates:** Advertising accepted; rates available upon request. **URL:** http://www.magic1019.com.

14552 ■ WMTI-FM - 106.1
201 Saint Charles Ave., Ste. 201
New Orleans, LA 70170
Phone: (504)581-7002
Format: Oldies. **Owner:** Citadel Broadcasting Corp., 7201 W Lake Mead Blvd., Ste. 400, Las Vegas, NV 89128-8366, Ph: (702)804-5200, Fax: (702)804-8250. **Operating Hours:** Continuous. **Ad Rates:** Advertising accepted; rates available upon request. **URL:** http://www.1061neworleans.com.

14553 ■ WNKV-FM - 91.1
PO Box 2098
Omaha, NE 68103-2098
Free: 800-525-5683
Format: Contemporary Christian. **Owner:** Educational Media Foundation, 2351 Sunset Blvd., Ste. 170-218, Rocklin, CA 95677, Ph: (800)434-8400. **URL:** http://www.klove.com.

14554 ■ WNOE-FM - 101.1
929 Howard Ave.
New Orleans, LA 70113
Phone: (504)679-7300
Fax: (504)679-7343
Free: 800-543-9663
Format: Country. **Networks:** Independent. **Founded:** 1968. **Operating Hours:** Continuous. **ADI:** New Orleans, LA. **Key Personnel:** Ray Romero, Dir. of Operations. **Wattage:** 100,000. **Ad Rates:** Noncommercial. **URL:** http://www.wnoe.com/main.html.

14555 ■ WODT-AM - 1280
929 Howard Ave.
New Orleans, LA 70113
Phone: (504)679-7300
Fax: (504)679-7339
Format: Gospel. **Operating Hours:** Continuous. **Key Personnel:** Dick Lewis, Gen. Mgr. **Ad Rates:** Advertising accepted; rates available upon request.

14556 ■ WODT-FM - 1280
929 Howard Ave.
New Orleans, LA 70113
Phone: (504)679-7300
Fax: (504)679-7339
Format: Sports. **Networks:** ABC. **Founded:** 1923. **Operating Hours:** Continuous; 100%. **ADI:** New Orleans, LA. **Key Personnel:** Dick Lewis, Gen. Mgr. **Wattage:** 5,000. **Ad Rates:** Noncommercial.

14557 ■ WQUE-FM - 93.3
929 Howard Ave.
New Orleans, LA 70113
Phone: (504)679-7300
Format: Urban Contemporary. **Networks:** Independent. **Founded:** 1949. **Formerly:** WDSU-FM. **Operating Hours:** Continuous; 100% local. **ADI:** New Orleans, LA. **Key Personnel:** Dick Lewis, Gen. Mgr. **Wattage:** 100,000. **Ad Rates:** Advertising accepted; rates available upon request. **URL:** http://www.q93.com.

14558 ■ WRBH-FM - 88.3
3606 Magazine St.
New Orleans, LA 70115-2545
Phone: (504)899-1144
Fax: (504)899-1165
Email: listen@wrbh.org
Format: Public Radio. **Owner:** Radio for the Blind and Print Handicapped Inc., at above address, New Orleans, LA 70115. **Founded:** 1975. **Operating Hours:** Continuous. **ADI:** New Orleans, LA. **Key Personnel:** Daniel Meyer, VP; Natalia Gonzalez, Exec. Dir., natalia@wrbh.org; David Benedetto, Dir. of Mktg., david@wrbh.org. **Wattage:** 51,000 ERP. **Ad Rates:** Underwriting

Circulation: ★ = AAM; △ or • = BPA; ♦ = CAC; ❑ = VAC; ⊕ = PO Statement; ‡ = Publisher's Report; Boldface figures = sworn; Light figures = estimated.

available. **URL:** http://www.wrbh.org.

14559 ■ WRNO-FM - 99.5
929 Howard Ave.
New Orleans, LA 70113
Phone: (504)679-7300
Email: news@wrno.com
Format: News; Information. **Operating Hours:** Continuous. **Wattage:** 100,000. **Ad Rates:** Advertising accepted; rates available upon request. **URL:** http://www.wrno.com.

14560 ■ WSHO-AM - 800
1001 Howard Ave., Ste. 4304
New Orleans, LA 70113-2045
Phone: (504)527-0800
Fax: (504)527-0881
Email: wsho@compuserve.com
Format: Religious; Contemporary Christian. **Operating Hours:** Continuous. **ADI:** New Orleans, LA. **Wattage:** 1,000. **Ad Rates:** Advertising accepted; rates available upon request. $25 for 60 seconds. **URL:** http://wsho.com.

14561 ■ WSMB-AM - 1350
1450 Poydras St., Ste. 500
New Orleans, LA 70112
Phone: (504)593-2100
Fax: (504)593-1850
Format: Talk; News. **Networks:** CBS. **Owner:** Entercom Communications Corp., at above address. **Founded:** 1925. **Operating Hours:** Continuous. **ADI:** New Orleans, LA. **Key Personnel:** John Andrews, Gen. Mgr.; Bob Christopher, Dir. of Operations. **Wattage:** 5,000. **Ad Rates:** Advertising accepted; rates available upon request.

14562 ■ WTIX-AM - 690
61 French Market Pl.
New Orleans, LA 70116
Phone: (504)522-6900
Fax: (504)525-0690
Format: Top 40. **Founded:** 1947. **Operating Hours:** Continuous. 50% network, 50% local. **Key Personnel:** Tony Ponseti, Gen. Mgr.; Jay Richards, Dir. of Programs. **Wattage:** 10,000. **Ad Rates:** $5-40 for 30 seconds; $5-60 for 60 seconds.

14563 ■ WTUL-FM - 91.5
Tulane University 1527, 6823 St. Charles Ave.
New Orleans, LA 70118
Phone: (504)865-5887
Format: Alternative/New Music/Progressive. **Networks:** Independent. **Owner:** Tulane University, at above address. **Founded:** 2005. **ADI:** New Orleans, LA. **Wattage:** 1,500 ERP. **Ad Rates:** Accepts Advertising. **URL:** http://www.wtulneworleans.com.

14564 ■ WUPL-TV - 54
1024 N Rampart St.
New Orleans, LA 70116
Phone: (504)529-4444
Ad Rates: Accepts Advertising. **URL:** http://wupltv.com.

14565 ■ WVUE-TV - 8
1025 S Jefferson Davis Pkwy.
New Orleans, LA 70125
Phone: (504)486-6161
Fax: (504)483-1212
Email: publicfile@fox8live.com
Format: Commercial TV. **Networks:** ABC; Fox. **Operating Hours:** Continuous; 25% network, 75% local. **ADI:** New Orleans, LA. **Key Personnel:** Jessica Lemoine, Contact. **Ad Rates:** Advertising accepted; rates available upon request. **URL:** http://www.fox8live.com.

14566 ■ WWL-AM - 870
400 Poydras St., 8th Fl.
New Orleans, LA 70130
Format: News; Talk; Sports. **Networks:** ABC; CBS. **Owner:** Entercom Communications Corp., at above address. **Founded:** 1922. **Operating Hours:** Continuous. **ADI:** New Orleans, LA. **Wattage:** 50,000. **Ad Rates:** Noncommercial. **URL:** http://www.wwl.com.

14567 ■ WWL-FM - 105.3
400 Poydras St., Ste. 800
New Orleans, LA 70130
Phone: (504)593-6376
Fax: (504)593-1850
Format: Sports; Talk; News. **Operating Hours:** Continuous. **Ad Rates:** Advertising accepted; rates available upon request. **URL:** http://www.wwl.com.

14568 ■ WWL-TV - 4
1024 N Rampart St.
New Orleans, LA 70116
Phone: (504)529-6298
Fax: (504)529-6472
URL: http://www.wwltv.com.

14569 ■ WWNO-FM - 89.9
2000 Lakeshore Dr.
2000 Lakeshore Dr., 4th Fl.
New Orleans, LA 70148
Phone: (504)280-7000
Fax: (504)280-6061
Email: comments@wwno.org
Format: Classical; Jazz; News; Public Radio. **Simulcasts:** KTLN-FM. **Networks:** National Public Radio (NPR); BBC World Service. **Owner:** University of New Orleans, 2000 Lakeshore Dr., New Orleans, LA 70148, Ph: (504)280-6000, Free: 888-514-4275. **Founded:** 1972. **Operating Hours:** Continuous. **ADI:** New Orleans, LA. **Key Personnel:** Robert Carroll, Chief Engineer, r.carroll@uno.edu; Ron Curtis, Operations Mgr., rcurtis@uno.edu; Jenni Lawson, Production Mgr., jlawson@uno.edu. **Local Programs:** *Classical Music*, Monday Wednesday Friday Thursday 8:00 p.m. - 11:00 p.m. 9:00 p.m.; *Le Show*, Sunday 8:00 p.m. - 9:00 p.m.; *Continuum*, Sunday 6:00 a.m. - 7:00 a.m. **Wattage:** 35,000 ERP. **Ad Rates:** Noncommercial. Combined underwriting rates available with KTLN-FM. **URL:** http://wwno.org.

14570 ■ WWOZ-FM - 90.7
PO Box 51840
New Orleans, LA 70151-1840
Phone: (504)568-1239
Fax: (504)558-9332
Email: feedback@wwoz.org
Format: Jazz; Blues; World Beat. **Owner:** Friends of WWOZ Inc., PO Box 51840, New Orleans, LA, Fax: (504)558-9332. **Founded:** 1980. **Operating Hours:** Continuous; 100% local. **Key Personnel:** David Freedman, Gen. Mgr.; Jorge Fuentes, Asst. Mgr.; Damond Jacob, Chief Engineer. **Wattage:** 4,000. **Ad Rates:** Noncommercial. **URL:** http://www.wwoz.org.

14571 ■ WYLD-AM - 940
929 Howard Ave.
New Orleans, LA 70113
Phone: (504)679-7300
Format: Religious; Gospel. **Founded:** 1949. **Operating Hours:** Continuous; 100% local. **ADI:** New Orleans, LA. **Key Personnel:** Darnetta Mahaffy, Sales Mgr., darnettamahaffy@clearchannel.com. **Wattage:** 10,000. **Ad Rates:** $40 for 30 seconds; $40-60 for 60 seconds. Combined advertising rates available with WYLD-FM, WQUE-FM, WODT-AM. **URL:** http://www.am940.com.

14572 ■ WYLD-FM - 98.5
929 Howard Ave.
New Orleans, LA 70113
Phone: (504)679-7300
Fax: (504)679-7345
Format: Urban Contemporary; Adult Contemporary. **Networks:** ABC. **Owner:** Clear Channel Radio, 200 E Basse Rd., San Antonio, TX 78209, Ph: (210)822-2828, Fax: (210)832-3428. **Founded:** 1949. **Operating Hours:** Continuous. **ADI:** New Orleans, LA. **Key Personnel:** Dick Lewis, Gen. Mgr. **Wattage:** 10,000 Day; 500 Night. **Ad Rates:** Advertising accepted; rates available upon request. **URL:** http://www.wyldfm.com/pages.

NEW ROADS

SEC LA. Pointe Coupee Parish. 6 mi. from Mississippi River, 22 mi. NW of Baton Rouge. Garment factory. Oil and gas. Commercial fisheries. Diversified farming. Pecans, corn, sugarcane, cotton.

14573 ■ K220EU-FM - 91.9
PO Box 391
Twin Falls, ID 83303
Fax: (208)736-1958
Free: 800-357-4226
Format: Religious; Contemporary Christian. **Owner:** CSN International, PO Box 391, Twin Falls, ID 83303, Ph: (208)736-1958, Fax: (208)736-1958, Free: 800-357-4226. **Key Personnel:** Don Mills, Music Dir., Prog. Dir.; Kelly Carlson, Dir. of Engg.; Ray Gorney, Asst. Dir. **URL:** http://www.csnradio.com.

OAK GROVE

NE LA. West Carroll Parish. 48 mi. NE of Monroe. Cotton. Cannery. Agriculture. Sweet potatoes, tomatoes, soybeans. Cattle.

14574 ■ KWCL-FM - 96.7
230 E Main St.
Oak Grove, LA 71263
Phone: (318)428-9670
Email: kwcl@bellsouth.net
Format: Oldies. **Networks:** ABC; Jones Satellite. **Founded:** 1973. **Operating Hours:** Continuous. **Wattage:** 23,000. **Ad Rates:** $4-5 for 30 seconds; $6-8 for 60 seconds. **URL:** http://www.kwclfm.com.

OPELOUSAS

SC LA. St. Landry Parish. 22 mi. N. of Lafayette. Manufactures lumber, brooms, drugs, perfume, salad oil, machinery. Cottonseed oil, meat processing and packing plants. Oil wells. Timber. Diversified farming. Cotton, corn, rice, jams.

14575 ■ KSLO-AM - 1230
PO Box 1150
Opelousas, LA 70571-1150
Phone: (337)942-2633
Fax: (337)942-2635
Format: News; Information; Country; Contemporary Country; Agricultural; French. **Networks:** ABC. **Owner:** KSLO Broadcasting Company Inc., at above address. **Founded:** 1947. **Operating Hours:** 5 a.m.-11 p.m.; 10% network, 90% local. **ADI:** Lafayette, LA. **Wattage:** 1,000. **Ad Rates:** $7.80-11.95 for 10 seconds; $11.95-16.85 for 30 seconds; $14.85-17.90 for 60 seconds. Combined advertising rates available with KOGM.

14576 ■ K39IN - 39
PO Box A
Santa Ana, CA 92711
Phone: (714)832-2950
Free: 888-731-1000
Owner: Trinity Broadcasting Network Inc., PO Box A, Santa Ana, CA 92711, Ph: (714)832-2950, Free: 888-731-1000.

PINEVILLE

C LA. Rapides Parish. Across Red River from Alexandria. Louisiana College. Saw, paper mills. Detergent and chemical plants. Commercial fisheries. Pine, hardwood timber. Diversified farming. Cotton, corn, potatoes.

14577 ■ Wildcat
Louisiana College
1140 College Dr.
Pineville, LA 71359
Phone: (318)487-7011
Free: 800-487-1906
Publication E-mail: wildcat@alex.lacollege.edu
Collegiate newspaper. **Freq:** Weekly during the academic year. **Print Method:** Offset. **Trim Size:** 11 1/2 x 15. **Cols./Page:** 4. **Col. Width:** 14 picas. **Col. Depth:** 196 agate lines. **URL:** http://wildcatsmedia.com. **Mailing address:** PO Box 566, Pineville, LA 71359. **Remarks:** Advertising accepted; rates available upon request. **Circ:** Free 1000.

14578 ■ KBKK-FM - 105.5
92 W Shamrock St.
Pineville, LA 71360
Phone: (318)487-1035
Format: Country. **Founded:** Sept. 05, 2006. **Wattage:** 6,000. **URL:** http://www.1055kbuck.com.

14579 ■ KEZP-FM - 104.3
92 W Shamrock St.
Pineville, LA 71360
Phone: (318)487-1035
Format: Alternative/New Music/Progressive. **Ad Rates:** Noncommercial.

14580 ■ KLAA-FM - 103.5
92 W Shamrock St.
Pineville, LA 71360
Phone: (318)487-1035
Format: Contemporary Country. **Networks:** Mutual Broadcasting System. **Owner:** Opus Broadcasting, 511 Rossanley Dr., Medford, OR 97501. **Formerly:** KISY-FM. **Operating Hours:** Continuous; 20% network, 80% local. **Wattage:** 50,000. **Ad Rates:** $10-47.75 for 60

seconds. **URL:** http://www.la103.com.

KWDF-AM - See Alexandria

14581 ■ KZLC-FM - 95.5
1140 College Dr.
Pineville, LA 71360
Phone: (318)487-7321
Format: Contemporary Christian. **Operating Hours:** Continuous.**Key Personnel:** Cheryl Clark, VP; Terry Martin, Director; Timothy Johnson, Exec. VP; Jeff Young, Contact. **URL:** http://www.lacollege.edu/about/kzlc-radio-lc.

PLAQUEMINE

S LA. Iberville Parish. On Mississippi River, 14 mi. SW of Baton Rouge. Lumber, sugar mills, moss gins, bottling works; foundry, chemical plants. Commercial fisheries. Oil wells; cypress, oak, ash timber. Diversified farming. Rice, sugarcane, corn.

14582 ■ Plaquemine Post-South
Plaquemine Publishing Inc.
58650 Belleview Dr.
Plaquemine, LA 70764
Phone: (225)687-3288
Fax: (225)687-1814
Publication E-mail: pscirculation@postsouth.com
Community newspaper. **Freq:** Weekly (Thurs.). **Print Method:** Offset. **Trim Size:** 14 x 23. **Cols./Page:** 6. **Col. Width:** 2 1/16 inches. **Col. Depth:** 21 inches. **Key Personnel:** Peter Pasqua, Editor; Glenn Stifflemire, Publisher. **USPS:** 576-480. **URL:** http://www.postsouth.com. **Ad Rates:** GLR $.40; BW $737.10; 4C $1,105.60; SAU $5.85; PCI $5.85. **Remarks:** Accepts advertising. **Circ:** (Not Reported).

14583 ■ KPAQ-FM - 88.1
PO Box 3206
Tupelo, MS 38803
Format: Religious. **Owner:** American Family Radio, at above address. **Wattage:** 2,900. **URL:** http://www.afa.net.

PONCHATOULA

SE LA. Tangipahoa Parish. 40 mi. NW of New Orleans. Lumber, veneer mills, brick, bottling works. Ships, fruit, vegetables. Cypress, hardwood timber. Poultry, truck, fruit farms. Strawberries, beans, peppers.

14584 ■ The Ponchatoula Times
The Ponchatoula Times
145 W Pine St., Ste. A
Ponchatoula, LA 70454-0743
Phone: (985)386-2877
Fax: (985)386-0458
Publication E-mail: editor@ponchatoula.com
Community newspaper. **Freq:** Weekly (Thurs.). **Print Method:** Offset. **Cols./Page:** 6. **Col. Depth:** 21 1/2 inches. **Key Personnel:** Bryan T. McMahon, Publisher. **Subscription Rates:** $25 Individuals in Parish; $25 Individuals senior in Parish; $30 Out of area; $30 Out of area senior. **URL:** http://www.ponchatoula.com/ptimes/index.php. **Ad Rates:** BW $708.21. **Remarks:** Accepts advertising. **Circ:** Paid ‡7400.

PORT ALLEN

SEC LA. West Baton Rouge Parish. 1 mi. W. of Baton Rouge. Chemical, iron, steel fabricating plants. Sugar mills. Diversified farming. Sugarcane, rice, corn, cotton.

14585 ■ The Louisiana Cattleman
Louisiana Cattlemen's Association
4921 I-10 Frontage Rd. W
Port Allen, LA 70767
Phone: (225)343-3491
Fax: (225)336-0002
Association magazine. **Freq:** Monthly. **Print Method:** Sheetfed Offset. **Trim Size:** 8 1/2 x 11. **Cols./Page:** 3. **Col. Width:** 13.5 picas. **Col. Depth:** 10 inches. **Key Personnel:** Cathy Berg, Editor. **USPS:** 588-320. **URL:** http://www.labeef.org/thelcamagazine.cfm. **Formerly:** The Louisiana Cattleman/The Louisiana Dairyman. **Ad Rates:** BW $625, Full page; BW $510, 2/3 page; BW $415, 1/2 page; BW $345, 1/3 page; BW $225, 1/4 page; BW $195, 1/6 page; BW $135, 1/8 page; BW $690, Inside back cover full page; 4C $1140, Full page; 4C $1025, 2/3 page; 4C $930, 1/2 page; 4C $860, 1/3 page; 4C $770, 1/4 page; 4C $1250, Outside back cover full page. **Remarks:** Accepts advertising. **Circ:** Paid ‡3900, Non-paid ‡800.

14586 ■ West Side Journal
West Side Journal
668 N Jefferson Ave.
Port Allen, LA 70767
Phone: (225)343-2540
Fax: (225)344-0923
Community weekly newspaper. **Freq:** Weekly (Thurs.). **Print Method:** Offset. **Cols./Page:** 6. **Col. Width:** 13 picas. **Col. Depth:** 21 inches. **URL:** http://www.thewestsidejournal.com. **Mailing address:** PO Box 260, Port Allen, LA 70767. **Remarks:** Advertising accepted; rates available upon request. **Circ:** 3000.

14587 ■ K237EW-FM - 95.3
PO Box 391
Twin Falls, ID 83303
Fax: (208)736-1958
Free: 800-357-4226
Format: Religious; Contemporary Christian. **Owner:** CSN International, PO Box 391, Twin Falls, ID 83303, Ph: (208)736-1958, Fax: (208)736-1958, Free: 800-357-4226. **Key Personnel:** Mike Kestler, President; Don Mills, Music Dir., Prog. Dir. **URL:** http://www.csnradio.com.

RUSTON

N LA. Lincoln Parish. 30 mi. W. of Monroe. Louisiana Tech University, Grambling State University. Manufactures soft drink bottles, chemicals, lumber, bricks, plywood, insulation, mop and broom handles, dairy and petroleum products. Timber, clay pits. Dairy, poultry, fruit, truck farms.

14588 ■ Arkansas Gardener
Carolina Gardener Inc.
PO Box 13070
Ruston, LA 71273
Fax: (318)251-8882
Free: 888-265-3600
Publisher's E-mail: contact@statebystategardening.com
Magazine featuring stories and information about equipment, strategies and other related information about gardening in Arkansas. **Freq:** 9/year. **Key Personnel:** Steve Giddings, Publisher; Jennifer Estes, Managing Editor, Associate Publisher. **Subscription Rates:** $24.95 Individuals; $43.95 Two years; $59.95 three years. **URL:** http://statebystategardening.com/ar. **Remarks:** Accepts classified advertising. **Circ:** (Not Reported).

14589 ■ Journal of the Academy of Marketing Science
Academy of Marketing Science
PO Box 3072
Ruston, LA 71272
Phone: (318)257-2612
Fax: (318)257-4253
Publication E-mail: advertising@sagepub.com
Professional journal on the science of marketing. **Freq:** Quarterly. **Print Method:** Offset. **Trim Size:** 8 1/2 x 11. **Cols./Page:** 2. **Key Personnel:** Robert W. Palmatier, Editor-in-Chief; George M. Zinkhan, Editor; G.T.M. Hult, Editor-in-Chief; Anne Hoekman, Managing Editor. **ISSN:** 0092--0703 (print); **EISSN:** 1552--7824 (electronic). **Subscription Rates:** Included in membership. **Alt. Formats:** Electronic publishing. **URL:** http://www.springer.com/business+%26+management/journal/11747. **Ad Rates:** BW $515; 4C $995. **Remarks:** Accepts advertising. **Circ:** ‡1500, 2000, ‡1500.

14590 ■ Ruston Daily Leader
Ruston Daily Leader
821 West California Avenue
Ruston, LA 71270
Phone: (318)255-4353
Fax: (318)255-4006
Publication E-mail: rslnew@ruston-leader.com
General newspaper. **Freq:** Daily and Sun. (eve.). **Print Method:** Offset. **Cols./Page:** 6. **Col. Width:** 25 nonpareils. **Col. Depth:** 294 agate lines. **Key Personnel:** Rick Hohlt, Publisher; Jeanie McCartney, Manager, Advertising. **Subscription Rates:** $138 Individuals home delivery; $25 Individuals home delivery for 2 months; $75 Individuals home delivery for 6 months. **URL:** http://www.rustonleader.com. **Ad Rates:** BW $75; SAU $5.85. **Remarks:** Accepts advertising. **Circ:** Combined 45000.

14591 ■ The Tech Talk
Louisiana Tech University
305 Wisteria St.
Ruston, LA 71272
Phone: (318)257-3036
Free: 800-LATECH-1
Publication E-mail: techtalk@latech.edu
Collegiate newspaper. **Founded:** 1925. **Freq:** Weekly (Thurs.). **Print Method:** Offset. **Cols./Page:** 6. **Col. Width:** 26 nonpareils. **Col. Depth:** 298 agate lines. **Key Personnel:** John Sadler, Editor. **Subscription Rates:** $25 Individuals. **URL:** http://www.thetechtalk.org. **Mailing address:** PO Box 3178, Ruston, LA 71272. **Ad Rates:** BW $1,750.58; 4C $1,970.58; PCI $13.73. **Remarks:** Accepts advertising. **Circ:** Paid ‡8000.

14592 ■ KAPI-FM - 88.3
PO Box 3206
Tupelo, MS 38803
Format: Religious. **Owner:** American Family Radio, at above address. **Wattage:** 300. **URL:** http://www.afr.net.

14593 ■ KLPI-FM - 89.1
100 Wisteria St.
Ruston, LA 71272
Phone: (318)257-4851
Format: Alternative/New Music/Progressive. **Owner:** Louisiana Tech University, 305 Wisteria St., Ruston, LA 71272, Ph: (318)257-3036, Free: 800-LATECH-1. **Founded:** 1966. **Operating Hours:** 8:00 a.m.-12:00 a.m. **Key Personnel:** Jedediah Wilson, Gen. Mgr.; Ross Beattie, Dir. of Programs. **Wattage:** 4,000. **Ad Rates:** Noncommercial. **Mailing address:** PO Box 8638, Ruston, LA 71272. **URL:** http://www.klpi.latech.edu.

14594 ■ KNBB-FM - 97.7
PO Box 430
Ruston, LA 71270
Phone: (318)255-5000
Fax: (318)255-5084
Free: 888-993-7762
Email: espn977@gmail.com
Format: Sports. **Key Personnel:** Louise Oxford, Contact. **Ad Rates:** Advertising accepted; rates available upon request. **URL:** http://www.espn977.com.

14595 ■ KPCH-FM - 97.7
500 N Monroe Ave.
Ruston, LA 71270
Phone: (318)255-5000
Fax: (318)255-5084
Free: 800-638-1075
Founded: 1984. **ADI:** Monroe, LA-El Dorado, AR. **Key Personnel:** Gary McKenney, Gen. Mgr., manager@z1075fm.com. **Wattage:** 50,000. **Ad Rates:** Accepts Advertising.

14596 ■ KRUS-AM
500 N Monroe Ave.
Ruston, LA 71270
Phone: (318)255-2530
Fax: (318)225-2100
Free: 800-638-1075
Format: Blues. **Networks:** AP. **Owner:** Communications Capital Inc., at above address. **Founded:** 1947. **Key Personnel:** James Cooper, Sports Dir., Music Dir. **Wattage:** 1,000. **Ad Rates:** $3.54-7.06 for 30 seconds; $7.06-11.77 for 60 seconds.

14597 ■ KXKZ-FM - 107.5
500 N Monroe St.
Ruston, LA 71270
Phone: (318)255-5000
Fax: (318)255-5084
Free: 800-638-1075
Format: Country. **Networks:** AP. **Owner:** Communcation Capital 2 Of La., at above address. **Founded:** 1965. **Operating Hours:** Continuous. **ADI:** Monroe, LA-El Dorado, AR. **Key Personnel:** Ed Hebert, Contact, ed@z1075fm.com. **Wattage:** 100,000. **Ad Rates:** $26 for 30 seconds; $34 for 60 seconds. $26 for 30 seconds; $35 for 60 seconds. **URL:** http://www.z1075fm.com.

SCHRIEVER

14598 ■ The Bayou Catholic
Diocese of Houma-Thibodaux

Circulation: ★ = AAM; △ or • = BPA; ♦ = CAC; ❑ = VAC; ⊕ = PO Statement; ‡ = Publisher's Report; Boldface figures = sworn; Light figures = estimated.

PO Box 505
Schriever, LA 70395
Phone: (985)850-3132
Fax: (985)868-7727
Publisher's E-mail: bayoucatholic@htdiocese.org
Official newspaper (tabloid) of the Diocese of Houma-Thibodaux. **Freq:** Weekly. **Print Method:** Offset. **Cols./Page:** 5. **Col. Width:** 11 picas. **Col. Depth:** 13 INS. **Key Personnel:** Mrs. Peggy Adams, Manager, Advertising; Mr. Louis Aguirre, MPS, Editor, General Manager; Mr. Glenn J. Landry, Business Manager. **ISSN:** 0274--8126 (print). **Subscription Rates:** $15 Individuals. **Ad Rates:** GLR $.96; BW $968.50; 4C $1,168.50; PCI $14.90. **Remarks:** Accepts advertising. **Circ:** Paid ‡33000.

SHREVEPORT

NW LA. Caddo Parish. On Red River, 196 mi. E. of Dallas, TX. Centenary College. Louisiana State University at Shreveport. L.S.U. School of Medicine. Baptist Christian College; Southern Univ. Shreveport branch. Manufactures trucks, transformers, electric components, paper products, glassware, chemicals, machinery, food and dairy products, feed. Oil refining. Lumber and woodworking plants. Sheet metal work. Iron and steel foundry. Gas and oil wells.

14599 ■ American Rose
American Rose Society
8877 Jefferson Paige Rd.
Shreveport, LA 71119-8817
Phone: (318)938-5402
Fax: (318)938-5405
Free: 800-637-6534
Publisher's E-mail: ars@ars-hq.org
Magazine concerning all aspects of rose growing. **Freq:** Bimonthly. **Print Method:** Offset. **Trim Size:** 8 1/4 x 10 7/8. **Cols./Page:** 3. **Col. Width:** 26 nonpareils. **Col. Depth:** 140 agate lines. **Key Personnel:** Beth Smiley, Managing Editor; Amanda Figlio, Associate Editor. **ISSN:** 0003--0899 (print). **Subscription Rates:** Included in membership. **URL:** http://www.rose.org/about-ars/american-rose. **Formerly**: The American Rose Magazine. **Mailing address:** PO Box 30000, Shreveport, LA 71130-0030. **Ad Rates:** GLR $.75; BW $773; 4C $1,049. **Remarks:** Accepts advertising. **Circ:** Paid ‡15000.

14600 ■ Centenary Today
Centenary College of Louisiana Alumni Association
PO Box 41188
Shreveport, LA 71134
Phone: (318)869-5115
Fax: (318)841-7266
Free: 800-259-6447
Publisher's E-mail: alumni@centenary.edu
Magazine featuring news, activities, programs, events, accomplishments and different stories about Centenary College of Louisiana. **Freq:** Semiannual. **Subscription Rates:** Free. **Alt. Formats:** PDF. **URL:** http://www.centenary.edu/magazine. **Remarks:** Advertising not accepted. **Circ:** 17000.

14601 ■ The Genie
Ark-La-Tex Genealogical Association
PO Box 4463
Shreveport, LA 71134-0463
Publisher's E-mail: altgenassn@gmail.com
Freq: Quarterly. **Subscription Rates:** free for members. **URL:** http://www.rootsweb.ancestry.com/~laaltga/genie.htm. **Remarks:** Advertising not accepted. **Circ:** (Not Reported).

14602 ■ International Journal of Innovation and Learning
Inderscience Publishers
c/o Dr. Binshan Lin, Editorial Board Member
Louisiana State University
BE321, College of Business Administration
One University Pl.
Shreveport, LA 71115
Publication E-mail: info@inderscience.com
Peer-reviewed journal presenting information on the current practice, content, technology, and services in the area of innovation and learning. **Freq:** 8/year. **Key Personnel:** Dr. Binshan Lin, Board Member; Dr. Kongkiti Phusavat, Editor-in-Chief; Prof. Dr. Pekka Kess, Editor. **ISSN:** 1471--8197 (print); **EISSN:** 1741--8089 (electronic). **Subscription Rates:** $1016 Individuals print or online for 1 user; $1727.20 Individuals online only for 2-3 users; $1415 Individuals print and online; $2540 Individuals online only for 4-5 users; $3302 Individuals online only for 6-7 users; $4013.20 Individuals online only for 8-9 users; $4673.60 Individuals online only for 10-14 users; $5334 Individuals online only for 15-19 users; $6299.20 Individuals online only for 20+ users. **URL:** http://www.inderscience.com/jhome.php?jcode=ijil. **Circ:** (Not Reported).

14603 ■ International Journal of Management and Enterprise Development
Inderscience Publishers
c/o Dr. Binshan Lin, Editorial Board Member
Dept. of Management & Marketing, Louisiana State University
BE321, College of Business Administration
One University Pl.
Shreveport, LA 71115
Publication E-mail: info@inderscience.com
Journal publishing articles that present current practice and research in the area of management and enterprise development. **Freq:** 4/yr. **Key Personnel:** Dr. Binshan Lin, Board Member; Prof. Zbigniew Pastuszak, Editor-in-Chief. **ISSN:** 1468--4330 (print); **EISSN:** 1741--8127 (electronic). **Subscription Rates:** $685 Individuals print or online for 1 user; $1164.50 Individuals online only for 2-3 users; $928 Individuals print and online; $1712.50 Individuals online only for 4-5 users; $2226.25 Individuals online only for 6-7 users; $2705.75 Individuals online only for 8-9 users; $3151 Individuals online only for 10-14 users; $3596.25 Individuals online only for 15-19 users; $4247 Individuals online only for 20+ users. **URL:** http://www.inderscience.com/jhome.php?jcode=ijmed. **Circ:** (Not Reported).

14604 ■ International Journal of Services and Standards
Inderscience Publishers
c/o Dr. Binshan Lin, Editorial Board Member
Dept. of Management & Marketing, Louisiana State University
BE321, College of Business Administration
One University Pl.
Shreveport, LA 71115
Publication E-mail: info@inderscience.com
Peer-reviewed journal publishing present current practice, models, and theory in both services and standards development, design, management, implementation and applications. **Freq:** Quarterly. **Key Personnel:** Dr. Binshan Lin, Board Member; Dr. Kai S. Koong, Editor-in-Chief; Prof. Zbigniew Pastuszak, Associate Editor. **ISSN:** 1740--8849 (print); **EISSN:** 1740--8857 (electronic). **Subscription Rates:** $685 Individuals print or online only for 1 user; $1164.50 Individuals online only for 2-3 users; $1712.50 Individuals online only for 4-5 users; $2226.25 Individuals online only for 6-7 users; $2705.75 Individuals online only for 8-9 users; $3151 Individuals online only for 10-14 users; $3596.25 Individuals online only for 15-19 users; $4247 Individuals online only for 20+ users; $928 Individuals print and online. **URL:** http://www.inderscience.com/jhome.php?jcode=ijss. **Circ:** (Not Reported).

14605 ■ The Journal of Ideology
Louisiana State University, Shreveport
1 University Pl.
Shreveport, LA 71115
Phone: (318)797-5000
Fax: (318)798-4120
Publisher's E-mail: ndolch@lsus.edu
Scholarly journal covering philosophy. **Freq:** Quarterly. **Key Personnel:** Dr. Norman A. Dolch, Editor; Alex S. Freedman, Founder; Stacey Martino, Assistant Editor; Dennis Peck, Associate Editor; Ivan Chapman, Founder; Larry Marshman, Associate Editor; Binshan Lin, Associate Editor. **ISSN:** 0783--9752 (print). **URL:** http://www.lsus.edu/offices-and-services/community-outreach/the-journal-of-ideology. **Formerly**: Q.J.I. **Remarks:** Advertising not accepted. **Circ:** (Not Reported).

14606 ■ SB Magazine: The Pulse of Shreveport-Bossier
SB Magazine Inc.
850 Stoner Ave.
Shreveport, LA 71101
Phone: (318)221-7264
Fax: (318)676-8850
Magazine containing interviews and articles regarding business, politics, sports, and personalities in North Louisiana. **Freq:** Monthly. **Key Personnel:** Kate Danner, Writer; Byron May, President. **Subscription Rates:** $16 Individuals; $28 Two years; $36 Individuals three years. **URL:** http://sbmag.net. **Remarks:** Accepts advertising. **Circ:** (Not Reported).

14607 ■ The Times
The Times
222 Lake St.
Shreveport, LA 71101
Phone: (318)459-3200
General newspaper. **Freq:** Mon.-Sun. (morn.). **Print Method:** Letterpress. **Cols./Page:** 6. **Col. Width:** 25 nonpareils. **Col. Depth:** 301 agate lines. **Subscription Rates:** $16.68 Individuals 7 days a week; per month; $11.27 Individuals weekends; per month; $7.60 Individuals Sundays only; per month. **URL:** http://www.shreveporttimes.com. **Ad Rates:** SAU $45.38. **Remarks:** Accepts advertising. **Circ:** Mon.-Fri. **★139000**, Sun. **★169000**, Sat. **★50635**.

14608 ■ KBCL-AM - 1070
316 Gregg St.
Shreveport, LA 71104
Phone: (318)861-1070
Format: Religious; News; Talk. **Owner:** Barnabas Center Ministries, 413 S Sharon Amity, Charlotte, NC 28211, Ph: (704)365-4545, Fax: (888)723-9330. **Founded:** 1957. **Operating Hours**: 6:30 a.m.-8 p.m.; 80% network, 20% local. **ADI**: Shreveport, LA-Texarkana, TX. **Key Personnel:** Leon McKee, Contact. **Wattage**: 250. **Ad Rates:** Noncommercial. **URL:** http://www.kbclthebridge.org.

14609 ■ KBSA-FM - 90.9
PO Box 5250
Shreveport, LA 71135
Phone: (318)797-5150
Fax: (318)797-5265
Free: 800-552-8502
Email: listenermail@redriverradio.org
Format: Public Radio. **Owner:** Red River Radio, 8675 Youree Dr., Shreveport, LA 71115, Fax: (318)798-0107. **Operating Hours**: Continuous. **Key Personnel:** Kermit Poling, Div. Dir., kpoling@lsus.edu. **Ad Rates:** Noncommercial; underwriting available. **URL:** http://www.redriverradio.org.

14610 ■ KBTT-FM - 103.7
208 N Thomas Dr.
Shreveport, LA 71107
Phone: (318)222-3122
Format: Hip Hop; Blues. **Founded:** Sept. 07, 2006. **URL:** http://www.kbtt.fm.

14611 ■ KDAQ-FM - 89.9
PO Box 5250
Shreveport, LA 71135
Phone: (318)798-0102
Fax: (318)797-5265
Free: 800-552-8502
Format: Public Radio; Jazz; Eclectic; Classical. **Networks:** National Public Radio (NPR). **Owner:** Red River Radio Network, 8675 Youree Dr., Shreveport, LA 71115, Ph: (318)798-0102, Fax: (318)798-0107, Free: 800-552-8502. **Founded:** 1984. **Operating Hours**: Continuous. **ADI**: Shreveport, LA-Texarkana, TX. **Key Personnel:** John Ellis, Contact; Kermit Poling, Gen. Mgr., kpoling@lsus.edu. **Wattage**: 100,000. **Ad Rates:** Noncommercial. **URL:** http://redriverradio.org/podcasts.

14612 ■ KDKS-FM - 102.1
208 N Thomas
Shreveport, LA 71137
Phone: (318)222-3122
Fax: (318)320-0102
Format: Hip Hop; Blues; Oldies. **Networks:** Independent. **Owner:** Dowe Co., Inc., at above address. **Founded:** Sept. 07, 2006. **Operating Hours:** Continuous. **Key Personnel:** Cary Camp, Mktg. Mgr., ccamp@radiogroupshreveport.com; Quinn Echols, Dir. of Programs, quinn.echols@alphamediausa.com; Melvin Jones, Sales Mgr., melvinjones@radiogroupshreveport.com. **Wattage**: 3,000. **Ad Rates:** Advertising accepted; rates available upon request. **URL:** http://www.kdks.fm.

14613 ■ KEEL-AM - 710
6341 Westport Ave.
Shreveport, LA 71129-2498
Phone: (318)688-1130
Format: News; Talk. **Networks:** CNN Radio. **Owner:** Townsquare Media Inc., 240 Greenwich Ave., Green-

wich, CT 06830-6507, Ph: (203)861-0900. **Founded:** 1922. **Operating Hours**: Continuous. **Key Personnel:** Lisa Janes, Gen. Mgr., lisajanes@townsquaremedia.com. **Wattage**: 50,000 Day ; 5,000 Night. **Ad Rates:** Advertising accepted; rates available upon request. **URL:** http://www.710keel.com.

14614 ■ KFLO-FM - 89.1
PO Box 7277
Shreveport, LA 71107
Phone: (318)550-2000
Fax: (318)550-2002
Email: info@miracle891.org
Format: Contemporary Christian. **Owner:** Family Life Education, 30 Arbor St., Hartford, CT 06106, Fax: (860)236-6721. **Key Personnel:** Dan Perkins, Operations Mgr., dperkins@miracle891.org; Joe Miot, Prog. Dir., jmiot@miracle891.org. **Wattage**: 20,000. **URL:** http://www.miracle891.org.

14615 ■ KLSA-FM - 90.7
One University Pl.
Shreveport, LA 71115
Phone: (318)797-5150
Fax: (318)797-5265
Free: 800-552-8502
Format: Public Radio. **Owner:** Louisiana State University, 1 E Campus Dr., Louisiana State University, Baton Rouge, LA 70803-1000, Ph: (225)578-3202, Fax: (225)578-5991. **Founded:** Sept. 19, 2006. **Operating Hours**: Continuous. **ADI**: Shreveport, LA-Texarkana, TX. **Wattage**: 100,000. **Ad Rates:** Noncommercial. **URL:** http://www.redriverradio.org.

14616 ■ KLTS-TV - 24
7733 Perkins Rd.
Baton Rouge, LA 70810
Phone: (225)767-5660
Free: 800-272-8161
Format: Public TV. **Simulcasts:** WLPB-TV Baton Rogue, LA. **Networks:** Public Broadcasting Service (PBS); Louisiana Public Broadcasting. **Owner:** Louisiana Public Broadcasting, 7733 Perkins Rd., Baton Rouge, LA 70810, Ph: (225)767-5660, Fax: (225)767-4288. **Founded:** 1978. **Operating Hours**: Continuous. **ADI**: Shreveport, LA-Texarkana, TX. **Key Personnel:** Clay Fourrier, Producer; Gary Allen, Producer; Ken Miller, Production Mgr.; Beth Courtney, CEO, President, bcourtney@lpb.org; Jason Viso, Div. Dir., jviso@lpb.org; Bob Neese, Contact, bneese@lpb.org. **Wattage**: 57,000. **Ad Rates:** Noncommercial. **URL:** http://beta.lpb.org.

14617 ■ KMSL-FM - 91.7
PO Box 3206
Tupelo, MS 38803
Format: Religious. **Owner:** American Family Radio, at above address. **Wattage**: 12,000. **URL:** http://www.afa.net.

14618 ■ KMSS-TV - 33
3519 Jewella Ave.
Shreveport, LA 71109
Phone: (318)631-5677
Fax: (318)631-4194
Email: info@kmsstv.com
Format: Commercial TV. **Networks:** Fox; Independent. **Owner:** Communications Corp., 700 Saint John St., Lafayette, LA 70501. **Founded:** Oct. 06, 1985. **Operating Hours**: Continuous; 26% network, 74% local. **ADI**: Shreveport, LA-Texarkana, TX. **Key Personnel:** Heather Evans, Mgr., hevans@ktalnews.tv; Mark McKay, VP. **Wattage**: 4,570,000. **Ad Rates:** $5-225 for 10 seconds; $6.50-360 for 15 seconds; $10-550 for 30 seconds; $20-1100 for 60 seconds. **URL:** http://www.kmsstv.com.

14619 ■ KOKA-AM - 980
208 N Thomas Dr.
Shreveport, LA 71107
Phone: (318)222-3122
Format: Religious. **Networks:** NBC; American Urban Radio. **Owner:** Cary D. Camp, 949 Poleman Rd., Shreveport, LA 71107. **Formerly**: KLMB-AM. **Operating Hours**: 6:00 a.m. - 5:00 p.m. Monday - Friday. **Key Personnel:** Cary D. Camp, Contact. **Wattage**: 5,000 ERP H; 079 ERP . **Ad Rates:** $18 for 30 seconds; $35 for 60 seconds. **URL:** http://www.koka.am.

14620 ■ KPXJ-TV - 21
312 E Kings Hwy.
Shreveport, LA 71104
Phone: (318)861-5800
Fax: (318)219-4680
Email: news@ktbs.com
Founded: 2004. **Key Personnel:** Cheryl May, Promotions Mgr., cmay@kpxj21.com; George Sirven, Station Mgr., gsirven@ktbs.com; Jan Elkins, Community Support, community@kpxj21.com. **Ad Rates:** Advertising accepted; rates available upon request. **URL:** http://www.ktbs.com.

14621 ■ KRUF-FM - 94.5
6341 Westport Ave.
Shreveport, LA 71129
Phone: (318)688-1130
Fax: (318)687-8574
Format: Contemporary Hit Radio (CHR). **Founded:** 1948. **Operating Hours**: Continuous. **Key Personnel:** Joan Williams, Dept. Mgr.; Lisa Janes, Operations Mgr.; Erin Bristol, Dir. of Sales, erinbristol@townsquaremedia; Johnette Robinson, Contact, johnetterobinson@townsquaremedia. **Wattage**: 100,000. **Ad Rates:** Advertising accepted; rates available upon request. **URL:** http://www.k945.com.

14622 ■ KRVQ-FM - 102.1
208 N Thomas Dr.
Shreveport, LA 71107
Phone: (318)222-3122
Format: Oldies. **Owner:** Ninety-Five Point Seven, Inc., at above address. **Founded:** Oct. 1998. **Operating Hours**: Continuous. **Key Personnel:** Howard Clark, Dir. of Programs; Buddy Barron, Dir. of Production; Cindy Delaney, Gen. Mgr.; Dick Howard, Sales Mgr. **Wattage**: 25,000. **Ad Rates:** $4-65 per unit. **URL:** http://www.kdks.fm/contact.

14623 ■ KSCL-FM - 91.3
2911 Centenary Blvd.
Shreveport, LA 71104
Phone: (318)869-5297
Fax: (318)869-5294
Format: Alternative/New Music/Progressive; Jazz; Ethnic; Urban Contemporary. **Networks:** Independent. **Owner:** Centenary College of Louisiana, 2911 Centenary Blvd., Shreveport, LA 71104, Ph: (318)869-5011, Free: 800-234-4448. **Founded:** 1976. **Operating Hours**: Noon - 12 a.m.; 100% local. **ADI**: Shreveport, LA-Texarkana, TX. **Key Personnel:** Marquette LaForest, Station Mgr.; Cara Lavender, Dir. of Programs; Zakk Owens, Music Dir. **Wattage**: 150. **Ad Rates:** Noncommercial. **URL:** http://www.extra.centenary.edu/kscl.

14624 ■ KSHV-TV - 45
3519 Jewella Ave.
Shreveport, LA 71109
Phone: (318)631-5677
Fax: (318)621-9688
Key Personnel: Ben Cothran, Operations Mgr.; Mike Halbrook, Promotions Mgr.; Isaac Turner, Dir. of Programs. **URL:** http://www.kshv.com.

14625 ■ KSLA-TV - 12
1812 Fairfield Ave.
Shreveport, LA 71101
Phone: (318)222-1212
Email: allkslasalesmanagers@ksla.com
Format: Commercial TV. **Networks:** CBS. **Owner:** Raycom Media Inc., 201 Monroe St., RSA Twr., 20th Fl., Montgomery, AL 36104-3731, Ph: (334)206-1400. **Founded:** 1955. **Operating Hours**: 5 a.m.-1:30 or 2 a.m. **ADI**: Shreveport, LA-Texarkana, TX. **Key Personnel:** Joe Sciortino, VP, Gen. Mgr.; James Smith, Gen. Mgr., VP, jamessmith@ksla.com. **Ad Rates:** Advertising accepted; rates available upon request. **URL:** http://www.ksla.com.

14626 ■ KSYB-AM - 1300
2807 Hilry Huckaby, III Ave.
Shreveport, LA 71107
Phone: (318)222-2744
Fax: (318)425-7507
Format: Gospel. **Networks:** Mutual Broadcasting System. **Owner:** Amistad Communications Inc., 66 State St., 1st Fl., Portland, ME 04101, Ph: (207)773-1956, Fax: (207)773-2087. **Founded:** 1975. **Formerly**: KFLO-AM. **Operating Hours**: Continuous. **ADI**: Shreveport, LA-Texarkana, TX. **Wattage**: 5,000. **Ad Rates:** $10-20 for 60 seconds. Combined advertising rates available with KBEF and KASO. **URL:** http://www.amistadradiogroup.com.

14627 ■ KTAL-FM - 98.1
208 N Thomas Dr.
Shreveport, LA 71137
Phone: (318)222-3122
Format: Classic Rock. **Owner:** Access 1 Communications, 11 Pennsylvania Plz., New York, NY 10001. **Founded:** 1945. **Operating Hours**: Continuous Monday - Friday; 12:00 p.m. - 2:00 p.m. Saturday; 10:00 a.m. - 2:00 p.m. Sunday. **ADI**: Shreveport, LA-Texarkana, TX. **Key Personnel:** Cary Camp, Gen. Mgr., cary.camp@alphamediausa.com; Greg Hanson, Prog. Dir., nuke@98rocks.fm. **Wattage**: 100,000 ERP. **Ad Rates:** Advertising accepted; rates available upon request. **URL:** http://www.98rocks.fm.

14628 ■ KTAL-TV - 6
3150 N Market St.
Shreveport, LA 71107
Phone: (318)629-6000
Fax: (318)629-6001
Free: 866-665-6000
Email: ktal@ktalnews.tv
Format: Commercial TV. **Networks:** NBC. **Founded:** 1953. **Operating Hours**: Continuous. **ADI**: Shreveport, LA-Texarkana, TX. **Key Personnel:** Mark Cummings, Gen. Mgr., VP, mcummings@ktalnews.tv. **Wattage**: 100,000. **Ad Rates:** Noncommercial. **URL:** http://www.arklatexhomepage.com.

14629 ■ KTBS-TV - 3
312 E Kings Hwy.
Shreveport, LA 71104
Phone: (318)861-5800
Fax: (318)219-4680
Email: ushare@ktbs.com
Format: Commercial TV; News. **Networks:** ABC. **Founded:** Sept. 03, 1955. **Operating Hours**: Continuous. **Key Personnel:** George Sirven, Station Mgr., gsirven@ktbs.com; Randy Bain, News Dir., rbain@ktbs.com. **Wattage**: 100,000. **Ad Rates:** Noncommercial. **URL:** http://www.ktbs.com.

14630 ■ K31HO - 31
PO Box A
Santa Ana, CA 92711
Phone: (714)832-2950
Free: 888-731-1000
Owner: Trinity Broadcasting Network Inc., PO Box A, Santa Ana, CA 92711, Ph: (714)832-2950, Free: 888-731-1000. **URL:** http://www.tbn.org.

14631 ■ KVKI-FM - 96.5
6341 W Port Ave.
Shreveport, LA 71129
Phone: (318)688-1130
Format: Adult Contemporary; Oldies. **Owner:** Townsquare Media Inc., 240 Greenwich Ave., Greenwich, CT 06830-6507, Ph: (203)861-0900. **Founded:** 1959. **Operating Hours**: Continuous. **Key Personnel:** Lisa Janes, Gen. Mgr., lisajanes@townsquaremedia.com. **Wattage**: 100,000. **Ad Rates:** Advertising accepted; rates available upon request. **URL:** http://www.965kvki.com.

14632 ■ KWKH-AM - 1130
6341 Westport Ave.
Shreveport, LA 71129
Phone: (318)688-1130
Format: Country. **Networks:** Mutual Broadcasting System. **Owner:** Townsquare Media Shreveport License L.L.C., 240 Greenwich Ave., Greenwhich, CT 06830, Ph: (203)861-0900. **Founded:** 1926. **Operating Hours**: Continuous. **Key Personnel:** Tom Benson, Contact; Lisa Janes, Gen. Mgr., lisajanes@townsquaremedia.com. **Wattage**: 50,000. **Ad Rates:** Advertising accepted; rates available upon request. **URL:** http://1130thetiger.com.

14633 ■ KXKS-FM - 93.7
6341 Westport Ave.
Shreveport, LA 71129-2498
Phone: (318)688-1130
Fax: (318)687-8574
Format: Country. **Owner:** Townsquare Media Shreveport License L.L.C., 240 Greenwich Ave., Greenwich, CT 06830, Ph: (203)861-0900. **Founded:** 1968. **Operating Hours**: Continuous. **Key Personnel:** Charlie Thomas, Gen. Mgr. **Wattage**: 95,000. **Ad Rates:** Advertising accepted; rates available upon request. **URL:**

Circulation: ★ = AAM; △ or • = BPA; ♦ = CAC; ❑ = VAC; ⊕ = PO Statement; ‡ = Publisher's Report; Boldface figures = sworn; Light figures = estimated.

http://www.mykisscountry937.com/main.php.

14634 ■ KYLA-FM
5700 W Oaks Blvd.
Rocklin, CA 95765
Free: 800-525-LOVE
Format: Contemporary Christian. **Owner:** Educational Media Foundation, 2351 Sunset Blvd., Ste. 170-218, Rocklin, CA 95677, Ph: (800)434-8400. **Wattage:** 690 ERP.

14635 ■ Red River Radio Network
8675 Youree Dr.
Shreveport, LA 71115
Phone: (318)798-0102
Fax: (318)798-0107
Free: 800-552-8502
Format: Bluegrass; News; Classical; Jazz; Talk. **Operating Hours:** Continuous. **ADI:** Shreveport, LA-Texarkana, TX. **Key Personnel:** Kermit Poling, Gen. Mgr. **Mailing address:** PO Box 5250, Shreveport, LA 71135. **URL:** http://www.redriverradio.org.

SLIDELL

SE LA. St. Tammany Parish. 22 mi. SE of Covington. Manufactures paint, chemicals. Meat packing plants. Shipbuilding. Steel fabricating. Lumber. Strawberries.

14636 ■ WGSO-AM - 990
2250 Gause Blvd. E, Ste. 205
Slidell, LA 70461-4235
Phone: (985)639-3820
Fax: (985)639-3869
Format: News; Talk; Information. **Networks:** CNN Radio. **Founded:** 1946. **Formerly:** WYAT-AM. **Operating Hours:** Continuous. **Key Personnel:** Harry Finch, Gen. Mgr., harry@wgso.com. **Wattage:** 1,000 Day; 400 Night. **Ad Rates:** Noncommercial.

14637 ■ WSLA-AM - 1560
PO Box 1175
Slidell, LA 70459
Format: News; Talk; Sports. **Owner:** MAPA Broadcasting, Inc., at above address. **Founded:** 1973. **Formerly:** WSDL-AM. **Key Personnel:** Paul Mayoral, President. **Wattage:** 1,000 KW. **Ad Rates:** $10 for 30 seconds. **URL:** http://wslaradio.com.

SPRINGHILL

14638 ■ KTKC-FM - 92.9
226 N Main St.
Springhill, LA 71075
Phone: (318)539-6000
Fax: (318)539-6002
Email: ktkc@ktkcfm.com
Format: Country. **Networks:** Louisiana; Satellite Music Network; ABC. **Owner:** Hunt Broadcasting, 805 Polk St., Mansfield, LA 71052, Fax: (318)871-2927. **Founded:** 1975. **Operating Hours:** 6 a.m.-midnight. **Key Personnel:** Leon Hunt, Owner. **Wattage:** 40,000. **Ad Rates:** Noncommercial. **URL:** http://www.ktkcfm.com.

SULPHUR

SW LA. Calcasieu Parish. 10 mi. W. of Lake Charles. Manufactures concrete and metal products, boats, plastics. Oil refinery. Agriculture. Rice, cattle.

14639 ■ Southwest Daily News
News Leader Inc.
716 E Napoleon St.
Sulphur, LA 70663
Phone: (337)527-7075
Community newspaper. **Founded:** 1939. **Freq:** Mon.-Sun. five days a week. **Print Method:** Offset. **Trim Size:** 13 5/8 x 21 7/8. **Cols./Page:** 6. **Col. Width:** 26 nonpareils. **Col. Depth:** 273 agate lines. **Key Personnel:** Rodrick Anderson, Editor; Marilyn Monroe, Editor; Lisa Kennedy, Manager. **USPS:** 507-520. **URL:** http://www.sulphurdailynews.com. **Ad Rates:** GLR $1.33; BW $1,518; 4C $2,068; SAU $12.05. **Remarks:** Accepts advertising. **Circ:** Combined ‡16000.

14640 ■ Carlyss Cablevision Inc.
153 W Dave Dugas Rd.
Sulphur, LA 70665
Phone: (337)583-2111
Free: 800-737-3900
Email: media@camtel.com
Owner: John Allen Henning, at above address. **Founded:** 1928. **Cities Served:** subscribing households 1,333. **URL:** http://www.camtel.com.

14641 ■ KEZM-AM - 1310
113 E Napoleon St.
Sulphur, LA 70663-3313
Phone: (337)527-3611
Fax: (337)527-0213
Email: kezm1310am@structurex.net
Format: Sports. **Founded:** 1955. **Operating Hours:** Continuous. **ADI:** Lake Charles, LA. **Key Personnel:** Bruce L. Merchant, Contact. **Wattage:** 500. **Ad Rates:** $4 for 30 seconds. **URL:** http://www.kezmonline.com.

THIBODAUX

SE LA. Lafourche Parish. On Bayou Lafourche, 45 mi. SW of New Orleans. Nicholls State University. Harvesting equipment factory. Sea food processing plant. Sugar refineries. Foundries. Ships vegetables. Oil, natural gas wells. Truck, dairy farms. Sugarcane, corn, vegetables.

14642 ■ Daily Comet
The Daily Comet
104 Hickory St.
Thibodaux, LA 70301
Phone: (985)448-7600
Publisher's E-mail: news@dailycomet.com
General newspaper. **Freq:** Daily (eve.). **Print Method:** Offset. **Cols./Page:** 6. **Col. Width:** 25 nonpareils. **Col. Depth:** 301 agate lines. **Key Personnel:** Dee Dee Thurston, Managing Editor, phone: (985)850-1149; David Simmon, Manager, Circulation, phone: (985)448-7621; Miles Forrest, Publisher, phone: (985)850-1123. **Subscription Rates:** $11.90 Individuals digital only/month; $14.50 Individuals 6-day print and digital/month. **URL:** http://www.dailycomet.com. **Mailing address:** PO Box 5238, Thibodaux, LA 70302. **Remarks:** Advertising accepted; rates available upon request. **Circ:** Mon.-Fri. *10501.

14643 ■ The Nicholls Worth
Nicholls State University
906 E 1st St.
Thibodaux, LA 70310
Free: 877-NICHOLLS
Publication E-mail: nw@nicholls.edu
Collegiate newspaper. **Freq:** Weekly (Thurs.). **Print Method:** Offset. **Cols./Page:** 5. **Col. Width:** 2 1/16 inches. **Col. Depth:** 13 13/16 inches. **Key Personnel:** Brian Griffin, Editor-in-Chief; Stef Steinbrenner, Managing Editor; Sloane Peterson, Business Manager. **URL:** http://thenichollsworth.com. **Ad Rates:** BW $260; SAU $3; PCI $4. **Remarks:** Advertising accepted; rates available upon request. **Circ:** ‡5500.

14644 ■ Sugar Bulletin
American Sugar Cane League of U.S.A. Inc.
206 E Bayon Rd.
PO Drawer 938
Thibodaux, LA 70301
Phone: (504)448-3707
Fax: (504)448-3722
News and information magazine for sugarcane growers and processors. **Founded:** 1922. **Freq:** Monthly. **Print Method:** Letterpress. **Cols./Page:** 2. **Col. Width:** 30 nonpareils. **Col. Depth:** 126 agate lines. **Key Personnel:** Charles J. Melancon, Jr., Editor. **Subscription Rates:** $15 Individuals. **URL:** http://www.amscl.org/sugar-bulletin-ad-rates. **Ad Rates:** BW $300. **Remarks:** Accepts advertising. **Circ:** ‡2000.

14645 ■ KNSU-FM - 91.5
PO Box 2664
Thibodaux, LA 70310
Phone: (985)448-5678
Email: knsupd@gmail.com
Format: Alternative/New Music/Progressive. **Owner:** Nicholls State University, 906 E 1st St., Thibodaux, LA 70310, Free: 877-NICHOLLS. **Founded:** 1972. **Formerly:** KVFG-FM. **Operating Hours:** 7 a.m.-2 a.m. Mon.-Thurs./7 a.m.-10 p.m. Fri/10 a.m.-10 p.m. **Wattage:** 250. **Ad Rates:** Noncommercial. **URL:** http://www.nicholls.edu.

14646 ■ KTIB-AM - 640
108 Green St.
Thibodaux, LA 70301
Phone: (985)447-6404
Fax: (985)447-6464
Format: Oldies; News. **Networks:** NewsTalk Radio. **Owner:** Delta Star Broadcasting, LLC, at above address. **Founded:** 1953. **Operating Hours:** Continuous. **Key Personnel:** Raymond Saadi, Gen. Mgr., VP. **Wattage:** 5,000 Day;1,000 Nigh. **Ad Rates:** Advertising accepted; rates available upon request. **URL:** http://www.ktib640.com/.

VILLE PLATTE

SC LA. Evangeline Parish. 48 mi. S. of Alexandria. Oil field products. Electric generators. Iron works. Agriculture. Cotton, corn, rice, yams.

14647 ■ KVPI-AM - 1050
PO Box J
Ville Platte, LA 70586
Phone: (337)363-2124
Format: Country. **Networks:** AP; Jones Satellite. **Owner:** Ville Platte Broadcasting Co., 809 W LaSalle St., Ville Platte, LA 70586-3129, Ph: (318)375-3258, Fax: (318)363-3574. **Founded:** 1953. **Operating Hours:** Sunrise-sunset; 100% local. **ADI:** Lafayette, LA. **Key Personnel:** Becky Vidrine, Contact; Bonnie Fontenot, Office Mgr. **Wattage:** 250. **Ad Rates:** $6.50-9.20 for 30 seconds; $10-15.50 for 60 seconds. Combined advertising rates available with KVPI-FM. **URL:** http://www.oldies925.com.

14648 ■ KVPI-FM - 92.5
809 W LaSalle St.
Ville Platte, LA 70586
Phone: (337)363-2124
Fax: (337)363-3574
Format: Oldies. **Networks:** Jones Satellite. **Owner:** Ville Platte Broadcasting Co., 809 W LaSalle St., Ville Platte, LA 70586-3129, Ph: (318)375-3258, Fax: (318)363-3574. **Founded:** 1967. **Operating Hours:** 6:00 a.m.-12:00 a.m. **ADI:** Lafayette, LA. **Key Personnel:** Bonnie Fontenot, Office Mgr.; Becky Vidrine, Contact; Danny Poullard, Contact. **Wattage:** 6,000. **Ad Rates:** $6.50-9.20 for 30 seconds; $10-15.50 for 60 seconds. **Mailing address:** PO Box J, Ville Platte, LA 70586. **URL:** http://www.oldies925.com.

VIVIAN

W LA. Caddo Parish. 32 mi. W. of Crowley. Manufactures mobile homes, garments, boats. Oil and gas refineries. Oil wells. Timber. Agriculture. Cotton, corn.

14649 ■ KNCB-AM - 1320
PO Box 1072
Vivian, LA 71082
Phone: (318)375-3278
Fax: (318)375-3329
Format: Country; Gospel. **Simulcasts:** 7:35 - noon. **Networks:** AP. **Owner:** North Caddo Broadcasting Co., 201 Airport Dr., Vivian, LA 71082-3403. **Founded:** 1966. **Operating Hours:** Pre-Sunrise - Sunset. **Wattage:** 005 KW. **Ad Rates:** $14 for 30 seconds; $18 for 60 seconds. Combined advertising rates available with KNCB-FM.

14650 ■ KNCB-FM - 105.3
17525 Hwy. 1 N
Vivian, LA 71082
Phone: (318)375-3278
Fax: (318)375-3329
Email: kncb@cs.com
Format: Country. **Networks:** ABC. **Owner:** North Caddo Broadcasting Co., 201 Airport Dr., Vivian, LA 71082-3403. **Founded:** 1996. **Operating Hours:** Continuous. **Key Personnel:** Ruby June Collins, Gen. Mgr., Operations Mgr.; Sherry Reece, Prog. Dir. **Wattage:** 3,200. **Ad Rates:** $14 for 30 seconds; $18 for 60 seconds. Combined advertising rates available with KNCB-AM.

WEST MONROE

N LA. Ouachita Parish. On the Ouachita River. Manufactures paper bags and boxes, cottonseed oil, veneer, syrup, concrete culverts, lumber. Commercial fisheries. Timber. Gas wells. Dairy, stock, poultry, truck farms. Cotton, corn.

14651 ■ The Ouachita Citizen
The Ouachita Citizen
1400 N 7th St.
West Monroe, LA 71294
Phone: (318)322-3161
Fax: (318)325-2285

Local newspaper. **Freq:** Weekly (Thurs.). **Print Method:** Offset. Uses mats. **Cols./Page:** 6. **Col. Width:** 2 1/16 inches. **Col. Depth:** 294 agate lines. **Key Personnel:** Sam Hanna, Jr., Publisher, phone: (318)396-0602. **ISSN:** 0746--7478 (print). **Subscription Rates:** $20.55 Individuals online only /year; $30.99 Individuals home delivery - regular , inside Franklin; $36.05 Out of state home delivery. **URL:** http://www.hannapub.com/ouachitacitizen. **Mailing address:** PO Box 758, West Monroe, LA 71294. **Remarks:** Advertising accepted; rates available upon request. **Circ:** ‡5200.

14652 ■ KARD-TV - 14
200 Pavilion Rd.
West Monroe, LA 71292
Phone: (318)323-1972
Format: Commercial TV. **Networks:** Fox. **Founded:** 1984. **Formerly**: KLAA-TV. **Operating Hours**: Continuous. **ADI**: Monroe, LA-El Dorado, AR. **Key Personnel:** Brian Jones, COO. **Ad Rates:** Noncommercial. **URL:** http://myarklamiss.com/.

14653 ■ KHLL-FM - 100.9
217 Gilliland Rd.
West Monroe, LA 71291
Phone: (318)322-1009
Format: Contemporary Christian. **Wattage**: 25,000. **Ad Rates:** Advertising accepted; rates available upon request. **URL:** http://www.hillradio.com.

14654 ■ KMBS-AM - 1310
PO Box 547
West Monroe, LA 71291-0547
Format: News; Sports; Talk; Information. **Owner:** Kay E. Morgan, 2103 Redwood, Monroe, LA 71201, Ph: (318)322-1127. **Founded:** 1956. **Formerly**: KUZN-AM. **Wattage**: 5,000 KW. **Ad Rates:** $14-18 per unit. **URL:** http://kmbs1310.net/.

14655 ■ KMCT-TV - 39
701 Parkwood Dr.
West Monroe, LA 71291
Phone: (318)322-1399
Fax: (318)323-3783
Free: 800-249-1399
Format: Commercial TV. **Networks:** Independent. **Owner:** Lamb Broadcasting Inc., at above address. **Founded:** 1986. **Operating Hours**: Continuous. **ADI**: Monroe, LA-El Dorado, AR. **Key Personnel:** Mike Reed, President. **Ad Rates:** Noncommercial.

14656 ■ KTVE-TV - 10
200 Pavilion Rd.
West Monroe, LA 71292-9487
Phone: (318)323-1972
Fax: (318)322-0926
Email: sales@nbc10news.net
Format: Commercial TV. **Networks:** NBC. **Owner:** Nexstar Broadcasting Group Inc., 545 E John Carpenter Fwy., Ste. 700, Irving, TX 75062, Ph: (972)373-8800. **Founded:** 1954. **Formerly**: KRBB-TV. **Operating Hours**: Continuous Mon.-Sat.; 5:30 a.m.-2:00 a.m. Sun. **ADI**: Monroe, LA-El Dorado, AR. **Key Personnel:** Randy Stone, Gen. Mgr., rstone@nbc10news.net. **URL:** http://www.myarklamiss.com.

WESTLAKE

SW LA. Calcasieu Parish. 4 mi. W. of Lake Charles. Oil refining, petrochemical, carbon black manufactured. Agriculture. Rice.

14657 ■ KAOK-AM - 1400
801 Columbia Southern Rd.
Westlake, LA 70669
Phone: (337)439-3300
Format: News; Talk. **Founded:** 1952. **Operating Hours:** 8:00 a.m. - 5:00 p.m. Monday - Wednesday. **ADI:** Lake Charles, LA. **Key Personnel:** Ed Prenergast, Contact. **Wattage**: 1,000 KW. **Ad Rates:** Advertising accepted; rates available upon request. $12-18 per unit. **URL:** http://www.kaok.com.

WINNFIELD

NWC LA. Winn Parish. 45 mi. NW of Alexandria. Lumber, creosote mills. Rock quarry, Oil wells. Truck farms. Corn, cattle.

14658 ■ KVCL-AM - 1270
304 KVCL Rd.
Winnfield, LA 71483
Phone: (318)628-5822
Fax: (318)628-7355
Format: Talk; News; Information. **Networks:** Mutual Broadcasting System; Louisiana. **Founded:** 1955. **Operating Hours**: Continuous. **Key Personnel:** Rhonda Leach, Gen. Mgr.; Michael Parker, Operations Mgr. **Wattage:** 1,000. **Ad Rates:** $20 for 30 seconds; $25 for 60 seconds. Combined advertising rates available with KVCL-FM. **URL:** http://www.kvclradio.com.

14659 ■ KVCL-FM - 92.1
605 San Antonio Ave.
Many, LA 71449
Phone: (318)628-5822
Fax: (318)628-7355
Format: Country. **Networks:** CNN Radio. **Owner:** Baldridge Dumas Communications, 605 San Antonio Ave., Many, LA 71449. **Founded:** 1955. **Operating Hours**: Continuous. **Key Personnel:** Mike Parker, Operations Mgr. **Wattage**: 10,000. **Ad Rates:** $23 for 30 seconds; $30 for 60 seconds. KVCL-AM. **URL:** http://www.wzlx.cbslocal.com.

WINNSBORO

NE LA. Franklin Parish. 39 mi. SE of Monroe. Fishing. Oil and gas wells. Cotton gins. Compress-warehouse. Sawmill. Timber. Stock, dairy, grain farms. Cotton, yams, beef, cattle.

14660 ■ The Franklin Sun
The Franklin Sun
514 Prairie St.
Winnsboro, LA 71295
Phone: (318)435-4521
Fax: (318)435-9220
Newspaper. **Freq:** Weekly (Wed.). **Print Method:** Offset. **Trim Size:** 6 x 21. **Cols./Page:** 6. **Col. Width:** 26 nonpareils. **Col. Depth:** 291 agate lines. **Subscription Rates:** $30.99 Individuals; $36.05 Out of state; $20.55 Individuals /year, online. **URL:** http://www.hannapub.com/franklinsun. **Ad Rates:** BW $648.90; PCI $5.15. **Remarks:** Accepts advertising. **Circ:** ‡6200.

ZACHARY

SEC LA. East Baton Rouge Parish. 15 mi. N. of Baton Rouge. Residential.

14661 ■ Zachary Plainsman-News
Louisiana Suburban Press
2060 Church St., Ste. E
Zachary, LA 70791
Phone: (225)654-6841
Fax: (225)654-8271
Local newspaper. **Freq:** Weekly (Thurs.). **Print Method:** Offset. **Cols./Page:** 6. **Col. Width:** 26 nonpareils. **Col. Depth:** 301 agate lines. **Key Personnel:** Stacy Gill, Editor; Kristi Lynch, Contact. **Subscription Rates:** $31 Individuals. **URL:** http://theadvocate.com/news/zachary. **Ad Rates:** GLR $.21; BW $703.05; 4C $903.05; PCI $5.45. **Remarks:** Accepts advertising. **Circ:** 2163.

Circulation: ★ = AAM; △ or • = BPA; ♦ = CAC; ❑ = VAC; ⊕ = PO Statement; ‡ = Publisher's Report; Boldface figures = sworn; Light figures = estimated.

AUBURN

Androscoggin Co. Androscoggin Co. (SE). 5 m W of Lewiston.

14662 ▪ The Orthodontic CYBERjournal
The Orthodontic CYBER journal
1 Willow Run
Auburn, ME 04210
Magazine covering orthodontics and dentofacial orthopedics. **Key Personnel:** Dr. Raymond Bedette, Publisher; Dr. Gary Roebuck, Publisher; Dr. Abraham Lifshitz, Editor-in-Chief; Dr. Larry W. White, Executive Editor. **Subscription Rates:** Free fonline. **Remarks:** Advertising accepted; rates available upon request. **Circ:** (Not Reported).

14663 ▪ WEZR-AM - 1240
555 Center St.
Auburn, ME 04210
Phone: (916)381-9463
Fax: (916)381-9458
Format: Oldies. **Founded:** 1870. **Operating Hours:** Continuous. **Ad Rates:** Advertising accepted; rates available upon request. **URL:** http://www.lewistonauburn.com.

14664 ▪ WMTW-TV - 8
99 Danville Corner Rd.
Auburn, ME 04210
Phone: (207)782-1800
Fax: (207)782-2165
Free: 800-248-6397
Email: wmtw@wmtw.com
Format: Commercial TV. **Networks:** ABC. **Founded:** 1954. **Operating Hours:** Continuous. **ADI:** Portland-Poland Spring, ME. **Key Personnel:** John MacMillan, Contact; David Butta, Contact. **Ad Rates:** Advertising accepted; rates available upon request. **URL:** http://www.wmtw.com.

14665 ▪ WMWX-FM - 99.9
PO Box 8
Auburn, ME 04212-0008
Email: themix@wmwx.com
Format: Adult Contemporary. **Networks:** Independent. **Founded:** 1978. **Formerly:** WWAV-FM; WKZS-FM. **Operating Hours:** Continuous; 100% local. **Key Personnel:** Ron Frizzell, Gen. Mgr.; Chrys Wilson, Sales Mgr.; Mac Dickson, Dir. of Programs; Eric Marenghi, Station Mgr. **Wattage:** 50,000. **Ad Rates:** $40-60 per unit.

AUGUSTA

SW ME. Kennebec Co. On Kennebec River, 26 mi. NE of Lewiston. State Capital. Founded 1628 as trading post of Plymouth colony. University of Maine at Augusta. Resort. Manufactures computers, wood and paper products, textiles, shoes; meat processing.

14666 ▪ The Christian Civic League Record
Christian Civic League
PO Box 5459
Augusta, ME 04330
Phone: (207)622-7634
Publisher's E-mail: info@cclmaine.org
Magazine on civic action. **Freq:** Monthly. **Print Method:** Offset. **Cols./Page:** 5. **Col. Width:** 22 nonpareils. **Col. Depth:** 182 agate lines. **URL:** http://www.cclmaine.org. **Remarks:** Advertising not accepted. **Circ:** Paid ‡2500, Non-paid ‡500.

14667 ▪ Journal of Maine Water Utilities Association
Maine Water Utilities Association
150 Capitol St., Ste. 5
Augusta, ME 04330
Phone: (207)623-9511
Fax: (207)623-9522
Publisher's E-mail: info@mwua.org
Association magazine. **Freq:** Annual. **Key Personnel:** Jeffrey L. McNelly, Executive Director. **Alt. Formats:** PDF. **URL:** http://www.mwua.org/journal.htm. **Remarks:** Advertising accepted; rates available upon request. **Circ:** 400.

14668 ▪ Kennebec Journal
Kennebec Journal
274 Western Ave.
Augusta, ME 04330
Phone: (207)623-3811
Fax: (207)623-2220
Free: 800-537-5508
General newspaper. **Freq:** Mon.-Sun. **Print Method:** Offset. **Cols./Page:** 6. **Col. Width:** 26 nonpareils. **Col. Depth:** 301 agate lines. **Key Personnel:** Anthony Ronzio, Editor, phone: (207)621-5678. **Subscription Rates:** $20 Individuals 7-day home delivery/month; $14 Individuals Friday Saturday & Sunday home delivery/month; $7.99 Individuals Sunday home delivery/month. **URL:** http://www.centralmaine.com. **Ad Rates:** PCI $11.06. **Remarks:** Accepts advertising. **Circ:** Mon.-Sat. ‡13026, Sun. ‡13068.

14669 ▪ Maine Fish and Wildlife
Maine Department of Inland Fisheries and Wildlife
41 State House Sta.
Augusta, ME 04333-0041
Phone: (207)287-8000
Fax: (207)287-8094
Publisher's E-mail: ifw.webmaster@maine.gov
Fish and wildlife conservation periodical. **Freq:** Quarterly. **Print Method:** Offset. **Trim Size:** 8 1/2 x 11. **Cols./Page:** 3 and 2. **Col. Width:** 27 and 42 nonpareils. **Col. Depth:** 133 agate lines. **Key Personnel:** Don Kleiner, Contact. **ISSN:** 0360--005X (print). **URL:** http://www.maine.gov. **Remarks:** Accepts advertising. **Circ:** Paid 12500, Non-paid 400.

14670 ▪ Maine Motor Transport News
Maine Motor Transport News
142 Whitten Rd.
Augusta, ME 04332-0857
Phone: (207)623-4128
Fax: (207)623-4096
Magazine on motor trucks. **Freq:** Bimonthly. **Print Method:** Letterpress. **Trim Size:** 8 3/8 x 10 7/8. **Cols./Page:** 3. **Col. Width:** 26 nonpareils. **Col. Depth:** 123 agate lines. **Key Personnel:** Brian Parke, Chief Executive Officer, President. **Subscription Rates:** $25 Members; $35 Nonmembers. **URL:** http://www.mmta.com/page/946-703/mmta-news-magazine. **Mailing address:** PO Box 857, Augusta, ME 04332-0857. **Ad Rates:** BW $363; 4C $613. **Remarks:** Accepts advertising. **Circ:** Paid 2452, Non-paid 1500.

14671 ▪ The Maine Sportsman: New England's Largest Outdoor Publication
The Maine Sportsman
183 State St., Ste. 101
Augusta, ME 04330
Phone: (207)622-4242
Fax: (207)622-4255
Free: 800-698-9501
Publication E-mail: info@mainesportsman.com
Magazine (tabloid) covering Maine hunting and fishing topics. **Freq:** Monthly. **Print Method:** Offset. **Trim Size:** 11 x 16. **Cols./Page:** 5. **Col. Width:** 1 7/8 inches. **Col. Depth:** 13 inches. **Subscription Rates:** $30 Individuals print; $49 Two years print; $14 Individuals online only; $38 Individuals print and online. **URL:** http://www.mainesportsman.com. **Remarks:** Accepts advertising. **Circ:** (Not Reported).

14672 ▪ Maine Trails: The Magazine of the Maine Better Transportation Assn
Maine Better Transportation Association
146 State St.
Augusta, ME 04330
Phone: (207)622-0526
Fax: (207)623-2928
Magazine informing association members and the business community about Maine transportation issues. **Freq:** Bimonthly. **Key Personnel:** Maria R. Fuentes, Executive Director. **Subscription Rates:** Included in membership. **URL:** http://www.mbtaonline.org/Newsroom/MaineTrailsMagazine/tabid/58/Default.aspx. **Formerly:** Transportation Infrastructure Issues with Maine. **Ad Rates:** BW $330, full page; BW $260, half page. **Remarks:** Accepts advertising. **Circ:** Controlled ‡1100.

14673 ▪ WABK-FM - 104.3
150 Whitten Rd.
Augusta, ME 04330
Phone: (207)623-9000
Email: wabk@clearchannel.com
Format: Oldies; Eighties. **Founded:** 1974. **Wattage:** 50,000. **Ad Rates:** Advertising accepted; rates available upon request. $19-39 for 30 seconds; $25-50 for 60 seconds. **URL:** http://www.big104fm.com.

14674 ▪ WCBB-TV - 10
1450 Lisbon St.
Lewiston, ME 04240
Fax: (207)783-5193
Free: 800-884-1717
Format: Public TV. **Simulcasts:** WMEB-TV; WMEM-TV; WMED-TV. **Networks:** Public Broadcasting Service (PBS). **Owner:** Maine Public Broadcasting Network, 1450 Lisbon St., Lewiston, ME 04240. **Founded:** 1961. **Formerly:** WCDB-TV. **Operating Hours:** 6 a.m.-12 a.m.; 90% network, 10% local. **Key Personnel:** Keith Shortall, News Dir.; Jim Dowe, CEO, President, jdowe@mpbn.net; Charles Beck, VP, Div. Dir. **Ad Rates:** Non-

Circulation: ★ = AAM; △ or • = BPA; ♦ = CAC; ❑ = VAC; ⊕ = PO Statement; ‡ = Publisher's Report; Boldface figures = sworn; Light figures = estimated.

commercial; underwriting available. **URL:** http://www.mpbn.net.

14675 ■ WEBB-FM - 98.5
56 Western Ave., Ste. 13
Augusta, ME 04330
Phone: (207)623-9898
Fax: (207)626-5948
Format: Country. **Simulcasts:** WTVL-AM. **Owner:** Citadel Broadcasting Corp., 7201 W Lake Mead Blvd., Ste. 400, Las Vegas, NV 89128-8366, Ph: (702)804-5200, Fax: (702)804-8250. **Key Personnel:** Andy Capwell, Prog. Dir., andy.capwell@townsquaremedia.com. **Wattage:** 61,000. **Ad Rates:** Noncommercial. **URL:** http://www.b985.fm.

14676 ■ WJZN-AM - 1490
56 Western Ave., Ste. 13
Augusta, ME 04330
Phone: (207)623-4735
Fax: (207)626-5948
Format: Oldies. **Simulcasts:** WTVL-AM. **Owner:** Citadel Broadcasting Corp., 7201 W Lake Mead Blvd., Ste. 400, Las Vegas, NV 89128-8366, Ph: (702)804-5200, Fax: (702)804-8250. **URL:** http://www.koolam.com.

14677 ■ WKCG-FM - 101.3
125 Community Dr., Ste. 201
Augusta, ME 04330
Phone: (207)623-9000
Format: Adult Contemporary. **Networks:** Jones Satellite. **Founded:** 1968. **Operating Hours:** Continuous; 99% local. **Wattage:** 50,000. **Ad Rates:** Noncommercial. **URL:** http://www.wvomfm.com.

14678 ■ WMDR-AM - 1340
160 Riverside Dr.
Augusta, ME 04330
Phone: (207)622-9467
Fax: (207)623-2874
Free: 888-825-1344
Format: Religious. **Owner:** Light of Life Ministries, Inc., at above address, Pittsburgh, PA 15212. **Ad Rates:** Advertising accepted; rates available upon request. **URL:** http://lightoflife.info.

14679 ■ WMDR-FM - 88.9
160 Riverside Dr.
Augusta, ME 04330
Phone: (207)622-1340
Format: Country; Religious; Gospel. **Owner:** Light of Life Ministries, Inc., at above address, Pittsburgh, PA 15212. **Operating Hours:** Continuous. **Wattage:** 50,000. **Ad Rates:** Noncommercial; underwriting available.

14680 ■ WMME-FM - 92.3
56 Western Ave., Ste. 13
Augusta, ME 04330
Phone: (207)623-4735
Format: Top 40. **Simulcasts:** WEZW-AM. **Owner:** Citadel Broadcasting Corp., 7201 W Lake Mead Blvd., Ste. 400, Las Vegas, NV 89128-8366, Ph: (702)804-5200, Fax: (702)804-8250. **Key Personnel:** Julie Beaulieu, Dir. of Sales, julie.beaulieu@townsquaremedia.com. **Wattage:** 50,000. **Ad Rates:** Noncommercial. **URL:** http://www.92moose.fm.

14681 ■ WTVL-AM - 1490
56 Western Ave., Ste. 1
Augusta, ME 04330
Phone: (207)623-4735
Format: Full Service. **Networks:** ABC. **Owner:** Citadel Communications Corp., San Diego, CA, Ph: (505)767-6700, Fax: (505)767-6767. **Founded:** 1946. **Key Personnel:** Jon Paradise, Dir. of Programs; Eric Leimbach, News Dir. **Wattage:** 1,000 ERP. **Ad Rates:** $15 for 30 seconds; $25 for 60 seconds. **URL:** http://koolam.com.

14682 ■ W264BQ-FM - 100.7
160 Bangor St.
Augusta, ME 04330
Phone: (207)622-1340
Email: wmdr@adelphia.net
Format: Contemporary Christian; Religious; Gospel. **Owner:** Light of Life Ministries, Inc., at above address, Pittsburgh, PA 15212. **Ad Rates:** Noncommercial.

14683 ■ WWWA-FM - 95.3
160 Riverside Dr.
Augusta, ME 04330
Phone: (207)622-1340
Free: 888-825-1344
Format: Religious. **Key Personnel:** Denise Lafountain, Station Mgr., denise@worshipradionetwork.org; Ryan Gagne, Dir. of Programs, ryan@worshipradionetwork.org; Randy Todd, Contact, randy@worshipradionetwork.org. **URL:** http://www.worshipradionetwork.org.

BANGOR

Penobscot Co. C ME. Penobscot Co. On Penobscot River, 60 mi. NE of Augusta. Bangor Theological Seminary. Husson College. University of Maine. Manufactures paper, footwear, wood products, lumber, electronics.

14684 ■ Bangor Daily News
Bangor Daily News
PO Box 1329
Bangor, ME 04402-1329
Phone: (207)990-8000
Free: 800-432-7964
Publisher's E-mail: bdnlib@bangordailynews.com
General newspaper. **Freq:** Mon.-Sat. (morn.). **Print Method:** Flexography. **Trim Size:** 13 x 21. **Cols./Page:** 6. **Col. Width:** 25 nonpareils. **Col. Depth:** 301 agate lines. **Key Personnel:** Richard Warren, Publisher; Mike Kearney, Director, Sales and Marketing; Michael J. Dowd, Editor-in-Chief. **ISSN:** 0892--8738 (print). **USPS:** 041-000. **URL:** http://bangordailynews.com. **Remarks:** Accepts advertising. **Circ:** (Not Reported).

14685 ■ The Blue Knights News
Blue Knights International Law Enforcement Motorcycle Club
38 Alden St.
Bangor, ME 04401-3421
Publisher's E-mail: international@blueknights.org
Freq: Quarterly. **URL:** http://www.blueknights.org/magazine.html. **Remarks:** Accepts advertising. **Circ:** (Not Reported).

14686 ■ International Journal of Environmentally Intelligent
Environmental Robots Inc.
407 Kenduskeag Ave.
Bangor, ME 04401
Publisher's E-mail: biomimetics@environmental-robots.com
Journal publishing information about the impact and the short-term as well as the long-term effects of design and manufacturing on the environment. **Key Personnel:** Mansour Ravandoust, Assistant Editor; Dr. Mohsen Shahinpoor, Editor-in-Chief. **URL:** http://www.ijecdm.com. **Formerly:** International Journal of Environmentally Conscious Design & Manufacturing. **Circ:** (Not Reported).

14687 ■ WABI-AM - 910
184 Target Industrial Cir.
Bangor, ME 04401
Phone: (207)947-9100
Fax: (207)942-8039
Format: Information; News. **Networks:** CNN Radio. **Founded:** 1924. **Operating Hours:** Continuous. **ADI:** Bangor, ME. **Key Personnel:** Josh Scroggins, Station Mgr.; Stacey Brann, Chief Engineer; Anthony Turner, Bus. Mgr. **Wattage:** 5,000. **Ad Rates:** $10-35 for 30 seconds; $12-40 for 60 seconds. Combined advertising rates available with WWBX-FM. **URL:** http://wabi.tv.

14688 ■ WABI-TV - 5
35 Hildreth St.
Bangor, ME 04401
Phone: (207)947-8321
Fax: (207)941-9378
Email: wabi@wabi.tv
Format: Commercial TV. **Networks:** CBS; NBC; ABC. **Owner:** Community Broadcasting Services, at above address. **Founded:** 1953. **Operating Hours:** Continuous. **Key Personnel:** Roger Gagne, Regional Mgr., rgagne@wabi.tv. **Wattage:** 12,000 ERP. **Ad Rates:** Advertising accepted; rates available upon request. **URL:** http://www.wabi.tv.

14689 ■ WBFB-FM - 104.7
184 Target Industrial Cir.
Bangor, ME 04401
Phone: (207)947-9100
Fax: (207)942-8039
Format: Contemporary Country. **Networks:** Independent. **Owner:** Clear Channel Communications Inc., at above address, Ph: (210)822-2828, Fax: (210)822-2299. **Founded:** 1986. **Formerly:** WWFX-FM. **Operating Hours:** Continuous; 100% local. **ADI:** Bangor, ME. **Key Personnel:** Josh Scroggins, Station Mgr.; Stacey Brann, Chief Engineer; Antony Turner, Bus. Mgr. **Wattage:** 50,000. **Ad Rates:** Noncommercial. **URL:** http://wbfb-fm.clearchannel.com.

14690 ■ WBGR-TV - 33
2881 Ohio St.
Bangor, ME 04401
Phone: (207)947-3300
Fax: (207)884-8333
Wattage: 1,000 ERP. **Ad Rates:** Advertising accepted; rates available upon request.

14691 ■ WEZQ-FM - 92.9
49 Acme Rd.
Brewer, ME 04412
Phone: (207)989-5631
Fax: (207)989-5685
Format: Adult Contemporary. **Owner:** Cumulus Broadcasting Inc., 3280 Peachtree Rd. NW, Ste. 2300, Atlanta, GA 30305-2447, Ph: (404)949-0700, Fax: (404)949-0740. **Key Personnel:** Bob Lacey, Contact; Sheri Lynch, Contact. **URL:** http://929theticket.com.

14692 ■ WHCF-FM - 88.5
1476 Broadway
Bangor, ME 04401
Phone: (207)947-2751
Fax: (207)947-0010
Email: contact@whcffm.com
Format: Contemporary Christian. **Owner:** Bangor Baptist Church, 1476 Broadway, Bangor, ME 04401, Ph: (207)947-6576, Fax: (207)990-8955. **Founded:** 1981. **Operating Hours:** Continuous Monday - Friday; 8:00 a.m. - 8:00 p.m. Saturday; 7:00 a.m. - 11:30 p.m. Sunday. **ADI:** Bangor, ME. **Key Personnel:** Tim Collins, Contact; Joe Polek, Contact; Tim Collins, Contact. **Wattage:** 35,000 ERP. **Ad Rates:** Noncommercial. **URL:** http://www.whcffm.com.

14693 ■ WHMX-FM
123 Hussan Ave.
Bangor, ME 04401
Phone: (207)262-1057
Fax: (207)947-0010
Email: contact@solutionfm.com
Format: Contemporary Christian. **Founded:** Sept. 15, 2006. **Key Personnel:** Mike Couchman, Contact, mike@solutionfm.com; Morgan Smith, Contact, morgan@solutionfm.com. **Wattage:** 48,000 ERP.

14694 ■ WHSN-FM - 89.3
One College Cir.
Bangor, ME 04401
Phone: (207)973-1011
Fax: (207)947-3987
Email: whsn@nescom.edu
Format: Alternative/New Music/Progressive. **Owner:** Husson College Trustees, 1 College Cir., Bangor, ME 04401, Ph: (207)941-7000. **Founded:** 1974. **ADI:** Bangor, ME. **Key Personnel:** Mark Nason, Dir. of Programs, mark@nescom.edu. **Wattage:** 3,000 ERP. **Ad Rates:** Noncommercial. **URL:** http://www.whsn-fm.com.

14695 ■ WKSQ-FM - 94.5
184 Target Industrial Cir.
Bangor, ME 04401
Phone: (207)947-9100
Format: Adult Contemporary. **Owner:** Blueberry Broadcasting, 184 Target Industrial Cir., Bangor, ME 04401, Ph: (207)947-9100. **Founded:** 1982. **Operating Hours:** Continuous. **ADI:** Bangor, ME. **Wattage:** 50,000. **Ad Rates:** $25-50 for 30 seconds. Combined advertising rates available with WBFB-FM & WLKE-FM. **URL:** http://www.kissfm.net.

14696 ■ WLBZ-TV - 2
329 Mt. Hope Ave.
Bangor, ME 04401
Phone: (207)942-4821
Email: newsdirector@wlbz2.com
Format: Commercial TV. **Networks:** NBC. **Owner:** Gannett Broadcasting, 7950 Jones Branch Dr., McLean, VA 22107-0150, Ph: (703)854-6000. **Founded:** 1954. **Operating Hours:** Continuous. **ADI:** Bangor, ME. **Key Personnel:** Bruce Glasier, Sports Dir. **Wattage:** 3,000 ERP. **Ad Rates:** Advertising accepted; rates available upon request. **URL:** http://www.wlbz2.com.

14697 ■ WMCM-FM - 103.3
184 Target Industrial Cir.
Bangor, ME 04401
Phone: (207)947-9100
Format: Country. **Networks:** ABC; Satellite Music Network. **Owner:** Blueberry Broadcasting, 184 Target Industrial Cir., Bangor, ME 04401, Ph: (207)947-9100. **Founded:** 1968. **Operating Hours**: Continuous; 90% network, 10% local. **Wattage**: 50,000. **Ad Rates:** Noncommercial. **URL:** http://www.971thebear.com.

14698 ■ WMED-FM - 89.7
63 Texas Ave.
Bangor, ME 04401
Fax: (207)942-2857
Free: 800-884-1717
Format: Public Radio. **Owner:** Maine Public Broadcasting Network, 1450 Lisbon St., Lewiston, ME 04240. **Key Personnel:** Jim Dowe, CEO, President, jdowe@mpbn.net; John Isacke, CFO, jisacke@mpbn.net; Keith Shortall, Gen. Mgr.; Charles Beck, Div. Dir. **Ad Rates:** Noncommercial. **URL:** http://www.mpbn.net.

WMEF-FM - See Fort Kent

14699 ■ WMEH-FM - 90.9
63 Texas Ave.
Bangor, ME 04401
Phone: (207)874-6570
Fax: (207)942-2857
Free: 800-884-1717
Format: Information; News; Classical; Jazz. **Owner:** Maine Public Broadcasting Network, 1450 Lisbon St., Lewiston, ME 04240. **Operating Hours**: Continuous. **Key Personnel:** Jim Dowe, CEO, President, jdowe@mpbn.net; Charles Beck, VP, Div. Dir., cbeck@mpbn.net; Keith Shortall, Dir. Pub. Aff., News Dir., kshortall@mpbn.net. **Ad Rates:** Noncommercial; underwriting available. **URL:** http://www.mpbn.net.

WMEM-FM - See Presque Isle

WMEP-FM - See Camden

WMEW-FM - See Waterville

14700 ■ W36CK - 36
PO Box A
Santa Ana, CA 92711
Phone: (714)832-2950
Free: 888-731-1000
Owner: Trinity Broadcasting Network Inc., PO Box A, Santa Ana, CA 92711, Ph: (714)832-2950, Free: 888-731-1000. **URL:** http://www.tbn.org.

14701 ■ WTOX-AM - 1450
1746 Broadway
Bangor, ME 04401
Phone: (207)794-6555
Fax: (207)794-3583
Format: Full Service. **Networks:** People's Network. **Owner:** Northland Communications Corp., Nine Boardwalk Pl., Seneca, SC 29678, Ph: (864)882-0002. **Founded:** 1989. **Formerly**: WLKN-AM; WKFM-FM. **Operating Hours**: Continuous. **ADI**: Bangor, ME. **Key Personnel:** Michael Dow, Operations Mgr.; Margaret Hayes, Gen. Mgr.; Lisa Jordon, News Dir.; Roger Parent, Sales Mgr.; Mitch Taylor, Dir. of Pub. Prog. & Svcs. **Wattage**: 1,000. **Ad Rates:** $2.55-4.35 for 30 seconds; $3.30-5.10 for 60 seconds. **Mailing address:** PO Box 9, Lincoln, ME 04457.

14702 ■ WVII-TV - 7
371 Target Industrial Cir.
Bangor, ME 04401
Phone: (207)945-6457
Format: Commercial TV. **Networks:** ABC. **Owner:** Bangor Communications L.L.C., 371-Target Industrial Cir., Bangor, ME 04401, Ph: (207)945-6457. **Founded:** 1965. **Operating Hours**: Continuous. **ADI**: Bangor, ME. **Wattage**: 316,000. **Ad Rates:** Noncommercial. **URL:** http://www.foxbangor.com.

14703 ■ WVOM-FM - 103.9
184 Target Industrial Cir.
Bangor, ME 04401
Phone: (207)947-9100
Format: Talk. **Ad Rates:** Noncommercial. **URL:** http://www.wvomfm.com.

14704 ■ WZLO 103.1 FM - 103.1
861 Broadway
Bangor, ME 04402-1929
Phone: (207)990-2800
Fax: (207)990-2444
Format: Adult Contemporary. **Networks:** ABC; AP. **Founded:** 1967. **Formerly**: WDME-FM. **Operating Hours**: Continuous. **Wattage**: 6,000. **Ad Rates:** $10-15 for 30 seconds; $12-18 for 60 seconds. Combined advertising rates available with WKIT-FM & WZON-AM. **Mailing address:** PO Box 1929, Bangor, ME 04402-1929. **URL:** http://www.zoneradio.com.

14705 ■ WZON-AM - 620
861 Broadway
Bangor, ME 04401
Phone: (207)990-2800
Fax: (207)990-2444
Free: 800-287-1003
Format: Sports. **Networks:** CBS; Mutual Broadcasting System; Talknet. **Owner:** The Zone Corp., at above address. **Founded:** 1926. **Operating Hours**: Continuous. **ADI**: Bangor, ME. **Key Personnel:** Ken Wood, Contact. **Wattage**: 5,000. **Ad Rates:** $7-20 for 30 seconds; $10-25 for 60 seconds. **URL:** http://www.zoneradio.com.

BAR HARBOR

SE ME. Hancock Co. On Mount Desert Island, 40 mi. SE of Bangor. Acadia National Park. Resort.

14706 ■ Bateau
Bateau Press
c/o Daniel Mahoney
105 Eden St.
Bar Harbor, ME 04609
Publisher's E-mail: info@bateaupress.org
Literary magazine covering poetry, flash fiction, short plays, mini reviews, comic strips, and graphic narratives. **Freq:** Semiannual. **Key Personnel:** James Grinwis, Editor; Ashley Schaffer, Managing Editor; Lynette Baker, Editor. **Subscription Rates:** $15 Single issue. **URL:** http://bateaupress.org. **Circ:** (Not Reported).

14707 ■ Human Ecology Review
Society for Human Ecology
c/o Barbara Carter, Secretary
105 Eden St.
Bar Harbor, ME 04609
Phone: (207)801-5632
Publisher's E-mail: info@societyforhumanecology.org
Journal highlighting peer-reviewed interdisciplinary research, essays, discussion papers, dialogue, and commentary on special topics relevant to human ecology. **Freq:** Semiannual Published September 2014. **ISSN:** 1074--4827 (print). **Subscription Rates:** $100 Institutions; $50 Single issue. **URL:** http://societyforhumanecology.org/human-ecology-homepage/human-ecology-review. **Remarks:** Advertising not accepted. **Circ:** (Not Reported).

14708 ■ Journal of Natural History Education and Experience
Natural History Network
PO Box 533
Bar Harbor, ME 04609
Publisher's E-mail: mail@naturalhistorynetwork.org
Alt. Formats: PDF. **URL:** http://naturalhistorynetwork.org/journal. **Remarks:** Advertising not accepted. **Circ:** (Not Reported).

BATH

Sagadahoc Co. S. ME. Sagadahoc Co. On Atlantic Ocean, 22 mi. SE of Lewiston. Marine museum. Shipbuilding. Trade center.

14709 ■ Coastal Journal
Coastal Journal
97 Commercial St.
Bath, ME 04530
Phone: (207)443-6241
Fax: (207)443-5605
Free: 800-649-6241
Community newspaper (tabloid). **Freq:** Weekly (Thurs.). **Print Method:** Offset. **Cols./Page:** 5 and 7. **Col. Width:** 2.069 and 1.442 inches. **Col. Depth:** 12 7/8 and 12 7/8 inches. **Key Personnel:** Bruce Hardina, Editor. **Subscription Rates:** Free. **URL:** http://www.coastaljournal.com. **Remarks:** Advertising accepted; rates available upon request. **Circ:** (Not Reported).

14710 ■ WJTO-AM
PO Box 308
Bath, ME 04530-0308
Phone: (207)443-6671
Founded: 1957. **Formerly**: WMMS-AM. **Wattage**: 1,000 Day; 006 Night.

BETHEL

W. ME. Oxford Co. On Androscoggin River, 33 mi. NW of Lewiston. Resort.

14711 ■ Bethel Citizen
Bethel Citizen
PO Box 109
Bethel, ME 04217
Phone: (207)824-2444
Fax: (207)824-2426
Free: 800-ABC-NEWS
Publication E-mail: news@bethelcitizen.com
Community newspaper. **Freq:** Weekly (Thurs.). **Print Method:** Offset. **Cols./Page:** 6. **Col. Width:** 24 nonpareils. **Col. Depth:** 294 agate lines. **Key Personnel:** Janice Bjorkland, Contact; Nancy Wight, Customer Service; Polly Davis, Assistant; Michael Daniels, Editor; Alison Aloisio, Reporter; Edward Snook, Publisher; Carri Frechette, Graphic Designer; Nancy Forest, Manager, Production. **Subscription Rates:** $46.30 Individuals in Maine & NH; $51.87 Individuals outside Maine & NH. **URL:** http://bethelcitizen.com. **Formerly**: The Bethel Oxford County Citizen. **Remarks:** Accepts advertising. **Circ:** (Not Reported).

BIDDEFORD

York Co. SE ME. York Co. On Saco River, 14 mi. SSW of Portland. Diversified manufacturing; textiles.

14712 ■ Aquaculture: An International Journal
Elsevier
c/o B.A. Costa-Pierre, Editor-in-Chief
University of New England
Marine Science Education and Research Ctr.
11 Hills Beach Rd.
Biddeford, ME 04005
Publisher's E-mail: t.reller@elsevier.com
Journal providing information on all aquatic food resources related directly or indirectly to human consumption. **Freq:** 16/yr. **Print Method:** Web press. **Trim Size:** 7 1/8 x 10. **Key Personnel:** B.A. Costa-Pierce, Editor-in-Chief; E.M. Donaldson, Advisor; G. Hulata, Editor. **ISSN:** 0044--8486 (print). **Subscription Rates:** $2715.20 Institutions ejournal; $8146 print. **URL:** http://www.journals.elsevier.com/aquaculture. **Circ:** (Not Reported).

14713 ■ Journal Tribune
Journal Publishing Corp.
457 Alfred Rd.
Biddeford, ME 04005
Phone: (207)282-1535
Fax: (207)282-3138
Publication E-mail: circulation@journaltribune.com
Independent general newspaper serving York County, ME. **Founded:** 1884. **Freq:** Daily (eve.) and Sat. (morn.). **Print Method:** Offset. **Trim Size:** 13 3/4 x 23 3/4. **Cols./Page:** 6. **Col. Width:** 2 1/16 inches. **Col. Depth:** 21.5 picas. **Key Personnel:** Nick Cowenhoven, Managing Editor; Al Edwards, Editor; Bruce Hardina, Publisher. **ISSN:** 0000-5720 (print). **USPS:** 005-720. **Subscription Rates:** $89 Individuals online, 365 days; $32.50 Individuals print, 13 weeks; $65 Individuals print, 26 weeks; $130 Individuals print, 52 weeks. **URL:** http://www.journaltribune.com. **Mailing address:** PO Box 627, Biddeford, ME 04005. **Ad Rates:** BW $1,644.75; 4C $475; SAU $12.75. **Remarks:** Accepts advertising. **Circ:** Mon.-Fri. ★**10000**.

14714 ■ WMEA-TV - 26
1450 Lisbon St.
Lewiston, ME 04240
Fax: (207)783-5193
Free: 800-884-1717
Format: Public TV. **Simulcasts:** WMEB-TV, WCBB-TV, WMEM-TV. **Networks:** Public Broadcasting Service (PBS). **Owner:** Maine Public Broadcasting Network, 1450 Lisbon St., Lewiston, ME 04240. **Founded:** Apr. 1974. **Operating Hours**: Continuous. **ADI**: Presque Isle, ME. **Key Personnel:** Jim Dowe, CEO, President,

Circulation: ★ = AAM; △ or • = BPA; ♦ = CAC; ❑ = VAC; ⊕ = PO Statement; ‡ = Publisher's Report; Boldface figures = sworn; Light figures = estimated.

jdowe@mpbn.net. **Wattage**: 692,000. **URL:** http://www.mpbn.net.

14715 ■ WSTG-FM - 94.3
Alfred Rd.
Business Park Pomerleau St.
Biddeford, ME 04005
Phone: (207)282-5121
Fax: (207)282-3228
Format: Soft Rock. **Networks:** ABC. **Owner:** Gold Coast Broadcasting, 2284 Victoria Ave., Ste. 2-G, Ventura, CA 93003, Ph: (805)289-1400, Fax: (805)644-7906. **Founded:** 1972. **Formerly**: WYJY; WSTQ-FM. **Operating Hours**: 5 a.m.-1 a.m. daily. **Key Personnel:** James M. McCann, President; Stephen McCann, VP; Richard Lutsk, VP. **Wattage**: 25,000 ERP. **Ad Rates:** $20 for 60 seconds. **Mailing address:** PO Box 667, Biddeford, ME 04005.

BOOTHBAY HARBOR

Lincoln Co. (S). 30 m NE of Portland. Summer resort. Shipyards, packing houses. Fisheries.

14716 ■ Boothbay Register
Maine-OK Enterprises
PO Box 357
Boothbay Harbor, ME 04538-0357
Phone: (207)633-4620
Fax: (207)633-7123
Publication E-mail: editorkburnham@boothbayregister.com
Community newspaper. **Freq:** Weekly (Thurs.). **Print Method:** Offset. **Trim Size:** 15 13/16 x 21. **Cols./Page:** 7. **Col. Width:** 2 1/16 INS. **Col. Depth:** 21 inches. **Key Personnel:** Mary D. Brewer, Managing Editor; Marylouise Cowan, Publisher; Pat Schmid, Office Manager. **USPS:** 061-120. **Subscription Rates:** $36.93 Individuals in Lincoln county; $54.86 Individuals outside Lincoln county; $52 Out of state. **URL:** http://www.boothbayregister.com. **Ad Rates:** PCI $11.25. **Remarks:** Advertising accepted; rates available upon request. **Circ:** (Not Reported).

BREWER

Penobscot Co. Penobscot Co. (SE). On Penobscot River opposite Bangor. Wood pulp, paper, brick.

14717 ■ WBZN-FM - 107.3
49 Acme Rd.
Brewer, ME 04412
Phone: (207)989-5631
Format: Contemporary Hit Radio (CHR). **Owner:** Cumulus Broadcasting Inc., 3280 Peachtree Rd. NW, Ste. 2300, Atlanta, GA 30305-2447, Ph: (404)949-0700, Fax: (404)949-0740. **Ad Rates:** Advertising accepted; rates available upon request. **URL:** http://z1073.com.

14718 ■ WDEA-AM - 1370
49 Acme Rd.
Brewer, ME 04412
Phone: (207)989-5631
Format: Big Band/Nostalgia. **Networks:** CBS; Mutual Broadcasting System; ABC. **Owner:** Cumulus Media Inc., 3280 Peachtree Rd. NW, Ste. 2300, Atlanta, GA 30305-2455, Ph: (404)949-0700, Fax: (404)949-0740. **Founded:** 1958. **Operating Hours**: Continuous. **Key Personnel:** Amy Rees, Contact; Fred Miller, Contact. **Wattage**: 5,000. **Ad Rates:** $5-17 for 30 seconds; $6-22 for 60 seconds. **URL:** http://wdea.am/help.

WEZQ-FM - See Bangor, ME

14719 ■ WQCB-FM - 106.5
49 Acme Rd.
Brewer, ME 04412
Phone: (207)989-5631
Email: jeff.tuttle@townsquaremedia.com
Format: Country. **Networks:** AP. **Owner:** Cumulus Media Inc., 3280 Peachtree Rd. NW, Ste. 2300, Atlanta, GA 30305-2455, Ph: (404)949-0700, Fax: (404)949-0740. **Founded:** 1985. **Operating Hours**: Continuous; 100% local. **Wattage**: 98,000. **Ad Rates:** $65 for 30 seconds; $70 for 60 seconds. **URL:** http://q1065.fm.

14720 ■ WWMJ-FM - 95.7
49 Acme Rd.
Brewer, ME 04412
Phone: (207)989-5631
Fax: (207)989-5685
Format: Classical. **Networks:** ABC. **Founded:** 1965. **Operating Hours**: Continuous. **Wattage**: 11,500. **Ad Rates:** Noncommercial.

BRUNSWICK

Cumberland Co. (SW). On Androscoggin River, 27 m NE of Portland. Bowdoin College (Co-educational). Summer resort. Naval Air Station. Manufactures paper, art supplies, shoes, children's clothing.

14721 ■ Bowdoin Magazine
Bowdoin College
5700 College Sta.
Brunswick, ME 04011-8448
Phone: (207)725-3000
Magazine for college alumni. **Freq:** Quarterly. **Print Method:** Offset. **Trim Size:** 8 1/8 x 10 7/8. **Cols./Page:** 3. **Col. Width:** 2 1/4 inches. **Col. Depth:** 9 3/4 inches. **Key Personnel:** Alison M. Bennie, Editor; Matthew J. O'Donnell, Associate Editor. **URL:** http://alumni.bowdoin.edu/gateway/magazine. **Remarks:** Accepts advertising. **Circ:** (Not Reported).

14722 ■ Brunswick Times Record
Times Record
3 Business Pky.
Brunswick, ME 04011
Phone: (207)729-3311
Fax: (207)729-5728
Newspaper with a Democratic orientation. **Freq:** Daily (eve.). **Print Method:** Offset. **Cols./Page:** 7. **Col. Width:** 24 nonpareils. **Col. Depth:** 301 agate lines. **Key Personnel:** Chris P. Miles, President, Publisher; Michelle Passmore, Director, Advertising; Robert Long, Managing Editor. **Subscription Rates:** $149 Individuals home subscription /year; $155 Individuals mail subscription (Maine and U.S.) /year. **URL:** http://www.timesrecord.com. **Mailing address:** PO Box 10, Brunswick, ME 04011-1302. **Remarks:** Accepts advertising. **Circ:** (Not Reported).

14723 ■ WBOR-FM - 91.1
Smith Union,Bowdoin College
Bowdoin College
Brunswick, ME 04011
Email: info@wbor.org
Format: Educational. **Owner:** Bowdoin College, 5700 College Sta., Brunswick, ME 04011-8448, Ph: (207)725-3000. **Operating Hours**: 7 a.m.-1 a.m. **Wattage**: 300. **Ad Rates:** Advertising accepted; rates available upon request. **URL:** http://www.wbor.org.

BURNHAM

14724 ■ WCHX-FM - 105.5
114 N Logan Blvd.
Burnham, ME 17009
Phone: (717)242-1055
Email: wchx@chx105.com
Format: Adult Contemporary. **Networks:** ABC. **Owner:** County of Mifflin, 20 N Wayne St., Lewistown, PA 17044, Ph: (717)248-6733, Fax: (717)248-3695. **Founded:** 1987. **Operating Hours**: Continuous; 3% network, 97% local. **Wattage**: 470. **Ad Rates:** $18 for 30 seconds. **URL:** http://www.chx105.com.

CALAIS

Washington Co. Washington Co. (SE). On St. Croix River, 90 m E of Bangor. Summer resort. Bridges to Milltown and St. Stephens, N.B. Manufactures furniture, lumber, pulpwood. Blueberries packed. Truck farms.

14725 ■ WMED-TV - 13
1450 Lisbon St.
Lewiston, ME 04240
Fax: (207)783-5193
Free: 800-884-1717
Format: Public TV. **Simulcasts:** WMEB-TV; WCBB-TV; WMEA-TV. **Networks:** Public Broadcasting Service (PBS). **Owner:** Maine Public Broadcasting Corp., 1450 Lisbon St., Lewiston, ME 04240. **Founded:** 1963. **Operating Hours**: Continuous. **Key Personnel:** Keith Shortall, Dir. of HR; Charles Beck, CFO. **Ad Rates:** Noncommercial. **URL:** http://www.mpbn.net.

CAMDEN

Knox Co. (S). On Penobscot Bay, 40 m E of Augusta. Resort. Manufactures felts, electronics, tents, leather and canvas products. Boat building & repairs.

14726 ■ The Camden Herald
Courier Publications
PO Box 248
Camden, ME 04843
Phone: (207)236-8511
Newspaper. **Freq:** Weekly (Thurs.). **Print Method:** Offset. **Cols./Page:** 6. **Col. Width:** 2 1/16 inches. **Col. Depth:** 294 agate lines. **Key Personnel:** David Grima, Editor; Kim Lincoln, Assistant Editor; Carolyn Flanagan, Office Manager. **Subscription Rates:** $37 Individuals in State; $60 Out of state; $37 Out of state e-edition only. **Formerly**: Coast Papers. **Ad Rates:** GLR $6; PCI $8. **Remarks:** Accepts advertising. **Circ:** 5000.

14727 ■ KMWorld: Creating and Managing the Knowledge-Based Enterprise
Information Today Inc.
22 Bayview St., 2nd Fl.
Camden, ME 04843
Phone: (207)236-8524
Fax: (207)236-6452
Publisher's E-mail: custserv@infotoday.com
Journal focusing on the applications of knowledge management solutions as they apply to business and corporations. **Freq:** Monthly. **Print Method:** Web offset. **Trim Size:** 10 7/16 x 13. **Key Personnel:** Hugh McKellar, Editor-in-Chief; Michael V. Zarrello, Director, Advertising; Sandra Haimila, Managing Editor; David Panara, Manager, Advertising; John Brokenshire, Chief Financial Officer; Andy Moore, Publisher; John C. Yersak, Vice President; Sue Hogan, Director; Joe Menendez, Manager, Marketing. **ISSN:** 1060-894X (print). **URL:** http://www.kmworld.com/conference/2015. **Formerly**: Imaging World. **Mailing address:** PO Box 1358, Camden, ME 04843. **Ad Rates:** BW $7,475; 4C $8,970. **Remarks:** Advertising accepted; rates available upon request. **Circ:** △**50,000**.

14728 ■ WMEP-FM - 90.5
65 Texas Ave.
Bangor, ME 04401
Fax: (207)942-2857
Free: 800-884-1717
Format: Public Radio. **Owner:** Maine Public Broadcasting Network, 1450 Lisbon St., Lewiston, ME 04240. **Operating Hours**: 5 a.m. - 1.30 a.m. **Key Personnel:** Jim Dowe, CEO, President, jdowe@mpbn.net; Charles Beck, VP, cbeck@mpbn.net; Keith Shortall, Dir. Pub. Aff. , News Dir., kshortall@mpbn.net. **Ad Rates:** Noncommercial; underwriting available. **URL:** http://www.mpbn.net.

CAPE ELIZABETH

14729 ■ The Cape Courier
The Cape Courier
PO Box 6242
Cape Elizabeth, ME 04107
Phone: (207)767-5023
Publisher's E-mail: info@capecourier.com
Community newspaper. **Freq:** Semimonthly. **Key Personnel:** Jess LeClair, Manager, Advertising; Sheila Zimmerman, Manager, Production; Patricia McCarthy, Editor. **Subscription Rates:** $21 Individuals inside Maine; $25 Out of area; $12 Individuals 6 months; $15 Students. **Alt. Formats:** PDF. **URL:** http://www.capecourier.com. **Ad Rates:** BW $660; PCI $11. **Remarks:** Accepts advertising. **Circ:** Combined 4700.

CARIBOU

Aroostook Co. Aroostook Co. (NE). 13 m N of Presque Isle. Potatoes, sugar beets.

14730 ■ WCXU-FM - 97.7
152 E Green Ridge Rd.
Caribou, ME 04736
Fax: (207)472-3221
Free: 800-660-9298
Email: channelxradio@yahoo.com
Format: Adult Contemporary. **Networks:** CNN Radio. **Owner:** Canxus Broadcasting Corp., 152 E Greenridge Rd., Caribou, ME 04736, Fax: (207)472-3221, Free: 800-660-9298. **Founded:** 1986. **Operating Hours**: Continuous; 15% network, 85% local. **ADI:** Presque Isle, ME. **Key Personnel:** Dennis Curley, President; Richard Chandler, Station Mgr., VP; Pamela Curley, Dir. of Traffic. **Local Programs**: *Oldies with Channel X,*

Saturday 7:00 p.m. - 12:00 a.m. **Wattage**: 6,000. **Ad Rates:** $10-15 for 30 seconds; $12-18 for 60 seconds. **URL:** http://www.channelxradio.com.

14731 ■ WCXX-FM - 102.3
152 E Green Ridge Rd.
Caribou, ME 04736
Phone: (207)473-7513
Fax: (207)472-3221
Free: 800-660-9298
Email: channelxradio@yahoo.com
Format: Adult Contemporary. **Simulcasts:** WCXU-FM and W276AY. **Networks:** CNN Radio. **Owner:** Canxus Broadcasting Corp., 152 E Greenridge Rd., Caribou, ME 04736, Fax: (207)472-3221, Free: 800-660-9298. **Founded:** 1988. **Operating Hours**: Continuous; 15% network, 85% local. **ADI**: Presque Isle, ME. **Key Personnel:** Dennis Curley, President; Richard Chandler, Station Mgr., VP; Douglas Christensen, News Dir.; Pamela Curley, Dir. of Traffic; Mark Stewart, Contact. **Wattage**: 3,000. **Ad Rates:** $10-15 for 30 seconds; $12-18 for 60 seconds. **URL:** http://www.channelxradio.com.

14732 ■ WFST-AM - 600
PO Box 600
Caribou, ME 04736
Phone: (207)492-6000
Fax: (207)493-3268
Email: wfst@wfst.net
Format: Religious. **Owner:** Northern Broadcast Ministries Inc., at above address. **Key Personnel:** John Stephenson, Mgr.; Dick Waugh, Program Mgr. **Ad Rates:** Noncommercial. **URL:** http://www.wfst.net.

14733 ■ W276AY-FM - 103.1
152 E Green Ridge Rd.
Caribou, ME 04736
Phone: (714)847-0809
Email: channelxradio@yahoo.com
Format: Adult Contemporary. **Ad Rates:** Advertising accepted; rates available upon request. **URL:** http://www.channelxradio.com.

CUSHING

14734 ■ QAJAQ - A Journal Dedicated to the Study of Northern Native Watercraft
Qajaq U.S.A.
88 Mason Cove Ln.
Cushing, ME 04563
Publisher's E-mail: info@qajaqusa.org
Journal promoting the traditions and techniques of Greenland-style kayaking. **Key Personnel:** Vernon Doucette, Editor. **Subscription Rates:** Included in membership; $29.99. **URL:** http://www.qajaqusa.org/Journal/Journal.html. **Remarks:** Advertising not accepted. **Circ:** (Not Reported).

DOVER FOXCROFT

14735 ■ The Piscataquis Observer
Northeast Publishing Co.
12 E Main St.
Dover Foxcroft, ME 04426-0030
Phone: (207)564-8355
Fax: (207)564-7056
Newspaper. **Freq:** Weekly (Wed.). **Print Method:** Offset. **Cols./Page:** 6. **Col. Width:** 26 nonpareils. **Col. Depth:** 301 agate lines. **Key Personnel:** Mark Putnam, Managing Editor, phone: (207)764-4471, fax: (207)764-4499. **Subscription Rates:** $41.15 Individuals in county; $52.64 Individuals in state; $52 Out of state. **URL:** http://www.observer-me.com. **Remarks:** Accepts advertising. **Circ:** (Not Reported).

EAST MACHIAS

14736 ■ Lighthouse Digest
Foghorn Publishing
PO Box 250
East Machias, ME 04630
Phone: (207)259-2121
Fax: (207)259-3323
Free: 800-668-7737
Publication E-mail: editor@lighthousedigest.com
Magazine covering historical stories, vintage stories, current events and lighthouse news from around the country. **Freq:** Bimonthly. **Print Method:** Offset. **Trim Size:** 13 x 21 1/2. **Cols./Page:** 6. **Col. Width:** 24 nonpareils. **Col. Depth:** 301 agate lines. **Key Personnel:** Timothy Harrison, Editor. **ISSN:** 1066-0038 (print). **Subscription Rates:** $34.95 Individuals; $59.95 Two years; $43 Canada; $75 Canada 2 years; $55 Other countries; $89 Other countries 2 years. **URL:** http://www.lighthousedigest.com; http://www.shop.foghornpublishing.com. **Ad Rates:** BW $1250. **Remarks:** Accepts advertising. **Circ:** (Not Reported).

EAST ORLAND

14737 ■ WERU-FM - 89.9
PO Box 170
East Orland, ME 04431
Phone: (207)469-6600
Fax: (207)469-8961
Email: info@weru.org
Format: Eclectic; Blues; Country; Jazz. **Founded:** 1843. **Operating Hours**: 18 hours Daily. **Key Personnel:** Greg Rossel, President; Willie Marquart, Mgr. of Fin., willie@weru.org; Matt Murphy, Gen. Mgr., matt@weru.org; Bruce Clark, Chief Engineer. **Wattage**: 15,000. **Ad Rates:** Advertising accepted; rates available upon request. **URL:** http://weru.org.

EASTPORT

Washington Co. Washington Co. (E). 80 m E of Bangor. Residential.

14738 ■ The Quoddy Tides
The Quoddy Tides
123 Water St.
Eastport, ME 04631
Phone: (207)853-4806
Fax: (207)853-4095
Publisher's E-mail: qtides@midmaine.com
Newspaper reporting community and marine news. **Freq:** Biweekly. **Print Method:** Offset. **Cols./Page:** 4. **Col. Width:** 14 picas. **Col. Depth:** 15 inches. **Key Personnel:** Edward French, Editor. **USPS:** 453-220. **Subscription Rates:** $35 Individuals Washington County; $45 Out of area; C$45 Canada. **URL:** http://www.quoddytides.com. **Mailing address:** PO Box 213, Eastport, ME 04631. **Remarks:** Accepts advertising. **Circ:** 5000.

ELLSWORTH

Hancock Co. Hancock Co. (SE). On Union River, 25 m S of Bangor. Summer resort. Fishing. Lumber mill. Timber. Truck, fruit, dairy, poultry farms. Blueberries.

14739 ■ The Ellsworth American
Ellsworth American Inc.
30 Water St.
Ellsworth, ME 04605
Phone: (207)667-2576
Fax: (207)667-7656
Publisher's E-mail: info@ellsworthamerican.com
Community newspaper. **Freq:** Weekly (Thurs.). **Print Method:** Offset. **Cols./Page:** 7. **Col. Width:** 26 nonpareils. **Col. Depth:** 298 agate lines. **Key Personnel:** Alan L. Baker, Publisher. **USPS:** 173-960. **Subscription Rates:** $31.95 Individuals Digital Only - 1 year; $4 Individuals Digital Only - 1 month; $45.25 Individuals Digital & Print Combo - One Year, Hancock County Delivery; $56.25 Individuals Digital & Print Combo - One Year, State of Maine Delivery; $63.25 Out of state Digital & Print Combo - One Year. **URL:** http://ellsworthamerican.com/newspaper. **Remarks:** Accepts advertising. **Circ:** Paid ⊕**10555**.

14740 ■ WBQI-FM - 107.7
98 Main St.
Ellsworth, ME 04605
Phone: (207)667-9800
Fax: (207)667-3900
Format: Classical. **Owner:** Nassau Broadcasting Partners L.P., 619 Alexander Rd., 3rd Fl., Princeton, NJ 08540-6000, Ph: (609)452-9696, Fax: (609)452-6017. **Key Personnel:** Scott Hooper, Dir. of Programs, shooper@nassaubroadcasting.com; Pat Collins, Gen. Mgr., pcollins@nassaubroadcasting.com; Stan Manning, Operations Mgr., smanning@nassaubroadcasting.com. **Ad Rates:** Advertising accepted; rates available upon request.

14741 ■ WLKE-FM - 99.1
PO Box 9494
Ellsworth, ME 04605
Phone: (207)667-7573
Format: Country. **Networks:** ABC. **Owner:** Blueberry Broadcasting L.L.C., PO Box 2600, Kennebunkport, ME 04046, Ph: (207)967-8094. **Founded:** 1992. **Operating Hours**: Continuous. **ADI**: Bangor, ME. **Wattage**: 45,000 ERP. **Ad Rates:** Advertising accepted; rates available upon request.

14742 ■ WNSX-FM
14 Westwood Dr.
Ellsworth, ME 04605
Phone: (207)667-0002
Fax: (207)667-0627
Format: Classic Rock. **Wattage**: 50,000 ERP.

FARMINGTON

Franklin Co. (W). 50 m NE of Lewiston. State Teachers College. Resort. Manufactures ear protectors, skewers, dowels. Dairy, fruit, truck farms. Sweet corn, string beans, apples.

14743 ■ The Beloit Poetry Journal
Beloit Poetry Journal
PO Box 151
Farmington, ME 04938
Publisher's E-mail: bpj@bpj.org
Magazine presenting new poems without bias as to school, length, form, or subject; including authors such as Albert Goldbarth, Karl Elder, Patricia Goedicke, and Lola Haskins; containing reviews of new books by and about poets. **Freq:** Quarterly. **Print Method:** Offset. **Trim Size:** 6 x 9. **Cols./Page:** 1. **Key Personnel:** Lee Sharkey, Senior Editor; John Rosenwald, Senior Editor; Melissa Crowe, Editor, Board Member. **ISSN:** 0005--8661 (print). **Subscription Rates:** $10 Individuals /year. **URL:** http://www.bpj.org. **Remarks:** Advertising not accepted. **Circ:** (Not Reported).

14744 ■ The Farmington Flyer
University of Maine at Farmington - UMF Mainestream
111 S St.
Farmington, ME 04938
Phone: (207)778-7050
Fax: (207)778-7275
Publisher's E-mail: studentlife@umf.maine.edu
Collegiate newspaper. **Founded:** 1929. **Freq:** 3/month. **Print Method:** Letterpress. Uses mats. **Trim Size:** 12 x 15. **Cols./Page:** 4. **Col. Width:** 23 nonpareils. **Col. Depth:** 189 agate lines. **Key Personnel:** Courtney Fowler, Editor-in-Chief. **Subscription Rates:** Free. **URL:** http://www2.umf.maine.edu/flyer/. **Formerly**: Mainestream. **Ad Rates:** GLR $11.25; BW $270; PCI $3. **Remarks:** Accepts advertising. **Circ:** Free ‡2000.

14745 ■ WKTJ-FM - 99.3
121 Broadway
Farmington, ME 04938
Phone: (207)778-3400
Fax: (207)778-3000
Format: Adult Contemporary; Full Service. **Owner:** Franklin Broadcasting Corp., 320 N Franklin St., Franklin, VA 23851, Ph: (757)562-3135, Fax: (757)562-2345. **Founded:** Dec. 21, 1959. **Operating Hours:** 6 a.m.-11:15 p.m. Mon.-Fri.; 6 a.m.-1 p.m. Sat. 7. **Key Personnel:** Bob Thomas, Contact; Steve Bull, Sales Mgr; Joel Wellington, Contact; Bob Thomas, Contact; Kathi Shrewsbury, Contact; Al Ibarguen, Contact. **Wattage**: 1,500 ERP. **Ad Rates:** $8-16 for 30 seconds; $9-18 for 60 seconds. **Mailing address:** PO Box 590, Farmington, ME 04938. **URL:** http://www.993KTJ.com.

14746 ■ WUMF-FM - 100.1
111 S St.
Farmington, ME 04938
Phone: (207)778-7050
Email: umfadmit@maine.edu
Format: Educational. **Founded:** 1864. **Key Personnel:** Darren Smart, Station Mgr. **Ad Rates:** Noncommercial. **URL:** http://www.umf.maine.edu.

FORT KENT

Aroostook Co. (N). 20 m S of Edmundston, New Brunswick. Residential.

Circulation: ★ = AAM; △ or • = BPA; ♦ = CAC; ❑ = VAC; ⊕ = PO Statement; ‡ = Publisher's Report; Boldface figures = sworn; Light figures = estimated.

14747 ■ WMEF-FM - 106.5
63 Texas Ave.
Bangor, ME 04401
Fax: (207)942-2857
Free: 800-884-1717
Format: Public Radio. **Owner:** Maine Public Broadcasting Network, 1450 Lisbon St., Lewiston, ME 04240. **Key Personnel:** Jim Dowe, CEO, President. **URL:** http://www.mpbn.net.

14748 ■ WUFX-FM - 92.1
23 University Dr.
Fort Kent, ME 04743
Phone: (207)834-7500
Free: 888-879-8635
Format: Full Service. **URL:** http://www.umfk.edu.

FREEPORT

14749 ■ WMSJ-FM - 89.3
PO Box 287
Freeport, ME 04032
Phone: (207)865-3448
Format: Contemporary Christian. **Owner:** Positive Radio Network, PO Box 287, Freeport, ME 04032, Ph: (207)865-3448. **Founded:** 1984. **Operating Hours:** Continuous. **Key Personnel:** Kenny Robinson, Dir. of Programs, kenny@positive.fm; Paula K., Sr. VP, paula@positive.fm. **Wattage:** 7,500. **Ad Rates:** $5 for 15 seconds. **URL:** http://www.positive.fm.

HARPSWELL

14750 ■ The Morganeer
Morgan 3/4 Group
388 High Head Rd.
Harpswell, ME 04079
Phone: (207)721-3206
Magazine containing studies regarding Morgan sports cars. **Freq:** Bimonthly. **Subscription Rates:** Included in membership. **URL:** http://www.morgan34.org/content.aspx?page_id=22&club_id=570267&module_id=19503. **Remarks:** Accepts advertising. **Circ:** (Not Reported).

14751 ■ WYFP-FM - 91.9
11530 Carmel Commons Blvd.
Charlotte, NC 28226
Phone: (704)523-5555
Free: 800-888-7077
Format: Religious. **Founded:** 1968. **Wattage:** 6,000. **Mailing address:** PO Box 7300, Charlotte, NC 28241. **URL:** http://www.bbnradio.org.

HOULTON

Aroostook Co. (N). Port of entry. 117 m NE of Bangor. Historic area. Manufactures wood products. Dairy. Agriculture. Potatoes, grain.

14752 ■ Polaris Cable
34 Military St.
Houlton, ME 04730
Phone: (207)532-2579
Email: sales@polariscable.com
Cities Served: Bridgewater, Danforth, Enfield, Hodgdon, Houlton, Howland, Island Falls, Littleton, Medway, Monticello, Oakfield, Oakfield, Passadumkeag, Patten, Smyrna, Maine; 218 channels. **URL:** http://www.polariscable.com.

14753 ■ WBCQ-FM - 94.7
39 Court St., Ste. 215
Houlton, ME 04730
Phone: (207)532-3600
Fax: (207)521-0056
Format: Country. **Owner:** County Communications, at above address. **Key Personnel:** Ken Holck, Contact. **Ad Rates:** Advertising accepted; rates available upon request. **URL:** http://www.wbcqfm.com/.

14754 ■ WHOU-FM - 100.1
39 Court St., Ste. 215
Houlton, ME 04730
Phone: (207)532-3600
Email: sales@whoufm.com
Format: Adult Contemporary. **Networks:** NBC. **Owner:** County Communications, at above address. **Founded:** 1950. **Formerly:** WHOU-AM; WHGS-AM. **Operating Hours:** Continuous. **Key Personnel:** David Moore, Owner, manager@whoufm.com; Barrett Quint, Chief Engineer, barrett@aroostookmedia.com. **Wattage:** 1,000. **Ad Rates:** $9.20-14.80 for 30 seconds; $4-18 for 60 seconds. **URL:** http://whoufm.yolasite.com.

KENNEBUNK

York Co. (SW). 25 m SW of Portland. Resort. Fishing community.

14755 ■ York County Coast Star
York County Coast Star Inc.
PO Box 979
Kennebunk, ME 04043
Phone: (207)985-2961
Fax: (207)985-9050
Free: 800-310-2961
Newspaper serving York County. **Freq:** Weekly (Thurs.). **Print Method:** Offset. **Cols./Page:** 6. **Col. Width:** 18 nonpareils. **Col. Depth:** 221 agate lines. **Key Personnel:** Howard Altschiller, Executive Editor. **Subscription Rates:** $73.95 Individuals 52 weeks. **URL:** http://www.seacoastonline.com/apps/pbcs.dll/section?category=NEWS14. **Ad Rates:** GLR $.31. **Remarks:** Accepts advertising. **Circ:** Thurs. 9724.

14756 ■ WBQQ-FM - 99.3
169 Port Rd.
Kennebunk, ME 04043
Phone: (207)967-0993
Fax: (207)967-8671
Format: Classical. **Owner:** Nassau Broadcasting Partners L.P., 619 Alexander Rd., 3rd Fl., Princeton, NJ 08540-6000, Ph: (609)452-9696, Fax: (609)452-6017. **Key Personnel:** Scott Hooper, Dir. of Programs, shooper@nassaubroadcasting.com; Pat Collins, Gen. Mgr., pcollins@nassaubroadcasting.com; Stan Manning, Operations Mgr., smanning@nassaubroadcasting.com. **Ad Rates:** Advertising accepted; rates available upon request.

14757 ■ WBQX-FM - 106.9
169 Port Rd.
Kennebunk, ME 04043
Phone: (207)967-0993
Fax: (207)967-8671
Format: Classical. **Owner:** Nassau Broadcasting Partners L.P., 619 Alexander Rd., 3rd Fl., Princeton, NJ 08540-6000, Ph: (609)452-9696, Fax: (609)452-6017. **Key Personnel:** Scott Hooper, Dir. of Programs, shooper@nassaubroadcasting.com. **URL:** http://wbqx.nh1media.com.

KINGFIELD

14758 ■ Paper Doll Studio
Original Paper Doll Artists Guild
PO Box 14
Kingfield, ME 04947
Phone: (207)265-2500
Free: 800-290-2928
Publisher's E-mail: opdag@yahoo.com
Freq: Quarterly. **URL:** http://www.opdag.com/studionews.html. **Remarks:** Advertising not accepted. **Circ:** 400.

LEWISTON

Androscoggin Co. Androscoggin Co. (SW). On Androscoggin River, 36 m N of Portland. Bates College. Lewiston and Auburn adjoin on opposite banks of Androscoggin River, forming practically one city in everything but government. Manufactures cotton, rayon and woolen textiles, woolen blankets, carpeting, shoes, lasts, spools, bobbins, bricks, wood products, machinery, store fixtures, belting and leather products, bleaching chemicals, electrical supplies and equipment, transistors, structural concrete. Brass and iron foundries.

14759 ■ Lewiston Sun-Journal
Sun-Journal
104 Park St.
Lewiston, ME 04240
Phone: (207)784-5411
Fax: (207)784-5955
Free: 800-482-0753
Publisher's E-mail: letters@sunjournal.com
General newspaper. **Freq:** Mon.-Sun. (morn.). **Print Method:** Offset. **Cols./Page:** 6. **Col. Width:** 26 nonpareils. **Col. Depth:** 294 agate lines. **Key Personnel:** James Costello, Sr., Publisher; Rex Rhoades, Executive Editor. **Subscription Rates:** $4.99 Individuals /week; print and digital bundle; $2.99 Individuals /week; digital only; $4.75 Individuals /week; print only. **URL:** http://www.sunjournal.com. **Remarks:** Accepts advertising. **Circ:** Mon.-Sat. ♦**26646**, Sun. ♦**28534**.

WCBB-TV - See Augusta

WMEA-TV - See Biddeford

WMEB-TV - See Orono

WMED-TV - See Calais

WMEM-TV - See Presque Isle

14760 ■ WRBC-FM - 91.5
Bates College
31 Frye St.
Lewiston, ME 04240
Phone: (207)777-7915
Format: Educational. **Owner:** Bates College, 2 Andrews Rd., Lewiston, ME 04240, Ph: (207)786-6255. **Founded:** 1873. **Operating Hours:** Continuous during school year; 8 a.m. - 12 p.m. during summer. **Wattage:** 120. **Ad Rates:** Noncommercial. **URL:** http://temporary.wrbcradio.com.

LINCOLN

Penobscot Co. (C). 40 m NE of Bangor. Paper machinery; Manufactures paper; Truck, poultry, dairy farms. Forest products; Recreation.

14761 ■ Lincoln News
Lincoln News
78 W Broadway
Lincoln, ME 04457
Phone: (207)794-6532
Fax: (207)794-2004
Community newspaper. **Freq:** Weekly (Thurs.). **Print Method:** Offset. **Trim Size:** 10 x 16. **Cols./Page:** 5. **Col. Width:** 2 inches. **Col. Depth:** 224 agate lines. **Key Personnel:** Colby Tenggren, Owner, Publisher. **USPS:** 313-780. **Subscription Rates:** $46.42 Individuals in-state; $50 Individuals out-of-state. **URL:** http://www.lincnews.com. **Mailing address:** PO Box 35, Lincoln, ME 04457. **Ad Rates:** BW $400; PCI $8. **Remarks:** Accepts advertising. **Circ:** ‡6300.

LINCOLNVILLE

14762 ■ Maine Organic Farmer and Gardener
Maine Organic Farmers and Gardeners Association
Waldo County
662 Slab City Rd.
Lincolnville, ME 04849
Publication E-mail: mofga@mofga.org
Freq: Quarterly. **Print Method:** Offset. **Cols./Page:** 6. **Col. Width:** 37 nonpareils. **Col. Depth:** 210 agate lines. **Key Personnel:** Jean English, Editor. **ISSN:** 0891--9194 (print). **URL:** http://www.mofga.org/Publications/MaineOrganicFarmerGardener/tabid/150/Default.aspx. **Remarks:** Advertising accepted; rates available upon request. **Circ:** (Not Reported).

MADAWASKA

Aroostook Co. (N). On St. John River, 2 m S of Edmunston, New Brunswick. Paper mill. Fishing tackle, perfumes, cosmetics manufactured. Dairy, truck farms. Potatoes.

14763 ■ St. John Valley Times
St. John Valley Times
160 Main St.
Madawaska, ME 04756
Phone: (207)728-3336
Fax: (207)433-1242
Free: 800-924-9041
Community newspaper. **Freq:** Weekly (Wed.). **Print Method:** Offset. **Trim Size:** 11 1/2 x 16. **Cols./Page:** 5. **Col. Width:** 2 inches. **Col. Depth:** 15 inches. **URL:** http://www.sjvalley-times.com. **Mailing address:** PO Box 419, Madawaska, ME 04756. **Ad Rates:** GLR $.87; BW $311.25; 4C $655.25; PCI $5.46. **Remarks:** Accepts advertising. **Circ:** Paid 6500, Free 20.

MEDWAY

14764 ■ W34CN - 34
PO Box A
Santa Ana, CA 92711
Phone: (714)832-2950
Free: 888-731-1000

Owner: Trinity Broadcasting Network Inc., PO Box A, Santa Ana, CA 92711, Ph: (714)832-2950, Free: 888-731-1000. **URL:** http://www.tbn.org.

MEXICO

14765 ■ WTBM-FM - 100.7
243 Main St.
Norway, ME 04268
Phone: (207)743-5911
Fax: (207)743-5913
Free: 800-386-2131
Format: Country. **Key Personnel:** Vic Hodgkins, Operations Mgr., vic@woxo.com; Jeremy Rush, Traffic Mgr., jeremy@woxo.com; Dick Gleason, Gen. Mgr., President, dickgleason@gmail.com. **Mailing address:** PO Box 72, Norway, ME 04268. **URL:** http://www.woxo.com.

MILLINOCKET

Penobscot Co. (C) 3 m N of Norcross. Residential.

14766 ■ WSYY-FM
PO Box 1240, LAKE Rd.
Millinocket, ME 04462
Email: wsyy@kai.net
Format: Country. **Wattage:** 23,500 ERP.

NEW GLOUCESTER

14767 ■ Healthcare Finance News
HIMSS Media
71 Pineland Dr., Ste. 203
New Gloucester, ME 04260
Phone: (207)688-6270
Fax: (207)688-6273
Newspaper delivering essential information, market data, and industry news. **Freq:** Monthly. **Key Personnel:** Richard Pizzi, Director, Editorial. **URL:** http://www.healthcarefinancenews.com. **Circ:** △**32302**.

14768 ■ Healthcare IT News
HIMSS Media
71 Pineland Dr., Ste. 203
New Gloucester, ME 04260
Phone: (207)688-6270
Fax: (207)688-6273
Newspaper covering healthcare information technology. **Freq:** Monthly. **Key Personnel:** Mike Miliard, Editor; Danielle Hartley, Publisher, Senior Vice President; Bernie Monegain, Editor. **URL:** http://www.healthcareitnews.com; http://www.himssmedia.com/media/healthcare-it-news/overview. **Remarks:** Accepts advertising. **Circ:** △**54100**.

NEWCASTLE

14769 ■ Lincoln County News
Lincoln County News
116 Mills Rd.
Newcastle, ME 04553
Phone: (207)563-3171
Fax: (207)563-3127
Publication E-mail: lcn@lincoln.midcoast.com
Newspaper with a Republican orientation. **Founded:** 1875. **Freq:** Weekly (Thurs.). **Print Method:** Offset. **Trim Size:** 16 1/2 x 22 1/2. **Cols./Page:** 7 and 6. **Col. Width:** 12.6 and 11 picas. **Col. Depth:** 21 and 21 inches. **Key Personnel:** Judith Finn, Editor; Christopher A. Roberts, Publisher; Samuel E. Roberts, Publisher; Ruth Hammond, Publisher; Peter Aguilar, Publisher. **USPS:** 313-500. **Subscription Rates:** $25 Individuals in county; $35 Out of area; $30 Individuals e-edition. **URL:** http://lincolncountynewsonline.com/index.asp. **Ad Rates:** GLR $.47; BW $882; 4C $985; SAU $5; PCI $6.50; BW $376; PCI $col. in. 5.35. **Remarks:** Accepts advertising. **Circ:** (Not Reported).

NOBLEBORO

14770 ■ Lincolnville Communications Inc.
133 Back Meadow Rd.
Nobleboro, ME 04555
Phone: (207)763-9911
Email: support@tidewater.net
Owner: Lincolnville Telephone Co., 133 Back Meadow Rd., Nobleboro, ME 04555, Ph: (207)763-9911, Fax: (207)763-9902. **Founded:** 1989. **Mailing address:** PO Box 200, Lincolnville Center, ME 04850. **URL:** http://www.lincolnvillecommunications.net.

NORWAY

Oxford Co. (W). 48 m NW of Portland. Summer resort. Timber. Manufactures shoes, snowshoes, wooden novelties, electronic parts, dowels, confectionery. Diversified farming. Sweet corn, beans.

14771 ■ Advertiser-Democrat
James Newspaper Inc.
1 Pikes Hill
Norway, ME 04268
Phone: (207)743-7011
Community newspaper. **Freq:** Weekly (Wed.). **Print Method:** Offset. **Trim Size:** 22 3/4 x 28. **Cols./Page:** 9. **Col. Width:** 16 nonpareils. **Col. Depth:** 297 agate lines. **Key Personnel:** A.M. Sheehan, Editor. **Subscription Rates:** $48.11 Individuals 57 weeks; Oxford County; $92.61 Individuals 114 weeks; Oxford County; $57.73 Individuals 57 weeks; other Maine counties; $110.65 Individuals 114 weeks; other Maine counties. **URL:** http://www.advertiserdemocrat.com. **Ad Rates:** GLR $.28; BW $708.75; SAU $6.75; PCI $4.50. **Remarks:** Accepts advertising. **Circ:** ‡7500.

14772 ■ WKTQ-AM - 1450
243 Main St.
Norway, ME 04268
Phone: (207)743-5911
Fax: (207)743-5913
Free: 800-386-2132
Email: gleasonmedia@gmail.com
Format: Religious. **Simulcasts:** WTME. **Networks:** USA Radio. **Founded:** 1955. **Operating Hours:** Continuous. **Key Personnel:** Dick Gleason, Gen. Mgr., President. **Wattage:** 1,000. **Ad Rates:** $7-13 for 30 seconds; $9-17 for 60 seconds. Combined advertising rates available with WOXO-FM, WTME-AM, WTBM-FM. **Mailing address:** PO Box 72, Norway, ME 04268. **URL:** http://www.wtme.com.

14773 ■ WOXO-FM - 92.7
243 Main St.
Norway, ME 04268
Phone: (207)743-5911
Fax: (207)743-5913
Free: 800-386-2132
Email: info@woxo.com
Format: Contemporary Country; Country. **Simulcasts:** WTBM. **Networks:** Independent. **Owner:** Gleason Marketing Services, 555 Center St., Auburn, ME 04210, Ph: (207)784-5868, Fax: (207)784-4700. **Founded:** 1970. **Formerly:** WNWY-FM. **Operating Hours:** Continuous. **Key Personnel:** Vic Hodgkins, Traffic Mgr., vic@woxo.com; Jeremy Rush, Station Mgr., jeremy@woxo.com. **Wattage:** 3,000. **Ad Rates:** $9.50-20 for 60 seconds. Combined advertising rates available with WTBM-FM, WKTQ-AM, WTME-AM. **Mailing address:** PO Box 72, Norway, ME 04268. **URL:** http://www.woxo.com.

WTBM-FM - See Mexico

14774 ■ WTME-AM - 780
243 Main St.
Norway, ME 04268
Phone: (207)743-5911
Fax: (207)743-5913
Free: 800-386-2132
Format: Talk; Gospel; Religious. **Simulcasts:** WKTQ-AM. **Networks:** USA Radio. **Owner:** Gleason Marketing Services, 555 Center St., Auburn, ME 04210, Ph: (207)784-5868, Fax: (207)784-4700. **Founded:** 1938. **Formerly:** WXGL-AM. **Operating Hours:** Continuous. **ADI:** Portland-Poland Spring, ME. **Key Personnel:** Richard Gleason, Gen. Mgr., President. **Wattage:** 1,000. **Ad Rates:** $7-13 for 30 seconds; $9-17 for 60 seconds. Combined advertising rates available with WOXO-FM, WTBM-FM. **Mailing address:** PO Box 72, Norway, ME 04268. **URL:** http://www.wtme.com/coverage.html.

OLD TOWN

Penobscot Co. (S). On Penobscot River, 12 m NE of Bangor. Manufactures shoes, paper, lumber, handles, canoes, boats, pulp products. Timber. Agriculture. Potatoes, truck crops.

14775 ■ WBZN-FM - 107.3
c/o Cumulus Broadcasting
3535 Piedmont Rd., Bldg.14, 14th Fl.
Atlanta, GA 30305
Phone: (404)949-0700
Fax: (404)949-0740
Format: Top 40. **Owner:** Cumulus Broadcasting Inc., 3280 Peachtree Rd. NW, Ste. 2300, Atlanta, GA 30305-2447, Ph: (404)949-0700, Fax: (404)949-0740. **Ad Rates:** Noncommercial. **URL:** http://www.wbzn-fm.com/.

ORONO

Penobscot Co. (C). On Penobscot River, 8 m NE of Bangor. University of Maine. Textile mill. Manufactures canvas goods, oars, paddles. Aquaculture (live bait). Agriculture. Hay, vegetables.

14776 ■ American Journal of Potato Research
Potato Association of America
c/o Lori Wing, Administrator
5719 Crossland Hall, Rm. 220
University of Maine
Orono, ME 04469-5719
Phone: (207)581-3042
Fax: (207)581-3015
Publisher's E-mail: umpotato@maine.edu
Peer-reviewed journal of the Potato Association of America. **Freq:** Bimonthly. **Print Method:** Offset. **Trim Size:** 8 1/2 x 11. **Cols./Page:** 2. **Col. Width:** 108 nonpareils. **Key Personnel:** John Bamberg, Editor-in-Chief. **ISSN:** 1099--209X (print); **EISSN:** 1874--9380 (electronic). **Subscription Rates:** $522 Institutions print & free access or e-only; $626 Institutions print & enchanced access. **URL:** http://www.springer.com/life+sciences/plant+sciences/journal/12230. **Formerly:** American Potato Journal. **Remarks:** Advertising not accepted. **Circ:** ‡1000.

14777 ■ WMEB-FM - 91.9
5748 Memorial Union
Orono, ME 04469-5748
Phone: (207)581-2333
Format: Sports; Talk. **Networks:** Independent. **Owner:** University of Maine, Orono, ME 04469, Ph: (207)581-1865, Fax: (207)581-1213, Free: 877-486-2364. **Founded:** 1963. **Operating Hours:** Continuous. **Key Personnel:** Jeff Mannix, Station Mgr., jeffrey.mannix@umit.maine.edu; Karen Sanborn, Dir. of Programs, karen.sanborn@umit.maine.edu; Emily Burnham, Music Dir., emily.burnham@umit.maine.edu. **Wattage:** 280. **Ad Rates:** Noncommercial. **URL:** http://www.umaine.edu.

14778 ■ WMEB-TV - 12
1450 Lisbon St.
Lewiston, ME 04240
Fax: (207)783-5193
Free: 800-884-1717
Format: Public TV. **Networks:** Public Broadcasting Service (PBS). **Owner:** Maine Public Broadcasting Network, 1450 Lisbon St., Lewiston, ME 04240. **Founded:** 1962. **Operating Hours:** Continuous. **Key Personnel:** Keith Shortall, Dir. of HR; Charles Beck, CFO. **Ad Rates:** Noncommercial; underwriting available. **URL:** http://www.mpbn.net.

ORRINGTON

14779 ■ WJCX-FM - 99.5
154 River Rd.
Orrington, ME 04474
Phone: (207)991-9555
Fax: (207)991-9553
Email: info@ccbangor.org
Format: Contemporary Christian; Talk. **Owner:** Calvary Chapel Bangor Maine, 154 River Rd., Orrington, ME 04474, Ph: (207)991-9555, Fax: (207)991-9553. **Founded:** 1996. **Operating Hours:** Continuous. **ADI:** Bangor, ME. **Wattage:** 6,000. **Ad Rates:** Noncommercial. **URL:** http://www.ccbangor.org.

PHIPPSBURG

14780 ■ The Hemingway Review
University of Idaho Press
c/o Susan F. Beegel
14 Terhune Dr.
Phippsburg, ME 04562
Phone: (207)389-2839

Circulation: ★ = AAM; △ or • = BPA; ♦ = CAC; ❑ = VAC; ⊕ = PO Statement; ‡ = Publisher's Report; Boldface figures = sworn; Light figures = estimated.

Fax: (207)389-2839
Publisher's E-mail: webmaster@jhupress.jhu.edu
Academic journal covering the work and life of Ernest Hemingway. **Freq:** Semiannual. **Print Method:** Photo offset. **Trim Size:** 6 x 9. **Key Personnel:** Susan F. Beegel, Editor. **ISSN:** 0276--3362 (print); **EISSN:** 1548--4815 (electronic). **URL:** http://muse.jhu.edu/journal/275; http://hemingwaysociety.org/?page_id=10. **Formerly:** Hemingway Notes. **Remarks:** Accepts advertising. **Circ:** Combined 1000, 1150.

PORTLAND

Cumberland Co. Cumberland Co. (SW). On Casco Bay, 108 m NE of Boston. Important port with extensive foreign and coastwise trade. Manufactures cans, confectionery, crackers and cakes, clay and foundry products, canned goods, fertilizer, potato chips, machinery, screen, elevators, furniture, clothing, paper and wood boxes, stoves, chemicals, hardware, yarn, shoes, sirups, jams, mattresses, paint, burial cases. Cooperage, sardine packing; cold storage plants.

14781 ■ AudioFile: The Audiobook Review
AudioFile
37 Silver St.
Portland, ME 04101
Phone: (207)774-7563
Fax: (207)775-3744
Publication E-mail: info@audiofilemagazine.com
Consumer magazine covering news, reviews and features on audiobooks. **Freq:** 6/year February/March, April/May, June/July, August/September, October/November, December/January. **Key Personnel:** Jennifer M. Dowell, Managing Editor; Robin F. Whitten, Editor; Elizabeth K. Dodge, Editor; Jennifer Steele, Art Director. **ISSN:** 1063--0244 (print). **Subscription Rates:** $19.95 Individuals 1 year; $26.95 Two years. **URL:** http://www.audiofilemagazine.com. **Ad Rates:** BW $2190; 4C $2920. **Remarks:** Accepts advertising. **Circ:** Combined 20,000.

14782 ■ The Cafe Review
Yes Books
589 Congress St.
Portland, ME 04101
Phone: (207)775-3233
Journal covering poetry, art, and book reviews. **Freq:** Quarterly. **Print Method:** Offset. **Key Personnel:** Steve Luttrell, Editor, Founder; Stacey Chase, Associate Editor. **ISSN:** 1069--7179 (print). **Subscription Rates:** $40 Individuals; $48 Other countries. **URL:** http://thecafereview.com. **Remarks:** Advertising not accepted. **Circ:** Controlled 500.

14783 ■ CIN: Computers, Informatics, Nursing
Lippincott Williams and Wilkins
c/o Leslie H. Nicoll, PhD, Ed.-in-Ch.
10A Beach St., Ste. 2
Portland, ME 04101
Phone: (207)553-7750
Fax: (207)553-7751
Publisher's E-mail: ronna.ekhouse@wolterskluwer.com
Journal covering computer applications in nursing--including practice, administration, and research. **Founded:** 1983. **Freq:** Bimonthly. **Print Method:** Sheetfed offset. **Trim Size:** 7 3/4 x 10 3/4. **Cols./Page:** 2. **Col. Width:** 40 nonpareils. **Col. Depth:** 127 agate lines. **Key Personnel:** Leslie H. Nicoll, PhD, Editor-in-Chief; Susan K. Shropshire, Associate. **ISSN:** 1538--2931 (print). **Subscription Rates:** $128 Individuals. **URL:** http://journals.lww.com/cinjournal/pages/default.aspx. **Formerly:** Computers in Nursing. **Remarks:** Accepts advertising. **Circ:** (Not Reported).

14784 ■ Maine History
Maine Historical Society
489 Congress St.
Portland, ME 04101
Phone: (207)774-1822
Fax: (207)775-4301
Publisher's E-mail: info@mainehistory.org
Scholarly journal covering local history. **Freq:** Semiannual January and July. **ISSN:** 1090--5413 (print). **Subscription Rates:** Included in membership; $30 Institutions /volume. **URL:** http://www.mainehistory.org/publications.shtml. **Remarks:** Advertising not accepted. **Circ:** (Not Reported).

14785 ■ Maine Sunday Telegram
Blethen Maine Newspapers
PO Box 1460
Portland, ME 04104
General Sunday newspaper. **Freq:** Sunday. **Print Method:** Flexography. **Cols./Page:** 6. **Col. Width:** 25 nonpareils. **Col. Depth:** 301 agate lines. **Key Personnel:** Cliff Schechtman, Executive Editor, phone: (207)791-6693. **Subscription Rates:** $9 Individuals /month. **URL:** http://www.pressherald.com. **Remarks:** Accepts advertising. **Circ:** Sun. ★**99116**.

14786 ■ National Fisherman
National Fisherman
PO Box 7438
Portland, ME 04112-7437
Phone: (207)842-5608
Fax: (207)842-5609
Publisher's E-mail: info@nationalfisherman.com
Magazine covering commercial fishing and boat building. **Founded:** 1903. **Freq:** Monthly. **Print Method:** Offset. **Trim Size:** 10 1/2 x 13. **Cols./Page:** 4. **Col. Width:** 28 nonpareils. **Col. Depth:** 189 agate lines. **Key Personnel:** Jerry Fraser, Publisher; Lincoln Bedrosian, Senior Editor; Chris Dimmerling, Manager, Sales. **ISSN:** 0027-9250 (print). **Subscription Rates:** $14.95 Individuals; $26.95 Two years; $37.95 Individuals 3 years; $5 Single issue. **URL:** http://www.nationalfisherman.com. **Ad Rates:** BW $3,685; 4C $4,950. **Remarks:** Accepts advertising. **Circ:** Paid △**31334**, Non-paid △**4332**.

14787 ■ Ocean Navigator: The Magazine of Marine Navigation & Ocean Voyaging
Navigator Publishing L.L.C.
58 Fore St.
Portland, ME 04101
Phone: (207)772-2466
Fax: (207)772-2879
Free: 866-918-6972
Publication E-mail: oceannavigator@pcspublink.com
Magazine on Marine navigation and offshore sailing equipment and techniques. **Freq:** 7/year. **Print Method:** Offset. **Trim Size:** 8 1/4 x 10 7/8. **Cols./Page:** 3. **Col. Width:** 26 nonpareils. **Col. Depth:** 140 agate lines. **Key Personnel:** Tim Queeney, Editor; Alex Agnew, Director, Advertising, Publisher. **ISSN:** 5669--8721 (print). **Subscription Rates:** $27.95 Individuals print; $44.95 Two years print; $14.95 Individuals online; $24.95 Two years online. **URL:** http://www.oceannavigator.com. **Mailing address:** PO Box 569, Portland, ME 04112. **Remarks:** Accepts advertising. **Circ:** Paid ‡43000, Non-paid ‡2000.

14788 ■ Portland: Maine's City Magazine
Portland
165 State St.
Portland, ME 04101
Phone: (207)775-4339
Fax: (207)775-2334
Magazine distributed in northern New England and Atlantic Canada featuring lifestyles, business news, real estate updates, performing arts, reviews, and fiction. **Freq:** 10/year. **Key Personnel:** Anna Nelson; Colin Sargent, Editor; Karen Gilbert, Director, Marketing. **ISSN:** 0887--5340 (print). **Subscription Rates:** $39 Out of state online (1 year); $58 Out of state online (2 years); $68 Out of state online (3 years); $41.15 Individuals online, in-state (1 year); $61.19 Individuals online, in-state (2 years); $71.74 Individuals online, in-state (3 years). **URL:** http://www.portlandmonthly.com/. **Ad Rates:** 4C $5,254, full page; 4C $3,149, half page. **Remarks:** Accepts advertising. **Circ:** Paid ‡10000.

14789 ■ Portland Press Herald
Blethen Maine Newspapers
PO Box 1460
Portland, ME 04104
Publication E-mail: circulation@pressherald.com
General newspaper. **Freq:** Daily. **Print Method:** Letterpress. **Cols./Page:** 6. **Col. Width:** 25 nonpareils. **Col. Depth:** 301 agate lines. **Key Personnel:** Dieter Bradbury, Editor, phone: (207)791-6329; Jeannine Guttman, Editor, Vice President, phone: (207)791-6310; Bill Thompson, Editor, phone: (207)791-6202; Cliff Schechtman, Managing Editor, phone: (207)791-6693. **Subscription Rates:** $9.99 Individuals /month (Sunday home delivery and 24/7 digital); $26 Individuals /month (7 day home delivery and 24/7 digital); $22 Individuals /month (Thursday-Sunday home delivery and 24/7 digital); $9.99 Individuals /month (digital only). **URL:** http://www.pressherald.com. **Feature Editors:** Eric Blom, *Editorials*, phone: (207)791-6450. **Remarks:** Accepts advertising. **Circ:** Mon.-Sat. ★**58054**, Sun. ★**90523**, Sat. ★**62284**.

14790 ■ Professional Mariner: Journal of the Maritime Industry
Navigator Publishing L.L.C.
58 Fore St.
Portland, ME 04101
Phone: (207)772-2466
Fax: (207)772-2879
Free: 866-918-6972
Journal for the licensed professional operators of commercial marine vessels of all kinds. **Freq:** 8/year. **Print Method:** Offset. **Trim Size:** 8 x 10 7/8. **Cols./Page:** 3. **Col. Width:** 26 nonpareils. **Col. Depth:** 140 agate lines. **Key Personnel:** Kim Norton, Designer; Alex Agnew, Director, Advertising, Publisher; John Gormley, Editor; Doreen Parlin, Business Manager; Larissa Dillman, Editor. **ISSN:** 1066-2774 (print). **Subscription Rates:** $19.95 Individuals 1 year, digital; $34.95 Individuals 2 years, digital; $44.95 Individuals 3 years, digital. **URL:** http://www.professionalmariner.com. **Mailing address:** PO Box 569, Portland, ME 04112. **Ad Rates:** BW $2995; 4C $4494. **Remarks:** Accepts advertising. **Circ:** Paid ‡25,400.

14791 ■ Seafood Business: The Magazine for Seafood Buyers
Diversified Business Communications Inc.
121 Free St.
Portland, ME 04101-3919
Phone: (207)842-5500
Publisher's E-mail: webmaster@divcom.com
Seafood industry magazine. **Freq:** Monthly. **Print Method:** Web offset. **Trim Size:** 10 7/8 x 14 1/2. **Cols./Page:** 3. **Col. Width:** 27 nonpareils. **Col. Depth:** 10 inches. **Key Personnel:** Fiona Robinson, Associate Publisher, Editor; Mary Larkin, Publisher; James Wright, Associate Editor. **ISSN:** 0889--3217 (print). **URL:** http://www.seafoodbusiness.com; http://www.seafoodsource.com/component/content/article/191-seafood-business/27627-seafood-business. **Formerly:** Seafood - Capital F. **Remarks:** Accepts advertising. **Circ:** (Not Reported).

14792 ■ Smart HomeOwner
Navigator Publishing L.L.C.
58 Fore St.
Portland, ME 04101
Phone: (207)772-2466
Fax: (207)772-2879
Free: 866-918-6972
Magazine covering information on innovate products, systems and building techniques. Core topics include energy efficiency, healthy home, environment friendly products, and home automation and electronics. **Freq:** Bimonthly February, April, June, August, October, and December. **Print Method:** Offset. **Trim Size:** 8 1/8 x 10 7/8. **Cols./Page:** 2 and 3. **Col. Width:** 42 and 27 nonpareils. **Col. Depth:** 140 agate lines. **Key Personnel:** Tim Queeney, Editor, Founder, phone: (207)822-4350; Tony Napolitano, Publisher, Representative, Advertising and Sales. **ISSN:** 0272-1732 (print). **Subscription Rates:** $19.95 Individuals. **URL:** http://www.smart-homeowner.com; http://www.navigatorpublishing.com. **Mailing address:** PO Box 569, Portland, ME 04112. **Remarks:** Accepts advertising. **Circ:** (Not Reported).

14793 ■ CTN-TV
516 Congress St.
Portland, ME 04101
Phone: (207)775-2900
Format: Music of Your Life; News; Talk; Information. **Owner:** Community Television Network, 516 Congress St., Portland, ME 04101, Ph: (207)775-2900. **Operating Hours:** 12:00 p.m. - 5:00 p.m. Monday - Thursday. **ADI:** Portland-Poland Spring, ME. **URL:** http://www.ctn5.org.

14794 ■ WBLM-FM - 102.9
1 City Ctr.
Portland, ME 04101
Phone: (207)774-6364
Fax: (207)774-8707
Format: Album-Oriented Rock (AOR); Classic Rock. **Networks:** Independent. **Owner:** Citadel Broadcasting Corp., 7201 W Lake Mead Blvd., Ste. 400, Las Vegas, NV 89128-8366, Ph: (702)804-5200, Fax: (702)804-

8250. **Founded:** 1973. **Operating Hours:** Continuous; 100% local. **ADI:** Portland-Poland Spring, ME. **Wattage:** 100,000. **Ad Rates:** Noncommercial. **URL:** http://www.wblm.com.

14795 ■ WCSH-TV - 6
1 Congress Sq.
Portland, ME 04101
Phone: (207)828-6666
Free: 800-464-1213
Format: Commercial TV; Public TV. **Networks:** NBC. **Owner:** Gannett Broadcasting, 7950 Jones Branch Dr., McLean, VA 22107-0150, Ph: (703)854-6000. **Founded:** 1953. **ADI:** Portland-Poland Spring, ME. **Wattage:** 1,000,000 ERP H. **Ad Rates:** Advertising accepted; rates available upon request. Combined advertising rates available with WLBZ-TV. **URL:** http://www.wcsh6.com.

14796 ■ WCYI-FM - 93.9
One City Ctr.
Portland, ME 04101
Email: wcyy@wcyy.com
Format: Alternative/New Music/Progressive. **Owner:** Citadel Broadcasting Corp., 7201 W Lake Mead Blvd., Ste. 400, Las Vegas, NV 89128-8366, Ph: (702)804-5200, Fax: (702)804-8250. **Key Personnel:** Mike Sambrook, Gen. Mgr. **Wattage:** 27,500. **Ad Rates:** Noncommercial. **URL:** http://www.wcyy.com.

14797 ■ WCYY-FM - 94.3
1 City Ctr., 3rd Fl.
Portland, ME 04101
Phone: (207)774-6364
Fax: (207)774-8707
Format: Alternative/New Music/Progressive. **Simulcasts:** WCYI-FM. **Networks:** Independent. **Owner:** Citadel Broadcasting Corp., 7201 W Lake Mead Blvd., Ste. 400, Las Vegas, NV 89128-8366, Ph: (702)804-5200, Fax: (702)804-8250. **Founded:** 1949. **Formerly:** WKFM-FM; WXGL-FM. **Operating Hours:** Continuous; 100% local. **ADI:** Portland-Poland Spring, ME. **Key Personnel:** Mike Marcello, Contact. **Wattage:** 50,000. **Ad Rates:** Noncommercial. **URL:** http://wcyy.com.

14798 ■ WFNK-FM - 107.5
477 Congress St.
3rd Fl., Annex
Portland, ME 04101
Phone: (207)797-0780
Fax: (207)253-1929
Free: 888-863-7265
Format: Oldies. **Owner:** Nassau Broadcasting, 619 Alexander Rd., 3rd Fl., Princeton, NJ 08540. **Operating Hours:** 5 a.m. to 12 a.m. Mon.-Fri.;7 p.m. to 12 p.m. Sat.-Sun. **Key Personnel:** Patrick Collins, Contact; Tim Gatz, Contact; Stan Manning, Contact. **Ad Rates:** Advertising accepted; rates available upon request. **URL:** http://www.1075frank.com.

14799 ■ WGME-TV - 13
81 Northport Dr.
Portland, ME 04103
Phone: (207)797-1313
Fax: (207)878-3505
Format: Commercial TV. **Networks:** CBS. **Owner:** Sinclair Broadcast Group Inc., 10706 Beaver Dam Rd., Hunt Valley, MD 21030, Ph: (410)568-1500, Fax: (410)568-1533. **Founded:** 1954. **Formerly:** WGAN-TV. **Operating Hours:** Continuous; 80% network, 20% local. **ADI:** Portland-Poland Spring, ME. **Key Personnel:** Kathleen Reynolds, Gen. Sales Mgr.; Craig Clark, Dept. Mgr.; Tom Humpage, News Dir. **Ad Rates:** $20-2000 per unit. **URL:** http://www.wgme.com.

14800 ■ WHOM-FM - 94.9
One City Ctr., 3rd Fl.
Portland, ME 04101
Phone: (207)774-6364
Fax: (207)774-8707
Free: 800-228-1949
Format: Adult Contemporary. **Networks:** ABC. **Founded:** 1958. **Formerly:** WMTW-FM. **Operating Hours:** Continuous. **ADI:** Portland-Poland Spring, ME. **Wattage:** 48,000. **Ad Rates:** $48-96 per unit. **URL:** http://www.pro.whom-fm.tritonflex.com.

14801 ■ WHTP - 104.7
477 Congress St., 3rd Flr. Annex
Portland, ME 04101
Phone: (207)797-0780
Fax: (207)774-4390
Format: Classical. **Owner:** Nassau Broadcasting Partners L.P., 619 Alexander Rd., 3rd Fl., Princeton, NJ 08540-6000, Ph: (609)452-9696, Fax: (609)452-6017. **Formerly:** WBQW-FM. **Key Personnel:** Pat Collins, Gen. Mgr., pcollins@nassaubroadcasting.com; Scott Hooper, Dir. of Programs, shooper@nassaubroadcasting.com. **URL:** http://www.wbqx.nh1media.com.

14802 ■ WHXQ-FM - 106.3
477 Congress St.
3rd Fl., Annex
Portland, ME 04101
Phone: (207)797-0780
Fax: (207)797-0368
Format: Classic Rock. **Owner:** Nassau Broadcasting Partners L.P., 619 Alexander Rd., 3rd Fl., Princeton, NJ 08540-6000, Ph: (609)452-9696, Fax: (609)452-6017. **Operating Hours:** Continuous. **Key Personnel:** Patrick Collins, Gen. Mgr., pcollins@nassaubroadcasting.com; Tim Gatz, Sales Mgr., tgatz@nassaubroadcasting.com; Stan Manning, Dir. of Programs, Promotions Dir., smanning@nassaubroadcasting.com. **Ad Rates:** Advertising accepted; rates available upon request.

14803 ■ WHXR-FM - 106.3
477 Congress St.
3rd Fl., Annex
Portland, ME 04101
Phone: (207)797-0780
Fax: (207)774-4390
Format: Classic Rock. **Owner:** Nassau Broadcasting Partners L.P., 619 Alexander Rd., 3rd Fl., Princeton, NJ 08540-6000, Ph: (609)452-9696, Fax: (609)452-6017. **Operating Hours:** Continuous. **Key Personnel:** Tim Gatz, Contact, tgatz@nassaubroadcasting.com. **Ad Rates:** Advertising accepted; rates available upon request. **URL:** http://whxr.nh1media.com.

14804 ■ WJBQ-FM - 97.9
One City Ctr., 3rd Fl.
Portland, ME 04101
Phone: (207)774-6364
Format: Contemporary Hit Radio (CHR); Top 40. **Networks:** Independent. **Owner:** Citadel Broadcasting Corp., 7201 W Lake Mead Blvd., Ste. 400, Las Vegas, NV 89128-8366, Ph: (702)804-5200, Fax: (702)804-8250. **Founded:** 1974. **Operating Hours:** Continuous; 100% local. **ADI:** Portland-Poland Spring, ME. **Key Personnel:** Barbara Cole, Gen. Sales Mgr. **Local Programs:** *Jeff Parsons*; *Q Morning Show*, Monday Tuesday Wednesday Thursday Friday Saturday 5:30 a.m. - 10:00 a.m. 6:00 a.m. - 10:00 a.m. **Wattage:** 50,000. **Ad Rates:** per unit. **URL:** http://www.wjbq.com.

14805 ■ WJJB-AM - 1440
779 Warren Ave.
Portland, ME 04103
Phone: (207)773-9695
Fax: (207)761-4406
Free: 866-811-9505
Format: Sports. **Key Personnel:** Dave Schumacher, Operations Mgr., shoe@thebigjab.com; Morgan Grumbach, Gen. Sales Mgr., morgan@atlanticcoastradio.com. **Ad Rates:** Noncommercial. **URL:** http://www.thebigjab.com.

14806 ■ WJJB-FM - 96.3
779 Warren Ave.
Portland, ME 04103
Phone: (207)773-9695
Fax: (207)761-4406
Free: 866-811-9505
Format: Sports. **Owner:** Atlantic Coast Radio L.L.C., 779 Warren Ave., Portland, ME 04103, Ph: (207)773-9695, Fax: (207)761-4406. **Operating Hours:** Continuous. **Key Personnel:** Dave Shoe, Operations Mgr., shoe@thebigjab.com; Morgan Grumbach, Gen. Sales Mgr. **Ad Rates:** Advertising accepted; rates available upon request. **URL:** http://www.thebigjab.com.

14807 ■ WLAM-AM - 1470
477 Congress St., 3rd Fl., Annex
Portland, ME 04101
Phone: (207)797-0780
Fax: (207)797-0368
Format: Oldies. **Simulcasts:** WLAM-FM. **Networks:** Westwood One Radio; ABC. **Owner:** Nassau Broadcasting, 619 Alexander Rd., 3rd Fl., Princeton, NJ 08540. **Founded:** 1947. **Formerly:** WJBQ-AM; WASY-AM. **Operating Hours:** Continuous; 85% network, 15% local. **ADI:** Portland-Poland Spring, ME. **Wattage:** 10,000 Day; 1,000 Night. **Ad Rates:** Advertising accepted; rates available upon request.

14808 ■ WLOB-AM - 1310
779 Warren Ave.
Portland, ME 04103-1007
Phone: (207)773-9695
Fax: (207)761-4406
Free: 877-393-8255
Format: News; Talk. **Simulcasts:** WLOB-FM. **Networks:** USA Radio. **Owner:** Atlantic Coast Radio L.L.C., 779 Warren Ave., Portland, ME 04103, Ph: (207)773-9695, Fax: (207)761-4406. **Founded:** 1956. **Operating Hours:** Continuous. **ADI:** Portland-Poland Spring, ME. **Key Personnel:** Morgan Grumbach, Sales Mgr., morgan@atlanticcoastradio.com; J.J. Jeffrey, Contact, newstalkwlob@yahoo.com. **Wattage:** 5,000. **Ad Rates:** Noncommercial. Combined advertising rates available with WLOB-FM. **URL:** http://www.wlobradio.com.

14809 ■ WLOB-FM - 96.3
779 Warren Ave.
Portland, ME 04103
Phone: (207)773-9695
Fax: (207)761-4406
Free: 877-393-8255
Format: News; Talk. **Networks:** USA Radio. **Owner:** Atlantic Coast Radio L.L.C., 779 Warren Ave., Portland, ME 04103, Ph: (207)773-9695, Fax: (207)761-4406. **ADI:** Portland-Poland Spring, ME. **Ad Rates:** Combined advertising rates available with WLOB-AM. **URL:** http://www.wlobradio.com.

14810 ■ WMEA-FM - 90.1
323 Marginal Way
Portland, ME 04101
Fax: (207)761-0318
Free: 800-884-1717
Format: Public Radio. **Owner:** Maine Public Broadcasting Network, 1450 Lisbon St., Lewiston, ME 04240. **Founded:** Sept. 14, 2006. **Key Personnel:** Jim Dowe, CEO, President, jdowe@mpbn.net; Mark Vogelzang, CFO; Charles Beck, VP, Div. Dir. **Ad Rates:** Noncommercial. **URL:** http://www.mpbn.net.

14811 ■ WMPG-FM - 90.9
96 Falmouth St.
Portland, ME 04104-9300
Phone: (207)780-4943
Format: Alternative/New Music/Progressive; Jazz. **Simulcasts:** W281AC. **Networks:** Pacifica. **Owner:** University of Southern Maine, PO Box 9300, Portland, ME 04104, Ph: (207)780-5670, Free: 800-800-4USM. **Founded:** 1971. **Operating Hours:** Continuous; 5% network; 95% local. **Key Personnel:** Jim Rand, Station Mgr.; Dale Robin Goodman, Dir. of Dev.; David Bunker, Dir. of Programs; Ron Raymond, Music Dir. **Wattage:** 110 Horizontal; 1,000 Vertical ERP. **Ad Rates:** Noncommercial. per unit. **URL:** http://www.wmpg.org.

14812 ■ WPFO-TV - 23
233 Oxford St., Ste. 35
Portland, ME 04101
Phone: (207)797-1313
Key Personnel: Rob Barry, Gen. Sales Mgr., rob@myfoxmaine.com; Barry Dodd, Director, bdodd@myfoxmaine.com. **Ad Rates:** Advertising accepted; rates available upon request. **URL:** http://www.myfoxmaine.com.

WRED-AM - See Westbrook

14813 ■ WRED-FM - 95.9
779 Warren Ave.
Portland, ME 04103
Phone: (207)773-9695
Fax: (207)761-4406
Email: info@redhot959.com
Format: Contemporary Hit Radio (CHR); Top 40. **Networks:** Westwood One Radio. **Owner:** Atlantic Coast Radio L.L.C., 779 Warren Ave., Portland, ME 04103, Ph: (207)773-9695, Fax: (207)761-4406. **Founded:** 1982. **Formerly:** WHYR-FM. **Operating Hours:** Continuous. **Wattage:** 6,000. **Ad Rates:** Advertising accepted; rates available upon request. Combined adver-

Circulation: ★ = AAM; △ or • = BPA; ♦ = CAC; ❑ = VAC; ⊕ = PO Statement; ‡ = Publisher's Report; Boldface figures = sworn; Light figures = estimated.

tising rates available with WJAB/WCLZ-FM, WLOB-AM, WLOB-FM. **URL:** http://atlanticcoastradio.com.

14814 ■ W32CA - 32
PO Box A
Santa Ana, CA 92711
Phone: (714)832-2950
Free: 888-731-1000
Owner: Trinity Broadcasting Network Inc., PO Box A, Santa Ana, CA 92711, Ph: (714)832-2950, Free: 888-731-1000.

PRESQUE ISLE

Aroostook Co. Aroostook Co. (N). 145 m N of Bangor. University of Maine at Presque Isle. Manufactures fertilizer, starch, barrels. Spruce timber. Agriculture, especially potatoes.

14815 ■ Maine Potato News
Maine Potato Board
744 Main St., Ste. 1
Presque Isle, ME 04769
Phone: (207)769-5061
Fax: (207)764-4148
Free: 800-553-5516
Publication E-mail: mainepotatoes@mainepotatoes.com
Newspaper reporting agriculture news for the potato industry. **Freq:** Monthly. **Print Method:** Web. **Cols./Page:** 5. **Col. Width:** 11.5 picas. **Col. Depth:** 13 inches. **Subscription Rates:** Free. **URL:** http://mainepotatoes.com/page/942/home. **Remarks:** Advertising accepted; rates available upon request. **Circ:** Free ‡6250.

14816 ■ WAGM-TV - 8
12 Brewer Rd.
Presque Isle, ME 04769
Phone: (207)764-4461
Fax: (207)764-5329
Free: 800-393-9246
Format: Commercial TV. **Networks:** CBS. **Owner:** Nepsk Inc., at above address. **Founded:** 1956. **Operating Hours:** 5:25 a.m.-2 a.m. **ADI:** Presque Isle, ME. **Key Personnel:** Kelly Landeen, VP, Gen. Mgr., klandeen@wagmtv.com; Rene Cloukey, Div. Dir., rcloukey@wagmtv.com. **Ad Rates:** $90 for 30 seconds. **URL:** http://wagmtv.com/contact.

14817 ■ WBPW-FM - 96.9
551 Main St.
Presque Isle, ME 04769
Phone: (207)769-6600
Format: Country. **Networks:** Westwood One Radio. **Owner:** Citadel Broadcasting Corp., 7201 W Lake Mead Blvd., Ste. 400, Las Vegas, NV 89128-8366, Ph: (702)804-5200, Fax: (702)804-8250. **Founded:** 1973. **Operating Hours:** Continuous. **ADI:** Presque Isle, ME. **Key Personnel:** Lisa Miles, Contact, lisa.miles@citcomm.com. **Wattage:** 100,000. **Ad Rates:** Advertising accepted; rates available upon request. Combined advertising rates available with WQHR WOZ1.

14818 ■ WEGP-AM - 1390
28 Houlton Rd.
Presque Isle, ME 04769
Phone: (207)762-6700
Fax: (207)762-3319
Format: Talk; News. **Networks:** Mutual Broadcasting System. **Operating Hours:** Continuous. **Key Personnel:** Patrick Patterson, Operations Mgr.; Carla Thibodeau, Gen. Mgr. **Wattage:** 5,000. **Ad Rates:** Advertising accepted; rates available upon request. **URL:** http://www.wegp.net.

14819 ■ WMEM-FM - 106.1
63 Texas Ave.
Bangor, ME 04401
Fax: (207)942-2857
Free: 800-884-1717
Format: Public Radio. **Owner:** Maine Public Broadcasting Network, 1450 Lisbon St., Lewiston, ME 04240. **Key Personnel:** Jim Dowe, CEO, President, jdowe@mpbn.net; Charles Beck, VP, cbeck@mpbn.net. **URL:** http://www.mpbn.net.

14820 ■ WMEM-TV - 10
1450 Lisbon St.
Lewiston, ME 04240
Fax: (207)783-5193
Free: 800-884-1717
Format: Public TV. **Simulcasts:** WMEB-TV, WCBB-TV; WMED-TV. **Networks:** Public Broadcasting Service (PBS). **Owner:** Maine Public Broadcasting Network, 1450 Lisbon St., Lewiston, ME 04240. **Founded:** 1963. **Operating Hours:** 6 a.m.-3:30 a.m. **ADI:** Presque Isle, ME. **Key Personnel:** Keith Shortall, News Dir.; Jim Dowe, CEO, President, jdowe@mpbn.net; Charles Beck, VP, Div. Dir. **Ad Rates:** Noncommercial. **URL:** http://www.mpbn.net.

14821 ■ WOZI-FM - 101.9
551 Main St.
Presque Isle, ME 04769
Phone: (207)769-6600
Format: Classic Rock; Oldies. **Owner:** Citadel Broadcasting Corp., 7201 W Lake Mead Blvd., Ste. 400, Las Vegas, NV 89128-8366, Ph: (702)804-5200, Fax: (702)804-8250. **Operating Hours:** Continuous. **ADI:** Presque Isle, ME. **Wattage:** 50,000. **Ad Rates:** Advertising accepted; rates available upon request. **URL:** http://www.1019therock.com.

14822 ■ WQHR-FM - 96.1
551 Main St.
Presque Isle, ME 04769
Phone: (207)769-6600
Format: Adult Contemporary. **Networks:** ABC. **Owner:** Citadel Broadcasting Corp., 7201 W Lake Mead Blvd., Ste. 400, Las Vegas, NV 89128-8366, Ph: (702)804-5200, Fax: (702)804-8250. **Founded:** 1995. **Operating Hours:** Continuous. **ADI:** Presque Isle, ME. **Wattage:** 100,000. **Ad Rates:** Advertising accepted; rates available upon request. Combined advertising rates available with WBPW WOZ1.

14823 ■ WUPI-FM - 92.1
181 Main St.
Presque Isle, ME 04769
Phone: (207)768-9711
Email: umpiwupi92.1@gmail.com
Format: Alternative/New Music/Progressive. **Owner:** University of Maine, Orono, ME 04469, Ph: (207)581-1865, Fax: (207)581-1213, Free: 877-486-2364. **Founded:** 1973. **Operating Hours:** Continuous. **ADI:** Presque Isle, ME. **Wattage:** 017. **Ad Rates:** Noncommercial. **URL:** http://www.wp.umpi.edu.

RANGELEY

14824 ■ Orgonomic Functionalism
Wilhelm Reich Infant Trust
Dodge Pond Rd.
Rangeley, ME 04970
Phone: (207)864-3443
Fax: (207)864-5156
Publisher's E-mail: wreich@rangeley.org
Literary magazine of works by Wilhelm Reich. **Freq:** occasional. **Key Personnel:** Mary Boyd Higgins, Editor. **ISSN:** 1054-075X (print). **Subscription Rates:** $8.95 Single issue; $50 all 6 issues. **URL:** http://www.wilhelmreichtrust.org/orgonomic_functionalism.html. **Mailing address:** PO Box 687, Rangeley, ME 04970. **Remarks:** Advertising not accepted. **Circ:** (Not Reported).

ROCKLAND

Knox Co. Knox Co. (S). On Penobscot Bay, 44 m E of Augusta. U.S. Coast Guard Base. Historic area. Museums. Commercial fishing industry.

14825 ■ Maine Boats, Homes & Harbors: The Magazine of the Coast
Maine Boats, Homes, & Harbors
218 S Main St.
Rockland, ME 04841
Phone: (207)594-8622
Fax: (207)593-0026
Publication E-mail: editor@maineboats.com
Consumer magazine covering living and boating on the Coast of Maine. **Freq:** 5/year. **Print Method:** Web Offset. **Trim Size:** 8 1/8 x 10 7/8. **Key Personnel:** John K. Hanson, Jr., Publisher; Peter Spectre, Editor. **ISSN:** 0894--8887 (print). **Subscription Rates:** $24.95 U.S.; $42.95 Canada; $60.95 Other countries; $39.95 Two years; $75.95 Canada 2 years; $111.95 Other countries 2 years. **Alt. Formats:** PDF. **URL:** http://www.maineboats.com. **Formerly:** Maine Boats & Harbors. **Mailing address:** PO Box 566, Rockland, ME 04841. **Ad Rates:** BW $3,555; 4C $4,860. **Remarks:** Accepts advertising. **Circ:** Combined 20000.

14826 ■ Wild Fibers
Wild Fibers
PO Box 1752
Rockland, ME 04841
Phone: (207)594-9455
Publication E-mail: info@wildfibersmagazine.com
Magazine for fiber enthusiasts. **Key Personnel:** Linda Cortright, Editor. **Subscription Rates:** $14.95 U.S. /year. **URL:** http://www.wildfibersmagazine.com. **Remarks:** Accepts advertising. **Circ:** (Not Reported).

14827 ■ WBYA-FM - 105.5
119 Tillson Ave.
Rockland, ME 04841
Phone: (207)594-9283
Fax: (207)594-1620
Format: Oldies. **Owner:** Nassau Broadcasting Partners L.P., 619 Alexander Rd., 3rd Fl., Princeton, NJ 08540-6000, Ph: (609)452-9696, Fax: (609)452-6017. **Key Personnel:** Stan Manning, Promotions Dir., Prog. Dir., smanning@nassaubroadcasting.com; Pat Collins, Gen. Mgr., pcollins@nassaubroadcasting.com. **Ad Rates:** Advertising accepted; rates available upon request. **URL:** http://wfnk.nh1media.com.

14828 ■ WRFR-FM - 93.3
20 Gay St.
Rockland, ME 04841
Phone: (207)594-0721
Email: wrfr93.3@gmail.com
Format: Country; Information. **Owner:** Penobscot School, 28 Gay St., Rockland, ME 04841, Ph: (207)594-1084, Free: 855-344-0414. **Operating Hours:** Continuous. **Ad Rates:** Noncommercial; underwriting available. **URL:** http://www.wrfr.org.

ROCKPORT

14829 ■ Down East Magazine: Maine At Its Best
Down East Enterprise Inc.
680 Commericial St.
Rockport, ME 04856
Phone: (207)594-9544
Free: 800-766-1670
Publication E-mail: editorial@downeast.com
The Magazine of Maine. **Freq:** Monthly. **Print Method:** Offset. **Trim Size:** 8 1/8 x 10 7/8. **Cols./Page:** 3. **Col. Width:** 27 nonpareils. **Col. Depth:** 140 agate lines. **Key Personnel:** John Viehman, Publisher; Paul Doiron, Editor-in-Chief; Thomas J. Giovanniello, Jr., Associate Publisher. **ISSN:** 0012--5776 (print). **Subscription Rates:** $33 Individuals /year (print and online); $28 Individuals /year (print); $19.99 Individuals /year (online). **URL:** http://www.downeast.com. **Mailing address:** PO Box 679, Rockport, ME 04843. **Remarks:** Advertising accepted; rates available upon request. **Circ:** (Not Reported).

14830 ■ Fly Rod & Reel: The Excitement of Fly-Fishing
Down East Enterprise Inc.
680 Commericial St.
Rockport, ME 04856
Phone: (207)594-9544
Free: 800-766-1670
Publisher's E-mail: editorial@downeast.com
All aspects of fly-fishing; travel, equipment, technique. **Freq:** Bimonthly. **Print Method:** Web offset. **Trim Size:** 8 1/8 x 10 7/8. **Cols./Page:** 3. **Col. Width:** 2 1/4 inches. **Col. Depth:** 10 inches. **Key Personnel:** Joseph Healy, Associate Publisher; Greg Thomas, Editor. **ISSN:** 1045--0149 (print). **Subscription Rates:** $19.95 U.S. 4 issues; $29.95 Other countries 4 issues. **URL:** http://www.flyrodreel.com. **Formerly:** Rod & Reel. **Mailing address:** PO Box 679, Rockport, ME 04843. **Ad Rates:** BW $2,730; 4C $4,115. **Remarks:** Accepts advertising. **Circ:** Paid ⋆54229.

SALSBURY COVE

14831 ■ MDIBL Bulletin
Mount Desert Island Biological Laboratory
159 Old Bar Harbor Rd.
Salsbury Cove, ME 04672
Phone: (207)288-3605
Fax: (207)288-2130
Publisher's E-mail: mdibl_info@mdibl.org
Scientific journal covering biological research. **Founded:**

1898. **Freq:** Annual. **Key Personnel:** Michael P. McKernan, Managing Editor. **URL:** http://www.mdibl.org/bulletin.php. **Mailing address:** PO Box 35, Salsbury Cove, ME 04672. **Remarks:** Advertising not accepted. **Circ:** (Not Reported).

SANFORD

14832 ■ WCDQ-FM - 92.1
PO Box 631
Sanford, ME 04073
Phone: (207)324-7271
Fax: (207)324-2464
Email: wcdq@wcdq.com
Format: Classic Rock. **Founded:** 1985. **Formerly:** WEBI-FM. **Operating Hours:** Continuous. **Key Personnel:** Becky Brown, Gen. Mgr., Contact; Russ Dumont, Dir. of Programs; Jonathan Smith, News Dir; Becky Brown, Contact. **Wattage:** 3,000. **Ad Rates:** $22-40 per unit. Combined advertising rates available with WSME-AM.

14833 ■ WSEW-FM - 88.7
PO Box 398
New Durham, NH 03855
Phone: (603)859-9170
Fax: (603)859-8172
Free: 888-512-1846
Email: wsew@wsew.org
Format: Religious; Contemporary Christian. **Operating Hours:** Continuous. **Ad Rates:** Noncommercial; underwriting available. **URL:** http://www.wsew.org.

14834 ■ WSME-AM - 1220
PO Box 631
Sanford, ME 04073
Phone: (207)324-7271
Fax: (207)324-2464
Email: wcdq@wcdq.com
Format: News; Talk. **Operating Hours:** Continuous. **Key Personnel:** Becky Brown, Sales Mgr.; Russ Dumont, Dir. of Programs. **Wattage:** 1,000. **Ad Rates:** $12-30 per unit. Combined advertising rates available with WCDQ-FM.

SCARBOROUGH

Cumberland Co. (SE). 5 m S of Westbrook.

14835 ■ Journal of Intercultural Disciplines
National Association of African American Studies
PO Box 6670
Scarborough, ME 04070
Phone: (207)839-8004
Fax: (207)839-3776
Journal covering information on academic field of understanding the experience and behavior of populations in United States of America and other countries. **Freq:** Semiannual spring and fall. **Subscription Rates:** $18 Individuals single copy; $45 Individuals /year; $100 Institutions /year for libraries, agencies, etc. **URL:** http://www.naaas.org/publications/journal-of-intercultural-disciplines. **Mailing address:** PO Box 6670, Scarborough, ME 04070-6670. **Remarks:** Advertising not accepted. **Circ:** 1000, 500.

SEARSPORT

14836 ■ The Polar Times
American Polar Society
PO Box 300
Searsport, ME 04974
Publisher's E-mail: aps@bluestreakme.com
Key Personnel: Capt. Cliff Bekkedahl, Managing Director. **Subscription Rates:** Included in membership. **URL:** http://www.americanpolar.org/polar-compendium/polar-times. **Circ:** (Not Reported).

SKOWHEGAN

Somerset Co. (SC). 15 m NNW of Waterville. Shoes, lumber, dairy, truck farms.

14837 ■ WFMX-FM - 107.9
PO Box 159
Skowhegan, ME 04976
Phone: (207)474-5171
Format: Adult Contemporary. **Owner:** Mountain Wireless Broadcasting, Inc., at above address, Waterville, ME. **Operating Hours:** Continuous. **Wattage:** 22,000 ERP. **Ad Rates:** Advertising accepted; rates available upon request. **URL:** http://www.mixmaine.com.

14838 ■ WSKW-AM - 1160
PO Box 159
Skowhegan, ME 04976
Phone: (207)474-5171
Fax: (207)474-3299
Email: maine.radio@verizon.net
Format: Sports; Talk. **Networks:** ESPN Radio. **Owner:** Mountain Wireless Inc. **Founded:** 1956. **Formerly:** WQMR-AM. **Operating Hours:** Continuous. **ADI:** Bangor, ME. **Wattage:** 10,000. **Ad Rates:** $12 per unit.

SOUTH PORTLAND

14839 ■ WBAE-AM - 1490
420 Western Ave.
South Portland, ME 04106
Phone: (207)774-4561
Format: News; Talk. **Owner:** Saga Communications Inc., 73 Kercheval Ave., Ste. 201, Grosse Pointe Farms, MI 48236, Ph: (313)886-7070, Fax: (313)886-7150. **URL:** http://www.am1490thebay.com.

14840 ■ WCLZ-FM - 98.9
420 Western Ave.
South Portland, ME 04106
Phone: (207)871-9259
Format: Adult Album Alternative. **Owner:** Saga Communications Inc., 73 Kercheval Ave., Ste. 201, Grosse Pointe Farms, MI 48236, Ph: (313)886-7070, Fax: (313)886-7150. **Formerly:** WTPN-FM. **Key Personnel:** Ethan Minton, Mgr., ethan@989wclz.com. **Wattage:** 50,000. **Ad Rates:** Advertising accepted; rates available upon request. **URL:** http://www.989wclz.com.

14841 ■ WGAN-AM - 560
420 Western Ave.
South Portland, ME 04106
Phone: (207)774-4561
Fax: (207)774-3788
Email: wgan@560wgan.com
Format: Talk; News. **Networks:** CBS. **Owner:** Saga Communications of New England Inc., 73 Kercheval Ave., Ste. 201, Grosse Pointe Farms, MI 48236, Ph: (313)886-7070. **Founded:** 1938. **Operating Hours:** 5 a.m.-4 a.m. **ADI:** Portland-Poland Spring, ME. **Key Personnel:** Jeff Wade, News Dir., Div. Mgr., jwade@portlandradiogroup.com. **Local Programs:** *The WGAN Eyeopener*, Monday 5:00 a.m.; *WGAN Morning News*, Monday Tuesday Wednesday Thursday Friday 5:00 a.m. - 9:00 a.m.; *Inside Maine*, Saturday 10:00 a.m. - 1:00 p.m. **Wattage:** 5,000. **Ad Rates:** Advertising accepted; rates available upon request. Combined advertising rates available with WZAN-AM. **URL:** http://www.wgan.com.

14842 ■ WMGX-FM
420 West Ave.
South Portland, ME 04106
Phone: (207)774-4561
Fax: (207)774-3788
Format: Adult Contemporary. **Owner:** Saga Communications of New England Inc., 420 Western Ave., South Portland, ME 04106, Ph: (207)774-4561, Fax: (207)774-3788. **Founded:** 1977. **Wattage:** 50,000 ERP. **URL:** http://coast931.com.

14843 ■ WPOR-AM - 1490
420 Western Ave.
South Portland, ME 04106
Phone: (313)886-7070
Email: wpor@cis.compuserve.com
Format: Talk; News; Information. **Simulcasts:** WPOR-FM. **Networks:** CBS. **Owner:** Saga Communications Inc., at above address. **Founded:** 1947. **Operating Hours:** Continuous. **ADI:** Portland-Poland Spring, ME. **Key Personnel:** Robert J. Gold, Gen. Mgr.; Bonnie Grant, Dir. of Sales; Jon Shannon, Dir. of Programs; Amy Rees, Sales Mgr. **Wattage:** 1,000. **Ad Rates:** $20-105 for 30 seconds; $25-120 for 60 seconds. **URL:** http://1490wbae.com.

14844 ■ WPOR-FM - 101.9
420 W Ave.
South Portland, ME 04106
Phone: (207)774-4561
Fax: (207)774-3788
Email: wpor@wpor.com
Format: Country; Talk; Information. **Owner:** Saga Communications Inc., 73 Kercheval Ave., Ste. 201, Grosse Pointe Farms, MI 48236, Ph: (313)886-7070, Fax: (313)886-7150. **Operating Hours:** Continuous. **Key Personnel:** Matty Jeff, Dir. of Programs, matty@wpor.com. **Ad Rates:** Advertising accepted; rates available upon request. **URL:** http://www.wpor.com.

14845 ■ WYNZ-FM - 100.9
420 Western Ave.
South Portland, ME 04106
Phone: (207)774-4561
Fax: (207)774-3788
Format: Oldies. **Networks:** CBS. **Owner:** Saga Communications of New England Inc., 420 Western Ave., South Portland, ME 04106, Ph: (207)774-4561, Fax: (207)774-3788. **Founded:** 1977. **Operating Hours:** Continuous. **ADI:** Portland-Poland Spring, ME. **Key Personnel:** Matty Jeff, Div. Mgr., matty@y1009.com. **Wattage:** 25,000. **Ad Rates:** Advertising accepted; rates available upon request. **URL:** http://www.rewind1009.com.

14846 ■ WZAN-AM - 970
420 Western Ave.
South Portland, ME 04106-1704
Phone: (207)774-4561
Format: Talk. **Networks:** CBS. **Owner:** Saga Communications of New England Inc., 73 Kercheval Ave., Ste. 201, Grosse Pointe Farms, MI 48236, Ph: (313)886-7070. **Founded:** 1925. **Formerly:** WYNZ-AM; WCSH-AM. **Operating Hours:** Continuous. **ADI:** Portland-Poland Spring, ME. **Key Personnel:** Warren Maddock, Sales Mgr., wmaddock@portlandradiogroup.com. **Wattage:** 5,000. **Ad Rates:** Advertising accepted; rates available upon request. Combined advertising rates available with WGAN. **URL:** http://www.970wzan.com.

SPRINGVALE

14847 ■ MetroCast Cablevision
102 Pleasant St.
Springvale, ME 04083
Phone: (207)324-3700
Fax: (207)490-1697
Free: 800-952-1001
Email: marketing@metrocast.com
Cities Served: Sanford, Maine; 68 channels. **URL:** http://www.metrocast.com.

STEUBEN

14848 ■ The Southeastern Naturalist
Eagle Hill Institute
59 Eagle Hill Rd.
Steuben, ME 04680-0009
Phone: (207)546-2821
Fax: (207)546-3042
Publication E-mail: office@eaglehill.us
Peer-reviewed interdisciplinary scientific journal covering field ecology, biology, behavior, biogeography, taxonomy, anatomy, physiology, geology and related fields in the southeastern United States. **Freq:** Quarterly. **Key Personnel:** Glen H. Mittelhauser, Board Member; Roger D. Applegate, Board Member. **ISSN:** 1528-7092 (print). **Subscription Rates:** $50 Individuals; $40 Students; $200 Institutions. **URL:** http://www.eaglehill.us/programs/journals/sena/southeastern-naturalist.shtml. **Mailing address:** PO Box 9, Steuben, ME 04680-0009. **Circ:** (Not Reported).

STONINGTON

Hancock Co. (SE). On Penobscot Bay, 65 m S of Bangor. Commercial fishing port. Sea food cannery, shipyards.

14849 ■ Commercial Fisheries News
Compass Publications Inc.-Fisheries Div.
PO Box 37
Stonington, ME 04681
Fax: (207)348-1059
Free: 800-989-5253
Publication E-mail: comfish@fish-news.com
Magazine for commercial fishermen. **Founded:** 1973. **Freq:** Monthly. **Print Method:** Web Offset. **Cols./Page:** 4. **Col. Width:** 28 nonpareils. **Col. Depth:** 210 agate lines. **Key Personnel:** Richard W. Martin, Publisher; Janice M. Plante, Associate Editor, phone: (607)277-5355, fax: (607)277-4949; Susan Jones, Managing Edi-

Circulation: ★ = AAM; △ or • = BPA; ♦ = CAC; ❑ = VAC; ⊕ = PO Statement; ‡ = Publisher's Report; Boldface figures = sworn; Light figures = estimated.

tor; Lorelei Stevens, Editor, phone: (508)432-2602, fax: (508)432-0609. **ISSN:** 0273-6713 (print). **Subscription Rates:** $21.95 Individuals print; $45 Individuals first class, print; $51.95 Canada first class, print; $87.95 Other countries first class, print; $15.95 Individuals online only; $25.95 Individuals print and online. **URL:** http://www.fish-news.com/cfn/. **Ad Rates:** BW $1,575; 4C $1,900. **Remarks:** Accepts advertising. **Circ:** 7037.

14850 ■ Fish Farming News
Compass Publications Inc.-Fisheries Div.
PO Box 37
Stonington, ME 04681
Fax: (207)348-1059
Free: 800-989-5253
Business newspaper for North American aquaculturists. **Freq:** Bimonthly. **Print Method:** Web offset. **Trim Size:** 10 x 13 1/2. **Cols./Page:** 4. **Col. Width:** 28 nonpareils. **Col. Depth:** 210 agate lines. **Key Personnel:** Stephen Rappaport, Writer; Richard W. Martin, Publisher, Editor; Lorelei Stevens, Editor; Susan Jones, Editor. **ISSN:** 1047--2525 (print). **Subscription Rates:** $14.95 Individuals print; $11.95 Individuals online; $20.95 Individuals print and online. **URL:** http://fish-news.com/ffn. **Ad Rates:** BW $1,090; 4C $1,490. **Remarks:** Accepts advertising. **Circ:** 7553.

14851 ■ Island Ad-Vantages
Penobscot Bay Press Inc.
69 Main St.
Stonington, ME 04681
Phone: (207)367-2200
Fax: (207)367-6397
Publication E-mail: ia@penobscotbaypress.com
Community newspaper. **Freq:** Weekly (Thurs.). **Print Method:** Offset. **Trim Size:** 11 x 17. **Cols./Page:** 4. **Col. Width:** 2 1/2 inches. **Col. Depth:** 15 inches. **Key Personnel:** Nat Barrows, Editor; Faith DeAmbrose, Managing Editor; Beverley Andrews, Manager, Circulation. **USPS:** 270-440. **Subscription Rates:** $34.50 Individuals; $49.50 Individuals in Maine; $59.95 Out of state. **URL:** http://islandadvantages.com. **Mailing address:** PO Box 36, Stonington, ME 04681. **Ad Rates:** BW $480; PCI $8. **Remarks:** Accepts advertising. **Circ:** 2750.

14852 ■ The Weekly Packet
Penobscot Bay Press Inc.
69 Main St.
Stonington, ME 04681
Phone: (207)367-2200
Fax: (207)367-6397
Publisher's E-mail: info@pbp.me
Community newspaper. **Freq:** Weekly (Thurs.). **Print Method:** Offset. **Trim Size:** 11 x 17. **Cols./Page:** 4. **Col. Width:** 2 1/2 inches. **Col. Depth:** 15 inches. **Key Personnel:** Beverley Andrews, Manager, Circulation; Nat Barrows, Editor. **USPS:** 624-320. **Subscription Rates:** $34.50 Individuals in-county; $49.50 Individuals in-state; $59.95 Out of state. **URL:** http://weeklypacket.com. **Mailing address:** PO Box 36, Stonington, ME 04681. **Remarks:** Accepts advertising. **Circ:** (Not Reported).

THOMASTON

14853 ■ WWBX-FM - 97.1
184 Target Industrial Cir.
Thomaston, ME 04861
Phone: (207)947-9100
Format: Top 40. **Founded:** Sept. 08, 2006. **Key Personnel:** Anthony Turner, Contact, anthonyturner@clearchannel.com; Josh Scroggins, Station Mgr., joshscroggins@clearchannel.com; Stacey Brann, Chief Engineer, staceybrann@clearchannel.com; Anthony Turner, Contact, anthonyturner@clearchannel.com. **URL:** http://www.971thebear.com.

TOPSHAM

Sagadahoc Co. (S). 28 m NE of Portland. Residential.

14854 ■ Journal of Maine Education
Maine Association for Supervision and Curriculum Development
50 Republic Ave.
Topsham, ME 04086
Phone: (207)522-8291
Fax: (207)725-8547
Publisher's E-mail: info@maineascd.org
Freq: Annual. **Key Personnel:** Michael Beaudoin, Board Member. **URL:** http://maineascd.org/journal-of-maine-education. **Remarks:** Accepts advertising. **Circ:** 900.

14855 ■ Slovene Studies
Society for Slovene Studies
c/o Raymond Miller, President
381 Cathance Rd.
Topsham, ME 04086
Journal containing studies regarding Slovene, the association and its members. **Freq:** Semiannual. **ISSN:** 0193- 1075 (print). **Subscription Rates:** Included in membership; $20 Nonmembers. **URL:** http://www.slovenestudies.com/index.php?lan=en&pg=p0&height=900. **Remarks:** Advertising not accepted. **Circ:** 500.

14856 ■ WBCI-FM - 105.9
122 Main St.
Topsham, ME 04086
Phone: (207)725-9224
Fax: (207)725-2686
Format: Talk; Religious. **Owner:** Blount Communications Group, 8 Lawrence Rd., Derry, NH 03038, Ph: (603)437-9337, Fax: (603)434-1035. **Founded:** Feb. 18, 1991. **Formerly:** WIGY-FM; WKRH-FM. **Operating Hours:** Continuous. **Wattage:** 50,000. **Ad Rates:** Noncommercial. **URL:** http://lifechangingradio.com/wbci.

WALDOBORO

Lincoln Co. (S) 10 m SE of Jefferson. Residential. Manufactures plastics.

14857 ■ Maine Antique Digest
Maine Antique Digest
911 Main St.
Waldoboro, ME 04572
Phone: (207)832-7534
Fax: (207)832-7341
Free: 800-752-8521
Publication E-mail: mad@maineantiquedigest.com
Tabloid featuring articles on art, antiques, and Americana. **Freq:** Monthly. **Print Method:** Offset. **Cols./Page:** 5. **Col. Width:** 21 nonpareils. **Col. Depth:** 210 agate lines. **USPS:** 019-630. **Subscription Rates:** $43 Individuals /year; print; $30 Individuals /year; online; $75 Other countries /year; print; $125 Canada /year; print; first class delivery; $135 Other countries /year; print; first class delivery. **URL:** http://www.maineantiquedigest.com. **Mailing address:** PO Box 1429, Waldoboro, ME 04572. **Ad Rates:** BW $913; PCI $17. **Remarks:** Accepts advertising. **Circ:** Paid ‡33000, Non-paid ‡1500.

WATERVILLE

Kennebec Co. Kennebec Co. (SWC). On Kennebec River, 18 m N of Augusta. Colby College. Thomas College. Summer resort. Manufactures pulp, worsted cloth, paper plates, shirts, fibre, meat, foundry products, monuments. Dairy, poultry, truck farms. Potatoes, corn, beans.

14858 ■ Colby
Colby College
4000 Mayflower Hill
Waterville, ME 04901-8440
Phone: (207)859-4000
Fax: (207)859-4349
Free: 800-723-3032
Publisher's E-mail: support@colby.edu
College alumni magazine. **Freq:** Quarterly. **Print Method:** Sheetfed Offset. **Trim Size:** 8 1/2 x 11. **Cols./Page:** 3. **Col. Width:** 26 nonpareils. **Col. Depth:** 133 agate lines. **Key Personnel:** Gerard E. Boyle, Managing Editor, phone: (207)859-4354. **URL:** http://www.colby.edu/magazine. **Remarks:** Advertising not accepted. **Circ:** Non-paid ‡26000.

14859 ■ Colby Echo
Colby College
4000 Mayflower Hill
Waterville, ME 04901-8440
Phone: (207)859-4000
Fax: (207)859-4349
Free: 800-723-3032
Publisher's E-mail: support@colby.edu
Collegiate newspaper. **Freq:** Weekly (Wed.) except in January and summer. **Print Method:** Offset. **Cols./Page:** 5. **Col. Width:** 23 nonpareils. **Col. Depth:** 220 agate lines. **Key Personnel:** Julianna Haubner, Editor-in-Chief. **Subscription Rates:** $60 Individuals 1 year; $100 Individuals 2 years. **URL:** http://colbyechonews.com. **Ad Rates:** PCI $6.75. **Remarks:** Accepts advertising. **Circ:** 3700.

14860 ■ WMEW-FM - 91.3
65 Texas Ave.
Bangor, ME 04401
Fax: (207)942-2857
Free: 800-884-1717
Format: Public Radio. **Owner:** Maine Public Broadcasting Network, 1450 Lisbon St., Lewiston, ME 04240. **Key Personnel:** Jim Dowe, CEO, President, jdowe@mpbn.net; Charles Beck, VP, cbeck@mpbn.net; Keith Shortall, Dir. Pub. Aff., kshortall@mpbn.net. **Ad Rates:** Noncommercial; underwriting available. **URL:** http://www.mpbn.net.

14861 ■ WMHB-FM - 89.7
4000 Mayflower Hill
Waterville, ME 04901-8840
Phone: (207)859-5450
Email: info@wmhb.org
Format: Alternative/New Music/Progressive; News. **Networks:** Independent. **Owner:** Mayflower Hill Broadcasting Inc. **Founded:** 1958. **Operating Hours:** Continuous; 100% local. **Wattage:** 110. **Ad Rates:** Underwriting available. **URL:** http://www.colby.edu/campus_cs/clubs/wmhb.

WESTBROOK

Cumberland Co. Cumberland Co. (SW). 6 m W of Portland. Manufactures corrugated paper boxes, coated printing and specialty paper. cotton and silk thread spinning, computers, solid tires, retreaded tires, shoes, dowels, cement blocks. Dairy, truck farms.

14862 ■ America Journal
America Journal
840 Main St.
Westbrook, ME 04092
Phone: (207)854-2577
Fax: (207)854-0018
Publisher's E-mail: sales@keepmecurrent.com
Community newspaper. **Freq:** Weekly (Wed.). **Print Method:** Offset. **Cols./Page:** 5. **Col. Width:** 11.5 picas. **Col. Depth:** 15 1/4 inches. **Key Personnel:** Jane Lord, Executive Editor; Lee Hews, Publisher. **ISSN:** 0092--119X (print). **URL:** http://www.keepmecurrent.com/american_journal. **Ad Rates:** GLR $0.9; BW $420; 4C $175; PCI $12.60. **Remarks:** excluding tobacco products. **Circ:** (Not Reported).

14863 ■ Journal of Intercultural Disciplines
National Association of Hispanic and Latino Studies
850 Main St.
Westbrook, ME 04092
Phone: (207)839-8004
Fax: (207)856-2800
Publisher's E-mail: natlaffiliates@earthlink.net
Journal covering information on academic field of understanding the experience and behavior of populations in United States of America and other countries. **Subscription Rates:** $45 Individuals; $100 Libraries; $18 Single issue. **URL:** http://www.naaas.org/publications/journal-of-intercultural-disciplines/. **Mailing address:** PO Box 6670, Scarborough, ME 04070-6670. **Remarks:** Advertising not accepted. **Circ:** (Not Reported).

14864 ■ Journal of Intercultural Disciplines
International Association of Asian Studies
850 Main St.
Westbrook, ME 04092
Phone: (207)839-8004
Fax: (207)839-3776
Journal covering information on academic field of understanding the experience and behavior of populations in United States of America and other countries. **Freq:** Semiannual spring and fall. **Subscription Rates:** $18 Individuals single copy; $45 Individuals /year; $100 Institutions /year for libraries, agencies, etc. **URL:** http://www.naaas.org/publications/journal-of-intercultural-disciplines. **Mailing address:** PO Box 6670, Scarborough, ME 04070-6670. **Remarks:** Advertising not accepted. **Circ:** 1000, 500.

14865 ■ Journal of Intercultural Disciplines
National Association of Native American Studies

850 Main St.
Westbrook, ME 04092
Phone: (207)839-8004
Fax: (207)839-3776
Journal covering information on academic field of understanding the experience and behavior of populations in United States of America and other countries. **Freq:** Semiannual spring and fall. **Subscription Rates:** $18 Individuals single copy; $45 Individuals /year; $100 Institutions /year for libraries, agencies, etc. **URL:** http://www.naaas.org/publications/journal-of-intercultural-disciplines. **Mailing address:** PO Box 6670, Scarborough, ME 04070-6670. **Remarks:** Advertising not accepted. **Circ:** 1000, 500.

14866 ■ Lakes Region Suburban Weekly
Lakes Region Suburban Weekly
840 Main St.
Westbrook, ME 04092
Phone: (207)854-2577
Fax: (207)854-0018
Community newspaper. **Freq:** Weekly. **Subscription Rates:** $35 Individuals in state; $35 Individuals snow bird; $50 Out of state; $65 Two years in-state; $65 Two years out-of-state. **URL:** http://www.keepmecurrent.com/. **Formerly**: Suburban News. **Mailing address:** PO Box 840, Westbrook, ME 04092. **Ad Rates:** BW $525; 4C $750. **Remarks:** Accepts advertising. **Circ:** Combined 8000.

14867 ■ WPME-TV - 35
4 Ledgeview Dr.
Westbrook, ME 04092
Phone: (207)774-0051
Fax: (207)774-6849
URL: http://www.ourmaine.com.

14868 ■ WPXT-TV - 51
Four Ledgeview Dr.
Westbrook, ME 04092
Phone: (207)774-0051
Fax: (207)774-6849
Free: 877-353-7634
Email: wpxt@ourmaine.com
Format: Commercial TV. **Founded:** 1986. **Formerly**: FOX 51. **Operating Hours**: Continuous. **ADI**: Portland-Poland Spring, ME. **Key Personnel:** Doug Finck, Gen. Mgr. **Wattage**: 3,020,000. **Ad Rates:** Noncommercial. Combined advertising rates available with UPN 35 WPME-TV. **URL:** http://ourmaine.com.

14869 ■ WRED-AM - 1440
779 Warren Ave.
Portland, ME 04103
Phone: (207)773-9695
Fax: (207)761-4406
Free: 866-811-9505
Format: Sports. **Owner:** Atlantic Coast Radio L.L.C., 779 Warren Ave., Portland, ME 04103, Ph: (207)773-9695, Fax: (207)761-4406. **Operating Hours:** Continuous. **Key Personnel:** Dave Schumacher, Operations Mgr.; Morgan Grumbach, Sales Mgr., morgan@atlanticcoastradio.com. **Ad Rates:** Advertising accepted; rates available upon request. **URL:** http://www.thebigjab.com.

WINDHAM

14870 ■ John Reich Journal
John Reich Collectors Society
c/o Stephen A. Crain, Secretary
PO Box 1680
Windham, ME 04062
Journal containing articles encouraging the study of numismatics and/or relating to early United States silver coins and also featuring new information about die varieties, die states of published die varieties, attribution methods, collections, collectors and many more. **Freq:** 3/year. **Subscription Rates:** Included in membership. **URL:** http://www.jrcs.org/jrcsjournals.html. **Remarks:** Advertising not accepted. **Circ:** (Not Reported).

YARMOUTH

Cumberland Co. (E). On Caseo Bay. 10 m N of Portland. Commercial fisheries.

14871 ■ Gourmet News
HME News
PO Box 998
Yarmouth, ME 04096
Phone: (207)846-0600
Fax: (207)846-0657
Business newspaper for the specialty food industry. **Freq:** Monthly. **Key Personnel:** Kate Seymour, Associate Publisher; Rocelle Aragon, Editor. **Subscription Rates:** Free to qualified subscribers. **Alt. Formats:** PDF. **URL:** http://www.gourmetnews.com. **Ad Rates:** BW $7930. **Remarks:** Accepts advertising. **Circ:** (Not Reported).

14872 ■ HME News: The Business Newspaper for Home Medical Equipment Providers
HME News
PO Box 998
Yarmouth, ME 04096
Phone: (207)846-0600
Fax: (207)846-0657
Business newspaper for home medical equipment providers. Editorial coverage focuses on industry news, mergers and acquisitions, governmental and regulatory impact on the HME industry, as well as product reviews and industry trend coverage. **Freq:** Monthly. **Key Personnel:** Elizabeth Beaulieu, Editor; Rick Rector, Publisher; Theresa Flaherty, Managing Editor. **Subscription Rates:** Free. **URL:** http://www.hmenews.com/#. **Remarks:** Accepts advertising. **Circ:** △**17,100**.

14873 ■ WYAR-FM - 88.3
PO Box 414
Yarmouth, ME 04096
Phone: (207)847-3169
Email: wyar@maine.rr.com
Format: Educational; Jazz; Oldies; Big Band/Nostalgia. **Owner:** Heritage Radio Society, Inc., at above address, Yarmouth, ME 04096. **Founded:** 1995. **Key Personnel:** Gary King, Founder; Wayne Newland, Producer. **Wattage**: 1,000. **Ad Rates:** Noncommercial. **URL:** http://www.wyar.org.

YORK

14874 ■ The York Weekly
James Carter Publications Inc.
15A Woodbridge Rd.
York, ME 03909
Phone: (207)363-4343
Fax: (207)351-2849
Publication E-mail: yorkweekly@seacoastonline.com
Community newspaper. **Freq:** Weekly (Wed.). **Print Method:** Offset. **Trim Size:** 11 1/2 x 15 1/2. **Cols./Page:** 6. **Col. Width:** 9 1/2 agate lines. **Col. Depth:** 14 1/2 inches. **Key Personnel:** Linda Holway, Director, Advertising; John Tabor, Publisher. **USPS:** 696-220. **Subscription Rates:** $69 Individuals 52 weeks; $39 Individuals 26 weeks; $29 Individuals 13 weeks. **URL:** http://www.seacoastonline.com/YorkWeekly. **Mailing address:** 15A Woodbridge Rd, York, ME 03909. **Ad Rates:** PCI $8.50. **Remarks:** Accepts advertising. **Circ:** ‡4315.

YORK CENTER

14875 ■ WXHT-FM - 95.3
PO Box 150
Portsmouth, NH 03802-0150
Phone: (603)430-9500
Fax: (603)430-9501
Networks: Independent. **Owner:** Atlantic Star Communications, at above address 7th Fl., Ste. 2. **Founded:** 1987. **Formerly**: WQMI-FM; WCQL-FM. **Operating Hours**: Continuous; 100% local. **ADI**: Boston-Worcester,MA-Derry-Manchester,NH. **Key Personnel:** Kim D. Jones, Gen. Mgr.; Glenn Stewart, Dir. of Programs; Charles Triest, Sales Mgr.; Kelly Brown, News Dir. **Wattage**: 6,000. **Ad Rates:** Advertising accepted; rates available upon request.

Circulation: ★ = AAM; △ or • = BPA; ♦ = CAC; ❑ = VAC; ⊕ = PO Statement; ‡ = Publisher's Report; Boldface figures = sworn; Light figures = estimated.

ABERDEEN

Harford Co. Harford Co. (NE). 2 m S of Havre de Grace.

14876 ■ The Bargaineer
Chesapeake Publishing Corp.
214 Belair Ave.
Aberdeen, MD 21001
Phone: (410)272-3131
Shopping guide. **Freq:** Weekly (Mon.). **Key Personnel:** Claudia Nimmo, General Manager. **Subscription Rates:** Free. **URL:** http://www.chespub.com/newsprs/bargaine.htm. **Mailing address:** PO Box 190, Aberdeen, MD 21001. **Circ:** Mon. ‡45000.

14877 ■ WAMD-AM
13321 New Hampshire Ave.
Silver Spring, MD 20904
Phone: (805)987-0400
Format: Oldies. **Networks:** ABC. **Owner:** Salem Media of New York LLC, at above address. **Founded:** 1957. **Key Personnel:** James V. McMahan, Contact. **Wattage:** 300 Day; 500 Night. **Ad Rates:** $20 for 30 seconds; $30 for 60 seconds.

ABINGDON

14878 ■ Journal of the AHVMA
American Holistic Veterinary Medical Association
33 Kensington Pky.
Abingdon, MD 21009
Phone: (410)569-0795
Fax: (410)569-2346
Publisher's E-mail: office@ahvma.org
Professional journal covering holistic veterinary medicine. **Freq:** 3/year. **Key Personnel:** Richard Palmquist, President. **Subscription Rates:** Included in membership. **URL:** http://www.ahvma.org. **Mailing address:** PO Box 630, Abingdon, MD 21009-0630. **Ad Rates:** BW $655; 4C $1,255. **Remarks:** Advertising accepted; rates available upon request. **Circ:** 1200.

ANNAPOLIS

Anne Arundel Co. Anne Arundel Co. (C). The State Capital. On Severn River, 2 m from Chesapeake Bay, 27 m SE of Baltimore. United States Naval Academy; St. John's College. Boat connections. Fish, crab and oyster industries. Boat yards; beverages, controls, concrete products manufactured. Trading center for residents of surrounding summer resorts.

14879 ■ The Capital
The Capital-Gazette Newspapers
888 Bestgate Rd., Ste 104
Annapolis, MD 21401
Phone: (410)268-5000
Fax: (410)268-4643
Publisher's E-mail: wcraft@capitalgazette.com
General newspaper. **Founded:** 1884. **Freq:** Daily and Sun. (eve.). **Print Method:** Offset. **Trim Size:** 13 5/8 x 22. **Cols./Page:** 6. **Col. Width:** 2 1/16 inches. **Col. Depth:** 21 inches. **Key Personnel:** Pat Richardson, Publisher. **Subscription Rates:** $212.23 Individuals 52 weeks; $107.32 Individuals 26 weeks; $54.99 Individuals 13 weeks. **URL:** http://www.capitalgazette.com/. **Remarks:** Accepts classified advertising. **Circ:** Mon.-Fri. ★**42825**, Sun. ★**44776**, Sat. ★**43320**.

14880 ■ Chesapeake Family
Jefferson Communications
929 W St., Ste. 210
Annapolis, MD 21401
Phone: (410)263-1641
Fax: (410)280-0255
Publisher's E-mail: editor@chesapeakefamily.com
Consumer parenting magazine. **Freq:** Monthly Latest Edition: August, 2016. **Print Method:** Web. **Trim Size:** 8 1/8 x 10 3/4. **Cols./Page:** 3. **Col. Width:** 2.25 inches. **Col. Depth:** 9 3/4 inches. **Key Personnel:** Donna Jefferson, Publisher; Mary McCarthy, Editor; Heather Grant, Art Director. **URL:** http://www.chesapeakefamily.com. **Formerly:** Chesapeake Children. **Ad Rates:** BW $2,600; 4C $2,650. **Remarks:** Accepts advertising. **Circ:** Controlled 40000.

14881 ■ Journal of Transportation Law, Logistics and Policy
Association of Transportation Law Professionals
c/o Lauren Michalski, Executive Director
PO Box 5407
Annapolis, MD 21403
Phone: (410)268-1311
Fax: (410)268-1322
Publisher's E-mail: info@atlp.org
Journal publishing articles dealing with transportation public policy, law and opinion. **Freq:** Quarterly. **Subscription Rates:** $100 U.S.; $105 Canada; $110 Other countries. **URL:** http://www.atlp.org/index.php?option=com_content&view=article&id=8:join-atlp&catid=9:membership&Itemid=137. **Remarks:** Accepts advertising. **Circ:** (Not Reported).

14882 ■ The Maryland Gazette
Capital Gazette Communications
888 Bestgate Rd., Ste. 104
Annapolis, MD 21401
Phone: (410)268-5000
Fax: (410)268-4643
Community newspaper. **Freq:** Semiweekly (Wed. and Sat.). **Print Method:** Offset. **Cols./Page:** 6. **Col. Width:** 26 nonpareils. **Col. Depth:** 301 agate lines. **Key Personnel:** Rick Hutzell, Editor, phone: (410)280-5938; Marty Padden, Manager, Advertising. **Subscription Rates:** $2.99 Individuals /week. **URL:** http://www.capitalgazette.com/maryland_gazette. **Ad Rates:** SAU $24.50. **Remarks:** Accepts advertising. **Circ:** (Not Reported).

14883 ■ Municipal Maryland
Maryland Municipal League
1212 West St.
Annapolis, MD 21401
Phone: (410)268-5514
Free: 800-492-7121
Publisher's E-mail: mml@mdmunicipal.org
Freq: 9/year latest issue: May/June 2015. **Print Method:** Offset. **Trim Size:** 8 1/2 x 11. **Cols./Page:** 2 and 3. **Col. Width:** 3.5 and 2 inches. **Col. Depth:** 9 3/8 inches. **Key Personnel:** Karen Bohlen, Editor. **Subscription Rates:** $40 Individuals; Included in membership. **Alt. Formats:** PDF. **URL:** http://www.mdmunicipal.org/index.aspx?NID=421. **Ad Rates:** BW $370; 4C $460. **Remarks:** Advertising accepted; rates available upon request. **Circ:** Paid ‡1750, Non-paid ‡190.

14884 ■ PassageMaker: The Trawler & Ocean Motorboat Magazine
Passage Maker Magazine
105 E Ave., Ste. 203
Annapolis, MD 21403
Phone: (410)990-9086
Fax: (410)990-9095
Magazine focusing on the practical and technical aspects of cruising. **Freq:** 8/year. **Key Personnel:** Peter Swanson, Editor-in-Chief; John Wooldridge, Board Member. **Subscription Rates:** $15.95 Individuals online; $29.95 Two years online; $43.95 Individuals print and online; $82.95 Two years print and online. **URL:** http://www.passagemaker.com. **Remarks:** Accepts advertising. **Circ:** 32,000.

14885 ■ Proceedings
United States Naval Institute
291 Wood Rd.
Annapolis, MD 21402
Phone: (410)268-6110
Fax: (410)571-1703
Free: 800-223-8764
Publisher's E-mail: customer@usni.org
Magazine on naval and maritime news. **Freq:** Monthly. **Print Method:** Offset. **Trim Size:** 7-7/8 x 10- 3/4. **Cols./Page:** 3. **Col. Width:** 12.5 picas. **Col. Depth:** 54 picas. **Key Personnel:** James M. Caiella, Associate Editor; Liese C. Doherty, Assistant Editor; Amy Voight, Editor; William Miller, Publisher; Kelly Erlinger, Creative Director, Manager, Production; Dave Sheehan, Manager, Advertising, phone: (410)295-1041, fax: (410)295-1049; Paul M. Merzlak, Editor-in-Chief. **ISSN:** 0041-798X (print). **URL:** http://www.usni.org/magazines/proceedings. **Ad Rates:** 4C $7,778. **Remarks:** Accepts advertising. **Circ:** Combined ‡61446.

14886 ■ Shipmate
United States Naval Academy Alumni Association
247 King George St.
Annapolis, MD 21402-1306
Phone: (410)295-4000
Publisher's E-mail: alumni@usna.com
Alumni magazine of the United States Naval Academy. **Freq:** 8/year. **Print Method:** Web press. **Trim Size:** 8 1/4 x 10 7/8. **Cols./Page:** 3 and 2. **Col. Width:** 27 and 42 nonpareils. **Col. Depth:** 136 agate lines. **ISSN:** 0488--6720 (print). **Subscription Rates:** Included in membership. **URL:** http://www.usna.com/Shipmate. **Ad Rates:** 4C $3995. **Remarks:** Accepts advertising. **Circ:** ‡42500.

14887 ■ Sierra Magazine: Explore, Enjoy and Protect the Planet
Sierra Club-California-Nevada-Hawaii Regional Field Office
c/o Joy Oakes, Staff Director
69 Franklin St.
Annapolis, MD 21401-2727
Phone: (410)268-7411

Circulation: ★ = AAM; △ or • = BPA; ♦ = CAC; ❑ = VAC; ⊕ = PO Statement; ‡ = Publisher's Report; Boldface figures = sworn; Light figures = estimated.

Fax: (410)268-1114
Publication E-mail: sierra.letters@sierraclub.org
Magazine featuring information about the Sierra Club and other environmental topics. **Freq:** Bimonthly. **Trim Size:** 8 x 10.5. **Key Personnel:** Bob Sipchen, Editor-in-Chief; Kristi Rummel, Director, Advertising. **URL:** http://www.sierraclub.org/sierra. **Remarks:** Accepts advertising. **Circ:** (Not Reported).

14888 ■ Starlights
International Star Class Yacht Racing Association
914 Bay Ridge Rd., Ste. 220
Annapolis, MD 21403
Phone: (443)458-5733
Fax: (443)458-5735
Publisher's E-mail: office@starclass.org
Journal containing organizational seminars, news, programs, Star Class racing yachts and sailboats. **Freq:** Quarterly. **Subscription Rates:** Included in membership. **Remarks:** Accepts advertising. **Circ:** 3800.

14889 ■ WBIS-AM - 1190
1610 West St., Ste. 209
Annapolis, MD 21401
Phone: (410)269-0700
Format: News; Talk. **Networks:** Business Radio. **Founded:** 1998. **Operating Hours:** Sunrise-sunset. **ADI:** Baltimore, MD. **Key Personnel:** Alan Pendleton, Gen. Mgr., alan@wbis1190.com. **Wattage:** 10,000. **Ad Rates:** Noncommercial.

14890 ■ WFSI-FM - 107.9
290 Hegenberger Rd.
Oakland, CA 94621
Free: 800-543-1495
Format: Religious. **Networks:** Family Stations Radio. **Owner:** Family Stations Inc., 290 Hegenberger Rd., Oakland, CA 94621, Free: 800-543-1495. **Founded:** 1959. **Operating Hours:** Continuous. **Wattage:** 50,000. **Ad Rates:** Noncommercial. **URL:** http://www.familyradio.org.

14891 ■ WHFS-FM - 105.7
1423 Clarkview Dr., Ste. 100
Baltimore, MD 21209
Phone: (410)825-1000
Format: Classic Rock; News; Sports; Information. **Owner:** CBS Radio Inc., at above address. **Key Personnel:** Mark Turley, Gen. Sales Mgr., mark.turley@cbsradio.com; Dave Labrozzi, Dir. of Programs, dave.labrozzi@cbsradio.com. **URL:** http://baltimore.cbslocal.com/station/1057-the-fan.

14892 ■ WMPT-TV - 22
11767 Owings Mills Blvd.
Owings Mills, MD 21117
Phone: (410)581-4097
Free: 800-627-6788
Email: comments@mpt.org
Format: Public TV. **Simulcasts:** WMPB, WCPB, WWPB, WGPT, WFPT. **Networks:** Public Broadcasting Service (PBS); Eastern Educational Television. **Owner:** Maryland Public Television, 11767 Owings Mills Blvd., Owings Mills, MD 21117, Ph: (410)356-5600, Fax: (410)581-6579, Free: 800-223-3678. **Founded:** 1969. **Operating Hours:** Continuous. **Key Personnel:** Tom Williams, Managing Dir.; Martin G. Jacobs, VP, CFO; Larry D. Unger, CEO, President; George R. Beneman, II, VP of Technology Dev. **Local Programs:** *MotorWeek*, Saturday Sunday Wednesday 5:00 p.m. 12:00 p.m. 7:30 p.m.; *Nova scienceNOW*, Wednesday 9:00 p.m.; *Antiques Roadshow*, Monday Tuesday Sunday Saturday 8:00 p.m. 12:00 a.m.; 3:00 a.m.; 5:00 p.m. 6:00 p.m.; *Artworks*, Thursday Sunday 8:30 p.m. 12:30 p.m. **Wattage:** 5,000,000. **Ad Rates:** Underwriting available. **URL:** http://www.mpt.org/home.

14893 ■ WNAV-AM - 1430
PO Box 6726
Annapolis, MD 21401
Phone: (410)263-1430
Fax: (410)268-5360
Email: news@wnav.com
Format: Adult Contemporary. **Networks:** CBS. **Owner:** Sajak Broadcasting Corp., 236 Admiral Dr., Annapolis, MD 21401, Ph: (410)263-1902, Fax: (410)268-5360, Free: 888-345 9628. **Founded:** 1949. **Operating Hours:** 5 a.m.-midnight. **Key Personnel:** Bill Lusby, Contact, billusby@wnav.com; Steve Hopp, Gen. Mgr., stevehopp@wnav.com. **Local Programs:** *Arts, Entertainment & More*, Friday 6:00 p.m. - 7:00 p.m.; *Weekend Morning*, Saturday 6:00 a.m. - 8:00 a.m.; *Morning Show*, Monday Tuesday Wednesday Thursday Friday 6:00 a.m. - 10:00 a.m.; *1430 Connection*, Friday Sunday 2:00 p.m. - 3:00 p.m. 7:00 a.m. - 7:30 a.m.; *In the Garden*, Saturday 8:00 a.m. - 10:00 a.m.; *Wonderful Words of Life*, Sunday 6:30 a.m. - 6:45 a.m.; *Crime Line*, Sunday 6:45 a.m. - 7:00 a.m.; *Family Chat Time*, Sunday 8:00 a.m. - 8:30 a.m.; *The Time Machine*, Saturday 3:00 p.m. - 7:00 p.m.; *Saturday Evening*, Saturday 7:00 p.m. - 12:00 a.m.; *Week in Review Weekend Headliner*, Saturday 5:00 a.m. - 6:00 a.m.; *Jewish Music, News and Views*, Sunday 9:00 a.m. - 9:30 a.m. **Wattage:** 5,000 Day; 1,000 Night. **Ad Rates:** Noncommercial. **URL:** http://www.1430wnav.com.

14894 ■ WRNR-FM - 103.1
112 Main St., 3rd Fl.
Annapolis, MD 21401
Phone: (410)626-0103
Fax: (410)267-7634
Free: 877-762-1031
Email: marketing@wrnr.com
Format: Adult Album Alternative. **Owner:** Empire Broadcasting Corp., 100 Saratoga Village Blvd., Ste. 21, Ballston Spa, NY 12020, Fax: (518)899-3057. **Founded:** 1976. **Operating Hours:** Continuous. **Key Personnel:** Steve Kingston, President, steve.kingston@wrnr.com; Bob Waugh, Prog. Dir., bobw@wrnr.com; Michael Hughes, VP. **Wattage:** 6,000. **Ad Rates:** Advertising accepted; rates available upon request. **URL:** http://www.wrnr.com.

ARNOLD

Anne Arundel Co. (C). 5 m N of Annapolis. Residential.

14895 ■ Campus Crier
Anne Arundel Community College
101 College Pky.
Arnold, MD 21012-1895
Phone: (410)777-2222
Fax: (410)777-7054
Publication E-mail: crier@mail.aacc.cc.md.us
Collegiate newspaper. **Freq:** Bimonthly. **Print Method:** Offset. **Cols./Page:** 4. **Col. Width:** 30 nonpareils. **Col. Depth:** 182 agate lines. **Key Personnel:** Derek Roper, Assistant Editor; Kimberly Stith, Editor. **Alt. Formats:** PDF. **URL:** http://www.aacc.edu. **Ad Rates:** BW $165; 4C $370; CNU $280. **Remarks:** Accepts advertising. **Circ:** ‡3000.

BALTIMORE

Baltimore city. An independent city not located in a county. On Patapsco River, 12 m from Chesapeake Bay. Important port connection with the sea through Chesapeake Bay and Chesapeake and Delaware Canal. Medical and cultural center, also trading, financial and manufacturing city. Johns Hopkins University and other universities and colleges; many private schools. Manufactures iron, steel, copper products, instruments, fertilizer, chemicals, tin ware, men's clothing, aircraft and parts, spices and flavoring extracts, malt and distilled beverages, soap and soap products, bakery products, electrical and electronic equipment and appliances, wire and cable. Boat and shipyards; dry docks; meat packing; printing and publishing; motor-vehicle assembling; sugar refining; vegetable canning; petroleum refining.

14896 ■ AACN Advanced Critical Care
Lippincott Williams & Wilkins
351 W Camden St.
Baltimore, MD 21201
Phone: (410)528-4000
Publisher's E-mail: info@aacn.org
Peer-reviewed journal for advanced practice critical care nurses. **Freq:** Quarterly. **Key Personnel:** Mary Fran Tracy, PhD, Editor-in-Chief. **ISSN:** 1559--7768 (print); **EISSN:** 1559--7776 (electronic). **Subscription Rates:** $130 U.S.; $139 Canada and Mexico; $263 Other countries; $533 Institutions; $541 Institutions, Canada and Mexico; $713 Institutions, other countries. **URL:** http://journals.lww.com/aacnadvancedcriticalcare/pages/default.aspx. **Formerly:** AACN Clinical Issues. **Remarks:** Advertising not accepted. **Circ:** 4000.

14897 ■ Accountability in Research
Taylor & Francis Group Journals
Dept. of Biochemistry & Molecular Biology
University of Maryland School of Medicine
108 N Greene St.
Baltimore, MD 21201-1503
Phone: (410)706-3327
Fax: (410)706-3189
Publisher's E-mail: customerservice@taylorandfrancis.com
Journal focusing on the examination and critical analysis of systems for maximizing integrity in the conduct of research. **Freq:** Bimonthly latest: Volume 23, 2016. **Key Personnel:** Adil E. Shamoo, PhD, Editor-in-Chief; Michael Davis, Board Member; Ruth H. Chadwick, Board Member. **ISSN:** 0898--9621 (print); **EISSN:** 1545--5815 (electronic). **Subscription Rates:** $434 Individuals print only; $1387 Institutions online only; $1585 Institutions print & online. **URL:** http://www.tandfonline.com/toc/gacr20/current. **Circ:** (Not Reported).

14898 ■ Addictive Disorders & Their Treatment
Lippincott Williams & Wilkins
351 W Camden St.
Baltimore, MD 21201
Phone: (410)528-4000
Peer-reviewed journal covering drug and alcohol addiction and developments in their treatment. **Freq:** Quarterly. **Key Personnel:** Pedro Ruiz, MD, Editor-in-Chief, phone: (713)500-2799, fax: (713)500-2757; Natalie McGroarty, Publisher. **ISSN:** 1531-5754 (print); **EISSN:** 1535-1122 (electronic). **Subscription Rates:** $185 Individuals; $194 Canada and Mexico; $207 Other countries; $541 Institutions; $549 Institutions, Canada and Mexico; $561 Institutions, other countries. **URL:** http://journals.lww.com/addictiondisorders/pages/default.aspx. **Remarks:** Accepts classified advertising. **Circ:** ‡156.

14899 ■ Advances in Neonatal Care
Lippincott Williams & Wilkins
351 W Camden St.
Baltimore, MD 21201
Phone: (410)528-4000
Peer-reviewed journal reporting on improvements in the care of infants and their families. **Freq:** Bimonthly. **Key Personnel:** Debra Brandon, PhD, Editor-in-Chief; Jacqueline M. McGrath, Editor-in-Chief. **ISSN:** 1536--0903 (print). **Subscription Rates:** $131 Individuals print; $367 Institutions; $150 Individuals Canada/Mexico; $381 Institutions Canada/Mexico; $223 Individuals UK/Australia; $475 Institutions UK/Australia. **URL:** http://journals.lww.com/advancesinneonatalcare/pages/default.aspx; http://www.lww.com/product/?1536-0903. **Ad Rates:** BW $2,355; 4C $1,700. **Remarks:** Advertising not accepted. **Circ:** ‡8497.

14900 ■ African American Review
John Hopkins University Press
2715 N Charles St.
Baltimore, MD 21218-4363
Phone: (410)516-6900
Fax: (410)516-6968
Publisher's E-mail: webmaster@jhupress.jhu.edu
Journal presenting essays on African American literature and culture. Contains interviews, poems, fiction, and book reviews. **Freq:** Quarterly. **Trim Size:** 7 x 10. **Key Personnel:** Aileen M. Keenan, Managing Editor; Nathan Grant, Editor. **ISSN:** 1062--4783 (print); **EISSN:** 1945--6182 (electronic). **Subscription Rates:** $40 Individuals; $105 Institutions; $72 Individuals 2 years; $210 Institutions 2 years; $45 Individuals online only; $81 Individuals 2 years online only. **URL:** http://www.press.jhu.edu/journals/african_american_review. **Formerly:** Negro American Literature Forum; Black American Literature Forum. **Ad Rates:** BW $400. **Remarks:** Advertising accepted; rates available upon request. **Circ:** Paid 2000.

14901 ■ Afro-American
Afro-American
2519 N Charles St.
Baltimore, MD 21218
Phone: (410)554-8200
Publisher's E-mail: editor@afro.com
Black community newspaper. **Key Personnel:** Dorothy Boulware, Editor; Kristin Gray, Managing Editor; John J. Oliver, Jr., Chairman of the Board, Publisher; Talibah Chikwendu, Executive Editor, phone: (410)554-8251. **Subscription Rates:** $12 Individuals. **URL:** http://www.afro.com. **Remarks:** Accepts advertising. **Circ:** (Not Reported).

14902 ■ Alternative Press Index
Alternative Press Center
PO Box 13127
Baltimore, MD 21203-3127
Phone: (312)451-8133
Publisher's E-mail: altpress@altpress.org
Index to alternative (progressive) periodicals in humanities, journalism, and social sciences. **Freq:** Semiannual April and October. **Print Method:** Offset. **Trim Size:** 8 1/2 x 11. **Cols./Page:** 3. **Col. Width:** 27 nonpareils. **Col. Depth:** 130 agate lines. **Key Personnel:** Charles D'Adamo, Senior Editor. **ISSN:** 0002--662X (print). **Subscription Rates:** $425 Institutions /year; $75 Individuals /year. **URL:** http://www.altpress.org/mod/pages/display/8/index.php?menu=pubs. **Remarks:** Advertising not accepted. **Circ:** Paid ‡550, Controlled ‡200, 650.

14903 ■ American Imago
Johns Hopkins University Press
2715 N Charles St.
Baltimore, MD 21218-4319
Phone: (410)516-6900
Fax: (410)516-6968
Free: 800-537-5487
Publisher's E-mail: webmaster@jhupress.jhu.edu
Scholarly journal covering aspects of psychology related to psychoanalysis, anthropology, philosophy, politics, art history, musicology, literary theory, and education. **Freq:** Quarterly. **Key Personnel:** Vera Camden, Editor; Paul Eisenstein, Editor; Louis Rose, Editor. **ISSN:** 0065--860X (print); **EISSN:** 1085--7931 (electronic). **Subscription Rates:** $180 Institutions /year (print); $45 Individuals /year (print); $360 Institutions two years (print); $81 Individuals two years (print); $55 Individuals /year (online); $99 Individuals two years (online). **URL:** http://www.press.jhu.edu/journals/american_imago. **Ad Rates:** BW $325. **Remarks:** Accepts advertising. **Circ:** 327.

14904 ■ American Journal of Mathematics
Johns Hopkins University Press
c/o Christopher Sogge, Ed.-in-Ch.
Dept. of Mathematics
Johns Hopkins University
3400 N Charles St.
Baltimore, MD 21218-2680
Publication E-mail: ajm@math.jhu.edu
Journal covering applied and pure mathematics. **Freq:** Bimonthly. **Print Method:** Offset. **Trim Size:** 6 x 9. **Cols./Page:** 1. **Col. Width:** 52 nonpareils. **Col. Depth:** 98 agate lines. **Key Personnel:** Freydoon Shahidi, Editor; Christopher Sogge, Editor-in-Chief. **ISSN:** 0002--9327 (print); **EISSN:** 1080--6377 (electronic). **Subscription Rates:** $110 Individuals print; $425 Institutions print; $850 Institutions print, 2 years; $198 Two years individual; $120 Individuals online. **URL:** http://www.press.jhu.edu/journals/american_journal_of_mathematics. **Ad Rates:** BW $275. **Remarks:** Accepts advertising. **Circ:** 699.

14905 ■ American Quarterly
Johns Hopkins University Press
2715 N Charles St.
Baltimore, MD 21218-4319
Phone: (410)516-6900
Fax: (410)516-6968
Free: 800-537-5487
Publication E-mail: american.quarterly@usc.edu
Journal on American culture. **Freq:** Quarterly. **Print Method:** Offset. **Trim Size:** 6 x 9. **Cols./Page:** 1. **Col. Width:** 26 picas. **Col. Depth:** 7 inches. **Key Personnel:** Cotten Seiler, Editor; Sarah Banet-Weiser, Editor; Jih-Fei Cheng, Managing Editor. **ISSN:** 0003--0678 (print); **EISSN:** 1080--6490 (electronic). **Subscription Rates:** $185 Institutions print; $370 Institutions print, 2 years; Included in membership; $38 Individuals. **URL:** http://www.press.jhu.edu/journals/american_quarterly/index.html; http://www.theasa.net/publications/page/american_quarterly; http://www.americanquarterly.org; http://muse.jhu.edu/journal/13. **Ad Rates:** BW $510, full page; BW $383, half page; BW $765, 2 page spread. **Remarks:** Accepts advertising. **Circ:** 4,513, 7,000.

14906 ■ AmericanStyle Magazine
The Rosen Group Inc.
3000 Chestnut Ave., Ste. 304
Baltimore, MD 21211
Phone: (410)889-2933
Fax: (410)243-7089
Publisher's E-mail: info@rosengrp.com
Consumer magazine covering art. **Freq:** Quarterly. **Trim Size:** 8 1/4 x 10 7/8. **Key Personnel:** Hope Daniels, Editor-in-Chief; Wendy Rosen, Publisher; Merle Honey Porter, Manager, Advertising. **ISSN:** 1078--8425 (print). **URL:** http://www.americanstyle.com. **Ad Rates:** BW $2568; 4C $3025. **Remarks:** Accepts advertising. **Circ:** (Not Reported).

14907 ■ Annals of Dyslexia
International Dyslexia Association
40 York Rd., 4th Fl.
Baltimore, MD 21204-5243
Phone: (410)296-0232
Fax: (410)321-5069
Publisher's E-mail: info@interdys.org
Freq: 3/year. **Trim Size:** 6 x 9. **Key Personnel:** Dr. Donald Compton, Editor-in-Chief. **ISSN:** 0736--9387 (print). **Subscription Rates:** Included in membership. **URL:** http://eida.org/annals-of-dyslexia/. **Formerly:** Bulletin of the Orton Society. **Remarks:** Advertising not accepted. **Circ:** 15,000.

14908 ■ Arethusa
Johns Hopkins University Press
2715 N Charles St.
Baltimore, MD 21218-4319
Phone: (410)516-6900
Fax: (410)516-6968
Free: 800-537-5487
Publisher's E-mail: webmaster@jhupress.jhu.edu
Journal on classics, literature, and cultural studies. **Freq:** 3/year. **Print Method:** Offset. **Trim Size:** 6 x 9. **Cols./Page:** 1. **Col. Width:** 26 picas. **Col. Depth:** 7 inches. **Key Personnel:** David Fredrick, Associate Editor; David Konstan, Associate Editor; Madeleine S. Kaufman, Managing Editor; John J. Peradotto, Associate Editor; Carolyn Higbie, Associate Editor; Martha Malamud, Editor. **ISSN:** 0004--0975 (print); **EISSN:** 1080--6504 (electronic). **Subscription Rates:** $40 Individuals print; $72 Two years print; $42 Individuals online; $81 Two years online; $120 Institutions print; $240 Two years print. **URL:** http://www.press.jhu.edu/journals/arethusa. **Ad Rates:** BW $325. **Remarks:** Accepts advertising. **Circ:** ‡315.

14909 ■ b: Baltimore's Daily Conversation Starts Here
Baltimore Sun Media Group
501 N Calvert St.
Baltimore, MD 21278
Free: 888-539-1280
Publisher's E-mail: customersatisfaction@baltsun.com
Newspaper covering entertainment, celebrity, and pop culture news for Baltimore's younger audience. **Freq:** Daily. **Key Personnel:** Luke Broadwater, Managing Editor; Anne Tallent, Editor, phone: (410)332-6250. **Subscription Rates:** Free. **URL:** http://baltimoresun.com. **Mailing address:** PO Box 1377, Baltimore, MD 21278. **Remarks:** Accepts advertising. **Circ:** Thurs. ♦**69222**.

14910 ■ Baltimore Afro-American
The Afro-American Co.
2519 N Charles St.
Baltimore, MD 21218
Phone: (410)554-8200
Free: 800-237-6892
Black community newspaper. **Freq:** Weekly (Sat.). **Cols./Page:** 6. **Col. Width:** 24 nonpareils. **Col. Depth:** 301 agate lines. **Key Personnel:** John J. Oliver, Jr., Chairman of the Board, Publisher; Ron Harris, Executive Editor. **Subscription Rates:** $40 Individuals print and online. **URL:** http://www.afro.com/section/baltimore-news. **Remarks:** Accepts advertising. **Circ:** (Not Reported).

14911 ■ Baltimore Business Journal
Baltimore Business Journal
1 E Pratt St., Ste. 205
Baltimore, MD 21202
Phone: (410)576-1161
Fax: (410)752-3112
Publisher's E-mail: baltimore@bizjournals.com
Newspaper reporting Baltimore business news. **Freq:** Weekly. **Print Method:** Offset. **Trim Size:** 11 1/4 x 15. **Cols./Page:** 4. **Key Personnel:** Ryan Sharrow, Managing Editor; John Dinkel, President, Publisher; Joanna Sullivan, Editor-in-Chief, phone: (410)454-0512. **Subscription Rates:** $96 Individuals print & online or digital issues only. **Online:** American City Business Journals Inc. American City Business Journals Inc. **URL:** http://www.bizjournals.com/baltimore. **Ad Rates:** BW $6,345; 4C $7,350. **Remarks:** Accepts advertising. **Circ:** (Not Reported).

14912 ■ The Baltimore Chronicle & Sentinel
The Baltimore Chronicle
PO Box 42581
Baltimore, MD 21284-2581
Publisher's E-mail: editor@baltimorechronicle.com
Local newspaper. **Freq:** Daily. **Print Method:** Web-only publication. **Trim Size:** 11 1/2 x 16. **Cols./Page:** 5. **Col. Width:** 11.5 picas. **Col. Depth:** 194 agate lines. **Key Personnel:** Alice Cherbonnier, Managing Editor; Uri Avnery, Writer. **Subscription Rates:** Free. **URL:** http://www.baltimorechronicle.com. **Remarks:** on website. **Circ:** Paid ‡450, Free ‡14000.

14913 ■ Baltimore City Paper
Times-Shamrock Communications
812 Park Ave.
Baltimore, MD 21201
Publication E-mail: lgardner@citypaper.com
Lifestyle and entertainment newspaper (tabloid). **Freq:** Weekly (Wed.). **Print Method:** Offset. **Cols./Page:** 5. **Col. Width:** 26 nonpareils. **Col. Depth:** 182 agate lines. **Key Personnel:** Lee Gardner, Editor; Athena Towery, Director, Production; Leslie Grim, Director, Advertising. **Subscription Rates:** Free. **URL:** http://www.citypaper.com. **Ad Rates:** BW $1975. **Remarks:** Accepts advertising. **Circ:** 50000.

14914 ■ The Baltimore Guide
R and B Publishing Co.
526 S Conkling St.
Baltimore, MD 21224
Phone: (410)732-6600
Fax: (410)732-6336
Publication E-mail: talkback@baltimoreguide.com
Community newspaper (tabloid). **Freq:** Weekly (Thurs.). **Print Method:** Offset. **Trim Size:** 10 1/4 x 13 3/4. **Cols./Page:** 5 and 6. **Col. Width:** 22 nonpareils. **Col. Depth:** 195 agate lines. **URL:** http://www.baltimoreguide.com. **Ad Rates:** GLR $1.15; BW $1120; 4C $1420; PCI $16.10. **Remarks:** Accepts advertising. **Circ:** (Not Reported).

14915 ■ Baltimore Magazine
Baltimore Magazine Advertising/Editorial/Business Offices
1000 Lancaster St., Ste. 400
Baltimore, MD 21202
Phone: (410)752-4200
Fax: (410)625-0280
Publication E-mail: smarge@baltimoremag.com
Publication covering regional news. **Freq:** Monthly. **Print Method:** Offset. Uses mats. **Trim Size:** 8 x 10 1/2. **Cols./Page:** 3. **Col. Width:** 26 nonpareils. **Col. Depth:** 140 agate lines. **Key Personnel:** Ken Iglehart, Managing Editor; Amanda Laine White-Iseli, Art Director; Stephen A. Geppi, Publisher; Richard M. Basoco, Chief Operating Officer, Editor. **ISSN:** 0005--4453 (print). **Subscription Rates:** $19.97 Individuals; $32.97 Individuals 2 years; $42.97 Individuals 3 years. **URL:** http://www.baltimoremagazine.net/this-month. **Remarks:** Accepts advertising. **Circ:** Paid ⋆**56000**.

14916 ■ The Baltimore Sun
Baltimore Sun Media Group
501 N. Calvert St.
Baltimore, MD 21278
Free: 888-539-1280
Publication E-mail: customersatisfaction@baltsun.com
General newspaper. **Freq:** Mon.-Sun. (morn.). **Print Method:** Offset. **Cols./Page:** 6. **Col. Width:** 25 nonpareils. **Col. Depth:** 294 agate lines. **Key Personnel:** Timothy E. Ryan, Publisher, Chief Executive Officer; Triffon G. Alatzas, Senior Vice President, Executive Editor, phone: (410)332-6154. **Online:** ProQuest L.L.C.; LexisNexis; Baltimore Sun Media Group Baltimore Sun Media Group. **Alt. Formats:** Handheld. **URL:** http://www.baltimoresun.com. **Mailing address:** PO Box 1377 , Baltimore, MD 21278. **Remarks:** Accepts advertising. **Circ:** Mon.-Fri. ⋆**195,561**, Sat. ⋆**246,056**, Sun. ⋆**343,552**.

Circulation: ⋆ = AAM; △ or • = BPA; ♦ = CAC; ❑ = VAC; ⊕ = PO Statement; ‡ = Publisher's Report; Boldface figures = sworn; Light figures = estimated.

14917 ■ Baltimore Times
Baltimore Publishing Group
2513 N Charles St.
Baltimore, MD 21215-4602
Publisher's E-mail: btimes@btimes.com
Community newspaper. **Freq:** Weekly (Fri.). **Print Method:** Photo offset. **Key Personnel:** Dena Wane, Director; Joy Bramble, Publisher. **Subscription Rates:** Free. **URL:** http://baltimoretimes-online.com. **Circ:** (Not Reported).

14918 ■ Baltimore's Child
Baltimore's Child
11 Dutton Ct.
Baltimore, MD 21228
Publisher's E-mail: info@baltimoreschild.com
Local parenting magazine. **Freq:** Monthly. **Key Personnel:** Joanne Giza, Publisher, Distribution Manager, phone: (410)542-4166, fax: (410)719-9342; Sharon Keech, Publisher, phone: (410)367-5884. **Subscription Rates:** Free. **URL:** http://baltimoreschild.com. **Remarks:** Accepts advertising. **Circ:** (Not Reported).

14919 ■ Behavioural Pharmacology
Lippincott Williams & Wilkins
351 W Camden St.
Baltimore, MD 21201
Phone: (410)528-4000
Publisher's E-mail: info@ebps.org
Peer-reviewed journal publishing original research, which studies the ways in which behavior is affected by any aspect of pharmacology. **Freq:** 8/year. **Key Personnel:** Louk Vanderschuren, Associate Editor; Jack Bergman, Associate Editor; Paul Willner, Editor. **ISSN:** 0955--8810 (print); **EISSN:** 1473--5849 (electronic). **Subscription Rates:** $574 Individuals; $565 Other countries; $2531 Institutions; $2616 Institutions, other countries; $288 Other countries in-training; $274 Canada and Mexico in-training; Included in membership. **URL:** http://journals.lww.com/behaviouralpharm/pages/default.aspx; http://www.ebps.org/publications/Pub_Behavioural.lasso. **Remarks:** Advertising not accepted. **Circ:** ‡127.

14920 ■ Better: Evidence-based Education
Johns Hopkins University Press
2715 N Charles St.
Baltimore, MD 21218-4319
Phone: (410)516-6900
Fax: (410)516-6968
Free: 800-537-5487
Publisher's E-mail: webmaster@jhupress.jhu.edu
Magazine for educators and policy makers interested in evidence-based education reform. **Key Personnel:** Robert Slavin, Editor-in-Chief. **ISSN:** 2041--921X (print). **Subscription Rates:** £10 Individuals online. **URL:** http://www.betterevidence.org. **Circ:** (Not Reported).

14921 ■ Biostatistics
Oxford University Press
c/o Scott L. Zeger, Founding Ed.
Dept. of Biostatistics
Johns Hopkins University
615 N Wolfe St.
Baltimore, MD 21205-2179
Fax: (410)955-3067
Publisher's E-mail: webenquiry.uk@oup.com
Journal publishing papers that develop and apply innovative statistical methods to problems of human health and disease including basic biomedical sciences, focusing on methods and applications. **Freq:** Quarterly. **Key Personnel:** Scott L. Zeger, Editor, Founder; Peter J. Diggle, Editor, Founder; Norman Breslow, Advisor, Board Member; Mitchell Gail, Advisor, Board Member; Sarah Darby, Advisor, Board Member; Adrian Bowman, Associate Editor; Niels Keiding, Advisor, Board Member. **ISSN:** 1465--4644 (print); **EISSN:** 1468--4357 (electronic). **Subscription Rates:** £245 Individuals print; $465 Individuals print; €367 Individuals print; £397 Institutions online; $769 Institutions online; €579 Institutions online; £490 Institutions print; $931 Institutions print; €735 Institutions print; £532 Institutions print and online; $1011 Institutions print and online; €799 Institutions print and online. **URL:** http://biostatistics.oxfordjournals.org. **Remarks:** Advertising accepted; rates available upon request. **Circ:** (Not Reported).

14922 ■ Blood Coagulation and Fibrinolysis: An International Journal in Haemostasis and Thrombosis
Lippincott Williams & Wilkins
c/o Dr. Evqueni L. Saenko, PhD, Editor
University of Maryland School of Medicine
Ctr. for Vascular & Inflammatory Diseases
800 W Baltimore St.
Baltimore, MD 21201
Phone: (410)706-8226
Fax: (410)706-8234
Peer-reviewed journal covering topics in haemostasis and thrombosis research today including blood coagulation, platelets, fibrinolysis, hemophilia, arterial disease and drug effects. **Freq:** 8/year. **Key Personnel:** Evqueni L. Saenko, PhD, Editor; Dr. Richard Marlar, Editor. **ISSN:** 0957--5235 (print); **EISSN:** 1473--5733 (electronic). **Subscription Rates:** $667 Individuals; $728 Other countries; $3690 Institutions; $3835 Institutions, other countries; $369 Individuals in-training. **URL:** http://journals.lww.com/bloodcoagulation/pages/default.aspx. **Circ:** ‡172.

14923 ■ Bulletin of the History of Medicine
Johns Hopkins University Press
2715 N Charles St.
Baltimore, MD 21218-4319
Phone: (410)516-6900
Fax: (410)516-6968
Free: 800-537-5487
Publisher's E-mail: webmaster@jhupress.jhu.edu
Official publication of the American Association for the History of Medicine. Journal covering the Social and Scientific aspects of the History of Medicine Worldwide. **Freq:** Quarterly. **Print Method:** Offset. **Trim Size:** 6 x 9. **Cols./Page:** 1. **Col. Width:** 52 nonpareils. **Col. Depth:** 102 agate lines. **Key Personnel:** Mary E. Fissell, Editor; Carolyn McLaughlin, Associate Editor; Randall M. Packard, Editor; Gert H. Brieger, Editor; Henry E. Sigerist, Founder. **ISSN:** 0007--5140 (print); **EISSN:** 1086--3176 (electronic). **Subscription Rates:** $190 Institutions print; $50 Individuals print; $65.01 Individuals online; $90 Two years print; $380 Institutions 2 years; print; $117.01 Two years online. **URL:** http://www.press.jhu.edu/journals/bulletin_of_the_history_of_medicine; http://muse.jhu.edu/journal/24. **Ad Rates:** BW $425; BW $500, full page; BW $375, half page. **Remarks:** Accepts advertising. **Circ:** 1573.

14924 ■ The Catholic Review
Cathedral Foundation Inc.
880 Park Ave.
Baltimore, MD 21201
Phone: (443)524-3150
Fax: (443)524-3155
Free: 888-768-9555
Publication E-mail: mail@catholicreview.org
Newspaper of the Archdiocese of Baltimore. **Freq:** Monthly. **Print Method:** Offset. **Trim Size:** 22 x 27 1/2. **Cols./Page:** 6. **Col. Width:** 2 1/16 inches. **Col. Depth:** 21 inches. **Key Personnel:** William E. Lori, Publisher. **ISSN:** 0008--8315 (print). **Subscription Rates:** $25 Individuals print and online; Free online. **URL:** http://www.catholicreview.org. **Ad Rates:** BW $2898; 4C $3398; PCI $34. **Remarks:** Accepts advertising. **Circ:** ‡65000.

14925 ■ The CEA Forum
College English Association
Johns Hopkins University Press
Journal Publishing Division
PO Box 19966
Baltimore, MD 21211-0966
Freq: Semiannual May and December. **Key Personnel:** Jamie Mcdaniel, Editor. **ISSN:** 0007--8034 (print). **Subscription Rates:** Included in membership. **URL:** http://www.cea-web.org/index.php?option=com_content&view=article&id=20:the-cea-forum-current-issues&catid=3:forum; http://journals.tdl.org/ceaforum/index.php/ceaforum. **Remarks:** Accepts advertising. **Circ:** (Not Reported).

14926 ■ Central Nervous System Agents in Medicinal Chemistry
Bentham Science Publishers Ltd.
Guilford Pharmaceuticals, Inc.
6611 Tributary St.
Baltimore, MD 21224
Publisher's E-mail: subscriptions@benthamscience.org
Journal covering all the latest and outstanding developments in medicinal chemistry and rational drug design for the discovery of new central nervous system agents. **Freq:** Quarterly. **Key Personnel:** Gregory S. Hamilton, Editor-in-Chief. **ISSN:** 1871--5249 (print); **EISSN:** 1875--6166 (electronic). **Subscription Rates:** $180 Individuals print; $520 print and online - academic; $680 print or online - academic; $1010 print and online - corporate; $1220 print or online - corporate. **URL:** http://benthamscience.com/journals/central-nervous-system-agents-in-medicinal-chemistry. **Formerly:** Current Medicinal Chemistry. Central Nervous System Agents. **Ad Rates:** BW $700; 4C $900. **Remarks:** Accepts advertising. **Circ:** ‡3000.

14927 ■ Circulation Research
Lippincott Williams and Wilkins
Circulation Research Editorial Office
2700 Lighthouse Point E, Ste. 230
Baltimore, MD 21224
Phone: (410)327-5005
Fax: (410)614-7660
Publisher's E-mail: ronna.ekhouse@wolterskluwer.com
Journal covering basic research on the cardiovascular system. **Founded:** 1953. **Freq:** Biweekly. **Key Personnel:** Prof. Roberto Bolli, MD, Editor. **ISSN:** 0009-7330 (print); **EISSN:** 1524-4571 (electronic). **Subscription Rates:** $717 Individuals print only; $1812 Institutions print only; $850 Individuals print only; other countries; $2091 Institutions print only; other countries; $707 Individuals online only. **URL:** http://www.lww.com/Product/0009-7330; http://circres.ahajournals.org/. **Ad Rates:** GLR $200; BW $720. **Remarks:** Accepts advertising. **Circ:** Paid ‡2900.

14928 ■ Clinical Dysmorphology
Lippincott Williams & Wilkins
351 W Camden St.
Baltimore, MD 21201
Phone: (410)528-4000
Peer-reviewed journal publishing case reports on the etiology, clinical delineation, genetic mapping and molecular embryology of birth defects. **Freq:** Quarterly. **Key Personnel:** Jill Clayton-Smith, Editor; Michael Baraitser, Editor; Dian Donnai, Editor. **ISSN:** 0962--8827 (print); **EISSN:** 1473--5717 (electronic). **Subscription Rates:** $415 Individuals; $423 Other countries; $1673 Institutions; $1745 Institutions, other countries; $201 Individuals in-training; $191 Canada and Mexico in-training. **URL:** http://journals.lww.com/clindysmorphol/pages/default.aspx. **Circ:** ‡199.

14929 ■ Cognitive and Behavioral Neurology
Lippincott Williams & Wilkins
c/o Barry Gordon, MD, Editor-in-Chief
The Johns Hopkins Medical Institutions
Baltimore, MD 21231
Phone: (410)955-8531
Fax: (410)955-0188
Peer-reviewed journal featuring original research articles, review articles, and brief reports covering diagnostic, therapeutic, and research work in areas such as pharmacotherapy, somatics, imaging, and EEG. **Freq:** 4/yr. **Print Method:** Sheetfed Offset. **Trim Size:** 8 1/4 x 11. **Key Personnel:** Harry Dean, Publisher; Barry Gordon, MD, Editor-in-Chief. **ISSN:** 1543--3633 (print); **EISSN:** 1537--0887 (electronic). **Subscription Rates:** $457 Individuals; $1074 Institutions; $487 Other countries individual; $1195 Institutions, other countries; $213 Individuals in-training; $202 Other countries in-training. **URL:** http://journals.lww.com/cogbehavneurol/pages/default.aspx; http://www.lww.com/Product/1543-3633. **Formerly:** Neuropsychiatry, Neuropsychology, and Behavioral Neurology. **Ad Rates:** BW $875; 4C $1525. **Remarks:** Accepts advertising. **Circ:** 116.

14930 ■ Configurations
Johns Hopkins University Press
2715 N Charles St.
Baltimore, MD 21218-4319
Phone: (410)516-6900
Fax: (410)516-6968
Free: 800-537-5487
Publisher's E-mail: webmaster@jhupress.jhu.edu
Journal on the relations of literature and the arts to the sciences and technology. **Freq:** Quarterly. **Print Method:** Offset. **Trim Size:** 6 x 9. **Cols./Page:** 1. **Col. Width:** 26 picas. **Col. Depth:** 7 inches. **Key Personnel:** Charles Bazerman, Board Member; Kenneth J. Knoespel, Editor; Sally Shuttleworth, Board Member; Bob Kowkabany,

Editor; Joseph Rouse, Board Member; Ronald Schleifer, Editor; Robert Markley, Editor. **ISSN:** 1063--1801 (print); **EISSN:** 1080--6520 (electronic). **Subscription Rates:** $35 Individuals print; 1 year; $63 Individuals print; 2 years; $40 Individuals online, 1 year; $72 Individuals online, 2 years; $110 Institutions print; 1 year; $220 Institutions print; 2 years. **URL:** http://www.press.jhu.edu/journals/configurations. **Ad Rates:** BW $325. **Remarks:** Accepts advertising. **Circ:** ‡492.

14931 ■ Continuum: Lifelong Learning in Neurology
Lippincott Williams & Wilkins
351 W Camden St.
Baltimore, MD 21201
Phone: (410)528-4000
Learning program of the American Academy of Neurology, giving neurologists information from the front lines of neurology. **Freq:** Bimonthly. **Key Personnel:** Aaron E. Miller, MD, Editor. **ISSN:** 1080--2371 (print); **EISSN:** 1538--6899 (electronic). **Subscription Rates:** $844 Individuals; $860 Other countries; $1438 Institutions; $1454 Institutions, other countries; $360 Individuals in-training; $454 Canada and Mexico in-training; $470 Other countries in-training. **URL:** http://journals.lww.com/continuum/Pages/default.aspx. **Circ:** (Not Reported).

14932 ■ Cornea: The Journal of Cornea and External Disease
Lippincott Williams & Wilkins
351 W Camden St.
Baltimore, MD 21201
Phone: (410)528-4000
Peer-reviewed journal offering the latest clinical and basic research on the cornea and the anterior segment of the eye. **Freq:** Monthly. **Print Method:** Sheetfed Offset. **Trim Size:** 8 1/8 x 10 7/8. **Key Personnel:** Alan Sugar, MD, Editor-in-Chief; Nina J. Chang, Publisher. **ISSN:** 0277-3740 (print); **EISSN:** 1536-4798 (electronic). **Subscription Rates:** $755 Individuals; $1815 Institutions; $336 Individuals in-training; $840 Other countries; $1730 Institutions, other countries; $338 Other countries in-training. **URL:** http://journals.lww.com/corneajrnl/pages/default.aspx; http://www.lww.com/Product/0277-3740. **Ad Rates:** BW $1,770; 4C $1,865. **Remarks:** Accepts advertising. **Circ:** 1138.

14933 ■ The Crisis
Crisis
4805 Mount Hope Dr.
Baltimore, MD 21215-3206
Magazine covering civil rights, current events, and the arts. **Freq:** Quarterly. **Print Method:** Offset. **Trim Size:** 8 1/2 x 11. **Cols./Page:** 3. **Col. Width:** 13 picas. **Subscription Rates:** $20 Individuals print and online; $12 Individuals print only; $10 Individuals online only. **URL:** http://www.thecrisismagazine.com. **Ad Rates:** 4C $10,000. **Remarks:** Accepts advertising. **Circ:** (Not Reported).

14934 ■ Current Molecular Medicine
Bentham Science Publishers Ltd.
The Sol Goldman Pancreatic Cancer Research Center, CRB-2, Ste. 345
Johns Hopkins University School of Medicine
1550 Orleans St.
Baltimore, MD 21231
Phone: (410)955-3511
Fax: (410)614-0671
Publisher's E-mail: subscriptions@benthamscience.org
Interdisciplinary journal focusing on current and comprehensive reviews on fundamental molecular mechanisms of disease pathogenesis, the development of molecular-diagnosis and/or novel approaches to rational treatment. **Freq:** 10/year. **Key Personnel:** David W. Li, Editor-in-Chief; David A. Frank, Associate Editor. **ISSN:** 1566--5240 (print); **EISSN:** 1875--5666 (electronic). **Subscription Rates:** $520 Individuals print; $2570 print and online - academic; $2340 print or online - academic; $5000 print and online - corporate; $4170 print or online - corporate. **URL:** http://benthamscience.com/journals/current-molecular-medicine. **Ad Rates:** BW $700; 4C $900. **Remarks:** Accepts advertising. **Circ:** ‡1000.

14935 ■ Current Opinion in Allergy and Clinical Immunology
Lippincott Williams & Wilkins
351 W Camden St.
Baltimore, MD 21201
Phone: (410)528-4000
Peer-reviewed journal empowering allergists and immunologists to put to good use vital clinical and research advances from throughout the world. **Freq:** Bimonthly. **Key Personnel:** Ian Burgess, Publisher; G. Walter Canonica, Editor; Mark Ballow, Editor. **ISSN:** 1528--4050 (print); **EISSN:** 1473--6322 (electronic). **Subscription Rates:** $458 Individuals; $1452 Institutions; $185 Individuals in-training. **URL:** http://journals.lww.com/co-allergy/pages/default.aspx. **Remarks:** Accepts advertising. **Circ:** ‡319.

14936 ■ Current Opinion in Clinical Nutrition and Metabolic Care
Lippincott Williams & Wilkins
351 W Camden St.
Baltimore, MD 21201
Phone: (410)528-4000
Peer-reviewed journal covering subjects such as protein metabolism and therapy, nutrition in the intensive care unit, anabolic and catabolic signals, assessment of nutritional status and analytical methods and nutraceutics. **Freq:** Bimonthly. **Key Personnel:** Yvon A. Carpentier, Editor; Luc A. Cynober, Editor. **ISSN:** 1363-1950 (print); **EISSN:** 1473-6519 (electronic). **Subscription Rates:** $497 Individuals; $1830 Institutions; $185 Individuals in-training; $515 Other countries; $1895 Institutions, other countries; $185 Other countries in-training. **URL:** http://journals.lww.com/co-clinicalnutrition/pages/default.aspx. **Remarks:** Accepts advertising. **Circ:** ‡195.

14937 ■ Current Opinion in Critical Care
Lippincott Williams & Wilkins
351 W Camden St.
Baltimore, MD 21201
Phone: (410)528-4000
Peer-reviewed journal covering subjects such as the respiratory system, neuroscience, cardiopulmonary resuscitation, the surgical patient, trauma and infectious diseases. **Freq:** Bimonthly. **Key Personnel:** Jean-Louis Vincent, MD, Editor; Ian Burgess, Publisher. **ISSN:** 1070--5295 (print); **EISSN:** 1531--7072 (electronic). **Subscription Rates:** $529 Individuals; $1795 Institutions; $1834 Institutions, other countries; $195 Individuals in-training. **URL:** http://journals.lww.com/co-criticalcare/pages/default.aspx. **Remarks:** Accepts advertising. **Circ:** ‡688.

14938 ■ Current Opinion in Endocrinology, Diabetes and Obesity
Lippincott Williams & Wilkins
351 W Camden St.
Baltimore, MD 21201
Phone: (410)528-4000
Peer-reviewed journal covering diabetes and endocrine pancreas, multihormonal systems disorders, obesity and nutrition, thyroid, adrenal cortex and other items. **Freq:** Bimonthly. **Key Personnel:** Lewis E. Braverman, MD, Editor; Ian Burgess, Publisher. **ISSN:** 1752--296X (print); **EISSN:** 1752--2978 (electronic). **Subscription Rates:** $430 U.S.; $445 Other countries; $1642 Institutions; $1664 Institutions, other countries; $195 Individuals in-training; $185 Canada and Mexico in-training; $195 Other countries in-training. **URL:** http://journals.lww.com/co-endocrinology/pages/default.aspx. **Formerly:** Current Opinion in Endocrinology and Diabetes. **Remarks:** Accepts advertising. **Circ:** ‡230.

14939 ■ Current Opinion in Hematology
Lippincott Williams & Wilkins
351 W Camden St.
Baltimore, MD 21201
Phone: (410)528-4000
Peer-reviewed journal covering subjects such as leukocytes, erythrocytes, hematopoietic growth factors, hematological malignancies and hemostasis and thrombosis. **Freq:** Bimonthly. **Key Personnel:** Thomas P. Stossel, MD, Editor; Ian Burgess, Publisher. **ISSN:** 1065--6251 (print); **EISSN:** 1531--7048 (electronic). **Subscription Rates:** $522 U.S.; $525 Other countries; $2016 Institutions; $2052 Institutions, other countries; $192 Other countries in-training; $182 Canada and Mexico in-training. **URL:** http://journals.lww.com/co-hematology/pages/default.aspx. **Remarks:** Accepts advertising. **Circ:** ‡702.

14940 ■ Current Opinion in Internal Medicine
Lippincott Williams & Wilkins
351 W Camden St.
Baltimore, MD 21201
Phone: (410)528-4000
Journal covering subjects such as cardiology, lipidology, organ transplantation, gastroenterology, clinical nutrition and metabolic care, nephrology and hypertension, rheumatology, allergy and clinical immunology, oncology. **Freq:** Bimonthly. **Key Personnel:** H.D. Humes, MD, Editor; Ian Burgess, Publisher. **ISSN:** 1535--5942 (print); **EISSN:** 1746--0956 (electronic). **URL:** http://www.co-internalmedicine.com/pt/re/cointernalmed/home.htm. **Circ:** (Not Reported).

14941 ■ Current Opinion in Nephrology and Hypertension
Lippincott Williams & Wilkins
351 W Camden St.
Baltimore, MD 21201
Phone: (410)528-4000
Peer-reviewed journal covering subjects such as circulation and hemodynamics, pathophysiology of hypertension, clinical nephrology, mineral metabolism, pharmacology and therapeutics, and other topics of relevance. **Freq:** Bimonthly. **Key Personnel:** Barry M. Brenner, MD, Editor; Ian Burgess, Publisher. **ISSN:** 1062--4821 (print); **EISSN:** 1473--6543 (electronic). **Subscription Rates:** $483 U.S.; $494 Other countries; $1812 Institutions; $1875 Institutions, other countries; $185 Other countries in-training; $185 Canada and Mexico in-training. **URL:** http://journals.lww.com/co-nephrolhypertens/pages/default.aspx. **Remarks:** Accepts advertising. **Circ:** ‡332.

14942 ■ Current Opinion in Organ Transplantation Online
Lippincott Williams & Wilkins
351 W Camden St.
Baltimore, MD 21201
Phone: (410)528-4000
Journal covering topics in the field of organ transplantation. **Freq:** Bimonthly. **Key Personnel:** Josep M. Grinyo, MD, Associate Editor; Linda S. Sher, MD, Editor. **ISSN:** 1087--2418 (print); **EISSN:** 1531--7013 (electronic). **Subscription Rates:** $242 Other countries online; $230 Canada and Mexico online. **URL:** http://journals.lww.com/co-transplantation/pages/default.aspx; http://www.lww.com/product/1531-7013. **Circ:** ‡628.

14943 ■ Current Opinion in Otolaryngology & Head and Neck Surgery
Lippincott Williams & Wilkins
351 W Camden St.
Baltimore, MD 21201
Phone: (410)528-4000
Peer-reviewed journal covering subjects such as the nose and paranasal sinuses, head and neck oncology, speech therapy and rehabilitation, facial plastic surgery, audiology and pediatric otolaryngology. **Freq:** Bimonthly. **Key Personnel:** Patrick J. Bradley, MBA, Editor; Paul J. Donald, MD, Editor; Ian Burgess, Publisher. **ISSN:** 1068--9508 (print); **EISSN:** 1531--6998 (electronic). **Subscription Rates:** $440 U.S. print; $471 Other countries print; $1526 Institutions print; $1568 Institutions, other countries print; $192 Other countries in-training - print; $182 Canada and Mexico in-training - print. **URL:** http://journals.lww.com/co-otolaryngology/pages/default.aspx. **Remarks:** Accepts advertising. **Circ:** ‡368.

14944 ■ Current Opinion in Pulmonary Medicine
Lippincott Williams & Wilkins
351 W Camden St.
Baltimore, MD 21201
Phone: (410)528-4000
Journal covering subjects such as asthma, obstructive, occupational, and environmental diseases, disorders of pulmonary circulation, neoplasms of the lung, sleep and respiratory neurobiology and cystic fibrosis. **Freq:** Bimonthly. **Key Personnel:** Om P. Sharma, MD, Editor; Ian Burgess, Publisher. **ISSN:** 1070--5287 (print); **EISSN:** 1531--6971 (electronic). **Subscription Rates:** $515 Individuals; $1645 Institutions; $1690 Institutions, other countries; $192 Other countries in-training; $182 Canada and Mexico in-training. **URL:** http://journals.lww.com/co-pulmonarymedicine/pages/default.aspx. **Remarks:** Accepts advertising. **Circ:** ‡251.

Circulation: ★ = AAM; △ or • = BPA; ♦ = CAC; ❑ = VAC; ⊕ = PO Statement; ‡ = Publisher's Report; Boldface figures = sworn; Light figures = estimated.

14945 ■ Current Opinion in Urology
Wolters Kluwer Health Inc.
Zuidpoolsingel 2
2400 BA Alphen aan den Rijn, Netherlands
Phone: 31 172 641-400
Peer-reviewed journal covering subjects such as benign prostatic hyperplasia, renal medicine and transplantation, functional reconstruction and trauma, oncology: bladder and testis and pediatric urology. **Freq:** 6/year. **Key Personnel:** Johannes Vieweg, Editor. **ISSN:** 0963--0643 (print); **EISSN:** 1473--6586 (electronic). **Subscription Rates:** $483 Individuals print; $328 Individuals online; $495 Other countries print; $312 Other countries online; $1802 Institutions print; $1869 Institutions, other countries print. **URL:** http://journals.lww.com/co-urology/pages/default.aspx. **Mailing address:** PO Box 1030, 2400 BA Alphen aan den Rijn, Netherlands. **Remarks:** Accepts advertising. **Circ:** ‡240.

14946 ■ The Daily Record: Business and Legal News of Maryland
The Daily Record CPN
11 E Saratoga St.
Baltimore, MD 21202
Phone: (443)524-8100
Publisher's E-mail: customerservice@thedolancompany.com
Daily Business Newspaper reporting news and features on business, real estate, technology, healthcare and law. **Freq:** Daily. **Print Method:** Web offset. **Trim Size:** 11 1/2 x 17 1/2. **Cols./Page:** 4. **Col. Width:** 2 5/16 inches. **Col. Depth:** 15 3/4 inches. **Key Personnel:** Frederick D. Godman, Senior Vice President; Tom Linthicum, Executive Editor; Paul Samuel, Associate Editor; Christopher Eddings, President. **USPS:** 145-120. **Subscription Rates:** $269 Individuals print and online - 1 year; $169 Individuals online - 1 year. **URL:** http://thedailyrecord.com. **Formerly**: Warfield's Business Record. **Ad Rates:** BW $2,868. **Remarks:** Accepts advertising. **Circ:** ‡7597, Free ‡1747.

14947 ■ Dirty Linen: Folk & World Music
Dirty Linen
PO Box 66600
Baltimore, MD 21239-6600
Phone: (410)583-7973
Fax: (410)337-6735
Free: 800-769-8044
Publication E-mail: info@dirtylinen.com
Consumer magazine covering folk and world music. **Freq:** Bimonthly. **Print Method:** Sheet Fed. **Trim Size:** 8 3/8 x 10 7/8. **Key Personnel:** Susan Hartman, Contact; Paul Hartman, Editor. **ISSN:** 1047--4315 (print). **Subscription Rates:** $25 Individuals; $45 Two years; $34 Canada; $62 Canada 2 years; $46 Other countries; $85 Other countries 2 years. **URL:** http://shop.dirtylinen.se. **Ad Rates:** BW $1,015; 4C $1,540. **Remarks:** Accepts advertising. **Circ:** Combined 12000.

14948 ■ Drug and Alcohol Dependence
Mosby Inc.
c/o Andraya Dolbee
Johns Hopkins Bayview Campus
Behavioral Pharmacology Research Unit
5510 Nathan Shock Dr.
Baltimore, MD 21224
Phone: (410)550-1977
Fax: (410)550-0030
Journal publishing original research, scholarly reviews, commentaries, and policy analyses in the area of drug, alcohol, and tobacco use and dependence. **Freq:** Monthly. **Key Personnel:** Eric C. Strain, Editor-in-Chief; F.J. Alvarez, Board Member; Andraya Dolbee, Office Manager; M.E. Ensminger, Board Member; S. Darke, Board Member; R. Ali, Board Member; W.K. Bickel, Board Member; K.T. Brady, Board Member. **ISSN:** 0376-8716 (print). **Subscription Rates:** $626 Individuals print and online; $4680 Institutions print. **URL:** http://www.journals.elsevier.com/drug-and-alcohol-dependence/#description; http://www.drugandalcoholdependence.com. **Circ:** (Not Reported).

14949 ■ Economia
Brookings Institution Press
The Johns Hopkins University Press
Journals Publishing Division
Baltimore, MD 21218-4319
Phone: (410)516-6989
Fax: (410)516-6968
Free: 800-548-1784
Publisher's E-mail: bibooks@brookings.edu
Journal of the Latin American and Caribbean Economic Association covering research in policy issues for economists and policymakers from the region. **Freq:** Semiannual Spring and Fall. **Key Personnel:** Catherine Mathieu-Canuto, Managing Editor; Roberto Rigobon, Editor; Eduardo Fernandez, Board Member; Jennifer Hooper, Associate Editor. **ISSN:** 1533-6239 (print). **Subscription Rates:** $100 Institutions; $114 Institutions, other countries; $60 Individuals; $74 Other countries. **URL:** http://muse.jhu.edu/journals/eco; http://www.brookings.edu/about/press/journals/economia. **Mailing address:** PO Box 19966, Baltimore, MD 21218-4319. **Circ:** (Not Reported).

14950 ■ Economic Opportunity Report
Business Publishers Inc.
PO Box 17592
Baltimore, MD 21297-1592
Fax: (800)508-2592
Free: 800-223-8720
Publisher's E-mail: custserv@bpinews.com
Journal containing information about developments that affect social programs. **Freq:** Monthly. **Key Personnel:** Amy Marchant, JD, Managing Editor. **ISSN:** 0013--2026 (print). **Subscription Rates:** $207 Individuals online. **URL:** http://www.bpinews.com/subscribe.htm. **Circ:** (Not Reported).

14951 ■ Eighteenth-Century Studies
Johns Hopkins University Press
2715 N Charles St.
Baltimore, MD 21218-4319
Phone: (410)516-6900
Fax: (410)516-6968
Free: 800-537-5487
Publisher's E-mail: asecs@wfu.edu
Magazine containing articles and reviews on eighteenth-century subjects, including a variety of languages and literatures, classics, drama, history, religion, philosophy, music, science, and political science. **Freq:** Quarterly. **Print Method:** Offset. **Trim Size:** 6 x 9. **Cols./Page:** 1. **Col. Width:** 52 nonpareils. **Col. Depth:** 93 agate lines. **Key Personnel:** Carolyn C. Guile, Editor; Steven Pincus, Editor. **ISSN:** 0013--2586 (print). **Subscription Rates:** $170 Institutions print; $340 Institutions print, 2 years; included in membership dues. **Alt. Formats:** PDF. **URL:** http://www.press.jhu.edu/journals/eighteenth-century_studies; http://muse.jhu.edu/journals/eighteenth-century_studies. **Ad Rates:** BW $400. **Remarks:** Accepts advertising. **Circ:** ‡2222, 4000.

14952 ■ Emergency Preparedness News
Business Publishers Inc.
PO Box 17592
Baltimore, MD 21297-1592
Fax: (800)508-2592
Free: 800-223-8720
Publisher's E-mail: custserv@bpinews.com
Journal containing information related to disaster management. **Freq:** Monthly. **Key Personnel:** Deborah Eby, Editor. **ISSN:** 0275--3782 (print). **Subscription Rates:** $247 Individuals online. **URL:** http://www.bpinews.com/subscribe.htm. **Circ:** (Not Reported).

14953 ■ The Emily Dickinson Journal
Johns Hopkins University Press
2715 N Charles St.
Baltimore, MD 21218-4319
Phone: (410)516-6900
Fax: (410)516-6968
Free: 800-537-5487
Publisher's E-mail: webmaster@jhupress.jhu.edu
Scholarly journal covering the author, poetry, and women's literature. **Freq:** Semiannual. **Trim Size:** 6 x 9. **Key Personnel:** Gary Lee Stonum, Advisor, Board Member; Suzanne Juhasz, Editor, Founder. **ISSN:** 1059--6879 (print); **EISSN:** 1096--858X (electronic). **Subscription Rates:** $45 Individuals /year (print); $115 Institutions /year (print); $230 Institutions two years (print); $81 Individuals two years (print); $55 Individuals /year (online); $99 Individuals two years (online). **URL:** http://www.press.jhu.edu/journals/emily_dickinson_journal. **Ad Rates:** BW $325. **Remarks:** Accepts advertising. **Circ:** Combined 351.

14954 ■ English Literary History
Johns Hopkins University Press
2715 N Charles St.
Baltimore, MD 21218-4319
Phone: (410)516-6900
Fax: (410)516-6968
Free: 800-537-5487
Publication E-mail: elh@jhu.edu
Journal covering the historical interpretation of major English and American literary works. **Freq:** Quarterly. **Print Method:** Offset. **Trim Size:** 6 x 9. **Cols./Page:** 1. **Col. Width:** 52 nonpareils. **Col. Depth:** 105 agate lines. **Key Personnel:** Simon During, Editor; Amanda Anderson, Editor; Frances Ferguson, Editor; Sharon Cameron, Editor; Richard Halpern, Editor. **ISSN:** 0013--8304 (print); **EISSN:** 1080--6547 (electronic). **Subscription Rates:** $50 Individuals print; $235 Institutions print; $470 Institutions print, 2 years; $90 Individuals print, 2 years; $60 Individuals online only; $108 Individuals online only, 2 years. **URL:** http://www.press.jhu.edu/journals/english_literary_history. **Also known as:** ELH. **Ad Rates:** BW $350. **Remarks:** Accepts advertising. **Circ:** 999.

14955 ■ The Erickson Tribune: Add More Living to Your Life
Erickson Living
701 Maiden Choice Ln.
Baltimore, MD 21228-5968
Phone: (410)242-2880
Fax: (410)737-8854
Free: 800-920-0856
Newspaper delivering feature articles of interest to retirees in Baltimore. **Freq:** Monthly. **Key Personnel:** Deborah Dasch, Editor-in-Chief. **Subscription Rates:** Free. **URL:** http://ericksontribune.com/. **Remarks:** Advertising accepted; rates available upon request. **Circ:** Non-paid ♦923070.

14956 ■ Evaluation & the Health Professions
SAGE Publications Inc.
c/o R. Barker Bausell, Founding Ed.
University of Maryland School of Nursing
Complementary Medicine Program, Office of Research
655 W Lombard St.
Baltimore, MD 21201
Publication E-mail: journals@sagepub.com
Journal providing information relating to research and practice in health settings. **Founded:** 1978. **Freq:** Quarterly. **Print Method:** Web Offset. **Trim Size:** 5 1/2 x 8 1/2. **Cols./Page:** 1. **Col. Width:** 50 nonpareils. **Col. Depth:** 100 agate lines. **Key Personnel:** James H. Derzon, Board Member; Mark R. Raymond, Board Member; Ariel Linden, Board Member; R. Barker Bausell, Editor, Founder; Carolyn F. Waltz, Editor, Founder. **ISSN:** 0163-2787 (print); **EISSN:** 1552-3918 (electronic). **Subscription Rates:** $842 Institutions combined (print & e-access); $926 Institutions current volume (print & all online content); $758 Institutions e-access; $842 Institutions backfile lease, e-access plus backfile; $1351 Institutions backfile purchase, e-access (content through 1998); $825 Institutions print only; $161 Individuals print only; $227 Institutions single print; $52 Individuals single print. **URL:** http://www.sagepub.com/journalsProdDesc.nav?prodId=Journal200787&. **Ad Rates:** BW $515; 4C $995. **Remarks:** Accepts advertising. **Circ:** Paid ‡500.

14957 ■ Evidence-Based Ophthalmology
Wolters Kluwer Health Inc.
Zuidpoolsingel 2
2400 BA Alphen aan den Rijn, Netherlands
Phone: 31 172 641-400
Peer-reviewed journal covering evidensed-based approach to eye care. **Freq:** Quarterly. **Key Personnel:** Peter J. Kertes, MD, Editor-in-Chief; Gary C. Brown, MD, Editor-in-Chief; Melissa M. Brown, MD, Editor-in-Chief. **ISSN:** 1555--9203 (print); **EISSN:** 155-5-9211 (electronic). **URL:** http://journals.lww.com/evidence-based-ophthalmology/Pages/default.aspx. **Mailing address:** PO Box 1030, 2400 BA Alphen aan den Rijn, Netherlands. **Circ:** (Not Reported).

14958 ■ Family & Community Health
Wolters Kluwer Health Inc.
Zuidpoolsingel 2
2400 BA Alphen aan den Rijn, Netherlands
Phone: 31 172 641-400
Peer-reviewed journal addressing the common goals of health care practitioners in teaching the essentials of self-care, family and community healthcare, and health promotion and maintenance. **Freq:** Quarterly. **Trim Size:** 6 7/8 x 10. **Key Personnel:** Bettina M. Beech, PhD,

Editor-in-Chief; Angeline Bushy, PhD, Board Member; Jeanette Lancaster, PhD, Board Member. **ISSN:** 0160--6379 (print); **EISSN:** 1550--5057 (electronic). **Subscription Rates:** $130 Individuals print; $142 Canada and Mexico print; $229 Individuals print - UK/ Australia; $240 Other countries print; $117 Elsewhere online; $464 Institutions print; $517 Institutions, Canada and Mexico print; $674 Institutions print - UK/ Australia; $708 Institutions, other countries print. **URL:** http://journals.lww.com/familyandcommunityhealth/Pages/default.aspx. **Mailing address:** PO Box 1030, 2400 BA Alphen aan den Rijn, Netherlands. **Ad Rates:** BW $895; 4C $1,380. **Remarks:** Accepts advertising. **Circ:** Paid 500.

14959 ■ Feminist Formations: A Publication of the National Women's Studies Association
John Hopkins University Press
2715 N Charles St.
Baltimore, MD 21218-4363
Phone: (410)516-6900
Fax: (410)516-6968
Publication E-mail: nwsaj@lsu.edu
Periodical containing feminist scholarship. **Founded:** 1988. **Freq:** 3/yr. **Key Personnel:** Dylan McCarthy Blackston, Managing Editor; Sandra K. Soto, Editor. **ISSN:** 2151-7363 (print). **Subscription Rates:** $40 Individuals print; $170 Institutions print; $45 Individuals online; $32 Members. **URL:** http://www.press.jhu.edu/journals/feminist_formations. **Formerly**: NWSA Journal. **Ad Rates:** BW $350. **Remarks:** Accepts advertising. **Circ:** 1,286.

14960 ■ Foot and Ankle Clinics
Mosby Inc.
Institute for Foot & Ankle Reconstruction at Mercy
Mercy Medical Ctr.
Baltimore, MD 21202
Journal publishing information on the diagnosis and treatment of conditions affecting the ankle and foot. **Freq:** Quarterly. **Key Personnel:** Mark S. Myerson, Editor. **ISSN:** 1083--7515 (print). **Subscription Rates:** $460 Individuals; $560 Institutions. **URL:** http://elsevier.com/journals/foot-and-ankle-clinics/1083-7515. **Remarks:** Accepts advertising. **Circ:** (Not Reported).

14961 ■ Future Reflections
National Organization of Parents of Blind Children
1800 Johnson St.
Baltimore, MD 21230
Phone: (410)659-9314
Magazine providing resources and information for parents and teachers as well as a positive philosophy about blindness. **Freq:** Quarterly. **Subscription Rates:** Free for members; $35 Canada and Mexico per year; $75 Other countries. **URL:** http://nfb.org/future-reflections. **Remarks:** Advertising not accepted. **Circ:** (Not Reported).

14962 ■ Gay Life
Gay and Lesbian Community Center of Baltimore
241 W Chase St.
Baltimore, MD 21201
Newspaper publishing news and articles of interest to the Baltimore gay community. **Freq:** Monthly. **Print Method:** Offset. **Trim Size:** 10 x 13.25. **Cols./Page:** 4. **Col. Width:** 14.25 picas. **Col. Depth:** 13.25 inches. **Key Personnel:** Craig Wiley, Executive Director. **Subscription Rates:** $50 Individuals; $100 Two years. **Formerly**: Baltimore Gay Paper. **Remarks:** Accepts advertising. **Circ:** Paid ‡3000, Free ‡10000.

14963 ■ The Gazette
Johns Hopkins University Press
2715 N Charles St.
Baltimore, MD 21218-4319
Phone: (410)516-6900
Fax: (410)516-6968
Free: 800-537-5487
Publication E-mail: gazette@jhu.edu
Tabloid containing articles on research and scholarly activities of faculty and information of general interest to faculty, students, and staff of the Johns Hopkins University. **Founded:** 1876. **Freq:** Bimonthly. **Print Method:** Offset. **Trim Size:** 11 1/2 x 16. **Cols./Page:** 4. **Col. Width:** 14 picas. **Key Personnel:** Lynna Bright; Lois Perschetz, Editor; Michael Buckley, Writer; Ann Stiller, Editor. **Subscription Rates:** Free. **URL:** http://hub.jhu.edu/gazette/about. **Formerly**: Johns Hopkins University Gazette. **Ad Rates:** BW $850. **Remarks:** Accepts advertising. **Circ:** Free ‡16000.

14964 ■ Generations
Jewish Museum of Maryland
15 Lloyd St.
Baltimore, MD 21202
Phone: (410)732-6400
Fax: (410)732-6451
Publisher's E-mail: info@jewishmuseummd.org
Magazine regarding the study and preservation of Maryland's Jewish history. **Freq:** Annual. **URL:** http://www.jewishmuseummd.org. **Remarks:** Advertising not accepted. **Circ:** (Not Reported).

14965 ■ Girls' Life
Monarch Services Inc.
4517 Harford Rd.
Baltimore, MD 21214
Phone: (410)254-9200
Fax: (410)254-0991
Free: 888-999-3222
Publisher's E-mail: letters@girlslife.com
The number one consumer magazine for girls ages 10 to 15. **Freq:** Bimonthly. **Key Personnel:** Karen Bokram, Editor, Publisher; Suzanne Long Teggler, Manager, Circulation. **ISSN:** 1078--3326 (print). **Subscription Rates:** $14.95 Individuals 1 year; $24.95 Two years; $29.95 Individuals 3 years; $14.98 Individuals online. **URL:** http://www.girlslife.com. **Ad Rates:** BW $14945; 4C $16606. **Remarks:** Accepts advertising. **Circ:** Paid **★500,000.**

14966 ■ Goucher Quarterly
Goucher College
1021 Dulaney Valley Rd.
Baltimore, MD 21204
Phone: (410)337-6000
Free: 800-GOUCHER
Publisher's E-mail: admissions@goucher.edu
College Alumni magazine. **Freq:** Quarterly. **Print Method:** Offset. **Trim Size:** 8.25 x 11. **Cols./Page:** 3 and 2. **Col. Width:** 27 and 42 nonpareils. **Col. Depth:** 133 agate lines. **USPS:** 223-920. **Alt. Formats:** PDF. **URL:** http://www.goucher.edu/goucher-quarterly. **Remarks:** Advertising not accepted. **Circ:** 18000.

14967 ■ The Greyhound
The Greyhound
4501 N Charles St.
Baltimore, MD 21210-2699
Phone: (410)617-2000
Free: 800-221-9107
Collegiate newspaper. **Freq:** Weekly (Tues.) during academic session. **Trim Size:** 11 X 17. **Cols./Page:** 5. **Col. Width:** 2 inches. **Col. Depth:** 15 inches. **Key Personnel:** Jenn Ruckel, Editor-in-Chief. **URL:** http://thegreyhound.org/site. **Remarks:** Adoption services. **Circ:** Free 3000.

14968 ■ Health Data Matrix
Lippincott Williams & Wilkins
351 W Camden St.
Baltimore, MD 21201
Phone: (410)528-4000
Freq: Bimonthly. **Key Personnel:** Lea Minkley-Sims, Editor; Jeff Rhodes, Manager, Sales, phone: (410)584-1952, fax: (410)584-8353. **ISSN:** 0745--2624 (print). **Subscription Rates:** $69.91 Individuals; $234.96 Institutions; $42.96 Individuals in-training; $179.96 Other countries; $334.96 Institutions, other countries; $67 Individuals; $203 Institutions; $157 Individuals international; $261 Institutions international; included in membership dues; $68.91 for individuals in U.S.; $217.96 for institutions in U.S.; $152.96 for individuals outside U.S. **URL:** http://www.ahdionline.org/Resources/Publications/tabid/161/Default.aspx; http://www.lww.com/product/?1936-2994. **Formerly**: Journal of the American Association for Medical Transcription. **Remarks:** Advertising accepted; rates available upon request. **Circ:** 10000, 10000.

14969 ■ Health Security
Mary Ann Liebert Inc., Publishers
c/o Jaclyn Fox, Mng. Ed.
Center for Biosecurity of the University of Pittsburgh Medical
Pier IV Bldg., Ste. 210
621 E Pratt St.
Baltimore, MD 21202
Phone: (443)573-3330
Fax: (443)573-3305
Publisher's E-mail: info@liebertpub.com
Peer-reviewed journal focusing on strategic, scientific and operational issues posed by biological weapons and bioterrorism. **Freq:** Bimonthly. **Key Personnel:** Crystal Franco, Associate Editor; Jennifer Nuzzo, Associate Editor; Gigi Kwik Gronvall, PhD, Associate Editor; Thomas V. Inglesby, MD, Editor-in-Chief; Tara O'Toole, MD, Editor, Founder; D. A. Henderson, MD, Editor-in-Chief. **ISSN:** 2326--5094 (print); **EISSN:** 2326--5108 (electronic). **Subscription Rates:** $719 Individuals print and online; $878 Other countries print and online; $648 Individuals online only. **URL:** http://www.liebertpub.com/overview/health-security/111. **Formerly**: Biosecurity and Bioterrorism: Biodefense Strategy, Practice, and Science. **Remarks:** Accepts advertising. **Circ:** (Not Reported).

14970 ■ The Hemingway Review
Johns Hopkins University Press
2715 N Charles St.
Baltimore, MD 21218-4319
Phone: (410)516-6900
Fax: (410)516-6968
Free: 800-537-5487
Publisher's E-mail: webmaster@jhupress.jhu.edu
Academic journal covering the work and life of Ernest Hemingway. **Freq:** Semiannual. **Print Method:** Photo offset. **Trim Size:** 6 x 9. **Key Personnel:** Susan F. Beegel, Editor. **ISSN:** 0276--3362 (print); **EISSN:** 1548--4815 (electronic). **URL:** http://muse.jhu.edu/journal/275; http://hemingwaysociety.org/?page_id=10. **Formerly**: Hemingway Notes. **Remarks:** Accepts advertising. **Circ:** Combined 1000, 1150.

14971 ■ Historically Speaking
Johns Hopkins University Press
2715 N Charles St.
Baltimore, MD 21218-4319
Phone: (410)516-6900
Fax: (410)516-6968
Free: 800-537-5487
Publisher's E-mail: webmaster@jhupress.jhu.edu
Journal covering all aspects of history, historiography and current affairs viewed in historical perspective. **Freq:** 5/yr. **Key Personnel:** Scott Hovey, Associate Editor. **ISSN:** 1941-4188 (print); **EISSN:** 1944-6438 (electronic). **Subscription Rates:** $140 Institutions print or electronic; $196 Institutions print + electronic. **URL:** http://muse.jhu.edu/journals/historically_speaking/. **Remarks:** Accepts advertising. **Circ:** ‡8500.

14972 ■ Holistic Nursing Practice
Lippincott Williams & Wilkins
351 W Camden St.
Baltimore, MD 21201
Phone: (410)528-4000
Peer-reviewed journal exploring emerging holistic approaches to nursing practice in clinical settings. **Freq:** Bimonthly. **Trim Size:** 7 x 10. **Cols./Page:** 2. **Col. Width:** 16 picas. **Col. Depth:** 45 picas. **Key Personnel:** Elizabeth Blunt, PhD, Board Member; Gloria F. Donnelly, PhD, Editor-in-Chief. **ISSN:** 0887-9311 (print); **EISSN:** 1550-5138 (electronic). **Subscription Rates:** $127 Individuals; $135 Canada and Mexico; $235 Other countries; $495 Institutions; $525 Institutions, Canada and Mexico; $676 Institutions, other countries; $72 U.S. in-training. **URL:** http://www.lww.com/product/?0887-9311; http://journals.lww.com/hnpjournal/pages/default.aspx. **Formerly**: Topics in Clinical Nursing. **Remarks:** Accepts advertising. **Circ:** 844, ‡844.

14973 ■ Hopkins Medicine
John Hopkins Medicine Marketing and Communications
901 S Bond St., Ste. 550
Baltimore, MD 21231
Phone: (410)955-6681
Fax: (410)955-8255
Magazine covering stories about treatment advances and medical research. **Freq:** 3/year. **Key Personnel:** Sue De Pasquale, Editor. **Subscription Rates:** $35 Individuals 3 years. **URL:** http://www.hopkinsmedicine.org/hmn/s04. **Circ:** (Not Reported).

14974 ■ House Rabbit Journal
House Rabbit Society- Maryland/DC/Northern Virginia Chapter
PO Box 50311
Baltimore, MD 21211

Circulation: ★ = AAM; △ or • = BPA; ♦ = CAC; ❑ = VAC; ⊕ = PO Statement; ‡ = Publisher's Report; Boldface figures = sworn; Light figures = estimated.

Phone: (410)889-4104
Publisher's E-mail: rabbit-center@rabbit.org
Contains information on rabbit diet, behavior, and environment. Features articles by veterinarians. **Freq:** 2 or 3 times a year. **Subscription Rates:** Included in membership. **URL:** http://rabbit.org/house-rabbit-journal-archive. **Remarks:** Advertising not accepted. **Circ:** 6000, 7000.

14975 ■ Imagine
Johns Hopkins University Press
2715 N Charles St.
Baltimore, MD 21218-4319
Phone: (410)516-6900
Fax: (410)516-6968
Free: 800-537-5487
Publisher's E-mail: webmaster@jhupress.jhu.edu
Periodical for 7th-12th graders who want to take an active role in their own education. Features student-written articles about challenging summer and extracurricular activities, expert college-planning advice, reviews of selective colleges, fascinating interviews, book reviews, puzzles, web resources, and more. **Freq:** 5/yr. **Key Personnel:** Melissa Hartman, Editor. **ISSN:** 1071-605X (print); **EISSN:** 1086-3230 (electronic). **Subscription Rates:** $40 Individuals print and online; $70 Institutions print and online; $30 Individuals print; $50 Institutions print; $50 Institutions online. **URL:** http://www.press.jhu.edu/journals/imagine/index.html. **Circ:** (Not Reported).

14976 ■ INFO Journal
International Fortean Organization
PO Box 50088
Baltimore, MD 21211
Publisher's E-mail: fortfest99@yahoo.com
Freq: 3/year. **ISSN:** 0019--0144 (print). **Subscription Rates:** Included in membership. **Remarks:** Advertising not accepted. **Circ:** (Not Reported).

14977 ■ Information Standards Quarterly
National Information Standards Organization
3600 Clipper Mill Rd., Ste. 302
Baltimore, MD 21211
Phone: (301)654-2512
Fax: (410)685-5278
Publisher's E-mail: nisohq@niso.org
Magazine covering information on communicating standards-based technology and practices in library, publishing and information technology. **Freq:** Quarterly. **Subscription Rates:** $130 Individuals /year; $165 Other countries /year; $36 Single issue. **URL:** http://www.niso.org/publications/isq/; http://www.niso.org. **Remarks:** Advertising not accepted. **Circ:** (Not Reported).

14978 ■ Ius Gentium
University of Baltimore School of Law
1401 N Charles St.
Baltimore, MD 21201
Phone: (410)837-4468
Fax: (410)837-4450
Publisher's E-mail: lawadmissions@ubalt.edu
Journal that facilitates analysis and the exchange of ideas about contemporary legal issues from a comparative perspective. **Freq:** Annual. **Key Personnel:** Mortimer Sellers, Editor. **ISSN:** 1534--6781 (print). **URL:** http://law.ubalt.edu/centers/cicl/publications/iusgentiumbookseries; http://www.springer.com/series/7888. **Remarks:** Accepts advertising. **Circ:** (Not Reported).

14979 ■ Johns Hopkins Magazine
Johns Hopkins University Press
2715 N Charles St.
Baltimore, MD 21218-4319
Phone: (410)516-6900
Fax: (410)516-6968
Free: 800-537-5487
Publication E-mail: jhmagazine@jhu.edu
Alumni magazine featuring general interest articles and medical updates. **Freq:** 5/year. **Print Method:** Offset. **Trim Size:** 8 1/4 x 10 7/8. **Cols./Page:** 3. **Col. Width:** 13 picas. **Col. Depth:** 9 3/8 inches. **Key Personnel:** Shaul Tsemach, Art Director; Dianne Macleod, Business Manager; Catherine Pierre, Editor; Dale Keiger, Editor. **Subscription Rates:** $20 Individuals; $25 Other countries; Free to qualified subscribers online. **URL:** http://magazine.jhu.edu. **Ad Rates:** BW $2250; 4C $3330. **Remarks:** Accepts advertising. **Circ:** Controlled ‡142000.

14980 ■ The Josephite Harvest
St. Joseph Society of the Sacred Heart
1130 N Calvert St.
Baltimore, MD 21202
Phone: (410)727-3386
Fax: (410)727-1006
Free: 866-346-6727
Publisher's E-mail: josephite1@aol.com
Magazine showcasing the work of the Josephite Apostolate. **Freq:** Quarterly. **Key Personnel:** Bill Murray, Contact, phone: (301)881-8180, fax: (301)881-8194. **ISSN:** 0021-7603 (print). **Subscription Rates:** $5 Individuals. **URL:** http://www.josephites.org/harvest-magazine/. **Remarks:** Advertising not accepted. **Circ:** (Not Reported).

14981 ■ Journal of Acquired Immune Deficiency Syndrome
Lippincott Williams & Wilkins
351 W Camden St.
Baltimore, MD 21201
Phone: (410)528-4000
Peer-reviewed journal covering recent research, results of clinical trials, documented case reports, and national policy issues. Contains a literature citation index. **Freq:** 15/yr. **Print Method:** Offset, Sheetfed. **Trim Size:** 8 1/4 x 11. **Cols./Page:** 2. **Key Personnel:** David D. Ho, MD, Editor-in-Chief; Paul A. Volberding, MD, Editor-in-Chief. **ISSN:** 1525--4135 (print); **EISSN:** 1077--9450 (electronic). **Subscription Rates:** $793 Individuals; $889 Canada and Mexico; $927 Other countries; $3014 Institutions; $3343 Institutions, Canada and Mexico; $3381 Institutions, other countries; $347 Individuals in-training; $330 Canada and Mexico in-training; $385 Other countries in-training. **URL:** http://journals.lww.com/jaids/pages/default.aspx; http://www.lww.com/Product/1525-4135. **Ad Rates:** BW $1650; 4C $1820. **Remarks:** Accepts advertising. **Circ:** 457.

14982 ■ The Journal of Ambulatory Care Management
Lippincott Williams & Wilkins
351 W Camden St.
Baltimore, MD 21201
Phone: (410)528-4000
Peer-reviewed journal providing applied information on the most important developments and issues in ambulatory care management. **Freq:** Quarterly. **Key Personnel:** Norbert Goldfield, MD, Editor. **ISSN:** 0148-9917 (print); **EISSN:** 1550-3267 (electronic). **Subscription Rates:** $130 Individuals print; $240 Other countries print; $499 Institutions print; $643 Institutions, other countries print; $89 Individuals in-training; $97 Other countries in-training. **URL:** http://journals.lww.com/ambulatorycaremanagement/pages/default.aspx. **Remarks:** Accepts advertising. **Circ:** ‡289.

14983 ■ Journal of Asian American Studies
Johns Hopkins University Press
2715 N Charles St.
Baltimore, MD 21218-4319
Phone: (410)516-6900
Fax: (410)516-6968
Free: 800-537-5487
Publisher's E-mail: webmaster@jhupress.jhu.edu
Scholarly journal covering Asian American studies. **Freq:** 3/year. **Key Personnel:** Pawan Dhingra, Board Member; Moon-Ho Jung, Board Member. **ISSN:** 1097--2129 (print); **EISSN:** 1096--8598 (electronic). **Subscription Rates:** $50 Individuals /year (print); $130 Institutions /year (print); $260 Institutions two years (print); $90 Individuals two years (print); $60 Individuals /year (online); $108 Individuals two years (online). **URL:** http://www.press.jhu.edu/journals/journal_of_asian_american_studies. **Ad Rates:** BW $400. **Remarks:** Accepts advertising. **Circ:** Combined 670.

14984 ■ Journal of Bioenergetics and Biomembranes
Springer Netherlands
c/o Dr. Peter L. Pedersen, Ed.
Dept. of Biological Chemistry
The Johns Hopkins University School of Medicine
725 N Wolfe St.
Baltimore, MD 21205
Journal focusing on biological membranes research. **Freq:** 6/year. **Print Method:** Offset. **Trim Size:** 6 x 9. **Cols./Page:** 1. **Col. Width:** 54 nonpareils. **Col. Depth:** 103 agate lines. **Key Personnel:** Dr. Daniel M. Raben, Editor-in-Chief. **ISSN:** 0145--479X (print); **EISSN:** 1573--6881 (electronic). **Subscription Rates:** $1441 Individuals print including free access or e-only. **URL:** http://www.springer.com/chemistry/organic+chemistry/journal/10863; http://link.springer.com/journal/10863. **Remarks:** Accepts advertising. **Circ:** (Not Reported).

14985 ■ Journal of Business & Technology Law
University of Maryland Francis King Carey School of Law
500 W Baltimore St.
Baltimore, MD 21201-1786
Phone: (410)706-7214
Fax: (410)706-4045
Publisher's E-mail: admissions@law.umaryland.edu
Journal focusing on matters at the intersection of business and technology. **Freq:** Semiannual. **Key Personnel:** Robert Walker, Editor-in-Chief. **ISSN:** 1941--5788 (print). **Subscription Rates:** $30 Individuals. **URL:** http://digitalcommons.law.umaryland.edu/jbtl. **Circ:** (Not Reported).

14986 ■ The Journal of Cardiovascular Nursing: Official Journal of the Preventive Cardiovascular Nurses Association
Lippincott Williams & Wilkins
351 W Camden St.
Baltimore, MD 21201
Phone: (410)528-4000
Peer-reviewed journal for advanced practice nurses in cardiovascular care, providing coverage of timely topics and practical information. **Freq:** 6/year. **Print Method:** Sheetfed. **Trim Size:** 7 7/8 x 10 7/8. **Key Personnel:** Barbara Riegel, Editor; Debra K. Moser, Editor. **ISSN:** 0889--4655 (print); **EISSN:** 1550--5049 (electronic). **Subscription Rates:** $136 Individuals print; $564 Institutions print; $144 Canada and Mexico print; $593 Institutions, Canada and Mexico print; $206 Other countries print; $812 Institutions, other countries print; $91 Elsewhere online. **URL:** http://journals.lww.com/jcnjournal/pages/default.aspx. **Ad Rates:** BW $945; 4C $1,455. **Remarks:** Accepts advertising. **Circ:** Paid 3424.

14987 ■ Journal of the Chinese Snuff Bottle Society
International Chinese Snuff Bottle Society
2601 N Charles St.
Baltimore, MD 21218-4514
Phone: (410)467-9400
Fax: (410)243-3451
Publisher's E-mail: icsbs.office@verizon.net
Journal featuring articles written by specialists in the field of Asian art specifically related to Chinese snuff bottles. Also including book reviews, auctions reports and news related to exhibitions and any other relevant information for collectors. **Freq:** 3/year. **Subscription Rates:** Included in membership; $20 Members /issue (back issue); $45 Nonmembers /issue (back issue). **URL:** http://www.snuffbottle.org/en/journals.aspx. **Ad Rates:** BW $1,250. **Remarks:** Accepts advertising. **Circ:** 525.

14988 ■ Journal of College Student Development
Johns Hopkins University Press
2715 N Charles St.
Baltimore, MD 21218-4319
Phone: (410)516-6900
Fax: (410)516-6968
Free: 800-537-5487
Publisher's E-mail: membership@counseling.org
Journal covering ideas for improving student services, research and development theory, professional issues, and ethics. **Founded:** 1959. **Freq:** Bimonthly. **Print Method:** Web offset. **Trim Size:** 7 x 10. **Cols./Page:** 2. **Col. Width:** 2 7/16 inches. **Key Personnel:** Debora L. Liddell, Editor. **ISSN:** 0897-5264 (print). **Subscription Rates:** $135 Individuals print; $75 Individuals online. **URL:** http://www.jcsdonline.org; http://www.press.jhu.edu/journals/journal_of_college_student_development/. **Ad Rates:** BW $335; BW $350. **Remarks:** Accepts advertising. **Circ:** Paid ‡9335, Non-paid ‡515, 501.

14989 ■ Journal of Colonialism and Colonial History
Johns Hopkins University Press
c/o Patricia W. Romero, Founding Ed.
Towson University
Baltimore, MD 21252

Publisher's E-mail: webmaster@jhupress.jhu.edu
Journal focusing on all aspects of the colonial experience, from living under imperial rules to the evolution of colonial rule. **Freq:** 3/week. **Key Personnel:** Patricia W. Romero, Editor, Founder; Clare Anderson, Editor. **ISSN:** 1532--5768 (print). **Subscription Rates:** $42 Individuals electronic; $75.60 Two years electronic. **URL:** http://www.press.jhu.edu/journals/journal_of_colonialism_and_colonial_history. **Circ:** (Not Reported).

14990 ■ Journal of Democracy
Johns Hopkins University Press
2715 N Charles St.
Baltimore, MD 21218-4319
Phone: (410)516-6900
Fax: (410)516-6968
Free: 800-537-5487
Publisher's E-mail: info@ned.org
Journal covering democratic regimes and movements around the world. **Freq:** Quarterly. **Trim Size:** 6 x 9. **Key Personnel:** Nancy Bermeo, Board Member; Yun-Han Chu, Board Member; Brent Kallmer, Managing Editor; Shaul Bakhash, Board Member; Daniel Brumberg, Board Member; Joao Carlos Espada, Board Member; Marc F. Plattner, Editor; Laurence Whitehead, Board Member; Larry Diamond, Editor. **ISSN:** 1045--5736 (print); **EISSN:** 1086--3214 (electronic). **Subscription Rates:** $45 Individuals print; $50 Individuals online; $170 Institutions print; $81 Individuals print; 2 years; $48.13 Individuals online; 2 years; $340 Institutions print; 2 years. **URL:** http://www.journalofdemocracy.org. **Ad Rates:** BW $400, full page; BW $300, half page. **Remarks:** Accepts advertising. **Circ:** 1750, 5000.

14991 ■ Journal of the Dermatology Nurses' Association
Lippincott Williams & Wilkins Society Journal Div.
351 W Camden St.
Baltimore, MD 21201-2436
Phone: (410)528-4000
Fax: (410)361-8034
Free: 800-638-3030
Publisher's E-mail: custserv@lww.com
Features state-of-the-art, peer-reviewed articles on all aspects of skin and wound care. **Freq:** Bimonthly. **Key Personnel:** Angela L. Borger, Editor-in-Chief. **ISSN:** 1945--760X (print); **EISSN:** 1945--7618 (electronic). **URL:** http://journals.lww.com/jdnaonline/Pages/default.aspx. **Ad Rates:** $2705-3715; $1130-2140. 4C $BW $. **Remarks:** Accepts advertising. **Circ:** 3138.

14992 ■ Journal of Early Christian Studies
North American Patristics Society
Johns Hopkins University
Press Journals Division
2715 N Charles St.
Baltimore, MD 21218
Free: 800-548-1784
Publisher's E-mail: info@patristics.org
Scholarly journal covering the study of Christianity. **Freq:** Quarterly. **Key Personnel:** Stephen Shoemaker, Editor. **ISSN:** 1067--6341 (print); **EISSN:** 1086--3184 (electronic). **Subscription Rates:** $50 Individuals /year (print); $180 Institutions /year (print); $360 Institutions two years (print); $90 Individuals two years (print); $65 Individuals online only; $117 Individuals two years - online only. **URL:** http://patristics.org/journal. **Ad Rates:** BW $350; BW $500, full page; BW $375, half page. **Remarks:** Accepts advertising. **Circ:** Combined 1328.

14993 ■ Journal of Early Christian Studies
Johns Hopkins University Press
2715 N Charles St.
Baltimore, MD 21218-4319
Phone: (410)516-6900
Fax: (410)516-6968
Free: 800-537-5487
Publisher's E-mail: info@patristics.org
Scholarly journal covering the study of Christianity. **Freq:** Quarterly. **Key Personnel:** Stephen Shoemaker, Editor. **ISSN:** 1067--6341 (print); **EISSN:** 1086--3184 (electronic). **Subscription Rates:** $50 Individuals /year (print); $180 Institutions /year (print); $360 Institutions two years (print); $90 Individuals two years (print); $65 Individuals online only; $117 Individuals two years - online only. **URL:** http://patristics.org/journal. **Ad Rates:** BW $350; BW $500, full page; BW $375, half page. **Remarks:** Accepts advertising. **Circ:** Combined 1328.

14994 ■ Journal of Fluorescence
Springer Netherlands
c/o Chris D. Geddes, PhD, Ed.-in-Ch.
Center for Fluorescence Spectros & Institute of Fluorescence
University of Maryland School of Medicine
Biotechnology Institute
Baltimore, MD 21201
Journal publishing peer-reviewed original articles that advance the practice of established spectroscopic technique. **Freq:** Bimonthly. **Key Personnel:** Susan L. Bane, Board Member; Amit Chattopadhyay, Editor; George Barisas, Board Member; Caroleann Aitken, Assistant; Joseph R. Lakowicz, Editor, Founder; Chris D. Geddes, PhD, Editor-in-Chief. **ISSN:** 1053-0509 (print). **Subscription Rates:** €1424 Institutions print or online; €1709 Institutions print & enchanced access. **URL:** http://link.springer.com/journal/10895. **Ad Rates:** BW $565. **Remarks:** Advertising accepted; rates available upon request. **Circ: 178.**

14995 ■ Journal of Glaucoma
Lippincott Williams & Wilkins
351 W Camden St.
Baltimore, MD 21201
Phone: (410)528-4000
Peer-reviewed journal addressing the spectrum of issues affecting definition, diagnosis, and management of the glaucomas. **Freq:** 9/year. **Print Method:** Sheetfed Offset. **Trim Size:** 8 1/4 x 11. **Key Personnel:** G.A. Cioffi, MD, Editor-in-Chief; Nina J. Chang, Publisher. **ISSN:** 1057-0829 (print); **EISSN:** 1536-481X (electronic). **Subscription Rates:** $579 Individuals; $1176 Institutions; $270 Individuals in-training; $613 Other countries individual; $1227 Institutions, other countries; $265 Other countries in-training. **URL:** http://journals.lww.com/glaucomajournal/pages/default.aspx; http://www.lww.com/Product/1057-0829. **Ad Rates:** BW $1375; 4C $1475. **Remarks:** Accepts advertising. **Circ:** 1,390.

14996 ■ The Journal of Head Trauma Rehabilitation
Lippincott Williams & Wilkins
351 W Camden St.
Baltimore, MD 21201
Phone: (410)528-4000
Peer-reviewed journal providing up-to-date information on the clinical management and rehabilitation of persons with traumatic brain injuries. **Founded:** 1985. **Freq:** Bimonthly. **Print Method:** Sheetfed. **Trim Size:** 7 3/4 x 10 3/4. **Key Personnel:** Bruce Caplan, PhD, Senior Editor; Jennifer E. Brogan, Vice President; John Corrigan, PhD, Editor-in-Chief. **ISSN:** 0885-9701 (print); **EISSN:** 1550-509X (electronic). **Subscription Rates:** $164 Individuals print; $300 Other countries print; $536 Institutions print; $776 Institutions, other countries print; $97 Individuals in-training; $179 Other countries in-training. **URL:** http://journals.lww.com/headtraumarehab/pages/default.aspx. **Ad Rates:** BW $900; 4C $1,385. **Remarks:** Accepts advertising. **Circ:** Paid 3060.

14997 ■ Journal of Health Care for the Poor and Underserved
Johns Hopkins University Press
2715 N Charles St.
Baltimore, MD 21218-4319
Phone: (410)516-6900
Fax: (410)516-6968
Free: 800-537-5487
Publisher's E-mail: webmaster@jhupress.jhu.edu
Peer-reviewed journal focusing on contemporary health care issues of medically underserved communities. **Freq:** Quarterly Latest edition: 2016, Volume 27. **Print Method:** Offset. **Trim Size:** 6 x 9. **Cols./Page:** 1. **Col. Width:** 4 3/4 inches. **Col. Depth:** 7 1/4 inches. **Key Personnel:** David Baines, Board Member; Claudia R. Baquet, Board Member; Gillian R. Barclay, Board Member; Virginia Brennan, PhD, Editor. **ISSN:** 1049--2089 (print); **EISSN:** 1548--6869 (electronic). **Subscription Rates:** $415 Institutions print; $830 Two years print; $80 Individuals print; $144 Two years print; $85 Individuals online; $153 Two years online. **URL:** http://www.press.jhu.edu/journals/journal_of_health_care_for_the_poor_and_underserved. **Ad Rates:** BW $325. **Remarks:** Accepts advertising. **Circ:** ‡768.

14998 ■ Journal of High Speed Networks
IOS Press Inc.
University of Maryland - Baltimore County
Dept. of Computer Science & Electrical Engineering
Maryland Ctr. for Telecommunications Research
1000 Hilltop Cir.
Baltimore, MD 21250
Phone: (410)455-3028
Publication E-mail: jhsn@csee.umbc.edu
Peer-reviewed journal serving as an archive for papers describing original results of lasting significance in both the theory and practice of high speed networks. **Freq:** Quarterly. **Key Personnel:** Francesco Palmieri, Editor-in-Chief; Prof. Deepinder Sidhu, Founder, Editor. **ISSN:** 0926--6801 (print); **EISSN:** 1875--8940 (electronic). **Subscription Rates:** €525 Institutions print & online; $700 Institutions print & online. **URL:** http://www.iospress.nl/journal/journal-of-high-speed-networks. **Circ:** (Not Reported).

14999 ■ Journal of the History of Childhood & Youth
Johns Hopkins University Press
2715 N Charles St.
Baltimore, MD 21218-4319
Phone: (410)516-6900
Fax: (410)516-6968
Free: 800-537-5487
Publisher's E-mail: webmaster@jhupress.jhu.edu
Peer-reviewed journal covering the development of childhood and youth cultures. **Freq:** 3/year. **Key Personnel:** Alice L. Hearst, Editor; James Marten, Editor. **ISSN:** 1939--6724 (print); **EISSN:** 1941--3599 (electronic). **Subscription Rates:** $103 Institutions print; $40 Individuals print; $206 Institutions print, two years; $72 Two years individual, print; $45 Individuals electronic only. **URL:** http://www.press.jhu.edu/journals/journal_of_the_history_of_childhood_and_youth; http://muse.jhu.edu/journal/400. **Ad Rates:** BW $325. **Remarks:** Accepts advertising. **Circ:** Combined ‡327.

15000 ■ Journal of the History of Philosophy
Johns Hopkins University Press
2715 N Charles St.
Baltimore, MD 21218-4319
Phone: (410)516-6900
Fax: (410)516-6968
Free: 800-537-5487
Publisher's E-mail: webmaster@jhupress.jhu.edu
Peer-reviewed history journal of Western philosophy (English, French, German, and Italian). **Freq:** Quarterly. **Print Method:** Offset. **Trim Size:** 6 1/4 x 10. **Cols./Page:** 1. **Col. Width:** 30 picas. **Col. Depth:** 45.5 picas. **Key Personnel:** Jack Zupko, Editor; Henry Southgate, Managing Editor; Steven Nadler, Editor. **ISSN:** 0022--5053 (print); **EISSN:** 1538--4586 (electronic). **Subscription Rates:** $63 Two years print, 2 years; $35 Individuals print; $138 Institutions print; $276 Institutions print, 2 years; $40.11 Individuals electronic access; $72.10 Individuals 2 years. **URL:** http://www.press.jhu.edu/journals/journal_of_the_history_of_philosophy. **Ad Rates:** BW $400, full page. **Remarks:** Accepts advertising. **Circ:** 805.

15001 ■ Journal of Immunotherapy
Lippincott Williams & Wilkins
351 W Camden St.
Baltimore, MD 21201
Phone: (410)528-4000
Publication E-mail: journalofimmunotherapy@gmail.com
Peer-reviewed journal featuring rapid publication of articles on immunomodulators, lymphokines, antibodies, cells, and cell products in cancer biology and therapy. **Freq:** 9/year. **Print Method:** Sheetfed Offset. **Trim Size:** 8 1/8 x 10 7/8. **Key Personnel:** David Myers, Publisher; Steven A. Rosenberg, PhD, Editor-in-Chief; Hannah Lee, Managing Editor, phone: (215)253-3551, fax: (215)220-3450. **ISSN:** 1524-9557 (print); **EISSN:** 1537-4513 (electronic). **Subscription Rates:** $865 Individuals; $3003 Institutions; $382 Individuals in-training; $989 Other countries individual; $3158 Institutions, other countries; $401 Other countries in-training. **URL:** http://journals.lww.com/immunotherapy-journal/pages/default.aspx; http://www.lww.com/Product/1524-9557. **Ad Rates:** BW $915; 4C $1320. **Remarks:** Accepts advertising. **Circ:** 379.

Circulation: ★ = AAM; △ or • = BPA; ♦ = CAC; ❑ = VAC; ⊕ = PO Statement; ‡ = Publisher's Report; Boldface figures = sworn; Light figures = estimated.

15002 ■ Journal of Information Technology Management
Association of Management/International Association of Management
c/o Dr. Al Bento, Ed.-in-Ch.
Merrick School of Business
University of Baltimore
1420 N Charles St.
Baltimore, MD 21201
Publisher's E-mail: aomgt@aom-iaom.org
Scholarly journal covering information technology in general language. **Freq:** Quarterly Annual. **Print Method:** Offset. **Trim Size:** 8 1/2 x 11. **Cols./Page:** 1. **Key Personnel:** Dr. Al Bento, Editor-in-Chief. **ISSN:** 1042--1319 (print). **Subscription Rates:** $150 Individuals U.S.; $350 Institutions U.S.; $210 Other countries; $410 Institutions, other countries. **URL:** http://jitm.ubalt.edu; http://www.aom-iaom.org/jitm.html. **Remarks:** Accepts advertising. **Circ:** (Not Reported).

15003 ■ Journal of Media Law & Ethics
University of Baltimore School of Law
1401 N Charles St.
Baltimore, MD 21201
Phone: (410)837-4468
Fax: (410)837-4450
Publisher's E-mail: lawadmissions@ubalt.edu
Peer-reviewed journal covering the understanding of media law and ethics and diversity in society. **Freq:** Quarterly. **Key Personnel:** Eric Easton, Editor. **ISSN:** 1940--9389 (print). **URL:** http://www.law.ubalt.edu/academics/publications/medialaw. **Circ:** (Not Reported).

15004 ■ Journal of Modern Greek Studies
Johns Hopkins University Press
2715 N Charles St.
Baltimore, MD 21218-4319
Phone: (410)516-6900
Fax: (410)516-6968
Free: 800-537-5487
Publisher's E-mail: webmaster@jhupress.jhu.edu
Peer-reviewed journal focusing on modern Greek studies. **Freq:** Semiannual May and October. **Print Method:** Offset. **Trim Size:** 6 x 9. **Cols./Page:** 1. **Col. Width:** 26 picas. **Col. Depth:** 7 inches. **Key Personnel:** Neni Panourgia, Editor. **ISSN:** 0738--1727 (print); **EISSN:** 1086--3265 (electronic). **Subscription Rates:** $50 Individuals print; 1 years; $90 Individuals print; 2 years; $55 Individuals online, 1 year; $138 Institutions print, 1 year; $276 Institutions print, 2 years. **URL:** http://www.press.jhu.edu/journals/journal_of_modern_greek_studies. **Ad Rates:** BW $325. **Remarks:** Accepts advertising. **Circ:** (Not Reported).

15005 ■ Journal of Nursing Care Quality
Lippincott Williams & Wilkins
351 W Camden St.
Baltimore, MD 21201
Phone: (410)528-4000
Peer-reviewed journal providing practicing nurses and those who play leadership roles in nursing care quality programs the latest on the utilization of quality principles and concepts in the practice setting. **Freq:** Quarterly. **Print Method:** Sheetfed. **Trim Size:** 6 7/8 x 10. **Cols./Page:** 2. **Col. Width:** 16 picas. **Col. Depth:** 45 picas. **Key Personnel:** Marilyn H. Oermann, PhD, Editor-in-Chief. **ISSN:** 1057--3631 (print); **EISSN:** 1550--5065 (electronic). **Subscription Rates:** $136 Individuals print; $543 Institutions print; $116 Elsewhere online; $156 Canada and Mexico print; $627 Institutions, Canada and Mexico print; $173 Individuals print - UK/ Australia; $715 Institutions print - UK/ Australia; $257 Other countries print; $747 Institutions, other countries print. **URL:** http://journals.lww.com/jncqjournal/pages/default.aspx. **Formerly**: Journal of Nursing Quality Assurance. **Mailing address:** PO Box 1030, 2400 BA Alphen aan den Rijn, Netherlands. **Ad Rates:** BW $900; 4C $1,385; BW $920; 4C $1,415. **Remarks:** Accepts advertising. **Circ:** 860, 1015.

15006 ■ Journal of Nursing Care Quality
Wolters Kluwer Health Inc.
Zuidpoolsingel 2
2400 BA Alphen aan den Rijn, Netherlands
Phone: 31 172 641-400
Peer-reviewed journal providing practicing nurses and those who play leadership roles in nursing care quality programs the latest on the utilization of quality principles and concepts in the practice setting. **Freq:** Quarterly. **Print Method:** Sheetfed. **Trim Size:** 6 7/8 x 10. **Cols./Page:** 2. **Col. Width:** 16 picas. **Col. Depth:** 45 picas. **Key Personnel:** Marilyn H. Oermann, PhD, Editor-in-Chief. **ISSN:** 1057--3631 (print); **EISSN:** 1550--5065 (electronic). **Subscription Rates:** $136 Individuals print; $543 Institutions print; $116 Elsewhere online; $156 Canada and Mexico print; $627 Institutions, Canada and Mexico print; $173 Individuals print - UK/ Australia; $715 Institutions print - UK/ Australia; $257 Other countries print; $747 Institutions, other countries print. **URL:** http://journals.lww.com/jncqjournal/pages/default.aspx. **Formerly**: Journal of Nursing Quality Assurance. **Mailing address:** PO Box 1030, 2400 BA Alphen aan den Rijn, Netherlands. **Ad Rates:** BW $900; 4C $1,385; BW $920; 4C $1,415. **Remarks:** Accepts advertising. **Circ:** 860, 1015.

15007 ■ Journal of Patient Safety
Wolters Kluwer Health Inc.
Zuidpoolsingel 2
2400 BA Alphen aan den Rijn, Netherlands
Phone: 31 172 641-400
Peer-reviewed journal focusing on presenting research advances and field applications in every area of patient safety. **Freq:** Quarterly. **Trim Size:** 8 1/2 x 11. **Key Personnel:** David Westfall Bates, MD, Editor-in-Chief. **ISSN:** 1549--8417 (print); **EISSN:** 1549--8425 (electronic). **Subscription Rates:** $290 Individuals print; $810 Institutions print; $246 Elsewhere online; $290 Canada and Mexico print; $901 Institutions, Canada and Mexico print; $305 Other countries print; $916 Institutions, other countries print. **URL:** http://journals.lww.com/journalpatientsafety/Pages/default.aspx. **Mailing address:** PO Box 1030, 2400 BA Alphen aan den Rijn, Netherlands. **Ad Rates:** BW $840; 4C $790. **Remarks:** Accepts advertising. **Circ:** 492.

15008 ■ Journal of Pediatric Hematology/ Oncology
Lippincott Williams & Wilkins
351 W Camden St.
Baltimore, MD 21201
Phone: (410)528-4000
Publication E-mail: jpho@ymail.com
Freq: 8/year 9/year. **Print Method:** Sheetfed Offset. **Trim Size:** 8 1/4 x 11. **Key Personnel:** Bruce M. Camitta, Editor-in-Chief; David Myers, Coordinator; Amy Newman, Coordinator; Barton A. Kamen, MD, Editor. **ISSN:** 1077-4114 (print); **EISSN:** 1536-3678 (electronic). **Subscription Rates:** $677 Individuals; $2167 Institutions; $237 Individuals in-training; $823 Other countries; $1997 Institutions, other countries; $256 Other countries in-training. **URL:** http://journals.lww.com/jpho-online/pages/default.aspx; http://www.lww.com/product/?1077-4114. **Ad Rates:** BW $1,405; 4C $1,525. **Remarks:** Accepts advertising. **Circ:** 277.

15009 ■ The Journal of Perinatal & Neonatal Nursing
Lippincott Williams & Wilkins
351 W Camden St.
Baltimore, MD 21201
Phone: (410)528-4000
Peer-reviewed journal offering information from top clinicians in perinatal and neonatal nursing. **Founded:** 1987. **Freq:** Quarterly. **Print Method:** Sheetfed. **Trim Size:** 7 3/4 x 10 3/4. **Key Personnel:** Diane J. Angelini, Editor-in-Chief; Susan Bakewell-Sachs, PhD, Editor. **ISSN:** 0893-2190 (print); **EISSN:** 1550-5073 (electronic). **Subscription Rates:** $129 Individuals print; $242 Other countries print; $443 Institutions print; $661 Institutions, other countries print; $86 Individuals in-training. **URL:** http://journals.lww.com/jpnnjournal/pages/default.aspx. **Ad Rates:** BW $1,220; 4C $1,300. **Remarks:** Accepts advertising. **Circ:** Paid 1171.

15010 ■ Journal of the Peripheral Nervous System: The Official Journal of the Peripheral Nerve Society and the Quantitative Sensory Testing Center
Wiley-Blackwell
c/o David R. Cornblath, Ed-in-Ch.
Johns Hopkins Hospital
Meyer 6-181a
601 N Caroline St.
Baltimore, MD 21287-7681
Phone: (410)955-2229
Fax: (410)502-6737
Publisher's E-mail: info@wiley.com
Journal on scientific and clinical aspects of the peripheral nervous system, in connection with the Peripheral Nerve Society. **Freq:** Quarterly. **Key Personnel:** David R. Cornblath, Editor-in-Chief; Amber Millen, Managing Editor. **ISSN:** 1085--9489 (print); **EISSN:** 1529--8027 (electronic). **Subscription Rates:** $675 Institutions print and online; £526 Institutions print and online; €668 Institutions print and online; $1026 Institutions, other countries print and online; $289 Individuals print and online; £235 Individuals print and online - UK, Europe (non-euro zone) and rest of the world; €350 Individuals print and online. **URL:** http://onlinelibrary.wiley.com/journal/10.1111/(ISSN)1529-8027. **Remarks:** Advertising accepted; rates available upon request. **Circ:** (Not Reported).

15011 ■ Journal of Radiology Nursing
Mosby Inc.
c/o Kathleen Gross, Ed.-in-Ch.
Greater Baltimore Medical Center
Dept. of Interventional Radiology
6701 N Charles St.
Baltimore, MD 21204
Phone: (443)849-2714
Journal publishing articles about patient care in the diagnostic and therapeutic imaging environments. **Freq:** Quarterly. **Trim Size:** 8 X 10 3/4. **Key Personnel:** Kathleen Gross, Editor-in-Chief; Maureen Hood, Board Member. **ISSN:** 1546--0843 (print). **Subscription Rates:** $102 U.S. online & print; $148 Canada online & print; $141 Other countries online & print; $87 Individuals online; $102 Students online & print; $148 Students, Canada online & print; $141 Students, other countries online & print; $87 Students online only. **URL:** http://www.radiologynursing.org; http://www.journals.elsevier.com/journal-of-radiology-nursing. **Ad Rates:** BW $1,325; 4C $1,225. **Remarks:** Accepts advertising. **Circ:** ‡2130.

15012 ■ Journal of Rehabilitation Research and Development
U.S. Department of Veterans Affairs Office of Research & Development Rehabilitation Research and Development Service
103 S Gay St., 5th Fl.
Baltimore, MD 21202
Phone: (410)962-1800
Peer-Reviewed journal containing scientific articles and clinical reports on rehabilitation research and development.Publishes original research papers from U.S and international researchers on all rehabilitation research disciplines. **Founded:** 1983. **Freq:** 10/year. **Key Personnel:** Robert L. Ruff, MD, Editor. **ISSN:** 0748-7711 (print). **Subscription Rates:** Free. **Alt. Formats:** PDF. **URL:** http://www.rehab.research.va.gov/jour/jourindx.html; http://www.research.va.gov/services/rrd.cfm. **Formerly**: Bulletin of Prosthetics Research. **Remarks:** Advertising not accepted. **Circ:** (Not Reported).

15013 ■ Journal of Spinal Disorders & Techniques
Lippincott Williams & Wilkins
351 W Camden St.
Baltimore, MD 21201
Phone: (410)528-4000
Peer-reviewed journal presenting thoroughly documented case reports and carefully selected literature review articles. **Freq:** 10/year. **Print Method:** Sheetfed Offset. **Trim Size:** 8 1/4 x 11. **Key Personnel:** Marcia Serepy, MD, Publisher; Thomas A. Zdeblick, Editor-in-Chief. **ISSN:** 1536-0652 (print); **EISSN:** 1539-2465 (electronic). **Subscription Rates:** $519 Individuals; $1188 Institutions; $252 Individuals in-training; $610 Other countries individual; $1409 Institutions, other countries; $274 Other countries in-training. **URL:** http://journals.lww.com/jspinaldisorders/pages/default.aspx; http://www.lww.com/Product/1536-0652. **Formerly**: Journal of Spinal Disorders. **Ad Rates:** BW $1470; 4C $1460. **Remarks:** Accepts advertising. **Circ:** 726.

15014 ■ Journal of Theoretical Probability
Springer Netherlands
c/o James Allen Fill, Editor-in-Chief
Johns Hopkins University
Baltimore, MD 21218-2680
Mathematics journal. **Freq:** Quarterly. **Print Method:** Offset. **Key Personnel:** Zhenqing Chen, Board Member; Uwe Einmahl, Board Member; S.G. Dani, Board Member; James Allen Fill, Editor-in-Chief; Arunava Mukherjea, Board Member. **ISSN:** 0894--9840 (print); **EISSN:**

1572--9230 (electronic). **Subscription Rates:** €1204 Institutions print & online; €1445 Institutions print & enhanced online; $1234 Institutions print & online; $1481 Institutions print & enhanced online. **URL:** http://www.springer.com/mathematics/probability/journal/10959. **Remarks:** Accepts advertising. **Circ:** Paid 350.

15015 ■ Journal of Women's History
Johns Hopkins University Press
2715 N Charles St.
Baltimore, MD 21218-4319
Phone: (410)516-6900
Fax: (410)516-6968
Free: 800-537-5487
Publication E-mail: womenshistory@uiuc.edu
Feminist journal on women's history. **Freq:** Quarterly. **Print Method:** offset. **Trim Size:** 6 x 9. **Cols./Page:** 1. **Col. Width:** 4 1/2 inches. **Col. Depth:** 8 inches. **Key Personnel:** Jean H. Quataert, Editor; Leila J. Rupp, Board Member, phone: (614)688-3092, fax: (614)292-2282. **ISSN:** 1042--7961 (print); **EISSN:** 1527--2036 (electronic). **Subscription Rates:** $50 Individuals print; $90 Two years print; $60 Individuals online; $108 Two years online; $155 Institutions print; $310 Two years print. **Online:** Project Muse. **URL:** http://muse.jhu.edu/journal/100; http://www.press.jhu.edu/journals/journal_of_womens_history. **Ad Rates:** BW $400. **Remarks:** Accepts advertising. **Circ:** (Not Reported).

15016 ■ Journal of Wound, Ostomy, and Continence Nursing
Lippincott Williams & Wilkins
351 W Camden St.
Baltimore, MD 21201
Phone: (410)528-4000
Journal for enterostomal therapy practitioners. Provides data relating to the care of persons with stomas, draining wounds, fistulas, pressure ulcers, and incontinence. Publishes text pages of originally submitted clinical studies from practitioners, educators, and researchers. **Print Method:** Offset. **Trim Size:** 8 1/8 x 10 7/8. **Cols./Page:** 2. **Col. Width:** 39 nonpareils. **Col. Depth:** 140 agate lines. **Key Personnel:** Mikel L. Gray, Editor-in-Chief; Gary Mawyer, Managing Editor. **ISSN:** 1071--5754 (print); **EISSN:** 1528--3976 (electronic). **Subscription Rates:** $118 Individuals; $184 Individuals U.K./Australia; $126 Canada and Mexico; $193 Other countries; $527 Institutions; $602 Institutions U.K./Australia; $498 Institutions, Canada and Mexico; $625 Institutions, other countries UK/Australia; $112 /year for individuals in U.S.; $481 /year for institutions in U.S.; $183 /year for individuals outside U.S.; $625 /year for institutions outside U.S. **Available online. URL:** http://journals.lww.com/jwocnonline/pages/default.aspx. **Formerly:** Journal of ET Nursing. **Ad Rates:** 4C $3060, for full page; 4C $2600, for half page; 4C $2275, for quarter page. **Remarks:** Accepts display and classified advertising. **Circ:** 6,200.

15017 ■ Kennedy Institute of Ethics Journal
Johns Hopkins University Press
2715 N Charles St.
Baltimore, MD 21218-4319
Phone: (410)516-6900
Fax: (410)516-6968
Free: 800-537-5487
Publisher's E-mail: littlem@georgetown.edu
Freq: Quarterly. **Trim Size:** 6 3/4 x 10. **Cols./Page:** 1. **Col. Width:** 4 3/4 inches. **Col. Depth:** 7 1/2 inches. **Key Personnel:** Rebecca Kukla, PhD, Editor-in-Chief; Dan W. Brock, PhD, Board Member; Lisa Sowle Cahill, PhD, Board Member; Arthur Caplan, PhD, Board Member; Alexander M. Capron, Board Member; Bernard Lo, MD, Board Member; James Childress, PhD, Board Member. **ISSN:** 1054--6863 (print); **EISSN:** 1086--3249 (electronic). **Subscription Rates:** $210 Institutions print; $420 Institutions print, 2 years. **Alt. Formats:** PDF. **URL:** http://kiej.georgetown.edu. **Ad Rates:** BW $325. **Remarks:** Accepts advertising. **Circ:** 1008.

15018 ■ Labor Herald
Labor Herald
4005 7 Mile Ln.
Baltimore, MD 21208-6116
Phone: (410)484-3832
Newspaper (tabloid) covering labor news. **Freq:** Biweekly. **Print Method:** Offset. **Trim Size:** 10 x 15. **Cols./Page:** 5. **Col. Width:** 22 nonpareils. **Col. Depth:** 210 agate lines. **Key Personnel:** Daniel Bernstein, Editor; Edward Burns, Manager, Advertising. **USPS:** 300-360. **Ad Rates:** GLR $1.20; BW $1,260; 4C $3,780; PCI $16.80. **Remarks:** Accepts advertising. **Circ:** ‡39850.

15019 ■ Lacrosse Magazine
U.S. Lacrosse
113 W University Pkwy.
Baltimore, MD 21210
Phone: (410)235-6882
Fax: (410)366-6735
Freq: Monthly. **Print Method:** Offset. **Trim Size:** 8.125 x 10.8125. **Cols./Page:** 3 and 2. **Col. Width:** 2.07 INS3.236 INS. **Col. Depth:** 9.342 INS9.342 INS. **Key Personnel:** Matt DaSilva, Editor-in-Chief. **ISSN:** 1050--5893 (print). **Subscription Rates:** $5 Members; $6 Nonmembers inclusive of postage; Included in membership. **URL:** http://www.laxmagazine.com/landing/index; http://www.uslacrosse.org/foundation/publications. **Ad Rates:** BW $4,600; 4C $1,420. **Remarks:** Advertising accepted; rates available upon request. **Circ:** Paid ‡250000.

15020 ■ Land Use Law Report
Business Publishers Inc.
PO Box 17592
Baltimore, MD 21297-1592
Fax: (800)508-2592
Free: 800-223-8720
Publisher's E-mail: custserv@bpinews.com
Journal containing information about the land use law. **Freq:** Monthly. **Key Personnel:** Amy Marchant, Managing Editor. **ISSN:** 1064-0401 (print). **Subscription Rates:** $297 Individuals online; $397 Individuals print and online. **URL:** http://www.bpinews.com/land-use-law.htm. **Circ:** (Not Reported).

15021 ■ Late Imperial China
Johns Hopkins University Press
2715 N Charles St.
Baltimore, MD 21218-4319
Phone: (410)516-6900
Fax: (410)516-6968
Free: 800-537-5487
Publisher's E-mail: webmaster@jhupress.jhu.edu
Scholarly journal covering history in China. **Freq:** Semiannual. **Trim Size:** 8 1/2 x 11. **Key Personnel:** Tobie Meyer-Fong, Editor; Janet Theiss, Editor. **ISSN:** 0884--3236 (print); **EISSN:** 1086--3257 (electronic). **Subscription Rates:** $40 Individuals /year (print); $128 Institutions /year (print); $256 Institutions two years (print); $72 Individuals two years (print); $50 Individuals /year (online); $90 Individuals two years (online). **URL:** http://www.press.jhu.edu/journals/late_imperial_china. **Ad Rates:** BW $275. **Remarks:** Accepts advertising. **Circ:** Combined 303.

15022 ■ The Law Forum
University of Baltimore School of Law
1401 N Charles St.
Baltimore, MD 21201
Phone: (410)837-4468
Fax: (410)837-4450
Publisher's E-mail: lawadmissions@ubalt.edu
College legal journal covering current law topics. **Freq:** Semiannual. **Key Personnel:** Katelyn Vu, Editor-in-Chief; Sarah Grago, Managing Editor; Molly Deere, Editor-in-Chief; Brittany King, Managing Editor. **ISSN:** 0811--5796 (print). **Subscription Rates:** Free. **URL:** http://law.ubalt.edu/academics/publications/lawforum/index.cfm. **Remarks:** Advertising not accepted. **Circ:** Controlled 8000.

15023 ■ Leviathan: A Journal of Melville Studies
Melville Society
c/o Johns Hopkins University Press
PO Box 19966
Baltimore, MD 21211-0966
Journal featuring a bounty of scholarly articles, notes, reviews, and creative writing of a critical, theoretical, cultural, or historical nature on the impressive body of work of American novelist and poet Herman Melville. **Freq:** 3/year March, June and October. **Key Personnel:** John Bryant, Advisor; Samuel Otter, Editor; Brian Yothers, Associate Editor. **ISSN:** 1525--6995 (print); **EISSN:** 1750--1849 (electronic). **Subscription Rates:** $145 Institutions print only; $30 Individuals print; $30 Members print. **URL:** http://melvillesociety.org/publications/leviathan-a-journal-of-melville-studies; http://www.press.jhu.edu/journals/leviathan. **Ad Rates:** BW $325, full page; BW $244, half page. **Remarks:** Accepts advertising. **Circ:** 500.

15024 ■ Leviathan: A Journal of Melville Studies
Johns Hopkins University Press
2715 N Charles St.
Baltimore, MD 21218-4319
Phone: (410)516-6900
Fax: (410)516-6968
Free: 800-537-5487
Journal featuring a bounty of scholarly articles, notes, reviews, and creative writing of a critical, theoretical, cultural, or historical nature on the impressive body of work of American novelist and poet Herman Melville. **Freq:** 3/year March, June and October. **Key Personnel:** John Bryant, Advisor; Samuel Otter, Editor; Brian Yothers, Associate Editor. **ISSN:** 1525--6995 (print); **EISSN:** 1750--1849 (electronic). **Subscription Rates:** $145 Institutions print only; $30 Individuals print; $30 Members print. **URL:** http://melvillesociety.org/publications/leviathan-a-journal-of-melville-studies; http://www.press.jhu.edu/journals/leviathan. **Ad Rates:** BW $325, full page; BW $244, half page. **Remarks:** Accepts advertising. **Circ:** 500.

15025 ■ Library Trends
Johns Hopkins University Press
2715 N Charles St.
Baltimore, MD 21218-4319
Phone: (410)516-6900
Fax: (410)516-6968
Free: 800-537-5487
Publisher's E-mail: webmaster@jhupress.jhu.edu
Peer-reviewed library and information science journal. **Freq:** Quarterly. **Print Method:** Letterpress and Offset. **Trim Size:** 6 x 9. **Cols./Page:** 1. **Col. Width:** 52 nonpareils. **Col. Depth:** 101 agate lines. **Key Personnel:** Boyd Rayward, Editor; Alistair Black, Editor; Cindy Ashwill, Managing Editor. **ISSN:** 0024--2594 (print); **EISSN:** 1559--0682 (electronic). **Subscription Rates:** $80 Individuals print; $144 Two years print, individual; $168 Institutions print, 1 year; $336 Institutions print, 2 years; $85 Individuals online, 1 year. **URL:** http://www.press.jhu.edu/journals/library_trends; http://muse.jhu.edu/journals/library_trends. **Ad Rates:** BW $400. **Remarks:** Accepts advertising. **Circ:** 1147.

15026 ■ Literature and Medicine
Johns Hopkins University Press
2715 N Charles St.
Baltimore, MD 21218-4319
Phone: (410)516-6900
Fax: (410)516-6968
Free: 800-537-5487
Publisher's E-mail: webmaster@jhupress.jhu.edu
Peer-reviewed journal exploring interfaces between literary and medical knowledge and understanding. **Freq:** Semiannual. **Print Method:** Offset. **Trim Size:** 6 x 9. **Cols./Page:** 1. **Col. Width:** 26 picas. **Col. Depth:** 7 inches. **Key Personnel:** Catherine Belling, Executive Editor. **ISSN:** 0278--9671 (print); **EISSN:** 1080--6571 (electronic). **Subscription Rates:** $40 Individuals print; $72 Two years print; $113 Institutions print; $226 Two years print; $45 Individuals online; $81 Two years online. **URL:** http://www.press.jhu.edu/journals/literature_and_medicine. **Ad Rates:** BW $325. **Remarks:** Accepts advertising. **Circ:** 262.

15027 ■ Maryland Bar Journal
Maryland State Bar Association
520 W Fayette St.
Baltimore, MD 21201
Phone: (410)685-7878
Fax: (410)685-1016
Free: 800-492-1964
Journal containing legal trends and informing members about updates and changes in different areas of the law. **Freq:** Bimonthly. **Key Personnel:** Patrick Tandy, Editor. **Subscription Rates:** $42 Nonmembers. **URL:** http://www.msba.org/publications/barjournal/default.aspx. **Remarks:** Accepts advertising. **Circ:** (Not Reported).

15028 ■ Maryland Historical Magazine
Maryland Historical Society
201 W Monument St.
Baltimore, MD 21201-4674
Phone: (410)685-3750

Circulation: ★ = AAM; △ or • = BPA; ♦ = CAC; ❑ = VAC; ⊕ = PO Statement; ‡ = Publisher's Report; Boldface figures = sworn; Light figures = estimated.

Magazine on Maryland history and culture. **Freq:** Quarterly. **Print Method:** Offset. **Trim Size:** 6 3/4 x 10. **Cols./Page:** 1. **Col. Width:** 5 inches. **Col. Depth:** 9 1/4 inches. **ISSN:** 0025--4528 (print). **Subscription Rates:** $50 Nonmembers print; Included in membership print; Free to qualified subscribers online. **URL:** http://www.mdhs.org/publications/maryland-historical-magazine; http://www.mdhs.org/publications. **Ad Rates:** BW $450. **Remarks:** Accepts advertising. **Circ:** ‡4500.

15029 ■ Maryland Journal of International Law
University of Maryland Francis King Carey School of Law
500 W Baltimore St.
Baltimore, MD 21201-1786
Phone: (410)706-7214
Fax: (410)706-4045
Publication E-mail: JIL @ law.umaryland.edu
Journal presenting balanced coverage on a broad range of topics related to international and comparative law. **Freq:** Annual. **Key Personnel:** Hannah He, Editor-in-Chief. **Subscription Rates:** $35 Individuals. **URL:** http://digitalcommons.law.umaryland.edu/mjil. **Circ:** (Not Reported).

15030 ■ Maryland Medicine
MedChi, Maryland State Medical Society
1211 Cathedral St.
Baltimore, MD 21201-5516
Fax: (410)547-0915
Free: 800-492-1056
Publisher's E-mail: members@medchi.org
Freq: Bimonthly Monthly. **Print Method:** Offset. **Trim Size:** 8 1/8 x 10 7/8. **Cols./Page:** 2. **Col. Width:** 42 nonpareils. **Col. Depth:** 132 agate lines. **ISSN:** 0025--4363 (print). **Subscription Rates:** $45 Individuals; $57 Other countries; $7 Single issue. **Alt. Formats:** PDF. **URL:** http://www.medchi.org; http://www.medchi.org/News-and-Publications/Maryland-Medicine-Journal. **Formerly:** Maryland Medical Journal. **Ad Rates:** BW $700; 4C $1,260. **Remarks:** Accepts advertising. **Circ:** ‡7500.

15031 ■ Maryland Poetry Review
Maryland State Poetry and Literary Society
Drawer H
Baltimore, MD 21228
Literary arts magazine. **Freq:** Annual. **Print Method:** Typeset. **Trim Size:** 7 x 11. **Key Personnel:** Rosemary Klein, Editor-in-Chief; Hugh Burgess, Assistant Editor; Dan Cuddy, Editor. **ISSN:** 0892-807X (print). **Subscription Rates:** $25 Two years; $15 Single issue. **Remarks:** Advertising not accepted. **Circ:** Paid 500.

15032 ■ Mechanisms of Ageing and Development
RELX Group P.L.C.
c/o V.A. Bohr, Ed.-in-Ch.
Laboratory of Molecular Gerontology National Institute on Aging
251 Bayview Blvd., Ste. 100
Baltimore, MD 21224
Phone: (410)558-8162
Fax: (410)558-8157
Publisher's E-mail: amsterdam@relx.com
Multidisciplinary journal concerned with underlying biological mechanisms in the process of ageing. **Founded:** 1972. **Freq:** 12/yr. **Key Personnel:** V.A. Bohr, Editor-in-Chief; T.B.L. Kirkwood, Associate Editor; E.S. Gonos, Associate Editor. **ISSN:** 0047-6374 (print). **Subscription Rates:** $1493.60 Institutions online; $314 Individuals print; $4662 Institutions print. **URL:** http://www.journals.elsevier.com/mechanisms-of-ageing-and-development. **Circ:** (Not Reported).

15033 ■ Medicine
Lippincott Williams and Wilkins
The Johns Hopkins Hospital
Division of Medical Genetics
Blalock 1007
600 N Wolfe St.
Baltimore, MD 21287-4922
Phone: (410)955-4864
Publisher's E-mail: ronna.ekhouse@wolterskluwer.com
Medical journal.Includes analytical reviews of Internal Medicine, Dermatology, Neurology, Pediatrics, and Psychiatry topics. **Founded:** 1922. **Freq:** Bimonthly 6/year. **Print Method:** Web offset. **Trim Size:** 8 1/8 x 10 7/8. **Cols./Page:** 2. **Col. Width:** 32 nonpareils. **Col. Depth:** 119 agate lines. **Key Personnel:** David B. Hellmann, MD, Editor-in-Chief, phone: (410)955-4864; Kerri Landis, Editor; Tom Pacific, Publisher. **ISSN:** 0025-7974 (print). **Subscription Rates:** $421 Individuals; $842 Two years; $1263 Individuals 3 years; $189 Individuals in-training. **URL:** http://journals.lww.com/md-journal/pages/default.aspx. **Ad Rates:** BW $880; 4C $1,700. **Remarks:** Accepts advertising. **Circ:** Paid ‡566.

15034 ■ Menckeniana: A Quarterly Review
Enoch Pratt Free Library
400 Cathedral St.
Baltimore, MD 21201-4401
Phone: (410)396-5430
Journal of the Enoch Pratt Free Library covering issues related to the author H.L. Mencken. **Freq:** Quarterly. **Key Personnel:** S.L. Harrison, Editor. **Subscription Rates:** $20 Individuals. **Alt. Formats:** PDF. **URL:** http://www.prattlibrary.org/menckeniana. **Circ:** (Not Reported).

15035 ■ The Mission Helper
Mission Helpers of the Sacred Heart
1001 W Joppa Rd.
Baltimore, MD 21204-3732
Phone: (410)823-8585
Publisher's E-mail: missionhelpercenter@missionhelpers.org
Magazine reporting on missionary activities. **Freq:** Semiannual. **Cols./Page:** 3. **Key Personnel:** Nancy Bowen, Editor; Jon Olexy, Managing Editor. **Alt. Formats:** PDF. **URL:** http://www.missionhelpers.org/?p=88. **Remarks:** Advertising not accepted. **Circ:** Controlled 8500.

15036 ■ MLN: Modern Language Notes
Johns Hopkins University Press
2715 N Charles St.
Baltimore, MD 21218-4319
Phone: (410)516-6900
Fax: (410)516-6968
Free: 800-537-5487
Publisher's E-mail: webmaster@jhupress.jhu.edu
Journal publishing critical studies in the modern languages (Italian, Hispanic, German, French) and recent work in comparative literature. **Freq:** 5/year. **Key Personnel:** Jacques Neefs, Editor; Elena Russo, Editor; Wilda Anderson, Editor. **ISSN:** 0026--7910 (print); **EISSN:** 1080--6598 (electronic). **Subscription Rates:** $230 Institutions 1 year - print; $50 Institutions 1 year - print; $460 Institutions 2 years - print; $90 Individuals 2 years - print; $60 Individuals 1 year - online; $108 Individuals 2 years - online. **URL:** http://www.press.jhu.edu/journals/modern_language_notes/index.html. **Ad Rates:** BW $400. **Remarks:** Accepts advertising. **Circ:** 727.

15037 ■ Molecular Medicine
Johns Hopkins University Press
2715 N Charles St.
Baltimore, MD 21218-4319
Phone: (410)516-6900
Fax: (410)516-6968
Free: 800-537-5487
Publisher's E-mail: webmaster@jhupress.jhu.edu
Journal covering research in molecular sciences for research scientists, molecular biologists, pharmaceutical scientists, clinical doctors, geneticists, and related professionals. **Founded:** 1994. **Freq:** Bimonthly. **Key Personnel:** Kevin J. Tracey, MD, Editor-in-Chief; Anthony Cerami, PhD, Editor-in-Chief. **ISSN:** 1076-1551 (print). **URL:** http://www.molmed.org. **Ad Rates:** BW $600; 4C $1,010. **Remarks:** Accepts advertising. **Circ:** 600.

15038 ■ The Montage
Essex Community College
7201 Rossville Blvd.
Baltimore, MD 21237-3898
Phone: (443)840-2222
Publisher's E-mail: contact@ccbcmd.edu
Collegiate magazine (tabloid). **Founded:** 1978. **Freq:** Triweekly (during the academic year). **Print Method:** Offset. **Trim Size:** 14 x 22. **Cols./Page:** 6. **Col. Width:** 2 inches. **URL:** http://www.ccbcmd.edu/services/newspapers.html. **Ad Rates:** GLR $5; BW $250; 4C $570; PCI $4.69. **Remarks:** Accepts advertising. **Circ:** ‡1000.

15039 ■ Music Monthly
Maryland Musician Publications
2807 Goodwood Rd.
Baltimore, MD 21214
Phone: (410)426-9000
Fax: (410)426-4100
Free: 800-854-4908
Publication E-mail: musicmonthly@comcast.net joe@renmediapublishing.com
Consumer magazine covering music, regionally and nationally. **Freq:** Monthly. **Print Method:** Web offset. **Trim Size:** 11 x 17. **Cols./Page:** 4. **Col. Width:** 2 1/4 inches. **Col. Depth:** 12 1/2 inches. **Key Personnel:** Kelly M. Connelly, Editor; Susan Mudd, Publisher. **Subscription Rates:** $25 Individuals. **Formerly:** Maryland Musician Magazine, Inc. **Ad Rates:** BW $800; 4C $2,500; CNU $900. **Remarks:** Accepts advertising. **Circ:** Controlled 35000.

15040 ■ Narrative Inquiry in Bioethics: A Journal of Qualitative Research
Johns Hopkins University Press
2715 N Charles St.
Baltimore, MD 21218-4319
Phone: (410)516-6900
Fax: (410)516-6968
Free: 800-537-5487
Publisher's E-mail: webmaster@jhupress.jhu.edu
Journal publishing information on bioethics. **Freq:** 3/year. **Trim Size:** 6.875 x 10. **Key Personnel:** James M. DuBois, PhD, Editor; Ana Iltis, PhD, Editor. **ISSN:** 2157--1732 (print); **EISSN:** 2157--1740 (electronic). **Subscription Rates:** $185 Institutions print; $50 Individuals print; $370 Institutions 2 years; $90 Individuals 2 years. **URL:** http://www.press.jhu.edu/journals/narrative_inquiry_in_bioethics. **Ad Rates:** BW $325. **Remarks:** Accepts advertising. **Circ:** ‡76.

15041 ■ Neurology Now: Healthy Living for Patients & their Families
Wolters Kluwer Health Inc.
Zuidpoolsingel 2
2400 BA Alphen aan den Rijn, Netherlands
Phone: 31 172 641-400
Journal featuring the latest advances in neurology research and treatment. **Freq:** Bimonthly. **Trim Size:** 8 1/8 x 10 7/8. **Key Personnel:** Orly Avitzur, Editor-in-Chief. **ISSN:** 1553--3271 (print); **EISSN:** 1553--328X (electronic). **URL:** http://journals.lww.com/neurologynow/pages/default.aspx. **Mailing address:** PO Box 1030, 2400 BA Alphen aan den Rijn, Netherlands. **Ad Rates:** BW $42,515; 4C $49,130. **Remarks:** Accepts advertising. **Circ:** 500000.

15042 ■ NeuroReport: For Rapid Communication of Neuroscience Research
Wolters Kluwer Health Inc.
Zuidpoolsingel 2
2400 BA Alphen aan den Rijn, Netherlands
Phone: 31 172 641-400
Peer-reviewed journal covering all aspects of neuroscience. **Freq:** 18/yr. **Key Personnel:** Giorgio Gabella, Board Member; Michael Jakowec, Editor; Patrick Stanton, Editor. **ISSN:** 0959--4965 (print); **EISSN:** 1473--558X (electronic). **Subscription Rates:** $1497 Individuals print; $7146 Institutions print; $1269 Individuals online; $6716 Institutions, other countries print; $1470 Other countries print; $7348 Institutions, other countries print. **URL:** http://journals.lww.com/neuroreport/Pages/aboutthejournal.aspx. **Mailing address:** PO Box 1030, 2400 BA Alphen aan den Rijn, Netherlands. **Remarks:** Accepts advertising. **Circ:** ‡171.

15043 ■ Neurosurgery Quarterly
Lippincott Williams & Wilkins
c/o Donlin M. Long, MD, Editor-in-Chief
Dept. of Neurological Surgery
The Johns Hopkins Hospital
600 N Wolfe St.
Baltimore, MD 21205
Phone: (410)955-2252
Fax: (410)955-6407
Peer-reviewed journal with worldwide developments in the diagnosis, management, and surgical treatment of neurological disorders. **Freq:** 4/yr. **Print Method:** Sheetfed Offset. **Trim Size:** 8 1/4 x 11. **Key Personnel:** Donlin M. Long, MD, Editor-in-Chief; Ali Gavenda, Publisher. **ISSN:** 1050--6438 (print); **EISSN:** 1534--4916 (electronic). **Subscription Rates:** $464 Individuals; $858 Institutions; $534 Other countries individual; $1010 Institutions, other countries; $179 Individuals in-training; $179 Other countries in-training. **URL:** http://journals.lww.com/neurosurgery-quarterly/pages/default.aspx; http://www.lww.com/Product/1050-6438. **Ad Rates:** BW

$1000; 4C $1375. **Remarks:** Accepts advertising. **Circ:** 154.

15044 ■ Nuclear Medicine Communications
Lippincott Williams & Wilkins
351 W Camden St.
Baltimore, MD 21201
Phone: (410)528-4000
Peer-reviewed journal publishing research and clinical work in all areas of nuclear medicine for an international readership. **Freq:** Monthly. **Key Personnel:** A.C. Perkins, PhD, Editor; P. Blower, Editor-in-Chief; S. Vinjamuri, MD, Editor-in-Chief; M.J. O'Doherty, Editor. **ISSN:** 0143-3636 (print); **EISSN:** 1473-5628 (electronic). **Subscription Rates:** $870 Individuals print; $876 Other countries print; $3288 Individuals print; $3412 Institutions print; $442 Individuals in-training. **URL:** http://journals.lww.com/nuclearmedicinecomm/pages/default.aspx. **Mailing address:** PO Box 1030, 2400 BA Alphen aan den Rijn, Netherlands. **Remarks:** Accepts advertising. **Circ:** ‡744.

15045 ■ Nuclear Medicine Communications
Wolters Kluwer Health Inc.
Zuidpoolsingel 2
2400 BA Alphen aan den Rijn, Netherlands
Phone: 31 172 641-400
Peer-reviewed journal publishing research and clinical work in all areas of nuclear medicine for an international readership. **Freq:** Monthly. **Key Personnel:** A.C. Perkins, PhD, Editor; P. Blower, Editor-in-Chief; S. Vinjamuri, MD, Editor-in-Chief; M.J. O'Doherty, Editor. **ISSN:** 0143-3636 (print); **EISSN:** 1473-5628 (electronic). **Subscription Rates:** $870 Individuals print; $876 Other countries print; $3288 Individuals print; $3412 Institutions print; $442 Individuals in-training. **URL:** http://journals.lww.com/nuclearmedicinecomm/pages/default.aspx. **Mailing address:** PO Box 1030, 2400 BA Alphen aan den Rijn, Netherlands. **Remarks:** Accepts advertising. **Circ:** ‡744.

15046 ■ Nursing Made Incredibly Easy!
Wolters Kluwer Health Inc.
Zuidpoolsingel 2
2400 BA Alphen aan den Rijn, Netherlands
Phone: 31 172 641-400
Peer-reviewed journal focusing on breaking down challenging clinical concepts and presenting them in more easily understood formats. **Freq:** 6/year. **Key Personnel:** Charlotte Davis, RN, Board Member. **ISSN:** 1544--5186 (print); **EISSN:** 1552--2032 (electronic). **Subscription Rates:** $54 Individuals print; $399 Institutions print; $64 Canada and Mexico print; $394 Institutions, Canada and Mexico print; $123 Other countries print; $453 Institutions print - UK/ Australia; $446 Institutions, other countries print; $42 Elsewhere online. **URL:** http://journals.lww.com/nursingmadeincrediblyeasy/Pages/default.aspx. **Mailing address:** PO Box 1030, 2400 BA Alphen aan den Rijn, Netherlands. **Remarks:** Accepts advertising. **Circ:** ‡28466.

15047 ■ Nursing2016
Wolters Kluwer Health Inc.
Zuidpoolsingel 2
2400 BA Alphen aan den Rijn, Netherlands
Phone: 31 172 641-400
Peer-reviewed journal created to provide practical, hands-on information to nurses. **Freq:** Monthly. **Key Personnel:** Elizabeth A. Ayello, Board Member. **ISSN:** 0360--4039 (print); **EISSN:** 1538--8689 (electronic). **Subscription Rates:** $29.90 Individuals print; $675.95 Institutions print; $61.95 Individuals print; $687.95 Institutions, Canada and Mexico print; $87.95 Individuals print - UK/ Australia; $729.95 Institutions print - UK/ Australia; $147.95 Other countries print; $716.95 Institutions, other countries print; $44 Elsewhere online. **URL:** http://journals.lww.com/nursing/Pages/default.aspx. **Formerly**: Nursing2014. **Mailing address:** PO Box 1030, 2400 BA Alphen aan den Rijn, Netherlands. **Circ:** 208639.

15048 ■ Obstetric Anesthesia Digest
Lippincott Williams & Wilkins
351 W Camden St.
Baltimore, MD 21201
Phone: (410)528-4000
Provides a summary of world literature in obstetric anesthesia through abstracts and commentaries, editorials, and case reports. **Founded:** 1981. **Freq:** 4/yr. **Print Method:** Web. **Trim Size:** 8 1/4 x 11. **Key Personnel:** Manuel C. Vallejo, MD; Curtis L. Baysinger, MD, Editor-in-Chief. **ISSN:** 0275-665X (print); **EISSN:** 1536-5395 (electronic). **Subscription Rates:** $344 Individuals U.S., Canada and Mexico; $357 Individuals other countries; $648 Institutions; $730 Institutions, Canada and Mexico; $743 Institutions, other countries; $162 U.S., Canada, and Mexico in-training; $175 Other countries in-training. **URL:** http://journals.lww.com/obstetricanesthesia/pages/default.aspx. **Ad Rates:** BW $1,135; 4C $1,650. **Remarks:** Accepts classified advertising. **Circ:** 336.

15049 ■ Office World News
Independent Office Products and Furniture Dealers Association
c/o Office Furniture Dealers Alliance
3601 E Joppa Rd.
Baltimore, MD 21234-3314
Phone: (410)930-8100
Fax: (410)931-8111
Freq: Bimonthly. **Remarks:** Accepts advertising. **Circ:** (Not Reported).

15050 ■ Older Americans Report
Business Publishers Inc.
PO Box 17592
Baltimore, MD 21297-1592
Fax: (800)508-2592
Free: 800-223-8720
Publisher's E-mail: custserv@bpinews.com
Journal containing information about the programs concerning the elderly people. **Freq:** Bimonthly. **Key Personnel:** Jan Mater-Cavagnaro, MA, Editor-in-Chief. **ISSN:** 0146-3640 (print). **Subscription Rates:** $449 Individuals; $349 Individuals online. **URL:** http://www.bpinews.com/spec_oar.htm. **Circ:** (Not Reported).

15051 ■ Oncology Times: The Oncology and Hematology Source
Lippincott Williams & Wilkins
351 W Camden St.
Baltimore, MD 21201
Phone: (410)528-4000
Newspaper for oncologists containing information on the latest issues in cancer care. **Freq:** 24/yr. **Trim Size:** 10 7/8 x 15. **Cols./Page:** 4. **Key Personnel:** George W. Sledge, Jr., Chairman. **ISSN:** 0276--2234 (print). **Subscription Rates:** $368.95 Individuals paperback; $512.95 Canada and Mexico paperback; $531.95 Other countries paperback; $689.95 Institutions paperback; $845.95 Institutions, Canada and Mexico paperback; $864.95 Institutions, other countries paperback. **URL:** http://journals.lww.com/oncology-times/pages/default.aspx. **Ad Rates:** BW $5,260; 4C $1,915. **Remarks:** Accepts classified advertising. **Circ:** 39918.

15052 ■ Otology & Neurotology
Lippincott Williams & Wilkins
c/o John K. Niparko, MD, Ed.-in-Ch.
Division of Otology, Neurotology & Skull Base Surgery
The Johns Hopkins Hospital
601 N Caroline St., JHOC-6223
Baltimore, MD 21287
Peer-reviewed journals covering topics related to clinical and basic science aspects of otology, neurotology, and skull base surgery. **Freq:** 9/year. **Print Method:** Sheetfed Offset. **Trim Size:** 8 1/4 x 11. **Key Personnel:** John K. Niparko, MD, Editor-in-Chief. **ISSN:** 1531--7129 (print); **EISSN:** 1537--4505 (electronic). **Subscription Rates:** $525 Individuals print. **URL:** http://journals.lww.com/otology-neurotology/Pages/default.aspx. **Formerly**: The American Journal of Otology. **Ad Rates:** BW $920; 4C $2,495. **Remarks:** Accepts advertising. **Circ:** 1267.

15053 ■ Perspectives on Language and Literacy
International Dyslexia Association
40 York Rd., 4th Fl.
Baltimore, MD 21204-5243
Phone: (410)296-0232
Fax: (410)321-5069
Publisher's E-mail: info@interdys.org
Magazine featuring practical articles for educators and other professionals dedicated to the identification and intervention of dyslexia and other reading problems. **Freq:** Quarterly. **Subscription Rates:** $15 Nonmembers single issue; Included in membership. **URL:** http://eida.org/perspectives/. **Also known as**: Perspectives. **Remarks:** Advertising not accepted. **Circ:** (Not Reported).

15054 ■ Pharmacogenetics and Genomics
Wolters Kluwer Health Inc.
Zuidpoolsingel 2
2400 BA Alphen aan den Rijn, Netherlands
Phone: 31 172 641-400
Peer-reviewed journal covering genetic variation in response to drugs and other chemicals in humans and animals. **Freq:** Monthly. **Key Personnel:** M. Schwab, Editor; M.J. Ratain, Editor. **ISSN:** 1744--6872 (print); **EISSN:** 1744--6880 (electronic). **Subscription Rates:** $628 Individuals print; $3226 Institutions print; $648 Other countries print; $3493 Institutions, other countries print; $733 Elsewhere online. **URL:** http://journals.lww.com/jpharmacogenetics/Pages/default.aspx. **Mailing address:** PO Box 1030, 2400 BA Alphen aan den Rijn, Netherlands. **Circ:** ‡214.

15055 ■ Philosophy and Literature
Johns Hopkins University Press
2715 N Charles St.
Baltimore, MD 21218-4319
Phone: (410)516-6900
Fax: (410)516-6968
Free: 800-537-5487
Publication E-mail: philandlit@bard.edu
Journal on the aesthetics of literature, theory of criticism, philosophical interpretation of literature. **Freq:** Semiannual. **Print Method:** Offset. **Trim Size:** 6 x 9. **Cols./Page:** 1. **Col. Width:** 26 picas. **Col. Depth:** 7 inches. **Key Personnel:** Patrick Henry, Editor; Denis Dutton, Editor, Founder; Garry Hagberg, Editor. **ISSN:** 0190--0013 (print); **EISSN:** 1086--329X (electronic). **Subscription Rates:** $40 Individuals print; 1 year; $72 Individuals print; 2 years; $50 Individuals online; 1 year; $90 Individuals online; 2 years; $130 Institutions print; 1 year. **URL:** http://www.press.jhu.edu/journals/philosophy_and_literature. **Ad Rates:** BW $325. **Remarks:** Accepts advertising. **Circ:** (Not Reported).

15056 ■ Philosophy, Psychiatry & Psychology
Johns Hopkins University Press
2715 N Charles St.
Baltimore, MD 21218-4319
Phone: (410)516-6900
Fax: (410)516-6968
Free: 800-537-5487
Publisher's E-mail: webmaster@jhupress.jhu.edu
Peer-reviewed scholarly journal covering overlap between philosophy, psychiatry, and psychology. **Freq:** Quarterly. **Key Personnel:** George J. Agich, Board Member; Kenneth F. Schaffner, Associate Editor; Gwen Adshead, Associate Editor; Jennifer Radden, Associate Editor; K.W.M. Fulford, Editor, Founder; John Z. Sadler, MD, Editor; Richard Gipps, Editor; Anita Avramides, Board Member; Michael A. Schwartz, Associate Editor. **ISSN:** 1071--6076 (print); **EISSN:** 108-6-3303 (electronic). **Subscription Rates:** $205 Institutions print - 1 year; $410 Institutions print - 2 years. **URL:** http://www.press.jhu.edu/journals/philosophy_psychiatry_and_psychology. **Ad Rates:** BW $275. **Remarks:** Accepts advertising. **Circ:** Paid 270.

15057 ■ Point of Care: The Journal of Near-Patient Testing & Technology
Wolters Kluwer Health Inc.
Zuidpoolsingel 2
2400 BA Alphen aan den Rijn, Netherlands
Phone: 31 172 641-400
Peer-reviewed journal focusing on the increasingly significant practice of "bedside" ancillary testing. **Freq:** Quarterly. **Trim Size:** 8 1/2 x 11. **Key Personnel:** Kent B. Lewandrowski, MD, Editor-in-Chief; James H. Nichols, PhD, Editor. **ISSN:** 1533--029X (print); **EISSN:** 1533--0303 (electronic). **Subscription Rates:** $225 Individuals print; $534 Institutions print; $231 Individuals print; $625 Institutions, Canada and Mexico print; $251 Other countries print; $645 Institutions, other countries print; $188 Elsewhere online. **URL:** http://journals.lww.com/poctjournal/Pages/default.aspx. **Mailing address:** PO Box 1030, 2400 BA Alphen aan den Rijn, Netherlands. **Ad Rates:** BW $1,100; 4C $1,215. **Remarks:** Accepts advertising. **Circ:** 298.

15058 ■ Port of Baltimore
Media Two
1014 W 36th St.
Baltimore, MD 21211
Phone: (410)828-0120

Circulation: ★ = AAM; △ or • = BPA; ♦ = CAC; ❑ = VAC; ⊕ = PO Statement; ‡ = Publisher's Report; Boldface figures = sworn; Light figures = estimated.

Fax: (410)825-1002
Publisher's E-mail: newbusiness@mediatwo.com
Maritime and shipping magazine. **Freq:** Bimonthly. **Print Method:** Web. **Trim Size:** 8 1/8 x 10 7/8. **Cols./Page:** 2 and 3. **Key Personnel:** Blaise Willig, Editor; Jonathan Witty, President. **Subscription Rates:** $10 Individuals /copy, (plus shipping and handling and tax). **URL:** http://www.pobdirectory.com. **Ad Rates:** BW $1,150; 4C $1,395. **Remarks:** Accepts advertising. **Circ:** Controlled ‡30000.

15059 ■ Portal: Libraries and the Academy
Johns Hopkins University Press
2715 N Charles St.
Baltimore, MD 21218-4319
Phone: (410)516-6900
Fax: (410)516-6968
Free: 800-537-5487
Publisher's E-mail: webmaster@jhupress.jhu.edu
Peer-reviewed scholarly journal covering academic information services for academic librarians. **Freq:** Quarterly. **Key Personnel:** Sarah M. Pritchard, Editor. **ISSN:** 1531--2542 (print); **EISSN:** 1530--7131 (electronic). **Subscription Rates:** $215 Institutions print; $55 Individuals print; $99 Two years print; $430 Institutions print - 2 years; $60 Individuals electronic; $108 Two years electronic. **URL:** http://press.jhu.edu/journals/portal_libraries_and_the_academy. **Ad Rates:** BW $325, full page; BW $244, half page; BW $406, cover 2 or 3; BW $488, 2-page spread. **Remarks:** Accepts advertising. **Circ:** Combined 187.

15060 ■ Postmodern Culture
Johns Hopkins University Press
2715 N Charles St.
Baltimore, MD 21218-4319
Phone: (410)516-6900
Fax: (410)516-6968
Free: 800-537-5487
Publisher's E-mail: webmaster@jhupress.jhu.edu
Scholarly journal covering humanities. **Freq:** 3/year. **Key Personnel:** Paula Geyh, Advisor, Board Member; Stuart Moulthrop, Advisor, Board Member; Wendy Chun, Board Member; David Herman, Board Member; James Berger, Board Member; Johanna Drucker, Board Member; Ellen McCallum, Editor; Heesok Chang, Board Member; James F. English, Advisor, Board Member; Eyal Amiran, Editor. **ISSN:** 1053--1920 (print). **Subscription Rates:** $40 Individuals /year; $70 Individuals two years. **URL:** http://www.press.jhu.edu/journals/postmodern_culture. **Remarks:** Accepts advertising. **Circ:** (Not Reported).

15061 ■ Psychiatric Genetics
Wolters Kluwer Health Inc.
Zuidpoolsingel 2
2400 BA Alphen aan den Rijn, Netherlands
Phone: 31 172 641-400
Peer-reviewed journal focusing on new areas of research, which have been opened up following the success of new technology in cloning many genes related to brain structure and function. **Freq:** 6/year. **Key Personnel:** Prof. John I. Nurnberger, Jr., Editor. **ISSN:** 0955--8829 (print); **EISSN:** 1473--5873 (electronic). **Subscription Rates:** $565 Individuals print; $1622 Institutions print; $591 Canada and Mexico print; $1680 Institutions, other countries print; $591 Other countries print. **URL:** http://journals.lww.com/psychgenetics/Pages/default.aspx. **Mailing address:** PO Box 1030, 2400 BA Alphen aan den Rijn, Netherlands. **Remarks:** Accepts advertising. **Circ:** ‡129.

15062 ■ Recreation News
Recreation News
1607 Sailaway Cir.
Baltimore, MD 21221
Phone: (410)638-6901
Fax: (410)638-6902
Newspaper focusing on recreational activities in the Mid-Atlantic area. **Founded:** Oct. 01, 1983. **Freq:** Monthly. **Print Method:** Offset. **Trim Size:** 10 3/8 x 14. **Cols./Page:** 6. **Col. Width:** 1 1/2 inches. **Col. Depth:** 14 inches. **Key Personnel:** Karl Teel, Publisher; Marvin Bond, Editor, phone: (410)944-4852. **ISSN:** 1056-9294 (print). **Subscription Rates:** $15 Individuals. **URL:** http://www.recreationnews.com. **Ad Rates:** BW $3677.52; 4C $4722.52; PCI $46. **Remarks:** Advertising accepted; rates available upon request. **Circ:** ‡106122.

15063 ■ Report on Preschool Programs
Business Publishers Inc.
PO Box 17592
Baltimore, MD 21297-1592
Fax: (800)508-2592
Free: 800-223-8720
Publisher's E-mail: custserv@bpinews.com
Journal containing information on child development programs. **Freq:** Monthly. **Key Personnel:** Chuck Dervarics, Editor. **ISSN:** 1544--9157 (print). **Subscription Rates:** $197 Individuals online. **URL:** http://www.bpinews.com/subscribe.htm. **Circ:** (Not Reported).

15064 ■ Reviews in American History
Johns Hopkins University Press
2715 N Charles St.
Baltimore, MD 21218-4319
Phone: (410)516-6900
Fax: (410)516-6968
Free: 800-537-5487
Publication E-mail: rah@mail.rochester.edu
Journal covering American economic, military, feminist, law, political, and religious history. **Freq:** Quarterly. **Print Method:** Offset. **Trim Size:** 4.75 x 7.5. **Cols./Page:** 1. **Col. Width:** 54 nonpareils. **Col. Depth:** 93 agate lines. **Key Personnel:** Denise Thompson-Slaughter, Managing Editor; Juliana Barr, Board Member; Thomas P. Slaughter, Editor. **ISSN:** 0048--7511 (print); **EISSN:** 1080--6628 (electronic). **Subscription Rates:** $45 Individuals print 1 year; $185 Institutions print 1 year; $370 Individuals print 2 years; $81 Institutions print 2 years; $55 Individuals online 1 year; $99 Individuals online 2 years. **URL:** http://www.press.jhu.edu/journals/reviews_in_american_history. **Ad Rates:** BW $425. **Remarks:** Accepts advertising. **Circ:** 1662.

15065 ■ Reviews in Medical Microbiology
Wolters Kluwer Health Inc.
Zuidpoolsingel 2
2400 BA Alphen aan den Rijn, Netherlands
Phone: 31 172 641-400
Peer-reviewed journal presenting the latest developments and techniques in medical microbiology, virology, mycology, parasitology, clinical microbiology, and hospital infection. **Freq:** Quarterly. **Key Personnel:** Phyllis Della-Latta, Editor-in-Chief, phone: (212)305-2929, fax: (212)305-8971; Curtis G. Gemmell, Editor. **ISSN:** 0954--139X (print); **EISSN:** 1473--5601 (electronic). **Subscription Rates:** $471 Individuals print; $1624 Institutions print; $461 Other countries print; $1780 Institutions, other countries print; $409 Elsewhere online. **URL:** http://journals.lww.com/revmedmicrobiol/Pages/default.aspx. **Mailing address:** PO Box 1030, 2400 BA Alphen aan den Rijn, Netherlands. **Remarks:** Accepts advertising. **Circ:** ‡88.

15066 ■ Robotica
Cambridge University Press
c/o Prof. Greg S. Chirikjian, Ed.-in-Ch.
Johns Hopkins University
Dept. of Mechanical Engineering
122 Latrobe Hall
Baltimore, MD 21218-2686
Publication E-mail: ad_sales@cambridge.org
Peer-reviewed journal on robotics studies. **Freq:** 8/year. **Key Personnel:** Prof. Greg S. Chirikjian, Editor-in-Chief. **ISSN:** 0263--5747 (print); **EISSN:** 1469--8668 (electronic). **Subscription Rates:** $1760 Institutions online only; £990 Institutions online only; $1722 Institutions online & print; £966 Institutions online & print; $393 Individuals online & print; £231 Individuals online & print; $45 Individuals article; £30 Individuals article. **URL:** http://journals.cambridge.org/action/displayJournal?jid=ROB. **Ad Rates:** BW $845. **Remarks:** Accepts advertising. **Circ:** ‡600.

15067 ■ Shakespeare Bulletin
Johns Hopkins University Press
2715 N Charles St.
Baltimore, MD 21218-4319
Phone: (410)516-6900
Fax: (410)516-6968
Free: 800-537-5487
Publisher's E-mail: webmaster@jhupress.jhu.edu
Peer-reviewed journal featuring Shakespeare and Renaissance drama. **Freq:** Quarterly. **Key Personnel:** Andrew James Hartley, Editor; Seymour Isenberg, Editor, Founder. **ISSN:** 0748--2558 (print); **EISSN:** 1931--1427 (electronic). **Subscription Rates:** $118 Institutions print; $236 Institutions print, two years; $35 Individuals print; $63 Two years individual, print; $40 Individuals online; $72 Individuals 2 years; online. **URL:** http://www.press.jhu.edu/journals/shakespeare_bulletin; http://muse.jhu.edu/journal/339. **Ad Rates:** BW $325. **Remarks:** Accepts advertising. **Circ:** Combined ‡293.

15068 ■ Shattered Wig Review
Shattered Wig Review
425 E 31st St.
Baltimore, MD 21218-3409
Phone: (410)243-6888
Literary journal covering alternative poetry, nonfiction, and visual arts. **Freq:** Semiannual. **Trim Size:** 8 1/2 x 8 1/2. **Key Personnel:** Sonny Bodkin, Editor. **Subscription Rates:** $10 Individuals; $6 Single issue. **Formerly:** The Gilded Watercress Annual. **Remarks:** Advertising not accepted. **Circ:** Combined 500.

15069 ■ Social Anarchism: A Journal of Theory and Practice
Social Anarchism
2743 Maryland Ave.
Baltimore, MD 21218
Publication E-mail: editors@socialanarchism.org
Journal featuring articles and essays focusing on anarchist theory and practice. **Freq:** Quarterly. **Key Personnel:** Howard Ehrlich, Editor. **ISSN:** 0196--4804 (print). **Subscription Rates:** $25 Individuals domestic; $40 Libraries; $50 Institutions; $32 Canada; $40 Other countries. **URL:** http://www.socialanarchism.org. **Remarks:** Advertising accepted; rates available upon request. **Circ:** (Not Reported).

15070 ■ South Central Review
Johns Hopkins University Press
2715 N Charles St.
Baltimore, MD 21218-4319
Phone: (410)516-6900
Fax: (410)516-6968
Free: 800-537-5487
Publisher's E-mail: webmaster@jhupress.jhu.edu
Interdisciplinary journal publishing a mix of scholarly articles, essays, interviews, and opinion pieces on literary criticism, film studies, philosophy and history, as well as current debates on important cultural and political topics. Official journal of the South Central Modern Language Association. **Freq:** 3/year. **Key Personnel:** Richard J. Golsan, Editor; Howard Marchitello, Associate Editor; Melanie Hawthorne, Advisor. **ISSN:** 0743--6831 (print); **EISSN:** 1549--3377 (electronic). **Subscription Rates:** $135 Institutions print; $270 Institutions print, 2 years. **URL:** http://www.press.jhu.edu/journals/south_central_review/index.html. **Ad Rates:** BW $325. **Remarks:** Accepts advertising. **Circ:** 569.

15071 ■ Techniques in Foot & Ankle Surgery
Wolters Kluwer Health Inc.
Zuidpoolsingel 2
2400 BA Alphen aan den Rijn, Netherlands
Phone: 31 172 641-400
Peer-reviewed journal covering the most innovative and successful surgical techniques for correction of foot and ankle disorders. **Freq:** Quarterly. **Trim Size:** 8 1/8 x 10 7/8. **Key Personnel:** Bruce E. Cohen, MD, Editor; W. Hodges Davis, MD, Editor; Robert B. Anderson, MD, Editor; Carroll Jones, MD, Editor; Vinod K. Panchbhavi, Editor-in-Chief. **ISSN:** 1536--0644 (print); **EISSN:** 1538--1943 (electronic). **Subscription Rates:** $250 Individuals print; $605 Institutions print; $264 Other countries print; $722 Institutions, other countries print; $211 Elsewhere online. **URL:** http://journals.lww.com/techfootankle/Pages/default.aspx. **Mailing address:** PO Box 1030, 2400 BA Alphen aan den Rijn, Netherlands. **Ad Rates:** BW $1,095; 4C $980. **Remarks:** Accepts advertising. **Circ:** 862.

15072 ■ Techniques in Neurosurgery
Lippincott Williams & Wilkins
351 W Camden St.
Baltimore, MD 21201
Phone: (410)528-4000
Provides a review of surgical procedures, anatomy, equipment, management strategies, outcomes, and developing technologies related to specific topics in neurosurgical techniques. **Freq:** 4/yr. **Print Method:** Sheetfed Offset. **Trim Size:** 8 1/4 x 11. **Key Personnel:** Christopher M. Loftus, MD, Editor-in-Chief, phone: (405)271-4912, fax: (405)271-3091; Maria McMichael, MD, Publisher; H. Hunt Batjer, MD, Editor-in-Chief,

phone: (312)908-8170, fax: (312)908-0225. **ISSN:** 1077-2855 (print); **EISSN:** 1534-5017 (electronic). **Ad Rates:** BW $870; 4C $1,130. **Remarks:** Accepts advertising. **Circ:** 909, Paid 842.

15073 ■ Techniques in Orthopaedics
Lippincott Williams & Wilkins
351 W Camden St.
Baltimore, MD 21201
Phone: (410)528-4000
Technique-oriented journal covering surgery, manipulations, and instruments being developed and applied in such areas as arthroscopy, arthroplasty, and trauma. **Freq:** Quarterly. **Print Method:** Sheetfed Offset. **Trim Size:** 8 1/4 x 11. **Cols./Page:** 2. **Col. Width:** 20 picas. **Col. Depth:** 52 picas. **Key Personnel:** Bruce D. Browner, MD, Editor-in-Chief. **ISSN:** 0885-9698 (print); **EISSN:** 2333-0600 (electronic). **USPS:** 801-263. **Subscription Rates:** $472 Individuals; $505 Canada and Mexico; $518 Other countries; $823 Institutions; $893 Institutions, Canada and Mexico; $906 Institutions, other countries; $209 U.S., Canada, and Mexico in-training; $222 Other countries in-training. **URL:** http://journals.lww.com/techortho/pages/default.aspx. **Ad Rates:** BW $1,225; 4C $1,465. **Remarks:** Accepts advertising. **Circ:** 269.

15074 ■ Techniques in Shoulder & Elbow Surgery
Lippincott Williams & Wilkins
351 W Camden St.
Baltimore, MD 21201
Phone: (410)528-4000
Peer-reviewed journal dealing with innovative and successful surgical techniques for correction of shoulder & elbow disorders. **Freq:** Quarterly. **Key Personnel:** Edward V. Craig, MD, Editor-in-Chief; David W. Altchek, MD, Board Member; Andrew Green, MD, Board Member. **ISSN:** 1523--9896 (print); **EISSN:** 1539--591X (electronic). **Subscription Rates:** $323 U.S., Canada, and Mexico print; $684 Institutions print; $337 Other countries print; $754 Institutions, other countries print; $309 Elsewhere online. **URL:** http://journals.lww.com/shoulderelbowsurgery/Pages/default.aspx. **Remarks:** Accepts advertising. **Circ:** ‡658.

15075 ■ Textual Cultures
Society for Textual Scholarship
c/o Gabrielle Dean, Treasurer
The Sheridan Libraries
Johns Hopkins University
3400 N Charles St.
Baltimore, MD 21218
Publication E-mail: textualcultures@gmail.com
Journal containing essays by scholars from numerous disciplines and focuses on issues of textual editing, redefinitions of textuality, the history of the book, material culture, and the fusion of codicology with literary, musicological, and art historical interpretation and iconography. **Freq:** Semiannual. **Key Personnel:** Dan O'Sullivan, Editor-in-Chief. **Subscription Rates:** Included in membership. **URL:** http://textualsociety.org/sts-journal-textual-cultures. **Remarks:** Advertising not accepted. **Circ:** (Not Reported).

15076 ■ Theatre Topics
Johns Hopkins University Press
2715 N Charles St.
Baltimore, MD 21218-4319
Phone: (410)516-6900
Fax: (410)516-6968
Free: 800-537-5487
Publisher's E-mail: webmaster@jhupress.jhu.edu
Peer-reviewed journal covering all aspects of theater. Published in cooperation with the Association for Theatre in Higher Education. **Freq:** Semiannual. **Key Personnel:** Kanta Kochhar-Lindgren, Editor; Harley Erdman, Board Member; Bob Kowkabany, Managing Editor; James Peck, Editor. **ISSN:** 1054--8378 (print); **EISSN:** 1086--3346 (electronic). **Subscription Rates:** $40 Individuals print; $95 Institutions print; $190 Institutions print, 2 years; $72 Individuals print, 2 years; $45 Individuals online; $81 Individuals online, 2 years. **URL:** http://www.press.jhu.edu/journals/theatre_topics; http://muse.jhu.edu/journal/200. **Ad Rates:** BW $400. **Remarks:** Accepts advertising. **Circ:** 1406.

15077 ■ Topics in Clinical Nutrition
Lippincott Williams & Wilkins
351 W Camden St.
Baltimore, MD 21201
Phone: (410)528-4000
Publisher's E-mail: orders@lww.com
Peer-reviewed journal addressing the challenges and problems of dietitians and others involved in dietary care in a health care setting. **Freq:** Quarterly. **Trim Size:** 7 x 10. **Cols./Page:** 2. **Col. Width:** 16 picas. **Col. Depth:** 45 picas. **Key Personnel:** Prof. Judith A. Gilbride, PhD, Editor; Elizabeth M. Young, MA, Associate Editor. **ISSN:** 0883-5691 (print); **EISSN:** 1550-5146 (electronic). **USPS:** 001-261. **Subscription Rates:** $123 Individuals; $129 Canada and Mexico; $238 Other countries; $503 Institutions; $528 Institutions, Canada and Mexico; $623 Institutions, other countries; $67 U.S. in-training; $152 Individuals UK/Australia. **URL:** http://journals.lww.com/topicsinclinicalnutrition/pages/default.aspx. **Remarks:** Accepts advertising. **Circ:** (Not Reported).

15078 ■ Topics in Geriatric Rehabilitation
Lippincott Williams & Wilkins
351 W Camden St.
Baltimore, MD 21201
Phone: (410)528-4000
Publisher's E-mail: orders@lww.com
Journal presenting clinical, basic, and applied research, as well as theoretical information, for the health care professional practicing in the area of geriatric rehabilitation. **Freq:** Quarterly. **Trim Size:** 7 x 10. **Cols./Page:** 2. **Col. Width:** 16 picas. **Col. Depth:** 45 picas. **Key Personnel:** Carole B. Lewis, PhD, Editor. **ISSN:** 0882-7524 (print); **EISSN:** 1550-2414 (electronic). **Subscription Rates:** $128 Individuals; $140 Canada and Mexico; $181 Other countries; $557 Institutions; $581 Institutions, Canada and Mexico; $720 Institutions, other countries; $148 Individuals UK/Australia; $589 Institutions UK/Australia; $62 U.S., Canada, and Mexico in-training; $70 Other countries in-training. **URL:** http://journals.lww.com/topicsingeriatricrehabilitation/pages/default.aspx; http://www.lww.com/product/?0882-7524. **Remarks:** Accepts advertising. **Circ:** (Not Reported).

15079 ■ Towson Times
Baltimore Sun Media Group
501 N Calvert St.
Baltimore, MD 21278
Free: 888-539-1280
Publisher's E-mail: customersatisfaction@baltsun.com
Community newspaper covering news, sports, businesses and community events. **Freq:** Weekly (Wed.). **Key Personnel:** Jim Joyner, Editor, phone: (410)332-6410. **ISSN:** 1041--0899 (print). **URL:** http://www.baltimoresun.com/news/maryland/baltimore-county/towson; http://baltimoresunmediagroup.com/media-portfolio/newspapers/the-towson-times. **Mailing address:** PO Box 1377, Baltimore, MD 21278. **Remarks:** Advertising accepted; rates available upon request. **Circ:** ‡35399.

15080 ■ Transactions of the American Philological Association
Johns Hopkins University Press
2715 N Charles St.
Baltimore, MD 21218-4319
Phone: (410)516-6900
Fax: (410)516-6968
Free: 800-537-5487
Publisher's E-mail: webmaster@jhupress.jhu.edu
Peer-reviewed journal featuring articles on classical studies. **Freq:** Semiannual. **Key Personnel:** Craig A. Gibson, Editor. **ISSN:** 0360-5949 (print); **EISSN:** 1533-0699 (electronic). **URL:** http://www.press.jhu.edu/journals/transactions_of_the_american_philological_association/. **Remarks:** Accepts advertising. **Circ:** Combined ‡3040.

15081 ■ Ultrasound Quarterly
Lippincott Williams & Wilkins
351 W Camden St.
Baltimore, MD 21201
Phone: (410)528-4000
Peer-reviewed journal with coverage of the newest, most sophisticated ultrasound techniques as well as in-depth analyses of important developments in the field. **Freq:** 4/yr. **Print Method:** Sheetfed Offset. **Trim Size:** 8 1/4 x 11. **Key Personnel:** Philip W. Ralls, MD, Editor-in-Chief; Matt Jozwiak, Publisher. **ISSN:** 0894--8771 (print); **EISSN:** 1536--0253 (electronic). **Subscription Rates:** $442 Individuals; $854 Institutions; $533 Other countries individual; $975 Institutions, other countries; $181 Individuals in-training; $195 Other countries in-training. **URL:** http://journals.lww.com/ultrasound-quarterly/pages/default.aspx. **Ad Rates:** BW $1010; 4C $1470. **Remarks:** Accepts advertising. **Circ:** 827.

15082 ■ University of Baltimore Journal of Land and Development
University of Baltimore School of Law
1401 N Charles St.
Baltimore, MD 21201
Phone: (410)837-4468
Fax: (410)837-4450
Publisher's E-mail: lawadmissions@ubalt.edu
Journal containing legal and policy analysis on issues related to land and development. **Key Personnel:** Greg Franklin, Editor-in-Chief. **URL:** http://law.ubalt.edu/academics/publications/landdevelopment. **Circ:** (Not Reported).

15083 ■ University of Maryland Law Journal of Race, Religion, Gender and Class
University of Maryland Francis King Carey School of Law
500 W Baltimore St.
Baltimore, MD 21201-1786
Phone: (410)706-7214
Fax: (410)706-4045
Publisher's E-mail: admissions@law.umaryland.edu
Journal that seeks to create a meaningful forum in which to explore the intersection between the law and its impact upon individuals and communities along the lines of race, religion, gender and class. **Freq:** Semiannual. **Key Personnel:** Eduardo S. Garcia, Editor-in-Chief; Daniel Murphy, Managing Editor. **ISSN:** 1554--4796 (print). **Subscription Rates:** $30 Individuals. **URL:** http://www.law.umaryland.edu/academics/journals/rrgc. **Circ:** (Not Reported).

15084 ■ Urbanite
Urbanite L.L.C.
2002 Clipper Park Rd., Ste. 400
Baltimore, MD 21211
Phone: (410)243-2050
Fax: (410)243-2115
Publication E-mail: mail@urbanitebaltimore.com
Magazine for the citizens of Baltimore. Encourages community involvement and celebrates Baltimore's storied past and promising future. **Freq:** Monthly. **Key Personnel:** Tracy Ward, Publisher; Jean M. Meconi, General Manager. **ISSN:** 1556--8105 (print). **Subscription Rates:** Free. **URL:** http://issuu.com/urbanitemagazine. **Remarks:** Accepts advertising. **Circ:** 154000.

15085 ■ USBE & Information Technology
Career Communications Group Inc.
729 E Pratt, Ste. 504
Baltimore, MD 21202
Phone: (410)244-7101
Magazine for black engineers, computer scientists, and professionals involved in the industry. **Freq:** Quarterly. **Print Method:** Offset. **Trim Size:** 8 1/2 x 11. **Key Personnel:** Tyrone D. Taborn, Publisher; Frank McCoy, Editor-in-Chief. **ISSN:** 1088--3444 (print). **Subscription Rates:** $26 Individuals. **URL:** http://www.blackengineer.com. **Formerly:** U.S. Black Engineer; U.S. Black Engineer & Information Technology. **Remarks:** call for rates. **Circ:** Non-paid 35000, Combined 130000.

15086 ■ Vegetarian Journal
Vegetarian Resource Group
PO Box 1463
Baltimore, MD 21203
Phone: (410)366-8343
Publisher's E-mail: vrg@vrg.org
Journal with recipes and news related to vegetarianism. **Freq:** Quarterly. **Trim Size:** 8 1/4 x 10 7/8. **Cols./Page:** 2 and 3. **Key Personnel:** Debra Wasserman, Editor. **ISSN:** 0885-7636 (print). **Subscription Rates:** $25 Members; $30 Individuals contributor; $50 Individuals supporter; $500 Individuals life; $35 Canada and Mexico; $45 Other countries. **Alt. Formats:** PDF. **URL:** http://www.vrg.org/journal. **Remarks:** Advertising not accepted. **Circ:** 24000.

15087 ■ VOLUNTAS
International Society for Third-Sector Research

Circulation: ★ = AAM; △ or • = BPA; ♦ = CAC; ❏ = VAC; ⊕ = PO Statement; ‡ = Publisher's Report; Boldface figures = sworn; Light figures = estimated.

Hampton House, No. 356
624 N Broadway
Baltimore, MD 21205-1900
Phone: (410)614-4678
Fax: (410)502-0397
Publisher's E-mail: istr@jhu.edu
Freq: 6/year. **ISSN:** 0957- 8765 (print); **EISSN:** 1573-7888 (electronic). **URL:** http://www.istr.org/?page=VOLUNTAS. **Remarks:** Advertising not accepted. **Circ:** (Not Reported).

15088 ■ VRG Vegetarian Journal
Vegetarian Resource Group
PO Box 1463
Baltimore, MD 21203
Phone: (410)366-8343
Publisher's E-mail: vrg@vrg.org
Freq: Quarterly. **ISSN:** 0885- 7636 (print). **Subscription Rates:** $25 Nonmembers; Included in membership; $35 Canada and Mexico; $45 Other countries. **Alt. Formats:** PDF. **URL:** http://www.vrg.org/journal/. **Remarks:** Advertising not accepted. **Circ:** (Not Reported).

15089 ■ WBAL-AM - 1090
3800 Hooper Ave.
Baltimore, MD 21211
Phone: (410)467-3000
Free: 800-767-9225
Email: news@wbal.com
Format: News; Talk; Sports. **Networks:** ABC; ESPN Radio. **Owner:** Hearst-Argyle Television Inc., at above address. **Founded:** 1925. **Operating Hours:** Continuous. **Key Personnel:** Lori Smyth, Promotions Dir.; Bob Cecil, Gen. Sales Mgr. **Local Programs:** *The C4 Show*, Monday Tuesday Wednesday Thursday Friday 9:00 a.m. - 1:00 p.m.; *Maryland's News Now*, Monday Tuesday Wednesday Thursday Friday 10:00 p.m. - 12:00 a.m. **Wattage:** 50,000. **Ad Rates:** Advertising accepted; rates available upon request. **URL:** http://www.wbal.com.

15090 ■ WBAL-TV - 11
3800 Hooper Ave.
Baltimore, MD 21211
Phone: (410)467-3000
Format: Commercial TV. **Networks:** NBC. **Owner:** Hearst Television Inc., 300 W 57th St., New York, NY 10019-3741, Ph: (212)887-6800, Fax: (212)887-6855. **Operating Hours:** Continuous. **ADI:** Baltimore, MD. **Ad Rates:** Advertising accepted; rates available upon request. **URL:** http://www.wbaltv.com.

15091 ■ WBFF-TV - 45
2000 W 41st St.
Baltimore, MD 21211
Phone: (410)467-4545
Email: news@foxbaltimore.com
Format: Commercial TV. **Networks:** Independent; Fox. **Owner:** Sinclair Broadcast Group Inc., 10706 Beaver Dam Rd., Hunt Valley, MD 21030, Ph: (410)568-1500, Fax: (410)568-1533. **Founded:** 1971. **Operating Hours:** Continuous. **ADI:** Baltimore, MD. **Wattage:** 400,000. **Ad Rates:** Noncommercial. **URL:** http://www.foxbaltimore.com.

15092 ■ WBJC-FM - 91.5
6776 Reisterstown Rd., Ste. 202
Baltimore, MD 21215-7893
Phone: (410)580-5800
Email: membership@wbjc.com
Format: Classical; Public Radio. **Networks:** National Public Radio (NPR). **Owner:** Baltimore City Community College, 2901 Liberty Heights Ave., Baltimore, MD 21215-7807, Ph: (410)462-8300, Free: 800-735-2258. **Founded:** 1952. **Operating Hours:** Continuous. **ADI:** Baltimore, MD. **Key Personnel:** Jonathan Palevsky, Prog. Dir.; Jim Ward, Dir. of Dev., jward@wbjc.com; Kati Harrison, Contact. **Local Programs:** *Face The Music*, Saturday 5:00 p.m. - 6:00 p.m.; *Live at the Concertgebouw*, Wednesday 11:00 p.m.; *WBJC Listener's Choice*, Friday 8:00 p.m. - 12:00 a.m.; *WBJC Operafest*, Saturday 1:00 p.m.; *Vocalise*, Saturday 8:00 p.m. - 9:00 p.m.; *Toccata*, Sunday 6:00 p.m. - 7:00 p.m.; *Past Masters*. **Wattage:** 50,000 ERP. **Ad Rates:** Noncommercial; underwriting available. Underwriting available. **URL:** http://www.wbjc.com.

15093 ■ WBMD-AM - 750
290 Hegenberger Rd.
Oakland, CA 94621
Free: 800-543-1495
Email: familyradio@familyradio.org
Format: Religious. **Networks:** Independent. **Owner:** Family Stations Inc., 290 Hegenberger Rd., Oakland, CA 94621, Free: 800-543-1495. **Founded:** 1946. **Operating Hours:** Sunrise-sunset. **ADI:** Baltimore, MD. **Wattage:** 1,000. **Ad Rates:** Advertising accepted; rates available upon request. **URL:** http://www.familyradio.org.

15094 ■ WCAO-AM - 600
711 W 40th St.
Baltimore, MD 21211
Phone: (410)366-7600
Format: Gospel; Religious. **Networks:** NBC. **Founded:** 1922. **Operating Hours:** Continuous. **ADI:** Baltimore, MD. **Key Personnel:** Lee Michaels, Prog. Dir. **Wattage:** 5,000. **Ad Rates:** Advertising accepted; rates available upon request. **URL:** http://www.heaven600.com.

15095 ■ WCBM-AM - 680
1726 Reisterstown Rd.
Baltimore, MD 21208
Phone: (410)580-6800
Fax: (410)580-6810
Free: 800-922-6680
Email: contactus@wcbm.com
Format: Talk. **Networks:** ABC. **Operating Hours:** Continuous. **Key Personnel:** Bob Pettit, Gen. Mgr., bpettit@wcbm.com; Frank Luber, Contact, drluber2002@yahoo.com; Sean Casey, Contact, sean@wcbm.com. **Local Programs:** *Les Kinsolving*, Monday Sunday 12:00 a.m. - 1:00 a.m. 10:00 p.m. - 12:00 a.m.; *Outdoorsman Radio Show*, Saturday 5:00 a.m. - 7:00 a.m.; *You Auto Know*, Saturday 8:00 a.m. - 10:00 a.m.; *Tom Moore Show*, Saturday 10:00 p.m. - 11:00 p.m.; *1-800-LAWCALL*, Monday Saturday 6:00 p.m. - 7:00 p.m. 12:00 a.m. - 1:00 a.m.; *Morning Show*, Monday Tuesday Wednesday Thursday Friday 5:00 a.m. - 9:00 a.m.; *Underwriters Corner*, Tuesday Thursday Saturday 6:00 p.m. - 7:00 p.m. 2:00 p.m. - 3:00 p.m.; *Money, Riches and Wealth*, Wednesday 6:00 p.m. - 7:00 p.m.; *The Savvy Investor*; *Review Preview*, Saturday 7:00 p.m. - 8:00 p.m.; *Radio Flea Market*, Sunday 7:00 a.m. - 8:00 a.m.; *Res-Q Health Line*, Sunday 8:00 a.m. - 9:00 a.m.; *All About Real Estate*, Sunday 12:00 p.m. - 1:00 p.m.; *21st Century Radio*, Sunday 8:00 p.m. - 10:00 p.m. **Wattage:** 50,000. **Ad Rates:** $20-120 per unit. **URL:** http://www.wcbm.com.

15096 ■ WDBB-TV - 17
2000 W 41St St.
Baltimore, MD 21211
Phone: (205)345-1117
Fax: (205)345-1173
Format: Commercial TV. **Networks:** Fox. **Owner:** Channel 17 Associates Ltd., at above address. **Founded:** 1983. **Operating Hours:** Continuous. **ADI:** Tuscaloosa, AL. **Key Personnel:** David DuBose, Gen. Mgr. **Ad Rates:** Advertising accepted; rates available upon request.

15097 ■ WEAA-FM - 88.9
1700 E Coldspring Ln.
Baltimore, MD 21251
Phone: (443)885-3564
Email: info@weaa.org
Format: Public Radio; Gospel; Jazz; News; Talk; World Beat. **Networks:** National Public Radio (NPR); AP; Corporation for Public Broadcasting; NBC; CNN Radio; Public Broadcasting Service (PBS). **Owner:** Morgan State University, 1700 E Cold Spring Ln., Baltimore, MD 21251, Ph: (443)885-3333, Fax: (443)885-8226. **Founded:** Jan. 10, 1977. **ADI:** Baltimore, MD. **Key Personnel:** Marcellus Shepard, Music Dir., Prog. Dir., marcellus.shepard@morgan.edu; Kevin F. Donohue, Contact, kdonohue@weaa.org. **Local Programs:** *In The Tradition*, Monday 8:00 p.m. - 11:00 p.m.; *Jazz After Hours*, Monday Tuesday Wednesday Thursday Friday 2:00 a.m. - 6:00 a.m.; *The Marc Steiner Show*, Monday Tuesday Wednesday Thursday Friday 10:00 a.m. - 12:00 p.m.; *Wealthy Radio*, Tuesday 7:00 p.m. - 8:00 p.m.; *Fiesta Musical*, Tuesday 8:00 p.m. - 11:30 p.m.; *Reggae, Roots & Culture*, Saturday 10:00 a.m. - 2:00 p.m.; *The Caribbean Affair*, Saturday 3:00 p.m. - 8:00 p.m.; *Real Questions*, Sunday 6:00 p.m. - 7:00 p.m.; *First Edition*, Monday Tuesday Wednesday Thursday Friday 5:00 p.m. - 7:00 p.m.; *Briefcase Radio*, Sunday 8:00 p.m. - 9:00 p.m.; *Final Call Radio Broadcast*, Sunday 11:00 p.m.; *Gospel Grace*, Sunday 5:00 a.m. - 5:00 p.m.; *Cool Vibes For Your Midday*, Monday Tuesday Wednesday Thursday Friday 12:00 p.m. - 2:00 p.m.; *The Friday Night Jazz Club*, Friday 8:00 p.m. - 12:00 a.m.; *Turning Back the Hands of Time*, Saturday 5:00 a.m. - 10:00 a.m. **Wattage:** 12,500 ERP. **Ad Rates:** Noncommercial. Underwriting available. **URL:** http://www.weaa.org.

15098 ■ WERQ-FM - 92.3
1705 Whitehead Rd.
Baltimore, MD 21207
Phone: (410)332-8200
Format: Urban Contemporary; Hip Hop; News. **Owner:** Radio One Inc., 1010 Wayne Ave., 14th Fl., Silver Spring, MD 20910, Ph: (301)306-1111, Fax: (302)636-5454. **Founded:** 1981. **Formerly:** WLPL-FM; WYST-FM. **Operating Hours:** Continuous. **ADI:** Baltimore, MD. **Key Personnel:** Howard Mazer, Gen. Mgr., hmazer@radio-one.com; Neke Howse, Dir. of Programs, neke92@aol.com. **Wattage:** 37,000. **Ad Rates:** Advertising accepted; rates available upon request. **URL:** http://92q.com.

WHFS-FM - See Annapolis, MD

15099 ■ WIYY-FM - 97.9
3800 Hooper Ave.
Baltimore, MD 21211
Phone: (410)889-0098
Fax: (410)675-7946
Free: 800-767-1098
Format: Album-Oriented Rock (AOR). **Networks:** ABC. **Owner:** Hearst Television Inc., 300 W 57th St., New York, NY 10019-3741, Ph: (212)887-6800, Fax: (212)887-6855. **Founded:** 1958. **Operating Hours:** Continuous. **ADI:** Baltimore, MD. **Key Personnel:** Hugues Jean, Contact, hjean@hearst.com; Lori Smyth, Contact, lsmyth@hearst.com; Dave Hill, Dir. of Programs, dshill@hearst.com. **Wattage:** 50,000 ERP. **Ad Rates:** Advertising accepted; rates available upon request. **URL:** http://www.98online.com.

15100 ■ WJFK-AM - 1300
1423 Clarkview Rd., Ste. 100
Baltimore, MD 21209
Format: Sports. **Simulcasts:** WJFK-FM. **Networks:** ABC; The Source. **Owner:** CBS Radio Inc., at above address. **Founded:** 1968. **Formerly:** WLIF-AM. **Operating Hours:** Continuous. **Key Personnel:** Dave Burgess, Dir. of Mktg., Promotions Dir., djburgess@cbs.com. **Wattage:** 5,000. **Ad Rates:** Noncommercial. **URL:** http://www.washington.cbslocal.com.

15101 ■ WJHU-FM
2216 N Charles St.
Baltimore, MD 21218
Email: mail@wypr.org
Format: Sports; News. **Owner:** Your Public Radio Corp., MD, Ph: (410)235-1660, Fax: (410)235-1161. **Founded:** 2002. **Operating Hours:** Continuous. **Key Personnel:** Anthony Brandon, President; Marc Steiner, Exec. VP. **Ad Rates:** Accepts Advertising. **URL:** http://www.wjhuradio.org.

15102 ■ WJZ-TV - 13
3725 Malden Ave.
Baltimore, MD 21211
Phone: (410)466-0013
Fax: (410)578-0642
Format: Commercial TV. **Networks:** CBS. **Owner:** CBS Corp., 51 W 52nd St., New York, NY 10019-6188, Ph: (212)975-4321, Fax: (212)975-4516, Free: 877-227-0787. **Operating Hours:** Continuous. **ADI:** Baltimore, MD. **Key Personnel:** Jay Newman, Gen. Mgr., VP. **Ad Rates:** Advertising accepted; rates available upon request. **URL:** http://baltimore.cbslocal.com.

15103 ■ WLIF-FM - 101.9
1423 Clarkview Rd., Ste. 100
Baltimore, MD 21209
Phone: (410)296-1019
Fax: (410)821-5482
Format: Adult Contemporary. **Networks:** Westwood One Radio. **Owner:** CBS Radio Inc., 1271 Avenue of the Americas, 44th Fl., New York, NY 10020-1401, Ph: (212)649-9600. **Founded:** 1970. **Operating Hours:** Continuous; 5% network, 95% local. **Key Personnel:** Jon Blum, Sales Mgr., jon.blum@cbsradio.com; Hal Martin, Promotions Dir., hmartin@cbs.com. **Wattage:** 13,500. **Ad Rates:** Advertising accepted; rates available upon request. **URL:** http://todays1019.cbslocal.com.

15104 ■ WMAR-TV - 2
6400 York Rd.
Baltimore, MD 21212
Phone: (410)377-2222
Format: Commercial TV. **Networks:** ABC. **Owner:** The E. W. Scripps Co., 312 Walnut St., Cincinnati, OH 45202, Ph: (513)977-3000. **Founded:** 1947. **Operating Hours:** Continuous. **ADI:** Baltimore, MD. **Key Personnel:** Bill Hooper, Gen. Mgr., VP, hooper@wmar.com. **URL:** http://www.abc2news.com.

15105 ■ WMPB-TV - 67
11767 Owings Mills Blvd.
Owings Mills, MD 21117
Phone: (410)356-5600
Free: 800-627-6788
Email: comments@mpt.org
Format: Public TV. **Simulcasts:** WMPT, WCPB, WWPB, WGPT, WFPT. **Networks:** Public Broadcasting Service (PBS); Eastern Educational Television. **Owner:** Maryland Public Television, 11767 Owings Mills Blvd., Owings Mills, MD 21117, Ph: (410)356-5600, Fax: (410)581-6579, Free: 800-223-3678. **Founded:** 1969. **Operating Hours:** Continuous. **ADI:** Baltimore, MD. **Key Personnel:** Tom Williams, Managing Dir.; Larry D. Unger, CEO, President; Martin G. Jacobs, CFO, VP; George R. Beneman, II, Sr. VP, Chief Tech. Ofc. **Local Programs:** *MotorWeek*, Sunday Saturday Wednesday 12:00 p.m. 5:00 p.m. 7:30 p.m.; *Art Works This Week*, Thursday Sunday 8:30 p.m. 12:30 p.m. **Wattage:** 1,000,000. **Ad Rates:** Noncommercial; underwriting available. **URL:** http://www.mpt.org/home.

15106 ■ WNUV-TV - 54
2000 W 41st St.
Baltimore, MD 21211
Phone: (410)467-4545
Fax: (410)467-5093
Format: Commercial TV. **Networks:** Warner Brothers Studios. **Founded:** 1982. **Operating Hours:** Continuous. **ADI:** Baltimore, MD. **Ad Rates:** Noncommercial. **URL:** http://www.cwbaltimore.com.

15107 ■ WOCT-FM - 104.3
711 W 40th St.
Baltimore, MD 21211
Phone: (410)366-7600
Format: Classic Rock. **Owner:** Capitol Broadcasting Company Inc., 2619 Western Blvd., Raleigh, NC 27606, Ph: (919)890-6000, Fax: (919)890-6095. **Formerly:** WBSB-FM; WSSF-FM. **Operating Hours:** Continuous. **ADI:** Baltimore, MD. **Key Personnel:** Ardie Gregory, Gen. Mgr.; Jay Supovitz, Gen. Sales Mgr; Terry Trouyet, Contact. **Wattage:** 29,000 ERP. **Ad Rates:** Accepts Advertising. **URL:** http://z1043.iheart.com.

15108 ■ WOLB-AM - 1010
1705 Whitehead Rd.
Baltimore, MD 21207
Phone: (410)332-8200
Format: Talk. **Simulcasts:** CNN at night and on weekends. **Networks:** CNN Radio. **Owner:** Radio One Inc., 1010 Wayne Ave., 14th Fl., Silver Spring, MD 20910, Ph: (301)306-1111, Fax: (302)636-5454. **Founded:** 1981. **Formerly:** WSID-AM; WYST-AM; WERQ-AM. **Operating Hours:** Continuous. **ADI:** Baltimore, MD. **Key Personnel:** Dave Willner, Sales Mgr., dwillner@radio-one.com; Howard Mazer, Gen. Mgr., hmazer@radio-one.com. **Wattage:** 1,000. **Ad Rates:** Advertising accepted; rates available upon request. **URL:** http://wolbbaltimore.newsone.com.

15109 ■ WPOC-FM - 93.1
711 W 40th St., Ste. 350
Baltimore, MD 21211
Phone: (410)366-7600
Format: Country. **Owner:** iHeartMedia Inc., 200 E Basse Rd., San Antonio, TX 78209, Ph: (210)832-3314. **Founded:** 1974. **Operating Hours:** Continuous. **ADI:** Baltimore, MD. **Key Personnel:** Tommy Chuck, Prog. Dir.; Meg Stevens, Prog. Dir., megstevens@clearchannel.com; Kevin Friedman, Sales Mgr., kevinfriedman@clearchannel.com. **Wattage:** 16,000. **Ad Rates:** Advertising accepted; rates available upon request. **URL:** http://www.wpoc.com.

15110 ■ WQSR-FM - 102.7
711 W 40th St.
Baltimore, MD 21211
Phone: (410)366-7600
Format: Oldies; Adult Contemporary. **Networks:** Independent. **Founded:** 1963. **Operating Hours:** Continuous. **ADI:** Baltimore, MD. **Wattage:** 50,000. **Ad Rates:** Advertising accepted; rates available upon request. **URL:** http://www.1027jackfm.com.

15111 ■ WRXS-FM - 106.9
2216 N Charles St.
Baltimore, MD 21218
Phone: (410)352-0001
Fax: (410)352-0005
Free: 877-797-1069
Format: Top 40. **Key Personnel:** Ron Gillenardo, President; Crystal Layton, VP. **Ad Rates:** Advertising accepted; rates available upon request.

15112 ■ WSMJ-FM - 104.3
711 W 40th St., Ste. 350
Baltimore, MD 21211
Phone: (410)366-7600
Fax: (410)235-3899
Format: Jazz. **Owner:** Citadel Broadcasting Corp., 7201 W Lake Mead Blvd., Ste. 400, Las Vegas, NV 89128-8366, Ph: (702)804-5200, Fax: (702)804-8250. **Key Personnel:** Lori Lewis, Dir. of Programs, llewis@smoothjazz1043.com; Angela Belton, Promotions Dir., angelabelton@clearchannel.com. **Wattage:** 8,000. **URL:** http://www.smoothjazz1043.com/amazon/buyme.php?asin=B000HT3Q3M.

15113 ■ WUTB-TV - 24
2000 W 41st St.
Baltimore, MD 21211
Phone: (410)358-2400
Fax: (410)764-7232
Format: Commercial TV. **Networks:** Home Shopping Network. **Formerly:** WHSW-TV. **Operating Hours:** Continuous. **ADI:** Baltimore, MD. **Key Personnel:** Brock Abernathy, Contact. **Ad Rates:** $25-75 for 30 seconds. **URL:** http://www.my24wutb.com/.

15114 ■ WWIN-AM - 1400
1705 Whitehead Rd.
Baltimore, MD 21207
Phone: (410)907-0320
Format: Gospel; Religious. **Networks:** Unistar. **Owner:** Radio One Inc., 1010 Wayne Ave., 14th Fl., Silver Spring, MD 20910, Ph: (301)306-1111, Fax: (302)636-5454. **Founded:** 1951. **Operating Hours:** Continuous. **ADI:** Baltimore, MD. **Key Personnel:** Howard Mazer, Gen. Mgr., hmazer@radio-one.com; Al Payne, Operations Mgr., apayne@radio-one.com; Dave Willner, Sales Mgr., dwillner@radio-one.com. **Wattage:** 3,000. **Ad Rates:** Advertising accepted; rates available upon request. **URL:** http://www.mybaltimorespirit.com.

15115 ■ WWIN-FM - 95.9
1705 White Head Rd.
Baltimore, MD 21207
Phone: (410)332-8200
Fax: (410)547-8783
Email: inquiry@radio-one.com
Format: Urban Contemporary; Adult Contemporary. **Networks:** Unistar. **Owner:** Radio One of Maryland Inc., 500 Princess Garden Pky., 7th Fl., Lanham, MD 20706, Ph: (301)306-1111. **Founded:** 1964. **Formerly:** WHTE-FM. **Operating Hours:** Continuous. **ADI:** Baltimore, MD. **Key Personnel:** Howard mazer, Gen. Mgr. **Wattage:** 3,000. **Ad Rates:** Noncommercial. **URL:** http://www.radio-one.com.

15116 ■ WWMX-FM - 106.5
1423 Clarkview Rd., Ste. 100
Baltimore, MD 21209
Phone: (410)825-1065
Format: Adult Contemporary. **Owner:** CBS Radio Inc., 40 W 57th St., New York, NY 10019, Ph: (212)846-3939, Fax: (212)315-2162. **Operating Hours:** Continuous. **Key Personnel:** Dave Labrozzi, VP, dave.labrozzi@cbsradio.com; Dave Burgess, Dir. of Mktg., Promotions Dir., djburgess@cbs.com; Tracy Brandys, Dir. of Sales, tracy.brandys@cbsradio.com. **Wattage:** 8,300. **Ad Rates:** $350-500 for 60 seconds. Co-owned stations WQSR; WLIF; WXYV; WJFK-AM. **URL:** http://mix1065fm.cbslocal.com.

15117 ■ WYPR-FM - 88.1
2216 N Charles St.
Baltimore, MD 21218
Phone: (410)235-1660
Fax: (410)235-1161
Email: frontdesk@wypr.org
Format: Public Radio. **Networks:** ABC. **Key Personnel:** Brian Crompwell, Bus. Mgr., bcrompwell@wypr.org; Andy Bienstock, Prog. Dir., VP, bienstock@wypr.org. **Wattage:** 15,000. **Ad Rates:** Accepts Advertising. **URL:** http://www.wypr.org.

15118 ■ WZFT-FM - 104.3
711 W 40th St.
Baltimore, MD 21211
Phone: (410)481-1043
Format: Top 40. **URL:** http://www.z1043.com.

BEL AIR

Harford Co. Harford Co. 23 m NE of Baltimore. Shoe factory. Horse breeding. Dairy.

15119 ■ Aegis: Your best source for Harford County news since 1856
Homestead Publishing Company Inc.
10 Hays St.
Bel Air, MD 21014
Phone: (410)838-4400
Free: 888-879-1710
Publication E-mail: news@theaegis.com
Community newspaper group. **Freq:** Semiweekly. **Print Method:** Offset. **Cols./Page:** 6. **Col. Width:** 26 nonpareils. **Col. Depth:** 294 agate lines. **Subscription Rates:** $66.48 Individuals home delivery in Harford/Cecil Counties; $48 Individuals online. **URL:** http://www.baltimoresun.com/news/maryland/harford/aegis. **Mailing address:** PO Box 189, Bel Air, MD 21014. **Ad Rates:** BW $3,700; 4C $2,281; SAU $15.52; PCI $15.52. **Remarks:** Accepts advertising. **Circ:** (Not Reported).

15120 ■ WHFC-FM - 91.1
401 Thomas Run Rd.
Bel Air, MD 21015
Phone: (443)412-2151
Free: 866-971-9432
Email: whfc@harford.edu
Format: Eclectic. **Owner:** Harford Community College, 401 Thomas Run Rd., Bel Air, MD 21015, Ph: (443)412-2000. **Founded:** 1972. **Operating Hours:** 7 a.m.-2 a.m. **Key Personnel:** Gary Helton, Station Mgr., ghelton@harford.edu. **Wattage:** 1,150. **Ad Rates:** $2.50-5.00 for 30 seconds. Harford Cable Network. **URL:** http://www.harford.edu.

BELTSVILLE

15121 ■ Knight Letter
Lewis Carroll Society of North America
11935 Beltsville Dr.
Beltsville, MD 20705
Freq: Semiannual. **Key Personnel:** Mahendra Singh, Editor-in-Chief. **ISSN:** 0193--886X (print). **Subscription Rates:** Included in membership. **URL:** http://www.lewiscarroll.org/publications/knightletter. **Remarks:** Advertising not accepted. **Circ:** (Not Reported).

BERLIN

15122 ■ Maryland Coast Dispatch
Maryland Coast Dispatch
PO Box 467
Berlin, MD 21811
Phone: (410)641-4561
Fax: (410)641-0966
Tabloid. **Freq:** Weekly. **Trim Size:** 10 x 13 1/2. **Cols./Page:** 4. **Col. Width:** 2 3/4 inches. **Col. Depth:** 13 1/2in INS. **Key Personnel:** J. Steven Green, Editor, Publisher; Patricia Lohmeyer, Office Manager. **Subscription Rates:** $35 Individuals 6 months; $54 Individuals; $90 Two years. **URL:** http://mdcoastdispatch.com. **Remarks:** Accepts advertising. **Circ:** Paid ‡25000.

15123 ■ WOCQ-FM - 103.9
20200 Dupont Blvd.
Georgetown, DE 19947
Phone: (302)856-2567
Fax: (302)856-7633
Format: Hip Hop; Blues. **Owner:** Great Scott Broadcasting, at above address, VA, Ph: (610)326-4000. **URL:** http://www.greatscottbroadcasting.com.

Circulation: ★ = AAM; △ or • = BPA; ♦ = CAC; ❑ = VAC; ⊕ = PO Statement; ‡ = Publisher's Report; Boldface figures = sworn; Light figures = estimated.

BETHESDA

Montgomery Co. (WC). Adjoins Washington, DC, on the East. Residential. Research and Development, Science and Medical center.

15124 ■ AABB News
American Association of Blood Banks
8101 Glenbrook Rd.
Bethesda, MD 20814-2749
Phone: (301)907-6977
Fax: (301)907-6895
Publisher's E-mail: aabb@aabb.org
Magazine covering information for blood banks, including calendar of events, employment listings, and government affairs update. **Freq:** Monthly. **ISSN:** 8756--6095 (print). **Subscription Rates:** Included in membership. **URL:** http://www.aabb.org/programs/publications/news/Pages/default.aspx. **Remarks:** Advertising accepted; rates available upon request. **Circ:** (Not Reported).

15125 ■ Addiction Biology
Wiley-Blackwell
c/o Dena Stringer, Editorial Secretary
NIAAA
10 Center Dr., 10CRC/1-5330
Bethesda, MD 20892-1108
Publication E-mail: addiction.biology@mail.nih.gov
Journal focusing on the action of drugs, of abuse and addictive processes. **Freq:** Quarterly. **Key Personnel:** Rainer Spanagel, PhD, Editor-in-Chief; Bill Carlezon, Editor; Stephen C. Heinrichs, Editor; Roberto Ciccocioppo, Editor; Markus Heilig, Editor; Christine Roggenkamp, Secretary; Dena Stringer, Secretary; Johan Franck, Editor; Rainer Spanagel, Editor-in-Chief. **ISSN:** 1355-6215 (print); **EISSN:** 1369-1600 (electronic). **Subscription Rates:** $1309 Institutions online only (The Americas); £793 Institutions online only (UK); €1006 Institutions online only (Europe); $1552 Institutions online only (rest of the world); £1234 Institutions online only; £748 Institutions online only; €949 Institutions online only; $1464 Institutions, other countries online only. **URL:** http://onlinelibrary.wiley.com/journal/10.1111/(ISSN)1369-1600. **Circ:** (Not Reported).

15126 ■ AFP Exchange: Turning Knowledge Into Performance
Association for Financial Professionals
4520 E West Hwy., Ste. 750
Bethesda, MD 20814
Phone: (301)907-2862
Fax: (301)907-2864
Trade magazine on treasury management with emphasis on the corporate point of view. **Freq:** Bimonthly. **Print Method:** Offset. **Trim Size:** 8 1/2 x 11. **Cols./Page:** 4. **Key Personnel:** Michael Connolly, Chairman. **ISSN:** 0731-1281 (print). **Subscription Rates:** $90 Nonmembers; free for members. **URL:** http://www.afponline.org/exchange. **Formerly**: Journal of Cash Management; TMA Journal. **Ad Rates:** BW $6950; BW $3800, 1/2 page. **Remarks:** Accepts advertising. **Circ:** 25,000.

15127 ■ AMAA Journal
American Medical Athletic Association
4405 E West Hwy., Ste. 405
Bethesda, MD 20814-4535
Phone: (301)913-9517
Fax: (301)913-9520
Free: 800-776-2732
Publisher's E-mail: amaa@americanrunning.org
Journal publishing original papers related to the medical aspects of sports, exercise and fitness. **Freq:** 3/year winter, spring/summer, and fall. **Subscription Rates:** Included in membership. **Alt. Formats:** PDF. **URL:** http://www.amaasportsmed.org/amaa_journal.htm. **Remarks:** Advertising not accepted. **Circ:** (Not Reported).

15128 ■ The American Journal of Gastroenterology
American College of Gastroenterology
6400 Goldsboro Rd., Ste. 200
Bethesda, MD 20817
Phone: (301)263-9000
Fax: (301)263-9025
Publisher's E-mail: info@acg.gi.org
Journal discussing clinically oriented original articles and major reviews of current gastroenterology topics. **Freq:** Monthly. **Print Method:** Offset. **Trim Size:** 8 3/8 x 10 7/8. **Cols./Page:** 2. **Col. Width:** 36 nonpareils. **Col. Depth:** 140 agate lines. **Key Personnel:** Eamonn M.M. Quigley, MD, Editor; Joel Richter, MD, Editor; Nicholas J. Talley, MD, Editor; William D. Chey, MD, Editor; Paul Moayyedi, PhD, Editor. **ISSN:** 0002--9270 (print); **EISSN:** 1572--0241 (electronic). **Subscription Rates:** $912 Individuals print + online (Americas); €726.41 Individuals print + online (Europe); £468 Other countries print + online; $820 Individuals online only (Americas); €655.07 Individuals online only (Europe); £422 Other countries online only; Included in membership. **URL:** http://www.nature.com/ajg/index.html; http://acgjournalcme.gi.org. **Remarks:** Accepts advertising. **Circ:** (Not Reported).

15129 ■ American Journal of Health System Pharmacy
American Society of Health-System Pharmacists
7272 Wisconsin Ave.
Bethesda, MD 20814
Phone: (301)664-8700
Fax: (301)657-1251
Free: 866-279-0681
Publisher's E-mail: custserv@ashp.org
Journal for pharmacists practicing in health-systems (acute care, ambulatory care, homecare, long term care, HMO's, PPOs, & PBMs). **Freq:** Semimonthly. **Print Method:** Offset. **Trim Size:** 8 1/8 x 10 7/8. **Cols./Page:** 2. **Col. Width:** 19 picas. **Col. Depth:** 55 picas. **Key Personnel:** Richard C. Talley, Editor-in-Chief; Maryam R. Mohassel, Managing Editor. **ISSN:** 1079--2082 (print). **Subscription Rates:** $393 Nonmembers; $491 Nonmembers other countries; $746 Nonmembers 2 years; $933 Nonmembers 2 years; $1060 Nonmembers other countries - 3 years; $1326 Nonmembers other countries - 3 years. **URL:** http://store.ashp.org/Store/ProductListing/ProductDetails.aspx?productId=3386. **Formerly**: American Journal of Hospital Pharmacy. **Ad Rates:** BW $4,155; 4C $2,415. **Remarks:** Accepts advertising. **Circ:** Combined ‡36525.

15130 ■ The American Journal of Occupational Therapy
The American Occupational Therapy Association, Inc.
4720 Montgomery Ln., Ste. 200
Bethesda, MD 20814-3449
Phone: (301)652-6611
Fax: (301)652-7711
Free: 800-729-2682
Publication E-mail: cdavis@aota.org
Peer-reviewed journal focuses on research, practice and health care issues in the field of occupational therapy. **Freq:** Bimonthly. **Cols./Page:** 3. **Key Personnel:** Chris Davis, Director. **ISSN:** 0272--9490 (print). **Subscription Rates:** $249 Individuals U.S.; $299 Institutions U.S.; $299 Individuals Canada; $349 Institutions Canada; $349 Individuals foreign (via airmail); $399 Institutions foreign (via airmail). **URL:** http://www.aota.org/Publications-News/AmericanJournalOfOccupationalTherapy.aspx. **Ad Rates:** 4C $1657. **Remarks:** Accepts advertising. **Circ:** ‡53000.

15131 ■ The American Journal of Pathology
American Society for Investigative Pathology
9650 Rockville Pke., Ste. E133
Bethesda, MD 20814
Phone: (301)634-7130
Fax: (301)634-7990
Publisher's E-mail: asip@asip.org
Journal publishing original experimental and clinical studies in diagnostic and experimental pathology. **Freq:** Monthly. **Print Method:** Waterless Web (text); Sheetfed offset (covers). **Trim Size:** 8 1/8 x 11. **Cols./Page:** 2. **Col. Width:** 39 nonpareils. **Col. Depth:** 140 agate lines. **Key Personnel:** Kevin A. Roth, Editor-in-Chief. **ISSN:** 0002--9440 (print). **Subscription Rates:** $487 Individuals print and online; $595 Other countries print and online. **URL:** http://www.asip.org/journals/ajp. **Ad Rates:** BW $1,250; SAU $415; BW $1405. **Remarks:** Accepts advertising. **Circ:** ‡2500, 550.

15132 ■ American Journal of Physiology: Renal Physiology
American Physiological Society
9650 Rockville Pke.
Bethesda, MD 20814-3991
Phone: (301)634-7164
Fax: (301)634-7241
Journal covering information on kidney and urinary tract physiology, epithelial cell biology and control of body fluid volume and composition. **Founded:** 1977. **Freq:** 24/yr. **Print Method:** Offset. **Trim Size:** 8 3/8 x 10 7/8. **Cols./Page:** 2. **Col. Width:** 21 picas. **Col. Depth:** 56 picas. **Key Personnel:** Gerard Apodaca, Associate Editor; P. Darwin Bell, Associate Editor; Jeffrey L. Garvin, Associate Editor; Lisa M. Satlin, Associate Editor; Thomas R. Kleyman, Editor-in-Chief. **ISSN:** 0363-6127 (print). **Subscription Rates:** $1210 Members print only; $1585 Members print only, Canada/Mexico; $1710 Members other, print only; $3115 Nonmembers print only; $3485 Nonmembers print only, Canada/Mexico; $3615 Nonmembers other, print only; $3215 Nonmembers print & online; $3570 Nonmembers print & online, Canada/Mexico; $3705 Nonmembers print & online, other; $3765 Nonmembers online only. **URL:** http://www.the-aps.org/mm/Publications/Journals/AJP-Renal. **Ad Rates:** BW $1070; 4C $2165. **Remarks:** Accepts advertising. **Circ:** Combined ‡750.

15133 ■ American Journal of Physiology Consolidated
American Physiological Society
9650 Rockville Pke.
Bethesda, MD 20814-3991
Phone: (301)634-7164
Fax: (301)634-7241
Physiology journal publishing articles from eight individual journals. **Freq:** Monthly. **Print Method:** Offset. **Trim Size:** 8 3/8 x 10 7/8. **Cols./Page:** 2. **Col. Width:** 21 picas. **Col. Depth:** 56 picas. **Key Personnel:** Jerry Dempsey, Editor; Ralph Fregosi, Associate Editor; Mark Hargreaves, Board Member; Andre De Troyer, Associate Editor; Matthew White, Associate Editor; Michael Joyner, Editor; Erik Richter, Associate Editor; Mark L. Goodwin, Manager; Margaret Reich, Director, Editor. **ISSN:** 0002--9513 (print). **Subscription Rates:** $3845 Individuals Tier 1, online only; $4650 Individuals Tier 2, online only; $5155 Individuals Tier3, online only; $4975 Individuals Tier 1, print and online (domestic); $5770 Individuals Tier 2, print and online (domestic); $3500 Individuals Tier 3, print and online (domestic); $5490 Individuals Tier 1, print and online (international); $6350 Individuals Tier 2, print and online (international); $7115 Individuals Tier 3, print and online (international); $6395 Individuals Tier 1-5, print only (domestic); $7035 Other countries Tier 1-5, print only. **URL:** http://ajpcon.physiology.org; http://www.the-aps.org; http://ebus.the-aps.org/EbusPPROD/Default.aspx?TabId=199. **Ad Rates:** BW $1,070. **Remarks:** Accepts advertising. **Circ:** Combined ‡2639.

15134 ■ Analytical Cellular Pathology
IOS Press Inc.
c/o Thomas Ried, Associate Editor
Section of Cancer Genomics
Genetics Br./CCR/NCI/NIH
Bldg. 50, Rm. 1408
Bethesda, MD 20892-8010
Publisher's E-mail: order@iospress.nl
Journal covering analytical and quantitative cytology and pathology. Covers diagnosis of disease using genetic and morphological approaches, methodological aspects of cytochemistry and histochemistry, in-situ hybridization, cell- and molecular biology, flow- and image-cytometry, and genetic and molecular diagnostics. **Freq:** Biweekly Fri. **Print Method:** Web offset. **Trim Size:** 10 x 14 1/2. **Cols./Page:** 4. **Col. Width:** 14 picas. **Key Personnel:** Thomas Ried, Associate Editor; Stanley Cohen, M.D., Editor-in-Chief. **ISSN:** 2210-7177 (print); **EISSN:** 2210-7185 (electronic). **Subscription Rates:** €184 Individuals online; $250 Individuals online; €735 Institutions online; $1000 Institutions online; €942 Institutions print and online; $1284 Institutions print and online; €795 Institutions print; $1084 Institutions print. **URL:** http://www.iospress.nl/journal/analytical-cellular-pathology/. **Formerly**: Cellular Oncology. **Remarks:** Advertising not accepted. **Circ:** (Not Reported).

15135 ■ Anatomical Record
American Association of Anatomists
9650 Rockville Pke.
Bethesda, MD 20814-3999
Phone: (301)634-7910
Fax: (301)634-7965
Publisher's E-mail: info@anatomy.org
Journal publishing new discoveries in the morphological aspects of molecular, cellular, systems, and evolutionary biology. **Freq:** Monthly. **Key Personnel:** Kurt H. Alber-

tine, PhD, Editor. **ISSN:** 1932--8486 (print); **EISSN:** 1932--8494 (electronic). **Subscription Rates:** $9830 Institutions print or online; $11796 Institutions print and online; $9998 Institutions, Canada and Mexico print only; $11964 Institutions, Canada and Mexico print and online; £5017 Institutions online only - UK; £7806 Institutions print and online - UK; £6505 Institutions print only; €6342 Institutions online only - Europe; €7806 Institutions print and online - Europe; €6505 Institutions print only; $12048 Institutions, other countries print and online; $10082 Institutions, other countries print only. **URL:** http://www.anatomy.org/publications/anatomical-record; http://onlinelibrary.wiley.com/journal/10.1002/(ISSN)1932-8494. **Remarks:** Advertising not accepted. **Circ:** (Not Reported).

15136 ■ APMA News
American Podiatric Medical Association
9312 Old Georgetown Rd.
Bethesda, MD 20814-1621
Phone: (301)581-9200
Non-scientific news for member podiatrists. **Freq:** 10/year. **Print Method:** Web heatset. **Trim Size:** 8 1/4 x 10 7/8. **Cols./Page:** 3. **Col. Width:** 2 3/16 inches. **Col. Depth:** 9 inches. **Key Personnel:** Gary Walchli, President; Stephen Tauber, Vice President; David Bubbins, Manager, Production. **ISSN:** 8750--2585 (print). **Subscription Rates:** Included in membership; $50 Non-members; $75 Individuals; $100 Other countries. **URL:** http://www.apma.org/workingforyou/content.cfm?ItemNumber=1371&navItemNumber=702. **Formerly:** American Podiatry Association News Report; APA Report. **Ad Rates:** $555-1675; $1090-2210. BW $1,420; 4C $2,295; BW $4C $. **Remarks:** Advertising accepted; rates available upon request. **Circ:** Paid 14858.

15137 ■ Aquatic Sciences and Fisheries Abstracts: Aquatic Sciences and Fisheries
Cambridge Scientific Abstracts L.P.
7200 Wisconsin Ave., Ste. 601
Bethesda, MD 20814
Phone: (301)961-6700
Fax: (301)961-6720
Free: 800-843-7751
Publisher's E-mail: sales@proquest.com
Journal containing information on the aquatic environments and marine pollution problems. **Freq:** Monthly. **Print Method:** Letterpress and Offset. **Trim Size:** 6 1/2 x 9. **ISSN:** 1045--6031 (print). **Circ:** (Not Reported).

15138 ■ ASFA Aquaculture Abstracts
Cambridge Scientific Abstracts L.P.
7200 Wisconsin Ave., Ste. 601
Bethesda, MD 20814
Phone: (301)961-6700
Fax: (301)961-6720
Free: 800-843-7751
Publisher's E-mail: sales@proquest.com
Scientific journal covering aquaculture. **Freq:** Monthly. **Print Method:** Letterset and Offset. **Trim Size:** 6 1/2 x 9. **ISSN:** 0022--2402 (print). **URL:** http://www.csa.com/e_products/printjalpha.php. **Circ:** (Not Reported).

15139 ■ ASFA Marine Biotechnology Abstracts
Cambridge Scientific Abstracts L.P.
7200 Wisconsin Ave., Ste. 601
Bethesda, MD 20814
Phone: (301)961-6700
Fax: (301)961-6720
Free: 800-843-7751
Publisher's E-mail: sales@proquest.com
Journal covering the application of molecular biology and molecular genetics to aquatic organisms. **Freq:** Monthly. **Print Method:** Web. **ISSN:** 1043-8971 (print). **URL:** http://search.proquest.com/asfamarine?accountid=14579. **Circ:** (Not Reported).

15140 ■ ASFA 1: Biological Sciences & Living Resources
Cambridge Scientific Abstracts L.P.
7200 Wisconsin Ave., Ste. 601
Bethesda, MD 20814
Phone: (301)961-6700
Fax: (301)961-6720
Free: 800-843-7751
Publisher's E-mail: sales@proquest.com
Scientific journal covering marine, freshwater, and brackish water environments. **Freq:** Monthly. **Print Method:** Letterpress. **Trim Size:** 6 1/2 x 9. **Cols./Page:** 2. **ISSN:** 0140--5373 (print). **URL:** http://proquest.libguides.com/asfa. **Circ:** (Not Reported).

15141 ■ ASFA 2: Ocean Technology, Policy & Non-Living Resources
Cambridge Scientific Abstracts L.P.
7200 Wisconsin Ave., Ste. 601
Bethesda, MD 20814
Phone: (301)961-6700
Fax: (301)961-6720
Free: 800-843-7751
Publisher's E-mail: sales@proquest.com
Scientific journal covering oceanography, offshore technology and operations. **Freq:** Monthly. **Print Method:** Letterpress and Offset. **Trim Size:** 6 1/2 x 9. **Cols./Page:** 2. **ISSN:** 0140--5381 (print). **URL:** http://proquest.libguides.com/asfa. **Circ:** (Not Reported).

15142 ■ ASHP Intersections
American Society of Health-System Pharmacists
7272 Wisconsin Ave.
Bethesda, MD 20814
Phone: (301)664-8700
Fax: (301)657-1251
Free: 866-279-0681
Publisher's E-mail: custserv@ashp.org
Freq: Quarterly. **URL:** http://www.ashpintersections.org. **Remarks:** Advertising not accepted. **Circ:** (Not Reported).

15143 ■ Association Trends
Martineau Corp.
8120 Woodmont Ave., Ste. 110
Bethesda, MD 20814-2743
Phone: (202)464-1662
Publication E-mail: associationtrends@associationtrends.com
Newspaper for staff professionals of volunteer organizations. Covers business, trade associations, and professional societies. **Freq:** Monthly. **Print Method:** Offset. **Trim Size:** 11 x 17. **Cols./Page:** 4. **Col. Width:** 28 nonpareils. **Col. Depth:** 224 agate lines. **Key Personnel:** Jill M. Cornish, Executive Editor; E. Francisco Dalere, Managing Editor. **ISSN:** 0196--1942 (print). **Subscription Rates:** $197 Individuals standard class; $497 Individuals informed executive; $897 Institutions executive suite (non-profit); $1097 Institutions executive suite (corporate); $197 Institutions News Delivery (for all); $497 Institutions Informed Executive (for all). **URL:** http://www.associationtrends.com. **Ad Rates:** BW $2,210; 4C $1,200. **Remarks:** Accepts advertising. **Circ:** Paid ‡4154, Free ‡2997.

15144 ■ The Autism Advocate
Autism Society
4340 East-West Hwy., Ste. 350
Bethesda, MD 20814
Free: 800-328-8476
Publisher's E-mail: info@autism-society.org
Freq: Quarterly. **ISSN:** 0047- 9101 (print). **Subscription Rates:** Included in membership. **URL:** http://www.autism-society.org/about-the-autism-society/publications/. **Remarks:** Accepts advertising. **Circ:** 60000.

15145 ■ Bacteriology: Microbiology Abstracts, Section B
Cambridge Scientific Abstracts L.P.
7200 Wisconsin Ave., Ste. 601
Bethesda, MD 20814
Phone: (301)961-6700
Fax: (301)961-6720
Free: 800-843-7751
Publisher's E-mail: sales@proquest.com
Scientific journal covering bacterial taxonomy and genetics, microbial ecology, vaccines, and immunology. **Freq:** Monthly. **Print Method:** Offset. **Trim Size:** 6 1/2 x 9. **Cols./Page:** 2. **ISSN:** 0300-8398 (print). **Subscription Rates:** $1595 Individuals print + web edition, (includes shipping); $1195 Individuals web edition. **URL:** http://www.proquest.com/customer-care/title-lists/ProQuest-Dialog-Prosheets.html. **Circ:** (Not Reported).

15146 ■ Bethesda Magazine
Bethesda Magazine
7768 Woodmont Ave., Ste. 204
Bethesda, MD 20814
Phone: (301)718-7787
Fax: (301)718-1875
Publisher's E-mail: customerservice@bethesdamagazine.com
Magazine covering restaurants, arts, schools, home design, home values, traffic and parking in and around the town of Bethesda. **Freq:** Bimonthly. **Key Personnel:** Steve Hull, Editor, Publisher. **Subscription Rates:** $19.95 Individuals. **URL:** http://www.bethesdamagazine.com. **Ad Rates:** 4C $3975; BW $3577.50. **Remarks:** Accepts advertising. **Circ:** ‡30000.

15147 ■ Calcium and Calcified Tissue Abstracts
Cambridge Scientific Abstracts L.P.
7200 Wisconsin Ave., Ste. 601
Bethesda, MD 20814
Phone: (301)961-6700
Fax: (301)961-6720
Free: 800-843-7751
Publisher's E-mail: sales@proquest.com
Scientific journal covering bone metabolism, tooth development, nerve transmission, and other calcium-related functions. **Freq:** Monthly. **Print Method:** Offset. **Trim Size:** 6 1/2 x 9. **Cols./Page:** 2. **ISSN:** 1069-5540 (print). **URL:** http://www.proquest.com/customer-care/title-lists/ProQuest-Dialog-Prosheets.html. **Circ:** (Not Reported).

15148 ■ CBE--Life Sciences Education
American Society for Cell Biology
8120 Woodmont Ave., Ste. 750
Bethesda, MD 20814
Phone: (301)347-9300
Fax: (301)347-9310
Publisher's E-mail: ascbinfo@ascb.org
Journal that focuses on life science education at the K-12, undergraduate, and graduate levels. **Freq:** Quarterly. **Key Personnel:** William B. Wood, Senior Editor; Malcolm Campbell, Senior Editor; Erin Dolan, Editor-in-Chief. **ISSN:** 1536--7509 (print). **Subscription Rates:** Free. **URL:** http://www.lifescied.org; http://www.ascb.org/index.php?option=com_content&view=article&id=602&Itemid=310. **Formerly:** Cell Biology Education. **Ad Rates:** 4C $700. **Remarks:** Accepts advertising. **Circ:** (Not Reported).

15149 ■ Cellular and Molecular Neurobiology
Springer Netherlands
c/o Juan M. Saavedra, MD, Editor
National Institute of Mental Health
Bethesda, MD 20892-0002
Scientific journal focusing on analysis of neuronal and brain function. **Freq:** Bimonthly. **Print Method:** Offset. **Key Personnel:** Edson X. Albuquerque, Board Member; Harold Gainer, Board Member; Nicolas G. Bazan, Board Member; Amitabha Chattopadhyay, Board Member; Juan M. Saavedra, MD, Editor; Masami Niwa, Associate Editor. **ISSN:** 0272--4340 (print); **EISSN:** 1573--6830 (electronic). **Subscription Rates:** €1981 Institutions print & online; €2377 Institutions print & enhanced access; $2100 Institutions print & online; $2520 Institutions print & enhanced access. **URL:** http://link.springer.com/journal/10571; http://www.springer.com/biomed/neuroscience/journal/10571. **Remarks:** Accepts advertising. **Circ:** (Not Reported).

15150 ■ Chemoreception Abstracts: Chemical Senses and Applied Techniques
Cambridge Scientific Abstracts L.P.
7200 Wisconsin Ave., Ste. 601
Bethesda, MD 20814
Phone: (301)961-6700
Fax: (301)961-6720
Free: 800-843-7751
Publication E-mail: sales@csa.com
Scientific journal covering the neurobiology, chemistry, and physiology of taste, smell, internal chemoreception, and chemotaxis. **Freq:** Monthly. **Print Method:** Offset. **Trim Size:** 6 1/2 x 9. **Cols./Page:** 2. **ISSN:** 0300-1261 (print). **URL:** http://www.proquest.com/customer-care/title-lists/ProQuest-Dialog-Prosheets.html. **Circ:** (Not Reported).

15151 ■ Clinical Gastroenterology and Hepatology
American Gastroenterological Association
4930 Del Ray Ave.
Bethesda, MD 20814
Phone: (301)654-2055
Fax: (301)654-5920

Circulation: ★ = AAM; △ or • = BPA; ♦ = CAC; ❑ = VAC; ⊕ = PO Statement; ‡ = Publisher's Report; Boldface figures = sworn; Light figures = estimated.

Journal publishing spectrum of themes in clinical gastroenterology and hepatology. **Freq:** Monthly. **Trim Size:** 8 1/4 x 11. **Key Personnel:** Hashem B. El-Serag. **ISSN:** 1542--3565 (print). **Subscription Rates:** $383 Individuals print and online; $197 Students print and online; $480 Canada print and online; $275 Students, other countries print and online; $467 Other countries online and print; $266 Students, other countries online and print. **Alt. Formats:** PDF. **URL:** http://www.cghjournal.org. **Ad Rates:** BW $2330; 4C $2020. **Remarks:** Accepts advertising. **Circ:** Combined ‡18425.

15152 ■ Communique
National Association of School Psychologists
4340 E West Hwy., Ste. 402
Bethesda, MD 20814
Phone: (301)657-0270
Fax: (301)657-0275
Free: 866-331-NASP
Membership newspaper of the National Association of School Psychologists.Each issue includes association news, legislative and practice developments, exemplary programs, reviews of books, tests, and software and job opportunities. **Freq:** 8/year. **Trim Size:** 10 3/4" x 14 1/2". **Key Personnel:** Margo Fuerst, Coordinator; John Desrochers, Editor; Susan Gorin, Executive Director, phone: (301)347-1640; Steven Landau, Associate Editor; Linda Morgan, Director, Production. **URL:** http://www.nasponline.org/publications/cq/39/8/index.aspx; http://www.nasponline.org/publications/cq/index.aspx?vol=42&issue=2. **Ad Rates:** 4C $4100, back cover - 4 color only; 4C $3800, inside back cover - 4 color only; 4C $2400, full page; 4C $1500, 1/2 page vertical or horizontal; 4C $1200, 1/4 page vertical; 4C $900, 1/8 page horizontal. **Remarks:** Accepts advertising. **Circ:** 25000.

15153 ■ Computer and Information Systems Abstracts Journal
Cambridge Scientific Abstracts L.P.
7200 Wisconsin Ave., Ste. 601
Bethesda, MD 20814
Phone: (301)961-6700
Fax: (301)961-6720
Free: 800-843-7751
Publisher's E-mail: sales@proquest.com
Journal covering computer and information sciences. Jointly published with Engineering Information Inc. **Freq:** Monthly. **Print Method:** Letterpress and Offset. **Trim Size:** 8 1/2 x 11. **Cols./Page:** 2. **Col. Width:** 42 nonpareils. **Col. Depth:** 133 agate lines. **ISSN:** 0191--9776 (print). **URL:** http://www.proquest.com/customer-care/title-lists/ProQuest-Dialog-Prosheets.html. **Circ:** (Not Reported).

15154 ■ Conference Papers Index
Cambridge Scientific Abstracts L.P.
7200 Wisconsin Ave., Ste. 601
Bethesda, MD 20814
Phone: (301)961-6700
Fax: (301)961-6720
Free: 800-843-7751
Publisher's E-mail: sales@proquest.com
Journal covering worldwide scientific and technical conferences. **Founded:** 1973. **Freq:** Bimonthly annual index. **Print Method:** Letterpress and Offset. **Trim Size:** 8 1/2 x 11. **Cols./Page:** 2. **Col. Width:** 43 nonpareils. **Col. Depth:** 126 agate lines. **Key Personnel:** Carla R. McMillan, Editor. **ISSN:** 0162-704X (print). **Online:** Dialog; STN International; Citadel; NlightN. **Alt. Formats:** Magnetic tape. **URL:** http://www.proquest.com/products-services/cpi-set-c.html; http://www.proquest.com. **Remarks:** Advertising not accepted. **Circ:** (Not Reported).

15155 ■ CSA Neurosciences Abstracts
Cambridge Scientific Abstracts L.P.
7200 Wisconsin Ave., Ste. 601
Bethesda, MD 20814
Phone: (301)961-6700
Fax: (301)961-6720
Free: 800-843-7751
Publisher's E-mail: sales@proquest.com
Scientific journal covering all aspects of vertebrate and invertebrate neuroscience, with special emphasis on neural diseases such as Alzheimer's. **Freq:** Monthly. **Print Method:** Offset. **Trim Size:** 6 1/2 x 9. **Cols./Page:** 2. **ISSN:** 0036-8075 (print). **URL:** http://www.proquest.com/customer-care/title-lists/ProQuest-Dialog-Prosheets.html. **Circ:** (Not Reported).

15156 ■ Developmental Dynamics
American Association of Anatomists
9650 Rockville Pke.
Bethesda, MD 20814-3999
Phone: (301)634-7910
Fax: (301)634-7965
Publisher's E-mail: info@anatomy.org
Journal providing a focus for communication among developmental biologists who study the progressive and dynamic emergence of form and function during embryonic development. **Freq:** Monthly 18/yr on wiley. **Key Personnel:** Parker B. Antin, Editor. **ISSN:** 1058--8388 (print); **EISSN:** 1097--0177 (electronic). **Subscription Rates:** $8111 Institutions online only; £4140 Institutions online only; €5233 Institutions online only. **URL:** http://www.anatomy.org/publications/developmental-dynamics; http://onlinelibrary.wiley.com/journal/10.1002/(ISSN)1097-0177. **Remarks:** Advertising not accepted. **Circ:** (Not Reported).

15157 ■ Drug Metabolism and Disposition
American Society for Pharmacology and Experimental Therapeutics
9650 Rockville Pke.
Bethesda, MD 20814-3995
Phone: (301)634-7060
Fax: (301)634-7061
Publisher's E-mail: ronna.ekhouse@wolterskluwer.com
Medical journal. **Founded:** 1973. **Freq:** Monthly. **Print Method:** Offset. **Trim Size:** 8 1/8 x 10 7/8. **Cols./Page:** 2. **Col. Width:** 32 nonpareils. **Col. Depth:** 119 agate lines. **Key Personnel:** Edward T. Morgan, Editor; Richard Dodenhoff, Director. **ISSN:** 0090-9556 (print). **Subscription Rates:** $437 Institutions online only (Tier 1); $478 Institutions online only (Tier 2); $533 Institutions online only (Tier 3). **URL:** http://dmd.aspetjournals.org/. **Mailing address:** PO Box 908, Philadelphia, PA 19106-3621. **Ad Rates:** BW $615. **Remarks:** Accepts advertising. **Circ:** Paid ‡500.

15158 ■ Ecology Abstracts
Cambridge Scientific Abstracts L.P.
7200 Wisconsin Ave., Ste. 601
Bethesda, MD 20814
Phone: (301)961-6700
Fax: (301)961-6720
Free: 800-843-7751
Publisher's E-mail: sales@proquest.com
Scientific journal about ecology. **Freq:** Monthly. **Print Method:** Offset. **Trim Size:** 6 1/2 x 9. **Cols./Page:** 2. **ISSN:** 0036- 8075 (print). **Subscription Rates:** $1550 Individuals print + web edition, (includes shipping); $1165 Individuals web edition. **URL:** http://www.proquest.com/customer-care/title-lists/ProQuest-Dialog-Prosheets.html. **Circ:** (Not Reported).

15159 ■ Education Week: American Education's Newspaper of Record
Editorial Projects in Education
6935 Arlington Rd., Ste. 100
Bethesda, MD 20814
Phone: (301)280-3100
Fax: (301)280-3200
Free: 800-346-1834
Publication E-mail: ew@epe.org
Professional newspaper for elementary and secondary school educators. **Founded:** 1981. **Freq:** 44/yr. **Print Method:** Offset. **Trim Size:** 10 3/4 x 14 5/8. **Cols./Page:** 5. **Key Personnel:** Virginia B. Edwards, Editor, President; Gregory Chronister, Executive Editor; Karen Diegmueller, Managing Editor. **ISSN:** 0277-4232 (print). **Subscription Rates:** $39 Individuals 20 issues plus digital access; $29 Individuals 6 months digital access; $89.94 Individuals /yr; print + digital; $79.94 Individuals /yr; digital only. **URL:** http://www.edweek.org/ew. **Ad Rates:** BW $8,605; 4C $11,220; PCI $120. **Remarks:** Accepts advertising. **Circ:** Paid ★**48540**.

15160 ■ EIS: Digests of Environmental Impact Statements
Cambridge Scientific Abstracts L.P.
7200 Wisconsin Ave., Ste. 601
Bethesda, MD 20814
Phone: (301)961-6700
Fax: (301)961-6720
Free: 800-843-7751
Publisher's E-mail: sales@proquest.com
Journal abstracting government environmental impact statements. **Freq:** Bimonthly. **ISSN:** 0364-1074 (print). **URL:** http://www.galileo.usg.edu/scholar/databases/zcei/?Welcome. **Circ:** (Not Reported).

15161 ■ Electrical Contractor
National Electrical Contractors Association
3 Bethesda Metro Ctr., Ste. 1100
Bethesda, MD 20814
Phone: (301)657-3110
Fax: (301)215-4500
Electrical engineering. **Freq:** Monthly. **Print Method:** Web. **Trim Size:** 8 1/8 x 10 7/8. **Cols./Page:** 3. **Col. Width:** 14 picas. **Col. Depth:** 57 picas. **Key Personnel:** Astra Hudson, Manager, Circulation; Donna L. Bailey, Associate Publisher; Timothy Johnson, Associate Editor; John W. Maisel, Publisher; Andrea Klee, Editor. **ISSN:** 0033--5118 (print). **Subscription Rates:** Free to qualified subscribers; $5 Single issue. **URL:** http://www.ecmag.com. **Ad Rates:** BW $10,490; 4C $2,390. **Remarks:** Accepts advertising. **Circ:** 90000.

15162 ■ Electronics & Communications Abstracts Journal
Cambridge Scientific Abstracts L.P.
7200 Wisconsin Ave., Ste. 601
Bethesda, MD 20814
Phone: (301)961-6700
Fax: (301)961-6720
Free: 800-843-7751
Publisher's E-mail: sales@proquest.com
Journal covering electronics and communications. Jointly published with Engineering Information Inc. **Freq:** Monthly. **Print Method:** Letterpress and Offset. **Trim Size:** 8 1/2 x 11. **Cols./Page:** 2. **Col. Width:** 42 nonpareils. **Col. Depth:** 133 agate lines. **ISSN:** 0361--3313 (print). **URL:** http://www.proquest.com/customer-care/title-lists/ProQuest-Dialog-Prosheets.html. **Circ:** (Not Reported).

15163 ■ Entomology Abstracts
Cambridge Scientific Abstracts L.P.
7200 Wisconsin Ave., Ste. 601
Bethesda, MD 20814
Phone: (301)961-6700
Fax: (301)961-6720
Free: 800-843-7751
Publisher's E-mail: sales@proquest.com
Journal containing information on the latest techniques and methodology, anatomy, physiology, etc. of insects and insect-like species. **Founded:** 1982. **Freq:** Monthly. **Print Method:** Offset. **Trim Size:** 6 1/2 x 9. **ISSN:** 0013-8924 (print). **Subscription Rates:** $1570 Individuals print + web edition, (includes shipping); $1180 Individuals web edition. **URL:** http://www.csa.com/factsheets/entomology-set-c.php. **Circ:** (Not Reported).

15164 ■ The FASEB Journal
Federation of American Societies for Experimental Biology
9650 Rockville Pke.
Bethesda, MD 20814
Phone: (301)634-7000
Fax: (301)634-7001
Publisher's E-mail: info@faseb.org
Journal on multidisciplinary life sciences research. **Freq:** Monthly. **Print Method:** Offset. **Trim Size:** 8 1/2 x 10 7/8. **Cols./Page:** 2. **Col. Width:** 42 nonpareils. **Col. Depth:** 133 agate lines. **Key Personnel:** Cody Mooneyhan, Managing Editor; Gerald Weissmann, MD, Editor-in-Chief; Mary Kiorpes Hayden, Manager, Production. **ISSN:** 0892--6638 (print); **EISSN:** 153-0-6860 (electronic). **Subscription Rates:** $444 Institutions U.S. and other countries (Tier 1 - online only); $999 Institutions U.S. and other countries (Tier 2 - online only); $1157 Institutions U.S. and other countries (Tier 3 - online only); $708 Institutions U.S. (Tier 1 - print & online); $754 Institutions, Canada and Mexico Tier 1 - print & online; $770 Institutions, other countries Tier 1 - print & online; $1245 Institutions U.S. (Tier 2 - print & online); $1290 Institutions, Canada and Mexico Tier 2 - print & online; $1306 Institutions, other countries Tier 2 - print & online; $1414 Institutions U.S. (Tier 3 - print & online); $1461 Institutions, Canada and Mexico Tier 3 - print & online; $1476 Institutions, other countries Tier 3 - print & online; $459 U.S. print & online; $504 Canada and Mexico print & online; $519 Other countries print & online; $331 U.S. member - print & online; $376 Canada and Mexico member - print & online; $391 Other countries member - print & online; $54 U.S. and other countries student - online only. **URL:** http://www.fasebj.

org. **Formerly**: Federation Proceedings. **Ad Rates:** BW $1,809; 4C $2,904. **Remarks:** Accepts advertising. **Circ:** 800.

15165 ■ Fisheries
American Fisheries Society
425 Barlow Pl., Ste. 110
Bethesda, MD 20814
Phone: (301)897-8616
Fax: (301)897-8096
Magazine covering fisheries management and aquatic resource issues. **Freq:** Monthly. **Trim Size:** 8.25 x 10. 875. **Key Personnel:** Madeleine Hall-Arber, Editor. **ISSN:** 0363--2415 (print); **EISSN:** 1548--8446 (electronic). **Subscription Rates:** $1530 Institutions American Fisheries Society Pack (online only); $486 Institutions Fisheries Infobase Online Pack (online only); $508 Institutions Fisheries Infobase (online only); $1791 Institutions American Fisheries Society Pack (print and online). **URL:** http://fisheries.org/2015/04/fisheries-magazine-april-2015. **Ad Rates:** BW $1,476; 4C $935. **Remarks:** Accepts advertising. **Circ:** ‡9500.

15166 ■ The Foot
The American College of Foot and Ankle Orthopedics and Medicine
5272 River Rd., Ste. 630
Bethesda, MD 20816
Phone: (301)718-6505
Fax: (301)656-0989
Free: 800-265-8263
Freq: Quarterly. **Key Personnel:** D.L. Lorimer, Executive Editor; T. Duckworth, Editor; Prof. R.J. Abboud, Editor-in-Chief. **ISSN:** 0958--2592 (print). **Subscription Rates:** $190 Individuals print; $583 Institutions print; $482.67 Institutions online. **URL:** http://www.journals.elsevier.com/the-foot; http://www.acfaom.org/about/publications. **Remarks:** Advertising not accepted. **Circ:** (Not Reported).

15167 ■ Forest Science
Society of American Foresters
5400 Grosvenor Ln.
Bethesda, MD 20814-2198
Fax: (301)897-3691
Free: 866-897-8720
Publisher's E-mail: membership@safnet.org
Magazine publishing research results covering silviculture, soils, biometry, diseases, recreation, photosynthesis, tree physiology, management, harvesting, and policy analysis. **Freq:** Bimonthly. **Print Method:** Offset. **Trim Size:** 7 x 9. **Cols./Page:** 1. **Col. Width:** 60 nonpareils. **Col. Depth:** 113 agate lines. **Key Personnel:** W. Keith Moser, Editor. **ISSN:** 0015--749X (print). **Subscription Rates:** $390 Nonmembers U.S. and Canada, print only; $1130 Institutions U.S. and Canada, print only; $490 Other countries print only, non-members; $1230 Institutions foreign, print only; $430 U.S. and Canada print and online, non-members; $1245 Institutions print and online, US and Canada; $530 Nonmembers other countries, print & online; $1345 Institutions other countries, print & online; $351 Nonmembers online only; $1055 Institutions online only. **URL:** http://www.safnet.org/publications/forscience/index.cfm. **Ad Rates:** BW $420. **Remarks:** Accepts advertising. **Circ:** 660.

15168 ■ Gastroenterology
Elsevier Inc.
1600 John F. Kennedy Blvd., Ste. 1800
Philadelphia, PA 19103-2899
Phone: (215)239-3900
Fax: (215)238-7883
Free: 800-523-1649
Publication E-mail: elspcs@elsevier.com
Medical journal examining all aspects of gastroenterlogy. **Freq:** Monthly 13/yr. **Print Method:** Offset. **Trim Size:** 8 1/4 x 11. **Cols./Page:** 2. **Col. Width:** 20 picas. **Col. Depth:** 56 picas. **Key Personnel:** David A. Brenner, Editor; M. Bishr Omary, Editor; Daniel K. Podolsky, Editor. **ISSN:** 0016--5085 (print). **Subscription Rates:** $658 U.S. print and online; $251 Students print and online; $997 Canada print and online; $597 Students, Canada print and online; $968 Other countries print and online; $562 Other countries print and online, students; $603 /year for individuals; $230 /year for students. **URL:** http://www.gastrojournal.org; http://www.gastro.org/journals-publications/gastroenterology. **Ad Rates:** $2485-2870, full page; $1880-2215, 1/2 page; $1320-1475, 1/4 page. BW $2,870; 4C $2,280. **Remarks:** Accepts advertising. **Circ:** Combined ‡14500, 20,000.

15169 ■ Health Affairs: The Policy Journal of the Health Sphere
Project HOPE
7500 Old Georgetown Rd., Ste. 600
Bethesda, MD 20814-6133
Phone: (301)656-7401
Fax: (301)654-2845
Publisher's E-mail: volunteers@projecthope.org
Peer-reviewed journal featuring health policy and health services research. **Freq:** Bimonthly. **Print Method:** Offset. **Trim Size:** 6 3/4 x 10. **Cols./Page:** 1. **Col. Width:** 62 nonpareils. **Col. Depth:** 112 agate lines. **Key Personnel:** Jane Hiebert-White, Publisher; John K. Iglehart, Editor; Donald E. Metz, Executive Editor. **ISSN:** 0278-2715 (print); **EISSN:** 1544-5208 (electronic). **Subscription Rates:** $596 Institutions print & online; $686 Institutions, other countries print & online; $542 Institutions online only; $621 Institutions all digital; $175 U.S. print and online; $265 Other countries print and online; $185 U.S. premium; $275 Other countries premium (print, online, mobile, iPad app); $145 Individuals digital (online, mobile, iPad app). **URL:** http://www.healthaffairs.org. **Remarks:** Advertising not accepted. **Circ:** Paid ‡10000.

15170 ■ Hearing Loss: The Journal of Self Help for Hard of Hearing People
Hearing Loss Association of America
7910 Woodmont Ave., Ste. 1200
Bethesda, MD 20814
Phone: (301)657-2248
Publisher's E-mail: info@hearingloss.org
Magazine covering all aspects of hearing loss as well as new technology.Contains latest information on products, services, research, and technology in the hearing care field. **Freq:** Bimonthly. **Trim Size:** 8 1/2 x 10 7/8. **Cols./Page:** 3. **Col. Width:** 2 1/4 inches. **Col. Depth:** 9 9/16 inches. **Key Personnel:** Barbara Kelley, Editor-in-Chief. **URL:** http://www.hearingloss.org/membership/hearing-loss-magazine/current-issue. **Formerly**: SHHH Journal. **Ad Rates:** GLR $10; BW $2,800; 4C $3,400. **Remarks:** Advertising accepted; rates available upon request. **Circ:** Paid 200000.

15171 ■ HLAA Hearing Loss
Hearing Loss Association of America
7910 Woodmont Ave., Ste. 1200
Bethesda, MD 20814
Phone: (301)657-2248
Publisher's E-mail: info@hearingloss.org
Freq: Bimonthly. **Key Personnel:** Barbara Kelley, Editor-in-Chief. **Subscription Rates:** Included in membership. **URL:** http://www.hearingloss.org/content/hearing-loss-magazine. **Ad Rates:** BW $3400. **Remarks:** Accepts advertising. **Circ:** (Not Reported).

15172 ■ International Journal for Ayurveda Research
U.S. National Institutes of Health National Center for Biotechnology Information PubMed Central
Bldg. 38A
Bethesda, MD 20894
Free: 888-346-3656
Publisher's E-mail: pubmedcentral@ncbi.nlm.nih.gov
Peer-reviewed journal covering ayurveda research. **Freq:** Quarterly. **Key Personnel:** Dr. U. M. Thatte, Executive Editor; Dr. N B Brindavanam, Associate Editor; Prof. K. K. Bhutani, Associate Editor; Dr. Ram Manohar, Associate Editor; Dr. Tanuja Nesari, Executive Editor; Dr. Supriya Bhalerao, Executive Editor. **ISSN:** 0974--7788 (print); **EISSN:** 0974--925X (electronic). **Subscription Rates:** Rs 600 Individuals print only; Rs 1200 Institutions print only; $60 Other countries print only; $120 Institutions, other countries print only. **URL:** http://www.ijaronline.com; http://www.ncbi.nlm.nih.gov/pubmed. **Circ:** (Not Reported).

15173 ■ Journal of Adhesion Science and Technology
The Adhesion Society
7101 Wisconsin Ave., Ste. 9901
Bethesda, MD 20814
Phone: (301)986-9700
Fax: (301)986-9795
Publisher's E-mail: Adhesionsociety@ascouncil.org
Journal focusing on the theories and mechanisms of adhesion covering adhesion principles in all areas of technology. **Freq:** Semimonthly. **Key Personnel:** I. Benedek, Board Member; A.K. Bhowmick, Board Member; A.D. Crocombe, Board Member; C. Cetinkaya, Board Member. **ISSN:** 0169--4243 (print); **EISSN:** 1568--5616 (electronic). **Subscription Rates:** $987 Individuals print ; $5057 Institutions online; $5779 Institutions print and online; $989 Individuals print and online. **URL:** http://www.tandfonline.com/toc/tast20/current. **Remarks:** Advertising not accepted. **Circ:** (Not Reported).

15174 ■ Journal of the American Medical Informatics Association
American Medical Informatics Association
4720 Montgomery Ln., Ste. 500
Bethesda, MD 20814
Phone: (301)657-1291
Fax: (301)657-1296
Publisher's E-mail: mail@amia.org
Journal publishing articles that assist physicians, informaticians, scientists, nurses, and other health care professionals develop and apply medical informatics to patient care, teaching, research, and health care administration. **Freq:** Bimonthly. **Print Method:** Web sheetfed. **Trim Size:** 8 1/2 x 10 7/8. **Key Personnel:** Lucila Ohno-Machado, MD, Editor-in-Chief; Kevin B. Johnson, MD, Associate Editor; Atul Butte, Associate Editor; Patricia F. Brennan, PhD, Associate Editor; Enrico Coiera, PhD, Associate Editor. **ISSN:** 1067--5027 (print); **EISSN:** 1527--974X (electronic). **Subscription Rates:** £245 Individuals print and online; $353467 Individuals print and online; €368 Individuals print and online; £194 Individuals online only; $369 Individuals online only; €291 Individuals online only. **URL:** http://jamia.oxfordjournals.org. **Ad Rates:** BW $1,380; 4C $1,745. **Remarks:** Accepts advertising. **Circ:** ‡3350.

15175 ■ Journal of the American Podiatric Medical Association
American Podiatric Medical Association
9312 Old Georgetown Rd.
Bethesda, MD 20814-1621
Phone: (301)581-9200
Peer-reviewed journal focusing on foot and ankle medicine. **Freq:** Bimonthly. **Print Method:** Offset. **Trim Size:** 8 1/8 x 10 7/8. **Cols./Page:** 2. **Col. Width:** 38 nonpareils. **Col. Depth:** 127 agate lines. **Key Personnel:** Noelle A. Boughanmi, Managing Editor. **ISSN:** 8750--7315 (print). **Subscription Rates:** $210 Institutions print and online; $245 Institutions, other countries print and online; $40 Individuals single issue; $210 Individuals print and online; $245 Other countries print and online. **URL:** http://www.japmaonline.org. **Ad Rates:** $1170-2305; $665-1800. BW $1,530; 4C $765; 4C $BW $. **Remarks:** Color advertising accepted; rates available upon request. **Circ:** Paid ‡13981, 14500.

15176 ■ Journal of Applied Physiology
American Physiological Society
9650 Rockville Pke.
Bethesda, MD 20814-3991
Phone: (301)634-7164
Fax: (301)634-7241
Journal covering respiratory, environmental, and exercise physiology. **Freq:** Monthly. **Print Method:** Offset. **Trim Size:** 8 3/8 x 10 7/8. **Cols./Page:** 2. **Col. Width:** 21 picas. **Col. Depth:** 56 picas. **Key Personnel:** Jerry Dempsey, Editor; Ralph Fregosi, Associate Editor; T.J. Barstow, Board Member; V. Brusasco, Board Member; Mark L. Goodwin, Manager; Peter Wagner, Editor-in-Chief. **ISSN:** 8750--7587 (print); **EISSN:** 1522--1601 (electronic). **Subscription Rates:** $2035 Institutions print only (tier 1-5); $2160 Institutions, other countries print only (tier 1-5); $1215 Institutions online only (tier 1); $1435 Institutions online only (tier 2); $1640 Institutions online only (tier 3); $1580 Institutions print and online (tier 1) domestic; $1845 Institutions print and online (tier 2) domestic; $2065 Institutions print and online (tier 3) domestic; $1680 Institutions, other countries print and online (tier 1); $1950 Institutions, other countries print and online (tier 2); $2185 Institutions, other countries print and online (tier 3). **URL:** http://jap.physiology.org. **Ad Rates:** BW $1,070; 4C $2,165. **Remarks:** Accepts advertising. **Circ:** Combined ‡970, 2400.

Circulation: ★ = AAM; △ or • = BPA; ♦ = CAC; ❑ = VAC; ⊕ = PO Statement; ‡ = Publisher's Report; Boldface figures = sworn; Light figures = estimated.

15177 ■ Journal of Aquatic Animal Health
American Fisheries Society
425 Barlow Pl., Ste. 110
Bethesda, MD 20814
Phone: (301)897-8616
Fax: (301)897-8096
Publication E-mail: eprzygod@fisheries.org
Journal featuring applied and basic research results relating to the causes, effects, treatments and prevention of disease, particularly of fish and shellfish. **Freq:** Quarterly. **Print Method:** Offset. **Trim Size:** 7 x 10. **Cols./Page:** 2. **Col. Width:** 16.5 picas. **Col. Depth:** 49 picas. **Key Personnel:** David Speare, Editor; Jeffrey Wolf, Editor. **ISSN:** 0899-7659 (print). **Subscription Rates:** $404 Institutions online only; $460 Institutions print and online. **URL:** http://fisheries.org/publications_goa/journal-of-aquatic-animal-health-guide-for-authors-2015. **Remarks:** Accepts advertising. **Circ:** Paid 1500.

15178 ■ The Journal of Cardiac Failure
Heart Failure Society of America
6707 Democracy Blvd., Ste. 925
Bethesda, MD 20817
Phone: (301)312-8635
Free: 888-213-4417
Publisher's E-mail: info@hfsa.org
Freq: Monthly. **ISSN:** 1071--9164 (print). **Subscription Rates:** $444 Individuals U.S.A. (print and online); $603 Individuals Canada (print and online); $585 Individuals other countries (print and online); $765 Institutions U.S.A. (print and online); $907 Institutions other countries (print and online). **URL:** http://www.hfsa.org/journal-of-cardiac-failure; http://www.onlinejcf.com. **Remarks:** Advertising not accepted. **Circ:** (Not Reported).

15179 ■ Journal of Chiropractic Education
Association of Chiropractic Colleges
4424 Montgomery Ave., Ste. 202
Bethesda, MD 20814
Free: 800-284-1062
Publisher's E-mail: info@chirocolleges.org
Journal covering issues in chiropractic education. **Freq:** Semiannual latest edition March 2016. **Key Personnel:** Dr. Bart Green, Editor-in-Chief. **ISSN:** 1042--5055 (print); **EISSN:** 2374--250X (electronic). **Subscription Rates:** $50 Individuals; $60 Libraries. **URL:** http://www.journalchiroed.com. **Remarks:** Accepts advertising. **Circ:** (Not Reported).

15180 ■ Journal of Forestry
Society of American Foresters
5400 Grosvenor Ln.
Bethesda, MD 20814-2198
Fax: (301)897-3691
Free: 866-897-8720
Publication E-mail: journal@safnet.org
Peer-reviewed journal of forestry serves to advance the profession by keeping professionals informed about significant developments and ideas in forest science, natural resource management, and forest policy. **Freq:** Bimonthly January, March, May, July, September, and November. **Print Method:** Offset. **Trim Size:** 8 1/4 x 10 7/8. **Cols./Page:** 3. **Col. Width:** 26 nonpareils. **Col. Depth:** 140 agate lines. **Key Personnel:** Michael Kilgore, Associate Editor; W. Keith Moser, Editor. **ISSN:** 0022--1201 (print). **Subscription Rates:** $206 Nonmembers U.S./Canada, print only; $449 Institutions U.S./Canada, print only; $373 Nonmembers online only; $555 Institutions online only; $421 Nonmembers U.S./Canada, print and online; $643 Institutions U.S./Canada, print and online; Included in membership with STUDENT-, GOLD-, and PLATINUM-level membership of the Society of American Foresters. **URL:** http://www.safnet.org/publications/jof/index.cfm. **Ad Rates:** BW $3255; 4C $3047. **Remarks:** Accepts advertising. **Circ:** 14000, 12000.

15181 ■ Journal of Histochemistry and Cytochemistry
Histochemical Society
9650 Rockville Pke.
Bethesda, MD 20814
Phone: (301)634-7026
Fax: (301)634-7099
Publisher's E-mail: mail@histochemicalsociety.org
Journal dealing with histochemistry and cytochemistry. **Freq:** Monthly. **Key Personnel:** Kevin A. Roth, Associate Editor; Denis G. Baskin, Executive Editor. **ISSN:** 0022--1554 (print); **EISSN:** 1551--5044 (electronic). **Subscription Rates:** £1135 Institutions print & e-access; £724 Institutions e-access only. **URL:** http://www.uk.sagepub.com/journals/Journal201999; http://jhc.sagepub.com/. **Remarks:** Advertising accepted; rates available upon request. **Circ:** (Not Reported).

15182 ■ Journal of Immunology
American Association of Immunologists
1451 Rockville Pke., Ste. 650
Bethesda, MD 20814
Phone: (301)634-7178
Fax: (301)634-7887
Publisher's E-mail: infoaai@aai.org
Medical and science journal. **Freq:** Semimonthly issues on September15,2016. **Print Method:** Web press. **Trim Size:** 8 3/8 x 10 7/8. **Cols./Page:** 2. **Col. Width:** 32 nonpareils. **Col. Depth:** 119 agate lines. **Key Personnel:** Pamela J. Fink, Ph.D., Editor-in-Chief; Peter E. Lipsky, MD, Editor; Elizabeth Mosko, Representative. **ISSN:** 0022- 1767 (print); **EISSN:** 1550- 6606 (electronic). **Subscription Rates:** $260 Individuals; Included in membership; $775 U.S. online only; $785 U.S. online and print; $1065 Other countries online and print. **URL:** http://www.jimmunol.org. **Ad Rates:** $1395-1890, for full page; $925-1260, for 1/2 page; $635-865, for 1/4 page. BW $1,085; 4C $1,885; BW $, for full pageBW $, for 1/2 pageBW $, for 1/4 page4C $645, for 2 color; 4C $730, for matched colors; 4C $1425, for 4 color. **Remarks:** Accepts display and classified advertising. **Circ:** Paid ‡9079, Non-paid ‡263, 3,460.

15183 ■ Journal of Interferon and Cytokine Research
International Cytokine and Interferon Society
c/o Federation of American Societies for Experimental Biology
9650 Rockville Pke.
Bethesda, MD 20814
Phone: (301)634-7250
Fax: (301)634-7455
Publisher's E-mail: icis@faseb.org
Freq: Monthly. **Key Personnel:** Ganes C. Sen, Editor-in-Chief. **ISSN:** 1079--9907 (print); **EISSN:** 1557--7465 (electronic). **Subscription Rates:** $1134 Individuals U.S. (print and online); $1314 Individuals other countries (print and online); $1123 Individuals online only. **URL:** http://www.liebertpub.com/jir. **Remarks:** Accepts advertising. **Circ:** (Not Reported).

15184 ■ Journal of Leukocyte Biology
Society for Leukocyte Biology
9650 Rockville Pke.
Bethesda, MD 20814
Phone: (301)634-7814
Fax: (301)634-7455
Publisher's E-mail: info@wiley.com
Biological research journal. **Freq:** Monthly. **Print Method:** Offset. Uses mats. **Cols./Page:** 1. **Col. Width:** 44 nonpareils. **Col. Depth:** 133 agate lines. **Key Personnel:** Luis J. Montaner, Editor-in-Chief; Gail Bishop, Board Member; Jill Suttles, Associate Editor; Carleton C. Stewart, Editor; Roberta Frederick, Manager, Advertising. **ISSN:** 0741--5400 (print); **EISSN:** 1938--3673 (electronic). **URL:** http://www.jleukbio.org; http://leukocytebiology.org/Resources/JLB-Journal.aspx. **Ad Rates:** BW $299. **Remarks:** Accepts advertising. **Circ:** 1415, 500, 100.

15185 ■ Journal of Neurophysiology
American Physiological Society
9650 Rockville Pke.
Bethesda, MD 20814-3991
Phone: (301)634-7164
Fax: (301)634-7241
Journal covering the nervous system and its functions. **Freq:** Semimonthly. **Print Method:** Offset. **Trim Size:** 8 3/8 x 10 7/8. **Cols./Page:** 2. **Col. Width:** 21 picas. **Col. Depth:** 56 picas. **Key Personnel:** R. Scheman, Director, Publications, Editor; Mark L. Goodwin, Manager; M. Frank, Executive Director; Bill Yates, Editor-in-Chief; Michele A. Basso, Assistant Editor. **ISSN:** 0022--3077 (print); **EISSN:** 1522--1598 (electronic). **Subscription Rates:** $1390 Institutions Tier 1, online only; $1635 Institutions Tier 2, online only; $1870 Institutions Tier 3, online only; $1800 Institutions Tier 1, domestic, print and online; $2090 Institutions Tier 2, domestic, print and online; $2360 Institutions Tier 3, domestic, print and online; $1955 Institutions, other countries Tier 1, print and online; $2260 Institutions, other countries Tier 2, print and online; $2530 Institutions, other countries Tier 3, print and online; $2325 Institutions Tiers 1-5, print only domestic; $2505 Institutions, other countries Tiers 1-5, print only. **Alt. Formats:** PDF. **URL:** http://jn.physiology.org; http://www.the-aps.org/mm/Publications/Journals/JN. **Ad Rates:** BW $905; 4C $2,000. **Remarks:** Accepts advertising. **Circ:** Paid ‡500.

15186 ■ Journal of Nuclear Cardiology
American Society of Nuclear Cardiology
4340 East-West Hwy., Ste. 1120
Bethesda, MD 20814-4578
Phone: (301)215-7575
Fax: (301)215-7113
Publisher's E-mail: info@asnc.org
Freq: Bimonthly. **ISSN:** 1071-3581 (print); **EISSN:** 1532-6551 (electronic). **Subscription Rates:** €491 Institutions print incl. free access; €589 Institutions print plus enhance access. **URL:** http://www.onlinejnc.com; http://www.asnc.org/content_112.cfm. **Remarks:** Accepts advertising. **Circ:** 4,000.

15187 ■ Journal of Pharmacology & Experimental Therapeutics
American Society for Pharmacology and Experimental Therapeutics
9650 Rockville Pke.
Bethesda, MD 20814-3995
Phone: (301)634-7060
Fax: (301)634-7061
Publisher's E-mail: info@aspet.org
Medical and pharmaceutical journal. **Freq:** Monthly. **Print Method:** Offset. **Trim Size:** 8 1/8 x 10 7/8. **Cols./Page:** 2. **Col. Width:** 32 nonpareils. **Col. Depth:** 119 agate lines. **Key Personnel:** David S. Miller, Associate Editor; Michael F. Jarvis, Editor; Jill Filler, Managing Editor; Richard Dodenhoff, Director. **ISSN:** 0022--3565 (print). **Subscription Rates:** $959 Institutions tire 1; $1049 Institutions tire 2; $1192 Institutions tire 3; Included in membership. **URL:** http://jpet.aspetjournals.org. **Ad Rates:** BW $775; 4C $1,095. **Remarks:** Accepts advertising. **Circ:** ‡650, 650.

15188 ■ Journal of Vegetation Science
International Association for Vegetation Science
9650 Rockville Pke.
Bethesda, MD 20814
Phone: (301)634-7255
Publisher's E-mail: admin@iavs.org
Journal covering botany. **Freq:** Bimonthly. **Key Personnel:** Alessandro Chiarucci, Editor-in-Chief. **ISSN:** 1100--9233 (print); **EISSN:** 1654--1103 (electronic). **Subscription Rates:** $2315 Institutions print and online; £1182 Institutions print and online, UK; €1502 Institutions print and online, Europe; $2315 Institutions, other countries print and online; $1929 Institutions print or online; €985 Institutions print or online, UK; €1251 Institutions print or online. Europe; $1929 Institutions, other countries print or online. **URL:** http://iavs.org/Publications/Journal-of-Vegetation-Science.aspx; http://onlinelibrary.wiley.com/journal/10.1111/(ISSN)1654-1103. **Remarks:** Advertising not accepted. **Circ:** (Not Reported).

15189 ■ Journal of Vertebrate Paleontology
Society of Vertebrate Paleontology
9650 Rockville Pke.
Bethesda, MD 20814
Phone: (301)634-7024
Fax: (301)634-7455
Publisher's E-mail: svp@vertpaleo.org
Peer-reviewed journal publishing studies on the evolution, functional morphology, taxonomy, phylogeny, biostratigraphy, paleoecology and paleobiogeography of fossil vertebrates. **Freq:** Bimonthly. **ISSN:** 0272-4634 (print). **Subscription Rates:** $140 Individuals print and online; $125 Individuals online; $60 Students undergraduate/graduate (print and online); $50 Students undergraduate/graduate (online). **URL:** http://vertpaleo.org/Publications/Journal-of-Vertebrate-Paleontology.aspx. **Remarks:** Advertising not accepted. **Circ:** (Not Reported).

15190 ■ The Journal of Wildlife Management
The Wildlife Society
5410 Grosvenor Ln., Ste. 200
Bethesda, MD 20814-2144
Phone: (301)897-9770
Fax: (301)530-2471
Publisher's E-mail: sales@allenpress.com
Journal covering wildlife management. **Freq:** 8/year.

Key Personnel: Evelyn Merrill, Editor-in-Chief. **ISSN:** 0022--541X (print); **EISSN:** 1937--2817 (electronic). **Subscription Rates:** $1061 U.S., Canada, and Mexico online only; £749 Institutions online only (U.K.); €864 Institutions online only (Europe zone); $1274 U.S., Canada, and Mexico print and online; £952 Institutions print and online (U.K.); €1100 Institutions print and online (Europe zone); $1061 U.S., Canada, and Mexico print only ; £793 Institutions print only (U.K.); €916 Institutions print only (Europe zone). **URL:** http://onlinelibrary.wiley.com/journal/10.1002/(ISSN)1937-2817. **Mailing address:** PO Box 368, Lawrence, KS 66044-0368. **Remarks:** Accepts advertising. **Circ:** 7000.

15191 ■ Law/Technology
World Jurist Association
7910 Woodmont Ave., Ste. 1440
Bethesda, MD 20814
Phone: (202)466-5428
Fax: (202)452-8540
Publisher's E-mail: wja@worldjurist.org
Freq: Quarterly. **ISSN:** 0278--3916 (print). **Subscription Rates:** $120 Institutions libraries, agencies and organizations; $120 Nonmembers; $100 Members. **URL:** http://worldjurist.org/publications/lawtechnology. **Ad Rates:** BW $1000, full page; BW $500, half page. **Remarks:** Accepts advertising. **Circ:** (Not Reported).

15192 ■ Microbiology Abstracts Section C: Algology, Mycology & Protozoology
Cambridge Scientific Abstracts L.P.
7200 Wisconsin Ave., Ste. 601
Bethesda, MD 20814
Phone: (301)961-6700
Fax: (301)961-6720
Free: 800-843-7751
Publisher's E-mail: sales@proquest.com
Scientific journal. **Freq:** Monthly except Dec. **Print Method:** Offset. **Trim Size:** 6 1/2 x 9. **Cols./Page:** 2. **ISSN:** 0301-2328 (print). **Subscription Rates:** $1525 Individuals print + web edition, (includes shipping); $1145 Individuals web edition. **URL:** http://www.csa.com/e_products/printjalpha.php. **Circ:** (Not Reported).

15193 ■ Military Medicine
AMSUS - The Society of the Federal Health Professionals
9320 Old Georgetown Rd.
Bethesda, MD 20814-1653
Phone: (301)897-8800
Fax: (301)530-5446
Free: 800-761-9320
Publisher's E-mail: amsus@amsus.org
Journal for professional personnel affiliated with the Federal medical services. **Freq:** Monthly. **Print Method:** Web press. **Trim Size:** 8 1/8 x 10 7/8. **Cols./Page:** 2 and 1. **Col. Width:** 3 l/2 and 7 inches. **Col. Depth:** 9 2/3 and 4 inches. **Key Personnel:** Capt. William H.J. Haffner, Editor; Mike Cowan, Publisher. **ISSN:** 0026--4075 (print). **Subscription Rates:** $170 Individuals print and online; $225 Other countries; $488 Institutions community college, nursing chool, community hospital/clinic; $650 Institutions research universities; $813 Institutions medical school, major teaching/research hospital; $30 Single issue. **URL:** http://publications.amsus.org. **Ad Rates:** BW $1970; 4C $1515. **Remarks:** Accepts advertising. **Circ: 8974**.

15194 ■ Molecular Biology of the Cell
American Society for Cell Biology
8120 Woodmont Ave., Ste. 750
Bethesda, MD 20814
Phone: (301)347-9300
Fax: (301)347-9310
Publisher's E-mail: ascbinfo@ascb.org
Journal publishing research articles on cell biology, genetics, and developmental biology. **Freq:** Semimonthly. **Key Personnel:** David G. Drubin, Editor-in-Chief; Mark J. Solomon, Associate Editor; Thomas D. Pollard, Editor. **ISSN:** 1059--1524 (print); **EISSN:** 1939--4586 (electronic). **Subscription Rates:** Included in membership; $626 Institutions. **URL:** http://www.molbiolcell.org. **Remarks:** Accepts advertising. **Circ:** (Not Reported).

15195 ■ Molecular Pharmacology: An International Journal
American Society for Pharmacology and Experimental Therapeutics
9650 Rockville Pke.
Bethesda, MD 20814-3995
Phone: (301)634-7060
Fax: (301)634-7061
Publisher's E-mail: info@aspet.org
Medical journal.Publishes key findings derived from the application of innovative structural biology, biochemistry, biophysics, physiology, genetics, and molecular biology to basic pharmacological problems that provide novel insights that are relevant to the broad fields of pharmacology and toxicology. **Freq:** Monthly. **Print Method:** Offset. **Trim Size:** 8 1/8 x 10 7/8. **Cols./Page:** 2. **Col. Width:** 32 nonpareils. **Col. Depth:** 119 agate lines. **Key Personnel:** Richard Dodenhoff, Director; Jill Filler, Managing Editor. **ISSN:** 0026--895X (print). **Subscription Rates:** $704 Institutions Tier 1; $769 Institutions Tier 2; $884 Institutions Tier 3. **URL:** http://molpharm.aspetjournals.org. **Ad Rates:** BW $921; 4C $1,871. **Remarks:** Accepts advertising. **Circ:** 425.

15196 ■ NACHC Community Health Forum
National Association of Community Health Centers
7501 Wisconsin Ave., Ste. 1100W
Bethesda, MD 20814
Phone: (301)347-0400
Freq: Bimonthly. **Subscription Rates:** $35 /year; Included in membership. **URL:** http://www.nachc.com/communityhealthforum.cfm. **Ad Rates:** $2333-2880, full page. **Remarks:** Accepts advertising. **Circ:** 3,000.

15197 ■ Nuclear Medicine and Biology: Official Journal of the Society of Radiopharmaceutical Sciences
Mosby Inc.
10432 Snow Point Dr.
Bethesda, MD 20814
Fax: (301)564-3022
Journal publishing original research covering all aspects of radiopharmaceutical chemistry: synthesis, radiopharmacy, in vitro and ex vivo testing, and in vivo evaluation of molecular probes for PET, SPECT, planar imaging, and autoradiography. **Freq:** Monthly. **Print Method:** Sheetfed. **Trim Size:** 8 1/4 x 11. **Key Personnel:** William C. Eckelman, Editor-in-Chief; L. Aloj, Editor; M.W. Brechbiel, Editor. **ISSN:** 0969--8051 (print). **Subscription Rates:** $598 Individuals print & online; $684 Other countries print & online; $598 Students print & online; $684 Students, other countries print & online. **URL:** http://www.nucmedbio.com; http://www.journals.elsevier.com/nuclear-medicine-and-biology/. **Ad Rates:** BW $1,490; 4C $1,565. **Remarks:** Accepts advertising. **Circ:** ‡660.

15198 ■ Nucleic Acids Abstracts
Cambridge Scientific Abstracts L.P.
7200 Wisconsin Ave., Ste. 601
Bethesda, MD 20814
Phone: (301)961-6700
Fax: (301)961-6720
Free: 800-843-7751
Publisher's E-mail: sales@proquest.com
Scientific journal covering molecular biology. **Freq:** Monthly. **Print Method:** Offset. **Trim Size:** 6 1/2 x 9. **Cols./Page:** 2. **ISSN:** 0031- 8655 (print). **Alt. Formats:** PDF. **URL:** http://www.proquest.com/customer-care/title-lists/ProQuest-Dialog-Prosheets.html. **Circ:** (Not Reported).

15199 ■ Oceanic Abstracts
Cambridge Scientific Abstracts L.P.
7200 Wisconsin Ave., Ste. 601
Bethesda, MD 20814
Phone: (301)961-6700
Fax: (301)961-6720
Free: 800-843-7751
Publisher's E-mail: sales@proquest.com
Journal covering oceanography, meteorology, marine biology, offshore engineering, living and non-living resources, law, ship technology, navigation and communications, the shipping industry, geology, geophysics, geochemistry, pollution, and conservation. **Founded:** 1981. **Freq:** Monthly. **Print Method:** Offset. **Trim Size:** 8 1/2 x 11. **Cols./Page:** 2. **Col. Width:** 42 nonpareils. **Col. Depth:** 133 agate lines. **ISSN:** 0748-1489 (print). **URL:** http://www.proquest.com/customer-care/title-lists/Title-Lists-CSA.html. **Circ:** (Not Reported).

15200 ■ OT Practice
The American Occupational Therapy Association, Inc.
4720 Montgomery Ln., Ste. 200
Bethesda, MD 20814-3449
Phone: (301)652-6611
Fax: (301)652-7711
Free: 800-729-2682
Publication E-mail: otpractice@aota.org
Professional magazine for occupational therapy practitioners. **Freq:** 22/ year. **Key Personnel:** Ted McKenna, Editor; Tracy Hammond, Manager, Advertising; Sarah Ely, Manager, Production. **ISSN:** 1084-4902 (print). **Subscription Rates:** $225 Individuals Individuals; $225 Institutions Institutions; $225 Canada Individuals; $225 Canada Institutions; $325 Other countries via air mail - Individuals; $380 Other countries via air mail - Institutions. **URL:** http://www.aota.org/en/Publications-News/OTP.aspx. **Formerly**: OT Week. **Ad Rates:** BW $2,572; 4C $3,072. **Remarks:** Accepts advertising. **Circ:** ‡36500.

15201 ■ OTJR: Occupation, Participation and Health
American Occupational Therapy Foundation
4720 Montgomery Ln., Ste. 202
Bethesda, MD 20814-3449
Phone: (240)292-1079
Fax: (240)396-6188
Publisher's E-mail: aotf@aotf.org
Peer-reviewed journal presenting original articles on occupational therapy research. **Freq:** Quarterly. **Key Personnel:** Prof. Sherrilene Classen, PhD, Editor. **ISSN:** 1539--4492 (print); **EISSN:** 1938--2383 (electronic). **Subscription Rates:** $124 Individuals print and online; $348 Institutions online; $379 Institutions print only; $387 Institutions print and online; $40 Individuals single print issue; $104 Institutions single print issue. **URL:** http://otj.sagepub.com. **Remarks:** Advertising not accepted. **Circ:** Paid 725.

15202 ■ Participation
IDB Family Association
1 Democracy Ctr., Ste. 110
6901 Rockledge Dr.
Bethesda, MD 20817
Phone: (301)493-6576
Fax: (301)493-6456
Publisher's E-mail: familya@iadb.org
Freq: Semiannual. **Subscription Rates:** Free. **Remarks:** Advertising not accepted. **Circ:** (Not Reported).

15203 ■ PDA Journal of Pharmaceutical Science and Technology
Parenteral Drug Association
Bethesda Towers, Ste. 150
4350 E West Hwy.
Bethesda, MD 20814-4485
Phone: (301)656-5900
Fax: (301)986-0296
Publisher's E-mail: info@pda.org
Peer-reviewed professional journal covering pharmaceutical science. **Freq:** Bimonthly. **Trim Size:** 8 1/4 x 11. **Cols./Page:** 2. **Key Personnel:** Richard V. Levy, PhD, Senior Vice President; Antonio Moreira, Associate Editor; Govind Rao, Editor-in-Chief. **ISSN:** 1079-7440 (print). **Subscription Rates:** $135 U.S.; $90 Other countries; $1195 Institutions 1-100 employees; $2095 Institutions 101-300 employees; $3695 Institutions 301-500 employees; Included in membership free online access. **URL:** http://journal.pda.org. **Formerly**: Journal of Parenteral Science and Technology. **Ad Rates:** BW $1,188; 4C $2,138. **Remarks:** Accepts advertising. **Circ:** 10500, Controlled 10000.

15204 ■ PE & RS Photogrammetric Engineering & Remote Sensing
ASPRS, The Imaging and Geospatial Information Society
5410 Grosvenor Ln., Ste. 210
Bethesda, MD 20814-2160
Phone: (301)493-0290
Fax: (301)493-0208
Publisher's E-mail: asprs@asprs.org
Peer-reviewed journal covering photogrammetry, remote sensing, geographic information systems, cartography, and surveying, global positioning systems, digital photogrammetry. **Freq:** Monthly. **Print Method:** Offset. **Trim Size:** 8 3/8 x 10 7/8. **Cols./Page:** 2 and 4. **Col. Width:** 21.5 and 9.6 picas. **Col. Depth:** 56 picas. **Key Personnel:** Michael Hauck, Publisher. **ISSN:** 0099--1112 (print). **Subscription Rates:** $1160 Individuals

Circulation: ★ = AAM; △ or • = BPA; ♦ = CAC; ❑ = VAC; ⊕ = PO Statement; ‡ = Publisher's Report; Boldface figures = sworn; Light figures = estimated.

print and online; $1224 Canada print and online; $1175 Other countries print and online; $899 U.S. digital; $944 Canada; $959 U.S. print; $1013 Canada print; $974 Other countries print. **URL:** http://www.asprs.org/Photogrammetric-Engineering-and-Remote-Sensing/PE-RS-Journals.html. **Remarks:** Accepts advertising. **Circ:** (Not Reported).

15205 ■ Pharmacoepidemiology and Drug Safety
International Society for Pharmacoepidemiology
5272 River Rd., Ste. 630
Bethesda, MD 20816
Phone: (301)718-6500
Fax: (301)656-0989
Publisher's E-mail: ispe@paimgmt.com
Freq: Monthly. **Key Personnel:** B.L. Strom, Editor. **ISSN:** 1053--8569 (print); **EISSN:** 1099--1557 (electronic). **Subscription Rates:** $2474 Institutions print or online; $2969 Institutions print and online; $1607 Individuals online only; £1264 Institutions print or online; £1517 Institutions print and online; €1599 Institutions print or online; €1919 Institutions print and online. **URL:** http://www.pharmacoepi.org/resources/journals.cfm; http://onlinelibrary.wiley.com/journal/10.1002/(ISSN)1099-1557. **Remarks:** Advertising accepted; rates available upon request. **Circ:** (Not Reported).

15206 ■ Pharmacological Reviews
American Society for Pharmacology and Experimental Therapeutics
9650 Rockville Pke.
Bethesda, MD 20814-3995
Phone: (301)634-7060
Fax: (301)634-7061
Publication E-mail: subscriptions@aspet.org
Medical journal.Contains important review articles on topics of high current interest. Topics covered have included biochemical and cellular pharmacology, drug metabolism and disposition, renal pharmacology, neuropharmacology, behavioral pharmacology, clinical pharmacology, and toxicology. **Freq:** Quarterly. **Print Method:** Offset. **Trim Size:** 8 1/8 x 10 7/8. **Cols./Page:** 2. **Col. Width:** 32 nonpareils. **Col. Depth:** 119 agate lines. **Key Personnel:** David R. Sibley, Editor. **ISSN:** 0031--6997 (print); **EISSN:** 1521--0081 (electronic). **Subscription Rates:** $286 Individuals Tier 1; $312 Individuals Tier 2; $377 Individuals Tier 3. **URL:** http://pharmrev.aspetjournals.org. **Ad Rates:** BW $790; 4C $1,465. **Remarks:** Accepts advertising. **Circ:** 600.

15207 ■ Physiological Genomics
American Physiological Society
9650 Rockville Pke.
Bethesda, MD 20814-3991
Phone: (301)634-7164
Fax: (301)634-7241
Published material related to the Human Genome Project and related materials. **Freq:** Semimonthly 24/yr. **Key Personnel:** Andy Greene, Editor-in-Chief; Julian Dow, Associate Editor; Andrew Greene, Editor-in-Chief; Victor J. Dzau, Editor, Founder; Bruce Aronow, Associate Editor. **ISSN:** 1094-8341 (print); **EISSN:** 1531--2267 (electronic). **Subscription Rates:** $335 Institutions Tier 1; $400 Institutions Tier 2; $455 Institutions Tier 3; $385 Institutions Tier 2, online only; $430 Institutions Tier 3, online only. **URL:** http://physiolgenomics.physiology.org; http://www.the-aps.org/mm/Publications/Journals/Physiol-Genomics. **Ad Rates:** BW $1,070; 4C $1,095; SAU $415. **Remarks:** Accepts advertising. **Circ:** ‡1700, 2,200.

15208 ■ Physiological Reviews
American Physiological Society
9650 Rockville Pke.
Bethesda, MD 20814-3991
Phone: (301)634-7164
Fax: (301)634-7241
Review journal covering physiology, biochemistry, nutrition, biophysics, and neuroscience. **Print Method:** Offset. **Trim Size:** 8 3/8 x 10 7/8. **Cols./Page:** 2. **Col. Width:** 21 picas. **Col. Depth:** 56 picas. **Key Personnel:** Mark L. Goodwin, Manager; Dennis Brown, Editor-in-Chief. **ISSN:** 0031-9333 (print); **EISSN:** 1522--1210 (electronic). **Subscription Rates:** $690 Individuals Tiers 1-5: print only, domestic; $730 Individuals Tiers 1-5: print only, international; $465 Individuals Tier 1, online only; $535 Individuals Tier 2: online only; $605 Individuals Tier 3: online only; $465 Individuals Tier 1: online, ; $555 Individuals Tier 2: online, ; $640 Individuals Tier 3: online, ; $590 Individuals Tier 1: print and online, domestic; $690 Individuals Tier 2: print and online, domestic; $770 Individuals Tier 3: print and online, domestic; $630 Other countries Tier 1, print and online; $725 Other countries Tier 2, print and online; $820 Other countries Tier 3, print and online; $760 Institutions Tiers 1-5, print only; $805 Other countries Tiers 1-5, print only. **URL:** http://physrev.physiology.org; http://www.the-aps.org/mm/Publications/Journals/PhysRev. **Ad Rates:** BW $1070; 4C $2165. **Remarks:** Accepts advertising. **Circ:** Paid ‡1050, ‡900.

15209 ■ Poet Lore
The Writer's Center
4508 Walsh St.
Bethesda, MD 20815
Phone: (301)654-8664
Fax: (240)223-0458
Poetry magazine. **Freq:** Semiannual. **Print Method:** Offset. **Trim Size:** 6 1/4 x 9. **Cols./Page:** 1. **Col. Width:** 60 nonpareils. **Col. Depth:** 100 agate lines. **Key Personnel:** David Lehman, Editor; Michele Wolf, Editor; David Wagoner, Editor; Jean Nordhaus, Editor; Tony Hoagland, Editor; Ethelbert E. Miller, Executive Editor; Jody Bolz, Executive Editor; Caitlin Hill, Managing Editor. **ISSN:** 0032--1966 (print). **Subscription Rates:** $25 Individuals /year; $9 Single issue. **URL:** http://www.writer.org/page.aspx?pid=664. **Remarks:** Advertising accepted; rates available upon request. **Circ:** Paid ‡600, Non-paid ‡10.

15210 ■ Pollution Abstracts
Cambridge Scientific Abstracts L.P.
7200 Wisconsin Ave., Ste. 601
Bethesda, MD 20814
Phone: (301)961-6700
Fax: (301)961-6720
Free: 800-843-7751
Publication E-mail: sales@csa.com
Journal covering environmental pollution. **Founded:** 1970. **Freq:** Monthly. **Print Method:** Letterpress and Offset. **Trim Size:** 8 1/2 x 11. **Cols./Page:** 2. **Col. Width:** 42 nonpareils. **Col. Depth:** 133 agate lines. **ISSN:** 0032-3624 (print). **URL:** http://www.csa.com/factsheets/pollution-set-c.php. **Circ:** (Not Reported).

15211 ■ Psychosomatics
Academy of Psychosomatic Medicine
5272 River Rd., Ste. 630
Bethesda, MD 20816-1453
Phone: (301)718-6520
Fax: (301)656-0989
Publisher's E-mail: info@apm.org
Freq: Bimonthly. **ISSN:** 0033--3182 (print). **Subscription Rates:** Included in membership; $282 Individuals in U.S. (online and print); $334 Individuals in Canada, Mexico and other countries (online and print); $154 Students in U.S. (online and print). **URL:** http://www.psychosomaticsjournal.com. **Ad Rates:** $375-1110; $815-1275. BW $4C $. **Remarks:** Accepts display advertising. **Circ:** (Not Reported).

15212 ■ RadTech Report
RadTech International North America
7720 Wisconsin Ave., Ste. 208
Bethesda, MD 20814
Phone: (240)497-1242
Publisher's E-mail: uveb@radtech.org
Freq: Bimonthly. **ISSN:** 1056- 0793 (print). **Subscription Rates:** Included in membership; $60 U.S., Canada, and Mexico /year for nonmembers; $95 Other countries /year for nonmembers. **URL:** http://www.radtech.org/magazinearchives. **Ad Rates:** BW $1,100. **Remarks:** Accepts advertising. **Circ:** 2000.

15213 ■ Risk Abstracts
Cambridge Scientific Abstracts L.P.
7200 Wisconsin Ave., Ste. 601
Bethesda, MD 20814
Phone: (301)961-6700
Fax: (301)961-6720
Free: 800-843-7751
Publisher's E-mail: sales@proquest.com
Journal covering the assessment and management of risk. **Founded:** 1990. **Freq:** Quarterly. **ISSN:** 0824-3336 (print). **URL:** http://ft.csa.com/factsheets/risk-set-c.php. **Circ:** (Not Reported).

15214 ■ RNA Journal
RNA Society
9650 Rockville Pke.
Bethesda, MD 20814-3998
Phone: (301)634-7166
Journal providing rapid communication of significant original research in all areas of the RNA structure and function in eukaryotic, prokaryotic, and viral systems. **Freq:** Monthly. **Subscription Rates:** Included in membership. **URL:** http://www.rnasociety.org/rna-journal/. **Remarks:** Accepts advertising. **Circ:** 40000.

15215 ■ School Psychology Review
National Association of School Psychologists
4340 E West Hwy., Ste. 402
Bethesda, MD 20814
Phone: (301)657-0270
Fax: (301)657-0275
Free: 866-331-NASP
Professional publication covering mental health and education. **Freq:** Quarterly. **Trim Size:** 7 x 10. **Key Personnel:** Thomas J. Power, Advisor; Matthew K. Burns, Editor; Shane Jimerson, Advisor; Susan M. Swearer, Advisor. **ISSN:** 0279--6015 (print). **URL:** http://www.nasponline.org/resources-and-publications/publications/about-spr. **Remarks:** Accepts advertising. **Circ:** (Not Reported).

15216 ■ Seminars in Hematology
Elsevier Inc.
c/o Neal S. Young, MD, Ed.
National Institutes of Health
Bethesda, MD 20892-0002
Publication E-mail: elspcs@elsevier.com
Medical journal covering articles of importance in clinical hematology and related fields for hematologists, internists, pathologists, blood banks, hospital staff, residents, and medical schools. **Freq:** Quarterly. **Print Method:** Web Offset. **Trim Size:** 8 1/4 x 11. **Cols./Page:** 1. **Col. Width:** 42 nonpareils. **Col. Depth:** 140 agate lines. **Key Personnel:** Photis Beris, MD, Editor; Neal S. Young, MD, Editor. **ISSN:** 0037--1963 (print). **Subscription Rates:** $367 Individuals; $578 Institutions. **URL:** http://journals.elsevier.com/seminars-in-hematology. **Ad Rates:** BW $2,060; 4C $1,700. **Remarks:** Accepts advertising. **Circ:** Combined ‡1214.

15217 ■ Teacher Magazine
Editorial Projects in Education
6935 Arlington Rd., Ste. 100
Bethesda, MD 20814
Phone: (301)280-3100
Fax: (301)280-3200
Free: 800-346-1834
Professional magazine for elementary and secondary school teachers. **Freq:** 9/year. **Print Method:** Offset. **Trim Size:** 10 3/4 x 14 5/8. **Cols./Page:** 5. **Key Personnel:** Virginia B. Edwards, Editor. **ISSN:** 1046--6193 (print). **URL:** http://www.edweek.org/tm/tb. **Remarks:** Accepts advertising. **Circ:** (Not Reported).

15218 ■ Toxicology Abstracts
Cambridge Scientific Abstracts L.P.
7200 Wisconsin Ave., Ste. 601
Bethesda, MD 20814
Phone: (301)961-6700
Fax: (301)961-6720
Free: 800-843-7751
Publisher's E-mail: sales@proquest.com
Scientific journal covering all aspects of toxicology. **Freq:** Monthly. **Print Method:** Offset. **Trim Size:** 6 1/2 x 9. **Cols./Page:** 2. **ISSN:** 0140-5365 (print). **URL:** http://www.proquest.com/customer-care/title-lists/ProQuest-Dialog-Prosheets.html. **Circ:** (Not Reported).

15219 ■ Transfusion
American Association of Blood Banks
8101 Glenbrook Rd.
Bethesda, MD 20814-2749
Phone: (301)907-6977
Fax: (301)907-6895
Publisher's E-mail: aabb@aabb.org
Freq: Monthly. **ISSN:** 0041- 1132 (print). **Subscription Rates:** Included in membership; $345 Individuals; $1097 Institutions. **URL:** http://www.aabb.org/programs/publications/Pages/transfusion.aspx; http://onlinelibrary.wiley.com/journal/10.1111/(ISSN)1537-2995. **Remarks:** Accepts advertising. **Circ:** 12,800.

15220 ■ Transfusion: Official Publication of the American Association of Blood Banks
American Association of Blood Banks
8101 Glenbrook Rd.
Bethesda, MD 20814-2749
Phone: (301)907-6977
Fax: (301)907-6895
Publisher's E-mail: aabb@aabb.org
Peer-reviewed journal publishing original manuscripts and preliminary reports in all fields relating to clinical transfusion, blood groups, immunology, genetics, anthropology and marrow and stem cell transplantation. **Freq:** Monthly. **Print Method:** Sheetfed offset. **Trim Size:** 8 5/8 x 11 1/8. **Cols./Page:** 2. **Col. Width:** 39 nonpareils. **Col. Depth:** 140 agate lines. **Key Personnel:** Paul M. Ness, Editor. **ISSN:** 0041-1132 (print); **EISSN:** 1537-2995 (electronic). **Subscription Rates:** $345 Individuals print + online; $329 Individuals online only; $1097 Institutions print + online; $914 Institutions online only; €468 Individuals print + online; €443 Individuals online only; £1049 Institutions print + online; £874 Institutions online only; £313 Individuals print + online, rest of world; £397 Individuals online only, rest of world; Free AABB members. **URL:** http://www.aabb.org/programs/publications/Pages/transfusion.aspx; http://onlinelibrary.wiley.com/journal/10.1111/(ISSN)1537-2995/issues. **Ad Rates:** GLR $12; BW $2,494; 4C $3,996. **Remarks:** Accepts advertising. **Circ:** Combined ‡10523.

15221 ■ U.S.A.E.: The National Independent Association Newspaper
Custom News Inc.
4341 Montgomery Ave.
Bethesda, MD 20814
Fax: (301)841-0040
Free: 800-627-8723
Publisher's E-mail: mail@usaenews.com
Weekly news of associations CVBs and hotels. **Freq:** Weekly (Tues.) except Christmas week. **Print Method:** Offset. **Trim Size:** 11 x 16. **Cols./Page:** 4. **Col. Width:** 14 picas. **Col. Depth:** 14 inches. **Key Personnel:** Anne Daly Heller, Publisher. **ISSN:** 0894--8194 (print). **USPS:** 702-930. **Subscription Rates:** $19.95 Individuals online; $150 Individuals print and online; $235 Individuals print and online (first class mail delivery). **URL:** http://www.usaenews.com. **Ad Rates:** BW $4,885; 4C $4,530. **Remarks:** Accepts advertising. **Circ:** 2000.

15222 ■ Virology and AIDS Abstracts
Cambridge Scientific Abstracts L.P.
7200 Wisconsin Ave., Ste. 601
Bethesda, MD 20814
Phone: (301)961-6700
Fax: (301)961-6720
Free: 800-843-7751
Publisher's E-mail: sales@proquest.com
Scientific journal which covers world scientific literature on human, animal, and plant viruses, with emphasis on AIDS. **Freq:** Monthly. **Print Method:** Offset. **Trim Size:** 6 1/2 x 9. **Cols./Page:** 2. **ISSN:** 0896-5919 (print). **Subscription Rates:** $1495 Individuals print + web edition, (includes shipping); $1120 Individuals web edition. **URL:** http://www.proquest.com/customer-care/title-lists/ProQuest-Dialog-Prosheets.html. **Circ:** (Not Reported).

15223 ■ Youth Theatre Journal
American Alliance for Theatre and Education
4908 Auburn Ave.
Bethesda, MD 20814
Phone: (301)200-1944
Fax: (301)280-1682
Publisher's E-mail: book.orders@tandf.co.uk
Peer-reviewed journal publishing ideas relating to practical and theoretical developments in the field of theatre and performance. **Freq:** Semiannual. **Key Personnel:** Drew Chappel, Editor; Gustave J. Weltsek, Board Member. **ISSN:** 0892--9092 (print); **EISSN:** 1948--4798 (electronic). **Subscription Rates:** $47 Individuals print only; $124 Institutions online only; $142 Institutions print and online. **URL:** http://www.tandfonline.com/toc/uytj20/current. **Remarks:** Accepts advertising. **Circ:** (Not Reported).

15224 ■ WCYK-AM - 810
7500 Old Georgetown Rd., 15th Fl.
Bethesda, MD 20814-6195
Phone: (434)978-4408
Free: 800-997-6534
Format: Country. **Simulcasts:** WCYK-FM. **Founded:** 1970. **Formerly:** WCNF-AM; WPED-AM. **Operating Hours:** Sunrise-sunset. **ADI:** Charlottesville, VA. **Key Personnel:** Bill Thomas, Dir. of Programs, billthomas@clearchannel.com; Pam Garrison, Promotions Dir., pamelad.garrison@clearchannel.com; Mike Chiumento, Gen. Sales Mgr.; Yon O'Conner, Account Mgr., yonoconner@clearchannel.com; Phil Robken, Gen. Mgr., philrobken@clearchannel.com; Steve Gaines, Gen. Mgr.; Vinnie Kice, Operations Mgr. **Wattage:** 1,000. **Ad Rates:** Noncommercial. $65 for 60 seconds.

BOWIE

Prince George's Co. Prince George's Co. (SC). 20 m SW of Baltimore. Bowie State College. Site of the Bowie Race Course. Steel mill. Dairy, poultry, truck farms.

15225 ■ The Bowie-Blade News
Capital Publishing Co.
6911 Laurel-Bowie Rd., Ste. 307
Bowie, MD 20715
Phone: (301)262-3700
Fax: (301)464-7027
Publication E-mail: letters@bladenews.com
Newspaper. **Freq:** Weekly (Thurs.). **Print Method:** Offset. **Cols./Page:** 6. **Col. Width:** 26 nonpareils. **Col. Depth:** 301 agate lines. **Key Personnel:** David Emanuel, Editor; Rick Osterfeld, Manager, Circulation. **Subscription Rates:** $156 By mail. **URL:** http://www.capitalgazette.com/bowie_bladenews. **Remarks:** Accepts advertising. **Circ:** Free ‡24988, Paid ‡72, Combined ‡25060.

BOYDS

15226 ■ Congressional Digest
Congressional Digest Corp.
PO Box 240
Boyds, MD 20841-0240
Phone: (301)916-1800
Fax: (240)599-7679
Publisher's E-mail: support@congressionaldigest.com
Unique 'Pro & Con' analysis shows you both sides of important Congressional controversies. Topics recently covered include Chemical Weapons Control, Deficit Reduction and Affirmation Action. **Freq:** 10/year. **Print Method:** Offset. **Trim Size:** 8 1/2 x 11. **Cols./Page:** 2. **Col. Width:** 42 nonpareils. **Col. Depth:** 140 agate lines. **ISSN:** 0010--5899 (print). **Subscription Rates:** $295 Individuals; $570 Individuals online. **URL:** http://congressionaldigest.com. **Remarks:** Advertising not accepted. **Circ:** (Not Reported).

BRUNSWICK

Frederick Co. Frederick Co. (N). 14 m SW of Frederick. Residential.

15227 ■ The Brunswick Citizen
Citizen Communications Inc.
101 W Potomac St.
Brunswick, MD 21716
Phone: (301)834-7722
Free: 877-834-6500
Publisher's E-mail: citizen@mip.net
Local newspaper. **Freq:** Weekly. **Print Method:** Offset. **Cols./Page:** 5. **Col. Width:** 24 nonpareils. **Col. Depth:** 14 agate lines. **Subscription Rates:** $15.50 Individuals in Frederick County 1 year; $23.50 Individuals the rest of Maryland 1 year; $32 Elsewhere 1 year; $25 Two years in Frederick County and Loudoun County; $39 Two years Other Maryland; $49 Two years elsewhere. **URL:** http://www.citizennewspapers.com/about_the_BC.html. **Ad Rates:** BW $371.95. **Remarks:** Accepts advertising. **Circ:** 3100.

15228 ■ The Middletown Valley Citizen
Citizen Communications Inc.
101 W Potomac St.
Brunswick, MD 21716
Phone: (301)834-7722
Free: 877-834-6500
Publisher's E-mail: citizen@mip.net
Community newspaper. **Freq:** Weekly. **Print Method:** Offset. **Cols./Page:** 5. **Col. Width:** 2 inches. **Col. Depth:** 14 inches. **ISSN:** 1056--7674 (print). **Subscription Rates:** $17.50 Individuals; $30 Two years. **URL:** http://www.citizennewspapers.com. **Remarks:** Accepts advertising. **Circ:** Paid ‡2000.

CALVERTON

15229 ■ Intermodal Insights
Intermodal Association of North America
11785 Beltsville Dr., Ste. 1100
Calverton, MD 20705
Phone: (301)982-3400
Publisher's E-mail: info@intermodal.org
Magazine containing latest news affecting the intermodal freight transportation industry. **Freq:** Monthly. **Subscription Rates:** Included in membership. **URL:** http://www.intermodal.org/business/advertising/advertising.php. **Remarks:** Accepts advertising. **Circ:** (Not Reported).

CAMBRIDGE

Dorchester Co. Dorchester Co. (SE). On Choptank River, 32 m W of Salisbury. Manufactures lumber, wire cloth, electronics, boats; vegetable, seafood canneries. Commercial fisheries. Oysters and crabs. Frozen fish processing. Metal casting. Printing and publishing. Farming. Tomatoes, wheat, corn, soybeans.

15230 ■ Dorchester/Eastern Shore Banner
Independent Newsmedia Inc.
103 Cedar St.
Cambridge, MD 21613
Phone: (410)228-3131
Publisher's E-mail: help@newszap.com
Community newspaper. **Freq:** Semiweekly (Wed. and Fri.). **Key Personnel:** Darel LaPrade, Publisher; Ed Dulin, President, Chief Executive Officer. **Subscription Rates:** $39 Individuals home delivery; $.50 Single issue. **URL:** http://www.dorchesterbanner.com. **Mailing address:** PO Box 580, Cambridge, MD 21613. **Remarks:** Accepts advertising. **Circ:** Paid ♦**2419**.

15231 ■ The Dorchester Star
Chesapeake Publishing Corp.
511 Poplar St.
Cambridge, MD 21613
Phone: (410)228-0222
Publication E-mail: dorchesterstar@chespub.com
Community newspaper. **Freq:** Weekly (Wed.). **Key Personnel:** David Fike, Publisher, phone: (443)245-5054; Gail Dean, Editor. **Subscription Rates:** $75 Individuals 52 weeks; online; $50 Individuals 26 weeks; online; $10.95 Individuals 4 weeks; online; $6.95 Individuals 4 weeks auto-renewing (online); $127 Individuals 52 weeks; print and online; $106 Individuals 40 weeks; print and online; $59 Individuals 20 weeks; print and online; $34 Individuals 10 weeks; print and online. **URL:** http://www.dorchesterstar.com; http://www.stardem.com/chespub/products/article_9d64f918-c1ae-11e3-80b1-0019bb2963f4.html. **Ad Rates:** GLR $.71; BW $9.95; 4C $12.45; PCI $8.95. **Remarks:** Accepts advertising. **Circ:** Non-paid ♦**12500**.

15232 ■ WAAI-FM - 100.9
2 Bay St.
Cambridge, MD 21613
Phone: (410)228-4800
Format: Country. **Networks:** AP. **Owner:** MTS Broadcasting L.L.C., 2 Bay St., Cambridge, MD 21613, Ph: (410)228-4800. **Founded:** 1989. **Operating Hours:** Continuous. **Key Personnel:** Troy Hill, Gen. Mgr., troydhill@verizon.net; Shane Walker, Operations Mgr., shanewalker25@comcast.net; Beverly Jones, Bus. Mgr., bjones211@comcast.net. **Wattage:** 1,300. **Ad Rates:** Noncommercial. **URL:** http://www.mtslive.com.

15233 ■ WCEM-AM - 1240
2 Bay St.
Cambridge, MD 21613
Phone: (410)228-4800
Format: Sports. **Networks:** ABC. **Owner:** MTS Broadcasting L.L.C., 2 Bay St., Cambridge, MD 21613, Ph: (410)228-4800. **Founded:** 1947. **Formerly:** WCMD-AM. **Operating Hours:** Continuous; 90% network, 10% local. **Key Personnel:** Troy Hill, Gen. Mgr., troydhill@verizon.net. **Wattage:** 1,000. **Ad Rates:** $6.50-20.75 for 30 seconds; $8.50-23.75 for 60 seconds. WCEM-FM; WAAI-FM; WTDK-FM. **URL:** http://www.mtslive.com.

15234 ■ WCEM-FM - 106.3
2 Bay St.
Cambridge, MD 21613

Circulation: ★ = AAM; △ or • = BPA; ♦ = CAC; ❑ = VAC; ⊕ = PO Statement; ‡ = Publisher's Report; Boldface figures = sworn; Light figures = estimated.

Phone: (410)376-3663
Fax: (410)228-0130
Format: Top 40; Full Service. **Owner:** MTS Broadcasting L.L.C., 2 Bay St., Cambridge, MD 21613, Ph: (410)228-4800. **Wattage:** 6,000. **Ad Rates:** Advertising accepted; rates available upon request. **URL:** http://www.mtslive.com.

15235 ■ WTDK-FM
2 Bay St.
Cambridge, MD 21613
Format: Oldies. **Founded:** 1306. **Wattage:** 3,900 ERP. **URL:** http://www.mtslive.com/.

CAMP SPRINGS

Prince George's Co. (SC). 5 m E of Washington, DC. Residential.

15236 ■ Seafarers LOG
Seafarers International Union
5201 Auth Way
Camp Springs, MD 20746
Phone: (301)899-0675
Fax: (301)899-7355
Monthly tabloid on maritime labor. **Freq:** Monthly Monday through Friday, 8 a.m. to 5 p.m. **Print Method:** Offset. **Cols./Page:** 4. **Col. Width:** 32 nonpareils. **Col. Depth:** 200 agate lines. **ISSN:** 1086--4636 (print). **Alt. Formats:** PDF. **URL:** http://www.seafarers.org/seafarerslog/seafarerslog.asp. **Remarks:** Advertising not accepted. **Circ:** Non-paid ‡43000.

CATONSVILLE

15237 ■ Arbutus Times
Patuxent Publishing Co.
757 Frederick Rd., Ste. 103
Catonsville, MD 21228
Phone: (410)788-4500
Publisher's E-mail: jquimby@patuxent.com
Suburban community newspaper. **Freq:** Weekly (Wed.). **Print Method:** Offset. **Cols./Page:** 5. **Col. Width:** 22 nonpareils. **Col. Depth:** 210 agate lines. **Key Personnel:** Keith Meisel, Editor. **Subscription Rates:** $24.95 Individuals; $37.95 Two years. **URL:** http://touch.baltimoresun.com; http://baltimoresunmediagroup.com/media-portfolio/newspapers/arbutus-times. **Remarks:** Accepts advertising. **Circ:** Combined ♦**1723.**

15238 ■ Catonsville Times
Patuxent Publishing Co.
757 Frederick Rd., Ste. 103
Catonsville, MD 21228
Phone: (410)788-4500
Publisher's E-mail: jquimby@patuxent.com
Suburban community newspaper. **Freq:** Weekly (Wed.). **Print Method:** Offset. **Trim Size:** 11 x 15. **Cols./Page:** 5. **Col. Width:** 11 picas. **Col. Depth:** 80.25 picas. **Key Personnel:** Keith Meisel, Editor. **Subscription Rates:** $24.95 Individuals; $37.95 Two years. **URL:** http://www.baltimoresun.com/news/maryland/baltimore-county/catonsville; http://baltimoresunmediagroup.com/media-portfolio/newspapers/catonsville-times. **Remarks:** Accepts advertising. **Circ:** Combined ♦**3150.**

15239 ■ Decision Analysis: A Journal of the Institute for Operation Research and the Management Sciences
Institute for Operations Research and the Management Sciences
5521 Research Park Dr., Ste. 200
Catonsville, MD 21228
Phone: (443)757-3500
Fax: (443)757-3515
Free: 800-446-3676
Publisher's E-mail: informs@informs.org
Peer-reviewed journal that aims to advance the theory, application, and teaching of all aspects of decision analysis. **Freq:** Quarterly. **Key Personnel:** L. Robin Keller, Associate Editor, phone: (949)824-6348. **ISSN:** 1545--8490 (print); **EISSN:** 1545--8504 (electronic). **Subscription Rates:** $430 Institutions online only; $488 Institutions print and online; $528 Institutions print and online, other countries; $35 Members online only; $85 Members print and online. **URL:** http://pubsonline.informs.org/journal/deca. **Circ:** (Not Reported).

15240 ■ Informs Transactions on Education
Institute for Operations Research and the Management Sciences
5521 Research Park Dr., Ste. 200
Catonsville, MD 21228
Phone: (443)757-3500
Fax: (443)757-3515
Free: 800-446-3676
Publisher's E-mail: informs@informs.org
Freq: 3/year. **EISSN:** 1532--0545 (electronic). **Subscription Rates:** Included in membership. **URL:** http://pubsonline.informs.org/journal/ited; http://www.informs.org/Find-Research-Publications/INFORMS-Journals. **Remarks:** Advertising not accepted. **Circ:** (Not Reported).

15241 ■ Management Science
Institute for Operations Research and the Management Sciences
5521 Research Park Dr., Ste. 200
Catonsville, MD 21228
Phone: (443)757-3500
Fax: (443)757-3515
Free: 800-446-3676
Publisher's E-mail: informs@informs.org
Disseminates scientific research focusing on the problems, interests, and concerns of the management science profession. **Freq:** Monthly. **Print Method:** Offset. **Trim Size:** 8.25 x 10.875. **Key Personnel:** Teck-Hua Ho, Editor, phone: (415)800-2823. **ISSN:** 0025--1909 (print); **EISSN:** 1526--5501 (electronic). **Subscription Rates:** $1115 Institutions print and online; $984 Institutions online only; $1235 Institutions, other countries print + online; $35 Members online; $140 Members print and online. **Online:** Institute for Operations Research and the Management Sciences Institute for Operations Research and the Management Sciences. **URL:** http://www.informs.org/Find-Research-Publications/Journals/Management-Science. **Ad Rates:** BW $1,000. **Remarks:** Accepts advertising. **Circ:** Paid 5000.

15242 ■ Manufacturing & Service Operations Management
Institute for Operations Research and the Management Sciences
5521 Research Park Dr., Ste. 200
Catonsville, MD 21228
Phone: (443)757-3500
Fax: (443)757-3515
Free: 800-446-3676
Publication E-mail: informs@informs.org
Freq: Quarterly. **Key Personnel:** Frances Moskwa; Stephen Graves, Editor; Kimberly Anoweck, Editor. **ISSN:** 1523--4614 (print); **EISSN:** 1526--5498 (electronic). **Subscription Rates:** $490 Institutions print and online; $530 Institutions, other countries print and online; $85 Members print and online; $429 Institutions online only; $35 Members online only; $350 Nonmembers print + online; $386 Other countries print + online; free for members. **Alt. Formats:** Print. **URL:** http://pubsonline.informs.org/journal/msom; http://www.informs.org/Recognize-Excellence/Community-Prizes-and-Awards/Manufacturing-and-Service-Operations-Management. **Remarks:** Advertising not accepted. **Circ:** (Not Reported).

15243 ■ Mathematics of Operations Research
Institute for Operations Research and the Management Sciences
5521 Research Park Dr., Ste. 200
Catonsville, MD 21228
Phone: (443)757-3500
Fax: (443)757-3515
Free: 800-446-3676
Publication E-mail: mathofor@gmail.com informs@informs.org
Journal on applications of mathematics in management. **Freq:** Quarterly. **Print Method:** Offset. **Trim Size:** 6 7/8 x 10. **Cols./Page:** 1. **Col. Width:** 62 nonpareils. **Col. Depth:** 117 agate lines. **Key Personnel:** Yinyu Ye, Editor; Imre Barany, Editor; Jim Dai, Editor; Uriel G. Rothblum, Editor-in-Chief; Stephen Siegforth, Editor. **ISSN:** 0364- 765X (print); **EISSN:** 1526- 5471 (electronic). **Subscription Rates:** $406 Institutions online only; $464 Institutions print and online; $500 Institutions, other countries print and online; $35 Members online only; $85 Members print and online. **URL:** http://pubsonline.informs.org/journal/moor; http://www.informs.org/Find-Research-Publications/Journals/Subscribe. **Remarks:** Advertising not accepted. **Circ:** ‡2,800.

15244 ■ Operations Management Education Review
Institute for Operations Research and the Management Sciences
5521 Research Park Dr., Ste. 200
Catonsville, MD 21228
Phone: (443)757-3500
Fax: (443)757-3515
Free: 800-446-3676
Publisher's E-mail: informs@informs.org
Journal covering high quality refereed operations management teaching materials, to enhance operations management education worldwide. **Freq:** Annual. **Print Method:** Offset. **Cols./Page:** 3. **Col. Width:** 14.25 picas. **Col. Depth:** 57 picas. **Key Personnel:** Carlos Condon, Board Member; James Cochran, Board Member; Ricardo Ernst, Board Member; James Blocher, Board Member; Gregory Dobson, Board Member; Jim Erskine, Board Member; Jose Luis Guerrero Cusumano, Board Member; Geraldo Ferrer, Board Member; Sum Chee Chuong, Board Member; Edward Davis, Board Member; Nigel Slack, Board Member. **ISSN:** 1649--7082 (print); **EISSN:** 2044--4567 (electronic). **Subscription Rates:** $390 Institutions print only; $395 Institutions print and electronic access; $160 Individuals electronic access; $175 Individuals print and electronic access; $375 Institutions electronic access. **URL:** http://www.neilsonjournals.com/OMER. **Remarks:** Advertising not accepted. **Circ:** (Not Reported).

15245 ■ Operations Research
Institute for Operations Research and the Management Sciences
c/o Kathleen Luckey, Managing Editor
INFORMS
5521 Research Park Dr., Ste. 200
Catonsville, MD 21228
Phone: (443)757-3583
Publisher's E-mail: informs@informs.org
Journal publishing new operations research for practitioners and Operations Research Society of America members. **Founded:** 1952. **Freq:** Bimonthly. **Print Method:** Offset. **Trim Size:** 8.125 x 10.875. **Cols./Page:** 2. **Col. Width:** 37 nonpareils. **Col. Depth:** 123 agate lines. **Key Personnel:** Stefanos Zenios, Editor-in-Chief. **ISSN:** 0030-364X (print). **Subscription Rates:** $643 Institutions print and online; $703 Institutions, other countries print and online; $110 Members print and online. **URL:** http://pubsonline.informs.org/journal/opre. **Ad Rates:** BW $1,000. **Remarks:** Accepts advertising. **Circ:** Paid ‡5300.

15246 ■ Organization Science: A Journal of the Institute of Operations Research and the Management Sciences
Institute for Operations Research and the Management Sciences
5521 Research Park Dr., Ste. 200
Catonsville, MD 21228
Phone: (443)757-3500
Fax: (443)757-3515
Free: 800-446-3676
Publisher's E-mail: informs@informs.org
Journal featuring innovative research on organizations drawing upon multiple disciplines. **Freq:** 6/year. **Print Method:** Offset. **Trim Size:** 6 7/8 x 10. **Cols./Page:** 1. **Col. Width:** 62 nonpareils. **Col. Depth:** 117 agate lines. **Key Personnel:** Katherine Bartol, Board Member; Gautam Ahuja, Senior Editor; Daniel A. Levinthal, Editor-in-Chief; Kathleen Luckey, Managing Editor, phone: (443)757-3583; Stephanie Myers, Editor, phone: (443)757-3514, fax: (443)757-3514; Jay Anand, Board Member. **ISSN:** 1047--7039 (print); **EISSN:** 1526--5455 (electronic). **Subscription Rates:** $475 Institutions online only; $541 Institutions print and online; $601 Institutions, other countries print & online; $35 Members online; $110 Members print and online; $475 U.S. corporate, online only; $541 U.S. corporate, print and online; $601 Other countries corporate, print and online. **URL:** http://pubsonline.informs.org/journal/orsc. **Remarks:** Accepts advertising. **Circ:** ‡1,700.

15247 ■ Transactions on Education
Institute for Operations Research and the Management Sciences
5521 Research Park Dr., Ste. 200
Catonsville, MD 21228
Phone: (443)757-3500
Fax: (443)757-3515

Free: 800-446-3676
Publication E-mail: informs@informs.org
Freq: Quarterly. **ISSN:** 0018--9359 (print). **Subscription Rates:** Currently, free of charge, however, may adopt a small subscription fee to become self-sustaining.; Included in membership. **URL:** http://pubsonline.informs.org/journal/ited; http://ieeexplore.ieee.org/xpl/aboutJournal.jsp?punumber=13. **Remarks:** Advertising not accepted. **Circ:** (Not Reported).

CHESTERTOWN

Kent Co. Kent Co. (NE). On Chester River, 45 m S of Wilmington, Del. Washington College. Summer & winter resort. Fertilizer and chemical factories; printing plant. Commercial fisheries. Diversified farming. Dairying. Wheat, corn, tomatoes.

15248 ■ Kent County News

Kent County News
223 High St.
Chestertown, MD 21620
Phone: (410)778-2011
Publisher's E-mail: news@stardem.com
Community newspaper. **Freq:** Weekly (Thurs.). **Print Method:** Offset. **Trim Size:** 13 x 21. **Cols./Page:** 6. **Col. Width:** 12.5 picas. **Col. Depth:** 21 inches. **Key Personnel:** Mary B. Burton, General Manager, Manager, Advertising; Kevin Hemstock, Editor. **USPS:** 292-660. **Subscription Rates:** $.99 Individuals online only 1 day; $2.99 Individuals online only 28 days; $20 Individuals print + online (182 days). **URL:** http://www.myeasternshoremd.com/kent_county_news. **Mailing address:** PO Box 30, Chestertown, MD 21620. **Ad Rates:** GLR $.70; BW $1121.40; 4C $1541.40; SAU $9.55; PCI $9. **Remarks:** Accepts advertising. **Circ:** 8500.

15249 ■ WCTR-AM - 1530

231 Flatland Rd.
Chestertown, MD 21620
Phone: (410)778-1530
Fax: (410)778-4800
Email: info@wctr.com
Format: Oldies; News; Sports; Adult Contemporary. **Networks:** CNN Radio. **Owner:** WCTR Broadcasting L.L.C., at above address, Chestertown, MD 21620. **Founded:** 1962. **Operating Hours:** Sunrise-sunset; 40% network, 60% local. **ADI:** Baltimore, MD. **Wattage:** 1,000. **Ad Rates:** $9.10-13.35 for 30 seconds; $10.35-17.65 for 60 seconds. **URL:** http://www.wctr.com.

CHEVERLY

15250 ■ Romani Studies: Continuing Journal of the Gypsy Lore Society

Gypsy Lore Society
5607 Greenleaf Rd.
Cheverly, MD 20785
Phone: (301)341-1261
Fax: (810)592-1768
Publisher's E-mail: gls.gypsyloresociety@gmail.com
Scholarly journal covering all branches of Romani/Gypsy studies. **Freq:** Semiannual. **Print Method:** offset. **Trim Size:** 6 x 9. **Key Personnel:** Yaron Matras, Editor; Victor A. Friedman, Board Member; Elena Marushiakova, Board Member. **ISSN:** 1528-0748 (print). **Subscription Rates:** Included in membership. **URL:** http://www.gypsyloresociety.org/gypsy-lore-society-publications/romani-studies. **Formerly:** Journal of the Gypsy Lore Society. **Ad Rates:** BW $50. **Remarks:** Accepts advertising. **Circ:** Paid 272.

CHEVY CHASE

Montgomery Co. Montgomery Co. (WC) on N.W. border of DC. Residential.

15251 ■ Journal of Addiction Medicine

American Society of Addiction Medicine
Upper Arcade, Ste. 101
4601 N Park Ave.
Chevy Chase, MD 20815-4520
Phone: (301)656-3920
Fax: (301)656-3815
Publisher's E-mail: email@asam.org
Journal focusing the needs of the professional practicing in the field of Addiction Medicine. **Freq:** 6/year. **Trim Size:** 8 1/8 x 10 7/8. **Key Personnel:** George F. Koob, PhD, Senior Editor; Michael A. Arends, Managing Editor; Natalie McGroarty, Publisher. **ISSN:** 1932- 0620 (print); **EISSN:** 1935- 3227 (electronic). **Subscription Rates:** $131 Individuals; $253 Institutions; $65 resident. **URL:** http://www.asam.org/Publication_home.html; http://journals.lww.com/journaladdictionmedicine/pages/default.aspx. **Ad Rates:** BW $1,125; 4C $1,565. **Remarks:** Accepts advertising. **Circ:** ‡3222.

15252 ■ Naturalist Quarterly

Audubon Naturalist Society of the Central Atlantic States
8940 Jones Mill Rd.
Chevy Chase, MD 20815
Phone: (301)652-9188
Fax: (301)951-7179
Publisher's E-mail: contact@anshome.org
Freq: Quarterly. **ISSN:** 0888--6555 (print). **Subscription Rates:** Included in membership. **Alt. Formats:** PDF. **URL:** http://www.audubonnaturalist.org/index.php/about-ans/naturalist-quarterly. **Circ:** (Not Reported).

15253 ■ WYRE-AM - 810

8785 Preston Pl.
Chevy Chase, MD 20815
Phone: (410)295-0722
Fax: (410)267-7634
Format: Country. **Networks:** ABC. **Owner:** Bay Broadcasting Corp., 112 Main St., Annapolis, MD 21401. **Founded:** 1946. **Formerly:** WASL-AM; WABW-AM. **Operating Hours:** Sunrise-sunset; 100% local. **Key Personnel:** Jacob Einstein, Gen. Mgr., Prog. Dir.; Sharon Narrigan, Sales Mgr.; John Rouse, Dir. of Programs. **Wattage:** 250. **Ad Rates:** $20-30 for 60 seconds.

CHURCHTON

15254 ■ WRYR-FM - 97.5

PO Box 205
Churchton, MD 20733
Phone: (410)867-9677
Format: Easy Listening. **Owner:** WRYR Community Radio Inc., PO Box 205, Churchton, MD 20733. **Ad Rates:** Noncommercial.

COCKEYSVILLE

15255 ■ Mason-Dixon ARRIVE

Stone House Publications
1242 Paper Mill Rd.
Cockeysville, MD 21030
Phone: (410)584-9960
Fax: (410)584-9166
Publication E-mail: info@mdarrive.com
Magazine presenting local stories on the history, people, and places of the Mason-Dixon area. **Freq:** Monthly. **Key Personnel:** Vicki K. Franz, President, Publisher; Gregory J. Alexander, Editor; Debbie Hanley, Office Manager. **Subscription Rates:** $28 Individuals; $15 Single issue. **URL:** http://www.mdarrive.com. **Remarks:** Accepts advertising. **Circ:** (Not Reported).

COLLEGE PARK

Prince George's Co. Prince George's Co. (SC). 8 m N of Washington, DC. University of Maryland. Electronic firms. Sheet metal works. Lumber mill.

15256 ■ American Journalism Review

American Journalism Review
University of Maryland
1117 Journalism Bldg.
College Park, MD 20742-7111
Phone: (301)405-8803
Fax: (301)405-8323
Free: 800-827-0771
Publication E-mail: editor@ajrumd.edu
Journalism review. **Freq:** Bimonthly. **Print Method:** Offset. **Trim Size:** 8 3/8 x 10 7/8. **Cols./Page:** 3. **Col. Width:** 14 nonpareils. **Key Personnel:** Lucy Dalglish, Publisher, Dean. **ISSN:** 1067--8654 (print). **URL:** http://ajr.org. **Formerly:** Washington Journalism Review. **Remarks:** Accepts advertising. **Circ:** (Not Reported).

15257 ■ Astronomy Letters

American Institute of Physics
1 Physics Ellipse
College Park, MD 20740
Phone: (516)576-2200
Fax: (516)349-7669
Free: 888-491-8833
Publication E-mail: pazh@maik.ru
Contains scientific papers on space experiments and theoretical research in the field of astronomy and astrophysics. **Key Personnel:** Rashid A. Sunyaev, Editor-in-Chief; Sergei. A Grebenev, Editor-in-Chief. **URL:** http://hea.iki.rssi.ru/pazh/; http://www.springer.com/astronomy/astronomy%2C+observations+and+techniques/journal/11443. **Circ:** (Not Reported).

15258 ■ Automation in Construction: An International Research Journal

Elsevier
c/o Miroslaw Skibniewski, Editor-in-Chief
University of Maryland
Department of Civil & Environmental Engineering
1188 Glenn L. Martin Hall
College Park, MD 20742-3021
Publisher's E-mail: t.reller@elsevier.com
Journal covering all stages of the construction life cycle from the initial design and architecture. **Freq:** Monthly. **Print Method:** Offset. **Trim Size:** 8 3/8 x 10 7/8. **Cols./Page:** 3. **Col. Width:** 13 picas. **Col. Depth:** 10 inches. **Key Personnel:** H. Li, Editor; Miroslaw Skibniewski, Editor-in-Chief; T. Bock, Board Member; E. Budny, Board Member; C. Eastman, Board Member. **ISSN:** 0926--5805 (print). **Subscription Rates:** $116 Individuals print; $486.40 Institutions ejournal; $1459 Individuals print. **URL:** http://www.journals.elsevier.com/automation-in-construction. **Circ:** (Not Reported).

15259 ■ Bulletin of the American Physical Society

American Physical Society
1 Physics Ellipse
College Park, MD 20740-3844
Phone: (301)209-3200
Fax: (301)209-0865
Magazine providing advance information and abstracts for meetings. **Freq:** Monthly. **Print Method:** Offset. **ISSN:** 0003--0503 (print). **URL:** http://www.aps.org/meetings/policies/baps.cfm. **Remarks:** Advertising not accepted. **Circ:** ‡39757.

15260 ■ CHAOS: An Interdisciplinary Journal of Nonlinear Science

American Institute of Physics
1 Physics Ellipse
College Park, MD 20740
Phone: (516)576-2200
Fax: (516)349-7669
Free: 888-491-8833
Publication E-mail: cha-edoffice@aip.org
Journal that is devoted to increasing the understanding of nonlinear phenomena and describing the manifestations in a manner comprehensible to researchers from a broad spectrum of disciplines. **Freq:** Quarterly. **Key Personnel:** David K. Campbell, Editor-in-Chief; Elizabeth Bradley, Editor. **ISSN:** 1054-1500 (print); **EISSN:** 1089-7682 (electronic). **Subscription Rates:** $815 Institutions print & online, domestic; $850 Institutions print & online; foreign surface freight; $65 Members online. **URL:** http://scitation.aip.org/content/aip/journal/chaos. **Remarks:** Advertising not accepted. **Circ:** (Not Reported).

15261 ■ Diamondback

University of Maryland
College Park, MD 20742
Phone: (301)405-1000
Publication E-mail: advertising@dbk.umd.edu
Collegiate newspaper. **Freq:** Weekly (Thurs.). **Print Method:** Offset. **Trim Size:** 13 x 21 1/4. **Cols./Page:** 6 and 6. **Col. Width:** 26 nonpareils and 2 1/16 agate lines. **Col. Depth:** 298 and 21 1/4 agate lines. **Key Personnel:** Mike King, Editor-in-Chief. **Subscription Rates:** Free in campus. **URL:** http://www.diamondbackonline.com. **Ad Rates:** BW $2138.20; SAU $13. **Remarks:** Accepts advertising. **Circ:** ‡20200.

15262 ■ Federal Register Index

The National Archives & Records Admin.
National Archives & Records Admin.
8601 Adelphi Rd.
College Park, MD 20740-6001
Phone: (301)837-0482
Fax: (301)837-0483
Free: 866-272-6272

Circulation: ★ = AAM; △ or • = BPA; ♦ = CAC; ❑ = VAC; ⊕ = PO Statement; ‡ = Publisher's Report; Boldface figures = sworn; Light figures = estimated.

Publisher's E-mail: orderstatus@nara.gov
Index to the Federal Register. **Freq:** Monthly. **Print Method:** Letterpress. **Cols./Page:** 3. **Col. Width:** 6 nonpareils. **Col. Depth:** 126 agate lines. **ISSN:** 0364--1406 (print). **URL:** http://www.archives.gov/federal-register. **Circ:** (Not Reported).

15263 ■ Feminist Studies
University of Maryland
University of Maryland
0103 Taliaferro Hall
College Park, MD 20742
Phone: (301)405-7415
Fax: (301)405-8395
Publication E-mail: info@feministstudies.org
Scholarly journal discussing women's studies issues. **Freq:** 3/year. **Print Method:** Perfect Bound. **Trim Size:** 6 x 9. **Key Personnel:** Karla Mantilla, Managing Editor; Claire G. Moses, Director, Editorial. **ISSN:** 0046--3663 (print). **Subscription Rates:** $40 Individuals print only; $350 Institutions print plus online; $20 Students print only; $65 Students, other countries. **URL:** http://www.feministstudies.org/home.html. **Ad Rates:** BW $450. **Remarks:** Accepts advertising. **Circ:** (Not Reported).

15264 ■ Foundations and Trends in Human-Computer Interaction
Now Publishers
c/o Ben Bederson, Ed.-in-Ch.
Human-Computer Interaction Lab
University of Maryland
3171 A.V. Williams Bldg.
College Park, MD 20742
Phone: (301)405-2764
Publisher's E-mail: zac.rolnik@nowpublishers.com
Academic journal that publishes new research in the field of human-computer interaction (HCI). **Freq:** Quarterly. **Key Personnel:** Ben Bederson, Editor. **ISSN:** 1551--3955 (print); **EISSN:** 1551--3963 (electronic). **Subscription Rates:** $480 Institutions online or print; €480 Other countries online or print; $570 Institutions print and online; €570 Other countries print and online. **URL:** http://www.nowpublishers.com/journals/HCI. **Circ:** (Not Reported).

15265 ■ Government Information Quarterly: An International Journal of Information Technology Management, Policies, and Practices
Elsevier Inc.
c/o J. Carlo Bertot, Associate Editor
College of Information Studies
Center for Library Innovation
University of Maryland, 4105 Hornbake Bldg.
College Park, MD 20742
Fax: (301)314-9145
Publisher's E-mail: healthpermissions@elsevier.com
Refereed scholarly journal. **Freq:** Quarterly. **Print Method:** Offset. **Trim Size:** 6 7/8 x 10. **Cols./Page:** 1. **Key Personnel:** T. Janowski, Editor-in-Chief; P.J. Birkinshaw, Board Member; P.T. Jaeger, Board Member; John Carlo Bertot, Associate Editor. **ISSN:** 0740--624X (print). **Subscription Rates:** $226 Individuals print; $946 Institutions print; $473.20 Institutions e-journal. **URL:** http://www.journals.elsevier.com/government-information-quarterly. **Circ:** (Not Reported).

15266 ■ International Journal of Document Analysis and Recognition
Springer-Verlag GmbH & Company KG
c/o David S. Doermann, Founding Ed.
Research Faculty
Language & Media Processing
University of Maryland
College Park, MD 20742
Phone: (301)405-1767
Fax: (301)314-2644
Publisher's E-mail: customerservice@springer.com
Journal publishing articles related to document analysis and recognition. Covering document image processing, handwriting models and analysis, storage and retrieval of documents etc. **Freq:** Quarterly. **Key Personnel:** David S. Doermann, Founder, Editor, Managing Editor; Simone Marinai, Editor-in-Chief. **ISSN:** 1433--2833 (print); **EISSN:** 1433--2825 (electronic). **Subscription Rates:** $358 Institutions print including free access or e-only; $430 Institutions print plus enhanced access; €325 Institutions print including free access or e-only; €390 Institutions print plus enhanced access. **URL:** http://www.springer.com/computer/image+processing/journal/10032. **Remarks:** Advertising accepted; rates available upon request. **Circ:** (Not Reported).

15267 ■ Journal of Arachnology
American Arachnological Society
University of Maryland
4112 Plant Science Bldg., Entomology
College Park, MD 20742-4454
Phone: (301)405-7519
Fax: (301)314-9290
Scientific journal of the American Arachnological Society. **Freq:** 3/year. **Key Personnel:** Prof. James E. Carrel, Editor-in-Chief, phone: (573)882-3037; Prof. Douglass H. Morse, Managing Editor, phone: (401)863-3152, fax: (401)863-2166. **ISSN:** 0160--8202 (print). **URL:** http://www.americanarachnology.org/JOA.html. **Remarks:** Advertising not accepted. **Circ:** (Not Reported).

15268 ■ Journal of Contemporary Athletics
Nova Science Publishers Inc.
c/o James H. Humphrey, Founding Editor
Dept. of Kinesiology
University of Maryland
College Park, MD 20742
Publisher's E-mail: nova.main@novapublishers.com
Journal that publishes material relevant to interscholastic, intercollegiate, club, and professional athletics. **Freq:** Quarterly. **Key Personnel:** James H. Humphrey, Editor, Founder; Dr. Dan Drane, PhD, Editor-in-Chief. **ISSN:** 1554--9933 (print). **Subscription Rates:** $295 Individuals. **URL:** http://www.novapublishers.com/catalog/product_info.php?products_id=1673. **Circ:** (Not Reported).

15269 ■ Journal of Experimental and Theoretical Physics
American Institute of Physics
1 Physics Ellipse
College Park, MD 20740
Phone: (516)576-2200
Fax: (516)349-7669
Free: 888-491-8833
Publisher's E-mail: sales@aip.org
Russian journal on the basic research level on gravitation and astrophysics, translated to English. **Freq:** Monthly. **Key Personnel:** A.F. Andreev, Editor-in-Chief. **ISSN:** 1063--7761 (print); **EISSN:** 1090--6509 (electronic). **Alt. Formats:** Electronic publishing. **URL:** http://www.springer.com/physics/particle+and+nuclear+physics/journal/11447; http://link.springer.com/journal/11447. **Circ:** (Not Reported).

15270 ■ Journal of Laser Applications
American Institute of Physics
1 Physics Ellipse
College Park, MD 20740
Phone: (516)576-2200
Fax: (516)349-7669
Free: 888-491-8833
Publisher's E-mail: sales@aip.org
Journal covering applications of lasers and electro-optics, including safety standards and education. **Freq:** Quarterly. **Key Personnel:** Reinhart Poprawe, Editor-in-Chief. **ISSN:** 1042--346X (print); **EISSN:** 1938--1387 (electronic). **Subscription Rates:** Included in membership. **URL:** http://jla.aip.org. **Ad Rates:** BW $900; BW $1,100. **Remarks:** Advertising accepted; rates available upon request. **Circ:** 1300, 1600.

15271 ■ Journal of Metamorphic Geology
Wiley-Blackwell
c/o Michael Brown, Ed.
Department of Geology
University of Maryland
College Park, MD 20742
Phone: (301)405-4365
Fax: (301)314-9661
Publisher's E-mail: info@wiley.com
Journal dedicated to wide spectrum of metamorphic geology right from individual crystals to lithospheric plates. **Freq:** 9/year. **Key Personnel:** Geoff Clarke, Editor; Michael Brown, Editor, phone: (301)405-4080; Doug Robinson, Editor; Donna L. Whitney, Editor; Richard White, Editor. **ISSN:** 0263--4929 (print); **EISSN:** 1525--1314 (electronic). **Subscription Rates:** $3358 Institutions print only; £1928 Institutions print only; €2448 Institutions print only; $4151 Institutions, other countries print only. **URL:** http://onlinelibrary.wiley.com/journal/10.1111/(ISSN)1525-1314. **Remarks:** Advertising accepted; rates available upon request. **Circ:** (Not Reported).

15272 ■ Journal of Optical Technology
American Institute of Physics
1 Physics Ellipse
College Park, MD 20740
Phone: (516)576-2200
Fax: (516)349-7669
Free: 888-491-8833
Publisher's E-mail: sales@aip.org
Russian journal on optics and space translated to English. **Freq:** Monthly. **Key Personnel:** A.S. Tibilov, Editor-in-Chief. **ISSN:** 1070--9762 (print); **EISSN:** 1091--0786 (electronic). **URL:** http://www.osapublishing.org/jot/journal/jot/about.cfm. **Formerly:** Soviet Journal of Optical Technology. **Remarks:** Advertising not accepted. **Circ:** ‡470.

15273 ■ Journal of Rheology
American Institute of Physics
1 Physics Ellipse
College Park, MD 20740
Phone: (516)576-2200
Fax: (516)349-7669
Free: 888-491-8833
Publisher's E-mail: rheology@aip.org
Contains detailed articles on the science of the deformation and flow of matter. Serves especially those in plastics, rubbers, paints, coatings, fibers, and structural materials. Includes abstracts from the Journal of the Society of Rheology, Japan. **Freq:** 6/year. **Print Method:** Offset. **Trim Size:** 8 1/2 x 11. **Cols./Page:** 1. **Col. Width:** 30 picas. **Col. Depth:** 126 agate lines. **Key Personnel:** Ralph H. Colby, Editor; Marcy Fowler, Assistant Editor. **ISSN:** 0148--6055 (print); **EISSN:** 1520--8516 (electronic). **URL:** http://www.rheology.org/sor/publications/j_rheology; http://scitation.aip.org/content/sor/journal/jor2. **Formerly:** Transactions of The Society of Rheology. **Ad Rates:** BW $1995; 4C $1140. **Remarks:** Accepts advertising. **Circ:** (Not Reported).

15274 ■ Journal of Vacuum Science and Technology A & B: Vacuum, Surfaces and Films
American Institute of Physics
1 Physics Ellipse
College Park, MD 20740
Phone: (516)576-2200
Fax: (516)349-7669
Free: 888-491-8833
Publisher's E-mail: sales@aip.org
Journal containing research review articles in all areas of vacuum science. **Freq:** Monthly. **Print Method:** Offset. **Trim Size:** 8 1/2 x 11. **Cols./Page:** 2. **Col. Width:** 41 nonpareils. **Col. Depth:** 136 agate lines. **Key Personnel:** Estella K. Stansbury, Assistant Editor; Eric Kay, Associate Editor; G. Parsons, Associate Editor; Eray Aydil, Editor-in-Chief. **ISSN:** 0022--5355 (print). **URL:** http://scitation.aip.org/content/avs/journal/jvst. **Ad Rates:** BW $1310; 4C $1240. **Remarks:** Accepts advertising. **Circ:** Paid ‡5400.

15275 ■ The Library Quarterly: A Journal of Investigation in Library and Information Studies
The University of Chicago Press
c/o John Carlo Bertot, Ed.
University of Maryland
College of Information Studies
4105 Hornbake Bldg., South Wing
College Park, MD 20742
Phone: (301)405-1741
Fax: (301)314-9145
Publication E-mail: lq@press.uchicago.edu
Research journal for library and information science scholars, practitioners, teachers, students, and those in related fields. **Freq:** Quarterly. **Trim Size:** 6 x 9. **Cols./Page:** 1. **Key Personnel:** Paul Jaeger, Editor; Joseph Tennis, Board Member. **ISSN:** 0024-2519 (print); **EISSN:** 1549-652X (electronic). **Subscription Rates:** $54 Individuals print and electronic; $48 Individuals electronic only; $49 Individuals print only; $27 Students electronic only; $97 Two years print and electronic; $49 Students electronic only, two years; $138 Individuals print and electronic, three years; $69 Students electronic only, three years. **URL:** http://www.press.uchicago.edu/ucp/journals/journal/lq.html; http://www.jstor.org/page/journal/libraryq/about.html. **Ad Rates:** BW $551. **Remarks:** Accepts advertising. **Circ:** 1062.

15276 ■ Lotus Remarque
Lotus, Ltd.
PO Box L
College Park, MD 20741
Phone: (301)982-4054
Fax: (301)982-4054
Publication E-mail: hq@lotuscarclub.org
Magazine for Lotus car owners. **Freq:** Bimonthly. **Print Method:** Offset. **Trim Size:** 8 1/2 x 11. **Cols./Page:** 2. **Col. Width:** 3 1/2 inches. **Col. Depth:** 10 inches. **Key Personnel:** Michael Gulley, Contact. **Subscription Rates:** $55 Individuals new member; $50 Individuals new member; $45 U.S. renewal; $50 Elsewhere renewal. **URL:** http://lotusltd.com/resources/documents-library. **Remarks:** Advertising accepted; rates available upon request. **Circ:** Paid ‡1250, Non-paid ‡45.

15277 ■ Low Temperature Physics
American Institute of Physics
1 Physics Ellipse
College Park, MD 20740
Phone: (516)576-2200
Fax: (516)349-7669
Free: 888-491-8833
Publication E-mail: fnt@ilt.kharkov.ua
Translation of Russian journal on experimental and theoretical work at low temperature physics. **Founded:** 1975. **Freq:** Monthly. **Print Method:** Offset. **Trim Size:** 8 3/8 x 11 1/4. **Cols./Page:** 2. **Col. Width:** 42 nonpareils. **Col. Depth:** 135 agate lines. **Key Personnel:** Viktor V. Eremenko, Editor. **ISSN:** 1063-777X (print). **Subscription Rates:** $4010 Institutions print and online; $4060 Canada and Mexico print and online, surface freight; $4070 By mail Europe and Asia; $221 Members online only. **URL:** http://scitation.aip.org/content/aip/journal/ltp. **Circ:** ‡150.

15278 ■ Medical Physics
American Institute of Physics
1 Physics Ellipse
College Park, MD 20740
Phone: (516)576-2200
Fax: (516)349-7669
Free: 888-491-8833
Publisher's E-mail: 2016.aapm@aapm.org
Journal focusing on the relationship of physics to human biology and medicine. **Freq:** Monthly. **Print Method:** Offset. **Trim Size:** 8 3/16 x 11. **Cols./Page:** 2. **Col. Width:** 41 nonpareils. **Col. Depth:** 136 agate lines. **Key Personnel:** Jeffrey Williamson; William R. Hendee, Editor; Penny Slattery, Manager. **ISSN:** 0094-2405 (print). **Subscription Rates:** $458 Members USA; $598 Members outside U.S.; $1454 Individuals all others; $1594 Other countries all others. **URL:** http://www.medphys.org. **Ad Rates:** BW $1610; 4C $1610. **Remarks:** Accepts advertising. **Circ:** 5300.

15279 ■ Networks: An International Journal
John Wiley & Sons Inc.
c/o Dr. B.L. Golden, Editor-in-Chief
Van Munching Hall
University of Maryland
College Park, MD 20742
Phone: (301)405-2232
Publisher's E-mail: info@wiley.com
Journal exploring applications and theory pertaining to innovations in design and use of computer networks, telecommunications, transportation systems, power grids, distribution systems, and other networks. **Freq:** 8/year. **Print Method:** Offset. **Trim Size:** 7 1/4 x 10 1/4. **Cols./Page:** 1. **Col. Width:** 84 nonpareils. **Col. Depth:** 140 agate lines. **Key Personnel:** Dr. B.L. Golden, Editor-in-Chief; Dr. D.R. Shier, Editor-in-Chief, phone: (864)656-1100; A. Proskurowski, Associate Editor; C. Alexopoulos, Associate Editor; R.K. Ahuja, Associate Editor; M. Mavronicolas, Associate Editor; S. Khuller, Associate Editor. **ISSN:** 0028--3045 (print); **EISSN:** 1097--0037 (electronic). **Subscription Rates:** $3485 Institutions print only; $3603 Institutions, Canada and Mexico print only; $3661 Institutions, other countries print only; $4182 Institutions print with online; $4324 Institutions, Canada and Mexico print with online; $4394 Institutions, other countries print with online. **URL:** http://onlinelibrary.wiley.com/journal/10.1002/(ISSN)1097-0037. **Ad Rates:** BW $772; 4C $1009. **Remarks:** Accepts advertising. **Circ:** Paid 1000.

15280 ■ Parallel Computing: Systems & Applications
RELX Group P.L.C.
c/o J. Hollingsworth, Editor-in-Chief
University of Maryland
Department of Computer Science
A.V. Williams Bldg.
College Park, MD 20742
Publisher's E-mail: amsterdam@relx.com
Journal publishing the theory and use of parallel computer systems. Includes vector, pipeline, array and fifth and future generation computers and neural computers. **Freq:** 10/year. **Key Personnel:** J. Hollingsworth, Editor-in-Chief; D. Trystram, Associate Editor. **ISSN:** 0167--8191 (print). **Subscription Rates:** $180 Individuals print; $1756.67 Institutions online; $2231 Institutions print. **URL:** http://www.journals.elsevier.com/parallel-computing. **Circ:** (Not Reported).

15281 ■ Physical Review A: Atomic, Molecular, and Optical Physics
American Physical Society
1 Physics Ellipse
College Park, MD 20740-3844
Phone: (301)209-3200
Fax: (301)209-0865
Physics journal. **Freq:** Monthly. **Print Method:** Letterpress and offset. **Trim Size:** 8 1/4 x 11 1/4. **Cols./Page:** 2. **Col. Width:** 41 nonpareils. **Col. Depth:** 140 agate lines. **Key Personnel:** Gordon W.F. Drake, Editor; Margaret Malloy, Managing Editor. **ISSN:** 1050--2947 (print). **URL:** http://www.aps.org/publications/apsnews/199704/online.cfm. **Remarks:** Advertising not accepted. **Circ:** 2200.

15282 ■ Physical Review B: Condensed Matter and Materials Physics
American Physical Society
1 Physics Ellipse
College Park, MD 20740-3844
Phone: (301)209-3200
Fax: (301)209-0865
Physics journal. **Freq:** Weekly. **Print Method:** Offset. **Trim Size:** 8 1/4 x 11 1/4. **Key Personnel:** Peter D. Adams, Editor. **ISSN:** 0163--1829 (print). **Subscription Rates:** $885 Institutions print and online (1958 to current); $1820 Institutions, other countries print and online (1958 to current); $60 Institutions online only. **URL:** http://journals.aps.org/prb. **Remarks:** Advertising not accepted. **Circ:** (Not Reported).

15283 ■ Physical Review D: Particles, Fields, Gravitation, and Cosmology
American Physical Society
1 Physics Ellipse
College Park, MD 20740-3844
Phone: (301)209-3200
Fax: (301)209-0865
Physics journal. **Freq:** Semimonthly. **Print Method:** Offset. **Trim Size:** 8 1/4 x 11 1/4. **Key Personnel:** Erick J. Weinberg, Editor. **ISSN:** 2470--0010 (print); **EISSN:** 2470--0029 (electronic). **Subscription Rates:** $885 Institutions print & online (1958-current); $1820 Institutions, other countries print & online (1958-current); $60 Institutions online only. **URL:** http://journals.aps.org/prd. **Remarks:** Advertising not accepted. **Circ:** 1900.

15284 ■ Physical Review E: Statistical, Nonlinear, and Soft Matter Physics
American Physical Society
1 Physics Ellipse
College Park, MD 20740-3844
Phone: (301)209-3200
Fax: (301)209-0865
Physics journal. **Freq:** Monthly. **Print Method:** Offset. **Trim Size:** 8 1/4 x 11 1/4. **Key Personnel:** Margaret Malloy, Associate Editor; Gene D. Sprouse, Editor-in-Chief. **ISSN:** 1539-3755 (print). **Subscription Rates:** $50 Members; $360 U.S. single issue; $395 Other countries single issue. **Alt. Formats:** CD-ROM. **URL:** http://journals.aps.org/pre. **Formerly:** Physical Review A. **Remarks:** Advertising not accepted. **Circ:** 1900.

15285 ■ Physical Review Letters
American Physical Society
1 Physics Ellipse
College Park, MD 20740-3844
Phone: (301)209-3200
Fax: (301)209-0865
Publication E-mail: prl@aps.org
Journal of physics research. **Freq:** Weekly. **Print Method:** Offset. **Trim Size:** 8 1/4 x 11 1/4. **Cols./Page:** 2. **Col. Width:** 41 nonpareils. **Col. Depth:** 130 agate lines. **Key Personnel:** Jack Sandweiss, Editor; George Basbas, Editor; Stanley G. Brown, Editor; Reinhardt B. Schuhmann, Editor. **ISSN:** 0031--9007 (print). **Subscription Rates:** $885 Institutions domestic (print and online); $1820 Institutions foreign (print and online); $60 Institutions online. **Alt. Formats:** CD-ROM. **URL:** http://journals.aps.org/prl. **Remarks:** Advertising not accepted. **Circ:** (Not Reported).

15286 ■ Physical Review Special Topics: Accelerators and Beams
American Physical Society
1 Physics Ellipse
College Park, MD 20740-3844
Phone: (301)209-3200
Fax: (301)209-0865
Publication E-mail: prstab@aps.org
Online physics journal. **Freq:** Monthly. **Print Method:** Online. **Key Personnel:** Frank Zimmermann, Editor. **ISSN:** 1098-4402 (print). **URL:** http://prst-ab.aps.org. **Remarks:** Advertising not accepted. **Circ:** (Not Reported).

15287 ■ Physics of Fluids
American Institute of Physics
1 Physics Ellipse
College Park, MD 20740
Phone: (516)576-2200
Fax: (516)349-7669
Free: 888-491-8833
Publication E-mail: pof@engineering.ucsb.edu
Journal focusing on fluid dynamics. **Freq:** Monthly. **Print Method:** Offset. **Trim Size:** 8 1/4 x 11 1/4. **Cols./Page:** 2. **Col. Width:** 41 nonpareils. **Col. Depth:** 138 agate lines. **Key Personnel:** Prof. L. Gary Leal, Editor; Prof. John Kim, Editor; E. John Hinch, Associate Editor. **ISSN:** 1070--6631 (print); **EISSN:** 1089--7666 (electronic). **Subscription Rates:** $3320 Institutions print & online; domestic; $3430 Institutions print & online; foreign surface; $3440 Institutions print & online; optional air; $105 /year for members; $1310 /year for nonmembers. **URL:** http://scitation.aip.org/content/aip/journal/pof2. **Remarks:** Advertising accepted; rates available upon request. **Circ:** (Not Reported).

15288 ■ Physics of Particles and Nuclei
American Institute of Physics
1 Physics Ellipse
College Park, MD 20740
Phone: (516)576-2200
Fax: (516)349-7669
Free: 888-491-8833
Publisher's E-mail: sales@aip.org
Russian journal on research in high-energy physics translated to English. **Freq:** Bimonthly. **Print Method:** Offset. **Trim Size:** 8 3/8 x 11 1/4. **Cols./Page:** 2. **Col. Width:** 42 nonpareils. **Col. Depth:** 135 agate lines. **Key Personnel:** Victor A. Matveev, Editor-in-Chief. **ISSN:** 1063--7796 (print); **EISSN:** 1531--8559 (electronic). **Subscription Rates:** $8749 Institutions print or e-only; $10499 Institutions print and enchanced access. **URL:** http://scitation.aip.org/content/aip/journal/ppn; http://www.springer.com/physics/particle+and+nuclear+physics/journal/11496. **Circ:** (Not Reported).

15289 ■ Physics Today
American Institute of Physics
1 Physics Ellipse
College Park, MD 20740
Phone: (516)576-2200
Fax: (516)349-7669
Free: 888-491-8833
Publisher's E-mail: sales@aip.org
Journal covering news of physics research and activities that affect physics. **Founded:** 1948. **Freq:** Monthly. **Print Method:** Letterpress. **Trim Size:** 8 x 10 1/2. **Cols./Page:** 3. **Col. Width:** 2 3/16 inches. **Col. Depth:** 140 agate lines. **Key Personnel:** Randolph A. Nana, Publisher. **ISSN:** 0031-9228 (print). **Subscription Rates:** $35 Individuals; $25 Members in affiliated societies. **URL:** http://scitation.aip.org/content/aip/magazine/physicstoday. **Ad Rates:** BW $10,340; 4C $1,700. **Remarks:** Advertising accepted; rates available upon

Circulation: ★ = AAM; △ or • = BPA; ♦ = CAC; ❑ = VAC; ⊕ = PO Statement; ‡ = Publisher's Report; Boldface figures = sworn; Light figures = estimated.

request. **Circ:** Combined ‡120000.

15290 ■ Quantum Electronics
American Institute of Physics
1 Physics Ellipse
College Park, MD 20740
Phone: (516)576-2200
Fax: (516)349-7669
Free: 888-491-8833
Russian journal on applications of lasers translated to English. **Freq:** Monthly. **Print Method:** Offset. **Trim Size:** 8 3/8 x 11 1/4. **Cols./Page:** 2. **Col. Width:** 42 nonpareils. **Col. Depth:** 135 agate lines. **Key Personnel:** O.N. Krokhin, Editor-in-Chief; I.B. Kovsh, Associate Editor; A.S. Semenov, Associate Editor. **ISSN:** 1063--7818 (print); **EISSN:** 1468--4799 (electronic). **Subscription Rates:** $4749 Individuals print & online; $4274 Individuals online only; $475 Single issue; £2639 Individuals print and online, rest of world; £2375 Individuals online, rest of world; £301 Single issue. **URL:** http://www.turpion.org/php/homes/pa.phtml?jrnid=qe. **Circ:** ‡450.

15291 ■ Research in Transportation Economics
RELX Group plc
Robert H. Smith School of Business
University of Maryland
College Park, MD 20742
Journal featuring economics research in the field of transportation. **Freq:** 6/yr. **Key Personnel:** G. Santos, Editor. **ISSN:** 0739-8859 (print). **Subscription Rates:** $727 Institutions print only. **URL:** http://www.journals.elsevier.com/research-in-transportation-economics/. **Circ:** (Not Reported).

15292 ■ Review of Scientific Instruments
American Institute of Physics
1 Physics Ellipse
College Park, MD 20740
Phone: (516)576-2200
Fax: (516)349-7669
Free: 888-491-8833
Publisher's E-mail: sales@aip.org
Journal covering articles on scientific instruments, apparatus, and techniques. **Freq:** Monthly. **Print Method:** Offset. **Trim Size:** 8 1/2 x 11. **Cols./Page:** 2. **Col. Width:** 41 nonpareils. **Col. Depth:** 136 agate lines. **Key Personnel:** John Clarke, Editor. **ISSN:** 0034--6748 (print); **EISSN:** 1089--7623 (electronic). **Online:** American Institute of Physics American Institute of Physics. **URL:** http://scitation.aip.org/content/aip/journal/rsi. **Ad Rates:** BW $900; 4C $990. **Remarks:** Accepts advertising. **Circ:** (Not Reported).

15293 ■ Reviews of Modern Physics
American Institute of Physics
1 Physics Ellipse
College Park, MD 20740
Phone: (516)576-2200
Fax: (516)349-7669
Free: 888-491-8833
Publisher's E-mail: sales@aip.org
Journal specializing in scholarly reviews of significant topics in physics. Also features colloquia and tutorial articles in rapidly developing fields of physics. **Freq:** Quarterly. **Trim Size:** 8 1/4 x 11. **Cols./Page:** 2. **Col. Width:** 20.5 picas. **Col. Depth:** 60 picas. **Key Personnel:** Gene D. Sprouse, Editor-in-Chief; Daniel T. Kulp, Director, Editorial. **ISSN:** 0034-6861 (print). **Subscription Rates:** $410 Institutions print and online; $685 Institutions print and online; $760 Institutions, other countries print and online. **URL:** http://www.aip.org. **Circ:** Paid 4,436.

15294 ■ SPS Observer
Sigma Pi Sigma
1 Physics Ellipse
College Park, MD 20740
Phone: (301)209-3007
Fax: (301)209-0839
Publisher's E-mail: sps@aip.org
Magazine containing interesting feature articles, physics problems, society news, announcements, meeting information, and breaking news in physics and related sciences. **Freq:** Quarterly. **Alt. Formats:** PDF. **URL:** http://www.spsobserver.org/. **Remarks:** Advertising not accepted. **Circ:** (Not Reported).

15295 ■ The SPS Observer
Society of Physics Students
1 Physics Ellipse
College Park, MD 20740
Phone: (301)209-3007
Publisher's E-mail: sps@aip.org
Freq: Quarterly. **Subscription Rates:** Included in membership. **URL:** http://www.spsobserver.org. **Remarks:** Advertising not accepted. **Circ:** 6000.

15296 ■ Technical Physics Letters
American Institute of Physics
1 Physics Ellipse
College Park, MD 20740
Phone: (516)576-2200
Fax: (516)349-7669
Free: 888-491-8833
Publisher's E-mail: sales@aip.org
Russian journal on the latest developments in all fields of physics translated to English. **Freq:** Semimonthly. **Print Method:** Offset. **Trim Size:** 8 3/8 x 11 1/4. **Cols./Page:** 2. **Col. Width:** 42 nonpareils. **Col. Depth:** 135 agate lines. **Key Personnel:** James R. Anderson, Editor; Zhores Alferov, Editor. **ISSN:** 1063--7850 (print); **EISSN:** 1090--6533 (electronic). **Subscription Rates:** $14448 Institutions incl. free access or e-only; $17338 Institutions plus enhanced access. **Alt. Formats:** Electronic publishing. **URL:** http://link.springer.com/journal/11455; http://www.springer.com/physics/classical+continuum+physics/journal/11455. **Circ:** (Not Reported).

15297 ■ A View from Within: A Case Study of Chinese Heritage Community Language Schools
National Foreign Language Center
Severn Bldg. 810
5245 Greenbelt Rd.
College Park, MD 20742
Phone: (301)405-9828
Fax: (301)405-9829
Subscription Rates: $10.95 each. **Mailing address:** PO Box 93, College Park, MD 20742. **Remarks:** Advertising not accepted. **Circ:** (Not Reported).

15298 ■ WMUC-FM - 88.1
3130 S Campus Dining Hall
College Park, MD 20742
Phone: (616)957-2570
Format: Eclectic. **Founded:** 1937. **Operating Hours:** Continuous. **Key Personnel:** Mario Pareja Lecaros, Gen. Mgr. **Ad Rates:** Advertising accepted; rates available upon request. **URL:** http://www.wmuc.umd.edu.

COLTONS POINT

15299 ■ Public Relations Review: A Global Journal of Research and Comment
Elsevier
c/o Ray E. Hiebert, Ed.
Communication Research Associates, Inc.
Coltons Point, MD 20626-0180
Publisher's E-mail: t.reller@elsevier.com
Communications journal covering public relations education, government, survey research, public policy, history, and bibliographies. **Freq:** 5/year. **Key Personnel:** Ray E. Hiebert, Editor-in-Chief. **ISSN:** 0363--8111 (print). **Subscription Rates:** $928 Institutions print or online; $242 Individuals print. **URL:** http://www.journals.elsevier.com/public-relations-review. **Mailing address:** PO Box 180, Coltons Point, MD 20626-0180. **Ad Rates:** BW $150. **Remarks:** Accepts advertising. **Circ:** Paid ‡1500, Non-paid ‡55.

COLUMBIA

Howard Co. (C). 20 m NE of Rockville. Howard Community College.

15300 ■ BaptistLIFE
Baptist Convention of Maryland/Delaware
10255 Old Columbia Rd.
Columbia, MD 21046
Phone: (410)290-5290
Free: 800-466-5290
Publisher's E-mail: jdixon@bcmd.org
News journal for Southern Baptists of Maryland and Delaware. **Freq:** Monthly. **Print Method:** Offset. **Trim Size:** 11 1/4 x 14 1/2. **Cols./Page:** 5. **Col. Width:** 1.9 inches. **Col. Depth:** 205 agate lines. **Key Personnel:** Bob Simpson, Editor; Irish White, Coordinator, Managing Editor; Lauren Rodriguez, Contact. **ISSN:** 0883--7864 (print). **Subscription Rates:** Free. **Alt. Formats:** PDF. **URL:** http://www.baptistlifeonline.org. **Formerly**: Bapist True Union. **Ad Rates:** PCI $18. **Remarks:** Accepts advertising. **Circ:** 24000.

15301 ■ Business Credit
National Association of Credit Management
8840 Columbia 100 Pky.
Columbia, MD 21045
Phone: (410)740-5560
Fax: (410)740-5574
Publisher's E-mail: nacm_national@nacm.org
Freq: 9/year. **ISSN:** 0897--0181 (print). **Subscription Rates:** $54 U.S. 1 year; $85 U.S. 2 years; $110 U.S. 3 years; $60 Canada 1 year; $95 Canada 2 years; $120 Canada 3 years; $65 Other countries 1 year; $100 Other countries 2 years; $130 Other countries 3 years; $7 Single issue. **URL:** http://www.nacm.org/business-credit-magazine.html. **Ad Rates:** 4C $3200. **Remarks:** Accepts advertising. **Circ:** 36800.

15302 ■ Business Credit: The Publication for Credit and Finance Professionals
National Association of Credit Management
8840 Columbia 100 Pky.
Columbia, MD 21045
Phone: (410)740-5560
Fax: (410)740-5574
Publisher's E-mail: nacm_national@nacm.org
Magazine covering finance, business risk management, providing information for the extension of credit, maintenance of accounts receivable, and cash asset management. **Freq:** 10/year. **Print Method:** Web offset. **Trim Size:** 8.125 x 10.875. **Cols./Page:** 3. **Col. Width:** 13 picas. **Col. Depth:** 67 picas. **Key Personnel:** Dan LaRusso, Contact, phone: (410)740-5560; Caroline Zimmerman, Director, Editorial. **ISSN:** 0897--0181 (print). **Subscription Rates:** $54 U.S. subscriber rate; $85 Two years subscriber rate; $60 Canada subscriber rate; $65 Two years Canada subscriber rate; $65 Other countries subscriber rate; $100 Two years foreign subscriber rate; $7 Single issue. **URL:** http://www.nacm.org/index.php?option=com_content&view=category&layout=blog&id=77&Itemid=188 . **Formerly**: Credit and Financial Management. **Ad Rates:** BW $4,400; 4C $5,375. **Remarks:** Accepts advertising. **Circ:** ‡20000.

15303 ■ Columbia Flier
Patuxent Publishing Co.
10750 Little Patuxent Pkwy.
Columbia, MD 21044-3106
Phone: (410)730-3990
Fax: (410)992-5339
Free: 877-886-1206
Publisher's E-mail: jquimby@patuxent.com
Suburban community newspaper. **Freq:** Weekly (Thurs.). **Print Method:** Offset. **Trim Size:** 10 1/4 x 11 1/2. **Cols./Page:** 5. **Col. Width:** 11 picas. **Col. Depth:** 80.25 picas. **Key Personnel:** Paul Milton, Executive Director. **ISSN:** 0192--7841 (print). **URL:** http://www.baltimoresun.com/news/maryland/howard/columbia; http://baltimoresunmediagroup.com/media-portfolio/newspapers/columbia-flier. **Mailing address:** PO Box L, Laurel, MD 20707. **Remarks:** Advertising accepted; rates available upon request. **Circ:** Combined ♦**37887**.

15304 ■ Columbia Union Visitor: Connecting Columbia Union Members
Columbia Union Conference of Seventh-day Adventists
5427 Twin Knolls Rd.
Columbia, MD 21045
Phone: (410)997-3414
Fax: (410)997-7420
Seventh-Day Adventist magazine. **Freq:** Monthly. **Print Method:** Web offset. **Trim Size:** 8 1/8 x 10 5/8. **Cols./Page:** 3 and 4. **Col. Width:** 26 and 20 nonpareils. **Col. Depth:** 136 agate lines. **Key Personnel:** Celeste Ryan, Editor. **Subscription Rates:** Free to members; $21 Nonmembers. **URL:** http://www.columbiaunion.org; http://www.columbiaunionvisitor.com. **Ad Rates:** BW $1500; 4C $2700. **Remarks:** Accepts advertising. **Circ:** Controlled ‡60000.

15305 ■ Emergency Medicine: The Practice Journal for Emergency Physicians
Cadmus Journal Services
8621 Robert Fulton Dr., Ste. 100
Columbia, MD 21046
Phone: (410)850-0500

Free: 800-257-5529
Trade magazine on the business of generating, transmitting and distributing electric power. **Freq:** 16/yr. **Print Method:** Web Offset. **Trim Size:** 7 7/8 x 10 3/4. **Cols./Page:** 3 and 2. **Col. Width:** 2 1/8 and 4 inches. **Col. Depth:** 10 inches. **Key Personnel:** Mark Branca, Publisher. **ISSN:** 0013--6654 (print). **Subscription Rates:** $830 Other countries; $184 Canada and Mexico; $570 Other countries surface mail; $329 Other countries air mail; $352 Institutions; $374 Institutions, Canada and Mexico; $406 Institutions, other countries; $67 Students; $42 Single issue US; $47 Single issue Canada & Mexico; $53 Single issue other countries; $47 U.S. back issues; $53 Canada and Mexico back issues; $59 Other countries back issues. **URL:** http://www.emed-journal.com. **Ad Rates:** BW $3,465; 4C $5,290. **Remarks:** Accepts advertising. **Circ:** Non-paid 48258.

15306 ■ Food Trade News
Best-Met Publishing Company Inc.
5537 Twin Knolls Rd., Ste. 438
Columbia, MD 21045
Phone: (410)730-5013
Fax: (410)740-4680
Publisher's E-mail: office@best-met.com
Newspaper for the retail supermarket industry. **Founded:** 1945. **Freq:** Monthly. **Print Method:** Offset. **Trim Size:** 10 x 14. **Cols./Page:** 5. **Col. Width:** 24 nonpareils. **Col. Depth:** 196 agate lines. **Key Personnel:** Beth Pripstein, Office Manager; Jeffrey W. Metzger, Publisher; Terri Maloney, Director, Editorial, Vice President. **ISSN:** 0015-6663 (print). **USPS:** 562-290. **Subscription Rates:** $69 Individuals. **URL:** http://best-met.com/newspaper/food-trade-news/. **Ad Rates:** BW $2656. **Remarks:** Accepts advertising. **Circ:** Controlled ‡27,555.

15307 ■ Food World
Best-Met Publishing Company Inc.
5537 Twin Knolls Rd., Ste. 438
Columbia, MD 21045
Phone: (410)730-5013
Fax: (410)740-4680
Publisher's E-mail: office@best-met.com
Regional food trade magazine (tabloid). **Freq:** Monthly published every first Monday of the month. **Print Method:** Offset. **Trim Size:** 10 x 10.5. **Cols./Page:** 5. **Col. Width:** 24 nonpareils. **Col. Depth:** 196 agate lines. **Key Personnel:** Terri Maloney, Director, Editorial, Vice President; Jeffrey W. Metzger, Publisher. **USPS:** 203-920. **Subscription Rates:** $69 Individuals /year. **URL:** http://best-met.com. **Ad Rates:** BW $3665.97. **Remarks:** Accepts advertising. **Circ:** ‡21572.

15308 ■ Howard County Times
Patuxent Publishing Co.
10750 Little Patuxent Pkwy.
Columbia, MD 21044-3106
Phone: (410)730-3990
Fax: (410)992-5339
Free: 877-886-1206
Publisher's E-mail: jquimby@patuxent.com
Community newspaper. **Freq:** Weekly (Thurs.). **Print Method:** Offset. **Trim Size:** 10 1/4 x 11 1/2. **Cols./Page:** 5. **Col. Width:** 11 picas. **Col. Depth:** 74 picas. **Key Personnel:** Paul Milton, Executive Director; Peter Pichaske, Editor. **ISSN:** 0748--5298 (print). **Subscription Rates:** $29.95 Individuals; $44.95 Two years. **URL:** http://www.baltimoresun.com/news/maryland/howard/?track=bs-subnav-local-ho; http://baltimoresunmediagroup.com/media-portfolio/newspapers/howard-county-times. **Mailing address:** PO Box L, Laurel, MD 20707. **Remarks:** Accepts advertising. **Circ:** Combined ♦**14787**.

15309 ■ International Journal of Flow Control
Multi-Science Publishing Company Ltd.
c/o Dr. Surya Raghu, Ed.-in-Ch.
Advanced Fluidics LLC
8860 Columbia Pky., Ste. 204
Columbia, MD 21045
Publication E-mail: flowcontroljournal@gmail.com
Journal covering topics on fluid flow control technology. **Freq:** Quarterly. **Key Personnel:** Dr. Surya Raghu, Editor-in-Chief. **ISSN:** 1756--8250 (print). **Subscription Rates:** £308 Individuals print and online; £299 Individuals print only; £278 Individuals online only. **URL:** http://www.multi-science.co.uk/ijfc.htm. **Circ:** (Not Reported).

15310 ■ JAMDA
AMDA - The Society for Post-Acute and Long-Term Care Medicine
11000 Broken Land Pky., Ste. 400
Columbia, MD 21044
Phone: (410)740-9743
Fax: (410)740-4572
Free: 800-876-2632
Publisher's E-mail: info@paltc.com
Freq: Monthly. **ISSN:** 1525--8610 (print). **Subscription Rates:** $289 U.S. print and online; $356 Other countries print and online; $246 Individuals online only; $124 Students print and online; $175 Students, other countries print and online; $105 Students online only. **URL:** http://www.jamda.com. **Remarks:** Accepts advertising. **Circ:** 8000.

15311 ■ The Journal of Histotechnology
National Society for HistoTechnology
8850 Stanford Blvd., Ste. 2900
Columbia, MD 21045
Phone: (443)535-4060
Fax: (443)535-4055
Publication E-mail: histo@nsh.org
Histotechnology and pathology journal. **Freq:** Quarterly. **Print Method:** Offset. **Trim Size:** 8 1/4 x 11. **Cols./Page:** 2. **Col. Width:** 39 nonpareils. **Col. Depth:** 133 agate lines. **Key Personnel:** Karen J.L. Burg, PhD, Editor-in-Chief. **ISSN:** 0147--8885 (print); **EISSN:** 2046--0236 (electronic). **Subscription Rates:** £148 Individuals print and online; $248 Institutions print and online. **URL:** http://cunninghamassociates.com/?page_id=805. **Ad Rates:** BW $1450; 4C $655. **Remarks:** Accepts advertising. **Circ:** Paid ‡4500.

15312 ■ The Official Guide to Howard County
Patuxent Publishing Co.
10750 Little Patuxent Pkwy.
Columbia, MD 21044-3106
Phone: (410)730-3990
Fax: (410)992-5339
Free: 877-886-1206
Publisher's E-mail: jquimby@patuxent.com
Magazine featuring visitor information on Howard County, Maryland. **Freq:** Weekly (Thurs.). **Trim Size:** 8 1/4 x 10 3/4. **Key Personnel:** Paul Milton, Executive Editor. **ISSN:** 0192--7841 (print). **URL:** http://essentials.baltimoresun.com/macro/patuxent/magazines.html; http://news.mywebpal.com. **Mailing address:** PO Box L, Laurel, MD 20707. **Ad Rates:** BW $4,922. **Remarks:** Accepts advertising. **Circ:** (Not Reported).

15313 ■ Porsche Panorama
Porsche Club of America
9689 Gerwig Ln., Unit 4C/D
Columbia, MD 21046
Phone: (410)381-0911
Fax: (410)381-0924
Publication E-mail: porpan@mindspring.com
Magazine for Porsche owners and members of the Porsche Club of America. **Freq:** Monthly. **Trim Size:** 8 3/8 x 10 7/8. **Col. Width:** 7 1/4 INS. **Key Personnel:** Betty Jo Turner, Editor-in-Chief. **ISSN:** 0147--3565 (print). **URL:** http://www.pca.org/panorama/edition/panorama-august-2015. **Mailing address:** PO Box 6400, Columbia, MD 21045. **Ad Rates:** BW $1,125; 4C $1,883. **Remarks:** Advertising accepted; rates available upon request. **Circ:** Combined ‡68500.

15314 ■ Regulatory Toxicology and Pharmacology
International Society of Regulatory Toxicology and Pharmacology
6546 Belleview Dr.
Columbia, MD 21046-1054
Phone: (410)992-9083
Fax: (410)740-9181
Key Personnel: Gio B. Gori, Editor. **ISSN:** 0273--2300 (print). **URL:** http://www.isrtp.org/nonmembers/manuscript.html; http://www.journals.elsevier.com/regulatory-toxicology-and-pharmacology. **Remarks:** Advertising not accepted. **Circ:** (Not Reported).

CRISFIELD

Somerset Co. Somerset Co. (SE). On Chesapeake Bay, 123 m S of Wilmington, Del. Important sea food shipping center. Manufactures brushes, sea food tools, nets, boxes, barrels, cutlery. Dairy, poultry, stock farms. Strawberries, tomatoes, potatoes.

15315 ■ Crisfield-Somerset County Times
Independent Newsmedia Inc.
914 W Main St.
Crisfield, MD 21817
Phone: (410)968-1188
Publisher's E-mail: help@newszap.com
Local newspaper. **Freq:** Weekly (Wed.). **Print Method:** Offset. **Trim Size:** 13 x 21 1/2. **Cols./Page:** 6. **Col. Width:** 26 nonpareils. **Col. Depth:** 301 agate lines. **Subscription Rates:** $26 Individuals online; $39 Individuals print; $2.95 Single issue back issue. **URL:** http://www.csctimes.com. **Ad Rates:** GLR $2.55; BW $1258; 4C $1458; PCI $9.75. **Remarks:** Accepts advertising. **Circ:** ‡1577.

CROFTON

15316 ■ Parma Eldalamberon
Elvish Linguistic Fellowship
2509 Ambling Cir.
Crofton, MD 21114
Freq: Annual. **Subscription Rates:** $35 Individuals. **URL:** http://www.eldalamberon.com/parma20.html. **Remarks:** Advertising not accepted. **Circ:** (Not Reported).

15317 ■ Vinyar Tengwar
Elvish Linguistic Fellowship
2509 Ambling Cir.
Crofton, MD 21114
Freq: Quarterly. **ISSN:** 1054--7606 (print). **URL:** http://www.elvish.org/VT. **Remarks:** Advertising not accepted. **Circ:** 125.

CUMBERLAND

Allegany Co. Allegany Co. (NW). On Potomac River, at terminal of Chesapeake & Ohio Canal, 130 m W of Baltimore. Alleghany Community College. Manufactures railroad equipment, brick, lumber, drills, plastics, steel shafting, glassware, boxes, macaroni, auto tires. Limestone quarries, coal mines.

15318 ■ Cumberland Times News
McLeansboro Times-Leader
19 Baltimore St.
Cumberland, MD 21502
Phone: (301)722-4600
Fax: (301)722-4870
General newspaper. **Freq:** Mon.-Sun. (morn.). **Print Method:** Offset. **Cols./Page:** 6. **Col. Width:** 25 nonpareils. **Col. Depth:** 301 agate lines. **Key Personnel:** Robin L. Quillon, Publisher; John D. Smith, Jr., Managing Editor; Jen James, Director, Advertising, phone: (301)722-4600; Joe O'Toole, Manager, Circulation, phone: (301)722-4600. **Subscription Rates:** $14.99 Individuals /month, total access; $11.99 Individuals /month, digital access. **URL:** http://www.times-news.com. **Mailing address:** PO Box 1662, Cumberland, MD 21502. **Ad Rates:** SAU $14.80. **Remarks:** Accepts advertising. **Circ:** Mon.-Fri. ★**27954**, Sun. ★**29869**, Sat. ★**28063**.

15319 ■ Cumberland Broadcasting Company Inc. - 1270
PO Box 1290
Cumberland, MD 21501
Phone: (301)724-5000
Email: info@wcbcradio.com
Format: News; Sports; Information. **Networks:** Westwood One Radio; ABC. **Operating Hours:** Continuous. **Wattage:** 5,000. **Ad Rates:** Advertising accepted; rates available upon request. **URL:** http://www.wcbcradio.com.

15320 ■ WCBC-AM - 1270
PO Box 1290
Cumberland, MD 21501
Phone: (301)724-5000
Email: info@wcbcradio.com
Format: News; Sports; Full Service. **Networks:** ABC. **Owner:** Cumberland Broadcasting Company Inc., PO Box 1290, Cumberland, MD 21501, Ph: (301)724-5000. **Founded:** Apr. 1976. **Operating Hours:** Continuous; 50% network, 50% local. **ADI:** Hagerstown, MD. **Wattage:** 5,000 Day; 1,000 Night. **Ad Rates:** $4.77-7.59 for 15 seconds; $9.53-15.18 for 30 seconds; $12.39-19.73 for 60 seconds. Combined advertising rates available with WCBC-FM. **URL:** http://www.wcbcradio.com.

Circulation: ★ = AAM; △ or • = BPA; ♦ = CAC; ❑ = VAC; ⊕ = PO Statement; ‡ = Publisher's Report; Boldface figures = sworn; Light figures = estimated.

15321 ■ WCBC-FM - 107.1
PO Box 1290
Cumberland, MD 21501
Phone: (301)724-5000
Email: info@wcbcradio.com
Format: Oldies. **Networks:** Jones Satellite. **Owner:** Cumberland Broadcasting Company Inc., PO Box 1290, Cumberland, MD 21501, Ph: (301)724-5000. **Founded:** 1990. **Formerly**: WKZG-FM. **Operating Hours**: Continuous. **Key Personnel:** Mary Clites, Gen. Mgr.; Bryan Gowans, News Dir; Andee Thompson, Contact. **Wattage**: 3,000. **Ad Rates:** Noncommercial. Combined advertising rates available with WCBC-AM. **URL:** http://www.wcbcradio.com.

15322 ■ WDZN-FM - 100.1
15 E Industrial Blvd.
Cumberland, MD 21502
Format: Educational. **Founded:** Sept. 07, 2006. **URL:** http://www.z100rock.com.

15323 ■ WKGO-FM - 106.1
350 Byrd Ave.
Cumberland, MD 21502
Phone: (301)722-6666
Fax: (301)722-0945
Format: Classic Rock. **Networks:** Westwood One Radio. **Founded:** 1962. **Operating Hours**: Continuous. **ADI**: Washington, DC. **Key Personnel**: Richard Cornwell, Gen. Sales Mgr., richcornwell@go106.com. **Wattage**: 4,000. **Ad Rates:** $16.00 for 30 seconds; $19.00 for 60 seconds. **URL:** http://www.go106.com.

15324 ■ WNTR-AM - 1230
15 E Industrial Pk.
Cumberland, MD 21502
Email: wrogwntr@miworld.net
Format: Sports; Information. **Networks:** NBC. **Owner:** Tschody Radio, at above address, Ph: (301)777-5400, Fax: (301)724-2571. **Founded:** 1948. **Formerly**: WALI-AM. **Operating Hours**: Continuous. **Key Personnel:** Geiger, Office Mgr.; JD Frye, Dir. of Programs; Rick Williams, Chief Engineer; Kevin Spencer, Asst. Dir.; Dick Yeden, Gen. Mgr; Patrick L. Sullivan, Contact. **Wattage**: 1,000. **Ad Rates:** $9-14 for 30 seconds; $10-17 for 60 seconds. **URL:** http://1390espn.com.

15325 ■ WQZK-FM - 94.1
15 E Industrial Blvd.
Cumberland, MD 21502
Phone: (301)759-1005
Format: Top 40. **Networks:** ABC; Jones Satellite; West Virginia Metro. **Owner:** Allegany Radio Corp., 15 East Industrial Blvd., Cumberland, MD 21502, Ph: (301)759-1005, Free: 866-440-9410. **Founded:** 1981. **Formerly**: WKLP-FM. **Operating Hours**: Continuous. **ADI**: Washington, DC. **Key Personnel:** Amy Ryan, Contact. **Wattage**: 50,000. **Ad Rates:** $5.50-10.35 for 15 seconds; $9-13.80 for 30 seconds; $12.80-17.25 for 60 seconds. Combined advertising rates available with WKIP. **URL:** http://www.941qzk.com.

15326 ■ WTBO-AM - 1450
350 Byrd Ave.
Cumberland, MD 21502
Phone: (301)722-6666
Fax: (301)722-0945
Format: News. **Simulcasts:** WTBO-FM. **Owner:** Dix Communications, at above address. **Founded:** 1928. **Operating Hours**: Continuous. **Wattage**: 1,000 Day; 1,000 Nig. **Ad Rates:** Accepts Advertising. **URL:** http://wtbocumberland.com/music/top-requests.

15327 ■ WVMD-FM - 99.5
15 E Industrial Blvd.
Cumberland, MD 21502
Phone: (301)759-1005
Fax: (301)759-3124
Format: Country; Bluegrass. **Owner:** Allegany Radio Corp., 15 East Industrial Blvd., Cumberland, MD 21502, Ph: (301)759-1005, Free: 866-440-9410. **URL:** http://www.tristateswolf.com.

DUNDALK

Baltimore Co. (N). 6 m E of Baltimore. Dundalk Community College. Ft. McHenry (historical site). Dundalk Marine Terminal. Auto body factory; steel plant; shipbuilding.

15328 ■ Dundalk Eagle
Kimbel Publication Inc.
PO Box 8936
Dundalk, MD 21222
Phone: (410)288-6060
Fax: (410)288-6963
Publication E-mail: info@dundalkeagle.com
Community newspaper. **Freq:** Weekly (Thurs.). **Print Method:** Offset. **Cols./Page:** 6. **Col. Width:** 20 nonpareils. **Col. Depth:** 210 agate lines. **Key Personnel:** David Fike, President, Publisher. **USPS:** 709-800. **Subscription Rates:** $19.08 Individuals print and online; in Baltimore County and Baltimore City; $27.56 Elsewhere print and online - Elsewhere in the US; $9.94 Individuals online (182 days). **URL:** http://www.dundalkeagle.com. **Ad Rates:** GLR $1; BW $1594; 4C $1902; PCI $15.40. **Remarks:** Advertising accepted; rates available upon request. **Circ:** Paid ‡20000, Free ‡1030.

EASTON

Talbot Co. Talbot Co. (E). On Tred Avon River, 38 m NW of Salisbury. Nurseries; canned goods, furniture, brick, tile, underwear manufactured. Seafood packing. Diversified farming. Wheat, soybeans, corn, tomatoes.

15329 ■ The Delmarva Farmer: The Agribusiness Newspaper of the Mid-Atlantic Region
American Farm Publications Inc.
PO Box 2026
Easton, MD 21601
Phone: (410)822-3965
Fax: (410)822-5068
Free: 800-634-5021
Publication E-mail: editorial@americanfarm.com
Newspaper (tabloid) featuring news of interest to agricultural concerns in Maryland, Delaware, Virginia, New Jersey, and Pennsylvania. **Freq:** Biweekly. **Print Method:** Offset. **Trim Size:** 11 1/4 x 14 1/2. **Cols./Page:** 4. **Col. Width:** 24 nonpareils. **Col. Depth:** 203 agate lines. **Key Personnel:** Bruce Hotchkiss, Senior Editor; E. Ralph Hostetter, Chairman, Publisher; Sean Clougherty, Managing Editor. **ISSN:** 0194--2964 (print). **Subscription Rates:** $35 Individuals; $60 Two years; $73 Individuals three years. **URL:** http://www.americanfarm.com/publications/the-delmarva-farmer. **Remarks:** Accepts advertising. **Circ:** Paid ‡8000, Free ‡3702.

15330 ■ The New Jersey Farmer: Growing with the Garden State
American Farm Publications Inc.
PO Box 2026
Easton, MD 21601
Phone: (410)822-3965
Fax: (410)822-5068
Free: 800-634-5021
Publication E-mail: tiffany@americanfarm.com
Tabloid featuring news of interest to agricultural concerns in New Jersey. **Freq:** Biweekly. **Print Method:** Offset. **Trim Size:** 11 1/4 x 14 1/2. **Cols./Page:** 4. **Col. Width:** 24 nonpareils. **Col. Depth:** 203 agate lines. **Key Personnel:** Ralph E. Hostetter, Chairman, Publisher; Bruce Hotchkiss, Senior Vice President. **ISSN:** 0898--8765 (print). **Subscription Rates:** $28 Individuals; $46 Two years; $58 Individuals 3 years. **URL:** http://www.americanfarm.com/publications/the-new-jersey-farmer. **Remarks:** Accepts advertising. **Circ:** Paid ‡2247, Controlled ‡2543.

15331 ■ Times/Record
Chesapeake Publishing Corp.
PO Box 600
Easton, MD 21601
Phone: (410)822-1500
Fax: (410)820-6512
Community newspaper. **Founded:** 1929. **Freq:** Weekly (Wed.). **Print Method:** Offset. **Cols./Page:** 6. **Col. Width:** 24 nonpareils. **Col. Depth:** 294 agate lines. **Key Personnel:** John Evans, Editor; Sean Venables, Editor; David Fike, Publisher, Vice President. **Subscription Rates:** $29 Individuals; $34 Individuals print & online. **Ad Rates:** SAU $5.10. **Remarks:** Accepts advertising. **Circ:** 4000.

15332 ■ Easton Cable
201 N Washington St.
Easton, MD 21601
Phone: (410)822-6110
Fax: (410)822-0743
Email: info@eastonutilities.com
Key Personnel: Hugh E. Grunden, PE., CEO, President; Paul Moeller, CFO, VP; Tracie Thomas, CPA., Controller. **Cities Served:** 70 channels. **Mailing address:** PO Box 1189, Easton, MD 21601. **URL:** http://eastonutilities.com.

15333 ■ WCEI-FM - 96.7
306 Port St.
Easton, MD 21601-4101
Phone: (410)822-3301
Fax: (410)822-0576
Email: studio@wceiradio.com
Format: Adult Contemporary. **Networks:** AP. **Owner:** First Media Radio L.L.C., at above address. **Founded:** 1975. **Formerly**: WEMD-FM. **Operating Hours**: Continuous. **Key Personnel:** Matt Spence, Dir. of Operations, matt@wceiradio.com; Tina Saddler, Office Mgr., tina@wceiradio.com; Stacie Monz, Gen. Mgr., stacie@wceiradio.com. **Wattage:** 25,000. **Ad Rates:** $25-55 for 30 seconds; $31-70 for 60 seconds. Combined advertising rates available with WCEI-AM; WEMD-AM. **URL:** http://www.wceiradio.com.

15334 ■ WDLZ-FM - 98.3
306 Port St.
Easton, MD 21601
Phone: (410)822-3301
Format: Soft Rock. **Networks:** North Carolina News; Westwood One Radio. **Owner:** First Media Radio L.L.C., at above address. **Founded:** 1965. **Formerly**: WBCG-FM. **Operating Hours**: 6 a.m.-midnight; 65% network, 35% local. **Wattage:** 3,000. **Ad Rates:** $4-10.50 per unit. Combined advertising rates available with WINX-AM, WSAY-FM.

15335 ■ WEMD-AM - 1460
306 Port St.
Easton, MD 21601-4101
Phone: (410)822-3301
Fax: (410)822-0576
Format: Talk; Big Band/Nostalgia; Easy Listening. **Networks:** AP. **Owner:** First Media Radio, LLC, 312 S Main St., Lexington, VA 24450, Ph: (540)463-2161. **Founded:** 1960. **Formerly**: WCEI-AM WEMD-AM; WCEI-AM. **Operating Hours**: Continuous. **Key Personnel:** Stacie Monz, Gen. Mgr., stacie@wceiradio.com; Matt Spence, Dir. of Operations, matt@wceiradio.com; Tina Saddler, Office Mgr., tina@wceiradio.com. **Wattage**: 1,000. **Ad Rates:** Noncommercial. Combined advertising rates available with WCEI-FM. **URL:** http://www.wceiradio.com.

WSMY-AM - See Weldon, NC

ELKRIDGE

15336 ■ IEEE Microwave Magazine
IEEE Microwave Theory and Techniques Society
c/o Edward C. Niehenke
Niehenke Consulting
5829 Bellanca Dr.
Elkridge, MD 21075
Phone: (410)796-5866
Publisher's E-mail: i.engelson@ieee.org
Magazine covering theory and techniques in the field of microwave. **Freq:** 11/year. **Key Personnel:** Alfy Riddle, Editor-in-Chief. **ISSN:** 1527--3342 (print). **URL:** http://ieeexplore.ieee.org/xpl/RecentIssue.jsp?punumber=6668; http://www.mtt.org/magazine.html. **Mailing address:** IEEE Admission and AdvancementPO Box 6804, Piscataway, NJ 08855-6804. **Remarks:** Accepts advertising. **Circ:** (Not Reported).

15337 ■ IEEE Transactions on Terahertz Science and Technology
IEEE Microwave Theory and Techniques Society
c/o Edward C. Niehenke
Niehenke Consulting
5829 Bellanca Dr.
Elkridge, MD 21075
Phone: (410)796-5866
Publication E-mail: thz.editors@ieee.org
Peer-reviewed journal covering terahertz science and applications. **Key Personnel:** Peter H. Siegel, Editor-in-Chief, phone: (818)952-6229. **URL:** http://www.mtt.org/terahertz. **Circ:** (Not Reported).

15338 ■ Journal of Forensic Nursing
International Association of Forensic Nurses

6755 Business Pky., Ste. 303
Elkridge, MD 21075-6740
Phone: (410)626-7805
Fax: (410)626-7804
Publisher's E-mail: info@forensicnurses.org
Peer-reviewed journal covering the field of forensic nursing. **Freq:** Quarterly. **Key Personnel:** Cindy Peternelj-Taylor, Editor-in-Chief; Paul Clements, Associate Editor. **ISSN:** 1556--3693 (print); **EISSN:** 1939--3938 (electronic). **Subscription Rates:** $97 Individuals Americas (print and online); £49 Other countries individual (print and online); €73 Individuals Euro zone (print and online); $264 Institutions Americas (print and online); £133 Institutions UK (print and online); €168 Institutions Europe (print and online); $257 Institutions, other countries print and online; $229 Institutions Americas (print or online only); £115 Institutions UK (print or online only); €146 Institutions Europe (print or online only); Included in membership. **URL:** http://journals.lww.com/forensicnursing/Pages/default.aspx. **Ad Rates:** 4C $1,540; BW $790. **Remarks:** Accepts advertising. **Circ:** 1000.

ELKTON

Cecil Co. Cecil Co. (NE). 18 m SW of Wilmington, Del. Clay, sand, gravel pits. Manufactures fireworks, explosives, plastics, rubber novelties, chemical compounds, hosiery, paper, dresses, boat building, rocket propellent, automotive parts. Agriculture. Dairy, beef.

15339 ■ Cecil Whig
Cecil Whig
601 N Bridge St.
Elkton, MD 21922
Phone: (410)398-3311
Free: 800-220-3311
Publisher's E-mail: accent@cecilwhig.com
General newspaper. **Freq:** Daily. **USPS:** 095-560. **Subscription Rates:** $81 Individuals print and online; $66 Individuals 40 weeks, print and online; $38 Individuals 20 weeks; $69 Individuals 365 days, online only; $50 Individuals 182 days, online only. **URL:** http://www.cecildaily.com. **Mailing address:** PO Box 429, Elkton, MD 21922. **Ad Rates:** GLR $.62; BW $1,001.70; 4C $1,251.70; PCI $8.70. **Remarks:** Accepts advertising. **Circ:** Mon.-Fri. ♦**14186**, Sun. ♦**30642**.

15340 ■ IEEE Industry Applications Magazine
IEEE - Industry Applications Society
c/o H. Landis Floyd, Ed.-in-Ch.
35 Gina Ct.
Elkton, MD 21921
Publisher's E-mail: ias-administrator@ieee.org
Professional magazine for electrical engineers in industry. **Founded:** 1995. **Freq:** Bimonthly. **Print Method:** Offset. **Trim Size:** 7 7/8 x 10 3/4. **Cols./Page:** 2. **Col. Width:** 3 3/8 inches. **Col. Depth:** 10 inches. **Key Personnel:** H. Landis Floyd, Editor-in-Chief. **ISSN:** 1077-2618 (print). **URL:** http://ieeexplore.ieee.org/xpl/RecentIssue.jsp?punumber=2943. **Ad Rates:** BW $2,725; 4C $990. **Remarks:** Accepts advertising. **Circ:** 10230.

15341 ■ The Mariner
The Mariner
601 Bridge St.
Elkton, MD 21921
Phone: (410)398-3311
Consumer magazine covering boating and leisure. **Freq:** Monthly 3rd friday. **Print Method:** Web offset. **Trim Size:** 10 x 11 1/8. **Cols./Page:** 5. **Col. Width:** 1 7/8 inches. **Col. Depth:** 11 1/8 inches. **Key Personnel:** Jean Korten Moser, Editor. **Alt. Formats:** PDF. **URL:** http://www.marinermagazine.com. **Remarks:** Accepts classified advertising. **Circ:** Combined ♦**45000**.

15342 ■ WOEL-FM - 89.9
3141 Old Elk Neck Rd.
Elkton, MD 21921
Phone: (410)398-3764
Format: Religious. **Networks:** USA Radio. **Owner:** Maryland Baptist Bible College, Maranatha Baptist Church 3141 Old Elk Neck Rd., Elkton, MD 21921-6822, Ph: (414)398-6667. **Founded:** 1978. **Operating Hours:** Continuous. **Wattage:** 3,000. **Ad Rates:** Noncommercial. **URL:** http://www.mbcmin.org.

ELLICOTT CITY

Howard Co. (E). Howard Co. (E).

15343 ■ Business Law Today
American Bar Association
c/o Arthur F. Fergenson, Ed.-in-Ch.
3545 Ellicott Mills Dr., Ste. 201
Ellicott City, MD 21043
Magazine of the business law section, ABA. **Freq:** Monthly. **Print Method:** Offset. **Trim Size:** 8 3/8 x 11. **Cols./Page:** 3. **Col. Width:** 2 3/16 inches. **Col. Depth:** 10 inches. **Key Personnel:** Arthur F. Fergenson, Editor-in-Chief; Paul L. Lion, Contact. **ISSN:** 1059-9436 (print). **Subscription Rates:** $28 Individuals. **Alt. Formats:** PDF. **URL:** http://www.americanbar.org/publications/blt/2015/08.html; http://www.americanbar.org/groups/business_law/publications.html. **Remarks:** Accepts advertising. **Circ:** Paid △**55000**.

15344 ■ International Journal of Emergency Mental Health
Chevron Publishing Corp.
3290 Pine Orchard Ln., Ste. F
Ellicott City, MD 21042
Phone: (410)750-9600
Fax: (410)750-9601
Publisher's E-mail: office@chevronpublishing.com
Peer-reviewed journal focusing on field of emergency mental health. **Freq:** Quarterly. **Trim Size:** 8 1/2 x 11. **Key Personnel:** Diane Gwin, Contact, phone: (410)740-0065. **ISSN:** 1522-4821 (print). **Subscription Rates:** $82 Individuals. **URL:** http://www.chevronpublishing.com/product.cfm?dispprodid=480. **Mailing address:** PO Box 6274, Ellicott City, MD 21042. **Ad Rates:** BW $500. **Remarks:** Accepts advertising. **Circ:** (Not Reported).

EMMITSBURG

15345 ■ Journal of Freshwater Ecology
Taylor & Francis Group Journals
c/o Jeffrey A. Simmons, Editor-in-Chief
Mount St. Mary's University
Emmitsburg, MD 21727
Publisher's E-mail: customerservice@taylorandfrancis.com
Peer-reviewed journal publishing a wide variety of original ecological studies, observations and techniques. **Freq:** Quarterly. **Key Personnel:** Dr. Jeffrey A. Simmons, Editor-in-Chief; Joseph A. Kawatski, Editor, Founder. **ISSN:** 0270--5060 (print); **EISSN:** 2156--6941 (electronic). **Subscription Rates:** $235 Institutions print and online; $206 Institutions online only. **URL:** http://www.tandfonline.com/toc/tjfe20/current. **Remarks:** Accepts advertising. **Circ:** (Not Reported).

15346 ■ WMTB-FM - 89.9
16300 Old Emmitsburg Rd.
Emmitsburg, MD 21727
Phone: (301)447-5239
Email: communications@msmary.edu
Format: Classical; Jazz; Rap; Album-Oriented Rock (AOR). **Owner:** Mount St. Mary's University, 16300 Old Emmitsburg RD., Emmitsburg, MD 21727, Ph: (301)447-6122, Fax: (301)447-5636, Free: 800-448-4347. **Founded:** 1977. **Operating Hours:** 10 a.m.-2a.m. Daily. **Wattage:** 010. **URL:** http://www.msmary.edu.

ESSEX

15347 ■ Avenue News
The Avenue Inc.
617-D Stemmers Run Rd.
Essex, MD 21221
Phone: (410)687-7775
Fax: (410)687-7881
Community newspaper (tabloid). **Freq:** Weekly (Thurs.). **Print Method:** Offset. **Cols./Page:** 6. **Col. Width:** 18 nonpareils. **Col. Depth:** 196 agate lines. **Key Personnel:** Amy Graziano, Editor; David Fike, Publisher, President. **URL:** http://www.avenuenews.com. **Ad Rates:** GLR $1.11; PCI $15.60. **Remarks:** Accepts advertising. **Circ:** (Not Reported).

FOREST HILL

15348 ■ Cemetery Dance
Cemetery Dance Publications
132-B Industry Ln., Ste. 7
Forest Hill, MD 21050
Phone: (410)588-5901
Fax: (410)588-5904
Publisher's E-mail: info@cemeterydance.com
Magazine covering short stories, articles, columns, interviews and news about horror, dark mystery, and suspense. **Freq:** Bimonthly. **Subscription Rates:** $27 U.S.; $49 Two years; $35 Canada; $66 Canada 2 years; $50 Other countries; $95 Two years 2 years. **URL:** http://www.cemeterydance.com/page/CDP/CTGY/MAGS. **Remarks:** Accepts advertising. **Circ:** (Not Reported).

FORT MEADE

15349 ■ All Hands: Magazine of the United States Navy
U.S. Government Publishing Office
6700 Taylor Ave.
Fort Meade, MD 20755
Phone: (301)222-6000
Publisher's E-mail: contactcenter@gpo.gov
General interest magazine covering the United States Navy. **Freq:** Monthly. **Print Method:** Letterpress and Offset. **Cols./Page:** 3. **Col. Width:** 28 nonpareils. **Col. Depth:** 122 agate lines. **ISSN:** 0002--5577 (print). **Circ:** (Not Reported).

15350 ■ Journal of Engineered Fibers & Fabrics
The Fiber Society
c/o Janice R. Gerde, Secretary
PO Box 564
Fort Meade, MD 20755-0564
Peer-reviewed journal publishing research on fibers, fabrics and related materials and applications. **Freq:** Quarterly. **ISSN:** 1558--9250 (print). **Subscription Rates:** Free. **URL:** http://www.jeffjournal.org. **Remarks:** Advertising not accepted. **Circ:** (Not Reported).

FORT WASHINGTON

Prince George's Co. (SC). 7 m S of Washington, DC. Residential.

15351 ■ Journal of Black Psychology
Association of Black Psychologists
7119 Allentown Rd., Ste. 203
Fort Washington, MD 20744
Phone: (301)449-3082
Fax: (301)449-3084
Publication E-mail: advertising@sagepub.com
Journal on psychology with an Afrocentric perspective. Official publication of the Association of Black Psychologists. **Freq:** Bimonthly Quarterly. **Print Method:** Offset. **Trim Size:** 5 1/2 x 8 1/2. **Key Personnel:** Kevin Cokley, Editor-in-Chief. **ISSN:** 0095--7984 (print); **EISSN:** 1552--4558 (electronic). **Subscription Rates:** £17 Single issue print; £80 Institutions print only; £98 Single issue print, Institutions; £492 Institutions e-access; £536 Institutions print only; £547 Institutions print and e-access; £602 Institutions current volume print and all online content; £1004 Institutions e-access (content through 1998); £516 Institutions (Print & E-access); £568 Institutions Backfile Lease, Combined Plus Backfile (Current Volume Print & All Online Content); £464 Institutions E-access; £516 Institutions Backfile Lease, E-access Plus Backfile (All Online Content) ; £947 Institutions E-access (Content through 1998) ; £506 Institutions print only; £78 Individuals print only; £93 Institutions single print ; £17 Individuals single print. **Alt. Formats:** PDF. **URL:** http://jbp.sagepub.com; http://uk.sagepub.com/en-gb/asi/journal-of-black-psychology/journal200978. **Ad Rates:** BW $875; 4C $1110, in addition to Black & White rate. **Remarks:** Accepts advertising. **Circ:** 2500.

15352 ■ Psych Discourse
Association of Black Psychologists
7119 Allentown Rd., Ste. 203
Fort Washington, MD 20744
Phone: (301)449-3082
Fax: (301)449-3084
Publisher's E-mail: abpsi@abpsi.org
Freq: Monthly. **Subscription Rates:** included in membership dues; $95 /year for nonmembers. **URL:** http://psychdiscourse.com/. **Remarks:** Advertising not accepted. **Circ:** 2500.

Circulation: ★ = AAM; △ or • = BPA; ♦ = CAC; ❑ = VAC; ⊕ = PO Statement; ‡ = Publisher's Report; Boldface figures = sworn; Light figures = estimated.

FREDERICK

Frederick Co. Frederick Co. (N). 45 m N of Baltimore. Frederick Community College. Hood College (Co-Ed). Manufactures glass containers, electronics, aluminum, clothing, foundry, dairy products, lime, fertilizer, lumber, bricks, flour. Agriculture. Dairying.

15353 ■ ACSM Bulletin: Promoting Advancement in the Collection, Analysis and Graphic Representation of Geo-Spatial Data
National Society of Professional Surveyors
5119 Pegasus Ct., Ste. Q
Frederick, MD 21704
Phone: (240)439-4615
Fax: (240)439-4952
Magazine on new techniques, developments, and projects in surveying, geodesy, GPS, cartography, LIS and GIS. **Freq:** Bimonthly. **Key Personnel:** Curtis W. Sumner, Executive Director; Ilse Genovese, Editor, phone: (240)632-9716, fax: (240)632-1321; John D. Hohol, Manager, Advertising, phone: (608)358-6511, fax: (608)237-2349. **ISSN:** 0747--9417 (print). **Subscription Rates:** $100 U.S.; $115 Other countries; $126 Individuals online + paper; $140 Individuals online + paper (International). **Ad Rates:** BW $1,945; 4C $2,512. **Remarks:** Accepts advertising. **Circ:** 8000.

15354 ■ Air Beat Magazine
Airborne Law Enforcement Association
50 Carroll Creek Way, Ste. 260
Frederick, MD 21701
Phone: (301)631-2406
Fax: (301)631-2466
Publishing articles pertaining to Airborne Public Safety. **Freq:** Bimonthly. **Subscription Rates:** $50 U.S. for nonmembers; $60 Canada and Mexico for nonmembers; $70 Other countries for nonmembers; Included in membership. **Alt. Formats:** PDF. **URL:** http://www.alea.org/Publications. **Remarks:** Accepts advertising. **Circ:** 8,000.

15355 ■ AOPA Flight Training
Aircraft Owners and Pilots Association
421 Aviation Way
Frederick, MD 21701
Phone: (301)695-2000
Fax: (301)695-2375
Free: 800-872-2672
Aviation magazine. **Freq:** Monthly. **Key Personnel:** Julie K. Boatman, Editor. **URL:** http://flighttraining.aopa.org/magazine. **Remarks:** Accepts advertising. **Circ:** (Not Reported).

15356 ■ AOPA Pilot
Aircraft Owners and Pilots Association
421 Aviation Way
Frederick, MD 21701
Phone: (301)695-2000
Fax: (301)695-2375
Free: 800-872-2672
Magazine for general aviation pilots and aircraft owners who are members of the Aircraft Owners and Pilots Assn. Articles are tailored to address the special informational requirements of both recreational and business pilots. **Freq:** Monthly. **Print Method:** Offset. **Trim Size:** 8 1/8 x 10 7/8. **Cols./Page:** 3. **Col. Width:** 2 1/4 inches. **Col. Depth:** 10 inches. **Key Personnel:** Thomas B. Haines, Associate Publisher, Editor-in-Chief. **ISSN:** 0001--2084 (print). **Subscription Rates:** Included in membership. **URL:** http://www.aopa.org/News-and-Video/AOPA-Pilot-Magazine. **Ad Rates:** BW $14210; 4C $23085. **Remarks:** Accepts advertising. **Circ:** Paid ★368865, 360253.

15357 ■ Employee Benefit Plan Review
Aspen Publishers, Inc.
7201 McKinney Cir.
Frederick, MD 21704
Phone: (301)698-7100
Fax: (800)901-9075
Free: 800-234-1660
Publication E-mail: editor@spencernet.com
Magazine serving decision-makers who administer, design, install, and service employee benefit plans. **Founded:** 1946. **Freq:** Monthly. **Print Method:** Web Offset. **Trim Size:** 8 3/8 x 10 7/8. **Cols./Page:** 2 and 3. **Col. Width:** 2 5/8 and 2 1/4 inches. **Col. Depth:** 115 agate lines. **Key Personnel:** Steven A. Meyerowitz, Editor-in-Chief; Richard Rubin, Publisher; Ellen Ros, Director, Editorial; Stephen A. Huth, Contact. **ISSN:** 0013-6808 (print). **Subscription Rates:** $395 Individuals. **URL:** http://www.aspenpublishers.com/Product.asp?catalog_name=Aspen&product_id=SS00136808. **Ad Rates:** BW $2300; 4C $3325. **Remarks:** Accepts advertising. **Circ:** (Not Reported).

15358 ■ Frederick Magazine
Diversions Publications Inc.
6 N East St., Ste. 301
Frederick, MD 21701
Phone: (301)662-8171
Publisher's E-mail: sales@fredmag.com
Consumer lifestyle magazine for mid-Maryland. **Freq:** Monthly. **Key Personnel:** Shawn Dewees, Publisher. **USPS:** 006-923. **Subscription Rates:** $24.95 Individuals; $39.95 Two years; $50.95 Individuals 3 years. **Alt. Formats:** Print. **URL:** http://fredmag.com. **Ad Rates:** 4C $2649. **Remarks:** Accepts advertising. **Circ:** Controlled 16000.

15359 ■ The Frederick-News Post
The Frederick News-Post
351 Ballenger Ctr. Dr.
Frederick, MD 21703
Phone: (301)662-1177
Fax: (301)662-6538
Publisher's E-mail: webmaster@fredericknewspost.com
General newspaper. **Freq:** Mon.-Sat. (morn.). **Print Method:** Offset. **Cols./Page:** 6. **Key Personnel:** Geordie Wilson, Publisher; Myron W. Randall, Editor, President. **Subscription Rates:** $26 Individuals /month, print and online; $7.99 Individuals /month - online only. **URL:** http://www.fredericknewspost.com. **Formerly:** The Frederick Post. **Ad Rates:** PCI $22.68. **Remarks:** Accepts advertising. **Circ:** Mon.-Sat. ★**39402**, Sun. ★**37591**.

15360 ■ Middletown-Brunswick Gazette
Post-Newsweek Media Inc.
c/o Molly Spence, Managing Editor
2A N Market St., 4th Fl.
Frederick, MD 21701
Community newspaper. **Freq:** Weekly (Thurs.). **Key Personnel:** Molly Spence, Managing Editor, phone: (301)846-2126, fax: (301)846-2124. **Subscription Rates:** Free. **URL:** http://www.gazette.net. **Remarks:** Accepts advertising. **Circ:** Free ■ **9693**.

15361 ■ Troubled Company Prospector: Profiles of Firms in Transition
Beard Group Inc.
PO Box 4250
Frederick, MD 21705
Phone: (240)629-3300
Fax: (240)629-3360
Publisher's E-mail: info@beardgroupinc.com
Professional magazine covering businesses showing signs of financial strain. **Freq:** Weekly. **Key Personnel:** Christopher Beard, Publisher, phone: (240)629-3300, fax: (240)629-3360. **ISSN:** 1062-2330 (print). **Subscription Rates:** $775 By mail six months subscription. **URL:** http://bankrupt.com/periodicals/tcp.html. **Remarks:** Advertising not accepted. **Circ:** (Not Reported).

15362 ■ The Word Among Us
Word Among Us Press
7115 Guilford Dr., Ste. 100
Frederick, MD 21704
Phone: (301)874-1700
Fax: (301)874-2190
Free: 800-775-9673
Publisher's E-mail: support@wau.org
Magazine containing articles to help Catholics read, understand, and act on the teachings of scripture and live the Christian life. **Freq:** Monthly. **Print Method:** Web. **Trim Size:** 5 3/8 x 8 3/8. **Cols./Page:** 2. **Col. Width:** 2 1/4 inches. **Col. Depth:** 7 inches. **ISSN:** 0742--4639 (print). **Subscription Rates:** $11.95 web edition; $33.20 U.S.; $33.20 Canada. **Remarks:** Advertising not accepted. **Circ:** Paid 200000.

15363 ■ WAFA-FM - 103.1
5742 Industry Ln.
Frederick, MD 21704
Phone: (301)620-7700
Fax: (301)696-0509
Format: Adult Contemporary. **Key Personnel:** Chris Elliott, Dir. of Programs; Larry Veihmeyer, Dir. of Sales; Barbara Smith, Promotions Dir., Dir. of Mktg. **Ad Rates:** Noncommercial. **URL:** http://www.key103radio.com.

15364 ■ WAFY-FM - 103.1
5742 Industry Ln.
Frederick, MD 21704
Phone: (301)620-7700
Fax: (301)696-0509
Format: Adult Contemporary. **Owner:** Nassau Broadcasting, 619 Alexander Rd., 3rd Fl., Princeton, NJ 08540. **Founded:** 1990. **Operating Hours:** Continuous. **Key Personnel:** Lillian Young, Bus. Mgr., lyoung@nassaubroadcasting.com. **Wattage:** 3,000. **Ad Rates:** Noncommercial. **URL:** http://www.key103radio.com.

15365 ■ WFMD-AM - 930
5966 Grove Hill Rd.
Frederick, MD 21703
Phone: (301)663-4181
Fax: (301)682-8018
Email: news@wfmd.com
Format: News; Talk. **Networks:** CBS; Fox; ABC. **Owner:** iHeartMedia Inc., 200 E Basse Rd., San Antonio, TX 78209, Ph: (210)832-3314. **Founded:** 1936. **Operating Hours:** Continuous. **Key Personnel:** Frank Mitchell, Prog. Dir., frankmitchell@clearchannel.com; Josh Brooks, Sales Mgr., joshbrooks@clearchannel.com. **Wattage:** 5,000 Day; 2,500 Nig. **Ad Rates:** Advertising accepted; rates available upon request. Combined advertising rates available with WFRE-FM. **URL:** http://www.wfmd.com.

15366 ■ WFPT-TV - 62
11767 Owings Mills Blvd.
Owings Mills, MD 21117
Phone: (410)356-5600
Fax: (410)581-4338
Free: 800-223-3678
Email: comments@mpt.org
Format: Public TV. **Simulcasts:** WMPB, WMPT, WCPB, WWPB, WGPT. **Networks:** Public Broadcasting Service (PBS). **Owner:** Maryland Public Television, 11767 Owings Mills Blvd., Owings Mills, MD 21117, Ph: (410)356-5600, Fax: (410)581-6579, Free: 800-223-3678. **Founded:** 1969. **Operating Hours:** Continuous. **Key Personnel:** Tom Williams, Managing Dir.; Martin G. Jacobs, VP, CFO; Steven Schupak, Exec. VP, COO; Larry D. Unger, CEO, President; George R. Beneman, II, Sr. VP, Chief Tech. Ofc. **Local Programs:** *MotorWeek*, Sunday Saturday Wednesday 12:00 p.m. 5:00 p.m. 7:30 p.m. **Wattage:** 3,300,000. **Ad Rates:** Noncommercial. **URL:** http://www.mpt.org/home.

15367 ■ WFRE-FM - 99.9
5966 Grove Hill Rd.
Frederick, MD 21703
Phone: (301)663-4181
Fax: (301)682-8018
Format: Country. **Owner:** iHeartMedia Inc., 200 E Basse Rd., San Antonio, TX 78209, Ph: (210)832-3314. **Founded:** Sept. 20, 2006. **Operating Hours:** Continuous. **Key Personnel:** Josh Brooks, Sales Mgr.; Michael Banks, Gen. Mgr. **Wattage:** 7,600 ERP. **Ad Rates:** Advertising accepted; rates available upon request. **URL:** http://www.wfre.com.

FROSTBURG

Allegany Co. Allegany Co. (NW). 30 m W of Cumberland.

15368 ■ Journal of the Alleghenies
Council of the Alleghenies
PO Box 514
Frostburg, MD 21532-0514
Phone: (301)689-3421
Journal covering local history. **Freq:** Annual. **Key Personnel:** Dr. Anthony Crosby, Editor. **Subscription Rates:** Included in membership. **URL:** http://www.counciloftheallegheniess.org/pub.htm. **Remarks:** Advertising not accepted. **Circ:** Paid 200.

15369 ■ WFRB-AM - 560
242 Finzel Rd.
Frostburg, MD 21532
Phone: (301)689-8871
Fax: (301)689-8880
Format: Talk. **Simulcasts:** WTBO-AM. **Networks:** CNN Radio. **Founded:** 1958. **Operating Hours:** Continuous. **ADI:** Washington, DC. **Wattage:** 5,000 Day 065 Night. **Ad Rates:** $8-10 for 30 seconds; $10-15 for 60 seconds. Combined advertising rates available with WTBO-AM. **URL:** http://talkradio560.com.

15370 ■ WFRB-FM - 105.3
242 Finzel Rd.
Frostburg, MD 21532
Phone: (301)689-8871
Fax: (301)689-8880
Format: Country. **Operating Hours:** Continuous. **Key Personnel:** Richard Cornwell, Gen. Sales Mgr., richcornwell@go106.com. **Wattage:** 13,500 ERP. **Ad Rates:** Advertising accepted; rates available upon request. **URL:** http://www.wfrb.com.

15371 ■ WFWM-FM - 91.9
101 Braddock Rd.
Frostburg, MD 21532-2303
Phone: (301)687-4143
Fax: (301)687-7040
Email: wfwm@frostburg.edu
Format: Jazz; Classical; Alternative/New Music/ Progressive; News. **Networks:** Independent; National Public Radio (NPR). **Owner:** Frostburg State University, 101 Braddock Rd., Frostburg, MD 21532-2303, Ph: (301)687-4000. **Founded:** 1989. **Operating Hours:** Continuous. **Key Personnel:** Chuck Dicken, Dir. of Sales. **Wattage:** 1,500. **Ad Rates:** Noncommercial. **URL:** http://www.wfwm.org.

15372 ■ WLIC-FM - 97.1
34 Springs Rd.
Grantsville, MD 21536
Phone: (301)895-3292
Fax: (301)895-3293
Email: info@hesalive.net
Format: Religious. **Networks:** USA Radio. **Owner:** He's Alive Inc., 34 Springs Rd., Grantsville, MD 21536, Ph: (301)895-3292, Fax: (301)895-3293. **Founded:** 1989. **Operating Hours:** 5:30 a.m.-midnight. **Wattage:** 145. **Ad Rates:** Noncommercial. **Mailing address:** PO Box 540, Grantsville, MD 21536. **URL:** http://www.hesalive.net.

FRUITLAND

15373 ■ W206AY-FM - 89.1
PO Box 391
Twin Falls, ID 83303
Fax: (208)736-1958
Free: 800-357-4226
Format: Religious; Contemporary Christian. **Owner:** CSN International, PO Box 391, Twin Falls, ID 83303, Ph: (208)736-1958, Fax: (208)736-1958, Free: 800-357-4226. **Key Personnel:** Kelly Carlson, Dir. of Engg.; Ray Gorney, Asst. Dir. **URL:** http://www.csnradio.com.

FULTON

15374 ■ Mid-Atlantic Builder
Maryland Building Industry Association
11825 W Market Pl.
Fulton, MD 20759
Phone: (301)776-6242
Publication E-mail: communications@homebuilders.org
Freq: Bimonthly. **Print Method:** Offset. **Trim Size:** 8 1/2 x 11. **Key Personnel:** Kristin Hoggle, Contact. **Subscription Rates:** Free; $35 Individuals premium (per month billed annually); $269 Individuals optimum (per month billed annually). **URL:** http://www.marylandbuilders.org/build-maryland.html; http://issuu.com/communications. **Ad Rates:** BW $1,440; 4C $2,100. **Remarks:** Accepts advertising. **Circ:** ‡6000.

GAITHERSBURG

Montgomery Co. Montgomery Co. (WC). 20 m NW of Washington, DC. Suburban community. Commercial and financial centers. Forest Oak (a tree known as a historical monument). Agri-business, research & development.

15375 ■ Aspen Hill Gazette
Post-Newsweek Media Inc.
9030 Comprint Ct.
Gaithersburg, MD 20877
Phone: (301)948-3120
Community newspaper. **Freq:** Weekly. **Key Personnel:** Melissa A. Chadwick, Editor, phone: (301)280-3006, fax: (301)670-7183. **Remarks:** Accepts advertising. **Circ:** Combined 8324.

15376 ■ Cartography and Geographic Information Science
Cartography and Geographic Information Society
Six Montgomery Village Ave., Ste. 403
Gaithersburg, MD 20879
Phone: (240)632-9522
Publisher's E-mail: curtis.sumner@acsm.net
Scholarly journal for cartographers and geographic information systems professionals. **Freq:** 5/year. **Key Personnel:** Scott M. Freundschuh, Executive Editor. **ISSN:** 1523--0406 (print); **EISSN:** 1545--0465 (electronic). **Subscription Rates:** $201 Institutions online; $230 Institutions print and online. **Alt. Formats:** PDF. **URL:** http://www.cartogis.org/publications/journal.php. **Formerly:** The American Cartographer. **Remarks:** Advertising not accepted. **Circ:** (Not Reported).

15377 ■ Dressage Today
Active Interest Media
656 Quince Orchard Rd., Ste. 600
Gaithersburg, MD 20878
Phone: (301)977-3900
Fax: (301)990-9015
Publication E-mail: dressage.today@equinetwork.com
Magazine for riders, with articles on both the practical and theoretical aspects of the riding discipline. Geared toward affluent, well-educated riders at every level of dressage. The average reader is a woman in her late 30s with a household income of more than $126,000 and a college degree. She is an experienced horse owner with 3 horses, one of whom is worth $19,000 on average. **Freq:** Monthly. **Key Personnel:** Philip Cooper, Director, Advertising; Jennifer Mellace, Editor. **Subscription Rates:** $19.95 Individuals. **URL:** http://dressagetoday.com/home. **Remarks:** Accepts advertising. **Circ:** Combined 32000.

15378 ■ EquiManagement
Active Interest Media
656 Quince Orchard Rd., Ste. 600
Gaithersburg, MD 20878
Phone: (301)977-3900
Fax: (301)990-9015
Publisher's E-mail: admin@aimmedia.com
Magazine publishing articles on marketing, finance, operations and human resources. **Freq:** Quarterly. **Key Personnel:** Kimberly S. Brown, Editor; David Andrick, Publisher. **URL:** http://www.aimmedia.com/equimanagement/; http://equimanagement.com. **Circ:** (Not Reported).

15379 ■ Equus
Primedia Equine Network
656 Quince Orchard Rd., Ste. 600
Gaithersburg, MD 20878
Phone: (301)977-3900
Fax: (301)990-9015
Publication E-mail: eqletters@equinetwork.com
Magazine featuring health, care, and understanding of horses. **Freq:** Monthly. **Print Method:** Offset. **Trim Size:** 8 x 10 1/2. **Cols./Page:** 3. **Col. Width:** 27 nonpareils. **Col. Depth:** 137 agate lines. **Key Personnel:** Bob Kliner, Associate Publisher; Deb Bennett, PhD, Editor; Laura Hillenbrand, Editor. **Subscription Rates:** $24.97 Two years; $14.97 Individuals 1 year; $48.97 Canada 2 years; $26.97 Canada 1 year; $72.97 Other countries 2 years; $38.97 Other countries 1 year. **URL:** http://www.equisearch.com/equus; http://equusmagazine.com. **Ad Rates:** BW $5050; 4C $8070. **Remarks:** Advertising accepted; rates available upon request. **Circ:** Paid ★**137418**.

15380 ■ Experimental Aging Research: An International Journal Devoted to the Scientific Study of the Aging Process
Routledge
c/o Julia Treland, Book Rev. Ed.
Gaithersburg, MD 20883-3429
Publisher's E-mail: book.orders@tandf.co.uk
International journal devoted to the scientific study of the aging process. **Freq:** 5/year. **Print Method:** Web Offset. **Trim Size:** 6 x 9. **Cols./Page:** 1. **Col. Width:** 4 1/2 inches. **Col. Depth:** 7 1/2 inches. **Key Personnel:** Julia Treland, Editor; Jeffrey W. Elias, Editor-in-Chief. **ISSN:** 0361-073X (print); **EISSN:** 1096-4657 (electronic). **Subscription Rates:** $219 Individuals print only; $834 Institutions online only; $953 Institutions print and online. **URL:** http://www.tandfonline.com/toc/uear20/current#.VHWfo9lwrlc. **Mailing address:** PO Box 83429, Gaithersburg, MD 20883-3429. **Remarks:** Accepts advertising. **Circ:** 1000.

15381 ■ Fire Protection Engineering Magazine
Society of Fire Protection Engineers
9711 Washingtonian Blvd., Ste. 380
Gaithersburg, MD 20878
Phone: (301)718-2910
Fax: (240)328-6225
Publisher's E-mail: info@sfpe.org
Freq: Quarterly. **Subscription Rates:** included in membership dues. **URL:** http://magazine.sfpe.org/. **Ad Rates:** BW $4390. **Remarks:** Accepts advertising. **Circ:** Combined ‡19300.

15382 ■ The Gazette
The Gazette
9030 Comprint Ct.
Gaithersburg, MD 20877
Phone: (301)948-3120
Publisher's E-mail: class@gazette.net
Community newspaper. **Founded:** Sept. 1993. **Freq:** Weekly (Wed.). **Print Method:** Web. **Trim Size:** 12 1/2 x 22. **Cols./Page:** 6. **Col. Width:** 2 3/8 inches. **Col. Depth:** 21 inches. **URL:** http://www.gazette.net/. **Formerly:** Country Gazette. **Ad Rates:** GLR $12; BW $440; 4C $990; SAU $10; PCI $10. **Remarks:** Accepts classified advertising. **Circ:** Free 6500.

15383 ■ The Germantown Gazette
Post-Newsweek Media Inc.
9030 Comprint Ct.
Gaithersburg, MD 20877
Phone: (301)948-3120
Newspaper. **Founded:** 1959. **Freq:** Weekly (Wed.). **Print Method:** Offset. Uses mats. **Trim Size:** 10 15/16 x 13. **Cols./Page:** 5. **Col. Width:** 26 nonpareils. **Col. Depth:** 182 agate lines. **Key Personnel:** Comfort Dorn, Editor, phone: (301)670-2071, fax: (301)670-2071. **URL:** http://www.gazette.net. **Formerly:** Gazette. **Ad Rates:** BW $1,710.80; 4C $2,210.80; SAU $26.32; PCI $26.32. **Remarks:** Advertising accepted; rates available upon request. **Circ:** Free ■ **29492**.

15384 ■ Journal of the American College of Dentists
American College of Dentists
839J Quince Orchard Blvd.
Gaithersburg, MD 20878-1614
Phone: (301)977-3223
Fax: (301)977-3330
Publisher's E-mail: office@acd.org
Journal reporting on ideas, advances, and opinions in dentistry. **Freq:** Quarterly. **Print Method:** Offset. **Trim Size:** 8 1/2 x 11. **Cols./Page:** 3. **Key Personnel:** David W. Chambers, Editor. **ISSN:** 0002--7979 (print). **Subscription Rates:** $30 Included in membership; $40 Nonmembers; $60 Other countries. **URL:** http://www.acd.org/publications.htm. **Remarks:** Advertising not accepted. **Circ:** Controlled ‡5000.

15385 ■ Journal of Forensic Sciences
American Academy of Forensic Sciences
c/o Susan Ballou, Secretary
100 Bureau Dr.
Gaithersburg, MD 20899-8102
Phone: (301)975-8750
Peer-reviewed journal covering the fields of forensic sciences. **Freq:** Bimonthly. **Key Personnel:** Michael Peat, Editor; Robert E. Gaensslen, PhD, Associate Editor. **ISSN:** 0022--1198 (print); **EISSN:** 1556--4029 (electronic). **Subscription Rates:** $651 Institutions online only; £401 Institutions online only, UK; €510 Institutions online only, Europe; $786 Institutions, other countries online only; $782 Institutions print and online; £482 Institutions print and online, UK; €612 Institutions print and online, Europe; $944 Institutions, other countries print and online; $403 Individuals print and online; £246 Individuals print and online, UK, Europe (non euro zone) and rest of the world; €367 Individuals print and online, Europe. **URL:** http://onlinelibrary.wiley.com/journal/10.1111/(ISSN)1556-4029; http://www.aafs.org/resources/journal-forensic-sciences. **Remarks:** Advertising not accepted. **Circ:** (Not Reported).

15386 ■ Journal of Physical and Chemical Reference Data
American Institute of Physics
National Institute of Standards & Technology
100 Bureau Dr., Mail Stop 2300
Gaithersburg, MD 20899-2300
Phone: (301)975-3774

Circulation: ★ = AAM; △ or • = BPA; ♦ = CAC; ❑ = VAC; ⊕ = PO Statement; ‡ = Publisher's Report; Boldface figures = sworn; Light figures = estimated.

Fax: (301)926-0416
Publication E-mail: jpcrd@nist.gov
Journal providing critically evaluated property data. **Freq:** Quarterly Bimonthly. **Key Personnel:** Donald R. Burgess, Jr., Editor; Allan H. Harvey, Editor; Robert L. Watters, Jr., Editor. **ISSN:** 0047-2689 (print); **EISSN:** 1529-7845 (electronic). **Subscription Rates:** $1700 Institutions tier 1, print & online; $1000 Institutions tier 1, online; $200 Individuals. **URL:** http://scitation.aip.org/content/aip/journal/jpcrd; http://www.nist.gov/srd/jpcrd.cfm. **Remarks:** Advertising not accepted. **Circ:** (Not Reported).

15387 ■ Kensington Gazette
Post-Newsweek Media Inc.
9030 Comprint Ct.
Gaithersburg, MD 20877
Phone: (301)948-3120
Community newspaper. **Freq:** Weekly (Wed.). **Key Personnel:** Melissa A. Chadwick, Editor, phone: (301)280-3006, fax: (301)670-7183. **Circ:** Combined 7158.

15388 ■ Machining Science & Technology
Taylor & Francis Group Journals
c/o Said Jahanmir, Exec. Ed.
Miti Heart Corp.
Gaithersburg, MD 20883
Publisher's E-mail: customerservice@taylorandfrancis.com
Trade Journal publishing scientific and technical papers related to machining and machining processes on all materials. **Founded:** 1997. **Freq:** 4/yr. **Print Method:** Offset. **Trim Size:** 8 1/4 x 10 7/8. **Cols./Page:** 1. **Key Personnel:** Said Jahanmir, Executive Editor; I.S. Jawahir, Editor; Dr. R. Stevenson, Advisor. **ISSN:** 1091-0344 (print); **EISSN:** 1532-2483 (electronic). **Subscription Rates:** $304 Individuals print only; $962 Institutions online only; $1099 Institutions print & online. **URL:** http://www.tandfonline.com/toc/lmst20/current#.U2G7IlHWI7o. **Mailing address:** PO Box 83610, Gaithersburg, MD 20883. **Ad Rates:** BW $890; 4C $1,935. **Remarks:** Accepts advertising. **Circ:** Paid 250.

15389 ■ Montgomery Village Gazette
Post-Newsweek Media Inc.
9030 Comprint Ct.
Gaithersburg, MD 20877
Phone: (301)948-3120
Community newspaper. **Freq:** Weekly (Wed.). **Key Personnel:** Lloyd Batzler, Editor. **Remarks:** Accepts advertising. **Circ:** Combined 9888.

15390 ■ Outdoor America
Izaak Walton League of America
707 Conservation Ln.
Gaithersburg, MD 20878
Phone: (301)548-0150
Publication E-mail: oa@iwla.org
Freq: Quarterly. **Print Method:** Offset. **Trim Size:** 8 1/4 x 10 7/8. **Cols./Page:** 3. **Col. Width:** 27 nonpareils. **Col. Depth:** 135 agate lines. **Key Personnel:** David W. Hoskins, Executive Director. **ISSN:** 0021-3314 (print). **Subscription Rates:** Included in membership. **Alt. Formats:** PDF. **URL:** http://www.iwla.org/news-events/outdoor-america/about-outdoor-america; http://www.iwla.org/index.php?ht=display/ContentDetails/i/92581/pid/203; http://www.iwla.org/index.php?ht=d/Contents/contenttype_id/16/pid/203/order/crt#cat_id_2305. **Mailing address:** c/o Mr. Tracy Longenecker, Membership Officer1911 Scull St., Lebanon, PA 17046-2780. **Ad Rates:** BW $1150; 4C $1600. **Remarks:** Accepts advertising. **Circ:** 45000.

15391 ■ Practical Horseman
Active Interest Media
656 Quince Orchard Rd., Ste. 600
Gaithersburg, MD 20878
Phone: (301)977-3900
Fax: (301)990-9015
Publication E-mail: practical.horseman@primedia.com
Magazine for riders training and competing in hunter/jumpers, dressage, eventing, driving and endurance. Features in-depth how-to articles that bring the top trainers and their insights to the reader. Also provides information on horse care and stable management. Read by horse owners and riders who often compete in more than one English discipline. Readers are primarily affluent, well-educated women who consider their horses an integral part of their lifestyle and have an average household income above $136,000. **Freq:** Monthly. **Key Personnel:** Sandra Oliynk, Editor; Philip Cooper, Director, Advertising. **Subscription Rates:** $19.95 Individuals; $29.95 Two years. **URL:** http://www.equisearch.com/magazines/practical-horseman. **Remarks:** Accepts advertising. **Circ:** Paid ★**58536**.

15392 ■ Quality Management in Health Care
Lippincott Williams and Wilkins
c/o Jean G. Carroll, PhD, Ed.
200 Orchard Ridge Dr.
Gaithersburg, MD 20878
Phone: (301)417-7617
Fax: (301)417-7550
Free: 800-638-8437
Publication E-mail: journals@ovid.com
Peer-reviewed journal providing a forum to explore and assist in the theoretical, technical, and strategic elements of quality management in health care. **Freq:** Quarterly. **Trim Size:** 7 3/4 x 10 3/4. **Cols./Page:** 2. **Col. Width:** 20 picas. **Col. Depth:** 54 picas. **Key Personnel:** Jean G. Carroll, PhD, Editor; Jean Gayton Carroll, PhD, Editor. **ISSN:** 1063--8628 (print); **EISSN:** 1550--5154 (electronic). **Subscription Rates:** $152 U.S. print; $172 Canada and Mexico print; $202 Individuals print - UK/Australia; $264 Other countries print; $538 Institutions print; $533 Institutions, Canada and Mexico print; $589 Institutions print - UK/Australia; $724 Institutions, other countries print; $76 Individuals print - In-Training. **URL:** http://journals.lww.com/qmhcjournal/pages/default.aspx; http://www.lww.com/product/?1063-8628. **Ad Rates:** 4C $2,490. **Remarks:** Accepts advertising. **Circ:** ‡349, ‡468.

15393 ■ The Rockville Gazette
Post-Newsweek Media Inc.
9030 Comprint Ct.
Gaithersburg, MD 20877
Phone: (301)948-3120
Community newspapers (tabloid). **Freq:** Weekly (Wed.). **Print Method:** Offset. **Trim Size:** 10 1/2 x 13. **Cols./Page:** 5. **Col. Width:** 26 nonpareils. **Col. Depth:** 182 agate lines. **Key Personnel:** Davis Kennedy, Editor; Judith Hruz, Managing Editor; Chuck Rheinsmith, Manager, Advertising. **Subscription Rates:** Free; $29.99 By mail. **Ad Rates:** BW $829.40; 4C $1179.40; PCI $12.76. **Remarks:** Accepts advertising. **Circ:** Free ■ **31872**.

15394 ■ Toxicology Mechanisms and Methods
Taylor & Francis Online
c/o Rakesh Dixit, Ed.-in-Ch.
Toxicology Dept., MedImmune Inc.
One MedImmune Way
Gaithersburg, MD 20878
Publisher's E-mail: support@tandfonline.com
Peer-reviewed journal containing original research on subjects dealing with the mechanisms by which foreign chemicals cause toxic tissue injury, including industrial compounds, environmental pollutants, hazardous wastes, drugs, pesticides, and chemical warfare agents, from molecular and cellular mechanisms of action to the consideration of mechanistic evidence in establishing regulatory policy and addressing aspects of the development, validation, and application of new and existing laboratory methods, techniques and equipment. **Freq:** 9/year. **Key Personnel:** Rakesh Dixit, PhD, Editor-in-Chief; Luis G. Valerio, PhD, Deputy, Editor-in-Chief; Carlos Palmeira, PhD, Associate Editor. **ISSN:** 1537--6516 (print); **EISSN:** 1537--6524 (electronic). **Subscription Rates:** $3093 Institutions online; $3256 Institutions print and online. **URL:** http://www.tandfonline.com/toc/itxm20/current. **Circ:** 225.

GAMBRILLS

15395 ■ Jones Communications
815 Rte. 3
Box 267
Gambrills, MD 21054
Phone: (410)987-3900
Fax: (410)923-3568
Founded: 1983. **Formerly:** Jones Intercable, Inc. **Cities Served:** subscribing households 51,500.

GERMANTOWN

15396 ■ Historical Archaeology
Society for Historical Archaeology
13017 Wisteria Dr., No. 395
Germantown, MD 20874
Phone: (301)972-9684
Fax: (866)285-3512
Publisher's E-mail: hq@sha.org
Freq: Quarterly. **ISSN:** 0440- 9213 (print). **Subscription Rates:** included in membership dues. **URL:** http://www.sha.org/index.php/view/page/journal. **Remarks:** Accepts advertising. **Circ:** (Not Reported).

15397 ■ Microcirculation
Microcirculatory Society
18501 Kingshill Rd.
Germantown, MD 20874
Phone: (301)760-7745
Journal featuring original contributions that are the result of investigations contributing significant new information relating to the microcirculation addressed at the intact animal, organ, cellular, or molecular level. **Freq:** Annual 8/yr. **Key Personnel:** William F. Jackson, PhD, Editor; Neil D. Granger, Editor; Steven J. Alexander, Board Member; Prof. William F. Jackson, PhD, Editor; Paul Kubes, Board Member; Jefferson C. Frisbee, Board Member, Editor-in-Chief; Daniel Beard, Board Member; Shawn Bearden, Board Member; Maria Sanz, Board Member. **ISSN:** 1073--9688 (print); **EISSN:** 1549--8719 (electronic). **Subscription Rates:** $1964 Institutions online only; £1199 Institutions online only; €1408 Institutions online only. **URL:** http://onlinelibrary.wiley.com/journal/10.1111/(ISSN)1549-8719. **Remarks:** Advertising not accepted. **Circ:** (Not Reported).

GLEN BURNIE

Anne Arundel Co. (C). 10 m S of Baltimore. Fort Meade. Furniture, toy, concrete block factories; sheet metal works; machinery, boat building; electronics. Diversified farming.

15398 ■ Maryland Music Educator
Maryland Music Educators Association
791 Aquahart Rd., Ste. 117
Glen Burnie, MD 21061
Publication E-mail: mmea.editor@gmail.com
Professional journal covering music education for the Maryland Music Educator's Association. **Freq:** Quarterly September (Fall Issue), November(Winter Issue), March (Spring Issue), and May (Summer Issue). **Print Method:** Offset. **Trim Size:** 8 1/2 x 11. **Cols./Page:** 3. **Col. Width:** 14 picas. **Key Personnel:** Felicia Burger Johnston, Editor. **ISSN:** 0025--4312 (print). **Subscription Rates:** $25 Nonmembers; Included in membership. **URL:** http://www.mmea-maryland.org/publications. **Remarks:** Accepts advertising. **Circ:** (Not Reported).

15399 ■ WFBR-AM - 1590
159 8th Ave. NW
Glen Burnie, MD 21061
Format: Ethnic. **Owner:** Multicultural Radio Broadcasting Inc., 27 William St., 11th Fl., New York, NY 10005, Ph: (212)966-1059, Fax: (212)966-9580. **Key Personnel:** John Gabel, Contact, johng@mrbi.net. **URL:** http://www.mrbi.net/radiogroup.htm.

GRANTSVILLE

15400 ■ WAIJ-FM - 90.3
PO Box 540
Grantsville, MD 21536
Phone: (301)895-3292
Fax: (301)895-3293
Email: info@hesalive.net
Format: Southern Gospel; Contemporary Christian. **Networks:** USA Radio. **Owner:** He's Alive Inc., 34 Springs Rd., Grantsville, MD 21536, Ph: (301)895-3292, Fax: (301)895-3293. **Founded:** 1984. **Operating Hours:** 5:30 a.m.-midnight. **Wattage:** 10,000. **Ad Rates:** Noncommercial. **URL:** http://www.hesalive.net.

WKJL-FM - See Clarksburg, WV

WLIC-FM - See Frostburg

WRIJ-FM - See Masontown, PA

15401 ■ WRWJ 88.1 FM - 88.1
34 Springs Rd.
Grantsville, MD 21536
Phone: (301)895-3292
Fax: (301)895-3293
Email: info@hesalive.net

Format: Religious. **Mailing address:** PO Box 540, Grantsville, MD 21536. **URL:** http://www.hesalive.net.

GRASONVILLE

Queen Anne's Co. (EC). 5 m SW of Queenstown.

15402 ■ Atlantic Broadband

330 Drummer Dr.
Grasonville, MD 21638
Free: 800-559-1746
Founded: 2003. **Key Personnel:** Patrick Bratton, CFO, Sr. VP; Almis J. Kuolas, Chief Tech. Ofc., Sr. VP; Leslie Brown, Sr. VP, Gen. Counsel. **Cities Served:** 223 community access channels. **URL:** http://www.atlanticbb.com.

GREENBELT

Prince George's Co. Prince Georges Co. (SC). 9 m NE of Washington, D. C. Residential.

15403 ■ American Journal of Alternative Agriculture

Henry A. Wallace Institute for Alternative Agriculture
9200 Edmonston Rd., Ste. 117
Greenbelt, MD 20770
Phone: (301)441-8777
Fax: (301)220-0164
Publisher's E-mail: info@eap.mcgill.ca
Journal covering agricultural science. **Freq:** Quarterly. **ISSN:** 0889--1893 (print). **Subscription Rates:** $24 Individuals U.S.; $26 Canada and Mexico; $28 Other countries; $44 Institutions U.S.; $46 Institutions Canada & Mexico; $48 Institutions, other countries; $12 Students U.S.; $14 Students Canada & Mexico; $16 Students, other countries. **URL:** http://eap.mcgill.ca/MagRack/AJAA/ajaa_ind.htm. **Circ:** (Not Reported).

15404 ■ Greenbelt News Review

Greenbelt Cooperative Publishing Association Inc.
15 Crescent Rd., Ste. 100
Greenbelt, MD 20770
Phone: (301)474-4131
Fax: (301)474-5880
Publication E-mail: newsreview@greenbelt.com
Community newspaper. **Freq:** Weekly (Thurs.). **Print Method:** Letterpress and offset. **Trim Size:** 11 x 17. **Cols./Page:** 5. **Col. Width:** 24 nonpareils. **Col. Depth:** 196 agate lines. **Key Personnel:** Mary Lou Williamson, Editor; Eileen Farnham, President; Diane Oberg, Business Manager. **Subscription Rates:** $45 Individuals; Free within the city of Greenbelt. **URL:** http://www.greenbeltnewsreview.com. **Ad Rates:** GLR $.58; BW $648; PCI $9.60. **Remarks:** Green ink available on last page; ask for details. **Circ:** Paid ‡100, Free ‡10900.

15405 ■ Journal of Oceanic Engineering

IEEE - Oceanic Engineering Society
c/o Stephen Holt, Web Administrator
National Aeronotics and Space Administration
Code 444 Bldg. 3, Rm. 144
8800 Greenbelt Rd.
Greenbelt, MD 20771
Professional journal covering oceanography and engineering. **Freq:** Quarterly. **Key Personnel:** N. Ross Chapman, Editor-in-Chief. **ISSN:** 0364--9059 (print). **URL:** http://www.oceanicengineering.org/page.cfm/cat/48/Description-of-Journal; http://www.oceanicengineering.org/page.cfm/cat/13/Journal-of-Oceanic-Engineering; http://ieeexplore.ieee.org/xpl/aboutJournal.jsp?punumber=48. **Remarks:** Advertising not accepted. **Circ:** (Not Reported).

15406 ■ Spectrum

National Association of Black Accountants, Inc.
7474 Greenway Center Dr., Ste. 1120
Greenbelt, MD 20770
Phone: (301)474-6222
Fax: (301)474-3114
Free: 888-571-2939
Publisher's E-mail: membership@nabainc.org
Professional magazine of the National Association of Black Accountants, Inc. **Founded:** June 1970. **Freq:** Annual. **Trim Size:** 8 1/2 x 11. **Cols./Page:** 2. **Col. Width:** 3 1/4 inches. **Col. Depth:** 9 inches. **Subscription Rates:** $20 Nonmembers. **URL:** http://www.nabainc.org/Publications/Publications/tabid/100/Default.aspx. **Ad Rates:** BW $6,000. **Remarks:** Accepts advertising. **Circ:** Controlled 22000.

HAGERSTOWN

Washington Co. Washington Co. (NW). 72 m NW of Baltimore. Hagerstown Junior College. Manufactures aircraft parts, truck engines, shoes, women's and children's dresses, sand blast and dust collecting equipment, furniture, ribbon, hosiery, underwear, leather goods, rubber heels and soles, cold storage doors, pipe organs and supplies, paper boxes, plastic pipes, paint, seashore erosion forms, creamery, mayonnaise products. Slate quarries.

15407 ■ American Jails

American Jail Association
1135 Professional Ct.
Hagerstown, MD 21740-5853
Phone: (301)790-3930
Fax: (301)790-2941
Magazine covering jails in the U.S. Includes advertisers' index, book reviews, calendar of events, state jail association news, foreign coverage, and military jail section. **Freq:** Bimonthly. **Subscription Rates:** Included in membership. **URL:** http://www.americanjail.org/prison-magazine. **Remarks:** Accepts advertising. **Circ:** (Not Reported).

15408 ■ Arteriosclerosis, Thrombosis, and Vascular Biology

American Heart Association - Dallas
PO Box 1590
Hagerstown, MD 21741
Phone: (301)223-2307
Fax: (301)223-2327
Free: 800-787-8985
Publisher's E-mail: calley.herth@heart.org
Freq: Monthly. **Print Method:** Offset. **Trim Size:** 8 1/8 x 10 7/8. **Cols./Page:** 2. **Col. Width:** 19 picas. **Col. Depth:** 57 picas. **Key Personnel:** Mark Taubman, Editor-in-Chief; Edward Fisher, Associate Editor; Melissa Arey, Managing Editor; Alan Daugherty, Editor-in-Chief. **ISSN:** 1079-5642 (print). **Subscription Rates:** $634 Individuals; $1502 Institutions; $313 Individuals in-training; $752 Other countries; $1512 Institutions, other countries; $372 Other countries in-training; $596 Individuals online; $286 Individuals online; in-training; $575 Individuals; $682 Other countries; $1253 Institutions; $1381 Institutions, other countries; $284 Individuals in-training; $337 Other countries in-training. **Alt. Formats:** PDF. **URL:** http://atvb.ahajournals.org; http://www.lww.com/product/?1079-5642. **Formerly:** Arteriosclerosis and Thrombosis: A Journal of Vascular Biology. **Ad Rates:** BW $685; 4C $2,010. **Remarks:** Accepts advertising. **Circ:** ★**3242**.

15409 ■ Infants and Young Children

Lippincott Williams and Wilkins
16522 Hunters Green Pky.
Hagerstown, MD 21740
Phone: (301)233-2300
Fax: (301)233-2398
Free: 800-638-3030
Publisher's E-mail: orders@lww.com
Interdisciplinary publication focusing on young children. **Freq:** Quarterly. **Trim Size:** 7 x 10. **Cols./Page:** 2. **Col. Width:** 16 inches. **Col. Depth:** 45 inches. **Key Personnel:** Mary Beth Bruder, PhD, Editor. **ISSN:** 0896--3746 (print). **Subscription Rates:** $134 U.S. print; $151 Canada and Mexico print; $182 Individuals print - UK/Australia; $249 Other countries print; $542 Institutions print; $508 Institutions, Canada and Mexico print; $528 Institutions print - UK/Australia; $715 Institutions, other countries print; $94 U.S. print - In-Training; $89 Canada and Mexico print - In-Training; $103 Other countries print - In-Training. **URL:** http://journals.lww.com/iycjournal/pages/default.aspx; http://www.lww.com/product/?0896-3746. **Remarks:** Advertising not accepted. **Circ:** (Not Reported).

15410 ■ International Journal of Evidence-based Healthcare

Lippincott Williams and Wilkins
16522 Hunters Green Pky.
Hagerstown, MD 21740
Phone: (301)233-2300
Fax: (301)233-2398
Free: 800-638-3030
Publisher's E-mail: orders@lww.com
Peer-reviewed journal publishing original scholarly work from the international Joanna Briggs Institute and Collaboration, which aims to advance the international understanding and development of evidence-based practice in nursing, midwifery, nutrition and dietetics, physiotherapy, occupational therapy, medical radiation, complimentary therapy, medicine and podiatry. **Freq:** Quarterly. **Key Personnel:** Hanan Khalil, Editor-in-Chief. **ISSN:** 1744-1609 (print). **Subscription Rates:** $148 Individuals print and online. **URL:** http://www.lww.com/webapp/wcs/stores/servlet/product_International-Journal-of-EvidenceBased-Healthcare_11851_-1_12551_Prod-17441609. **Remarks:** Accepts advertising. **Circ:** (Not Reported).

15411 ■ Journal of Perinatal and Neonatal Nursing

Lippincott Williams and Wilkins
16522 Hunters Green Pky.
Hagerstown, MD 21740
Phone: (301)233-2300
Fax: (301)233-2398
Free: 800-638-3030
Publisher's E-mail: orders@lww.com
Journal on issues and practical concerns in perinatal and neonatal clinical practice. **Founded:** 1987. **Freq:** 4/year. **Key Personnel:** Susan Bakewell-Sachs, Editor; Diane J. Angelini, Editor. **ISSN:** 0893-2190 (print). **Subscription Rates:** $129 Individuals; $135 Canada and Mexico; $242 Other countries; $443 Institutions; $469 Institutions, Canada and Mexico; $661 Institutions, other countries. **URL:** http://journals.lww.com/jpnnjournal/pages/default.aspx. **Ad Rates:** BW $1,220; 4C $1,300. **Remarks:** Accepts advertising. **Circ:** Paid 2000.

15412 ■ Liberty

Review and Herald Publishing
55 W Oak Ridge Dr.
Hagerstown, MD 21740-7390
Phone: (301)393-3000
Publisher's E-mail: info@rhpa.org
Magazine concerning religious freedom. **Founded:** 1888. **Freq:** Bimonthly. **Print Method:** Offset. **Trim Size:** 8 1/8 x 10 5/8. **Cols./Page:** 3. **Col. Width:** 40 nonpareils. **Col. Depth:** 131 agate lines. **ISSN:** 0024-2055 (print). **Subscription Rates:** $7.95 Individuals. **URL:** http://www.libertymagazine.org/. **Remarks:** Advertising not accepted. **Circ:** 200000.

15413 ■ Listen: Celebrating Positive Choices

Health Connection
55 W Oak Ridge Dr.
Hagerstown, MD 21740-7301
Phone: (301)790-9735
Fax: (888)294-8405
Free: 800-548-8700
Publication E-mail: editor@listenmagazine.org
Magazine promoting drug awareness and other teen issues. **Freq:** Monthly Sept.-May. **Print Method:** Offset. **Trim Size:** 8 x 10 5/8. **Cols./Page:** 2. **Col. Width:** 47 nonpareils. **Col. Depth:** 127 agate lines. **Key Personnel:** Celeste Perrino-Walker, Editor, phone: (301)393-4082; Julie Haines, Manager, Circulation. **ISSN:** 0024--435X (print). **Subscription Rates:** $35.90 Individuals. **URL:** http://www.listenmagazine.org. **Remarks:** Advertising not accepted. **Circ:** ‡35000.

15414 ■ Message: A Christian Magazine of Contemporary Issues

Review and Herald Publishing
55 W Oak Ridge Dr.
Hagerstown, MD 21740-7390
Phone: (301)393-3000
Publisher's E-mail: info@rhpa.org
Religious magazine for African-Americans. **Founded:** 1898. **Freq:** Bimonthly. **Print Method:** Offset. **Trim Size:** 8.125 x 10.625. **Cols./Page:** 3. **Col. Width:** 2 1/8 inches. **Col. Depth:** 9 1/4 inches. **Key Personnel:** Washington Johnson, Editor, phone: (301)393-4100, fax: (301)393-4103; Pat Harris, Assistant Editor, phone: (301)393-4099; Samuel Thomas, Jr., Director, Marketing, phone: (301)393-3182. **ISSN:** 0026-0231 (print). **Subscription Rates:** $17.95 Individuals. **URL:** http://www.messagemagazine.org. **Formerly:** Message Magazine. **Ad Rates:** BW $2,060; 4C $2,540. **Remarks:** Accepts advertising. **Circ:** Paid ‡75000.

15415 ■ The Morning Herald

The Herald-Mail Co.
100 Summit Ave.
Hagerstown, MD 21740

Circulation: ★ = AAM; △ or • = BPA; ♦ = CAC; ❑ = VAC; ⊕ = PO Statement; ‡ = Publisher's Report; Boldface figures = sworn; Light figures = estimated.

Phone: (301)733-5131
Free: 800-626-6397
Publication E-mail: news@herald-mail.com
General newspaper. **Freq:** Daily. **Print Method:** Offset. **Cols./Page:** 6. **Col. Width:** 26 nonpareils. **Col. Depth:** 301 agate lines. **Key Personnel:** Brittney Hamilton, Director, Advertising; Dave Elliott, Director, Product Development. **Subscription Rates:** $152 Individuals 12 months, 7-day home delivery; $77.52 Individuals 6 months, 7-day home delivery; $39.15 Individuals 3 months, 7-day home delivery; $65.89 Individuals digital only. **URL:** http://www.heraldmailmedia.com/?module=displaystory&story_id=132605&format=html. **Remarks:** Accepts advertising. **Circ:** Mon.-Sat. ‡31957, Sun. ‡36778.

15416 ■ The Nontrad Journal
Association for Non-Traditional Students in Higher Education
19134 Olde Waterford Rd.
Hagerstown, MD 21742
Phone: (301)992-2901
Fax: (301)766-9162
Publisher's E-mail: president@antsheboardofdirectors.org
Peer-reviewed journal serving as a forum for introducing and presenting new research in education, and critiquing existing research. **Freq:** Annual. **Subscription Rates:** Included in membership; $18.95 Nonmembers hard copy; $7.95 Nonmembers electronic copy. **URL:** http://www.myantshe.org/page-1858413. **Remarks:** Advertising not accepted. **Circ:** (Not Reported).

15417 ■ Nurse Educator
J.B. Lippincott Co.
PO Box 1600
Hagerstown, MD 21741
Phone: (301)223-2300
Fax: (301)223-2400
Free: 800-638-3030
Publisher's E-mail: customerservice@lww.com
Journal containing information on both the practical and the theoretical aspects of nursing education. **Freq:** Bimonthly. **Key Personnel:** Marilyn H. Oermann, PhD, Editor-in-Chief. **ISSN:** 0363--3624 (print); **EISSN:** 1538--9855 (electronic). **Subscription Rates:** $154 Individuals print only; $161 Canada and Mexico print only; $298 Other countries print only; $281 Individuals UK/Australia - print only; $683 Institutions print only; $712 Institutions, Canada and Mexico print only; $828 Institutions, other countries print only; $133 Individuals online only. **URL:** http://journals.lww.com/nurseeducatoronline/Pages/default.aspx. **Remarks:** Accepts advertising. **Circ:** (Not Reported).

15418 ■ Topics in Clinical Nutrition
Lippincott Williams and Wilkins
16522 Hunters Green Pky.
Hagerstown, MD 21740
Phone: (301)233-2300
Fax: (301)233-2398
Free: 800-638-3030
Publisher's E-mail: orders@lww.com
Peer-reviewed journal addressing the challenges and problems of dietitians and others involved in dietary care in a health care setting. **Freq:** Quarterly. **Trim Size:** 7 x 10. **Cols./Page:** 2. **Col. Width:** 16 picas. **Col. Depth:** 45 picas. **Key Personnel:** Prof. Judith A. Gilbride, PhD, Editor; Elizabeth M. Young, MA, Associate Editor. **ISSN:** 0883-5691 (print); **EISSN:** 1550-5146 (electronic). **USPS:** 001-261. **Subscription Rates:** $123 Individuals; $129 Canada and Mexico; $238 Other countries; $503 Institutions; $528 Institutions, Canada and Mexico; $623 Institutions, other countries; $67 U.S. in-training; $152 Individuals UK/Australia. **URL:** http://journals.lww.com/topicsinclinicalnutrition/pages/default.aspx. **Remarks:** Accepts advertising. **Circ:** (Not Reported).

15419 ■ Topics in Geriatric Rehabilitation
Lippincott Williams and Wilkins
16522 Hunters Green Pky.
Hagerstown, MD 21740
Phone: (301)233-2300
Fax: (301)233-2398
Free: 800-638-3030
Publisher's E-mail: orders@lww.com
Journal presenting clinical, basic, and applied research, as well as theoretical information, for the health care professional practicing in the area of geriatric rehabilitation. **Freq:** Quarterly. **Trim Size:** 7 x 10. **Cols./Page:** 2. **Col. Width:** 16 picas. **Col. Depth:** 45 picas. **Key Personnel:** Carole B. Lewis, PhD, Editor. **ISSN:** 0882-7524 (print); **EISSN:** 1550-2414 (electronic). **Subscription Rates:** $128 Individuals; $140 Canada and Mexico; $181 Other countries; $557 Institutions; $581 Institutions, Canada and Mexico; $720 Institutions, other countries; $148 Individuals UK/Australia; $589 Institutions UK/Australia; $62 U.S., Canada, and Mexico in-training; $70 Other countries in-training. **URL:** http://journals.lww.com/topicsingeriatricrehabilitation/pages/default.aspx; http://www.lww.com/product/?0882-7524. **Remarks:** Accepts advertising. **Circ:** (Not Reported).

15420 ■ Topics in Language Disorders
Lippincott Williams and Wilkins
16522 Hunters Green Pky.
Hagerstown, MD 21740
Phone: (301)233-2300
Fax: (301)233-2398
Free: 800-638-3030
Publisher's E-mail: orders@lww.com
Peer-reviewed journal providing information to practicing professionals dealing with the language disabled. **Freq:** Quarterly. **Trim Size:** 7 x 10. **Cols./Page:** 2. **Col. Width:** 16 picas. **Col. Depth:** 45 picas. **Key Personnel:** Nickola Wolf Nelson, PhD, Editor-in-Chief; Katharine G. Butler, PhD, Editor. **ISSN:** 0271--8294 (print); **EISSN:** 1550--3259 (electronic). **Subscription Rates:** $134 Individuals print; $528 Institutions print; $152 Individuals print; $616 Institutions print; $184 Individuals print; $631 Institutions print; $249 Other countries print; $801 Institutions, other countries print; $115 Elsewhere online. **URL:** http://journals.lww.com/topicsinlanguagedisorders/pages/default.aspx. **Remarks:** Accepts advertising. **Circ:** Paid 3278, Non-paid 78.

15421 ■ Vibrant Life: Physical health, mental clarity, spiritual balance
Review and Herald Publishing
55 W Oak Ridge Dr.
Hagerstown, MD 21740-7390
Phone: (301)393-3000
Publisher's E-mail: info@rhpa.org
Christian magazine for 25- to 45-year olds. Emphasizes preventative medicine and covers physical, mental, and spiritual health topics. **Freq:** Bimonthly. **Print Method:** Offset. **Trim Size:** 8.125 x 10.625. **Cols./Page:** 3. **Col. Width:** 26 nonpareils. **Col. Depth:** 129 agate lines. **Key Personnel:** Genia Blumberg, Advertising Executive, phone: (301)393-3170, fax: (301)393-4055. **ISSN:** 0749--3509 (print). **Subscription Rates:** $19.95 Individuals; $26.95 Other countries. **URL:** http://www.vibrantlife.com. **Formerly**: Life & Health. **Ad Rates:** BW $886; 4C $1,440. **Remarks:** Accepts advertising. **Circ:** Combined 30000.

15422 ■ Antietam Cable TV
1000 Willow Cir.
Hagerstown, MD 21740
Phone: (301)797-5000
Email: info@antietamcable.com
Owner: Schurz Communications Inc., 1301 E Douglas Rd., Mishawaka, IN 46545, Ph: (574)247-7237. **Founded:** 1966. **Key Personnel:** Brian Lynch, Gen. Mgr. **Cities Served:** Hagerstown, Maryland: subscribing households 38,500; 50 channels; 1 community access channel. **Postal Areas Served:** 21740. **URL:** http://www.antietamcable.com.

15423 ■ WHAG-TV - 25
13 E Washington St.
Hagerstown, MD 21740
Phone: (301)797-4408
Fax: (301)733-1735
Format: Commercial TV. **Networks:** NBC. **Owner:** Nexstar Broadcasting Group Inc., 545 E John Carpenter Fwy., Ste. 700, Irving, TX 75062, Ph: (972)373-8800. **Founded:** 1970. **Operating Hours**: Continuous; 50% network, 50% local. **ADI**: Hagerstown, MD. **Key Personnel:** Mark Kraham, News Dir., mkraham@whag.com; Hugh Breslin, Gen. Mgr., hbreslin@whag.com. **Ad Rates:** $5-4000 per unit. **URL:** http://www.your4state.com/news.

15424 ■ WJAL-TV - 68
Swamp Fox Rd.
Box 1975
Hagerstown, MD 21742
Phone: (717)375-4000
Fax: (717)375-4052
Free: 800-811-4959
Format: Commercial TV. **Owner:** Entravision Communications Corporation, 2425 Olympic Blvd., Ste. 6000 W, Santa Monica, CA 90404-4030, Ph: (310)447-3870, Fax: (310)447-3899. **Founded:** 1987. **Operating Hours**: Continuous. **ADI**: Hagerstown, MD. **Key Personnel:** Steve Ullom, Sr. VP; Donna Jeter, Operations Mgr., djeter@entravision.com; David Richards, Contact, engineering@wjal.com. **Wattage:** 4,000,000. **Ad Rates:** $25-90 for 30 seconds. **URL:** http://www.wjal.com.

15425 ■ WJEJ-AM - 1240
1135 Haven Rd.
Hagerstown, MD 21742
Phone: (301)739-2323
Fax: (301)797-7408
Free: 800-265-0057
Email: wjej@myactv.net
Format: Full Service; Easy Listening; Oldies. **Networks:** CBS. **Owner:** Hagerstown Broadcasting Co., Inc., 1135 Haven Rd., Hagerstown, MD 21742. **Founded:** 1932. **Operating Hours**: Continuous; 10% network, 90% local. **ADI**: Hagerstown, MD. **Key Personnel:** John T. Staub, Gen. Mgr., Owner; Joanna Staub, Asst. Mgr. **Local Programs**: *The EnvironMinute*, Monday Tuesday Wednesday Thursday Friday 12:33 p.m.; *America's Future*, Monday Tuesday Wednesday Thursday Friday 12:45 p.m.; *Contemporary Retirement*, Wednesday 9:30 a.m. - 10:00 a.m.; *The Old Farmer's Almanac Radio Report*, Monday Tuesday Wednesday Thursday Friday Saturday, 5:45 a.m.; 10:45 a.m.; *The WJEJ Radio Phone Party*, Monday Tuesday Wednesday Thursday Friday 11:06 a.m. - 11:36 a.m. **Wattage**: 1,000. **Ad Rates:** $10-15 for 30 seconds; $14-21 for 60 seconds. **URL:** http://www.wjejradio.com.

15426 ■ WWEG-FM - 106.9
880 Commonwealth Ave.
Hagerstown, MD 21740
Phone: (301)733-4500
Fax: (301)733-0040
Free: 800-222-1069
Format: Oldies. **Networks:** Independent. **Owner:** Nassau Broadcasting, 619 Alexander Rd., 3rd Fl., Princeton, NJ 08540. **Founded:** 1957. **Formerly**: WARK-FM; WARX-FM. **Operating Hours**: Continuous; 10% Network, 90% Local. **ADI**: Hagerstown, MD. **Key Personnel:** Kym McKay, Contact, kmckay@nassaubroadcasting.com; Mike Krafthofer, Contact, mkrafthofer@nassaubroadcasting.com; Chris Elliott, Div. Mgr. **Wattage**: 15,500. **Ad Rates:** $20-50 for 30 seconds; $25-45 for 60 seconds. **URL:** http://www.1069theeagle.com.

15427 ■ WWMD-FM - 104.7
1135 Haven Rd.
Hagerstown, MD 21742
Phone: (301)739-2323
Fax: (301)797-7408
Free: 800-265-0057
Format: Easy Listening. **Owner:** Hagerstown Broadcasting Co., Inc., 1135 Haven Rd., Hagerstown, MD 21742. **Founded:** 1946. **Formerly**: WJEJ-FM. **Operating Hours**: 5 a.m.-2 a.m.; 1% network, 99% local. **ADI**: Hagerstown, MD. **Key Personnel:** John T. Staub, Gen. Mgr., President, Contact; Dan Wilson, Sales Mgr.; Louis J. Scally, Chief Engineer; Tom Bradley, News Dir.; Kenneth Forsythe, Promotions Mgr.; Jackie Hall, Traffic Mgr; John T. Staub, Contact. **Wattage**: 75,000. **Ad Rates:** $13-18 for 30 seconds; $16-25 for 60 seconds. Combined advertising rates available with WJEJ-AM.

15428 ■ WWPB-TV - 31
11767 Owings Mills Blvd.
Owings Mills, MD 21117
Phone: (410)356-5600
Free: 800-627-6788
Email: comments@mpt.org
Format: Public TV. **Simulcasts:** WMPB, WMPT, WCPB, WGPT, WFPT. **Networks:** Public Broadcasting Service (PBS). **Owner:** Maryland Public Television, 11767 Owings Mills Blvd., Owings Mills, MD 21117, Ph: (410)356-5600, Fax: (410)581-6579, Free: 800-223-3678. **Founded:** 1969. **Operating Hours**: Continuous. **Key Personnel:** Larry D. Unger, CEO, President; Steven Schupak, Exec. VP, COO; George R. Beneman, II, Sr. VP, Chief Tech. Ofc.; Tom Williams, Managing Dir.;

Martin G. Jacobs, VP, CFO. **Local Programs:** *Motor-Week*, Sunday Saturday Wednesday 12:00 p.m. 5:00 p.m. 7:30 p.m. **Wattage:** 4,070,000. **Ad Rates:** Noncommercial; underwriting available. **URL:** http://www.mpt.org/home.

HALETHORPE

15429 ■ WRBS-FM - 95.1
3500 Commerce Dr.
Halethorpe, MD 21227
Phone: (410)247-4100
Fax: (410)247-4533
Free: 866-304-9727
Email: info@951shinefm.com
Format: Religious. **Owner:** Peter & John Ministries, 3500 Commerce Dr., Halethorpe, MD 21227. **Founded:** 1964. **Operating Hours:** Continuous; 5% network, 95% local. **ADI:** Baltimore, MD. **Local Programs:** *Psalm 95*, Sunday 9:00 p.m. - 10:00 p.m.; *Sounds of Life*, Sunday 11:00 a.m. - 11:30 a.m.; *Positive Music*, Monday Tuesday Wednesday Thursday Friday 10:00 a.m. - 3:00 p.m. **Wattage:** 50,000. **Ad Rates:** Noncommercial. **URL:** http://www.wrbs.com.

HAMPSTEAD

15430 ■ Maryland Beverage Journal
Beverage Journal Inc.
PO Box 159
Hampstead, MD 21074-0159
Phone: (410)796-5455
Fax: (410)796-5511
Publisher's E-mail: spatten@beerwineliquor.com
Trade magazine for the beer, wine and liquor industry in Maryland. **Freq:** Monthly. **Print Method:** Offset. **Trim Size:** 8.375 x 10.875. **Cols./Page:** 3. **Col. Width:** 2 3/8 inches. **Col. Depth:** 10 inches. **Key Personnel:** Stephen Patten, Associate Publisher. **USPS:** 783-300. **Subscription Rates:** $45 Individuals 1 year; print + online, (plus MD sales tax (if applicable)); $75 Individuals 2 years; print + online, (plus MD sales tax (if applicable)); $100 Individuals 3 years; print + online, (plus MD sales tax (if applicable)). **URL:** http://www.beveragejournalinc.com/new. **Ad Rates:** BW $595; 4C $970. **Remarks:** Accepts advertising. **Circ:** Paid ‡4600, Controlled ‡1800.

Washington DC Beverage Journal - See Washington, DC

HANOVER

15431 ■ Journal of American College Health
American College Health Association
1362 Mellon Rd., Ste. 180
Hanover, MD 21076-3198
Phone: (410)859-1500
Fax: (410)859-1510
Publisher's E-mail: membership@acha.org
Freq: 8/year. **Print Method:** Offset. **Trim Size:** 8 1/2 x 11. **Cols./Page:** 2. **Col. Width:** 3 3/8 inches. **Col. Depth:** 9 1/2 inches. **Key Personnel:** Teri Aronowitz, PhD, Executive Editor. **ISSN:** 0744--8481 (print); **EISSN:** 1940--3208 (electronic). **Subscription Rates:** $416 Institutions online only; $475 Institutions print and online. **URL:** http://www.tandfonline.com/toc/vach20/current. **Ad Rates:** BW $600; 4C $2,170. **Remarks:** Accepts advertising. **Circ:** 3420.

15432 ■ Pennysaver
Pennysaver
1342 Charwood Rd.
Hanover, MD 21076
Fax: (410)684-6188
Free: 888-899-8992
Shopper. **Founded:** Aug. 22, 1979. **Freq:** Weekly. **Print Method:** Offset. **Trim Size:** 7 1/2 x 10 1/2. **Cols./Page:** 4. **Col. Width:** 9 picas. **Col. Depth:** 60 picas. **Key Personnel:** Chris Shertzer, Vice President, Sales; Mary Brown, Director, Sales. **URL:** http://www.mdpennysaver.com. **Formerly:** Maryland Pennysaver. **Remarks:** Accepts advertising. **Circ:** Combined ‡1211526.

HARWOOD

15433 ■ Aerosphere Air and Space Magazine
Aerosphere
4422 Cobalt Dr.
Harwood, MD 20776
Publication E-mail: info@aerosphere.com
Aviation and space magazine. **Key Personnel:** Carlton W. Austin, Publisher, Director, Editorial; John Carlisle, Editor; Jeff Pardo, Editor. **Subscription Rates:** Free. **URL:** http://www.aerosphere.com. **Remarks:** Advertising not accepted. **Circ:** (Not Reported).

HAVRE DE GRACE

15434 ■ WASA-AM - 1330
PO Box 164
Havre de Grace, MD 21078-0164
Phone: (410)939-0800
Fax: (410)321-8863
Format: Country. **Networks:** USA Radio. **Founded:** 1948. **Operating Hours:** 6 a.m.-midnight. **Key Personnel:** Kurt M. Elasavage, President; Donald P. Kampes, VP; Brain J. Marks, Dir. of Programs. **Wattage:** 5,000. **Ad Rates:** $5.50-7.25 for 30 seconds; $10-13.50 for 60 seconds.

15435 ■ WJSS-AM - 1330
1605 Level Rd.
Havre de Grace, MD 21078
Phone: (410)939-9446
Email: wjss@comcast.net
Format: Religious. **Key Personnel:** Ronald Reeves, Gen. Mgr.; Shamaar Guess, Production Mgr.; Nicole Rossi, News Dir. **Wattage:** 5,000. **Ad Rates:** Advertising accepted; rates available upon request. **URL:** http://www.smashhits.fm/whgm-advertising-contact-form.

15436 ■ WXCY-FM - 103.7
707 Revolution St.
Havre de Grace, MD 21078
Phone: (410)939-1100
Fax: (888)766-1104
Free: 800-788-WXCY
Email: loyallistener@wxcyfm.com
Format: Country. **Owner:** Delmarva Broadcasting Co., 2727 Shipley Rd., Wilmington, DE 19803, Ph: (302)478-2700, Fax: (302)478-0100. **Founded:** 1960. **Formerly:** WHDG-FM. **Operating Hours:** Continuous. **Key Personnel:** Bob Bloom, Gen. Mgr. **Wattage:** 37,000. **Ad Rates:** $40-45 for 30 seconds; $50-55 for 60 seconds. **Mailing address:** PO Box 269, Havre de Grace, MD 21078. **URL:** http://www.wxcyfm.com.

HUNT VALLEY

15437 ■ WZBA-FM - 100.7
11350 McCormick Rd., Ste. 701
Executive Plz. III
Hunt Valley, MD 21031
Phone: (410)771-8484
Fax: (410)771-1616
Format: Classic Rock. **Networks:** ABC. **Formerly:** WTIR-FM; WGRX-FM. **Operating Hours:** Continuous. **Key Personnel:** Jefferson Ward, Gen. Mgr.; Dan Michaels, Prog. Dir. **Wattage:** 2,700. **Ad Rates:** Advertising accepted; rates available upon request. **URL:** http://www.thebayonline.com.

HYATTSVILLE

Prince George's Co. Prince George's Co. (SC). 7 m NE of Washington, DC. Manufactures cinder blocks, auto bodies, plastics, motor vehicles, aircraft parts, bricks. Residential. Truck, dairy, poultry, fruit farms.

15438 ■ National Vital Statistics Report
National Center for Health Statistics
Metro IV Bldg.
3311 Toledo Rd.
Hyattsville, MD 20782
Phone: (301)458-4500
Fax: (301)458-4020
Free: 800-232-4636
Publisher's E-mail: edward.sondik@cdc.hhs.gov
Magazine covering population studies; includes vital statistics on mortality, natality, marriage, and divorce. **Founded:** 1950. **Freq:** Monthly. **Print Method:** Offset. **Cols./Page:** 2. **Col. Width:** 42 nonpareils. **Col. Depth:** 123 agate lines. **URL:** http://www.cdc.gov/nchs/products/nvsr.htm. **Formerly:** Monthly Vital Statistics Report. **Remarks:** Advertising not accepted. **Circ:** Non-paid ‡9000.

15439 ■ WHFS-FM - 99.1
8201 Corporate Dr., Ste. 550
Hyattsville, MD 20785
Phone: (301)306-0991
Fax: (301)731-0431
Free: 800-321-WHFS
Format: Alternative/New Music/Progressive. **Owner:** CBS Radio, New York, NY, Ph: (614)249-7676, Fax: (614)249-6995. **Founded:** 1968. **Operating Hours:** Continuous. **ADI:** Washington, DC. **Key Personnel:** Phil Zachary, Gen. Mgr., VP; Bill Parshall, Gen. Sales Mgr.; Robert Benjamin, Dir. of Programs; Bob Waugh, Music Dir. **Wattage:** 50,000. **URL:** http://www.whfs.com.

JB ANDREWS

15440 ■ Air Power History
Air Force Historical Foundation
1602 California Ave., Ste. F-162
JB Andrews, MD 20762
Phone: (301)736-1959
Freq: Quarterly. **Subscription Rates:** $35 /year for individuals; $45 /year for institutions. **URL:** http://afhistoricalfoundation.org/resources/Air_Power_History.asp. **Mailing address:** PO Box 790, Clinton, MD 20735-0790. **Remarks:** Accepts advertising. **Circ:** 7000.

LA PLATA

Charles Co. Charles Co. (SW). 25 m S of Washington, DC. Charles County Community College. Bottling works. Timber. Tobacco. Metal works. Diversified farming.

15441 ■ WDLE-FM - 107.1
PO Box 1670
La Plata, MD 20646
Free: 800-322-1071
Format: Adult Contemporary. **Networks:** CBS. **Owner:** Southernwood Media Corp., at above address, Ph: (301)754-9901. **Founded:** 1978. **Formerly:** WCTD-FM. **Operating Hours:** Continuous; 2% network; 98% local. **ADI:** Salisbury, MD. **Key Personnel:** Thom Walsh, Dir. of Programs; Ernest Colburn, Operations Mgr.; Jill Flemming, News Dir.; Troy Hill, Music Dir; Gary Kleiman, Contact. **Wattage:** 3,000. **Ad Rates:** $4-13 for 30 seconds; $7-16 for 60 seconds.

15442 ■ WSMD-FM - 98.3
PO Box 2470
La Plata, MD 20646-2470
Phone: (301)884-8255
Networks: ABC. **Owner:** Somar Communications Inc., at above address. **Founded:** 1988. **Operating Hours:** Continuous. **Key Personnel:** Cheryl White, Contact. **Wattage:** 3,000 ERP. **URL:** http://www.star983.com.

LANDOVER

15443 ■ Annals of Biomedical Engineering
Biomedical Engineering Society
8201 Corporate Dr., Ste. 1125
Landover, MD 20785-2224
Phone: (301)459-1999
Fax: (301)459-2444
Free: 877-871-2637
Journal containing professional articles and abstracts from biomedical literature. **Freq:** Monthly 12/yr. **Trim Size:** 8 1/4 x 10 7/8. **Key Personnel:** Kyriacos Athanasiou, Editor-in-Chief. **ISSN:** 0090--6964 (print); **EISSN:** 1573--9686 (electronic). **Subscription Rates:** $1786 Institutions print incl. Free Access OR e-only for the Americas; €1570 Institutions print incl. Free Access OR e-only for the Americas. **URL:** http://bmes.org/annals; http://www.springer.com/biomed/journal/10439. **Remarks:** Accepts advertising. **Circ:** 5000.

15444 ■ DECISIVE
Decisive Media
8201 Corporate Dr., Ste. 500
Landover, MD 20785
Phone: (301)850-2858
Bilingual magazine that covers the interests of Latino car buyers. **Freq:** Quarterly. **Key Personnel:** Karen Payton, Chief Operating Officer. **URL:** http://www.decisivemagazine.com. **Formerly:** Latinos on Wheels. **Remarks:** Accepts advertising. **Circ:** 720000.

LANHAM

Prince George's Co. (SC) 4 m S College Park. Residential.

Circulation: ⋆ = AAM; △ or • = BPA; ♦ = CAC; ❑ = VAC; ⊕ = PO Statement; ‡ = Publisher's Report; Boldface figures = sworn; Light figures = estimated.

15445 ■ Collections Journal: A Journal for Museum and Archives Professionals
AltaMira Press
4501 Forbes Blvd., Ste. 200
Lanham, MD 20706
Phone: (301)459-3366
Fax: (301)429-5748
Free: 800-462-6420
Publication E-mail: info@altamirapress.com
Journal that offers information on handling, preserving, researching, and organizing museum and archive collections. **Freq:** Quarterly. **Key Personnel:** Gary Edson, Board Member; Julee Decker, Editor. **ISSN:** 1550--1906 (print). **Subscription Rates:** $43 Individuals; $99 Institutions museum; $149 Institutions non-museum; $12.50 Individuals single issue; $25 Institutions single issue; museum; $40 Institutions single issue; non-museum. **URL:** http://rowman.com/Page/JMAP. **Ad Rates:** BW $350. **Remarks:** Accepts advertising. **Circ:** (Not Reported).

15446 ■ Journal of Evidence-Based Practices for Schools
The Rowman & Littlefield Publishing Group Inc.
4501 Forbes Blvd., Ste. 200
Lanham, MD 20706
Phone: (301)459-3366
Fax: (301)429-5748
Free: 800-462-6420
Publisher's E-mail: customercare@rowman.com
Journal publishing articles for educators and school psychologists. **Freq:** Semiannual. **Key Personnel:** Brian Wilhoit, Editor. **ISSN:** 1523--4738 (print). **Subscription Rates:** $75 Individuals; $90 Institutions; $100 Other countries; $115 Institutions, other countries. **URL:** http://rowman.com/page/je. **Circ:** (Not Reported).

15447 ■ Journal for Vascular Ultrasound
Society for Vascular Ultrasound
4601 Presidents Dr., Ste. 260
Lanham, MD 20706-4831
Phone: (301)459-7550
Fax: (301)459-5651
Free: 800-788-8346
Publisher's E-mail: svuinfo@svunet.org
Freq: Quarterly March, June, September, December. **ISSN:** 1044- 4122 (print). **Subscription Rates:** $165 U.S. and Canada; $200 Other countries; $265 Institutions US and Canada; $300 Institutions, other countries. **URL:** http://account.svunet.org/i4a/pages/index.cfm?pageid=3337. **Ad Rates:** BW $1,800, full page; BW $1,000, half page. **Remarks:** Accepts advertising. **Circ:** 5,500.

15448 ■ Labor Studies Journal
United Association for Labor Education
PO Box 598
Lanham, MD 20703
Phone: (202)585-4393
Publisher's E-mail: info@uale.org
Journal exploring the role of the trade union movement in forging American economic and social policy. **Freq:** Quarterly March, June, September, December. **Print Method:** Offset. **Trim Size:** 5 x 9. **Key Personnel:** Bob Bruno; Bruce Nissen, Advisor; Lynn Feekin, Editor; Michelle Kaminski, Editor. **ISSN:** 0160-449X (print); **EISSN:** 1538-9758 (electronic). **Subscription Rates:** $66 Individuals print; $119 Institutions single copy; $432 Institutions print; $397 Institutions electronic; $441 Institutions print and electronic; $21 Individuals Single Print Issue. **URL:** http://us.sagepub.com/en-us/nam/labor-studies-journal/journal201857; http://uale.org/labor-studies-journal; http://www.sagepub.com/journals/Journal201857/subscribe. **Ad Rates:** BW $515; 4C $995. **Remarks:** Accepts advertising. **Circ:** Paid ‡800.

15449 ■ The National AMVET
AMVETS
4647 Forbes Blvd.
Lanham, MD 20706-4380
Phone: (301)459-9600
Fax: (301)459-7924
Free: 877-726-8387
Publication E-mail: amvets@amvets.org
Freq: Quarterly. **Print Method:** Offset. **Trim Size:** 8 1/8 x 10 7/8. **Cols./Page:** 3. **Col. Width:** 13 picas. **Col. Depth:** 55.5 picas. **Key Personnel:** Richard W. Flanagan, Contact. **ISSN:** 0027--853X (print). **Subscription Rates:** Included in membership; $20 Nonmembers; $34 Nonmembers 2 years; $48 Nonmembers 3 years. **URL:** http://www.amvets.org/american-veteran-magazine. **Ad Rates:** BW $1953; 4C $3161; PCI $150; 4C $5700, full page; 4C $3100, half page. **Remarks:** Accepts advertising. **Circ:** Paid ‡175000, Controlled ‡4000, 300000.

15450 ■ Pro Ecclesia: A Journal of Catholic and Evangelical Theology
The Rowman & Littlefield Publishing Group Inc.
4501 Forbes Blvd., Ste. 200
Lanham, MD 20706
Phone: (301)459-3366
Fax: (301)429-5748
Free: 800-462-6420
Publisher's E-mail: customercare@rowman.com
Journal publishing biblical, liturgical, historical and doctrinal articles. **Freq:** Quarterly. **Key Personnel:** Joseph Mangina, Editor. **ISSN:** 1063--8512 (print). **Subscription Rates:** $45 Individuals; $110 Institutions; $75 Other countries; $25 Students. **URL:** http://rowman.com/page/ProEcclesia; http://www.e-ccet.org/pro-ecclesia. **Circ:** (Not Reported).

15451 ■ Teacher Education and Practice
The Rowman & Littlefield Publishing Group Inc.
4501 Forbes Blvd., Ste. 200
Lanham, MD 20706
Phone: (301)459-3366
Fax: (301)429-5748
Free: 800-462-6420
Publisher's E-mail: customercare@rowman.com
Peer-reviewed journal publishing research on the field of teaching profession. **Freq:** Quarterly. **Key Personnel:** Patrick Jenlink, Editor. **ISSN:** 1063--8512 (print). **Subscription Rates:** $66 Individuals; $170 Institutions; $91 Other countries; $195 Institutions, other countries. **URL:** http://rowman.com/page/TEP. **Circ:** (Not Reported).

15452 ■ Teacher Librarian: The Journal of School Library Professionals K-12
Teacher Librarian
4501 Forbes Blvd., Ste. 200
Lanham, MD 20706
Phone: (301)459-3366
Fax: (301)429-5748
Publication E-mail: tlibrarian@ggpubs.com
Journal covering issues for library professionals working with children and young adults. **Freq:** 5/year. **Print Method:** Web offset. **Key Personnel:** David Loertscher, Editor; Elizabeth Marcoux, Editor. **ISSN:** 0315-8888 (print). **Subscription Rates:** $60 U.S. and Canada 1 year print & digital; $120 U.S. and Canada 2 year print & digital; $180 U.S. and Canada 3 year print & digital; $75 Other countries 1 year print & digital; $150 Other countries 2 year print & digital; $225 Other countries 3 year print & digital. **URL:** http://www.teacherlibrarian.com. **Formerly**: Emergency Librarian. **Ad Rates:** BW $1,200; 4C $1,725. **Remarks:** Accepts advertising. **Circ:** Combined 26000.

15453 ■ WARW-FM - 94.7
4200 Parliament Pl., Ste. 300
Lanham, MD 20706
Format: Classic Rock. **Networks:** CBS. **Owner:** CBS Radio Inc., 1271 Avenue of the Americas, 44th Fl., New York, NY 10020-1401, Ph: (212)649-9600. **Founded:** 1946. **Formerly**: WJMD-FM. **Operating Hours**: Continuous. **Wattage**: 50,000 ERP. **Ad Rates:** Noncommercial. **URL:** http://www.947freshfm.cbslocal.com.

15454 ■ WIAD-FM - 94.7
4200 Parliament Pl., Ste. 300
Lanham, MD 20706
Phone: (301)683-0947
Format: Adult Album Alternative. **Founded:** Feb. 02, 2007. **Formerly**: WTGB-FM. **Key Personnel:** Jennifer Touchette, Sales Mgr., jennifer.touchette@cbsradio.com; Cindy Friedman, Gen. Sales Mgr., cindy.friedman@cbsradio.com. **Wattage**: 50,000. **URL:** http://www.947freshfm.cbslocal.com.

15455 ■ WKYS-FM - 93.9
5900 Princess Garden Pkwy., 8th Fl.
Lanham, MD 20706
Phone: (301)306-1111
Fax: (301)306-9540
Format: Hip Hop. **Networks:** Independent. **Owner:** Radio One Licenses L.L.C., 1010 Wayne Ave., 14th Fl., Silver Spring, MD 20910. **Founded:** 1947. **Operating Hours**: Continuous; 100% local. **ADI**: Washington, DC. **Key Personnel:** Lou Hernandez, Dir. of Production, lhernandez@radio-one.com; Quon Wilson, Promotions Dir., qwilson@radio-one.com; Cynthia Bullock, Traffic Mgr., cbullock@radio-one.com. **Wattage**: 24,500. **Ad Rates:** Noncommercial. **URL:** http://kysdc.com.

15456 ■ WOL-AM - 1450
5900 Princess Garden Pky., 5th Fl.
Lanham, MD 20706
Format: News; Talk. **Simulcasts:** WOLB-AM. **Networks:** ABC; Shadow Traffic. **Owner:** Radio One Inc., 1010 Wayne Ave., 14th Fl., Silver Spring, MD 20910, Ph: (301)306-1111, Fax: (302)636-5454. **Founded:** 1924. **Operating Hours**: Continuous. **ADI**: Washington, DC. **Key Personnel:** Jeff Wilson, Gen. Mgr., jeffwilson@radio-one.com; Alfred Liggins, President; Cathy Hughes, Owner. **Wattage**: 370 KW. **Ad Rates:** Combined advertising rates available with WMMJ-FM. **URL:** http://woldcnews.newsone.com.

WPGC-FM - See Washington, DC

15457 ■ WPGC 95.5 FM - 1580
4200 Parliament Pl., Ste. 300
Lanham, MD 20706
Phone: (301)918-2377
Format: Gospel. **Networks:** CBS; AP. **Owner:** CBS Radio Inc., 40 W 57th St., New York, NY 10019, Ph: (212)846-3939, Fax: (212)315-2162. **Founded:** May 1954. **Formerly**: WPGC-AM. **Operating Hours**: Continuous; 50% network, 50% local. **Key Personnel:** Ivy Savoy Smith, Contact, isavoy@wpgc955.com. **Wattage**: 50,000 Day; 292 Night. **Ad Rates:** $15-55 per unit. **URL:** http://wpgc.cbslocal.com.

15458 ■ WPRS-FM - 104.1
5900 Princess Garden Pkwy., 5th Fl.
Lanham, MD 20706
Phone: (301)306-1111
Format: Contemporary Christian. **Owner:** Radio One Inc., 1010 Wayne Ave., 14th Fl., Silver Spring, MD 20910, Ph: (301)306-1111, Fax: (302)636-5454. **Founded:** 1947. **Formerly**: WQQW; WGMS-FM. **Operating Hours**: Sunrise-sunset. **ADI**: Washington, DC. **Key Personnel:** Chris Wegmann, Gen. Mgr. **Ad Rates:** Advertising accepted; rates available upon request. **URL:** http://www.radio-one.com.

15459 ■ WYCB-AM - 1340
5900 Princess Garden Pkwy.
Lanham, MD 20706
Email: inquiry@radio-one.com
Format: Gospel; Religious. **Networks:** Mutual Broadcasting System. **Owner:** Radio One Inc., 1010 Wayne Ave., 14th Fl., Silver Spring, MD 20910, Ph: (301)306-1111, Fax: (302)636-5454. **Founded:** 1978. **Operating Hours**: Continuous. **ADI**: Washington, DC. **Key Personnel:** Chris Wegmann, Gen. Mgr. **URL:** http://www.radio-one.com.

LARGO

15460 ■ Young Innovators
Educators Serving the Community
9701 Apollo Dr., Ste. 301
Largo, MD 20774-4783
Phone: (301)498-2899
Fax: (301)362-4360
Publisher's E-mail: info@eduserc.org
Magazine featuring articles on workforce development, corporate diversity, job readiness skills, corporate promotion of educational programs and community-based programs. **Freq:** Quarterly. **Subscription Rates:** Included in membership; $22 /year. **URL:** http://www.eduserc.org/about-us. **Ad Rates:** 4C $2,000; BW $1,600. **Remarks:** Accepts advertising. **Circ:** (Not Reported).

LAUREL

Prince George's Co. Prince George's Co. (SC). 16 m NE of Washington, DC. Manufactures paints, electric housewares, fans. Diversified farming. Dairy products.

15461 ■ Clinton-Fort Washington Gazette
Post-Newsweek Media Inc.
c/o Alison Walker, Asst. Mng. Ed.

13501 Virginia Manor Rd.
Laurel, MD 20707
Community newspaper. **Freq:** Weekly (Thurs.). **Key Personnel:** Alison Walker, Assistant Managing Editor, phone: (240)473-7544, fax: (240)473-7501. **Subscription Rates:** Free. **URL:** http://www.gazette.net/. **Remarks:** Accepts advertising. **Circ:** Free ■ **31780.**

15462 ■ Fertility Today
Fertility Today
PO Box 117
Laurel, MD 20725-0117
Phone: (410)715-8559
Magazine that provides information on matters of fertility and infertility. **Freq:** Quarterly. **Print Method:** Offset. **Key Personnel:** Diana Broomfield, MD, Chief Executive Officer, Founder. **Subscription Rates:** $27.80 U.S.; $34 Canada; $42 Other countries; $55.60 Two years; $68 Canada 2 years; $84 Other countries 2 years; $6.95 U.S. per issue; $8.50 Canada per issue; $10.50 Other countries per issue. **URL:** http://www.fertilitytoday.org. **Ad Rates:** 4C $4250. **Remarks:** Advertising accepted; rates available upon request. **Circ:** 225000.

15463 ■ Free Press
Free Press
615 Main St.
Laurel, MD 20707
Phone: (301)725-2000
Fax: (301)317-8736
Community newspaper. **Founded:** 1947. **Freq:** Weekly (Thurs.). **Print Method:** Letterpress and offset. Uses mats. **Trim Size:** 11 x 15. **Cols./Page:** 5 and 6. **Col. Width:** 24 11 and 20 nonpareils picas. **Col. Depth:** 231 80.25 and 224 agate lines picas. **Key Personnel:** Veda F. Ponikvar, Editor; Jim Joyner, Editor; S. Zekeorunsky, Publisher; Christy K. Kass, Editor. **Subscription Rates:** $18 Individuals; $23 Out of area. **Ad Rates:** GLR $33. 00; PCI $4.60. **Remarks:** Advertising accepted; rates available upon request. **Circ:** ‡3550, Paid 25, Free 22252, ‡3000.

15464 ■ Greenbelt Gazette
Post-Newsweek Media Inc.
c/o Jeff Lyles, Managing Editor
13501 Virginia Manor Rd.
Laurel, MD 20707
Community newspaper. **Freq:** Weekly (Thurs.). **Key Personnel:** Jeff Lyles, Managing Editor, phone: (240)473-7508, fax: (240)473-7501. **Subscription Rates:** Free. **URL:** http://www.gazette.net. **Remarks:** Accepts advertising. **Circ:** Free ■ **5857.**

15465 ■ Hobie Hotline
International Hobie Class Association
c/o Rich McVeigh, President
15800 Bond Mill Rd.
Laurel, MD 20707-3257
Phone: (301)435-7795
Freq: Bimonthly. **Subscription Rates:** $11.97 /year. **Alt. Formats:** PDF. **URL:** http://www.hobiecat.com/hobie-cat-racing/#hotline-magazines. **Remarks:** Accepts advertising. **Circ:** (Not Reported).

15466 ■ Hyattsville-Port Towns Gazette
Post-Newsweek Media Inc.
c/o Jeff Lyles, Managing Editor
13501 Virginia Manor Rd.
Laurel, MD 20707
Community newspaper. **Freq:** Weekly (Thurs.). **Key Personnel:** Jeff Lyles, Managing Editor, phone: (240)473-7508, fax: (240)473-7501. **Subscription Rates:** Free. **URL:** http://www.gazette.net. **Remarks:** Accepts advertising. **Circ:** Free ■ **18243.**

15467 ■ Johns Hopkins APL Technical Digest
Johns Hopkins University Applied Physics Laboratory
11100 Johns Hopkins Rd.
Laurel, MD 20723-6099
Phone: 240 228-5000
Fax: 240 228-1093
Publication E-mail: technicaldigest@jhuapl.edu
Technical journal covering research and programs at Johns Hopkins University Applied Physics Laboratory. **Freq:** Quarterly. **Key Personnel:** David M. Silver, Editor-in-Chief. **ISSN:** 0270--5214 (print). **URL:** http://techdigest.jhuapl.edu; http://www.jhuapl.edu/techdigest. **Remarks:** Advertising not accepted. **Circ:** Controlled ⊕**4330.**

15468 ■ The Journal of Spelean History
American Spelean History Association
6304 Kaybro St.
Laurel, MD 20707
Phone: (301)725-5877
Publisher's E-mail: asha@caves.org
Journal covering spelean history for cave explorers. **Freq:** Semiannual. **Trim Size:** 8 1/2 x 11. **Key Personnel:** Greg Brick, Editor. **ISSN:** 0022--4693 (print). **Subscription Rates:** $2.50 Single issue; $2 Individuals. **URL:** http://caves.org/section/asha. **Remarks:** Advertising not accepted. **Circ:** Paid ‡120, Non-paid ‡20, 125.

15469 ■ Journal of Ultrasound in Medicine: Official Journal of the American Institute of Ultrasound in Medicine
American Institute of Ultrasound in Medicine
14750 Sweitzer Ln., Ste. 100
Laurel, MD 20707-5906
Phone: (301)498-4100
Fax: (301)498-4450
Free: 800-638-5352
Publisher's E-mail: admin@aium.org
Journal covering research and practical, basic and clinical aspects of ultrasound, advances in the field, appropriate techniques, and equipment modifications. **Freq:** Monthly. **Print Method:** Offset. **Trim Size:** 8.25 x 10.875. **Cols./Page:** 2. **Col. Width:** 17.8 picas. **Col. Depth:** 53 picas. **Key Personnel:** Flemming Forsberg, Editor; Wesley Lee, Editor; Levon N. Nazarian, MD, Editor-in-Chief. **ISSN:** 0278--4297 (print); **EISSN:** 1550--9613 (electronic). **Subscription Rates:** $573 Institutions online only; $315 U.S. AIUM Physician Member - Print + Online; $360 Canada and Mexico AIUM Physician Member - Print + Online; $390 Other countries AIUM Physician Member - Print + Online; $165 U.S. AIUM Nonphysician Member - Print + Online; $210 Canada and Mexico AIUM Nonphysician Member - Print + Online; $240 Other countries AIUM Nonphysician Member - Print + Online; $380 U.S. Non-Member Individual - Print + Online; $430 Canada and Mexico Non-Member Individual - Print + Online; $445 Other countries Non-Member Individual - Print + Online; $610 U.S. Institution - Print + Online; $660 Canada and Mexico Institution - Print + Online; $675 Other countries Institution - Print + Online. **URL:** http://www.jultrasoundmed.org. **Ad Rates:** 4C $3300, full page; 4C $2700, half page; BW $2500, full page; BW $1900, half page. **Remarks:** Accepts advertising. **Circ:** 10000.

15470 ■ Largo-Lanham Gazette
Post-Newsweek Media Inc.
c/o Alison Walker, Assistant Managing Editor
13501 Virginia Manor Rd.
Laurel, MD 20707
Community newspaper. **Freq:** Weekly (Thurs.). **Key Personnel:** Alison Walker, Assistant Managing Editor, phone: (240)473-7544, fax: (240)473-7501. **Subscription Rates:** Free. **URL:** http://www.gazette.net. **Remarks:** Accepts advertising. **Circ:** Free ■ **30033.**

15471 ■ Laurel Gazette
Post-Newsweek Media Inc.
c/o Jeff Lyles, Managing Editor
13501 Virginia Manor Rd.
Laurel, MD 20707
Community newspaper. **Freq:** Weekly (Thurs.). **Key Personnel:** Jeff Lyles, Managing Editor, phone: (240)473-7508, fax: (240)473-7501. **Subscription Rates:** Free. **URL:** http://www.gazette.net. **Remarks:** Accepts advertising. **Circ:** Free ■ **26783.**

15472 ■ Management and Organization Review
International Association for Chinese Management Research
c/o Xiaomeng Zhang, Executive Secretary
8636 Waterside Ct.
Laurel, MD 20723
Phone: (316)978-6788
Fax: (316)978-3349
Publisher's E-mail: info@iacmr.org
Journal publishing research on the management and organization of Chinese companies and multinational companies operating in China. **Freq:** 3/year March, July and November. **Key Personnel:** Anne Tsui, Editor-in-Chief. **ISSN:** 1740- 8776 (print); **EISSN:** 1740- 8784 (electronic). **Subscription Rates:** $102 Individuals print and online subscription; $693 Institutions print subscription; $797 Institutions print and online subscription; $693 Institutions online subscription; Included in membership. **URL:** http://www.iacmr.org/v2en/List.asp?navid=38. **Mailing address:** PO Box 88, Wichita, KS 67260. **Remarks:** Advertising not accepted. **Circ:** (Not Reported).

15473 ■ Proceedings of the Entomological Society of Washington
Entomological Society of Washington
c/o Abigail Kula, Treasurer
8305 Mary Lee Ln.
Laurel, MD 20723
Phone: (240)425-2198
Scientific journal for publication of original research on insects. **Freq:** Quarterly January, April, July, and October. **Print Method:** Offset. **Trim Size:** 6 7/8 x 10. **Cols./Page:** 2. **Col. Width:** 31 1/2 nonpareils. **Col. Depth:** 112 agate lines. **Key Personnel:** Matthew L. Buffington, Editor; Robert R. Kula, Board Member. **ISSN:** 0013--8797 (print). **Subscription Rates:** Included in membership. **URL:** http://www.entsocwash.org/default.asp?Action=Show_Proceedings. **Remarks:** Advertising accepted; rates available upon request. **Circ:** ‡800.

15474 ■ Ultrasound in Medicine & Biology
World Federation for Ultrasound in Medicine and Biology
14750 Sweitzer Ln., Ste. 100
Laurel, MD 20707-5906
Phone: (301)498-4100
Fax: (301)498-4450
Publisher's E-mail: t.reller@elsevier.com
Journal publishing original contributions on significant advances in clinical diagnostic, interventional and therapeutic applications, new and improved clinical techniques, the physics, engineering and technology of ultrasound in medicine and biology, and the interactions between ultrasound and biological materials, including bioeffects. **Freq:** Monthly. **Key Personnel:** Christy K. Holland, Editor-in-Chief; Denis N. White, Editor, Founder; Rose M. Randolph, Managing Editor. **ISSN:** 0301-5629 (print). **Subscription Rates:** $523 Individuals print and online; $554 Students Canada and other Countries (print and online; $508 Individuals; $2272 Institutions; $538 Other countries; $2389 Institutions, other countries; $2389 Institutions, Canada. **URL:** http://www.umbjournal.org; http://www.journals.elsevier.com/ultrasound-in-medicine-and-biology. **Mailing address:** PO Box 945, New York, NY 10159-0945. **Remarks:** Accepts advertising. **Circ:** (Not Reported).

15475 ■ The Upper Marlboro Star
Post-Newsweek Media Inc.
c/o Alison Walker, Assistant Managing Editor
13501 Virginia Manor Rd.
Laurel, MD 20707
Community newspaper. **Freq:** Weekly (Thurs.). **Key Personnel:** Alison Walker, Assistant Managing Editor, phone: (240)473-7544, fax: (240)473-7501. **Subscription Rates:** Free. **URL:** http://www.gazette.net. **Remarks:** Accepts advertising. **Circ:** Free ■ **14821.**

15476 ■ Wheaton Gazette
Post-Newsweek Media Inc.
c/o Sophie Yarborough, Ed.
13501 Virginia Manor Rd.
Laurel, MD 20707
Community newspaper. **Freq:** Weekly (Wed.). **Key Personnel:** Sophie Yarborough, Editor, phone: (240)473-7561, fax: (240)473-7501. **Subscription Rates:** Free. **URL:** http://www.gazette.net/. **Remarks:** Accepts advertising. **Circ:** Free ■ **25301.**

15477 ■ WILC-AM - 900
13499 Baltimore Blvd., Ste. 200
Laurel, MD 20707
Phone: (301)419-2122
Fax: (301)419-2409
Format: Hispanic; Adult Contemporary. **Networks:** Independent. **Owner:** ZGS Broadcasting Holdings, Inc., at above address. **Founded:** 1985. **Formerly:** WLMD-AM. **Operating Hours:** 6 a.m.-10 p.m. **Key Personnel:** Wendy Thomson, Gen. Mgr., wthompson@zgsgroup.com. **Wattage:** 1,900. **Ad Rates:** $15-30 for 15 seconds; $25-48 for 30 seconds; $30-60 for 60 seconds. **URL:** http://www.radioviva900.com/reglas.php.

Circulation: ★ = AAM; △ or • = BPA; ♦ = CAC; ❑ = VAC; ⊕ = PO Statement; ‡ = Publisher's Report; Boldface figures = sworn; Light figures = estimated.

LAVALE

15478 ■ WWPN-FM - 101.1
PO Box 3382
Lavale, MD 21502-3382
Format: Contemporary Christian. **Ad Rates:** Advertising accepted; rates available upon request. **URL:** http://www.spirit101.com.

LINTHICUM

15479 ■ AUA News
American Urological Association
1000 Corporate Blvd.
Linthicum, MD 21090
Phone: (410)689-3700
Fax: (410)689-3800
Free: 866-746-4282
Publisher's E-mail: aua@auanet.org
Professional Journal covering clinical and socioeconomic issues regarding urology for urologists. **Freq:** Monthly. **Trim Size:** 10 7/8 x 15. **Key Personnel:** Robert C. Flanigan, MD, Editor. **ISSN:** 1088--7350 (print). **Subscription Rates:** $110 Nonmembers; $135 Institutions nonmembers; Included in membership. **URL:** http://www.auanet.org/education/aua-news.cfm. **Ad Rates:** GLR $225; BW $4,140; 4C $2,475. **Remarks:** Accepts advertising. **Circ:** Paid 14749, Free 1021, Paid ‡15235, 13000.

LINTHICUM HEIGHTS

15480 ■ Journal of Urology
Elsevier
American Urological Association
Publications Department
1000 Corporate Blvd.
Linthicum Heights, MD 21090
Phone: (410)689-3922
Fax: (410)689-3800
Publication E-mail: publications@auanet.org
Medical journal. **Freq:** Monthly. **Print Method:** Web. **Trim Size:** 8 1/8 x 10 7/8. **Key Personnel:** William D. Steers, MD, Editor-in-Chief; Badrinath Konety, Associate Editor; Deborah R. Erickson, Associate Editor. **ISSN:** 0022--5347 (print). **Subscription Rates:** $1092 Individuals print + online; $1462 Other countries print + online; $870 Students, other countries print + online; $465 Students print + online; $1158 Individuals print + online (/year); $1550 Other countries print and online; $493 Students print and online; $922 Students, other countries print and online. **URL:** http://www.jurology.com; http://www.auanet.org/education/journal-of-urology.cfm; http://www.journals.elsevier.com/the-journal-of-urology. **Ad Rates:** BW $150; 4C $1,960. **Remarks:** Accepts advertising. **Circ:** 16700, Non-paid ‡423.

LOCH LYNN HEIGHTS

15481 ■ WMSG-AM - 1050
407 Lothian St.
Loch Lynn Heights, MD 21550
Phone: (301)334-1100
Fax: (301)334-9400
Email: office@wkhj.com
Format: Country; Gospel. **Networks:** ABC. **Founded:** 1963. **Operating Hours**: 6 a.m.-11 p.m. **Wattage**: 1,000 Day; 075 Night. **Ad Rates:** $2.75-5.70 for 10 seconds; $4.05-8.15 for 30 seconds; $5.50-11.35 for 60 seconds. $2.75-$5.70 Tennessee; $4.05-$8.15 for 30 seconds; $5.50-$11.35 for 60 seconds. Combined advertising rates available with. **URL:** http://www.wmsg.com.

LUTHERVILLE

15482 ■ True Grit
Jack Russell Terrier Club of America
PO Box 4527
Lutherville, MD 21094-4527
Phone: (410)561-3655
Fax: (410)560-2563
Magazine covering topics like agility, behavior, breeding, conformation, grooming, go-to-ground, hunting and hunting stories, JRTCA history, Kennel Club recognition, obedience, racing, rescue, trailing and various veterinary and medical articles. **Freq:** Quarterly. **Subscription Rates:** Included in membership. **URL:** http://www.therealjackrussell.com/jrtca/truegrit.php. **Remarks:** Advertising accepted; rates available upon request. **Circ:** 5000.

MECHANICSVILLE

15483 ■ Kilt and Harp
Scottish Harp Society of America
PO Box 681
Mechanicsville, MD 20659
Publisher's E-mail: president@shsa.org
Freq: Quarterly. **Subscription Rates:** included in membership dues. **URL:** http://www.shsa.org/2014/03/16/spring-kilt-and-harp-is-here. **Remarks:** Accepts advertising. **Circ:** 250.

15484 ■ WMDM-AM - 1690
28095 Three Notch Rd., Ste. 2-B
Mechanicsville, MD 20659
Format: Oldies. **Simulcasts:** WMDM-FM 97.7. **Networks:** ABC; Westwood One Radio; Talknet. **Founded:** 1953. **Formerly**: WPTX-AM. **Operating Hours**: Continuous. **Key Personnel:** Alisa Riley, Gen. Mgr., alisa_riley@hotmail.com; Tomas Cuellar, Operations Mgr., tc@olg.com; Stacy Reynolds, Dir. of Programs, stacy@olg.com. **Wattage**: 5,000 Day; 1,000 Night.

15485 ■ WMDM-FM - 97.7
28095 Three Notch Rd., No. 2B
Mechanicsville, MD 20659
Format: Contemporary Hit Radio (CHR). **Networks:** ABC; Westwood One Radio. **Owner:** Somar Communications Inc., at above address. **Founded:** 1976. **Operating Hours**: Continuous. **Wattage**: 3,000. **Ad Rates:** Noncommercial. **URL:** http://www.977therocket.com.

15486 ■ WSMD-FM - 98.3
28095 Three Notch Rd., Ste. 2-B
Mechanicsville, MD 20659
Phone: (301)884-5550
Fax: (301)884-0280
Free: 800-782-7983
Format: Classic Rock; News; Sports. **Networks:** ABC. **Founded:** 1988. **Formerly**: WQMR-FM. **Operating Hours**: Continuous. **Wattage**: 3,000 ERP. **Ad Rates:** Noncommercial. WKIK-FM, WMDM-FM, WPTX-AM. **URL:** http://www.star983.com.

MONTGOMERY

15487 ■ Comcast Cable
50 W Gude Dr.
Rockville, MD 20850-1150
Phone: (301)424-4400
Free: 800-266-2278
Email: we_can_help@comcast.com
Founded: 1984. **Formerly**: Cable TV of Montgomery. **Key Personnel:** David A. Scott, COO, President. **Cities Served:** Montgomery and Prince Georges counties. **URL:** http://www.comcast.com.

MOUNTAIN LAKE PARK

Garrett Co. Garrett Co. (NW). 3 m S of Oakland. Residential.

15488 ■ WKHJ-FM - 104.5
PO Box 2337
Mountain Lake Park, MD 21550
Phone: (301)334-4272
Fax: (301)334-2152
Format: Adult Contemporary. **Networks:** CNN Radio. **Owner:** Southern Highlands Inc., at above address. **Founded:** 1990. **Operating Hours**: Continuous. **ADI:** Pittsburgh, PA. **Key Personnel:** Terry King, Contact; Terry King, Contact. **Wattage**: 6,000. **Ad Rates:** Noncommercial. **URL:** http://www.1045khj.com.

MYERSVILLE

15489 ■ JADARA: A Journal for Professionals Networking for Excellence in Service Delivery for Individuals Who Are Deaf or Hard of Hearing
American Deafness and Rehabilitation Association
PO Box 480
Myersville, MD 21773-0480
Fax: (301)293-8969
Publisher's E-mail: adaraorgn@comcast.net
Journal focusing on original research, news, and resources on deafness and rehabilitation.Publishes manuscripts containing original scholarly research or practice in the field of deafness with school, community, clinical, social service, or other related applications. **Freq:** 3/year. **Trim Size:** 6 x 10. **Key Personnel:** Charlene Crump, President; Caroline M. Kobek Pezzarossi, Editor-in-Chief. **ISSN:** 0899--9228 (print). **Alt. Formats:** PDF. **URL:** http://www.adara.org/index.php/publications. **Remarks:** Advertising accepted; rates available upon request. **Circ:** Paid 1200.

NEW MARKET

15490 ■ Applied Spectroscopy
Society for Applied Spectroscopy
168 W Main St., No. 300
New Market, MD 21774
Phone: (301)694-8122
Fax: (301)694-6860
Publisher's E-mail: sasadmin@s-a-s.org
Magazine covering spectroscopic emission and absorption. **Freq:** Monthly. **Print Method:** Letterpress and offset. **Cols./Page:** 2. **Col. Width:** 32 nonpareils. **Col. Depth:** 119 agate lines. **Key Personnel:** Michael Blades, Editor-in-Chief; Peter Griffiths, Editor; Bonnie A. Saylor, Executive Director. **ISSN:** 0003--7028 (print); **EISSN:** 1943--3530 (electronic). **Subscription Rates:** £919 Institutions e-access; £721 Institutions print only; £736 Institutions print & online; £66 Institutions single print issue. **URL:** http://www.s-a-s.org/4DCGI/cms/review.html?Action=CMS_Document&DocID=28&MenuKey=journal; http://uk.sagepub.com/en-gb/asi/applied-spectroscopy/journal202492. **Ad Rates:** BW $700; 4C $1375. **Remarks:** Accepts advertising. **Circ:** ‡6500.

NEW WINDSOR

15491 ■ Airborne Quarterly
American Airborne Association
10301 McKinstry Mill Rd.
New Windsor, MD 21776-7903
Phone: (410)775-7733
Fax: (410)775-7760
Free: 888-567-2927
Publisher's E-mail: eagle187@hughes.net
Freq: Quarterly. **URL:** http://www.americanairborneassn.org/ABQuarterly.htm. **Remarks:** Advertising not accepted. **Circ:** (Not Reported).

OAKLAND

Garrett Co. Garrett Co. (NW). 50 m SW of Cumberland. Summer & winter resorts. Maple sugar and syrup, wood products, lens manufactured. Feed, lumber, flour mills. Dairy, truck, grain farms. Potatoes, buckwheat, corn & green beans.

15492 ■ The Republican
Sincell Publishing Company Inc.
108 S Second St.
Oakland, MD 21550-1520
Phone: (301)334-3963
Fax: (301)334-5904
Publication E-mail: newsroom@therepublicannews.com
Community newspaper. **Founded:** Mar. 04, 1877. **Freq:** Weekly (Thurs.). **Print Method:** Offset. **Cols./Page:** 8. **Col. Width:** 22 nonpareils. **Col. Depth:** 294 agate lines. **Key Personnel:** Donald W. Sincell, Editor, Manager; Lisa Rook, Manager, Advertising. **Subscription Rates:** $37.10 Individuals inside Maryland, print; $44.10 Individuals inside Maryland, print and online; $21.20 Individuals inside Maryland, 3 months; $35 Individuals outside Maryland, print; $25 Individuals outside Maryland, 6 months, print; $24 Individuals outside Maryland, 3 months, print; $42 Individuals Armed Forces Personnel, out of state, print and online. **URL:** http://www.therepublicannews.com/. **Mailing address:** PO Box 326, Oakland, MD 21550-0326. **Ad Rates:** GLR $4.10; BW $579.60; 4C $929.60; PCI $4.25. **Remarks:** Accepts advertising. **Circ:** Paid ★10210.

15493 ■ WGPT-TV - 36
11767 Owings Mills Blvd.
Owings Mills, MD 21117
Phone: (410)356-5600
Free: 800-627-6788
Email: comments@mpt.org
Format: Public TV. **Simulcasts:** WMPB, WMPT, WCPB, WWPB, WFPT. **Networks:** Public Broadcasting Service (PBS). **Owner:** Maryland Public Television, 11767 Ow-

ings Mills Blvd., Owings Mills, MD 21117, Ph: (410)356-5600, Fax: (410)581-6579, Free: 800-223-3678. **Operating Hours**: Continuous. **Key Personnel:** Steven Schupak, Sr. VP; Larry D. Unger, CEO, President. **Wattage**: 250,000. **Ad Rates:** Noncommercial. **URL:** http://www.mpt.org/home.

15494 ■ WXIE-FM - 92.3
PO Box 271
Oakland, MD 21550
Phone: (301)334-1100
Fax: (301)334-5800
Format: Classic Rock. **Networks:** ABC. **Owner:** Oakland Media Group, Oakland, MD. **Founded:** 1966. **Operating Hours:** Continuous. **Key Personnel:** James Butscher, Contact. **Wattage:** 990. **Ad Rates:** $2.75-5.70 for 10 seconds; $4.05-8.15 for 30 seconds; $5.50-11.35 for 60 seconds. $2.75-$5.70 Tennessee; $4.05-$8.15 for 30 seconds; $5.50-$11.35 for 60 seconds. Combined advertising rates available with.

OCEAN CITY

Worcester Co. Worchester Co. (SE). on Atlantic Ocean, 23 m E of Salisbury. Summer beach resort. Light industries. Commercial and sport fishing.

15495 ■ Oceana Magazine
Oceana Magazine
12505 Coastal Hwy., Ste. 201
Ocean City, MD 21842
Phone: (410)250-5700
Online guide for lodgings, restaurants, entertainment, fishing reports, discount coupons and more at Ocean City, Maryland and the nearby Delaware resorts. **Freq:** Quarterly. **Alt. Formats:** PDF. **URL:** http://oceana.org. **Remarks:** Accepts advertising. **Circ:** Non-paid ‡27000.

15496 ■ WEES-FM - 107.9
Gold Coast Mall
Ocean City, MD 21842
Phone: (410)289-5882
Format: Educational; Oldies. **Operating Hours:** Continuous. **Ad Rates:** Noncommercial; underwriting available. **URL:** http://www.wees.org.

15497 ■ WOCM-FM - 98.1
117 W 49th St.
Ocean City, MD 21842
Phone: (410)723-3683
Email: sales@ocean98.com
Format: Adult Album Alternative. **Owner:** Irie Radio, Inc., at above address. **Founded:** 1993. **Formerly**: WSBL-FM. **Operating Hours**: Continuous. **ADI**: Salisbury, MD. **Wattage**: 3,000. **Ad Rates:** $5-10 for 30 seconds; $8-12 for 60 seconds. **URL:** http://www.ocean98.com.

15498 ■ WQMR-FM - 101.1
7200 Coastal Hwy., Ste. 101
Ocean City, MD 21843
Phone: (410)524-6862
Fax: (410)524-6808
Free: 800-524-5596
Format: Talk; News; Information. **Operating Hours**: Continuous. **Key Personnel:** Jack Gillen, Gen. Mgr., President, jack@wqmr.com; Kevin Bresnahan, Bus. Mgr., VP, kevin@wqmr.com; Dave Kettinger, Sales Mgr., dave@wqmr.com; Heather Renee Shingleton, Account Exec., Dir. of Production, News Dir., heather@wqmr.com; Paulo McKenzie, Account Exec., paulo@wqmr.com. **Ad Rates:** Advertising accepted; rates available upon request. **Mailing address:** PO Box 856, Ocean City, MD 21843.

15499 ■ WSUX-FM - 98.3
11500 Coastal Hwy.
Ocean City, MD 21842
Phone: (302)629-6636
Fax: (302)846-9898
Owner: South Jersey Radio, at above address, Ph: (906)653-1400. **Founded:** 1971. **Wattage**: 3,000. **Ad Rates:** $10-24 for 30 seconds; $14-28 for 60 seconds.

OWINGS MILLS

Baltimore Co. (N). 3m N of Pikesville. Light industrial.

15500 ■ American Journal of Physical Medicine and Rehabilitation
Association of Academic Physiatrists
10461 Mill Run Cir., Ste. 730
Owings Mills, MD 21117
Phone: (410)654-1000
Fax: (410)654-1001
Journal containing scholarly research in physical medicine and rehabilitation within an academic environment. **Freq:** Monthly. **ISSN:** 0894--9115 (print). **Subscription Rates:** Included in membership. **URL:** http://www.physiatry.org/?page=AJPMR_journal. **Remarks:** Accepts advertising. **Circ:** (Not Reported).

WCPB-TV - See Salisbury
WFPT-TV - See Frederick
WGPT-TV - See Oakland
WMPB-TV - See Baltimore
WMPT-TV - See Annapolis
WWPB-TV - See Hagerstown

OXON HILL

15501 ■ Journal of Child Nutrition & Management
School Nutrition Association
120 Waterfront St., Ste. 300
National Harbor
Oxon Hill, MD 20745-1142
Phone: (301)686-3100
Fax: (301)686-3115
Free: 800-877-8822
Publisher's E-mail: servicecenter@schoolnutrition.org
Journal covering school food service facilities, food quality and production, management, program evaluation, and nutrition standards. **Freq:** Semiannual fall and spring. **Key Personnel:** Patricia Montague; Carolyn Bedhar, PhD, Editor. **ISSN:** 0160--6271 (print). **URL:** http://schoolnutrition.org/JCNM. **Remarks:** Advertising accepted; rates available upon request. **Circ:** (Not Reported).

15502 ■ School Nutrition
School Nutrition Association
120 Waterfront St., Ste. 300
National Harbor
Oxon Hill, MD 20745-1142
Phone: (301)686-3100
Fax: (301)686-3115
Free: 800-877-8822
Publisher's E-mail: servicecenter@schoolnutrition.org
Freq: 11/year combined issue in June/July. **ISSN:** 0160--6271 (print). **Subscription Rates:** Included in membership; $90 Nonmembers. **URL:** http://schoolnutrition.org/snmagazine. **Ad Rates:** 4C $6811. **Remarks:** Accepts advertising. **Circ:** (Not Reported).

15503 ■ School Nutrition: Positive Identification
School Nutrition Association
120 Waterfront St., Ste. 300
National Harbor
Oxon Hill, MD 20745-1142
Phone: (301)686-3100
Fax: (301)686-3115
Free: 800-877-8822
Publisher's E-mail: servicecenter@schoolnutrition.org
Magazine for school foodservice operators. **Freq:** 11/year. **Print Method:** Offset. **Trim Size:** 8 3/8 x 10 7/8. **Cols./Page:** 3 and 2. **Col. Width:** 26 and 41 nonpareils. **Col. Depth:** 140 agate lines. **Key Personnel:** Patricia Fitzgerald, Editor. **ISSN:** 1075--3885 (print). **Subscription Rates:** $90 Individuals. **URL:** http://www.schoolnutrition.org/SNMagazine. **Formerly**: School Food Service Journal; School Foodservice & Nutrition. **Ad Rates:** 4C $6811. **Remarks:** Accepts advertising. **Circ:** Combined 55000.

15504 ■ WWGB-AM - 1030
6710 Oxon Hill Rd., Ste. 100, Indian Head
Oxon Hill, MD 20745
Phone: (301)749-1444
Fax: (301)749-7244
Email: radio@wwgb.com
Format: Religious. **URL:** http://www.wwgb.com.

POCOMOKE CITY

Worcester Co. Worcester Co. (SE). On Pocomoke River, 21 m S of Salisbury. Tourism, Shopping and docking areas. Manufactures flour, feed, canned goods, crates, baskets, fertilizer, foundry products, lumber. Pine and oak timber. Diversified farming. Poultry, potatoes, corn, beans, tomatoes.

15505 ■ WKHW-FM - 106.5
20200 DuPont Blvd.
Georgetown, DE 19947
Phone: (302)856-2567
Fax: (302)856-7633
Format: Classic Rock. **Owner:** Great Scott Broadcasting, at above address, VA, Ph: (610)326-4000. **URL:** http://www.greatscottbroadcasting.com/eeo.php.

POTOMAC

Montgomery Co. (WC). 5 m S. of Rockville. Residential.

15506 ■ WCTN-AM
100-25 Queens Blvd.
Forest Hills, NY 11375
Phone: (718)335-3333
Fax: (301)299-5301
Email: wctn@wctn.net
Format: Religious. **Networks:** USA Radio; Moody Broadcasting; Ambassador Inspirational Radio. **Owner:** Win Radio Broadcasting Corp., at above address. **Founded:** 1973. **Key Personnel:** Dr. Richard S. Yoon, President. **Wattage**: 2,500 Day; 350 Night. **Ad Rates:** $20-35 for 30 seconds; $25-40 for 60 seconds.

PRINCE FREDERICK

Calvert Co. (S). On Patuxent River, 41 m SE of Washington, DC. Tourism. Fish, crab industries. Agriculture. Tobacco, corn.

15507 ■ The Calvert County Recorder
Southern Maryland Newspapers
PO Box 485
Prince Frederick, MD 20678
Phone: (301)855-1029
Fax: (410)535-1214
Community newspaper. **Freq:** Semiweekly (Wed. and Fri.). **Print Method:** Offset. **Trim Size:** 13 x 21. **Cols./Page:** 6. **Col. Width:** 28 nonpareils. **Col. Depth:** 294 agate lines. **Subscription Rates:** $12.60 Individuals home delivery and online - 90 days; $19.99 Individuals online only - 1 year. **URL:** http://www.somdnews.com/recorder. **Ad Rates:** GLR $6.22; BW $783.12; 4C $1,283.12; PCI $6.22. **Remarks:** Accepts advertising. **Circ:** Paid ♦**10015**, Non-paid ♦**233**, Combined ♦**10924**.

15508 ■ WMJS-FM - 102.1
3950 Hallowing Point
Box 547
Prince Frederick, MD 20678
Format: Soft Rock. **Founded:** 1971. **Operating Hours**: Continuous. **Key Personnel:** Ada Gollub, Sales Mgr.; Melvin Gollub, Gen. Mgr. **Wattage**: 082 ERP. **Ad Rates:** Noncommercial. $10-13 for 30 seconds; $17.80-32 for 60 seconds. Underwriting available. **URL:** http://www.wmjs.org/.

PRINCE GEORGES

15509 ■ Prince George's Sentinel
Chesapeake Publishing Corp.
9458 Lanham-Severn Rd.
Seabrook, MD 20706
Phone: (301)306-9500
Publication E-mail: editor-pg@thesentinel.com
Community newspaper. Includes legal ads and notices. **Freq:** Weekly (Thurs.). **Print Method:** Offset. **Trim Size:** 11 x 15. **Cols./Page:** 5. **Col. Width:** 22 nonpareils. **Col. Depth:** 190 agate lines. **Key Personnel:** Lynn G. Kapiloff, Chief Executive Officer. **Subscription Rates:** Free; $10.50 By mail. **URL:** http://www.thesentinel.com/pgs/. **Formerly**: Prince Georges Post-Sentinel. **Ad Rates:** BW $861; PCI $13. **Remarks:** Accepts advertising. **Circ:** (Not Reported).

PRINCESS ANNE

Somerset Co. Somerset Co. (SE). On Manokin River, 12 m S of Salisbury. University of Maryland-Eastern Shore. Fruit and vegetable canneries. Manufactures needles, shirts, lumber, modular homes, flour, feed. Nurseries. Agriculture. Poultry. Potatoes, strawberries, tomatoes, beans.

Circulation: ★ = AAM; △ or • = BPA; ♦ = CAC; ❑ = VAC; ⊕ = PO Statement; ‡ = Publisher's Report; Boldface figures = sworn; Light figures = estimated.

15510 ■ WESM-FM - 91.3
Backbone Rd.
Princess Anne, MD 21853
Phone: (410)651-8001
Fax: (410)651-8005
Free: 866-651-8001
Email: wesm913@umes.edu
Format: Jazz; Blues; Gospel. **Networks:** Public Radio International (PRI); National Public Radio (NPR). **Owner:** University of Maryland Eastern Shore, Office of Academic Affairs John T. Williams Hall 11868 Academic Oval, Princess Anne, MD 21853-1299, Ph: (410)651-2200. **Founded:** 1987. **Operating Hours:** Continuous. **Key Personnel:** Stephen Williams, Gen. Mgr. **Wattage:** 50,000. **Ad Rates:** Noncommercial; underwriting available. **URL:** http://www.wesm913.org.

15511 ■ WOLC-FM - 102.5
PO Box 130
Princess Anne, MD 21853
Phone: (410)543-9652
Fax: (410)651-9652
Free: 877-569-9652
Format: Religious. **Networks:** Ambassador Inspirational Radio; SkyLight Satellite; Sun Radio. **Owner:** Maranantha and Associates Inc., 7716 Capron Ct., Lorton, VA 22079, Ph: (703)944-5483. **Founded:** 1976. **Operating Hours:** Continuous; 40% network, 60% local. **Key Personnel:** Dave Wilson, Coord.; Ron Hall, Sales Mgr.; Debbie Byrd, Gen. Mgr., dbyrd@wolc.org; Rodney Baylous, Dir. of Programs, rbaylous@wolc.org. **Local Programs:** *Delmarva Headlines*, Monday Tuesday Wednesday Thursday Friday, 7:03 a.m. - 7:15 a.m.; 8:02 a.m. - 8:25 a.m.; 5:02 p.m. -5:15 a.m.; *Our Daily Bread*, Monday Tuesday Wednesday Thursday Friday 6:25 a.m. - 6:45 a.m.; *SRN News*, Monday Tuesday Wednesday Thursday Friday, 6:00 a.m. - 6:25 a.m.; 7:00 a.m.; 7:02 a.m. - 7:03 a.m.; 8:00 a.m. - 8:02 a.m.; 9:00 a.m. - 9:02; 11:00 a.m. - 11:30 a.m.; 12:00 p.m. - 12:02 p.m.; 2:00 p.m. - 2:04 p.m.; 3:00 p.m. - 3:30 p.m.; 4:00 p.m. - 4:02 p.m.; 5:00 p.m. - 5:02 p.m. ; *Insights*, Monday Tuesday Wednesday Thursday Friday 7:44 a.m. - 7:45 a.m.; *The Point*, Monday Tuesday Wednesday Thursday Friday 8:25 a.m. - 8:45; *Family News in Focus*, Monday Tuesday Wednesday Thursday Friday 9:02 a.m. - 9:05 a.m.; *The Dobson Family Minute*, Monday Tuesday Wednesday Thursday Friday 4:30 p.m. - 5:00 p.m.; *Peace With God*, Sunday 1:00 p.m.; *Joy in the Morning*, Monday Tuesday Wednesday Thursday Friday 6:00 a.m. - 9:00 a.m.; *Joy Ride*, Monday Tuesday Wednesday Thursday Sunday 3:00 p.m. - 6:30 p.m. **Wattage:** 50,000. **Ad Rates:** Noncommercial. **URL:** http://www.wolc.org.

PRINCETON

15512 ■ WQPM-AM - 1300
15395 91st Ave., N
Maple Grove, MN 55369
Phone: (763)389-1300
Format: Contemporary Country. **Networks:** ABC. **Owner:** Milestone Radio L.L.C., 14443 Armstrong Blvd NW, Ramsey, MN 55303, Ph: (763)420-3598. **Founded:** 1967. **Formerly:** WKPM-AM. **Operating Hours:** Continuous; 2% network, 98% local. **Key Personnel:** Neil Freeman, Dir. of Programs. **Wattage:** 1,000. **Ad Rates:** Advertising accepted; rates available upon request.

RIDERWOOD

15513 ■ Orienteering North America
Orienteering USA
c/o Glen Schorr, Executive Director
PO Box 505
Riderwood, MD 21139
Phone: (410)802-1125
Publisher's E-mail: gjs@orienteeringusa.org
Freq: Bimonthly. **ISSN:** 0886- 1080 (print). **Subscription Rates:** Included in membership; $27 Other countries 6 issues + 1 digital issue first-class mail only; $20 U.S. 6 issues + 1 digital issue; $23 Canada 6 issues + 1 digital issue first-class mail only; $40 U.S. 12 issues + 2 digital issues; $46 Canada 12 issues + 2 digital issues first-class mail only; $54 Other countries 12 issues + 2 digital issues first-class mail only. **URL:** http://www.us.orienteering.org/ona-magazine. **Remarks:** Accepts advertising. **Circ:** 2300.

ROCKVILLE

Montgomery Co. Montgomery Co. (WC). 17 m N of Washington, D.C. Residential & commercial. Research and development center.

15514 ■ Adventure Tales
Wildside Press L.L.C.
9710 Traville Gateway Dr., Ste. 234
Rockville, MD 20850
Phone: (301)762-1305
Fax: (301)762-1306
Magazine focusing on adventure-oriented fiction. **Freq:** Quarterly. **Subscription Rates:** $35 Individuals. **URL:** http://www.wildsidebooks.com/Adventure-Tales_c_312.html. **Circ:** (Not Reported).

15515 ■ Alpha Omegan: Journal of Alpha Omega International Dental Fraternity
Alpha Omega International Dental Fraternity
50 W Edmonston Dr., No. 206
Rockville, MD 20852
Phone: (301)738-6400
Fax: (301)738-6403
Free: 877-368-6326
Publisher's E-mail: headquarters@ao.org
Journal covering scientific issues of interest to the fraternity of dentist. **Freq:** Semiannual. **ISSN:** 0002--6417 (print). **Subscription Rates:** Included in membership. **URL:** http://www.ao.org/ourpublications#alphaomegan. **Circ:** (Not Reported).

15516 ■ American Heritage
American Heritage
416 Hungerford Dr., Ste. 216
Rockville, MD 20850-4127
Phone: (240)453-0900
Free: 800-777-1222
Publisher's E-mail: mail@americanheritage.com
Magazine on the political, cultural, and social aspects of American history. **Freq:** Bimonthly. **Print Method:** Web offset. **Trim Size:** 8 1/2 x 10 7/8. **Cols./Page:** 3. **Col. Width:** 13.5 picas. **Col. Depth:** 55.5 picas. **Key Personnel:** Robert Jenkins, Director, Sales; John F. Ross, Executive Editor. **ISSN:** 0002--8738 (print). **Subscription Rates:** $17.95 Individuals; $29.95 Two years; $23.95 Canada; $35.95 Two years. **URL:** http://www.americanheritage.com/. **Remarks:** Accepts advertising. **Circ:** Paid ★**344797**.

15517 ■ American Journal of Audiology
American Speech-Language-Hearing Association
2200 Research Blvd.
Rockville, MD 20850-3289
Phone: (301)296-5700
Fax: (301)296-8580
Free: 800-638-8255
Publisher's E-mail: actioncenter@asha.org
Professional journal covering issues in the field of speech and hearing. **Freq:** Semiannual June and December. **Key Personnel:** Dr. Sheila R. Pratt, Editor; Harvey Abrams, Reviewer; Dana Boatman, Associate Editor. **ISSN:** 1059-0889 (print). **Subscription Rates:** Free online access to members; $49 Nonmembers online only; $137 Nonmembers institutions; online only. **URL:** http://aja.asha.org. **Remarks:** Accepts advertising. **Circ:** 8670.

15518 ■ American Journal of Speech Language Pathology
American Speech-Language-Hearing Association
2200 Research Blvd.
Rockville, MD 20850-3289
Phone: (301)296-5700
Fax: (301)296-8580
Free: 800-638-8255
Publisher's E-mail: actioncenter@asha.org
Professional journal covering issues in speech, language, and hearing. **Freq:** Quarterly. **Print Method:** Offset. **Trim Size:** 8 1/8 x 10 7/8. **Key Personnel:** Dr. Krista Wilkinson, PhD, Editor; Diane L. Kendall, PhD, Associate Editor. **ISSN:** 1058--0360 (print); **EISSN:** 1558--9110 (electronic). **Subscription Rates:** $300 Institutions domestic; $360 Institutions foreign; $122 Nonmembers domestic; $146 Nonmembers foreign; $73 Members domestic; $83 Members foreign. **URL:** http://ajslp.pubs.asha.org. **Remarks:** Advertising accepted; rates available upon request. **Circ:** 37715.

15519 ■ American Medical Writers Association Journal
American Medical Writers Association
30 W Gude Dr., Ste. 525
Rockville, MD 20850-4347
Phone: (240)238-0940
Fax: (301)294-9006
Publisher's E-mail: amwa@amwa.org
Journal covering issues for medical writers. **Freq:** Quarterly. **ISSN:** 0090--046X (print). **Subscription Rates:** $75 Nonmembers. **URL:** http://www.amwa.org/journal. **Formerly:** AMWA Journal. **Ad Rates:** BW $750; 4C $1,250. **Remarks:** Advertising accepted; rates available upon request. **Circ:** (Not Reported).

15520 ■ ASBMB Today
American Society for Biochemistry and Molecular Biology
11200 Rockville Pke., Ste. 302
Rockville, MD 20852-3110
Phone: (240)283-6600
Fax: (301)881-2080
Publisher's E-mail: asbmb@asbmb.org
Freq: Monthly. **URL:** http://www.asbmb.org/asbmbtoday. **Remarks:** Accepts advertising. **Circ:** (Not Reported).

15521 ■ The ASHA Leader
American Speech-Language-Hearing Association
2200 Research Blvd.
Rockville, MD 20850-3289
Phone: (301)296-5700
Fax: (301)296-8580
Free: 800-638-8255
Publisher's E-mail: actioncenter@asha.org
Newsmagazine for and about speech-language pathologists, audiologists, and speech, language, and hearing scientists. **Founded:** Sept. 1959. **Freq:** Semiannual (June/July combined). **Key Personnel:** Carol Polovoy, Managing Editor; Bridget Murray Law, Managing Editor. **Subscription Rates:** $103 Individuals domestic; $136 Individuals other countries; $154 Institutions domestic; $193 Institutions foreign. **URL:** http://www.asha.org/publications/archive/magazine.htm. **Formerly:** Asha. **Ad Rates:** BW $5,015; 4C $6,015. **Remarks:** Accepts advertising. **Circ:** (Not Reported).

15522 ■ Aviation Today: For Corporate, Commercial and Private Aircraft Owners and Operators
Access Intelligence L.L.C.
4 Choke Cherry Rd., 2nd Fl.
Rockville, MD 20850
Phone: (301)354-2000
Fax: (301)309-3847
Free: 800-777-5006
Publisher's E-mail: info@accessintel.com
Aviation magazine for aircraft owners/operators. **Freq:** Monthly. **Print Method:** Offset. **Trim Size:** 8 1/8 x 10 7/8. **Cols./Page:** 3. **Col. Width:** 26 nonpareils. **Col. Depth:** 140 agate lines. **Key Personnel:** Paul Leighton; Joe Rasone, Publisher. **ISSN:** 0828-9344 (print). **Subscription Rates:** Free to qualified subscribers. **URL:** http://www.aviationtoday.com. **Formerly:** Aviation Trade. **Mailing address:** PO Box 9187, Gaithersburg, MD 20898. **Ad Rates:** BW $1,655; 4C $2,694; PCI $45. **Remarks:** Accepts advertising. **Circ:** Controlled ‡17000, Paid ‡1000.

15523 ■ Avionics Magazine
Access Intelligence L.L.C.
4 Choke Cherry Rd., 2nd Fl.
Rockville, MD 20850
Phone: (301)354-2000
Fax: (301)309-3847
Free: 800-777-5006
Publication E-mail: av@omeda.com
Magazine about aviation electronics for commercial and military aircraft. **Freq:** Monthly. **Print Method:** Offset. **Trim Size:** 8 1/8 x 10 7/8. **Cols./Page:** 3. **Col. Width:** 26 nonpareils. **Col. Depth:** 126 agate lines. **Key Personnel:** Tish Drake, Publisher; Emily Feliz, Editor, phone: (301)354-1820. **ISSN:** 0273--7639 (print). **Subscription Rates:** Free to qualified subscribers. **URL:** http://www.aviationtoday.com/av. **Mailing address:** PO Box 9187, Gaithersburg, MD 20898. **Remarks:** Accepts classified advertising. **Circ:** △**19000**.

15524 ■ AWT Analyst
Association of Water Technologies
9707 Key West Ave., Ste. 100
Rockville, MD 20850
Phone: (301)740-1421
Fax: (301)990-9771
Publisher's E-mail: awt@awt.org
Magazine featuring new technologies in the areas of cooling, boiler and wastewater treatment. **Freq:** Quarterly. **Subscription Rates:** included in membership dues; $100 for nonmembers in U.S.; $125 for nonmembers in Canada, Mexico; $200 for nonmembers in other countries. **URL:** http://www.awt.org/resources/analyst.cfm. **Remarks:** Accepts advertising. **Circ:** 3,000.

15525 ■ Biophysical Journal
Biophysical Society
11400 Rockville Pke., Ste. 800
Rockville, MD 20852
Phone: (240)290-5600
Fax: (240)290-5555
Publisher's E-mail: society@biophysics.org
Journal focusing on biophysics. **Freq:** Semimonthly. **Print Method:** Offset. **Trim Size:** 8 1/2 x 11. **Cols./Page:** 2. **Col. Width:** 39 nonpareils. **Col. Depth:** 124 agate lines. **ISSN:** 0006--3495 (print). **URL:** http://www.biophysics.org/Meetings/Exhibits/AdvertisingOpportunities/BiophysicalJournal/tabid/2263/Default.aspx. **Ad Rates:** BW $1,100; 4C $1,600. **Remarks:** Accepts advertising. **Circ:** (Not Reported).

15526 ■ CableFAX
Access Intelligence L.L.C.
4 Choke Cherry Rd., 2nd Fl.
Rockville, MD 20850
Phone: (301)354-2000
Fax: (301)309-3847
Free: 800-777-5006
Publisher's E-mail: info@accessintel.com
Publication focusing on enhancing efficiency of cable operations through good business practices. **Freq:** Bimonthly. **Key Personnel:** Mike Grebb, Executive Editor; Amy Abbey, Associate Publisher; Joann Fato, Manager, Production. **URL:** http://www.cable360.net/cablefaxmag/. **Formerly**: CableWORLD. **Mailing address:** PO Box 9187, Gaithersburg, MD 20898. **Remarks:** Accepts advertising. **Circ:** △**12000**.

15527 ■ Challenge Magazine
Disabled Sports USA
451 Hungerford Dr., Ste. 100
Rockville, MD 20850
Phone: (301)217-0960
Fax: (301)217-0968
Publisher's E-mail: information@dsusa.org
Magazine providing information on sports for people with physical disabilities.Provides adaptive sports information to adults and children with disabilities, including those who are visually impared, amputees, spinal cord injured, and those who have multiple sclerosis, head injury, cerebral palsy, autism and other related intellectual disabilities. **Freq:** 3/yr. **Key Personnel:** Kirk Bauer, Executive Director, phone: (301)217-9838; Huayra Gomez-Garcia, Executive Assistant. **ISSN:** 1940-526X (print). **Subscription Rates:** $40. **URL:** http://www.disabledsportsusa.org/resources/challenge-magazine/. **Formed by the merger of:** Handicapped Sport Report. **Remarks:** Accepts advertising. **Circ:** Paid 30000.

15528 ■ Chemical Engineering
Access Intelligence L.L.C.
4 Choke Cherry Rd., 2nd Fl.
Rockville, MD 20850
Phone: (301)354-2000
Fax: (301)309-3847
Free: 800-777-5006
Publisher's E-mail: info@accessintel.com
Chemical process industries magazine. **Founded:** 1902. **Freq:** Monthly. **Print Method:** Offset. **Trim Size:** 7 7/8 x 10 3/4. **Cols./Page:** 3. **Col. Width:** 27 nonpareils. **Col. Depth:** 140 agate lines. **Key Personnel:** Rebekkah J. Marshall, Editor-in-Chief, phone: (310)401-1971; Dorothy Lozowski, Managing Editor, phone: (212)621-4678. **Subscription Rates:** $109.97 Individuals print; $136.97 Canada; $239 Other countries. **URL:** http://www.chemengonline.com/. **Mailing address:** PO Box 9187, Gaithersburg, MD 20898. **Ad Rates:** BW $10,540; 4C $2,400. **Remarks:** Accepts advertising. **Circ:** △**63100**.

15529 ■ Chemical Week
Access Intelligence L.L.C.
4 Choke Cherry Rd., 2nd Fl.
Rockville, MD 20850
Phone: (301)354-2000
Fax: (301)309-3847
Free: 800-777-5006
Publisher's E-mail: info@accessintel.com
Chemical process industries magazine. **Founded:** 1914. **Freq:** Weekly (Wed.). **Print Method:** Offset. **Cols./Page:** 3. **Col. Width:** 25 nonpareils. **Col. Depth:** 154 agate lines. **Key Personnel:** Lyn Tattum, Publisher; Robert Westervelt, Editor-in-Chief. **Subscription Rates:** $299.97 Individuals print; $353.97 Canada print; $715 Other countries print; $299.97 Other countries digital only. **URL:** http://www.chemweek.com/home/. **Mailing address:** PO Box 9187, Gaithersburg, MD 20898. **Ad Rates:** BW $10,193; 4C $13,862; PCI $220. **Remarks:** Advertising accepted; rates available upon request. **Circ:** (Not Reported).

15530 ■ Civil War Chronicles
American Heritage
416 Hungerford Dr., Ste. 216
Rockville, MD 20850-4127
Phone: (240)453-0900
Free: 800-777-1222
Publisher's E-mail: mail@americanheritage.com
Magazine chronicling the Civil War. **Freq:** Quarterly. **Key Personnel:** Richard Snow, Editor; Malcolm S. Forbes, Jr., Publisher. **URL:** http://www.americanheritage.com/CivilWar. **Circ:** (Not Reported).

15531 ■ Clinical Endocrinology News
Quadrant Healthcom
5635 Fishers Ln., Ste. 6000
Rockville, MD 20852
Publisher's E-mail: stephen.stoneburn@qhc.com
Newspaper containing news and commentary about clinical development in the field of clinical endocrinology. **Freq:** Monthly. **Key Personnel:** Mary Jo M. Dales, MD, Executive Director. **Subscription Rates:** $131 U.S. 1 year; $246 U.S. 2 years; $353 U.S. 3 years; $211 Canada and Mexico 1 year; $389 Canada and Mexico 2 years; $587 Canada and Mexico 3 years; $239 Other countries 1 year; $461 Other countries 2 years; $676 Other countries 3 years; $39 Institutions Student/Resident. **URL:** http://www.clinicalendocrinologynews.com. **Remarks:** Accepts advertising. **Circ:** △**13929**.

15532 ■ Clinical Neurology News
International Medical News Group
5635 Fishers Ln., Ste. 6000
Rockville, MD 20852
Phone: (240)221-2400
Newspaper for neurology specialists. **Freq:** Monthly. **Key Personnel:** Alicia Ault, Reporter; Renee Matthews, Senior Editor; Alan J. Imhoff, President; Lorinda Bullock, Associate Editor; Richard Franki, Associate Editor; Jay C. Cherniak, Associate Editor; Lori Buckner Farmer, Senior Editor. **URL:** http://www.clinicalneurologynews.com. **Remarks:** Accepts classified advertising. **Circ:** Combined △**15044**.

15533 ■ Clinical Psychiatry News
International Medical News Group
5635 Fishers Ln., Ste. 6000
Rockville, MD 20852
Free: 877-524-9337
Publication E-mail: cpnews@elsevier.com
Medical and psychiatry tabloid. **Freq:** Monthly. **Print Method:** Offset. **Trim Size:** 11 1/4 x 14 3/8. **Cols./Page:** 4. **Col. Width:** 14 picas. **Col. Depth:** 13 1/4 inches. **Key Personnel:** Denise Fulton, Executive Editor; Alan J. Imhoff, President; Gina Henderson, Senior Editor. **ISSN:** 0270--6644 (print). **Subscription Rates:** $109 Individuals; $173 Other countries. **URL:** http://journals.elsevierhealth.com/periodicals/cpnews. **Ad Rates:** BW $6,350; 4C $8,315. **Remarks:** Accepts advertising. **Circ:** Non-paid △**37345**.

15534 ■ Contemporary Issues in Communication Science and Disorders
National Student Speech Language Hearing Association
2200 Research Blvd., No. 322
Rockville, MD 20850-3289
Phone: (301)296-5700
Fax: (301)296-8580
Free: 800-498-2071
Publisher's E-mail: nsslha@asha.org
Journal containing topics pertaining to the processes and disorders of speech, language, and hearing and to the diagnosis and treatment of such disorders, as well as articles on educational and professional issues in the discipline. **Freq:** Semiannual. **ISSN:** 0736--0312 (print). **Alt. Formats:** PDF. **URL:** http://www.asha.org/Publications/cicsd. **Remarks:** Accepts advertising. **Circ:** (Not Reported).

15535 ■ Dermatology News™
International Medical News Group
5635 Fishers Ln., Ste. 6000
Rockville, MD 20852
Publication E-mail: sknews@elsevier.com
Dermatology/allergy tabloid. **Freq:** Monthly. **Print Method:** Offset. **Trim Size:** 11 1/4 x 14 3/8. **Cols./Page:** 4. **Col. Width:** 14 picas. **Col. Depth:** 13 1/4 inches. **Key Personnel:** Neil S. Goldberg, Advisor; Leslie S. Baumann, MD, Advisor; David E. Cohen, MD, Advisor; Suzanne M. Connolly, MD, Advisor; Adelaide A. Hebert, Advisor; Richard G. Glogau, MD, Advisor; Amy Pfeiffer, Senior Editor; Mary Jo M. Dales, Editor-in-Chief. **Subscription Rates:** $109 Individuals; $173 Other countries. **URL:** http://www.edermatologynews.com. **Formerly**: Skin & Allergy News: News and Views that Matter to Dermatology. **Ad Rates:** BW $2760; 4C $6530. **Remarks:** Accepts advertising. **Circ:** Controlled △**13344**.

15536 ■ Direct
Access Intelligence L.L.C.
4 Choke Cherry Rd., 2nd Fl.
Rockville, MD 20850
Phone: (301)354-2000
Fax: (301)309-3847
Free: 800-777-5006
Publisher's E-mail: corporatecustomerservice@penton.com
Trade magazine covering marketing for direct marketing practitioners. **Founded:** 1988. **Freq:** 16/yr. **URL:** http://chiefmarketer.com/direct-marketing. **Remarks:** Accepts advertising. **Circ:** ‡46537.

15537 ■ DS/USA Challenge
Disabled Sports USA
451 Hungerford Dr., Ste. 100
Rockville, MD 20850
Phone: (301)217-0960
Fax: (301)217-0968
Publisher's E-mail: information@dsusa.org
Freq: 3/year. **ISSN:** 1940--526X (print). **Subscription Rates:** Free to qualified subscribers. **Alt. Formats:** PDF. **URL:** http://www.disabledsportsusa.org/resources/challenge-magazine. **Remarks:** Advertising not accepted. **Circ:** 22000.

15538 ■ Family Practice News
International Medical News Group
5635 Fishers Ln., Ste. 6000
Rockville, MD 20852
Free: 877-524-9337
Publication E-mail: fpnews@frontlinemedcom.com
Family physician medical tabloid. **Freq:** 24/yr. **Print Method:** Offset. **Trim Size:** 11 1/4 x 14 3/8. **Cols./Page:** 4. **Col. Width:** 14 picas. **Col. Depth:** 13 1/4 inches. **Key Personnel:** Mary Jo Dales, Contact; Denise Fulton, Executive Editor; Alan J. Imhoff, President, Chief Executive Officer. **ISSN:** 0300--7073 (print). **Subscription Rates:** $169 U.S.; $249 Canada and Mexico; $308 Other countries surface mail; $396 Other countries air mail; $352 Institutions; $426 Institutions, Canada and Mexico; $494 Institutions, other countries; $49 Students; $28 Single issue current; $36 Single issue back issues; $36 Canada and Mexico current; $41 Canada and Mexico back issues; $41 Other countries current; $45 Other countries back issues. **URL:** http://www.familypracticenews.com. **Ad Rates:** BW $11,995; 4C $14,590. **Remarks:** Accepts advertising. **Circ:** Non-paid △**82147**.

15539 ■ Groundwork
Landscape Contractors Association of Maryland, District of Columbia and Virginia
9707 Key W Ave., Ste. 100
Rockville, MD 20850-3992
Phone: (301)948-0810

Circulation: ★ = AAM; △ or • = BPA; ♦ = CAC; ❑ = VAC; ⊕ = PO Statement; ‡ = Publisher's Report; Boldface figures = sworn; Light figures = estimated.

Fax: (301)990-9771
Publisher's E-mail: lca@mgmtsol.com
Magazine containing publications meant for only members of the Landscape Contractors Association of Maryland, District of Columbia and Virginia. **Freq:** Monthly. **URL:** http://www.lcamddcva.org/about/sponsoropp.cfm. **Remarks:** Accepts advertising. **Circ:** (Not Reported).

15540 ■ Hospitalist News
Quadrant Healthcom
5635 Fishers Ln., Ste. 6000
Rockville, MD 20852
Free: 877-524-9336
Publisher's E-mail: stephen.stoneburn@qhc.com
Newspaper featuring clinical, health policy, and regulatory news specifically tailored to the practice needs of hospitalists. **Freq:** Monthly. **Key Personnel:** Lori Buckner Farmer, Managing Editor. **Subscription Rates:** $120 U.S.; $120 Other countries. **URL:** http://www.ehospitalistnews.com; http://www.ehospitalistnews.com/news.html. **Remarks:** Accepts advertising. **Circ:** Non-paid △**20351**.

15541 ■ H.P. Lovecraft's Magazine of Horror
Wildside Press L.L.C.
9710 Traville Gateway Dr., Ste. 234
Rockville, MD 20850
Phone: (301)762-1305
Fax: (301)762-1306
Magazine covering the writings of H.P. Lovecraft. **Freq:** Quarterly. **Key Personnel:** John Gregory Betancourt, Publisher. **ISSN:** 1552--8642 (print). **Subscription Rates:** varies. **URL:** http://wildsidepress.com/h-p-lovecrafts-magazine-of-horror. **Circ:** (Not Reported).

15542 ■ IEEE Circuits and Devices
Institute of Electrical and Electronics Engineers
c/o Dr. Ronald Waynant, Ed.-in-Ch.
12725 Twinbrook Pkwy, Rm. 267
Rockville, MD 20857
Phone: (301)827-4688
Fax: (301)827-4677
Publisher's E-mail: society-info@ieee.org
Publication featuring information on electro-optics, PC components and programs for engineers, and application oriented articles. **Freq:** Bimonthly. **Print Method:** Web Offset. **Trim Size:** 7 7/8 x 10 3/4. **Key Personnel:** Dr. Ronald Waynant, Editor-in-Chief; Susan Schneiderman, Manager, Business Development, phone: (732)562-3946, fax: (732)981-1855. **ISSN:** 8755--3996 (print). **URL:** http://ieeexplore.ieee.org/xpl/RecentIssue.jsp?punumber=101. **Remarks:** Advertising accepted; rates available upon request. **Circ:** (Not Reported).

15543 ■ The IHS Primary Care Provider
U.S. Department of Health and Human Services Indian Health Service
Reyes Bldg.
801 Thompson Ave., Ste. 400
Rockville, MD 20852-1627
Phone: (301)443-6394
Fax: (301)443-4794
Journal for health care professionals, physicians, nurses, pharmacists, dentists, and dietitians. **Freq:** Monthly. **Key Personnel:** John F. Saari, MD, Editor. **Subscription Rates:** Included in membership. **URL:** http://www.ihs.gov/provider. **Remarks:** Advertising not accepted. **Circ:** 8000.

15544 ■ In-Motion
Access Intelligence L.L.C.
4 Choke Cherry Rd., 2nd Fl.
Rockville, MD 20850
Phone: (301)354-2000
Fax: (301)309-3847
Free: 800-777-5006
Publisher's E-mail: info@accessintel.com
Magazine covering information on talent, technology, and services of film and video production. **Founded:** Aug. 02, 1995. **Key Personnel:** Nic Paget-Clarke, Editor, Publisher; Roberto Flores, Editor; Alice Lovelace, Editor. **URL:** http://www.inmotionmagazine.com. **Mailing address:** PO Box 9187, Gaithersburg, MD 20898. **Remarks:** Accepts advertising. **Circ:** (Not Reported).

15545 ■ In Vivo
Elsevier Business Intelligence
5635 Fishers Ln., Ste. 6000
Rockville, MD 20852
Phone: (240)221-4500
Fax: (240)221-4400
Free: 800-332-2181
Publisher's E-mail: fdc.customer.service@fdcreports.com
Publication covering the global health care market. Covers company strategy, marketplace trends, industry events, deal making, and management issues. **Freq:** Monthly except July/August. **Trim Size:** 8.5 x 11. **Key Personnel:** Nancy Dvorin, Managing Editor. **ISSN:** 0733-1398 (print). **Subscription Rates:** $1905 Individuals online. **URL:** http://www.elsevierbi.com/publications/in-vivo. **Ad Rates:** BW $6,500; 4C $6,500. **Remarks:** Accepts advertising. **Circ:** Paid ‡10000.

15546 ■ Inside Laboratory Management
AOAC International
2275 Research Blvd., Ste. 300
Rockville, MD 20850-3250
Phone: (301)924-7077
Fax: (301)924-7089
Free: 800-379-2622
Publisher's E-mail: aoac@aoac.org
Professional magazine covering analytical laboratory management. **Freq:** Bimonthly. **Print Method:** Web offset. **Trim Size:** 8 1/2 x 11. **Key Personnel:** Tien Milor, Managing Editor. **ISSN:** 1092--2059 (print). **URL:** http://www.aoac.org/imis15_prod/AOAC/Publications/Inside_Laboratory_Management__ILM_/AOAC_Member/Publications/ILM/AOAC_ILM_CCO.aspx. **Remarks:** Accepts advertising. **Circ:** (Not Reported).

15547 ■ Interactive Learning Environments
Routledge
c/o Dr. Joseph Psotka, Ed.
US Army Research Institute
1436 Fallsmead Way
Rockville, MD 20854-5535
Publisher's E-mail: book.orders@tandf.co.uk
Peer-reviewed journal publishing articles on all aspects of the design and use of interactive learning environments. **Freq:** 8/year. **Key Personnel:** Dr. Joseph Psotka, Editor; Dr. S.L. Greener, Editor. **ISSN:** 1049--4820 (print); **EISSN:** 1744--5191 (electronic). **Subscription Rates:** $400 Individuals print; $1155 Institutions online; $1320 Institutions print and online. **URL:** http://www.tandfonline.com/toc/nile20/current. **Remarks:** Advertising accepted; rates available upon request. **Circ:** (Not Reported).

15548 ■ Internal Medicine News
International Medical News Group
5635 Fishers Ln., Ste. 6100
Rockville, MD 20852
Phone: (240)221-2400
Publication E-mail: imnews@elsevier.com
Publication covering clinical developments for practicing internists. **Freq:** Semimonthly. **Key Personnel:** Denise Fulton, Executive Editor; Alan J. Imhoff, President; Terry Rudd, Managing Editor. **Subscription Rates:** $174 Individuals; $317 Other countries. **URL:** http://www.internalmedicinenews.com. **Ad Rates:** BW $5,805; 4C $7,565. **Remarks:** Accepts advertising. **Circ:** Paid △**106644**.

15549 ■ Journal of AOAC International: An International Journal of Analytical Sciences
AOAC International
2275 Research Blvd., Ste. 300
Rockville, MD 20850-3250
Phone: (301)924-7077
Fax: (301)924-7089
Free: 800-379-2622
Publisher's E-mail: aoac@aoac.org
Peer-reviewed journal on Analytical chemistry and microbiology. **Freq:** Bimonthly. **Print Method:** Offset. **Trim Size:** 8 1/4 x 11. **Cols./Page:** 2. **Col. Width:** 40 nonpareils. **Col. Depth:** 139 agate lines. **Key Personnel:** Catherine Wattenberg, Editor; Robert Rathbone, Director. **ISSN:** 1060--3271 (print); **EISSN:** 1944--7922 (electronic). **Subscription Rates:** $470 Individuals member, within North America; $570 Individuals member, outside North America; $690 Individuals nonmember, within North America; $810 Individuals nonmember, outside North America; $500 Institutions member, within North America; $630 Institutions member, outside North America; $750 Institutions nonmember, within North America; $870 Institutions nonmember, outside North America. **URL:** http://www.aoac.org/imis15_prod/AOAC/Publications/Journal_Of_AOAC/AOAC_Member/Publications/Journal_of_AOAC/The_Journal_of_AOAC.aspx. **Formerly:** Journal of the Association of Official Analytical Chemists. **Remarks:** Accepts advertising. **Circ:** (Not Reported).

15550 ■ The Journal of Biological Chemistry
American Society for Biochemistry and Molecular Biology
11200 Rockville Pke., Ste. 302
Rockville, MD 20852-3110
Phone: (240)283-6600
Fax: (301)881-2080
Publisher's E-mail: asbmb@asbmb.org
Biochemistry journal. **Freq:** Weekly. **Print Method:** Web press. **Trim Size:** 8 3/8 x 10 7/8. **Cols./Page:** 2. **Col. Width:** 32 nonpareils. **Col. Depth:** 119 agate lines. **Key Personnel:** Guengerich F. Peter, Editor-in-Chief; Herbert Tabor, Editor. **ISSN:** 0021--9258 (print); **EISSN:** 1083--351X (electronic). **Subscription Rates:** Included in membership online access. **URL:** http://www.jbc.org; http://www.jbc.org/content/current. **Ad Rates:** BW $1525; 4C $2620. **Remarks:** Accepts advertising. **Circ:** ‡3300, 7000.

15551 ■ Journal of Compensation and Benefits
Thomson Reuters (Legal) Inc.
1455 Research Blvd.
Rockville, MD 20850
Phone: (301)545-4000
Free: 800-874-4337
Magazine offering practical guidance on compensation and employee benefits issues. **Freq:** Bimonthly. **Print Method:** Offset. **Trim Size:** 7 3/4 x 10 7/8. **Cols./Page:** 2. **Col. Width:** 18.5 picas. **Col. Depth:** 125 agate lines. **Key Personnel:** Jeffrey D. Mamorsky, Editor. **ISSN:** 0893--780X (print). **Subscription Rates:** $972 Individuals. **URL:** http://legalsolutions.thomsonreuters.com/law-products/Treatises/Journal-of-Compensation-and-Benefits/p/100000474. **Remarks:** Accepts advertising. **Circ:** Paid 2816, Non-paid 1509.

15552 ■ Journal of Speech, Language, and Hearing Research
American Speech-Language-Hearing Association
2200 Research Blvd.
Rockville, MD 20850-3289
Phone: (301)296-5700
Fax: (301)296-8580
Free: 800-638-8255
Publisher's E-mail: actioncenter@asha.org
Journal covering research in language, speech and hearing. **Freq:** Bimonthly. **Print Method:** Offset. **Trim Size:** 8 1/8 x 10 7/8. **Key Personnel:** Pam Leppin, Advertising Representative, phone: (301)296-8683; Nancy Tye-Murray, Dr., Editor. **ISSN:** 1092--4388 (print); **EISSN:** 1558--9102 (electronic). **Subscription Rates:** $727 Institutions print; $872 Institutions, other countries print; $599 Institutions online ; $212 Individuals online. **URL:** http://jslhr.pubs.asha.org. **Remarks:** Accepts advertising. **Circ:** ‡17475.

15553 ■ Journal of Vision
Association for Research in Vision and Ophthalmology
1801 Rockville Pke., Ste. 400
Rockville, MD 20852-5622
Phone: (240)221-2900
Fax: (240)221-0370
Publisher's E-mail: arvo@arvo.org
Peer-reviewed journal offers articles concerning visual function in humans and other organisms. **Freq:** Continuous. **Key Personnel:** Denis G. Pelli, Associate Editor; Dennis M. Levi, OD, PhD, Editor-in-Chief. **ISSN:** 1534--7362 (print). **Subscription Rates:** Free. **URL:** http://www.journalofvision.org. **Remarks:** Advertising not accepted. **Circ:** (Not Reported).

15554 ■ Language, Speech, and Hearing Services in Schools
American Speech-Language-Hearing Association
2200 Research Blvd.
Rockville, MD 20850-3289
Phone: (301)296-5700
Fax: (301)296-8580
Free: 800-638-8255
Publisher's E-mail: actioncenter@asha.org
Journal pertaining to speech, hearing, and language services for children, particularly in schools. **Freq:** Quarterly. **Print Method:** Offset. **Trim Size:** 8 1/8 x 10 7/8. **Cols./Page:** 2. **Col. Width:** 20 picas. **Col. Depth:**

55 picas. **Key Personnel:** Ann Packman, Associate Editor; C. Melanie Schuele, Editor. **ISSN:** 0161--1461 (print); **EISSN:** 1558--9129 (electronic). **Subscription Rates:** $300 Institutions; $360 Institutions, other countries; $122 Nonmembers; $146 Nonmembers other countries; $73 Members; $73 Members other members. **URL:** http://lshss.asha.org. **Remarks:** Accepts advertising. **Circ:** 52340.

15555 ■ Latvian Dimensions
American Latvian Association
400 Hurley Ave.
Rockville, MD 20850-3121
Phone: (301)340-1914
Publisher's E-mail: alainfo@alausa.org
Magazine featuring reviews of timely issues in Latvia and current affairs in the U.S. **Freq:** 3/year. **ISSN:** 1069--9595 (print). **Subscription Rates:** Included in membership. **Alt. Formats:** Download; PDF. **URL:** http://www.alausa.org/lv/citi/latvian-dimensions. **Ad Rates:** BW $500. **Remarks:** Accepts advertising. **Circ:** (Not Reported).

15556 ■ Molecular and Cellular Proteomics
American Society for Biochemistry and Molecular Biology
11200 Rockville Pke., Ste. 302
Rockville, MD 20852-3110
Phone: (240)283-6600
Fax: (301)881-2080
Publisher's E-mail: asbmb@asbmb.org
Journal that publishes research articles on molecular and cellular proteomics. **Freq:** Monthly. **Trim Size:** 8 3/8 x 10 7/8. **Key Personnel:** Dr. Ralph A. Bradshaw, Associate Editor; A. Burlingame, Associate Editor. **ISSN:** 1535--9476 (print); **EISSN:** 1535--9484 (electronic). **URL:** http://www.mcponline.org; http://www.asbmb.org/publications/molecularandcellularproteomics. **Ad Rates:** BW $1,010; 4C $2,105. **Remarks:** Accepts advertising. **Circ:** 800.

15557 ■ Montgomery County Story
Montgomery County Historical Society
111 W Montgomery Ave.
Rockville, MD 20850
Phone: (301)340-2825
Fax: (301)340-2871
Publisher's E-mail: info@montgomeryhistory.org
Journal containing articles on Montgomery county history. **Freq:** Semiannual. **Subscription Rates:** $3 Individuals; $5 By mail. **URL:** http://montgomeryhistory.org/montgomerycountystory. **Remarks:** Advertising not accepted. **Circ:** (Not Reported).

15558 ■ Ob.Gyn. News: Tabloid Covering Obstetrics and Gynecology Distributed to Ob/Gyns
International Medical News Group
5635 Fishers Ln., Ste. 6000
Rockville, MD 20852
Free: 800-480-4851
Publication E-mail: obnews@elsevier.com
Obstetrics and gynecology tabloid distributed to obstetricians and gynecologists. **Freq:** Semimonthly. **Print Method:** Offset. **Trim Size:** 11 1/4 x 14 3/8. **Cols./Page:** 4. **Col. Width:** 14 picas. **Col. Depth:** 13 1/4 inches. **Key Personnel:** Catherine Hackett, Senior Editor; Mary Jo M. Dales, Editor-in-Chief; Denise Fulton, Executive Editor; Alan J. Imhoff, President; Kathy Scarbeck, Executive Editor. **Subscription Rates:** $174 Individuals domestic; $217 Individuals Canada/Mexico; $317 Individuals other countries - surface mail; $408 Individuals other countries - air mail; $363 Institutions USA; $439 Institutions Canada/Mexico; $509 Institutions other countries; $50 Students; $29 Single issue current issue - US; $36 Single issue back issue - US. **URL:** http://www.obgynnews.com. **Ad Rates:** BW $8750; 4C $3635. **Remarks:** Advertising accepted; rates available upon request. **Circ:** Non-paid △**37824**, ‡42320.

15559 ■ Oceanography
The Oceanography Society
PO Box 1931
Rockville, MD 20849-1931
Phone: (301)251-7708
Fax: (301)251-7709
Publisher's E-mail: info@tos.org
Magazine publishing articles that chronicle all aspects of ocean science and its applications. **Freq:** Quarterly every March, June, September and December. **Key Personnel:** Ellen Kappel, Editor. **ISSN:** 1042-8275 (print). **Subscription Rates:** Included in membership; $195 Libraries per year; $40 Nonmembers. **Alt. Formats:** PDF. **URL:** http://tos.org/publications; http://tos.org/oceanography. **Remarks:** Accepts advertising. **Circ:** 1,500.

15560 ■ Oncology Issues
Association of Community Cancer Centers
11600 Nebel St., Ste. 201
Rockville, MD 20852-2557
Phone: (301)984-9496
Fax: (301)770-1949
Journal providing essential business information needed by oncology healthcare providers. **Freq:** Bimonthly. **Trim Size:** 8 x 10 3/4. **Key Personnel:** Amanda Patton, Associate Editor; Monique J. Marino, Managing Editor; Christian Downs, Editor-in-Chief. **Subscription Rates:** $59.99 Individuals /year; $159.99 Institutions /year; $159.99 Libraries /year. **URL:** http://www.accc-cancer.org/oncology_issues/. **Ad Rates:** $5410-5590, for full page; $4565-4730, for 1/2 page (h); $4565-4730, for 1/2 page (v); $3920-4035, for 1/4 page; $2705-2885, for full page; $1030-1860, for 1/2 page (h); $1860-2030, for 1/2 page (v); $1215-1320, for 1/4 page. 4C $, for full page4C $, for 1/2 page (h)4C $, for 1/2 page (v)4C $, for 1/4 pageBW $, for full pageBW $, for 1/2 page (h)BW $, for 1/2 page (v)BW $, for 1/4 pageBW $2,670; 4C $2,500. **Remarks:** Accepts advertising. **Circ:** 18,000, 16881.

15561 ■ Operations & Fulfillment
Access Intelligence L.L.C.
4 Choke Cherry Rd., 2nd Fl.
Rockville, MD 20850
Phone: (301)354-2000
Fax: (301)309-3847
Free: 800-777-5006
Publisher's E-mail: corporatecustomerservice@penton.com
Magazine for direct-to-customer operations and fulfillment professionals, covering receiving, warehousing, picking, packing, and shipping. **Freq:** 10/year. **Key Personnel:** Jim Tierney, Writer; Melissa Dowling, Editor-in-Chief, phone: (203)358-4221; Tim Parry, Writer, phone: (203)358-4161. **Alt. Formats:** Download. **URL:** http://multichannelmerchant.com/opsandfulfillment. **Remarks:** Accepts advertising. **Circ:** (Not Reported).

15562 ■ Optometric Education
Association of Schools and Colleges of Optometry
6110 Executive Blvd., Ste. 420
Rockville, MD 20852
Phone: (301)231-5944
Fax: (301)770-1828
Optometric journal. **Freq:** 3/year. **Print Method:** Offset. **Trim Size:** 8 1/2 x 11. **Cols./Page:** 3. **Col. Width:** 29 nonpareils. **Col. Depth:** 136 agate lines. **Key Personnel:** Aurora Denial, Editor; James Kundart, Editor; Elizabeth Hoppe, Secretary. **ISSN:** 1933--8880 (print). **Subscription Rates:** $30 Individuals; $40 Other countries. **URL:** http://journal.opted.org. **Formerly:** Journal of Optometric Education. **Ad Rates:** BW $725; 4C $1395. **Remarks:** Advertising accepted; rates available upon request. **Circ:** ‡2800.

15563 ■ Pediatric News
International Medical News Group
5635 Fishers Ln., Ste. 6000
Rockville, MD 20852
Free: 877-524-9337
Publication E-mail: rhnews@elsevier.com
Tabloid covering pediatric medicine and distributed to pediatricians. **Founded:** 1967. **Freq:** Monthly. **Print Method:** Offset. **Trim Size:** 11 1/4 x 14 3/8. **Cols./Page:** 4. **Col. Width:** 14 picas. **Col. Depth:** 13 1/4 inches. **Key Personnel:** Catherine Cooper Nellist, Managing Editor; Mary Jo M. Dales, Editor-in-Chief; Alan J. Imhoff, President, Chief Executive Officer; Kathy Scarbeck, Executive Editor; Amy Pfeiffer, Director, Communications. **Subscription Rates:** $109 Individuals; $173 Other countries. **URL:** http://www.epediatricnews.com. **Ad Rates:** BW $4,750; 4C $2,350. **Remarks:** Accepts advertising. **Circ:** Non-paid △**49994**.

15564 ■ Pharmacopeial Forum
United States Pharmacopeial Convention
12601 Twinbrook Pky.
Rockville, MD 20852-1790
Phone: (301)881-0666
Free: 800-227-8772
Publisher's E-mail: custsvc@usp.org
Journal on drug standards. **Freq:** Bimonthly. **Print Method:** Offset. **Trim Size:** 8 1/2 x 11. **Cols./Page:** 2 and 1. **Col. Width:** 38 and 76 nonpareils. **Col. Depth:** 136 agate lines. **ISSN:** 0363--4655 (print). **Subscription Rates:** $469 Individuals. **URL:** http://www.usp.org/products/PF. **Remarks:** Advertising not accepted. **Circ:** (Not Reported).

15565 ■ The Plant Cell
American Society of Plant Biologists
15501 Monona Dr.
Rockville, MD 20855-2768
Phone: (301)251-0560
Fax: (301)279-2996
Publisher's E-mail: info@aspb.org
Academic research journal reporting major advances in plant cellular and molecular biology. **Freq:** Monthly. **Print Method:** Sheet-fed, Letterpress. **Trim Size:** 8 3/8 x 10 7/8. **Cols./Page:** 2. **Col. Width:** 19 picas. **Col. Depth:** 51 picas. **Key Personnel:** Nancy A. Winchester, Director, Publications, phone: (301)296-0904; Cathie Martin, Editor-in-Chief, phone: (44)1603 452571, fax: (44)1603 456844; Patti Lockhart, Managing Editor, phone: (301)296-0908, fax: (301)296-0909; Susan Entwistle, Manager, Production, phone: (301)296-0906, fax: (301)309-9196; Annette Kessler, Manager, phone: (301)296-0910, fax: (301)279-2996; Nancy Eckardt, Senior Editor. **ISSN:** 1040--4651 (print). **Subscription Rates:** $215 Members print; $150 Students print; $450 Nonmembers. **Alt. Formats:** PDF. **URL:** http://www.plantcell.org; http://www.aspb.org/publications/aspb-journals. **Ad Rates:** BW $1430; 4C $2570. **Remarks:** Advertising accepted; rates available upon request. **Circ:** ‡1,600.

15566 ■ Regulatory Focus
Regulatory Affairs Professionals Society
5635 Fishers Ln., Ste. 550
Rockville, MD 20852
Phone: (301)770-2920
Fax: (301)841-7956
Publisher's E-mail: raps@raps.org
Freq: Monthly. **ISSN:** 1097- 2668 (print). **Subscription Rates:** Included in membership. **URL:** http://www.raps.org/focus-online.aspx. **Remarks:** Accepts advertising. **Circ:** 8,900.

15567 ■ Rheumatology News
Quadrant Healthcom
5635 Fishers Ln., Ste. 6000
Rockville, MD 20852
Free: 877-524-9336
Publication E-mail: rhnews@elsevier.com
Newspaper featuring news regarding the field of rheumatology. **Freq:** Monthly. **Key Personnel:** Sally Koch Kubetin, Senior Editor; Jeff Evans, Managing Editor. **Subscription Rates:** $135 U.S. 1 year; $246 U.S. 2 years; $353 U.S. 3 years; $211 Canada and Mexico 1 year; $389 Canada and Mexico 2 years; $587 Canada and Mexico 3 years; $239 Other countries 1 year; $461 Other countries 2 years; $676 Other countries 3 years; $39 Institutions Student/Resident. **URL:** http://www.rheumatologynews.com. **Remarks:** Accepts advertising. **Circ:** Non-paid △**8381**.

15568 ■ The Rose Sheet
Elsevier Business Intelligence
5635 Fishers Ln., Ste. 6000
Rockville, MD 20852
Phone: (240)221-4500
Fax: (240)221-4400
Free: 800-332-2181
Publication E-mail: roseeditor@fdcreports.com
Trade journal for executives in the toiletries, fragrance, cosmetic, and skin care industries. **Freq:** Weekly (Mon.). **Trim Size:** 8 1/2 x 11. **Cols./Page:** 1. **Key Personnel:** Ryan Nelson, Managing Editor, phone: (240)221-4416. **ISSN:** 0279--1110 (print). **Subscription Rates:** $2370 Individuals online access. **URL:** http://www.pharmamedtechbi.com/publications/the-rose-sheet. **Remarks:** Advertising accepted; rates available upon request. **Circ:** (Not Reported).

15569 ■ Rotor & Wing
Access Intelligence L.L.C.

Circulation: ★ = AAM; △ or • = BPA; ♦ = CAC; ❑ = VAC; ⊕ = PO Statement; ‡ = Publisher's Report; Boldface figures = sworn; Light figures = estimated.

4 Choke Cherry Rd., 2nd Fl.
Rockville, MD 20850
Phone: (301)354-2000
Fax: (301)309-3847
Free: 800-777-5006
Publisher's E-mail: info@accessintel.com
Magazine covering helicopters. **Freq:** Monthly. **Print Method:** Offset. **Trim Size:** 8 x 10 3/4. **Cols./Page:** 3. **Col. Width:** 27 nonpareils. **Col. Depth:** 140 agate lines. **ISSN:** 0191--6408 (print). **Subscription Rates:** $99 U.S. 1 year (print); $129 Canada 1 year (print); $149 Other countries 1 year (print); $188 U.S. 2 years (print); $228 Canada 2 years (print); $278 Other countries 2 years (print). **Online:** Access Intelligence L.L.C. Access Intelligence L.L.C. **URL:** http://www.aviationtoday.com/rw. **Mailing address:** PO Box 9187, Gaithersburg, MD 20898. **Ad Rates:** BW $8,650; 4C $1,765. **Remarks:** Accepts advertising. **Circ:** △**30000**.

15570 ■ Selenology
American Lunar Society
c/o Andrew Martin
722 Mapleton Rd.
Rockville, MD 20850
Freq: Quarterly. **Subscription Rates:** Included in membership; $15 Nonmembers /year. **URL:** http://eselenology.offworldventures.com. **Remarks:** Advertising not accepted. **Circ:** 200.

15571 ■ The Sentinel
Gazette Printing Company Inc.
22 W Jefferson St., Ste. 309
Rockville, MD 20850
Phone: (301)388-0788
Publisher's E-mail: info@gazettenews.com
Community newspaper. **Founded:** 1852. **Freq:** Weekly (Sat.). **Print Method:** Offset. **Cols./Page:** 5. **Col. Width:** 1 7/8 inches. **Col. Depth:** 16 inches. **USPS:** 676-110. **URL:** http://www.thesentinel.com/. **Ad Rates:** BW $416; 4C $666; SAU $12.94. **Remarks:** Accepts advertising. **Circ:** Free ‡13000.

15572 ■ Strange Magazine
Strange Magazine
11772 Parklawn Dr.
Rockville, MD 20852
Phone: (301)570-7561
Fax: (301)570-7562
Publication E-mail: strange1@strangemag.com
Consumer magazine covering strange phenomena. **Freq:** Semiannual. **Print Method:** Web offset. **Trim Size:** 8 3/16 x 10 11/16. **ISSN:** 0894--8968 (print). **Subscription Rates:** Free. **URL:** http://www.strangemag.com. **Remarks:** Accepts advertising. **Circ:** Combined 15500.

15573 ■ Surgery News
Elsevier Society News Group
5635 Fishers Ln., Ste. 6000
Rockville, MD 20852
Publisher's E-mail: postmaster@facs.org
Newspaper that provides coverage of clinical, regulatory, legislative, and financial aspects of surgery and medicine. **Freq:** Monthly. **Key Personnel:** Alan Imhoff, President, Publisher, phone: (973)290-8216; Mary Jo Dales, Executive Director, phone: (240)221-2470; Mark Branca, Director, phone: (973)290-8246, fax: (973)290-8250. **ISSN:** 1553--6785 (print). **Subscription Rates:** $199 Individuals; $230 Individuals. **URL:** http://www.esng-meded.com; http://www.acssurgerynews.com; http://www.esng-meded.com/surgerynews/index.php. **Remarks:** Accepts advertising. **Circ:** △**36000**.

15574 ■ Transportation Leader
Taxicab, Limousine & Paratransit Association
3200 Tower Oaks Blvd., Ste. 220
Rockville, MD 20852
Phone: (301)984-5700
Fax: (301)984-5703
Publisher's E-mail: info@tlpa.org
Magazine for owners and operators of taxicab, limousine, livery, van, and minibus fleets. Includes information on vehicles, marketing, public relations, legal issues, industry meetings and conventions, industry products and more. **Freq:** Quarterly. **Print Method:** Sheet-fed offset. **Trim Size:** 8 1/2 x 11. **ISSN:** 0040--0426 (print). **Subscription Rates:** $16 Individuals. **URL:** http://www.tlpa.org/Publications. **Formerly:** Taxicab Management; Taxi and Livery Management. **Ad Rates:** BW $1980. **Remarks:** Accepts advertising. **Circ:** ‡6000.

15575 ■ Via Satellite: The Leader in Global Satellite Coverage
Access Intelligence L.L.C.
4 Choke Cherry Rd., 2nd Fl.
Rockville, MD 20850
Phone: (301)354-2000
Fax: (301)309-3847
Free: 800-777-5006
Publisher's E-mail: info@accessintel.com
Communication satellite industry magazine. **Freq:** 13/yr. **Print Method:** Web. **Trim Size:** 7.875 x 10.750. **Cols./Page:** 3. **Col. Width:** 2 1/4 inches. **Col. Depth:** 9 3/4 inches. **Key Personnel:** Joe Rosone, Vice President; Julie Samuel, Director. **ISSN:** 1041--0643 (print). **Subscription Rates:** $89 Individuals; $99 Canada; $129 Other countries. **URL:** http://www.satellitetoday.com. **Mailing address:** PO Box 9187, Gaithersburg, MD 20898. **Ad Rates:** BW $9,815; 4C $10,565; PCI $60. **Remarks:** Accepts advertising. **Circ:** 30000.

15576 ■ Washington Jewish Week
Washington Jewish Week
11900 Parklawn Dr, Suite 300
Rockville, MD 20852
Phone: (301)230-2222
Publication E-mail: publisher@washingtonjewishweek.com
Jewish interests Newspaper. **Freq:** Weekly. **Print Method:** Offset. **Cols./Page:** 5. **Col. Width:** 27 nonpareils. **Col. Depth:** 200 agate lines. **Key Personnel:** Larry Fishbein, Publisher; Meredith Jacobs, Editor. **URL:** http://washingtonjewishweek.com. **Ad Rates:** GLR $37.80; BW $2,565; PCI $36.15. **Remarks:** Accepts advertising. **Circ:** ‡13000.

15577 ■ Weird Tales
Wildside Press L.L.C.
9710 Traville Gateway Dr., Ste. 234
Rockville, MD 20850
Phone: (301)762-1305
Fax: (301)762-1306
Magazine focusing on dark fantasy literature. **Key Personnel:** John Harlacher, Creative Director, Publisher; Marvin Kaye, Editor. **Subscription Rates:** $20 Individuals basic; $35 Individuals deluxe. **Alt. Formats:** E-book. **URL:** http://www.wildsidebooks.com/Weird-Tales-Magazine_c_236.html; http://weirdtalesmagazine.com. **Circ:** (Not Reported).

Comcast Cable - See Montgomery, MD

15578 ■ WASH-FM - 97.1
1801 Rockville Pke.
Rockville, MD 20852
Phone: (240)747-2700
Free: 866-927-4361
Format: Jazz. **Founded:** 1948. **Operating Hours:** Continuous. **ADI:** Washington, DC. **Key Personnel:** Aaron Hyland, Sales Mgr.; Bill Cahill, Dir. of Programs, billcahill@clearchannel.com; Kim Sauer, Promotions Dir., kim@hot995.com; Ivan Blank, Sales Mgr., ivanblank@clearchannel.com. **Wattage:** 23,500. **Ad Rates:** Advertising accepted; rates available upon request. **URL:** http://www.washfm.com/music/playlist.

15579 ■ WBIG-FM - 100.3
1801 Rockville Pke.
Rockville, MD 20852
Phone: (240)747-2700
Free: 800-493-1003
Format: Oldies. **Owner:** Chancellor Media Licensee Co., at above address. **Founded:** 1993. **Operating Hours:** Continuous. **ADI:** Washington, DC. **Key Personnel:** James Howard, Dir. of Programs; Aaron Hyland, Sales Mgr. **Wattage:** 36,000. **Ad Rates:** Noncommercial. **URL:** http://www.wbig.com.

15580 ■ WIHT-FM - 99.5
1801 Rockville Pke., 6th Fl.
Rockville, MD 20852
Phone: (240)747-2700
Free: 877-995-4681
Format: Top 40. **Owner:** iHeartMedia Inc., 200 E Basse Rd., San Antonio, TX 78209, Ph: (210)832-3314. **Founded:** 1960. **Formerly:** WGAY-FM; WJMO-FM. **Operating Hours:** Continuous. **ADI:** Baltimore, MD. **Key Personnel:** Toby Knapp, Asst. Dir., tk@hot995.com; Ken Roberts, Gen. Sales Mgr., kenroberts@clearchannel.com; Aaron Hyland, Sales Mgr., bethcohen@clearchannel.com. **Wattage:** 21,000. **Ad Rates:** Advertising accepted; rates available upon request. **URL:** http://www.hot995.com.

15581 ■ WLXE-AM - 1600
12216 Parklawn Dr.
Rockville, MD 20852
Format: Hispanic. **Owner:** Multicultural Radio Broadcasting Inc., 27 William St., 11th Fl., New York, NY 10005, Ph: (212)966-1059, Fax: (212)966-9580. **Key Personnel:** John Gabel, Contact, johng@mrbi.net.

15582 ■ WMZQ-FM - 98.7
1801 Rockville Pke., 5th Fl.
Rockville, MD 20852
Phone: (240)747-2700
Free: 800-505-0098
Format: Country. **Owner:** iHeartMedia Inc., 200 E Basse Rd., San Antonio, TX 78209, Ph: (210)832-3314. **Founded:** 1977. **Operating Hours:** Continuous. **Key Personnel:** Aaron Hyland, Dir. of Programs, Sales Mgr., megstevens@clearchannel.com. **Ad Rates:** Advertising accepted; rates available upon request. **URL:** http://www.wmzq.com.

15583 ■ WSPZ-AM
1801 Rockville Pke.
Rockville, MD 20852
Phone: (205)339-3700
Fax: (205)339-3704
Founded: 1936. **Key Personnel:** Matt Jones, Dir. of Programs.

15584 ■ WTEM-AM - 980
1801 Rockville Pke.
Rockville, MD 20852
Phone: (301)230-0980
Founded: 1946. **Formerly**: WGMS-AM. **Wattage**: 50,000 Day; 5,000 Night.

15585 ■ WWDC-FM - 101.1
1801 Rockville Pke.
Rockville, MD 20852
Phone: (240)747-2700
Format: Album-Oriented Rock (AOR). **Networks:** Independent. **Owner:** iHeartMedia Inc., 200 E Basse Rd., San Antonio, TX 78209, Ph: (210)832-3314. **Founded:** 1947. **Operating Hours:** Continuous. **Key Personnel:** Greg Roche, Music Dir., roche@dc101.com; James Howard, Prog. Dir., james@dc101.com. **Wattage**: 22,500. **Ad Rates:** Advertising accepted; rates available upon request. **URL:** http://www.dc101.com.

15586 ■ WWXT-FM - 92.7
1801 Rockville Pke., Ste. 401
Rockville, MD 20852
Phone: (301)230-3510
Format: Sports. **Owner:** Red Zebra Broadcasting, at above address. **Operating Hours**: Continuous. **URL:** http://www.espn980.com.

15587 ■ WXTR-AM
1801 Rockville Pke., Ste. 405
Rockville, MD 20852
Phone: (301)230-3500
Owner: Red Zebra Broadcasting Licensee, LLC, at above address. **Ad Rates:** Advertising accepted; rates available upon request.

SAINT MARYS CITY

15588 ■ WSMC-FM - 91.7
47645 College Dr.
Lower Charles Hall
Saint Marys City, MD 20686-3001
Phone: (240)895-2000
Format: Eclectic. **Networks:** Independent. **Owner:** St. Marys College of Maryland, 47645 College Dr., Saint Marys City, MD 20686-3001, Ph: (240)895-2000. **Founded:** 1975. **Formerly**: WSMC-AM. **Operating Hours**: 14 hours Daily. **Key Personnel:** Jim Guest, Gen. Mgr., ejguest@osprey.smcm.edu; Robyn Felmming, Dir. of Programs; Sarah Loff, Music Dir. **Wattage**: 010. **URL:** http://www.smcm.edu.

SALISBURY

Wicomico Co. Wicomico Co. (SE). On Wicomico River, 100 m S of Wilmington, Del. Salisbury State College. Wor-Wic Technical Community College. Manufactures printed computer forms, plastics, feeds, frozen foods, service station pumps and hoists, food processors. Industrial and commercial centers; retail and wholesale center.

15589 ■ The Daily Times
Delmarva Media Group
618 Beam St.
Salisbury, MD 21801
Phone: (410)749-7171
General newspaper. **Founded:** 1923. **Freq:** Daily. **Print Method:** Offset. **Cols./Page:** 6. **Col. Width:** 24 nonpareils. **Col. Depth:** 301 agate lines. **Key Personnel:** Greg Bassett, General Manager, Publisher, phone: (410)749-7171; Nikki Lavigne, Manager, Circulation; Robb Scott, Director, Advertising. **Subscription Rates:** $12.39 Individuals; $8.65 Individuals weekends (Thurs. - Sun.); $6.40 Individuals Wednesday and Sunday; $4.35 Individuals Sundays only. **URL:** http://www.delmarvanow.com/apps/pbcs.dll/frontpage. **Formerly:** The Daily News. **Remarks:** Accepts advertising. **Circ:** Mon.-Sat. ***25,984**, Sun. ***29931**.

15590 ■ Delaware Coast Press
Gannett Company Inc.
618 Beam St.
Salisbury, MD 21801
Phone: (410)749-7171
Community newspaper (tabloid). **Freq:** Weekly (Wed.). **Print Method:** Offset. **Cols./Page:** 5. **Col. Width:** 10 13/16 inches. **Col. Depth:** 13 inches. **Key Personnel:** James Fisher, Contact. **Subscription Rates:** $12.39 Individuals 7 days a week/month; $8.65 Individuals weekends/month; $6.40 Individuals Wednesday & Sunday/month; $4.35 Individuals Sunday only. **Ad Rates:** 4C $231; SAU $9; PCI $7.30. **Remarks:** Accepts advertising. **Circ:** Combined ♦**13889**.

15591 ■ The Flyer
Salisbury State University
CB 3183
Salisbury University
Salisbury, MD 21801
Phone: (410)543-6058
Fax: (410)677-5359
Collegiate newspaper. **Founded:** 1949. **Freq:** Weekly. **Print Method:** Offset. **Cols./Page:** 4. **Col. Depth:** 13 inches. **Key Personnel:** Sarah Lake, Editor-in-Chief; Sean Gossard, Editor; Megan McCarthy, Manager, Advertising, phone: (410)543-6192, fax: (410)677-5359. **Subscription Rates:** $10 Individuals semester. **URL:** http://www.thesuflyer.com/index.html. **Ad Rates:** BW $200. **Remarks:** Accepts advertising. **Circ:** Free ‡2,000.

15592 ■ Literature Film Quarterly
Salisbury University
1101 Camden Ave.
Salisbury, MD 21801
Phone: (410)543-6000
Publication E-mail: litfilmquart@salisbury.edu
Magazine covering film adaptations of literature. **Freq:** Quarterly. **Print Method:** Offset. **Trim Size:** 6 x 9. **Cols./Page:** 1. **Col. Width:** 52 nonpareils. **Col. Depth:** 105 agate lines. **Key Personnel:** Brenda J. Grodzicki, Business Manager, Editor; David T. Johnson, Editor; Elsie M. Walker, Editor. **ISSN:** 0090--4260 (print). **Subscription Rates:** $90 U.S. institutions and libraries; $40 Individuals U.S. and foreign; $100 Institutions and libraries, air mail; $15 Single issue current issue; $10 Single issue back issue. **URL:** http://www.salisbury.edu/lfq. **Ad Rates:** BW $200. **Remarks:** Accepts advertising. **Circ:** ‡800.

15593 ■ The Metropolitan Magazine
Pyramid Design Inc.
205 W Main St.
Salisbury, MD 21801
Free publication. **Freq:** Monthly. **URL:** http://www.themetropolitanmagazine.com. **Circ:** Free ■ **28000**.

15594 ■ Somerset Herald
Gannett Company Inc.
618 Beam St.
Salisbury, MD 21801
Phone: (410)749-7171
Publication E-mail: herald@shore-source.com
Community newspaper. **Freq:** Weekly (Wed.). **Print Method:** Offset. **Cols./Page:** 6. **Col. Width:** 12 picas. **Col. Depth:** 21 1/2 inches. **Key Personnel:** Liz Holland, Editor, phone: (410)651-1600; Robert Scott, Director, Advertising. **ISSN:** 8756--6397 (print). **URL:** http://www.delmarvanow.com. **Formerly:** Marylander & Herald. **Ad Rates:** GLR $7.28; BW $729; 4C $1135; PCI $6.60. **Remarks:** Accepts advertising. **Circ:** (Not Reported).

15595 ■ WBOC-TV - 16
1729 N Salisbury Blvd.
Salisbury, MD 21801
Phone: (410)749-1111
Fax: (410)749-2361
Email: wboc@wboc.com
Format: Commercial TV. **Networks:** CBS. **Owner:** Thomas Draper, at above address. **Founded:** 1954. **Operating Hours:** Continuous. **ADI:** Salisbury, MD. **Wattage:** 4,000,000 VIS/400,000 AUR. **Ad Rates:** $25-900 per unit. **URL:** http://www.wboc.com.

15596 ■ WCPB-TV - 28
11767 Owings Mills Blvd.
Owings Mills, MD 21117
Phone: (410)356-5600
Free: 800-627-6788
Email: comments@mpt.org
Format: Public TV. **Simulcasts:** WMPB, WMPT, WWPB, WGPT, WFPT. **Networks:** Public Broadcasting Service (PBS). **Owner:** Maryland Public Television, 11767 Owings Mills Blvd., Owings Mills, MD 21117, Ph: (410)356-5600, Fax: (410)581-6579, Free: 800-223-3678. **Founded:** 1969. **Operating Hours:** Continuous. **Key Personnel:** Tom Williams, Managing Dir.; Larry D. Unger, CEO, President; Steven Schupak, Exec. VP, COO; George R. Beneman, II, Sr. VP, Chief Tech. Ofc.; Martin G. Jacobs, VP, CFO. **Local Programs:** *MotorWeek*, Sunday Saturday Wednesday 12:00 p.m. 5:00 p.m. 7:30 p.m. **Wattage:** 2,300,000. **Ad Rates:** Noncommercial. **URL:** http://www.mpt.org/home.

15597 ■ WDIH-FM - 90.3
PO Box 186
Salisbury, MD 21803
Phone: (410)736-4257
Email: wdihradio@gmail.com
Format: Adult Contemporary. **Owner:** Salisbury Educational Broadcasting Foundation, at above address. **Founded:** 1988. **ADI:** Hagerstown, MD. **Wattage:** 378. **Ad Rates:** Noncommercial. **URL:** http://www.wdihradio90-3.org.

WICO-AM - See Salisbury, MD

15598 ■ WICO-AM - 1320
919 Ellegood St.
Salisbury, MD 21801-8433
Phone: (410)219-3500
Email: wico@wicoam.com
Format: Talk; News. **Networks:** NBC; Daynet; ABC. **Owner:** Delmarva Broadcasting Co., 2727 Shipley Rd., DE 19810. **Founded:** 1957. **Operating Hours:** Continuous. **ADI:** Salisbury, MD. **Wattage:** 1,000 Day ; 028 Night. **Ad Rates:** Advertising accepted; rates available upon request. Combined advertising rates available with WICO-FM; WQJZ-FM. **Mailing address:** PO Box 909, Salisbury, DE 21801-8433. **URL:** http://www.wicoam.com.

15599 ■ WICO-FM - 97.5; 92.5
PO Box 909
Salisbury, MD 21803
Phone: (410)219-3500
Email: wico@wicoam.com
Format: Contemporary Country; Talk. **Simulcasts:** WXJN-FM. **Networks:** Independent; Meadows Racing. **Owner:** Delmarva Broadcasting Co., 2727 Shipley Rd., Wilmington, DE 19803, Ph: (302)478-2700, Fax: (302)478-0100. **Founded:** 1969. **Operating Hours:** Continuous. **ADI:** Salisbury, MD. **Key Personnel:** Joe Beail, Gen. Sales Mgr., joeb@radiocenter.com; Michael Reath, Gen. Mgr., miker@radiocenter.com. **Wattage:** 4,500. **Ad Rates:** Advertising accepted; rates available upon request. Combined advertising rates available with WICO-AM, WQJZ-FM. **URL:** http://www.wicotalk.com.

15600 ■ WJDY-AM - 1470
1633 N Division St.
Salisbury, MD 21801-3805
Free: 844-289-7234
Format: News; Information. **Founded:** 1958. **ADI:** Salinas-Monterey, CA. **Wattage:** 5,000 KW. **Ad Rates:** Advertising accepted; rates available upon request. **URL:** http://newsradio1470.iheart.com/.

15601 ■ WKZP-FM - 95.9
351 Tilghman Rd.
Salisbury, MD 21801
Phone: (410)572-1923
Format: Album-Oriented Rock (AOR). **Key Personnel:** Chris Walus, Gen. Mgr. **Wattage:** 2,000. **Ad Rates:** Noncommercial.

15602 ■ WLBW-FM - 92.1
351 Tilghman Rd.
Salisbury, MD 21804
Phone: (410)742-1923
Fax: (410)742-2329
Format: Oldies. **Founded:** Sept. 07, 2006. **Key Personnel:** Paul Burton, Gen. Sales Mgr., paulburton@clearchannel.com; Douglas Hillard, Gen. Mgr. **Wattage:** 6,000. **Ad Rates:** Noncommercial.

15603 ■ WMDT-TV - 47
202 Downtown Plz.
Salisbury, MD 21801
Phone: (410)742-4747
Fax: (410)742-5767
Format: Commercial TV. **Networks:** ABC. **Founded:** 1980. **Operating Hours:** Continuous. **ADI:** Salisbury, MD. **Key Personnel:** Kathleen McLain, Gen. Mgr., kathleen_mclain@wmdt.com; Phil Bankert, Sales Mgr., phil_bankert@wmdt.com; Sarah Truitt, News Dir., sarah_truitt@wmdt.com. **Ad Rates:** Advertising accepted; rates available upon request. **Mailing address:** PO Box 4009, Salisbury, MD 21801. **URL:** http://www.wmdt.com.

15604 ■ WQHQ-FM - 104.7
351 Tilghman Rd.
Salisbury, MD 21804-1920
Phone: (410)742-1923
Free: 800-762-0105
Format: Adult Contemporary. **Networks:** Independent. **Founded:** 1965. **Operating Hours:** Continuous. **ADI:** Hagerstown, MD. **Key Personnel:** Chris Walus, Div. Pres.; Paul Burton, Sr. VP of Sales, paulburton@clearchannel.com. **Wattage:** 50,000. **Ad Rates:** Advertising accepted; rates available upon request. **URL:** http://www.q105fm.com.

15605 ■ WSBY-FM - 98.9
351 Tilghman Rd.
Salisbury, MD 21804
Phone: (410)742-1923
Format: Urban Contemporary. **Ad Rates:** Noncommercial. **URL:** http://mymagic989.iheart.com.

15606 ■ WSCL-FM - 89.5
PO Box 2596
Salisbury, MD 21802
Phone: (410)543-6895
Fax: (410)548-6000
Free: 800-543-6895
Format: Classical; News; Public Radio. **Networks:** National Public Radio (NPR); AP; Public Radio International (PRI); BBC World Service. **Owner:** Salisbury University Foundation Inc., 1308 Camden Ave., Salisbury, MD 21801, Ph: (410)543-6175. **Founded:** 1987. **Operating Hours:** Continuous; 20% network, 80% local, **ADI:** Salisbury, MD. **Key Personnel:** Mary Kramer, Contact; Marc Steiner, Contact; Mike Miller, President; Dana Whitehair, Gen. Mgr.; Don Rush, Prog. Dir., dwroeck@salisbury.edu. **Wattage:** 33,000. **Ad Rates:** Noncommercial; underwriting available. **URL:** http://delmarvapublicradio.net.

15607 ■ WSDL-FM - 90.7
PO Box 2596
Salisbury, MD 21802
Phone: (410)543-6895
Format: Public Radio. **Networks:** National Public Radio (NPR); AP; Public Radio International (PRI); BBC World Service. **Owner:** Salisbury State University Foundation, Inc., 1101 Camden Avenue, Salisbury, MD 21801, Ph: (410)543-6000. **Founded:** Sept. 16, 2006. **Operating Hours:** Continuous. **Wattage:** 18,500. **Ad Rates:** Noncommercial. **URL:** http://www.delmarvapublicradio.net.

15608 ■ WTGM-AM - 960
351 Tilghman Rd.
Salisbury, MD 21804
Phone: (410)742-1923
Format: Sports. **Networks:** Westwood One Radio; ESPN Radio. **Founded:** 1930. **Formerly:** WBOC-AM. **Operating Hours:** Continuous; 20% local, 80% network. **ADI:** Salisbury, MD. **Wattage:** 5,000. **Ad Rates:** Noncommercial.

Circulation: ★ = AAM; △ or • = BPA; ♦ = CAC; ❑ = VAC; ⊕ = PO Statement; ‡ = Publisher's Report; Boldface figures = sworn; Light figures = estimated.

15609 ■ WWFG-FM - 99.9
351 Tilghman Rd.
Salisbury, MD 21804
Phone: (410)742-1923
Format: Country. **Networks:** Independent. **Founded:** 1978. **Formerly:** WKHI-FM. **Operating Hours:** Continuous; 100% local. **ADI:** Hagerstown, MD. **Wattage:** 38,000. **Ad Rates:** Noncommercial. **URL:** http://www.froggy999.com.

15610 ■ WXSU-FM - 96.3
PO Box 3151
Salisbury, MD 21801
Phone: (410)543-6195
Email: wxsu@gulls.salisbury.edu
Format: Hip Hop; Album-Oriented Rock (AOR); Information. **Operating Hours:** 14 hours Daily. **Ad Rates:** Noncommercial; underwriting available. **URL:** http://www.orgs.salisbury.edu.

SEABROOK

Prince George's Co. (SC). 5 m. E of College Park. Residential.

Prince George's Sentinel - See Prince Georges

SEVERNA PARK

Anne Arundel Co. (C) 7 m N. of Annapolis. Residential.

15611 ■ AMA Alliance Today
American Medical Association Alliance
550 M Ritchie Highway 271
Severna Park, MD 21146
Free: 800-549-4619
Publisher's E-mail: admin@amaalliance.org
Magazine for the families of physicians. **Freq:** Bimonthly three times a year. **Print Method:** Offset. **Trim Size:** 8 3/8 x 10 7/8. **Cols./Page:** 3. **Col. Width:** 27 nonpareils. **Col. Depth:** 140 agate lines. **Key Personnel:** Rosetta Gervasi, Editor; Jo Posselt, Executive Director. **ISSN:** 0163--0512 (print). **Subscription Rates:** $7 Individuals; Included in membership. **Alt. Formats:** PDF. **Formerly:** MD's Wife; Facets. **Remarks:** Accepts advertising. **Circ:** (Not Reported).

15612 ■ Marine Electronics Journal
National Marine Electronics Association
692 Ritchie Hwy., Ste. 104
Severna Park, MD 21146-3919
Phone: (410)975-9425
Fax: (410)975-9450
Publication E-mail: info@nmea.org
Professional journal covering marine electronics. **Freq:** 6/year. **Key Personnel:** James W. Fullilove, Editor; Bruce J. Cole, Manager, Advertising. **URL:** http://www.marineelectronicsjournal.com/content/about_us/mej.asp. **Ad Rates:** BW $2290; 4C $3220. **Remarks:** Advertising accepted; rates available upon request. **Circ:** (Not Reported).

15613 ■ Sacred Dance Guild Journal
Sacred Dance Guild
550M Ritchie Hwy., No. 271
Severna Park, MD 21146
Free: 877-422-8678
Publication E-mail: journal@sacreddanceguild.org
Scholarly journal covering liturgical dance. **Freq:** Triennial. **Key Personnel:** Toni Intravaia, Editor. **ISSN:** 1043--5328 (print). **URL:** http://sdgjournal.wordpress.com. **Ad Rates:** BW $100. **Remarks:** Accepts advertising. **Circ:** (Not Reported).

SILVER SPRING

Montgomery Co. (WC). Adjoins Washington, DC., on the north. Computer industry; instrument factory. Nurseries.

15614 ■ Advances in Pulmonary Hypertension
Pulmonary Hypertension Association
801 Roeder Rd., Ste. 1000
Silver Spring, MD 20910
Phone: (301)565-3004
Fax: (301)565-3994
Free: 800-748-7274
Publisher's E-mail: pha@phassociation.org
Journal containing up-to-date information regarding diagnosis, pathophysiology and treatment of pulmonary hypertension. Featuring history of individuals who have made major contributions to the field via dedication to patient care, innovative research, and furthering the mission of the PH community to cure pulmonary hypertension. **Freq:** Quarterly. **Key Personnel:** Myung Park, Editor-in-Chief. **ISSN:** 1933-088X (print). **Subscription Rates:** Free. **URL:** http://www.phaonlineuniv.org/Journal/index.cfm?navItemNumber=532. **Remarks:** Advertising not accepted. **Circ:** 31000, 36000.

15615 ■ Adventist Review
General Conference of Seventh-Day Adventists
12501 Old Columbia Pke.
Silver Spring, MD 20904
Phone: (301)680-6000
Seventh Day Adventist magazine. **Freq:** Monthly. **Print Method:** Offset. **Trim Size:** 8 1/8 x 10 3/8. **Cols./Page:** 4. **Col. Width:** 21 nonpareils. **Col. Depth:** 135 agate lines. **Key Personnel:** Bill Knott, Editor, Publisher; Gerald Klingbeil, Associate Editor. **ISSN:** 0161--1119 (print). **Subscription Rates:** $12.95 Individuals print and online; $7.95 Individuals online only. **URL:** http://www.adventistreview.org. **Ad Rates:** BW $1032; 4C $1432. **Remarks:** Accepts advertising. **Circ:** Paid ‡30000.

15616 ■ Air Transport World
Penton Business Media, Inc.
The Blair Bldg., Ste. 700
8380 Colesville Rd.
Silver Spring, MD 20910
Phone: (301)755-0200
Fax: (301)514-3909
Magazine for world airline management. **Freq:** Monthly. **Print Method:** Offset. **Trim Size:** 7 3/4 x 10 3/4. **Cols./Page:** 3. **Col. Width:** 28 nonpareils. **Col. Depth:** 138 agate lines. **Key Personnel:** Kathryn M. Young, Managing Editor; Dr. Edvaldo Pereira Lima, Editor. **ISSN:** 0002--2543 (print). **Subscription Rates:** $69 Individuals /year (online). **URL:** http://atwonline.com. **Remarks:** Accepts advertising. **Circ:** (Not Reported).

15617 ■ American Hiker: The magazine of America Hiking Society
American Hiking Society
1422 Fenwick Ln.
Silver Spring, MD 20910
Phone: (301)565-6704
Fax: (301)565-6714
Free: 800-972-8608
Publisher's E-mail: info@americanhiking.org
Magazine covering hiking for members. **Freq:** Quarterly. **Subscription Rates:** Included in membership. **URL:** http://www.americanhiking.org. **Remarks:** Advertising accepted; rates available upon request. **Circ:** 10000.

15618 ■ The American Nurse
American Nurses Association
8515 Georgia Ave., Ste. 400
Silver Spring, MD 20910-3492
Phone: (301)628-5000
Fax: (301)628-5001
Free: 800-284-2378
Publication E-mail: adsales@ana.org
Newspaper (tabloid) for the nursing profession. **Freq:** Bimonthly. **Print Method:** Web/heat-set. **Trim Size:** 11 3/8 x 16. **Cols./Page:** 4. **Col. Width:** 28 nonpareils. **Col. Depth:** 200 agate lines. **ISSN:** 0098--1486 (print). **URL:** http://www.theamericannurse.org. **Ad Rates:** BW $7675; 4C $6745; PCI $117. **Remarks:** Accepts advertising. **Circ:** ‡210000.

15619 ■ Blurt
MMVIII Blurt Magazine
140 Southwood Ave.
Silver Spring, MD 20901
Magazine presenting indie music and entertainment. **Freq:** Quarterly. **Key Personnel:** Scott Crawford, Founder; Fred Mills, Editor; Randy Harward, Senior Editor. **Subscription Rates:** $12 Individuals. **URL:** http://blurtonline.com. **Circ:** (Not Reported).

15620 ■ Dance Education in Practice
National Dance Education Organization
8609 2nd Ave., Ste. 203-B
Silver Spring, MD 20910
Phone: (301)585-2880
Fax: (301)585-2888
Contains practical approaches to dance education and teaching that provide educators with models of new ideas, strategies, and content they can apply to their own practice. **Freq:** Quarterly. **ISSN:** 2373--4833 (print); **EISSN:** 2373--4841 (electronic). **Subscription Rates:** $138 Institutions online; $158 Institutions print and online; Included in membership. **URL:** http://www.tandfonline.com/toc/udep20/current. **Circ:** (Not Reported).

15621 ■ In Transit
Amalgamated Transit Union
1000 New Hampshire Ave.
Silver Spring, MD 20903
Phone: (301)431-7100
Fax: (301)431-7117
Free: 888-240-1196
Amalgamated transit union magazine. **Freq:** Bimonthly. **Print Method:** Offset. **Trim Size:** 8 1/2 x 11. **Cols./Page:** 4. **Col. Width:** 13 picas. **Col. Depth:** 60 picas. **URL:** http://www.atu.org/media/intransit. **Remarks:** Advertising not accepted. **Circ:** Non-paid 175000.

15622 ■ International Body Psychotherapy Journal
United States Association for Body Psychotherapy
8639 B 16th St., Ste. 119
Silver Spring, MD 20910
Phone: (202)466-1619
Publication E-mail: admin@usabp.org
Academic journal that seeks to support, promote and stimulate the exchange of ideas, scholarship and research within the field of body psychotherapy as well as an interdisciplinary exchange with related fields of clinical practice and inquiry. **Freq:** Semiannual spring and fall. **Key Personnel:** Jill van der Aa, Managing Editor; Jacqueline A. Carleton, PhD, Editor-in-Chief, phone: (212)987-4969, fax: (212)427-0264. **ISSN:** 1538--960X (print). **Alt. Formats:** PDF. **URL:** http://usabp.org/ibpjournal. **Formerly:** USA Body Psychotherapy Journal. **Remarks:** Accepts advertising. **Circ:** (Not Reported).

15623 ■ JazzTimes: America's Jazz Magazine
Jazz Times
10801 Margate Rd.
Silver Spring, MD 20901
Phone: (617)315-9154
Magazine incorporating all genres of jazz music for professionals and fans. **Freq:** 10/year. **Print Method:** Web offset. **Trim Size:** 8 1/2 x 10 3/4. **Cols./Page:** 3. **Col. Width:** 2 1/4 inches. **Col. Depth:** 10 inches. **Key Personnel:** Jeff Sabin, Director, Advertising; Lee Mergner, Publisher, phone: (617)315-9151. **ISSN:** 0272--572X (print). **Subscription Rates:** $29.99 Individuals; $55.98 Two years; $34.99 Canada; $60.98 Canada 2 years, incl. of postage & GST; $54.99 Other countries; $80.98 Other countries 2 years; $34.99 Individuals print and digital; $63.98 Two years print and digital; $20 Individuals online. **URL:** http://jazztimes.com. **Remarks:** Accepts advertising. **Circ:** Paid ‡80898, Non-paid ‡9000.

15624 ■ Journal of the American Society for Information Science and Technology
American Society for Information Science and Technology
8555 16th St., Ste. 850
Silver Spring, MD 20910
Phone: (301)495-0900
Fax: (301)495-0810
Publisher's E-mail: asist@asist.org
Journal containing reports of research and development in the subjects and applications in information science and technology. **Freq:** Monthly. **Subscription Rates:** $3172 U.S. institutions; print only; $3884 U.S. institutions; print and online; $3175 U.S. institutions; online only. **URL:** http://www.asis.org/jasist.html. **Remarks:** Advertising not accepted. **Circ:** (Not Reported).

15625 ■ Journal of Dance Education
National Dance Education Organization
8609 2nd Ave., Ste. 203-B
Silver Spring, MD 20910
Phone: (301)585-2880
Fax: (301)585-2888
Freq: Quarterly. **Key Personnel:** Wendy Oliver, Editor. **ISSN:** 1529--0824 (print). **Subscription Rates:** Included in membership. **URL:** http://www.ndeo.org/content.aspx?page_id=22&club_id=893257&module_id=53093. **Remarks:** Advertising accepted; rates available upon request. **Circ:** (Not Reported).

15626 ■ Journal of Midwifery & Women's Health
American College of Nurse-Midwives

8403 Colesville Rd., Ste. 1550
Silver Spring, MD 20910
Phone: (240)485-1800
Fax: (240)485-1818
Publisher's E-mail: info@wiley.com
Freq: Bimonthly. **Trim Size:** 8 X 10 3/4. **Key Personnel:** Deanne R. Williams, Editor; Linda V. Walsh, PhD, Associate Editor; Frances E. Likis, Editor-in-Chief; Mary K. Barger, Associate Editor; Maureen Shannon, Editor. **ISSN:** 1526--9523 (print); **EISSN:** 1542--2011 (electronic). **Subscription Rates:** $200 Individuals print + online (The Americas); £142 Individuals print + online (UK); €164 Individuals print + online (Europe - non Euro zone); €164 Individuals print + online (Europe - Euro zone); $656 Institutions print + online (The Americas); £465 Institutions print + online (UK); €534 Institutions print + online (Europe); $546 Institutions online or print; £387 Institutions online or print; €445 Institutions online or print. **URL:** http://onlinelibrary.wiley.com/journal/10.1111/(ISSN)1542-2011; http://www.midwife.org/Journal-of-Midwifery-Women-s-Health. **Ad Rates:** BW $2035; 4C $1545. **Remarks:** Accepts advertising. **Circ:** ‡7194.

15627 ■ Journal of Music Therapy
American Music Therapy Association
8455 Colesville Rd., Ste. 1000
Silver Spring, MD 20910
Phone: (301)589-3300
Fax: (301)589-5175
Publisher's E-mail: info@musictherapy.org
Freq: Quarterly. **ISSN:** 0022--2917 (print). **Subscription Rates:** $317 Institutions print and online; $292 Institutions print only; $253 Institutions online only. **URL:** http://www.musictherapy.org/research/pubs/#The_Journal_of_Music_Therapy. **Remarks:** Advertising not accepted. **Circ:** (Not Reported).

15628 ■ Journal of National Black Nurses Association
National Black Nurses Association
8630 Fenton St., Ste. 330
Silver Spring, MD 20910-3803
Phone: (301)589-3200
Fax: (301)589-3223
Publisher's E-mail: info@nbna.org
Freq: Semiannual. **URL:** http://www.nbna.org/nbna%20journal. **Remarks:** Advertising not accepted. **Circ:** (Not Reported).

15629 ■ Journal of the National Medical Association
National Medical Association
8403 Colesville Rd., Ste. 920
Silver Spring, MD 20910
Phone: (202)347-1895
Journal on specialized clinical research related to the health problems of African-Americans and other minorities. Recognizes significant contributions by black physicians and others involved with minority health issues and health disparities. **Freq:** Monthly. **Print Method:** Web offset. **Trim Size:** 8 1/8 x 10 7/8. **Cols./Page:** 2. **Key Personnel:** Dr. William E. Lawson, Editor-in-Chief. **ISSN:** 0027--9684 (print). **Subscription Rates:** $125 Individuals; $275 Institutions; $50 Individuals intern, resident, fellow, student; $22 Single issue; $35. **URL:** http://ww.nmanet.org/index.php/publications/how-to-submit-a-manuscript. **Ad Rates:** BW $6,150; 4C $8,545. **Remarks:** Accepts advertising. **Circ:** 42000, 28000.

15630 ■ JPEN: Journal of Parenteral and Enteral Nutrition
American Society for Parenteral and Enteral Nutrition
8630 Fenton St., Ste. 412
Silver Spring, MD 20910-3805
Phone: (301)587-6315
Fax: (301)587-2365
Publisher's E-mail: aspen@nutr.org
Scientific peer review journal on nutrition.Publishes original, peer-reviewed studies that define the cutting edge of basic and clinical research in the field. **Freq:** Bimonthly. **Print Method:** Web Press. **Trim Size:** 8 3/8 x 10 7/8. **Cols./Page:** 2. **Col. Width:** 32 nonpareils. **Col. Depth:** 119 agate lines. **Key Personnel:** Pamela Charney, PhD, Board Member; Deborah A. Andris, RN, Associate Editor; James Barone, MD, Associate Editor; Kelly A. Tappenden, PhD, Editor-in-Chief. **ISSN:** 0148--6071 (print); **EISSN:** 194-1-2444 (electronic). **Subscription Rates:** £235 Institutions print & e-access; £230 Institutions print only; £212 Institutions e-access; £112 Individuals print & e-access; £42 Single issue institution; £24 Single issue. **URL:** http://pen.sagepub.com. **Ad Rates:** BW $1,925; 4C $3,725. **Remarks:** Accepts advertising. **Circ:** Combined ‡6560.

15631 ■ Lab Matters
Association of Public Health Laboratories
8515 Georgia Ave., Ste. 700
Silver Spring, MD 20910
Phone: (240)485-2745
Fax: (240)485-2700
Publisher's E-mail: info@aphl.org
Freq: Quarterly. **URL:** http://www.aphl.org/aboutaphl/publications/lab-matters/pages/default.aspx. **Ad Rates:** 4C $1950. **Remarks:** Accepts advertising. **Circ:** (Not Reported).

15632 ■ LCWR Occasional Papers
Leadership Conference of Women Religious
8808 Cameron St.
Silver Spring, MD 20910-4152
Phone: (301)588-4955
Fax: (301)587-4575
Subscription Rates: $5 Single issue summer 2014/summer 2015/ winter 2015; $4 Single issue winter 2014/summer 2013/winter 2012/winter 2011/summer 2011. **URL:** http://lcwr.org/publications/occasional-papers. **Remarks:** Advertising not accepted. **Circ:** (Not Reported).

15633 ■ NADmag
National Association of the Deaf
8630 Fenton St., Ste. 820
Silver Spring, MD 20910
Phone: (301)587-1788
Fax: (301)587-1791
Publication E-mail: nadmagads@nad.org
Magazine for deaf and hard of hearing people, and their parents and educators. **Freq:** Bimonthly. **Trim Size:** 8 1/2 x 11. **Key Personnel:** Howard A. Rosenblum, Chief Executive Officer; Shane H. Feldman, Chief Operating Officer. **Subscription Rates:** Included in membership. **URL:** http://www.nad.org/advertise. **Formerly:** The NAD Broadcaster. **Ad Rates:** BW $1,400; BW $850, employment advertisement. **Remarks:** Accepts advertising. **Circ:** 7000.

15634 ■ NCP: Nutrition in Clinical Practice
American Society for Parenteral and Enteral Nutrition
8630 Fenton St., Ste. 412
Silver Spring, MD 20910-3805
Phone: (301)587-6315
Fax: (301)587-2365
Publisher's E-mail: aspen@nutr.org
Clinical nutrition journal. **Freq:** 6/year February, April, June, August, October, December. **Print Method:** Sheet Fed. **Trim Size:** 8 3/8 x 10 7/8. **Cols./Page:** 2. **Col. Width:** 32 nonpareils. **Col. Depth:** 119 agate lines. **Key Personnel:** Jeanette Hasse, PhD, Editor-in-Chief; Vincent T. Armenti, MD, Board Member; Kenneth A. Kudsk, MD, Board Member; Gail Cresci, Board Member; Charles M. Mueller, PhD, Board Member. **ISSN:** 0884--5336 (print). **Subscription Rates:** £255 Institutions print and e-access; £230 Institutions e-access; £250 Institutions print only; £100 Individuals print and e-access; £46 Institutions single print issue; £22 Individuals single print issue. **URL:** http://www.nutritioncare.org; http://ncp.sagepub.com. **Ad Rates:** BW $1,925; 4C $3,725. **Remarks:** Accepts advertising. **Circ:** Combined ‡5820.

15635 ■ Obesity
The Obesity Society
8757 Georgia Ave., Ste. 1320
Silver Spring, MD 20910-3757
Phone: (301)563-6526
Fax: (301)563-6595
Free: 800-974-3084
Publisher's E-mail: customerservice@oxon.blackwellpublishing.com
Scientific journal covering obesity research. **Freq:** Monthly 5/year. **Trim Size:** 8 1/2 x 11. **Key Personnel:** Eric Ravussin, PhD, Editor-in-Chief; Donna H. Ryan, MD, Associate, Editor-in-Chief. **ISSN:** 1930--7381 (print); **EISSN:** 1930--739X (electronic). **Subscription Rates:** $707 Institutions print or online - The Americas/USA/Canada & Mexico/ROW; $849 Institutions print and online - The Americas/USA/Canada & Mexico/ROW; £455 Institutions print or online - UK; £546 Institutions print and online - UK; €527 Institutions print or online - Europe; €633 Institutions print and online - Europe. **URL:** http://onlinelibrary.wiley.com/journal/10.1002/(ISSN)1930-739X; http://www.obesity.org/publications/obesity-journal.htm. **Formerly:** Obesity Research. **Mailing address:** PO Box 1354, Oxford OX4 2ZG, United Kingdom. **Ad Rates:** BW $920; 4C $1,870. **Remarks:** Accepts advertising. **Circ:** Paid 1200.

15636 ■ Pastoral Music
National Association of Pastoral Musicians
962 Wayne Ave., Ste. 210
Silver Spring, MD 20910-4461
Phone: (240)247-3000
Fax: (240)247-3001
Publication E-mail: headquarters@napfe.org
Pastoral music magazine. **Freq:** Bimonthly. **Print Method:** Offset. **Trim Size:** 8 1/2 x 11. **Cols./Page:** 3. **Col. Width:** 26 nonpareils. **Col. Depth:** 136 agate lines. **Key Personnel:** Dr. Gordon E. Truitt, Senior Editor; Dr. Michael J. McMahon, President; Andrea Schellman, Assistant Editor. **ISSN:** 0363--6569 (print). **Subscription Rates:** $31 Individuals; Included in membership. **Alt. Formats:** Download; PDF. **URL:** http://www.npm.org/pastoral_music/archives.html; http://www.npm.org/pastoral_music. **Ad Rates:** BW $850; PCI $100. **Remarks:** Accepts advertising. **Circ:** 9000.

15637 ■ Performance Improvement
International Society for Performance Improvement
PO Box 13035
Silver Spring, MD 20910
Phone: (301)587-8570
Fax: (301)587-8573
Publisher's E-mail: info@ispi.org
Freq: 10/year. **Subscription Rates:** $95 U.S., Canada, and Mexico; $135 Other countries. **URL:** http://ispi.org/ISPI/Resources/Performance_Improvement_Journal.aspx. **Remarks:** Accepts advertising. **Circ:** 6000.

15638 ■ Performance Improvement Quarterly
International Society for Performance Improvement
PO Box 13035
Silver Spring, MD 20910
Phone: (301)587-8570
Fax: (301)587-8573
Publisher's E-mail: info@wiley.com
Peer-reviewed journal covering the interdisciplinary field of human performance technology. **Freq:** Quarterly. **Key Personnel:** Ingrid Guerra-López, Editor. **ISSN:** 0898--5952 (print); **EISSN:** 1937--8327 (electronic). **Subscription Rates:** $256 Institutions online only - US, Canada, Mexico and other countries; $134 Institutions online only - UK; €168 Institutions online only - Europe; $256 Institutions print and online; $348 Institutions, Canada and Mexico print and online; £207 Institutions print and online - UK; €260 Institutions print and online - Europe; $382 Institutions, other countries print and online; $256 U.S., Canada, and Mexico print only - Institution; $65 U.S., Canada, and Mexico print only - individual; £47 Individuals print only - UK; €59 Individuals print only - Europe; $89 Other countries print only; Included in membership online access; $52 Members print; in North America; $65 Members print; outside North America; $89 Institutions nonmembers (rest of the world); print only; $327 Institutions nonmembers (USA); print + online; $377 Institutions nonmembers in Canada and Mexico (print + online); £220 Institutions nonmembers (UK); print + online; €275 Institutions nonmembers (Europe); print + online; $420 Institutions nonmembers (rest of the world); print + online. **URL:** http://onlinelibrary.wiley.com/journal/10.1002/(ISSN)1937-8327; http://ispi.org/ISPI/Resources/Performance_Improvement_Quarterly.aspx. **Remarks:** Accepts advertising. **Circ:** (Not Reported).

15639 ■ Prensa Hispana
The Spanish Speaking Community of Maryland Inc.
8519 Piney Branch Rd.
Silver Spring, MD 20901
Phone: (301)587-7217
Fax: (301)589-1397
Publication E-mail: prensa_hispana@hotmail.com
Community newspaper (Spanish). **Freq:** Monthly. **Trim Size:** 11 x 17. **Key Personnel:** Emilio Perche Rivas, Editor; Roberto Cubero, Editor, Owner, Contact. **Subscription Rates:** $15. **Ad Rates:** BW $1,170.00; SAU $10 x 13; PCI $18.00. **Remarks:** Advertising accepted;

Circulation: ★ = AAM; △ or • = BPA; ♦ = CAC; ❑ = VAC; ⊕ = PO Statement; ‡ = Publisher's Report; Boldface figures = sworn; Light figures = estimated.

rates available upon request. **Circ:** Free 30000.

15640 ■ Prout Journal
Proutist Universal
2005 Wheaton Haven Ct.
Silver Spring, MD 20902
Phone: (202)239-1171
Fax: (202)207-3525
Journal containing articles about ecology, economy, culture, ethics, spirituality, science, politics and health. **Freq:** Quarterly. **Key Personnel:** Marc Friedlander, Editor-in-Chief. **URL:** http://www.proutjournal.org. **Remarks:** Advertising not accepted. **Circ:** (Not Reported).

15641 ■ Science Weekly
Science Weekly Inc.
2141 Industrial Pkwy., Ste. 202
Silver Spring, MD 20904-7824
Phone: (301)680-8804
Fax: (301)680-9240
Free: 800-493-3559
Publisher's E-mail: info@scienceweekly.com
Publication covering science and mathematics. **Freq:** Weekly. **ISSN:** 0890--0388 (print). **Subscription Rates:** $20 Individuals; $5.95 Students minimum of 20 copies. **Online:** Gale. **Mailing address:** PO Box 70638, Bethesda, MD 20813-0638. **Circ:** (Not Reported).

15642 ■ Social Education
National Council for the Social Studies
8555 16th St., Ste. 500
Silver Spring, MD 20910
Phone: (301)588-1800
Fax: (301)588-2049
Free: 800-683-0812
Publisher's E-mail: membership@ncss.org
Official journal of the National Council for the Social Studies. **Freq:** 6/year September; October; November/December; January/February; March/April; and May/June. **Print Method:** Web offset. **Trim Size:** 8.75 x 11.5. **Cols./Page:** 3. **Col. Width:** 2 1/8 inches. **Col. Depth:** 8 1/2 inches. **Key Personnel:** Steven Lapham, Associate Editor; Michael Simpson, Director, Publications. **ISSN:** 0037--7724 (print). **Subscription Rates:** $170 Individuals electronic + print; $160 Individuals electronic access; $74 Individuals print. **URL:** http://www.socialstudies.org/publications/socialeducation#gsc.tab=0. **Ad Rates:** BW $2,300; 4C $2,800. **Remarks:** Advertising accepted; rates available upon request. **Circ:** Paid ‡29000, 20000.

15643 ■ Social Studies and the Young Learner
National Council for the Social Studies
8555 16th St., Ste. 500
Silver Spring, MD 20910
Phone: (301)588-1800
Fax: (301)588-2049
Free: 800-683-0812
Publisher's E-mail: membership@ncss.org
Peer-reviewed magazine covering social studies education for grades K-6. **Freq:** Quarterly September/October; November/December; January/February; and March/April. **Print Method:** Web offset. **Trim Size:** 8.75 x 11.5. **Cols./Page:** 3. **Col. Width:** 2 1/8 inches. **Col. Depth:** 8 1/2 inches. **Key Personnel:** Andrea Libresco, Editor; Jeannette Balantic, Editor. **ISSN:** 1056--0300 (print). **Subscription Rates:** $107 Individuals digital; $118 Individuals digital and print; $47 Individuals print. **URL:** http://www.socialstudies.org/ssyl; http://www.socialstudies.org/publications/ssyl. **Ad Rates:** BW $1,000; 4C $1,500. **Remarks:** Accepts advertising. **Circ:** (Not Reported).

15644 ■ The Veteran
Associates of Vietnam Veterans of America
8719 Colesville Rd., Ste. 100
Silver Spring, MD 20910
Phone: (301)585-4000
Fax: (301)585-0519
Free: 800-882-1316
Magazine featuring Vietnam Veteran and family issues. **Freq:** Bimonthly. **Subscription Rates:** $4 Individuals. **URL:** http://vva.org/publications/the-vva-veteran. **Remarks:** Accepts advertising. **Circ:** (Not Reported).

15645 ■ Vision
National Catholic Office for the Deaf
c/o Arrow Bookkeeping
8737 Colesville Rd., Ste. 501
Silver Spring, MD 20910
Phone: (301)577-1684
Publisher's E-mail: info@ncod.org
Journal for persons involved in ministry with deaf people. **Founded:** 1977. **Freq:** Quarterly. **Print Method:** 2 issues offset, 2 issues website. **Trim Size:** 7 1/2 x 10. **Subscription Rates:** $20 Individuals; $35 Two years; $30 Other countries; $55 Two years other countries. **URL:** http://www.ncod.org/visionmagazine.php. **Formerly:** Listening. **Ad Rates:** BW $300. **Remarks:** Advertising accepted; rates available upon request. **Circ:** (Not Reported).

15646 ■ The Washington Diplomat
The Washington Diplomat Inc.
PO Box 1345
Silver Spring, MD 20915
Phone: (301)933-3552
Fax: (301)949-0065
Publisher's E-mail: sales@washdiplomat.com
Newspaper for the international and diplomatic community in Washington, D.C. **Freq:** Monthly. **Key Personnel:** Victor Shiblie, Editor-in-Chief, Publisher; Anna Gawel, Managing Editor; Fuad Shiblie, Director, Operations. **Subscription Rates:** $29 Individuals; $49 Two years. **URL:** http://www.washdiplomat.com. **Formerly:** Embassy Flash. **Remarks:** Advertising accepted; rates available upon request. **Circ:** (Not Reported).

15647 ■ Washington Gardener
Washington Gardener
826 Philadelphia Ave.
Silver Spring, MD 20910
Phone: (301)588-6894
Fax: (301)768-4029
Publisher's E-mail: editor@washingtongardener.com
Magazine covering gardening and landscaping for the Washington, D.C., metropolitan area. **Freq:** Bimonthly. **Key Personnel:** Kathy Jentz, Editor. **Subscription Rates:** $20 Individuals. **URL:** http://washingtongardener.blogspot.com. **Remarks:** Accepts advertising. **Circ:** (Not Reported).

15648 ■ Radio One Licenses L.L.C.
1010 Wayne Ave., 14th Fl.
Silver Spring, MD 20910
Email: inquiry@radio-one.com
Format: News; Eclectic; Talk. **Simulcasts:** WAMJ-FM, WPZS-FM, WFXC-FM, WKJS-FM. **Key Personnel:** Jay Schneider, Chief Tech. Ofc., Exec. VP; Jay Stevens, Sr. VP; Peter D. Thompson, Exec. VP, CFO. **Ad Rates:** Accepts Advertising. **URL:** http://radio-one.com.

WAMD-AM - See Aberdeen, MD

15649 ■ WAMJ-FM
101 Wayne Ave.
Silver Spring, MD 20910
Phone: (404)832-7200
Fax: (404)688-7686
Format: Adult Contemporary. **Owner:** Radio One Inc., 1010 Wayne Ave., 14th Fl., Silver Spring, MD 20910, Ph: (301)306-1111, Fax: (302)636-5454. **Key Personnel:** Wayne Brown, Gen. Mgr.

WCBQ-AM - See Oxford, NC

15650 ■ WFXC-FM
1010 Wayne Ave., 14Th Fl.
Silver Spring, MD 20910
Format: Urban Contemporary. **Wattage:** 8,000 ERP.

15651 ■ WFXK-FM - 104.3
1010 Wayne Ave., 14th Fl.
Silver Spring, MD 20910
Format: Urban Contemporary. **Key Personnel:** Gary Weiss, Gen. Mgr. **Ad Rates:** Advertising accepted; rates available upon request. **URL:** http://foxync.hellobeautiful.com.

15652 ■ WIZF-FM
1010 Wayne Ave.
Silver Spring, MD 20910
Format: Hip Hop. **Founded:** 1206. **Wattage:** 2,500 ERP.

15653 ■ WMET-AM - 1160
8121 Georgia Ave., Ste. 806
Silver Spring, MD 20910
Free: 866-369-1160
Format: World Beat. **Simulcasts:** media general cable 17 audio. **Networks:** Business Radio. **Owner:** IDT Media, 102580 Santa Monica BLVD, Los Angeles, CA. **Founded:** 1983. **Operating Hours:** Continuous. **Key Personnel:** Yube Levin, Gen. Mgr., ylevin@wmet1160.com; Bob Appel, Sales Mgr., bappel@wmet1160.com; Jim Cuddy, Dir. of Production, jcuddy@wmet1160.com. **Wattage:** 50,000 Day; 1,000 Night. **Ad Rates:** $15; $40-60 for 30 seconds; $50-60 for 60 seconds. www.businessradio1150.com through broadcast.com/yahoo!. **URL:** http://www.wmet1160.com.

15654 ■ WMMJ-FM - 102.3
8515 Georgia Ave., 9th Fl.
Silver Spring, MD 20910
Phone: (301)306-1111
Format: Blues. **Networks:** ABC. **Owner:** Radio One Licenses L.L.C., 1010 Wayne Ave., 14th Fl., Silver Spring, MD 20910. **Founded:** 1987. **Operating Hours:** Continuous. **ADI:** Washington, DC. **Key Personnel:** Jeff Wilson, Gen. Mgr., jeffwilson@radio-one.com; Cynthia Bullock, Traffic Mgr., cbullock@radio-one.com. **Local Programs:** *My Majic DC*, Sunday Monday Tuesday Wednesday Thursday Friday Saturday 12:00 a.m. - 6:00 a.m. **Wattage:** 3,000. **Ad Rates:** Noncommercial. **URL:** http://www.mymajicdc.com.

15655 ■ WNNL-FM
1010 Wayne Ave., 14Th Fl.
Silver Spring, MD 20910
Format: Gospel. **Wattage:** 7,900 ERP. **Ad Rates:** Advertising accepted; rates available upon request.

15656 ■ WOLB-AM
1010 Wayne Ave., 14Th Fl.
Silver Spring, MD 20910
Format: Talk. **Founded:** Sept. 07, 2006. **ADI:** Baltimore, MD. **Wattage:** 250 Day; 030 Night.

15657 ■ WPHI-FM
1010 Wayne Ave., 14Th Fl.
Silver Spring, MD 20910
Phone: (610)276-1100
Fax: (610)276-1139
Format: Urban Contemporary; Hip Hop; Blues. **Owner:** Radio One Inc., 1010 Wayne Ave., 14th Fl., Silver Spring, MD 20910, Ph: (301)306-1111, Fax: (302)636-5454. **Founded:** 1980. **Formerly:** WDRE-FM; WIBF-FM. **Key Personnel:** Andrew Rosen, Gen. Mgr., arosen@radio-one.com. **Wattage:** 780 ERP. **Ad Rates:** $200 per unit.

15658 ■ WPZE-FM
1010 Wayne Ave., 14Th Fl.
Silver Spring, MD 20910
Phone: (404)765-9750
Fax: (404)688-7686
Format: Gospel. **Key Personnel:** Wayne Brown, Gen. Mgr. **Wattage:** 3,000 ERP.

15659 ■ WTMW-TV - 14
962 Wayne Ave.
Silver Spring, MD 20910-4433
Owner: Urban Broadcasting Corp., at above address.

15660 ■ WWRC-AM - 980
8121 Georgia Ave.
Silver Spring, MD 20910-4933
Phone: (301)587-4900
Fax: (301)587-5759
Format: Talk. **Networks:** CNN Radio. **Owner:** Evergreen Media Corp., Dallas, TX, Ph: (214)869-9020. **Founded:** 1923. **Operating Hours:** Continuous. **ADI:** Washington, DC. **Key Personnel:** Shandelle Barton, Promotions Dir.; Dennis Reese, Sales Mgr.; Eric Jennings, Bus. Mgr.; Diana Silman, Dir. of Programs; David Howard, Gen. Sales Mgr.; Melissa Kelly, Sales Mgr.; Bob Deutsch, Promotions Mgr.; Leslie Brown, Bus. Mgr; Dianne Robinson, Contact. **Wattage:** 50,000 daytime/5,000 night. **Ad Rates:** Advertising accepted; rates available upon request.

STEVENSVILLE

15661 ■ Aside World
World Sidesaddle Federation
PO Box 161
Stevensville, MD 21666-0161
Phone: (918)683-0539
Fax: (410)643-1497
Publisher's E-mail: info@sidesaddle.com
Magazine covering horseback riding. **Freq:** Quarterly. **URL:** http://www.sidesaddle.com/membership.shtml. **Remarks:** Advertising accepted; rates available upon request. **Circ:** 350.

TAKOMA PARK

Prince George's Co.

15662 ■ WGTS-FM - 91.9
7600 Flower Ave.
Takoma Park, MD 20912
Phone: (301)891-4200
Fax: (301)270-9191
Free: 800-400-1432
Email: donations@wgts919.com
Format: Contemporary Christian. **Founded:** 1948. **Operating Hours:** 12am-8.41pm- Mon.-Fri.; Continuous-Sat.-Sun. **Key Personnel:** John Konrad, Gen. Mgr., VP; Becky Alignay, Dir. of Programs; Ben Milton, Music Dir. **Wattage:** 23,700. **Ad Rates:** Noncommercial; underwriting available. **URL:** http://www.wgts.org.

THURMONT

Frederick Co. Frederick Co. (N). 17 m N of Frederick. Catoctin Mountain National Park. Manufactures shoes, clothing, salesbooks. Graineries. Dairy and poultry farms. Wheat, truck crops, peaches, apples.

15663 ■ WTHU-AM - 1450
10 Radio Ln.
Thurmont, MD 21788-1645
Phone: (301)637-6736
Format: News; Talk; Sports. **Founded:** 1968. **Formerly:** WFCO-AM. **Key Personnel:** Chuck Walmer, Contact. **Wattage:** 500 Daytime; 400 Nig. **Ad Rates:** Advertising accepted; rates available upon request. $8-14 for 30 seconds. **URL:** http://www.wthu.org/.

TIMONIUM

15664 ■ Discovery Medicine
Discovery Medicine
10 Gerard Ave., Ste. 201
Timonium, MD 21093
Phone: (443)808-5005
Free: 888-833-0526
Publisher's E-mail: service@discoverymedicine.com
Online journal that publishes articles on diseases, biology, new diagnostics, and treatments for medical professionals. **Freq:** Monthly. **Key Personnel:** Noel R. Rose, MD, Editor-in-Chief; Peter H. Rheinstein, MD, Publisher; Benjamin Yang, MD, Executive Editor. **ISSN:** 1539--6509 (print). **Subscription Rates:** $139 Individuals 1 year (personal); $1399 Institutions 1 year. **URL:** http://www.discoverymedicine.com. **Remarks:** Advertising not accepted. **Circ:** (Not Reported).

15665 ■ Journal of Behavioral Optometry
Optometric Extension Program Foundation
2300 York Rd., Ste. 113
Timonium, MD 21093
Phone: (410)561-3791
Fax: (410)252-1719
Freq: 6/year. **ISSN:** 1045--8395 (print). **Alt. Formats:** PDF. **URL:** http://www.oepf.org/journals. **Remarks:** Accepts advertising. **Circ:** (Not Reported).

15666 ■ Mid-Atlantic Thoroughbred
Maryland Horse Breeders Association
30 E Padonia Rd., Ste. 303
Timonium, MD 21093
Phone: (410)252-2100
Fax: (410)560-0503
Publisher's E-mail: info@marylandthoroughbred.com
Magazine for people in the thoroughbred industry. The sport of racing and the agriculture of breeding in the Mid-Atlantic region. Edited to serve a readership comprised of breeders, trainers, owners and enthusiasts. **Freq:** Monthly. **Print Method:** Web offset. **Trim Size:** 8 1/8 x 10 7/8. **Cols./Page:** 4. **Col. Width:** 10 picas. **Col. Depth:** 56 picas. **Key Personnel:** James B. Steel, Jr., Advisor; Joe Clancy, Editor. **ISSN:** 1056-3245 (print). **Subscription Rates:** $36 Individuals; $65 Two years; $127 Other countries; $86 Individuals three years. **URL:** http://midatlantictb.com/cms. **Mailing address:** PO Box 427, Timonium, MD 21094. **Ad Rates:** GLR $7; BW $755; 4C $1,840; PCI $50. **Remarks:** Accepts advertising. **Circ:** Paid ‡10500.

TOWSON

Baltimore Co. (NC) 5 m North of Baltimore. Goucher College; Towson State University.

15667 ■ ASAIO Journal
Lippincott Williams and Wilkins
605 Worcester Rd.
Towson, MD 21286
Phone: (410)321-5031
Fax: (410)321-1456
Publisher's E-mail: ronna.ekhouse@wolterskluwer.com
Journal publishing peer-reviewed articles on the theory, design, fabrication, laboratory evaluation, and clinical use of artificial kidneys, heart, lungs, liver, pancreas, and blood vessels. Official publication of the American Society of Internal Organs (ASAIO). **Freq:** Bimonthly. **Print Method:** Sheetfed offset. **Trim Size:** 8 1/8 x 10 7/8. **Key Personnel:** Mark S. Slaughter, MD, Editor; Marjory Spraycar, Managing Editor. **ISSN:** 1058--2916 (print); **EISSN:** 1538--943x (electronic). **Subscription Rates:** $909 Individuals print; 1 year; $1542 Institutions print; 1 year; $261 Individuals print; 1 year - in-training; $1387 Canada and Mexico print; 1 year; $1425 Other countries print; 1 year; $2226 Institutions, Canada and Mexico print; 1 year; $2264 Institutions, other countries print; 1 year. **URL:** http://journals.lww.com/asaiojournal/pages/default.aspx. **Ad Rates:** BW $980; 4C $1,180. **Remarks:** Accepts advertising. **Circ:** 642.

15668 ■ The Baltimore Messenger
Patuxent Publishing Co.
409 Washington Ave.
Towson, MD 21204
Phone: (410)337-2400
Fax: (410)337-2490
Publisher's E-mail: jquimby@patuxent.com
Community newspaper. **Freq:** Weekly (Thurs.). **Print Method:** Offset. **Cols./Page:** 5 and 7. **Col. Width:** 11 picas. **Col. Depth:** 182 agate lines. **Key Personnel:** Larry Perl, Editor. **ISSN:** 1041--0899 (print). **Subscription Rates:** $24.95 Individuals; $37.50 Two years. **URL:** http://www.explorebaltimorecounty.com/publications/ms; http://baltimoresunmediagroup.com/media-portfolio/newspapers/baltimore-messenger. **Remarks:** Accepts advertising. **Circ:** **♦2405**.

15669 ■ Journal of Community Psychology
John Wiley & Sons Inc.
c/o Raymond P. Lorion, PhD, Editor
College of Education
Towson University
8000 York Rd.
Towson, MD 21252-0001
Publisher's E-mail: info@wiley.com
Peer-reviewed journal focusing research, evaluation, assessment and intervention and review articles that deal with human behavior in community settings. **Freq:** 8/year. **Print Method:** Offset. **Trim Size:** 7 1/4 x 10 1/4. **Cols./Page:** 1. **Col. Width:** 32 picas. **Col. Depth:** 51 picas. **Key Personnel:** Raymond P. Lorion, PhD, Editor; J.R. Newbrough, PhD, Editor; Peter Benson, PhD, Board Member; Michael B. Blank, Associate Editor; Anne Mulvey, PhD, Board Member; Maury Nation, PhD, Board Member; Ronald W. Manderscheid, PhD, Board Member; Maritza Montero, Board Member; David Mandell, Board Member. **ISSN:** 0090--4392 (print); **EISSN:** 1520--6629 (electronic). **Subscription Rates:** $1188 Institutions online. **URL:** http://onlinelibrary.wiley.com/journal/10.1002/(ISSN)1520-6629. **Ad Rates:** BW $772; 4C $1009. **Remarks:** Accepts advertising. **Circ:** (Not Reported).

15670 ■ Journal of Surgical Orthopaedic Advances
Data Trace Publishing Co.
110 W Rd., Ste. 227
Towson, MD 21204-2341
Phone: (410)494-4994
Fax: (410)494-0515
Free: 800-342-0454
Publisher's E-mail: info@datatrace.com
Peer-reviewed journal containing orthopaedic information. **Freq:** Quarterly. **Key Personnel:** L. Andrew Koman, MD, Editor. **ISSN:** 1548-825X (print). **URL:** http://www.datatrace.com/medical/JSOA_print.htm. **Mailing address:** PO Box 1239, Brooklandville, MD 21022. **Ad Rates:** BW $1200; 4C $1400. **Remarks:** Accepts advertising. **Circ:** (Not Reported).

15671 ■ Metropolitan Universities Journal
Coalition of Urban and Metropolitan Universities
8000 York Rd.
Towson, MD 21252
Phone: (410)704-3700
Publisher's E-mail: cumu@towson.edu
Freq: Quarterly. **Subscription Rates:** $55 Individuals; $95 Two years; $105 Institutions; $185 Institutions 2 years. **URL:** http://www.cumuonline.org/?page=journal. **Remarks:** Advertising not accepted. **Circ:** (Not Reported).

15672 ■ Monthly Digest
Baltimore County Volunteer Firemen's Association
700 E Joppa Rd.
Towson, MD 21286-5500
Phone: (410)887-4885
Fax: (410)832-8507
Journal containing information about the Baltimore County Volunteer Firemen's Association, including summary of meeting minutes, officers, and committee reports. **Freq:** Monthly. **URL:** http://www.bcvfa.org. **Circ:** (Not Reported).

15673 ■ North County News
Patuxent Publishing Co.
409 Washington Ave.
Towson, MD 21204
Phone: (410)337-2400
Fax: (410)337-2490
Publisher's E-mail: jquimby@patuxent.com
Community newspaper. **Founded:** 1989. **Freq:** Weekly (Wed.). **Key Personnel:** Elizabeth Eck, Editor, phone: (410)332-6463. **URL:** http://www.explorebaltimorecounty.com/publications/nc. **Remarks:** Accepts advertising. **Circ:** Non-paid **♦16679**.

15674 ■ Northeast Reporter
Patuxent Publishing Co.
409 Washington Ave.
Towson, MD 21204
Phone: (410)337-2400
Fax: (410)337-2490
Publisher's E-mail: jquimby@patuxent.com
Community newspaper. **Founded:** 1945. **Freq:** Weekly (Wed.). **Key Personnel:** Elizabeth Eck, Managing Editor. **URL:** http://www.explorebaltimorecounty.com/publications/re. **Remarks:** Accepts advertising. **Circ:** (Not Reported).

15675 ■ The Towerlight
Towson University
8000 York Rd.
Towson, MD 21252-0001
Phone: (410)704-2000
Publication E-mail: editor@thetowerlight.com
Community newspaper. **Freq:** Weekly. **Print Method:** Offset. **Cols./Page:** 5. **Key Personnel:** Carley Milligan, Editor-in-Chief, phone: (410)704-5141; Cody Boteler, Senior Editor; Mike Raymond, General Manager, phone: (410)704-5153. **URL:** http://www.thetowerlight.com. **Ad Rates:** 4C $840. **Remarks:** Accepts advertising. **Circ:** ‡10000.

15676 ■ WMJF-TV - 16
Media Ctr.
8000 York Rd.
Towson, MD 21252
Phone: (410)704-8788
Fax: (410)704-3744
Owner: Towson University, 8000 York Rd., Towson, MD 21252-0001, Ph: (410)704-2000. **Key Personnel:** Dr. John MacKerron, Gen. Mgr.

15677 ■ WNST-AM - 1570
1550 Hart Rd.
Towson, MD 21286
Phone: (410)821-9678
Email: info@wnst.net
Format: Sports. **Founded:** 1998. **Ad Rates:** Advertising accepted; rates available upon request. **URL:** http://www.wnst.net.

15678 ■ WTMD-FM - 89.7
8000 York Rd.
Towson, MD 21252
Phone: (410)704-8938
Fax: (410)704-8936
Email: wtmd@towson.edu
Format: Adult Album Alternative. **Networks:** AP. **Owner:** Towson University, 8000 York Rd., Towson, MD 21252-0001, Ph: (410)704-2000. **Founded:** 1976. **Formerly:** WCVT-FM. **Operating Hours:** Continuous. **Local Programs:** *Altered Fridays*, Friday 4:00 p.m.; *Stuck in the Jam*, Sunday 9:00 p.m. - 11:00 p.m.; *TMD Roadhouse*,

Circulation: ★ = AAM; △ or • = BPA; ♦ = CAC; ❑ = VAC; ⊕ = PO Statement; ‡ = Publisher's Report; Boldface figures = sworn; Light figures = estimated.

Friday 7:00 p.m.; *National Shows.* **Wattage:** 10,000. **Ad Rates:** Noncommercial. **URL:** http://www.wtmd.org.

UPPER MARLBORO

Prince George's Co. Prince George's Co. (SC). 18 m E of Washington, DC. Packing plants. Agriculture. Tobacco, corn, feed, wheat.

15679 ■ The Machinist
International Association of Machinists and Aerospace Workers
9000 Machinists Pl.
Upper Marlboro, MD 20772-2687
Phone: (301)967-4500
Publisher's E-mail: websteward@iamaw.org
Tabloid containing information on employment and technology. **Freq:** Monthly. **Print Method:** Offset. **Trim Size:** 11 1/2 x 16 1/4. **Key Personnel:** Robert J. Kalaski, Editor. **Remarks:** Advertising not accepted. **Circ:** 750000.

WALDORF

Charles Co. (S) 20 m S.E. of Washington, DC.

15680 ■ Accident Reconstruction Journal
Victor T. Craig
PO Box 234
Waldorf, MD 20604-0234
Phone: (301)843-1371
Fax: (301)843-1371
Technical periodic on the subject of traffic collision investigation and reconstruction. Each issue includes six feature articles, approximately twenty traffic safety news reports, eight technical practice problems with solutions presented in the back, a comprehensive list of upcoming classes, conferences and seminars, and occasional book and course reviews. **Freq:** Bimonthly. **Trim Size:** 8 1/2 x 11. **Key Personnel:** Victor Craig, Editor; Victor T. Craig, Editor. **ISSN:** 1057-8153 (print). **Subscription Rates:** $49 hard copy, second class mail; $29 digital via email; $69 hard copy plus digital; $62 Canada, hard copy via surface mail; $69 Canada, hard copy via air mail; $82 Canada, hard copy plus digital; $69 Western Europe, hard copy via surface mail; $82 Western Europe, hard copy via air mail; $71 Pacific Rim, hard copy via surface mail; $82 Pacific Rim, hard copy via air mail; $39 Individuals U.S. and Canada; $69 Two years. **Ad Rates:** BW $399. **Remarks:** Advertising accepted; rates available upon request. **Circ:** Combined 2800.

15681 ■ Enquirer Gazette
Southern Maryland Newspapers
7 Industrial Park Cir.
Waldorf, MD 20602
Phone: (301)645-9480
Publication E-mail: rperry@somdnews.com
Community newspaper. **Freq:** Weekly (Thurs.). **Print Method:** Offset. **Cols./Page:** 6. **Col. Width:** 30 nonpareils. **Col. Depth:** 294 agate lines. **Key Personnel:** Rob Perry, Editor, phone: (443)231-3387. **Subscription Rates:** $14.95 By mail. **URL:** http://www.somdnews.com/enquirer_gazette. **Remarks:** Accepts advertising. **Circ:** Combined ♦**2414**.

15682 ■ The Enterprise
Southern Maryland Newspapers
7 Industrial Park Cir.
Waldorf, MD 20602
Phone: (301)645-9480
Publisher's E-mail: somdcirc@somdnews.com
Community newspaper. **Founded:** 1884. **Freq:** Semiweekly (Wed. and Fri.). **Key Personnel:** Karen Acton, Publisher; Rick Boyd, Editor. **Subscription Rates:** $44.41 Individuals by carrier; $47.41 By mail. **URL:** http://www.somdnews.com/section/news08. **Remarks:** Advertising accepted; rates available upon request. **Circ:** Paid ♦**14447**.

15683 ■ Maryland Independent
Southern Maryland Newspapers
7 Industrial Park Cir.
Waldorf, MD 20602
Phone: (301)645-9480
Publisher's E-mail: somdcirc@somdnews.com
County newspaper. **Freq:** Semiweekly (Wed. and Fri.). **Key Personnel:** Rob Perry, Editor, phone: (443)231-3387. **Subscription Rates:** $44.41 Individuals. **URL:** http://www.somdnews.com/independent. **Circ:** Paid ♦**17371**.

15684 ■ The Southern Maryland Wedding Guide: Planning a Southern Maryland Wedding just Got Better
The Southern Maryland Wedding Guide L.L.C.
3195 Old Washington Rd.
Waldorf, MD 20602
Phone: (301)274-2440
Publisher's E-mail: info@somdweddings.com
Bridal magazine featuring wedding planning and services in the Southern Maryland area. **Key Personnel:** Kimberly Bean, Chief Executive Officer, Founder. **URL:** http://www.somdweddings.com. **Circ:** (Not Reported).

WELCOME

15685 ■ Ethical Human Psychology and Psychiatry
International Society for Ethical Psychology and Psychiatry
5884 Joshua Pl.
Welcome, MD 20693
Freq: 3/year. **Subscription Rates:** $85 Individuals print; $210 Institutions print; $80 Individuals online; $200 Institutions online. **URL:** http://www.springerpub.com/ethical-human-psychology-and-psychiatry.html. **Remarks:** Accepts advertising. **Circ:** (Not Reported).

WESTMINSTER

Carroll Co. Carroll Co. (N). 28 m NW of Baltimore. Western Maryland College; Carroll County Farm Museum. Manufactures car assembly parts, clothing, fertilizer, soft drinks. Crafts distribution. Meat packing. Agriculture. Dairy products, peaches, apples.

15686 ■ Carroll County Times
Landmark Community Newspapers L.L.C.
201 Railroad Ave.
Westminster, MD 21158
Phone: (410)875-5400
Free: 877-228-4637
Publisher's E-mail: marketing@lcni.com
General newspaper. **Freq:** Daily. **Print Method:** Offset. **Trim Size:** 13 3/4 x 22 3/4. **Cols./Page:** 6. **Col. Width:** 24 nonpareils. **Col. Depth:** 301 agate lines. **Key Personnel:** Trish McCarthy Carroll, Publisher, phone: (410)857-7885; Paul Milton, Editor, phone: (410)857-7878; Wayne Carter, Editor, phone: (410)857-7879. **Subscription Rates:** $129.01 Individuals Mon.-Sun.; $73.67 Individuals 6 months; Mon.-Sun.; $41.34 Individuals 3 months; Mon.-Sun.; $51.63 Individuals Sunday only; $27.56 Individuals 6 months; Sunday only; $15.32 Individuals 3 months; Sunday only. **URL:** http://www.carrollcountytimes.com. **Mailing address:** PO Box 346, Westminster, MD 21158. **Ad Rates:** 4C $1699. **Remarks:** Accepts advertising. **Circ:** Mon.-Sat. ★**24297**, Sun. ★**26634**.

15687 ■ Community Times
Landmark Community Newspapers L.L.C.
201 Railroad Ave.
Westminster, MD 21158
Phone: (410)848-4400
Free: 877-228-4637
Publication E-mail: ctimes@lcniofmd.com
Community newspaper. **Freq:** Daily and Sun. **Print Method:** Letterpress and Offset. **Cols./Page:** 6. **Col. Width:** 24 nonpareils. **Col. Depth:** 300 agate lines. **Key Personnel:** Baxter Smith, Editor, phone: (410)751-5916. **Subscription Rates:** $1.99 Individuals /week - (in zip codes 21071, 21133, 21163, 21117, 21136); $0.99 Individuals digital - 10 days. **URL:** http://www.carrollcountytimes.com/publications/community_times. **Mailing address:** PO Box 346, Westminster, MD 21158. **Ad Rates:** BW $1338; 4C $1658; SAU $10.92. **Remarks:** Accepts advertising. **Circ:** (Not Reported).

15688 ■ The McDaniel Free Press
The McDaniel Free Press
2 College Hill
Westminster, MD 21157
Phone: (410)848-7000
Fax: (410)857-2752
Publication E-mail: phoenix@mcdaniel.edu
Collegiate newspaper. **Founded:** 1922. **Freq:** Bimonthly. **Print Method:** Letterpress and offset. **Trim Size:** 10 1/4 x 15. **Cols./Page:** 5. **Col. Width:** 24 nonpareils. **Col. Depth:** 196 agate lines. **Key Personnel:** Melanie Ojwang, Editor-in-Chief; Josh Ambrose, Advisor. **Subscription Rates:** $15 Individuals. **URL:** http://www.mcdaniel.edu. **Formerly:** The Phoenix; The Gold Bug; The Scrimshaw. **Ad Rates:** GLR $.15; BW $472.50; PCI $6.30. **Remarks:** Accepts advertising. **Circ:** ‡1,500.

15689 ■ WTTR-AM - 1470
101 WTTR Ln.
Westminster, MD 21158
Phone: (410)848-5511
Fax: (410)876-5095
Email: info@wttr.com
Format: Full Service; Sports; Agricultural; Oldies. **Networks:** Fox. **Owner:** Sajak Broadcasting Corp., 236 Admiral Dr., Annapolis, MD 21401, Ph: (410)263-1902, Fax: (410)268-5360, Free: 888-345 9628. **Founded:** 1953. **Operating Hours:** Continuous. **ADI:** Baltimore, MD. **Wattage:** 1,000 Day 1,000 Nig. **Ad Rates:** Advertising accepted; rates available upon request. **URL:** http://www.wttr.com.

WHEATON

Montgomery Co. (WC). 5 m N of Washington, DC. Residential

15690 ■ Bilingual Research Journal
National Association for Bilingual Education
c/o Ana G. Mendez University System
1106 Veirs Mills Rd., No. L-1
Wheaton, MD 20902
Phone: (240)450-3700
Fax: (240)450-3799
Journal covering bilingual research. **Freq:** 4/yr. **ISSN:** 1523--5882 (print); **EISSN:** 1523--5890 (electronic). **Subscription Rates:** $103 Individuals print only; $300 Institutions online only; $343 Institutions print and online. **URL:** http://www.nabe.org/Publications; http://www.tandfonline.com/loi/ubrj20/#.V0KOajWrS0O. **Remarks:** Advertising accepted; rates available upon request. **Circ:** (Not Reported).

15691 ■ WACA-AM - 1540
2730 University Blvd. W, Ste. 200
Wheaton, MD 20902
Phone: (301)942-3500
Fax: (301)942-7798
Format: Hispanic. **URL:** http://radioamerica.net.

WILLIAMSPORT

Washington Co. Washington Co. (NW). 5 m S of Hagerstown.

15692 ■ WCRH-FM - 90.5
PO Box 439
Williamsport, MD 21795
Phone: (301)582-0282
Email: crm@cedarridge.org
Format: Religious. **Networks:** Moody Broadcasting; Ambassador Inspirational Radio. **Owner:** Cedar Ridge Ministries, 12146 Cedar Ridge Rd., Williamsport, MD 21795, Ph: (301)582-0282. **Founded:** 1976. **Operating Hours:** Continuous; 50% network, 50% local. **ADI:** Hagerstown, MD. **Key Personnel:** Jeffrey Bean, Director; Michael Gardner, Chairman; Jeff Semler, V. Ch. **Wattage:** 10,000. **Ad Rates:** Noncommercial. **URL:** http://cedarridgeministries.org.

WORTON

15693 ■ WKHS-FM - 90.5
PO Box 905
Worton, MD 21678
Phone: (410)778-4249
Fax: (410)778-3802
Format: Jazz. **Simulcasts:** WXPN. **Owner:** Kent County Board of Education, 215 Washington Ave., Chestertown, MD 21620, Ph: (410)778-1595. **Founded:** 1973. **Operating Hours:** Continuous. **Key Personnel:** Steve Kramarck, Station Mgr. **Wattage:** 17,500 ERP. **Ad Rates:** Accepts Advertising. **URL:** http://www.wkhsradio.org/.

ACTON

NE MA. Middlesex Co. 18 mi. NW of Cambridge. Manufactures concrete, chemical products, motors, generators, mechanical measuring and controlling instruments, calculators, textiles. Truck, poultry, fruit, dairy farms.

15694 ■ WHAB-FM
96 Charter Rd.
Acton, MA 01720-2931
Phone: (508)264-4700
Fax: (508)263-8409
Format: Eclectic. **Founded:** 1979. **Key Personnel:** Patrick Mullaney, Dir. of Programs. **Wattage:** 008 ERP.

ALLSTON

15695 ■ Cablevision of Boston
28 Travis St.
Allston, MA 02134
Fax: (617)787-6606
Owner: Cablevision Systems Corp., 11020 Flatlands Ave., Brooklyn, NY 11207. **Founded:** 1982. **Cities Served:** Suffolk County.

AMESBURY

15696 ■ New England Cablevision Inc.
194 Rear Main St.
Amesbury, MA 01913
Owner: Diversified Communications, PO Box 7437, Portland, ME 04112, Ph: (207)842-5400, Fax: (207)842-5405. **Founded:** 1982. **Cities Served:** subscribing households 12,500. **URL:** http://corp.sec.state.ma.us/CorpWeb/CorpSearch/CorpSummary.aspx?FEIN=010343576&SEARCH_TYPE=1.

AMHERST

WC MA. Hampshire Co. 4 mi. E. of Connecticut River, 14 mi. N. of Holyoke. Amherst College (coed); Hampshire College (co-ed). University of Massachusetts. Publishing industry. Dairy and poultry farms. Tobacco, onions, apples.

15697 ■ Amherst
Amherst College
PO Box 5000
Amherst, MA 01002-5000
Phone: (413)542-2000
College alumni publication. **Freq:** Quarterly Winter, Spring, Summer and Fall. **Print Method:** Offset. **Cols./Page:** 3. **Col. Width:** 26 nonpareils. **Col. Depth:** 130 agate lines. **Key Personnel:** Emily Gold Boutilier, Editor, phone: (413)542-8275; Betsy Cannon Smith, Editor, phone: (413)542-2031; Suzanne Auerbach, Director. **URL:** http://www.amherst.edu/aboutamherst/magazine. **Circ:** (Not Reported).

15698 ■ Amherst Bulletin
H.S. Gere & Sons Inc.
9 East Pleasant St.
Amherst, MA 01002
Phone: (413)549-2000
General newspaper. **Freq:** Weekly. **Print Method:** Offset. **Trim Size:** 13 3/4 x 22 3/4. **Cols./Page:** 6. **Col. Width:** 24 agate lines. **Col. Depth:** 301 nonpareils. **Key Personnel:** Jim Foudy, Publisher; Debra Scherban, Editor. **ISSN:** 0192-8449 (print). **Subscription Rates:** $147 Individuals; $260 By mail. **URL:** http://www.amherstbulletin.com; http://www.gazettenet.com. **Ad Rates:** BW $1104; 4C $1554; PCI $11.05. **Remarks:** Accepts advertising. **Circ:** Controlled 13,000.

15699 ■ Amherst Student
Amherst College
Amherst College
Box 1912
Amherst, MA 01002
Phone: (413)542-2304
Fax: (413)542-2305
College newspaper. **Freq:** Weekly (Wed.). **Print Method:** Web. **Trim Size:** 10 x 16. **Cols./Page:** 2. **Key Personnel:** Mary Byrne, Publisher; Nazir Khan, Editor-in-Chief; Emmett Knowlton, Editor-in-Chief. **Subscription Rates:** $40 Individuals /semester; $75 Individuals /year. **URL:** http://amherststudent.amherst.edu. **Ad Rates:** BW $560; PCI $7. **Remarks:** Accepts advertising. **Circ:** Controlled 2500.

15700 ■ Cineaste: America's Leading Magazine on the Art and Politics of the Cinema
Cineaste Publishers Inc.
c/o Barbara Saltz, Advertising Representative
6 University Dr., Ste. 206, PMB 161
Amherst, MA 01002
Phone: (413)230-3488
Fax: (413)230-3367
Motion Pictures see also. **Freq:** Quarterly. **Print Method:** Offset. **Trim Size:** 8 1/2 x 11. **Cols./Page:** 2 and 3. **Col. Width:** 21 and 13.5 picas. **Col. Depth:** 137 agate lines. **Key Personnel:** Richard Porton, Board Member; Barbara Saltz, Advertising Representative; Dan Georgakas, Editor; Gary Crowdus, Editor-in-Chief, Founder; Cynthia Lucia, Board Member; Rahul Hamid, Board Member. **ISSN:** 0009--7004 (print). **Subscription Rates:** $22 Individuals; $27 Other countries. **URL:** http://www.cineaste.com. **Ad Rates:** BW $500; 4C $750. **Remarks:** Accepts advertising. **Circ:** 11000.

15701 ■ The Common
Amherst College
PO Box 5000
Amherst, MA 01002-5000
Phone: (413)542-2000
Publication E-mail: info@thecommononline.org
Journal featuring essays, documentaries, fiction and poetry. **Freq:** Semiannual fall and spring. **Key Personnel:** Jennifer Acker, Editor. **Subscription Rates:** $24 Individuals print; $42 Two years print; $30 Individuals print and digital; $52 Two years print and digital; $12 Individuals digital; $20 Two years digital. **URL:** http://www.thecommononline.org; http://www.amherst.edu/arts/the-common. **Circ:** (Not Reported).

15702 ■ Critical Reviews in Food Science & Nutrition
Taylor & Francis Group Journals
c/o Fergus M. Clydesdale, Editor
Department of Food Science
College of Natural Resources & the Environment
University of Massachusetts at Amherst
Amherst, MA 01003
Publisher's E-mail: customerservice@taylorandfrancis.com
Journal focusing on current technology, food science, and human nutrition. **Freq:** 12/yr. **Key Personnel:** Fergus M. Clydesdale, Editor; Ken Lee, Advisor; Joseph Hotchkiss, Advisor; C.Y. Lee, Advisor; John W. Erdman, Jr., Advisor. **ISSN:** 1040--8398 (print); **EISSN:** 1549--7852 (electronic). **Subscription Rates:** $4855 Institutions print and online; $4248 Institutions online only; $489 Individuals print only. **URL:** http://www.tandfonline.com/toc/bfsn20/current. **Circ:** (Not Reported).

15703 ■ English Literary Renaissance
Massachusetts Center for Interdisciplinary Renaissance Studies
650 E Pleasant St.
Amherst, MA 01002
Phone: (413)577-3600
Publisher's E-mail: renaissance@english.umass.edu
Scholarly journal covering literature in England from 1485-1666. **Freq:** 3/year. **Key Personnel:** Arthur F. Kinney, Editor. **ISSN:** 0013--8312 (print); **EISSN:** 1475--6757 (electronic). **Subscription Rates:** $284 U.S. online; £169 Institutions online - UK; €216 Institutions online - Europe; $341 U.S. print and online; £203 Institutions print and online - UK; €260 Institutions print and online - Europe; $284 U.S. and other countries print; £169 Institutions print - UK; €216 Institutions print - Europe; $44 Individuals print and online; €44 Individuals print and online - UK, Europe; £27 Individuals print and online - ROW; $23 Students print and online; £17 Students print and online - UK, Europe and Rest of the World. **URL:** http://www.umass.edu/renaissance/; http://onlinelibrary.wiley.com/journal/10.1111/(ISSN)1475-6757. **Mailing address:** PO Box 2300, Amherst, MA 01004. **Ad Rates:** BW $100. **Remarks:** Accepts advertising. **Circ:** Combined 1450.

15704 ■ Equity & Excellence in Education
Routledge
c/o Maurianne Adams, Editor
University of Massachusetts
370 Hills S, 111 Thatcher Rd.
Amherst, MA 01003
Publisher's E-mail: book.orders@tandf.co.uk
Journal publishing essays that describe and assess practical efforts to achieve educational equity and are contextualized within an appropriate literature review. **Freq:** Quarterly. **Key Personnel:** Maurianne Adams, Editor. **ISSN:** 1066--5684 (print); **EISSN:** 1547--3457 (electronic). **Subscription Rates:** $109 Individuals print only; $243 Institutions online only; $278 Institutions print and online. **URL:** http://www.tandfonline.com/toc/ueee20/current. **Circ:** (Not Reported).

15705 ■ Food Biotechnology
Taylor & Francis Group Journals
Department of Food Sciences
University of Massachusetts
340 Chenoweth Laboratory
Box 31410
Amherst, MA 01003

Circulation: ★ = AAM; △ or • = BPA; ♦ = CAC; ❑ = VAC; ⊕ = PO Statement; ‡ = Publisher's Report; Boldface figures = sworn; Light figures = estimated.

Publisher's E-mail: customerservice@taylorandfrancis.com
Peer-reviewed journal focusing on recent developments and applications of modern genetics as well as enzyme, cell, tissue, and organ-based biological processes to produce and improve foods, food ingredients, and functional foods. **Freq:** Quarterly. **Key Personnel:** Dr. Kalidas Shetty, Editor; R. Gonzalez, Board Member; M.P. Davidson, Board Member; D.G. Hoover, Board Member. **ISSN:** 0890--5436 (print); **EISSN:** 1532--4249 (electronic). **Subscription Rates:** $2421 Institutions print and online; $2118 Institutions online only; $600 Individuals print only. **URL:** http://tandfonline.com/toc/lfbt20/current. **Circ:** (Not Reported).

15706 ■ The Indicator
Amherst College
PO Box 5000
Amherst, MA 01002-5000
Phone: (413)542-2000
Publication E-mail: theindicator@amherst.edu
Journal on social and political issues. **Key Personnel:** Karl Teo Molin, Editor. **Subscription Rates:** $35 Individuals. **URL:** http://www.amherst.edu/campuslife/studentgroups/indicator. **Circ:** (Not Reported).

15707 ■ Journal of Alternative Investments
Chartered Alternative Investment Analyst Association
100 University Dr.
Amherst, MA 01002-2357
Phone: (413)253-7373
Fax: (413)253-4494
Publisher's E-mail: info@caia.org
Freq: Quarterly. **Key Personnel:** Hossein Kazemi, Editor-in-Chief. **Subscription Rates:** $845 Individuals; $1437 Two years; $2028 Individuals 3 years. **URL:** http://www.iijournals.com/toc/jai/current. **Remarks:** Advertising not accepted. **Circ:** (Not Reported).

15708 ■ The Journal of Alternative Investments
Institutional Investor Inc. Journals Group
c/o Thomas Schneeweis, Ed.
University of Massachusetts
Amherst, MA 01003
Phone: (413)545-5641
Fax: (413)545-3858
Publication E-mail: jai@som.umass.edu
Journal covering research on investing in and managing alternative investments, including commodities, hedge funds, private equity, funds of funds, futures, oil and gas and timber for money managers of alternative investments and institutional investors. **Freq:** Quarterly. **Print Method:** Web offset. **Trim Size:** 8 3/8" x 10 7/8". **Key Personnel:** Hossein Kazemi, Editor-in-Chief. **ISSN:** 1520-3255 (print). **Subscription Rates:** $1185 Individuals; $2015 Two years; $2844 Individuals 3 years. **URL:** http://www.iijournals.com/toc/jai/current. **Ad Rates:** BW $5,532; 4C $9,133. **Remarks:** Accepts advertising. **Circ:** (Not Reported).

15709 ■ Massachusetts Daily Collegian
University of Massachusetts
109 Munson Hall
Amherst, MA 01003
Phone: (413)545-0444
Fax: (413)545-3082
Collegiate newpaper in New England. **Freq:** Daily. **Print Method:** Offset. **Cols./Page:** 6. **Col. Width:** 12.5 picas. **Col. Depth:** 21 inches. **URL:** http://dailycollegian.com. **Ad Rates:** BW $2,394; 4C $500; PCI $19. **Remarks:** Advertising accepted; rates available upon request. **Circ:** Free ‡17000.

15710 ■ The Massachusetts Review
University of Massachusetts
109 Munson Hall
Amherst, MA 01003
Phone: (413)545-0444
Fax: (413)545-3082
Magazine of literature, arts, and current affairs. **Freq:** Quarterly. **Print Method:** Offset. **Trim Size:** 6 x 9. **Cols./Page:** 1. **Col. Width:** 6 inches. **Key Personnel:** David Lenson, Editor; Aaron Hellem, Managing Editor. **ISSN:** 0025--4878 (print). **Subscription Rates:** $29 Individuals; $55 Two years; $48 Other countries; $93 Two years overseas; $35 Libraries; $68 Two years library. **URL:** http://www.massreview.org. **Ad Rates:** BW $125. **Remarks:** Accepts advertising. **Circ:** Paid ‡1400, Non-paid ‡300.

15711 ■ Pakn Treger
Yiddish Book Center
Harry and Jeanette Weinberg Bldg.
1021 West St.
Amherst, MA 01002
Phone: (413)256-4900
Fax: (413)256-4700
Publisher's E-mail: yiddish@bikher.org
Freq: Semiannual. **Subscription Rates:** included in membership dues; $6 for nonmembers. **Alt. Formats:** E-book. **URL:** http://www.yiddishbookcenter.org/pakn-treger. **Remarks:** Accepts advertising. **Circ:** 30000.

15712 ■ Peregrine
Amherst Writers and Artists Press Inc.
190 University Dr., Ste. 1
Amherst, MA 01002-3818
Phone: (413)253-3307
Publication E-mail: peregrine@amherstwriters.com
Literary journal covering poetry, fiction, essays. **Founded:** 1984. **Freq:** Annual. **Trim Size:** 6 x 9. **ISSN:** 0890-622X (print). **Subscription Rates:** $12 Single issue sample issue; $15 Individuals current copy. **URL:** http://www.amherstwriters.com/index.php/awa-press/peregrine. **Mailing address:** PO Box 1076, Amherst, MA 01004. **Remarks:** Advertising not accepted. **Circ:** (Not Reported).

15713 ■ Pesticide Biochemistry and Physiology
RELX Group P.L.C.
c/o J.M. Clark, Ed.
University of Massachusetts
Dept. of Veterinary & Animal Sciences
311B Morrill 1 N
Amherst, MA 01003
Publisher's E-mail: amsterdam@relx.com
Journal publishing scientific articles pertaining to the mode action of plant protection agents, such as insecticides, fungicides, herbicides, similar compounds including nonlethal pest control agents, biosynthesis of pheromones, hormones, and plant resistance agents. **Freq:** 9/yr. **Trim Size:** 6 7/8 x 10. **Key Personnel:** J.M. Clark, Editor. **ISSN:** 0048--3575 (print). **Subscription Rates:** $1964 Institutions print; $509 Individuals print; $818.33 Institutions online. **URL:** http://www.journals.elsevier.com/pesticide-biochemistry-and-physiology. **Remarks:** Accepts advertising. **Circ:** (Not Reported).

15714 ■ Review of Radical Political Economics
Union for Radical Political Economics
c/o Frances Boyes
University of Massachusetts
418 N Pleasant St.
Amherst, MA 01002-1735
Phone: (413)577-0806
Fax: (413)577-0261
Publisher's E-mail: sales@pfp.sagepub.com
Academic journal containing information on radical political economics. **Freq:** Quarterly. **Trim Size:** 7 x 10. **Cols./Page:** 1. **Col. Width:** 30 picas. **Col. Depth:** 42 picas. **Key Personnel:** David Barkin, Editor; Enid Arvidson, Managing Editor. **ISSN:** 0486--6134 (print); **EISSN:** 1552--8502 (electronic). **Subscription Rates:** £348 Institutions e-access; £379 Institutions print only; £387 Institutions print and e-access; £104 Institutions single print issue. **URL:** http://rrp.sagepub.com. **Remarks:** Accepts advertising. **Circ:** 2400.

15715 ■ UMASS Magazine: The Magazine for Alumni & Friends of the University
University of Massachusetts
109 Munson Hall
Amherst, MA 01003
Phone: (413)545-0444
Fax: (413)545-3082
Magazine containing collegiate and alumni news. **Freq:** Quarterly. **Print Method:** Web Offset. **Trim Size:** 8 x 10 3/4. **Cols./Page:** 3. **Col. Width:** 28 nonpareils. **Col. Depth:** 210 agate lines. **Key Personnel:** Patricia Sullivan, Managing Editor; Robert Lindquist, Executive Officer. **URL:** http://umassmag.com. **Formerly:** Contact, Massachusetts Magazine. **Ad Rates:** BW $3600; 4C $5040. **Remarks:** Accepts advertising. **Circ:** Free ‡200000, ‡190000.

15716 ■ Veterinary Immunology and Immunopathology: An International Journal of Comparative Immunology
Mosby Inc.
University of Massachusetts
Amherst, MA 01003-9305
Journal publishing articles on fundamental research on animal immune systems, new techniques and developments in veterinary immunodiagnosis, immunogenetics, immunology and immunopathology of parasitic and infectious disease, and clinical immunology in animals. **Freq:** 14/yr. **Trim Size:** 8 1/4 X 11. **Key Personnel:** C.L. Baldwin, Editor-in-Chief; Dr. J. Naessens, Editor-in-Chief. **ISSN:** 0165--2427 (print). **Subscription Rates:** $4173.60 Institutions e-journal; $4173 Individuals print. **URL:** http://www.journals.elsevier.com/veterinary-immunology-and-immunopathology. **Ad Rates:** BW $1610; 4C $2875. **Remarks:** Accepts advertising. **Circ:** ‡125.

15717 ■ WAMH-FM - 89.3
Amherst College
Campus Ctr.
Amherst, MA 01002-5000
Phone: (413)542-2224
Email: wamh@amherst.edu
Format: Full Service. **Networks:** Independent. **Founded:** 1948. **Formerly:** WAMF-FM. **Operating Hours:** Continuous; 100% local. **Key Personnel:** Ashley Hogan, Gen. Mgr.; Dan Correia, Chief Engineer. **Wattage:** 150. **URL:** http://www.www3.amherst.edu/~wamh.

15718 ■ WFCR-FM - 88.5
Hampshire House
University of Massachusetts
131 County Cir.
Amherst, MA 01003-9257
Phone: (413)545-0100
Fax: (413)545-2546
Email: radio@wfcr.org
Format: Classical; Jazz; News; Folk; Public Radio. **Networks:** National Public Radio (NPR); Public Radio International (PRI). **Owner:** University of Massachusetts Amherst, 37 Mather Dr., Amherst, MA 01002, Ph: (413)545-0111, Fax: (413)545-3880. **Founded:** 1961. **Operating Hours:** Continuous. **ADI:** Springfield, MA. **Key Personnel:** Martin Miller, Gen. Mgr., miller@wfcr.org; John Montanari, Music Dir.; Chuck Dube, Chief Engineer, cld@wfcr.org. **Wattage:** 13,000. **Ad Rates:** Noncommercial. **URL:** http://www.nepr.net.

15719 ■ WMUA-FM - 91.1
University of Massachusetts
105 Campus Ctr.
Amherst, MA 01003
Phone: (413)545-2876
Fax: (413)545-0682
Format: Alternative/New Music/Progressive. **Networks:** AP. **Founded:** 1949. **Operating Hours:** Continuous. **Local Programs:** *The Jazz Garden*, Monday 9:00 a.m. - 12:00 p.m.; *Writer's Voice*, Friday 4:00 p.m. - 5:00 p.m.; *Poetry a la Carte*, Wednesday 5:00 p.m. - 5:30 p.m.; *Jazz in Silhouette*, Friday 9:00 a.m. - 12:00 p.m.; *Oblivion Express*, Tuesday 6:00 a.m. - 8:00 a.m.; *Fresh Sounds*, Tuesday 9:00 a.m. - 12:00 p.m.; *Acoustic Cafe*, Sunday 2:00 p.m. - 4:00 p.m.; *Mnemonics*, Thursday 8:00 p.m. - 10:00 p.m.; *Polka Bandstand*, Saturday 8:30 a.m. - 12:00 p.m.; *Cheap Thrills*; *Melting Point*, Tuesday 12:00 p.m. - 2:00 p.m.; *Underground Spiritual Game*, Saturday 6:00 p.m. - 8:00 p.m.; *Nothing to Say and Saying It*. **Wattage:** 450. **Ad Rates:** Noncommercial. **URL:** http://www.wmua.org.

ANDOVER

NE MA. Essex Co. 3 mi. S. of Lawrence. Manufactures electronics, card cloth, dyestuffs and chemicals.

15720 ■ Il Tridente
RMS Media Group, Inc.
300 Brickstone Sq., Ste. 904
Andover, MA 01810
Phone: (978)623-8020
Fax: (978)824-3975
Publisher's E-mail: info@rmsmg.com
Magazine for Maserati enthusiasts. **URL:** http://www.rmsmg.com/work/iltridente.html. **Circ:** (Not Reported).

15721 ■ New York Stock Exchange
RMS Media Group, Inc.
300 Brickstone Sq., Ste. 904
Andover, MA 01810
Phone: (978)623-8020
Fax: (978)824-3975

Publisher's E-mail: info@rmsmg.com
Magazine highlighting the business communities. **URL:** http://rmsmg.com/work.html. **Circ:** 100000.

15722 ■ Northshore
RMS Media Group, Inc.
300 Brickstone Sq., Ste. 904
Andover, MA 01810
Phone: (978)623-8020
Fax: (978)824-3975
Publication E-mail: info@rmsmg.com
Magazine covering the lifestyle and people of North Shore section of New England. **Freq:** 8/year. **URL:** http://rmsmg.com/work.html. **Circ:** (Not Reported).

15723 ■ Ocean Home
RMS Media Group, Inc.
300 Brickstone Sq., Ste. 904
Andover, MA 01810
Phone: (978)623-8020
Fax: (978)824-3975
Publisher's E-mail: info@rmsmg.com
Magazine for oceanfront property owners and home buyers. **Freq:** Bimonthly. **URL:** http://rmsmg.com/work.html. **Circ:** (Not Reported).

15724 ■ WPAA-FM - 91.7
180 Main St.
Andover, MA 01810
Phone: (978)749-4000
Fax: (978)749-4415
Email: wpaa@aol.com
Format: Eclectic. **Owner:** Phillips Academy, at above address. **Founded:** 1965. **Operating Hours:** Weekdays: 6:30-8 a.m., 5 p.m.-midnight Weekends 8:00 a.m.-midnight. **Key Personnel:** Kelly Sinclair, Exec. Dir.; Kelly Trainor, Gen. Mgr. **Wattage:** 10,000. **Ad Rates:** Advertising accepted; rates available upon request. **URL:** http://www.andover.edu/About/AdministrationGovernance/Pages/Trustees.aspx.

ATHOL

C. MA. Worcester Co. 29 mi. W. of Fitchburg. Manufactures mechanical tools, drills, cutters, shoes, artificial leather, leather findings, celluloid goods, wooden toys, textile machinery, window blinds, furniture, metal and wooden novelties, plastic extrusions, paper boxes.

15725 ■ Athol Daily News
Athol Press
225 Exchange St.
Athol, MA 01331
Phone: (978)249-3535
Publication E-mail: newsroom@atholdailynews.com
General newspaper. **Print Method:** Offset. **Cols./Page:** 6. **Col. Width:** 25 nonpareils. **Col. Depth:** 294 agate lines. **Key Personnel:** Jacki Caron, Manager, Advertising; Lisa Arnot, Office Manager. **Subscription Rates:** $171.60 Individuals home delivery; $202.80 By mail; $99.99 Individuals online. **URL:** http://atholdailynews.com. **Mailing address:** PO Box 1000, Athol, MA 01331. **Remarks:** Accepts advertising. **Circ:** ‡4300.

ATTLEBORO

SE MA. Bristol Co. 8 mi. N. of Pawtucket, RI. Manufactures jewelry and jewelry findings, bleach, dyes, reinforced paper, gold and silver plate, tools, nuclear fuel, electronic components, optical goods, paper boxes, rubber stamps, metal specialties, labels and seals, badges.

15726 ■ MJSA Journal
Manufacturing Jewelers and Suppliers of America
8 Hayward St.
Attleboro, MA 02703
Phone: (508)316-2132
Fax: (508)316-1429
Publisher's E-mail: info@mjsa.org
Magazine covering all aspects of jewelry making. **Freq:** Monthly. **URL:** http://www.mjsa.org/publicationsmedia/mjsa_journal. **Ad Rates:** BW $3197; 4C $4862. **Remarks:** Accepts advertising. **Circ:** (Not Reported).

15727 ■ The Sun Chronicle
The Sun Chronicle
34 S Main St.
Attleboro, MA 02703-0600
Phone: (508)222-7000
Fax: (508)236-0462
Publication E-mail: news@thesunchronicle.com
General newspaper. **Freq:** Daily (eve.), Sat. and Sun. (morn.). **Print Method:** Offset. **Cols./Page:** 6. **Col. Width:** 2 1/6 inches. **Col. Depth:** 21 1/4 inches. **Key Personnel:** Oreste D'Arconte, Publisher; Mike Kirby, Editor. **Subscription Rates:** $226 Individuals; $112.75 Individuals 6 months; $56.50 Individuals 3 months. **URL:** http://www.thesunchronicle.com. **Mailing address:** PO Box 600, Attleboro, MA 02703-0600. **Ad Rates:** PCI $17.68. **Remarks:** Accepts advertising. **Circ:** Mon.-Sat. ★**17,799**, Sun. ★**18,655**.

15728 ■ WARA-AM - 1320
45 West St.
Attleboro, MA 02703
Email: talk@am1320wara.com
Format: Eclectic. **Founded:** 1950. **Operating Hours:** 6:00 a.m. - 12:00 p.m. , 8:00 p.m. - 10:00 p.m. Monday - Friday, 7:00 a.m. - 8:00 a.m. , 9:00 a.m. - 12:00 p.m. Saturday. **Key Personnel:** Joseph Mangiacotti, Contact. **Wattage:** 5,000 KW. **Ad Rates:** Noncommercial. Underwriting available. **URL:** http://www.wararadio.com/.

AUBURNDALE

15729 ■ The Oxfordian
Shakespeare Oxford Fellowship
PO Box 66083
Auburndale, MA 02466
Publisher's E-mail: info@shakespeareoxfordfellowship.org
Freq: Annual Summer/Fall. **Key Personnel:** Michael Egan, Editor. **ISSN:** 1521--3641 (print). **Subscription Rates:** Included in membership. **URL:** http://www.shakespeareoxfordfellowship.org/the-oxfordian. **Remarks:** Advertising not accepted. **Circ:** (Not Reported).

BARRE

C. MA. Worcester Co. 22 mi. NW of Worcester. Machine shop and foundry. Dairy farms.

15730 ■ Barre Gazette
Turley Publications
5 Exchange St.
Barre, MA 01005
Phone: (978)355-4000
Fax: (978)355-6274
Publisher's E-mail: support@turley.com
Community newspaper. **Freq:** Weekly (Thurs.). **Print Method:** Offset. **Trim Size:** 13 x 21. **Cols./Page:** 8. **Col. Width:** 1 1/2 inches. **Col. Depth:** 294 agate lines. **Key Personnel:** Ellie Downer, Editor; Patrick H. Turley, Publisher, phone: (413)283-8393. **USPS:** 044-560. **Subscription Rates:** $33 Individuals; $44 Two years; $38 Out of area; $54 Out of area 2 years. **URL:** http://barregazette.turley.com/. **Mailing address:** PO Box 448, Barre, MA 01005. **Ad Rates:** GLR $.334; BW $1008; 4C $1308; PCI $6. **Remarks:** Accepts advertising. **Circ:** 2,666.

15731 ■ The Natural Farmer: Publication of the Northeast Organic Farming Association
Northeast Organic Farming Association, Massachusetts Chapter
411 Sheldon Rd.
Barre, MA 01005
Phone: (978)355-2853
Fax: (978)355-4046
Publisher's E-mail: info@nofamass.org
Newspaper featuring farming issues. **Freq:** Quarterly. **ISSN:** 1077--2294 (print). **Alt. Formats:** PDF. **URL:** http://www.nofa.org/tnf/index.php. **Ad Rates:** BW $360; 4C $500. **Remarks:** Accepts advertising. **Circ:** (Not Reported).

BELMONT

NE MA. Middlesex Co. 6 mi. NW of Boston. (Branch of Boston P.O.) Residential.

15732 ■ Sons of Italy News: New England's Largest Italian-American Newspaper
Grand Lodge of Massachusetts, Order of the Sons of Italy
93 Concord Ave.
Belmont, MA 02478-4061
Phone: (617)489-5234
Fax: (617)489-5371
Publication E-mail: newspaper@osiama.org
Fraternal magazine. **Freq:** Bimonthly. **Print Method:** Offset. **Cols./Page:** 5. **Col. Width:** 22 nonpareils. **Col. Depth:** 210 agate lines. **Key Personnel:** Pamela Donnaruma, Editor. **ISSN:** 0038-1446 (print). **Subscription Rates:** $2 Individuals. **URL:** http://www.osiama.org/newspaper.html. **Ad Rates:** BW $500. **Remarks:** Accepts advertising. **Circ:** (Not Reported).

BERNARDSTON

15733 ■ Shropshire Voice
American Shropshire Registry Association
c/o Becky Peterson, Secretary
41 Bell Rd.
Bernardston, MA 01337
Phone: (413)624-9652
Publisher's E-mail: shropsec@hotmail.com
Freq: 3/year. **Subscription Rates:** $5 Single issue; $15 Individuals. **URL:** http://shropshires.org/text/shropshire-voice.html. **Ad Rates:** BW $125; 4C $250. **Remarks:** Accepts advertising. **Circ:** (Not Reported).

BEVERLY

NE MA. Essex Co. On an inlet of the Atlantic Ocean, 20 mi. NE of Boston. Summer resort. Manufactures shoe machinery and findings, wood and metal products, textiles, sails, electronic tubes.

15734 ■ Dialogues in Pediatric Urology
The Society for Pediatric Urology
500 Cummings Ctr., Ste. 4550
Beverly, MA 01915
Phone: (978)927-8330
Fax: (978)524-0498
Freq: 6/year. **Subscription Rates:** $50 /year for nonmembers; included in membership dues. **URL:** http://spuonline.org/journal.cgi. **Remarks:** Advertising not accepted. **Circ:** (Not Reported).

15735 ■ Georgetown Record
GateHouse Media Inc.
72 Cherry Hill Dr.
Beverly, MA 01915
Phone: (978)739-8506
Fax: (978)739-8501
Publication E-mail: georgetown@cnc.com
Community newspaper (tabloid). **Freq:** Weekly (Thurs.). **Print Method:** Offset. **Trim Size:** 11 3/8 x 17. **Cols./Page:** 5. **Col. Width:** 2 1/16 inches. **Col. Depth:** 16 inches. **Key Personnel:** Rosemary Herbert, Editor. **USPS:** 746-610. **Subscription Rates:** $66 Individuals residents of Georgetown; $85 Out of area. **URL:** http://www.wickedlocal.com/georgetown/. **Circ:** (Not Reported).

15736 ■ Hamilton-Wenham Chronicle
GateHouse Media Inc.
72 Cherry Hill Dr.
Beverly, MA 01915
Publication E-mail: hamilton-wenham@cnc.com
Community newspaper (tabloid). **Freq:** Weekly (Wed.). **Print Method:** Offset. **Trim Size:** 11 3/8 x 17. **Cols./Page:** 5. **Col. Width:** 2 1/16 inches. **Col. Depth:** 16 inches. **Key Personnel:** Sam Trapani, Editor, phone: (978)739-8542; Chris Hurley, Editor, phone: (978)739-8515. **USPS:** 068-550. **Subscription Rates:** $69.95 Individuals; $89.95 Out of area. **URL:** http://hamilton.wickedlocal.com. **Ad Rates:** BW $980; 4C $1,480; SAU $12.25; PCI $12.25. **Remarks:** Accepts advertising. **Circ:** Combined 60253.

15737 ■ Hand
American Association for Hand Surgery
500 Cummings Ctr., Ste. 4550
Beverly, MA 01915
Phone: (978)927-8330
Fax: (978)524-8890
Journal providing multidisciplinary expertise from surgical, medical, hand therapy and other health care professional specialties to advance the quality of care and health of patients with hand and upper extremity pathologies. **Freq:** Quarterly. **ISSN:** 1558- 9447 (print); **EISSN:** 1558- 9455 (electronic). **Subscription Rates:** Included in membership; $311 Nonmembers. **URL:** http://handsurgery.org/Hand/; http://link.springer.com/journal/11552. **Remarks:** Accepts advertising. **Circ:** 900.

15738 ■ Journal of Gastrointestinal Surgery
Society for Surgery of the Alimentary Tract

Circulation: ★ = AAM; △ or • = BPA; ♦ = CAC; ❑ = VAC; ⊕ = PO Statement; ‡ = Publisher's Report; Boldface figures = sworn; Light figures = estimated.

500 Cummings Ctr., Ste. 4550
Beverly, MA 01915
Phone: (978)927-8330
Fax: (978)524-8890
Publisher's E-mail: info@detroitautoscene.com
Contains articles on the latest developments in gastrointestinal surgery. **Freq:** Monthly. **ISSN:** 1091--255X (print); **EISSN:** 1873--4626 (electronic). **Subscription Rates:** Included in membership; $636 Institutions print or online. **URL:** http://www.ssat.com/cgi-bin/Journal-of-GI-Surgery.cgi; http://www.ahpba.org/resources/links.phtml; http://www.springer.com/medicine/surgery/journal/11605. **Remarks:** Accepts advertising. **Circ:** (Not Reported).

15739 ■ Journal of Investigative Medicine
American Federation for Medical Research
500 Cummings Ctr., Ste. 4550
Beverly, MA 01915-6534
Phone: (978)927-8330
Fax: (978)524-8890
Medical journal. **Freq:** Bimonthly. **Print Method:** Letterpress and offset. **Trim Size:** 8 1/8 x 10 7/8. **Cols./Page:** 2. **Col. Width:** 33 nonpareils. **Col. Depth:** 122 agate lines. **Key Personnel:** Veronica M. Catanese, M.D., Editor-in-Chief; Jennifer Coates, Manager, Sales, phone: (905)522-7017, fax: (905)522-7839. **ISSN:** 1081-5589 (print). **Subscription Rates:** $266 Individuals print; $292.60 Individuals online; $319.20 Individuals print and online; $349 Institutions, other countries print. **Available online. URL:** http://www.afmr.org; http://afmr.org/journal.cgi; http://www.afmr.org/journal.cgi. **Remarks:** Accepts advertising. **Circ:** ‡14000.

15740 ■ Marblehead Home and Style
North of Boston Media Group
32 Dunham Rd.
Beverly, MA 01915
Phone: (978)338-1234
Publisher's E-mail: sales@nobmg.com
Magazine featuring home styles. **Key Personnel:** Karen Andreas, Publisher. **Subscription Rates:** $15 Individuals. **URL:** http://www.nobmg.com/information.php#marblehead; http://www.marbleheadhomeandstyle.com. **Remarks:** Accepts advertising. **Circ:** (Not Reported).

15741 ■ North Andover Citizen
GateHouse Media Inc.
72 Cherry Hill Dr.
Beverly, MA 01915
Phone: (978)739-1320
Fax: (978)739-8501
Publication E-mail: northandover@wickedlocal.com
Community newspaper (tabloid). **Freq:** Weekly (Fri.). **Print Method:** Offset. **Trim Size:** 11 3/8 x 17. **Cols./Page:** 4. **Col. Width:** 30 nonpareils. **Col. Depth:** 182 agate lines. **Key Personnel:** Donna Capodelupo, Editor, phone: (978)739-8506; Pete Chianca, Editor-in-Chief; Joe McConnel, Editor, phone: (978)739-1324. **USPS:** 450-630. **Subscription Rates:** $62 Individuals; $85 Out of area. **URL:** http://northandover.wickedlocal.com. **Ad Rates:** BW $644; SAU $8.05. **Remarks:** Accepts advertising. **Circ:** (Not Reported).

15742 ■ Operative Techniques in Thoracic and Cardiovascular Surgery
American Association for Thoracic Surgery
500 Cummings Ctr., Ste. 4550
Beverly, MA 01915-6183
Phone: (978)927-8330
Fax: (978)524-0498
Official journal of the American Association for Thoracic Surgery covering techniques in cardiovascular and thoracic surgery. **Freq:** Quarterly. **Print Method:** Sheetfed. **Trim Size:** 9 x 12. **Key Personnel:** Fred A. Crawford, Jr., Editor-in-Chief. **ISSN:** 1522--2942 (print). **Subscription Rates:** $361 Individuals print and online; $307 Individuals online only; $182 Students print and online; $155 Students online only. **URL:** http://www.optechtcs.com; http://www.journals.elsevier.com/operative-techniques-in-thoracic-and-cardiovascular-surgery; http://www.sciencedirect.com/science/journal/15222942. **Ad Rates:** $315-1215; $575-1500. BW $1040; 4C $1380; BW $4C $. **Remarks:** Accepts display advertising. **Circ:** ‡1020, 900.

15743 ■ Plastic Surgical Nursing
American Society of Plastic Surgical Nurses
500 Cummings Ctr., Ste. 4550
Beverly, MA 01915
Fax: (978)524-0498
Free: 877-337-9315
Freq: Quarterly. **Trim Size:** 7 7/8 x 10 7/8. **Key Personnel:** Tracey Hotta, Editor; Jill Jones, Board Member; Susan Lamp, Board Member. **ISSN:** 0741--5206 (print); **EISSN:** 1550--1841 (electronic). **Subscription Rates:** $90 Individuals print; $533 Institutions print; $98 Canada and Mexico print; $560 Institutions, Canada and Mexico print; $110 Individuals print - UK/ Australia; $670 Institutions, other countries; $194 Other countries print. **URL:** http://journals.lww.com/psnjournalonline/pages/default.aspx. **Ad Rates:** BW $1,505; 4C $1,230. **Remarks:** Accepts advertising. **Circ:** 1204.

15744 ■ Retail Merchandiser: The Authority on Mass, Drug & Specialty Retailing
Phoenix Media Corp.
100 Cummings Ctr., Ste. 211-C
Beverly, MA 01915
Phone: (978)338-6545
Trade publication covering the retail industry. **Freq:** Monthly. **Key Personnel:** Russ Gager, Editor, Manager, phone: (312)676-1128. **URL:** http://www.retail-merchandiser.com. **Remarks:** Accepts advertising. **Circ:** (Not Reported).

The Salem News - See Salem

15745 ■ Seminars in Thoracic and Cardiovascular Surgery
American Association for Thoracic Surgery
500 Cummings Ctr., Ste. 4550
Beverly, MA 01915-6183
Phone: (978)927-8330
Fax: (978)524-0498
Scholarly journal covering thoracic and cardiovascular surgery for the practicing surgeon. **Freq:** Quarterly. **Print Method:** Sheetfed. **Trim Size:** 8 1/4 x 11. **Key Personnel:** Harvey Pass, MD, Editor. **ISSN:** 1043--0679 (print). **Subscription Rates:** $342 Individuals print and online; $291 Individuals online only; $179 Students print and online; $147 Students online only. **URL:** http://www.semthorcardiovascsurg.com; http://www.journals.elsevier.com/seminars-in-thoracic-and-cardiovascular-surgery. **Ad Rates:** $385-1325; $670-1565. BW $1180; 4C $1475; BW $4C $. **Remarks:** Accepts display advertising. **Circ:** Combined ‡1285, 781.

15746 ■ WBOQ-FM - 104.9
8 Enon St.
Beverly, MA 01915
Phone: (978)927-1049
Fax: (978)921-2635
Free: 800-370-1049
Email: sales@northshore1049.com
Format: Oldies. **Networks:** Concert Music Network (CMN). **Owner:** Westport Communications L.L.C., at above address. **Founded:** 1964. **Formerly**: WVCA-FM. **Operating Hours:** Continuous. **Key Personnel:** Todd Tanger, President, todd@wboq.com. **Local Programs:** *Good Time Favorites*, Saturday 9:30 a.m. - 1:00 p.m.; *Beatle Brunch with Joe Johnson*, Sunday 12:00 p.m. 1:00 p.m. **Wattage**: 3,200. **Ad Rates:** Noncommercial. **URL:** http://www.northshore1049.com.

BILLERICA

NC MA. Middlesex Co. 6 mi. S. of Lowell.

15747 ■ Campfire Chatter
North American Family Campers Association
PO Box 345
Billerica, MA 01821
Phone: (781)584-6443
Freq: Monthly. **ISSN:** 0410--4889 (print). **Subscription Rates:** Included in membership. **URL:** http://www.nafca.org/chatter.html. **Remarks:** Accepts advertising. **Circ:** (Not Reported).

BOSTON

E. MA. Suffolk Co. On Massachusetts Bay. The State Capital. Noted educational center with more than 200 private schools and colleges in Boston and immediate vicinity. Many historical features. Important seaport. Foremost fishing port and wool market. The industrial center of New England and center of one of the largest suburban areas in the United States. More than 200,000,000 pounds of fish are landed annually. Extensive fish freezing and cold storage plants. Important industries; printing and publishing, ship building, sugar refining, manufacture of boots and shoes; electrical machinery, textiles, bakery products, confectionery, cutlery, leather, plastics, chemicals, furniture, wooden and paper boxes, foundry and machine shop products, woolens, worsteds, meat packing.

15748 ■ Adweek/New England
Adweek L.P.
100 Boylston St., Ste. 210
Boston, MA 02116
Phone: (617)482-2921
Free: 800-641-2030
Publisher's E-mail: info@adweek.com
News magazine serving the advertising, marketing, and media industries in New England. **Freq:** Weekly. **Print Method:** Offset. **Trim Size:** 8 3/8 x 10 7/8. **Cols./Page:** 3. **Key Personnel:** James Cooper, Executive Editor; Alison Fahey, Executive Director. **ISSN:** 0888--0840 (print). **Subscription Rates:** $69 Individuals print and online - weekly; $49 Individuals online only- weekly. **URL:** http://www.adweek.com. **Remarks:** Accepts advertising. **Circ:** Paid ‡19976.

15749 ■ AGNI
AGNI Magazine
Boston University Creative Writing Program
236 Bay State Rd.
Boston, MA 02215
Publisher's E-mail: agni@bu.edu
Journal of literature and ideas. **Freq:** Semiannual April and October. **Key Personnel:** William Pierce, Senior Editor; Sven Birkerts, Editor; Askold Melnyczuk, Editor, Founder. **ISSN:** 0191--3352 (print). **Subscription Rates:** $20 Individuals one year - Canada add $5 for shipment & international add $10 for shipment; $38 Two years plus free back issue. - Canada add $5 for shipment & international add $10 for shipment; $53 Individuals three years (plus two free back issues) - Canada add $5 for shipment & international add $10 for shipment; $25 Institutions one year - Canada add $5 for shipment & international add $10 for shipment; $50 Institutions two years - Canada add $5 for shipment & international add $10 for shipment; $75 Institutions three years - Canada add $5 for shipment & international add $10 for shipment. **URL:** http://www.bu.edu/agni/subscribe.html. **Formerly:** AGNI Review. **Ad Rates:** BW $500. **Remarks:** Accepts advertising. **Circ:** (Not Reported).

15750 ■ AMC Outdoors: The Magazine of the Appalachian Mountain Club
Appalachian Mountain Club
5 Joy St.
Boston, MA 02108-1403
Phone: (617)523-0655
Fax: (617)523-0722
Publication E-mail: amcpublications@outdoors.org
Outdoor recreation and conservation magazine. **Freq:** Monthly. **Print Method:** Web. **Trim Size:** 8 x 10 3/4. **Cols./Page:** 3. **Col. Width:** 40 nonpareils. **Col. Depth:** 126 agate lines. **Key Personnel:** John D. Judge, President; Walter Gaff, Senior Vice President; Kevin Breunig, Vice President, Communications, Vice President, Marketing. **ISSN:** 1067--5604 (print). **Subscription Rates:** $18 Individuals; $32 Two years; $42 Individuals 3 years; Included in membership. **URL:** http://www.outdoors.org/publications/index.cfm; http://www.outdoors.org/publications/outdoors; http://www.outdoors.org/publications/outdoors/index.cfm. **Formerly**: Appalachian Bulletin; AMC Guide to Outdoor Adventures. **Ad Rates:** GLR $1.95; BW $2,403; 4C $3,390; PCI $45. **Remarks:** Accepts advertising. **Circ:** Paid ‡94000, Non-paid ‡1000.

15751 ■ American Ancestors
New England Historic Genealogical Society
101 Newbury St.
Boston, MA 02116
Phone: (617)536-5740
Fax: (617)536-7307
Free: 888-296-3447
Publication E-mail: magazine@nehgs.org
Magazine of the New England Historic Genealogical Society. **Freq:** Quarterly. **Trim Size:** 8.375 x 11. **Key Personnel:** Ralph J. Crandall, Executive Director. **ISSN:** 1527-9405 (print). **Subscription Rates:** $79.95 Individuals includes membership; $99.95 Individuals family.

URL: http://www.newenglandancestors.org/publications/nea.asp. **Formerly**: New England Ancestors. **Ad Rates:** BW $500; 4C $1,100. **Remarks:** Accepts advertising. **Circ:** Paid 30000, 21000.

15752 ■ American Journal of Archaeology
Archaeological Institute of America
656 Beacon St., 6th Fl.
Boston, MA 02215-2006
Phone: (617)353-9361
Fax: (617)353-6550
Publisher's E-mail: aia@aia.bu.edu
Professional journal covering archaeological subjects. **Freq:** Quarterly. **Key Personnel:** Madeleine J. Donachie, Director. **ISSN:** 0002--9114 (print). **Subscription Rates:** included in membership dues; $80 Individuals print; $295 Institutions print; $50 Students print; $90 Individuals print & electronic; $60 Students print & electronic; $325 Institutions print & electronic; $120 Other countries print & electronic; $295 Institutions online; $80 Individuals online; $50 Students online. **URL:** http://www.archaeological.org/webinfo.php?page=10041; http://www.ajaonline.org. **Remarks:** Advertising not accepted. **Circ:** (Not Reported).

15753 ■ American Journal of Clinical Oncology
Lippincott Williams & Wilkins
c/o David E. Wazer, Editor-in-Chief
Tufts University School of Medicine
Tufts Medical Ctr., Dept. of Radiation Oncology
800 Washington St.
Boston, MA 02111
Peer-reviewed journal covering ongoing research in cancer treatment. **Freq:** 6/year. **Print Method:** Sheetfed Offset. **Trim Size:** 8 1/4 x 11. **Key Personnel:** David Myers, MD, Publisher; David E. Wazer, MD, Editor-in-Chief. **ISSN:** 0277-3732 (print); **EISSN:** 1537-453X (electronic). **Subscription Rates:** $668 Individuals; $1500 Institutions; $202 in training; $823 Individuals international; $1640 Institutions international; $231 Other countries in-training. **URL:** http://journals.lww.com/amjclinicaloncology/pages/default.aspx; http://www.lww.com/Product/0277-3732. **Ad Rates:** BW $1,270; 4C $1,460. **Remarks:** Accepts advertising. **Circ:** Combined 493.

15754 ■ American Journal of Hematology
c/o Carlo Brugnara, Ed.-in-Ch.
Children's Hospital Boston
Harvard Medical School
300 Longwood Ave. BA 760
Boston, MA 02115
Medical research journal. **Freq:** Monthly. **Print Method:** Offset. **Trim Size:** 8 1/2 x 11 1/4. **Cols./Page:** 1. **Col. Width:** 85 nonpareils. **Col. Depth:** 130 agate lines. **Key Personnel:** Carlo Brugnara, Editor-in-Chief; Mark Fleming, Advisor; Patrick G. Gallagher, Advisor. **ISSN:** 0361--8609 (print); **EISSN:** 1096--8652 (electronic). **Subscription Rates:** $6425 Institutions print or online - USA online only - Canada & Mexico/ROW; $7710 Institutions USA; print and online; $352 Individuals print only - USA/Canada & Mexico; $7912 Institutions, Canada and Mexico print and online; $6593 Institutions, Canada and Mexico print only; £3280 Institutions UK; online only; £4091 Institutions UK; print and online; £3409 Institutions UK; print only; $436 Individuals print only - UK, Europe and Rest of the World; €4146 Institutions Europe; online only; €5171 Institutions Europe; print and online; €4309 Institutions Europe'; print only; $8013 Institutions, other countries print and online; $6677 Institutions, other countries print only. **URL:** http://onlinelibrary.wiley.com/journal/10.1002/(ISSN)1096-8652. **Ad Rates:** BW $980; 4C $1,545. **Remarks:** Accepts advertising. **Circ:** Paid 547.

15755 ■ The American Journal of Human Genetics
Elsevier Inc.
c/o Cynthia C. Morton, Editor
Brigham & Women's Hospital
New Research Bldg., Rm. 160A
77 Ave., Louis Pasteur
Boston, MA 02115
Publisher's E-mail: healthpermissions@elsevier.com
Journal devoted to research and review on heredity in man and the application of genetic principles in medicine, psychology, anthropology, and social sciences. **Freq:** Monthly. **Print Method:** Offset. **Trim Size:** 8-1/4 x 10-7/8. **Cols./Page:** 1. **Col. Width:** 58 nonpareils. **Col. Depth:** 107 agate lines. **Key Personnel:** Joshua Akey, Associate Editor; Sara B. Cullinan, PhD, Editor; Kerry E. Evans, Managing Editor; David Nelson, Editor. **ISSN:** 0002--9297 (print). **Subscription Rates:** $1072.20 Institutions online. **URL:** http://www.journals.elsevier.com/the-american-journal-of-human-genetics. **Ad Rates:** BW $525; 4C $1420. **Remarks:** Accepts advertising. **Circ:** ‡4400.

15756 ■ American Journal of Kidney Diseases
Elsevier Inc.
Tufts Medical Center, Box 391
800 Washington St.
Boston, MA 02111
Phone: (617)636-0599
Fax: (617)636-0598
Publisher's E-mail: healthpermissions@elsevier.com
Medical journal specialised for renal functions. **Freq:** Monthly. **Print Method:** Offset. **Trim Size:** 8 1/4 x 11. **Cols./Page:** 2. **Col. Width:** 45 nonpareils. **Col. Depth:** 138 agate lines. **Key Personnel:** Andrew S. Levey, MD, Editor-in-Chief; Daniel E. Weiner, MD, Editor; Nijse Dorman, PhD, Managing Editor. **ISSN:** 0272- 6386 (print). **Subscription Rates:** Included in membership; $621 Individuals online and print; $311 Students online and print; $851 Other countries online and print; $410 Students, other countries online and print. **Alt. Formats:** Download. **URL:** http://www.ajkd.org. **Remarks:** Advertising accepted; rates available upon request. **Circ:** 3,000.

15757 ■ American Journal of Law & Medicine
American Society of Law, Medicine and Ethics
765 Commonwealth Ave., Ste. 1634
Boston, MA 02215-1401
Phone: (617)262-4990
Fax: (617)437-7596
Publisher's E-mail: bulawaid@bu.edu
Law review publishing scholarly and professional articles, student cases and notes, and annotations of recent healthcare-related court decisions. **Freq:** Quarterly. **Print Method:** Web/Perfect bound. **Trim Size:** 6 3/4 x 10. **Cols./Page:** 1. **Col. Width:** 29.5 picas. **Col. Depth:** 49 picas. **Key Personnel:** Tanya Beroukhim, Editor-in-Chief; Kevin Outterson, Editor-in-Chief; Edward J. Hutchinson, Editor; Ted Hutchinson, Director, Publications, Executive Director; Katie Kenney Johnson, Director, Conferences. **ISSN:** 0098--8588 (print); **EISSN:** 2375--835X (electronic). **Subscription Rates:** £198 Institutions print only; £182 Institutions online only; £202 Institutions print and online; £54 Single issue. **URL:** http://aslme.org/index.php; http://www.bu.edu/ajlm. **Remarks:** Advertising accepted; rates available upon request. **Circ:** 3000.

15758 ■ American Journal of Law & Medicine
Boston University School of Law
765 Commonwealth Ave.
Boston, MA 02215
Phone: (617)353-3160
Publisher's E-mail: bulawaid@bu.edu
Law review publishing scholarly and professional articles, student cases and notes, and annotations of recent healthcare-related court decisions. **Freq:** Quarterly. **Print Method:** Web/Perfect bound. **Trim Size:** 6 3/4 x 10. **Cols./Page:** 1. **Col. Width:** 29.5 picas. **Col. Depth:** 49 picas. **Key Personnel:** Tanya Beroukhim, Editor-in-Chief; Kevin Outterson, Editor-in-Chief; Edward J. Hutchinson, Editor; Ted Hutchinson, Director, Publications, Executive Director; Katie Kenney Johnson, Director, Conferences. **ISSN:** 0098--8588 (print); **EISSN:** 2375--835X (electronic). **Subscription Rates:** £198 Institutions print only; £182 Institutions online only; £202 Institutions print and online; £54 Single issue. **URL:** http://aslme.org/index.php; http://www.bu.edu/ajlm. **Remarks:** Advertising accepted; rates available upon request. **Circ:** 3000.

15759 ■ Appalachia Journal
Appalachian Mountain Club
5 Joy St.
Boston, MA 02108-1403
Phone: (617)523-0655
Fax: (617)523-0722
Journal containing articles on hiking, climbing, canoeing, kayaking, Appalachian Mountain history, and the environment. Includes poetry, short fiction, and essays. **Freq:** Semiannual June and December. **Key Personnel:** Henry Schreiber, Director; John D. Judge, President. **ISSN:** 0003--6587 (print). **Subscription Rates:** $18 Individuals; $32 Two years; $42 Individuals three years. **URL:** http://www.outdoors.org/publications/appalachia. **Remarks:** Accepts advertising. **Circ:** (Not Reported).

15760 ■ Archaeology
Archaeological Institute of America
656 Beacon St., 6th Fl.
Boston, MA 02215-2006
Phone: (617)353-9361
Fax: (617)353-6550
Publication E-mail: general@archaeology.org
Archaeological magazine of worldwide discovery, excavations and ancient cult uses. **Freq:** Bimonthly. **Print Method:** Offset. **Trim Size:** 8 x 10 1/2. **Cols./Page:** 3. **Col. Width:** 25 nonpareils. **Col. Depth:** 140 agate lines. **Key Personnel:** Peter A. Young, Editor-in-Chief, phone: (718)472-3050; Meegan Daly, Director, Advertising; Jarrett A. Lobell, Executive Editor. **ISSN:** 0003--8113 (print). **Subscription Rates:** $14.97 U.S.; $29.97 Other countries. **URL:** http://www.archaeology.org/. **Ad Rates:** BW $9,265; 4C $12,490. **Remarks:** Accepts classified advertising. **Circ:** Paid ★**225000**, 175000, 200000.

15761 ■ Archaeology's Dig: The Archeology magazine for kids
Archaeological Institute of America
656 Beacon St., 6th Fl.
Boston, MA 02215-2006
Phone: (617)353-9361
Fax: (617)353-6550
Publisher's E-mail: aia@aia.bu.edu
Consumer magazine covering archaeology for children. **Freq:** 9/yr. **Remarks:** Accepts advertising. **Circ:** (Not Reported).

15762 ■ Arion: A Journal of Humanities and the Classics
Boston University
1 Silber Way
Boston, MA 02215
Phone: (617)353-2000
Publication E-mail: arion@bu.edu
Literary journal covering poetry, translations, and reviews. **Freq:** 3/year. **Key Personnel:** Herbert Golder, Editor-in-Chief; Nicholas Poburko, Managing Editor; Robert Alter, Board Member. **ISSN:** 0095-5909 (print). **Subscription Rates:** $32.50 Individuals 1 year; $57.50 Two years; $13 Single issue back issues; $18 Single issue international; $9 Out of country /year for shipping and handling. **URL:** http://www.bu.edu/arion. **Remarks:** Accepts advertising. **Circ:** Paid 425.

15763 ■ Atlantic Coast In-House
Lawyers Weekly Publications
10 Milk St., Ste. 1000
Boston, MA 02111
Phone: (617)451-7300
Publication that focuses on topics of interest to in-house lawyers practicing along the Atlantic coast. **Freq:** Bimonthly. **Key Personnel:** Henriette Campagne, Publisher; Charlene Smith, Director, Advertising. **URL:** http://www.newenglandinhouse.com. **Ad Rates:** BW $3,061; 4C $400. **Remarks:** Accepts advertising. **Circ:** ‡11000.

15764 ■ Banker & Tradesman
The Warren Group
280 Summer St., 8th Fl.
Boston, MA 02210-1131
Phone: (617)428-5100
Fax: (617)428-5120
Free: 800-356-8805
Publisher's E-mail: customer_service@thewarrengroup.com
Real estate, financial and general business news tabloid. **Freq:** Weekly (Wed.). **Print Method:** Offset. **Trim Size:** 11 3/8 x 16 7/8. **Cols./Page:** 4. **Col. Width:** 28 nonpareils. **Col. Depth:** 217 agate lines. **Key Personnel:** Vincent Michael Valvo, Editor-in-Chief, Publisher; Timothy Warren, Jr., Chief Executive Officer, Publisher; David B. Lovins, Chief Operating Officer, President. **Subscription Rates:** $379 Individuals print & online; $679 Two years print & online ; $299 Individuals online only; 539 Two years online only. **URL:** http://bankerandtradesman.com. **Ad Rates:** BW $990; 4C

Circulation: ★ = AAM; △ or • = BPA; ♦ = CAC; ❑ = VAC; ⊕ = PO Statement; ‡ = Publisher's Report; Boldface figures = sworn; Light figures = estimated.

$2350; PCI $40. **Remarks:** Accepts advertising. **Circ:** Paid ‡4,900.

15765 ■ Bay Windows
Bay Windows
28 Damrell St., Ste. 204
Boston, MA 02127
Phone: (617)266-6670
Magazine covering gay male and lesbian news and literature. **Freq:** Weekly (Thurs.). **Trim Size:** 10 x 12.75. **Key Personnel:** Jeff Coakley, Publisher. **Subscription Rates:** $115 By mail first class; $55 By mail 3rd class. **URL:** http://www.baywindows.com. **Ad Rates:** BW $1381. **Remarks:** Accepts advertising. **Circ:** ■ **20000**.

15766 ■ Berklee Today: A Forum for Contemporary Music and Musicians
Berklee College of Music
1140 Boylston St.
Boston, MA 02215
Phone: (617)266-1400
Fax: (617)747-2047
Publisher's E-mail: admissions@berklee.edu
College alumni magazine covering music and music industry issues. **Freq:** Quarterly. **Trim Size:** 9 x 10 7/8. **Key Personnel:** Mark Small, Editor; Stephen Croes, Board Member. **ISSN:** 1052-3839 (print). **URL:** http://www.berklee.edu/berklee-today/spring-2016. **Ad Rates:** BW $1,400; 4C $1,800. **Remarks:** Accepts advertising. **Circ:** Non-paid ‡48000.

15767 ■ Boston Bar Journal
Boston Bar Association
16 Beacon St.
Boston, MA 02108
Phone: (617)742-0615
Fax: (617)523-0127
Publication E-mail: bsashin@bostonbar.org bbj@bostonbar.org
Journal for lawyers on important matters of legal interest. **Freq:** Quarterly. **Key Personnel:** Carol Head, Editor, phone: (617)341-7700. **URL:** http://www.bostonbar.org/about-us/library/boston-bar-journal. **Remarks:** Accepts advertising. **Circ:** (Not Reported).

15768 ■ Boston Business Journal
Boston Business Journal
160 Federal St., 12th Fl.
Boston, MA 02110-1700
Phone: (617)330-1000
Fax: (617)330-1015
Publisher's E-mail: boston@bizjournals.com
Business newspaper specializing in local and regional business for upper management and CEO's of large and mid-sized businesses. **Freq:** Weekly. **Print Method:** Offset. **Trim Size:** 10 1/8 x 13 1/2. **Cols./Page:** 4. **Col. Width:** 14.3 picas. **Key Personnel:** George Donnelly, Executive Editor, phone: (617)316-3221; Greg Walsh, Associate Editor, phone: (617)316-3229; Eric Convey, Managing Editor, phone: (617)316-3235; Craig M. Douglas, Managing Editor, phone: (617)316-3223. **ISSN:** 0746--4975 (print). **Subscription Rates:** $111 Individuals print and online. **Online:** American City Business Journals Inc. **URL:** http://www.bizjournals.com/boston. **Ad Rates:** BW $3,595; 4C $4,600. **Remarks:** Accepts advertising. **Circ:** Paid ★**16098**.

15769 ■ Boston Common
Niche Media L.L.C.
745 Boylston St., Ste. 602
Boston, MA 02116
Phone: (617)266-3390
Fax: (617)266-3722
Luxury lifestyle and entertainment magazine covering Boston. **Freq:** 5/year. **Print Method:** Web offset. **Trim Size:** 10 x 12. **Key Personnel:** Glen Kelly, Publisher. **Subscription Rates:** $15 Individuals; $4.99 Individuals. **URL:** http://www.bostoncommon-magazine.com. **Ad Rates:** 4C $18,025. **Remarks:** Accepts advertising. **Circ:** ★**50000**.

15770 ■ The Boston Globe
The New York Times Co.
135 Morrissey Blvd.
Boston, MA 02205-5819
Phone: (617)929-2000
Publisher's E-mail: national@nytimes.com
General newspaper. **Founded:** 1872. **Freq:** Mon.-Sun. (morn.). **Print Method:** Offset. Uses mats. **Cols./Page:** 6. **Col. Width:** 24 nonpareils. **Col. Depth:** 294 agate lines. **Key Personnel:** Martin Baron, Editor. **Subscription Rates:** $886.08 By mail in New England, 7-day; $600.60 By mail in New England, Mon-Sat.; $1007.50 Out of area by mail, 7-day; $2281.76 Other countries by mail, 7-day; $626.60 By mail student & military, 7-day. **URL:** http://www.bostonglobe.com. **Mailing address:** PO Box 55819, Boston, MA 02205-5819. **Ad Rates:** SAU $184.25. **Remarks:** Accepts advertising. **Circ:** Mon.-Fri. ★**414225**, Sat. ★**401744**, Sun. ★**652146**.

15771 ■ Boston Herald
ProQuest L.L.C.
70 Fargo St.
Boston, MA 02210
Phone: (617)426-3000
Publisher's E-mail: info@proquest.com
General newspaper. **Freq:** Daily. **Print Method:** Letterpress. Uses mats. **Cols./Page:** 5. **Col. Width:** 17 nonpareils. **Col. Depth:** 200 agate lines. **Key Personnel:** Joe Dwinell, Managing Editor, phone: (617)619-6493; Patrick J. Purcell, Publisher; Joe Sciacca, Editor-in-Chief. **Subscription Rates:** $258.44 Individuals print; 7-day delivery (52 weeks). **Online:** ProQuest L.L.C. ProQuest L.L.C.; LexisNexis; Boston Herald Inc. Boston Herald Inc. **Alt. Formats:** Handheld. **URL:** http://www.bostonherald.com. **Remarks:** Accepts advertising. **Circ:** Mon.-Fri. ★**182350**, Sat. ★**143282**, Sun. ★**105629**.

15772 ■ Boston Magazine
Boston Magazine
300 Massachusetts Ave.
Boston, MA 02115
Phone: (617)262-9700
Fax: (617)262-4925
Publisher's E-mail: editor@bostonmagazine.com
Magazine covering business, politics, and lifestyle in the Boston metropolitan area. **Freq:** Monthly. **Print Method:** Offset. **Trim Size:** 8 x 10 7/8. **Cols./Page:** 3. **Col. Width:** 27 nonpareils. **Col. Depth:** 140 agate lines. **Subscription Rates:** $9.95 Individuals; $15.95 Two years. **URL:** http://www.bostonmagazine.com. **Ad Rates:** BW $13,210; 4C $18,880. **Remarks:** Accepts advertising. **Circ:** ‡106144.

15773 ■ Boston Magazine's Concierge
Echo Media
900 Circle 75 Pky., Ste. 1600
Atlanta, GA 30339
Phone: (770)955-3535
Fax: (770)955-3599
Publisher's E-mail: salesinfo@echo-media.com
Magazine for discerning travelers. **Freq:** Monthly. **URL:** http://echomedia.com/medias/details/5625. **Remarks:** Accepts advertising. **Circ:** 127824.

15774 ■ Boston Magazine's Elegant Wedding
Echo Media
900 Circle 75 Pky., Ste. 1600
Atlanta, GA 30339
Phone: (770)955-3535
Fax: (770)955-3599
Publisher's E-mail: salesinfo@echo-media.com
Magazine for brides. **Freq:** Semiannual. **URL:** http://echomedia.com/medias/details/5623. **Remarks:** Advertising not accepted. **Circ:** 60000.

15775 ■ Boston Magazine's Home & Garden
Boston Magazine
300 Massachusetts Ave.
Boston, MA 02115
Phone: (617)262-9700
Fax: (617)262-4925
Publisher's E-mail: editor@bostonmagazine.com
Magazine offering information on homes and garden design in the Boston area. **Freq:** Monthly. **Key Personnel:** James Burnett, Editor; Jennifer L. Johnson, Managing Editor. **ISSN:** 1544--8797 (print). **Subscription Rates:** $9.95 Individuals. **URL:** http://www.bostonmagazine.com/index.html. **Remarks:** Accepts advertising. **Circ:** (Not Reported).

15776 ■ Boston Metro
Echo Media
900 Circle 75 Pky., Ste. 1600
Atlanta, GA 30339
Phone: (770)955-3535
Fax: (770)955-3599
Publisher's E-mail: salesinfo@echo-media.com
Newspaper of Boston metropolitan area. **Freq:** Daily. **Subscription Rates:** Free. **URL:** http://echomedia.com/medias/details/5320. **Remarks:** Accepts advertising. **Circ:** (Not Reported).

15777 ■ Boston-Panorama Magazine
Key Magazines Inc.
332 Congress St.
Boston, MA 02210
Phone: (617)423-3400
Fax: (617)423-7108
Publisher's E-mail: info@keymilwaukee.com
Travelers' magazine covering Boston, Massachusetts area. **Freq:** 26/yr. **Key Personnel:** Tim Montgomery, Publisher. **Subscription Rates:** $49 Individuals. **URL:** http://www.keymagazine.com/boston/index.html; http://www.bostonguide.com/. **Remarks:** Accepts advertising. **Circ:** (Not Reported).

15778 ■ The Boston Phoenix
The Phoenix Media/Communications Group
126 Brookline Ave.
Boston, MA 02215
Phone: (617)536-5390
Fax: (617)536-1463
Publisher's E-mail: letters@phx.com
Metropolitan newspaper. **Freq:** Weekly (Thurs.). **Print Method:** Offset. **Trim Size:** 11 x 17. **Cols./Page:** 6. **Col. Width:** 11 picas. **Col. Depth:** 16 inches. **Key Personnel:** Carly Carioli, Editor; Stephen Mindich, Publisher. **URL:** http://thephoenix.com/boston. **Ad Rates:** GLR $6.43; BW $8,385; 4C $9,635; PCI $87.35. **Remarks:** Accepts advertising. **Circ:** Combined ■ **97520**.

15779 ■ Boston Seniority
City of Boston Commission on Affairs of the Elderly
One City Hall Sq.
Boston, MA 02201-2010
Newspaper for senior Bostonians. **Freq:** Monthly. **Trim Size:** 8 1/2 x 11. **Cols./Page:** 3. **Col. Width:** 2 5/16 inches. **Col. Depth:** 9 3/4 inches. **Key Personnel:** Martha Rios, Editor; Tula Mahl, Editor. **Subscription Rates:** Free. **URL:** http://www.boston.gov/departments/elderly-commission/boston-seniority-magazine. **Remarks:** Accepts advertising. **Circ:** Free ‡20.

15780 ■ Boston Spirit
Boston Spirit
301 Massachusetts Ave.
Boston, MA 02115
Phone: (781)223-8538
Fax: (617)209-1134
Publisher's E-mail: publisher@bostonspiritmagazine.com
Magazine that offers information on gay and lesbian community in Boston. **Freq:** Bimonthly. **Key Personnel:** James A. Lopata, Editor-in-Chief; David Zimmerman, Publisher. **Subscription Rates:** Free. **URL:** http://bostonspiritmagazine.com. **Remarks:** Accepts advertising. **Circ:** (Not Reported).

15781 ■ BOSTONIA
Boston University
1 Silber Way
Boston, MA 02215
Phone: (617)353-2000
Publisher's E-mail: askus@bu.edu
Boston University alumni magazine. **Freq:** 3/year. **Print Method:** Web offset. **Trim Size:** 8 1/8 x 10 7/8. **Cols./Page:** 3. **Col. Width:** 27 nonpareils. **Col. Depth:** 129 1/2 agate lines. **Key Personnel:** Cynthia K. Buccini, Managing Editor; Art Jahnke, Editor. **ISSN:** 0264--1441 (print). **URL:** http://www.bu.edu/bostonia/fall14; http://www.bu.edu/bostonia/about-bostonia. **Remarks:** Advertising not accepted. **Circ:** (Not Reported).

15782 ■ Bulletin of the American Schools of Oriental Research
American Schools of Oriental Research
Boston University
656 Beacon St., 5th Fl.
Boston, MA 02215
Phone: (617)353-6570
Fax: (617)353-6575
Publisher's E-mail: asor@bu.edu
Journal on Near Eastern studies. **Freq:** Quarterly. **Print Method:** Offset. **Trim Size:** 8 1/2 x 11. **Cols./Page:** 2. **Col. Width:** 36 nonpareils. **Col. Depth:** 120 agate lines. **Key Personnel:** Eric H. Cline, Editor. **ISSN:** 0003-097X (print). **Subscription Rates:** $290 Institutions; $322 Institutions, other countries. **URL:** http://www.asor.org/

pubs/basor. **Ad Rates:** BW $500. **Remarks:** Accepts advertising. **Circ:** ‡2000.

15783 ■ Bulletin of the AMS
American Meteorological Society
45 Beacon St.
Boston, MA 02108-3693
Phone: (617)227-2425
Fax: (617)742-8718
Publication E-mail: letterstotheeditor@ametsoc.org
Magazine containing official American Meteorological Society professional articles, membership news, and book reviews. **Freq:** Monthly. **Key Personnel:** Jeff Rosenfeld, Editor-in-Chief; Keith L. Seitter, Executive Director. **ISSN:** 1520--0477 (print). **Subscription Rates:** $175 Nonmembers print only; Included in membership; Free online. **Online:** American Meteorological Society American Meteorological Society. **URL:** http://www2.ametsoc.org/ams/index.cfm/publications/bulletin-of-the-american-meteorological-society-bams; http://journals.ametsoc.org/toc/bams/current. **Ad Rates:** BW $1,230; 4C $2,680. **Remarks:** Accepts advertising. **Circ:** ‡12585.

15784 ■ The Bulletin of Symbolic Logic
Association for Symbolic Logic
c/o Akihiro Kanamori
Department of Mathematics
Boston University
Boston, MA 02215
Publisher's E-mail: asl@vassar.edu
Journal covering all aspects of logic, including mathematical or philosophical logic; logic in computer science or linguistics; history and philosophy of logic; and application of logic to other fields. **Freq:** Quarterly. **Key Personnel:** Patricia Blanchette, Editor; Frank Wagner, Editor; Hannes Leitgeb, Editor. **ISSN:** 1079--8986 (print). **Subscription Rates:** Included in membership. **URL:** http://www.aslonline.org/journals-bulletin.html. **Ad Rates:** BW $300. **Remarks:** Accepts advertising. **Circ:** ‡2500, ‡2500, 2500.

15785 ■ Cancer Causes and Control: An International Journal of Studies of Cancer in Human Populations
Springer Netherlands
c/o Graham A. Colditz, Ed. Emeritus
Channing Laboratory
Harvard University
Boston, MA 02115
Medical journal covering investigation into the causes, control, and subsequent prevention of cancer. **Freq:** Monthly. **Key Personnel:** Immaculata De Vivo, Editor-in-Chief; Edward Giovannucci, Editor-in-Chief; Graham A. Colditz, Editor. **ISSN:** 0957--5243 (print); **EISSN:** 1573--7225 (electronic). **Subscription Rates:** €3076 Institutions print & online; €3691 Institutions print & enchanced access; $3241 Institutions print & online; $3889 Institutions print & enhanced access. **URL:** http://www.springer.com/biomed/cancer/journal/10552. **Remarks:** Accepts advertising. **Circ:** (Not Reported).

15786 ■ Cardiology in Review
Lippincott Williams & Wilkins
c/o Patrick T. O'Gara, MD, Editor-in-Chief
Harvard Medical School
75 Francis St.
Boston, MA 02115
Peer-reviewed journal offering reviews on the conditions and problems encountered by practicing cardiologists. **Freq:** Bimonthly. **Trim Size:** 8 1/8 x 10 7/8. **Key Personnel:** Patrick T. O'Gara, MD, Editor-in-Chief; William H. Frishman, MD, Editor-in-Chief; Alexandra Gavenda, Publisher. **ISSN:** 1061--5377 (print); **EISSN:** 1538--4683 (electronic). **Subscription Rates:** $401 Individuals; $518 Canada and Mexico; $534 Other countries; $989 Institutions; $1170 Institutions, Canada and Mexico; $1186 Institutions, other countries. **URL:** http://journals.lww.com/cardiologyinreview/pages/default.aspx. **Ad Rates:** BW $985; 4C $995. **Remarks:** Accepts advertising. **Circ:** 214.

15787 ■ The Christian Science Journal
Christian Science Publishing Society
210 Massachusetts Ave.
Boston, MA 02115
Phone: (617)450-2000
Publisher's E-mail: info@ChristianScience.com
Freq: Monthly. **Print Method:** Offset. **Trim Size:** 8 1/8 x 10 3/4. **Cols./Page:** 1 and 3. **Col. Width:** 28.75 and 12.3 picas. **Col. Depth:** 58.3 picas. **Key Personnel:** Marilyn Jones, Managing Editor. **ISSN:** 0009--5613 (print). **Subscription Rates:** $99 Individuals; $49.50 Individuals 6 months; $24.75 Individuals 3 months. **URL:** http://journal.christianscience.com. **Remarks:** Advertising not accepted. **Circ:** (Not Reported).

15788 ■ The Christian Science Monitor
Christian Science Publishing Society
210 Massachusetts Ave.
Boston, MA 02115
Phone: (617)450-2000
Publisher's E-mail: info@ChristianScience.com
National daily newspaper. **Founded:** 1908. **Freq:** Daily (morn.). **Print Method:** Offset. **Trim Size:** 11 x 14. **Cols./Page:** 6. **Col. Width:** 20 nonpareils. **Col. Depth:** 192 agate lines. **Key Personnel:** Marshall Ingwerson, Editor; Jonathan Wells, Publisher; John Yemma, Editor; David Cook, Senior Editor; Clayton Jones, Writer. **Subscription Rates:** $66.75 Individuals; $85 Canada; $140 Other countries; $5.99 Individuals /month, print and digital; 4.99 /month, digital. **Alt. Formats:** Handheld. **URL:** http://www.csmonitor.com/. **Ad Rates:** BW $5,600; 4C $6,000; PCI $195. **Remarks:** Advertising accepted; rates available upon request. **Circ:** Mon.-Fri. ★**53203**.

15789 ■ Christian Science Quarterly
Christian Science Publishing Society
210 Massachusetts Ave.
Boston, MA 02115
Phone: (617)450-2000
Publisher's E-mail: info@ChristianScience.com
Freq: Quarterly. **Subscription Rates:** $20 /year. **URL:** http://christianscience.com/prayer-and-health/inspirational-media/publications. **Remarks:** Advertising not accepted. **Circ:** (Not Reported).

15790 ■ Christian Science Quarterly Bible Lessons
Christian Science Publishing Society
210 Massachusetts Ave.
Boston, MA 02115
Phone: (617)450-2000
Publisher's E-mail: info@ChristianScience.com
Religious magazine for daily study of the Bible. Editions printed in Danish, Dutch, English, French, Greek, German, Indonesian, Italian, Japanese, Norwegian, Polish, Portuguese, Spanish, and Swedish; also a monthly English Braille edition. **Freq:** Quarterly. **Print Method:** Offset. **Trim Size:** 4.625 x 9.5. **Cols./Page:** 1. **ISSN:** 0145--7365 (print). **Subscription Rates:** $12.95 Individuals 4 weeks (4 issues). **Alt. Formats:** CD-ROM; Electronic publishing; PDF. **URL:** http://christianscience.com/bible-lessons. **Remarks:** Advertising not accepted. **Circ:** (Not Reported).

15791 ■ Christian Science Sentinel: Exploring the World of Spirituality and Healing
Christian Science Publishing Society
210 Massachusetts Ave.
Boston, MA 02115
Phone: (617)450-2000
Publisher's E-mail: info@ChristianScience.com
Christian Science magazine. Inspiring non-fiction and testimonies of Christian healing. **Freq:** 52/yr. **Print Method:** Offset. **Trim Size:** 8 1/8 x 10 3/8. **Cols./Page:** 3. **Col. Width:** 17.5 picas. **Col. Depth:** 56 picas. **ISSN:** 0009--563X (print). **Subscription Rates:** $90 Individuals; $49.50 Canada 6 months; $24.75 Other countries 3 months. **URL:** http://sentinel.christianscience.com. **Remarks:** Advertising not accepted. **Circ:** Paid ⊕**35000**.

15792 ■ Circulation
Lippincott Williams and Wilkins
560 Harrison Ave., Ste. 502
Boston, MA 02118
Phone: (617)542-5100
Fax: (617)542-6539
Publication E-mail: circ@circulationjournal.org
Journal containing original articles on cardiovascular, clinical, and laboratory investigation. **Founded:** Jan. 1950. **Freq:** Semimonthly. **Print Method:** Offset. **Trim Size:** 8 1/4 x 10 7/8. **Cols./Page:** 2. **Col. Width:** 38 nonpareils. **Col. Depth:** 130 agate lines. **Key Personnel:** Karen Barry, Managing Editor; Joseph Loscalzo, PhD, Editor-in-Chief. **ISSN:** 0009-7322 (print); **EISSN:** 1524-4539 (electronic). **Subscription Rates:** $596 Individuals print; $1506 Institutions print; $913 Individuals print; other countries; $2042 Institutions print; other countries; $586 Individuals online only. **URL:** http://circ.ahajournals.org/. **Remarks:** Accepts classified advertising. **Circ:** Paid 7406.

15793 ■ Civil Engineering Practice: Journal of the Boston Society of Civil Engineers
Boston Society of Civil Engineers Section
The Engineering Ctr.
1 Walnut St.
Boston, MA 02108-3616
Phone: (617)227-5551
Fax: (617)227-6783
Publisher's E-mail: bsces@engineers.org
Professional magazine covering civil engineering. **Freq:** Semiannual. **Print Method:** Sheetfed offset. **Trim Size:** 7 1/4 x 10. **Cols./Page:** 2. **Col. Width:** 17 picas. **Col. Depth:** 61 picas. **ISSN:** 0886--9685 (print). **Subscription Rates:** $27.50 Individuals /copy. **URL:** http://www.bsces.org/news. **Formerly**: Journal of the Boston Society of Civil Engineers. **Remarks:** Accepts advertising. **Circ:** Paid 3250.

15794 ■ Club Business International
International Health, Racquet and Sportsclub Association
70 Fargo St.
Boston, MA 02210
Phone: (617)951-0055
Fax: (617)951-0056
Free: 800-228-4772
Publisher's E-mail: info@ihrsa.org
Magazine covering health and fitness industry. **Freq:** Monthly. **Subscription Rates:** $35.95 Members U.S.; $129.95 Members international. **URL:** http://www.ihrsa.org/cbi-magazine. **Remarks:** Accepts advertising. **Circ:** ‡23010.

15795 ■ Cognitive Therapy & Research
Springer Netherlands
c/o Stefan Hofmann, Ed.
Dept. of Psychology
648 Beacon St., 6th Fl.
Boston University
Boston, MA 02215
Journal focusing on cognitive psychology. **Freq:** Bimonthly. **Print Method:** Offset. **Trim Size:** 6 x 9. **Cols./Page:** 1. **Col. Width:** 54 nonpareils. **Col. Depth:** 103 agate lines. **Key Personnel:** Keith S. Dobson, Board Member; Michael Zvolensky, Associate Editor; David M. Fresco, Associate Editor; Albert Bandura, Board Member; Stefan G. Hofmann, Editor-in-Chief; Edward C. Chang, Associate Editor. **ISSN:** 0147-5916 (print); **EISSN:** 1573-2819 (electronic). **Subscription Rates:** $1656 Institutions print or online; $1987 Institutions print & enchanced access. **URL:** http://www.springer.com/medicine/journal/10608; http://link.springer.com/journal/10608. **Remarks:** Advertising accepted; rates available upon request. **Circ:** (Not Reported).

15796 ■ Congregational Library Bulletin
Congregational Library and Archives
14 Beacon St., 2nd Fl.
Boston, MA 02108
Phone: (617)523-0470
Fax: (617)523-0491
Publisher's E-mail: circ@14beacon.org
Journal covering religious works of the library. **Freq:** Triennial. **Key Personnel:** Harold F. Worthley, Director. **ISSN:** 0010--5821 (print). **Alt. Formats:** PDF. **URL:** http://www.congregationallibrary.org/members/bulletins. **Remarks:** Advertising not accepted. **Circ:** Paid 925.

15797 ■ Continental Magazine
The Pohly Co.
867 Boylston St. 5Th Fl.
Boston, MA 02116
Phone: (617)451-1700
Fax: (617)338-7767
Free: 800-383-0888
Publisher's E-mail: info@pohlyco.com
Inflight magazine for Continental Airlines. **Freq:** Monthly. **Key Personnel:** Diana Pohly, President, Chief Executive Officer, phone: (617)451-1700; Michael Buller, Contact. **Subscription Rates:** Free on flights. **URL:** http://www.pohlyco.com/case-studies/motion-zone/continental-airlines-magazine. **Ad Rates:** BW $28655;

Circulation: ★ = AAM; △ or • = BPA; ♦ = CAC; ❑ = VAC; ⊕ = PO Statement; ‡ = Publisher's Report; Boldface figures = sworn; Light figures = estimated.

4C $35800. **Remarks:** Accepts advertising. **Circ:** Non-paid 334000.

15798 ■ Critical Pathways in Cardiology: A Journal of Evidence-Based Medicine
Lippincott Williams & Wilkins
c/o Christopher P. Cannon, MD, Editor-in-Chief
350 Longwood Ave., 1st Fl.
Boston, MA 02115
Phone: (617)278-0146
Fax: (617)734-7329
Publication E-mail: cpc@partners.org
Peer-reviewed journal providing a single source for the diagnostic and therapeutic protocols in use at hospitals worldwide for patients with cardiac disorders. **Freq:** Quarterly March, June, September, December. **Trim Size:** 8 1/8 x 10 7/8. **Key Personnel:** Christopher P. Cannon, MD, Editor-in-Chief; Benjamin A. Steinberg, MD, Managing Editor; Alexandra Gavenda, Publisher. **ISSN:** 1535--282X (print); **EISSN:** 1535--2811 (electronic). **Subscription Rates:** $295 U.S.; $290 Canada and Mexico; $303 Other countries; $572 Institutions; $687 Institutions, Canada and Mexico; $700 Institutions, other countries. **URL:** http://journals.lww.com/critpathcardio/pages/default.aspx. **Ad Rates:** BW $970; 4C $1,025. **Remarks:** Accepts advertising. **Circ:** 841.

15799 ■ Design Management Review
Design Management Institute
38 Chauncy St., Ste. 800
Boston, MA 02111
Phone: (617)338-6380
Freq: Quarterly. **Subscription Rates:** $842 Institutions print and online; £448 Institutions print and online; €604 Institutions print and online; $99 Individuals print and online; £59 Individuals print and online. **URL:** http://www.dmi.org/?page=Review. **Remarks:** Accepts advertising. **Circ:** 7500.

15800 ■ Digital Journal of Ophthalmology
Harvard University Press
Massachusetts Eye & Ear Infirmary
243 Charles St.
Boston, MA 02114
Publication E-mail: djo@meei.harvard.edu djo@harvard.edu
Journal for ophthalmologists, health and eye care providers, vision scientists and ophthalmic patients. Publishes ophthalmic information. **Key Personnel:** Carolyn Kloek, MD, Board Member; Aaron Savar, MD, Editor; Ankoor Shah, PhD, Editor-in-Chief; Stacey C. Brauner, MD, Board Member; Joan Miller, MD, Board Member; Dean Cestari, MD, Board Member; George Papaliodis, MD, Board Member; Melanie Kazlas, MD, Board Member; Demetrio Vavvas, PhD, Board Member. **ISSN:** 1542--8958 (print). **Subscription Rates:** Free. **URL:** http://www.djo.harvard.edu. **Remarks:** Advertising not accepted. **Circ:** (Not Reported).

15801 ■ DMI Academic Review
Design Management Institute
38 Chauncy St., Ste. 800
Boston, MA 02111
Phone: (617)338-6380
Scholarly journal covering design in products, communication, and environments for organizational use worldwide. **Freq:** Quarterly. **Key Personnel:** Rachel Cooper, Editor; Roberto Verganti, Editor. **ISSN:** 1045-7194 (print). **Subscription Rates:** $29 Individuals. **URL:** http://dmi.site-ym.com/?page=Review. **Remarks:** Accepts advertising. **Circ:** (Not Reported).

15802 ■ Dollars & Sense: The Magazine of Economic Justice
Economic Affairs Bureau
1 Milk St., 5th Fl.
Boston, MA 02109
Phone: (617)447-2177
Fax: (617)447-2179
Publication E-mail: dollars@dollarsandsense.org
Magazine providing left-wing perspectives on current economic affairs. **Freq:** 6/year. **Print Method:** Offset. **Trim Size:** 8 1/2 x 11. **Cols./Page:** 2. **Col. Width:** 20 picas. **Col. Depth:** 8 3/4 inches. **Key Personnel:** Chris Sturr, Editor; Paul Piwko, Business Manager; Amy Gluckman, Editor. **ISSN:** 0012--5245 (print). **Subscription Rates:** $19.95 Individuals; $29 Canada; $43 Other countries; $45 Institutions; $5 Single issue. **URL:** http://www.dollarsandsense.org. **Ad Rates:** BW $550. **Remarks:** Accepts advertising. **Circ:** ‡8000.

15803 ■ DVS Guide
Descriptive Video Service
1 Guest St.
Boston, MA 02135
Phone: (617)300-5400
Magazine listing updates and programs available from the Descriptive Video Service, a free national service that makes television programs, cable programming and movies accessible to blind or visually impaired individuals. **Freq:** Quarterly. **Mailing address:** PO Box 55785, Boston, MA 02135-5875. **Remarks:** Advertising not accepted. **Circ:** Combined 24688.

15804 ■ El Mundo
Caribe Communication
408 S Huntington Ave.
Boston, MA 02130
Phone: (617)522-5060
Fax: (617)524-5886
Publisher's E-mail: ads@elmundoboston.com
Community newspaper (Spanish). **Founded:** 1972. **Freq:** Weekly. **Print Method:** Offset. **Cols./Page:** 5. **Col. Width:** 11 picas. **Col. Depth:** 16 inches. **Subscription Rates:** $70 Individuals. **URL:** http://www.elmundoboston.com. **Remarks:** Accepts advertising. **Circ:** 30000.

15805 ■ El Planeta
The Phoenix Media/Communications Group
126 Brookline Ave.
Boston, MA 02215
Phone: (617)536-5390
Fax: (617)536-1463
Publisher's E-mail: letters@phx.com
Newspaper in Spanish serving the Hispanic community in Massachusetts. **Freq:** Weekly (Fri.). **Key Personnel:** Marcela Garcia, Editor, phone: (617)937-5900, fax: (617)859-8201; Raul Medina, Manager, Sales; Michael Johnson, Manager, Circulation. **Subscription Rates:** Free. **URL:** http://elplaneta.com. **Ad Rates:** BW $2250; 4C $400. **Remarks:** Accepts advertising. **Circ:** Free ■ **50,000.**

15806 ■ The Episcopal Times
Episcopal Diocese of Massachusetts
138 Tremont St.
Boston, MA 02111
Phone: (617)482-5800
Free: 800-472-4428
Publisher's E-mail: ccris2@yahoo.com
Religious newspaper. **Freq:** 8/year. **Print Method:** Offset. **Trim Size:** 11 x 12. **Cols./Page:** 4. **Col. Width:** 28 nonpareils. **Col. Depth:** 196 agate lines. **Key Personnel:** Lynn Clark, Director; Tracy Sukraw, Director, Communications, Editor. **Alt. Formats:** PDF. **Ad Rates:** BW $1,000. **Remarks:** Accepts advertising. **Circ:** ‡33000.

15807 ■ Foodservice East
The Newbury Street Group Inc.
93 Massachusetts Ave., Ste. 306
Boston, MA 02115
Phone: (617)267-2224
Fax: (617)267-5554
Compact Tabloid covering trends and analysis of the foodservice industry in the Northeast. A business-to-business publication featuring news, analysis and trends for the Northeast food service professional. **Freq:** Quarterly. **Print Method:** Offset. **Trim Size:** 10 7/8 x 14 1/2. **Cols./Page:** 5. **Col. Width:** 11.5 picas. **Col. Depth:** 190 agate lines. **Key Personnel:** Susan Holaday, Editor; Richard E. Dolby, Publisher. **ISSN:** 0885--6877 (print). **Subscription Rates:** $30 Individuals; $5 Single issue. **URL:** http://www.foodserviceeast.com. **Ad Rates:** BW $2,891; 4C $3,756; PCI $50. **Remarks:** Accepts advertising. **Circ:** ‡22241.

15808 ■ Gay and Lesbian Review Worldwide
Gay & Lesbian Review Inc.
PO Box 180300
Boston, MA 02118
Phone: (617)421-0082
Publication E-mail: info@glreview.com
Periodical covering gay and lesbian issues and literature. **Freq:** Bimonthly. **Key Personnel:** Stephen Hemrick, Manager, Advertising. **ISSN:** 1532--1118 (print). **Subscription Rates:** $23 Individuals print only; $18.99 Individuals online only. **URL:** http://www.glreview.org. **Formerly:** Harvard Gay and Lesbian Review. **Ad Rates:** 4C $1,235, full page; 4C $750, half page; 4C $450, quarter page; 4C $230, business card; 4C $1,550, back cover; 4C $1,375, inside cover. **Remarks:** Accepts advertising. **Circ:** 11000.

15809 ■ Genomics
RELX Group P.L.C.
Dana-Farber Cancer Institute
Boston, MA 02115
Publisher's E-mail: amsterdam@relx.com
Journal promoting of all facets of human and mouse genetic analysis. **Freq:** Monthly. **Trim Size:** 8 1/2 x 11. **Key Personnel:** J. Quackenbush, Editor-in-Chief; F.H. Ruddle, Editor, Founder. **ISSN:** 0888--7543 (print). **Subscription Rates:** $656 Individuals print; $1303 Institutions print; $543 Institutions online. **URL:** http://www.journals.elsevier.com/genomics. **Remarks:** Accepts advertising. **Circ:** (Not Reported).

15810 ■ The Guide: Gay Travel, Entertainment, Politics and Sex
Fidelity Publishing - The Guide
PO Box 990593
Boston, MA 02199
Phone: (617)266-8557
Fax: (617)266-1125
Consumer magazine covering travel, entertainment, politics and sex for gay men. **Freq:** Monthly. **ISSN:** 1047-8906 (print). **Subscription Rates:** $30 Individuals standard mail; $45 Individuals first class mail; $75 Individuals air mail; C$45 Canada airmail; €90 Other countries airmail. **URL:** http://www.guidemag.com. **Ad Rates:** BW $10200. **Remarks:** Accepts advertising. **Circ:** Combined 30,000.

15811 ■ Harvard Business Review
Harvard Business Review Press
60 Harvard Way
Boston, MA 02163
Phone: (617)783-7400
Free: 800-795-5200
Publisher's E-mail: custserv@hbsp.harvard.edu
Magazine for business executives. **Founded:** July 01, 2006. **Freq:** Monthly. **Print Method:** Offset. **Trim Size:** 8 3/16 x 10 3/4. **Cols./Page:** 3 and 2. **Col. Width:** 27 and 41 nonpareils. **Col. Depth:** 140 agate lines. **Key Personnel:** Henry J. Boye, Publisher; C. Bielaszka-DuVernay, Managing Editor; Janice Obuchowski, Coordinator. **ISSN:** 0017-8012 (print). **Subscription Rates:** $89 U.S.; $99 U.S. all access; $109 Canada; $119 Canada all access. **URL:** http://hbr.org/. **Ad Rates:** BW $33,081; 4C $41,224. **Remarks:** Accepts advertising. **Circ:** Paid ★**238045.**

15812 ■ The Herald of Christian Science
Christian Science Publishing Society
210 Massachusetts Ave.
Boston, MA 02115
Phone: (617)450-2000
Publisher's E-mail: info@ChristianScience.com
Christian Science magazine with articles and testimonies of Christian healing (German, French, Spanish, Portuguese, Norwegian, Swedish, Danish, Dutch, Italian, Indonesian, Japanese, and Greek). **Freq:** Monthly. **Print Method:** Offset. **Trim Size:** 8 1/4 x 7 3/4. **Cols./Page:** 1. **Col. Width:** 50 nonpareils. **Col. Depth:** 91 agate lines. **ISSN:** 0145--7578 (print). **URL:** http://herald.christianscience.com. **Remarks:** Advertising not accepted. **Circ:** (Not Reported).

15813 ■ The Horn Book Guide
The Horn Book Inc.
56 Roland St., Ste. 200
Boston, MA 02129
Phone: (617)628-0225
Fax: (617)628-0882
Free: 800-325-1170
Publisher's E-mail: info@hbook.com
Critical reviews of approximately 4,000 children's and young adult books each year. **Freq:** Semiannual. **Trim Size:** 8 1/2 x 11. **Key Personnel:** Roger Sutton, Editor-in-Chief; Rachel L. Smith, Reviewer; Elissa Gershowitz, Senior Editor; Lolly Robinson, Manager, Production; Bridget McCaffrey, Reviewer; Kitty Flynn, Executive Editor; Katie Bircher, Associate Editor; Andrew Thorne, Vice President, Marketing. **ISSN:** 1044--405X (print). **Subscription Rates:** $49 Individuals. **URL:** http://www.hbook.com/horn-book-guide. **Ad Rates:** BW $1499; 4C

$1999. **Remarks:** Accepts advertising. **Circ:** (Not Reported).

15814 ■ The Horn Book Magazine: About Books for Children and Young Adults
The Horn Book Inc.
56 Roland St., Ste. 200
Boston, MA 02129
Phone: (617)628-0225
Fax: (617)628-0882
Free: 800-325-1170
Publisher's E-mail: info@hbook.com
Journal devoted to children's and young adult literature. **Freq:** Bimonthly. **Print Method:** Offset. **Trim Size:** 6 x 9. **Cols./Page:** 1. **Col. Width:** 48 nonpareils. **Col. Depth:** 98 agate lines. **Key Personnel:** Andrew Thorne, Vice President, Marketing; Roger Sutton, Editor-in-Chief; Lolly Robinson, Manager, Production. **ISSN:** 0018--5078 (print). **Subscription Rates:** $49 Individuals; $66 Canada and Mexico; $70 Other countries. **URL:** http://www.hbook.com/horn-book-magazine-2. **Ad Rates:** 4C $2,150, full page; 4C $1,382, half page; BW $1,654, full page; BW $1,063, half page. **Remarks:** Accepts advertising. **Circ:** Combined 16000.

15815 ■ The Huntington News
Northeastern University
360 Huntington Ave.
Boston, MA 02115
Phone: (617)373-2000
Collegiate newspaper (tabloid). **Freq:** Weekly (Thurs.). **Print Method:** Offset. **Trim Size:** 10 x 16. **Cols./Page:** 5. **Col. Width:** 2 inches. **Col. Depth:** 16 inches. **Key Personnel:** Sam Haas, Editor-in-Chief. **URL:** http://huntnewsnu.com. **Formerly**: The Northeastern News. **Remarks:** Accepts advertising. **Circ:** (Not Reported).

15816 ■ International Journal of Pattern Recognition and Artificial Intelligence
World Scientific Publishing Company Private Ltd.
c/o P.S.P. Wang, Editor-in-Chief
Northeastern University
College of Computer Science
360 Huntington Ave.
Boston, MA 02115
Publisher's E-mail: wspc@wspc.com.sg
Peer-reviewed journal publishing both applications and theory-oriented articles on new developments in the fields of pattern recognition and artificial intelligence. **Freq:** 8/year. **Key Personnel:** X. Jiang, Editor-in-Chief; J.K. Aggarwal, Associate Editor; P.S.P. Wang, Editor-in-Chief. **ISSN:** 0218--0014 (print); **EISSN:** 1793--6381 (electronic). **Subscription Rates:** $2148 Institutions and libraries; print & electronic; $1917 Institutions and libraries; electronic only; £1580 Institutions and libraries; print & electronic; £1410 Institutions and libraries; electronic only; S$3524 Institutions and libraries; print & electronic; S$3144 Institutions and libraries; electronic only. **URL:** http://www.worldscientific.com/worldscinet/ijprai. **Remarks:** Advertising accepted; rates available upon request. **Circ:** (Not Reported).

15817 ■ The Jewish Advocate
The Jewish Advocate
15 School St.
Boston, MA 02108
Phone: (617)367-9100
Fax: (617)367-9310
Publisher's E-mail: businessoffice@thejewishadvocate.com
Local Jewish community newspaper. **Freq:** Weekly. **Key Personnel:** Daniel M. Kimmel, Editor. **Subscription Rates:** $44 Individuals print only; $50 Individuals print and online; $24 Individuals online only; $79.95 Two years print only; $89 Two years print and online; $36 Two years online only; $99.95 Individuals three years; $109 Individuals three years; $48 Individuals three years. **URL:** http://www.thejewishadvocate.com. **Remarks:** Accepts advertising. **Circ:** 22000.

15818 ■ Joslin Magazine
Joslin Diabetes Center
1 Joslin Pl.
Boston, MA 02215
Phone: (617)732-2400
Publisher's E-mail: diabetes@joslin.harvard.edu
Freq: Quarterly. **Subscription Rates:** included in membership dues. **Remarks:** Advertising not accepted. **Circ:** (Not Reported).

15819 ■ Journal of Aging and Social Policy
Routledge Journals Taylor & Francis Group
University of Massachusetts-Boston
Gerontology Institute
100 Morrissey Blvd.
Boston, MA 02125-3393
Forum for analysis, argument, research, and advocacy of social policy as it affects the aging population. **Founded:** 1989. **Freq:** Quarterly. **Trim Size:** 6 x 8 3/8. **Key Personnel:** Francis G. Caro, Editor; Robert Geary, Managing Editor. **ISSN:** 0895-9420 (print). **Subscription Rates:** $141 Individuals online; $157 Individuals print & online; $704 Institutions online; $805 Institutions print & online. **URL:** http://www.tandf.co.uk/journals/WASP. **Ad Rates:** BW $315; 4C $550. **Remarks:** Accepts advertising. **Circ:** 448.

15820 ■ Journal of Archaeology
Archaeological Institute of America - Boston
Boston University
656 Beacon St., 6th Fl.
Boston, MA 02215
Phone: (617)353-9361
Publisher's E-mail: aia@aia.bu.edu
Journal of the Archaeological Institute of America, Boston. **Freq:** Quarterly January, April, July, and October. **Key Personnel:** Madeleine J. Donachie, Director; Sheila Dillon, Editor-in-Chief. **Subscription Rates:** $295 Institutions print or online; $325 Institutions print and online; $80 Individuals print or online; $90 Individuals print and online; $50 Students print or online; $60 Students print and online. **URL:** http://www.ajaonline.org. **Remarks:** Accepts advertising. **Circ:** (Not Reported).

15821 ■ Journal of the Atmospheric Sciences
American Meteorological Society
45 Beacon St.
Boston, MA 02108-3693
Phone: (617)227-2425
Fax: (617)742-8718
Publisher's E-mail: amsinfo@ametsoc.org
Peer-reviewed journal covering research related to the physics, dynamics, and chemistry of the atmosphere of the earth and other planets. **Freq:** Monthly. **Print Method:** Offset. **Trim Size:** 8 1/4 x 10 7/8. **Cols./Page:** 3 and 2. **Col. Width:** 30 and 39 nonpareils. **Col. Depth:** 140 agate lines. **Key Personnel:** Dr. Ka Kit Tung, Editor-in-Chief, phone: (206)685-3794, fax: (206)685-1440; Ming Cai, Editor; Wojtek Grabowski, Editor; Joanna D. Haigh, Editor; Prof. Robert Houze, Editor; Dr. Rolando Garcia, Editor; Prof. J.Michael Wallace, Editor. **ISSN:** 0022--4928 (print); **EISSN:** 1520--0469 (electronic). **Subscription Rates:** $2480 Individuals print and online; $920 Individuals online only. **Online:** American Meteorological Society American Meteorological Society. **URL:** http://journals.ametsoc.org/loi/atsc. **Remarks:** Advertising not accepted. **Circ:** (Not Reported).

15822 ■ Journal of Clinical Psychopharmacology
Lippincott Williams and Wilkins
Tufts University
School of Medicine
Dept. of Pharmacology & Experimental Therapeutics
136 Harrison Ave.
Boston, MA 02111
Phone: (617)636-2178
Publisher's E-mail: ronna.ekhouse@wolterskluwer.com
Medical journal. **Freq:** 6/year. **Print Method:** Offset. **Trim Size:** 8 1/8 x 10 7/8. **Cols./Page:** 2. **Col. Width:** 32 nonpareils. **Col. Depth:** 119 agate lines. **Key Personnel:** David J. Greenblatt, MD, Editor-in-Chief; Richard I. Shader, MD, Editor-in-Chief; Natalie McGroarty, Publisher. **ISSN:** 0271--0749 (print); **EISSN:** 1533--712X (electronic). **Subscription Rates:** $461 Individuals; $882 Two years; $1323 Individuals 3 years. **Alt. Formats:** Download. **URL:** http://journals.lww.com/psychopharmacology/pages/default.aspx. **Ad Rates:** BW $1,200; 4C $2,320. **Remarks:** Accepts advertising. **Circ:** 544.

15823 ■ Journal of Electrostatics: Fundamentals, Applications and Hazards
RELX Group P.L.C.
c/o M.N. Horenstein, Ed.
Department of Electrical & Computer Engineering
Boston University
44 Cumington St.
Boston, MA 02215
Publisher's E-mail: amsterdam@relx.com
Journal dealing with all aspects of static electricity, its applications as well as dangers posed. **Freq:** 6/year. **Key Personnel:** M.N. Horenstein, Editor. **ISSN:** 0304--3886 (print). **Subscription Rates:** $264 Individuals print; $2661 Institutions print; $2218.67 Institutions ejournal. **URL:** http://www.journals.elsevier.com/journal-of-electrostatics. **Circ:** (Not Reported).

15824 ■ Journal of Functional Programming
Cambridge University Press
c/o Dr. Matthias Felleisen, Editor-in-Chief
Northeastern University
College of Computer Science
360 Huntingdon Ave.
Boston, MA 02115
Publication E-mail: ad_sales@cambridge.org
Peer-reviewed journal on computer science. **Freq:** Bimonthly. **Key Personnel:** Jeremy Gibbons, Editor-in-Chief; Dr. Matthias Felleisen, Editor-in-Chief. **ISSN:** 0956--7968 (print). **Subscription Rates:** $642 Institutions online only; £411 Institutions online only. **URL:** http://journals.cambridge.org/action/displayJournal?jid=JFP. **Ad Rates:** BW $845. **Remarks:** Accepts advertising. **Circ:** 400.

15825 ■ Journal of Haitian Studies
Haitian Studies Association
University of Massachusetts Boston
McCormack Hall, Rm. 2-211
100 Morrissey Blvd.
Boston, MA 02125-3393
Publication E-mail: johs@cbs.ucsb.edu
Freq: Semiannual. **Key Personnel:** Roberto Strongman, Assistant Editor; Claudine Michel, Editor. **ISSN:** 1090--3488 (print). **Subscription Rates:** $30 Individuals one year; $50 Institutions one year; $80 Institutions two years. **URL:** http://www.research.ucsb.edu/cbs/publications/johs; http://www.research.ucsb.edu/cbs/publications/johs/index.html; http://www.umb.edu/haitianstudies/johs. **Remarks:** Advertising not accepted. **Circ:** 103, 103.

15826 ■ Journal of Haitian Studies
University of California, Santa Barbara Center for Black Studies Research
4603 South Hall
Santa Barbara, CA 93106-3140
Phone: (805)893-3914
Fax: (805)893-7243
Publication E-mail: johs@cbs.ucsb.edu
Freq: Semiannual. **Key Personnel:** Roberto Strongman, Assistant Editor; Claudine Michel, Editor. **ISSN:** 1090--3488 (print). **Subscription Rates:** $30 Individuals one year; $50 Institutions one year; $80 Institutions two years. **URL:** http://www.research.ucsb.edu/cbs/publications/johs; http://www.research.ucsb.edu/cbs/publications/johs/index.html; http://www.umb.edu/haitianstudies/johs. **Remarks:** Advertising not accepted. **Circ:** 103, 103.

15827 ■ Journal of Hydrometeorology
American Meteorological Society
45 Beacon St.
Boston, MA 02108-3693
Phone: (617)227-2425
Fax: (617)742-8718
Publisher's E-mail: amsinfo@ametsoc.org
Peer-reviewed journal covering research related to the modeling, observing, and forecasting of processes related to water and energy fluxes and storage terms. **Freq:** Bimonthly. **Key Personnel:** L. Ruby Leung, Editor; Christa Peters-Lidard, Editor-in-Chief. **ISSN:** 1525--755X (print). **URL:** http://www.ametsoc.org/ams/index.cfm/publications/journals/journal-of-hydrometeorology; http://www.ametsoc.org/ams/index.cfm/publications/journals. **Circ:** (Not Reported).

15828 ■ The Journal of Infectious Diseases
The University of Chicago Press
225 Friend St., 7th Fl.
Boston, MA 02114-1812
Phone: (617)367-1848
Fax: (617)367-2624
Publication E-mail: jid@press.uchicago.edu
Medical journal presenting new research in infectious diseases, providing new information from clinical,

Circulation: ★ = AAM; △ or • = BPA; ♦ = CAC; ❑ = VAC; ⊕ = PO Statement; ‡ = Publisher's Report; Boldface figures = sworn; Light figures = estimated.

epidemiologic, and lab experience. **Founded:** 1904. **Freq:** Semimonthly. **Print Method:** Offset. **Trim Size:** 8 1/4 x 10 7/8. **Cols./Page:** 2. **Col. Width:** 36 nonpareils. **Col. Depth:** 116 agate lines. **Key Personnel:** William Schaffner, Associate Editor; Michael Hughes, Editor; David C. Hooper, Editor; Ann M. Arvin, Associate Editor; Peter Densen, Associate Editor; Richard J. Whitley, Associate Editor; Jane R. Schwebke, Associate Editor; Joseph A. Kovacs, Associate Editor; Martin Hirsch, Editor; Lee Powers, Managing Editor. **ISSN:** 0022-1899 (print); **EISSN:** 1537-6613 (electronic). **Subscription Rates:** $161 Individuals print and electronic; $81 Other countries electronic only; $81 Individuals special electronic only; $777 Institutions print and electronic; $647 Institutions electronic only; $666 Institutions print only. **URL:** http://www.jstor.org/stable/1412649. **Ad Rates:** BW $730; 4C $2000. **Remarks:** Accepts advertising. **Circ:** 10,553.

15829 ■ The Journal of Law, Medicine & Ethics
American Society of Law, Medicine and Ethics
765 Commonwealth Ave., Ste. 1634
Boston, MA 02215-1401
Phone: (617)262-4990
Fax: (617)437-7596
Publication E-mail: publications@aslme.org
Peer-reviewed journal publishing research at the intersection of law, health policy, ethics, and medicine. **Freq:** Quarterly. **Print Method:** Web, Perfect Bound. **Trim Size:** 8 1/2 x 11. **Cols./Page:** 2 and 3. **Col. Width:** 20 and 13 picas. **Col. Depth:** 54 picas. **Key Personnel:** Ted Hutchinson, Director, Publications; Katie Kenney Johnson, Director, Conferences. **ISSN:** 1073--1105 (print); **EISSN:** 1748--720X (electronic). **Subscription Rates:** £457 Institutions online; £508 Institutions print and online; £498 Institutions print; $137 Institutions Single Print Issue; Included in membership. **URL:** http://www.aslme.org/Publications. **Formerly**: Law, Medicine & Health Care. **Ad Rates:** BW $695. **Remarks:** Color advertising not accepted. **Circ:** ‡5000.

15830 ■ Journal of Monetary Economics
RELX Group P.L.C.
c/o Robert G. King, Ed.
Department of Economics
Boston University
270 Bay State Rd.
Boston, MA 02215
Publisher's E-mail: amsterdam@relx.com
A broad base journal on monetary economics. **Freq:** 8/year. **Key Personnel:** Robert G. King, Editor; Charles I. Plosser, Editor. **ISSN:** 0304--3932 (print). **Subscription Rates:** $141 Individuals print; $3336 Institutions print; 2779.33 ejournal. **URL:** http://www.journals.elsevier.com/journal-of-monetary-economics. **Circ:** (Not Reported).

15831 ■ Journal of Official Statistics
Walter de Gruyter Inc.
121 High St., 3rd Fl.
Boston, MA 02110
Phone: (857)284-7073
Fax: (857)284-7358
Publisher's E-mail: service@degruyter.com
Journal featuring research articles in the area of survey and statistical methodology. **Freq:** Quarterly. **Key Personnel:** Stefan Lundgren, Publisher. **EISSN:** 2001--7367 (electronic). **Subscription Rates:** $42. **URL:** http://www.degruyter.com/view/j/jos. **Remarks:** Advertising not accepted. **Circ:** (Not Reported).

15832 ■ Journal of Science & Technology Law
Boston University School of Law
765 Commonwealth Ave.
Boston, MA 02215
Phone: (617)353-3160
Publication E-mail: jstl@bu.edu
Journal focusing on science and technology law. **Key Personnel:** Young J. Yoon; Emily Crim, Managing Editor; Grant Gendron, Managing Editor. **Subscription Rates:** $50 Individuals; $55 Other countries; $25 Individuals /back issue; $27.50 Other countries /back issue. **Online:** Boston University School of Law Boston University School of Law; LexisNexis; Westlaw. **URL:** http://www.bu.edu/jostl. **Circ:** (Not Reported).

15833 ■ Journal of Thoracic Imaging
Lippincott Williams & Wilkins
c/o Phillip M. Boiselle, MD, Ed.-in-Ch.
Beth Israel Deaconess Medical Ctr.
330 Brookline Ave.
Boston, MA 02215
Phone: (617)667-1636
Fax: (617)667-0665
Peer-reviewed journal on all aspects of the diagnosis of chest disease using imaging techniques. **Freq:** Bimonthly. **Trim Size:** 8 1/4 x 11. **Cols./Page:** 2. **Col. Width:** 20 picas. **Col. Depth:** 54 picas. **Key Personnel:** Phillip M. Boiselle, MD, Editor-in-Chief. **ISSN:** 0883-5993 (print). **Subscription Rates:** $644 Individuals; $771 Canada and Mexico; $785 Other countries; $1145 Institutions; $1364 Institutions, Canada and Mexico; $1378 Institutions, other countries; $316 U.S., Canada, and Mexico in-training; $330 Other countries in-training. **URL:** http://journals.lww.com/thoracicimaging/pages/default.aspx. **Ad Rates:** BW $1,025; 4C $1,445. **Remarks:** Accepts advertising. **Circ:** 825.

15834 ■ Journal of Transnational Management
International Management Development Association
c/o Kip Becker, PhD, Ed.
Boston University
Metropolitan College
808 Commonwealth Ave.
Boston, MA 02215
Publisher's E-mail: imda-l@umassd.edu
Journal on transnational management development issues. **Freq:** Quarterly. **Trim Size:** 6 x 8 3/8. **Key Personnel:** Kip Becker, PhD, Editor; Erdener Kaynak, Editor, Founder. **ISSN:** 1547-5778 (print); **EISSN:** 1547-5786 (electronic). **Subscription Rates:** $620 Institutions online; $138 Individuals online; $709 Institutions print & online; $148 Individuals print & online; included in membership dues. **URL:** http://www.tandfonline.com/toc/wtnm20/current#.Ve6Wu9Kqqkp; http://www.bu.edu/goglobal/a/goglobal_zulfiqar/zulfiqar_index.html; http://www.tandfonline.com/loi/wtnm20?open=9&repitition=1#.Ve6XXdKqqko. **Formerly**: Journal of Transnational Management Development. **Ad Rates:** BW $315; 4C $550. **Remarks:** Accepts advertising. **Circ:** Paid 107.

15835 ■ Lawyer's Journal: Massachusetts Bar Association
Massachusetts Bar Association
20 West St.
Boston, MA 02111-1204
Phone: (617)338-0500
Publication E-mail: lawjournal@massbar.org
Professional journal covering legal issues. **Freq:** Monthly. **Key Personnel:** Andrea Barter, Editor; Bill Archambeault, Manager, Periodicals; Robert L. Holloway, Jr., Treasurer; Jenny Wong, Editor; Marilyn J. Wellington, Executive Director; Denise Squillante, President; Douglas K. Sheff, Vice President; Kate O'Toole, Communications Specialist; Martin W. Healy, Editor, General Counsel. **Subscription Rates:** Free. **Alt. Formats:** Download; PDF. **URL:** http://www.massbar.org/publications/lawyers-journal. **Remarks:** Advertising accepted; rates available upon request. **Circ:** Controlled 19000.

15836 ■ Massachusetts Bar Association Lawyers Journal
Massachusetts Bar Association
20 West St.
Boston, MA 02111-1204
Phone: (617)338-0500
Publication E-mail: lawjournal@massbar.org
communications@massbar.org
Professional newspaper covering law. **Freq:** Monthly. **Key Personnel:** Bill Archambeault, Editor; Jason M. Scally, Editor. **Subscription Rates:** $30 Nonmembers; $20 Members. **URL:** http://www.massbar.org/publications/lawyers-journal. **Remarks:** Advertising accepted; rates available upon request. **Circ:** (Not Reported).

15837 ■ Massachusetts Beverage Business
New Beverage Publications Inc.
55 Clarendon St.
Boston, MA 02116-6067
Phone: (617)598-1900
Fax: (617)598-1940
Publisher's E-mail: jfsilva@beveragebusiness.com
Publication for the retail beverages industry. **Freq:** Monthly. **Print Method:** Offset. **Trim Size:** 8 1/2 x 11. **Cols./Page:** 3. **Col. Width:** 27 nonpareils. **Col. Depth:** 140 agate lines. **Key Personnel:** Ben Stone, Director, Advertising, Director, Marketing, phone: (617)598-1922, fax: (617)598-1941; P.J. Stone, Creative Director, Executive Editor, phone: (617)598-1911; Maia Merill, Managing Editor, phone: (617)598-1910. **ISSN:** 1090--9214 (print). **USPS:** 333-200. **Subscription Rates:** $76 Individuals Standard mail; $196 Individuals Express delivery. **URL:** http://www.beveragebusiness.com. **Formerly**: Massachusetts Beverage Price Journal. **Ad Rates:** BW $1350; 4C $1800. **Remarks:** Accepts advertising. **Circ:** Paid ‡7,485, Non-paid ‡560.

15838 ■ Massachusetts Law Review
Massachusetts Bar Association
20 West St.
Boston, MA 02111-1204
Phone: (617)338-0500
Journal containing scholarly review and analysis of the law in Massachusetts (federal and state). **Freq:** Quarterly. **Key Personnel:** Victor N. Baltera, Board Member. **ISSN:** 0163--1411 (print). **Alt. Formats:** PDF. **URL:** http://www.massbar.org/publications/massachusetts-law-review. **Remarks:** Accepts advertising. **Circ:** (Not Reported).

15839 ■ Massachusetts Lawyers Weekly
Lawyers Weekly Publications
10 Milk St., Ste. 1000
Boston, MA 02111
Phone: (617)451-7300
Newspaper (tabloid) reporting Massachusetts legal news. **Freq:** Weekly. **Print Method:** Offset full run. **Trim Size:** 11 x 17. **Cols./Page:** 4. **Key Personnel:** Henriette Campagne, Editor, phone: (617)218-8192; Suzette Bocamazo, Editor, phone: (617)218-8191. **ISSN:** 0196--7509 (print). **Subscription Rates:** $379 Individuals; $684 Two years. **URL:** http://masslawyersweekly.com. **Ad Rates:** 4C $4,400. **Remarks:** Advertising accepted; rates available upon request. **Circ:** ‡16000.

15840 ■ Menopause: The Journal of the North American Menopause Society
Lippincott Williams & Wilkins
c/o Diane K. Barker, Mng. Ed.
55 Fruit St., FH524B
Boston, MA 02114
Phone: (617)724-1372
Fax: (617)724-0988
Peer-reviewed journal devoted to the exploration of subjects pertaining to menopause. **Freq:** Monthly. **Print Method:** Sheetfed Offset. **Trim Size:** 8 1/4 x 11. **Key Personnel:** Diane K. Barker, Managing Editor; Isaac Schiff, MD, Editor-in-Chief, phone: (617)726-3001, fax: (617)726-7548. **ISSN:** 1072--3714 (print); **EISSN:** 1530--0374 (electronic). **URL:** http://journals.lww.com/menopausejournal/Pages/default.aspx. **Ad Rates:** BW $1,630; 4C $3,155. **Remarks:** Accepts advertising. **Circ:** Paid 1817.

15841 ■ Michigan Medical Law Report
Lawyers Weekly Publications
10 Milk St., Ste. 1000
Boston, MA 02111
Phone: (617)451-7300
Publication covering legal topics of interest to doctors and health care providers in Michigan. **Freq:** Quarterly. **Key Personnel:** Gary Gosselin, Editor; Douglas Levy, Associate Editor. **Subscription Rates:** $339 Individuals print and digital; $199 Individuals digital. **URL:** http://milawyersweekly.com/mi-medical-law-report. **Remarks:** Accepts advertising. **Circ:** (Not Reported).

15842 ■ Midwest In-House
Lawyers Weekly Publications
10 Milk St., Ste. 1000
Boston, MA 02111
Phone: (617)451-7300
Publication that focuses on topics of interest to in-house lawyers practicing in the Midwest. **Freq:** Bimonthly. **Key Personnel:** Paul Boynton, Publisher. **URL:** http://newenglandinhouse.com. **Ad Rates:** BW $2,878; 4C $400. **Remarks:** Accepts advertising. **Circ:** (Not Reported).

15843 ■ Missouri Medical Law Report
Lawyers Weekly Publications
10 Milk St., Ste. 1000
Boston, MA 02111
Phone: (617)451-7300
Publication covering legal topics of interest to doctors and health care providers in Missouri. **Freq:** Quarterly. **Key Personnel:** Richard Gard, Publisher. **Subscription**

Rates: $357.01 Individuals online. **URL:** http://www.momedicallaw.com. **Remarks:** Accepts advertising. **Circ:** (Not Reported).

15844 ■ Modern Judaism: A Journal of Jewish Ideas and Experience
Oxford University Press
Center for Judaic Studies
Boston University
147 Bay State Rd.
Boston, MA 02215
Phone: (617)353-8089
Fax: (617)353-7710
Publisher's E-mail: webenquiry.uk@oup.com
Journal providing a distinctive, interdisciplinary forum for discussion of the modern Jewish experience, focusing on topics pertinent to the understanding of Jewish life today and the forces that have shaped that experience. **Freq:** 3/year. **Key Personnel:** Prof. Steven T. Katz, Editor; Deborah Lipstadt, Board Member; Sander Gilman, Board Member; Jehuda Reinharz, Board Member; Arnold Eisen, Board Member; Michael A. Meyer, Board Member; Irving Greenberg, Board Member; Paul Mendes-Flohr, Board Member. **ISSN:** 0276--1114 (print); **EISSN:** 1086--3273 (electronic). **Subscription Rates:** £85 Institutions online; $192 Institutions online; €185 Institutions online; £98 Institutions print; $219 Institutions print; €212 Institutions print; £105 Institutions print and online; $240 Institutions print and online; €230 Institutions print and online; £40 Individuals print; $92 Individuals print; €89 Individuals print; £22 Students print; $49 Students print; €47 Students print; £22 Individuals print - senior; $49 Individuals print - senior; €47 Individuals print - senior. **URL:** http://mj.oxfordjournals.org. **Remarks:** Advertising accepted; rates available upon request. **Circ:** (Not Reported).

15845 ■ New England Economic Indicators
Federal Reserve Bank of Boston
600 Atlantic Ave.
Boston, MA 02210-2204
Phone: (617)973-3000
Fax: (877)888-2520
Free: 888-851-1920
Publication E-mail: boston.library@bos.frb.org
Statistical publication. **Freq:** Quarterly. **Trim Size:** 8 1/2 x 11. **Key Personnel:** Robert Clifford, Editor. **ISSN:** 0458--4448 (print). **URL:** http://www.bostonfed.org/economic/neei. **Mailing address:** PO Box 55882, Boston, MA 02205-5882. **Remarks:** Advertising not accepted. **Circ:** (Not Reported).

15846 ■ New England Historical and Genealogical Register
New England Historic Genealogical Society
101 Newbury St.
Boston, MA 02116
Phone: (617)536-5740
Fax: (617)536-7307
Free: 888-296-3447
Publisher's E-mail: administration@nehgs.org
Scholarly journal focusing on genealogy and history. **Freq:** Quarterly. **Print Method:** Offset. **Trim Size:** 6 x 9. **Cols./Page:** 1. **Col. Width:** 48 nonpareils. **Col. Depth:** 98 agate lines. **Key Personnel:** Henry B. Hoff, Editor. **ISSN:** 0028--4785 (print). **URL:** http://www.americanancestors.org/the-register. **Ad Rates:** BW $425. **Remarks:** Accepts advertising. **Circ:** ‡20000, 21000.

15847 ■ New England Home
New England Home
530 Harrison Ave., Ste. 302
Boston, MA 02118
Phone: (203)849-9345
Free: 800-609-5154
Publisher's E-mail: info@nehomemag.com
Magazine that showcases architecture and design of luxury New England homes. **Freq:** Bimonthly. **Key Personnel:** Erin Marvin, Managing Editor; Kyle Hoepner, Editor-in-Chief; Kathy Bush-Dutton, Publisher; Glenn Sadin, Manager, Production. **Subscription Rates:** $19.95 Individuals; $38 Two years. **Remarks:** Advertising accepted; rates available upon request. **Circ:** (Not Reported).

15848 ■ New England In-House
Lawyers Weekly Publications
10 Milk St., Ste. 1000
Boston, MA 02111
Phone: (617)451-7300
Publication that focuses on topics of interest to in-house lawyers practicing in New England. **Freq:** Quarterly. **Key Personnel:** Henriette Campagne, Publisher; Charlene Smith, Vice President, Sales. **Subscription Rates:** Free. **URL:** http://www.newenglandinhouse.com. **Ad Rates:** BW $3,015; 4C $495. **Remarks:** Accepts advertising. **Circ:** ‡6000.

15849 ■ New England Journal on Criminal and Civil Confinement
New England Law Boston
154 Stuart St.
Boston, MA 02116
Phone: (617)451-0010
Publisher's E-mail: admit@nesl.edu
Journal addressing important constitutional and policy issues in the areas of criminal justice and civil confinement. **Freq:** Semiannual. **Key Personnel:** Tifanei N. Ressl-Moyer, Editor-in-Chief. **Subscription Rates:** $25 Individuals /year. **URL:** http://www.nesl.edu/students/ne_journal_ccc.cfm. **Circ:** (Not Reported).

15850 ■ The New England Journal of Higher Education
New England Board of Higher Education
45 Temple Pl.
Boston, MA 02111
Phone: (617)357-9620
Fax: (617)338-1577
Publication E-mail: info@nebhe.org
Journal of higher education and economic development. **Founded:** 1986. **Freq:** Quarterly. **Trim Size:** 8 1/2 x 11 1/2. **Key Personnel:** John O. Harney, Executive Editor. **ISSN:** 0895-6405 (print). **URL:** http://www.nebhe.org/thejournal/; http://www.nebhe.org/content/view/33/70/; http://www.nebhe.org/nejhe-archives. **Formerly:** Connection. **Ad Rates:** 4C $2,500; BW $1,600. **Remarks:** Accepts advertising. **Circ:** Controlled 12000.

15851 ■ The New England Journal of Medicine
Massachusetts Medical Society
10 Shattuck St.
Boston, MA 02115-6094
Phone: (617)734-9800
Fax: (617)739-9864
Publication E-mail: nejmcust@mms.org nejmintlcust@mms.org
Journal for the medical profession. **Freq:** Weekly. **Key Personnel:** Ronald W. Dunlap, M.D., President; Jeffrey M. Drazen, MD, Editor-in-Chief; Gregory D. Curfman, MD, Executive Editor; Stephen Morrissey, PhD, Managing Editor. **ISSN:** 0028-4793 (print). **Subscription Rates:** $149 Individuals online only; $179 Individuals print & online; $139 Students print & online; $49 Students online only. **Online:** ProQuest L.L.C.; LexisNexis; Massachusetts Medical Society Massachusetts Medical Society; Ovid Technologies Inc. **Alt. Formats:** CD-ROM. **URL:** http://www.nejm.org. **Remarks:** Accepts advertising. **Circ:** △**160453**.

15852 ■ New England Law Review
New England School of Law
154 Stuart St.
Boston, MA 02116
Phone: (617)451-0010
Publication E-mail: lawreview@nesl.edu
Professional journal covering law. **Freq:** Quarterly. **Key Personnel:** Janie Reilly; Michael Martucci, Editor-in-Chief. **ISSN:** 0028--4823 (print). **Subscription Rates:** $35 Individuals; $15 Single issue; $40 Other countries. **URL:** http://www.nesl.edu/students/law_review.cfm. **Remarks:** Advertising not accepted. **Circ:** (Not Reported).

15853 ■ The New England Quarterly: A Historical Review of New England Life and Letters
Northeastern University
360 Huntington Ave.
Boston, MA 02115
Phone: (617)373-2000
Publication E-mail: neq@neu.edu
Journal carrying articles in the fields of literature, history, and culture relating to New England. **Freq:** Quarterly March, June, September, and December. **Print Method:** Offset. **Trim Size:** 4 1/2 x 7. **Cols./Page:** 1. **Col. Width:** 4 inches. **Col. Depth:** 7 inches. **Key Personnel:** Jonathan Chu, Editor. **ISSN:** 0028--4866 (print); **EISSN:** 1937--2213 (electronic). **Subscription Rates:** $45 Individuals print and online; $121 Institutions print and online; $25 Students online; $40 Individuals online only; $104 Institutions online only. **Alt. Formats:** PDF. **URL:** http://www.northeastern.edu/neq; http://colonialsociety.org/neq.html. **Ad Rates:** BW $400. **Remarks:** Color advertising not accepted. **Circ:** Paid ‡2200.

15854 ■ Northeastern University Law Journal
Northeastern University School of Law
416 Huntington Ave.
Boston, MA 02115
Phone: (617)373-5149
Journal covering articles with a social justice consciousness. **Key Personnel:** Mary Donahue, Editor-in-Chief. **Subscription Rates:** $20 Individuals; $12 Single issue. **URL:** http://nulj.org. **Circ:** (Not Reported).

15855 ■ NPSF Journal of Patient Safety
National Patient Safety Foundation
268 Summer St., 6th Fl.
Boston, MA 02210
Phone: (617)391-9900
Fax: (617)391-9999
Publisher's E-mail: info@wolterskluwer.com
Journal presenting research advances and field applications within the area of patient safety. **Freq:** Quarterly. **Key Personnel:** David Westfall Bates, MD, Editor-in-Chief. **ISSN:** 1549--8417 (print); **EISSN:** 1549--8425 (electronic). **Subscription Rates:** $277 Individuals; $740 Institutions. **URL:** http://www.npsf.org/?page=publications_. **Remarks:** Accepts advertising. **Circ:** (Not Reported).

15856 ■ Nutrition Today
Lippincott Williams and Wilkins
c/o Frances Stern Nutrition Ctr.
New England Medical Ctr.
Boston, MA 02111
Phone: (617)636-5273
Publication E-mail: nutoday@aol.com
Health science journal. **Freq:** Bimonthly. **Print Method:** Web offset. **Trim Size:** 8 1/2 x 11. **Cols./Page:** 3. **Col. Width:** 27 nonpareils. **Col. Depth:** 137 agate lines. **Key Personnel:** Johanna Dwyer, Editor; Kathleen M. Phelan, Publisher. **ISSN:** 0029-666X (print). **Subscription Rates:** $109 Individuals; $430 Institutions; $62 Individuals in-training; $219 Other countries; $586 Institutions, other countries. **URL:** http://journals.lww.com/nutritiontodayonline/pages/default.aspx. **Mailing address:** PO Box 783, 750 Washington St., Boston, MA 02111. **Ad Rates:** BW $1,255. **Remarks:** Accepts advertising. **Circ:** Paid 1594.

15857 ■ The Oncologist: The International Peer-Reviewed journal for the Practicing Oncologist/Hematologist
AlphaMed Press
c/o Bruce A. Chabner, Ed.-in-Ch.
Massachusetts General Hospital
55 Fruit St.
Boston, MA 02114
Publication E-mail: theoncologist@cambeywest.com
Journal covering clinical oncology. **Freq:** Monthly. **Print Method:** Offset. **Trim Size:** 11 x 14 1/2. **Cols./Page:** 4 and 3. **Col. Width:** 36 and 28 nonpareils. **Col. Depth:** 210 agate lines. **Key Personnel:** Patrick G. Johnston, Senior Editor; Bruce A. Chabner, Editor-in-Chief; H.M. Pinedo, Senior Editor; Martin J. Murphy, Jr., Executive Editor; Ann Murphy, Managing Editor. **ISSN:** 1083--7159 (print); **EISSN:** 1549--490X (electronic). **Subscription Rates:** $420 Institutions online; $500 Institutions print and online. **URL:** http://theoncologist.alphamedpress.org. **Ad Rates:** BW $2875. **Remarks:** Accepts advertising. **Circ:** △**16507**.

15858 ■ Panorama
Jerome Press Publications Inc.
332 Congress St.
Boston, MA 02210
Visitor's guide distributed for guests at 63 hotels in the Boston area. **Founded:** 1951. **Freq:** Biweekly. **Print Method:** Offset. **Trim Size:** 5 5/8 x 8 3/8. **Cols./Page:** 2. **Col. Width:** 2 5/16 inches. **Col. Depth:** 7 3/4 inches. **ISSN:** 0048-282X (print). **Subscription Rates:** $49 Individuals; $1.89 Single issue. **URL:** http://www.panoramamagazine.com/panoramamagazine/. **Ad**

Circulation: ★ = AAM; △ or • = BPA; ♦ = CAC; ❑ = VAC; ⊕ = PO Statement; ‡ = Publisher's Report; Boldface figures = sworn; Light figures = estimated.

Rates: BW $490; 4C $640. **Remarks:** Accepts advertising. **Circ:** Non-paid ‡28745.

15859 ■ Particulate Science and Technology: An International Journal
Taylor & Francis Group Journals
c/o Dr. Malay K. Mazumder, Editor-in-Chief
Boston University
Department of Electrical & Computer Engineering
8 St. Mary's St.
Boston, MA 02215
Phone: (617)997-7049
Fax: (617)353-6440
Publisher's E-mail: customerservice@taylorandfrancis.com
Journal publishing original research and review material dealing with particulate science and technology. **Freq:** Bimonthly. **Print Method:** Offset Uses mats. **Trim Size:** 7 x 10. **Key Personnel:** Virendra M. Puri, Editor-in-Chief, phone: (814)865-7792, fax: (814)863-1031; Dr. Malay K. Mazumder, Editor-in-Chief. **ISSN:** 0272--6351 (print); **EISSN:** 1548--0046 (electronic). **Subscription Rates:** $646 Individuals print only; $1436 Institutions online only; $1641 Individuals print and online. **URL:** http://www.tandfonline.com/toc/upst20/current. **Remarks:** Accepts advertising. **Circ:** ‡150.

15860 ■ Paths of Progress
Dana-Farber Cancer Institute
450 Brookline Ave.
Boston, MA 02115
Phone: (617)632-4090
Publication E-mail: pathsofprogress@dfci.harvard.edu
Freq: Semiannual. **Alt. Formats:** PDF. **URL:** http://www.jimmyfund.org/about-us/news-and-publications/publications/paths-of-progress. **Remarks:** Advertising not accepted. **Circ:** (Not Reported).

15861 ■ Pharmacotherapy: The Journal of Human Pharmacology and Drug Therapy
Pharmacotherapy Publications Inc.
750 Washington Ave.
Boston, MA 02111
Phone: (617)636-5390
Fax: (617)636-5318
Publisher's E-mail: accp@accp.com
Magazine presenting original research articles on all aspects of human pharmacology and reviews of articles on drugs and drug therapy. **Freq:** Monthly. **Print Method:** Offset. **Trim Size:** 8 1/8 x 10 7/8. **Cols./Page:** 2. **Col. Width:** 37 nonpareils. **Col. Depth:** 135 agate lines. **Key Personnel:** C. Lindsay DeVane, Editor-in-Chief; Denise E. Gibson, Managing Editor. **ISSN:** 0277--0008 (print); **EISSN:** 1875--9114 (electronic). **Subscription Rates:** $572 U.S., Canada, and Mexico online only - Institutions; $687 U.S., Canada, and Mexico print and online - institutions; $572 U.S., Canada, and Mexico print only - institutions; $126 U.S., Canada, and Mexico online only - personal; $170 U.S., Canada, and Mexico print and online - personal; $82 U.S., Canada, and Mexico online only - student; $115 U.S., Canada, and Mexico print and online - student; £370 Institutions print or online - UK; £444 Institutions print and online - UK; £84 Individuals online only - UK; £113 Individuals print and online - UK; £54 Students online only - UK; £84 Students print and online - UK; €429 Institutions print or online - Europe; €515 Institutions print and online - Europe; €95 Individuals online only - Europe; €129 Individuals print and online - Europe; €61 Students online only - Europe; €95 Students print and online - Europe. **URL:** http://onlinelibrary.wiley.com/journal/10.1002/(ISSN)1875-9114; http://www.accp.com/bookstore/th_journal.aspx. **Ad Rates:** BW $1,920. **Remarks:** Accepts advertising. **Circ:** 10766.

15862 ■ Plastics News: Crains' International Newspaper for the Plastics Industry
Crain Communications Inc.
101 Federal Street, Suite 1900, Room 1612
Boston, MA 02110
Publisher's E-mail: info@crain.com
Magazine (tabloid) for the plastics industry providing business news. **Freq:** Weekly. **Print Method:** Saddle Stitch. **Trim Size:** 10 7/8 x 14 1/2. **Cols./Page:** 5. **Col. Width:** 14 inches. **Key Personnel:** Don Loepp, Editor, phone: (313)446-6767; Robert Grace, Associate Publisher. **ISSN:** 1042-802X (print). **Subscription Rates:** $89 U.S. print + web; $160 Two years print + web; $292 Other countries print + web; $89 Individuals web only; $139 Canada print + web; $250 Canada two years, print + web; $526 Two years other countries. **URL:** http://www.plasticsnews.com. **Ad Rates:** BW $9,720; 4C $12,805; PCI $274. **Remarks:** Advertising accepted; rates available upon request. **Circ:** 45000.

15863 ■ Post-Gazette
Post-Gazette
PO Box 130135
Boston, MA 02113
Phone: (617)227-8929
Fax: (617)227-5307
Publisher's E-mail: postgazette@aol.com
Newspaper. **Freq:** Weekly (Fri.). **Print Method:** Offset. **Cols./Page:** 5. **Col. Width:** 23 nonpareils. **Col. Depth:** 223 agate lines. **Key Personnel:** Pamela Donnaruma, Publisher. **Subscription Rates:** $30 Individuals. **URL:** http://www.bostonpostgazette.com . **Ad Rates:** PCI $20; BW $1,600. **Remarks:** Accepts advertising. **Circ:** Paid 15900.

15864 ■ Providence Phoenix
The Phoenix Media/Communications Group
126 Brookline Ave.
Boston, MA 02215
Phone: (617)536-5390
Fax: (617)536-1463
Publication E-mail: feedback@phx.com
Statewide newspaper. **Freq:** Weekly. **Print Method:** Web offset. **Trim Size:** 10 x 14. **Cols./Page:** 6. **Col. Width:** 1 1/2 inches. **Col. Depth:** 14 inches. **Key Personnel:** Stephen L. Brown, Associate Publisher; Lou Papineau, Managing Editor; David Scharfenberg, Editor. **Subscription Rates:** $49 Individuals 6 months, bulk; $89 Individuals bulk; $175 Individuals 6 months, first class; $289 Individuals first class. **URL:** http://thephoenix.com/providence. **Formerly:** The Phoenix's Newspaper; NewPaper. **Ad Rates:** GLR $2.87; BW $3,381; 4C $4,180; PCI $45. **Remarks:** Accepts advertising. **Circ:** Free ‡64000, 107000.

15865 ■ Psychiatric Rehabilitation Journal
Psychiatric Rehabilitation Journal
940 Commonwealth Ave. W
Boston, MA 02215
Phone: (617)353-3549
Fax: (617)353-7700
Publisher's E-mail: prj@bu.edu
Journal discussing issues, programs, and research on psychiatric rehabilitation.Publishes original contributions related to the rehabilitation, psychosocial treatment, and recovery of people with serious mental illnesses. **Freq:** Quarterly. **Trim Size:** 8 1/2 x 11. **Key Personnel:** William A. Anthony, PhD, Editor; Kenneth J. Gill, Board Member; Kathleen Furlong-Norman, Managing Editor. **ISSN:** 1095-158X (print). **Subscription Rates:** $85 Members; $85 Students; $165 Nonmembers; $512 Institutions; $109 Other countries; $194 Other countries surface; $561 Institutions, other countries surface; $123 By mail; $207 By mail; $576 By mail. **URL:** http://www.apa.org/pubs/journals/prj/; http://www.psychrehabassociation.org. **Formerly:** Psychosocial Rehabilitation Journal/Innovations & Research. **Ad Rates:** BW $275, full page; BW $230, 1/2 page; BW $325, cover 3; BW $380, cover 4. **Remarks:** Advertising accepted; rates available upon request. **Circ:** 230.

15866 ■ Raven: A Journal of Vexillology
North American Vexillological Association
PO Box 55701
Boston, MA 02205-5071
Freq: Annual. **ISSN:** 1071- 0043 (print). **Subscription Rates:** included in membership dues; $40. **URL:** http://www.nava.org/nava-publications/raven. **Remarks:** Advertising not accepted. **Circ:** 450.

15867 ■ Review of Banking & Financial Law
Boston University School of Law
765 Commonwealth Ave.
Boston, MA 02215
Phone: (617)353-3160
Publisher's E-mail: bulawaid@bu.edu
Journal reporting banking and financial law. **Freq:** Semiannual. **Key Personnel:** Laura Goldsmith, Editor-in-Chief. **Subscription Rates:** $173 Individuals. **Online:** Boston University School of Law Boston University School of Law. **Alt. Formats:** PDF. **URL:** http://www.bu.edu/rbfl. **Circ:** (Not Reported).

15868 ■ The Review of Network Economics
CRA International Inc.
200 Clarendon St.
Boston, MA 02116-5092
Phone: (617)425-3000
Fax: (617)425-3132
Journal covering new research in network economics and related subjects, including topics in the economics of networks, regulation, competition law, industrial organization etc. **Freq:** Quarterly Mar., June, Sept., and Dec. **Key Personnel:** Julian Wright, Managing Editor; John Panzar, Editor. **Subscription Rates:** $427 Institutions online; €316 Institutions online; $237 Individuals online; €99 Individuals online; $427 Institutions print; €316 Institutions print; $427 Individuals print; €316 Individuals print; $512 Institutions print + online; €379 Institutions print + online; $512 Individuals print + online; €379 Individuals print + online. **URL:** http://www.degruyter.com/view/j/rne. **Circ:** (Not Reported).

15869 ■ Rubber & Plastics News
Crain Communications Inc.
101 Federal Street, Suite 1900, Room 1612
Boston, MA 02110
Publisher's E-mail: info@crain.com
Rubber industry newspaper (tabloid). **Freq:** Biweekly. **Print Method:** Offset. **Trim Size:** 10 7/8 x 14 1/2. **Cols./Page:** 4. **Col. Width:** 2 5/16 inches. **Col. Depth:** 13 1/2 inches. **ISSN:** 0300--6123 (print). **Subscription Rates:** $99 Individuals; $138 Canada; $140 Other countries. **Online:** Crain Communications Inc. Crain Communications Inc. **URL:** http://crain.com/brands/rubber-plastics-news. **Remarks:** Accepts advertising. **Circ:** Paid △**3725**, Non-paid △**12386**.

15870 ■ Salamander: A Magazine for Poetry, Fiction and Memoirs
Salamander Inc.
English Dept.
Suffolk University
41 Temple St.
Boston, MA 02114
Magazine featuring poetry, fiction, memoir, and works in translation. **Freq:** Semiannual. **Key Personnel:** Jennifer Barber, Editor-in-Chief. **Subscription Rates:** $15 Individuals print; $10 Individuals online; $17 Individuals print + online; $9 Single issue. **URL:** http://salamandermag.org. **Circ:** (Not Reported).

15871 ■ Simmons Review
Simmons College
300 The Fenway
Boston, MA 02115
Phone: (617)521-2000
Collegiate alumni magazine. **Freq:** 3/year. **Print Method:** Offset. **Trim Size:** 8 1/2 x 11. **Cols./Page:** 2. **Col. Width:** 39 nonpareils. **Col. Depth:** 128 agate lines. **Key Personnel:** Allyson Irish, Director, Public Relations, phone: (617)521-2324. **ISSN:** 0049--0512 (print). **Remarks:** Advertising not accepted. **Circ:** Non-paid 35000.

15872 ■ Smith Alumnae Quarterly
Alumnae Association of Smith College
PO Box 340029
Boston, MA 02241-0429
Publisher's E-mail: alumnae@smith.edu
College alumnae magazine. **Freq:** Quarterly. **Print Method:** Offset. **Trim Size:** 8 1/2 x 11. **Cols./Page:** 3. **Col. Width:** 28 nonpareils. **Col. Depth:** 133 agate lines. **Key Personnel:** Elise Gibson, Managing Editor; Cheryl Dellecese, Associate Director; John MacMillan, Editor. **USPS:** 499-000. **URL:** http://saqonline.smith.edu. **Remarks:** Advertising not accepted. **Circ:** ‡40000.

15873 ■ South Carolina Lawyers Weekly
Lawyers Weekly Publications
10 Milk St., Ste. 1000
Boston, MA 02111
Phone: (617)451-7300
Publication covering legal issues in South Carolina. **Freq:** Weekly. **Key Personnel:** Tonya Mathis, Publisher; Frederick Horlbeck, Writer. **Subscription Rates:** $329 Individuals print & online. **URL:** http://sclawyersweekly.com. **Ad Rates:** BW $1,280; 4C $350. **Remarks:** Accepts advertising. **Circ:** (Not Reported).

15874 ■ The Standard: New England's Insurance Weekly
Standard Publishing Corp.
155 Federal St., 13th Fl.
Boston, MA 02110

Phone: (617)457-0600
Fax: (617)457-0608
Free: 800-682-5759
Publication E-mail: stnd@earthlink.net
Trade newspaper covering insurance events, legislation, regulatory hearings, and court sessions for independent insurance agents in New England. **Freq:** Weekly (Fri.). **Print Method:** Offset. **Trim Size:** 8 1/2 x 11. **Cols./Page:** 3. **Col. Width:** 2.25 picas. **Col. Depth:** 140 agate lines. **Key Personnel:** Erin L. Ayers, Editor; John C. Cross, Esq., President, Publisher; Susanne E. Dillman, Manager, Advertising. **ISSN:** 0038--9390 (print). **Subscription Rates:** $97.50 Individuals U.S. **URL:** http://www.spcpub.com/page.cfm?name=The_Standard; http://www.spcpub.com/page_insurance_publications.cfm. **Ad Rates:** BW $2705; 4C $750. **Remarks:** Accepts advertising. **Circ:** 4625.

15875 ■ Statistics in Medicine
John Wiley & Sons Inc.
c/o Ralph D'Agostino, Ed.
Department of Mathematics, Boston University
111 Cummington St.
Boston, MA 02215
Publisher's E-mail: info@wiley.com
Journal covering all aspects of the collection, analysis, presentation and interpretation of medical data. **Freq:** 30/yr. **Trim Size:** 10 1/4 x 7 7/8. **Key Personnel:** Ralph D'Agostino, Editor; T. Colton, Editor, Founder; Petra Macaskill, Editor; A.L. Johnson, Editor, Founder; L.S. Freedman, Editor, Founder; Paul Albert, Associate Editor; Alexei A. Dmitrienko, Associate Editor. **ISSN:** 0277--6715 (print); **EISSN:** 1097--0258 (electronic). **Subscription Rates:** $8002 Institutions online or print - USA/Canada & Mexico/ROW; $9603 Institutions print & online - USA/Canada & Mexico/ROW; £4087 Institutions online or print - UK; £4905 Institutions print & online - UK; €5165 Institutions online or print - Europe; €6198 Institutions print & online - Europe. **URL:** http://onlinelibrary.wiley.com/journal/10.1002/(ISSN)1097-0258. **Ad Rates:** BW $720; 4C $2,020. **Remarks:** Advertising accepted; rates available upon request. **Circ:** Paid 12600.

15876 ■ Studies in Romanticism
Boston University
1 Silber Way
Boston, MA 02215
Phone: (617)353-2000
Publisher's E-mail: askus@bu.edu
Literary journal. **Freq:** Quarterly. **Print Method:** Offset. **Trim Size:** 6 x 9 1/8. **Cols./Page:** 1. **Col. Width:** 53 nonpareils. **Col. Depth:** 96 agate lines. **Key Personnel:** Deborah Swedberg, Managing Editor; Charles Rzepka, Editor. **ISSN:** 0039--3762 (print). **Subscription Rates:** $28 Individuals; $75 Institutions; $85 Other countries; $7 Single issue. **URL:** http://www.bu.edu/sir. **Remarks:** Accepts advertising. **Circ:** ‡1800.

15877 ■ Suffolk Journal of Health and Biomedical Law
Suffolk University Law School
David J. Sargent Hall
120 Tremont St.
Boston, MA 02108-4977
Phone: (617)573-8000
Journal covering articles in various fields of health and biomedical law. **Freq:** Semiannual. **Key Personnel:** Sara Frank, Editor-in-Chief. **Subscription Rates:** $35 Individuals /year; $15 Single issue. **URL:** http://www.suffolk.edu/law/student-life/22350.php. **Circ:** (Not Reported).

15878 ■ Syndicated Columnists Weekly
National Braille Press Inc.
88 Saint Stephen St.
Boston, MA 02115
Phone: (617)425-2400
Fax: (617)437-0456
Publisher's E-mail: orders@nbp.org
Newspaper covering syndicated columnists from major U.S. papers in Braille. **Freq:** Weekly. **Key Personnel:** Kesel Wilson. **Subscription Rates:** $24 Individuals; $45 Two years. **Alt. Formats:** Download. **URL:** http://www.nbp.org/ic/nbp/publications/periodicals.html. **Remarks:** Advertising not accepted. **Circ:** Combined 1,500.

15879 ■ Tire Business: Your Number One information resource
Crain Communications Inc.
101 Federal Street, Suite 1900, Room 1612
Boston, MA 02110
Publisher's E-mail: info@crain.com
Newspaper (tabloid) serving independent tire dealers, retreaders, tire wholesalers and others allied to the tire industry. **Freq:** Semiweekly. **Print Method:** Offset. **Trim Size:** 10 7/8 x 14 1/2. **Cols./Page:** 5. **Col. Width:** 1 7/8 inches. **Col. Depth:** 13 1/2 inches. **Key Personnel:** Keith E. Crain, Director, Editorial; Sigmund J. Mikolajczyk, Managing Editor; Chris Harris, Associate Publisher, Director, Sales; Dave Zielasko, Editor, Publisher, Vice President. **ISSN:** 0746-9070 (print). **Subscription Rates:** $79 Individuals annual - print; Included in membership online - online subscribers only. **URL:** http://www.tirebusiness.com. **Ad Rates:** BW $5,797; 4C $7,797; PCI $105.50. **Remarks:** Accepts advertising. **Circ:** Paid ★**8869**, Non-paid ★**19768**.

15880 ■ Transplant Infectious Disease
Wiley-Blackwell
c/o Betsy L. Barr, Admin. Ed.
Massachusetts General Hospital
GRB 1008-D
55 Fruit St.
Boston, MA 02114
Phone: (617)726-3465
Fax: (617)726-3731
Publisher's E-mail: info@wiley.com
Journal dealing with prevention and treatment of infection complicating organ and bone marrow transplantation in connection with Transplantation Society. **Freq:** Bimonthly. **Key Personnel:** Robert H. Rubin, Editor, Founder; Emily Blumberg, MD, Editor; Andreas H. Groll, Editor. **ISSN:** 1398--2273 (print); **EISSN:** 1399--3062 (electronic). **Subscription Rates:** $914 Institutions online only; £546 Institutions online only; €693 Institutions online only; $1067 Institutions, other countries online only; $465 Individuals online only; £234 Individuals online only; £234 Individuals online only; Europe (non-Euro zone); $348 Individuals online only; Europe (Euro zone); $234 Individuals online only; other countries. **URL:** http://www.blackwellpublishing.com/journal.asp?ref=1398-2273. **Remarks:** Advertising accepted; rates available upon request. **Circ:** (Not Reported).

15881 ■ UU World: The Magazine of the Unitarian Universalist Association
Unitarian Universalist Association
24 Farnsworth St.
Boston, MA 02210-1262
Phone: (617)742-2100
Fax: (617)367-3237
Publication E-mail: world@uua.org
Religious news magazine. **Freq:** Quarterly. **Print Method:** Offset. **Trim Size:** 8 1/8 x 10 1/2. **Cols./Page:** 3. **Col. Width:** 2 3/16 inches. **Col. Depth:** 9 3/8 inches. **Key Personnel:** Kenneth Sutton, Managing Editor; Robert Delboy, Art Director; Michelle Bates Deakin, Editor; Christopher L. Walton, Editor; Scott Ullrich, Business Manager. **ISSN:** 0892--2462 (print). **Subscription Rates:** $20 Individuals; $38 Two years; $57 Individuals for three years; $22 Other countries; Included in membership. **URL:** http://www.uua.org/publications/uuworld. **Formerly:** World Magazine; UUA World. **Remarks:** Accepts advertising. **Circ:** Controlled ‡126000, Combined ‡126,000.

15882 ■ Virginia Medical Law Report
Lawyers Weekly Publications
10 Milk St., Ste. 1000
Boston, MA 02111
Phone: (617)451-7300
Publication covering legal issues that concern doctors and health care providers in Virginia. **Freq:** Bimonthly. **Subscription Rates:** $29.95 Individuals non-medical professional - print and online. **URL:** http://www.vamedicallaw.com. **Remarks:** Accepts advertising. **Circ:** (Not Reported).

15883 ■ WORK: A Journal of Prevention, Assessment and Rehabilitation
IOS Press Inc.
c/o Karen Jacobs, Ed.-in-Ch.
Boston University
Sargent College of Health & Rehabilitation Sciences
635 Commonwealth Ave.
Boston, MA 02215
Publisher's E-mail: order@iospress.nl
Peer-reviewed journal covering the entire scope of interdisciplinary and international work practice in which the first goal is injury or disability prevention. **Freq:** 12/yr. **Key Personnel:** Karen Jacobs, Editor-in-Chief, phone: (617)353-7516, fax: (617)353-2926. **ISSN:** 1051-9815 (print); **EISSN:** 1875-9270 (electronic). **Subscription Rates:** $1662 Institutions print & online; €1248 Institutions print & online; $311 Individuals online only; €235 Individuals online only. **URL:** http://www.iospress.nl/loadtop/load.php?isbn=10519815. **Circ:** (Not Reported).

15884 ■ The WorldPaper: Global Perspectives from Local Sources
World Times Inc.
225 Franklin St., 26th Fl.
Boston, MA 02210
Phone: (617)439-5400
Fax: (617)439-5415
Publisher's E-mail: info@worldtimes.com
An international editorial supplement on global issues to newspapers and magazines featuring writers who write about their native countries (English, Spanish, Russian, Chinese, Japanese). **Freq:** Weekly. **Cols./Page:** 3. **Key Personnel:** Axel Leblois, President; Christine Leblois, Publisher; Peter Orne, Editor. **URL:** http://www.worldtimes.com/wp.html. **Remarks:** Accepts advertising. **Circ:** Paid 1800000.

15885 ■ Continental Cablevision Inc.
The Pilot House, Lewis Wharf
Boston, MA 02110
Phone: (617)742-9500
Founded: 1963. **Key Personnel:** Amos B. Hostetter, Jr., Chairman, CEO; Timothy P. Neher, V. Ch. **Cities Served:** subscribing households 3,000,000. **URL:** http://continentalstory.com/wp-content/uploads/2015/11/CCI-ebook-Final.pdf.

15886 ■ WAAF-AM - 1440
20 Guest St.
Boston, MA 02135-2040
Phone: (617)779-5400
Fax: (617)931-1073
Format: Adult Contemporary. **Networks:** ABC; Univision. **Founded:** 1926. **Operating Hours:** Continuous. **Wattage:** 5,000. **Ad Rates:** Noncommercial. **URL:** http://www.waaf.com.

15887 ■ WAAF-FM - 97.7
20 Guest St., 3rd Fl.
Boston, MA 02135-2040
Phone: (617)779-5400
Fax: (617)931-1073
Format: Classic Rock. **Owner:** Entercom Communications Corp., 401 City Ave., Ste. 809, Bala Cynwyd, PA 19004-1130, Ph: (610)660-5610, Fax: (610)660-5620. **Operating Hours:** Continuous. **Ad Rates:** Advertising accepted; rates available upon request. **URL:** http://www.waaf.com.

15888 ■ WBCN-FM - 104.1
83 Leo Birmingham Pkwy.
Boston, MA 02135
Format: Alternative/New Music/Progressive. **Networks:** Independent. **Owner:** CBS Radio Inc., 40 W 57th St., New York, NY 10019, Ph: (212)846-3939, Fax: (212)315-2162. **Founded:** 1968. **Operating Hours:** Continuous. **ADI:** Boston-Worcester,MA-Derry-Manchester,NH. **Wattage:** 50,000. **Ad Rates:** Advertising accepted; rates available upon request. **URL:** http://wbcn.com.

15889 ■ WBOS-FM - 92.9
55 Morrissey Blvd.
Boston, MA 02125-3315
Phone: (617)822-9600
Format: Album-Oriented Rock (AOR). **Networks:** Independent. **Owner:** Greater Media Inc., 35 Braintree Hill Pk., Ste. 300, Braintree, MA 02184-8708, Ph: (781)348-8600, Fax: (781)348-8695. **Founded:** 1954. **Operating Hours:** Continuous. **ADI:** Boston-Worcester,MA-Derry-Manchester,NH. **Key Personnel:** Ken West, Prog. Dir. **Wattage:** 50,000. **Ad Rates:** $200-350 per unit. **URL:** http://www.myradio929.com.

Circulation: ★ = AAM; △ or • = BPA; ♦ = CAC; ❑ = VAC; ⊕ = PO Statement; ‡ = Publisher's Report; Boldface figures = sworn; Light figures = estimated.

15890 ■ WBPR-FM - 91.9
100 Morrissey Blvd.
Boston, MA 02125-3393
Phone: (617)287-6900
Fax: (617)287-6916
Free: 800-573-2100
Email: wumb@umb.edu
Format: Folk; Jazz. **Owner:** University of Massachusetts, 100 Morrissey Blvd., Boston, MA 02125-3393, Ph: (617)287-5000. **Key Personnel:** Patricia Monteith, Gen. Mgr., pat.monteith@umb.edu. **Ad Rates:** Noncommercial. **URL:** http://www.wumb.org.

15891 ■ WBPX-TV - 32
1120 Soldiers Field Rd.
Boston, MA 02134
Phone: (617)787-6868
Fax: (617)787-4114
Format: Commercial TV. **Owner:** ION Media Networks, at above address. **Founded:** July 1993. **Formerly:** WABU-TV. **Operating Hours:** Continuous. **ADI:** Boston-Worcester,MA-Derry-Manchester,NH. **Key Personnel:** Dian McLaughlin, Contact, diannemclaughlin@ionmedia.com. **Local Programs:** *7 News Today in New England*, Monday Tuesday Wednesday Thursday Friday Saturday Sunday 5:00 a.m. - 7:00 a.m.; 9:00 a.m. - 10:00 a.m. 6:00 a.m. - 7:00 a.m.; 9:00 a.m. - 11:00 a.m. 9:00 a.m. - 10:30 a.m. **Ad Rates:** Advertising accepted; rates available upon request. **URL:** http://www.iontelevision.com/.

15892 ■ WBZ-AM - 1030
1170 Soldiers Field Rd.
Boston, MA 02134
Phone: (617)787-7000
Format: News; Talk. **Networks:** ABC; AP. **Owner:** CBS Radio Inc., 40 W 57th St., New York, NY 10019, Ph: (212)846-3939, Fax: (212)315-2162. **Founded:** 1921. **Operating Hours:** Continuous. **ADI:** Boston-Worcester,MA-Derry-Manchester,NH. **Key Personnel:** Chris Hill, Gen. Sales Mgr., chris.hill@cbsradio.com; Peter Casey, News Dir., Prog. Dir., peter.casey@cbsradio.com. **Wattage:** 50,000. **Ad Rates:** Advertising accepted; rates available upon request. **URL:** http://www.boston.cbslocal.com.

15893 ■ WBZ-TV - 4
1170 Soldiers Field Rd.
Boston, MA 02134
Phone: (617)787-7000
Fax: (617)787-7390
Format: Commercial TV. **Networks:** CBS. **Owner:** CBS Corp., 51 W 52nd St., New York, NY 10019-6188, Ph: (212)975-4321, Fax: (212)975-4516, Free: 877-227-0787. **Founded:** 1948. **Operating Hours:** Continuous. **ADI:** Boston-Worcester,MA-Derry-Manchester,NH. **Key Personnel:** Ed Piette, Gen. Mgr., President. **Ad Rates:** Advertising accepted; rates available upon request. **URL:** http://boston.cbslocal.com.

15894 ■ WERS-FM - 88.9
120 Boylston St.
Boston, MA 02116
Phone: (617)824-8890
Email: info@wers.org
Format: Eclectic. **Networks:** Independent. **Owner:** Emerson College, 120 Boylston St., Boston, MA 02116-4624, Ph: (617)824-8542, Fax: (617)824-8535. **Founded:** 1949. **Operating Hours:** 6 a.m.-2 a.m.; 100% local. **ADI:** Boston-Worcester,MA-Derry-Manchester,NH. **Key Personnel:** Jack Casey, Gen. Mgr.; Howard D. Simpson, Operations Mgr. **Wattage:** 4,000. **Ad Rates:** Noncommercial. **URL:** http://www.wers.org.

15895 ■ WFPB-AM - 1170
University of Massachusetts Boston
100 Morrissey Blvd.
Boston, MA 02125-3393
Phone: (617)287-6900
Fax: (617)287-6916
Free: 800-573-2100
Email: wumb@umb.edu
Format: Jazz. **Key Personnel:** Patricia Monteith, Gen. Mgr., pat.monteith@umb.edu; Grady Moates, Dir. of Sales; Patty Domeniconi, Div. Dir. **Ad Rates:** Noncommercial. **URL:** http://www.wumb.org.

15896 ■ WFPB-FM - 91.9
University of Massachusetts Boston
100 Morrissey Blvd.
Boston, MA 02125-3393
Phone: (617)287-6900
Fax: (617)287-6916
Free: 800-573-2100
Format: Jazz. **Key Personnel:** Grady Moates, Dir. of Engg.; Patty Domeniconi, Dir. of Admin., Dir. of Operations, patty.domeniconi@umb.edu. **Ad Rates:** Advertising accepted; rates available upon request. **URL:** http://wumb.org.

15897 ■ WGBH-FM - 89.7
One Guest St.
Boston, MA 02135
Phone: (617)300-5400
Email: events@wgbh.org
Format: Public Radio. **Networks:** National Public Radio (NPR); Public Radio International (PRI). **Owner:** WGBH Educational Foundation, One Guest St., Boston, MA 02135, Ph: (617)300-5400, Fax: (617)300-1026. **Founded:** 1951. **Operating Hours:** Continuous. **Key Personnel:** Jonathan C. Abbott, President; Margaret Drain, VP. **Local Programs:** *Classics in the Morning*; *Jazz with Eric in the Evening*, Friday Saturday Sunday 9:00 p.m. - 12:00 a.m. **Wattage:** 100,000. **Ad Rates:** Noncommercial. **URL:** http://www.wgbh.org.

15898 ■ WGBH-TV - 2
1 Guest St.
Boston, MA 02135
Phone: (617)300-5400
Format: Public TV. **Networks:** Public Broadcasting Service (PBS). **Owner:** WGBH Educational Foundation, One Guest St., Boston, MA 02135, Ph: (617)300-5400, Fax: (617)300-1026. **Founded:** 1955. **Operating Hours:** 6 a.m.-1 a.m. **ADI:** Boston-Worcester,MA-Derry-Manchester,NH. **Key Personnel:** Susan L. Kantrowitz, Gen. Counsel, VP; Jonathan C. Abbott, CEO, President. **Ad Rates:** Noncommercial. **URL:** http://www.wgbh.org.

15899 ■ WHDH-TV - 7
7 Bulfinch Pl.
Boston, MA 02114
Phone: (617)725-0763
Format: Commercial TV; News. **Networks:** NBC. **Owner:** Sunbeam Television Corp., 1401 79th Street Cswy., Miami, FL 33141-4104. **Formerly:** WNEV-TV. **Operating Hours:** Continuous. **Key Personnel:** Patricia Markham, Traffic Mgr., pmarkham@whdh.com; Ross Kramer, Dir. of Bus. Dev., Dir. of Mktg., rkramer@whdh.com. **Local Programs:** *Urban Update*. **Ad Rates:** Advertising accepted; rates available upon request. **URL:** http://www1.whdh.com/.

15900 ■ WKLB-FM - 102.5
55 Morrissey Blvd.
Boston, MA 02125
Phone: (617)822-6880
Fax: (617)822-6659
Free: 888-819-1025
Format: Country; Jazz. **Networks:** Westwood One Radio. **Founded:** Sept. 07, 2006. **Formerly:** WSSH-FM. **Operating Hours:** Continuous. **ADI:** Boston-Worcester,MA-Derry-Manchester,NH. **Key Personnel:** Bill Garcia, Dir. of Programs; Ginny Rogers, Music Dir., grogers@wklb.com. **Wattage:** 50,000. **Ad Rates:** Advertising accepted; rates available upon request. $75-400 for 60 seconds; $175-350 per unit. **URL:** http://www.wklb.com.

15901 ■ WLVI-TV - 56
Seven Bulfinch Pl.
Boston, MA 02114
Fax: (617)248-0653
Free: 800-280-8477
Email: news@whdh.com
Format: Commercial TV. **Networks:** Warner Brothers Studios. **Owner:** Sunbeam Television Corp., 1401 79th Street Cswy., Miami, FL 33141-4104. **Founded:** Dec. 1966. **Operating Hours:** Continuous. **ADI:** Boston-Worcester,MA-Derry-Manchester,NH. **Local Programs:** *The Steve Wilkos Show*, Monday Tuesday Wednesday Thursday Friday 12:00 p.m.; 3:00 a.m.; *The Wendy Williams Show*, Monday 10:00 a.m. **Wattage:** 120 KW. **Ad Rates:** Advertising accepted; rates available upon request. **URL:** http://www.whdh.com.

15902 ■ WMEX-AM - 1150
330 Stuart St.
Boston, MA 02116
Phone: (617)542-0241
Fax: (617)542-5809
Format: Adult Contemporary. **Simulcasts:** WMJX-FM. **Networks:** ABC. **Owner:** Greater Media Inc., 35 Braintree Hill Pk., Ste. 300, Braintree, MA 02184, Ph: (781)348-8600. **Founded:** 1979. **Operating Hours:** Continuous. **ADI:** Boston-Worcester,MA-Derry-Manchester,NH. **Key Personnel:** Nancy Quill, Music Dir.; Sue Oberg, Dir. of Traffic; Peter Smyth, Gen. Mgr.; Don Kelley, Operations Mgr.; Frank Kelley, Gen. Sales Mgr.; Jaime Weiser, Promotions Dir; Candy Oteri, Contact; Molly O'Brien, Contact; Tim Stansky, Contact; Alex Klemmer, Contact. **Wattage:** 5,000.

15903 ■ WMFP-TV - 62
One Beacon St. 35th Fl.
Boston, MA 02108
Phone: (978)717-5633
Format: Public TV; Information. **Networks:** Independent. **Owner:** Shop At Home Inc., at above address, Ph: (423)688-0300, Fax: (423)689-5067. **Founded:** 1987. **Operating Hours:** Continuous. **Key Personnel:** Bill Desmond, Chief Engineer. **Wattage:** 1,000,000 Horizontal. **URL:** http://www.wmfp-tv.com/.

15904 ■ WMJX-FM - 106.7
55 Morrissey Blvd.
Boston, MA 02125
Phone: (617)822-9600
Format: Adult Contemporary. **Simulcasts:** WMEX-AM. **Owner:** Greater Media Inc., 35 Braintree Hill Pk., Ste. 300, Braintree, MA 02184-8708, Ph: (781)348-8600, Fax: (781)348-8695. **Founded:** 1981. **Operating Hours:** Continuous. **ADI:** Boston-Worcester,MA-Derry-Manchester,NH. **Key Personnel:** Don Kelley, Dir. of Programs, VP, dkelley@magic1067.com. **Local Programs:** *Bedtime Magic*; *Boston Life*, Sunday 7:00 a.m.; *Exceptional Women*, Sunday 7:30 a.m. **Wattage:** 50,000. **Ad Rates:** Noncommercial. **URL:** http://www.magic1067.com.

15905 ■ WMKK-FM - 93.7
20 Guest St., 3rd Fl.
Boston, MA 02135
Phone: (617)779-5800
Format: Eclectic. **Owner:** Entercom Communications Corp., 401 City Ave., Ste. 809, Bala Cynwyd, PA 19004-1130, Ph: (610)660-5610, Fax: (610)660-5620. **Key Personnel:** Pat Paxton, Div. Pres.; Michael Doyle, Div. Pres.; Weezie Kramer, Group Pres.; Gary Kurtz, Gen. Sales Mgr., gkurtz@entercom.com. **URL:** http://www.entercom.com.

15906 ■ WNEF-FM - 91.7
University of Massachusetts Boston, 100 Morrissey Blvd.
Boston, MA 02125-3393
Format: Jazz. **Ad Rates:** Noncommercial. **URL:** http://www.wumb.org.

15907 ■ WNKS-FM - 95.1
116 Huntington Ave.
Boston, MA 02116
Format: Contemporary Hit Radio (CHR). **Owner:** EZ Charlotte, Inc., at above address. **Founded:** July 15, 1975. **Formerly:** WEOJ-FM. **Operating Hours:** Continuous. **Key Personnel:** Bill Schoening, Gen. Mgr.; Keith Cornwell, Sales Mgr.; Brian Bridgeman, Dir. of Programs. **Wattage:** 100,000. **URL:** http://www.kiss951.com.

15908 ■ WODS-FM - 103.3
83 Leo Birmingham Pkwy.
Boston, MA 02135
Phone: (617)746-1300
Format: Oldies. **Networks:** CBS. **Owner:** CBS Radio Inc., 1271 Avenue of the Americas, 44th Fl., New York, NY 10020-1401, Ph: (212)649-9600. **Founded:** 1948. **Formerly:** WMRQ-FM; WHTT-FM; WEEI-FM. **Operating Hours:** Continuous. **Key Personnel:** Dan Baptiste, Sales Mgr., dan.baptiste@cbsradio.com; Doreen Wong, Sales Mgr.; Barbara Jean Scanell, Gen. Mgr.; Jay Beau Jones, Dir. of Programs, jaybeau.jones@cbsradio.com; Patti Taylor, Gen. Mgr. of Sales & Mktg.; Karalyn Mallozzi, Dir. of Mktg. **Wattage:** 16,000. **Ad Rates:** Noncommercial. **URL:** http://www.mix1041.cbslocal.com.

15909 ■ WPXG-TV - 21
1120 Soldiers Field Rd.
Boston, MA 02134
Phone: (617)787-6868
Fax: (617)787-4004

Email: diannemclaughlin@ionmedia.com
Owner: ION Media Networks, at above address. **Key Personnel:** William L. Watson, VP. **URL:** http://www.ionmedia.tv/page.php?p=stations&station=162.

15910 ■ WRBB-FM - 104.9
360 Huntington Ave.
No. 174, Curry Student Ctr.
Boston, MA 02115
Phone: (617)373-4338
Format: Eclectic. **Owner:** Northeastern University, 360 Huntington Ave., Boston, MA 02115, Ph: (617)373-2000. **Founded:** 1970. **Operating Hours:** Continuous. **Wattage:** 019. **Ad Rates:** Noncommercial; underwriting available. **URL:** http://www.wrbbsports.com.

15911 ■ WRKO-AM - 680
20 Guest St., Third Fl.
Boston, MA 02135
Phone: (617)779-3400
Free: 877-469-4322
Format: Talk. **Networks:** ABC. **Founded:** 1922. **Operating Hours:** Continuous. **ADI:** Boston-Worcester,MA-Derry-Manchester,NH. **Key Personnel:** John Capuano, Gen. Sales Mgr.; Jason Wolfe, Dir. of Programs. **Local Programs:** *Bill Kelly's Financial*, Saturday Sunday 9:00 a.m. - 12:00 p.m. 2:00 p.m. - 3:00 p.m.; *Howie Carr, Finneran's Forum*, Monday Tuesday Wednesday Thursday Friday 7:30 a.m. **Wattage:** 50,000. **Ad Rates:** Advertising accepted; rates available upon request. **URL:** http://www.wrko.com.

15912 ■ WROR-FM - 105.7
55 Morrissey Blvd.
Boston, MA 02125-3315
Phone: (617)822-9600
Fax: (617)822-6459
Format: Adult Contemporary. **Owner:** Greater Boston Radio, Inc., at above address, Braintree, MA; CBS Radio Inc., 1271 Avenue of the Americas, 44th Fl., New York, NY 10020-1401, Ph: (212)649-9600. **Wattage:** 23,000 ERP. **Ad Rates:** Advertising accepted; rates available upon request; Noncommercial. **URL:** http://www.wror.com.

15913 ■ WSBK-TV - 38
1170 Soldiers Field Rd.
Boston, MA 02134
Phone: (617)787-7000
Format: Commercial TV. **Networks:** United Paramount Network; Independent. **Owner:** CBS Corp., 51 W 52nd St., New York, NY 10019-6188, Ph: (212)975-4321, Fax: (212)975-4516, Free: 877-227-0787. **Founded:** 1964. **Operating Hours:** Continuous; 100% local. **ADI:** Boston-Worcester,MA-Derry-Manchester,NH. **Key Personnel:** Ed Piette, Gen. Mgr., President; Helyn Wynyard, Contact. **Ad Rates:** Noncommercial. **URL:** http://boston.cbslocal.com.

15914 ■ WTBU-AM - 640
640 Commonwealth Ave.
Boston, MA 02215
Phone: (617)353-6401
Email: news@wtburadio.org
Format: Full Service; Eclectic. **Owner:** Boston University College of Communication, 640 Commonwealth Ave., Boston, MA 02215, Ph: (617)353-3450, Fax: (617)353-3405. **Founded:** Oct. 1999. **Operating Hours:** 7 a.m. to 1 a.m. **Ad Rates:** Advertising accepted; rates available upon request. **URL:** http://www.wtburadio.org.

15915 ■ WTBU-FM - 89.3
640 Commonweath Ave.
Boston, MA 02215
Phone: (617)353-6400
Format: Eclectic; News; Sports. **Owner:** Boston University, at above address. **Founded:** 1999. **Ad Rates:** Noncommercial. **URL:** http://www.wtburadio.org/.

15916 ■ WTKK-FM - 96.9
55 Morrissey Blvd.
Boston, MA 02125
Phone: (617)822-9600
Fax: (617)822-6871
Format: Talk. **Key Personnel:** Grace Blazer, Dir. of Programs, gblazer@969wtkk.com; Nika Desautels, Gen. Sales Mgr., ndesautels@969wtkk.com. **Ad Rates:** Noncommercial. **URL:** http://www.wtkk.com.

15917 ■ WUMB-FM - 91.9
University of Massachusetts Boston
100 Morrissey Blvd.
Boston, MA 02125-3393
Phone: (617)287-6900
Fax: (617)287-6916
Free: 800-573-2100
Email: wumb@umb.edu
Format: Folk. **Networks:** National Public Radio (NPR); AP. **Owner:** University of Massachusetts Amherst, 37 Mather Dr., Amherst, MA 01002, Ph: (413)545-0111, Fax: (413)545-3880. **Founded:** 1982. **Operating Hours:** Continuous; 90% local; 10% NRP, PRI. **ADI:** Boston-Worcester,MA-Derry-Manchester,NH. **Key Personnel:** Patricia A. Monteith, Gen. Mgr., pat.monteith@umb.edu; Grady Moates, Dir. of Engg. **Wattage:** 1,000. **Ad Rates:** Noncommercial. **URL:** http://www.wumb.org.

15918 ■ WUNI-TV - 27
33 4th Ave.
Needham, MA 02494
Phone: (781)433-2727
Format: Commercial TV; Hispanic. **Networks:** Univision. **Owner:** Entravision Communication Corp., 2425 Olympic Blvd. W, Ste. 6000, Santa Monica, CA 90404. **Operating Hours:** Continuous. **ADI:** Boston-Worcester,MA-Derry-Manchester,NH. **Key Personnel:** Alex Von Lichtenberg, Gen. Mgr., alexvl@entravision.com. **Local Programs:** *Noticias Nueva Inglaterra*, Monday Tuesday Wednesday Thursday Friday 6:00 p.m.; 11:00 p.m. **Ad Rates:** Advertising accepted; rates available upon request. **URL:** http://www.wunitv.com.

15919 ■ WUNR-AM - 1600
160 N Washington St.
Boston, MA 02114-2142
Phone: (617)367-9003
Fax: (617)367-2265
Format: Ethnic. **Networks:** Independent. **Founded:** 1948. **ADI:** Boston-Worcester,MA-Derry-Manchester,NH. **Key Personnel:** Jane A. Clarke, Contact; Stephen C. Lalli, Contact; Suzanne Pellegrini, Contact. **Wattage:** 20,000 Daytime;2,000. **Ad Rates:** Advertising accepted; rates available upon request. $15-26 for 30 seconds; $19-32 for 60 seconds. **URL:** http://www.wunr.com/.

15920 ■ WZLX-FM - 100.7
83 Leo M. Birmingham Pky.
Boston, MA 02135
Phone: (617)746-5100
Fax: (617)746-5102
Format: Classic Rock. **Founded:** 1979. **Operating Hours:** Continuous. **ADI:** Boston-Worcester,MA-Derry-Manchester,NH. **Key Personnel:** Mike Thomas, Dir. of Programs, mikethomas@wzlx.com. **Local Programs:** *K & M Show*, Monday Tuesday Wednesday Thursday Friday 5:30 a.m. - 10:00 a.m. **Wattage:** 20,000. **Ad Rates:** Noncommercial. **URL:** http://wzlx.cbslocal.com.

BRAINTREE

E. MA. Norfolk Co. 10 mi. S. of Boston. Historical area. Manufactures leather goods, pipes, valves, linoleum, rubber tile, petroleum products, beverages, potato chips. Shipbuilding.

15921 ■ The Pilot: Official newspaper of the Archdiocese of Boston
Archdiocese of Boston
66 Brooks Dr.
Braintree, MA 02184
Phone: (617)254-0100
Fax: (617)783-4564
Official Roman Catholic Archdiocesan newspaper of Boston. **Freq:** Weekly (Fri.). **Print Method:** Offset. **Cols./Page:** 5. **Col. Width:** 9 7/8 inches. **Col. Depth:** 13 inches. **Key Personnel:** Bernard Law, Publisher; Rev. Peter V. Conley, Editor. **Subscription Rates:** $39 Individuals. **URL:** http://www.thebostonpilot.com. **Ad Rates:** GLR $1.60; BW $1,500; PCI $22.40. **Remarks:** Accepts advertising. **Circ:** 31000.

15922 ■ WSMA-FM - 90.5
PO Box 391
Twin Falls, ID 83303
Fax: (208)736-1958
Free: 800-357-4226
Format: Religious; Contemporary Christian. **Owner:** CSN International, PO Box 391, Twin Falls, ID 83303, Ph: (208)736-1958, Fax: (208)736-1958, Free: 800-357-4226. **Key Personnel:** Kelly Carlson, Dir. of Engg.; Ray Gorney, Asst. Dir. **URL:** http://www.csnradio.com.

BREWSTER

15923 ■ Journal of Human Development and Capabilities: A Multi-Disciplinary Journal for People-Centered Development
Human Development and Capability Association
PO Box 1051
Brewster, MA 02631
Publisher's E-mail: admin@hd-ca.org
Freq: Quarterly. **ISSN:** 1945--2829 (print); **EISSN:** 1945--2837 (electronic). **Subscription Rates:** Included in membership; $173 Individuals print only; $637 Institutions online only; $728 Institutions print and online. **URL:** http://tandfonline.com/loi/cjhd20#.U-iCgHKSwX1; http://hd-ca.org/publication-and-resources/journal-of-human-development-and-capabilities. **Remarks:** Advertising not accepted. **Circ:** (Not Reported).

BRIDGEWATER

SE MA. Plymouth Co. 7 mi. S. of Brockton. State College. Shoe, leatherboard and nail factories; foundry; brickyard; machine shops. Truck, poultry, dairy farms. Potatoes, corn, tomatoes.

15924 ■ Contemporary Justice Review
Justice Studies Association
c/o Jo-Ann Della Giustina, President
Dept. of Criminal Justice
Bridgewater State University
Maxwell Library, Rm. 311E
Bridgewater, MA 02325
Journal featuring: social and restorative justice theory; restorative justice demonstration projects; peacemaking criminology; state crimes and healing from genocide; peaceful methods of conflict resolution; truth and reconciliation commissions; environmental justice; critiques of criminal justice institutions and law; structural issues of justice in the family, school, and workplace; utopian visions of a just society; and non-violent, needs-meeting solutions to needs-denying, power-based social arrangements. **Freq:** Quarterly. **Key Personnel:** Daniel Okada, Editor-in-Chief. **ISSN:** 1028--2580 (print); **EISSN:** 1477--2248 (electronic). **Subscription Rates:** $145 Individuals /year (print only); $458 Institutions /year (online only); $523 Institutions /year (print and online). **URL:** http://www.justicestudies.org/Justice-Pub.html; http://www.tandfonline.com/action/aboutThisJournal?show=aimsScope&journalCode=gcjr&&#.VEhl_Slwrld. **Remarks:** Accepts advertising. **Circ:** (Not Reported).

15925 ■ The Journal of International Women's Studies
Bridgewater State University
131 Summer St.
Bridgewater, MA 02325
Phone: (508)531-1000
Publication E-mail: jiws@bridgew.edu
Journal focusing on the relationship between feminist theory and various forms of organizing for scholars, activists, and students. **Key Personnel:** Dr. Catherine Ndinda, Editor; Diana Fox, Executive Editor. **EISSN:** 1539--8706 (electronic). **Subscription Rates:** Free. **URL:** http://vc.bridgew.edu/jiws. **Circ:** (Not Reported).

15926 ■ WBIM-FM - 91.5
Bridgewater State College
109 Campus Ctr.
Bridgewater, MA 02325
Phone: (508)531-1000
Fax: (508)531-1786
Format: Alternative/New Music/Progressive. **Owner:** Bridgewater State University, 131 Summer St., Bridgewater, MA 02325, Ph: (508)531-1000. **Founded:** 1971. **Operating Hours:** midnight. **Key Personnel:** Ali Linden, Dir. of Programs, wbimpd@gmail.com; Evan Dardano, Music Dir., wbimmd@gmail.com. **Wattage:** 180. **Ad Rates:** Noncommercial. **URL:** http://www.bridgew.edu.

BRIGHTON

C. MA. Suffolk Co. District of Boston.

15927 ■ WEEI-AM - 850
20 Guest St., 3rd Fl.
Brighton, MA 02135-2040
Phone: (617)779-3500

Circulation: ★ = AAM; △ or • = BPA; ♦ = CAC; ❑ = VAC; ⊕ = PO Statement; ‡ = Publisher's Report; Boldface figures = sworn; Light figures = estimated.

Format: Sports. **Networks:** CBS. **Founded:** 1924. **Operating Hours**: Continuous. **ADI**: Boston-Worcester,MA-Derry-Manchester,NH. **Local Programs**: *Big Show*, Monday Tuesday Wednesday Thursday Friday 2:00 p.m. - 6:00 p.m.; *Planet Mikey*, Monday Tuesday Wednesday Thursday Friday 6:00 p.m. - 10:00 p.m.; *John Ryder*. **Wattage**: 50,000. **Ad Rates:** Advertising accepted; rates available upon request. **URL:** http://www.weei.com.

15928 ■ WGBX-TV - 43
1 Guest St.
Brighton, MA 02135
Phone: (617)300-5400
Email: events@wgbh.org
Format: Public TV. **Networks:** Public Broadcasting Service (PBS). **Owner:** WGBH Educational Foundation, One Guest St., Boston, MA 02135, Ph: (617)300-5400, Fax: (617)300-1026. **Founded:** 1967. **Operating Hours**: Continuous. **ADI**: Boston-Worcester,MA-Derry-Manchester,NH. **Key Personnel:** Jon Abbott, CEO. **Ad Rates:** Noncommercial; underwriting available. **URL:** http://www.wgbh.org.

15929 ■ WKAF-FM - 97.7
20 Guest St.
Brighton, MA 02135-2040
Phone: (617)779-5400
Format: Album-Oriented Rock (AOR). **Owner:** Entercom Communications Corp., 401 City Ave., Ste. 809, Bala Cynwyd, PA 19004-1130, Ph: (610)660-5610, Fax: (610)660-5620. **URL:** http://www.bostonradio.org/stations/19633.

15930 ■ WVEI-AM - 1440
20 Guest St., Third Fl.
Brighton, MA 02135-2040
Phone: (617)779-0850
Fax: (617)779-3557
Free: 888-525-0850
Format: Sports. **Ad Rates:** Noncommercial. **URL:** http://www.weei.com.

BROCKTON

SE MA. Plymouth Co. 20 mi. S. of Boston. Manufactures shoe findings and tools, textiles, boxes, metal products, plastics, electronics, machine tools.

15931 ■ The Enterprise
Enterprise
1324 Belmont St., Unit 102
Brockton, MA 02301
Phone: (508)586-6200
Publisher's E-mail: newsroom@enterprisenews.com
Community newspaper. **Founded:** 1880. **Freq:** Daily (eve.), Sat. and Sun. (morn.). **Print Method:** Letterpress and flexography. **Cols./Page:** 6. **Col. Width:** 2 1/16 inches. **Col. Depth:** 21 inches. **Key Personnel:** Chazy Dowaliby, Editor, phone: (508)427-4036; Steve Damish, Managing Editor, phone: (508)427-4022. **ISSN:** 0744-2114 (print). **Subscription Rates:** $72 Individuals 12 weeks; Monday-Sunday; Print plus full digital access to the Enterprise website, and access to the E-Paper and mobile apps; $60 Individuals 1 year; Monda-Sunday; Access to the E-Paper and mobile apps; $42 Individuals 12 weeks; Friday-Sunday; Print; $26.40 Individuals 12 weeks; Sunday Only; Print; $1.50 Individuals all access /week. **URL:** http://www.enterprisenews.com/. **Ad Rates:** GLR $2.88; BW $5,081.58; 4C $5,506.58; PCI $40.35; GLR $3.01; BW $5,312.16; 4C $5,737.16; PCI $42.16. **Remarks:** Accepts advertising. **Circ:** Mon.-Fri. ★**32998**, Sat. ★**36601**, Sun. ★**39353**.

15932 ■ WXBR-AM - 1460
60 Main St.
Brockton, MA 02301
Phone: (508)525-4550
Format: Full Service. **Networks:** CNN Radio. **Founded:** 1946. **Formerly**: WBET-AM. **Operating Hours**: Continuous; 5% network, 95% local. **ADI**: Boston-Worcester,MA-Derry-Manchester,NH. **Wattage**: 5,000 Day; 1,000 Night. **Ad Rates:** Noncommercial. **URL:** http://www.radioazure.com.

BROOKLINE

E. MA. Norfolk Co. 3 mi. SW of Boston. (Branch of Boston P.O.) Residential. Manufactures greeting cards, shades and curtains.

15933 ■ Cook's Country
Boston Common Press
17 Sta. St.
Brookline, MA 02445
Phone: (617)232-1000
Magazine that offers information and recipes on country style cooking. **Freq:** Bimonthly. **Key Personnel:** Christopher Kimball, Editor. **Subscription Rates:** $19.95 Individuals. **URL:** http://www.cookscountry.com. **Circ:** (Not Reported).

15934 ■ Cook's Illustrated
Boston Common Press
17 Sta. St.
Brookline, MA 02445
Phone: (617)232-1000
Consumer magazine covering cooking. **Freq:** Bimonthly. **URL:** http://www.cooksillustrated.com. **Remarks:** Advertising not accepted. **Circ:** (Not Reported).

15935 ■ Edible Boston
Edible Communities Inc.
288 Washington St. No. 363
Brookline, MA 02445
Phone: (617)278-9114
Publication E-mail: info@edibleboston.net
Magazine featuring the local food in Boston. **Freq:** Quarterly. **Key Personnel:** Ilene Bezahler, Editor, Publisher. **Subscription Rates:** $35 Individuals one year; $65 Two years. **URL:** http://edibleboston.com. **Ad Rates:** 4C $3360. **Remarks:** Advertising accepted; rates available upon request. **Circ:** (Not Reported).

15936 ■ Greek Orthodox Theological Review
Holy Cross Orthodox Press
50 Goddard Ave.
Brookline, MA 02445
Fax: (617)850-1430
Free: 800-245-0599
Publication E-mail: gotr@hchc.edu
Academic journal for the Orthodox Christian community and theologians. **Freq:** Quarterly. **Print Method:** Offset. **Trim Size:** 6 x 9. **Cols./Page:** 1. **Col. Width:** 55 nonpareils. **Col. Depth:** 81 agate lines. **Key Personnel:** George D. Dragas, Editor. **ISSN:** 0017--3894 (print). **URL:** http://www.hchc.edu/community/administrative_offices/holy.cross.orthodox.press/2321; http://www.hchc.edu/community/administrative_offices/holy.cross.orthodox.press/the-greek-orthodox-theological-review. **Remarks:** Advertising not accepted. **Circ:** ‡800.

15937 ■ International Journal of Infectious Diseases
International Society for Infectious Diseases
9 Babcock St., 3rd Fl.
Brookline, MA 02446
Phone: (617)277-0551
Fax: (617)278-9113
Publisher's E-mail: support@elsevier.com
Professional medical journal covering disease control in less-developed countries. **Freq:** Monthly. **Print Method:** Sheetfed Offset. **Trim Size:** 8 1/8 x 10 7/8. **Key Personnel:** Craig Lee, Editor; Annette Fowler, Administrator; Maria Guzman, Editor; William Cameron, Editor-in-Chief. **ISSN:** 1201--9712 (print). **Subscription Rates:** $40 Members; $243 Nonmembers. **URL:** http://www.ijidonline.com; http://www.isid.org/publications/ijid.shtml. **Ad Rates:** BW $1545; 4C $3080. **Remarks:** Advertising not accepted. **Circ:** (Not Reported).

15938 ■ Journal of the History of Dentistry
American Academy of the History of Dentistry
c/o Marc B. Ehrlich, Secretary
1371 Beacon St.
Brookline, MA 02446
Publisher's E-mail: info@histden.org
Trade journal covering the history of dentistry. **Freq:** 3/year. **Key Personnel:** David Chernin, Editor; Peter Meyerhof, DDS, President. **ISSN:** 0007--5132 (print). **Subscription Rates:** $125 Institutions Print Edition Only; $150 Institutions, other countries Print Edition Only; $250 Institutions Print Edition *plus Online Access to Back Issues* (from 1980-2013) U.S./other countries. **URL:** http://www.histden.org/drupal/journal. **Formerly**: Bulletin of the History of Dentistry. **Remarks:** Accepts advertising. **Circ:** (Not Reported).

BURLINGTON

NE MA. Middlesex Co. 12 mi. NW of Boston. Northeastern University. Electronic and computer industry.

15939 ■ American Journal of Preventive Medicine
Elsevier Inc.
30 Corporate Dr.
4th Fl.
Burlington, MA 01803
Phone: (781)313-4700
Fax: (781)313-4880
Publisher's E-mail: info@aptrweb.org
Journal Covering basic and applied sciences that contribute to the promotion of health and the prevention of disease, disability, and premature death. **Freq:** Monthly. **Print Method:** Offset. **Trim Size:** 8 1/2 x 11. **Key Personnel:** Matthew L. Boulton, MD, Editor-in-Chief; R.B. Wallace, MD, Associate Editor; Jillian Morgan, Managing Editor. **ISSN:** 0749--3797 (print). **Subscription Rates:** $421 Other countries print and online; $393 Individuals print and online; $421 Canada print and online; Free to members. **URL:** http://www.ajpmonline.org; http://www.journals.elsevier.com/american-journal-of-preventive-medicine. **Ad Rates:** 4C $1,535. **Remarks:** Accepts advertising. **Circ:** Paid ‡2740.

15940 ■ Energy Economics
JAI Press Inc.
30 Corporate Dr., 4th Fl.
Burlington, MA 01803
Phone: (781)313-4700
Fax: (781)313-4880
Covers financial and developmental aspects in the energy industry. **Freq:** 8/year. **Trim Size:** 7 x 10. **Key Personnel:** B.W. Ang, Editor-in-Chief; J. Weyant, Editor-in-Chief; Richard S.J. Tol, Editor-in-Chief. **ISSN:** 0140--9883 (print). **Subscription Rates:** $145 Individuals print; $1577.33 Institutions online; $1893 Institutions print; €1223 Institutions for European countries and Iran. **URL:** http://www.journals.elsevier.com/energy-economics. **Formed by the merger of**: Journal of Energy, Finance and Development. **Remarks:** Accepts advertising. **Circ:** (Not Reported).

15941 ■ IHRIM.link
International Association for Human Resource Information Management
PO Box 1086
Burlington, MA 01803
Phone: (781)791-9488
Free: 800-804-3983
Publisher's E-mail: information@ihrim.org
Publication by the International Association for Human Resource Information Management (IHRIM) covering human resources for professionals. **Freq:** Bimonthly. **Key Personnel:** Tom Faulkner, Managing Editor, Publisher. **Subscription Rates:** $29.50 Members print and online; $69.50 Nonmembers print and online. **URL:** http://www.ihrimpublications.com. **Remarks:** Accepts advertising. **Circ:** (Not Reported).

15942 ■ IHRIM.Wire
International Association for Human Resource Information Management
PO Box 1086
Burlington, MA 01803
Phone: (781)791-9488
Free: 800-804-3983
Publisher's E-mail: information@ihrim.org
Publication by the International Association for Human Resource Information Management (IHRIM) covering human resources for professionals. **Freq:** Monthly. **Key Personnel:** Lynne Mealy, Chief Executive Officer, President; Tom Faulkner, Managing Editor, Publisher, phone: (512)374-9961. **URL:** http://www.ihrim.org/Publications_Overview.html. **Ad Rates:** BW $1000; 4C $1700. **Remarks:** Accepts advertising. **Circ:** (Not Reported).

15943 ■ Journal of Purchasing and Supply Management
Butterworth-Heinemann
30 Corporate Dr., Ste. 400
Burlington, MA 01803
Free: 800-545-2522
Publisher's E-mail: usbkinfo@elsevier.com
Journal encouraging the development of conceptual thinking and practical approaches within the field of purchasing and supply management. **Freq:** Quarterly. **Key Personnel:** Dr. A. Ancarani, Editor; Dr. G.A. Zsidisin, Editor. **ISSN:** 1478--4092 (print). **Subscription**

Rates: $137 Individuals print; $276.53 Institutions eJournal; $903 Institutions print. **URL:** http://ees.elsevier.com/jpsm/; http://store.elsevier.com/product.jsp?isbn=14784092. **Formerly**: European Journal of Purchasing and Supply Management. **Circ:** (Not Reported).

15944 ■ Journal of Retailing and Consumer Services
Butterworth-Heinemann
30 Corporate Dr., Ste. 400
Burlington, MA 01803
Free: 800-545-2522
Publisher's E-mail: usbkinfo@elsevier.com
Journal focusing on consumer behavior and decision making by managers and policy makers. **Freq:** 6/year. **Key Personnel:** Prof. Harry Timmermans, Editor; G. Birtwistle, Board Member; A. Borgers, Board Member. **ISSN:** 0969--6989 (print). **Subscription Rates:** $356 Individuals print; $427.20 Institutions ejournal; $1394 Institutions print. **URL:** http://www.journals.elsevier.com/journal-of-retailing-and-consumer-services; http://store.elsevier.com/product.jsp?isbn=09696989. **Circ:** (Not Reported).

15945 ■ The Knee
Butterworth-Heinemann
30 Corporate Dr., Ste. 400
Burlington, MA 01803
Free: 800-545-2522
Publisher's E-mail: usbkinfo@elsevier.com
Journal centering on anatomy, biochemistry of bone and soft tissues, surgery and rehabilitation. **Freq:** 6/year. **Print Method:** Sheetfed Offset. **Trim Size:** 210 x 297. **Key Personnel:** Caroline Hing; Simon Donell, Editor-in-Chief; Michael Ries, Editor-in-Chief; A.A. Amis, Board Member; P. Walker, Board Member; N.J. Fiddian, Board Member; J. Minns, Board Member; J. Bellemans, Board Member; James Stiehl, Editor-in-Chief. **ISSN:** 0968--0160 (print). **Subscription Rates:** $233 Individuals online only; $259 Individuals print + online. **URL:** http://secure.jbs.elsevierhealth.com/action/ecommerce?code=thekne-site; http://www.thekneejournal.com/issue/S0968-0160(11)X0007-8#. **Ad Rates:** BW $1,570; 4C $1,575. **Remarks:** Accepts advertising. **Circ:** (Not Reported).

15946 ■ Seminars in Colon and Rectal Surgery
Elsevier Inc.
c/o David J. Schoetz, Jr., Ed.-in-Ch.
The Lahey Clinic
41 Mall Rd.
Burlington, MA 01805
Phone: (781)744-8889
Publisher's E-mail: healthpermissions@elsevier.com
Journal covering colon and rectal surgery. **Freq:** Quarterly. **Trim Size:** 8 1/4 x 11. **Key Personnel:** David J. Schoetz, Jr., Editor-in-Chief. **ISSN:** 1043--1489 (print). **Subscription Rates:** $311 Individuals online and print; $421 Other countries online and print; $280 Individuals online only; $311 Students online and print; $421 Students, other countries online and print. **URL:** http://www.journals.elsevier.com/seminars-in-colon-and-rectal-surgery. **Ad Rates:** BW $1,130; 4C $1,360. **Remarks:** Accepts advertising. **Circ:** Paid ‡365.

15947 ■ Transport Policy
Butterworth-Heinemann
30 Corporate Dr., Ste. 400
Burlington, MA 01803
Free: 800-545-2522
Publisher's E-mail: usbkinfo@elsevier.com
Journal providing a bridge between theory and practice in transport policy development and implementation. **Freq:** 6/year. **Key Personnel:** R. Vickerman, Editor-in-Chief; A. Sumalee, Editor. **ISSN:** 0967--070X (print). **Subscription Rates:** $188 Individuals print; $324.80 Institutions ejournal; $1065 Institutions print. **URL:** http://www.journals.elsevier.com/transport-policy; http://store.elsevier.com/product.jsp?isbn=0967070X. **Circ:** (Not Reported).

15948 ■ Ultrasonics Sonochemistry
Butterworth-Heinemann
30 Corporate Dr., Ste. 400
Burlington, MA 01803
Free: 800-545-2522
Publisher's E-mail: usbkinfo@elsevier.com
Journal centering on ultrasonics sonochemistry. **Freq:** 6/year. **Key Personnel:** D.J. Casadonte, Jr., Editor; S. Koda, Editor; T.J. Mason, Editor-in-Chief. **ISSN:** 1350--4177 (print). **Subscription Rates:** $251 Individuals print ; $401.33 Institutions ejournal; $1317 Institutions print. **URL:** http://www.journals.elsevier.com/ultrasonics-sonochemistry; http://store.elsevier.com/product.jsp?issn=13504177. **Circ:** (Not Reported).

CAMBRIDGE

NE MA. Middlesex Co. On Charles River, 3 mi. W. of Boston. (Branch of Boston P.O.) Harvard University; Massachusetts Institute of Technology; Radcliffe College. Manufactures rubber goods, electrical machinery, foundry products, furniture. Printing, publishing and electronic research industries.

15949 ■ Advances in Mathematics
RELX Group P.L.C.
Massachusetts Institute of Technology
Cambridge, MA 02139
Publisher's E-mail: amsterdam@relx.com
Journal reporting significant advances in all areas of pure mathematics. **Founded:** 1967. **Freq:** 18/yr. **Trim Size:** 6 x 9. **Key Personnel:** Tomasz S. Mrowka, Editor; Michael J. Hopkins, Editor; Gang Tian, Editor. **ISSN:** 0001-8708 (print). **Subscription Rates:** $3899 Institutions print. **URL:** http://www.journals.elsevier.com/advances-in-mathematics. **Remarks:** Accepts advertising. **Circ:** (Not Reported).

15950 ■ Algebra & Number Theory
Mathematical Sciences Publishers
c/o Bjorn Poonen, Managing Editor
Massachusetts Institute of Technology, No. 2-244
Dept. of Mathematics
77 Massachusetts Ave.
Cambridge, MA 02139-4307
Publisher's E-mail: contact@mathscipub.org
Peer-reviewed journal covering algebra and number theory. **Freq:** 10/year. **Key Personnel:** Bjorn Poonen, Managing Editor, fax: (510)642-8204. **ISSN:** 1937--0652 (print); **EISSN:** 1944--7833 (electronic). **Subscription Rates:** $325 Individuals electronic only; $520 Individuals print and electronic. **URL:** http://msp.berkeley.edu/ant/about/cover/cover.html; http://msp.org/publications/journals/#ant. **Circ:** (Not Reported).

15951 ■ American Journal of Human Biology: The Official Journal of the Human Biology Association
Wiley-Blackwell
c/o Peter T. Ellison, Editor
Department of Anthropology
Harvard University
11 Divinity Ave.
Cambridge, MA 02138
The official journal of the Human Biology Council. **Freq:** Bimonthly. **Print Method:** Offset. **Trim Size:** 8 1/4 x 11. **Key Personnel:** Peter T. Ellison, Editor; Cynthia M. Beall, Board Member; Lynnette Leidy Sievert, Editor-in-Chief. **ISSN:** 1042--0533 (print); **EISSN:** 1520--6300 (electronic). **Subscription Rates:** $2162 Institutions online only; £1104 Institutions online only; €1395 Institutions online only; $2162 Institutions, other countries online only. **URL:** http://onlinelibrary.wiley.com/journal/10.1002/(ISSN)1520-6300. **Ad Rates:** BW $772; 4C $1,009. **Remarks:** Accepts advertising. **Circ:** 5600.

15952 ■ AppendX
Appendx
PO Box 382806
Cambridge, MA 02238
Phone: (617)495-4115
Fax: (617)495-8916
Publisher's E-mail: appendx@gsd.harvard.edu
Professional journal covering architecture criticism. **Freq:** Annual. **Trim Size:** 8 x 10. **Key Personnel:** Darell W. Fields, Executive Editor; Jeannie Kim, Managing Editor. **URL:** http://www.appendx.org. **Remarks:** Accepts advertising. **Circ:** (Not Reported).

15953 ■ Asian American Policy Review
Nieman Foundation for Journalism at Harvard
Harvard University
Walter Lippmann House
1 Francis Ave.
Cambridge, MA 02138
Phone: (617)495-2237
Publication E-mail: asian_american_policy_review@hks.harvard.edu
Journal covering Asian Pacific American public policy. **Freq:** Annual. **Key Personnel:** Martha Foley, Publisher; Uyen Doan, Editor-in-Chief. **ISSN:** 1062--1830 (print). **Subscription Rates:** $20 Individuals. **URL:** http://isites.harvard.edu/icb/icb.do?keyword=k74751. **Ad Rates:** BW $200. **Remarks:** Accepts advertising. **Circ:** Combined 700.

15954 ■ Asian Economic Papers
The MIT Press
1 Rogers St.
Cambridge, MA 02142-1493
Phone: (617)253-5646
Fax: (617)258-6779
Free: 800-356-0343
Publisher's E-mail: sales@mitpress.mit.edu
Journal promoting high-quality analyses of the economic issues central to Asian countries and offers creative solutions to the region's current problems by drawing on the work of economists worldwide. Comprises selected articles and summaries of discussions from the meetings of the Asian Economic Panel. Provides a unique and useful resource to economists and informed nonspecialists concerned with specific Asian issues, particular Asian economies, and interactions between Asia and other regions. Strives to anticipate developments that will affect Asian economies, encourage discussions of these trends, and explore individual country or regional responses that minimize negative repercussions on neighboring economies. **Freq:** 3/year. **Trim Size:** 6 x 9. **Key Personnel:** Wing Thye Woo, Editor; Jeffrey D. Sachs, Board Member; Naoyuki Yoshino, Editor; Sung-Chun Jung, Editor. **ISSN:** 1535--3516 (print); **EISSN:** 1536--0083 (electronic). **Subscription Rates:** $48 Individuals electroniconly; $53 Individuals print & electronic ; $184 Institutions electronic only; $213 Institutions print & electronic ; $20 Students electronic only; $24 Students print & electronic. **URL:** http://www.mitpressjournals.org/loi/asep. **Ad Rates:** BW $350. **Remarks:** Accepts advertising. **Circ:** Controlled ‡400.

15955 ■ Cancer Cell
Cell Press
600 Technology Sq.
Cambridge, MA 02139
Phone: (617)661-7057
Fax: (617)661-7061
Free: 866-314-2355
Publication E-mail: cancer@cell.com
Peer-reviewed journal that publishes reports of results in any area of cancer research, from molecular and cellular biology to clinical oncology. **Freq:** Monthly. **Trim Size:** 8.375 x 10.875. **Key Personnel:** Li-Kuo Su, Editor; Emilie Marcus, Chief Executive Officer. **ISSN:** 1535--6108 (print). **URL:** http://www.cell.com/cancer-cell/home. **Remarks:** Accepts advertising. **Circ:** (Not Reported).

15956 ■ Catalyst: The Magazine of the Union of Concerned Scientists
Union of Concerned Scientists
2 Brattle Sq.
Cambridge, MA 02138-3780
Phone: (617)547-5552
Fax: (617)864-9405
Publisher's E-mail: ucs@ucsusa.org
Magazine covering UCS issues (energy policy, arms control, nuclear power safety, transportation policy, climate change, biodiversity, invasive species, antibiotic use in livestock agriculture, genetically modified foods, forest conservation). **Founded:** 2002. **Freq:** Semiannual. **Trim Size:** 8 1/2 x 11. **ISSN:** 1539-3410 (print). **Subscription Rates:** $25 Individuals. **URL:** http://www.ucsusa.org/publications/catalyst/. **Formerly**: Nucleus. **Mailing address:** PO Box 9105, Cambridge, MA 02238-9105. **Remarks:** Advertising not accepted. **Circ:** Paid 50000.

15957 ■ Cell
Cell Press
600 Technology Sq.
Cambridge, MA 02139
Phone: (617)661-7057
Fax: (617)661-7061
Free: 866-314-2355
Publication E-mail: celleditor@cell.com
Peer-reviewed journal on molecular and cell biology. **Founded:** 1974. **Freq:** 26/yr. **Print Method:** Sheetfed. **Trim Size:** 8 1/8 x 10 7/8. **Cols./Page:** 2. **Col. Width:**

Circulation: ★ = AAM; △ or • = BPA; ♦ = CAC; ❑ = VAC; ⊕ = PO Statement; ‡ = Publisher's Report; Boldface figures = sworn; Light figures = estimated.

40 nonpareils. **Col. Depth:** 120 agate lines. **Key Personnel:** Emilie Marcus, Editor; Elena Porro, Senior Editor; Meredith Adinolfi, Managing Editor. **ISSN:** 0092-8674 (print). **Subscription Rates:** $246 U.S. and Canada individual, print and online; $371 Other countries individual, print and online. **URL:** http://www.cell.com/cell/home. **Remarks:** Advertising accepted; rates available upon request. **Circ:** Combined ‡21000.

15958 ■ Cell Metabolism
Cell Press
600 Technology Sq.
Cambridge, MA 02139
Phone: (617)661-7057
Fax: (617)661-7061
Free: 866-314-2355
Publication E-mail: metabolism@cell.com
Peer-reviewed journal that publishes reports of results in any area of metabolic biology, from molecular and cellular biology to translational studies. **Freq:** Monthly. **Key Personnel:** Nikla Emambokus, Editor; Emilie Marcus, Chief Executive Officer. **ISSN:** 1550--4131 (print). **Subscription Rates:** $217 U.S. and other countries online or print; $212 Individuals online and print - U.S; $311 Other countries online and print. **URL:** http://www.cell.com/cell-metabolism/home. **Remarks:** Accepts advertising. **Circ:** (Not Reported).

15959 ■ Communications in Mathematical Physics
Springer Netherlands
c/o H.-T. Yau, Editor-in-Chief
Department of Mathematics
Harvard University
1 Oxford St.
Cambridge, MA 02138
Journal featuring mathematical physics. **Freq:** 3/year. **Print Method:** Offset. **Trim Size:** 11 x 13 3/4. **Cols./Page:** 5. **Col. Width:** 22 nonpareils. **Col. Depth:** 175 agate lines. **Key Personnel:** H.T. Yau, Editor-in-Chief; Prof. M. Aizenman, Board Member; Prof. A. Connes, Board Member; Prof. Y. Kawahigashi, Board Member; P.T. Chrusciel, Board Member; N.A. Nekrasov, Board Member; J.L. Lebowitz, Advisor, Board Member. **ISSN:** 0010--3616 (print); **EISSN:** 1432--0916 (electronic). **URL:** http://www.springer.com/physics/theoretical%2C+mathematical+%26+computational+physics/journal/220. **Circ:** (Not Reported).

15960 ■ Computer Music Journal
The MIT Press
1 Rogers St.
Cambridge, MA 02142-1493
Phone: (617)253-5646
Fax: (617)258-6779
Free: 800-356-0343
Publication E-mail: cmj@mitpress.mit.edu
Peer-reviewed journal for musicians, composers, scientists, engineers, and computer enthusiasts interested in contemporary and electronic music and computer generated sound. **Founded:** 1977. **Freq:** Quarterly Spring, Summer, Fall and Winter. **Print Method:** Offset. **Trim Size:** 8 1/2 x 11. **Cols./Page:** 2. **Col. Width:** 36 nonpareils. **Col. Depth:** 126 agate lines. **Key Personnel:** Douglas Keislar, Editor; Keeril Makan, Managing Editor; George Tzanetakis, Associate Editor; James Harley, Associate Editor; John Chowning, Advisor; Lonce Wyse, Associate Editor; Brett Terry, Associate Editor; Pierre Boulez, Advisor. **ISSN:** 0148-9267 (print). **Subscription Rates:** $70 Individuals print & online; $63 Individuals online; $357 Institutions print & online; $308 Institutions online only; $42 Students print and electronic access, retired; $37 Students electronic access, retired. **Alt. Formats:** PDF. **URL:** http://www.mitpressjournals.org/loi/comj. **Ad Rates:** BW $450. **Remarks:** Accepts advertising. **Circ:** 1000.

15961 ■ Cultural Survival Quarterly: World Report on The Rights of Indigenous Peoples and Ethnic Minorities
Cultural Survival
2067 Massachusetts Ave.
Cambridge, MA 02140
Phone: (617)441-5400
Fax: (617)441-5417
Publisher's E-mail: culturalsurvival@culturalsurvival.org
Magazine for general public and policy makers intended to stimulate action for ethnic minorities and indigenous peoples. **Freq:** Quarterly. **Trim Size:** 8 3/8 x 10 7/8. **Cols./Page:** 3. **Col. Width:** 13.5 picas. **Key Personnel:** Mark Cherrington, Editor. **ISSN:** 0740--3291 (print). **Subscription Rates:** Free for members. **URL:** http://www.culturalsurvival.org/publications/csq/index.cfm. **Remarks:** Accepts advertising. **Circ:** (Not Reported).

15962 ■ Cultural Survival Voices
Cultural Survival
2067 Massachusetts Ave.
Cambridge, MA 02140
Phone: (617)441-5400
Fax: (617)441-5417
Publisher's E-mail: culturalsurvival@culturalsurvival.org
General newspaper. **Key Personnel:** Mark Camp, Editor. **URL:** http://www.culturalsurvival.org/our-voices-on-the-air. **Remarks:** Advertising not accepted. **Circ:** (Not Reported).

15963 ■ Daedalus
American Academy of Arts and Sciences
136 Irving St.
Cambridge, MA 02138
Publication E-mail: daedalus@amacad.org
Interdisciplinary journal. **Freq:** Quarterly. **Print Method:** Offset. **Trim Size:** 7 x 10. **Cols./Page:** 2. **Col. Width:** 52 nonpareils. **Col. Depth:** 103 agate lines. **Key Personnel:** Phyllis Bendell, Director, Publications, Managing Editor. **ISSN:** 0011--5266 (print); **EISSN:** 1548--6192 (electronic). **Subscription Rates:** $37 Single issue; $133 Institutions online; $148 Institutions print and online. **Alt. Formats:** PDF. **URL:** http://www.amacad.org/content/publications/publicationListing.aspx?i=135; http://www.mitpressjournals.org/loi/daed. **Remarks:** Accepts advertising. **Circ:** ‡2200.

15964 ■ Developmental Cell
Cell Press
600 Technology Sq.
Cambridge, MA 02139
Phone: (617)661-7057
Fax: (617)661-7061
Free: 866-314-2355
Publication E-mail: devcelleditor@cell.com
Peer-reviewed journal that covers and publishes research in the fields of cell biology and developmental biology. **Freq:** Monthly. **Key Personnel:** Deborah Sweet, Director, Publications; Emilie Marcus, Chief Executive Officer. **ISSN:** 1534--5807 (print). **Subscription Rates:** $217 U.S. and other countries online or print; $212 U.S. online; $311 Other countries online and print. **URL:** http://www.cell.com/developmental-cell/home. **Remarks:** Accepts advertising. **Circ:** (Not Reported).

15965 ■ Econometrica
Econometric Society
Massachusetts Institute of Technology
Department of Economics
50 Memorial Dr.
Cambridge, MA 02142-1347
Phone: (617)253-1927
Fax: (617)253-1330
Publication E-mail: econometrica@econometricsociety.org
Journal concerning economic theory in relation to statistics and mathematics. **Founded:** 1933. **Freq:** Bimonthly. **Key Personnel:** Daron Acemoglu, Editor, phone: (617)253-1927, fax: (617)253-1330; Geri Mattson, Managing Editor, phone: (410)391-2564, fax: (410)391-2542. **ISSN:** 0012-9682 (print). **Subscription Rates:** $746 Institutions print and premiun online; £480 Institutions print and premiun online; $586 Institutions online only; £373 Institutions online only; Included in membership. **URL:** http://www.econometricsociety.org/tocs.asp. **Ad Rates:** BW $350. **Remarks:** Advertising accepted; rates available upon request. **Circ:** ‡7000.

15966 ■ Ed.
Harvard Graduate School of Education
44 R. Brattle St.
Third Fl.
Cambridge, MA 02138
Phone: (617)496-4822
Fax: (617)495-1863
Magazine for the Harvard Graduate School of Education. **Freq:** Semiannual. **Trim Size:** 8 1/2 x 11. **Cols./Page:** 2. **Key Personnel:** Jill Anderson, Contact; Jane Buchbinder, Editor. **URL:** http://www.gse.harvard.edu/news_events/ed/index.html. **Formerly:** Harvard Education Buletin. **Remarks:** Accepts advertising. **Circ:** (Not Reported).

15967 ■ European Journal of Psychological Assessment
Hogrefe & Huber Publishers
875 Massachusetts Ave., 7th Fl.
Cambridge, MA 02139-3015
Fax: (617)354-6875
Free: 866-823-4726
Publisher's E-mail: president@eapa-homepage.org
Journal covering articles on theoretical and applied developments in psychology. **Freq:** Quarterly. **Print Method:** Offset. **Trim Size:** 8 1/4 x 11. **Key Personnel:** Karl Schweizer, Editor-in-Chief; Itziar Alonso-Arbiol, Editor; Michael Schreiner, Assistant Editor; Antonio Godoy, Associate Editor. **ISSN:** 1015--5759 (print); **EISSN:** 2151--2426 (electronic). **Subscription Rates:** $434 Institutions; $208 Individuals; $151 Members; $109 Single issue. **URL:** http://www.eapa-homepage.org/journal; http://us.hogrefe.com/products/journals/ejpa. **Mailing address:** PO Box 90153, 5000 LE Tilburg, Netherlands. **Remarks:** Accepts advertising. **Circ:** (Not Reported).

15968 ■ Evolutionary Computation
The MIT Press
1 Rogers St.
Cambridge, MA 02142-1493
Phone: (617)253-5646
Fax: (617)258-6779
Free: 800-356-0343
Publisher's E-mail: sales@mitpress.mit.edu
Journal providing an international forum for facilitating and enhancing the exchange of information among researchers involved in both the theoretical and practical aspects of computational systems of an evolutionary nature. Publishes both theoretical and practical developments of computational systems drawing their inspiration from nature, with particular emphasis on evolutionary algorithms (EAs), including, but not limited to, genetic algorithms (GAs), evolution strategies (ESs), evolutionary programming (EP), genetic programming (GP), classifier systems (CSs), and other natural computation techniques. **Freq:** Quarterly. **Key Personnel:** Hans-Georg Beyer, Editor-in-Chief. **ISSN:** 1063--6560 (print); **EISSN:** 1530--9304 (electronic). **Subscription Rates:** $80 Individuals online only; $430 Institutions online only; $40 Students online only; retired; $22 Individuals single issue; $121 Institutions single issue. **URL:** http://www.mitpressjournals.org/loi/evco. **Remarks:** Accepts advertising. **Circ:** (Not Reported).

15969 ■ eWeek
ZDNet
1 Athenaeum St.
Cambridge, MA 02142
Publication covering electronic business. **Freq:** Monthly. **Key Personnel:** Jason Brooks, Executive Editor. **ISSN:** 1530--6283 (print). **Subscription Rates:** $125 Individuals; $155 Canada; $195 Other countries airmail; $85 Individuals digital. **Online:** Gale. **URL:** http://www.eweek.com. **Ad Rates:** BW $63,535; 4C $76,668. **Remarks:** Accepts advertising. **Circ:** *400100.

15970 ■ The ExChange
Alexander Technique International
1692 Massachusetts Ave., 3rd Fl.
Cambridge, MA 02138
Phone: (617)497-5151
Fax: (617)497-2615
Free: 888-668-8996
Publisher's E-mail: alexandertechnique@verizon.net
Freq: 3/year. **Subscription Rates:** $35. **Remarks:** Advertising not accepted. **Circ:** (Not Reported).

15971 ■ 15 Minutes
Harvard Crimson Inc.
14 Plympton St.
Cambridge, MA 02138
Phone: (617)576-6565
Fax: (617)576-7860
Publisher's E-mail: letters@thecrimson.com
Arts and entertainment tabloid. **Freq:** Weekly (Thurs.). **Print Method:** Offset. **Cols./Page:** 4. **Col. Width:** 27 nonpareils. **Col. Depth:** 168 agate lines. **Key Personnel:** Nicholas P. Fandos, Managing Editor. **Subscription Rates:** $350 Individuals premium plus; $250 Individuals premium. **URL:** http://www.thecrimson.com/section/fm. **Ad Rates:** BW $1,000; 4C $1,500. **Remarks:** Accepts advertising. **Circ:** Non-paid ‡10000.

15972 ■ Global Environmental Politics
The MIT Press
1 Rogers St.
Cambridge, MA 02142-1493
Phone: (617)253-5646
Fax: (617)258-6779
Free: 800-356-0343
Publisher's E-mail: sales@mitpress.mit.edu
Peer-reviewed journal covering the relationship between global political forces and environmental change, including the role of states, multilateral institutions and agreements, trade, international finance, corporations, inequalities, non-governmental organizations, science and technology, and grassroots movements. GEP brings a strong focus to bear on the implications of local-global interactions for environmental management as well as the implications of environmental change for world politics. Each issue is divided into two sections, Current Debates and Research Articles. Current Debates are short provocative commentaries on topics in international and comparative environmental politics. Research Articles are full-length papers that contain original theoretical and empirical contributions to research on environmental politics. GEP breaks new ground in political science, international relations, sociology, history, human geography, public policy, science and technology studies, environmental ethics, law, economics, and environmental science. **Freq:** Quarterly. **Key Personnel:** Stacy D. VanDeveer, Editor; Jennifer Clapp, Board Member; Matthew Paterson, Board Member. **ISSN:** 1526--3800 (print); **EISSN:** 1536--0091 (electronic). **Subscription Rates:** $257 Institutions online only; $300 Institutions print and online; $75 Institutions single issue. **URL:** http://www.mitpressjournals.org/loi/glep. **Ad Rates:** BW $300. **Remarks:** Accepts advertising. **Circ:** 250.

15973 ■ Harvard Advocate
Harvard Advocate
21 S St.
Cambridge, MA 02138
Publisher's E-mail: contact@theharvardadvocate.com
Literary journal. **Freq:** Quarterly. **Print Method:** Letterpress and offset. **Cols./Page:** 2 and 3. **Col. Width:** 26 and 41 nonpareils. **Col. Depth:** 133 agate lines. **Key Personnel:** Julian Lucas, Editor. **ISSN:** 0017-8004 (print). **Subscription Rates:** $35 Individuals domestic; $69 Two years domestic; $45 Institutions, other countries; $75 Institutions, other countries 8 issues. **URL:** http://theharvardadvocate.com. **Ad Rates:** BW $325. **Remarks:** Accepts advertising. **Circ:** Paid ‡300, Non-paid ‡3000.

15974 ■ Harvard Business Law Review
Harvard University Law School
1563 Massachusetts Ave.
Cambridge, MA 02138
Phone: (617)495-3109
Publisher's E-mail: jdadmiss@law.harvard.edu
Journal featuring topics discussing the intersection of law and business. **Freq:** Annual. **Key Personnel:** Della Fok, Editor-in-Chief; Jordan Weber, Editor-in-Chief. **ISSN:** 2164--3601 (print); **EISSN:** 2164--361X (electronic). **URL:** http://www.hblr.org. **Circ:** (Not Reported).

15975 ■ Harvard Crimson
Harvard Crimson Inc.
14 Plympton St.
Cambridge, MA 02138
Phone: (617)576-6565
Fax: (617)576-7860
Publication E-mail: news@thecrimson.com
Collegiate newspaper. **Freq:** Daily (morn.) Mon.- Fri., except on federal and University holidays. **Print Method:** Letterpress and offset. **Cols./Page:** 6. **Col. Width:** 27 nonpareils. **Col. Depth:** 294 agate lines. **Key Personnel:** Nicholas P. Fandos, Writer. **Subscription Rates:** $250 Individuals Sept.-Oct.; $225 Individuals Nov.-Dec.; $175 Individuals Jan.-Feb.; $125 Individuals Mar.-Apr.; $50 Individuals May. **Ad Rates:** BW $2,016; PCI $16. **Remarks:** Accepts advertising. **Circ:** ‡10000.

15976 ■ Harvard Design Magazine: Architecture, Landscape Architecture, Urban Design and Planning
Harvard Design Magazine
48 Quincy St.
Cambridge, MA 02138
Phone: (617)495-7814
Fax: (617)496-3391
Publication E-mail: hdm@gsd.harvard.edu
Magazine providing 'critical explorations of key contemporary issues and practices related to the built environment.' Includes essays, photographic and design portfolios, book reviews and debates. **Freq:** Semiannual. **Key Personnel:** Meghan Ryan, Coordinator; William Saunders, Editor. **ISSN:** 1093--4421 (print). **Subscription Rates:** $32 Individuals; $38 Other countries; $18 Single issue; $21 Other countries single issue. **URL:** http://www.harvarddesignmagazine.org. **Ad Rates:** BW $2,000; 4C $4,000. **Remarks:** Accepts advertising. **Circ:** 12000..

15977 ■ Harvard Divinity Bulletin
Harvard Divinity School
45 Francis Ave.
Cambridge, MA 02138
Phone: (617)495-5761
Magazine featuring articles, reviews, and opinion pieces on religion and contemporary life, religion and the arts, religious history, and the study of religion. **Freq:** Quarterly spring, summer, autumn and winter. **Key Personnel:** Wendy S. McDowell, Senior Editor; Susan Lloyd McGarry, Managing Editor. **Subscription Rates:** $8 Individuals /copy. **URL:** http://bulletin.hds.harvard.edu/receive-the-bulletin. **Remarks:** Accepts advertising. **Circ:** 21000.

15978 ■ Harvard Educational Review
Harvard Graduate School of Education
44 R. Brattle St.
Third Fl.
Cambridge, MA 02138
Phone: (617)496-4822
Fax: (617)495-1863
Publication E-mail: hepg@harvard.edu
Scholarly journal in education; publishes articles and book reviews. **Freq:** Quarterly. **Print Method:** Offset. **Trim Size:** 6 3/4 x 10. **Cols./Page:** 1. **Col. Width:** 5 inches. **Col. Depth:** 7 1/2 inches. **Key Personnel:** Kolajo Paul Afolabi, Editor; Candice Bocala, Editor; Raygine DiAquoi, Editor. **ISSN:** 0017-8055 (print); **EISSN:** 1943-5045 (electronic). **Subscription Rates:** $410 Institutions print & online; $426 Canada print & online; $479 Other countries print & online; $367 Institutions online only; $59 Individuals print & online; $84 Canada print & online; $99 Other countries print & online; $39 Individuals online only. **URL:** http://www.hepg.org/her-home. **Ad Rates:** BW $525. **Remarks:** Accepts advertising. **Circ:** ‡6500.

15979 ■ Harvard Environmental Law Review
Harvard University Law School
1563 Massachusetts Ave.
Cambridge, MA 02138
Phone: (617)495-3109
Publisher's E-mail: jdadmiss@law.harvard.edu
Journal featuring topics related to climate change, air and water pollution regulation, land use, law and economics, administrative law and international environmental law. **Freq:** Semiannual. **Key Personnel:** Samantha Caravello, Editor-in-Chief. **Subscription Rates:** $42 Individuals; $52 Other countries. **URL:** http://harvardelr.com. **Circ:** (Not Reported).

15980 ■ Harvard Human Rights Journal
Harvard Society for Law and Public Policy
Harvard Law School
Caspersen Student Center
1585 Massachusetts Ave., Ste. 3039
Cambridge, MA 02138
Publication E-mail: hlshrj@gmail.com
Journal on international human rights in association with Harvard Human Rights Program. **Freq:** Annual. **Key Personnel:** Brianna Dollinger, Editor-in-Chief. **Subscription Rates:** $32 Individuals domestic; $37 Other countries. **URL:** http://harvardhrj.com/. **Circ:** (Not Reported).

15981 ■ Harvard Human Rights Journal
Harvard University Law School
1563 Massachusetts Ave.
Cambridge, MA 02138
Phone: (617)495-3109
Publisher's E-mail: jdadmiss@law.harvard.edu
Journal covering on a broad range of topics related to human rights, international human rights law, and international humanitarian law. **Freq:** Annual. **Key Personnel:** Brianna Dollinger, Editor-in-Chief. **URL:** http://harvardhrj.com. **Circ:** (Not Reported).

15982 ■ The Harvard Independent
Nieman Foundation for Journalism at Harvard
59 Sheppard St.
Cambridge, MA 02138
Collegiate newspaper. **Freq:** Weekly (Thurs.). **Print Method:** Offset. **Cols./Page:** 4. **Col. Width:** 25 nonpareils. **Col. Depth:** 196 agate lines. **Key Personnel:** Faith Zhang, Editor-in-Chief. **Subscription Rates:** Free; $15 Individuals. **URL:** http://www.harvardindependent.com. **Ad Rates:** BW $168, per week; PCI $3. **Remarks:** Accepts advertising. **Circ:** ‡8000.

15983 ■ Harvard International Law Journal
Harvard University Law School
1563 Massachusetts Ave.
Cambridge, MA 02138
Phone: (617)495-3109
Publisher's E-mail: jdadmiss@law.harvard.edu
Journal covering a wide variety of topics in public and private international law. **Key Personnel:** Becca Donaldson, Editor-in-Chief. **URL:** http://www.harvardilj.org. **Circ:** (Not Reported).

15984 ■ Harvard International Review
Harvard International Review
59 Shepard St.
Box 205
Cambridge, MA 02138
Phone: (617)495-9607
Fax: (617)496-4472
Publication E-mail: contact@hir.harvard.edu
Publication focusing on current international events. **Freq:** Quarterly. **Key Personnel:** Ashley Collins, Editor-in-Chief; Sarah Moon, Associate. **ISSN:** 0739--1854 (print). **Subscription Rates:** $22 Individuals; $40 Two years; $30 Institutions; $48 Two years institutions; $32 Other countries; $60 Other countries two years; $40 Institutions, other countries; $58 Institutions, other countries two years. **URL:** http://hir.harvard.edu. **Ad Rates:** BW $995; 4C $1495. **Remarks:** Accepts advertising. **Circ:** (Not Reported).

15985 ■ Harvard Journal of Asiatic Studies
Harvard-Yenching Institute
Vanserg Hall, Ste. 20
25 Francis Ave.
Cambridge, MA 02138
Phone: (617)495-4050
Fax: (617)496-7206
Publisher's E-mail: yenching@fas.harvard.edu
Scholarly journal covering languages, literature, cultures, and the history of Eastern and Central Asia. **Founded:** 1936. **Freq:** Semiannual. **Print Method:** Photo offset. **Trim Size:** 6 1/8 x 9 1/8. **Key Personnel:** Joanna Handlin Smith, Editor, phone: (617)495-2758, fax: (617)495-7798. **ISSN:** 0073-0548 (print). **Subscription Rates:** $36 Individuals; $60 Institutions; $48 Other countries; $72 Institutions, other countries. **URL:** http://www.hjas.org/. **Remarks:** Advertising not accepted. **Circ:** Paid 1500.

15986 ■ Harvard Journal of Law & Gender
Harvard Society for Law and Public Policy
1585 Massachusetts Ave.
Cambridge, MA 02138
Fax: (617)300-8659
Publication E-mail: hlsjlg@mail.law.harvard.edu
Law journal discussing legal issues concerning women's interests in the background of political, economic, historical, and sociological scenario. Topics include domestic violence, sexual harassment, reproductive rights and women in the uniform. **Freq:** Semiannual. **Key Personnel:** Suria Bahadue, Editor-in-Chief; Deanna Parrish, Editor-in-Chief. **ISSN:** 0270-1456 (print). **Subscription Rates:** $42 Individuals; $52 Other countries. **URL:** http://harvardjlg.com/. **Formerly:** Harvard Women's Law Journal. **Circ:** (Not Reported).

Circulation: ★ = AAM; △ or • = BPA; ♦ = CAC; ❑ = VAC; ⊕ = PO Statement; ‡ = Publisher's Report; Boldface figures = sworn; Light figures = estimated.

15987 ■ Harvard Journal of Law & Gender
Harvard University Law School
1563 Massachusetts Ave.
Cambridge, MA 02138
Phone: (617)495-3109
Publisher's E-mail: jdadmiss@law.harvard.edu
Journal exploring the interconnections between race, class, sexuality, and gender in the law. **Key Personnel:** Suria Bahadue, Editor-in-Chief. **ISSN:** 0270--1456 (print). **URL:** http://harvardjlg.com. **Circ:** (Not Reported).

15988 ■ Harvard Journal of Law and Public Policy
Federalist Society for Law and Public Policy Studies
1585 Massachusetts Ave.
Cambridge, MA 02138
Fax: (617)300-8659
Publication E-mail: jlpp@mail.law.harvard.edu
Professional journal covering law. **Freq:** 3/year. **Cols./Page:** 1. **Key Personnel:** Patrick Swiber, Editor-in-Chief. **ISSN:** 0193--4872 (print). **Subscription Rates:** $55 U.S.; $75 Other countries; $55 Individuals. **URL:** http://www.harvard-jlpp.com; http://www.fed-soc.org/publications. **Remarks:** Advertising not accepted. **Circ:** (Not Reported).

15989 ■ Harvard Journal of Law & Technology
Harvard Society for Law and Public Policy
Harvard Law School
28 Pound Hall
Cambridge, MA 02138
Phone: (617)495-3606
Fax: (617)495-8828
Publication E-mail: jolt@mail.law.harvard.edu
Law journal. **Freq:** Semiannual. **Key Personnel:** Ariel Simms, Editor-in-Chief. **ISSN:** 0897--3393 (print). **Subscription Rates:** $95 Individuals. **URL:** http://jolt.law.harvard.edu. **Circ:** (Not Reported).

15990 ■ Harvard Journal on Legislation
Harvard University Law School
1563 Massachusetts Ave.
Cambridge, MA 02138
Phone: (617)495-3109
Publisher's E-mail: jdadmiss@law.harvard.edu
Journal covering range of legislative topics including Affirmative Action, punitive damages, family law, executive agency regulation, and anti-terrorism legislation. **Freq:** Semiannual. **Key Personnel:** Grace Signorelli, Managing Editor. **Subscription Rates:** $42 Individuals; $52 Other countries. **URL:** http://www.harvardjol.com. **Circ:** (Not Reported).

15991 ■ Harvard Journal on Racial and Ethnic Justice
Harvard University Law School
1563 Massachusetts Ave.
Cambridge, MA 02138
Phone: (617)495-3109
Publisher's E-mail: jdadmiss@law.harvard.edu
Journal publishing manuscripts that address social and economic issues affecting racial and ethnic minorities. **Freq:** Annual. **Key Personnel:** Catherine Howard, Editor-in-Chief. **Subscription Rates:** $32 Individuals; $37 Other countries. **URL:** http://hjrej.com. **Circ:** (Not Reported).

15992 ■ Harvard Law Review
Harvard Law Review
Gannett House
1511 Massachusetts Ave.
Cambridge, MA 02138
Phone: (617)495-7889
Fax: (617)495-5053
Journal publishing legal scholarship. **Freq:** 8/year Nov.-June. **Print Method:** Offset. **Cols./Page:** 1. **Col. Width:** 78 nonpareils. **Col. Depth:** 136 agate lines. **Key Personnel:** Michael Arthus, Board Member; Denis O'Brien, Director, Finance, Specialist, Circulation; Jennifer Heath, Web Administrator. **ISSN:** 0017-811X (print). **Subscription Rates:** $60 Individuals; $200 Institutions; $110 Two years individuals; $375 Two years institutions; $150 Individuals three years; $525 Institutions three years; $5 Single issue; $15 Institutions single issue; $85 Other countries; $225 Institutions, other countries; $160 Other countries two years; $425 Institutions, other countries two years. **URL:** http://harvardlawreview.org. **Ad Rates:** BW $350. **Remarks:** Accepts advertising. **Circ:** 4000.

15993 ■ Harvard Magazine
Harvard Magazine Inc.
7 Ware St.
Cambridge, MA 02138-4037
Phone: (617)495-5746
Fax: (617)495-0324
Publisher's E-mail: harvard_magazine@harvard.edu
Alumni magazine. **Freq:** Bimonthly. **Print Method:** Offset. **Trim Size:** 8 3/8 x 10 7/8. **Cols./Page:** 3. **Col. Width:** 26 nonpareils. **Col. Depth:** 135 agate lines. **Key Personnel:** Elizabeth Gudrais, Associate Editor; John S. Rosenberg, Editor; Jean Martin, Senior Editor; Irina Kuksin, Publisher; Jonathan S. Shaw, Managing Editor; Felecia Carter, Director. **ISSN:** 0095-2427 (print). **Subscription Rates:** $27 U.S.; $44 Two years; $35 Canada and Mexico; $55 Other countries. **Ad Rates:** BW $12,570; 4C $18,360. **Remarks:** Accepts advertising. **Circ:** △**245737**.

15994 ■ Harvard Political Review
Institute of Politics Harvard University
Student Organization Center at Hilles
59 Shepard St.
Cambridge, MA 02138
Journal on politics and public policy in both domestic and international contexts. **Freq:** Quarterly. **Key Personnel:** Flavia Cuervo, Publisher. **URL:** http://harvardpolitics.com. **Mailing address:** PO Box 174, Cambridge, MA 02138. **Remarks:** Advertising accepted; rates available upon request. **Circ:** ‡2000.

15995 ■ Harvard Review
Lamont Library Level 5
Harvard University
Harvard Yard
Cambridge, MA 02138
Phone: (617)495-2452
Publication E-mail: info@harvardreview.org
Literary journal covering fiction, nonfiction, book reviews, and poetry. **Freq:** Semiannual. **Key Personnel:** Christina Thompson, Editor; Laura Healy, Managing Editor. **ISSN:** 1077--2901 (print). **Subscription Rates:** $20 Individuals domestic; $50 Individuals domestic 3-years; $80 Individuals domestic 5-years; $30 Institutions domestic; $32 Other countries; $40 Institutions, other countries international; $80 Other countries 3 years; $128 Other countries 5 years. **URL:** http://hcl.harvard.edu/harvardreview. **Ad Rates:** BW $500. **Remarks:** Accepts advertising. **Circ:** Controlled 2300.

15996 ■ The Harvard Salient
Turley Publications
PO Box 381053
Cambridge, MA 02238-1053
Publication E-mail: salient@hcs.harvard.edu
Voice of conservation at America's premier university. **Freq:** Biweekly. **Print Method:** Offset. **Cols./Page:** 4. **Col. Width:** 2 1/4 inches. **Col. Depth:** 15 inches. **Key Personnel:** Patrick T. Brennan, Managing Editor; Michael P.H. Stanley, Publisher; Michael E. Cowett, Editor. **URL:** http://www.hcs.harvard.edu/~salient/site/Harvard_Salient.html. **Ad Rates:** BW $200; 4C $500; PCI $5. **Remarks:** Accepts advertising. **Circ:** 4,500.

15997 ■ Harvard Science Review
Harvard University Press
79 Garden St.
Cambridge, MA 02138
Phone: (617)495-2600
Fax: (617)495-5898
Publication E-mail: hsr@hcs.harvard.edu harvard.sci.review@gmail.com
A science journal. **Freq:** Semiannual. **Trim Size:** 8 1/2 x 11. **Key Personnel:** Caitlin Andrews, Co-President. **ISSN:** 1062--7022 (print). **URL:** http://harvardsciencereview.com. **Remarks:** Accepts advertising. **Circ:** (Not Reported).

15998 ■ Harvard Theological Review
Harvard Divinity School
45 Francis Ave.
Cambridge, MA 02138
Phone: (617)495-5761
Publication E-mail: htr@hds.harvard.edu
Scholarly magazine covering theology, ethics, and history. **Freq:** Quarterly. **Key Personnel:** Margaret Studier, Managing Editor. **ISSN:** 0017--8160 (print). **URL:** http://www.hds.harvard.edu/faculty-research/research-publications/harvard-theological-review. **Ad Rates:** BW $200. **Remarks:** Accepts advertising. **Circ:** 1500.

15999 ■ Harvard Ukrainian Studies
American Association for Ukrainian Studies
34 Kirkland St.
Cambridge, MA 02138
Journal publishing articles in all fields of Ukrainian studies with an emphasis on the humanities. **Subscription Rates:** Included in membership. **URL:** http://www.huri.harvard.edu/pubs/hus.html. **Remarks:** Advertising not accepted. **Circ:** (Not Reported).

16000 ■ Harvard University Gazette
Harvard University Gazette
Smith Campus Center
1350 Massachusetts Ave.
Cambridge, MA 02138
Phone: (617)495-1585
Fax: (617)495-0754
Publisher's E-mail: media@harvard.edu
Community newspaper. **Freq:** Monthly. **Key Personnel:** Terry Murphy, Managing Editor; Jim Concannon, Editor. **ISSN:** 0364-7692 (print). **Alt. Formats:** PDF. **URL:** http://news.harvard.edu/gazette. **Remarks:** Advertising not accepted. **Circ:** 30150.

16001 ■ IEEE Control Systems Magazine
IEEE Control Systems Society
c/o Richard D. Braatz, Editor-in-Chief
Massachusetts Institute of Technology
77 Massachusetts Ave., Rm. 66-372
Cambridge, MA 02139
Magazine covering theory, analysis, design and all aspects of control systems. **Freq:** Bimonthly. **Key Personnel:** Jonathan How, Editor-in-Chief. **ISSN:** 0272--1708 (print). **URL:** http://ieeexplore.ieee.org/xpl/RecentIssue.jsp?reload=true&punumber=37. **Remarks:** Accepts advertising. **Circ:** (Not Reported).

16002 ■ Information and Computation
RELX Group P.L.C.
c/o A.R. Meyer, Ed.-in-Ch.
Massachusetts Institute for Technology
Computer Science & Artificial Intelligence Lab.
32 Vassar St., G32-624
Cambridge, MA 02139-3594
Phone: (617)253-6024
Publisher's E-mail: amsterdam@relx.com
Journal publishing original papers on theoretical computer sciences and computational aspects of information theory. **Freq:** Monthly. **Trim Size:** 8 1/2 x 11. **Key Personnel:** A.R. Meyer, Editor-in-Chief. **ISSN:** 0890--5401 (print). **Subscription Rates:** $85 Individuals print only; $876.27 Institutions eJournal; $1315 Institutions print only. **URL:** http://www.journals.elsevier.com/information-and-computation/. **Remarks:** Accepts advertising. **Circ:** (Not Reported).

16003 ■ InterJournal
New England Complex Systems Institute
283 Main St., Ste. 319
Cambridge, MA 02142
Phone: (617)547-4100
Fax: (617)661-7711
Publisher's E-mail: news@necsi.edu
Journal covering the fields of science and engineering. **Key Personnel:** Y. Bar-Yam, Managing Editor. **ISSN:** 1081--0625 (print). **URL:** http://www.interjournal.org; http://www.necsi.edu/education/books-pub.html; http://necsi.edu/publications/journals.html. **Remarks:** Advertising not accepted. **Circ:** (Not Reported).

16004 ■ International Security
The MIT Press
Belfer Ctr. for Science & International Affairs
Harvard University
79 John F. Kennedy St.
Cambridge, MA 02138
Phone: (617)495-1914
Fax: (617)495-8963
Publication E-mail: is@harvard.edu
Peer-reviewed journal of essays on international affairs and issues of defense, security, arms control, and use of force, from all political viewpoints. **Founded:** 1976. **Freq:** Quarterly. **Trim Size:** 6 3/4 x 10. **Cols./Page:** 1. **Col. Width:** 74 nonpareils. **Col. Depth:** 133 agate lines. **Key Personnel:** Diane J. McCree, Managing Editor; Owen R. Cote, Jr., Editor; Steven E. Miller, Editor-in-Chief; Sean M. Lynn-Jones, Editor. **ISSN:** 0162-2889 (print). **Subscription Rates:** $59 Individuals print and

online; $52 Individuals online; $30 Students print and online, retired; $27 Students online; $273 Institutions print and online; $240 Institutions online only. **URL:** http://www.mitpressjournals.org/loi/isec; http://belfercenter.ksg.harvard.edu/project/58/quarterly_journal.html. **Ad Rates:** BW $600. **Remarks:** Accepts advertising. **Circ:** ‡2100.

16005 ■ Journal of the American Association of Variable Star Observers
American Association of Variable Star Observers
49 Bay State Rd.
Cambridge, MA 02138
Phone: (617)354-0484
Fax: (617)354-0665
Publication E-mail: aavso@aavso.org
Scientific journal covering variable star astronomy and related topics and association news. **Freq:** Semiannual June/December. **Key Personnel:** John R. Percy, Editor; Elizabeth Waagen, Associate Editor; Michael Saladyga, Editor. **ISSN:** 0271--9053 (print); **EISSN:** 2380--3606 (electronic). **URL:** http://www.aavso.org/apps/jaavso. **Remarks:** Advertising not accepted. **Circ:** (Not Reported).

16006 ■ Journal of Cold War Studies
The MIT Press
1 Rogers St.
Cambridge, MA 02142-1493
Phone: (617)253-5646
Fax: (617)258-6779
Free: 800-356-0343
Publisher's E-mail: sales@mitpress.mit.edu
Peer-reviewed journal featuring articles based on archival research in the former communist world and in western countries cold war studies. **Freq:** Quarterly winter, spring, summer, fall. **Trim Size:** 6 x 9. **Key Personnel:** Eliot A. Cohen, Board Member; Mark Kramer, Editor; Hannes Adomeit, Board Member; Aleksei Filitov, Board Member; John Lewis Gaddis, Board Member; Lawrence Freedman, Board Member; Ethan B. Kapstein, Board Member; Roderick MacFarquhar, Board Member; Donald Kagan, Board Member. **ISSN:** 1520--3972 (print); **EISSN:** 1531--3298 (electronic). **URL:** http://www.mitpressjournals.org/loi/jcws. **Ad Rates:** BW $350. **Remarks:** Accepts advertising. **Circ:** Combined 450.

16007 ■ Journal of Differential Geometry
International Press of Boston Inc.
Dept. of Mathematics
Harvard University
Cambridge, MA 02138
Publisher's E-mail: ipb-orders@intlpress.com
Academic journal devoted to research in differential geometry and related subjects. **Freq:** 9/year. **Key Personnel:** Gerhard Huisken, Associate Editor; Jun Li, Editor; S.T. Yau, Editor-in-Chief; Richard Hamilton, Editor; Simon K. Donaldson, Editor; Cao Huai-Dong, Managing Editor; Richard M. Schoen, Editor; Robert Bartnik, Associate Editor. **ISSN:** 0022--040X (print); **EISSN:** 1945--743X (electronic). **Subscription Rates:** $1429 Institutions print + online; $1545 Institutions, other countries print + online; $1070 Institutions online; $439 Individuals print; $577 Other countries print. **URL:** http://intlpress.com/site/pub/pages/journals/items/jdg/_home/_main. **Remarks:** Accepts advertising. **Circ:** Combined 1250.

16008 ■ Journal of Individual Differences
Hogrefe & Huber Publishers
875 Massachusetts Ave., 7th Fl.
Cambridge, MA 02139-3015
Fax: (617)354-6875
Free: 866-823-4726
Publisher's E-mail: customerservice@hogrefe-publishing.com
Journal covering differences between humans and animals with respect to their behavior, emotion, cognition, and developmental aspects. **Freq:** Quarterly. **Print Method:** Offset litho. **Trim Size:** 8 1/4 x 11. **Key Personnel:** Thomas Rammsayer, Associate Editor; Burkhard Brocke, Board Member; Aljoscha Neubauer, Associate Editor; Sam Gosling, Associate Editor; Philip J. Corr, Associate Editor; Juergen Hennig, PhD, Editor-in-Chief. **ISSN:** 1614--0001 (print); **EISSN:** 2151--2299 (electronic). **Subscription Rates:** $324 Institutions; $159 Individuals; $81 Single issue print and online + postage and handling. **URL:** http://us.hogrefe.com/products/journals/jid. **Remarks:** Accepts advertising. **Circ:** (Not Reported).

16009 ■ Journal of Psychophysiology
Hogrefe & Huber Publishers
875 Massachusetts Ave., 7th Fl.
Cambridge, MA 02139-3015
Fax: (617)354-6875
Free: 866-823-4726
Publisher's E-mail: customerservice@hogrefe-publishing.com
Journal covering psycho physiological measures on human subjects. **Freq:** Quarterly. **Print Method:** Letterpress. **Trim Size:** 7 x 10. **Cols./Page:** 2. **Col. Width:** 30 nonpareils. **Col. Depth:** 110 agate lines. **Key Personnel:** Michael Falkenstein, Editor-in-Chief. **ISSN:** 0269-8803 (print); **EISSN:** 2151-2124 (electronic). **Subscription Rates:** $369 Institutions; $274 Individuals; $118 Members of SPR; €294 Institutions; €198 Individuals; €90 Members of SPR; €45 Members FEPS special rate; £224 Institutions; £163 Individuals; £72 Members of SPR; £36 Members FEPS special rate; $93 Single issue online; €69 Single issue online; £56 Single issue online. **URL:** http://www.hogrefe.com/periodicals/journal-of-psychophysiology/. **Remarks:** Advertising not accepted. **Circ:** (Not Reported).

16010 ■ Journal of Public Economics
RELX Group P.L.C.
c/o R. Chetty, Ed.
Harvard University
Cambridge, MA 02142
Publisher's E-mail: amsterdam@relx.com
Journal covering the problems of public economics and focusing on the application of modern economic theory and methods of quantitative analysis. **Freq:** 12/yr. **Key Personnel:** R. Chetty, Editor; H.J. Kleven, Editor. **ISSN:** 0047--2727 (print). **Subscription Rates:** $273 Individuals print; $3975 Institutions print; $3312.67 Institutions ejournal. **URL:** http://www.journals.elsevier.com/journal-of-public-economics. **Circ:** (Not Reported).

16011 ■ Land Lines
Lincoln Institute of Land Policy
113 Brattle St.
Cambridge, MA 02138-3407
Phone: (617)661-3016
Fax: (617)661-7235
Free: 800-526-3873
Publisher's E-mail: help@lincolninst.edu
Providing summarizes on findings and examines the aspects of community land trust that may help to explain the sustainability and success of community land trust home ownership. **Freq:** Quarterly latest Edition 2014. **Alt. Formats:** PDF. **Remarks:** Advertising not accepted. **Circ:** 8000.

16012 ■ Linguistic Inquiry
The MIT Press
c/o Samuel Jay Keyser, Ed.-in-Ch.
MIT Linguistics & Philosophy
77 Mass Ave., 32-D770
Cambridge, MA 02139
Publisher's E-mail: sales@mitpress.mit.edu
Journal on advanced linguistics research and theory, including phonology, syntax, semantics, and morphology. **Freq:** Quarterly Winter, Spring, Summer, Fall. **Print Method:** Offset. **Trim Size:** 6 3/4 x 9 1/4. **Cols./Page:** 1. **Col. Width:** 60 nonpareils. **Col. Depth:** 98 agate lines. **Key Personnel:** Anne Mark, Managing Editor; Prof. Samuel Jay Keyser, Editor-in-Chief, phone: (617)253-1917; Eric Reuland, Editor; Charlotte Gibbs, Manager. **ISSN:** 0024-3892 (print); **EISSN:** 1530-9150 (electronic). **Subscription Rates:** $87 Individuals print and online; $81 Individuals online only; $600 Institutions print and online; $405 Institutions online only; $50 Students print and online, retired; $46 Students online only, retired. **URL:** http://www.mitpressjournals.org/loi/ling. **Ad Rates:** BW $400. **Remarks:** Accepts advertising. **Circ:** 1100.

16013 ■ Methodology: European Journal of Research Methods for the Behavioral and Social Sciences
Hogrefe & Huber Publishers
875 Massachusetts Ave., 7th Fl.
Cambridge, MA 02139-3015
Fax: (617)354-6875
Free: 866-823-4726
Publisher's E-mail: customerservice@hogrefe-publishing.com
Journal that offers the exchange of methodological research and applications in the different fields, including new methodological approaches, review articles, software information, and instructional papers that can be used in teaching. **Freq:** Quarterly. **Key Personnel:** Joop Hox, PhD, Board Member. **ISSN:** 1614--1881 (print); **EISSN:** 1614--2241 (electronic). **Subscription Rates:** $304 Institutions; $149 Individuals; $76 Single issue. **URL:** http://www.hogrefe.com/periodicals/methodology. **Circ:** (Not Reported).

16014 ■ MIT Sloan
MIT Sloan School of Management
30 Memorial Dr.
Cambridge, MA 02142
Phone: (617)258-5434
Alumni magazine for MIT's Sloan School of Management. **Freq:** Semiannual. **Subscription Rates:** Free to qualified subscribers. **URL:** http://mitsloan.mit.edu/alumnimagazine. **Circ:** (Not Reported).

16015 ■ MIT Sloan Management Review
Sloan Management Review
One Charles Pk.EE20-600 6th Fl.
Cambridge, MA 02139-4307
Phone: (617)253-7170
Fax: (617)258-9739
Free: 877-727-7170
Publication covering issues in business. **Freq:** Quarterly. **ISSN:** 1532-9194 (print). **Subscription Rates:** $75 Individuals. **Online:** Gale. **URL:** http://sloanreview.mit.edu/. **Ad Rates:** BW $4,481, full page; BW $3,809, 2/3 page vertical; BW $3,360, 1/2 page vertical or horizontal; BW $3,137, 1/3 page vertical. **Circ:** (Not Reported).

16016 ■ Modernism/Modernity
Johns Hopkins University Press
c/o Prof. Jeffrey Schnapp, Ed.
Harvard University
Dept. of Romance Languages & Literatures
Boylston Hall 423
Cambridge, MA 02138
Publication E-mail: modernism-modernity@stanford.edu
Scholarly journal covering modernist studies, including art, music, architecture, literary theory, history and related areas. **Freq:** Quarterly. **Trim Size:** 5.5 x 8. **Key Personnel:** Jeffrey T. Schnapp, Advisor, Board Member; Debra Rae Cohen, Editor. **ISSN:** 1071--6068 (print); **EISSN:** 1080--6601 (electronic). **Subscription Rates:** $180 Institutions print - 1 year (4 issues); $50 Individuals print - 1 year (4 issues) (does not include MSA membership); $360 Institutions print - 2 years (8 issues) ; $90 Two years print - 8 issues (does not include MSA membership); $45 Students 12 months subscription - retired or adjunct faculty member & students ; $65 Individuals 12 months - regular member; $60 Individuals electronic; $108 Two years electronic. **Alt. Formats:** PDF. **URL:** http://www.press.jhu.edu/journals/modernism_modernity; http://muse.jhu.edu/journals/modernism-modernity. **Ad Rates:** BW $275. **Remarks:** Accepts advertising. **Circ:** Combined 1136.

16017 ■ Molecular Cell
Cell Press
600 Technology Sq.
Cambridge, MA 02139
Phone: (617)661-7057
Fax: (617)661-7061
Free: 866-314-2355
Publication E-mail: molecule@cell.com
Peer-reviewed journal on molecular biology. **Freq:** Bimonthly. **Key Personnel:** John Pham, Editor. **ISSN:** 1097--2765 (print). **Subscription Rates:** $270 U.S. individual, print and online; $278 Canada individual, print and online; $278 U.S. and other countries individual, online only; $408 Other countries individual, print and online. **URL:** http://www.cell.com/molecular-cell/home. **Remarks:** Accepts advertising. **Circ:** (Not Reported).

16018 ■ Nature Chemical Biology
Nature Publishing Group
25 First St., Ste. 104
Cambridge, MA 02141
Phone: (617)475-9273
Fax: (646)563-7109

Circulation: ★ = AAM; △ or • = BPA; ♦ = CAC; ❑ = VAC; ⊕ = PO Statement; ‡ = Publisher's Report; Boldface figures = sworn; Light figures = estimated.

Publication E-mail: chembio@us.nature.com
Multidisciplinary journal providing an international forum for the timely publication of significant new research at the interface between chemistry and biology. **Freq:** Monthly. **Key Personnel:** Terry L. Sheppard, Editor-in-Chief. **ISSN:** 1552-4450 (print); **EISSN:** 1552-4469 (electronic). **Subscription Rates:** $175 Individuals print & online; $273 Two years print & online; $59 Individuals online only. **URL:** http://www.nature.com/nchembio/index.html. **Circ:** (Not Reported).

16019 ■ Neuron
Cell Press
600 Technology Sq.
Cambridge, MA 02139
Phone: (617)661-7057
Fax: (617)661-7061
Free: 866-314-2355
Publication E-mail: neuron@cell.com
Peer-reviewed journal encompassing all areas of neuroscience. **Freq:** Biweekly. **Print Method:** Web Press. **Trim Size:** 8.125 x 10.875. **Key Personnel:** Ben A. Barres, Board Member; David J. Anderson, Board Member; Susan K. McConnell, Board Member; Cori Bargmann, Board Member; Yasushi Miyashita, Board Member; Philippe Ascher, Board Member; Laurence F. Abbott, Board Member; Earl K. Miller, Board Member; Robert C. Malenka, Board Member. **ISSN:** 0896-6273 (print). **Subscription Rates:** $265 U.S. and other countries online only; $245 Canada online only; $257 U.S. and Canada print and online; $265 Canada print and online; $389 Other countries online and print. **URL:** http://www.cell.com/neuron/home. **Remarks:** Advertising accepted; rates available upon request. **Circ:** ‡2678.

16020 ■ Nieman Reports
Nieman Foundation for Journalism at Harvard
Harvard University
Walter Lippmann House
1 Francis Ave.
Cambridge, MA 02138
Phone: (617)495-2237
Publication E-mail: nreditor@harvard.edu nreports@harvard.edu
Trade magazine covering journalism. **Freq:** Quarterly. **Key Personnel:** James Geary, Editor. **ISSN:** 0028--9817 (print). **USPS:** 430-650. **Subscription Rates:** $25 Individuals 1 year; $40 Two years; $35 Other countries 1 year; $60 Other countries 2 years. **URL:** http://niemanreports.org/about-nieman-reports. **Remarks:** Advertising not accepted. **Circ:** Combined 5,822, 1350.

16021 ■ Nuclear Instruments and Methods in Physics Research Section A: Accelerators, Spectrometers, Detectors and Associated Equipment
RELX Group P.L.C.
c/o W. Barletta, Coordinating Editor
Massachusetts Institute of Technology
Cambridge, MA 02139
Publisher's E-mail: amsterdam@relx.com
Journal publishing articles on design, manufacturing and performance of scientific instruments with a focus on large scale facilities. **Freq:** 36/yr. **Key Personnel:** W. Barletta, Coordinator, Education Resources; R. Klanner, Editor; F. Sauli, Editor; F. Parmigiani, Editor; D. Wehe, Editor. **ISSN:** 0168--9002 (print). **Subscription Rates:** $8737.33 Institutions online; $11095 Institutions print. **URL:** http://www.journals.elsevier.com/nuclear-instruments-and-methods-in-physics-research-section-a-accelerators-spectrometers-detectors-and-associated-equipment. **Remarks:** Advertising accepted; rates available upon request. **Circ:** (Not Reported).

16022 ■ Perspective: Harvard-Radcliffe's Liberal Monthly
Perspective
PO Box 2439
Cambridge, MA 02238
Political magazine written and published by students. **Freq:** Monthly. **Trim Size:** 10 x 16. **Cols./Page:** 4. **Col. Width:** 2 1/4 inches. **Col. Depth:** 16 inches. **Key Personnel:** Dylan Matthews, Editor-in-Chief; Ian Kumekawa, Managing Editor; Lucy Caplan, Managing Editor. **URL:** http://www.perspy.com/. **Ad Rates:** BW $325. **Remarks:** Accepts advertising. **Circ:** Controlled 4000.

16023 ■ Psyche: Journal of Entomology
Cambridge Entomological Club
26 Oxford St.
Cambridge, MA 02138-2902
Publisher's E-mail: hindawi@hindawi.com
Entomology academic journal. **Freq:** Quarterly. **Print Method:** Offset. **Trim Size:** 6 x 9. **Cols./Page:** 1. **Col. Width:** 48 nonpareils. **Col. Depth:** 84 agate lines. **Key Personnel:** K Horton, Managing Editor. **ISSN:** 0033-2615 (print). **Subscription Rates:** $495. **URL:** http://www.hindawi.com/journals/psyche; http://eciton.org/pysche. **Remarks:** Advertising not accepted. **Circ:** 700.

16024 ■ Q: The Journal of Sexual Orientation and Public Policy at Harvard
John F. Kennedy School of Government Harvard University
79 John F. Kennedy St.
Cambridge, MA 02138
Phone: (617)495-1100
Publication E-mail: qjournal@ksg.harvard.edu
Journal covering sexual orientation and public policy at Harvard University. **Freq:** Annual. **Key Personnel:** Christine Connare, President, phone: (617)496-9987. **ISSN:** 1532-5385 (print). **Subscription Rates:** $15 Individuals. **URL:** http://www.hks.harvard.edu/qjournal. **Circ:** (Not Reported).

16025 ■ The Quarterly Journal of Economics
The MIT Press
Harvard University
Littauer Ctr., Rm. 227
1875 Cambridge St.
Cambridge, MA 02138
Phone: (617)496-3293
Publication E-mail: qje_admin@editorialexpress.com
Journal of analytical articles in economic theory. **Founded:** 1886. **Freq:** Quarterly February, May, August and November. **Print Method:** Offset. **Trim Size:** 6 x 9. **Cols./Page:** 1. **Key Personnel:** Trina Ott, Assistant Editor; Lawrence F. Katz, Editor; Robert J. Barro, Editor. **ISSN:** 0033-5533 (print). **Subscription Rates:** $67 Individuals print; $36 Individuals print, senior citizen and student; $675 Institutions print and online; $621 Institutions print only; $540 Institutions online; £389 Institutions print and online. **URL:** http://qje.oxfordjournals.org. **Ad Rates:** BW $400. **Remarks:** Accepts advertising. **Circ:** ‡3000.

16026 ■ Radcliffe Magazine
Harvard University Radcliffe Institute for Advanced Study
10 Garden St.
Cambridge, MA 02138
Publisher's E-mail: info@radcliffe.harvard.edu
Alumni magazine. **Freq:** Semiannual. **Print Method:** Offset. **Trim Size:** 8 1/2 x 10 7/8. **Cols./Page:** 4. **Col. Width:** 34 nonpareils. **Col. Depth:** 140 agate lines. **Key Personnel:** Pat Harrison, Editor, Manager, Periodicals, phone: (617)495-8116; Alison Franklin, Director, Communications, phone: (617)496-3078. **ISSN:** 2153--2338 (print); **EISSN:** 2153--2346 (electronic). **Alt. Formats:** PDF. **Formerly:** Radcliffe Quarterly: A Magazine of the Radcliffe Institute for Advanced Study. **Remarks:** Advertising not accepted. **Circ:** Free ‡33500.

16027 ■ Review of Economics and Statistics
The MIT Press
Harvard Kennedy School
79 JFK St., Box 134
Cambridge, MA 02138
Phone: (617)495-2111
Fax: (617)495-5147
Publication E-mail: restat@hks.harvard.edu
Economics journal. **Freq:** Quarterly. **Print Method:** Offset. **Trim Size:** 8 1/2 x 11. **Cols./Page:** 2. **Col. Width:** 36 nonpareils. **Col. Depth:** 119 agate lines. **Key Personnel:** Asim Ijaz Khwaja, Editor; Guido Kuersteiner, Associate Editor; Edward Miguel, Associate Editor; Mark W. Watson, Editor; Philippe Aghion, Editor; Christopher Carroll, Associate Editor. **ISSN:** 0034-6535 (print). **Subscription Rates:** $79 Individuals print and online; $71 Individuals online only; $646 Institutions print and online; $553 Institutions online; $42 Students print and online, retired; $39 Students online only, retired. **URL:** http://www.mitpressjournals.org/loi/rest. **Ad Rates:** BW $350. **Remarks:** Accepts advertising. **Circ:** 1400.

16028 ■ Sky & Telescope: The Essential Magazine of Astronomy
Sky Publishing Corp.
Cambridge, MA 02140
Phone: (617)864-7360
Fax: (617)864-6117
Free: 800-253-0245
Publisher's E-mail: online@skyandtelescope.com
Magazine on astronomy and space science. **Freq:** Monthly. **Print Method:** Offset. **Trim Size:** 8 3/16 x 10 7/8. **Cols./Page:** 3. **Col. Width:** 2 5/16 inches. **Col. Depth:** 9 7/8 inches. **Key Personnel:** Robert Naeye, Senior Editor; Dennis di Cicco, Senior Editor. **ISSN:** 0037-6604 (print). **Subscription Rates:** $37.95 Individuals print; $29.95 Individuals digital. **Ad Rates:** BW $5,455; 4C $7,920. **Remarks:** Accepts advertising. **Circ:** Paid ‡90055.

16029 ■ Sloan Management Review
Massachusetts Institute of Technology Department of Urban Studies and Planning Community Innovators Lab
1 Charles Pk.
EE20-600 6th Fl.
Cambridge, MA 02142
Phone: (877)727-7170
Fax: (617)258-9739
Publication E-mail: smr-help@mit.edu
Business journal highlighting trends and practical techniques for managers. **Freq:** Quarterly. **Print Method:** Offset. **Trim Size:** 8 3/8 x 10 13/16. **Cols./Page:** 2. **Col. Width:** 19.5 picas. **Col. Depth:** 125 agate lines. **Key Personnel:** Mike Barette, Contact, phone: (617)258-5661. **ISSN:** 0019-848X (print). **Subscription Rates:** $75 U.S. Digital and Print; $69 U.S. Digital Only. **URL:** http://sloanreview.mit.edu. **Ad Rates:** BW $4,481. **Remarks:** Accepts advertising. **Circ:** ‡20000.

16030 ■ Social Science History
Social Science History Association
History Faculty
Massachusetts Institute of Technology, E51-255
77 Massachusetts Ave.
Cambridge, MA 02139
Phone: (617)253-4955
Fax: (617)253-9406
Publication E-mail: socialsciencehistory@mit.edu
Journal featuring historical analysis. **Freq:** Quarterly. **Print Method:** Offset. **Trim Size:** 6 x 9. **Cols./Page:** 1. **Col. Width:** 52 nonpareils. **Col. Depth:** 86 agate lines. **Key Personnel:** Jeffrey K. Beemer, Associate Editor; Anne McCants, Editor. **ISSN:** 0145--5532 (print). **Subscription Rates:** $160 Institutions electronic; $192 Institutions print; $70 Individuals; $25 Students. **URL:** http://www.dukeupress.edu/Social-Science-History. **Ad Rates:** BW $225. **Remarks:** Accepts advertising. **Circ:** ‡1234.

16031 ■ Speculum: A Journal of Medieval Studies
Medieval Academy of America
17 Dunster St., Ste. 202
Cambridge, MA 02138
Phone: (617)491-1622
Fax: (617)492-3303
Publisher's E-mail: inf@themedievalacademy.org
Scholarly journal containing reviews and articles pertaining to all disciplines of medieval studies. **Freq:** Quarterly. **Print Method:** Offset. **Trim Size:** 6 3/4 x 10. **Cols./Page:** 1. **Col. Width:** 58 nonpareils. **Col. Depth:** 115 agate lines. **Key Personnel:** Paul E. Szarmach, Editor; Jacqueline Brown, Associate Editor. **ISSN:** 0038-7134 (print); **EISSN:** 2040-8072 (electronic). **Subscription Rates:** $254 Institutions online & print; £154 Institutions, other countries online & print; $193 Institutions online only; £117 Institutions, other countries online only. **URL:** http://www.medievalacademy.org/?page=Speculum; http://journals.cambridge.org/action/displayJournal?jid=SPC. **Ad Rates:** BW $400. **Remarks:** Color advertising not accepted. **Circ:** ‡5950, 5770.

16032 ■ The Tech
The Tech
84 Massachusetts Ave., Ste. 483
Cambridge, MA 02139-4300
Phone: (617)253-1541
Fax: (617)258-8226
Publication E-mail: general@the-tech.mit.edu
Collegiate newspaper (tabloid). **Founded:** Nov. 17, 1881. **Freq:** Semiweekly. **Print Method:** Offset. **Trim Size:** 10 x 16. **Cols./Page:** 5. **Col. Width:** 80 inches. **Key Personnel:** Jeff Guo, Editor-in-Chief; Greg Steinbrecher, Business Manager. **ISSN:** 0148-9607 (print). **Subscription Rates:** $50 Individuals; $90 Two years; $200 Other countries air mail. **URL:** http://tech.mit.edu/.

Mailing address: PO Box 397029, Cambridge, MA 02139-7029. **Ad Rates:** BW $1200. **Remarks:** tobacco. **Circ:** Combined ‡21308.

16033 ■ Technology Review
Technology Review
1 Main St., 13th Fl.
Cambridge, MA 02142
Phone: (617)253-8250
Fax: (617)258-5850
Publication E-mail: trcomments@mit.edu
Magazine reviewing new developments in technology with an emphasis on economic, political, and social implications. Not a new product publication. **Freq:** 6/year. **Print Method:** Offset. **Trim Size:** 8 x 10 3/4. **Cols./Page:** 2 and 3. **Col. Width:** 3.25 and 2.5 picas. **Col. Depth:** 9.5 picas. **Key Personnel:** John Benditt, Editor, phone: (617)258-7888, fax: (617)258-8778; R. Bruce Journey, Chief Executive Officer, Publisher, phone: (617)253-2708. **Subscription Rates:** $29.95 Individuals; $39.95 Other countries. **Alt. Formats:** Download; PDF. **URL:** http://www.technologyreview.com. **Ad Rates:** BW $20,054; 4C $26,738, 4-Color. **Remarks:** Advertising accepted; rates available upon request. **Circ:** Paid 221784.

16034 ■ Transition: An International Review
Indiana University Press
104 Mt. Auburn St., 3R
Cambridge, MA 02138
Phone: (617)496-2845
Fax: (617)496-2877
Publication E-mail: transit@fas.harvard.edu
International review of ethnicity, culture and politics. **Freq:** Triennial. **Trim Size:** 6 7/8 x 9 3/4. **Cols./Page:** 2. **Col. Width:** 2 1/2 inches. **Col. Depth:** 7 13/16 inches. **Key Personnel:** Henry Louis Gates, Jr., Publisher; Vincent Brown, Editor; Tommie Shelby, Editor. **ISSN:** 0041-1191 (print); **EISSN:** 1527-8042 (electronic). **Subscription Rates:** $39.50 Individuals print ; $43.50 Individuals print and electronic; $156.50 Institutions electronic and print; $313 Institutions 2 years; electronic and print; $35.50 Individuals electronic only; $103.50 Institutions electronic only; $115 Institutions print only. **URL:** http://www.jstor.org/action/showPublication?journalCode=transition&. **Remarks:** Accepts advertising. **Circ:** Paid 1100, Non-paid 200.

16035 ■ VooDoo Magazine: The M.I.T. Journal of Humour
VooDoo Magazine
MIT
MIT, Rm. 50-309
77 Massachusetts Ave.
Cambridge, MA 02139
Publisher's E-mail: voodoo@mit.edu
Collegiate humor magazine containing articles and comics. **Freq:** 3/yr. **Print Method:** web offset. **Trim Size:** 8 x 10 3/4. **Cols./Page:** 2. **ISSN:** 1066-2499 (print). **Subscription Rates:** $10 Individuals; $3 Single issue. **Ad Rates:** BW $600; 4C $3,000; PCI $10. **Remarks:** Accepts advertising. **Circ:** Non-paid 8000.

16036 ■ WCRI Research Briefs
Workers Compensation Research Institute
955 Massachusetts Ave.
Cambridge, MA 02139
Phone: (617)661-9274
Fax: (617)661-9284
Publisher's E-mail: wcri@wcrinet.org
Magazine concerning original research on workers' compensation. **Freq:** Monthly. **Subscription Rates:** $79 Individuals. **URL:** http://www.wcrinet.org/order_research_brief.html; http://www.wcrinet.org/order_publications.html. **Remarks:** Advertising not accepted. **Circ:** (Not Reported).

16037 ■ Women's Policy Journal of Harvard: Women's Policy Journal of Harvard
John F. Kennedy School of Government Harvard University
79 John F. Kennedy St.
Cambridge, MA 02138
Phone: (617)495-1100
Publication E-mail: wpjh@hks.harvard.edu
Journal that covers a specific subject, with an emphasis on policy making in that specific area. **Freq:** Annual. **Key Personnel:** Martha Foley, Publisher; Dr. Richard Parker, Faculty Advisor; Courtney Walsh, Editor-in-Chief. **ISSN:** 1534-0473 (print). **Subscription Rates:** $20 Individuals; $40 Institutions; $10 Students. **URL:** http://isites.harvard.edu/icb/icb.do?keyword=k74754. **Ad Rates:** BW $300. **Remarks:** Accepts advertising. **Circ:** (Not Reported).

16038 ■ WHRB-FM - 95.3
389 Harvard St.
Cambridge, MA 02138-3900
Phone: (617)495-4818
Email: mail@whrb.org
Format: Classical. **Owner:** Harvard Radio Broadcasting Inc., 389 Harvard St. , Cambridge, MA 02138-3900, Ph: (617)495-4818. **Founded:** 1939. **Operating Hours:** Continuous. **Local Programs:** *Sunday Night at the Opera*, Sunday 8:00 p.m. - 12:00 a.m.; *The Darker Side*, Saturday Monday 9:00 p.m. - 7:00 a.m. 12:00 a.m. - 5:00 a.m.; *Record Hospital*, Monday Tuesday Wednesday Thursday Friday Saturday 10:00 p.m. - 12:00 a.m. 12:00 a.m. - 5:00 a.m.; 10:00 p.m. - 12:00 a.m. 12:00 a.m. - 5:00 a.m.; *The Jazz Spectrum*, Monday Tuesday Wednesday Thursday Friday 5:00 a.m. - 1:00 p.m.; *Hillbilly at Harvard*, Saturday 9:00 a.m. - 1:00 p.m.; *Blues Hangover*, Saturday Sunday 5:00 a.m. - 9:00 a.m. 7:00 a.m. - 11:00 a.m.; *From Across the Yard*, Sunday 12:30 p.m.; *Classical Music Interlude*, Saturday Sunday Monday 1:00 p.m.; 6:00 p.m. 12:30 p.m. 7:00 p.m.; *Crimson Sportstalk*, Sunday 1:00 p.m. - 2:00 p.m. **Wattage:** 1,450 ERP. **Ad Rates:** Noncommercial. **URL:** http://www.whrb.org.

16039 ■ WJIB-AM
443 Concord Ave.
Cambridge, MA 02138
Phone: (617)868-7400
Format: Adult Contemporary. **Owner:** Bob Bittner Broadcasting, Inc., at above address. **Founded:** 1991. **Formerly:** WLVG-AM; WCAS-AM. **Key Personnel:** Bob Bittner, Gen. Mgr. **Wattage:** 250 Day; 005 Night. **URL:** http://www.wjib.org.

16040 ■ WMBR-FM - 88.1
3 Ames St.
Cambridge, MA 02142
Phone: (617)253-4000
Format: Alternative/New Music/Progressive. **Networks:** Independent. **Owner:** Technology Broadcasting Corp., Walker Memorial Bldg., 50-030 142 Memorial Dr. , Cambridge, MA 02142, Ph: (617)253-4000. **Founded:** 1961. **Formerly:** WTBS-FM. **Operating Hours:** 6 a.m.-2:30 a.m.; 95% local. **Key Personnel:** Linda Pinkow, News Dir.; Nancy Masley, Office Mgr., office-manager@wmbr.org; Ken Field, Contact. **Local Programs:** *Breakfast of Champions*, Monday Tuesday Wednesday Thursday Friday 8:00 a.m. - 10:00 a.m.; *Lost & Found*, Monday Tuesday Wednesday Thursday Friday 12:00 p.m. - 2:00 p.m.; *WMBR Nightly News*, Monday Tuesday Wednesday Thursday Friday 5:30 p.m.; *What's Left*, Friday 6:00 p.m. - 7:00 p.m.; *Nooks & Crannies*, Wednesday 11:00 p.m.; *The Show Show*, Saturday 8:00 p.m. - 10:00 p.m.; *Late Risers' Club*, Monday Tuesday Wednesday Thursday Friday 10:00 a.m. - 12:00 p.m.; *James Dean Death Car Experience*, Saturday 6:00 p.m. - 8:00 p.m. **Wattage:** 720. **Ad Rates:** Noncommercial; underwriting available. **URL:** http://www.wmbr.org.

16041 ■ WRCA-AM - 1330
552 Massachusettes Ave., Ste. 201
Cambridge, MA 02139-4088
Phone: (617)492-3300
Email: wrca1330@aol.com
Format: Ethnic; Religious. **Networks:** Independent. **Owner:** Beasley Broadcasting of Naples Florida, 3033 Riviera Dr., Ste. 200, Naples, FL 34103, Ph: (239)263-5000, Fax: (239)263-8191. **Founded:** 1948. **Formerly:** WDLW-AM. **Operating Hours:** Continuous. **Key Personnel:** Stu Fink, Mgr. **Wattage:** 5,000. **Ad Rates:** $35 for 60 seconds. **URL:** http://www.1330wrca.com.

CANTON

E. MA. Norfolk Co. 15 mi. SW of Boston. Residential.

16042 ■ Historical Journal of Film, Radio and Television
International Association for Media and History
c/o Cynthia Miller, Treasurer
484 Bolivar St.
Canton, MA 02021
Publisher's E-mail: iamhist.web@gmail.com
Journal including research articles, extensive book reviews, and a comments section. **Freq:** Quarterly. **Key Personnel:** Jo Fox, Associate Editor; Brett Bowles, Associate Editor; Roel Vande Winkel, Editor; David Culbert, Editor; Ian Jarvie, Associate Editor. **ISSN:** 0143--9685 (print); **EISSN:** 1465--3451 (electronic). **Subscription Rates:** $1622 Institutions print and online; $1419 Institutions online; $537 Individuals online. **URL:** http://iamhist.org/historical-journal-of-film-radio-television; http://www.tandfonline.com/toc/chjf20/current#.U2B-qYHWLto. **Remarks:** Accepts advertising. **Circ:** (Not Reported).

CENTERVILLE

16043 ■ Citroen Quarterly
Citroen Quarterly Car Club
PO Box 611
Centerville, MA 02632-0611
Publisher's E-mail: citroenquarterly@comcast.net
Freq: Quarterly. **Subscription Rates:** $20 /year in U.S.; $30 /year outside U.S. and Canada (airmail). **Remarks:** Accepts advertising. **Circ:** (Not Reported).

16044 ■ Citroen Quarterly Archives
Citroen Quarterly Car Club
PO Box 611
Centerville, MA 02632-0611
Publisher's E-mail: citroenquarterly@comcast.net
Journal providing technical, contemporary, historical information and insights on automobiles. **Subscription Rates:** $3.50 /issue in North America; $6 /issue outside North America. **Remarks:** Advertising not accepted. **Circ:** (Not Reported).

CHARLESTOWN

SE MA. Middlesex Co. On Boston Harbor.

16045 ■ WLLH-AM
529 Main St., Ste. 200
Charlestown, MA 02129
Owner: Mega Communications, LLC., at above address. **Founded:** 1934. **Ad Rates:** Advertising accepted; rates available upon request.

CHATHAM

SE MA. Barnstable Co. On Atlantic Ocean, 18 mi. E. of Barnstable. Resort town.

16046 ■ The Cape Cod Chronicle
Hyora Publications Inc.
60-C Munson Meeting Way
Chatham, MA 02633
Phone: (508)945-2220
Fax: (508)945-2579
Publisher's E-mail: twood@capecodchronicle.com
Community newspaper. **Freq:** Weekly (Thurs.). **Key Personnel:** Deb DeCosta, Manager, Advertising; William F. Galvin, Managing Editor; Timothy J. Wood, Editor; Henry C. Hyora, Publisher. **Remarks:** Accepts advertising. **Circ:** 10650.

CHELSEA

16047 ■ WESX-AM - 1230
90 Everett Ave.
Chelsea, MA 02150
Phone: (617)884-4500
Format: Big Band/Nostalgia; Oldies; Adult Contemporary; Talk; News; Sports. **Networks:** AP. **Owner:** Principle Broadcast Network, 90 Everett Ave., Chelsea, MA 02150-2337. **Founded:** 1939. **Operating Hours:** Controlled; 5%network, 95% local. **Key Personnel:** Angel Rivas, Dir. of Operations, Dir. of Sales; Charles Rodrigues, Gen. Mgr; Joel L. De Assis, Contact. **Local Programs:** *Show do Leandrinho*; *Radio Mania*, Monday Tuesday Wednesday Thursday Friday 9:00 a.m. - 10:00 a.m.; *Litwin Polka Variety Show*, Sunday 11:00 a.m. - 12:00 p.m.; *Community Outreach*, Sunday 7:00 a.m. - 8:00 a.m.; *A Hora do Milagre*, Monday Wednesday Friday 12:00 p.m. - 1:00 p.m. **Wattage:** 1,000. **Ad Rates:** Noncommercial. **URL:** http://www.wesx1230am.com.

16048 ■ WJDA-AM - 1300
90 Everett Ave.
Chelsea, MA 02150

Circulation: ★ = AAM; △ or • = BPA; ♦ = CAC; ❑ = VAC; ⊕ = PO Statement; ‡ = Publisher's Report; Boldface figures = sworn; Light figures = estimated.

Phone: (617)884-4500
Email: info@wjda1300.com
Format: News; Sports. **Networks:** Independent. **Owner:** North Shore Broadcasting Co., 200 E Thomas St., Hammond, LA 70401. **Founded:** 1947. **Operating Hours:** Continuous Mon-Sat.; 6 a.m.-11 p.m. Sun. **Wattage:** 1,000. **Ad Rates:** $16-24 for 30 seconds; $20-30 for 60 seconds. **URL:** http://www.wjda1300am.com.

CHESTNUT HILL

NE MA. Middlesex Co. 6 mi. SW of Boston. (Branch of Boston P.O.) Residential.

16049 ■ Boston College Law Review
Boston College
140 Commonwealth Ave.
Chestnut Hill, MA 02467
Phone: (617)552-8000
Publication E-mail: bcpubs@bc.edu
Journal covering articles relating to legal issues. **Freq:** 5/year published in January, March, May, September and November. **Key Personnel:** David A. Libardoni, Editor-in-Chief. **ISSN:** 0161-6587 (print). **Subscription Rates:** $40 Individuals; $10 Single issue. **URL:** http://www.bc.edu/schools/law/lawreviews/bclawreview.html. **Circ:** (Not Reported).

16050 ■ The Heights: The Independent Student Newspaper of Boston College
Boston College
140 Commonwealth Ave.
Chestnut Hill, MA 02467
Phone: (617)552-8000
Publication E-mail: editor@bcheights.com
Collegiate newspaper. **Freq:** Weekly (Tues.). **Print Method:** Offset. **Cols./Page:** 5. **Col. Width:** 24 nonpareils. **Col. Depth:** 196 agate lines. **Key Personnel:** Eleanor Hildebrandt, Editor-in-Chief. **Subscription Rates:** $17.99 Individuals; $54.99 Individuals semester long package. **URL:** http://bcheights.com. **Ad Rates:** PCI $13.40. **Remarks:** Accepts advertising. **Circ:** Free 10000.

16051 ■ Massachusetts Civil Service Commission Reporter
Landlaw Specialty Publishers
675 VFW Pky., No. 354
Chestnut Hill, MA 02467-3656
Fax: (617)608-2798
Free: 800-637-6330
Publisher's E-mail: contact@landlaw.com
Professional magazine covering civil service and law. **Freq:** Bimonthly. **ISSN:** 1522--6689 (print). **Subscription Rates:** $100 Individuals print or online - deluxe starter; $225 Individuals print or online - deluxe standard; $300 Individuals basic online. **URL:** http://www.landlaw.com/massachusetts-civil-service-commission-reporter.asp. **Formerly**: Massachusetts Civil Service Reporter. **Remarks:** Advertising not accepted. **Circ:** (Not Reported).

16052 ■ MCAD Reporter
Landlaw Specialty Publishers
675 VFW Pky., No. 354
Chestnut Hill, MA 02467-3656
Fax: (617)608-2798
Free: 800-637-6330
Publisher's E-mail: contact@landlaw.com
Professional magazine covering discrimination law. **Freq:** Monthly. **Print Method:** Three ring binder. **Trim Size:** 8 1/2 x 11. **ISSN:** 0199--5235 (print). **Subscription Rates:** $100 Individuals; $300 Individuals online; $225 Individuals deluxe rate. **URL:** http://www.landlaw.com/mcad-massachusetts-commission-against-discrimination-reporter.asp. **Also known as**: Massachusetts Discrimination Law Reporter. **Remarks:** Advertising not accepted. **Circ:** (Not Reported).

16053 ■ Method: Journal of Lonergan Studies
Lonergan Institute at Boston College
140 Commonwealth Ave.
Chestnut Hill, MA 02467
Phone: (617)552-8095
Publisher's E-mail: legeres@bc.edu
Scholarly journal covering the writings of Bernard Lonergan. **Freq:** Semiannual April & October. **Trim Size:** 6 x 9. **Key Personnel:** Patrick Byrne, Editor; Mark Morelli, Editor; Charles Hefling, Editor. **Subscription Rates:** $16 Individuals; $25 Institutions library. **URL:** http://bclonergan.org/publications/method-journal-of-lonergan-studies. **Remarks:** Advertising not accepted. **Circ:** Combined 500.

16054 ■ Philosophy & Social Criticism: An International, Inter-disciplinary Quarterly Journal
Boston College
140 Commonwealth Ave.
Chestnut Hill, MA 02467
Phone: (617)552-8000
International journal focusing on continental thought, American philosophy, ethics, law, hermeneutics, literary theory, cultural critique, politics, modernity and postmodernity. **Freq:** Monthly. **Key Personnel:** David M. Rasmussen, Editor. **ISSN:** 0191--4537 (print); **EISSN:** 1481--734x (electronic). **Subscription Rates:** $18 Individuals print, single issue; $137 Individuals print; $302 Institutions single, print issue; $2519 Institutions e-access; $2743 Institutions print; $2799 Institutions print and e-access. **URL:** http://psc.sagepub.com; http://us.sagepub.com/en-us/nam/journal/philosophy-social-criticism. **Remarks:** Accepts advertising. **Circ:** (Not Reported).

16055 ■ WZBC-FM - 90.3
Boston College
McElroy Commons 107
Chestnut Hill, MA 02467
Phone: (617)552-3511
Fax: (617)552-1738
Format: Educational. **Networks:** Independent. **Owner:** Boston College Board of Trustees, 140 Commonwealth Ave., Chestnut Hill, MA 02467, Ph: (617)552-4686, Fax: (617)552-1738. **Founded:** 1960. **Formerly**: WVBC-FM. **Operating Hours**: 7 a.m.-6 a.m.; 100% local. **Key Personnel:** Neil Patch, Project Mgr., wzbcmusic@gmail.com; Matt Keilson, Dir. of Programs, wzbcpd@gmail.com; Samantha Tilney, Promotions Dir., zbcpromo@gmail.com. **Wattage:** 1,000. **Ad Rates:** Noncommercial. **URL:** http://www.bc.edu/bc_org/svp/st_org/wzbc.

CHICOPEE

SW MA. Hampden Co. 4 mi. S. of Holyoke. Residential.

16056 ■ National Engineer: Magazine of the National Association of Power Engineers
National Association of Power Engineers
1 Springfield St.
Chicopee, MA 01013
Phone: (413)592-6273
Fax: (413)592-1998
Publisher's E-mail: nape@powerengineers.com
Magazine featuring information on new technology, repairs and maintenance, education, news and safety tips. **Freq:** Bimonthly. **Print Method:** Offset. **Trim Size:** 8 1/2 x 11. **Cols./Page:** 3. **Col. Width:** 26 nonpareils. **Col. Depth:** 140 agate lines. **Key Personnel:** Barry Battista, Committee Chairman. **ISSN:** 0027--9218 (print). **Subscription Rates:** Included in membership. **URL:** http://www.powerengineers.com/Membership. **Ad Rates:** BW $787; 4C $1312; PCI $50. **Remarks:** Accepts advertising. **Circ:** Paid ‡5422, Controlled ‡56.

16057 ■ WWLP-TV - 22
1 Broadcast Ctr.
Chicopee, MA 01013
Phone: (413)377-2200
Format: Commercial TV. **Networks:** NBC. **Operating Hours**: 6 a.m.-1:30 a.m. **ADI**: Springfield, MA. **Key Personnel:** Amy Phillips, Producer. **URL:** http://wwlp.com.

CLINTON

C. MA. Worcester Co. On Nashua River, 12 mi. N. of Worchester. Manufactures flashlights, metal, concrete and wire goods, dyestuffs, chemicals, plastics, cereals, books, carpets, looms, furniture, radiators, luminous signs. Fruit, dairy, poultry farms. Apples, peaches.

16058 ■ The Item
The Coulter Press
156 Church St.
Clinton, MA 01510
Phone: (978)368-0176
Fax: (978)368-1151
Publisher's E-mail: info@telegram.com
General newspaper. **Founded:** 1893. **Freq:** Biweekly. **Print Method:** Offset. **Trim Size:** 11.625″ x 21 1/2″. **Cols./Page:** 6. **Col. Width:** 25 nonpareils. **Col. Depth:** 300 agate lines. **Key Personnel:** Gary Hutner, Publisher; Jan Gottesman, Editor. **USPS:** 118-580. **Subscription Rates:** $29 Individuals; $39 Out of state. **URL:** http://www.telegram.com/section/coulter/. **Ad Rates:** BW $1,046; PCI $9.40. **Remarks:** Accepts advertising. **Circ:** ‡5700.

CONCORD

NE MA. Middlesex Co. On Concord River, 20 mi. NW of Boston. Rich in historical and literary interest. Dairy, poultry, truck and fruit farms.

16059 ■ About Action Unlimited
Action Unlimited
100-1 Domino Dr.
Concord, MA 01742
Phone: (978)371-2442
Fax: (978)287-5046
Publisher's E-mail: ads@actionunlimited.com
Community newspaper. **Freq:** Weekly. **Print Method:** Offset. **Trim Size:** 7.375 X 10. **Cols./Page:** 4. **Col. Depth:** 10 INS. **Key Personnel:** Carol Margraf Toomey, Publisher; Joe Toomey, Manager, Circulation; Pam Kaplan, Director, Advertising. **Subscription Rates:** Free. **URL:** http://www.actionunlimited.com. **Remarks:** Accepts advertising. **Circ:** (Not Reported).

16060 ■ Burlington Union
GateHouse Media Inc.
PO Box 9191
Concord, MA 01742
Publication E-mail: burlington@wickedlocal.com
Community newspaper. **Freq:** Weekly (Thurs.). **Print Method:** Offset. **Cols./Page:** 9. **Col. Width:** 21 nonpareils. **Col. Depth:** 294 agate lines. **Key Personnel:** Chuck Goodrich, Publisher; Kathleen Cordeiro, Editor-in-Chief, phone: (978)371-5736. **URL:** http://burlington.wickedlocal.com. **Ad Rates:** GLR $.32. **Circ:** (Not Reported).

16061 ■ Chelmsford Independent
GateHouse Media Inc.
150 Baker Ave. Ext., Ste. 101
Concord, MA 01742
Phone: (978)256-7196
Fax: (978)371-5212
Publication E-mail: chelmsford@cnc.com
Community newspaper. **Freq:** Weekly (Thurs.). **Print Method:** Offset. **Cols./Page:** 7. **Col. Width:** 28 nonpareils. **Col. Depth:** 196 agate lines. **Key Personnel:** Steve Tobey, Editor, phone: (978)371-5741; Jesse Floyd, Editor, phone: (978)371-5751; Chuck Goodrich, Publisher. **USPS:** 677-030. **Subscription Rates:** $65 Individuals; $85 Out of area. **URL:** http://chelmsford.wickedlocal.com. **Mailing address:** PO Box 9191, Concord, MA 01742. **Ad Rates:** PCI $7.80. **Remarks:** Accepts advertising. **Circ:** (Not Reported).

16062 ■ Concord Journal
GateHouse Media Inc.
150 Baker Ave. Ext., Ste. 305
Concord, MA 01742
Phone: (508)369-2800
Community newspaper. **Freq:** Weekly (Thurs.). **Print Method:** Offset. **Cols./Page:** 6. **Col. Width:** 20 nonpareils. **Col. Depth:** 294 agate lines. **Key Personnel:** Cheryl Lecesse, Editor, phone: (978)371-5742; Steve Tobey, Editor, phone: (978)371-5741; Chuck Goodrich, Publisher. **USPS:** 127-760. **Subscription Rates:** $77 Individuals; $85 Out of country. **URL:** http://concord.wickedlocal.com. **Mailing address:** PO Box 9191, Concord, MA 01742. **Ad Rates:** PCI $12.50. **Remarks:** Accepts advertising. **Circ:** (Not Reported).

16063 ■ Lincoln Journal
GateHouse Media Inc.
150 Baker Ave. Ext., Ste. 101
Concord, MA 01742
Community newspaper. **Founded:** 1965. **Freq:** Weekly (Thurs.). **Print Method:** Offset. **Cols./Page:** 6. **Col. Width:** 20 nonpareils. **Col. Depth:** 294 agate lines. **Key Personnel:** Chuck Goodrich, Publisher; Stephen Tobey, Editor, phone: (978)371-5741. **USPS:** 000-076. **Subscription Rates:** $69 Individuals; $85 Out of area. **URL:** http://lincoln.wickedlocal.com. **Ad Rates:** PCI $12.50. **Remarks:** Accepts advertising. **Circ:** (Not Reported).

16064 ■ Littleton Independent
GateHouse Media Inc.

150 Baker Ave. Ext., Ste. 101
Concord, MA 01742
Phone: (978)952-6106
Community newspaper. **Founded:** 1960. **Freq:** Weekly (Thurs.). **Print Method:** Offset. **Cols./Page:** 6. **Col. Width:** 20 nonpareils. **Col. Depth:** 294 agate lines. **Key Personnel:** Nathan Lamb, Editor, phone: (978)371-5759; Chuck Goodrich, Publisher; Steve Tobey, Editor, phone: (978)371-5471. **USPS:** 315-800. **Subscription Rates:** $68 Individuals; $85 Out of area. **URL:** http://littleton.wickedlocal.com. **Ad Rates:** BW $786; 4C $1186; SAU $7.80; PCI $7. **Circ:** (Not Reported).

16065 ■ Maynard Beacon
GateHouse Media Inc.
150 Baker Ave. Ext., Ste. 101
Concord, MA 01742
Phone: (978)897-7535
Fax: (978)371-5220
Community newspaper. **Freq:** Weekly (Thurs.). **Print Method:** Offset. **Cols./Page:** 6. **Col. Width:** 20 nonpareils. **Col. Depth:** 294 agate lines. **Key Personnel:** Doug Hastings, Editor, phone: (781)674-7724; Chuck Goodrich, Publisher. **USPS:** 006-152. **Subscription Rates:** $59 Out of area. **URL:** http://maynard.wickedlocal.com. **Mailing address:** PO Box 9191, Concord, MA 01742. **Ad Rates:** BW $2000; 4C $2400; SAU $16.70; PCI $16.70. **Remarks:** Accepts advertising. **Circ:** (Not Reported).

16066 ■ Vibration Magazine
World Wide Essence Society
PO Box 285
Concord, MA 01742
Phone: (978)369-8454
Publisher's E-mail: wwes@essences.com
Freq: Quarterly. **Subscription Rates:** Free. **URL:** http://www.essences.com/vibration/about.html. **Remarks:** Advertising not accepted. **Circ:** (Not Reported).

16067 ■ WIQH-FM - 88.3
500 Walden St.
Concord, MA 01742
Phone: (978)369-2440
Email: wiqh@colonial.net
Format: Album-Oriented Rock (AOR); Alternative/New Music/Progressive; Jazz. **Owner:** Concord-Carlisle Regional School District, 500 Walden St., Concord, MA 01742, Ph: (978)318-1400. **Founded:** 1971. **Operating Hours:** 1 p.m.-10 p.m. **Key Personnel:** Ned Roos, Station Mgr. **Wattage:** 100. **Ad Rates:** Noncommercial. **URL:** http://www.wiqh.org.

CUMMAQUID

16068 ■ Edible Cape Cod
Edible Communities Inc.
PO Box 515
Cummaquid, MA 02637
Phone: (508)375-9883
Publication E-mail: info@ediblecapecod.com
Magazine focusing on the local food of Cape Cod. **Freq:** Quarterly. **Key Personnel:** Tracy Anderson, Contact; Dianne Langland, Editor. **Subscription Rates:** $32 Individuals. **URL:** http://ediblecapecod.com. **Ad Rates:** BW $1600. **Remarks:** Accepts advertising. **Circ:** (Not Reported).

16069 ■ The International Educator: Official Publication of the International Educator's Institute
TIE - The International Educator
PO Box 513
Cummaquid, MA 02637-0513
Free: 877-375-6668
Publication E-mail: tie@tieonline.com
Newspaper reporting job listings from schools around the world. Includes information on salary, benefits, terms and conditions of employment, and application instructions also news on global education and general education information. **Freq:** 5/year. **Print Method:** Web-set. **Trim Size:** 10.75 x 13.75. **Cols./Page:** 5. **Col. Width:** 2 inches. **Col. Depth:** 16 inches. **Key Personnel:** Daniel Lincoln, Editor; Julianne Thrasher, Director. **ISSN:** 1044--3509 (print). **Subscription Rates:** $49 U.S. and Canada print and online; $59 Other countries print and online. **URL:** http://www.tieonline.com. **Ad Rates:** BW $3280; 4C $3906. **Remarks:** Accepts advertising. **Circ:** 14000.

DANVERS

NE MA. Essex Co. 3 mi. N. of Peabody. Residential.

16070 ■ Danvers Herald
GateHouse Media Inc.
75 Sylvan St., C 105
Danvers, MA 01923
Phone: (978)774-0505
Fax: (978)739-8501
Publication E-mail: danvers@wickedlocal.com
Community newspaper (tabloid). **Freq:** Weekly (Thurs.). **Print Method:** Offset. **Trim Size:** 11 3/8 x 17. **Cols./Page:** 5. **Col. Width:** 2 1/16 inches. **Col. Depth:** 16 inches. **Key Personnel:** Pete Chianca, Editor-in-Chief. **Subscription Rates:** $22.95 Individuals. **URL:** http://danvers.wickedlocal.com. **Ad Rates:** BW $644; SAU $8.05. **Remarks:** Accepts advertising. **Circ:** (Not Reported).

16071 ■ Melrose Free Press
GateHouse Media Inc.
75 Sylvan St., C 105,
Danvers, MA 01923
Phone: (978)739-1314
Fax: (978)739-8501
Publication E-mail: melrose@wickedlocal.com
Community newspaper (tabloid). **Founded:** 1901. **Freq:** Weekly (Thurs.). **Print Method:** Offset. **Trim Size:** 14 x 22 3/4. **Cols./Page:** 6. **Col. Width:** 2 inches. **Col. Depth:** 21 inches. **Key Personnel:** Chris Hurley, Editor, phone: (978)739-8515; Peter Chianca, Editor-in-Chief, phone: (978)739-1346. **USPS:** 338-340. **Subscription Rates:** $59 Individuals; $85 Out of area. **URL:** http://melrose.wickedlocal.com. **Formerly:** Melrose Observer; Prime Times. **Ad Rates:** BW $644; PCI $8.05. **Remarks:** Accepts classified advertising. **Circ:** (Not Reported).

16072 ■ North of Boston
GateHouse Media Inc.
75 Sylvan St., C 105
Danvers, MA 01923
Publication E-mail: northshore@wickedlocal.com
Community newspaper (tabloid). **Freq:** Weekly (Sun.). **Print Method:** Offset. **Trim Size:** 11 3/8 x 17. **Cols./Page:** 5. **Col. Width:** 2 1/16 inches. **Col. Depth:** 16 inches. **Key Personnel:** Peter Chianca, Editor-in-Chief; Charles F. Goodrich, Publisher. **Subscription Rates:** Free. **URL:** http://northofboston.wickedlocal.com. **Ad Rates:** GLR $1.59; BW $2,232; SAU $27.90. **Remarks:** Accepts advertising. **Circ:** (Not Reported).

16073 ■ Nova Review
Nova Media Inc.
222 Rosewood Dr.
Danvers, MA 01923-4520
Phone: (978)750-8400
Publication E-mail: trund@netonecom.net
Journal publishing social issue and political criticism, art and health issues especially regarding drug culture plus rehabilitation techniques. Ebooks available for down loading on site. **Key Personnel:** Thomas J. Rundquist, Editor. **ISSN:** 1079--8374 (print). **URL:** http://www.novamediainc.com. **Ad Rates:** BW $150; 4C $200; SAU $10; CNU $10; PCI $10. **Remarks:** Accepts advertising. **Circ:** Non-paid 20000.

16074 ■ Saugus Advertiser
GateHouse Media Inc.
75 Sylvan St., C 105
Danvers, MA 01923
Phone: (978)739-1395
Fax: (978)739-8501
Publication E-mail: saugus@wickedlocal.com
Community newspaper. **Freq:** Weekly. **Print Method:** Offset. **Trim Size:** 14 x 22 3/4. **Cols./Page:** 6. **Col. Width:** 2 inches. **Col. Depth:** 21 inches. **Key Personnel:** David Winder, Manager, Production, phone: (978)739-1371; Joe McConnell, Editor, phone: (978)739-1324. **USPS:** 609-400. **Subscription Rates:** $85 Individuals 1 year. **URL:** http://saugus.wickedlocal.com; http://saugusadvertiser.mypapertoday.com/in-town/#top. **Ad Rates:** BW $1,544; 4C $2,044; SAU $12.25; PCI $12.25. **Remarks:** Accepts classified advertising. **Circ:** (Not Reported).

16075 ■ Scleroderma Voice
Scleroderma Foundation
300 Rosewood Dr., Ste. 105
Danvers, MA 01923
Phone: (978)463-5843
Fax: (978)463-5809
Free: 800-722-4673
Publisher's E-mail: sfinfo@scleroderma.org
Freq: Quarterly. **Subscription Rates:** Included in membership. **URL:** http://www.scleroderma.org/site/PageServer?pagename=patients_voice#.Vujd3NKrSig. **Remarks:** Advertising not accepted. **Circ:** (Not Reported).

16076 ■ Tri-Town Transcript
GateHouse Media Inc.
75 Sylvan St., Ste. C 105
Danvers, MA 01923
Phone: (978)739-1393
Fax: (978)739-8501
Community newspaper (tabloid). **Founded:** 1960. **Freq:** Weekly (Thurs.). **Print Method:** Offset. Uses mats. **Trim Size:** 11 3/8 x 17. **Cols./Page:** 5. **Col. Width:** 2 1/16 inches. **Col. Depth:** 16 inches. **Key Personnel:** Kathryn O'Brien, Editor, phone: (978)739-1393; Chuck Goodrich, Publisher. **USPS:** 311-430. **Subscription Rates:** $85 Out of state; $61 Individuals local. **URL:** http://media.wickedlocal.com/interactive/circ/boxford.html. **Ad Rates:** BW $644; SAU $8.05; PCI $8.05. **Remarks:** Accepts advertising. **Circ:** (Not Reported).

DARTMOUTH

16077 ■ ADVANCE for Physician Assistants
Association of Family Practice Physician Assistants
77 Wollcott Ave.
Dartmouth, MA 02747
Phone: (774)206-6774
Fax: (508)998-6001
Publisher's E-mail: info@afppa.org
Targets practicing physician assistants and physician assistant students with senior status. **Freq:** Monthly. **Print Method:** Web Offset. **Trim Size:** 8 3/8 x 10 7/8. **Cols./Page:** 3. **Col. Width:** 2 3/16 inches. **Col. Depth:** 9 1/2 inches. **Key Personnel:** Jennifer Ford, Associate Editor; Michael Gerchufsky, Editor; Maryann Kurkowski, Manager, Circulation, Manager, Subscriptions; Terri Castrinoes, Assistant Manager; Maria Senior, Exhibition Manager. **ISSN:** 1096--6315 (print). **Subscription Rates:** Free for members. **Remarks:** Accepts advertising. **Circ:** (Not Reported).

DEDHAM

E. MA. Norfolk Co. On Charles River, 9 mi. SW of Boston. Residential. Manufactures control mechanisms, greeting cards, corrugated boxes.

16078 ■ The Dedham Times
The Dedham Times
395 Washington St.
Dedham, MA 02026
Phone: (781)329-5553
Fax: (781)329-8291
Publisher's E-mail: dtimes@rcn.com
Community newspaper. **Freq:** Weekly (Fri.). **Trim Size:** 11 1/4 x 17. **Cols./Page:** 5. **Col. Width:** 1 7/8 inches. **Key Personnel:** James E. Heald, General Manager. **Subscription Rates:** $34 Individuals; $40 Out of area. **URL:** http://www.dedhamtimes.com. **Ad Rates:** BW $375; 4C $485; PCI $10. **Remarks:** Advertising accepted; rates available upon request. **Circ:** Paid 3000.

16079 ■ Journal of Unitarian Universalist History
Unitarian Universalist History and Heritage Society
70 High St.
Dedham, MA 02026
Publisher's E-mail: membership@uuhhs.org
Freq: Annual. **Subscription Rates:** Included in membership; $15 others. **URL:** http://uuhhs.org/journal-of-uu-history. **Remarks:** Advertising not accepted. **Circ:** 500.

16080 ■ WFXT-TV - 25
25 Fox Dr.
Dedham, MA 02027-9125
Phone: (781)467-2525
Fax: (781)467-7212
Format: Commercial TV. **Networks:** Fox. **Owner:** Fox Broadcasting Co., PO Box 900, Beverly Hills, CA 90213. **Founded:** Oct. 10, 1977. **Formerly:** WXNE-TV. **Operating Hours:** Continuous; 21% network, 79% local. **ADI:** Boston-Worcester,MA-Derry-Manchester,NH. **Key**

Circulation: ★ = AAM; △ or • = BPA; ♦ = CAC; ❑ = VAC; ⊕ = PO Statement; ‡ = Publisher's Report; Boldface figures = sworn; Light figures = estimated.

Personnel: Debby Pellerin, Dir. of Traffic; Bill Holbrook, VP of Engg. **Local Programs**: *Fox 25 News*, Monday Tuesday Wednesday Thursday Friday Saturday. **Ad Rates:** Advertising accepted; rates available upon request. **URL:** http://www.myfoxboston.com.

DEVENS

16081 ■ The Public Spirit
Nashoba Publications Inc.
78 Barnum Rd.
Devens, MA 01434
Phone: (978)772-0777
Fax: (978)772-4012
Community newspaper. **Founded:** 1869. **Freq:** Weekly (Wed.). **Print Method:** Offset. **Cols./Page:** 8. **Col. Width:** 24 nonpareils. **Col. Depth:** 294 agate lines. **Key Personnel:** Bill Walker, Director, Operations; Kate Walsh, Managing Editor; Ken Blanchette, Editor. **Subscription Rates:** $30.54 Individuals; $51.08 Two years; $32.50 Out of state. **URL:** http://www.nashobapublishing.com/ayer. **Ad Rates:** GLR $.267. **Remarks:** Accepts classified advertising. **Circ:** 12,000.

DORCHESTER

SE MA. Suffolk Co. Ward of city of Boston.

16082 ■ AIRSPACE
Association of Independents in Radio
1452 Dorchester Ave., 2nd Fl.
Dorchester, MA 02122
Phone: (617)825-4400
Fax: (617)825-4422
Publisher's E-mail: join@airmedia.org
Journal featuring information about radio movement. **Freq:** Quarterly. **Key Personnel:** Samantha Schongalla, Manager. **Subscription Rates:** free for members. **Remarks:** Accepts advertising. **Circ:** (Not Reported).

DUDLEY

16083 ■ WNRC-FM - 97.5
124 Center Rd.
Dudley, MA 01571
Phone: (508)213-1560
Free: 800-470-3379
Email: helpdesk@nichols.edu
Format: Eclectic. **Ad Rates:** Noncommercial. **URL:** http://www.nichols.edu.

DUXBURY

SE MA. Plymouth Co. On Duxbury Bay, 30 mi. SE of Boston. Residential.

16084 ■ Duxbury Clipper
Duxbury Clipper
11 S Station St.
Duxbury, MA 02331
Phone: (781)934-2811
Publisher's E-mail: editor@duxburyclipper.com
Community newspaper (tabloid). **Freq:** Weekly. **Print Method:** Offset. **Trim Size:** 11 1/2 x 17. **Cols./Page:** 5. **Col. Width:** 1.9 inches. **Col. Depth:** 15 1/2 inches. **Key Personnel:** Gillian Smith, Editor. **USPS:** 163-260. **Subscription Rates:** $42 Individuals Duxbury only including web access; $74 Two years Duxbury only including web access; $35 Individuals senior citizens; Duxbury only including web access; $80 Out of area. **URL:** http://www.duxburyclipper.com. **Remarks:** Accepts advertising. **Circ:** Paid ‡4400.

EAST LONGMEADOW

SW MA. Hampden Co. 12 mi. S. of Westfield. Residential.

16085 ■ The Reminder
Journal/Express Inc.
280 North Main St.
East Longmeadow, MA 01028
Shopper. **Founded:** 1940. **Freq:** Weekly (Tues.). **Print Method:** Offset. **Trim Size:** 10.194" x 13". **Cols./Page:** 6. **Col. Width:** 12 picas. **Col. Depth:** 294 agate lines. **Key Personnel:** Chris Maza, Assistant Managing Editor. **URL:** http://www.thereminder.com/. **Ad Rates:** PCI $6.75. **Remarks:** Accepts advertising. **Circ:** Combined ‡45300.

16086 ■ The Reminder
The Reminder
280 N Main St.
East Longmeadow, MA 01028
Publication E-mail: online@ffdailyreminder.com
Newspaper (tabloid). **Founded:** 1946. **Freq:** Daily (eve.) not on Sat. and Sun. **Subscription Rates:** $350 By mail plus GST; $250 By mail plus GST; $400 Other countries by mail + GST. **URL:** http://www.thereminder.com. **Ad Rates:** GLR $.56; BW $401.63; 4C $861.63. **Remarks:** Accepts advertising. **Circ:** Paid 3800.

16087 ■ WAQY-FM - 102.1
45 Fisher Ave.
East Longmeadow, MA 01028
Phone: (413)525-4141
Fax: (413)525-4334
Format: Classic Rock. **Simulcasts:** WAQY-FM. **Owner:** Saga Communications Inc., at above address. **Founded:** 1947. **Formerly**: WIXY-AM. **Operating Hours**: Sunrise-sunset. **Key Personnel:** Rob Cressman, Dir. of Programs, rcressman@lazer993.com; Alex Byrne, Contact, Mgr., Sales Mgr., alex@springfieldrocks.com; Alex Byrne, Contact, alex@springfieldrocks.com. **Wattage**: 2,500. **Ad Rates:** Advertising accepted; rates available upon request. **URL:** http://www.rock102.com.

16088 ■ WKFM-FM - 104.7
PO Box 187
East Longmeadow, MA 01028-0187
Phone: (413)487-1500
Format: Classic Rock. **Networks:** Independent. **Owner:** WKFM on Syracuse, Inc., at above address. **Founded:** 1961. **Operating Hours**: Continuous; 100% local. **ADI**: Syracuse, NY. **Key Personnel:** Eric Mastel, Gen. Sales Mgr.; Brian Illes, Dir. of Programs; Lois Burns, News Dir; Jay Sterin, Contact. **Wattage**: 50,000.

16089 ■ WLZX-FM - 99.3
45 Fisher Ave.
East Longmeadow, MA 01028
Format: Album-Oriented Rock (AOR); Classic Rock. **Owner:** Saga Communications Inc., at above address. **Operating Hours**: Continuous. **Key Personnel:** Pat Kelly, Contact, pat@lazer993.com. **Ad Rates:** Advertising accepted; rates available upon request. **URL:** http://www.lazer993.com.

EAST SANDWICH

16090 ■ WSDH-FM - 91.5
365 Quaker Meetinghouse Rd., Ste. A
East Sandwich, MA 02537
Phone: (508)888-1054
Fax: (508)833-8023
Owner: Sandwich Public Schools, at above address. **Founded:** 1977. **Wattage**: 310 ERP. **Ad Rates:** Accepts Advertising. **URL:** http://www.sandwich.k12.ma.us/.

EASTHAM

16091 ■ Wreck & Rescue
U.S. Life-Saving Service Heritage Association
PO Box 1031
Eastham, MA 02642
Free: 844-875-7742
Publisher's E-mail: info@uslife-savingservice.org
Freq: Quarterly Winter, Spring, Summer, Fall. **Subscription Rates:** Included in membership. **URL:** http://uslife-savingservice.org/publications/wreck-and-rescue. **Remarks:** Advertising not accepted. **Circ:** (Not Reported).

EASTHAMPTON

SE MA. Hampshire Co. 12 mi. NNW of Springfield.

16092 ■ Edible Pioneer Valley
Edible Communities Inc.
19 Hill Ave.
Easthampton, MA 01027
Phone: (413)203-1739
Free: 866-373-4299
Publication E-mail: info@ediblepioneervalley.com
Magazine featuring the local food of Pioneer Valley region. **Freq:** Quarterly. **Trim Size:** 7.5 x 9.5. **Subscription Rates:** $28 Individuals; $52 Two years. **URL:** http://ediblepioneervalley.com. **Ad Rates:** 4C $1900. **Remarks:** Accepts advertising. **Circ:** (Not Reported).

EDGARTOWN

SE MA. Dukes Co. On E. shore of Martha's Vineyard Island. Ferry connections with Woods Hole via Vineyard Haven. Summer resort. Shell fisheries, deep water fishing industry.

16093 ■ Martha's Vineyard Magazine
Martha's Vineyard Magazine
34 S Summer St.
Edgartown, MA 02539
Phone: (508)627-4311
Fax: (508)627-7444
Free: 877-850-0409
Publisher's E-mail: info@mvmagazine.com
Magazine covering the history, art, poetry, lifestyles, and culture of Martha's Vineyard. **Freq:** 7/year. **Print Method:** Web offset. **Trim Size:** 8 1/8 x 10 7/8. **Cols./Page:** 3. **Col. Width:** 2 1/4 inches. **Col. Depth:** 9 5/16 inches. **Key Personnel:** Nicole M. Miller, Editor; Joe Pitt, General Manager. **ISSN:** 1052-5785 (print). **Subscription Rates:** $17.95 Individuals; $33.50 Two years; $49.95 Individuals 3 years; $32.95 Other countries 1 year; $63.50 Other countries 2 years; $94.95 Other countries 3 years. **URL:** http://www.mvmagazine.com. **Mailing address:** PO Box 66, Edgartown, MA 02539. **Ad Rates:** BW $2,590; 4C $2,590. **Remarks:** Accepts advertising. **Circ:** Paid ■ **3408**, Non-paid ■ **593**.

16094 ■ Vineyard Gazette
Vineyard Gazette Inc.
34 S Summer St.
Edgartown, MA 02539
Phone: (508)627-4311
Fax: (508)627-7444
Free: 877-850-0409
Publication E-mail: news@mvgazette.con
Resort and local newspaper. **Freq:** Tues. & Fri. (summers only), plus Friday yr.-round. **Print Method:** Offset. **Cols./Page:** 7. **Col. Width:** 26 nonpareils. **Col. Depth:** 294 agate lines. **USPS:** 659-940. **Subscription Rates:** $41 Individuals; $74 Two years; $53 Elsewhere; $98 Elsewhere 2 years; $385 Other countries USA; $29.99 Individuals online only. **URL:** http://vineyardgazette.com. **Mailing address:** PO Box 66, Edgartown, MA 02539. **Ad Rates:** BW $3,124; PCI $23.80. **Remarks:** Accepts advertising. **Circ:** 13500.

FAIRHAVEN

16095 ■ WBSM-AM - 1420
22 Sconticut Neck Rd.
Fairhaven, MA 02719
Phone: (508)996-0500
Format: Talk; News; Sports. **Networks:** CBS; AP. **Owner:** Citadel Broadcasting Corp., 7201 W Lake Mead Blvd., Ste. 400, Las Vegas, NV 89128-8366, Ph: (702)804-5200, Fax: (702)804-8250. **Founded:** 1949. **Operating Hours**: Continuous; 20% network, 80% local. **Key Personnel:** Mark Stachowski, Mgr., mark.stachowski@townsquaremedia.com; Michael Rock, Dir. of Sales, michael.rock@townsquaremedia.com. **Local Programs**: *Spooky SouthCoast*, Saturday 10:00 p.m. - 12:00 a.m.; *Scott Reiniche*; *Ken Pittman*; *Phil Paleologos*, Monday Tuesday Wednesday Thursday Friday 6:00 a.m. - 10:00 a.m.; *Pete Braley in the Morning*, Monday Tuesday Wednesday Thursday Friday 6:00 a.m. - 10:00 a.m.; *Secrets To Healthy Living*, Sunday 9:00 a.m. - 10:00 a.m. **Wattage**: 5,000 Day; 1,000 Night. **Ad Rates:** $24-30 for 30 seconds; $24-45 for 60 seconds. **URL:** http://www.wbsm.com.

16096 ■ WFHN-FM - 107
22 Sconticut Neck Rd.
Fairhaven, MA 02719
Phone: (508)999-6690
Fax: (508)999-1420
Format: Contemporary Hit Radio (CHR); Top 40. **Networks:** Independent. **Owner:** Citadel Communications Corp., San Diego, CA, Ph: (505)767-6700, Fax: (505)767-6767. **Founded:** 1989. **Operating Hours**: Continuous; 100% local. **Key Personnel:** Mark Stachowski, Mgr., mark.stachowski@townsquaremedia.com; Michael Rock, Music Dir.; Deborah Soares, Promotions Dir.; Colleen Jackson, Traffic Mgr. **Wattage**: 3,000. **Ad Rates:** $26-43 for 30 seconds; $32-48 for 60 seconds. **URL:** http://www.fun107.com.

FALL RIVER

SE MA. Bristol Co. On Tauton River, at mouth of Mount Hope Bay, 18 mi. SE of Providence, RI. Foreign and domestic trade. Manufactures cotton goods, thread and yarns, rayon and silk products, textiles, lighting fixtures curtains, rubber and latex products, paper boxes, plastics, textile machinery, luggage, rope and cord, leather belting, fiberglass boats. Cotton, cloth bleaching plants.

16097 ■ The Anchor
Diocese of Fall River
887 Highland Ave.
Fall River, MA 02720
Phone: (508)675-7151
Fax: (508)675-7048
Publisher's E-mail: info@fallriverdiocese.org
Catholic newspaper (tabloid). **Founded:** Apr. 11, 1957. **Freq:** Weekly (Fri.). **Print Method:** Offset. **Cols./Page:** 5. **Col. Width:** 22 nonpareils. **Col. Depth:** 204 agate lines. **Key Personnel:** David B. Jolivet, Editor. **USPS:** 545-020. **URL:** http://www.anchornews.org. **Mailing address:** PO Box 7, Fall River, MA 02720. **Ad Rates:** GLR $.85; BW $500; 4C $1,000; PCI $17.50. **Remarks:** Accepts advertising. **Circ:** Paid 27000.

16098 ■ O'Jornal
GateHouse Media Inc.
10 Purchase St.
Fall River, MA 02720
Phone: (508)678-3844
Bilingual newspaper covering news and events relevant to the Portuguese and Brazilian communities in Southern New England. **Freq:** Weekly (Fri.). **Key Personnel:** Ric Oliviera, Publisher. **Subscription Rates:** Free. **URL:** http://ojornal.com. **Remarks:** Accepts advertising. **Circ:** Non-paid ♦**9913**.

16099 ■ WHTB-AM - 1400
456 Rock St.
Fall River, MA 02722
Phone: (508)678-9727
Fax: (508)673-0310
Owner: SNE Broadcasting Ltd., 10 N Main St., Fall River, MA 02720-2120. **Founded:** 1948. **Formerly:** WALE-AM. **Wattage:** 1,000. **Ad Rates:** Advertising accepted; rates available upon request.

FALMOUTH

E. MA. Barnstable Co. On sea coast, 39 mi. SE of New Bedford. Resort. Marine Biological Laboratory and Oceanographic Institution. Commercial fisheries. Agriculture. Strawberries, cranberries.

16100 ■ The Bourne Enterprise
Falmouth Publishing Co.
50 Depot Ave.
Falmouth, MA 02540
Phone: (508)548-4700
Fax: (508)540-8407
Free: 800-286-7744
Local newspaper. **Freq:** Weekly. **Print Method:** Offset. **Trim Size:** 14 x 23. **Cols./Page:** 6. **Col. Width:** 21 nonpareils. **Col. Depth:** 294 agate lines. **Key Personnel:** John Paradise, Managing Editor; Dan Crowley, Director, Sports. **Subscription Rates:** $33 Individuals; $40 Out of area; $60.50 Two years; $75 Two years Out of county mail. **URL:** http://www.capenews.net/bourne. **Ad Rates:** BW $1,169; SAU $7.25; PCI $7.25. **Remarks:** Accepts advertising. **Circ:** (Not Reported).

16101 ■ Enterprise Newspapers
Falmouth Publishing Co.
50 Depot Ave.
Falmouth, MA 02540
Phone: (508)548-4700
Fax: (508)540-8407
Free: 800-286-7744
Community newspaper. **Freq:** Weekly (Fri.). **Print Method:** Offset. **Cols./Page:** 6. **Col. Depth:** 21 inches. **Key Personnel:** Bill Hough, Editor; John R. Paradise, Managing Editor. **ISSN:** 0747-0142 (print). **Subscription Rates:** $44 Individuals 1 year; in-county; print & online; $60 Individuals 1 year; out of county; print & online; $80 Individuals 2 years; in-county; print & online; $110 Individuals 2 years; out of county; print & online. **Formerly:** Arts and Entertainment Tourist Guide. **Ad Rates:** BW $576; 4C $856; SAU $11.85; PCI $10.59. **Remarks:** Accepts advertising. **Circ:** Combined ■ **70928**.

FEEDING HILLS

16102 ■ Southwick Suffield News
Turley Publications
23 Southwick St.
Feeding Hills, MA 01030
Phone: (413)786-7747
Fax: (413)786-8457
Publisher's E-mail: support@turley.com
Community newspaper serving townspeople of Southwick and Suffield. **Freq:** Weekly (Fri.). **Key Personnel:** Tim Kane, Editor. **URL:** http://southwicknewsonline.com. **Remarks:** Accepts advertising. **Circ:** 6000.

16103 ■ WLCQ-FM - 99.7
522 Springfield St.
Feeding Hills, MA 01030
Free: 877-843-7997
Email: contact@wlcq.com
Format: Contemporary Christian. **URL:** http://www.wlcq.com.

FITCHBURG

C. MA. Worcester Co. On Nashua River, 46 mi. NW of Boston. Fitchburg State College. Manufactures electrical equipment, paper, shoes, cotton and woolen goods, saws, machine knives, plastic goods, screen plates, curtains, air conditioning equipment, boxes, luggage, textiles, brass and iron castings, furniture, hardware.

16104 ■ The Guide
North Central Massachusetts Chamber of Commerce
860 South St.
Fitchburg, MA 01420
Phone: (978)353-7600
Fax: (978)353-4896
Publisher's E-mail: chamber@massweb.org
Journal of the North Central Massachusetts Chamber of Commerce. **Freq:** Semiannual fall/winter and spring/summer edition. **URL:** http://www.northcentralmass.com/services/publications/default.cfm. **Circ:** (Not Reported).

16105 ■ Sentinel & Enterprise
Sentinel and Enterprise
808 Main St.
Fitchburg, MA 01420
Phone: (978)343-6911
Fax: (978)342-1158
Publisher's E-mail: news@sentinelandenterprise.com
General newspaper. **Founded:** 1838. **Freq:** Daily (eve.). **Key Personnel:** Charles St. Amand, Editor; Tom Kirk, Publisher; Dennis West, Manager, Circulation. **Subscription Rates:** $276.60 Individuals print and online; $223.60 Individuals Wed thru Sun, print and online; $156 Individuals Sunday, print and online; $171.60 Individuals Thursday, Saturday and Sunday, print and online. **URL:** http://www.sentinelandenterprise.com/. **Mailing address:** PO Box 730, Fitchburg, MA 01420. **Ad Rates:** GLR $1.30; BW $2,101.41; 4C $2,411.41; SAU $16.29; PCI $15.66. **Remarks:** Accepts advertising. **Circ:** Mon.-Sat. ★**16158**, Sun. ★**17495**.

16106 ■ WFGL-AM - 960
356 Broad St.
Fitchburg, MA 01420
Free: 888-310-7729
Email: info@renewfm.org
Format: Religious. **Owner:** Calvary Radio Network, 3000 W MacArthur Blvd., Ste. 500, Santa Ana, CA 92707, Ph: (219)548-5800, Free: 866-303-9457. **Founded:** 1994. **Operating Hours:** Continuous. **Key Personnel:** George Small, Gen. Mgr. **Wattage:** 2,500. **Ad Rates:** Noncommercial. **URL:** http://www.renewfm.org.

16107 ■ WPKZ-AM - 1280
762 Water St.
Fitchburg, MA 01420
Phone: (978)343-3766
Fax: (978)345-6397
Email: sales@wpkz.net
Format: Sports; Talk; Information. **Networks:** ABC. **Owner:** Central Broadcasting Company L.L.C., at above address. **Founded:** 1941. **Formerly:** WEIM-AM. **Operating Hours:** Continuous; 15% network, 85% local. **ADI:** Boston-Worcester,MA-Derry-Manchester,NH. **Wattage:** 5,000. **Ad Rates:** $20-40 for 30 seconds; $40-50 for 60 seconds. **URL:** http://www.wpkz.net.

16108 ■ WXPL-FM - 91.3
160 Pearl St.
Fitchburg, MA 01420
Phone: (978)665-3000
Email: parkingservices@fitchburgstate.edu
Format: Alternative/New Music/Progressive. **Owner:** Fitchburg State University. **Founded:** 1985. **Formerly:** WFRC-FM. **Operating Hours:** 8:30 a.m.- 2 a.m. **Key Personnel:** Dave Donahue, Dir. of Public Rel., ddonahu@student.fitchburgstate.edu. **Wattage:** 110. **Ad Rates:** Noncommercial. **URL:** http://www.fitchburgstate.edu.

FLORENCE

16109 ■ International Journal of Testing
Routledge Journals Taylor & Francis Group
c/o Stephen G. Sireci, Ed.
43 Whittier St.
Florence, MA 01062
Journal covering research, theory, and practice in testing and assessment in psychology, education, counseling, human resource management, and related disciplines for scholars, professionals and graduate student interested in test development and test use. **Freq:** Quarterly. **Key Personnel:** Mark J. Gierl, Editor; Rob R. Meijer, Editor; Stephen G. Sireci, Editor. **ISSN:** 1530--5058 (print); **EISSN:** 1532--7574 (electronic). **Subscription Rates:** $437 Institutions online only; $83 Individuals print and online; $499 Institutions print and online. **URL:** http://www.tandfonline.com/toc/hijt20/current. **Ad Rates:** BW $325. **Remarks:** Accepts advertising. **Circ:** (Not Reported).

16110 ■ Option
Folk Education Association of America
73 Willow St.
Florence, MA 01062
Phone: (413)489-1012
Publisher's E-mail: folkedu@gmail.com
Freq: Semiannual. **Subscription Rates:** included in membership dues; $8 for nonmembers (2 volumes set). **Remarks:** Accepts advertising. **Circ:** 250.

FRAMINGHAM

NE MA. Middlesex Co. 21 mi. SW of Boston. State College. Residential. Retailing center.

16111 ■ Ashland TAB
GateHouse Media Inc.
33 New York Ave.
Framingham, MA 01701
Fax: (508)626-4400
Publication E-mail: ashland@cnc.com
Community newspaper (tabloid). **Founded:** Oct. 1988. **Freq:** Weekly. **Print Method:** Offset. **Trim Size:** 10 x 16. **Cols./Page:** 7. **Col. Width:** 8 picas. **Key Personnel:** Richard Lodge, Editor-in-Chief, phone: (508)626-3871. **Subscription Rates:** $46 Individuals; $63 Out of area. **URL:** http://ashland.wickedlocal.com; http://media.wickedlocal.com/interactive/circ/ashland.html. **Formerly:** The Ashland/Holliston Gazette. **Remarks:** Accepts classified advertising. **Circ:** (Not Reported).

16112 ■ Australian Macworld
IDG Communications Inc.
492 Old Connecticut Path
Framingham, MA 01701
Phone: (508)872-0080
Fax: (508)988-7888
Magazine dedicated to the Macintosh computers. **Freq:** Monthly. **Print Method:** Offset. **Trim Size:** 8 1/2 x 11. **Cols./Page:** 3. **Col. Width:** 27 nonpareils. **Col. Depth:** 133 agate lines. **Key Personnel:** Liana Pappas, Publisher; Dave Bullard, Editor-in-Chief. **ISSN:** 0744--2548 (print). **URL:** http://www.idg.com/www/IDGProducts.nsf/ByKey/Australia_Publication_Macworld-Australia; http://www.macworld.com.au. **Remarks:** Accepts advertising. **Circ:** 14000.

16113 ■ Business World Czech Republic
IDG Communications Inc.
492 Old Connecticut Path
Framingham, MA 01701
Phone: (508)872-0080
Fax: (508)988-7888
Magazine devoted to business executives. **Freq:** Monthly. **Print Method:** Offset. **Trim Size:** 8 1/2 x 11.

Circulation: ★ = AAM; △ or • = BPA; ♦ = CAC; ❑ = VAC; ⊕ = PO Statement; ‡ = Publisher's Report; Boldface figures = sworn; Light figures = estimated.

Cols./Page: 3. **ISSN:** 0098--342X (print). **URL:** http://www.idg.com/www/IDGProducts.nsf/ByKey/Czech-Republic_Publication_CIO-Business-World; http://businessworld.cz. **Remarks:** Accepts advertising. **Circ:** 7000.

16114 ■ CE Pro
EH Publishing Inc.
111 Speen St., Ste. 200
Framingham, MA 01701-2000
Phone: (508)663-1500
Fax: (508)663-1599
Publisher's E-mail: moe@ehpub.com
Magazine for professionals in the electronic systems business. **Freq:** Monthly. **Key Personnel:** Jason Knott, Editor; Steve Crowe, Editor; Tom LeBlanc, Writer. **Subscription Rates:** $40 Canada; $50 Other countries. **URL:** http://www.cepro.com; http://www.ehpub.com/custom_electronics. **Remarks:** Accepts advertising. **Circ:** △**30000**.

16115 ■ CEO & CIO China
IDG Communications Inc.
492 Old Connecticut Path
Framingham, MA 01701
Phone: (508)872-0080
Fax: (508)988-7888
Magazine covering technical and business concerns. **Freq:** Semimonthly. **Print Method:** Offset. Uses mats. **Trim Size:** 8 1/4 x 11. **Cols./Page:** 3. **Col. Width:** 27 nonpareils. **Col. Depth:** 133 agate lines. **URL:** http://www.idg.com/www/IDGProducts.nsf/ByKey/People's-Republic-of-China_Publication_CEO-&-CIO-China; http://www.ceocio.com.cn. **Remarks:** Accepts advertising. **Circ:** 198000.

16116 ■ Channel World Belgium
IDG Communications Inc.
492 Old Connecticut Path
Framingham, MA 01701
Phone: (508)872-0080
Fax: (508)988-7888
Magazine providing information on hard- and software and/or services, product information, sales and marketing strategies, market analysis. **Freq:** Monthly. **Print Method:** Letterpress. **Cols./Page:** 1. **Col. Width:** 76 nonpareils. **Col. Depth:** 112 agate lines. **ISSN:** 0272--7846 (print). **Ad Rates:** 4C $3429. **Remarks:** Accepts advertising. **Circ:** 6,000.

16117 ■ ChannelPro
EH Publishing Inc.
111 Speen St., Ste. 200
Framingham, MA 01701-2000
Phone: (508)663-1500
Fax: (508)663-1599
Publisher's E-mail: moe@ehpub.com
Magazine for resellers, integrators, system builders, and information technology professionals. **Freq:** Monthly. **Key Personnel:** Michael Siggins, Editor, phone: (919)325-0108; Cecilia Galvin, Managing Editor, phone: (919)325-0109. **Subscription Rates:** $39.99 Canada; $59.99 Other countries. **URL:** http://www.channelprosmb.com; http://www.ehpub.com/information_technology. **Remarks:** Accepts advertising. **Circ:** Non-paid 35000.

16118 ■ China Computerworld
IDG Communications Inc.
492 Old Connecticut Path
Framingham, MA 01701
Phone: (508)872-0080
Fax: (508)988-7888
Newspaper in China. **Freq:** Weekly. **Print Method:** Offset. **Cols./Page:** 4. **Col. Width:** 28 nonpareils. **Col. Depth:** 205 agate lines. **ISSN:** 0745--9327 (print). **URL:** http://www.idg.com/www/IDGProducts.nsf/ByKey/People's-Republic-of-China_Publication_China-Computerworld. **Remarks:** Accepts advertising. **Circ:** 246000.

16119 ■ CIO Asia
IDG Communications Inc.
492 Old Connecticut Path
Framingham, MA 01701
Phone: (508)872-0080
Fax: (508)988-7888
Journal focusing on IT strategy and return on IT investment. **Freq:** Bimonthly. **Print Method:** Offset. **Trim Size:** 6 3/4 x 9 7/8. **Cols./Page:** 2. **Col. Width:** 27 nonpareils. **Col. Depth:** 112 agate lines. **ISSN:** 0190--2725 (print). **URL:** http://www.idg.com/www/IDGProducts.nsf/ByKey/Asia-Pacific_WebSite_CIO-Asia-Online; http://www.cio-asia.com. **Remarks:** Accepts advertising. **Circ:** (Not Reported).

16120 ■ CIO Australia
IDG Communications Inc.
492 Old Connecticut Path
Framingham, MA 01701
Phone: (508)872-0080
Fax: (508)988-7888
Magazine focusing on IT strategies and control of the purchase of technology products and services and the success of IT and business executives. **Freq:** Quarterly. **Print Method:** Offset. Uses mats. **Trim Size:** 8 1/2 x 11. **Cols./Page:** 4. **Col. Width:** 2 1/4 inches. **Col. Depth:** 7 inches. **ISSN:** 0037--7996 (print). **URL:** http://www.idg.com/www/IDGProducts.nsf/ByKey/Australia_Publication_CIO-Australia; http://www.cio.com.au. **Remarks:** Accepts advertising. **Circ:** 10000.

16121 ■ CIO Bulgaria
IDG Communications Inc.
492 Old Connecticut Path
Framingham, MA 01701
Phone: (508)872-0080
Fax: (508)988-7888
Magazine devoted to highly targeted readers with case studies, analyses and insight into enterprise management concepts for the information era. **Freq:** Monthly. **Print Method:** Offset. **Trim Size:** 6 x 8 3/8. **Cols./Page:** 1. **Col. Width:** 50 nonpareils. **Col. Depth:** 98 agate lines. **ISSN:** 1542--6432 (print). **URL:** http://www.idg.com/www/IDGProducts.nsf/ByKey/Bulgaria_Publication_CIO-Bulgaria; http://cio.bg. **Remarks:** Accepts advertising. **Circ:** 4000.

16122 ■ CIO France
IDG Communications Inc.
492 Old Connecticut Path
Framingham, MA 01701
Phone: (508)872-0080
Fax: (508)988-7888
Magazine devoted to IT managers, managers in organization, innovation, purchasing and finance. **Freq:** Bimonthly. **Print Method:** Offset. **Trim Size:** 8 1/8 x 10 7/8. **Cols./Page:** 12. **ISSN:** 1091--0808 (print). **Remarks:** Accepts advertising. **Circ:** (Not Reported).

16123 ■ CIO India
IDG Communications Inc.
492 Old Connecticut Path
Framingham, MA 01701
Phone: (508)872-0080
Fax: (508)988-7888
Magazine focusing on high level information on IT executives. **Freq:** Monthly. **Print Method:** Offset. **Trim Size:** 8 1/4 x 10 3/4. **Cols./Page:** 3 and 2. **Col. Width:** 13.5 and 21.5 picas. **Col. Depth:** 10 inches. **Key Personnel:** Subdhir Kamath, Vice President, Sales. **ISSN:** 8750--9210 (print). **URL:** http://www.idg.com/www/IDGProducts.nsf/ByKey/India_Publication_CIO-India. **Remarks:** Accepts advertising. **Circ:** (Not Reported).

16124 ■ CIO IT-Strategie fur Manager
IDG Communications Inc.
492 Old Connecticut Path
Framingham, MA 01701
Phone: (508)872-0080
Fax: (508)988-7888
Magazine addressing business decision-makers who are responsible for the strategic deployment of IT within their companies. **Freq:** 8/year. **Print Method:** Offset. **Trim Size:** 8 3/8 x 10 7/8. **Cols./Page:** 3. **Col. Width:** 28 nonpareils. **Col. Depth:** 140 agate lines. **ISSN:** 0037--7333 (print). **URL:** http://www.idg.com/www/IDGProducts.nsf/ByKey/Germany_Publication_CIO--IT-Strategie-für-Manager; http://www.cio.de. **Remarks:** Accepts advertising. **Circ:** 10000.

16125 ■ CIO Korea
IDG Communications Inc.
492 Old Connecticut Path
Framingham, MA 01701
Phone: (508)872-0080
Fax: (508)988-7888
Magazine providing information on IT products, solution and services. **Freq:** Monthly. **Print Method:** Offset. Uses mats. **Trim Size:** 6 x 9. **Cols./Page:** 1. **Col. Width:** 4 1/4 inches. **Col. Depth:** 7 3/8 inches. **ISSN:** 0039--7709 (print). **URL:** http://www.idg.com/www/IDGProducts.nsf/ByKey/South-Korea_WebSite_CIO-Korea; http://www.ciokorea.com. **Remarks:** Accepts advertising. **Circ:** (Not Reported).

16126 ■ CIO Magazine: The Magazine for Information Executives
CXO Media Inc.
492 Old Connecticut Path
Framingham, MA 01701-4584
Phone: (508)872-0080
Fax: (508)879-7784
Free: 888-434-5478
Publisher's E-mail: stozeski@idglist.com
Publication for Chief Information Officers (CIOs) and other senior-level IT executives. **Freq:** 18/yr. **Print Method:** Web Offset. **Trim Size:** 8 3/4 x 10 7/8. **Cols./Page:** 4. **Key Personnel:** Maryfran Johnson, Editor-in-Chief; Elana Varon, Executive Editor. **ISSN:** 0894--9301 (print). **Subscription Rates:** $129 U.S. and Canada print; $195 Other countries print; $29 Individuals digital. **URL:** http://www.cio.com/magazine. **Mailing address:** PO Box 9208, Framingham, MA 01701-4584. **Ad Rates:** BW $28,035; 4C $36,330. **Remarks:** Accepts advertising. **Circ:** Non-paid △**140000**.

16127 ■ CIO Sweden
IDG Communications Inc.
492 Old Connecticut Path
Framingham, MA 01701
Phone: (508)872-0080
Fax: (508)988-7888
Magazine covering information on the success of IT strategy and business executives in achieving corporate goals. **Freq:** 9/year. **Print Method:** Offset. **Trim Size:** 6 3/4 x 9 7/8. **Cols./Page:** 2. **Col. Width:** 27 nonpareils. **Col. Depth:** 112 agate lines. **ISSN:** 0092--055X (print). **URL:** http://www.idg.com/www/IDGProducts.nsf/ByKey/Sweden_Publication_CIO-Sweden; http://cio.idg.se. **Remarks:** Accepts advertising. **Circ:** (Not Reported).

16128 ■ CIO Taiwan
IDG Communications Inc.
492 Old Connecticut Path
Framingham, MA 01701
Phone: (508)872-0080
Fax: (508)988-7888
Magazine providing information on advanced concepts, detailed analysis and valuable real-life information. **Freq:** Bimonthly. **Print Method:** Offset. Uses mats. **Trim Size:** 8 1/2 x 11. **Cols./Page:** 3. **Col. Width:** 26 nonpareils. **Col. Depth:** 133 agate lines. **ISSN:** 8756--3894 (print). **URL:** http://www.idg.com/www/IDGProducts.nsf/ByKey/Taiwan_Publication_CIO-Taiwan; http://www.cio.com.tw. **Remarks:** Accepts advertising. **Circ:** (Not Reported).

16129 ■ CMO China
IDG Communications Inc.
492 Old Connecticut Path
Framingham, MA 01701
Phone: (508)872-0080
Fax: (508)988-7888
Magazine providing information on promotion of brand and brand management. **Freq:** Monthly. **Print Method:** Letterpress. **Cols./Page:** 2. **Col. Width:** 40 nonpareils. **Col. Depth:** 112 agate lines. **ISSN:** 0041--2155 (print). **Remarks:** Accepts advertising. **Circ:** (Not Reported).

16130 ■ Computer News Middle East
IDG Communications Inc.
492 Old Connecticut Path
Framingham, MA 01701
Phone: (508)872-0080
Fax: (508)988-7888
Magazine focusing on government, oil, banking and education. **Freq:** Monthly. **Print Method:** Offset. **Trim Size:** 8 1/4 x 10 7/8. **Cols./Page:** 3. **Col. Width:** 27 nonpareils. **Col. Depth:** 134 agate lines. **Key Personnel:** Dominic De Sousa, Publisher. **ISSN:** 0041--2538 (print). **Subscription Rates:** $735 Individuals. **URL:** http://idg.com/www/IDGProducts.nsf/ByKey/Middle-East-Africa_WebSite_ComputerNewsME.com; http://www.cnmeonline.com. **Remarks:** Accepts advertising. **Circ:** (Not Reported).

16131 ■ Computer Sweden
IDG Communications Inc.
492 Old Connecticut Path
Framingham, MA 01701
Phone: (508)872-0080
Fax: (508)988-7888
Newspaper covering information on technology for managers and professionals. **Freq:** Weekly. **Print Method:** Offset. **Trim Size:** 8 1/4 x 10 7/8. **Cols./Page:** 3. **Col. Width:** 26 nonpareils. **Col. Depth:** 134 agate lines. **ISSN:** 0195--0363 (print). **URL:** http://www.idg.com/www/IDGProducts.nsf/ByKey/Sweden_Publication_Computer-Sweden; http://computersweden.idg.se. **Remarks:** Accepts advertising. **Circ:** 38000.

16132 ■ ComputerPartner Austria
IDG Communications Inc.
492 Old Connecticut Path
Framingham, MA 01701
Phone: (508)872-0080
Fax: (508)988-7888
Magazine for Austria's IT channel. **Freq:** Monthly. **Print Method:** Letterpress. **Cols./Page:** 2. **Col. Width:** 40 nonpareils. **Col. Depth:** 112 agate lines. **ISSN:** 0895--8211 (print). **URL:** http://www.idg.com/www/IDGProducts.nsf/ByKey/Austria_Publication_ComputerPartner-Austria; http://www.computerpartner.at. **Remarks:** Accepts advertising. **Circ:** 6000.

16133 ■ Computerworld
101communications LLC
PO Box 9171
Framingham, MA 01701
Phone: (508)879-0700
Newspaper for information systems executives. **Freq:** Weekly. **Print Method:** Offset. Uses mats. **Trim Size:** 10 3/8 x 13. **ISSN:** 0010-4841 (print). **Subscription Rates:** $129 Individuals; $129 Canada; $295 Other countries; $250 Individuals Mexico/Central/South America; $29 Individuals digital edition. **URL:** http://www.computerworld.com. **Ad Rates:** BW $25,280; 4C $34,045. **Remarks:** Accepts advertising. **Circ:** (Not Reported).

16134 ■ Computerworld Colombia
IDG Communications Inc.
492 Old Connecticut Path
Framingham, MA 01701
Phone: (508)872-0080
Fax: (508)988-7888
Magazine devoted to managers and information technology professionals. **Freq:** Monthly. **URL:** http://computerworld.co. **Remarks:** Accepts advertising. **Circ:** (Not Reported).

16135 ■ Computerworld Czech Republic
IDG Communications Inc.
492 Old Connecticut Path
Framingham, MA 01701
Phone: (508)872-0080
Fax: (508)988-7888
Newspaper for information technology professionals. **Freq:** Semimonthly. **URL:** http://computerworld.cz. **Remarks:** Accepts advertising. **Circ:** (Not Reported).

16136 ■ Computerworld Romania
IDG Communications Inc.
492 Old Connecticut Path
Framingham, MA 01701
Phone: (508)872-0080
Fax: (508)988-7888
Magazine featuring Romanian and worldwide computer markets, trends, statistics and new software products. **Freq:** Quarterly. **URL:** http://www.computerworld.ro. **Remarks:** Accepts advertising. **Circ:** (Not Reported).

16137 ■ Computerworld Szamitastechnika
IDG Communications Inc.
492 Old Connecticut Path
Framingham, MA 01701
Phone: (508)872-0080
Fax: (508)988-7888
Magazine covering market analysis, test reports and news on international as well as domestic information technology markets. **Freq:** Semimonthly. **URL:** http://computerworld.hu. **Remarks:** Accepts advertising. **Circ:** (Not Reported).

16138 ■ Computerworld Top 100
IDG Communications Inc.
492 Old Connecticut Path
Framingham, MA 01701
Phone: (508)872-0080
Fax: (508)988-7888
Magazine for analyzing trends and events of information technology business. **Freq:** Annual. **URL:** http://computerworld.bg/supplement/top100. **Remarks:** Accepts advertising. **Circ:** (Not Reported).

16139 ■ Computerworld Venezuela
IDG Communications Inc.
492 Old Connecticut Path
Framingham, MA 01701
Phone: (508)872-0080
Fax: (508)988-7888
Newspaper devoted to IT readers in Venezuela. **Freq:** Monthly. **URL:** http://www.computerworld.net.ve. **Remarks:** Accepts advertising. **Circ:** (Not Reported).

16140 ■ Control Engineering China
IDG Communications Inc.
492 Old Connecticut Path
Framingham, MA 01701
Phone: (508)872-0080
Fax: (508)988-7888
Magazine devoted to Chinese control engineers. **Freq:** Monthly. **URL:** http://www.macworld.co.uk/about/idg.cfm. **Remarks:** Accepts advertising. **Circ:** 20000.

16141 ■ CSO Magazine
CXO Media Inc.
492 Old Connecticut Path
Framingham, MA 01701-4584
Phone: (508)872-0080
Fax: (508)879-7784
Free: 888-434-5478
Publisher's E-mail: stozeski@idglist.com
Magazine providing information of security executives. **Founded:** Sept. 01, 2002. **Freq:** 10/year. **Key Personnel:** Bob Bragdon, Publisher. **Subscription Rates:** $70 U.S. and Canada Professional; $95 Other countries. **URL:** http://www.csoonline.com. **Mailing address:** PO Box 9208, Framingham, MA 01701-4584. **Ad Rates:** BW $13130. **Remarks:** Accepts advertising. **Circ:** 27,000.

16142 ■ Dagens Miljo
IDG Communications Inc.
492 Old Connecticut Path
Framingham, MA 01701
Phone: (508)872-0080
Fax: (508)988-7888
Magazine focusing on environmental benefits social responsibility and issues. **Freq:** Monthly. **URL:** http://www.aktuellhallbarhet.se/detta-ar-dagens-miljo. **Remarks:** Accepts advertising. **Circ:** (Not Reported).

16143 ■ Dealer World Espana
IDG Communications Inc.
492 Old Connecticut Path
Framingham, MA 01701
Phone: (508)872-0080
Fax: (508)988-7888
Magazine covering all possible channels of IT distribution. **Freq:** Monthly. **URL:** http://www.dealerworld.es/home. **Remarks:** Accepts advertising. **Circ:** (Not Reported).

16144 ■ Digital Power
IDG Communications Inc.
492 Old Connecticut Path
Framingham, MA 01701
Phone: (508)872-0080
Fax: (508)988-7888
Magazine providing digital products information. **Freq:** Monthly. **Remarks:** Accepts advertising. **Circ:** (Not Reported).

16145 ■ Distributique
IDG Communications Inc.
492 Old Connecticut Path
Framingham, MA 01701
Phone: (508)872-0080
Fax: (508)988-7888
Magazine providing business information for resellers, distributors, software houses and manufacturers. **Freq:** Weekly. **Print Method:** Offset. **Trim Size:** 8 1/4 x 10 7/8. **Cols./Page:** 3 and 2. **Col. Width:** 26 and 40 nonpareils. **Col. Depth:** 140 agate lines. **ISSN:** 0149--4147 (print). **URL:** http://www.distributique.com. **Remarks:** Accepts advertising. **Circ:** (Not Reported).

16146 ■ Electronic Design & Application World
IDG Communications Inc.
492 Old Connecticut Path
Framingham, MA 01701
Phone: (508)872-0080
Fax: (508)988-7888
Magazine providing coverage of technology design and applications information in three fields - electronics, telecommunications and computers. **Freq:** Monthly. **Print Method:** Offset. **Trim Size:** 11 x 16 1/2. **Cols./Page:** 5. **Col. Width:** 11 picas. **Col. Depth:** 210 agate lines. **ISSN:** 0193--1474 (print). **USPS:** 635-480. **URL:** http://www.idg.com/news/idg-announces-the-launch-of-electronic-design-application-world-in-china. **Remarks:** Accepts advertising. **Circ:** (Not Reported).

16147 ■ Electronic Engineering & Product World
IDG Communications Inc.
492 Old Connecticut Path
Framingham, MA 01701
Phone: (508)872-0080
Fax: (508)988-7888
Magazine devoted to business and technology decision makers in the Chinese electronics industry. **Freq:** Semimonthly. **Print Method:** Web offset. **Trim Size:** 211 X 276 mm. **URL:** http://www.eepw.com.cn. **Remarks:** Accepts advertising. **Circ:** (Not Reported).

16148 ■ Electronic House
EH Publishing Inc.
111 Speen St., Ste. 200
Framingham, MA 01701-2000
Phone: (508)663-1500
Fax: (508)663-1599
Publisher's E-mail: moe@ehpub.com
Magazine providing high-tech information on whole-house control, home theaters, house-wide music systems, security, wiring for the future, zoned heating and cooling, and remote monitoring. **Freq:** 11/year. **Print Method:** Offset. **Trim Size:** 8 x 10 7/8. **Key Personnel:** Lisa Montgomery, Editor; Arlen Schweiger, Managing Editor. **ISSN:** 0886--6643 (print). **URL:** http://www.electronichouse.com/tag/electronic-house-magazine. **Remarks:** Accepts advertising. **Circ:** (Not Reported).

16149 ■ Electronic House Ideas
EH Publishing Inc.
111 Speen St., Ste. 200
Framingham, MA 01701-2000
Phone: (508)663-1500
Fax: (508)663-1599
Publisher's E-mail: moe@ehpub.com
Magazine featuring electronic ideas for homeowners. **Freq:** Quarterly. **Subscription Rates:** $19.95 U.S. **URL:** http://www.electronichouseideas.com; http://www.ehpub.com/promotional_opportunities. **Circ:** Paid 70000.

16150 ■ Electronic Products China
IDG Communications Inc.
492 Old Connecticut Path
Framingham, MA 01701
Phone: (508)872-0080
Fax: (508)988-7888
Journal covering information on electronics products in China. **Freq:** Monthly. **URL:** http://www.epc.com.cn. **Remarks:** Accepts advertising. **Circ:** (Not Reported).

16151 ■ Framingham State College Magazine
Alumni Association - Framingham State College
100 State St.
Framingham, MA 01701-9101
Phone: (508)626-4012
Fax: (508)626-4036
Publisher's E-mail: alumni@framingham.edu
Freq: 3/year. **Mailing address:** PO Box 9101, Framingham, MA 01701-9101. **Remarks:** Advertising not accepted. **Circ:** 33000.

16152 ■ Framingham TAB
GateHouse Media Inc.
33 New York Ave.
Framingham, MA 01701
Fax: (508)626-4400
Publication E-mail: framingham@cnc.com
Community newspaper (tabloid). **Freq:** Weekly. **Print Method:** Offset. **Trim Size:** 10 x 16. **Cols./Page:** 7. **Col. Width:** 8 picas. **Key Personnel:** Phil Maddocks,

Circulation: ⋆ = AAM; △ or • = BPA; ♦ = CAC; ❑ = VAC; ⊕ = PO Statement; ‡ = Publisher's Report; Boldface figures = sworn; Light figures = estimated.

Editor; Richard Lodge, Editor-in-Chief, phone: (508)626-3871. **Subscription Rates:** Free. **URL:** http://framingham.wickedlocal.com. **Remarks:** Accepts classified advertising. **Circ:** (Not Reported).

16153 ■ GamePro
IDG Communications Inc.
492 Old Connecticut Path
Framingham, MA 01701
Phone: (508)872-0080
Fax: (508)988-7888
Magazine that provides video game reviews, tips, and cheat codes. **Freq:** Monthly. **Subscription Rates:** $17.97 Individuals; $27.97 Two years. **URL:** http://www.idg.com/www/IDGProducts.nsf/ByKey/Germany_Publication_GamePro; http://www.gamepro.de/. **Circ:** ‡17676.

16154 ■ Holliston TAB
GateHouse Media Inc.
33 New York Ave.
Framingham, MA 01701
Fax: (508)626-4400
Publication E-mail: holliston@cnc.com
Community newspaper (tabloid). **Founded:** 1988. **Freq:** Weekly. **Print Method:** Offset. **Trim Size:** 10 x 16. **Cols./Page:** 7. **Col. Width:** 8 picas. **Key Personnel:** Richard Lodge, Editor-in-Chief; Jeff Adair, Editor. **Subscription Rates:** $46 Individuals; $63 Out of area. **URL:** http://holliston.wickedlocal.com. **Formerly**: The Ashland Holliston Gazette. **Remarks:** Accepts classified advertising. **Circ:** (Not Reported).

16155 ■ InfoWorld Mexico
IDG Communications Inc.
492 Old Connecticut Path
Framingham, MA 01701
Phone: (508)872-0080
Fax: (508)988-7888
Magazine providing technical analysis and solutions on products of information technology. **Freq:** Semimonthly. **Print Method:** Offset. **Trim Size:** 8 1/4 x 11 5/8. **Cols./Page:** 2. **Col. Width:** 18 picas. **Col. Depth:** 60 picas. **Key Personnel:** Ricardo Vargas, Consultant; Mireya Cortes, Consultant; Ricardo Castro Romo, Director General; Claudia Mercado Arceo, Editor; Juan Carlos Garcia, Reporter; Karla Torres, Manager, Circulation; Jorge Torres, Consultant. **ISSN:** 1047--5354 (print). **Remarks:** Accepts advertising. **Circ:** (Not Reported).

16156 ■ Internetworld Sweden
IDG Communications Inc.
492 Old Connecticut Path
Framingham, MA 01701
Phone: (508)872-0080
Fax: (508)988-7888
Magazine targeting internet developments and successful web ventures. **Freq:** Bimonthly. **Print Method:** Offset. **Trim Size:** 11 1/2 x 16. **Cols./Page:** 5. **Col. Width:** 11.7 picas. **Col. Depth:** 210 agate lines. **ISSN:** 0193--1474 (print). **URL:** http://internetworld.idg.se. **Remarks:** Accepts advertising. **Circ:** (Not Reported).

16157 ■ IT-Bransjen
IDG Communications Inc.
492 Old Connecticut Path
Framingham, MA 01701
Phone: (508)872-0080
Fax: (508)988-7888
Magazine devoted to channel workers. **Freq:** Monthly. **Print Method:** Offset. **Trim Size:** 7 3/4 x 10 3/4. **Cols./Page:** 3. **Col. Width:** 28 nonpareils. **Col. Depth:** 138 agate lines. **ISSN:** 0002--2543 (print). **URL:** http://www.cw.no/it-bransjen. **Remarks:** Accepts advertising. **Circ:** (Not Reported).

16158 ■ IT Karriere
IDG Communications Inc.
492 Old Connecticut Path
Framingham, MA 01701
Phone: (508)872-0080
Fax: (508)988-7888
Journal providing information to IT professionals. **Freq:** Bimonthly. **Also known as:** IT Career. **Remarks:** Accepts advertising. **Circ:** (Not Reported).

16159 ■ IT.Branschen
IDG Communications Inc.
492 Old Connecticut Path
Framingham, MA 01701
Phone: (508)872-0080
Fax: (508)988-7888
Business magazine for the IT industry. **Freq:** 9/year. **URL:** http://www.idg.com/www/IDGProducts.nsf/ByKey/Sweden_Publication_IT.Branschen; http://www.projektmedia.se/it-branschen. **Remarks:** Accepts advertising. **Circ:** 12000.

16160 ■ Kino Domowe-Magazyn DVD
IDG Communications Inc.
492 Old Connecticut Path
Framingham, MA 01701
Phone: (508)872-0080
Fax: (508)988-7888
Magazine devoted to technology decision- makers worldwide. **Freq:** Monthly. **Remarks:** Accepts advertising. **Circ:** (Not Reported).

16161 ■ Live Sound! International
EH Publishing Inc.
Live Sound International
111 Speen St.
Framingham, MA 01701
Fax: (866)449-3761
Publisher's E-mail: moe@ehpub.com
Performance audio magazine for any live sound application. **Founded:** Jan. 1991. **Freq:** 12/yr. **Print Method:** Web offset. **Trim Size:** 7 7/8 x 10 3/4. **Cols./Page:** 3. **Col. Width:** 2 1/4 INS. **Col. Depth:** 9 1/2 INS. **Key Personnel:** Keith Clark, Editor-in-Chief; Pat Brown, Consultant; Kevin McPherson, Publisher. **ISSN:** 1077-5447 (print). **USPS:** 011-619. **Subscription Rates:** $60 Canada and Mexico; $140 Other countries. **URL:** http://www.livesoundint.com. **Formerly**: REP. **Ad Rates:** BW $36,450; 4C $4,647. **Remarks:** Accepts advertising. **Circ:** Paid 2800, Non-paid 7950.

16162 ■ MetroWest Daily News
GateHouse Media Inc.
33 New York Ave.
Framingham, MA 01701-8857
Phone: (508)626-4412
Fax: (508)626-4400
Community newspaper. **Freq:** Daily. **Key Personnel:** Nancy Olesin, Editor, phone: (508)626-4446; Art Davidson, Editor, phone: (508)626-4403; Richard Lodge, Editor-in-Chief, phone: (508)626-3871. **Subscription Rates:** $9.20 Individuals 1 month; $119.60 Individuals. **URL:** http://www.metrowestdailynews.com. **Formerly**: Metrowest. **Circ:** (Not Reported).

16163 ■ Modern Materials Handling
EH Publishing Inc.
111 Speen St., Ste. 200
Framingham, MA 01701
Publication E-mail: webmaster@mmh.com
Publication featuring materials handling. **Founded:** 1946. **Freq:** 14/yr. **Print Method:** Offset. Uses mats. **Cols./Page:** 3 and 2. **Col. Width:** 27 and 40 nonpareils. **Col. Depth:** 140 agate lines. **Key Personnel:** Noel P. Bodenburg, Managing Editor, phone: (860)217-0474; Bob Trebilcock, Executive Editor, phone: (603)357-0484; Lorie King Rogers, Associate Editor, phone: (603)355-2233; Sara Pearson Specter, Editor. **Subscription Rates:** Free. **URL:** http://www.mmh.com. **Ad Rates:** BW $58,984; 4C $21,110. **Remarks:** Accepts advertising. **Circ:** Combined △**80094**.

Natick Bulletin - See Natick

16164 ■ Natick Bulletin and TAB
GateHouse Media Inc.
33 New York Ave.
Framingham, MA 01701
Fax: (508)626-4400
Community newspaper. **Freq:** Weekly. **Print Method:** Offset. **Trim Size:** 10 x 16. **Cols./Page:** 8. **Col. Width:** 8 picas. **Col. Depth:** 16 inches. **Key Personnel:** Philip Maddocks, Editor, phone: (508)626-4437; Richard Lodge, Contact, phone: (508)626-3871. **Subscription Rates:** $61 Individuals. **URL:** http://natick.wickedlocal.com. **Remarks:** Accepts classified advertising. **Circ:** (Not Reported).

16165 ■ Network World
SYS-CON Media
492 Old Connecticut Path
Framingham, MA 01701
Free: 800-622-1108
Publisher's E-mail: info@sys-con.com
Magazine for Linux administrators and developers. **Founded:** 1986. **Freq:** Monthly. **Key Personnel:** Tim Greene, Senior Editor; John Dix, Editor-in-Chief. **URL:** http://www.linuxworld.com/?source=nwwfooter. **Formerly**: LinuxWorld. **Mailing address:** PO Box 9208, Framingham, MA 01701. **Ad Rates:** 4C $11,070. **Remarks:** Accepts advertising. **Circ:** (Not Reported).

16166 ■ Network World: The Newsweekly of Enterprise Network Computing
Network World Inc./IDG
492 Old Connecticut Path
Framingham, MA 01701
Publisher's E-mail: networkworld@theygsgroup.com
The newsweekly of enterprise network computing. **Founded:** Mar. 24, 1986. **Freq:** 5/yr. **Print Method:** Offset. **Trim Size:** 10 9/16 x 13 1/4. **Cols./Page:** 5. **Col. Width:** 1 13/16 inches. **Col. Depth:** 14 inches. **Key Personnel:** John Dix, Editor-in-Chief; Adam Dennison, Publisher. **ISSN:** 0887-7661 (print). **Subscription Rates:** $129 Individuals; $160.50 Canada; $150 Central and South America; $300 Other countries; $59 digital subscription. **URL:** http://www.networkworld.com. **Formerly**: Computer World on Communications; On Communications. **Mailing address:** PO Box 9208, Framingham, MA 1701. **Ad Rates:** 4C $20,720. **Remarks:** Accepts advertising. **Circ:** Non-paid △**170075**.

16167 ■ New England Wild
New England Wild Flower Society
180 Hemenway Rd.
Framingham, MA 01701
Phone: (508)877-7630
Fax: (508)877-3658
Publisher's E-mail: information@newenglandwild.org
Magazine covering native plants and their habitats including conservation, horticulture and education. **Freq:** Annual. **Subscription Rates:** Included in membership. **URL:** http://www.newenglandwild.org/membership/magazines. **Remarks:** Advertising not accepted. **Circ:** (Not Reported).

16168 ■ Remedies for Life
IDG Communications Inc.
492 Old Connecticut Path
Framingham, MA 01701
Phone: (508)872-0080
Fax: (508)988-7888
Magazine delivering authoritative, insightful editorial coverage dedicated to the science and promise of dietary supplements. **Freq:** Monthly. **Print Method:** Offset. **Cols./Page:** 3. **Col. Width:** 27 nonpareils. **Col. Depth:** 116 agate lines. **ISSN:** 0362--4048 (print). **URL:** http://www.remediesmagazine.com. **Remarks:** Accepts advertising. **Circ:** (Not Reported).

16169 ■ Security Sales & Integration
EH Publishing Inc.
111 Speen St., Ste. 200
Framingham, MA 01701-2000
Phone: (508)663-1500
Fax: (508)663-1599
Publication E-mail: secsales@bobit.com info@securitysales.com
Magazine covering the security industry. **Freq:** Monthly. **Print Method:** Offset. **Trim Size:** 8 x 10 7/8. **Cols./Page:** 3. **Col. Width:** 13 picas. **Col. Depth:** 10 inches. **Key Personnel:** Steven Nesbitt, Publisher, Manager, Sales; Rodney Bosch, Senior Editor; Scott Goldfine, Editor-in-Chief. **ISSN:** 1204--831X (print). **Subscription Rates:** Free. **URL:** http://www.securitysales.com/topic/tag/SSI_Magazine. **Formerly**: Alarm Installer and Dealer. **Ad Rates:** 4C $6,168. **Remarks:** Accepts advertising. **Circ:** 28000.

16170 ■ Sudbury Town Crier
GateHouse Media Inc.
33 New York Ave.
Framingham, MA 01701
Fax: (508)626-4400
Community newspaper. **Founded:** 1997. **Freq:** Weekly. **Print Method:** Offset. **Trim Size:** 10 x 16. **Cols./Page:** 5. **Col. Width:** 12 picas. **Key Personnel:** Jeff Adair, Editor, phone: (508)626-3926. **Subscription Rates:** $68 Individuals. **URL:** http://sudbury.wickedlocal.com. **Formerly**: The Wayland/Sudbury Gazette; The Sudbury Tab. **Remarks:** Accepts classified advertising. **Circ:** (Not Reported).

16171 ■ Wayland Town Crier
GateHouse Media Inc.
33 New York Ave.
Framingham, MA 01701
Fax: (508)626-4400
Publication E-mail: wayland@wickedlocal.com
Community newspaper (tabloid). **Freq:** Weekly (Thurs.). **Print Method:** Offset. **Trim Size:** 10 x 16. **Cols./Page:** 7. **Col. Width:** 8 picas. **Key Personnel:** Michael Wyner, Editor, phone: (508)626-4441. **URL:** http://wayland.wickedlocal.com. **Remarks:** Accepts classified advertising. **Circ:** (Not Reported).

16172 ■ Weston Town Crier & TAB
GateHouse Media Inc.
33 New York Ave.
Framingham, MA 01701
Fax: (508)626-4400
Publication E-mail: weston@cnc.com
Community newspaper (tabloid). **Freq:** Weekly (Thurs.). **Print Method:** Offset. **Trim Size:** 10 x 16. **Cols./Page:** 7. **Col. Width:** 8 picas. **Key Personnel:** Michael Wyner, Editor, phone: (508)626-4441; Richard Lodge, Editor-in-Chief. **Subscription Rates:** $71 Individuals. **URL:** http://weston.wickedlocal.com. **Remarks:** Advertising not accepted. **Circ:** (Not Reported).

16173 ■ WBIX-AM - 1060
100 Mt. Wayte Ave.
Framingham, MA 01702
Phone: (508)424-2568
Free: 877-639-1060
Email: wbixam1060@yahoo.com
Format: News; Talk. **Key Personnel:** Jim Harris, Gen. Sales Mgr., jim_wbix@comcast.net. **Ad Rates:** Advertising accepted; rates available upon request.

16174 ■ WDJM-FM - 91.3
Framingham State College
100 State St.
Framingham, MA 01701-9101
Phone: (508)626-4500
Format: Alternative/New Music/Progressive. **Networks:** Independent. **Owner:** Framingham State College, 100 State St., Framingham, MA 01701-9101, Ph: (508)626-4500, Fax: (508)626-4017. **Founded:** 1972. **Formerly:** WFSB-FM. **Operating Hours:** 9 a.m.-2 a.m.; 100% local. **Wattage:** 100. **Ad Rates:** Noncommercial. **Mailing address:** PO Box 9101, Framingham, MA 01701-9101. **URL:** http://www.framingham.edu.

16175 ■ WSRO-AM - 650
100 Mt. Wayte Ave.
Framingham, MA 01702
Phone: (508)820-0001
Format: Ethnic; Tejano; Religious; Gospel; Contemporary Christian. **Operating Hours:** Continuous. **Ad Rates:** Advertising accepted; rates available upon request. **URL:** http://www.wsro.com.

FRANKLIN

NE MA. Norfolk Co. 8 mi. E. of Milford. Residential.

16176 ■ Glass Scene
Glass New England
PO Box 389
Franklin, MA 02038-0389
Phone: (508)528-6211
Fax: (508)528-6211
Trade publication covering news for glass installers who sell and repair architectural and auto glass. **Freq:** Quarterly. **Print Method:** Offset. **Trim Size:** 8 x 11. **Key Personnel:** Jay Kruza, Editor. **Subscription Rates:** $15. **Ad Rates:** BW $650. **Remarks:** Accepts advertising. **Circ:** Paid 1200.

16177 ■ WGAO-FM - 88.3
99 Main St.
Franklin, MA 02038
Phone: (508)541-1518
Fax: (508)541-1941
Format: Contemporary Christian; Eclectic; Album-Oriented Rock (AOR); Classic Rock; Alternative/New Music/Progressive. **Networks:** AP. **Founded:** 1975. **Operating Hours:** 8 a.m.- 12 a.m. 10% network, 90% local. **Key Personnel:** Richard Pezzuolo, Contact. **Wattage:** 175. **Ad Rates:** Noncommercial. **URL:** http://www.dean.edu.

GARDNER

C. MA. Worcester Co. 58 mi. W. of Boston. Environmental control systems, molded plastics, foundry and machine shop products, steel and metal tubing, yarn. Dairy farms.

16178 ■ The Gardner News
The Gardner News Inc.
309 Central St.
Gardner, MA 01440
Phone: (978)632-8000
Fax: (978)630-5410
General newspaper. **Founded:** 1869. **Freq:** Mon.-Sat. (eve.). **Print Method:** Offset. **Cols./Page:** 8. **Col. Width:** 21 nonpareils. **Col. Depth:** 301 agate lines. **Key Personnel:** Alberta S. Bell, President, Publisher, phone: (978)632-8000. **Subscription Rates:** $187 Individuals home delivery; $300 Individuals mail. **URL:** http://thegardnernews.com/. **Mailing address:** PO Box 340, Gardner, MA 01440. **Ad Rates:** GLR $.48; BW $1,075; 4C $1,375; SAU $9; PCI $6.25. **Remarks:** Accepts advertising. **Circ:** (Not Reported).

16179 ■ WGAW-AM - 1340
362 Green St.
Gardner, MA 01440
Phone: (978)632-1340
Format: Talk. **Ad Rates:** Advertising accepted; rates available upon request. **URL:** http://www.wgaw1340.com.

GEORGETOWN

16180 ■ Manufacturer's Mart
Manufacturers' Mart Publications
PO Box 310
Georgetown, MA 01833
Fax: (978)352-4829
Free: 800-835-0017
Publisher's E-mail: info@manufacturersmart.com
Publication for manufacturing and production engineers. **Freq:** Monthly. **Print Method:** Offset. **Cols./Page:** 4. **Col. Width:** 30 nonpareils. **Col. Depth:** 193 agate lines. **URL:** http://www.manufacturersmart.com. **Circ:** Combined 28442.

GLOUCESTER

NE MA. Essex Co. On S. side of Cape Ann Peninsula, 28 mi. NE of Boston. Summer resort. Catching, canning, freezing and shipping of fish, especially cod, haddock, halibut, mackerel and ocean perch. Manufactures glue, nets and seines, ink, isinglass, cod liver oil, oiled clothing, paint, wooden boxes, textiles.

16181 ■ Cape Ann
North of Boston Media Group
36 Whittemore St.
Gloucester, MA 01930
Phone: (978)283-7000
Fax: (978)282-4397
Free: 800-836-7800
Publisher's E-mail: sales@nobmg.com
Local magazine featuring the North of Boston living in Cape Ann region. **Freq:** Quarterly. **Key Personnel:** Karen Andreas, Publisher; Marybeth Callahan, Manager, Advertising. **Subscription Rates:** $15 Individuals. **URL:** http://www.capeannmagazine.com. **Remarks:** Accepts advertising. **Circ:** (Not Reported).

16182 ■ The Noise: Rock Around Boston
The Noise
PO BOX 353
Gloucester, MA 01931
Phone: (617)331-9637
Publication E-mail: tmax@thenoise-boston.com
Fanzine covering bands based in New England ONLY - with a focus on the Boston music scene. **Freq:** 9/year. **Print Method:** Web offset. **Trim Size:** 8 3/8 x 10 3/4. **Cols./Page:** 2. **Col. Width:** 3 5/8 INS. **Col. Depth:** 10 INS. **Key Personnel:** Francis Dimenno, Editor; T. Max, Editor; Mike Baldino, Associate Editor; Joe Coughlin, Associate Editor; Kier Byrnes, Associate Editor. **Subscription Rates:** $24 Individuals; $40 Other countries. **URL:** http://www.thenoise-boston.com. **Ad Rates:** BW $440. **Remarks:** Accepts advertising. **Circ:** Paid ‡5000.

16183 ■ Old-House Interiors
Gloucester Publishers
108 E Main St.
Gloucester, MA 01930
Phone: (978)283-3200
Publisher's E-mail: info@oldhouseinteriors.com
Consumer magazine covering interior design for period homes. **Freq:** Bimonthly. **Print Method:** web offset. **Trim Size:** 8 3/6 x 10 7/8. **Key Personnel:** Bill O'Donnell, Publisher; Patricia Poore, Editor-in-Chief. **ISSN:** 1079--3941 (print). **Subscription Rates:** $29.95 Individuals print and online; $16.99 Individuals digital; $24.95 Individuals print. **URL:** http://www.oldhouseinteriors.com. **Ad Rates:** BW $3,000; 4C $3,750. **Remarks:** Accepts advertising. **Circ:** Paid 120000.

GREAT BARRINGTON

W. MA. Berkshire Co. On Housatonic River, 20 mi. SW of Pittsfield. Summer resort. Paper mills; log homes. Manufactures nuclear components. Dairy, poultry farms.

16184 ■ Berkshire Record
Berkshire Record
21 Elm St.
Great Barrington, MA 01230
Phone: (413)528-5380
Fax: (413)528-9449
Publication E-mail: berkrec@bcn.net
Community newspaper. **Freq:** Weekly (Fri.). **Print Method:** Web offset. **Trim Size:** 14 x 23. **Cols./Page:** 6. **Col. Width:** 6 inches. **Col. Depth:** 21 1/2 inches. **Key Personnel:** Ed Shepardson, Managing Editor. **USPS:** 004-483. **Subscription Rates:** $25 Individuals 26 weeks; $30 Out of area 26 weeks; $40 Individuals 52 weeks; $50 Out of area 52 weeks. **URL:** http://www.berkshirerecord.net. **Ad Rates:** 4C $1500; SAU $9.10; CNU $9.10; PCI $7.90; BW $1100. **Remarks:** Accepts advertising. **Circ:** Paid ‡12000.

16185 ■ Orion
Orion Magazine
187 Main St.
Great Barrington, MA 01230
Phone: (413)528-4422
Free: 888-909-6568
Publication E-mail: orionmag@pcspublink.com
Magazine centering on cultural issues related to nature. **Founded:** 1982. **Freq:** Bimonthly. **ISSN:** 1058-3130 (print). **Subscription Rates:** $35 Individuals; $59 Two years; $79 Individuals 3 years. **URL:** http://www.orionmagazine.org/. **Formerly:** Orion Nature Quarterly, Orion: People and Nature. **Remarks:** Advertising not accepted. **Circ:** Paid ‡20000, Controlled ‡200.

16186 ■ Southern Berkshire Shopper's Guide
Southern Berkshire Shopper's Guide
141 W Ave.
Great Barrington, MA 01230
Phone: (413)528-0095
Fax: (413)528-4805
Shopper. **Freq:** Weekly (Thurs.). **Print Method:** Offset. **Trim Size:** 15/8 x 16. **Cols./Page:** 6. **Col. Width:** 20 nonpareils. **Col. Depth:** 224 agate lines. **Key Personnel:** Eunice Raifstanger, Publisher; Jean Raifstanger, Business Manager. **URL:** http://shoppersguide-inc.com. **Ad Rates:** GLR $5.50; BW $528; PCI $8.50. **Remarks:** Accepts advertising. **Circ:** Controlled ‡22,500.

16187 ■ WAMQ-FM - 105.1
PO Box 66600
Albany, NY 12206
Phone: (518)465-5233
Fax: (518)432-6974
Free: 800-323-9262
Email: mail@wamc.org
Format: Public Radio. **Key Personnel:** Alan Chartock, President, alan@wamc.org. **Ad Rates:** Noncommercial. **URL:** http://wamc.org.

16188 ■ WSBS-AM - 860
425 Stockbridge Rd.
Great Barrington, MA 01230
Phone: (413)528-0860
Fax: (413)528-2162
Email: fun@wsbs.com
Format: Adult Contemporary; Full Service. **Owner:** Vox Communications Group. **Founded:** 1956. **Operating Hours:** Continuous. **Key Personnel:** Peter Berry, Mktg. Mgr., VP, peterb@live959.com; Jesse Stewart, Prog. Dir., jesse@wsbs.com; Dave Isby, Sales Mgr., Station

Circulation: ★ = AAM; △ or • = BPA; ♦ = CAC; ❑ = VAC; ⊕ = PO Statement; ‡ = Publisher's Report; Boldface figures = sworn; Light figures = estimated.

Mgr., disby@wsbs.com; Karen Negrini, Dir. of Traffic. **Wattage:** 2,700 Day; 004 Night. **Ad Rates:** Advertising accepted; rates available upon request. WNAW-AM; WMNB-FM. **URL:** http://www.wsbs.com.

GREENFIELD

NW MA. Franklin Co. On Connecticut River, 20 mi. N. of Northampton. Franklin Co. (NW). On Connecticut River, 20 m N of Northampton. Manufactures dies, machine tools, grinding and finishing machinery, sterling silver tableware, shovels, rakes, paper boxes. Agriculture. Corn, cucumbers, squash, cabbage, apples, potatoes.

16189 ■ Markers
Association for Gravestone Studies
101 Munson St., Ste. 108
Greenfield, MA 01301
Phone: (413)772-0836
Publisher's E-mail: info@gravestonestudies.org
Freq: Annual. **ISSN:** 0277- 8726 (print). **Subscription Rates:** $9 Members; $20 Nonmembers. **URL:** http://gravestonestudies.org/publicatons/markers. **Remarks:** Advertising not accepted. **Circ:** 500.

16190 ■ The Recorder
The Recorder
14 Hope St.
Greenfield, MA 01302
Phone: (413)772-0261
Fax: (413)774-5511
Publisher's E-mail: letters@recorder.com
General newspaper. **Founded:** Feb. 01, 1792. **Freq:** Mon.-Sat. (morn.). **Print Method:** Offset. **Trim Size:** 13 3/4 x 22 3/4. **Cols./Page:** 6. **Col. Width:** 25 nonpareils. **Col. Depth:** 298 agate lines. **Key Personnel:** George Forcier, Managing Editor. **Subscription Rates:** $3.40 Individuals by carrier, print and online/week; $8 Individuals online. **URL:** http://www.recorder.com. **Ad Rates:** SAU $8.65. **Remarks:** Accepts advertising. **Circ:** (Not Reported).

16191 ■ WGAM-AM - 1520
267 Main St.
Greenfield, MA 01301
Fax: (413)772-2322
Format: Easy Listening. **Owner:** Radio Skutnik Inc., at above address. **Founded:** 1980. **Formerly**: WPOE-AM; Howard Communication Co. **Operating Hours**: Sunrise-sunset; 80% network, 20% local. **Key Personnel:** Ed Skutnik, Station Mgr. **Wattage:** 10,000. **Ad Rates:** $15-20 for 30 seconds; $20-40 for 60 seconds. **Mailing address:** PO Box 520, Greenfield, MA 01301.

16192 ■ WHAI-AM
98.3 Fm Whai Studios, 81 Woodard Rd.
Greenfield, MA 01301
Phone: (413)774-4301
Fax: (413)773-5637
Owner: Saga Communications Inc., at above address. **Founded:** 1938. **Key Personnel:** Dan Guin, Gen. Mgr., dan@whai.com; Nick Danjer, Dir. of Programs, nick@whai.com. **Ad Rates:** $7.50-21.65 for 15 seconds; $10.70-30.90 for 30 seconds; $14-38.60 for 60 seconds. **URL:** http://whai.com/common/longformrules.php.

16193 ■ WHAI-FM - 98.3
81 Woodard Rd.
Greenfield, MA 01301
Phone: (413)774-4301
Fax: (413)773-5637
Email: info@whai.com
Format: Adult Contemporary. **Owner:** Saga Communications Inc., at above address. **Founded:** 1948. **Operating Hours**: 7:00 p.m. - Midnight. **Key Personnel:** Dan Guin, Gen. Mgr., dan@whai.com; Nick Danjer, Mgr., nick@whai.com. **Wattage**: 2,000 ERP. **Ad Rates:** Advertising accepted; rates available upon request. **URL:** http://www.whai.com.

16194 ■ WIZZ-AM - 1520
PO Box 983
Greenfield, MA 01302
Phone: (413)774-5757
Fax: (413)625-8274
Format: Big Band/Nostalgia. **Key Personnel:** Dan Ferriera, Chief Engineer, danf@wizzradio.com. **Wattage:** 10,000. **Ad Rates:** Advertising accepted; rates available upon request. **URL:** http://www.wizzradio.com.

16195 ■ WLPV-FM - 107.9
450 Davis St.
Greenfield, MA 01301
Format: Contemporary Christian. **Operating Hours**: Continuous. **Wattage**: 100. **URL:** http://www.wlpv1079online.com.

16196 ■ WPVQ-FM - 95.3
81 Woodard Rd.
Greenfield, MA 01301
Format: Country. **Owner:** Saga Communications Inc., 73 Kercheval Ave., Ste. 201, Grosse Pointe Farms, MI 48236, Ph: (313)886-7070, Fax: (313)886-7150. **Operating Hours**: Continuous. **Key Personnel:** Dan Guin, Gen. Mgr., dan@whai.com; Nick Danjer, Dir. of Programs, nick@whai.com. **Wattage**: 570. **Ad Rates:** Advertising accepted; rates available upon request. **URL:** http://www.bear953.com.

HAMILTON

NE MA. Essex Co. 3 mi. NE of Wenham. Residential.

16197 ■ WGAW-AM
PO Box 403
Hamilton, MA 01936-0403
Phone: (978)632-1340
Format: Adult Contemporary. **Networks:** AP. **Founded:** 1946. **Key Personnel:** Mark Rossi, Contact. **Wattage**: 1,000. **URL:** http://www.wgaw1340.com/.

HANOVER

SE MA. Plymouth Co. 30 mi. S. of Boston. Residential.

16198 ■ Foundations and Trends in Accounting
Now Publishers
PO Box 1024
Hanover, MA 02339
Phone: (781)871-0245
Publisher's E-mail: zac.rolnik@nowpublishers.com
Academic journal publishing new research in all branches of accounting. **Freq:** Quarterly. **Key Personnel:** Stefan J. Reichelstein, Editor-in-Chief. **ISSN:** 1554--0642 (print); **EISSN:** 1554--0650 (electronic). **Subscription Rates:** $480 Institutions online - U.S; €480 Institutions online; $480 Institutions print; €480 Other countries print; $570 Institutions print and online; €570 Other countries print and online. **URL:** http://www.nowpublishers.com/acc. **Circ:** (Not Reported).

16199 ■ Foundations and Trends in Communications and Information Theory
Now Publishers
PO Box 1024
Hanover, MA 02339
Phone: (781)871-0245
Publisher's E-mail: zac.rolnik@nowpublishers.com
Academic journal covering new research in the field of information processing and electronic communication. **Freq:** Quarterly. **Key Personnel:** Sergio Verdu, Editor-in-Chief, phone: (609)258-5315. **ISSN:** 1567--2190 (print); **EISSN:** 1567--2328 (electronic). **Subscription Rates:** $480 Institutions print only, additional 50 for pph; €480 Institutions, other countries print only, additional 50 for pph; $570 Institutions print and online, additional 50 for pph; €570 Institutions, other countries print and online, additional 50 for pph; $480 Institutions online only; €480 Institutions, other countries online only. **URL:** http://www.nowpublishers.com/CIT. **Circ:** (Not Reported).

16200 ■ Foundations and Trends in Computer Graphics and Vision
Now Publishers
PO Box 1024
Hanover, MA 02339
Phone: (781)871-0245
Publisher's E-mail: zac.rolnik@nowpublishers.com
Academic journal publishing new research and reports in the field of computer graphics. **Freq:** Quarterly. **Key Personnel:** Brian Curless, Editor-in-Chief; Luc Van Gool, Editor-in-Chief; Richard Szeliski, Board Member. **ISSN:** 1572--2740 (print); **EISSN:** 1572--2759 (electronic). **Subscription Rates:** $480 Institutions online only; €480 Institutions, other countries online only; $480 Institutions print (+50pph); €480 Institutions, other countries print (+50pph); $570 Institutions print and online (+50pph); €570 Institutions, other countries print and online (+50pph). **URL:** http://www.nowpublishers.com/CGV. **Circ:** (Not Reported).

16201 ■ Foundations and Trends in Databases
Now Publishers
PO Box 1024
Hanover, MA 02339
Phone: (781)871-0245
Publisher's E-mail: zac.rolnik@nowpublishers.com
Journal dedicated to the management of large volumes of data. **Freq:** Monthly. **Print Method:** Offset. **Trim Size:** 10 7/16 x 13 3/4. **Cols./Page:** 4. **Key Personnel:** Surajit Chaudhuri, Editor; Minos Garofalakis, Editor; Joseph M. Hellerstein, Editor-in-Chief. **ISSN:** 1931--7883 (print); **EISSN:** 1931--7891 (electronic). **Subscription Rates:** $480 Institutions print or online; €480 Institutions, other countries print or online; $570 Institutions print and online; €570 Institutions print and online. **URL:** http://www.nowpublishers.com/DBS. **Circ:** (Not Reported).

16202 ■ Foundations and Trends in Entrepreneurship
Now Publishers
PO Box 1024
Hanover, MA 02339
Phone: (781)871-0245
Publisher's E-mail: zac.rolnik@nowpublishers.com
Academic journal publishing new research in the area of entrepreneurship, including start-ups, gender and ethnicity, government programs, small business, and other topics. **Freq:** Bimonthly. **Key Personnel:** David B. Audretsch, Editor-in-Chief; Mike Wright, Editor-in-Chief; Albert N. Link, Editor-in-Chief. **ISSN:** 1551--3114 (print); **EISSN:** 1551--3122 (electronic). **Subscription Rates:** $600 Institutions online; €600 Institutions, other countries online; $600 Institutions print (+75pph); €600 Institutions, other countries print (+75pph); $710 Institutions print and online (+75pph); €710 Institutions, other countries print and online (+75pph). **URL:** http://www.nowpublishers.com/ENT. **Circ:** (Not Reported).

16203 ■ Foundations and Trends in Finance
Now Publishers
PO Box 1024
Hanover, MA 02339
Phone: (781)871-0245
Publisher's E-mail: zac.rolnik@nowpublishers.com
Academic journal that covers corporate finance, financial markets, asset pricing, and derivatives. **Freq:** Quarterly. **Key Personnel:** Sheridan Titman, Editor-in-Chief. **ISSN:** 1567--2395 (print); **EISSN:** 1567--2409 (electronic). **Subscription Rates:** $480 Institutions online; €480 Institutions, other countries online; $480 Institutions print (+50pph); €480 Institutions, other countries print (+50pph); $570 Institutions print and online (+50pph); €570 Institutions, other countries print and online (+50pph). **URL:** http://www.nowpublishers.com/FIN. **Circ:** (Not Reported).

16204 ■ Foundations and Trends in Information Retrieval
Now Publishers
PO Box 1024
Hanover, MA 02339
Phone: (781)871-0245
Publisher's E-mail: zac.rolnik@nowpublishers.com
Academic journal that publishes new research in the field of information retrieval. **Freq:** 5/year. **Key Personnel:** Mark Sanderson, Editor-in-Chief; Douglas W. Oard, Editor-in-Chief. **ISSN:** 1554--0669 (print); **EISSN:** 1554--0677 (electronic). **Subscription Rates:** $540 Institutions online or print; €540 Other countries online or print; $630 Institutions print and online; €630 Other countries online and print. **URL:** http://www.nowpublishers.com/journals/INR. **Circ:** (Not Reported).

16205 ■ Foundations and Trends in Marketing
Now Publishers
PO Box 1024
Hanover, MA 02339
Phone: (781)871-0245
Publisher's E-mail: zac.rolnik@nowpublishers.com
Journal covering business to business marketing, Bayesian models, behavioral decision making, branding and brand equity, channel management, choice modeling, comparative market structure and competitive marketing strategy. **Freq:** Weekly. **Print Method:** Offset. **Trim Size:** 10 1/2 x 14. **Cols./Page:** 5. **Col. Width:** 11 picas. **Col. Depth:** 13 inches. **Key Personnel:** David Bell, Editor; Jehoshua Eliashberg, Editor-in-Chief; Amitava Chattopadhyay, Editor; Pradeep Chintagunta,

Editor. **ISSN:** 1555--0753 (print); **EISSN:** 1555--0761 (electronic). **Subscription Rates:** $480 Institutions print or online; €480 Institutions, other countries print or online; $570 Institutions print and online; €570 Institutions, other countries print and online. **URL:** http://www.nowpublishers.com/MKT. **Remarks:** Advertising not accepted. **Circ:** (Not Reported).

16206 ■ Foundations and Trends in Microeconomics
Now Publishers
PO Box 1024
Hanover, MA 02339
Phone: (781)871-0245
Publisher's E-mail: zac.rolnik@nowpublishers.com
Academic journal that publishes current research in all areas of economics. **Freq:** Quarterly. **Key Personnel:** W. Kip Viscusi, Editor-in-Chief. **ISSN:** 1547--9846 (print); **EISSN:** 1547--9854 (electronic). **Subscription Rates:** $480 Institutions online; €480 Institutions, other countries online; $480 Institutions print (+50pph); €480 Institutions, other countries print (+50pph); $570 Institutions print and online (+50pph); €570 Institutions, other countries print and online (+50pph). **URL:** http://www.nowpublishers.com/MIC. **Circ:** (Not Reported).

16207 ■ Foundations and Trends in Networking
Now Publishers
PO Box 1024
Hanover, MA 02339
Phone: (781)871-0245
Publisher's E-mail: zac.rolnik@nowpublishers.com
Academic journal publishing new research in computer networking. **Freq:** Quarterly. **Key Personnel:** Anthony Ephremides, Editor-in-Chief, phone: (301)405-3641; Francois Baccelli, Editor. **ISSN:** 1554--057X (print); **EISSN:** 1554--0588 (electronic). **Subscription Rates:** $480 Institutions online or print; €480 Other countries print or online; $570 Institutions print and online; €570 Other countries print and online. **URL:** http://www.nowpublishers.com/NET. **Circ:** (Not Reported).

16208 ■ Foundations and Trends in Signal Processing
Now Publishers
PO Box 1024
Hanover, MA 02339
Phone: (781)871-0245
Publisher's E-mail: zac.rolnik@nowpublishers.com
Journal covering survey and tutorial articles on the foundations, algorithms, methods, and applications of signal processing. **Freq:** Quarterly. **Print Method:** Web offset. **Trim Size:** 8 1/2 x 11. **Cols./Page:** 2 and 3. **Col. Width:** 30 and 44 nonpareils. **Col. Depth:** 133 agate lines. **Key Personnel:** Robert M. Gray, Founder, Editor; Yonina Eldar, Editor-in-Chief. **ISSN:** 1932--8346 (print); **EISSN:** 1932--8354 (electronic). **Subscription Rates:** $480 Institutions print or online; €480 Institutions, other countries print or online; $570 Institutions print and online; €570 Institutions, other countries print and online. **URL:** http://www.nowpublishers.com/SIG. **Circ:** (Not Reported).

16209 ■ Foundations and Trends in Technology, Information and Operations Management
Now Publishers
PO Box 1024
Hanover, MA 02339
Phone: (781)871-0245
Publisher's E-mail: zac.rolnik@nowpublishers.com
Journal that publishes articles in the area of business and technology, including B2B commerce, supply chain management, logistics, facility location, and competitive operations. **Freq:** Quarterly. **Key Personnel:** Charles Corbett, Editor-in-Chief. **ISSN:** 1571--9545 (print); **EISSN:** 1571--9553 (electronic). **Subscription Rates:** $480 Institutions online; €480 Institutions, other countries online; $480 Institutions print (+50pph); €480 Institutions, other countries print (+50pph); $570 Institutions print and online (+50pph); €570 Institutions, other countries print and online (+50pph). **URL:** http://www.nowpublishers.com/TOM. **Circ:** (Not Reported).

16210 ■ Foundations and Trends in Theoretical Computer Science
Now Publishers
PO Box 1024
Hanover, MA 02339
Phone: (781)871-0245
Publisher's E-mail: zac.rolnik@nowpublishers.com
Academic computer science journal. **Freq:** Quarterly. **Key Personnel:** Madhu Sudan, Editor-in-Chief. **ISSN:** 1551--305X (print); **EISSN:** 1551--3068 (electronic). **Subscription Rates:** $480 Institutions online; €480 Institutions, other countries online; $480 Institutions print (+50pph); €480 Institutions, other countries print (+50pph); $570 Institutions print and online (+50pph); €570 Institutions, other countries print and online (+50pph). **URL:** http://www.nowpublishers.com/TCS. **Circ:** (Not Reported).

16211 ■ Foundations and Trends in Web Science
Now Publishers
PO Box 1024
Hanover, MA 02339
Phone: (781)871-0245
Publisher's E-mail: zac.rolnik@nowpublishers.com
Academic journal publishing new research in web science, including: content management, data mining, HCI, emergent behavior, semantic web, standards, and mobile/pervasive web. **Freq:** Semiannual. **Key Personnel:** Wendy Hall, Editor-in-Chief; Nigel Shadbolt, Editor-in-Chief. **ISSN:** 1555--077X (print); **EISSN:** 1555--0788 (electronic). **Subscription Rates:** $355 Institutions online or print; $355 Other countries print or online; $400 Institutions print and online; €400 Other countries online and print. **URL:** http://www.nowpublishers.com/journals/WEB. **Circ:** (Not Reported).

16212 ■ Quarterly Journal of Political Science
Now Publishers
PO Box 1024
Hanover, MA 02339
Phone: (781)871-0245
Publisher's E-mail: zac.rolnik@nowpublishers.com
Journal focusing on positive political science and contemporary political economy. **Freq:** Quarterly. **Key Personnel:** Scott Ashworth, Editor-in-Chief; Keith Krehbiel, Editor; Nolan McCarty, Editor; John Huber, Editor. **ISSN:** 1554--0626 (print); **EISSN:** 1554--0634 (electronic). **Subscription Rates:** $480 Institutions online only; €480 Institutions, other countries online only; $530 Institutions print inly; €530 Institutions, other countries print only; $620 Institutions print and online; $620 Institutions, other countries print and online; $100 U.S. print only; $150 U.S. print only; $170 U.S. print and online. **URL:** http://www.nowpublishers.com/QJPS. **Remarks:** Advertising not accepted. **Circ:** (Not Reported).

HARWICH

16213 ■ Harwich Oracle
GateHouse Media Inc.
5 Namskaket Rd.
Harwich, MA 02645
Community newspaper. **Freq:** Weekly (Wed.). **Print Method:** Offset. **Trim Size:** 11 x 16 1/2. **Cols./Page:** 5. **Col. Width:** 21 inches. **Col. Depth:** 224 agate lines. **Key Personnel:** Matt Rice, Editor, phone: (508)247-3261. **Subscription Rates:** $57 Out of area; $26 Individuals. **URL:** http://harwich.wickedlocal.com. **Ad Rates:** GLR $.50; BW $564; 4C $1164; PCI $7.05. **Remarks:** Accepts classified advertising. **Circ:** (Not Reported).

16214 ■ WCCT-FM
351 Pleasant Lake Ave.
Harwich, MA 02645
Phone: (508)432-4500
Fax: (508)432-7916
Format: News; Eclectic. **Networks:** National Public Radio (NPR). **Founded:** 1989.

HAVERHILL

NE MA. Essex Co. On Merrimack River, 33 mi. N. of Boston. Manufactures shoes, heels, soles, counters, plastics, chemicals leather goods, coin operated machines, paper boxboard, electric coils, machinery.

16215 ■ The Haverhill Gazette
Eagle-Tribune Publishing Co.
181 Merrimack St.
Haverhill, MA 01831
Phone: (978)373-1000
Publisher's E-mail: direland@eagletribune.com
Community newspaper. **Freq:** Weekly (Thurs.). **Print Method:** Offset. **Cols./Page:** 5. **Col. Width:** 1 15/16 inches. **Col. Depth:** 12 3/4 inches. **Key Personnel:** Donna Capodelupo, Editor, phone: (978)556-8528; Al Getler, Publisher, phone: (978)946-2110. **Subscription Rates:** $19.99 Individuals; $35 Out of area; $39.98 Two years; $59.97 Individuals three years. **URL:** http://www.hgazette.com. **Mailing address:** PO Box 991, Haverhill, MA 01831. **Remarks:** Accepts advertising. **Circ:** ‡3900.

16216 ■ WXRV-FM - 92.5
30 How St.
Haverhill, MA 01830
Phone: (978)374-4733
Fax: (978)373-8023
Free: 800-352-9250
Email: info@wxrv.com
Format: Adult Album Alternative. **Networks:** Westwood One Radio. **Owner:** Northeast Broadcasting Co., at above address. **Founded:** 1959. **Formerly:** WLYT-FM. **Operating Hours:** Continuous. **Key Personnel:** Donald St. Sauveur, Gen. Mgr. **Wattage:** 25,000. **Ad Rates:** Advertising accepted; rates available upon request. **URL:** http://www.theriverboston.com.

HINGHAM

16217 ■ Cohasset Mariner
GateHouse Media Inc.
73 South St.
Hingham, MA 02043
Phone: (781)749-0031
Fax: (781)749-2931
Publication E-mail: cohasset@wickedlocal.com
Community newspaper. **Freq:** Weekly (Thurs.). **Print Method:** Offset. **Trim Size:** 11 3/8 x 17. **Cols./Page:** 6. **Col. Width:** 18 nonpareils. **Col. Depth:** 217 agate lines. **Key Personnel:** Mark Olivieri, Publisher, phone: (781)837-4504; Mary Ford, Editor, phone: (781)741-2933; William Wassersug, Editor, phone: (781)837-4577. **Subscription Rates:** $64 Individuals; $89.95 Out of area. **URL:** http://cohasset.wickedlocal.com. **Ad Rates:** BW $767.25; 4C $1,167.25; SAU $8.25. **Remarks:** Accepts advertising. **Circ:** (Not Reported).

HOLDEN

C. MA. Worcester Co. 8 mi. NNW of Worcester.

16218 ■ The Landmark: Your Weekly Newspaper Serving the Wachusett Region
The Landmark
1105A Main St.
Holden, MA 01520
Phone: (508)829-5981
Fax: (508)829-5984
Publication E-mail: editor@thelandmark.com
Community newspaper serving a five town region. **Freq:** Weekly. **Print Method:** Offset. **Trim Size:** 11 x 16. **Cols./Page:** 6. **Col. Width:** 1 9/16 inches. **Col. Depth:** 15 1/2 inches. **Key Personnel:** L.L. Lehans, Associate Editor; Thomas Signa, Controller; Barbara Brown, General Manager. **USPS:** 303-930. **Subscription Rates:** $42 Individuals in state; $55 Out of state 1 year; $72 Two years in state; $39 Individuals senior, in state (1 years); $68 Two years senior, in state. **URL:** http://www.thelandmark.com. **Formerly:** The Holden Landmark. **Mailing address:** PO Box 546, Holden, MA 01520. **Remarks:** Accepts classified advertising. **Circ:** (Not Reported).

16219 ■ Warship International
International Naval Research Organization
PO Box 48
Holden, MA 01520-0048
Phone: (508)799-9229
Publication E-mail: editor@warship.org
Navy historical magazine. **Founded:** 1964. **Freq:** Quarterly. **Print Method:** Offset. **Trim Size:** 8.5″ x 11″. **Cols./Page:** 2. **Col. Width:** 46 nonpareils. **Col. Depth:** 134 agate lines. **ISSN:** 0043-0374 (print). **Subscription Rates:** $8.25 Single issue. **URL:** http://www.warship.org/wi.htm. **Remarks:** Accepts advertising. **Circ:** Paid 3000, Non-paid 62.

HOLLISTON

NE MA. Middlesex Co. 12 mi. W. of Quincy. Residential.

Circulation: ★ = AAM; △ or • = BPA; ♦ = CAC; ❑ = VAC; ⊕ = PO Statement; ‡ = Publisher's Report; Boldface figures = sworn; Light figures = estimated.

16220 ■ Journal of the New England Water Works Association
New England Water Works Association
125 Hopping Brook Rd.
Holliston, MA 01746
Phone: (508)893-7979
Fax: (508)893-9898
Technical journal reporting on association events as well as meetings and information of interest to the waterworks industry. **Freq:** Quarterly. **Print Method:** Offset. **Trim Size:** 7 1/4 x 10. **Cols./Page:** 2. **Col. Width:** 3 inches. **Col. Depth:** 8 inches. **Key Personnel:** Peter C. Karalekas, Jr., Editor. **ISSN:** 0028--4939 (print). **Subscription Rates:** Included in membership. **URL:** http://www.newwa.org/Publications/Journal,TheSource,Currents.aspx. **Ad Rates:** BW $445; 4C $1,300. **Remarks:** Accepts advertising. **Circ:** Paid ‡2800, Non-paid ‡243.

16221 ■ WHHB-FM - 99.9
370 Hollis St.
Holliston, MA 01746
Phone: (508)429-0654
Fax: (508)429-0653
Format: Eclectic; Alternative/New Music/Progressive. **Owner:** Holliston High School, 370 Hollis St, Holliston, MA 01746, Ph: (508)429-0677, Fax: (508)429-8225. **Founded:** 1969. **Operating Hours**: Daily, 6:00 a.m. - 7:30 a.m., 2:00 p.m. - 10:00 p.m. **Wattage**: 017. **Ad Rates:** Noncommercial. **URL:** http://www.holliston.k12.ma.us.

HOLYOKE

SW MA. Hampden Co. On Connecticut River, 10 mi. N. of Springfield. Prominent in the manufacturing of fine writing papers and paper converting. Manufactures air compressors, air conditioners, electronics, cotton, silk, rayon, synthetic fabrics, fabricated steel products, leather belting, detergent, optical and paper mill equipment, roller chains, rubber products, sporting goods.

16222 ■ Tracings
Sisters of Providence
Five Gamelin St.
Holyoke, MA 01040
Phone: (413)536-7511
Fax: (413)536-7917
Publisher's E-mail: sisters@sisofprov.org
Tabloid spreading mission awareness and reporting on the activities of the Sisters of Providence. **Founded:** 1980. **Freq:** Quarterly. **URL:** http://www.sisofprov.org/html/news.html. **Remarks:** Advertising not accepted. **Circ:** Free ‡3250.

16223 ■ WCCH-FM - 103.5
303 Homestead Ave.
Holyoke, MA 01040
Phone: (413)538-7000
Fax: (413)552-2045
Email: 1035wcch@hcc.edu
Format: Adult Contemporary. **Owner:** Holyoke Community College, 303 Homestead Ave., Holyoke, MA 01040, Ph: (413)538-7000. **Operating Hours**: 6 a.m.-11 p.m. **Wattage**: 009. **Ad Rates:** Noncommercial. **URL:** http://www.hcc.edu/life/student_clubs.html.

HOPKINTON

16224 ■ Mequoda Library
Mequoda Group L.L.C.
77 Main St.
Hopkinton, MA 01748
Electronic magazine that aims to provide a source for the latest research on website publishing and Internet marketing. **Freq:** Biweekly. **Key Personnel:** Don Nicholas, Executive Director; Amanda McArthur, Specialist, Media Resources. **Subscription Rates:** Free. **URL:** http://www.mequoda.com. **Circ:** (Not Reported).

HUDSON

NE MA. Middlesex Co. 5 mi. NW of Malboro. Manufactures footwear, aircraft parts and auxiliary equipment, woolens, rubber products, hand and edge tools, electronic equipment, lumber, nonferous castings, machine parts. Truck, poultry, fruit, dairy farms.

16225 ■ A-R Cable Investments, Inc.
577 Main St.
Hudson, MA 01749
Phone: (508)562-1675
Fax: (508)562-7591
Owner: Cablevision Systems Corp., One Media Crossways, Woodbury, NY 11797, Ph: (516)364-8450, Fax: (516)393-1780. **Formerly**: A-R Cable Services Inc. **Key Personnel:** Audrey M. Hall, Gen. Mgr., ahall@cablevision.com; David Green, Director, dgreen@cablevision.com; Carl Andersen, Dir. of Sales & Mktg., candersl@cablevision.com; Tom Garcia, Dir. of Engg., tgarcia@cablevision.com. **Cities Served:** Acton, Hudson, Maynard, Stow, Sudbury, Massachusetts: subscribing households 18,708; 69 channels; 2 community access channels.

HULL

16226 ■ The Highlander: The Magazine of Scottish Heritage
The Highlander
87 Highland Ave.
Hull, MA 02045
Phone: (781)925-0600
Fax: (781)925-1439
Publication E-mail: nray@highlandermagazine.com
Scottish history and culture, publication. **Freq:** 6/year January, March, May, July, September and November. **Print Method:** Offset. **Trim Size:** 8 1/2 x 11. **Cols./Page:** 3. **Col. Width:** 2 1/4 inches. **Col. Depth:** 10 inches. **ISSN:** 0161--5378 (print). **Subscription Rates:** $34.95 U.S.; $66 Two years; $49.95 Canada; $96 Canada 2 years; $54.95 Other countries; $106 Other countries 2 years. **URL:** http://www.highlandermagazine.com/inside.html. **Ad Rates:** BW $840. **Remarks:** Advertising accepted; rates available upon request. **Circ:** (Not Reported).

HYANNIS

E. MA. Barnstable Co. 45 mi. SE of Boston. Manufactures lumber, packaging machinery, bayberry candles. Fisheries. Summer resort. Agriculture. Cranberries.

16227 ■ The Barnstable Patriot
Ottawa Newspaper Inc.
4 Ocean St.
Hyannis, MA 02601
Phone: (508)771-1427
Fax: (508)790-3997
Publication E-mail: info@barnstablepatriot.com
emaroney@barnstablepatriot.com
Community newspaper. **Founded:** June 26, 1830. **Freq:** Weekly (Fri.). **Print Method:** Offset. **Cols./Page:** 6. **Col. Width:** 21 nonpareils. **Col. Depth:** 126 agate lines. **Key Personnel:** David Still, II, Editor; Barbara J. Hennigan, Business Manager; Edward F. Maroney, Associate Editor. **USPS:** 044-480. **Subscription Rates:** $29 Individuals; $53 Two years. **URL:** http://barnstablepatriot.com/home2. **Mailing address:** PO Box 1208, Hyannis, MA 02601. **Ad Rates:** PCI $12.75. **Remarks:** Accepts advertising. **Circ:** ‡4791.

16228 ■ Cape Cod Times
Cape Cod Times
319 Main St.
Hyannis, MA 02601
Phone: (508)775-1200
Fax: (508)771-3292
Free: 800-286-2233
Publisher's E-mail: news@capecodonline.com
General newspaper. **Founded:** 1936. **Freq:** Mon.-Sun. (morn.). **Print Method:** Offset. **Trim Size:** 13 x 21 1/4. **Cols./Page:** 6. **Col. Width:** 12.5 picas. **Col. Depth:** 21 1/4 inches. **Key Personnel:** Paul Pronovost, Editor-in-Chief. **USPS:** 089-120. **Subscription Rates:** $332 Individuals Mon-Sun, prepaid; $273 Individuals Fri-Sat-Sun, delivery. **URL:** http://www.capecodonline.com. **Formerly**: Cape Cod Standard Times. **Feature Editors:** Tim Miller, *Entertainment*, phone: (508)862-1140, tmiller@capecodonline.com. **Ad Rates:** SAU $31.88; PCI $31.88. **Remarks:** Accepts advertising. **Circ:** Mon.-Sat. ★**50521**, Sun. ★**58454**.

16229 ■ Cape Cod Broadcasting Media
737 W Main St.
Hyannis, MA 02601
Phone: (508)771-1224
Format: News; Country; Contemporary Country. **Networks:** NBC; ABC. **Ad Rates:** Advertising accepted; rates available upon request. **URL:** http://www.ccbmedia.com.

16230 ■ WCIB-FM - 101.9
154 Barnstable Rd.
Hyannis, MA 02601
Phone: (508)778-2888
Free: 877-266-5102
Format: Oldies. **Owner:** Qantum Communications Corp., LLC, at above address. **Founded:** 1971. **Operating Hours**: Continuous. **ADI**: Boston-Worcester,MA-Derry-Manchester,NH. **Wattage**: 50,000. **Ad Rates:** Advertising accepted; rates available upon request. **URL:** http://www.cool102.com.

16231 ■ WCOD-FM - 106
154 Barnstable Rd.
Hyannis, MA 02601
Phone: (508)778-2888
Free: 888-770-9263
Email: mcv@qantumcapecod.com
Format: Contemporary Hit Radio (CHR). **Owner:** Qantum of Cape Cod L.L.C., at above address, Hyannis, MA 02601. **Founded:** 1967. **Operating Hours**: Continuous; 100% local. **ADI**: Boston-Worcester,MA-Derry-Manchester,NH. **Wattage**: 50,000. **Ad Rates:** $30-70 per unit. **URL:** http://www.106wcod.com.

16232 ■ WFCC-FM - 107.5
737 W Main St.
Hyannis, MA 02601
Phone: (508)771-1224
Format: Classical. **Networks:** Concert Music Network (CMN). **Owner:** Cape Cod Broadcasting Media, 737 W Main St., Hyannis, MA 02601, Ph: (508)771-1224. **Founded:** 1987. **Operating Hours**: 6 a.m.-midnight. **Wattage**: 50,000. **Ad Rates:** Advertising accepted; rates available upon request. **URL:** http://www.wfcc.com.

16233 ■ WKPE-FM - 103.9
737 W Main St.
Hyannis, MA 02601
Owner: Cape Cod Broadcasting Media, 737 W Main St., Hyannis, MA 02601, Ph: (508)771-1224. **Founded:** 1970. **Wattage**: 5,500. **Ad Rates:** $50-120 for 30 seconds; $50-125 for 60 seconds.

16234 ■ WOCN-FM - 104.7
737 W Main St.
Hyannis, MA 02601
Phone: (508)771-1224
Fax: (508)775-2605
Free: 800-896-9626
Format: Adult Contemporary; News. **Networks:** CBS. **Owner:** Cape Cod Broadcasting Media, 737 W Main St., Hyannis, MA 02601, Ph: (508)771-1224. **Founded:** 1994. **Operating Hours**: Continuous. **ADI**: Boston-Worcester,MA-Derry-Manchester,NH. **Key Personnel:** Wayne White, Operations Mgr., Prog. Dir., wayne@ocean1047.com; Kate Watt, Promotions Dir., katewatt@capecodbroadcasting.com. **Wattage**: 50,000. **Ad Rates:** Noncommercial. **URL:** http://www.ocean1047.com.

16235 ■ WQRC-FM - 99.9
737 W Main St.
Hyannis, MA 02601
Phone: (508)771-1224
Format: Adult Contemporary. **Networks:** AP. **Owner:** Cape Cod Broadcasting Media, 737 W Main St., Hyannis, MA 02601, Ph: (508)771-1224. **Founded:** 1970. **Operating Hours**: Continuous; 2% network, 98% local. **ADI**: Boston-Worcester,MA-Derry-Manchester,NH. **Key Personnel:** Gregory D. Bone, Contact; Michelle Lorraine, Promotions Dir., michellelorraine@capecodbroadcasting.com; Stephen M. Colella, Dir. of Sales, stephencolella@capecodbroadcasting.com; Wayne W. White, Operations Mgr., waynewhite@capecodbroadcasting.com; Dennis Hanley, CFO; Gregory D. Bone, Contact. **Local Programs**: *Squeaky Clean Morning Show*; *Sunday Journal*, Sunday 7:00 a.m.; *Intelligence for your life*, Monday Tuesday Wednesday Thursday Friday Saturday 8:00 p.m. - 1:00 a.m. **Wattage**: 50,000. **Ad Rates:** $60-120 per unit. **URL:** http://www.wqrc.com.

16236 ■ WRZE-FM - 96.3
154 Barnstable Rd.
Hyannis, MA 02601
Phone: (508)778-2888
Fax: (508)778-9651
Free: 800-388-ROSE

Format: Top 40; Alternative/New Music/Progressive; Contemporary Hit Radio (CHR). **Key Personnel:** Steve McVie, Operations Mgr., mcv@qantumcapecod.com. **Ad Rates:** Noncommercial. **URL:** http://www.therose.net.

16237 ■ WXTK-FM - 95.1
154 Barnstable Rd.
Hyannis, MA 02601
Phone: (508)778-2888
Email: news@95wxtk.com
Format: News; Talk. **Owner:** Quantum of Cape Cod, at above address, Hyannis, MA. **Operating Hours:** Continuous. **Key Personnel:** Steve McVie, Dir. of Operations, mcv@qantumcapecod.com. **Wattage:** 50,000. **Ad Rates:** Advertising accepted; rates available upon request. **URL:** http://www.95wxtk.com.

INDIAN ORCHARD

16238 ■ Titanic Commutator
Titanic Historical Society, Inc.
PO Box 51053
Indian Orchard, MA 01151-0053
Phone: (413)543-4770
Fax: (413)583-3633
Publisher's E-mail: titanicinfo@titanichistoricalsociety.org
Freq: Quarterly. **Subscription Rates:** Included in membership. **URL:** http://www.titanichistoricalsociety.org/membership/commutator.html. **Remarks:** Accepts advertising. **Circ:** (Not Reported).

IPSWICH

NE MA. Essex Co. 25 mi. N. of Boston. Summer resort. Manufactures electronic and electrical products, leather. Shellfish industries.

16239 ■ Computer Science Index
EBSCO Information Services
10 Estes St.
Ipswich, MA 01938
Phone: (978)356-6500
Fax: (978)356-6565
Free: 800-653-2726
Publisher's E-mail: information@ebscohost.com
A bibliography of computer-related publications. **Founded:** 1971. **ISSN:** 0270-4846 (print). **URL:** http://www.ebsco.com/home/whatsnew/csi.asp; http://www.epnet.com. **Formerly**: Computer Literature Index. **Mailing address:** PO Box 682, Ipswich, MA 01938-2106. **Circ:** Controlled 500.

16240 ■ Criminal Justice Abstracts
EBSCO Information Services
10 Estes St.
Ipswich, MA 01938
Phone: (978)356-6500
Fax: (978)356-6565
Free: 800-653-2726
Publisher's E-mail: information@ebscohost.com
Legal and social science journal. Contains abstracts of books, articles, and reports on crime and justice published worldwide. **Freq:** Quarterly. **Print Method:** Offset. **Trim Size:** 6 x 9. **Cols./Page:** 1. **Col. Width:** 54 nonpareils. **Col. Depth:** 98 agate lines. **Key Personnel:** Judith A. Ryder, Editor; Leslie Bachman, Senior Editor. **ISSN:** 0146--9177 (print). **URL:** http://www.ebscohost.com/academic/criminal-justice-abstracts. **Formerly**: Crime and Delinquency Literature. **Mailing address:** PO Box 682, Ipswich, MA 01938-2106. **Remarks:** Accepts advertising. **Circ:** (Not Reported).

16241 ■ Educational Administration Abstracts
EBSCO Information Services
10 Estes St.
Ipswich, MA 01938
Phone: (978)356-6500
Fax: (978)356-6565
Free: 800-653-2726
Publisher's E-mail: information@ebscohost.com
Journal providing educational administration abstracts. **Founded:** 1966. **Freq:** Quarterly. **Print Method:** Offset. **Trim Size:** 5 1/2 x 8 1/2. **Cols./Page:** 1. **Col. Width:** 50 nonpareils. **Col. Depth:** 100 agate lines. **Key Personnel:** Susan Twombly, PhD, Commissioner; John C. Daresh, PhD, Commissioner; Charles Butler, PhD, Commissioner; Francis Stage, PhD, Commissioner; Carol Merz, PhD, Commissioner; Lynn Arney, EdD, Commissioner. **ISSN:** 0013-1601 (print). **Subscription Rates:** $876 Institutions print only; $193 Individuals print only; $241 Single issue institutional; print; $63 Single issue individual; print. **URL:** http://www.ebscohost.com/academic/educational-administration-abstracts. **Mailing address:** PO Box 682, Ipswich, MA 01938-2106. **Ad Rates:** BW $480. **Remarks:** Accepts advertising. **Circ:** Paid 300.

16242 ■ Family Studies Abstracts
EBSCO Information Services
10 Estes St.
Ipswich, MA 01938
Phone: (978)356-6500
Fax: (978)356-6565
Free: 800-653-2726
Publisher's E-mail: information@ebscohost.com
Journal containing family studies abstracts. **Freq:** Quarterly. **Print Method:** Offset. **Trim Size:** 5 1/2 x 8 1/2. **Cols./Page:** 1. **Col. Width:** 50 nonpareils. **Col. Depth:** 100 agate lines. **ISSN:** 0164--0283 (print). **Subscription Rates:** $999 Institutions print only; $215 Individuals print only; $275 Single issue institutional; $70 Single issue individual. **URL:** http://www.ebscohost.com/academic/family-studies-abstracts. **Mailing address:** PO Box 682, Ipswich, MA 01938-2106. **Ad Rates:** BW $445; 4C $895. **Remarks:** Accepts advertising. **Circ:** Paid ‡300.

16243 ■ Horn and Whistle
Horn and Whistle Enthusiasts Group
c/o Eric C. Larson, Publisher
2 Abell Ave.
Ipswich, MA 01938
Official Journal of the Horn & Whistle Enthusiasts Group. **Freq:** Quarterly. **Trim Size:** 8 x 11. **Cols./Page:** 2 and 4. **Col. Width:** 21 picas. **Col. Depth:** 9 1/2 inches. **Key Personnel:** Eric C. Larson, Publisher. **Subscription Rates:** $25 U.S. and Canada; $30 Other countries; $10 Individuals online. **Remarks:** Accepts advertising. **Circ:** (Not Reported).

16244 ■ Human Resources Abstracts
EBSCO Information Services
10 Estes St.
Ipswich, MA 01938
Phone: (978)356-6500
Fax: (978)356-6565
Free: 800-653-2726
Publisher's E-mail: information@ebscohost.com
Journal of abstracts on employment and labor relations. **Freq:** Quarterly. **Print Method:** Offset. **Trim Size:** 5 1/2 x 8 1/2. **Cols./Page:** 1. **Col. Width:** 50 nonpareils. **Col. Depth:** 100 agate lines. **ISSN:** 0099-2453 (print). **Subscription Rates:** $1173 Institutions print only; $266 Individuals print only; $323 Institutions single print; $86 Individuals single print. **URL:** http://www.ebscohost.com/academic/human-resources-abstracts. **Mailing address:** PO Box 682, Ipswich, MA 01938-2106. **Ad Rates:** BW $445; 4C $490. **Remarks:** Accepts advertising. **Circ:** Paid ‡500.

16245 ■ Internet & Personal Computing Abstracts
EBSCO Information Services
10 Estes St.
Ipswich, MA 01938
Phone: (978)356-6500
Fax: (978)356-6565
Free: 800-653-2726
Publisher's E-mail: information@ebscohost.com
Abstracts journal covering 120 publications on the Internet and personal computers. **Freq:** Quarterly. **ISSN:** 1529-7705 (print). **Subscription Rates:** $235 Individuals; $442 Two years; $245 Canada and Mexico; $260 Elsewhere. **URL:** http://www.ebscohost.com/public/internet-personal-computing-abstracts. **Formerly**: MCA. **Also known as:** Micro Computer Abstracts. **Mailing address:** PO Box 682, Ipswich, MA 01938-2106. **Remarks:** Advertising not accepted. **Circ:** (Not Reported).

16246 ■ Ipswich Chronicle
GateHouse Media Inc.
72 Cherry Hill Dr.
Ipswich, MA 01938
Community newspaper (tabloid). **Freq:** Weekly (Thurs.). **Print Method:** Offset. **Trim Size:** 11 3/8 x 17. **Cols./Page:** 5. **Col. Width:** 2 1/16 inches. **Col. Depth:** 16 inches. **Key Personnel:** Daniel Mac Alpine, Editor, phone: (978)739-1303; Joshua Boyd, Editor, phone: (978)739-8512. **USPS:** 269-640. **Subscription Rates:** $69.95 Individuals; $89.95 Out of area. **URL:** http://ipswich.wickedlocal.com. **Ad Rates:** BW $980; 4C $1,480; PCI $12.25. **Remarks:** Accepts advertising. **Circ:** Combined 60253.

16247 ■ Race Relations Abstracts
EBSCO Information Services
10 Estes St.
Ipswich, MA 01938
Phone: (978)356-6500
Fax: (978)356-6565
Free: 800-653-2726
Publisher's E-mail: information@ebscohost.com
Scholarly journal covering race relations, including discrimination, education, employment, health, politics, law and legislation. **Freq:** Quarterly. **ISSN:** 0307--9201 (print). **URL:** http://www.ebscohost.com/academic/race-relations-abstracts. **Formerly**: SAGE Race Relations Abstracts. **Mailing address:** PO Box 682, Ipswich, MA 01938-2106. **Remarks:** Accepts advertising. **Circ:** (Not Reported).

16248 ■ Social Sciences Index
EBSCO Information Services
10 Estes St.
Ipswich, MA 01938
Phone: (978)356-6500
Fax: (978)356-6565
Free: 800-653-2726
Publisher's E-mail: custserv@hwwilson.com
Index of social sciences periodicals. **Freq:** Monthly. **Print Method:** Offset. **Trim Size:** 6 3/4 x 10 1/8. **Cols./Page:** 2. **Col. Width:** 30 nonpareils. **Col. Depth:** 123 agate lines. **ISSN:** 0019--2872 (print). **URL:** http://www.ebscohost.com/academic/social-sciences-index-retrospective. **Remarks:** Advertising not accepted. **Circ:** (Not Reported).

16249 ■ Urban Studies Abstracts
EBSCO Information Services
10 Estes St.
Ipswich, MA 01938
Phone: (978)356-6500
Fax: (978)356-6565
Free: 800-653-2726
Publisher's E-mail: information@ebscohost.com
Journal containing abstracts on urban studies. **Freq:** Quarterly February, May, August, November. **Print Method:** Offset. **Trim Size:** 5 1/2 x 8 1/2. **Cols./Page:** 1. **Col. Width:** 50 nonpareils. **Col. Depth:** 100 agate lines. **ISSN:** 0090-5747 (print). **Subscription Rates:** $967 Institutions print only; $261 Individuals print only; $266 Institutions single print; $85 Individuals single print. **URL:** http://www.ebscohost.com/academic/urban-studies-abstracts. **Mailing address:** PO Box 682, Ipswich, MA 01938-2106. **Ad Rates:** BW $445; 4C $895. **Remarks:** Accepts advertising. **Circ:** Paid ‡300.

16250 ■ Violence & Abuse Abstracts
EBSCO Information Services
10 Estes St.
Ipswich, MA 01938
Phone: (978)356-6500
Fax: (978)356-6565
Free: 800-653-2726
Publisher's E-mail: information@ebscohost.com
Journal covering all aspects of violence and abuse. **Freq:** Quarterly. **Print Method:** Offset. **Trim Size:** 5 1/2 x 8 1/2. **Cols./Page:** 1. **Col. Width:** 50 nonpareils. **Col. Depth:** 100 agate lines. **ISSN:** 1077--2197 (print). **URL:** http://www.ebscohost.com/academic/violence-abuse-abstracts. **Mailing address:** PO Box 682, Ipswich, MA 01938-2106. **Remarks:** Accepts advertising. **Circ:** (Not Reported).

JAMAICA PLAIN

16251 ■ Arnoldia: Magazine of the Arnold Arboretum
Arnold Arboretum Harvard University
125 Arborway
Jamaica Plain, MA 02130-3500
Phone: (617)524-1718
Fax: (617)524-1418
Publication E-mail: arnoldia@arnarb.harvard.edu
Journal of the Arnold Arboretum covering horticulture, botany, and the history of landscape design. **Freq:**

Circulation: ★ = AAM; △ or • = BPA; ♦ = CAC; ❑ = VAC; ⊕ = PO Statement; ‡ = Publisher's Report; Boldface figures = sworn; Light figures = estimated.

Quarterly. **Key Personnel:** Michele Levy, Director, Communications, phone: (617)645-6672; Arnold Arboretum, Manager, Circulation. **ISSN:** 0042-633 (print). **Alt. Formats:** PDF. **URL:** http://arnoldia.arboretum.harvard.edu. **Remarks:** Advertising not accepted. **Circ:** 4450.

KINGSTON

16252 ■ Edible South Shore
Edible Communities Inc.
c/o Hart Design LLC
15 Evergreen St.
Kingston, MA 02364-1425
Phone: (781)582-1726
Fax: (781)582-1726
Publication E-mail: info@ediblesouthshore.com
Magazine covering the local food of Plymouth and Bristol Counties. **Freq:** Quarterly. **Key Personnel:** Laurie Hepworth, Publisher; Michael Hart, Creative Director, Publisher. **URL:** http://ediblesouthshore.com. **Remarks:** Accepts advertising. **Circ:** (Not Reported).

LANCASTER

16253 ■ Earth Sciences History
History of Earth Sciences Society
c/o David Spanagel, Treasurer
PO Box 70
Lancaster, MA 01523
Journal promoting historical work on all areas of the earth sciences including geology, geography, geophysics, oceanography, paleontology, meteorology, and climatology. **Freq:** Semiannual. **ISSN:** 0736--623X (print); **EISSN:** 1944--6187 (electronic). **Subscription Rates:** Included in membership. **URL:** http://www.historyearthscience.org/journal.html. **Circ:** (Not Reported).

LAWRENCE

NE MA. Essex Co. On Merrimack River, 27 mi. NW of Boston. Manufactures electronics, paper products, rubber products, leather goods, textiles, rugs, shoes, soap, chemicals, mattresses, plastics, machinery, boxes, boats, furniture, cosmetics.

16254 ■ The Long Story
The Long Story
18 Eaton St.
Lawrence, MA 01843
Phone: (978)686-7638
Literary magazine covering fiction and poetry. **Freq:** Semiannual. **Key Personnel:** R.P. Burnham, Editor. **ISSN:** 0741--4242 (print). **Subscription Rates:** $15 Individuals; $8 Individuals single copy; $14 Individuals; $25 Other countries air mail. **Alt. Formats:** PDF. **URL:** http://www.longstorylitmag.com/longstorylitmag/LongStory.html. **Remarks:** Advertising not accepted. **Circ:** Combined 1100.

LEXINGTON

NE MA. Middlesex Co. 11 mi. NW of Boston. (Branch of Boston P.O.) Residential town of historical interest. Research, light industry. Nurseries.

16255 ■ Arlington Advocate
Arlington Chamber of Commerce
9 Meriam St.
Lexington, MA 02420
Phone: (781)674-7726
Fax: (781)674-7735
Publisher's E-mail: info@arlcc.org
Freq: Weekly (Thurs.) Periodic. **Print Method:** Offset. **Trim Size:** 13 3/4 x 22 1/2. **Cols./Page:** 6. **Col. Width:** 12 nonpareils. **Col. Depth:** 21 inches. **Key Personnel:** Andrew Levin, Editor; Chuck Goodrich, Publisher; Doug Hastings, Editor, phone: (781)674-7724. **URL:** http://arlington.wickedlocal.com. **Ad Rates:** BW $1418.76; 4C $1718.76; SAU $12.44. **Remarks:** Advertising not accepted. **Circ:** (Not Reported).

16256 ■ Belmont Citizen-Herald
GateHouse Media Inc.
9 Meriam St.
Lexington, MA 02420
Local newspaper. **Freq:** Weekly (Thurs.). **Print Method:** Offset. **Cols./Page:** 6. **Col. Width:** 2 1/16 inches. **Col. Depth:** 21 1/2 inches. **Key Personnel:** Chuck Goodrich, Publisher; Mark Goodman, Editor, phone: (978)371-5739. **URL:** http://belmont.wickedlocal.com/. **Ad Rates:** BW $1512; 4C $1812; SAU $12. **Remarks:** Accepts advertising. **Circ:** (Not Reported).

16257 ■ CryoGas International: Over 35 Years of Reporting on Cryogenics, Industrial Gases, and Related Systems
J.R. Campbell and Associates Inc.
Five Militia Dr.
Lexington, MA 02421
Phone: (781)862-0624
Fax: (781)863-9411
Publisher's E-mail: cgi@cryogas.com
Professional magazine focusing on the business of industrial gases. **Freq:** Monthly 11/yr (Aug. and Sept. issues combined). **Print Method:** Offset. **Trim Size:** 8 1/2 x 11. **Cols./Page:** 2. **Col. Width:** 3 2/5 inches. **Col. Depth:** 9 inches. **Key Personnel:** John T. Miaskowski, Manager, Sales, phone: (440)572-4744, fax: (440)572-3389; Agnes H. Baker, Managing Editor; John R. Campbell, Publisher; Melissa Martel, Manager, Circulation. **ISSN:** 1052-0139 (print). **Subscription Rates:** $150 Individuals; $200 Other countries. **URL:** http://www.gasworld.com/magazines/cryogas. **Formerly:** Cryogenic Information Report. **Ad Rates:** 4C $3,090. **Remarks:** Accepts advertising. **Circ:** (Not Reported).

16258 ■ Lexington Minuteman
GateHouse Media Inc.
9 Meriam St.
Lexington, MA 02420
Community newspaper. **Freq:** Weekly (Thurs.). **Print Method:** Offset. **Cols./Page:** 6. **Col. Width:** 20 nonpareils. **Col. Depth:** 294 agate lines. **Key Personnel:** Chuck Goodrich, Publisher; Ben Aaronson, Editor, phone: (781)674-7725; Doug Hastings, Editor, phone: (781)674-7724. **USPS:** 331-340. **Subscription Rates:** $74 Individuals; $85 Out of area. **URL:** http://lexington.wickedlocal.com. **Ad Rates:** PCI $12.50. **Remarks:** Accepts advertising. **Circ:** (Not Reported).

16259 ■ The Northern Light: A Window for Freemasonry
Supreme Council, Scottish Rite, NMJ, USA
33 Marrett Rd
Lexington, MA 02421
Phone: (781)862-4410
Fax: (781)863-1833
Free: 800-814-1432
Publication E-mail: editor@supremecouncil.org
Magazine containing articles of interest to Masons and their families. **Freq:** Quarterly. **Print Method:** Offset. **Trim Size:** 8 1/8 x 10 7/8. **Cols./Page:** 3. **Col. Width:** 27 nonpareils. **Col. Depth:** 136 agate lines. **Key Personnel:** Alan Foulds, Editor, phone: (781)465-3320. **ISSN:** 1088--4416 (print). **Subscription Rates:** Included in membership. **Alt. Formats:** Download; PDF. **URL:** http://www.scottishritenmj.org/members-center/the-northern-light. **Mailing address:** PO Box 519, Lexington, MA 02420-0519. **Remarks:** Advertising not accepted. **Circ:** (Not Reported).

16260 ■ Oil and Energy: Serving the Independent Fuel and Heating Contractor
New England Fuel Institute
238 Bedford St., Ste. 2
Lexington, MA 02420
Phone: (617)924-1000
Fax: (617)924-1022
Publication E-mail: oil.energy@gstone.biz
Magazine for the independent fuel and heating contractor. **Freq:** Monthly. **Print Method:** Sheet fed Offset. **Trim Size:** 8 1/8 x 10 7/8. **Cols./Page:** 3. **Col. Width:** 13 picas. **Col. Depth:** 10 inches. **Key Personnel:** Steven Andrews, Managing Editor. **ISSN:** 0044--0205 (print). **Subscription Rates:** $40 Canada members; $60 Other countries members; $30 Nonmembers. **URL:** http://oilandenergyonline.com. **Formerly:** Yankee Oilman Magazine. **Ad Rates:** BW $1765; 4C $2575. **Remarks:** Advertising accepted; rates available upon request. **Circ:** Controlled ‡6605, Paid ‡2045.

16261 ■ WIN News: Women's International Network News
Women's International Network
187 Grant St.
Lexington, MA 02420-2126
Publication E-mail: winnews@igc.org
Journal by, for, and about women, reporting on the status of women and women's rights around the globe. **Freq:** Quarterly winter, spring, summer, autumn. **Print Method:** Letterpress and offset. **Trim Size:** 7 x 11. **Cols./Page:** 2. **Col. Width:** 36 nonpareils. **Col. Depth:** 140 agate lines. **Key Personnel:** Marcia L. Williams, Publisher; Fran P. Hosken, Editor. **ISSN:** 0145--7985 (print). **Subscription Rates:** $35 Individuals 4 issues ; $48 Institutions; $52 Canada and Mexico; $10 Individuals air mail; $15 Single issue back issues per year; Included in membership. **URL:** http://www.feminist.com/win.htm. **Remarks:** Accepts advertising. **Circ:** ‡1100.

LITTLETON

NE MA. Middlesex Co. 4 mi. N. of Harvard. Residential.

16262 ■ Behavior and Philosophy
Cambridge Center for Behavioral Studies
550 Newtown Rd., Ste. 950
Littleton, MA 01460
Phone: (978)369-2227
Fax: (978)369-8584
Free: 866-509-0467
Journal focusing on the study of philosophical, metaphysical, and methodological foundations of the study of behavior, brain, and mind. **Key Personnel:** Erik Arntzen, Editor. **ISSN:** 1053--8348 (print). **Alt. Formats:** Download; PDF. **URL:** http://www.behavior.org/resource.php?id=319; http://www.behavior.org/scholarship.php?tab=Journal; http://www.behavior.org/interest.php?id=2&tab=Journal&scholar&journ=bap#tabs. **Mailing address:** PO Box 7067, Beverly, MA 01915. **Remarks:** Accepts advertising. **Circ:** (Not Reported).

16263 ■ Behavioral Technology Today
Cambridge Center for Behavioral Studies
550 Newtown Rd., Ste. 950
Littleton, MA 01460
Phone: (978)369-2227
Fax: (978)369-8584
Free: 866-509-0467
Journal disseminating results of behavioral research, of importance to the general public. **Key Personnel:** H.S. Pennypacker, Editor; Murray Sidman, Editor. **ISSN:** 1532--9518 (print). **Alt. Formats:** Download; PDF. **URL:** http://www.behavior.org/scholarship.php?tab=Journal&journ=btt; http://www.behavior.org/interest.php?id=2&tab=Journal&scholar&journ=btt#tabs. **Mailing address:** PO Box 7067, Beverly, MA 01915. **Remarks:** Accepts advertising. **Circ:** (Not Reported).

LONGMEADOW

16264 ■ WRCX-FM - 102.1
45 Fisher Ave. E
Longmeadow, MA 01106
Phone: (413)525-4141
Fax: (413)525-4334
Format: Eclectic. **Owner:** Radio Continental, Rivadavia 835, Capital Federal, Argentina. **Ad Rates:** Advertising accepted; rates available upon request. **URL:** http://rock102.com.

LOWELL

NE MA. Middlesex Co. On Merrimack River, at mouth of Concord River, 25 mi. NW of Boston. University of Lowell. Urban National Cultural Park. Manufactures textile machines, knit products, plastics, textiles. Electronic printing and publishing industries.

16265 ■ Lowell Sun
Lowell Sun Publishing Co.
491 Dutton St.
Lowell, MA 01854
Phone: (978)458-7100
Free: 800-359-1300
Publisher's E-mail: moneil@mediaonene.com
General newspaper. **Founded:** 1878. **Freq:** Daily (eve.), Sat. and Sun. (morn.). **Print Method:** Letterpress. **Cols./Page:** 6. **Col. Width:** 25 nonpareils. **Col. Depth:** 301 agate lines. **Key Personnel:** Mark O'Neil, President, Publisher, phone: (978)970-4807; James Campanini, Editor, phone: (978)970-4621. **USPS:** 321-180. **Subscription Rates:** $208 Individuals; $91 Individuals Sunday delivery. **URL:** http://www.lowellsun.com. **Remarks:** Accepts advertising. **Circ:** Mon.-Fri. ★**47367**, Sat. ★**41577**, Sun. ★**50116**.

16266 ■ UMASS Lowell Connector: Umass Lowell's only student run news-paper
University of Massachusetts at Lowell

1 University Ave.
Lowell, MA 01854
Phone: (978)934-4000
Publication E-mail: connector@uml.edu
Collegiate newspaper. **Founded:** 1950. **Freq:** Weekly. **Print Method:** Broadsheet. **Trim Size:** 11 x 21. **Cols./Page:** 6. **Col. Depth:** 1 agate lines. **Key Personnel:** Christopher Tran, Editor-in-Chief. **URL:** http://umlconnector.com. **Formerly**: The Text. **Remarks:** Accepts advertising. **Circ:** Free ‡3000.

16267 ■ The Valley Dispatch
The Dispatch News
491 Dutton St. Sq.
Lowell, MA 01854
Phone: (978)459-1300
Local newspaper. **Freq:** Weekly (Fri.). **Print Method:** Offset. **Trim Size:** 10 x 16. **Cols./Page:** 8. **Col. Width:** 1 1/8 inches. **Col. Depth:** 224 agate lines. **Key Personnel:** Mark O'Neil, President, Publisher, phone: (978)970-4807; Mike Sheehan, Manager, Circulation, phone: (978)970-4855; James Campanini, Editor, phone: (978)970-4621. **ISSN:** 8750-1341 (print). **URL:** http://www.thevalleydispatch.com/. **Remarks:** Accepts classified advertising. **Circ:** 17922.

16268 ■ WCAP-AM - 980
243 Central St.
Lowell, MA 01852
Phone: (978)454-0404
Fax: (978)458-9124
Format: News; Sports; Talk. **Simulcasts:** WCVB-TV. **Networks:** ABC; Fox. **Founded:** 1951. **Operating Hours**: Continuous. **Key Personnel:** Mary Treen, Traffic Mgr., mary@980wcap.com. **Local Programs**: *The Beatles and Before*, Monday Thursday Tuesday Wednesday Friday Sunday 12:15 a.m. - 5:30 a.m. 12:15 a.m. - 5:30 a.m.; 7:00 p.m. - 12:00 a.m. 12:15 a.m. - 5:30 a.m.; 7:00 p.m. - 9:00 p.m. 12:15 a.m. - 5:30 a.m.; 7:00 p.m. - 10:00 p.m. 12:15 a.m. - 6:30 a.m.; 1:00 p.m. - 2:00 p.m.; *Paying Attention!*, Saturday 10:00 a.m. - 12:00 p.m.; *Good Night with Dick Summer*, Sunday Monday Tuesday Wednesday Thursday Friday Saturday 12:00 a.m. - 12:15 a.m.; *Merrimack Valley Radio in the Morning*, Monday Tuesday Wednesday Thursday Friday 6:00 a.m. - 10:00 a.m. **Wattage:** 5,000. **Ad Rates:** Advertising accepted; rates available upon request. **URL:** http://www.980wcap.com.

16269 ■ WJUL-FM - 91.5
1 University Ave.
Lowell, MA 01854
Phone: (978)934-4970
Email: wjul@uml.edu
Format: Religious. **Owner:** University of Massachusetts at Lowell, 1 University Ave., Cumnock Hall, Ste. 110, MA 01854-5104. **Founded:** 1952. **Formerly**: WLTI-FM. **Operating Hours**: 5 a.m.-4 a.m. **Key Personnel:** Abram Taber, Gen. Mgr., gm@wuml.org; Nate Osit, Station Mgr., sm@wuml.org; Patrick Murphy, Music Dir., md@wuml.org; Gretchen Lewis, Music Dir., Dir. of Programs, asstmd@wuml.org; Nate Walsh, Chief Engineer, beeffajitas@earthlink.net; Kelly Andreoni, Contact. **Wattage**: 1,400 ERP. **Ad Rates:** Noncommercial. **URL:** http://www.wuml.org.

16270 ■ WUML-FM - 91.5
One University Ave.
Lowell, MA 01854
Phone: (978)934-4969
Email: info@wuml.org
Format: Information. **URL:** http://www.wuml.org.

LUNENBURG

16271 ■ WCMX-AM - 1000
194 Electric Ave.
Lunenburg, MA 01462
Phone: (978)582-8282
Fax: (978)582-4978
Format: Religious. **Owner:** Twin City Baptist Temple Inc., at above address. **Founded:** 1967. **Formerly**: WLMS-AM. **Operating Hours**: 6 a.m.-7 p.m.; 100% local. **Key Personnel:** Nathan Burke, Station Mgr. **Wattage**: 1,000. **Ad Rates:** Noncommercial. **URL:** http://www.hope1000.net.

LYNN

NE MA. Essex Co. On Massachusetts Bay, 10 mi. NE of Boston. Large trade center. Manufactures electrical and electronic equipment, aircraft jet engines, steam turbines and gears, shoes and allied products, shoe welding, folding, and taping machinery, incandescent lamps, leather goods and dressing, plastics, rubber goods moulds, wire and foundry products, upholstery springs. Lobster fisheries.

16272 ■ The Daily Item
The Daily Item
38 Exchange St.
Lynn, MA 09103
Publication E-mail: internet@dailyitem.com
General newspaper. **Founded:** 1877. **Freq:** Mon.-Sat. (morn.). **Print Method:** Offset. **Trim Size:** 14 x 22 3/4. **Cols./Page:** 6. **Col. Width:** 12.5 picas. **Col. Depth:** 294 agate lines. **Key Personnel:** Gary Grossman, Publisher. **Subscription Rates:** $65 By mail 13 weeks. **URL:** http://www.dailyitem.com; http://www.itemlive.com. **Ad Rates:** GLR $15.26; BW $1,922.76; 4C $2,187.76; SAU $15.26. **Remarks:** Accepts advertising. **Circ:** ‡21,220, ‡25,300.

16273 ■ WFNX-FM - 99.9
25 Exchange St.
Lynn, MA 01901
Phone: (781)595-9369
Format: Alternative/New Music/Progressive. **Simulcasts:** WFEX-FM. **Owner:** Phoenix Media Group, 126 Brookline Ave., Boston, MA 02215, Ph: (617)536-5390, Fax: (617)536-1463. **Founded:** 1983. **Operating Hours**: Continuous. **Wattage:** 1,850. **Ad Rates:** Advertising accepted; rates available upon request. Combined advertising rates available with WFEX-FM, WPHX-FM, and WWRX-FM. **URL:** http://www.wfnx.com.

LYNNFIELD

N. MA. Essex Co. 12 mi. NE of Boston. Residential.

16274 ■ New England Bride
New England Bride Inc.
29 Durham Dr.
Lynnfield, MA 01940
Phone: (978)535-4186
Fax: (978)535-3090
Free: 800-241-5458
Magazine for brides-to-be in six New England states. **Freq:** Monthly. **Print Method:** Offset. **Trim Size:** 8 1/8 x 10 7/8. **Cols./Page:** 3. **Col. Width:** 27 nonpareils. **Col. Depth:** 140 agate lines. **Key Personnel:** Laura Catizone, Associate Publisher, phone: (800)241-5458; Thomas J. Parello, Publisher. **ISSN:** 1539--2120 (print). **Subscription Rates:** $36 Individuals; $10 Individuals 1st copy (add $5 for each additional copy). **Ad Rates:** BW $3,560. **Remarks:** Accepts advertising. **Circ:** Non-paid ‡15075.

MALDEN

NE MA. Middlesex Co. On Malden River, 5 mi. N. of Boston. (Branch of Boston P.O.) Manufactures rubber boots, fire hoses, paints, varnishes, drugs, radio and electronic parts, shoes, spices, sheet steel, aluminum products, auto bodies, seat covers, draperies, furniture.

16275 ■ Abacus: A Journal of Accounting, Finance and Business Studies
Wiley-Blackwell
350 Main St.
Commerce Pl.
Malden, MA 02148-5018
Phone: (781)388-8200
Fax: (781)388-8210
Free: 800-216-2552
Journal covering academic and professional aspects of accounting, finance and business. **Freq:** Quarterly. **Key Personnel:** S. Jones, Editor-in-Chief; J. Baxter, Board Member; A. Charitou, Associate Editor. **ISSN:** 0001--3072 (print); **EISSN:** 1467--6281 (electronic). **Subscription Rates:** $733 Institutions America, online only - annual; £514 Institutions U.K, online only - annual; £587 Institutions Europe, Euro and non-euro zone, online only - annual; $569 Institutions Australia and New Zealand, online only - annual; $1003 Institutions ROW, online only - annual; $880 Institutions America, print and online - annual; £617 Institutions U.K, print and online - annual; €705 Institutions Europe, euro and non-euro zone, print and online - annual; $683 Institutions Australia and New Zealand, print and online - annual; $1204 Institutions ROW, print and online - annual; $733 Institutions America, print only - annual; £514 Institutions U.K, print only - annual; €587 Institutions Europe, euro and non-euro zone, print only - annual; $569 Institutions Australia and New Zealand, print only - annual; $1003 Institutions ROW, print only - annual; $166 Individuals America, online and print - annual; £117 Individuals ROW, U.K and Europe (non-euro zone), online and print - annual; €146 Individuals Europe, online and print - annual; A$164 Individuals Australia and New Zealand, online and print - annual. **URL:** http://onlinelibrary.wiley.com/journal/10.1111/(ISSN)1467-6281. **Remarks:** Accepts advertising. **Circ:** (Not Reported).

16276 ■ Academic Emergency Medicine: Official Journal of the Society for Academic Emergency Medicine
Wiley-Blackwell
350 Main St.
Commerce Pl.
Malden, MA 02148-5018
Phone: (781)388-8200
Fax: (781)388-8210
Free: 800-216-2552
Journal of emergency medicine. **Freq:** Monthly. **Print Method:** Web - Sheetfed. **Trim Size:** 8 1/4 x 10 7/8. **Key Personnel:** Jeffrey A. Kline, Editor-in-Chief; David C. Cone, MD, Editor; Carey D. Chisholm, MD, Editor; Roger J. Lewis, MD, Reviewer; Mark Hauswald, MD, Associate, Senior Editor. **ISSN:** 1069--6563 (print); **EISSN:** 1553--2712 (electronic). **Subscription Rates:** $367 Institutions online only; $441 Institutions print + online; $202 Individuals print + online; $111 Members print + online; £196 Institutions online only; £236 Institutions print + online; £101 U.S. and other countries print + online; £57 Members U.K., Europe & rest of the world - print + online; €246 Institutions online only; €296 Institutions print + online; €154 Individuals print + online; €84 Members print + online; $377 Institutions, other countries online only; $453 Institutions, other countries print + online. **URL:** http://onlinelibrary.wiley.com/journal/10.1111/(ISSN)1553-2712. **Remarks:** Accepts advertising. **Circ:** (Not Reported).

16277 ■ Acta Crystallographica Section A: Foundations of Crystallography
Wiley-Blackwell
350 Main St.
Commerce Pl.
Malden, MA 02148-5018
Phone: (781)388-8200
Fax: (781)388-8210
Free: 800-216-2552
Publisher's E-mail: execsec@iucr.org
Publication covering crystallogrphy in English, French, German and Russian. **Freq:** Bimonthly. **Key Personnel:** Dr. Vladimir E. Dmitrienko, Editor; Prof. Samar Hasnain, Editor-in-Chief. **ISSN:** 0108--7673 (print); **EISSN:** 2053--2733 (electronic). **Subscription Rates:** $993 Institutions online only, The Americas; £593 Institutions online only, UK; €753 Institutions online only, Europe; $993 Institutions, other countries online only; $251 Individuals online only; £150 Individuals online only, UK and Europe (non-euro zone); €225 Individuals online only, Europe; 150 Other countries online only. **URL:** http://journals.iucr.org/a/journalhomepage.html; http://onlinelibrary.wiley.com/journal/10.1111/(ISSN)2053-2733. **Remarks:** Advertising accepted; rates available upon request. **Circ:** (Not Reported).

16278 ■ Advanced Functional Materials: Combining Chemtronics and Journal of Molecular Electronics
Wiley-Blackwell
350 Main St.
Commerce Pl.
Malden, MA 02148-5018
Phone: (781)388-8200
Fax: (781)388-8210
Free: 800-216-2552
Journal on advanced electronic and optic technologies for chemists, physicists, materials scientists, and bioengineers. **Freq:** 48/yr. **Key Personnel:** Joern Ritterbusch, Editor-in-Chief. **ISSN:** 1616--301X (print); **EISSN:** 1616--3028 (electronic). **Subscription Rates:** $11099

Circulation: ★ = AAM; △ or • = BPA; ♦ = CAC; ❑ = VAC; ⊕ = PO Statement; ‡ = Publisher's Report; Boldface figures = sworn; Light figures = estimated.

Institutions print and online; $11099 Institutions, Canada and Mexico print and online; £5664 Institutions print and online; €9194 Institutions print and online; $11099 Institutions, other countries print and online. **URL:** http://onlinelibrary.wiley.com/journal/10.1002/(ISSN)1616-3028. **Formerly**: Advanced Materials for Optics and Electronics. **Remarks:** Accepts advertising. **Circ:** (Not Reported).

16279 ■ Africa Research Bulletin: Economic, Financial and Technical Series
Wiley-Blackwell
350 Main St.
Commerce Pl.
Malden, MA 02148-5018
Phone: (781)388-8200
Fax: (781)388-8210
Free: 800-216-2552
Journal focusing on political and economic developments throughout Africa. **Freq:** Monthly. **Key Personnel:** Virginia Baily, Editor; Veronica Hoskins, Editor. **ISSN:** 0001--9852 (print); **EISSN:** 1467--6346 (electronic). **Subscription Rates:** $2795 Institutions print and online; £1475 Institutions print and online; €1872 Institutions print and online; $1876 Institutions print and online; Africa; $3263 Institutions, other countries print and online; $2329 Institutions print or online; £1229 Institutions print or online; $2719 Institutions, other countries print or online; $1563 Institutions Africa; print or online. **URL:** http://www.wiley.com/WileyCDA/WileyTitle/productCd-ARBE.html; http://onlinelibrary.wiley.com/journal/10.1111/(ISSN)1467-6346. **Remarks:** Accepts advertising. **Circ:** (Not Reported).

16280 ■ Africa Research Bulletin: Political, Social and Cultural Series
Wiley-Blackwell
350 Main St.
Commerce Pl.
Malden, MA 02148-5018
Phone: (781)388-8200
Fax: (781)388-8210
Free: 800-216-2552
Journal focusing on political and economic developments throughout Africa. **Freq:** Monthly. **Key Personnel:** Virginia Baily, Editor; Elizabeth Oliver, Editor; Veronica Hoskins, Editor. **ISSN:** 0001--9844 (print); **EISSN:** 1467--825X (electronic). **Subscription Rates:** $2795 Institutions print and online; £1475 Institutions print and online; €1872 Institutions print and online; $1876 Institutions print and online; Africa; $3263 Institutions, other countries print and online; $2329 Institutions print or online; £1229 Institutions print or online; $2719 Institutions, other countries print or online. **URL:** http://as.wiley.com/WileyCDA/WileyTitle/productCd-ARBP.html; http://onlinelibrary.wiley.com/journal/10.1111/(ISSN)1467-825X. **Remarks:** Accepts advertising. **Circ:** (Not Reported).

16281 ■ African Development Review
Wiley-Blackwell
350 Main St.
Commerce Pl.
Malden, MA 02148-5018
Phone: (781)388-8200
Fax: (781)388-8210
Free: 800-216-2552
Journal focusing on the study and analysis of development policy in Africa. **Freq:** Quarterly. **Key Personnel:** Kupukile Mlambo, Editor; Leonce Ndikumana, Managing Editor; John C. Anyanwu, Editor. **ISSN:** 1017--6772 (print); **EISSN:** 1467--8268 (electronic). **Subscription Rates:** $514 Institutions print and online; £305 Institutions print and online; €389 Institutions print and online; $102 Individuals print and online; £61 Individuals print and online; €93 Individuals print and online. **URL:** http://onlinelibrary.wiley.com/journal/10.1111/%28ISSN%291467-8268. **Remarks:** Accepts advertising. **Circ:** (Not Reported).

16282 ■ American Journal on Addictions
Wiley-Blackwell
350 Main St.
Commerce Pl.
Malden, MA 02148-5018
Phone: (781)388-8200
Fax: (781)388-8210
Free: 800-216-2552
Peer-reviewed journal encouraging research on the etiology, prevention, identification, and treatment of substance abuse and covering a wide variety of topics ranging from codependence to genetics, epidemiology to dual diagnostics, etiology to neuroscience. **Freq:** Bimonthly. **Key Personnel:** Thomas R. Kosten, MD, Editor. **ISSN:** 1055--0496 (print); **EISSN:** 1521--0391 (electronic). **Subscription Rates:** $986 Institutions online ; $334 Individuals online. **URL:** http://onlinelibrary.wiley.com/journal/10.1111/(ISSN)1521-0391; http://as.wiley.com/WileyCDA/WileyTitle/productCd-AJA6.html. **Ad Rates:** BW $500; 4C $700. **Remarks:** Advertising not accepted. **Circ:** ‡1047.

16283 ■ Analytic Philosophy
Wiley-Blackwell
350 Main St.
Commerce Pl.
Malden, MA 02148-5018
Phone: (781)388-8200
Fax: (781)388-8210
Free: 800-216-2552
Journal covering all areas of analytic philosophy. **Freq:** Quarterly. **Key Personnel:** David Sosa, Editor. **ISSN:** 2153--9596 (print); **EISSN:** 2153--960x (electronic). **Subscription Rates:** $867 Institutions; £400 Institutions UK; €509 Institutions Europe; $1009 Institutions, other countries; $1041 Institutions print and online; £480 Institutions print and online, UK; €611 Institutions print and online, Europe; $1211 Institutions, other countries print and online; $157 Individuals print and online; £77 Individuals print and online, UK and Europe (non euro zone); €114 Individuals print and online, Europe; £94 Other countries print and online. **URL:** http://onlinelibrary.wiley.com/journal/10.1111/(ISSN)2153-960X/issues. **Formerly**: Philosophical Books. **Remarks:** Accepts advertising. **Circ:** (Not Reported).

16284 ■ Andrology
Blackwell Publishing Inc.
350 Main St.
Malden, MA 02148
Phone: (781)388-8200
Fax: (781)388-8210
Free: 800-216-2522
Publisher's E-mail: info@andrologysociety.org
Journal publishing papers on publishes papers on all aspects of andrology, ranging from basic molecular research to the results of clinical investigations. **Freq:** Bimonthly. **Print Method:** Sheetfed offset. **Trim Size:** 8 1/2 x 11. **Cols./Page:** 2. **Col. Width:** 39 nonpareils. **Col. Depth:** 140 agate lines. **Key Personnel:** Arthur Burnett, Associate Editor; Ewa Rajpert-De Meyts, Editor-in-Chief. **ISSN:** 2047--2919 (print); **EISSN:** 2047--2927 (electronic). **Subscription Rates:** $1634 Institutions print and online; £886 Institutions print and online; €1324 Institutions print and online; $1910 Institutions, other countries print and online; $1361 Institutions print or online; £738 Institutions print or online; €1103 Institutions print or online; $1591 Institutions, other countries print or online. **URL:** http://onlinelibrary.wiley.com/journal/10.1111/(ISSN)2047-2927?globalMessage=0; http://onlinelibrary.wiley.com/journal/10.1111/(ISSN)2047-2927. **Formed by the merger of**: Journal of Andrology; International Journal of Andrology: The Official Journal of the European Academy of Andrology. **Ad Rates:** BW $600; 4C $870. **Remarks:** Accepts advertising. **Circ:** 1120, ‡1200.

16285 ■ Annals of Anthropological Practice
Blackwell Publishing Inc.
350 Main St.
Malden, MA 02148
Phone: (781)388-8200
Fax: (781)388-8210
Free: 800-216-2522
Publisher's E-mail: journaladsusa@bos.blackwellpublishing.com
Journal focusing on information relevant to the advancement of professionals in the field from the National Association for the Practice of Anthropology (NAPA). **Freq:** Semiannual. **Key Personnel:** John Brett, Editor. **ISSN:** 2153--957X (print); **EISSN:** 2153--9588 (electronic). **Subscription Rates:** $74 Institutions online; $73 Institutions, other countries online; £39 Institutions online; €48 Institutions online. **URL:** http://onlinelibrary.wiley.com/journal/10.1111/(ISSN)2153-9588; http://practicinganthropology.org/publications/annals. **Formerly**: NAPA Bulletin. **Remarks:** Accepts advertising. **Circ:** 950.

16286 ■ Annals of Noninvasive Electrocardiology
Wiley-Blackwell
350 Main St.
Commerce Pl.
Malden, MA 02148-5018
Phone: (781)388-8200
Fax: (781)388-8210
Free: 800-216-2552
Medical journal covering noninvasive electrocardiology for professionals. **Freq:** Quarterly. **Key Personnel:** Shlomo Stern, MD, Editor-in-Chief; Wojciech Zareba, Editor-in-Chief. **ISSN:** 1082--720X (print); **EISSN:** 1542--474X (electronic). **Subscription Rates:** $545 Institutions; £420 Institutions UK; €535 Institutions Europe; $821 Institutions rest of the world. **URL:** http://onlinelibrary.wiley.com/journal/10.1111/(ISSN)1542-474X. **Ad Rates:** BW $800; 4C $1735. **Remarks:** Accepts advertising. **Circ:** (Not Reported).

16287 ■ Annals of Noninvasive Electrocardiology
Blackwell Publishing Inc.
350 Main St.
Malden, MA 02148
Phone: (781)388-8200
Fax: (781)388-8210
Free: 800-216-2522
Medical journal covering noninvasive electrocardiology for professionals. **Freq:** Quarterly. **Key Personnel:** Shlomo Stern, MD, Editor-in-Chief; Wojciech Zareba, Editor-in-Chief. **ISSN:** 1082--720X (print); **EISSN:** 1542--474X (electronic). **Subscription Rates:** $545 Institutions; £420 Institutions UK; €535 Institutions Europe; $821 Institutions rest of the world. **URL:** http://onlinelibrary.wiley.com/journal/10.1111/(ISSN)1542-474X. **Ad Rates:** BW $800; 4C $1735. **Remarks:** Accepts advertising. **Circ:** (Not Reported).

16288 ■ Anthropology of Work Review
Blackwell Publishing Inc.
350 Main St.
Malden, MA 02148
Phone: (781)388-8200
Fax: (781)388-8210
Free: 800-216-2522
Publisher's E-mail: journaladsusa@bos.blackwellpublishing.com
Journal discussing various aspects in the development of work processes. Published for The Society for the Anthropology of Work. **Freq:** 3/year. **Key Personnel:** Sarah Lyon, Editor. **ISSN:** 0883--024X (print); **EISSN:** 1548--1417 (electronic). **Subscription Rates:** $83 Institutions print & online; $69 Institutions online only; $67 Institutions, other countries online; $81 Institutions, other countries print and online. **URL:** http://onlinelibrary.wiley.com/journal/10.1111/(ISSN)1548-1417; http://saw.americananthro.org/?page_id=67; http://www.wiley.com/WileyCDA/WileyTitle/productCd-AWR.html. **Remarks:** Accepts advertising. **Circ:** 500.

16289 ■ Antipode: A Radical Journal of Geography
Wiley-Blackwell
350 Main St.
Commerce Pl.
Malden, MA 02148-5018
Phone: (781)388-8200
Fax: (781)388-8210
Free: 800-216-2552
Journal focusing on key geographical ideas such as space, scale, place and landscape. **Freq:** 5/year. **Key Personnel:** Sharad Chari, Editor. **ISSN:** 0066--4812 (print); **EISSN:** 1467--8330 (electronic). **Subscription Rates:** $1226 Individuals online; $1472 Institutions print and online; $1226 Institutions print; $102 Individuals print and online; £733 Institutions online; £880 Institutions print and online; £733 Institutions print; £74 Individuals print and online; €929 Institutions online; €1115 Institutions print and online; €929 Institutions print; €110 Individuals print and online; $1434 Institutions online - rest of the world; $1721 Institutions print and online - rest of the world; $1434 Institutions print - rest of the world; $74 Individuals print and online - rest of the world. **URL:** http://onlinelibrary.wiley.com/journal/10.1111/(ISSN)1467-8330. **Remarks:** Accepts

advertising. **Circ:** (Not Reported).

16290 ■ The Aristotelian Society Supplementary Volume
Wiley-Blackwell
350 Main St.
Commerce Pl.
Malden, MA 02148-5018
Phone: (781)388-8200
Fax: (781)388-8210
Free: 800-216-2552
Journal containing the Symposia to be read at the Annual Joint Session of the Mind Association and the Aristotelian Society. **Freq:** Annual. **Key Personnel:** Mathew Soteriou, Editor. **ISSN:** 0309--7013 (print); **EISSN:** 1467--8349 (electronic). **URL:** http://onlinelibrary.wiley.com/journal/10.1111/(ISSN)1467-8349. **Remarks:** Accepts advertising. **Circ:** (Not Reported).

16291 ■ Art History
Wiley-Blackwell
350 Main St.
Commerce Pl.
Malden, MA 02148-5018
Phone: (781)388-8200
Fax: (781)388-8210
Free: 800-216-2552
Journal focusing on all aspects, areas and periods of the history of art, from a diversity of perspectives. **Freq:** 5/year. **Key Personnel:** Genevieve Warwick, Editor; David Peters, Editor; David Peters Corbett, Board Member; Gavin Parkinson, Editor; Christine Riding, Editor. **ISSN:** 0141--6790 (print); **EISSN:** 1467--8365 (electronic). **Subscription Rates:** $1301 Institutions print or online; £678 Institutions print or online, UK; €860 Institutions print or online, Europe; $1519 Institutions, other countries print or online; $1562 Institutions print and online; £814 Institutions print and online, UK; €1032 Institutions print and onlilne, Europe; $1823 Institutions, other countries print and online; $319 Individuals print and online; £152 Individuals print and online - UK and Europe (non-euro zone); €227 Individuals print and online; £193 Other countries print and online. **Online:** Blackwell Publishing Inc. Blackwell Publishing Inc. **URL:** http://onlinelibrary.wiley.com/journal/10.1111/(ISSN)1467-8365; http://www.aah.org.uk/art-history. **Remarks:** Accepts advertising. **Circ:** (Not Reported).

16292 ■ Asia Pacific Journal of Human Resources
Wiley-Blackwell
350 Main St.
Commerce Pl.
Malden, MA 02148-5018
Phone: (781)388-8200
Fax: (781)388-8210
Free: 800-216-2552
Publisher's E-mail: journaladsusa@bos.blackwellpublishing.com
Journal focusing on human resources in the Australasian region. **Freq:** Quarterly. **Key Personnel:** Timothy Bartram, Editor-in-Chief; Helen De Cieri, Board Member; Wayne F. Cascio, Board Member; Malcolm Rimmer, Editor; Robin Kramar, Associate Editor; Peter Boxall, Associate Editor. **ISSN:** 1038--4111 (print); **EISSN:** 1744--7941 (electronic). **Subscription Rates:** $881 Institutions print and online; £478 Institutions print and online; €554 Institutions print and online; $881 Institutions, other countries print and online; $734 Institutions print or online; £398 Institutions print or online; €461 Institutions print or online; $734 Institutions, other countries print or online. **Online:** Gale. **URL:** http://onlinelibrary.wiley.com/journal/10.1111/(ISSN)1744-7941. **Remarks:** Accepts advertising. **Circ:** (Not Reported).

16293 ■ Asia Pacific Viewpoint
Wiley-Blackwell
350 Main St.
Commerce Pl.
Malden, MA 02148-5018
Phone: (781)388-8200
Fax: (781)388-8210
Free: 800-216-2552
Journal focusing on academic research in geography and allied disciplines on the economic and social development of the Asia Pacific. **Freq:** 3/year. **Key Personnel:** Assoc. Prof. Lisa Law, Editor-in-Chief; Prof. Warwick E. Murray, Board Member; Dr. Andrew McGregor, Board Member. **ISSN:** 1360--7456 (print); **EISSN:** 1467--8373 (electronic). **Subscription Rates:** $324 Institutions online; $389 Institutions print and online; $324 Institutions print; $85 Individuals print and online; £232 Institutions online; £279 Institutions print or online; £232 Institutions print; £59 Individuals print and online; €294 Institutions online; €353 Institutions print and online; €294 Institutions print; €74 Individuals print and online. **URL:** http://onlinelibrary.wiley.com/journal/10.1111/(ISSN)1467-8373. **Remarks:** Accepts advertising. **Circ:** (Not Reported).

16294 ■ Asian Economic Policy Review
Wiley-Blackwell
350 Main St.
Commerce Pl.
Malden, MA 02148-5018
Phone: (781)388-8200
Fax: (781)388-8210
Free: 800-216-2552
Journal covering international economics and economic policy with a primary focus on Asia. **Freq:** Semiannual. **Print Method:** Offset. **Trim Size:** 8 1/2 x 11. **Cols./Page:** 3. **Key Personnel:** Colin McKenzie, Managing Editor; Akira Kojima, Associate Editor; Shujiro Urata, Editor. **ISSN:** 1832--8105' (print); **EISSN:** 1748--3131 (electronic). **Subscription Rates:** $380 Institutions print and online; £227 Institutions print and online; €287 Institutions print and online; $437 Institutions, other countries print and online; $80 Individuals print and online; £53 Individuals print and online; €63 Individuals print and online. **URL:** http://onlinelibrary.wiley.com/journal/10.1111/%28ISSN%291748-3131. **Circ:** (Not Reported).

16295 ■ Austral Entomology
Wiley-Blackwell
350 Main St.
Commerce Pl.
Malden, MA 02148-5018
Phone: (781)388-8200
Fax: (781)388-8210
Free: 800-216-2552
Journal focusing on the biology, ecology, taxonomy and control of insects and arachnids within an Australian context. Official publication of the Australian Entomological Society. **Freq:** Quarterly. **Key Personnel:** Dr. MF Braby, Editor. **ISSN:** 1326-6756 (print); **EISSN:** 2052-1758 (electronic). **URL:** http://as.wiley.com/WileyCDA/WileyTitle/productCd-AEN.html. **Formerly:** Australian Journal of Entomology. **Remarks:** Accepts advertising. **Circ:** (Not Reported).

16296 ■ Australasian Journal of Dermatology
Wiley-Blackwell
350 Main St.
Commerce Pl.
Malden, MA 02148-5018
Phone: (781)388-8200
Fax: (781)388-8210
Free: 800-216-2552
Peer-reviewed journal focusing on all aspects of clinical practice and research in dermatology including dermatopathology and mycology. **Freq:** Quarterly. **Key Personnel:** Marius Rademaker, Editor; Stephen Shumack, Board Member. **ISSN:** 0004--8380 (print); **EISSN:** 1440--0960 (electronic). **Subscription Rates:** $808 Institutions online; $970 Institutions print and online; $808 Institutions print; $269 Individuals print and online; £500 Institutions online; £600 Institutions print and online; £500 Institutions print; £166 Individuals print and online; €634 Institutions online; €761 Institutions print and online; €634 Institutions print; €248 Individuals print and online. **URL:** http://onlinelibrary.wiley.com/journal/10.1111/(ISSN)1440-0960. **Remarks:** Accepts advertising. **Circ:** (Not Reported).

16297 ■ Australian Accounting Review
Wiley-Blackwell
350 Main St.
Commerce Pl.
Malden, MA 02148-5018
Phone: (781)388-8200
Fax: (781)388-8210
Free: 800-216-2552
Publisher's E-mail: cpalibrary@cpaaustralia.com.au
Peer-reviewed journal providing in-depth discussion and critical analysis of developments affecting professionals in all areas of finance, accounting, and business. **Freq:** Quarterly. **Key Personnel:** Linda English, Editor. **ISSN:** 1035--6908 (print); **EISSN:** 1835--2561 (electronic). **Subscription Rates:** $365 Institutions online; $438 Institutions print & online; $146 Individuals print & online. **URL:** http://wiley.com/WileyCDA/WileyTitle/productCd-AUAR.html; http://www.cpaaustralia.com.au/media/australian-accounting-review; http://onlinelibrary.wiley.com/journal/10.1111/(ISSN)1835-2561; http://ordering.onlinelibrary.wiley.com/subs.asp?ref=1035-6908. **Mailing address:** GPO Box 2820, Melbourne, VIC 3001, Australia. **Remarks:** Advertising not accepted. **Circ:** (Not Reported).

16298 ■ The Australian Economic Review
Wiley-Blackwell
350 Main St.
Commerce Pl.
Malden, MA 02148-5018
Phone: (781)388-8200
Fax: (781)388-8210
Free: 800-216-2552
Journal focusing on applied economics. **Freq:** Quarterly. **Key Personnel:** Prof. Ross Williams, Editor; Prof. Orley Ashenfelter, Associate Editor; John Freebairn, Associate Editor; Prof. Ian McDonald, Editor; Prof. Nicholas Barr, Associate Editor; Prof. Richard Blundell, Associate Editor. **ISSN:** 0004-9018 (print); **EISSN:** 1467-8462 (electronic). **Subscription Rates:** $123 Individuals U.S. print and online; $50 Students U.S. print and online; $698 Institutions U.S. print and standard online; $608 Institutions U.S. print or online; £491 Institutions print and online; £426 Institutions print or online. **URL:** http://www.wiley.com/WileyCDA/WileyTitle/productCd-AERE.html. **Remarks:** Accepts advertising. **Circ:** (Not Reported).

16299 ■ Australian Endodontic Journal
Wiley-Blackwell
350 Main St.
Commerce Pl.
Malden, MA 02148-5018
Phone: (781)388-8200
Fax: (781)388-8210
Free: 800-216-2552
Journal covering dentistry. **Freq:** 3/year. **Print Method:** Offset. **Trim Size:** 8 x 10 3/4. **Cols./Page:** 3. **Col. Width:** 26 nonpareils. **Col. Depth:** 96 agate lines. **Key Personnel:** Dr. Ralph Reid, Editor-in-Chief; Dr. Christine Yu, Editor. **ISSN:** 1329--1947 (print); **EISSN:** 1747--4477 (electronic). **Subscription Rates:** $271 Institutions online; £156 Institutions online; €201 Institutions online; $307 Institutions, other countries online. **URL:** http://onlinelibrary.wiley.com/journal/10.1111/(ISSN)1747-4477. **Remarks:** Accepts advertising. **Circ:** (Not Reported).

16300 ■ The Australian Journal of Agriculture and Resource Economics
Wiley-Blackwell
350 Main St.
Commerce Pl.
Malden, MA 02148-5018
Phone: (781)388-8200
Fax: (781)388-8210
Free: 800-216-2552
Publication E-mail: ajare@blackwellpublishingasia.com
Journal focusing on agricultural and resource economics. **Freq:** Quarterly. **Key Personnel:** Ross Cullen, Associate Editor; Geoffrey Kerr, Associate Editor. **ISSN:** 1364--985X (print); **EISSN:** 1467--8489 (electronic). **Subscription Rates:** $650 Institutions online; $780 Institutions print and online; $650 Institutions print; £421 Institutions online; £506 Institutions print and online; £421 Institutions print; €537 Institutions online; €645 Institutions print and online; €537 Institutions print; $549 Institutions online - Australia and New Zealand; $659 Institutions print and online - Australia and New Zealand; $549 Institutions print - Australia and New Zealand; $823 Institutions online - rest of the world; $988 Institutions print and online - rest of the world; $823 Institutions print - rest of the world. **URL:** http://onlinelibrary.wiley.com/journal/10.1111/(ISSN)1467-8489. **Remarks:** Accepts advertising. **Circ:** (Not Reported).

Circulation: ★ = AAM; △ or • = BPA; ♦ = CAC; ❑ = VAC; ⊕ = PO Statement; ‡ = Publisher's Report; Boldface figures = sworn; Light figures = estimated.

16301 ■ Australian Journal of Politics & History
Wiley-Blackwell
350 Main St.
Commerce Pl.
Malden, MA 02148-5018
Phone: (781)388-8200
Fax: (781)388-8210
Free: 800-216-2552
Journal focusing on the politics and history of Australia and modern Europe, intellectual history, political history, and the history of political thought. **Freq:** Quarterly. **Key Personnel:** Matt Mcdonald, Editor; Andrew Bonnell, Editor. **ISSN:** 0004--9522 (print); **EISSN:** 1467--8497 (electronic). **Subscription Rates:** $446 Institutions online; $536 Institutions print and online; $446 Institutions print; $102 Individuals print and online; £312 Institutions online; £375 Institutions print and online; £312 Institutions print; £73 Individuals print and online; €397 Institutions online; €477 Institutions print and online; €397 Institutions print; €73 Individuals print and online; $323 Institutions online - Australia and New Zealand; $388 Institutions print - Australia and New Zealand; A$125 Individuals print and online; $607 Institutions online - rest of the world; $729 Institutions print and online - rest of the world; $607 Institutions print - rest of the world; £73 Individuals print and online; $323 Institutions print only - Australia and New Zealand. **URL:** http://as.wiley.com/WileyCDA/WileyTitle/productCd-AJPH.html; http://onlinelibrary.wiley.com/journal/10.1111/(ISSN)1467-8497. **Remarks:** on request. **Circ:** (Not Reported).

16302 ■ Australian Journal of Politics & History
Blackwell Publishing Inc.
350 Main St.
Malden, MA 02148
Phone: (781)388-8200
Fax: (781)388-8210
Free: 800-216-2522
Journal focusing on the politics and history of Australia and modern Europe, intellectual history, political history, and the history of political thought. **Freq:** Quarterly. **Key Personnel:** Matt Mcdonald, Editor; Andrew Bonnell, Editor. **ISSN:** 0004--9522 (print); **EISSN:** 1467--8497 (electronic). **Subscription Rates:** $446 Institutions online; $536 Institutions print and online; $446 Institutions print; $102 Individuals print and online; £312 Institutions online; £375 Institutions print and online; £312 Institutions print; £73 Individuals print and online; €397 Institutions online; €477 Institutions print and online; €397 Institutions print; €73 Individuals print and online; $323 Institutions online - Australia and New Zealand; $388 Institutions print - Australia and New Zealand; A$125 Individuals print and online; $607 Institutions online - rest of the world; $729 Institutions print and online - rest of the world; $607 Institutions print - rest of the world; £73 Individuals print and online; $323 Institutions print only - Australia and New Zealand. **URL:** http://as.wiley.com/WileyCDA/WileyTitle/productCd-AJPH.html; http://onlinelibrary.wiley.com/journal/10.1111/(ISSN)1467-8497. **Remarks:** on request. **Circ:** (Not Reported).

16303 ■ Australian Journal of Public Administration
Wiley-Blackwell
350 Main St.
Commerce Pl.
Malden, MA 02148-5018
Phone: (781)388-8200
Fax: (781)388-8210
Free: 800-216-2552
Journal focusing on federal, state, local and intergovernmental public sector settings. **Freq:** Quarterly. **Key Personnel:** John Wanna, Editor. **ISSN:** 0313--6647 (print); **EISSN:** 1467--8500 (electronic). **Subscription Rates:** $328 Institutions online; $394 Institutions print and online; $328 Institutions print; $85 Individuals print and online; £228 Institutions online; £274 Institutions print and online; £228 Institutions print; £58 Individuals print and online; €288 Institutions online; €346 Institutions print and online; €70 Individuals print and online; $211 Institutions online - Australia and New Zealand; $254 Institutions print and online - Australia and New Zealand; $211 Institutions print - Australia and New Zealand; A$114 Individuals print and online - Australia and New Zealand; $443 Institutions online - rest of the world; $532 Institutions print and online - rest of the world; $443 Institutions print - rest of the world; £58 Individuals print and online; Included in membership included in membership dues. **URL:** http://onlinelibrary.wiley.com/journal/10.1111/(ISSN)1467-8500; http://www.ipaa.org.au/publications. **Remarks:** Accepts advertising. **Circ:** (Not Reported).

16304 ■ Australian Journal of Rural Health
Wiley-Blackwell
350 Main St.
Commerce Pl.
Malden, MA 02148-5018
Phone: (781)388-8200
Fax: (781)388-8210
Free: 800-216-2552
Journal focusing on rural health in Australia. Geared toward general practitioners, nurses, allied health professionals, pharmacists, health administrators, universities, rural health units and libraries. **Freq:** Bimonthly Semiannual. **Key Personnel:** Prof. James Dunbar, Board Member; Prof. Prasuna Reddy, Deputy; Peter Brown, Manager; David Perkins, Editor. **ISSN:** 1038--5282 (print); **EISSN:** 1440--1584 (electronic). **Subscription Rates:** $1619 Institutions print and online; £1001 Institutions print and online; €1275 Institutions print and online; A$952 Institutions print and online - Australia and New Zealand; $1961 Institutions, other countries print and online; $188 Individuals print and online; £117 Other countries print and online; €175 Individuals print and online; A$300 Individuals print and online - Australia and New Zealand; $1349 Institutions print or online; The Americas; £834 Institutions print or online; UK; €1062 Institutions print or online; Europe; A$793 Institutions print or online; Australia & New Zealand; $1634 Institutions, other countries rest of the world, print or online ; A$952 Institutions, Canada print and online; Australia & New Zealand; £117 Individuals print and online; UK, Europe (non-euro zone) and rest of the world. **URL:** http://onlinelibrary.wiley.com/journal/10.1111/(ISSN)1440-1584. **Remarks:** Accepts advertising. **Circ:** (Not Reported).

16305 ■ Barnlakaren
Wiley-Blackwell
350 Main St.
Commerce Pl.
Malden, MA 02148-5018
Phone: (781)388-8200
Fax: (781)388-8210
Free: 800-216-2552
Journal of the Swedish Pediatric Society, focusing on pediatric research. **Freq:** Bimonthly. **Key Personnel:** Viveca Karlsson, Editor; Hugo Lagerkrantz, Advisor. **ISSN:** 1651--0534 (print). **Subscription Rates:** $37 Nonmembers print only, Americas; €22 Nonmembers print only; £22 Nonmembers rest of world, print only. **URL:** http://as.wiley.com/WileyCDA/WileyTitle/productCd-BKN.html. **Circ:** (Not Reported).

16306 ■ Basic and Applied Pathology
Wiley-Blackwell
350 Main St.
Commerce Pl.
Malden, MA 02148-5018
Phone: (781)388-8200
Fax: (781)388-8210
Free: 800-216-2552
Journal covering the fields of experimental, anatomical, clinical, molecular, forensic and legal, and toxicological pathology in humans and animals. **Freq:** Quarterly. **Key Personnel:** Jeong-Wook Seo, Editor-in-Chief; Jae Hak Park, Associate Editor. **EISSN:** 1755--9294 (electronic). **URL:** http://onlinelibrary.wiley.com/journal/10.1111/%28ISSN%291755-9294. **Remarks:** Accepts advertising. **Circ:** (Not Reported).

16307 ■ Basin Research
Wiley-Blackwell
350 Main St.
Commerce Pl.
Malden, MA 02148-5018
Phone: (781)388-8200
Fax: (781)388-8210
Free: 800-216-2552
Journal focusing on sedimentary basin systems. **Freq:** Bimonthly. **Key Personnel:** W. Cavazza, Board Member; J.F. Dewey, Board Member; Michelle Kominz, Editor; D.W. Burbank, Board Member; H.D. Sinclair, Board Member; Richard Davies, Editor; Cynthia Ebinger, Editor-in-Chief. **ISSN:** 0950--091X (print); **EISSN:** 1365--2117 (electronic). **Subscription Rates:** $2504 Institutions print and online; £1359 Institutions print and online; €1722 Institutions print and online; $2921 Institutions, other countries print and online; $271 Individuals print and online; £147 Individuals print and online; €219 Individuals print and online; £162 Other countries print and online. **URL:** http://onlinelibrary.wiley.com/journal/10.1111/(ISSN)1365-2117. **Remarks:** Accepts advertising. **Circ:** (Not Reported).

16308 ■ Bioethics: Journal of the International Association of Bioethics
Wiley-Blackwell
350 Main St.
Commerce Pl.
Malden, MA 02148-5018
Phone: (781)388-8200
Fax: (781)388-8210
Free: 800-216-2552
Publisher's E-mail: journaladsusa@bos.blackwellpublishing.com
Journal focusing on the subject of bioethics for all those working in philosophy, medicine, law, sociology, public policy, education and related fields. **Freq:** 9/year. **Key Personnel:** Prof. Ruth Chadwick, Editor; Prof. Udo Schuklenk, Editor. **ISSN:** 0269--9702 (print); **EISSN:** 1467--8519 (electronic). **URL:** http://onlinelibrary.wiley.com/journal/10.1111/(ISSN)1467-8519. **Remarks:** Accepts advertising. **Circ:** (Not Reported).

16309 ■ Biological Journal of the Linnean Society
Wiley-Blackwell
350 Main St.
Commerce Pl.
Malden, MA 02148-5018
Phone: (781)388-8200
Fax: (781)388-8210
Free: 800-216-2552
Journal focusing on the process of organic evolution in the broadest sense. **Freq:** Monthly. **Key Personnel:** J.A. Allen, Editor. **ISSN:** 0247--4066 (print); **EISSN:** 1095--8312 (electronic). **Subscription Rates:** $7471 Institutions online only; £3977 Institutions online only; €5050 Institutions online only; $8567 Institutions, other countries online only. **URL:** http://onlinelibrary.wiley.com/journal/10.1111/(ISSN)1095-8312. **Remarks:** Accepts advertising. **Circ:** (Not Reported).

16310 ■ Biotropica
Wiley-Blackwell
350 Main St.
Commerce Pl.
Malden, MA 02148-5018
Phone: (781)388-8200
Fax: (781)388-8210
Free: 800-216-2552
Journal focusing on original research on the ecology and conservation of tropical ecosystems and on the evolution, behavior, and ecology of tropical organisms. **Freq:** Bimonthly. **Key Personnel:** Jaboury Ghazoul, Editor; Emilio Bruna, Editor-in-Chief. **ISSN:** 0006--3606 (print); **EISSN:** 1744--7429 (electronic). **Subscription Rates:** $566 Institutions online only; $347 Institutions online only; €440 Institutions online only; $286 Institutions online only; Developing World; $678 Institutions, other countries online only. **URL:** http://onlinelibrary.wiley.com/journal/10.1111/(ISSN)1744-7429. **Ad Rates:** 4C $600. **Remarks:** Accepts advertising. **Circ:** (Not Reported).

16311 ■ Bipolar Disorders: An International Journal of Psychiatry and Neurosciences
Wiley-Blackwell
350 Main St.
Commerce Pl.
Malden, MA 02148-5018
Phone: (781)388-8200
Fax: (781)388-8210
Free: 800-216-2552
Journal focusing on research of relevance for the basic mechanisms, clinical aspects, or treatment of bipolar disorders. **Freq:** 8/year. **Key Personnel:** Roy K.N. Chengappa, Editor-in-Chief, phone: (412)802-6930, fax: (412)802-6931; Samuel Gershon, Editor-in-Chief. **ISSN:** 1398--5647 (print); **EISSN:** 1399--5618 (electronic).

Subscription Rates: $1045 Institutions online only; £623 Institutions online only; €791 Institutions online only; $1217 Institutions, other countries online only; $324 Individuals online only; £195 Other countries online only; €291 Individuals online only. **URL:** http://onlinelibrary.wiley.com/journal/10.1111/(ISSN)1399-5618. **Remarks:** Accepts advertising. **Circ:** (Not Reported).

16312 ■ Birth
Wiley-Blackwell
350 Main St.
Commerce Pl.
Malden, MA 02148-5018
Phone: (781)388-8200
Fax: (781)388-8210
Free: 800-216-2552
Journal focusing on issues and practices in the care of childbearing women, infants, and families. **Freq:** Quarterly. **Trim Size:** 8 1/4 x 10 7/8. **Key Personnel:** Marian MacDorman, Editor; Diony Young, Editor, phone: (585)243-0087, fax: (585)243-0087. **ISSN:** 0730--7659 (print); **EISSN:** 1523--536X (electronic). **Subscription Rates:** $791 Institutions print & online; $836 Institutions, Canada and Mexico print & online; £611 Institutions print & online; €773 Institutions print & online; $1193 Institutions, other countries print & online; $125 Individuals print & online; $141 Canada and Mexico print & online; £115 Other countries print & online; €169 Individuals print & online. **URL:** http://onlinelibrary.wiley.com/journal/10.1111/(ISSN)1523-536X. **Ad Rates:** BW $700; 4C $975. **Remarks:** Accepts advertising. **Circ:** Paid ‡1119.

16313 ■ BJOG
Wiley-Blackwell
350 Main St.
Commerce Pl.
Malden, MA 02148-5018
Phone: (781)388-8200
Fax: (781)388-8210
Free: 800-216-2552
Journal focusing on all areas of obstetrics and gynaecology, including contraception, urogynaecology, fertility, oncology and clinical practice. **Freq:** 13/yr. **Key Personnel:** Khalid Khan, Editor-in-Chief; Philip J. Steer, Editor; Michael Marsh, Deputy, Editor-in-Chief; Elizabeth Hay, Managing Editor. **ISSN:** 1470--0328 (print); **EISSN:** 1471--0528 (electronic). **Subscription Rates:** $1006 Institutions print and online; £603 Institutions print and online; €764 Institutions print and online; $1296 Institutions, other countries print and online; $307 Individuals print and online; £185 Individuals print and online; €274 Individuals print and online; £202 Other countries print and online. **URL:** http://onlinelibrary.wiley.com/journal/10.1111/(ISSN)1471-0528. **Remarks:** Accepts advertising. **Circ:** (Not Reported).

16314 ■ BJU International
Wiley-Blackwell
350 Main St.
Commerce Pl.
Malden, MA 02148-5018
Phone: (781)388-8200
Fax: (781)388-8210
Free: 800-216-2552
Journal focusing on urology and nephrology. **Freq:** 12/year. **Key Personnel:** Audrai O'Dwyer, Managing Editor; Prokar Dasgupta, Editor-in-Chief. **ISSN:** 1464--4096 (print); **EISSN:** 1464--410X (electronic). **Subscription Rates:** $1898 Institutions print & online; £1030 Institutions print & online; €1310 Institutions print & online; $2216 Institutions, other countries print & online; $414 Individuals print & online; £228 Individuals print & online; €335 Individuals print & online; £247 Other countries print & online. **URL:** http://onlinelibrary.wiley.com/journal/10.1111/(ISSN)1464-410X. **Remarks:** Accepts advertising. **Circ:** (Not Reported).

16315 ■ British Journal of Clinical Pharmacology
Wiley-Blackwell
350 Main St.
Commerce Pl.
Malden, MA 02148-5018
Phone: (781)388-8200
Fax: (781)388-8210
Free: 800-216-2552
Publisher's E-mail: info@bps.ac.uk
Journal focusing on all aspects of drug action in humans. **Founded:** 1974. **Freq:** Monthly. **Key Personnel:** J.M. Ritter, Editor; A. Cohen, Editor-in-Chief; James M. Ritter, Editor-in-Chief; R. Bies, Board Member. **ISSN:** 0306-5251 (print); **EISSN:** 1365-2125 (electronic). **Subscription Rates:** $365 Individuals online; $174 Members AS-CPT, online; $3169 Institutions online; $354 Individuals online, Americas; €288 Individuals online, Europe; £192 Individuals online, non-Euro zone; £212 Other countries online; $168 Members online; €151 Members online; £101 Members online; $2989 Institutions Americas; online; £1619 Institutions UK; online; £2056 Institutions Europe; online. **URL:** http://onlinelibrary.wiley.com/journal/10.1111/(ISSN)1365-2125. **Remarks:** Advertising accepted; rates available upon request. **Circ:** (Not Reported).

16316 ■ British Journal of Dermatology
Wiley-Blackwell
350 Main St.
Commerce Pl.
Malden, MA 02148-5018
Phone: (781)388-8200
Fax: (781)388-8210
Free: 800-216-2552
Journal focusing on the pathology of the skin. **Freq:** Monthly. **Key Personnel:** John English, Advisor; J. Caulfield, Manager; A.V. Anstey, Editor. **ISSN:** 0007-0963 (print); **EISSN:** 1365-2133 (electronic). **Subscription Rates:** $467 Individuals print & online; $443 Individuals online only; $325 Members print & online; $3599 Institutions print & online; $2999 Institutions print or online. **URL:** http://www.wiley.com/WileyCDA/WileyTitle/productCd-BJD.html. **Remarks:** Accepts advertising. **Circ:** (Not Reported).

16317 ■ British Journal of Educational Technology
Wiley-Blackwell
350 Main St.
Commerce Pl.
Malden, MA 02148-5018
Phone: (781)388-8200
Fax: (781)388-8210
Free: 800-216-2552
Journal focusing on developments in international educational and training technology. **Freq:** Bimonthly. **Key Personnel:** Nick Rushby, Editor. **ISSN:** 0007--1013 (print); **EISSN:** 1467--8535 (electronic). **Subscription Rates:** $2031 Institutions print & online; £1031 Institutions print & online; €1306 Institutions print & online; $2370 Institutions, other countries print & online; $242 Individuals print & online; £117 Individuals print & online; €174 Individuals print & online; £145 Other countries print & online. **URL:** http://onlinelibrary.wiley.com/journal/10.1111/(ISSN)1467-8535. **Remarks:** Accepts advertising. **Circ:** (Not Reported).

16318 ■ British Journal of Haematology
Wiley-Blackwell
350 Main St.
Commerce Pl.
Malden, MA 02148-5018
Phone: (781)388-8200
Fax: (781)388-8210
Free: 800-216-2552
Freq: Semimonthly. **Key Personnel:** Finbarr E. Cotter, Editor-in-Chief; Deborah Rund, Editor. **ISSN:** 0007--1048 (print); **EISSN:** 1365--2141 (electronic). **Subscription Rates:** $3722 Institutions print & online; £2012 Institutions print & online; €2554 Institutions print & online; $4340 Institutions, other countries print & online; $385 Individuals print & online; £209 Individuals print & online; £313 Individuals print & online; $231 Other countries print & online. **URL:** http://onlinelibrary.wiley.com/journal/10.1111/(ISSN)1365-2141. **Remarks:** Advertising accepted; rates available upon request. **Circ:** (Not Reported).

16319 ■ British Journal of Industrial Relations
Wiley-Blackwell
350 Main St.
Commerce Pl.
Malden, MA 02148-5018
Phone: (781)388-8200
Fax: (781)388-8210
Free: 800-216-2552
Journal focusing on industrial relations. **Freq:** Quarterly. **Key Personnel:** John Godard, Executive Editor; Ben Roberts, Editor, Founder. **ISSN:** 0007--1080 (print); **EISSN:** 1467--8543 (electronic). **USPS:** 146-78543. **Subscription Rates:** $1367 Institutions print & online; £654 Institutions print & online; €830 Institutions print & online; $1554 Institutions, other countries print & online; $59 Students print & online; £29 Students print & online; €38 Students print & online; £36 Students, other countries print & online; $205 Individuals print & online; £85 Individuals print & online; €107 Individuals print & online; £117 Individuals print & online. **URL:** http://onlinelibrary.wiley.com/journal/10.1111/(ISSN)1467-8543. **Remarks:** Accepts advertising. **Circ:** (Not Reported).

16320 ■ British Journal of Learning Disabilities
Wiley-Blackwell
350 Main St.
Commerce Pl.
Malden, MA 02148-5018
Phone: (781)388-8200
Fax: (781)388-8210
Free: 800-216-2552
Journal focusing on debates and developments in research, policy and practice within the learning disability field. **Freq:** Quarterly. **Key Personnel:** Prof. Duncan Mitchell, Editor; Prof. Bob Gates, Editor-in-Chief. **ISSN:** 1354--4187 (print); **EISSN:** 1468--3156 (electronic). **Subscription Rates:** $857 Institutions print & online; £470 Institutions print & online; €592 Institutions print & online; $1001 Institutions, other countries print & online; $131 Individuals print & online; £73 Individuals print & online; €109 Individuals print & online; £82 Other countries print & online. **URL:** http://onlinelibrary.wiley.com/journal/10.1111/(ISSN)1468-3156. **Remarks:** Accepts advertising. **Circ:** 3500.

16321 ■ British Journal of Management
Wiley-Blackwell
350 Main St.
Commerce Pl.
Malden, MA 02148-5018
Phone: (781)388-8200
Fax: (781)388-8210
Free: 800-216-2552
Official journal of the British Academy of Management. **Freq:** Quarterly. **Key Personnel:** David Otley, Editor; Celeste Wilderom, Board Member; Matthew Robson, Board Member; Pawan S. Budhwar, Editor-in-Chief; Mustafa Ozbilgin, Board Member; Mark J.F. Wouters, Board Member; Emma Missen, Managing Editor, phone: 44 1277 215940; Veronique Ambrosini, Board Member; Catherine Cassell, Board Member; Astrid Homan, Board Member; Robert Ford, Board Member. **ISSN:** 1045--3172 (print); **EISSN:** 1467--8551 (electronic). **USPS:** 146-78551. **URL:** http://onlinelibrary.wiley.com/journal/10.1111/(ISSN)1467-8551. **Remarks:** Accepts advertising. **Circ:** (Not Reported).

16322 ■ The British Journal of Politics & International Relations
Wiley-Blackwell
350 Main St.
Commerce Pl.
Malden, MA 02148-5018
Phone: (781)388-8200
Fax: (781)388-8210
Free: 800-216-2552
Publisher's E-mail: journaladsusa@bos.blackwellpublishing.com
Journal focusing on political science in Britain. **Freq:** Quarterly. **Key Personnel:** John Peterson, Editor-in-Chief; Alan Convery, Editor-in-Chief. **ISSN:** 1369--1481 (print); **EISSN:** 1467--856x (electronic). **USPS:** 146-7856X. **URL:** http://onlinelibrary.wiley.com/journal/10.1111/(ISSN)1467-856X. **Remarks:** Advertising accepted; rates available upon request. **Circ:** (Not Reported).

16323 ■ The British Journal of Sociology
Wiley-Blackwell
350 Main St.
Commerce Pl.
Malden, MA 02148-5018
Phone: (781)388-8200
Fax: (781)388-8210
Free: 800-216-2552
Publication E-mail: bjs@lse.ac.uk
Journal focusing on sociological scholarship. **Freq:**

Circulation: ★ = AAM; △ or • = BPA; ♦ = CAC; ❑ = VAC; ⊕ = PO Statement; ‡ = Publisher's Report; Boldface figures = sworn; Light figures = estimated.

Quarterly. **Key Personnel:** Nigel Dodd, Editor-in-Chief; Richard Wright, Board Member. **ISSN:** 0007--1315 (print); **EISSN:** 1468--4446 (electronic). **Subscription Rates:** $951 Institutions print and online; £524 Institutions print and online; €668 Institutions print and online; $1024 Institutions, other countries print and online; $82 Individuals print and online; £46 Other countries print and online; €57 Individuals print and online; $52 Students print and online; £28 Students, other countries print and online; €36 Students print and online. **URL:** http://onlinelibrary.wiley.com/journal/10.1111/(ISSN)1468-4446. **Remarks:** on request. **Circ:** (Not Reported).

16324 ■ British Journal of Special Education
Wiley-Blackwell
350 Main St.
Commerce Pl.
Malden, MA 02148-5018
Phone: (781)388-8200
Fax: (781)388-8210
Free: 800-216-2552
Journal focusing on the whole range of learning difficulties relating to children in mainstream and special schools. **Freq:** Quarterly. **Key Personnel:** Graham Hallett, Editor; Fiona Hallett, Editor. **ISSN:** 0952--3383 (print); **EISSN:** 1467--8578 (electronic). **USPS:** 146-78578. **Subscription Rates:** $890 Institutions print and online; £470 Institutions print and online; €591 Institutions print and online; $1034 Institutions print and online. **URL:** http://onlinelibrary.wiley.com/journal/10.1111/(ISSN)1467-8578. **Remarks:** Advertising accepted; rates available upon request. **Circ:** (Not Reported).

16325 ■ Bulletin of Economic Research
Blackwell Publishing Inc.
350 Main St.
Malden, MA 02148
Phone: (781)388-8200
Fax: (781)388-8210
Free: 800-216-2522
Publisher's E-mail: customerservice@oxon.blackwellpublishing.com
Journal focusing on the entire field of economics, econometrics and economic history. **Freq:** Quarterly. **Key Personnel:** Gabriel Talmain, Board Member; Klaus G. Zauner, Editor; Gianni De Fraja, Board Member; Giacomo Bonanno, Associate Editor; Gulcin Ozkan, Managing Editor; Hassan Molana, Associate Editor; George Norman, Associate Editor; Christina Atanasova, Associate Editor; David Newbery, Associate Editor. **ISSN:** 0307--3378 (print); **EISSN:** 1467--8586 (electronic). **Subscription Rates:** $1274 Institutions print or online; £571 Institutions print or online; £60 Individuals print + online; £686 Institutions print + online; $99 Individuals print + online; €90 Individuals print + online; £60 Individuals print + online; $1529 Institutions print + online; €873 Institutions print + online; $1784 Institutions, other countries print + online. **URL:** http://onlinelibrary.wiley.com/journal/10.1111/(ISSN)1467-8586. **Mailing address:** PO Box 1354, Oxford OX4 2ZG, United Kingdom. **Remarks:** Accepts advertising. **Circ:** (Not Reported).

16326 ■ Bulletin of Latin American Research
Wiley-Blackwell
350 Main St.
Commerce Pl.
Malden, MA 02148-5018
Phone: (781)388-8200
Fax: (781)388-8210
Free: 800-216-2552
Journal focusing on Latin America from all academic disciplines in the general fields of the social sciences and humanities. **Freq:** Quarterly January, March, June and September. **Key Personnel:** Dr. Geoffrey Kantaris, Editor; Prof. Tony Kapcia, Editor. **ISSN:** 0261--3050 (print); **EISSN:** 1470--9856 (electronic). **Subscription Rates:** $1589 Institutions print & online; $1544 Institutions, other countries print or online; $1324 Institutions print or online; £863 Institutions print & online; $1853 Institutions, other countries print & online; £719 Institutions print or online; €1096 Institutions print & online; €913 Institutions print or online; $52 Individuals print and online (joint member); $44 Members print and online; $23 Students print and online; $1110 Institutions print only. **URL:** http://onlinelibrary.wiley.com/journal/10.1111/(ISSN)1470-9856; http://www.slas.org.uk/pubs/blar.htm; http://lasa.international.pitt.edu/members/other-publications. **Remarks:** Accepts advertising. **Circ:** (Not Reported).

16327 ■ Business Ethics: A European Review
Wiley-Blackwell
350 Main St.
Commerce Pl.
Malden, MA 02148-5018
Phone: (781)388-8200
Fax: (781)388-8210
Free: 800-216-2552
Journal focusing on ethics in business. **Freq:** Quarterly. **Key Personnel:** Dr. David Campbell, Board Member; Dima Jamali, Editor. **ISSN:** 0962--8770 (print); **EISSN:** 1467--8608 (electronic). **Subscription Rates:** $90 Members Americas (print and online), APA/EBEN and Society for Business Ethics ; £56 Members UK and non Euro zone (print and online), APA/EBEN and Society for Business Ethics ; €82 Members Euro zone (print and online), APA/EBEN and Society for Business Ethics ; $166 Members Americas (print and online), British Philosophical Association; £100 Members UK (print and online), British Philosophical Association; €150 Members Europe (print and online only), British Philosophical Association; $1902 Institutions print or online; £1134 Institutions print or online; €1439 Institutions print or online; $2218 Institutions print or online; $2283 Institutions print and online; £1361 Institutions print and online; €1727 Institutions print and online; $2662 Institutions print and online. **URL:** http://onlinelibrary.wiley.com/journal/10.1111/(ISSN)1467-8608. **Remarks:** Advertising accepted; rates available upon request. **Circ:** (Not Reported).

16328 ■ Business and Society Review
Wiley-Blackwell
350 Main St.
Commerce Pl.
Malden, MA 02148-5018
Phone: (781)388-8200
Fax: (781)388-8210
Free: 800-216-2552
Journal focusing on a wide range of ethical issues concerning the relationships between business, society, and the public good. **Freq:** Quarterly. **Key Personnel:** Robert E. Frederick, Editor, phone: (781)891-2747, fax: (781)891-2988; Michael W. Hoffman, Executive Director; John R. Boatright, Board Member. **ISSN:** 0045--3609 (print); **EISSN:** 1467--8594 (electronic). **Subscription Rates:** $404 Institutions print or online; £322 Institutions print or online; €402 Institutions print or online; $624 Institutions, other countries print or online; $485 Institutions print and online; £387 Institutions print and online; €483 Institutions print and online; $749 Institutions, other countries print and online. **URL:** http://onlinelibrary.wiley.com/journal/10.1111/(ISSN)1467-8594. **Remarks:** Accepts advertising. **Circ:** (Not Reported).

16329 ■ Business Strategy Review
Wiley-Blackwell
350 Main St.
Commerce Pl.
Malden, MA 02148-5018
Phone: (781)388-8200
Fax: (781)388-8210
Free: 800-216-2552
Journal focusing on research, ideas, and issues animating the global business environment. **Freq:** Quarterly. **Key Personnel:** Stuart Crainer, Editor. **ISSN:** 0955-5419 (print); **EISSN:** 1467-8616 (electronic). **Subscription Rates:** £378 Institutions print & online; £315 Institutions print or online; €478 Institutions print & online; $436 Institutions print & online; $363 Institutions print or online. **URL:** http://onlinelibrary.wiley.com/journal/10.1111/(ISSN)1467-8616. **Remarks:** Accepts advertising. **Circ:** (Not Reported).

16330 ■ The Canadian Geographer
Wiley-Blackwell
350 Main St.
Commerce Pl.
Malden, MA 02148-5018
Phone: (781)388-8200
Fax: (781)388-8210
Free: 800-216-2552
Publication covering geography in Canada. **Freq:** Quarterly. **Key Personnel:** Lawrence D. Berg, Board Member; Nadine Schuurman, Editor. **ISSN:** 0008-3658 (print); **EISSN:** 1541-0064 (electronic). **Subscription Rates:** $458 Institutions print or online; $550 Institutions print and online; $236 Institutions, Canada and Mexico print or online; $284 Institutions, Canada and Mexico print and online; £356 Institutions print or online; £428 Institutions print and online; €452 Institutions print or online; €543 Institutions print and online; $695 Institutions, other countries print or online; $834 Institutions, other countries print and online. **URL:** http://www.cag-acg.ca/en/the_canadian_geographer.html; http://onlinelibrary.wiley.com/journal/10.1111/(ISSN)1541-0064. **Ad Rates:** BW $350. **Remarks:** Accepts advertising. **Circ:** (Not Reported).

16331 ■ Canadian Journal of Agricultural Economics
Blackwell Publishing Inc.
350 Main St.
Malden, MA 02148
Phone: (781)388-8200
Fax: (781)388-8210
Free: 800-216-2522
Publisher's E-mail: journaladsusa@bos.blackwellpublishing.com
Peer-reviewed journal provides farm management and agri-food related topics concerning agribusiness. **Freq:** Quarterly. **Print Method:** Sheet Offset. **Trim Size:** 6 3/4 x 9 3/4. **Cols./Page:** 1. **Col. Width:** 31 picas. **Col. Depth:** 45 picas. **Key Personnel:** Bishnu Saha, Editor; Jill Hobbs, Editor; Sian Mooney, Editor; Wuyang Hu, Editor; James F. Nolan, Editor; Elwin G. Smith, Editor; Cornelis G. van Kooten, Editor. **ISSN:** 0008-3976 (print); **EISSN:** 1744-7976 (electronic). **Subscription Rates:** $334 Institutions print or online; £199 Institutions print or online; $299 Institutions, Canada and Mexico print or online; €251 Institutions print or online; $387 Institutions, other countries print or online; $359 Institutions, Canada and Mexico print & online; £239 Institutions print & online; €302 Institutions print & online; $465 Institutions, other countries print & online; $401 Institutions print + online. **URL:** http://www.wiley.com/WileyCDA/WileyTitle/productCd-CJAG.html; http://onlinelibrary.wiley.com/journal/10.1111/(ISSN)1744-7976; http://caes.usask.ca/cjae/; http://caes.usask.ca/cjae/index.php. **Also known as:** Revue canadienne d'agroeconomie. **Ad Rates:** BW $450. **Remarks:** Advertising accepted; rates available upon request. **Circ:** Paid 1000.

16332 ■ Canadian Journal of Economics
Blackwell Publishing Inc.
350 Main St.
Malden, MA 02148
Phone: (781)388-8200
Fax: (781)388-8210
Free: 800-216-2522
Publisher's E-mail: journaladsusa@bos.blackwellpublishing.com
Journal of the Canadian Economics Association addressing decisions of economic and public policy. **Freq:** Quarterly. **Print Method:** Offset. Uses mats. **Trim Size:** 6 x 9. **Cols./Page:** 1. **Col. Width:** 54 nonpareils. **Col. Depth:** 98 agate lines. **Key Personnel:** Francisco Ruge-Murcia, Managing Editor; Michael Baker, Editor. **ISSN:** 0008--4085 (print); **EISSN:** 1540--5982 (electronic). **Subscription Rates:** $348 U.S. and other countries print or online; $418 U.S. and other countries print and online; £209 Institutions print or online; £251 Institutions print and online; €265 Institutions print or online; €318 Institutions print and online; $410 Other countries print or online; $492 Other countries print and online. **URL:** http://onlinelibrary.wiley.com/journal/10.1111/(ISSN)1540-5982; http://www.wiley.com/WileyCDA/WileyTitle/productCd-CAJE.html. **Remarks:** Accepts advertising. **Circ:** (Not Reported).

16333 ■ Cancer Science
Wiley-Blackwell
350 Main St.
Commerce Pl.
Malden, MA 02148-5018
Phone: (781)388-8200
Fax: (781)388-8210
Free: 800-216-2552
Journal focusing on the fields of basic, translational and clinical cancer. Formerly the Japanese Journal of Cancer Research. **Freq:** Monthly. **Key Personnel:** Hiroyuki Mano, Editor; Yusuke Nakamura, Editor-in-Chief;

Takashi Nishimura, Associate Editor; Kohei Miyazono, Editor-in-Chief, Deputy; Richard J. Ablin, Associate Editor; Takashi Sugimura, Editor; Ryuzo Ueda, Associate Editor; Takao Yamori, Associate Editor. **ISSN:** 1347-9032 (print); **EISSN:** 1349-7006 (electronic). **Subscription Rates:** $1340 Institutions online only; £798 Institutions online only; €1014 Institutions online only; $1562 Institutions, other countries online only. **URL:** http://onlinelibrary.wiley.com/journal/10.1111/(ISSN)1349-7006; http://www.wiley.com/bw/journal.asp?ref=1347-9032&site=1. **Remarks:** Accepts advertising. **Circ:** (Not Reported).

16334 ■ Cardiovascular Therapeutics
Wiley-Blackwell
350 Main St.
Commerce Pl.
Malden, MA 02148-5018
Phone: (781)388-8200
Fax: (781)388-8210
Free: 800-216-2552
Journal focusing on reviews on the pharmacology, pharmacokinetics, toxicology and clinical trials of new or potential cardiovascular drugs. **Freq:** Bimonthly. **Key Personnel:** Chim Lang, Editor. **ISSN:** 1755--5914 (print); **EISSN:** 1755--5922 (electronic). **Subscription Rates:** $674 Institutions online only; £464 Institutions online only; €588 Institutions online only; $907 Institutions, other countries online only; $290 Individuals online only; £175 Individuals online only; €262 Individuals online only. **URL:** http://onlinelibrary.wiley.com/journal/10.1111/(ISSN)1755-5922. **Formerly**: Cardiovascular Drug Reviews. **Circ:** (Not Reported).

16335 ■ Cell Biology International
Wiley-Blackwell
350 Main St.
Commerce Pl.
Malden, MA 02148-5018
Phone: (781)388-8200
Fax: (781)388-8210
Free: 800-216-2552
Scholarly journal covering cell biology for plant and animal scientists. **Freq:** Monthly. **Key Personnel:** D.N. Wheatley, Associate Editor; C. Jensen, Associate Editor; I.L. Cameron, Assistant Editor; Colin Green, Associate Editor; Sergio Schenkman, Editor-in-Chief. **ISSN:** 0165--6995 (print); **EISSN:** 1095--8355 (electronic). **Subscription Rates:** $1609 U.S. and other countries online; £953 Institutions online; €1161 Institutions online. **URL:** http://onlinelibrary.wiley.com/journal/10.1002/(ISSN)1095-8355. **Circ:** (Not Reported).

16336 • ■ Cell Proliferation
Wiley-Blackwell
350 Main St.
Commerce Pl.
Malden, MA 02148-5018
Phone: (781)388-8200
Fax: (781)388-8210
Free: 800-216-2552
Journal focusing on studies of all aspects of cell proliferation and differentiation in normal and abnormal states; control systems and mechanisms operating at inter- and intracellular, molecular and genetic levels; modification by and interactions with chemical and physical agents; mathematical modelling; and the development of new techniques. **Freq:** Bimonthly. **Key Personnel:** Dr. C. Sarraf, Editor. **ISSN:** 0960--7722 (print); **EISSN:** 1365--2184 (electronic). **Subscription Rates:** $2720 Institutions online only; £1473 Institutions online only; $3175 Institutions, other countries online only; $428 Individuals online only; £226 Individuals online only (UK); £3175 Other countries online only. **URL:** http://onlinelibrary.wiley.com/journal/10.1111/(ISSN)1365-2184. **Remarks:** Advertising not accepted. **Circ:** (Not Reported).

16337 ■ Centaurus
Wiley-Blackwell
350 Main St.
Commerce Pl.
Malden, MA 02148-5018
Phone: (781)388-8200
Fax: (781)388-8210
Free: 800-216-2552
Publisher's E-mail: info@ceramic.co.za
Journal focusing on the study of the history of science. International Magazine of the History of Mathematics. **Freq:** Quarterly. **Key Personnel:** Ida Stamhuis, Editor; Peter Barker, Associate Editor. **ISSN:** 0008--8994 (print); **EISSN:** 1600--0498 (electronic). **Subscription Rates:** $827 Institutions print or online; £491 Institutions print or online; €623 Institutions print or online; $959 Institutions, other countries print or online; $993 Institutions print and online; £590 Institutions print and online; €748 Institutions print and online; $1151 Institutions, other countries print and online. **URL:** http://onlinelibrary.wiley.com/journal/10.1111/(ISSN)1600-0498. **Remarks:** Accepts advertising. **Circ:** (Not Reported).

16338 ■ Chemical Biology & Drug Design
Blackwell Publishing Inc.
350 Main St.
Malden, MA 02148
Phone: (781)388-8200
Fax: (781)388-8210
Free: 800-216-2522
Publisher's E-mail: journaladsusa@bos.blackwellpublishing.com
Peer-reviewed journal containing new concepts, insight and new findings within the scope of chemical biology and drug design. **Freq:** Monthly. **Key Personnel:** David Selwood, Editor-in-Chief. **ISSN:** 1747--0277 (print); **EISSN:** 1747--0285 (electronic). **Subscription Rates:** $2299 Institutions online only; $1245 Institutions online only, UK; €1581 Institutions online only, Europe; $2438 Institutions, other countries online only; $244 Individuals online only; £146 Individuals online only, UK and Europe (non euro zone); €220 Individuals online only; £146 Other countries online only. **URL:** http://onlinelibrary.wiley.com/journal/10.1111/(ISSN)1747-0285. **Remarks:** Accepts advertising. **Circ:** (Not Reported).

16339 ■ Child and Adolescent Mental Health
Wiley-Blackwell
350 Main St.
Commerce Pl.
Malden, MA 02148-5018
Phone: (781)388-8200
Fax: (781)388-8210
Free: 800-216-2552
Journal focusing on the exchange of clinical experience, ideas and research. **Freq:** Quarterly. **Key Personnel:** Crispin Day, Editor; Jacqueline Barnes, Editor; Tamsin Ford, Editor. **ISSN:** 1475--357X (print); **EISSN:** 1475--3588 (electronic). **Subscription Rates:** $315 Institutions print or online; £189 Institutions print or online; €238 Institutions print or online; $366 Institutions, other countries print or online; $378 Institutions print and online; £227 Institutions print and online; €286 Institutions print and online; $440 Institutions, other countries print and online; $83 Individuals print and online; £52 Individuals print and online; €74 Individuals print and online. **URL:** http://onlinelibrary.wiley.com/journal/10.1111/(ISSN)1475-3588. **Formerly:** Child Psychology & Psychiatry Review. **Ad Rates:** BW $500. **Remarks:** Accepts advertising. **Circ:** (Not Reported).

16340 ■ Child Development
Wiley-Blackwell
350 Main St.
Commerce Pl.
Malden, MA 02148-5018
Phone: (781)388-8200
Fax: (781)388-8210
Free: 800-216-2552
Journal focusing on topics in the field of child development. **Freq:** Bimonthly. **Key Personnel:** Jeffrey J. Lockman, Editor-in-Chief; Adam Martin, Managing Editor. **ISSN:** 0009--3920 (print); **EISSN:** 1467--8624 (electronic). **Subscription Rates:** $1047 Institutions print and online; £749 Institutions print and online; €951 Institutions print and online; $1463 Institutions, other countries print and online; $872 Institutions print or online; £624 Institutions print or online; €729 Institutions print or online; $1219 Institutions, other countries print or online. **URL:** http://onlinelibrary.wiley.com/journal/10.1111/(ISSN)1467-8624. **Ad Rates:** BW $625. **Remarks:** Accepts advertising. **Circ:** (Not Reported).

16341 ■ Child Development Perspectives
Blackwell Publishing Inc.
350 Main St.
Malden, MA 02148
Phone: (781)388-8200
Fax: (781)388-8210
Free: 800-216-2522
Publisher's E-mail: journaladsusa@bos.blackwellpublishing.com
Journal covering the field of developmental sciences. **Freq:** 3/year. **ISSN:** 1750--8592 (print); **EISSN:** 1750--8606 (electronic). **Subscription Rates:** $64 Individuals print & online; £85 Individuals print & online, UK and Europe (non euro zone); €86 Individuals print & online, Europe; $90 Other countries print & online. **URL:** http://onlinelibrary.wiley.com/journal/10.1111/(ISSN)1750-8606. **Remarks:** Accepts advertising. **Circ:** (Not Reported).

16342 ■ China & World Economy
Wiley-Blackwell
350 Main St.
Commerce Pl.
Malden, MA 02148-5018
Phone: (781)388-8200
Fax: (781)388-8210
Free: 800-216-2552
Journal focusing on the problems faced and progress made by China in its interaction with the world economy. **Freq:** Bimonthly. **Print Method:** Offset. **Cols./Page:** 5. **Col. Width:** 12 picas. **Col. Depth:** 15 inches. **Key Personnel:** Xiaoming Feng, Managing Editor; Yongding Yu, Editor-in-Chief; Hung-gay Fung, Associate, Editor-in-Chief; Shaoqing Sun, Contact; Zhinan Zhang, Contact. **ISSN:** 1671--2234 (print); **EISSN:** 1749--124X (electronic). **Subscription Rates:** $725 Institutions print and online; £431 Institutions print and online; €548 Institutions print and online; $843 Institutions, other countries print and online; $127 Individuals print and online; £71 Individuals print and online. **URL:** http://onlinelibrary.wiley.com/journal/10.1111/%28ISSN%291749-124X. **Circ:** (Not Reported).

16343 ■ City & Community
Blackwell Publishing Inc.
350 Main St.
Malden, MA 02148
Phone: (781)388-8200
Fax: (781)388-8210
Free: 800-216-2522
Publisher's E-mail: journaladsusa@bos.blackwellpublishing.com
Official journal of the Community and Urban Sociology Section covering research and theory about communities and metropolitan areas. **Freq:** Quarterly. **Key Personnel:** Hilary Silver, Editor. **ISSN:** 1535--6841 (print); **EISSN:** 1540--6040 (electronic). **Subscription Rates:** $99 Individuals print & online; $52 Students print & online; $564 Institutions print & online; $641 Institutions, other countries print or online; $470 Institutions print or online; €129 Individuals print & online. **URL:** http://www.wiley.com/WileyCDA/WileyTitle/productCd-CICO.html; http://onlinelibrary.wiley.com/journal/10.1111/(ISSN)1540-6040. **Ad Rates:** BW $300. **Remarks:** Accepts advertising. **Circ:** (Not Reported).

16344 ■ Clinical Endocrinology: The Clinical Journal of the Society for Endocrinology
Wiley-Blackwell
350 Main St.
Commerce Pl.
Malden, MA 02148-5018
Phone: (781)388-8200
Fax: (781)388-8210
Free: 800-216-2552
Journal focusing on the clinical aspects of endocrinology, including the clinical application of molecular endocrinology. **Freq:** Monthly. **Key Personnel:** J.S. Bevan, Senior Editor; S.J. Judd, Senior Editor. **ISSN:** 0300--0664 (print); **EISSN:** 1365--2265 (electronic). **Subscription Rates:** $3374 Institutions print or online; £1823 Institutions print or online; €2313 Institutions print or online; $3937 Institutions, other countries print or online; $4049 Institutions print and online; £2188 Institutions print and online; €2776 Institutions print and online; $4725 Institutions, other countries print and online. **URL:** http://onlinelibrary.wiley.com/journal/10.1111/(ISSN)1365-2265. **Remarks:** Accepts advertising. **Circ:** (Not Reported).

16345 ■ Clinical and Experimental Ophthalmology
Wiley-Blackwell

Circulation: ★ = AAM; △ or • = BPA; ♦ = CAC; ❑ = VAC; ⊕ = PO Statement; ‡ = Publisher's Report; Boldface figures = sworn; Light figures = estimated.

350 Main St.
Commerce Pl.
Malden, MA 02148-5018
Phone: (781)388-8200
Fax: (781)388-8210
Free: 800-216-2552
Journal focusing on all aspects of clinical practice and research in ophthalmology and vision science. Official journal of The Royal Australian and New Zealand College of Ophthalmologists. **Freq:** 9/year. **Key Personnel:** Prof. Charles N.J. McGhee, Associate Editor; Ms. Victoria Cartwright, Managing Editor. **ISSN:** 1442--6404 (print); **EISSN:** 1442--9071 (electronic). **Subscription Rates:** $975 Institutions print or online; £606 Institutions print or online; €768 Institutions print or online; A$740 Institutions print or online; $1184 Institutions, other countries print or online; $1170 Institutions print and online; £728 Institutions print and online; €922 Institutions print and online; A$888 Institutions print and online; $1421 Institutions, other countries print and online; $345 Individuals print and online; £213 Individuals print and online; €318 Individuals print and online; A$404 Individuals print and online. **URL:** http://onlinelibrary.wiley.com/journal/10.1111/(ISSN)1442-9071. **Remarks:** Advertising accepted; rates available upon request. **Circ:** (Not Reported).

16346 ■ Clinical and Experimental Optometry
Wiley-Blackwell
350 Main St.
Commerce Pl.
Malden, MA 02148-5018
Phone: (781)388-8200
Fax: (781)388-8210
Free: 800-216-2552
Publisher's E-mail: customerservice@oxon.blackwellpublishing.com
Peer-reviewed journal covering the field of clinical optometry and vision science. **Freq:** Bimonthly. **Key Personnel:** Prof. Barry H. Collin, Editor; Prof. Raymond Applegate, Board Member; Prof. Robert F. Hess, Board Member; Prof. David Atchison, Board Member; Prof. Nathan Efron, Board Member; Dr. Erica Fletcher, Associate Editor. **ISSN:** 0816-4622 (print); **EISSN:** 1444-0938 (electronic). **Subscription Rates:** $463 Institutions online only; £277 Institutions online only; €348 Institutions online only; $537 Institutions online only; $556 Institutions print + online; £333 Institutions print + online; €418 Institutions print + online; $645 Institutions print + online. **URL:** http://onlinelibrary.wiley.com/journal/10.1111/(ISSN)1444-0938. **Mailing address:** PO Box 1354, Oxford OX4 2ZG, United Kingdom. **Remarks:** Advertising accepted; rates available upon request. **Circ:** (Not Reported).

16347 ■ Clinical and Experimental Pharmacology and Physiology
Wiley-Blackwell
350 Main St.
Commerce Pl.
Malden, MA 02148-5018
Phone: (781)388-8200
Fax: (781)388-8210
Free: 800-216-2552
Journal focusing on results of clinical and experimental work in pharmacology and physiology. **Freq:** Monthly. **Key Personnel:** Ding-Feng Su; Roger Evans. **ISSN:** 0305--1870 (print); **EISSN:** 1440--1681 (electronic). **Subscription Rates:** $3039 Institutions online; £1612 Institutions, other countries online; €2428 Institutions, other countries online; $3744 Institutions rest of the world, online. **URL:** http://onlinelibrary.wiley.com/journal/10.1111/(ISSN)1440-1681. **Remarks:** Accepts advertising. **Circ:** (Not Reported).

16348 ■ Clinical Implant Dentistry and Related Research
Wiley-Blackwell
350 Main St.
Commerce Pl.
Malden, MA 02148-5018
Phone: (781)388-8200
Fax: (781)388-8210
Free: 800-216-2552
Journal featuring the scientific and technical developments within clinical implant dentistry and related subjects. **Freq:** Quarterly. **Key Personnel:** William Becker, Editor-in-Chief; Lars Sennerby, Editor-in-Chief; Ignace Naert, Board Member; Luiz A. Salata, Board Member; Else Marie Pinholt, Board Member. **ISSN:** 1523--0899 (print); **EISSN:** 1708--8208 (electronic). **Subscription Rates:** $507 Institutions print and online; $562 Institutions, Canada print and online; £286 Institutions print and online; €364 Institutions print or online; $557 Institutions, other countries print and online; $246 Individuals print and online; $273 Canada print and online; £137 Individuals print and online. **URL:** http://onlinelibrary.wiley.com/journal/10.1111/%28ISSN%291708-8208. **Circ:** (Not Reported).

16349 ■ Clinical Otolaryngology
Wiley-Blackwell
350 Main St.
Commerce Pl.
Malden, MA 02148-5018
Phone: (781)388-8200
Fax: (781)388-8210
Free: 800-216-2552
Journal focusing on clinical and clinically-oriented research. **Freq:** Bimonthly. **Key Personnel:** G.G. Browning, Editor; Terry Jones, Editor-in-Chief. **ISSN:** 0307-7772 (print). **Subscription Rates:** $243 Members print and online; $2500 Institutions print and online; $2173 Institutions print or online; $145 Members online only; £133 Members print and online; £81 Members online only; £1353 Institutions print and online; £1176 Institutions print or online. **URL:** http://www.wiley.com/WileyCDA/WileyTitle/productCd-COA.html. **Formerly:** Clinical Otolaryngology and Allied Sciences. **Remarks:** Accepts advertising. **Circ:** (Not Reported).

16350 ■ The Clinical Respiratory Journal
Blackwell Publishing Inc.
350 Main St.
Malden, MA 02148
Phone: (781)388-8200
Fax: (781)388-8210
Free: 800-216-2522
Publisher's E-mail: journaladsusa@bos.blackwellpublishing.com
Peer-reviewed journal featuring clinical research in all areas of respiratory medicine. **Freq:** Quarterly. **Key Personnel:** Chen Wang, Editor-in-Chief. **ISSN:** 1752--6981 (print); **EISSN:** 1752--699X (electronic). **Subscription Rates:** £296 Institutions UK (online); $542 Institutions Americas (online only); €374 Institutions Europe (online only); $575 Institutions, other countries online only. **URL:** http://onlinelibrary.wiley.com/journal/10.1111/(ISSN)1752-699X. **Remarks:** Advertising accepted; rates available upon request. **Circ:** (Not Reported).

16351 ■ The Clinical Teacher
Wiley-Blackwell
350 Main St.
Commerce Pl.
Malden, MA 02148-5018
Phone: (781)388-8200
Fax: (781)388-8210
Free: 800-216-2552
Journal focusing on medical education. **Freq:** Quarterly. **Key Personnel:** Steve Trumble, Editor-in-Chief; Sue Symons, Manager. **ISSN:** 1743--4971 (print); **EISSN:** 1743--498X (electronic). **Subscription Rates:** $215 Individuals online only; $671 Institutions online only; £118 Individuals online only; £367 Institutions online only; £130 Individuals rest of the world, online only; £782 Institutions rest of world, online only. **URL:** http://onlinelibrary.wiley.com/journal/10.1111/(ISSN)1743-498X. **Remarks:** Accepts advertising. **Circ:** (Not Reported).

16352 ■ Clinical Transplantation
Wiley-Blackwell
350 Main St.
Commerce Pl.
Malden, MA 02148-5018
Phone: (781)388-8200
Fax: (781)388-8210
Free: 800-216-2552
Journal focusing on organ or tissue transplants, including: kidney, intestine, liver, pancreas, heart, heart valves, lung, bone marrow, cornea, skin, bone, and cartilage, viable or stored. **Freq:** Bimonthly. **Key Personnel:** David E.R. Sutherland, Editor-in-Chief. **ISSN:** 0902--0063 (print); **EISSN:** 1399--0012 (electronic). **Subscription Rates:** $1832 Institutions online only; £1095 Institutions online only; €1390 Institutions online only; $2143 Institutions, other countries online only; $742 Individuals online only; £443 Individuals online only; €662 Individuals online only. **URL:** http://onlinelibrary.wiley.com/journal/10.1111/(ISSN)1399-0012. **Remarks:** Advertising accepted; rates available upon request. **Circ:** (Not Reported).

16353 ■ CNS Neuroscience & Therapeutics
Wiley-Blackwell
350 Main St.
Commerce Pl.
Malden, MA 02148-5018
Phone: (781)388-8200
Fax: (781)388-8210
Free: 800-216-2552
Journal covering reviews on the pharmacology, pharmacokinetics, toxicology and clinical trials of new drugs affecting the central nervous system. The reviews cover the pharmacology, pharmacokinetics, toxicology, and clinical experience with these drugs. **Freq:** Monthly. **Print Method:** Offset. **Cols./Page:** 4. **Col. Width:** 21 3/5 nonpareils. **Col. Depth:** 10 inches. **Key Personnel:** Ding-Feng Su, Editor-in-Chief; Jun Chen, Associate Editor; Jian-Sheng Lin, Associate Editor. **ISSN:** 1755--5930 (print); **EISSN:** 1755--5949 (electronic). **Subscription Rates:** $1031 Institutions print and online; £711 Institutions print and online; €898 Institutions print and online; $1384 Institutions, other countries print and online. **URL:** http://onlinelibrary.wiley.com/journal/10.1111/%28ISSN%291755-5949. **Formerly:** CNS Drug Reviews. **Circ:** (Not Reported).

16354 ■ Cognitive Science: A Multidisciplinary Journal
Wiley-Blackwell
350 Main St.
Commerce Pl.
Malden, MA 02148-5018
Phone: (781)388-8200
Fax: (781)388-8210
Free: 800-216-2552
Publisher's E-mail: journaladsusa@bos.blackwellpublishing.com
Journal publishing articles in all areas of cognitive science, on such topics as knowledge representation, inference, memory processes, learning, problem solving, planning, perception, and other areas of multidisciplinary concern. **Freq:** 8/year. **Key Personnel:** Arthur B. Markman, Reviewer; John R. Anderson, Reviewer; Richard P. Cooper, Executive Editor. **ISSN:** 0364--0213 (print); **EISSN:** 1551--6709 (electronic). **URL:** http://onlinelibrary.wiley.com/journal/10.1111/(ISSN)1551-6709. **Ad Rates:** BW $800. **Remarks:** Accepts advertising. **Circ:** (Not Reported).

16355 ■ Coloration Technology
Wiley-Blackwell
350 Main St.
Commerce Pl.
Malden, MA 02148-5018
Phone: (781)388-8200
Fax: (781)388-8210
Free: 800-216-2552
Peer-reviewed journal covering reviews on topics related to coloration. **Freq:** Bimonthly. **Print Method:** Offset. **Trim Size:** 10 1/2 x 16. **Cols./Page:** 5. **Col. Width:** 2 inches. **Col. Depth:** 16 inches. **Key Personnel:** Peter Duffield, Board Member; Catherine Barber, Managing Editor; Andrew Towns, Editor-in-Chief; Artur Cavaco-Paulo, Board Member; Bob Christie, Board Member; Geoff Collins, Board Member. **ISSN:** 1472--3581 (print); **EISSN:** 1478--4408 (electronic). **USPS:** 659-530. **Subscription Rates:** $785 Institutions online only; £394 Institutions online only; €501 Institutions online only; $845 Institutions, other countries online only; $942 Institutions print and online; £473 Institutions print and online; €602 Institutions print and online; $1014 Institutions, other countries print and online; $740 Institutions U.S - online only; £371 Institutions U.K - online only; €472 Institutions Europe (Euro and non-Euro zone) - online only; $797 Institutions, other countries online only; $888 Institutions U.S - print and online; £446 Institutions U.K - print and online; €567 Institutions Europe (Euro and non-Euro zone) - print and online; $597 Institutions print and online; $495 Members U.S - online only; £250 Members U.K - online only; €372 Members Europe (Euro and non-Euro zone) - online only; £271 Members rest of the world - online only; $614 Members U.S. - print and online; £312 Members U.K and Europe (non-

Euro zone) - print and online; €463 Members Europe - print and online; £393 Members rest of the world - print and online. **URL:** http://onlinelibrary.wiley.com/journal/10.1111/(ISSN)1478-4408; http://www.sdc.org.uk/resources/publications/coloration-technology. **Remarks:** Advertising not accepted. **Circ:** (Not Reported).

16356 ■ Communication, Culture & Critique
Wiley-Blackwell
350 Main St.
Commerce Pl.
Malden, MA 02148-5018
Phone: (781)388-8200
Fax: (781)388-8210
Free: 800-216-2552
Journal covering the qualitative research examining the role of communication and cultural criticism in today's world. **Freq:** Quarterly. **Key Personnel:** Radhika Parameswaran, Editor. **ISSN:** 1753--9129 (print); **EISSN:** 1753--9137 (electronic). **Subscription Rates:** $119 Individuals print & online; £86 Individuals print & online, UK and Europe (non euro zone); €127 Individuals print & online; £86 Out of area print & online. **URL:** http://onlinelibrary.wiley.com/journal/10.1111/(ISSN)1753-9137. **Remarks:** Accepts advertising. **Circ:** (Not Reported).

16357 ■ Communication Theory
Wiley-Blackwell
350 Main St.
Commerce Pl.
Malden, MA 02148-5018
Phone: (781)388-8200
Fax: (781)388-8210
Free: 800-216-2552
Journal covering the theoretical development of communication from across a wide array of disciplines, such as communication studies, sociology, psychology, political science, cultural and gender studies, philosophy, linguistics, and literature. **Freq:** Quarterly. **Print Method:** Offset. **Trim Size:** 12.5 x 22. **Cols./Page:** 6. **Col. Width:** 11 picas. **Col. Depth:** 21 inches. **Key Personnel:** Karin Gwinn Wilkins, Editor; Angharad Valdivia, Board Member; Donnalyn Pompper, Board Member. **ISSN:** 1050--3293 (print); **EISSN:** 1468--2885 (electronic). **USPS:** 152-700. **Subscription Rates:** $85 Individuals print and online; £53 Other countries print and online; €77 Individuals print and online; £53 Individuals U.K, Europe (non-Euro zone) and Rest of the World - print and online. **URL:** http://onlinelibrary.wiley.com/journal/10.1111/%28ISSN%291468-2885; http://onlinelibrary.wiley.com/doi/10.1111/comt.2015.25.issue-1/issuetoc. **Ad Rates:** BW $445; SAU $5.25; PCI $4.95. **Remarks:** Accepts advertising. **Circ:** (Not Reported).

16358 ■ Community Dentistry and Oral Epidemiology
Wiley-Blackwell
350 Main St.
Commerce Pl.
Malden, MA 02148-5018
Phone: (781)388-8200
Fax: (781)388-8210
Free: 800-216-2552
Journal focusing on community dentistry. **Freq:** Bimonthly. **Key Personnel:** John A. Spencer, Editor-in-Chief. **ISSN:** 0301--5661 (print); **EISSN:** 1600--0528 (electronic). **Subscription Rates:** $994 Institutions print or online; £593 Institutions print or online; €750 Institutions print or online; $1159 Institutions, other countries print or online; $1193 Institutions print and online; £7112 Institutions print and online; €900 Institutions print and online; $1391 Institutions, other countries print and online. **URL:** http://onlinelibrary.wiley.com/journal/10.1111/(ISSN)1600-0528. **Remarks:** Accepts advertising. **Circ:** (Not Reported).

16359 ■ Computer Graphics Forum
Wiley-Blackwell
350 Main St.
Commerce Pl.
Malden, MA 02148-5018
Phone: (781)388-8200
Fax: (781)388-8210
Free: 800-216-2552
Journal focusing on computer graphics. **Freq:** 8/year. **Key Personnel:** Hao Zhang, Editor. **ISSN:** 0167--7055 (print); **EISSN:** 1467--8659 (electronic). **Subscription Rates:** $1224 Institutions online only; £745 Institutions online only; €944 Institutions online only; $1347 Institutions, other countries online only. **URL:** http://onlinelibrary.wiley.com/journal/10.1111/(ISSN)1467-8659. **Remarks:** Accepts advertising. **Circ:** (Not Reported).

16360 ■ Congenital Heart Disease: Clinical Studies from Fetus to Adulthood
Blackwell Publishing Inc.
350 Main St.
Malden, MA 02148
Phone: (781)388-8200
Fax: (781)388-8210
Free: 800-216-2522
Publisher's E-mail: journaladsusa@bos.blackwellpublishing.com
Journal featuring articles on congenital heart disease in children and adults. **Freq:** Bimonthly. **Key Personnel:** Douglas S. Moodie, Editor-in-Chief; Elizabeth Brenner, Managing Editor. **ISSN:** 1747--079X (print); **EISSN:** 1747--0803 (electronic). **Subscription Rates:** $736 Institutions online; £414 Institutions online, UK; €522 Institutions online, Europe; $802 Institutions, other countries online; $346 Individuals online ; £217 Individuals online, UK and Europe (non euro zone); €289 Individuals online; $217 Other countries online. **URL:** http://onlinelibrary.wiley.com/journal/10.1111/(ISSN)1747-0803. **Remarks:** Accepts advertising. **Circ:** (Not Reported).

16361 ■ Conservation Biology
Wiley-Blackwell
350 Main St.
Commerce Pl.
Malden, MA 02148-5018
Phone: (781)388-8200
Fax: (781)388-8210
Free: 800-216-2552
Journal focusing on the key issues contributing to the study and preservation of species and habitats. **Freq:** Bimonthly. **Key Personnel:** Ken Paige, Editor; Ellen Main, Senior Editor. **ISSN:** 0888--8892 (print); **EISSN:** 1523--1739 (electronic). **USPS:** 152-31739. **Subscription Rates:** $1341 Institutions print and online; $1384 Institutions, Canada and Mexico print and online; £1152 Institutions print and online; €1463 Institutions print and online; $2256 Institutions, other countries print and online; $1117 Institutions print or online; $1153 Institutions, Canada and Mexico print or online; £960 Institutions print or online; €1219 Institutions print or online; $1880 Institutions, other countries print or online. **URL:** http://onlinelibrary.wiley.com/journal/10.1111/(ISSN)1523-1739. **Ad Rates:** BW $700; 4C $850. **Remarks:** Accepts advertising. **Circ:** (Not Reported).

16362 ■ Constellations: An International Journal of Critical and Democratic Theory
Wiley-Blackwell
350 Main St.
Commerce Pl.
Malden, MA 02148-5018
Phone: (781)388-8200
Fax: (781)388-8210
Free: 800-216-2552
Publisher's E-mail: journaladsusa@bos.blackwellpublishing.com
Peer-reviewed journal committed to publishing the best contemporary critical and democratic theory. **Freq:** Quarterly. **Key Personnel:** Andrew Arato, Editor, phone: (212)229-5700, fax: (212)229-5595; Nancy Fraser, Member; Ian Zuckerman, Member. **ISSN:** 1351--0487 (print); **EISSN:** 1467--8675 (electronic). **Subscription Rates:** $1347 Institutions print or online; £706 Institutions print or online; €896 Institutions print or online; $1701 Institutions, other countries print or online; $1617 Institutions print and online; £848 Institutions print and online; €1076 Institutions print and online; $2042 Institutions, other countries print and online; $52 Individuals print and online; £31 Individuals print and online; €51 Individuals print and online. **URL:** http://onlinelibrary.wiley.com/journal/10.1111/(ISSN)1467-8675. **Remarks:** Advertising accepted; rates available upon request. **Circ:** (Not Reported).

16363 ■ Creativity and Innovation Management
Wiley-Blackwell
350 Main St.
Commerce Pl.
Malden, MA 02148-5018
Phone: (781)388-8200
Fax: (781)388-8210
Free: 800-216-2552
Journal focusing on the theory and practice of organizing imagination and innovation. **Freq:** Quarterly. **Key Personnel:** Petra de Weerd-Nederhof, Editor; Olaf Fisscher, Editor; Klaasjan Visscher, Editor. **ISSN:** 0963--1690 (print); **EISSN:** 1467--8691 (electronic). **Subscription Rates:** $1610 Institutions print or online; £959 Institutions print or online; €1219 Institutions print or online; $1876 Institutions, other countries print or online; $1932 Institutions print and online; £1151 Institutions print and online; €1463 Institutions print and online; $2252 Institutions, other countries print and online. **URL:** http://onlinelibrary.wiley.com/journal/10.1111/(ISSN)1467-8691. **Remarks:** Advertising accepted; rates available upon request. **Circ:** (Not Reported).

16364 ■ Criminology & Public Policy
Wiley-Blackwell
350 Main St.
Commerce Pl.
Malden, MA 02148-5018
Phone: (781)388-8200
Fax: (781)388-8210
Free: 800-216-2552
Journal focusing on policy discussions of criminology research findings and the study of criminal justice policy and practice. **Freq:** Quarterly. **Key Personnel:** Natasha A. Frost, Board Member; Tom Blomberg, Editor. **ISSN:** 1538--6473 (print); **EISSN:** 1745--9133 (electronic). **Subscription Rates:** $405 Institutions print and online; $337 Institutions online only; $494 Institutions, other countries print and online; $411 Institutions, other countries online only. **URL:** http://onlinelibrary.wiley.com/journal/10.1111/(ISSN)1745-9133. **Remarks:** Advertising accepted; rates available upon request. **Circ:** (Not Reported).

16365 ■ Critical Quarterly
Wiley-Blackwell
350 Main St.
Commerce Pl.
Malden, MA 02148-5018
Phone: (781)388-8200
Fax: (781)388-8210
Free: 800-216-2552
Journal focusing on literary criticism, cultural studies, poetry and fiction. **Freq:** Quarterly. **Key Personnel:** Colin MacCabe, Editor; Nigella Lawson, Managing Editor; Kate Mellor, Managing Editor; Joanna Jellinek, Publisher; Shalini Puri, Associate Editor. **ISSN:** 0011--1562 (print); **EISSN:** 1467--8705 (electronic). **Subscription Rates:** $595 Institutions print or online; £318 Institutions print or online; €401 Institutions print or online; $695 Institutions, other countries print or online; $714 Institutions print and online; £382 Institutions print and online; €482 Institutions print and online; $834 Institutions, other countries print and online; $64 Individuals print and online; £38 Individuals print and online; €58 Individuals print and online. **URL:** http://onlinelibrary.wiley.com/journal/10.1111/(ISSN)1467-8705. **Remarks:** Advertising accepted; rates available upon request. **Circ:** (Not Reported).

16366 ■ CrossCurrents
Blackwell Publishing Inc.
350 Main St.
Malden, MA 02148
Phone: (781)388-8200
Fax: (781)388-8210
Free: 800-216-2522
Publisher's E-mail: journaladsusa@bos.blackwellpublishing.com
Journal. **Founded:** 1950. **Freq:** Quarterly. **Key Personnel:** Charles Henderson, Executive Director. **ISSN:** 0011-1953 (print). **Subscription Rates:** $44 Individuals print and online; $103 Institutions seminaries, print and online; $210 Institutions print and online; $183 Institutions online only. **URL:** http://www.wiley.com/WileyCDA/WileyTitle/productCd-CROS.html. **Formerly:** CrossCurrents/Religion and Intellectual Life. **Ad Rates:** BW $400. **Remarks:** Accepts advertising. **Circ:** Paid ‡4000, Controlled ‡400.

Circulation: ★ = AAM; △ or • = BPA; ♦ = CAC; ❑ = VAC; ⊕ = PO Statement; ‡ = Publisher's Report; Boldface figures = sworn; Light figures = estimated.

16367 ■ Curtis's Botanical Magazine
Wiley-Blackwell
350 Main St.
Commerce Pl.
Malden, MA 02148-5018
Phone: (781)388-8200
Fax: (781)388-8210
Free: 800-216-2552
Journal focusing on botanicals. **Freq:** Quarterly. **Key Personnel:** Martyn Rix, Editor. **ISSN:** 1355-4905 (print); **EISSN:** 1467-8748 (electronic). **Subscription Rates:** $122 Individuals print & online; $89 Members print & online; $930 Institutions print & online; €557 Institutions print or online; $808 Institutions print or online; €97 Individuals print & online; £61 Individuals print & online; £505 Institutions print & online; €643 Institutions print & online; £439 Institutions print or online. **URL:** http://onlinelibrary.wiley.com/journal/10.1111/(ISSN)1467-8748. **Remarks:** Accepts advertising. **Circ:** (Not Reported).

16368 ■ Cytopathology
Wiley-Blackwell
350 Main St.
Commerce Pl.
Malden, MA 02148-5018
Phone: (781)388-8200
Fax: (781)388-8210
Free: 800-216-2552
Journal focusing on cytology that will increase knowledge and understanding of the aetiology, diagnosis and management of human disease. **Freq:** Bimonthly. **Key Personnel:** Dr. Gray W. Oxford, Advisor; Dr. Amanda Herbert, Editor. **ISSN:** 0956--5507 (print); **EISSN:** 1365--2303 (electronic). **Subscription Rates:** $1507 Institutions print or online; £818 Institutions print or online; €1039 Institutions print or online; $1758 Institutions, other countries print or online; $1809 Institutions print and online; £982 Institutions print and online; €1247 Institutions print and online; $2110 Institutions, other countries print and online. **URL:** http://onlinelibrary.wiley.com/journal/10.1111/(ISSN)1365-2303. **Remarks:** Advertising accepted; rates available upon request. **Circ:** (Not Reported).

16369 ■ Decision Sciences Journal of Innovative Education
Wiley-Blackwell
350 Main St.
Commerce Pl.
Malden, MA 02148-5018
Phone: (781)388-8200
Fax: (781)388-8210
Free: 800-216-2552
Peer-reviewed journal covering the field of decision sciences. **Freq:** Quarterly. **Key Personnel:** Vijay R. Kannan, Editor; Chetan S. Sankar. **ISSN:** 1540-4595 (print); **EISSN:** 1540-4609 (electronic). **Subscription Rates:** $558 Institutions Americas (print and online); £418 Institutions UK (print and online); €530 Institutions Europe (print and online); $789 Institutions, other countries print and online; $485 Institutions Americas (print or online only); £363 Institutions UK (print or online only); €462 Institutions Europe (print or online only); $687 Institutions, other countries print or online only. **URL:** http://onlinelibrary.wiley.com/journal/10.1111/(ISSN)1540-4609. **Remarks:** Advertising not accepted. **Circ:** (Not Reported).

16370 ■ The Developing Economies
Wiley-Blackwell
350 Main St.
Commerce Pl.
Malden, MA 02148-5018
Phone: (781)388-8200
Fax: (781)388-8210
Free: 800-216-2552
Journal featuring research articles dealing with empirical and comparative studies on social sciences relating to the developing countries. **Freq:** Quarterly. **Key Personnel:** Shujiro Urata, Editor; Shin-ichi Fukuda, Editor. **ISSN:** 0012--1533 (print); **EISSN:** 1746--1049 (electronic). **Subscription Rates:** $264 Institutions online; £158 Institutions online, UK; €200 Institutions online, Europe; $306 Institutions, other countries online; $317 Institutions print and online; £190 Institutions print and online, UK; €240 Institutions print and online, Europe; $368 Institutions, other countries Europe (online only). **Alt. Formats:** PDF. **URL:** http://onlinelibrary.wiley.com/journal/10.1111/(ISSN)1746-1049; http://www.ide.go.jp/English/Publish/Periodicals/De/backnumber.html. **Remarks:** Accepts advertising. **Circ:** (Not Reported).

16371 ■ Developing World Bioethics
Wiley-Blackwell
350 Main St.
Commerce Pl.
Malden, MA 02148-5018
Phone: (781)388-8200
Fax: (781)388-8210
Free: 800-216-2552
Journal publishing case studies, teaching materials, news in brief, and legal backgrounds to bioethics scholars and students in developing and developed countries alike. **Freq:** 3/yr. **Key Personnel:** Andy F. Visser, Managing Editor; Derrick Aarons, Board Member; Willem Landman, Board Member; Prof. Udo Schuklenk, PhD, Editor. **ISSN:** 1471-8731 (print); **EISSN:** 1471-8847 (electronic). **Subscription Rates:** $1960 Institutions print or online; $2352 Institutions print & online; $263 Individuals print & online. **URL:** http://onlinelibrary.wiley.com/journal/10.1111/(ISSN)1471-8847. **Remarks:** Accepts advertising. **Circ:** (Not Reported).

16372 ■ Development and Change
Wiley-Blackwell
350 Main St.
Commerce Pl.
Malden, MA 02148-5018
Phone: (781)388-8200
Fax: (781)388-8210
Free: 800-216-2552
Journal focusing on development studies and social change. **Freq:** Bimonthly. **Key Personnel:** Ashwani Saith, Editor; Paula E. Bownas, Managing Editor. **ISSN:** 0012-155X (print). **Subscription Rates:** $50 Students print and online; $1283 Institutions print and online; $1069 Institutions print or online; £766 Institutions print and online; £638 Institutions print or online. **URL:** http://as.wiley.com/WileyCDA/WileyTitle/productCd-DECH.html; http://onlinelibrary.wiley.com/journal/10.1111/(ISSN)1467-7660. **Remarks:** Accepts advertising. **Circ:** (Not Reported).

16373 ■ Development, Growth and Differentiation: Official Journal of the Japanese Society of Developmental Biologists
Wiley-Blackwell
350 Main St.
Commerce Pl.
Malden, MA 02148-5018
Phone: (781)388-8200
Fax: (781)388-8210
Free: 800-216-2552
Publisher's E-mail: journaladsusa@bos.blackwellpublishing.com
Journal focusing on aspects of developmental phenomena in all kinds of organisms, including plants and microorganisms. **Freq:** 9/year. **Key Personnel:** Harukazu Nakamura, Editor-in-Chief; Kiyokazu Agata, Board Member; Koji Tamura, Board Member. **ISSN:** 0012--1592 (print); **EISSN:** 1440--169X (electronic). **Subscription Rates:** $2076 Institutions online only; £1284 Institutions online only - UK; €1630 Institutions online only - Europe; $2512 Institutions, other countries online only. **URL:** http://onlinelibrary.wiley.com/journal/10.1111/(ISSN)1440-169X. **Remarks:** Accepts advertising. **Circ:** (Not Reported).

16374 ■ Development Policy Review
Wiley-Blackwell
350 Main St.
Commerce Pl.
Malden, MA 02148-5018
Phone: (781)388-8200
Fax: (781)388-8210
Free: 800-216-2552
Peer-reviewed journal focusing on links between research and policy in international development. **Freq:** Bimonthly. **Key Personnel:** Pilar Domingo, Editor. **ISSN:** 0950-6764 (print). **Subscription Rates:** $95 Individuals print and online; $70 Members IDS, SID and DSA, print and online; $61 Students print and online; $1112 Institutions print and online; $926 Institutions print or online; £664 Institutions print and online; £553 Institutions print or online; £57 Individuals print and online. **URL:** http://as.wiley.com/WileyCDA/WileyTitle/productCd-DPR.html. **Remarks:** Accepts advertising. **Circ:** (Not Reported).

16375 ■ Developmental Science
Wiley-Blackwell
350 Main St.
Commerce Pl.
Malden, MA 02148-5018
Phone: (781)388-8200
Fax: (781)388-8210
Free: 800-216-2552
Journal focusing on scientific developmental psychology from leading thinkers in the field. **Freq:** Bimonthly. **Key Personnel:** Mark H. Johnson, Board Member; Denis Mareschal, Editor; Thomas Gaston, Managing Editor. **ISSN:** 1363--755X (print); **EISSN:** 1467--7687 (electronic). **Subscription Rates:** $1941 Institutions, other countries online only; $103 Members online only; $64 Students online only; $1667 Institutions online only. **URL:** http://onlinelibrary.wiley.com/journal/10.1111/(ISSN)1467-7687. **Remarks:** Accepts advertising. **Circ:** (Not Reported).

16376 ■ Diabetes, Obesity and Metabolism
Wiley-Blackwell
350 Main St.
Commerce Pl.
Malden, MA 02148-5018
Phone: (781)388-8200
Fax: (781)388-8210
Free: 800-216-2552
Journal focusing on clinical and experimental pharmacology studies related to diabetes, obesity and metabolism, including evaluations of new glucose and weight-lowering drugs, new therapeutic developments in the management and prevention of diabetic complications, e.g. growth factors and biotechnology products for foot ulcers, and clinical trials involving established medicines, e.g. optimal treatment of hypertension, lipids or infection in the diabetic population. **Freq:** Monthly. **Key Personnel:** Prof. A. Garber, Editor; Prof. R. Donnelly, Editor-in-Chief. **ISSN:** 1462--8902 (print); **EISSN:** 1463--1326 (electronic). **Subscription Rates:** $1660 Institutions online only; £900 Institutions online only; €1143 Institutions online only; $1937 Institutions, other countries online only; $196 Individuals online only; £109 Individuals online only - UK and Europe (non-euro zone); €161 Individuals online only; £120 Other countries online only. **URL:** http://onlinelibrary.wiley.com/journal/10.1111/(ISSN)1463-1326. **Remarks:** Accepts advertising. **Circ:** (Not Reported).

16377 ■ Diabetic Medicine: One of the leading Clinical Diabetes Journals in the world
Wiley-Blackwell
350 Main St.
Commerce Pl.
Malden, MA 02148-5018
Phone: (781)388-8200
Fax: (781)388-8210
Free: 800-216-2552
Publisher's E-mail: journaladsusa@bos.blackwellpublishing.com
Journal focusing on basic and applied research of direct relevance to clinical diabetes and its scope ranges from fundamental research to delivery of better health care. **Freq:** Monthly. **Key Personnel:** A. Ceriello, Associate Editor; C. Acerini, Associate Editor. **ISSN:** 0742--3071 (print); **EISSN:** 1464--5491 (electronic). **Subscription Rates:** $3700 Institutions print and online; £2004 Institutions print and online; €2548 Institutions print and online; $4318 Institutions, other countries print and online; $539 Individuals print and online; £324 Individuals print and online - UK, Europe (non-euro zone) and rest of the world; €483 Other countries print and online. **URL:** http://onlinelibrary.wiley.com/journal/10.1111/(ISSN)1464-5491. **Remarks:** Accepts advertising. **Circ:** (Not Reported).

16378 ■ Dialectica: The Official Journal of the European Society for Analytic Philosophy
Wiley-Blackwell
350 Main St.
Commerce Pl.
Malden, MA 02148-5018
Phone: (781)388-8200
Fax: (781)388-8210
Free: 800-216-2552
Publisher's E-mail: journaladsusa@bos.blackwellpublishing.com
Journal focusing on theoretical and systematic philosophy. **Freq:** Quarterly. **Key Personnel:** Marcel

Weber, Editor. **ISSN:** 0012--2017 (print); **EISSN:** 1746--8361 (electronic). **Subscription Rates:** $711 Institutions print and online; £388 Institutions print and online; €492 Institutions print and online; $418 Institutions print and online - developing country; $826 Institutions, other countries print and online; £87 Individuals print and online - UK and Europe (non-euro zone); €70 Individuals print and online; £52 Other countries print and online. **URL:** http://onlinelibrary.wiley.com/journal/10.1111/(ISSN)1746-8361. **Remarks:** Accepts advertising. **Circ:** (Not Reported).

16379 ■ Dialog
Wiley-Blackwell
350 Main St.
Commerce Pl.
Malden, MA 02148-5018
Phone: (781)388-8200
Fax: (781)388-8210
Free: 800-216-2552
Journal investigating the intersections between contemporary social issues and the mission of the Lutheran church. **Freq:** Quarterly. **Key Personnel:** Kristin Johnston Largen, Editor; Christine Little, Managing Editor. **ISSN:** 0012-2033 (print); **EISSN:** 1540-6385 (electronic). **Subscription Rates:** $59 Individuals print & online; $32 Students print & online; $50 Members print & online; $359 Institutions print & online; $573 Institutions, other countries print & online; $282 Institutions print or online; €80 Individuals print & online; £54 Individuals print & online; €52 Students print & online; £33 Students print & online. **URL:** http://www.wiley.com/WileyCDA/WileyTitle/productCd-DIAL.html. **Ad Rates:** BW $475. **Remarks:** Accepts advertising. **Circ:** (Not Reported).

16380 ■ Digest of Middle East Studies
Blackwell Publishing Inc.
350 Main St.
Malden, MA 02148
Phone: (781)388-8200
Fax: (781)388-8210
Free: 800-216-2522
Publisher's E-mail: journaladsusa@bos.blackwellpublishing.com
Peer-reviewed scholarly journal covering Middle East affairs. **Freq:** Biennial. **Trim Size:** 6 x 9. **Cols./Page:** 1. **Col. Width:** 4 1/4 inches. **Col. Depth:** 7 inches. **Key Personnel:** Mohammed M. Aman, PhD, Editor-in-Chief, phone: (414)229-3315, fax: (414)229-3314; Mary Jo Aman, Associate Editor. **ISSN:** 1060--4367 (print); **EISSN:** 1949--3606 (electronic). **Subscription Rates:** $2088 Institutions online; £1535 Institutions online; €1951 Institutions online; non-Euro zone; €1951 Institutions online; Euro zone; $3004 Institutions, other countries online. **URL:** http://onlinelibrary.wiley.com/journal/10.1111/(ISSN)1949-3606. **Remarks:** Accepts advertising. **Circ:** Paid 1000.

16381 ■ Digestive Endoscopy
Wiley-Blackwell
350 Main St.
Commerce Pl.
Malden, MA 02148-5018
Phone: (781)388-8200
Fax: (781)388-8210
Free: 800-216-2552
Journal publishing original articles that offer significant contributions to knowledge in the broad field of endoscopy. **Freq:** Bimonthly. **Key Personnel:** Choitsu Sakamoto, Editor-in-Chief. **ISSN:** 0915--5635 (print); **EISSN:** 1443--1661 (electronic). **Subscription Rates:** $261 Individuals print & online; $1470 Institutions print & online; $1225 Institutions print or online; €244 Individuals print & online; £858 Institutions print & online; £758 Institutions print or online; £165 Individuals print + online. **URL:** http://www.wiley.com/WileyCDA/WileyTitle/productCd-DEN.html; http://onlinelibrary.wiley.com/journal/10.1111/(ISSN)1443-1661. **Remarks:** Accepts advertising. **Circ:** (Not Reported).

16382 ■ Disasters
Wiley-Blackwell
350 Main St.
Commerce Pl.
Malden, MA 02148-5018
Phone: (781)388-8200
Fax: (781)388-8210
Free: 800-216-2552
Journal aiming to provide a forum for academics, policymakers and practitioners for high-quality research and practice related to natural disasters and complex political emergencies around the world. **Freq:** Quarterly. **Key Personnel:** Helen Young, Editor; David Alexander, Editor; Richard Jones, Assistant Editor; Paul Harvey, Board Member. **ISSN:** 0361-3666 (print); **EISSN:** 1467-7717 (electronic). **Subscription Rates:** $103 Individuals print & online; $174 Two years print & online; $61 Individuals print & online; $91 Members ALNAP/DSA/ENN, print & online; $55 Students print & online; $1016 Institutions print & online; €93 Individuals print & online; €156 Two years print & online; £605 Institutions print & online. **URL:** http://onlinelibrary.wiley.com/journal/10.1111/(ISSN)1467-7717. **Remarks:** Accepts advertising. **Circ:** (Not Reported).

16383 ■ Diseases of the Esophagus
Wiley-Blackwell
350 Main St.
Commerce Pl.
Malden, MA 02148-5018
Phone: (781)388-8200
Fax: (781)388-8210
Free: 800-216-2552
Journal covering covers all aspects of the esophagus - etiology, investigation and diagnosis, and both medical and surgical treatment. **Freq:** 8/year. **Trim Size:** A4. **Key Personnel:** Andre Duranceau, Editor-in-Chief; John Pandolfino, Editor-in-Chief; Zach DeBoer, Managing Editor. **ISSN:** 1120--8694 (print); **EISSN:** 1442--2050 (electronic). **URL:** http://onlinelibrary.wiley.com/journal/10.1111/(ISSN)1442-2050; http://www.isde.net. **Remarks:** Accepts advertising. **Circ:** (Not Reported).

16384 ■ Diversity and Distributions
Wiley-Blackwell
350 Main St.
Commerce Pl.
Malden, MA 02148-5018
Phone: (781)388-8200
Fax: (781)388-8210
Free: 800-216-2552
Journal publishing papers on a wide range of themes relating to the study of biodiversity. **Freq:** Monthly. **Key Personnel:** Janet Franklin, Editor-in-Chief. **ISSN:** 1366--9516 (print); **EISSN:** 1472--4642 (electronic). **URL:** http://onlinelibrary.wiley.com/journal/10.1111/(ISSN)1472-4642. **Remarks:** Accepts advertising. **Circ:** (Not Reported).

16385 ■ Early Intervention in Psychiatry
Blackwell Publishing Inc.
350 Main St.
Malden, MA 02148
Phone: (781)388-8200
Fax: (781)388-8210
Free: 800-216-2522
Publisher's E-mail: journaladsusa@bos.blackwellpublishing.com
Journal covering the study of early intervention for the full range of psychiatric disorders and mental health problems. **Freq:** Quarterly. **Key Personnel:** Prof. Patrick D. McGorry, Editor-in-Chief; Dr. Rosemary Purcell, Managing Editor; Dr. Jean Addington, Associate Editor. **ISSN:** 1751--7885 (print); **EISSN:** 1751--7893 (electronic). **Subscription Rates:** $325 Institutions online only; £173 Institutions online only, UK; €217 Institutions online only, Europe; $332 Institutions, other countries online. **URL:** http://onlinelibrary.wiley.com/journal/10.1111/(ISSN)1751-7893. **Remarks:** Accepts advertising. **Circ:** (Not Reported).

16386 ■ Early Medieval Europe
Wiley-Blackwell
350 Main St.
Commerce Pl.
Malden, MA 02148-5018
Phone: (781)388-8200
Fax: (781)388-8210
Free: 800-216-2552
Journal publishing information and debate on the history of Europe from the later Roman Empire to the eleventh century. The journal is a thoroughly interdisciplinary forum, encouraging the discussion of archaeology, numismatics, paleography, diplomatic, literature, onomastics, art history, linguistics and epigraphy, as well as more traditional historical approaches. It covers Europe in its entirety, including material on Iceland, Ireland, the British Isles, Scandinavia and Continental Europe (both west and east). **Freq:** Quarterly. **Key Personnel:** Prof. Paul Fouracre, Editor; Dr. Paul Dutton, Editor; Dr. Antonio Sennis, Editor. **ISSN:** 0963--9462 (print); **EISSN:** 1468--0254 (electronic). **Subscription Rates:** $1038 Institutions print and online; £581 Institutions print and online; €736 Institutions print and online; $1208 Institutions, other countries print and online; $123 Individuals print and online; £68 Individuals print and online - UK, Europe (non-euro zone) and rest of the world; €102 Individuals print and online; $68 Students print and online; £44 Students print and online - UK, Europe (non-euro zone) and rest of the world; €61 Students print and online. **URL:** http://onlinelibrary.wiley.com/journal/10.1111/(ISSN)1468-0254. **Remarks:** Accepts advertising. **Circ:** (Not Reported).

16387 ■ Earth Surface Processes and Landforms: The Journal of the British Geomorphological Research Group
Wiley-Blackwell
350 Main St.
Commerce Pl.
Malden, MA 02148-5018
Phone: (781)388-8200
Fax: (781)388-8210
Free: 800-216-2552
Publisher's E-mail: info@wiley.com
Journal containing important research papers on all aspects of geomorphology. **Freq:** 15/yr. **Key Personnel:** Prof. M.J. Kirkby, Associate Editor; Prof. S.N. Lane, Editor; Steve Darby, Advisor; Massimo Rinaldi, Board Member; Greg Tucker, Board Member. **ISSN:** 019-7-9337 (print); **EISSN:** 1096--9837 (electronic). **Subscription Rates:** $6735 Institutions print and online; £3438 Institutions print and online; €4346 Institutions print and online; $6735 Institutions, other countries print and online. **URL:** http://onlinelibrary.wiley.com/journal/10.1002/(ISSN)1096-9837. **Remarks:** Accepts advertising. **Circ:** (Not Reported).

16388 ■ Echocardiography: A Journal of Cardiovascular Ultrasound and Allied Techniques
Wiley-Blackwell
350 Main St.
Commerce Pl.
Malden, MA 02148-5018
Phone: (781)388-8200
Fax: (781)388-8210
Free: 800-216-2552
Journal providing information for clinical and academic cardiologists on performing and interpreting M-mode, 2-D, and Doppler echocardiograms in adults and children. **Freq:** 10/year. **Key Personnel:** Navin C. Nanda, MD, Editor-in-Chief. **ISSN:** 0742--2822 (print); **EISSN:** 1540--8175 (electronic). **Subscription Rates:** $1312 Institutions online only; $365 Individuals online only; £995 Institutions online only; £301 Individuals online only; €1264 Institutions online only; €301 Individuals online only. **URL:** http://onlinelibrary.wiley.com/journal/10.1111/(ISSN)1540-8175. **Remarks:** Advertising accepted; rates available upon request. **Circ:** ‡2449.

16389 ■ Ecography
Wiley-Blackwell
350 Main St.
Commerce Pl.
Malden, MA 02148-5018
Phone: (781)388-8200
Fax: (781)388-8210
Free: 800-216-2552
Journal publishing papers centered towards pattern and diversity in ecology, which includes studies in biodiversity, biogeography, ecological conservation and natural history of species. **Freq:** Monthly. **Key Personnel:** Carsten Rahbek, Editor-in-Chief; Maria Persson, Managing Editor; Miguel B. Araujo, Editor-in-Chief. **ISSN:** 0906--7590 (print); **EISSN:** 1600--0587 (electronic). **Subscription Rates:** $137 Individuals online only; $127 Members print plus online; $991 Institutions online only; $1146 Institutions, other countries online only; £86 Other countries online only. **URL:** http://onlinelibrary.wiley.com/journal/10.1111/(ISSN)1600-0587. **Circ:** (Not Reported).

Circulation: ★ = AAM; △ or • = BPA; ♦ = CAC; ❑ = VAC; ⊕ = PO Statement; ‡ = Publisher's Report; Boldface figures = sworn; Light figures = estimated.

16390 ■ Ecological Entomology
Blackwell Publishing Inc.
350 Main St.
Malden, MA 02148
Phone: (781)388-8200
Fax: (781)388-8210
Free: 800-216-2522
Publisher's E-mail: info@royensoc.co.uk
Journal publishing articles on conversation issues. **Freq:** Bimonthly. **Key Personnel:** Francis S. Gilbert, Editor; Rebeca B. Rosengaus, Editor. **ISSN:** 0307--6946 (print); **EISSN:** 1365--2311 (electronic). **Subscription Rates:** $3068 Institutions print & online; the Americas; $2556 Institutions print only or online only; the Americas; £1656 Institutions print & online; UK; £1379 Institutions print only or online only; UK; €2108 Institutions print & online; Europe; €1756 Institutions print only or online only; Europe; $3578 Institutions, other countries print & online; $2981 Institutions, other countries print only or online only; rest of the world. **URL:** http://as.wiley.com/WileyCDA/WileyTitle/productCd-EEN.html; http://www.royensoc.co.uk/publications/Ecological_Entomology.htm; http://onlinelibrary.wiley.com/journal/10.1111/(ISSN)1365-2311. **Remarks:** Accepts advertising. **Circ:** (Not Reported).

16391 ■ Ecological Management and Restoration
Wiley-Blackwell
350 Main St.
Commerce Pl.
Malden, MA 02148-5018
Phone: (781)388-8200
Fax: (781)388-8210
Free: 800-216-2552
Journal publishing information about the science and practice of ecosystem restoration and management for land managers. **Freq:** 3/yr. **Key Personnel:** Dr. Tein McDonald, Editor. **ISSN:** 1442-7001 (print); **EISSN:** 1442-8903 (electronic). **Subscription Rates:** $113 Individuals print and online; $512 Institutions print and online; $445 Institutions print or online; £317 Institutions print and online; £275 Institutions print or online; $422 Institutions print and online, Australia/New Zealand; $367 Institutions print or online, Australia/New Zealand. **URL:** http://as.wiley.com/WileyCDA/WileyTitle/productCd-EMR.html. **Remarks:** Accepts advertising. **Circ:** (Not Reported).

16392 ■ Ecology of Freshwater Fish
Wiley-Blackwell
350 Main St.
Commerce Pl.
Malden, MA 02148-5018
Phone: (781)388-8200
Fax: (781)388-8210
Free: 800-216-2552
Journal publishing articles on all aspects of fish ecology and fishery sciences in lakes, rivers and estuaries, including ecologically oriented studies of behaviour, genetics and physiology and the conservation, development and management of recreational and commercial fisheries. **Freq:** Quarterly. **Key Personnel:** Asbjorn Vollestad, Editor; David C. Heins, Editor; Javier Lobon-Cervia, Editor. **ISSN:** 0906--6691 (print); **EISSN:** 1600--0633 (electronic). **Subscription Rates:** $1084 Institutions online only; £647 Institutions online only; €820 Institutions online only; $1263 Institutions, other countries online only. **URL:** http://onlinelibrary.wiley.com/journal/10.1111/(ISSN)1600-0633. **Remarks:** Accepts advertising. **Circ:** (Not Reported).

16393 ■ Ecology Letters
Wiley-Blackwell
350 Main St.
Commerce Pl.
Malden, MA 02148-5018
Phone: (781)388-8200
Fax: (781)388-8210
Free: 800-216-2552
Journal serving as a forum for the rapid publication of ecology research. **Freq:** Monthly. **Key Personnel:** Tim Coulson, Editor-in-Chief; Michael Hochberg, Editor, Founder; Priyanga Amarasekare, Editor; Marti J. Anderson, Editor. **ISSN:** 1461-023X (print); **EISSN:** 1461-0248 (electronic). **Subscription Rates:** $3124 Institutions online only; $3644 Institutions, other countries online only; $299 Individuals online only; £1691 Institutions online only; £163 Individuals online only. **URL:** http://onlinelibrary.wiley.com/journal/10.1111/(ISSN)1468-0254. **Remarks:** Accepts advertising. **Circ:** (Not Reported).

16394 ■ Econometrics Journal
Blackwell Publishing Inc.
350 Main St.
Malden, MA 02148
Phone: (781)388-8200
Fax: (781)388-8210
Free: 800-216-2522
Publisher's E-mail: journaladsusa@bos.blackwellpublishing.com
Journal publishing articles on all aspects of econometrics: Applied, Computational, Methodological, and Theoretical. **Freq:** 3/yr. **Key Personnel:** Richard J. Smith, Managing Editor. **ISSN:** 1368-4221 (print); **EISSN:** 1368-423X (electronic). **Subscription Rates:** €63 Individuals print only; €237 Institutions print only; $73 Individuals print only; $351 Institutions print only; £44 Individuals print only; £186 Institutions print only. **URL:** http://as.wiley.com/WileyCDA/WileyTitle/productCd-ECTJ.html. **Remarks:** Accepts advertising. **Circ:** (Not Reported).

16395 ■ Economic Affairs: Journal of the Institute of Economic Affairs
Wiley-Blackwell
350 Main St.
Commerce Pl.
Malden, MA 02148-5018
Phone: (781)388-8200
Fax: (781)388-8210
Free: 800-216-2552
Publisher's E-mail: journaladsusa@bos.blackwellpublishing.com
Journal or those interested in the application of economic principles to practical affairs. **Freq:** Quarterly. **Key Personnel:** Philip Booth, Editor; Dr. Richard Wellings, Editor. **ISSN:** 0265--0665 (print); **EISSN:** 1468--0270 (electronic). **Subscription Rates:** $90 Individuals print plus online; $666 Students print plus online; $585 Institutions print plus online; $487 Institutions print or online; €58 Individuals print plus online; €50 Students print plus online; £51 Other countries print plus online; £41 Students, other countries print plus online. **URL:** http://onlinelibrary.wiley.com/journal/10.1111/(ISSN)1468-0270. **Remarks:** Accepts advertising. **Circ:** (Not Reported).

16396 ■ Economic Inquiry
Wiley-Blackwell
350 Main St.
Commerce Pl.
Malden, MA 02148-5018
Phone: (781)388-8200
Fax: (781)388-8210
Free: 800-216-2552
Publication E-mail: journals@weai.org
Journal covering research in all areas of economics. **Freq:** Quarterly. **Print Method:** Offset. **Trim Size:** 6 7/8 x 10. **Cols./Page:** 2. **Key Personnel:** R. Preston McAfee, Editor; Wesley W. Wilson, Editor; Prof. R. Preston McAfee, Editor. **ISSN:** 0095-2583 (print); **EISSN:** 1465-7295 (electronic). **Subscription Rates:** $491 Institutions print and online; €378 Institutions print and online; £298 Institutions print and online; $409 Institutions online only; €315 Institutions online only; £248 Institutions online only; $450 Institutions print and online; $534 Institutions, other countries print and online; €346 Institutions print and online; £248 Institutions, other countries online; $485 Institutions, other countries online only; £273 Institutions UK (print and online). **URL:** http://www.weai.org/EI; http://onlinelibrary.wiley.com/journal/10.1111/(ISSN)1465-7295; http://onlinelibrary.wiley.com/journal/10.1111/%28ISSN%291465-7295. **Formerly:** Western Economic Journal. **Ad Rates:** BW $350. **Remarks:** Accepts advertising. **Circ:** Paid 3500, 3400.

16397 ■ The Economic Journal
Wiley-Blackwell
350 Main St.
Commerce Pl.
Malden, MA 02148-5018
Phone: (781)388-8200
Fax: (781)388-8210
Free: 800-216-2552
Publication covering economics. **Freq:** 8/year. **Key Personnel:** Martin Cripps, Managing Editor; Andrea Galeotti, Managing Editor; Rachel Griffith, Managing Editor; Morten Ravn, Managing Editor; Kjell Salvanes, Managing Editor; Frederic Vermeulen, Managing Editor. **ISSN:** 0013--0133 (print); **EISSN:** 1468--0297 (electronic). **Subscription Rates:** $910 Institutions print and online, The Americas; €728 Institutions print and online; £573 Institutions print, online; $347 Institutions print and online (developing world, Americas); $420 Institutions print or online (developing world, ROW). **URL:** http://onlinelibrary.wiley.com/journal/10.1111/%28ISSN%291468-0297; http://as.wiley.com/WileyCDA/WileyTitle/productCd-ECOJ.html; http://www.res.org.uk/view/economichome.html; http://onlinelibrary.wiley.com/doi/10.1111/ecoj.12187/abstract. **Remarks:** Advertising accepted; rates available upon request. **Circ:** (Not Reported).

16398 ■ The Economic Journal
Blackwell Publishing Inc.
350 Main St.
Malden, MA 02148
Phone: (781)388-8200
Fax: (781)388-8210
Free: 800-216-2522
Publication covering economics. **Freq:** 8/year. **Key Personnel:** Martin Cripps, Managing Editor; Andrea Galeotti, Managing Editor; Rachel Griffith, Managing Editor; Morten Ravn, Managing Editor; Kjell Salvanes, Managing Editor; Frederic Vermeulen, Managing Editor. **ISSN:** 0013--0133 (print); **EISSN:** 1468--0297 (electronic). **Subscription Rates:** $910 Institutions print and online, The Americas; €728 Institutions print and online; £573 Institutions print, online; $347 Institutions print and online (developing world, Americas); $420 Institutions print or online (developing world, ROW). **URL:** http://onlinelibrary.wiley.com/journal/10.1111/%28ISSN%291468-0297; http://as.wiley.com/WileyCDA/WileyTitle/productCd-ECOJ.html; http://www.res.org.uk/view/economichome.html; http://onlinelibrary.wiley.com/doi/10.1111/ecoj.12187/abstract. **Remarks:** Advertising accepted; rates available upon request. **Circ:** (Not Reported).

16399 ■ Economic Notes
Wiley-Blackwell
350 Main St.
Commerce Pl.
Malden, MA 02148-5018
Phone: (781)388-8200
Fax: (781)388-8210
Free: 800-216-2552
Journal presenting key issues in the fields of finance and monetary economics. **Freq:** 3/year. **Key Personnel:** Luca Fiorito, Managing Editor; Alberto Dalmazzo, Editor. **ISSN:** 0391--5026 (print); **EISSN:** 1468--0300 (electronic). **Subscription Rates:** $576 Institutions print and online; £346 Institutions print and online; €440 Institutions print and online; $672 Institutions, other countries print and online; $73 Individuals print and online; £48 Individuals print and online - UK, Europe (non-euro zone) and other countries; €64 Individuals print and online. **URL:** http://onlinelibrary.wiley.com/doi/10.1111/ecno.v45.1/issuetoc. **Remarks:** Accepts advertising. **Circ:** (Not Reported).

16400 ■ Economic Outlook
Wiley-Blackwell
350 Main St.
Commerce Pl.
Malden, MA 02148-5018
Phone: (781)388-8200
Fax: (781)388-8210
Free: 800-216-2552
Journal detailing the forecast detailing the forecast over the next five years for all of the key UK macroeconomic indicators. **Freq:** Quarterly. **Key Personnel:** Adrian Cooper, Editor. **ISSN:** 1040-489X (print); **EISSN:** 1468-0319 (electronic). **Subscription Rates:** $2823 Institutions print & online; $2352 Institutions online; £1680 Institutions print & online; £1400 Institutions online. **URL:** http://as.wiley.com/WileyCDA/WileyTitle/productCd-ECOL.html. **Remarks:** Accepts advertising. **Circ:** (Not Reported).

16401 ■ Economic Record
Wiley-Blackwell
350 Main St.
Commerce Pl.
Malden, MA 02148-5018

Phone: (781)388-8200
Fax: (781)388-8210
Free: 800-216-2552
Publication covering economics. **Freq:** Quarterly in March, June, September and December. **Key Personnel:** Garry Barrett, Editor. **ISSN:** 0013--0249 (print); **EISSN:** 1475--4932 (electronic). **Subscription Rates:** $455 Institutions print and online; £354 Institutions print and online; €453 Institutions print + online (Euro zone); $545 Institutions print + online (Australia and NZ); $694 Institutions print + online (rest of the world); $578 Institutions, other countries print or online. **URL:** http://onlinelibrary.wiley.com/journal/10.1111/(ISSN)1475-4932; http://www.wiley.com/WileyCDA/WileyTitle/productCd-ECOR.html. **Remarks:** Advertising accepted; rates available upon request. **Circ:** (Not Reported).

16402 ■ Economic Record
Blackwell Publishing Inc.
350 Main St.
Malden, MA 02148
Phone: (781)388-8200
Fax: (781)388-8210
Free: 800-216-2522
Publication covering economics. **Freq:** Quarterly in March, June, September and December. **Key Personnel:** Garry Barrett, Editor. **ISSN:** 0013--0249 (print); **EISSN:** 1475--4932 (electronic). **Subscription Rates:** $455 Institutions print and online; £354 Institutions print and online; €453 Institutions print + online (Euro zone); $545 Institutions print + online (Australia and NZ); $694 Institutions print + online (rest of the world); $578 Institutions, other countries print or online. **URL:** http://onlinelibrary.wiley.com/journal/10.1111/(ISSN)1475-4932; http://www.wiley.com/WileyCDA/WileyTitle/productCd-ECOR.html. **Remarks:** Advertising accepted; rates available upon request. **Circ:** (Not Reported).

16403 ■ Economica
Wiley-Blackwell
350 Main St.
Commerce Pl.
Malden, MA 02148-5018
Phone: (781)388-8200
Fax: (781)388-8210
Free: 800-216-2552
Journal publishing research in all branches of economics. **Freq:** Quarterly. **ISSN:** 0013--0427 (print); **EISSN:** 1468--0335 (electronic). **Subscription Rates:** $699 Institutions print and online; £406 Institutions print and online; €514 Institutions print and online; $792 Institutions, other countries print and online; $76 Individuals print and online; £50 Individuals print and online - UK, Europe (non-euro zone) and rest of the world; €62 Individuals print and online; $53 Students print and online; £33 Students print and online - UK, Europe (non-euro zone) and rest of the world; €45 Students print and online. **URL:** http://onlinelibrary.wiley.com/journal/10.1111/(ISSN)1468-0335. **Remarks:** Accepts advertising. **Circ:** (Not Reported).

16404 ■ Economica
Blackwell Publishing Inc.
350 Main St.
Malden, MA 02148
Phone: (781)388-8200
Fax: (781)388-8210
Free: 800-216-2522
Journal publishing research in all branches of economics. **Freq:** Quarterly. **ISSN:** 0013--0427 (print); **EISSN:** 1468--0335 (electronic). **Subscription Rates:** $699 Institutions print and online; £406 Institutions print and online; €514 Institutions print and online; $792 Institutions, other countries print and online; $76 Individuals print and online; £50 Individuals print and online - UK, Europe (non-euro zone) and rest of the world; €62 Individuals print and online; $53 Students print and online; £33 Students print and online - UK, Europe (non-euro zone) and rest of the world; €45 Students print and online. **URL:** http://onlinelibrary.wiley.com/journal/10.1111/(ISSN)1468-0335. **Remarks:** Accepts advertising. **Circ:** (Not Reported).

16405 ■ Economics & Politics
Wiley-Blackwell
350 Main St.
Commerce Pl.
Malden, MA 02148-5018
Phone: (781)388-8200
Fax: (781)388-8210
Free: 800-216-2552
Journal focusing on analytical political economy, broadly defined as the study of economic phenomena and policy in models that include political processes. **Freq:** 3/year. **Key Personnel:** Peter Rosendorff, Editor; Jagdish Bhagwati, Editor, Founder. **ISSN:** 0954--1985 (print); **EISSN:** 1468--0343 (electronic). **Subscription Rates:** $1576 Institutions print and online; £794 Institutions print and online; €1006 Institutions print and online; $1835 Institutions, other countries print and online; $118 Individuals print and online; £71 Individuals print and online - UK, Europe (non-euro zone) and rest of the world; €106 Individuals print and online. **URL:** http://onlinelibrary.wiley.com/journal/10.1111/(ISSN)1468-0343. **Remarks:** Accepts advertising. **Circ:** (Not Reported).

16406 ■ Economics of Transition
Wiley-Blackwell
350 Main St.
Commerce Pl.
Malden, MA 02148-5018
Phone: (781)388-8200
Fax: (781)388-8210
Free: 800-216-2552
Journal publishing articles on the economics of transition and institutional development. **Freq:** Quarterly. **Key Personnel:** Philippe Aghion, Managing Editor; Sergei Guriev, Editor. **ISSN:** 0967--0750 (print); **EISSN:** 1468--0351 (electronic). **Subscription Rates:** $1079 Institutions print and online; £648 Institutions print and online; €824 Institutions print and online; $160 Institutions print and online, developing world; $1266 Institutions, other countries print and online; $123 Individuals print and online; £76 Individuals print and online - UK, Europe (non-euro zone), developing world and rest of the world; €111 Individuals print and online. **URL:** http://onlinelibrary.wiley.com/journal/10.1111/(ISSN)1468-0351. **Remarks:** Accepts advertising. **Circ:** (Not Reported).

16407 ■ Educational Measurement: Issues and Practice
Wiley-Blackwell
350 Main St.
Commerce Pl.
Malden, MA 02148-5018
Phone: (781)388-8200
Fax: (781)388-8210
Free: 800-216-2552
Freq: Quarterly. **Key Personnel:** Howard Everson, Editor; Susan M. Brookhart, Advisor, Board Member. **ISSN:** 073-1-1745 (print); **EISSN:** 1745--3992 (electronic). **URL:** http://onlinelibrary.wiley.com/journal/10.1111/(ISSN)1745-3992. **Ad Rates:** BW $450. **Remarks:** Accepts advertising. **Circ:** 2600.

16408 ■ Educational Theory
Wiley-Blackwell
350 Main St.
Commerce Pl.
Malden, MA 02148-5018
Phone: (781)388-8200
Fax: (781)388-8210
Free: 800-216-2552
Journal fostering the continuing development of educational theory and to encourage wide and effective discussion of theoretical problems within the educational profession. **Freq:** Bimonthly. **Key Personnel:** Joyce Atkinson, Managing Editor. **ISSN:** 0013--2004 (print); **EISSN:** 1741--5446 (electronic). **Subscription Rates:** $77 Individuals print & online; $353 Institutions print & online; €383 Institutions print & online; $294 Institutions print or online; €93 Individuals print & online; £303 Institutions print & online; €319 Institutions print or online; £252 Institutions print or online; £62 Individuals print & online. **URL:** http://onlinelibrary.wiley.com/journal/10.1111/(ISSN)1741-5446. **Ad Rates:** BW $200. **Remarks:** Accepts advertising. **Circ:** (Not Reported).

16409 ■ Emergency Medicine Australasia
Wiley-Blackwell
350 Main St.
Commerce Pl.
Malden, MA 02148-5018
Phone: (781)388-8200
Fax: (781)388-8210
Free: 800-216-2552
Peer-reviewed journal covering reports, reviews and opinions on the research and clinical practice of emergency care. **Freq:** Bimonthly. **Key Personnel:** Geoff Hughes, Editor-in-Chief. **ISSN:** 1742--6731 (print); **EISSN:** 1742--6723 (electronic). **Subscription Rates:** $243 Individuals print + online (Americas); £151 Individuals print + online (UK, Europe and rest of the world); A$252 Individuals print + online (Australia and New Zealand); $1259 Institutions print + online (Americas); £778 Institutions print + online (UK); €986 Institutions print + online (Europe); A$1041 Institutions print + online (Australia and New Zealand); $1049 Institutions print or online (Americas); £648 Institutions print or online (UK); €821 Institutions print or online (Europe); A$867 Institutions print or online (Australia and New Zealand); $1265 Institutions print or online (rest of the world). **URL:** http://www.acem.org.au/Standards-Publications/EMA.aspx; http://onlinelibrary.wiley.com/journal/10.1111/(ISSN)1742-6723. **Ad Rates:** BW $1690; 4C $3300. **Remarks:** Accepts advertising. **Circ:** (Not Reported).

16410 ■ Endodontic Topics
Wiley-Blackwell
350 Main St.
Commerce Pl.
Malden, MA 02148-5018
Phone: (781)388-8200
Fax: (781)388-8210
Free: 800-216-2552
Journal for endodontists and general practitioners with interest in endodontics. **Freq:** Semiannual. **Key Personnel:** Martin Trope, Editor, Founder; Markus Haapasalo, Editor-in-Chief. **ISSN:** 1601--1538 (print); **EISSN:** 1601--1546 (electronic). **Subscription Rates:** $729 Institutions online only; £437 Institutions online only; €553 Institutions online only; $852 Institutions, other countries online only; $186 Individuals online only; £114 Individuals online only - UK, Europe (non-euro zone) and rest of the world; $167 Individuals online only. **URL:** http://onlinelibrary.wiley.com/journal/10.1111/(ISSN)1601-1546. **Remarks:** Accepts advertising. **Circ:** (Not Reported).

16411 ■ Entomologia Experimental et Applicata
Wiley-Blackwell
350 Main St.
Commerce Pl.
Malden, MA 02148-5018
Phone: (781)388-8200
Fax: (781)388-8210
Free: 800-216-2552
Journal publishing original research papers in the fields of experimental biology and ecology of insects and other terrestrial arthropods, with both pure and applied scopes. **Freq:** Monthly. **Key Personnel:** Dr. M.J. Stout, Editor; Dr. D. Raubenheimer, Editor. **ISSN:** 0013--8703 (print); **EISSN:** 1570--7458 (electronic). **Subscription Rates:** $4391 Institutions print plus online; $3659 Institutions print or online; €38 Members online only; £2378 Institutions print plus online; £1981 Institutions print or online; $5121 Institutions, other countries print & online; $4267 Institutions, other countries print or online. **URL:** http://onlinelibrary.wiley.com/journal/10.1111/(ISSN)1570-7458. **Remarks:** Accepts advertising. **Circ:** (Not Reported).

16412 ■ Entomologia Experimentalis et Applicata
Blackwell Publishing Inc.
350 Main St.
Malden, MA 02148
Phone: (781)388-8200
Fax: (781)388-8210
Free: 800-216-2522
Publisher's E-mail: journaladsusa@bos.blackwellpublishing.com
Journal covering the fields of experimental biology and ecology of insects and other terrestrial arthropods, with both pure and applied scopes. **Freq:** Monthly. **Key Personnel:** Leo W. Beukeboom, Editor-in-Chief. **ISSN:** 0013--8703 (print); **EISSN:** 1570--7458 (electronic). **Subscription Rates:** $4142 Institutions Americas (print and online); £2242 Institutions UK (print and online); €2848 Institutions Europe (print and online); $4830 Institutions, other countries print and online; $3451

Circulation: ★ = AAM; △ or • = BPA; ♦ = CAC; ❑ = VAC; ⊕ = PO Statement; ‡ = Publisher's Report; Boldface figures = sworn; Light figures = estimated.

Institutions Americas (print or online only); £1868 Institutions UK (print or online only); €2373 Institutions Europe (print or online only); $4025 Institutions, other countries print or online only. **URL:** http://onlinelibrary.wiley.com/journal/10.1111/(ISSN)1570-7458. **Remarks:** Advertising accepted; rates available upon request. **Circ:** (Not Reported).

16413 ■ Entomological Research
Wiley-Blackwell
350 Main St.
Commerce Pl.
Malden, MA 02148-5018
Phone: (781)388-8200
Fax: (781)388-8210
Free: 800-216-2552
Journal covering entomology. Topics covered include insects, mites, ticks or other arthropods of economic importance in agriculture, forestry, stored products, biological control, medicine, animal health and natural resource management. **Freq:** Bimonthly. **Print Method:** Offset. **Trim Size:** 6 7/8 x 10. **Cols./Page:** 2. **Col. Width:** 32 nonpareils. **Col. Depth:** 112 agate lines. **Key Personnel:** Yeon Jae Bae, Board Member; Yeon Soo Han, Editor-in-Chief. **ISSN:** 1738--2297 (print); **EISSN:** 1748--5967 (electronic). **Subscription Rates:** $572 Institutions online only; £334 Institutions online only; €423 Institutions online only; $651 Institutions, other countries online only. **URL:** http://onlinelibrary.wiley.com/journal/10.1111/%28ISSN%291748-5967. **Circ:** (Not Reported).

16414 ■ Entomological Science
Wiley-Blackwell
350 Main St.
Commerce Pl.
Malden, MA 02148-5018
Phone: (781)388-8200
Fax: (781)388-8210
Free: 800-216-2552
Journal publishing original research papers and reviews from any entomological discipline or from directly allied fields in ecology, behavioral biology, physiology, biochemistry, development, genetics, systematic, morphology, evolution and general entomology. **Freq:** Quarterly March, June, September and December. **Key Personnel:** Takao Itioka, Associate Editor; Jun-Ichi Kojima, Board Member; Hideharu Numata, Board Member. **ISSN:** 1343--8786 (print); **EISSN:** 1479--8298 (electronic). **Subscription Rates:** $910 Institutions online only; £564 Institutions online only; €715 Institutions online only; $1104 Institutions, other countries online only. **URL:** http://onlinelibrary.wiley.com/journal/10.1111/(ISSN)1479-8298. **Remarks:** Accepts advertising. **Circ:** (Not Reported).

16415 ■ Environmental Microbiology
Wiley-Blackwell
350 Main St.
Commerce Pl.
Malden, MA 02148-5018
Phone: (781)388-8200
Fax: (781)388-8210
Free: 800-216-2552
Journal publishing article on the study of microbial processes in the environment, microbial communities and microbial interactions. **Freq:** Monthly. **Key Personnel:** Kenneth N. Timmis, Editor. **ISSN:** 1462--2912 (print); **EISSN:** 1462--2920 (electronic). **Subscription Rates:** $5808 Institutions print only; £3144 Institutions print only; €3995 Institutions print only; $6777 Institutions, other countries print only. **URL:** http://onlinelibrary.wiley.com/journal/10.1111/(ISSN)1462-2920; http://www.sfam.org.uk/en/journals/environmental-microbiology.cfm. **Remarks:** Accepts advertising. **Circ:** (Not Reported).

16416 ■ Epilepsia
Blackwell Publishing Inc.
350 Main St.
Malden, MA 02148
Phone: (781)388-8200
Fax: (781)388-8210
Free: 800-216-2522
Publisher's E-mail: journaladsusa@bos.blackwellpublishing.com
Journal covering current clinical and research results and aspects of epilepsies. **Freq:** Monthly. **Print Method:** Offset Sheet-fed. **Trim Size:** 8 1/4 x 11. **Cols./Page:** 2. **Key Personnel:** Gary W. Mathern, Editor-in-Chief. **ISSN:** 0013--9580 (print); **EISSN:** 1528--1167 (electronic). **Subscription Rates:** $1952 Institutions print or online; $2343 Institutions print and online; $692 Individuals online only; $728 Individuals print and online; £1360 Institutions print or online UK; £1632 Institutions print and online UK; £611 Individuals online only UK; £644 Individuals print and online UK; €1727 Institutions print or online Europe; €2073 Institutions print and online Europe; €611 Individuals online only Europe; €965 Individuals print and online Europe; $2663 Institutions, other countries print or online; $3196 Institutions, other countries print and online. **URL:** http://as.wiley.com/WileyCDA/WileyTitle/productCd-EPI.html; http://onlinelibrary.wiley.com/journal/10.1111/(ISSN)1528-1167. **Remarks:** Accepts advertising. **Circ:** (Not Reported).

16417 ■ EPPO Bulletin: A journal of regulatory plant protection
Wiley-Blackwell
350 Main St.
Commerce Pl.
Malden, MA 02148-5018
Phone: (781)388-8200
Fax: (781)388-8210
Free: 800-216-2552
Publisher's E-mail: journaladsusa@bos.blackwellpublishing.com
Journal publishing research findings on all aspects of plant protection, but particularly those of immediate concern to government plant protection services. **Freq:** 3/year. **Key Personnel:** Martin Ward, Editor-in-Chief. **ISSN:** 0250--8052 (print); **EISSN:** 1365--2338 (electronic). **Subscription Rates:** $1690 Institutions print + online; $1408 Institutions print or online; £916 Institutions print & online; £763 Institutions print or online; €1163 Institutions print plus online; €969 Institutions print or online; $1968 Institutions, other countries print & online; $1640 Institutions, other countries print or online. **URL:** http://onlinelibrary.wiley.com/doi/10.1111/epp.2014.44.issue-1/issuetoc. **Remarks:** Accepts advertising. **Circ:** (Not Reported).

16418 ■ Ethology
Wiley-Blackwell
350 Main St.
Commerce Pl.
Malden, MA 02148-5018
Phone: (781)388-8200
Fax: (781)388-8210
Free: 800-216-2552
Journal publishing original contributions from all branches of behavioural research on all species of animals, both in the field and lab. **Freq:** Monthly. **Key Personnel:** Jutta Schneider, Editor-in-Chief; Susan A. Foster, Board Member, Editor. **ISSN:** 0179--1613 (print); **EISSN:** 1439--0310 (electronic). **Subscription Rates:** $3614 Institutions print and online; £2148 Institutions print and online; €2729 Institutions print and online; $4631 Institutions, other countries print and online; $205 Individuals print and online; £129 Individuals print and online - UK, Europe (non-euro zone) and rest of the world; €192 Individuals print and online. **URL:** http://onlinelibrary.wiley.com/journal/10.1111/(ISSN)1439-0310. **Remarks:** Accepts advertising. **Circ:** (Not Reported).

16419 ■ EuroChoices
Wiley-Blackwell
350 Main St.
Commerce Pl.
Malden, MA 02148-5018
Phone: (781)388-8200
Fax: (781)388-8210
Free: 800-216-2552
Peer-reviewed journal covering topical European agri-food and rural resource issues. **Freq:** 3/year. **Key Personnel:** Prof. John Davis, Editor-in-Chief; Csaba Csaki, Editor. **ISSN:** 1478--0917 (print); **EISSN:** 1746--692x (electronic). **Subscription Rates:** $253 Institutions; £154 Institutions UK; €196 Institutions Europe; $297 Institutions, other countries; $304 Institutions print and online; £185 Institutions print and online, UK; €236 Institutions print and online, Europe; $357 Institutions, other countries print and online; $54 Individuals print and online; £30 Individuals print and online, UK and Europe (non euro zone); €48 Individuals print and online; £30 Other countries print and online. **URL:** http://onlinelibrary.wiley.com/journal/10.1111/(ISSN)1746-692X. **Remarks:** Accepts advertising. **Circ:** (Not Reported).

16420 ■ European Financial Management
Wiley-Blackwell
350 Main St.
Commerce Pl.
Malden, MA 02148-5018
Phone: (781)388-8200
Fax: (781)388-8210
Free: 800-216-2552
Journal publishing research from around the world, providing a forum for both executives and academics concerned with the financial management of European corporations and financial institutions. **Freq:** 5/year. **Key Personnel:** Prof. John A. Doukas, Founder, Managing Editor, phone: (757)683-5521, fax: (757)683-5639; Julian Franks, Editor; Pekka Hietala, Editor. **ISSN:** 1354--7798 (print); **EISSN:** 1468--036X (electronic). **Subscription Rates:** $208 Members print & online; $99 Students print & online; $2843 Institutions print & online; $2369 Institutions print or online; €185 Members print & online; €90 Students print & online; £1692 Institutions print & online; £1410 Institutions print or online. **URL:** http://onlinelibrary.wiley.com/journal/10.1111/(ISSN)1468-036X. **Remarks:** Accepts advertising. **Circ:** (Not Reported).

16421 ■ European Journal of Cancer Care
Wiley-Blackwell
350 Main St.
Commerce Pl.
Malden, MA 02148-5018
Phone: (781)388-8200
Fax: (781)388-8210
Free: 800-216-2552
Journal focusing on cancer care across Europe and internationally. **Freq:** Bimonthly. **Key Personnel:** Stephen J. O'Connor, Editor. **ISSN:** 0961--5423 (print); **EISSN:** 1365--2354 (electronic). **Subscription Rates:** $1370 Institutions online only; £744 Institutions online only; €945 Institutions online only; $1595 Institutions, other countries online only; $269 Individuals online only; £144 Individuals online only; €217 Individuals online only; $160 Individuals online only - rest of the world. **URL:** http://onlinelibrary.wiley.com/journal/10.1111/(ISSN)1365-2354. **Remarks:** Advertising accepted; rates available upon request. **Circ:** (Not Reported).

16422 ■ European Journal of Clinical Investigation
Wiley-Blackwell
350 Main St.
Commerce Pl.
Malden, MA 02148-5018
Phone: (781)388-8200
Fax: (781)388-8210
Free: 800-216-2552
Journal publishing publishes papers in the field of clinical investigation, provided they contribute to the advancement of knowledge in this field. **Freq:** Monthly. **Key Personnel:** John P.A. Ioannidis, Editor-in-Chief. **ISSN:** 0014--2972 (print); **EISSN:** 1365--2362 (electronic). **Subscription Rates:** $2761 Institutions online only; £1479 Institutions online only; €1901 Institutions online only; $3220 Institutions, other countries online only. **URL:** http://onlinelibrary.wiley.com/journal/10.1111/(ISSN)1365-2362. **Remarks:** Advertising accepted; rates available upon request. **Circ:** (Not Reported).

16423 ■ European Journal of Dental Education
Wiley-Blackwell
350 Main St.
Commerce Pl.
Malden, MA 02148-5018
Phone: (781)388-8200
Fax: (781)388-8210
Free: 800-216-2552
Journal focusing on dental education. **Freq:** Quarterly. **Key Personnel:** Prof. Michael Manogue, Editor-in-Chief. **ISSN:** 1396--5883 (print); **EISSN:** 1600--0579 (electronic). **Subscription Rates:** $955 Institutions print or online; £568 Institutions print or online; €719 Institutions print or online; $1111 Institutions, other countries print or online; $1146 Institutions print and online; £682 Institutions print and online; €863 Institutions print and online; $1334 Institutions, other countries print and

online; $393 Individuals print and online; £240 Individuals print and online; €357 Individuals print and online. **URL:** http://onlinelibrary.wiley.com/journal/10.1111/(ISSN)1600-0579. **Remarks:** Advertising accepted; rates available upon request. **Circ:** (Not Reported).

16424 ■ European Journal of Education
Wiley-Blackwell
350 Main St.
Commerce Pl.
Malden, MA 02148-5018
Phone: (781)388-8200
Fax: (781)388-8210
Free: 800-216-2552
Journal examining and comparing education politics, trends, reforms, and programs of European countries in an international perspective. **Freq:** Quarterly. **Key Personnel:** Jean Gordon, Editor; Jean-Pierre Jallade, Editor. **ISSN:** 0141-8211 (print); **EISSN:** 1465-3435 (electronic). **Subscription Rates:** $3108 Institutions, other countries print & online; $2662 Institutions print & online; $2702 Institutions, other countries print or online; $2314 Institutions print or online; €1752 Institutions print or online; €2015 Institutions print & online; $307 Members print & online; £1382 Institutions print or online; £1588 Institutions print & online. **URL:** http://onlinelibrary.wiley.com/journal/10.1111/(ISSN)1465-3435. **Remarks:** Accepts advertising. **Circ:** (Not Reported).

16425 ■ European Journal of Haematology
Wiley-Blackwell
350 Main St.
Commerce Pl.
Malden, MA 02148-5018
Phone: (781)388-8200
Fax: (781)388-8210
Free: 800-216-2552
Journal focusing on basic and clinical information in haematology. **Freq:** Monthly. **Key Personnel:** Niels Borregaard, Editor-in-Chief. **ISSN:** 0902--4441 (print); **EISSN:** 1600--0609 (electronic). **Subscription Rates:** $2342 Institutions print & online; €1770 Institutions print & online; $1951 Institutions print or online; £1396 Institutions print & online; €1475 Institutions print or online; £1163 Institutions print or online. **URL:** http://onlinelibrary.wiley.com/journal/10.1111/(ISSN)1600-0609/issues. **Remarks:** Advertising accepted; rates available upon request. **Circ:** (Not Reported).

16426 ■ European Journal of Oral Sciences
Wiley-Blackwell
350 Main St.
Commerce Pl.
Malden, MA 02148-5018
Phone: (781)388-8200
Fax: (781)388-8210
Free: 800-216-2552
Journal focusing on research papers within clinical dentistry, on all basic science aspects of structure, chemistry, developmental biology, physiology and pathology of relevant tissues, as well as on microbiology, biomaterials and the behavioural sciences as they relate to dentistry. **Freq:** Bimonthly. **Key Personnel:** Prof. Anders Linde, Editor-in-Chief; Prof. Wouter Beertsen, Editor. **ISSN:** 0909--8836 (print); **EISSN:** 1600--0722 (electronic). **Subscription Rates:** $1121 Institutions print & online; $934 Institutions print or online; €706 Institutions print or online; £670 Institutions print & online; €848 Institutions print & online; £558 Institutions print or online. **URL:** http://as.wiley.com/WileyCDA/WileyTitle/productCd-EOS.html; http://onlinelibrary.wiley.com/journal/10.1111/%28ISSN%291600-0722. **Remarks:** Advertising accepted; rates available upon request. **Circ:** (Not Reported).

16427 ■ European Journal of Political Research
Blackwell Publishing Inc.
350 Main St.
Malden, MA 02148
Phone: (781)388-8200
Fax: (781)388-8210
Free: 800-216-2522
Publisher's E-mail: journaladsusa@bos.blackwellpublishing.com
Journal focusing on specializes in articles articulating theoretical and comparative perspectives in political science, and welcomes both quantitative and qualitative approaches. **Freq:** 6/year 8/year. **Key Personnel:** Yannis Papadopoulos, Editor; Claudio M. Radaelli, Editor. **ISSN:** 0304--4130 (print); **EISSN:** 1475--6765 (electronic). **Subscription Rates:** $57 Individuals print & online; $1765 Institutions print & online; €1027 Institutions print or online; $1471 Institutions print or online; £971 Institutions, other countries print & online; €1233 Institutions print & online; £809 Institutions, other countries print or online; €51 Individuals print & online; £32 Individuals print & online; Included in membership; $33 Individuals European Consortium for Political Research Member (print and online); £22 Individuals European Consortium for Political Research Member (print and online); €30 Individuals European Consortium for Political Research Member (print and online); £22 Other countries European Consortium for Political Research Member (print and online). **URL:** http://as.wiley.com/WileyCDA/WileyTitle/productCd-EJPR.html; http://ecpr.eu/Publications/Journals/EJPR.aspx; http://onlinelibrary.wiley.com/journal/10.1111/%28ISSN%291475-6765; http://ordering.onlinelibrary.wiley.com/subs.asp?ref=0304-4130. **Remarks:** Advertising accepted; rates available upon request. **Circ:** (Not Reported).

16428 ■ European Journal of Soil Science
Wiley-Blackwell
350 Main St.
Commerce Pl.
Malden, MA 02148-5018
Phone: (781)388-8200
Fax: (781)388-8210
Free: 800-216-2552
Journal publishing the latest significant findings of research, the description of new techniques, and up-to-date authoritative and critical reviews over the whole field of soil science and its applications. **Freq:** Bimonthly. **Key Personnel:** Steve Jarvis, Editor-in-Chief; Ian Grieve, Editor; R.M. Lark, Associate Editor; G.J.D. Kirk, Associate Editor. **ISSN:** 1351--0754 (print); **EISSN:** 1365--2389 (electronic). **Subscription Rates:** $2306 Institutions, other countries print & online; $1977 Institutions print & online; $1636 Institutions print or online; £888 Institutions print or online; £1072 Institutions print & online; €1128 Institutions print or online; €1364 Institutions print & online. **URL:** http://as.wiley.com/WileyCDA/WileyTitle/productCd-EJSS.html; http://www.soils.org.uk/european-journal-soil-science-access; http://onlinelibrary.wiley.com/journal/10.1111/(ISSN)1365-2389; http://onlinelibrary.wiley.com/journal/10.1111/%28ISSN%291365-2389. **Remarks:** Advertising accepted; rates available upon request. **Circ:** (Not Reported).

16429 ■ European Law Journal: Review of European Law in Context
Wiley-Blackwell
350 Main St.
Commerce Pl.
Malden, MA 02148-5018
Phone: (781)388-8200
Fax: (781)388-8210
Free: 800-216-2552
Publisher's E-mail: journaladsusa@bos.blackwellpublishing.com
Journal focusing on developed specifically to express and develop the study and understanding of European law in its social, cultural, political and economic context. **Freq:** Bimonthly. **Key Personnel:** Francis Snyder, Editor-in-Chief; Bruno de Witte, Advisor; Carol Harlow, Advisor. **ISSN:** 1351--5993 (print); **EISSN:** 1468--0386 (electronic). **Subscription Rates:** £1352 Institutions print & online; $68 Members print & online; £1126 Institutions print or online; $2260 Institutions print & online; €1712 Institutions print & online; $1883 Institutions print or online. **URL:** http://www.wiley.com/WileyCDA/WileyTitle/productCd-EULJ.html; http://onlinelibrary.wiley.com/journal/10.1111/%28ISSN%291468-0386. **Remarks:** Advertising accepted; rates available upon request. **Circ:** (Not Reported).

16430 ■ Experimental Dermatology
Wiley-Blackwell
350 Main St.
Commerce Pl.
Malden, MA 02148-5018
Phone: (781)388-8200
Fax: (781)388-8210
Free: 800-216-2552
Journal providing a vehicle for the rapid publication of innovative and definitive reports, letters to the editor and review articles covering all aspects of experimental dermatology. **Freq:** Monthly. **Key Personnel:** Ralf Paus, Editor; Thomas A. Luger, Editor. **ISSN:** 0906--6705 (print); **EISSN:** 1600--0625 (electronic). **Subscription Rates:** $384 Individuals online; $1214 Institutions online; £242 Individuals online; £726 Institutions online. **URL:** http://onlinelibrary.wiley.com/journal/10.1111/%28ISSN%291600-0625. **Remarks:** Advertising accepted; rates available upon request. **Circ:** (Not Reported).

16431 ■ Expert Systems
Wiley-Blackwell
350 Main St.
Commerce Pl.
Malden, MA 02148-5018
Phone: (781)388-8200
Fax: (781)388-8210
Free: 800-216-2552
Journal focusing on artificial intelligence and advanced computing. The journal's readers include knowledge engineers, artificial intelligence researchers, project managers, computer scientists and managers. **Freq:** 5/yr. **Key Personnel:** Lucia Rapanotti, Board Member; Jon G. Hall, Editor-in-Chief. **ISSN:** 0266-4720 (print); **EISSN:** 1468-0394 (electronic). **Subscription Rates:** £585 Institutions online only; $982 Institutions online only; €742 Institutions online only; $1144 Institutions, other countries online only. **URL:** http://onlinelibrary.wiley.com/journal/10.1111/%28ISSN%291468-0394. **Remarks:** Accepts advertising. **Circ:** (Not Reported).

16432 ■ Family Process
Wiley-Blackwell
350 Main St.
Commerce Pl.
Malden, MA 02148-5018
Phone: (781)388-8200
Fax: (781)388-8210
Free: 800-216-2552
Journal focusing on theory and practice, philosophical underpinnings, qualitative and quantitative clinical research, and training in couple and family therapy, family interaction, and family relationships with networks and larger systems. **Freq:** Quarterly. **Key Personnel:** Jay Lebow, Editor. **ISSN:** 0014--7370 (print); **EISSN:** 1545--5300 (electronic). **Subscription Rates:** $87 Individuals print and online; $83 Individuals online only; $36 Students print and online; $34 Students online only; $640 Institutions print and online; $533 Institutions online only; £73 Other countries print and online; £468 Institutions UK, print and online; €554 Institutions Europe, print and online. **URL:** http://onlinelibrary.wiley.com/journal/10.1111/(ISSN)1545-5300. **Ad Rates:** BW $350. **Remarks:** Accepts advertising. **Circ:** (Not Reported).

16433 ■ Financial Accountability and Management
Wiley-Blackwell
350 Main St.
Commerce Pl.
Malden, MA 02148-5018
Phone: (781)388-8200
Fax: (781)388-8210
Free: 800-216-2552
Journal focusing on new thinking and research in the financial accountability, accounting, and financial and resource management of all types of governmental and other non-profit organizations and services. **Freq:** Quarterly. **Key Personnel:** Prof. Irvine Lapsley, Editor; Willie Seal, Board Member; Audrey Marsh, Assistant Editor; Mahmoud Ezzamel, Board Member; Gwyn Bevan, Board Member. **ISSN:** 0267--4424 (print); **EISSN:** 1468--0408 (electronic). **Subscription Rates:** €897 Institutions Europe, print & online; $1497 Institutions print & online; $1247 Institutions print or online; $1453 Institutions, other countries print or online; £706 Institutions print & online; $1744 Institutions, other countries print & online; £588 Institutions print or online; €747 Institutions print or online. **URL:** http://www.wiley.com/WileyCDA/WileyTitle/productCd-FAAM.html; http://onlinelibrary.wiley.com/journal/10.1111/(ISSN)1468-0408. **Remarks:** Advertising accepted; rates available

Circulation: ★ = AAM; △ or • = BPA; ♦ = CAC; ❑ = VAC; ⊕ = PO Statement; ‡ = Publisher's Report; Boldface figures = sworn; Light figures = estimated.

upon request. **Circ:** (Not Reported).

16434 ■ Financial Markets, Institutions & Instruments
Wiley-Blackwell
350 Main St.
Commerce Pl.
Malden, MA 02148-5018
Phone: (781)388-8200
Fax: (781)388-8210
Free: 800-216-2552
Journal focusing on the academic and professional finance communities. **Freq:** 5/yr. **Key Personnel:** Mary Jaffier, Managing Editor; Anthony Saunders, Editor. **ISSN:** 0963-8008 (print); **EISSN:** 1468-0416 (electronic). **Subscription Rates:** €830 Institutions print & online; $874 Institutions print & online; £654 Institutions print & online; $728 Institutions print or online; €691 Institutions Europe, print or online; $1066 Institutions, other countries print or online; $1280 Institutions, other countries print & online. **URL:** http://onlinelibrary.wiley.com/journal/10.1111/(ISSN)1468-0416. **Ad Rates:** BW $325. **Remarks:** Accepts advertising. **Circ:** (Not Reported).

16435 ■ The Financial Review
Wiley-Blackwell
350 Main St.
Commerce Pl.
Malden, MA 02148-5018
Phone: (781)388-8200
Fax: (781)388-8210
Free: 800-216-2552
Journal focusing on empirical, theoretical and methodological research providing new insights into all areas of financial economics. **Freq:** Quarterly. **Key Personnel:** Bonnie F. Van Ness, Editor; Robert A. Van Ness, Editor. **ISSN:** 0732-8516 (print). **Subscription Rates:** $507 Institutions print & online; €464 Institutions print & online; $441 Institutions print or online; £367 Institutions print & online; €403 Institutions print or online; £318 Institutions print or online. **URL:** http://onlinelibrary.wiley.com/journal/10.1111/(ISSN)1540-6288. **Ad Rates:** BW $361. **Remarks:** Accepts advertising. **Circ:** 800.

16436 ■ Fiscal Studies
Wiley-Blackwell
350 Main St.
Commerce Pl.
Malden, MA 02148-5018
Phone: (781)388-8200
Fax: (781)388-8210
Free: 800-216-2552
Journal focusing on public economics and fiscal policy. **Freq:** Quarterly. **Key Personnel:** Claire Crawford, Managing Editor; Joel Slemrod, Advisor, Board Member; Thomas Crossley, Editor; Eric French, Editor; Judith Payne, Editor; Richard Blundell, Advisor, Board Member. **ISSN:** 0143--5671 (print); **EISSN:** 1475--5890 (electronic). **Subscription Rates:** $924 Institutions, other countries print & online; $770 Institutions, other countries online or print; $661 Institutions online or print; £476 Institutions print & online; $794 Institutions print & online; £396 Institutions print or online; Included in membership. **URL:** http://onlinelibrary.wiley.com/journal/10.1111/(ISSN)1475-5890; http://www.ifs.org.uk/publications/fiscalStudies; http://www.wiley.com/bw/journal.asp?ref=0143-5671&site=1; http://www.ifs.org.uk/publications/?sorting=newest&q=&partial_results=1&year_published[start]=&year_published[end]=&author=&page=1&. **Remarks:** Advertising accepted; rates available upon request. **Circ:** 1500.

16437 ■ Fish and Fisheries
Wiley-Blackwell
350 Main St.
Commerce Pl.
Malden, MA 02148-5018
Phone: (781)388-8200
Fax: (781)388-8210
Free: 800-216-2552
Journal focusing on the broad field of the biology of fish and their exploitation and conservation at a professional level. **Freq:** Quarterly. **Key Personnel:** Prof. Tony J. Pitcher, Editor; Prof. Paul J.B. Hart, Editor. **ISSN:** 1467--2960 (print); **EISSN:** 1467--2979 (electronic). **Subscription Rates:** €1085 Institutions print & online; $232 Members print & online; $1572 Institutions print & online; $1310 Institutions print or online; $1527 Institutions, other countries print or online; €904 Institutions print or online; £128 Members print & online; £857 Institutions print & online; $1833 Institutions, other countries print & online; £714 Institutions print or online. **URL:** http://onlinelibrary.wiley.com/journal/10.1111/(ISSN)1467-2979. **Remarks:** Advertising accepted; rates available upon request. **Circ:** (Not Reported).

16438 ■ Fisheries Management and Ecology
Wiley-Blackwell
350 Main St.
Commerce Pl.
Malden, MA 02148-5018
Phone: (781)388-8200
Fax: (781)388-8210
Free: 800-216-2552
Peer-reviewed journal focusing on all aspects of the management, ecology and conservation of inland, estuarine and coastal fisheries. **Freq:** Bimonthly. **Key Personnel:** Ian G. Cowx, Editor; Hal L. Schramm, Editor. **ISSN:** 0969--997X (print); **EISSN:** 1365--2400 (electronic). **Subscription Rates:** €1451 Institutions print & online; $267 Members print & online; $2106 Institutions print & online; $2043 Institutions, other countries print & online; $1755 Institutions print or online; €1209 Institutions print or online; £142 Members print & online; £1142 Institutions print & online; $2452 Institutions, other countries print & online; £951 Institutions print or online. **URL:** http://onlinelibrary.wiley.com/journal/10.1111/(ISSN)1365-2400. **Remarks:** Advertising accepted; rates available upon request. **Circ:** (Not Reported).

16439 ■ Fisheries Oceanography
Wiley-Blackwell
350 Main St.
Commerce Pl.
Malden, MA 02148-5018
Phone: (781)388-8200
Fax: (781)388-8210
Free: 800-216-2552
Journal focusing on fisheries science. The international journal of the Japanese Society for Fisheries Oceanography. **Freq:** Bimonthly. **Key Personnel:** Dr. David Checkley, Jr., Editor-in-Chief. **ISSN:** 1054--6006 (print); **EISSN:** 1365--2419 (electronic). **Subscription Rates:** $433 Individuals print & online; $21006 Institutions print & online; €1448 Institutions print & online; $1755 Institutions print or online; £1140 Institutions print & online. **URL:** http://onlinelibrary.wiley.com/journal/10.1111/(ISSN)1365-2419. **Remarks:** Advertising accepted; rates available upon request. **Circ:** (Not Reported).

16440 ■ Foreign Policy Analysis
Wiley-Blackwell
350 Main St.
Commerce Pl.
Malden, MA 02148-5018
Phone: (781)388-8200
Fax: (781)388-8210
Free: 800-216-2552
Journal focusing on the processes, outcomes, and theories of foreign policy. **Freq:** Quarterly. **Key Personnel:** A. Cooper Drury, Editor-in-Chief; Marijke Breuning, Board Member; Ralph Carter, Board Member; Douglas A. Van Belle, Board Member; Valerie Hudson, Board Member; Alex Mintz, Board Member; Julie Kaarbo, Associate Editor; Cooper A. Drury, Editor-in-Chief. **ISSN:** 1743--8586 (print); **EISSN:** 1743--8594 (electronic). **Subscription Rates:** $2264 Institutions print or online; $2718 Institutions print and online; £2187 Institutions print or online; £2624 Institutions print and online; €2196 Institutions print or online; €2636 Institutions print and online. **URL:** http://fpa.oxfordjournals.org. **Remarks:** Advertising accepted; rates available upon request. **Circ:** (Not Reported).

16441 ■ Forest Pathology
Blackwell Publishing Inc.
350 Main St.
Malden, MA 02148
Phone: (781)388-8200
Fax: (781)388-8210
Free: 800-216-2522
Publisher's E-mail: journaladsusa@bos.blackwellpublishing.com
Peer-reviewed journal covering forest pathological problems occurring in any part of the world. **Freq:** Bimonthly. **Key Personnel:** Dr. Ottmar Holdenrieder, Editor; Dr. Steve Woodward, Editor-in-Chief; Dr. Marie-Laure Desprez-Loustau, Editor. **ISSN:** 1437--4781 (print); **EISSN:** 1439--0329 (electronic). **Subscription Rates:** $1587 Institutions online only; £947 Institutions online only; €1203 Institutions online only; $2034 Other countries print and online. **URL:** http://www.wiley.com/bw/journal.asp?ref=1437-4781&site=1. **Remarks:** Advertising accepted; rates available upon request. **Circ:** (Not Reported).

16442 ■ Freshwater Biology
Wiley-Blackwell
350 Main St.
Commerce Pl.
Malden, MA 02148-5018
Phone: (781)388-8200
Fax: (781)388-8210
Free: 800-216-2552
Journal focusing on all aspects of the ecology of inland surface waters, including rivers and lakes, connected ground waters, flood plains and other wetlands. **Freq:** Monthly. **Key Personnel:** Alan G. Hildrew, Editor; Colin R. Townsend, Editor. **ISSN:** 0046--5070 (print); **EISSN:** 1365--2427 (electronic). **Subscription Rates:** $444 Individuals print & online; $9560 Institutions print & online; €5479 Institutions print or online; $7966 Institutions print or online; £242 Individuals print & online; £5177 Institutions print & online; €6575 Institutions print & online; £4314 Institutions print or online. **URL:** http://onlinelibrary.wiley.com/journal/10.1111/(ISSN)1365-2427. **Remarks:** Advertising accepted; rates available upon request. **Circ:** (Not Reported).

16443 ■ Functional Ecology
Wiley-Blackwell
350 Main St.
Commerce Pl.
Malden, MA 02148-5018
Phone: (781)388-8200
Fax: (781)388-8210
Free: 800-216-2552
Journal focusing on the fields of physiological, biophysical and evolutionary ecology. **Freq:** Bimonthly. **Key Personnel:** Edith Allen, Associate Editor; Charles W. Fox, Editor; Liz Baker, Managing Editor. **ISSN:** 0269--8463 (print); **EISSN:** 1365--2435 (electronic). **Subscription Rates:** $1931 Institutions online only; $2252 Institutions, other countries online only; €1325 Institutions online only; £1045 Institutions online only. **URL:** http://onlinelibrary.wiley.com/journal/10.1111/(ISSN)1365-2435. **Remarks:** Advertising accepted; rates available upon request. **Circ:** (Not Reported).

16444 ■ Fundamental & Clinical Pharmacology
Wiley-Blackwell
350 Main St.
Commerce Pl.
Malden, MA 02148-5018
Phone: (781)388-8200
Fax: (781)388-8210
Free: 800-216-2552
Journal focusing on important and novel developments in fundamental as well as clinical research relevant to drug therapy. **Freq:** Bimonthly. **Key Personnel:** Pascal Bousquet, Editor-in-Chief. **ISSN:** 0767--3981 (print); **EISSN:** 1472--8206 (electronic). **Subscription Rates:** $1567 Institutions online only; £851 Institutions online only; €1082 Institutions online only; $1827 Institutions, other countries online only. **URL:** http://onlinelibrary.wiley.com/journal/10.1111/(ISSN)1472-8206. **Remarks:** Advertising accepted; rates available upon request. **Circ:** (Not Reported).

16445 ■ GCB Bioenergy
Wiley-Blackwell
350 Main St.
Commerce Pl.
Malden, MA 02148-5018
Phone: (781)388-8200
Fax: (781)388-8210
Free: 800-216-2552
Journal covering all aspects of current and potential biofuel production. **Freq:** Bimonthly. **Key Personnel:** Steve Long, Editor; Rachel Shekar, Executive Editor. **ISSN:** 1757--1693 (print); **EISSN:** 1757--1707 (electronic). **Subscription Rates:** $6619 Institutions print & online; $5756 Institutions print or online; $446 Individuals print & online. **URL:** http://onlinelibrary.wiley.com/journal/10.1111/(ISSN)1757-1707/issues. **Remarks:** Accepts

advertising. **Circ:** (Not Reported).

16446 ■ Gender & History
Wiley-Blackwell
350 Main St.
Commerce Pl.
Malden, MA 02148-5018
Phone: (781)388-8200
Fax: (781)388-8210
Free: 800-216-2552
Journal focusing on established as the major international journal for research and writing on the history of gender and sexuality. **Freq:** 3/year. **Key Personnel:** Michele Mitchell, Contact; Karen Adler, Editor; Regina Kunzel, Editor. **ISSN:** 0953--5233 (print); **EISSN:** 1468--0424 (electronic). **Subscription Rates:** $56 Individuals print and online; $51 Members print and online, student; $1144 Institutions print and online; €874 Institutions print and online; £36 Individuals print and online (UK and non-Euro zone); £32 Members print and online (UK and non-Euro zone); £31 Students print and online (UK, non-Euro zone developing countries, and rest of the world). **URL:** http://onlinelibrary.wiley.com/journal/10.1111/(ISSN)1468-0424. **Remarks:** Advertising accepted; rates available upon request. **Circ:** (Not Reported).

16447 ■ Gender, Work and Organization
Wiley-Blackwell
350 Main St.
Commerce Pl.
Malden, MA 02148-5018
Phone: (781)388-8200
Fax: (781)388-8210
Free: 800-216-2552
Journal focusing on social science research. **Freq:** Bimonthly. **Key Personnel:** David Knights, Editor-in-Chief; Deborah Kerfoot, Editor-in-Chief. **ISSN:** 0968--6673 (print); **EISSN:** 1468--0432 (electronic). **Subscription Rates:** $73 Individuals print and online (The Americas); $62 Members print and online (The Americas); $50 Students print and online (The Americas); $1827 Institutions print and online (The Americas); €1152 Institutions print or online (Europe Euro zone and non-Euro zone); €64 Individuals print & online (Europe Euro zone); €57 Members print & online (Europe Euro zone); €44 Students print & online (Europe Euro zone); €1383 Institutions print & online (Europe Euro zone and non-Euro zone). **URL:** http://onlinelibrary.wiley.com/journal/10.1111/(ISSN)1468-0432. **Remarks:** Advertising accepted; rates available upon request. **Circ:** (Not Reported).

16448 ■ Genes, Brain and Behavior
Wiley-Blackwell
350 Main St.
Commerce Pl.
Malden, MA 02148-5018
Phone: (781)388-8200
Fax: (781)388-8210
Free: 800-216-2552
Journal focusing on research in behavioral and neural genetics in its broadest sense. **Freq:** 8/year. **Key Personnel:** Wim E. Crusio, Editor-in-Chief, Founder; Christine van Broeckhoven, Associate Editor; Daniel Goldowitz, Associate Editor; Steven De Belle, Board Member; Joseph Takahashi, Board Member; Enrico Alleva, Board Member; Michael F. Miles, Board Member; Gene E. Robinson, Board Member; Maja Bucan, Board Member; Greg Gibson, Board Member. **ISSN:** 1601--1848 (print); **EISSN:** 1601--183X (electronic). **Subscription Rates:** $11164 Institutions online (The Americas); €802 Institutions online (Europe Euro and non Euro zone); $1359 Institutions, other countries online; £630 Institutions online (UK). **URL:** http://onlinelibrary.wiley.com/journal/10.1111/(ISSN)1601-183X; http://www.ibangs.org/news; http://onlinelibrary.wiley.com/doi/10.1111/gbb.2016.15.issue-2/issuetoc. **Remarks:** Advertising accepted; rates available upon request. **Circ:** (Not Reported).

16449 ■ Genes to Cells
Wiley-Blackwell
350 Main St.
Commerce Pl.
Malden, MA 02148-5018
Phone: (781)388-8200
Fax: (781)388-8210
Free: 800-216-2552
Journal focusing on works aimed at understanding the basic mechanisms underlying biological events. **Freq:** Monthly. **Key Personnel:** Mitsuhiro Yanagida, Editor-in-Chief; Helen M. Blau, Editor; Anne Ephrussi, Editor. **ISSN:** 1356--9597 (print); **EISSN:** 1365--2443 (electronic). **Subscription Rates:** $3262 Institutions online only (The Americas); €2325 Institutions online only (Europe Euro and non-Euro zone); £1831 Institutions online only (UK); $3583 Institutions, other countries online only; $71 Members online only (The Americas); £46 Members online only (UK, Europe non Euro zone, and the rest of the world); €52 Institutions online only (Europe Euro zone). **URL:** http://onlinelibrary.wiley.com/journal/10.1111/(ISSN)1365-2443. **Remarks:** Advertising accepted; rates available upon request. **Circ:** (Not Reported).

16450 ■ Geobiology
Wiley-Blackwell
350 Main St.
Commerce Pl.
Malden, MA 02148-5018
Phone: (781)388-8200
Fax: (781)388-8210
Free: 800-216-2552
Journal focusing on the relationship between life and the Earth's physical and chemical environment. **Freq:** 6/year. **Key Personnel:** Kurt Konhauser, Editor-in-Chief. **ISSN:** 1472--4677 (print); **EISSN:** 1472--4669 (electronic). **Subscription Rates:** €691 Institutions Europe (Euro and non-Euro zone), online; $1003 Institutions online (The Americas); $1169 Institutions online, rest of the world; £547 Institutions U.K. , online. **URL:** http://onlinelibrary.wiley.com/journal/10.1111/(ISSN)1472-4669. **Remarks:** Advertising accepted; rates available upon request. **Circ:** (Not Reported).

16451 ■ Geofluids
Wiley-Blackwell
350 Main St.
Commerce Pl.
Malden, MA 02148-5018
Phone: (781)388-8200
Fax: (781)388-8210
Free: 800-216-2552
Journal focusing on original research into the role of fluids in mineralogical, chemical, and structural evolution of the Earth's crust. **Freq:** Quarterly. **Key Personnel:** Steve Ingebritsen, Board Member; Richard Worden, Editor; Bruce Yardley, Board Member. **ISSN:** 1468--8115 (print); **EISSN:** 1468--8123 (electronic). **Subscription Rates:** $177 Individuals online; $1141 Institutions online; €144 Individuals online; €790 Institutions online; £621 Institutions online; £98 Individuals online. **URL:** http://onlinelibrary.wiley.com/journal/10.1111/(ISSN)1468-8123. **Remarks:** Advertising accepted; rates available upon request. **Circ:** (Not Reported).

16452 ■ Geografiska Annaler: Series B, Human Geography
Wiley-Blackwell
350 Main St.
Commerce Pl.
Malden, MA 02148-5018
Phone: (781)388-8200
Fax: (781)388-8210
Free: 800-216-2552
Publisher's E-mail: journaladsusa@bos.blackwellpublishing.com
Journal covering all theoretical and empirical aspects of human and economic geography. **Freq:** Quarterly. **Key Personnel:** Orjan Sjoberg, Editor; Örjan Sjöberg, Editor-in-Chief. **ISSN:** 0435--3684 (print); **EISSN:** 1468--0467 (electronic). **Subscription Rates:** $83 Individuals print & online; $57 Students print & online (The Americas); $951 Institutions, other countries print & online; €515 Institutions print or online (Europe Euro and non-Euro zone); £52 Individuals print and online; £32 Students print and online. **URL:** http://onlinelibrary.wiley.com/journal/10.1111/(ISSN)1468-0467; http://ssag.se/publikationer/geografiska-annaler-b. **Remarks:** Advertising accepted; rates available upon request. **Circ:** (Not Reported).

16453 ■ Geographical Journal
Blackwell Publishing Inc.
350 Main St.
Malden, MA 02148
Phone: (781)388-8200
Fax: (781)388-8210
Free: 800-216-2522
Publisher's E-mail: membership@rgs.org
Journal focusing on original research and scholarship in physical and human geography. **Freq:** Quarterly. **Key Personnel:** Prof. Maano Ramutsindela, Board Member; Dr. Emma Mawdsley, Board Member; Dr. Frances Harris, Editor; Prof. Mark Maslin, Board Member; Klaus Dodds, Editor. **ISSN:** 0016--7398 (print); **EISSN:** 1475--4959 (electronic). **Subscription Rates:** $405 Institutions online or print; $486 Institutions print + online (The Americas); £241 Institutions online or print; £290 Institutions print + online; $470 Institutions, other countries online or print; $564 Institutions, other countries print + online; €305 Institutions print or online; €366 Institutions print + online. **URL:** http://onlinelibrary.wiley.com/journal/10.1111/(ISSN)1475-4959; http://www.geography.sav.sk/en1/index.php?option=com_content&view=article&id=81&Itemid=30&lang=. **Remarks:** Advertising accepted; rates available upon request. **Circ:** (Not Reported).

16454 ■ Geographical Research
Blackwell Publishing Inc.
350 Main St.
Malden, MA 02148
Phone: (781)388-8200
Fax: (781)388-8210
Free: 800-216-2522
Publisher's E-mail: customerservice@oxon.blackwellpublishing.com
Journal focusing on advancing geographical research across the discipline. **Freq:** Quarterly. **Key Personnel:** Kevin Dunn, Advisor, Board Member; Iain Hay, Editor-in-Chief; Wayne Stephenson, Editor; Brian Finlayson, Editor; Amanda Davies, Editor. **ISSN:** 1745--5863 (print); **EISSN:** 1745--5871 (electronic). **Subscription Rates:** $592 Institutions online or print; $711 Institutions print + online (The Americas); $861 Individuals print + online (rest of the world); £466 Institutions online or print; £560 Institutions print + online; £68 Individuals print + online; €466 Institutions print or online, Europe. **URL:** http://onlinelibrary.wiley.com/journal/10.1111/(ISSN)1745-5871. **Formerly**: Australian Geographical Studies. **Mailing address:** PO Box 1354, Oxford OX4 2ZG, United Kingdom. **Remarks:** Advertising accepted; rates available upon request. **Circ:** (Not Reported).

16455 ■ Geography Compass
Wiley-Blackwell
350 Main St.
Commerce Pl.
Malden, MA 02148-5018
Phone: (781)388-8200
Fax: (781)388-8210
Free: 800-216-2552
Journal featuring research articles on the field of geography. **Freq:** Monthly. **Key Personnel:** Michael Bradshaw, Editor-in-Chief. **EISSN:** 1749--8198 (electronic). **Subscription Rates:** $1613 Institutions; £964 Institutions UK; €1225 Institutions Europe; $766 Institutions developing world; $1888 Institutions, other countries UK (online only); $87 Individuals; £47 Individuals UK and Europe (non euro zone); €57 Individuals Europe; £47 Individuals developing world; £47 Other countries. **URL:** http://onlinelibrary.wiley.com/journal/10.1111/(ISSN)1749-8198. **Remarks:** Accepts advertising. **Circ:** (Not Reported).

16456 ■ Geology Today
Wiley-Blackwell
350 Main St.
Commerce Pl.
Malden, MA 02148-5018
Phone: (781)388-8200
Fax: (781)388-8210
Free: 800-216-2552
Journal for earth scientists. **Freq:** Bimonthly. **Key Personnel:** Prof. Peter Doyle, Editor; Dr. Eric Robinson, Advisor. **ISSN:** 0266--6979 (print); **EISSN:** 1365--2451 (electronic). **Subscription Rates:** $119 Individuals print and online; $85 Members print and online; $51 Students print and online; $1532 Institutions print & online; $1790 Institutions, other countries print and online; £827 Institutions print & online; £64 Individuals print & online. **URL:** http://onlinelibrary.wiley.com/journal/10.1111/

Circulation: ★ = AAM; △ or • = BPA; ♦ = CAC; ❑ = VAC; ⊕ = PO Statement; ‡ = Publisher's Report; Boldface figures = sworn; Light figures = estimated.

(ISSN)1365-2451. **Remarks:** Advertising accepted; rates available upon request. **Circ:** (Not Reported).

16457 ■ Geophysical Prospecting
Wiley-Blackwell
350 Main St.
Commerce Pl.
Malden, MA 02148-5018
Phone: (781)388-8200
Fax: (781)388-8210
Free: 800-216-2552
Journal focusing on research on the science of geophysics as it applies to exploration. **Freq:** Bimonthly. **Key Personnel:** Tijmen Jan Moser, Editor-in-Chief; Mohammed N. Alfaraj, Editor; Philip N. Armstrong, Editor; Claudio Bagaini, Editor; Angus I. Best, Editor. **ISSN:** 0016--8025 (print); **EISSN:** 1365--2478 (electronic). **Subscription Rates:** $2012 Institutions print or online; £1090 Institutions print or online, UK; €1385 Institutions print or online, Europe; $2347 Institutions, other countries print or online; $2415 Institutions print and online; £1307 Institutions print and online, UK; €1662 Institutions print and online, Europe; $2817 Institutions, other countries print and online. **URL:** http://onlinelibrary.wiley.com/journal/10.1111/(ISSN)1365-2478. **Ad Rates:** 4C €1,825, full page bleed; 4C €1,725, full page non-bleed; 4C €1,250, half page horizontal or vertical. **Remarks:** Accepts advertising. **Circ:** ‡8841, ‡8841.

16458 ■ Geostandards & Geoanalytical Research
Blackwell Publishing Inc.
350 Main St.
Malden, MA 02148
Phone: (781)388-8200
Fax: (781)388-8210
Free: 800-216-2522
Publisher's E-mail: journaladsusa@bos.blackwellpublishing.com
Peer-reviewed journal covering the field of geology. **Freq:** Quarterly. **Key Personnel:** Thomas C. Meisel, Editor-in-Chief. **ISSN:** 1639--4488 (print); **EISSN:** 1751--908X (electronic). **Subscription Rates:** $1140 Institutions Americas (print and online); £628 Institutions UK (print and online); €797 Institutions Europe (print and online); $1227 Institutions, other countries print and online; $950 Institutions Americas (online only); £523 Institutions UK (online only); €664 Institutions Europe (online only); $1022 Institutions, other countries online only; $211 Individuals print and online; £120 Individuals print and online. **URL:** http://onlinelibrary.wiley.com/journal/10.1111/(ISSN)1751-908X. **Remarks:** Advertising accepted; rates available upon request. **Circ:** (Not Reported).

16459 ■ Geriatrics & Gerontology
Wiley-Blackwell
350 Main St.
Commerce Pl.
Malden, MA 02148-5018
Phone: (781)388-8200
Fax: (781)388-8210
Free: 800-216-2552
Journal focusing on the growing importance of the subject area in developed economies and their particular significance to a country like Japan with a large aging population. **Freq:** Quarterly. **Key Personnel:** Kentaro Shimokado, Editor-in-Chief; Hajime Orimo, Editor-in-Chief; Hidetada Sasaki, Editor-in-Chief. **ISSN:** 1444--1586 (print); **EISSN:** 1447--0594 (electronic). **Subscription Rates:** $509 Institutions online only; £315 Institutions online only, UK; €386 Institutions online only, Europe; $614 Institutions, other countries online only. **URL:** http://onlinelibrary.wiley.com/journal/10.1111/(ISSN)1447-0594. **Remarks:** Accepts advertising. **Circ:** (Not Reported).

16460 ■ Geriatrics & Gerontology International
Wiley-Blackwell
350 Main St.
Commerce Pl.
Malden, MA 02148-5018
Phone: (781)388-8200
Fax: (781)388-8210
Free: 800-216-2552
Official journal of the Japanese Geriatrics Society, reflecting the growing importance of the subject area in developed economies and its particular significance to a country like Japan with a large aging population. **Freq:** Quarterly. **Key Personnel:** Hidetada Sasaki, Editor-in-Chief; Tsutomu Chiba, Board Member; Yoshinori Doi, Board Member; Yasuyoshi Ouchi, Associate Editor; Hidetoshi Endo, Board Member; Fumio Eto, Board Member; Takashi Inamatsu, Board Member; Toshio Ogihara, Associate Editor; Kentaro Shimokado, Editor-in-Chief. **ISSN:** 1444--1586 (print); **EISSN:** 1447--0594 (electronic). **Subscription Rates:** $509 Institutions online; £315 Institutions online; €386 Institutions online; $614 Institutions, other countries online. **URL:** http://onlinelibrary.wiley.com/journal/10.1111/(ISSN)1447-0594. **Remarks:** Accepts advertising. **Circ:** (Not Reported).

16461 ■ German Economic Review
Wiley-Blackwell
350 Main St.
Commerce Pl.
Malden, MA 02148-5018
Phone: (781)388-8200
Fax: (781)388-8210
Free: 800-216-2552
Journal focusing on original research of general interest in a broad range of economic disciplines, including macro- and microeconomics, public economics, business administration and finance. **Freq:** Quarterly. **Key Personnel:** Mathias Hoffmann, Editor; Wolfgang Leininger, Editor. **ISSN:** 1465-6485 (print); **EISSN:** 1468-0475 (electronic). **Subscription Rates:** $69 Individuals print & online; $235 Institutions print & online; $298 Institutions, other countries print & online; $211 Institutions print or online; €68 Individuals print & online; £153 Institutions print & online; $298 Institutions, other countries print or online; £139 Institutions print or online. **URL:** http://www.wiley.com/WileyCDA/WileyTitle/productCd-GEER.html. **Remarks:** Accepts advertising. **Circ:** (Not Reported).

16462 ■ German Life and Letters
Wiley-Blackwell
350 Main St.
Commerce Pl.
Malden, MA 02148-5018
Phone: (781)388-8200
Fax: (781)388-8210
Free: 800-216-2552
Journal publishing articles dealing with literary and non-literary concerns in the German-speaking world. **Freq:** Quarterly. **Key Personnel:** Dr. Rebecca Braun, Editor; Dr. Margaret Littler, Editor. **ISSN:** 0016--8777 (print); **EISSN:** 1468--0483 (electronic). **Subscription Rates:** $871 Institutions print or online; £508 Institutions print or online; €644 Institutions print or online; $1158 Institutions, other countries print or online; $1046 Institutions print and online; £610 Institutions print and online, UK; €773 Institutions print and online, Europe; $1390 Institutions, other countries print and online; $78 Individuals print and online; £53 Other countries print and online; €80 Individuals print and online, Europe. **URL:** http://onlinelibrary.wiley.com/journal/10.1111/(ISSN)1468-0483. **Remarks:** Accepts advertising. **Circ:** (Not Reported).

16463 ■ Gerodontology
Wiley-Blackwell
350 Main St.
Commerce Pl.
Malden, MA 02148-5018
Phone: (781)388-8200
Fax: (781)388-8210
Free: 800-216-2552
Journal focusing on dental care for gerodontology. **Freq:** Quarterly. **Key Personnel:** Michael MacEntee, Editor-in-Chief; James P. Newton, Editor. **ISSN:** 0734--0664 (print); **EISSN:** 1741--2358 (electronic). **Subscription Rates:** $766 Institutions print or online; £458 Institutions print or online, UK; €580 Institutions print or online, Europe; $892 Institutions, other countries print or online; $920 Institutions print and online; £550 Institutions print and online, UK; €696 Institutions print and online, Europe; $1071 Institutions, other countries print and online; $280 Individuals print and online; £156 Individuals print and online, UK and Europe (non-euro zone); €230 Individuals print and online, Europe; £167 Other countries print and online. **URL:** http://onlinelibrary.wiley.com/journal/10.1111/(ISSN)1741-2358. **Remarks:** Accepts advertising. **Circ:** (Not Reported).

16464 ■ Global Change Biology
Wiley-Blackwell
350 Main St.
Commerce Pl.
Malden, MA 02148-5018
Phone: (781)388-8200
Fax: (781)388-8210
Free: 800-216-2552
Journal focusing on promoting understanding of the interface between all aspects of current environmental change and biological systems, including rising tropospheric O3 and CO2 concentrations, climate change, loss of biodiversity, and eutrophication. **Freq:** Monthly. **Key Personnel:** Steve Long, Editor; Rachel Shekar, Executive Editor; Harry Smith, Founder. **ISSN:** 1354--1013 (print); **EISSN:** 1365--2486 (electronic). **Subscription Rates:** $6469 Institutions online only; $6102 Institutions print only; $7730 Institutions print and online; $474 Individuals print and online. **URL:** http://onlinelibrary.wiley.com/journal/10.1111/(ISSN)1365-2486. **Remarks:** Accepts advertising. **Circ:** (Not Reported).

16465 ■ Global Ecology and Biogeography: A Journal of Macroecology
Wiley-Blackwell
350 Main St.
Commerce Pl.
Malden, MA 02148-5018
Phone: (781)388-8200
Fax: (781)388-8210
Free: 800-216-2552
Publisher's E-mail: journaladsusa@bos.blackwellpublishing.com
Journal focusing on the emerging field of macroecology: the study of broad, consistent patterns in the ecological characteristics of organisms and ecosystems. **Freq:** Monthly. **Key Personnel:** Prof. David J. Currie, Editor, phone: (613)562-5800, fax: (613)562-5486; Martin T. Sykes, Senior Editor; Brian Mcgill, Editor-in-Chief. **ISSN:** 1466--822X (print); **EISSN:** 1466--8238 (electronic). **Subscription Rates:** $8844 Institutions online only; $10613 Institutions print and online; $8844 Institutions print only; $684 Individuals print and online. **URL:** http://onlinelibrary.wiley.com/journal/10.1111/(ISSN)1466-8238. **Remarks:** Accepts advertising. **Circ:** (Not Reported).

16466 ■ Global Networks
Wiley-Blackwell
350 Main St.
Commerce Pl.
Malden, MA 02148-5018
Phone: (781)388-8200
Fax: (781)388-8210
Free: 800-216-2552
Journal focusing on high quality, peer-reviewed research on global networks, transnational affairs and practices and their relation to wider theories of globalization. **Freq:** Quarterly. **Key Personnel:** Dr. Alisdair Rogers, Editor; Prof. Steve Vertovec, Editor; Prof. Robin Cohen, Editor. **ISSN:** 1470-2266 (print); **EISSN:** 1471-0374 (electronic). **Subscription Rates:** $95 Individuals print and online; $59 Students print and online; $77 Members print and online; $890 Institutions print and online; $741 Institutions print or online. **URL:** http://onlinelibrary.wiley.com/journal/10.1111/(ISSN)1471-0374. **Remarks:** Accepts advertising. **Circ:** (Not Reported).

16467 ■ Governance
Wiley-Blackwell
350 Main St.
Commerce Pl.
Malden, MA 02148-5018
Phone: (781)388-8200
Fax: (781)388-8210
Free: 800-216-2552
Journal focusing on peer-reviewed articles that take an international or comparative approach to public policy and administration. **Freq:** Quarterly. **Key Personnel:** Robert H. Cox, Editor; Clay Wescott, Editor; Michael Barzelay, Editor. **ISSN:** 0952--1895 (print); **EISSN:** 1468--0491 (electronic). **Subscription Rates:** $936 Institutions online only; £722 Institutions online only, UK; €913 Institutions online only, Europe; $1408 Institutions, other countries online only. **URL:** http://onlinelibrary.wiley.com/journal/10.1111/(ISSN)1468-0491. **Ad Rates:** BW $350. **Remarks:** Accepts advertising. **Circ:** (Not Reported).

16468 ■ Grass and Forage Science
Wiley-Blackwell
350 Main St.
Commerce Pl.
Malden, MA 02148-5018
Phone: (781)388-8200
Fax: (781)388-8210
Free: 800-216-2552
Journal focusing on journal that publishes the results of research and development in all aspects of grass and forage production, management and utilization, occasional reviews of the state of knowledge on relevant topics, and book reviews. **Freq:** Quarterly. **Key Personnel:** Kevin Smith, Editor; Alan Hopkins, Editor. **ISSN:** 0142--5242 (print); **EISSN:** 1365--2494 (electronic). **Subscription Rates:** $1764 Institutions print or online; £961 Institutions print or online, UK; €1221 Institutions print or online, Europe; $2058 Institutions, other countries print or online; $2117 Institutions print and online; £1154 Institutions print and online, UK; €1466 Institutions print and online, Europe; $2470 Institutions, other countries print and online. **URL:** http://onlinelibrary.wiley.com/journal/10.1111/(ISSN)1365-2494. **Remarks:** Accepts advertising. **Circ:** (Not Reported).

16469 ■ Grassland Science
Wiley-Blackwell
350 Main St.
Commerce Pl.
Malden, MA 02148-5018
Phone: (781)388-8200
Fax: (781)388-8210
Free: 800-216-2552
Journal focusing on original research papers, review articles and short reports in all aspects of grassland science, with an aim of presenting and sharing knowledge, ideas and philosophies on better management and use of grasslands, forage crops and turf plants for both agricultural and non-agricultural purposes across the world. **Freq:** Quarterly. **Key Personnel:** Masahiko Hirata, President; Bryan Kindiger, Board Member; Toshihiko Yamada, Editor-in-Chief; Shuichi Sugiyama, Board Member; Shinro Yamamoto, Board Member. **ISSN:** 1744--6961 (print); **EISSN:** 1744--697X (electronic). **Subscription Rates:** $529 Institutions online only; £273 Institutions online only, UK; €348 Institutions online only, Europe; $529 Institutions, other countries online only. **URL:** http://onlinelibrary.wiley.com/journal/10.1111/(ISSN)1744-697X. **Remarks:** Advertising accepted; rates available upon request; Accepts classified advertising. **Circ:** Paid 1400.

16470 ■ Ground Water
Wiley-Blackwell
350 Main St.
Commerce Pl.
Malden, MA 02148-5018
Phone: (781)388-8200
Fax: (781)388-8210
Free: 800-216-2552
Journal focusing exclusively on ground water. **Freq:** Bimonthly. **Key Personnel:** Franklin W. Schwartz, Advisor; Mark Bakker, PhD, Associate Editor; Hendrik M. Haitjema, PhD, Editor-in-Chief; Yongje Kim, PhD, Advisor. **ISSN:** 0017--467X (print); **EISSN:** 1745--6584 (electronic). **Subscription Rates:** $771 Institutions print or online; £464 Institutions print or online, UK; €588 Institutions print or online, Europe; $905 Institutions, other countries print or online; $926 Institutions print and online; £557 Institutions print and online, UK; €706 Institutions print and online, Europe; $1086 Institutions, other countries print and online. **URL:** http://onlinelibrary.wiley.com/journal/10.1111/(ISSN)1745-6584. **Remarks:** Accepts advertising. **Circ:** (Not Reported).

16471 ■ Ground Water Monitoring & Remediation
Wiley-Blackwell
350 Main St.
Commerce Pl.
Malden, MA 02148-5018
Phone: (781)388-8200
Fax: (781)388-8210
Free: 800-216-2552
Journal devoted to advancing the practice of the ground water monitoring and remediation field by combining forward thinking academic research with practical solutions from industry leaders. **Freq:** Quarterly. **Print Method:** Offset. **Trim Size:** 8 1/8 x 10 7/8. **Cols./Page:** 2. **Col. Width:** 26 nonpareils. **Col. Depth:** 152 agate lines. **Key Personnel:** Paul Johnson, Editor; Michael J. Barcelona, Associate Editor; David Huntley, Associate Editor; Neil R. Thomson, PhD, Editor; Paul C. Johnson, Editor; Richard L. Johnson, Associate Editor; David W. Major, Editor; William G. Rixey, Editor. **ISSN:** 1069--3629 (print); **EISSN:** 1745--6592 (electronic). **Subscription Rates:** $359 Institutions print or online; £297 Institutions print or online, UK; €374 Institutions print or online, Europe; $578 Institutions, other countries print or online; $431 Institutions print and online; £357 Institutions print and online, UK; €449 Institutions print and online, Europe; $694 Institutions, other countries print and online. **URL:** http://onlinelibrary.wiley.com/journal/10.1111/(ISSN)1745-6592; http://www.ngwa.org/pubs/gwmr/Pages/default.aspx. **Formerly:** Ground Water Monitoring Review. **Ad Rates:** BW $2,110; 4C $2,960. **Remarks:** Accepts advertising. **Circ:** ‡15500.

16472 ■ Growth and Change
Wiley-Blackwell
350 Main St.
Commerce Pl.
Malden, MA 02148-5018
Phone: (781)388-8200
Fax: (781)388-8210
Free: 800-216-2552
Journal focusing on urban and regional policy. **Freq:** Quarterly. **Key Personnel:** Dan Rickman, Editor. **ISSN:** 0017--4815 (print); **EISSN:** 1468--2257 (electronic). **Subscription Rates:** $428 Institutions online only; £350 Institutions online only; €445 Institutions online only; $686 Institutions, other countries online only; $105 Individuals online only; £95 Individuals online only, UK and Europe (non-euro zone) and rest of the world; €140 Individuals online only, Europe. **URL:** http://onlinelibrary.wiley.com/journal/10.1111/(ISSN)1468-2257. **Ad Rates:** BW $350. **Remarks:** Accepts advertising. **Circ:** 350.

16473 ■ Haemophilia
Wiley-Blackwell
350 Main St.
Commerce Pl.
Malden, MA 02148-5018
Phone: (781)388-8200
Fax: (781)388-8210
Free: 800-216-2552
Journal focusing on the exchange of information regarding the comprehensive care of haemophilia. **Freq:** 6/year. **Key Personnel:** Craig M. Kessler, Editor; Christine A. Lee, Board Member; M. Makris, Editor. **ISSN:** 1351--8216 (print); **EISSN:** 1365--2516 (electronic). **Subscription Rates:** $1624 Institutions print or online; £881 Institutions print or online, UK; €1118 Institutions print or online, Europe; $1895 Institutions, other countries print or online; $1949 Institutions print and online; £1058 Institutions print and online, UK; €1342 Institutions print and online, Europe; $2274 Institutions, other countries print and online; $400 Individuals print and online; £217 Individuals print and online, UK and Europe (non-euro zone); €322 Individuals print and online, Europe; £240 Individuals print and online. **URL:** http://onlinelibrary.wiley.com/journal/10.1111/(ISSN)1365-2516. **Remarks:** Accepts advertising. **Circ:** (Not Reported).

16474 ■ Headache: The Journal of Head and Face Pain
Wiley-Blackwell
350 Main St.
Commerce Pl.
Malden, MA 02148-5018
Phone: (781)388-8200
Fax: (781)388-8210
Free: 800-216-2552
Freq: 10/year. **Print Method:** Offset. **Trim Size:** 8 1/4 x 10 3/4. **Cols./Page:** 2. **Col. Width:** 42 nonpareils. **Col. Depth:** 151 agate lines. **Key Personnel:** Thomas N. Ward, MD, Editor-in-Chief; John F. Rothrock, MD, Senior Editor, Advisor; Jason Roberts, Associate Editor. **ISSN:** 0017--8748 (print); **EISSN:** 1526--4610 (electronic). **Subscription Rates:** $576 Institutions print or online; £476 Institutions print or online, UK; €605 Institutions print or online, Europe; $930 Institutions, other countries print or online; $692 Institutions print and online; £572 Institutions print and online, UK; €726 Institutions print and online, Europe; $1116 Institutions, other countries print and online; $273 Individuals online only; £234 Individuals online only - UK, Europe (non-euro zone) and rest of the world; €350 Individuals online only, Europe; $288 Individuals print and online; £247 Individuals print and online - UK, Europe (non-euro zone) and rest of the world; €370 Individuals print and online, Europe. **URL:** http://onlinelibrary.wiley.com/journal/10.1111/(ISSN)1526-4610; http://www.headachejournal.org/view/0/index.html. **Ad Rates:** BW $1070; 4C $1220; BW $2,737; 4C $3,912. **Remarks:** Accepts advertising. **Circ:** ‡1266, ‡1006, Paid 30000.

16475 ■ Health Expectations
Wiley-Blackwell
350 Main St.
Commerce Pl.
Malden, MA 02148-5018
Phone: (781)388-8200
Fax: (781)388-8210
Free: 800-216-2552
Journal focusing on critical thinking and informed debate about all aspects of public participation in health care and health policy. **Freq:** Quarterly. **Key Personnel:** Carolyn Chew-Graham, Editor; Carolyn Graham, Editor-in-Chief; Angela Coulter, Board Member. **ISSN:** 1369--6513 (print); **EISSN:** 1369--7625 (electronic). **URL:** http://onlinelibrary.wiley.com/journal/10.1111/(ISSN)1369-7625. **Remarks:** Accepts advertising. **Circ:** (Not Reported).

16476 ■ Health Information & Libraries Journal
Wiley-Blackwell
350 Main St.
Commerce Pl.
Malden, MA 02148-5018
Phone: (781)388-8200
Fax: (781)388-8210
Free: 800-216-2552
Journal focusing on management and libraries. **Freq:** Quarterly. **Key Personnel:** Penny Bonnett, Assistant Editor; Mario J. Grant, Editor. **ISSN:** 1471--1834 (print); **EISSN:** 1471--1842 (electronic). **Subscription Rates:** $1071 Institutions print or online; £582 Institutions print or online, UK; €738 Institutions print or online, Euro; $1250 Institutions, other countries print or online; $1286 Institutions print and online; £699 Institutions print and online, UK; €886 Institutions print and online, Europe; $1500 Institutions, other countries print and online. **URL:** http://onlinelibrary.wiley.com/journal/10.1111/(ISSN)1471-1842. **Remarks:** Accepts advertising. **Circ:** (Not Reported).

16477 ■ Health and Social Care in the Community
Wiley-Blackwell
350 Main St.
Commerce Pl.
Malden, MA 02148-5018
Phone: (781)388-8200
Fax: (781)388-8210
Free: 800-216-2552
Journal focusing on the common ground between health and social care in the community. **Freq:** Bimonthly. **Key Personnel:** Karen Luker, Editor; Karen Chalmers, Editor. **ISSN:** 0966--0410 (print); **EISSN:** 1365--2524 (electronic). **Subscription Rates:** $1436 Institutions print or online; £778 Institutions print or online, UK; €988 Institutions print or online, Europe; $1676 Institutions, other countries print or online; $1724 Institutions print and online; £934 Institutions print and online, UK; €1186 Institutions print and online, Europe; $2012 Institutions, other countries print and online; $246 Individuals print and online; £135 Individuals print and online, UK and Europe (non-euro zone); €200 Individuals print and online; £149 Other countries print and online; $183 Students print and online; £100 Students print and online, UK and Europe (non-euro zone); €150 Students print and online, Europe; £113 Students, other countries print and online. **URL:** http://onlinelibrary.wiley.com/journal/10.1111/(ISSN)1365-2524. **Remarks:** Advertising not accepted. **Circ:** (Not Reported).

16478 ■ Helicobacter
Wiley-Blackwell
350 Main St.
Commerce Pl.
Malden, MA 02148-5018

Circulation: ★ = AAM; △ or • = BPA; ♦ = CAC; ❑ = VAC; ⊕ = PO Statement; ‡ = Publisher's Report; Boldface figures = sworn; Light figures = estimated.

Phone: (781)388-8200
Fax: (781)388-8210
Free: 800-216-2552
Journal focusing on Helicobacter pylori in peptic ulcer, gastric adenocarcinoma, and primary gastric lymphoma. **Freq:** Bimonthly. **Key Personnel:** David Y. Graham, Editor-in-Chief, phone: (713)795-0232, fax: (713)790-1040; Leif P. Andersen, Board Member; Masahiro Asaka, Board Member. **ISSN:** 1083--4389 (print); **EISSN:** 1523--5378 (electronic). **Subscription Rates:** $1863 Institutions online only; £1012 Institutions online only; €1284 Institutions online only; $2177 Institutions online only; $357 Institutions online only; £195 Institutions online only; €290 Institutions online only; £213 Institutions online only. **URL:** http://onlinelibrary.wiley.com/journal/10.1111/(ISSN)1523-5378. **Remarks:** Accepts advertising. **Circ:** (Not Reported).

16479 ■ Hemodialysis International: The Official Journal of the International Society for Hemodialysis
Wiley-Blackwell
350 Main St.
Commerce Pl.
Malden, MA 02148-5018
Phone: (781)388-8200
Fax: (781)388-8210
Free: 800-216-2552
Journal focusing on clinical and experimental topics related to dialysis. **Freq:** Quarterly. **Key Personnel:** John Daugirdas, Editor-in-Chief; Christopher R. Blagg, MD, Editor; Bernard Canaud, MD, Associate Editor; Madhukar Misra, MD, Board Member. **ISSN:** 1492--7535 (print); **EISSN:** 1542--4758 (electronic). **Subscription Rates:** $391 Institutions print or online; £308 Institutions print or online, UK; €391 Institutions print or online, Europe; $599 Institutions, other countries print or online; $470 Institutions print and online; £370 Institutions print and online; €470 Institutions print and online; $719 Institutions, other countries print and online. **URL:** http://onlinelibrary.wiley.com/journal/10.1111/(ISSN)1542-4758. **Ad Rates:** BW $500; 4C $1150. **Remarks:** Accepts advertising. **Circ: 3500.**

16480 ■ Hereditas
Wiley-Blackwell
350 Main St.
Commerce Pl.
Malden, MA 02148-5018
Phone: (781)388-8200
Fax: (781)388-8210
Free: 800-216-2552
Journal focusing on all sections of the genetics discipline. **Freq:** Bimonthly. **Key Personnel:** Stefan Baumgartner, Editor-in-Chief; Petter Oscarsson, Board Member. **ISSN:** 0018--0661 (print); **EISSN:** 1601--5223 (electronic). **URL:** http://onlinelibrary.wiley.com/journal/10.1111/(ISSN)1601-5223; http://hereditasjournal.biomedcentral.com. **Remarks:** Accepts advertising. **Circ:** (Not Reported).

16481 ■ The Heythrop Journal
Wiley-Blackwell
350 Main St.
Commerce Pl.
Malden, MA 02148-5018
Phone: (781)388-8200
Fax: (781)388-8210
Free: 800-216-2552
Journal focusing on theology and philosophy. **Freq:** Bimonthly. **Key Personnel:** Patrick Madigan, Editor; J. McDade, Chairperson. **ISSN:** 0018--1196 (print); **EISSN:** 1468--2265 (electronic). **Subscription Rates:** $663 Institutions print or online; £371 Institutions print or online; €471 Institutions print or online; $325 Institutions print or online, developing World; $774 Institutions, other countries print or online; $796 Institutions print and online; £446 Institutions print and online; €566 Institutions print and online; $390 Institutions print and online, developing World; $929 Institutions, other countries print and online; $119 Individuals print and online; £61 Individuals print and online - UK and Europe (non-euro zone); €93 Individuals print and online, Europe; £71 Other countries print and online. **URL:** http://onlinelibrary.wiley.com/journal/10.1111/(ISSN)1468-2265. **Remarks:** Accepts advertising. **Circ:** (Not Reported).

16482 ■ Higher Education Quarterly
Wiley-Blackwell
350 Main St.
Commerce Pl.
Malden, MA 02148-5018
Phone: (781)388-8200
Fax: (781)388-8210
Free: 800-216-2552
Journal focusing on policy, strategic management and ideas in higher education. **Freq:** Quarterly. **Key Personnel:** Prof. Lee Harvey, Editor; Dr. Celia Whitchurch, Editor. **ISSN:** 0951--5224 (print); **EISSN:** 1468--2273 (electronic). **Subscription Rates:** $888 Institutions print or online; £438 Institutions print or online; €556 Institutions print or online; $1034 Institutions, other countries print or online; $1066 Institutions print and online; £526 Institutions print and online; €668 Institutions print and online; $1241 Institutions, other countries print and online; $175 Individuals print and online; £85 Individuals print and online; €125 Individuals print and online; £105 Other countries print and online. **URL:** http://onlinelibrary.wiley.com/journal/10.1111/(ISSN)1468-2273. **Remarks:** Accepts advertising. **Circ:** (Not Reported).

16483 ■ Histopathology
Wiley-Blackwell
350 Main St.
Commerce Pl.
Malden, MA 02148-5018
Phone: (781)388-8200
Fax: (781)388-8210
Free: 800-216-2552
Journal focusing on advances in pathology. **Freq:** Monthly. **Key Personnel:** Alastair D. Burt, Editor. **ISSN:** 0309--0167 (print); **EISSN:** 1365--2559 (electronic). **Subscription Rates:** $3299 Institutions online only; $3959 Institutions print and online; $430 Individuals print and online; $3299 Institutions print only. **URL:** http://onlinelibrary.wiley.com/journal/10.1111/(ISSN)1365-2559. **Remarks:** Accepts advertising. **Circ:** (Not Reported).

16484 ■ Historical Research: The Bulletin of the Institute of Historical Research
Wiley-Blackwell
350 Main St.
Commerce Pl.
Malden, MA 02148-5018
Phone: (781)388-8200
Fax: (781)388-8210
Free: 800-216-2552
Journal focusing on history from Britain to the Far East and from the early middle ages to the twentieth century. **Freq:** Quarterly. **Key Personnel:** Lawrence Goldman, Editor-in-Chief; Dr. Jane Winters, Executive Editor; Dr. Julie Spraggon, Editor. **ISSN:** 0950--3471 (print); **EISSN:** 1468--2281 (electronic). **Subscription Rates:** $611 Institutions print or online; £270 Institutions print or online; €342 Institutions print or online; $713 Institutions, other countries print or online; $734 Institutions print and online; £324 Institutions print and online; €411 Institutions print and online; $856 Institutions, other countries print and online; $119 Individuals print and online; £57 Individuals print and online; €86 Individuals print and online; £71 Other countries print and online. **URL:** http://onlinelibrary.wiley.com/journal/10.1111/(ISSN)1468-2281. **Remarks:** Accepts advertising. **Circ:** (Not Reported).

16485 ■ History of Education Quarterly
Wiley-Blackwell
350 Main St.
Commerce Pl.
Malden, MA 02148-5018
Phone: (781)388-8200
Fax: (781)388-8210
Free: 800-216-2552
Journal covering the field of education. **Freq:** Quarterly. **Key Personnel:** James D. Anderson, Senior Editor; Yoon K. Pak, Editor; Christopher M. Span, Editor. **ISSN:** 0018-2680 (print); **EISSN:** 1748-5959 (electronic). **Subscription Rates:** $189 Institutions Americas (print and online); £122 Institutions UK (print and online); €155 Institutions Europe (print and online); $237 Institutions, other countries print and online; $165 Institutions Americas (online only); £106 Institutions UK (online only); €135 Institutions Europe (online only); $206 Institutions, other countries online only. **URL:** http://www.wiley.com/WileyCDA/WileyTitle/productCd-HOEQ.html. **Remarks:** Accepts advertising. **Circ:** (Not Reported).

16486 ■ History: The Journal of the Historical Association
Wiley-Blackwell
350 Main St.
Commerce Pl.
Malden, MA 02148-5018
Phone: (781)388-8200
Fax: (781)388-8210
Free: 800-216-2552
Publisher's E-mail: customerservice@oxon.blackwellpublishing.com
Journal focusing on broad chronological coverage with a wide geographical spread of articles featuring contributions from social, political, cultural, economic and ecclesiastical historians. **Freq:** Quarterly. **Key Personnel:** Emma Griffin, Editor. **ISSN:** 0018--2648 (print); **EISSN:** 1468--229X (electronic). **Subscription Rates:** $767 Institutions print or online; £435 Institutions print or online, UK; €549 Institutions print or online, Europe; $895 Institutions, other countries print and online; $921 Institutions print and online; £522 Institutions print and online; €659 Institutions print and online, Europe; $1074 Institutions, other countries print and online; $161 Individuals print and online; £97 Other countries print and online; €142 Individuals print and online, Europe. **URL:** http://onlinelibrary.wiley.com/journal/10.1111/(ISSN)1468-229X. **Mailing address:** PO Box 1354, Oxford OX4 2ZG, United Kingdom. **Remarks:** Accepts advertising. **Circ:** (Not Reported).

16487 ■ History and Theory: Studies in the Philosophy of History
Wiley-Blackwell
350 Main St.
Commerce Pl.
Malden, MA 02148-5018
Phone: (781)388-8200
Fax: (781)388-8210
Free: 800-216-2552
Journal focusing on the nature of history. **Freq:** Quarterly. **Key Personnel:** Brian C. Fay, Senior Editor; Richard T. Vann, Senior Editor; Philip Pomper, Editor; Julia Perkins, Managing Editor, phone: (860)685-3292; David Gary Shaw, Associate Editor; Ethan Kleinberg, Executive Editor. **ISSN:** 0018--2656 (print); **EISSN:** 1468--2303 (electronic). **Subscription Rates:** $373 Institutions print or online; £288 Institutions print or online; €365 Institutions print or online; $559 Institutions, Canada print or online; $448 Institutions print and online; £346 Institutions print and online; €438 Institutions print and online; $671 Free to qualified subscribers print and online; $56 Individuals print and online; £49 Other countries print and online; €73 Individuals print and online. **URL:** http://onlinelibrary.wiley.com/journal/10.1111/(ISSN)1468-2303. **Ad Rates:** BW $425. **Remarks:** Accepts advertising. **Circ:** (Not Reported).

16488 ■ HIV Medicine
Wiley-Blackwell
350 Main St.
Commerce Pl.
Malden, MA 02148-5018
Phone: (781)388-8200
Fax: (781)388-8210
Free: 800-216-2552
Publisher's E-mail: bhiva@bhiva.org
Peer-reviewed journal publishing original articles and guidelines on all aspects of HIV treatment and diagnosis. **Freq:** Monthly 10/yr. **Key Personnel:** Brian Gazzard, Editor; Jens Lundgren, Editor. **ISSN:** 1464--2662 (print); **EISSN:** 1468--1293 (electronic). **Subscription Rates:** $1922 Institutions print or online; £1042 Institutions print or online; €1322 Institutions print or online; $2241 Institutions print or online; $2307 Institutions print and online; £1251 Institutions print and online; €1587 Institutions print and online; £2690 Institutions, other countries print and online; $337 Individuals print and online; £202 Other countries print and online; €303 Individuals print and online. **URL:** http://onlinelibrary.wiley.com/journal/10.1111/(ISSN)1468-1293; http://www.bhiva.org/HIVMedicineJournal.aspx. **Remarks:** Accepts advertising. **Circ:** (Not Reported).

16489 ■ Human Communication Research
Wiley-Blackwell
350 Main St.

Commerce Pl.
Malden, MA 02148-5018
Phone: (781)388-8200
Fax: (781)388-8210
Free: 800-216-2552

Interpersonal communication journal. **Founded:** 1974. **Freq:** Quarterly 4/yr. **Print Method:** Offset. **Trim Size:** 6 x 9. **Cols./Page:** 1 and 5. **Col. Width:** 50 nonpareils. **Col. Depth:** 100 agate lines and 1 3/4 inches. **Key Personnel:** John A. Courtright, Editor-in-Chief; Prof. Howard Giles, Board Member; James E. Katz, Editor; Tamara Afifi, Board Member; Walid Afifi, Associate Editor; James P. Dillard, Editor. **ISSN:** 0360-3989 (print). **Subscription Rates:** $115 Individuals print and online; $1736 Institutions print and online; $1446 Institutions online only; $84 Individuals print + online; €93 Individuals print + online; £62 Individuals print + online; $61 Individuals; $209 Institutions; $111 Individuals print and online; €119 Individuals print and online; £80 Individuals print and online. **URL:** http://cscc.scu.edu/trends/journals/hcr.html; http://as.wiley.com/WileyCDA/WileyTitle/productCd-HCRE.html; http://hcr.oupjournals.org/; http://onlinelibrary.wiley.com/journal/10.1111/(ISSN)1468-2958. **Ad Rates:** BW $479; BW $445. **Remarks:** Advertising accepted; rates available upon request. **Circ:** Paid ‡6,200.

16490 ■ Human Resource Management Journal
Wiley-Blackwell
350 Main St.
Commerce Pl.
Malden, MA 02148-5018
Phone: (781)388-8200
Fax: (781)388-8210
Free: 800-216-2552

Peer-reviewed journal focusing on people management in the areas of economics, politics and sociology. **Freq:** Quarterly. **Key Personnel:** Adrian Wilkinson, Editor-in-Chief; Mick Marchington, Editor; David Collings, Editor-in-Chief; Scott A. Snell, Advisor; Jaap Paauwe, Editor. **ISSN:** 0954--5395 (print); **EISSN:** 1748--8583 (electronic). **Subscription Rates:** $337 Individuals print + online; $725 Institutions print + online; $604 Institutions online only; $843 Institutions, other countries print + online; $702 Institutions, other countries online only; €281 Individuals print + online; £436 Institutions print + online; £363 Institutions online only; €548 Institutions print + online; €456 Institutions online only. **URL:** http://onlinelibrary.wiley.com/journal/10.1111/(ISSN)1748-8583. **Circ:** (Not Reported).

16491 ■ Hypatia: A Journal of Feminist Philosophy
Blackwell Publishing Inc.
350 Main St.
Malden, MA 02148
Phone: (781)388-8200
Fax: (781)388-8210
Free: 800-216-2522
Publication E-mail: hypatia@uw.edu

Journal for scholarly research at the intersection of philosophy and women's studies. **Freq:** Quarterly. **Trim Size:** 6 x 9. **Key Personnel:** Sally J. Scholz, Editor. **ISSN:** 0887--5367 (print); **EISSN:** 1527--2001 (electronic). **Subscription Rates:** $60 Individuals print + online; $353 Institutions print + online; $294 Institutions print or online; £31 Individuals print + online; $50 Students print + online; $437 Institutions, other countries print + online; $364 Institutions, other countries print or online. **URL:** http://onlinelibrary.wiley.com/journal/10.1111/(ISSN)1527-2001. **Remarks:** Advertising accepted; rates available upon request. **Circ:** (Not Reported).

16492 ■ Ibis
Blackwell Publishing Inc.
350 Main St.
Malden, MA 02148
Phone: (781)388-8200
Fax: (781)388-8210
Free: 800-216-2522

Journal focusing on research activity in ornithological science. **Freq:** Quarterly. **Key Personnel:** Paul F. Donald, PhD, Editor-in-Chief; Rauri C.K. Bowie, Editor; Dan Chamberlain, Editor. **ISSN:** 0019--1019 (print); **EISSN:** 1474--919X (electronic). **Subscription Rates:** $1154 Institutions print and online; £623 Institutions print or online; €795 Institutions print and online; $1343 Institutions, other countries print or online. **URL:** http://onlinelibrary.wiley.com/journal/10.1111/(ISSN)1474-919X. **Remarks:** Accepts advertising. **Circ:** (Not Reported).

16493 ■ Immunological Reviews
Blackwell Publishing Inc.
350 Main St.
Malden, MA 02148
Phone: (781)388-8200
Fax: (781)388-8210
Free: 800-216-2522
Publisher's E-mail: journaladsusa@bos.blackwellpublishing.com

Journal aiming to a broad and continuously updated survey of advances in basic immunology and their clinical applications. **Freq:** Bimonthly. **Key Personnel:** John Cambier, Editor-in-Chief; Rafi Ahmed, Board Member. **ISSN:** 0105--2896 (print); **EISSN:** 1600--065X (electronic). **Subscription Rates:** $1630 Institutions online only; £974 Institutions online only; €1236 Institutions online only; $1905 Institutions, other countries online only; $661 Individuals online only; £367 Individuals online only - UK and Europe (non-Euro zone); €549 Individuals online only; £367 Other countries online only. **URL:** http://onlinelibrary.wiley.com/journal/10.1111/(ISSN)1600-065X. **Remarks:** Accepts advertising. **Circ:** (Not Reported).

16494 ■ Immunology
Blackwell Publishing Inc.
350 Main St.
Malden, MA 02148
Phone: (781)388-8200
Fax: (781)388-8210
Free: 800-216-2522
Publisher's E-mail: onlinecommunity@immunology.org

Journal publishing original work in all areas of immunology. **Freq:** Monthly. **Key Personnel:** Prof. Stephen Anderton, Associate Editor; Dr. Stephen Jameson, Board Member; Prof. Danny Altmann, Editor-in-Chief. **ISSN:** 0019--2805 (print); **EISSN:** 1365--2567 (electronic). **Subscription Rates:** $2626 Institutions print or online; £1422 Institutions print or online; €1807 Institutions print or online; $3064 Institutions, other countries print or online; $3152 Institutions print and online; £1707 Institutions print and online; €2169 Institutions print and online; $3677 Institutions, other countries print and online. **URL:** http://onlinelibrary.wiley.com/journal/10.1111/(ISSN)1365-2567. **Remarks:** Accepts advertising. **Circ:** 4500.

16495 ■ Indoor Air
Blackwell Publishing Inc.
350 Main St.
Malden, MA 02148
Phone: (781)388-8200
Fax: (781)388-8210
Free: 800-216-2522
Publisher's E-mail: journaladsusa@bos.blackwellpublishing.com

Freq: Bimonthly. **Key Personnel:** Jan Sundell, Editor; William Nazaroff, Editor-in-Chief; Yuguo Li, Associate Editor. **ISSN:** 0905--6947 (print); **EISSN:** 1600--0668 (electronic). **Subscription Rates:** $1052 Institutions online only; £628 Institutions online only; €798 Institutions online only; $1227 Institutions, other countries online only. **URL:** http://onlinelibrary.wiley.com/journal/10.1111/(ISSN)1600-0668. **Remarks:** Accepts advertising. **Circ:** (Not Reported).

16496 ■ Industrial Relations: A Journal of Economy and Society
Blackwell Publishing Inc.
350 Main St.
Malden, MA 02148
Phone: (781)388-8200
Fax: (781)388-8210
Free: 800-216-2522
Publisher's E-mail: journaladsusa@bos.blackwellpublishing.com

Journal focusing on corporate restructuring and downsizing, the changing employment relationship in union and nonunion settings, high performance work systems, the demographics of the workplace, and the impact of globalization on national labor markets. **Freq:** Quarterly. **Key Personnel:** Chris Riddell, Editor. **ISSN:** 0019-8676 (print). **Subscription Rates:** $68 Individuals U.S. print and online; $34 Students U.S. print and online; £68 Individuals print and online; £47 Students print and online; $427 Institutions U.S. print and online; $68 Other countries print and online; $372 Institutions U.S. print or online; £373 Institutions print and online; $706 Institutions, other countries print and online; £325 Institutions print or online. **URL:** http://as.wiley.com/WileyCDA/WileyTitle/productCd-IREL.html. **Ad Rates:** BW $464. **Remarks:** Accepts advertising. **Circ:** (Not Reported).

16497 ■ Industrial Relations Journal
Wiley-Blackwell
350 Main St.
Commerce Pl.
Malden, MA 02148-5018
Phone: (781)388-8200
Fax: (781)388-8210
Free: 800-216-2552

Peer-reviewed journal covering human resources and labor relations. **Freq:** Bimonthly. **Key Personnel:** Peter Nolan, Editor-in-Chief; Peter Prowse, Editor; Linda Dickens, Board Member; John Benson, Board Member; Kim Hoque, Board Member. **ISSN:** 0019--8692 (print); **EISSN:** 1468--2338 (electronic). **Subscription Rates:** $99 Students print and online; $131 Members BUIRA: print and online; €90 Students print and online. **URL:** http://onlinelibrary.wiley.com/journal/10.1111/(ISSN)1468-2338. **Remarks:** Accepts advertising. **Circ:** (Not Reported).

16498 ■ Influenza and Other Respiratory Viruses
Blackwell Publishing Inc.
350 Main St.
Malden, MA 02148
Phone: (781)388-8200
Fax: (781)388-8210
Free: 800-216-2522
Publisher's E-mail: journaladsusa@bos.blackwellpublishing.com

Journal covering influenza and other respiratory viruses. **Freq:** Bimonthly. **Key Personnel:** Alan W. Hampson, Editor-in-Chief; John Wood, Senior Editor. **ISSN:** 1750--2640 (print); **EISSN:** 1750--2659 (electronic). **Subscription Rates:** £420 Institutions UK (online only); $837 Institutions Americas (online only); €534 Institutions Europe (online only); $904 Institutions, other countries online only. **URL:** http://onlinelibrary.wiley.com/journal/10.1111/(ISSN)1750-2659. **Remarks:** Accepts advertising. **Circ:** (Not Reported).

16499 ■ infocus Magazine
Wiley-Blackwell
350 Main St.
Commerce Pl.
Malden, MA 02148-5018
Phone: (781)388-8200
Fax: (781)388-8210
Free: 800-216-2552

Journal providing a platform for scientists and technologists from all fields which use any type of microscope, with a focus on optical, mechanical and electronic features of design of all types of light, electron, X-ray and ion microscopes and microanalysers. **Freq:** Quarterly. **Key Personnel:** Allison Winton, Contact, phone: 44 1865 254764; Timothy F. Watson, Editor; Adrian P. Burden, Editor; Laura Kingsbury, Editor, phone: 44 1865 254767. **ISSN:** 1750--4740 (print); **EISSN:** 1365--3067 (electronic). **Subscription Rates:** $664 Institutions print only; £356 Institutions print only; $774 Institutions, other countries print only; €452 Institutions print only. **URL:** http://as.wiley.com/WileyCDA/WileyTitle/productCd-INFM.html; http://www.rms.org.uk/study-read/infocus-magazine.html. **Formerly**: Proceedings of the Royal Microscopical Society. **Ad Rates:** 4C £870. **Remarks:** Advertising accepted; rates available upon request. **Circ:** (Not Reported).

16500 ■ Information Systems Journal
Blackwell Publishing Inc.
350 Main St.
Malden, MA 02148
Phone: (781)388-8200
Fax: (781)388-8210
Free: 800-216-2522
Publisher's E-mail: journaladsusa@bos.blackwellpublishing.com

Journal focusing on the study of, and interest in, informa-

Circulation: ★ = AAM; △ or • = BPA; ♦ = CAC; ❑ = VAC; ⊕ = PO Statement; ‡ = Publisher's Report; Boldface figures = sworn; Light figures = estimated.

tion systems. **Freq:** Bimonthly. **Key Personnel:** Guy Fitzgerald, Editor, Founder; David Avison, Editor, Founder; Philip Powell, Editor-in-Chief. **ISSN:** 1350--1917 (print); **EISSN:** 1365--2575 (electronic). **Subscription Rates:** $1751 Institutions print and online; £953 Institutions print and online; €1208 Institutions print and online; $2045 Institutions, other countries print and online; $1459 Institutions print or online; £794 Institutions print or online; €1006 Institutions print or online; $1704 Institutions, other countries print or online. **URL:** http://onlinelibrary.wiley.com/journal/10.1111/(ISSN)1365-2575. **Remarks:** Accepts advertising. **Circ:** (Not Reported).

16501 ■ Insect Molecular Biology
Blackwell Publishing Inc.
350 Main St.
Malden, MA 02148
Phone: (781)388-8200
Fax: (781)388-8210
Free: 800-216-2522
Publisher's E-mail: journaladsusa@bos.blackwellpublishing.com
Journal focusing on molecular genetic techniques to the study of insects. **Freq:** Bimonthly. **Key Personnel:** Prof. Paul Eggleston, PhD, Editor; Anthony A. James, Board Member; Prof. David A. O'Brochta, PhD, Editor. **ISSN:** 0962--1075 (print); **EISSN:** 1365--2583 (electronic). **Subscription Rates:** $2912 Institutions print and online; £1576 Institutions print and online; €2001 Institutions print and online; $3394 Institutions, other countries print and online; $2426 Institutions print or online; £1313 Institutions print or online; €1667 Institutions print or online; $2828 Institutions, other countries print or online. **URL:** http://onlinelibrary.wiley.com/journal/10.1111/(ISSN)1365-2583. **Remarks:** Accepts advertising. **Circ:** (Not Reported).

16502 ■ Insect Science
Wiley-Blackwell
350 Main St.
Commerce Pl.
Malden, MA 02148-5018
Phone: (781)388-8200
Fax: (781)388-8210
Free: 800-216-2552
Journal focusing on adaptation and evolutionary biology of insects from their molecules to ecosystems including: ecology and IPM; behaviour and social biology; molecular biology; physiology, biochemistry and toxicology; genetics and development; and systematics and evolution. **Freq:** Bimonthly. **Key Personnel:** Yun Xian Zhao, Managing Editor; Mu Mu Wang, Managing Editor; Le Kang, Editor-in-Chief; D. Ren, Board Member; K.Y. Zhu, Board Member; D. Denlinger, Board Member; S.J. Simpson, Board Member. **ISSN:** 1672--9609 (print); **EISSN:** 1744--7917 (electronic). **Subscription Rates:** $752 Institutions online only; £449 Institutions online only; €571 Institutions online only; $878 Institutions, other countries online only. **URL:** http://onlinelibrary.wiley.com/journal/10.1111/(ISSN)1744-7917. **Remarks:** Advertising accepted; rates available upon request. **Circ:** (Not Reported).

16503 ■ Insect Science
Blackwell Publishing Inc.
350 Main St.
Malden, MA 02148
Phone: (781)388-8200
Fax: (781)388-8210
Free: 800-216-2522
Journal focusing on adaptation and evolutionary biology of insects from their molecules to ecosystems including: ecology and IPM; behaviour and social biology; molecular biology; physiology, biochemistry and toxicology; genetics and development; and systematics and evolution. **Freq:** Bimonthly. **Key Personnel:** Yun Xian Zhao, Managing Editor; Mu Mu Wang, Managing Editor; Le Kang, Editor-in-Chief; D. Ren, Board Member; K.Y. Zhu, Board Member; D. Denlinger, Board Member; S.J. Simpson, Board Member. **ISSN:** 1672--9609 (print); **EISSN:** 1744--7917 (electronic). **Subscription Rates:** $752 Institutions online only; £449 Institutions online only; €571 Institutions online only; $878 Institutions, other countries online only. **URL:** http://onlinelibrary.wiley.com/journal/10.1111/(ISSN)1744-7917. **Remarks:** Advertising accepted; rates available upon request. **Circ:** (Not Reported).

16504 ■ Integrative Zoology
Wiley-Blackwell
350 Main St.
Commerce Pl.
Malden, MA 02148-5018
Phone: (781)388-8200
Fax: (781)388-8210
Free: 800-216-2552
Journal covering zoology. **Freq:** Quarterly. **Print Method:** Offset. **Trim Size:** 8 1/2 x 11. **Cols./Page:** 3. **Col. Width:** 30 nonpareils. **Col. Depth:** 140 agate lines. **Key Personnel:** Zhibin Zhang, Editor-in-Chief; John Buckeridge, Editor-in-Chief. **ISSN:** 1749--4877 (print). **Subscription Rates:** $973 Institutions online only; £640 Institutions online only; $973 Institutions, other countries online only; €722 Institutions online only. **URL:** http://onlinelibrary.wiley.com/journal/10.1111/(ISSN)1749-4877. **Circ:** (Not Reported).

16505 ■ Internal Medicine Journal
Blackwell Publishing Inc.
350 Main St.
Malden, MA 02148
Phone: (781)388-8200
Fax: (781)388-8210
Free: 800-216-2522
Publisher's E-mail: racp@racp.edu.au
Journal focusing on the study and research of human disease. **Freq:** Monthly. **Key Personnel:** Jeff Szer, Editor-in-Chief; Virginia Savickis, Manager. **ISSN:** 1444--0903 (print); **EISSN:** 1445--5994 (electronic). **Subscription Rates:** $1852 Institutions print and online; £1145 Institutions print and online; €1452 Institutions print and online - Europe (non-Euro and Euro zone); A$1185 Institutions print and online - Australia and New Zealand; $2241 Institutions, other countries print and online; $1543 Institutions print and online; £954 Institutions print and online; €1210 Institutions print and online - Europe (non-Euro and Euro zone); A$1185 Institutions print and online - Australia and New Zealand; $1867 Institutions, other countries print and online; $374 Individuals print and online; £232 Individuals print and online - UK, Europe (non-Euro zone) and rest of the world; €348 Individuals print and online; A$373 Individuals print and online; Free for members. **URL:** http://onlinelibrary.wiley.com/journal/10.1111/(ISSN)1445-5994; http://www.racp.edu.au/page/publications/internal-medicine-journal/. **Remarks:** Accepts advertising. **Circ:** (Not Reported).

16506 ■ International Affairs
Blackwell Publishing Inc.
350 Main St.
Malden, MA 02148
Phone: (781)388-8200
Fax: (781)388-8210
Free: 800-216-2522
Publisher's E-mail: contact@chathamhouse.org
Journal covering international relations. Published for the Royal Institute of International Affairs, UK. **Freq:** Bimonthly January, March, May, July, September and November. **Key Personnel:** Caroline Soper, Editor; Sabine Wolf, Editor; Andrew Dorman, Editor; Katy Taylor, Assistant Editor. **ISSN:** 0020--5850 (print); **EISSN:** 1468--2346 (electronic). **Subscription Rates:** $758 Institutions online; the Americas; £454 Institutions online; UK; €577 Institutions online; Europe; $889 Institutions online; Rest of the World; $910 Institutions print and online; The Americas; £545 Institutions print and online; UK; €693 Institutions print and online; Europe; $1067 Institutions print and online; Rest of the World; $758 Institutions print; The Americas; £454 Institutions print; UK; €577 Institutions print; Europe; $889 Institutions print; Rest of the World; $89 Individuals print or online; The Americas; £82 Individuals print and online; UK; €82 Individuals print and online; Europe (non-Euro zone); £122 Individuals print and online; Europe (Euro zone); £82 Individuals print and online; Rest of the World; $60 Students print and online; The Americas; £34 Students print and online; UK and Europe (non-Europe zone); €53 Students print and online; Europe; £34 Students print and online; Rest of the World; $804 Institutions U.S. - online only; £482 Institutions U.K. - online only; €612 Institutions Europe (Euro and non-Euro zone) - online only; $943 Institutions online only; rest of the world; $965 Institutions U.S. - print and online; £579 Institutions U.K. - print and online; €735 Institutions Europe (Euro and non-Euro zone) - print and online; $1132 Institutions rest of the world - print and online; $804 Institutions U.S. - print only; £482 Institutions U.K. - print only; €612 Institutions Europe (Euro and non-Euro zone) - print only; $943 Institutions rest of the world - print only; $92 Individuals U.S. - print and online; £85 Individuals U.K. and Europe (non-Euro zone) - print and online; €126 Individuals Europe (Euro zone) - print and online; £85 Individuals rest of the world - print and online; $62 Students U.S. - print and online; £36 Students U.K. and Europe (non-Euro zone) - print and online; €55 Students Europe - print and online; £36 Students, other countries print and online; Included in membership. **URL:** http://onlinelibrary.wiley.com/journal/10.1111/(ISSN)1468-2346; http://www.chathamhouse.org/publications/ia/subscribe; http://journals.cambridge.org; http://www.chathamhouse.org/publications/ia; http://ordering.onlinelibrary.wiley.com/subs.asp?ref=1468-2346&doi=10.1111/(ISSN)1468-2346. **Remarks:** Accepts advertising. **Circ:** (Not Reported).

16507 ■ International Economic Review
Blackwell Publishing Inc.
350 Main St.
Malden, MA 02148
Phone: (781)388-8200
Fax: (781)388-8210
Free: 800-216-2522
Publisher's E-mail: journaladsusa@bos.blackwellpublishing.com
Journal focusing on modern quantitative economics. **Freq:** Quarterly. **Key Personnel:** Masaki Aoyagi, Editor; Harold L. Cole, Editor. **ISSN:** 0020-6598 (print). **Subscription Rates:** $83 Individuals print and online; $37 Students print and online; $688 Institutions print and online; $601 Institutions print or online; £436 Institutions, other countries print and online; £414 Institutions, other countries print or online; £61 Individuals print and online; £35 Students print and online. **URL:** http://www.wiley.com/bw/journal.asp?ref=0020-6598&site=1. **Ad Rates:** BW $386. **Remarks:** Accepts advertising. **Circ:** 2,300.

16508 ■ International Endodontic Journal
Blackwell Publishing Inc.
350 Main St.
Malden, MA 02148
Phone: (781)388-8200
Fax: (781)388-8210
Free: 800-216-2522
Journal focusing on endodontology. **Freq:** Monthly. **Key Personnel:** Prof. Paul M.H. Dummer, Editor-in-Chief; J.L. Gutmann, Board Member. **ISSN:** 0143--2885 (print); **EISSN:** 1365--2591 (electronic). **Subscription Rates:** $2753 Institutions print and online; £1494 Institutions print and online; €1896 Institutions print and online; $3214 Institutions, other countries print and online; $608 Individuals print and online; £331 Individuals print and online - UK, Europe (non-Euro zone) and rest of the world; €494 Individuals print and online; Included in membership. **URL:** http://onlinelibrary.wiley.com/journal/10.1111/(ISSN)1365-2591; http://www.britishendodonticsociety.org.uk/profession/member_benefits.html. **Remarks:** Accepts advertising. **Circ:** (Not Reported).

16509 ■ International Finance
Blackwell Publishing Inc.
350 Main St.
Malden, MA 02148
Phone: (781)388-8200
Fax: (781)388-8210
Free: 800-216-2522
Publisher's E-mail: journaladsusa@bos.blackwellpublishing.com
Journal focusing on bridging the gap between theory and finance. **Freq:** 3/year. **Key Personnel:** Dr. Benn Steil, Editor. **ISSN:** 1367--0271 (print); **EISSN:** 1468--2362 (electronic). **Subscription Rates:** $1338 Institutions print or online; £798 Institutions print or online; €1012 Institutions print or online; $1559 Institutions, other countries print or online; $1606 Institutions print and online; £958 Institutions print and online; €1215 Institutions print and online; $1871 Institutions, other countries print and online. **URL:** http://onlinelibrary.wiley.com/journal/10.1111/(ISSN)1468-2362. **Remarks:** Accepts advertising. **Circ:** (Not Reported).

16510 ■ International Journal of Applied Linguistics
Blackwell Publishing Inc.
350 Main St.
Malden, MA 02148
Phone: (781)388-8200
Fax: (781)388-8210
Free: 800-216-2522
Publisher's E-mail: journaladsusa@bos.blackwellpublishing.com
Journal focusing on articles that focus on the mediation between expertise about language and experience of language. **Freq:** 3/year. **Key Personnel:** Janina Brutt-Griffler, Editor; Daniel Perrin, Editor. **ISSN:** 0802--6106 (print); **EISSN:** 1473--4192 (electronic). **Subscription Rates:** $438 Institutions print or online; £264 Institutions print or online; €332 Institutions print or online; $514 Institutions print or online; $526 Institutions print and online; £317 Institutions print and online; €399 Institutions print and online; $514 Institutions, other countries print and online. **URL:** http://onlinelibrary.wiley.com/journal/10.1111/(ISSN)1473-4192. **Remarks:** Accepts advertising. **Circ:** (Not Reported).

16511 ■ International Journal of Art & Design Education
Blackwell Publishing Inc.
350 Main St.
Malden, MA 02148
Phone: (781)388-8200
Fax: (781)388-8210
Free: 800-216-2522
Publisher's E-mail: info@nsead.org
Journal publishing articles about art and design education at all levels. **Freq:** 3/year. **Key Personnel:** Dr. Sandra Hiett, Editor; Jeff Adams, Editor. **ISSN:** 1476--8062 (print); **EISSN:** 1476--8070 (electronic). **Subscription Rates:** $1954 Institutions print and online; £969 Institutions print and online; €1229 Institutions print and online; $2276 Institutions, other countries print and online; $150 Individuals print and online; £90 Individuals print and online - UK, Europe (non-euro zone) and rest of the world; €133 Individuals print and online. **URL:** http://onlinelibrary.wiley.com/journal/10.1111/(ISSN)1476-8070. **Formerly:** Journal of Arts and Design Education. **Remarks:** Advertising accepted; rates available upon request. **Circ:** 2800, 2800.

16512 ■ International Journal of Auditing
Blackwell Publishing Inc.
350 Main St.
Malden, MA 02148
Phone: (781)388-8200
Fax: (781)388-8210
Free: 800-216-2522
Publisher's E-mail: journaladsusa@bos.blackwellpublishing.com
Journal focusing on global auditing perspectives. **Freq:** 3/year. **Key Personnel:** David Hay, Editor-in-Chief; Thomas McKee, Board Member, Editor. **ISSN:** 1090--6738 (print); **EISSN:** 1099--1123 (electronic). **Subscription Rates:** $1332 Institutions print and online; £795 Institutions print and online; €1007 Institutions print and online; $1554 Institutions, other countries print and online; $97 Individuals print or online; £59 Individuals print or online - UK, Europe (non-euro zone) and rest of the world; €89 Individuals print or online. **URL:** http://onlinelibrary.wiley.com/journal/10.1111/(ISSN)1099-1123. **Remarks:** Accepts advertising. **Circ:** (Not Reported).

16513 ■ International Journal of Clinical Practice
Blackwell Publishing Inc.
350 Main St.
Malden, MA 02148
Phone: (781)388-8200
Fax: (781)388-8210
Free: 800-216-2522
Publisher's E-mail: journaladsusa@bos.blackwellpublishing.com
Journal focusing on publishes high-calibre, timely, clinically focused material for a global general medical audience, including original data from clinical investigations plus educational review and discussion of related and otherwise topical clinical concerns. **Freq:** 13/yr. **Key Personnel:** Graham Jackson, Editor; Leslie Citrome, MD, Editor-in-Chief. **ISSN:** 1368--5031 (print); **EISSN:** 1742--1241 (electronic). **Subscription Rates:** $747 Institutions online only; £306 Institutions online only; €385 Institutions online only; $871 Institutions, other countries online only; $89 Individuals online only; £57 Individuals online only - UK, Europe (non-euro zone) and rest of the world; €70 Other countries online only. **URL:** http://onlinelibrary.wiley.com/journal/10.1111/(ISSN)1742-1241. **Remarks:** Accepts advertising. **Circ:** (Not Reported).

16514 ■ International Journal of Consumer Studies
Blackwell Publishing Inc.
350 Main St.
Malden, MA 02148
Phone: (781)388-8200
Fax: (781)388-8210
Free: 800-216-2522
Publisher's E-mail: journaladsusa@bos.blackwellpublishing.com
Journal providing an international forum for academic and research papers with a focus on how consumers can enhance their security and well being. **Freq:** Bimonthly. **Key Personnel:** Katherine Hughes, Editor. **ISSN:** 1470--6423 (print); **EISSN:** 1470--6431 (electronic). **Subscription Rates:** $2081 Institutions print and online; £1131 Institutions print and online; €1434 Institutions print and online; $2428 Institutions, other countries print and online; $247 Individuals print and online; £135 Individuals print and online - UK and Europe (non-euro zone); €201 Individuals print and online; $149 Other countries print and online; $186 Students print and online; £101 Students print and online - UK and Europe (non-euro zone)'; €152 Students print and online ; £111 Students, other countries print and online. **URL:** http://onlinelibrary.wiley.com/journal/10.1111/(ISSN)1470-6431. **Remarks:** Accepts advertising. **Circ:** (Not Reported).

16515 ■ International Journal of Cosmetic Science
Blackwell Publishing Inc.
350 Main St.
Malden, MA 02148
Phone: (781)388-8200
Fax: (781)388-8210
Free: 800-216-2522
Journal presenting scientific research, both pure and applied, in: cosmetics, toiletries, perfumery and allied fields. **Freq:** Bimonthly. **Key Personnel:** Karl Lintner, Editor-in-Chief. **ISSN:** 0142--5463 (print); **EISSN:** 1468--2494 (electronic). **Subscription Rates:** $2624 Institutions print or online; £1419 Institutions print or online; €1802 Institutions print or online; $3062 Institutions, other countries print or online; $3149 Institutions print and online; £1702 Institutions print and online; €2162 Institutions print and online; $3674 Institutions, other countries print and online; Included in membership; £1418 Institutions print only; €1801 Institutions print only; $3061 Institutions, other countries print only. **URL:** http://onlinelibrary.wiley.com/journal/10.1111/(ISSN)1468-2494; http://www.scs.org.uk/content.aspx?pageid=448. **Remarks:** Advertising accepted; rates available upon request. **Circ:** (Not Reported).

16516 ■ International Journal of Dairy Technology
Blackwell Publishing Inc.
350 Main St.
Malden, MA 02148
Phone: (781)388-8200
Fax: (781)388-8210
Free: 800-216-2522
Publisher's E-mail: journaladsusa@bos.blackwellpublishing.com
Freq: Quarterly. **Key Personnel:** Dr. John Tuohy, Editor; Ian McDougall, Editor. **ISSN:** 1364--727X (print); **EISSN:** 1471--0307 (electronic). **Subscription Rates:** $1479 Institutions print and online; £801 Institutions print and online; €1016 Institutions print and online; $1731 Institutions, other countries print and online; $1232 Institutions print or online; £667 Institutions print or online; €846 Institutions print or online; $1442 Institutions, other countries print or online. **URL:** http://onlinelibrary.wiley.com/journal/10.1111/(ISSN)1471-0307/issues. **Remarks:** Accepts advertising. **Circ:** (Not Reported).

16517 ■ International Journal of Dermatology
Blackwell Publishing Inc.
350 Main St.
Malden, MA 02148
Phone: (781)388-8200
Fax: (781)388-8210
Free: 800-216-2522
Publisher's E-mail: journaladsusa@bos.blackwellpublishing.com
Journal focusing on aspects of the diagnosis and management of skin diseases. **Freq:** Monthly. **Key Personnel:** Dr. Rokea A. el-Azhary, Editor-in-Chief; Lawrence E. Gibson, Editor-in-Chief; David Mehregan, Editor; George T. Reizner, Board Member. **ISSN:** 0011-9059 (print). **Subscription Rates:** $377 Individuals print & online; $2182 Institutions print and online; $1897 Institutions print or online; £1301 Institutions print and online; £1129 Institutions print or online; £226 Individuals print and online; €338 Individuals print and online. **URL:** http://onlinelibrary.wiley.com/journal/10.1111/(ISSN)1365-4632. **Remarks:** Accepts advertising. **Circ:** (Not Reported).

16518 ■ International Journal of Economic Theory
Blackwell Publishing Inc.
350 Main St.
Malden, MA 02148
Phone: (781)388-8200
Fax: (781)388-8210
Free: 800-216-2522
Publisher's E-mail: journaladsusa@bos.blackwellpublishing.com
Journal publishing articles for international audiences in all fields of economic theory. **Freq:** Quarterly. **Key Personnel:** Kazuo Nishimura, Managing Editor; Makoto Yano, Managing Editor; Marcus Berliant, Editor; Robert Becker, Associate Editor. **ISSN:** 1742--7355 (print); **EISSN:** 1742--7363 (electronic). **Subscription Rates:** $700 Institutions print and online; £431 Institutions print and online; €549 Institutions print and online; $845 Institutions, other countries print and online; $583 Institutions print or online; £359 Institutions print or online; €457 Institutions print or online; $704 Institutions, other countries print or online; $191 Individuals print and online; £119 Individuals print and online - UK, Europe (non-euro zone) and rest of the world; €149 Other countries print and online. **URL:** http://onlinelibrary.wiley.com/journal/10.1111/(ISSN)1742-7363. **Remarks:** Advertising accepted; rates available upon request. **Circ:** (Not Reported).

16519 ■ International Journal of Experimental Pathology
Blackwell Publishing Inc.
350 Main St.
Malden, MA 02148
Phone: (781)388-8200
Fax: (781)388-8210
Free: 800-216-2522
Publisher's E-mail: journaladsusa@bos.blackwellpublishing.com
Journal reporting original experimental investigations into the biogenesis and progression of pathologic processes which afford new insights into the basic mechanisms underlying human disease. **Freq:** Bimonthly. **Key Personnel:** David R. Katz, Editor; Prof. Malcolm Alison, Associate Editor. **ISSN:** 0959--9673 (print); **EISSN:** 1365--2613 (electronic). **Subscription Rates:** $1222 Institutions online only; £667 Institutions online only; €847 Institutions online only; $1424 Institutions, other countries online only; $91 Individuals online only; £59 Individuals online only - UK, Europe (non-euro zone) and rest of the world; €73 Other countries online only. **URL:** http://onlinelibrary.wiley.com/journal/10.1111/(ISSN)1365-2613. **Remarks:** Accepts advertising. **Circ:** (Not Reported).

16520 ■ International Journal of Food Science and Technology
Blackwell Publishing Inc.
350 Main St.
Malden, MA 02148
Phone: (781)388-8200
Fax: (781)388-8210
Free: 800-216-2522
Publisher's E-mail: info@ifst.org

Circulation: ★ = AAM; △ or • = BPA; ♦ = CAC; ❑ = VAC; ⊕ = PO Statement; ‡ = Publisher's Report; Boldface figures = sworn; Light figures = estimated.

Journal publishing a wide range of subjects relating to food technology, ranging from pure research in the various sciences associated with food to practical experiments designed to improve technical processes. **Freq:** Monthly. **Key Personnel:** Prof. Charles Brennan, Editor-in-Chief; Prof. Christopher Smith, Board Member; Dr. Niall Young, Board Member. **ISSN:** 0950--5423 (print); **EISSN:** 1365--2621 (electronic). **Subscription Rates:** $4014 Institutions print and online; £2175 Institutions print and online; €2760 Institutions print and online; $4683 Institutions, other countries print and online; $3345 Institutions print or online; £1812 Institutions print or online; €2300 Institutions print or online; $3902 Institutions, other countries print or online. **URL:** http://onlinelibrary.wiley.com/journal/10.1111/(ISSN)1365-2621; http://www.ifst.org/knowledge-centre-publications/international-journal-food-science-technology. **Remarks:** Accepts advertising. **Circ:** (Not Reported).

16521 ■ International Journal of Gynecological Cancer
Blackwell Publishing Inc.
350 Main St.
Malden, MA 02148
Phone: (781)388-8200
Fax: (781)388-8210
Free: 800-216-2522
Publisher's E-mail: journaladsusa@bos.blackwellpublishing.com
Journal presenting papers from throughout the global community of researchers covering many topics related to gynecological cancer. **Freq:** Bimonthly. **Key Personnel:** Uziel Beller, MD, Editor-in-Chief; Gillian M. Thomas, MD, Associate Editor. **ISSN:** 1048-891X (print). **Subscription Rates:** $882 Individuals; $2188 Institutions; $508 Individuals in training; $1077 Other countries; $2188 Institutions, other countries; $508 Other countries in training. **URL:** http://journals.lww.com/ijgc/pages/default.aspx. **Ad Rates:** BW $471; 4C $989. **Remarks:** Accepts advertising. **Circ: 1600.**

16522 ■ International Journal of Immunogenetics: Official Journal of the British Society for Histocompatibility and Immunogenetics
Blackwell Publishing Inc.
350 Main St.
Malden, MA 02148
Phone: (781)388-8200
Fax: (781)388-8210
Free: 800-216-2522
Publisher's E-mail: journaladsusa@bos.blackwellpublishing.com
Journal publishing original contributions on the genetic control of components of the immune system and their interactions in both humans and experimental animals. **Freq:** Bimonthly. **Key Personnel:** Frederico Garrido, Board Member; Dr. P.J. Travers, Editor. **ISSN:** 1744--3121 (print); **EISSN:** 1744--313X (electronic). **Subscription Rates:** $2871 Institutions print and online; £1556 Institutions print and online; €1974 Institutions print and online; $3348 Institutions, other countries print and online; $2392 Institutions print or online; £1296 Institutions print or online; €1645 Institutions print or online; $2790 Institutions, other countries print or online. **URL:** http://onlinelibrary.wiley.com/journal/10.1111/(ISSN)1744-313X. **Remarks:** Accepts advertising. **Circ:** (Not Reported).

16523 ■ International Journal of Japanese Sociology
Blackwell Publishing Inc.
350 Main St.
Malden, MA 02148
Phone: (781)388-8200
Fax: (781)388-8210
Free: 800-216-2522
Publisher's E-mail: journaladsusa@bos.blackwellpublishing.com
Journal focusing on improving understanding of all aspects of Japanese society. **Freq:** Annual. **Key Personnel:** Daishiro Nomiya, Editor-in-Chief. **ISSN:** 0918--7545 (print); **EISSN:** 1475--6781 (electronic). **Subscription Rates:** $224 Institutions print and online; £143 Institutions print and online; €183 Institutions print and online; $275 Institutions, other countries print and online; $186 Institutions print or online; £119 Institutions print or online; €152 Institutions print or online; $229 Institutions, other countries print or online. **URL:** http://onlinelibrary.wiley.com/journal/10.1111/(ISSN)1475-6781. **Remarks:** Accepts advertising. **Circ:** (Not Reported).

16524 ■ International Journal of Laboratory Hematology
Blackwell Publishing Inc.
350 Main St.
Malden, MA 02148
Phone: (781)388-8200
Fax: (781)388-8210
Free: 800-216-2522
Publisher's E-mail: journaladsusa@bos.blackwellpublishing.com
Journal focusing on new developments, research topics and the practice of clinical and laboratory haematology. **Freq:** Bimonthly. **Key Personnel:** Dr. Steve Kitchen, Associate Editor; Szu-Hee Lee, Editor-in-Chief. **ISSN:** 1751--5521 (print); **EISSN:** 1751--553X (electronic). **Subscription Rates:** $2255 Institutions print or online; £1219 Institutions print or online; €1549 Institutions print or online; $2630 Institutions, other countries print or online; $2706 Institutions print and online; £1463 Institutions print and online; €1859 Institutions print and online; $3156 Institutions, other countries print and online. **URL:** http://onlinelibrary.wiley.com/journal/10.1111/(ISSN)1751-553X. **Formerly:** Clinical and Laboratory Haematology. **Remarks:** Accepts advertising. **Circ:** (Not Reported).

16525 ■ International Journal of Management Reviews
Blackwell Publishing Inc.
350 Main St.
Malden, MA 02148
Phone: (781)388-8200
Fax: (781)388-8210
Free: 800-216-2522
Publisher's E-mail: journaladsusa@bos.blackwellpublishing.com
Journal serving as a reference tool for business academics and doctoral students. **Freq:** Quarterly. **Key Personnel:** Prof. Oswald Jones, Editor-in-Chief; Emma Missen, Managing Editor. **ISSN:** 1460--8545 (print); **EISSN:** 1468--2370 (electronic). **Subscription Rates:** $113 Individuals print and online; £76 Individuals print and online - UK, Europe (non-euro zone) and rest of the world; €88 Other countries print and online; $67 Members print and online; £51 Members print and online - UK, Europe (non-euro zone) and rest of the world; €57 Members print and online; $57 Students print and online; £36 Students print and online - UK, Europe (non-euro zone) and rest of the world; €44 Students, other countries print and online. **URL:** http://onlinelibrary.wiley.com/journal/10.1111/(ISSN)1468-2370. **Remarks:** Accepts advertising. **Circ:** (Not Reported).

16526 ■ International Journal of Mental Health Nursing: The Official Journal of the Australian College of Mental Health Nurses Inc.
Blackwell Publishing Inc.
350 Main St.
Malden, MA 02148
Phone: (781)388-8200
Fax: (781)388-8210
Free: 800-216-2522
Publisher's E-mail: journaladsusa@bos.blackwellpublishing.com
Journal focusing on current trends and developments in mental health practice and research. **Freq:** Bimonthly. **Key Personnel:** Kim Usher, Editor-in-Chief. **ISSN:** 1445--8330 (print); **EISSN:** 1447--0349 (electronic). **Subscription Rates:** $838 Institutions print and online; £514 Institutions print and online; €652 Institutions print and online; A$657 Institutions print and online - Australia and New Zealand; $1005 Institutions, other countries print and online; $195 Individuals print and online; £121 Individuals print and online - UK, Europe (non-euro zone) and rest of the world; €180 Individuals print and online; A$200 Individuals print and online - Australia and New Zealand. **URL:** http://onlinelibrary.wiley.com/journal/10.1111/(ISSN)1447-0349. **Remarks:** Accepts advertising. **Circ:** (Not Reported).

16527 ■ International Journal of Nautical Archaeology
Blackwell Publishing Inc.
350 Main St.
Malden, MA 02148
Phone: (781)388-8200
Fax: (781)388-8210
Free: 800-216-2522
Publisher's E-mail: journaladsusa@bos.blackwellpublishing.com
Journal covering all aspects of nautical archaeological research, exploring humankind's use and development of water transport from prehistory to the recent past. **Freq:** Semiannual. **Key Personnel:** Miranda Richardson, Editor. **ISSN:** 1057-2414 (print). **Subscription Rates:** $123 Individuals print & online; $860 Institutions print & online; $747 Institutions print or online; £602 Institutions print and online; £523 Institutions print or online; £81 Individuals print and online. **URL:** http://onlinelibrary.wiley.com/journal/10.1111/(ISSN)1095-9270. **Remarks:** Accepts advertising. **Circ:** (Not Reported).

16528 ■ International Journal of Nursing Practice
Blackwell Publishing Inc.
350 Main St.
Malden, MA 02148
Phone: (781)388-8200
Fax: (781)388-8210
Free: 800-216-2522
Publisher's E-mail: journaladsusa@bos.blackwellpublishing.com
Journal publishing articles about advances the international understanding and development of nursing, both as a profession and as an academic discipline. **Freq:** Bimonthly. **Key Personnel:** Alan Pearson, Editor-in-Chief. **ISSN:** 1322--7114 (print); **EISSN:** 1440--172X (electronic). **Subscription Rates:** $1233 Institutions, Canada online only; £763 Institutions online only; €969 Institutions online only; A$998 Institutions online only, Australia & New Zealand; 1494 Dh Institutions, other countries online only. **URL:** http://onlinelibrary.wiley.com/journal/10.1111/(ISSN)1440-172X. **Remarks:** Accepts advertising. **Circ:** (Not Reported).

16529 ■ International Journal of Nursing Terminologies and Classifications
Blackwell Publishing Inc.
350 Main St.
Malden, MA 02148
Phone: (781)388-8200
Fax: (781)388-8210
Free: 800-216-2522
Journal publishing articles reflecting knowledge development related to nursing terminology and classification for diagnoses, interventions, and outcomes; use of nursing language in practice and education; the processes of clinical judgment and knowledge presentation; and the use of nursing language and classification in research, practice, and education. **Freq:** Quarterly. **Key Personnel:** Jane Flanagan, Editor; Heather Herdman, Chief Executive Officer, Executive Director; Shigemi Kamitsuru, Chairman; Takako Egawa, PhD, Board Member. **ISSN:** 2047--3087 (print); **EISSN:** 2047--3095 (electronic). **Subscription Rates:** $274 Institutions online only; £181 Institutions online only; €229 Institutions online only; $349 Institutions, other countries online only; Included in membership; $291 Institutions online only; £192 Institutions online only; €243 Institutions Europe: online only. **URL:** http://onlinelibrary.wiley.com/journal/10.1111/(ISSN)2047-3095/issues; http://www.nanda.org/nanda-international-journal-of-nursing-knowledge.html. **Formerly:** International Journal of Nursing Terminologies and Classification. **Remarks:** Advertising accepted; rates available upon request. **Circ:** (Not Reported).

16530 ■ International Journal of Older People Nursing
Wiley-Blackwell
350 Main St.
Commerce Pl.
Malden, MA 02148-5018
Phone: (781)388-8200
Fax: (781)388-8210
Free: 800-216-2552
Journal covering gerontological nursing. **Freq:** Quarterly. **Print Method:** Offset. **Cols./Page:** 4. **Col. Width:** 2 1/4 inches. **Col. Depth:** 16 inches. **Key Personnel:** Jackie Bridges, Board Member; Brendan McCormack, Board Member; Tanya McCance, Board Member; Jan Dewing, Board Member; Sarah H. Kagan, Editor-in-Chief. **ISSN:** 1748--3735 (print); **EISSN:** 1748--3743 (electronic). **Subscription Rates:** $594 Individuals online; £324

Institutions online; €411 Institutions online; $688 Institutions, other countries online; $131 Individuals online; £86 Individuals online; €99 Individuals online; £86 Other countries online. **URL:** http://onlinelibrary.wiley.com/journal/10.1111/(ISSN)1748-3743. **Remarks:** Accepts advertising. **Circ:** (Not Reported).

16531 ■ International Journal of Paediatric Dentistry
Blackwell Publishing Inc.
350 Main St.
Malden, MA 02148
Phone: (781)388-8200
Fax: (781)388-8210
Free: 800-216-2522
Publisher's E-mail: journaladsusa@bos.blackwellpublishing.com
Journal publishing papers on all aspects of paediatric dentistry: preventive, restorative and orthodontic treatment for children, behavioural management, and aspects of community dentistry related to children. **Freq:** Bimonthly. **Key Personnel:** Chris Deery, Editor-in-Chief. **ISSN:** 0960--7439 (print); **EISSN:** 1365--263X (electronic). **Subscription Rates:** $2103 Institutions print and online; £1143 Institutions print and online; €1451 Institutions print and online; $2453 Institutions, other countries print and online; $1752 Institutions print or online; £952 Institutions print or online; €1209 Institutions print or online; $2044 Institutions, other countries print or online. **URL:** http://onlinelibrary.wiley.com/journal/10.1111/(ISSN)1365-263X. **Remarks:** Accepts advertising. **Circ:** (Not Reported).

16532 ■ International Journal of Selection and Assessment
Blackwell Publishing Inc.
350 Main St.
Malden, MA 02148
Phone: (781)388-8200
Fax: (781)388-8210
Free: 800-216-2522
Publisher's E-mail: journaladsusa@bos.blackwellpublishing.com
Journal publishing articles related to all aspects of personnel selection, staffing, and assessment in organizations. **Freq:** Quarterly. **Key Personnel:** Jesus F. Salgado, Board Member, Editor; Deniz S. Ones, Board Member, Editor; Chockalingam Viswesvaran, Editor. **ISSN:** 0965--075X (print); **EISSN:** 1468--2389 (electronic). **Subscription Rates:** $1391 Institutions print and online; £832 Institutions print and online; €1053 Institutions print and online; $1623 Institutions, other countries print and online; $144 Individuals print and online; £89 Individuals print and online - UK, Europe (non-euro zone) and rest of the world; €131 Other countries print and online; $113 Students print and online; £67 Students print and online - UK, Europe (non-euro zone) and rest of the world; €100 Students print and online. **URL:** http://onlinelibrary.wiley.com/journal/10.1111/(ISSN)1468-2389. **Remarks:** Accepts advertising. **Circ:** (Not Reported).

16533 ■ International Journal of Social Welfare
Blackwell Publishing Inc.
350 Main St.
Malden, MA 02148
Phone: (781)388-8200
Fax: (781)388-8210
Free: 800-216-2522
Publisher's E-mail: journaladsusa@bos.blackwellpublishing.com
Journal publishing articles about major social forces of a global nature such as demographic trends, migration patterns and the globalization of the economy are reshaping social welfare policies and social work practices the world over. **Freq:** Quarterly. **Key Personnel:** Ake Bergmark, Editor-in-Chief; Sven Hessle, Editor; Noella Bickham, Managing Editor. **ISSN:** 1369--6866 (print); **EISSN:** 1468--2397 (electronic). **Subscription Rates:** $1076 Institutions online only; £644 Institutions online only; €818 Institutions online only; $1260 Institutions, other countries online only; $106 Individuals online only; £64 Individuals online only - UK, Europe (non-euro zone) and rest of the world; €96 Other countries online only. **URL:** http://onlinelibrary.wiley.com/journal/10.1111/(ISSN)1468-2397/issues. **Remarks:** Accepts advertising. **Circ:** (Not Reported).

16534 ■ International Journal of Systematic Theology
Blackwell Publishing Inc.
350 Main St.
Malden, MA 02148
Phone: (781)388-8200
Fax: (781)388-8210
Free: 800-216-2522
Publisher's E-mail: journaladsusa@bos.blackwellpublishing.com
Journal publishing articles and reviews of books on constructive Christian theology. **Freq:** Quarterly. **Key Personnel:** Prof. John Webster, Editor; Dr. Paul T. Nimmo, Editor. **ISSN:** 1463--1652 (print); **EISSN:** 1468--2400 (electronic). **Subscription Rates:** $963 Institutions print and online; £576 Institutions print and online; €729 Institutions print and online; A$470 Institutions print and online - developing world; $1124 Institutions, other countries print and online; $111 Individuals print and online; £65 Individuals print and online - UK, Europe (non-euro zone) and rest of the world; €98 Individuals print and online; $54 Students print and online; £27 Students print and online - UK and Europe (non-euro zone); €32 Students print and online; $54 Other countries print and online. **URL:** http://onlinelibrary.wiley.com/journal/10.1111/(ISSN)1468-2400. **Remarks:** Accepts advertising. **Circ:** (Not Reported).

16535 ■ International Journal of Training and Development
Blackwell Publishing Inc.
350 Main St.
Malden, MA 02148
Phone: (781)388-8200
Fax: (781)388-8210
Free: 800-216-2522
Publisher's E-mail: journaladsusa@bos.blackwellpublishing.com
Journal focusing on improving national and corporate economic performance. **Freq:** Quarterly. **Key Personnel:** Paul Lewis, Editor-in-Chief; William J. Rothwell, Editor; Linda Miller, Editor. **ISSN:** 1360--3736 (print); **EISSN:** 1468--2419 (electronic). **Subscription Rates:** $1308 Institutions print and online; £779 Institutions print and online; €987 Institutions print and online; $1522 Institutions, other countries print and online; $166 Individuals print and online; £100 Individuals print and online - UK, Europe (non-euro zone) and rest of the world; €150 Individuals print and online; $90 Students print and online; £56 Students print and online - UK, Europe (non-euro zone) and rest of the world; €82 Students, other countries print and online. **URL:** http://onlinelibrary.wiley.com/journal/10.1111/(ISSN)1468-2419. **Remarks:** Accepts advertising. **Circ:** (Not Reported).

16536 ■ International Journal of Urban and Regional Research
Wiley-Blackwell
350 Main St.
Commerce Pl.
Malden, MA 02148-5018
Phone: (781)388-8200
Fax: (781)388-8210
Free: 800-216-2552
Publication on urban and regional development. Presents comparative research; examines the social basis of approaches to planning and state intervention; demonstrates links between sociology, political economy, history, social anthropology, demography, and geography. Analyzes diversity of patterns of urbanization worldwide. Events and Debates section covers current policy developments, citizen initiatives, and alternative solutions. Includes reports on research trends, initiatives, and conference reports. **Freq:** Bimonthly. **Key Personnel:** Roger Keil, Advisor, Board Member; Talja Blokland, Advisor; Marisol Garcia, Advisor, Board Member; Jeremy Seekings, Advisor; Neil Brenner, Board Member; Takashi Machimura, Advisor, Board Member; Terry McBride, Managing Editor; Matthew Gandy, Editor. **ISSN:** 0309--1317 (print); **EISSN:** 1468--2427 (electronic). **Subscription Rates:** $1158 Institutions print or online - USA; £618 Institutions print or online - UK; €787 Institutions print or online - Europe; $1301 Institutions, other countries print or online; $1390 Institutions print and online - USA; £742 Institutions print and online - UK; €945 Institutions print and online - Europe; $1562 Institutions, other countries print and online; $101 Individuals print and online - USA; £97 Individuals print and online - UK; €142 Individuals print and online - Europe; £97 Other countries print and online; $50 Students print and online - USA; £31 Students print and online - UK, Europe (non-euro zone) and rest of the world; €51 Students print and online - Europe. **URL:** http://onlinelibrary.wiley.com/journal/10.1111/(ISSN)1468-2427. **Remarks:** Accepts advertising. **Circ:** (Not Reported).

16537 ■ International Journal of Urban and Regional Research
Blackwell Publishing Inc.
350 Main St.
Malden, MA 02148
Phone: (781)388-8200
Fax: (781)388-8210
Free: 800-216-2522
Publication on urban and regional development. Presents comparative research; examines the social basis of approaches to planning and state intervention; demonstrates links between sociology, political economy, history, social anthropology, demography, and geography. Analyzes diversity of patterns of urbanization worldwide. Events and Debates section covers current policy developments, citizen initiatives, and alternative solutions. Includes reports on research trends, initiatives, and conference reports. **Freq:** Bimonthly. **Key Personnel:** Roger Keil, Advisor, Board Member; Talja Blokland, Advisor; Marisol Garcia, Advisor, Board Member; Jeremy Seekings, Advisor; Neil Brenner, Board Member; Takashi Machimura, Advisor, Board Member; Terry McBride, Managing Editor; Matthew Gandy, Editor. **ISSN:** 0309--1317 (print); **EISSN:** 1468--2427 (electronic). **Subscription Rates:** $1158 Institutions print or online - USA; £618 Institutions print or online - UK; €787 Institutions print or online - Europe; $1301 Institutions, other countries print or online; $1390 Institutions print and online - USA; £742 Institutions print and online - UK; €945 Institutions print and online - Europe; $1562 Institutions, other countries print and online; $101 Individuals print and online - USA; £97 Individuals print and online - UK; €142 Individuals print and online - Europe; £97 Other countries print and online; $50 Students print and online - USA; £31 Students print and online - UK, Europe (non-euro zone) and rest of the world; €51 Students print and online - Europe. **URL:** http://onlinelibrary.wiley.com/journal/10.1111/(ISSN)1468-2427. **Remarks:** Accepts advertising. **Circ:** (Not Reported).

16538 ■ International Journal of Urological Nursing
Blackwell Publishing Inc.
350 Main St.
Malden, MA 02148
Phone: (781)388-8200
Fax: (781)388-8210
Free: 800-216-2522
Publisher's E-mail: journaladsusa@bos.blackwellpublishing.com
Peer-reviewed journal containing articles related to urological disorders. **Freq:** 3/year. **Key Personnel:** Rachel Busuttil Leaver, Editor; Jerome Marley, Associate Editor. **ISSN:** 1749--7701 (print); **EISSN:** 1749--771x (electronic). **Subscription Rates:** $448 Institutions; £245 Institutions UK; €309 Institutions Europe; $522 Institutions Australia and New Zealand; $522 Institutions, other countries; $538 Institutions print and online; £294 Institutions print and online, UK; €371 Institutions print and online, Europe; $627 Institutions print and online, Australia, New Zealand and other countries; $164 Individuals print and online; £245 Individuals print and online, UK; €309 Individuals print and online, Europe; $522 Individuals print and online, Australia, New Zealand and other countries. **URL:** http://onlinelibrary.wiley.com/journal/10.1111/(ISSN)1749-771X. **Circ:** (Not Reported).

16539 ■ International Journal of Urology
Blackwell Publishing Inc.
350 Main St.
Malden, MA 02148
Phone: (781)388-8200
Fax: (781)388-8210
Free: 800-216-2522
Publisher's E-mail: office@urol.or.jp

Circulation: ★ = AAM; △ or • = BPA; ♦ = CAC; ❑ = VAC; ⊕ = PO Statement; ‡ = Publisher's Report; Boldface figures = sworn; Light figures = estimated.

Journal focusing on urology. **Freq:** Monthly. **Key Personnel:** Mototsugu Oya, Editor; Prof. Akihiko Okuyama, Editor; Yoshio Aso, Editor; Haruki Kume, Board Member; Norio Nonomura, Editor-in-Chief. **ISSN:** 0919--8172 (print); **EISSN:** 1442--2042 (electronic). **Subscription Rates:** $2145 Institutions print and online; £1325 Institutions print and online; €1683 Institutions print and online; $2594 Institutions, other countries print and online; $1787 Institutions print or online; £1104 Institutions print or online; €1402 Institutions print or online; $2161 Institutions, other countries print or online; $20 Members online only. **URL:** http://onlinelibrary.wiley.com/journal/10.1111/(ISSN)1442-2042; http://www.urol.or.jp/en/journal.html. **Remarks:** Advertising accepted; rates available upon request. **Circ:** (Not Reported).

16540 ■ International Labour Review
Wiley-Blackwell
350 Main St.
Commerce Pl.
Malden, MA 02148-5018
Phone: (781)388-8200
Fax: (781)388-8210
Free: 800-216-2552
Publisher's E-mail: ilo@ilo.org
Publication covering human resources and labor relations. **Freq:** Quarterly. **Key Personnel:** Mark Lansky, Managing Editor; Marie-Christine Nallet, Editor. **ISSN:** 0020-7780 (print); **EISSN:** 1564-913X (electronic). **Subscription Rates:** £235 Institutions print and online; $431 Institutions print and online; €298 Institutions print and online; €102 Individuals; £68 Individuals; $123 Individuals. **URL:** http://www.ilo.org/public/english/revue/; http://onlinelibrary.wiley.com/journal/10.1111/(ISSN)1564-913X. **Circ:** (Not Reported).

16541 ■ International Migration
Blackwell Publishing Inc.
350 Main St.
Malden, MA 02148
Phone: (781)388-8200
Fax: (781)388-8210
Free: 800-216-2522
Publisher's E-mail: journaladsusa@bos.blackwellpublishing.com
Journal focusing on migration issues as analyzed by demographers, economists, sociologists, political scientists and other social scientists from all parts of the world. **Freq:** Bimonthly. **Key Personnel:** Dr. Howard Duncan, Editor. **ISSN:** 0020--7985 (print); **EISSN:** 1468--2435 (electronic). **Subscription Rates:** $582 Institutions online only; £349 Institutions online only; €443 Institutions online only; $390 Institutions online only, developing world; $682 Institutions, other countries online only; $60 Individuals online only; £39 Individuals online only - UK, Europe (non-euro zone) and rest of the world; €59 Individuals online only. **URL:** http://onlinelibrary.wiley.com/journal/10.1111/(ISSN)1468-2435. **Remarks:** Accepts advertising. **Circ:** (Not Reported).

16542 ■ International Nursing Review
Blackwell Publishing Inc.
350 Main St.
Malden, MA 02148
Phone: (781)388-8200
Fax: (781)388-8210
Free: 800-216-2522
Publisher's E-mail: icn@icn.ch
Journal focusing on current concerns and issues of modern day nursing and health care from an international perspective. **Freq:** Quarterly. **Key Personnel:** James Buchan, Board Member; Sue Turale, Editor. **ISSN:** 0020--8132 (print); **EISSN:** 1466--7657 (electronic). **Subscription Rates:** $606 Institutions print and online; £329 Institutions print and online; €417 Institutions print and online; $708 Institutions, other countries print and online; $141 Individuals print and online; £79 Individuals print and online - UK, Europe (non-euro zone) and rest of the world; €115 Individuals print and online; $505 Institutions print only or online only; $82 Members print and online; American Nurses Association and Canadian Nurses Association. **URL:** http://onlinelibrary.wiley.com/journal/10.1111/(ISSN)1466-7657; http://www.icn.ch/publications/international-nursing-review-inr. **Remarks:** Accepts advertising. **Circ:** (Not Reported).

16543 ■ International Review of Finance
Blackwell Publishing Inc.
350 Main St.
Malden, MA 02148
Phone: (781)388-8200
Fax: (781)388-8210
Free: 800-216-2522
Publisher's E-mail: journaladsusa@bos.blackwellpublishing.com
Journal focusing on research on all aspects of financial economics, with a particular emphasis on the financial markets and institutions of emerging markets. **Freq:** Quarterly. **Key Personnel:** Naifu Chen, Advisor; Takao Kobayashi, Advisor; Bruce D. Grundy, Advisor; Sheridan Titman, Advisor; Henry Cao, Editor. **ISSN:** 1369--412X (print). **Subscription Rates:** $748 Institutions print and online; £496 Institutions print and online; €628 Institutions print and online; $962 Institutions, other countries print and online; $623 Institutions print or online; £413 Institutions print or online; €523 Institutions print or online; $801 Institutions, other countries print or online. **URL:** http://onlinelibrary.wiley.com/journal/10.1111/(ISSN)1468-2443. **Remarks:** Accepts advertising. **Circ:** (Not Reported).

16544 ■ International Social Security Review
Blackwell Publishing Inc.
350 Main St.
Malden, MA 02148
Phone: (781)388-8200
Fax: (781)388-8210
Free: 800-216-2522
Publisher's E-mail: journaladsusa@bos.blackwellpublishing.com
Journal publishing articles on social security issues around the world. **Freq:** Quarterly. **Key Personnel:** Roddy McKinnon, Editor. **ISSN:** 0020-871X (print). **Subscription Rates:** $77 Individuals print and online; $409 Institutions print and online; $355 Institutions print or online; €71 Individuals print and online; £49 Individuals print and online; £244 Institutions print and online; £212 Institutions print or online. **URL:** http://onlinelibrary.wiley.com/journal/10.1111/(ISSN)1468-246X. **Remarks:** Accepts advertising. **Circ:** (Not Reported).

16545 ■ International Studies Quarterly
Blackwell Publishing Inc.
350 Main St.
Malden, MA 02148
Phone: (781)388-8200
Fax: (781)388-8210
Free: 800-216-2522
Publisher's E-mail: journaladsusa@bos.blackwellpublishing.com
Freq: Quarterly. **Key Personnel:** Daniel H. Nexon, Editor; William R. Thompson, Board Member, Editor; Brett Ashley Leeds, Board Member. **ISSN:** 0020--8833 (print); **EISSN:** 1468--2478 (electronic). **URL:** http://www.isanet.org/Publications/ISQ. **Ad Rates:** BW $550. **Remarks:** Accepts advertising. **Circ:** (Not Reported).

16546 ■ International Transactions in Operational Research
Blackwell Publishing Inc.
350 Main St.
Malden, MA 02148
Phone: (781)388-8200
Fax: (781)388-8210
Free: 800-216-2522
Publisher's E-mail: journaladsusa@bos.blackwellpublishing.com
Journal focusing on the practice of Operational Research (OR) and Management Science internationally. **Freq:** Bimonthly. **Key Personnel:** Peter Bell, Board Member; Vicky Mabin, Board Member; Celso Ribeiro, Editor. **ISSN:** 0969--6016 (print); **EISSN:** 1475--3995 (electronic). **Subscription Rates:** $2297 Institutions print and online; £1367 Institutions print and online; €1737 Institutions print and online; $1047 Institutions print and online, developing world; $2679 Institutions, other countries print and online; $159 Individuals print and online; £96 Individuals print and online - UK, Europe (non-euro zone) and rest of the world; €141 Individuals print and online. **URL:** http://onlinelibrary.wiley.com/journal/10.1111/(ISSN)1475-3995. **Remarks:** Accepts advertising. **Circ:** (Not Reported).

16547 ■ International Wound Journal
Blackwell Publishing Inc.
350 Main St.
Malden, MA 02148
Phone: (781)388-8200
Fax: (781)388-8210
Free: 800-216-2522
Publisher's E-mail: journaladsusa@bos.blackwellpublishing.com
Journal focusing on providing the best quality information, research data and education on all aspects of wounds and wound healing. **Freq:** Bimonthly. **Key Personnel:** Prof. Keith Harding, Editor-in-Chief; Dr. Douglas Queen, Editor. **ISSN:** 1742--4801 (print); **EISSN:** 1742--481X (electronic). **Subscription Rates:** $869 Institutions online only; £471 Institutions online only; €596 Institutions online only; $1014 Institutions, other countries online only; $174 Individuals online only; £95 Individuals online only - UK and Europe (non-euro zone); €141 Individuals online only; £106 Other countries online only. **URL:** http://onlinelibrary.wiley.com/journal/10.1111/(ISSN)1742-481X. **Remarks:** Accepts advertising. **Circ:** (Not Reported).

16548 ■ Invertebrate Biology
Blackwell Publishing Inc.
350 Main St.
Malden, MA 02148
Phone: (781)388-8200
Fax: (781)388-8210
Free: 800-216-2522
Scientific journal covering the biology of invertebrate animals and research in the fields of cell and molecular biology, ecology, physiology, systematics, genetics, biogeography and behavior. **Freq:** Quarterly. **Trim Size:** 8 1/2 x 11. **Key Personnel:** Bruno Pernet, Editor-in-Chief; Maria Byrne, Board Member. **ISSN:** 1077--8306 (print); **EISSN:** 1744--7410 (electronic). **Subscription Rates:** $364 Institutions; £221 Institutions UK; €280 Institutions Europe; $430 Institutions, other countries; $437 Institutions print and online; £266 Institutions print and online, UK; €336 Institutions print and online, Europe; $516 Institutions, other countries print and online. **URL:** http://amicros.org/?page_id=2; http://onlinelibrary.wiley.com/journal/10.1111/(ISSN)1744-7410. **Formerly:** Transactions of the American Microscopial Society. **Remarks:** Advertising not accepted. **Circ:** (Not Reported).

16549 ■ The Island Arc
Wiley-Blackwell
350 Main St.
Commerce Pl.
Malden, MA 02148-5018
Phone: (781)388-8200
Fax: (781)388-8210
Free: 800-216-2552
Journal focusing on earth science research activities in the western Pacific rim and Asia, as well as in other parts of the world. **Freq:** Quarterly. **Key Personnel:** Tetsuji Muto, Editor-in-Chief; Susumu Umino, Editor-in-Chief. **ISSN:** 1038-4871 (print); **EISSN:** 1440-1738 (electronic). **Subscription Rates:** £933 Institutions print and online; $1512 Institutions print and online; $1829 Institutions print and online, rest of the world. **URL:** http://as.wiley.com/WileyCDA/WileyTitle/productCd-IAR.html. **Remarks:** Accepts advertising. **Circ:** (Not Reported).

16550 ■ Japan Journal of Nursing Science
Wiley-Blackwell
350 Main St.
Commerce Pl.
Malden, MA 02148-5018
Phone: (781)388-8200
Fax: (781)388-8210
Free: 800-216-2552
Journal focusing on health care and nursing. Official English language journal of the Japan Academy of Nursing Science. **Freq:** Semiannual. **Key Personnel:** William L. Holzemer, Editor-in-Chief; Misuzu F. Gregg, Associate Editor. **ISSN:** 1742--7932 (print); **EISSN:** 1742--7924 (electronic). **Subscription Rates:** $360 Institutions online only; £220 Institutions online only; €280 Institutions online only; $431 Institutions, other countries online only; $67 Individuals online only; £36 Individuals online only; €54 Individuals online only; £76 Other countries Japan, online only; £36 Other countries online only. **URL:** http://onlinelibrary.wiley.com/journal/10.1111/

(ISSN)1742-7924. **Remarks:** Accepts advertising. **Circ:** (Not Reported).

16551 ■ The Japanese Economic Review
Wiley-Blackwell
350 Main St.
Commerce Pl.
Malden, MA 02148-5018
Phone: (781)388-8200
Fax: (781)388-8210
Free: 800-216-2552
Journal focusing on economic analysis across the whole field of economics from researchers both within and outside Japan. **Freq:** Quarterly. **Key Personnel:** Fumio Hayashi, Editor; Hitoshi Matsushima, Editor. **ISSN:** 1352--4739 (print); **EISSN:** 1468--5876 (electronic). **Subscription Rates:** $336 Institutions print or online; £235 Institutions print or online; €299 Institutions print or online; $202 Institutions print or online; $471 Institutions, other countries print or online; $403 Institutions print and online; £282 Institutions print and online; €359 Institutions print and online; $242 Institutions print and online; $565 Institutions, other countries print and online. **URL:** http://onlinelibrary.wiley.com/journal/10.1111/(ISSN)1468-5876. **Formerly:** The Economic Studies Quarterly. **Ad Rates:** BW $260. **Remarks:** Accepts advertising. **Circ:** (Not Reported).

16552 ■ Japanese Psychological Research
Wiley-Blackwell
350 Main St.
Commerce Pl.
Malden, MA 02148-5018
Phone: (781)388-8200
Fax: (781)388-8210
Free: 800-216-2552
Journal focusing on analysis of problem-orientated research in the field of psychology. **Freq:** Quarterly. **Key Personnel:** Prof. Jun-ichi Abe, Editor; Prof. Makoto Miyatani, Executive Editor. **ISSN:** 0021--5368 (print); **EISSN:** 1468--5884 (electronic). **URL:** http://onlinelibrary.wiley.com/journal/10.1111/(ISSN)1468-5884. **Remarks:** Accepts advertising. **Circ:** (Not Reported).

16553 ■ JCMS: Journal of Common Market Studies
Wiley-Blackwell
350 Main St.
Commerce Pl.
Malden, MA 02148-5018
Phone: (781)388-8200
Fax: (781)388-8210
Free: 800-216-2552
Publisher's E-mail: journaladsusa@bos.blackwellpublishing.com
Forum for the development and evaluation of theoretical and empirical issues in the politics and economics of European integration, focusing on developments within the EU. **Freq:** 5/year. **Key Personnel:** Michelle Cini, Editor; Amy Verdun, Editor; Iain Begg, Board Member. **ISSN:** 0021--9886 (print); **EISSN:** 1468--5965 (electronic). **Subscription Rates:** $1952 Institutions print or online; £968 Institutions print or online; €1227 Institutions print or online; $2278 Institutions, other countries print or online; $2343 Institutions print and online; £1162 Institutions print and online; €1473 Institutions print and online; $2734 Institutions, other countries print and online; $314 Individuals print and online; £157 Individuals print and online; €233 Individuals print and online; £188 Other countries print and online. **URL:** http://onlinelibrary.wiley.com/journal/10.1111/(ISSN)1468-5965. **Ad Rates:** BW $275. **Remarks:** Accepts advertising. **Circ:** (Not Reported).

16554 ■ Journal of Advanced Nursing
Wiley-Blackwell
350 Main St.
Commerce Pl.
Malden, MA 02148-5018
Phone: (781)388-8200
Fax: (781)388-8210
Free: 800-216-2552
Peer-reviewed scientific journal featuring research and scholarship of contemporary relevance for the advancement of evidence-based nursing, midwifery, and healthcare. **Freq:** Monthly. **Key Personnel:** Jane Noyes, Editor; Roger Watson, Editor-in-Chief; Di Sinclair, Managing Editor. **ISSN:** 0309--2402 (print); **EISSN:** 1365--2648 (electronic). **Subscription Rates:** $3501 Institutions print or online; $4202 Institutions print and online; $401 Individuals online only; $420 Individuals print and online. **URL:** http://onlinelibrary.wiley.com/journal/10.1111/(ISSN)1365-2648. **Remarks:** Accepts advertising. **Circ:** (Not Reported).

16555 ■ Journal of Advanced Transportation
Wiley-Blackwell
350 Main St.
Commerce Pl.
Malden, MA 02148-5018
Phone: (781)388-8200
Fax: (781)388-8210
Free: 800-216-2552
Peer-reviewed journal covering transportation technology and engineering. **Freq:** Quarterly. **Key Personnel:** Jacek Zak, Editor; S.C. Wirasinghe, Editor-in-Chief; William H.K. Lam, Editor-in-Chief. **ISSN:** 0197--6729 (print); **EISSN:** 2042--3195 (electronic). **Subscription Rates:** £549 Institutions print & online; €646 Institutions print & online; $897 Institutions, other countries print & online. **URL:** http://onlinelibrary.wiley.com/journal/10.1002/(ISSN)2042-3195. **Remarks:** Advertising not accepted. **Circ:** Combined 355.

16556 ■ Journal of Agrarian Change
Wiley-Blackwell
350 Main St.
Commerce Pl.
Malden, MA 02148-5018
Phone: (781)388-8200
Fax: (781)388-8210
Free: 800-216-2552
Journal focusing on agrarian political economy. **Freq:** Quarterly. **Key Personnel:** Deborah Johnston, Editor; Cristobal Kay, Editor. **ISSN:** 1471--0358 (print); **EISSN:** 1471--0366 (electronic). **Subscription Rates:** $899 Institutions online only; £537 Institutions online only; €680 Institutions online only; $288 Institutions online only, Bangladesh and Pakistan; $397 Institutions online only; $1046 Institutions, other countries online only. **URL:** http://onlinelibrary.wiley.com/journal/10.1111/(ISSN)1471-0366. **Remarks:** Accepts advertising. **Circ:** (Not Reported).

16557 ■ Journal of Agronomy and Crop Science
Wiley-Blackwell
350 Main St.
Commerce Pl.
Malden, MA 02148-5018
Phone: (781)388-8200
Fax: (781)388-8210
Free: 800-216-2552
Journal focusing on the field of general and special science of yield and quality of field and fodder crops. **Freq:** Bimonthly. **Key Personnel:** Dr. J.M. Greef, Editor-in-Chief. **ISSN:** 0931--2250 (print); **EISSN:** 1439--037X (electronic). **Subscription Rates:** $2341 Institutions print or online; £1268 Institutions print or online; €1612 Institutions print or online; $2731 Institutions print or online; $2810 Institutions print and online; £1522 Institutions print and online; €1935 Institutions print and online; $3278 Institutions, other countries print and online; $166 Individuals print and online; £99 Other countries print and online; €147 Individuals print and online. **URL:** http://onlinelibrary.wiley.com/journal/10.1111/(ISSN)1439-037X. **Remarks:** Accepts advertising. **Circ:** (Not Reported).

16558 ■ Journal of the American Geriatrics Society
Blackwell Publishing Inc.
350 Main St.
Malden, MA 02148
Phone: (781)388-8200
Fax: (781)388-8210
Free: 800-216-2522
Publisher's E-mail: journaladsusa@bos.blackwellpublishing.com
Medical journal reporting developments in the clinical fields of geriatric medicine and gerontology. **Freq:** Monthly. **Key Personnel:** Thomas T. Yoshikawa, Editor; William Applegate, Editor; Joseph G. Ouslander, Executive Editor. **ISSN:** 0002--8614 (print); **EISSN:** 1532--5415 (electronic). **Subscription Rates:** $1134 Institutions USA; print or online; $1361 Institutions USA; print and online; $409 Individuals USA; online only; $450 Individuals USA; print and online; £893 Institutions UK; print or online; £1072 Institutions UK; print and online; £353 Individuals UK and Europe(non-Euro zone) and Rest of the World; online only; £391 Individuals UK and Europe(non-Euro zone) and Rest of the World; print and online; €530 Individuals Europe (Euro zone); online only; €583 Individuals Europe (Euro zone); print and online; $1746 Institutions, other countries print or online; $2096 Institutions, other countries print and online. **URL:** http://onlinelibrary.wiley.com/journal/10.1111/(ISSN)1532-5415; http://www.americangeriatrics.org/publications/shop_publications/journals. **Ad Rates:** BW $2008; 4C $1150. **Remarks:** Accepts advertising. **Circ:** (Not Reported).

16559 ■ The Journal of Analytical Psychology
Wiley-Blackwell
350 Main St.
Commerce Pl.
Malden, MA 02148-5018
Phone: (781)388-8200
Fax: (781)388-8210
Free: 800-216-2552
Journal focusing on international developments and current controversies in analytical psychology and Jungian thinking. **Freq:** 5/year. **Key Personnel:** Warren Colman, Editor; William Owen, Editor-in-Chief; David M. Sedgwick, Editor-in-Chief. **ISSN:** 0021--8774 (print); **EISSN:** 1468--5922 (electronic). **Subscription Rates:** $746 Institutions print or online; $896 Institutions print and online; $198 Individuals print and online. **URL:** http://onlinelibrary.wiley.com/journal/10.1111/(ISSN)1468-5922. **Remarks:** Accepts advertising. **Circ:** (Not Reported).

16560 ■ Journal of Anatomy
Wiley-Blackwell
350 Main St.
Commerce Pl.
Malden, MA 02148-5018
Phone: (781)388-8200
Fax: (781)388-8210
Free: 800-216-2552
Journal focusing on contributions to understanding development, evolution and function through a broad range of anatomical approaches. **Freq:** Monthly. **Key Personnel:** Julia Clarke, Editor-in-Chief; Edward Fenton, Managing Editor. **ISSN:** 0021--8782 (print); **EISSN:** 1469--7580 (electronic). **Subscription Rates:** $3146 Institutions print or online; £1703 Institutions print or online; €2164 Institutions print or online; $3669 Institutions, other countries print or online; $3776 Institutions print and online; £2044 Institutions print and online; €2597 Institutions print and online; $4403 Institutions, other countries print and online. **URL:** http://onlinelibrary.wiley.com/journal/10.1111/(ISSN)1469-7580. **Remarks:** Accepts advertising. **Circ:** 1050.

16561 ■ Journal of Animal Breeding and Genetics
Wiley-Blackwell
350 Main St.
Commerce Pl.
Malden, MA 02148-5018
Phone: (781)388-8200
Fax: (781)388-8210
Free: 800-216-2552
Journal focusing on the progress of research in animal production, quantitative genetics, biology, and evolution of domestic animals. **Freq:** Bimonthly. **Key Personnel:** Dr. Asko Maki-Tanila, Executive Editor; Dr. I. Misztal, Editor. **ISSN:** 0931--2668 (print); **EISSN:** 1439--0388 (electronic). **Subscription Rates:** $2252 Institutions print or online; £1221 Institutions print or online; €1546 Institutions print or online; $2627 Institutions, other countries print or online; $2703 Institutions print and online; £1466 Institutions print and online; €1856 Institutions print and online; $3153 Institutions, other countries print and online; $577 Individuals print and online; £313 Individuals print and online; €467 Individuals print and online, UK and Europe; £345 Other countries print and online. **URL:** http://onlinelibrary.wiley.com/journal/10.1111/(ISSN)1439-0388. **Remarks:** Accepts advertising. **Circ:** (Not Reported).

Circulation: ★ = AAM; △ or • = BPA; ♦ = CAC; ❑ = VAC; ⊕ = PO Statement; ‡ = Publisher's Report; Boldface figures = sworn; Light figures = estimated.

16562 ■ Journal of Animal Physiology and Animal Nutrition
Blackwell Publishing Inc.
350 Main St.
Malden, MA 02148
Phone: (781)388-8200
Fax: (781)388-8210
Free: 800-216-2522
Publisher's E-mail: journaladsusa@bos.blackwellpublishing.com
Journal featuring articles on research in the fields of animal physiology, physiology and biochemistry of nutrition, animal nutrition, feed technology, and feed preservation. **Freq:** Bimonthly. **Key Personnel:** Geert Janssens, Editor; Andrea Fascetti, Editor; Michael Goldberg, Editor. **ISSN:** 0931--2439 (print); **EISSN:** 1439--0396 (electronic). **Subscription Rates:** $2265 Institutions; £1226 Institutions UK; €1558 Institutions Europe; $2641 Institutions, other countries; $2718 Institutions print and online; £1472 Institutions print and online, UK; €1870 Institutions print and online, Europe; $3170 Institutions, other countries print and online; $518 Individuals print and online; £281 Individuals print and online, UK and Europe (non euro zone); €420 Individuals print and online, Europe (euro zone); £309 Other countries print and online. **URL:** http://onlinelibrary.wiley.com/journal/10.1111/(ISSN)1439-0396. **Circ:** (Not Reported).

16563 ■ Journal of Animal Psychology and Nutrition
Wiley-Blackwell
350 Main St.
Commerce Pl.
Malden, MA 02148-5018
Phone: (781)388-8200
Fax: (781)388-8210
Free: 800-216-2552
Journal focusing on research in the fields of animal physiology, physiology and biochemistry of nutrition, animal feeding, feed technology, and food preservation. **Freq:** Bimonthly. **Key Personnel:** Ellen Kienzle, Editor; Geert Janssens, Editor; Michael Kreuzer, Editor. **ISSN:** 0931--2439 (print); **EISSN:** 1439--0396 (electronic). **Subscription Rates:** $2265 Institutions print or online; £1226 Institutions print or online; €1558 Institutions print or online; $2641 Institutions, other countries print or online; $2718 Institutions print and online; £1472 Institutions print and online; €1870 Institutions print and online; $3170 Institutions, other countries print and online; $518 Individuals print and online; £281 Individuals print and online; €420 Individuals print and online; £309 Individuals print and online. **URL:** http://onlinelibrary.wiley.com/journal/10.1111/(ISSN)1439-0396/earlyview. **Remarks:** Accepts advertising. **Circ:** (Not Reported).

16564 ■ Journal of Applied Biobehavioral Research
Blackwell Publishing Inc.
350 Main St.
Malden, MA 02148
Phone: (781)388-8200
Fax: (781)388-8210
Free: 800-216-2522
Publisher's E-mail: journaladsusa@bos.blackwellpublishing.com
Journal featuring findings of behavioral science research. **Freq:** Quarterly. **Key Personnel:** Robert J. Gatchel, PhD, Editor. **ISSN:** 1071--2089 (print); **EISSN:** 1751--9861 (electronic). **Subscription Rates:** $215 Institutions online only; £121 Institutions online only, UK; €154 Institutions online only, Europe; $236 Institutions, other countries online only. **URL:** http://onlinelibrary.wiley.com/journal/10.1111/(ISSN)1751-9861. **Circ:** (Not Reported).

16565 ■ Journal of Applied Corporate Finance
Wiley-Blackwell
350 Main St.
Commerce Pl.
Malden, MA 02148-5018
Phone: (781)388-8200
Fax: (781)388-8210
Free: 800-216-2552
Journal focusing on risk management, corporate strategy, corporate governance and capital structure. **Freq:** Quarterly. **Key Personnel:** Klaus Eder, Editor; Nadia Everaert, Editor. **ISSN:** 1078--1196 (print); **EISSN:** 1745--6622 (electronic). **Subscription Rates:** $117 Individuals U.S. print and online; $41 Students U.S. print and online; $88 Institutions U.S. alumni; $608 Institutions U.S. print and online; $506 Institutions U.S. print or online; £372 Institutions print + online; £310 Institutions print or online; £65 Other countries print + online; €472 Institutions print + online; €393 Institutions print or online; €97 Individuals print or online, Euro zone; $728 Institutions, other countries print + online. **URL:** http://www.wiley.com/WileyCDA/WileyTitle/productCd-JACF.html; http://www.wiley.com/bw/journal.asp?ref=1078-1196&site=1. **Formerly**: Midland, Continental Journal of Applied Corporate Finance. **Remarks:** Accepts advertising. **Circ:** (Not Reported).

16566 ■ Journal of Applied Ecology
Wiley-Blackwell
350 Main St.
Commerce Pl.
Malden, MA 02148-5018
Phone: (781)388-8200
Fax: (781)388-8210
Free: 800-216-2552
Journal focusing on ecological science and environmental management. **Freq:** Bimonthly. **Key Personnel:** Prof. E.J. Milner-Gulland, Executive Editor; EJ Milner-Gulland, Editor; Marc Cadotte, Executive Editor; Mark Whittingham, Senior Editor. **ISSN:** 0021--8901 (print); **EISSN:** 1365--2664 (electronic). **Subscription Rates:** $1755 Institutions print or online; £951 Institutions print or online; €1207 Institutions print or online; $2046 Institutions, other countries print or online; $2106 Institutions print and online; £1142 Institutions print and online; €1449 Institutions print and online; $2456 Institutions print and online. **URL:** http://onlinelibrary.wiley.com/journal/10.1111/(ISSN)1365-2664; http://www.britishecologicalsociety.org/publications/journals/journal-of-applied-ecology; http://www.journalofappliedecology.org/view/0/index.html. **Remarks:** Accepts advertising. **Circ:** (Not Reported).

16567 ■ Journal of Applied Entomology
Wiley-Blackwell
350 Main St.
Commerce Pl.
Malden, MA 02148-5018
Phone: (781)388-8200
Fax: (781)388-8210
Free: 800-216-2552
Journal focusing on entomology. **Freq:** 10/year. **Key Personnel:** Dr. Stefan Vidal, Editor; Christine Denys, Managing Editor. **ISSN:** 0931--2048 (print); **EISSN:** 1439--0418 (electronic). **Subscription Rates:** $3455 Institutions print or online; £2056 Institutions print or online; €2611 Institutions print or online; $4429 Institutions, other countries print or online; $4146 Institutions print and online; £2468 Institutions print and online; €3134 Institutions print and online; $5315 Institutions print and online; $230 Individuals print and online; $151 Individuals print and online; €225 Individuals print and online; £165 Other countries print and online. **URL:** http://onlinelibrary.wiley.com/journal/10.1111/(ISSN)1439-0418. **Remarks:** Accepts advertising. **Circ:** (Not Reported).

16568 ■ Journal of Applied Ichthyology
Wiley-Blackwell
350 Main St.
Commerce Pl.
Malden, MA 02148-5018
Phone: (781)388-8200
Fax: (781)388-8210
Free: 800-216-2552
Journal focusing on ichthyology, aquaculture, and marine fisheries; ichthyopathology and ichthyoimmunology; environmental toxicology using fishes as test organisms; basic research on fishery management; and aspects of integrated coastal zone management in relation to fisheries and aquaculture. **Freq:** Bimonthly. **Key Personnel:** Harald Rosenthal, Editor-in-Chief; Dietrich Schnack, Editor. **ISSN:** 0175--8659 (print); **EISSN:** 1439--0426 (electronic). **Subscription Rates:** $1622 Institutions online only; £879 Institutions online only; €1115 Institutions online only; $1889 Institutions, other countries online only; $524 Individuals online only; £314 Individuals online only; €469 Individuals online only; £314 Individuals online only. **URL:** http://onlinelibrary.wiley.com/journal/10.1111/(ISSN)1439-0426; http://wscs.info/publications/jai.aspx. **Remarks:** Accepts advertising. **Circ:** (Not Reported).

16569 ■ Journal of Applied Microbiology
Wiley-Blackwell
350 Main St.
Commerce Pl.
Malden, MA 02148-5018
Phone: (781)388-8200
Fax: (781)388-8210
Free: 800-216-2552
Journal focusing on all aspects of applied microbiology; including environmental, food, agricultural, medical, pharmaceutical, veterinary, taxonomy, soil, systematics, water and biodeterioration. **Freq:** Monthly. **Key Personnel:** A. Gilmour, Editor-in-Chief; L. Baillie, Editor; Prof. Arthur Gilmour, Editor-in-Chief. **ISSN:** 1364--5072 (print); **EISSN:** 1365--2672 (electronic). **Subscription Rates:** $7137 Institutions print + online; £3864 Institutions print + online; €4906 Institutions print + online (Euro and non Euro zone); $8324 Institutions, other countries print + online; $5947 Institutions print or online; £3220 Institutions print or online; €4088 Institutions print or online (Euro and non Euro zone); $6936 Institutions, other countries print or online. **URL:** http://onlinelibrary.wiley.com/journal/10.1111/(ISSN)1365-2672; http://www.sfam.org.uk/en/journals/journal-of-applied-microbiology.cfm. **Remarks:** Accepts advertising. **Circ:** (Not Reported).

16570 ■ Journal of Applied Philosophy
Wiley-Blackwell
350 Main St.
Commerce Pl.
Malden, MA 02148-5018
Phone: (781)388-8200
Fax: (781)388-8210
Free: 800-216-2552
Journal focusing on philosophical research. **Freq:** Quarterly. **Key Personnel:** Christopher Bennett, Editor. **ISSN:** 0264--3758 (print); **EISSN:** 1468--5930 (electronic). **Subscription Rates:** $1098 Institutions print or online; $1319 Institutions print and online; $188 Individuals print and online; £658 Institutions print or online; £790 Institutions print and online; £113 Other countries print and online; €834 Institutions print or online; €1001 Institutions print and online; A$1027 Institutions print or online; A$1233 Institutions print and online; $1284 Institutions, other countries print or online; $1541 Institutions, other countries print and online; included in membership dues. **URL:** http://onlinelibrary.wiley.com/journal/10.1111/(ISSN)1468-5930; http://www.appliedphil.org/view/publications.html; http://onlinelibrary.wiley.com/journal/10.1111/(ISSN)1468-5930;jsessionid=A30956C91752AA0BD4BCDF62B6055D24.f01t04. **Remarks:** Accepts advertising. **Circ:** (Not Reported).

16571 ■ Journal of Applied Research in Intellectual Disabilities
Wiley-Blackwell
350 Main St.
Commerce Pl.
Malden, MA 02148-5018
Phone: (781)388-8200
Fax: (781)388-8210
Free: 800-216-2552
Peer-reviewed journal focusing on applied research in intellectual disabilities. **Freq:** Bimonthly. **Key Personnel:** Chris Hatton, Editor; Peter Langdon, Editor. **ISSN:** 1360-2322 (print). **Subscription Rates:** $167 Individuals U.S. print and online; $130 Members IASSID, U.S. print and online; $1117 Institutions, other countries print & online; $1008 Institutions U.S. print and online; $876 Institutions U.S. print or online; £548 Institutions print and online; £475 Institutions print or online; £92 Individuals print and online. **URL:** http://www.wiley.com/WileyCDA/WileyTitle/productCd-JAR.html. **Remarks:** Accepts advertising. **Circ:** (Not Reported).

16572 ■ Journal of Applied Social Psychology
Wiley-Blackwell
350 Main St.
Commerce Pl.
Malden, MA 02148-5018
Phone: (781)388-8200
Fax: (781)388-8210
Free: 800-216-2552

Publisher's E-mail: journaladsusa@bos.blackwellpublishing.com
Journal devoted to applications of experimental behavioral science research to problems of society. Topics covered include organizational and leadership psychology, safety, health, and gender issues, perceptions of war and natural hazards, jury deliberation, performance, AIDS, cancer, heart disease, exercise, and sports. **Freq:** Monthly. **Print Method:** Offset. **Cols./Page:** 5. **Col. Width:** 12 picas. **Col. Depth:** 12 inches. **Key Personnel:** Richard J. Crisp, PhD, Editor-in-Chief. **ISSN:** 0021--9029 (print); **EISSN:** 1559--1816 (electronic). **USPS:** 122-940. **Subscription Rates:** $1950 Institutions print or online; $2340 Institutions print + online; £1111 Institutions print or online; £1334 Institutions print + online; €1410 Institutions print or online; €1692 Institutions print + online; $2172 Institutions, other countries print or online; $2607 Institutions, other countries print + online. **URL:** http://onlinelibrary.wiley.com/journal/10.1111/%28ISSN%291559-1816. **Ad Rates:** BW $850. **Remarks:** Accepts advertising. **Circ:** (Not Reported).

16573 ■ Journal of Avian Biology
Wiley-Blackwell
350 Main St.
Commerce Pl.
Malden, MA 02148-5018
Phone: (781)388-8200
Fax: (781)388-8210
Free: 800-216-2552
Journal focusing on all areas of ornithology, with an emphasis on ecology, behaviour and evolutionary biology. **Freq:** Bimonthly. **Key Personnel:** Thomas Alerstam, Editor-in-Chief; Dr. Johan Nilsson, Managing Editor; Peter Arcese, Editor. **ISSN:** 0908--8857 (print); **EISSN:** 1600--048X (electronic). **Subscription Rates:** $549 Institutions online only; £328 Institutions online only; €419 Institutions online only; $643 Institutions online only; $119 Individuals online only; £71 Individuals online only; €107 Individuals online only. **URL:** http://onlinelibrary.wiley.com/journal/10.1111/(ISSN)1600-048X. **Remarks:** Accepts advertising. **Circ:** (Not Reported).

16574 ■ Journal of Biogeography
Wiley-Blackwell
350 Main St.
Commerce Pl.
Malden, MA 02148-5018
Phone: (781)388-8200
Fax: (781)388-8210
Free: 800-216-2552
Journal focusing on biogeography. **Freq:** Monthly. **Key Personnel:** David R. Bellwood, Associate Editor; Mark Bush, Associate Editor; Robert J. Whittaker, Technical Manager; Brad Hawkins, Editor-in-Chief. **ISSN:** 0305--0270 (print); **EISSN:** 1365--2699 (electronic). **URL:** http://onlinelibrary.wiley.com/journal/10.1111/(ISSN)1365-2699. **Remarks:** Accepts advertising. **Circ:** (Not Reported).

16575 ■ Journal of Business Finance and Accounting
Wiley-Blackwell
350 Main St.
Commerce Pl.
Malden, MA 02148-5018
Phone: (781)388-8200
Fax: (781)388-8210
Free: 800-216-2552
Journal focusing on finance and economic aspects of accounting. **Freq:** 10/year. **Key Personnel:** P.F. Pope, Editor; A.W. Stark, Editor; M. Walker, Editor; Andrew Stark, Editor; Peter F. Pope, Editor; Martin Walker, Editor; Paul Andre, Associate Editor. **ISSN:** 0306--686X (print); **EISSN:** 1468--5957 (electronic). **Subscription Rates:** $3058 Institutions print and online; £1605 Institutions print and online; €2036 Institutions print and online; $3570 Institutions, other countries print and online; $289 Individuals print and online; £141 Individuals print and online; €212 Individuals print and online; £174 Other countries print and online. **URL:** http://onlinelibrary.wiley.com/journal/10.1111/(ISSN)1468-5957. **Remarks:** Accepts advertising. **Circ:** (Not Reported).

16576 ■ The Journal of Child Psychology and Psychiatry
Wiley-Blackwell
350 Main St.
Commerce Pl.
Malden, MA 02148-5018
Phone: (781)388-8200
Fax: (781)388-8210
Free: 800-216-2552
Journal focusing on child and adolescent psychology and psychiatry. **Freq:** Monthly. **Key Personnel:** Prof. Edmund Sonuga-Barke, Editor-in-Chief; Tobias Banaschewski, Editor; Stephen Petrill, Editor. **ISSN:** 0021-9630 (print); **EISSN:** 1469-7610 (electronic). **Subscription Rates:** $1171 Institutions U.S. print and online; $1018 Institutions U.S. print or online; £696 Institutions print and online; £605 Institutions print or online. **URL:** http://onlinelibrary.wiley.com/journal/10.1111/(ISSN)1469-7610. **Remarks:** Accepts advertising. **Circ:** (Not Reported).

16577 ■ Journal of Chinese Philosophy
Wiley-Blackwell
350 Main St.
Commerce Pl.
Malden, MA 02148-5018
Phone: (781)388-8200
Fax: (781)388-8210
Free: 800-216-2552
Journal focusing on Chinese philosophy. **Freq:** Quarterly. **Key Personnel:** Chung-Ying Cheng, Editor-in-Chief; Linyu Gu, Associate Executive, Editor; Lauren Pfister, Associate Editor. **ISSN:** 0301--8121 (print); **EISSN:** 1540--6253 (electronic). **Subscription Rates:** $1251 Institutions print and online; £903 Institutions print and online; €1145 Institutions print and online; $1764 Institutions, other countries print and online; $110 Individuals print and online; £91 Other countries print and online; €133 Institutions print and online. **URL:** http://onlinelibrary.wiley.com/journal/10.1111/(ISSN)1540-6253. **Ad Rates:** 4C $250. **Remarks:** Accepts advertising. **Circ:** (Not Reported).

16578 ■ Journal of Clinical Nursing
Wiley-Blackwell
350 Main St.
Commerce Pl.
Malden, MA 02148-5018
Phone: (781)388-8200
Fax: (781)388-8210
Free: 800-216-2552
Publication E-mail: jcn@oxon.blackwellpublishing.com
Peer-reviewed scientific journal that seeks to promote the development and exchange of knowledge that is directly relevant to spheres of nursing and midwifery practice. **Freq:** 24/yr. **Key Personnel:** Debra Jackson, Editor-in-Chief. **ISSN:** 0962--1067 (print); **EISSN:** 1365--2702 (electronic). **Subscription Rates:** $3400 Institutions print and online; £1841 Institutions print and online; €2340 Institutions print and online; $3964 Institutions, other countries print and online; $454 Individuals print and online; £248 Individuals print and online; €371 Individuals print and online; £272 Individuals print and online; $248 Students print and online; £135 Students print and online; €200 Students print and online; £150 Students, other countries print and online. **URL:** http://onlinelibrary.wiley.com/journal/10.1111/(ISSN)1365-2702. **Remarks:** Accepts advertising. **Circ:** (Not Reported).

16579 ■ Journal of Clinical Periodontology
Wiley-Blackwell
350 Main St.
Commerce Pl.
Malden, MA 02148-5018
Phone: (781)388-8200
Fax: (781)388-8210
Free: 800-216-2552
Focuses on scientific and clinical progress in the field of Periodontology and allied disciplines. **Freq:** Monthly. **Key Personnel:** Dr. Maurizio Tonetti, Editor-in-Chief; B.G. Loos, Board Member; Prof. Maurizio Tonetti, Editor; Jan Lindhe, Editor. **ISSN:** 0303--6979 (print); **EISSN:** 1600--051X (electronic). **Subscription Rates:** $1775 Institutions print and online; £1058 Institutions print and online; €1343 Institutions print and online; $2070 Institutions, other countries print and online. **URL:** http://onlinelibrary.wiley.com/journal/10.1111/(ISSN)1600-051X; http://www.bsperio.org.uk/links.php. **Remarks:** Accepts advertising. **Circ:** (Not Reported).

16580 ■ The Journal of Clinical Pharmacology
Wiley-Blackwell
350 Main St.
Commerce Pl.
Malden, MA 02148-5018
Phone: (781)388-8200
Fax: (781)388-8210
Free: 800-216-2552
Journal focusing on clinical information about the safety, tolerability, efficacy, therapeutic applications, toxicology, and total evaluation of new and established drugs for humans. **Freq:** Monthly. **Key Personnel:** Joseph S. Bertino, Jr., Editor; Rajesh Krishna, Board Member; Hartmut Derendorf, Associate Editor; Marjory M. Spraycar, Managing Editor. **ISSN:** 0091--2700 (print); **EISSN:** 1552--4604 (electronic). **Subscription Rates:** $1182 Institutions online only ; C$1182 Institutions, Canada and Mexico online only; £768 Institutions online only; €888 Institutions online only; $1182 Institutions, other countries online only. **URL:** http://onlinelibrary.wiley.com/journal/10.1002/(ISSN)1552-4604. **Remarks:** Accepts advertising. **Circ:** (Not Reported).

16581 ■ Journal of Clinical Pharmacy and Therapeutics
Wiley-Blackwell
350 Main St.
Commerce Pl.
Malden, MA 02148-5018
Phone: (781)388-8200
Fax: (781)388-8210
Free: 800-216-2552
Publisher's E-mail: journaladsusa@bos.blackwellpublishing.com
Journal focusing on all aspects of drug development and drug use. **Freq:** Bimonthly. **Key Personnel:** Alain Li Wan Po, Editor-in-Chief; Martin Kendall, Editor. **ISSN:** 0269--4727 (print); **EISSN:** 1365--2710 (electronic). **Subscription Rates:** $2729 Institutions print and online; £1478 Institutions print or online; €1876 Institutions print and online; $3192 Institutions print and online. **URL:** http://onlinelibrary.wiley.com/journal/10.1111/(ISSN)1365-2710. **Remarks:** Accepts advertising. **Circ:** (Not Reported).

16582 ■ Journal of Computer Assisted Learning
Wiley-Blackwell
350 Main St.
Commerce Pl.
Malden, MA 02148-5018
Phone: (781)388-8200
Fax: (781)388-8210
Free: 800-216-2552
Peer-reviewed journal focusing on the whole range of uses of information and communication technology to support learning and knowledge exchange. **Freq:** Bimonthly. **Key Personnel:** Paul A. Kirschner, Editor-in-Chief. **ISSN:** 0266--4909 (print); **EISSN:** 1365--2729 (electronic). **Subscription Rates:** $2112 Institutions print and online; £1170 Institutions print and online; €1484 Institutions print and online; $2514 Institutions, other countries print and online; $261 Individuals print and online; £140 Other countries print and online ; €210 Institutions print and online. **URL:** http://onlinelibrary.wiley.com/journal/10.1111/(ISSN)1365-2729. **Remarks:** Accepts advertising. **Circ:** (Not Reported).

16583 ■ Journal of Computer-Mediated Communication
Wiley-Blackwell
350 Main St.
Commerce Pl.
Malden, MA 02148-5018
Phone: (781)388-8200
Fax: (781)388-8210
Free: 800-216-2552
Peer-reviewed journal focusing on computer mediated research on social science via the Internet. **Freq:** Quarterly. **Key Personnel:** Naomi Baron, Board Member. **ISSN:** 1083-6101 (print). **Subscription Rates:** $1568 Institutions Combined Subscription with Communication Theory and Communication, Culture & Critique and Human Communication Research and Journal of Communication. **URL:** http://onlinelibrary.wiley.com/journal/10.1111/(ISSN)1083-6101. **Remarks:**

Circulation: ★ = AAM; △ or • = BPA; ♦ = CAC; ❑ = VAC; ⊕ = PO Statement; ‡ = Publisher's Report; Boldface figures = sworn; Light figures = estimated.

Advertising not accepted. **Circ:** (Not Reported).

16584 ■ Journal of Contingencies and Crisis Management
Wiley-Blackwell
350 Main St.
Commerce Pl.
Malden, MA 02148-5018
Phone: (781)388-8200
Fax: (781)388-8210
Free: 800-216-2552
Publication E-mail: jccm@fsw.vu.nl
Journal focusing on contingency planning, scenario analysis and crisis management in both corporate and public sectors. **Freq:** Quarterly. **Key Personnel:** Dr. Ira Helsloot, Editor; Prof. Alexander Kouzmin, Editor, Founder; Uriel Rosenthal, Editor, Founder. **ISSN:** 0966--0879 (print); **EISSN:** 1468--5973 (electronic). **Subscription Rates:** $1191 Institutions print and online; £711 Institutions print and online; €903 Institutions print and online; $1386 Institutions, other countries print and online; $131 Individuals print and online; £80 Other countries print and online; €118 Individuals print and online. **URL:** http://onlinelibrary.wiley.com/journal/10.1111/(ISSN)1468-5973. **Remarks:** Accepts advertising. **Circ:** (Not Reported).

16585 ■ Journal of Cosmetic Dermatology
Wiley-Blackwell
350 Main St.
Commerce Pl.
Malden, MA 02148-5018
Phone: (781)388-8200
Fax: (781)388-8210
Free: 800-216-2552
Journal focusing on all aspects of cosmetic dermatology. **Freq:** Quarterly. **Key Personnel:** Zoe Diana Draelos, MD, Editor; Marc Avram, MD, Associate Editor; Anthony Benedetto, Associate Editor. **ISSN:** 1473--2130 (print); **EISSN:** 1473--2165 (electronic). **Subscription Rates:** $1338 Institutions print and online; £728 Institutions print and online; €921 Institutions print and online; $1420 Institutions, other countries print and online; $268 Individuals print and online; £146 Other countries print and online; €217 Individuals print and online; $277 Individuals print and online, The Americas; $1419 Institutions print and online, The Americas; Included in membership. **URL:** http://onlinelibrary.wiley.com/journal/10.1111/(ISSN)1473-2165; http://www.iacdworld.org/home-in.htm. **Ad Rates:** BW $910; 4C $989. **Remarks:** Accepts advertising. **Circ:** **650**.

16586 ■ Journal of Cutaneous Pathology
Wiley-Blackwell
350 Main St.
Commerce Pl.
Malden, MA 02148-5018
Phone: (781)388-8200
Fax: (781)388-8210
Free: 800-216-2552
Journal focusing on dermatopathology and cutaneous pathology. **Freq:** 12/yr. **Key Personnel:** Timothy H. McCalmont, Editor-in-Chief. **ISSN:** 0303-6987 (print). **Subscription Rates:** $566 Individuals U.S. print and online; $538 Individuals U.S. online only; $1780 Institutions U.S. print and online; $1548 Institutions U.S. print or online; €506 Individuals print and online; €483 Individuals online only; £1062 Institutions print and online; £924 Institutions print or online. **URL:** http://www.wiley.com/WileyCDA/WileyTitle/productCd-CUP.html. **Remarks:** Accepts advertising. **Circ:** (Not Reported).

16587 ■ Journal der Deutschen Dermatologischen Gesellschaft
Wiley-Blackwell
350 Main St.
Commerce Pl.
Malden, MA 02148-5018
Phone: (781)388-8200
Fax: (781)388-8210
Free: 800-216-2552
Publisher's E-mail: journaladsusa@bos.blackwellpublishing.com
German-language journal. **Freq:** Monthly. **Key Personnel:** Dr. Sergij Goerdt, Editor-in-Chief; Prof. Michael P. Schon, Editor. **ISSN:** 1610--0379 (print); **EISSN:** 1610--0387 (electronic). **Subscription Rates:** $1136 Institutions print or online; $1364 Institutions print and online; $493 Individuals print and online. **URL:** http://onlinelibrary.wiley.com/journal/10.1111/(ISSN)1610-0387. **Remarks:** Accepts advertising. **Circ:** (Not Reported).

16588 ■ Journal of Digestive Diseases
Wiley-Blackwell
350 Main St.
Commerce Pl.
Malden, MA 02148-5018
Phone: (781)388-8200
Fax: (781)388-8210
Free: 800-216-2552
Journal focusing on research relating to the esophagus, stomach, small intestine, colon, liver, biliary tract and pancreas. Official English-language journal of the Chinese Society of Gastroenterology and the Chinese Medical Association Shanghai Branch. **Freq:** Monthly. **Key Personnel:** Shu Dong Xiao, Editor-in-Chief. **ISSN:** 1751--2972 (print); **EISSN:** 1751--2980 (electronic). **Subscription Rates:** $928 Institutions print & online; £477 Institutions print & online; $773 Institutions print or online; £397 Institutions print or online. **URL:** http://onlinelibrary.wiley.com/journal/10.1111/(ISSN)1751-2980. **Formerly:** Chinese Journal of Digestive Diseases. **Remarks:** Accepts advertising. **Circ:** (Not Reported).

16589 ■ Journal of Ecology
Wiley-Blackwell
350 Main St.
Commerce Pl.
Malden, MA 02148-5018
Phone: (781)388-8200
Fax: (781)388-8210
Free: 800-216-2552
Journal focusing on all aspects of the ecology of plants (i.e. in both aquatic and terrestrial ecosystems and focusing on plant communities, populations or individuals, as well as studies of the interactions between plants and their environment or plants and other organisms). **Freq:** Bimonthly. **Key Personnel:** Michael J. Hutchings, Editor; David J. Gibson, Executive Editor; Richard D. Bardgett, Editor. **ISSN:** 0022--0477 (print); **EISSN:** 1365--2745 (electronic). **Subscription Rates:** $2273 Institutions print and online; £1230 Institutions print and online; €1566 Institutions print and online; $2652 Institutions, other countries print and online; $1894 Individuals print and online; £1025 Individuals print and online; €1305 Individuals print and online; $2210 Other countries print and online; $1894 Institutions print or online; £1025 Institutions print or online; €1305 Institutions print or online; $2210 Institutions, other countries print or online. **URL:** http://onlinelibrary.wiley.com/journal/10.1111/(ISSN)1365-2745; http://www.wiley.com/bw/journal.asp?ref=0022-0477&site=1; http://www.britishecologicalsociety.org/publications/journals/journal-of-ecology. **Ad Rates:** BW $900; 4C $2,250. **Remarks:** Accepts advertising. **Circ:** (Not Reported).

16590 ■ Journal of Economic Surveys
Wiley-Blackwell
350 Main St.
Commerce Pl.
Malden, MA 02148-5018
Phone: (781)388-8200
Fax: (781)388-8210
Free: 800-216-2552
Journal focusing on economics, econometrics, economic history and business. economics. **Freq:** 5/year. **Key Personnel:** Donald A.R. George, Managing Editor; Leslie T. Oxley, Editor-in-Chief; Colin J. Roberts, Founder, Editor; Stuart T. Sayer, Founder, Editor; Iris Claus, Managing Editor. **ISSN:** 0950--0804 (print); **EISSN:** 1467--6419 (electronic). **Subscription Rates:** $1469 Institutions print and online; £897 Institutions print and online; €1137 Institutions print and online; $2054 Institutions, other countries print or online; $144 Individuals print and online; £89 Other countries print and online; €131 Individuals print and online; $68 Students print and online; £44 Students, other countries print and online; €61 Students print and online. **URL:** http://onlinelibrary.wiley.com/journal/10.1111/(ISSN)1467-6419. **Remarks:** Accepts advertising. **Circ:** (Not Reported).

16591 ■ Journal of Educational Measurement
Wiley-Blackwell
350 Main St.
Commerce Pl.
Malden, MA 02148-5018
Phone: (781)388-8200
Fax: (781)388-8210
Free: 800-216-2552
Journal covering testing in education. **Freq:** Quarterly. **Key Personnel:** Barbara G. Dodd, Board Member; Jimmy dela Torre, Editor; Brian Clauser, Board Member. **ISSN:** 0022--0655 (print); **EISSN:** 1745--3984 (electronic). **Subscription Rates:** $671 Institutions print and online; $559 Institutions print or online; £414 Institutions print and online; £345 Institutions print or online; €525 Institutions print and online; €437 Institutions print or online; $804 Institutions, other countries print and online; $670 Institutions, other countries print or online. **URL:** http://onlinelibrary.wiley.com/journal/10.1111/(ISSN)1745-3984. **Remarks:** Accepts advertising. **Circ:** (Not Reported).

16592 ■ Journal of Empirical Legal Studies
Wiley-Blackwell
350 Main St.
Commerce Pl.
Malden, MA 02148-5018
Phone: (781)388-8200
Fax: (781)388-8210
Free: 800-216-2552
Journal focusing on law and law-related fields, including civil justice, corporate law, criminal justice, domestic relations, economics, finance, health care, political science, psychology, public policy, securities regulation, and sociology. **Freq:** Quarterly. **Key Personnel:** Theodore Eisenberg, Founder, Editor; Michael Heise, PhD, Editor; Jeffrey J. Rachlinski, PhD, Editor. **ISSN:** 1740-1453 (print); **EISSN:** 1740-1461 (electronic). **Subscription Rates:** $675 Institutions U.S. print & online; $50 Members print & online; $675 Institutions U.S. print or online; £516 Institutions print & online; $1007 Institutions, other countries print & online; £516 Institutions print or online. **URL:** http://www.wiley.com/WileyCDA/WileyTitle/productCd-JELS.html. **Ad Rates:** BW $225. **Remarks:** Accepts advertising. **Circ:** (Not Reported).

16593 ■ The Journal of Eukaryotic Microbiology
Wiley-Blackwell
350 Main St.
Commerce Pl.
Malden, MA 02148-5018
Phone: (781)388-8200
Fax: (781)388-8210
Free: 800-216-2552
Journal focusing on protists, including lower algae and fungi. **Freq:** Bimonthly. **Key Personnel:** Roberto Docampo, Editor-in-Chief. **ISSN:** 1066-5234 (print); **EISSN:** 1550-7408 (electronic). **Subscription Rates:** $491 Institutions print & online; €381 Institutions print & online; $427 Institutions print or online; £300 Institutions print & online; €331 Institutions print or online; £261 Institutions print or online. **URL:** http://as.wiley.com/WileyCDA/WileyTitle/productCd-JEU.html. **Ad Rates:** 4C $600. **Remarks:** Accepts advertising. **Circ:** (Not Reported).

16594 ■ Journal of Evaluation in Clinical Practice
Wiley-Blackwell
350 Main St.
Commerce Pl.
Malden, MA 02148-5018
Phone: (781)388-8200
Fax: (781)388-8210
Free: 800-216-2552
Journal focusing on clinical practice across medicine, nursing and the allied health professions. **Freq:** Bimonthly. **Key Personnel:** Prof. Andrew Miles, Editor-in-Chief. **ISSN:** 1356--1294 (print); **EISSN:** 1365--2753 (electronic). **Subscription Rates:** $1906 Institutions online only; £1031 Institutions online only; €1309 Institutions online only; $2217 Institutions, other countries online only. **URL:** http://onlinelibrary.wiley.com/journal/10.1111/(ISSN)1365-2753. **Remarks:** Accepts advertising. **Circ:** (Not Reported).

16595 ■ Journal of Evolutionary Biology
Wiley-Blackwell
350 Main St.
Commerce Pl.
Malden, MA 02148-5018
Phone: (781)388-8200
Fax: (781)388-8210

Free: 800-216-2552
Peer-reviewed journal focusing on micro- and macro-evolution of all types of organisms. **Freq:** Bimonthly. **Key Personnel:** Michael G. Ritchie, Editor-in-Chief. **ISSN:** 1010-061X (print). **Subscription Rates:** $3654 Institutions U.S. print and online; $3177 Institutions U.S., print or online; €2166 Institutions print or online; €2491 Institutions print & online; $3825 Institutions, other countries print & online; £1961 Institutions print and online; £1706 Institutions print or online. **URL:** http://onlinelibrary.wiley.com/journal/10.1111/(ISSN)1420-9101. **Remarks:** Accepts advertising. **Circ:** (Not Reported).

16596 ■ Journal of Family Theory & Review
Wiley-Blackwell
350 Main St.
Commerce Pl.
Malden, MA 02148-5018
Phone: (781)388-8200
Fax: (781)388-8210
Free: 800-216-2552
Journal covering all areas of family theory. **Freq:** Quarterly. **Key Personnel:** Robert M. Milardo, PhD, Editor. **ISSN:** 1756--2570 (print); **EISSN:** 1756--2589 (electronic). **Subscription Rates:** $161 Individuals print & online; £130 Individuals print & online, UK, Europe (non euro zone) and other countries; €194 Individuals print & online, Europe; $68 Students print & online; £65 Students print & online, UK, Europe (non euro zone) and other countries; €97 Students print & online, Europe. **URL:** http://onlinelibrary.wiley.com/journal/10.1111/(ISSN)1756-2589. **Circ:** (Not Reported).

16597 ■ Journal of Family Therapy
Wiley-Blackwell
350 Main St.
Commerce Pl.
Malden, MA 02148-5018
Phone: (781)388-8200
Fax: (781)388-8210
Free: 800-216-2552
Journal focusing on human relationships in systems such as couples, families, professional networks, and wider groups. Publishes articles on theory, research, clinical practice and training. **Freq:** Quarterly. **Key Personnel:** Mark Rivett, Editor; Alan Carr, PhD, Associate Editor; Howard Liddle, PhD, Associate Editor; Reenee Singh, Editor. **ISSN:** 0163--4445 (print); **EISSN:** 1467--6427 (electronic). **Subscription Rates:** $857 Institutions print and online; £472 Institutions print and online; €599 Institutions print and online; $999 Institutions, other countries print and online; $102 Individuals online only; £61 Other countries online only; €92 Individuals online only. **URL:** http://onlinelibrary.wiley.com/journal/10.1111/(ISSN)1467-6427. **Remarks:** Accepts advertising. **Circ:** (Not Reported).

16598 ■ The Journal of Financial Research
Wiley-Blackwell
350 Main St.
Commerce Pl.
Malden, MA 02148-5018
Phone: (781)388-8200
Fax: (781)388-8210
Free: 800-216-2552
Journal focusing on investment and portfolio management, capital markets and institutions, and corporate finance, corporate governance, and capital investment. **Freq:** Quarterly. **Key Personnel:** Scott E. Hein, Editor; Jeffrey M. Mercer, Editor; Drew B. Winters, Associate Editor. **ISSN:** 0270-2592 (print). **Subscription Rates:** $561 Institutions print and online; €530 Institutions print or online; $487 Institutions print or online; £482 Institutions print and online; €610 Institutions print and online; £418 Institutions print or online. **URL:** http://as.wiley.com/WileyCDA/WileyTitle/productCd-JFIR.html. **Ad Rates:** 4C $300. **Remarks:** Accepts advertising. **Circ:** (Not Reported).

16599 ■ Journal of Fish Diseases
Wiley-Blackwell
350 Main St.
Commerce Pl.
Malden, MA 02148-5018
Phone: (781)388-8200
Fax: (781)388-8210
Free: 800-216-2552
Journal focusing on all aspects of disease in both wild and cultured fish and shellfish. **Freq:** Monthly. **Key Personnel:** R.J. Roberts, Editor. **ISSN:** 0140-7775 (print); **EISSN:** 1365-2761 (electronic). **Subscription Rates:** $3753 Institutions U.S. print and online; $3127 Institutions U.S. print or online; £2031 Institutions print & online; £1692 Institutions print or online. **URL:** http://www.wiley.com/WileyCDA/WileyTitle/productCd-JFD.html. **Remarks:** Accepts advertising. **Circ:** (Not Reported).

16600 ■ Journal of Flood Risk Management
Wiley-Blackwell
350 Main St.
Commerce Pl.
Malden, MA 02148-5018
Phone: (781)388-8200
Fax: (781)388-8210
Free: 800-216-2552
Peer-reviewed journal covering all areas related to flood risk. **Freq:** Quarterly. **Key Personnel:** Paul Samuels, Editor-in-Chief; Jim Hall, Associate Editor. **EISSN:** 1753--318X (electronic). **Subscription Rates:** £901 Institutions FTE-Large, online only; €1108 Institutions FTE-Large, online only; $1279 Institutions, other countries FTE-Large, online only; $336 Individuals online only; £237 Individuals U.K.; €292 Individuals Europe (Euro and non-Euro zone). **URL:** http://onlinelibrary.wiley.com/journal/10.1111/(ISSN)1753-318X. **Remarks:** Advertising accepted; rates available upon request. **Circ:** (Not Reported).

16601 ■ Journal of Food Biochemistry
Wiley-Blackwell
350 Main St.
Commerce Pl.
Malden, MA 02148-5018
Phone: (781)388-8200
Fax: (781)388-8210
Free: 800-216-2552
Peer-reviewed journal focusing on the effects of handling, storage, and processing on the biochemical aspects of food tissues, systems, and bioactive compounds in the diet. **Freq:** Bimonthly. **Key Personnel:** Norman F. Haard, Editor; Benjamin Kofi Simpson, Editor. **ISSN:** 0145--8884 (print); **EISSN:** 1745--4514 (electronic). **Subscription Rates:** $598 Institutions online only; £411 Institutions online only; €517 Institutions online only; $798 Institutions, other countries online only. **URL:** http://onlinelibrary.wiley.com/journal/10.1111/(ISSN)1745-4514. **Remarks:** Accepts advertising. **Circ:** (Not Reported).

16602 ■ Journal of Forensic Sciences
Wiley-Blackwell
350 Main St.
Commerce Pl.
Malden, MA 02148-5018
Phone: (781)388-8200
Fax: (781)388-8210
Free: 800-216-2552
Peer-reviewed journal covering the fields of forensic sciences. **Freq:** Bimonthly. **Key Personnel:** Michael Peat, Editor; Robert E. Gaensslen, PhD, Associate Editor. **ISSN:** 0022--1198 (print); **EISSN:** 1556--4029 (electronic). **Subscription Rates:** $651 Institutions online only; £401 Institutions online only, UK; €510 Institutions online only, Europe; $786 Institutions, other countries online only; $782 Institutions print and online; £482 Institutions print and online, UK; €612 Institutions print and online, Europe; $944 Institutions, other countries print and online; $403 Individuals print and online; £246 Individuals print and online, UK, Europe (non euro zone) and rest of the world; €367 Individuals print and online, Europe. **URL:** http://onlinelibrary.wiley.com/journal/10.1111/(ISSN)1556-4029; http://www.aafs.org/resources/journal-forensic-sciences. **Remarks:** Advertising not accepted. **Circ:** (Not Reported).

16603 ■ Journal of Hepato-Biliary-Pancreatic Sciences
Wiley-Blackwell
350 Main St.
Commerce Pl.
Malden, MA 02148-5018
Phone: (781)388-8200
Fax: (781)388-8210
Free: 800-216-2552
Publishes original articles in the English language dealing with clinical investigations of and basic research on all aspects of the field of hepatic, biliary, and pancreatic surgery. **Freq:** Monthly. **Key Personnel:** Tadahiro Takada, Editor-in-Chief; Jiro Fujimoto, Board Member; B.J. Ammori, Board Member; Fumihiko Miura, Associate Editor; John L. Cameron, Board Member. **ISSN:** 1868--6974 (print); **EISSN:** 1868--6982 (electronic). **Subscription Rates:** $634 Institutions print or online; €497 Institutions Europe; print or online; £404 Institutions UK; print or online; $761 Institutions print & online; £485 Institutions UK; print & online; €597 Institutions Europe; print & online. **URL:** http://onlinelibrary.wiley.com/journal/10.1002/(ISSN)1868-6982. **Formerly:** Journal of Hepato-Biliary-Pancreatic Surgery. **Remarks:** Accepts advertising. **Circ:** (Not Reported).

16604 ■ Journal of Historical Sociology
Wiley-Blackwell
350 Main St.
Commerce Pl.
Malden, MA 02148-5018
Phone: (781)388-8200
Fax: (781)388-8210
Free: 800-216-2552
Periodical focusing on history. **Freq:** Quarterly. **Key Personnel:** Derek Sayer, Managing Editor; Wong Yoke-Sum, Managing Editor; Rod Bantjes, Editor; Richard Biernacki, Editor; Bruce Curtis, Editor; Claude Denis, Editor. **ISSN:** 0952--1909 (print); **EISSN:** 1467--6443 (electronic). **Subscription Rates:** $159 Members print and online; €141 Members print and online; £96 Members print and online; $1359 Institutions print and online; $1132 Institutions print, online; $1586 Institutions, other countries print and online; $1321 Institutions, other countries print, online; €718 Institutions print or online; €862 Institutions print and online. **URL:** http://onlinelibrary.wiley.com/journal/10.1111/(ISSN)1467-6443. **Remarks:** Accepts advertising. **Circ:** (Not Reported).

16605 ■ Journal of Hospital Medicine
Wiley-Blackwell
350 Main St.
Commerce Pl.
Malden, MA 02148-5018
Phone: (781)388-8200
Fax: (781)388-8210
Free: 800-216-2552
Journal on hospital medicine. **Freq:** Monthly. **Trim Size:** 8 1/4 x 10 7/8. **Key Personnel:** Andrew Auerbach, MD, Editor-in-Chief. **ISSN:** 1553--5592 (print); **EISSN:** 1553--5606 (electronic). **Subscription Rates:** $1479 Institutions print or online, large; $1775 Institutions print + online, large. **URL:** http://onlinelibrary.wiley.com/journal/10.1002/(ISSN)1553-5606; http://www.hospitalmedicine.org/Web/Media_Center/Web/Media_Center/Media_Center.aspx; http://onlinelibrary.wiley.com/journal/10.1002/%28ISSN%291553-5606/issues. **Ad Rates:** BW $2070; 4C $300. **Remarks:** Accepts advertising. **Circ:** Paid △**10007**.

16606 ■ Journal of Human Nutrition and Dietetics
Wiley-Blackwell
350 Main St.
Commerce Pl.
Malden, MA 02148-5018
Phone: (781)388-8200
Fax: (781)388-8210
Free: 800-216-2552
Peer-reviewed journal covering applied nutrition and dietetics in connection with the British Dietetic Association. **Freq:** Bimonthly. **Key Personnel:** A. Anderson, Board Member; Angela Madden, Editor, phone: 44 1707 286494. **ISSN:** 0952--3871 (print); **EISSN:** 1365--277X (electronic). **Subscription Rates:** $1296 Institutions online; £704 Institutions online; €892 Institutions online, euro and non euro zone ; $1509 Individuals online, ROW; $270 Individuals online; £147 Individuals online; €147 Individuals online,non euro zone ; €220 Individuals online, euro zone ; $163 Individuals online, ROW; Included in membership. **URL:** http://onlinelibrary.wiley.com/journal/10.1111/(ISSN)1365-277X; http://www.bda.uk.com/membership/publications/hnd_journal. **Remarks:** Advertising ac-

Circulation: ★ = AAM; △ or • = BPA; ♦ = CAC; ❑ = VAC; ⊕ = PO Statement; ‡ = Publisher's Report; Boldface figures = sworn; Light figures = estimated.

cepted; rates available upon request. **Circ:** (Not Reported).

16607 ■ Journal of Industrial Ecology
Wiley-Blackwell
350 Main St.
Commerce Pl.
Malden, MA 02148-5018
Phone: (781)388-8200
Fax: (781)388-8210
Free: 800-216-2552
Scholarly journal covering industrial ecology worldwide. **Freq:** Bimonthly. **Trim Size:** 7 x 10. **Key Personnel:** Reid Lifset, Editor-in-Chief; Helge Brattebo, Editor. **ISSN:** 1088--1980 (print); **EISSN:** 1530--9290 (electronic). **Subscription Rates:** $591 Institutions online only; £303 Institutions online only; €381 Institutions online only; £591 Institutions, other countries online only. **URL:** http://onlinelibrary.wiley.com/journal/10.1111/(ISSN)1530-9290; http://www.is4ie.org/jie. **Ad Rates:** BW $350. **Remarks:** Accepts advertising. **Circ:** Combined 1100.

16608 ■ Journal of Industrial Economics
Wiley-Blackwell
350 Main St.
Commerce Pl.
Malden, MA 02148-5018
Phone: (781)388-8200
Fax: (781)388-8210
Free: 800-216-2552
Publication covering economics. **Freq:** Quarterly. **Key Personnel:** Kai-Uwe Kuhn, Advisor; Patrick Legros, Managing Editor; Jan Stevenson, Editor. **ISSN:** 0022--1821 (print); **EISSN:** 1467--6451 (electronic). **Subscription Rates:** $103 Individuals print + online; $44 Students print + online; $468 Institutions print + online; $390 Institutions print, online; €390 Institutions print and online; €325 Institutions print, online; $651 Institutions, other countries print + online; $542 Institutions, other countries print, online; £309 Institutions print + online; £257 Institutions print, online. **URL:** http://onlinelibrary.wiley.com/journal/10.1111/(ISSN)1467-6451. **Remarks:** Accepts advertising. **Circ:** (Not Reported).

16609 ■ Journal of International Financial Management & Accounting
Wiley-Blackwell
350 Main St.
Commerce Pl.
Malden, MA 02148-5018
Phone: (781)388-8200
Fax: (781)388-8210
Free: 800-216-2552
Journal covering research focusing on international aspects of financial management and reporting, banking and financial services, auditing and taxation. **Freq:** 3/year. **Key Personnel:** Prof. Frederick Choi, Editor, phone: (212)998-0047, fax: (212)995-4221; Prof. Richard Levich, Editor, phone: (212)998-0422, fax: (212)995-4220; Sidney Gray, Associate Editor. **ISSN:** 0954--1314 (print); **EISSN:** 1467--646X (electronic). **Subscription Rates:** $1159 Institutions print or online; £617 Institutions print or online; €782 Institutions print or online, euro and non euro zone; $1352 Institutions, other countries print or online; $1391 Institutions print and online; £741 Institutions print and online; €939 Institutions print and online, euro and non euro zone; $1623 Institutions print and online, ROW. **URL:** http://onlinelibrary.wiley.com/journal/10.1111/(ISSN)1467-646X. **Remarks:** Advertising accepted; rates available upon request. **Circ:** (Not Reported).

16610 ■ Journal of Law and Society
Wiley-Blackwell
350 Main St.
Commerce Pl.
Malden, MA 02148-5018
Phone: (781)388-8200
Fax: (781)388-8210
Free: 800-216-2552
Law periodical. **Freq:** Quarterly. **Key Personnel:** Prof. Philip A. Thomas, Editor, phone: 44 29 20874368; Peter Alldridge, Advisor, Board Member; Robert Lee, Assistant Editor; Stewart Field, Assistant Editor; Richard K. Lewis, Assistant Editor; Reza Banakar, Advisor, Board Member. **ISSN:** 0263--323X (print); **EISSN:** 1467--6478 (electronic). **Subscription Rates:** $83 Individuals print and online; €74 Individuals print and online; £52 Individuals print and online; $57 Members print and online; £32 Students print and online; $1516 Institutions print and online; $1263 Institutions print, online; €945 Institutions print and online; €787 Institutions print, online; $1766 Institutions, other countries print and online. **URL:** http://onlinelibrary.wiley.com/journal/10.1111/(ISSN)1467-6478. **Remarks:** Accepts advertising. **Circ:** (Not Reported).

16611 ■ Journal of Legal Studies Education
Wiley-Blackwell
350 Main St.
Commerce Pl.
Malden, MA 02148-5018
Phone: (781)388-8200
Fax: (781)388-8210
Free: 800-216-2552
Journal covering legal education issues. **Freq:** Semiannual. **Key Personnel:** Tonia Murphy, Editor; Debra Burke, Editor-in-Chief; Lucien J. Dhooge, Editor, Advisor; Robert C. Bird, Editor; Ronnie Cohen, Editor; Vincent A. Carrafiello, Editor; Mark S. Blodgett, Editor; Konrad S. Lee, Editor. **ISSN:** 0896--5811 (print); **EISSN:** 1744--1722 (electronic). **Subscription Rates:** $904 U.S. print and online; £615 Institutions print + online; €779 Institutions print and online; $1200 Other countries print + online; $753 U.S. online or print; £512 Institutions online or print; €649 Institutions online or print; $1000 Other countries online or print. **URL:** http://onlinelibrary.wiley.com/journal/10.1111/(ISSN)1744-1722. **Remarks:** Advertising accepted; rates available upon request. **Circ:** (Not Reported).

16612 ■ Journal of Management Studies
Wiley-Blackwell
350 Main St.
Commerce Pl.
Malden, MA 02148-5018
Phone: (781)388-8200
Fax: (781)388-8210
Free: 800-216-2552
General business publication. **Freq:** 8/year. **Key Personnel:** Steven W. Floyd, Board Member; Mike Wright, Board Member; Timothy Clark, Board Member; Andrew Delios, Board Member; Joep Cornelissen, Board Member. **ISSN:** 0022--2380 (print); **EISSN:** 1467--6486 (electronic). **Subscription Rates:** $248 Individuals print and online, America; €225 Individuals print and online, Europe; £151 Individuals print and online, rest of World; $157 Members print and online, America; €140 Members print and online, Europe; £94 Members print and online, rest of World; $3213 Institutions print and online, America; €1940 Institutions print and online, Europe; £1529 Institutions print and online, UK; $3748 Institutions, other countries print and online. **URL:** http://onlinelibrary.wiley.com/journal/10.1111/(ISSN)1467-6486. **Remarks:** Accepts advertising. **Circ:** (Not Reported).

16613 ■ Journal of Neurochemistry: Official Journal of the International Society for Neurochemistry
Blackwell Publishing Inc.
350 Main St.
Malden, MA 02148
Phone: (781)388-8200
Fax: (781)388-8210
Free: 800-216-2522
Publisher's E-mail: journaladsusa@bos.blackwellpublishing.com
Journal providing coverage of significant advances in neurochemistry and molecular and cellular biology. **Freq:** Semimonthly. **Key Personnel:** Jorg B. Schulz, Editor-in-Chief; Sean Murphy, Editor-in-Chief. **ISSN:** 0022-3042 (print); **EISSN:** 1471-4159 (electronic). **Subscription Rates:** $6097 Institutions online only; $1136 Individuals online only; $25 Members online only; £3299 Institutions online only; £677 Individuals online only; €4190 Institutions online only. **URL:** http://onlinelibrary.wiley.com/journal/10.1111/(ISSN)1471-4159; http://as.wiley.com/WileyCDA/WileyTitle/productCd-JNC2.html. **Ad Rates:** BW $900; 4C $2,250. **Remarks:** Accepts advertising. **Circ:** 2333.

16614 ■ Journal of Nursing Scholarship
Wiley-Blackwell
350 Main St.
Commerce Pl.
Malden, MA 02148-5018
Phone: (781)388-8200
Fax: (781)388-8210
Free: 800-216-2552
Peer-reviewed journal covering nursing. **Freq:** Quarterly. **Trim Size:** 8 1/2 x 11. **Key Personnel:** Susan Gennaro, Editor; Sabina De Geest, PhD, Associate Editor. **ISSN:** 1527--6546 (print); **EISSN:** 1547--5069 (electronic). **Subscription Rates:** $368 Institutions print and online; £267 Institutions print and online; €341 Institutions print and online; $522 Institutions, other countries print and online; $79 Individuals print and online; £60 Individuals print and online - UK, Europe (non euro zone) and rest of the world; €89 Individuals print and online; Included in membership; $82 Individuals print and online; $325 Institutions online only. **URL:** http://onlinelibrary.wiley.com/journal/10.1111/(ISSN)1547-5069; http://www.nursingsociety.org/learn-grow/publications/journal-of-nursing-scholarship. **Ad Rates:** BW $2,785. **Remarks:** Accepts advertising. **Circ:** 130000.

16615 ■ Journal of Phycology: An International Journal of Algal Research
Blackwell Publishing Inc.
350 Main St.
Malden, MA 02148
Phone: (781)388-8200
Fax: (781)388-8210
Free: 800-216-2522
Publisher's E-mail: journaladsusa@bos.blackwellpublishing.com
Journal presenting research on algae. **Freq:** Bimonthly. **Print Method:** Letterpress and offset. **Cols./Page:** 2. **Col. Width:** 39 nonpareils. **Col. Depth:** 133 agate lines. **Key Personnel:** Debashish Bhattacharya, Editor; Christopher E. Lane, Board Member; Charles D. Amsler, Associate Editor. **ISSN:** 0022--3646 (print); **EISSN:** 1529--8817 (electronic). **Subscription Rates:** $977 Institutions online only; $1173 Institutions print and online; $977 Institutions print only; £581 Institutions online only; £765 Institutions print and online; £637 Institutions print only. **URL:** http://onlinelibrary.wiley.com/journal/10.1111/(ISSN)1529-8817. **Ad Rates:** BW $550; 4C $850. **Remarks:** Accepts advertising. **Circ:** ‡1900.

16616 ■ Journal of Policy and Practice in Intellectual Disabilities
Wiley-Blackwell
350 Main St.
Commerce Pl.
Malden, MA 02148-5018
Phone: (781)388-8200
Fax: (781)388-8210
Free: 800-216-2552
Publisher's E-mail: customerservice@oxon.blackwellpublishing.com
Journal is a forum for description of evidence-based policy and practice related to people with intellectual and developmental disabilities. **Freq:** Quarterly. **Key Personnel:** Matthew P. Janicki, PhD, Editor. **ISSN:** 1741-1122 (print); **EISSN:** 1741-1130 (electronic). **Subscription Rates:** $129 Individuals print + online; $557 Institutions print + online; $485 Institutions print or online; £428 Institutions print + online; $80 Individuals ASSID member; £99 Individuals print + online; £371 Institutions print, online; €542 Institutions print + online; €470 Institutions print or online; €149 Individuals print + online. **URL:** http://onlinelibrary.wiley.com/journal/10.1111/(ISSN)1741-1130. **Mailing address:** PO Box 1354, Oxford OX4 2ZG, United Kingdom. **Remarks:** Advertising not accepted. **Circ:** (Not Reported).

16617 ■ The Journal of Political Philosophy
Wiley-Blackwell
350 Main St.
Commerce Pl.
Malden, MA 02148-5018
Phone: (781)388-8200
Fax: (781)388-8210
Free: 800-216-2552
Journal focusing on political philosophy. **Freq:** Quarterly. **Key Personnel:** Robert E. Goodin, Editor, phone: 61 261 252156; Geoffrey Brennan, Associate Editor; Claus Offe, Associate Editor; Philip Pettit, Associate Editor; Jeremy Waldron, Associate Editor; Carole Pateman, Associate Editor; Chandran Kukathas, Associate Editor; John Dryzek, Associate Editor; Anne Phillips, Board Member. **ISSN:** 0963--8016 (print); **EISSN:** 1467--9760 (electronic). **Subscription Rates:** $74 Individuals print + online; £50 Individuals print + online; £50 Individuals print + online; €68 Individuals print + online; $50

Individuals print + online, ROW; $1244 Institutions print + online, America; £902 Institutions print + online, UK; €1140 Institutions print + online; $1762 Institutions print + online, ROW; $1036 Institutions print or online, The America's; £751 Institutions print or online, UK; €950 Institutions print or online, euro and non euro zone ; $1468 Institutions print or online, ROW. **URL:** http://onlinelibrary.wiley.com/journal/10.1111/(ISSN)1467-9760. **Remarks:** Advertising accepted; rates available upon request. **Circ:** (Not Reported).

16618 ■ Journal of Popular Culture
Blackwell Publishing Inc.
350 Main St.
Malden, MA 02148
Phone: (781)388-8200
Fax: (781)388-8210
Free: 800-216-2522
Publisher's E-mail: kdvorak@houston.rr.com
Journal covering all aspects of mass culture. **Freq:** Bimonthly. **Print Method:** Offset. **Trim Size:** 6 x 9. **Cols./Page:** 1. **Col. Width:** 27 nonpareils. **Col. Depth:** 7 1/2 inches. **Key Personnel:** Gary C. Hoppenstand, Editor. **ISSN:** 0022-3840 (print); **EISSN:** 1540-5931 (electronic). **Subscription Rates:** $356 Institutions online 6 issues; €351 Institutions online; $543 Institutions, other countries online; $428 Institutions print and online; £333 Institutions print and online; €422 Institutions print and online; 652 Institutions, other countries print and online; $356 Institutions America; print or online; £227 Institutions print or online; €351 Institutions print; $543 Institutions, other countries print and online. **URL:** http://as.wiley.com/WileyCDA/WileyTitle/productCd-JPCU.html; http://pcaaca.org/journals/; http://onlinelibrary.wiley.com/journal/10.1111/(ISSN)1540-5931. **Ad Rates:** BW $475. **Remarks:** Color advertising not accepted. **Circ:** ‡3500, 3300.

16619 ■ Journal of Popular Music Studies
Wiley-Blackwell
350 Main St.
Commerce Pl.
Malden, MA 02148-5018
Phone: (781)388-8200
Fax: (781)388-8210
Free: 800-216-2552
Peer-reviewed journal dedicated to research on popular music throughout the world and approached from a variety of positions. **Freq:** Quarterly. **Key Personnel:** Gus Stadler, Editor-in-Chief. **ISSN:** 1524--2226 (print); **EISSN:** 1533--1598 (electronic). **Subscription Rates:** $368 Institutions; £307 Institutions UK; €391 Institutions Europe; $598 Institutions, other countries; $442 Institutions print and online; £369 Institutions print and online, UK; €470 Institutions print and online, Europe; $718 Institutions, other countries print and online. **URL:** http://onlinelibrary.wiley.com/journal/10.1111/(ISSN)1533-1598. **Ad Rates:** BW $350. **Remarks:** Accepts advertising. **Circ:** (Not Reported).

16620 ■ Journal of Prosthodontics
Wiley-Blackwell
350 Main St.
Commerce Pl.
Malden, MA 02148-5018
Phone: (781)388-8200
Fax: (781)388-8210
Free: 800-216-2552
Professional journal covering dentistry. **Freq:** 8/year. **Print Method:** Sheetfed Offset. **Trim Size:** 8 1/4 x 10 7/8. **Key Personnel:** David Felton, Editor-in-Chief. **ISSN:** 1059--941X (print); **EISSN:** 1532--849X (electronic). **Subscription Rates:** $246 Individuals print and online; $777 Institutions print and online; €825 Institutions print and online; £652 Institutions print and online; $647 Institutions online or print; €687 Institutions online or print; Included in membership. **URL:** http://as.wiley.com/WileyCDA/WileyTitle/productCd-JOPR.html; http://onlinelibrary.wiley.com/journal/10.1111/(ISSN)1532-849X. **Ad Rates:** BW $1,490; 4C $1,395. **Remarks:** Accepts advertising. **Circ:** Paid ‡3184.

16621 ■ Journal of Public Economic Theory
Wiley-Blackwell
350 Main St.
Commerce Pl.
Malden, MA 02148-5018
Phone: (781)388-8200
Fax: (781)388-8210
Free: 800-216-2552
Peer-reviewed journal focusing on research in the field of public economics. **Freq:** Bimonthly. **Key Personnel:** Myrna Holtz Wooders, Editor, phone: (615)343-0462, fax: (615)343-8495; Reinhard Selten, Advisor, Editor; Martin Shubik, Editor; John Ledyard, Advisor, Editor; Rod Garrat, Associate Editor; James Mirrlees, Advisor, Editor; Roger Guesnerie, Advisor, Editor. **ISSN:** 1097--3923 (print); **EISSN:** 1467--9779 (electronic). **Subscription Rates:** $1231 Institutions online only; £910 Institutions online only; €1155 Institutions online only; $1781 Institutions, other countries online only. **URL:** http://onlinelibrary.wiley.com/journal/10.1111/(ISSN)1467-9779. **Remarks:** Accepts advertising. **Circ:** (Not Reported).

16622 ■ Journal of Renal Care
Blackwell Publishing Inc.
350 Main St.
Malden, MA 02148
Phone: (781)388-8200
Fax: (781)388-8210
Free: 800-216-2522
Publisher's E-mail: journaladsusa@bos.blackwellpublishing.com
Peer-reviewed journal covering the field of healthcare for kidney disease. **Freq:** Quarterly. **Key Personnel:** Nicola Thomas, Editor. **ISSN:** 1755-6678 (print). **Subscription Rates:** $178 Individuals Americas (print and online); £90 Individuals non-Euro zone (print and online); €133 Individuals Euro zone (print and online); £96 Other countries individual (print and online); $616 Institutions Americas (print and online); £309 Institutions UK (print and online); €393 Institutions Europe (print and online); $667 Institutions, other countries print and online; $536 Institutions Americas (print or online only); £269 Institutions UK (print or online only). **URL:** http://www.wiley.com/WileyCDA/WileyTitle/productCd-JORC.html. **Circ:** (Not Reported).

16623 ■ Journal of Research on Adolescence: The Official Journal of the Society for Research on Adolescence
Blackwell Publishing Inc.
350 Main St.
Malden, MA 02148
Phone: (781)388-8200
Fax: (781)388-8210
Free: 800-216-2522
Publisher's E-mail: journaladsusa@bos.blackwellpublishing.com
Journal focusing on the second decade of life. **Freq:** Quarterly. **Key Personnel:** Nancy G. Guerra, Editor; Paul Boxer, Associate Editor. **ISSN:** 1050--8392 (print); **EISSN:** 1532--7795 (electronic). **Subscription Rates:** $893 Institutions online only; $169 Individuals online only. **URL:** http://onlinelibrary.wiley.com/journal/10.1111/%28ISSN%291532-7795; http://www.s-r-a.org/journal-research-adolescence/about-jra. **Ad Rates:** BW $425. **Remarks:** Accepts advertising. **Circ:** (Not Reported).

16624 ■ Journal of Sleep Research
Wiley-Blackwell
350 Main St.
Commerce Pl.
Malden, MA 02148-5018
Phone: (781)388-8200
Fax: (781)388-8210
Free: 800-216-2552
Peer-reviewed journal covering the field of sleep and wakefulness. **Freq:** Quarterly. **Key Personnel:** Derk-Jan Dijk, Editor; Claudio Bassetti, Associate Editor; Tom de Boer, Associate Editor. **ISSN:** 0962-1105 (print). **Subscription Rates:** $193 Members print + online (National societies); €158 Members print + online (National societies); £105 Members print + online (National societies); £114 Members print + online (National societies, rest of world); $842 Institutions print + online; £458 Institutions print + online; €584 Institutions print + online; $983 Institutions, other countries print + online; $732 Institutions print or online; $854 Institutions, other countries print or online. **URL:** http://www.wiley.com/bw/journal.asp?ref=0962-1105. **Remarks:** Advertising accepted; rates available upon request. **Circ:** (Not Reported).

16625 ■ Journal for Specialists in Pediatric Nursing
Wiley-Blackwell
350 Main St.
Commerce Pl.
Malden, MA 02148-5018
Phone: (781)388-8200
Fax: (781)388-8210
Free: 800-216-2552
Peer-reviewed journal focusing on nurses who specialize in the care of children and families. **Freq:** Quarterly. **Key Personnel:** Kristen Overstreet, Managing Editor; Nancy Ryan-Wenger, Editor-in-Chief. **ISSN:** 1539--0136 (print); **EISSN:** 1744--6155 (electronic). **Subscription Rates:** $258 Institutions online only; £180 Institutions online only; €227 Institutions online only; $347 Institutions, other countries online only; $231 Individuals online only; £162 Other countries online only; €203 Individuals. **URL:** http://onlinelibrary.wiley.com/journal/10.1111/(ISSN)1744-6155. **Ad Rates:** BW $1,000; 4C $975. **Remarks:** Accepts advertising. **Circ:** (Not Reported).

16626 ■ Journal of Supreme Court History
Wiley-Blackwell
350 Main St.
Commerce Pl.
Malden, MA 02148-5018
Phone: (781)388-8200
Fax: (781)388-8210
Free: 800-216-2552
Journal containing the collection and preservation of the history of the Supreme Court of the United States. **Freq:** 3/year. **Key Personnel:** Melvin I. Urofsky, Editor; Clare Cushman, Managing Editor. **ISSN:** 1059--4329 (print); **EISSN:** 1540--5818 (electronic). **Subscription Rates:** $236 Institutions; £183 Institutions; €231 Institutions; $352 Institutions, other countries; $284 Institutions print and online; £220 Institutions print and online, UK; €278 Institutions print and online, Europe; $423 Institutions, other countries print and online. **URL:** http://onlinelibrary.wiley.com/journal/10.1111/(ISSN)1540-5818. **Circ:** (Not Reported).

16627 ■ Journal for the Theory of Social Behaviour
Wiley-Blackwell
350 Main St.
Commerce Pl.
Malden, MA 02148-5018
Phone: (781)388-8200
Fax: (781)388-8210
Free: 800-216-2552
Journal focusing on the links between social structures and human agency embedded in behavioural practices. **Freq:** Quarterly. **Key Personnel:** Alex Gillespie, Editor. **ISSN:** 0021--8308 (print); **EISSN:** 1468--5914 (electronic). **Subscription Rates:** $875 Institutions print or online; £539 Institutions print or online; €684 Institutions print or online; $1260 Institutions print or online; $1050 Institutions print and online; £647 Institutions print and online; €821 Institutions print and online; $1512 Institutions, other countries print and online; $137 Individuals print and online; £92 Individuals print and online; €135 Individuals print and online; £113 Other countries print and online. **URL:** http://onlinelibrary.wiley.com/journal/10.1111/(ISSN)1468-5914. **Remarks:** Accepts advertising. **Circ:** (Not Reported).

16628 ■ Journal of Thrombosis and Haemostasis
Blackwell Publishing Inc.
350 Main St.
Malden, MA 02148
Phone: (781)388-8200
Fax: (781)388-8210
Free: 800-216-2522
Publication E-mail: editorjth@abdn.ac.uk
Journal that publishes research papers on thrombosis, bleeding disorders and vascular biology. **Freq:** Monthly. **Trim Size:** 8 1/4 10 7/8. **Key Personnel:** Prof. Mike Greaves, Editor-in-Chief; W. Aird, Associate Editor; Prof. David Lane, Editor-in-Chief. **ISSN:** 1538-7933 (print); **EISSN:** 1538-7836 (electronic). **Subscription Rates:** $593 Individuals print + online; €704 Individuals print + online; £470 Individuals print + online; $1534 Institutions print and online; $2252 Institutions, other countries print & online; $1278 Institutions print only; £1151 Institutions print and online; £959 Institutions print only; $1278

Circulation: ★ = AAM; △ or • = BPA; ♦ = CAC; ❑ = VAC; ⊕ = PO Statement; ‡ = Publisher's Report; Boldface figures = sworn; Light figures = estimated.

Institutions online only; Included in membership. **URL:** http://as.wiley.com/WileyCDA/WileyTitle/productCd-JTH.html; http://www.isth.org/?page=JTH; http://onlinelibrary.wiley.com/journal/10.1111/%28ISSN%291538-7836. **Ad Rates:** BW $1,405; 4C $1,230. **Remarks:** Accepts advertising. **Circ: 3076.**

16629 ■ Journal of the World Aquaculture Society
Wiley-Blackwell
350 Main St.
Commerce Pl.
Malden, MA 02148-5018
Phone: (781)388-8200
Fax: (781)388-8210
Free: 800-216-2552
Peer-reviewed journal featuring papers on the culture of aquatic plants and animals. **Freq:** Bimonthly. **Key Personnel:** Carl Webster, Editor; Sungchul Bai, Associate Editor; Dominique Bureau, Associate Editor; Carole Engle, Editor. **ISSN:** 0893--8849 (print); **EISSN:** 1749--7345 (electronic). **Subscription Rates:** £378 Institutions UK (print and online); $564 Institutions Americas (print and online); €432 Institutions Europe (print and online); $667 Institutions, other countries print and online; £315 Institutions UK (print or online only); $519 Institutions Americas (print or online only); €398 Institutions Europe (print or online only); $614 Institutions online, ROW; $623 Institutions print and online ; €478 Institutions print and online ; $737 Institutions print and online, ROW. **URL:** http://onlinelibrary.wiley.com/journal/10.1111/(ISSN)1749-7345; http://www.was.org/View/Journal-of-the-World-Aquaculture-Society.aspx. **Remarks:** Advertising not accepted. **Circ:** (Not Reported).

16630 ■ KYKLOS: International Review for Social Sciences
Wiley-Blackwell
350 Main St.
Commerce Pl.
Malden, MA 02148-5018
Phone: (781)388-8200
Fax: (781)388-8210
Free: 800-216-2552
Publisher's E-mail: customerservice@oxon.blackwellpublishing.com
Journal covering social sciences. **Freq:** Quarterly. **Key Personnel:** Rene L. Frey, Editor, Managing Editor; Bruno S. Frey, Managing Editor; Reiner Eichenberger, Managing Editor. **ISSN:** 0023--5962 (print); **EISSN:** 1467--6435 (electronic). **Subscription Rates:** $956 Institutions print or online; $1148 Institutions print + online; $65 Students print + online; £571 Institutions print or online; £686 Institutions print + online; £40 Students print + online; €726 Institutions print or online; €872 Institutions print + online; €60 Students print + online; $1116 Institutions, other countries print or online; $1340 Institutions, other countries print and online. **URL:** http://onlinelibrary.wiley.com/journal/10.1111/(ISSN)1467-6435. **Mailing address:** PO Box 1354, Oxford OX4 2ZG, United Kingdom. **Remarks:** Accepts advertising. **Circ:** (Not Reported).

16631 ■ Lakes & Reservoirs: Research and Management
Blackwell Publishing Inc.
350 Main St.
Malden, MA 02148
Phone: (781)388-8200
Fax: (781)388-8210
Free: 800-216-2522
Publisher's E-mail: journaladsusa@bos.blackwellpublishing.com
Peer-reviewed journal covering the research on the management and conservation of lakes and reservoirs. **Freq:** Quarterly. **Key Personnel:** W. Rast, Editor-in-Chief; T. Watanabe, Advisor. **ISSN:** 1320--5331 (print); **EISSN:** 1440--1770 (electronic). **Subscription Rates:** $954 Institutions online only; £593 Institutions online only, UK; €754 Institutions online only, Europe; $1159 Institutions, other countries online only. **URL:** http://onlinelibrary.wiley.com/journal/10.1111/(ISSN)1440-1770. **Remarks:** Accepts advertising: **Circ:** (Not Reported).

16632 ■ Language Learning
Blackwell Publishing Inc.
350 Main St.
Malden, MA 02148
Phone: (781)388-8200
Fax: (781)388-8210
Free: 800-216-2522
Publisher's E-mail: journaladsusa@bos.blackwellpublishing.com
Journal focusing on the understanding of language learning. **Freq:** Quarterly. **Key Personnel:** Nick C. Ellis, Editor; Lourdes Ortega, Editor; Scott Jarvis, Associate Editor. **ISSN:** 0023--8333 (print); **EISSN:** 1467--9922 (electronic). **Subscription Rates:** $546 Institutions; £420 Institutions UK; €530 Institutions; $818 Institutions, other countries; $656 Institutions print and online; £504 Institutions print and online, UK; €636 Institutions print and online, Europe; $982 Institutions, other countries print and online; $128 Individuals print and online; €147 Individuals print and online, UK and Europe (non euro zone); €146 Individuals print and online, Europe; £128 Other countries print and online; $64 Students print and online; £38 Students print and online, UK, Europe (non euro zone) and other countries; €58 Students print and online, Europe. **URL:** http://onlinelibrary.wiley.com/journal/10.1111/(ISSN)1467-9922. **Remarks:** Accepts advertising. **Circ:** (Not Reported).

16633 ■ Law & Policy
Wiley-Blackwell
350 Main St.
Commerce Pl.
Malden, MA 02148-5018
Phone: (781)388-8200
Fax: (781)388-8210
Free: 800-216-2552
Peer-reviewed journal publishing articles on law & policy. **Freq:** Quarterly. **Key Personnel:** Jesse Morse, Managing Editor; Keith Hawkins, Board Member; Murray Levine, Board Member; Nancy Reichman, Editor. **ISSN:** 0265--8240 (print); **EISSN:** 1467--9930 (electronic). **Subscription Rates:** $661 Institutions online only; £530 Institutions online only; €671 Institutions online only; $1035 Institutions, other countries online only; $63 Individuals online only; £48 Individuals online only; £48 Individuals online only; €66 Individuals online only. **URL:** http://onlinelibrary.wiley.com/journal/10.1111/(ISSN)1467-9930. **Remarks:** Accepts advertising. **Circ:** (Not Reported).

16634 ■ Learning Disabilities Research and Practice
Blackwell Publishing Inc.
350 Main St.
Malden, MA 02148
Phone: (781)388-8200
Fax: (781)388-8210
Free: 800-216-2522
Publisher's E-mail: journaladsusa@bos.blackwellpublishing.com
Publishes articles addressing the nature and characteristics of LD students, promising research, program development, assessment practices, and teaching methodologies from different disciplines. **Freq:** Quarterly. **Key Personnel:** Diane Haager, PhD, Editor. **ISSN:** 0938--8982 (print); **EISSN:** 1540--5826 (electronic). **Subscription Rates:** $687 Institutions; £527 Institutions; €668 Institutions; $1031 Institutions, other countries; $825 Institutions print and online; £633 Institutions print and online - UK; €802 Institutions print and online - Europe; $1238 Institutions, other countries print and online; $82 Individuals print and online; £63 Individuals print and online - UK, Europe (non-euro zone) and rest of the world; €94 Individuals print and online - Europe. **URL:** http://onlinelibrary.wiley.com/journal/10.1111/(ISSN)1540-5826. **Ad Rates:** BW $550. **Remarks:** Accepts advertising. **Circ:** 12500.

16635 ■ Lethaia: An International Journal of Palaeontology and Stratigraphy
Wiley-Blackwell
350 Main St.
Commerce Pl.
Malden, MA 02148-5018
Phone: (781)388-8200
Fax: (781)388-8210
Free: 800-216-2552
Publisher's E-mail: journaladsusa@bos.blackwellpublishing.com
Journal emphasizing new developments and discoveries in palaeobiological and biostratigraphical research. **Freq:** Quarterly. **Key Personnel:** Peter Doyle, Editor-in-Chief; David A.T. Harper, Editor. **ISSN:** 0024--1164 (print); **EISSN:** 1502--3931 (electronic). **Subscription Rates:** $567 Institutions print and online; £273 Institutions print and online; €359 Institutions print and online; $549 Institutions, other countries print and online. **URL:** http://onlinelibrary.wiley.com/journal/10.1111/(ISSN)1502-3931. **Circ:** (Not Reported).

16636 ■ Linguistics Abstracts
Wiley-Blackwell
350 Main St.
Commerce Pl.
Malden, MA 02148-5018
Phone: (781)388-8200
Fax: (781)388-8210
Free: 800-216-2552
Journal containing abstracts in English of linguistics articles. **Freq:** Quarterly. **Key Personnel:** Benjamin V. Tucker, Editor. **ISSN:** 0267--5498 (print); **EISSN:** 1368--5295 (electronic). **Subscription Rates:** $2710 Institutions online only. **URL:** http://www.linguisticsabstracts.com; http://www.wiley.com/WileyCDA/WileyTitle/productCd-LABS.html. **Remarks:** Accepts advertising. **Circ:** (Not Reported).

16637 ■ Liver Transplantation: An Issue of Clinics in Liver Disease
Wiley-Blackwell
350 Main St.
Commerce Pl.
Malden, MA 02148-5018
Phone: (781)388-8200
Fax: (781)388-8210
Free: 800-216-2552
Publisher's E-mail: info@wiley.com
Official journal of the American Association for the Study of Liver Diseases and the International Liver Transplantation Society. **Freq:** Monthly. **Trim Size:** 8 1/4 x 11. **Key Personnel:** John Lake, Editor; John Roberts, Editor. **ISSN:** 1527--6465 (print); **EISSN:** 1527--6473 (electronic). **Subscription Rates:** $445 Individuals online only; $487 Individuals print and online; $445 Individuals print only; $3491 Institutions print and online; $2909 Institutions online only; $2909 Institutions print only. **URL:** http://onlinelibrary.wiley.com/journal/10.1002/(ISSN)1527-6473; http://as.wiley.com/WileyCDA/PressRelease/pressReleaseId-62057.html. **Ad Rates:** BW $950; 4C $1575. **Remarks:** Accepts advertising. **Circ:** Paid 5370.

16638 ■ Malden Evening News
Eastern Middlesex Press Publications Inc.
277 Commercial St.
Malden, MA 02148
Phone: (617)321-8000
Fax: (617)321-8008
Publication E-mail: newsmerc@user1.channel1.com
General newspaper. **Freq:** Daily (eve.). **Print Method:** Offset. **Cols./Page:** 6. **Col. Width:** 25 nonpareils. **Col. Depth:** 294 agate lines. **Key Personnel:** Tom Daly, General Manager. **Subscription Rates:** $118 Individuals. **URL:** http://www.maldennews.com. **Formerly:** Daily News Mercury. **Ad Rates:** BW $1,512; 4C $2,312; SAU $12. **Remarks:** Accepts advertising. **Circ:** ‡15000.

16639 ■ Marine Mammal Science
Wiley-Blackwell
350 Main St.
Commerce Pl.
Malden, MA 02148-5018
Phone: (781)388-8200
Fax: (781)388-8210
Free: 800-216-2552
Journal covering the research on marine mammals. **Freq:** Quarterly. **Key Personnel:** Daryl J. Boness, Editor. **ISSN:** 0824--0469 (print); **EISSN:** 1748--7692 (electronic). **Subscription Rates:** $359 Institutions online only; £223 Institutions online only, UK; €280 Institutions online only, Europe; $429 Institutions, other countries online only. **URL:** http://onlinelibrary.wiley.com/journal/10.1111/(ISSN)1748-7692; http://www.marinemammalscience.org/journal. **Remarks:** Accepts advertising. **Circ:** (Not Reported).

16640 ■ Mathematical Finance: An International Journal of Mathematics, Statistics, and Financial
Blackwell Publishing Inc.
350 Main St.
Malden, MA 02148
Phone: (781)388-8200
Fax: (781)388-8210
Free: 800-216-2522
Publisher's E-mail: journaladsusa@bos.blackwellpublishing.com
Journal containing latest theoretical developments in the fields of finance, economics, mathematics, and statistics. **Freq:** Quarterly. **Trim Size:** 9 3/4 x 6 3/4. **Key Personnel:** Jerome Detemple, Editor. **ISSN:** 0960--1627 (print). **Subscription Rates:** $216 Individuals print & online; $1961 Institutions print & online; $1634 Institutions print or online; €263 Individuals print & online; $3002 Institutions, other countries print & online; $2501 Institutions, other countries print or online; £177 Individuals print & online; €1947 Institutions print & online; €1622 Institutions print or online. **URL:** http://onlinelibrary.wiley.com/journal/10.1111/(ISSN)1467-9965. **Ad Rates:** BW $350. **Remarks:** Accepts advertising. **Circ:** ‡800.

16641 ■ Microcirculation
Wiley-Blackwell
350 Main St.
Commerce Pl.
Malden, MA 02148-5018
Phone: (781)388-8200
Fax: (781)388-8210
Free: 800-216-2552
Journal featuring original contributions that are the result of investigations contributing significant new information relating to the microcirculation addressed at the intact animal, organ, cellular, or molecular level. **Freq:** Annual 8/yr. **Key Personnel:** William F. Jackson, PhD, Editor; Neil D. Granger, Editor; Steven J. Alexander, Board Member; Prof. William F. Jackson, PhD, Editor; Paul Kubes, Board Member; Jefferson C. Frisbee, Board Member, Editor-in-Chief; Daniel Beard, Board Member; Shawn Bearden, Board Member; Maria Sanz, Board Member. **ISSN:** 1073--9688 (print); **EISSN:** 1549--8719 (electronic). **Subscription Rates:** $1964 Institutions online only; £1199 Institutions online only; €1408 Institutions online only. **URL:** http://onlinelibrary.wiley.com/journal/10.1111/(ISSN)1549-8719. **Remarks:** Advertising not accepted. **Circ:** (Not Reported).

16642 ■ Middle East Policy
Blackwell Publishing Inc.
350 Main St.
Malden, MA 02148
Phone: (781)388-8200
Fax: (781)388-8210
Free: 800-216-2522
Publisher's E-mail: journaladsusa@bos.blackwellpublishing.com
Publication covering politics and the Middle East. **Founded:** 1982. **Freq:** Quarterly. **Print Method:** pdf files to film. **Trim Size:** 6.75 x 10. **Key Personnel:** Anne Joyce, Editor. **ISSN:** 1061-1924 (print); **EISSN:** 1475-4967 (electronic). **Subscription Rates:** $304 Institutions print or online; $365 Institutions print and online; $63 Individuals print and online; $49 Members print and online; £239 Institutions print or online; £287 Institutions print and online; £54 Individuals print and online; £43 Members print and online; €305 Institutions print or online; €366 Institutions print and online. **URL:** http://as.wiley.com/WileyCDA/WileyTitle/productCd-MEPO.html; http://onlinelibrary.wiley.com/journal/10.1111/(ISSN)1475-4967. **Ad Rates:** BW $450; 4C $500. **Remarks:** Accepts advertising. **Circ:** (Not Reported).

16643 ■ Mind, Brain, and Education
Blackwell Publishing Inc.
350 Main St.
Malden, MA 02148
Phone: (781)388-8200
Fax: (781)388-8210
Free: 800-216-2522
Publisher's E-mail: journaladsusa@bos.blackwellpublishing.com
Peer-reviewed journal featuring articles concerned with brain and behavioral issues relevant to the broad field of education. **Freq:** Quarterly. **Key Personnel:** Kurt W. Fischer, PhD, Editor-in-Chief; David B. Daniel, PhD, Managing Editor; pat levitt, Editor-in-Chief. **ISSN:** 1751--2271 (print); **EISSN:** 1751--228x (electronic). **Subscription Rates:** $333 Institutions; €214 Institutions UK; €270 Institutions Europe; $416 Institutions, other countries; $400 Institutions print and online; £257 Institutions print and online, UK; €324 Institutions print and online, Europe; $500 Institutions, other countries print and online; $150 Individuals print and online; £88 Individuals print and online, UK and Europe (non euro zone); €129 Individuals print and online, Europe; £88 Individuals print and online. **URL:** http://onlinelibrary.wiley.com/journal/10.1111/(ISSN)1751-228X. **Remarks:** Accepts advertising. **Circ:** (Not Reported).

16644 ■ The Modern Law Review
Wiley-Blackwell
350 Main St.
Commerce Pl.
Malden, MA 02148-5018
Phone: (781)388-8200
Fax: (781)388-8210
Free: 800-216-2552
Peer-reviewed journal publishing articles relating to common law jurisdictions. **Freq:** Bimonthly. **Key Personnel:** Martin Loughlin, Member; Julia Black, Editor; W.R. Cornish, Board Member; J.S. Anderson, Board Member; M.R. Chesterman, Board Member. **ISSN:** 0026-7961 (print); **EISSN:** 1468-2230 (electronic). **Subscription Rates:** $468 Institutions online only; £263 Institutions online only; €333 Institutions online only; $562 Institutions print and online; £316 Institutions print and online; €400 Institutions print and online; $113 Individuals print and online; £68 Individuals print and online; €102 Individuals print and online; $18 Students print and online; £11 Students print and online; €13 Students print and online; $70 Individuals print and online - teacher; £30 Individuals print and online - teacher; €42 Individuals print and online - teacher. **URL:** http://onlinelibrary.wiley.com/journal/10.1111/(ISSN)1468-2230; http://as.wiley.com/WileyCDA/WileyTitle/productCd-MLR.html. **Remarks:** Accepts advertising. **Circ:** (Not Reported).

16645 ■ Modern Theology
Wiley-Blackwell
350 Main St.
Commerce Pl.
Malden, MA 02148-5018
Phone: (781)388-8200
Fax: (781)388-8210
Free: 800-216-2552
Peer-reviewed journal covering philosophy and religion. **Freq:** Quarterly. **Key Personnel:** Nicholas Lash, Board Member; Lewis Ayres, Board Member; Sarah Coakley, Board Member; Catherine Pickstock, Associate Editor; Gregory L. Jones, Associate Editor; William T. Cavanaugh, Editor, phone: (773)325-7680; David Ford, Board Member; James J. Buckley, Associate Editor. **ISSN:** 0266-7177 (print); **EISSN:** 1468-0025 (electronic). **Subscription Rates:** $965 Institutions print or online; £585 Institutions print or online; €741 Institutions print or online; $568 Institutions print or online - Developing World; $1313 Institutions, other countries print or online; $1158 Institutions print and online; £702 Institutions print and online; €890 Institutions print and online; $682 Institutions print and online - Developing World; $1576 Institutions, other countries print and online; $88 Individuals print and online; £58 Individuals print and online; €86 Individuals print and online; $60 Individuals print and online, rest of the world. **Online:** Gale. **URL:** http://onlinelibrary.wiley.com/journal/10.1111/(ISSN)1468-0025; http://as.wiley.com/WileyCDA/WileyTitle/productCd-MOTH.html. **Remarks:** Accepts advertising. **Circ:** (Not Reported).

16646 ■ Molecular Carcinogenesis
Wiley-Blackwell
350 Main St.
Commerce Pl.
Malden, MA 02148-5018
Phone: (781)388-8200
Fax: (781)388-8210
Free: 800-216-2552
Medical research journal. **Freq:** Monthly. **Print Method:** Offset. **Trim Size:** 8 1/2 x 11 1/4. **Key Personnel:** John DiGiovanni, Editor-in-Chief; Stuart H. Yuspa, Executive Editor; Lawrence A. Loeb, Associate Editor; Mariano Barbacid, Associate Editor; Jill Pelling, Associate Editor; Jesus Paramio, Associate Editor. **ISSN:** 0899--1987 (print); **EISSN:** 1098--2744 (electronic). **Subscription Rates:** $4026 Institutions print only; $4832 Institutions print with online; $5033 Institutions, Canada and Mexico print with online; $5134 Institutions, other countries print with online. **URL:** http://onlinelibrary.wiley.com/journal/10.1002/(ISSN)1098-2744. **Ad Rates:** BW $772; 4C $1009. **Remarks:** Accepts advertising. **Circ:** 4550.

16647 ■ Molecular Oral Microbiology
Wiley-Blackwell
350 Main St.
Commerce Pl.
Malden, MA 02148-5018
Phone: (781)388-8200
Fax: (781)388-8210
Free: 800-216-2552
Journal covering the fundamental and applied aspects of oral infections. **Freq:** Bimonthly. **Key Personnel:** Howard F. Jenkinson, Editor-in-Chief; Richard J. Lamont, Editor. **ISSN:** 2041--1006 (print); **EISSN:** 2041--1014 (electronic). **Subscription Rates:** $1152 Institutions print or online; £686 Institutions print or online, UK; €872 Institutions print or online, Europe; $1343 Institutions, other countries print or online; $1383 Institutions print and online; £824 Institutions print and online, UK; €1047 Institutions print and online, Europe; $1612 Institutions, other countries print and online; $436 Individuals print and online; £260 Individuals print and online - UK, Europe (non-euro zone) and rest of the world; €389 Individuals print and online. **URL:** http://onlinelibrary.wiley.com/doi/10.1111/omi.2015.30.issue-6/issuetoc. **Formerly:** Oral Microbiology and Immunology. **Remarks:** Advertising accepted; rates available upon request. **Circ:** (Not Reported).

16648 ■ Monographs of the Society for Research in Child Development
Blackwell Publishing Inc.
350 Main St.
Malden, MA 02148
Phone: (781)388-8200
Fax: (781)388-8210
Free: 800-216-2522
Publisher's E-mail: journaladsusa@bos.blackwellpublishing.com
Monographs presenting research studies and findings in child development. **Freq:** 3/year. **Print Method:** Offset. **Trim Size:** 6 x 9. **Cols./Page:** 1. **Col. Width:** 54 nonpareils. **Col. Depth:** 100 agate lines. **Key Personnel:** Patricia J. Bauer, Editor; Adam Martin, Managing Editor, phone: (734)926-0615, fax: (734)926-0606. **ISSN:** 0037--976X (print); **EISSN:** 1540--5834 (electronic). **Subscription Rates:** $1047 Institutions print + online; £749 Institutions print + online; €951 Institutions print + online; $1463 Institutions, other countries print + online; $872 Institutions print or online; £624 Institutions print or online; €792 Institutions print or online; $1219 Institutions, other countries print or online. **URL:** http://onlinelibrary.wiley.com/journal/10.1111/(ISSN)1540-5834; http://as.wiley.com/WileyCDA/WileyTitle/productCd-MONO.html. **Remarks:** Accepts advertising. **Circ:** (Not Reported).

16649 ■ The Muslim World
Blackwell Publishing Inc.
350 Main St.
Malden, MA 02148
Phone: (781)388-8200
Fax: (781)388-8210
Free: 800-216-2522
Publisher's E-mail: info@hartsem.edu
Journal of Islamic studies, addressing Christian-Muslim relations. **Freq:** Quarterly. **Key Personnel:** Steven Blackburn, Associate Editor; Dr. Yahya M. Michot, Editor; Nicolas Mumejian, Managing Editor. **ISSN:** 0027--4909 (print); **EISSN:** 1478--1913 (electronic). **Subscription Rates:** $51 Individuals print & online; $45 Students print & online; $430 Institutions print & online; $358 Institutions print or online; €58 Individuals print & online; $570 Institutions, other countries print & online; $475 Institutions, other countries print or online; £245 Institutions print or online; £294 Institutions print and online; £42 Individuals print and online; £28 Students print and online; €308 Institutions print or online; €370 Institutions print and online; $33 Members American Academy

Circulation: ★ = AAM; △ or • = BPA; ♦ = CAC; ❑ = VAC; ⊕ = PO Statement; ‡ = Publisher's Report; Boldface figures = sworn; Light figures = estimated.

of Religion, America (print and online); $213 Members Association of British Theological and Philosophical Libraries, America (print and online); £28 Members American Academy of Religion, UK (print and online); £145 Members Association of British Theological and Philosophical Libraries, UK and Europe - nonEuro zone (print and online); €58 Individuals Europe - Euro zone (print and online); £28 Members American Academy of Religion, Europe - nonEuro zone (print and online); €45 Members American Academy of Religion, Europe - Euro zone (print and online); €216 Members Association of British Theological and Philosophical Libraries, Europe - Euro zone (print and online); €32 Students Europe - Euro zone (print and online); $101 Institutions developing world (print or online); $122 Institutions developing world (print and online); £28 Members American Academy of Religion, Developing World (print and online); £145 Members Association of British Theological and Philosophical Libraries, Developing World (print and online). **URL:** http://www.wiley.com/WileyCDA/WileyTitle/productCd-MUWO.html; http://www.hartsem.edu/macdonald-center/the-muslim-world-journal; http://onlinelibrary.wiley.com/journal/10.1111/(ISSN)1478-1913. **Remarks:** Accepts advertising. **Circ:** ‡1000, 1000.

16650 ■ Nations and Nationalism
Blackwell Publishing Inc.
350 Main St.
Malden, MA 02148
Phone: (781)388-8200
Fax: (781)388-8210
Free: 800-216-2522
Publisher's E-mail: journaladsusa@bos.blackwellpublishing.com
Journal focusing on the study of nationalism. **Freq:** Quarterly. **Key Personnel:** Anthony D. Smith, Editor-in-Chief. **ISSN:** 1354--5078 (print); **EISSN:** 1469--8129 (electronic). **Subscription Rates:** $131 Individuals print + online - The Americas; £92 Individuals print + online - UK/Europe(non euro zone)/ROW; €139 Individuals print + online - Europe (euro zone); $112 Members print + online - The Americas - American Historical Association/American Political Science Association Member; £80 Members print + online - UK/Europe(non euro zone)/ROW - American Historical Association/American Political Science Association Member; €119 Members print + online - Europe (euro zone) - American Historical Association/American Political Science Association Member. **URL:** http://as.wiley.com/WileyCDA/WileyTitle/productCd-NANA.html; http://onlinelibrary.wiley.com/journal/10.1111/(ISSN)1469-8129. **Remarks:** Accepts advertising. **Circ:** (Not Reported).

16651 ■ Negotiation Journal
Wiley-Blackwell
350 Main St.
Commerce Pl.
Malden, MA 02148-5018
Phone: (781)388-8200
Fax: (781)388-8210
Free: 800-216-2552
Journal focusing on the development of better strategies for resolving differences through the give-and-take process of negotiation. **Freq:** Quarterly. **Key Personnel:** Michael Wheeler, Editor; Daniel Druckman, Associate Editor; Carrie Menkel-Meadow, Associate Editor. **ISSN:** 0748-4526 (print); **EISSN:** 1571-9979 (electronic). **Subscription Rates:** £62 Other countries print and online; $83 Individuals Americas (print and online); €93 Individuals Euro zone (print and online); £785 Institutions UK (print and online); $1065 Institutions Americas (print and online); €995 Institutions Europe (print and online); $1065 Institutions, other countries print and online; £680 Institutions UK (print or online only); $930 Institutions Americas (print or online only); €865 Institutions Europe (print or online only). **URL:** http://www.wiley.com/WileyCDA/WileyTitle/productCd-NEJO.html. **Remarks:** Accepts advertising. **Circ:** (Not Reported).

16652 ■ Neuromodulation
Wiley-Blackwell
350 Main St.
Commerce Pl.
Malden, MA 02148-5018
Phone: (781)388-8200
Fax: (781)388-8210
Free: 800-216-2552
Journal publishing scientific and clinical information focusing on neuromodulation, in connection with the International Neuromodulation Society and the International Functional Electrical Stimulation Society (IFESS). **Freq:** Quarterly. **Key Personnel:** Robert Levy, MD, Editor-in-Chief; Tia Sofatzis, Managing Editor. **ISSN:** 1094-7159 (print). **Subscription Rates:** $210 Individuals print & online; $437 Institutions print & online; £335 Institutions print & online; $397 Institutions online only; €264 Individuals print & online; €426 Institutions print & online; €386 Institutions online only. **URL:** http://www.wiley.com/bw/journal.asp?ref=1094-7159. **Remarks:** Advertising accepted; rates available upon request. **Circ:** (Not Reported).

16653 ■ Nursing for Women's Health: An AWHONN Publication
Wiley-Blackwell
350 Main St.
Commerce Pl.
Malden, MA 02148-5018
Phone: (781)388-8200
Fax: (781)388-8210
Free: 800-216-2552
Publisher's E-mail: journaladsusa@bos.blackwellpublishing.com
Pee-reviewed journal covering practice management resources and industry trends in women's health. **Freq:** Bimonthly. **Print Method:** Web offset. **Trim Size:** 8 3/8 x 10 3/8. **Key Personnel:** Carolyn Davis Cockey, Executive Editor; Mary C. Brucker, PhD, Editor; Jennifer P. Hellwig, MS, Managing Editor. **ISSN:** 1751--4851 (print); **EISSN:** 1751--486X (electronic). **Formerly:** AWHONN Lifelines. **Remarks:** Accepts advertising. **Circ:** (Not Reported).

16654 ■ Obesity Reviews
Wiley-Blackwell
350 Main St.
Commerce Pl.
Malden, MA 02148-5018
Phone: (781)388-8200
Fax: (781)388-8210
Free: 800-216-2552
Publisher's E-mail: enquiries@worldobesity.org
Journal publishing papers from all disciplines related to obesity. **Freq:** Monthly. **Key Personnel:** David A. York, Editor; Dr. David B. Allison, Board Member. **ISSN:** 1467--7881 (print); **EISSN:** 1467--789X (electronic). **Subscription Rates:** $1317 Institutions print and online; £719 Institutions print and online; €915 Institutions print and online; $1538 Institutions, other countries print and online; $251 Individuals print and online; £135 Individuals print and online - UK and Europe (non euro zone); €202 Individuals print and online; £152 Other countries print and online. **URL:** http://onlinelibrary.wiley.com/journal/10.1111/(ISSN)1467-789X; http://www.worldobesity.org/what-we-do/publications/obesityreviews. **Remarks:** Accepts advertising. **Circ:** (Not Reported).

16655 ■ Oil and Energy Trends: A Monthly Publication of International Energy Statistics and Analysis
Wiley-Blackwell
350 Main St.
Commerce Pl.
Malden, MA 02148-5018
Phone: (781)388-8200
Fax: (781)388-8210
Free: 800-216-2552
Magazine providing latest information on all major energy statistics. **Freq:** Monthly. **Key Personnel:** Francisco R. Parra, Editor, Founder; Paul McDonald, Consultant, Editor; Anna Smart, Editor, phone: (124)377-0191. **ISSN:** 0950--1045 (print); **EISSN:** 1744--7992 (electronic). **Subscription Rates:** $5383 Institutions print or online; £3183 Institutions print or online; €4043 Institutions print or online; $6235 Institutions, other countries print or online; $6460 Institutions print and online; £3820 Institutions print and online; €4852 Institutions print and online; $7482 Institutions, other countries print and online. **URL:** http://onlinelibrary.wiley.com/journal/10.1111/(ISSN)1744-7992. **Remarks:** Accepts advertising. **Circ:** (Not Reported).

16656 ■ OPEC Energy Review: Energy Economics and Related Issues
Wiley-Blackwell
350 Main St.
Commerce Pl.
Malden, MA 02148-5018
Phone: (781)388-8200
Fax: (781)388-8210
Free: 800-216-2552
Magazine focusing on energy economics and related issues, such as economic development and the environment. **Freq:** Quarterly. **Key Personnel:** Prof. Sadek Boussena, Editor. **ISSN:** 1753--0229 (print); **EISSN:** 1753--0237 (electronic). **Subscription Rates:** $210 Individuals print + online; €188 Individuals print + online (Euro zone); £127 Individuals print + online (non-Euro zone); $1036 Institutions print + online; £618 Institutions print + online (UK); €783 Institutions print + online (Europe); £515 Institutions print or online (UK); $863 Institutions print or online; $1006 Institutions, other countries print + online; €652 Institutions print + online. **URL:** http://onlinelibrary.wiley.com/journal/10.1111/(ISSN)1753-0237. **Formerly:** OPEC Review. **Remarks:** Advertising accepted; rates available upon request. **Circ:** (Not Reported).

16657 ■ Oxford Bulletin of Economics & Statistics
Wiley-Blackwell
350 Main St.
Commerce Pl.
Malden, MA 02148-5018
Phone: (781)388-8200
Fax: (781)388-8210
Free: 800-216-2552
Publication covering economics. **Freq:** Bimonthly. **Key Personnel:** David Hendry, Editor; Anindya Banerjee, Editor; Jonathan Temple, Editor. **ISSN:** 0305--9049 (print); **EISSN:** 1468--0084 (electronic). **Subscription Rates:** $164 Individuals print + online; $1474 Institutions print + online; $1228 Institutions print or online; €146 Individuals print + online; €918 Institutions print + online; €765 Institutions print or online; £99 Other countries print + online, individuals; $1722 Institutions, other countries print + online; $1435 Institutions, other countries print or online; £724 Institutions print + online. **URL:** http://onlinelibrary.wiley.com/journal/10.1111/(ISSN)1468-0084. **Remarks:** Advertising accepted; rates available upon request. **Circ:** (Not Reported).

16658 ■ Pacific Philosophical Quarterly
Wiley-Blackwell
350 Main St.
Commerce Pl.
Malden, MA 02148-5018
Phone: (781)388-8200
Fax: (781)388-8210
Free: 800-216-2552
Publication covering philosophy and religion. **Freq:** Quarterly. **Key Personnel:** Rima Basu, Managing Editor. **ISSN:** 0279--0750 (print); **EISSN:** 1468--0114 (electronic). **Subscription Rates:** $111 Individuals print + online; £60 Individuals print + online; €90 Individuals print + online; £65 Other countries print + online; $652 Institutions print + online; £449 Institutions print + online; €473 Institutions print, online. **URL:** http://onlinelibrary.wiley.com/journal/10.1111/(ISSN)1468-0114. **Remarks:** Advertising accepted; rates available upon request. **Circ:** (Not Reported).

16659 ■ Pacing and Clinical Electrophysiology
Blackwell Publishing Inc.
350 Main St.
Malden, MA 02148
Phone: (781)388-8200
Fax: (781)388-8210
Free: 800-216-2522
Publisher's E-mail: journaladsusa@bos.blackwellpublishing.com
Peer-reviewed journal in the field of pacing and implantable cardioversion defibrillation, featuring original didactic papers and cases reports related to daily practice. **Freq:** Monthly. **Print Method:** Offset. **Trim Size:** 8 1/2 x 11 1/8. **Cols./Page:** 2. **Col. Width:** 39 nonpareils. **Col. Depth:** 140 agate lines. **Key Personnel:** S. Serge Barold, Associate Editor; John D. Fisher, Editor-in-Chief; Melvin M. Scheinman, Associate Editor. **ISSN:** 0147--8389 (print); **EISSN:** 1540--8159 (electronic). **Subscription Rates:** $434 Individuals print and online; £372 Individuals print or online; €558 Individuals print and online; $1460 Institutions print and online; £1137 Institutions print and online; €1442 Institu-

tions print and online; $2222 Other countries print and online; $1216 Institutions Americas (print or online only); €1201 Institutions Europe (print or online only); £947 Institutions UK (print or online only). **URL:** http://www.wiley.com/WileyCDA/WileyTitle/productCd-PACE.html; http://onlinelibrary.wiley.com/journal/10.1111/(ISSN)1540-8159. **Ad Rates:** BW $1239; 4C $1160. **Remarks:** Advertising accepted; rates available upon request. **Circ:** Paid ‡382.

16660 ■ Pain Practice
Blackwell Publishing Inc.
350 Main St.
Malden, MA 02148
Phone: (781)388-8200
Fax: (781)388-8210
Free: 800-216-2522
Publisher's E-mail: journaladsusa@bos.blackwellpublishing.com
Journal that offers information about pain research, evaluation methods, and techniques of pain management. **Freq:** Bimonthly. **Key Personnel:** Craig T. Hartrick, Editor-in-Chief; Pedro Bejarano, Board Member; Ramsin Benyamin, Board Member; Honorio Benzon, Managing Editor; Allen Burton, Board Member. **ISSN:** 1530-7085 (print); **EISSN:** 1533-2500 (electronic). **Subscription Rates:** $170 Individuals print and online; €219 Individuals print and online; $170 Individuals online only; $532 Institutions print and online; €510 Institutions print and online; $463 Institutions print or online; £404 Institutions print and online; $787 Institutions, other countries print and online; £350 Institutions print or online; £146 Individuals print and online. **URL:** http://as.wiley.com/WileyCDA/WileyTitle/productCd-PAPR.html. **Ad Rates:** BW $808; 4C $1,000. **Remarks:** Accepts advertising. **Circ:** **1700**.

16661 ■ Palaeontology
Wiley-Blackwell
350 Main St.
Commerce Pl.
Malden, MA 02148-5018
Phone: (781)388-8200
Fax: (781)388-8210
Free: 800-216-2552
Journal covering various paleontological topics such as paleozoology, paleobotany, systematic studies, paleoecology, micropaleontology, paleobiogeography, functional morphology, stratigraphy, taxonomy, taphonomy, paleoenvironmental reconstruction, paleoclimate analysis, and biomineralisation studies published in connection with paleontological association. **Freq:** Bimonthly. **Key Personnel:** Dr. Andrew Smith, Editor-in-Chief. **ISSN:** 0031--0239 (print); **EISSN:** 1475--4983 (electronic). **Subscription Rates:** Included in membership. **URL:** http://onlinelibrary.wiley.com/journal/10.1111/(ISSN)1475-4983; http://www.palass.org/publications/palaeontology-journal. **Remarks:** Advertising accepted; rates available upon request. **Circ:** (Not Reported).

16662 ■ Parasite Immunology
Wiley-Blackwell
350 Main St.
Commerce Pl.
Malden, MA 02148-5018
Phone: (781)388-8200
Fax: (781)388-8210
Free: 800-216-2552
Journal covering research on all aspects of parasite immunology in human and animal hosts. Publishes original work on all parasites, mainly helminths, protozoa and ectoparasites. **Freq:** Monthly. **Key Personnel:** Eleanor Riley, Editor; Richard Grencis, Editor. **ISSN:** 0141--9838 (print); **EISSN:** 1365--3024 (electronic). **Subscription Rates:** $226 Individuals online only; £146 Other countries online only; £146 Individuals online only (Europe - non Euro zone and UK); €176 Individuals online only (Europe - Euro zone); $2890 Institutions online only; £1566 Institutions online only; €1989 Institutions online only; $3373 Institutions, other countries online only. **URL:** http://onlinelibrary.wiley.com/journal/10.1111/(ISSN)1365-3024. **Remarks:** Advertising accepted; rates available upon request. **Circ:** (Not Reported).

16663 ■ Peace & Change: A Journal of Peace Research
Wiley-Blackwell
350 Main St.
Commerce Pl.
Malden, MA 02148-5018
Phone: (781)388-8200
Fax: (781)388-8210
Free: 800-216-2552
Magazine publishing articles on peace-related topics such as peace movements and activism, conflict resolution, nonviolence, internationalism, race and gender issues, cross-cultural studies, economic development, the legacy of imperialism, and the post-Cold War upheaval. **Freq:** Quarterly. **Key Personnel:** Kevin Clements, Board Member; Sandi E. Cooper, Board Member; Mohammed Abu-Nimer, Board Member; Elavie Ndura-Ouedraogo, Board Member; Lee Smithey, Board Member. **ISSN:** 0149--0508 (print); **EISSN:** 1468--0130 (electronic). **Subscription Rates:** $549 Institutions print or online; £423 Institutions print or online; $827 Institutions, other countries print or online; $659 Institutions print and online; £508 Institutions print and online; $993 Institutions, other countries print and online; $125 Individuals print and online; £100 Other countries print and online; €536 Institutions print or online; €644 Institutions print and online; £100 Individuals print and online (UK and Europe non-Euro zone); €150 Individuals print and online (Europe - Euro zone). **URL:** http://onlinelibrary.wiley.com/journal/10.1111/(ISSN)1468-0130; http://www.peacehistorysociety.org/journal.php; http://www.peacejusticestudies.org/resources. **Remarks:** Accepts advertising. **Circ:** (Not Reported).

16664 ■ Pediatric Anesthesia
Wiley-Blackwell
350 Main St.
Commerce Pl.
Malden, MA 02148-5018
Phone: (781)388-8200
Fax: (781)388-8210
Free: 800-216-2552
Peer-reviewed journal covering all areas relevant to anesthesia and intensive care in new-borns, infants and children. **Freq:** Monthly. **Key Personnel:** B. Anderson, Associate Editor; N.S. Morton, Editor; A. Davidson, Editor-in-Chief. **ISSN:** 1155--5645 (print); **EISSN:** 1460--9592 (electronic). **Subscription Rates:** $2302 Institutions print or online; £1247 Institutions print or online; €1583 Institutions print or online; $2685 Institutions, other countries print or online; $2763 Institutions print + online; £1497 Institutions print + online; €1900 Institutions print + online; $3222 Institutions, other countries print + online; $554 Individuals print + online; £299 Individuals print + online; €446 Individuals print + online; £329 Other countries print + online; $173 Students print + online; £103 Students print + online; €119 Students print + online; £103 Students, other countries print + online. **URL:** http://onlinelibrary.wiley.com/journal/10.1111/(ISSN)1460-9592. **Remarks:** Advertising accepted; rates available upon request. **Circ:** (Not Reported).

16665 ■ Pediatric Diabetes
Wiley-Blackwell
350 Main St.
Commerce Pl.
Malden, MA 02148-5018
Phone: (781)388-8200
Fax: (781)388-8210
Free: 800-216-2552
Journal devoted to disseminate new knowledge relating to the epidemiology, etiology, pathogenesis, management, complications and prevention of diabetes in childhood and adolescence. **Freq:** 8/year. **Key Personnel:** Mark A. Sperling, Editor-in-Chief; Silva Arslanian, Associate Editor; Thomas Danne, Associate Editor. **ISSN:** 1399--543X (print); **EISSN:** 1399--5448 (electronic). **Subscription Rates:** $1006 Institutions online; £633 Institutions online; €806 Institutions online; $1241 Institutions online; $211 Individuals online; £127 Individuals online - UK and Europe (non-euro zone); €188 Individuals online; $245 Other countries online. **URL:** http://onlinelibrary.wiley.com/journal/10.1111/(ISSN)1399-5448. **Remarks:** Accepts advertising. **Circ:** (Not Reported).

16666 ■ Pediatrics International
Wiley-Blackwell
350 Main St.
Commerce Pl.
Malden, MA 02148-5018
Phone: (781)388-8200
Fax: (781)388-8210
Free: 800-216-2552
Journal publishing articles of scientific research in pediatrics and child health delivery. **Freq:** Bimonthly. **Key Personnel:** Atsushi Manabe, Editor-in-Chief; Norikazu Shimizu, Board Member; Yoshiyuki Ohtomo, Editor; Junko Takita, Editor; Susumu Kanzaki, Board Member. **ISSN:** 1328--8067 (print); **EISSN:** 1442--200X (electronic). **Subscription Rates:** $1121 Institutions online only; £694 Institutions online only; €881 Institutions online only; $1359 Institutions, other countries online only. **URL:** http://onlinelibrary.wiley.com/journal/10.1111/(ISSN)1442-200X; http://www.jpeds.or.jp/modules/en/index.php?content_id=4. **Formerly:** Acta Paediatrica Japonica. **Remarks:** Advertising accepted; rates available upon request. **Circ:** (Not Reported).

16667 ■ Periodontology 2000
Wiley-Blackwell
350 Main St.
Commerce Pl.
Malden, MA 02148-5018
Phone: (781)388-8200
Fax: (781)388-8210
Free: 800-216-2552
Journal comprising monographs useful for periodontists and general practitioners with interest in periodontics. **Freq:** 3/year. **Key Personnel:** Jorgan Slots, Editor-in-Chief; Mark P. Bartold, Board Member; Ian L.C. Chapple, Board Member. **ISSN:** 0906--6713 (print); **EISSN:** 1600--0757 (electronic). **Subscription Rates:** $470 Individuals print + online; €422 Individuals print + online; $282 Individuals print + online; $1131 Institutions print + online; $942 Institutions print or online; €856 Institutions print + online; $1314 Institutions, other countries print + online; $1095 Institutions, other countries print or online; £672 Institutions print + online; £560 Institutions print or online; €713 Institutions print or online. **URL:** http://onlinelibrary.wiley.com/journal/10.1111/(ISSN)1600-0757. **Remarks:** Advertising accepted; rates available upon request. **Circ:** (Not Reported).

16668 ■ Personnel Psychology: A Journal of Applied Research
Blackwell Publishing Inc.
350 Main St.
Malden, MA 02148
Phone: (781)388-8200
Fax: (781)388-8210
Free: 800-216-2522
Publisher's E-mail: customerservice@oxon.blackwellpublishing.com
Journal covering empirical research on personnel, including test validation, selection, labor-management relations, training, compensation, and reward systems. Also publishes related book reviews. **Freq:** Quarterly. **Key Personnel:** Bradford S. Bell, Editor; Ann Marie Ryan, Board Member; Frederick P. Morgeson, Board Member; Michael J. Burke, Board Member; Lilian Eby, Board Member. **ISSN:** 0031--5826 (print); **EISSN:** 1744--6570 (electronic). **Subscription Rates:** $105 Individuals print & online; $80 Members print & online; $699 Institutions print & online; $582 Institutions print or online; £59 Individuals print & online; £47 Members print & online; £449 Institutions print & online; €92 Individuals print & online; €473 Institutions print & online; €70 Students print & online. **URL:** http://as.wiley.com/WileyCDA/WileyTitle/productCd-PEPS.html; http://onlinelibrary.wiley.com/journal/10.1111/(ISSN)1744-6570. **Mailing address:** PO Box 1354, Oxford OX4 2ZG, United Kingdom. **Ad Rates:** BW $300. **Remarks:** Accepts display advertising. **Circ:** Paid 2392.

16669 ■ Perspektiven der Wirtschaftspolitik
Blackwell Publishing Inc.
350 Main St.
Malden, MA 02148
Phone: (781)388-8200
Fax: (781)388-8210
Free: 800-216-2522
Publisher's E-mail: journaladsusa@bos.blackwellpublishing.com
Journal covering the field of economics and neighbouring disciplines. **Freq:** Quarterly. **Key Personnel:** Lars P. Feld, Editor; Lutz Arnold, Editor; Franz W. Wagner,

Circulation: ★ = AAM; △ or • = BPA; ♦ = CAC; ❑ = VAC; ⊕ = PO Statement; ‡ = Publisher's Report; Boldface figures = sworn; Light figures = estimated.

Editor. **ISSN:** 1465--6493 (print); **EISSN:** 1468--2516 (electronic). **URL:** http://onlinelibrary.wiley.com/journal/10.1111/(ISSN)1468-2516. **Remarks:** Accepts advertising. **Circ:** (Not Reported).

16670 ■ Photodermatology, Photoimmunology and Photomedicine
Wiley-Blackwell
350 Main St.
Commerce Pl.
Malden, MA 02148-5018
Phone: (781)388-8200
Fax: (781)388-8210
Free: 800-216-2552
Journal providing a focal point for dissemination of investigations on direct and indirect effects of electromagnetic radiation (ultraviolet, visible and infrared) entering through skin. The thrust areas include aging, carcinogenesis, immunology, instrumentation and optics, lasers, photodynamic therapy, photosensitivity, pigmentation and therapy. **Freq:** Bimonthly. **Key Personnel:** Thomas M. Runger, Editor-in-Chief; James Ferguson, Board Member; Warwick L. Morison, Advisor; Ryoichi Kamide, Board Member; Craig Elmets, Board Member; Ponciano Cruz, Board Member; Rik Roelandts, Board Member; Goren Wennersten, Editor, Founder. **ISSN:** 0905--4383 (print); **EISSN:** 1600--0781 (electronic). **Subscription Rates:** $954 Institutions print and online; $1118 Institutions, other countries print and online; $795 Institutions print or online; $931 Institutions, other countries print or online; €728 Institutions print and online; €606 Institutions print or online; £572 Institutions print and online; £476 Institutions print or online. **URL:** http://onlinelibrary.wiley.com/journal/10.1111/(ISSN)1600-0781. **Remarks:** Advertising accepted; rates available upon request. **Circ:** (Not Reported).

16671 ■ Phycological Research
Wiley-Blackwell
350 Main St.
Commerce Pl.
Malden, MA 02148-5018
Phone: (781)388-8200
Fax: (781)388-8210
Free: 800-216-2552
Journal encouraging exchange of information on research phycology in terms of phylogenetics and taxonomy, ecology and population biology, morphology, cellular and molecular biology, physiology and biochemistry, genetics, photobiology, biotechnology, and fisheries. The journal published in connection with the Japanese Society of Phycology. **Freq:** Quarterly. **Key Personnel:** Mitsunobu Kamiya, Editor-in-Chief; Daisuke Honda, Associate Editor. **ISSN:** 1322--0829 (print); **EISSN:** 1440--1835 (electronic). **Subscription Rates:** $975 Institutions online only; $1176 Institutions, other countries online only; €765 Institutions online only; £604 Institutions online only. **URL:** http://onlinelibrary.wiley.com/journal/10.1111/(ISSN)1440-1835. **Remarks:** Advertising accepted; rates available upon request. **Circ:** (Not Reported).

16672 ■ Physiological Entomology
Wiley-Blackwell
350 Main St.
Commerce Pl.
Malden, MA 02148-5018
Phone: (781)388-8200
Fax: (781)388-8210
Free: 800-216-2552
Peer-reviewed journal on physiology insects and other arthropods. **Freq:** Quarterly. **Key Personnel:** Jim Hardie, Editor; Graham Goldsworthy, Advisor; H. Numata, Advisor; J.S. Bale, Advisor; T.C. Baker, Advisor; S.B. Vinson, Advisor; R. Galun, Advisor; A.E. Douglas, Advisor. **ISSN:** 0307-6962 (print). **Subscription Rates:** $1110 Institutions print + online; $1295 Institutions, other countries print + online; £600 Institutions print + online; £522 Institutions print, online; $1126 Institutions, other countries print, online; $965 Institutions print, online. **URL:** http://www.wiley.com/bw/journal.asp?ref=0307-6962&site=1. **Remarks:** Advertising accepted; rates available upon request. **Circ:** (Not Reported).

16673 ■ Pigment Cell and Melanoma Research
Wiley-Blackwell
350 Main St.
Commerce Pl.
Malden, MA 02148-5018
Phone: (781)388-8200
Fax: (781)388-8210
Free: 800-216-2552
Peer-reviewed journal dealing with all aspects of pigment cells or melanocytes including development, cell and molecular biology, genetics and melanoma. **Freq:** Bimonthly. **Key Personnel:** Marcus Bosenberg, Board Member; Zeev Ronai, Board Member; Heinz Arnheiter, Editor-in-Chief; Mickey Marks, Board Member; David Parichy, Board Member. **ISSN:** 1755--1471 (print); **EISSN:** 1755--148X (electronic). **Subscription Rates:** $1173 Institutions print or online; £701 Institutions print or online; €891 Institutions print or online; $1370 Institutions, other countries print or online; $1408 Institutions print and online; £842 Institutions print and online; €1070 Institutions print and online; $1644 Institutions, other countries print and online; $126 Individuals print only; £152 Individuals print only; €229 Individuals print only. **URL:** http://onlinelibrary.wiley.com/journal/10.1111/(ISSN)1755-148X. **Formerly:** Pigment Cell Research. **Remarks:** Advertising accepted; rates available upon request. **Circ:** (Not Reported).

16674 ■ Plant Breeding
Wiley-Blackwell
350 Main St.
Commerce Pl.
Malden, MA 02148-5018
Phone: (781)388-8200
Fax: (781)388-8210
Free: 800-216-2552
Peer-reviewed journal covering all aspects of plant breeding especially in crop plants. **Freq:** Bimonthly. **Key Personnel:** Prof. Christian Jung, Editor; Dr. Jens Leon, Editor-in-Chief, phone: 49 228 732877; Frank Ordon, Prof., Editor-in-Chief. **ISSN:** 0179--9541 (print); **EISSN:** 1439--0523 (electronic). **Subscription Rates:** $2838 Institutions print or online; £1691 Institutions print or online; €2147 Institutions print or online; $3637 Institutions, other countries print or online; $3406 Institutions print and online; £2030 Institutions print and online; €2577 Institutions print and online; $4365 Institutions, other countries print and online; $217 Individuals print and online; £134 Individuals print and online; €201 Individuals print and online. **URL:** http://onlinelibrary.wiley.com/journal/10.1111/(ISSN)1439-0523. **Remarks:** Advertising accepted; rates available upon request. **Circ:** (Not Reported).

16675 ■ Plant, Cell & Environment
Wiley-Blackwell
350 Main St.
Commerce Pl.
Malden, MA 02148-5018
Phone: (781)388-8200
Fax: (781)388-8210
Free: 800-216-2552
Journal covering plant biochemistry, molecular biology, biophysics, cell physiology, whole plant physiology, crop physiology and physiological ecology. **Freq:** Monthly. **Key Personnel:** Keith Mott, Editor-in-Chief; Stephen P. Long, Editor; Tom Sharkey, Editor. **ISSN:** 0140--7791 (print); **EISSN:** 1365--3040 (electronic). **Subscription Rates:** $7045 Institutions; £3813 Institutions UK; €4843 Institutions Europe; $8218 Institutions, other countries; $8454 Institutions print and online; £4576 Institutions print and online, UK; €5812 Institutions print and online, Europe; $9862 Institutions, other countries print and online; $333 Individuals print and online; £180 Individuals print and online, UK and Europe (non euro zone); €268 Individuals print and online; £198 Other countries print and online. **URL:** http://onlinelibrary.wiley.com/journal/10.1111/(ISSN)1365-3040. **Remarks:** Accepts advertising. **Circ:** (Not Reported).

16676 ■ Plant Species Biology
Wiley-Blackwell
350 Main St.
Commerce Pl.
Malden, MA 02148-5018
Phone: (781)388-8200
Fax: (781)388-8210
Free: 800-216-2552
Peer-reviewed journal covering the study of plant species and their biological aspects. **Freq:** 3/year. **Key Personnel:** William F. Grant, Editor-in-Chief; Masashi Ohara, Editor-in-Chief; Shoichi Kawano, Editor-in-Chief; Shu-Miaw Chaw, Board Member; Teruyoshi Nagamitsu, Associate Editor; Makoto Kato, Associate Editor; E.R. Alvarez-Buylla, Board Member; David W. Inouye, Board Member; Hong-Ya Gu, Board Member; Michael J. Hutchings, Board Member. **ISSN:** 0913--557X (print); **EISSN:** 1442--1984 (electronic). **Subscription Rates:** $668 Institutions online only; £412 Institutions online only; €522 Institutions online only; $803 Institutions, other countries online only. **URL:** http://onlinelibrary.wiley.com/journal/10.1111/(ISSN)1442-1984. **Remarks:** Advertising accepted; rates available upon request. **Circ:** (Not Reported).

16677 ■ Presidential Studies Quarterly
Blackwell Publishing Inc.
350 Main St.
Malden, MA 02148
Phone: (781)388-8200
Fax: (781)388-8210
Free: 800-216-2522
Publisher's E-mail: journaladsusa@bos.blackwellpublishing.com
Publication covering political science and history. **Freq:** Quarterly. **Key Personnel:** Carolyn Allen-Bates, Managing Editor; George C. Edwards, III, Editor. **ISSN:** 0360-4918 (print); **EISSN:** 1741-5705 (electronic). **Subscription Rates:** $516 Institutions print or online; $620 Institutions print + online; £334 Institutions print or online; £401 Institutions print + online; €424 Institutions print or online; €509 Institutions print + online; $655 Institutions, other countries print or online; $786 Institutions, other countries print + online. **URL:** http://www.wiley.com/WileyCDA/WileyTitle/productCd-PSQ.html; http://onlinelibrary.wiley.com/journal/10.1111/(ISSN)1741-5705. **Ad Rates:** BW $480. **Remarks:** Color advertising not accepted. **Circ:** (Not Reported).

16678 ■ Psychophysiology: The International Journal of the Society for Psychophysiological Research
Blackwell Publishing Inc.
350 Main St.
Malden, MA 02148
Phone: (781)388-8200
Fax: (781)388-8210
Free: 800-216-2522
Publisher's E-mail: journaladsusa@bos.blackwellpublishing.com
Journal concerning psychology, physiology, psychosomatic medicine. **Freq:** Bimonthly. **Print Method:** Offset. **Trim Size:** 6 7/8 x 10. **Cols./Page:** 2. **Col. Width:** 17 picas. **Col. Depth:** 54 picas. **Key Personnel:** Monica Fabiani, PhD, Editor. **ISSN:** 0048--5772 (print); **EISSN:** 1469--8986 (electronic). **URL:** http://onlinelibrary.wiley.com/journal/10.1111/(ISSN)1469-8986. **Ad Rates:** BW $950. **Remarks:** Accepts advertising. **Circ:** ‡2200.

16679 ■ Public Health Nursing
Wiley-Blackwell
350 Main St.
Commerce Pl.
Malden, MA 02148-5018
Phone: (781)388-8200
Fax: (781)388-8210
Free: 800-216-2552
Journal publishing contributions on public health, with a particular emphasis on matters relating to public health professionals. **Freq:** Bimonthly. **Key Personnel:** Bobbie Berkowitz, PhD, Board Member. **ISSN:** 0737--1209 (print); **EISSN:** 1525--1446 (electronic). **Subscription Rates:** $881 Institutions print or online; $850 Institutions, Canada and Mexico print or online; £675 Institutions print or online; €856 Institutions print or online; $1316 Institutions, other countries print or online; $1058 Institutions print + online; $1020 Institutions, Canada and Mexico print + online; £810 Institutions print + online; €1028 Institutions print + online; $1580 Institutions, other countries print + online; $225 Individuals print + online (America, Canada and Mexico); £254 Individuals print + online (UK and Rest of the World); €381 Individuals print + online; $163 Students print + online (America, Canada and Mexico); £129 Students print + online (UK and Rest of the World); €192 Students print + online. **URL:** http://onlinelibrary.wiley.com/journal/10.1111/(ISSN)1525-1446. **Ad Rates:** BW $505. **Remarks:** Advertising accepted; rates available upon request. **Circ:** ‡275.

16680 ■ Ratio: An International Journal of Analytic Philosophy
Wiley-Blackwell
350 Main St.
Commerce Pl.
Malden, MA 02148-5018
Phone: (781)388-8200
Fax: (781)388-8210
Free: 800-216-2552
Publisher's E-mail: customerservice@oxon.blackwellpublishing.com
Journal covering analytical philosophy. **Freq:** Quarterly. **Key Personnel:** Brad Hooker, Associate Editor; Emma Borg, Associate Editor; Alice Drewery, Associate Editor; David S. Oderberg, Editor. **ISSN:** 0034--0006 (print); **EISSN:** 1467--9329 (electronic). **Subscription Rates:** $155 Individuals print + online; £73 Individuals print + online; €107 Individuals print + online; £93 Other countries print + online; $1431 Institutions print + online; £668 Institutions print + online; €845 Institutions print + online; $1665 Institutions, other countries print + online; $1192 Institutions print or online; £556 Institutions print or online; €704 Institutions print or online; $1387 Institutions, other countries print or online; $125 Members print + online; £59 Members print + online; €89 Members print + online; £76 Members print + online - rest of the world. **URL:** http://onlinelibrary.wiley.com/journal/10.1111/(ISSN)1467-9329. **Mailing address:** PO Box 1354, Oxford OX4 2ZG, United Kingdom. **Remarks:** Advertising accepted; rates available upon request. **Circ:** (Not Reported).

16681 ■ Restoration Ecology
Wiley-Blackwell
350 Main St.
Commerce Pl.
Malden, MA 02148-5018
Phone: (781)388-8200
Fax: (781)388-8210
Free: 800-216-2552
Journal publishing research articles concerned with the halting and reversing of ecological damage. **Freq:** Bimonthly. **Key Personnel:** Mark Briggs, Board Member; Stuart Allison, Board Member; Brandon Bestelmeyer, Board Member; James Aronson, Board Member; Roger Anderson, Board Member; Darren Ryder, Board Member; John Scullion, Board Member. **ISSN:** 1061--2971 (print); **EISSN:** 1526--100X (electronic). **Subscription Rates:** $904 Institutions online only; £686 Institutions online only; $930 Institutions, Canada and Mexico online only; €871 Institutions online only; $1342 Institutions, other countries online only. **URL:** http://onlinelibrary.wiley.com/journal/10.1111/(ISSN)1526-100X. **Remarks:** Advertising accepted; rates available upon request. **Circ:** (Not Reported).

16682 ■ Review of Development Economics: An Essential Resource for any Development Economist
Wiley-Blackwell
350 Main St.
Commerce Pl.
Malden, MA 02148-5018
Phone: (781)388-8200
Fax: (781)388-8210
Free: 800-216-2552
Publisher's E-mail: customerservice@oxon.blackwellpublishing.com
Journal publishing articles on current growth problems of developing countries, including the transition economies. **Freq:** Quarterly. **Key Personnel:** Kaushik Basu, Board Member; Sajal Lahiri, Editor; Timothy Besley, Board Member; Abhijit Banerjee, Board Member; Jeffrey B. Nugent, Board Member; Elias Dinopoulos, Editor; Martin Ravallion, Board Member; Jorge Braga, Board Member. **ISSN:** 1363--6669 (print); **EISSN:** 1467--9361 (electronic). **Subscription Rates:** $1164 Institutions print or online; $1397 Institutions print + online; $1543 Institutions, other countries print or online; $1852 Institutions, other countries print + online; £790 Institutions print or online; £948 Institutions print + online; €1002 Institutions print or online; €1203 Institutions print + online. **URL:** http://onlinelibrary.wiley.com/journal/10.1111/(ISSN)1467-9361. **Mailing address:** PO Box 1354, Oxford OX4 2ZG, United Kingdom. **Remarks:** Advertising accepted; rates available upon request. **Circ:** (Not Reported).

16683 ■ Review of European Comparative & International Environmental Law
Wiley-Blackwell
350 Main St.
Commerce Pl.
Malden, MA 02148-5018
Phone: (781)388-8200
Fax: (781)388-8210
Free: 800-216-2552
Publisher's E-mail: customerservice@oxon.blackwellpublishing.com
Journal publishing articles on International and European Community environmental law and policy including climate change, international trade and the environment, international water law, environmental liability, waste management and the protection of biodiversity. **Freq:** 3/year. **Key Personnel:** Hugh Wilkins, Board Member; Harro van Asselt, Editor. **ISSN:** 2050--0386 (print); **EISSN:** 2050--0394 (electronic). **Subscription Rates:** $1628 Institutions print and online; £1086 Institutions print and online; €1377 Institutions print and online; $414 Institutions developing world - print and online; $2120 Institutions, other countries print and online. **URL:** http://onlinelibrary.wiley.com/journal/10.1002/(ISSN)2050-0394. **Formerly:** Review of European Community & International Environmental Law. **Mailing address:** PO Box 1354, Oxford OX4 2ZG, United Kingdom. **Remarks:** Advertising accepted; rates available upon request. **Circ:** (Not Reported).

16684 ■ Review of Income and Wealth
Wiley-Blackwell
350 Main St.
Commerce Pl.
Malden, MA 02148-5018
Phone: (781)388-8200
Fax: (781)388-8210
Free: 800-216-2552
Association journal covering research on national and economic and social accounting as related to the measurement and analysis of income and wealth. **Freq:** Quarterly. **Key Personnel:** Conchita D'Ambrosio, Managing Editor; Robert J. Hill, Managing Editor; Stephan Klasen, Board Member. **ISSN:** 0034--6586 (print); **EISSN:** 1475--4991 (electronic). **Subscription Rates:** £232 Institutions print & online; $368 Institutions print & online; $306 Institutions print or online; £193 Institutions print or online; $452 Institutions, other countries print & online; $376 Institutions, other countries print or online. **URL:** http://onlinelibrary.wiley.com/journal/10.1111/(ISSN)1475-4991. **Remarks:** Advertising accepted; rates available upon request. **Circ:** ‡1400.

16685 ■ Review of International Economics
Wiley-Blackwell
350 Main St.
Commerce Pl.
Malden, MA 02148-5018
Phone: (781)388-8200
Fax: (781)388-8210
Free: 800-216-2552
Journal containing articles on international economics including novel and controversial ideas. **Freq:** 5/year. **Key Personnel:** Peter H. Egger, Editor-in-Chief. **ISSN:** 0965--7576 (print); **EISSN:** 1467--9396 (electronic). **Subscription Rates:** $1359 Institutions print or online; £928 Institutions print or online; €1177 Institutions print or online; $1815 Institutions, other countries print or online; $1631 Institutions print + online; £1114 Institutions print + online; €1413 Institutions print + online; $2178 Institutions, other countries print + online; $103 Individuals print + online; £85 Individuals print + online; €125 Individuals print + online. **URL:** http://onlinelibrary.wiley.com/journal/10.1111/(ISSN)1467-9396. **Remarks:** Accepts advertising. **Circ:** (Not Reported).

16686 ■ Review of Policy Research
Wiley-Blackwell
350 Main St.
Commerce Pl.
Malden, MA 02148-5018
Phone: (781)388-8200
Fax: (781)388-8210
Free: 800-216-2552
Peer-reviewed journal focusing on the research outcomes and consequences of policy change in domestic and comparative contexts. **Freq:** Bimonthly. **Key Personnel:** Christopher Gore, Editor; Christopher J. Bosso, Board Member; Sandra Braman, Board Member; Thomas Bernauer, Board Member. **ISSN:** 1541-132X (print). **Subscription Rates:** $1676 Institutions print + online; £1232 Institutions print + online; $1457 Institutions print, online; £1071 Institutions print, online; €1566 Institutions print + online; €1361 Institutions print, online; $2414 Institutions, other countries print + online; $2099 Institutions, other countries print, online. **URL:** http://www.wiley.com/bw/journal.asp?ref=1541-132X&site=1. **Remarks:** Advertising accepted; rates available upon request. **Circ:** (Not Reported).

16687 ■ Review of Urban & Regional Development Studies: Journal of the Applied Regional Science Conference
Wiley-Blackwell
350 Main St.
Commerce Pl.
Malden, MA 02148-5018
Phone: (781)388-8200
Fax: (781)388-8210
Free: 800-216-2552
Publication E-mail: rurds@e.okayama-u.ac.jp
Journal containing thorough empirical analysis, stressing theoretical and methodological issues, others policy relevance and the operational aspects of the academic disciplines. **Freq:** 3/year. **Key Personnel:** Tatsuaki Kuroda, Editor; Phillip McCann, Editor; Ryohei Nakamura, Board Member. **ISSN:** 0917--0553 (print); **EISSN:** 1467--940X (electronic). **Subscription Rates:** $446 Institutions print or online; £315 Institutions print or online; €399 Institutions print or online; $286 Institutions print or online (Japan); $614 Institutions, other countries print or online; $536 Institutions print + online; £378 Institutions print + online; €479 Institutions print + online; $344 Institutions print + online (Japan); $737 Institutions, other countries print + online. **URL:** http://onlinelibrary.wiley.com/journal/10.1111/(ISSN)1467-940X. **Mailing address:** PO Box 1354, Oxford OX4 2ZG, United Kingdom. **Remarks:** Advertising accepted; rates available upon request. **Circ:** (Not Reported).

16688 ■ Risk Management & Insurance Review
Wiley-Blackwell
350 Main St.
Commerce Pl.
Malden, MA 02148-5018
Phone: (781)388-8200
Fax: (781)388-8210
Free: 800-216-2552
Journal covering articles in the field of risk and insurance. It contains original research involving applications and applied techniques, research literature, business practice, and public policy along with articles discussing and evaluating instructional techniques. **Freq:** Semiannual. **Key Personnel:** Martin Shubik, Associate Editor; Patricia Born, Editor. **ISSN:** 1098--1616 (print); **EISSN:** 1540--6296 (electronic). **Subscription Rates:** $287 Institutions print + online; £225 Institutions print + online; $239 Institutions print or online; £187 Institutions print or online; €285 Institutions print + online; $437 Institutions, other countries print + online; $364 Institutions, other countries print or online; €237 Institutions print or online; £176 Institutions online only - UK; €223 Institutions online only - Europe (euro and non-euro zone); $343 Institutions online only - ROW; $270 Institutions print and online - U.S; $212 Institutions print and online - UK; £268 Institutions print and online - Europe (euro and non-euro zone); €412 Institutions print and online - ROW; £176 Institutions print and online - UK. **URL:** http://onlinelibrary.wiley.com/journal/10.1111/(ISSN)1540-6296; http://www.fox.temple.edu/cms_academics/phd/risk-management-and-insurance. **Remarks:** Accepts advertising. **Circ:** (Not Reported).

16689 ■ Scandinavian Political Studies
Wiley-Blackwell
350 Main St.
Commerce Pl.
Malden, MA 02148-5018
Phone: (781)388-8200
Fax: (781)388-8210
Free: 800-216-2552
Journal focusing on policy and electoral issues affecting the Scandinavian countries, in connection with the Nordic Political Science Association. **Freq:** Quarterly. **Key Personnel:** Åse Gornitzka, Editor; Carl Henrik Knutsen, Editor. **ISSN:** 0080--6757 (print); **EISSN:**

Circulation: ★ = AAM; △ or • = BPA; ♦ = CAC; ❑ = VAC; ⊕ = PO Statement; ‡ = Publisher's Report; Boldface figures = sworn; Light figures = estimated.

1467--9477 (electronic). **Subscription Rates:** $505 Institutions print or online; £302 Institutions print or online - UK; €380 Institutions print or online - Europe; $588 Institutions, other countries print or online; $606 Institutions print + online; £363 Institutions print + online - UK; €456 Institutions print + online - Europe; $706 Institutions, other countries print + online; $87 Individuals print + online; £53 Other countries print or online - UK/non euro zone/ROW; €81 Individuals print and online - euro zone; $58 Members Nordic Political Science Association Member: Print + Online; £34 Members Nordic Political Science Association Member: Print + Online - UK/non euro zone/ROW; €53 Members Nordic Political Science Association Member: Print + Online - euro zone; $56 Students Print + Online ; £33 Students Print + Online - UK/non euro zone/ROW; €51 Students Print + Online - euro zone. **URL:** http://onlinelibrary.wiley.com/journal/10.1111/(ISSN)1467-9477. **Remarks:** Advertising accepted; rates available upon request. **Circ:** (Not Reported).

16690 ■ Scottish Journal of Political Economy
Wiley-Blackwell
350 Main St.
Commerce Pl.
Malden, MA 02148-5018
Phone: (781)388-8200
Fax: (781)388-8210
Free: 800-216-2552
Journal featuring research articles in the field of economics. **Freq:** 5/year. **Key Personnel:** Tim Barmby, Editor. **ISSN:** 0036--9292 (print); **EISSN:** 1467--9485 (electronic). **Subscription Rates:** $639 Institutions; £329 Institutions; €416 Institutions; $741 Institutions, other countries; $767 Institutions print and online; £395 Institutions print and online, UK; €500 Institutions print and online, Europe; $890 Institutions, other countries print and online; $105 Individuals print and online; £62 Individuals print and online, UK, Europe (non euro zone) and rest of the world; €93 Individuals print and online. **URL:** http://onlinelibrary.wiley.com/journal/10.1111/(ISSN)1467-9485. **Remarks:** Accepts advertising. **Circ:** (Not Reported).

16691 ■ Singapore Journal of Tropical Geography
Wiley-Blackwell
350 Main St.
Commerce Pl.
Malden, MA 02148-5018
Phone: (781)388-8200
Fax: (781)388-8210
Free: 800-216-2552
Geography journal. **Freq:** 3/year. **Key Personnel:** Victor R. Savage. **ISSN:** 0129--7619 (print); **EISSN:** 1467--9493 (electronic). **Subscription Rates:** $380 Institutions online only; £267 Institutions online only; €337 Institutions online only; $518 Institutions, other countries online only. **URL:** http://onlinelibrary.wiley.com/journal/10.1111/(ISSN)1467-9493. **Ad Rates:** BW $260. **Remarks:** Accepts advertising. **Circ:** (Not Reported).

16692 ■ Social Anthropology
Blackwell Publishing Inc.
350 Main St.
Malden, MA 02148
Phone: (781)388-8200
Fax: (781)388-8210
Free: 800-216-2522
Publisher's E-mail: journaladsusa@bos.blackwellpublishing.com
Journal focusing on anthropological studies. **Freq:** Quarterly. **Key Personnel:** Mark Maguire, Editor; David Berliner, Editor. **ISSN:** 0964-0282 (print); **EISSN:** 1469-0282 (electronic). **Subscription Rates:** $555 Institutions print and online, The Americas; $501 Institutions online, The Americas; $91 Individuals print + online, America; £299 Institutions online, UK; £333 Institutions print + online, UK; £54 Individuals print + online, UK; €380 Institutions online, Europe; €422 Institutions print + online, Europe; £54 Individuals print + online, Europe-(non Euro zone); €81 Individuals print + online, Europe(Euro zone). **URL:** http://as.wiley.com/WileyCDA/WileyTitle/productCd-SOCA.html; http://onlinelibrary.wiley.com/journal/10.1111/(ISSN)1469-8676. **Ad Rates:** BW $625. **Remarks:** Accepts advertising. **Circ:** Paid ‡2100, Non-paid ‡41.

16693 ■ Social Issues and Policy Review
Wiley-Blackwell
350 Main St.
Commerce Pl.
Malden, MA 02148-5018
Phone: (781)388-8200
Fax: (781)388-8210
Free: 800-216-2552
Journal containing theoretical and empirical reviews of topics and programs of research that are directly relevant to understanding and addressing social issues and public policy. **Freq:** Annual. **Key Personnel:** Samuel L. Gaertner, Editor; Rupert Brown, Editor. **ISSN:** 1751--2395 (print); **EISSN:** 1751--2409 (electronic). **Subscription Rates:** $1092 Institutions print & online; $1311 Institutions print or online; $117 Individuals print & online; $31 Students print & online. **URL:** http://onlinelibrary.wiley.com/journal/10.1111/(ISSN)1751-2409. **Remarks:** Accepts advertising. **Circ:** (Not Reported).

16694 ■ Social Science Quarterly
Wiley-Blackwell
350 Main St.
Commerce Pl.
Malden, MA 02148-5018
Phone: (781)388-8200
Fax: (781)388-8210
Free: 800-216-2552
Journal featuring articles about current research in political science, history, sociology, economics, and women's studies. **Freq:** 5/yr. **Print Method:** Offset. **Trim Size:** 6 x 9. **Cols./Page:** 1. **Col. Width:** 54 nonpareils. **Col. Depth:** 105 agate lines. **Key Personnel:** Keith Gaddie, Editor; Kim Gaddie, Managing Editor; Kelly Damphousse, Editor. **ISSN:** 0038-4941 (print); **EISSN:** 1540-6237 (electronic). **Subscription Rates:** $51 Members online only; The Americas and Europe (Euro zone); $417 Institutions online only; the Americas; £377 Institutions online only; UK; €477 Institutions online only; Europe (Euro and non-Euro zones); $735 Institutions online only; rest of the world. **URL:** http://onlinelibrary.wiley.com/journal/10.1111/(ISSN)1540-6237; http://socialsciencequarterly.org. **Circ:** (Not Reported).

16695 ■ Sociological Methodology
Blackwell Publishing Inc.
350 Main St.
Malden, MA 02148
Phone: (781)388-8200
Fax: (781)388-8210
Free: 800-216-2522
Publisher's E-mail: customer@asanet.org
Scholarly publication covering methods of research in the social sciences, including conceptualizations and modeling, research design, data collection, and related issues. **Freq:** Annual August. **Key Personnel:** Tim Futing Liao, Editor; Lisa Savage, Managing Editor; Tim Liao, Editor. **ISSN:** 0081--1750 (print); **EISSN:** 1467--9531 (electronic). **Subscription Rates:** $45 Members; $30 Students; $425 Institutions print/online; $383 Institutions online only. **URL:** http://www.asanet.org/journals/sm/sm.cfm. **Remarks:** Advertising not accepted. **Circ:** (Not Reported).

16696 ■ The Sociological Quarterly
Wiley-Blackwell
350 Main St.
Commerce Pl.
Malden, MA 02148-5018
Phone: (781)388-8200
Fax: (781)388-8210
Free: 800-216-2552
Journal publishing research and theory in all areas of sociological inquiry, focusing on publishing sociological research and writing. **Freq:** Quarterly. **Key Personnel:** Betty A. Dobratz, Editor; Lisa K. Waldner, Editor; Peter Kivisto, Editor, Advisor; Patricia Adler, Editor, Advisor. **ISSN:** 0038--0253 (print); **EISSN:** 1533--8525 (electronic). **Subscription Rates:** $670 Institutions print + online; $558 Institutions print or online; £405 Institutions print + online; £337 Institutions print or online; €512 Institutions print + online; €426 Institutions print or online; $785 Institutions, other countries print and online; $654 Institutions, other countries print or online; free online access for members. **URL:** http://onlinelibrary.wiley.com/journal/10.1111/(ISSN)1533-8525. **Remarks:** Accepts display advertising. **Circ:** 2,000.

16697 ■ The Sociological Review
Wiley-Blackwell
350 Main St.
Commerce Pl.
Malden, MA 02148-5018
Phone: (781)388-8200
Fax: (781)388-8210
Free: 800-216-2552
Journal covering sociology and social work. **Freq:** Quarterly. **Key Personnel:** Sarah Green, Editor. **ISSN:** 0038--0261 (print); **EISSN:** 1467--954X (electronic). **Subscription Rates:** $70 Individuals print and online; €64 Individuals print and online; £45 Other countries print and online, individuals; $809 Institutions print and online; £418 Institutions print and online; $942 Institutions, other countries print and online; $674 Institutions online; £348 Institutions online; €440 Institutions online; $785 Institutions, other countries online. **Online:** Gale. **URL:** http://onlinelibrary.wiley.com/journal/10.1111/(ISSN)1467-954X. **Remarks:** Accepts advertising. **Circ:** (Not Reported).

16698 ■ Studia Linguistica
Wiley-Blackwell
350 Main St.
Commerce Pl.
Malden, MA 02148-5018
Phone: (781)388-8200
Fax: (781)388-8210
Free: 800-216-2552
Journal covering the field of general linguistics. **Freq:** 3/year. **Key Personnel:** Christer Platzack, Editor; Arthur Holmer, Editor. **ISSN:** 0039--3193 (print); **EISSN:** 1467--9582 (electronic). **Subscription Rates:** $698 Institutions; £378 Institutions; €480 Institutions; $808 Institutions, other countries; $838 Institutions print and online; £454 Institutions print and online; €576 Institutions print and online; $970 Institutions, other countries print and online; $135 Individuals print and online; £83 Individuals print and online, UK, Europe (non euro zone) and rest of the world; €123 Individuals print and online; $55 Students print and online; £32 Students print and online, UK, Europe (non euro zone) and rest of the world; €38 Students print and online. **URL:** http://onlinelibrary.wiley.com/journal/10.1111/(ISSN)1467-9582. **Remarks:** Accepts advertising. **Circ:** (Not Reported).

16699 ■ Surgical Practice
Blackwell Publishing Inc.
350 Main St.
Malden, MA 02148
Phone: (781)388-8200
Fax: (781)388-8210
Free: 800-216-2522
Publisher's E-mail: journaladsusa@bos.blackwellpublishing.com
Peer-reviewed journal featuring papers in all fields of surgery and surgery-related disciplines. **Freq:** Quarterly. **Key Personnel:** Paul B.S. Lai, Editor-in-Chief; Samuel PY Kwok, Chairman; Miranda KY Chan, Editor. **ISSN:** 1744--1625 (print); **EISSN:** 1744--1633 (electronic). **Subscription Rates:** $611 Institutions; £377 Institutions UK; €477 Institutions Europe; $736 Institutions, other countries; $734 Institutions print and online; £453 Institutions print and online, UK; €573 Institutions print and online, Europe; $884 Institutions, other countries print and online. **URL:** http://onlinelibrary.wiley.com/journal/10.1111/(ISSN)1744-1633. **Remarks:** Accepts advertising. **Circ:** (Not Reported).

16700 ■ Syntax: A Journal of Theoretical, Experimental and Interdisciplinary Research
Blackwell Publishing Inc.
350 Main St.
Malden, MA 02148
Phone: (781)388-8200
Fax: (781)388-8210
Free: 800-216-2522
Publisher's E-mail: journaladsusa@bos.blackwellpublishing.com
Journal covering formal syntactic theory and theoretically-oriented descriptive work on particular languages and comparative grammar. **Freq:** Quarterly. **Key Personnel:** David Adger, Editor; Suzanne Flynn, Editor, phone: (617)253-7821, fax: (617)253-6189; Elizabeth Laurencot, Managing Editor. **ISSN:** 1368--

0005 (print); **EISSN:** 1467--9612 (electronic). **Subscription Rates:** $93 Individuals print + online; $52 Students print + online; $77 Members print + online; $580 Institutions print or online; $696 Institutions print + online. **URL:** http://onlinelibrary.wiley.com/journal/10.1111/(ISSN)1467-9612. **Remarks:** Accepts advertising. **Circ:** (Not Reported).

16701 ■ Systematic Entomology
Wiley-Blackwell
350 Main St.
Commerce Pl.
Malden, MA 02148-5018
Phone: (781)388-8200
Fax: (781)388-8210
Free: 800-216-2552
Journal containing taxonomic papers on insects. **Freq:** Quarterly. **Key Personnel:** Peter S. Cranston, Editor; Lars Vilhelmsen, Editor. **ISSN:** 0307--6970 (print); **EISSN:** 1365--3113 (electronic). **Subscription Rates:** $2314 Institutions; £1251 Institutions UK; €1592 Institutions; $2701 Institutions, other countries; $2777 Institutions print and online; £1502 Institutions print and online, UK; €1911 Institutions print and online, Europe; $3242 Institutions, other countries print and online. **URL:** http://onlinelibrary.wiley.com/journal/10.1111/(ISSN)1365-3113. **Remarks:** Accepts advertising. **Circ:** (Not Reported).

16702 ■ Veterinary Anaesthesia and Analgesia
Wiley-Blackwell
350 Main St.
Commerce Pl.
Malden, MA 02148-5018
Phone: (781)388-8200
Fax: (781)388-8210
Free: 800-216-2552
Peer-reviewed journal covering all branches of anaesthesia and the pain relief in animals. **Freq:** Bimonthly. **Key Personnel:** Shannon Axiak, Editor; Cynthia M. Trim, Editor; Peter J. Pascoe, Editor; K.W. Clarke, Editor. **ISSN:** 1467--2987 (print); **EISSN:** 1467--2995 (electronic). **Subscription Rates:** $1142 Institutions print and online; £622 Institutions print and online; €788 Institutions print and online; $1334 Institutions, other countries print and online; $951 Institutions print or online; £518 Individuals print and online; $278 Individuals print and online; €229 Individuals print and online; $165 Other countries print and online; $210 Individuals print + online; €172 Individuals print + online; £114 Individuals print + online; £125 Other countries print + online; $691 Institutions print + online; $628 Institutions print or online; £374 Institutions print + online; £340 Institutions print or online; $807 Institutions, other countries print + online; $733 Institutions, other countries print or online. **URL:** http://onlinelibrary.wiley.com/journal/10.1111/(ISSN)1467-2995; http://www.wiley.com/bw/journal.asp?ref=1467-2987; http://www.acvaa.org/Links. **Formerly:** Journal of Veterinary Anaesthesia. **Ad Rates:** BW £400; 4C £900. **Remarks:** Advertising accepted; rates available upon request. **Circ:** 400.

16703 ■ Veterinary Ophthalmology
Blackwell Publishing Inc.
350 Main St.
Malden, MA 02148
Phone: (781)388-8200
Fax: (781)388-8210
Free: 800-216-2522
Publisher's E-mail: office16@acvo.org
Freq: Bimonthly. **Key Personnel:** David A. Wilkie, Editor. **ISSN:** 1463--5216 (print); **EISSN:** 1463--5224 (electronic). **Subscription Rates:** $1157 Institutions; £846 Institutions UK; €1075 Institutions Europe; $1656 Institutions, other countries; $1389 Institutions print and online; £1016 Institutions print and online; €1290 Institutions print and online; $1988 Institutions, other countries print and online; $224 Individuals print and online; £158 Individuals print and online, UK, Europe (non euro zone) and Rest of the world; €226 Individuals print and online, Europe; $217 Individuals print only; £798 Institutions print or online; £153 Individuals print only; €1014 Institutions print or online; €219 Individuals print only; $1562 Institutions, other countries print or online. **Alt. Formats:** PDF. **URL:** http://onlinelibrary.wiley.com/journal/10.1111/(ISSN)1463-5224; http://www.acvo.org/new/public/publications/ophtho_journal.shtml. **Remarks:** Accepts advertising. **Circ:** (Not Reported).

16704 ■ Weed Research
Wiley-Blackwell
350 Main St.
Commerce Pl.
Malden, MA 02148-5018
Phone: (781)388-8200
Fax: (781)388-8210
Free: 800-216-2552
Freq: Bimonthly. **Key Personnel:** Jon Marshall, Editor-in-Chief. **ISSN:** 0043--1737 (print); **EISSN:** 1365--3180 (electronic). **Subscription Rates:** $1650 Institutions print or online; £893 Institutions print or online, UK; €1132 Institutions print or online, Europe; $1923 Institutions, other countries print or online; $1980 Institutions print and online; £1072 Institutions print and online, UK; €1359 Institutions print and online, Europe; $2308 Institutions, other countries print and online. **URL:** http://www.ewrs.org/weedresearch.asp; http://onlinelibrary.wiley.com/journal/10.1111/(ISSN)1365-3180. **Remarks:** Advertising not accepted. **Circ:** (Not Reported).

16705 ■ Working USA: The Journal of Labor and Society
Blackwell Publishing Inc.
350 Main St.
Malden, MA 02148
Phone: (781)388-8200
Fax: (781)388-8210
Free: 800-216-2522
Publisher's E-mail: journaladsusa@bos.blackwellpublishing.com
Peer-reviewed journal focusing on the labor movement and related topics. **Freq:** Quarterly. **Trim Size:** 7 x 10. **Key Personnel:** David Reynolds, Board Member; Immanuel Ness, Editor; Joseph Wilson, Board Member; Bill Fletcher, Jr., Board Member. **ISSN:** 1089--7011 (print); **EISSN:** 1743--4580 (electronic). **Subscription Rates:** $464 Institutions online; $57 Individuals online; $40 Students online. **URL:** http://onlinelibrary.wiley.com/journal/10.1111/(ISSN)1743-4580. **Ad Rates:** BW $750. **Remarks:** Accepts advertising. **Circ:** Paid 2143, Controlled 5000.

16706 ■ World Englishes
Blackwell Publishing Inc.
350 Main St.
Malden, MA 02148
Phone: (781)388-8200
Fax: (781)388-8210
Free: 800-216-2522
Publisher's E-mail: journaladsusa@bos.blackwellpublishing.com
Journal focusing on the usage of English varieties globally. **Freq:** Quarterly. **Key Personnel:** Daniel R. Davis, Editor; Braj B. Kachru, Advisor, Founder. **ISSN:** 0883--2919 (print); **EISSN:** 1467--971X (electronic). **Subscription Rates:** $204 Individuals print + online; $117 Members print + online; $1922 Institutions print + online; $1601 Institutions print or online. **URL:** http://onlinelibrary.wiley.com/journal/10.1111/(ISSN)1467-971X. **Circ:** (Not Reported).

16707 ■ Worldviews on Evidence-Based Nursing
Blackwell Publishing Inc.
350 Main St.
Malden, MA 02148
Phone: (781)388-8200
Fax: (781)388-8210
Free: 800-216-2522
Publisher's E-mail: journaladsusa@bos.blackwellpublishing.com
Peer-reviewed journal that offers research, policy and practice, education and management for nursing. **Freq:** Quarterly. **Key Personnel:** Jo Rycroft-Malone, Editor; Tracey Bucknall, Associate Editor; Bernadette Mazurek Melnyk, Associate Editor. **ISSN:** 1545--102X (print); **EISSN:** 1741--6787 (electronic). **Subscription Rates:** $518 Institutions online or print; $622 Institutions print + online; $170 Individuals online; $179 Individuals online and print; £379 Institutions print or online; £455 Institutions print and online; £124 Individuals online; £130 Individuals print and online; €476 Institutions print or online; €572 Institutions print and online; €185 Individuals online; €194 Individuals print and online; $734 Other countries print or online; $881 Other countries print and online. **URL:** http://as.wiley.com/WileyCDA/WileyTitle/productCd-WVN.html; http://onlinelibrary.wiley.com/journal/10.1111/%28ISSN%291741-6787. **Remarks:** Accepts advertising. **Circ:** (Not Reported).

16708 ■ The Yale Review
Blackwell Publishing Inc.
350 Main St.
Malden, MA 02148
Phone: (781)388-8200
Fax: (781)388-8210
Free: 800-216-2522
Publisher's E-mail: customerservice@oxon.blackwellpublishing.com
Public affairs articles, literature, book reviews, poetry, and critical articles on literature and culture. **Freq:** Quarterly. **Print Method:** Offset. **Trim Size:** 6 x 9 1/8. **Cols./Page:** 1. **Col. Width:** 26 picas. **Col. Depth:** 44 picas. **Key Personnel:** Claude Rawson, Board Member; Susan Bianconi, Managing Editor; J.D. McClatchy, Editor, phone: (203)432-0499, fax: (203)432-0510; Susan Biaconi, Managing Editor. **ISSN:** 0044--0124 (print); **EISSN:** 1467--9736 (electronic). **Subscription Rates:** $203 Institutions online or print; $244 Institutions print & online; $43 Individuals print & online; $32 Members print & online; $306 Institutions, other countries online or print; $368 Institutions, other countries print & online; £46 Other countries print and online; £34 Other countries print & online - members. **Online:** Gale. **URL:** http://as.wiley.com/WileyCDA/WileyTitle/productCd-YREV.html; http://www.wiley.com/bw/journal.asp?ref=0044-0124&site=1. **Mailing address:** PO Box 1354, Oxford OX4 2ZG, United Kingdom. **Ad Rates:** BW $450. **Remarks:** Accepts advertising. **Circ:** ‡6000.

MARBLEHEAD

16709 ■ Marblehead Reporter
GateHouse Media Inc.
11 State St.
Marblehead, MA 01945
Publication E-mail: marblehead@wickedlocal.com
Community newspaper. **Freq:** Weekly (Thurs.). **Print Method:** Offset. **Trim Size:** 11 3/8 x 17. **Cols./Page:** 5. **Col. Width:** 2 1/16 inches. **Col. Depth:** 16 inches. **Key Personnel:** Kris Olson, Editor, phone: (781)639-4806; Joe McConnell, Editor, phone: (978)739-1324. **Subscription Rates:** $73.95 Individuals; $93.95 Out of area. **URL:** http://marblehead.wickedlocal.com. **Ad Rates:** GLR $3.20; BW $800; 4C $1,250; SAU $12.45. **Remarks:** Accepts advertising. **Circ:** (Not Reported).

16710 ■ Swampscott Reporter
GateHouse Media Inc.
11 State St.
Marblehead, MA 01945
Publication E-mail: swampscott@cnc.com
swampscott@wickedlocal.com
Community newspaper (broadsheet). **Freq:** Weekly (Thurs.). **Print Method:** Offset. Uses mats. **Trim Size:** 12 1/2 x 22 1/2. **Cols./Page:** 6. **Col. Width:** 2 inches. **Col. Depth:** 21 inches. **Key Personnel:** Jeff Pope, Editor, phone: (781)639-4803; Joshua Boyd, Editor, phone: (978)739-8512. **ISSN:** 0893--3634 (print). **Subscription Rates:** $65 Individuals; $85 Out of area. **URL:** http://swampscott.wickedlocal.com/?refresh=true. **Ad Rates:** BW $740; SAU $11.50. **Remarks:** Accepts advertising. **Circ:** (Not Reported).

MARLBOROUGH

NE MA NE MA. Middlesex Co Middlesex Co. 27 mi. W. of Boston 5 mi. S. of Hudson. Manufactures shoes and slippers, miners lamps, paper, wire and foundry products, electronic equipment, feed. Metal stampings. Dairy and fruit farms.

16711 ■ Marlborough Enterprise
GateHouse Media Inc.
40 Mechanic St.
Marlborough, MA 01752
Fax: (508)490-7471
Publication E-mail: marlborough@wickedlocal.com
Local newspaper. **Freq:** Weekly (Fri.). **Print Method:** Offset. **Cols./Page:** 5. **Col. Width:** 12 picas. **Col. Depth:** 13 inches. **Key Personnel:** Richard Lodge, Editor-in-Chief, phone: (508)626-3871; Art Davidson, Editor, phone: (508)626-4403. **USPS:** 330-360. **URL:** http://marlborough.wickedlocal.com. **Ad Rates:** PCI $8.

Circulation: ★ = AAM; △ or • = BPA; ♦ = CAC; ❑ = VAC; ⊕ = PO Statement; ‡ = Publisher's Report; Boldface figures = sworn; Light figures = estimated.

30. **Remarks:** Accepts classified advertising. **Circ:** (Not Reported).

Southborough Villager - See Southborough

16712 ■ The Westborough News
The Westborough News
40 Mechanics St.
Marlborough, MA 01752
Phone: (508)490-7475
Fax: (508)490-7471
Publication E-mail: westboroevents@wickedlocal.com
Community newspaper. **Freq:** Weekly. **Print Method:** Offset. **Cols./Page:** 6. **Col. Width:** 9.5 picas. **Col. Depth:** 16 inches. **Key Personnel:** Richard Lodge, Editor-in-Chief; Kelleigh Welch, Editor; Linda Vahey, Manager, Circulation. **ISSN:** 0893--3782 (print). **Subscription Rates:** $23 Individuals; $85 Out of area. **URL:** http://westborough.wickedlocal.com. **Ad Rates:** PCI $7. 50. **Remarks:** Accepts advertising. **Circ:** Paid 4300.

16713 ■ The Woodland Steward
Massachusetts Land League
c/o Massachusetts Forest Alliance
249 Lakeside Ave.
Marlborough, MA 01752-4503
Phone: (617)455-9918
Publisher's E-mail: massforests@verizon.net
Journal featuring information about woodlands owners. **Freq:** Quarterly. **Alt. Formats:** PDF. **URL:** http://massforestalliance.org/steward. **Remarks:** Accepts advertising. **Circ:** (Not Reported).

MARSHFIELD

SE MA. Plymouth Co. 30 mi. SE of Boston. Residential.

16714 ■ Abington Mariner
GateHouse Media Inc.
165 Enterprise Dr.
Marshfield, MA 02050
Phone: (781)837-3500
Fax: (781)837-4543
Community newspaper. **Freq:** Weekly (Fri.). **Print Method:** Offset. **Trim Size:** 11 3/8 x 17. **Cols./Page:** 5. **Col. Width:** 15 1/2 inches. **Col. Depth:** 2 1/8 inches. **Key Personnel:** Mark Olivieri, Publisher, phone: (781)837-4504; Seth Jacobson, Editor, phone: (781)837-4558; Paul Harber, Editor, phone: (781)837-4579. **USPS:** 088-760. **Subscription Rates:** $39 Individuals; $63 Out of area. **URL:** http://abington.wickedlocal.com. **Formerly**: Abington/Rockland Mariner. **Ad Rates:** BW $942; 4C $1,300; PCI $8.25. **Circ:** (Not Reported).

16715 ■ Hanover Mariner
GateHouse Media Inc.
165 Enterprise Dr.
Marshfield, MA 02050
Phone: (781)837-4500
Fax: (781)837-4543
Community newspaper. **Freq:** Weekly (Wed.). **Print Method:** Offset. **Trim Size:** 11 3/8 x 17. **Cols./Page:** 5. **Col. Width:** 2 1/8 inches. **Col. Depth:** 15 1/2 inches. **Key Personnel:** Mark Olivieri, Publisher, phone: (781)837-4504; Matthew Gill, Contact, phone: (781)837-4575. **Subscription Rates:** $65 Individuals by mail; $85 Out of area by mail. **URL:** http://hanover.wickedlocal.com. **Ad Rates:** BW $942.40; 4C $1,300; PCI $8.25. **Circ:** (Not Reported).

16716 ■ Marshfield Mariner
GateHouse Media Inc.
165 Enterprise Dr.
Marshfield, MA 02050
Phone: (781)837-4500
Fax: (781)837-4543
Community newspaper. **Freq:** Weekly (Wed.). **Print Method:** Offset. **Trim Size:** 11 3/8 x 17. **Cols./Page:** 5. **Col. Width:** 2 1/8 inches. **Col. Depth:** 15 1/2 inches. **Key Personnel:** Mark Olivieri, Publisher, phone: (781)837-4504; Gregory Mathis, Editor-in-Chief, phone: (781)837-4560; Bill Fonda, Contact, phone: (781)837-4562. **Subscription Rates:** $64 Individuals by mail; $85 Out of area by mail. **URL:** http://marshfield.wickedlocal.com. **Ad Rates:** BW $942.40; 4C $1,300; PCI $8.25. **Circ:** (Not Reported).

16717 ■ Norwell Mariner
GateHouse Media Inc.
165 Enterprise Dr.
Marshfield, MA 02050
Phone: (781)837-4500
Fax: (781)837-4543
Community newspaper. **Freq:** Weekly (Wed.). **Print Method:** Offset. **Trim Size:** 11 3/8 x 17. **Cols./Page:** 5. **Col. Width:** 2 1/8 inches. **Col. Depth:** 15 1/2 inches. **Key Personnel:** Mark Olivieri, Publisher, phone: (781)837-4504; Gregory Mathis, Editor-in-Chief, phone: (781)837-4560; Matthew J. Gill, Contact, phone: (781)837-4575. **Subscription Rates:** $63 Individuals by mail; $85 Out of area by mail. **URL:** http://norwell.wickedlocal.com. **Ad Rates:** GLR $11.78; BW $942.40; 4C $1,300; PCI $8.25. **Circ:** (Not Reported).

16718 ■ Pembroke Mariner & Express
GateHouse Media Inc.
165 Enterprise Dr.
Marshfield, MA 02050
Phone: (781)837-3500
Fax: (781)837-4543
Publication E-mail: pembroke@wickedlocal.com
Community newspaper. **Freq:** Weekly (Fri.). **Print Method:** Offset. **Trim Size:** 16 1/2 x 11. **Cols./Page:** 5. **Col. Width:** 21 nonpareils. **Col. Depth:** 224 agate lines. **Key Personnel:** Mark Olivieri, Publisher, phone: (781)837-4504; Dana Forsythe, Editor, phone: (781)837-4559; Anne Finn, Manager, Advertising, phone: (781)837-4505. **URL:** http://pembroke.wickedlocal.com. **Formerly**: Pembroke Reporter. **Ad Rates:** GLR $.49; BW $560; 4C $960; PCI $7.45. **Remarks:** .49. **Circ:** Paid 1441.

16719 ■ Pembroke Mariner & Reporter
GateHouse Media Inc.
165 Enterprise Dr.
Marshfield, MA 02050
Phone: (781)837-4500
Fax: (781)837-4543
Community newspaper. **Freq:** Weekly. **Print Method:** Offset. **Trim Size:** 11 3/8 x 17. **Cols./Page:** 5. **Col. Width:** 2 1/8 inches. **Col. Depth:** 15 1/2 inches. **Key Personnel:** Mark Olivieri, Publisher, phone: (781)837-4504; Dana Forsythe, Editor, phone: (781)837-4559. **Subscription Rates:** $56 Individuals by mail; $85 Out of area by mail. **URL:** http://pembroke.wickedlocal.com. **Ad Rates:** BW $942.40; 4C $1,300; PCI $8.25. **Circ:** (Not Reported).

16720 ■ Scituate Mariner
GateHouse Media Inc.
165 Enterprise Dr.
Marshfield, MA 02050
Phone: (781)837-4500
Fax: (781)837-4543
Community newspaper. **Freq:** Weekly (Thurs.). **Print Method:** Offset. **Trim Size:** 11 3/8 x 17. **Cols./Page:** 5. **Col. Width:** 2 1/8 inches. **Col. Depth:** 15 1/2 inches. **Key Personnel:** Nancy White, Editor, phone: (781)837-4562; William Wassersug, Editor, phone: (781)837-4577. **Subscription Rates:** $69 Individuals by mail; $85 Out of area by mail. **URL:** http://scituate.wickedlocal.com. **Ad Rates:** BW $942.40; 4C $1,300; PCI $8.25. **Circ:** (Not Reported).

16721 ■ WATD-FM - 95.9
130 Enterprise Dr.
Marshfield, MA 02050
Phone: (781)837-1166
Fax: (781)837-1978
Format: Adult Contemporary. **Networks:** Independent. **Owner:** Marshfield Broadcasting Co., at above address, Ph: (781)837-4900, Fax: (781)837-1825. **Founded:** 1977. **Operating Hours**: Continuous. **Key Personnel:** Carol Perry, Owner, cperry@959watd.com. **Local Programs**: *Round Midnight Jazz Show*, Sunday 12:00 a.m. - 5:30 a.m.; *The Money Mavericks.* **Wattage**: 3,000. **Ad Rates:** $22-35 for 30 seconds; $24-40 for 60 seconds. **URL:** http://www.959watd.com.

MATTAPAN

16722 ■ Survival News
Survivors, Inc.
95 Standard St.
Mattapan, MA 02126
Phone: (617)298-7311
Fax: (617)296-4276
Publisher's E-mail: masswelf@aol.com
Newspaper containing articles about social issues. **Freq:** Semiannual. **Print Method:** Web offset. **Cols./Page:** 2. **Col. Width:** 5 inches. **Col. Depth:** 15 1/2 inches. **Key Personnel:** Diane Dujon, Editor; Dottie Stevens, Contact. **Subscription Rates:** $1 Single issue; $10 By mail; $25 Institutions. **Alt. Formats:** PDF. **URL:** http://www.survivorsinc.org. **Remarks:** Advertising accepted; rates available upon request. **Circ:** Paid 750, Free ⊕**9000.**

MATTAPOISETT

16723 ■ The Wanderer
Wanderer Communication Inc.
55 County Rd., Rte. 6
Mattapoisett, MA 02739
Phone: (508)758-9055
Fax: (508)758-4845
Publication E-mail: news@wanderer.com
Community newspaper. **Freq:** Weekly. **Subscription Rates:** $58 Individuals first class mail. **URL:** http://www.wanderer.com. **Mailing address:** PO Box 102, Mattapoisett, MA 02739. **Ad Rates:** BW $136; 4C $196. **Remarks:** Advertising accepted; rates available upon request. **Circ:** (Not Reported).

MAYNARD

NE MA. Middlesex Co. 18 mi. NW of Cambridge. Residential.

16724 ■ WAVM-FM - 91.7
1 Tiger Dr.
Maynard, MA 01754
Phone: (978)897-5179
Email: wavmstudio@gmail.com
Format: Full Service. **Owner:** Maynard High School, 1 Tiger Dr., Maynard, MA 01754. **Ad Rates:** Noncommercial. **URL:** http://wavm.org.

MEDFIELD

16725 ■ Saxophone Journal
Dorn Publications Inc.
PO Box 206
Medfield, MA 02052
Phone: (508)359-1015
Fax: (508)359-7988
Publisher's E-mail: dornpub@dornpub.com
Trade magazine for professional saxophone players. **Freq:** Bimonthly. **Subscription Rates:** $47.50 Individuals; $62.50 Out of country; $90 Two years; $120 Two years out of country; $8 Single issue with CD + 5.25 for postage. **Alt. Formats:** DVD; Download; PDF. **URL:** http://www.dornpub.com/saxophonejournal.html. **Remarks:** Accepts advertising. **Circ:** (Not Reported).

MEDFORD

NE MA. Middlesex Co. On Mystic River, 5 mi. NW of Boston. (Branch of Boston P.O.); Tufts University. Manufactures paper boxes, leather, textile oil and soap, wire and iron products, jointing compounds, wax and polish, valves, waterproof sheeting, mattresses, commercial pumps, containers, concrete blocks, dental materials, fruit syrup, truck and trailer bodies.

16726 ■ The Fletcher Forum of World Affairs
Fletcher School of Law & Diplomacy
160 Packard Ave.
Medford, MA 02155-5815
Phone: (617)627-3700
Fax: (617)627-3712
Publication E-mail: forum@tufts.edu
Journal of contemporary, legal, political, economic, and diplomatic aspects of international affairs. **Freq:** Semiannual. **Key Personnel:** Julia Radice, Editor-in-Chief. **ISSN:** 1046-1868 (print). **Subscription Rates:** $20 Individuals 1 year; $38 Individuals 2 years; $55 Individuals 3 years; $50 Institutions 1 year; $95 Institutions 2 years; $140 Institutions 3 years; 40 Individuals 1 year; other countries; 78 Individuals 2 years; other countries; 115 Individuals 3 years; other countries; 70 Institutions, other countries 1 year; 130 Institutions, other countries 2 years; 175 Institutions, other countries 3 years. **URL:** http://www.fletcherforum.org. **Remarks:** Advertising accepted; rates available upon request. **Circ:** Paid 2000.

16727 ■ FORESIGHT: The International Journal of Applied Forecasting
International Institute of Forecasters
53 Tesla Ave.
Medford, MA 02155

Phone: (781)234-4077
Publisher's E-mail: forecasters@forecasters.org
Journal containing objective, practical articles, case studies and special features on budgeting and financial planning, S&OP, marketing, demand planning, supply chain, logistics or production planning. **Freq:** Quarterly. **ISSN:** 1555- 9068 (print). **Subscription Rates:** $95 U.S.; $107 Canada and Mexico; $119 Other countries; $195 Libraries; $395 Institutions corporate site license; $165 U.S. 2 years; $189 Canada and Mexico 2 years; $213 Other countries 2 years; $345 Libraries 2 years; $695 Institutions 2 years. **URL:** http://forecasters.org/foresight/. **Remarks:** Accepts advertising. **Circ:** 600.

16728 ■ Local Environment
Routledge Journals Taylor & Francis Group
c/o Julian Agyeman, Editor in Chief
Dept. of Urban & Environmental Policy & Planning
Tufts University
Medford, MA 02155
Journal focusing on local environmental, justice and sustainability policy, politics and action. **Freq:** Monthly. **Print Method:** Offset. **Trim Size:** 8 1/8 x 10 7/8. **Cols./Page:** 5. **Key Personnel:** Julian Agyeman, Editor-in-Chief; Sue Buckingham, Advisor; Katerina Eckerberg, Advisor; Harriet Bulkeley, Advisor; Anna Davies, Advisor. **ISSN:** 1354--9839 (print); **EISSN:** 1469--6711 (electronic). **Subscription Rates:** $1707 Institutions online only; $1951 Institutions print and online. **URL:** http://www.tandfonline.com/toc/cloe20/current; http://www.tandfonline.com/loi/cloe20. **Remarks:** Advertising not accepted. **Circ:** (Not Reported).

16729 ■ Tufts Magazine
Tufts University Alumni Association
Office Of Alumni Relations
80 George St., Ste. 100-3
Medford, MA 02155
Phone: (617)627-3532
Fax: (617)627-3938
Free: 800-843-2586
Publication E-mail: tuftsmagazine@tufts.edu
Magazine containing articles regarding Tufts Alumni. **Freq:** Quarterly. **ISSN:** 1535- 5063 (print). **Subscription Rates:** Free. **URL:** http://www.tufts.edu/alumni/magazine/winter2015. **Remarks:** Advertising not accepted. **Circ:** 80000.

16730 ■ WJMN-FM - 94.5
10 Cabot Rd., Ste. 302
Medford, MA 02155
Phone: (781)663-2500
Fax: (781)290-0722
Format: Contemporary Hit Radio (CHR); Hip Hop. **Networks:** Independent. **Founded:** 1948. **Operating Hours:** Continuous. **Key Personnel:** Tom McConnell, Gen. Mgr. **Wattage:** 9,200. **Ad Rates:** Advertising accepted; rates available upon request. **URL:** http://jamn945.com.

16731 ■ WMFO-FM - 91.5
PO Box 65
Medford, MA 02155
Phone: (617)627-3800
Format: Full Service. **Owner:** Tufts University, 419 Boston Ave., Medford, MA 02155, Ph: (617)628-5000. **Founded:** 1970. **Formerly:** WTUR-AM. **Operating Hours:** Continuous; 100% local. **Key Personnel:** Andy Sayler, Contact. **Wattage:** 125. **Ad Rates:** Noncommercial. **URL:** http://www.wmfo.org.

16732 ■ WXKS-AM - 1430
10 Cabot Rd., Ste. 302
Medford, MA 02155
Phone: (781)396-1430
Fax: (781)290-0722
Format: Hispanic. **Networks:** Independent. **Founded:** 1952. **Operating Hours:** Continuous. **Wattage:** 5,000 Day; 1,000 Night. **Ad Rates:** Noncommercial. **URL:** http://www.kiss108.com.

16733 ■ WXKS-FM - 108
10 Cabot Rd., Ste. 302
Medford, MA 02155
Phone: (781)396-1430
Fax: (781)290-0722
Format: Contemporary Hit Radio (CHR). **Networks:** Independent. **Owner:** iHeartMedia Inc., 200 E Basse Rd., San Antonio, TX 78209, Ph: (210)832-3314. **Founded:** 1979. **Operating Hours:** Continuous. **ADI:** Boston-Worcester,MA-Derry-Manchester,NH. **Wattage:** 50,000. **Ad Rates:** Advertising accepted; rates available upon request. **URL:** http://www.kiss108.com//main.html.

MELROSE

NE MA. Middlesex Co. 8 mi. N. of Boston. Manufactures chemicals, radios, electronics, lighting.

16734 ■ Intermezzo: Intermezzo
Intermezzo
99 Essex St.
Melrose, MA 02176
Phone: (781)665-7717
Fax: (781)665-7712
Publisher's E-mail: rtully@intermezzomagazine.com
Magazine that aims to explore a variety of fine life experiences in international cuisine, wine and spirits, kitchen and home decor, wellness, leisure and travel. **Freq:** Bimonthly. **Print Method:** Web Offset. **Trim Size:** 8 x 10 3/4. **Subscription Rates:** $23 Individuals; $35 Two years; $49 Canada; $79 Other countries. **URL:** http://www.intermezzomagazine.com. **Remarks:** Accepts advertising. **Circ:** (Not Reported).

METHUEN

W. MA. Essex Co. 9 mi. NE of Lowell. Industrial.

16735 ■ WCCM-AM
462 Merrimack S
Methuen, MA 01844
Phone: (973)328-5000
Fax: (978)687-1180
Email: info@1110wccmam.com
Format: Alternative/New Music/Progressive; News; Talk; Sports. **Networks:** AP; CNN Radio; ESPN Radio. **Owner:** Costa Eagle Radio, at above address. **Founded:** 1947. **Formerly:** Curt Gowdy Broadcasting. **Key Personnel:** Chris Fenwick, Contact; PJ Costa, Contact, pjc@costaeagleradio.com. **Local Programs:** *Hotline*. **Wattage:** 5,000 Day. **Ad Rates:** Noncommercial. $17-30 for 30 seconds; $20-45 for 60 seconds.

16736 ■ WCEC-AM - 1490
462 Merrimack St.
Methuen, MA 01844
Phone: (978)659-0071
Format: Hispanic; News; Talk; Sports. **Owner:** Costa Eagle Broadcasting, 462 Merrimack St., Methuen, MA 01844, Fax: (978)687-1180. **Operating Hours:** Continuous. **Wattage:** 1,000. **URL:** http://wcec1490am.com.

16737 ■ WNNW-AM - 800
462 Merrimack St.
Methuen, MA 01844
Phone: (978)686-9966
Free: 888-887-6937
Format: Hispanic. **URL:** http://www.power800am.com.

MILFORD

C. MA. Worcester Co. 12 mi. SW of Framington. Manufactures computers, rubber goods, elastic webbing, ceramic tile, glass, tools, concrete, dies, metal stampings, construction materials, paints. Dairy, truck farms.

16738 ■ Milford Daily News
GateHouse Media Inc.
197 Main St.
Milford, MA 01757
Publication E-mail: delivery@mypapertoday.com
milforddailynews@wickedlocal.com
General newspaper. **Freq:** Mon.-Sun. **Print Method:** Offset Uses mats. **Trim Size:** 13 x 21 1/2. **Cols./Page:** 6. **Col. Width:** 2 1/16 inches. **Col. Depth:** 301 agate lines. **Key Personnel:** Elizabeth Banks, Managing Editor. **USPS:** 144-320. **Subscription Rates:** $76.95 Individuals 12 weeks (Monday-Sunday; all access); $74.95 Individuals 1 year (Monday-Sunday; e-paper); $52.95 Individuals 12 weeks (Thursday-Sunday); $31.95 Individuals 12 weeks (Sunday only). **Alt. Formats:** Electronic publishing. **URL:** http://www.milforddailynews.com; http://milford.wickedlocal.com. **Ad Rates:** GLR $1.32; SAU $12.35. **Remarks:** Accepts advertising. **Circ:** (Not Reported).

16739 ■ WMRC-AM - 1490
258 Main St.
Milford, MA 01757
Phone: (508)473-1490
Email: news@wmrcdailynews.com
Format: Full Service. **Owner:** First Class Radio Inc., 3316 W Chain Of Rocks Rd., Ste. 2, Granite City, IL 62040, Ph: (618)797-3266, Fax: (618)797-3267, Free: 866-723-4605. **Key Personnel:** Rick Michaels, Operations Mgr., rick@wmrcradio.com; Tom McAuliffe, II, Owner, mrclink1490@aol.com. **Local Programs:** *The Town Crier*, Monday Tuesday Wednesday Thursday Friday; *The Unforgettable 45s*, Monday Tuesday Wednesday Thursday Friday 8:30 a.m.; *The Voice of Portugal*, Sunday 8:00 a.m.; *Sports Buzz*, Saturday 10:00 a.m.; *The WMRC Daybreak Morning Show*, Monday Tuesday Wednesday Thursday Friday 5:00 p.m.; *Music from the 70's, 80's, 90's and Today*, Monday Tuesday Wednesday Thursday Friday 9:00 a.m. - 5:00 p.m.; *The Paul Parent Garden Show*, Sunday 6:00 a.m. - 10:00 a.m. **Wattage:** 1,000. **Ad Rates:** Advertising accepted; rates available upon request. $14-20 for 30 seconds; $17-24 for 60 seconds. **Mailing address:** PO Box 421, Milford, MA 01757. **URL:** http://www.wmrcdailynews.com.

MILTON

E. MA. Norfolk Co. 6 mi. S. of Boston. (Branch of Boston P.O.) Residential. Manufactures crackers, cocoa, chocolate, ice cream.

16740 ■ WMLN-FM - 91.5
1071 Blue Hill Ave.
Milton, MA 02186
Phone: (617)333-0500
Fax: (617)333-2114
Format: Alternative/New Music/Progressive; News; Sports. **Networks:** NBC; CNN Radio. **Owner:** Curry College, 1071 Blue Hill Ave., Milton, MA 02186, Ph: (617)333-2075, Fax: (617)333-2114. **Founded:** 1975. **Operating Hours:** Continuous; 5% network, 95% local. **Key Personnel:** Alan Frank, Contact, afrank@post03.curry.edu. **Wattage:** 170. **Ad Rates:** Noncommercial. **URL:** http://www.curry.edu.

MOUNT HERMON

16741 ■ WNMH-FM - 91.5
One Lamplighter Way
Mount Hermon, MA 01354
Phone: (413)498-3000
Fax: (413)498-3010
Email: info@nmhschool.org
Format: News; Contemporary Hit Radio (CHR); Alternative/New Music/Progressive. **Networks:** ABC. **Owner:** Northfield-Mount Herman School. **Founded:** 1984. **Formerly:** WMHS-FM. **Operating Hours:** Continuous. **Key Personnel:** Bill Hattendorf, Contact, bhattendorf@nmhschool.org. **Wattage:** 235. **Ad Rates:** Noncommercial. **URL:** http://www.nmhschool.org.

NANTUCKET

SE MA. Nantucket Co. On N. shore of Nantucket Island, 25 mi. SE of Hyannis. Boat connections. Resort.

16742 ■ The Inquirer and Mirror
The Inquirer and Mirror Inc.
PO Box 1198
Nantucket, MA 02554-1198
Phone: (508)228-0001
Fax: (508)325-5089
Publication E-mail: newsroom@inkym.com
Community newspaper. **Founded:** June 23, 1821. **Freq:** Weekly (Thurs.). **Print Method:** Offset. **Cols./Page:** 8. **Col. Width:** 22 nonpareils. **Col. Depth:** 287 agate lines. **Key Personnel:** Marianne R. Stanton, Editor; Joshua H. Balling, Assistant Editor; Greg Derr, Director, Production. **ISSN:** 0891-8686 (print). **Subscription Rates:** $69 Individuals; $69 Individuals on-island; $119 Two years on-island; $75 Individuals off-island; $289 Individuals off-island first class mail; $129 Two years off-island; $840 Individuals foreign; $45 Individuals military; $6.75 Single issue; $21 Individuals nantucket today; $38 Two years nantucket today. **URL:** http://www.ack.net. **Remarks:** Accepts advertising. **Circ:** Paid 10609, Non-paid 187.

Circulation: ★ = AAM; △ or • = BPA; ♦ = CAC; ❑ = VAC; ⊕ = PO Statement; ‡ = Publisher's Report; Boldface figures = sworn; Light figures = estimated.

16743 ■ Nantucket Magazine
Nantucket Journal Inc.
PO Box 142
Nantucket, MA 02554
Phone: (508)228-1515
Consumer magazine covering Nantucket Island. **Freq:** Quarterly. **Print Method:** 9 1/2 X 13. **Trim Size:** 9.5 X 13. **Key Personnel:** Bruce A. Percelay, Publisher; Fifi Greenberg, Director, Advertising. **ISSN:** 1074--1763 (print). **URL:** http://www.n-magazine.com. **Formerly:** Nantucket Journal. **Remarks:** Advertising accepted; rates available upon request. **Circ:** Combined 8864.

16744 ■ Yesterday's Island
Yesterday's Island Inc.
One Skyline Dr.
Nantucket, MA 02554-2860
Phone: (508)228-9165
Fax: (508)228-1348
Publisher's E-mail: info@nantucket.net
Tourist guide. **Freq:** Weekly. **Print Method:** Offset. Cols 5. **Col. Width:** 24 nonpareils. **Col. Depth:** 224 agate lines. **Key Personnel:** Suzanne M. Daub, Editor; Jerry T. Daub, Publisher. **Subscription Rates:** $25 Individuals. **Mailing address:** PO Box 626, Nantucket, MA 02554-2860. **Ad Rates:** GLR $1. **Remarks:** Accepts advertising. **Circ:** Non-paid 350000.

NATICK

NE MA. Middlesex Co. 18 mi. W. of Boston. Manufactures electronic equipment, boxes and boxboard, baseballs, softballs, band saws, machine parts, electric clocks. Foundry.

16745 ■ Natick Bulletin
GateHouse Media Inc.
33 New York Ave.
Framingham, MA 01701
Publication E-mail: natick@cnc.com
Newspaper. **Freq:** Weekly (Fri.). **Print Method:** Offset. **Cols./Page:** 6. **Col. Width:** 20 nonpareils. **Col. Depth:** 224 agate lines. **Key Personnel:** Ian B. Murphy, Editor; Richard Lodge, Editor-in-Chief. **Subscription Rates:** $65.95 Individuals. **URL:** http://natick.wickedlocal.com/?refresh=true. **Ad Rates:** GLR $.62. **Remarks:** Accepts advertising. **Circ:** (Not Reported).

NEEDHAM

E. MA. Norfolk Co. 12 mi. SW of Boston. (Branch of Boston P.O.) Manufactures knit goods, dental and surgical instruments, textiles, electronic products.

16746 ■ Bedford Minuteman
GateHouse Media Inc.
254 Second Ave.
Needham, MA 02492
Phone: (781)433-8366
Community newspaper. **Freq:** Weekly (Thurs.). **Print Method:** Offset. **Cols./Page:** 6. **Col. Width:** 21 nonpareils. **Col. Depth:** 294 agate lines. **Key Personnel:** Eileen Kennedy, Editor; Kathleen Cordeir, Editor-in-Chief, phone: (978)371-5736; Chuck Goodrich, Publisher. **USPS:** 047-740. **Subscription Rates:** $69 Individuals; $85 Out of area. **URL:** http://bedford.wickedlocal.com. **Ad Rates:** PCI $8.80. **Remarks:** Accepts advertising. **Circ:** (Not Reported).

16747 ■ Billerica Minuteman
GateHouse Media Inc.
254 Second Ave.
Needham, MA 02492
Phone: (781)433-8366
Publication E-mail: billerica.events@cnc.com
Community newspaper. **Freq:** Weekly (Thurs.). **Print Method:** Offset. **Cols./Page:** 6. **Col. Width:** 21 nonpareils. **Col. Depth:** 294 agate lines. **Key Personnel:** Max Bowen, Editor, phone: (978)371-5726; Chuck Goodrich, Publisher. **USPS:** 925-740. **Subscription Rates:** $65 Individuals; $85 Out of area. **URL:** http://billerica.wickedlocal.com. **Ad Rates:** SAU $6.50. **Remarks:** Accepts advertising. **Circ:** (Not Reported).

16748 ■ Bio - IT World
Bio-It World Inc.
250 First Ave., Ste. 300
Needham, MA 02494-2887
Phone: (508)628-4700
Fax: (508)628-4766
Publisher's E-mail: subscribe-ecliniqua@newsletters.bio-itworld.com
Online magazine that covers application of technology products and services to enable the life sciences R&D value chain in pharmaceutical, biotechnology, healthcare, government, and academic research organizations, spanning basic research, drug discovery and development, clinical trials, and regulatory compliance. **Freq:** Monthly. **Key Personnel:** Kevin Davies, PhD, Editor-in-Chief. **ISSN:** 1538--5728 (print). **Subscription Rates:** Free. **URL:** http://www.bio-itworld.com. **Remarks:** Accepts advertising. **Circ:** (Not Reported).

16749 ■ Brookline TAB
GateHouse Media Inc.
254 Second Ave.
Needham, MA 02494
Phone: (781)433-8334
Community newspaper (tabloid). **Freq:** Weekly (Tues.). **Print Method:** Offset. **Trim Size:** 10 x 16. **Cols./Page:** 7. **Col. Width:** 8 picas. **Key Personnel:** Erin Clossey, Editor, phone: (781)433-8334; Chuck Goodrich, Publisher. **URL:** http://brookline.wickedlocal.com. **Remarks:** Accepts advertising. **Circ:** (Not Reported).

16750 ■ Cambridge Chronicle
GateHouse Media Inc.
254 Second Ave.
Needham, MA 02494
Publication E-mail: cambridge@wickedlocal.com
Community newspaper. **Founded:** 1846. **Freq:** Weekly (Thurs.). **Print Method:** Offset. **Cols./Page:** 6. **Col. Width:** 26 nonpareils. **Col. Depth:** 294 agate lines. **Key Personnel:** David L. Harris, Managing Editor, phone: (617)629-3387; Greg Reibman, Publisher, phone: (781)433-8345. **Subscription Rates:** $31 Individuals Available to residents of Cambridge only. **URL:** http://cambridge.wickedlocal.com. **Ad Rates:** GLR $3.75; BW $2,432; SAU $19.30; PCI $19.30. **Remarks:** Accepts advertising. **Circ:** (Not Reported).

16751 ■ Choral Director: The Choral Director's Management Magazine
Symphony Publishing Group
21 Highland Cir., Ste. 1
Needham, MA 02494
Fax: (781)453-9389
Free: 800-964-5150
Magazine for school choir directors. **Freq:** Bimonthly. **Key Personnel:** Christian Wissmuller, Executive Editor; Laurie Guptill, Manager, Production. **URL:** http://www.choraldirectormag.com. **Ad Rates:** BW $2700. **Remarks:** Accepts advertising. **Circ:** ‡16000.

16752 ■ Dover-Sherborn Press
GateHouse Media Inc.
254 Second Ave.
Needham, MA 02494
Community newspaper (tabloid). **Founded:** Oct. 1985. **Freq:** Weekly (Thurs.). **Print Method:** Offset. **Trim Size:** 10 x 16. **Cols./Page:** 7. **Col. Width:** 8 picas. **Key Personnel:** Greg Reibman, Publisher, phone: (781)433-8345. **Subscription Rates:** $63 Individuals; $85 Out of area. **URL:** http://buy.mypapertoday.com/page43.html. **Formerly:** The Dover/Sherborn Gazette; The Dover TAB. **Remarks:** Accepts classified advertising. **Circ:** (Not Reported).

16753 ■ International Journal of Case Method Research and Application
World Association for Case Method Research and Application
23 Mackintosh Ave.
Needham, MA 02492-1218
Phone: (781)444-8982
Fax: (781)444-1548
Publisher's E-mail: wacra@rcn.com
Freq: Quarterly. **ISSN:** 1554-7752 (print). **Subscription Rates:** Included in membership. **URL:** http://www.wacra.org. **Remarks:** Accepts advertising. **Circ:** 2,000.

16754 ■ Needham Times
GateHouse Media Inc.
254 2nd Ave.
Needham, MA 02494
Publication E-mail: needham@suburbanworld.com
Local newspaper. **Freq:** Weekly (Thurs.). **Print Method:** Offset. **Trim Size:** 11 x 17. **Cols./Page:** 6. **Col. Width:** 10 1/4 picas. **Col. Depth:** 16 inches. **Key Personnel:** Valentina Zic, Editor, phone: (781)433-8366; Emily Cataneo, Reporter; Greg Reibman, Publisher. **Subscription Rates:** $30 Out of area; $22 Students. **URL:** http://needham.wickedlocal.com. **Ad Rates:** PCI $10.98. **Remarks:** Advertising accepted; rates available upon request. **Circ:** Free 11700.

16755 ■ Newton TAB
GateHouse Media Inc.
254 Second Ave.
Needham, MA 02494
Community newspaper (tabloid). **Freq:** Weekly (Tues.). **Print Method:** Offset. **Trim Size:** 10 x 16. **Cols./Page:** 7. **Col. Width:** 8 picas. **Key Personnel:** Greg Reibman, Publisher, phone: (781)433-8345; Gail Spector, Editor, phone: (781)433-8367. **Subscription Rates:** $52 Individuals 52 weeks; $70 Out of area; $26 Individuals online; $62 Individuals print + online. **URL:** http://newton.wickedlocal.com/?refresh=true. **Circ:** (Not Reported).

16756 ■ School Band and Orchestra
Symphony Publishing Group
21 Highland Cir., Ste. 1
Needham, MA 02494
Fax: (781)453-9389
Free: 800-964-5150
Magazine for school band directors that offers information on building and enhancing school music programs. **Freq:** Monthly. **Trim Size:** 8.25 x 11.125. **Key Personnel:** Christian Wissmuller, Associate Editor; Laurie Guptill, Manager, Production; Sidney L. Davis, Publisher. **URL:** http://sbomagazine.com. **Ad Rates:** BW $2750; 4C $3250. **Remarks:** Accepts advertising. **Circ:** (Not Reported).

16757 ■ Wellesley Townsman
GateHouse Media Inc.
254 Second Ave.
Needham, MA 02494
Community newspaper (tabloid). **Freq:** Weekly (Thurs.). **Print Method:** Offset. **Trim Size:** 10 x 16. **Cols./Page:** 7. **Col. Width:** 8 picas. **Key Personnel:** Cathy Brauner, Editor, phone: (781)431-2003. **Subscription Rates:** $82 Individuals. **URL:** http://wellesley.wickedlocal.com. **Circ:** (Not Reported).

16758 ■ West Roxbury Transcript
GateHouse Media Inc.
254 Second Ave.
Needham, MA 02492
Phone: (781)433-8366
Community newspaper. **Freq:** Weekly (Thurs.). **Print Method:** Offset. **Cols./Page:** 6. **Col. Width:** 25 nonpareils. **Col. Depth:** 300 agate lines. **Key Personnel:** Greg Reibman, Publisher, phone: (781)433-8345; Julie Cohen, Editor, phone: (781)433-8384. **Subscription Rates:** $89.95 Out of area; $66.95 Individuals. **URL:** http://west-roxbury.wickedlocal.com. **Ad Rates:** BW $2,142; 4C $2,802. **Remarks:** Accepts advertising. **Circ:** Paid 4032, Free 190.

16759 ■ WBNW-AM - 1120
144 Gould St.
Needham, MA 02494
Free: 888-205-2263
Format: News. **Owner:** Money Matters Radio Inc., at above address, Needham, MA 02494. **Founded:** July 1998. **Key Personnel:** Jason Wolfe, Contact; Tucker Silva, Contact. **Wattage:** 5,000 Watts. **Ad Rates:** Noncommercial.

WUNI-TV - See Boston

NEEDHAM HEIGHTS

NE MA. Norfolk Co. 10 mi. E. of Wellesley.

16760 ■ WCVB-TV - 5
5 TV Pl.
Needham Heights, MA 02494
Phone: (781)449-0400
Format: Commercial TV. **Networks:** ABC. **Owner:** Hearst Television Inc., 300 W 57th St., New York, NY 10019-3741, Ph: (212)887-6800, Fax: (212)887-6855. **Founded:** 1972. **Operating Hours:** Continuous. **ADI:** Boston-Worcester,MA-Derry-Manchester,NH. **Key Personnel:** Bill Fine, Gen. Mgr.; Karen Colbert, Asst. GM; Andrew Vrees, News Dir; Liz Cheng, Contact; Karen Holmes Ward, Contact. **Wattage:** 100,000. **Ad Rates:** Advertising accepted; rates available upon request. **URL:** http://www.wcvb.com.

NEW BEDFORD

SE MA. Bristol Co. On Buzzards Bay at mouth of Acushnet River, 56 mi. S. of Boston. Bridge to Fairhaven. Port of entry, with good harbor. Resort. Shopping center for Cape Cod, Martha's Vineyard and Nantucket. One of the largest fishing ports on the Atlantic coast. Freezing plants. Manufactures fine cotton and silk goods, tire fabrics, drills, screws, copper, eyelets and tacks, capacitors, rubber goods, paper products, rope, twine, lubricating oil, paint, electrical goods, golf balls, textile-mill supplies and machinery, cable, wire, camera film.

16761 ■ WFHL-FM - 88.1
71 William St.
New Bedford, MA 02740
Phone: (508)991-7600
Fax: (508)991-2060
Email: info@radiowfhl.com
Format: Religious. **Mailing address:** PO Box 3025, New Bedford, MA 02741. **URL:** http://www.radiowfhl.com.

16762 ■ WJFD-FM - 97.3
651 Orchard St., Ste. 300
New Bedford, MA 02744
Phone: (508)997-2929
Format: Music of Your Life. **Owner:** West Islip Fire Department, 309 Union Blvd., West Islip, NY 11795, Fax: (877)610-8041, Free: 877-610-8041. **Founded:** 1949. **Operating Hours:** Continuous. **ADI:** Providence, RI-New Bedford, MA. **Key Personnel:** Claudia Bernier, Mgr., claudia@wjfd.com; Cristiano Raposo, Contact, cris@wjfd.com; Jorge Morais, Contact, jorge@wjfd.com. **Wattage:** 50,000 ERP. **Ad Rates:** Noncommercial. **URL:** http://www.wjfd.com.

16763 ■ WTKL-FM - 91.1
PO Box 2098
Omaha, NE 68103
Free: 800-525-5683
Email: info@klove.com
Format: Contemporary Christian. **Owner:** Educational Media Foundation, 5700 W Oaks Blvd., CA 95765, Free: 800-800434-8400. **URL:** http://www.klove.com.

NEWBURYPORT

NE MA. Essex Co. On Merrimac River, 3 mi. from ocean, 35 mi. NE of Boston. Major historic sights. Manufactures electronics, semi-conductors, silverware, machine shop products. Fisheries. Truck farms.

16764 ■ ALN Magazine
Online Learning Consortium
PO Box 1238
Newburyport, MA 01950-8238
Phone: (617)716-1414
Fax: (888)898-6209
Publisher's E-mail: info@onlinelearning-c.org
Remarks: Advertising not accepted. **Circ:** (Not Reported).

16765 ■ Journal of Participatory Medicine
Society for Participatory Medicine
PO Box 1183
Newburyport, MA 01950-1183
Publisher's E-mail: info@participatorymedicine.org
ISSN: 2152- 7202 (print). **Subscription Rates:** Free. **URL:** http://www.jopm.org. **Remarks:** Advertising not accepted. **Circ:** (Not Reported).

16766 ■ Newburyport Daily News
Eagle-Tribune Publishing Co.
23 Liberty St.
Newburyport, MA 01950
Phone: (978)462-6666
Fax: (978)465-8505
Publisher's E-mail: direland@eagletribune.com
General newspaper. **Freq:** Mon.-Sat. (eve.). **Cols./Page:** 6. **Col. Width:** 25 nonpareils. **Col. Depth:** 294 agate lines. **Key Personnel:** Shiela Smith, Publisher; John Macone, Editor, phone: (978)462-6666. **Subscription Rates:** $20.99 Individuals total access/month ; $16.99 Individuals digital access/month. **URL:** http://www.newburyportnews.com. **Ad Rates:** PCI $23.95. **Remarks:** Accepts advertising. **Circ:** (Not Reported).

16767 ■ Online Learning
Online Learning Consortium
PO Box 1238
Newburyport, MA 01950-8238
Phone: (617)716-1414
Fax: (888)898-6209
Publisher's E-mail: hello@cnie-rcie.ca
Freq: Quarterly 4/year. **Key Personnel:** Gregory W. Hislop, Associate Editor; Peter Shea, Editor-in-Chief. **ISSN:** 1939--5256 (print); **EISSN:** 1092--8235 (electronic). **Subscription Rates:** $185 Members; $49.95 Single issue; $210 Nonmembers; $185 Individuals for print; $49.95 Individuals single issue (print). **Alt. Formats:** PDF. **URL:** http://olc.onlinelearningconsortium.org/publications/olj_main; http://onlinelearningconsortium.org/read/online-learning-journal/. **Formerly:** Journal of Asynchronous Learning Networks; Asynchronous Learning Networks. **Remarks:** Advertising accepted; rates available upon request. **Circ:** (Not Reported).

16768 ■ WNBP-AM - 1450
1 Merrimac St.
Newburyport, MA 01950
Phone: (978)462-1450
Fax: (978)462-0333
Format: Big Band/Nostalgia; Oldies. **Networks:** AP. **Founded:** 1957. **Operating Hours:** Continuous. **Key Personnel:** Carl Strube, Gen. Mgr., carl@wnbp.com; Win Damon, Contact, win@wnbp.com. **Wattage:** 1,000. **Ad Rates:** Noncommercial. **URL:** http://www.wnbp.com.

NEWTON

NE MA. Middlesex Co. 7 mi. SW of Boston. (Branch of Boston P.O.) Andover Newton Theological School; Boston College; Mt. Ida Jr. College; Aquinas Jr. College; LaSell Jr. College. Residential. Manufactures radio tubes, railway signals, yarn, knit goods, electronics, fans, plastics.

16769 ■ Boston College Environmental Affairs Law Review
Boston College Law School
885 Centre St.
Newton, MA 02459
Phone: (617)552-8550
Fax: (617)552-2615
Publisher's E-mail: bclawadm@bc.edu
Academic journal covering environmental law. **Print Method:** Docutech. **Trim Size:** 6 x 9. **ISSN:** 0190-7034 (print). **URL:** http://lawdigitalcommons.bc.edu/ealr/about.html. **Remarks:** Advertising not accepted. **Circ:** Paid 800.

16770 ■ Boston College Journal of Law & Social Justice
Boston College Law School
885 Centre St.
Newton, MA 02459
Phone: (617)552-8550
Fax: (617)552-2615
Publication E-mail: bcpubs@bc.edu
Journal dealing with legal issues. **Freq:** Semiannual. **Key Personnel:** Hilary Weddell, Editor-in-Chief. **Subscription Rates:** $35 Individuals plus 10.00 for foreign mailing; $10 Single issue plus 1.00 for foreign mailing. **Alt. Formats:** PDF. **URL:** http://jlsj.bclawreview.org/about-us/. **Formerly:** Boston College Third World Law Journal. **Circ:** (Not Reported).

16771 ■ Boston College Journal of Law and Social Justice
Boston College Law School
885 Centre St.
Newton, MA 02459
Phone: (617)552-8550
Fax: (617)552-2615
Publisher's E-mail: bclawadm@bc.edu
Journal covering articles on issues affecting underrepresented populations, human and civil rights, immigration, women and children, and issues of disproportionate economic impact. **Freq:** Semiannual. **Key Personnel:** Erica Coray, Editor-in-Chief. **ISSN:** 0276--3583 (print). **URL:** http://jlsj.bclawreview.org. **Circ:** (Not Reported).

16772 ■ CIO Decisions
TechTarget Inc.
275 Grove St.
Newton, MA 02466
Phone: (617)431-9200
Fax: (617)431-9201
Free: 888-274-4111
Publisher's E-mail: techtargetwebsite@techtarget.com
Magazine covering topics of interest to Chief Information Officers. **Freq:** Monthly. **URL:** http://www.techtarget.com/html/ipad_support.html. **Remarks:** Accepts advertising. **Circ:** (Not Reported).

16773 ■ Golfdom
Questex L.L.C.
P.O Box 2090
Skokie, IL 60076-7990
Phone: (847)763-4942
Fax: (847)763-9694
Publisher's E-mail: info@questex.com
Magazine for greenkeepers, club managers and golf professionals. **Founded:** 1999. **Freq:** Monthly. **Print Method:** web offset. **Trim Size:** 7 3/4 x 10 1/2. **Col. Width:** 10 INS. **Key Personnel:** Seth Jones, Editor-in-Chief; Beth Geraci, Senior Editor. **Subscription Rates:** $48 Individuals; $70 Canada and Mexico; $105 Other countries; $69 Two years; $101 Canada and Mexico Two years; $152 Other countries Two years. **URL:** http://www.golfdom.com. **Mailing address:** P.O Box 2090, Skokie, IL 60076-7990. **Ad Rates:** BW $4,820. **Remarks:** Accepts advertising. **Circ:** Non-paid ■ **23147**, Paid ■ **48**.

16774 ■ GPWA Times
Gambling Portal Webmasters Association
95 Wells Ave.
Newton, MA 02459
Phone: (617)332-2850
Fax: (617)964-2280
Publisher's E-mail: sales@gpwa.org
Subscription Rates: Included in membership. **URL:** http://www.gpwa.org/magazine/. **Ad Rates:** BW $1,500. **Remarks:** Accepts advertising. **Circ:** (Not Reported).

16775 ■ Hotel Management
Questex L.L.C.
275 Grove St., Ste. 2-130
Newton, MA 02466
Phone: (617)219-8300
Fax: (617)219-8310
Free: 888-552-4346
Publisher's E-mail: info@questex.com
Magazine (tabloid) covering the global lodging industry. **Freq:** 11/year. **Print Method:** Offset. **Trim Size:** 11 x 15. **Cols./Page:** 4. **Col. Width:** 27 nonpareils. **Col. Depth:** 196 agate lines. **Key Personnel:** Jason Q. Freed, Senior Editor, phone: (216)706-3727; Ruthanne Terrero, Director, Editorial, Vice President; Stephanie Ricca, Editor-in-Chief. **ISSN:** 0018--6082 (print). **Subscription Rates:** $74 U.S. /yr; $98 Canada and Mexico /yr; $169 Other countries /yr. **URL:** http://www.hotelmanagement.net/hotel-management-magazine-subscription. **Formerly:** Hotel & Motel Management. **Remarks:** Advertising accepted; rates available upon request. **Circ:** Non-paid ■ **46409**.

16776 ■ Information Security
TechTarget Inc.
275 Grove St.
Newton, MA 02466
Phone: (617)431-9200
Fax: (617)431-9201
Free: 888-274-4111
Publisher's E-mail: techtargetwebsite@techtarget.com
Magazine covering information security topics. **Freq:** Monthly. **Key Personnel:** Peter S. Tippett, Publisher; Sarah L. Cain, Managing Editor. **URL:** http://searchsecurity.techtarget.com/ezine/Information-Security-magazine. **Remarks:** Accepts advertising. **Circ:** (Not Reported).

16777 ■ LP-Gas
Questex L.L.C.
275 Grove St., Ste. 2-130
Newton, MA 02466
Phone: (617)219-8300
Fax: (617)219-8310
Free: 888-552-4346
Publisher's E-mail: info@questex.com
Magazine serving the licensed petroleum gas industry. **Founded:** 1940. **Freq:** Monthly. **Print Method:** Letterpress and offset. **Trim Size:** 7 3/4 x 10 1/2. **Cols./Page:** 3. **Col. Width:** 26 nonpareils. **Col. Depth:** 140 agate lines. **Key Personnel:** Brian Kanaba, Publisher, phone: (216)706-3745, fax: (216)706-3710; Patrick Hyland, Editor-in-Chief, phone: (216)706-3724; Sean Carr, Publisher, phone: (216)706-3726. **ISSN:** 0024-7103 (print). **Subscription Rates:** $55 Individuals; $63 Canada and Mexico; $138 Other countries. **URL:** http://

Circulation: ★ = AAM; △ or • = BPA; ♦ = CAC; ❑ = VAC; ⊕ = PO Statement; ‡ = Publisher's Report; Boldface figures = sworn; Light figures = estimated.

www.lpgasmagazine.com. **Ad Rates:** BW $4600. **Remarks:** Accepts advertising. **Circ:** Non-paid ■ **12,066**, Paid ■ **864**, Combined ■ **12,930**.

16778 ■ Nightclub & Bar Magazine
Questex L.L.C.
275 Grove St., Ste. 2-130
Newton, MA 02466
Phone: (617)219-8300
Fax: (617)219-8310
Free: 888-552-4346
Publisher's E-mail: info@questex.com
Trade magazine covering management, lighting, sound, food, beverage, promotions, current trends, and other bar industry news. **Freq:** 9/yr. **Print Method:** Offset. **Trim Size:** 8 1/8 x 10 7/8. **Cols./Page:** 3. **Col. Width:** 13 picas. **Col. Depth:** 58 picas. **Key Personnel:** Donna Hood Crecca, Publisher, Director, Editorial, phone: (631)265-3839; Jon Taffer, President. **ISSN:** 0893-4117 (print). **Subscription Rates:** $30 Individuals; $45 Canada and Mexico; $85 Other countries. **URL:** http://www.nightclub.com. **Ad Rates:** BW $3,828; 4C $5,055. **Remarks:** Accepts advertising. **Circ:** Free ■ **21544**, Paid ■ **306**.

16779 ■ Plays: The Drama Magazine for Young People
Plays Magazine
897 Washington St.
Newton, MA 02460
Phone: (617)630-9100
Fax: (617)630-9101
Free: 800-630-5755
Publisher's E-mail: customerservice@playsmagazine.com
Magazine for schools, libraries or drama groups containing one-act plays for holiday celebrations and special patriotic occasions, plays with modern settings and modern situations. Features comedies, dramas, skits, puppet plays, and dramatized classics. **Freq:** 7/year. **Key Personnel:** Elizabeth Preston, Editor. **USPS:** 473-810. **Subscription Rates:** $59 U.S.; $71 Canada air mail; $84 Other countries; $109 Two years; C$133 Two years Canada; $159 Other countries airmail; 2 years. **URL:** http://www.playsmagazine.com . **Mailing address:** PO Box 600160, Newton, MA 02460. **Ad Rates:** BW $1,000; PCI $80. **Remarks:** Accepts advertising. **Circ:** ‡9000.

16780 ■ Storage
TechTarget Inc.
275 Grove St.
Newton, MA 02466
Phone: (617)431-9200
Fax: (617)431-9201
Free: 888-274-4111
Publisher's E-mail: techtargetwebsite@techtarget.com
Magazine covering storage and data recovery solutions. **Freq:** Monthly. **Key Personnel:** Jillian Coffin, Publisher. **URL:** http://searchstorage.techtarget.com. **Remarks:** Accepts advertising. **Circ:** (Not Reported).

16781 ■ WNTN-AM - 1550
143 Rumford Ave.
Newton, MA 02466
Phone: (617)969-1550
Email: info@wntn.com
Format: Talk; Ethnic. **Networks:** Independent. **Owner:** Colt Communications L.L.C., at above address. **Founded:** 1968. **Operating Hours:** Sunrise-sunset; 100% local. **Key Personnel:** Rob Rudnick, Gen. Mgr.; Sybil Tonkonogy, Dir. Pub. Aff.; Leo Sullivan, Chief Engineer. **Local Programs:** *1550 Today*, Saturday 8:00 a.m. - 9:00 a.m.; *Grecian Echoes*, Monday Tuesday Wednesday Thursday Friday Sunday 7:00 a.m. - 11:00 a.m. 7:00 a.m. - 12:00 p.m.; *Frugal Yankee*, Tuesday Friday 11:00 a.m. - 11:30 a.m.; *Abundant Life*, Saturday 7:00 a.m. - 7:30 a.m.; *Radio Compas*, Saturday 8:30 a.m. - 10:30 a.m.; *Jhankar*, Saturday 10:30 a.m. - 12:00 p.m.; *Huskies Radio*; *The Benchwarmers*, Sunday 12:00 p.m. - 1:00 p.m.; *Arabic Baptist Church*, Sunday 2:00 p.m. - 3:00 p.m.; *Gallerie Haitienne*, Sunday 3:00 p.m. - 5:00 p.m. **Wattage:** 10,000. **Ad Rates:** Noncommercial. **URL:** http://wntn.com.

NEWTON HIGHLANDS

SE MA. Middlesex Co. 7 mi. W. of Boston.

16782 ■ Organic Preparations and Procedures International: The New Journal for Organic Synthesis
Organic Preparations and Procedures Inc.
PO Box 610009
Newton Highlands, MA 02461-0009
Scholarly journal covering organic synthesis. **Freq:** 6/year. **Key Personnel:** Prof. J.P. Anselme, Executive Editor; Fabienne J. Madsen, Manager, Advertising; J.A. Moore, Associate Editor; James A. Moore, Associate Editor. **ISSN:** 0030-4948 (print); **EISSN:** 1945-5453 (electronic). **Subscription Rates:** $108 Single issue. **URL:** http://www.oppint.com; http://www.tandfonline.com/toc/uopp20/.U5UgetIW2qY. **Remarks:** Advertising accepted; rates available upon request. **Circ:** (Not Reported).

NEWTON UPPER FALLS

16783 ■ InterfaithFamily.com
InterfaithFamily.com Inc.
90 Oak St., 4th Fl.
Newton Upper Falls, MA 02464-1439
Phone: (617)581-6860
Fax: (617)965-7772
Publisher's E-mail: help@interfaithfamily.com
Webzine offering a Jewish perspective on choices faced by interfaith families. **Freq:** Biweekly. **Key Personnel:** Edmund Case, Chief Executive Officer, phone: (617)581-6805. **URL:** http://www.interfaithfamily.com/web_magazine_table_of_contents/Web_Magazine_Issue_212__-_Growing_Up_in_an_Interfaith_Family.shtml. **Mailing address:** PO Box 428, Newton Upper Falls, MA 02464-1439. **Remarks:** Advertising accepted; rates available upon request. **Circ:** 11000.

16784 ■ Sh'ma: A Journal of Jewish Responsibility
Jewish Family and Life!
90 Oak St.
Newton Upper Falls, MA 02464
Phone: (617)965-7700
Fax: (617)965-7772
Free: 877-568-7462
Publisher's E-mail: marketing@jflmedia.com
Jewish interest publication. **Freq:** Monthly except July & August. **Print Method:** Offset. **Trim Size:** 8 x 11. **Cols./Page:** 2. **Col. Width:** 36 nonpareils. **Col. Depth:** 119 agate lines. **Key Personnel:** Susan Berrin, Editor; Josh Rolnick, Publisher. **ISSN:** 0049--0385 (print). **Subscription Rates:** $29 U.S. 1 year - 10 issues; $39 Other countries 1 year - 10 issues; $49 Two years US - 20 issues; $59 Two years other countries - 20 issues; Free digital edition. **URL:** http://www.shma.com. **Mailing address:** PO Box 9129, Newton Upper Falls, MA 02464. **Remarks:** Accepts advertising. **Circ:** Paid ‡6287, Non-paid ‡377.

NEWTONVILLE

Middlesex Co. 7 mi. W. of Boston. Residential.

16785 ■ Dante Studies
Dante Society of America
PO Box 600616
Newtonville, MA 02460
Phone: (617)831-9288
Publisher's E-mail: info@sunypress.edu
Scholarly journal covering literature. **Freq:** Annual. **Trim Size:** 6 x 9. **Key Personnel:** Justin Steinberg, Editor-in-Chief. **ISSN:** 0070--2862 (print). **Subscription Rates:** $100 Institutions print - 2 years; $50 Institutions print - 1 year. **URL:** http://www.press.jhu.edu/journals/dante_studies; http://dantesociety.org/publications/dante-studies. **Remarks:** Advertising not accepted. **Circ:** 700.

NORFOLK

NE MA. Norfolk Co. 2 mi. S. of Rockville.

16786 ■ The Journal of Interdisciplinary History
The MIT Press
c/o Ed Freedman, Mng. Ed.
147 North St.
Norfolk, MA 02056-1535
Phone: (508)863-0702
Publication E-mail: edtyct@verizon.net
Journal includes substantive articles, research notes, review essays, and book reviews relating historical research and work in economics and demographics. **Freq:** Quarterly. **Print Method:** Offset. **Trim Size:** 5 7/8 x 9. **Cols./Page:** 1. **Col. Width:** 54 nonpareils. **Col. Depth:** 105 agate lines. **Key Personnel:** Robert I. Rotberg, Editor; Ed Freedman, Managing Editor; Theodore K. Rabb, Editor. **ISSN:** 0022-1953 (print); **EISSN:** 1530-9169 (electronic). **Subscription Rates:** $63 Individuals print and online; $58 Individuals online; $359 Institutions print and online; $310 Institutions online; $33 Students print and online, retired; $29 Students online only, retired. **URL:** http://www.mitpressjournals.org/loi/jinh. **Ad Rates:** BW $400. **Remarks:** Accepts advertising. **Circ:** 600.

NORTH ADAMS

W. MA. Berkshire Co. Near W. end of Hoosac tunnel, 18 mi. NE of Pittsfield. State College; Williams College. Limestone quarries. Manufactures electronics components, wire, machinery, textiles, shoes, papers, chemical products.

16787 ■ WJJW-FM - 91.1
375 Church St.
North Adams, MA 01247
Phone: (413)662-5000
Format: Educational; Alternative/New Music/Progressive. **Networks:** Independent. **Owner:** Massachusetts College of Liberal Arts, 375 Church St., North Adams, MA 01247, Ph: (413)662-5000. **Founded:** 1974. **Operating Hours:** 7 a.m.-3 a.m. **Wattage:** 423. **Ad Rates:** Noncommercial. **URL:** http://www.mcla.edu.

16788 ■ WUPE-AM - 1110
466 Curran Hwy.
North Adams, MA 01247
Phone: (413)663-6567
Fax: (413)662-2143
Format: Oldies. **Owner:** Vox Communications, 211 Jason St., Pittsfield, MA 01201, Ph: (413)499-3333, Fax: (413)442-1590. **Key Personnel:** Pete Barry, Mktg. Mgr., President; Larry Kratka, News Dir. **URL:** http://www.wupe.com.

16789 ■ WUPE-FM - 100.1
466 Curran Hwy.
North Adams, MA 01247
Phone: (413)663-6567
Fax: (413)662-2143
Email: news@wupe.com
Format: Easy Listening; Full Service. **Networks:** AP. **Owner:** Vox Communications, 211 Jason St., Pittsfield, MA 01201, Ph: (413)499-3333, Fax: (413)442-1590; Vox Radio Group Co., Inc., at above address. **Founded:** 1964. **Formerly:** WMNB-FM; WMNB-AM. **Operating Hours:** 5:30 a.m.-midnight Mon.-Sat.; 7 a.m.-midnight Sun. **Key Personnel:** Pete Barry, Mktg. Mgr., President, peterb@live959.com; Bob Heck, Bus. Mgr., Traffic Mgr., traffic@live959.com. **Wattage:** 1,000. **Ad Rates:** Noncommercial. $18-25 for 30 seconds; $23-30 for 60 seconds. Combined advertising rates available with WMNB-FM, WSBS-AM. **URL:** http://www.wupe.com.

NORTH ANDOVER

NE MA. Essex Co. 12 mi. NE of Lowell. Residential.

16790 ■ The Andovers
North of Boston Media Group
100 Turnpike St.
North Andover, MA 01845
Phone: (978)946-2000
Fax: (978)685-1588
Publisher's E-mail: sales@nobmg.com
Local magazine focusing on Andover communities, history, culture, and values. **Key Personnel:** Karen Andreas, Publisher. **Subscription Rates:** $15 Individuals. **URL:** http://www.theandoversmagazine.com. **Remarks:** Accepts advertising. **Circ:** Controlled 4500.

16791 ■ The Eagle-Tribune
Eagle-Tribune Publishing Co.
100 Turnpike St.
North Andover, MA 01845
Phone: (978)946-2000
Fax: (978)687-6045
Publication E-mail: news@eagletribune.com
General newspaper. **Freq:** Daily and Sun. **Print Method:** Offset. **Trim Size:** 13 x 21 1/2. **Cols./Page:** 6. **Col. Width:** 2 1/16 inches. **Col. Depth:** 21 1/2 inches. **Key Personnel:** Al Getler, Publisher, phone: (978)946-2000; Al White, Editor, phone: (978)946-2479; Gretchen Put-

nam, Managing Editor, phone: (978)946-2337. **Subscription Rates:** $23.88 Individuals 12 weeks, home delivery; $15 Individuals 12 weekends, home delivery; $11.88 Individuals 12 sundays, home delivery. **Formerly:** Lawrence Eagle-Tribune. **Ad Rates:** BW $4,586; 4C $4,981; PCI $35.55. **Remarks:** Advertising accepted; rates available upon request. **Circ:** Mon.-Fri. ‡44012.

16792 ■ Mobile Electronics Magazine: Serving the Mobile Electronics Industry
Bobit Business Media
85 Flagship Dr., Ste. F
North Andover, MA 01845
Publication E-mail: info@me-mag.com info@mobile-electronics.com
Technical journal of automotive electronics. Covers installation of autosound, security, mobile video, navigation, and radar detectors. **Freq:** Monthly. **Print Method:** Offset. **Trim Size:** 7 7/8 x 10 3/4. **Cols./Page:** 3. **Col. Width:** 2 3/16 inches. **Col. Depth:** 10 inches. **Key Personnel:** Travis Weeks, Publisher, phone: (951)371-8519; Greg Basich, Executive Editor; Mary Reimer, Manager, Production, phone: (310)533-2517, fax: (310)533-2501; Chris Cook, Editor, phone: (310)533-2443; Joni Owens, Publisher, phone: (310)533-2530. **ISSN:** 0087-2287 (print). **URL:** http://www.me-mag.com. **Formerly:** Installation News; Mobile Electronics Retailer. **Ad Rates:** BW $3,652; 4C $4,458; PCI $75. **Remarks:** Accepts advertising. **Circ:** Combined 22000.

16793 ■ Newburyport
North of Boston Media Group
100 Turnpike St.
North Andover, MA 01845
Phone: (978)946-2000
Fax: (978)685-1588
Publication E-mail: sales@newburyportmagazine.com
Lifestyle community magazine. **Key Personnel:** Cathy Giannoccaro, Manager, Advertising, phone: (978)462-6666. **URL:** http://www.nobmg.com/information.php#newburyport. **Ad Rates:** 4C $1,675. **Remarks:** Accepts advertising. **Circ:** 4,500.

NORTH ATTLEBORO

16794 ■ DC Velocity
Agile Business Media L.L.C.
Tower Sq., No. 4
500 E Washington St.
North Attleboro, MA 02760
Phone: (508)316-9002
Magazine catering to the information needs of business professionals in large distribution center operations. **Freq:** Monthly. **Key Personnel:** Peter Bradley, Director, Editorial, phone: (617)942-1790; Gary Master, Publisher, phone: (412)596-7837, fax: (719)495-7072; Toby Gooley, Senior Editor, phone: (617)299-1189. **URL:** http://www.dcvelocity.com. **Remarks:** Accepts advertising. **Circ:** Non-paid △**50200**.

16795 ■ On Deck!
Navy & Marine Living History Association, Inc.
41 Kelley Blvd.
North Attleboro, MA 02760-4734
Subscription Rates: Free. **URL:** http://navyandmarine.org/ondeck/index.htm. **Remarks:** Advertising not accepted. **Circ:** (Not Reported).

16796 ■ PCMI Journal: Member's Only Edition
Photo Chemical Machining Institute
11 Robert Toner Blvd., No. 234
North Attleboro, MA 02763
Phone: (508)385-0085
Fax: (508)232-6005
Publisher's E-mail: info@pcmi.org
Freq: Quarterly. **Subscription Rates:** $150 Individuals online. **URL:** http://pcmi.org/PCMI_store/index.php. **Remarks:** Advertising not accepted. **Circ:** (Not Reported).

16797 ■ Photo Chemical Machining Institute--Journal
Photo Chemical Machining Institute
11 Robert Toner Blvd., No. 234
North Attleboro, MA 02763
Phone: (508)385-0085
Fax: (508)232-6005
Publisher's E-mail: info@pcmi.org
Freq: Quarterly. **Subscription Rates:** $60 Nonmembers. **Remarks:** Accepts advertising. **Circ:** 600.

16798 ■ Spray Etching of Stainless Steel
Photo Chemical Machining Institute
11 Robert Toner Blvd., No. 234
North Attleboro, MA 02763
Phone: (508)385-0085
Fax: (508)232-6005
Publisher's E-mail: info@pcmi.org
Freq: Semiannual. **Subscription Rates:** €137.95 Individuals. **Remarks:** Advertising not accepted. **Circ:** (Not Reported).

NORTH DARTMOUTH

16799 ■ Benchmarking: An International Journal
Emerald Group Publishing Limited
c/o Prof. Angappa Gunasekaran, Ed.
Dept. of Management
University of Massachusetts, Dartmouth
285 Old W port Rd.
North Dartmouth, MA 02747-2300
Publisher's E-mail: emerald@emeraldinsight.com
Journal reviewing different approaches to benchmarking. **Freq:** Bimonthly. **Key Personnel:** Prof. Angappa Gunasekaran, Editor; Prof. Ronald E. McGaughey, Editor; Patti Davis, Publisher. **ISSN:** 1463--5771 (print). **URL:** http://www.emeraldgrouppublishing.com/products/journals/journals.htm?id=BIJ. **Circ:** (Not Reported).

16800 ■ International Journal of Business Information Systems
Inderscience Publishers
c/o Prof. Angappa Gunasekaran, Ed.-in-Ch.
University of Massachusetts - Dartmouth
Charlton College of Business
285 Old Westport Rd.
North Dartmouth, MA 02747-2300
Publication E-mail: info@inderscience.com
Peer-reviewed journal covering general areas of business information systems. **Freq:** 12/yr. **Key Personnel:** Prof. Angappa Gunasekaran, Editor-in-Chief. **ISSN:** 1746--0972 (print); **EISSN:** 1746--0980 (electronic). **Subscription Rates:** $1415 Individuals print or online for 1 user; $2405.50 Individuals online only for 2-3 users; $1981 Individuals print and online; $3537.50 Individuals online only for 4-5 users; $4598.75 Individuals online only for 6-7 users; $5589.25 Individuals online only for 8-9 users; $6509 Individuals online only for 10-14 users; $7428.75 Individuals online only for 15-19 users; $8773 Individuals online only for 20+ users. **URL:** http://www.inderscience.com/jhome.php?jcode=ijbis. **Circ:** (Not Reported).

16801 ■ International Journal of Indian Culture and Business Management
Inderscience Publishers
c/o Prof. Angappa Gunasekaran, Ed.-in-Ch.
University of Massachusetts-Dartmouth
Department of Decision & Information Sciences, Charlton College of Business
285 Old Westport Rd.
North Dartmouth, MA 02747-2300
Publication E-mail: info@inderscience.com
Journal covering field of new developments in Indian culture and their implications on business. **Freq:** 8/year. **Key Personnel:** Prof. Angappa Gunasekaran, Editor-in-Chief. **ISSN:** 1753--0806 (print); **EISSN:** 1753--0814 (electronic). **Subscription Rates:** $1016 Individuals print; $1415 Individuals print & online. **URL:** http://www.inderscience.com/jhome.php?jcode=ijicbm. **Circ:** (Not Reported).

16802 ■ International Journal of Industrial and Systems Engineering
Inderscience Publishers
University of Massachusetts - Dartmouth
Dept. of Decision & Information Sciences
Charlton College of Business
285 Old Westport Rd.
North Dartmouth, MA 02747-2300
Publication E-mail: info@inderscience.com
Journal covering industrial and systems engineering. **Freq:** 12/yr. **Key Personnel:** Prof. Thomas Boucher, Board Member; Prof. Stephen Bush, Board Member; Prof. Richard Booth, Board Member; Prof. Ghaleb Abbasi, Board Member; Prof. Theodore Allen, Board Member; Prof. Ronald Askin, Board Member; Prof. Chris Backhouse, Board Member; Prof. Pat Banerjee, Board Member; Layek Abdel-Malek, Board Member; Prof. Robert W. Brennan, Board Member; Prof. Angappa Gunasekaran, Editor-in-Chief. **ISSN:** 1748--5037 (print); **EISSN:** 1748--5045 (electronic). **Subscription Rates:** $1415 Individuals print or online; $1981 Individuals online and print. **URL:** http://www.inderscience.com/jhome.php?jcode=ijise. **Circ:** (Not Reported).

16803 ■ International Journal of Information and Operations Management Education
Inderscience Publishers
c/o Prof. Daniel Braha, Editorial Board Member
University of Massachusetts - Dartmouth
Dept. of Management
285 Old Westport Rd.
North Dartmouth, MA 02747-2300
Publication E-mail: info@inderscience.com
Peer-reviewed journal publishinb research and practice of innovation and lifetime learning in information systems and operations management. **Freq:** Quarterly. **Key Personnel:** Dr. Harm-Jan Steenhuis, Editor-in-Chief; Prof. Bradley T. Ewing, Board Member; Prof. Mark A. Thompson, Board Member. **ISSN:** 1744--2303 (print); **EISSN:** 1744--2311 (electronic). **Subscription Rates:** $685 Individuals print and online for 1 user; $1164.50 Individuals online only for 2-3 users; $928 Individuals print and online; $1712.50 Individuals online only for 4-5 users; $2226.25 Individuals online only for 6-7 users; $2705.75 Individuals online only for 8-9 users; $3151 Individuals online only for 10-14 users; $3596.25 Individuals online only for 15-19 users; $4247 Individuals online only for 20+ users. **URL:** http://www.inderscience.com/jhome.php?jcode=ijiome. **Circ:** (Not Reported).

16804 ■ International Journal of Logistics Systems and Management
Inderscience Publishers
c/o Prof. Angappa Gunasekaran, Ed.-in-Ch.
University of Massachusetts - Dartmouth
Charlton School of Business
285 Old Westport Rd.
North Dartmouth, MA 02747-2300
Publication E-mail: info@inderscience.com
Journal proposing and fostering discussion on the development of logistics resources, with emphasis on the implications that logistics strategies and systems have on organisational productivity and competitiveness in the global and electronic markets. **Freq:** 12/yr. **Key Personnel:** Prof. Angappa Gunasekaran, Editor-in-Chief. **ISSN:** 1742--7967 (print); **EISSN:** 1742--7975 (electronic). **Subscription Rates:** €1415 Individuals print or online for 1 user; €2405.50 Individuals online only for 2-3 users; €1981 Individuals print and online; €3537.50 Individuals online only for 4-5 users; €4598.75 Individuals online only for 6-7 users; €5589.25 Individuals online only for 8-9 users; €6509 Individuals online only for 10-14 users; €7428.75 Individuals online only for 15-19 users; €8773 Individuals online only for 20+ users. **URL:** http://www.inderscience.com/jhome.php?jcode=ijlsm. **Circ:** (Not Reported).

16805 ■ International Journal of Mathematics in Operational Research
Inderscience Enterprises Ltd.
c/o Prof. Angappa Gunasekaran, Ed.-in-Ch.
Department of Decision & Information Sciences
Charlton College of Business, University of Massachusetts - Dartmouth
285 Old Westport Rd.
North Dartmouth, MA 02747-2300
Publisher's E-mail: copyright@inderscience.com
Peer-reviewed journal covering mathematical theory and applications in operational research and management science. **Freq:** Bimonthly. **Key Personnel:** Prof. Angappa Gunasekaran, Editor-in-Chief. **ISSN:** 1757--5850 (print); **EISSN:** 1757--5869 (electronic). **Subscription Rates:** $1016 Individuals print only - annual (includes surface mail); or online (for single user only); $1415 Individuals print and online. **URL:** http://www.inderscience.com/jhome.php?jcode=ijmor. **Circ:** (Not Reported).

16806 ■ International Journal of Operational Research
Inderscience Publishers
c/o Prof. Angappa Gunasekaran, Ed.-in-Ch.
University of Massachusetts
Charlton College of Business
285 Old Westport Rd.

Circulation: ★ = AAM; △ or • = BPA; ♦ = CAC; ❑ = VAC; ⊕ = PO Statement; ‡ = Publisher's Report; Boldface figures = sworn; Light figures = estimated.

North Dartmouth, MA 02747-2300
Publication E-mail: info@inderscience.com
Peer-reviewed journal covering new theory and application of operations research (OR) techniques and models that include inventory, queuing, transportation, game theory, scheduling, project management, mathematical programming, decision-support systems, multi-criteria decision making, artificial intelligence, neural network, fuzzy logic, expert systems, and simulation. **Freq:** 12/yr. **Key Personnel:** Prof. Angappa Gunasekaran, Editor-in-Chief; Prof. Siau Ching Lenny Koh, Associate Editor. **ISSN:** 1745--7645 (print); **EISSN:** 1745--7653 (electronic). **Subscription Rates:** $1415 Individuals print or online only for 1 user; $2405.50 Individuals online only for 2-3 users; $1981 Individuals print and online; $3537.50 Individuals online only for 4-5 users; $4598.75 Individuals online only for 6-7 users; $5589.25 Individuals online only for 8-9 users; $6509 Individuals online only for 10-14 users; $7428.75 Individuals online only for 15-19 users; 8773 ¥ Individuals online only for 20+ users. **URL:** http://www.inderscience.com/jhome.php?jcode=ijor. **Circ:** (Not Reported).

16807 ■ International Journal of Procurement Management
Inderscience Publishers
c/o Prof. Angappa Gunasekaran, Ed.-in-Ch.
University of Massachusetts-Dartmouth
Department of Decision & Information Sciences, Charlton College of Business
285 Old Westport Rd.
North Dartmouth, MA 02747-2300
Publication E-mail: info@inderscience.com
Journal covering development of procurement resources. **Freq:** 6/year. **Key Personnel:** Prof. Angappa Gunasekaran, Editor-in-Chief. **ISSN:** 1753--8432 (print); **EISSN:** 1753--0806 (electronic). **Subscription Rates:** $820 Individuals print or online only for 1 user; $1394 Individuals online only for 2-3 users; $1147 Individuals print and online; $2050 Individuals online only for 4-5 users; $2665 Individuals online only for 6-7 users; $3239 Individuals online only for 8-9 users; $3772 Individuals online only for 10-14 users; $4305 Individuals online only for 15-19 users; $4084 Individuals online only for 20 users. **URL:** http://www.inderscience.com/jhome.php?jcode=ijpm. **Circ:** (Not Reported).

16808 ■ International Journal of Productivity and Quality Management
Inderscience Publishers
c/o Prof. Angappa Gunasekaran, Ed.-in-Ch.
University of Massachusetts
Charlton College of Business
285 Old Westport Rd.
North Dartmouth, MA 02747-2300
Publication E-mail: info@inderscience.com
Peer-reviewd journal covering strategies, techniques and tools for productivity and quality management and improvement in 21st century manufacturing and service organisations. **Freq:** 8/year. **Key Personnel:** Prof. Angappa Gunasekaran, Editor-in-Chief. **ISSN:** 1746--6474 (print); **EISSN:** 1746--6482 (electronic). **Subscription Rates:** $1415 Individuals print or online only for 1 user; $2405.50 Individuals online only for 2-3 users; $1981 Individuals print and online; $3537.50 Individuals online only for 4-5 users; $4598.75 Individuals online only for 6-7 users; $5589.25 Individuals online only for 8-9 users; $6509 Individuals online only for 10-14 users; $7428.75 Individuals online only for 15-19 users; $8773 Individuals online only for 20+ users. **URL:** http://www.inderscience.com/jhome.php?jcode=ijpqm. **Circ:** (Not Reported).

16809 ■ International Journal of Services and Operations Management
Inderscience Publishers
c/o Prof. Angappa Gunasekaran, Ed.-in-Ch.
University of Massachusetts
Charlton College of Business
285 Old Westport Rd.
North Dartmouth, MA 02747-2300
Publication E-mail: info@inderscience.com
Peer-reviewed journal covering areas of service and manufacturing operations management. **Freq:** Monthly. **Key Personnel:** Prof. Angappa Gunasekaran, Editor-in-Chief. **ISSN:** 1744--2370 (print); **EISSN:** 1744--2389 (electronic). **Subscription Rates:** $1415 Individuals print or online only for 1 user; $2405.50 Individuals print and online; $3537.50 Individuals online only for 4-5 users; $4598.75 Individuals online only for 6-7 users; $5589.25 Individuals online only for 8-9 users; $6509 Individuals online only for 10-14 users; $7428.75 Individuals online only for 15-19 users; $8773 Individuals online only for 20+ users; $1981 Individuals print and online. **URL:** http://www.inderscience.com/jhome.php?jcode=ijsom. **Circ:** (Not Reported).

NORTH EASTON

E. MA. Bristol Co. 5 mi. S. of Stoughton. Stonehill College. Residential.

16810 ■ The Summit
Stonehill College
320 Washington St.
North Easton, MA 02356
Phone: (508)565-1000
Publisher's E-mail: marketing@stonehill.edu
Collegiate newspaper. **Founded:** 1948. **Freq:** Weekly (during the academic year). **Print Method:** Offset. **Cols./Page:** 5. **Col. Width:** 24 nonpareils. **Col. Depth:** 224 agate lines. **Key Personnel:** Winslow Cilfone, Editor. **USPS:** 010-795. **Remarks:** Advertising accepted; rates available upon request. **Circ:** Free 1700.

16811 ■ WSHL-FM - 91.3
320 Washington St.
North Easton, MA 02357
Phone: (508)565-1919
Email: development@stonehill.edu
Format: Alternative/New Music/Progressive; Hip Hop; Sports. **Owner:** Stonehill College, 320 Washington St., Easton, MA 02357, Ph: (508)565-1000. **Founded:** 1973. **Operating Hours:** Continuous. **Wattage:** 100. **Ad Rates:** Noncommercial. **URL:** http://www.stonehill.edu.

NORTH FALMOUTH

16812 ■ CORPUS Reports
CORPUS
2 Adamian Dr.
North Falmouth, MA 02556
Phone: (508)523-4032
Publisher's E-mail: corpus6431@me.com
Journal containing reports about Corpus Association. **Freq:** Bimonthly. **Subscription Rates:** Included in membership. **URL:** http://www.corpus.org/index.cfm?fuseaction=category.display&Category_ID=17. **Remarks:** Accepts advertising. **Circ:** 3000.

NORTH QUINCY

16813 ■ WEZE-AM - 590
500 Victory Rd., 2nd Fl.
North Quincy, MA 02171
Phone: (617)328-0880
Fax: (617)328-0375
Format: Religious. **Owner:** Salem Communication, Boston, 500 Victory Rd., Second Fl., Quincy, MA 02171, Ph: (617)328-0880. **Founded:** 1922. **Operating Hours:** Continuous. **Key Personnel:** Pat Ryan, Gen. Mgr.; Pauline Rockwell, Bus. Mgr., pauliner@salemradioboston.com. **Wattage:** 5,000. **Ad Rates:** Noncommercial. **URL:** http://www.wezeradio.com.

16814 ■ WTTT-AM - 1150
500 Victory Rd.
North Quincy, MA 02171
Format: News; Talk. **Owner:** Salem Media Group Inc., 4880 Santa Rosa Rd., Camarillo, CA 93012, Ph: (805)987-0400, Fax: (805)384-4520. **Operating Hours:** Continuous. **Key Personnel:** Pat Ryan, Gen. Sales Mgr., patr@salemradioboston.com. **Ad Rates:** Advertising accepted; rates available upon request. **URL:** http://www.talk1150.com.

NORTHAMPTON

WC MA. Hampshire Co. 17 mi. NW of Springfield. Smith College (women). Manufactures cutlery, wire cable, toothbrushes, caskets, optical merchandise, indelible ink, tracer paper. Agriculture. Tobacco, onions, potatoes.

16815 ■ Contact Quarterly
Contact Collaborations Inc.
PO Box 603
Northampton, MA 01061
Phone: (413)586-1181
Fax: (413)586-9055
Publisher's E-mail: info@contactquarterly.com
Journal featuring dance, improvisation, performance, and contemporary movement arts. **Freq:** Semiannual January & May. **Key Personnel:** Nancy Stark Smith, Editor. **Subscription Rates:** $30 Individuals; $42 Other countries; $28 Students; $41 Students, other countries; $45 U.S. libraries & institutions; $56 Other countries libraries & institutions; $15 Individuals online. **URL:** http://www.contactquarterly.com/index.php. **Ad Rates:** BW $475. **Circ:** (Not Reported).

16816 ■ Daily Hampshire Gazette
H.S. Gere & Sons Inc.
115 Conz St.
Northampton, MA 01061
Phone: (413)584-5000
Publication E-mail: newsroom@gazettenet.com
General newspaper. **Freq:** Daily. **Print Method:** Offset. **Trim Size:** 12 1/4 x 22 3/4. **Cols./Page:** 6. **Col. Width:** 1.83 inches. **Col. Depth:** 21 1/2 inches. **Key Personnel:** Larry Parnass, Editor; Jim Foudy, Publisher. **ISSN:** 0739--3506 (print). **Subscription Rates:** $2.41 Individuals online access/week; $3.60 Individuals print & online/week ; $1 Individuals one day access. **URL:** http://www.gazettenet.com. **Ad Rates:** GLR $.98; BW $2,121; 4C $2,571; SAU $16.44; PCI $16.44. **Remarks:** Accepts advertising. **Circ:** Mon.-Fri. ★**18001**, Sat. ★**19082**.

16817 ■ Mammalian Species
American Society of Mammalogists
c/o Virginia Hayssen, Ed.
Smith College
Clark Science Center
Northampton, MA 01063-0100
Phone: (413)585-3856
Fax: (413)585-3786
Publisher's E-mail: asm@allenpress.com
Scholarly journal covering the biology of mammalian species, including fossil history, genetics, systematics, anatomy, physiology, behavior, conservation, and ecology. **Freq:** Bimonthly. **Key Personnel:** Virginia Hayssen, Editor. **ISSN:** 1545-1410 (print); **EISSN:** 1545-1410 (electronic). **Subscription Rates:** £205 Institutions online only; $388 Institutions online only; €307 Institutions online only; £241 Institutions print and online; $437 Institutions print and online; €362 Institutions print and online; £69 Individuals online only; $131 Individuals online only; €104 Individuals online only. **URL:** http://www.mammalsociety.org/publications/mammalian-species. **Circ:** (Not Reported).

16818 ■ The Sophian: The Student Press of Smith College
Smith College
7 College Ln.
Northampton, MA 01063
Phone: (413)584-2700
Publication E-mail: sophian@smith.edu
Collegiate newspaper. **Freq:** Weekly. **Trim Size:** 11 x 17. **Cols./Page:** 5. **Col. Width:** 2 inches. **Col. Depth:** 16 inches. **Key Personnel:** Sandy Gu, Associate Editor; Joanna Johnson, Editor-in-Chief; Gina Charusombat, Managing Editor. **Subscription Rates:** $30 Individuals semester; $50 Individuals. **URL:** http://www.thesmithsophian.com. **Remarks:** Accepts advertising. **Circ:** ‡3500.

16819 ■ WEIB-FM - 106.3
Eight N King St.
Northampton, MA 01060
Phone: (413)585-1112
Fax: (413)585-9138
Format: Jazz. **Owner:** Cutting Edge Broadcasting Inc., 8 N King St. , Northampton, MA 01060, Ph: (413)585-5750, Fax: (413)585-9138. **Key Personnel:** Carol Moore-Cutting, Gen. Mgr. **Ad Rates:** Advertising accepted; rates available upon request. **URL:** http://www.weibfm.com/home.htm.

16820 ■ WHMP-AM - 1400
15 Hampton Ave.
Northampton, MA 01060
Phone: (413)586-7400
Fax: (413)585-0927
Format: News; Information. **Networks:** CBS. **Owner:** Saga Communications Inc., at above address. **Founded:** 1950. **Operating Hours:** Continuous. **Wattage:** 1,000. **URL:** http://www.whmp.com.

16821 ■ WHMP-FM - 99.3
15 Hampton Ave.
Northampton, MA 01060
Phone: (413)586-7400
Fax: (413)585-0927
Format: Contemporary Hit Radio (CHR). **Owner:** Saga Communicatins, 73 Kercheval Ave., Grosse Pointe Farms, MI 48236. **Founded:** 1956. **Key Personnel:** Dave Musante, Sales Mgr., dmus@whmp.com; Chris Collins, Dir. of Programs, collins@whmp.com. **Wattage:** 3,000. **URL:** http://whmp.com/contact-us/.

16822 ■ WOZQ-FM - 91.9
Campus Ctr., 106, Smith College
100 Elm St.
Northampton, MA 01063
Phone: (413)585-4977
Email: wozq@smith.edu
Format: Oldies. **Owner:** Smith College, 7 College Ln., Northampton, MA 01063, Ph: (413)584-2700. **Founded:** 1949. **Operating Hours:** Continuous. **Ad Rates:** Noncommercial. **URL:** http://www.sophia.smith.edu.

16823 ■ WRSI-FM - 93.9
15 Hampton Ave.
Northampton, MA 01060
Phone: (413)586-7400
Fax: (413)585-0927
Format: Alternative/New Music/Progressive. **Owner:** Saga Communication Inc., 73 Kercheval Ave., Ste. 201, Grosse Pointe Farms, MI 48236, Ph: (313)886-7070, Fax: (313)886-7150. **Founded:** 1981. **Operating Hours:** Continuous. **Key Personnel:** Chris Belmonte, Dept. Mgr., monte@wrsi.com; Edward Christian, President; Scott Howard, Contact, scooter@wrsi.com; Scott Howard, Contact, scooter@wrsi.com. **Local Programs:** *The Back Porch*, Sunday 9:00 a.m. - 12:00 p.m. **Wattage:** 2,500. **Ad Rates:** $25-35 for 60 seconds. Combined advertising rates available with WSSH, WHDQ, WKXE, WNHV, WTSV. **URL:** http://wrsi.com/contact-93-3-the-river.

NORTON

SE MA. Bristol Co. 8 mi. NW of Taunton. Wheaton College (women). Pine, oak timber. Manufactures paper and wooden boxes, box boards. Agriculture. Turkeys.

16824 ■ Berkeley Studies
International Berkeley Society
26 E Main St.
Dept. of Philosophy
Wheaton College
Norton, MA 02766
Freq: Annual. **URL:** http://internationalberkeleysociety.org/berkeley-studies. **Remarks:** Accepts advertising. **Circ:** (Not Reported).

16825 ■ Wheaton Wire
Wheaton College
26 E Main St.
Norton, MA 02766-2322
Phone: (508)286-8200
Publication E-mail: wire@wheatonma.edu
Collegiate newspaper (tabloid). **Freq:** Daily during the academic year. **Print Method:** Offset. **Trim Size:** 9 1/2 x 14. **Cols./Page:** 5. **Key Personnel:** Shannon Witter, Managing Editor; Mandi DeGroff, Editor-in-Chief; Annmarie Hanson, Business Manager. **Subscription Rates:** $25 Individuals per year; $15 Individuals per semester. **URL:** http://www.wheatonwire.com. **Ad Rates:** BW $200; PCI $5. **Remarks:** Accepts advertising. **Circ:** (Not Reported).

NORWELL

NE MA. Plymouth Co. 12 mi. ENE of Brockton. Agriculture.

16826 ■ Air Space and Law
Kluwer Academic/Plenum Publishing Corp.
101 Philip Dr.
Norwell, MA 02061
Phone: (781)871-6600
Fax: (781)871-6528
Publisher's E-mail: kluwer@wkap.com
Journal covering issues dealing with all aspects of air space and law. **Freq:** Bimonthly. **Key Personnel:** Mark Franklin, Editor; Henry A. Wassenbergh, Board Member; Berend J.H. Crans, Editor. **ISSN:** 0927-3379 (print). **Alt. Formats:** PDF. **URL:** http://www.kluwerlawonline.com/toc.php?pubcode=AILA. **Circ:** (Not Reported).

16827 ■ Anatomical Science International: The Official Journal of the Japanese Association of Anatomists
Springer
101 Philip Dr., Assinippi Pk.
Norwell, MA 02061
Phone: (781)871-6600
Fax: (781)878-0449
Journal focusing on morphological sciences in animals and humans. Official English journal of the Japanese Association of Anatomists. Formerly titled Kaibogaku Zasshi. **Freq:** Quarterly. **Key Personnel:** Hiroshi Abe, Managing Editor. **ISSN:** 1447--6959 (print); **EISSN:** 1447--073X (electronic). **Subscription Rates:** $469 Institutions includes free access or e-only; $563 Institutions including enhanced access. **URL:** http://www.springer.com/medicine/internal/journal/12565. **Remarks:** Accepts advertising. **Circ:** (Not Reported).

16828 ■ Chromosome Research: Cytogenetics, Genomics, Chromatin and the Nucleus
Kluwer Academic/Plenum Publishing Corp.
101 Philip Dr.
Norwell, MA 02061
Phone: (781)871-6600
Fax: (781)871-6528
Publisher's E-mail: kluwer@wkap.com
Journal covering all aspects of chromosome and nuclear biology worldwide. **Freq:** Quarterly. **Key Personnel:** Conly L. Rieder, Editor-in-Chief; Jiming Jiang, Associate Editor; Wendy Bickmore, Associate Editor. **ISSN:** 0967--3849 (print); **EISSN:** 1573--6849 (electronic). **Subscription Rates:** €1897 Institutions print including free access or e-only; €2276 Institutions print plus enhanced access. **URL:** http://www.springer.com/life+sciences/cell+biology/journal/10577. **Circ:** (Not Reported).

16829 ■ DDIN International
Larson Worldwide Inc.
95 Mt. Blue St.
Norwell, MA 02061-1015
Trade magazine covering diecutting process. **Freq:** Quarterly. **Print Method:** Web offset. **Trim Size:** 8 1/2 x 11. **Cols./Page:** 3. **Key Personnel:** Robert Larson, Contact. **ISSN:** 1078-6902 (print). **Subscription Rates:** $50 U.S. Mexico; $90 Two years in U.S.A. and Mexico; $75 Other countries; $140 Two years other countries; $60 Canada; $110 Two years Canada. **Formerly:** DDIN North America. **Ad Rates:** GLR $75; BW $1,365; 4C $2,015. **Remarks:** Accepts advertising. **Circ:** Combined 6000.

16830 ■ Educational Technology Research and Development: A Bi-monthly Publication of the Association for Educational Communications & Technology
Springer
101 Philip Dr., Assinippi Pk.
Norwell, MA 02061
Phone: (781)871-6600
Fax: (781)878-0449
Journal for the educational community. Combines case studies, practices, and developmental theories. **Freq:** Bimonthly. **Print Method:** Offset. **Trim Size:** 7 x 10. **Cols./Page:** 2. **Col. Width:** 29 nonpareils. **Col. Depth:** 114 agate lines. **Key Personnel:** J.M. Spector, Editor-in-Chief. **ISSN:** 1042-1629 (print). **Subscription Rates:** $250 Institutions includes free access or e-only; $45 Members includes enhanced access. **URL:** http://www.springer.com/education+%26+language/learning+%26+instruction/journal/11423. **Formerly:** Educational Communication Technology Journal. **Circ:** (Not Reported).

16831 ■ Integrated Pest Management
Kluwer Academic/Plenum Publishing Corp.
101 Philip Dr.
Norwell, MA 02061
Phone: (781)871-6600
Fax: (781)871-6528
Publisher's E-mail: kluwer@wkap.com
Journal covering all aspects of pest management, including chemical control, host resistance, and cultural control. **Freq:** Quarterly. **Key Personnel:** Zuzana Bernhart, Editor-in-Chief. **ISSN:** 1353--5226 (print); **EISSN:** 1572--9745 (electronic). **Subscription Rates:** €244.19 Individuals eBook; €259 Individuals hardcover/softcover. **URL:** http://www.springer.com/gp/book/9781402089893. **Circ:** (Not Reported).

16832 ■ Intertax
Kluwer Academic/Plenum Publishing Corp.
101 Philip Dr.
Norwell, MA 02061
Phone: (781)871-6600
Fax: (781)871-6528
Publisher's E-mail: kluwer@wkap.com
Journal covering tax information worldwide. **Freq:** Monthly. **Key Personnel:** Alexander Rust, Editor; Michael A. Olesnicky, Associate Editor; Mary Walsh, Associate Editor; Otmar Thommes, Associate Editor; Fred C. De Hosson, Editor-in-Chief. **ISSN:** 0927--5940 (print); **EISSN:** 1573--6970 (electronic). **URL:** http://www.kluwerlawonline.com/toc.php?pubcode=TAXI. **Remarks:** Advertising not accepted. **Circ:** (Not Reported).

16833 ■ Journal of International Arbitration
Kluwer Academic/Plenum Publishing Corp.
101 Philip Dr.
Norwell, MA 02061
Phone: (781)871-6600
Fax: (781)871-6528
Publisher's E-mail: sales@kluwerlaw.com
Publication covering the informational needs of those involved in arbitration worldwide. **Freq:** 6/year. **Key Personnel:** Friven Guanhua Yeoh, Assistant Editor; Dr. Michael J. Moser, Editor. **ISSN:** 0255--8106 (print). **Alt. Formats:** PDF. **URL:** http://www.kluwerlawonline.com/toc.php?pubcode=JOIA. **Circ:** (Not Reported).

16834 ■ Journal of NeuroVirology
Springer
101 Philip Dr., Assinippi Pk.
Norwell, MA 02061
Phone: (781)871-6600
Fax: (781)878-0449
Features articles on basic and clinical research in neurovirology. **Freq:** Bimonthly. **Key Personnel:** Kamel Khalili, Editor-in-Chief. **ISSN:** 1355--0284 (print); **EISSN:** 1538--2443 (electronic). **Subscription Rates:** $99 Individuals; Included in membership; €63.02 Individuals online only. **URL:** http://www.jneurovirol.com; http://www.springer.com/biomed/neuroscience/journal/13365. **Remarks:** Accepts advertising. **Circ:** (Not Reported).

16835 ■ Journal of Signal Processing Systems
Springer
101 Philip Dr., Assinippi Pk.
Norwell, MA 02061
Phone: (781)871-6600
Fax: (781)878-0449
Journal covering signal processing systems with VLSI circuits. **Freq:** 9/year. **Key Personnel:** S.y. Kung, Editor-in-Chief. **ISSN:** 1939--8018 (print); **EISSN:** 1939--8115 (electronic). **Subscription Rates:** $2960 Institutions print incl. free access or e-only; $3552 Institutions print plus enhanced access; €2772 Institutions print incl. free access or e-only; €3326 Institutions print plus enhanced access. **URL:** http://www.springer.com/engineering/signals/journal/11265. **Formerly:** Journal of VLSI Signal Processing-Systems for Signal, Image, and Video Technology: The Journal of DSP Technologies. **Circ:** (Not Reported).

16836 ■ Journal of Supercomputing: An International Journal of High-Performance Computer Design, Analysis
Kluwer Academic/Plenum Publishing Corp.
101 Philip Dr.
Norwell, MA 02061
Phone: (781)871-6600
Fax: (781)871-6528
Publisher's E-mail: kluwer@wkap.com
Journal covering high-performance computer design, analysis, and use worldwide. **Freq:** 3/year. **Key Personnel:** Hamid R. Arabnia, Editor; David H. Bailey, Board Member; Narsingh Deo, Board Member. **ISSN:** 0920--8542 (print); **EISSN:** 1573--0484 (electronic). **Subscription Rates:** $2416 Institutions print incl. free access or e-only; $2899 Institutions print plus enhanced access; £2346 Institutions print incl. free access or e-only; 2815 Institutions print plus enhanced access. **URL:** http://www.springer.com/computer/swe/journal/11227. **Circ:** (Not Reported).

Circulation: ★ = AAM; △ or • = BPA; ♦ = CAC; ❑ = VAC; ⊕ = PO Statement; ‡ = Publisher's Report; Boldface figures = sworn; Light figures = estimated.

16837 ■ Letters in Peptide Science
Springer
101 Philip Dr., Assinippi Pk.
Norwell, MA 02061
Phone: (781)871-6600
Fax: (781)878-0449
Research journal covering all aspects of peptide science. **Freq:** Bimonthly. **Key Personnel:** Fernando Albericio, Editor; Jane V. Aldrich, Editor; Dr. Fernando Albericio, Editor-in-Chief, phone: (34)3 402 9058, fax: (34)3 339 7878; Ben M. Dunn, Editor; Gregg B. Fields, Editor; Yasutsugu Shimonishi, Editor; John D. Wade, Editor. **ISSN:** 0929--5666 (print); **EISSN:** 1573--496X (electronic). **Subscription Rates:** $39.95 Individuals; €34.95 Individuals; £29.95 Individuals. **Online:** Kluwer Online. **URL:** http://link.springer.com/article/10.1023/B:LIPS.0000014283.12037.02. **Circ:** (Not Reported).

16838 ■ New England Real Estate Journal
East Coast Publications
New England & New York Real Estate Journal
57 Washington St.
Norwell, MA 02061
Phone: (781)878-4540
Fax: (781)871-1853
Free: 800-654-4993
Publication E-mail: nerej@rejournal.com
Newspaper publishing commercial, industrial, and investment real estate news. **Freq:** Weekly (Fri.). **Print Method:** Offset. **Trim Size:** 10 1/4 x 16. **Cols./Page:** 5. **Col. Width:** 2 inches. **Col. Depth:** 16 inches. **Key Personnel:** Joanne Connolly, Publisher; Jeff Keller, Publisher; Julie Santos, Publisher. **ISSN:** 0028--4890 (print). **Subscription Rates:** $69.50 Individuals. **URL:** http://nerej.com. **Ad Rates:** BW $2,195; 4C $2,995. **Remarks:** Accepts advertising. **Circ:** Paid ‡40000.

16839 ■ New York Real Estate Journal
East Coast Publications
17 Accord Park Dr., Ste. 205
Norwell, MA 02061-1629
Phone: (781)878-4540
Fax: (781)871-1853
Free: 800-654-4993
Publication E-mail: info@nyrej.com
Commercial real estate journal. **Freq:** Biweekly. **Print Method:** Web offset. **Trim Size:** 10 1/4 x 13 1/4. **Cols./Page:** 5. **Col. Width:** 2 inches. **Col. Depth:** 13 inches. **Key Personnel:** Maxine Ramos, Publisher. **ISSN:** 1057-2104 (print). **Subscription Rates:** $49.50 Individuals. **URL:** http://nyrej.com. **Mailing address:** PO Box 55, Accord, MA 02018. **Ad Rates:** BW $1,995; 4C $2,595. **Remarks:** Advertising accepted; rates available upon request. **Circ:** Paid 27000.

16840 ■ Positivity: An International Journal Devoted to the Theory and Applications of Positivity in Analysis
Kluwer Academic/Plenum Publishing Corp.
101 Philip Dr.
Norwell, MA 02061
Phone: (781)871-6600
Fax: (781)871-6528
Publisher's E-mail: kluwer@wkap.com
Journal covering the theory and applications of positivity in analysis worldwide. **Freq:** Quarterly. **Key Personnel:** T. Ando, Board Member; W. Arendt, Board Member; Ben de Pagter, Editor-in-Chief. **ISSN:** 1385-1292 (print); **EISSN:** 1572-9281 (electronic). **Subscription Rates:** €459 Institutions print incl. free access or e-only ; €551 Institutions print plus enhanced access ; $498 Institutions print incl. free access or e-only ; $598 Institutions print plus enhanced access. **URL:** http://www.springer.com/birkhauser/mathematics/journal/11117; http://link.springer.com/journal/volumesAndIssues/11117. **Circ:** (Not Reported).

16841 ■ Reaction Kinetics, Mechanisms & Catalysis
Kluwer Academic/Plenum Publishing Corp.
101 Philip Dr.
Norwell, MA 02061
Phone: (781)871-6600
Fax: (781)871-6528
Publisher's E-mail: kluwer@wkap.com
Journal covering research in reaction kinetics and related topics. **Freq:** Semiannual. **Key Personnel:** J.M. Basset, Board Member; M. Bartok, Board Member; G. Bazsa, Board Member; Prof. Istvan Fabian, Editor-in-Chief. **ISSN:** 1878--5190 (print); **EISSN:** 1878--5204 (electronic). **Subscription Rates:** €3814 Institutions print incl. free access or e-only; €4577 Institutions print plus enhanced access; $4017 Institutions print incl. free access or e-only; $4820 Institutions print plus enhanced access. **URL:** http://www.springer.com/chemistry/catalysis/journal/11144. **Formerly:** Reaction Kinetics and Catalysis Letters. **Circ:** (Not Reported).

16842 ■ Reanimation
Springer
101 Philip Dr., Assinippi Pk.
Norwell, MA 02061
Phone: (781)871-6600
Fax: (781)878-0449
Journal focusing on reanimation. **Freq:** 8/year. **Print Method:** Heat-set web offset. **Trim Size:** 8 1/8 x 10 7/8. **Cols./Page:** 2 and 3. **Col. Width:** 40 and 26 nonpareils. **Col. Depth:** 140 agate lines. **Key Personnel:** Bruno Megarbane, Editor-in-Chief. **ISSN:** 1624--0693 (print). **Subscription Rates:** $398 Institutions; €308 Institutions. **Alt. Formats:** Electronic publishing. **URL:** http://www.springer.com/medicine/critical+care+and+emergency+medicine/journal/13546. **Circ:** (Not Reported).

16843 ■ Russian Physics Journal
Kluwer Academic/Plenum Publishing Corp.
101 Philip Dr.
Norwell, MA 02061
Phone: (781)871-6600
Fax: (781)871-6528
Publisher's E-mail: kluwer@wkap.com
Translation of Izvestiya VUZ. Fizika covering specialized research in applied physics. **Freq:** Monthly. **Print Method:** Offset. **Cols./Page:** 1. **Col. Width:** 85 nonpareils. **Col. Depth:** 126 agate lines. **Key Personnel:** E.F. Dudarev, Associate Editor; T.S. Portnova, Secretary; V.G. Bagrov, Board Member; Alexander I. Potekaev, Editor-in-Chief; V.I. Gaman, Associate Editor; G.F. Karavaev, Board Member. **ISSN:** 1064--8887 (print); **EISSN:** 1573--9228 (electronic). **Subscription Rates:** €6969 Institutions print + free online access; €8363 Institutions print + enhanced access. **URL:** http://www.springer.com/physics/journal/11182. **Formerly:** Soviet Physics Journal. **Remarks:** Advertising not accepted. **Circ:** (Not Reported).

16844 ■ Strength of Materials
Kluwer Academic/Plenum Publishing Corp.
101 Philip Dr.
Norwell, MA 02061
Phone: (781)871-6600
Fax: (781)871-6528
Publisher's E-mail: kluwer@wkap.com
The journal focuses on the strength of materials and structural components subjected to different types of force and thermal loadings, the limiting strength criteria of structures, and the theory of strength of structures. **Freq:** Bimonthly. **Print Method:** Offset. **Key Personnel:** J.D. Landes, Advisor, Board Member; A.O. Khotsyanovskii, Secretary; N.A. Makhutov, Advisor, Board Member; Andrea Carpinteri, Advisor, Board Member; N.F. Morozov, Advisor, Board Member; V.A. Strizhalo, Associate Editor; V.T. Troshchenko, Board Member. **ISSN:** 0039--2316 (print); **EISSN:** 1573--9325 (electronic). **Subscription Rates:** €6036 Institutions print or electronic; €7243 Institutions print and enhanced access; $6310 Institutions print or electronic; $7572 Institutions print and enhanced access. **URL:** http://www.springer.com/materials/characterization+%26+evaluation/journal/11223. **Remarks:** Advertising not accepted. **Circ:** (Not Reported).

NORWOOD

E. MA. Norfolk Co. 3 mi. S. of Dedham. Residential.

16845 ■ Journal of Electronic Defense: Official Publication of the Association of Old Crows
Horizon House Publications Inc.
685 Canton St.
Norwood, MA 02062
Phone: (781)769-9750
Fax: (781)769-5037
Free: 800-966-8526
Publication E-mail: editor@crows.org
Defense electronics magazine. **Freq:** Monthly. **Print Method:** Offset. **Trim Size:** 7 13/16 x 10 3/4. **Cols./Page:** 3. **Col. Width:** 26 nonpareils. **Col. Depth:** 140 agate lines. **Key Personnel:** John Knowles, Editor-in-Chief, phone: (978)509-1450. **Subscription Rates:** $200 Individuals; 350 Other countries. **URL:** http://www.crows.org/jed/jed.html. **Ad Rates:** BW $7,650; 4C $9,090. **Remarks:** Accepts advertising. **Circ:** (Not Reported).

16846 ■ Journal of Infusion Nursing: The Official Publication of the Infusion Nurses Society
Infusion Nurses Society
c/o Mary Alexander, Ed.
315 Norwood Park S
Norwood, MA 02062
Phone: (781)440-9408
Fax: (781)440-9409
Publisher's E-mail: ins@ins1.org
Medical journal covering infusion nursing. **Freq:** 6/year. **Print Method:** Web Offset. **Trim Size:** 7 3/4 x 10 3/4. **Key Personnel:** Mary Alexander, Editor; Dorothy Lohmann, Managing Editor. **ISSN:** 1533--1458 (print); **EISSN:** 1539--0667 (electronic). **Subscription Rates:** $155 U.S.; $525 Institutions; $76 Individuals in training; $169 Canada and Mexico; $521 Institutions, Canada and Mexico; $214 Individuals UK/Australia; $591 Institutions UK/Australia; $296 Other countries; $639 Institutions, other countries. **URL:** http://journals.lww.com/journalofinfusionnursing/pages/default.aspx; http://www.lww.com/product/?1533-1458. **Ad Rates:** $1030-2735; $710-1610. GLR $30; BW $2,600; 4C $1,610; BW $1,380; BW $4C $. **Remarks:** Accepts advertising. **Circ:** Paid 7014, 7420.

16847 ■ Microwave Journal: Microwave - RF & Lightwave Technology
Horizon House Publications Inc.
685 Canton St.
Norwood, MA 02062
Phone: (781)769-9750
Fax: (781)769-5037
Free: 800-966-8526
Publication E-mail: mwj@mwjournal.com
Electronic engineering magazine. **Freq:** Monthly. **Print Method:** Offset. **Trim Size:** 7 13/16 x 10 3/4. **Cols./Page:** 3 and 2. **Col. Width:** 26 and 40 nonpareils. **Col. Depth:** 140 agate lines. **Key Personnel:** Carl Sheffres, Publisher. **ISSN:** 0192--6225 (print). **Subscription Rates:** Free. **URL:** http://www.mwjournal.com. **Ad Rates:** BW $7,540. **Remarks:** Accepts advertising. **Circ:** 50000.

16848 ■ Telecom Engine: Service Provider Technologies and Applications
Horizon House Publications Inc.
685 Canton St.
Norwood, MA 02062
Phone: (781)769-9750
Fax: (781)769-5037
Free: 800-966-8526
Provides a global perspective on the communications industry. Readership is predominantly in the service provider industry. **Freq:** Monthly. **Print Method:** Offset. **Trim Size:** 8 3/16 x 10 7/8. **Cols./Page:** 3. **Col. Width:** 2 1/8 inches. **Col. Depth:** 10 inches. **Key Personnel:** Christopher Snow, Associate Editor; Jared Bazzy, Executive Editor. **ISSN:** 0278--4831 (print). **USPS:** 296-270. **Subscription Rates:** $120 Individuals; $185 Individuals; $10 Single issue; $200 Individuals foreign; $370 Individuals foreign; $20 Single issue. **URL:** http://www.telecomengine.com. **Formerly:** Telecommunications Magazine. **Ad Rates:** BW $14,576. **Remarks:** Advertising accepted; rates available upon request. **Circ:** (Not Reported).

ORANGE

NC MA. Franklin Co. 5 mi. N. of Wendell Depot.

16849 ■ WCAT-AM - 700
660 E Main St.
Orange, MA 01364
Format: Talk; News. **Owner:** PS Broadcasting, Inc., at above address. **Founded:** 1956. **Formerly:** WPNS-AM. **Operating Hours:** Sunrise-sunset; 75% network, 25% local. **Key Personnel:** Jean Partridge, Gen. Mgr., President. **Wattage:** 2,500. **Ad Rates:** $6-9 for 30 seconds; $7-12 for 60 seconds. **Mailing address:** PO Box 90, Orange, MA 01364.

16850 ■ WJDF-FM - 97.3
11 S Main St., Ste. 401
Orange, MA 01364-0973
Phone: (978)544-5335
Fax: (978)544-2131
Email: info@wjdf.com
Format: Adult Contemporary. **Key Personnel:** Fred Deane, Music Dir.; Jay Deane, Dir. of Programs; Donn Deane, Gen. Mgr. **Ad Rates:** Advertising accepted; rates available upon request. **Mailing address:** PO Box 973, Orange, MA 01364-0973. **URL:** http://www.wjdf.com/images/mainpage.htm.

ORLEANS

E. MA. Barnstable Co. 40 mi. SE of Plymouth. Fishing.

16851 ■ Cape Codder
GateHouse Media Inc.
5 Namskaket Rd.
Orleans, MA 02653
Local newspaper. **Freq:** Weekly (Fri.). **Print Method:** Offset. **Cols./Page:** 5. **Col. Width:** 20 nonpareils. **Col. Depth:** 224 agate lines. **Key Personnel:** Mark Olivieri, Publisher, phone: (508)247-3260; Carol K. Dumas, Managing Editor, phone: (508)247-3255; Matt Rice, Editor, phone: (508)247-3261. **Subscription Rates:** $69.95 Individuals; $89.95 Out of area. **URL:** http://brewster.wickedlocal.com. **Ad Rates:** SAU $15.55. **Remarks:** Accepts advertising. **Circ:** (Not Reported).

PALMER

SW MA. Hampden Co. 15 mi. E. of Springfield. Manufactures plastic products, wire goods, metal culverts, ladders, cosmetics, fire trucks, brushes. Dairy, poultry, fruit farms. Apples.

16852 ■ Chicopee Register
Turley Publications
24 Water St.
Palmer, MA 01069
Phone: (413)283-8393
Free: 800-824-6548
Publisher's E-mail: support@turley.com
Community newspaper serving city of Chicopee. **Freq:** Weekly (Thurs.). **URL:** http://chicopeeregister.turley.com. **Remarks:** Accepts advertising. **Circ:** 13,000.

16853 ■ Journal Register
Turley Publications
24 Water St.
Palmer, MA 01069
Phone: (413)283-8393
Free: 800-824-6548
Publisher's E-mail: support@turley.com
Newspaper. **Founded:** 1850. **Freq:** Weekly (Thurs.). **Print Method:** Letterpress and Offset. **Cols./Page:** 8. **Col. Width:** 20 nonpareils. **Col. Depth:** 294 agate lines. **Key Personnel:** Doug Farmer, Editor; Tim Kane, Executive Editor. **Subscription Rates:** $10 Individuals; $9 Individuals 12 weeks 10% off; $9 Individuals 13-25 weeks 15% off; $8 Individuals 26-38weeks 20% off; $8 Individuals 39-52 weeks 25% off. **URL:** http://www.palmerjr.com. **Ad Rates:** GLR $.183; PCI $9.25. **Remarks:** Accepts advertising. **Circ:** 5200.

16854 ■ The New England Antiques Journal
Turley Publications
24 Water St.
Palmer, MA 01069
Phone: (413)283-8393
Free: 800-824-6548
Publisher's E-mail: support@turley.com
Magazine covering antiques, arts, historic preservation, restoration, artisanship and more. **Freq:** Monthly. **Trim Size:** 8.125 x 10.75. **Col. Width:** 2 1/8 inches. **Col. Depth:** 11 3/4 inches. **Key Personnel:** John Fiske, Editor-in-Chief; Charlann Griswold, Manager, Circulation. **ISSN:** 0897-5795 (print). **Subscription Rates:** $15.95 Individuals; $25.95 Two years; $15.95 Individuals gift subscription; $25.95 Two years two years gift subscription; $32 Canada; $63 Individuals European (surface price); $142 Individuals European (air mail); $54 Canada two years. **URL:** http://www.antiquesjournal.com. **Ad Rates:** BW $899; 4C $1,199. **Remarks:** Accepts advertising. **Circ:** Paid 25000.

16855 ■ Quaboag Current
Turley Publications
24 Water St.
Palmer, MA 01069
Phone: (413)283-8393
Free: 800-824-6548
Publisher's E-mail: support@turley.com
Community newspaper serving the towns of West Brookfield, East Brookfield, North Brookfield, Warren, West Warren, and New Braintree. **Freq:** Weekly. **Key Personnel:** Eileen Kennedy, Editor. **URL:** http://quaboagcurrent.com. **Remarks:** Accepts advertising. **Circ:** 3500.

16856 ■ Tantasqua Town Common
Turley Publications
24 Water St.
Palmer, MA 01069
Phone: (413)283-8393
Free: 800-824-6548
Publication E-mail: towncommon@turley.com
Community newspaper serving Tantasqua. **Freq:** Weekly. **Key Personnel:** Tim Kane, Executive Editor; Beth Baker, Director, Advertising. **URL:** http://thetantasquatowncommon.com. **Remarks:** Accepts advertising. **Circ:** 10100, ‡3000.

16857 ■ WARE-AM - 1250
3 Converse St., Ste. 101
Palmer, MA 01069-1538
Phone: (413)289-2300
Fax: (413)289-2323
Format: Oldies; Talk. **Networks:** AP. **Owner:** Success Signal Broadcasting Inc., at above address. **Founded:** 1946. **Operating Hours:** Continuous; 5% network; 95% local. **Key Personnel:** Bruce Marshall, Contact, bruce.marshall3@verizon.net. **Wattage:** 5,000. **Ad Rates:** $10-18 for 60 seconds. **URL:** http://www.realoldies1250.com.

PAXTON

16858 ■ WSRS-FM - 96.1
96 Stereo Ln.
Paxton, MA 01612
Phone: (508)757-9696
Fax: (508)757-1779
Format: Adult Contemporary. **Networks:** Independent. **Owner:** iHeartMedia Inc., 200 E Basse Rd., San Antonio, TX 78209, Ph: (210)832-3314. **Founded:** 1940. **Operating Hours:** Continuous. **ADI:** Boston-Worcester,MA-Derry-Manchester,NH. **Key Personnel:** Dan Kelleher, Chief Engineer, dankelleher@clearchannel.com; Sean Davey, Dir. of Mktg., Mktg. Mgr., seandavey@clearchannel.com; Joel Palmer, Dir. of Production, joelpalmer@clearchannel.com; Joe Flynn, Sales Mgr., joeflynn@clearchannel.com; Tom Holt, Dir. of Programs, tomholt@clearchannel.com. **Wattage:** 25,000. **Ad Rates:** Noncommercial. **URL:** http://www.wsrs.com.

16859 ■ WTAG-AM - 580
58 Stereo Ln.
Paxton, MA 01612
Phone: (508)795-0580
Fax: (508)757-1779
Format: Talk; Sports. **Networks:** CBS. **Owner:** Clear Channel Communications Inc., at above address, Ph: (210)822-2828, Fax: (210)822-2299. **Founded:** 1924. **Operating Hours:** Continuous. **ADI:** Boston-Worcester,MA-Derry-Manchester,NH. **Key Personnel:** Kevin Johnson, Producer; Joe Flynn, Prog. Dir., joeflynn@clearchannel.com; Dan Kelleher, Station Mgr., danielkelleher@clearchannel.com. **Wattage:** 5,000. **Ad Rates:** Noncommercial. **URL:** http://www.wtag.com.

PEABODY

NE MA. Essex Co. 15 mi. NE of Boston. Tanning, finishing of leather and sheepskin. Manufactures gelatin, corrugated boxes, nails, shoe machinery, fibre and leather innersoles, resinous chemicals, plastics.

16860 ■ North Shore Golf
Suburban Publishing Corp.
10 First Ave.
Peabody, MA 01961
Phone: (978)532-5880
Fax: (978)532-4250
Free: 800-221-2078
Publisher's E-mail: ads@weeklynews.net
Magazine featuring golf in North Shore. **Freq:** Bimonthly. **Trim Size:** 8.25 x 10.625. **Key Personnel:** Richard Ayer, Publisher; Bob Albright, Editor. **Subscription Rates:** $12 Individuals. **URL:** http://www.suburbanpublishing.com. **Ad Rates:** BW $1,995. **Remarks:** Accepts advertising. **Circ:** (Not Reported).

16861 ■ Peabody-Lynnfield Edition
Suburban Publishing Corp.
10 First Ave.
Peabody, MA 01961
Phone: (978)532-5880
Fax: (978)532-4250
Free: 800-221-2078
Publisher's E-mail: ads@weeklynews.net
Community newspaper. **Freq:** Weekly (Thurs.). **Print Method:** Offset. **Trim Size:** 11 3/8 x 17. **Key Personnel:** Richard H. Ayer, Chief Executive Officer, President; Bill Smith, Editor; Jim Downey, Manager, Circulation. **Ad Rates:** GLR $19.50; SAU $17.15. **Remarks:** Accepts advertising. **Circ:** (Not Reported).

PETERSHAM

16862 ■ Rhodora: Journal of the New England Botanical Club
New England Botanical Club
c/o Dr. Elizabeth Farnsworth, Ed.-in-Ch.
324 N Main St.
Petersham, MA 01366
Phone: (978)249-6771
Publication E-mail: rhodora@allenpress.com
Peer-reviewed journal devoted primarily to the flora of North America. **Freq:** Quarterly. **Print Method:** Offset. **Trim Size:** 6 x 9. **Cols./Page:** 1. **Col. Width:** 24 picas. **Col. Depth:** 41 picas. **Key Personnel:** Dr. Elizabeth Farnsworth, Senior Editor; Nishanta Rajakaruna, Editor-in-Chief. **ISSN:** 0035-4902 (print). **Subscription Rates:** Included in membership; $120 Institutions print & online. **URL:** http://www.rhodorajournal.org/loi/rhod; http://www.rhodora.org/rhodora/aboutrhodora.html. **Remarks:** Advertising not accepted. **Circ:** Paid 800, Non-paid 15.

PITTSFIELD

W. MA. Berkshire Co. 58 mi. NW of Springfield. Publishing center. Summer and winter resorts. Manufactures electrical equipment, wooden pallets and skids, textiles, machinery, cement blocks, steel fabric, tools and dies, paper, control systems, plastics, missiles.

16863 ■ The Berkshire Eagle
New England Newspapers Inc.
75 S Church St.
Pittsfield, MA 01202
Phone: (413)447-7311
General newspaper. **Founded:** 1789. **Freq:** Daily and Sun. **Print Method:** Offset. **Trim Size:** 12 1/2 x 22 1/2. **Cols./Page:** 6. **Col. Width:** 12.3 picas. **Col. Depth:** 21 1/4 inches. **Key Personnel:** Tara Caccamo, Manager, Circulation, phone: (413)496-6351; Kevin Moran, Managing Editor, phone: (413)496-6215. **ISSN:** 0895-8193 (print). **Subscription Rates:** $3 Individuals /week, all access digital or all access + sunday print; $4 Individuals /week, all access, wednesday,saturday and sunday, print; $7 Individuals /week, all access + 7day print. **URL:** http://www.berkshireeagle.com. **Mailing address:** PO Box 1171, Pittsfield, MA 01202. **Remarks:** Accepts advertising. **Circ:** Mon.-Sat. ★**31207**, Sun. ★**35445**.

16864 ■ Photonics Spectra
Laurin Publishing Company Inc.
100 W St.
Pittsfield, MA 01201-4949
Phone: (413)499-0514
Fax: (413)442-3180
Free: 800-553-0051
Publisher's E-mail: photonics@laurin.com
Magazine covering optics, fiber, electro-optics, lasers, imaging and optical computing. **Founded:** 1967. **Freq:** Monthly. **Print Method:** Offset. **Trim Size:** 8 1/4 x 10 7/8. **Cols./Page:** 3 and 2. **Col. Width:** 26 and 40 nonpareils. **Col. Depth:** 140 agate lines. **Key Personnel:** Heidi Miller, Manager, Circulation. **ISSN:** 0731-1230 (print). **URL:** http://www.photonics.com/Splash.aspx?PID=5. **Mailing address:** PO Box 4949, Pittsfield, MA 01202-4949. **Ad Rates:** BW $11,295; 4C $13,345. **Remarks:** Accepts advertising. **Circ:** Non-paid △**95667**.

Circulation: ★ = AAM; △ or • = BPA; ♦ = CAC; ❑ = VAC; ⊕ = PO Statement; ‡ = Publisher's Report; Boldface figures = sworn; Light figures = estimated.

16865 ■ Pittsfield Gazette
The Pittsfield Gazette Inc.
PO Box 2236
Pittsfield, MA 01202
Phone: (413)443-2010
Publisher's E-mail: pittsfieldgazette@verizon.net
Community newspaper. **Freq:** Weekly (Thurs.). **Trim Size:** 10.5 x 14. **Cols./Page:** 5. **Col. Width:** 11/12 inches. **URL:** http://pittsfieldgazette.com. **Ad Rates:** PCI $8. **Remarks:** Accepts advertising. **Circ:** (Not Reported).

16866 ■ WBEC-AM - 1420
211 Jason St.
Pittsfield, MA 01201
Phone: (413)499-3333
Fax: (413)442-1590
Format: Full Service; News; Talk. **Networks:** ABC. **Founded:** 1947. **Operating Hours:** Continuous. **ADI:** Albany-Schenectady-Troy, NY. **Key Personnel:** Peter Barry, Mktg. Mgr., VP, peterb@live959.com; Todd Lee, Operations Mgr., todd@wupe.com. **Wattage:** 1,000. **Ad Rates:** Advertising accepted; rates available upon request. **URL:** http://www.live959.com.

16867 ■ WBEC-FM - 95.9
211 Jason St.
Pittsfield, MA 01201
Phone: (413)499-3333
Fax: (413)442-1590
Email: contest@live959.com
Format: News. **Founded:** 1963. **Key Personnel:** Peter Barry, VP, Mgr., peterb@live959.com. **Wattage:** 1,000 ERP. **Ad Rates:** Advertising accepted; rates available upon request. AM1420 & WZEC-FM in Bennington VT. **URL:** http://www.live959.com.

16868 ■ WBRK-AM - 1340
100 N St.
Pittsfield, MA 01201
Phone: (413)442-1553
Fax: (413)445-5294
Email: wbrk@wbrk.com
Format: Adult Contemporary. **Networks:** CBS. **Founded:** 1936. **Operating Hours:** Continuous. **Key Personnel:** Len Bean, VP; Robert Shade, VP of Sales; Willard Hodgkins, III, President; Cheryl Tripp-Cleveland, VP; Mike Bunn, Contact; Rick Beltaire, Contact. **Wattage:** 1,000. **Ad Rates:** $9.75 for 30 seconds; $30.50 for 60 seconds. **URL:** http://www.wbrk.com.

16869 ■ WBRK-FM - 101.7
100 North St.
Pittsfield, MA 01201
Phone: (413)442-1553
Fax: (413)445-5294
Email: wbrk@wbrk.com
Format: Full Service; Oldies; Talk. **Networks:** CBS; Westwood One Radio; ABC. **Key Personnel:** Bob Shade, Sports Dir., bob@wbrk.com; Willard Hodgkins, III, President, chip@wbrk.com. **Wattage:** 3,000 ERP. **URL:** http://wbrk.com.

16870 ■ WTBR-FM - 89.7
Taconic High School
96 Valentine Rd.
Pittsfield, MA 01201
Phone: (413)448-9607
Fax: (413)769-2930
Format: Educational; Eclectic. **Networks:** American Public Radio (APR). **Founded:** 1978. **Operating Hours:** 7 a.m. to 12 a.m. Mon-Fri; Continuous Sat-Sun. **Wattage:** 400. **Ad Rates:** Noncommercial; underwriting available; Noncommercial. **URL:** http://www.wtbrfm.com.

16871 ■ WUHN-AM - 1110
211 Jason St.
Pittsfield, MA 01201
Phone: (413)499-3333
Fax: (413)442-1590
Email: news@wupe.com
Format: Classical. **Owner:** Vox Radio Group Co., Inc., at above address. **Founded:** 1971. **Operating Hours:** Sunrise-sunset. **Key Personnel:** Peter Barry, Mktg. Mgr., President, peterb@live959.com; Larry Kratka, News Dir., news@wupe.com. **Wattage:** 5,000. **Ad Rates:** Noncommercial. **URL:** http://www.wupe.com.

16872 ■ WUPE-FM - 95.9
1350 West St.
Pittsfield, MA 01201
Format: Adult Contemporary. **Networks:** Westwood One Radio. **Owner:** Weiner Broadcasting, Inc., at above address. **Founded:** 1975. **Operating Hours:** Continuous. **Key Personnel:** Philip Weiner, Gen. Mgr. **Wattage:** 1,000. **URL:** http://www.wupe.com/contact-us/eeo-2015.

PLYMOUTH

SE MA. Plymouth Co. On Plymouth Bay, 37 mi. SE of Boston. Rich in historical interest, oldest town in New England. Landing place of the Pilgrims in 1620. Museums, whale watches, fishing boats.

16873 ■ Duxbury Reporter
MPG Newspapers
9 Long Pond Rd.
Plymouth, MA 02360
Community newspaper. **Freq:** Weekly (Fri.). **Print Method:** Offset. **Trim Size:** 16 1/2 x 11. **Cols./Page:** 5. **Col. Width:** 21 nonpareils. **Col. Depth:** 224 agate lines. **Key Personnel:** Gregory Mathis, Editor-in-Chief; Tim Oliver, Manager, Sales; Ryan Wood, Editor; Mark Olivieri, Publisher. **URL:** http://duxbury.wickedlocal.com. **Remarks:** Accepts advertising. **Circ:** (Not Reported).

16874 ■ Wareham Courier
GateHouse Media Inc.
182 Standish Ave.
Plymouth, MA 02360
Phone: (508)591-6624
Fax: (508)591-6601
Publication E-mail: wareham@wickedlocal.com
Community newspaper. **Freq:** Weekly (Thurs.). **Print Method:** Offset. **Cols./Page:** 5. **Col. Width:** 21 nonpareils. **Col. Depth:** 224 agate lines. **Key Personnel:** Mark Olivieri, Publisher, phone: (781)837-4506; Frank Mulligan, Editor, phone: (508)591-6628; Gregory Mathis, Editor-in-Chief, phone: (781)837-4560. **URL:** http://wareham.wickedlocal.com. **Ad Rates:** GLR $.67; BW $750; 4C $1,350; PCI $9.38. **Remarks:** Accepts advertising. **Circ:** Paid ‡1664.

16875 ■ WPLM-AM - 1390
17 Columbus Rd.
Plymouth, MA 02360
Phone: (508)746-1390
Fax: (508)830-1128
Free: 877-327-9991
Format: News. **Simulcasts:** WPLM-FM. **Networks:** Westwood One Radio. **Owner:** Plymouth Rock Broadcasting Corp., Not Available. **Founded:** 1955. **Operating Hours:** Continuous. **ADI:** Boston-Worcester,MA-Derry-Manchester,NH. **Key Personnel:** Alan W. Anderson, Gen. Mgr. **Wattage:** 5,000. **Mailing address:** PO Box 991, Boston, MA 02118. **URL:** http://www.easy991.com.

16876 ■ WPLM-FM - 99.1
17 Columbus Rd.
Plymouth, MA 02360
Format: Easy Listening. **Founded:** 1961. **Wattage:** 50,000. **Ad Rates:** Noncommercial; Advertising accepted; rates available upon request.

PLYMPTON

16877 ■ Vintage Bike
Triumph International Owners Club
PO Box 158
Plympton, MA 02367-0158
Phone: (508)946-1939
Fax: (508)946-1145
Magazine featuring British motorcycles in general and Triumph in particular. **Freq:** Quarterly. **Subscription Rates:** $24 4 issues; $42.50 Two years 8 issues; $30 Canada and Mexico 4 issues; $35 Out of country 4 issues. **URL:** http://vintagebikemagazine.com. **Remarks:** Accepts advertising. **Circ:** 2800.

PROVINCETOWN

E. MA. Barnstable Co. At tip of Cape Cod, 55 mi. by water SE of Boston. Historic spot where the Mayflower first landed. Summer theatre and resort. Boat building. Artist colony.

16878 ■ WOMR-FM - 92.1
494 Commercial St.
Provincetown, MA 02657
Phone: (508)487-2619
Fax: (508)487-5524
Free: 800-921-9667
Email: info@womr.org
Format: Eclectic; Information. **Founded:** 1982. **Operating Hours:** Continuous. **Key Personnel:** Chris Boles, Mgr., chris@womr.org. **Local Programs:** *On a Lark or Dixieland Jazz etc.*, Sunday 9:00 a.m. - 12:00 p.m.; *Counterspin*, Monday Tuesday 9:00 p.m. - 9:30 a.m. 5:00 a.m. - 5:30 a.m.; *The Old Songs Home*, Monday 9:30 a.m. - 12:30 p.m.; *Cafe Classicale*, Monday 1:00 p.m. - 4:00 p.m.; *The Fiddle and the Harp*, Monday 5:00 p.m. - 8:00 p.m.; *The Joe Poire Show*, Thursday; *Alternative Radio*, Monday Thursday 8:00 p.m. - 9:00 p.m. 3:00 a.m. - 4:00 a.m.; *TUC Radio*, Tuesday 4:00 a.m. - 4:30 a.m.; *Sea Change Radio*, Tuesday 4:30 a.m. - 5:00 a.m.; *Jazz Odyssey*, Tuesday 5:00 p.m. - 8:00 p.m.; *Low Tide Lounge*, Wednesday 9:30 a.m. - 12:30 p.m.; *The Anne Levine Show*, Monday 12:00 a.m. - 1:00 a.m.; *Jazz Juice*, Wednesday 1:00 p.m. - 4:00 p.m.; *Bradford Street Bluegrass*, Wednesday 5:00 p.m. - 8:00 p.m.; *Planetary Radio*, Thursday 4:00 a.m. - 4:30 a.m.; *Spiritual Awakening*, Thursday 5:00 a.m. - 6:00 a.m.; *New Dimensions*, Thursday 6:00 a.m. - 7:00 a.m.; *Making Contact*, Friday 5:00 a.m. - 5:30 a.m.; *Straight, No Chaser*, Wednesday 1:00 p.m. - 4:00 p.m.; *Charted Course*, Thursday 9:00 p.m. - 12:00 a.m.; *FM Odyssey*, Monday Friday 1:00 a.m. - 3:00 a.m. 12:00 a.m. - 2:00 a.m.; *Jazz Inspired*, Thursday Friday 2:00 a.m. - 3:00 a.m. 3:00 a.m. - 4:00 a.m.; *Sprouts*; *The English Breakfast*, Tuesday 6:00 a.m. - 9:00 a.m.; *Friday Folk*, Friday 9:30 a.m. - 12:30 p.m.; *Memory Lane*, Saturday 6:00 a.m. - 10:00 a.m.; *WOMR Opera House*, Saturday 2:00 p.m. - 6:00 p.m.; *Issues in the News*, Tuesday 9:00 a.m. - 9:30 a.m.; *Kitchen Sink*, Saturday 6:00 p.m. - 9:00 p.m.; *The Soul Funky Train*, Thursday 1:00 p.m. - 4:00 p.m.; *Joyride Media*, Sunday 4:00 a.m. - 5:00 a.m.; *Squid Jigger's Blend*, Wednesday 6:00 a.m. - 9:00 a.m.; *Free Speech Radio News*, Overnight; *Thursday First Light*, Thursday 5:00 a.m. - 9:00 a.m.; *Nauset Teens*, Saturday 10:00 a.m. - 12:00 p.m.; *This Way Out*, Tuesday 5:30 a.m. - 6:00 a.m.; *My Little Corner of the World*, Wednesday 6:30 a.m. - 8:30 a.m.; *Counter Spin*, Monday 9:00 a.m. - 9:30 a.m.; *Global Soul*, Saturday 12:00 a.m. - 3:00 a.m.; *Bluegrass Review*, Wednesday 3:00 a.m. - 4:00 a.m.; *Democracy Now!*, Monday Tuesday Wednesday Thursday Friday 400 p.m. - 5:00 p.m.; *Community Partners on the Air*, Wednesday 12:30 p.m. - 1:00 p.m.; *Talking Back*, Tuesday 9:00 a.m. - 9:30 a.m.; *The Fiddle and the Harp*, Monday 5:00 p.m. - 8:00 p.m.; *Sounds of America*, Thursday 5:00 p.m. - 8:00 p.m.; *Psychedelic Oyster*, Monday 9:00 p.m. - 12:00 p.m.; *Night Flight*, Tuesday 9:00 p.m. - 12:00 a.m.; *Mary's Ukulele Show*, Wednesday 8:00 p.m. - 8:30 p.m.; *Brand New Day*, Tuesday 6:00 a.m. - 9:00 a.m.; *Art of the Song*, Tuesday 3:00 a.m. - 4:00 a.m.; *FolkScene*, Monday 4:00 a.m. - 6:00 a.m.; *The Latest Score*, Tuesday 1:00 p.m. - 4:00 p.m.; *For a Better State of Mind*, Tuesday 8:00 p.m. - 9:00 p.m.; *T Bird's Blues Ride with T-Bird*, Thursday 9:30 a.m. - 12:30 p.m.; *My Dumb 'ol Radio Show or Monuments of Mars*, Friday; *WoodSong's Old-Time Radio Hour*, Sunday 5:00 a.m. - 6:00 a.m.; *The Old Country Blues Buffet or Sitting In*, Sunday 1:00 p.m. - 4:00 p.m.; *Arts Week and the Poets Corner*, Thursday 12:30 p.m. - 1:00 p.m.; *Sands of Time or Herb Talk*, Friday 9:00 a.m. - 9:30 a.m. **Wattage:** 6,000 ERP. **Mailing address:** PO Box 975, Provincetown, MA 02657. **URL:** http://www.womr.org.

QUINCY

E. MA. Norfolk Co. On the sea coast, 8 mi. S. of Boston. Eastern Nazarene College. Ship building yards. Manufactures weighing, packaging, mattress and surfacing machinery, plastics, paper, rubber products, iron products, electron tubes, crystal diodes, chemicals, paint, gears, telephones, builders' supplies. Foundry.

16879 ■ American Journal of Transportation
Fleur de Lis Publishing Inc.
1354 Hancock St., Ste. 300
Quincy, MA 02169
Free: 800-599-6358
Professional magazine covering international commerce for shippers, transportation professionals and regulators. **Freq:** Weekly (Mon.). **Key Personnel:** George Lauriat, Editor-in-Chief; William Bourbon, Publisher. **ISSN:** 1529-1820 (print). **Subscription Rates:** $138 Individuals;

$236 Two years; $187 Canada and Mexico; $318 Two years Canada and Mexico; $278 Other countries; $520 Other countries two years. **URL:** http://www.ajot.com/. **Ad Rates:** BW $3600; 4C $4500. **Remarks:** Accepts advertising. **Circ:** Paid 32,715.

16880 ■ Amour Creole
Amour Creole
PO Box 961666
Quincy, MA 02169
Phone: (617)286-4994
Fax: (888)824-0005
Free: 888-828-4442
Publisher's E-mail: info@amourcreole.com
Magazine featuring Haitian style, entertainment, and current issues. **Freq:** Quarterly. **Key Personnel:** Esther Lafontant, Founder, Publisher; Jourdan Wittly, Founder. **Subscription Rates:** $14.97 Individuals 1 year; $29.94 Individuals 2 years; $19.97 Canada 1 year; $39.94 Canada 2 years; $86.97 Other countries 1 year. **URL:** http://amourcreole.com. **Remarks:** Advertising accepted; rates available upon request. **Circ:** 250000.

16881 ■ The Best of Northeast Golf
Madavor Media
85 Quincy Ave., Ste. B
Quincy, MA 02169
Phone: (617)536-0100
Fax: (617)536-0102
Free: 800-437-5828
Publisher's E-mail: info@madavor.com
Magazine delivering informative, interesting, and well-written articles about courses, people, places, and events that promote and grow the game of golf. **Freq:** Annual. **Key Personnel:** Susan Fitzgerald, Publisher; Kathryn Peck, Director, Editorial. **Circ:** (Not Reported).

16882 ■ Fire Technology
National Fire Protection Association
1 Batterymarch Pk.
Quincy, MA 02169-7471
Phone: (617)770-3000
Fax: (617)770-0700
Publisher's E-mail: stds_admin@nfpa.org
Peer-reviewed scientific journal covering fire protection research and applications. **Freq:** Quarterly. **Print Method:** Offset. **Trim Size:** 6 x 9. **Cols./Page:** 1. **Col. Width:** 27 picas. **Col. Depth:** 45 picas. **Key Personnel:** John M. Watts, Jr., Editor; Kathleen M. Robinson, Director, Editorial; Elizabeth Weckman, Board Member. **ISSN:** 0015--2684 (print). **Subscription Rates:** €877 Institutions print incl. free access or e-only ; €1052 Institutions print plus enhanced access; $949 Institutions print incl. free access or e-only; $1139 Institutions print plus enhanced access. **URL:** http://www.nfpa.org/member-access/fire-technology. **Remarks:** Advertising not accepted. **Circ:** ‡4000.

16883 ■ International Figure Skating
Madavor Media
85 Quincy Ave., Ste. B
Quincy, MA 02169
Phone: (617)536-0100
Fax: (617)536-0102
Free: 800-437-5828
Publisher's E-mail: info@madavor.com
News magazine for figure skating. **Freq:** Bimonthly. **Print Method:** Web. **Trim Size:** 8 1/2 x 11. **Key Personnel:** Miene Smith, Manager, Sales, fax: (617)536-0102. **ISSN:** 1070--9568 (print). **Subscription Rates:** $29.99 U.S. 1 year; $52.98 U.S. 2 years; $34.99 Canada 1 year; $60.98 Canada 2 years; $54.99 Other countries 1 year; $80.98 Other countries 2 years. **Ad Rates:** BW $2,415; 4C $3,675. **Remarks:** Accepts advertising. **Circ:** Paid 70000.

16884 ■ New England Hockey Journal
Seamans Media Inc.
1400 Hancock St., 7th Fl.
Quincy, MA 02169
Phone: (617)773-9955
Fax: (617)773-6688
Publisher's E-mail: feedback@nyhockeyjournal.com
Magazine covering hockey events in New England. **Freq:** Monthly. **Key Personnel:** Eric Seamans, Publisher. **URL:** http://www.seamansmedia.com/magazines. **Ad Rates:** 4C $2899. **Remarks:** Accepts advertising. **Circ:** (Not Reported).

16885 ■ New York Golf
Madavor Media
85 Quincy Ave., Ste. B
Quincy, MA 02169
Phone: (617)536-0100
Fax: (617)536-0102
Free: 800-437-5828
Publisher's E-mail: info@madavor.com
Magazine delivering informative, interesting, and well-written articles about courses, people, places, and events that promote and grow the game of golf. **Freq:** Semiannual. **Key Personnel:** Susan Fitzgerald, Publisher; Kathryn Peck, Director, Editorial. **Circ:** (Not Reported).

16886 ■ NFPA Journal
National Fire Protection Association
1 Batterymarch Pk.
Quincy, MA 02169-7471
Phone: (617)770-3000
Fax: (617)770-0700
Publication E-mail: nfpajournal@nfpa.org
Magazine concerning fire protection, prevention. Features technical, scientific and industrial applications of fire protection, suppression, investigations and education. **Freq:** Bimonthly. **Print Method:** Offset. **Trim Size:** 8 1/8 x 10 7/8. **Cols./Page:** 3. **Col. Width:** 13.6 picas. **Col. Depth:** 57.5 picas. **Key Personnel:** Scott Sutherland, Executive Editor. **ISSN:** 1054--8793 (print). **Subscription Rates:** Included in membership. **URL:** http://www.nfpa.org/newsandpublications/nfpa-journal/about-nfpa-journal; http://www.nfpa.org/newsandpublications/nfpa-journal/2015/january-february-2015. **Formerly:** Fire Journal; Fire Command. **Ad Rates:** BW $6750; PCI $300; 4C $9,200. **Remarks:** Accepts advertising. **Circ:** ‡79000.

16887 ■ The Patriot Ledger
The Patriot Ledger
400 Crown Colony Dr.
Quincy, MA 02169-0930
Phone: (617)786-7000
Fax: (617)786-7384
Publication E-mail: newsroom@ledger.com
General newspaper. **Founded:** Jan. 07, 1837. **Freq:** Daily (eve.). **Print Method:** Letterpress. **Trim Size:** 13 x 22. **Cols./Page:** 6. **Col. Width:** 2 1/16 inches. **Col. Depth:** 22 inches. **Key Personnel:** Chazy Dowaliby, Editor, phone: (617)786-7013, fax: (617)786-7393. **Subscription Rates:** $79.95 Individuals digital; $1.50 Individuals All access; One week. **URL:** http://www.patriotledger.com/. **Ad Rates:** GLR $3.88; BW $7,175.52; SAU $54.36. **Remarks:** Accepts advertising. **Circ:** Mon.-Fri. ⋆**55000**, Sat. ⋆**63000**.

16888 ■ The Writer Magazine: The Pioneer (Oldest) Magazine for Writers
Madavor Media
85 Quincy Ave., Ste. B
Quincy, MA 02169
Phone: (617)536-0100
Fax: (617)536-0102
Free: 800-437-5828
Magazine for free-lance writers. Publishing practical information and advice on how to write publishable material and where to sell it. **Freq:** Monthly. **Print Method:** Saddle-Stitched; Computer to Plate, Full Run. **Trim Size:** 8 1/4 x 10 3/4. **Cols./Page:** 3. **Key Personnel:** Alicia Anstead, Editor-in-Chief. **ISSN:** 0043--9517 (print). **Subscription Rates:** $32.95 Individuals; $42.95 Canada; $61 Two years; $44.95 Other countries. **URL:** http://www.writermag.com. **Mailing address:** PO Box 1612, Waukesha, WI 53187-1612. **Ad Rates:** BW $1,957; 4C $2,794. **Remarks:** Accepts advertising. **Circ:** Paid 28844.

16889 ■ Atlantic Broadband
2 Batterymarch Pk., Ste. 205
Quincy, MA 02169
Phone: (617)786-8800
Fax: (617)786-8803
Free: 888-536-9600
Key Personnel: David J. Keefe, Sr. VP, Gen. Mgr.; Patrick Bratton, CFO; Edward T. Holleran, Jr., VP; Almis J. Kuolas, Chief Tech. Ofc. **Cities Served:** 283 channels. **URL:** http://www.atlanticbb.com.

16890 ■ WILD-AM - 1090
500 Victory Rd., 2nd Fl.
Quincy, MA 02171-3139
Phone: (617)472-9447
Fax: (617)472-9474
Format: Talk. **Networks:** American Urban Radio; ABC. **Owner:** Radio One Inc., 1010 Wayne Ave., 14th Fl., Silver Spring, MD 20910, Ph: (301)306-1111, Fax: (302)636-5454. **Founded:** May 1946. **Operating Hours:** Sunrise-sunset. **Wattage:** 5,000 Day; 1,000 Night. **Ad Rates:** $72 for 30 seconds; $90 for 60 seconds. **URL:** http://www.bostonradio.org/stations/47413.html.

16891 ■ WROL-AM - 950
500 Victory Rd.
Quincy, MA 02171
Phone: (617)328-0880
Fax: (617)328-0375
Email: contactus@salemradioboston.com
Format: Religious; Ethnic; Contemporary Christian. **Owner:** Salem Media Group Inc., 4880 Santa Rosa Rd., Camarillo, CA 93012, Ph: (805)987-0400, Fax: (805)384-4520. **Operating Hours:** Continuous. **Key Personnel:** Pat Ryan, Gen. Mgr., patr@salemradioboston.com; Phil Boyce, Sr. VP; Michael Miller, Sr. VP. **Ad Rates:** Advertising accepted; rates available upon request. **URL:** http://www.salem.cc.

16892 ■ WWZN-AM
308 Victory Rd.
Quincy, MA 02171
Phone: (617)237-1200
Fax: (617)237-1177
Ad Rates: Noncommercial.

RANDOLPH

E. MA. Norfolk Co. 14 mi. S. of Boston. Residential. Manufactures paper boxes, business machines.

16893 ■ Randolph Herald
MPG Newspapers
370 Paramount Dr., Ste. 3
Raynham, MA 02767
Community newspaper. **Freq:** Weekly (Wed.). **Print Method:** Offset. **Cols./Page:** 6. **Col. Width:** 9.5 picas. **Col. Depth:** 16 inches. **Key Personnel:** Mark Olivieri, Publisher; Alice Coyle, Managing Editor; Linda Vahey, Manager, Circulation. **URL:** http://www.wickedlocal.com/randolph. **Ad Rates:** PCI $10.95. **Remarks:** Accepts advertising. **Circ:** Combined ‡3169.

RAYNHAM

16894 ■ Bridgewater Independent
MPG Newspapers
370 Paramount Dr., Ste. 3
Raynham, MA 02767
Phone: (508)967-3520
Fax: (508)967-3501
Community newspaper. **Founded:** 1812. **Freq:** Weekly (Wed.). **Print Method:** Offset. **Cols./Page:** 6. **Col. Width:** 1 9/16 inches. **Col. Depth:** 16 inches. **Key Personnel:** Mark Olivieri, Publisher. **USPS:** 064-980. **URL:** http://bridgewater.wickedlocal.com/. **Formerly:** Bridgewater Townsman. **Ad Rates:** PCI $10.95. **Remarks:** Accepts advertising. **Circ:** Combined ‡2455.

16895 ■ Lakeville Call
GateHouse Media Inc.
370 Paramount Dr., Unit 3
Raynham, MA 02767
Phone: (508)967-3520
Fax: (508)967-3501
Community newspaper. **Freq:** Weekly (Wed.). **Key Personnel:** Mark Olivieri, Publisher, phone: (781)837-4504; Alice Coyle, Managing Editor, phone: (508)967-3505. **URL:** http://lakeville.wickedlocal.com. **Remarks:** Accepts advertising. **Circ:** Non-paid ♦**2300**.

16896 ■ Mansfield News
GateHouse Media Inc.
370 Paramount Dr., Unit 3
Raynham, MA 02767
Phone: (508)967-3510
Fax: (508)967-3501
Community newspaper. **Freq:** Weekly (Fri.). **Print Method:** Offset. **Trim Size:** 13 x 16. **Cols./Page:** 5. **Col. Width:** 2 1/16 inches. **Col. Depth:** 16 inches. **Key Personnel:** Mark Olivieri, Publisher, phone: (781)837-

Circulation: ⋆ = AAM; △ or • = BPA; ♦ = CAC; ❑ = VAC; ⊕ = PO Statement; ‡ = Publisher's Report; Boldface figures = sworn; Light figures = estimated.

4504; Donna Whitehead, Editor, phone: (508)967-3510; John Quattrucci, Editor, phone: (508)967-3527. **USPS:** 328-280. **Subscription Rates:** $55 Individuals resident's of Mansfield; $85 Out of state. **URL:** http://mansfield.wickedlocal.com. **Ad Rates:** BW $460; SAU $5.75. **Remarks:** Accepts advertising. **Circ:** (Not Reported).

Randolph Herald - See Randolph

16897 ■ Raynham Call
GateHouse Media Inc.
370 Paramount Dr., Unit 3
Raynham, MA 02767
Phone: (508)967-3520
Fax: (508)967-3501
Community newspaper. **Freq:** Weekly (Wed.). **Key Personnel:** Mark Olivieri, Publisher, phone: (781)837-4504; Alice Coyle, Managing Editor, phone: (508)967-3505; Linda Vahey, Manager, Circulation. **Subscription Rates:** $15 Individuals. **URL:** http://raynham.wickedlocal.com. **Remarks:** Accepts advertising. **Circ:** Combined ‡2354.

16898 ■ Stoughton Journal
GateHouse Media Inc.
370 Paramount Dr., Ste. 3
Raynham, MA 02767
Phone: (508)967-3515
Fax: (508)967-3501
Community newspaper. **Freq:** Weekly (Fri.). **Print Method:** Offset. **Trim Size:** 11 3/8 x 17. **Cols./Page:** 5. **Col. Width:** 1 7/8 inches. **Col. Depth:** 16 inches. **Key Personnel:** Mark Olivieri, Publisher, phone: (781)837-4504; Stuart Green, Editor, phone: (508)967-3515; John Quattrucci, Editor, phone: (508)967-3527. **Subscription Rates:** $45.95 Individuals by mail; $89.95 Out of area by mail. **URL:** http://stoughton.wickedlocal.com. **Ad Rates:** BW $942.40; 4C $1,300; PCI $8.25. **Circ:** (Not Reported).

REVERE

E. MA. Suffolk Co. On Massachusetts Bay, 6 mi. NE of Boston. (Branch of Boston P.O.) Summer resort. Residential. Manufactures air conditioning, electrical controls, heating equipment, paint, furniture, textiles, wood heels, electric pumps, hotel, restaurant, kitchen, and farm equipment, machine parts, chemicals, spices, beverages, brass.

16899 ■ The Beacon Hill Times
Independent Newspaper Group
385 Broadway, Ste. 105
Revere, MA 02151
Phone: (781)485-0588
Fax: (781)485-1403
Newspaper covering two neighborhoods, Beacon Hill and Charles River Park, in the Boston, MA, area. **Freq:** Weekly (Tues.). **Print Method:** web. **Trim Size:** 11 x 17. **Key Personnel:** Karen Cord Taylor, Editor; Jacqueline Harris, Managing Director. **URL:** http://www.beaconhilltimes.com. **Ad Rates:** BW $1,240; 4C $1,540. **Remarks:** Accepts advertising. **Circ:** 9000.

16900 ■ Chelsea Record
Independent Newspaper Group
385 Broadway, Ste. 105
Revere, MA 02151
Phone: (781)485-0588
Fax: (781)485-1403
Community newspaper. **Freq:** Weekly (Thurs.). **Print Method:** Photo Offset. **URL:** http://www.chelsearecord.com. **Remarks:** Advertising accepted; rates available upon request. **Circ:** Paid 2900.

16901 ■ East Boston Sun Transcript
Independent Newspaper Group
385 Broadway, Ste. 105
Revere, MA 02151
Phone: (781)485-0588
Fax: (781)485-1403
Community newspaper. **Freq:** Weekly (Wed.). **Print Method:** Photo Offset. **Subscription Rates:** Free. **URL:** http://www.eastietimes.com; http://www.eastietimes.com/pages. **Remarks:** Advertising accepted; rates available upon request. **Circ:** Non-paid 10300.

16902 ■ The Everett Independent
Independent Newspaper Group
385 Broadway, Ste. 105
Revere, MA 02151
Phone: (781)485-0588
Fax: (781)485-1403
Community newspaper. **Freq:** Weekly (Wed.). **Key Personnel:** Stephen Quigley, President; Cary Shuman, Editor-in-Chief; Joshua Resnek, Vice President. **URL:** http://everettindependent.com. **Circ:** Non-paid ‡12500.

16903 ■ Winthrop Sun Transcript
Independent Newspaper Group
385 Broadway, Ste. 105
Revere, MA 02151
Phone: (781)485-0588
Fax: (781)485-1403
Community newspaper. **Freq:** Weekly (Thurs.). **Print Method:** Photo Offset. **URL:** http://www.winthroptranscript.com. **Remarks:** Advertising accepted; rates available upon request. **Circ:** (Not Reported).

16904 ■ Comcast
41 Marble St.
Revere, MA 02151
Free: 800-266-2278
Email: we_can_help@comcast.com
Owner: Comcast Corp., 1 Comcast Ctr., Philadelphia, PA 19103-2838, Ph: (215)665-1700, Fax: (215)981-7790, Free: 800-266-2278. **Founded:** May 2000. **Key Personnel:** Brian L. Roberts, Chairman, CEO. **Cities Served:** 183 channels. **URL:** http://www.comcast.com.

RICHMOND

16905 ■ upstreet: A Literary Magazine
Ledgetop Publishing
PO Box 105
Richmond, MA 01254-0105
Phone: (413)441-9702
Publication E-mail: editor@upstreet-mag.org
Magazine featuring best new fiction, poetry and creative nonfiction. **Freq:** Annual. **Key Personnel:** Vivian Dorsel, Editor, Publisher. **URL:** http://www.upstreet-mag.org/welcome_layers.html. **Circ:** (Not Reported).

ROCKLAND

16906 ■ Mid Atlantic Real Estate Journal: The Most Comprehensive Source for Commercial Real Estate News
NJPA Real Estate Journal
PO Box 26
Rockland, MA 02370
Phone: (781)871-5298
Fax: (781)871-5299
Free: 800-584-1062
Publisher's E-mail: editor@njpajournal.com
Publication covering real estate markets in New Jersey and Pennsylvania. **Freq:** Semimonthly. **Key Personnel:** Linda Christman, Chief Executive Officer, Publisher; Ben Summers, Editor-in-Chief. **Subscription Rates:** $99 Individuals print; $148.50 Two years print. **URL:** http://www.njpajournal.com. **Formerly:** NJPA Real Estate Journal. **Ad Rates:** BW $1,295; 4C $1895. **Remarks:** Accepts advertising. **Circ:** Controlled 25000.

16907 ■ WRPS-FM - 88.3
52 Mackinlay Wy.
Rockland, MA 02370
Phone: (781)871-0724
Format: Educational. **Founded:** 1974. **Operating Hours:** Continuous. **Key Personnel:** David Cable-Murphy, Gen. Mgr. **Wattage:** 100. **Ad Rates:** Noncommercial. **URL:** http://wrps883rockland.wordpress.com.

ROYALSTON

16908 ■ Pioneer
Raivaaja Publishing Co.
PO Box 88
Royalston, MA 01368-0088
Phone: (978)343-3822
Publication E-mail: editor@raivaaja.org
Newspaper serving the Finnish-American community (Finnish and English). **Founded:** 1905. **Freq:** Weekly (Wed.). **Print Method:** Offset. **Cols./Page:** 5. **Col. Width:** 11 picas. **Col. Depth:** 88 picas. **ISSN:** 1059-4779 (print). **Subscription Rates:** $33 Individuals U.S.; $38 Other countries. **URL:** http://www.raivaaja.org. **Also known as:** Raivaaja. **Ad Rates:** GLR $.70; BW $500; PCI $4.50. **Remarks:** Accepts advertising. **Circ:** ‡2000.

RUSSELL

16909 ■ Russell Municipal Cable TV
65 Main St.
Russell, MA 01071
Phone: (413)862-6204
Email: information@russellma.net
Owner: Town of Russell, Massachusetts, at above address. **Founded:** 1987. **Cities Served:** subscribing households 470.

RUTLAND

16910 ■ Military Collector and Historian
Company of Military Historians
PO Box 910
Rutland, MA 01543-0910
Phone: (508)799-9229
Publisher's E-mail: cmhhq@aol.com
Freq: Quarterly. **Subscription Rates:** Included in membership. **URL:** http://www.military-historians.org/publications/journal/journal.htm. **Remarks:** Advertising not accepted. **Circ:** (Not Reported).

SALEM

Essex Co. On the Atlantic Ocean, 16 mi. NE of Boston. State College. One of the oldest cities in the state. Manufactures incandescent bulbs, fluorescent tubes and fixtures, games, confectionery, leather shoes, steam valves, chemicals, leather novelties, mattresses. Lobster fisheries.

16911 ■ The Jewish Journal/North of Boston: Serving the Communities North of Boston
North Shore Jewish Press
27 Congress St., Ste. 501
Salem, MA 01970
Phone: (978)745-4111
Fax: (978)745-5333
Publication E-mail: editorial@jewishjournal.org
Jewish newspaper. **Freq:** Biweekly. **Print Method:** Offset. **Trim Size:** 11 x 17. **Cols./Page:** 5. **Col. Width:** 1 3/4 inches. **Col. Depth:** 16 inches. **Key Personnel:** Barbara Schneider, Publisher; Susan Jacobs, Editor; Chester Baker, Business Manager. **ISSN:** 1040--0095 (print). **Subscription Rates:** Free. **URL:** http://boston.forward.com. **Ad Rates:** BW $1276; PCI $20.85. **Remarks:** Accepts advertising. **Circ:** 13000, 13500.

16912 ■ Quick Fiction: Precious Little Fiction in 500 Words (Or Less)
Quick Fiction
PO Box 4445
Salem, MA 01970
Literary journal that publishes narrative stories and prose less than 500 words. **Freq:** Semiannual. **Key Personnel:** Jennifer Pieroni, Editor-in-Chief; Adam Pieroni, Publisher. **URL:** http://www.quickfiction.org. **Remarks:** Accepts advertising. **Circ:** (Not Reported).

16913 ■ The Salem News
Eagle-Tribune Publishing Co.
32 Dunham Rd.
Beverly, MA 01915
Phone: (978)922-1234
Fax: (978)927-4524
Publisher's E-mail: direland@eagletribune.com
General newspaper. **Founded:** 1880. **Freq:** Mon.-Sat. (eve.). **Print Method:** Offset. **Trim Size:** 13 13/16 x 22 1/2. **Cols./Page:** 6. **Col. Width:** 2 1/32 inches. **Col. Depth:** 21 inches. **Key Personnel:** Helen Gifford, Managing Editor, phone: (978)338-2508; Karen Andreas, Publisher, phone: (978)338-2671; David Olson, Editor, phone: (978)338-2531. **Subscription Rates:** $17.99 Individuals Total access per month.; $14.99 Individuals Digital. **URL:** http://www.salemnews.com. **Formerly:** Salem Evening News; Beverly Times; Peabody Times. **Ad Rates:** GLR $6.54; BW $205; SAU $26.56; PCI $23.25. **Remarks:** Accepts advertising. **Circ:** Mon.-Fri. ‡27825.

16914 ■ The Salem State Log
Salem State University
352 Lafayette St.
Salem, MA 01970
Phone: (978)542-6000
Collegiate newspaper. **Freq:** Semimonthly. **Print Method:** Offset. **Cols./Page:** 5. **Col. Width:** 22 nonpareils. **Col. Depth:** 224 agate lines. **Key Personnel:** Dr. Nancy D. Harrington, President; Dr. Peggy Dil-

lon, Contact. **URL:** http://salemstatelog.org; http://www.salemstate.edu/log. **Ad Rates:** GLR $.36; BW $360; PCI $7. **Remarks:** Accepts advertising. **Circ:** Free ‡4000.

16915 ■ WMWM-FM - 91.7
352 Lafayette St.
Salem, MA 01970-5353
Phone: (978)542-8500
Email: wmwmsalem@gmail.com
Format: Alternative/New Music/Progressive. **Networks:** Independent. **Owner:** Salem State College Board of Trustees, 352 Lafayette St., Salem, MA 01970, Ph: (978)542-6000. **Founded:** 1968. **Operating Hours:** 7 a.m.-12 a.m. **Local Programs:** *The Juke Joint*, Sunday 12:00 p.m. - 3:00 p.m.; *MoodSwings*, Sunday 6:00 p.m. - 9:00 p.m.; *The Alternative Ulster*, Tuesday; *Uncle Henry's Basement*, Saturday 6:00 p.m. - 9:00 p.m. **Wattage:** 130. **Ad Rates:** Noncommercial. **URL:** http://www.wmwmsalem.com/.

SANDWICH

NW MA. Barnstable Co. S. of Cape Cod. Glass manufacturing. Cape Cod's oldest settlement.

16916 ■ Sandwich Broadsider
Community Newspaper
923 G, Rte. 6A
Yarmouth Port, MA 02675
Phone: (508)375-4947
Fax: (508)375-4903
Community newspaper. **Freq:** Weekly (Thurs.). **Print Method:** Offset. **Trim Size:** 11 x 16 1/2. **Cols./Page:** 5. **Col. Width:** 21 inches. **Col. Depth:** 224 agate lines. **Key Personnel:** John Basile, Managing Editor, phone: (508)375-4945; Mark Olivieri, Publisher. **USPS:** 387-010. **Subscription Rates:** $24 Individuals. **URL:** http://sandwich.wickedlocal.com. **Formerly:** Village Broadsider. **Ad Rates:** GLR $48; BW $532; 4C $1,132; PCI $6.65. **Remarks:** Accepts advertising. **Circ:** (Not Reported).

SEEKONK

16917 ■ WRIB-AM - 1220
95 Sagamore Rd.
Seekonk, MA 02771
Phone: (508)336-4110
Format: Ethnic; Religious. **Networks:** Independent. **Owner:** Carter Broadcasting Corp., 50 Braintree Hill Pk., Ste. 308, Braintree, MA 02184, Ph: (617)423-0210. **Founded:** 1946. **Operating Hours:** 6 a.m.-10 p.m. **Key Personnel:** John Pierce, Gen. Mgr. **Wattage:** 1,000. **URL:** http://www.wstl.us.

SHARON

E. MA. Norfolk Co. 17 mi. SW of Boston. Residential. Manufactures electronics, steel dies. Stamping mills. Resort.

16918 ■ Sharon Advocate
GateHouse Media Inc.
254 Second Ave.
Sharon, MA 02067
Publication E-mail: sharon@wickedlocal.com
Community newspaper. **Freq:** Weekly (Thurs.). **Print Method:** Offset. **Trim Size:** 14 3/16 x 21 5/16. **Cols./Page:** 6. **Col. Width:** 2 1/16 inches. **Col. Depth:** 21 1/2 inches. **Key Personnel:** Phil Salisbury, Editor, phone: (781)433-8364; Chuck Goodrich, Publisher, phone: (781)433-8345; Tom Fargo, Editor, phone: (781)433-8372. **USPS:** 491-900. **URL:** http://sharon.wickedlocal.com. **Ad Rates:** GLR $7.75; BW $892.50; PCI $6.50. **Remarks:** Accepts advertising. **Circ:** (Not Reported).

16919 ■ TDM Review
Association for Commuter Transportation
1 Chestnut Sq., 2nd Fl.
Sharon, MA 02067
Phone: (202)792-8501
Publisher's E-mail: info@actweb.org
Magazine containing topics regarding Transportation Demand Management. **Freq:** Quarterly. **Subscription Rates:** Included in membership. **Alt. Formats:** PDF. **URL:** http://actweb.org/news-publications/tdm-review/. **Remarks:** Accepts advertising. **Circ:** (Not Reported).

SHEFFIELD

SW MA. Berkshire Co. 24 mi. S. of Pittsfield. Resort.

16920 ■ WBSL-FM - 91.7
245 N Undermountian Rd.
Sheffield, MA 01257
Phone: (413)229-8511
Fax: (413)229-1028
Format: Educational; Public Radio. **Owner:** Berkshire Schools, 14259 Claridon Troy Rd., Burton, OH 44021, Ph: (440)834-3380. **Founded:** 1972. **Operating Hours:** 6:45-8:00 a.m. Mon-Fri; 7:00-11:00 p.m. Sun. **Key Personnel:** James Harris, Dir. of Comm. **Wattage:** 250. **Ad Rates:** Noncommercial. **URL:** http://www.berkshireschool.org.

SHELBURNE FALLS

NW MA. Franklin Co. 8 mi. NW of Greenfield. Residential. Agriculture.

16921 ■ Charlemont TV
56 Bridge St.
Shelburne Falls, MA 01370
Phone: (413)625-6040
Key Personnel: John Peffer, Contact, john@charlemonttv.com; Terri Peffer, Contact, terri@charlemonttv.com. **Cities Served:** Charlemont, Massachusetts; Readsboro, Vermont. **URL:** http://www.charlemonttv.com/directions.html.

SHREWSBURY

NC MA. Worcester Co. 10 mi. S. of Boylston.

16922 ■ Shrewsbury Electric and Cable Operations
100 Maple Ave.
Shrewsbury, MA 01545
Phone: (508)841-8500
Owner: SELCO. **Founded:** 1983. **Formerly:** Shrewsbury Electric Light Plant. **Key Personnel:** Tom Josie, Gen. Mgr., tjosie@ci.shrewsbury.ma.us; John Terrasi, Contact, jterrasi@ci.shrewsbury.ma.us; Jeffrey Black, Contact, jblack@ci.shrewsbury.ma.us. **Cities Served:** subscribing households 11,508. **URL:** http://www.selco.shrewsburyma.gov.

SOMERSET

SE MA. Bristol Co. On Taunton River, 6 mi. N. of Fall River. (Branch of Fall River P.O.) Residential.

16923 ■ WSAR-AM - 1480
One Home St.
Somerset, MA 02725
Phone: (508)678-9727
Fax: (508)673-0310
Format: Talk; News; Sports. **Networks:** ABC. **Founded:** Apr. 1921. **Operating Hours:** Continuous; 25% network, 75% local. **Key Personnel:** Robert Melfi, Mgr., Promotions Dir., Sales Mgr.; Mary Murphy, Office Mgr., mary@wsar.com. **Local Programs:** *Underreported*, Friday 10:00 a.m.; *The WSAR Newsroom*, Monday Tuesday Wednesday Thursday Friday 12:00 p.m. - 1:00 p.m.; *Law Talk*, Tuesday 1:00 p.m. - 2:00 p.m.; *Tony From the Right*, Saturday 11:00 a.m. - 1:00 p.m.; *The Bristol County Breakfast Club*, Monday Tuesday Wednesday Thursday Friday 5:00 a.m. - 9:00 a.m. **Wattage:** 5,000. **Ad Rates:** $20-40 for 60 seconds. Combined advertising rates available with WHTB-AM. **URL:** http://www.wsar.com.

SOMERVILLE

NE MA. Middlesex Co. Suburb of Boston on the Mystic River. (Branch of Boston P.O.) Manufactures paper products, caskets, industrial oil and tanning materials, vinegar, ladders and woodenware, spraying equipment, furniture, metal stamps, tools and dies, novelties, ornamental iron, suitcases and bags, wagon and truck bodies, piano tuners' supplies, textiles, brooms, food processing and packaging.

16924 ■ Communications in Information and Systems
International Press of Boston Inc.
387 Somerville Ave.
Somerville, MA 02143
Phone: (617)623-3016
Fax: (617)623-3101
Publisher's E-mail: ipb-orders@intlpress.com
Journal dealing with communications in information and systems. **Freq:** Quarterly. **Key Personnel:** Stephen S.T. Yau, Editor-in-Chief; Wing-Shing Wong, Editor-in-Chief. **ISSN:** 1526--7555 (print); **EISSN:** 2163--4548 (electronic). **URL:** http://intlpress.com/site/pub/pages/journals/items/cis/_home/_main. **Mailing address:** PO Box 502, Somerville, MA 02143-2950. **Circ:** (Not Reported).

16925 ■ The Concord Review
National History Club
PO Box 441812
Somerville, MA 02144
Phone: (781)248-7921
Journal featuring the academic research work of secondary students. **Freq:** Quarterly. **Key Personnel:** Will Fitzhugh, Founder, President. **Subscription Rates:** Included in membership. **Alt. Formats:** E-book. **URL:** http://www.tcr.org. **Circ:** (Not Reported).

16926 ■ Homology, Homotopy and Applications
International Press
387 Somerville Ave.
Somerville, MA 02143
Phone: (617)623-3016
Fax: (617)623-3101
Publisher's E-mail: ipb-info@intlpress.com
Peer-reviewed journal devoted to homology and homotopy in algebra and topology and their applications to field of mathematics. **Freq:** Semiannual. **Key Personnel:** Gunnar Carlsson, Editor-in-Chief; J. Daniel Christensen, Managing Editor. **ISSN:** 1532--0073 (print); **EISSN:** 1532--0081 (electronic). **URL:** http://intlpress.com/site/pub/pages/journals/items/hha/_home/_main/index.html. **Mailing address:** PO Box 43502, Somerville, MA 02143. **Remarks:** Accepts advertising. **Circ:** (Not Reported).

16927 ■ Journal of Symplectic Geometry
International Press
387 Somerville Ave.
Somerville, MA 02143
Phone: (617)623-3016
Fax: (617)623-3101
Publisher's E-mail: ipb-info@intlpress.com
Journal that focuses on the impact of symplectic geometry in mathematics. **Freq:** Quarterly March, June, September, and December. **Key Personnel:** Simon Donaldson, Managing Editor; Victor Guillemin, Managing Editor; Tomasz Mrowka, Managing Editor. **ISSN:** 1527--5256 (print); **EISSN:** 1540--2347 (electronic). **Subscription Rates:** $567 Individuals print + online; $616 Other countries; $332 Individuals online. **URL:** http://intlpress.com/site/pub/pages/journals/items/jsg/_home/_main. **Mailing address:** PO Box 43502, Somerville, MA 02143. **Circ:** (Not Reported).

16928 ■ Malden Observer
GateHouse Media Inc.
20-40 Holland St., Ste. 404
Somerville, MA 02144
Phone: (781)393-1827
Fax: (781)393-1821
Publication E-mail: malden@wickedlocal.com
Community newspaper (tabloid). **Founded:** 1988. **Freq:** Weekly (Fri.). **Print Method:** Offset. **Cols./Page:** 6. **Col. Width:** 2 1/16 inches. **Col. Depth:** 21 inches. **Key Personnel:** Chris Hurley, Editor; Natalie Miller, Editor, phone: (781)393-1827; Marlene Switzer, Editor-in-Chief. **USPS:** 001-093. **Subscription Rates:** $45 Individuals; $85 Out of area. **URL:** http://malden.wickedlocal.com. **Formerly:** Prime Times. **Ad Rates:** BW $1,352; 4C $1,852; SAU $16.90; PCI $16.90. **Remarks:** Accepts classified advertising. **Circ:** (Not Reported).

16929 ■ Methods and Applications of Analysis
International Press of Boston Inc.
387 Somerville Ave.
Somerville, MA 02143
Phone: (617)623-3016
Fax: (617)623-3101
Publisher's E-mail: ipb-orders@intlpress.com
Academic journal covering research in applied mathematics with applications to the sciences. **Freq:** Quarterly. **Key Personnel:** Russel Caflisch, Editor; Didier Bresch, Editor; Xin Zhou-Ping, Editor-in-Chief; Yau Shing-Tung, Editor-in-Chief; Peter Lax, Editor. **ISSN:** 1073--2772 (print); **EISSN:** 1945--0001 (electronic). **Subscription Rates:** $543 Institutions print only; $571 Institutions, other countries print only; $485 Institutions

Circulation: ★ = AAM; △ or • = BPA; ♦ = CAC; ❑ = VAC; ⊕ = PO Statement; ‡ = Publisher's Report; Boldface figures = sworn; Light figures = estimated.

online only. **URL:** http://intlpress.com/site/pub/pages/journals/items/maa/_home/_main. **Mailing address:** PO Box 502, Somerville, MA 02143-2950. **Ad Rates:** GLR $50; BW $250; 4C $500. **Remarks:** Accepts advertising. **Circ:** Combined 100.

16930 ■ Socialist Standard: Journal of the Socialist Party of Great Britain
World Socialist Party of the United States
PO Box 440247
Somerville, MA 02144
Publisher's E-mail: joinwspus@wspus.org
Freq: Monthly. **Subscription Rates:** $16.50 /year for individuals; $30 /year for institutions. **URL:** http://wspus.org/2011/02/socialist-standard-211. **Remarks:** Advertising not accepted. **Circ:** (Not Reported).

16931 ■ Somerville Journal
GateHouse Media Inc.
80 Central St.
Somerville, MA 02143
Publication E-mail: somerville@wickedlocal.com
Community newspaper. **Freq:** Weekly (Thurs.). **Print Method:** Offset. **Cols./Page:** 6. **Col. Width:** 26 nonpareils. **Col. Depth:** 294 agate lines. **Key Personnel:** Dan Atkinson, Editor, phone: (617)629-3385; Chuck Goodrich, Publisher. **URL:** http://somerville.wickedlocal.com. **Ad Rates:** GLR $3.75; BW $2,431.80; SAU $19.30; PCI $19.30. **Remarks:** Accepts advertising. **Circ:** (Not Reported).

16932 ■ The Somerville News
The Somerville News
699 Broadway
Somerville, MA 02144
Phone: (617)666-4010
Fax: (617)628-0422
Publisher's E-mail: news@thesomervilletimes.com
Community newspaper. **Freq:** Weekly (Wed.). **Print Method:** Letterpress. **Trim Size:** 10 x 16. **Cols./Page:** 5. **Col. Width:** 22 nonpareils. **Col. Depth:** 220 agate lines. **Key Personnel:** George P. Hassett, Editor; Bobbie Toner, Director, Advertising, phone: (617)666-4010. **Alt. Formats:** PDF. **Ad Rates:** BW $1,320; SAU $10.95; PCI $15.07. **Remarks:** Accepts advertising. **Circ:** Combined ‡14000.

16933 ■ Watertown TAB & Press
GateHouse Media Inc.
80 Central St.
Somerville, MA 02143
Publication E-mail: watertown@wickedlocal.com
Community newspaper. **Freq:** Weekly (Fri.). **Print Method:** Offset. **Cols./Page:** 6. **Col. Width:** 26 nonpareils. **Col. Depth:** 294 agate lines. **Key Personnel:** Chuck Goodrich, Publisher; Dana Forsythe, Editor, phone: (781)433-8331. **URL:** http://watertown.wickedlocal.com. **Ad Rates:** GLR $3.75; BW $1,688.40; SAU $13.40; PCI $13.40. **Remarks:** Accepts advertising. **Circ:** (Not Reported).

SOUTH DENNIS

16934 ■ Best Read Guide Cape Cod
Best Read Guide-Cape Cod
900 Rte. 134
South Dennis, MA 02660
Phone: (508)385-0003
Fax: (508)385-2777
Magazine offering tourism information on the city of Cape Cod, Massachusetts including attractions, lodging, dining, etc. **Freq:** 6/yr. **Trim Size:** 5 1/4 x 7 1/2. **Key Personnel:** Pat Brooks, Manager, Sales, phone: (508)432-1567. **URL:** http://bestreadguidecapecod.com. **Ad Rates:** BW $3,196; 4C $3,396. **Remarks:** Accepts advertising. **Circ:** (Not Reported).

SOUTH EASTON

16935 ■ WXRB-FM - 95.1
501 Washington St., Apt. 2A
South Easton, MA 02375
Phone: (508)213-2138
Email: wxrbfm@yahoo.com
Format: Oldies. **Networks:** CBS. **Owner:** WXRB/FM Educational Broadcasting Inc., at above address. **Operating Hours:** Continuous. **Key Personnel:** Peter Q. George, Gen. Mgr. **Wattage:** 014 ERP H. **Ad Rates:** Accepts Advertising. **URL:** http://www.wxrbfm.com.

SOUTH HADLEY

WC MA. Hampshire Co. 4 mi. N. of Holyoke. Mount Holyoke College (women). Residential.

16936 ■ The Holyoke Sun
Turley Publications
138 College St., Ste. B
South Hadley, MA 01075
Phone: (413)612-2310
Fax: (413)592-3568
Publisher's E-mail: support@turley.com
Community newspaper serving Greater Holyoke. **Freq:** Weekly (Fri.). **Key Personnel:** Kristin Will, Editor; Tim Kane, Executive Editor. **URL:** http://holyokesunonline.com. **Remarks:** Accepts advertising. **Circ:** 7000.

16937 ■ Town Reminder
Turley Publications
138 College St., Ste. B
South Hadley, MA 01075
Phone: (413)536-5333
Fax: (413)536-5334
Publication E-mail: townreminder@turley.com
Community newspaper serving South Hadley, Granby, Chicopee, Holyoke, and Ludlow. **Freq:** Weekly (Fri.). **Key Personnel:** Kristin Will, Associate Editor; Tim Kane, Executive Editor. **URL:** http://townreminderonline.com. **Remarks:** Accepts advertising. **Circ:** 11800.

16938 ■ WMHC-FM - 91.5
Blanchard Student Ctr.
South Hadley, MA 01075
Phone: (413)538-2019
Fax: (413)538-2431
Email: info@massbroadcasters.org
Format: Educational. **Owner:** Mount Holyoke College, 50 College St., South Hadley, MA 01075, Ph: (413)538-2000, Fax: (413)538-2391, Free: 800-642-4483. **Founded:** 1940. **Operating Hours:** midnight. **Ad Rates:** Noncommercial. **URL:** http://www.massbroadcasters.org.

SOUTH HAMILTON

16939 ■ WNSH-AM - 1570
PO Box 2443
South Hamilton, MA 01982
Phone: (508)954-1282
Fax: (978)468-1954
Email: kwillcox@wnsh.com
Format: Full Service; Ethnic; Adult Contemporary; Top 40; Oldies; Middle-of-the-Road (MOR). **Networks:** Independent. **Owner:** Willow Farm Inc., at above address. **Founded:** 1967. **Formerly:** WMLO-AM. **Operating Hours:** Continuous. **Key Personnel:** Keating Willcox, Gen. Mgr. **Wattage:** 50,000. **Ad Rates:** $179 for 30 seconds; $360 for 60 seconds.

SOUTHBOROUGH

S. MA. Worcester Co. 4 mi. SE of Marlborough. Residential.

16940 ■ Southborough Villager
GateHouse Media Inc.
40 Mechanic St.
Marlborough, MA 01752
Fax: (508)490-7471
Publication E-mail: northboro-southboro@wickedlocal.com
Community newspaper. **Freq:** Weekly (Fri.). **Print Method:** Offset. **Cols./Page:** 6. **Col. Width:** 12 picas. **Col. Depth:** 21 inches. **Key Personnel:** Glenda Hazard, Editor, phone: (508)490-7454; Richard Lodge, Editor-in-Chief, phone: (508)626-3871. **USPS:** 528-250. **URL:** http://southborough.wickedlocal.com. **Ad Rates:** PCI $5. **Remarks:** Accepts advertising. **Circ:** (Not Reported).

SOUTHBRIDGE

C. MA. Worcester Co. 21 mi. S. of Worcester. Manufactures optical goods, cutlery, worsteds. Dairy farms.

16941 ■ Blackstone Valley Tribune
Stonebridge Press and Villager Newspapers
25 Elm St.
Southbridge, MA 01550
Phone: (508)764-4325
Fax: (508)764-8102
Free: 800-367-9898
Community newspaper. **Freq:** Semiweekly (Wed. and Fri.). **Print Method:** Offset. **Cols./Page:** 6. **Col. Width:** 19 nonpareils. **Col. Depth:** 189 agate lines. **Key Personnel:** Frank G. Chilinski, Publisher; Adam Minor, Editor. **Alt. Formats:** PDF. **URL:** http://www.blackstonevalleytribune.com/118975.113119body.lasso?publication=BLA. **Mailing address:** PO Box 90, Southbridge, MA 01550. **Ad Rates:** GLR $8; BW $1175; 4C $1975; PCI $10.50. **Circ:** Wed. ‡5300, Fri. ‡12996.

16942 ■ The Southbridge Evening News
Stonebridge Press and Villager Newspapers
25 Elm St.
Southbridge, MA 01550
Phone: (508)764-4325
Fax: (508)764-8102
Free: 800-367-9898
Publication E-mail: fchilinski@stonebridgepress.com
General newspaper. **Founded:** 1923. **Freq:** Daily. **Print Method:** Offset. **Cols./Page:** 6. **Col. Width:** 1 1/2 inches. **Col. Depth:** 16 inches. **Key Personnel:** Frank G. Chilinski, President, Publisher; Julie Clarke, Manager, Production; Walter Bird, Jr., Editor, phone: (508)909-4107, fax: (508)764-8015. **USPS:** 504-380. **Subscription Rates:** $48 Individuals web access.; $60 Individuals print and web access; Home delivery of the newspaper in the towns of Southbridge, Sturbridge, Charlton, Brimfield, Holland, Fiskdale and Wales.; $120 Individuals print and web access; Mail delivery of the newspaper in all other Worcester County towns.; $197.50 Individuals print and web access; Mail delivery of the newspaper to out of Worcester County locations. **URL:** http://www.southbridgeeveningnews.com; http://www.southbridgeeveningnews.com/118975.113119body.lasso?publication=SOU. **Formerly:** The News. **Mailing address:** PO Box 90, Southbridge, MA 01550. **Ad Rates:** GLR $10; BW $1,099; PCI $9. **Remarks:** Accepts advertising. **Circ:** Paid ‡5400.

16943 ■ The Winchendon Courier
Stonebridge Press and Villager Newspapers
25 Elm St.
Southbridge, MA 01550
Phone: (508)764-4325
Fax: (508)764-8102
Free: 800-367-9898
Newspaper. **Freq:** Weekly (Wed.). **Print Method:** Offset. **Cols./Page:** 8. **Col. Depth:** 301 agate lines. **Key Personnel:** Ruth DeAmicis, Editor. **Subscription Rates:** $8 Individuals basic; $6 Individuals every week. **Alt. Formats:** PDF. **URL:** http://www.winchendoncourier.com; http://www.stonebridgepress.com/118975.113119body.lasso?publication=WIN. **Formerly:** Jaffrey-Rindge Chronicles. **Mailing address:** PO Box 90, Southbridge, MA 01550. **Ad Rates:** PCI $6. **Remarks:** Accepts classified advertising. **Circ:** (Not Reported).

16944 ■ WESO-AM - 970
100 Foster St.
Southbridge, MA 01550
Phone: (508)909-0970
Fax: (508)764-2682
Owner: Money Matters Radio Inc., at above address, Needham, MA 02494. **Founded:** 1955. **Wattage:** '1,000 Day 021 Night. **Ad Rates:** $13-22.05 for 30 seconds; $16.25-27.50 for 60 seconds.

SPRINGFIELD

SW MA. Hampden Co. On Connecticut River, 98 mi. SW of Boston. American International College; Springfield College; Western New England College; Springfield Technical Community College. Manufactures electrical machinery and equipment, computer components, games toys, school supplies, fibre products, matches, drop forgings, proprietary medicine, machine tools, firearms, packaging machinery, stationery, chains, textiles, saws, plastics, chemicals and allied products, leather goods, wire, castings and patterns, brass and brass goods, tools.

16945 ■ Issues in Accounting Education
American Accounting Association
c/o Lori Holder-Webb, Ed.
Western New England University
Department of Accounting and Finance
1215 Wilbraham Rd.
Springfield, MA 01119
Phone: (413)782-1496
Fax: (413)796-2068

Publication E-mail: lholderwebb@wne.edu
Freq: Quarterly. **Trim Size:** 7 x 10. **Key Personnel:** Sandy Hilton, Associate Editor; Lori Holder-Webb, Editor; Beverly Jackling, Associate Editor. **ISSN:** 0739--3172 (print). **Subscription Rates:** $390 Individuals print only; $874 Individuals print package of three association wide journals. **URL:** http://aaahq.org/Research/AAA-Journals/Issues-in-Accounting-Education. **Remarks:** Advertising accepted; rates available upon request. **Circ:** 5500.

16946 ■ Pediatric Exercise Science
Human Kinetics Inc.
c/o Thomas W. Rowland, MD, Consulting Ed.
Baystate Medical Center
Springfield, MA 01199
Phone: (413)794-7350
Fax: (413)784-5995
Publisher's E-mail: info@hkusa.com
Journal stimulating better understanding and greater awareness of the importance of childhood exercise to scientists, health-care providers, and physical educators. **Freq:** Quarterly February, May, August, November. **Key Personnel:** Thomas W. Rowland, MD, Editor; Bareket Falk, Editor. **ISSN:** 0899-8493 (print); **EISSN:** 1543-2920 (electronic). **Subscription Rates:** $101 Individuals online and print; $609 Institutions online and print; $81 Students online and print; $81 Individuals online; $499 Institutions online; $61 Students online. **URL:** http://journals.humankinetics.com/PES. **Circ:** (Not Reported).

16947 ■ Yellow Jacket
American International College
1000 State St.
Springfield, MA 01109
Phone: (413)205-3201
Free: 800-242-3142
Publisher's E-mail: inquiry@aic.edu
Collegiate newspaper. **Founded:** 1934. **Freq:** Semimonthly (during the academic year). **Print Method:** Offset. **Trim Size:** 11 x 14. **Cols./Page:** 4. **Col. Width:** 24 nonpareils. **Col. Depth:** 185 agate lines. **URL:** http://aicyellowjacket.com. **Ad Rates:** BW $200; PCI $20. **Remarks:** Accepts advertising. **Circ:** 800.

16948 ■ ABC-40-TV - 40
1300 Liberty St.
Springfield, MA 01104
Phone: (413)733-4040
Fax: (413)788-7640
Format: Commercial TV. **Networks:** ABC. **Founded:** 1953. **Formerly**: WGGB-TV. **Operating Hours**: Continuous. **ADI**: Springfield, MA. **Key Personnel:** John Gormally, Owner, President; David Baer, News Dir., dbaer@wggb.com. **Ad Rates:** $50-1500 per unit. **URL:** http://www.wggb.com.

16949 ■ Comcast Cable
3303 Main St.
Springfield, MA 01107
Free: 800-266-2278
Email: we_can_help@comcast.com
Owner: Continental Cablevision Inc., The Pilot House, Lewis Wharf, Boston, MA 02110, Ph: (617)742-9500. **Founded:** 1963. **Formerly**: Continental Cablevision, Inc. of Springfield. **Key Personnel:** David A. Scott, CFO, Exec. VP; David N. Watson, Exec. VP; Neil Smith, President. **Cities Served:** Hampden County. **URL:** http://www.comcast.com.

16950 ■ WACE-AM - 730
PO Box 1
Springfield, MA 01101
Phone: (413)594-6654
Email: wace@waceradio.com
Format: Religious; Talk. **Networks:** Independent. **Owner:** Carter Broadcasting Corp., 50 Braintree Hill Pk., Ste. 308, Braintree, MA 02184, Ph: (617)423-0210. **Founded:** 1946. **Operating Hours**: Continuous. **Local Programs**: *Miracle Revival Hour*, Monday Tuesday Wednesday Thursday Friday 6:15 a.m. - 6:30 a.m.; 9:45 a.m. - 10:00 a.m.; *Songtime USA*, Monday Tuesday Wednesday Thursday Friday 7:00 a.m. - 8:00 a.m.; 3:00 p.m. - 4:00 p.m.; *Breakthrough Ministries*, Monday Tuesday Wednesday Thursday Friday 8:30 a.m. - 8:45 a.m.; *Information Radio Network*, Monday Tuesday Wednesday Thursday Friday Saturday Sunday 5:00 p.m. 4:00 p.m.; *Fullness Of Truth*, Thursday Sunday 12:00 p.m. 8:30 a.m.; *Faith and Inspiration*, Saturday 8:00 a.m. - 8:30 a.m.; *Outreach Broadcast*, Saturday 10:00 a.m. - 10:30 a.m.; *Jesus Is Our Shepherd*, Saturday Monday 9:00 a.m. - 9:30 a.m. 12:00 p.m.; *Irish Hours*, Saturday 11:00 a.m. - 1:00 p.m. **Wattage**: 5,000. **Ad Rates:** Advertising accepted; rates available upon request. **URL:** http://www.waceradio.com.

16951 ■ WACM-AM - 1490
230 Park Ave.
New York, NY 10169
Phone: (646)435-5781
Format: Hispanic. **Networks:** Spanish Broadcasting System. **Owner:** Davidson Media Group, at above address. **Founded:** 1949. **Operating Hours**: Continuous. **Key Personnel:** Felix Perez, President, fperez@davidsonmediagroup.com. **Wattage**: 470. **Ad Rates:** Noncommercial.

16952 ■ WAIC-FM - 91.9
1000 State St.
Springfield, MA 01109
Free: 800-242-3142
Email: inquiry@aic.edu
Format: Educational; Contemporary Hit Radio (CHR). **Networks:** Independent. **Owner:** American International College. **Founded:** 1950. **Operating Hours**: 6 a.m.-midnight; 100% local. **ADI**: Springfield, MA. **Wattage**: 440. **Ad Rates:** Noncommercial. **URL:** http://www.aic.edu.

16953 ■ WDMR-TV - 65
PO Box 2631
Springfield, MA 01101-2631
Email: channel13@home.com
Networks: Telemundo. **Owner:** Channel 13 Televisions, Inc., 886 Maple Ave., Hartford, CT 06114, Ph: (860)956-1303, Fax: (860)956-1303, Free: 860-956-6834. **Founded:** June 13, 1990. **Formerly**: WBX-TV. **ADI**: Springfield, MA. **Key Personnel:** William Newton, Gen. Mgr; Lucio C. Ruzzier, Contact. **Wattage**: 15,000 ERP. **Ad Rates:** Advertising accepted; rates available upon request.

16954 ■ WGBB-TV - 40
1300 Liberty St.
Springfield, MA 01104
Phone: (413)733-4040
Fax: (413)788-7640
Email: newstips@wggb.com
Key Personnel: John Gormally, Owner. **URL:** http://www.wggb.com.

16955 ■ WGBY-TV - 57
44 Hampden St.
Springfield, MA 01103
Free: 800-781-9429
Email: feedback@wgby.org
Format: Public TV. **Networks:** Public Broadcasting Service (PBS). **Owner:** WGBH Educational Foundation, One Guest St., Boston, MA 02135, Ph: (617)300-5400, Fax: (617)300-1026. **Founded:** 1971. **Operating Hours**: Continuous. **ADI**: Springfield, MA. **Key Personnel:** Rusell J. Peotter, Gen. Mgr; Charley Rose, Contact. **Wattage**: 50,000 H. **Ad Rates:** Noncommercial. **URL:** http://www.wgby.org.

16956 ■ WHYN-AM - 560
1331 Main St., 4th Fl.
Springfield, MA 01103
Phone: (413)781-1011
Format: News; Talk. **Owner:** iHeartMedia Inc., 200 E Basse Rd., San Antonio, TX 78209, Ph: (210)832-3314. **Operating Hours**: Continuous. **ADI**: Springfield, MA. **Wattage**: 5,000 ERP. **Ad Rates:** Noncommercial. **URL:** http://www.whyn.com.

16957 ■ WHYN-FM - 93.1
1331 Main St., 4th Fl.
Springfield, MA 01103
Phone: (413)781-1011
Fax: (413)734-4434
Free: 888-293-9310
Email: advertising@mix931.com
Format: Adult Contemporary. **Simulcasts:** WHYN-AM 560. **Owner:** iHeartMedia Inc., 200 E Basse Rd., San Antonio, TX 78209, Ph: (210)832-3314. **Key Personnel:** Sean Davey, Contact, seandavey@clearchannel.com; Sean Davey, Contact, seandavey@clearchannel.com. **Wattage**: 8,600. **Ad Rates:** Advertising accepted; rates available upon request. **URL:** http://www.mix931.com.

16958 ■ WMAS-AM - 1450
1000 Hall of Fame Ave.
Springfield, MA 01105
Phone: (413)737-1414
Fax: (413)737-1488
Free: 800-937-9627
Email: events@947wmas.com
Format: Oldies. **Networks:** Mutual Broadcasting System; ABC. **Founded:** 1932. **Operating Hours**: Continuous; 5% network, 95% local. **ADI**: Springfield, MA. **Key Personnel:** Craig Swimm, Gen. Mgr. **Wattage**: 1,000. **Ad Rates:** Noncommercial. **URL:** http://www.947wmas.com.

16959 ■ WMAS-FM - 94.7
1000 Hall of Fame Ave.
Springfield, MA 01105
Phone: (413)737-1414
Fax: (413)737-1488
Free: 800-YES-WMAS
Format: Adult Contemporary. **Networks:** Independent. **Owner:** Citadel Communications Corp., San Diego, CA, Ph: (505)767-6700, Fax: (505)767-6767. **Founded:** 1947. **Operating Hours**: Continuous; 5% network, 95% local. **ADI**: Springfield, MA. **Key Personnel:** Craig Swimm, Contact; Craig Swimm, Contact. **Wattage**: 50,000. **Ad Rates:** Advertising accepted; rates available upon request. **URL:** http://www.947wmas.com.

16960 ■ WNEK-FM
1215 Wibraham Rd.
Springfield, MA 01119
Phone: (413)782-1582
Owner: Western New England College. **Founded:** 1970. **Formerly**: WTRZ-FM. **ADI**: Springfield, MA. **Ad Rates:** Noncommercial.

16961 ■ WNNZ-AM - 640
1331 Main St.
Springfield, MA 01103
Phone: (413)781-1011
Fax: (413)734-4434
Format: Sports. **Networks:** Unistar; CBS; ABC. **Founded:** 1987. **Operating Hours**: Continuous; 100% local. **ADI**: Springfield, MA. **Key Personnel:** Sean Davey, Gen. Mgr. **Wattage**: 50,000. **Ad Rates:** $35-60 for 30 seconds; $35-60 for 60 seconds. **URL:** http://www.clearchannel.com.

16962 ■ WPKX-FM - 97.9
1331 Main St., 4th Fl.
Springfield, MA 01103
Phone: (413)736-9759
Free: 800-345-9759
Format: Country. **Operating Hours**: Continuous. **Ad Rates:** Advertising accepted; rates available upon request. **URL:** http://www.mykix1009.com.

16963 ■ WRNX-FM - 100.9
1331 Main St., 4th Fl.
Springfield, MA 01103
Phone: (413)536-1009
Format: Adult Album Alternative. **Networks:** AP. **Owner:** iHeartMedia Inc., 200 E Basse Rd., San Antonio, TX 78209, Ph: (210)832-3314. **Founded:** 1963. **Operating Hours**: 8:30 a.m.-5:00 p.m. **Key Personnel:** Glenn Cardinal, Gen. Mgr.; Donnie Moorhouse, Dir. of Programs; Tom Pluta, Gen. Sales Mgr.; Sean Davey, Dir. of Mktg., Mktg. Mgr. **Wattage**: 5,000. **Ad Rates:** $60 for 60 seconds; $12-19 per unit. **URL:** http://www.mykix1009.com.

16964 ■ WSCB-FM - 89.9
263 Alden St.
Springfield, MA 01109-3797
Phone: (413)748-3000
Format: Eclectic. **Owner:** Springfield College, 263 Alden St., Springfield, MA 01109-3797, Ph: (413)748-3000, Free: 800-343-1257. **Founded:** 1958. **Operating Hours**: Continuous. **ADI**: Springfield, MA. **Wattage**: 100. **Ad Rates:** Noncommercial.

16965 ■ WSHM-TV - 3
One Monarch Pl., Ste. 300
Springfield, MA 01144
Phone: (413)736-4333
Fax: (413)523-4934
Email: sales@cbs3springfield.com

Circulation: ★ = AAM; △ or • = BPA; ♦ = CAC; ❑ = VAC; ⊕ = PO Statement; ‡ = Publisher's Report; Boldface figures = sworn; Light figures = estimated.

Owner: Meredith Corp., 1716 Locust St., Des Moines, IA 50309-3038, Ph: (515)284-3000. **URL:** http://www.cbs3springfield.com.

16966 ■ WSPR-AM
PO Box 1270
Springfield, MA 01102
Phone: (413)732-4182
Fax: (413)733-7423
Free: 800-232-1270
Format: Talk. **Networks:** AP; ABC; Mutual Broadcasting System. **Owner:** DYCOM, Inc., at above address. **Founded:** 1936. **Key Personnel:** Daniel C. Yorke, Contact. **Wattage:** 1,000 Day. **Ad Rates:** $15-40 per unit.

16967 ■ WSPR-AM - 1270
230 Park Ave.
10 Fl., Office 106
New York, NY 10169
Phone: (646)435-5781
Format: World Beat. **Owner:** Davidson Media Group, at above address. **Operating Hours:** Continuous. **Key Personnel:** Sanjay Sanghoee, Owner, sanjay@davidsonmediagroup.com. **Wattage:** 5,000. **Ad Rates:** Advertising accepted; rates available upon request. **URL:** http://www.davidsonmediagroup.com/print.php?id=member_stations_19&id2=s.

16968 ■ WTCC-FM - 90.7
One Armory Sq.
Springfield, MA 01102-9000
Phone: (413)755-6822
Format: Educational. **Owner:** Springfield Technical Community College, 1 Armory Sq., Ste. 1, Springfield, MA 01102-9000, Ph: (413)755-6344, Fax: (413)755-6306. **Founded:** Aug. 19, 1971. **Operating Hours:** 12 a.m.-11 p.m. Mon.-Sun. **Key Personnel:** David P. Fontaine, President; Bret F. Coughlin, Contact; Maria P. Goncalves, Contact. **Wattage:** 4,000. **Ad Rates:** Noncommercial. **Mailing address:** PO Box 9000, Springfield, MA 01102-9000. **URL:** http://www.wtccfm.org.

STOCKBRIDGE

W. MA. Berkshire Co. 10 mi. S. of Pittsfield. Residential.

16969 ■ Marian Helper
Association of Marian Helpers
Marians of the Immaculate Conception
Eden Hill
Stockbridge, MA 01263
Phone: (413)298-3931
Free: 800-462-7426
Publisher's E-mail: eadm@marian.org
Freq: Quarterly. **Key Personnel:** David Came, Executive Editor. **Subscription Rates:** Free for North American association members; Included in membership. **Alt. Formats:** PDF. **URL:** http://secure.marianweb.net/marian.org/marianhelper/index.php?; http://www.marian.org/marianhelper/. **Formerly:** Marian Helpers Bulletin; Association of Marian Helpers Bulletin. **Remarks:** Advertising not accepted. **Circ:** Controlled 650000, 6000.

STONEHAM

NE MA. Middlesex Co. 9 mi. N. of Boston. (Branch of Boston P.O.) Manufactures electronics, shoes, chemicals, upholstered furniture, confectionery, window shades, golf balls.

16970 ■ The Stoneham Independent
Woburn Daily Times Inc.
200F Main St., Ste. 343
Stoneham, MA 02180
Phone: (781)438-1660
Fax: (781)438-6762
Publication E-mail: news@stonehamindependent.com
Community newspaper. **Freq:** Weekly (Wed.). **Print Method:** Offset. **Trim Size:** 11.6 x 21. **Key Personnel:** Al Turco, Editor; Mark Haggerty, General Manager; Joe Haggerty, Contact. **USPS:** 522-400. **URL:** http://homenewshere.com/stoneham_independent. **Ad Rates:** PCI $12.35. **Remarks:** Accepts advertising. **Circ:** Paid ‡3000.

STOUGHTON

E. MA. Norfolk Co. 19 mi. S. of Boston. Manufactures woolen knit goods, elastic webbing, shoes, rubber specialties, plastics, machine tools, raincoats.

16971 ■ Pythian International
The Order of Knights of Pythias
Supreme Lodge Knights of Pythias
458 Pearl St.
Stoughton, MA 02072-1655
Fax: (781)341-0496
Magazine containing information about the Knights of Pythias. **Freq:** Quarterly. **Key Personnel:** Bob Epstein, Editor-in-Chief. **URL:** http://pythias.org/index.php?option=com_content&view=article&id=65&Itemid=70. **Circ:** (Not Reported).

STOW

16972 ■ Association Meetings: The Independent Voice of the Association Industry
Information Data Products Group of Penton Media Inc.
c/o Regina McGee
132 Great Rd., Ste. 120
Stow, MA 01775-1189
Magazine for association meeting planners. **Freq:** Bimonthly. **Print Method:** Offset. Uses mats. **Trim Size:** 8 1/8 x 11. **Cols./Page:** 3. **Col. Width:** 27 nonpareils. **Col. Depth:** 140 agate lines. **Key Personnel:** Sue Pelletier, Editor, phone: (978)448-0377; Melissa Fromento, General Manager, phone: (212)204-4237; Betsy Bair, Director, Editorial, phone: (978)448-0582. **ISSN:** 8750--1686 (print). **Subscription Rates:** $65 Canada; $98 Other countries. **Ad Rates:** BW $6,750; 4C $9,825. **Remarks:** Accepts advertising. **Circ:** Paid ‡19300.

16973 ■ Corporate Meetings & Incentives: The Senior Executives Guide to Decision Making
Information Data Products Group of Penton Media Inc.
c/o Barbara Scofidio, Ed.
132 Great Rd., Ste. 120
Stow, MA 01775-1189
Magazine for executives and travel professionals responsible for choosing sites and destinations for meeting and incentive travel programs. **Freq:** Monthly. **Print Method:** Web offset. **Trim Size:** 8 1/8 x 10 7/8. **Cols./Page:** 3. **Col. Width:** 27 nonpareils. **Col. Depth:** 140 agate lines. **Key Personnel:** Barbara Scofidio, Editor, phone: (978)448-8211; Melissa Fromento, General Manager, phone: (212)204-4237; Betsy Bair, Director, Editorial, phone: (978)448-0582; David Kovaleski, Writer, phone: (617)782-0121. **ISSN:** 0745--1636 (print). **Subscription Rates:** $97 Canada; $123 Free to qualified subscribers in USA; $123 Other countries. **URL:** http://meetingsnet.com/corporate-meetings. **Ad Rates:** BW $7,375; 4C $9,825. **Remarks:** Accepts advertising. **Circ:** 36283.

STURBRIDGE

SW MA. Worcester Co. 18 mi. SW of Worcester. Industrial.

16974 ■ Old Sturbridge Village
Old Sturbridge Village
1 Old Sturbridge Village Rd.
Sturbridge, MA 01566
Phone: (508)347-3362
Fax: (508)347-0375
Free: 800-733-1830
Publisher's E-mail: info@osv.org
Magazine covering museum research, collections, and programs for museum members. **Freq:** 3/year. **Trim Size:** 8 1/2 x 11. **ISSN:** 0485--6724 (print). **URL:** http://www.osv.org/visitor-magazines-annual-reports. **Formerly:** Rural Visitor. **Remarks:** Accepts advertising. **Circ:** (Not Reported).

SUDBURY

NE MA. Middlesex Co. 16 mi. W. of Cambridge. Residential. Manufactures machinery equipment. Nurseries.

16975 ■ AHRA Radiology Management
AHRA: The Association for Medical Imaging Management
490B Boston Post Rd., Ste. 200
Sudbury, MA 01776
Phone: (978)443-7591
Free: 800-334-2472
Publisher's E-mail: memberservices@ahraonline.org
Journal publishing research and best practices on healthcare management issues specific to medical imaging. **Freq:** 6/year. **Subscription Rates:** $100 U.S.; $115 Canada; $135 Other countries; Included in membership. **URL:** http://www.ahraonline.org/radiologymanagement. **Remarks:** Accepts advertising. **Circ:** (Not Reported).

16976 ■ The Concord Review
The Concord Review Inc.
730 Boston Post Rd., Ste. 24
Sudbury, MA 01776
Phone: (978)443-0022
Free: 800-331-5007
Journal featuring the academic research work of secondary students. **Freq:** Quarterly. **Key Personnel:** Will Fitzhugh, Founder, President. **Subscription Rates:** Included in membership. **Alt. Formats:** E-book. **URL:** http://www.tcr.org. **Circ:** (Not Reported).

16977 ■ WYAJ-FM
Lincoln Sundbury Regional High School
390 Lincoln Rd.
Sudbury, MA 01776
Phone: (978)443-3531
Fax: (978)443-8824
Format: Full Service; Alternative/New Music/Progressive. **Networks:** Independent. **Owner:** Sudbury Valley Broadcasting Foundation, at above address. **Founded:** 1979. **Wattage:** 004 ERP. **URL:** http://www.lsrhs.net.

TEWKSBURY

NE MA. Middlesex Co. 5 mi. SE of Lowell. Manufactures printing inks, wood products. Nurseries.

16978 ■ Tewksbury Advocate
GateHouse Media Inc.
150 Baker Ave., Ste. 101
Tewksbury, MA 01876
Community newspaper. **Founded:** 1957. **Freq:** Weekly (Thurs.). **Print Method:** Offset. **Cols./Page:** 6. **Col. Width:** 21 nonpareils. **Col. Depth:** 294 agate lines. **Key Personnel:** Chuck Goodrich, Publisher; Mac McEntire, Editor, phone: (978)371-5744; Michael Liuzza, Editor, phone: (978)371-5748. **Subscription Rates:** $38 Individuals; $85 Out of area. **URL:** http://media.wickedlocal.com/interactive/circ/tewksbury.html; http://buy.mypapertoday.com/page98.html. **Formerly:** Merrimack Valley Advertiser. **Mailing address:** PO Box 9191, Tewksbury, MA 01876. **Ad Rates:** BW $2,413; PCI $19.15. **Remarks:** Accepts advertising. **Circ:** (Not Reported).

TISBURY

SE MA. Dukes Co. On Martha's Vineyard.

16979 ■ WVVY-FM - 93.7
PO Box 1989
Tisbury, MA 02568
Phone: (508)693-9379
Format: News; Talk. **Owner:** Marthas Vineyard Community Radio Inc., PO BOX 1989, Tisbury, MA 02568, Ph: (508)693-9379. **URL:** http://www.wvvy.org.

TOPSFIELD

16980 ■ IDA Journal of Desalination and Water Reuse
International Desalination Association
94 Central St., Ste. 200
Topsfield, MA 01983-1838
Phone: (978)887-0410
Fax: (978)887-0411
Publisher's E-mail: info@idadesal.org
Journal providing topical articles on all areas of desalination and water reuse. **Freq:** Quarterly. **ISSN:** 1947--7953 (print); **EISSN:** 2051--6452 (electronic). **Subscription Rates:** £217 Individuals online only; £310 Institutions online only; $458 Institutions online only. **URL:** http://idadesal.org/publications/ida-journal-of-desalination-water-reuse; http://www.maneyonline.com/loi/ida. **Mailing address:** PO Box 387, Topsfield, MA 01983-0587. **Remarks:** Accepts advertising. **Circ:** (Not Reported).

16981 ■ Perspectives on Science and Christian Faith
American Scientific Affiliation
218 Boston St., Ste. 208
Topsfield, MA 01983-2210
Phone: (978)887-8833
Fax: (978)887-8755
Publisher's E-mail: asa@asa3.org

Journal containing articles about science and Christian faith. **Freq:** Quarterly. **Key Personnel:** James Peterson, Editor. **Subscription Rates:** $50 Individuals; $85 Institutions; $20 Students; Included in membership. **URL:** http://network.asa3.org/?page=PSCF. **Remarks:** Accepts advertising. **Circ:** (Not Reported).

16982 ■ Perspectives on Science and Christian Faith: Journal of the ASA
American Scientific Affiliation
218 Boston St., Ste. 208
Topsfield, MA 01983-2210
Phone: (978)887-8833
Fax: (978)887-8755
Publisher's E-mail: asa@asa3.org
Academic science and Christian theology journal. **Freq:** Quarterly. **Print Method:** Offset. **Trim Size:** 8 1/2 x 11. **Cols./Page:** 2. **Col. Width:** 19 picas. **Col. Depth:** 22 picas. **Key Personnel:** Arie Leegwater, Editor; Lyn Berg, Managing Editor. **ISSN:** 0892-2675 (print). **Subscription Rates:** $50 Individuals; $85 Institutions; $20 Students. **Alt. Formats:** PDF. **URL:** http://network.asa3.org/?page=PSCF. **Formerly**: Journal of the American Scientific Affiliation. **Ad Rates:** BW $410; PCI $35. **Remarks:** Advertising accepted; rates available upon request. **Circ:** ‡2500.

16983 ■ WBMT-FM - 88.3
20 Endicott Rd.
Topsfield, MA 01983-2013
Format: Classic Rock; Music of Your Life; Sports; Talk; Jazz; Religious. **Owner:** Masconomet Regional High School, 20 Endicott Rd., Boxford, MA 01921, Ph: (508)887-2323. **Founded:** 1978. **Key Personnel:** Mike Sanger, Contact; Rebecca Schricker, Contact. **Wattage**: 660 ERP. **Ad Rates:** Accepts Advertising. **URL:** http://www.wbmtrocks.com/.

UXBRIDGE

16984 ■ Spirit of Change Magazine
Spirit of Change
PO Box 405
Uxbridge, MA 01569
Phone: (508)278-9640
Fax: (508)278-9641
Publisher's E-mail: info@spiritofchange.org
Consumer magazine covering holistic health and New Age issues. **Freq:** Quarterly. **Print Method:** Web. **Key Personnel:** Michella Bedrosian, Director, Advertising; Carol Bedrosian, Editor. **Subscription Rates:** $20 Individuals 2 years. **URL:** http://www.spiritofchange.org. **Ad Rates:** BW $1,460; 4C $1,760. **Remarks:** Accepts advertising. **Circ:** Combined 75000.

VINEYARD HAVEN

16985 ■ The Martha's Vineyard Times
Martha's Vineyard Times
PO Box 518
Vineyard Haven, MA 02568-0518
Phone: (508)693-6100
Fax: (508)693-6000
Publisher's E-mail: service@edgartownmarine.com
Community newspaper. **Freq:** Weekly (Thurs.). **Key Personnel:** Douglas Cabral, Editor; Nelson Sigelman, Managing Editor; Peter Oberfest, Publisher. **URL:** http://www.mvtimes.com. **Ad Rates:** BW $2250, full page; BW $1350, half page. **Remarks:** Accepts advertising. **Circ:** (Not Reported).

16986 ■ WMVY-FM - 92.7
57 Carrolls Way
Vineyard Haven, MA 02568
Phone: (508)693-5000
Fax: (508)693-8211
Format: Adult Album Alternative. **Owner:** Aritaur Communications Inc., at above address. **Founded:** 1981. **Operating Hours**: Continuous. **Key Personnel:** Greg Orcutt, Gen. Mgr., gorcutt@mvyradio.com; Joseph V. Gallagher, President, joe@aritaur.com. **Wattage**: 3,000. **Ad Rates:** Noncommercial. **Mailing address:** PO Box 1148, Vineyard Haven, MA 02568. **URL:** http://www.mvyradio.com.

WAKEFIELD

NE MA NE MA. Middlesex Co Middlesex Co. 10 mi. N. of Boston 10 mi. N. of Boston. Manufactures shoes, textiles, lead, iron pipe. Residential. Manufactures footwear, window screens, iron pipe, plastics.

16987 ■ Feldenkrais Journal
Feldenkrais Guild of North America
401 Edgewater Pl., Ste. 600
Wakefield, MA 01880
Freq: Annual. **Subscription Rates:** $15 Individuals. **URL:** http://www.feldenkrais.com/the-feldenkrais-journal. **Remarks:** Advertising not accepted. **Circ:** (Not Reported).

16988 ■ North Reading Transcript
Great Oak Publications Inc.
26 Albion St.
Wakefield, MA 01880
Phone: (781)245-0080
Community newspaper. **Freq:** Weekly (Thurs.). **Print Method:** Offset. **Cols./Page:** 5. **Col. Width:** 26 nonpareils. **Col. Depth:** 224 agate lines. **USPS:** 394-700. **Subscription Rates:** $28 Individuals /year in North Reading Residents only. **URL:** http://wp.localheadlinenews.com/?page_id=177. **Ad Rates:** GLR $.50; BW $480; 4C $920; SAU $7; PCI $7. **Remarks:** Advertising accepted; rates available upon request. **Circ:** (Not Reported).

16989 ■ The Wakefield Daily Item
Wakefield Item Co.
26 Albion St.
Wakefield, MA 01880
Phone: (781)245-0080
Fax: (781)246-0061
Publisher's E-mail: circulation@wakefielditem.com
General newspaper. **Freq:** Daily (eve.). **Key Personnel:** Peter Rossi, Editor. **URL:** http://wp.localheadlinenews.com/?page_id=119. **Ad Rates:** PCI $8.20. **Remarks:** Accepts advertising. **Circ:** (Not Reported).

WALPOLE

E. MA. Norfolk Co. 12 mi. SW of Braintree. Residential.

16990 ■ Journal Asiatique
PEETERS - Leuven
141 Endean Dr.
Walpole, MA 02032
Publication E-mail: peeters@peeters-us.com
Journal covering orientalist philology and history, humanities and the social sciences. **Freq:** Semiannual. **Key Personnel:** Christina Scherrer-Schaub, Managing Editor; G. Colas, Editor. **ISSN:** 0012--762X (print); **EISSN:** 1783--1504 (electronic). **URL:** http://poj.peeters-leuven.be/content.php?url=journal.php&code=ja. **Remarks:** Advertising accepted; rates available upon request. **Circ:** (Not Reported).

16991 ■ The Walpole Times
The Walpole Times
7 West St.
Walpole, MA 02081
Publication E-mail: editor@walpoletimes.com
Community newspaper. **Freq:** Weekly (Thurs.). **Print Method:** Offset. **Cols./Page:** 6. **Col. Width:** 26 nonpareils. **Col. Depth:** 294 agate lines. **Key Personnel:** Keith Ferguson, Editor, phone: (508)921-1857; Keith Lewis, Editor; Greg Reibman, Publisher. **URL:** http://walpole.wickedlocal.com. **Ad Rates:** GLR $.41; BW $787.50; PCI $5.75. **Remarks:** Accepts advertising. **Circ:** Paid 5700, Free 121.

16992 ■ WSRB-FM - 91.5
275 Common St.
Walpole, MA 02081
Format: Top 40; Album-Oriented Rock (AOR); Classic Rock; Alternative/New Music/Progressive. **Networks:** Independent. **Owner:** Town of Walpole, 135 School St., Walpole, MA 02081, Ph: (508)660-7289, Fax: (508)660-1167. **Founded:** 1974. **Formerly**: WWWA-FM. **Operating Hours:** 2:00-5:00 p.m. **Wattage**: 010.

WALTHAM

NE MA. Middlesex Co. 10 mi. W. of Boston. Brandeis University; Bentley College. Manufactures radio and TV transmitting apparatus, x-ray, electronic components, photographic equipment, computing equipment, soft drinks, machinery.

16993 ■ Bentley Observer
Bentley College - Marketing and Communication Department
175 Forest St.
Waltham, MA 02452
Phone: (781)891-2000
College and alumni news magazine. **Freq:** 3/year. **Print Method:** Sheetfed offset. **Key Personnel:** Susan Simpson, Editor; Caleb Cochran, Managing Editor. **Alt. Formats:** PDF. **URL:** http://www.bentley.edu/observer/about-observer. **Remarks:** Advertising not accepted. **Circ:** Controlled 52000.

16994 ■ Contemporary Jewry
Association for the Social Scientific Study of Jewry
c/o Prof. Leonard Saxe, Treasurer
Cohen Center for Modern Jewish Studies
Brandeis University
415 South St.
Waltham, MA 02453
Publisher's E-mail: assjtreasurer@gmail.com
Journal publishing articles on the social scientific study of Jewry. **Freq:** 3/year. **ISSN:** 0147--1694 (print). **URL:** http://www.contemporaryjewry.org/8.html. **Remarks:** Accepts advertising. **Circ:** 300.

16995 ■ The Journal of Strategic Information Systems
RELX Group P.L.C.
c/o Bob Galliers, Ed.-in-Ch.
Bentley University
Waltham, MA 02452-4705
Publisher's E-mail: amsterdam@relx.com
Journal focusing on the management, business and organizational issues associated with the introduction of information systems. **Freq:** 4/yr. **Key Personnel:** Bob Galliers, Editor-in-Chief; Sirkka Jarvenpaa, Editor-in-Chief. **ISSN:** 0963--8687 (print). **Subscription Rates:** $199 Individuals print; $925 Institutions print; $772 Institutions ejournal. **URL:** http://www.journals.elsevier.com/the-journal-of-strategic-information-systems. **Circ:** (Not Reported).

16996 ■ The Justice: The Independent Student Newspaper of Brandeis University Since 1949
Brandeis University
415 South St.
Waltham, MA 02453
Phone: (781)736-2000
Collegiate newspaper. **Freq:** Weekly (Tues.) during school year. **Print Method:** Offset. **Cols./Page:** 5. **Col. Width:** 22 nonpareils. **Col. Depth:** 224 agate lines. **Key Personnel:** Nashrah Rahman, Managing Editor, phone: (781)736-3567; Emily Kraus, Editor-in-Chief. **Subscription Rates:** Free for students living in Waltham. **URL:** http://www.thejustice.org; http://www.brandeis.edu/information/campus.html. **Ad Rates:** PCI $250, Student Groups; PCI $350, Non-Profit/On-Campus; PCI $1425, Off-Campus/Local. **Remarks:** Accepts advertising. **Circ:** Paid 300, Free 4200.

16997 ■ Mosaic
Educational Development Center, Inc.
43 Foundry Ave.
Waltham, MA 02453-8313
Phone: (617)969-7100
Fax: (617)969-5979
Publication E-mail: mosaic@edc.org
Journal covering issues in education. **Freq:** 2-3/yr. **URL:** http://main.edc.org/newsroom/mosaic. **Remarks:** Advertising not accepted. **Circ:** 4000.

16998 ■ Transgender Tapestry
International Foundation for Gender Education
272 Carroll St. NW
Waltham, MA 02454
Phone: (202)207-8364
Publisher's E-mail: office@ifge.org
Freq: Quarterly. **Subscription Rates:** $55 Other countries /year; $40 U.S. /year; $75 Two years. **URL:** http://www.ifge.org/tgmag/tgmagtop.htm. **Remarks:** Advertising accepted; rates available upon request. **Circ:** (Not Reported).

16999 ■ The Vanguard
Bentley College
175 Forest St.
Waltham, MA 02452-4713
Phone: (781)891-2000
Publisher's E-mail: ag_hrsupport@bentley.edu

Circulation: ★ = AAM; △ or • = BPA; ♦ = CAC; ❑ = VAC; ⊕ = PO Statement; ‡ = Publisher's Report; Boldface figures = sworn; Light figures = estimated.

College newspaper (tabloid). **Founded:** 1975. **Freq:** Weekly (Thurs.) during academic year. **Print Method:** Offset. **Trim Size:** 11 x 17. **Cols./Page:** 5. **Col. Width:** 11 picas. **Col. Depth:** 16 inches. **Key Personnel:** Mideno Bayagbona, Editor. **URL:** http://www.vanguardngr.com. **Formerly:** The Inferno. **Ad Rates:** GLR $8; BW $8. **Remarks:** Accepts advertising. **Circ:** Free ‡4,000.

17000 ■ Your Teen
Your Teen
c/o Susan Borison
Brandeis University
415 South St.
Waltham, MA 02453
Phone: (781)736-2000
Publication E-mail: info@yourteenmag.com
Magazine featuring parenting articles and offers open forum for parents of teens. **Freq:** 6/year. **Key Personnel:** Susan Borison, Editor-in-Chief, Publisher; Stephanie Silverman, Managing Editor, Publisher. **Subscription Rates:** $15 Individuals. **URL:** http://yourteenmag.com. **Circ:** 22000.

17001 ■ WBRS-FM - 100.1
415 S St.
Waltham, MA 02453-2728
Phone: (781)736-4786
Email: gm@wbrs.org
Format: Eclectic. **Owner:** Trustees of Brandeis University, PO Box 549110, Waltham, MA 02453, Ph: (781)736-2000. **Founded:** 1968. **Key Personnel:** Jackie Benowitz, Gen. Mgr., gm@wbrs.org; Daniel Hammerschlag, Dir. of Programs, pd@wbrs.org; Diego Medrano, Tech. Dir., tech@wbrs.org; Michael Zonenashvili, Music Dir., music@wbrs.org; Jesse Manning, Sports Dir., sports@wbrs.org. **Wattage**: 025 ERP. **Ad Rates:** Noncommercial. **URL:** http://www.wbrs.org.

17002 ■ WCRB-FM - 99.5
750 South St.
Waltham, MA 02453
Phone: (781)893-7080
Fax: (781)893-0038
Owner: Nassau Broadcasting Partners, L.P., at above address. **Founded:** 1947. **Local Programs:** *Kids Classical*, Saturday 8:30 a.m. - 9:30 a.m. **Wattage:** 27,000 ERP. **Ad Rates:** $75-300 for 30 seconds; $75-300 for 60 seconds. Combined advertising rates available with WFCC, WKPE-FM, WCRI, WCNX-AM. **URL:** http://www.wcrb.com.

WARE

WC MA. Hampshire Co. 27 mi. NE of Springfield. Manufactures cotton goods, woolens, gummed paper, iron castings, hydraulic equipment, ice skates, athletic shoes.

17003 ■ Ware River News
Turley Publications
80 Main St.
Ware, MA 01082
Phone: (413)967-3505
Fax: (413)967-6009
Publisher's E-mail: support@turley.com
Community newspaper. **Freq:** Weekly (Thurs.). **Print Method:** Offset. **Cols./Page:** 8. **Col. Width:** 18 nonpareils. **Col. Depth:** 294 agate lines. **Key Personnel:** Tim Kane, Editor. **USPS:** 666-100. **Subscription Rates:** $31 Individuals. **URL:** http://www.warenewsonline.com. **Ad Rates:** GLR $.33; BW $1,058; PCI $9.25. **Remarks:** Accepts advertising. **Circ:** 4429.

WATERTOWN

NE MA. Middlesex Co. 8 mi. W. of Boston. (Branch of Boston P.O.) Fisher Jr. College; Perkins School for the Blind. Residential. Manufactures fabricated metal products, electrical and other machinery, medical instruments, rubber products, electronic equipment, chemical products.

17004 ■ Antiques and Fine Art
Pure Imaging, Inc.
570 Arsenal St.
Watertown, MA 02472
Phone: (617)926-1007
Fax: (617)926-0104
Publisher's E-mail: mail@pureimaging.com
Magazine focusing on antiques and fine art. **Freq:** Bimonthly. **URL:** http://www.antiquesandfineart.com. **Remarks:** Accepts advertising. **Circ:** (Not Reported).

17005 ■ The Armenian Weekly
Hairenik Association
80 Bigelow Ave.
Watertown, MA 02472
Phone: (617)926-3974
Fax: (617)926-1750
Publication E-mail: armenianweekly@hairenik.com
Tabloid on Armenian interests. **Freq:** Weekly (Sat.). **Print Method:** Offset. **Trim Size:** 10 x 16. **Cols./Page:** 5. **Key Personnel:** Khatchig Mouradian, Editor. **ISSN:** 0148--2971 (print). **Subscription Rates:** $75 Individuals. **URL:** http://armenianweekly.com. **Ad Rates:** BW $450; PCI $10. **Remarks:** Color advertising not accepted. **Circ:** Paid ‡2200, Free ‡300, 3000.

17006 ■ Haytoug/Hoki
Armenian Youth Federation
80 Bigelow Ave.
Watertown, MA 02472
Phone: (617)923-1933
Fax: (617)924-1933
Publisher's E-mail: ce@ayf.org
Freq: Quarterly. **Subscription Rates:** Free. **URL:** http://ayfwest.org/programs/haytoug/archive/; http://ayfwest.org/programs/haytoug/. **Remarks:** Accepts advertising. **Circ:** (Not Reported).

WEBSTER

C. MA. Worcester Co. On French River, 18 mi. S. of Worcester. Lake resort. Manufactures textiles, shoes. Dairy, fruit farms.

17007 ■ WGFP-AM - 940
27 Douglas Rd.
Webster, MA 01570
Phone: (508)949-3456
Email: sales@coolcountry940.com
Format: Country. **Networks:** ABC. **Founded:** 1980. **Operating Hours:** 6 a.m.-6 p.m.; 70% network, 30% local. **ADI:** Boston-Worcester,MA-Derry-Manchester,NH. **Wattage:** 1,000. **Ad Rates:** Advertising accepted; rates available upon request. **URL:** http://www.coolcountry940.com/newweb.

WELLESLEY

E. MA. Norfolk Co. 15 mi. SW of Boston. Wellesley College (women); Babson College (men); Mass. Bay Community College.

17008 ■ Advanced Transportation Technology News
BCC Research
49 Walnut Park, Bldg. 2
Wellesley, MA 02481
Phone: (781)489-7301
Fax: (781)489-7308
Free: 866-285-7215
Publisher's E-mail: information@bccresearch.com
Publication covering technology and related news for the transportation industry. **Freq:** Monthly. **ISSN:** 1077--6877 (print). **Subscription Rates:** $2250 Individuals hard copy mail delivery. **URL:** http://www.bccresearch.com/market-research/advanced-transportation-technologies. **Circ:** (Not Reported).

17009 ■ Babson Alumni Magazine
Babson College
231 Forest St.
Wellesley, MA 02457-0310
Phone: (781)235-1200
Magazine for college alumni and parents. **Freq:** Quarterly. **Print Method:** Web press. **Trim Size:** 8 3/4 x 11. **Cols./Page:** 2 and 4. **Col. Width:** 26 nonpareils. **Col. Depth:** 135 agate lines. **Key Personnel:** Donna Coco, Editor; Sharman Andersen, Editor; John Crawford, Associate Editor. **USPS:** 898-140. **Subscription Rates:** Free to alumni & parents. Downloadable to App store. **URL:** http://magazine.babson.edu. **Formerly:** Babson Bulletin. **Remarks:** Advertising not accepted. **Circ:** Controlled 32000.

17010 ■ Wellesley Magazine
Wellesley College
106 Central St.
Wellesley, MA 02481
Phone: (781)283-1000
Magazine for college alumnae. **Freq:** Quarterly November, January, May, and July. **Print Method:** Offset. **Cols./Page:** 3. **Col. Width:** 30 nonpareils. **Col. Depth:** 133 agate lines. **Key Personnel:** Laura Katz, Editor. **Subscription Rates:** Free to all alumnae, honorary members of the Association, and to the Trustees of the College. **URL:** http://magazine.wellesley.edu. **Formerly:** Alumnae Magazine. **Ad Rates:** BW $1,800. **Remarks:** Accepts advertising. **Circ:** ‡34000.

17011 ■ The Women's Review of Books: Book Review
Wellesley College
Center for Research on Women
Wellesley College
Wellesley, MA 02481
Magazine on feminist thinking and writing. **Freq:** Monthly (except August). **Print Method:** Offset. **Trim Size:** 10 x 15. **Cols./Page:** 4. **Col. Width:** 28 nonpareils. **Col. Depth:** 210 agate lines. **Key Personnel:** Linda Gardiner, Editor, phone: (781)283-2535; Anita D. McClellan, Manager, Advertising, phone: (781)283-2560; Amy Hoffman, Customer Service, Editor-in-Chief, phone: (781)283-2087; Amanda Nash, Editor. **ISSN:** 0738--1433 (print); **EISSN:** 1949--0410 (electronic). **Subscription Rates:** $46 Individuals North America; $133 Institutions North America; $110 Other countries airmail; $219 Institutions, other countries airmail. **Alt. Formats:** CD-ROM; Microform. **URL:** http://www.wcwonline.org/Women-s-Review-of-Books/womens-review-of-books. **Ad Rates:** BW $2781. **Remarks:** Color advertising not accepted. **Circ:** Paid ‡12000, Non-paid ‡500.

17012 ■ WZLY-FM - 91.5
Wellesley College
Schneider Ctr.
106 Central St.
Wellesley, MA 02481
Phone: (781)283-2690
Format: Eclectic. **Networks:** AP. **Owner:** Wellesley College, 106 Central St., Wellesley, MA 02481, Ph: (781)283-1000. **Founded:** 1942. **Operating Hours:** 9 a.m.-3 a.m. **Key Personnel:** Julia Orlov, Music Dir., md@wzly.net; Hilary Allen, Gen. Mgr., gm@wzly.net. **Wattage:** 010. **Ad Rates:** Noncommercial. **URL:** http://www.wzly.net.

WELLESLEY HILLS

17013 ■ Contingency Planning and Recovery Journal
Management Advisory Publications
PO Box 81151
Wellesley Hills, MA 02481-0001
Phone: (781)235-2895
Fax: (781)235-5446
Publisher's E-mail: info@masp.com
Business magazine for managers, disaster recovery planners, auditors, security officers and contingency planning coordinators, users dependent on computers, LAN Administrators, and year 2000 project managers. Covers contingency planning, business process continuity, disaster recovery and business resumption. **Freq:** Quarterly. **Print Method:** Offset. **Trim Size:** 8 1/2 x 11. **Cols./Page:** 2. **Col. Width:** 3.4 inches. **Col. Depth:** 9 inches. **ISSN:** 0899--4595 (print). **Subscription Rates:** $75 Individuals North America; $96 Other countries. **URL:** http://www.masp.com/publications/CPR-J.html. **Remarks:** Accepts advertising. **Circ:** (Not Reported).

WEST BARNSTABLE

SE MA. Barnstable Co. 10 mi. SE of Hyannis.

17014 ■ WKKL-FM - 90.7
2240 Iyannough Rd.
West Barnstable, MA 02668
Phone: (508)375-4030
Email: wkklmusic@capecod.edu
Format: Eclectic. **Networks:** Independent. **Owner:** Cape Cod Community College, 2240 Iyannough Rd., West Barnstable, MA 02668, Ph: (508)362-2131, Free: 877-846-3672. **Founded:** 1977. **Operating Hours:** 10 a.m.-4 p.m. Mon.-Fri.;10 a.m.-1 p.m. Sat.-Sun.; NPR 1 a.m. **Key Personnel:** Bob Paluzzi, Dir. of Production. **Wattage:** 305. **Ad Rates:** Noncommercial. **URL:** http://www.capecod.edu/web/wkkl-90.7.

WEST SPRINGFIELD

WC MA. Hampden Co. Across Connecticut River from Springfield. Manufactures paper, boxes, plastic products, wire, electronic equipment, fabricated metal products. Smelting and machine works, bindery. Agriculture.

17015 ■ The Agawam Advertiser News
Turley Publications
38 Union St., Ste. 52
West Springfield, MA 01089
Phone: (413)786-7747
Fax: (413)786-8457
Publisher's E-mail: support@turley.com
Community newspaper serving Agawam and Feeding Hills. **Freq:** Weekly (Thurs.). **Key Personnel:** Michael J. Ballway, Managing Editor. **Subscription Rates:** $35 Individuals in-state; $40 Out of state; $15 Two years in-state; $25 Two years out of state. **URL:** http://agawamadvertisernews.turley.com. **Ad Rates:** PCI $10.75; 4C $50, up to 20 column inches. **Remarks:** Accepts advertising. **Circ:** 5200.

WEST YARMOUTH

17016 ■ WFQR-FM - 101.1
278 S Sea Ave.
West Yarmouth, MA 02673
Phone: (508)775-5678
Fax: (508)862-6329
Ad Rates: Advertising accepted; rates available upon request.

17017 ■ WFRQ-FM - 101.1
278 S Sea Ave.
West Yarmouth, MA 02673
Phone: (508)775-5678
Fax: (508)862-6329
Format: Eclectic. **Owner:** Nassau Broadcasting Partners L.P., 619 Alexander Rd., 3rd Fl., Princeton, NJ 08540-6000, Ph: (609)452-9696, Fax: (609)452-6017. **Operating Hours:** Continuous. **Ad Rates:** Advertising accepted; rates available upon request.

17018 ■ WPXC-FM - 102.9
278 S Sea Ave.
West Yarmouth, MA 02673
Phone: (508)775-5678
Fax: (508)862-6329
Free: 800-445-7499
Owner: Nassau Broadcasting Partners L.P., 619 Alexander Rd., 3rd Fl., Princeton, NJ 08540-6000, Ph: (609)452-9696, Fax: (609)452-6017. **Founded:** 1987. **Wattage:** 6,800. **Ad Rates:** Advertising accepted; rates available upon request.

WESTBOROUGH

C. MA. Worcester Co. 3 mi. SE of Woodville. Residential.

17019 ■ BioProcess International
Informa Healthcare
One Research Dr., Ste. 400A
Westborough, MA 01581
Phone: (508)616-5550
Fax: (212)202-4567
Publication E-mail: info@bioprocessintl.com
Journal that aims to provide the global industrial biotherapeutic community with information detailing the business, politics, ethics, applications, products, and services required to successfully drive biopharmaceuticals. **Freq:** Monthly. **Key Personnel:** Brian Caine, Publisher; S. Anne Montgomery, Editor-in-Chief. **URL:** http://www.bioprocessintl.com. **Ad Rates:** BW $6,610; 4C $11,480. **Remarks:** Accepts advertising. **Circ:** △**30010**.

17020 ■ District Energy
International District Energy Association
24 Lyman St., Ste. 230
Westborough, MA 01581-2841
Phone: (508)366-9339
Fax: (508)366-0019
Publisher's E-mail: idea@districtenergy.org
Magazine featuring information for district energy industry professionals. **Freq:** Quarterly. **Print Method:** Offset. **Trim Size:** 8.375 x 10.875. **Cols./Page:** 2. **Col. Width:** 40 nonpareils. **Col. Depth:** 133 agate lines. **Key Personnel:** Rob Thornton, Contact. **ISSN:** 1077-6222 (print). **Subscription Rates:** $50 Nonmembers; $75 Nonmembers other countries; $40 Members; $65 Members other countries; $50 Individuals; $75 Institutions. **URL:** http://www.districtenergy.org/district-energy-magazine-overview. **Formerly:** District Heating & Cooling. **Ad Rates:** 4C $850. **Remarks:** Accepts advertising. **Circ:** 6,000.

17021 ■ Massachusetts Wildlife
Massachusetts Department of Fish and Game Division of Fisheries and Wildlife
1 Rabbit Hill Rd.
Westborough, MA 01581
Phone: (508)389-6300
Magazine featuring articles and photos on the environment, conservation, fishing, hunting, natural history and everything relating to the outdoors in Massachusetts. **Freq:** Quarterly. **Subscription Rates:** $6 Individuals; $10 Two years. **URL:** http://www.mass.gov/eea/agencies/dfg/dfw/publications/massachusetts-wildlife-magazine.html. **Circ:** (Not Reported).

WESTFIELD

SW MA. Hampden Co. 10 mi. W. of Springfield. State College. Manufactures bicycles, boilers, plastic molds, rifles, sports arms, machinery, fish line, abrasives, paper, foundry products, whips, whip lashes, brass valves, brushes and polishes, metal nuts, cigars, digital computers. Agriculture. Tobacco.

17022 ■ Historical Journal of Massachusetts
Westfield State University
577 Western Ave.
Westfield, MA 01086-1630
Phone: (413)572-5300
Publication E-mail: masshistoryjournal@westfield.ma.edu
Scholarly journal covering local history. **Freq:** Semiannual January and June. **Key Personnel:** Dr. Mara Dodge, Director, Editorial; Lynn D. Martin, Associate Editor, phone: (413)572-5344; Dr. Fred Cooksey, Associate Editor. **ISSN:** 0276--8313 (print). **Subscription Rates:** $18 Individuals /year; $58 Other countries. **URL:** http://www.wsc.mass.edu/mhj. **Remarks:** Accepts advertising. **Circ:** (Not Reported).

17023 ■ The Longmeadow News
Westfield News Advertiser Inc.
62-64 School St.
Westfield, MA 01085-2835
Phone: (413)562-4181
Fax: (413)562-4185
Community newspaper. **Freq:** Weekly (Thurs.). **Print Method:** Offset. Uses mats. **Cols./Page:** 4. **Col. Width:** 16 nonpareils. **Col. Depth:** 224 agate lines. **USPS:** 746-869. **URL:** http://www.longmeadow.org. **Ad Rates:** PCI $5.50. **Remarks:** Accepts advertising. **Circ:** ‡1930.

17024 ■ WSKB-FM - 89.5
577 W Ave.
Westfield, MA 01086
Format: Alternative/New Music/Progressive. **Owner:** Westfield State University, 577 Western Ave., Westfield, MA 01086-1630, Ph: (413)572-5300. **Founded:** 1968. **Operating Hours:** 8 a.m.-2 a.m.; 100% local. **Wattage:** 100. **Ad Rates:** Noncommercial. **URL:** http://wskb895.wordpress.com.

WESTFORD

17025 ■ Graduating Engineer & Computer Careers
Alloy Education
Two LAN Dr., Ste. 100
Westford, MA 01886
Phone: (978)692-5092
Fax: (978)692-4174
Publisher's E-mail: hshulick@alloyeducation.com
Magazine focusing on employment, education, and career development for entry-level engineers and computer scientists. **Freq:** Quarterly. **Print Method:** Offset. **Trim Size:** 8 x 10 3/4. **Cols./Page:** 3. **Col. Width:** 26 nonpareils. **Col. Depth:** 140 agate lines. **Key Personnel:** Matt Summer, Vice President, Sales and Marketing; Tim Clancy, Publisher; Ann Morley, Manager, Sales; Hector Barrera, Account Executive. **ISSN:** 0193--2276 (print). **URL:** http://www.graduatingengineer.com; http://www.graduatingengineer.com/about-the-magazine. **Formerly:** Graduating Engineer. **Remarks:** Accepts advertising. **Circ:** Non-paid 65000.

WESTMINSTER

17026 ■ Button
Button
PO Box 77
Westminster, MA 01473
Consumer magazine covering poetry, fiction, and literature. **Founded:** June 1993. **Freq:** Annual. **Key Personnel:** S. Cragin, Publisher. **Subscription Rates:** $5 Individuals 4 issues; $2.50 Single issue. **URL:** http://www.moonsigns.net/Button-frame.htm. **Ad Rates:** BW $50. **Remarks:** Accepts advertising. **Circ:** Combined 1200.

WESTON

NE MA. Middlesex Co. 12 mi. W. of Boston. Regis College (women). Residential.

17027 ■ Activities Directors' Quarterly for Alzheimer's & Other Dementia Patients
Prime National Publishing Corp.
470 Boston Post Rd.
Weston, MA 02493-1529
Phone: (781)899-2702
Fax: (781)899-4900
Free: 800-743-7206
Publisher's E-mail: radjr@pnpco.com
Trade journal for activities directors working with patients with Alzheimer's disease and other forms of dementia. **Freq:** Quarterly. **Print Method:** Offset. **Trim Size:** 8 3/8 x 10 7/8. **Key Personnel:** Linda L. Buettner, PhD, Editor-in-Chief. **ISSN:** 1531--7277 (print). **URL:** http://www.pnpco.com/pn08000.html. **Ad Rates:** BW $1195; 4C $1295. **Remarks:** Advertising accepted; rates available upon request. **Circ:** (Not Reported).

17028 ■ American Journal of Disaster Medicine
Prime National Publishing Corp.
470 Boston Post Rd.
Weston, MA 02493-1529
Phone: (781)899-2702
Fax: (781)899-4900
Free: 800-743-7206
Publisher's E-mail: radjr@pnpco.com
Peer-reviewed journal covering disaster and emergency medicine. **Freq:** Quarterly. **Trim Size:** 8 3/8 x 10 7/8. **Key Personnel:** Susan M. Briggs, MD, Editor-in-Chief. **ISSN:** 1932--149X (print). **Subscription Rates:** $335 Individuals print only; $445 Institutions; $544 Libraries. **URL:** http://pnpco.com/pn03000.html. **Ad Rates:** 4C $2,995. **Remarks:** Accepts advertising. **Circ:** 350.

17029 ■ American Journal of Recreation Therapy
Prime National Publishing Corp.
470 Boston Post Rd.
Weston, MA 02493-1529
Phone: (781)899-2702
Fax: (781)899-4900
Free: 800-743-7206
Publisher's E-mail: radjr@pnpco.com
Journal covering recreation therapy for professional looking to treat individuals with an illness or disability. **Freq:** Quarterly. **Print Method:** Offset. **Trim Size:** 8 3/8 x 10 7/8. **Key Personnel:** Candace Ashton-Shaeffer, PhD, Board Member; Nancy E. Richeson, Editor-in-Chief, Managing Editor. **Subscription Rates:** $167 Individuals USA; $202 Individuals Canada; $256 Individuals other countries; $75 Individuals single issue; $171 Institutions USA; $207 Institutions Canada; $261 Institutions other countries. **URL:** http://www.pnpco.com/pn10000.html. **Ad Rates:** BW $1425. **Remarks:** Advertising accepted; rates available upon request. **Circ:** (Not Reported).

17030 ■ Journal of Emergency Management
Prime National Publishing Corp.
470 Boston Post Rd.
Weston, MA 02493-1529
Phone: (781)899-2702
Fax: (781)899-4900
Free: 800-743-7206
Publisher's E-mail: radjr@pnpco.com
Journal for fire, police, town/city management, and emergency managers covering natural disasters, terrorism, and catastrophic accidents. **Freq:** Bimonthly. **Print Method:** Offset. **Trim Size:** 8.375 x 10.875. **Key**

Circulation: ★ = AAM; △ or • = BPA; ♦ = CAC; ❑ = VAC; ⊕ = PO Statement; ‡ = Publisher's Report; Boldface figures = sworn; Light figures = estimated.

Personnel: William L. Waugh, Jr., Editor-in-Chief; Barbara Audley, Board Member; Wayne B. Blanchard, PhD, Board Member; Anthony E. Brown, PhD, Board Member; Paul A. Bott, Board Member; Michael W. Brand, PhD, Board Member; Richard A. Bissell, PhD, Board Member; Hilda J. Blanco, PhD, Board Member. **ISSN:** 1543--5865 (print). **URL:** http://www.pnpco.com/pn06001.html. **Ad Rates:** BW $2870; 4C $1395. **Remarks:** Advertising accepted; rates available upon request. **Circ:** (Not Reported).

17031 ■ Journal of Neurodegeneration and Regeneration
Prime National Publishing Corp.
470 Boston Post Rd.
Weston, MA 02493-1529
Phone: (781)899-2702
Fax: (781)899-4900
Free: 800-743-7206
Publisher's E-mail: radjr@pnpco.com
Journal covering developments in understanding the molecular mechanisms of neurodegeneration, neuroprotection and neuroregeneration. **Freq:** Bimonthly. **Trim Size:** 8 3/8 x 10 7/8. **Key Personnel:** Cathy M. Helgason, MD, Editor-in-Chief; Philippe Taupin, Editor-in-Chief. **ISSN:** 1932--1481 (print). **Subscription Rates:** $155 Individuals; $168 Canada; $189 Other countries. **URL:** http://pnpco.com/pn02000.html. **Ad Rates:** BW $5,275. **Remarks:** Accepts advertising. **Circ:** (Not Reported).

WEYMOUTH

E. MA. Norfolk Co. 15 mi. SE of Boston. (Branch of Boston P.O.) Manufactures shoes, shoe counters, belting, electronics components, paper boxes, industrial resins and chemicals.

17032 ■ Braintree Forum
GateHouse Media Inc.
91 Washington St.
Weymouth, MA 02188-1702
Phone: (781)682-4850
Fax: (781)682-4851
Community newspaper. **Freq:** Weekly (Thurs.). **Print Method:** Offset. **Cols./Page:** 6. **Col. Width:** 18 nonpareils. **Col. Depth:** 224 agate lines. **Key Personnel:** Mark Olivieri, Publisher, phone: (781)837-4504; Cathy Conley, Managing Editor, phone: (781)682-4850; Paul Harber, Editor, phone: (781)837-4579. **URL:** http://braintree.wickedlocal.com. **Ad Rates:** BW $767; 4C $1,167; PCI $8.25. **Remarks:** Accepts advertising. **Circ:** (Not Reported).

17033 ■ Holbrook Sun
GateHouse Media Inc.
91 Washington St.
Weymouth, MA 02188
Phone: (781)682-4850
Fax: (781)682-4851
Community newspaper. **Freq:** Weekly. **Print Method:** Offset. **Trim Size:** 8 1/2 x 11. **Cols./Page:** 4 and 6. **Col. Width:** 14.5 and 9 picas. **Col. Depth:** 15 1/2 inches. **Key Personnel:** Mark Olivieri, Publisher, phone: (781)837-4504; Gregory Mathis, Editor-in-Chief, phone: (781)682-4850. **USPS:** 247-120. **Subscription Rates:** $55 Individuals; $85 Out of area. **URL:** http://media.wickedlocal.com/interactive/circ/holbrook.html. **Ad Rates:** BW $767; 4C $1,167; PCI $8.25. **Remarks:** Accepts classified advertising. **Circ:** (Not Reported).

17034 ■ Continental Cablevision
83 Moore Rd.
Weymouth, MA 02189
Email: ccnctv3@aol.com
Owner: Continental Cablevision Inc., The Pilot House, Lewis Wharf, Boston, MA 02110, Ph: (617)742-9500. **Founded:** 1973. **Key Personnel:** Brian Lambert, Gen. Mgr.; Barrett Lester, Mgr. **Cities Served:** Lawrence, Methvew, North Andover, Massachusetts: subscribing households 34,000; 64 channels; 1 community access channel; 10 hours per week community access programming. **URL:** http://corp.sec.state.ma.us/CorpWeb/CorpSearch/CorpSummary.aspx?FEIN=000543760&SEARCH_TYPE=1.

WILBRAHAM

17035 ■ Wilbraham-Hampden Times
Turley Publications
2341 Boston Rd.
Wilbraham, MA 01095
Phone: (413)682-0007
Fax: (413)682-0013
Publisher's E-mail: support@turley.com
Community newspaper serving Wilbraham and Hampden. **Freq:** Weekly (Thurs.). **Key Personnel:** Charles F. Bennett, Editor; Tim Kane, Executive Editor. **URL:** http://wilbrahamtimes.com. **Remarks:** Accepts advertising. **Circ:** 9338.

WILLIAMSTOWN

W. MA. Berkshire Co. On Hoosac River, 18 mi. N. of Pittsfield. Williams College. Manufactures wire.

17036 ■ Gastronomica: The Journal of Food and Culture
University of California Press - Journals and Digital Publishing Division
c/o Dara Goldstein, Ed.
Williams College
Hollander Hall
85 Mission Park Dr.
Williamstown, MA 01267
Publisher's E-mail: library@ucpressjournals.com
Peer-reviewed scholarly journal covering food studies, including history, literature, representation and cultural impact of food in cultures worldwide. **Freq:** Quarterly February, May, August and November. **Trim Size:** 8 1/2 x 11. **Key Personnel:** Melissa L. Caldwell, Editor. **ISSN:** 1529--3262 (print); **EISSN:** 1533--8622 (electronic). **Subscription Rates:** $284 Institutions online only; $22 Individuals online only, student/retired; $44 Individuals online only; $96 Institutions online only, single issue; $15 Individuals online only, single issue; $357 Institutions print and online; $59 Individuals print and online. **URL:** http://gcfs.ucpress.edu. **Ad Rates:** BW $894. **Remarks:** Accepts advertising. **Circ:** 9300.

17037 ■ Williams Alumni Review
Society of Alumni of Williams College
75 Park St.
Williamstown, MA 01267
Phone: (413)597-4151
Publisher's E-mail: alumni.relations@williams.edu
Magazine for collegiate alumni, parents, and friends. **Freq:** Quarterly. **Print Method:** Web. **Trim Size:** 8 3/8 x 10 7/8. **Cols./Page:** 2 and 3. **Col. Width:** 40 and 26 nonpareils. **Col. Depth:** 138 agate lines. **Key Personnel:** Francesca B. Shanks, Assistant Editor; Amy T. Lovett, Editor, phone: (413)597-4981; Jennifer Grow, Assistant Editor. **USPS:** 684-580. **Subscription Rates:** Free. **Alt. Formats:** PDF. **URL:** http://magazine.williams.edu. **Remarks:** Advertising not accepted. **Circ:** Free ‡30417.

17038 ■ The Williams Record
Williams College
Hopkins Hall
880 Main St.
Williamstown, MA 01267
Phone: (413)597-3131
Publication E-mail: wiliamsrecordeic@gmail.com
Collegiate newspaper. **Freq:** 11/year. **Print Method:** Offset. **Cols./Page:** 6. **Col. Width:** 2 1/8 inches. **Col. Depth:** 21 1/4 inches. **Key Personnel:** Emily Dugdale, Editor; Ben Eastburn, Manager, Production; Matthew Piltch, Editor-in-Chief. **USPS:** 684-680. **Subscription Rates:** $45 Individuals one semester (11 issues); $78 Two years one year (22 issues); $145 Individuals two years (44 issues); $185 Individuals three years (66 issues); $225 Individuals four years (88 issues). **URL:** http://williamsrecord.com. **Ad Rates:** BW $1,100; PCI $10. **Remarks:** Accepts advertising. **Circ:** Free ‡3000.

17039 ■ WCFM-FM - 91.9
Baxter Hall
Williams College
Williamstown, MA 01267
Phone: (413)597-3265
Format: Full Service. **Owner:** President and Trustees of Williams College, 880 Main St., Williamstown, MA 01267, Ph: (413)597-4233, Fax: (413)597-4015. **Founded:** 1941. **Operating Hours:** Continuous. **Key Personnel:** Joe Leidy, Gen. Mgr. **Ad Rates:** Noncommercial. **URL:** http://wcfm.williams.edu.

WINCHESTER

NE MA. Middlesex Co. 8 mi. NW of Boston. Residential. Manufactures pointers for automotive instrument panels.

17040 ■ The Quarterly Review of Wines: The Wine Magazine
Q.R.W. Inc.
24 Garfield Ave.
Winchester, MA 01890
Consumer magazine on fine wines and selected spirits. **Freq:** Quarterly. **Print Method:** Web offset. **Trim Size:** 8 1/2 x 10 7/8. **Cols./Page:** 3. **Col. Width:** 2.25 picas. **Col. Depth:** 9 3/4 inches. **Key Personnel:** Richard L. Elia, Publisher. **ISSN:** 0740-1248 (print). **Subscription Rates:** $17.95 Individuals; $29.95 Two years; $25.95 Canada; $49.95 Other countries European. **Ad Rates:** GLR $175; BW $7000; 4C $10,000. **Remarks:** Accepts advertising. **Circ:** Combined ‡150000.

17041 ■ Winchester Star
GateHouse Media Inc.
9 Meriam St.
Winchester, MA 01890
Phone: (781)674-7740
Publication E-mail: winchester@wickedlocal.com
Local newspaper. **Founded:** 1880. **Freq:** Weekly (Thurs.). **Print Method:** Offset. **Trim Size:** 13 3/4 x 22 1/2. **Cols./Page:** 6. **Col. Width:** 2 1/16 inches. **Col. Depth:** 21 inches. **Key Personnel:** Chuck Goodrich, Publisher; Stephen Tobey, Editor, phone: (978)371-5741. **Subscription Rates:** $69 Individuals; $85 Out of area. **URL:** http://winchester.wickedlocal.com. **Ad Rates:** BW $1,370; SAU $10.87. **Remarks:** Accepts classified advertising. **Circ:** Combined 69131.

WOBURN

NE MA. Middlesex Co. 10 mi. NW of Boston. Manufactures mattresses, plastics, chemical and aluminum products, leather, leatherworking machinery, gears, tools, electronics, automotive parts, rubber rolls, belt knives and band saws. Floriculture.

17042 ■ Daily Times Chronicle
Woburn Daily Times Inc.
1 Arrow Dr.
Woburn, MA 01801
Phone: (781)933-3700
Fax: (781)932-3321
Suburban community newspaper. **Freq:** Daily (eve.). **Print Method:** Offset. **Cols./Page:** 6. **Col. Width:** 2 1/16 inches. **Col. Depth:** 294 agate lines. **Key Personnel:** James D. Haggerty, III, Publisher; Thomas R. Kirk, Sr., Director, Advertising; Peter M. Haggerty, Publisher. **USPS:** 689-360. **Subscription Rates:** $164 Individuals; $216 By mail. **URL:** http://homenewshere.com/daily_times_chronicle. **Ad Rates:** GLR $1.16; BW $2,041; 4C $450; SAU $15; PCI $15. **Remarks:** Accepts advertising. **Circ:** Mon.-Fri. ‡10,590.

17043 ■ Middlesex East Update
Woburn Daily Times Inc.
1 Arrow Dr.
Woburn, MA 01801
Phone: (781)933-3700
Fax: (781)932-3321
Community newspaper. **Freq:** Weekly (Wed.). **Print Method:** Photo offset. **Key Personnel:** Richard Haggerty, General Manager. **Subscription Rates:** Free. **URL:** http://homenewshere.com/middlesex_east. **Circ:** Non-paid 5011.

17044 ■ Wilmington-Tewksbury Town Crier
Daily Times
1 Arrow Dr.
Woburn, MA 01801
Phone: (978)658-2346
Fax: (978)658-2266
Publication E-mail: office@yourtowncrier.com
Community newspaper. **Freq:** Weekly. **Print Method:** Offset. **Cols./Page:** 6. **Col. Width:** 12 picas. **Col. Depth:** 21 inches. **Key Personnel:** Jamie Pote, Editor. **USPS:** 635-340. **Subscription Rates:** $33 Individuals in town; $42 Single issue, Canada out of town; $61 Two years; $80 Individuals 3 years. **URL:** http://www.homenewshere.com. **Remarks:** Accepts advertising. **Circ:** (Not Reported).

17045 ■ WAZN-AM - 1470
500 W Cummings Pk., Ste. 2600
Woburn, MA 01801
Phone: (781)938-0869
Fax: (781)983-0933
Format: Ethnic. **Owner:** Multicultural Radio Broadcast-

ing Inc., 27 William St., 11th Fl., New York, NY 10005, Ph: (212)966-1059, Fax: (212)966-9580. **ADI:** Boston-Worcester,MA-Derry-Manchester,NH. **Key Personnel:** Jim Glogowski, Contact, jimg@mrbi.net. **Wattage:** 1,400 day; 3,400 night.

17046 ■ WLYN-AM - 1360
500 W Cummings Pk.
Woburn, MA 01801
Format: Ethnic. **Simulcasts:** WAZN. **Networks:** Independent. **Owner:** Multicultural Radio Broadcasting Inc., 27 William St., 11th Fl., New York, NY 10005, Ph: (212)966-1059, Fax: (212)966-9580. **Founded:** 1947. **Operating Hours:** Continuous. **Key Personnel:** Jim Glogowski, Contact, jimg@mrbi.net. **Wattage:** 700. **Ad Rates:** Combined advertising rates available with WAZN.

WOODS HOLE

SW MA. Barnstable Co. 16 mi. ESE of New Bedford. Whaling, goat guilding. Residential.

17047 ■ Journal of Eukaryotic Microbiology
International Society of Protistologists
c/o Virginia Edgcomb, President
Woods Hole Oceanographic Institution
Geology and Geophysics Dept.
220 McLean Laboratory, MS 8
Woods Hole, MA 02543
Phone: (508)274-0963
Professional journal covering zoology. **Founded:** 1954. **Freq:** Bimonthly. **Key Personnel:** Roberto Docampo, Editor-in-Chief. **Subscription Rates:** $483 Institutions online only; £295 Institutions online only (UK); €374 Institutions online only (Europe); $577 Other countries. **URL:** http://onlinelibrary.wiley.com/journal/10.1111/(ISSN)1550-7408. **Remarks:** Accepts advertising. **Circ:** (Not Reported).

17048 ■ Oceanus Magazine: Reports on Research at the Woods Hole Oceanographic Institution
Woods Hole Oceanographic Institution
266 Woods Hole Rd.
Woods Hole, MA 02543-1050
Phone: (508)289-2252
Publication E-mail: oceanuseditor@whoi.edu
Oceanus is both an on-line magazine and a semiannual print magazine published by Woods Hole Oceanographic Institution. **Freq:** 3/yr. **Print Method:** Sheetfed. **Trim Size:** 8 1/2 x 11. **Cols./Page:** 2. **Col. Width:** 17 picas. **Col. Depth:** 59 picas. **Key Personnel:** Kate Madin, Editor, Writer; Lonny Lippsett, Managing Editor. **ISSN:** 0029-8182 (print). **Subscription Rates:** $8 Individuals; $23 Out of area. **URL:** http://www.whoi.edu/oceanus. **Remarks:** Advertising not accepted. **Circ:** Controlled 5000.

17049 ■ Z Magazine
Z Communications
18 Millfield St.
Woods Hole, MA 02543
Phone: (508)548-9063
Fax: (508)457-0626
Political magazine. **Founded:** 1988. **Freq:** Monthly. **Trim Size:** 8 x 10 3/4. **Cols./Page:** 2 and 3. **Col. Width:** 3 1/4 and 2 1/8 inches. **Col. Depth:** 9 1/4 inches. **Key Personnel:** Eric Sargent, Editor; Michael Albert, Editor; Lydia Sargent, Editor. **ISSN:** 1056-5507 (print). **Subscription Rates:** $33 Individuals. **URL:** http://www.zcommunications.org/zmag. **Remarks:** Advertising accepted; rates available upon request. **Circ:** (Not Reported).

17050 ■ WCAI-FM - 90.1
PO Box 82
Woods Hole, MA 02543
Phone: (508)548-9600
Free: 866-999-4626
Email: wcai@capeandislands.org
Format: Talk; News. **Networks:** National Public Radio (NPR). **Owner:** WGBH Educational Foundation, One Guest St., Boston, MA 02135, Ph: (617)300-5400, Fax: (617)300-1026. **Operating Hours:** Continuous. **Key Personnel:** Jay Allison, Sales Mgr. **Wattage:** 6,500. **Ad Rates:** Noncommercial. **URL:** http://www.capeandislands.org.

17051 ■ WNAN-FM - 91.1
PO Box 82
Woods Hole, MA 02543
Phone: (508)548-9600
Fax: (508)548-5517
Free: 866-999-4626
Email: cainan@wgbh.org
Format: Public Radio. **Key Personnel:** Jay Allison, Exec. Producer, Founder. **Ad Rates:** Noncommercial. **URL:** http://www.capeandislands.org.

WORCESTER

C. MA. Worcester Co. 40 mi. W. of Boston. College of the Holy Cross (Catholic); Clark University; Worcester Polytechnic Institute; Assumption College; State College; other schools. Manufacturing.

17052 ■ The Catholic Free Press
Roman Catholic Diocese of Worcester
51 Elm St.
Worcester, MA 01609
Publication E-mail: editor@catholicfreepress.org
Religious newspaper. **Freq:** Annual. **Print Method:** Offset. **Cols./Page:** 6. **Col. Width:** 26 nonpareils. **Col. Depth:** 294 agate lines. **Key Personnel:** Margaret M. Russel, Executive Editor. **ISSN:** 0008-8056 (print). **Subscription Rates:** $30 Individuals one year (paper and eEdition); $50 Individuals two year (paper and eEdition; $30 Individuals one year (eEdition only); $30 Individuals one year (paper only). **URL:** http://www.catholicfreepress.org. **Ad Rates:** GLR $.89; BW $150; SAU $15.85. **Remarks:** Accepts advertising. **Circ:** ‡24500.

17053 ■ Common-place: The Interactive Journal of Early American Life
American Antiquarian Society
185 Salisbury St.
Worcester, MA 01609-1634
Phone: (508)755-5221
Fax: (508)753-3311
Publisher's E-mail: library@americanantiquarian.org
Contains American history, literature, and culture to 1900, including original research, book reviews, regular columns, and blogs. **Freq:** Quarterly. **Key Personnel:** Anna Mae Duane, Editor; Walter Woodward, Editor. **ISSN:** 1544--824X (print). **URL:** http://www.americanantiquarian.org/common-place-quarterly-online-magazine-early-american-history-and-culture. **Remarks:** Advertising not accepted. **Circ:** (Not Reported).

17054 ■ Economic Geography
Economic Geography
950 Main St.
Worcester, MA 01610
Publisher's E-mail: econgeography@clarku.edu
Peer-reviewed journal publishing articles that deepen the understanding of significant economic geography issues around the world. **Founded:** Mar. 1925. **Freq:** Quarterly. **Print Method:** Offset printing. **Trim Size:** 7 x 10. **Cols./Page:** 2. **Col. Width:** 30 nonpareils. **Col. Depth:** 112 agate lines. **Key Personnel:** Hilary Laraba, Managing Editor; Henry Wai-Chung Yeung, Editor, phone: (656)516-6810, fax: (656)777-3091; Yuko Aoyama, PhD, Editor, phone: (503)793-7403; Amy K. Glasmeier, Board Member; Bjorn T. Asheim, Board Member. **ISSN:** 0013-0095 (print). **Subscription Rates:** $358 Institutions online only; $430 Institutions print and online; $358 Institutions print only; $66 Individuals online only; $74 Individuals print and online; $66 Individuals print only; $34 Students online only; $40 Students print and online; $34 Students print only. **URL:** http://www.clarku.edu/econgeography. **Remarks:** Advertising not accepted. **Circ:** ‡1600.

17055 ■ The Fifty Plus Advocate
Mar-Len Publications
131 Lincoln St.
Worcester, MA 01605
Phone: (508)752-2512
Fax: (508)752-9057
Newspaper for senior citizens. **Freq:** Biweekly. **Print Method:** Offset. **Cols./Page:** 6. **Col. Width:** 22 nonpareils. **Col. Depth:** 224 agate lines. **Key Personnel:** Sondra Shapiro, Assistant Publisher, Executive Editor. **Ad Rates:** BW $4,023; 4C $5,223. **Remarks:** Accepts advertising. **Circ:** Free 72000, Paid 1303.

17056 ■ Hartford Business Journal
New England Business Media L.L.C.
172 Shrewsbury St., Ste. 2
Worcester, MA 01604
Phone: (508)755-8004
Covers business and industry in the greater Hartford area of Connecticut. **Freq:** Weekly. **Subscription Rates:** $84.95. **URL:** http://www.hartfordbusiness.com. **Remarks:** Accepts advertising. **Circ:** (Not Reported).

17057 ■ Idealistic Studies: An Interdisciplinary Journal of Philosophy
Philosophy Documentation Center
c/o Prof. Gary Overvold, Ed.
Department of Philosophy
Clark University
950 Main St.
Worcester, MA 01610-1407
Phone: (508)793-7416
Publication E-mail: govervold@clarku.edu
Peer-reviewed scholarly journal covering the tradition and legacy of philosophical Idealism. **Freq:** 3/year. **Key Personnel:** Prof. Gary Overvold, Editor. **ISSN:** 0046--8541 (print); **EISSN:** 2153--8239 (electronic). **Subscription Rates:** $64 Institutions print only; $35 Individuals print or online; $22 Institutions single/back issues; $12 Individuals single/back issues; $215 Institutions online only; $250 Institutions print and online; $30 Members online. **URL:** http://www.pdcnet.org/idstudies. **Remarks:** Accepts advertising. **Circ:** (Not Reported).

17058 ■ International Journal of Entrepreneurship and Small Business
Inderscience Publishers
c/o Prof. Frank Hoy, Honorary Ch. Ed.
Worcester Polytechnic Institute
Department of Management
Worcester, MA 01609-2280
Publication E-mail: info@inderscience.com
Journal publishing and fostering discussion on international, cross-cultural and comparative academic research about entrepreneurs, including corporate intrapreneurs and founders of domestic new ventures. **Freq:** 12/yr. **Key Personnel:** Prof. Frank Hoy, Editor; Prof. Louis Jacques Filion, Associate Editor; Prof. Jan M. Ulijn, Associate Editor. **ISSN:** 1476--1297 (print); **EISSN:** 1741--8054 (electronic). **Subscription Rates:** $1415 Individuals online only for 1 user; $2405 Individuals online only for 2-3 users; $1981 Individuals print and online; $3537.50 Individuals online only for 4-5 users; $4598.75 Individuals online only for 6-7 users; $5589.25 Individuals online only for 8-9 users; $6509 Individuals online only for 10-14 users; $7428.75 Individuals online only for 15-19 users; $8773 Individuals online only for 20+ users. **URL:** http://www.inderscience.com/jhome.php?jcode=ijesb. **Circ:** (Not Reported).

17059 ■ International Journal of Immunological Studies
Inderscience Enterprises Ltd.
c/o Prof. Demetri Kantarelis, Editor
Department of Economics & Global Studies
Assumption College
500 Salisbury St.
Worcester, MA 01609-1296
Publisher's E-mail: copyright@inderscience.com
Peer-reviewed journal covering research in all aspects of immunology. **Freq:** Quarterly. **Key Personnel:** Dr. Borros Arneth, Editor-in-Chief. **ISSN:** 1754--1441 (print); **EISSN:** 1754--145X (electronic). **Subscription Rates:** $420 Individuals print only - annual (includes surface mail); or online (for single user only); $510 Individuals print and online. **URL:** http://www.inderscience.com/jhome.php?jcode=ijis. **Circ:** (Not Reported).

17060 ■ Journal of Clinical Apheresis
American Society for Apheresis
c/o Robert Weinstein, MD, Ed.-in-Ch.
University of Massachusetts Medical School
UMass Memorial Medical Center
55 Lake Ave. N
Worcester, MA 01655
Publication E-mail: apheresis@townisp.com
Journal covering issues in blood collection. **Freq:** 6/year. **Key Personnel:** Robert Weinstein, MD, Editor-in-Chief. **ISSN:** 0733--2459 (print); **EISSN:** 1098--1101 (electronic). **Subscription Rates:** Included in membership; $2084 U.S. and other countries online; £1065 Institutions online; €1345 Institutions online; $384

Circulation: ★ = AAM; △ or • = BPA; ♦ = CAC; ❑ = VAC; ⊕ = PO Statement; ‡ = Publisher's Report; Boldface figures = sworn; Light figures = estimated.

Individuals online; $408 Individuals U.K and Europe. **URL:** http://onlinelibrary.wiley.com/journal/10.1002/%28ISSN%291098-1101. **Remarks:** Advertising accepted; rates available upon request. **Circ:** (Not Reported).

17061 ■ Mainebiz
New England Business Media L.L.C.
172 Shrewsbury St., Ste. 2
Worcester, MA 01604
Phone: (508)755-8004
Covers the news, trends, data, politics, and personalities of Maine's business community. **Freq:** Biweekly. **Subscription Rates:** $47.95. **URL:** http://www.mainebiz.biz. **Remarks:** Accepts advertising. **Circ:** (Not Reported).

17062 ■ Natural Resource Modeling
Blackwell Publishing Inc.
c/o Catherine A. Roberts, Editor
Department of Mathematics & Computer Science
Colorado of Holy Cross
Worcester, MA 01610
Publisher's E-mail: journaladsusa@bos.blackwellpublishing.com
Journal focusing on mathematical modeling of natural resource systems. **Freq:** Quarterly. **Key Personnel:** Catherine A. Roberts, Editor. **ISSN:** 0890--8575 (print); **EISSN:** 1939--7445 (electronic). **URL:** http://www.wiley.com/WileyCDA/WileyTitle/productCd-NRM2,subjectCd-MA81.html. **Circ:** (Not Reported).

17063 ■ The Scarlet: The Student Newspaper of Clark University
Clark University Press
950 Main St.
Worcester, MA 01610
Phone: (508)793-7711
Fax: (508)793-8834
Free: 800-462-5275
Publication E-mail: scarlet@clarku.edu
Collegiate newspaper. **Freq:** Weekly (Thurs.) (during the academic year). **Print Method:** Offset. **Cols./Page:** 5. **Col. Width:** 1 3/4 inches. **Col. Depth:** 30 nonpareils. **URL:** http://www.clarkscarlet.com. **Remarks:** Accepts advertising. **Circ:** Free 2000.

17064 ■ School Arts Magazine: The Art Education Magazine
Davis Publications Inc.
50 Portland St.
Worcester, MA 01608
Phone: (508)754-7201
Fax: (508)753-3834
Free: 800-533-2847
Publisher's E-mail: sasubmissions@davisart.com
Magazine publishing articles on art and craft teaching. **Freq:** 10/year. **Print Method:** Offset. **Trim Size:** 8 1/8 x 10 7/8. **Cols./Page:** 3. **Col. Width:** 27 nonpareils. **Col. Depth:** 140 agate lines. **Key Personnel:** Nancy Walkup, Editor. **ISSN:** 0036-6463 (print). **Subscription Rates:** $24.95 Individuals; $39.95 Two years. **URL:** http://www.davisart.com/Portal/SchoolArts/SAdefault.aspx. **Ad Rates:** BW $1,813; 4C $2,363. **Remarks:** Accepts advertising. **Circ:** Paid 23829.

17065 ■ Tech News: The Student Newspaper of Worcester Polytechnic Institute
Worcester Polytechnic Institute
100 Institute Rd.
Worcester, MA 01609-2280
Phone: (508)831-5000
Fax: (508)831-5824
Publication E-mail: technews@wpi.edu
Collegiate newspaper. **Freq:** Weekly during academic year. **Print Method:** Letterpress. **Trim Size:** 8 1/2 x 11. **Cols./Page:** 4. **Col. Width:** 2 3/8 inches. **Col. Depth:** 16 inches. **Key Personnel:** Moriah Knock, Contact. **ISSN:** 1093-0081 (print). **URL:** http://www.wpi.edu/News/TechNews/about.shtml. **Formerly:** Newspeak; WPI Newspeak. **Remarks:** Accepts advertising. **Circ:** Paid ‡100, Free ‡2650.

17066 ■ Telegram & Gazette
Worchester Telegram & Gazette Corp.
20 Franklin St.
Worcester, MA 01608
Phone: (508)793-9100
Fax: (508)793-9313
Publisher's E-mail: info@telegram.com
General newspaper. **Freq:** Daily. **Print Method:** Flex. **Trim Size:** 13 3/4 x 22 3/4. **Cols./Page:** 6. **Col. Width:** 2 1/16 inches. **Col. Depth:** 21 1/2 inches. **Key Personnel:** Bruce Gaultney, Publisher, phone: (508)793-9111; Leah Lamson, Editor, phone: (508)793-9120; Susan E. Burtchell, Director, Advertising, phone: (508)793-9296; Anthony J. Simollardes, Director, phone: (508)793-9324. **USPS:** 005-046. **Subscription Rates:** $96.59 Individuals seven days home delivery (super saver); $51.74 Individuals thursday thru sunday (super saver); $94.25 Individuals seven days home delivery (standard); $49.40 Individuals thursday thru sunday (standard); $89.70 Individuals seven days home delivery (non-digital); $44.85 Individuals thursday thru sunday (non-digital). **Formed by the merger of:** Worcester Telegram; The Evening Gazette; The Saturday Paper; The Sunday Telegram. **Feature Editors:** Karen Webber, *Features*, phone: (508)793-9232, kwebber@telegram.com; Nancy Campbell, phone: (508)793-9227, ncampbell@telegram.com. **Ad Rates:** BW $11,491.20; 4C $12,341.20; SAU $104.75; CNU $13,199; PCI $104.75. **Remarks:** Accepts advertising. **Circ:** Mon.-Sat. ★100001, Sun. ★115996.

17067 ■ Worcester Business Journal
New England Business Media L.L.C.
172 Shrewsbury St., Ste. 2
Worcester, MA 01604
Phone: (508)755-8004
Covers the news, trends, data, politics, and personalities of the Central Massachusetts business community. **Freq:** Biweekly. **Key Personnel:** Peter Stanton, Chief Executive Officer, Publisher. **Subscription Rates:** $54.95 Individuals 1 year - 24 issues; $89.95 Individuals 2 years - 58 issues; $124.95 Individuals 3 years - 87 issues. **URL:** http://www.wbjournal.com. **Remarks:** Accepts advertising. **Circ:** (Not Reported).

17068 ■ Worcester Magazine: Worcester's Alternative News-weekly
Worcester Publishing Ltd.
172 Shrewsbury St., Ste. 2
Worcester, MA 01604
Phone: (508)755-8004
Publisher's E-mail: editorial@wbjournal.com
Regional tabloid. **Freq:** Weekly. **Print Method:** Offset. **Trim Size:** 11 x 15. **Cols./Page:** 4. **Col. Width:** 28 nonpareils. **Col. Depth:** 238 agate lines. **Key Personnel:** Gareth Charter, Publisher; Jeremy Shulkin, Writer; Doreen Manning, Editor. **ISSN:** 0191-4960 (print). **Subscription Rates:** $47 Individuals third class mail; $125 Individuals first class mail. **URL:** http://worcestermag.com. **Ad Rates:** BW $2,750. **Remarks:** Accepts advertising. **Circ:** Controlled ‡27354.

17069 ■ WPI Journal
Worcester Polytechnic Institute Alumni Association
100 Institute Rd.
Worcester, MA 01609-2280
Phone: (508)831-5600
Fax: (508)831-5791
Publication E-mail: wpijournal@wpi.edu
Contains information on the activities of the alumni. **Freq:** Quarterly. **Print Method:** Offset. **Trim Size:** 8 1/2 x 11. **Cols./Page:** 3. **Col. Width:** 27 nonpareils. **Col. Depth:** 133 agate lines. **Key Personnel:** Doreen Manning, Editor; Peggy Isaacson, Associate Editor; Joan Killough-Miller, Associate Editor. **ISSN:** 1538-5094 (print). **Subscription Rates:** Included in membership; free. **URL:** http://www.wpi.edu/news/wpi-journal.html. **Formerly:** Transformations. **Remarks:** Advertising not accepted. **Circ:** (Not Reported).

17070 ■ WPI Journal
Worcester Polytechnic Institute
100 Institute Rd.
Worcester, MA 01609-2280
Phone: (508)831-5000
Fax: (508)831-5824
Publication E-mail: wpijournal@wpi.edu
Contains information on the activities of the alumni. **Freq:** Quarterly. **Print Method:** Offset. **Trim Size:** 8 1/2 x 11. **Cols./Page:** 3. **Col. Width:** 27 nonpareils. **Col. Depth:** 133 agate lines. **Key Personnel:** Doreen Manning, Editor; Peggy Isaacson, Associate Editor; Joan Killough-Miller, Associate Editor. **ISSN:** 1538-5094 (print). **Subscription Rates:** Included in membership; free. **URL:** http://www.wpi.edu/news/wpi-journal.html. **Formerly:** Transformations. **Remarks:** Advertising not accepted. **Circ:** (Not Reported).

17071 ■ WCHC-FM - 88.1
One College St.
Box G
Worcester, MA 01610
Phone: (508)793-2474
Email: wchc@g.holycross.edu
Format: Eclectic. **Owner:** College of the Holy Cross, 1 College St., Worcester, MA 01610, Ph: (508)793-2011. **Founded:** 1948. **Operating Hours:** Continuous. **Key Personnel:** Chrissy McCue, Dir. of Programs. **Wattage:** 100. **Ad Rates:** Noncommercial. **Mailing address:** PO Box G, Worcester, MA 01610. **URL:** http://www.college.holycross.edu/wchc.

17072 ■ WCRN-AM - 830
82 Franklin St.
Worcester, MA 01608
Format: Big Band/Nostalgia; News; Talk; Sports. **Owner:** Carter Broadcasting Corp., 50 Braintree Hill Pk., Ste. 308, Braintree, MA 02184, Ph: (617)423-0210. **Key Personnel:** Chris Thompson, Gen. Sales Mgr., chris@wcrnradio.com. **Wattage:** 50,000. **Ad Rates:** Advertising accepted; rates available upon request. **URL:** http://www.wcrnradio.com.

17073 ■ WCUW-FM - 91.3
910 Main St.
Worcester, MA 01610
Phone: (508)753-2284
Email: wcuw@wcuw.org
Format: Eclectic. **Networks:** Independent. **Owner:** WCUW Inc., 910 Main St., Worcester, MA 01610, Ph: (508)753-2284. **Founded:** 1973. **Operating Hours:** Continuous; 100% local. **ADI:** Boston-Worcester,MA-Derry-Manchester,NH. **Wattage:** 630. **Ad Rates:** Noncommercial. **URL:** http://www.wcuw.org.

17074 ■ WCUW Inc. - 91.3
910 Main St.
Worcester, MA 01610
Phone: (508)753-2284
Email: wcuw@wcuw.org
Format: Ethnic; Eclectic. **Networks:** Independent. **Operating Hours:** Continuous. **Wattage:** 630 ERP. **Ad Rates:** Noncommercial. **URL:** http://www.wcuw.org.

17075 ■ WICN-FM - 90.5
50 Portland St.
Worcester, MA 01608
Phone: (508)752-0700
Format: Jazz; Folk; Bluegrass; News. **Networks:** National Public Radio (NPR); Public Radio International (PRI). **Owner:** WICN Public Radio Inc., Worcester, MA 01608, Ph: (508)752-0700, Free: 855-752-0700. **Founded:** 1969. **Operating Hours:** Continuous; 40% network, 60% local. **ADI:** Boston-Worcester,MA-Derry-Manchester,NH. **Key Personnel:** Thomas Lucci, Gen. Mgr., toml@wicn.org; Joe Zupan, Host, jzupan@wicn.org. **Local Programs:** *The Jazz Matinee*, Monday Tuesday Wednesday Thursday Friday Saturday 3:00 p.m. - 6:00 p.m. 2:00 p.m. - 6:00 p.m. 12:00 p.m. - 4:00 p.m.; *Soul Serenade*, Monday 7:00 p.m. - 10:00 p.m.; *A Tasteful Blend*, Thursday. **Wattage:** 8,100. **Ad Rates:** Noncommercial; underwriting available. **URL:** http://www.wicn.org.

17076 ■ WICN Public Radio Inc. - 90.5
Worcester, MA 01608
Phone: (508)752-0700
Free: 855-752-0700
Email: membership@wicn.org
Format: Public Radio. **Networks:** National Public Radio (NPR). **Operating Hours:** Continuous. **ADI:** Boston-Worcester,MA-Derry-Manchester,NH. **Wattage:** 1,100 ERP. **Ad Rates:** Noncommercial. **URL:** http://www.wicn.org.

17077 ■ WLAT-AM
122 Green St., Ste. 2r
Worcester, MA 01604
Phone: (860)524-0001
Fax: (860)548-1922
Format: Hispanic. **Owner:** Freedom Communications of Connecticut, Inc., 360 Lexington Ave., New York, NY 10017, Ph: (646)227-1320, Fax: (646)227-1337. **Founded:** 1939. **Formerly:** WNAQ-AM. **Key Personnel:** Oscar Nieves, Contact. **Wattage:** 5,000 Day; 2,800 Nig. **Ad Rates:** $10-39 for 30 seconds; $13-45 for 60 seconds.

17078 ■ WORC-AM
108 Grove St., No. 17A
Worcester, MA 01605-2629
Phone: (508)799-0581
Fax: (508)756-4851
Format: Talk. **Networks:** USA Radio. **Owner:** Davis Radio Corp., at above address. **Founded:** 1925. **Key Personnel:** Rich Green, Dir. of Programs, Contact; Mike Roberts, News Dir., mike@worc.com; Rich Green, Contact. **Wattage**: 5,000 Day; 1,000 Nig. **Ad Rates:** $17-50 per unit.

17079 ■ WORC-FM - 98.9
250 Commercial St., Winsor Bldg., 5th Fl.
250 Commercial St.
Worcester, MA 01608
Phone: (508)752-1045
Fax: (508)973-0824
Format: Oldies. **Simulcasts:** WORC-AM 1310. **Networks:** AP. **Owner:** Cumulus Media Inc., 3280 Peachtree Rd. NW, Ste. 2300, Atlanta, GA 30305-2455, Ph: (404)949-0700, Fax: (404)949-0740. **Operating Hours**: Continuous; 10% network, 90% local. **Wattage**: 1,870. **Ad Rates:** Noncommercial. **URL:** http://www.nashicon989.com.

17080 ■ WVNE-AM - 760
70 James St., Ste. 201
Worcester, MA 01603
Phone: (508)831-9863
Fax: (508)831-7964
Format: Religious. **Networks:** USA Radio; Sun Radio; Ambassador Inspirational Radio. **Owner:** Blount Communication Group, 8 Lawrence Rd., Derry, NH 03038, Ph: (603)437-9337, Fax: (603)434-1035. **Founded:** 1990. **Operating Hours**: Sunrise-sunset. **Wattage**: 25,000 Day; 8,600 Night. **Ad Rates:** $10-18 for 30 seconds; $14-26 for 60 seconds. Combined advertising rates available with WARV, WFIF, WDER, WBCI-FM. **URL:** http://lifechangingradio.com/wvne/.

17081 ■ WWFX-FM - 100.1
250 Commercial St.
250 Commercial St., Ste. 530
Worcester, MA 01608
Phone: (508)752-1045
Fax: (508)973-0824
Format: Classic Rock; Oldies. **Networks:** AP. **Operating Hours**: Continuous; 10% network, 90% local. **Wattage**: 2,850. **Ad Rates:** Advertising accepted; rates available upon request. **URL:** http://www.pikefm.com.

17082 ■ WXLO-FM - 104.5
250 Commercial St.
Worcester, MA 01608
Phone: (508)752-1045
Fax: (508)793-0824
Email: show@wxlo.com
Format: Adult Contemporary. **Networks:** CNN Radio. **Owner:** Citadel Broadcasting Corp., 7201 W Lake Mead Blvd., Ste. 400, Las Vegas, NV 89128-8366, Ph: (702)804-5200, Fax: (702)804-8250. **Founded:** 1979. **Operating Hours**: Continuous. **Key Personnel:** Jen Carter, Contact; Rick Brackett, Contact. **Wattage**: 37,000 ERP. **Ad Rates:** Advertising accepted; rates available upon request. **URL:** http://www.wxlo.com.

YARMOUTH PORT

17083 ■ Lake City News & Post
Community Newspaper
923 G Rte. 6A
Yarmouth Port, MA 02675
Phone: (508)375-4947
Community newspaper. **Freq:** Weekly (Wed.). **Trim Size:** 129. **Cols./Page:** 6. **Col. Width:** 2 inches. **Col. Depth:** 21 1/2 inches. **Ad Rates:** BW $774; 4C $1044; PCI $6. **Remarks:** Advertising accepted; rates available upon request. **Circ:** Mon.-Sat. 4258.

Sandwich Broadsider - See Sandwich

17084 ■ South Shore Living
Rabideau Publishing L.L.C.
PO Box 208
Yarmouth Port, MA 02675
Phone: (508)771-6549
Fax: (508)771-3769
Publisher's E-mail: events@capecodmagazine.com
Local magazine covering life in the Boston area's south shore communities. **Freq:** Monthly. **Trim Size:** 8.125 x 10.875. **Key Personnel:** Michael J. Rabideau, Publisher; Maria Ferri, Managing Editor; Liz Rabideau, Associate Publisher. **Subscription Rates:** $14.95 Individuals; $24.95 Two years. **URL:** http://www.ssliving.com. **Remarks:** Accepts advertising. **Circ:** (Not Reported).

17085 ■ Village Journal
Community Newspaper
923 G Rte. 6A
Yarmouth Port, MA 02675
Phone: (508)375-4947
Community newspaper. **Freq:** Weekly. **Print Method:** Offset. **Trim Size:** 10 3/8 x 15 5/16. **Cols./Page:** 6. **Col. Width:** 1 5/8 inches. **Col. Depth:** 15 inches. **Key Personnel:** Michael H. Stines, Editor. **USPS:** 999-840. **Subscription Rates:** $14; $19 off Cape. **Formerly**: The Village Advertiser. **Ad Rates:** BW $540; PCI $6. **Remarks:** Accepts advertising. **Circ:** Paid 2950, Free 100.

Circulation: ★ = AAM; △ or • = BPA; ♦ = CAC; ❏ = VAC; ⊕ = PO Statement; ‡ = Publisher's Report; Boldface figures = sworn; Light figures = estimated.

ADRIAN

Lenawee Co. Lenawee Co. (S). 34 m NW of Toledo, Ohio. Adrian College. Sienna Heights College. Manufactures aluminum extrusions, plastic injection moldings, dust filters, coil springs, auto accessories, chains, cables, electric specialties, paper, chemicals, automotive soft-trim, machine tools. Agriculture. Wheat, corn, specialty corps, livestock.

17086 ■ The Daily Telegram
GateHouse Media Inc.
133 N Winter St.
Adrian, MI 49221
Phone: (517)265-5111
Fax: (517)263-4152
General newspaper. **Founded:** 1892. **Freq:** Daily (eve.). **Print Method:** Offset. **Cols./Page:** 6. **Col. Width:** 2 inches. **Col. Depth:** 21 1/2 inches. **Key Personnel:** Paul J. Heidbreder, Publisher; Mark Lenz, Editor; Jeff Stahl, Manager, Circulation. **Subscription Rates:** $8.99 Individuals monthly; $2 Individuals digital and home delivery - per week. **URL:** http://www.lenconnect.com. **Formerly:** Adrian Daily Telegram. **Ad Rates:** BW $168; 4C $304; SAU $13.22. **Remarks:** Advertising accepted; rates available upon request. **Circ:** (Not Reported).

17087 ■ The National Gleaner Forum
Gleaner Life Insurance Society
5200 W US Highway 223
Adrian, MI 49221-9461
Fax: (517)265-7745
Free: 800-992-1894
Publisher's E-mail: gleaner@gleanerlife.org
Fraternal insurance magazine. **Freq:** Quarterly. **Print Method:** Offset. **Trim Size:** 5 3/8 x 8. **Cols./Page:** 2. **Col. Width:** 26 nonpareils. **Col. Depth:** 95 agate lines. **USPS:** 373-200. **Subscription Rates:** Included in membership. **Alt. Formats:** Download; PDF. **URL:** http://www.gleanerlife.org/portal/Collection.aspx?cid=2147483653&aud=Member. **Mailing address:** PO Box 1894, Adrian, MI 49221-7894. **Remarks:** Advertising not accepted. **Circ:** ⊕**31000**.

17088 ■ Reconstruction: Studies in Contemporary Culture
Reconstruction
c/o Davin Heckman
Siena Hts. University
English Department
1247 E Siena Heights Dr.
Adrian, MI 49221
Online journal devoted to postmodern science. **Freq:** Quarterly. **Key Personnel:** Davin Heckman, Editor; Marc Ouellette, Managing Editor; Alan Clinton, Editor. **ISSN:** 1547--4348 (print). **Subscription Rates:** Free online. **URL:** http://reconstruction.eserver.org/upcoming.shtml. **Circ:** (Not Reported).

17089 ■ WABJ-AM - 1490
121 W Maumec
Adrian, MI 49221
Phone: (517)265-1500
Fax: (517)263-4525
Format: News; Talk. **Owner:** Friends Communication of Michigan Inc., at above address. **Founded:** 1947. **Ad Rates:** Noncommercial.

17090 ■ WLEN-FM - 103.9
PO Box 687
Adrian, MI 49221
Phone: (517)263-1039
Fax: (517)265-5362
Email: info@wlen.com
Format: Adult Contemporary. **Networks:** CNN Radio. **Owner:** Lenawee Broadcasting Co., 242 W Maumee, Adrian, MI 49221-2022. **Founded:** 1965. **Operating Hours:** Continuous; 10% network, 90% local. **ADI:** Detroit, MI. **Key Personnel:** Julie Koehn, Contact; Dale Gaertner, Prog. Dir.; Steve Barkway, Sports Dir. **Wattage:** 3,000. **Ad Rates:** Noncommercial. **URL:** http://www.wlen.com.

17091 ■ WQTE-FM - 95.3
121 W Maunee St.
Adrian, MI 49221
Phone: (517)265-1500
Fax: (517)263-4525
Format: Country. **Owner:** Friends Communications of Michigan Inc., at above address. **Founded:** 1976. **Ad Rates:** Advertising accepted; rates available upon request.

17092 ■ WVAC-FM - 107.9
110 S Madison St.
Adrian, MI 49221
Phone: (517)265-5161
Free: 800-877-2246
Format: Full Service. **Networks:** Independent. **Owner:** Adrian College, 110 S Madison St., Adrian, MI 49221, Ph: (517)265-5161, Free: 800-877-2246. **Founded:** 1983. **Operating Hours:** Continuous; 100% local. **Wattage:** 010. **Ad Rates:** Noncommercial. **URL:** http://www.adrian.edu.

ALBION

Calhoun Co. Calhoun Co. (S). 20 m W of Jackson. Albion College. Manufactures pearlitic and malleable castings, bakery equipment, casters, counterweights, conveyors, screw products, fiberglass insulation, computer cabinetry, wire shelving. Oil exploration and oil well services. Agriculture. Wheat, corn, apples, soybeans.

17093 ■ Morning Star: The Shopping Guide
Salesmen Publications
125 E Cass St.
Albion, MI 49224
Phone: (517)629-2127
Publisher's E-mail: info@salesmanpublications.com
Shopper. **Freq:** Weekly (Wed.). **Print Method:** Offset. **Trim Size:** 11 3/8 x 16 3/4. **Cols./Page:** 6. **Col. Width:** 19 nonpareils. **Col. Depth:** 224 agate lines. **Key Personnel:** George R. Raymond, Editor. **Subscription Rates:** $189 Individuals; $309 Two years; $409 Individuals 3 years; $22.95 Individuals monthly. **URL:** http://www.morningstar.com/?byrefresh=yes; http://www.salesmanpublications.com/MorningStar.html. **Ad Rates:** BW $345; PCI $4. **Remarks:** Color advertising accepted; rates available upon request. **Circ:** Free 9,366.

17094 ■ WBJW-FM - 91.7
PO Box 4164
Evansville, IN 47724
Fax: (812)768-5552
Free: 800-264-5550
Format: Religious. **Owner:** Thy Word Network, PO Box 4164, Evansville, IN 47724. **Key Personnel:** Floyd Turner, Chief Engineer. **Ad Rates:** Noncommercial. **URL:** http://www.thyword.us.

ALLEGAN

Allegan Co. Allegan Co. (SW). On Kalamazoo River 23 m NW of Kalamazoo. Manufactures chairs, electric heating, pipe fittings, auto parts, drugs, electronics, cement blocks and vaults; commercial printing plant. Fruit, dairy, Christmas tree, poultry farms. Onions, celery.

17095 ■ Allegan Flashes
Flashes Publishers Inc.
595 Jenner Dr.
Allegan, MI 49010-1567
Phone: (269)673-2141
Shopper. **Freq:** Weekly (Mon.). **Print Method:** Offset. **Trim Size:** 11 3/8 x 13 3/4. **Cols./Page:** 4. **Col. Width:** 2 7/16 inches. **Col. Depth:** 12 1/2 inches. **Key Personnel:** Peter Esser, Publisher, phone: (616)546-4259; Debbie Sloan, Manager, phone: (269)276-4364. **URL:** http://www.flashespublishers.com/node/10. **Ad Rates:** GLR $6; BW $946.56; 4C $225; PCI $9.15. **Remarks:** Advertising accepted; rates available upon request. **Circ:** ‡75,600.

17096 ■ Holland Flashes Shopping Guide
Flashes Publishers Inc.
595 Jenner Dr.
Allegan, MI 49010-1567
Phone: (269)673-2141
Shopper/weekly newspaper. **Freq:** Weekly (Mon.). **Print Method:** Offset. **Trim Size:** 10 3/8 x 12 1/2. **Cols./Page:** 4. **Col. Width:** 2 7/16 inches. **Col. Depth:** 12 1/2 inches. **Key Personnel:** Peter Esser, Publisher, phone: (616)546-4259; Debbie Sloan, Manager, phone: (269)673-1720. **Ad Rates:** GLR $8; BW $738; 4C $220; PCI $7.38. **Remarks:** Accepts advertising. **Circ:** (Not Reported).

17097 ■ Kalamazoo Flashes
Flashes Publishers Inc.
595 Jenner Dr.
Allegan, MI 49010-1567
Phone: (269)673-2141
Shopping guide. **Freq:** Weekly. **Print Method:** Offset. **Key Personnel:** Peter Esser, Publisher, phone: (616)546-4259. **Formerly:** Kalamazoo, Westside, Village, & Portage Flashes. **Remarks:** Accepts advertising. **Circ:** (Not Reported).

17098 ■ Senior Times
Flashes Publishers Inc.
595 Jenner Dr.
Allegan, MI 49010-1567
Phone: (269)673-2141
Newspaper for senior citizens in Kalamazoo, MI. **Founded:** 1989. **Freq:** 13/yr. **Print Method:** Offset. **Trim Size:** 10 3/8 x 16. **Cols./Page:** 6. **Col. Width:** 1 5/8

Circulation: ★ = AAM; △ or • = BPA; ♦ = CAC; ❑ = VAC; ⊕ = PO Statement; ‡ = Publisher's Report; Boldface figures = sworn; Light figures = estimated.

inches. **Col. Depth:** 16 inches. **Key Personnel:** Deb Lunsford, Manager, Circulation. **URL:** http://www.flashespublishers.com/. **Ad Rates:** BW $1150. **Remarks:** Accepts classified advertising. **Circ:** (Not Reported).

ALMA

Gratiot Co. Gratiot Co. (C). 36 m W of Saginaw. Alma College. Manufactures automotive supplies, recreational boat products, plastic, beet sugar, dairy products, Oil refineries. Agriculture. Beans, sugar beets, corn.

17099 ■ Michigan Academician
Michigan Academy of Science, Arts, & Letters
Alma College, Centennial House
614 W Superior St.
Alma, MI 48801-1599
Phone: (989)463-7969
Fax: (989)463-7970
Publisher's E-mail: michiganacademy@alma.edu
Publication covering the humanities, science and technology. **Freq:** Quarterly. **Print Method:** Offset. **Trim Size:** 6 x 9. **Key Personnel:** Kathleen Duke. **ISSN:** 0026--2005 (print). **Online:** Gale. **URL:** http://netforum.avectra.com/eweb/DynamicPage.aspx?Site=MASAL&WebCode=academician. **Remarks:** Advertising not accepted. **Circ:** Paid ⊕**850**.

17100 ■ WFYC-AM - 1280
PO Box 665
Alma, MI 48801-0669
Phone: (517)463-3175
Format: Sports. **Founded:** 1948. **Operating Hours:** Continuous. **ADI:** Flint-Saginaw-Bay City, MI. **Key Personnel:** James Sommerville, Contact. **Wattage:** 1,000. **Ad Rates:** for 30 seconds; for 60 seconds. Combined advertising rates available with WQBX-FM.

17101 ■ WMLM-AM - 1520
4170 N State Rd.
Alma, MI 48801
Phone: (989)463-4013
Email: info@wmlm.com
Owner: Siefker Broadcasting Corp., at above address. **Founded:** 1977. **Wattage:** 1,000 KW. **Ad Rates:** $7-11 for 30 seconds; $7.50-20 for 60 seconds. **URL:** http://www.wmlm.com/.

17102 ■ WQAC-FM - 90.9
614 W Superior St.
Alma, MI 48801
Phone: (989)463-7333
Format: Eclectic. **Ad Rates:** Noncommercial.

17103 ■ WQBX-FM - 104.9
5310 N State Rd.
Alma, MI 48801
Phone: (989)463-3175
Fax: (989)463-6674
Email: wqbxfm@gmail.com
Format: Adult Contemporary. **Owner:** Jacom, Inc., at above address. **Founded:** 1948. **Formerly:** WFYC-FM. **Operating Hours:** Continuous. **ADI:** Flint-Saginaw-Bay City, MI. **Key Personnel:** Susan Sommerville, Contact. **Wattage:** 6,000. **Ad Rates:** $15-20 for 60 seconds. Combined advertising rates available with WFYC-AM. **Mailing address:** PO Box 665, Alma, MI 48801. **URL:** http://www.wqbx.biz/contact.html.

ALMONT

17104 ■ Unsearchable Riches: A Bimonthly Magazine for God and His Word
Concordant Publishing Concern Inc.
PO Box 449
Almont, MI 48003
Phone: (810)798-3563
Publisher's E-mail: email@concordant.org
Magazine presenting exposition of scripture, both Old and New Testaments. **Freq:** Bimonthly. **Print Method:** Offset. **Trim Size:** 5 x 7 1/2. **Cols./Page:** 1. **Col. Width:** 48 nonpareils. **Col. Depth:** 81 agate lines. **ISSN:** 0042--0476 (print). **Subscription Rates:** $1 Individuals personal; $20 Individuals gift; $15 Individuals U.R. Index, cross reference. **Alt. Formats:** PDF. **URL:** http://www.concordant.org/ur/index.html. **Remarks:** Advertising not accepted. **Circ:** ‡2000.

ALPENA

Alpena Co. Alpena Co. (NE). On Thunder Bay, 125 m N of Bay City. Summer resort. Limestone quarries. Manufactures paper, cement. Fisheries; timber. Farming. Potatoes, raspberries.

17105 ■ Alpena News
Alpena News Publishing Co.
130 Park Pl.
Alpena, MI 49707
Phone: (989)354-3111
Fax: (989)354-2096
Free: 800-448-0254
General newspaper. **Freq:** Mon.-Sat. (morn.). **Print Method:** Offset. **Trim Size:** 6 x 21 1/2. **Cols./Page:** 6. **Col. Width:** 1 7/8 inches. **Col. Depth:** 301 agate lines. **Key Personnel:** Bill Speer, Editor; Kathy Burton, Business Manager; Steve Murch, Managing Editor. **USPS:** 014-600. **Subscription Rates:** $52 Individuals monday thru saturday, home delivery + digital; $74.75 By mail monday thru saturday, in-state delivery + digital; $81.25 Out of state monday thru saturday, mail delivery + digital. **Mailing address:** PO Box 367, Alpena, MI 49707. **Ad Rates:** GLR $20.23; BW $12.75; 4C $230; SAU $20.23; PCI $12.75. **Remarks:** Accepts advertising. **Circ:** Mon.-Sat. ★**10,697**.

17106 ■ Alpena Star
Morningstar Publications
431 N Ripley Blvd.
Alpena, MI 49707
Phone: (989)356-2121
Fax: (989)354-8275
Free: 800-368-4131
Shopper (tabloid). **Freq:** Weekly. **Print Method:** Offset Uses mats. **Trim Size:** 11 1/8 x 17 1/2. **Cols./Page:** 6. **Col. Width:** 21 nonpareils. **Col. Depth:** 224 agate lines. **URL:** http://flashpageturn.com/?PID=1000553. **Formerly:** Alpena Star Advertiser. **Mailing address:** PO Box 464, Alpena, MI 49707. **Remarks:** Accepts advertising. **Circ:** 19800.

17107 ■ WATZ-AM - 1450
123 Prentiss St.
Alpena, MI 49707
Phone: (989)354-8400
Fax: (989)354-3436
Email: watz@watz.com
Format: News; Talk; Sports. **Networks:** ABC. **Owner:** Midwestern Broadcasting Co., 314 E. Front St., Traverse City, MI 49684. **Founded:** 1946. **Operating Hours:** 5:30 a.m.-1 a.m. **ADI:** Alpena, MI. **Key Personnel:** Susie Martin, Music Dir., martins@watz.com; Mike Centala, Gen. Mgr., mcentala@watz.com; Bruce Johnson, News Dir. **Wattage:** 1,000. **Ad Rates:** $6 for 30 seconds; $9 for 60 seconds. Combined advertising rates available with WATZ-FM. **URL:** http://www.watz.com.

17108 ■ WATZ-FM - 99.3
123 Prentiss St.
Alpena, MI 49707
Phone: (989)354-8400
Fax: (989)354-3436
Email: watz@watz.com
Format: Contemporary Country. **Networks:** ABC. **Owner:** WATZ, 123 Prentiss St., Alpena, MI 49707, Ph: (989)354-8400, Fax: (989)354-3436. **Founded:** 1967. **Operating Hours:** Continuous. **ADI:** Alpena, MI. **Key Personnel:** Steve Wright, Dir. of Operations; Bruce Johnson, News Dir.; Mike Centala, Gen. Mgr., mcentala@watz.com. **Wattage:** 50,000 ERP. **Ad Rates:** $7-11.50 for 10 seconds; $13-17 for 30 seconds; $17-23 for 60 seconds. Combined advertising rates available with WATZ-AM. **URL:** http://www.watz.com.

17109 ■ WBKB-TV - 11
1390 N Bagley St.
Alpena, MI 49707
Phone: (989)356-3434
Format: Commercial TV. **Networks:** CBS. **Owner:** Thunder Bay Broadcasting Corp., 1390 N Bagley St., Alpena, MI 49707-8101. **Founded:** 1975. **Operating Hours:** Continuous. **ADI:** Alpena, MI. **Key Personnel:** Stephanie Parkinson, Contact. **Ad Rates:** Advertising accepted; rates available upon request. **URL:** http://wbkb11.com.

17110 ■ WCML-TV - 6
1999 E Campus Dr.
Mount Pleasant, MI 48859
Phone: (989)774-3105
Fax: (989)774-4427
Free: 800-727-9268
Format: Public TV. **Networks:** Public Broadcasting Service (PBS). **Owner:** Central Michigan University, 1200 S Franklin St., Mount Pleasant, MI 48859, Ph: (989)774-4000. **Founded:** 1975. **Operating Hours:** midnight. **ADI:** Alpena, MI. **Key Personnel:** David Nicholas, News Dir., nicho1d@cmich.edu; Rick Schudiske, Asst. GM, Director, schud1ra@cmich.edu; Ray Ford, Dir. of Programs, ford1r@cmich.edu. **Ad Rates:** Noncommercial. **URL:** http://www.wcmu.org.

17111 ■ W18BT - 18
PO Box A
Santa Ana, CA 92711
Phone: (714)832-2950
Free: 888-731-1000
Owner: Trinity Broadcasting Network Inc., PO Box A, Santa Ana, CA 92711, Ph: (714)832-2950, Free: 888-731-1000. **URL:** http://www.tbn.org.

17112 ■ WHAK-FM - 99.9
1491 M-32 W
Alpena, MI 49707
Email: info@999thewave.com
Format: Oldies. **Ad Rates:** Noncommercial.

17113 ■ WHSB-FM - 107.7
1491 M-32 W
Alpena, MI 49707
Phone: (989)354-4611
Fax: (989)354-4014
Format: Adult Contemporary. **Networks:** Jones Satellite. **Owner:** Edwards Group Inc., 125 Eagles Nest Dr., Seneca, SC 29678, Ph: (864)882-3272, Fax: (864)882-3718. **Founded:** 1964. **Operating Hours:** Continuous. **ADI:** Alpena, MI. **Key Personnel:** Darrel Kelly, Gen. Mgr., dkelly@truenorthradionetwork.com; Phil Heimerl, News Dir., news@truenorthradionetwork.com. **Wattage:** 100,000. **Ad Rates:** Noncommercial. Combined advertising rates available with WHAK-AM; WHAK-FM. **URL:** http://www.truenorthradionetwork.com.

17114 ■ WMLQ-FM - 96.7
123 Prentiss St.
Alpena, MI 49707
Phone: (989)354-8400
Fax: (517)734-7804
Format: Big Band/Nostalgia; Full Service. **Networks:** Satellite Music Network; ABC. **Owner:** President - John D. Degroat, at above address. **Founded:** 1984. **Operating Hours:** 12:00 a.m.-10:00 p.m Monday – Friday ; 1:00 a.m. - 10:00 p.m Saturday – Sunday. **ADI:** Alpena, MI. **Key Personnel:** Ken Smolinski, Station Mgr. **Ad Rates:** $6-11 for 30 seconds; $8-13 for 60 seconds. **URL:** http://www.watz.com.

17115 ■ WRGZ-FM - 96.7
123 Prentiss St.
Alpena, MI 49707
Phone: (989)354-8400
Fax: (989)354-3436
Email: watz@watz.com
Format: Country. **Key Personnel:** Mike Centala, Gen. Mgr., mcentala@watz.com. **URL:** http://www.watz.com.

17116 ■ WVXA-FM - 96.7
123 Prentiss St.
Alpena, MI 49707
Fax: (989)354-3436
Email: wvxa@xstarnet.com
Format: Public Radio. **Key Personnel:** Carolyn Heinzel, Contact. **Wattage:** 26,000. **Ad Rates:** Noncommercial. **URL:** http://www.watz.com.

17117 ■ WWTH-FM - 100.7
1491 M-32 W
Alpena, MI 49707
Phone: (989)354-4611
Fax: (989)354-4104
Free: 800-743-6424
Email: info@1007thundercountry.com
Format: Country. **Owner:** Edwards Communications, LLC, 125 Eagles Nest Dr., Seneca, SC 29678. **Wattage:** 20,500. **Ad Rates:** Advertising accepted; rates available upon request. **URL:** http://truenorthradionetwork.com.

ANN ARBOR

Washtenaw Co. Washtenaw Co. (SE). On Huron River, 38 m W of Detroit. University of Michigan. Manufactures ball bearings, springs, baling presses, drill heads, tapping and reaming machinery, advertising novelties, precision instruments, awnings. Major high technology center in robotics, computers.

17118 ■ Ann Arbor Observer
Ann Arbor Observer Co.
2390 Winewood
Ann Arbor, MI 48103
Phone: (734)769-3175
Fax: (734)769-3375
Publisher's E-mail: editor@aaobserver.com
City magazine offering in-depth features, profiles, historical articles, items on new business, restaurant reviews, and a listing of events and exhibits. **Freq:** Monthly. **Print Method:** Offset. **Trim Size:** 10 1/2 x 13 1/2. **Key Personnel:** John Hilton, Editor; Patricia Garcia, Publisher; Jean Morgan, Business Manager. **Subscription Rates:** Individuals free to all permanent residents of the Ann Arbor ZIP codes and school district.; $20 Individuals; $35 Two years; $10 Individuals digital. **URL:** http://annarborobserver.com/articles/front_page.html. **Ad Rates:** BW $3,285. **Remarks:** Accepts advertising. **Circ:** Paid ‡60,000.

17119 ■ Austrian Studies
ITHAKA
301 E Liberty, Ste. 400
Ann Arbor, MI 48104-2262
Phone: (734)887-7000
Fax: (734)998-9113
Publisher's E-mail: support@jstor.org
Journal covering distinctive cultural traditions of the Habsburg Empire and the Austrian Republic. **Freq:** Annual. **Key Personnel:** Deborah Holmes, Editor. **ISSN:** 1350-7532 (print). **Subscription Rates:** £76 Institutions, other countries; $177 Institutions. **URL:** http://maney.co.uk/index.php/journals/aus/. **Circ:** (Not Reported).

17120 ■ BioMatters: Driving Biosciences Industry Growth
MichBio
3520 Green Ct., Ste. 175
Ann Arbor, MI 48105-1175
Phone: (734)527-9150
Fax: (734)302-4933
Publisher's E-mail: info@michbio.org
Magazine chronicling Michigan's bioscience industry. **Freq:** Semiannual. **Key Personnel:** Stephen Rapundalo, PhD, President; Jayne Berkaw, Editor. **Subscription Rates:** Included in membership. **Alt. Formats:** PDF. **URL:** http://www.michbio.org/?page=24. **Mailing address:** PO Box 130199, Ann Arbor, MI 48113-0199. **Remarks:** Accepts advertising. **Circ:** (Not Reported).

17121 ■ Called: The Lifestyle Magazine for Female Pastors and Women of Ministry
DuCille Inc.
PO Box 1141
Ann Arbor, MI 48106
Fax: (866)384-5037
Free: 866-384-5037
Publisher's E-mail: publisher@calledmagazine.com
Magazine targeting female pastors including profiles of female church leaders, fashion and beauty, marriage, ministerial marketing, spiritual issues, humor, food, and finance. **Freq:** Quarterly. **Trim Size:** 9 x 10 7/8. **Key Personnel:** Marsha DuCille, Director, Editorial, Publisher. **Subscription Rates:** $13.99 Individuals 1 year; $19.99 Individuals 2 years; $10.95 Single issue. **URL:** http://calledmagazine.com. **Remarks:** Accepts advertising. **Circ:** (Not Reported).

17122 ■ Child Development Perspectives
Society for Research in Child Development
2950 S State St., Ste. 401
Ann Arbor, MI 48104
Phone: (734)926-0600
Fax: (734)926-0601
Publisher's E-mail: journaladsusa@bos.blackwellpublishing.com
Journal covering the field of developmental sciences. **Freq:** 3/year. **ISSN:** 1750--8592 (print); **EISSN:** 1750--8606 (electronic). **Subscription Rates:** $64 Individuals print & online; £85 Individuals print & online, UK and Europe (non euro zone); €86 Individuals print & online, Europe; $90 Other countries print & online. **URL:** http://onlinelibrary.wiley.com/journal/10.1111/(ISSN)1750-8606. **Remarks:** Accepts advertising. **Circ:** (Not Reported).

17123 ■ The Clinical Neuropsychologist
American Academy of Clinical Neuropsychology
Dept. of Psychiatry
University of Michigan Health System
1500 E Medical Center Dr.
Ann Arbor, MI 48109-5295
Phone: (734)936-8269
Fax: (734)936-9761
Freq: 8/year. **ISSN:** 1744--4144 (print); **EISSN:** 1385--4046 (electronic). **Subscription Rates:** $728 for individuals (print only); $1874 for institutions (print and electronic). **URL:** http://www.theaacn.org/journals.aspx; http://www.tandfonline.com/toc/ntcn20/current. **Remarks:** Advertising not accepted. **Circ:** (Not Reported).

17124 ■ Comparative Studies in Society & History
Cambridge University Press
c/o David Akin, Mng. Ed.
University of Michigan
1007 E Huron
Ann Arbor, MI 48109-1690
Publication E-mail: cssh@atsumich.edu
Peer-reviewed journal focusing on anthropology, sociology, history, political science. **Freq:** Quarterly. **Key Personnel:** Diane Owen Hughes, Member; David Akin, Managing Editor; Thomas Trautmann, Member; Andrew Shryock, Editor. **ISSN:** 0010--4175 (print); **EISSN:** 1475--2999 (electronic). **Subscription Rates:** $64 Individuals print only; $301 Institutions online & print; $244 Institutions online only; £38 Individuals print only; £191 Institutions online & print; £156 Institutions online only; £38 Institutions online only. **URL:** http://journals.cambridge.org/action/displayJournal?jid=CSS; http://journals.cambridge.org/action/displayIssue?jid=CSS&tab=currentissue; http://cssh.lsa.umich.edu. **Ad Rates:** BW $960. **Remarks:** Accepts advertising. **Circ:** Combined ‡2000, 2000.

17125 ■ Dimensions
University of Michigan Taubman College of Architecture and Urban Planning
2000 Bonisteel Blvd., Rm. 2150
Ann Arbor, MI 48109-2069
Phone: (734)764-1300
Fax: (734)763-2322
Journal featuring the architectural work produced by students, fellows, and visiting lecturers. **Freq:** Annual. **ISSN:** 1074-6536 (print). **Subscription Rates:** $15 Students. **URL:** http://taubmancollege.umich.edu/architecture/publications/dimensions. **Circ:** (Not Reported).

17126 ■ Education About Asia
Association for Asian Studies
825 Victors Way, Ste. 310
Ann Arbor, MI 48108
Phone: (734)665-2490
Fax: (734)665-3801
Freq: 3/year Spring, Fall and Winter. **Subscription Rates:** $20 Members U.S.; $30 Members outside U.S.; $8 Members single copy; $30 Nonmembers; $37 Nonmembers outside U.S.; $8 Nonmembers single copy. **URL:** http://www.asian-studies.org/Publications/EAA/About. **Remarks:** Accepts advertising. **Circ:** (Not Reported).

17127 ■ Education Digest
Prakken Publications Inc.
2851 Boardwalk Dr.
Ann Arbor, MI 48104
Phone: (734)975-2800
Fax: (734)975-2787
Free: 800-530-9673
Magazine covering educational products. **Freq:** Monthly. **Print Method:** Offset. **Trim Size:** 8 3/8 x 10 7/8. **Cols./Page:** 3. **Col. Width:** 27 nonpareils. **Col. Depth:** 140 agate lines. **Key Personnel:** Pam Moore, Managing Editor; Vanessa Ravelli, Manager, Circulation. **ISSN:** 0046--1482 (print). **Subscription Rates:** $58 Individuals; $78 Other countries. **URL:** http://www.eddigest.com. **Ad Rates:** BW $775. **Remarks:** Accepts advertising. **Circ:** (Not Reported).

17128 ■ The Education Digest: Essential Readings Condensed for Quick Review
Prakken Publications Inc.
2851 Boardwalk Dr.
Ann Arbor, MI 48104
Phone: (734)975-2800
Fax: (734)975-2787
Free: 800-530-9673
Journal containing condensed articles from educational publications focusing on key issues, policies, practices, and research, with regular monthly columns and features aimed primarily at professional educators. **Freq:** 9/yr (Sept. through May). **Print Method:** Web Offset. **Trim Size:** 5 1/2 x 8. **Cols./Page:** 2. **Col. Width:** 24 nonpareils. **Col. Depth:** 92 agate lines. **Key Personnel:** Pam Moore, Managing Editor. **ISSN:** 0013-127X (print). **Subscription Rates:** $53.20 Individuals US agency; $73.20 Other countries Foreign/Canadian Agency; $58 Individuals; $78 Other countries. **URL:** http://www.eddigest.com. **Ad Rates:** BW $775; 4C $400; PCI $50. **Remarks:** Accepts advertising. **Circ:** 10,000.

17129 ■ Endangered Species UPDATE
University of Michigan School of Natural Resources & Environment
440 Church St.
Ann Arbor, MI 48109-1041
Phone: (734)764-6453
Publication E-mail: esupdate@umich.edu
Technical environmental journal. **Freq:** Quarterly. **Key Personnel:** Megan Banka, Editor; David Faulkner, Assistant Editor. **ISSN:** 1081--3705 (print). **URL:** http://www.umich.edu/~esupdate. **Remarks:** Advertising not accepted. **Circ:** (Not Reported).

17130 ■ FOUND
FOUND Magazine
3455 Charing Cross Rd.
Ann Arbor, MI 48108-1911
Publisher's E-mail: info@foundmagazine.com
Consumer magazine covering found items. **Freq:** Triennial. **Key Personnel:** Davy Rothbart, Editor; James Molenda, Managing Editor; Sarah Locke, Senior Editor. **Subscription Rates:** $5 Single issue. **URL:** http://foundmagazine.com. **Remarks:** Accepts advertising. **Circ:** (Not Reported).

17131 ■ IEEE Transactions on Geoscience and Remote Sensing
IEEE - Geoscience and Remote Sensing Society
c/o Dr. Kamal Sarabandi, President
Dept. of Electrical Eng. and Computer Science
Ann Arbor, MI 48109-2122
Phone: (734)936-1575
Fax: (734)647-2106
Publisher's E-mail: webmaster@grss-ieee.org
Journal focusing on the theory, concepts, and techniques of science and engineering as applied to sensing the land, oceans, atmosphere, and space, including the processing, interpretation, and dissemination of this information. **Freq:** Monthly. **Key Personnel:** Prof. Antonio J. Plaza, Editor. **ISSN:** 0196--2892 (print). **Subscription Rates:** Included in membership. **URL:** http://www.grss-ieee.org/publications/transactions. **Remarks:** Advertising not accepted. **Circ:** (Not Reported).

17132 ■ International Journal of Legal Information
International Association of Law Libraries
c/o Barbara Garavaglia, Secretary
University of Michigan Law Library
801 Monroe St.
Ann Arbor, MI 48109
Phone: (734)764-9338
Fax: (734)764-5863
Professional journal covering foreign, comparative, and international law. Official publication of the International Association of Law Libraries. **Freq:** 3/year. **Key Personnel:** Thomas Mills, Editor; Mark Engsberg, Editor. **ISSN:** 0731--1265 (print). **Subscription Rates:** Included in membership. **Alt. Formats:** Microfiche. **URL:** http://iall.org/journal-ijli. **Formerly**: International Journal of Law Libraries. **Remarks:** Advertising not accepted. **Circ:** Paid 600.

17133 ■ ISR Sampler
Institute for Social Research
426 Thompson St.
Ann Arbor, MI 48104-2321
Phone: (734)764-8354
Fax: (734)647-4575
Publisher's E-mail: umisr-info@umich.edu
Alt. Formats: Download; PDF. **URL:** http://home.isr.umich.edu/news/isrsampler/. **Mailing address:** PO Box 1248, Ann Arbor, MI 48106-1248. **Remarks:** Advertising not accepted. **Circ:** (Not Reported).

Circulation: ★ = AAM; △ or • = BPA; ♦ = CAC; ❑ = VAC; ⊕ = PO Statement; ‡ = Publisher's Report; Boldface figures = sworn; Light figures = estimated.

17134 ■ Journal of the American Oriental Society
American Oriental Society
Hatcher Graduate Library
University of Michigan
Ann Arbor, MI 48109-1190
Phone: (734)764-7555
Fax: (734)647-4760
Oriental studies journal. **Freq:** Quarterly. **Print Method:** Offset. **Trim Size:** 8 1/4 x 10. **Cols./Page:** 2. **Col. Width:** 30 nonpareils. **Col. Depth:** 104 agate lines. **Key Personnel:** Stephanie W. Jamison, Editor-in-Chief; Peri Bearman, Associate Editor; Gary Beckman, Associate Editor. **ISSN:** 0003--0279 (print). **Subscription Rates:** $35 Individuals /issue; Included in membership. **URL:** http://www.americanorientalsociety.org/publications/journal-of-the-american-oriental-society-jaos. **Ad Rates:** BW $250. **Remarks:** Accepts advertising. **Circ:** ‡2300.

17135 ■ Journal for Anthroposophy
Anthroposophical Society in America
1923 Geddes Ave.
Ann Arbor, MI 48104
Phone: (734)662-9355
Fax: (734)662-1727
Publisher's E-mail: info@anthroposophy.org
Journal containing valuable articles, poems, and visual artwork in the field of philosophy, anthroposophy, and consciousness studies. **Freq:** Semiannual. **Subscription Rates:** $15 Single issue; $85 Individuals set of ten + shipping included. **URL:** http://www.anthroposophy.org/communications/journal-for-anthroposophy. **Remarks:** Accepts advertising. **Circ:** (Not Reported).

17136 ■ The Journal of Asian Studies
Association for Asian Studies
825 Victors Way, Ste. 310
Ann Arbor, MI 48108
Phone: (734)665-2490
Fax: (734)665-3801
Journal containing articles and book reviews by Asian and Western specialists. **Freq:** Quarterly May, August, February, November. **Print Method:** Web offset. **Trim Size:** 10 x 7 1/2. **Cols./Page:** 1. **Key Personnel:** Jeffrey N. Wasserstrom, Editor; Jennifer H. Munger, Managing Editor. **ISSN:** 0021-9118 (print); **EISSN:** 1752-0401 (electronic). **Subscription Rates:** $208 U.S., Canada, and Mexico institution; print and online bundle; $197 U.S., Canada, and Mexico institution; online only; Free members; £117 Elsewhere + VAT, print and online; £112 Elsewhere + VAT, online only; $55 U.S., Canada, and Mexico back issue; £32 Elsewhere back issue; $248 Institutions print and online; $236 Institutions online only; £145 Institutions print and online; £140 Institutions online only. **URL:** http://www.aasianst.org; http://www.asian-studies.org/publications/JAS.htm. **Ad Rates:** 4C $800. **Remarks:** Accepts advertising. **Circ:** 8,000.

17137 ■ Journal of Behavioral Decision Making
John Wiley and Sons Ltd.
c/o Frank J. Yates, Assoc. Ed.
Department of Psychology
University of Michigan
525 E University Ave.
Ann Arbor, MI 48109-1109
Journal on behavioral decision making for practitioners and researchers in cognitive and social psychology, management science, experimental economics, and organizational behavior. **Freq:** 5/year. **Key Personnel:** George Wright, Editor; Lehman Benson, III, Editor; Jonathan Baron, Board Member; Fergus Bolger, Editor. **ISSN:** 0894--3257 (print); **EISSN:** 1099--0771 (electronic). **Subscription Rates:** $1791 Institutions, other countries print and online; £915 Institutions print and online; €1157 Institutions print and online; $311 Other countries print only; £176 Individuals print only; $321 Individuals print in U.S., Canada, Mexico, and rest of the world; £182 Individuals print in U.K. **URL:** http://onlinelibrary.wiley.com/journal/10.1002/(ISSN)1099-0771; http://www.sjdm.org/links.html. **Remarks:** Accepts advertising. **Circ:** (Not Reported).

17138 ■ Journal of Electronic Publishing
University of Michigan Press
839 Greene St.
Ann Arbor, MI 48104-3209
Phone: (734)764-4388
Fax: (734)615-1540
Free: 800-621-2736
Publication E-mail: jep-info@umich.edu
Journal discussing on electronic publishing. **Key Personnel:** Shana Kimball, Board Member; Maria Bonn, Editor. **ISSN:** 1080--2711 (print). **Subscription Rates:** Free. **URL:** http://www.journalofelectronicpublishing.org. **Circ:** (Not Reported).

17139 ■ Journal of Research on Adolescence
Society for Research on Adolescence
2950 S State St., Ste. 401
Ann Arbor, MI 48104
Phone: (734)926-0700
Fax: (734)926-0701
Publisher's E-mail: info@s-r-a.org
Freq: Quarterly. **ISSN:** 1050--8392 (print); **EISSN:** 1532--7795 (electronic). **Subscription Rates:** $893 Institutions online only; $169 Individuals online only. **URL:** http://www.s-r-a.org/journal-research-adolescence; http://onlinelibrary.wiley.com/journal/10.1111/%28ISSN%291532-7795/earlyview. **Remarks:** Advertising not accepted. **Circ:** (Not Reported).

17140 ■ Medical Dosimetry
American Association of Medical Dosimetrists
c/o Lon Marsh, Ed.-in-Ch.
University of Michigan Hospital
Division of Radiation Oncology, UH-B2C490
1500 E Medical Center Dr.
Ann Arbor, MI 48109-0010
Publisher's E-mail: aamd@medicaldosimetry.org
Professional medical magazine. **Freq:** Quarterly. **Trim Size:** 8 1/4 x 11. **Key Personnel:** Lon Marsh, Editor-in-Chief; T. Pawlicki, Associate Editor. **ISSN:** 0958--3947 (print). **Subscription Rates:** $224 Individuals U.S./Canada/International (online+print) personal/students; Included in membership. **Online:** Hanley & Belfus Inc. **URL:** http://www.meddos.org; http://www.medicaldosimetry.org/publications/journal.cfm. **Remarks:** Accepts advertising. **Circ:** (Not Reported).

17141 ■ Michigan Alumnus
Alumni Association of the University of Michigan
200 Fletcher St.
Ann Arbor, MI 48109-1007
Phone: (734)764-0384
Free: 800-847-4764
College alumni magazine. **Freq:** Quarterly. **Print Method:** Web. **Trim Size:** 8 3/8 x 10 7/8. **Cols./Page:** 3. **Col. Width:** 40 nonpareils. **Col. Depth:** 134 agate lines. **Key Personnel:** Steve C. Grafton, Chief Executive Officer, President; Barbara Scott, Vice President, Communications, Vice President, Marketing. **Subscription Rates:** Included in membership. **URL:** http://alumni.umich.edu/join/alumnus-preview. **Ad Rates:** BW $2625; 4C $2625. **Remarks:** Accepts advertising. **Circ:** 100,000.

17142 ■ The Michigan Daily
The Michigan Daily
420 Maynard St.
Ann Arbor, MI 48109
Phone: (734)418-4115
Publication E-mail: news@michigandaily.com
Collegiate newspaper. **Freq:** Daily Monday through Friday during the fall and winter. **Print Method:** Letter press. **Trim Size:** 11.375 x 13.625. **Cols./Page:** 6. **Col. Width:** 26 nonpareils. **Col. Depth:** 301 agate lines. **Key Personnel:** Zach Yancer, Business Manager; Stephen Steinberg, Editor-in-Chief; Nick Spar, Managing Editor; Nicole Aber, Managing Editor. **Subscription Rates:** $2 Single issue additional copy; $200 By mail fall term; $200 Individuals winter term; $225 By mail year round; Free E-newsletters. **Remarks:** Accepts advertising. **Circ:** ‡15,000.

17143 ■ Michigan Feminist Studies
University of Michigan - Women's Studies Department
Rm. 1122, Lane Hall
204 S State St.
Ann Arbor, MI 48109-1290
Phone: (734)763-2047
Fax: (734)647-4943
Publication E-mail: mfs.editors@umich.edu
Interdisciplinary, feminist journal produced and edited by graduate students at the University of Michigan. **Freq:** Annual. **Key Personnel:** Laura Hirshfield, Editor; Jessica Ott, Editor; Hillary Brass, Editor. **ISSN:** 1055--856X (print). **Subscription Rates:** $50 Individuals 5 years; $40 Institutions 1 year; $100 Institutions 3 years. **URL:** http://sitemaker.umich.edu/michigan.feminist.studies/home. **Formerly:** Occasional Papers in Women's Studies. **Ad Rates:** BW $50. **Remarks:** Accepts advertising. **Circ:** Controlled 250.

17144 ■ Michigan Journal of Environmental and Administrative Law
University of Michigan Law School
Hutchins Hall
625 S State St.
Ann Arbor, MI 48109-1215
Phone: (734)764-1358
Journal publishing notes and articles relating to environmental and administrative law. **Freq:** Annual. **Key Personnel:** Sarah Stellberg, Editor-in-Chief. **URL:** http://www.mjeal-online.org; http://www.law.umich.edu/journalsandorgs/Pages/orgs.aspx. **Circ:** (Not Reported).

17145 ■ Michigan Journal of Gender & Law
University of Michigan Michigan Journal of Gender & Law
Office of Student Affairs
625 S State St.
Ann Arbor, MI 48109-1215
Phone: (734)764-0516
Publication E-mail: maureen@umich.edu
Journal covering feminist law, gender issues and related issues of race, class, sexual orientation and culture. **Freq:** Semiannual. **Print Method:** PDF file. **Trim Size:** 8 1/2 x 11. **Key Personnel:** Greer Donley, Editor-in-Chief. **ISSN:** 1095-8835 (print). **Subscription Rates:** $35 Individuals; $40 Other countries. **URL:** http://repository.law.umich.edu/mjgl; http://www.law.umich.edu/journalsandorgs/studentorganizations/Pages/mjgl.aspx. **Remarks:** Accepts advertising. **Circ:** (Not Reported).

17146 ■ Michigan Journal of Gender and Law
University of Michigan Law School
Hutchins Hall
625 S State St.
Ann Arbor, MI 48109-1215
Phone: (734)764-1358
Journal providing a forum for exploring how gender issues and related issues of race, class, sexual orientation, gender identity and culture impact law and society. **Freq:** Semiannual. **Key Personnel:** Emily Suran, Editor-in-Chief. **ISSN:** 1095--8835 (print). **Subscription Rates:** $35 U.S.; $40 Other countries. **URL:** http://repository.law.umich.edu/mjgl. **Circ:** (Not Reported).

17147 ■ Michigan Journal of International Law
University of Michigan Law School
Hutchins Hall
625 S State St.
Ann Arbor, MI 48109-1215
Phone: (734)764-1358
Journal publishing articles that address issues of international law. **Freq:** Quarterly. **Key Personnel:** Luca Winer, Editor-in-Chief. **URL:** http://www.mjilonline.org. **Circ:** (Not Reported).

17148 ■ Michigan Journal of Race and Law
University of Michigan Law School
Hutchins Hall
625 S State St.
Ann Arbor, MI 48109-1215
Phone: (734)764-1358
Journal serving as a forum for the exploration of issues relating to race and law. **Freq:** Semiannual. **Key Personnel:** Aaron W. Walker, Editor-in-Chief. **Subscription Rates:** $35 Individuals /year; $40 Other countries /year. **URL:** http://mjrl.org. **Circ:** (Not Reported).

17149 ■ Michigan Law Review
Michigan Law Review
Hutchins Hall
625 S State St.
Ann Arbor, MI 48109-1215
Phone: (734)764-0542
Fax: (734)647-5817
Publisher's E-mail: mlr.articles@umich.edu
Legal journal. **Freq:** October, November, December, February, March, April, May, and June. **Print Method:** Offset. **Trim Size:** 6 3/4 x 10. **Cols./Page:** 1. **Col. Width:** 56 nonpareils. **Col. Depth:** 106 agate lines. **Key Personnel:** Maureen Bishop, Manager; Charles E. Weikel, Managing Editor; Amy Murphy, Editor-in-Chief. **ISSN:** 0026-2234 (print). **Subscription Rates:** $60 Individuals; $70 Other countries; $10 Single issue; $16 Individuals book review; $12 Individuals special issues. **URL:** http://michiganlawreview.org. **Remarks:** Advertising not accepted. **Circ:** ‡2,040.

17150 ■ Michigan Mathematical Journal
University of Michigan Dept. of Mathematics
2084 E Hall
530 Church St.
Ann Arbor, MI 48109-1043
Phone: (734)647-4462
Fax: (734)763-0937
Publication E-mail: Michigan.Math.J@umich.edu
Scholarly journal covering research in mathematics. **Freq:** Quarterly. **Trim Size:** 6 x 9. **Cols./Page:** 1. **Col. Width:** 4 1/2 inches. **Col. Depth:** 7 1/2 inches. **Key Personnel:** Mircea Mustata, Managing Editor. **ISSN:** 0026--2285 (print); **EISSN:** 1945--2365 (electronic). **Subscription Rates:** $250 Institutions print and online; $125 Individuals print and online. **URL:** http://lsa.umich.edu/math/centers-outreach/michigan-mathematical-journal.html. **Remarks:** Advertising not accepted. **Circ:** Paid 900.

17151 ■ Michigan Middle School Journal
Michigan Association of Middle School Educators
1390 Eisenhower Pl.
Ann Arbor, MI 48108
Phone: (734)677-5678
Fax: (734)677-2407
Magazine containing reports of current best teaching practices and issues concerning middle school level education. **Freq:** Annual. **Key Personnel:** Alecia Powell, Manager. **Subscription Rates:** included in membership dues. **URL:** http://mamse.org/publications. **Remarks:** Accepts advertising. **Circ:** (Not Reported).

17152 ■ Michigan Municipal Review: The Official Magazine of the Michigan Municipal League
Michigan Municipal League
1675 Green Rd.
Ann Arbor, MI 48105
Phone: (734)662-3246
Free: 800-653-2483
Magazine for the exchange of ideas and information between officials of Michigan's cities and villages. **Freq:** Bimonthly. **Print Method:** Offset. **Trim Size:** 8 1/2 x 11. **Cols./Page:** 3. **Col. Width:** 13 picas. **Col. Depth:** 57 picas. **Key Personnel:** Jeanette Westhead, Contact; George D. Goodman, Publisher; Kim Cekola, Editor. **ISSN:** 0026-2331 (print). **Subscription Rates:** $24 Individuals six issues; $4 Single issue. **Alt. Formats:** PDF. **URL:** http://www.mml.org/resources/publications/mmr/index.html. **Ad Rates:** BW $1,000. **Remarks:** Accepts advertising. **Circ:** ‡10000.

17153 ■ Michigan Quarterly Review
University of Michigan
0576 Rackham Bldg.
915 E Washington St.
Ann Arbor, MI 48109-1070
Publication E-mail: mqr@umich.edu
Journal publishing cultural and literary commentary and reviews, essays, memoirs, fiction, and poetry. **Freq:** Quarterly. **Print Method:** Offset. **Trim Size:** 6 x 9. **Cols./Page:** 1. **Col. Width:** 52 nonpareils. **Col. Depth:** 103 agate lines. **Key Personnel:** Jonathan Freedman, Editor; Vicki Lawrence, Managing Editor. **ISSN:** 0026-2420 (print); **EISSN:** 1558-7266 (electronic). **Subscription Rates:** $25 Individuals; $30 Other countries; $45 Two years; $50 Other countries two years. **URL:** http://www.michiganquarterlyreview.com. **Mailing address:** 0576 Rackham Bldg.915 E Washington St., Ann Arbor, MI 48109-1070. **Ad Rates:** BW $100; CNU $100. **Remarks:** Accepts advertising. **Circ:** ‡1,200.

17154 ■ Molecular Pharmaceutics
American Chemical Society
c/o Gordon L. Amidon, PhD, Ed.-in-Ch.
Prof. of Pharmaceutical Sciences
College of Pharmacy, The University of Michigan
428 Church St., Rm. 2012
Ann Arbor, MI 48109-1065
Phone: (734)764-9313
Fax: (202)513-8735
Publisher's E-mail: help@acs.org
Scholarly journal dealing with chemical and biological sciences related to drug development. **Freq:** 6/year. **Key Personnel:** Carston R. Wagner, Executive Editor, phone: (612)625-2614, fax: (202)354-4582; Kyung-Dall Lee, Associate Editor; Gordon L. Amidon, PhD, Editor-in-Chief. **ISSN:** 1543--8384 (print); **EISSN:** 1543--8392 (electronic). **URL:** http://pubs.acs.org/journal/mpohbp. **Remarks:** Accepts advertising. **Circ:** (Not Reported).

17155 ■ Plainsong and Medieval Music
Cambridge University Press
c/o Prof. James Borders, Ed.
University of Michigan
School of Music, Theatre & Dance
1100 Baits Dr.
Ann Arbor, MI 48109-2085
Publisher's E-mail: newyork@cambridge.org
Journal on medieval music. **Freq:** Semiannual. **Key Personnel:** Dr. Helen Deeming, Member; Prof. James Borders, Editor. **ISSN:** 0961--1371 (print); **EISSN:** 1474--0087 (electronic). **Subscription Rates:** $233 Institutions print and online; £143 Institutions print and online; $207 Institutions online only; £124 Institutions online only. **URL:** http://journals.cambridge.org/action/displayJournal?jid=PMM. **Ad Rates:** BW $785. **Remarks:** Accepts advertising. **Circ:** ‡400.

17156 ■ Planning for Higher Education
Society for College and University Planning
1330 Eisenhower Pl.
Ann Arbor, MI 48108
Phone: (734)669-3270
Publisher's E-mail: info@scup.org
Magazine on higher education. **Freq:** Quarterly September, December, March, and June. **Key Personnel:** Claire L. Turcotte, PhD, Managing Editor, phone: (734)699-3289; Terry Calhoun, Director, phone: (734)764-2003. **ISSN:** 0736--0983 (print). **Subscription Rates:** Included in membership. **URL:** http://www.scup.org/page/phe. **Remarks:** Accepts advertising. **Circ:** (Not Reported).

17157 ■ Reviews of Geophysics
American Geophysical Union
c/o Mark B. Moldwin, Editor-in-Chief
University of Michigan
Atmospheric, Oceanic & Space Sciences Space Research Bldg.
2455 Hayward St.
Ann Arbor, MI 48109-2143
Phone: (734)647-3370
Publisher's E-mail: service@agu.org
Professional journal covering scientific work in geophysics. **Freq:** Quarterly. **Key Personnel:** Mark B. Moldwin, Editor-in-Chief; Mark B. Moldwin, Editor-in-Chief; Fabio Florindo, Editor; Gregory Okin, Editor, phone: (310)746-6964. **ISSN:** 8755--1209 (print); **EISSN:** 1944--9208 (electronic). **Subscription Rates:** $644 U.S. and other countries online; large; $426 U.S. and other countries online; medium; $304 U.S. and other countries online; small; £406 Institutions online; large; £269 Institutions online; medium; £193 Institutions online; small; €471 Institutions online; large; €312 Institutions online; medium; €223 Institutions online; small. **URL:** http://agupubs.onlinelibrary.wiley.com/agu/journal/10.1002/(ISSN)1944-9208. **Remarks:** Advertising not accepted. **Circ:** (Not Reported).

17158 ■ SIAM Journal on Control and Optimization
Society for Industrial and Applied Mathematics
c/o Anthony M. Bloch, Editor-in-Chief
University of Michigan
530 Church St.
Ann Arbor, MI 48109
Publisher's E-mail: service@siam.org
Journal covering mathematical theory and application of control. **Freq:** Bimonthly. **Print Method:** Offset. **Trim Size:** 6 x 9. **Cols./Page:** 1. **Col. Width:** 31 picas. **Col. Depth:** 50 picas. **Key Personnel:** Henk Nijmeijer, Editor; Qing Zhang, Editor; Anthony M. Bloch, Editor-in-Chief; Helene Frankowska, Editor. **ISSN:** 0363--0129 (print); **EISSN:** 1095--7138 (electronic). **Subscription Rates:** $129 Members domestic; $135 Members foreign; $115 Members electronic only (1997 - present); $959 Individuals list price. **Online:** Society for Industrial and Applied Mathematics Society for Industrial and Applied Mathematics. **URL:** http://www.siam.org/journals/sicon.php. **Remarks:** Accepts advertising. **Circ:** ‡1312.

17159 ■ Tech Directions: Linking Education to Careers
Prakken Publications Inc.
2851 Boardwalk Dr.
Ann Arbor, MI 48104
Phone: (734)975-2800
Fax: (734)975-2787
Free: 800-530-9673
Magazine covering issues, programs, and projects in industrial education, technology education, trade and industry, and vocational-technical career education. Articles are geared for teacher and administrator use and reference from elementary school through postsecondary levels. **Freq:** Monthly (Aug. through May). **Print Method:** Web offset. **Trim Size:** 8 x 10 7/8. **Cols./Page:** 3 and 2. **Col. Width:** 27 and 41 nonpareils. **Col. Depth:** 140 agate lines. **Key Personnel:** Tonya L. White, Contact; Susanne Peckham, Managing Editor. **ISSN:** 1062-9351 (print). **Subscription Rates:** $30 Individuals U.S.; $27 Institutions U.S.; $50 Individuals Canada; $47 Institutions Canada. **Formerly:** School Shop; School Shop/Tech Directions. **Ad Rates:** BW $2756; 4C $800; PCI $100. **Remarks:** Accepts advertising. **Circ:** (Not Reported).

17160 ■ University of Michigan Journal of Law Reform
University of Michigan Law School
Hutchins Hall
625 S State St.
Ann Arbor, MI 48109-1215
Phone: (734)764-1358
Journal promoting legal reform. **Freq:** Quarterly. **Key Personnel:** Jessica Shaffer, Editor-in-Chief. **Subscription Rates:** $40 Individuals; $45 Other countries; $15 Single issue. **URL:** http://mjlr.org. **Circ:** (Not Reported).

17161 ■ WAAM-AM - 1600
4230 Packard Rd.
Ann Arbor, MI 48108
Phone: (734)971-1600
Fax: (734)973-2916
Email: support@waamradio.com
Format: Talk; News. **Owner:** Ann Arbor First Ventures, LP, at above address. **Founded:** 1947. **Operating Hours:** Continuous. **ADI:** Lansing (Ann Arbor), MI. **Key Personnel:** Dan Martin, Operations Mgr., dan@waamradio.com. **Local Programs:** *On The Edge with Thayrone*, Monday Tuesday Wednesday Thursday Friday 3:00 p.m. - 6:00 p.m.; *Bone Conduction Music Show*, Saturday Sunday 4:00 p.m. - 6:00 p.m. 7:00 p.m. - 11:00 p.m.; *Speaking of Art*, Saturday 3:00 p.m. - 4:00 p.m.; *The Appliance Doctor*, Saturday 8:00 a.m. - 10:00 a.m.; *Bill O'Reilly*; *Neil Cavuto's Money Report*. **Wattage:** 5,000 Day; 5,000 Nig. **Ad Rates:** Advertising accepted; rates available upon request. **URL:** http://www.waamradio.com.

17162 ■ WBCM-AM - 1440
PO Box 504
Ann Arbor, MI 48106-9902
Phone: (734)930-5200
Format: Religious. **Founded:** 1925. **Operating Hours:** Continuous. **Key Personnel:** Mark Dewitt, Station Mgr. **Wattage:** 5,000. **Ad Rates:** $3-18 for 30 seconds; $6-21 for 60 seconds. **URL:** http://avemariaradio.net.

17163 ■ WCBN-FM - 88.3
515 Thompson St.
Ann Arbor, MI 48109-1316
Phone: (734)647-4122
Email: training@wcbn.org
Format: Jazz; Educational; Reggae. **Founded:** 1972. **Operating Hours:** 6 a.m.-3 p.m. **Key Personnel:** Liz Wason, Gen. Mgr.; Cory Levinson, Asst. GM; Kristin Sumrall, Prog. Dir.; James Rocker, Music Dir.; Rushi Vyas, Sports Dir.; Aaron Smith, Music Dir; Bennett Stein, Contact. **Wattage:** 200. **Ad Rates:** Noncommercial. **URL:** http://www.wcbn.org.

WFUM-FM - See Flint

17164 ■ WPXD-TV - 31
3975 Varsity Dr.
Ann Arbor, MI 48108
Phone: (734)973-7900
Fax: (734)973-7906
Owner: ION Media Networks Inc., 601 Clearwater Park Rd., West Palm Beach, FL 33401-6233, Ph: (561)659-4122, Fax: (561)659-4252. **Founded:** 1981.

17165 ■ WQKL-FM - 107.1
1100 Victors Way, Ste. 100
Ann Arbor, MI 48108
Phone: (734)998-1071
Format: Adult Album Alternative. **Owner:** Cumulus Broadcasting Inc., 3280 Peachtree Rd. NW, Ste. 2300,

Circulation: ★ = AAM; △ or • = BPA; ♦ = CAC; ❑ = VAC; ⊕ = PO Statement; ‡ = Publisher's Report; Boldface figures = sworn; Light figures = estimated.

Atlanta, GA 30305-2447, Ph: (404)949-0700, Fax: (404)949-0740. **Founded:** 1988. **Operating Hours**: Continuous; 5% network, 95% local. **Key Personnel:** Matt Spaulding, Mktg. Mgr., matt.spaulding@cumulus.com.; Chris Ammel, Dir. of Programs, chris@annarbors107one.com. **Wattage**: 3,000. **Ad Rates:** $60 for 30 seconds; $75 for 60 seconds. WWWW-FM, WTKA-AM, WCAS-AM. **URL:** http://www.annarbors107one.com.

17166 ■ WTKA-AM - 1050
1100 Victors Way, Ste. 100
Ann Arbor, MI 48108
Phone: (734)302-8100
Email: studio@wtka.com
Format: Talk; Sports. **Owner:** Cumulus Media Inc., 3280 Peachtree Rd. NW, Ste. 2300, Atlanta, GA 30305-2455, Ph: (404)949-0700, Fax: (404)949-0740. **Founded:** 1947. **Operating Hours**: Continuous. **ADI**: Lansing (Ann Arbor), MI. **Key Personnel:** Scott Meier, Contact; Brian Cowan, Contact; Ira Weintraub, Sports Dir., Exec. Producer. **Local Programs**: *The Michigan Insider*, Monday Tuesday Wednesday Thursday Friday 6:00 a.m. - 10:00 a.m; *Ann Arbor's BIG SHOW*, Monday Tuesday Wednesday Thursday Friday 3:00 p.m. - 6:00 p.m. **Wattage**: 10,000 Day; 500 Nigh. **Ad Rates:** Advertising accepted; rates available upon request. **URL:** http://www.wtka.com.

17167 ■ WUOM-FM - 91.7
535 W William St., Ste. 110
Ann Arbor, MI 48103
Phone: (734)764-9210
Fax: (734)647-3488
Free: 888-258-9866
Email: michigan.radio@umich.edu
Format: Public Radio. **Owner:** University of Michigan, 500 S State St., Ann Arbor, MI 48109, Ph: (734)764-1817. **Founded:** 1948. **Operating Hours**: Continuous. **Key Personnel:** Steve Chrypinski, Dir. of Mktg., steveski@umich.edu; Vincent Duffy, News Dir., vduffy@umich.edu. **Ad Rates:** Noncommercial. **URL:** http://www.michiganradio.org.

WVGR-FM - See Grand Rapids

17168 ■ WWCM-AM - 990
PO Box 504
Ann Arbor, MI 48106-9902
Phone: (734)930-3169
Email: ahqe50c@prodigy.com
Founded: 1962. **Formerly**: WYNZ-AM. **Key Personnel:** Steve Clarke, Dir. of Production; Henry Root, Operations Mgr.; Michael P. Jones, Gen. Mgr.; Lou Velker, Gen. Mgr.; Daniel Poole, President; Chris Yates, Gen. Sales Mgr.; Janet Raeburn, Office Mgr; Hugh Duncan, Contact; Hugh Duncan, Contact. **Wattage**: 9,200 day; 250 night . **Ad Rates:** $14 for 30 seconds; $28 for 60 seconds. **URL:** http://avemariaradio.net.

AUBURN HILLS

Oakland Co. Oakland County. (SE). E. of Pontiac.

17169 ■ Audi
Audi of America Inc.
c/o Audi Customer Experience Center
3800 Hamlin Rd.
Auburn Hills, MI 48326
Free: 800-822-2834
Publisher's E-mail: bf@autohuset-glostrup.dk
Magazine featuring Audi products, technologies, lifestyle and vision. **URL:** http://www.audiusa.com/myaudi/audi-magazine. **Remarks:** Accepts advertising. **Circ:** (Not Reported).

17170 ■ WAHS-FM
2800 Waukegan S
Auburn Hills, MI 48326-3261
Phone: (248)852-9427
Fax: (248)852-0595
Format: Educational. **Founded:** 1976. **Wattage**: 2,400 ERP. **Ad Rates:** Noncommercial.

BAD AXE

Huron Co. Huron Co. (E). 55 m NE of Saginaw. Summer resort. Creameries; metal working, seat belt assembling factories. Diversified farming. Wheat, dairying, navy beans, beef cattle.

17171 ■ Huron Daily Tribune
Huron Daily Tribune
211 N Heisterman St.
Bad Axe, MI 48413
Phone: (989)269-6461
Fax: (989)269-9893
General newspaper. **Freq:** Daily Saturday. **Print Method:** Offset. **Cols./Page:** 6. **Col. Width:** 22 nonpareils. **Col. Depth:** 301 agate lines. **Key Personnel:** Jenny Anderson, Publisher; John Frazier, Editor; Vicki Yaroch, Director, Advertising. **Subscription Rates:** $195 Individuals home delivery (52 weeks); $14 Individuals EZ pay home delivery (1 week); $234 Individuals mail (52 weeks); $65 Individuals e-Edition (52 weeks). **Ad Rates:** PCI $19.30. **Remarks:** Accepts advertising. **Circ:** Mon.-Fri. ★**7,051**, Sun. ★**7,548**.

17172 ■ The Thumb Blanket
County Press
55 Westland Dr.
Bad Axe, MI 48413
Phone: (989)269-9918
Fax: (989)269-7730
Publication E-mail: hcveditor@mihomepaper.com
Shopping guide. **Freq:** Weekly (Sun.). **Print Method:** Offset. **Trim Size:** 11 1/4 x 16. **Cols./Page:** 6. **Col. Width:** 21 nonpareils. **Col. Depth:** 210 agate lines. **Key Personnel:** Chris Ogryski, Editor; Jack Guza, Publisher; Duane Wurst, Manager, Production; Brian Schwartz, Manager, Circulation. **Subscription Rates:** $22 Individuals; $42 Two years; $31 Out of area. **URL:** http://huroncountypress.mihomepaper.com. **Remarks:** Accepts advertising. **Circ:** Non-paid 18,859.

17173 ■ WLEW-AM - 1340
935 S Van Dyke Rd.
Bad Axe, MI 48413
Phone: (989)269-9931
Fax: (989)269-7702
Format: Contemporary Country. **Networks:** CNN Radio. **Owner:** Thumb Broadcasting Inc., 935 S Van Dyke Rd., Bad Axe, MI 48413. **Founded:** 1950. **Operating Hours**: Continuous; 100% local. **ADI**: Flint-Saginaw-Bay City, MI. **Wattage**: 1,000. **Ad Rates:** Noncommercial. Combined advertising rates available with WLEW-FM. **URL:** http://thumbnet.net.

17174 ■ WLEW-FM - 102.1
935 S Van Dyke Rd.
Bad Axe, MI 48413
Phone: (989)269-9931
Fax: (989)269-7702
Email: info@thumbnet.net
Format: Classical; Oldies. **Networks:** CNN Radio. **Owner:** Thumb Broadcasting Inc., 935 S Van Dyke Rd., Bad Axe, MI 48413. **Founded:** 1950. **Operating Hours**: Continuous; 100% local. **ADI**: Flint-Saginaw-Bay City, MI. **Wattage**: 50,000. **Ad Rates:** $14.40 for 30 seconds; $18 for 60 seconds. **URL:** http://www.thumbnet.net.

BALDWIN

Lake Co. Lake Co. (W). 33 m SW of Cadillac.

17175 ■ W201CF-FM - 88.1
PO Box 391
Twin Falls, ID 83303
Fax: (208)736-1958
Free: 800-357-4226
Format: Religious; Contemporary Christian. **Owner:** CSN International, PO Box 391, Twin Falls, ID 83303, Ph: (208)736-1958, Fax: (208)736-1958, Free: 800-357-4226. **Key Personnel:** Kelly Carlson, Dir. of Engg.; Ray Gorney, Asst. Dir. **URL:** http://www.csnradio.com.

BARAGA

17176 ■ WCUP-FM - 105.7
PO Box 550
Baraga, MI 49908
Phone: (906)487-7625
Fax: (906)483-4910
Free: 877-987-7625
Format: Country. **Key Personnel:** John Preston, Sales Mgr. **Ad Rates:** Noncommercial. **URL:** http://www.keepitintheup.com.

17177 ■ WGLI-FM - 98.7
PO Box 550
Baraga, MI 49908
Phone: (906)487-7625
Fax: (906)353-9200
Free: 888-377-9287
Format: Album-Oriented Rock (AOR). **Operating Hours**: Continuous. **Ad Rates:** Advertising accepted; rates available upon request. **URL:** http://www.keepitintheup.com/wgli_fm.

BATTLE CREEK

Calhoun Co. Calhoun Co. (S). On Kalamazoo River, 45 m SW of Lansing. Manufactures pumps, auto valves, brass and hardware goods, steel and wire specialties, cartons, box board, animal foods, cookies, cereal, materials handling equipment, packaging machines.

17178 ■ Battle Creek Enquirer
Gannett Company Inc.
155 W Van Buren St.
Battle Creek, MI 49015
Free: 800-333-4139
General newspaper. **Founded:** 1900. **Freq:** Daily (eve.), Sat. and Sun. (morn.). **Print Method:** Urbanite Offset press. **Trim Size:** 13 x 21 1/4. **Cols./Page:** 6. **Col. Width:** 25 nonpareils. **Col. Depth:** 308 agate lines. **Key Personnel:** Michael McCullough, Editor, General Manager, phone: (269)966-0670. **Subscription Rates:** $9.50 Individuals digital only; $13.50 Individuals digital and print. **URL:** http://www.battlecreekenquirer.com. **Ad Rates:** GLR $20.35; BW $252; 4C $545; SAU $27. **Remarks:** Accepts advertising. **Circ:** Mon.-Sat. 15,854, Sun. 23,270.

17179 ■ Battle Creek Shopper News
J-Ad Graphics.
1361 E Columbia Ave.
Battle Creek, MI 49014
Phone: (269)965-3955
Fax: (269)968-8586
Free: 800-870-7083
Community newspaper (tabloid). **Freq:** Weekly (Thurs.). **Print Method:** Offset. **Trim Size:** 10 3/8 x 16. **Cols./Page:** 6. **Col. Width:** 1 5/8 inches. **Col. Depth:** 16 inches. **Key Personnel:** Donna Hazel, Contact; Shelly Sulser, Editor; Fred Jacobs, Publisher. **Subscription Rates:** Free; $36 By mail. **URL:** http://thebattlecreekshopper.com. **Formerly**: Beacon Preview. **Ad Rates:** BW $705.60; 4C $855.60; PCI $8.80. **Remarks:** Accepts advertising. **Circ:** Free ‡50,020.

17180 ■ The Scene
Scene Publications
4642 Capital Ave., SW
Battle Creek, MI 49015-9350
Phone: (269)979-1411
Fax: (269)979-3474
Publication E-mail: info@scenenewspaper.com
Community newspaper. **Freq:** Monthly. **Key Personnel:** James Moran, Publisher, phone: (920)418-1777; Jim Lundstrom, Editor. **URL:** http://new.scenenewspaper.com/. **Formerly**: The Valley Scene. **Remarks:** Accepts advertising. **Circ:** Non-paid 30000.

17181 ■ WBCK-AM - 930
70 W Michigan Ave., Ste. 700
Battle Creek, MI 49017
Phone: (269)963-5555
Format: News; Talk; Full Service. **Owner:** Cumulus Broadcasting Inc., 3280 Peachtree Rd. NW, Ste. 2300, Atlanta, GA 30305-2447, Ph: (404)949-0700, Fax: (404)949-0740. **Founded:** 1948. **Operating Hours**: Continuous - Monday - Friday; 8:00 a.m. - 7:00 p.m. Saturday; 8:00 a.m. - 4:00 p.m. Sunday. **ADI**: Grand Rapids-Kalamazoo-Battle Creek, MI. **Key Personnel:** Tom Forde, News Dir., tom.forde@cumulus.com; Tim Collins, Operations Mgr., tim.collins@cumulus.com. **Wattage**: 5,000 KW. **Ad Rates:** Advertising accepted; rates available upon request. **URL:** http://go955.com.

17182 ■ WBXX-FM
390 Golden Ave.
Battle Creek, MI 49015
Phone: (269)963-5555
Format: Adult Contemporary. **Founded:** 1976. **Key Personnel:** Jack McDevitt, Gen. Mgr.; John Patrick, Dir. of Programs, jpatrick@slearchannel.com. **Wattage**: 6,000 ERP. **Ad Rates:** $23-25 for 60 seconds. **URL:** http://1049theedge.com.

17183 ■ WNWN-FM - 98.5
25 W Michigan Ave., 4th Fl.
Battle Creek, MI 49017

Phone: (269)968-1991
Fax: (269)968-1881
Format: Contemporary Country. **Networks:** ABC. **Owner:** Midwest Communications Inc., 904 Grand Ave., Wausau, WI 54403, Ph: (715)842-1437, Fax: (715)842-7061. **Founded:** 1949. **Operating Hours**: Continuous. **ADI**: Grand Rapids-Kalamazoo-Battle Creek, MI. **Key Personnel:** Peter Tanz, Gen. Mgr.; P.J. Lacey, Dir. of Programs; Jim Whelan, News Dir.; Cindy Ireland, Sales Mgr. **Wattage**: 50,000. **Ad Rates:** Noncommercial. Combined advertising rates available with WFAT-FM.

BAY CITY

Bay Co. Bay Co. (EC). On Saginaw River, 12 m N of Saginaw. Fisheries. Oil wells. Manufactures hoisting and conveying machinery, space capsule components, cement, power shovels, welding machines, boats, lumber, cigars, transformers, water pipes, canned goods, sausage, nut products, trailers, furniture, toys, automobile parts. Iron foundries; shipyards; petroleum, sugar refineries; petro chemicals.

17184 ■ Bay City Democrat & Bay County Legal News
Bay City Democrat & Bay County Legal News
309 9th St.
Bay City, MI 48708
Phone: (989)893-6344
Fax: (989)893-2991
Publisher's E-mail: bcdem@sbcglobal.net
Community and legal newspaper. **Freq:** Weekly (Thurs.). **Cols./Page:** 6. **Col. Width:** 2 inches. **Col. Depth:** 18 1/2 inches. **Key Personnel:** Scott E. DeVeau, Editor. **Alt. Formats:** PDF. **URL:** http://bclegalnews.com/legal-news/#. **Mailing address:** PO Box 278, Bay City, MI 48708. **Circ:** Mon.-Sat. 51,600.

17185 ■ The Bay City Times
The Bay City Times
311 5th St.
Bay City, MI 48708-5853
Phone: (989)894-9632
Publisher's E-mail: webmaster@mlive.com
General newspaper. **Freq:** Tuesday, Thursday, Friday & Sunday. **Print Method:** Letterpress. **Cols./Page:** 6. **Col. Width:** 24 nonpareils. **Col. Depth:** 298 agate lines. **Key Personnel:** Cynthia Orr, Director, Advertising, phone: (989)894-9674; Matt Sharp, Publisher; Mike Krygier, Manager, Circulation, phone: (989)895-3552; Kevin Dykema. **Subscription Rates:** $13.92 Individuals every four weeks. **URL:** http://members.mlive.com/index.aspx?siteCode=BCT. **Ad Rates:** GLR $2.81; BW $6666.12; 4C $7286.12; PCI $31.37. **Remarks:** Accepts advertising. **Circ:** Mon.-Sat. ★**33,614**, Sun. ★**43,478**.

17186 ■ WCHW-FM - 91.3
1624 Columbus Ave.
Bay City, MI 48708
Phone: (989)892-1741
Fax: (989)892-7946
Format: Album-Oriented Rock (AOR). **Founded:** 1973. **Operating Hours**: 8:00 am - 5:00 pm; Mon. - Fri. **ADI**: Flint-Saginaw-Bay City, MI. **Wattage**: 110. **Ad Rates:** Noncommercial. **URL:** http://www.wchwonline.freewebspace.com.

BENTON HARBOR

Berrien Co. Berrien Co. (SW). On Lake Michigan 35 m NW of South Bend, Ind. Manufactures steel and malleable castings, processed food, construction machinery, veneer and paper-packing machinery, vacuum pumps, corrugated containers, appliances, recreational vehicles. Fruit packing and shipping. Boating and sport fishing. Grapes, peaches, apples, cherries.

17187 ■ Mid-West Family Broadcast Group
580 E Napier Ave.
Benton Harbor, MI 49022
URL: http://midwestfamilybroadcasting.com/madison.

17188 ■ WHFB-AM - 1060
2100 Fairplain Ave.
Benton Harbor, MI 49022
Phone: (269)932-8097
Fax: (269)879-9813
Format: Full Service. **Operating Hours**: Continuous. **Key Personnel:** Ric Federighi, Gen. Mgr., Partner, ric@whfbradio.com. **Wattage**: 5,000. **Ad Rates:** Advertising accepted; rates available upon request. **URL:** http://www.whfbradio.com.

17189 ■ WHFB-FM - 99.9
107 Water St., Ste. 204
Benton Harbor, MI 49022
Phone: (574)247-4343
Fax: (574)239-4231
Format: Country. **Founded:** 1947. **Key Personnel:** Bill Gamble, Operations Mgr., Prog. Dir., bgamble@wsbtradio.com; Tom Weidle, Gen. Mgr., President; Dan Mason, Dir. of Programs; Lindy Bartholmey, Sales Mgr.; Ed Skonie, News Dir.; Michele Stone, Promotions Dir. **Wattage**: 50,000 ERP. **Ad Rates:** $27-41 per unit. **URL:** http://newcountry999.com.

17190 ■ WIRX-FM - 107.1
580 E Napier Ave.
Benton Harbor, MI 49022
Phone: (269)925-1111
Fax: (269)925-1011
Format: Album-Oriented Rock (AOR). **Owner:** Mid-West Family Broadcast Group, 580 E Napier Ave., Benton Harbor, MI 49022. **Founded:** 1966. **Operating Hours**: Continuous. **ADI**: South Bend-Elkhart, IN. **Key Personnel:** Bob Bucholtz, Gen. Mgr.; Dave Doetsch, VP, Gen. Mgr.; Paul Layendecker, Operations Mgr.; Gayle Olson, President; Sue Patzer, Promotions Dir.; Phil McDonald, Div. Dir., pmcdonald@wsjm.com; Terry Green, Tech. Dir. **Wattage**: 1,200. **Ad Rates:** Advertising accepted; rates available upon request. **Mailing address:** PO Box 107, Saint Joseph, MI 49085. **URL:** http://www.wirx.com.

17191 ■ WSJM-AM - 1400
580 E Napier Ave.
Benton Harbor, MI 49022
Phone: (269)925-1111
Fax: (269)925-1011
Email: news@wsjm.com
Format: News; Talk; Sports. **Owner:** WSJM, Inc., at above address, Benton Harbor, MI 49022. **Founded:** 1956. **Operating Hours**: Continuous. **Key Personnel:** Gayle Olson, President. **Wattage**: 880. **Ad Rates:** Advertising accepted; rates available upon request. **Mailing address:** PO Box 107, Saint Joseph, MI 49085. **URL:** http://www.wsjm.com.

17192 ■ W216BX-FM - 91.1
PO Box 391
Twin Falls, ID 83303
Fax: (208)736-1958
Free: 800-357-4226
Format: Religious; Contemporary Christian. **Owner:** CSN International, PO Box 391, Twin Falls, ID 83303, Ph: (208)736-1958, Fax: (208)736-1958, Free: 800-357-4226. **Key Personnel:** Kelly Carlson, Dir. of Engg.; Ray Gorney, Asst. Dir. **URL:** http://www.csnradio.com.

17193 ■ WYTZ-FM - 97.5
580 E Napier Ave.
Benton Harbor, MI 49022
Phone: (269)925-1111
Fax: (269)925-1011
Format: Country. **Key Personnel:** Gayle Olson, President, golson@wirx.com; Jim Gifford, News Dir., gifford@wsjm.com; Paul Layendecker, Dir. of Operations, paul@wcsy.com; Sue Patzer, Promotions Dir., spatzer@theradiostations.com; Dave Doetsch, Gen. Mgr., VP, daved@wirx.com. **URL:** http://www.975ycountry.com.

BERRIEN SPRINGS

Berrien Co. Berrien Co. (SW). On St. Joseph River 20 m N of South Bend, Ind. Andrews University. Summer resort. Manufactures electrical parts, tools, die cast. Salmon fishing center. Vegetable and fruit farms.

17194 ■ Lake Union Herald
Lake Union Conference of Seventh-day Adventists
PO Box 287
Berrien Springs, MI 49103-0287
Phone: (269)473-8200
Fax: (269)471-7920
Religious magazine containing news for members of Seventh-day Adventist Church in the Great Lakes area. **Freq:** Monthly. **Trim Size:** 8 x 10.625. **Cols./Page:** 4. **Col. Width:** 1.625 inches. **Key Personnel:** Gary Burns, Editor; Don Livesay, Publisher; Judi Doty, Manager, Circulation. **ISSN:** 0194--908X (print). **Subscription Rates:** $12.50 Individuals. **URL:** http://herald.lakeunion.org. **Ad Rates:** BW $2,627. **Remarks:** members only. **Circ:** 41000.

17195 ■ NEAS Bulletin
Near East Archaeological Society
Andrews University
Horn Archaeological Museum
9047 Old US 31
Berrien Springs, MI 49104-0990
Phone: (269)471-3273
Freq: Annual. **ISSN:** 0739--0068 (print). **Subscription Rates:** Included in membership. **URL:** http://www.cbrgroup.org/pages.asp?pageid=106095. **Remarks:** Accepts advertising. **Circ:** 400.

17196 ■ WAUS-FM - 90.7
Andrews University
Berrien Springs, MI 49104
Phone: (269)471-3400
Fax: (269)471-3804
Free: 800-553-9287
Email: waus@andrews.edu
Format: Classical. **Networks:** Public Radio International (PRI); BBC World Service; AP. **Owner:** Andrews University, 8975 US 31, Berrien Springs, MI 49104, Ph: (616)471-7771. **Founded:** 1971. **Operating Hours**: Continuous; 20% network. **ADI**: South Bend-Elkhart, IN. **Wattage**: 50,000. **Ad Rates:** Noncommercial. **URL:** http://www.waus.org.

BIG RAPIDS

Mecosta Co. Mecosta Co. (WC). On Muskegon River, 56 m N of Grand Rapids. Ferris State College. Manufactures furniture, saw-filing machinery, tools, butter, shoes, gloves. Summer resort. Natural gas and oil wells. Dairy, fruit, grain farms. Beans, potatoes.

17197 ■ Ferris State Torch: Truth, Fairness and accuracy since 1931
Ferris State University
1201 S State St.
Big Rapids, MI 49307
Phone: (231)591-2340
Fax: (231)591-2325
Free: 800-562-9130
Publication E-mail: orchads@ferris.edu
Collegiate newspaper. **Freq:** Weekly. **Print Method:** Offset. **Trim Size:** 9 3/4 x 15. **Cols./Page:** 5. **Col. Width:** 23 nonpareils. **Col. Depth:** 196 agate lines. **Key Personnel:** Antonio Coleman, Editor-in-Chief, phone: (231)591-5978; Steve Fox, Advisor, phone: (231)591-2529; Laura Anger, Business Manager, phone: (231)591-2609. **Subscription Rates:** $45 By mail. **URL:** http://fsutorch.com. **Ad Rates:** PCI $6.75. **Remarks:** Accepts advertising. **Circ:** Free ‡6000.

17198 ■ Lake County Star
The Pioneer Group
115 N Michigan Ave.
Big Rapids, MI 49307
Phone: (231)796-4831
Weekly community newspaper. **Founded:** 1873. **Freq:** Weekly (Thurs.). **Print Method:** Offset, Web. **Cols./Page:** 5. **Col. Width:** 1 7/8 inches. **Col. Depth:** 10 inches. **Subscription Rates:** $33 Individuals in County; $55.20 Out of area; $75 Out of state; $33 Individuals Online. **URL:** http://www.pioneergroup.net/; http://lakecountystar.com/. **Ad Rates:** GLR $6.35; 4C $150; SAU $7.75. **Circ:** Thurs. ‡2900.

17199 ■ The Pioneer
The Pioneer Group
115 N Michigan Ave.
Big Rapids, MI 49307
Phone: (231)796-4831
General newspaper. **Founded:** Apr. 17, 1862. **Freq:** 6-days/week. **Print Method:** Offset. **Trim Size:** 14 x 22 3/4. **Cols./Page:** 9. **Col. Width:** 21 nonpareils. **Col. Depth:** 399 agate lines. **Key Personnel:** Jack A. Batdorff, Chairman of the Board; John A. Batdorff, II, Chief Executive Officer, President. **ISSN:** 8750-5533 (print). **Subscription Rates:** $148.80 Individuals in County; $183 Out of area; $241.20 Out of state. **URL:** http://www.pioneergroup.com. **Ad Rates:** SAU $9.35; PCI $5.35. **Remarks:** Accepts advertising. **Circ:** Paid 5859, Free 24.

Circulation: ★ = AAM; △ or • = BPA; ♦ = CAC; ❑ = VAC; ⊕ = PO Statement; ‡ = Publisher's Report; Boldface figures = sworn; Light figures = estimated.

17200 ■ River Valley News Shopper
The Pioneer Group
115 N Michigan Ave.
Big Rapids, MI 49307
Phone: (231)796-4831
Shopping guide with local news and features. **Founded:** 1865. **Freq:** Weekly (Mon.). **Print Method:** Offset. **Cols./Page:** 5. **Col. Width:** 1 7/8 inches. **Col. Depth:** 16 inches. **Key Personnel:** John Norton, Publisher. **Subscription Rates:** Free. **URL:** http://rivervalleyshopper.com. **Formerly**: The Record. **Ad Rates:** GLR $9.45; BW $756; 4C $906; SAU $6.50. **Remarks:** Accepts advertising. **Circ:** Mon. ‡21000.

17201 ■ Tri-County Shoppers Guide
The Pioneer Group
115 N Michigan Ave.
Big Rapids, MI 49307
Phone: (231)796-4831
Shopper. **Freq:** Weekly (Mon.). **Print Method:** Offset. **Trim Size:** 10 1/16 x 16. **Cols./Page:** 5. **Col. Width:** 16 nonpareils. **Col. Depth:** 224 agate lines. **Key Personnel:** John Norton, Publisher. **Subscription Rates:** $138 Individuals; $165 Out of country; $213 Out of state. **URL:** http://tricountynewsshopper.com. **Ad Rates:** GLR $8; BW $908; 4C $1,068; PCI $11.35. **Remarks:** Accepts advertising. **Circ:** Mon. ‡18,200.

17202 ■ Charter Communications
1100 E Maple St.
Big Rapids, MI 49307
Free: 888-438-2427
Key Personnel: Mary Jo Moehle, VP of Investor Rel. **Cities Served:** 42 channels. **URL:** http://www.charter.com.

17203 ■ WBRN-AM - 1460
18720 16 Mile Rd.
Big Rapids, MI 49307
Phone: (231)796-7000
Fax: (231)796-7951
Format: News; Talk; Sports. **Networks:** ESPN Radio; Westwood One Radio. **Owner:** Mentor Partners Inc., at above address. **Founded:** 1953. **Operating Hours**: Continuous. **Key Personnel:** Jeff Scarpelli, Gen. Mgr., wybr@wybr.com; Paul Cicchini, News Dir., news@wbrn.com; Diane Scarpelli, Sales Mgr.; Mark Wittkoski, Chief Engineer. **Wattage**: 5,000. **Ad Rates:** $13.60 for 30 seconds; $17 for 60 seconds. **URL:** http://www.wbrn.com.

17204 ■ WBRN-FM - 100.9
18720 16 Mile Rd.
Big Rapids, MI 49307
Phone: (231)796-7000
Fax: (231)796-7951
Email: wbrnfm@wbrn.com
Format: Adult Contemporary; Classic Rock. **Networks:** Jones Satellite; AP. **Owner:** RH Communications, Inc., 10203 Birchridge Dr., Ste. D, Humble, TX 77338. **Founded:** 1964. **Operating Hours**: Continuous; 100% local. **Key Personnel:** Robert J. Hampson, Jr., Gen. Mgr., President; Monte D. Johnson, Operations Mgr.; William Beckwith, Dir. of Programs; George Keen, Chief Engineer; Carol Ann Wells, Sales Mgr.; Brian Goodenow, Dir. of Operations. **Local Programs**: *The John Gibson Show*, Saturday 1:00 p.m. - 2:00 p.m. **Wattage**: 6,000. **Ad Rates:** $13.60 for 30 seconds; $17 for 60 seconds. **URL:** http://www.wbrn.com/.

17205 ■ WDEE-FM - 97.3
PO Box 722
Big Rapids, MI 49307
Phone: (231)796-9730
Email: sunny@sunny973.com
Format: Oldies. **Ad Rates:** Noncommercial. **URL:** http://www.sunny973.com.

17206 ■ WWBR-FM - 100.9
18720 16 Mile Rd.
Big Rapids, MI 49307
Phone: (231)796-7000
Fax: (231)796-7951
Format: Country. **Owner:** Mentor Partners Inc., at above address. **Key Personnel:** Diane Scarpelli, Sales Mgr.; Jeff Scarpelli, Gen. Mgr. **URL:** http://www.bigcountry1009.com.

17207 ■ WYBR-FM - 102.3
18720 16 Mile Rd.
Big Rapids, MI 49307
Phone: (231)796-7000
Fax: (231)796-7951
Format: Adult Contemporary. **Owner:** Mentor Partners Inc., at above address. **Key Personnel:** Jeff Scarpelli, Gen. Mgr.; Diane Scarpelli, Sales Mgr.; Mark Wittkoski, Chief Engineer. **Ad Rates:** Advertising accepted; rates available upon request. **URL:** http://www.wybr.com.

BINGHAM FARMS

17208 ■ CIDR-FM - 93.9
30100 Telegraph Rd., Ste. 460
Bingham Farms, MI 48025
Phone: (248)646-8484
Fax: (248)646-1070
Email: advertising@939theriverradio.com
Format: Adult Album Alternative. **Owner:** Ctvglobemedia Inc., 9 Channel Nine Ct., Scarborough, ON, Canada M1S 4B5, Ph: (416)332-5000, Free: 866-690-6179. **Founded:** 1932. **Formerly**: CKLW-FM, The River. **Operating Hours**: Continuous. **ADI:** Detroit, MI. **Key Personnel:** Phat Matt, Dir. of Programs. **Wattage:** 100,000. **Ad Rates:** Advertising accepted; rates available upon request. Combined advertising rates available with CIMX. **URL:** http://www.939theriverradio.com.

17209 ■ CIMX-FM - 88.7
30100 Telegraph, Ste. 460
Bingham Farms, MI 48025
Phone: (248)646-8484
Email: advertising@89xradio.com
Format: Album-Oriented Rock (AOR). **Owner:** CHUM Group, 1331 Yonge St., Toronto, ON, Canada M4T 1Y1, Ph: (416)925-6666, Fax: (416)926-4026. **Key Personnel:** Cal Cagno, Promotions Dir., cal@89xradio.com. **Ad Rates:** Advertising accepted; rates available upon request. **URL:** http://www.89xradio.com.

17210 ■ Comcast Cablevision of Flint
30600 Telegraph Rd., Ste. 2345
Bingham Farms, MI 48025
Phone: (810)235-9200
Fax: (810)235-9205
Free: 800-266-2278
Owner: Comcast Corp., 1 Comcast Ctr., Philadelphia, PA 19103-2838, Ph: (215)665-1700, Fax: (215)981-7790, Free: 800-266-2278. **Founded:** 1966. **Cities Served:** Genesee and Oakland Counties.

BIRMINGHAM

Oakland Co. Oakland Co. (SE). 15 m N of Detroit. Manufactures automobile bodies, plastic products, electrical components, orthopedic supplies, garage doors.

17211 ■ Edible Wow
Edible Communities Inc.
PO Box 247
Birmingham, MI 48012
Phone: (248)739-1429
Fax: (248)593-6162
Publication E-mail: info@ediblewow.com
Magazine focusing on the local food of Southeastern Michigan. **Freq:** Quarterly. **Key Personnel:** Kate Harper, Publisher; Robb Harper, Publisher. **Subscription Rates:** $28 Individuals. **URL:** http://ediblewow.com. **Remarks:** Accepts advertising. **Circ:** (Not Reported).

BLOOMFIELD

17212 ■ WJCO-AM - 1510
1700 N Woodward Ave.
Bloomfield, MI 48301
Format: Country; News. **Networks:** CBS; Motor Racing. **Founded:** 1963. **Operating Hours**: Sunrise-sunset. **Key Personnel:** Zail Greenbain, Contact; Brian Shapiro, Contact; Michael Bruening, Contact. **Wattage**: 5,400. **Ad Rates:** $15-25 per unit. **URL:** http://www.dleg.state.mi.us/bcs_corp/dt_corp.asp?id_nbr=040438&name_entity=WJCO,%20INC.

BLOOMFIELD HILLS

Oakland Co Oakland Co. Oakland Co. (SC). 20 m NW of Detroit.

17213 ■ CAM Magazine: The Voice of the Construction Industry
Construction Association of Michigan
43636 Woodward Ave.
Bloomfield Hills, MI 48302
Phone: (248)972-1000
Fax: (248)972-1001
Publisher's E-mail: marketing@cam-online.com
Magazine featuring construction industry trends and information. **Freq:** Monthly. **Print Method:** Sheetfed offset. **Trim Size:** 8 1/2 x 11. **Cols./Page:** 3. **Col. Width:** 14 picas. **Col. Depth:** 9 1/2 inches. **Key Personnel:** Cathy Jones, Contact, phone: (248)969-2171; David Miller, Associate Editor; Amanda Tackett, Director, Publications, Managing Editor; Mary Krempsky, Associate Editor; Kevin Koehler, President. **ISSN:** 0883-7880 (print). **Subscription Rates:** $40 Individuals; $75 Two years. **URL:** http://www.cam-online.com/Magazine.aspx; http://www.cam-online.com/Publications/CAMMagazine.aspx. **Mailing address:** PO Box 3204, Bloomfield Hills, MI 48302. **Ad Rates:** BW $1,070; 4C $1,760. **Remarks:** Advertising accepted; rates available upon request. **Circ:** 3600.

17214 ■ Traffic Injury Prevention
Taylor & Francis Group Journals
c/o David C. Viano, Ed.-in-Ch.
ProBiomechanics LLC
265 Warrington Rd.
Bloomfield Hills, MI 48304-2952
Phone: (248)645-5832
Fax: (248)645-5598
Publisher's E-mail: customerservice@taylorandfrancis.com
Journal dealing with traffic safety, crash causation, injury prevention and treatment. **Freq:** 8/yr. **Key Personnel:** Alessandro Calvi, Associate Editor; David C. Viano, Editor-in-Chief. **ISSN:** 1538--9588 (print); **EISSN:** 1538--957X (electronic). **Subscription Rates:** $347 Individuals print only; $1381 Institutions online only; $1578 Institutions print and online. **URL:** http://www.tandfonline.com/toc/gcpi20/current. **Remarks:** Advertising not accepted. **Circ:** (Not Reported).

17215 ■ WBFH-FM - 88.1
4175 Andover Rd.
Bloomfield Hills, MI 48302
Phone: (248)341-5690
Format: Educational; Adult Contemporary. **Founded:** Oct. 01, 1976. **Operating Hours:** Continuous. **Key Personnel:** Pete Bowers, Station Mgr. **Wattage:** 360. **Ad Rates:** Noncommercial. **URL:** http://www.bloomfield.org.

BLOOMINGDALE

17216 ■ Bloomingdale Telephone Co.
101 W Kalamazoo St.
Bloomingdale, MI 49026
Phone: (269)521-7300
Free: 800-377-3130
Email: helpdesklevel1@bloomingdalecom.net
Founded: 1955. **Key Personnel:** Richard Godfrey, VP; Robert Remington, President. **Cities Served:** 37 channels. **Mailing address:** PO Box 187, Bloomingdale, MI 49026. **URL:** http://www.bloomingdalecom.net.

BOYNE CITY

Charlevoix Co. Charlevoix Co. (N). On Lake Charlevoix, 42 m NE of Traverse City. Tourism. Year-round resort. Light industry.

17217 ■ Seaway Review: The International Business Transportation Magazine of the Great Lakes/St. Lawrence System
Harbor House Publishers Inc.
221 Water St.
Boyne City, MI 49712
Phone: (231)582-2814
Fax: (866)906-3392
Free: 800-491-1760
Publisher's E-mail: harbor@harborhouse.com
Magazine on maritime transportation, business, and international and economic news and analyses. **Freq:** Quarterly March, June, September, December. **Print Method:** Offset. **Trim Size:** 8 3/4 x 11 1/4. **Cols./Page:** 3 and 2. **Col. Width:** 20 and 28 nonpareils. **Col. Depth:** 140 agate lines. **Key Personnel:** Janenne Irene Pung, Editor; Tina Felton, Business Manager; Michelle Cortright, Publisher; Amanda Korthase, Manager, Circulation; Lisa Liebgott, Manager, Production. **ISSN:** 0037-0487 (print). **Subscription Rates:** $32 Individuals 1

year, print only; $53 Individuals 2 years, print only; $75 Individuals 3 years, print only; $38 Individuals 1 year, print and online; $63 Individuals 2 years, print and online; $90 Individuals 3 years, print and online; $47 Other countries print only, 1 year; $68 Other countries print only, 2 years; $100 Other countries print only, 3 years; $20 Individuals online only, 1 year; $53 Other countries 1 year, print and online; $78 Other countries 2 years, print and online; $115 Other countries 3 years, print and online. **URL:** http://www.greatlakes-seawayreview.com. **Ad Rates:** BW $2895; 4C $2950. **Remarks:** Accepts advertising. **Circ:** 6,000.

BRIGHTON

Livingston Co. Livingston Co. (SE). 18 miles north of Ann Arbor. Summer resort. Manufactures metal stamps for auto industry, furnace pipes, trailers. Agriculture. Potatoes, beans.

17218 ■ The Engravers Journal
The Engravers Journal
10087 Spencer Rd.
Brighton, MI 48114-7524
Publication E-mail: info@engraversjournal.com
facebook@engraversjournal.com
Magazine covering awards, trophies, signs and advertising specialties, published for the advancement of the recognition and identification industry. **Freq:** Monthly. **Print Method:** Offset. Uses mats. **Trim Size:** 8 3/8 x 10 7/8. **Cols./Page:** 2 and 3. **Col. Width:** 2 1/8 and 43 nonpareils. **Col. Depth:** 114 agate lines. **Key Personnel:** Mike Davis, Publisher; Sonja Davis, General Manager. **Subscription Rates:** $55 Individuals print or online; $99 Two years print or online; $132 Individuals three years (print or online); $65 Individuals print and online; $119 Two years print and online); $162 Individuals three years (print and online); $69 Canada print or online; $124 Canada two years (print or online); $180 Canada three years (print or online); $79 Canada print and online; $144 Canada two years (print and online); $210 Canada three years (print and online); $125 Other countries print only (Air Mail) or digital edition only; $219 Other countries two years [print only (Air Mail) or digital edition only]; $135 Other countries print and online; $239 Other countries two years (print and online). **URL:** http://www.engraversjournal.com. **Mailing address:** PO Box 318, Brighton, MI 48116-0318. **Ad Rates:** BW $1380; 4C $1905. **Remarks:** Accepts advertising. **Circ:** (Not Reported).

BROOKLYN

Jackson Co. Jackson Co. (S). 16 m SE of Jackson. Resort. Factories. Diversified farming.

17219 ■ The Brooklyn Exponent
The Brooklyn Exponent
160 S Main St.
Brooklyn, MI 49230
Phone: (517)592-2122
Fax: (517)592-3241
Local newspaper. **Founded:** Sept. 01, 1881. **Freq:** Weekly (Tues.). **Print Method:** Web. **Cols./Page:** 5. **Col. Width:** 23 nonpareils. **Col. Depth:** 224 agate lines. **Key Personnel:** Jeff Steers, Editor; Matt Schepeler, Publisher. **Subscription Rates:** $35 Individuals print only (annual); $35 Individuals online only (annual); 45 Individuals print and online (annual). **URL:** http://www.theexponent.com. **Formerly:** The Exponent. **Ad Rates:** 4C $800; PCI $5.75. **Remarks:** Accepts advertising. **Circ:** Paid ‡6,000.

BUCHANAN

Berrien Co. Berrien Co. (SW). On St. Joseph River 15 m NW of South Bend, Ind. Resort. Manufactures lawn and patio furniture, hydraulic parts, microphones and accessories, public address equipment, loudspeakers, respirators and goggles, aircraft parts, wood, metal, plastic, lollipops, flour and syrup; packaging and finishing plants; tool & die, machining fabricator, metalizing shops; forgings.

17220 ■ Berrien County Record
Berrien County Record
206 Main St.
Buchanan, MI 49107
Phone: (269)695-3878
Fax: (269)695-3880
Publisher's E-mail: bcrnews@bcrnews.net
Community newspaper. **Freq:** Weekly (Wed.). **Print Method:** Offset. **Cols./Page:** 6. **Col. Width:** 12.25 picas. **Col. Depth:** 21 1/2 inches. **USPS:** 051-600. **Subscription Rates:** $30 Individuals in county; $35 Out of area other. **URL:** http://www.bcrnews.net. **Ad Rates:** BW $600; 4C $90; SAU $6; PCI $4.80. **Remarks:** Advertising accepted; rates available upon request. **Circ:** Paid 2,600, Free 350.

17221 ■ Heartcry: A Journal on Revival and Spiritual Awakening
Life Action Revival Ministries
2727 Niles-Buchanan Rd.
Buchanan, MI 49107
Phone: (269)697-8600
Fax: (269)695-2474
Publisher's E-mail: info@lifeaction.org
Journal containing biographical sketches of key revival leaders and crisp abridgements of the best revival-related sermons and manuscripts. **Freq:** Quarterly. **Subscription Rates:** $3.95 /copy. **URL:** http://www.lifeaction.org/revival-resources/heart-cry-journal/. **Mailing address:** PO Box 31, Buchanan, MI 49107-0031. **Remarks:** Advertising not accepted. **Circ:** (Not Reported).

17222 ■ Spirit of Revival
Life Action Revival Ministries
2727 Niles-Buchanan Rd.
Buchanan, MI 49107
Phone: (269)697-8600
Fax: (269)695-2474
Publisher's E-mail: info@lifeaction.org
Freq: 1-2/year. **Subscription Rates:** $2.50 Single issue /copy. **URL:** http://www.lifeaction.org/revival-resources/spirit-revival-magazine/. **Mailing address:** PO Box 31, Buchanan, MI 49107-0031. **Remarks:** Advertising not accepted. **Circ:** 60000.

BURTON

17223 ■ Subterranean Magazine
Subterranean Press
PO Box 190106
Burton, MI 48519
Phone: (810)232-1489
Fax: (810)232-1447
Publisher's E-mail: subpress@gmail.com
Magazine covering horror, suspense, and dark mystery genres. **Freq:** Quarterly. **Key Personnel:** Ellen Datlow, Editor. **URL:** http://subterraneanpress.com/magazine. **Mailing address:** PO Box 190106, Burton, MI 48519. **Circ:** (Not Reported).

17224 ■ WCRZ-FM - 107.9
3338 E Bristol Rd.
Burton, MI 48529
Phone: (810)743-1080
Format: Adult Contemporary. **Networks:** CBS. **Owner:** Regent Communication Inc., 2000 5th 3rd Ctr. 511 Walnut St., Cincinnati, OH 45202, Ph: (513)651-1190. **Founded:** 1961. **Operating Hours:** Continuous. **Key Personnel:** Kristine Sikkema, Dir. of Sales, kristine.sikkema@townsquaremedia.com. **Wattage:** 50,000. **Ad Rates:** Noncommercial. **URL:** http://www.wcrz.com.

17225 ■ WFNT-AM - 1470
3338 E Bristol Rd.
Burton, MI 48529
Phone: (810)743-1080
Fax: (810)742-5170
Free: 866-860-1470
Format: Bluegrass. **Key Personnel:** Zoe Burdine-Fly, Gen. Mgr., zoe.burdine-fly@townsquaremedia.com. **Ad Rates:** Noncommercial. **URL:** http://www.wfnt.com.

17226 ■ WQUS-FM - 103.1
3338 E Bristol Rd.
Burton, MI 48529
Phone: (810)743-1080
Fax: (810)742-5170
Free: 866-313-1031
Format: Classic Rock. **Owner:** Townsquare Media Inc., 2000 Fifth Third Ctr. 511 Walnut St., Cincinnati, OH 45202, Ph: (513)651-1190. **Operating Hours:** Continuous. **Key Personnel:** Jay Patrick, Dir. of Programs, jaypatrick@wcrz.com; Kelly Quinn, Gen. Mgr., kelly.quinn@townsquaremedia.com. **Ad Rates:** Advertising accepted; rates available upon request. **URL:** http://www.us103.com.

17227 ■ WRCL-FM - 93.7
3338 E Bristol Rd.
Burton, MI 48529
Format: Hip Hop. **Ad Rates:** Advertising accepted; rates available upon request. **URL:** http://www.club937.com.

17228 ■ WWBN-FM - 101.5
3338 E Bristol Rd.
Burton, MI 48529
Phone: (810)743-1080
Fax: (810)742-5170
Free: 800-225-5324
Format: Album-Oriented Rock (AOR). **Networks:** Independent. **Owner:** Townsquare Media Inc., 240 Greenwich Ave., Greenwich, CT 06830-6507, Ph: (203)861-0900. **Founded:** 1953. **Operating Hours:** Continuous. **ADI:** Flint-Saginaw-Bay City, MI. **Wattage:** 1,800. **Ad Rates:** $15-95 for 60 seconds. Combined advertising rates available with WCRZ, WFNT, WQUS, WRCL, WLSP. **URL:** http://www.banana1015.com.

CADILLAC

Wexford Co. Wexford Co. (NW). 95 m N of Grand Rapids. Manufactures tables, rubber goods, malleable iron, heaters, boats, machined products, refrigerators, vacuum cleaners, interior auto parts, lumber. Dairy, poultry, truck farms. Potatoes, beans, wheat. Summer and winter resort.

17229 ■ Cadillac News
Cadillac News
130 N Mitchell St.
Cadillac, MI 49601
Phone: (231)775-6565
Fax: (231)775-8790
Publisher's E-mail: customerservice@cadillacnews.com
General newspaper. **Freq:** Mon.-Sat. (morn.). **Print Method:** Offset. **Trim Size:** 14 x 22 3/4. **Cols./Page:** 6. **Col. Width:** 1.833 inches. **Col. Depth:** 21 1/2 inches. **Key Personnel:** Christopher Huckle, Publisher, phone: (231)779-5200; Matthew Seward, Managing Editor, phone: (231)779-4126; Sandy Smith, Business Manager, phone: (231)779-4133. **USPS:** 082-500. **Subscription Rates:** $1.95 Individuals monthly (print); $7.95 Individuals monthly (online). **Mailing address:** PO Box 640, Cadillac, MI 49601-0640. **Remarks:** alcoholic beverages. **Circ:** Mon.-Fri. ‡10,218, Sat. ‡11,500, Free ‡20,225.

17230 ■ WBYW-FM - 89.7
PO Box 567
Cadillac, MI 49601
Free: 877-278-5512
Format: Contemporary Christian; Country; News. **Networks:** Independent. **Founded:** 1978. **Formerly:** WEHB-FM. **ADI:** Traverse City-Cadillac, MI. **Key Personnel:** Al Lane, Contact. **Wattage:** 3,200 ERP. **URL:** http://www.strongtowerradio.org.

17231 ■ WCMV-TV - 27
1999 E Campus Dr.
Mount Pleasant, MI 48859
Phone: (989)774-3105
Fax: (989)774-4427
Free: 800-727-9268
Format: Public TV. **Networks:** Public Broadcasting Service (PBS). **Owner:** Central Michigan University, 1200 S Franklin St., Mount Pleasant, MI 48859, Ph: (989)774-4000. **Founded:** 1984. **Operating Hours:** 6 a.m.-midnight; 90% network, 10% local. **ADI:** Traverse City-Cadillac, MI. **Key Personnel:** Kim Walters, Gen. Sales Mgr.; Ray Ford, Dir. of Programs, ford1r@cmich.edu; David Nicholas, Dir. of Dev., nicho1d@cmich.edu. **Ad Rates:** Noncommercial. **URL:** http://www.wcmu.org.

17232 ■ WFQX-TV - 33
PO Box 282
Cadillac, MI 49601
Phone: (231)775-9813
Format: Commercial TV. **Simulcasts:** WFVX-TV. **Networks:** Fox; United Paramount Network. **Founded:** 1983. **Formerly:** WGKI-TV. **Operating Hours:** Continuous; 25% network, 75% local. **ADI:** Traverse City-Cadillac, MI. **Local Programs:** *FOX 32 News at 10 PM*, Monday Tuesday Wednesday Thursday Friday 10:00

Circulation: ★ = AAM; △ or • = BPA; ♦ = CAC; ❑ = VAC; ⊕ = PO Statement; ‡ = Publisher's Report; Boldface figures = sworn; Light figures = estimated.

p.m. **Wattage:** 776,000. **Ad Rates:** $25-600 for 30 seconds.

17233 ■ WFUP-TV - 45
PO Box 282
Cadillac, MI 49601
Phone: (231)775-9813
Email: info@mifox32.com
Networks: Fox. **Owner:** Cadillac Telecasting Company, 2132 Tower Rd, Boyne Falls, MI 49713, Ph: (231)549-5459. **Founded:** 1993. **URL:** http://www.mifox32.com.

17234 ■ WFVX-TV - 45
7669 S 45 Rd.
Cadillac, MI 49601
Phone: (616)775-9813
Fax: (616)775-1898
Email: info@fox33.net
Format: Commercial TV. **Simulcasts:** WFQX-TV. **Networks:** Fox; United Paramount Network. **Founded:** 1989. **Formerly:** WGKU-TV. **Operating Hours:** Continuous. **ADI:** Traverse City-Cadillac, MI. **Key Personnel:** Carol Donohue, Sales Mgr.; Greg Buzzell, Chief Engineer; Jean Joseph, Bus. Mgr.; Julia Horchner, Program Mgr. **Wattage:** 851,000. **Ad Rates:** $25-600 for 30 seconds.

17235 ■ WLXV-FM - 96.7
7825 S Mackinaw Trl.
Cadillac, MI 49601-9746
Phone: (231)775-1263
Fax: (231)779-2844
Format: Adult Contemporary. **Owner:** MacDonald Garber Broadcasting, Inc., 2095 US 131, South Petoskey, MI 49770. **Founded:** 1974. **Formerly:** WWLZ-FM; WITW-FM. **Operating Hours:** Continuous. **Key Personnel:** Greg Marshall, Gen. Mgr. **Wattage:** 25,000. **Ad Rates:** Noncommercial. WATT. **URL:** http://www.mix96cadillac.com.

17236 ■ WOLW-FM - 91.1
PO Box 695
Gaylord, MI 49734-0695
Fax: (989)732-8171
Free: 800-545-8857
Format: Religious. **Simulcasts:** WPHN-FM & WHST-FM. **Networks:** Moody Broadcasting. **Owner:** The Ministries Of Northern Christian Radio Inc., PO Box 695, Gaylord, MI 49734, Fax: (989)732-8171, Free: 800-545-8857. **Founded:** 1988. **Operating Hours:** Continuous; 60% local, 40% network. **ADI:** Traverse City-Cadillac, MI. **Key Personnel:** George Lake, CEO. **Wattage:** 50,000. **Ad Rates:** Noncommercial. **URL:** http://www.ncradio.org.

17237 ■ WWTV-TV - 9
PO Box 627
Cadillac, MI 49601
Phone: (231)775-3478
Email: info@9and10news.com
Format: Commercial TV; News. **Simulcasts:** WWUP-TV Channel 10. **Networks:** CBS. **Owner:** Heritage Broadcasting Group, 22320 N 130th Ave., Tustin, MI 49688-8564, Ph: (231)775-3478, Fax: (231)775-3671. **Founded:** 1954. **Operating Hours:** Continuous. **Local Programs:** *Michigan This Morning*; *You Saw It*. **Wattage:** 316,000 visual; 31,600 aural. **Ad Rates:** Advertising accepted; rates available upon request. Combined advertising rates available with WWUP-TV. **URL:** http://www.9and10news.com.

17238 ■ WWUP-TV - 10
PO Box 627
Cadillac, MI 49601
Phone: (231)775-3478
Free: 800-782-7910
Owner: Heritage Broadcasting Group. **Founded:** Sept. 06, 2006. **Ad Rates:** Noncommercial. **URL:** http://www.9and10news.com.

CANTON

17239 ■ WSDP-FM - 88.1
46181 Joy Rd.
Canton, MI 48187
Phone: (734)416-7732
Format: Contemporary Hit Radio (CHR); Full Service. **Owner:** Plymouth-Canton Community Schools, at above address. **Founded:** 1972. **Operating Hours:** Continuous. **Key Personnel:** Bill Keith, Station Mgr.; Derek Harbison, Dir. of Production. **Wattage:** 300 ERP. **Ad Rates:** Noncommercial. Underwriting available. **URL:** http://www.881theescape.com/.

CARO

Tuscola Co. Tuscola Co. (E). 30 m E of Saginaw. Manufactures plastic blow moldings, custom injection molding, concrete, read-mix, boat docks, hoists, lawn furniture, sugar production, refining. Agriculture. Sugar beets, beans, grains, corn.

17240 ■ Tuscola County Advertiser
Tuscola Today
344 N State St.
Caro, MI 48723
Phone: (989)673-3181
Local newspaper. **Freq:** Semiweekly (Wed. and Sat.). **Print Method:** Offset. **Cols./Page:** 8. **Col. Width:** 18 nonpareils. **Col. Depth:** 294 agate lines. **Key Personnel:** Amy Joles, Editor; Tim Murphy, Publisher; Tina Morris, Business Manager. **Subscription Rates:** $39.95 Individuals; $47.95 Out of area. **Ad Rates:** GLR $.28; BW $848.40; 4C $1088.40; SAU $5.87; PCI $5.05. **Remarks:** Accepts advertising. **Circ:** Wed. 8,423, Sat. 7,709.

17241 ■ WKYO-AM - 1360
1521 W Caro Rd.
Caro, MI 48723
Phone: (989)672-1360
Fax: (989)673-0256
Owner: Edwards Communications, LLC, 125 Eagles Nest Dr., Seneca, SC 29678. **Founded:** 1962. **Wattage:** 1,000 KW. **Ad Rates:** Accepts Advertising. **URL:** http://www.realcountryonline.com/home.asp.

17242 ■ W207BX-FM - 89.3
PO Box 391
Twin Falls, ID 83303
Fax: (208)736-1958
Free: 800-357-4226
Format: Religious; Contemporary Christian. **Owner:** CSN International, PO Box 391, Twin Falls, ID 83303, Ph: (208)736-1958, Fax: (208)736-1958, Free: 800-357-4226. **URL:** http://www.csnradio.com.

CASS CITY

Tuscola Co. Tuscola Co. (E). 38 m E of Bay City. Manufactures carburetors, electric fuel pumps, industrial screens, wire cable, crates, auto stamping, elevators. Dairy, stock, poultry, grain farms.

17243 ■ Cass City Chronicle
Cass City Chronicle
6550 Main St.
Cass City, MI 48726
Phone: (989)872-2010
Fax: (989)872-3810
Publisher's E-mail: chronicle@cchronicle.net
Community newspaper. **Freq:** Weekly (Tues.). **Print Method:** Offset. **Cols./Page:** 8. **Col. Width:** 19 nonpareils. **Col. Depth:** 294 agate lines. **Key Personnel:** Tom Montgometry, Editor; Harmony Doerr, Office Manager. **Subscription Rates:** $23.10 Individuals Tuscola, Sanilac and Huron counties; $27.50 Individuals in Michigan; $29.70 Other countries; $37.40 Two years Tuscola, Sanilac and Huron counties; $45.10 Two years in Michigan; $49.50 Two years other countries; $51.70 Individuals Tuscola, Sanilac and Huron counties (Three years); $59.40 Individuals in Michigan (Three years); $63.80 Individuals other countries (Three years); $22 Individuals e-mail subscription. **Ad Rates:** SAU $6.97. **Remarks:** Accepts advertising. **Circ:** ‡3,100.

CEDAR

17244 ■ Critical Asian Studies
Critical Asian Studies
3693 S Bay Bluffs Dr.
Cedar, MI 49621-9434
Phone: (231)228-7116
Fax: (928)223-5511
Peer-reviewed journal focusing on Asian studies. **Freq:** Quarterly. **Print Method:** Offset. **Trim Size:** 8 1/4 x 10. **Cols./Page:** 2. **Col. Width:** 42 nonpareils. **Col. Depth:** 130 agate lines. **Key Personnel:** Patricio Abinales, Editor; Thomas P. Fenton, Editor; Martin Hart-Landsberg, Editor. **ISSN:** 0007--4810 (print). **Subscription Rates:** $109 Individuals U.S.; $337 Institutions online; $385 Institutions print and online; £242 Institutions print and online; £212 Institutions online; £68 Individuals. **URL:** http://criticalasianstudies.org. **Formerly:** Bulletin of Concerned Asian Scholars. **Remarks:** Advertising accepted; rates available upon request. **Circ:** 1000.

CHARLOTTE

Eaton Co. Eaton Co. (S). 16 m SW of Lansing. Manufactures furniture, culverts, glass bottles, road machinery, tape recorders, aluminum moldings, iron castings, lumber, flour. Grain farms. Wheat, corn, beans.

17245 ■ Eaton County Quest
Eaton County Genealogical Society
100 W Lawrence Ave.
Charlotte, MI 48813
Phone: (517)543-8792
Fax: (517)543-6999
Publisher's E-mail: ecgsoc@gmail.com
Magazine containing historical and genealogical information of Eaton County. **Freq:** 3/year. **Key Personnel:** Marcy Cousino, Corresponding Secretary. **ISSN:** 0107--5881 (print). **Subscription Rates:** $4.50 Individuals back issue. **URL:** http://www.miegs.org/Publications.shtml. **Mailing address:** PO Box 337, Charlotte, MI 48813-0337. **Circ:** (Not Reported).

17246 ■ Eaton Rapids Community News
Lansing State Journal
239 S Cochran Ave.
Charlotte, MI 48813
Phone: (517)541-2505
Fax: (517)543-3677
Shopper. **Founded:** Feb. 1993. **Freq:** Weekly. **Print Method:** Offset. **Trim Size:** 11 1/4 x 17. **Cols./Page:** 6. **Col. Width:** 9.5 picas. **Col. Depth:** 16 inches. **Key Personnel:** Rachel S. Greco, Editor. **Subscription Rates:** $25 Individuals 7 days a week (daily); $19 Individuals weekends (Thursday - Sunday); $12 Individuals Sundays only; $12 Individuals Digital. **URL:** http://www.lansingstatejournal.com/news/communities-eaton-rapids/. **Formerly:** The Advantage; Eaton County News. **Circ:** Paid 1305, Non-paid 120193.

17247 ■ WLCM-AM - 1390
1613 Lawrence Hwy
Charlotte, MI 48813
Phone: (517)543-8200
Fax: (517)543-7779
Format: Religious. **Owner:** Christian Broadcasting System Ltd., 5201 S Saginaw, Flint, MI 48507, Ph: (810)694-4146. **Founded:** 1956. **Formerly:** WNNY-AM; WNLF-AM; WGWY-AM; WCER-AM. **Operating Hours:** 6am-sunset. **ADI:** Lansing (Ann Arbor), MI. **Key Personnel:** Jeff Frank, Station Mgr. **Wattage:** 5,000 daytime; 070 nightime. **Ad Rates:** Noncommercial. Combined advertising rates available with WLQV, WSNL, WLYV. **Mailing address:** PO Box 338, Charlotte, MI 48813. **URL:** http://www.wlcmradio.com.

CHEBOYGAN

Cheboygan Co. Cheboygan Co. (N). On the Straits of Mackinac, 40 m N of Petroskey. Boat connections. Sumer resort. Manufactures tools, dies, auto parts, camera cases, mining machinery parts, taps, tank chocks, wooden boxes and crates, fisheries. Timber. Farming. Dairy products, cattle.

17248 ■ Daily Tribune
Cheboygan Daily Tribune Inc.
308 N Main St.
Cheboygan, MI 49721
Phone: (231)627-7144
Publisher's E-mail: newsusa@newsusa.com
Local newspaper. **Founded:** 1875. **Freq:** Daily. **Print Method:** Offset. **Cols./Page:** 6. **Col. Width:** 25 nonpareils. **Col. Depth:** 294 agate lines. **Key Personnel:** Zac Britton, Editor; Shawna Jankoviak, Contact. **Subscription Rates:** $140 Individuals within 497 zip 52 weeks; $170 Out of state 497 zip 52 weeks; $80 Individuals 497 zip 26 weeks; $100 Out of state 497 zip 26 weeks; $50 Individuals 497 zip 13 weeks; $70 Out of state 497 zip 13 weeks. **URL:** http://www.cheboygannews.com. **Ad Rates:** BW $100; 4C $280; PCI $8.05. **Remarks:** Accepts advertising. **Circ:** ‡4665.

17249 ■ Shoppers Fair
Cheboygan Daily Tribune Inc.
308 N Main St.
Cheboygan, MI 49721

Phone: (231)627-7144
Publisher's E-mail: newsusa@newsusa.com
Shopper. **Freq:** Weekly (Sat.). **Print Method:** Offset. **Cols./Page:** 5. **Col. Width:** 21 nonpareils. **Col. Depth:** 224 agate lines. **URL:** http://www.cheboygannews.com. **Ad Rates:** GLR $.39; BW $470; SAU $5.88; PCI $5.60. **Remarks:** Accepts advertising. **Circ:** ‡14500.

WAVC-FM - See Mio

17250 ■ WCBY-AM - 1240
1356 Mackinaw Ave.
Cheboygan, MI 49721
Phone: (231)627-2341
Fax: (231)627-7000
Format: Middle-of-the-Road (MOR). **Simulcasts:** WIDG. **Networks:** ABC. **Owner:** Northern Star Broadcasting L.L.C., 514 Munson Ave., MI 49686. **Founded:** 1954. **Operating Hours:** Continuous. **Key Personnel:** Mary Reynolds, Gen. Mgr., VP of Sales & Mktg. **Wattage:** 1,000. **Ad Rates:** Noncommercial. Combined advertising rates available with WGFM, WMKC, WLJZ. **URL:** http://www.nsbroadcasting.com.

17251 ■ WCKC-FM - 107.1
1356 Mackinaw Ave.
Cheboygan, MI 49721
Phone: (231)627-2341
Fax: (231)627-7000
Free: 888-751-BEAR
Format: Classic Rock. **Owner:** Northern Star Broadcasting L.L.C., 514 Munson Ave., MI 49686. **Key Personnel:** Tim Logan, Dir. of Programs, tim@classicrockthebear.com; Mary Reynolds, Gen. Mgr., mary@nsbroadcasting.com. **Wattage:** 6,000. **Ad Rates:** Noncommercial. **URL:** http://www.classicrockthebear.com.

17252 ■ WGFM-FM - 105.1
1356 Mackinaw Ave.
Cheboygan, MI 49721
Fax: (231)627-7000
Format: Classic Rock. **Wattage:** 100,000. **Ad Rates:** Advertising accepted; rates available upon request. **URL:** http://www.classicrockthebear.com.

17253 ■ WGFN-FM - 98.1
1356 Mackinaw Ave.
Cheboygan, MI 49721-1003
Phone: (231)627-2341
Fax: (231)627-7000
Format: Classic Rock. **Key Personnel:** Tim Logan, Gen. Mgr., tim@classicrockthebear.com. **URL:** http://www.classicrockthebear.com.

WIAN-AM - See Marquette

WIDG-AM - See Saint Ignace

17254 ■ WIHC-FM - 97.9
1356 Mackinaw Ave.
Cheboygan, MI 49721
Phone: (231)627-2341
Format: Classic Rock. **Ad Rates:** Noncommercial.

17255 ■ WMKC-FM
1356 Mackinaw Ave.
Cheboygan, MI 49721
Format: Country. **Wattage:** 100,000 ERP. **Ad Rates:** Noncommercial.

CHELSEA

Washtenaw Co. Washtenaw Co. (SE). 15 m W of Ann Arbor. Manufactures screw-machine products, prepared baking mixes, auto accessories. Automobile proving ground. Diversified farming. Dairy products, eggs, livestock.

17256 ■ The Chelsea Standard
Heritage Newspapers Inc.
20750 W Old US 12, Hwy. 12
Chelsea, MI 48118
Phone: (734)475-1371
Publisher's E-mail: subscribe@heritage.com
Community newspaper. **Freq:** Weekly (Thurs.). **Print Method:** Offset. **Trim Size:** 13 3/4 x 22 3/4. **Cols./Page:** 6. **Col. Width:** 2 1/16 inches. **Col. Depth:** 301 agate lines. **Key Personnel:** Michelle Rogers, Managing Editor. **Subscription Rates:** $35 Individuals mail; $64 Two years mail; $19.50 Individuals 6 months, mail. **Remarks:** Accepts advertising. **Circ:** Thurs. ♦**2437**.

17257 ■ The Dexter Leader
Heritage Newspapers Inc.
20750 W Old US 12, Hwy. 12
Chelsea, MI 48118
Phone: (734)475-1371
Publisher's E-mail: subscribe@heritage.com
Community newspaper. **Freq:** Weekly (Thurs.). **Print Method:** Offset. **Trim Size:** 13 3/4 x 22 3/4. **Cols./Page:** 6. **Col. Width:** 2 1/16 inches. **Col. Depth:** 301 agate lines. **Key Personnel:** Michelle Rogers, Managing Editor. **Subscription Rates:** $35 Individuals; $64 Two years mail; $19.50 Individuals 6 months, mail. **Remarks:** Accepts advertising. **Circ:** ‡3500.

CLARE

Isabella Co. Clare Co. (NC). 50 m NW of Saginaw. Manufactures custom machinery, electronic components, automotive wire harness, auto interior products, plastic extrusion, cheese. Meat, poultry packing plant. Gas, oil wells. Stock, dairy, fruit farms.

17258 ■ Clare County Review: Mid-Michigan's Most Widely Circulated Newspaper
Clare County Review
2141 E Ludington Dr.
Clare, MI 48617
Phone: (989)386-4414
Fax: (989)386-2412
Publisher's E-mail: info@clarecountyreview.com
Community newspaper. **Freq:** Weekly. **Key Personnel:** Al Iacco, Manager, Advertising; Mike Wilcox, Editor, Publisher; Patricia A. Maurer, Correspondent. **URL:** http://www.clarecountyreview.com. **Formerly:** Farwell News and Review. **Ad Rates:** BW $1,164; 4C $1,259.50; SAU $10.50; PCI $9.75. **Remarks:** Accepts classified advertising. **Circ:** ‡10000.

CLINTON TOWNSHIP

17259 ■ Advisor & Source Newspapers
Advisor & Source Newspapers
19176 Hall Rd., Ste. 200
Clinton Township, MI 48038
Phone: (586)716-8100
Fax: (586)716-8533
Publication E-mail: jody.mcveigh@advisorsource.com
Community newspaper. **Freq:** Weekly (Sun.). **Print Method:** Offset. **Cols./Page:** 6. **Col. Width:** 2 1/16 inches. **Col. Depth:** 21 inches. **Key Personnel:** Jody McVeigh, Editor. **URL:** http://www.sourcenewspapers.com. **Formerly:** Romeo-Washington Advisor. **Ad Rates:** BW $1,717.07; 4C $1,966.07; SAU $13.63. **Remarks:** Accepts advertising. **Circ:** Combined ‡9502.

17260 ■ Long Life
Immortalist Society
24355 Sorrentino Ct.
Clinton Township, MI 48035-3229
Phone: (586)791-5961
Publisher's E-mail: immsoc@aol.com
Magazine covering topics and activities of individuals and organizations that educate the public about cryonics done by the Immortalist Society. **Freq:** Quarterly. **Alt. Formats:** PDF. **Circ:** (Not Reported).

17261 ■ Macomb County Legal News
Advisor & Source Newspapers
19176 Hall Rd., Ste. 200
Clinton Township, MI 48038
Phone: (586)716-8100
Fax: (586)716-8533
Legal newspaper. **Freq:** Weekly (Fri.). **Print Method:** Offset. **Cols./Page:** 6. **Col. Width:** 25 nonpareils. **Col. Depth:** 301 agate lines. **Key Personnel:** Suzanne Favale, Publisher, phone: (248)577-6109; Paul Arlon, Director, Advertising, phone: (248)556-7719; Brad Thompson, President; Melanie Deeds, Editor, phone: (586)463-4300. **ISSN:** 0024-9289 (print). **Subscription Rates:** $45 Individuals. **URL:** http://www.legalnews.com/macomb/. **Ad Rates:** BW $1490; SAU $11.55. **Remarks:** Accepts advertising. **Circ:** (Not Reported).

17262 ■ The Macomb Daily
The Macomb Daily
19176 Hall Rd., 2nd Fl.
Clinton Township, MI 48038
Phone: (586)469-4510
Publisher's E-mail: onlineads@21stcenturynewspapers.com
General newspaper. **Freq:** Daily. **Print Method:** Offset. **Cols./Page:** 6. **Col. Width:** 12.6 picas. **Col. Depth:** 21.5 inches. **Key Personnel:** Niky Hachigian, Editor; Ken Kish, Managing Editor. **Subscription Rates:** $210.60 Individuals home delivery. **URL:** http://www.macombdaily.com. **Feature Editors:** Debbie Komar, debbie.komar@macombdaily.com. **Ad Rates:** BW $5721.15; 4C $6326.15; SAU $44.35. **Circ:** Mon.-Fri. ⋆**48,741**, Sat. ⋆**41,260**, Sun. ⋆**59,863**.

17263 ■ WADL-TV - 38
35000 Adell Dr.
Clinton Township, MI 48035
Phone: (586)790-3838
Format: Commercial TV. **Simulcasts:** WJBK-TV. **Networks:** Independent. **Owner:** Adell Broadcasting Corp., at above address. **Founded:** 1989. **ADI:** Detroit, MI. **Key Personnel:** Frank Adell, Contact. **URL:** http://www.wadldetroit.com/contact-us.

CLIO

Genesee Co. Genesee Co. (SC). 20 m N of Flint.

17264 ■ WEYI-TV - 25
2225 W Willard Rd.
Clio, MI 48420
Phone: (810)687-1000
Fax: (810)687-4925
Format: Commercial TV. **Networks:** CBS. **Owner:** Sinclair Broadcast Group Inc., 10706 Beaver Dam Rd., Hunt Valley, MD 21030, Ph: (410)568-1500, Fax: (410)568-1533. **Founded:** 1953. **Formerly:** WKNX-TV. **Operating Hours:** Continuous; 95% network, 5% local. **ADI:** Flint-Saginaw-Bay City, MI. **Key Personnel:** Mary Speer, Contact, mspeer@nbc25.net. **Ad Rates:** Advertising accepted; rates available upon request.

COLDWATER

S. MI. Branch Co. 32 mi. S. of Battle Creek. Lake resort. Manufactures iron castings, automotive seatings and springs, store fixtures, fishing equipment, wood products. Molybdenum. Stock yard. Dairy, grain, stock farms.

17265 ■ The Daily Reporter
GateHouse Media Inc.
15 W Pearl St.
Coldwater, MI 49036
Community newspaper. **Founded:** 1961. **Freq:** Daily (eve.). **Print Method:** Offset. **Trim Size:** 14 x 22 3/4. **Cols./Page:** 6. **Col. Width:** 2 1/16 inches. **Col. Depth:** 21 inches. **Key Personnel:** Heather Jeffrey, Executive Editor; Cassandra Harmon, Business Manager; Gary Baker, Editor; Karen Allard, Manager, Circulation; David Ferro, Publisher. **URL:** http://www.thedailyreporter.com/. **Ad Rates:** BW $882; 4C $1,092; SAU $7; PCI $7. **Remarks:** Accepts advertising. **Circ:** Paid ‡4783.

17266 ■ Great Lakes Trail Rider
Cycle Conservation Club of Michigan
c/o Lewis Shuler, Executive Director
PO Box 486
Coldwater, MI 49036-0486
Freq: Monthly. **Subscription Rates:** Free for members. **URL:** http://www.cycleconservationclub.org/members/GLTR.html. **Remarks:** Accepts advertising. **Circ:** (Not Reported).

17267 ■ WTVB-AM - 1590
182 N Angola Rd.
Coldwater, MI 49036
Phone: (517)279-1590
Fax: (517)279-4695
Format: Oldies; Full Service. **Networks:** ABC; Satellite Music Network. **Owner:** Midwest Communications Inc., 904 Grand Ave., Wausau, WI 54403, Ph: (715)842-1437, Fax: (715)842-7061. **Founded:** 1947. **Operating Hours:** Continuous; 60% network, 40% local. **Key Personnel:** Ken Delaney, Contact, ken.delaney@mwcradio.com. **Wattage:** 5,000. **Ad Rates:** $10-20.50 for 30 seconds; $14-24 for 60 seconds. **URL:** http://wtvbam.com/local-sports-live.

Circulation: ⋆ = AAM; △ or • = BPA; ♦ = CAC; ❑ = VAC; ⊕ = PO Statement; ‡ = Publisher's Report; Boldface figures = sworn; Light figures = estimated.

CRYSTAL

17268 ■ Crystal Cable TV
122 Lake St.
Crystal, MI 48818
Phone: (989)235-6100
Owner: Rex Skea, 1033 Senator Rd., Crystal, MI 48818, Ph: (989)235-6695. **Founded:** 1988. **Key Personnel:** Rex Skea, President, rskea@glccmi.com; Mark Winslow, Gen. Mgr., markw@glccmi.com. **Cities Served:** subscribing households 600. **Mailing address:** PO Box 365, Crystal, MI 48818.

DAVISON

Genesee Co. Genesee Co. (SEC). 9 m E of Flint. Dairy, stock, poultry, truck, grain farms. Wheat, corn, beans.

17269 ■ The Davison Index
The Davison Index
220 N Main St.
Davison, MI 48423-0100
Phone: (810)653-3511
Fax: (810)667-6309
Free: 866-348-8439
Publisher's E-mail: ads@mihomepaper.com
Newspaper. **Freq:** Weekly. **Print Method:** Offset. **Trim Size:** 11 3/8 x 16 1/4. **Cols./Page:** 6. **Col. Width:** 20 nonpareils. **Col. Depth:** 210 agate lines. **URL:** http://davisonindex.mihomepaper.com. **Ad Rates:** GLR $.37; BW $540; PCI $6. **Remarks:** Advertising accepted; rates available upon request. **Circ:** 11000.

DEARBORN

Wayne Co. Wayne Co. (SE). 10 m W of Detroit. Manufactures automobiles, truck, airplane motors, plane parts, joints, cold rolled strip steel, tools, dies, stampings, bricks, road paving mixtures.

17270 ■ AAA Living
AAA Automobile Club of Michigan
1 Auto Club Dr.
Dearborn, MI 48126
Free: 800-222-6424
Magazine covering travel, recreation and lifestyle activities in Michigan, the U.S., and around the world. Also reports on highway and home safety. **Freq:** Bimonthly 6/yr. **Print Method:** Offset. **Trim Size:** 7 7/8 x 10 7/8. **Cols./Page:** 3. **Col. Width:** 28 nonpareils. **Col. Depth:** 138 agate lines. **ISSN:** 0745--1798 (print). **URL:** http://michigan.aaa.com/magazine/aaaliving.aspx. **Formerly**: Michigan Living. **Ad Rates:** BW $51,061; 4C $60,072. **Remarks:** Accepts advertising. **Circ:** Paid ★**1026777**.

17271 ■ International Journal of Vehicle Safety
Inderscience Publishers
c/o Dr. Jesse Ruan, Ed.-in-Ch.
Ford Scientific Research Laboratory
Ford Motor Co.
2101 Village Rd.
Dearborn, MI 48124
Publication E-mail: ijvs@inderscience.com
Journal covering the subjects of passive and active safety in road traffic as well as traffic related public health issues, from impact biomechanics to vehicle crashworthiness, and from crash avoidance to intelligent highway systems. **Freq:** Quarterly. **Key Personnel:** Dr. Jesse Ruan, Editor-in-Chief; Dr. Cliff C. Chou, Editor; Prof. Remy Willinger, Editor. **ISSN:** 1479--3105 (print); **EISSN:** 1479--3113 (electronic). **Subscription Rates:** $685 Individuals print or online; $928 Individuals print and online. **URL:** http://www.inderscience.com/jhome.php?jcode=ijvs. **Circ:** (Not Reported).

17272 ■ Journal of Manufacturing Systems
Society of Manufacturing Engineers
1 SME Dr.
Dearborn, MI 48128-2408
Phone: (313)425-3000
Fax: (313)425-3400
Free: 800-733-4763
Publication E-mail: publications@sme.org
Freq: Quarterly. **Print Method:** Offset. **Trim Size:** 8 1/2 x 11. **Cols./Page:** 2. **Col. Width:** 20 picas. **Col. Depth:** 8 3/4 inches. **Key Personnel:** S.J. Hu, Editor; J.G. Bollinger, Editor; R. Suri, Editor. **ISSN:** 0278--6125 (print). **Subscription Rates:** $1039 Institutions print; $520 Institutions e-journal. **URL:** http://www.journals.elsevier.com/journal-of-manufacturing-systems. **Mailing address:** PO Box 930, Dearborn, MI 48121-0930. **Remarks:** Accepts classified advertising. **Circ:** Paid 1500.

17273 ■ WHFR-FM - 89.3
5101 Evergreen Rd.
Dearborn, MI 48128
Phone: (313)845-9676
Fax: (313)317-4034
Free: 800-585-9676
Email: whfr@hfcc.edu
Format: Eclectic; Information. **Networks:** Public Radio International (PRI). **Owner:** Henry Ford College, 5101 Evergreen Rd., Dearborn, MI 48128, Ph: (313)845-9600, Fax: (313)845-6464, Free: 800-585-4322. **Founded:** 1985. **Operating Hours**: Continuous; 63% local, 37% network. **Key Personnel:** Lara Hrycaj, Operations Mgr., whfr-om@hfcc.edu. **Wattage**: 270 ERP. **Ad Rates:** Noncommercial. Underwriting available. **URL:** http://whfr.fm.

DEARBORN HEIGHTS

17274 ■ Leaves
Mariannhill Mission Society
23715 Ann Arbor Trl.
Dearborn Heights, MI 48127
Phone: (313)561-7140
Fax: (313)561-9486
Magazine providing religious and spiritual encouragement for families. **Founded:** 1938. **Freq:** Monthly. **Print Method:** Offset. **Key Personnel:** Rev. Thomas Heier, Editor-in-Chief. **ISSN:** 0714-4113 (print). **Subscription Rates:** Free. **URL:** http://www.mariannhill.us/leaves.html. **Remarks:** Advertising not accepted. **Circ:** Free 75000.

DETROIT

Wayne Co (SE). On Detroit River, 18 m above Lake Erie. One of the most important ports on the Great Lakes. Bridge and tunnels connecting Detroit with Windsor, Canada. Wayne State University, University of Detroit; professional and technological schools and colleges. Noted for the world's largest manufacture of automobiles and auto products. Also manufactures gray iron and machine tools and fixtures, ranges and heating devices, pharmaceuticals, computing machines, foundry products, paints, varnishes, lacquers, chemicals, beer, pleasure boats, paper and twine, air conditioning equipment, aircraft bearings and cushions,bolts, screws, nuts, boilers, tanks, ball bearings, tools, steel plates, flues and tubes, rubber goods. Meat packing. Shipyards. Salt, alkali mines.

17275 ■ ACSM's Health & Fitness Journal
Lippincott Williams and Wilkins
c/o Steven J. Keteyian, PhD, Ed.-in-Ch.
Division of Cardiovascular Medicine
Henry Ford Hospital
6525 2nd Ave.
Detroit, MI 48202
Phone: (313)972-1920
Fax: (313)972-1921
Publication E-mail: adixon@lww.com
Professional journal covering health and fitness for fitness instructors, personal trainers, exercise leaders, program managers and other health and fitness professionals. **Freq:** Bimonthly. **Trim Size:** 8 1/8 x 10 7/8. **Key Personnel:** Lori A. Tish, Managing Editor, phone: (317)634-8932, fax: (317)634-8927; David Myers, Publisher; Steven J. Keteyian, PhD, Editor-in-Chief. **ISSN:** 1091--5397 (print); **EISSN:** 1536--593X (electronic). **Subscription Rates:** $88 Individuals; $197 Institutions; $82 Individuals in-training; $106 Other countries; $197 Institutions; $198 Institutions, other countries; $101 Individuals in-training. **URL:** http://journals.lww.com/acsm-healthfitness/pages/default.aspx. **Ad Rates:** BW $1,385; 4C $1,195. **Remarks:** Accepts advertising. **Circ:** 9294.

17276 ■ The Adcrafter: The Voice of Advertising in Detroit
Adcraft Club of Detroit
15 E Kirby St., Ste. 418
Detroit, MI 48202
Phone: (313)872-7850
Publisher's E-mail: adcraft@adcraft.org
Magazine for the advertising industry. **Freq:** Monthly. **Print Method:** Offset. **Trim Size:** 8 1/2 x 11. **Cols./Page:** 3. **Col. Width:** 14 picas. **Col. Depth:** 9.5 inches. **ISSN:** 0001--8066 (print). **Subscription Rates:** $30 Individuals online; $100 Individuals print. **URL:** http://www.adcraft.org/adcrafter. **Ad Rates:** BW $900; 4C $1980; PCI $35. **Remarks:** Accepts advertising. **Circ:** ‡2500.

17277 ■ Against the Current
Center for Changes
7012 Michigan Ave.
Detroit, MI 48210
Phone: (313)841-0160
Fax: (313)841-8884
Publication E-mail: cfc@igc.org
Magazine oriented toward movements for social and political change. Emphasizes labor, national minorities, feminist issues, and international solidarity. Supports socialist democracy and workers' control, worldwide. **Freq:** Bimonthly. **Print Method:** Offset. **Trim Size:** 8 1/2 x 11. **Cols./Page:** 3. **Col. Width:** 27 nonpareils. **Col. Depth:** 133 agate lines. **Key Personnel:** Robert Brenner, Editor; Dianne Feeley, Editor; David Finkel, Editor. **ISSN:** 0739--4853 (print). **Subscription Rates:** $25 Individuals; $45 Individuals 2 years; $30 Individuals supporting; $55 Individuals 2 years, supporting. **URL:** http://www.solidarity-us.org/atc. **Formerly**: Changes Socialist Monthly. **Remarks:** Accepts advertising. **Circ:** Paid ‡1600.

17278 ■ Automotive News
Crain Communications Inc.
1155 Gratiot Ave.
Detroit, MI 48207-2732
Phone: (313)446-6000
Publisher's E-mail: info@crain.com
Tabloid reporting on all facets of the automotive and truck industry, as well as related businesses. **Founded:** 1925. **Freq:** Weekly. **Print Method:** Offset. **Trim Size:** 11 x 14 1/2. **Cols./Page:** 5. **Col. Width:** 2 inches. **Col. Depth:** 196 agate lines. **Key Personnel:** Richard Johnson, Editor, phone: (313)446-0371; Jason Stein, Publisher, Editor. **Subscription Rates:** $159 Individuals print and digital online; $99 Individuals digital/online; $699 Individuals data center only (full access); $199 Individuals data center only (limited access). **URL:** http://www.autonews.com. **Ad Rates:** BW $15,510; 4C $19,930; PCI $218. **Remarks:** Accepts advertising. **Circ:** Paid ★**76100**.

17279 ■ AutoWeek
Crain Communications Inc.
1155 Gratiot Ave.
Detroit, MI 48207-2732
Phone: (313)446-6000
Publisher's E-mail: info@crain.com
Magazine for car enthusiasts, includes news coverage and features on vehicles, personalities, and events. Provides coverage of Formula One, CART, NASCAR, and IMSA races. **Freq:** Weekly. **Print Method:** Letterpress and Offset. **Trim Size:** 8 1/4 x 10 3/4. **Cols./Page:** 3. **Col. Width:** 2 1/4 inches. **Col. Depth:** 140 agate lines. **Key Personnel:** K.C. Crain, Publisher, Vice President, phone: (313)446-1681; Ken Ross, Art Director; Wes Raynal, Executive Editor, phone: (313)446-0332; Cheryl L. Blahnik, Assistant Director. **ISSN:** 0192--9674 (print). **Subscription Rates:** $29.95 Individuals 24 issues. **Online:** Crain Communications Inc. Crain Communications Inc. **URL:** http://autoweek.com. **Ad Rates:** BW $21805; 4C $33964. **Remarks:** Accepts classified advertising. **Circ:** ‡275000.

17280 ■ Bulletin of the Detroit Institute of Arts
Detroit Institute of Arts
5200 Woodward Ave.
Detroit, MI 48202
Phone: (313)833-7900
Publisher's E-mail: membership@dia.org
Scholarly journal covering the collection of the Detroit Institute of Arts. **Freq:** Semiannual. **Print Method:** Sheetfed offset. **Trim Size:** 8 1/4 x 11 1/2. **Cols./Page:** 3. **Col. Width:** 2 1/8 inches. **Col. Depth:** 9 1/4 inches. **Key Personnel:** Tracee Glab, Assistant Editor. **ISSN:** 0011--9636 (print). **Subscription Rates:** $15 Nonmembers; $13.50 Members. **Alt. Formats:** PDF. **URL:** http://www.dia.org/learn/bulletin.aspx. **Remarks:** Advertising not accepted. **Circ:** Combined 5500.

17281 ■ Business Insurance
Crain Communications Inc.
1155 Gratiot Ave.
Detroit, MI 48207-2732

Phone: (313)446-6000
Publisher's E-mail: info@crain.com
International newsweekly reporting on corporate risk and employee benefit management news. **Freq:** Weekly. **Print Method:** Offset. **Trim Size:** 10 7/8 x 14 1/2. **Cols./Page:** 5. **Col. Width:** 11.5 picas. **Col. Depth:** 14 inches. **Key Personnel:** Paul Bomberger, Managing Editor; Paul D. Winston, Associate Publisher, Director, Editorial. **ISSN:** 0007--6864 (print). **Subscription Rates:** $799 Individuals data + print and digital; $99 Individuals print & digital; $125 Individuals digital edition. **Online:** Lexis-Nexis; Crain Communications Inc. Crain Communications Inc. **URL:** http://www.businessinsurance.com. **Remarks:** Accepts advertising. **Circ:** (Not Reported).

17282 ■ Canton Observer
Observer & Eccentric Newspapers
615 W Lafayette Blvd., 2nd Level
Detroit, MI 48226
Free: 866-887-2737
Community newspaper. **Freq:** Weekly (Thurs. and Sun.). **Print Method:** Offset. **Cols./Page:** 6. **Col. Width:** 11 picas. **Col. Depth:** 21 1/2 inches. **Key Personnel:** Peter Neill, Publisher; Susan Rosiek, Executive Editor, Publisher, phone: (313)222-5397; Joe Bauman, Managing Editor. **Subscription Rates:** $7 Individuals monthly. **URL:** http://www.hometownlife.com/news/observer-canton. **Remarks:** Accepts advertising. **Circ:** Sun. ♦**9282**.

17283 ■ Crain's Cleveland Business
Crain Communications Inc.
1155 Gratiot Ave.
Detroit, MI 48207-2732
Phone: (313)446-6000
Publisher's E-mail: info@crain.com
Metropolitan business newspaper serving seven counties. **Freq:** Weekly. **Print Method:** Offset. **Trim Size:** 10 1/4 x 14. **Cols./Page:** 5. **Col. Width:** 25 nonpareils. **Col. Depth:** 196 agate lines. **Key Personnel:** Mark Dodosh, Editor, phone: (216)771-5358; Scott Suttell, Managing Editor, phone: (216)771-5227; Brian Tucker, Director, Editorial, Publisher, phone: (216)771-5174. **Subscription Rates:** $39 Individuals 1 year, print. **Online:** LexisNexis; Crain Communications Inc. Crain Communications Inc. **URL:** http://www.crainscleveland.com. **Remarks:** Accepts advertising. **Circ:** Paid ⋆**20,585**.

17284 ■ Crain's Detroit Business
Crain Communications Inc.
1155 Gratiot Ave.
Detroit, MI 48207-2732
Phone: (313)446-6000
Publisher's E-mail: info@crain.com
Local business tabloid covering Wayne, Macomb, Oakland, Livingston, and Washtenaw counties. **Freq:** Weekly (Mon.) 52 issues. **Print Method:** Offset. **Trim Size:** 11 x 14 3/4. **Cols./Page:** 5. **Col. Width:** 2 inches. **Col. Depth:** 14 inches. **Key Personnel:** Jennette Smith, Managing Editor, phone: (313)446-1622; Mary Kramer, Publisher, phone: (313)446-0399; Keith Crain, Editor-in-Chief. **ISSN:** 0882--1992 (print). **Subscription Rates:** $59 Individuals print edition; $36 Individuals online edition. **Online:** Crain Communications Inc. Crain Communications Inc. **URL:** http://www.crainsdetroit.com. **Ad Rates:** GLR $84; BW $12,390; 4C $13,374; PCI $900. **Remarks:** Accepts advertising. **Circ:** Paid ⋆**29000**.

17285 ■ Crain's New York Business
Crain Communications Inc.
1155 Gratiot Ave.
Detroit, MI 48207-2732
Phone: (313)446-6000
Publisher's E-mail: info@crain.com
Regional business tabloid. **Freq:** Weekly. **Print Method:** Offset. **Trim Size:** 10 7/8 x 14 1/2. **Cols./Page:** 5. **Col. Width:** 2 inches. **Col. Depth:** 14 inches. **Key Personnel:** Glenn Coleman, Editor; Greg David, Columnist, phone: (212)210-0270. **ISSN:** 8756--789X (print). **Subscription Rates:** $39.95 Individuals digital only/year; $49.95 Individuals print and digital/year. **Online:** Crain Communications Inc. Crain Communications Inc. **URL:** http://www.crainsnewyork.com. **Ad Rates:** PCI $682.50. **Remarks:** Accepts advertising. **Circ:** ⋆**59866**.

17286 ■ Criticism: A Quarterly for Literature and the Arts
Wayne State University Press
The Leonard N Simons Bldg. 4809 Woodward Ave.
Detroit, MI 48201-1309
Phone: (313)577-6120
Fax: (313)577-6131
Free: 800-978-7323
Publication E-mail: criticism.at.wayne@gmail.com
Journal on literature and the arts. **Freq:** Quarterly. **Print Method:** Offset. **Trim Size:** 6 x 9. **Cols./Page:** 1. **Col. Width:** 4 1/4 inches. **Col. Depth:** 6 5/8 inches. **Key Personnel:** Jonathan Flatley, Associate Editor, phone: (313)577-8301; Lara Langer Cohen, Associate Editor; Marie Buck, Board Member. **ISSN:** 0011--1589 (print); **EISSN:** 1536--0342 (electronic). **Subscription Rates:** $64 Individuals online or print additional $60.00 is charged for postage to addresses outside the U.S.; $75 Individuals print and online additional $60.00 is charged for postage to addresses outside the U.S.; $29 Individuals senior/student - print or online additional $60.00 is charged for postage to addresses outside the U.S.; $41 Individuals senior/student - print and online additional $60.00 is charged for postage to addresses outside the U.S.; $179 Institutions print additional $60.00 is charged for postage to addresses outside the U.S. **URL:** http://wsupress.wayne.edu/journals/detail/criticism; http://digitalcommons.wayne.edu/criticism. **Ad Rates:** BW $200. **Remarks:** Accepts advertising. **Circ:** ‡1,200.

17287 ■ Decode
Encode Media Group
PO Box 13158
Detroit, MI 48213
Phone: (313)312-0670
Fax: (313)838-9988
Publisher's E-mail: info@encodeonline.com
Entertainment lifestyle magazine. **Freq:** 4/yr. **Trim Size:** 4 7/8 x 7 1/4. **Cols./Page:** 2. **Col. Width:** 12 picas. **Col. Depth:** 90 agate lines. **Key Personnel:** Paul Martin, Associate Publisher; Arvell Jones, Publisher. **Subscription Rates:** $6 U.S. and Canada. **URL:** http://bigcityman.wix.com/encode. **Ad Rates:** BW $4,050; 4C $5,400. **Remarks:** Accepts advertising. **Circ:** Paid ‡50000, Combined ‡250000.

17288 ■ Detroit Free Press
McClatchy Newspapers Inc.
615 W Lafayette
Detroit, MI 48226
Phone: (313)222-6400
Fax: (313)222-5981
Publisher's E-mail: pensions@mcclatchy.com
General newspaper. Publishes combined weekend and holiday editions with the Detroit News under 1989 Joint Operating Agreement. **Founded:** May 01, 1831. **Freq:** 3/week Thursday, Friday and Sunday. **Print Method:** Offset. **Cols./Page:** 6. **Col. Width:** 13 picas. **Col. Depth:** 21 3/4 inches. **Key Personnel:** David Hunke, Chief Executive Officer; Laura Varon Brown, Editor; Steve Dorsey, Assistant Managing Editor; Nancy Laughlin, Managing Editor; Nancy Andrews, Managing Editor; Ron Dzwonkowski, Associate Editor. **URL:** http://www.freep.com. **Remarks:** Accepts advertising. **Circ:** ⋆**1119200**, ⋆**1662500**, ⋆**679484**.

17289 ■ The Detroit Jewish News
The Detroit Jewish News
29200 Northwestern Hwy., Ste. 110
Southfield, MI 48034
Phone: (248)354-6060
Jewish interest newspaper. **Freq:** Weekly (Fri.). **Print Method:** Offset. **Trim Size:** 11 x 14. **Cols./Page:** 4. **Col. Depth:** 13 inches. **Key Personnel:** Kevin Browett, Chief Operating Officer; Arthur M. Horwitz, Publisher, Executive Editor; Robert Sklar, Editor. **USPS:** 275-520. **URL:** http://www.thejewishnews.com. **Ad Rates:** BW $2,090; 4C $2,525; PCI $47.50. **Remarks:** Accepts advertising. **Circ:** (Not Reported).

17290 ■ Detroit Legal News
Detroit Legal News Publishing L.L.C.
2001 W Lafayette
Detroit, MI 48216-1852
Phone: (248)577-6100
Fax: (248)577-6111
Free: 800-875-5275
Legal and financial newspaper. **Freq:** Daily Monday-Friday. **Print Method:** Offset. **Trim Size:** 15 1/2 x 22. **Cols./Page:** 7. **Col. Width:** 1 7/8 inches. **Col. Depth:** 21 inches. **Key Personnel:** Brad Thompson, President; Tom Kirvan, Editor-in-Chief, phone: (248)556-7703; Suzanne Favale, Publisher, phone: (248)577-6109; Paul Arlon, Director, Advertising, phone: (248)556-7719. **USPS:** 155-580. **Subscription Rates:** $80 Individuals one county access to web + 1 paper; $210 Individuals three county access to web + 3 papers; $350 Individuals all county access to web + 9 papers. **Alt. Formats:** PDF. **URL:** http://www.legalnews.com/detroit. **Remarks:** Advertising accepted; rates available upon request. **Circ:** ⊕**1850**.

17291 ■ The Detroit News
Digital First Media
615 W Lafayette Blvd.
Detroit, MI 48226
Phone: (313)222-2300
Fax: (313)496-5400
General newspaper. **Founded:** 1873. **Freq:** 3/week. **Print Method:** Offset. **Cols./Page:** 6. **Col. Width:** 2 1/16 inches. **Col. Depth:** 22 1/4 inches. **Key Personnel:** Nolan Finley, Editor, phone: (313)222-2064; Gary Miles, Managing Editor, phone: (313)222-2594; Jonathan Wolman, Editor, phone: (313)222-2110; Marti Davenport, Editor. **Subscription Rates:** $20 Individuals weekends (Thursday through Sunday); $15 Individuals Sundays only. **URL:** http://www.detnews.com. **Remarks:** Accepts advertising. **Circ:** (Not Reported).

17292 ■ Detroit Society for Genealogical Research Magazine
Detroit Society for Genealogical Research Inc.
The Burton Historical Collection
Detroit Public Library
5201 Woodward Ave.
Detroit, MI 48202-4093
Phone: (313)833-1480
Genealogy magazine. **Freq:** Quarterly. **Print Method:** Letterpress and offset. **Trim Size:** 8 1/2 x 11. **Cols./Page:** 1. **Key Personnel:** William Ruddock, Editor. **ISSN:** 0011--9687 (print). **Subscription Rates:** Included in membership. **Alt. Formats:** PDF. **URL:** http://dsgr.org/clist.php?nm=60. **Remarks:** Advertising not accepted. **Circ:** ‡900.

17293 ■ Detroiter: A Publication of the Detroit Regional Chamber
Detroit Regional Chamber
1 Woodward Ave., Ste. 1900
Detroit, MI 48232-0840
Phone: (313)964-4000
Fax: (313)964-0183
Free: 866-627-5463
Publisher's E-mail: members@detroitchamber.com
Magazine focusing on Metro Detroit business news. **Freq:** Quarterly. **Print Method:** Offset. **Trim Size:** 7 3/8 x 9 7/8. **Cols./Page:** 3. **Col. Width:** 28 nonpareils. **Col. Depth:** 139 agate lines. **ISSN:** 0011--9709 (print). **Subscription Rates:** $14 Members; $18 Nonmembers; $4 Single issue. **URL:** http://www.detroitchamber.com/news-media/detroiter-magazine. **Mailing address:** PO Box 33840, Detroit, MI 48232-0840. **Ad Rates:** 4C $3345; BW $2335. **Remarks:** Accepts advertising. **Circ:** Paid 13000, Controlled 3000.

17294 ■ Farmington Observer
Observer & Eccentric Newspapers
615 W Lafayette Blvd., 2nd Level
Detroit, MI 48226
Free: 866-887-2737
Community newspaper. **Freq:** Weekly (Thurs. and Sun.). **Print Method:** Offset. **Cols./Page:** 6. **Col. Width:** 11 picas. **Col. Depth:** 21 1/2 inches. **Key Personnel:** Susan Rosiek, Executive Editor, Publisher, phone: (313)222-5397; Joe Bauman, Managing Editor. **Subscription Rates:** $7 Individuals monthly. **URL:** http://www.hometownlife.com/news/observer-farmington. **Remarks:** Accepts advertising. **Circ:** Thurs. ♦**10816**, Sun. ♦**10920**.

17295 ■ Garden City Observer
Observer & Eccentric Newspapers
615 W Lafayette Blvd., 2nd Level
Detroit, MI 48226
Free: 866-887-2737
Community newspaper. **Freq:** Semiweekly (Thurs. and Sun.). **Print Method:** Offset. **Cols./Page:** 6. **Col. Width:** 11 picas. **Col. Depth:** 21 1/2 inches. **Key Personnel:** Susan Rosiek, Executive Editor, Publisher; Joe Bauman, Managing Editor. **Subscription Rates:** $7 Individu-

Circulation: ⋆ = AAM; △ or • = BPA; ♦ = CAC; ❑ = VAC; ⊕ = PO Statement; ‡ = Publisher's Report; Boldface figures = sworn; Light figures = estimated.

als monthly. **URL:** http://www.hometownlife.com/news/observer-garden-city. **Remarks:** Accepts advertising. **Circ:** Thurs. ♦**3330**, Sun. ♦**3540**.

17296 ■ Human Biology: The International Journal of Population Biology and Genetics
Wayne State University Press
The Leonard N Simons Bldg. 4809 Woodward Ave.
Detroit, MI 48201-1309
Phone: (313)577-6120
Fax: (313)577-6131
Free: 800-978-7323
Publisher's E-mail: theresa.martinelli@wayne.edu
Journal on population genetics, evolutionary and genetic demography, and behavioral genetics. **Freq:** Quarterly. **Print Method:** Offset. **Trim Size:** 6 x 9. **Cols./Page:** 1. **Col. Width:** 4 1/2 inches. **Col. Depth:** 7 inches. **Key Personnel:** Michael Crawford, Associate Editor; Franz Manni, PhD, Executive Editor; Evelyne Heyer, PhD, Editor-in-Chief; Dario Demarchi, Board Member. **ISSN:** 0018--7143 (print); **EISSN:** 1534--6617 (electronic). **Subscription Rates:** $430 Institutions online (for 12-month access); $162 Individuals online (for 12-month access) or print (for 1 volume year); $56 Students and senior, online (for 12-month access) or print (for 1 volume year); $436 Individuals print and online (for 6 issues + 12-month access); $174 Individuals print and online (for 6 issues + 12-month access); $68 Students and seniors, print and online (for 6 issues + 12-month access); $418 Institutions print (for 1 volume year). **URL:** http://www.wsupress.wayne.edu/journals/detail/human-biology. **Ad Rates:** BW $125. **Remarks:** Advertising not accepted. **Circ:** 1,800.

17297 ■ Huntington Woods/Berkley Mirror
Detroit Free Press
615 W Lafayette, 2nd Level
Detroit, MI 48226
Phone: (313)222-6751
Fax: (313)223-3318
Publisher's E-mail: smason@hometownlife.com
Community newspaper. **Freq:** Weekly (Thurs.). **Print Method:** Offset. **Key Personnel:** Choya Jordan, Manager, Marketing; Susan Rosiek, Executive Editor; Bill Emerick, Editor. **URL:** http://archive.hometownlife.com/section/NEWS14/Huntington-Woods. **Ad Rates:** GLR $9.04; BW $519.80; 4C $300. **Remarks:** Accepts advertising. **Circ:** (Not Reported).

17298 ■ Industry Focus: Industry Focus
Crain Communications Inc.
1155 Gratiot Ave.
Detroit, MI 48207-2732
Phone: (313)446-6000
Publisher's E-mail: info@crain.com
Magazine that covers industrial development, finance, and future technology. **Freq:** 10/yr. **Key Personnel:** Regis J. Coccia, Editor. **Subscription Rates:** $97 Individuals included with business focus. **URL:** http://www.businessinsurance.com/article1000150. **Remarks:** Accepts advertising. **Circ:** (Not Reported).

17299 ■ International Journal of Whole Schooling
Whole Schooling Press
Wayne State University
217 Education
Detroit, MI 48202
Phone: (313)577-1607
Publisher's E-mail: wholeschooling@twmi.rr.com
International, refereed academic journal dedicated to exploring ways to improve learning and schooling for all children. **Key Personnel:** Dianne Chambers, Editor. **ISSN:** 1710--2146 (print). **Subscription Rates:** Free. **URL:** http://www.wholeschooling.net/Journal_of_Whole_Schooling/IJWSIndex.html. **Circ:** (Not Reported).

17300 ■ Journal of American Ethnic History
University of Illinois Press
c/o John J. Bukowczyk, Editor
Department of History
Wayne State University
3094 Faculty/Admin. Bldg.
Detroit, MI 48202
Publisher's E-mail: uipress@uillinois.edu
Journal addressing various aspects of American immigration and ethnic history including background of emigration, ethnic and racial groups, Native Americans, and immigration policies. **Freq:** Quarterly. **Print Method:** Offset. **Trim Size:** 6 x 9. **Key Personnel:** John J. Bukowczyk, Editor. **ISSN:** 0278-5927 (print); **EISSN:** 1936-4695 (electronic). **Subscription Rates:** $45 Individuals print or online; $257 Institutions print or online; $310 Institutions print + online; $25 Students print or online; $35 Students print + online; $10 Individuals Canada/Mexico; $35 Individuals other countries; $20 Single issue individuals; $50 Single issue institutions; included in membership dues. **URL:** http://www.press.uillinois.edu/journals/jaeh.html; http://iehs.org/online/jaeh. **Ad Rates:** BW $350. **Remarks:** Accepts advertising. **Circ:** 700, 450, 830.

17301 ■ Journal of Law in Society
Wayne State University Law School
42. W. Warren Ave.
Detroit, MI 48202
Phone: (313)577-3933
Publisher's E-mail: lawinquire@wayne.edu
Journal providing scholarly discourse on the intersection of law and society. **Freq:** Semiannual. **Key Personnel:** Steve Knox, Editor-in-Chief. **Subscription Rates:** $25 Individuals /year; $15 Single issue /issue. **URL:** http://law.wayne.edu/journal-of-law-society. **Circ:** (Not Reported).

17302 ■ Journal of the Neurological Sciences
Mosby Inc.
Dept. of Neurology
Wayne State University School of Medicine
Detroit Medical Center
8D University Health Center
Detroit, MI 48201
Journal providing a medium for the prompt publication of studies on the interface between clinical neurology and the basic sciences. **Freq:** Semimonthly. **Key Personnel:** Robert P. Lisak, Editor; R.A. Lewis, Editor; Prof. John D. England, Editor-in-Chief. **ISSN:** 0022--510X (print). **Subscription Rates:** $6722.40 Institutions online; $6722 Institutions print. **URL:** http://www.jns-journal.com; http://www.journals.elsevier.com/journal-of-the-neurological-sciences. **Circ:** (Not Reported).

17303 ■ Livonia Observer
Observer & Eccentric Newspapers
615 W Lafayette Blvd., 2nd Level
Detroit, MI 48226
Free: 866-887-2737
Community newspaper. **Freq:** Semiweekly (Sun. and Thurs.). **Print Method:** Offset. **Cols./Page:** 6. **Col. Width:** 11 picas. **Col. Depth:** 21 1/2 inches. **Key Personnel:** Susan Rosiek, Executive Editor, Publisher, phone: (313)222-5397; Sue Mason, Editor; Joe Bauman, Managing Editor. **Subscription Rates:** $7 Individuals monthly. **URL:** http://www.hometownlife.com/news/observer-livonia. **Remarks:** Accepts advertising. **Circ:** Thurs. ♦**13542**, Sun. ♦**13999**.

17304 ■ Marvels & Tales: Journal of Fairy-Tale Studies
Wayne State University Press
The Leonard N Simons Bldg. 4809 Woodward Ave.
Detroit, MI 48201-1309
Phone: (313)577-6120
Fax: (313)577-6131
Free: 800-978-7323
Publisher's E-mail: theresa.martinelli@wayne.edu
Peer-reviewed multidisciplinary journal dealing with fairy-tale studies with scholarly inputs from literature, folklore, gender studies, children's literature, social and cultural history, anthropology, film studies, ethnic studies, art and music history, and others. **Freq:** Semiannual Spring and Fall. **Key Personnel:** Anne E. Duggan, Associate Editor. **ISSN:** 1521--4281 (print); **EISSN:** 1536--1802 (electronic). **Subscription Rates:** $42 Individuals online; $25 Students or seniors (print or online); $110 Institutions print; $44 Individuals print; $53 Individuals print and online; $37 Students or seniors (print and online). **URL:** http://www.wsupress.wayne.edu/journals/detail/marvels-tales. **Ad Rates:** BW $100. **Remarks:** Accepts advertising. **Circ:** (Not Reported).

17305 ■ Merrill-Palmer Quarterly: Journal of Developmental Psychology
Wayne State University Press
The Leonard N Simons Bldg. 4809 Woodward Ave.
Detroit, MI 48201-1309
Phone: (313)577-6120
Fax: (313)577-6131
Free: 800-978-7323
Publisher's E-mail: theresa.martinelli@wayne.edu
Journal presenting original experimental, theoretical, and review papers on issues of human development. **Freq:** Quarterly. **Print Method:** Offset. **Trim Size:** 6 x 9. **Cols./Page:** 1. **Col. Width:** 26. picas. **Col. Depth:** 42 picas. **Key Personnel:** Dr. Gary Ladd, Editor. **ISSN:** 0272--930X (print); **EISSN:** 1535--0266 (electronic). **Subscription Rates:** $124 Individuals print + online; $50 print + online; student/Senior; $38 print or online; student/Senior; $271 Institutions print; $112 Individuals print or online. **URL:** http://wsupress.wayne.edu/journals/detail/merrill-palmer-quarterly. **Ad Rates:** BW $300. **Remarks:** Accepts advertising. **Circ:** Paid ‡1200, Non-paid ‡100.

17306 ■ Metro Times: News, Arts, and Entertainment in Metro Detroit
Metro Times Inc.
733 St. Antoine
Detroit, MI 48226
Phone: (313)961-4060
Fax: (313)961-6598
Publication E-mail: letters@metrotimes.com
Newspaper. **Freq:** Weekly. **Print Method:** Offset. **Trim Size:** 10 3/8 x 13. **Cols./Page:** 6. **Col. Width:** 20 nonpareils. **Col. Depth:** 182 agate lines. **Key Personnel:** John J. Badanjek, Publisher. **Subscription Rates:** $150 Individuals; $160 Canada. **URL:** http://www.metrotimes.com. **Remarks:** Accepts advertising. **Circ:** Free ■ **75840**, Paid ■ **24**, Combined ■ **75864**, Controlled ■ **629100**.

17307 ■ Michigan Chronicle
Real Times Inc.
535 Grisworld St., Ste. 1300
Detroit, MI 48226
Phone: (313)963-8100
Black community newspaper. **Freq:** Weekly (Wed.). **Print Method:** Offset. **Cols./Page:** 6. **Col. Width:** 21 nonpareils. **Col. Depth:** 126 inches. **Key Personnel:** Hiram Jackson, Publisher. **Subscription Rates:** $50 Individuals 1 year. **URL:** http://michronicleonline.com; http://www.realtimesmedia.com/index.php/newspapers. **Ad Rates:** GLR $37.75; BW $4,756.50; 4C $1,147.90. **Remarks:** Advertising accepted; rates available upon request. **Circ:** Paid ■ **24944**.

17308 ■ North Korean Review
McFarland & CPI, Publishers
c/o Suk-Hi Kim, Editor
College of Business Administration
University of Detroit Mercy
4001 W McNichols Rd.
Detroit, MI 48221
Phone: (313)993-1264
Fax: (313)993-1673
Publisher's E-mail: info@mcfarlandpub.com
Journal covering culture, history, economics, business, religion, politics, and international relations in North Korea. **Freq:** Semiannual. **Key Personnel:** Prof. Suk-Hi Kim, Editor; Rhonda Herman, Publisher; Bernhard Seliger, Associate Editor. **ISSN:** 1551--2789 (print). **Subscription Rates:** $120 Institutions postpaid; $100 Institutions, other countries postpaid; $40 Individuals postpaid. **URL:** http://www.mcfarlandbooks.com/customers/journals/north-korean-review. **Circ:** (Not Reported).

17309 ■ NSM Magazine
National Socialist Movement
PO Box 13768
Detroit, MI 48213
Phone: (651)659-6307
Publisher's E-mail: nsm88secretary@gmail.com
Magazine containing articles, news, and events of activism and rallying, as part of condemning violence against White Americans of non-Jewish descent. **Freq:** Quarterly. **Subscription Rates:** $16 /year; $4.50 Single issue /issue. **Alt. Formats:** PDF. **URL:** http://www.nsm88.org/stormtrooper/index.html. **Remarks:** Accepts advertising. **Circ:** (Not Reported).

17310 ■ Pediatric Radiology
Springer-Verlag GmbH & Company KG
c/o Dr. T.L. Slovis, Mng. Ed.
Children's Hospital
Children's Research Center of Michigan
3901 Beaubien Blvd.
Detroit, MI 48201
Publication E-mail: pedradeditor@med.wayne.edu
Journal providing information on latest research and

growth in all areas of pediatric imaging and in related fields published in connection with European Society of Pediatric Radiology, the Society for Pediatric Radiology, and the Asian and Oceanic Society for Pediatric Radiology. Covers advances in technology, methodology, apparatus and auxiliary equipment, and modifications of standard techniques. **Freq:** Monthly. **Key Personnel:** Peter J. Strouse, Managing Editor; Dr. T.L. Slovis, Managing Editor; Dr. G. Sebag, Managing Editor. **ISSN:** 0301-0449 (print). **Subscription Rates:** €2332 Institutions print + online; €2798 Institutions print + enchanced access. **URL:** http://www.springer.com/medicine/radiology/journal/247. **Remarks:** Advertising accepted; rates available upon request. **Circ:** 1650.

17311 ■ Plymouth Observer
Observer & Eccentric Newspapers
615 W Lafayette Blvd., 2nd Level
Detroit, MI 48226
Free: 866-887-2737
Community newspaper. **Freq:** Semiweekly (Thurs. and Sun.). **Print Method:** Offset. **Cols./Page:** 6. **Col. Width:** 11 picas. **Col. Depth:** 21 1/2 inches. **Key Personnel:** Susan Rosiek, Executive Editor, Publisher; Hugh Gallagher, Managing Editor; Joe Bauman, Managing Editor. **Subscription Rates:** $7 Individuals monthly. **URL:** http://www.hometownlife.com/news/observer-plymouth. **Remarks:** Accepts advertising. **Circ:** Thurs. ♦**5,007**, Sun. ♦**5,078**.

17312 ■ Pontiac Excitement: An Official General Motors Magazine
GP Sandy
PO Box 33172
Detroit, MI 48232-5172
Free: 800-762-2737
Publisher's E-mail: info@sandycorp.com
Consumer magazine covering news for Pontiac automobile owners. **Freq:** Triennial. **Print Method:** Web Offset. **Trim Size:** 8 1/8 x 10 3/4. **URL:** http://wwww23.pontiac.com/showHome.do. **Formerly**: Pontiac Driving Excitement; Pontiac Excitement. **Ad Rates:** 4C $29,000. **Remarks:** Accepts advertising. **Circ:** Non-paid 850000.

17313 ■ Post Identity
University of Detroit Mercy
4001 W McNichols Rd.
Detroit, MI 48221-3038
Phone: (313)993-1000
Free: 800-635-5020
Publisher's E-mail: admissions@udmercy.edu
Peer-reviewed journal focusing on humanities. **Freq:** Annual. **Key Personnel:** Tim Dugdale, Associate Editor; Nicholas Rombes, Editor; Rosemary Weatherston, Editor. **URL:** http://liberalarts.udmercy.edu/pi. **Circ:** (Not Reported).

17314 ■ Redford Observer
Observer & Eccentric Newspapers
615 W Lafayette Blvd., 2nd Level
Detroit, MI 48226
Free: 866-887-2737
Community newspaper. **Freq:** Semiweekly Thurs. and Sun. **Print Method:** Offset. **Cols./Page:** 6. **Col. Width:** 11 picas. **Col. Depth:** 21 1/2 inches. **Key Personnel:** Dave Varga, Editor; Susan Rosiek, Executive Editor, Publisher, phone: (313)222-5397; Joe Bauman, Managing Editor. **Subscription Rates:** $7 Individuals monthly. **URL:** http://www.hometownlife.com/news/observer-redford. **Remarks:** Accepts advertising. **Circ:** Thurs. ♦**4,363**, Sun. ♦**4,567**.

17315 ■ Reverie: Midwest African American Literature
Aquarius Press
PO Box 23096
Detroit, MI 48223
Journal featuring literature by African Americans. **Freq:** Quarterly. **Key Personnel:** Lita Hooper, Editor-in-Chief. **Subscription Rates:** $10 Individuals. **Circ:** (Not Reported).

17316 ■ Rubber & Plastics News
Crain Communications Inc.
1155 Gratiot Ave.
Detroit, MI 48207-2732
Phone: (313)446-6000
Publisher's E-mail: info@crain.com
Rubber industry newspaper (tabloid). **Freq:** Biweekly. **Print Method:** Offset. **Trim Size:** 10 7/8 x 14 1/2. **Cols./Page:** 4. **Col. Width:** 2 5/16 inches. **Col. Depth:** 13 1/2 inches. **ISSN:** 0300--6123 (print). **Subscription Rates:** $99 Individuals; $138 Canada; $140 Other countries. **Online:** Crain Communications Inc. Crain Communications Inc. **URL:** http://crain.com/brands/rubber-plastics-news. **Remarks:** Accepts advertising. **Circ:** Paid △**3725**, Non-paid △**12386**.

17317 ■ Solidarity
United Auto Workers
Solidarity House
8000 E Jefferson Ave.
Detroit, MI 48214
Phone: (313)926-5000
Free: 800-243-8829
Magazine covering labor, economic, social, and political affairs affecting union members. Includes book and film reviews. **Freq:** Bimonthly. **Print Method:** Web. **Trim Size:** 8 1/2 x 11. **Cols./Page:** 4. **Col. Width:** 11 picas. **Col. Depth:** 60 picas. **ISSN:** 0164--856X (print). **Subscription Rates:** Included in membership. **URL:** http://www.uaw.org/page/solidarity-magazine. **Remarks:** Advertising not accepted. **Circ:** (Not Reported).

17318 ■ The South End
Wayne State University Student Newspapers Publishing Board
Student Ctr.
5221 Gullen Mall, Rm. 369
Detroit, MI 48202
Phone: (313)577-3497
Collegiate newspaper. **Founded:** 1918. **Freq:** Daily Monthly Online In print, every first Wednesday of months during the fall and winter semesters. **Print Method:** Offset. **Cols./Page:** 5. **Col. Width:** 20 nonpareils. **Col. Depth:** 189 agate lines. **Key Personnel:** Steve Krause, Managing Editor; Briana Valleskey, Editor-in-Chief. **Subscription Rates:** Free. **URL:** http://thesouthend.wayne.edu/. **Formerly**: The Daily Collegian. **Remarks:** Advertising accepted; rates available upon request. **Circ:** Free ‡10000.

17319 ■ South Oakland Eccentric
Observer & Eccentric Newspapers
615 W Lafayette Blvd., 2nd Level
Detroit, MI 48226
Free: 866-887-2737
Community newspaper. **Founded:** 1939. **Freq:** Semiweekly (Thurs. and Sun.). **Print Method:** Offset. **Cols./Page:** 6. **Col. Width:** 11 picas. **Col. Depth:** 21 1/2 inches. **Key Personnel:** Joe Bauman, Managing Editor; Susan Rosiek, Executive Editor, Publisher, phone: (313)222-5397. **Subscription Rates:** $4.25 Individuals monthly with EZ pay. **URL:** http://www.hometownlife.com/news/eccentric-south-oakland/. **Formerly**: Southfield Eccentric; Mirror. **Remarks:** Accepts advertising. **Circ:** Sun. ♦**14,278**.

17320 ■ Stem Cells and Development
Mary Ann Liebert Inc., Publishers
c/o Graham C. Parker, Children's Research Center of Michigan
The Carman & Ann Adams Dept. of Pediatrics
Wayne State University School of Medicine
Children's Hospital of Michigan, 3901 Beaubien
Detroit, MI 48201
Phone: (313)993-3843
Fax: (313)745-0282
Publisher's E-mail: info@liebertpub.com
Peer-reviewed medical journal covering the latest in stem cell development. **Freq:** 24/yr. **Print Method:** Offset. **Trim Size:** 8 1/2 x 11. **Cols./Page:** 2. **Col. Width:** 3 1/4 inches. **Col. Depth:** 9 1/2 inches. **Key Personnel:** Marc A. Williams, PhD, Associate Editor; Graham C. Parker, PhD, Editor-in-Chief. **ISSN:** 1547--3287 (print); **EISSN:** 1557--8534 (electronic). **Subscription Rates:** $457 Individuals print and online; $558 Other countries print and online; $422 Individuals online only; $3535 Institutions print and online; $4066 Institutions, other countries print and online; $3119 Institutions print only; $3587 Institutions, other countries print only; $3466 Institutions online only. **URL:** http://www.liebertpub.com/overview/stem-cells-and-development/125. **Formerly**: Journal of Hemotherapy; Journal of Hematotherapy & Stem Cell Research. **Ad Rates:** BW $1,095; 4C $1,845. **Remarks:** Advertising accepted; rates available upon request. **Circ:** (Not Reported).

17321 ■ Struggle: A Magazine of Proletarian Revolutionary Literature
Tim Hall
PO Box 13261
Detroit, MI 48213-0261
Publisher's E-mail: timhall11@yahoo.com
Literary magazine covering poetry, fiction, essays, and related literature. **Freq:** Quarterly. **Print Method:** Xerox. **Trim Size:** 8 1/2 x 5 1/2. **Key Personnel:** Tim Hall, Editor. **ISSN:** 1094--9399 (print). **Subscription Rates:** $2 Single issue 36-page issues; $3 Single issue 36-page issues by mail; $4 Single issue 72-page double issues; $5 Single issue 72-page double issues by mail; $10 Single issue a sub of four single issues; $12 Institutions a sub of four single issues; $15 Other countries a sub of four single issues. **URL:** http://www.strugglemagazine.net. **Remarks:** Advertising not accepted. **Circ:** Combined 600.

17322 ■ Waste & Recycling News
Crain Communications Inc.
1155 Gratiot Ave.
Detroit, MI 48207-2732
Phone: (313)446-6000
Publisher's E-mail: info@crain.com
Trade newspaper covering waste management. **Freq:** Biweekly. **Key Personnel:** KC Crain, Publisher, Vice President; John Campanelli, Editor; Douglas Fisher, Managing Editor. **URL:** http://webcache.googleusercontent.com/search?q=cache:xgPwR_icNCwJ:test.crain.com/news_and_events/waste_%26_recycling_news_launches_curbside_live_weekly_newscast.html+&cd=1&hl=en&ct=clnk&gl=ph. **Formerly**: Waste News. **Remarks:** Advertising accepted; rates available upon request. **Circ:** Paid 45281.

17323 ■ Wayne State Magazine
Wayne State University
42 W Warren Ave.
Detroit, MI 48202
Phone: (313)577-2424
Alumni magazine. **Freq:** Quarterly. **Print Method:** Web Press. **Trim Size:** 8 1/2 x 11. **Cols./Page:** 3. **Col. Width:** 13 picas. **Col. Depth:** 7 inches. **Key Personnel:** Peggy O'Connor, Editor. **URL:** http://alumni.wayne.edu/s/1536/gid2/wn/index.aspx?sid=1536&gid=2&pgid=598. **Ad Rates:** BW $900; 4C $900. **Remarks:** Accepts advertising. **Circ:** Non-paid 18000.

17324 ■ Westland Observer
Observer & Eccentric Newspapers
615 W Lafayette Blvd., 2nd Level
Detroit, MI 48226
Free: 866-887-2737
Community newspaper. **Freq:** Semiweekly (Thurs. and Sun.). **Print Method:** Offset. **Cols./Page:** 6. **Col. Width:** 11 picas. **Col. Depth:** 21 1/2 inches. **Key Personnel:** Susan Rosiek, Executive Editor, Publisher, phone: (313)222-5397; Joe Bauman, Managing Editor. **Subscription Rates:** $7 Individuals monthly. **URL:** http://www.hometownlife.com/news/observer-wayne-westland. **Remarks:** Accepts advertising. **Circ:** Thurs. ♦**7,139**, Sun. ♦**7,619**.

17325 ■ Booth American Co.
333 W Fort St.
Detroit, MI 48226
Phone: (313)202-3360
Fax: (313)202-3390
Founded: 1939. **Key Personnel:** Richard Lesley, Contact. **Cities Served:** Kernville, California; Madeira, Florida; Bingham Farms, Birmingham, Bloomfield Hill, Jackson, Michigan; Boone, North Carolina; Andersonville, South Carolina; Watertown, South Dakota; Blacksburg, Blacksburg, Salem, Virginia: subscribing households 141,761.

17326 ■ Comcast Cablevision of Detroit Inc.
12775 Lyndon St.
Detroit, MI 48227-3982
Phone: (313)934-2600
Fax: (313)934-9490
Founded: 1963. **Formerly**: Barden Cablevision. **Key Personnel:** Robert Hood, Operations Mgr.; Steve Burke, COO; John Barden, Contact. **Cities Served:** subscribing households 4,100. **URL:** http://www.comcast.com.

Circulation: ★ = AAM; △ or • = BPA; ♦ = CAC; ❑ = VAC; ⊕ = PO Statement; ‡ = Publisher's Report; Boldface figures = sworn; Light figures = estimated.

17327 ■ 96.3 WDVD-FM - 96.3
3011 W Grand Blvd., Ste. 800, Fisher Bldg.
Fisher Bldg.
Detroit, MI 48202
Phone: (313)871-3030
Fax: (313)871-8974
Format: Adult Contemporary; Top 40. **Networks:** ABC. **Owner:** Citadel Broadcasting Corp., 7201 W Lake Mead Blvd., Ste. 400, Las Vegas, NV 89128-8366, Ph: (702)804-5200, Fax: (702)804-8250. **Founded:** 1948. **Formerly:** WHYT-FM; WPLT-FM. **Operating Hours:** 5.30 a.m.-12 a.m. **Wattage:** 20,000. **Ad Rates:** Noncommercial. **URL:** http://www.963wdvd.com.

17328 ■ WCHB-AM - 1200
3250 Franklin St.
Detroit, MI 48207
Phone: (313)259-2000
Fax: (313)259-7011
Format: Religious; News; Talk. **Networks:** Independent. **Owner:** Radio One Inc., 1010 Wayne Ave., 14th Fl., Silver Spring, MD 20910, Ph: (301)306-1111, Fax: (302)636-5454. **Founded:** 1956. **Operating Hours:** Continuous; 2% network, 98% local. **Wattage:** 1,000. **Ad Rates:** Noncommercial. **URL:** http://wchbnewsdetroit.com.

17329 ■ WCSX-FM - 94.7
1 Radio Plaza Dr.
Detroit, MI 48220
Phone: (248)398-9470
Email: sales@wcsx.com
Format: Classic Rock. **Owner:** Greater Media Inc., 35 Braintree Hill Pk., Ste. 300, Braintree, MA 02184-8708, Ph: (781)348-8600, Fax: (781)348-8695. **Operating Hours:** Continuous. **Local Programs:** *Ken Calvert Show*, Saturday 8:00 a.m. - 12:00 p.m.; *Uncle Buck*, Monday Tuesday Wednesday Thursday Friday 12:00 a.m. - 5:30 a.m.; *Deminski and Doyle.* **Wattage:** 13,500 ERP. **Ad Rates:** Noncommercial. **URL:** http://www.wcsx.com.

17330 ■ WDET-FM - 101.9
4600 Cass Ave.
Detroit, MI 48201
Phone: (313)577-4146
Fax: (313)577-1300
Email: wdetfm@wdet.org
Format: Alternative/New Music/Progressive; Jazz; News; Folk; Blues. **Networks:** National Public Radio (NPR). **Owner:** Wayne State University, 42 W Warren Ave., Detroit, MI 48202, Ph: (313)577-2424. **Founded:** 1949. **Operating Hours:** Continuous; 25% network, 75% local. **ADI:** Detroit, MI. **Key Personnel:** Jerome Vaughn, News Dir., jvaughn@wdet.com; Carmen Garcia, Dir. of Dev. **Wattage:** 48,000. **Ad Rates:** Noncommercial; underwriting available. **URL:** http://wdet.org.

17331 ■ WDIV-TV - 4
550 W Lafayette Blvd.
Detroit, MI 48226-3140
Phone: (313)222-0444
Format: Commercial TV; News. **Networks:** NBC. **Formerly:** WWJ-TV. **Operating Hours:** Continuous. **Key Personnel:** Gary Macko, Sales Mgr., gmacko@wdiv.com. **Ad Rates:** Noncommercial. **URL:** http://www.clickondetroit.com.

17332 ■ WDMK-FM - 105.9
3250 Franklin St.
Detroit, MI 48207
Phone: (313)259-2000
Fax: (313)259-7011
Format: Urban Contemporary. **Owner:** Radio One Inc., 1010 Wayne Ave., 14th Fl., Silver Spring, MD 20910, Ph: (301)306-1111, Fax: (302)636-5454. **Operating Hours:** Continuous. **Ad Rates:** Advertising accepted; rates available upon request. **URL:** http://www.kissdetroit.com.

17333 ■ WDRJ-AM - 1440
2994 E Grand Blvd.
Detroit, MI 48202
Key Personnel: Tim Gallagher, President.

17334 ■ WDRQ-FM - 93.1
3011 W Grand Blvd., Ste. 800
Fisher Bldg.
Detroit, MI 48202-3086
Phone: (313)873-9893
Format: Contemporary Hit Radio (CHR). **Networks:** Independent. **Owner:** Cumulus Media Inc., 3280 Peachtree Rd. NW, Ste. 2300, Atlanta, GA 30305-2455, Ph: (404)949-0700, Fax: (404)949-0740. **Founded:** 1947. **Operating Hours:** Continuous; 100% local. **Wattage:** 26,500. **Ad Rates:** Noncommercial. **URL:** http://www.nashfm931.com.

17335 ■ WDTR-FM - 90.9
123 Selden St., Ste. 250
Detroit, MI 48201
Phone: (313)494-2087
Format: Information; Educational. **Owner:** Northland Community Broadcasters, 148 E Grand River, Williamston, MI 48895, Ph: (313)494-1000, Free: 888-887-7139. **Founded:** 1948. **Operating Hours:** 6:30 a.m.-8:30 p.m.; 95% local. 8:30 to 8:30 p.m weekends. **ADI:** Detroit, MI. **Wattage:** 47,000. **Ad Rates:** Noncommercial. **URL:** http://www.wrcjfm.org.

17336 ■ WEXL-AM - 1340
12300 Radio Pl.
Detroit, MI 48228
Phone: (313)837-1340
Fax: (313)272-5045
Format: Religious; Gospel. **Networks:** Independent. **Owner:** Crawford Broadcasting Co., 725 Skippack St., Ste. 210, Blue Bell, PA 19422. **Founded:** 1923. **Operating Hours:** Continuous. **Wattage:** 1,000. **Ad Rates:** Noncommercial. **URL:** http://wexl1340.com.

17337 ■ WGPR-FM - 107.5
3146 E Jefferson Ave.
Detroit, MI 48207
Phone: (313)259-8862
Format: Urban Contemporary. **Networks:** CBS. **Owner:** WGPR, Inc., at above address, Detroit, MI. **Founded:** 1961. **Operating Hours:** Continuous. **ADI:** Detroit, MI. **Wattage:** 50,000. **Ad Rates:** $39-88 for 30 seconds; $44-110 for 60 seconds.

17338 ■ WHTD-FM - 102.7
3250 Franklin St.
Detroit, MI 48207
Phone: (313)259-2000
Fax: (313)259-7011
Format: Hip Hop. **ADI:** Detroit, MI. **Ad Rates:** Advertising accepted; rates available upon request. **URL:** http://www.hothiphopdetroit.com.

17339 ■ WJLB-FM - 97.9
242 John R St.
Detroit, MI 48226
Phone: (248)324-5800
Fax: (313)298-7098
Email: workwithus@iheartmedia.comt
Networks: CBS. **Founded:** 1939. **Operating Hours:** Continuous; 100% local. **ADI:** Detroit, MI. **Wattage:** 50,000 ERP. **Ad Rates:** Advertising accepted; rates available upon request. **URL:** http://www.fm98wjlb.com.

17340 ■ WJR-AM - 760
3011 W Grand Blvd., Ste. 800
Detroit, MI 48202
Phone: (313)875-4440
Format: News; Talk. **Owner:** ABC Radio, 125 W End Ave., New York, NY 10023. **Founded:** 1922. **Operating Hours:** Continuous. **Local Programs:** *The Mark Dantonio Show*, Thursday 7:00 p.m. - 8:00 p.m.; *Paul W. Smith*, Monday Tuesday Wednesday Thursday Friday 5:30 a.m. - 9:00 a.m. **Wattage:** 50,000. **Ad Rates:** Advertising accepted; rates available upon request. **URL:** http://www.wjr.com.

17341 ■ WJZZ-FM - 105.9
3250 Franklin St.
Detroit, MI 48207
Phone: (313)871-0590
Fax: (313)871-8770
Format: Jazz. **Networks:** Independent. **Owner:** Bell Broadcasting Co., at above address. **Founded:** 1963. **Formerly:** WCHD-FM. **Operating Hours:** Continuous; 100% local. **ADI:** Detroit, MI. **Key Personnel:** Mary Bell, President; Wendell Cox, VP; Eric B. Bass, Gen. Sales Mgr.; Terry Arnold, Dir. of Programs; Treva Bass, Chief Engineer; Robert Bass, Contact; Deborah F. Copeland, Contact. **Wattage:** 20,000. **Ad Rates:** $50-270 for 30 seconds; $50-300 for 60 seconds.

17342 ■ WMUZ-FM - 103.5
12300 Radio Pl.
Detroit, MI 48228
Phone: (313)272-3434
Fax: (313)272-5045
Email: station@wmuz.com
Format: Religious; Contemporary Christian; Talk. **Networks:** Independent. **Owner:** Crawford Broadcasting Co., 2821 S Parker Rd., Ste. 1205, Denver, CO 80014, Ph: (303)433-5500, Fax: (303)433-1555. **Founded:** 1958. **Operating Hours:** Continuous. **ADI:** Detroit, MI. **Wattage:** 50,000. **Ad Rates:** Advertising accepted; rates available upon request. **URL:** http://wmuz.com.

17343 ■ WMYD-TV - 20
27777 Franklin Rd., Ste. 1220
Southfield, MI 48037-0020
Phone: (248)355-2020
Format: Commercial TV. **Networks:** Warner Brothers Studios; CNN Radio. **Founded:** 1968. **Operating Hours:** Continuous; 100% local. **ADI:** Detroit, MI. **Key Personnel:** Ed Fernandez, Gen. Mgr. **Wattage:** 1,200,000. **Ad Rates:** Advertising accepted; rates available upon request. **URL:** http://www.tv20detroit.com.

17344 ■ WRCJ-FM - 90.9
123 Selden St., Ste. 250.
Detroit, MI 48201
Phone: (313)494-2087
Format: Jazz; Classical. **Owner:** Detroit Public Schools, 3011 W Grand Blvd., Fisher Bldg., Ste. 1101, Detroit, MI 48202, Ph: (313)873-7860, Fax: (313)873-3284. **Operating Hours:** Continuous. **Key Personnel:** Roger Sherman, Contact. **Ad Rates:** Advertising accepted; rates available upon request. **URL:** http://www.wrcjfm.org/contact-us/.

17345 ■ WRIF-FM - 101
One Radio Plaza Rd.
Detroit, MI 48220
Phone: (248)547-0101
Fax: (248)542-8800
Email: sales@wrif.com
Format: Album-Oriented Rock (AOR). **Owner:** Greater Media Inc., 35 Braintree Hill Pk., Ste. 300, Braintree, MA 02184-8708, Ph: (781)348-8600, Fax: (781)348-8695. **Founded:** 1971. **Operating Hours:** Continuous. **ADI:** Detroit, MI. **Local Programs:** *Night Call*, Sunday 11:00 p.m. - 1:00 a.m. **Wattage:** 27,200. **Ad Rates:** Noncommercial. **URL:** http://www.wrif.com.

17346 ■ WTVS-TV - 56
1 Clover Ct.
Detroit, MI 48202
Phone: (248)305-3900
Email: email@dptv.org
Format: Public TV. **Networks:** Public Broadcasting Service (PBS); BBC World Service. **Owner:** Detroit Educational Television Foundation, at above address. **Founded:** 1953. **Operating Hours:** Continuous; 60% network, 5% local, 35% other. **Key Personnel:** Rich Homberg, Gen. Mgr., President, rhomberg@dptv.org. **Local Programs:** *American Black Journal*, Sunday Wednesday 9:30 a.m. 7:30 p.m. **Wattage:** 1,550,000. **Ad Rates:** Noncommercial. **URL:** http://www.dptv.org.

17347 ■ WUDL-LD - 66
PO Box A
Santa Ana, CA 92711
Phone: (714)832-2950
Free: 888-731-1000
Email: comments@tbn.org
Owner: Trinity Broadcasting Network Inc., PO Box A, Santa Ana, CA 92711, Ph: (714)832-2950, Free: 888-731-1000. **Formerly:** W66BV. **URL:** http://www.tbn.org.

17348 ■ WUDT-TV - 23
645 Griswold St., Ste. 3000
Detroit, MI 48226
Phone: (313)263-0263
Fax: (313)263-0283
Owner: Equity Broadcasting Co., at above address.

17349 ■ WUFL-AM - 1030
7355 N Oracle Rd.
Tucson, AZ 85704
Free: 800-776-1070
Format: Religious. **Owner:** Family Life Broadcasting System, PO Box 35300, Tucson, AZ 85740, Free: 800-776-1070. **Founded:** 1988. **Operating Hours:** Sunrise-

sunset. **Wattage:** 5,000. **Ad Rates:** Noncommercial. **URL:** http://www.myflr.org.

DOWAGIAC

Cass Co. Cass Co. (SW). 15 m N of Niles. Manufactures evaporators, condensers, auto parts, die castings, louver doors, laminated wood products, kitchen appliances, pallets, steel tanks. Nurseries. Summer resort. Timber. Diversified farming. Wheat, fruit, corn.

17350 ■ WDOW-AM
26914 Marcellus Hwy.
Dowagiac, MI 49047
Phone: (269)782-5106
Owner: Langford Broadcasting, LLC, at above address. **Founded:** 1960. **Key Personnel:** Larry Langford, Gen. Mgr., Owner. **Ad Rates:** $7.50-10 for 30 seconds; $10.50-12 for 60 seconds. Combined advertising rates available with WDOW-FM. **URL:** http://www.wdowradio.com/.

17351 ■ WGTO-AM
26914 Marcellus Hwy.
Dowagiac, MI 49047
Phone: (269)362-4009
Email: wgto910am@aol.com
Format: Oldies. **Founded:** Sept. 14, 2006. **Wattage:** 1,000 Day; 035 Night. **Ad Rates:** Noncommercial. **URL:** http://www.wgtoradio.com/.

DURAND

Shiawassee Co. Shiawassee Co. (SEC). 15 m W of Flint. Manufactures gravel screens, mattresses, auto and machinery parts, sport vehicles. Grain elevators. Agriculture. Wheat, dairying, cattle raising.

17352 ■ Michigan Grange News
Michigan State Grange
404 S Oak St.
Durand, MI 48429
Phone: (989)288-4546
Publisher's E-mail: msgrange1873@yahoo.com
Freq: Bimonthly Monthly. **Print Method:** Copy. **Trim Size:** 8 1/2 x 11. **Cols./Page:** 3. **Col. Width:** 42 nonpareils. **Col. Depth:** 140 agate lines. **Key Personnel:** Roland G. Winter, President, phone: (269)781-2500. **USPS:** 345-580. **Subscription Rates:** Included in membership. **Alt. Formats:** PDF. **URL:** http://www.michiganstategrange.org/uploads/mgn_--May-June_2014.pdf. **Formerly:** Michigan Patron. **Ad Rates:** BW $140. **Remarks:** Accepts advertising. **Circ:** ‡1,300.

EAST JORDAN

17353 ■ Michigan Snowmobiler
Michigan Snowmobiler
PO Box 417
East Jordan, MI 49727
Phone: (231)536-2371
Fax: (231)536-7691
Publication E-mail: publisher@michsnowmag.com
Magazine on snowmobiling. **Freq:** Semiannual 6/yr (monthly, Sept.-Feb.). **Print Method:** Web offset. **Trim Size:** 9 13/16 x 12. **Cols./Page:** 5. **Col. Width:** 1 13/16 inches. **Col. Depth:** 12 inches. **ISSN:** 0746--2298 (print). **Subscription Rates:** $15 Individuals add $19.00 per year - Canadian and other foreign; $25 Two years add $19.00 per year - Canadian and other foreign. **URL:** http://www.michsnowmag.com. **Ad Rates:** BW $1500, full page; BW $900, half page; BW $555, quarter page; PCI $40. **Remarks:** Accepts advertising. **Circ:** ‡26,000.

EAST LANSING

Ingham Co. Ingham Co. (S). Adjoins Lansing. Michigan State University. Residential. Nuclear and cancer research. Computer software development. Technical instrumentation.

17354 ■ Agricultural Economics Report
Michigan State University Department of Agricultural, Food, and Resource Economics
Justin S. Morrill Hall of Agriculture
446 W Circle Dr., Rm. 202
East Lansing, MI 48824-1039
Phone: (517)355-4563
Fax: (517)432-1800
Publisher's E-mail: afre@anr.msu.edu
Publication covering farm management and agricultural economics for researchers. **Freq:** Irregular. **Trim Size:** 8 1/2 x 11. **ISSN:** 0065--4442 (print). **Alt. Formats:** PDF. **URL:** http://www.afre.msu.edu. **Remarks:** Advertising not accepted. **Circ:** Non-paid 15.

17355 ■ Communication Outlook: Quarterly International Magazine
Michigan State University Artificial Language Laboratory
405 Computer Ctr.
East Lansing, MI 48824-1042
Phone: (517)353-5399
Fax: (517)353-4766
Publication E-mail: artlang@pilot.msu.edu
Magazine reporting on the newest developments in the application of technology for neurologically impaired persons. **Freq:** Quarterly. **Key Personnel:** Rebecca Ann Baird, Editor; Deanna Hoopingarner, Associate Editor. **Subscription Rates:** $18 Individuals North and South America; $24 Other countries; $5 Single issue. **URL:** http://www.msu.edu/~artlang/CommOut.html. **Remarks:** Advertising accepted; rates available upon request. **Circ:** Paid 1500.

17356 ■ Contagion: Journal of Violence, Mimesis, and Culture
Michigan State University Press
1405 S Harrison Rd., Ste. 25, Manly Miles Bldg.
East Lansing, MI 48823-5245
Phone: (517)355-9543
Fax: (517)432-2611
Journal covering the theory and applications of the mimetic model in anthropology, economics, literature, philosophy, psychology, religion, and sociology. **Freq:** Monthly. **Print Method:** Offset. **Trim Size:** 8 1/2 x 11. **Cols./Page:** 2. **Col. Width:** 41 nonpareils. **Col. Depth:** 136 agate lines. **Key Personnel:** William A. Johnsen, Editor. **ISSN:** 1075--7201 (print); **EISSN:** 1930--1200 (electronic). **Subscription Rates:** $44 Individuals USA (print only); $40 Individuals USA (online only); $49 Individuals USA (print and online); $54 Individuals other countries (print only); $40 Individuals other countries (online only); $60 Individuals other countries (print and online); $131 Institutions USA (print only); $141 Institutions other countries (print only). **Alt. Formats:** PDF. **URL:** http://msupress.org/journals/cont. **Ad Rates:** BW $250. **Remarks:** Color advertising not accepted. **Circ:** (Not Reported).

17357 ■ CR: The New Centennial Review: Interdisciplinary Perspectives on the Americas
Michigan State University Press
1405 S Harrison Rd., Ste. 25, Manly Miles Bldg.
East Lansing, MI 48823-5245
Phone: (517)355-9543
Fax: (517)432-2611
Journal covering America's comparative studies for a different future. **Key Personnel:** Scott Michaelsen, Editor; David E. Johnson, Editor. **URL:** http://msupress.org/journals/cr. **Ad Rates:** BW $250. **Remarks:** Accepts advertising. **Circ:** (Not Reported).

17358 ■ FOLKLORICA: Journal of the Slavic and East European Folklore Association
Slavic, East European, and Eurasian Folklore Association
c/o Shannon Spasova
Dept. of Linguistics and Germanic, Slavic, Asian and African Languages, Michigan State University
B-331 Wells Hall
619 Red Cedar Rd.
East Lansing, MI 48824-3402
Publisher's E-mail: SEEFA@lsv.uky.edu
Freq: Annual. **Key Personnel:** Jeanmarie Rouhier-Willoughby, Editor. **ISSN:** 1920-0242 (print). **Subscription Rates:** $35 Institutions /year (print and online); $10 Students /year (print and online); $45 Institutions /year (print and online); Free Gratis Only for those international scholars unable to pay the membership fee. **URL:** http://journals.ku.edu/index.php/folklorica. **Remarks:** Advertising not accepted. **Circ:** (Not Reported).

17359 ■ Fourth Genre: Explorations in Nonfiction
Michigan State University Press
1405 S Harrison Rd., Ste. 25, Manly Miles Bldg.
East Lansing, MI 48823-5245
Phone: (517)355-9543
Fax: (517)432-2611
Journal devoted to publishing notable, innovative work in nonfiction. **Freq:** Semiannual. **Print Method:** Offset. **Cols./Page:** 6. **Col. Width:** 25 nonpareils. **Col. Depth:** 294 agate lines. **Key Personnel:** Ned Stuckey-French, Editor; Michael Steinberg, Editor, Founder. **Subscription Rates:** $45 Individuals print; $40 Individuals electronic (PDF); $50 Individuals print and electronic (PDF); $66 Other countries print; $40 Other countries electronic (PDF); $74 Other countries print and electronic (PDF); $26 Students print or electronic (PDF); $47 Students print and electronic (PDF); $135 Institutions print; $156 Institutions, other countries print. **Alt. Formats:** PDF. **URL:** http://msupress.org/journals/fg/?id=50-214-6. **Ad Rates:** BW $250. **Remarks:** Accepts advertising. **Circ:** Paid 509, 14,182.

17360 ■ French Colonial History
Michigan State University Press
1405 S Harrison Rd., Ste. 25, Manly Miles Bldg.
East Lansing, MI 48823-5245
Phone: (517)355-9543
Fax: (517)432-2611
Peer-reviewed journal covering all aspects of French colonization and history of all French colonies. **Freq:** Annual. **Key Personnel:** Jeremy Rich, Board Member. **ISSN:** 1539--3402 (print). **Subscription Rates:** $49 Individuals print + online; $60 Other countries print + online; $131 Institutions print; $141 Institutions, other countries print; $44 Individuals print; $54 Individuals print; $40 Individuals pdf. **Alt. Formats:** PDF. **URL:** http://msupress.org/journals/fch; http://msupress.org/journals/fch/?id=50-214-8. **Ad Rates:** BW $250. **Remarks:** Accepts advertising. **Circ:** (Not Reported).

17361 ■ International Journal of Comparative and Applied Criminal Justice
Michigan State University - College of Social Science - School of Criminal Justice
Baker Hall, Rm. 560
655 Auditorium Rd.
East Lansing, MI 48824
Phone: (517)355-2197
Fax: (517)432-1787
Scholarly journal covering research in criminal justice. **Freq:** Quarterly. **Key Personnel:** Mahesh Nalla, PhD, Editor-in-Chief. **ISSN:** 0192--4036 (print); **EISSN:** 2157--6475 (electronic). **Subscription Rates:** $293 Institutions print and online; $256 Institutions online; $75 Individuals print. **URL:** http://www.tandfonline.com/toc/rcac20/current#.VQdfq9KUfId. **Remarks:** Advertising not accepted. **Circ:** Paid 400.

17362 ■ International Tax and Public Finance
International Institute of Public Finance
c/o John D. Wilson, Ed.-in-Ch.
Dept. of Economics
Michigan State University
East Lansing, MI 48824-1316
Journal covering tax and public finance worldwide. **Freq:** Bimonthly. **Key Personnel:** Robert Chirinko, Editor-in-Chief; Michael Smart, Associate Editor; Ruud A. De Mooij, Editor; D. Dharmapala, Associate Editor; E. Janeba, Associate Editor; Alan Auerbach, Associate Editor; Timothy Besley, Associate Editor; David E. Wildasin, Associate Editor; Robin Boadway, Associate Editor; Ronald B. Davies, Editor-in-Chief; Lans Bovenberg, Associate Editor; Deborah Swenson, Associate Editor. **ISSN:** 0927--5940 (print); **EISSN:** 1573--6970 (electronic). **Subscription Rates:** $1457 Institutions print including free access; $1748 Institutions print plus enhanced access; €1401 Institutions print including free access; €1681 Institutions print plus enhanced access. **URL:** http://link.springer.com/journal/10797; http://www.iipf.org/relpub.htm. **Remarks:** Accepts advertising. **Circ:** (Not Reported).

17363 ■ Journal of Animal and Natural Resource Law
Michigan State University College of Law
Law College Bldg.
648 N Shaw Ln.
East Lansing, MI 48824-1300
Phone: (517)432-6800
Fax: (517)432-6801
Journal educating both members of the legal community and the public at large about issues in the cutting edge field of Animal and Natural Resource Law. **Freq:** Annual. **Key Personnel:** Claire Corsey, Editor-in-Chief. **URL:** http://www.msujanrl.org. **Circ:** (Not Reported).

17364 ■ Journal of Empirical Finance
RELX Group P.L.C.

Circulation: ★ = AAM; △ or • = BPA; ♦ = CAC; ❑ = VAC; ⊕ = PO Statement; ‡ = Publisher's Report; Boldface figures = sworn; Light figures = estimated.

c/o R.T. Baillie, Ed.
Michigan State University
Dept. of Economics
110 Marshal Adams Hall
East Lansing, MI 48824
Phone: (517)355-1864
Fax: (517)432-1068
Publisher's E-mail: amsterdam@relx.com
Journal providing a common platform for exchange of ideas in econometrics and finance. **Freq:** 5/year. **Key Personnel:** R.T. Baillie, Editor; G. Bekaert, Advisor; F.C. Palm, Editor; Th.J. Vermaelen, Editor; C.C.P. Wolff, Editor. **ISSN:** 0927--5398 (print). **Subscription Rates:** $91 Individuals print; $970 Institutions print; $808.67 Institutions ejournal. **URL:** http://www.journals.elsevier.com/journal-of-empirical-finance. **Circ:** (Not Reported).

17365 ■ Journal of International Business Studies
Academy of International Business
Eppley Ctr.
Michigan State University
645 N Shaw Ln., Rm. 7
East Lansing, MI 48824
Phone: (517)432-1452
Fax: (517)432-1009
Publisher's E-mail: jibs@msb.edu
Scholarly business journal, covering topics from e-commerce to foreign markets. **Freq:** 9/year. **Key Personnel:** John Cantwell, Editor-in-Chief. **ISSN:** 0047--8210 (print); **EISSN:** 1478--6990 (electronic). **Subscription Rates:** $572 Institutions print; £356 Institutions, other countries; £356 Institutions print; $137 Individuals print + online; £219 Individuals print + online. **URL:** http://www.palgrave-journals.com/jibs/index.html; http://aib.msu.edu/jibs. **Remarks:** Advertising accepted; rates available upon request. **Circ:** Paid 4200.

17366 ■ Journal of International Financial Markets, Institutions and Money
RELX Group P.L.C.
c/o G.G. Booth, Ed.
Michigan State University
315 Eppley Center
East Lansing, MI 48824
Publisher's E-mail: amsterdam@relx.com
Journal dealing with all aspects of international financial markets, institutions and money. **Freq:** 6/year. **Key Personnel:** G.G. Booth, Editor; S. Benninga, Associate Editor. **ISSN:** 1042-4431 (print). **Subscription Rates:** $80 Individuals print; $585 Institutions print; $584.80 Institutions ejournal. **URL:** http://www.journals.elsevier.com/journal-of-international-financial-markets-institutions-and-money. **Circ:** (Not Reported).

17367 ■ Journal of Research in Science Teaching: The Official Journal of the National Association for Research in Science Teaching
John Wiley & Sons Inc.
Michigan State University
326 Erickson Hall
East Lansing, MI 48824
Phone: (517)432-4862
Fax: (517)432-2795
Publisher's E-mail: info@wiley.com
Journal featuring original articles of research related to philosophy, historical perspective, teaching strategies, curriculum development, and other topics relevant to science education. **Freq:** 10/year. **Print Method:** Offset. **Trim Size:** 7 1/4 x 10 1/4. **Cols./Page:** 1. **Col. Width:** 78 nonpareils. **Col. Depth:** 140 agate lines. **Key Personnel:** Joseph Krajcik, Editor; Dr. Robert Geier, Assistant Editor; Dr. Angela Calabrese Barton, Editor; Douglas W. Huffman, Board Member. **ISSN:** 0022--4308 (print); **EISSN:** 1098--2736 (electronic). **Subscription Rates:** $2215 Institutions print or online; $2658 Institutions print and online; $2215 Institutions, Canada and Mexico online; $2836 Institutions, Canada and Mexico print and online; $2363 Institutions, Canada and Mexico print; £1132 Institutions online; £1494 Institutions print and online; £1245 Institutions print; €1430 Institutions online; €1889 Institutions print and online; €1574 Institutions print; $2215 Institutions, other countries online; $2925 Institutions, other countries print and online; $2437 Institutions, other countries print. **URL:** http://onlinelibrary.wiley.com/journal/10.1002/(ISSN)1098-2736; http://as.wiley.com/WileyCDA/WileyTitle/productCd-TEA.html. **Ad Rates:** BW $1575; 4C $1230. **Remarks:** Accepts advertising. **Circ:** 19950, 92.

17368 ■ Journal for the Study of Radicalism
Michigan State University Press
1405 S Harrison Rd., Ste. 25, Manly Miles Bldg.
East Lansing, MI 48823-5245
Phone: (517)355-9543
Fax: (517)432-2611
Journal engaging in serious, scholarly exploration of the forms, representations, meanings and historical influences of radical social movements. **Freq:** Semiannual. **Key Personnel:** Ann Larabee, Board Member; Arthur Versluis, Editor. **ISSN:** 1930--1189 (print). **Subscription Rates:** $40 Individuals pdf. **Alt. Formats:** PDF. **URL:** http://msupress.org/journals/jsr; http://msupress.org/journals/jsr/?id=50-214-5. **Ad Rates:** BW $250. **Remarks:** Accepts advertising. **Circ:** (Not Reported).

17369 ■ Journal of West African History
Michigan State University Press
1405 S Harrison Rd., Ste. 25, Manly Miles Bldg.
East Lansing, MI 48823-5245
Phone: (517)355-9543
Fax: (517)432-2611
Peer-reviewed journal that contains research on the social, cultural, economic, and political history of West Africa. **Freq:** Semiannual. **Subscription Rates:** $40 Individuals electronic edition. **URL:** http://msupress.org/journals/jwah. **Remarks:** Accepts advertising. **Circ:** (Not Reported).

17370 ■ MEA Voice
Michigan Education Association
1216 Kendale Blvd.
East Lansing, MI 48826-2573
Phone: (517)332-6551
Fax: (517)337-5587
Free: 800-292-1934
Publisher's E-mail: webmaster@mea.org
Educational magazine for teachers union. **Founded:** Sept. 01, 1969. **Freq:** Quarterly. **Print Method:** Web press. **Trim Size:** 8 3/8 x 10 7/8. **Key Personnel:** Brenda Ortega, Editor. **ISSN:** 0883-573X (print). **URL:** http://www.mea.org/voice. **Formerly**: Teacher's Voice; Voice. **Mailing address:** PO Box 2573, East Lansing, MI 48826-2573. **Remarks:** Accepts display and classified advertising. **Circ:** ‡160000.

17371 ■ Michigan Medicine: The Journal of the Michigan State Medical Society
Michigan State Medical Society
120 W Saginaw St.
East Lansing, MI 48823
Phone: (517)337-1351
Publisher's E-mail: msms@msms.org
Medical magazine. **Freq:** Bimonthly. **Print Method:** Web offset. **Trim Size:** 8 1/4 x 10 7/8. **Cols./Page:** 3. **Col. Width:** 26 nonpareils. **Col. Depth:** 136 agate lines. **Key Personnel:** Sheri Greenhoe, Director, Communications, phone: (517)336-7603. **ISSN:** 0026--2293 (print). **Subscription Rates:** $93.50 Individuals; $176.72 Two years; $79.48 Institutions; $150.21 Two years. **URL:** http://msms.org/MichiganMedicine. **Ad Rates:** BW $1,775; 4C $1,952. **Remarks:** Advertising accepted; rates available upon request. **Circ:** ‡14000.

17372 ■ Michigan State University Journal of Medicine and Law
Michigan State University College of Law
Law College Bldg.
648 N Shaw Ln.
East Lansing, MI 48824-1300
Phone: (517)432-6800
Fax: (517)432-6801
Journal containing articles on cutting edge and controversial topics in the health law field. **Freq:** Semiannual. **Key Personnel:** Natalie F. Weiss, Editor-in-Chief. **Subscription Rates:** $18 Individuals /year; $28 Other countries /year. **URL:** http://www.msu.edu/~msujml. **Circ:** (Not Reported).

17373 ■ MidAmerica
Society for the Study of Midwestern Literature
c/o Mr. Roger J. Bresnahan, PhD, Secretary/Treasurer
Michigan State University
Bessey Hall, Rm. 235
434 Farm Ln.
East Lansing, MI 48824
Contains the annual bibliography of primary and secondary works of Midwestern literature. **Freq:** Annual. **Key Personnel:** Marcia Noe, Editor. **Alt. Formats:** PDF. **URL:** http://www.ssml.org/publications/midamerica. **Remarks:** Advertising not accepted. **Circ:** (Not Reported).

17374 ■ Midwestern Miscellany
Society for the Study of Midwestern Literature
c/o Mr. Roger J. Bresnahan, PhD, Secretary/Treasurer
Michigan State University
Bessey Hall, Rm. 235
434 Farm Ln.
East Lansing, MI 48824
Journal covering Midwestern literature study. **Freq:** Semiannual. **Alt. Formats:** PDF. **URL:** http://www.ssml.org/publications/midwestern_miscellany. **Remarks:** Advertising not accepted. **Circ:** (Not Reported).

17375 ■ MSU Alumni Magazine
Michigan State University Alumni Association
535 Chestnut Rd., Rm. 300
East Lansing, MI 48824
Phone: (517)355-8314
Fax: (517)355-5265
Free: 877-678-2586
Publication E-mail: msuaa@msualum.edu
Alumni association magazine. **Freq:** Quarterly (during the academic year). **Print Method:** Offset. **Cols./Page:** 3 and 2. **Col. Width:** 28 and 40 nonpareils. **Col. Depth:** 133 agate lines. **Key Personnel:** Paula Davenport, Editor. **URL:** http://alumni.msu.edu/magazine. **Ad Rates:** BW $1000; 4C $1800. **Remarks:** Advertising accepted; rates available upon request. **Circ:** 37000.

17376 ■ Northeast African Studies
Michigan State University Press
1405 S Harrison Rd., Ste. 25, Manly Miles Bldg.
East Lansing, MI 48823-5245
Phone: (517)355-9543
Fax: (517)432-2611
Scholarly journal covering Northeast African studies. **Freq:** Semiannual. **Cols./Page:** 1. **Key Personnel:** Lee V. Cassanelli, Editor; Natalie Eidenier, Editor. **ISSN:** 0740--9133 (print). **Subscription Rates:** $63 U.S. 1 Year (2 issues) - Print Edition Individuals; $84 Other countries 1 Year (2 issues) - Print Edition Individuals; $57 Individuals 1 Year (2 issues) - Electronic (PDF) Edition U.S. and International; $69 U.S. 1 Year (2 issues) - Print & Electronic (PDF) Edition Individuals; $92 Other countries 1 Year (2 issues) - Print & Electronic (PDF) Edition Individuals; $189 Institutions 1 Year (2 issues) - Print Edition U.S.; $210 Institutions 1 Year (2 issues) - Print Edition International. **Alt. Formats:** PDF. **URL:** http://msupress.msu.edu/journals/neas/. **Ad Rates:** BW $250. **Remarks:** Accepts advertising. **Circ:** (Not Reported).

17377 ■ Packaging Technology and Science: An International Journal
John Wiley & Sons Inc.
c/o Diana Twede, Ed.-in-Ch.
School of Packaging
Michigan State University
East Lansing, MI 48824
Publisher's E-mail: info@wiley.com
Journal contains information about packaging technology and science. **Freq:** 8/year. **Trim Size:** 7 7/8 x 10 1/4. **Key Personnel:** A.L. Brody, Board Member; Y. Dagel, Editor; David Shires, Editor-in-Chief; Diana Twede, Editor-in-Chief; K. Cooksey, Board Member. **ISSN:** 0894--3214 (print); **EISSN:** 1099--1522 (electronic). **Subscription Rates:** $3290 Institutions online or print - USA/Canada & Mexico/ROW; $3948 Institutions print & online - USA/Canada & Mexico/ROW; £1680 Institutions online or print - UK; £2016 Institutions print & online - UK; €2124 Institutions online or print - Europe; €2549 Institutions print & online - Europe. **URL:** http://onlinelibrary.wiley.com/journal/10.1002/(ISSN)1099-1522. **Ad Rates:** BW $940; 4C $2,240. **Remarks:** Advertising accepted; rates available upon request. **Circ:** 2800.

17378 ■ Phytopathology: An International Journal of the American Phytopathological Society
American Phytopathological Society
c/o George W. Sundin, Editor-in-Chief
Michigan State University
Plant, Soil, and Microbial Sciences Dept.
578 Wilson Rd.
East Lansing, MI 48824-1311
Phone: (517)355-4573
Fax: (517)353-5598
Publisher's E-mail: aps@scisoc.org

Plant pathology journal reporting original research. **Freq:** Monthly. **Print Method:** Sheet-fed offset. **Trim Size:** 8 1/2 x 11. **Cols./Page:** 2. **Col. Width:** 42 nonpareils. **Col. Depth:** 120 agate lines. **Key Personnel:** George W. Sundin, Editor-in-Chief; Peter J. Balint-Kurti, Senior Editor; Thomas J. Baum, Senior Editor. **ISSN:** 0031-949X (print). **Subscription Rates:** $895 Institutions and libraries; print; U.S.; $1009 Institutions, other countries and libraries; print. **URL:** http://apsjournals.apsnet.org/loi/phyto. **Ad Rates:** BW $1040. **Remarks:** Accepts advertising. **Circ:** 5,000.

17379 ■ The Plant Journal
Wiley-Blackwell
c/o Christoph Benning, Ed.-in-Ch.
Michigan State University
Department of Biochemistry & Molecular Biology
215 Biochemistry
East Lansing, MI 48824-1319
Phone: (517)355-1609
Fax: (517)353-9334
Publisher's E-mail: info@wiley.com
Journal devoted to research works on modern plant biology. **Freq:** Semimonthly. **Key Personnel:** Christoph Benning, Editor-in-Chief. **ISSN:** 0960--7412 (print); **EISSN:** 1365--313X (electronic). **Subscription Rates:** $7342 Institutions print and online; £3972 Institutions print and online; €5043 Institutions print and online; $8567 Institutions, other countries print and online; $544 Individuals print and online; £297 Individuals print and online - UK and Europe (non-euro zone); €443 Individuals print and online; £325 Other countries print and online. **URL:** http://onlinelibrary.wiley.com/journal/10.1111/(ISSN)1365-313X. **Remarks:** Accepts advertising. **Circ:** (Not Reported).

17380 ■ Real Analysis Exchange
Michigan State University Press
1405 S Harrison Rd., Ste. 25, Manly Miles Bldg.
East Lansing, MI 48823-5245
Phone: (517)355-9543
Fax: (517)432-2611
Journal covering geometric measure theory. **Freq:** Semiannual. **Key Personnel:** David Preiss, Associate Editor; Marianna Csornyei, Editor; Steve Jackson, Editor; Lee Larson, Managing Editor; Paul D. Humke, Editor-in-Chief; Manav Das, Editor; Krzysztof Ciesielski, Editor; Zoltan Buczolich, Editor. **Subscription Rates:** $82 Individuals print; $75 Individuals electronic (PDF); $90 Individuals print and electronic (PDF); $103 Other countries print; $75 Other countries electronic (PDF); $119 Other countries print and electronic (PDF); $246 Institutions print; $222 Institutions, other countries and U.S, online; $271 Institutions print and online; $267 Institutions, other countries print; $294 Institutions, other countries print and online. **Alt. Formats:** PDF. **URL:** http://msupress.org/journals/raex/?Page=home. **Ad Rates:** BW $250. **Remarks:** Accepts advertising. **Circ:** (Not Reported).

17381 ■ Red Cedar Review
Michigan State University Press
1405 S Harrison Rd., Ste. 25, Manly Miles Bldg.
East Lansing, MI 48823-5245
Phone: (517)355-9543
Fax: (517)432-2611
Student-run literary digest containing poetry, short fiction, and creative non-fiction from both veteran and emerging writers. **Freq:** Annual. **Key Personnel:** Natalie Eidenier, Editor; Amelia Larson, Editor. **ISSN:** 0034-1967 (print). **Subscription Rates:** $73 Individuals print; $66 Individuals electronic; $81 Individuals print & electronic; $219 Institutions print; $113 Other countries print only; $66 Other countries electronic; $125 Other countries print and electronic; $259 Institutions, other countries print only. **URL:** http://msupress.org/journals/rcr. **Ad Rates:** GLR $50; BW $250; SAU $100. **Remarks:** Accepts advertising. **Circ:** (Not Reported).

17382 ■ Rhetoric & Public Affairs
Michigan State University Press
1405 S Harrison Rd., Ste. 25, Manly Miles Bldg.
East Lansing, MI 48823-5245
Phone: (517)355-9543
Fax: (517)432-2611
Journal covering history, theory, and criticism of public discourse. **Freq:** Quarterly. **Key Personnel:** Martin J. Medhurst, Editor. **Subscription Rates:** $78 Individuals print only; $71 Individuals electronic only; $87 Individuals print and electronic; $234 Institutions print only; $277 Institutions, other countries print; $121 Other countries print only; $71 Other countries electronic only; $134 Other countries print and electronic. **URL:** http://msupress.org/journals/rpa. **Ad Rates:** BW $250. **Remarks:** Accepts advertising. **Circ:** (Not Reported).

17383 ■ The State News
State News Inc.
435 E Grand River Ave.
East Lansing, MI 48823
Phone: (517)432-3000
Fax: (517)432-3005
Publisher's E-mail: feedback@statenews.com
Collegiate newspaper. **Founded:** 1906. **Freq:** daily during fall and spring & three times weekly during summer. **Print Method:** Offset. **Trim Size:** 14 x 22 7/8. **Cols./Page:** 6. **Col. Width:** 25 nonpareils. **Col. Depth:** 294 agate lines. **Key Personnel:** Colleen Curran, Manager, Advertising; Celeste Bott, Editor-in-Chief. **USPS:** 520-260. **Subscription Rates:** $125 Individuals One full year.; $75 Individuals One semester only (Fall or Spring).; $60 Individuals Summer semester only. **URL:** http://www.statenews.com. **Remarks:** Accepts advertising. **Circ:** Mon.-Fri. ‡27500.

17384 ■ WDBM-FM - 89
G-4 Holden Hall
East Lansing, MI 48825
Phone: (517)884-8900
Email: training@impact89fm.org
Format: Eclectic. **Founded:** 1988. **Operating Hours:** Continuous; 100% local. **Wattage:** 2,000. **Ad Rates:** Noncommercial. **URL:** http://www.impact89fm.org.

17385 ■ WKAR-AM - 870
283 Communications Arts & Sciences Bldg.
East Lansing, MI 48824-1212
Phone: (517)432-3120
Fax: (313)432-3858
Email: mail@wkar.org
Format: Talk; News. **Networks:** National Public Radio (NPR); Public Radio International (PRI). **Owner:** Michigan State University Board of Trustee, 220 Trowbridge Rd, East Lansing, MI 48824, Ph: (517)355-1855. **Founded:** 1922. **Operating Hours:** Sunrise-sunset; 50% network, 50% local. **ADI:** Lansing (Ann Arbor), MI. **Key Personnel:** Gary Blievernicht, Tech. Svcs. Mgr., garyb@wkar.org; Diane Hutchens, Contact, diane@wkar.org. **Wattage:** 10,000. **Ad Rates:** Noncommercial. **URL:** http://wkar.org/programs/current-sports-al-martin-am-870-newstalk.

17386 ■ WKAR-FM - 90.5
Michigan State University, Communication Arts & Sciences Bldg., 404 Wilson Rd., Rm. 212
Michigan State University
East Lansing, MI 48824-1212
Phone: (517)432-9527
Fax: (517)353-7124
Email: mail@wkar.org
Format: Classical. **Owner:** MSU Broadcasting Services, at above address. **Operating Hours:** Continuous. **Key Personnel:** Nancy Gilleo, Bus. Mgr., nancy@wkar.org; Cindy Herfindahl, Dir. of Dev., cindy@wkar.org. **Ad Rates:** Advertising accepted; rates available upon request. **URL:** http://www.wkar.org.

17387 ■ WKAR-TV - 23
404 Wilson Rd., Rm. 212, Communication Arts & Sciences Bldg.
Michigan State University
East Lansing, MI 48824-1212
Phone: (517)884-4700
Fax: (517)432-3858
Email: ivs@wkar.org
Format: Public TV. **Networks:** Public Broadcasting Service (PBS). **Owner:** Michigan State University, East Lansing, MI 48824, Ph: (517)355-1855, Fax: (517)353-1647. **Founded:** 1954. **Operating Hours:** 6:45 a.m.-12:30 a.m.; 95% network, 5% local. **ADI:** Lansing (Ann Arbor), MI. **Key Personnel:** DeAnne Hamilton, Contact, deanne@wkar.org; Nancy Gilleo, Bus. Mgr., nancy@wkar.org; Gary Blievernicht, Dir. of Engg., garyb@wkar.org; Phil Barrie, Contact, philb@wkar.org; Phil Barrie, Contact, philb@wkar.org. **Ad Rates:** Noncommercial. **URL:** http://www.wkar.org.

EAST TAWAS

Iosco Co. Iosco Co. (NE). On Saginaw Bay, 55 m NE of Bay City. Tourism. Industrial pattern and plastic plants. Rock mining. Agriculture.

17388 ■ Iosco County News Herald
News-Press Publishing Company Inc.
110 W State St.
East Tawas, MI 48730
Phone: (989)362-3456
Fax: (989)362-6601
Publisher's E-mail: editor@iosconews.com
Community newspaper. **Freq:** Weekly (Wed.). **Print Method:** Offset. **Trim Size:** 11 x 17 1/2. **Cols./Page:** 5. **Col. Width:** 24 nonpareils. **Col. Depth:** 231 agate lines. **Key Personnel:** John Morris, Editor; Holly Nelson, Editor. **USPS:** 268-520. **Subscription Rates:** $52 Individuals print; $20 Individuals online. **Mailing address:** PO Box 72, East Tawas, MI 48730. **Ad Rates:** GLR $5.22; SAU $5.22. **Remarks:** Accepts advertising. **Circ:** (Not Reported).

EASTPOINTE

Macomb Co. (SE) 10 m SE of Warren. Residential.

17389 ■ Propeller
American Power Boat Association
17640 E 9 Mile Rd.
Eastpointe, MI 48021-2563
Phone: (586)773-9700
Fax: (586)773-6490
Publisher's E-mail: apbahq@apba.org
Freq: 5/year. **ISSN:** 0194- 6218 (print). **Subscription Rates:** Included in membership; $25 U.S. and Canada; $55 Other countries. **URL:** http://www.apba.org/propeller. **Mailing address:** PO Box 377, Eastpointe, MI 48021-0377. **Remarks:** Accepts advertising. **Circ:** 6500.

ELMIRA

Otrego Co. (N). 40 m SW of Cheboygan. Residential.

17390 ■ WSRT-FM - 106.7
1020 Hastings St., Ste. 102
Traverse City, MI 49686
Phone: (231)947-0003
Format: Soft Rock; Talk. **Operating Hours:** Continuous. **Key Personnel:** Dennis Winslow, Dir. of Programs; Charlie Ferguson, Gen. Mgr., charlie@wklt.com. **Ad Rates:** Advertising accepted; rates available upon request. **URL:** http://www.wklt.com.

ELSIE

Clinton Co. Clinton Co. (SC). 16 m NW of Owosso. Diversified farming. Dairy products, grain, sugar beets.

17391 ■ WOES-FM - 91.3
8989 Colony Rd.
Elsie, MI 48831
Phone: (989)862-4237
Format: Polka. **Owner:** Ovid-Elsie Area Schools, at above address. **Founded:** 1978. **Operating Hours:** Continuous. **Key Personnel:** Jim Dorman, Contact; George Bishop, Contact; Kevin Somers, Contact; Jim Dorman, Contact. **Wattage:** 553. **Ad Rates:** Noncommercial. **URL:** http://www.oe.k12.mi.us/~woes/woes.htm.

ERIE

17392 ■ The Vegetable Growers News
Michigan Vegetable Council
PO Box 277
Erie, MI 48133
Phone: (734)848-8899
Fax: (734)848-8899
Publisher's E-mail: mivegcouncil@charter.net
Freq: Monthly. **Print Method:** Offset. **Trim Size:** 11 x 15. **Cols./Page:** 4. **Key Personnel:** Matt Milkovich, Managing Editor; Kimberly Warren, Associate Publisher, Director, Editorial; Matt McCallum, Chief Executive Officer, Publisher. **Subscription Rates:** $9.95 Individuals online (one year); $15.50 Individuals U.S. print and online (one year); $35.50 Individuals U.S. print and online (three years); $56 Individuals Canadian print and online (one year); $100 Individuals international print and online (one year). **URL:** http://vegetablegrowersnews.com. **Formerly:** The Great

Circulation: ★ = AAM; △ or • = BPA; ♦ = CAC; ❑ = VAC; ⊕ = PO Statement; ‡ = Publisher's Report; Boldface figures = sworn; Light figures = estimated.

Lakes Vegetable Grower News. **Ad Rates:** BW $870; 4C $3,005. **Remarks:** Accepts advertising. **Circ:** △**15220**, 14000.

ESCANABA

Delta Co. Delta Co. (S Up. Penin.). On Lake Michigan, 56 m N of Memominee. Vacation areas. Parks. Historical landmarks. Lumber and ore shipping center. Manufactures paper, pre-cut buildings, plastic packaging, yardsticks, paint paddles, truck cranes, electric motors, forest harvesting equipment, torsional vibration dampers, foundry products, beverages. Fisheries; timber. Dairy, beef, mink, poultry, potato, bean & strawberry farms.

17393 ■ The Daily Press
The Daily Press
600 Ludington St.
Escanaba, MI 49829
Phone: (906)786-2021
Free: 800-743-0609
General newspaper. **Founded:** 1909. **Freq:** Daily (eve.) and Sat. (morn.). **Print Method:** Offset. **Key Personnel:** Brian Rowell, Managing Editor. **Subscription Rates:** $185.70 Individuals home delivery; $217.90 By mail in state; $234.60 Out of state mail. **URL:** http://www.dailypress.net. **Ad Rates:** PCI $10.03. **Remarks:** Accepts advertising. **Circ:** Mon.-Fri. ★**8993**.

17394 ■ WCHT-AM - 600
524 Ludington St., Ste. 300
Escanaba, MI 49829
Phone: (906)789-0600
Free: 800-866-0097
Format: Talk; News. **Founded:** 1958. **Formerly**: WLST-AM; WBDN-AM. **Operating Hours**: Continuous. **Key Personnel:** Richard A. Duerson, Gen. Mgr., VP. **Wattage**: 570 day; 134 night. **Ad Rates:** $6.50-9 for 15 seconds; $7.50-10 for 30 seconds; $8.50-15 for 60 seconds. **URL:** http://radioresultsnetwork.com.

17395 ■ WCMM-FM - 102.5
524 Ludington St., Ste. 300
Escanaba, MI 49829
Phone: (906)789-4102
Format: Country. **Key Personnel:** Marc Tall, Contact, marc@radioresultnetwork.com. **Ad Rates:** Noncommercial. **URL:** http://www.wcmmradio.com.

17396 ■ WDBC-AM - 680
604 Ludington St.
Escanaba, MI 49829
Phone: (906)786-3800
Fax: (906)789-9959
Free: 800-676-9801
Format: News; Talk; Adult Contemporary. **Networks:** Jones Satellite; Westwood One Radio. **Owner:** KMB Broadcasting, at above address. **Founded:** 1941. **Operating Hours**: Continuous. **Wattage:** 10,000. **Ad Rates:** $6.50-9.50 for 15 seconds; $9.50-15.50 for 30 seconds; $10.50-25 for 60 seconds. Combined advertising rates available with WYKX-FM. **URL:** http://www.kmbbroadcasting.com/wdbc.

17397 ■ WGKL-FM - 105.5
524 Ludington St., Ste. 300
Escanaba, MI 49829
Phone: (906)789-9700
Fax: (906)789-9701
Format: Oldies. **Ad Rates:** Advertising accepted; rates available upon request. **URL:** http://www.wgklradio.com.

17398 ■ WGLQ-FM - 97.1
524 Ludington St., Ste. 300
Escanaba, MI 49829
Phone: (906)789-9700
Fax: (906)789-9701
Email: rrnews@radioresultsnetwork.com
Format: Contemporary Hit Radio (CHR). **Networks:** ABC. **Owner:** Lakes Radio Inc., at above address. **Founded:** 1976. **Formerly**: WKZY-FM. **Operating Hours**: Continuous; 5% network, 95% local. **ADI**: Green Bay-Appleton (Suring), WI. **Wattage:** 100,000. **Ad Rates:** Noncommercial. **URL:** http://www.wglqradio.com.

17399 ■ WMXG-FM - 106.3
1101 A Ludington St.
Escanaba, MI 49829
Wattage: 50,000. **Ad Rates:** Noncommercial.

17400 ■ W20BZ - 20
PO Box A
Santa Ana, CA 92711
Phone: (714)832-2950
Free: 888-731-1000
Owner: Trinity Broadcasting Network Inc., PO Box A, Santa Ana, CA 92711, Ph: (714)832-2950, Free: 888-731-1000. **URL:** http://www.tbn.org.

17401 ■ WYKX-FM - 104.7
604 Ludington St.
Escanaba, MI 49829
Phone: (906)786-3800
Fax: (906)789-9959
Free: 800-676-9801
Format: Country. **Owner:** KMB Broadcasting, at above address. **Founded:** 1978. **Operating Hours**: Continuous. **Local Programs**: *Trails and Tales*, Saturday 9:00 a.m. **Wattage:** 100,000. **Ad Rates:** Noncommercial. Combined advertising rates available with WDBC-AM. **URL:** http://kmbbroadcasting.com/wykx.

FARMINGTON HILLS

Oakland Co. Oakland Co. (SC). 14 m SSW of Pontiac.

17402 ■ ACI Structural Journal: Journal of the American Concrete Institute
American Concrete Institute
38800 Country Club Dr.
Farmington Hills, MI 48331-3439
Phone: (248)848-3700
Fax: (248)848-3701
Journal containing information on structural design and analysis of concrete elements and structures; includes design and analysis theory, and related ACI standards and committee reports. **Freq:** Bimonthly. **Print Method:** Offset. **Trim Size:** 8 1/8 x 10 7/8. **Cols./Page:** 2. **Col. Width:** 40 nonpareils. **Col. Depth:** 140 agate lines. **Key Personnel:** Daniel W. Falconer, Managing Director; Jeri A. Kolodziej, Manager; Renee J. Lewis, Director; Douglas J. Sordyl, Managing Director; John W. Nehasil, Managing Director; Rex C. Donahey, Editor-in-Chief; William R. Tolley, Executive Vice President. **ISSN:** 0889--3241 (print). **Subscription Rates:** $167 Individuals print; $176 Other countries print; $167 Individuals online; Included in membership. **URL:** http://www.concrete.org/Publications/ACIStructuralJournal.aspx. **Remarks:** Advertising not accepted. **Circ:** ‡16400.

17403 ■ Ash at Work
American Coal Ash Association
38800 Country Club Dr.
Farmington Hills, MI 48331
Phone: (720)870-7897
Fax: (720)870-7889
Publisher's E-mail: info@acaa-usa.org
Magazine covering information on all facets of the coal combustion products industry. **Freq:** Semiannual. **Subscription Rates:** Free. **Alt. Formats:** PDF. **URL:** http://www.acaa-usa.org/Publications/Ash-at-Work. **Ad Rates:** BW $1297.29; 4C $1915.29. **Remarks:** Accepts advertising. **Circ:** 12,000.

17404 ■ Concrete Abstracts
American Concrete Institute
38800 Country Club Dr.
Farmington Hills, MI 48331-3439
Phone: (248)848-3700
Fax: (248)848-3701
Magazine summarizing and indexing U.S. and international publications that report developments in concrete and concrete technology. **Founded:** July 1971. **Freq:** Bimonthly. **ISSN:** 0045-8007 (print). **URL:** http://www.concrete.org. **Remarks:** Advertising not accepted. **Circ:** ‡676.

17405 ■ Concrete International
American Concrete Institute
38800 Country Club Dr.
Farmington Hills, MI 48331-3439
Phone: (248)848-3700
Fax: (248)848-3701
Publication E-mail: concrete@networkmediapartners.com
Trade magazine covering engineering, construction, structural design, and the technology of concrete. **Founded:** Jan. 1979. **Freq:** Monthly. **ISSN:** 0162-4075 (print). **URL:** http://concreteinternational.com/pages/index.asp. **Formerly**: Concrete International: Design & Construction. **Ad Rates:** BW $3,675; 4C $4,950; PCI $140. **Remarks:** Accepts advertising. **Circ:** (Not Reported).

17406 ■ Humanistic Judaism
Society for Humanistic Judaism
28611 W 12 Mile Rd.
Farmington Hills, MI 48334
Phone: (248)478-7610
Fax: (248)478-3159
Publisher's E-mail: info@shj.org
Freq: Quarterly. **ISSN:** 0441--4195 (print). **Subscription Rates:** $21 Individuals; $31 Canada and Mexico; $43 Other countries; $30 Institutions libaries and organizations; $40 Institutions, Canada and Mexico libraries and organizations; $52 Institutions, other countries libraries and organizations. **URL:** http://www.shj.org/store/hj-journal. **Remarks:** Advertising not accepted. **Circ:** (Not Reported).

17407 ■ Journal of the American College of Neuropsychiatrists
American College of Osteopathic Neurologists and Psychiatrists
28595 Orchard Lake Rd., Ste. 200
Farmington Hills, MI 48334
Phone: (248)553-6207
Fax: (248)553-6222
Publisher's E-mail: acn-aconp@msn.com
Professional journal covering medical developments, research, case studies, and analysis of political actions in neuropsychiatrics. **Freq:** Semiannual. **Circ:** (Not Reported).

17408 ■ PTI Journal
Post-Tensioning Institute
38800 Country Club Dr.
Farmington Hills, MI 48331
Phone: (248)848-3180
Fax: (248)848-3181
Publisher's E-mail: technical.inquiries@post-tensioning.org
Freq: Semiannual. **Subscription Rates:** Included in membership. **URL:** http://www.post-tensioning.org/pti_journal.php. **Remarks:** Accepts advertising. **Circ:** (Not Reported).

17409 ■ Supercharger
SAE Detroit Section
28535 Orchard Lake Rd., Ste. 200
Farmington Hills, MI 48334
Phone: (248)324-4445
Free: 877-606-7323
Publisher's E-mail: info@sae-detroit.org
Magazine containing subjects of current interest for members of the Society of Automotive Engineers. **Founded:** 1927. **Freq:** Monthly (1/month Oct.-May). **Print Method:** Offset. **Trim Size:** 5 1/2 x 8 1/2. **Cols./Page:** 2. **Col. Width:** 2 inches. **Col. Depth:** 7 inches. **URL:** http://www.sae-detroit.org/supercharger. **Ad Rates:** BW $1,600; 4C $3,000. **Remarks:** Accepts advertising. **Circ:** Paid 17988.

17410 ■ WDFN-AM - 1130
27675 Halsted Rd.
Farmington Hills, MI 48331
Phone: (248)324-5800
Format: Sports. **Owner:** iHeartMedia Inc., 200 E Basse Rd., San Antonio, TX 78209, Ph: (210)832-3314. **Founded:** 1939. **Operating Hours**: Continuous. **Wattage:** 50,000. **Ad Rates:** Advertising accepted; rates available upon request. **URL:** http://www.wdfn.com.

17411 ■ WDTW-AM - 1310
27675 Halsted Rd.
Farmington Hills, MI 48331
Phone: (248)324-5800
Free: 800-783-7412
Format: Talk. **Networks:** CNN Radio. **Owner:** Clear Channel Radio, 200 E Basse Rd., San Antonio, TX 78209, Ph: (210)822-2828, Fax: (210)832-3428. **Founded:** 1946. **Formerly**: WXDX-AM. **Operating Hours**: midnight. **ADI**: Detroit, MI. **Wattage**: 5,000. **Ad Rates:** Noncommercial.

17412 ■ WDTW-FM - 106.7
27675 Halsted Rd.
Farmington Hills, MI 48331
Free: 877-988-1067
Format: Adult Contemporary. **ADI**: Detroit, MI. **Wattage**: 61,000. **URL:** http://www.thedrocks.com.

17413 ■ WKQI-FM - 95.5
12 Mile Rd.
Farmington Hills, MI 48331
Phone: (313)298-9595
Free: 800-329-9536
Email: programming@channel955.com
Format: Top 40. **Founded:** 1949. **Operating Hours**: Continuous. **ADI**: Detroit, MI. **Key Personnel:** Jeff Luckoff, Gen. Sales Mgr., jluckoff@clearchannel.com. **Wattage**: 100,000. **Ad Rates:** Noncommercial.

17414 ■ WMXD-FM - 92.3
27675 Halsted Rd.
Farmington Hills, MI 48331
Phone: (248)324-5800
Format: Adult Contemporary; Urban Contemporary. **Networks:** Independent. **Owner:** iHeartMedia Inc., 200 E Basse Rd., San Antonio, TX 78209, Ph: (210)832-3314. **Founded:** 1964. **Formerly**: WVAE-FM. **Operating Hours**: Continuous. **ADI**: Detroit, MI. **Key Personnel:** Gayle Halebian Lewkow, Gen. Sales Mgr. **Wattage**: 50,000. **Ad Rates:** Noncommercial. **URL:** http://www.mix923fm.com//main.html.

17415 ■ WNIC-FM - 100.3
27675 Halstead Rd.
Farmington Hills, MI 48331
Phone: (248)324-5800
Fax: (248)848-0297
Format: Adult Contemporary. **Owner:** iHeartMedia Inc., 200 E Basse Rd., San Antonio, TX 78209, Ph: (210)832-3314. **Founded:** 1946. **Operating Hours**: Continuous. **Wattage**: 32,000. **Ad Rates:** Noncommercial. **URL:** http://www.wnic.com.

FENTON

Genesee Co. Genesee Co. (SEC). 16 m S of Flint. Tools, dies, machine tools, automotive accessories and parts, chemicals, plastics manufactured. Dairy, fruit, poultry, grain farms.

17416 ■ Tri-County Times
Tri-County Times
256 N Fenway Dr.
Fenton, MI 48430
Phone: (810)629-8282
Fax: (810)629-9227
Publisher's E-mail: news@tctimes.com
Community newspaper. **Founded:** Apr. 1994. **Freq:** Semiweekly (Wed. and Sun.). **Trim Size:** 10 X 14. **Key Personnel:** Sharon Stone, Editor; Vera Hogan, Contact. **Subscription Rates:** $55 Individuals. **URL:** http://www.tctimes.com/. **Remarks:** Accepts advertising. **Circ:** Sun. 24875, Wed. 13825.

FERNDALE

Oakland Co. Oakland Co. (SE). 9 m N of Detroit. Castings, forgings. Residential.

17417 ■ Fifth Estate
Fifth Estate
PO Box 201016
Ferndale, MI 48220
Publication E-mail: fe@fifthestate.org
Magazine covering anarchism and radical environmentalism. **Freq:** Quarterly. **Print Method:** Web Offset. **Cols./Page:** 4. **ISSN:** 0015-0800 (print). **Subscription Rates:** $14 Individuals; $20 Canada and Mexico; Free for prisoners & soldiers; $20 Libraries & institutions; $24 Other countries; $1000 police & government agencies. **URL:** http://fifthestate.org/fepages/contact.html. **Remarks:** Advertising not accepted. **Circ:** Paid 5000.

17418 ■ Metro Parent Magazine
Metro Parent Publishing Group
22041 Woodward Ave.
Ferndale, MI 48220
Phone: (248)398-3400
Fax: (248)399-4215
Consumer magazine covering parenting in Southeast Michigan. **Freq:** Monthly. **Key Personnel:** Alyssa Martina, President, Publisher; Julia Elliott, Editor-in-Chief; Kim Kovelle, Managing Editor. **URL:** http://www.metroparent.com/magazine. **Remarks:** Accepts advertising. **Circ:** Free ■ **66421**.

17419 ■ WDTK-AM - 1400
2 Radio Plz.
Ferndale, MI 48220-2129
Phone: (248)581-1234
Format: Talk; News. **Operating Hours**: Continuous. **Ad Rates:** Advertising accepted; rates available upon request. **URL:** http://www.wdtkam.com.

17420 ■ WMGC-FM - 105.1
One Radio Plz.
Ferndale, MI 48220
Phone: (248)414-5600
Fax: (248)542-8800
Email: feedback@detroitsports1051.com
Format: Adult Contemporary. **Ad Rates:** Advertising accepted; rates available upon request. **URL:** http://www.detroitsports1051.com.

17421 ■ WOMC-FM - 104.3
2201 Woodward Hts.
Ferndale, MI 48220
Phone: (248)546-9600
Format: Oldies. **Networks:** Westwood One Radio. **Owner:** CBS Radio Inc., 1271 Avenue of the Americas, 44th Fl., New York, NY 10020-1401, Ph: (212)649-9600. **Founded:** 1948. **Operating Hours**: Continuous. **ADI**: Detroit, MI. **Key Personnel:** Scott Walker, Dir. of Programs, scott.walker@cbsradio.com; Dina McCutcheon, Contact, dina.mccutcheon@cbsradio.com11. **Wattage**: 190,000. **Ad Rates:** Advertising accepted; rates available upon request. **URL:** http://womc.cbslocal.com.

17422 ■ WYCD-FM - 99.5
2201 Woodward Heights Blvd.
Ferndale, MI 48220
Phone: (248)546-9600
Format: Country. **Owner:** CBS Radio Inc., 40 W 57th St., New York, NY 10019, Ph: (212)846-3939, Fax: (212)315-2162. **Founded:** 1960. **Key Personnel:** Debbie Kenyon, Gen. Mgr., VP; Tim Roberts, Prog. Dir.; Greg Smith, Sales Mgr.; Jay Jennings, Gen. Sales Mgr.; Patti Taylor, Sales Mgr. **URL:** http://wycd.cbslocal.com.

FLINT

Genesee Co. Genesee Co. (SEC). On Flint River, 55 m NW of Detroit. Manufactures recreational vehicles, pick-up trucks, automobiles, auto bodies and accessories, highway supplies, structural steel,, chemical, paint, corrugated boxes, plastic plumbing fittings & pipes, tools, dies, storage tanks, tents, awnings; foundry.

17423 ■ The Clio Messenger
The Flint Journal
200 E First St.
Flint, MI 48502-1925
Publisher's E-mail: applause@flintjournal.com
Community newspaper. **Freq:** Weekly. **Subscription Rates:** Free. **URL:** http://www.mlive.com/clio/. **Remarks:** Accepts advertising. **Circ:** Combined 8889.

17424 ■ The Davison Flagstaff
The Flint Journal
200 E First St.
Flint, MI 48502-1925
Publisher's E-mail: applause@flintjournal.com
Community newspaper. **Freq:** Weekly. **Key Personnel:** Marjory Raymer, Editor, phone: (810)766-6118. **URL:** http://www.mlive.com/davison/. **Remarks:** Accepts advertising. **Circ:** Combined 8808.

17425 ■ The Flint Journal
The Flint Journal
200 E First St.
Flint, MI 48502-1925
Publisher's E-mail: applause@flintjournal.com
General newspaper. **Freq:** Sundays, Tuesdays, Thursdays and Fridays. **Print Method:** Letterpress. **Cols./Page:** 6. **Col. Width:** 25 nonpareils. **Col. Depth:** 308 agate lines. **Key Personnel:** Tom Eason, Director, Advertising, phone: (810)766-6381, fax: (810)767-8922; Brian Masck, Director, phone: (810)766-6477; Matthew Sharp, Publisher; Mike Pastorino, Manager, Circulation; Marjory Raymer, Editor. **Subscription Rates:** $12.94 Individuals 4 weeks; $11.20 Individuals digital - 4 weeks; $11.20 Individuals digital and print - 4 weeks; $9.39 Individuals Sunday only; $12.50 Individuals e-replica - 4 weeks. **URL:** http://members.mlive.com/index.aspx?siteCode=FJNL; http://www.mlive.com/#/0. **Feature Editors:** Michael Riha, phone: (810)766-6189, mriha@flintjournal.com. **Remarks:** Accepts advertising. **Circ:** Mon.-Fri. ★**167,821**, Sun. ★**217,145**.

17426 ■ The Flint Township News
The Flint Journal
200 E First St.
Flint, MI 48502-1925
Publisher's E-mail: applause@flintjournal.com
Community newspaper. **Freq:** Semiweekly (Thur. and Sun.). **URL:** http://www.mlive.com/flinttownship/. **Circ:** Combined 10779.

17427 ■ The Flushing Observer
The Flint Journal
200 E 1st St.
Flint, MI 48502
Phone: (810)766-6100
Publisher's E-mail: applause@flintjournal.com
Suburban newspaper. **Freq:** Weekly. **Print Method:** Offset. **Cols./Page:** 6. **Col. Depth:** 294 agate lines. **Key Personnel:** Marjory Raymer, Editor, phone: (810)766-6118. **URL:** http://www.mlive.com/flushing. **Ad Rates:** BW $834; 4C $1284; PCI $6.62. **Remarks:** Accepts advertising. **Circ:** ‡7,500.

The Grand Blanc News - See Grand Blanc

17428 ■ Michigan Chess
Michigan Chess Association
c/o Jeff Aldrich, Membership Secretary
PO Box 40
Flint, MI 48501
Phone: (810)955-7271
Magazine containing news and articles on chess. **Freq:** Bimonthly. **Subscription Rates:** Included in membership. **Alt. Formats:** CD-ROM; PDF. **URL:** http://206.130.103.122/interim/magazine/index.html. **Remarks:** Accepts advertising. **Circ:** 1100.

17429 ■ The Swartz Creek News
The Flint Journal
200 E First St.
Flint, MI 48502-1925
Publisher's E-mail: applause@flintjournal.com
Community newspaper. **Freq:** Weekly (Sun.). **Key Personnel:** Laura Angus, Editor. **URL:** http://www.mlive.com/swartzcreek/. **Circ:** Combined 10779.

17430 ■ Nash FM 95.1 - 95.1
6317 Taylor Dr.
Flint, MI 48507
Phone: (810)238-7300
Format: Public Radio; Full Service; Eclectic. **Networks:** American Public Radio (APR). **Founded:** 1953. **Formerly**: WFBE-FM. **Operating Hours**: 5 a.m.-1 a.m.; 45% network, 55% local. **ADI**: Flint-Saginaw-Bay City, MI. **Wattage**: 50,000. **Ad Rates:** Advertising accepted; rates available upon request. **URL:** http://www.nashfm951.com.

17431 ■ WDZZ-FM - 92.7
6317 Taylor Dr.
Flint, MI 48507
Phone: (810)238-7300
Fax: (810)743-2500
Format: Urban Contemporary; Blues. **Owner:** Cumulus Broadcasting Inc., 3280 Peachtree Rd. NW, Ste. 2300, Atlanta, GA 30305-2447, Ph: (404)949-0700, Fax: (404)949-0740. **Founded:** 1979. **Operating Hours**: 6:00 a.m. - Midnight Monday - Saturday; 6:00 a.m. - 3:00 p.m. Sunday. **ADI**: Flint-Saginaw-Bay City, MI. **Key Personnel:** Donna Luce, Dir. of Mktg. **Wattage**: 3,000 ERP. **Ad Rates:** Advertising accepted; rates available upon request. Combined advertising rates available with WFDF-AM. **URL:** http://www.wdzz.com.

17432 ■ WFLT-AM
317 South Averill Ave.
Flint, MI 48506
Phone: (810)239-5733
Fax: (810)239-7134
Format: Religious; Gospel. **Networks:** Independent. **Founded:** 1955. **Key Personnel:** Victoria Bennett, Traffic Mgr. **Wattage**: 500 Day; 142 Night. **Ad Rates:** $12.50-20 for 30 seconds; $15-25 for 60 seconds.

17433 ■ WFUM-FM - 91.1
535 W William St., Ste. 110
Ann Arbor, MI 48103
Phone: (734)764-9210
Fax: (734)647-3488

Circulation: ★ = AAM; △ or • = BPA; ♦ = CAC; ❑ = VAC; ⊕ = PO Statement; ‡ = Publisher's Report; Boldface figures = sworn; Light figures = estimated.

Free: 888-258-9866
Email: michigan.radio@umich.edu
Format: Public Radio. **Simulcasts:** WUOM-FM. **Networks:** National Public Radio (NPR). **Owner:** University of Michigan Board of Regents, 500 S State St., Ann Arbor, MI 48109. **Founded:** 1985. **Operating Hours:** Continuous. **Key Personnel:** Vincent Duffy, News Dir., vduffy@umich.edu; Steve Chrypinski, Dir. of Mktg., steveski@umich.edu; Tamar Charney, Dir. of Programs. **Wattage:** 17,500. **Ad Rates:** Noncommercial. Combined advertising rates available with WCRZ-FM. **URL:** http://michiganradio.org.

17434 ■ WKUF-FM - 94.3
1700 W Third Ave.
Flint, MI 48504
Phone: (810)762-9500
Fax: (810)762-9948
Free: 800-955-4464
Email: wkuf@kettering.edu
Format: News; Talk; Blues; Hip Hop. **Owner:** Kettering University, 1700 University Ave., Flint, MI 48504, Ph: (810)762-9500. **Operating Hours:** Continuous. **Ad Rates:** Advertising accepted; rates available upon request. **URL:** http://www.kettering.edu.

17435 ■ WLSP-AM - 1530
240 Greenwich Ave.
511 Walnut St.
Greenwich, CT 06830
Phone: (203)861-0900
Format: Talk; News. **Networks:** ESPN Radio; Westwood One Radio. **Owner:** Townsquare Media Inc., 240 Greenwich Ave., Greenwich, CT 06830-6507, Ph: (203)861-0900. **Founded:** 1962. **Formerly:** WDEY-AM; WWGZ-AM. **Operating Hours:** Sunrise-sunset. **ADI:** Detroit, MI. **Wattage:** 5,000. **Ad Rates:** Noncommercial.

17436 ■ WOWE-FM
444 Church St.
Flint, MI 48502
Format: Oldies. **Wattage:** 3,000 ERP.

17437 ■ WRSR-FM - 103.9
G-4511 Miller Rd.
Flint, MI 48507
Phone: (810)238-7300
Fax: (810)743-2500
Format: Classic Rock. **Owner:** Cumulus Broadcasting Inc., 3280 Peachtree Rd. NW, Ste. 2300, Atlanta, GA 30305-2447, Ph: (404)949-0700, Fax: (404)949-0740. **URL:** http://www.classicfox.com.

17438 ■ WSNL-AM - 600
5210 S Saginaw Rd.
Flint, MI 48507
Phone: (810)694-4146
Fax: (810)694-0661
Format: Religious; Talk. **Networks:** Independent; USA Radio. **Owner:** Christian Broadcasting System Ltd., 5201 S Saginaw, Flint, MI 48507, Ph: (810)694-4146. **Founded:** 1946. **Formerly:** WTAC-AM. **Operating Hours:** Continuous. **Key Personnel:** Graham Parker, Station Mgr. **Wattage:** 1,000. **Ad Rates:** $16-22 for 30 seconds; $18-24 for 60 seconds. **URL:** http://www.wsnlradio.com.

17439 ■ WWCK-AM - 1570
6317 Taylor Dr.
Flint, MI 48507
Phone: (810)238-7300
Fax: (810)424-3595
Format: Talk. **Networks:** Independent. **Owner:** Cumulus Media Inc., 3280 Peachtree Rd. NW, Ste. 2300, Atlanta, GA 30305-2455, Ph: (404)949-0700, Fax: (404)949-0740. **Founded:** 1946. **Operating Hours:** Continuous. **ADI:** Flint-Saginaw-Bay City, MI. **Wattage:** 3,000. **Ad Rates:** Noncommercial. **URL:** http://www.supertalk1570.com.

17440 ■ WWCK-FM - 105.5
6317 Taylor Dr.
Flint, MI 48507
Phone: (810)251-5105
Fax: (810)725-2500
Format: Contemporary Hit Radio (CHR); News. **Owner:** Cumulus Broadcasting Inc., 3280 Peachtree Rd. NW, Ste. 2300, Atlanta, GA 30305-2447, Ph: (404)949-0700, Fax: (404)949-0740. **Operating Hours:** 5:00 a.m. - Midnight Monday - Friday; 8:00 a.m. - Midnight Saturday; 10:00 a.m. - Midnight Sunday. **ADI:** Flint-Saginaw-Bay City, MI. **Wattage:** 25,000 ERP. **Ad Rates:** Advertising accepted; rates available upon request. **URL:** http://www.wwck.com.

FLUSHING

Genesee Co. Genessee Co. (SEC). On Flint River, 10 m W of Flint. Tool and die factory. Diversified farming. Dairy products, beans, grain.

17441 ■ The Catholic Times: Authorized Publication of the Diocese of Lansing
G.L.S. Diocesan Reports, Inc.
104 1/2 E Main St.
Flushing, MI 48433
Publisher's E-mail: gm@catholicweekly.org
Religious newspaper covering the local, national, and international church. **Freq:** Weekly (Fri.). **Print Method:** Offset. **Trim Size:** 13 3/8 x 22 3/4. **Cols./Page:** 8. **Col. Width:** 9 picas. **Col. Depth:** 294 agate lines. **Key Personnel:** Mark A. Myczkowiak, General Manager, President; Mark Haney, Executive Director. **USPS:** 007-686. **Subscription Rates:** $29.95 Individuals. **Alt. Formats:** PDF. **URL:** http://www.colsdioc.org/Offices/TheCatholicTimes.aspx. **Formerly:** The Catholic Weekly. **Ad Rates:** GLR $.52; BW $1176; 4C $1576; PCI $7.25. **Remarks:** Accepts advertising. **Circ:** Paid ‡12,000.

FRANKENMUTH

Saginaw Co. Saginaw Co. (EC). 15 m S of Saginaw. Residential.

17442 ■ Frankenmuth News
Frankenmuth News
527 N Franklin St., Ste. A
Frankenmuth, MI 48734
Phone: (989)652-3246
Fax: (989)652-2417
Local newspaper. **Freq:** Weekly (Wed.). **Print Method:** Offset. **Cols./Page:** 6. **Col. Width:** 12 nonpareils. **Col. Depth:** 301 agate lines. **Key Personnel:** Vanessa Sanders, Web Administrator; Vicky Hayden, Manager, Advertising; Scott Wenzel, Editor; Steve Grainger, Publisher. **USPS:** 207-960. **Subscription Rates:** $37 Individuals Saginaw & Tuscola County; $40 Out of area other Michigan residents; $42 Out of state; $25 Individuals online. **Mailing address:** PO Box 252, Frankenmuth, MI 48734. **Ad Rates:** GLR $.45; BW $663; 4C $500; SAU $5.20; PCI $6. **Remarks:** Accepts advertising. **Circ:** ‡5,100.

FRANKFORT

Benzie Co. Benzie Co. (NW). On Lake Michigan, 20 m S of Traverse City. Residential.

17443 ■ Benzie County Record-Patriot
The Pioneer Group
417 Main St.
Frankfort, MI 49635
Phone: (616)352-9659
Fax: (616)352-7874
Publication E-mail: recpat@pioneergroup.com
Community newspaper. **Freq:** Weekly (Wed.). **Print Method:** Offset. **Cols./Page:** 5. **Col. Width:** 21 nonpareils. **Col. Depth:** 182 agate lines. **Key Personnel:** Jack Batdorff, II, Chief Executive Officer, President. **Subscription Rates:** $2.50 Individuals RecordPatriot.com - Daily Pass Online Edition; $2.95 Individuals RecordPatriot.com - Monthly (+Free Trial first month) Online Edition; $35.40 Individuals RecordPatriot.com - 12 Months (+Free Trial) Online Edition; $23.95 Individuals Print Edition (6 months) Benzie County; $35.40 Individuals Print Edition(12 months) Benzie County; $30.90 Individuals Print Edition (6 months) Michigan, outside of Benzie County; $46.80 Individuals Print Edition(12 months) Michigan, outside of Benzie County; $38.15 Individuals Print Edition (6 months) Outside Michigan; $61.80 Individuals Print Edition(12 months) Outside Michigan. **URL:** http://recordpatriot.com; http://pioneergroup.com/newspapers. **Mailing address:** PO Box 673, Frankfort, MI 49635. **Ad Rates:** SAU $6.50. **Remarks:** Advertising accepted; rates available upon request. **Circ:** Wed. ‡4200.

17444 ■ WBNZ-FM - 99.3
1532 Forrester Rd.
Frankfort, MI 49635
Phone: (231)352-9603
Fax: (231)352-7877
Free: 800-974-9269
Format: Adult Contemporary; News; Sports. **Owner:** Fort Bend Broadcasting Co., at above address. **Founded:** 1978. **Operating Hours:** Continuous. **ADI:** Traverse City-Cadillac, MI. **Wattage:** 50,000. **Ad Rates:** $7-12 for 30 seconds; $9-14 for 60 seconds.

FREEPORT

Barry Co. Barry Co. (SW). 9 m N. of Hastings. Residential.

17445 ■ Freeport News
Freeport News
129 Division St.
Freeport, MI 49325
Phone: (242)352-8321
Fax: (242)351-5893
Community newspaper. **Freq:** Mon.-Sat. **Print Method:** Letterpress. **Cols./Page:** 5. **Col. Width:** 24 nonpareils. **Col. Depth:** 224 agate lines. **Key Personnel:** Ollie Ferguson, General Manager; Hubert Russell, Manager, Circulation. **Alt. Formats:** PDF. **Remarks:** Accepts advertising. **Circ:** ‡18,000.

FREMONT

Newaygo Co. Newaygo Co. (W). 25 m NE of Muskegon. Manufactures canned baby food, pickles, apple juice, lubricants, insecticides. Dairy, poultry, fruit farms.

17446 ■ Etruscan Studies
Etruscan Foundation
PO Box 26
Fremont, MI 49412-0026
Phone: (231)519-0675
Fax: (231)924-0777
Publisher's E-mail: office@etruscanfoundation.org
Peer-reviewed journal publishing details activities in all areas of research and study related to the Etruscan civilization with articles contributed by scholars around the world. **Freq:** Annual. **Subscription Rates:** Included in membership. **URL:** http://www.etruscanfoundation.org/publications.htm. **Remarks:** Advertising not accepted. **Circ:** (Not Reported).

17447 ■ Hi-Lites Shoppers Guide
Hi-Lites Graphics Inc.
1212 Locust St.
Fremont, MI 49412
Phone: (616)924-0630
Fax: (616)924-5580
Free: 800-482-5262
Shopper (tabloid). **Freq:** Weekly (Sun.). **Print Method:** Offset. **Trim Size:** 11 x 17. **Cols./Page:** 6. **Col. Width:** 20 nonpareils. **Col. Depth:** 244 agate lines. **Subscription Rates:** Free. **URL:** http://www.hi-lites.net. **Ad Rates:** BW $700; 4C $150; PCI $6.75. **Remarks:** Accepts advertising. **Circ:** Free 20,000.

17448 ■ Times-Indicator
T.I. Publications
44 W Main St.
Fremont, MI 49412-0007
Phone: (231)924-4400
Fax: (231)924-4066
Local newspaper covering Newaygo County and adjacent areas. **Freq:** Weekly (Wed.). **Print Method:** Offset. **Cols./Page:** 8. **Col. Width:** 18 nonpareils. **Col. Depth:** 301 agate lines. **Key Personnel:** Debby Reinhold, Manager, Advertising; Richard C. Wheater, Sr., Editor. **Subscription Rates:** $35 Individuals in Newaygo County and surrounding townships; $45 Individuals West Michigan Area; $58 Out of area; $64 Two years in Newaygo County; $82 Two years in West Michigan; $110 Two years OOA; $27 Individuals in Newaygo County (6 months); $31 Individuals West Michigan Area (6 months); $35 Out of area 6 months. **Mailing address:** PO Box 7, Fremont, MI 49412-0007. **Ad Rates:** BW $590; 4C $800; SAU $7.25. **Remarks:** Accepts classified advertising. **Circ:** 7,500.

GAGETOWN

17449 ■ WCTP-FM - 88.5
4330 Farver Rd.
Gagetown, MI 48735
Phone: (989)315-8043
Fax: (989)872-3700
Email: info@wctpradiofm.com

Format: Gospel. **Owner:** Plonta Broadcasting, at above address. **Formerly:** WPEE-FM. **Wattage:** 6,000 ERP. **URL:** http://www.wctpradiofm.com/.

GALESBURG

17450 ■ Climax Telephone Co.
13800 E Michigan Ave.
Galesburg, MI 49053
Phone: (269)746-4411
Fax: (269)746-9914
Free: 800-627-5287
Email: info@ctstelecom.com
Key Personnel: Joe Vernon, Contact, jvernon@ctstelecom.com; Chad Collver, Contact, ccollver@ctstelecom.com; John Carlson, Contact, jcarlson@ctstelecom.com. **Cities Served:** 35 channels. **URL:** http://www.ctstelecom.com.

GAYLORD

Otsego Co. Otsego Co. (N). 70 m W of Alpena. Hay fever resort. Hardwood timber.

17451 ■ Gaylord Herald Times
Otsego County Herald Times Inc.
2058 S Otsego Ave.
Gaylord, MI 49734
Phone: (989)732-1111
Fax: (989)732-3490
Free: 800-968-2544
Community newspaper. **Freq:** Semiweekly (Wed. and Sat.). **Print Method:** Offset. **Cols./Page:** 6. **Col. Width:** 1.83 nonpareils. **Col. Depth:** 301 agate lines. **Key Personnel:** Chris Engle, Reporter; Doug Caldwell, Publisher; Paul Gunderson, General Manager; Jeremy Speer, Editor; Cathy Landry, Editor. **Subscription Rates:** $63 Individuals Otsego, Crawford, Montmorency, Antrim and Cheboygan Counties; $99.45 Out of area. **Ad Rates:** PCI $8.34; PCI $10.20. **Remarks:** Advertising accepted; rates available upon request. **Circ:** Paid ‡7,010, Free ‡140.

17452 ■ Northern Star
Morningstar Publications
1966 S Otsego Ave.
Gaylord, MI 49735
Phone: (989)732-5125
Fax: (989)732-9323
Shopper (tabloid). **Founded:** 1960. **Freq:** Weekly. **Print Method:** Offset. Uses mats. **Trim Size:** 11 1/8 x 17 1/2. **Cols./Page:** 6. **Col. Width:** 21 nonpareils. **Col. Depth:** 224 agate lines. **URL:** http://www.21stcenturynewspapers.com/paper.asp?par=51. **Remarks:** Accepts advertising. **Circ:** 19800.

17453 ■ WBLW-FM - 88.1
PO Box 177
Gaylord, MI 49735
Phone: (989)705-7464
Free: 800-485-1910
Format: Religious. **Owner:** Grace Baptist Church, 232 S Townline Rd., Gaylord, MI 49735, Ph: (939)732-5676. **Key Personnel:** Tim Ramsey, Station Mgr; Bob Pierce, Contact. **Ad Rates:** Noncommercial. **URL:** http://www.wblwradio.com.

WHST-FM - See Tawas City

17454 ■ WKPK-FM - 88.3
PO Box 190
Gaylord, MI 49735
Email: peak1067@gt11.com
Format: News; Religious; Contemporary Christian; Information. **Owner:** Northern Radio of Gaylord, at above address. **Founded:** 1972. **Formerly:** WWRM-FM. **Wattage:** 15,000 ERP Vertical. **Ad Rates:** $15-22 per unit. **URL:** http://www.smile.fm.

17455 ■ WMJZ-FM - 101.5
3687 Old 27 S
Gaylord, MI 49734
Phone: (989)732-9515
Fax: (989)732-6202
Format: Eclectic; Information. **Key Personnel:** Kent Smith, Gen. Mgr., kent@radioeagle.com; Chip Arledge, Dir. of Programs, chip@radioeagle.com; Mike Reling, Operations Mgr., mike@radioeagle.com. **Mailing address:** PO Box 1766, Gaylord, MI 49734. **URL:** http://www.radioeaglegaylord.com.

WOLW-FM - See Cadillac

17456 ■ WPHN-FM - 90.5
PO Box 695
Gaylord, MI 49734-0695
Fax: (989)732-8171
Free: 800-545-8857
Format: Religious; Gospel. **Simulcasts:** WOLW-FM, WHST-FM. **Networks:** Moody Broadcasting. **Owner:** The Ministries Of Northern Christian Radio Inc., PO Box 695, Gaylord, MI 49734, Fax: (989)732-8171, Free: 800-545-8857. **Founded:** 1985. **Operating Hours:** Continuous; 20% network, 80% local. **Wattage:** 100,000. **Ad Rates:** Noncommercial. **URL:** http://www.ncradio.org.

WTHN-FM - See Sault Sainte Marie

17457 ■ W221CA-FM - 92.1
7119 M-68
Indian River, MI 49749
Phone: (231)238-8500
Fax: (231)238-0803
Format: Religious. **Owner:** Baraga Broadcasting Inc., at above address, Traverse City, MI 49684. **Operating Hours:** Continuous. **Key Personnel:** Brian Brachel, Station Mgr., wavetech@chartermi.net; Tom McMahon, Contact, tom@utmi.net; Tom McMahon, Contact, tom@utmi.net. **URL:** http://www.baragabroadcasting.com.

GLADWIN

Gladwin Co. Gladwin Co. (NEC). 40 m NW of Bay City. Manufactures pickup campers, precision tools, automotive parts, plastics. Stock, dairy farms. Lake resort.

17458 ■ Gladwin County Record and Beaverton Clarion
Gladwin County Record and Beaverton Clarion
700 E Cedar
Gladwin, MI 48624
Phone: (989)426-9411
Fax: (989)426-2023
Community newspaper. **Freq:** Weekly (Wed.). **Print Method:** Offset. **Trim Size:** 13 x 21 1/2. **Cols./Page:** 6. **Col. Width:** 2 inches. **Col. Depth:** 21 1/2 inches. **Key Personnel:** Stephanie Buffman, Editor. **USPS:** 219-100. **Subscription Rates:** $32 Individuals in County - print and online; $57.60 Two years print and online; $38 Out of area print and online; $68.40 Two years within Michigan - print and online; $28 Individuals online access only. **Mailing address:** PO Box 425, Gladwin, MI 48624. **Ad Rates:** GLR $8.45; BW $1064.70; 4C $1064.70; SAU $8.45; PCI $8.45. **Remarks:** Accepts advertising. **Circ:** Paid ‡8,200, Free ‡60.

17459 ■ WGDN-AM - 1350
3601 W Woods Rd.
Gladwin, MI 48624
Phone: (989)426-1031
Fax: (989)426-9436
Format: Religious. **Simulcasts:** WGDN-FM. **Networks:** USA Radio. **Owner:** Apple Broadcasting Co., Inc., at above address. **Founded:** 1974. **Operating Hours:** 5 a.m.-midnight. Sunrise-sunset. **Wattage:** 250. **Ad Rates:** $6 for 30 seconds; $7 for 60 seconds. **URL:** http://www.103country.com.

17460 ■ WGDN-FM - 103.1
3601 W Woods Rd.
Gladwin, MI 48624
Phone: (989)426-1031
Fax: (989)426-1031
Format: Country. **Networks:** USA Radio. **Founded:** 1987. **Formerly:** WGMM-FM. **Operating Hours:** Continuous. **ADI:** Flint-Saginaw-Bay City, MI. **Wattage:** 25,000. **Ad Rates:** $10 for 30 seconds; $12 for 60 seconds. **URL:** http://www.103country.com.

GRAND BLANC

Genesee Co. Genesee Co. (SEC). 6 m S of Flint. Residential.

17461 ■ The Grand Blanc News
The Flint Journal
200 E First St.
Flint, MI 48502-1925
Publisher's E-mail: applause@flintjournal.com
Community newspaper. **Freq:** Semiweekly (Thurs. and Sun.). **URL:** http://www.mlive.com/grandblanc/. **Circ:** Combined 13935.

17462 ■ WFDF-AM - 910
2467 E Hill Rd., Ste. C
Grand Blanc, MI 48439
Phone: (248)304-4381
Free: 877-870-5678
Format: Talk; Sports; News. **Networks:** CBS; Satellite Music Network. **Owner:** Radio Disney Group L.L.C., 77 W 66th St., 16th Fl., New York, NY 10023-6201. **Founded:** 1922. **Formerly:** WFCF-AM. **Operating Hours:** Continuous. **ADI:** Flint-Saginaw-Bay City, MI. **Wattage:** 50,000. **Ad Rates:** Advertising accepted; rates available upon request.

GRAND HAVEN

Ottawa Co. Ottawa Co (W). On Lake Michigan at the mouth of Grand River, 12 m S of Muskegon. Resort. Manufactures printing equipment, auto parts, pneumatic tools, plastic products, plumbing fixtures, metal & office furniture. Tannery. Agriculture. Potatoes, blueberries, celery. Evergreen farms.

17463 ■ Grand Haven Tribune
Grand Haven Publishing Corp.
101 N 3rd St.
Grand Haven, MI 49417
Phone: (616)842-6400
Fax: (616)842-9584
Publisher's E-mail: news@grandhaventribune.com
General newspaper. **Freq:** Daily (eve.) and Sat. (morn.). **Print Method:** Offset. **Trim Size:** 13 x 21. **Cols./Page:** 6. **Col. Width:** 12.3 picas. **Col. Depth:** 21 inches. **Key Personnel:** Fred Van den Brand, Editor; Paul Bedient, Manager, Advertising, Contact. **Subscription Rates:** $65; $86 Out of area. **URL:** http://www.grandhaventribune.com. **Ad Rates:** BW $9.65; SAU $11.35. **Remarks:** Accepts advertising. **Circ:** Mon.-Sat. 10135.

17464 ■ Charter Communications
315 Davis St.
Grand Haven, MI 49417-1830
Free: 888-438-2427
Key Personnel: Neil Smit, CEO, President; Michael J. Lovett, COO, Exec. VP. **Cities Served:** 72 channels. **URL:** http://www.charter.com.

17465 ■ WGHN-AM - 1370
1 S Harbor Dr.
Grand Haven, MI 49417
Phone: (616)842-8110
Fax: (616)842-4350
Format: Sports. **Simulcasts:** WGHN-FM. **Networks:** CBS. **Owner:** WGHN Inc., at above address. **Founded:** 1956. **Operating Hours:** 6:00 a.m. - Midnight. **ADI:** Grand Rapids-Kalamazoo-Battle Creek, MI. **Key Personnel:** Walt Zerlaut, News Dir., walt@wghn.com; Vicki Coulson, Contact, vicki@wghn.com. **Wattage:** 500 Day; 022 Night. **URL:** http://www.wghn.com.

17466 ■ WGHN-FM - 92.1
1 S Harbor Dr.
Grand Haven, MI 49417
Phone: (616)842-8110
Fax: (616)842-4350
Format: Adult Contemporary. **Simulcasts:** WGHN-AM. **Networks:** CBS. **Owner:** WGHN Inc., at above address. **Founded:** 1969. **Operating Hours:** Continuous; 5% network, 95% local. **ADI:** Grand Rapids-Kalamazoo-Battle Creek, MI. **Key Personnel:** Walt Zerlaut, News Dir., walt@wghn.com. **Wattage:** 3,000. **Ad Rates:** $13-21 per unit. **URL:** http://www.wghn.com.

GRAND RAPIDS

Kent Co. Kent Co. (W). On Grand River, 140 m NW of Detroit. Aquinas College, Calvin College, Grand Valley State College (Seidman Graduate School of Business), Grand Rapids Junior College, Davenport Business College. Lake resort. Furniture center of the country; wholesale fruit and produce center. Also manufactures metal products, veneer and lumber products, gases and welding equipment, typewriters, calculators, auto upholstery, bakery products, valves, fittings, paper products, varnishes, lacquers, paints, refrigerators, plumbing and bathroom fixtures, auto bodies, parts, tires, brass, iron products, knit underwear; gypsum gravel pits.

Circulation: ★ = AAM; △ or • = BPA; ♦ = CAC; ❑ = VAC; ⊕ = PO Statement; ‡ = Publisher's Report; Boldface figures = sworn; Light figures = estimated.

17467 ■ The Banner
Faith Alive Christian Resources
2850 Kalamazoo Ave. SE
Grand Rapids, MI 49560
Phone: (616)224-0728
Fax: (888)642-8606
Free: 800-333-8300
Publication E-mail: info@thebanner.org
Magazine of the Christian Reformed Church in America. **Founded:** 1865. **Freq:** Bimonthly. **Print Method:** Offset. **Trim Size:** 8 1/2 x 11. **Cols./Page:** 3 and 4. **Col. Depth:** 10 inches. **Key Personnel:** Joyce Kane, Assistant Editor; Bob De Moor, Editor-in-Chief. **ISSN:** 0005-5557 (print). **URL:** http://www.thebanner.org. **Ad Rates:** BW $3245; 4C $3370. **Remarks:** Accepts advertising. **Circ:** Paid ‡90,000, Controlled ‡255.

17468 ■ Chimes
Calvin College
3201 Burton SE
Grand Rapids, MI
Phone: (616)526-6000
Fax: (616)526-7069
Free: 800-688-0122
Publication E-mail: chimes@calvin.edu
Collegiate newspaper. **Founded:** 1907. **Freq:** Weekly (Fri.). **Print Method:** Offset. **Cols./Page:** 5. **Col. Width:** 24 nonpareils. **Col. Depth:** 210 agate lines. **Key Personnel:** Lauren Stauffer, Contact; Sarah Potter, Contact; Griffin Jackson, Editor. **Subscription Rates:** Free. **URL:** http://www.calvin.edu/chimes/. **Remarks:** Accepts advertising. **Circ:** Paid ‡90, Free ‡3,500.

17469 ■ Christian Home & School
Christian Schools International
3350 E Paris Ave. SE
Grand Rapids, MI 49512
Phone: (616)957-1070
Fax: (616)957-5022
Free: 800-635-8288
Publisher's E-mail: info@csionline.org
Magazine addressing issues of concern to contemporary Christian families; particularly aimed at parents who support Christian education. **Freq:** Annual Three times (March, May and November). **Print Method:** offset. **Trim Size:** 8 1/2 x 11. **Cols./Page:** 3. **Col. Width:** 13.5 picas. **Col. Depth:** 55 picas. **Key Personnel:** Dave Koetje, Chief Executive Officer, President. **ISSN:** 0095-5389 (print). **Subscription Rates:** $11.95 U.S.; $13.95 Individuals Canada; $21.95 U.S. two years; $25.95 Two years Canada; $20 Individuals foreign. **URL:** http://www.csionline.org/christian_home_and_school. **Ad Rates:** GLR $10; BW $1950; 4C $2600. **Remarks:** Advertising accepted; rates available upon request. **Circ:** 70,000, 90,000.

17470 ■ The Collegiate
Grand Rapids Community College
143 Bostwick Ave. NE
Grand Rapids, MI 49503-3295
Phone: (616)234-4000
Publication E-mail: collegiate@grcc.edu
Collegiate tabloid. **Freq:** Monthly 13/yr (during the academic year). **Print Method:** Offset. **Trim Size:** 10 x 15.25. **Cols./Page:** 6. **Col. Width:** 24 nonpareils. **Col. Depth:** 213 agate lines. **Key Personnel:** Austin Metz, Editor-in-Chief. **URL:** http://thecollegiatelive.com. **Ad Rates:** BW $520; SAU $3.50; PCI $20. **Remarks:** Accepts advertising. **Circ:** Free ‡2,500.

17471 ■ E-quip
Dynamic Youth Ministries
Calvinist Cadet Corps
1333 Alger St. SE
Grand Rapids, MI 49507
Phone: (616)241-5616
Fax: (616)241-5558
Publisher's E-mail: info@calvinistcadets.org
Freq: Quarterly. **Subscription Rates:** Members available to members only. **Mailing address:** PO Box 7259, Grand Rapids, MI 49510. **Remarks:** Advertising not accepted. **Circ:** (Not Reported).

17472 ■ Faith and Philosophy: Journal of the Society of Christian Philosophers
Society of Christian Philosophers
Dept. of Philosophy
Calvin College
1845 Knollcrest Cir. SE
Grand Rapids, MI 49546-4402
Publication E-mail: faithandphilosophy@asbury.edu
Scholarly refereed journal covering the philosophy of religion with special emphasis on issues relevant to philosophy and Christianity. **Freq:** Quarterly. **Trim Size:** 6 x 9. **ISSN:** 0739--7046 (print). **Subscription Rates:** $79 Institutions plus annual postage of Canada - $18, and all other non-U.S. add $18; $45 Individuals plus annual postage of Canada - $18, and all other non-U.S. add $18; $25 Students plus annual postage of Canada - $18, and all other non-U.S. add $18; $12 Single issue back issues. **URL:** http://www.faithandphilosophy.com. **Ad Rates:** BW $175. **Remarks:** Accepts advertising. **Circ:** Paid 2000.

17473 ■ Grand Rapids Family Magazine
Gemini Publications
549 Ottawa Ave. NW, Ste. 201
Grand Rapids, MI 49503-1444
Phone: (616)459-4545
Fax: (616)459-4800
Publisher's E-mail: info@geminipub.com
Magazine for West Michigan families. **Freq:** Monthly. **Key Personnel:** Randy Prichard, Manager, Advertising and Sales. **Subscription Rates:** $12 Individuals 1 year; $20 Two years; $25 Individuals 3 years. **URL:** http://www.grfamily.com. **Remarks:** Accepts advertising. **Circ:** 15000.

17474 ■ Grand Rapids Magazine
Gemini Publications
549 Ottawa Ave. NW, Ste. 201
Grand Rapids, MI 49503-1444
Phone: (616)459-4545
Fax: (616)459-4800
Publication E-mail: info@geminipub.com
Regional general interest magazine. **Freq:** Monthly. **Print Method:** Offset. **Trim Size:** 8 3/8 x 10 7/8. **Cols./Page:** 3. **Col. Width:** 28 nonpareils. **Col. Depth:** 140 agate lines. **Key Personnel:** Carole Valade, Editor; Randy Prichard, Manager, Sales. **ISSN:** 1055-5145 (print). **USPS:** 997-340. **Subscription Rates:** $24 Individuals; $2 Single issue; $34 Two years; $4.95 Individuals single copy newsstand price. **URL:** http://www.grmag.com/home.htm; http://www.geminipub.com/publications.htm. **Ad Rates:** BW $2350; 4C $2750. **Circ:** Paid 10,950.

17475 ■ The Grand Rapids Press
MLive Media Group
169 Monroe Ave. NW, Ste. 100
Grand Rapids, MI 49503
Phone: (616)222-5411
Free: 800-878-1400
Publication E-mail: grnews@mlive.com
General newspaper. **Freq:** Daily. **Print Method:** Letterpress. **Cols./Page:** 6. **Col. Width:** 24 nonpareils. **Col. Depth:** 308 agate lines. **Key Personnel:** Julie Hoogland, Editor; Tanda Gmiter, Producer; Kate Nagengast, Producer; Nate Reens, Producer. **Online:** MLive Media Group MLive Media Group. **Alt. Formats:** Handheld. **URL:** http://www.mlive.com/grand-rapids. **Ad Rates:** SAU $34.83. **Remarks:** Accepts advertising. **Circ:** Mon.-Sat. ★**135,902**, Sun. ★**186,047**.

17476 ■ The Grand Rapids Times
The Grand Rapids Times
2016 Eastern SE
Grand Rapids, MI 49510
Phone: (616)245-8737
Fax: (616)245-1026
Publication E-mail: staff@grtimes.com
Newspaper targeted for black population in Grand Rapids, Muskegon, Battle Creek and Kalamazoo, Michigan. **Freq:** Weekly. **Print Method:** Web offset. **Trim Size:** 9 5/16 x 15. **Cols./Page:** 5. **Col. Width:** 2 inches. **Col. Depth:** 15 inches. **Key Personnel:** Patricia Pulliam, Publisher, Editor-in-Chief. **Subscription Rates:** $25 Individuals; $40 Two years. **Mailing address:** PO Box 7258, Grand Rapids, MI 49510. **Ad Rates:** BW $450; 4C $750; SAU $5.99; PCI $13.50. **Remarks:** Accepts advertising. **Circ:** (Not Reported).

17477 ■ The Jackson Citizen Patriot
MLive Media Group
169 Monroe NW, Ste. 100
Grand Rapids, MI 49503
Free: 800-878-1400
Publisher's E-mail: pwest@mlive.com
General newspaper. **Freq:** Daily (eve.). **Print Method:** Offset. **Cols./Page:** 6. **Col. Width:** 25 nonpareils. **Col. Depth:** 304 agate lines. **Key Personnel:** Sara Scott, Editor. **Subscription Rates:** $11.08 Individuals online. **URL:** http://www.mlive.com/jackson. **Ad Rates:** SAU $21.22. **Remarks:** Advertising accepted; rates available upon request. **Circ:** Mon.-Sat. ★**33,325**, Sun. ★**38,197**.

17478 ■ Journal of Markets & Morality
Action Institute for the Study of Religion and Liberty
98 E Fulton St.
Grand Rapids, MI 49503
Phone: (616)454-3080
Fax: (616)454-9454
Free: 800-345-2286
Publication E-mail: webmaster@acton.org
Journal focusing on the relationship between economics and morality from both social science and theological perspectives. **Freq:** Semiannual. **Key Personnel:** Jordan J. Ballor, Executive Editor; Kenneth L. Grasso, Board Member; Dylan Pahman, Managing Editor; Ian R. Harper, Board Member. **Subscription Rates:** $30 Individuals print and online /yr.; $40 Other countries print and online /yr.; $65 Institutions print and online /yr.; $75 Institutions, other countries print and online /yr. **URL:** http://www.marketsandmorality.com/index.php/mandm. **Remarks:** Advertising accepted; rates available upon request. **Circ:** (Not Reported).

17479 ■ Journals of Jim Elliot
Baker Publishing
6030 E Fulton Rd.
Grand Rapids, MI 49301
Phone: (616)676-9185
Fax: (800)398-3111
Free: 800-877-2665
Publisher's E-mail: orders@bakerpublishinggroup.com
Journal featuring the life story of Jim Elliot. **Key Personnel:** Elisabeth Elliot, Contact. **Subscription Rates:** $20 Single issue. **URL:** http://www.bakerpublishinggroup.com/books/the-journals-of-jim-elliot/228880. **Circ:** (Not Reported).

17480 ■ Kalamazoo Gazette
MLive Media Group
169 Monroe NW, Ste. 100
Grand Rapids, MI 49503
Free: 800-878-1400
Publisher's E-mail: pwest@mlive.com
General newspaper. **Freq:** Daily. **Print Method:** Letterpress. **Cols./Page:** 6. **Col. Width:** 24 nonpareils. **Col. Depth:** 308 agate lines. **URL:** http://www.mlive.com/kalamazoo. **Ad Rates:** 4C $265; 4C $210. **Remarks:** Accepts advertising. Sunday: Color: $265 Monday-Saturday: Color: $210. **Circ:** Mon.-Fri. ★**54,363**, Sat. ★**58,499**, Sun. ★**71,437**.

17481 ■ Lake Michigan Circle Tour & Lighthouse Guide
West Michigan Tourist Association
741 Kenmoor Ave., Ste. E
Grand Rapids, MI 49546
Phone: (616)245-2217
Fax: (616)954-3924
Publisher's E-mail: travel@wmta.org
Magazine of the West Michigan Tourist Association, featuring a guide to Lake Michigan's shoreline. **Freq:** Annual. **Subscription Rates:** Free; free. **Alt. Formats:** CD-ROM. **URL:** http://www.wmta.org/publications-24. **Remarks:** Accepts advertising. **Circ:** 75000.

17482 ■ Local 951 Journal
United Food and Commercial Workers - Local 951
3270 Evergreen Dr. NE
Grand Rapids, MI 49525-9580
Phone: (616)361-7683
Fax: (616)447-1000
Free: 800-999-0951
Publisher's E-mail: information@ufcwlocal951.com
Magazine containing membership information pertaining to the United Food and Commercial Workers AFL-CIO, Local 951. **Freq:** Quarterly. **Subscription Rates:** Free; free. **Remarks:** Advertising not accepted. **Circ:** 35000.

17483 ■ Michigan Blue: Michigan's Lakestyle Magazine
Gemini Publications
549 Ottawa Ave. NW, Ste. 201
Grand Rapids, MI 49503-1444
Phone: (616)459-4545
Fax: (616)459-4800
Publisher's E-mail: info@geminipub.com

Lifestyle magazine featuring homes products, pastimes, seasons, and sentiments of lakefront living. **Freq:** Bimonthly. **Key Personnel:** John Zwarensteyn, Publisher; Lisa Jensen, Editor. **Subscription Rates:** $18 Individuals; $28 Two years; $38 Individuals three years. **URL:** http://www.miblu emag.com. **Circ:** (Not Reported).

17484 ■ Michigan Golf
Gemini Publications
549 Ottawa Ave. NW, Ste. 201
Grand Rapids, MI 49503-1444
Phone: (616)459-4545
Fax: (616)459-4800
Publication E-mail: info@geminipub.com
Magazine promoting golf in Michigan. **Freq:** Semiannual. **Subscription Rates:** $15 Individuals 4 years; $5 Single issue. **URL:** http://www.michigangolfmagazine.com. **Circ:** 160000.

17485 ■ Our Daily Bread
Our Daily Bread Ministries
PO Box 2222
Grand Rapids, MI 49501-2222
Religious magazine. **Freq:** Quarterly. **Subscription Rates:** Free. **URL:** http://ourdailybread.org. **Remarks:** Advertising not accepted. **Circ:** Non-paid ⊕**1600000**.

17486 ■ Pedagogy
Duke University Press
Department of English
Calvin College
1795 Knollcrest Cir. SE
Grand Rapids, MI 49546
Phone: (616)526-6598
Fax: (616)526-8508
Publication E-mail: pedagogy@calvin.edu
Journal covering teaching in the field of undergraduate and graduate English studies. **Freq:** 3/year. **Key Personnel:** Jennifer L. Holberg, Editor, Founder; Marcy Taylor, Editor, Founder; Mark C. Long, Associate Editor. **ISSN:** 1531--4200 (print); **EISSN:** 1533--6255 (electronic). **Subscription Rates:** $25 Individuals; $18 Students. **URL:** http://muse.jhu.edu/journals/pedagogy; http://www.dukeupress.edu/Pedagogy. **Ad Rates:** BW $250, full page; BW $200, half page. **Remarks:** Accepts advertising. **Circ:** 330.

17487 ■ Primerus Paradigm
International Society of Primerus Law Firms
171 Monroe Ave. NW, Ste. 750
Grand Rapids, MI 49503
Phone: (616)454-9939
Fax: (616)458-7099
Free: 800-968-2211
Magazine publishing information for International Society of Primerus Law Firms members. **Freq:** Quarterly. **Alt. Formats:** PDF. **URL:** http://www.primerus.com/primerus-paradigm-magazine.htm. **Remarks:** Advertising not accepted. **Circ:** (Not Reported).

17488 ■ The Saint: Aquinas College Student Press
Aquinas College Publications Board
1607 Robinson Rd. SE
Grand Rapids, MI 49506-1799
Phone: (616)632-8900
Fax: (616)732-4487
Publisher's E-mail: registrar@aquinas.edu
Collegiate newspaper. **Freq:** Biweekly. **Print Method:** Offset. **Trim Size:** 11 1/4 x 14 1/2. **Cols./Page:** 5. **Col. Width:** 1 3/4 inches. **Col. Depth:** 13 inches. **Key Personnel:** Dan Treul, Editor-in-Chief; Brian Dowling, Editor; John Taylor, Business Manager. **Subscription Rates:** Free; $5 By mail. **Formerly:** Aquinas Sunrise; Aquinas Times. **Ad Rates:** BW $140; GLR $10. **Remarks:** Accepts classified advertising. **Circ:** 2,330.

17489 ■ Tasters Guild
Tasters Guild International
1515 Michigan NE
Grand Rapids, MI 49503
Phone: (616)454-7815
Fax: (616)459-9969
Journal providing association news plus articles on wine, food, recipes, tasting notes and travel. **Freq:** 3/year. **URL:** http://www.tastersguild.com. **Remarks:** Advertising not accepted. **Circ:** (Not Reported).

17490 ■ WAYG-FM - 89.9
1159 E Beltline NE
Grand Rapids, MI 49525
Phone: (616)942-1500
Email: info@wcsg.org
Format: Contemporary Christian. **Owner:** Cornerstone University, 1001 E Beltline Ave. NE, Grand Rapids, MI 49525. **Key Personnel:** Rich Anderson, Contact. **Ad Rates:** Noncommercial. **URL:** http://www.wcsg.org.

17491 ■ WBBL-AM - 1340
60 Monroe Ctr. NW, 3rd Fl.
Grand Rapids, MI 49503
Phone: (616)774-8461
Fax: (616)451-3299
Free: 800-785-1073
Format: Sports. **Owner:** Citadel Broadcasting Corp., 7201 W Lake Mead Blvd., Ste. 400, Las Vegas, NV 89128-8366, Ph: (702)804-5200, Fax: (702)804-8250. **Founded:** 1940. **Operating Hours:** Continuous. **ADI:** Grand Rapids-Kalamazoo-Battle Creek, MI. **Key Personnel:** Bret Bakita, Dir. of Programs, onthebench@wbbl.com; Matt Hanlon, Dir. of Mktg., Mktg. Mgr. **Wattage:** 1,000. **Ad Rates:** Noncommercial. **URL:** http://www.wbbl.com.

17492 ■ WBFX-FM - 101.3
77 Monroe Ctr., Ste. 1000
Grand Rapids, MI 49503
Phone: (616)459-1919
Fax: (616)732-3303
Format: Classic Rock. **Networks:** ABC. **Founded:** 1973. **Formerly:** WCUZ-FM. **Operating Hours:** Continuous; 100% local. **Key Personnel:** Tim Feagan, Gen. Mgr., timfeagan@clearchannel.com; Kelly Norton, Dir. of Sales, kellynorton@iheartmedia.com. **Wattage:** 50,000. **Ad Rates:** Noncommercial. **URL:** http://www.1013thebrew.com//main.html.

17493 ■ WBMX-AM - 640
1345 Thomas St. S
Grand Rapids, MI 49506-2651
Format: Adult Contemporary; Middle-of-the-Road (MOR); News. **ADI:** Grand Rapids-Kalamazoo-Battle Creek, MI. **Key Personnel:** David Bradley, Contact; Robert S. Van Prooyen, Contact; David Bradley, Contact. **Wattage:** 1,000 day; 250 night.

WCSG-FM - See Kalamazoo

17494 ■ WFGR-FM - 98.7
50 Monroe Ave. NW, Ste. 500
Grand Rapids, MI 49503
Phone: (616)459-9889
Format: Oldies; Classical. **Key Personnel:** Russ Hines, Gen. Mgr., Russ.Hines@townsquaremedia.com; Tom Cook, Mgr., Tom.Cook@townsquaremedia.com; James Thomas, Dir. of Sales, James.Thomas@townsquaremedia.com; Bruce Parrott, Contact, brucep@gogrand.com. **Ad Rates:** Noncommercial. **URL:** http://www.wfgr.com.

17495 ■ WFUR-AM - 1570
PO Box 1808
Grand Rapids, MI 49501
Phone: (616)451-9387
Format: News; Contemporary Christian; Gospel; Information. **Networks:** USA Radio. **Founded:** 1948. **Operating Hours:** Continuous Monday - Friday, 9:30 a.m. - 8:00 p.m. Saturday, 7:00 a.m. - 4:00 p.m. Sunday. **ADI:** Grand Rapids-Kalamazoo-Battle Creek, MI. **Key Personnel:** William E. Kuiper, Sr., Owner; William Kuiper, Contact. **Wattage:** 1,000 KW. **Ad Rates:** $6-10 for 30 seconds; $7.50-12 for 60 seconds. Combined advertising rates available with WFUR-FM, WKPR-AM. **URL:** http://www.wfuramfm.com/.

17496 ■ WFUR-FM - 102.9
399 Garfield Rd.
Grand Rapids, MI 49504
Phone: (616)451-9387
Format: Religious. **Networks:** USA Radio. **Founded:** 1947. **Operating Hours:** Continuous. **Key Personnel:** William E. Kuiper, Gen. Mgr. **Wattage:** 50,000. **Ad Rates:** $14.50-20 for 30 seconds; $18.50-24 for 60 seconds. **URL:** http://www.wfuramfm.com/history.html.

17497 ■ WGRD-AM - 1410
38 Fulton West
Grand Rapids, MI 49503
Phone: (616)459-4114
Fax: (616)459-6887
Format: Alternative/New Music/Progressive; Talk. **Owner:** Townsquare Media Inc., 240 Greenwich Ave., Greenwich, CT 06830-6507, Ph: (203)861-0900. **Founded:** 1947. **Operating Hours:** Sunrise-sunset. **ADI:** Grand Rapids-Kalamazoo-Battle Creek, MI. **Key Personnel:** Phil Catlett, VP; Joel Schaaf, Station Mgr. **Wattage:** 1,000. **URL:** http://wgrd.com.

17498 ■ WGRD-FM - 97.9
50 Monroe Ave. NW, Ste. 500
Grand Rapids, MI 49503
Phone: (616)459-4111
Fax: (616)459-6887
Free: 800-WGR-D979
Format: Alternative/New Music/Progressive. **Networks:** American Ag Net. **Owner:** Townsquare Media Inc., 2000 Fifth Third Ctr. 511 Walnut St., Cincinnati, OH 45202, Ph: (513)651-1190. **Founded:** 1962. **Operating Hours:** Continuous. **Wattage:** 13,000. **Ad Rates:** Noncommercial. $10-200 per unit. **URL:** http://www.wgrd.com.

17499 ■ WGVK-TV - 52
301 W Fulton Ave.
Grand Rapids, MI 49504-6492
Phone: (616)331-6666
Format: Public TV. **Networks:** Public Broadcasting Service (PBS). **Owner:** Grand Valley State University, 1 Campus Dr., Allendale, MI 49401-9403, Ph: (616)331-5000. **Founded:** 1972. **Operating Hours:** 6:30 a.m.-1 a.m.; 90% network, 10% local. **ADI:** Grand Rapids-Kalamazoo-Battle Creek, MI. **Key Personnel:** Michael Walenta, Gen. Mgr. **Ad Rates:** Noncommercial. **URL:** http://www.wgvu.org.

17500 ■ WGVU-AM - 850
301 Fulton St. W
Grand Rapids, MI 49504-6492
Phone: (616)331-6666
Fax: (616)957-5137
Email: businessdevelopment@wgvu.org
Format: Jazz; News; Talk; Information. **Networks:** AP; American Public Radio (APR); National Public Radio (NPR); USA Radio; International Broadcasting; CNN Radio. **Owner:** Grand Valley State University, at above address. **Founded:** 1954. **Formerly:** WMAX-AM. **Operating Hours:** Continuous. **ADI:** Grand Rapids-Kalamazoo-Battle Creek, MI. **Key Personnel:** Michael T. Walenta, Gen. Mgr. **Wattage:** 1,000. **Ad Rates:** Advertising accepted; rates available upon request; Noncommercial. $8-40 for 30 seconds; $10-50 for 60 seconds. **URL:** http://www.wgvu.org.

17501 ■ WGVU-TV - 35
301 W Fulton Ave.
Grand Rapids, MI 49504-6492
Phone: (616)331-6666
Free: 800-442-2771
Email: business@wgvu.org
Format: Public TV. **Networks:** Public Broadcasting Service (PBS). **Owner:** Grand Valley State University, 1 Campus Dr., Allendale, MI 49401-9403, Ph: (616)331-5000. **Founded:** 1972. **Operating Hours:** 6:30 a.m.-1:00 a.m.; 90% network, 10% local. **ADI:** Grand Rapids-Kalamazoo-Battle Creek, MI. **Key Personnel:** Michael T. Walenta, Gen. Mgr. **Local Programs:** *Ask The...*, Thursday Friday 6:00 p.m. 1:30 p.m.; 9:00 p.m.; *Family Health Matters*, Sunday 3:00 p.m.; *West Michigan Week*, Friday Sunday 8:00 p.m. 10:00 p.m.; 10:00 a.m. **Ad Rates:** Noncommercial; underwriting available. **URL:** http://www.wgvu.org.

17502 ■ WHTS-FM - 105.3
60 Monroe Ctr. NW, Ste. 300
Grand Rapids, MI 49503
Phone: (616)774-8461
Format: Top 40. **Owner:** Citadel Broadcasting Corp., 7201 W Lake Mead Blvd., Ste. 400, Las Vegas, NV 89128-8366, Ph: (702)804-5200, Fax: (702)804-8250. **Founded:** 1980. **Formerly:** WPXR-FM. **Operating Hours:** Continuous. **Key Personnel:** Jack Spade, Dir. of Programs, jack.spade@citcomm.com; Kate Conley, Gen. Sales Mgr., kate.conley@citcomm.com. **Wattage:** 39,000. **Ad Rates:** $25-75 per unit. **URL:** http://www.y-103.com.

Circulation: ★ = AAM; △ or • = BPA; ♦ = CAC; ❑ = VAC; ⊕ = PO Statement; ‡ = Publisher's Report; Boldface figures = sworn; Light figures = estimated.

17503 ■ WJNZ-AM - 1140
1919 Eastern SE
Grand Rapids, MI 49507
Phone: (616)475-4299
Fax: (616)475-4335
Format: Urban Contemporary; Blues. **Networks:** American Urban Radio; ABC. **Owner:** Goodrich Radio Marketing Inc., at above address. **Founded:** 1977. **Formerly:** WKWM-AM. **Operating Hours:** Continuous. **ADI:** Grand Rapids-Kalamazoo-Battle Creek, MI. **Wattage:** 10,000. **Ad Rates:** $17-28 for 60 seconds.

17504 ■ WKPR-AM - 1440
399 Garfield Rd.
Grand Rapids, MI 49504
Phone: (616)451-9387
Format: Full Service; Contemporary Christian; Gospel; Information. **Networks:** USA Radio. **Owner:** Kalamazoo Broadcasting Co., Inc., WFUR Radio 399 Garfield Ave. SW, Grand Rapids, MI 49501, Ph: (616)451-9387. **Founded:** 1960. **ADI:** Grand Rapids-Kalamazoo-Battle Creek, MI. **Key Personnel:** Tad Odell, Contact. **Wattage:** 2,700 Day 024 Night. **Ad Rates:** $6-7 for 30 seconds; $7-8 for 60 seconds. **URL:** http://www.wfuramfm.com.

17505 ■ WLAV-FM - 96.9
60 Monroe Ctr. NW, 3rd Fl.
Grand Rapids, MI 49503
Phone: (616)459-9797
Free: 800-882-9528
Format: Classic Rock. **Owner:** Citadel Broadcasting Corp., 7201 W Lake Mead Blvd., Ste. 400, Las Vegas, NV 89128-8366, Ph: (702)804-5200, Fax: (702)804-8250. **Operating Hours:** Continuous. **ADI:** Grand Rapids-Kalamazoo-Battle Creek, MI. **Wattage:** 50,000 ERP. **Ad Rates:** Noncommercial; Advertising accepted; rates available upon request. **URL:** http://www.wlav.com.

17506 ■ WLHT-FM - 95.7
50 Monroe Ave. NW, Ste. 500
Grand Rapids, MI 49503
Phone: (616)770-8957
Format: Adult Contemporary; Information. **Owner:** Townsquare Media Inc., 240 Greenwich Ave., Greenwich, CT 06830-6507, Ph: (203)861-0900. **Founded:** 1962. **Operating Hours:** Continuous. **ADI:** Grand Rapids-Kalamazoo-Battle Creek, MI. **Key Personnel:** Russ Hines, Gen. Mgr., russ.hines@townsquaremedia.com; Tom Cook, Div. Mgr., tom.cook@townsquaremedia.com; James Thomas, Dir. of Sales, james.thomas@townsquaremedia.com. **Wattage:** 41,000. **Ad Rates:** Noncommercial. Combined advertising rates available with WNWZ-AM, WTRV-FM, WFGR-FM, WGRD-FM. **URL:** http://www.mychannel957.com.

17507 ■ WMJH-AM - 810
2422 Burton, SE
Grand Rapids, MI 49546
Phone: (616)863-6770
Email: sima@birach.com
Format: Big Band/Nostalgia. **Ad Rates:** Noncommercial.

17508 ■ WNWZ-AM - 1410
50 Monroe Ave. NW, Ste. 500
Grand Rapids, MI 49503
Phone: (616)451-4800
Format: Hispanic. **Networks:** CNN Radio. **Owner:** Townsquare Media Inc., 2000 Fifth Third Ctr. 511 Walnut St., Cincinnati, OH 45202, Ph: (513)651-1190. **Founded:** 1962. **Formerly:** WRCV-AM. **Operating Hours:** Continuous. **Key Personnel:** Russ Hines, Gen. Mgr., russ.hines@townsquaremedia.com; James Thomas, Dir. of Sales, james.thomas@townsquaremedia.com. **Wattage:** 1,000. **Ad Rates:** Noncommercial. WLHT. **URL:** http://touch1410.com.

17509 ■ WODJ-FM - 107.3
60 Monroe Center St. NW, 10th Fl.
Grand Rapids, MI 49503-2916
Phone: (616)774-8461
Fax: (616)956-3424
Email: wodj@wodj.com
Format: Oldies. **Networks:** Westwood One Radio. **Founded:** 1989. **Operating Hours:** Continuous. **ADI:** Grand Rapids-Kalamazoo-Battle Creek, MI. **Key Personnel:** Len O'Kelly, Dir. of Programs; Nancy Faasse, Bus. Mgr., Sales Mgr., nfaasse@wodj.com; Tom Wilson, Dir. of Production; Scott Fredericks, Promotions Dir. **Wattage:** 50,000. **Ad Rates:** $55-90 for 60 seconds. Combined advertising rates available with WSNX, WKWM, WSHZ, WMHG, WMRR.

17510 ■ WOOD-AM - 1300
77 Monroe Center St. NW, Ste. 1000
Grand Rapids, MI 49503
Phone: (616)459-1919
Free: 866-290-2899
Format: News; Talk; Information. **Simulcasts:** WOOD-FM 105.7. **Networks:** Independent. **Owner:** iHeartMedia Inc., 200 E Basse Rd., San Antonio, TX 78209, Ph: (210)832-3314. **Founded:** 1924. **Formerly:** WEBK-AM. **Operating Hours:** Continuous. **ADI:** Grand Rapids-Kalamazoo-Battle Creek, MI. **Key Personnel:** Tim Feagan, Gen. Mgr., timfeagan@iheartmedia.com; Kelly Iris, Contact, kellyiris@clearchannel.com; Rod Kackley, News Dir., rodkackley@clearchannel.com; Kelly Norton, Dir. of Sales, kellynorton@iheartmedia.com. **Local Programs:** *The David Carrier Show*, Sunday 7:00 a.m. - 9:00 a.m. **Wattage:** 5,000. **Ad Rates:** Advertising accepted; rates available upon request. **URL:** http://www.woodradio.com.

17511 ■ WOOD-FM - 105.7
77 Monroe Center, Ste. 1000
Grand Rapids, MI 49503
Phone: (616)459-1919
Fax: (616)723-3303
Free: 877-759-1057
Format: Adult Contemporary. **Networks:** Independent. **Owner:** iHeartMedia Inc., 200 E Basse Rd., San Antonio, TX 78209, Ph: (210)832-3314. **Founded:** 1962. **Operating Hours:** Continuous; 100% local. **ADI:** Grand Rapids-Kalamazoo-Battle Creek, MI. **Key Personnel:** Tim Feagan, Gen. Mgr., timfeagan@iheartmedia.com; Kelly Norton, Dir. of Sales, kellynorton@iheartmedia.com; Dave Taft, Prog. Dir., davetaft@iheartmedia.com. **Wattage:** 265,000. **Ad Rates:** Advertising accepted; rates available upon request. **URL:** http://www.westmichiganstar.com//main.html.

17512 ■ WOOD-TV - 8
120 College Ave. SE
Grand Rapids, MI 49503
Phone: (616)456-8888
Fax: (269)968-9341
Email: cc@wotv.com
Format: Commercial TV. **Networks:** NBC; ABC. **Owner:** Media General Inc., 333 E Franklin St., Richmond, VA 23219, Ph: (804)649-6000, Fax: (502)259-5537. **Founded:** 1949. **Formerly:** WOTV-TV; WUHQ-TV. **Operating Hours:** Continuous; 44% network, 56% local. **ADI:** Grand Rapids-Kalamazoo-Battle Creek, MI. **Key Personnel:** Jack Doles, Sports Dir., jack.doles@woodtv.com. **Wattage:** 5,000,000. **Ad Rates:** Advertising accepted; rates available upon request. **URL:** http://www.woodtv.com.

17513 ■ WPRR-AM - 1680
3777 44th St.
Grand Rapids, MI 49512
Phone: (616)656-2619
Fax: (616)656-2158
Email: info@publicrealityradio.org
Format: Public Radio. **Formerly:** WDSS-AM. **Operating Hours:** Continuous. **Key Personnel:** Rick Tormala, Contact, rick@publicrealityradio.org. **Wattage:** 10,000 Daytime; 680. **Ad Rates:** Accepts Advertising. **URL:** http://www.publicrealityradio.org.

17514 ■ WSNX-FM - 104.5
77 Monroe Ctr., Ste. 1000
Grand Rapids, MI 49503-2912
Phone: (616)459-1919
Free: 877-320-1045
Format: Top 40. **Founded:** 1971. **Formerly:** WTRU-FM. **Operating Hours:** Continuous. **Key Personnel:** Eric O'Brien, Dir. of Programs, eob@wsnx.com. **Wattage:** 32,000. **Ad Rates:** Advertising accepted; rates available upon request. **URL:** http://www.1045snx.com.

17515 ■ WTKG-AM - 1230
77 Monroe Center St. NW, Ste. 1000
Grand Rapids, MI 49503
Phone: (616)459-1919
Format: Talk. **Networks:** ABC; Westwood One Radio; People's Network; USA Radio. **Owner:** iHeartMedia Inc., 200 E Basse Rd., San Antonio, TX 78209, Ph: (210)832-3314. **Founded:** 1945. **Formerly:** WJEF-AM; WCUZ-AM. **Operating Hours:** Continuous. **ADI:** Grand Rapids-Kalamazoo-Battle Creek, MI. **Key Personnel:** Tim Feagan, Gen. Mgr., timfeagan@clearchannel.com. **Wattage:** 1,000. **Ad Rates:** Advertising accepted; rates available upon request. **URL:** http://www.wtkg.com.

17516 ■ WTNR-FM - 94.5
60 Monroe Center NW, 3rd Fl.
Grand Rapids, MI 49503
Phone: (616)774-8461
Format: Country. **Owner:** Citadel Broadcasting Corp., 7201 W Lake Mead Blvd., Ste. 400, Las Vegas, NV 89128-8366, Ph: (702)804-5200, Fax: (702)804-8250. **Key Personnel:** Marcus Bradman, Promotions Dir., marcus.bradman@citcomm.com. **Ad Rates:** Advertising accepted; rates available upon request. **URL:** http://www.nashfm945.com.

17517 ■ WTRV-FM - 100.5
50 Monroe Ave. NW, Ste. 500
Grand Rapids, MI 49503
Phone: (616)451-4800
Format: Easy Listening; Adult Contemporary. **Owner:** Townsquare Media Inc., 2000 Fifth Third Ctr. 511 Walnut St., Cincinnati, OH 45202, Ph: (513)651-1190. **Founded:** 1997. **Operating Hours:** Continuous. **Key Personnel:** Russ Hines, Gen. Mgr., russ.hines@townsquaremedia.com; Tom Cook, Dept. Mgr., tom.cook@townsquaremedia.com; James Thomas, Dir. of Sales, james.thomas@townsquaremedia.com. **Wattage:** 3,500. **Ad Rates:** Noncommercial. WLHT, WGRD, WFGR, WNWZ-AM. **URL:** http://www.rivergrandrapids.com.

17518 ■ WVGR-FM - 104.1
535 W William St., Ste. 110
Ann Arbor, MI 48103
Phone: (734)764-9210
Fax: (734)647-3488
Free: 888-258-9866
Email: michigan.radio@umich.edu
Format: Public Radio. **Networks:** National Public Radio (NPR); Public Radio International (PRI). **Founded:** 1961. **Operating Hours:** Continuous. **Key Personnel:** Steve Chrypinski, Dir. of Mktg., steveski@umich.edu; Vincent Duffy, News Dir., vduffy@umich.edu. **Wattage:** 108,000. **Ad Rates:** Noncommercial. **URL:** http://www.michiganradio.org.

17519 ■ WVTI-FM - 96.1
77 Monroe Center, Ste. 1000
Grand Rapids, MI 49503
Phone: (616)459-1919
Fax: (616)732-3303
Format: Adult Contemporary. **Formerly:** WAKX-FM. **Operating Hours:** Continuous. **Key Personnel:** Kate Folkertsma, Bus. Mgr. **Wattage:** 50,000 Horizontal ERP; 45,000 Vertical ERP. **Ad Rates:** Noncommercial. **URL:** http://www.961maxfm.com.

17520 ■ WXMI-TV - 17
3117 Plaza Dr. NE
Grand Rapids, MI 49525
Phone: (616)364-8722
Format: Commercial TV. **Networks:** Fox; Independent. **Owner:** The Tribune Media Co., 435 N Michigan Ave., Chicago, IL 60611-4066, Ph: (312)222-9100, Fax: (312)222-4206, Free: 800-874-2863. **Founded:** 1982. **Operating Hours:** 6 a.m.-2 a.m.; 99% network and syndicated, 1% local. **ADI:** Grand Rapids-Kalamazoo-Battle Creek, MI. **Ad Rates:** Advertising accepted; rates available upon request. **URL:** http://www.fox17online.com.

17521 ■ WXSP-TV - 15
120 College Ave. SE
Grand Rapids, MI 49503
Phone: (616)456-8888
Founded: Sept. 07, 2006. **URL:** http://www.woodtv.com.

17522 ■ WYCE-FM - 88.1
711 Bridge St. NW
Grand Rapids, MI 49504
Phone: (616)742-9923
Format: Eclectic. **Owner:** Grand Rapids Cable Access Center, 711 Bridge St. NW, Grand Rapids, MI 49504, Ph: (616)459-4788. **Founded:** 1984. **Operating Hours:** Continuous; 100% local. **ADI:** Grand Rapids-Kalamazoo-Battle Creek, MI. **Key Personnel:** Pete Bruinsma, Prog. Dir., pete@grcmc.org; Matt Jarrells, Dir. Ed., matt@grcmc.org; Nicole Leach, Contact, nicole@grcmc.org. **Wattage:** 1,000. **Ad Rates:** Noncommercial. **URL:** http://www.grcmc.org.

17523 ■ WZPX-TV - 43
2610 Horizon Dr. SE, Ste. E
Grand Rapids, MI 49546
Phone: (616)222-4343
Fax: (616)493-2677
Key Personnel: Brandon Burgess, Chairman, CEO. **Ad Rates:** Noncommercial. **URL:** http://www.ionmedia.tv.

17524 ■ WZZM-TV - 13
645 Three Mile
Grand Rapids, MI 49544
Phone: (616)559-1300
Fax: (616)785-1301
Email: sales@wzzm13.com
Format: Commercial TV. **Networks:** ABC. **Owner:** Gannett Company Inc., 7950 Jones Branch Dr., McLean, VA 22107-0150, Ph: (703)854-6089. **Operating Hours:** 6 a.m.-12:30 a.m. or sign off. **ADI:** Grand Rapids-Kalamazoo-Battle Creek, MI. **Key Personnel:** Chuck Mikowski, Tech. Dir., VP. **Ad Rates:** Advertising accepted; rates available upon request. **URL:** http://www.wzzm13.com.

GRAYLING

Crawford Co. Crawford Co. (N). On Au Sable River, 44 m E of Traverse City. Historical Museum. Summer-winter tourist attraction. Hunting, trout fishing, skiing, snowmobiling. Logging. Timber. Agriculture.

17525 ■ Crawford County Avalanche
Crawford County Avalanche
102 Michigan Ave.
Grayling, MI 49738
Phone: (989)348-6811
Fax: (989)348-6806
Publication E-mail: avalanche@i2k.net
Community newspaper. **Freq:** Weekly (Thurs.). **Print Method:** Offset. **Cols./Page:** 6. **Col. Width:** 21 nonpareils. **Col. Depth:** 294 agate lines. **Key Personnel:** Linda Golnick, General Manager. **Subscription Rates:** $20 Individuals; $30 Out of area; $60 Other countries; $18 Individuals Senior citizen; $28 Out of area Senior citizen; $58 Other countries Senior citizen. **Mailing address:** PO Box 490, Grayling, MI 49738. **Ad Rates:** BW $554.40; 4C $814.40; SAU $4.40; PCI $4.40. **Remarks:** Accepts advertising. **Circ:** ‡5,000.

17526 ■ WGRY-AM - 1230
6514 Old Lake Rd.
Grayling, MI 49738
Phone: (989)348-6171
Fax: (989)348-6181
Format: Country; Adult Contemporary. **Networks:** Jones Satellite; AP. **Owner:** Gannon Broadcasting Systems, Inc., at above address, Grayling, MI. **Founded:** 1970. **Operating Hours**: Continuous; 99% network, 1% local. **ADI**: Traverse City-Cadillac, MI. **Key Personnel:** William S. Gannon, Gen. Mgr., Owner, billgannon@i2k.net. **Wattage:** 750. **Ad Rates:** $12-17 for 30 seconds; $14-21 for 60 seconds. Combined advertising rates available with WQON-FM & WGRY-FM: $16-$23 for 30 seconds; $19-$28 for 60 seconds. **URL:** http://www.i2k.net.

17527 ■ WGRY-FM - 100.3
6514 Old Lake Rd.
Grayling, MI 49738
Phone: (989)348-6171
Fax: (989)348-6181
Format: Country. **Networks:** Jones Satellite; AP. **Owner:** Gannon Broadcasting Systems, Inc., at above address, Grayling, MI. **Founded:** 1989. **Operating Hours**: Continuous; 96% network, 4% local. **ADI**: Traverse City-Cadillac, MI. **Key Personnel:** William S. Gannon, Gen. Mgr., Owner, billgannon@i2k.net. **Wattage**: 60,000. **Ad Rates:** $12-17 for 30 seconds; $14-21 for 60 seconds. Combined advertising rates available with WQON-FM & WGRY-AM: $16-23 for 30 seconds; $19-28 for 60 seconds. **URL:** http://www.i2k.net.

17528 ■ WQON-FM - 101.1
6514 Old Lake Rd.
Grayling, MI 49738
Phone: (989)348-6171
Fax: (989)348-6181
Format: Adult Contemporary. **Founded:** 1977. **Key Personnel:** Sheryl Coyne, President, CEO; Bob Ditmer, Contact. **Wattage**: 6,000. **Ad Rates:** Noncommercial. **URL:** http://www.q100-fm.com.

GREENVILLE

Montcalm Co. Montcalm Co. (SC). 32 m NE of Grand Rapids. Resort. Manufactures refrigerators, freezers, precision plastic dies, fertilizers, auto bearings, foundry products; frozen food processing. Diversified farming. Potatoes, beans.

17529 ■ The Daily News
The Daily News
109 N Lafayette St.
Greenville, MI 48838
Phone: (616)754-9301
Fax: (616)754-8559
Publisher's E-mail: news@staffordgroup.com
General newspaper. **Founded:** 1854. **Freq:** Daily (eve.) and Sat. (morn.). **Print Method:** Offset. **Trim Size:** 14 x 22 3/4. **Cols./Page:** 8. **Col. Width:** 9 picas. **Col. Depth:** 21 inches. **Key Personnel:** Rob Stafford, President, Publisher; Carol Pettengill, Manager, Circulation; Darrin Clark, Managing Editor. **USPS:** 144-220. **URL:** http://thedailynews.cc. **Remarks:** Accepts classified advertising. **Circ:** (Not Reported).

17530 ■ Charter Communications
1202 W Benton St.
Greenville, MI 48838-2126
Free: 888-438-2427
Owner: Charter Communications Inc., 400 Atlantic St., Stamford, CT 06901, Ph: (203)905-7801. **Founded:** 1976. **Cities Served:** Belding, Carson City, Cedar Springs, Fowler, Grant, Howard City, Ionia, Kent City, Newaygo, Rockford, Sparta, Stanton, Stanton, Michigan: subscribing households 30,000; 200 channels; 3 community access channels; 504 hours per week community access programming. **URL:** http://www.charter.com.

GROSSE ILE

Wayne Co. (SE). 17 m S of Detroit. Small business area; industrial park.

17531 ■ The American Revenuer
American Revenue Association
PO Box 74
Grosse Ile, MI 48138-0074
Phone: (734)676-2649
Fax: (734)676-2959
Publisher's E-mail: revenuer@omnitelcom.com
Magazine on collecting revenue and Cinderella stamps. **Freq:** Quarterly. **Print Method:** Offset. **Trim Size:** 8 1/2 x 11. **Cols./Page:** 2. **Col. Width:** 40. nonpareils. **Col. Depth:** 129 agate lines. **Key Personnel:** Kenneth Trettin, Editor; Robert Hohertz, President, phone: (610)926-6200; Hermann Ivester, Vice President. **ISSN:** 0163--1608 (print). **Subscription Rates:** Included in membership. **Alt. Formats:** PDF. **URL:** http://revenuer.org/revenuer.html. **Ad Rates:** BW $120; 4C $400. **Remarks:** Accepts advertising. **Circ:** Paid 1300, Non-paid 10.

17532 ■ The Penny Post
Carriers and Locals Society, Inc.
PO Box 74
Grosse Ile, MI 48138
Phone: (734)676-2649
Fax: (734)676-2959
Freq: Quarterly. **Alt. Formats:** PDF. **URL:** http://www.pennypost.org/penny_post.html. **Circ:** (Not Reported).

GROSSE POINTE

Wayne Co. Wayne Co. (SE). 8 m NE of Detroit.

17533 ■ Journal of the Royal College of Physicians and Surgeons
Royal College of Physicians & Surgeons of the United States of America
485 Allard Rd.
Grosse Pointe, MI 48236
Phone: (313)882-0641
Fax: (313)882-0979
Publisher's E-mail: info@rcpsus.com
Freq: Semiannual. **URL:** http://www.rcpsus.com/become-a-member/journals. **Mailing address:** PO Box 36081, Grosse Pointe, MI 48236. **Remarks:** Accepts advertising. **Circ:** (Not Reported).

GROSSE POINTE FARMS

Wayne Co. Wayne Co. (NE). On Lake St. Clair. 10 m E of Detroit.

17534 ■ KBAI-AM - 930
73 Kercheval Ave.
Grosse Pointe Farms, MI 48236
Phone: (313)886-7070
Fax: (313)886-7150
Format: Big Band/Nostalgia. **Networks:** NBC. **Founded:** 1969. **Operating Hours**: Continuous. **Key Personnel:** Sandra Hertz, Operations Mgr., Contact; Bill Bordeaux, Chief Engineer; Chris Forgy, Gen. Mgr; Sandra Hertz, Contact. **Wattage**: 1,000 Day;500 Night. **Ad Rates:** $10 for 30 seconds; $12 for 60 seconds. $10 for 30 seconds; $12 for 60 seconds. Combined advertising rates available with KWAV-FM. **URL:** http://sagacom.com.

17535 ■ Saga Communications of Arkansas L.L.C.
73 Kercheval Ave.
Grosse Pointe Farms, MI 48236
Email: interactive@sagacom.com
Format: News; Eclectic; Sports; Talk. **Networks:** Fox; CBS; NBC; ABC. **Founded:** 1986. **Key Personnel:** Bob Lawrence, VP; Tom Atkins, Dir. of Engg.; Edward Christian, President, CEO. **URL:** http://sagacom.com.

GROSSE POINTE WOODS

17536 ■ Grosse Pointe News: Complete Newspaper coverage of all the Pointes
Anteebo Publishers
21316 Mack Ave.
Grosse Pointe Woods, MI 48236
Publisher's E-mail: editor@grossepointenews.com
Community newspaper. **Freq:** Weekly (Thurs.). **Print Method:** Offset. **Trim Size:** 11 5/8 x 21. **Cols./Page:** 6. **Col. Width:** 26 nonpareils. **Col. Depth:** 294 agate lines. **Key Personnel:** Robert G. Liggett, Jr., Chairman, Publisher; Peter J. Birkner, Manager, Advertising, phone: (313)882-3500; Joe Warner, Editor, General Manager. **USPS:** 230-400. **Subscription Rates:** $39.50 Individuals print and online; $72 Two years print and online; $99.50 Individuals print and online (three years); $35 Individuals online. **Ad Rates:** BW $3060.54; 4C $3260.54; SAU $24.29; PCI $25.88. **Remarks:** Accepts advertising. **Circ:** ‡11,050.

HANCOCK

17537 ■ WMPL-AM - 920
326 Quincy St.
Hancock, MI 49930
Phone: (906)482-1330
Fax: (906)482-1540
Format: News; Sports. **Owner:** J and J Broadcasting Inc., 222 South Lawrence St., Ironwood, MI 49938, Fax: (906)932-2485. **Operating Hours**: Continuous. **Local Programs**: *Mitch In The Morning*, Monday Tuesday Wednesday Thursday Friday 6:00 a.m. - 8:00 a.m.; *The Jan Tucker Show*, Monday Tuesday Wednesday Thursday Friday 9:00 a.m. - 10:30 a.m.; *The Super Saver Hotline*, Monday Tuesday Wednesday Thursday Friday 11:00 a.m. - 12:00 p.m.; *Overnights*, Monday Tuesday Wednesday Thursday Friday 12:00 a.m. - 6:00 a.m.; *Yahoo! Sports Radio*, Monday Tuesday Wednesday Thursday Friday Sunday 6:00 p.m. - 1:00 a.m. 1:00 p.m. - 1:00 a.m.; 11:00 a.m. - 1:00 a.m.; *The Watchdog On Wall Street*, Saturday 8:00 a.m. - 10:00 a.m. **Wattage**: 1,000. **Ad Rates:** $2-3.50 for 15 seconds; $3.50-6.50 for 30 seconds; $6-12 for 60 seconds. **Mailing address:** PO Box 547, Hancock, MI 49930. **URL:** http://www.wmpl920.com.

HARBOR SPRINGS

17538 ■ WCMW-FM - 103.9
1999 E Campus Dr.
Mount Pleasant, MI 48859
Phone: (989)774-3105
Fax: (989)774-4427
Free: 800-727-9268
Format: Public Radio. **Founded:** Sept. 07, 2006. **Key Personnel:** David Nicholas, News Dir., nicho1d@cmich.edu; John Sheffler, Div. Dir., sheff1@cmich.edu; Kim Walters, Contact, walte1kj@cmich.edu; Kim Walters,

Circulation: ★ = AAM; △ or • = BPA; ♦ = CAC; ❏ = VAC; ⊕ = PO Statement; ‡ = Publisher's Report; Boldface figures = sworn; Light figures = estimated.

Contact, walte1kj@cmich.edu. **Ad Rates:** Noncommercial. **URL:** http://www.wcmu.org.

HARRISON

Clare Co. Clare Co. (C). Mid Michigan Community College. Summer resort.

17539 ■ Clare County Cleaver: In the Heart of Michigan's Vacationland
Clare County Cleaver
183 W Main St.
Harrison, MI 48625
Phone: (517)539-7496
Fax: (517)539-5901
Publisher's E-mail: cccleaver@sbcglobal.net
General newspaper. **Freq:** Weekly. **Print Method:** Offset. **Key Personnel:** Genine Hopkins, Reporter, phone: (989)539-1352; Dale Price, Specialist, Advertising and Sales, phone: (989)620-7980. **Subscription Rates:** $24 Individuals Clare County; $26 Out of area; $48 Two years Clare County; $52 Out of area two years; $24 Individuals online. **URL:** http://clarecountycleaver.net; http://clarecountycleaver.net/subdept.html. **Mailing address:** PO Box 436, Harrison, MI 48625. **Remarks:** Advertising accepted; rates available upon request. **Circ:** (Not Reported).

HARRISVILLE

Alcona Co. Alcona Co. (NE). On Lake Huron, 30 m S of Alpena. Nurseries. Precision tool factories. Sand and gravel plants. Agriculture. Dairy and beef cattle.

17540 ■ Alcona County Review
Alcona County Review
111 Lake St.
Harrisville, MI 48740
Phone: (989)724-6384
Fax: (989)724-6655
Free: 877-873-8439
Publisher's E-mail: editor@alconareview.com
Community newspaper. **Freq:** Weekly (Wed.). **Print Method:** Web. **Trim Size:** 11 1/2. **Cols./Page:** 5. **Col. Width:** 2 inches. **Col. Depth:** 16 inches. **Key Personnel:** John D. Boufford, Manager, Production; Cheryl L. Peterson, Editor; Eileen Roe, Manager, Circulation. **USPS:** 001-290. **Subscription Rates:** $25 Individuals; $47 Two years; $32 Out of area; $61 Out of area two years; $29 Individuals snowbird; $55 Two years snowbird; $20 Individuals online. **Alt. Formats:** PDF. **Mailing address:** PO Box 548, Harrisville, MI 48740. **Ad Rates:** BW $520; PCI $6.50. **Remarks:** Accepts advertising. **Circ:** ‡3,400.

HART

Oceana Co. Oceana Co. (W). 37 m N of Muskegon. Summer & winter resort. Manufactures canned goods. Frozen fruit & vegetable packing plants. Agriculture. Cherries, prunes, plums, apples, asparagus, beans, douglas firs.

17541 ■ Oceana's Herald-Journal
Oceana's Herald
123 S State St.
Hart, MI 49420-0190
Phone: (231)873-5602
Publication E-mail: info@oceanheraldjournal.com
Community newspaper. **Freq:** Weekly (Thurs.). **Print Method:** Offset. **Trim Size:** 15 x 22. **Cols./Page:** 6. **Col. Width:** 13 picas. **Col. Depth:** 21 inches. **Key Personnel:** Mary Sanford, Editor, phone: (231)873-5602; Julie Payment, Manager, Circulation. **Subscription Rates:** $43.50 Individuals Oceana County; $50 Out of area; $59 Out of state; $43.50 Individuals e-Edition; $1.25 Single issue. **URL:** http://www.shorelinemedia.net/oceanas_herald_journal. **Ad Rates:** BW $768.60; 4C $976.80; PCI $6.10. **Remarks:** Accepts advertising. **Circ:** ‡7,560.

17542 ■ WCXT-FM
220 Polk
Hart, MI 49420
Phone: (269)925-1111
Fax: (269)925-1011
Format: Adult Contemporary. **Founded:** 1983. **Key Personnel:** Mark Waters, Dir. of Programs. **Wattage:** 3,700 ERP. **URL:** http://www.983thecoast.com.

HASLETT

Ingham Co. (S). 5m E of Lansing. Residential.

17543 ■ Michigan Florist: A publication of the Michigan Floral Association
Michigan Floral Association
1152 Haslett Rd.
Haslett, MI 48840
Phone: (517)575-0110
Fax: (517)575-0115
Magazine for retail florists, wholesalers and growers; covering products, industry services, floral arrangements, floral business, and related concerns. **Freq:** Bimonthly. **Print Method:** Offset. **Trim Size:** 8 1/2 x 11. **Cols./Page:** 3. **Col. Width:** 2 1/4 inches. **Col. Depth:** 10 inches. **Key Personnel:** Heidi Anderson, Editor. **ISSN:** 0026-217X (print). **Subscription Rates:** $50 Members; $5 Single issue. **URL:** http://www.michiganfloral.org. **Ad Rates:** BW $720; 4C $995. **Remarks:** Accepts advertising. **Circ:** Controlled ‡1500.

HASTINGS

Barry Co. Barry Co. (SW). 26 m NW of Battle Creek. Lake resort. Manufactures piston rings, oil additives, commercial presses, railroad car seals, sprinkler equipment, furniture, machinery, fiber glass products, awnings, aluminum die castings and siding. Diversified farming.

17544 ■ WBCH-AM - 1220
119 W State St.
Hastings, MI 49058
Phone: (269)945-3414
Free: 800-523-1872
Email: wbch@wbch.com
Format: Hot Country. **Networks:** ABC; Westwood One Radio. **Owner:** WBCH AM, 119 W State St., Hastings, MI 49058, Ph: (269)945-3414, Free: 800-523-1872. **Founded:** 1958. **Operating Hours:** Continuous. **ADI:** Grand Rapids-Kalamazoo-Battle Creek, MI. **Wattage:** 250. **Ad Rates:** Advertising accepted; rates available upon request. **Mailing address:** PO Box 88, Hastings, MI 49058. **URL:** http://www.wbch.com.

17545 ■ WBCH-FM - 100.1
119 W State St.
Hastings, MI 49058
Phone: (269)945-3414
Free: 800-523-1872
Email: wbch@wbch.com
Format: Country. **Networks:** ABC. **Owner:** Barry Broadcasting Co., at above address. **Founded:** 1958. **Operating Hours:** Continuous. **ADI:** Grand Rapids-Kalamazoo-Battle Creek, MI. **Wattage:** 3,000. **Ad Rates:** Noncommercial. **Mailing address:** PO Box 88, Hastings, MI 49058. **URL:** http://www.wbch.com.

HIGHLAND

Oakland Co.

17546 ■ Minas Tirith Evening Star
American Tolkien Society
PO Box 97
Highland, MI 48357
Publication E-mail: editor@americantolkiensociety.org
Journal covering issues related to the author J.R.R. Tolkien. **Freq:** Quarterly. **ISSN:** 1063--0848 (print). **Subscription Rates:** Included in membership. **Alt. Formats:** PDF. **URL:** http://www.americantolkiensociety.org/MTES.htm. **Remarks:** Advertising accepted; rates available upon request. **Circ:** (Not Reported).

HIGHLAND PARK

Wayne Co.

17547 ■ WHPR-FM - 88.1
15851 Woodward Ave.
Highland Park, MI 48203
Phone: (313)868-6612
Format: Music of Your Life; Talk. **Owner:** R.J.'s Late Night Entertainment Corp., at above address. **Founded:** 1954. **Operating Hours:** Continuous. **Key Personnel:** R.J. Watkins, Contact; Geo. Hutcherson, Contact; Henry Tyler, Contact. **Wattage:** 044 ERP. **URL:** http://www.fm881whpr.com.

HILLSDALE

Hillsdale Co. Hillsdale Co. (S). 33 m S of Jackson. Hillsdale College. Lake resort. Manufactures automotive stereo speakers, personal shower, plastic products, dies, tools, fixtures, flour products, sausage, sealants and adhesives, automotive parts, auto paint test panels, playground equipment, stadium lights, recreation equipment. Agriculture.

17548 ■ Hillsdale Daily News
GateHouse Media Inc.
33 McCollum St.
Hillsdale, MI 49242-0287
Phone: (517)437-7351
General newspaper. **Freq:** Daily. **Print Method:** Offset. **Trim Size:** 13 3/4 x 22 3/4. **Cols./Page:** 6. **Col. Width:** 2 1/16 inches. **Col. Depth:** 21 1/2 inches. **Key Personnel:** Roxanne Morgret, Manager, Circulation, phone: (517)437-7351; Michael Clutter, Editor; David Ferro, Publisher. **USPS:** 245-700. **Subscription Rates:** $4.99 Individuals monthly; $2.21 Individuals digital - weekly. **URL:** http://www.hillsdale.net. **Remarks:** Accepts advertising. **Circ:** (Not Reported).

17549 ■ WCSR-AM - 1340
PO Box 273
Hillsdale, MI 49242
Phone: (517)437-4444
Fax: (517)437-7461
Format: Adult Contemporary; Full Service. **Networks:** AP. **Owner:** WCSR Inc., 170 N West St., Hillsdale, MI 49242-1224. **Founded:** 1955. **Operating Hours:** Continuous. **ADI:** Lansing (Ann Arbor), MI. **Key Personnel:** Russell Martin, News Dir.; Mike Flynn, Gen. Mgr., VP. **Wattage:** 500 Day; 250 Night. **Ad Rates:** $11-18.25 for 30 seconds; $13.75-22.50 for 60 seconds. **URL:** http://www.radiohillsdale.com.

17550 ■ WCSR-FM - 92.1
PO Box 273
Hillsdale, MI 49242
Phone: (517)437-4444
Fax: (517)437-7461
Email: wcsrinc@comcast.net
Format: Adult Contemporary. **Networks:** AP. **Owner:** WCSR Inc., 170 N West St., Hillsdale, MI 49242-1224. **Founded:** 1955. **Operating Hours:** Continuous; 99% local, 1% network. **ADI:** Lansing (Ann Arbor), MI. **Key Personnel:** Russell Martin, News Dir.; Mike Flynn, Gen. Mgr., VP. **Wattage:** 6,000. **Ad Rates:** $11-18.25 for 30 seconds; $13.75-22.50 for 60 seconds. **URL:** http://www.radiohillsdale.com.

HOLLAND

Ottawa Co. Ottawa Co. (W). On Macatawa Bay, 25 m SW of Grand Rapids. Lake resort. Hope College; Western Theological Seminary. Manufactures mobile home furnaces, office furniture, boats, canned goods, springs, floor clocks, chemicals, die castings, bearings, bolts, novelties, concrete, woodworking machinery, metal, lifesavers. Hatcheries. Agriculture. Celery, onions, fruit, tulip bulbs.

17551 ■ Group Tour Magazine Northeastern Region
Group Tour Media
2465 112th Ave.
Holland, MI 49424-9657
Phone: (616)393-2077
Fax: (616)393-0085
Free: 800-767-3489
Trade magazine covering the regional group tour industry. **Freq:** Quarterly February, May, August and November. **Print Method:** Web press. **Trim Size:** 8.875 x 11.25. **Key Personnel:** David Hoekman, Managing Editor; Amanda Black, Writer. **Subscription Rates:** Free. **URL:** http://www.grouptour.com/magazine/group-tour-magazine. **Formerly:** Group Tour Magazine New England Region. **Ad Rates:** 4C $5590. **Remarks:** Accepts advertising. **Circ:** Controlled 15184.

17552 ■ Group Tour Magazine Southeastern Region
Group Tour Media
2465 112th Ave.
Holland, MI 49424-9657
Phone: (616)393-2077
Fax: (616)393-0085
Free: 800-767-3489
Trade magazine covering the regional group tour industry. **Freq:** Quarterly March, June, September and December. **Print Method:** Web press. **Trim Size:** 8.375 x 11.25. **Key Personnel:** David Hoekman, Managing Editor. **Subscription Rates:** Free. **URL:** http://www.

grouptour.com/magazine/group-tour-magazine. **Ad Rates:** 4C $5760. **Remarks:** Accepts advertising. **Circ:** Controlled 15184.

17553 ■ Group Tour Magazine Western Region
Group Tour Media
2465 112th Ave.
Holland, MI 49424-9657
Phone: (616)393-2077
Fax: (616)393-0085
Free: 800-767-3489
Trade magazine covering the regional group tour industry. **Freq:** Quarterly January, April, July and October. **Print Method:** Web press. **Key Personnel:** David Hoekman, Managing Editor; Rick Martinez, Editor. **Subscription Rates:** Free. **URL:** http://www.grouptour.com/magazine/group-tour-magazine. **Ad Rates:** 4C $5760. **Remarks:** Accepts advertising. **Circ:** Controlled 15361.

17554 ■ Student Group Tour Magazine
Group Tour Media
2465 112th Ave.
Holland, MI 49424-9657
Phone: (616)393-2077
Fax: (616)393-0085
Free: 800-767-3489
Magazine covering group tour opportunities for student groups. **Freq:** 3/year. **Key Personnel:** David Hoekman, Managing Editor; Elly Devries, Publisher. **Subscription Rates:** Free to active group youth travel planner. **URL:** http://www.studentgrouptourmagazine.com. **Ad Rates:** BW $6,160. **Remarks:** Accepts advertising. **Circ:** Combined 16126.

17555 ■ WHTC-AM - 1450
87 Central Ave.
Holland, MI 49423
Phone: (616)392-3121
Fax: (616)392-8066
Format: Full Service. **Networks:** CBS. **Owner:** Midwest Communications Inc., 904 Grand Ave., Wausau, WI 54403, Ph: (715)842-1437, Fax: (715)842-7061. **Founded:** 1948. **Operating Hours**: Continuous Daily; 5% network, 95% local. **ADI**: Grand Rapids-Kalamazoo-Battle Creek, MI. **Key Personnel:** Gary Stevens, News Dir. **Local Programs:** *Words Of Hope*, Sunday 8:00 a.m.; *The VanHoutons*, Sunday 8:45 a.m. - 9:00 a.m.; *Trinity Church Service*, Sunday 9:30 a.m. - 10:45 a.m.; *Hope Church Service*, Sunday 11:00 a.m. - 12:00 p.m.; *Red's Place*, Saturday 6:00 a.m. - 7:00 a.m.; *WHTC Outdoor Show*, Saturday 7:00 a.m. - 8:00 a.m.; *WHTC Computer Talk*, Saturday 8:00 a.m. - 9:00 a.m.; *Talk of the Town*, Monday Tuesday Wednesday Thursday Friday 9:30 a.m. - 11:30 a.m. **Wattage**: 1,000. **Ad Rates:** $25 for 30 seconds; $29 for 60 seconds. **URL:** http://www.whtc.com.

17556 ■ WTHS-FM - 89.9
PO Box 9000
Holland, MI 49422-9000
Phone: (616)395-7878
Email: wths@hope.edu
Format: Full Service; Alternative/New Music/Progressive. **Networks:** Mutual Broadcasting System. **Founded:** 1956. **Formerly**: WTAS-FM. **Operating Hours**: Continuous. **Key Personnel:** Dave Murray, Advisor, Operator, murrayd@hope.edu; Kevin Watson, Gen. Mgr., kevin.watson@hope.edu; Jack Miller, Dir. of Production. **Wattage**: 1,000. **Ad Rates:** Noncommercial. **URL:** http://wths.hope.edu.

17557 ■ WYVN-FM - 92.7
87 Central Ave.
Holland, MI 49423
Phone: (616)392-3121
Fax: (616)392-8066
Format: Classic Rock. **Owner:** Midwest Communications Inc., 904 Grand Ave., Wausau, WI 54403, Ph: (715)842-1437, Fax: (715)842-7061. **Key Personnel:** Gary Stevens, News Dir., g.stevens@mwcradio.com; Brent Alan, Contact, brent.alan@mwcradio.com; Kevin Oswald, Contact, kevin.oswald@mwcradio.com. **Ad Rates:** Advertising accepted; rates available upon request. **URL:** http://www.927thevan.com.

HOLT

17558 ■ WJXQ-FM - 106.1
2495 Cedar St.
Holt, MI 48842
Phone: (517)363-2106
Fax: (517)699-1880
Format: Album-Oriented Rock (AOR); Classic Rock; Heavy Metal. **Key Personnel:** Scott Truman, Sales Mgr., scott.truman@mwcradio.com. **URL:** http://www.q106fm.com.

17559 ■ WJZL-FM - 92.9
2495 Cedar St.
Holt, MI 48842
Email: wjzl@wjzlonline.com
Format: Jazz. **Key Personnel:** Scott Truman, Sales Mgr., struman@mmrglansing.com; Drew Henderson, Dir. of Programs, dhenderson@mmrglansing.com. **Ad Rates:** Advertising accepted; rates available upon request. **URL:** http://929wlmi.com.

17560 ■ WQTX-FM - 92.1
2495 Cedar St.
Holt, MI 48842
Phone: (517)699-0111
Fax: (517)699-1880
Free: 866-360-4487
Format: Country. **Owner:** Rubber City Radio Group, 1795 W Market St., Akron, OH 44313, Ph: (330)370-2000, Free: 800-589-6499. **Ad Rates:** Advertising accepted; rates available upon request. **URL:** http://www.big921.com.

17561 ■ WVIC-FM - 94.1
2495 N Cedar St.
Holt, MI 48842
Phone: (517)699-0111
Fax: (517)699-1880
Format: Soft Rock. **Owner:** Midwest Communications Inc., 904 Grand Ave., Wausau, WI 54403, Ph: (715)842-1437, Fax: (715)842-7061. **Founded:** Dec. 1993. **Formerly**: WIBM-FM; WBHR-FM; WXIK-FM. **Operating Hours**: Continuous. **ADI**: Lansing (Ann Arbor), MI. **Wattage**: 50,000. **Ad Rates:** Noncommercial. **URL:** http://www.941wvic.com.

HOMER

Calhoun Co. Calhoun Co. (S). 23 m SW of Jackson. Manufactures plastics, custom packaging machines. Foundry. Machine shop. Farming. Wheat, corn, hay.

17562 ■ The Homer Index
The Homer Index
119 W Main St.
Homer, MI 49245
Community newspaper. **Freq:** Weekly (Wed.). **Print Method:** Offset. **Trim Size:** 13 x 21 1/2. **Cols./Page:** 6. **Col. Width:** 26 nonpareils. **Col. Depth:** 308 agate lines. **Key Personnel:** Sharon Warner, General Manager, Manager, Advertising; Mike Warner, Editor, Manager, Advertising and Sales, Publisher; Portia Hyde, Compositor; Mike Clutter, Editor. **ISSN:** 0891-1398 (print). **Subscription Rates:** $30 Individuals print or online; $36 Individuals Calhoun or Hillsdale County MI (print and online); $39 Individuals Outside Calhoun or Hillsdale County MI (print and online); $33 Individuals Outside Calhoun or Hillsdale County MI (print only). **URL:** http://www.homerindex.com. **Ad Rates:** GLR $.14; BW $327.60; SAU $3.06; PCI $2.60. **Remarks:** Accepts advertising. **Circ:** 1,700.

HOUGHTON

Houghton Co. Houghton Co. (NW Up. Penin.). On Portage Lake, with ship canal to Lake Superior. Michigan Technological University, Suomi College. Summer & winter recreation Lumber mills. Fisheries. Copper mines. Farming.

17563 ■ The Daily Mining Gazette
The Daily Mining Gazette
PO Box 368
Houghton, MI 49931
Phone: (906)482-1500
Fax: (906)482-2726
Free: 800-682-7607
General newspaper. **Freq:** Mon.-Sat. except New Year's Day, Thanksgiving and Christmas. **Print Method:** Offset. **Trim Size:** 13 x 21 1/2. **Cols./Page:** 6. **Col. Width:** 27 nonpareils. **Col. Depth:** 301 agate lines. **Key Personnel:** Larry Holcombe, Managing Editor, phone: (906)483-2210; Michael Scott, Publisher, phone: (906)483-2230; Yvonne Robillard, Manager, Advertising, phone: (906)483-2220. **Subscription Rates:** $205.40 Individuals for 52 weeks Monday through Saturday home delivery, carrier + Digital; $17.15 Individuals Monday through Saturday home delivery, carrier - Easy Pay + Digital; $23 By mail Monday through Saturday home delivery, mail - Easy Pay + Digital; $68.90 Individuals Monday through Saturday home delivery, USPS mail + Digital. **Ad Rates:** PCI $15.45. **Remarks:** Accepts advertising. **Circ:** Mon.-Fri. ★**8,672**, Sat. ★**8,670**.

17564 ■ IEEE Engineering in Medicine and Biology Magazine
Institute of Electrical and Electronics Engineers
Michigan Technological University
Department of Biomedical Engineering
1400 Townsend Dr.
Houghton, MI 49931
Phone: (906)487-2772
Fax: (906)487-1717
Publisher's E-mail: society-info@ieee.org
Professional magazine covering engineering in medicine and biology. **Founded:** Mar. 1982. **Freq:** Bimonthly. **Print Method:** Web offset, saddle-stitch. **Trim Size:** 7-7/8 X 10-3/4. **Key Personnel:** Michael Neuman, Editor-in-Chief. **ISSN:** 0739-5175 (print). **URL:** http://ieeexplore.ieee.org/xpl/RecentIssue.jsp?punumber=51. **Remarks:** Accepts advertising. **Circ:** Paid ‡7983.

17565 ■ Michigan Tech Lode
Michigan Technological University
1400 Townsend Dr.
Houghton, MI 49931-1295
Phone: (906)487-1885
Collegiate newspaper. **Freq:** Weekly. **Print Method:** Offset. **Trim Size:** 2 x 21. **Cols./Page:** 6. **Col. Width:** 2 INS. **Col. Depth:** 21 1/2 INS. **Key Personnel:** Erika Peabody, Editor-in-Chief; Cameron Schwach, Editor; Abhishek Gupta, Business Manager. **Subscription Rates:** Free. **URL:** http://www.mtulode.com. **Ad Rates:** PCI $10; BW $230; 4C $320. **Remarks:** Advertising accepted; rates available upon request. **Circ:** Free 5,000.

17566 ■ Mineral Processing and Extractive Metallurgy Review
Taylor & Francis Group Journals
c/o Komar S. Kawatra, Ed.-in-Ch.
Chemical Engineering Dept.
Michigan Technological University
1400 Townsend Dr.
Houghton, MI 49931
Fax: (906)487-3213
Publisher's E-mail: customerservice@taylorandfrancis.com
Journal publishing papers dealing with both applied and theoretical aspects of extractive and process metallurgy and mineral processing. **Freq:** 6/year. **Key Personnel:** Francis W. Petersen, Board Member; Hassan El-Shall, Board Member; Komar S. Kawatra, Editor-in-Chief; Cyril O'Connor, Board Member; Dimitrios Panias, Board Member; Hanumantha Rao Kota, Board Member. **ISSN:** 0882--7508 (print); **EISSN:** 1547--7401 (electronic). **Subscription Rates:** $964 Individuals print only; $3051 Institutions online only; $3487 Institutions print and online. **URL:** http://www.tandfonline.com/toc/gmpr20/current. **Circ:** (Not Reported).

17567 ■ Sensor Letters
American Scientific Publishers
c/o Dr. Keat G. Ong, Ed.
Michigan Technological University
1400 Townsend Dr.
Houghton, MI 49931
Publisher's E-mail: order@aspbs.com
Peer-reviewed journal covering the fundamental and applied research aspects on sensor science and technology in all fields of science, engineering and medicine. **Freq:** Monthly. **Key Personnel:** Dr. Keat G. Ong, Editor; Prof. Ahmad Umar, PhD, Editor-in-Chief. **ISSN:** 1546--198X (print); **EISSN:** 1546--1971 (electronic). **URL:** http://www.aspbs.com/sensorlett. **Remarks:** Advertising not accepted. **Circ:** (Not Reported).

Circulation: ★ = AAM; △ or • = BPA; ♦ = CAC; ❑ = VAC; ⊕ = PO Statement; ‡ = Publisher's Report; Boldface figures = sworn; Light figures = estimated.

17568 ■ Houghton Broadcasting
313 E Montezuma Ave.
Houghton, MI 49931
Phone: (906)482-7700
Fax: (906)482-7751
Key Personnel: Jeff Harju, Gen. Mgr., jharju@up.net; Kevin Ericson, Traffic Mgr.; Sarah Rousseau, Office Mgr. **URL:** http://www.kbear102.com.

17569 ■ WCCY-AM - 1400
313 Montezuma Ave.
Houghton, MI 49931-2112
Phone: (906)482-7700
Fax: (906)482-7751
Free: 800-320-0137
Format: News; Sports. **Networks:** ABC. **Owner:** Heartland Communications Group L.L.C., 909 N Railroad St., Eagle River, WI 54521, Ph: (920)882-4750, Fax: (920)882-4751. **Founded:** 1929. **Formerly**: WHDF-AM. **Operating Hours:** Continuous; 20% network, 80% local. **ADI**: Marquette, MI. **Key Personnel:** Sarah Rousseau, Office Mgr.; Kevin Ericson, Operations Mgr., Prog. Dir.; Jeff Harju, Gen. Mgr., jharju@up.net. **Wattage**: 1,000. **Ad Rates:** $7.50-11.90 for 60 seconds. **URL:** http://www.wccy.com.

17570 ■ WHKB-FM - 102.3
313 E Montezuma Ave.
Houghton, MI 49931
Phone: (906)482-7700
Fax: (906)482-7751
Format: Country. **Key Personnel:** Kevin Ericson, Operations Mgr., Traffic Mgr., Dir. of Programs; Jeff Harju, Gen. Mgr., jharju@up.net; Sarah Rousseau, Office Mgr., houghtonradio@up.net. **Wattage**: 6,000. **Ad Rates:** Noncommercial. **URL:** http://www.kbear102.com.

17571 ■ WMTU-FM - 91.9
G03 Wadsworth Hall
1703 Townsend Dr.
Houghton, MI 49931-1193
Phone: (906)487-2333
Format: Eclectic. **Ad Rates:** Noncommercial. **URL:** http://www.wmtu.mtu.edu.

17572 ■ WOLV-FM - 97.7
313 E Montezuma Ave.
Houghton, MI 49931
Phone: (906)482-7700
Fax: (906)482-7751
Format: Adult Contemporary. **Owner:** Houghton Broadcasting, 313 E Montezuma Ave., Houghton, MI 49931, Ph: (906)482-7700, Fax: (906)482-7751. **Founded:** 1981. **Formerly**: WHUH-FM; WOLF-FM. **Operating Hours:** Continuous. **ADI**: Marquette, MI. **Key Personnel:** Jeff Harju, Gen. Mgr., jharju@up.net; Kevin Ericson, Operations Mgr.; Sarah Rousseau, Office Mgr. **Wattage**: 6,500. **Ad Rates:** $10-16.50 for 60 seconds. **URL:** http://www.thewolf.com.

17573 ■ W27CQ - 27
PO Box A
Santa Ana, CA 92711
Phone: (714)832-2950
Free: 888-731-1000
Owner: Trinity Broadcasting Network Inc., PO Box A, Santa Ana, CA 92711, Ph: (714)832-2950, Free: 888-731-1000.

HOUGHTON LAKE

Roscommon Co. (NC). On Houghton Lake, 65 m NW of Bay City. Resort.

17574 ■ The Houghton Lake Resorter
The Houghton Lake Resorter
PO Box 248
Houghton Lake, MI 48629
Phone: (989)366-5341
Fax: (989)366-4472
Publisher's E-mail: news@houghtonlakeresorter.com
Local newspaper. **Freq:** Weekly (Thurs.). **Print Method:** Offset. **Trim Size:** 14 x 22 3/4. **Cols./Page:** 6. **Col. Width:** 24 nonpareils. **Col. Depth:** 301 agate lines. **Key Personnel:** Thomas W. Hamp, Editor; Eric M. Hamp, Managing Editor; Patty Tribelhorn, Manager, Advertising. **Subscription Rates:** $25 Individuals; $30 Out of area; $.75 Single issue. **Ad Rates:** GLR $.34; BW $774; 4C $1301; SAU $6; PCI $6.80. **Remarks:** Accepts classified advertising. **Circ:** ‡12,000.

HOWELL

Livingston Co. Livingston Co. (SE). 50 m NW of Detroit. Manufactures asphalt, metal abrasives and castings, chemicals, building supplies, dies, auto parts and accessories. Truck farming. Horse breeding.

17575 ■ Great Lakes Christmas Tree Journal
Michigan Christmas Tree Association
c/o Marsha Gray, Executive Director
PO Box 377
Howell, MI 48844
Phone: (517)545-9971
Fax: (517)545-4501
Free: 800-589-8733
Magazine of the Michigan Christmas Tree Assn. **Freq:** Quarterly January, April, July and October. **Cols./Page:** 3. **Col. Width:** 2 1/4 INS. **Col. Depth:** 10 INS. **Key Personnel:** Marsha Gray, Editor, Executive Director. **Subscription Rates:** $25 Nonmembers Ontario, Illinois, Indiana and Michigan; Included in membership. **URL:** http://www.mcta.org/members/great-lakes-journal. **Formerly**: Michigan Christmas Tree Journal. **Ad Rates:** BW $375; 4C $750; PCI $25. **Remarks:** Advertising accepted; rates available upon request. **Circ:** 1,200.

17576 ■ Home Town News
Hometown Newspapers
323 E Grand River
Howell, MI 48843
Phone: (517)548-2000
Publisher's E-mail: calendar@livingstondaily.com
Community newspaper. **Freq:** Weekly. **URL:** http://www.hometownnews.com. **Circ:** Paid 10503, Free 11321.

17577 ■ Livingston County Press and Argus
Hometown Newspapers
323 E Grand River
Howell, MI 48843
Phone: (517)548-2000
Publisher's E-mail: calendar@livingstondaily.com
Community newspaper. **Freq:** Weekly (Wed.). **Print Method:** Offset. **Trim Size:** 13 3/4 x 22 1/2. **Cols./Page:** 6. **Col. Width:** 2 1/16 inches. **Col. Depth:** 21 1/2 inches. **Subscription Rates:** $14 Single issue Sunday thru Friday per month; $7.75 Single issue Sundays. **Ad Rates:** BW $1,200; 4C $1,400; SAU $9.30; PCI $9.30. **Remarks:** Accepts advertising. **Circ:** Mon.-Fri. ★**14234**, Sun. ★**16715**.

17578 ■ The Vintage Triumph
Vintage Triumph Register
PO Box 655
Howell, MI 48844
Freq: Bimonthly. **URL:** http://www.vtr.org/tvt. **Remarks:** Advertising not accepted. **Circ:** (Not Reported).

17579 ■ WHMI-FM - 93.5
1277 Parkway Dr.
Howell, MI 48843
Phone: (517)546-0860
Fax: (517)546-1758
Free: 888-946-4935
Email: whmi@whmi.com
Format: Adult Contemporary; News; Sports. **Networks:** ABC. **Owner:** Livingston Radio Company Inc., at above address. **Founded:** 1977. **Operating Hours:** Continuous. **ADI:** Detroit, MI. **Key Personnel:** Debbie Platt, Sales Mgr., dplatt@whmi.com. **Wattage:** 5,200. **Ad Rates:** Advertising accepted; rates available upon request. **Mailing address:** PO Box 935, Howell, MI 48843. **URL:** http://www.whmi.com.

HUDSON

Lenawee Co. Lenawee Co. (S). 19 m W of Adrian. Manufactures screw machine products, aluminum castings. Irrigation system and diversified farming.

17580 ■ Bi-County Herald
Bi-County Herald
115 S Church St.
Hudson, MI 49247
Phone: (517)448-2201
Publication E-mail: bch@tc3net.com
Shopper. **Freq:** Weekly (Tues.). **Print Method:** Offset. **Cols./Page:** 8. **Col. Width:** 20 nonpareils. **Col. Depth:** 301 agate lines. **Subscription Rates:** Free; $25 By mail. **Alt. Formats:** CD-ROM. **URL:** http://www.bicountyherald.com/cms. **Ad Rates:** GLR $3.75; SAU $3; GLR $6.45; BW $4.60. **Remarks:** Accepts advertising. **Circ:** Free ‡12442.

17581 ■ Hudson Post Gazette
Hudson Post Gazette
113 S Market St.
Hudson, MI 49247
Phone: (517)448-2611
Community newspaper. **Freq:** Weekly (Thurs.). **Key Personnel:** Wes Boyd, Editor; Amanda Boyd, Business Manager; Bill Mullaly, Reporter. **USPS:** 253-600. **Subscription Rates:** $25 Individuals in Lenawee and Hillsdale Counties print; $28 Elsewhere print; $18 Individuals Online only - 1 year. **Alt. Formats:** PDF. **URL:** http://www.hudsonpg.com. **Mailing address:** PO Box 70, Hudson, MI 49247. **Ad Rates:** SAU $4.50. **Remarks:** Accepts advertising. **Circ:** 2,000.

INDIAN RIVER

Cheboygan Co. (N). 22 m W of Petoskey. Resort. Boating. Light manufacturing.

17582 ■ WTCK-FM - 90.9
7119 M-68
Indian River, MI 49749
Phone: (231)238-8500
Fax: (231)238-0803
Format: Religious. **Owner:** Baraga Broadcasting Inc., at above address, Traverse City, MI 49684. **Operating Hours:** Continuous. **Key Personnel:** Brian Brachel, Station Mgr., wavetech@chartermi.net; Fr. Harry Speckman, President, frharry@utmi.net; Tom McMahon, Contact, tom@utmi.net; Tom McMahon, Contact, tom@utmi.net. **URL:** http://www.baragabroadcasting.com.

W236BZ-FM - See Mackinaw City

W221CA-FM - See Gaylord

INTERLOCHEN

17583 ■ Grand Traverse Woman
Grand Traverse Woman L.L.C.
2492 Reynolds Rd.
Interlochen, MI 49643
Phone: (231)276-5105
Publisher's E-mail: info@grandtraversewoman.com
Magazine that aims to serve women ages 25 and older who live, work and play in Northern Michigan with articles on health, family, career, and education. **Freq:** Bimonthly. **Trim Size:** 10 x 13. **Key Personnel:** Kandace Chapple, Editor, phone: (231)275-3134; Kerry Winkler, Account Manager, Publisher. **Mailing address:** PO Box 22, Interlochen, MI 49643. **Ad Rates:** BW $745. **Remarks:** Accepts advertising. **Circ:** 10000.

17584 ■ WIAA-FM - 88.7
9900 Diamond Park Rd.
Interlochen, MI 49643-0199
Phone: (231)276-7472
Fax: (231)276-7464
Free: 800-681-5912
Email: ipr@interlochen.org
Format: Classical. **Simulcasts:** WIZY-FM. **Networks:** Michigan Public Radio; Public Radio International (PRI); National Public Radio (NPR); AP. **Owner:** Interlochen Center for the Arts, 9900 Diamond Park Rd., Interlochen, MI 49643, Ph: (231)276-7200, Free: 800-681-5912. **Founded:** 1963. **Operating Hours:** Continuous. **Wattage:** 100,000. **Ad Rates:** Noncommercial. **Mailing address:** PO Box 199, Interlochen, MI 49643-0199. **URL:** http://www.interlochen.org.

17585 ■ WIAB-FM - 88.5
PO Box 199
Interlochen, MI 49643-0199
Phone: (231)276-4400
Fax: (231)276-4417
Email: ipr@interlochen.org
Format: News; Public Radio; Classical. **Owner:** Interlochen Center for the Arts, 9900 Diamond Park Rd., Interlochen, MI 49643, Ph: (231)276-7200, Free: 800-681-5912. **Ad Rates:** Advertising accepted; rates available upon request. **URL:** http://www.interlochen.org.

17586 ■ WICA-FM - 91.5
PO Box 199
Interlochen, MI 49643-0199
Phone: (231)276-4400
Fax: (231)276-4417
Free: 800-441-9422
Email: ipr@interlochen.org

Format: News. **Networks:** National Public Radio (NPR); Public Radio International (PRI); Michigan Public Radio. **Owner:** Interlochen Public Radio, 9350 Lyon St., Interlochen, MI 49643-0199, Free: 800-441-9422. **Founded:** Sept. 2000. **Operating Hours:** Continuous. **Key Personnel:** Thom Paulson, Gen. Mgr., VP, paulsontm@interlochen.org; Peter Payette, News Dir., payettepc@interlochen.org. **URL:** http://interlochenpublicradio.org.

17587 ■ WICV-FM - 100.9
PO Box 199
Interlochen, MI 49643-0199
Phone: (231)276-4400
Fax: (231)276-4417
Email: ipr@interlochen.org
Format: Classical. **Networks:** National Public Radio (NPR); Public Radio International (PRI); Michigan Public Radio. **Owner:** Interlochen Center for the Arts, 9900 Diamond Park Rd., Interlochen, MI 49643, Ph: (231)276-7200, Free: 800-681-5912. **Founded:** 1989. **Operating Hours:** Continuous. **Key Personnel:** Thom Paulson, Gen. Mgr., VP, paulsontm@interlochen.org; Peter Payette, News Dir., payettepc@interlochen.org. **URL:** http://interlochenpublicradio.org.

IONIA

Ionia Co. Ionia Co. (C). 5 m N of Saranar.

17588 ■ Sentinel-Standard
Liberty Group Michigan Holdings Inc.
114 N Depot St.
Ionia, MI 48846
Phone: (616)527-2100
General newspaper. **Founded:** 1866. **Freq:** Daily except Monday and Sunday and six postal holidays. **Key Personnel:** Cindy Conrad, Publisher, phone: (616)527-2100; Lori Kilchermann, Editor. **Subscription Rates:** $99 Individuals; $120 Out of country. **URL:** http://www.sentinel-standard.com. **Remarks:** Accepts advertising. **Circ:** (Not Reported).

17589 ■ WION-AM - 1430
1150 Haynor Rd.
Ionia, MI 48846
Phone: (616)527-9466
Fax: (616)775-5908
Email: office@i1430.com
Format: News; Middle-of-the-Road (MOR). **Networks:** ABC; Jones Satellite. **Owner:** Packer Radio WION LLC, at above address. **Founded:** 1953. **Operating Hours:** Continuous; 60% network, 40% local. **Key Personnel:** Jim Carlyle, Mgr., carlyle@i1430.com; Jim Aaron, Music Dir. **Wattage:** 5,000. **Ad Rates:** $8-15 for 30 seconds; $10-20 for 60 seconds. **URL:** http://www.i1430.com.

IRON MOUNTAIN

Dickinson Co. Dickinson Co. (SW Up. Penin.) 53 m NW of Escanaba. Summer resort. Chemicals, lumber, mine and marine machinery manufactured. Pulp mill, timber. Dairy, fruit, truck farms. Potatoes, hay, apples.

17590 ■ Northside TV Corp.
521 Vulcan St.
Iron Mountain, MI 49801
Phone: (906)774-1351
Email: voipsupport@ccisystems.com
Cities Served: 58 channels. **URL:** http://www.upnorthcable.com.

17591 ■ WIMK-FM - 93.1
101 E Kent St.
Iron Mountain, MI 49801
Phone: (906)774-4321
Fax: (906)774-7799
Format: Classic Rock. **Operating Hours:** Continuous. **Key Personnel:** Dennise Bakran, Account Mgr. **Ad Rates:** Advertising accepted; rates available upon request. **URL:** http://www.rockthebear.com.

17592 ■ WJNR-FM - 101.5
212 W J St.
Iron Mountain, MI 49801-4646
Free: 800-742-5507
Format: Full Service; Country. **Owner:** Results Broadcasting Inc., 1456 E Green Bay St., Shawano, WI 54166, Ph: (715)524-2194, Fax: (715)524-9980, Free: 800-236-9824. **Operating Hours:** Continuous. **Key Personnel:** Trisha Peterson, Gen. Mgr. **Ad Rates:** Advertising accepted; rates available upon request. **URL:** http://www.frogcountry.com.

17593 ■ WMIQ-AM - 1450
101 E Kent St.
Iron Mountain, MI 49801
Phone: (906)774-4321
Fax: (906)779-7799
Format: News; Talk; Sports. **Owner:** Northern Star Broadcasting L.L.C., 514 Munson Ave., MI 49686. **Founded:** 1947. **Operating Hours:** 5:00 a.m. - 8:00 p.m. Monday - Friday. **Wattage:** 1,000 KW. **Ad Rates:** $2-8 for 15 seconds; $3-10 for 30 seconds; $4.50-13 for 60 seconds. Combined advertising rates available with WIMK, WZNL. **URL:** http://talk1450.com.

17594 ■ WOBE-FM - 100.7
212 W J St.
Iron Mountain, MI 49801-4646
Owner: Results Broadcasting of Michigan Inc., at above address. **Founded:** 1972. **Key Personnel:** Trisha Peterson, Gen. Mgr. **Wattage:** 100,000. **Ad Rates:** $8-20 for 30 seconds; $15-30 for 60 seconds.

17595 ■ WUPK-FM - 94.1
101 E Kent St.
Iron Mountain, MI 49801
Phone: (906)774-4321
Fax: (906)774-7799
Format: Alternative/New Music/Progressive; Sports. **Operating Hours:** Continuous. **Key Personnel:** Dennise Bakran, Account Mgr., Sales Mgr. **Ad Rates:** Advertising accepted; rates available upon request. **URL:** http://www.rockthebear.com.

IRON RIVER

17596 ■ Iron County Reporter
Northland Publishers Inc.
PO Box 311
Iron River, MI 49935
Phone: (906)265-9927
Fax: (906)265-5755
Publisher's E-mail: sales@ironcountyreporter.com
Community newspaper. **Freq:** Weekly (Wed.). **Print Method:** Offset. **Key Personnel:** Allyce Westphal, Editor; Margaret Christensen, Publisher; Nan Borske, Office Manager. **Subscription Rates:** $45 Individuals in Iron county; $55 Individuals outside Iron county; $26 Individuals in Iron county (6 months); $31 Individuals out of iron county (6 months); $25 Individuals E-Edition. **URL:** http://www.ironcountyreporter.com. **Formerly:** Iron River Reporter. **Ad Rates:** BW $725; 4C $600; SAU $4.45; PCI $5.80. **Remarks:** Accepts advertising. **Circ:** ‡7,200.

17597 ■ Iron River Cooperative TV Antenna Corp.
316 N 2nd Ave.
Iron River, MI 49935
Phone: (906)265-3810
Email: ircable@ironriver.tv
Founded: Sept. 07, 2006. **Cities Served:** 53 channels. **URL:** http://www.ironriver.tv.

17598 ■ WIKB-AM - 1230
809 W Genesee St.
Iron River, MI 49935
Phone: (906)265-5104
Fax: (906)265-3486
Format: Oldies. **Networks:** NBC. **Owner:** Heartland Communication Group, 313 E Montezuma Ave., Houghton, MI 49931. **Founded:** 1949. **Operating Hours:** 5 a.m.-11 p.m. Mon.-Sat., 7 a.m.-10 p.m. Sun.; 3% network. **Key Personnel:** Mike Eakin, Gen. Mgr.; Leslie Howell, Office Mgr.; Mo Michael, Dir. of Programs. **Wattage:** 1,000. **Ad Rates:** Advertising accepted; rates available upon request. **URL:** http://www.wikb.com.

17599 ■ WIKB-FM - 99.1
809 W Genesee St.
Iron River, MI 49935
Phone: (906)265-9622
Fax: (906)265-3486
Format: Adult Contemporary; News; Sports. **Owner:** Heartland Communications Group, LLC, 313 E Montezuma Ave., Houghton, MI 49931. **Founded:** Nov. 15, 1981. **Operating Hours:** Continuous. **Key Personnel:** Mike Eakin, Gen. Mgr.; Mo Michael, Dir. of Programs; Leslie Howell, Office Mgr. **Ad Rates:** Advertising accepted; rates available upon request. **URL:** http://www.wikb.com.

IRONWOOD

Gogebic Co. Gogebic Co. (NW Up Penin.) 90 m E of Duluth, Mn. Gogebic Community College. Summer & winter recreation. Manufactures floor wax, polishes, cleaners, soaps, concrete blocks and shapes, hardwood and softwood lumber, molded rubber products, gloves, mittens, men's sport shirts, sauge, luncheon meats, truck campers and toppers, dairy products, tools; copper mining and smelting, meat packing.

17600 ■ Ironwood Daily Globe
Globe Publishing Co.
118 E McLeod Ave.
Ironwood, MI 49938
Phone: (906)932-2211
Fax: (906)932-5358
Free: 800-236-2887
Publisher's E-mail: jantuck@jamadots.com
General newspaper. **Freq:** Mon.-Sat. (eve.). **Print Method:** Offset. **Cols./Page:** 6. **Col. Width:** 2 inches. **Col. Depth:** 301 agate lines. **Key Personnel:** Marissa Casari, Specialist, Circulation. **Subscription Rates:** $19 Individuals Online-only subscription 1 month; $40 Individuals Online-only subscription 3 months; $75 Individuals Online-only subscription 6 moths; $125 Individuals Online-only subscription 1 year; All print edition orders must be phoned in. **Mailing address:** PO Box 548, Ironwood, MI 49938. **Ad Rates:** SAU $8.22. **Remarks:** Advertising accepted; rates available upon request. **Circ:** Paid ‡5,296.

17601 ■ North Country Sun
North Country Sun Inc.
216 E Aurora
Ironwood, MI 49938
Phone: (906)932-3530
Fax: (906)932-3074
Publisher's E-mail: evergreen@charterinternet.com
Shopper. **Freq:** Weekly (Mon.). **Print Method:** Offset. **Trim Size:** 11 1/2 x 17 1/2. **Cols./Page:** 6. **Col. Width:** 19 nonpareils. **Col. Depth:** 231 agate lines. **Subscription Rates:** $65 Individuals. **Alt. Formats:** PDF. **URL:** http://www.greatnortherncon.com/papers/north.html. **Mailing address:** PO Box 425, Ironwood, MI 49938. **Ad Rates:** BW $693; 4C $893; PCI $7. **Remarks:** Accepts advertising. **Circ:** ‡15,774.

17602 ■ Charter Communications
115 E McLeod Ave.
Ironwood, MI 49938-2119
Free: 888-438-2427
Key Personnel: Paul G. Allen, Chairman; Michael J. Lovett, COO, Exec. VP; Neil Smit, CEO, President; Marwan Fawaz, Chief Tech. Ofc., Exec. VP. **Cities Served:** 16 channels. **URL:** http://www.charter.com.

17603 ■ WHRY-AM - 1450
209 Harrison St.
Ironwood, MI 49938
Phone: (906)932-5234
Fax: (906)932-1548
Format: Oldies. **Ad Rates:** Noncommercial. **URL:** http://www.wupm-whry.com.

17604 ■ WIMI-FM - 99.7
222 S Lawrence St.
Ironwood, MI 49938
Phone: (906)932-2411
Fax: (906)932-2485
Email: traffic@wimifm.com
Format: Adult Contemporary. **Networks:** CNN Radio. **Owner:** Quicksilver Broadcasting L.L.C., at above address. **Founded:** 1974. **Operating Hours:** Continuous. **Wattage:** 100,000. **Ad Rates:** Noncommercial. **URL:** http://www.wimifm.com.

17605 ■ WJMS-AM - 590
222 S Lawrence St.
Ironwood, MI 49938
Phone: (906)932-2411
Fax: (906)932-2485
Format: Country. **Owner:** Quicksilver Broadcasting L.L.C., at above address. **Founded:** 1931. **Wattage:** 5,000 Day; 1,000 Nig. **Ad Rates:** Advertising accepted; rates available upon request. **URL:** http://www.wjmsam.com.

Circulation: ★ = AAM; △ or • = BPA; ♦ = CAC; ❑ = VAC; ⊕ = PO Statement; ‡ = Publisher's Report; Boldface figures = sworn; Light figures = estimated.

17606 ■ WUPM-FM - 107
209 Harrison St.
Ironwood, MI 49938
Phone: (906)932-5234
Fax: (906)932-1548
Format: Contemporary Hit Radio (CHR). **Networks:** ABC. **Owner:** Big G Little o Inc., 209 Harrison St., Ironwood, MI 49938-1713. **Founded:** 1977. **Operating Hours:** Continuous. **Wattage:** 53,000. **Ad Rates:** Advertising accepted; rates available upon request. Combined advertising rates available with WHRY-AM.

ITHACA

Gratiot Co. Gratiot Co. (C). 40 m N of Lansing. Frontier Festival City. Shoe, modular housing, automotive & airplane parts manufactured. Grain elevators, dairy, poultry farms. Beans, sugar beets, corn.

17607 ■ Gratiot County Herald
MacDonald Publications
123 N Main St.
Ithaca, MI 48847
Phone: (989)875-4151
Fax: (989)875-3159
Publication E-mail: gcherald@gcherald.com
Local newspaper. **Freq:** Weekly (Thurs.). **Print Method:** Offset. **Cols./Page:** 5. **Col. Width:** 18 nonpareils. **Col. Depth:** 301 agate lines. **Key Personnel:** Tom MacDonald, Publisher; Greg Nelson, Editor; DeAnna Coffin, Office Manager. **Subscription Rates:** $40 Individuals; $30 Individuals online only subscriptions. **URL:** http://gcherald.com. **Mailing address:** PO Box 10, Ithaca, MI 48847. **Ad Rates:** GLR $0.60; BW $532; 4C $932; SAU $6.65. **Remarks:** Accepts advertising. **Circ:** ‡7400.

JACKSON

Jackson Co. Jackson Co. (S). 72 m W of Detroit. Manufactures auto and aircraft parts and accessories, tires, confectionery, grinding wheels, air conditioning and refrigeration equipment, flexible hose lines and fittings, extracts and flavoring, carbon and alloy steel.

17608 ■ Jackson County Legal News
Detroit Legal News Publishing L.L.C.
304 Francis St.
Jackson, MI 49204
Phone: (517)782-0825
Fax: (517)782-4996
Legal newspaper. **Freq:** Weekly (Mon.). **Print Method:** Offset. **Cols./Page:** 5. **Col. Width:** 22 nonpareils. **Col. Depth:** 224 agate lines. **Key Personnel:** Suzanne Favale, Publisher, phone: (248)577-6109; Brad Thompson, President. **USPS:** 271-860. **Subscription Rates:** $80 Individuals One county access to web + 1 paper (valid for new subscriber).; $210 Individuals Three county access to web + 3 papers (valid for new subscriber).; $350 Individuals All county access to web + 9 papers (valid for new subscriber). **URL:** http://www.legalnews.com/jackson. **Mailing address:** PO Box 1090, Jackson, MI 49204. **Ad Rates:** PCI $3. **Remarks:** Accepts advertising. **Circ:** 1,900.

17609 ■ Photo Marketing Magazine
Professional School Photographers Association International
3000 Picture Pl.
Jackson, MI 49201
Phone: (517)788-8100
Fax: (517)788-8371
Free: 800-762-9287
Publisher's E-mail: m.bell@bellphoto.com
Freq: Monthly. **Subscription Rates:** $15 /year, for those in the photo industry only. **URL:** http://www.pmai.org/Magazine/. **Remarks:** Accepts advertising. **Circ:** 22000.

17610 ■ WIBM-AM - 1450
1700 Glenshire Dr.
Jackson, MI 49201
Phone: (517)787-9546
Format: Sports. **Networks:** ESPN Radio. **Owner:** Jackson Radio Works Inc., 1700 Glenshire Dr., Jackson, MI 49201. **Founded:** 1925. **Formerly:** WCXI-AM. **Operating Hours:** Continuous. **Local Programs:** *Fantasy Focus*, Sunday 7:00 a.m. - 8:30 a.m.; *The John Kincade Show*, Sunday 11:30 a.m. - 1:00 p.m.; *ESPN GameDay*, Sunday 1:00 p.m. - 4:00 p.m.; *The Baseball Show*, Sunday 4:00 p.m. - 7:30 p.m.; *The Scott Van Pelt Show*, Monday Tuesday Wednesday Thursday Friday 1:00 p.m. - 4:00 p.m. **Wattage:** 810. **Ad Rates:** Noncommercial. Combined advertising rates available with WKHM-AM, WKHM-FM. **URL:** http://wkhm.com.

17611 ■ WKHM-AM - 970
3905 Clinton Way
Jackson, MI 49201
Phone: (517)787-9546
Format: News; Talk. **Owner:** Jackson Radio Works Inc., 1700 Glenshire Dr., Jackson, MI 49201. **Founded:** 1952. **Operating Hours:** Continuous. **Local Programs:** *AM Jackson*, Monday Tuesday Wednesday Thursday Friday 6:00 a.m. - 10:00 a.m.; *Church of God*, Sunday 8:30 a.m. - 9:00 a.m.; 11:30 a.m. - 12:00 p.m.; *The Handyman Show*, Saturday 10:00 a.m. - 12:00 p.m. **Wattage:** 1,000 Day; 1,000 Nig. **Ad Rates:** Advertising accepted; rates available upon request. **URL:** http://www.wkhm.com.

17612 ■ WKHM-FM - 105.3
1700 Glenshire Dr.
Jackson, MI 49201
Phone: (517)787-9546
Fax: (517)787-7517
Format: Adult Contemporary; Contemporary Hit Radio (CHR). **Owner:** Jackson Radio Works Inc., 1700 Glenshire Dr., Jackson, MI 49201. **Key Personnel:** Jamie McKibbin, Operations Mgr., Program Mgr., jamie@k1053.com. **URL:** http://www.k1053.com.

JENISON

Ottawa Co. (W). 25 m of Grand Haven. Sawmill; bedding, concrete-mason manufactured. Dairy, poultry, tulip bulbs, fruit farming.

17613 ■ East Grand Rapids Cadence
Advance Newspapers
2141 Port Sheldon Rd.
Jenison, MI 49429
Phone: (616)669-2700
Free: 800-439-0960
Publication E-mail: retailsales@advancenewspapers.com
Community newspaper. **Founded:** 1966. **Freq:** Weekly (Wed.). **Print Method:** Web. **Trim Size:** 10 3/8 x 15 7/8. **Cols./Page:** 6. **Col. Width:** 1 5/8 picas. **Key Personnel:** Mike Wyngarden, Managing Editor, phone: (616)669-2700; Joel Holland, Publisher. **URL:** http://www.advancenewspapers.com/news.html. **Formerly:** East Grand Rapids Advance. **Mailing address:** PO Box 9, Jenison, MI 49429. **Ad Rates:** BW $998; 4C $1123; PCI $71.75. **Remarks:** Accepts advertising. **Circ:** Free ■ **44,275**.

17614 ■ The Enigma
National Puzzlers' League
2507 Almar St.
Jenison, MI 49428
Freq: Monthly. **Subscription Rates:** $18 /year; $25 /year for overseas or large type edition. **Alt. Formats:** PDF. **URL:** http://enigma.puzzlers.org/; http://www.puzzlers.org/dokuwiki/doku.php?id=mini:start. **Remarks:** Advertising not accepted. **Circ:** 400.

17615 ■ Forest Hills Advance
Advance Newspapers
2141 Port Sheldon Rd.
Jenison, MI 49429
Phone: (616)669-2700
Free: 800-439-0960
Publication E-mail: retailsales@advancenewspapers.com
Community newspaper. **Freq:** Weekly (Wed.). **Print Method:** Web. **Trim Size:** 10 3/8 x 15 7/8. **Cols./Page:** 6. **Col. Width:** 1 5/8 picas. **Key Personnel:** Joel Holland, Publisher; Mike Wyngarden, Managing Editor; Tara Berghuis, Manager, Production; Karen Waite, Editor. **URL:** http://www.advancenewspapers.com. **Formerly:** Ada/Cascada Forest Hills Advance. **Mailing address:** PO Box 9, Jenison, MI 49429. **Ad Rates:** BW $883; 4C $1,008; PCI $9.20. **Remarks:** Accepts advertising. **Circ:** Free ■ **15062**, Paid ■ **96**.

17616 ■ Grand Valley Advance
Advance Newspapers
2141 Port Sheldon Rd.
Jenison, MI 49429
Phone: (616)669-2700
Free: 800-439-0960
Publication E-mail: retailsales@advancenewspapers.com
Suburban community newspaper (tabloid). **Founded:** 1966. **Freq:** Weekly (Tues.). **Print Method:** Offset. **Trim Size:** 10 3/8 x 15 7/8. **Cols./Page:** 6. **Col. Width:** 1 5/8 nonpareils. **Key Personnel:** Joel Holland, Publisher; Mike Wyngarden, Editor. **URL:** http://www.advancenewspapers.com/news.html. **Mailing address:** PO Box 9, Jenison, MI 49429. **Ad Rates:** BW $898; 4C $1,023; PCI $9.35. **Remarks:** Accepts advertising. **Circ:** Free ■ **37376**, Paid ■ **5446**, Combined ■ **42822**.

17617 ■ Kentwood Advance
Advance Newspapers
2141 Port Sheldon Rd.
Jenison, MI 49429
Phone: (616)669-2700
Free: 800-439-0960
Publisher's E-mail: news@advancenewspapers.com
Suburban newspaper (tabloid). **Freq:** Weekly (Tues.). **Print Method:** Web. **Trim Size:** 10 3/8 x 15 7/8. **Cols./Page:** 6. **Col. Width:** 1 5/8 nonpareils. **Col. Depth:** 224 agate lines. **Key Personnel:** Karen Waite, Editor, phone: (616)669-2700; Mike Wyngarden, Editor; Jeanne Anderson, Contact; Signe Tanner, Contact. **URL:** http://www.mlive.com/advancenewspapers. **Mailing address:** PO Box 9, Jenison, MI 49429. **Ad Rates:** BW $1,138; 4C $1,263; PCI $11.85. **Remarks:** Accepts advertising. **Circ:** Free ■ **16453**, Paid ■ **207**.

17618 ■ On the Town: The Arts and Entertainment Magazine of West Michigan
On the Town
PO Box 499
Jenison, MI 49429-0499
Phone: (616)669-1366
Fax: (616)662-4060
Publication E-mail: townmag@mail.iserv.net
Arts and entertainment magazine for West Michigan. **Freq:** Monthly. **Print Method:** Web offset. **Trim Size:** 10 1/8 x 12. **Cols./Page:** 4. **Col. Width:** 2 1/4 inches. **Col. Depth:** 12 3/4 inches. **Key Personnel:** Joel Holland, Publisher, phone: (616)669-2700; Joanne N. Bailey-Boorsma, Editor, phone: (616)699-1366. **URL:** http://www.on-the-town.com/main.html. **Ad Rates:** BW $1,698; 4C $1,945. **Remarks:** Advertising accepted; rates available upon request. **Circ:** ■ **30000**.

17619 ■ The Standard Bearer
Reformed Free Publishing Association
1894 Georgetown Center Dr.
Jenison, MI 49428-7137
Phone: (616)457-5970
Publisher's E-mail: mail@rfpa.org
Freq: Semimonthly. **ISSN:** 0362--4692 (print). **Subscription Rates:** $11.50 Individuals print; $17.50 Other countries print; $35 Other countries print; $23 Individuals online. **URL:** http://rfpa.org/pages/the-standard-bearer. **Remarks:** Advertising not accepted. **Circ:** (Not Reported).

Walker/Westside Advance - See Walker

17620 ■ Wyoming Advance
Advance Newspapers
2141 Port Sheldon Rd.
Jenison, MI 49429
Phone: (616)669-2700
Free: 800-439-0960
Publication E-mail: retailsales@advancenewspapers.com
Community tabloid newspaper. **Freq:** Weekly (Tues.). **Print Method:** Web. **Trim Size:** 10 3/8 x 15 7/8. **Cols./Page:** 6. **Col. Width:** 15/8 nonpareils. **Key Personnel:** Karen Waite, Editor; Sheila McGrath, Editor; Mike Wyngarden, Contact; Larry Hirt, Contact. **Mailing address:** PO Box 9, Jenison, MI 49429. **Ad Rates:** BW $1,334; 4C $1,738; PCI $13.90. **Remarks:** Accepts advertising. **Circ:** Free ■ **20651**, Paid ■ **1168**.

KALAMAZOO

Kalamazoo Co. Kalamazoo Co. (SW). 141 m W of Detroit and 142 m E of Chicago. Kalamazoo College; Western Michigan University; Nazareth College; Kalamazoo Valley Community College. Extensive paper and paper product manufacturers; silos, fishing tackle, drill presses, golf, tools, auto shop equipment, auto parts, air conditioning equipment, furnace blowers, stampings, printing ink business forms, forgings, gas heaters, musical instruments, railroad maintenance of way equipment, paint, essential oils, surgical and hospital equipment, pharmaceuticals, meat products, chemicals, truck transmissions, taxicabs, automobiles, school furniture, aircraft and missile controls; oil refinery.

17621 ■ Comparative Drama
Western Michigan University
1903 W Michigan Ave.
Kalamazoo, MI 49008
Phone: (269)387-1000
Publication E-mail: comparative-drama@wmich.edu
Journal for comparative and interdisciplinary study of drama. **Freq:** Quarterly (Spring, Summer, Fall, and Winter). **Print Method:** Offset. **Trim Size:** 6 x 9. **Cols./Page:** 1. **Col. Width:** 4 1/8 inches. **Col. Depth:** 7 inches. **Key Personnel:** Robert C. Evans, Advisor; Sander M. Goldberg, Advisor; Brian Johnston, Advisor; Dr. Eve Salisbury, Senior Editor. **ISSN:** 0010-4078 (print). **Subscription Rates:** $25 Individuals; $30 Out of country; $45 Institutions libraries; $75 Two years institution and libraries; $55 Institutions, other countries libraries; $90 Two years institution and libraries, outside U.S.; $37 Individuals agency; $60 Two years agency; $45 Other countries agency; $70 Two years agency, outside U.S. **URL:** http://www.wmich.edu/compdr. **Remarks:** Advertising not accepted. **Circ:** Paid ‡850, Controlled ‡50.

17622 ■ Coonhound Bloodlines: The Complete Magazine for the Houndsman and Coon Hunter
United Kennel Club
100 E Kilgore Rd.
Kalamazoo, MI 49002-5584
Phone: (269)343-9020
Fax: (269)343-7037
Publication E-mail: ads@ukcdogs.com
Magazine about coonhound field trials and hunting; including information about training, veterinary care, upcoming events, stories, event results and rules. Features articles by the nation's top trainers. **Freq:** Monthly. **Print Method:** Web Offset Lithography, Perfect Bound. **Trim Size:** 8 1/8 x 10 7/8. **Cols./Page:** 2 and 3. **Col. Width:** 43 and 28 nonpareils. **Col. Depth:** 136 1/2 agate lines. **Key Personnel:** Kelly Ballema, Manager, Production; Vicki Rand, Editor. **USPS:** 017-690. **Subscription Rates:** $40 Other countries 1 year; $30 Individuals U.S.; $70 Two years foreign; $54 Two years; $7 Individuals sample issue, current yr. back issue; $10 Individuals back issue, 70's; $8 Individuals back issue, 80's; $8 Individuals back issue, 90's; $7 Individuals back issue, 2000; $70 Other countries 2 years. **URL:** http://www.ukcdogs.com/Web.nsf/WebPages/Publications/CoonhoundBloodlines. **Ad Rates:** BW $220; 4C $400; PCI $18. **Remarks:** Accepts advertising. **Circ:** 18000.

17623 ■ Hunting Retriever
United Kennel Club
100 E Kilgore Rd.
Kalamazoo, MI 49002-5584
Phone: (269)343-9020
Fax: (269)343-7037
Publisher's E-mail: registration@ukcdogs.com
Magazine featuring hunting retrievers. **Freq:** Bimonthly. **Print Method:** Offset. **Trim Size:** 8 1/2 x 11. **Cols./Page:** 3. **Col. Width:** 2 3/8 inches. **Col. Depth:** 9 3/4 inches. **Key Personnel:** Vicki Rand, Editor; Kelly Ballema, Manager, Production. **ISSN:** 8750-6629 (print). **Subscription Rates:** $25 Individuals 1 year; $30 Other countries 1 year; $50 Individuals 2 years; $60 Individuals 2 years. **URL:** http://www.ukcdogs.com/Web.nsf/WebPages/Publications/HuntingRetriever. **Ad Rates:** BW $150; 4C $375; PCI $15. **Remarks:** Accepts advertising. **Circ:** Paid 5000, Non-paid 50, 4000.

17624 ■ Journal of Sociology and Social Welfare
Journal of Sociology and Social Welfare
Western Michigan University, School of Social Work
1903 W Michigan Ave.
Kalamazoo, MI 49008-5354
Phone: (269)387-1000
Publisher's E-mail: swrk-jssw@wmich.edu
Journal presenting a broad range of articles which analyze social welfare institutions, policies, or problems from a social scientific perspective. **Freq:** Quarterly March, June, September and December. **Print Method:** Offset. **Trim Size:** 6 x 9. **Cols./Page:** 1. **Col. Width:** 4.25 inches. **Col. Depth:** 7 inches. **Key Personnel:** Frederick MacDonald, Managing Editor; Robert D. Leighninger, Jr., Editor; Robert Moroney, Associate Editor. **ISSN:** 0191-5096 (print). **Subscription Rates:** $52 Individuals print & online; $64 Other countries print & online; $96 Institutions print & online; $108 Institutions, other countries print & online; $44 Individuals online only; $88 Institutions online only. **URL:** http://www.wmich.edu/socialworkjournal. **Remarks:** Advertising not accepted. **Circ:** ‡650.

17625 ■ Medieval Prosopography at Medieval Institute Publications: History and Collective Biography
Western Michigan University
1903 W Michigan Ave.
Kalamazoo, MI 49008
Phone: (269)387-1000
Publisher's E-mail: helpdesk@wmich.edu
Scholarly journal covering biography and history in the medieval period. **Freq:** Annual. **Print Method:** Traditional. **Trim Size:** 7 x 10. **Cols./Page:** 1. **Key Personnel:** Patricia Hollahan, PhD, Managing Editor; Thomas P. Krol, Editor; Theresa Whitaker, Director, Exhibits, Editor. **ISSN:** 0198--9405 (print). **Subscription Rates:** $34.95 Individuals; $775 Institutions. **URL:** http://wmich.edu/medievalpublications/journals/prosopography. **Remarks:** Advertising not accepted. **Circ:** (Not Reported).

17626 ■ Public Affairs Quarterly
University of Illinois Press
c/o Fritz Allhoff, Editor
Western Michigan University
Department of Philosophy
Kalamazoo, MI 49008
Publisher's E-mail: uipress@uillinois.edu
Scholarly journal covering social and political philosophy. **Freq:** Quarterly. **Key Personnel:** Nicholas Rescher, Executive Editor, fax: (412)383-7506. **ISSN:** 0887--0373 (print); **EISSN:** 2152--0542 (electronic). **Subscription Rates:** $60 Individuals print only; $336 Institutions print or online; $377 Institutions print + online; $40 Individuals single issues; $90 Institutions single issues. **URL:** http://www.press.uillinois.edu/journals/paq.html. **Ad Rates:** BW $225. **Remarks:** Accepts advertising. **Circ:** 250.

17627 ■ Western Herald
Western Michigan University
1903 W Michigan Ave.
Kalamazoo, MI 49008
Phone: (269)387-1000
Publisher's E-mail: helpdesk@wmich.edu
Collegiate newspaper. **Founded:** 1916. **Freq:** Weekly (Thurs.) during the academic year. **Print Method:** Offset. **Cols./Page:** 6. **Col. Width:** 26 nonpareils. **Col. Depth:** 294 agate lines. **Key Personnel:** Brian Abbott, General Manager; Nicole Taylor, Manager, Advertising; Nora Strehl, Editor-in-Chief. **Subscription Rates:** $12 Individuals; $10 Individuals student organization/non-profit. **URL:** http://westernherald.com. **Ad Rates:** 4C $290. **Remarks:** Accepts advertising. **Circ:** Combined 12,500.

17628 ■ WMU, The Magazine
Western Michigan University
1903 W Michigan Ave.
Kalamazoo, MI 49008
Phone: (269)387-1000
Publication E-mail: ask-wmu@wmich.edu
University and Alumni magazine. **Freq:** Quarterly. **Print Method:** Offset. **Trim Size:** 8 1/4 x 10 3/4. **Cols./Page:** 3. **Col. Width:** 40 nonpareils. **Col. Depth:** 224 agate lines. **Key Personnel:** Cheryl P. Roland, Executive Director, phone: (269)387-8412; David H. Smith, Contact, phone: (269)387-8431. **ISSN:** 0279-3628 (print). **Subscription Rates:** Free to alumni association members. **URL:** http://www.wmich.edu/magazine. **Formerly:** The Westerner. **Remarks:** Advertising not accepted. **Circ:** Free 50,000.

17629 ■ WPC News
WPC Club
Box 3504
Kalamazoo, MI 49003-3504
Fax: (269)694-2818
Freq: Bimonthly. **Subscription Rates:** Included in membership. **Remarks:** Accepts advertising. **Circ:** (Not Reported).

17630 ■ SBM Communications
517 E Kalamazoo Ave.
Kalamazoo, MI 49007
Founded: 1981. **Formerly:** Cable TV of Kalamazoo. **Cities Served:** Kalamazoo, Michigan: subscribing households 50; 26 channels; 6 community access channels. **URL:** http://www.dleg.state.mi.us/bcs_corp/dt_corp.asp?id_nbr=273811&name_entity=S.B.M.%20COMMUNICATIONS,%20INC.

17631 ■ WCSG-FM - 91.3; 91.3
1159 E Beltline Ave. NE
Grand Rapids, MI 49525-5805
Phone: (616)942-1500
Free: 800-968-4543
Email: info@wcsg.org
Format: Adult Contemporary; Contemporary Christian. **Networks:** Fox. **Owner:** Cornerstone University, 1001 E Beltline Ave. NE, Grand Rapids, MI 49525. **Founded:** 1973. **Operating Hours**: 5:00 a.m. - 11:00 p.m. Monday - Friday; 6:00 a.m. - 7:00 p.m. Saturday; Midnight - 9:00 p.m. Sunday. **ADI**: Grand Rapids-Kalamazoo-Battle Creek, MI. **Key Personnel:** John Balyo, Contact; Becky Carlson, Contact; Joel Hill, Contact; Rich Anderson, Contact. **Wattage**: 37,000 ERP. **Ad Rates:** Noncommercial. **URL:** http://www.wcsg.org.

17632 ■ WIDR-FM - 89.1
1501 Faunce Student Services Bldg.
Kalamazoo, MI 49008
Phone: (269)387-6301
Format: Alternative/New Music/Progressive. **Networks:** Independent. **Owner:** Western Michigan University, 1903 W Michigan Ave., Kalamazoo, MI 49008, Ph: (269)387-1000. **Founded:** 1952. **Operating Hours**: Continuous; 100% local. **Key Personnel:** Johanna Kelly, Gen. Mgr. **Wattage**: 100. **Ad Rates:** Noncommercial. **URL:** http://www.widrfm.org.

17633 ■ WKDS-FM - 89.9
606 East Kilgore Road
606 E Kilgore Rd.
Kalamazoo, MI 49001
Format: Full Service. **Networks:** Independent. **Owner:** Kalamazoo Public Schools, 1220 Howard St., Kalamazoo, MI 49008, Ph: (269)337-0100. **Founded:** 1983. **Operating Hours**: 8 a.m.-6 p.m.; 100% local. **Key Personnel:** Carol Fletcher, Dir. of Programs. **Wattage**: 100. **Ad Rates:** Noncommercial. **URL:** http://www.wkds.4t.com.

17634 ■ WKFR-FM - 103.3
4154 Jennings Dr.
Kalamazoo, MI 49048
Phone: (269)344-0111
Format: Contemporary Hit Radio (CHR); Alternative/New Music/Progressive. **Networks:** Westwood One Radio. **Owner:** Cumulus Broadcasting Inc., 3280 Peachtree Rd. NW, Ste. 2300, Atlanta, GA 30305-2447, Ph: (404)949-0700, Fax: (404)949-0740. **Operating Hours**: Continuous. **Key Personnel:** Kate Conley, Gen. Mgr. **Local Programs**: *The Billy Bush Show*; *Retro Lunch*, Monday Tuesday Wednesday Thursday Friday 12:00 p.m. **Wattage**: 50,000. **Ad Rates:** Advertising accepted; rates available upon request. Combined advertising rates available with WKMI and WRKR. **URL:** http://www.wkfr.com.

17635 ■ WKZO-AM - 590
4200 W Main St.
Kalamazoo, MI 49006
Phone: (269)345-7121
Fax: (269)345-1436
Free: 800-742-6590
Format: News; Sports; Talk. **Networks:** CBS; ESPN Radio. **Owner:** Midwest Communications Inc., 904 Grand Ave., Wausau, WI 54403, Ph: (715)842-1437, Fax: (715)842-7061. **Founded:** 1931. **Operating Hours**: Continuous. **ADI**: Grand Rapids-Kalamazoo-Battle Creek, MI. **Wattage**: 5,000. **Ad Rates:** Advertising accepted; rates available upon request. Combined advertising rates available with WQLR-FM & WQSN-AM, WKLZ-AM. **URL:** http://www.wkzo.com.

17636 ■ WLLA-TV - 64
7048 E Kilgore Rd.
Kalamazoo, MI 49003
Format: Commercial TV. **Networks:** Independent. **Owner:** Christian Faith Broadcast Inc., 3809 Maple Ave.,

Circulation: ★ = AAM; △ or • = BPA; ♦ = CAC; ❑ = VAC; ⊕ = PO Statement; ‡ = Publisher's Report; Boldface figures = sworn; Light figures = estimated.

Castalia, OH 44824, Ph: (419)684-5311, Fax: (419)684-5378. **Operating Hours**: Continuous. **ADI**: Grand Rapids-Kalamazoo-Battle Creek, MI. **Wattage**: 2,500,000. **Ad Rates:** $12-75 for 30 seconds. **URL:** http://www.wlla.com.

17637 ■ WMUK-FM - 102.1
1903 W Michigan Ave.
Kalamazoo, MI 49008-5351
Phone: (269)387-5715
Fax: (269)387-4630
Email: online@wmuk.org
Format: Public Radio. **Networks:** National Public Radio (NPR); Public Radio International (PRI). **Owner:** Western Michigan University, 1903 W Michigan Ave., Kalamazoo, MI 49008, Ph: (269)387-1000. **Founded:** 1951. **Formerly**: WMCR-FM. **ADI**: Grand Rapids-Kalamazoo-Battle Creek, MI. **Local Programs**: *Grassroots*, Sunday 10:00 a.m. - 12:00 p.m. ; *Car Talk*, Saturday 10:00 am. - 11:00 a.m.; *Bob Edwards Weekend*, Sunday Saturday 4:00 p.m. - 5:00 p.m. 8:00 a.m. - 10:00 a.m.; *Millennium of Music*, Wednesday 9:00 p.m.; *Studio 360*, Saturday 1:00 p.m.; *Pipedreams*, Tuesday 9:00 p.m.; *MidDay Classical*. **Wattage**: 49,000 ERP. **Ad Rates:** Advertising accepted; rates available upon request. **URL:** http://www.wmuk.org.

17638 ■ WNWN-AM - 1560
4200 W Main St.
Kalamazoo, MI 49006
Phone: (269)345-7121
Fax: (269)345-1436
Format: Urban Contemporary; Oldies. **URL:** http://www.go955.com.

17639 ■ WQLR-AM - 1660
4200 W Main St.
Kalamazoo, MI 49006
Phone: (269)345-7121
Fax: (269)345-1436
Format: Sports. **Networks:** ESPN Radio; Fox. **Owner:** Midwest Communications Inc., 904 Grand Ave., Wausau, WI 54403, Ph: (715)842-1437, Fax: (715)842-7061. **Founded:** 1985. **Formerly**: WQSN-AM. **Operating Hours**: Continuous. **ADI**: Grand Rapids-Kalamazoo-Battle Creek, MI. **Local Programs**: *Petros and Money*, Monday Tuesday Wednesday Thursday Friday 7:00 p.m. - 10:00 p.m.; *Race Day on Fox*, Sunday 6:00 a.m. - 8:00 a.m. **Wattage**: 10,000 a Day; 1,000 Night. **Ad Rates:** Advertising accepted; rates available upon request. Combined advertising rates available with WQLR-FM, WKZO-AM, WKLZ-AM. **URL:** http://1660thefan.com.

17640 ■ WRKR-FM - 107.7
4154 Jennings Dr.
Kalamazoo, MI 49048
Phone: (269)344-0111
Format: Classic Rock; Talk; News. **Networks:** ABC. **Owner:** Cumulus Media Inc., 3280 Peachtree Rd. NW, Ste. 2300, Atlanta, GA 30305-2455, Ph: (404)949-0700, Fax: (404)949-0740. **Founded:** 1988. **Formerly**: Crystal Radio Group Inc. **Operating Hours**: Continuous. **Key Personnel:** Mike McKelly, Div. Mgr., mike.mckelly@townsquaremedia.com; Dave Benson, Contact; Kate Conley, Gen. Mgr., kate.conley@townsquaremedia.com. **Wattage**: 50,000. **Ad Rates:** Advertising accepted; rates available upon request. Combined advertising rates available with WKMI-AM, WKFR-FM. **URL:** http://www.wrkr.com.

17641 ■ WVFM-FM - 106.5
4200 W Main St.
Kalamazoo, MI 49006
Phone: (269)373-1065
Fax: (269)345-1436
Format: Top 40. **Owner:** Midwest Communications Inc., 904 Grand Ave., Wausau, WI 54403, Ph: (715)842-1437, Fax: (715)842-7061. **Founded:** 1972. **Operating Hours**: Continuous. **Wattage**: 33,000. **Ad Rates:** Noncommercial. Combined advertising rates available with WKZO-AM, WQSN-AM, WKLZ-AM. **URL:** http://www.myfm1065.com.

17642 ■ WWMT-TV - 3
590 W Maple St.
Kalamazoo, MI 49008
Phone: (269)388-3333
Free: 800-875-3333
Email: program@wwmt.com
Format: Commercial TV; News. **Networks:** CBS. **Owner:** Freedom Communication Inc., 17666 Fitch, Irvine, CA 92614-6022, Ph: (949)253-2300, Fax: (949)474-7675. **Founded:** 1950. **Formerly**: WKZO-TV. **Operating Hours**: Continuous. **ADI**: Grand Rapids-Kalamazoo-Battle Creek, MI. **Ad Rates:** Advertising accepted; rates available upon request. **URL:** http://www.wwmt.com.

17643 ■ WYZO-FM - 96.5
4200 W Main St.
Kalamazoo, MI 49006
Phone: (269)345-7121
Fax: (269)345-4136
Format: Country. **Networks:** Unistar. **Owner:** Midwest Radio Group, 904 Grand Ave., Wausau, WI 54403, Ph: (715)842-1437, Fax: (715)842-7061. **Founded:** 1986. **Formerly**: WHEZ-AM; WFAT-FM. **Operating Hours**: Continuous. **ADI**: Grand Rapids-Kalamazoo-Battle Creek, MI. **Wattage**: 3,400. **Ad Rates:** $30-80 for 60 seconds. Combined advertising rates available with WNWN-FM.

KALKASKA

Kalkaska Co. Kalkaska Co. (C).

17644 ■ The Leader and the Kalkaskian
The Leader and the Kalkaskian
318 N Cedar St.
Kalkaska, MI 49646
Phone: (231)258-4600
Fax: (231)258-4603
County newspaper. **Freq:** Weekly (Wed.). **Print Method:** Offset. **Trim Size:** 13 1/4 x 21. **Cols./Page:** 5. **Col. Width:** 2 1/16 inches. **Col. Depth:** 21 inches. **Key Personnel:** Byrce Martin, Editor; Lee Hill, Office Manager. **ISSN:** 5454-2000 (print). **Subscription Rates:** $34.50 Individuals in county; $42 Out of country. **URL:** http://morningstarpublishing.com/leader_and_kalkaskian; http://www.morningstarpublishing.com/leader_and_kalkaskian. **Remarks:** Accepts advertising. **Circ:** 3,900.

KINGSFORD

17645 ■ WEUL-FM - 98.1
130 Carmen Dr.
Marquette, MI 49855
Phone: (906)249-1423
Free: 800-359-9673
Format: Religious. **Owner:** Gospel Opportunities Inc., 130 Carmen Dr., Marquette, MI 49855-9380, Ph: (906)249-1423, Free: 800-359-9673. **Founded:** 1990. **ADI:** Marquette, MI. **Key Personnel:** Curt Marker, Mgr.; Andy Larsen, News Dir. **Wattage**: 240. **Ad Rates:** Noncommercial. **URL:** http://www.whwl.net.

L'ANSE

Baraga Co. Baraga Co. (N Up. Penin.). On L'Anse Bay, 50 m NW of Marquette. Paper board, road building machinery manufactured. Lumber mills. Fisheries. Timber. Grain farms. Summer resort.

17646 ■ Kippis!
Finnish North American Literature Association
c/o Beth L. Virtanen, President
PO Box 212
L'Anse, MI 49946
Publisher's E-mail: admin@finnala.com
Freq: Semiannual winter and summer. **Subscription Rates:** Free. **URL:** http://www.finnala.com/Kippis.html. **Ad Rates:** BW $100, full page; BW $50, half page. **Remarks:** Accepts advertising. **Circ:** (Not Reported).

LAKE ORION

Oakland Co. Oakland Co. (SE). 11 m N of Pontiac. Aviation and auto parts factory. Lake resort. Residential. Dairy, poultry, grain farms. Potatoes, corn, beans.

17647 ■ Lake Orion Review
30 N Broadway
Lake Orion, MI 48362
Phone: (248)693-8331
Fax: (248)693-5712
Publication E-mail: lakeorionreview@sbcglobal.net
Newspaper. **Freq:** Weekly (Wed.). **Print Method:** Offset. **Cols./Page:** 6. **Col. Width:** 18 nonpareils. **Col. Depth:** 210 agate lines. **Key Personnel:** Dan Shriner, Editor; Joe Saint Henry, Editor; Don Rush, Assistant Publisher; Eric Lewis, Manager, Advertising; Jackie Nowicki, Manager, Advertising; James A. Sherman, Jr., Publisher. **URL:** http://www.lakeorionreview.com. **Ad Rates:** BW $396; SAU $7.90; PCI $6. **Remarks:** Advertising accepted; rates available upon request. **Circ:** 2700.

LAKEVIEW

17648 ■ WRIZ-FM - 106.3
420 Lincoln Ave.
Lakeview, MI 48850-0259
Format: Adult Contemporary; Contemporary Hit Radio (CHR); New Age. **Founded:** 1989. **Key Personnel:** Gerald Rehead, Contact. **Wattage**: 3,000. **Mailing address:** PO Box 259, Lakeview, MI 48850-0259.

LANSE

17649 ■ L'Anse Sentinel
The L'Anse Sentinel Inc.
202 N Main St.
Lanse, MI 49946
Phone: (906)524-6194
Fax: (906)524-6197
Publisher's E-mail: sentinel@up.net
Local newspaper. **Freq:** Weekly (Wed.). **Print Method:** Offset. **Cols./Page:** 6. **Col. Width:** 30 nonpareils. **Col. Depth:** 301 agate lines. **Key Personnel:** Joseph Schutte, Manager, Advertising; Barry Drue, Editor; Ed Danner, Publisher. **Subscription Rates:** $48 Individuals Baraga, Marquette, Houghton County; $52 Elsewhere; $57 Out of area; 29 Individuals Baraga, Marquette, Houghton County (6 months); 31 Elsewhere (6 months); 33 Out of area (6 months). **Mailing address:** PO Box 7, Lanse, MI 49946. **Ad Rates:** GLR $.36; SAU $8.20. **Remarks:** Accepts advertising. **Circ:** ‡4,241.

LANSING

Ingham Co. Ingham Co. (S). The State Capital. On Grand River, 84 m NW of Detroit. Michigan State University (East Lansing). Manufactures automobiles, auto castings and forgings, auto wheels, plastics, chemicals, fertilizers, tools and dies, stampings, aerial photography equipment.

17650 ■ Delta Waverly Community News
Lansing State Journal
120 E Lenawee
Lansing, MI 48933
Phone: (517)377-1001
Free: 800-234-1719
Community newspaper. **Freq:** Weekly (Sun.). **Print Method:** Offset. **Trim Size:** 10 1/4 x 16. **Cols./Page:** 6. **Col. Width:** 9.5 picas. **Col. Depth:** 16 inches. **Key Personnel:** Barb Modrack, Editor. **Subscription Rates:** $12 Individuals monthly. **URL:** http://www.lansingstatejournal.com/news/communities-delta-waverly. **Formerly**: Delta Waverly News Herald. **Ad Rates:** GLR $2.58; BW $626; 4C $776; SAU $8.47; PCI $6.52. **Remarks:** Accepts advertising. **Circ:** (Not Reported).

17651 ■ DeWitt Bath Review
Lansing State Journal
120 E Lenawee
Lansing, MI 48933
Phone: (517)377-1001
Free: 800-234-1719
Community newspaper. **Freq:** Weekly (Sun.). **Print Method:** Offset. **Cols./Page:** 6. **Col. Width:** 9.5 picas. **Col. Depth:** 224 agate lines. **Key Personnel:** Tom Thelen, Editor, phone: (517)541-2512, fax: (517)543-3677. **Subscription Rates:** $12 Individuals digital per month; $12 Individuals digital and print per month. **URL:** http://www.lansingstatejournal.com/news/communities-dewitt-bath. **Ad Rates:** GLR $.66; BW $744; 4C $999; SAU $9.30; PCI $10.40. **Remarks:** Accepts advertising. **Circ:** (Not Reported).

17652 ■ The Grand Ledge Independent: Grand Ledge Independent
Lansing State Journal
120 E Lenawee
Lansing, MI 48933
Phone: (517)377-1001
Free: 800-234-1719
Community newspaper. **Freq:** Weekly (Tues.). **Print Method:** Offset. **Cols./Page:** 6. **Col. Width:** 9.5 picas. **Col. Depth:** 16 inches. **Subscription Rates:** $12

Individuals digital - monthly; $12 Individuals digital and print - monthly. **URL:** http://www.lansingstatejournal.com/news/communities-grand-ledge. **Ad Rates:** GLR $2.58; BW $615; 4C $776; SAU $10; PCI $6.25. **Remarks:** Accepts advertising. **Circ:** (Not Reported).

17653 ■ The Historical Society of Michigan Chronicle
Historical Society of Michigan
5815 Executive Dr.
Lansing, MI 48911
Phone: (517)324-1828
Fax: (517)324-4370
Free: 800-692-1828
Publisher's E-mail: hsm@hsmichigan.org
Freq: 6/year. **Subscription Rates:** $4.95 Single issue; Included in membership. **URL:** http://www.hsmichigan.org/publications/michiganhistory. **Ad Rates:** BW $375. **Remarks:** Accepts advertising. **Circ:** 4500.

17654 ■ Holt Community News
Lansing State Journal
120 E Lenawee
Lansing, MI 48933
Phone: (517)377-1001
Free: 800-234-1719
Community newspaper. **Freq:** Weekly. **Key Personnel:** Stephanie Angel, Managing Editor; Will Kangas, Reporter. **URL:** http://www.lansingstatejournal.com/news/communities-holt. **Remarks:** Advertising accepted; rates available upon request. **Circ:** (Not Reported).

17655 ■ Ingham County Community News
Lansing State Journal
120 E Lenawee
Lansing, MI 48919
Phone: (517)377-1112
Community newspaper. **Freq:** Weekly. **Key Personnel:** Kurt Madden, Editor. **Subscription Rates:** $10 Individuals Thursday to Sunday; $7.50 Individuals Sunday only; $13.50 Individuals Monday to Sunday. **URL:** http://www.lansingstatejournal.com/news/communities-mason. **Remarks:** Advertising accepted; rates available upon request. **Circ:** (Not Reported).

17656 ■ Journal of the American Society of Podiatric Medical Assistants
American Society of Podiatric Medical Assistants
1000 W St. Joseph Hwy., Ste. 200
Lansing, MI 48915
Fax: (517)485-9408
Free: 888-882-7762
Publisher's E-mail: aspmaex@aol.com
Professional journal covering issues in podiatry. **Freq:** Quarterly. **Key Personnel:** Karen Keathley, Executive Director. **Subscription Rates:** Included in membership. **Remarks:** Advertising accepted; rates available upon request. **Circ:** (Not Reported).

17657 ■ Journey with Olds
Oldsmobile Club of America
PO Box 80318
Lansing, MI 48908-0318
Phone: (314)878-5651
Publisher's E-mail: webmaster@oldsmobileclub.org
Magazine featuring car collection. **Freq:** Monthly. **URL:** http://www.oldsmobileclub.org/resources/monthly-magazine. **Remarks:** Accepts advertising. **Circ:** 6500.

17658 ■ Lansing City Community News
Lansing State Journal
120 E Lenawee
Lansing, MI 48933
Phone: (517)377-1001
Free: 800-234-1719
Community newspaper. **Freq:** Daily. **Key Personnel:** Will Kangas, Editor. **Subscription Rates:** $10 Individuals /month, Thursday to Sunday; $7.50 Individuals /month, Sundays only; $13.50 Individuals /month, Monday to Sunday. **URL:** http://www.lansingstatejournal.com/news. **Remarks:** Advertising accepted; rates available upon request. **Circ:** (Not Reported).

17659 ■ Lansing State Journal
Lansing State Journal
120 E Lenawee
Lansing, MI 48933
Phone: (517)377-1001
Free: 800-234-1719
General newspaper. **Founded:** 1855. **Freq:** Daily. **Print Method:** Letterpress. **Cols./Page:** 7. **Col. Width:** 26 nonpareils. **Col. Depth:** 308 agate lines. **Key Personnel:** Brian Priester, Publisher; Michael Hirten, Executive Editor, phone: (517)377-1076; Stephanie Angel, Editor, phone: (517)377-1017. **Subscription Rates:** $12 Individuals digital; $12 Individuals digital and print. **URL:** http://www.lansingstatejournal.com. **Remarks:** Accepts advertising. **Circ:** Mon.-Fri. ★**44,888**, Sun. ★**68,344**, Sat. ★**48,865**.

17660 ■ Michigan Banker Magazine
Michigan Banker Magazine
1430 E Michigan Ave.
Lansing, MI 48906
Phone: (517)484-0775
Fax: (517)484-4676
Free: 800-288-4248
Magazine reporting banking news. Aimed exclusively at Michigan's commercial banking industry. **Freq:** Monthly. **Print Method:** Sheet-fed offset. **Trim Size:** 8 1/2 x 11. **Cols./Page:** 3. **Col. Width:** 14 picas. **Col. Depth:** 10 inches. **Key Personnel:** Bill Perry, Editor; Greg O'Neil, Chief Executive Officer, Publisher. **ISSN:** 0193-0257 (print). **Subscription Rates:** $92.50 Individuals. **URL:** http://mybankermag.com. **Formerly:** Michigan Banking and Business News. **Ad Rates:** BW $785; 4C $590; PCI $25. **Remarks:** Accepts advertising. **Circ:** Paid ‡650.

17661 ■ Michigan Bar Journal
State Bar of Michigan
306 Townsend St.
Lansing, MI 48933-2012
Phone: (517)346-6300
Fax: (517)482-6248
Free: 800-968-1442
Publisher's E-mail: gconyers@mail.michbar.org
Legal magazine. **Freq:** Monthly. **Print Method:** Web offset. **Trim Size:** 8 1/2 x 11. **Cols./Page:** 3. **Col. Width:** 28 nonpareils. **Col. Depth:** 136 agate lines. **Key Personnel:** Linda Novak, Editor. **ISSN:** 0164-3576 (print). **Subscription Rates:** $60 Nonmembers; $70 Other countries members. **URL:** http://www.michbar.org/journal/home. **Ad Rates:** BW $1,250. **Remarks:** Accepts advertising. **Circ:** ‡31,600.

17662 ■ Michigan Bicyclist
League of Michigan Bicyclists
416 S Cedar St., Ste. A
Lansing, MI 48912
Phone: (517)334-9100
Fax: (517)334-9111
Free: 888-642-4537
Freq: Quarterly. **Key Personnel:** Rich Moeller, Executive Director; John Lindenmayer, Editor. **URL:** http://www.lmb.org/index.php?option=com_content&view=category&layout=blog&id=37&Itemid=35. **Remarks:** Accepts advertising. **Circ:** 3000.

17663 ■ Michigan Country Lines
Michigan Electric Cooperative Association
201 Townsend St. Suite 900
Lansing, MI
Phone: (517)351-6322
Fax: (517)351-6396
Publisher's E-mail: info@countrylines.com
Magazine on rural lifestyles and home energy use. **Freq:** Monthly except Aug. and Dec. **Trim Size:** 8 x 10 3/4. **Key Personnel:** Gail Knudtson, Editor; Michael W. Peters, Chief Executive Officer, President. **USPS:** 591-710. **URL:** http://www.countrylines.com. **Ad Rates:** BW $6,710; 4C $7,110. **Remarks:** Accepts advertising. **Circ:** (Not Reported).

17664 ■ Michigan Farm News: Michigan's Only Statewide Farm Newspaper
Michigan Farm Bureau
7373 W Saginaw Hwy.
Lansing, MI 48917
Phone: (517)323-7000
Free: 800-292-2680
Publisher's E-mail: mfbweb@michfb.com
Agribusiness publication for Michigan farmers. **Freq:** 3/week. **Print Method:** Web offset. **Trim Size:** 11 x 17. **Cols./Page:** 4. **Col. Width:** 2 3/8 inches. **Col. Depth:** 10 inches. **Key Personnel:** Dennis Rudat, Publisher, Director; Paul Jackson, Editor. **URL:** http://www.michfb.com/MI/FarmNews/Default.aspx. **Remarks:** Accepts advertising. **Circ:** (Not Reported).

17665 ■ Michigan Food News
Michigan Grocers Association
221 N Walnut St.
Lansing, MI 48933-1121
Phone: (517)372-6800
Fax: (517)372-3002
Free: 800-947-6237
Freq: Monthly 11 times/year including a combined October-November edition. **Print Method:** Sheet fed offset. **Trim Size:** 10 x 14. **Cols./Page:** 5. **Col. Width:** 17 nonpareils. **Col. Depth:** 224 agate lines. **Key Personnel:** Lisa Reibsome, Editor. **Subscription Rates:** $30 Nonmembers; Included in membership; $25 /year for nonmembers. **URL:** http://www.michigangrocers.org/members-only/mifoodnew. **Ad Rates:** BW $850; 4C $1,500; PCI $25. **Remarks:** Accepts advertising. **Circ:** Controlled 5,000, 9000.

17666 ■ Michigan Historical Review
Central Michigan University Clarke Historical Library
5815 Executive Dr.
Lansing, MI 48911
Phone: (517)332-1828
Fax: (517)324-4370
Free: 800-366-3703
Publication E-mail: mihisrev@cmich.edu
Publication covering history and literature. **Freq:** Semiannual. **Key Personnel:** Dave Macleod, Editor, phone: (989)774-6567. **ISSN:** 0890--1686 (print). **Subscription Rates:** $20 Individuals 25 foreign; $10 Single issue; $30 Institutions 35 foreign; Included in membership. **Online:** Gale. **URL:** http://www.cmich.edu/library/clarke/PublicPrograms/The_Michigan_Historical_Review/Pages/default.aspx; http://www.hsmichigan.org/publications/michigan-historical-review. **Circ:** (Not Reported).

17667 ■ Michigan Master Plumber and Mechanical Contractor
Michigan Plumbing and Mechanical Contractors Association
PO Box 13100
Lansing, MI 48901-3100
Phone: (517)484-5500
Fax: (517)484-5225
Publisher's E-mail: info@mpmca.org
Magazine for plumbing contractors and mechanical contractors. **Freq:** Quarterly. **Print Method:** Offset. Uses mats. **Trim Size:** 8 1/2 x 11. **Cols./Page:** 3. **Col. Width:** 42 nonpareils. **Col. Depth:** 140 agate lines. **Key Personnel:** Brett Glatfelter, Director, Advertising; Walter P. Maner, III, Executive Director. **URL:** http://www.mpmca.org/magazine.htm. **Ad Rates:** BW $425; 4C $990. **Remarks:** Accepts advertising. **Circ:** Controlled ‡3,100.

17668 ■ The Michigan Optometrist
Michigan Optometric Association
530 W Ionia St., Ste. A
Lansing, MI 48933
Phone: (517)482-0616
Fax: (517)482-1611
Freq: Bimonthly. **Print Method:** Offset. **Trim Size:** 8 1/2 x 11. **Cols./Page:** 2. **Col. Width:** 39 nonpareils. **Col. Depth:** 126 agate lines. **Key Personnel:** William D. Dansby, CAE, Editor; Cindy Schnetzler, Executive Director. **ISSN:** 1071-1627 (print). **USPS:** 345-500. **Subscription Rates:** $25 Individuals; $4 Single issue; Included in membership. **Alt. Formats:** PDF. **URL:** http://www.themoa.org/aws/MOA/pt/sp/optometrists_membership. **Ad Rates:** BW $400; PCI $16. **Remarks:** Accepts advertising. **Circ:** Combined ‡1200.

17669 ■ Michigan Out-of-Doors
Michigan United Conservation Clubs
2101 Wood St.
Lansing, MI 48912-3728
Phone: (517)371-1041
Free: 800-777-6720
Publisher's E-mail: membership@mucc.org
Freq: 10/year Monthly Six bi-monthly print editions and four digital-only editions. **Print Method:** Offset. **Trim Size:** 8 1/8 x 10 3/4. **Cols./Page:** 3. **Col. Width:** 27 nonpareils. **Col. Depth:** 196 agate lines. **Key Personnel:** Dennis Muchmore, Executive Director, phone: (517)346-6455; Tony Hansen, Editor, phone: (517)346-6483. **ISSN:** 0026-2382 (print). **Subscription Rates:**

Circulation: ★ = AAM; △ or • = BPA; ♦ = CAC; ❑ = VAC; ⊕ = PO Statement; ‡ = Publisher's Report; Boldface figures = sworn; Light figures = estimated.

$30 Individuals; $50 Two years. **URL:** http://www.mucc.org/michigan_out_of_doors; http://mucc.org/michigan-outofdoors-magazine/. **Mailing address:** PO Box 30235, Lansing, MI 48912-3728. **Ad Rates:** GLR $5.36; BW $3135; 4C $3905; PCI $75. **Remarks:** Accepts advertising. **Circ:** (Not Reported).

17670 ■ Michigan Pharmacist
Michigan Pharmacists Association
408 Kalamazoo Plz.
Lansing, MI 48933
Phone: (517)484-1466
Fax: (517)484-4893
Publisher's E-mail: MPA@MichiganPharmacists.org
Regional professional magazine for hospital, independent, community and consultant pharmacists, pharmacy students and technicians, and pharmaceutical representatives, wholesalers and companies. **Freq:** Quarterly (January, April, July and October). **Print Method:** Offset. **Trim Size:** 8 1/2 x 11. **Cols./Page:** 3 and 2. **Col. Width:** 28 and 42 nonpareils. **Col. Depth:** 140 agate lines. **Key Personnel:** Leah Godzina, Director, Communications; La Vone Swanson, Associate Director. **ISSN:** 1045-6481 (print). **Subscription Rates:** Included in membership. **URL:** http://www.michiganpharmacists.org/publications; http://www.michiganpharmacists.org/membership. **Formerly:** Journal Michigan Pharmacist. **Ad Rates:** BW $1,200. **Remarks:** Accepts advertising. **Circ:** ‡3,200.

17671 ■ Tracks Magazine
Michigan United Conservation Clubs
2101 Wood St.
Lansing, MI 48912-3728
Phone: (517)371-1041
Free: 800-777-6720
Publication E-mail: education@mucc.org
Wildlife magazine which discusses conservation issues (targeted at young audience). **Freq:** 9/year. **Print Method:** Web offset. **Trim Size:** 8 1/2 x 11. **Key Personnel:** Erin McDonough, Executive Director; Shaun McKeon, Editor. **ISSN:** 0238-8810 (print). **Subscription Rates:** $10 family. **URL:** http://mucc.org/home/education-programs/tracks-magazine. **Mailing address:** PO Box 30235, Lansing, MI 48912-3728. **Remarks:** Advertising not accepted. **Circ:** Paid 62000.

17672 ■ WFMK-FM - 99.1
3420 Pine Tree Rd.
Lansing, MI 48911
Phone: (517)394-7272
Free: 800-618-9365
Format: Adult Contemporary. **Networks:** Independent. **Owner:** Citadel Broadcasting Corp., 7201 W Lake Mead Blvd., Ste. 400, Las Vegas, NV 89128-8366, Ph: (702)804-5200, Fax: (702)804-8250. **Founded:** 1959. **Operating Hours**: Continuous; 100% local. **ADI**: Lansing (Ann Arbor), MI. **Key Personnel:** Josh Strickland, Dept. Mgr., josh.strickland@townsquaremedia.com; Zoe Burdine-Fly, Gen. Mgr. **Wattage**: 28,000. **Ad Rates:** $90 for 30 seconds; $100 for 60 seconds. **URL:** http://www.99wfmk.com.

17673 ■ WHTV-TV - 18
2820 E Saginaw St.
Lansing, MI 48912
Phone: (517)372-9497
Key Personnel: Lori Harper, Station Mgr. **URL:** http://www.my18.tv.

17674 ■ WHZZ-FM - 101.7
600 W Cavanaugh Rd.
Lansing, MI 48910-5254
Phone: (517)393-1320
Fax: (517)393-0882
Format: Contemporary Hit Radio (CHR). **Owner:** MacDonald Broadcasting Co., 2000 Whittier Ave., Saginaw, MI 48601-2271. **Founded:** 1947. **Operating Hours**: Continuous. **ADI**: Lansing (Ann Arbor), MI. **Key Personnel:** Cindy Tuck, Gen. Mgr., cindytuck@macdonaldbroadcasting.com; Mark Price, Dir. of Production, lansing.production@macdonaldbroadcasting.com. **Wattage**: 3,000. **Ad Rates:** Noncommercial. **URL:** http://www.1017mikefm.com.

17675 ■ WILS-AM - 1320
600 W Cavanaugh Rd.
Lansing, MI 48910
Phone: (517)393-1320
Fax: (517)393-0882
Format: Talk. **Owner:** MacDonald Broadcasting Co., 2000 Whittier Ave., Saginaw, MI 48601-2271. **Operating Hours**: Continuous. **ADI**: Lansing (Ann Arbor), MI. **Key Personnel:** Dave Horski, Contact. **Wattage**: 25,000. **Ad Rates:** Advertising accepted; rates available upon request. $15-25 per unit. **URL:** http://www.1320wils.com.

17676 ■ WILX-TV - 10
500 American Rd.
Lansing, MI 48911
Phone: (517)393-0110
Fax: (517)393-8555
Email: comments@wilx.com
Format: Commercial TV. **Simulcasts:** WEYI-TV, WEYI-TV. **Networks:** NBC. **Owner:** Gray Television Inc., 4370 Peachtree Rd. NE, No. 400, Atlanta, GA 30319-3054, Ph: (404)266-8333. **Founded:** 1959. **Operating Hours**: Continuous. **Key Personnel:** Kevin Ragan, News Dir., kevin.ragan@wilx.com. **Wattage**: 30,000 ERP H. **Ad Rates:** Advertising accepted; rates available upon request. **URL:** http://www.wilx.com.

17677 ■ WITL-FM - 100.7
3420 Pine Tree Rd.
Lansing, MI 48911
Phone: (517)394-7272
Free: 800-968-7744
Format: Country. **Networks:** ABC. **Owner:** Citadel Broadcasting Corp., 7201 W Lake Mead Blvd., Ste. 400, Las Vegas, NV 89128-8366, Ph: (702)804-5200, Fax: (702)804-8250. **Founded:** 1964. **Operating Hours**: Continuous. **Key Personnel:** Chris Tyler, Dir. of Programs, chris.tyler@citcomm.com; Jordan Lee, Contact, jordan.lee@citcomm.com; Jordan Lee, Contact, jordan.lee@citcomm.com. **Wattage**: 50,000. **Ad Rates:** $23-79 for 30 seconds; $26-94 for 60 seconds. **URL:** http://www.witl.com.

17678 ■ WJIM-AM - 1240
3420 Pine Tree Rd.
Lansing, MI 48911
Format: News; Talk. **Networks:** ABC. **Owner:** Citadel Broadcasting Corp., 7201 W Lake Mead Blvd., Ste. 400, Las Vegas, NV 89128-8366, Ph: (702)804-5200, Fax: (702)804-8250. **Operating Hours**: Continuous. **ADI**: Lansing (Ann Arbor), MI. **Local Programs:** *Health and Wellness Solutions*, Saturday 9:00 a.m. - 11:00 a.m.; *Absolute Truth with Tim Fair*, Tuesday Thursday Sunday 6:00 p.m.; 8:00 p.m.; 10:00 p.m. 9:00 a.m.; *Somewhere In Time with Art Bell*; *The Travel Queen Jane DeGrow*, Sunday 2:00 p.m. - 4:00 p.m. **Wattage**: 1,000. **Ad Rates:** $25-50 for 60 seconds. Combined advertising rates available with WJIM-FM; WMMQ-FM; WVFN-AM; WFMK-FM; WITL-FM. **URL:** http://www.wjimam.com.

17679 ■ WJIM-FM - 97.5
3420 Pine Tree Rd.
Lansing, MI 48911
Phone: (517)394-7272
Format: Top 40. **Owner:** Citadel Broadcasting Corp., 7201 W Lake Mead Blvd., Ste. 400, Las Vegas, NV 89128-8366, Ph: (702)804-5200, Fax: (702)804-8250. **Founded:** 1960. **Operating Hours**: Continuous. **ADI**: Lansing (Ann Arbor), MI. **Wattage**: 45,000. **Ad Rates:** $75-100 for 60 seconds. Combined advertising rates available with WJIM-AM, WITL-FM, WMMQ-FM, WVFN, and WFMK. **URL:** http://wjimam.com.

17680 ■ WLAJ-TV - 53
2820 E Saginaw St.
Lansing, MI 48912
Phone: (517)394-5300
Fax: (517)394-7599
Founded: 1990. **URL:** http://wlns.com.

17681 ■ WLGH-FM - 88.1
148 E Grand River Rd.
Williamston, MI 48895
Free: 888-887-7139
Email: 411@smile.fm
Format: Easy Listening. **Owner:** Superior Communications, Inc., at above address, White Plains, NY. **Mailing address:** PO Box 388, Williamston, MI 48895. **URL:** http://www.smile.fm.

17682 ■ WLNS-TV - 6
2820 E Saginaw St.
Lansing, MI 48912
Phone: (517)372-8282
Fax: (517)372-1507
Email: chief@wlns.com
Format: Full Service. **Networks:** CBS; ABC. **Founded:** 1950. **Operating Hours**: Continuous. **ADI**: Lansing (Ann Arbor), MI. **Key Personnel:** Steve South, Gen. Sales Mgr. **Wattage**: 984,000 ERP. **Ad Rates:** Accepts Advertising. **URL:** http://www.wlns.com.

17683 ■ WLNZ-FM - 89.7
400 N Capitol, Ste. 001
Lansing, MI 48933
Format: Alternative/New Music/Progressive. **Networks:** Public Radio International (PRI); AP; National Public Radio (NPR). **Owner:** Lansing Community College, PO Box 40010, Lansing, MI 48901-7210, Ph: (517)483-1957, Free: 800-644-4522. **Founded:** 1961. **Formerly**: WLCC-FM. **Operating Hours**: Continuous. **Key Personnel:** Lyle Laylin, Engineer. **Wattage**: 420. **Ad Rates:** Noncommercial. **Mailing address:** PO Box 40010, Lansing, MI 48901-7210. **URL:** http://www.lcc.edu.

17684 ■ WMMQ-FM - 94.9
3420 Pine Tree Rd.
Lansing, MI 48911
Phone: (517)363-4949
Fax: (517)394-7272
Format: Classic Rock. **Owner:** BB Broadcasting, Inc., 2301 W Big Beaver Rd., Ste. 921, Troy, MI 48084; Citadel Broadcasting Corp., 7201 W Lake Mead Blvd., Ste. 400, Las Vegas, NV 89128-8366, Ph: (702)804-5200, Fax: (702)804-8250. **Founded:** 1963. **Formerly**: WVIC-FM; WCER-FM. **Operating Hours**: Continuous. **ADI**: Lansing (Ann Arbor), MI. **Key Personnel:** Deb Hart, Contact, deb@wmmq.com; Joey Pants, Contact, joey@wmmq.com. **Wattage**: 50,000. **Ad Rates:** $75-125 for 30 seconds; for 60 seconds. Combined advertising rates available with WJIM-AM/FM, WVFN-AM, WITL-FM, WFMK-FM. **URL:** http://wmmq.com.

17685 ■ WQHH-FM - 96.5
600 W Cavanaugh
Lansing, MI 48910
Phone: (517)393-1320
Fax: (517)393-0882
Format: Hip Hop; Blues. **Owner:** MacDonald Broadcasting Co., 2000 Whittier Ave., Saginaw, MI 48601-2271. **Founded:** 1988. **Operating Hours**: Continuous. **ADI**: Lansing (Ann Arbor), MI. **Key Personnel:** Cindy Tuck, Gen. Mgr., cindytuck@macdonaldbroadcasting.com. **Wattage**: 6,000. **Ad Rates:** Noncommercial. Combined advertising rates available with WXLA-AM. **URL:** http://www.power965fm.com.

17686 ■ WSRQ-FM - 100.1
3105 S Martin Luther King Jr. Blvd.
Lansing, MI 48910-2939
Email: radiooperations@excite.com
Format: Alternative/New Music/Progressive; Contemporary Hit Radio (CHR). **Simulcasts:** WTCU-FM. **Networks:** Westwood One Radio. **Owner:** Fort Bend Broadcasting, PO Box 948, Houston, TX 77001, Ph: (713)227-2600, Fax: (713)227-2606. **Founded:** 1987. **Formerly**: WRQT-FM; WZTU-FM. **Operating Hours**: Continuous. **ADI**: Traverse City-Cadillac, MI. **Key Personnel:** D. Schaberg, VP of Operations, Contact, dcs1037@aol.com; D. Schaberg, Contact. **Wattage**: 3,000. **Ad Rates:** $15 for 30 seconds; $20 for 60 seconds. Combined advertising rates available with WTCU-FM. **URL:** http://www.sarasotatalkradio.com/.

17687 ■ WSYM-TV - 47
600 W St. Joseph St., Ste. 47
Lansing, MI 48933
Phone: (517)484-7747
Fax: (517)484-3144
Email: 47today@fox47news.com
Format: News. **Networks:** Fox. **Owner:** Journal Broadcast Group Inc., 333 W State St., Milwaukee, WI 53203-1305, Ph: (414)332-9611, Fax: (414)967-5400. **Founded:** 1982. **Formerly**: WFSL-TV. **Operating Hours**: Continuous. **ADI**: Lansing (Ann Arbor), MI. **Key Personnel:** Gary Baxter, Gen. Mgr., VP, gbaxter@fox47news.com; David Giles, VP, Gen. Counsel; Kip Bohne, Contact, kbohne@fox47news.com. **Local Programs:** *Fox 47 News at 10*, Monday Tuesday Wednesday Thursday Friday Saturday Sunday 10:00 p.m.; *Melinda's Garden Moment*. **URL:** http://www.jrn.com/fox47news.

17688 ■ WVFN-AM - 730
3420 Pine Tree Rd.
Lansing, MI 48911
Phone: (517)394-7272
Format: Sports; Talk. **Networks:** ESPN Radio. **Owner:** Citadel Broadcasting Corp., 7201 W Lake Mead Blvd., Ste. 400, Las Vegas, NV 89128-8366, Ph: (702)804-5200, Fax: (702)804-8250. **Founded:** 1964. **Formerly:** WVIC-AM. **Operating Hours:** Continuous. **ADI:** Lansing (Ann Arbor), MI. **Key Personnel:** Matt Hanlon, Contact, matt.hanlon@citcomm.com; Zoe Burdine-Fly, Gen. Mgr., zoe.burdine-fly@townsquaremedia.com; Matt Hanlon, Contact, matt.hanlon@citcomm.com. **Local Programs:** *Staudt on Sports*, Monday Tuesday Wednesday Thursday Friday 9:00 a.m.; *The Huge Show*, Monday Tuesday Wednesday Thursday Friday 7:00 p.m. - 9:00 p.m.; *Mad Dog in the Morning*, Monday Tuesday Wednesday Thursday Friday 6:00 a.m. - 9:00 a.m.; *Pardon the Interruption*, Monday Tuesday Wednesday Thursday Friday 5:30 p.m. - 6:00 p.m. **Wattage:** 500 Day; 050 Night. **Ad Rates:** $10-40 for 60 seconds. Combined advertising rates available with WMMQ-FM, WFMK-FM, WJIM-AM, WJIM-FM, WITL-FM. **URL:** http://www.thegame730am.com.

17689 ■ WXLA-AM - 1180
600 W Cavanaugh
Lansing, MI 48917
Phone: (517)393-1320
Format: Adult Contemporary; Oldies. **Networks:** Independent. **Owner:** MacDonald Broadcasting Company Inc., at above address. **Founded:** 1977. **Operating Hours:** Sunrise-sunset. **ADI:** Lansing (Ann Arbor), MI. **Key Personnel:** Cindy Tuck, Gen. Mgr., cindytuck@macdonaldbroadcasting.com. **Wattage:** 1,000. **Ad Rates:** Noncommercial.

LAPEER

Lapeer Co. Lapeer Co. (SE). 20 m E of Flint. Lake resort. Manufactures gray iron castings, trailers, boxes, automotive accessories, aircraft specialties. Dairy, grain farms.

17690 ■ County Press
County Press
1521 Imlay City Rd.
Lapeer, MI 48446
Phone: (810)664-0811
Free: 800-994-0811
County newspaper. **Freq:** Semiweekly (Wed. and Sun.). **Print Method:** Offset. **Cols./Page:** 6. **Col. Width:** 25 nonpareils. **Col. Depth:** 300 agate lines. **Key Personnel:** Jeff Hogan, Editor; Deanna Sera, Director, Advertising; Wes Smith, Publisher. **Subscription Rates:** $20 Individuals; $60 Out of country. **URL:** http://thecountypress.mihomepaper.com. **Formerly:** Lapeer County Press. **Mailing address:** PO Box 220, Lapeer, MI 48446. **Ad Rates:** GLR $1.06; BW $2570; 4C $3087; SAU $20.40. **Remarks:** Accepts advertising. **Circ:** (Not Reported).

17691 ■ Charter Communications
1122 S Lapeer Rd., Ste. C
Lapeer, MI 48446
Free: 888-438-2427
Founded: 1993. **Cities Served:** 41 channels. **URL:** http://www.charter.com.

17692 ■ WMPC-AM - 1230
923 S Main St.
Lapeer, MI 48446
Phone: (810)664-6211
Format: Gospel. **Networks:** SkyLight Satellite; AP; Moody Broadcasting. **Owner:** Calvary Bible Church, 855 S Drake Rd., Kalamazoo, MI 49009, Ph: (269)372-1130, Fax: (269)372-2581. **Founded:** 1926. **Operating Hours:** Continuous; 50% network, 50% local. **Key Personnel:** Debbie Webb, Contact; Debbie Webb, Contact. **Local Programs:** *Creation Moments*; *Little Brown Church*, Monday Tuesday Wednesday Thursday Friday 12:00 p.m.; *Discover the Word*, Monday Tuesday Wednesday Thursday Friday 7:30 p.m. **Wattage:** 1,000. **Ad Rates:** Noncommercial. **Mailing address:** PO Box 104, Lapeer, MI 48446. **URL:** http://www.wmpc.org.

LIVONIA

Wayne Co. Wayne Co. (SE). 20 m W of Detroit. Manufactures tools, dies, stampings, paint, laminated glass, auto bodies and transmissions. Nursery.

17693 ■ Everythingpeople
American Society of Employers
19575 Victor Pky., Ste. 100
Livonia, MI 48152
Phone: (248)353-4500
Fax: (734)402-0462
Magazine focusing on developments both inside and outside the HR profession. **Freq:** Monthly. **URL:** http://www.aseonline.org/News/EverythingPeople-This-Week. **Remarks:** Advertising not accepted. **Circ:** (Not Reported).

17694 ■ The Hearing Professional: Official Journal of the International Hearing Society
International Hearing Society
16880 Middlebelt Rd., Ste. 4
Livonia, MI 48154
Phone: (734)522-7200
Fax: (734)522-0200
Magazine publishing technical articles and product announcements on hearing aids and hearing. Contains business information, and news for hearing health professionals. Includes annual index, chapter news, and book reviews. **Freq:** Quarterly. **Print Method:** Offset. **Trim Size:** 8 1/2 x 11. **Cols./Page:** 3. **Col. Width:** 28 nonpareils. **Col. Depth:** 133 agate lines. **Key Personnel:** Alan Lowell, President; Kathleen Mennillo, Executive Director, phone: (734)522-7200; Kara Nacarato, Editor. **ISSN:** 0004-7473 (print). **Subscription Rates:** Included in membership; $45 /year for nonmembers outside U.S.; $35 /year for nonmembers in U.S. **URL:** http://www.ihsinfo.org/ihsV2/sign_in/index.cfm?urlreferrer=/IhsV2/hearing_professional. **Ad Rates:** BW $1155; 4C $1808; PCI $80. **Remarks:** Advertising accepted; rates available upon request. **Circ:** 3,300.

17695 ■ Journal of Transcultural Nursing
Transcultural Nursing Society
Madonna University
36600 Schoolcraft Rd.
Livonia, MI 48150
Fax: (734)793-2457
Free: 888-432-5470
Publisher's E-mail: staff@tcns.org
Journal focusing on topics that affect nursing and health care clinical practice, research, education, and theory development. **Freq:** Bimonthly. **Key Personnel:** Marilyn Douglas, Editor; Marjory Spraycar, Managing Editor; Norma Cuellar, Editor-in-Chief. **ISSN:** 1043--6596 (print); **EISSN:** 1552--7832 (electronic). **Subscription Rates:** £562 Institutions print & e-access; £618 Institutions current volume print & all online content; £506 Institutions e-access; £562 Institutions all online content; £430 Institutions e-access (content through 1998); £551 Institutions print only; £93 Individuals print only; £101 Institutions single print; £20 Individuals single print. **URL:** http://tcn.sagepub.com; http://uk.sagepub.com/en-gb/asi/journal-of-transcultural-nursing/journal200814. **Remarks:** Advertising accepted; rates available upon request. **Circ:** (Not Reported).

17696 ■ The MacGuffin
Schoolcraft College
18600 Haggerty Rd.
Livonia, MI 48152
Phone: (734)462-4400
Publication E-mail: macguffin@schoolcraft.edu
Literary magazine featuring poetry, short fiction, and creative non-fiction. **Freq:** 3/year. **Trim Size:** 6 x 9. **Key Personnel:** Gordon Krupsky, Managing Editor; Elizabeth Kircos, Editor; Carol Was, Editor; Steven A. Dolgin, Editor. **URL:** http://www.schoolcraft.edu/a-z-index/the-macguffin#.V-94NtR97s1. **Circ:** (Not Reported).

17697 ■ Nonprofit World
Society for Nonprofit Organizations
PO Box 510354
Livonia, MI 48151
Phone: (734)451-3582
Fax: (734)451-5935
Publisher's E-mail: info@snpo.org
Freq: Quarterly. **Subscription Rates:** $49 Individuals electronic; $69 Individuals; $150 Institutions. **Alt. Formats:** CD-ROM. **URL:** http://www.snpo.org/publications/nonprofitworld.php. **Ad Rates:** BW $990. **Remarks:** Accepts advertising. **Circ:** (Not Reported).

17698 ■ Resource Book
Right to Life - Lifespan
32540 Schoolcraft Rd., Ste. 100
Livonia, MI 48150-4305
Phone: (734)524-0162
Fax: (734)524-0166
Journal containing current educational and legislative information about anti-abortionary interest. **Freq:** Annual. **Trim Size:** 7 x 10. **Subscription Rates:** free upon request; Free free upon request. **URL:** http://www.rtllifespan.org/ls/resourcebook.wml; http://www.rtl-lifespan.org. **Remarks:** Advertising not accepted. **Circ:** (Not Reported).

17699 ■ Scrap & Stamp Arts
Scott Advertising & Publishing Co.
30595 Eight Mile Rd.
Livonia, MI 48152
Phone: (248)477-6650
Fax: (248)477-6795
Free: 800-458-8237
Publisher's E-mail: contactus@scottpublications.com
Consumer magazine covering rubber stamping for hobbyists. **Freq:** 8/year. **Subscription Rates:** $29.90 U.S. 1 year; $55 U.S. 2 years; $45.90 Other countries 1 year; $87 Other countries 2 years. **URL:** http://scottpublications.com/ssa. **Formerly:** Stamping Arts & Crafts. **Remarks:** Accepts advertising. **Circ:** (Not Reported).

17700 ■ Soft Dolls & Animals
Scott Advertising & Publishing Co.
30595 Eight Mile Rd.
Livonia, MI 48152
Phone: (248)477-6650
Fax: (248)477-6795
Free: 800-458-8237
Publisher's E-mail: contactus@scottpublications.com
Magazine covering fabric dolls, teddy bears, and other fabric figures for hobbyists and crafters. **Freq:** Bimonthly. **Subscription Rates:** $29.95 U.S. 1 year; $53.90 U.S. 2 years; $41.95 Other countries 1 year; $77.90 Other countries 2 years; $7.99 Single issue. **URL:** http://scottpublications.com/sdamag. **Remarks:** Accepts advertising. **Circ:** (Not Reported).

17701 ■ Bright House Networks
14525 Farmington Rd.
Livonia, MI 48154
Free: 866-898-9101
Owner: Bright House Networks, 117 S Mill St., Ste. I, Tehachapi, CA 93561, Free: 877-424-9246. **Cities Served:** Wayne County. **URL:** http://www.brighthouse.com.

LOWELL

17702 ■ Lowell Ledger
Lowell Ledger
105 N Broadway
Lowell, MI 49331-0128
Phone: (616)897-9261
Fax: (616)897-4809
Community newspaper. **Freq:** Weekly. **Cols./Page:** 6. **Col. Width:** 9 1/2 picas. **Col. Depth:** 16 inches. **Key Personnel:** Roger K. Brown, Editor. **Subscription Rates:** $25 Individuals zip codes that begin with 493 or 495; $36 Out of state outside 493 or 495 zip codes. **URL:** http://lowellbuyersguide.com. **Mailing address:** PO Box 128, Lowell, MI 49331-0128. **Circ:** 2,200.

LUDINGTON

Mason Co. Mason Co. (W). On Lake Michigan, 90 m NW of Grand Rapids. Resort. Manufactures tool boxes, printer's and railway equipment, wood pallets, plastic products, games and toys, pine and oak furniture, electical equipment, motor and refrigerator parts, chemicals. Fisheries. Agriculture. Fruits and vegetables.

17703 ■ Ludington Daily News
Ludington Daily News
202 N Rath Ave.
Ludington, MI 49431-0340
Phone: (231)845-5181
Fax: (231)843-4011
Free: 800-748-0407
Publisher's E-mail: sports@ludingtondailynews.com

Circulation: ★ = AAM; △ or • = BPA; ♦ = CAC; ❑ = VAC; ⊕ = PO Statement; ‡ = Publisher's Report; Boldface figures = sworn; Light figures = estimated.

General newspaper. **Freq:** Daily. **Print Method:** Offset. **Cols./Page:** 6. **Col. Width:** 24 nonpareils. **Col. Depth:** 301 agate lines. **Key Personnel:** John Walker, Manager, Advertising; Jeffrey N. Evans, Publisher; Steve Begnoche, Managing Editor. **Subscription Rates:** $17.30 Individuals Mason County, Branch & Pentwater (Home Delivery Rates) 4 weeks; $49.35 Individuals Mason County, Branch & Pentwater (Home Delivery Rates) 12 weeks; $96.60 Individuals Mason County, Branch & Pentwater (Home Delivery Rates) 24 weeks; $202.60 Out of area Mason County, Branch & Pentwater - 1 year; $27.70 Out of area 4 weeks; $78.95 Out of area 12 weeks; $154.70 By mail 24 weeks; $324.25 By mail 1 year; $10.25 Individuals e-edition - 4 weeks; $29.15 Individuals e-edition - 12 weeks; $57 Individuals e-edition - 24 weeks; $119.65 Individuals e-edition - 1 year. **URL:** http://www.shorelinemedia.net/ludington_daily_news. **Mailing address:** PO Box 340, Ludington, MI 49431-0340. **Ad Rates:** PCI $11. **Remarks:** Advertising accepted; rates available upon request. **Circ:** Mon.-Sat. ★**7,537**.

17704 ■ WKLA-FM - 106.3
5941 W US 10
Ludington, MI 49431
Phone: (231)843-3438
Fax: (231)843-1886
Free: 888-843-1063
Format: Adult Contemporary. **Networks:** ABC. **Owner:** Lake Michigan Broadcasting, at above address. **Founded:** 1971. **Operating Hours:** Continuous. **ADI:** Traverse City-Cadillac, MI. **Wattage:** 6,000. **Ad Rates:** Noncommercial. Combined advertising rates available with WKLA-AM: $6.60-$12 for 30 seconds, $8.25-$15 for 60 seconds.

17705 ■ WKZC-FM - 95
5941 W U.S. 10
Ludington, MI 49431
Phone: (231)843-3438
Format: Country. **Networks:** ABC. **Owner:** Lake Michigan Broadcasting, at above address. **Founded:** 1983. **Operating Hours:** Continuous. **Wattage:** 25,000. **Ad Rates:** $3.96-13.20 for 30 seconds; $4.95-16.50 for 60 seconds.

17706 ■ WMOM-FM - 102.7
206 E Ludington Ave.
Ludington, MI 49431
Phone: (231)845-9666
Format: Adult Contemporary. **Ad Rates:** Advertising accepted; rates available upon request. **URL:** http://www.wmom.fm.

WMTE-AM - See Manistee

17707 ■ WWKR-FM - 94.1
5399 Wallace Ln.
Ludington, MI 49431
Phone: (231)843-0941
Fax: (231)843-9411
Email: info@94k-rock.com
Format: Classic Rock. **Ad Rates:** Advertising accepted; rates available upon request. **Mailing address:** PO Box 855, Ludington, MI 49431. **URL:** http://www.94k-rock.com.

LUPTON

17708 ■ WMSD-FM - 90.9
2906 E Heath
Lupton, MI 48635
Phone: (989)473-4616
Free: 866-473-9673
Format: Religious. **Operating Hours:** Continuous. **Wattage:** 5,000. **Ad Rates:** Noncommercial. **URL:** http://www.wmsdradio.com.

MACKINAC ISLAND

Mackinac Co. Mackinac Co. (E. Up. Penin.) On Straits of Mackinac, 45 m SW of Sault Sainte Marie. Tourism. Historical. Ferry boats from St. Ignace and Mackinaw City.

17709 ■ The Mackinac Island Town Crier: A Weekly Newspaper Serving the Makinac Island Community
The St. Ignace News
7529 Market St.
Mackinac Island, MI 49757
Phone: (906)847-3788
Publisher's E-mail: sales@stignacenews.com
Community newspaper. **Freq:** 18 consecutive weeks from mid-May to mid-September and once in October, December, February, and April. **Print Method:** Offset. **Trim Size:** 11 1/2 x 17. **Cols./Page:** 5. **Col. Width:** 12 picas. **Col. Depth:** 16 inches. **Key Personnel:** Wesley H Maurer, Jr., Publisher; Mary R. Maurer, Business Manager; Ellen Paquin, Editor. **USPS:** 324-060. **Subscription Rates:** $30 Individuals print; $35 Out of state print; $20 Individuals online; $5 Individuals weekly (online); $50 Individuals print and online; $55 Out of state print and online. **URL:** http://www.mackinacislandnews.com. **Mailing address:** PO Box 532, Mackinac Island, MI 49757. **Ad Rates:** GLR $.40; BW $440; PCI $5.50. **Remarks:** Advertising accepted; rates available upon request. **Circ:** ‡2,700.

MACKINAW CITY

17710 ■ W236BZ-FM - 95.3
7119 M-68
Indian River, MI 49749
Phone: (231)238-0815
Fax: (231)238-0803
Free: 866-799-9825
Format: Religious. **Owner:** Baraga Broadcasting Inc., at above address, Traverse City, MI 49684. **Formerly:** W237CF-FM. **Operating Hours:** Continuous. **Key Personnel:** Tom McMahon, Contact, tom@utmi.net; Tom McMahon, Contact, tom@utmi.net. **Mailing address:** PO Box 1109, Indian River, MI 49749. **URL:** http://www.place123.net.

MADISON HEIGHTS

17711 ■ Better Investing
National Association of Investors Corporation
711 W 13 Mile Rd.
Madison Heights, MI 48071
Phone: (248)583-6242
Fax: (248)583-4880
Free: 877-275-6242
Publisher's E-mail: service@betterinvesting.org
Magazine focusing on investing in long-term common stock. **Freq:** 10/year Monthly. **Print Method:** Web offset. **Trim Size:** 8 x 10 7/8. **Cols./Page:** 3. **Col. Width:** 27 nonpareils. **Col. Depth:** 138 agate lines. **Key Personnel:** Adam Ritt, Editor. **ISSN:** 0006- 016X (print). **Subscription Rates:** $22 Individuals 10 issues; Included in membership; $31 /year for nonmembers; $1.50 /issue for nonmembers; e-magazine; included in membership dues. **URL:** http://www.betterinvesting.org/Public/StartLearning/BI+Mag/default.htm. **Ad Rates:** GLR $18; BW $6,645; 4C $13,350; PCI $252. **Remarks:** Accepts advertising. **Circ:** Paid ★**198964**, 386000.

MANISTEE

Manistee Co. Manistee Co. (W). On Lake Michigan, 20 m N of Ludington. Tourist area. Historical museums. Fishing & boating. Produce oil and gas. Heavy industry. Agriculture. Fruit orchards.

17712 ■ Manistee News Advocate
The Pioneer Group
75 W Maple St.
Manistee, MI 49660
Phone: (231)723-3592
Fax: (616)723-4733
Publication E-mail: mnainfo@pioneergroup.com
Local newspaper. **Freq:** Daily. **Print Method:** Web offset. **Trim Size:** 6 x 21 1/2. **Cols./Page:** 8. **Col. Width:** 25 nonpareils. **Col. Depth:** 294 agate lines. **Key Personnel:** Marilyn Barker, Manager, Advertising. **Subscription Rates:** $2.50 Individuals Online Edition ManisteeNews.com - Daily Pass; $9.45 Individuals Online Edition ManisteeNews.com - Monthly (+Free Trial for the first month); $113.40 Individuals Online Edition ManisteeNews.com - 12 Months (+Free Trial for the first month); $41.25 Individuals Print Edition Manistee County (3-Months); $80.50 Individuals Print Edition Manistee County(6-Months); $151.80 Individuals Print Edition Manistee County(12-Months); $51 Individuals Print Edition Michigan, outside of Manistee County (3-Months); $96.40 Individuals Print Edition Michigan, outside of Manistee County(6-Months); $183 Individuals Print Edition Michigan, outside of Manistee County(12-Months); $67.40 Individuals Print Edition Outside Michigan (3-Months); $127.50 Individuals Print Edition Outside Michigan(6-Months); $241.20 Individuals Print Edition Outside Michigan(12-Months). **URL:** http://manisteenews.com; http://pioneergroup.com. **Mailing address:** PO Box 317, Manistee, MI 49660. **Ad Rates:** BW $838.50; 4C $1,238.50; SAU $8.50. **Remarks:** Accepts advertising. **Circ:** ‡5000.

17713 ■ West Shore Shoppers Guide
The Pioneer Group
75 W Maple St.
Manistee, MI 49660
Phone: (231)723-3592
Fax: (616)723-4733
Free: 888-723-3592
Shopper. **Freq:** Weekly (Sun.). **Print Method:** Offset. **Trim Size:** 12 x 13. **Cols./Page:** 6. **Col. Width:** 13 nonpareils. **Col. Depth:** 78 agate lines. **URL:** http://westshoreshoppersguide.com; http://pioneergroup.com/advertise. **Mailing address:** PO Box 317, Manistee, MI 49660. **Ad Rates:** SAU $8.50. **Remarks:** Accepts advertising. **Circ:** ‡13,000.

17714 ■ WCMW-TV - 21
c/o WCMU-TV
1999 E Campus Dr.
Mount Pleasant, MI 48859
Phone: (989)774-3105
Fax: (989)774-4427
Free: 800-727-9268
Format: Public TV. **Networks:** Public Broadcasting Service (PBS). **Owner:** Central Michigan University, 1200 S Franklin St., Mount Pleasant, MI 48859, Ph: (989)774-4000. **Founded:** 1984. **Operating Hours:** 6 a.m.-midnight; 90% network, 10% local. **ADI:** Traverse City-Cadillac, MI. **Key Personnel:** Ray Ford, Prog. Dir., ford1r@cmich.edu. **Ad Rates:** Noncommercial. **URL:** http://www.wcmu.org.

17715 ■ WMTE-AM
359 River St.
Manistee, MI 49660
Phone: (616)723-9906
Fax: (616)723-9908
Free: 800-968-1480
Format: Middle-of-the-Road (MOR). **Networks:** ABC. **Owner:** Chickering & Assoc. Broadcast Group, at above address, Ph: (616)843-3438, Fax: (616)843-1886. **Founded:** 1947. **Wattage:** 1,000. **Ad Rates:** $3.96-13.20 for 30 seconds; $4.95-16.50 for 60 seconds.

17716 ■ WMTE-AM - 1340
5941 W US 10
Ludington, MI 49431
Phone: (231)843-3438
Format: News; Talk. **Networks:** ABC; ESPN Radio. **Owner:** Lake Michigan Broadcasting, at above address. **Founded:** 1951. **Operating Hours:** Continuous. **Wattage:** 1,000. **Ad Rates:** Noncommercial. $8-12 for 30 seconds; $12-14 for 60 seconds. Combined advertising rates available with WKLA-AM, WKLA-FM, WKZC-FM, WMTE-FM.

MANISTIQUE

Schoolcraft Co. Schoolcraft Co. (EC Up. Penin.). On Lake Michigan, 45 m E of Escanaba. Lake resort. Marina. Manufactures lumber, paper, pulp, lime. Fisheries. Hardwood timber. Agriculture. Potatoes, oats, hay.

17717 ■ Pioneer-Tribune
Pioneer-Tribune
212 Walnut St.
Manistique, MI 49854
Phone: (906)341-5200
Publisher's E-mail: newsroom@pioneertribune.com
Community newspaper. **Freq:** Weekly (Thurs.). **Print Method:** Offset. **Cols./Page:** 8. **Col. Depth:** 300 agate lines. **Key Personnel:** Lisa A. Demers, Publisher; Rick B. Demers, Business Manager; Paul Olson, Editor. **Subscription Rates:** $38 Individuals print or online; $5 Individuals 10 day online sunscription; $48 Out of state print. **Ad Rates:** GLR $4.50; BW $420. **Remarks:** Advertising accepted; rates available upon request. **Circ:** 4,000.

17718 ■ WTIQ-AM - 1490
7876 W County Rd. 442
Manistique, MI 49854

Phone: (906)341-1490
Email: wtiq@chartermi.net
Format: Hip Hop; Classic Rock. **Networks:** ABC. **Owner:** Lakes Radio, Inc., PO Box 352, Rice Lake, WI 54868, Ph: (715)234-2131. **Founded:** 1964. **Wattage:** 1,000 KW. **Ad Rates:** Accepts Advertising. **URL:** http://www.wtiqradio.com.

MARLETTE

Sanilac Co. Samilac Co. (E). 40 m NE of Flint. Residential.

17719 ■ Leader
Leader
Box 338
Marlette, MI 48453
Phone: (517)635-2435
Fax: (517)635-3769
Publisher's E-mail: bglover@carrolsweb.com
Community newspaper. **Founded:** 1961. **Freq:** Weekly (Wed.). **Print Method:** Offset. Uses mats. **Cols./Page:** 5 and 6. **Col. Width:** 24 and 24 nonpareils. **Col. Depth:** 224 and 301 agate lines. **Key Personnel:** John Frazier, Contact. **Subscription Rates:** $7.50 Individuals; $13 Individuals. **Ad Rates:** GLR $.12; SAU $6.50. **Remarks:** Accepts advertising. **Circ:** ‡315, ‡2000.

MARQUETTE

Marquette Co. Marquette Co. (NWC, Up. Penin.). On Lake Superior, 60 m N of Escanaba. Northern Michigan University. Center and chief port of iron industry of upper Michigan. Manufactures foundry products, woodenware and wood novelties, mining machinery, lumber, sausage, beverages. Fisheries; timber. Diversified farming. Summer resort.

17720 ■ Action Shopper
Action Shopper
249 W Washington St.
Marquette, MI 49855
Phone: (906)228-8920
Fax: (906)228-5777
Publisher's E-mail: classifieds@actionshopperonline.com
Free shopper. **Founded:** May 16, 1972. **Freq:** Weekly (Wed.). **Print Method:** Offset. **Trim Size:** 11 1/4 x 15. **Cols./Page:** 7. **Col. Width:** 8 picas. **Col. Depth:** 223 agate lines. **URL:** http://www.greatnorthernconn.com/papers/marquette.html. **Mailing address:** PO Box 610, Marquette, MI 49855. **Ad Rates:** GLR $10.40; BW $812.25; 4C $1037.25; PCI $9.26. **Remarks:** Advertising accepted; rates available upon request. **Circ:** 22,300.

17721 ■ The Mining Journal
The Mining Journal
249 W Washington
Marquette, MI 49855
Phone: (906)228-2500
Fax: (906)228-3273
Free: 800-562-7811
General newspaper. **Founded:** 1846. **Freq:** Daily (eve.), Sat. and Sun. (morn.). **Print Method:** Offset. **Trim Size:** 13 3/4 x 22 3/4. **Cols./Page:** 6. **Col. Width:** 25 nonpareils. **Col. Depth:** 301 agate lines. **Key Personnel:** Dan Weingarten, Editor; Bud Sargent, Managing Editor; David Bond, Art Director; Jerry Newhouse, Manager, Circulation; Dave Schneider, Editor; Emily Xu, Accountant; James Reevs, Publisher. **Subscription Rates:** $58.70 Individuals home delivery - carrier 7 days; $54.60 Individuals home delivery - motor route 7 days; $75 Individuals home delivery - mail 7 days; $90 Out of state home delivery - motor route 7 days. **URL:** http://www.miningjournal.net. **Ad Rates:** GLR $.89; BW $1607.34; 4C $2107.34; SAU $12.46; PCI $12.46. **Remarks:** Accepts advertising. **Circ:** Mon.-Fri. ★**14,263**, Sun. ★**15,842**, Sat. ★**14,780**, ★**11,618**, △**13,904**.

17722 ■ Northern Magazine
Northern Michigan University Alumni Association
1401 Presque Isle Ave.
Marquette, MI 49855
Phone: (906)227-2610
Free: 877-GRA-DNMU
Publisher's E-mail: alumni@nmu.edu
Magazine featuring news about NMU's faculty, programs, events, activities and accomplishments of NMU alumni. **Freq:** 3/year. **Subscription Rates:** $15 /year. **Alt. Formats:** PDF. **URL:** http://www.nmu.edu/communicationsandmarketing/northernmagazine. **Formerly:** Northern Horizons. **Remarks:** Accepts advertising. **Circ:** 40000.

17723 ■ The UP Catholic: The Newspaper of the Diocese of Marquette
Roman Catholic Diocese of Marquette
PO Box 1000
Marquette, MI 49855
Phone: (906)225-1141
Fax: (906)225-0437
Catholic newspaper. **Freq:** Semimonthly. **Print Method:** Offset. **Cols./Page:** 5. **Col. Width:** 10 13/16 inches. **Col. Depth:** 13 inches. **Key Personnel:** John Fee, II, Editor, phone: (906)227-9128; Mr. Stephen Gretzinger, Manager, Advertising; Bishop Alexander K. Sample, Publisher. **ISSN:** 1063--4525 (print). **USPS:** 916-360. **Subscription Rates:** $20 U.S. **Ad Rates:** BW $75; 4C $125; PCI $13.42. **Remarks:** Advertising accepted; rates available upon request. **Circ:** Paid ‡22000.

17724 ■ Great Lakes Radio Inc.
3060 US 41 W
Marquette, MI 49855
Phone: (906)228-6800
Fax: (906)228-8128
Format: Adult Contemporary; Oldies; Eighties; Country; Sports; Classic Rock. **Founded:** 1992. **Key Personnel:** Todd Noordyk, Gen. Mgr.; Walt Lindala, Mgr. **URL:** http://www.greatlakesshopping.com.

WEUL-FM - See Kingsford

17725 ■ WHCH-FM - 98.3
3060 US 41 W
Marquette, MI 49855
Phone: (906)228-6800
Format: Classic Rock; Full Service. **Networks:** AP; Jones Satellite. **Owner:** Great Lakes Radio Inc., 3060 US 41 W, Marquette, MI 49855, Ph: (906)228-6800, Fax: (906)228-8128. **Founded:** 1974. **Formerly:** WQXO-FM. **Operating Hours:** Continuous. **ADI:** Marquette, MI. **Key Personnel:** Todd Noordyk, Gen. Mgr., todd@greatlakesradio.org; Devin Lawrence, Dir. of Programs; Walt Lindala, News Dir. **Wattage:** 2,600 ERP. **Ad Rates:** Advertising accepted; rates available upon request. **URL:** http://wrup.com.

WHWG-FM - See Trout Lake

17726 ■ WHWL-FM - 95.7
130 Carmen Dr.
Marquette, MI 49855
Phone: (906)249-1423
Free: 800-359-9673
Format: Religious. **Owner:** Gospel Opportunities Inc., 130 Carmen Dr., Marquette, MI 49855-9380, Ph: (906)249-1423, Free: 800-359-9673. **Founded:** 1975. **Operating Hours:** 5:50 a.m.-midnight. **ADI:** Marquette, MI. **Key Personnel:** Curt Marker, Mgr.; Andy Larsen, News Dir. **Wattage:** 100,000. **Ad Rates:** Noncommercial. **URL:** http://www.whwl.net.

17727 ■ WIAN-AM - 1240
1356 Mackinaw Ave.
Cheboygan, MI 49721
Phone: (231)627-2341
Email: info@nsbroadcasting.com
Format: News; Talk; Sports. **Simulcasts:** WDMJ-AM. **Networks:** ABC. **Owner:** Northern Star Broadcasting, 3250 Racquet Club Dr., Traverse City, MI 49684, Ph: (231)922-4981. **Founded:** 1947. **Formerly:** WJPD-AM. **Operating Hours:** Continuous; 98% network. **ADI:** Marquette, MI. **Wattage:** 1,000. **Ad Rates:** $10-15 for 60 seconds. **URL:** http://www.nsbroadcasting.com.

17728 ■ WJPD-FM - 92.3
1009 W Ridge St., Ste. A
Marquette, MI 49855
Phone: (906)225-1313
Fax: (906)225-1324
Email: wjpd@wjpd.com
Format: Country. **Operating Hours:** Continuous. **Key Personnel:** Bill Curtis, Gen. Mgr., bill@rock101.net. **Wattage:** 100,000 ERP. **Ad Rates:** Advertising accepted; rates available upon request. **URL:** http://www.wjpd.com.

17729 ■ WKQS-FM - 101.9
3060 US, 41 W
Marquette, MI 49855
Phone: (906)227-7777
Format: Adult Contemporary. **Networks:** ABC. **Founded:** Jan. 04, 1997. **Operating Hours:** Continuous. **Wattage:** 12,000. **Ad Rates:** Noncommercial. **URL:** http://www.wkqsfm.com.

17730 ■ WMQT-FM - 107.7
121 N Front St.
Marquette, MI 49855
Phone: (906)225-9100
Fax: (906)225-5577
Format: Adult Contemporary. **Owner:** Taconite Broadcasting Inc., at above address. **Founded:** 1974. **Operating Hours:** Continuous. **ADI:** Marquette, MI. **Key Personnel:** Tom Mogush, Gen. Mgr., Gen. Sales Mgr., tom@wmqt.com; Jim Koski, Dir. of Programs, jim@wmqt.com; Jill Trudeau, Production Mgr., jill@wmqt.com. **Wattage:** 100,000. **Ad Rates:** $20-26 for 30 seconds; $24-36 for 60 seconds. Combined advertising rates available with WZAM-AM. **URL:** http://www.wmqt.com.

17731 ■ WNMU-FM - 90.1
1401 Presque Ilse Ave.
Marquette, MI 49855
Phone: (906)227-2600
Free: 800-227-9668
Email: pr90@nmu.edu
Format: Public Radio. **Networks:** National Public Radio (NPR). **Owner:** Northern Michigan University, 1401 Presque Isle Ave., Marquette, MI 49855-5301, Ph: (906)227-1000. **Founded:** 1963. **ADI:** Marquette, MI. **Key Personnel:** Eric Smith, Gen. Mgr., esmith@nmu.edu; Evelyn Massaro, Station Mgr., emassaro@nmu.edu; Stan Wright, Operations Mgr., swright@nmu.edu; Nicole Walton, News Dir., nwalton@nmu.edu. **Local Programs:** *Sound Spectrum*, Monday Saturday 3:00 a.m. 10:00 p.m.; *Nature Watch*, Monday Tuesday Wednesday Thursday Friday 9:00 a.m.; *Humoresque*, Monday Tuesday Wednesday Thursday Friday 9:35 a.m. - 12:00 p.m.; *Classical Guitar Alive*, Monday 12:00 p.m.; *Sounds Choral*, Thursday 12:00 p.m.; *Savannah Music Festival*; *Marketplace Money*, Wednesday Saturday 4:00 a.m. 11:00 a.m.; *In the Pines*, Thursday Sunday 3:30 p.m. 9:00 p.m.; *Night Studio*, Monday Tuesday Wednesday Thursday Friday Monday Friday 2:00 a.m. 10:06 p.m.; *Weekday*, Monday Tuesday Wednesday Thursday Friday 3:00 p.m. **Wattage:** 100,000 ERP. **Ad Rates:** Accepts Advertising. **URL:** http://www.wnmufm.org.

17732 ■ WNMU-TV - 13
1401 Presque Isle Ave.
Marquette, MI 49855
Free: 800-227-9668
Format: Public TV. **Simulcasts:** WNMU-FM. **Networks:** Public Broadcasting Service (PBS). **Owner:** Northern Michigan University, 1401 Presque Isle Ave., Marquette, MI 49855-5301, Ph: (906)227-1000. **Founded:** 1972. **Operating Hours:** Continuous. **ADI:** Marquette, MI. **Key Personnel:** Eric Smith, Gen. Mgr., esmith@nmu.edu; Bruce Turner, Station Mgr., bturner@nmu.edu; Evelyn Massaro, Station Mgr., emassaro@nmu.edu. **Local Programs:** *Ask The...*, Thursday Friday 8:00 p.m. 12:00 p.m.; *High School Bowl*, Monday Saturday 12:00 p.m. 8:00 p.m.; *Media Meet*, Saturday Sunday 6:30 p.m. 7:30 p.m. **Wattage:** 15,400 ERP H. **Ad Rates:** Noncommercial. **URL:** http://wnmutv.nmu.edu.

17733 ■ WPIQ-FM - 99.9
3060 US 41 W
Marquette, MI 49855
Phone: (906)228-6800
Email: frontdesk@greatlakesradio.org
Format: Talk; Sports. **Networks:** Jones Satellite. **Operating Hours:** Continuous. **Key Personnel:** Todd Noordyk, Gen. Mgr.; Walt Lindala, News Dir.; Mark Evans, Sports Dir.; Staci Zanetti, Traffic Mgr. **Wattage:** 6,000. **Ad Rates:** Noncommercial. **URL:** http://wrup.com.

17734 ■ WRUP-FM - 98.3
2025 US 41 W
Marquette, MI 49855
Phone: (906)228-6800
Format: Classic Rock; Country. **Networks:** Jones Satellite. **Owner:** Great Lakes Radio Inc., 3060 US 41 W, Marquette, MI 49855, Ph: (906)228-6800, Fax:

Circulation: ★ = AAM; △ or • = BPA; ♦ = CAC; ❑ = VAC; ⊕ = PO Statement; ‡ = Publisher's Report; Boldface figures = sworn; Light figures = estimated.

(906)228-8128. **Founded:** 1974. **Operating Hours:** Continuous; 80% network, 20% local. **Wattage:** 100,000. **Ad Rates:** Advertising accepted; rates available upon request. **URL:** http://www.wrup.com.

17735 ■ W17CS - 17
PO Box A
Santa Ana, CA 92711
Phone: (714)832-2950
Free: 888-731-1000

Owner: Trinity Broadcasting Network Inc., PO Box A, Santa Ana, CA 92711, Ph: (714)832-2950, Free: 888-731-1000.

17736 ■ WSHN-FM - 100.1
1921 W Ridge St.
Marquette, MI 49855
Phone: (231)924-4700
Email: wshn@riverview.net

Owner: Noordyk Broadcasting, Inc., at above address. **Founded:** 1960. **ADI:** Grand Rapids-Kalamazoo-Battle Creek, MI. **Key Personnel:** John Russell, News Dir. **Wattage:** 5,000. **Ad Rates:** Accepts Advertising.

17737 ■ WUPG-FM - 96.7
715 W Washington St., Ste. 1
Marquette, MI 49855
Phone: (906)225-0656
Fax: (906)225-0656

Format: Information; Full Service. **Key Personnel:** Kent Smith, Gen. Mgr., kent@radioeagle.com; Chip Arledge, Dir. of Programs, chip@radioeagle.com. **URL:** http://www.radioeaglemarquette.com.

17738 ■ WUPX-FM - 91.5
1204 University Ctr.
Marquette, MI 49855
Phone: (906)227-1844

Format: Country. **Owner:** Northern Michigan University, 1401 Presque Isle Ave., Marquette, MI 49855-5301, Ph: (906)227-1000. **Founded:** 1970. **Formerly:** WBKX-FM. **Operating Hours:** Continuous. **ADI:** Marquette, MI. **Wattage:** 1,700 ERP. **Ad Rates:** Accepts Advertising. **URL:** http://www.wupx.com.

17739 ■ WZAM-AM - 970
121 N Front St., Ste. A
Marquette, MI 49855
Phone: (906)225-9100
Fax: (906)225-5577

Format: Sports. **Founded:** 1959. **Formerly:** WMVN-AM. **Operating Hours:** 6 a.m.-7 p.m. **Key Personnel:** Tom Mogush, Contact, tom@wmqt.com; Casey Ford, Dir. of Programs, casey@espn970.com; Tom Mogush, Contact, tom@wmqt.com. **Wattage:** 5,000. **Ad Rates:** Noncommercial.

MARSHALL

Calhoun Co. Calhoun Co. (S). On Kalamazoo River, 13 m E of Battle Creek. Historical Landmarks. Manufactures packaging equipment, auto parts and trailers, refrigerator cabinets, trusses, pre-fabricated homes, boxes, automatic doors, castings, cheese. Agriculture. Onions, livestock, grain.

17740 ■ WMLY-FM - 93.1
PO Box 61
Marshall, MI 49068
Email: wb8out@sbcglobal.net

Format: Religious; News; Talk; Contemporary Christian. **Operating Hours:** Continuous. **Wattage:** 090 ERP. **URL:** http://www.lifetalk.net/stationInfo.html?id=58.

MASON

Ingham Co. Ingham Co. (C). 12 m S of Lansing. Plastics, dairy products and beans.

17741 ■ Healthy & Fit: Healthy Solutions. Fit Results. A Better You
Healthy and Fit
PO Box 26
Mason, MI 48854
Phone: (517)244-1844

Magazine that provides editorials, tips, and advice for Michigan's health and fitness enthusiasts. **Freq:** Monthly. **Key Personnel:** Tim Kissman, Publisher, phone: (517)244-1844. **Subscription Rates:** $10 Individuals. **URL:** http://www.healthyandfitmagazine.com. **Remarks:** Accepts advertising. **Circ:** (Not Reported).

17742 ■ WUNN-AM - 1110
PO Box 35300
Tucson, AZ 85740
Free: 800-776-1070

Format: Religious. **Owner:** Family Life Communications, Inc., 7355 N Oracle Rd., Tucson, AZ 85704, Ph: (520)544-5950, Fax: (520)742-6979, Free: 800-776-1070. **Founded:** 1967. **Operating Hours:** Sunrise-sunset; 80% network, 20% local. **Wattage:** 1,000. **Ad Rates:** Noncommercial. **URL:** http://www.myflr.org.

MAYVILLE

Tuscola Co. Tuscola Co. (E). 30 m SE of Saginaw. Concrete block, chloride chemical factories; engine parts shop. Diversified farming. Beans, corn, potatoes, sugar beets. Dairy farms.

17743 ■ Mayville Monitor
Mayville Monitor
PO Box 299
Mayville, MI 48744-0299

Community newspaper. **Freq:** Weekly (Thurs.). **Print Method:** Offset. **Trim Size:** 11 1/2 x 16. **Cols./Page:** 6. **Col. Width:** 9.5 picas. **Col. Depth:** 15 inches. **Key Personnel:** Gale Langford, Editor. **USPS:** 334-680. **Subscription Rates:** $15 Individuals in County; $18 Out of area; $24 Out of state. **Alt. Formats:** PDF. **URL:** http://www.mayvillelibrary.org. **Ad Rates:** BW $315; 4C $496; SAU $4; PCI $3.50. **Remarks:** Accepts advertising. **Circ:** Paid 1,000.

17744 ■ TAMS Journal
Token and Medal Society, Inc.
c/o Kathy Freeland, Secretary
PO Box 195
Mayville, MI 48744-0195
Phone: (989)843-5247
Publisher's E-mail: tokens@idahovandals.com

Magazine on tokens and medals (numismatic items). **Founded:** Apr. 1961. **Freq:** 6/year. **Print Method:** Letterpress. **Trim Size:** 8 1/2 x 11. **Cols./Page:** 2. **Col. Width:** 42 nonpareils. **Col. Depth:** 140 agate lines. **Key Personnel:** Stephen Bobbitt, Editor. **Subscription Rates:** $25 Individuals. **URL:** http://www.tokenandmedal.org/page2/page2.html. **Ad Rates:** BW $75. **Remarks:** Accepts advertising from members only. **Circ:** ‡1,200.

MENOMINEE

Menominee Co. Menominee Co. (SW Up. Penin.). On Green Bay and Menominee River, opposite Marinette, Wis. Summer resort. Manufactures lumber, furniture, paper, electrical appliances, sporting goods, helicopters, pressure vessels, sawmill machinery, boilers, saws, cheese; foundry castings. Commercial fisheries. Dairy farms.

17745 ■ WAGN-AM - 1340
413 10th Ave.
Menominee, MI 49858
Phone: (906)863-5551
Fax: (906)863-5679

Format: News; Talk. **Networks:** ABC; Mutual Broadcasting System; Westwood One Radio. **Founded:** 1953. **Operating Hours:** Continuous. **ADI:** Green Bay-Appleton (Suring), WI. **Key Personnel:** Barb VanDeHei, Sales Mgr., barbvandehei@baycitiesradio.net. **Wattage:** 1,000. **Ad Rates:** Noncommercial.

17746 ■ WHYB-FM - 103.7
413 10th Ave.
Menominee, MI 49858
Phone: (906)863-5551
Fax: (906)863-5679

Format: Oldies. **Networks:** Westwood One Radio. **Owner:** Bay Cities Radio, at above address. **Founded:** 1984. **Formerly:** WCJL-FM. **Operating Hours:** Continuous. **ADI:** Green Bay-Appleton (Suring), WI. **Key Personnel:** Chris Bernier, Gen. Mgr. **Wattage:** 7,000. **Ad Rates:** $15-30 for 30 seconds. WSFQ.

MIDLAND

Midland Co. Midland Co. (EC). 18 m W of Bay City. Manufactures chemicals, plastics, silicones, tools, cement products. Oil refinery. Oil, gas wells. Diversified farming. Beans, sugar beets.

17747 ■ Midland Daily News
Hearst Corp.
124 S McDonald St.
Midland, MI 48640
Phone: (989)835-7171
Fax: (989)835-9151
Publication E-mail: info@mdn.net

General newspaper. **Freq:** Daily (eve.). **Print Method:** Offset. **Cols./Page:** 6. **Col. Width:** 25 nonpareils. **Col. Depth:** 301 agate lines. **Key Personnel:** Jenny L. Anderson, Publisher, phone: (989)839-4260; John Telfer, II, Editor, phone: (989)839-4240; Ralph Wirtz, Managing Editor, phone: (989)839-4241; Tim Neuman, Manager, Production, phone: (989)839-4277. **USPS:** 347-700. **Subscription Rates:** $15 Out of state weekend mail delivery, 4 weeks; $21 Out of state daily mail delivery, 4 weeks; $136.50 Individuals daily mail delivery, 26 weeks; $13 Individuals in state, weekend mail delivery, 4 weeks; $18.20 Individuals in state, daily mail delivery, 4 weeks; $42.25 Individuals in state, weekend mail delivery, 13 weeks; $52 Out of state weekend mail delivery, 13 weeks; $104 Out of state weekend mail delivery, 26 weeks; $59.15 Individuals daily mail delivery, 13 weeks. **URL:** http://www.ourmidland.com. **Ad Rates:** GLR $1.75; BW $2277; 4C $2752; PCI $17.65. **Remarks:** Advertising accepted; rates available upon request. **Circ:** Mon.-Sat. ★**16,161**, Sun. ★**17,797**.

17748 ■ WMPX-AM - 1490
PO Box 1689
Midland, MI 48641
Phone: (989)631-1490
Fax: (989)631-6357
Free: 877-658-1490
Email: sales@wmpxwmrx.com

Format: Adult Contemporary. **Networks:** ABC. **Founded:** 1948. **Operating Hours:** Continuous Mon.-Sat.; 5 a.m.-midnight Sun. **Wattage:** 1,000. **URL:** http://www.wmpxwmrx.com.

17749 ■ WMRX-FM - 97.7
1510 Bayliss St.
Midland, MI 48640
Phone: (989)631-1490
Fax: (989)631-6357
Free: 877-658-1490
Email: sales@wmpxwmrx.com

Format: Classical. **Networks:** Satellite Music Network. **Founded:** 1984. **Operating Hours:** Continuous (Mon.-Sat.); 5 a.m.-midnight Sun. **Wattage:** 4,100. **Ad Rates:** Noncommercial. **Mailing address:** PO Box 1689, Midland, MI 48641. **URL:** http://www.wmpxwmrx.com.

17750 ■ WYLZ-FM - 100.9
825 E Main St.
Midland, MI 48640
Email: wheelz@citcomm.com

Format: Classic Rock. **Simulcasts:** WILZ-FM. **Networks:** ABC. **Owner:** Citadel Broadcasting Corp., 7201 W Lake Mead Blvd., Ste. 400, Las Vegas, NV 89128-8366, Ph: (702)804-5200, Fax: (702)804-8250. **Key Personnel:** Stan Parman, Dir. of Programs, stan.parman@citcomm.com; Tom Clark, Dir. of Sales, tom.clark@citcomm.com; Chris Monk, Gen. Mgr., chris.monk@citcomm.com. **Wattage:** 2,600. **Ad Rates:** $35-75 for 60 seconds. **URL:** http://www.espn1009.com.

MIO

Oscoda Co. (NE). On Au Sable River, 65 m SW of Alpena. Resort. Pine, hardwood timber. Diversified farming. Hay, livestock.

17751 ■ WAVC-FM - 93.9
1356 Mackinaw Ave.
Cheboygan, MI 49721-1003
Phone: (231)627-2341
Fax: (231)627-7000

Format: Country. **Owner:** Northern Star Broadcasting L.L.C., 514 Munson Ave., MI 49686. **Key Personnel:** Susan Melton, Prog. Dir. **URL:** http://www.1029bigcountry.com.

MONROE

Monroe Co. Monroe Co. (SE). On Lake Erie, 18 m N of Toledo, Ohio. Resort. Port facilities. Manufactures paper products, fibreboard and fibre shipping containers, auto parts, glass, commercial stokers, cement; rolling steel mill. Nuclear Power Plant. Stone quarries. Nurseries. Diversified farming.

17752 ■ IHM Connections
IHM Sisters
610 W Elm Ave.
Monroe, MI 48162-7909
Phone: (734)241-3660
Fax: (734)240-9801
Publisher's E-mail: communications@ihmsisters.org
Newspaper covering activities of the IHM Sisters and their associates in ministry. **Freq:** Semiannual. **Print Method:** Offset. **Cols./Page:** 4. **Alt. Formats:** PDF. **URL:** http://ihmsisters.org/private/highlights/connections. **Remarks:** Advertising not accepted. **Circ:** Paid 1250.

17753 ■ IHM Quarterly
IHM Sisters
610 W Elm Ave.
Monroe, MI 48162-7909
Phone: (734)241-3660
Fax: (734)240-9801
Publication E-mail: communications@ihmsisters.org
Quarterly newsletter. **Freq:** Quarterly Winter, Spring, Summer and Fall. **Key Personnel:** Holly Knight, Contact; Molly Hunt, Editor. **URL:** http://ihmsisters.org/publications/ihm-quarterly; http://ihmsisters.org/publications. **Remarks:** Advertising not accepted. **Circ:** (Not Reported).

17754 ■ The Monroe Evening News/The Monroe Sunday News
Monroe Publishing Co.
20 W First St.
Monroe, MI 48161
Phone: (734)242-1100
Fax: (734)242-0937
General newspaper. **Freq:** Daily. **Print Method:** Web atlas offset press. **Trim Size:** 13 3/4 x 23 3/4. **Cols./Page:** 6. **Col. Width:** 26 nonpareils. **Col. Depth:** 21 inches. **Key Personnel:** Grattan Gray, Chairman of the Board; Lonnie Peppler-Moyer, Publisher; Deborah Saul, Editor, phone: (734)240-5748; Shirley Hyden, Officer, Human Resources; Zewicky David, Manager, Circulation, phone: (734)240-5025. **USPS:** 359-400. **Subscription Rates:** $167.96 daily and Sunday; $104 Sunday/weekend/Friday-Sunday only. **URL:** http://www.monroenews.com. **Ad Rates:** PCI $18.51. **Remarks:** Accepts advertising. **Circ:** Mon.-Sat. ★**21,387**, Sun. ★**24,351**.

17755 ■ Monroe Magazine
Monroe Publishing Co.
20 W First St.
Monroe, MI 48161
Phone: (734)242-1100
Fax: (734)242-0937
Magazine highlighting the good life in Monroe County. **Freq:** Quarterly. **Key Personnel:** Deborah Saul, Editor. **URL:** http://www.monroenews.com. **Circ:** (Not Reported).

17756 ■ Charter Communications
1145 S Telegraph Rd.
Monroe, MI 48161-5590
Free: 888-438-2427
Key Personnel: Neil Smit, CEO, President; Michael J. Lovett, COO, Exec. VP. **Cities Served:** 52 channels. **URL:** http://www.charter.com.

17757 ■ River Raisin Cable
899 S Telegraph Rd.
Monroe, MI 48161
Cities Served: subscribing households 16,451. **URL:** http://www.dleg.state.mi.us/bcs_corp/dt_corp.asp?id_nbr=363327&name_entity=RIVER%20RAISIN%20CABLEVISION%20INC.

17758 ■ WTWR-FM - 98.3
14930 LaPlaisance Rd., Ste. 113
Monroe, MI 48161
Phone: (734)242-6600
Fax: (734)242-6599
Free: 888-578-0098
Format: Contemporary Hit Radio (CHR); Top 40. **Networks:** Independent. **Owner:** Cumulus Broadcasting Inc., 3280 Peachtree Rd. NW, Ste. 2300, Atlanta, GA 30305-2447, Ph: (404)949-0700, Fax: (404)949-0740. **Founded:** 1982. **Operating Hours**: Continuous; 100% local. **Key Personnel:** Brent Dingman, Contact, brent.dingman@cumulus.com; Brent Dingman, Contact, brent.dingman@cumulus.com. **Wattage:** 3,400. **Ad Rates:** $38 for 30 seconds; $38 for 60 seconds.

17759 ■ WYDM-FM - 97.5
1555 S Rasinville Rd.
Monroe, MI 48161
Phone: (734)265-3549
Email: dream975@monroeccc.edu
Format: Adult Contemporary. **Founded:** 1978. **Formerly:** WEJY-FM. **Operating Hours**: 6:30 a.m.-8 p.m. Mon.-Fri. **Wattage**: 010. **Ad Rates:** Noncommercial. **URL:** http://profile.infofree.com.

MORENCI

Lenawee Co. Lenawee Co. (S). 20 m SW of Adrian. Manufactures rubber, chemicals, broaching and screw machine products. Diversified farming. Corn, wheat, oats. Dairying.

17760 ■ The Morenci Observer
State Line Observer
120 N St.
Morenci, MI 49256
Phone: (517)458-6811
Fax: (517)458-6811
Publisher's E-mail: editor@statelineobserver.com
Community newspaper. **Freq:** Weekly (Wed.). **Print Method:** Offset. **Cols./Page:** 6. **Col. Width:** 26 nonpareils. **Col. Depth:** 294 agate lines. **Key Personnel:** David G. Green, Editor, phone: (517)458-6811. **Subscription Rates:** $28 Individuals. **URL:** http://statelineobserver.com. **Ad Rates:** BW $340; SAU $6; PCI $4.75. **Remarks:** Accepts advertising. **Circ:** Paid ‡2,280.

MOUNT CLEMENS

Macomb Co. Macomb Co. (SE). On Clinton River, 20 m N of Detroit. Manufactures dinnerware, plastics, seat belts, paint, vinyl, boat sails, dies, metal auto parts, tools.

17761 ■ American Road
Mock Turtle Press
PO Box 46519
Mount Clemens, MI 48046
Phone: (206)369-5782
Fax: (586)468-7483
Free: 877-285-5434
Publisher's E-mail: sales@mockturtlepress.com
Magazine that features articles about historic United States highways. **Freq:** Quarterly. **Key Personnel:** Becky Repp, General Manager. **Subscription Rates:** $16.95 Individuals; $16.95 Other countries plus shipping fee. **URL:** http://www.americanroadmagazine.com. **Remarks:** Accepts advertising. **Circ:** (Not Reported).

17762 ■ Bar Briefs
Macomb County Bar Association
40 N Main St., Rm. 435
Mount Clemens, MI 48043
Phone: (586)468-2940
Fax: (586)468-6926
Publisher's E-mail: mcba@macombbar.org
Magazine of Macomb County Bar Association, containing timely legal articles. **Freq:** Monthly. **URL:** http://www.macombbar.org/?page=7. **Remarks:** Accepts advertising. **Circ:** (Not Reported).

17763 ■ The Daily Tribune
The Daily Tribune Publishing Inc.
100 Macomb Daily Dr.
Mount Clemens, MI 48043-5802
Phone: (586)783-0315
Fax: (586)469-2892
Free: 888-622-6629
General newspaper. **Founded:** 1902. **Freq:** Daily except Saturday. **Print Method:** Offset. **Cols./Page:** 6. **Col. Width:** 25 nonpareils. **Col. Depth:** 301 agate lines. **Key Personnel:** Richard Kelly, Executive Editor, phone: (586)783-0372; Mike Beeson, Managing Editor. **Subscription Rates:** $132 Individuals by carrier, print and online; $80 Individuals 80; $230 Out of area by mail outside 50 miles radius ot Mt. Pleasant. **URL:** http://www.dailytribune.com/. **Ad Rates:** PCI $17.70; BW $569. **Remarks:** Accepts classified advertising. **Circ:** Mon.-Fri. ★**9396**, Sun. ★**10339**.

MOUNT PLEASANT

Isabella Co. Isabella Co. (C). 48 m W of Bay City. Central Michigan University Tourism. Horse racing. Manufactures gasoline, motor oil, bathroom fixtures, commercial kitchen equipment, condensed milk, flour, automobile hardware. Oil wells. Diversified farming. Sugar beets, corn, oats.

17764 ■ Central Michigan Life
Central Michigan University
1200 S Franklin St.
Mount Pleasant, MI 48859
Phone: (989)774-4000
Collegiate newspaper. **Freq:** 3/week Monday, Wednesday, Friday. **Print Method:** Offset. **Cols./Page:** 6 and 6. **Col. Width:** 28 nonpareils and 2 1/8 inches. **Col. Depth:** 294 agate lines and 21 inches. **Key Personnel:** Eric Dresden, Editor-in-Chief; John Manzo, Editor. **Subscription Rates:** $65 Individuals. **URL:** http://www.cm-life.com. **Ad Rates:** GLR $11.40; BW $1436.40; 4C $1676.40; PCI $11.55. **Remarks:** Accepts advertising. **Circ:** 13,500.

17765 ■ International Journal of Computer and Information Science
International Association for Computer and Information Science
735 Meadowbrook Dr.
Mount Pleasant, MI 48858
Phone: (989)774-3811
Publisher's E-mail: acis@acisinternational.org
Journal covering the latest developments in the fields of computer and information science. **Freq:** Quarterly. **Key Personnel:** Tokuro Matsuo, Editor-in-Chief. **ISSN:** 1525--9293 (print). **Subscription Rates:** Free. **URL:** http://www.acisinternational.org/ijcis.html. **Remarks:** Advertising not accepted. **Circ:** (Not Reported).

17766 ■ Michigan Oil and Gas News
Michigan Oil and Gas Association
PO Box 250
Mount Pleasant, MI 48804-0250
Phone: (989)772-5181
Fax: (989)773-2970
Magazine reporting drilling activities in Michigan; includes permit information. **Freq:** Weekly (Fri.). **Print Method:** Offset. **Trim Size:** 8 1/2 x 11. **Cols./Page:** 3. **Col. Width:** 27 nonpareils. **Col. Depth:** 140 agate lines. **USPS:** 405-780. **Subscription Rates:** $180 Individuals electronic or print; $90 Individuals electronic or print. **URL:** http://www.michiganoilandgas.org. **Remarks:** Advertising accepted; rates available upon request. **Circ:** ‡700, Non-paid ‡40.

17767 ■ The Morning Sun
Morning Star Publishing Co.
711 W Pickard
Mount Pleasant, MI 48858
Phone: (989)779-6000
Fax: (989)779-6051
General newspaper. **Founded:** 1864. **Freq:** Daily (morn.) Sun.-Fri. **Print Method:** Offset. **Cols./Page:** 8. **Col. Width:** 1 1/2 inches. **Col. Depth:** 301 agate lines. **Key Personnel:** Jeremy H. Dickman, Editor, phone: (989)779-6056; Christine Fox-Mortimer, Manager, Circulation; Don Negus, Director, Advertising, phone: (989)779-6118; Linda Gittleman, Reporter, phone: (989)463-6071; Rick Mills, Executive Editor, phone: (989)779-6003; Mindy Norton, Editor, phone: (989)779-6065; Al Frattura, President, Publisher, phone: (989)779-6001; Jim Lahde, Editor. **Subscription Rates:** $234.52 Individuals home delivery. **URL:** http://www.themorningsun.com. **Ad Rates:** BW $2495; 4C $2730; SAU $11.96; PCI $14.85. **Remarks:** Accepts advertising. **Circ:** Mon.-Fri. ★**10,515**, Sat. ★**10,030**, Sun. ★**12,014**.

17768 ■ Presque Isle Star
Morningstar Publications
711 W Pickard St.
Mount Pleasant, MI 48858
Phone: (989)779-6000
Fax: (989)779-6051
Shopper (tabloid). **Freq:** Weekly. **Print Method:** Offset. Uses mats. **Trim Size:** 11 1/8 x 17 1/2. **Cols./Page:** 6. **Col. Width:** 21 nonpareils. **Col. Depth:** 224 agate lines. **URL:** http://www.server-jbmultimedia.net/JRC-MS-PresqueIsleStar/sitebase/index.aspx?adgroupid=226768&view=double&fh=535&TrackString=TYPE_desktop_VIEW_Flip+Page+View_GROUPTITLE_Presque+Isle+Star. **Formerly**: The Northern Advertiser. **Remarks:** Accepts advertising. **Circ:** 6,000.

Circulation: ★ = AAM; △ or • = BPA; ♦ = CAC; ❑ = VAC; ⊕ = PO Statement; ‡ = Publisher's Report; Boldface figures = sworn; Light figures = estimated.

17769 ■ WCFX-FM - 95.3
5847 Venture Way
Mount Pleasant, MI 48858
Phone: (989)772-4173
Fax: (989)773-1236
Free: 800-621-9595
Format: Contemporary Hit Radio (CHR); Top 40. **Simulcasts:** WABX-AM. **Networks:** Michigan. **Founded:** 1967. **Operating Hours**: Continuous. **Key Personnel:** Kent Bergstrom, Operations Mgr.; Jim Spangenberg, Gen. Mgr., jim.spangenberg@wcfx.com; Angie Evans, Dir. of Production. **Wattage**: 6,000. **Ad Rates:** Noncommercial. **URL:** http://www.wcfx.com.

17770 ■ WCMB-FM - 95.7
1999 E Campus Dr.
Mount Pleasant, MI 48859
Phone: (989)774-3105
Fax: (989)774-4427
Free: 800-727-9268
Format: Public Radio. **Owner:** CMU Public Broadcasting, 1999 E Campus Dr., Mount Pleasant, MI 48859, Ph: (989)774-3105, Fax: (989)774-4427, Free: 800-727-9268. **Key Personnel:** Edward Grant, Gen. Mgr., grant1eb@cmich.edu. **Ad Rates:** Noncommercial. **URL:** http://www.wcmu.org.

17771 ■ WCML-FM - 91.7
1999 E Campus Dr.
Mount Pleasant, MI 48859
Phone: (989)774-3105
Fax: (989)774-4427
Free: 800-727-9268
Format: Talk; News; Classical. **Networks:** National Public Radio (NPR); Public Radio International (PRI). **Owner:** Central Michigan University, 1200 S Franklin St., Mount Pleasant, MI 48859, Ph: (989)774-4000. **Founded:** 1978. **Operating Hours**: Continuous. **ADI**: Alpena, MI. **Key Personnel:** Kim Walters, Dir. of Programs, Director, Dir. of Bus. Dev., ford1r@cmich.edu; David Nicholas, News Dir., nicho1d@cmich.edu; Ed Grant, Gen. Mgr., grant1eb@cmich.edu. **Wattage**: 100,000. **Ad Rates:** Noncommercial. **URL:** http://www.wcmu.org.

WCML-TV - See Alpena

17772 ■ WCMU-FM - 89.5
1999 E Campus Dr.
Mount Pleasant, MI 48859
Phone: (989)774-3105
Fax: (989)774-4427
Free: 800-727-9268
Format: Jazz; Blues; News; Classical; Public Radio. **Networks:** National Public Radio (NPR); Public Radio International (PRI). **Owner:** Central Michigan University, 1200 S Franklin St., Mount Pleasant, MI 48859, Ph: (989)774-4000. **Founded:** 1964. **Operating Hours**: Continuous; 25% network, 75% local. **ADI**: Flint-Saginaw-Bay City, MI. **Key Personnel:** David Nicholas, News Dir.; Ray Ford, Contact, ford1r@cmich.edu; Ray Ford, Contact, ford1r@cmich.edu. **Wattage**: 100,000. **Ad Rates:** Noncommercial. **URL:** http://www.wcmu.org.

17773 ■ WCMU-TV - 14
Central Michigan University
3965 E Broomfield
Mount Pleasant, MI 48859
Phone: (989)774-3105
Fax: (989)774-4427
Free: 800-727-9268
Format: Public TV; News; Talk. **Networks:** Public Broadcasting Service (PBS). **Owner:** Central Michigan University, 1200 S Franklin St., Mount Pleasant, MI 48859, Ph: (989)774-4000. **Founded:** 1967. **Operating Hours**: Continuous. **Key Personnel:** Ed Grant, Station Mgr., monte.higgins@cmich.edu; Rick Schudiske, Program Mgr; Linda Hyde, Contact; Monte Higgins, Contact. **Wattage**: 450,000 ERP Horizont. **Ad Rates:** Noncommercial. Underwriting available. **URL:** http://www.wcmu.org/.

WCMV-TV - See Cadillac

WCMW-FM - See Harbor Springs

WCMW-TV - See Manistee

17774 ■ WCMZ-FM - 98.3
1999 E Campus Dr.
Mount Pleasant, MI 48859
Format: Public Radio. **Key Personnel:** Edward Grant, Gen. Mgr.; Kim Walters, Dir. of Dev.; Randy Kapenga, Tech. Dir.; Shannon Peak, Asst. Mgr. **URL:** http://wcmu.org.

17775 ■ WMHW-FM - 91.5
344 Moore Hall, Central Michigan University
Mount Pleasant, MI 48859
Phone: (989)774-4000
Email: wmhw@cmich.edu
Format: Alternative/New Music/Progressive. **Owner:** Central Michigan University, 1200 S Franklin St., Mount Pleasant, MI 48859, Ph: (989)774-4000. **Founded:** 1963. **Operating Hours**: Continuous; 100% local. **Key Personnel:** Chad Roberts, Contact, rober2cj@cmich.edu. **Wattage**: 300. **Ad Rates:** Noncommercial. **URL:** http://www.wmhw.org.

17776 ■ WMMI-AM - 830
4895 E Wing Rd.
Mount Pleasant, MI 48858
Phone: (989)772-9664
Format: News; Talk. **Networks:** Michigan Public Radio. **Owner:** Central Michigan Communications Inc., 1200 S Franklin St., Mount Pleasant, MI 48859, Ph: (989)774-4000. **Founded:** 1987. **Operating Hours**: Sunrise-sunset; 90% network, 10% local. **Key Personnel:** Tina Sawyer, Contact; Tina Sawyer, Contact. **Wattage**: 1,000. **Ad Rates:** Noncommercial. Combined advertising rates available with WCZY-FM: 15 $14.25-16.00; 30 $16.00-$17.75. **URL:** http://www.wczy.net.

WWCM-FM - See Standish

MUNISING

Alger Co. Alger Co. (NC Up. Penin.). 44 m E of Marquette. Manufactures paper, lumber, wood products, tools & dies. Fisheries; timber. Dairy, stock, poultry, fruit farms. Lake resorts.

17777 ■ WQXO-AM - 1400
101 E Munising Ave.
Munising, MI 49862
Phone: (906)387-4000
Email: calendar@wqxo.com
Format: Oldies. **Simulcasts:** W286BC-FM. **Networks:** ABC; Fox; NBC. **Owner:** Great Lakes Radio Inc., 3060 US 41 W, Marquette, MI 49855, Ph: (906)228-6800, Fax: (906)228-8128. **Founded:** 1955. **Operating Hours**: Continuous. **Key Personnel:** Todd Noordyk, Gen. Mgr. **Wattage**: 1,000. **Ad Rates:** Noncommercial. **URL:** http://wqxo.com.

MUSKEGON

Muskegon Co. Muskegon Co. (W). On Muskegon Lake and Lake Michigan, 40 m NW of Grand Rapids. Great Lakes and foreign shipping lines. Manufactures automobile and airplane motors, piston rings, iron castings, office, school, laboratory equipment, auto, truck, trailer and airplane parts, bowling and billard equipment, chemicals, cranes, hoists, wire, machine tools, dies, paper, meat products, coil springs, boilers, chlorine gas, gasoline dispensing equipment, bearings, metal fabricating, wood products. Resort.

17778 ■ Miniature Collector
Scott Advertising & Publishing Co.
2145 W Sherman Blvd.
Muskegon, MI 49441
Phone: (231)755-2200
Fax: (231)755-1003
Publisher's E-mail: contactus@scottpublications.com
Magazine for collectors and makers of dollhouses, dollhouse furnishings, and other miniatures. Articles include profiles of top artists, visits to private and public collections, and how-to projects. **Freq:** Monthly. **Print Method:** Offset. **Trim Size:** 8 1/2 x 11. **Cols./Page:** 3. **Col. Width:** 26 nonpareils. **Col. Depth:** 140 agate lines. **Key Personnel:** Ruth Keessen, Publisher. **ISSN:** 0199--9184 (print). **Subscription Rates:** $39.95 Individuals; $63.95 Other countries; $74.95 Two years; $122.95 Other countries two years. **URL:** http://www.scottpublications.com/mcmag. **Remarks:** Advertising accepted; rates available upon request. **Circ:** (Not Reported).

17779 ■ The Muskegon Chronicle & The Sunday Chronicle
The Muskegon Chronicle & The Sunday Chronicle
981 Third St.
Muskegon, MI 49443
Phone: (231)722-3161
General newspaper. **Freq:** Daily (eve.), Sat. and Sun. (morn.). **Print Method:** Letterpress. **Trim Size:** 13 1/2 x 22 3/4. **Cols./Page:** 6. **Col. Width:** 25 nonpareils. **Col. Depth:** 308 agate lines. **Key Personnel:** Steve Westphal, General Manager, phone: (231)725-6301; Sheila Reinecke, Director, Advertising and Sales, phone: (231)725-6312; Linda Allard, Manager, Operations, phone: (231)725-6310; Cindy Fairfield, Editor, phone: (231)725-6370; Tom Kendra, Editor, phone: (231)725-6364. **Subscription Rates:** $14.55 Individuals by carrier; 7 day; $15.05 Individuals by motor route; 7 day. **Ad Rates:** GLR $34.37; BW $4,175.96; 4C $4,900.96; GLR $40.12; BW $4,874.58; 4C $5,599.58. **Remarks:** Accepts advertising. **Circ:** Mon.-Fri. ★**41114**, Sun. ★**45583**, Sat. ★**42094**.

17780 ■ WHEY-FM - 88.9
PO Box 1511
Muskegon, MI 49443
Phone: (231)563-6280
Format: Contemporary Christian. **Owner:** Muskegon Community Radio Service Broadcasting Company, Inc., 1433 Simonelli Rd, Muskegon, MI 49445. **Wattage**: 1,000. **URL:** http://www.muskegoncommunityradio.com/88.9.

17781 ■ WKBZ-AM - 1090
3565 Green St.
Muskegon, MI 49444
Phone: (231)733-2600
Fax: (231)733-7461
Format: News; Talk. **Networks:** CBS; Mutual Broadcasting System. **Founded:** 1926. **Operating Hours**: Continuous. **Key Personnel:** Mark Dixon, Dir. of Programs, markdixon@clearchannel.com; Tim Feagan, Gen. Mgr., timfeagan@clearchannel.com; Dave Taft, Dir. of Operations, davetaft@clearchannel.com. **Local Programs**: *Polka Melodies*, Saturday Sunday 9:00 a.m. - 12:00 p.m. 10:00 a.m. - 12:00 p.m.; *Doug Stephan Good Day*, Saturday 6:00 a.m. - 7:00 a.m. **Wattage**: 1,000. **Ad Rates:** Advertising accepted; rates available upon request. **URL:** http://www.newstalk1090.com.

17782 ■ WMRR-FM - 101.7
3565 Green St.
Muskegon, MI 49444
Phone: (231)733-2600
Fax: (231)733-7461
Format: Classic Rock; Album-Oriented Rock (AOR). **Owner:** Clear Channel Inc., 200 E Basse Rd., San Antonio, TX 78209, Ph: (612)336-9700, Fax: (612)336-9701. **Founded:** 1992. **Operating Hours**: Continuous. **ADI**: Grand Rapids-Kalamazoo-Battle Creek, MI. **Key Personnel:** Andy O'Riley, Dir. of Programs, andyoriley@clearchannel.com; Paul Boscarino, Gen. Sales Mgr., paulboscarino@clearchannel.com; Bruce Law, Dir. of Sales, brucelaw@clearchannel.com; Brian Thomas, Prog. Dir., bthomas@rock1017fm.com; Dave Taft, Operations Mgr.; Tim Feagan, Gen. Mgr., timfeagan@clearchannel.com. **Wattage**: 12,000. **Ad Rates:** $15-55 for 60 seconds. WMUS-FM, WSHZ-FM, WMGH-AM, WMUS-AM. **URL:** http://www.rock1017fm.com.

17783 ■ WMUS-AM - 1090
3565 Green St.
Muskegon, MI 49444
Phone: (231)733-2600
Fax: (231)733-7461
Format: Contemporary Country; News; Talk. **Networks:** ABC. **Founded:** 1947. **Operating Hours**: Sunrise-sunset. **Key Personnel:** Tim Feagan, Gen. Mgr., timfeagan@clearchannel.com; Mark Dixon, Prog. Dir., mark@107mus.com. **Wattage**: 1,000. **Ad Rates:** Noncommercial. Combined advertising rates available with WMUS-FM. **URL:** http://www.107mus.com//main.html.

17784 ■ WMUS-FM - 107
3565 Green St.
Muskegon, MI 49444
Phone: (231)733-2600
Fax: (231)733-7461
Free: 800-222-WMUS
Format: Country. **Simulcasts:** WMUS-AM. **Networks:** ABC. **Owner:** Clear Channel Inc., 200 E Basse Rd., San Antonio, TX 78209, Ph: (612)336-9700, Fax: (612)336-9701. **Founded:** 1947. **Operating Hours**: 6am to 11pm. **ADI**: Grand Rapids-Kalamazoo-Battle Creek, MI. **Key Personnel:** Tim Feagan, Gen. Mgr.,

timfeagan@clearchannel.com. **Wattage:** 50,000. **Ad Rates:** $15-100 for 60 seconds. Combined advertising rates available with WMUS-AM. **URL:** http://www.107mus.com//main.html.

17785 ■ WSHZ-FM
3565 Green St.
Muskegon, MI 49444
Phone: (231)733-6108
Fax: (231)733-7461
Simulcasts: WMUS-FM, WMUS-AM, WMRR-FM, WMHG-AM. **Owner:** Clear Channel Inc., 200 E Basse Rd., San Antonio, TX 78209, Ph: (612)336-9700, Fax: (612)336-9701. **Founded:** 1999. **Ad Rates:** Noncommercial.

17786 ■ WUVS-FM
1877 Peck St.
Muskegon, MI 49441
Phone: (231)727-5007
Fax: (231)725-0027
Format: Urban Contemporary; Jazz. **Key Personnel:** Paul Billings, Dir. of Programs, pa@1037thebeat.com; Rose Reese, Operations Mgr., rosie@1037thebeat.com; Robert Billings, Music Dir., rb@1037thebeat.com. **Wattage:** 100 ERP. **Ad Rates:** Noncommercial.

MUSKEGON HEIGHTS

Muskegon Co. Muskegon Co. (WC). 2 m S of Roosevelt Park.

17787 ■ WLAW-FM - 92.5
3375 Merriam St., Ste. 201
Muskegon Heights, MI 49444
Phone: (231)830-0176
Format: Country. **Owner:** Cumulus Media Inc., 3280 Peachtree Rd. NW, Ste. 2300, Atlanta, GA 30305-2455, Ph: (404)949-0700, Fax: (404)949-0740. **Key Personnel:** Jon Russell, Operations Mgr., jon.russell@cumulus.com; Kevin Matthews, Dir. of Programs, kevin.matthews@cumulus.com. **URL:** http://www.Muskegonnashicon.com.

17788 ■ WLCS-FM - 98.3
3375 Merriam, Ste. 201
Muskegon Heights, MI 49444
Phone: (231)830-0176
Fax: (231)830-0104
Format: Oldies. **Networks:** ABC. **Founded:** 1983. **Formerly:** WIMM-FM. **Operating Hours:** Continuous. **ADI:** Grand Rapids-Kalamazoo-Battle Creek, MI. **Key Personnel:** Bob Bolton, Gen. Mgr., VP, bobbolton1@aol.com. **Wattage:** 3,000. **Ad Rates:** $24 for 30 seconds; $26 for 60 seconds. Combined advertising rates available with WEFG-FM & WUBR-AM. **URL:** http://www.983wlcs.com.

17789 ■ WVIB-FM - 100.1
3375 Merriam St., Ste. 201
Muskegon Heights, MI 49444
Phone: (231)830-0176
Fax: (231)830-0104
Format: Adult Contemporary; Blues. **Owner:** Citadel Broadcasting Corp., 7201 W Lake Mead Blvd., Ste. 400, Las Vegas, NV 89128-8366, Ph: (702)804-5200, Fax: (702)804-8250. **Key Personnel:** Jon Russell, Operations Mgr., jon.russell@cumulus.com. **URL:** http://www.v100fm.com.

NEGAUNEE

17790 ■ City of Negaunee Cable TV
100 Silver St.
Negaunee, MI 49866
Phone: (906)475-7400
Fax: (906)475-0178
Email: cmsecretary@cityofnegaunee.com
Cities Served: 44 channels. **Mailing address:** PO Box 70, Negaunee, MI 49866. **URL:** http://www.cityofnegaunee.com.

17791 ■ WLUC-TV - 6
177 U.S. 41 E
Negaunee, MI 49866
Phone: (906)475-4161
Fax: (906)475-4824
Free: 800-562-9776
Email: tv6news@wluctv6.com
Format: Commercial TV. **Networks:** NBC. **Owner:** Sinclair Broadcast Group Inc., 10706 Beaver Dam Rd., Hunt Valley, MD 21030, Ph: (410)568-1500, Fax: (410)568-1533. **Founded:** 1956. **Operating Hours:** 5:30 a.m.-2 a.m. **ADI:** Marquette, MI. **Wattage:** 100,000. **Ad Rates:** Advertising accepted; rates available upon request. **URL:** http://www.uppermichiganssource.com.

NEW BALTIMORE

Macomb Co. Macomb Co. (SE). On Lake St. Clair, 10 m NE of Mt. Clemens. Manufactures plastics, screw machine products. Fishing.

17792 ■ The Voice
The Voice
51180 Bedfort St.
New Baltimore, MI 48047
Phone: (586)716-8100
Fax: (586)716-8918
Free: 800-561-2248
Publisher's E-mail: editor@voicenews.com
Community newspaper. **Founded:** 1979. **Freq:** Weekly. **Print Method:** Offset. **Cols./Page:** 6. **Col. Width:** 9.5 picas. **Col. Depth:** 13 1/2 inches. **Key Personnel:** Rene Allard, Manager, Circulation; Jeff Payne, Editor; Debbie Loggins, General Manager. **USPS:** 503-110. **Subscription Rates:** $13 Individuals 3 months; $20 Individuals 6 months; $26 Individuals 9 months; $30 Individuals; $50 Two years. **URL:** http://www.voicenews.com/. **Ad Rates:** PCI $5.15. **Remarks:** Accepts advertising. **Circ:** 1125.

NEWBERRY

Luce Co. Luee Co. (NC). 2 m E of Dollarville.

17793 ■ Newberry News
Newberry News Inc.
316 Newberry Ave.
Newberry, MI 49868
Phone: (906)293-8401
Fax: (906)293-8815
Publisher's E-mail: nbynews@att.net
Community newspaper. **Freq:** Weekly (Wed.). **Cols./Page:** 6. **Col. Width:** 1.83 inches. **Col. Depth:** 21 inches. **Key Personnel:** Jim Diem, Editor; Nancy Diem, Manager, Advertising; Mary Gordon, Business Manager. **USPS:** 383-980. **Subscription Rates:** $40 Individuals online one year; $5 Individuals online one week; $54 Individuals print - local; $50 Individuals print - seasonal; $82 Individuals print & online - local; $94 Individuals print and online - national; $23 Students print or online. **URL:** http://newberrynews.our-hometown.com. **Mailing address:** PO Box 46, Newberry, MI 49868. **Ad Rates:** BW $75; SAU $3; PCI $3.70. **Remarks:** Accepts advertising. **Circ:** 3,600.

17794 ■ WMJT-FM - 96.7
210 W John St.
Newberry, MI 49868
Phone: (906)293-1400
Fax: (906)293-5161
Format: Contemporary Hit Radio (CHR); Information. **Key Personnel:** Teri Petrie, Sales Mgr., teri@radioeagle.com. **Ad Rates:** Advertising accepted; rates available upon request. **Mailing address:** PO Box 486, Newberry, MI 49868. **URL:** http://www.radioeaglenewberry.com.

17795 ■ WNBY-AM - 1450
Hwy. M-123 S
Newberry, MI 49868
Phone: (906)293-3221
Simulcasts: WNBY-FM. **Owner:** Sovereign Communications, 898 Meander Rd., Portsmouth, VA 23707. **Founded:** 1966. **Key Personnel:** Gerald Feutz, Contact; Sandy Feutz, Contact; Vickie Holcomb, Contact. **Wattage:** 1,000 Daytime; 1,000. **Ad Rates:** $7 for 30 seconds; $9 for 60 seconds. **Mailing address:** PO Box 501, Newberry, MI 49868. **URL:** http://www.1450wnby.com.

NILES

Cass Co. Berrien Co. (SW). On St. Joseph River, 10 m N of South Bend, Ind. Manufactures book paper, paper dress patterns, injection molded steering wheels, wire specialties, steel cables and tanks, store fixtures, industrial fans, freezers, kitchen units, moveable office partitions. Agriculture. Wheat, dairy products, fruit.

17796 ■ Argus
Argus
217 N 4th St.
Niles, MI 49120
Publisher's E-mail: info@argusinteractive.com
Newspaper. **Founded:** 1875. **Freq:** Weekly (Thurs.). **Print Method:** Offset. **Cols./Page:** 8. **Col. Width:** 15 nonpareils. **Col. Depth:** 294 agate lines. **URL:** http://www.edwardsburgargus.com. **Circ:** 1800.

17797 ■ Dowagiac Daily News: Online Edition
Leader Publications
217 Fourth St.
Niles, MI 49120
Phone: (269)683-2101
Fax: (269)683-2175
Community newspaper. **Freq:** Daily (eve.). **Print Method:** Offset. **Cols./Page:** 8. **Col. Width:** 22 nonpareils. **Col. Depth:** 294 agate lines. **Key Personnel:** Scott Novak, Editor; Michael Caldwell, Publisher. **URL:** http://www.leaderpub.com/category/news/dowagiac-news. **Ad Rates:** PCI $3.93. **Remarks:** Accepts advertising. **Circ:** (Not Reported).

17798 ■ Edwardsburg Argus
Boone Newspapers Inc.
217 N 4th St.
Niles, MI 49120
Newspaper covering the Southwestern Michigan. **Freq:** Weekly (Thurs.). **URL:** http://www.leaderpub.com/category/news/edwardsburg. **Remarks:** Accepts advertising. **Circ:** (Not Reported).

17799 ■ Niles Daily Star
Argus
217 N 4th St.
Niles, MI 49120
Publisher's E-mail: info@argusinteractive.com
General newspaper. **Freq:** Mon.-Sat. (morn.). **Print Method:** Offset. **Cols./Page:** 8. **Col. Width:** 21 nonpareils. **Col. Depth:** 294 agate lines. **Key Personnel:** Scott Novak, Editor; Bob Bell, Manager, Production; Katie Rohman, Managing Editor; Rhonda Rauen, Manager, Accounting. **Subscription Rates:** $7.50 Individuals per month; home delivery; $10.50 By mail per month. **URL:** http://www.leaderpub.com/category/news/niles/. **Ad Rates:** PCI $4.80. **Remarks:** Accepts advertising. **Circ:** (Not Reported).

17800 ■ WSMK-FM - 99.1
925 N 5th St.
Niles, MI 49120
Fax: (269)683-7759
Format: Blues. **Ad Rates:** Advertising accepted; rates available upon request. **URL:** http://www.wsmk99.com.

NOVI

Oakland Co Oakland Co. Oakland Co. (SW). NW of Detroit.

17801 ■ BMWE Journal
Brotherhood of Maintenance of Way Employees Division of the International Brotherhood of Teamsters
41475 Gardenbrook Rd.
Novi, MI 48375-1328
Phone: (248)662-2660
Fax: (248)662-2659
Publisher's E-mail: contactus@bmwe.org
Railroad labor tabloid. **Freq:** Bimonthly. **Print Method:** Offset. **Key Personnel:** Freddie N. Simpson, Editor, President; Perry K. Geller, Sr., Secretary, Treasurer. **ISSN:** 1049--3921 (print). **Subscription Rates:** $20 Individuals. **Alt. Formats:** PDF. **URL:** http://www.bmwe.org/journalarchive.shtm. **Remarks:** Advertising not accepted. **Circ:** ‡60000.

17802 ■ The Constructivist
Association for Constructivist Teaching
23900 Greening Dr.
Novi, MI 48375
Journal containing knowledgeable articles about the Constructivist movement. **Alt. Formats:** PDF. **URL:** http://sites.google.com/site/assocforconstructteaching/journal; http://sites.google.com/site/assocforconstructteaching/journal/the-constructivist-archive. **Remarks:** Advertising not accepted. **Circ:** (Not Reported).

Circulation: ★ = AAM; △ or • = BPA; ♦ = CAC; ❑ = VAC; ⊕ = PO Statement; ‡ = Publisher's Report; Boldface figures = sworn; Light figures = estimated.

17803 ■ WOVI-FM - 89.5
25345 Taft Rd.
Novi, MI 48374
Phone: (248)449-1526
Fax: (248)449-1519
Format: Adult Album Alternative. **Networks:** Independent. **Owner:** Novi Community School District, 25345 Taft Rd., Novi, MI 48374, Ph: (248)449-1200. **Founded:** 1978. **Operating Hours**: Continuous; 100% local. **Wattage**: 100 ERP. **Ad Rates:** Noncommercial.

OAK PARK

17804 ■ WHND-AM - 560
22150 Greenfield Rd. No. 200
Oak Park, MI 48237
Format: Oldies. **Networks:** Unistar. **Owner:** Radio Group, Inc., 640 Fifth Ave., New York, NY 10019. **Founded:** 1956. **Formerly**: WQTE-AM. **Operating Hours**: Sunrise-sunset. **Wattage**: 500. **Ad Rates:** Advertising accepted; rates available upon request. **URL:** http://www.560theanswer.com/.

OKEMOS

Ingham Co. (S). 8 m E of Lansing. Manufactures wooden furniture, dies and tools, storage batteries. Agriculture. Grain, wheat, corn.

17805 ■ Journal of the Michigan Dental Association
Michigan Dental Association
3657 Okemos Rd., Ste. 200
Okemos, MI 48864-3927
Phone: (517)372-9070
Fax: (517)372-0008
Free: 800-589-2632
Journal of The Michigan Dental Association. **Freq:** Monthly. **Print Method:** Offset. **Trim Size:** 8 1/2 x 11. **Cols./Page:** 3. **Col. Width:** 13 picas. **Col. Depth:** 62 picas. **URL:** http://www.smilemichigan.com/pro/Classified-Ads-Journal/MDA-Journal. **Ad Rates:** BW $585; 4C $1225. **Remarks:** Accepts advertising. **Circ:** Paid 6,601.

17806 ■ Kappa Omicron Nu FORUM
Kappa Omicron Nu
1749 Hamilton Rd., Ste. 106
Okemos, MI 48864
Phone: (517)351-8335
Publisher's E-mail: info@kon.org
Journal featuring articles, stories, concepts, researches and studies about philosophy and other relevant subjects. Highlights philosophy as the center of underlying belief systems of the world. **Freq:** Semiannual. **ISSN:** 1546- 2676 (print). **Subscription Rates:** $10 Individuals 1 year; $30 Individuals 3 years; $50 Individuals 5 years. **Alt. Formats:** PDF. **URL:** http://www.kon.org/archives/forum/forum_archives.html. **Remarks:** Advertising not accepted. **Circ:** (Not Reported).

17807 ■ Triad: The Journal of the Michigan Osteopathic Association
Michigan Osteopathic Association
445 Woodlake Cir.
Okemos, MI 48864
Phone: (517)347-1555
Fax: (517)347-1566
Free: 800-657-1556
Publisher's E-mail: moa@mi-osteopathic.org
Professional journal of the Michigan Osteopathic Association. **Freq:** Quarterly. **Trim Size:** 8 3/8 x 10 7/8. **Key Personnel:** Getchen Christensen, Director, Advertising; Cheri Rugh, Managing Editor; Mark E. Sikorski, DO, Editor-in-Chief. **ISSN:** 1046-4948 (print). **Subscription Rates:** Members. **URL:** http://www.mi-osteopathic.org. **Ad Rates:** BW $900; 4C $1,483. **Remarks:** Accepts advertising. **Circ:** (Not Reported).

OLIVET

Eaton Co. Eaton Co. (S). 18 m NE of Battle Creek. Olivet College. Machine tools, steel fabricating, fittings, hydraulic tube bending manufactured. Dairy, stock, poultry farms. Onions. Lake resort.

17808 ■ Shipherd's Record: Olivet College Alumni & Friends Magazine
Olivet College
320 S Main St.
Olivet, MI 49076
Free: 800-456-7189
Publisher's E-mail: admissions@olivetcollege.edu
College alumni magazine. **Freq:** Semiannual. **Print Method:** Offset. **Trim Size:** 16 1/4 x 11 1/4. **Cols./Page:** 3. **Col. Width:** 28 nonpareils. **Col. Depth:** 134 agate lines. **Key Personnel:** Steven M. Corey, PhD, President; Molly Goaley, Managing Editor. **USPS:** 407-860. **URL:** http://www.olivetcollege.edu. **Remarks:** Accepts advertising. **Circ:** Non-paid 12,000.

17809 ■ WOCR-FM - 89.7
320 S Main St.
Olivet, MI 49076-9406
Phone: (269)749-7635
Free: 800-456-7189
Email: wocr@olivetcollege.edu
Format: Eclectic; Information; Sports. **Networks:** Independent. **Owner:** Olivet College, 320 S Main St., Olivet, MI 49076, Free: 800-456-7189. **Founded:** 1975. **Operating Hours:** 12 hours Daily. 100% local. **Key Personnel:** Donald L. Tuski, PhD, President. **Wattage:** 110. **Ad Rates:** Noncommercial. **URL:** http://www.olivetcollege.edu.

ONTONAGON

Ontonagon Co. Ontonagon Co. (NW Up. Penin.). On Lake Superior, 122 m W of Marquette. Lumber and pulp manufactured. Silver and copper mines. Timber. Agriculture. Potatoes, hay, dairying. Resort.

17810 ■ The Ontonagon Herald
The Ontonagon Herald
326 River St.
Ontonagon, MI 49953
Phone: (906)884-2826
Fax: (906)884-2939
Publisher's E-mail: maureen@ontonagonherald.com
Community newspaper. **Freq:** Weekly (Wed.). **Print Method:** Web offset. **Trim Size:** 14 x 22. **Cols./Page:** 6. **Col. Width:** 2 1/16 inches. **Col. Depth:** 21 inches. **Key Personnel:** Maureen Guzek, Editor. **Subscription Rates:** $42.95 Individuals in county; $52.95 Out of area. **URL:** http://www.ontonagonherald.com. **Ad Rates:** BW $693; 4C $812; PCI $5.50. **Remarks:** Advertising accepted; rates available upon request. **Circ:** 3,750.

17811 ■ WOAS-FM - 88.5
701 Parker Ave.
Ontonagon, MI 49953-1949
Format: Educational. **Networks:** Independent. **Owner:** Ontonagon Area School District, 701 Parker Ave., Ontonagon, MI 49953, Ph: (906)813-0614. **Founded:** 1979. **Wattage:** 009 ERP. **Ad Rates:** Noncommercial. **URL:** http://www.woas-fm.org.

17812 ■ WUPY-FM - 101.1
622 River St.
Ontonagon, MI 49953-1422
Phone: (906)884-9668
Fax: (906)884-4985
Free: 800-524-9879
Format: News; Sports; Country. **Owner:** S & S Broadcasting, at above address. **Founded:** 1986. **Operating Hours:** Midnight - 7:00 p.m. Monday - Friday; Midnight - 10:00 p.m. Saturday; Midnight - 8:00 p.m. Sunday. **Wattage:** 100,000 ERP. **URL:** http://www.wupy101.com.

OSCODA

17813 ■ Oscoda Press
News Press Publishing Co.
311 S State St.
Oscoda, MI 48750
Phone: (989)739-2054
Fax: (989)739-3201
Publisher's E-mail: editor1@oscodapress.com
Local newspaper. **Freq:** Weekly (Wed.). **Cols./Page:** 5. **Col. Width:** 11.5 picas. **Col. Depth:** 16 inches. **Key Personnel:** Jason Ogden, Reporter; Ben Murphy, Director, Sports; Holly Nelson, Editor; Karen Rouse, Reporter; Jim Dunn, Publisher; John Morris, Editor. **USPS:** 412-840. **Subscription Rates:** $55 Individuals in county; $65 Out of state; $60 Elsewhere in Michigan; $50 Individuals online e-edition; $20 Individuals access to e-edition with print. **URL:** http://www.iosconews.com/oscoda_press/. **Mailing address:** PO Box 663, Oscoda, MI 48750. **Ad Rates:** SAU $4.20. **Remarks:** Accepts advertising. **Circ:** 5,900.

OTSEGO

Allegan Co. Allegan Co. (SW). 15 m NW of Kalamazoo. Manufactures paper, polishing and grinding, auto engine testing equipment, plastic film, brass, dairy products. Diversified farming.

17814 ■ Shoppers Guide
Community Shoppers Guide Inc.
117 N Farmer St.
Otsego, MI 49078-0168
Phone: (269)694-9431
Fax: (269)694-9145
Shopper. **Founded:** 1945. **Freq:** Weekly (Sat.). **Print Method:** Offset. **Trim Size:** 10 1/2 x 16. **Cols./Page:** 4. **Col. Width:** 2.5 inches. **Col. Depth:** 16 inches. **URL:** http://www.communityshoppersguide.net. **Ad Rates:** BW $784; 4C $984; PCI $12.25. **Remarks:** Accepts advertising. **Circ:** Free ‡13,000, ‡4,283.

17815 ■ WQXC-FM - 100.9
706 E Allegan
Otsego, MI 49078
Phone: (269)343-1111
Fax: (269)692-6861
Format: Oldies. **Networks:** AP. **Owner:** Forum Communications Co., 203 Henrietta Ave. S, Park Rapids, MN 56470. **Founded:** 1981. **Operating Hours**: Continuous. **ADI**: Grand Rapids-Kalamazoo-Battle Creek, MI. **Key Personnel:** Todd Overhuel, Dir. of Programs, overhuel@wqxc.com; Tom Flynn, Gen. Mgr., tflynn@wqxc.com; Tim Bontrager, Sales Mgr., timb@wqxc.com. **Wattage:** 3,000. **Ad Rates:** Advertising accepted; rates available upon request. **Mailing address:** PO Box 80, Otsego, MI 49078-0080. **URL:** http://www.wqxc.com.

17816 ■ WZUU-FM - 92.5
PO Box 80
Otsego, MI 49078
Phone: (269)343-1717
Format: Contemporary Hit Radio (CHR). **Operating Hours**: Continuous. **Key Personnel:** Scotty Melvin, Dir. of Programs, scottybud@wzuu.com; Tim Bontrager, Sales Mgr., timb@wqxc.com%20; Tom Flynn, Gen. Mgr. **Ad Rates:** Advertising accepted; rates available upon request. **URL:** http://www.wzuu.com.

OWOSSO

Shiawassee Co. Shiawassee Co. (SEC). 25 m W of Flint. Manufactures electric motors, storage batteries, auto trim, abrasives, power brakes, furniture, steel tanks. Agriculture. Vegetables, grain, livestock.

17817 ■ The Argus-Press
The Argus-Press Co.
201 E Exchange St.
Owosso, MI 48867
Phone: (989)725-5136
Fax: (989)725-6376
General newspaper. **Freq:** Daily. **Print Method:** Offset. **Trim Size:** 13 3/4 x 22 3/4. **Cols./Page:** 6. **Col. Width:** 12 picas. **Col. Depth:** 301 agate lines. **Key Personnel:** Dan Basso, Managing Editor; Michael T. Kruszkowski, Director, Advertising; Richard E. Campbell, Chairman, Editor; Thomas E. Campbell, Publisher. **USPS:** 416-280. **Subscription Rates:** $25 3 months. **URL:** http://www.argus-press.com. **Ad Rates:** GLR $.75; BW $1341.60; 4C $1626.60; SAU $10.40. **Remarks:** Advertising accepted; rates available upon request. **Circ:** Paid ‡12,000.

17818 ■ WJSZ-FM - 92.5
103 N Washington St.
Owosso, MI 48867
Phone: (989)725-1925
Fax: (989)725-7925
Email: studio@z925.com
Format: Music of Your Life; Contemporary Hit Radio (CHR). **Key Personnel:** Rod Krol, President, studio@z925.com. **URL:** http://z925.com.

17819 ■ WOAP-AM - 1080
2301 N M-52
Owosso, MI 48867
Phone: (989)725-8196
Fax: (989)725-6626
Owner: 1090 Investments, LLC, 32500 Parklane Ave., Garden City, MI 48135, Ph: (734)525-1111, Fax: (734)525-3608. **Founded:** 1948. **Operating Hours**: 9:00

a.m. - Midnight Monday - Friday, 9:00 a.m. - Midnight Saturday - Sunday. **Wattage:** 1,000 KW. **Ad Rates:** $18-25 for 60 seconds; $18-25 for 60 seconds. **Mailing address:** PO Box 128, Owosso, MI 48867. **URL:** http://www.woapradio.com.

PAW PAW

Van Buren Co. Van Buren Co. (SW). 17 m W of Kalamazoo. Manufactures fish bait, fruit packages, canned goods, health foods, wine. Nurseries. Diversified farming. Grapes, apples, asparagus. Lake resort.

17820 ■ The Courier-Leader
The Courier-Leader
32280 E Red Arrow Hwy.
Paw Paw, MI 49079
Phone: (269)657-5080
Fax: (269)657-5723
Publication E-mail: vineyardpress@vineyardpress.biz
Newspaper covering local agriculture and industry. **Freq:** Weekly (Fri.). **Print Method:** Offset. **Cols./Page:** 6. **Col. Width:** 12 1/2 nonpareils. **Col. Depth:** 290 agate lines. **Key Personnel:** Robin Racette-Griffin, Editor; Steven A. Racette, General Manager. **USPS:** 564-620. **Subscription Rates:** $22 Individuals. **URL:** http://www.pawpawcourierleader.com. **Mailing address:** PO Box 129, Paw Paw, MI 49079. **Ad Rates:** BW $567; 4C $300; SAU $4.84; PCI $7. **Remarks:** Accepts advertising. **Circ:** Paid ‡3,200.

PETOSKEY

Emmet Co. Emmet Co. (N). On Little Traverse Bay, 69 m NE of Traverse City. Summer resort. Manufactures log homes, cutting blocks, concrete masonry, plastic bags, auto lock nuts. Limestone quarries. Agriculture. Potatoes, apples.

17821 ■ The Graphic
Petoskey News-Review, Super Shopper, and Graphic
319 State St.
Petoskey, MI 49770
Phone: (231)347-2544
Fax: (231)347-6833
Publisher's E-mail: petoskeynews@petoskeynews.com
Entertainment resort newspaper. **Founded:** 1960. **Freq:** Weekly. **Print Method:** Offset. **Trim Size:** 11 3/8 x 14. **Cols./Page:** 5. **Col. Width:** 5 inches. **Col. Depth:** 13 inches. **Key Personnel:** Maggie Peterson, Editor, phone: (231)439-9397. **Subscription Rates:** Free. **URL:** http://www.petoskeynews.com; http://www.petoskeynews.com/graphic/. **Mailing address:** PO Box 528, Petoskey, MI 49770. **Ad Rates:** BW $2,083.90; 4C $2,725.90; SAU $32.06; PCI $32.06. **Remarks:** Advertising accepted; rates available upon request. **Circ:** Free 17000.

17822 ■ Petoskey News-Review
Petoskey News-Review, Super Shopper, and Graphic
319 State St.
Petoskey, MI 49770
Phone: (231)347-2544
Fax: (231)347-6833
Publisher's E-mail: petoskeynews@petoskeynews.com
Local newspaper. **Freq:** Daily 5/week. **Print Method:** Offset. **Trim Size:** 14 x 22 3/4. **Cols./Page:** 6. **Col. Width:** 12 picas. **Col. Depth:** 21 inches. **Key Personnel:** Christy Lyons, Director, Advertising, phone: (231)439-9329; Doug Caldwell, Publisher; Jeremy McBain, Editor. **USPS:** 387-660. **Subscription Rates:** $15.95 Individuals 1 month; $47.95 Individuals 3 months; $93.75 Individuals 6 months; $182.25 Individuals 1 year; $89 Out of area 3 months; $172 Out of area 6 months; $331 Out of area 1 year. **URL:** http://www.petoskeynews.com. **Mailing address:** PO Box 528, Petoskey, MI 49770. **Ad Rates:** GLR $32.06; BW $4136; 4C $4778; PCI $32.06. **Remarks:** Advertising accepted; rates available upon request. **Circ:** Mon.-Thurs. ★**8,994**, Fri. ★**10,717**.

17823 ■ The Social Contract
Social Contract Press
445 E Mitchell St.
Petoskey, MI 49770
Phone: (231)347-1171
Fax: (231)347-1185
Free: 800-352-4843
Freq: Quarterly. **Subscription Rates:** Free. **URL:** http://www.thesocialcontract.com/artman2/publish. **Remarks:** Advertising not accepted. **Circ:** 1500.

17824 ■ Super Shopper
Petoskey News-Review, Super Shopper, and Graphic
319 State St.
Petoskey, MI 49770
Phone: (231)347-2544
Fax: (231)347-6833
Publisher's E-mail: petoskeynews@petoskeynews.com
Shopper. **Founded:** 1972. **Freq:** Weekly (Sun.). **Print Method:** Offset. **Trim Size:** 14 x 22 3/4. **Cols./Page:** 6. **Col. Width:** 12 picas. **Col. Depth:** 21 inches. **Key Personnel:** Ken Winter, Contact; Lisa Kelso, Manager, Advertising. **URL:** http://www.petoskeynews.com. **Mailing address:** PO Box 528, Petoskey, MI 49770. **Ad Rates:** BW $4136; 4C $4777; SAU $32.06; PCI $32.06. **Remarks:** Advertising accepted; rates available upon request. **Circ:** (Not Reported).

17825 ■ 1270AM/102.3FM WMKT - 1270
PO Box 286
Petoskey, MI 49770
Phone: (231)347-8713
Fax: (231)347-8782
Email: greg.marshall@wmktthetalkstation.com
Format: Talk; News. **Key Personnel:** Greg Marshall, Contact, marshall@1270wmkt.com. **Wattage:** 1,000. **URL:** http://wmktthetalkstation.com.

17826 ■ WATT-AM - 1240
PO Box 286
Petoskey, MI 49770
Phone: (231)775-1263
Fax: (231)779-2844
Format: Talk; News. **Networks:** Westwood One Radio. **Owner:** MacDonald Garber Broadcasting Inc., 2095 US 131 S, Petoskey, MI 49770, Ph: (231)347-8713, Fax: (231)347-9920. **Founded:** 1945. **Operating Hours:** Continuous. **ADI:** Traverse City-Cadillac, MI. **Key Personnel:** Trish Garber, Gen. Mgr. **Wattage:** 1,000. **Ad Rates:** Noncommercial. Combined advertising rates available with WLXV.

17827 ■ WJML-AM - 1110
2175 Click Rd.
Petoskey, MI 49770
Phone: (231)348-5000
Free: 800-228-9565
Email: talk@wjml.com
Format: News; Talk. **Networks:** CBS. **Owner:** Stone Communications, Inc., 9 Chenery Ter., Belmont, MA 02478. **Founded:** Dec. 06, 1966. **Operating Hours:** Continuous. **ADI:** Traverse City-Cadillac, MI. **Wattage:** 10,000. **Ad Rates:** $16-22 for 60 seconds. WWKK. **URL:** http://wjml.com.

17828 ■ WKHQ-FM - 105.9
PO Box 286
Petoskey, MI 49770
Phone: (231)347-8713
Fax: (231)347-9920
Free: 877-947-1106
Format: Music of Your Life; News. **Owner:** MacDonald Garber Broadcasting, Inc., 2095 US 131, South Petoskey, MI 49770. **Founded:** 1980. **Key Personnel:** Dave B. Goode, Contact, david.goode@106khq.com. **Wattage:** 100,000 ERP. **Ad Rates:** $12-29 for 30 seconds; $17-34 for 60 seconds. **URL:** http://www.106khq.com/.

17829 ■ WKLZ-FM
322 Bay St.
Petoskey, MI 49770-2407
Phone: (616)348-2000
Fax: (616)348-7002
Format: Adult Contemporary; Soft Rock. **Networks:** AP; ABC. **Owner:** Petoskey Broadcasting, at above address. **Founded:** 1965. **Formerly:** WJML-FM. **Wattage:** 100,000 ERP. **URL:** http://wklt.com.

17830 ■ WLXT-FM - 96.3
2095 US 131 S
Petoskey, MI 49770
Fax: (231)347-8782
Free: 800-968-9636
Email: traffic@lite96.com
Format: Adult Contemporary. **Owner:** MacDonald Garber Broadcasting, Inc., 2095 US 131, South Petoskey, MI 49770. **Operating Hours:** Continuous. **Key Personnel:** Heather Leigh, Contact. **Wattage:** 100,000. **Ad Rates:** Noncommercial. **URL:** http://www.lite96.com.

17831 ■ WMBN-AM - 1340
PO Box 286
Petoskey, MI 49770
Phone: (231)347-8713
Format: Sports. **Founded:** 1947. **Operating Hours:** Continuous. **Key Personnel:** Chick Watkins, Contact; Dan Armstrong, Contact; Mark Haden, Contact. **Wattage:** 1,000. **Ad Rates:** Noncommercial.

PITTSFORD

Hillsdale Co. (SC). 5 m W of Hudson.

17832 ■ WPCJ-FM - 91.1
9400 Beecher Rd.
Pittsford, MI 49271
Phone: (517)523-3427
Format: News; Religious; Information. **Owner:** Pittsford Educational Broadcasting Foundation, at above address. **Founded:** 1985. **Operating Hours:** 12:00 a.m. - 10:31 p.m. Monday - Friday, 12:00 a.m. - 10:34 p.m. Saturday - Sunday. **Key Personnel:** Richard Krage, Station Mgr. **Wattage:** 270 ERP. **Ad Rates:** Accepts Advertising. **URL:** http://www.freedomfarm.info/.

PLAINWELL

Allegan Co. Allegan Co. (SE). 11 m N of Kalamazoo. Resort, aluminum products, onions.

17833 ■ WAKV-AM
213 Gilkey St.
Plainwell, MI 49080
Email: vintage@net-link.net
Format: Oldies. **Wattage:** 1,000 Day; 101 Night. **Ad Rates:** Advertising accepted; rates available upon request.

PLYMOUTH

Wayne Co. Wayne Co. (SE). 9 m NW of Wayne. Residential.

17834 ■ La Vita Lamborghini Magazine
Lamborghini Club of America
PO Box 701963
Plymouth, MI 48170
Phone: (734)216-4455
Fax: (925)253-9397
Publisher's E-mail: info@lamborghiniclubamerica.com
Magazine for Lamborghini owners. **Freq:** Quarterly. **Subscription Rates:** $50. **URL:** http://lavitalamborghini.com. **Formerly:** Lamborghini Club America Magazine. **Ad Rates:** BW $2900, two page spread; BW $1750, full page; BW $900, 1/2 page. **Remarks:** Accepts advertising. **Circ:** Controlled 1000.

PONTIAC

Oakland Co. Oakland Co. (SE). 26 m NW of Detroit. Lake resort region. Manufactures autos, trucks, buses, auto bodies, parts and accessories, rubber moulded products, trailers, paint, varnish, lacquer, dairy, iron products, boats, plastic, housewares, electronic circuit boards.

17835 ■ The Fear Finder
Halloween Events Inc.
18 S Perry St.
Pontiac, MI 48342
Phone: (248)332-7662
Publisher's E-mail: ed@fearfinder.com
Newspaper covering local Halloween events and news. **Freq:** Annual. **Print Method:** Photo offset. **Trim Size:** 11 3/8 x 14. **URL:** http://www.fearfinder.com. **Ad Rates:** BW $5443; 4C $6443. **Remarks:** Accepts advertising. **Circ:** Combined 500000.

17836 ■ Oakland Press: Serving Oakland County
Oakland Press
48 W Huron St.
Pontiac, MI 48342
Phone: (248)332-8181
General newspaper. **Freq:** Mon.-Sun. (morn.). **Print Method:** Letterpress. **Cols./Page:** 6. **Col. Width:** 2 1/16 inches. **Col. Depth:** 21 1/2 inches. **Key Personnel:** Kevin Haezebroeck, Publisher; Michelle Mills, Director, Advertising; Glenn Gilbert, Executive Editor. **Subscription Rates:** $54 Individuals 12-week home delivery;

Circulation: ★ = AAM; △ or • = BPA; ♦ = CAC; ❑ = VAC; ⊕ = PO Statement; ‡ = Publisher's Report; Boldface figures = sworn; Light figures = estimated.

$234 Individuals 52-week home delivery. **URL:** http://www.theoaklandpress.com. **Feature Editors:** Allan P. Adler, phone: (248)745-4626, allan.adler@oakpress.com; Alissa Malerman, phone: (248)745-4607, alissa.malerman@oakpress.com; Matt Myftiu, phone: (248)745-4617, matt.myftiu@oakpress.com; Tim Thompson, phone: (248)745-4655, tim.thompson@oakpress.com; Jeff Kuehn, *Editorials*, phone: (248)745-4682, jeff.kuehn@oakpress.com. **Ad Rates:** SAU $31.50. **Remarks:** Accepts advertising. **Circ:** Mon.-Fri. ***66,459**, Sat. ***63,130**, Sun. ***76,678**.

PORT HURON

St. Clair Co. St. Clair Co. (E). On St. Clair River and Lake Huron, 56 m NE of Detroit. Important rail and St. Lawrence Seaway shipping terminal. Manufactures chicory, copper wire and pipe, paper, woodworking machinery, auto parts, salt, sugar, castings, marine and industrial motors, brass products, industrial tape, conveyor, fishing equipment. Elevators. Fisheries.

17837 ■ Times Herald
The Times Herald Co.
911 Military St.
Port Huron, MI 48061-5009
Phone: (810)985-7171
Fax: (810)989-6294
Publisher's E-mail: customerservice@thetimesherald.com
General newspaper. **Founded:** 1869. **Freq:** Daily (eve.). **Print Method:** Offset. **Cols./Page:** 6. **Col. Width:** 25 nonpareils. **Col. Depth:** 301 agate lines. **Key Personnel:** Lori Driscoll, General Manager, phone: (810)989-6236; Shawn Bumeder, Publisher, phone: (810)989-6280. **Subscription Rates:** $16.09 Individuals daily; month; $10.22 Individuals weekends, month; $7.61 Individuals Sunday only, month. **URL:** http://www.thetimesherald.com. **Mailing address:** PO Box 5009, Port Huron, MI 48061-5009. **Ad Rates:** BW $2702.87; 4C $3097.87; SAU $24.65. **Remarks:** Accepts advertising. **Circ:** Mon.-Sat. ***27,707**, Sun. ***38,349**.

17838 ■ Woman's Life
Woman's Life Insurance Society
1338 Military St.
Port Huron, MI 48060-5423
Phone: (810)985-5191
Fax: (810)985-6970
Free: 800-521-9292
Publisher's E-mail: website@womanslife.org
Magazine for members of Woman's Life Insurance Society, a fraternal benefit society. **Freq:** Quarterly. **Print Method:** Offset. **Trim Size:** 8 3/8 x 10 7/8. **Cols./Page:** 3. **Col. Width:** 13 picas. **Col. Depth:** 53 picas. **Key Personnel:** Wendy L. Krabach, Managing Editor; Janice U. Whipple, Editor. **ISSN:** 0027-5689 (print). **Subscription Rates:** Free to members. **URL:** http://www.womanslife.org; http://www.womanslife.org/about-us/media-center. **Formerly**: Review. **Mailing address:** PO Box 5020, Port Huron, MI 48061-5020. **Remarks:** Advertising not accepted. **Circ:** Non-paid 32,000, 30000.

17839 ■ WBTI-FM - 96.9
808 Huron Ave.
Port Huron, MI 48060
Phone: (810)982-9000
Fax: (810)987-9380
Format: Adult Contemporary. **Networks:** Independent. **Owner:** Liggett Communications L.L.C., at above address. **Founded:** 1991. **Operating Hours**: Continuous. **Key Personnel:** Ben Coburn, Dir. of Programs, bcoburn@radiofirst.net. **Wattage**: 3,000. **Ad Rates:** Advertising accepted; rates available upon request. WPHM-AM; WHLX-AM, WHLS-AM, WSAQ-FM. **URL:** http://www.wbti.com.

17840 ■ WGRT-FM - 102.3
624 Grand River Ave.
Port Huron, MI 48060
Phone: (810)987-3200
Fax: (810)987-3325
Format: Adult Contemporary. **Networks:** ABC. **Owner:** Port Huron Family Radio Inc., at above address. **Founded:** 1991. **Operating Hours**: Continuous. **Wattage**: 3,000. **Ad Rates:** Noncommercial. **URL:** http://www.wgrt.com.

17841 ■ WHLS-AM - 1450
808 Huron Ave.
Port Huron, MI 48060
Phone: (810)982-9000
Fax: (810)987-9380
Owner: Liggett Communications L.L.C., at above address. **Founded:** 1938. **Wattage**: 1,000 KW. **Ad Rates:** $6-24.50 for 30 seconds; $7-27.50 for 60 seconds. Combined advertising rates available with WSAQ-FM, WPHM-AM, WBTI-AM, WHLX-AM. **Mailing address:** PO Box 807, Port Huron, MI 48060. **URL:** http://www.whls.net.

17842 ■ WHLX-AM - 1590
808 Huron Ave.
Port Huron, MI 48060
Phone: (810)982-9000
Fax: (810)987-9380
Format: Oldies. **Simulcasts:** WHLS-AM. **Owner:** Liggett Communications L.L.C., at above address. **Founded:** 1952. **Formerly**: WSMA-AM; WIFN-AM; WHYT-AM; WDOG-AM. **Operating Hours**: Continuous. **Wattage**: 1,000. **Ad Rates:** Advertising accepted; rates available upon request. Combined advertising rates available with WBTI-FM, WPHM-AM,WSAO-FM, WHLS-AM.

17843 ■ WNFA-FM - 88.3
2865 Maywood Dr.
Port Huron, MI 48060
Format: Religious; Contemporary Christian. **Networks:** Moody Broadcasting; SkyLight Satellite; USA Radio. **Owner:** Wonderful News Radio, 2865 Maywood Dr., Port Huron, MI 48060, Ph: (810)985-3260, Free: 800-989-9637. **Founded:** 1986. **Operating Hours**: Continuous; 50% network, 50% local. **Key Personnel:** Ellyn Davey, Music Dir., ellyn@wnradio.com; Brian Smith, Dir. of Production, brian@wnradio.com; Lori McNaughton, Operations Mgr., lori@wnradio.com. **Wattage**: 1,300. **Ad Rates:** Noncommercial. **URL:** http://power883.com.

17844 ■ WNFR-FM - 90.7
2865 Maywood Dr.
Port Huron, MI 48060
Phone: (810)985-3260
Free: 800-989-9637
Format: Religious. **Founded:** 1986. **Key Personnel:** Brian Smith, Station Mgr., brian@wnradio.com; Lori McNaughton, Operations Mgr., lori@wnradio.com; Allen Klaski, Dir. of Production. **Ad Rates:** Noncommercial. **URL:** http://www.907hopefm.com.

17845 ■ Wonderful News Radio - 90.7
2865 Maywood Dr.
Port Huron, MI 48060
Phone: (810)985-3260
Free: 800-989-9637
Format: Gospel; Contemporary Christian. **Founded:** 1986. **Operating Hours**: Midnight - 8:00 p.m. Monday - Sunday. **Wattage**: 42,000 ERP. **Ad Rates:** Noncommercial. **URL:** http://www.907hopefm.com.

17846 ■ WPHM-AM - 1380
808 Huron Ave.
Port Huron, MI 48060
Fax: (810)987-9380
Format: News; Talk. **Networks:** NBC; ESPN Radio; ABC. **Operating Hours**: Continuous. **Wattage**: 5,000 Day5,000 Nigh. **Ad Rates:** Advertising accepted; rates available upon request. **URL:** http://www.wphm.net.

17847 ■ WSAQ-FM - 107.1
808 Huron Ave.
Port Huron, MI 48060
Phone: (810)987-9000
Format: Contemporary Country. **Networks:** Westwood One Radio. **Owner:** Liggett Communications L.L.C., at above address. **Founded:** 1964. **Operating Hours**: Continuous. **Wattage**: 6,000 ERP. **Ad Rates:** Noncommercial. Combined advertising rates available with WHLS-AM, WHLX-AM, WBTI-FM, WPHM-AM. **URL:** http://www.wsaq.com.

17848 ■ WSGR-FM
323 Erie St.
Port Huron, MI 48061-5015
Phone: (810)984-5064
Format: Eclectic. **Founded:** 1971. **Key Personnel:** John Hill, Gen. Mgr. **Wattage**: 120 ERP.

PORTAGE

Kalamazoo Co. Kalamazoo Co. (SW). 10 m S of Kalamazoo.

17849 ■ The Analysis of Verbal Behavior
Association for Behavior Analysis
550 W Centre Ave.
Portage, MI 49024
Phone: (269)492-9310
Journal publishing articles on behavior analysis and behaviorism as a philosophy. **Freq:** Semiannual. **ISSN:** 0889--9401 (print). **Subscription Rates:** $43 Students members, print and online; $55 Members print and online. **URL:** http://www.abainternational.org/journals/the-analysis-of-verbal-behavior.aspx. **Remarks:** Advertising not accepted. **Circ:** (Not Reported).

17850 ■ The Behavior Analyst
Association for Behavior Analysis
550 W Centre Ave.
Portage, MI 49024
Phone: (269)492-9310
Publication E-mail: mnormand@pacific.edu
Journal containing articles on theoretical, experimental and applied topics in behavior analysis. **Freq:** Semiannual. **Key Personnel:** Matthew Normand, Editor. **ISSN:** 0738--6729 (print). **Subscription Rates:** $28 Students members, print and online; $66 Members print and online; $25 Students online; $35 Members online. **URL:** http://www.abainternational.org/journals/the-behavior-analyst.aspx. **Remarks:** Advertising not accepted. **Circ:** (Not Reported).

17851 ■ NAFI Mentor
National Association of Flight Instructors
3101 E Milham Ave.
Portage, MI 49002
Free: 866-806-6156
Publisher's E-mail: nafi@nafinet.org
Freq: Bimonthly. **Subscription Rates:** Included in membership. **URL:** http://www.nafinet.org/publications/index.aspx. **Remarks:** Accepts advertising. **Circ:** (Not Reported).

17852 ■ NETA World
International Electrical Testing Association
3050 Old Centre Ave., Ste. 102
Portage, MI 49024
Phone: (269)488-6382
Fax: (269)488-6383
Publisher's E-mail: neta@netaworld.org
Trade magazine for the electrical testing and maintenance industry. **Freq:** Quarterly. **Subscription Rates:** Included in membership; $40 Nonmembers. **URL:** http://www.netaworld.org; http://www.netaworld.org/neta-world-journal. **Remarks:** Advertising accepted; rates available upon request. **Circ:** Controlled 25000, 6000.

PRUDENVILLE

17853 ■ WTWS-FM - 92.1
PO Box 468
Prudenville, MI 48651
Phone: (989)366-5364
Fax: (989)366-6200
Format: Country. **Ad Rates:** Advertising accepted; rates available upon request. **URL:** http://www.ilovethetwister.com.

17854 ■ WUPS-FM - 98.5
PO Box 468
Prudenville, MI 48651
Phone: (989)366-5364
Fax: (989)366-6200
Free: 800-968-4636
Email: info@wups.com
Format: Classic Rock. **Networks:** ABC. **Owner:** Coltrace Communications Inc., at above address. **Founded:** 1953. **Formerly**: WJGS-FM. **Operating Hours**: Continuous; 2% network, 98% local. **Wattage**: 100,000. **Ad Rates:** $20-38 for 30 seconds; $22-40 for 60 seconds. **URL:** http://www.wups.com.

17855 ■ WVXH-FM - 92.1
PO Box 468
Prudenville, MI 48651
Phone: (989)366-6095
Fax: (989)366-6200
Format: Talk; Eclectic; Public Radio. **Owner:** Xavier University, Cincinnati, OH. **Founded:** 1975. **Formerly**:

WKKM-FM. **Operating Hours**: Continuous. **Wattage:** 920 ERP. **Ad Rates:** Advertising accepted; rates available upon request. **URL:** http://ilovethetwister.com.

ROCHESTER

Oakland Co. Oakland Co. (SE). 8 m E of Pontiac. Manufactures drills, broaching machines, blotting paper, cement blocks, data processing machines, iron castings.

17856 ■ International Journal of Reliability and Safety
Inderscience Publishers
c/o Prof. Zissimos P. Mourelatos, Ed.-in-Ch.
Dept. of Mechanical Engineering
Oakland University
Rochester, MI 48309-4478
Publisher's E-mail: editor@inderscience.com
Journal providing an authoritative source of information and an international forum in the field of reliability and safety. **Freq:** Quarterly. **Key Personnel:** Prof. Zissimos P. Mourelatos, Editor-in-Chief; Prof. Lambros Katafygiotis, Associate Editor; Prof. Sankaran Mahadevan, Associate Editor. **ISSN:** 1479--389X (print); **EISSN:** 1479--3903 (electronic). **Subscription Rates:** €520 Individuals print or online only for 1 user; €882 Individuals online only for 2-3 users; €706 Individuals print and online; €1292 Individuals online only for 4-5 users; €1680 Individuals online only for 6-7 users; €2048 Individuals online only for 8-9 users; €2390 Individuals online only for 10-14 users; €2709 Individuals online only for 15-19 users; €3171 Individuals online only for 20+ users. **Circ:** (Not Reported).

17857 ■ WXOU-FM - 88.3
69 Oakland Center
Rochester, MI 48309
Phone: (248)370-4273
Email: generalmanager@wxou.org
Format: Educational; Full Service; Alternative/New Music/Progressive. **Owner:** Oakland University, 2200 N Squirrel Rd., Rochester, MI 48309-4401, Ph: (248)370-2100. **Founded:** 1972. **Operating Hours**: Continuous. **Local Programs**: *The Erik Anderson Program*, Friday 9:00 p.m. - 11:00 p.m. ; *Technology Today*, Saturday 5:00 p.m. - 6:00 p.m.; *The Electric Johnson*, Monday 10:00 p.m. - 12:00 a.m.; *Self-Proclamed Music Snob*; *Unfolded Gospel*, Tuesday 9:00 a.m. - 11:00 a.m.; *Metal Meltdown*, Sunday 10:00 p.m. - 11:00 p.m.; *The One O'Clock Takeover*, Tuesday 1:00 p.m. - 3:00 p.m.; *Reggae Revolver*, Tuesday 8:00 p.m. - 9:00 p.m.; *Outsight Radio Hours*, Tuesday 10:00 p.m. - 12:00 a.m.; *Frampton's Watermelon*, Monday 4:00 p.m. - 5:00 p.m.; *Cinema Serenade*; *The Old Front Porch Show*, Tuesday 5:00 p.m. - 7:00 p.m. **Wattage**: 110. **Ad Rates:** Noncommercial. **URL:** http://www.wxou.org.

ROGERS CITY

Presque Isle Co. Presque Isle Co. (NE). On Lake Huron, 40 m N of Alpena. Resorts. Museum. Boat harbor. World's largest limestone quarry. Limestone crushing plant. Timber. Agriculture. Potatoes, beans, livestock.

17858 ■ Presque Isle County Advance
Presque Newspaper Inc.
PO Box 50
Rogers City, MI 49779
Phone: (989)734-2105
Community newspaper. **Freq:** Weekly (Thurs.). **Print Method:** Offset. **Cols./Page:** 8. **Col. Width:** 20 nonpareils. **Col. Depth:** 294 agate lines. **Key Personnel:** Beth Kowalski, General Manager; Peter Jakey, Managing Editor. **USPS:** 097--050. **Subscription Rates:** $32 Individuals Presque Isle, Alpena, Montmorency, and Cheboygan Counties; $36 Out of area; $43 Out of state; $50 Canada; $65 Other countries; $.75 Single issue. **URL:** http://demo.piadvance.com. **Ad Rates:** GLR $500; BW $1,144; 4C $1,750; SAU $5; PCI $3.50. **Remarks:** Accepts advertising. **Circ:** 4400.

ROMEO

Macomb Co. Macomb Co. (SE). 23 m NE of Pontiac. Manufactures auto parts, plastic products, seat belts, tractors and tractor equipment. Agriculture. Fruit, dairy products.

17859 ■ The Countryman
The Romeo Observer
124 W St. Clair
Romeo, MI 48065-0096
Phone: (586)752-3524
Fax: (586)752-0548
Community newspaper. **Freq:** Weekly. **Print Method:** Offset. **Trim Size:** 2 1/16. **Cols./Page:** 6. **Col. Width:** 11.9 inches. **Col. Depth:** 21 1/2 inches. **Key Personnel:** Dennis A. Setter, Managing Editor; Melvin E. Bleich, Editor; Chris Gray, Writer; Robert Bleich, Manager, Circulation; Cheryl Jackson, Office Manager; Linda Lindberg, Advertising Representative; Karen Setter, Assistant Editor. **Subscription Rates:** £38 Individuals 1 year; £15.50 Individuals 6 issues; £3.70 Single issue. **URL:** http://www.countrymanmagazine.co.uk/magazine.html. **Mailing address:** PO Box 96, Romeo, MI 48065-0096. **Ad Rates:** BW $1,613; 4C $1,863; SAU $8.70. **Remarks:** Accepts advertising. **Circ:** Non-paid ‡2200.

17860 ■ The Romeo Observer
The Romeo Observer
124 W St. Clair
Romeo, MI 48065-0096
Phone: (586)752-3524
Fax: (586)752-0548
Community newspaper. **Freq:** Weekly (Wed.). **Print Method:** Offset. **Cols./Page:** 6. **Col. Width:** 11.9 picas. **Col. Depth:** 301 agate lines. **Key Personnel:** Sandy Bombassei, Contact; Rocio Knittel, Contact; Chris Gray, Writer; Karen Setter, Assistant Editor; Cheryl Jackson, Office Manager; Melvin E. Bleich, Editor; Dennis A. Setter, Managing Editor; Robert Bleich, Manager, Circulation. **USPS:** 470-340. **Subscription Rates:** $21 Individuals in Michigan; $27 Out of state outside of Michigan. **Mailing address:** PO Box 96, Romeo, MI 48065-0096. **Ad Rates:** GLR $18; BW $1,613; 4C $1,863. **Remarks:** Accepts advertising. **Circ:** (Not Reported).

ROYAL OAK

Oakland Co. Oakland Co. (SE). 10 m N of Detroit. Tools, paint, mattresses, hydraulic mechanisms, automotive parts manufactured. Residential.

17861 ■ Better Investing
National Association of Investors Corporation
PO Box 220
Royal Oak, MI 48068-0220
Phone: (248)583-6242
Fax: (248)583-4880
Free: 877-275-6242
Publisher's E-mail: service@betterinvesting.org
Magazine focusing on investing in long-term common stock. **Freq:** 10/year Monthly. **Print Method:** Web offset. **Trim Size:** 8 x 10 7/8. **Cols./Page:** 3. **Col. Width:** 27 nonpareils. **Col. Depth:** 138 agate lines. **Key Personnel:** Adam Ritt, Editor. **ISSN:** 0006- 016X (print). **Subscription Rates:** $22 Individuals 10 issues; Included in membership; $31 /year for nonmembers; $1.50 /issue for nonmembers; e-magazine; included in membership dues. **URL:** http://www.betterinvesting.org/Public/StartLearning/BI+Mag/default.htm. **Ad Rates:** GLR $18; BW $6,645; 4C $13,350; PCI $252. **Remarks:** Accepts advertising. **Circ:** Paid ⋆**198964**, 386000.

17862 ■ Big City Blues Magazine
Big City Blues Magazine
PO Box 1805
Royal Oak, MI 48068-1805
Phone: (248)582-1544
Fax: (248)582-8242
Publication E-mail: blues@bigcitybluesmag.com
Consumer magazine covering blues music. **Freq:** Bimonthly. **Trim Size:** 8.25 x 10.5. **Key Personnel:** Robert Whitall, Jr., Editor-in-Chief, Publisher; Shirley Mae Owens, Editor. **Subscription Rates:** $40 Individuals; $70 Two years; $100 Individuals 3 years; $50 Canada; $90 Other countries. **Ad Rates:** BW $824. **Remarks:** Accepts advertising. **Circ:** (Not Reported).

17863 ■ Clear
Clear Magazine
433 N Washington Ave.
Royal Oak, MI 48067
Phone: (248)544-2532
Fax: (248)544-0008
Publisher's E-mail: info@clearmag.com
Contemporary fashion and design magazine. **Freq:** Bimonthly. **Key Personnel:** Emin Kadi, Publisher; Anna Carnick, Editor. **URL:** http://www.clearmag.com. **Remarks:** Accepts advertising. **Circ:** Controlled ‡170000.

17864 ■ HOUR Detroit: Metropolitan Detroit's Monthly Magazine
HOUR Media
117 W Third St.
Royal Oak, MI 48067
Phone: (248)691-1800
Fax: (248)691-4531
Consumer magazine covering local lifestyle, entertainment, fashion and food. **Freq:** Monthly. **Key Personnel:** George Bulanda, Managing Editor, phone: (248)691-1800; John Balardo, Publisher; Rebecca Powers, Editor; Ann Duke, Director, Advertising. **Subscription Rates:** $17.95 U.S. 1 year 12 issues; $83.95 Canada 1 year 12 issues; $29.95 U.S. 2 years 24 issues; $161.95 Canada 2 years 24 issues; $39.95 U.S. 3 years 36 issues; $237.95 Canada 3 years 36 issues. **URL:** http://www.hourdetroit.com. **Also known as**: Hour Detroit Magazine. **Remarks:** Advertising accepted; rates available upon request. **Circ:** ⋆**45000**.

17865 ■ Metro Times
Real Detroit Weekly L.L.C.
615 S Washington Ave., Second Fl.
Royal Oak, MI 48067
Phone: (248)591-7325
Fax: (248)544-9893
Community newspaper covering local music and entertainment. **Founded:** Feb. 11, 1999. **Freq:** Weekly (Wed.). **Print Method:** Web press. **Trim Size:** 9.75 x 10.5. **Key Personnel:** John J. Badanjek, Editor-in-Chief; Adam O'Connor, Editor; Alysa Zavala, Managing Editor. **Subscription Rates:** Free. **URL:** http://metrotimes.com. **Formerly**: Real Detroit Weekly. **Ad Rates:** BW $2,195; 4C $2,595; SAU $19. **Remarks:** Accepts advertising. **Circ:** Free ‡65000.

17866 ■ Road & Travel Magazine
Caldwell Communications Inc.
811 N Main St., Ste. 105
Royal Oak, MI 48067
Phone: (248)546-4646
Fax: (248)546-6550
Lifestyle magazine specializing in auto, travel, and safety topics aimed at upscale women consumers between 29-59. **Freq:** Weekly. **Key Personnel:** Courtney Caldwell, Founder, Editor-in-Chief, Publicist. **URL:** http://www.roadandtravel.com/company/companylanding/landing.htm. **Remarks:** Accepts advertising. **Circ:** (Not Reported).

17867 ■ WOWF-FM - 99.5
306 S Washington, Ste. 500
Royal Oak, MI 48067
Phone: (810)398-1100
Fax: (810)543-3699
Format: Contemporary Country. **Networks:** NBC; The Source. **Owner:** Alliance Broadcasting, at above address. **Founded:** 1988. **Formerly**: WDFX-FM. **Operating Hours**: Continuous; 5% network, 95% local. **ADI:** Detroit, MI. **Key Personnel:** Betty Pazdernik, Gen. Mgr. **Wattage**: 21,000. **Ad Rates:** $115-300 per unit.

17868 ■ W208BB-FM - 89.5
PO Box 391
Twin Falls, ID 83303
Fax: (208)736-1958
Free: 800-357-4226
Format: Religious; Contemporary Christian. **Owner:** CSN International, PO Box 391, Twin Falls, ID 83303, Ph: (208)736-1958, Fax: (208)736-1958, Free: 800-357-4226. **URL:** http://www.csnradio.com.

SAGINAW

Saginaw Co. Saginaw Co. (EC). On Saginaw River, 92 m NW of Detroit. Manufactures auto parts, power steering, measuring instruments; heavy machine tools, boilers, dairy, meat, graphite, sheet metal products, conveyor equipment; seed cleaners; saw mill and baking machinery; portable wash tubs; aluminum, bronze, brass, iron castings, salt, chemicals. Beet sugar refinery. Grain and bean elevators.

17869 ■ The American Dance Circle
Lloyd Shaw Foundation
2124 Passolt St.
Saginaw, MI 48603

Circulation: ⋆ = AAM; △ or • = BPA; ♦ = CAC; ❑ = VAC; ⊕ = PO Statement; ‡ = Publisher's Report; Boldface figures = sworn; Light figures = estimated.

Magazine covering dance descriptions, dance history, and foundation activities. **Freq:** Quarterly March, June, September, and December. **Subscription Rates:** Included in membership. **Alt. Formats:** Download; PDF. **URL:** http://www.lloydshaw.org/american-dance-circle.html. **Remarks:** Advertising accepted; rates available upon request. **Circ:** (Not Reported).

17870 ■ The Catholic Weekly: Official Publication of the Dioceses of Saginaw and Gaylord
G.L.S. Diocesan Reports, Inc.
1520 Court St.
Saginaw, MI 48602-4067
Phone: (989)793-7661
Fax: (989)793-7663
Publisher's E-mail: gm@catholicweekly.org
Religious newspaper covering the local, national, and international church. **Freq:** Weekly (Fri.). **Print Method:** Offset. **Trim Size:** 13 3/8 x 22 3/4. **Cols./Page:** 8. **Col. Width:** 9 picas. **Col. Depth:** 294 agate lines. **Key Personnel:** Mark Haney, Executive Editor; Mark A. Myczkowiak, General Manager, President. **USPS:** 376-750. **Subscription Rates:** $29.95 Individuals. **URL:** http://www.catholicweekly.org. **Ad Rates:** BW $1,218; 4C $1,438; PCI $7.75. **Remarks:** Accepts advertising. **Circ:** Paid ⊕**11508**, Free ⊕**583**.

17871 ■ The Saginaw News
The Saginaw News
100 S Michigan Ave., Ste. 3
Saginaw, MI 48602
Phone: (989)671-1202
Publisher's E-mail: sanews@mlive.com
General newspaper. **Freq:** Daily (eve.). **Print Method:** Letterpress. **Cols./Page:** 6. **Col. Width:** 24 nonpareils. **Col. Depth:** 308 agate lines. **Key Personnel:** Matt Sharp, Publisher. **USPS:** 475-440. **Subscription Rates:** $8 Individuals online only. **URL:** http://www.mlive.com/saginaw. **Ad Rates:** PCI $41.89. **Remarks:** Color advertising accepted; rates available upon request. **Circ:** Mon.-Sat. ★**44143**, Sun. ★**54090**.

17872 ■ WCEN-FM - 94.5
1795 Tittabawassee Rd.
Saginaw, MI 48604
Phone: (989)752-3456
Free: 877-945-WCEN
Format: Country. **Networks:** Mutual Broadcasting System. **Founded:** 1963. **Operating Hours:** Continuous. **ADI:** Flint-Saginaw-Bay City, MI. **Wattage:** 100,000. **Ad Rates:** $26-36 for 60 seconds. $20-$30 per unit. Combined advertising rates available with WCEN-AM. **URL:** http://www.945themoose.com.

17873 ■ WGER-FM - 106.3
1795 Tittabawassee Rd.
Saginaw, MI 48604
Phone: (989)752-3456
Fax: (989)754-5046
Email: scott@mix1063fm.com
Format: Adult Contemporary; Soft Rock. **Founded:** 1964. **Operating Hours:** Continuous; 100% local. **ADI:** Flint-Saginaw-Bay City, MI. **Wattage:** 3,000. **Ad Rates:** $25-55 for 30 seconds. **URL:** http://www.mix1063fm.com.

17874 ■ WHEELZ-FM - 104.5
1740 Champagne Dr. N
Saginaw, MI 48604
Phone: (989)776-2100
Free: 877-943-3591
Format: Classic Rock. **Networks:** ABC; CNN Radio. **Owner:** Cumulus Media Inc., 3280 Peachtree Rd. NW, Ste. 2300, Atlanta, GA 30305-2455, Ph: (404)949-0700, Fax: (404)949-0740. **Operating Hours:** Continuous. **ADI:** Flint-Saginaw-Bay City, MI. **Wattage:** 2,900 ERP. **Ad Rates:** Advertising accepted; rates available upon request. Combined advertising rates available with WIOG FM/WKQZ FM/WHNN FM. **URL:** http://www.wheelz1045.com.

17875 ■ WHNN-FM - 96.1
1740 Champagne Dr. N
Saginaw, MI 48604-9239
Phone: (989)298-9466
Format: Oldies. **Networks:** Westwood One Radio. **Owner:** Cumulus Media Inc., 3280 Peachtree Rd. NW, Ste. 2300, Atlanta, GA 30305-2455, Ph: (404)949-0700, Fax: (404)949-0740. **Founded:** 1947. **Operating Hours:** Continuous; 5% network, 95% local. **ADI:** Flint-Saginaw-Bay City, MI. **Wattage:** 100,000. **Ad Rates:** $40-100 per unit. **URL:** http://www.whnn.com.

17876 ■ WIOG-FM - 102.5
1740 Champagne Dr. N
Saginaw, MI 48604-9239
Phone: (989)776-2100
Free: 877-330-9464
Format: Top 40. **Owner:** Cumulus Media Inc., 3280 Peachtree Rd. NW, Ste. 2300, Atlanta, GA 30305-2455, Ph: (404)949-0700, Fax: (404)949-0740. **Founded:** 1969. **Operating Hours:** Continuous. **Key Personnel:** Tom Clark, Contact, tom.clark@cumulus.com. **Ad Rates:** Advertising accepted; rates available upon request. **URL:** http://www.wiog.com.

17877 ■ WKCQ-FM - 98.1
2000 Whittier St.
Saginaw, MI 48601-2271
Phone: (989)752-8161
Fax: (989)752-8102
Free: 800-262-0098
Email: kevinprofitt@98fmkcq.com
Format: Country. **Networks:** ABC. **Owner:** MacDonald Broadcasting Co., 2000 Whittier Ave., Saginaw, MI 48601-2271. **Founded:** 1962. **Operating Hours:** Continuous. **ADI:** Flint-Saginaw-Bay City, MI. **Key Personnel:** Dr. John Richards, Music Dir.; Kevin Profitt, Contact; Kenneth H. MacDonald, Contact. **Wattage:** 50,000. **Ad Rates:** Advertising accepted; rates available upon request. **URL:** http://www.98fmkcq.com.

17878 ■ WKQZ-FM - 93.3
1740 Champagne Dr. N
Saginaw, MI 48604-9239
Format: Full Service. **Owner:** Citadel Broadcasting Corp., 7201 W Lake Mead Blvd., Ste. 400, Las Vegas, NV 89128-8366, Ph: (702)804-5200, Fax: (702)804-8250. **Operating Hours:** Continuous; 100% local. **Wattage:** 39,000. **Ad Rates:** Noncommercial; Advertising accepted; rates available upon request.

17879 ■ WNEM-AM - 1250
107 N Franklin St.
Saginaw, MI 48607-1263
Phone: (989)755-8191
Fax: (989)758-2111
Email: wnem@wnem.com
Format: News. **Networks:** Sun Radio. **Owner:** Meredith Corp., 1716 Locust St., Des Moines, IA 50309-3038, Ph: (515)284-3000. **Founded:** 1947. **Formerly:** WKNX-AM. **Operating Hours:** Continuous. **Key Personnel:** Wesley Goheen, Producer. **Wattage:** 1,000 Day 129 Night. **Ad Rates:** $12-15 for 30 seconds; $15-18 for 60 seconds. **URL:** http://www.wnem.com.

17880 ■ WNEM-TV - 5
107 N Franklin St.
Saginaw, MI 48607
Phone: (989)758-8191
Fax: (989)758-2111
Format: Commercial TV. **Networks:** CBS. **Owner:** Meredith Corp., 1716 Locust St., Des Moines, IA 50309-3038, Ph: (515)284-3000. **Founded:** 1954. **Operating Hours:** Continuous. **ADI:** Flint-Saginaw-Bay City, MI. **Key Personnel:** Brandon Allendorfer, Contact, brandon.allendorfer@wnem.com; Ian Rubin, Contact, ian.rubin@wnem.com. **Ad Rates:** Noncommercial. **URL:** http://www.wnem.com.

17881 ■ WSAM-AM - 1400
2000 Whittier St.
Saginaw, MI 48601
Phone: (989)752-8161
Format: Soft Rock. **Networks:** ABC. **Owner:** MacDonald Broadcasting Co., 2000 Whittier Ave., Saginaw, MI 48601-2271. **Founded:** 1940. **Operating Hours:** Continuous. **ADI:** Flint-Saginaw-Bay City, MI. **Wattage:** 1,000. **Ad Rates:** Advertising accepted; rates available upon request. **URL:** http://www.thebay104fm.com.

17882 ■ WSGW-AM - 790
1795 Tittabawassee Rd.
Saginaw, MI 48604
Phone: (989)752-3456
Free: 866-790-9749
Format: News; Talk. **Networks:** CBS. **Owner:** NextMedia, 6312 S Fiddlers Green Cir., Ste. 205 E, Greenwood Village, CO 80111, Ph: (303)694-9118, Fax: (303)694-4940. **Founded:** 1950. **Operating Hours:** Continuous. **ADI:** Flint-Saginaw-Bay City, MI. **Key Personnel:** Dave Maurer, Prog. Dir., dave@wsgw.com; Shannone Dunlap, Gen. Mgr. **Wattage:** 5,000 Day; 1,000 Nig. **Ad Rates:** Advertising accepted; rates available upon request. WGER-FM, WTLZ-FM, WTCF-FM, WCEN-FM. **URL:** http://www.wsgw.com.

17883 ■ WSGW-FM - 100.5
1795 Tittabawassee Rd.
Saginaw, MI 48604
Phone: (989)752-3456
Free: 866-790-9749
Format: News; Talk; Sports. **Operating Hours:** Continuous. **Key Personnel:** Shannone Dunlap, Gen. Mgr., VP, sdunlap@nextmediagroup.com; Dave Maurer, Operations Mgr., Prog. Dir., dave@wsgw.com. **Ad Rates:** Advertising accepted; rates available upon request. **URL:** http://www.fmtalk1005.com.

17884 ■ WTLZ-FM - 107.1
1795 Tittabawassee Rd.
Saginaw, MI 48604-9431
Phone: (989)921-7107
Fax: (989)754-5046
Format: Urban Contemporary. **Networks:** ABC; Satellite Radio. **Owner:** NextMedia, 6312 S Fiddlers Green Cir., Ste. 205 E, Greenwood Village, CO 80111, Ph: (303)694-9118, Fax: (303)694-4940. **Founded:** 1988. **Operating Hours:** Continuous; 10% network, 90% local. **ADI:** Flint-Saginaw-Bay City, MI. **Key Personnel:** Dave Maurer, Operations Mgr., dmaurer@nextmediagroup.net; Shannone Dunlap, Gen. Mgr., sdunlap@nextmediagroup.net; Yvonne Daniels, Dir. of Programs, yvonne@kisswtlz.com. **Wattage:** 6,000. **Ad Rates:** Noncommercial.

SAINT CLAIR SHORES

Macomb Co. Macomb Co. (SE). 12 m N of Detroit on Lake Saint Clair. Manufactures tools, dies, valves, machinery and pipe fittings.

17885 ■ The Journal of Teaching in Travel and Tourism
International Society of Travel and Tourism Educators
23220 Edgewater St.
Saint Clair Shores, MI 48082
Phone: (586)294-0208
Fax: (586)294-0208
Journal publishing manuscripts relating to travel and tourism education at various levels ranging from professional schools to degree granting universities. **Freq:** Quarterly. **ISSN:** 1531--3220 (print); **EISSN:** 1531--3239 (electronic). **Subscription Rates:** $116 Individuals online only; $405 Institutions online only; $121 Individuals print and online; $486 Institutions print and online. **URL:** http://www.istte.org/journal.html; http://www.tandfonline.com/toc/wttt20/current. **Remarks:** Advertising not accepted. **Circ:** (Not Reported).

SAINT IGNACE

Mackinac Co. Mackinac Co. (E Up Penin.). On Straits of Mackinac, 50 m S of Sault Sante Marie. Summer resort. Boat connections to Mackinac Island. Father Marquette National Park. Fisheries. Timber.

17886 ■ The St. Ignace News
The St. Ignace News
359 Reagon St.
Saint Ignace, MI 49781
Phone: (906)643-9150
Fax: (906)643-9122
Publisher's E-mail: sales@stignacenews.com
Community newspaper. **Freq:** Weekly (Thurs.). **Print Method:** Offset. **Cols./Page:** 6. **Col. Width:** 12.5 picas. **Col. Depth:** 294 agate lines. **Key Personnel:** Wesley H. Maurer, Jr., Editor; Ellen Paquin, Editor; Wendy Colegrove, Manager, Circulation; Sherry Cece, Manager; Mary R. Maurer, Associate Publisher; Tammy Matson, Contact. **USPS:** 462-380. **Subscription Rates:** $48 Individuals local; $60 Individuals Michigan Residents (Not Local); $75 Individuals Out-of-State; $35 Individuals online; $5 Individuals online; $83 Individuals print and online(local); $95 Individuals Michigan Residents ; $110 Individuals Out-of-State. **URL:** http://www.stignacenews.com. **Mailing address:** PO Box 277, Saint Ignace, MI 49781. **Ad Rates:** GLR $.55; BW $864; SAU $7.73. **Remarks:** Accepts advertising. **Circ:** 7000.

17887 ■ WIDG-AM - 940
1356 Mackinaw Ave.
Cheboygan, MI 49721
Phone: (231)627-2341
Fax: (231)627-7000
Format: Sports. **Networks:** AP. **Owner:** Northern Star Broadcasting L.L.C., 514 Munson Ave., MI 49686. **Founded:** 1966. **Operating Hours**: Continuous; 10% network, 90% local. **ADI**: Traverse City-Cadillac, MI. **Key Personnel:** Mary Reynolds, Gen. Mgr., VP of Sales & Mktg., mary@nsbroadcasting.com; Tammy Johnson, Contact; Tammy Johnson, Contact. **Wattage**: 5,000. **Ad Rates:** $6-16 per unit. Combined advertising rates available with WMKC. **URL:** http://www.nsbroadcasting.com.

SAINT JOHNS

Clinton Co. Clinton Co. (SC). 18 m N of Lansing. Manufactures farm implement parts, iron castings, piston rings and bushings, bearings, chemicals, apple products. Hatchery. Diversified farming. Livestock, beans, peppermint.

17888 ■ Michigan Farmer
Farm Progress Companies Inc.
c/o Jennifer Vincent, Editor
710 W Pk. St.
Saint Johns, MI 48879
Phone: (989)224-1235
Publisher's E-mail: circhelp@farmprogress.com
Agricultural magazine. **Freq:** 15/yr. **Print Method:** Offset. **Trim Size:** 8 1/2 x 10 3/4. **Cols./Page:** 3. **Key Personnel:** Jennifer Vincent, Editor; Frank Holdmeyer, Executive Editor, phone: (515)278-7782, fax: (515)278-7796; John Otte, Editor, phone: (515)278-7785, fax: (515)278-7797. **ISSN:** 0126-2158 (print). **Subscription Rates:** $29.95 Individuals; $48.95 Two years; $64.95 Individuals Three years. **URL:** http://farmprogress.com/michigan-farmer. **Remarks:** Accepts advertising. **Circ:** (Not Reported).

17889 ■ St. Johns Reminder
St. Johns Reminder
109 W Higham St.
Saint Johns, MI 48879-0473
Phone: (989)224-8356
Fax: (989)224-9458
Publication E-mail: sjreminder@michigannewspapers.com
Shopper/Community News. **Freq:** Weekly (Sat.). **Print Method:** Offset. **Cols./Page:** 6. **Col. Width:** 20 nonpareils. **Col. Depth:** 294 agate lines. **Key Personnel:** Jim O'Rourke, Publisher. **Subscription Rates:** $32 Individuals. **URL:** http://www.morningstarpublishing.com/about_us/stjohns. **Ad Rates:** GLR $.33; BW $355.20; 4C $606.40; PCI $3.70. **Remarks:** Accepts advertising. **Circ:** (Not Reported).

17890 ■ WWSJ-AM - 1580
1363 W Parks Rd.
Saint Johns, MI 48879
Phone: (989)224-7911
Email: sales@joy1580.com
Format: Gospel. **Owner:** Larry and Helen Harp, Wayne and Elmira Hill, 815 Maryland NE, Grand Rapids, MI 49505. **Founded:** 1959. **Formerly**: WRBJ-AM. **Operating Hours**: Continuous. **ADI**: Lansing (Ann Arbor), MI. **Key Personnel:** Michael McFadden, Contact, michael@joy1580.com; Larry Harp, Gen. Mgr., gm@1580.com; Gloria Jones, Contact, gloria@joy1580.com; Michael McFadden, Contact, michael@joy1580.com. **Local Programs**: *Mid Morning Gospel Jamz*, Monday Tuesday Wednesday Thursday Friday 11:00 a.m. - 3:00 p.m.; *Afternoon Praise*, Monday Tuesday Wednesday Thursday Friday 3:00 p.m. - 6:00 p.m.; *Serving Up Soul*, Saturday 11:00 a.m. - 3:00 p.m.; *The Bobby Jones Countdown*, Saturday 3:00 p.m - 5:00 p.m.; *Gospel Cafe*, Saturday 7:00 a.m. - 11:00 a.m.; *The Big Brother CJ Radio Show*, Monday Tuesday Wednesday Thursday Friday 6:00 p.m. - 7:00 p.m. **Wattage**: 1,000 Night 003 Day. **Ad Rates:** $10 for 30 seconds; $15 for 60 seconds. **URL:** http://www.joy1580.com.

SAINT JOSEPH

Berrien Co. Berrien Co. (W). On Lake Michigan 35 m NW of South Bend, Ind. Resort. Manufactures auto, tractor, and aircraft brakes, rubber goods, paper products, home appliances, electronic equipment, plastics, aluminum and zinc castings, auto jacks, electric furnaces, beverages, lab equipment. Fruit farms.

17891 ■ Applied Engineering in Agriculture
American Society of Agricultural and Biological Engineers
2950 Niles Rd.
Saint Joseph, MI 49085-8607
Phone: (269)429-0300
Fax: (269)429-3852
Free: 800-371-2723
Publisher's E-mail: hq@asabe.org
Peer-reviewed journal focused on practical applications of current research related to engineering for agricultural, food and biological systems. **Freq:** Bimonthly. **Trim Size:** 8 1/2 x 11. **Key Personnel:** Donna M. Hull, Director, Publications. **ISSN:** 0883--8542 (print). **Subscription Rates:** accessible only to members. **Alt. Formats:** Download; PDF. **URL:** http://www.asabe.org/publications/order-publications/periodicals.aspx. **Remarks:** Advertising not accepted. **Circ:** (Not Reported).

17892 ■ The Herald-Palladium
The Herald-Palladium
3450 Hollywood Rd.
Saint Joseph, MI 49085
Phone: (269)429-2400
Fax: (269)429-4398
Publication E-mail: eaccounts@TheHP.com
General newspaper. **Freq:** Daily (eve.), Sat. and Sun. (morn.). **Print Method:** Offset. **Trim Size:** 13 3/4 x 22 3/4. **Cols./Page:** 6. **Col. Width:** 26 nonpareils. **Col. Depth:** 301 agate lines. **Key Personnel:** David Holgate, Publisher; Larry Hall, Manager, Operations; Dave Brown, Managing Editor, phone: (269)429-4298. **USPS:** 387-440. **Subscription Rates:** $1 Individuals 1 day; $27.50 Individuals 4 weeks; $87.50 Individuals 13 weeks; $164 Individuals 26 weeks; 311 52 Weeks. **URL:** http://www.heraldpalladium.com. **Mailing address:** PO Box 128, Saint Joseph, MI 49085. **Remarks:** Accepts advertising. **Circ:** Mon.-Sat. ★**22894**, Sun. ★**25445**.

17893 ■ Resource: Engineering and Technology for a Sustainable World
American Society of Agricultural and Biological Engineers
2950 Niles Rd.
Saint Joseph, MI 49085-8607
Phone: (269)429-0300
Fax: (269)429-3852
Free: 800-371-2723
Publisher's E-mail: hq@asabe.org
Freq: 6/year. **ISSN:** 1076--3333 (print). **Subscription Rates:** $110 Nonmembers /yr ; $24 Members /yr. **URL:** http://www.asabe.org/publications/resource-magazine.aspx. **Remarks:** Accepts advertising. **Circ:** 7000.

17894 ■ Resource: Resource Engineering and Technology for a Sustainable World
American Society of Agricultural and Biological Engineers
2950 Niles Rd.
Saint Joseph, MI 49085-8607
Phone: (269)429-0300
Fax: (269)429-3852
Free: 800-371-2723
Publisher's E-mail: hq@asabe.org
Magazine covering technology for food and agriculture. **Founded:** 1994. **Key Personnel:** Sue Mitrovich, Editor, phone: (269)932-7013; Donna M. Hull, Director, Publications, phone: (269)932-7026. **ISSN:** 1076-3333 (print). **Subscription Rates:** $90 Nonmembers; $10.75 Single issue for non-members; $24 Single issue for members. **URL:** http://www.asabe.org/publications/resource-magazine.aspx. **Formerly**: Agricultural Engineering. **Ad Rates:** BW $995; 4C $1,295. **Remarks:** Accepts advertising. **Circ:** (Not Reported).

17895 ■ Transactions of the ASABE
American Society of Agricultural and Biological Engineers
2950 Niles Rd.
Saint Joseph, MI 49085-8607
Phone: (269)429-0300
Fax: (269)429-3852
Free: 800-371-2723
Publisher's E-mail: hq@asabe.org
Agricultural engineering peer-reviewed research journal. **Freq:** Bimonthly. **Print Method:** Offset. **Trim Size:** 8 1/2 x 11. **Cols./Page:** 2. **Col. Width:** 40 nonpareils. **Col. Depth:** 140 agate lines. **Key Personnel:** Paul Heinemann, Contact; James A. Lindley, Contact; Donna M. Hull, Director. **ISSN:** 2151-0032 (print). **URL:** http://www.asabe.org/publications/authors/journal-description-and-criteria.aspx. **Remarks:** Advertising not accepted. **Circ:** ‡1200.

17896 ■ WCNF-FM - 94.9
PO Box 107
Saint Joseph, MI 49085
Phone: (269)934-9830
Format: Adult Contemporary. **Founded:** June 07, 2006. **Key Personnel:** Gayle Olson, President; Jim Gifford, News Dir. **Ad Rates:** Advertising accepted; rates available upon request.

SALINE

Washtenaw Co. Washtenaw Co. (SE). 9 m S of Ann Arbor. Manufactured auto, plastic parts. Diversified farming. Residential.

17897 ■ Manchester Enterprise
Heritage Newspapers Inc.
106 W Michigan Ave.
Saline, MI 48176
Phone: (734)429-7380
Publication E-mail: subscribe@heritage.com
Community newspaper. **Founded:** 1867. **Freq:** Weekly (Thurs.). **Print Method:** Offset. **Cols./Page:** 5. **Col. Width:** 23 nonpareils. **Col. Depth:** 224 agate lines. **Key Personnel:** Michelle Rogers, Managing Editor. **USPS:** 327-460. **Subscription Rates:** $26 Individuals 26 weeks; $52 Individuals 52 weeks; $104 Individuals 104 weeks. **URL:** http://www.heritage.com/manchester_enterprise/. **Remarks:** Accepts advertising. **Circ:** Paid ♦**847**.

17898 ■ Milan News-Leader
Heritage Newspapers Inc.
106 W Michigan Ave.
Saline, MI 48176
Phone: (734)429-7380
Publication E-mail: editor@milannews.com
Community newspaper. **Freq:** Weekly (Thurs.). **Print Method:** Offset. **Trim Size:** 11 1/4 x 15. **Cols./Page:** 6. **Col. Width:** 1 5/8 inches. **Col. Depth:** 14 inches. **Key Personnel:** Michelle Rogers, Managing Editor. **Subscription Rates:** $31.20 Individuals. **URL:** http://www.heritage.com/milan_news_leader. **Formed by the merger of**: Milan News; Milan Leader. **Remarks:** Accepts classified advertising. **Circ:** Paid ♦**807**.

17899 ■ The Saline Reporter
Heritage Newspapers Inc.
106 W Michigan Ave.
Saline, MI 48176
Phone: (734)429-7380
Publication E-mail: westadvertising@heritage.com
Community newspaper. **Freq:** Weekly (Thurs.). **Print Method:** Offset. **Cols./Page:** 8. **Col. Width:** 20 nonpareils. **Col. Depth:** 294 agate lines. **Key Personnel:** Michelle Rogers, Managing Editor. **URL:** http://www.salinereporter.com. **Remarks:** Accepts classified advertising. **Circ:** Thurs. ♦**2563**.

17900 ■ Ypsilanti Courier
Heritage Newspapers Inc.
106 W Michigan Ave.
Saline, MI 48176
Phone: (734)429-7380
Publication E-mail: editor@ypsilanticourier.com
Community newspaper. **Freq:** Weekly (Thurs.). **Key Personnel:** Michelle Rogers, Managing Editor. **Subscription Rates:** $35 Individuals. **URL:** http://www.heritage.com/ypsilanti_courier. **Remarks:** Accepts advertising. **Circ:** Combined ‡5511.

17901 ■ WLBY-AM - 1290
Clear Channel
200 Basse Rd.
San Antonio, TX 78209
Phone: (734)302-8100
Format: Big Band/Nostalgia. **Owner:** Clear Channel Inc., 200 E Basse Rd., San Antonio, TX 78209, Ph: (612)336-9700, Fax: (612)336-9701. **Wattage**: 500. **URL:** http://www.1290wlby.com/.

Circulation: ★ = AAM; △ or • = BPA; ♦ = CAC; ❑ = VAC; ⊕ = PO Statement; ‡ = Publisher's Report; Boldface figures = sworn; Light figures = estimated.

SANDUSKY

Sanilac Co. Sanilac Co. (E). 50 m NW of Port Huron. Culvert pipes, steel bridges, road machinery, rubber products manufactured. Hydraulic jacks plant; pallet factory. Dairy, poultry, grain farms.

17902 ■ Sanilac County News
Sanilac County News
65 S Elk St.
Sandusky, MI 48471-0072
Community newspaper. **Freq:** Weekly (Wed.). **Print Method:** Offset. **Cols./Page:** 7. **Col. Width:** 62 picas. **Col. Depth:** 196 agate lines and 14 inches. **Key Personnel:** Eric Levine, Editor, phone: (810)648-4000; Carol Seifferlein. **Subscription Rates:** $24 Individuals print only, in county, one year; $43 Out of area out of county, one year; $20 Individuals online only, one year; $12 Individuals 6 months; $8 Out of area online and print subscription, one year. **URL:** http://sanilaccountynews.mihomepaper.com. **Mailing address:** PO Box 72, Sandusky, MI 48471-0072. **Ad Rates:** BW $906.5; 4C $995; SAU $1,425. **Remarks:** Accepts advertising. **Circ:** Paid ‡6800.

17903 ■ Sanilac Broadcasting Co.
19 S Elk St.
Sandusky, MI 48471
Free: 877-257-0925
Format: Country; Soft Rock. **Networks:** ABC. **Founded:** 1968. **Key Personnel:** Bob Armstrong, Gen. Mgr. **Ad Rates:** Advertising accepted; rates available upon request. **URL:** http://www.sanilacbroadcasting.com.

17904 ■ WBGV-FM - 92.5
19 S Elk St.
Sandusky, MI 48471
Phone: (810)648-2700
Fax: (810)648-3242
Free: 877-257-0925
Format: Country. **Owner:** Sanilac Broadcasting Co., 19 S Elk St., Sandusky, MI 48471, Free: 877-257-0925. **Founded:** Sept. 02, 1999. **Key Personnel:** Bob Armstrong, Gen. Mgr., boba@sanilacbroadcasting.com; Stan Grabitz, Prog. Dir., stang@sanilacbroadcasting.com; Renae Davis, News Dir., renaed@sanilacbroadcasting.com. **Ad Rates:** Advertising accepted; rates available upon request. **URL:** http://www.sanilacbroadcasting.com.

17905 ■ WMIC-AM - 660
19 S Elk St.
Sandusky, MI 48471
Phone: (810)648-2700
Fax: (810)648-3242
Free: 877-257-0925
Format: Full Service; Contemporary Country. **Networks:** ABC. **Owner:** Sanilac Broadcasting Co., 19 S Elk St., Sandusky, MI 48471, Free: 877-257-0925. **Founded:** 1968. **Operating Hours:** 6 a.m.-sunset. **ADI:** Flint-Saginaw-Bay City, MI. **Key Personnel:** Bob Armstrong, Gen. Mgr., boba@sanilacbroadcasting.com; Stan Grabitz, Dir. of Programs, stang@sanilacbroadcasting.com; Renae Davis, News Dir., renaed@sanilacbroadcasting.com. **Wattage:** 1,000. **Ad Rates:** $8-12 for 30 seconds; $10-14 for 60 seconds. Combined advertising rates available with WTGV-FM & WBGV-FM. **URL:** http://www.sanilacbroadcasting.com.

17906 ■ WTGV-FM - 97.7
19 S Elk St.
Sandusky, MI 48471
Format: Easy Listening. **Networks:** ABC. **Owner:** Sanilac Broadcasting Co., 19 S Elk St., Sandusky, MI 48471, Free: 877-257-0925. **Founded:** 1971. **Operating Hours:** Continuous. **ADI:** Flint-Saginaw-Bay City, MI. **Key Personnel:** Renae Davis, News Dir., renaed@sanilacbroadcasting.com. **Wattage:** 3,000. **Ad Rates:** $8-12 for 30 seconds; $10-14 for 60 seconds. Combined advertising rates available with WTGV-FM, WBGV-FM. **URL:** http://www.sanilacbroadcasting.com.

SAUGATUCK

Allegan Co. Allegan Co. (SW). On the Kalamazoo River, about a half mile inland from Lake Michigan, 12 m SW of Holland. Resort. Fisheries. Fruit, truck farms.

17907 ■ The Commercial Record
Kaechele Publications Inc.
3217 Blue Star Hwy.
Saugatuck, MI 49453
Phone: (269)857-2570
Fax: (269)857-4637
Community newspaper. **Founded:** 1868. **Freq:** Weekly (Thurs.). **Print Method:** Offset. **Cols./Page:** 5. **Col. Width:** 2 1/8 inches. **Col. Depth:** 16 inches. **Key Personnel:** Cheryl Kaechele, Publisher; Scott Sullivan, Editor. **USPS:** 125-700. **Subscription Rates:** $33 Individuals; $39 Out of area; $45 Out of state; $55 Two years; $66 Out of area 2 years; $72 Out of state 2 years; $82 Out of state. **URL:** http://commercialrecord.org/; http://www.allegannews.com/commercial-record. **Mailing address:** PO Box 246, Saugatuck, MI 49453. **Ad Rates:** SAU $6.61. **Remarks:** Accepts advertising. **Circ:** (Not Reported).

SAULT SAINTE MARIE

Chippewa Co. Chippewa Co. (Ex. NE Up. Penin.). On St. Mary's River International Boundry Line, and St. Mary's Falls Canal, at Eastern end of Lake Superior. Lake Superior State College. Tourism, Manufactures plastics, metals, lumber, dairy products, beverages. Light industry. Drydock facilities. Fisheries; Timber. Dairy, stock farms. Hay, buckwheat, potatoes, livestock.

17908 ■ Sault Ste. Marie Evening News
Sault Ste. Marie Evening News
109 Arlington St.
Sault Sainte Marie, MI 49783
Phone: (906)632-2235
Fax: (906)632-1222
General newspaper. **Freq:** Daily. **Key Personnel:** Cathy Kaiser, Manager, Advertising; Howard Kaiser, Publisher; Kate Hoornstra, Manager, Circulation. **Subscription Rates:** $4.99 Individuals /month, online only; $3 Individuals /week, print and online. **URL:** http://www.sooeveningnews.com. **Ad Rates:** BW $17.92, national open rate; BW $13.77, local open rate; BW $8.30, pick-up open rate. **Remarks:** Accepts advertising. **Circ:** 5750.

17909 ■ WDMJ-AM - 1320
PO Box 1230
Sault Sainte Marie, MI 49783
Phone: (906)225-1313
Format: News; Talk; Sports. **Simulcasts:** WIAN-AM. **Networks:** ABC. **Owner:** Northern Star Broadcasting L.L.C., 514 Munson Ave., MI 49686. **Founded:** 1931. **Operating Hours:** Continuous; 2% network, 98% local. **ADI:** Marquette, MI. **Key Personnel:** Tammy Johnson, Contact, tjohnson@nsbroadcasting.com. **Wattage:** 5,000. **Ad Rates:** $10-15 for 60 seconds.

17910 ■ WKNW-AM
PO Box 1230
Sault Sainte Marie, MI 49783
Phone: (906)632-1400
Fax: (906)635-1216
Format: Talk; News; Sports. **Networks:** Mutual Broadcasting System; NBC; CBS; EFM. **Owner:** Northern Star Broadcasting L.L.C., 514 Munson Ave., MI 49686. **Founded:** 1990. **Wattage:** 1,000 Day; 950 Night. **Ad Rates:** $6-10 for 60 seconds.

17911 ■ WLSO 90.1 FM - 90.1
Cisler Student Ctr., Ste. 105, 680 W Easterday Ave.
Sault Sainte Marie, MI 49783
Phone: (906)635-7504
Format: Alternative/New Music/Progressive; Heavy Metal; Hip Hop; Country. **Owner:** Lake Superior State University, 650 W Easterday Ave., Sault Sainte Marie, MI 49783, Ph: (906)632-6841, Fax: (906)635-2111. **Founded:** 1993. **Ad Rates:** Noncommercial. **URL:** http://wlso.lssu.edu.

17912 ■ WNBY-FM - 93.7
PO Box 1230
Sault Sainte Marie, MI 49783
Phone: (906)293-3221
Fax: (906)293-8275
Format: Oldies. **Networks:** ABC; Satellite Music Network; Jones Satellite. **Owner:** Sandy Feutz, at above address. **Founded:** 1966. **Operating Hours:** Continuous. **Key Personnel:** Gerald Feutz, Contact; Saundra Feutz, Contact; Vickie Holcomb, Contact. **Wattage:** 6,000. **Ad Rates:** $9.50 for 30 seconds; $12 for 60 seconds.

17913 ■ WSOO-AM - 1230
PO Box 1230
Sault Sainte Marie, MI 49783
Phone: (906)632-2231
Fax: (906)632-4411
Format: News; Sports. **Networks:** ABC; Michigan. **Owner:** Sovereign Communications, 898 Meander Rd., Portsmouth, VA 23707. **Founded:** 1940. **Operating Hours:** Continuous. **Key Personnel:** Tom Ewing, Gen. Mgr., tewing@up.net. **Wattage:** 1,000. **Ad Rates:** Noncommercial. **URL:** http://www.1230wsoo.com.

17914 ■ WSUE-FM - 101.3
PO Box 1230
Sault Sainte Marie, MI 49783
Phone: (906)632-2231
Fax: (906)632-4411
Email: info@rock101.net
Format: Classic Rock. **Founded:** 1940. **Operating Hours:** Continuous. **Key Personnel:** Mark San Angelo, Operations Mgr., mark@rock101.net. **Wattage:** 100,000. **Ad Rates:** Advertising accepted; rates available upon request. **URL:** http://www.rock101.net.

17915 ■ WTHN-FM - 102.3
PO Box 695
Gaylord, MI 49734
Fax: (989)732-8171
Free: 800-545-8857
Format: Religious. **Operating Hours:** Continuous. **Key Personnel:** John Rakis, Contact, jrakis@ncradio.org; George Lake, CEO, glake@ncradio.org; John Rakis, Contact, jrakis@ncradio.org. **Ad Rates:** Advertising accepted; rates available upon request. **URL:** http://www.thepromisefm.com.

17916 ■ WYSS-FM - 99.5
1402 Ashmun St.
Sault Sainte Marie, MI 49783
Phone: (906)635-0995
Fax: (906)635-1216
Format: Alternative/New Music/Progressive. **Owner:** Northern Star Broadcasting L.L.C., 1356 Mackinaw Ave., Cheboygan, MI 49721, Ph: (231)627-2341, Fax: (231)627-7000. **Founded:** 1972. **Formerly:** WSMM-FM. **Operating Hours:** Continuous. **ADI:** Traverse City-Cadillac, MI. **Wattage:** 100,000. **Ad Rates:** Noncommercial. **URL:** http://www.yesfm.net.

SCHOOLCRAFT

17917 ■ WOFR-FM - 89.5
290 Hegenberger Rd.
Oakland, CA 94621
Free: 800-543-1495
Format: Religious. **Owner:** Family Stations Inc., 290 Hegenberger Rd., Oakland, CA 94621, Free: 800-543-1495. **URL:** http://www.wofr.org.

SHELBY TOWNSHIP

17918 ■ The Basenji: Devoted to Basenjis Worldwide Since 1964
AWA, LLC
PO Box 2017
Chesterfield, VA 23832
Magazine providing dog breed information. **Freq:** 6/year. **Print Method:** Offset. **Trim Size:** 8 1/2 x 11. **Cols./Page:** 2. **Col. Width:** 42 nonpareils. **Col. Depth:** 136 agate lines. **Key Personnel:** Lisa Auerback, Editor. **ISSN:** 0094--9744 (print). **URL:** http://www.thebasenjionline.com/tbm. **Ad Rates:** BW $75, full inside page; 4C $135, full inside page. **Remarks:** Accepts advertising. **Circ:** ‡1450.

17919 ■ Inky Trail News
Inky Trail News
50416 Schoenherr Rd., No. 111
Shelby Township, MI 48315
Newspaper covering crafts, hobbies, entertainment, and penpals for women. **Freq:** Bimonthly. **Print Method:** Tabloid. **Trim Size:** 11 x 13. **Key Personnel:** Wendy Fisher, Editor. **ISSN:** 1087--4399 (print). **Subscription Rates:** $15 Individuals; $3 Single issue. **URL:** http://inky-trails-news.com/default.aspx. **Ad Rates:** BW $20. **Remarks:** Accepts advertising. **Circ:** 500.

SIX LAKES

17920 ■ The Purple Heart Magazine
Ladies Auxiliary of the Military Order of the Purple Heart United States of America
c/o Jan Knapp, President
PO Box 150
Six Lakes, MI 48886
Phone: (231)881-0735
Publisher's E-mail: jknapp@purpleheartmi.com
Magazine containing well-written articles about some of the activities of The Military Order of the Purple Heart around the country. **Freq:** Bimonthly. **Subscription Rates:** Included in membership. **URL:** http://www.purpleheart.org/MemberBenefits.aspx. **Remarks:** Advertising not accepted. **Circ:** (Not Reported).

SOUTH HAVEN

Van Buren Co. Van Buren Co. (SW). 24 m NW of PAW PAW. Residential.

17921 ■ le Despencer
Spencer Historical and Genealogical Society
68281 Birch St.
South Haven, MI 49090-9780
Publisher's E-mail: registrar@spencersociety.org
Journal containing Spencer genealogical articles, editorial comments, and past announcements. **Freq:** Quarterly. **Subscription Rates:** Included in membership. **Alt. Formats:** Download; PDF. **URL:** http://myshgs.org/2013/10. **Remarks:** Advertising not accepted. **Circ:** (Not Reported).

17922 ■ WCSY-FM - 103.7
11637 M-140 Hwy., Ste. B
South Haven, MI 49090
Phone: (269)637-6397
Fax: (269)637-2675
Format: Oldies. **Owner:** Mid-West Family Broadcasting Group, 730 Rayovac Dr., Madison, WI 53711, Ph: (608)273-1000. **Operating Hours**: Continuous. **Key Personnel:** Paul Layendecker, Operations Mgr.; Dave Doetsch, VP, Gen. Mgr.; Bob Bucholtz, Gen. Sales Mgr., bbucholtz@wsjm.com; Gayle Olson, VP, Gen. Mgr; Jim Gifford, Contact, news@wsjm.com. **Ad Rates:** Advertising accepted; rates available upon request. **URL:** http://www.wcsy.com.

SOUTH LYON

Oakland Co. Oakland Co. (SE). 15 m N of Ann Arbor. Seamless steel tubes, plastics, windows, doors manufactured. Horses. Farming. Potatoes, grain, hay.

17923 ■ The South Lyon Herald
Gannett Company Inc.
101 N Lafayette
South Lyon, MI 48178
Phone: (248)437-2011
Fax: (248)437-3386
Community newspaper. **Freq:** Weekly (Thurs.). **Print Method:** Offset. **Trim Size:** 13 3/4 x 22 1/2. **Cols./Page:** 6. **Col. Width:** 2 1/16 inches. **Col. Depth:** 21 1/2 inches. **Key Personnel:** Kurt Kuban, Editor. **USPS:** 503-600. **Subscription Rates:** $5 By mail per month. **URL:** http://www.hometownlife.com/news/hometown-south-lyon. **Ad Rates:** BW $819.15; 4C $1019.15; SAU $6.35. **Remarks:** Accepts advertising. **Circ:** (Not Reported).

SOUTHFIELD

Oakland Co. Oakland Co. (SE). 3 m N of Detroit. Manufactures precision tools, metal stampings, golf clubs, foundation garments, electro magnetic devices, storm windows.

17924 ■ Clinical Neuropharmacology
Lippincott Williams & Wilkins
c/o Peter A. LeWitt, MD, Editor-in-Chief
Henry Ford Hospital
Franklin Pointe Medical Ctr.
26400 W 12 Mile Rd., Ste. 115
Southfield, MI 48034
Phone: (248)355-2452
Peer-reviewed journal featuring both classic neurologic disorders as well as those disorders often called psychiatric. **Freq:** 6/year. **Print Method:** Sheetfed Offset. **Trim Size:** 8 1/8 x 10 7/8. **Key Personnel:** Peter A. LeWitt, MD, Editor-in-Chief; Harry Dean, Publisher. **ISSN:** 0362-5664 (print); **EISSN:** 1537-162X (electronic). **Subscription Rates:** $566 U.S.; $1422 Institutions; $648 Other countries individual; $1498 Institutions, other countries; $248 Individuals in-training; $264 Other countries in-training. **URL:** http://journals.lww.com/clinicalneuropharm/pages/default.aspx; http://www.lww.com/Product/0362-5664. **Ad Rates:** BW $950; 4C $1,555. **Remarks:** Accepts advertising. **Circ:** 159.

The Detroit Jewish News - See Detroit

17925 ■ Health Care Weekly Review
The Martin Group Inc.
24901 Northwestern Hwy., Ste. 316A
Southfield, MI 48075
Phone: (248)440-6080
Fax: (248)352-4801
Professional newspaper covering the health care industry. **Freq:** Weekly. **Key Personnel:** Mark Spiess, Publisher; David Martin, Editor-in-Chief. **Subscription Rates:** $49 Individuals. **Remarks:** Accepts advertising. **Circ:** 10,000.

17926 ■ Journal of Hospital Librarianship
Routledge Journals Taylor & Francis Group
c/o Carole M. Gilbert, Editor-in-Chief
Providence Hosp & Med Ctr.
16001 W Nine Mile Rd.
Southfield, MI 48075
Professional journal covering developments and advancements in hospital librarianship. **Freq:** Quarterly. **Trim Size:** 6 x 8 3/8. **Key Personnel:** Helen-Ann Brown Epstein, Associate Editor; Carole M. Gilbert, Editor-in-Chief. **ISSN:** 1532--3269 (print); **EISSN:** 1532--3277 (electronic). **Subscription Rates:** $122 Individuals online only; $139 Individuals print and online; $248 Institutions online only; $283 Institutions print and online. **URL:** http://www.tandfonline.com/toc/whos20/current. **Remarks:** Accepts advertising. **Circ:** (Not Reported).

17927 ■ Michigan Journal of Counseling and Development
Michigan Counseling Association
PO Box 2287
Southfield, MI 48037
Phone: (313)312-4622
Publisher's E-mail: michigancounselingassociation@gmail.com
Journal containing timely articles and research in the field of counseling. **Freq:** Semiannual. **Subscription Rates:** Included in membership. **URL:** http://www.michigancounselingassociation.com/benefits-of-membership.html. **Remarks:** Advertising not accepted. **Circ:** (Not Reported).

17928 ■ Reiki News Magazine
International Center for Reiki Training
21421 Hilltop St., Unit No. 28
Southfield, MI 48033
Phone: (248)948-8112
Fax: (248)948-9534
Free: 800-332-8112
Magazine that publishes articles on every aspect of Reiki practice. **Freq:** Quarterly. **Key Personnel:** Corey Bippes, Manager, Advertising. **ISSN:** 1539--6533 (print). **Subscription Rates:** $17 U.S.; $20 Canada; $25 Other countries; $16 U.S. perpetual subscription; $19 Canada perpetual subscription; $24 Other countries perpetual subscription. **URL:** http://www.reikiwebstore.com/SearchResult.cfm?CategoryID=10. **Ad Rates:** BW $825; 4C $1320. **Remarks:** Accepts advertising. **Circ:** 50000.

17929 ■ Reiki News Magazine
Vision Publications
21421 Hilltop St., Ste. 28
Southfield, MI 48033
Phone: (248)948-8112
Fax: (248)948-9534
Free: 800-332-8112
Magazine that publishes articles on every aspect of Reiki practice. **Freq:** Quarterly. **Key Personnel:** Corey Bippes, Manager, Advertising. **ISSN:** 1539--6533 (print). **Subscription Rates:** $17 U.S.; $20 Canada; $25 Other countries; $16 U.S. perpetual subscription; $19 Canada perpetual subscription; $24 Other countries perpetual subscription. **URL:** http://www.reikiwebstore.com/SearchResult.cfm?CategoryID=10. **Ad Rates:** BW $825; 4C $1320. **Remarks:** Accepts advertising. **Circ:** 50000.

17930 ■ Technology Century
Engineering Society of Detroit
20700 Civic Center Dr., Ste. 450
Southfield, MI 48076
Phone: (248)353-0735
Fax: (248)353-0736
Publisher's E-mail: esd@esd.org
Freq: Quarterly. **ISSN:** 8750--7811 (print). **Subscription Rates:** Included in membership; $25 Nonmembers /year. **Alt. Formats:** Download; PDF. **URL:** http://ww2.esd.org/PUBLICATIONS/TechnologyCentury.htm. **Ad Rates:** BW $1,800; BW $1,500, corporate member. **Remarks:** Accepts advertising. **Circ:** 6000.

17931 ■ Ward's Auto World
Ward's Communications
3000 Town Ctr., St. 2750
Southfield, MI 48075-1245
Phone: (248)357-0800
Fax: (248)357-0810
Publisher's E-mail: wards@wardsauto.com
Business magazine containing news and analysis for middle and upper management within all disciplines of the automotive OEM. **Founded:** 1965. **Freq:** Monthly. **Print Method:** Web offset. **Trim Size:** 8 x 10 3/4. **Cols./Page:** 2 and 3. **Col. Width:** 40 and 26 nonpareils. **Col. Depth:** 130 agate lines. **Key Personnel:** Drew Winter, Senior Editor; Tom Murphy, Senior Editor. **ISSN:** 0043-0315 (print). **Subscription Rates:** $69 Individuals U.S.A and Mexico; $85 Canada; $104 Other countries. **URL:** http://wardsauto.com/about/waw/; http://wardsauto.com/wardsauto-world/magazine. **Remarks:** Accepts advertising. **Circ:** △**68133**.

17932 ■ Ward's Automotive Yearbook
Ward's Communications
3000 Town Ctr., St. 2750
Southfield, MI 48075-1245
Phone: (248)357-0800
Fax: (248)357-0810
Publisher's E-mail: wards@wardsauto.com
Trade journal featuring articles and statistics on the automotive industry including sales, production, and development. **Freq:** Annual Latest Edition 2014. **Trim Size:** 8 1/4 x 11. **Key Personnel:** Barb Liske, Contact, phone: (248)799-2645; Rebecca Hughes, Contact; Alan K. Binder, Editor, phone: (248)799-2612. **Subscription Rates:** $625 Individuals 2014 yearbook; digital download or CD-ROM or printed book. **Alt. Formats:** CD-ROM. **URL:** http://wardsauto.com/subscriptions/auto-yearbook; http://wardsauto.com. **Remarks:** Accepts advertising. **Circ:** Paid 5000, 5000.

Birach Broadcasting Corp. - See Saint Louis, MO

17933 ■ Continental Cablevision
27800 Franklin Rd.
Southfield, MI 48034
Phone: (248)350-0102
Fax: (248)353-0141
Owner: Continental Cablevision Inc., The Pilot House, Lewis Wharf, Boston, MA 02110, Ph: (617)742-9500. **Founded:** 1982.

17934 ■ KTFX-AM - 1340
21700 Northwestern Hwy., Twr. 14, Ste. 1190
Southfield, MI 48075
Phone: (248)557-3500
Email: love1340am@sbcglobal.net
Format: News; Country; Talk; Religious. **Owner:** K95.5 Inc., 1600 W Jackson, Hugo, OK 74743. **Founded:** 1961. **Formerly**: KTOW-AM. **Wattage**: 500 Day; 1,000 Night. **Ad Rates:** Accepts Advertising. **URL:** http://www.birach.com.

KTUV-AM - See Little Rock, AR

17935 ■ WBRD-AM - 1420
21700 Northwestern Hwy., Twr. 14, Ste. 1190
Southfield, MI 48075
Format: Gospel. **URL:** http://www.birach.com.

WCND-AM - See Shelbyville, KY

17936 ■ WCXI-AM - 1160
21700 Northwest Hwy., Twr. 14, Ste. 1190
Southfield, MI 48075
Phone: (248)557-3500
Fax: (248)557-2950
Format: Country. **Founded:** Nov. 15, 1985. **Key Personnel:** Brenda Charette, Operations Mgr. **Wattage**: 1,000. **Ad Rates:** Noncommercial. **URL:** http://www.birach.com.

Circulation: ★ = AAM; △ or • = BPA; ♦ = CAC; ❑ = VAC; ⊕ = PO Statement; ‡ = Publisher's Report; Boldface figures = sworn; Light figures = estimated.

17937 ■ WCXN-AM - 1170
21700 NW Hwy. Tower 14, Ste. 1190
Southfield, MI 48075
Phone: (248)557-3500
Fax: (248)577-2950
Email: sima@birach.com
Format: Hispanic. **Owner:** Birach Broadcasting Group, 580 W Clark Rd., Ypsilanti, MI 48198. **Founded:** 1985. **Operating Hours**: Sunrise-sunset. **Wattage**: 10,000. **Ad Rates:** $15-25 for 30 seconds. **URL:** http://www.birach.com/wcxn.htm.

17938 ■ WJBK-TV - 2
16550 W 9 Mile Rd.
Southfield, MI 48037-2000
Format: Commercial TV; News; Sports. **Networks:** Fox. **Founded:** Oct. 24, 1948. **Operating Hours**: Continuous. **ADI**: Detroit, MI. **Key Personnel:** Sheila Bruce, Contact, sheila.bruce@foxtv.com. **Local Programs**: *FOX 2 News Morning*, Monday Tuesday Wednesday Tuesday Friday 5:30 p.m.; *FOX 2 News Weekend*, Saturday Sunday 7:30 p.m. **Wattage**: 100,000 ERP. **Ad Rates:** Advertising accepted; rates available upon request. **Mailing address:** PO Box 2000, Southfield, MI 48037-2000. **URL:** http://www.myfoxdetroit.com.

17939 ■ WKBD-TV - 50
26905 W 11 Mile Rd.
Southfield, MI 48033
Phone: (248)355-7000
Format: Sports. **Simulcasts:** TV Simulcasts with WWJ-TV. **Networks:** United Paramount Network; CBS. **Owner:** CBS Corp., 51 W 52nd St., New York, NY 10019-6188, Ph: (212)975-4321, Fax: (212)975-4516, Free: 877-227-0787. **Founded:** 1965. **Operating Hours**: Continuous; 5% network, 95% local. **ADI**: Detroit, MI. **Key Personnel:** Trey Fabacher, Station Mgr., VP. **Wattage**: 2,300 KW. **Ad Rates:** $25-10000 for 30 seconds. WWJ-TV. **URL:** http://cwdetroit.cbslocal.com.

17940 ■ WKRK-FM - 97.1
15600 W Twelve Mile Rd.
Southfield, MI 48076
Phone: (248)395-9797
Fax: (248)423-7725
Format: Talk. **Networks:** CBS. **Owner:** CBS Radio Stations Inc., 1515 Broadway, New York, NY 10036, Ph: (212)846-3939. **Founded:** 1941. **Formerly**: WYST-FM; WJOI-FM. **Operating Hours**: Controlled; 100% local. **ADI**: Detroit, MI. **Key Personnel:** Terry Lieberman, Dir. of Programs, terry.lieberman@971fm.com. **Wattage**: 15,000. **Ad Rates:** Advertising accepted; rates available upon request. **URL:** http://www.infinitybroadcasting.com.

WMYD-TV - See Detroit

17941 ■ WPON-AM - 1460
21700 Northwestern Hwy., Twr. 14, Ste. 1190
Southfield, MI 48075
Phone: (248)557-3500
Fax: (248)557-2950
Email: wpon@wpon.com
Format: Oldies; Talk. **Networks:** Independent. **Owner:** Birach Broadcasting Corp., at above address. **Founded:** 1940. **Operating Hours**: Continuous; 100% local. **Local Programs**: *20 Grand Review*, Monday 4:00 p.m.; *Sports Talk 60*, Friday 9:00 a.m. - 11:00 a.m.; *Voice of Pakistan*, Sunday 11:00 a.m. - 12:00 p.m. **Wattage**: 1,000. **Ad Rates:** $12-20 for 10 seconds; $22-30 for 30 seconds; $28-40 for 60 seconds. **URL:** http://www.wpon.com.

17942 ■ WVMV-FM - 98.7
26455 American Dr.
Southfield, MI 48034
Phone: (248)455-7350
Format: Jazz. **Key Personnel:** Tim Roberts, Prog. Dir., tim.roberts@cbsradio.com. **Ad Rates:** Advertising accepted; rates available upon request. **URL:** http://987ampradio.cbslocal.com.

17943 ■ WWJ-AM - 950
26495 American Dr.
Southfield, MI 48034
Phone: (248)327-2900
Fax: (248)304-4970
Email: wwjnewsroom@cbsradio.com
Format: News; Sports. **Networks:** CBS; AP. **Owner:** CBS Radio Inc., 1271 Avenue of the Americas, 44th Fl., New York, NY 10020-1401, Ph: (212)649-9600. **Founded:** 1920. **Operating Hours**: Continuous; 10% network, 90% local. **Wattage**: 50,000. **Ad Rates:** Noncommercial. **URL:** http://www.detroit.cbslocal.com.

17944 ■ WWJ-TV - 62
26905 W 11 Mile Rd.
Southfield, MI 48033
Phone: (248)355-7000
Email: wwjnewsroom@cbsradio.com
Founded: Dec. 11, 1994. **Ad Rates:** Noncommercial. **URL:** http://www.detroit.cbslocal.com.

17945 ■ WXYT-AM - 1270
26495 American Dr.
Southfield, MI 48034
Phone: (248)455-7200
Format: Sports. **Networks:** CNN Radio. **Owner:** CBS Radio Inc., 1271 Avenue of the Americas, 44th Fl., New York, NY 10020-1401, Ph: (212)649-9600. **Founded:** 1925. **Formerly**: WXYZ-AM. **Operating Hours**: Continuous. **Wattage**: 50,000. **Ad Rates:** $150 for 60 seconds. **URL:** http://detroit.cbslocal.com.

17946 ■ WXYZ-TV - 7
20777 W 10 Mile Rd.
Southfield, MI 48037
Phone: (248)827-7777
Free: 800-825-0770
Format: Commercial TV. **Networks:** ABC. **Owner:** Scripps-Howard Broadcasting Inc., 312 Walnut St., Cincinnati, OH 45202, Ph: (513)977-3035. **Founded:** 1948. **Operating Hours**: Continuous; 45% network, 55% local. **ADI**: Detroit, MI. **Key Personnel:** Ed Fernandez, Gen. Mgr., VP. **Ad Rates:** Advertising accepted; rates available upon request. **URL:** http://www.wxyz.com.

SOUTHGATE

Wayne Co.

17947 ■ Heritage Sunday
Heritage Newspapers Inc.
1 Heritage Dr., Ste. 100
Southgate, MI 48195
Phone: (734)246-0800
Community newspaper. **Freq:** Weekly (Sun.). **URL:** http://www.heritage.com. **Remarks:** Accepts advertising. **Circ:** (Not Reported).

17948 ■ The Ile Camera
Heritage Newspapers Inc.
1 Heritage Dr., Ste. 100
Southgate, MI 48195
Phone: (734)246-0800
Local newspaper. **Freq:** Weekly (Fri.). **Print Method:** Offset. Uses mats. **Cols./Page:** 5. **Col. Width:** 11.5 picas. **Col. Depth:** 13 inches. **Key Personnel:** Lena Khzouz, Editor. **Subscription Rates:** $35 By mail; $18.50 By mail 6 months. **URL:** http://thenewsherald.com/ile_camera. **Remarks:** Accepts classified advertising. **Circ:** Paid ‡3,500.

17949 ■ The News-Herald
Heritage Newspapers Inc.
1 Heritage Dr., Ste. 100
Southgate, MI 48195
Phone: (734)246-0800
Community newspaper. **Founded:** 1879. **Freq:** 3/week Wednesdays & Sundays. **Print Method:** Offset. **Cols./Page:** 6. **Col. Width:** 11 picas. **Col. Depth:** 21 1/2 inches. **Key Personnel:** Karl Ziomek, Editor. **Subscription Rates:** $138 Individuals Downriver only, Wednesday and Sunday; $69.30 Individuals 6 months (Downriver only), Wednesdays & Sundays; $103.95 Individuals 9 months (Downriver only), Wednesdays & Sundays; $34.65 Individuals 3 months (Downriver only), Wednesdays & Sundays. **URL:** http://www.thenewsherald.com. **Ad Rates:** BW $7,305. **Remarks:** Accepts advertising. **Circ:** Combined ♦**40613**, Combined ♦**38008**.

17950 ■ Press & Guide
Heritage Newspapers Inc.
1 Heritage Dr., Ste. 100
Southgate, MI 48195
Phone: (734)246-0800
Community newspaper. **Freq:** Semiweekly (Wed. and Sun.). **Print Method:** Offset. **Trim Size:** 13 3/4 x 22 1/2. **Cols./Page:** 6. **Col. Width:** 2 1/16 inches. **Col. Depth:** 21 inches. **Key Personnel:** Jason Alleyne, Editor. **Subscription Rates:** $10.63 Individuals /month. **URL:** http://www.pressandguide.com. **Remarks:** Accepts advertising. **Circ:** Combined ‡9351, Combined ‡10784.

17951 ■ The Suburban News
Heritage Newspapers Inc.
1 Heritage Dr., Ste. 100
Southgate, MI 48195
Phone: (734)246-0800
Suburban newspaper. **Founded:** Feb. 07, 1973. **Freq:** Daily. **Print Method:** Offset. **Cols./Page:** 6. **Col. Width:** 2 1/8 inches. **Col. Depth:** 21 inches. **Key Personnel:** Ellen Dooley, Editor; Christine Unish, Assistant Editor; Ted Meadowcroft, Manager, Circulation. **URL:** http://www.nj.com/suburbannews/. **Ad Rates:** BW $1076; 4C $1526; PCI $8.54. **Remarks:** Accepts advertising. **Circ:** Non-paid 92,454.

17952 ■ Warrendale-West Detroit Press & Guide
Heritage Newspapers Inc.
1 Heritage Dr., Ste. 100
Southgate, MI 48195
Phone: (734)246-0800
Community newspaper. **Freq:** Semiweekly (Wed. and Sun.). **URL:** http://www.pressandguide.com. **Remarks:** Accepts advertising. **Circ:** Sun. ‡20000, Wed. ‡25000.

SPARTA

Kent Co. Kent Co. (W). 15 m N of Grand Rapids. Manufactures piston rings, waxed paper products, furniture. Dairy, fruit farms. Apples.

17953 ■ Fresh Cut
Great American Publishing Co.
75 Applewood Dr. Ste. A
Sparta, MI 49345
Phone: (616)887-9008
Fax: (616)887-2666
Magazine for people involved in the fresh-cut produce trade, focusing on all aspects of the industry. Targeted to produce processors, retail and wholesale grocers, distributors, brokers, foodservice operators, and other buyers and end users of the fresh-cut products. **Freq:** Monthly. **Print Method:** Offset. **Trim Size:** 8 3/8 x 10 7/8. **Cols./Page:** 3. **Col. Width:** 1 1/16 inches. **Col. Depth:** 10 inches. **Key Personnel:** Matt McCallum, Publisher; Scott Christie, Managing Editor; Kimberly Warren, Associate Publisher. **ISSN:** 1072-2831 (print). **Subscription Rates:** $25 Individuals print and digital; $56 Canada print and digital; $100 Other countries print and digital. **URL:** http://produceprocessing.net. **Mailing address:** PO Box 128, Sparta, MI 49345. **Ad Rates:** BW $2,500; 4C $3,100; PCI $140. **Remarks:** Accepts advertising. **Circ:** Combined 17497.

17954 ■ The Fruit Growers News
Great American Publishing Co.
75 Applewood Dr. Ste. A
Sparta, MI 49345
Phone: (616)887-9008
Fax: (616)887-2666
Agricultural tabloid. **Freq:** Monthly. **Print Method:** Offset. **Trim Size:** 11 x 15. **Cols./Page:** 4. **Key Personnel:** Sally Ostman, Office Manager; Matt Milkovich, Managing Editor; Dick Lehnert, Managing Editor; Kimberly Warren, Associate Publisher, Director, Editorial; Matt McCallum, Publisher. **Subscription Rates:** $9.95 Individuals. **URL:** http://fruitgrowersnews.com. **Formerly**: The Great Lakes Fruit Growers News. **Mailing address:** PO Box 128, Sparta, MI 49345. **Remarks:** Accepts advertising. **Circ:** (Not Reported).

17955 ■ Party & Paper Retailer
Great American Publishing Co.
75 Applewood Dr. Ste. A
Sparta, MI 49345
Phone: (616)887-9008
Fax: (616)887-2666
Trade magazine for retailers of paper tableware, decorations, stationery, greeting cards, balloons, and other party-related items. **Freq:** Monthly. **Print Method:** Web Offset. **Trim Size:** 8 1/4 x 10 7/8. **Cols./Page:** 3. **Col. Width:** 2 1/4 inches. **Col. Depth:** 7 inches. **Key Personnel:** Matt McCallum, Chief Executive Officer; Abby Heugel, Managing Editor. **ISSN:** 0899--6008 (print). **Subscription Rates:** $19.95 U.S. print and online; $56 Canada print and online; $100 Other countries print and online; $9.95 Individuals US, Canada and other Countries; online. **URL:** http://partypaper.com. **Mailing address:** PO Box 128, Sparta, MI 49345. **Remarks:** Advertising accepted; rates available upon request. **Circ:** (Not Reported).

17956 ■ Spudman Magazine: Voice of the Potato Industry
Great American Publishing Co.
75 Applewood Dr. Ste. A
Sparta, MI 49345
Phone: (616)887-9008
Fax: (616)887-2666
Magazine for potato growers and managers involved in packing, shipping, buying, and processing. **Freq:** 8/year. **Print Method:** Offset. **Trim Size:** 7.75 x 10.75. **Cols./Page:** 3. **Col. Width:** 28 nonpareils. **Col. Depth:** 140 agate lines. **Key Personnel:** Matt McCallum, Chief Executive Officer, Publisher; Sally Ostman, Office Manager; Bill Schaefer, Managing Editor, phone: (208)234-2634. **ISSN:** 0038--8661 (print). **Subscription Rates:** $9.95 Other countries online, 1 year; $56 Canada print and online; $100 Other countries print and online; Free U.S. **URL:** http://spudman.com. **Formerly**: Supdman. **Mailing address:** PO Box 128, Sparta, MI 49345. **Remarks:** Advertising accepted; rates available upon request. **Circ:** (Not Reported).

17957 ■ The Vegetable Growers News
Great American Publishing Co.
75 Applewood Dr. Ste. A
Sparta, MI 49345
Phone: (616)887-9008
Fax: (616)887-2666
Publisher's E-mail: mivegcouncil@charter.net
Freq: Monthly. **Print Method:** Offset. **Trim Size:** 11 x 15. **Cols./Page:** 4. **Key Personnel:** Matt Milkovich, Managing Editor; Kimberly Warren, Associate Publisher, Director, Editorial; Matt McCallum, Chief Executive Officer, Publisher. **Subscription Rates:** $9.95 Individuals online (one year); $15.50 Individuals U.S. print and online (one year); $35.50 Individuals U.S. print and online (three years); $56 Individuals Canadian print and online (one year); $100 Individuals international print and online (one year). **URL:** http://vegetablegrowersnews.com. **Formerly**: The Great Lakes Vegetable Grower News. **Ad Rates:** BW $870; 4C $3,005. **Remarks:** Accepts advertising. **Circ:** △**15220**, 14000.

SPRING ARBOR

Jackson Co. (S). 10 m SW of Jackson. Manufactures motor vehicle parts, miscellaneous plastic and wood products. Diversified farming. Wheat, corn, beans.

17958 ■ KTGG-AM - 1540
106 E Main St.
Spring Arbor, MI 49283-9799
Phone: (517)968-0011
Free: 800-968-0011
Format: Contemporary Christian. **Networks:** SkyLight Satellite. **Owner:** Spring Arbor University, at above address. **Founded:** 1985. **Operating Hours:** Sunrise-sunset; 100% local. **Key Personnel:** Charles H. Webb, President, charles.webb@arbor.edu. **Wattage:** 450 Day ; 185 Night. **Ad Rates:** Noncommercial. **URL:** http://www.arbor.edu.

17959 ■ WJKN-FM
106 E Main St.
Spring Arbor, MI 49283
Phone: (517)750-6540
Format: Contemporary Christian. **Owner:** Spring Arbor University, at above address. **Founded:** Sept. 06, 2005.

17960 ■ WSAE-FM
106 E Main St.
Spring Arbor, MI 49283
Phone: (517)750-6540
Fax: (517)750-6619
Free: 888-346-6336
Email: info@home.fm
Format: Contemporary Christian. **Networks:** SkyLight Satellite. **Owner:** Spring Arbor College Communications, at above address. **Founded:** 1963. **Key Personnel:** Malachi Crane, Gen. Mgr.; Rachel Ryder, Dir. of Programs, rachel@home.fm; Dave Benson, Chief Engineer. **Wattage**: 3,900 ERP. **Ad Rates:** Underwriting available.

STANDISH

Arenac Co. Arenac Co. (E). 28 m N of Bay City. Diversified industry and agriculture. Tourism.

17961 ■ Arenac County Independent
Arenac County Independent
1010 W Cedar St.
Standish, MI 48658
Phone: (989)846-4531
Fax: (989)846-9868
Publication E-mail: info@ogemawherald.com
Community newspaper. **Freq:** Weekly (Wed.). **Print Method:** Offset. **Cols./Page:** 6. **Col. Width:** 25 nonpareils. **Col. Depth:** 301 agate lines. **Key Personnel:** Liz Gorske, Publisher. **URL:** http://www.arenacindependent.com. **Mailing address:** PO Box 699, Standish, MI 48658. **Ad Rates:** GLR $.27; BW $709.50; SAU $5.50. **Remarks:** Advertising accepted; rates available upon request. **Circ:** ‡6156.

17962 ■ WWCM-FM - 96.9
1999 E Campus Dr.
Mount Pleasant, MI 48859
Phone: (989)774-3105
Fax: (989)774-4427
Free: 800-727-9268
Format: Public Radio. **Owner:** CMU Public Broadcasting, 1999 E Campus Dr., Mount Pleasant, MI 48859, Ph: (989)774-3105, Fax: (989)774-4427, Free: 800-727-9268. **Ad Rates:** Underwriting available. **URL:** http://www.wcmu.org.

STURGIS

St. Joseph Co. St. Joseph Co. (S). 35 m NE of Elkhart, Ind. Manufactures carbon salesbooks, Venetian blinds, drapery, hardware, novelty paper products, carbon paper, steel-seating equipment, furniture, acrylic & acrylic mirrors, elastic bandages, mobile homes, camper trailers, business trucks, grey-iron castings, grass shears. Diversified farming. Lake resort.

WBET-FM - See Sturgis, MI

17963 ■ WBET-FM - 99.3
7080 S Nottawa
Sturgis, MI 49091
Phone: (269)651-2383
Fax: (269)659-1111
Email: wbet@wbetfm.com
Format: Oldies. **Simulcasts:** WMSH-AM. **Networks:** ABC; Jones Satellite. **Owner:** Swick Broadcasting Co. Inc., at above address. **Founded:** 1951. **Formerly**: WSTR-FM; WMSH-FM. **Operating Hours**: Continuous. **Wattage**: 3,000. **Ad Rates:** $6-12 for 30 seconds; $7-15 for 60 seconds. Combined advertising rates available with WTHD-FM, WLKI-FM. **URL:** http://www.wbetfm.com.

SUNFIELD

Eaton Co. Eaton Co. (NW). 22 m W of Lansing.

17964 ■ The Sunfield Sentinel
Sunfield Sentinel Publishing
135 Main
Sunfield, MI 48890
Phone: (517)566-8500
Farming community newspaper. **Freq:** Weekly. **Print Method:** Offset. **Cols./Page:** 6. **Col. Width:** 12 picas. **Col. Depth:** 280 agate lines. **Key Personnel:** Connie Speaks, Editor; Art Kimball, Publisher. **URL:** http://www.sunprintpublishing.com. **Ad Rates:** BW $240; PCI $3. **Remarks:** Color advertising not accepted. **Circ:** ‡900.

SWARTZ CREEK

17965 ■ Fireplug
Michigan State Firemen's Association
9001 Miller Rd., Ste. 10
Swartz Creek, MI 48473
Phone: (810)635-9513
Fax: (810)445-2858
Publisher's E-mail: office@msfassoc.net
Trade magazine for firefighters. **Freq:** Quarterly. **Print Method:** Offset. **Trim Size:** 8 1/2 x 11. **Key Personnel:** Paul Wayco, Editor-in-Chief. **ISSN:** 0273-6101 (print). **URL:** http://msfassoc.org/?page_id=19. **Mailing address:** PO Box 405, Swartz Creek, MI 48473. **Ad Rates:** BW $345; 4C $517. **Remarks:** Accepts advertising. **Circ:** 4500.

TAWAS CITY

Iosco Co. Iosco Co. (NE). On Saginaw Bay, 50 m NE of Bay City. Auto accessories, wood preserving factories. Gypsum quarries. Agriculture. Summer resort.

17966 ■ The Northeastern Shopper
The Northeastern Shopper
129 E North St.
Tawas City, MI 48764-0447
Phone: (989)362-6111
Fax: (989)362-7080
Free: 800-800-5713
Shopper. **Freq:** Sunday. **Print Method:** Offset. **Trim Size:** 11 x 17. **Cols./Page:** 6. **Col. Width:** 21 nonpareils. **Col. Depth:** 224 agate lines. **URL:** http://www.morningstarpublishing.com/about_us/northeasternnorth. **Ad Rates:** BW $1237.44; PCI $12.89. **Remarks:** Accepts advertising. **Circ:** Free 23000.

17967 ■ WHST-FM - 106.1
PO Box 695
Gaylord, MI 49734-0695
Fax: (989)732-8171
Free: 800-545-8857
Format: Contemporary Christian. **Owner:** The Ministries Of Northern Christian Radio Inc., PO Box 695, Gaylord, MI 49734, Fax: (989)732-8171, Free: 800-545-8857. **Founded:** 1973. **Formerly**: WDBI-FM. **Operating Hours**: Continuous. **Key Personnel:** Lorie Lewis, Accountant; Aubrey Wilson, Secretary, awilson@ncradio.org; John Rakis, Dir. of Dev. **Wattage**: 25,000. **Ad Rates:** Noncommercial. **URL:** http://www.ncradio.org.

17968 ■ WIOS-AM - 1480
PO Box 549
Tawas City, MI 48764
Phone: (989)362-3417
Fax: (989)362-4544
Email: sales@wkjc.com
Format: Easy Listening; Talk; News. **Networks:** ABC. **Owner:** Carroll Broadcasting Inc., 523 Meadow Rd., Tawas City, MI 48764, Ph: (989)362-3417, Fax: (989)362-4544, Free: 800-585-3515. **Founded:** 1958. **Operating Hours**: Sunrise-sunset. **ADI**: Flint-Saginaw-Bay City, MI. **Key Personnel:** Kevin Allen, Contact; John Carroll, Jr., Gen. Mgr.; Tim Carroll, Sales Mgr; Kevin Allen, Contact. **Wattage**: 1,000. **Ad Rates:** Noncommercial. Combined advertising rates available with WKJC-FM. **URL:** http://www.wiosradio.com.

17969 ■ WKJC-FM - 104.7
523 Meadow Rd.
Tawas City, MI 48764-0549
Phone: (989)362-3417
Fax: (989)362-4544
Email: sales@wkjc.com
Format: Country. **Simulcasts:** ABC, ESPN, Freeform, ABCNews.com,. **Owner:** Carroll Broadcasting Inc., 523 Meadow Rd., Tawas City, MI 48764, Ph: (989)362-3417, Fax: (989)362-4544, Free: 800-585-3515. **Operating Hours**: Continuous. **Key Personnel:** John Carroll, Jr., Gen. Mgr.; Tim Carroll, Sales Mgr., VP. **Wattage**: 50,000 ERP. **Ad Rates:** Noncommercial; Advertising accepted; rates available upon request. **Mailing address:** PO Box 549, Tawas City, MI 48764-0549. **URL:** http://www.wkjc.com.

TAYLOR

Wayne Co.

17970 ■ WZGX-AM
23300 Goddard Rd.
Taylor, MI 48180
Phone: (205)428-0146
Fax: (205)426-3178
Format: Hispanic. **Networks:** Spanish Broadcasting System; Spanish Information Service. **Owner:** Bessemer Radio, Inc., at above address. **Founded:** 1950. **Formerly**: WSMQ-AM; WBCO-AM; WYAM-AM; WENN-AM. **Key Personnel:** Raul Ortal, Contact, raulortal@aol.com. **Wattage**: 1,000. **Ad Rates:** $4-25 for 30 seconds; $8-50 for 60 seconds.

TECUMSEH

Lenawee Co. Lenawee Co. (S). 10 m N of Adrian. Manufactures electrical refrigeration units, auto parts, protective systems, corrugated containers, boats. Ships sand, gravel. Diversified farming.

17971 ■ The Tecumseh Herald
The Tecumseh Herald

Circulation: ★ = AAM; △ or • = BPA; ♦ = CAC; ❑ = VAC; ⊕ = PO Statement; ‡ = Publisher's Report; Boldface figures = sworn; Light figures = estimated.

110 E Logan St.
Tecumseh, MI 49286
Phone: (517)423-2174
Community newspaper. **Freq:** Weekly (Thurs.). **Print Method:** Offset. **Cols./Page:** 6. **Col. Width:** 18 nonpareils. **Col. Depth:** 294 agate lines. **Key Personnel:** James C. Lincoln, Editor, President, Publisher; Jean Oatman, Manager, Advertising. **Subscription Rates:** $39 Individuals. **URL:** http://www.tecumsehherald.com. **Mailing address:** PO Box 218, Tecumseh, MI 49286. **Ad Rates:** BW $1,334.55; PCI $11.15. **Remarks:** Accepts advertising. **Circ:** ‡4100.

THREE OAKS

Berrien Co. Berrien Co. (SW). 5 m N of South Bend, In. Residential.

17972 ■ Harbor County Guide
Harbor Country Chamber of Commerce
15311 Three Oaks Rd.
Three Oaks, MI 49128
Phone: (269)469-5409
Fax: (269)820-2006
Publisher's E-mail: chamber@harborcountry.org
Magazine covering business and tourist information about the eight communities of Harbor County. **Freq:** Annual. **Subscription Rates:** Free. **Circ:** (Not Reported).

THREE RIVERS

St. Joseph Co. St. Joseph Co. (S). 25 m S of Kalamazoo. Manufactures paper containers, hydramatic motors, boxboard, steam traps, copper cable, camper trailers, blankets, auto springs, steel fabricators, electric saws, fur. Nursery. Farming. Dairy products, stock.

17973 ■ Three Rivers Commercial-News
Three Rivers Commercial News
124 N Main St.
Three Rivers, MI 49093
Phone: (269)279-7488
Fax: (269)279-6007
Local newspaper. **Freq:** Daily (eve.) and Sat. (morn.). **Print Method:** Offset. **Cols./Page:** 8. **Col. Width:** 18 nonpareils. **Col. Depth:** 301 agate lines. **Key Personnel:** Dirk Milliman, II, Editor; Barb England, General Manager; Elena Hines, Managing Editor. **URL:** http://www.threeriversnews.com. **Ad Rates:** GLR $6.35; BW $860; 4C $1,080; SAU $7.10; PCI $5.30. **Remarks:** Accepts advertising. **Circ:** Paid 4503, Free ‡17100.

17974 ■ WLKM-AM
59750 Constantine Rd.
Three Rivers, MI 49093
Phone: (269)278-1815
Fax: (269)273-7975
Owner: Impact Radio, LLC, at above address. **Founded:** 1962. **Ad Rates:** $3 for 30 seconds; $4.50 for 60 seconds. **URL:** http://www.wlkm.com/about-us/contact-us.

17975 ■ WLKM-FM - 95.9
59750 Constantine Rd.
Three Rivers, MI 49093
Phone: (269)278-1815
Fax: (269)273-7975
Email: info@wlkm.com
Format: News; Oldies. **Networks:** Michigan Farm Radio; CNN Radio. **Owner:** Impact Radio, LLC, at above address. **Founded:** 1975. **Operating Hours:** Continuous. **ADI:** Grand Rapids-Kalamazoo-Battle Creek, MI. **Wattage:** 3,000. **Ad Rates:** $8.30-13.80 for 30 seconds; $9.70-16.15 for 60 seconds. **URL:** http://www.wlkm.com.

TRAVERSE CITY

Leelanau Co. Grand Traverse Co. (NW). On Grand Traverse Bay, 150 m N of Grand Rapids. Resort. Northwestern Michigan College. Manufactures boron carbide products, clothing, cone gears, fish lures, wall accessories and furniture components, canned fruits, frozen pies and desserts, wine, automotive parts, electrical components. Agriculture. Cherries, apples.

17976 ■ CALF News Magazine: Cattle Feeder
CALF News Magazine Ltd.
PO Box 1810
Traverse City, MI 49685-1810
Phone: (308)452-3207
Magazine for commercial feedlot operators (1,000 head or more). **Freq:** Monthly. **Print Method:** Offset. **Trim Size:** 8 1/2 x 11. **Cols./Page:** 3. **Col. Width:** 28 nonpareils. **Col. Depth:** 140 agate lines. **Key Personnel:** Betty Jo Gigot, Editor, phone: (620)272-6862, fax: (620)275-7333; Patti Wilson, Manager, Sales, phone: (308)440-0059; Larisa Willrett, Editor, Manager, Circulation. **Subscription Rates:** $40 Individuals; $70 Two years; $50 Other countries; $90 Other countries 2 years; $90 Individuals three years; $120 Other countries three years. **URL:** http://www.calfnews.net. **Ad Rates:** BW $1,945; 4C $3,075; PCI $120. **Remarks:** Accepts advertising. **Circ:** 7400.

17977 ■ Edible Grande Traverse
Edible Communities Inc.
PO Box 930
Traverse City, MI 49685
Phone: (231)360-3663
Publication E-mail: info@ediblegrandetraverse.com
Magazine featuring the local food of Northwest Lower Michigan. **Freq:** 5/year. **Key Personnel:** Charlie Wunsch, Publisher; Barb Tholin, Publisher. **Subscription Rates:** $28 Individuals; $7 Single issue. **URL:** http://www.ediblecommunities.com/grandetraverse. **Ad Rates:** 4C $2200. **Remarks:** Accepts advertising. **Circ:** (Not Reported).

17978 ■ The Home Shop Machinist
The Home Shop Machinist
PO Box 629
Traverse City, MI 49685
Free: 800-447-7367
Magazine for the amateur small shop machinist. **Freq:** Bimonthly. **Print Method:** Offset. **Trim Size:** 8 1/2 x 11. **Key Personnel:** Gretchen Christensen, Manager, Advertising; Daron Klooster, Managing Editor. **ISSN:** 0744-6640 (print). **Subscription Rates:** $29.95 Individuals 1 year; $55.95 Individuals 2 years; $77.95 Individuals 3 years. **URL:** http://www.homeshopmachinist.net/home. **Ad Rates:** BW $310; 4C $2,340. **Remarks:** Advertising accepted; rates available upon request. **Circ:** Paid ‡34500, Non-paid ‡92.

17979 ■ Independent Publisher Online: The Voice of The Independent Publishing Industry
Jenkins Group Inc.
1129 Woodmere Ave., Ste. B
Traverse City, MI 49686
Phone: (231)933-0445
Fax: (231)933-0448
Free: 800-706-4636
Online magazine containing book reviews and articles about independent publishing. **Freq:** Monthly. **Key Personnel:** Jim Barnes, Editor. **Subscription Rates:** Free. **URL:** http://www.independentpublisher.com. **Formerly:** Small Press; Independent Publisher. **Remarks:** Advertising accepted; rates available upon request. **Circ:** (Not Reported).

17980 ■ Just Labs: A Celebration of the Labrador Retriever
VP Demand Creation Services
2779 Aero Park Dr.
Traverse City, MI 49685
Phone: (231)946-3712
Fax: (231)946-3289
Free: 800-327-7377
Publisher's E-mail: service@villagepress.com
Magazine devoted to Labrador dogs. **Freq:** 6/year. **Print Method:** Sheet Fed Offset. **Trim Size:** 8 1/8 x 10 3/4. **Cols./Page:** 5. **Col. Width:** 26 nonpareils. **Col. Depth:** 196 agate lines. **Key Personnel:** Jason Smith, Editor; Jill LaCross, Managing Editor. **Subscription Rates:** $23.95 U.S. /year; $32.95 Canada /year; $38.95 Other countries /year. **URL:** http://www.justlabsmagazine.com. **Mailing address:** PO Box 968, Traverse City, MI 49685. **Ad Rates:** BW $2397; 4C $2876. **Remarks:** Accepts advertising. **Circ:** (Not Reported).

17981 ■ Live Steam & Outdoor Railroading
VP Demand Creation Services
PO Box 1810
Traverse City, MI 49685-1810
Free: 800-447-7367
Publisher's E-mail: service@villagepress.com
Magazine covering steam powered engines for hobbyists. **Freq:** Bimonthly. **Print Method:** Offset. **Trim Size:** 8 1/8 x 10 3/4. **Cols./Page:** 3. **Col. Width:** 14 picas. **Col. Depth:** 60 picas. **Key Personnel:** Gretchen Christensen, Manager, Advertising; Neil Knopf, Editor. **ISSN:** 0364-5177 (print). **Subscription Rates:** $39.95 1 year; $74.95 2 year; $104.95 3 year; $56.95 1 year; C$49.95 1 year; C$93.95 2 year; C$103.95 3 year; C$62.95 1 year; 52.95 Other countries 1 year; 98.95 Other countries 2 year; 134.95 Other countries 3 year; 86.95 Other countries 1 year. **URL:** http://www.livesteam.net. **Formerly:** Live Steam Newsletter; Live Steam: The Bimonthly Magazine for all Live Steamers and Large Scale Railroaders. **Ad Rates:** BW $707; 4C $950. **Remarks:** Advertising accepted; rates available upon request. **Circ:** Paid ‡11764, Non-paid ‡107.

17982 ■ Machinist's Workshop
VP Demand Creation Services
2779 Aero Park Dr.
Traverse City, MI 49685
Phone: (231)946-3712
Fax: (231)946-3289
Free: 800-327-7377
Publisher's E-mail: service@villagepress.com
Magazine describing metal working techniques and projects for hobby machinists. **Freq:** 6/year. **Print Method:** Offset. **Trim Size:** 8 1/2 x 11. **Cols./Page:** 3. **Col. Width:** 2 1/2 inches. **Col. Depth:** 10 inches. **Key Personnel:** George Bulliss, Editor; Gretchen Christensen, Manager, Advertising. **ISSN:** 0897--070X (print). **Subscription Rates:** $26.95 Individuals one year; $55.95 Individuals two years; $77.95 Individuals 3 years. **URL:** http://www.homeshopmachinist.net. **Formerly:** Projects in Metal. **Mailing address:** PO Box 968, Traverse City, MI 49685. **Ad Rates:** BW $704. **Remarks:** Accepts advertising. **Circ:** Paid ‡19,911, Non-paid ‡91.

17983 ■ The Pointing Dog Journal
VP Demand Creation Services
2779 Aero Park Dr.
Traverse City, MI 49685
Phone: (231)946-3712
Fax: (231)946-3289
Free: 800-327-7377
Publisher's E-mail: service@villagepress.com
Magazine covering tips on nutrition, healthcare, and first-aid for sporting dogs. **Freq:** Bimonthly. **Print Method:** Offset. **Trim Size:** 8 1/2 x 11. **Cols./Page:** 3. **Col. Width:** 27 nonpareils. **Col. Depth:** 140 agate lines. **Key Personnel:** Jason Smith, Managing Editor. **ISSN:** 0160--8894 (print). **Subscription Rates:** $26.95 Individuals; $35.95 Canada; $43.95 Other countries. **URL:** http://www.pointingdogjournal.com/?noredirect=true. **Mailing address:** PO Box 968, Traverse City, MI 49685. **Ad Rates:** BW $2397; 4C $2876. **Remarks:** Accepts advertising. **Circ:** (Not Reported).

17984 ■ The Retriever Journal
VP Demand Creation Services
2779 Aero Park Dr.
Traverse City, MI 49685
Phone: (231)946-3712
Fax: (231)946-3289
Free: 800-327-7377
Publisher's E-mail: service@villagepress.com
Magazine devoted to retrievers. Including training advice, feature stories on hunting experiences with retrievers, health and safety features, and hunting destinations. **Freq:** Bimonthly. **Print Method:** Offset. **Trim Size:** 13 3/4 x 22 7/8. **Cols./Page:** 6. **Col. Width:** 25 nonpareils. **Col. Depth:** 301 agate lines. **Key Personnel:** John Roddy, Director, Advertising and Sales; Jason Smith, Managing Editor. **Subscription Rates:** $26.95 Individuals; $35.95 Canada; $43.95 Other countries. **URL:** http://www.retrieverjournal.com/?noredirect=true. **Mailing address:** PO Box 968, Traverse City, MI 49685. **Remarks:** Accepts advertising. **Circ:** (Not Reported).

17985 ■ The S.A.R. Magazine
Michigan Society, Sons of the American Revolution
6432 Mission Ridge Rd.
Traverse City, MI 49686
Magazine containing historical articles on the Revolutionary War. Also includes Sons of the American Revolution, Michigan Society chapter activities and news. **Freq:** Quarterly. **Key Personnel:** Steve Vest, Editor. **Subscription Rates:** $10 Individuals; $3 Single issue. **URL:** http://www.sar.org/News/SAR-Magazine-now-available-line. **Remarks:** Accepts advertising. **Circ:** (Not Reported).

17986 ■ Traverse City Record-Eagle
Dow Jones Local Media Group Inc.
120 W Front St.
Traverse City, MI 49684
Phone: (231)946-2000
Publication E-mail: nronquist@record-eagle.com
General newspaper. **Freq:** Daily (morn.). **Print Method:** Offset. **Trim Size:** 12 1/2 x 21. **Cols./Page:** 6. **Col. Width:** 21 nonpareils. **Col. Depth:** 300 agate lines. **Key Personnel:** Frank Senger, Publisher, phone: (231)933-1403, fax: (231)946-8273; Michael Casuscelli, Publisher, phone: (231)933-1403; Bill Thomas, Editor, phone: (231)933-1467; Rich Roxbury, Manager, Circulation, phone: (231)933-1422. **Subscription Rates:** $21.99 Individuals /month; total access; $16.99 By mail /month; digital class. **URL:** http://www.record-eagle.com. **Feature Editors:** Jodee Taylor, phone: (231)933-1511, features@record-eagle.com. **Ad Rates:** GLR $3.19; BW $3,708.75; 4C $4,411.80; SAU $21; PCI $34.20. **Remarks:** Accepts classified advertising. **Circ:** Mon.-Sat. ★**28183**, Sun. ★**38464**, 20,000.

17987 ■ Traverse, Northern Michigan's Magazine
Prism Publications Inc.
148 E Front St.
Traverse City, MI 49684
Phone: (231)941-8174
Fax: (231)941-8391
Free: 800-678-3416
Publication E-mail: traverse@traversemagazine.com
Regional lifestyle features magazine. **Freq:** Monthly. **Print Method:** Offset. **Trim Size:** 8 3/8 x 10 7/8. **Cols./Page:** 3. **Key Personnel:** Diane Kolak, Art Director; Rachel North, Director, Marketing; Deborah W. Fellows, Founder. **ISSN:** 1071--3719 (print). **Subscription Rates:** $24 Individuals; $44 Two years; $64 Individuals 3 years. **URL:** http://www.mynorth.com. **Formerly**: TRAVERSE the Magazine. **Ad Rates:** BW $2,628.75; 4C $3,505. **Remarks:** Accepts advertising. **Circ:** ‡30000.

17988 ■ KBAL-AM - 1410
13999 S West Bay Shore Dr.
Traverse City, MI 49684
Phone: (231)947-3220
Format: Big Band/Nostalgia. **Networks:** Voice of Southwest Agriculture; Westwood One Radio. **Owner:** Roy Henderson, 1110 West William Cannon Dr., Austin, TX 78745, Ph: (512)383-1112. **Founded:** 1954. **Operating Hours**: Continuous. **Key Personnel:** Shay Hardy, Gen. Mgr., Prog. Dir., kbal@centex.net; Ti Martin, Music Dir., timartin@kbalradio.com. **Wattage**: 800; 250 overnight. **Ad Rates:** Advertising accepted; rates available upon request. Fixed position add $5.00 per spot.

17989 ■ KBAL-FM - 106.1
13999 S West Bay Shore Dr.
Traverse City, MI 49684
Phone: (231)947-3220
Format: Country. **Networks:** Voice of Southwest Agriculture; Texas State. **Owner:** Roy E. Henderson, at above address. **Founded:** 1996. **Operating Hours**: Continuous. **Key Personnel:** Shay Hardy, Gen. Mgr., Prog. Dir., kbal@centex.net; T.I. Martin, Music Dir., timartin@kbalradio.com. **Wattage**: 3,000. **Ad Rates:** Noncommercial. Combined advertising rates available with KBAL-AM. **URL:** http://sansabaradio.com/index.html.

17990 ■ KTWL-FM - 105.3
13999 SW Bayshore Dr.
Traverse City, MI 49684
Phone: (231)947-3220
Format: Classic Rock; Oldies. **Owner:** Roy E. Henderson, at above address. **Operating Hours**: Continuous. **Key Personnel:** Ryan Henderson, Gen. Mgr., ryan@ktwl.com. **Ad Rates:** Advertising accepted; rates available upon request.

17991 ■ WBCM-FM - 93.5
314 E Front St.
Traverse City, MI 49684
Phone: (231)947-7675
Fax: (231)929-3988
Email: wtcm@wtcmradio.com
Format: Country. **Owner:** WBCM Radio Inc., 314 E Front St., Traverse City, MI 49684. **Founded:** 1978. **Formerly**: WCLX-FM; WTCM-FM. **Key Personnel:** Joel Franck, News Dir., joelfranck@wtcmi.com. **Wattage**: 14,000 ERP. **Ad Rates:** $8 for 30 seconds; $10 for 60 seconds. **URL:** http://www.wtcmi.com/.

17992 ■ WBYB-FM - 94.3
745 S Garfield Ave.
Traverse City, MI 49685
Phone: (616)947-0003
Fax: (616)947-4290
Free: 888-442-8943
Format: Country. **Owner:** Northern Michigan Radio, Inc., at above address. **Founded:** Nov. 25, 1997. **Formerly**: WIAR-FM. **Operating Hours**: Continuous. **Key Personnel:** D. C. Cavender, Dir. of Programs, dccav@hotmail.com; Susan Melton, Promotions Dir., susancole@yahoo.com; A. J. Allan, Director. **Wattage**: 15,000. **URL:** http://www.10943.com.

17993 ■ WCCW-FM - 107.5
Radio Ctr.
300 E Front St., Ste. 450
Traverse City, MI 49684
Phone: (231)946-6211
Format: Oldies. **Networks:** ABC. **Owner:** Midwestern Broadcasting Co., 314 E. Front St., Traverse City, MI 49684. **Founded:** 1960. **Operating Hours**: Continuous. **ADI**: Traverse City-Cadillac, MI. **Key Personnel:** Dave Gauthier, Contact, davegauthier@wccwi.com. **Wattage**: 50,000. **Ad Rates:** $20-32 for 30 seconds; $28-40 for 60 seconds. Combined advertising rates available with WCCW-AM, WKJF-AM. **URL:** http://www.wccwi.com.

17994 ■ WGTU-TV - 29
8513 M-72 W
Traverse City, MI 49684
Phone: (231)947-7770
Format: Commercial TV. **Simulcasts:** WGTQ. **Networks:** ABC. **Owner:** Barrington Broadcasting Group, LLC, 2500 W Higgins Rd., Ste. 155, Hoffman Estates, IL 60169. **Founded:** 1971. **Operating Hours**: Continuous. **ADI**: Traverse City-Cadillac, MI. **Wattage**: 1,303,000. **Ad Rates:** Noncommercial. Combined advertising rates available with WGTQ. **URL:** http://www.upnorthlive.com.

17995 ■ WJZJ-FM - 95.5
3250 Racquet Dr.
Traverse City, MI 49684
Phone: (231)922-4981
Ad Rates: Advertising accepted; rates available upon request.

17996 ■ WJZQ-FM - 92.9
314 E Front St.
Traverse City, MI 49684
Phone: (231)947-7675
Fax: (231)929-3988
Format: Jazz. **Ad Rates:** Noncommercial. **URL:** http://www.101theone.com.

17997 ■ WKLT-FM - 97.5
1020 Hastings St.
Traverse City, MI 49686
Phone: (231)947-0003
Free: 800-968-9558
Email: ida@wklt.com
Format: Album-Oriented Rock (AOR); Classic Rock. **Simulcasts:** WKLZ-FM. **Owner:** Northern Radio of Michigan Inc., at above address. **Founded:** 1979. **Operating Hours**: 6:00 a.m. - Midnight. **ADI**: Traverse City-Cadillac, MI. **Key Personnel:** Terri Ray, Contact. **Local Programs**: *Lunch at the Leetsville*, Monday Tuesday Wednesday Thursday Friday 12:00 p.m. - 1:00 p.m. **Wattage**: 32,000 ERP. **Ad Rates:** Advertising accepted; rates available upon request. Combined advertising rates available with WKPK-FM, WBYB-FM, WAIR-FM. **URL:** http://wklt.com.

17998 ■ WLDR-FM - 101.9
13999 SW Bayshore Dr.
Traverse City, MI 49684
Phone: (231)947-3220
Fax: (231)947-7201
Format: Country. **Simulcasts:** WOUF-FM. **Networks:** Westwood One Radio; CBS. **Owner:** Fort Bend Broadcasting, 1110 W Westilliam Cannon Dr., Brenham, TX 77834-0037. **Founded:** 1966. **Operating Hours:** Continuous. **ADI**: Traverse City-Cadillac, MI. **Key Personnel:** Susan Melton, Contact; Dave Maxson, News Dir., dave.maxson@wldr.com; Lori McFarlan, Gen. Mgr., lori.mcfarlan@wldr.com; Roy Henderson, Owner; Susan Melton, Contact; D.C. Cavender, Contact. **Wattage**: 100,000. **Ad Rates:** $24-32 for 60 seconds. Combined advertising rates available with WLDR-AM. **URL:** http://www.sunnycountry.fm.

17999 ■ WLJN-AM - 1400
PO Box 1400
Traverse City, MI 49685-1400
Phone: (231)946-1400
Fax: (231)946-3959
Free: 800-968-1400
Email: info@newreleasetuesday.com
Format: Religious; Talk. **Networks:** Moody Broadcasting. **Owner:** Good News Media Inc., PO Box 1408, Traverse City, MI 49685, Ph: (231)946-3959, Fax: (231)946-1400. **Founded:** Dec. 23, 1982. **Operating Hours:** 12 a.m.-11 p.m. Mon.-Fri.; 6 a.m.-11 p.m. Sat. **ADI**: Traverse City-Cadillac, MI. **Wattage**: 640. **Ad Rates:** Noncommercial. **URL:** http://www.newreleasetuesday.com.

18000 ■ WLJN-FM - 89.9
PO Box 1400
Traverse City, MI 49685-1400
Phone: (231)946-1400
Fax: (231)946-3959
Free: 800-968-1400
Email: info@newreleasetuesday.com
Format: Religious; News. **Networks:** Moody Broadcasting. **Owner:** Good News Media Inc., PO Box 1408, Traverse City, MI 49685, Ph: (231)946-3959, Fax: (231)946-1400. **Founded:** Dec. 23, 1982. **Operating Hours:** Continuous; 55% network, 45% local. **ADI**: Traverse City-Cadillac, MI. **Key Personnel:** Don Parker, Contact, donp@wljn.com. **Wattage**: 39,000. **Ad Rates:** Underwriting available. **URL:** http://www.newreleasetuesday.com.

18001 ■ WLJW-AM - 1370
PO Box 1400
Traverse City, MI 49685-1400
Phone: (231)946-1400
Fax: (231)946-3959
Email: office@goodnewsmediainc.org
Format: Religious. **Founded:** Dec. 23, 1982. **Operating Hours:** Continuous. **Key Personnel:** Brian Harcey, Gen. Mgr., brianh@wljn.com; Pete Lathrop, Dir. of Programs, petel@wljn.com; Don Parker, Chief Engineer, donp@wljn.com. **Ad Rates:** Advertising accepted; rates available upon request. **Mailing address:** PO Box 1400, Traverse City, MI 49685-1408. **URL:** http://www.wljn.com.

18002 ■ WNMC-FM - 90.7
1701 E Front St.
Traverse City, MI 49686
Phone: (231)995-1090
Format: Jazz; Ethnic; Alternative/New Music/Progressive; Talk; Folk; Public Radio. **Networks:** IBS. **Owner:** Northwestern Michigan College, at above address. **Founded:** 1967. **Operating Hours**: 20 hours Daily; 100% local. **ADI**: Traverse City-Cadillac, MI. **Key Personnel:** Bob Brown, Music Dir.; James Walker, Music Dir.; Eric Hines, Station Mgr. **Local Programs**: *Folk Aire*, Tuesday Saturday 7:00 p.m. - 9:00 p.m. 2:00 p.m. - 4:00 p.m.; *Highway 49*, Friday 8:00 p.m. - 9:00 p.m.; *Mornings on WNMC*. **Wattage**: 600. **Ad Rates:** $5 per unit. **URL:** http://www.wnmc.org.

18003 ■ WPBN-TV - 7
8513 M-72 W
Traverse City, MI 49684
Phone: (231)947-7770
Fax: (231)947-0354
Free: 800-968-7770
Format: Commercial TV. **Networks:** NBC. **Founded:** 1954. **Operating Hours**: Continuous; 70% network, 30% local. **ADI**: Traverse City-Cadillac, MI. **Key Personnel:** Jill Saarela, CEO, President, jsaarela@upnorthlive.com; Betsy Bard, Gen. Sales Mgr., bbard@upnorthlive.com; Todd Harrison, Gen. Mgr. **Ad Rates:** Noncommercial. **URL:** http://www.upnorthlive.com.

WSRT-FM - See Elmira

18004 ■ WTCM-AM - 580
314 E Front St.
Traverse City, MI 49684
Phone: (231)947-7675
Fax: (231)929-3988

Circulation: ★ = AAM; △ or • = BPA; ♦ = CAC; ❑ = VAC; ⊕ = PO Statement; ‡ = Publisher's Report; Boldface figures = sworn; Light figures = estimated.

Format: Talk; News. **Owner:** Midwestern Broadcasting Co., 314 E. Front St., Traverse City, MI 49684. **Founded:** 1941. **Operating Hours:** Continuous. **ADI:** Traverse City-Cadillac, MI. **Key Personnel:** Ross Biederman, President. **Wattage:** 50,000. **Ad Rates:** Advertising accepted; rates available upon request. $25-44 for 30 seconds; $29-50 for 60 seconds. **Mailing address:** PO Box 472, Traverse City, MI 49684. **URL:** http://www.wtcmradio.com.

18005 ■ WTOM-TV - 4
8513 M-72 W
Traverse City, MI 49684
Phone: (231)947-7770
Fax: (231)947-0354
Free: 800-968-7770
Format: Commercial TV. **Networks:** NBC. **Owner:** Sinclair Broadcast Group Inc., 10706 Beaver Dam Rd., Hunt Valley, MD 21030, Ph: (410)568-1500, Fax: (410)568-1533. **Founded:** 1954. **Operating Hours:** Continuous. **ADI:** Traverse City-Cadillac, MI. **Key Personnel:** Jill Saarela, CEO, President, jsaarela@upnorthlive.com; Betsy Bard, Gen. Sales Mgr., bbard@upnorthlive.com. **Ad Rates:** Advertising accepted; rates available upon request. **URL:** http://www.upnorthlive.com.

18006 ■ WWKK-AM - 750
13999 S West Bay Shore Dr.
Traverse City, MI 49684
Phone: (231)947-3220
Format: News; Talk. **Owner:** Stone Communications, Inc., 9 Chenery Ter., Belmont, MA 02478. **Founded:** June 16, 2000. **Operating Hours:** Continuous. **ADI:** Traverse City-Cadillac, MI. **Wattage:** 1,000. **Ad Rates:** Noncommercial.

TROUT LAKE

18007 ■ WHWG-FM - 89.9
130 Carmen Dr.
Marquette, MI 49855
Phone: (906)249-1423
Free: 800-359-9673
Format: Religious; Gospel. **Owner:** Gospel Opportunities Inc., 130 Carmen Dr., Marquette, MI 49855-9380, Ph: (906)249-1423, Free: 800-359-9673. **Founded:** 1999. **Key Personnel:** Andy Larsen, News Dir. **Wattage:** 500. **Ad Rates:** Noncommercial. **URL:** http://www.whwl.net.

TROY

Oakland Co. Oakland Co. (SE). 12 m N of Detroit. Light industry. Residential.

18008 ■ Air Conditioning, Heating and Refrigeration News
BNP Media
2401 W Big Beaver Rd., Ste. 700
Troy, MI 48084
Phone: (248)362-3700
Fax: (248)362-5103
Free: 800-952-6643
Publisher's E-mail: asm@halldata.com
Tabloid for HVAC and commercial refrigeration contractors, wholesalers, manufacturers, engineers, and owners/managers. **Freq:** Weekly. **Key Personnel:** Kyle Gargaro, Editor-in-Chief; Mike Murphy, Publisher, phone: (248)244-6446, fax: (248)244-2905. **ISSN:** 0002-2276 (print). **URL:** http://www.achrnews.com. **Remarks:** Accepts advertising. **Circ:** (Not Reported).

18009 ■ Al Hakeem
National Arab American Medical Association
2265 Livernois Rd., Ste. 720
Troy, MI 48083
Phone: (248)646-3661
Fax: (248)646-0617
Publisher's E-mail: naama@naama.com
Freq: 3/year. **Subscription Rates:** Included in membership. **Alt. Formats:** PDF. **URL:** http://www.naama.com/resources. **Remarks:** Accepts advertising. **Circ:** 2500.

18010 ■ Appliance Design
BNP Media
2401 W Big Beaver Rd., Ste. 700
Troy, MI 48084
Phone: (248)362-3700
Fax: (248)362-5103
Free: 800-952-6643
Publisher's E-mail: asm@halldata.com
Magazine on appliance technology, design for manufacturing, and design trends. **Freq:** Monthly. **Print Method:** Offset. **Trim Size:** 7 7/8 x 10 7/8. **Key Personnel:** Darrell Dal Pozzo, Publisher, phone: (630)694-4342; Seth M. Fisher, Editor-in-Chief. **ISSN:** 0003--679X (print). **Subscription Rates:** Included in membership. **URL:** http://www.appliancedesign.com; http://www.bnpmedia.com/Articles/Publications/Manufacturing. **Formerly:** Appliance Manufacturer. **Ad Rates:** BW $4,975; 4C $7,620. **Remarks:** Accepts advertising. **Circ:** △**28267**.

18011 ■ Assembly Magazine
BNP Media
2401 W Big Beaver Rd., Ste. 700
Troy, MI 48084-3333
Phone: (248)362-3700
Fax: (248)362-0317
Publisher's E-mail: asm@halldata.com
Magazine focusing on assembly of hard goods, including electronic and mechanical products. **Freq:** Monthly. **Print Method:** Web Offset. **Key Personnel:** Austin Weber, Senior Editor, phone: (630)694-4013; Thomas A. Esposito, Publisher, phone: (610)436-4220; John Sprovieri, Editor-in-Chief, phone: (847)405-4068, fax: (847)405-4068; Christopher Sheehy, Manager, Circulation, phone: (503)251-7442. **ISSN:** 1050--8171 (print). **Subscription Rates:** Free to qualified subscribers. **URL:** http://www.assemblymag.com; http://www.assemblymag.com/publications/3. **Formerly:** Assembly Engineering. **Ad Rates:** 4C $8,689. **Remarks:** Accepts classified advertising. **Circ:** Controlled △**54,000**, △**56114**.

18012 ■ Beverage Industry
BNP Media
2401 W Big Beaver Rd., Ste. 700
Troy, MI 48084
Phone: (248)362-3700
Fax: (248)362-5103
Free: 800-952-6643
Publisher's E-mail: asm@halldata.com
Magazine (tabloid) for management of multiple beverage markets, including soft drinks, bottled water, beer, juice, wine, and non-carbonated drinks. **Freq:** Monthly. **Print Method:** Offset. **Trim Size:** 10 1/2 x 13-7/8. **Cols./Page:** 4 and 5. **Key Personnel:** Jennifer Zegler, Editor; Steven Pintarelli, Publisher, phone: (203)267-3388; Jessica Jacobsen, Managing Editor. **ISSN:** 0148-6187 (print). **Subscription Rates:** subscription needed. **Alt. Formats:** PDF. **URL:** http://www.bevindustry.com. **Ad Rates:** BW $6,420. **Remarks:** Accepts advertising. **Circ:** Paid 34001.

18013 ■ Candy Industry: The Global Magazine of Chocolate Confectionery
BNP Media
2401 W Big Beaver Rd., Ste. 700
Troy, MI 48084
Phone: (248)362-3700
Fax: (248)362-5103
Free: 800-952-6643
Publisher's E-mail: asm@halldata.com
Magazine serving candy industry management. **Freq:** Monthly. **Print Method:** Offset. **Trim Size:** 8 x 10 3/4. **Cols./Page:** 3. **Col. Width:** 27 nonpareils. **Col. Depth:** 140 agate lines. **Key Personnel:** Diana Rotman, Manager, Sales, phone: (847)405-4116; Kristine Collins, Publisher, phone: (847)224-8944; Bernard Pacyniak, Editor-in-Chief, phone: (847)405-4004; Dee Wakefield, Manager, Marketing, phone: (207)938-1199. **ISSN:** 0745-1032 (print). **Subscription Rates:** subscription required. **Alt. Formats:** PDF. **URL:** http://www.candyindustry.com. **Ad Rates:** BW $4,540; 4C $1,540. **Remarks:** Advertising accepted; rates available upon request. **Circ:** Combined △**13501**.

18014 ■ Casino Journal
BNP Media
2401 W Big Beaver Rd., Ste. 700
Troy, MI 48084
Phone: (248)362-3700
Fax: (248)362-5103
Free: 800-952-6643
Publisher's E-mail: asm@halldata.com
Trade publication covering the casino gaming industry. **Freq:** Monthly. **Subscription Rates:** Free. **Circ:** (Not Reported).

18015 ■ DBusiness
Hour Media L.L.C.
5750 New King Dr. Ste. 100
Troy, MI 48098
Phone: (248)691-1800
Fax: (248)691-4531
Covers business topics pertaining to Detroit, Michigan. **Freq:** Bimonthly. **Subscription Rates:** $9.95. **URL:** http://www.dbusiness.com. **Remarks:** Accepts advertising. **Circ:** (Not Reported).

18016 ■ Engineered Systems: Practical Applications for Innovative HVAC Mechanical System Engineers
BNP Media
PO Box 2600
Troy, MI 48007
Fax: (248)502-1038
Publisher's E-mail: asm@halldata.com
Publication focusing on heating and cooling systems design, operations, and maintenance for commercial, industrial, and institutional applications; bulleting automation and airflow management. **Freq:** Monthly. **Key Personnel:** Robert C. Beverly, Editor, phone: (434)974-6986, fax: (248)502-1038; Peter Moran, Publisher, phone: (914)882-7033, fax: (248)502-1052; Caroline Fritz, Managing Editor, phone: (419)754-7467, fax: (248)502-2084. **ISSN:** 0891-9976 (print). **URL:** http://www.esmagazine.com; http://www.bnpmedia.com/Articles/Publications/HVACR. **Ad Rates:** GLR $93; BW $8,030; 4C $9,525; PCI $120. **Remarks:** Accepts advertising. **Circ:** Controlled △**48400**.

18017 ■ Environmental Design and Construction
BNP Media
2401 W Big Beaver Rd., Ste. 700
Troy, MI 48084
Phone: (248)362-3700
Fax: (248)362-5103
Free: 800-952-6643
Publisher's E-mail: asm@halldata.com
Periodical covering issues in architecture and construction. **Freq:** Monthly. **Key Personnel:** Jeff Bagwell, Manager, Production, phone: (248)244-6481, fax: (248)283-6589; Michelle Clark Hucal, Associate Publisher, phone: (248)244-1280, fax: (248)786-1394; Diana Brown, Publisher, phone: (248)244-6258. **ISSN:** 1095--8932 (print). **URL:** http://www.bnpmedia.com/Articles/Publications/Architecture. **Remarks:** Advertising accepted; rates available upon request. **Circ:** Non-paid △**28500**.

18018 ■ Flexible Packaging: The Indispensable Tool for Converters & Printers of Flexible Packaging
BNP Media
2401 W Big Beaver Rd., Ste. 700
Troy, MI 48084
Phone: (248)362-3700
Fax: (248)362-5103
Free: 800-952-6643
Publisher's E-mail: asm@halldata.com
Magazine covering flexible packaging. **Trim Size:** 8 x 10 3/4. **Key Personnel:** Randy Green, Publisher, phone: (248)786-6498; Erin J. Wolford, Editor-in-Chief. **URL:** http://www.flexpackmag.com. **Ad Rates:** BW $5000; 4C $1410. **Remarks:** Accepts advertising. **Circ:** (Not Reported).

18019 ■ Floor Trends
BNP Media
2401 W Big Beaver Rd., Ste. 700
Troy, MI 48084
Phone: (248)362-3700
Fax: (248)362-5103
Free: 800-952-6643
Publisher's E-mail: asm@halldata.com
Trade magazine covering color & design trends for both commercial & residential professionals in the floor covering industry. **Freq:** 6/year. **Print Method:** Offset, Web. **Trim Size:** 8 1/2 x 10 7/8. **Cols./Page:** 2. **Col. Width:** 40 nonpareils. **Col. Depth:** 140 agate lines. **Key Personnel:** Michael Chmielecki, Associate Editor; Matthew Spieler, Editor. **ISSN:** 1521--8031 (print). **URL:** http://www.floortrendsmag.com. **Formerly:** Western Floors; National Floor Trends Magazine. **Remarks:** Accepts advertising. **Circ:** 20,000.

18020 ■ Independent Provisioner
BNP Media
2401 W Big Beaver Rd., Ste. 700
Troy, MI 48084
Phone: (248)362-3700
Fax: (248)362-5103
Free: 800-952-6643
Publisher's E-mail: asm@halldata.com
Magazine focusing on meat and poultry processors. **Freq:** Bimonthly. **Trim Size:** 8 X 10 3/4. **Key Personnel:** Sam Gazdziak, Editor-in-Chief, phone: (770)777-0058; Rick Parsons, Associate Publisher, phone: (407)302-7952. **URL:** http://www.provisioneronline.com. **Ad Rates:** BW $4020; 4C $1490. **Remarks:** Accepts advertising. **Circ:** 10000.

18021 ■ ISHN
BNP Media
2401 W Big Beaver Rd., Ste. 700
Troy, MI 48084
Phone: (248)362-3700
Fax: (248)362-5103
Free: 800-952-6643
Publication E-mail: ishn@halldata.com
Business-to-business magazine for safety and health managers at high-hazard worksites in manufacturing, construction, health facilities, and service industries. Content covering OSHA and EPA regulations, howto features, safety and health management topics, and the latest product news. **Freq:** Monthly. **Key Personnel:** Dave Johnson, Editor, phone: (610)666-0261, fax: (610)666-1906; Maureen Brady, Managing Editor, phone: (610)409-0954, fax: (248)502-1087; Randy Green, Publisher, phone: (248)244-6498, fax: (248)244-6439. **Subscription Rates:** Free. **URL:** http://www.ishn.com; http://www.ishn.com/publications/3. **Remarks:** Accepts advertising. **Circ:** △**71400**.

18022 ■ Journal of Advanced Manufacturing Systems
World Scientific Publishing Company Inc.
c/o Dr. Gopalan Mukundan, Managing Editor
Chrysler LLC
6508 Shoreline Dr.
Troy, MI 48085
Phone: (248)838-4901
Publisher's E-mail: wspc@wspc.com
Journal focusing on product development, process planning, resource planning, applications, and tools in the areas related to advanced manufacturing. **Freq:** Semiannual. **Key Personnel:** Dr. Gopalan Mukundan, Managing Editor; Dr. Bernie Nadel, Associate Editor, phone: (248)557-2274, fax: (248)557-2109; Dr. Nezih Yaramanoglu, Associate Editor, phone: (49)30 46777510, fax: (49)30 46777511; Prof. Hojjat Adeli, Associate Editor; Prof. Suren N. Dwivedi, Associate Editor, phone: (337)989-7262, fax: (337)989-7272; Prof. Vijay Kumar Jain, Associate Editor. **ISSN:** 0219--6867 (print); **EISSN:** 1793--6896 (electronic). **Subscription Rates:** $741 Institutions electronic + print; $661 Institutions electronic only; £544 Institutions electronic + print; £486 Institutions electronic only. **URL:** http://www.worldscientific.com/worldscinet/jams. **Circ:** (Not Reported).

18023 ■ Meat & Deli Retailer
BNP Media
2401 W Big Beaver Rd., Ste. 700
Troy, MI 48084
Phone: (248)362-3700
Fax: (248)362-5103
Free: 800-952-6643
Publisher's E-mail: asm@halldata.com
Magazine for professionals in the meat and deli industry. **Freq:** 9/year. **Key Personnel:** Peter Hansen, Regional Manager; Brion Palmer, Publisher; Richard Mitchell, Editor; Patricia Catini, Designer; Rosemary Weiss, Manager, Production. **ISSN:** 1555--8339 (print). **URL:** http://www.bnpmedia.com/Articles/Publications/FoodRetail. **Ad Rates:** BW $4,160. **Remarks:** Accepts advertising. **Circ:** (Not Reported).

18024 ■ Metro Detroit Weddings
Hour Media L.L.C.
5750 New King Dr. Ste. 100
Troy, MI 48098
Phone: (248)691-1800
Fax: (248)691-4531
Covers wedding services, products, and locations in the Detroit area. **Freq:** Semiannual. **Subscription Rates:** Free. **URL:** http://www.detroitwed.com. **Remarks:** Accepts advertising. **Circ:** (Not Reported).

18025 ■ Motor Magazine
Motor Information Systems
1301 W Long Lake Rd., Ste. 300
Troy, MI 48098
Free: 800-426-6867
Publisher's E-mail: motormagazine@motor.com
Magazine for the automotive aftermarket trade, professional technicians, and shop owners. **Freq:** Monthly. **Key Personnel:** John Lypen, Editor-in-Chief; Paul M. Eckstein, Managing Editor. **ISSN:** 0027--1748 (print). **Subscription Rates:** Free in U.S.; $60 Other countries surface mail; $120 Other countries airmail; $96 Two years other countries; surface mail; $216 Two years other countries; airmail. **URL:** http://www.motor.com. **Remarks:** Advertising accepted; rates available upon request. **Circ:** Combined ★**135782**.

18026 ■ Paint & Coatings Industry: PCI
Paint and Coatings Industry
2401 W Big Beaver Rd., Ste. 700
Troy, MI 48084
Fax: (248)244-3915
Trade journal. **Freq:** Monthly. **Print Method:** Offset. **Trim Size:** 8 x 10 3/4. **Cols./Page:** 2. **Col. Width:** 3 INS. **Key Personnel:** Donna M. Campbell, Publisher, phone: (610)650-4050, fax: (248)502-1091; Brian Biddle, Manager, Production, phone: (847)405-4104, fax: (248)244-3915; Kristin Johansson, Editor, phone: (248)641-0592, fax: (248)502-2094; Karen Parker, Associate Editor, phone: (248)229-2681; Darlene R. Brezinski, PhD, Editor. **ISSN:** 0884--3848 (print). **USPS:** 751-390. **Subscription Rates:** Free. **URL:** http://www.pcimag.com. **Ad Rates:** BW $4,250; 4C $5,375; PCI $125. **Remarks:** Advertising accepted; rates available upon request. **Circ:** Combined △**19034**.

18027 ■ Point of Beginning
BNP Media
2401 W Big Beaver Rd., Ste. 700
Troy, MI 48084
Phone: (248)362-5103
Fax: (248)362-5103
Publication E-mail: pob@halldata.com macleodb@bnpmedia.com
Magazine printing technical, business, trade, and general interest news for mapping and surveying professionals. **Freq:** Monthly. **Print Method:** Offset. **Trim Size:** 8 1/4 x 10 3/4. **Cols./Page:** 3 and 2. **Col. Width:** 26 and 40 nonpareils. **Col. Depth:** 10 inches. **Key Personnel:** Kimberly J. Schwartz, Senior Editor, phone: (248)244-6465, fax: (248)786-1398; Diana Brown, Publisher, phone: (248)244-6258, fax: (248)244-3911; Dan Murfey, Publisher, phone: (248)244-1277, fax: (248)244-3913; Christine L. Grahl, Editor; Karen Scally, Associate Editor; Lindsay Nagy, Manager, Production. **ISSN:** 0739-3865 (print). **URL:** http://www.pobonline.com. **Ad Rates:** BW $7,770; 4C $1,450. **Remarks:** Advertising accepted; rates available upon request. **Circ:** Controlled △**38005**.

18028 ■ Pollution Engineering
BNP Media
2401 W Big Beaver Rd., Ste. 700
Troy, MI 48084
Phone: (248)362-3700
Fax: (248)362-5103
Free: 800-952-6643
Publisher's E-mail: asm@halldata.com
Magazine focusing on pollution control, air, water, solid waste, and toxic/hazardous waste. **Key Personnel:** Roy Bigham, Managing Editor, phone: (248)244-6252, fax: (248)786-1356; Sarah Harding, Publisher, phone: (216)280-4467, fax: (248)283-6583. **Remarks:** Accepts advertising. **Circ:** Combined △**30847**.

18029 ■ Retail Confectioner
BNP Media
2401 W Big Beaver Rd., Ste. 700
Troy, MI 48084
Phone: (248)362-3700
Fax: (248)362-5103
Free: 800-952-6643
Publisher's E-mail: asm@halldata.com
Magazine covering the field of confectionery and snack food retailing and distribution. **Trim Size:** 8 x 10 3/4. **Key Personnel:** Kristine Collins, Publisher; Deborah Cassell, Executive Editor, phone: (847)405-4050. **URL:** http://www.bnpmedia.com/CDA/Articles/Publications/FoodRetail/BNP_GUID_9-5-2006_A_10000000000000174973. **Formerly:** Confection & Snack Retailing. **Ad Rates:** 4C $5,080. **Remarks:** Accepts advertising. **Circ:** (Not Reported).

18030 ■ Roofing Contractor
BNP Media
2401 W Big Beaver Rd., Ste. 700
Troy, MI 48084
Phone: (248)362-3700
Fax: (248)362-5103
Free: 800-952-6643
Publisher's E-mail: asm@halldata.com
Trade magazine on roofing and insulation. **Freq:** Monthly. **Print Method:** Offset. **Trim Size:** 8 3/8 x 11 1/4. **Cols./Page:** 3. **Col. Width:** 30 nonpareils. **Col. Depth:** 140 agate lines. **Key Personnel:** Jill Bloom, Publisher, phone: (248)244-6253, fax: (248)244-3949; Greg Ettling, Senior Editor, phone: (630)694-4334, fax: (630)694-4002; Jenn Nagel, Manager, Production, phone: (248)619-6471, fax: (248)244-2040; Chris King, Editor, phone: (248)244-6497. **ISSN:** 0273--5954 (print). **URL:** http://www.roofingcontractor.com. **Remarks:** Accepts advertising. **Circ:** (Not Reported).

18031 ■ SDM Dealer/Installer Marketplace
BNP Media
2401 W Big Beaver Rd., Ste. 700
Troy, MI 48084
Phone: (248)362-3700
Fax: (248)362-5103
Free: 800-952-6643
Publisher's E-mail: asm@halldata.com
Trade magazine covering products and services in the security market for dealers and installers. **Freq:** Monthly. **Key Personnel:** Laura Stepanek, Editor, phone: (630)694-4027, fax: (630)227-0214; Mark McCourt, Publisher. **Subscription Rates:** Free to qualified subscribers. **URL:** http://www.sdmmag.com. **Remarks:** Advertising accepted; rates available upon request. **Circ:** Combined 28505.

18032 ■ Snack Food and Wholesale Bakery
BNP Media
2401 W Big Beaver Rd., Ste 700
Troy, MI 48084
Publication E-mail: sfwb@halldata.com
Trade publication covering the snack food and bakery industries. **Freq:** Monthly. **Print Method:** Web Offset. **Trim Size:** 8 7/8 x 10 3/4. **Key Personnel:** Chris Luke, Publisher, phone: (908)917-4171; Lauren R. Hartman, Editor, phone: (847)405-4015. **ISSN:** 1096-4835 (print). **Subscription Rates:** $85 Individuals. **URL:** http://www.snackandbakery.com. **Ad Rates:** BW $4,390. **Remarks:** Accepts advertising. **Circ:** △**14000**.

18033 ■ Snips Magazine
BNP Media
2401 W Big Beaver Rd., Ste. 700
Troy, MI 48084
Phone: (248)362-3700
Fax: (248)362-5103
Free: 800-952-6643
Publisher's E-mail: asm@halldata.com
Magazine for the sheet metal, warm-air heating, ventilating and air conditioning industry. Provides helpful hints for contractors. **Freq:** Monthly. **Print Method:** Offset. **Trim Size:** 8 x 10 3/4. **Cols./Page:** 3 and 2. **Col. Width:** 27 and 41 nonpareils. **Col. Depth:** 140 agate lines. **Key Personnel:** Sally Fraser, Publisher, phone: (248)244-6240; Michael McConnell, Editor, phone: (248)244-6416; Christina Kopah, Manager, Circulation. **ISSN:** 0037--7457 (print). **Subscription Rates:** Free. **URL:** http://www.snipsmag.com; http://www.bnpmedia.com/Articles/Publications/HVACR. **Ad Rates:** BW $4185; 4C $5415. **Remarks:** Accepts advertising. **Circ:** △**20000**.

18034 ■ Stagnito's New Products Magazine
BNP Media
2401 W Big Beaver Rd., Ste. 700
Troy, MI 48084
Phone: (248)362-3700
Fax: (248)362-5103
Free: 800-952-6643
Publisher's E-mail: asm@halldata.com

Circulation: ★ = AAM; △ or • = BPA; ♦ = CAC; ❑ = VAC; ⊕ = PO Statement; ‡ = Publisher's Report; Boldface figures = sworn; Light figures = estimated.

Magazine covering new products of all types. **Freq:** Monthly. **Key Personnel:** Nick Roskelly, Managing Editor, phone: (847)405-4109. **URL:** http://www.newproductsonline.com. **Ad Rates:** BW $4,850; 4C $6,250. **Remarks:** Accepts advertising. **Circ:** (Not Reported).

18035 ■ Structural Engineering and Design: News, Views & Industry Trends
BNP Media
2401 W Big Beaver Rd., Ste. 700
Troy, MI 48084
Phone: (248)362-3700
Fax: (248)362-5103
Free: 800-952-6643
Publisher's E-mail: asm@halldata.com
Professional magazine covering industry news, trends, new products, technical instruction, code developments, and new techniques for structural engineers. **Founded:** Feb. 2000. **Freq:** Weekly. **Trim Size:** 8 1/8 x 10 7/8. **Key Personnel:** Jennifer Goupil, Editor, phone: (206)547-1548. **ISSN:** 1525-6251 (print). **Subscription Rates:** $10 Individuals online; $100 Individuals print and online. **URL:** http://www.gostructural.com. **Formerly**: Structural Engineer. **Ad Rates:** BW $4,792.50; 4C $5,325. **Remarks:** Accepts advertising. **Circ:** Non-paid 34000.

18036 ■ Supply House Times
BNP Media
2401 W Big Beaver Rd., Ste. 700
Troy, MI 48084
Phone: (248)362-3700
Fax: (248)362-5103
Free: 800-952-6643
Publisher's E-mail: asm@halldata.com
Trade magazine for wholesalers in plumbing, heating, cooling, piping, and water systems. Areas of major emphasis include: warehousing, materials handling, inventory control, accounting, data processing, merchandising, salesmanship and general management. **Freq:** Monthly. **Print Method:** Offset. **Trim Size:** 8 1/2 x 11. **Cols./Page:** 3. **Col. Width:** 26 nonpareils. **Col. Depth:** 140 agate lines. **Key Personnel:** Jean Eslick, Regional Manager; Scott Franz, Publisher, phone: (937)748-9975, fax: (248)502-2083; Mike Miazga, Editor, phone: (847)405-4056, fax: (248)502-9001; John McNally, Senior Editor. **URL:** http://www.supplyht.com. **Circ:** (Not Reported).

18037 ■ Sustainable Facility
BNP Media
2401 W Big Beaver Rd., Ste. 700
Troy, MI 48084
Phone: (248)362-3700
Fax: (248)362-5103
Free: 800-952-6643
Publisher's E-mail: asm@halldata.com
Magazine reporting on the energy management market as it relates to commercial, industrial, and institutional facilities. **Freq:** Monthly. **Print Method:** Heat set web offset. **Trim Size:** 10 7/8 x 14 3/4. **Cols./Page:** 5. **Col. Width:** 1 7/8 inches. **Col. Depth:** 12 7/8 inches. **Key Personnel:** Jeff Bagwell, Manager, Production; Derrick Teal, Editor; Michelle Hucal, Associate Publisher. **ISSN:** 0162--9131 (print). **URL:** http://www.bnpmedia.com/Articles/Publications/Architecture. **Formerly**: Energy User News. **Remarks:** Advertising accepted; rates available upon request. **Circ:** (Not Reported).

18038 ■ Sustainable Home: A Special Section in Environmental Design Construction
BNP Media
2401 W Big Beaver Rd., Ste. 700
Troy, MI 48084
Phone: (248)362-3700
Fax: (248)362-5103
Free: 800-952-6643
Publisher's E-mail: asm@halldata.com
Magazine covering the latest news and information for the green residential marketplace. **Key Personnel:** Diana Brown, Publisher, phone: (248)244-6258; Michelle Hucal, Senior Editor, phone: (248)244-1280, fax: (248)362-5103. **URL:** http://www.sustainablehomemag.com. **Circ:** (Not Reported).

18039 ■ Walls & Ceilings: Voice of the Industry since 1938
BNP Media
2401 W Big Beaver Rd., Ste. 700
Troy, MI 48084
Phone: (248)362-3700
Fax: (248)362-5103
Free: 800-952-6643
Publisher's E-mail: asm@halldata.com
Trade magazine for contractors, suppliers, and distributors of drywall, plaster, stucco, EIFS, acoustics, metal framing, and ceilings. **Freq:** Monthly. **Print Method:** Offset. **Trim Size:** 8 3/8 x 10 7/8. **Cols./Page:** 3. **Col. Width:** 2 1/6 inches. **Col. Depth:** 10 inches. **Key Personnel:** Amy Tuttle, Manager, Sales, Publisher, fax: (517)589-8618; Mark Fowler, Director, Editorial. **ISSN:** 0043--0161 (print). **Subscription Rates:** Free. **URL:** http://www.bnpmedia.com/Articles/Publications/Architecture; http://www.wconline.com. **Ad Rates:** 4C $6120. **Remarks:** Advertising accepted; rates available upon request. **Circ:** Combined △33500.

18040 ■ WCAR-AM - 1090
PO Box 4905
Troy, MI 48099
Phone: (734)525-1111
Free: 877-327-1090
Format: Religious. **Owner:** Michigan Catholic Radio, at above address. **Formerly**: WIID-AM. **Operating Hours**: Continuous. **ADI**: Detroit, MI. **Wattage:** 500. **Ad Rates:** $28 for 30 seconds; $54 for 60 seconds. **URL:** http://catholicradio.org.

TWIN LAKE

Muskegon Co. (WC). 5 m S of Whitehall.

18041 ■ Blue Lake Fine Arts Camp
300 E Crystal Lake Rd.
Twin Lake, MI 49457
Phone: (231)894-1966
Fax: (231)893-5120
Free: 800-221-3796
Email: international@bluelake.org
Format: Jazz; Classical. **Networks:** National Public Radio (NPR). **Founded:** 1922. **Key Personnel:** Dave Myers, VP of Dev.; Louis Smith, Treasurer; Paul Boscarino, Gen. Mgr. **Ad Rates:** Underwriting available. **URL:** http://bluelake.org.

18042 ■ WBLU-FM - 88.9
300 E Crystal Lake Rd.
Twin Lake, MI 49457
Phone: (231)894-5656
Fax: (231)893-2457
Free: 800-889-9258
Email: international@bluelake.org
Format: Public Radio; Classical; Jazz. **Owner:** Blue Lake Public Radio, 300 E Crystal Lake Rd. , Twin Lake, MI 49457, Ph: (231)894-1966. **Founded:** 1922. **Key Personnel:** Bill McFarlin, VP of Dev.; Dave Berndt, Bus. Mgr. **Ad Rates:** Noncommercial. **URL:** http://bluelake.org/radio.html.

18043 ■ WBLV-FM - 90.3
300 E Crystal Lake Rd.
Twin Lake, MI 49457
Phone: (231)894-5656
Fax: (231)893-2457
Free: 800-221-3796
Email: radio@bluelake.org
Format: Public Radio; Classical; Jazz. **Simulcasts:** WBLU-FM. **Networks:** National Public Radio (NPR); American Public Radio (APR); Michigan Public Radio. **Owner:** Blue Lake Fine Arts Camp, 300 E Crystal Lake Rd., Twin Lake, MI 49457, Ph: (231)894-1966, Fax: (231)893-5120, Free: 800-221-3796. **Founded:** 1982. **Operating Hours**: Continuous; 21% network, 79% local. **Key Personnel:** Bill McFarlin, VP; Dave Myers, Gen. Mgr.; James Niblock, VP. **Wattage:** 100,000. **Ad Rates:** Noncommercial; underwriting available. $8-20 per unit; $12-25 per unit; $12-25 per unit. **URL:** http://www.bluelake.org.

UNION LAKE

Oakland Co. (SE). 10 m SW of Pontiac. Light industry. Resort. Apples. Dairy farms.

18044 ■ Highland Spinal Column Newsweekly
Spinal Column Publications
PO Box 14
Union Lake, MI 48387-0014
Phone: (248)360-7355
Publisher's E-mail: news@thescngroup.com
Local newspaper. **Freq:** Weekly. **Print Method:** Offset. **Trim Size:** 10 1/2 x 15. **Cols./Page:** 8. **Col. Width:** 7 picas. **Col. Depth:** 14 inches. **Key Personnel:** Jim Stevenson, Publisher. **URL:** http://www.spinalcolumnonline.com. **Ad Rates:** GLR $4.75; BW $1485; PCI $9.50. **Remarks:** Accepts advertising. **Circ:** Combined ‡50887.

18045 ■ Milford Spinal Column Newsweekly
Spinal Column Publications
PO Box 14
Union Lake, MI 48387-0014
Phone: (248)360-7355
Publisher's E-mail: news@thescngroup.com
Local newspaper. **Freq:** Weekly (Wed.). **Print Method:** Offset. **Trim Size:** 10 1/2 x 15. **Cols./Page:** 8. **Col. Width:** 7 picas. **Col. Depth:** 14 inches. **Key Personnel:** Susan Fancy, Publisher; Tim Dmoch, Editor; Dennis Boggs, Manager, Circulation. **URL:** http://www.spinalcolumnonline.com. **Ad Rates:** GLR $4.59; BW $514; PCI $9.18. **Remarks:** Accepts advertising. **Circ:** Free ‡50,000.

18046 ■ Novi Spinal Column Newsweekly
Spinal Column Publications
PO Box 14
Union Lake, MI 48387-0014
Phone: (248)360-7355
Publisher's E-mail: news@thescngroup.com
Local newspaper. **Freq:** Weekly. **Print Method:** Offset. **Trim Size:** 10 1/2 x 15. **Cols./Page:** 8. **Col. Width:** 7 picas. **Col. Depth:** 14 inches. **Key Personnel:** Susan Fancy, Publisher; Tim Dmoch, Editor. **URL:** http://www.spinalcolumnonline.com. **Ad Rates:** GLR $5.82; BW $652; PCI $11.64. **Remarks:** Accepts advertising. **Circ:** Free ‡4,150.

18047 ■ Waterford Spinal Column Newsweekly
Spinal Column Publications
PO Box 14
Union Lake, MI 48387-0014
Phone: (248)360-7355
Publication E-mail: editor@scnmail.com
Local newspaper. **Freq:** Weekly (Wed.). **Print Method:** Weekly (Wed.). **Trim Size:** 10 1/2 x 15. **Cols./Page:** 8. **Col. Width:** 7 picas. **Col. Depth:** 14 inches. **Key Personnel:** Dennis Boggs, Manager, Circulation; Jim Stevenson, Publisher. **URL:** http://www.spinalcolumnonline.com. **Ad Rates:** GLR $7.75; BW $868.88; PCI $15.50. **Remarks:** Accepts advertising. **Circ:** Free ‡50000.

18048 ■ West Bloomfield Spinal Column Newsweekly
Spinal Column Publications
PO Box 14
Union Lake, MI 48387-0014
Phone: (248)360-7355
Publisher's E-mail: news@thescngroup.com
Local newspaper. **Freq:** Weekly. **Print Method:** Offset. **Trim Size:** 10 1/2 x 15. **Cols./Page:** 8. **Col. Width:** 7 picas. **Col. Depth:** 14 inches. **Key Personnel:** Jim Stevenson, Publisher. **URL:** http://www.spinalcolumnonline.com. **Ad Rates:** GLR $8.11; BW $1,545; PCI $16.22. **Remarks:** Accepts advertising. **Circ:** Free ‡52216.

UNIVERSITY CENTER

Bay Co.

18049 ■ The Delta Collegiate
Delta College
1961 Delta Rd.
University Center, MI 48710
Phone: (989)686-9000
Publisher's E-mail: info@delta.edu
Collegiate newspaper. **Freq:** Weekly. **Print Method:** Offset. **Cols./Page:** 5. **Col. Width:** 23 nonpareils. **Col. Depth:** 196 agate lines. **Key Personnel:** Ashley Niedzwiecki, Editor-in-Chief; Karen Randolph, Advisor. **URL:** http://deltacollegiate.altervista.org. **Ad Rates:** BW $300; PCI $7. **Remarks:** Color advertising not accepted. **Circ:** Free ‡3,500.

18050 ■ WDCP-TV - 35
1961 Delta Rd.
University Center, MI 48710
Free: 877-472-7677
Email: wdcq@alpha.delta.edu
Format: Public TV. **Networks:** Public Broadcasting Service (PBS). **Owner:** Delta College, 1961 Delta Rd., University Center, MI 48710, Ph: (989)686-9000. **Founded:** 1986. **Formerly**: WUCX-TV. **Operating Hours**: 6:30 a.m.-12:30 a.m. **Key Personnel:** Pam Clark, Station Mgr., pnclark@alpha.delta.edu; Kent Wieland, Program Mgr., kwwielan@alpha.delta.edu; Tom Bennett, Production Mgr., tjbennet@alpha.delta.edu; Tom Garnett, Chief Engineer, tggarnet@alpha.delta.edu. **URL:** http://www.deltabroadcasting.org.

18051 ■ WDCQ-TV
Delta Rd.
University Center
University Center, MI 48710
Fax: (989)686-0155
Free: 877-472-7677
Email: wdcq@alpha.delta.edu
Format: Public TV; News. **Networks:** Independent. **Owner:** Delta College, 1961 Delta Rd., University Center, MI 48710, Ph: (989)686-9000. **Founded:** 1962. **Formerly**: WUCM-TV. **Operating Hours**: Continuous. **Wattage**: 200,000 ERP. **URL:** http://www.deltabroadcasting.org/home/#.V6N4ytJ97IV.

VASSAR

Tuscola Co. Tuscola Co. (E). 19 m E of Saginaw. Auto castings, plastic products, tools, dies manufactured. Diversified farming. Potatoes, sugar beets, beans.

18052 ■ Cass River Trader
Bilbey Publications L.L.C.
5881 W Frannkenmuth Rd.
Vassar, MI 48768
Phone: (989)823-8651
Fax: (989)823-2531
Publication E-mail: ads@cassrivertrader.com kidsville@kidsvillemi.com
Shopper. **Freq:** Weekly (Mon.). **Print Method:** Offset. **Trim Size:** 11 1/2 x 16. **Cols./Page:** 6. **Col. Width:** 20 nonpareils. **Col. Depth:** 210 agate lines. **URL:** http://www.cassrivertrader.com. **Ad Rates:** BW $535; 4C $350; PCI $5.95. **Remarks:** Advertising accepted; rates available upon request. **Circ:** Free 20000.

WALKER

18053 ■ Walker/Westside Advance
Advance Newspapers
2141 Port Sheldon Rd.
Jenison, MI 49429
Phone: (616)669-2700
Free: 800-439-0960
Publication E-mail: retailsales@advancenewspapers.com
Suburban community newspaper (tabloid). **Freq:** Weekly (Tues.). **Print Method:** Web. **Trim Size:** 10 3/8 x 15 7/8. **Cols./Page:** 6. **Col. Width:** 1 5/8 nonpareils. **Key Personnel:** Mike Wyngarden, Editor; Karen Waite, Editor. **Subscription Rates:** $25. **URL:** http://www.mlive.com/walker. **Mailing address:** PO Box 9, Jenison, MI 49429. **Ad Rates:** BW $1,358.40; 4C $1,483.40; PCI $14.15. **Remarks:** Accepts advertising. **Circ:** Combined ‡198885.

18054 ■ W214AY-FM - 90.7
PO Box 391
Twin Falls, ID 83303
Fax: (208)736-1958
Free: 800-357-4226
Format: Religious; Contemporary Christian. **Owner:** CSN International, PO Box 391, Twin Falls, ID 83303, Ph: (208)736-1958, Fax: (208)736-1958, Free: 800-357-4226. **Key Personnel:** Kelly Carlson, Dir. of Engg.; Ray Gorney, Asst. Dir. **URL:** http://www.csnradio.com.

WARREN

Macomb Co Macomb Co. Macomb Co. (SE). 4 m S of Sterling Heights. Manufacture machinery, aluminum, auto accessories, chemicals, electronics. Agriculture.

18055 ■ Academic Psychiatry
Springer Publishing Company Inc.
31201 Chicago Rd. S A101
Warren, MI 48093
Phone: (586)939-6800
Fax: (586)939-5850
Journal contributing to the efforts in furthering psychiatry as a profession and to knowledge pool of medicine. **Freq:** 6/year. **Trim Size:** 8 1/8 x 10 7/8. **Key Personnel:** Alan K. Louie, MD, Associate Editor; Laura Weiss Roberts, MD, Editor-in-Chief; John H. Coverdale, MD, Editor. **ISSN:** 1042--9670 (print); **EISSN:** 1545--7230 (electronic). **Subscription Rates:** $543 Institutions print including free access or e-only; $652 Members print plus enhanced access. **URL:** http://www.springer.com/medicine/psychiatry/journal/40596. **Ad Rates:** BW $1070; 4C $1200. **Remarks:** Advertising accepted; rates available upon request. **Circ:** 1050.

18056 ■ Advertiser Times
C & G Publishing
13650 Eleven Mile Rd.
Warren, MI 48089
Phone: (586)498-8000
Fax: (586)498-9631
Community newspaper. **Freq:** Biweekly. **Key Personnel:** Gregg Demers, Director, Editorial, phone: (586)498-1042; David Wallace, Editor. **Subscription Rates:** Free. **URL:** http://www.candgnews.com/Staff-Boxes/Ad-Times.asp. **Remarks:** Accepts advertising. **Circ:** Non-paid ♦**26295.**

18057 ■ Archives of Pharmacal Research
Springer Publishing Company Inc.
31201 Chicago Rd. S A101
Warren, MI 48093
Phone: (586)939-6800
Fax: (586)939-5850
Publishes research reports in the pharmaceutical-biomedical sciences. **Freq:** Monthly. **Key Personnel:** Seo-kyong Lee, Editor-in-Chief. **ISSN:** 0253--6269 (print); **EISSN:** 1976--3786 (electronic). **Subscription Rates:** €1579 Institutions print incl. free access or e-only; €1895 Institutions print plus enhanced access; $2114 Institutions print incl. free access or e-only; $2537 Institutions print plus enhanced access. **URL:** http://www.springer.com/biomed/pharmacology+%26+toxicology/journal/12272; http://www.psk.or.kr/home/kor/article/submission/default.asp?globalmenu=3&localmenu=1; http://link.springer.com/journal/12272. **Remarks:** Advertising accepted; rates available upon request. **Circ:** (Not Reported).

18058 ■ Birmingham-Bloomfield Eagle
C & G Publishing
13650 Eleven Mile Rd.
Warren, MI 48089
Phone: (586)498-8000
Fax: (586)498-9631
Community newspaper. **Freq:** Weekly. **Key Personnel:** Gregg Demers, Director, Editorial, phone: (586)498-1042; Annie Bates, Editor, phone: (586)498-1071. **Subscription Rates:** Free. **URL:** http://www.candgnews.com/Staff-Boxes/Eagle.asp. **Remarks:** Accepts advertising. **Circ:** Non-paid ♦**33231.**

18059 ■ Detroit Auto Scene
Springer Publications
31201 Chicago Rd. S, Ste. A-101
Warren, MI 48093
Phone: (586)939-6800
Fax: (586)939-5850
Publication E-mail: info@detroitautoscene.com
Local newspaper. **Freq:** Weekly (Mon.). **Print Method:** Offset. **Trim Size:** 13 x 26. **Cols./Page:** 6. **Col. Width:** 891 picas. **Col. Depth:** 21 inches. **Subscription Rates:** Free. **Formerly**: New Center News; Renaissance Times--New Center News. **Ad Rates:** BW $1031.20. **Remarks:** Accepts advertising. **Circ:** Free 8000.

18060 ■ Eastsider
C & G Publishing
13650 Eleven Mile Rd.
Warren, MI 48089
Phone: (586)498-8000
Fax: (586)498-9631
Community newspaper. **Founded:** 1982. **Freq:** Biweekly. **Cols./Page:** 4. **Col. Width:** 10 5/16 inches. **Col. Depth:** 13 1/2 inches. **Key Personnel:** Gregg Demers, Director, Editorial, phone: (586)498-1042. **URL:** http://www.candgnews.com/Staff-Boxes/Eastsider.asp. **Ad Rates:** BW $1,331. **Remarks:** Accepts advertising. **Circ:** Non-paid ♦**30,830.**

18061 ■ Farmington Press
C & G Publishing
13650 Eleven Mile Rd.
Warren, MI 48089
Phone: (586)498-8000
Fax: (586)498-9631
Community newspaper. **Founded:** 2008. **Freq:** Weekly. **Key Personnel:** Gregg Demers, Director, Editorial, phone: (586)498-1042; Annie Bates, Editor, phone: (586)498-1071. **Subscription Rates:** Free. **URL:** http://www.candgnews.com/Staff-Boxes/Farmington.asp. **Remarks:** Accepts advertising. **Circ:** Non-paid ♦**38204.**

18062 ■ Fraser-Clinton Township Chronicle
C & G Publishing
13650 Eleven Mile Rd.
Warren, MI 48089
Phone: (586)498-8000
Fax: (586)498-9631
Community newspaper. **Freq:** Biweekly. **Cols./Page:** 4. **Col. Width:** 10 5/16 inches. **Col. Depth:** 13 1/2 inches. **Key Personnel:** Jon Malavolti, Editor. **URL:** http://www.candgnews.com/newspaper/fraserclintonchronicle. **Ad Rates:** BW $953. **Remarks:** Accepts advertising. **Circ:** Non-paid ♦**30,747.**

18063 ■ Graphene Technology
Springer Publications
31201 Chicago Rd. S, Ste. A-101
Warren, MI 48093
Phone: (586)939-6800
Fax: (586)939-5850
Peer-reviewed journal that focuses on graphene and the translation of research into commercial applications. **ISSN:** 2365--6301 (print); **EISSN:** 2365--631X (electronic). **Subscription Rates:** Free. **URL:** http://www.springer.com/materials/nanotechnology/journal/41127. **Circ:** (Not Reported).

18064 ■ Graphene Technology
The Graphene Council
Peer-reviewed journal that focuses on graphene and the translation of research into commercial applications. **ISSN:** 2365--6301 (print); **EISSN:** 2365--631X (electronic). **Subscription Rates:** Free. **URL:** http://www.springer.com/materials/nanotechnology/journal/41127. **Circ:** (Not Reported).

18065 ■ Grosse Pointe Times
C & G Publishing
13650 Eleven Mile Rd.
Warren, MI 48089
Phone: (586)498-8000
Fax: (586)498-9631
Community newspaper. **Freq:** Biweekly. **Cols./Page:** 4. **Col. Width:** 10 5/16 inches. **Col. Depth:** 13 1/2 inches. **Key Personnel:** Gregg Demers, Director, Editorial, phone: (586)498-1042; Elaine Myers, Manager, Advertising, phone: (586)218-5012. **URL:** http://www.candgnews.com/newspaper/grossepointetimes. **Ad Rates:** BW $1,072. **Remarks:** Accepts advertising. **Circ:** Non-paid ♦**18,827.**

18066 ■ International Journal of Human Factors Modelling and Simulation
Inderscience Publishers
c/o Dr. Shih-Ken Chen, Ed.-in-Ch.
30500 Mound Rd.
Warren, MI 48090-9055
Publication E-mail: info@inderscience.com
Journal aiming to promote knowledge of human factors particularly the advancement of that field using computational methods, seeking to initiate and support international activities and cooperation in this field. **Freq:** Quarterly. **Key Personnel:** Dr. Shih-Ken Chen, Editor-in-Chief. **ISSN:** 1742--5549 (print); **EISSN:** 1742--5557 (electronic). **Subscription Rates:** $685 Individuals print or online for 1 user; $1164.50 Individuals online only for 2-3 users; $928 Individuals print and online; $1712.50 Individuals online only for 4-5 users; $2226.25 Individuals online only for 6-7 users; $2705.75 Individuals online only for 8-9 users; $3151 Individuals online only for 10-14 users; $3596.25 Individuals online only for 15-19 users; $4247 Individuals online only for 20+ users. **URL:** http://www.inderscience.com/jhome.php?jcode=ijhfms. **Circ:** (Not Reported).

Circulation: ★ = AAM; △ or • = BPA; ♦ = CAC; ❑ = VAC; ⊕ = PO Statement; ‡ = Publisher's Report; Boldface figures = sworn; Light figures = estimated.

18067 ■ The Journal
C & G Publishing
13650 Eleven Mile Rd.
Warren, MI 48089
Phone: (586)498-8000
Fax: (586)498-9631
Community newspaper. **Freq:** Weekly. **Cols./Page:** 4. **Col. Width:** 10 5/16 inches. **Col. Depth:** 13 1/2 inches. **URL:** http://www.candgnews.com/Contact.asp. **Ad Rates:** BW $1,270. **Remarks:** Accepts advertising. **Circ:** ‡31590.

18068 ■ Journal of Cancer Education
Springer Publications
31201 Chicago Rd. S, Ste. A-101
Warren, MI 48093
Phone: (586)939-6800
Fax: (586)939-5850
Publisher's E-mail: info@detroitautoscene.com
Official journal of the American Association for Cancer Education (AACE) and the European Association for Cancer Education (EACE). Publishing original contributions dealing with the varied aspects of cancer education. **Freq:** Quarterly. **Key Personnel:** Richard E. Gallagher, Associate Editor; Joseph F. O'Donnell, Editor, phone: (603)650-1755; Robert M. Chamberlain, Associate Editor; Arthur M. Michalek, PhD, Editor-in-Chief. **ISSN:** 0885--8195 (print); **EISSN:** 1543--0154 (electronic). **Subscription Rates:** €487 Institutions print incl. free access or e-only ; €584 Institutions print plus enhanced access ; $658 Institutions print incl. free access or e-only ; $790 Institutions print plus enhanced access. **URL:** http://www.springer.com/biomed/cancer/journal/13187. **Ad Rates:** BW $350. **Remarks:** Accepts advertising. **Circ:** (Not Reported).

18069 ■ Journal of Gastrointestinal Surgery
Springer Publications
31201 Chicago Rd. S, Ste. A-101
Warren, MI 48093
Phone: (586)939-6800
Fax: (586)939-5850
Publisher's E-mail: info@detroitautoscene.com
Contains articles on the latest developments in gastrointestinal surgery. **Freq:** Monthly. **ISSN:** 1091--255X (print); **EISSN:** 1873--4626 (electronic). **Subscription Rates:** Included in membership; $636 Institutions print or online. **URL:** http://www.ssat.com/cgi-bin/Journal-of-GI-Surgery.cgi; http://www.ahpba.org/resources/links.phtml; http://www.springer.com/medicine/surgery/journal/11605. **Remarks:** Accepts advertising. **Circ:** (Not Reported).

18070 ■ Macomb Township Chronicle
C & G Publishing
13650 Eleven Mile Rd.
Warren, MI 48089
Phone: (586)498-8000
Fax: (586)498-9631
Community newspaper. **Freq:** Weekly. **Key Personnel:** Jon Malavolti, Editor; Gregg Demers, Director, Editorial, phone: (586)498-1042. **Subscription Rates:** Free. **URL:** http://www.candgnews.com/Staff-Boxes/Macomb.asp. **Remarks:** Accepts advertising. **Circ:** Non-paid ♦**27358**.

18071 ■ Madison-Park News
C & G Publishing
13650 Eleven Mile Rd.
Warren, MI 48089
Phone: (586)498-8000
Fax: (586)498-9631
Community newspaper. **Freq:** Biweekly. **Cols./Page:** 4. **Col. Width:** 10 5/16 inches. **Col. Depth:** 13 1/2 inches. **Key Personnel:** Gregg Demers, Director, Editorial, phone: (586)498-1042; Annie Bates, Editor, phone: (586)498-1071; Susan Shanley, Editor, phone: (586)498-1048. **URL:** http://www.candgnews.com/newspaper/madisonparknews. **Ad Rates:** BW $706. **Remarks:** Accepts advertising. **Circ:** ‡19,568.

18072 ■ Molecular Neurobiology
Springer Publishing Company Inc.
31201 Chicago Rd. S A101
Warren, MI 48093
Phone: (586)939-6800
Fax: (586)939-5850
Journal devoted to neuroscientists. **Freq:** Bimonthly. **Key Personnel:** Nicolas G. Bazan, MD, Editor-in-Chief; Bertil Fredholm, Advisor; William Agnew, Advisor; Rene Anand, Advisor; Piu Chan, Advisor; Susan Amara, Advisor; Eric A. Barnard, Advisor; Colin J. Barnstable, Advisor. **ISSN:** 0893--7648 (print); **EISSN:** 1559--1182 (electronic). **Subscription Rates:** €1578 Institutions print and electronic; €1894 Institutions print and enhanced access; $1919 Institutions print and electronic; $2303 Institutions print and enhanced access. **URL:** http://www.springer.com/biomed/neuroscience/journal/12035. **Remarks:** Advertising not accepted. **Circ:** (Not Reported).

18073 ■ Purinergic Signalling
Springer Publications
31201 Chicago Rd. S, Ste. A-101
Warren, MI 48093
Phone: (586)939-6800
Fax: (586)939-5850
Publisher's E-mail: info@detroitautoscene.com
Academic journal publishing in the field of purinergic signalling and its implications for health and disease. **Freq:** Quarterly. **Key Personnel:** Prof. Geoffrey Burnstock, Editor-in-Chief. **ISSN:** 1573--9538 (print); **EISSN:** 1573--9546 (electronic). **Subscription Rates:** $538 Institutions electronic. **URL:** http://www.springer.com/biomed/journal/11302. **Remarks:** Accepts advertising. **Circ:** (Not Reported).

18074 ■ Rochester Post
C & G Publishing
13650 Eleven Mile Rd.
Warren, MI 48089
Phone: (586)498-8000
Fax: (586)498-9631
Community newspaper. **Freq:** Weekly. **Key Personnel:** Gregg Demers, Director, Editorial, phone: (586)498-1042; Annie Bates, Editor, phone: (586)498-1071. **Subscription Rates:** Free. **URL:** http://www.candgnews.com/Staff-Boxes/Post.asp. **Remarks:** Accepts advertising. **Circ:** Non-paid ♦**38663**.

18075 ■ Royal Oak Review
C & G Publishing
13650 Eleven Mile Rd.
Warren, MI 48089
Phone: (586)498-8000
Fax: (586)498-9631
Community newspaper. **Freq:** Weekly. **Key Personnel:** David Wallace, Editor; Gregg Demers, Director, Editorial, phone: (586)498-1042. **Subscription Rates:** Free. **URL:** http://www.candgnews.com/Staff-Boxes/Royal-Oak.asp. **Remarks:** Accepts advertising. **Circ:** Non-paid ♦**32670**.

18076 ■ St. Clair Shores Sentinel
C & G Publishing
13650 Eleven Mile Rd.
Warren, MI 48089
Phone: (586)498-8000
Fax: (586)498-9631
Community newspaper. **Freq:** Weekly. **Cols./Page:** 4. **Col. Width:** 10 5/16 inches. **Col. Depth:** 13 1/2 inches. **Key Personnel:** Gregg Demers, Director, Editorial, phone: (586)498-1042; Barry Bernard, Manager, Production, phone: (586)498-1036. **Alt. Formats:** PDF. **URL:** http://www.candgnews.com/newspaper/stclairshoressentinel. **Ad Rates:** BW $1,331. **Remarks:** Advertising accepted; rates available upon request. **Circ:** Non-paid ♦**27,358**.

18077 ■ Shelby Utica News
C & G Publishing
13650 Eleven Mile Rd.
Warren, MI 48089
Phone: (586)498-8000
Fax: (586)498-9631
Community newspaper. **Freq:** Daily. **Cols./Page:** 4. **Col. Width:** 10 5/16 inches. **Col. Depth:** 13 1/2 inches. **Key Personnel:** Gregg Demers, Director, Editorial, phone: (586)498-1042; Barry Bernard, Manager, Production, phone: (586)498-1036; Susan Shanley, Editor, phone: (586)498-1048. **Alt. Formats:** PDF. **URL:** http://www.candgnews.com/Staff-Boxes/Shelby.asp. **Ad Rates:** BW $1,000. **Remarks:** Accepts advertising. **Circ:** ‡30,088.

18078 ■ Southfield Sun
C & G Publishing
13650 Eleven Mile Rd.
Warren, MI 48089
Phone: (586)498-8000
Fax: (586)498-9631
Community newspaper. **Freq:** Weekly. **Key Personnel:** Gregg Demers, Director, Editorial, phone: (586)498-1042; Annie Bates, Editor, phone: (586)498-1071. **Subscription Rates:** Free. **URL:** http://www.candgnews.com/Staff-Boxes/Sun.asp. **Remarks:** Accepts advertising. **Circ:** Non-paid ♦**33088**.

18079 ■ Sterling Heights Sentry
C & G Publishing
13650 Eleven Mile Rd.
Warren, MI 48089
Phone: (586)498-8000
Fax: (586)498-9631
Community newspaper. **Freq:** Weekly. **Key Personnel:** Gregg Demers, Director, Editorial, phone: (586)498-1042; Annie Bates, Editor, phone: (586)498-1071. **Subscription Rates:** Free. **URL:** http://www.candgnews.com/Staff-Boxes/Sterling.asp. **Remarks:** Accepts advertising. **Circ:** Non-paid ♦**48049**.

18080 ■ Tech Center News
Springer Publications
31201 Chicago Rd. S, Ste. A-101
Warren, MI 48093
Phone: (586)939-6800
Fax: (586)939-5850
Publisher's E-mail: info@detroitautoscene.com
Newspaper containing automotive and business news for the business community, including General Motors Technical Center, in Warren, Michigan. **Freq:** Weekly. **Print Method:** Offset. **Trim Size:** 13 x 26. **Cols./Page:** 6. **Col. Width:** 891 picas. **Col. Depth:** 21 inches. **Subscription Rates:** Free. **URL:** http://www.techcenternews.com. **Ad Rates:** 4C $250; SAU $13.50; PCI $13.50. **Remarks:** Accepts advertising. **Circ:** Controlled ‡5000.

18081 ■ Troy Times
C & G Publishing
13650 Eleven Mile Rd.
Warren, MI 48089
Phone: (586)498-8000
Fax: (586)498-9631
Community newspaper. **Freq:** Biweekly. **Cols./Page:** 4. **Col. Width:** 10 5/16 inches. **Col. Depth:** 13 1/2 inches. **Key Personnel:** Gregg Demers, Director, Editorial, phone: (586)498-1042; Annie Bates, Editor, phone: (586)498-1071; Susan Shanley, Editor, phone: (586)498-1048. **URL:** http://www.candgnews.com/newspaper/troytimes. **Ad Rates:** BW $1,184. **Remarks:** Accepts advertising. **Circ:** Non-paid ♦**31,404**.

18082 ■ U.S. Auto Scene
Springer Publications
31201 Chicago Rd. S, Ste. A-101
Warren, MI 48093
Phone: (586)939-6800
Fax: (586)939-5850
Publisher's E-mail: info@detroitautoscene.com
Automotive newspaper. **Freq:** Weekly. **Print Method:** Offset. **Cols./Page:** 6. **Col. Width:** 891 picas. **Col. Depth:** 21 inches. **Subscription Rates:** Free. **URL:** http://usautoscene.net. **Ad Rates:** 4C $250; SAU $22.56; PCI $8.90. **Remarks:** Accepts advertising. **Circ:** 8000.

18083 ■ Warren Weekly
C & G Publishing
13650 Eleven Mile Rd.
Warren, MI 48089
Phone: (586)498-8000
Fax: (586)498-9631
Community newspaper. **Freq:** Weekly. **Cols./Page:** 4. **Col. Width:** 10 5/16 inches. **Col. Depth:** 13 1/2 inches. **Key Personnel:** Barry Bernard, Manager, Production, phone: (586)498-1036; Gregg Demers, Director, Editorial, phone: (586)498-1042. **URL:** http://www.candgnews.com/newspaper/warrenweekly. **Remarks:** Accepts advertising. **Circ:** Non-paid ♦**55,505**.

18084 ■ West Bloomfield Beacon
C & G Publishing
13650 Eleven Mile Rd.
Warren, MI 48089
Phone: (586)498-8000
Fax: (586)498-9631
Community newspaper. **Freq:** Weekly. **Key Personnel:** Gregg Demers, Director, Editorial, phone: (586)498-1042; Annie Bates, Editor, phone: (586)498-1071. **Subscription Rates:** Free. **URL:** http://www.candgnews.

com/Staff-Boxes/Beacon.asp. **Remarks:** Accepts advertising. **Circ:** Non-paid ♦**27135**.

18085 ■ Woodward Talk
C & G Publishing
13650 Eleven Mile Rd.
Warren, MI 48089
Phone: (586)498-8000
Fax: (586)498-9631
Community newspaper. **Freq:** Weekly. **Key Personnel:** David Wallace, Editor; Gregg Demers, Director, Editorial, phone: (586)498-1042. **Subscription Rates:** Free. **URL:** http://www.candgnews.com/Staff-Boxes/Talk.asp. **Remarks:** Accepts advertising. **Circ:** Non-paid ♦**20107**.

18086 ■ WPHS-FM - 89.1
30333 Hoover Rd.
Warren, MI 48093
Phone: (586)698-4501
Fax: (586)751-3755
Format: Alternative/New Music/Progressive. **Owner:** Warren Consolidated Schools, at above address. **Founded:** 1964. **Operating Hours:** Continuous. **Wattage:** 100. **Ad Rates:** Noncommercial. **URL:** http://www.wphs891.weebly.com.

WATERVLIET

Berrien Co. Berrien Co. (SW). 20 m SW of Kalamazoo. Residential.

18087 ■ Tri-City Record
Tri-City Record
PO Box 7
Watervliet, MI 49098
Phone: (269)463-6397
Publication E-mail: record@tricityrecord.com
Local newspaper. **Freq:** Weekly (Thurs.). **Print Method:** Offset. **Cols./Page:** 6. **Col. Width:** 12.3 picas. **Col. Depth:** 21.5 inches. **Key Personnel:** Karl B. Bayer, Editor; Amy Loshbough, Business Manager. **USPS:** 869-340. **Subscription Rates:** $32 Individuals year. **URL:** http://www.tricityrecord.com. **Ad Rates:** GLR $7; BW $903; 4C $125; SAU $6; PCI $14.25; 4C $65. **Remarks:** Advertising accepted; rates available upon request. **Circ:** Paid ‡2300.

WEST BLOOMFIELD

18088 ■ Building Business & Apartment Management
Home Builders Association of Southeastern Michigan
2075 Walnut Lake Rd.
West Bloomfield, MI 48323
Phone: (248)737-4477
Construction and apartment industry magazine. **Founded:** 1937. **Freq:** Monthly. **Print Method:** Web Offset. **Trim Size:** 8 1/2 x 10 7/8. **Cols./Page:** 3. **Col. Width:** 21 INS. **Col. Depth:** 140 INS. **Key Personnel:** Susan Adler Shanteau, Editor. **Subscription Rates:** $48 Individuals. **Alt. Formats:** PDF. **URL:** http://www.builders.org/bbam-magazine.php. **Formerly:** Bildor. **Ad Rates:** BW $1,450; 4C $1,650. **Remarks:** Accepts advertising. **Circ:** Paid ‡3000.

18089 ■ The Flooring Contractor
Floor Covering Installation Contractors Association
7439 Millwood Dr.
West Bloomfield, MI 48322
Phone: (248)661-5015
Fax: (248)661-5018
Publisher's E-mail: info@fcica.com
Freq: Quarterly. **Subscription Rates:** Free. **URL:** http://www.fcica.com/press-room/the-flooring-contractor. **Remarks:** Accepts advertising. **Circ:** (Not Reported).

18090 ■ Mortuary Management
Abbott and Hast Publications
2361 Horseshoe Dr.
West Bloomfield, MI 48322
Phone: (248)737-9294
Fax: (248)737-9296
Free: 800-453-1199
Publisher's E-mail: info@abbottandhast.com
Trade magazine for the funeral service industry. **Freq:** Monthly. **Key Personnel:** Greg Abbott, General Manager. **ISSN:** 0027--1268 (print). **Subscription Rates:** $43 Individuals /year domestic; $68 Two years domestic; $93 Individuals 3 years (domestic); $52 Other countries /year; $81 Other countries 2 years. **URL:** http://www.abbottandhast.com/mm.html; http://www.mortuarymanagement.com. **Ad Rates:** BW $1250, full page; BW $710, half page; 4C $2095, full page; 4C $1280, half page. **Remarks:** Accepts advertising. **Circ:** Paid ⊕**9500**.

18091 ■ WBLD-FM
4510 Walnut Lake Rd.
West Bloomfield, MI 48323
Format: Eclectic. **Owner:** West Bloomfield Board of Education, 5810 Commerce Rd., West Bloomfield, MI 48324, Ph: (248)865-6420, Fax: (248)865-6421. **Founded:** 1974. **Key Personnel:** Paul S. Townley, Station Mgr. **Wattage:** 044 ERP. **Ad Rates:** Noncommercial.

WEST BRANCH

Ogemaw Co. Ogemaw Co. (NE). 52 m NW of Bay City. Lake resort. Hunting, fishing, boating. Manufactures auto parts, crude oil, dairy products, flour, feed. Oil wells. Grain, stock, fruit farms.

18092 ■ WBMI-FM - 105.5
PO Box 807
West Branch, MI 48661
Phone: (248)434-1341
Fax: (248)434-1329
Founded: 1972. **Wattage:** 6,000. **Ad Rates:** Accepts Advertising. **URL:** http://www.wbmiradio.com/.

WHITEHALL

Muskegon Co. Muskegon Co. (WC). 5 m N of Twin Lake.

18093 ■ White Lake Beacon
White Lake Beacon
432 Spring St.
Whitehall, MI 49461
Phone: (231)894-5356
Fax: (231)894-2174
Community newspaper. **Freq:** Weekly (Sun.). **Print Method:** Offset. **Trim Size:** 15 x 21. **Cols./Page:** 6. **Col. Width:** 28 nonpareils. **Col. Depth:** 199 agate lines. **Subscription Rates:** $44 Individuals carrier; $49 By mail; $53.50 within the state; $62.50 Out of state; $44 Individuals online (1 year). **URL:** http://www.shorelinemedia.net/white_lake_beacon. **Mailing address:** PO Box 98, Whitehall, MI 49461. **Ad Rates:** BW $945; 4C $1,125; SAU $7.50. **Remarks:** Accepts advertising. **Circ:** Paid ‡815, Free ‡9885.

WILLIAMSTON

Ingham Co. Ingham Co. (S). 14 m E of Lansing. Brick, tile, mobile homes manufactured. Grain, poultry, dairy farms. Alfalfa, corn.

18094 ■ Out Your Backdoor
Out Your Backdoor
4686 Meridian Rd.
Williamston, MI 48895
Phone: (517)347-1689
Fax: (517)347-7884
Magazine focusing on bicycling, adventure, culture, the outdoors, hobbies, and sports. **Freq:** Monthly. **Print Method:** Web offset. **Trim Size:** 8.25 x 11. **Cols./Page:** 2. **Col. Width:** 3 inches. **Col. Depth:** 7 1/2 inches. **Key Personnel:** Jeff Potter, Editor. **URL:** http://www.outyourbackdoor.com. **Remarks:** Advertising not accepted. **Circ:** Paid 1000, Non-paid 4000.

WAIR-FM - See Lake City, CO

18095 ■ WJOH-FM - 91.5
148 E Grand River Rd.
Williamston, MI 48895
Free: 888-887-7139
Email: 411@smile.fm
Format: Religious; Contemporary Christian. **Founded:** 1978. **Operating Hours:** Continuous. **Ad Rates:** Advertising accepted; rates available upon request. **Mailing address:** PO Box 388, Williamston, MI 48895. **URL:** http://www.smile.fm.

18096 ■ WJOJ-FM - 89.7
148 East Grand River Rd.
Williamston, MI 48895
Free: 888-887-7139
Email: 411@smile.fm
Format: Contemporary Christian. **Owner:** Superior Communications, Inc., at above address, White Plains, NY. **Mailing address:** PO Box 388, Williamston, MI 48895. **URL:** http://www.smile.fm.

WLGH-FM - See Lansing

18097 ■ WTAC-FM - 89.7
148 E Grand River
Williamston, MI 48895
Free: 888-887-7139
Email: 411@smile.fm
Format: Contemporary Christian. **Owner:** Superior Communications Inc., 704 E Gude Dr., Rockville, MD 20850, Ph: (301)762-7878. **Wattage:** 15,000. **Ad Rates:** Advertising accepted; rates available upon request. **Mailing address:** PO Box 388, Williamston, MI 48895. **URL:** http://smile.fm.

WIXOM

18098 ■ Signal
Detroit Educational Television Foundation
1 Clover Ct.
Wixom, MI 48393-2247
Phone: (248)305-3900
Publisher's E-mail: email@dptv.org
Detroit public television program guide. **Freq:** Monthly or bimonthly. **Trim Size:** 8 1/8 x 10 7/8. **USPS:** 000-183. **Subscription Rates:** $40 Individuals. **URL:** http://detroitpublictv.org/support/benefits.shtml. **Formerly:** Signal 56. **Ad Rates:** BW $1,600; 4C $2,000. **Remarks:** Color advertising accepted; rates available upon request. **Circ:** ‡60000.

WYOMING

Kent Co. Kent Co. (WC). 5 m S of Grand Rapids.

18099 ■ WYGR-AM - 1530
1303 Chicago Dr. SW
Wyoming, MI 49509
Phone: (616)475-9947
Fax: (888)924-1146
Email: wygr1530@yahoo.com
Format: Hip Hop; Blues. **Simulcasts:** WYGR-FM. **Owner:** WYGR Broadcasting. **Founded:** 1964. **Operating Hours:** Sunrise-sunset. **Key Personnel:** Roland Rusticus, Gen. Mgr., roland.rusticus@wygr.net. **Local Programs:** *La Furia*, Sunday 7:00 a.m. - 9:00 a.m.; *The Polka Pops*, Saturday Sunday 12:00 p.m. - 3:00 p.m.; *Eighth Reformed Church*, Sunday 9:30 a.m. - 10:30 a.m. **Wattage:** 500 Day; 250 Night. **Mailing address:** PO Box 9591, Wyoming, MI 49509. **URL:** http://www.wygr.net.

YPSILANTI

Washtenaw Co. Washtenaw Co. (SE). On Huron River, 8 m E of Ann Arbor. Eastern Michigan University, Cleary College. Manufactures auto parts, automobiles, paper, plastics, ladders, sheet metal machinery. Diversified farming. Corn, oats, wheat.

18100 ■ Eastern
Eastern Michigan University
202 Welch Hall
Ypsilanti, MI 48197
Phone: (734)487-2211
Fax: (734)483-9744
Publication E-mail: exemplar@emich.edu
Magazine that offers information about Michigan State to prospective students. **Freq:** 3/year. **ISSN:** 1549--5361 (print). **Subscription Rates:** Free. **URL:** http://www.emich.edu/easternmag. **Formerly:** Exemplar. **Remarks:** Advertising not accepted. **Circ:** (Not Reported).

18101 ■ Eastern Echo
Eastern Michigan University
228 King Hall
Ypsilanti, MI 48197
Phone: (734)487-1010
Fax: (734)487-1241
Collegiate newspaper. **Freq:** 3/week Monday, Wednesday, and Friday. **Print Method:** Offset. **Cols./Page:** 6. **Col. Width:** 12 picas. **Col. Depth:** 294 agate lines. **Key Personnel:** Brian Peterson, Manager, Advertising; Katrese Stafford, Editor-in-Chief; Lukas Burch, Editor. **URL:** http://www.easternecho.com. **Ad Rates:** PCI $13; 4C $200. **Remarks:** Accepts classified advertising. **Circ:** Free ‡10000.

Circulation: ★ = AAM; △ or • = BPA; ♦ = CAC; ❑ = VAC; ⊕ = PO Statement; ‡ = Publisher's Report; Boldface figures = sworn; Light figures = estimated.

18102 ■ International Journal of Information Systems and Change Management
Inderscience Enterprises Ltd.
c/o Prof. David C. Chou, Editor-in-Chief
Dept. of Computer Information Systems
College of Business
E Michigan University
Ypsilanti, MI 48197
Publisher's E-mail: copyright@inderscience.com
Peer-reviewed journal covering the general field of information systems and change management theories, methodologies, modeling, processes and tools, with emphasis on the management, problem-solving and strategies for dealing with business changes. **Freq:** 4/yr. **Print Method:** Offset. **Cols./Page:** 5. **Col. Width:** 1 7/8 inches. **Col. Depth:** 14 1/2 inches. **Key Personnel:** Prof. Injazz J. Chen, Board Member; Dr. Shaw K. Chen, Board Member; Prof. Chen H. Chung, Board Member; Chao-Hsien Chu, Board Member; Prof. David C. Chou, Editor-in-Chief. **ISSN:** 1479-3121 (print); **EISSN:** 1479-313X (electronic). **Subscription Rates:** €520 Individuals print or online; €706 Individuals print and online. **URL:** http://www.inderscience.com/jhome.php?jcode=ijiscm. **Remarks:** Advertising not accepted. **Circ:** (Not Reported).

18103 ■ JNT
Eastern Michigan University
202 Welch Hall
Ypsilanti, MI 48197
Phone: (734)487-2211
Fax: (734)483-9744
Publication E-mail: jnt@emich.edu
Peer-reviewed journal covering essays that explore narrative issues from a variety of interdisciplinary, cross-cultural, and critical contexts. **Freq:** 3/year. **Print Method:** Offset. **Cols./Page:** 6. **Col. Width:** 18 nonpareils. **Col. Depth:** 224 agate lines. **Key Personnel:** Andrea Kaston, Editor; Abby Coykendall, Editor; Joseph Csicsila, Board Member; Paul Bruss, Board Member; Ian Wojcik-Andrews, Board Member; James A. Knapp, Board Member; Laura George, Board Member; Craig Dionne, Board Member; Martin Shichtman, Board Member. **Subscription Rates:** $30 Individuals 3 issues; $35 Institutions libraries, 3 issues; $10 add for shipping outside US; $8 Single issue. **URL:** http://www.emich.edu/english/jnt. **Remarks:** Advertising not accepted. **Circ:** (Not Reported).

18104 ■ Journal of Narrative Theory
Eastern Michigan University
202 Welch Hall
Ypsilanti, MI 48197
Phone: (734)487-2211
Fax: (734)483-9744
Publication E-mail: jnt@emich.edu
Journal providing a forum for the theoretical exploration of narrative in all its forms. **Freq:** 3/yr. **Key Personnel:** Craig Dionne, Board Member; Abby Coykendall, Editor. **Subscription Rates:** $30 Individuals; $35 Institutions; $8 Single issue. **URL:** http://www.emich.edu/english/jnt. **Circ:** (Not Reported).

18105 ■ Michigan Golfer
Great Lakes Sports Publications Inc.
4007 Carpenter Rd., No. 366
Ypsilanti, MI 48197
Phone: (734)507-0241
Fax: (734)434-4765
Publisher's E-mail: info@glsp.com
Magazine highlighting golfing scene in Michigan. Includes calendar of events. **Freq:** Quarterly. **Trim Size:** 8 3/8 x 10 3/4. **Cols./Page:** 3. **Col. Width:** 2 1/4 inches. **Col. Depth:** 9 3/4 inches. **Key Personnel:** Dave Foley, Editor; Mike Duff, Editor; Cheryl Clark, Chief Financial Officer; Scott Sullivan, Editor; Jennie McCafferty, Associate Publisher, Producer; Art McCafferty, Chief Executive Officer, Publisher. **ISSN:** 1071-2313 (print). **Alt. Formats:** PDF. **URL:** http://www.michigangolfer.com; http://michigangolfer.com. **Ad Rates:** 4C $550. **Remarks:** Accepts advertising. **Circ:** ‡16,000.

18106 ■ Michigan Runner & Fitness Sports
Great Lakes Sports Publications Inc.
4007 Carpenter Rd., No. 366
Ypsilanti, MI 48197
Phone: (734)507-0241
Fax: (734)434-4765
Publisher's E-mail: info@glsp.com
Publication featuring statewide calendar of events, event previews, and general interest information for Michigan runners. **Freq:** 6/yr. **Print Method:** Offset. **Trim Size:** 8 1/16 x 10 1/2. **Cols./Page:** 6. **Col. Width:** 2 5/8 inches. **Col. Depth:** 9 1/2 inches. **Key Personnel:** Art McCafferty, Chief Executive Officer, Publisher; Scott Sullivan, Editor; Dave Foley, Editor; Mike Duff, Editor; Jennie McCafferty, Associate Publisher. **ISSN:** 0279-1773 (print). **Subscription Rates:** $17 U.S. continental U.S.; $42 Other countries Alaska, Hawaii, Canada and U.S. possessions; $3 Single issue; $5 By mail back issues. **URL:** http://michiganrunner.net; http://www.michiganrunner.tv. **Ad Rates:** GLR $10.0; BW $075; 4C $1350; PCI $18.75. **Remarks:** Accepts advertising. **Circ:** ‡7,000.

18107 ■ Sociological Practice
Association for Applied and Clinical Sociology
c/o Fonda Martin, Executive Officer
Eastern Michigan University
Dept. of Sociology, Anthropology, and Criminology
926 E Forest Ave.
Ypsilanti, MI 48198
Phone: (734)845-1206
Publisher's E-mail: sac_aacs@emich.edu
Freq: Annual. **Remarks:** Advertising not accepted. **Circ:** (Not Reported).

18108 ■ WEMU-FM - 89.1
PO Box 980350
Ypsilanti, MI 48198-0350
Phone: (734)487-2229
Fax: (734)487-1015
Free: 888-299-8910
Format: Public Radio. **Networks:** National Public Radio (NPR); Michigan Public Radio. **Owner:** Eastern Michigan University, 202 Welch Hall, Ypsilanti, MI 48197, Ph: (734)487-2211, Fax: (734)483-9744. **Founded:** 1965. **Operating Hours:** Continuous; 27% network, 73% local. **Key Personnel:** Linda Yohn, Operations Mgr.; Clark Smith, News Dir. **Wattage:** 16,000. **Ad Rates:** Noncommercial; underwriting available. **URL:** http://www.wemu.org.

18109 ■ WSDS-AM - 1480
580 W Clark Rd.
Ypsilanti, MI 48198
Phone: (734)484-0078
Format: Country. **Simulcasts:** Jones Radio Network. **Networks:** Mutual Broadcasting System; Jones Satellite. **Founded:** 1962. **Formerly:** WYSI-AM. **Operating Hours:** 5:30 a.m.-midnight weekdays; 7 a.m.-midnight Sun.; 6 a.m.-midnight, Sat. **Wattage:** 750 Day; 3,500 Night. **Ad Rates:** Noncommercial.

ZEELAND

Ottawa Co Ottawa Co. Ottawa Co. (SC). 21 m WSW of Grand Rapids. Poultry.

18110 ■ WGNB-FM - 89.3
3764 84th Ave.
Zeeland, MI 49464
Phone: (616)772-7300
Email: wgnb@moody.edu
Format: Religious. **Networks:** Moody Broadcasting; Sun Radio. **Owner:** The Moody Bible Institute of Chicago, 820 N Lasalle St., Chicago, IL 60610, Ph: (312)329-4000, Free: 800-356-6639. **Founded:** 1989. **Operating Hours:** Continuous; 40% network, 60% local. **ADI:** Grand Rapids-Kalamazoo-Battle Creek, MI. **Key Personnel:** Scott Curtis, Operations Mgr.; Jack Haveman, Station Mgr. **Wattage:** 30,000. **Ad Rates:** Noncommercial. **Mailing address:** PO Box 40, Zeeland, MI 49464. **URL:** http://www.moodyradiowestmichigan.fm.

18111 ■ WGNR-FM - 88.9
PO Box 9516
Zeeland, MI 49464
Phone: (616)772-7300
Fax: (616)772-9663
Free: 800-968-8930
Format: Religious. **Networks:** Moody Broadcasting. **Owner:** Moody Bible Institute, 820 N LaSalle Blvd., Chicago, IL 60610, Free: 800-356-6639. **Founded:** 1979. **Operating Hours:** Continuous; 40% network, 60% local. **Key Personnel:** Scott Keegan, Contact. **Wattage:** 3,000. **Ad Rates:** Noncommercial.

18112 ■ WPNW-AM - 1260
Lanser Broadcasting, 425 Centerstone Ct.
Zeeland, MI 49464-2247
Phone: (616)931-9930
Fax: (616)931-1280
Email: traffic@jq99.com
Format: News; Talk. **Owner:** Lanser Broadcasting Inc., at above address. **Founded:** 1956. **Formerly:** WJBL-AM. **Operating Hours:** Continuous. **ADI:** Grand Rapids-Kalamazoo-Battle Creek, MI. **Key Personnel:** Brad Lanser, Contact, bradl@jq99.com; Brad Lanser, Contact, bradl@jq99.com. **Wattage:** 10,000 Day; 1,000 Night. **Ad Rates:** $8-15 for 15 seconds; $10-23 for 30 seconds; $13-27 for 60 seconds. $12-$20 for 15 seconds; $22-$48 for 30 seconds; $28-$58 for 60 seconds. Combined advertising rates available with WJQK-FM. **URL:** http://www.1260thepledge.com.

ADA

NW MN. Norman Co. 45 mi. NE of Fargo, ND. Feed manufacturer. Elevators. Agriculture. Grain, potatoes, sugar beets, sunflowers, soybeans. Dairy products.

18113 ■ KRJB-FM - 106.5
312 W Main St.
Ada, MN 56510
Phone: (218)784-2844
Fax: (218)784-3749
Free: 800-569-4171
Format: Full Service; Country; Agricultural. **Networks:** CNN Radio. **Owner:** R&J Broadcasting Inc., 312 W Main St., Ada, MN 56510, Ph: (218)784-2844, Fax: (218)784-3749, Free: 800-569-4171. **Founded:** 1985. **Formerly:** KMCA-FM. **Operating Hours:** Continuous; 15% network, 85% local. **Local Programs:** *Kaleidoscope*, Monday Tuesday Wednesday Thursday Friday 9:00 a.m. - 9:30 a.m.; *Good News Fellowship Program*, Sunday 8:00 a.m. - 8:30 a.m.; *The Confessional Lutheran*, Sunday 10:30 a.m. - 11:00 a.m.; *Red River Farm Network Market*, Monday Tuesday Wednesday Thursday Friday 6:30 a.m.; 9:30 a.m.; 10:30 a.m.; 11:30 a.m.; 12:30 p.m.; 1:45 p.m. **Wattage:** 100,000. **Ad Rates:** $9 for 30 seconds; $18 for 60 seconds. Combined advertising rates available with KMAV-AM & FM; KRJM-FM. **URL:** http://rjbroadcasting.com/.

18114 ■ R&J Broadcasting Inc.
312 W Main St.
Ada, MN 56510
Phone: (218)784-2844
Fax: (218)784-3749
Free: 800-569-4171
Format: Full Service; Information. **Networks:** NBC; ABC. **URL:** http://www.rjbroadcasting.com.

ADRIAN

SW MN. Nobles Co. 40 mi. E. of Sioux Fall, SD. Nobles Co. Creamery. Plastics, cement block factory; elevator. Grain, stock, dairy, poultry farms.

18115 ■ Nobles County Review
Nobles County Review
PO Box 160
Adrian, MN 56110
Phone: (507)483-2213
Publisher's E-mail: ncreview@frontier.com
Community newspaper. **Freq:** Weekly (Wed.). **Print Method:** Offset. **Trim Size:** 15 x 21. **Cols./Page:** 8. **Col. Width:** 21 nonpareils. **Col. Depth:** 21 inches. **URL:** http://www.noblescountyreview.net. **Formerly:** Ellsworth Voice. **Ad Rates:** GLR $3.50; BW $450; PCI $3.25. **Remarks:** Color advertising accepted; rates available upon request. **Circ:** ‡1400.

AITKIN

NEC MN. Aitkin Co. On Mississippi River, 88 mi. SW of Duluth. Aitkin Co. Summer & winter resort. Manufactures pallets, wooden boxes, crates. Timber. Truck, turkey, grain, wild rice, dairy farms.

18116 ■ Aitkin Independent Age
Messenger Publications Inc.
213 Minnesota Ave. N
Aitkin, MN 56431
Phone: (218)927-3761
Fax: (218)927-3763
Free: 800-450-3761
Publication E-mail: age@aitkinage.com
County newspaper. **Freq:** Weekly. **Print Method:** Offset. **Cols./Page:** 6. **Col. Width:** 1 7/8 inches. **Col. Depth:** 21 1/2 inches. **Key Personnel:** Ann Schwartz, Editor. **USPS:** 010-620. **Subscription Rates:** $33 Individuals; $39 Out of area; $46 Out of state. **URL:** http://www.messagemedia.co/aitkin. **Ad Rates:** GLR $9; BW $1,080; 4C $1,216; SAU $9.50; PCI $10.05. **Circ:** Paid ‡5200.

18117 ■ KFGI-FM - 101.5
PO Box 140
Aitkin, MN 56431
Phone: (218)927-2100
Fax: (218)927-4090
Free: 800-450-5546
Email: froggy@mlecmn.net
Format: Country. **Key Personnel:** Terry Dee, Gen. Mgr.; Tom Martin, News Dir.; Rick Skogs, Music Dir.; Rick Eby, Chief Engineer. **Ad Rates:** Noncommercial. **URL:** http://www.kkinradio.com/samfm.htm.

18118 ■ KKIN-AM - 930
PO Box 140
Aitkin, MN 56431
Phone: (218)927-2100
Fax: (218)927-4090
Free: 800-450-5546
Email: kkinradio@embarqmail.com
Format: Music of Your Life. **Networks:** Jones Satellite. **Owner:** Quarnstrom Stations, PO Box 9115, Fargo, ND 58106. **Founded:** 1961. **Operating Hours:** Continuous. **ADI:** Duluth, MN-Superior, WI. **Key Personnel:** Tom Martin, News Dir. **Wattage:** 2,500. **Ad Rates:** Noncommercial. **URL:** http://www.kkinradio.com.

18119 ■ KKIN-FM - 94.3
PO Box 140
Aitkin, MN 56431
Phone: (218)927-2100
Fax: (218)927-4090
Email: kkinradio@embarqmail.com
Format: Country. **Operating Hours:** Continuous. **Key Personnel:** Tom Martin, Gen. Mgr. **Ad Rates:** Advertising accepted; rates available upon request. **URL:** http://www.kkinradio.com.

18120 ■ KLKS-FM - 100.1
PO Box 140
Aitkin, MN 56431
Phone: (218)927-2100
Fax: (218)927-4090
Free: 800-450-5546
Format: Full Service. **Networks:** CNN Radio. **Founded:** 1984. **Key Personnel:** Tom Kenow, Sales Mgr., klksale@uslink.net; Bob Bundgaard, Contact; Diane Anderson, Contact. **Wattage:** 5,200 ERP. **Ad Rates:** Accepts Advertising. **URL:** http://www.kkinradio.com.

ALBANY

C MN. Stearns Co. 20 mi. NW of Saint Cloud. Residential.

18121 ■ The Munising News: News articles and links for Munising, Michigan
Peterson Publishing Inc.
22967 350th St.
Albany, MN 56307
Community newspaper. **Freq:** Weekly (Mon.). **Print Method:** Offset. **Trim Size:** 15 1/4 x 21 1/2. **Cols./Page:** 9. **Col. Width:** 21 nonpareils. **Col. Depth:** 301 agate lines. **URL:** http://www.munising.com; http://greatnorthernconn.com/papers/munising.html. **Ad Rates:** GLR $6; BW $903; 4C $225; SAU $7; PCI $4. **Remarks:** Accepts advertising. **Circ:** ‡3,000, 8000.

18122 ■ Stearns-Morrison Enterprise
Stearn-Morrison
561 Railroad Ave.
Albany, MN 56307
Phone: (320)352-6577
Fax: (320)352-5647
Publication E-mail: aenterprise@albanytel.com
Newspaper. **Freq:** Weekly (Tues.). **Print Method:** Offset. **Cols./Page:** 7. **Col. Width:** 24 nonpareils. **Col. Depth:** 294 agate lines. **URL:** http://www.albanyenterprise.com. **Ad Rates:** PCI $13.48; 4C $110. **Remarks:** Accepts advertising. **Circ:** 4500.

18123 ■ KASM-AM - 1150
PO Box 160
Albany, MN 56307
Phone: (320)845-2184
Fax: (320)845-2187
Free: 800-950-2148
Format: Talk; Ethnic; Country; Polka; Agricultural; Big Band/Nostalgia. **Networks:** Independent. **Owner:** Star-Com Inc., at above address. **Founded:** 1950. **Operating Hours:** Daytime; 100% local. **ADI:** Minneapolis-St. Paul, MN. **Key Personnel:** Randy Rothstein, Office Mgr. **Wattage:** 2,500. **Ad Rates:** Advertising accepted; rates available upon request.

ALBERT LEA

SC MN. Freeborn Co. 100 mi. S. of Minneapolis. Freeborn Co. Manufactures stoves, lamps, meat, dairy products, road machinery, beverages, hay tools, poultry equipment, iron shears, store fixtures. Diversified farming.

18124 ■ Albert Lea Tribune
Boone Newspapers Inc.
808 W Front St.
Albert Lea, MN 56007
Phone: (507)373-1411
Fax: (507)373-0333
Newspaper covering the local news, sports, business, and entertainment in Albert Lea region. **Freq:** 6 days a week. **Key Personnel:** Tim Engstrom, Editor, phone: (507)379-3433. **Subscription Rates:** $129 in town delivery; $183 out of town, motor delivery; $198 By mail. **URL:** http://www.albertleatribune.com. **Remarks:** Accepts advertising. **Circ:** (Not Reported).

Circulation: ⋆ = AAM; △ or • = BPA; ♦ = CAC; ❑ = VAC; ⊕ = PO Statement; ‡ = Publisher's Report; Boldface figures = sworn; Light figures = estimated.

18125 ■ Freeborn County Shopper
Boone Newspapers Inc.
110 Pearl St.
Albert Lea, MN 56007
Phone: (507)373-1310
Fax: (507)373-4253
Newspaper covering Albert Lea and a large share of Southern Minnesota and Northern Iowa. **Freq:** Weekly (Tues.). **Key Personnel:** Julia Thompson, General Manager. **URL:** http://www.freeborncountyshopper.com. **Remarks:** Accepts advertising. **Circ:** 17082.

18126 ■ The NAVTA Journal
National Association of Veterinary Technicians in America
PO Box 1227
Albert Lea, MN 56007
Fax: (507)489-4518
Free: 888-996-2882
Freq: Bimonthly. **ISSN:** 1552--4663 (print). **Subscription Rates:** Included in membership. **Alt. Formats:** PDF. **URL:** http://www.navta.net/?page=overview. **Remarks:** Advertising accepted; rates available upon request. **Circ:** 8000.

18127 ■ Tribune
Albert Lea Publishing Co.
808 W Front St., Ste. 60
Albert Lea, MN 56007
Phone: (507)373-1411
Fax: (507)373-0333
Publisher's E-mail: news@albertleatribune.com
General newspaper. **Founded:** 1897. **Freq:** Daily and Sun. (eve.). **Print Method:** Offset. **Cols./Page:** 6. **Col. Width:** 25 nonpareils. **Col. Depth:** 301 agate lines. **Key Personnel:** Tim Engstrom, Managing Editor; Scott Schmeltzer, Publisher; Crystal Miller, Manager, Advertising. **Subscription Rates:** $129 Individuals in Albert Lea; $183 Out of area; $198 By mail. **URL:** http://www.albertleatribune.com. **Ad Rates:** SAU $9.55; PCI $19.25. **Remarks:** Accepts advertising. **Circ:** (Not Reported).

18128 ■ KATE-AM - 1450
Skyline Plz.
1633 W Main St.
Albert Lea, MN 56007
Phone: (507)373-2338
Fax: (507)373-4736
Free: 888-516-5088
Format: News; Information; Talk. **Networks:** ABC; Minnesota News. **Owner:** Three Eagles Communications, 3800 Cornhusker Hwy., Lincoln, NE 68504, Ph: (402)466-1234, Fax: (402)467-4095. **Founded:** 1937. **Operating Hours:** Continuous. **ADI:** Rochester, MN-Mason City, IA-Austin, MN. **Key Personnel:** Aaron Worm, Sports Dir., Prog. Dir., aworm@albertlea.threeeagles.com. **Wattage:** 1,000. **Ad Rates:** Advertising accepted; rates available upon request. Combined advertising rates available with KCPI-FM. **URL:** http://www.myalbertlea.com.

18129 ■ KCPI-FM - 94.9
1633 West Main St.
1633 W Main St.
Albert Lea, MN 56007
Phone: (507)373-2338
Fax: (507)373-4736
Free: 888-516-5088
Format: Soft Rock. **Owner:** Three Eagles Communications, 3800 Cornhusker Hwy., Lincoln, NE 68504, Ph: (402)466-1234, Fax: (402)467-4095. **Founded:** 1974. **Operating Hours:** Continuous. **ADI:** Rochester, MN-Mason City, IA-Austin, MN. **Key Personnel:** Aaron Worm, Sports Dir., aworm@albertlea.threeeagles.com. **Wattage:** 5,000. **Ad Rates:** Noncommercial. Combined advertising rates available with KATE-AM. **URL:** http://www.myalbertlea.com.

18130 ■ K40JT - 40
PO Box A
Santa Ana, CA 92711
Phone: (714)832-2950
Owner: Trinity Broadcasting Network Inc., PO Box A, Santa Ana, CA 92711, Ph: (714)832-2950, Free: 888-731-1000.

18131 ■ KQPR-FM - 96.1
109 E Clark St.
Albert Lea, MN 56007
Phone: (507)373-9401
Fax: (507)373-9045
Free: 866-835-9696
Email: kqpr@power96rocker.com
Format: Classic Rock. **Wattage:** 25,000 ERP. **Ad Rates:** Noncommercial. KQPR will accept no advertising which is placed with an intent to discriminate on the basis of race, gender or ethnicity. **Mailing address:** PO Box 1106, Albert Lea, MN 56007. **URL:** http://www.power96rocker.com.

ALDEN

SC MN. Freeborn Co. 25 mi. W. of Austin. Residential.

18132 ■ The Alden Advance
The Alden Advance
150 E Main
Alden, MN 56009
Phone: (507)874-3440
Fax: (507)874-3440
Publication E-mail: editor@aldenadvance.com
Community newspaper. **Freq:** Weekly (Thurs.). **Print Method:** Offset. **Cols./Page:** 6. **Col. Width:** 2 1/8 inches. **Col. Depth:** 21 1/2 inches. **Key Personnel:** Beth Zeller, Editor. **ISSN:** 0898-526X (print). **Subscription Rates:** $25 Individuals a year for Freeborn and Faribault Counties; $30 Out of area elsewhere. **URL:** http://aldenadvance.com. **Mailing address:** PO Box 485, Alden, MN 56009. **Ad Rates:** BW $283.80; PCI $4.64; GLR $.28. **Remarks:** Accepts advertising. **Circ:** ‡642.

ALEXANDRIA

WC MN. Douglas Co. 65 mi. NW of Saint Cloud. Resort. Manufactures aircraft & parts, abrasives, plastics and concrete products. Diversified farming. Dairying, soybeans, beef cattle, hogs, corn.

18133 ■ Alexandria Lakes Area Visitor Guide
Alexandria Lakes Area Chamber of Commerce
206 Broadway St.
Alexandria, MN 56308
Phone: (320)763-3161
Free: 800-235-9441
Publisher's E-mail: info@alexandriamn.org
Magazine containing information on lodging and attractions in Alexandria, MN area. **Freq:** Annual. **Subscription Rates:** Free; Included in membership. **URL:** http://www.alexandriamn.org/visit-alexandria/Visitor-Center.aspx. **Remarks:** Advertising not accepted. **Circ:** (Not Reported).

18134 ■ The Echo/Press
Echo Press
225 7th Ave. E
Alexandria, MN 56308-0549
Phone: (320)763-3133
Fax: (320)763-3258
Publisher's E-mail: echo@echopress.com
Community newspaper. **Freq:** Semiweekly (Wed. and Fri.). **Print Method:** Offset. **Trim Size:** 13 x 21 1/2. **Cols./Page:** 6. **Col. Width:** 29 nonpareils. **Col. Depth:** 301 agate lines. **Key Personnel:** Al Edenloff, Editor; Jody Hanson, General Manager, Publisher; Diann Drew, Business Manager. **Subscription Rates:** $64 Individuals local; $75.95 Individuals local plus TV spotlight; $57.60 Individuals senior citizen; $69.55 Individuals senior citizen plus TV spotlight; $73.55 Elsewhere Minnesota; $80.25 Out of state. **URL:** http://www.echopress.com. **Formerly:** Lake Region Echo/Press. **Mailing address:** PO Box 549, Alexandria, MN 56308-0549. **Remarks:** Accepts advertising. **Circ:** Combined 10,500.

18135 ■ Lakeland Shopping Guide
Echo Press
225 7th Ave. E
Alexandria, MN 56308-0549
Phone: (320)763-3133
Fax: (320)763-3258
Publisher's E-mail: echo@echopress.com
Shopper. **Freq:** Weekly (Sun.). **Print Method:** Offset. **Trim Size:** 10 1/4 x 15. **Cols./Page:** 6. **Col. Width:** 20 nonpareils. **Col. Depth:** 210 agate lines. **Key Personnel:** Jody Hanson, Publisher; Al Edenloff, Editor; Lynn Mounsdon, Distribution Manager, Manager, Circulation. **Subscription Rates:** Free to distribution area. **URL:** http://www.echopress.com/content/lakeland-shopping-guide; http://www.forumcomm.com/portfolio/echo-press. **Mailing address:** PO Box 549, Alexandria, MN 56308-0549. **Ad Rates:** BW $990; 4C $1265; SAU $8; PCI $11. **Remarks:** Accepts advertising. **Circ:** Free ■ **25,478**, 27,000.

18136 ■ KIKV-FM - 100.7
604 3rd Ave. W
Alexandria, MN 56308
Phone: (320)762-2154
Fax: (320)762-2156
Format: Country; News. **Networks:** ABC; Linder Farm. **Founded:** 1970. **Operating Hours:** Continuous. **Key Personnel:** Dave Vagle, Gen. Mgr. **Wattage:** 100,000. **Ad Rates:** Advertising accepted; rates available upon request. Combined advertising rates available with KULO-FM. **Mailing address:** PO Box 1024, Alexandria, MN 56308. **URL:** http://www.alexandriaradio.net.

18137 ■ KXRA-AM - 1490
1312 Broadway St.
Alexandria, MN 56308
Phone: (320)763-3131
Fax: (320)763-5641
Email: thefolks@kxra.com
Format: Talk. **Ad Rates:** Advertising accepted; rates available upon request. **Mailing address:** PO Box 69, Alexandria, MN 56308. **URL:** http://www.voiceofalexandria.com.

18138 ■ KXRA-FM - 92.3
1312 Broadway St.
Alexandria, MN 56308
Phone: (320)763-3131
Fax: (320)763-5641
Email: thefolks@kxra.com
Format: Classic Rock. **Ad Rates:** Advertising accepted; rates available upon request. **Mailing address:** PO Box 69, Alexandria, MN 56308. **URL:** http://www.voiceofalexandria.com.

18139 ■ KXRZ-FM - 99.3
1312 Broadway
Alexandria, MN 56308
Phone: (320)763-3131
Email: thefolks@kxra.com
Format: Classic Rock; News; Sports. **Owner:** Access Broadcasting Inc., 2432 Brittany St., Eugene, OR 97405, Ph: (541)431-0036. **Wattage:** 6,000. **Ad Rates:** Advertising accepted; rates available upon request. **URL:** http://www.voiceofalexandria.com.

ANNANDALE

18140 ■ Annandale Advocate
Annandale Advocate
PO Box 417
Annandale, MN 55302
Phone: (320)274-2424
Community newspaper. **Freq:** Weekly (Wed.). **Cols./Page:** 6. **Col. Width:** 12.2 picas. **Col. Depth:** 21 1/2 inches. **Key Personnel:** Steve Prinsen, Publisher; Chuck Sterling, Editor. **Subscription Rates:** $11 Individuals 3 months; $20 Individuals 6 months; $34 Individuals 1 year; $40 Out of state 1 year; $68 Two years. **URL:** http://annandaleadvocate.com. **Circ:** Controlled 2,800.

APPLE VALLEY

18141 ■ Group Facilitation: A Research and Applications Journal
International Association of Facilitators
15050 Cedar Ave. S, No. 116-353
Apple Valley, MN 55124
Phone: (952)891-3541
Free: 800-281-9948
Publisher's E-mail: office@iaf-world.org
Journal consisting of topics and reviews focused on art and science of group facilitation, organizational learning and development, and group and system dynamics. **Freq:** Semiannual. **Key Personnel:** Stephen Thorpe, Dr., Editor. **Subscription Rates:** Included in membership. **URL:** http://www.iaf-world.org/site/publications/find/iaf/covers. **Remarks:** Advertising not accepted. **Circ:** (Not Reported).

APPLETON

SW MN. Swift Co. On Pomme de Terre River, 150 mi. W. of Minneapolis. Electronic plant. Elevator. Grain, dairy, stock, poultry farms. Wheat, oats, corn, beans, soybeans.

18142 ■ Appleton Press
Appleton Press
241 W Snelling Ave.
Appleton, MN 56208
Phone: (320)289-1323
Publication E-mail: news@appletonpress.com
Newspaper with a Democratic orientation. **Freq:** Weekly (Wed.). **Print Method:** Offset. **Cols./Page:** 6. **Col. Width:** 26 nonpareils. **Col. Depth:** 301 agate lines. **URL:** http://www.mnnews.com/newspapers/appleton.html. **Ad Rates:** BW $509.60; SAU $2.40. **Remarks:** Accepts advertising. **Circ:** ‡2105.

18143 ■ Pioneer Public Television - 10
120 W Schlieman Ave.
Appleton, MN 56208
Phone: (320)289-2622
Fax: (320)289-2634
Free: 800-726-3178
Email: yourtv@pioneer.org
Format: Educational. **Networks:** Public Broadcasting Service (PBS). **Founded:** 1966. **Formerly:** KWCM-TV. **Operating Hours:** Continuous. **Key Personnel:** Glen Cerny, Station Mgr., gcerny@pioneer.org; Jon Panzer, Dir. of Engg., Dir. of Operations, jpanzer@pioneer.org. **URL:** http://www.pioneer.org/2016-writers-contest.html.

ARLINGTON

SC MN. Sibley Co. 40 mi. N. of Mankato. Manufactures canned vegetables, cement blocks and silos. Heating equipment. Electric transformer rebuilding.

18144 ■ Arlington Enterprise
Arlington Enterprise
402 W Alden St.
Arlington, MN 55307
Phone: (507)964-5547
Fax: (507)964-2423
Publication E-mail: info@arlingtonmnnews.com
Community newspaper. **Freq:** Weekly (Thurs.). **Print Method:** Offset. **Trim Size:** 8 x 11 1/2. **Cols./Page:** 7. **Col. Width:** 28 nonpareils. **Col. Depth:** 301 agate lines. **Key Personnel:** Joyce Ramige, Publisher; Kurt Menk, Editor. **USPS:** 031-980. **Subscription Rates:** $33 Individuals in Minnesota, print; $38 Out of state print; $1 Single issue online; $10 Individuals 6 months, online; $15 Individuals 9 months, online; $20 Individuals 12 months, online. **URL:** http://www.mnnews.com/newspapers/arlington.html; http://www.arlingtonmnnews.com/about_us. **Mailing address:** PO Box 388, Arlington, MN 55307. **Ad Rates:** BW $325; SAU $2.75; PCI $4.70. **Remarks:** Color advertising accepted; rates available upon request. **Circ:** 1400.

ASKOV

EC MN. Pine Co. 47 mi. SW of Duluth. Nursery. Agriculture. Dairy products, eggs.

18145 ■ Askov American
Askov American
PO Box 275
Askov, MN 55704
Phone: (320)838-3151
Fax: (320)838-3152
Publication E-mail: askovamerican@scicable.com
Community newspaper. **Freq:** Weekly (Thurs.). **Print Method:** Offset. **Cols./Page:** 7. **Col. Width:** 12 picas. **Col. Depth:** 21.5 inches. **USPS:** 034-140. **URL:** http://www.askovamerican.com. **Ad Rates:** GLR $.20; BW $425; PCI $4. **Remarks:** Accepts advertising. **Circ:** ‡1936.

AUSTIN

SE MN. Mower Co. 100 mi. S. of Minneapolis. Meat packing and canned foods. Manufactures paper boxes, concrete products, business forms, water pollution control equipment, burial vaults, folding cartons, plastic pipes, animal feed, fertilizers. Dairy, stock, truck, poultry farms.

18146 ■ Austin Daily Herald
Austin Daily Herald
310 Second St. NE
Austin, MN 55912
Phone: (507)433-8851
Fax: (507)437-8644
Publisher's E-mail: newsroom@austindailyherald.com
General newspaper. **Freq:** Daily and Sun. (eve.). **Print Method:** Offset. **Cols./Page:** 6. **Col. Width:** 25 nonpareils. **Col. Depth:** 295 agate lines. **Key Personnel:** Dave Churchill, Publisher, phone: (507)434-2201. **Subscription Rates:** $9.75 Individuals in town (carrier), per month; $11.70 Individuals in town (motor) / out of town, per month; $16 By mail per month. **URL:** http://www.austindailyherald.com. **Mailing address:** PO Box 578, Austin, MN 55912. **Ad Rates:** SAU $7.62. **Remarks:** Accepts advertising. **Circ:** Mon.-Fri. 8,500, Sun. 8,440.

18147 ■ Mower County Shopper
Boone Newspapers Inc.
3405 W Oakland Ave.
Austin, MN 55912
Phone: (507)437-7731
Fax: (507)437-7733
Newspaper serving as shopping guide for Austin resident and local merchants. **Freq:** Weekly (Tues.). **Subscription Rates:** Free. **URL:** http://www.boonenewspapers.com/community/mower.shtml. **Remarks:** Accepts advertising. **Circ:** ‡17500.

18148 ■ Someplace Special
Austin Area Chamber of Commerce
329 N Main St., Ste. 102
Austin, MN 55912
Phone: (507)437-4561
Fax: (507)437-4869
Free: 888-319-5655
Publisher's E-mail: admin@austincoc.com
Magazine containing community information about the Austin, MN area. **Subscription Rates:** Included in membership. **URL:** http://www.austincoc.com/member-benefits.html. **Remarks:** Advertising not accepted. **Circ:** (Not Reported).

18149 ■ KAAL-TV - 6
1701 10th Pl. NE
Austin, MN 55912
Phone: (507)437-6666
Fax: (507)433-9560
Email: news@kaaltv.com
Format: Commercial TV. **Networks:** ABC. **Owner:** Hubbard Broadcasting Inc., 3415 University Ave., Saint Paul, MN 55114-2099, Ph: (651)646-5555, Fax: (651)642-4172. **Founded:** July 27, 1953. **Operating Hours:** Continuous. **ADI:** Rochester, MN-Mason City, IA-Austin, MN. **Key Personnel:** Chris Mans, Sales Mgr., cmans@kaaltv.com; Bill Klein, Sales Mgr., bklein@kaaltv.com. **Wattage:** 8,300 ERP. **Mailing address:** PO Box 577, Austin, MN 55912. **URL:** http://www.kaaltv.com.

18150 ■ KAUS-AM - 1480
18431 State Highway 105
Austin, MN 55912
Phone: (507)437-7666
Format: News; Talk; Sports. **Operating Hours:** Continuous. **Ad Rates:** Advertising accepted; rates available upon request. **URL:** http://www.myaustinminnesota.com.

18151 ■ KAUS-FM - 99.9
18431 State Hwy. 105
Austin, MN 55912
Phone: (507)437-7666
Fax: (507)437-7669
Free: 800-321-1480
Format: Country. **Owner:** Three Eagles of Luverne, Inc., at above address. **Operating Hours:** Continuous. **ADI:** Rochester, MN-Mason City, IA-Austin, MN. **Key Personnel:** Bob Mithuen, Gen. Mgr., rmithuen@digity.me; Scott Fuller, Prog. Dir., sfuller@digity.me. **Wattage:** 100,000. **Ad Rates:** Advertising accepted; rates available upon request. **URL:** http://www.myuscountry.com.

18152 ■ KSMQ-TV - 15
2000 8th Ave. NW
Austin, MN 55912
Phone: (507)481-2095
Free: 800-658-2539
Format: Educational. **Networks:** Public Broadcasting Service (PBS). **Founded:** 1972. **Operating Hours:** Sunrise-sunset. **Ad Rates:** Noncommercial. **URL:** http://www.ksmq.org.

BAGLEY

NW MN. Clearwater Co. 170 mi. W. of Duluth. Hunting, fishing & camping. Lumber mills. Timber. Agriculture. Potatoes, wild rice, alfalfa seed, sunflower. Lake resort.

18153 ■ Bagley Public Utilities
18 main Ave.
Bagley, MN 56621
Phone: (218)694-2300
Email: bagleypu@qutel.com
Owner: Bagley Public Utilities, at above address. **Founded:** 1976. **Cities Served:** subscribing households 534. **URL:** http://www.bagleymn.us/index.asp?sec=%7b8065fd0e-6f13-4704-a2db-98edfa3b8d6d%7d&type=b_basic&persistdesign=none.

BALATON

SW MN. Lyon Co. 70 mi. NE of Sioux Falls, SD. Creamery; elevators. Dairy, poultry, grain, beef raising farms.

18154 ■ Balaton-Press-Tribune
Balaton Publishing
PO Box 310
Balaton, MN 56115
Phone: (507)734-5421
Fax: (507)734-2316
Publication E-mail: balatonpublishing@yahoo.com
Community newspaper. **Freq:** Weekly (Wed.). **Print Method:** Offset. **Cols./Page:** 6. **Col. Width:** 14 picas. **Col. Depth:** 21.5 inches. **Key Personnel:** Jennifer Ringkob, Editor; Seth Schmidt, Publisher. **Subscription Rates:** $22 Individuals; $28 Out of area. **URL:** http://www.mnnews.com/newspapers/balaton.html. **Formerly:** Balaton-Russell-Press-Tribune-Record. **Ad Rates:** BW $367.65; SAU $2.52; PCI $2.85. **Remarks:** Accepts advertising. **Circ:** ‡454.

BATTLE LAKE

WC MN. Otter Tail Co. On a lake of the same name, 17 mi E. of Fergus Falls. Resort. Elevators. Grain, dairy, poultry farms.

18155 ■ Battle Lake Review
Review Enterprises Inc.
114 Lake Ave.
Battle Lake, MN 56515-4049
Phone: (218)864-5952
Fax: (218)864-5212
Publication E-mail: blreview@arvig.net
Community newspaper. **Freq:** Weekly (Wed.). **Print Method:** Offset. **Cols./Page:** 7. **Col. Width:** 28 nonpareils. **Col. Depth:** 301 agate lines. **Key Personnel:** Jon A. Tamke, Editor. **URL:** http://www.mnnews.com/newspapers/battlelake.html. **Ad Rates:** GLR $.25; SAU $5.80; PCI $4.80. **Remarks:** Accepts advertising. **Circ:** Combined ‡2026.

BAUDETTE

NW MN. Lake of the Woods Co. On Rainy River, 180 mi NW of Duluth. Pharmaceutical laboratory. Summer resort. Timber. Dairy, grain farms. Grass seed, seed potatoes.

18156 ■ The Baudette Region
The Baudette Region
110 W Main St.
Baudette, MN 56623
Phone: (218)634-1722
Fax: (218)634-1224
Publication E-mail: norlight@wiktel.com
Community newspaper. **Freq:** Weekly (Wed.). **Print Method:** Offset. **Trim Size:** 13 x 21 1/2. **Cols./Page:** 6. **Col. Width:** 12 picas. **Key Personnel:** Penny Mio, Editor; Cindy Olson, Office Manager. **USPS:** 045-500. **Subscription Rates:** $32 Individuals; $45 Out of area. **URL:** http://www.mnnews.com/newspapers/baudette.html. **Ad Rates:** GLR $5.30; BW $495; SAU $5.30. **Remarks:** Advertising accepted; rates available upon request. **Circ:** Paid 1669, 2400.

BAXTER

18157 ■ In-Fisherman: The Journal of Freshwater Fishing
InterMedia Outdoors
7819 Highland Scenic Rd.
Baxter, MN 56425-8011
Phone: (218)829-1648
Publisher's E-mail: privacycoordinator@imoutdoors.com

Circulation: ★ = AAM; △ or • = BPA; ♦ = CAC; ❑ = VAC; ⊕ = PO Statement; ‡ = Publisher's Report; Boldface figures = sworn; Light figures = estimated.

Magazine for freshwater anglers, from beginners to professionals. **Freq:** 12/yr. **Print Method:** Offset. **Trim Size:** 7 x 9 7/16. **Cols./Page:** 3. **Col. Width:** 2 1/8 inches. **Col. Depth:** 9 7/16 inches. **Key Personnel:** Jim Besenfelder, Director, Advertising, phone: (218)824-2518; Steve Hoffman, Publisher. **ISSN:** 0276-9905 (print). **Subscription Rates:** $29 Individuals 1 year; $55 Individuals 2 years. **URL:** http://www.in-fisherman.com. **Ad Rates:** BW $10670; 4C $14410. **Remarks:** Accepts advertising. **Circ:** Paid ★220,784.

18158 ■ KBLB-FM - 93.3
13225 Dogwood Dr. S
Baxter, MN 56425
Phone: (218)822-2933
Fax: (218)828-1119
Format: Country. **Key Personnel:** Mike Boen, Gen. Mgr. **Wattage:** 100,000 Watt. **Ad Rates:** Advertising accepted; rates available upon request.

18159 ■ KLIZ-FM - 107.5
13225 Dogwood Dr. S
Baxter, MN 56425
Phone: (218)829-1075
Fax: (218)828-1119
Email: kliz_1075@hotmail.com
Format: Classic Rock; News; Album-Oriented Rock (AOR). **Operating Hours:** Continuous. **Key Personnel:** Mike Boen, Gen. Mgr., biggermike@brainerd.net. **Wattage:** 10,000. **Ad Rates:** Advertising accepted; rates available upon request. **URL:** http://www.brainerdradio.net.

18160 ■ KUAL-FM - 103.5
13225 Dogwood Dr. S
Baxter, MN 56425
Phone: (218)822-7625
Fax: (218)828-1119
Email: cooloIdies@cool1035.com
Format: Oldies. **Key Personnel:** Mike Boen, Gen. Mgr., biggermike@brainerd.net. **URL:** http://www.cool1035.com.

18161 ■ WJJY-FM - 106.7
13225 Dogwood Dr., S
Baxter, MN 56425
Phone: (218)828-1067
Fax: (218)828-1119
Email: wjjy@1067wjjy.com
Format: Adult Contemporary. **Networks:** Mutual Broadcasting System. **Founded:** 1978. **Operating Hours:** Continuous; 15% network, 85% local. **Key Personnel:** Mike Boen, Gen. Mgr., biggermike@brainerd.net. **Wattage:** 100,000. **Ad Rates:** Advertising accepted; rates available upon request. **Mailing address:** PO Box 746, Brainerd, MN 56401-0746. **URL:** http://www.1067wjjy.com.

BELGRADE

18162 ■ Belgrade Observer
Belgrade Observer
303 Washburn Ave.
Belgrade, MN 56312-0279
Community newspaper. **Freq:** Weekly (Mon.). **Cols./Page:** 5. **Col. Width:** 11.5 picas. **Col. Depth:** 15 inches. **Subscription Rates:** $16 Individuals local; $14 Individuals; $0.50 Single issue. **URL:** http://www.belgradearea.com/index.htm. **Mailing address:** PO Box 279, Belgrade, MN 56312-0279. **Circ:** 1200.

BELLE PLAINE

18163 ■ Belle Plaine Herald
Belle Plaine Herald
113 E Main St.
Belle Plaine, MN 56011
Phone: (952)873-2261
Fax: (952)873-2262
Publisher's E-mail: bpherald@frontiernet.net
Community newspaper. **Freq:** Weekly (Wed.). **Cols./Page:** 6. **Col. Width:** 14 picas. **Col. Depth:** 21 inches. **Key Personnel:** Edward Townsend, Publisher. **Subscription Rates:** $26 Individuals print & online 1 year; $30 Out of state print & online 1 year; $5 Individuals online only 1 month; $15 Individuals online only 6 months; $22 Individuals online only 1 year. **URL:** http://www.belleplaineherald.com. **Circ:** 3,500.

18164 ■ International Journal of Listening
International Listening Association
Dr. Nan Johnson-Curiskis, Executive Director
943 Park Dr.
Belle Plaine, MN 56011
Phone: (952)594-5697
Journal focusing on aspects of listening in a variety of contexts, including professional, interpersonal, public/political, media or mass communication, educational, intercultural and international. **Freq:** 3/year. **Key Personnel:** Pamela Cooper, Editor. **ISSN:** 1090--4018 (print); **EISSN:** 1932--586X (electronic). **Subscription Rates:** Included in membership; $109 Individuals print only; $433 Institutions online only; $495 Institutions print and online; $109 Individuals print and online. **URL:** http://www.listen.org/IJL_TF; http://www.tandfonline.com/loi/hijl20#.VMz0EFXF8z. **Remarks:** Advertising not accepted. **Circ:** (Not Reported).

BEMIDJI

NW MN. Beltrami Co. On Lake Bemidji, 140 mi. NE of Fargo, ND. Bemidji State University. Summer resort, in center of The Thousand Lakes region. Computer industry. Woolen mills. Forestry & timber products. Lumber, cement, bricks, woolen goods.

18165 ■ The Bemidji Pioneer
Forum Communications Co.
1320 Neilson Ave. SE
Bemidji, MN 56619
Phone: (218)333-9200
Fax: (218)333-9819
Publication E-mail: jmail@bemidjipioneer.com
Newspaper featuring news and sports on a local, state, and national level. **Freq:** Daily Tuesday-Sunday. **Key Personnel:** Molly Miron, Editor; Tom Siemers, Manager, Circulation; Dennis Doeden, Publisher. **Subscription Rates:** $160 Individuals by carrier; $14.50 Individuals 1 month; $43.50 Individuals 3 months; $87 Individuals 6 months; $160 Individuals; $16 By mail 1 month; $49.50 By mail 3 months; $99 By mail 6 months; $182 By mail. **URL:** http://www.bemidjipioneer.com. **Mailing address:** PO Box 455, Bemidji, MN 56619. **Remarks:** Accepts advertising. **Circ:** Paid ‡7585, Sun. ‡9242.

18166 ■ KAWE-TV - 9
1500 Birchmont Dr. NE
Bemidji, MN 56601
Phone: (218)751-3407
Fax: (218)751-3142
Free: 800-292-0922
Format: Commercial TV. **Networks:** Public Broadcasting Service (PBS). **Owner:** Lakeland Public Television, 108 Grant Ave. NE, Bemidji, MN 56601, Ph: (218)751-3407, Fax: (218)751-3142, Free: 800-292-0922. **Founded:** June 1980. **Operating Hours:** Continuous. **Key Personnel:** Bill Sanford, Dir. of Engg., Gen. Mgr., bsanford@lakelandptv.org. **Ad Rates:** Advertising accepted; rates available upon request. **URL:** http://www.lptv.org.

18167 ■ KBHP-FM - 101.1
PO Box 1656
Bemidji, MN 56619-1656
Phone: (218)444-1500
Free: 888-775-2101
Format: Country; Contemporary Country. **Simulcasts:** KBUN-AM. **Networks:** ABC; Minnesota News. **Owner:** Paul Bunyan Broadcasting Co., 502 Beltrami Ave. NW, Bemidji, MN 56601. **Founded:** 1972. **Operating Hours:** Continuous. **Wattage:** 100,000. **Ad Rates:** Advertising accepted; rates available upon request. Combined advertising rates available with KBUN-AM. **URL:** http://www.kb101fm.com/home.html.

18168 ■ KBSB-FM - 89.7
1500 Birchmont Dr. N
Bemidji, MN 56601
Phone: (218)755-2059
Fax: (218)755-4119
Format: News; Sports; Information. **Owner:** Bemidji State University, at above address. **Founded:** 1968. **Operating Hours:** Continuous. **Key Personnel:** Nick Stoltman, Sales Mgr., Station Mgr., nick@beaverbroadcasting.com. **Wattage:** 120 ERP Horizontal. **Ad Rates:** $5 for 30 seconds; $8 for 60 seconds. Combined advertising rates available with KDRS-FM; KBSU-TV. **Mailing address:** PO Box 11, Bemidji, MN 56601. **URL:** http://www.bemidjistate.edu/.

18169 ■ KBUN-AM - 1450
PO Box 1656
Bemidji, MN 56619
Phone: (218)444-1500
Fax: (218)751-8091
Format: Sports; Talk. **Networks:** Mutual Broadcasting System; ESPN Radio; Minnesota News. **Owner:** Paul Bunyan Broadcasting Co., 502 Beltrami Ave. NW, Bemidji, MN 56601. **Founded:** 1946. **Operating Hours:** Continuous. **ADI:** Minneapolis-St. Paul, MN. **Key Personnel:** Kev Jackson, Prog. Dir. **Wattage:** 1,000. **Ad Rates:** Advertising accepted; rates available upon request. Combined advertising rates available with KBHP-FM. **URL:** http://www.kbunam.com.

18170 ■ KCRB-FM - 88.5
PO Box 578
Bemidji, MN 56619-0578
Phone: (218)751-8864
Fax: (218)751-8640
Format: Classical. **Networks:** Minnesota Public Radio; National Public Radio (NPR); American Public Radio (APR). **Owner:** Minnesota Public Radio Inc., 480 Cedar St., Saint Paul, MN 55101, Ph: (651)290-1500, Free: 800-228-7123. **Founded:** 1982. **Operating Hours:** Continuous; 97% network, 3% local. **Wattage:** 95,000. **Ad Rates:** Noncommercial. **URL:** http://www.minnesota.publicradio.org/radio/stations/knbjkcrb.

18171 ■ K42FH - 42
PO Box A
Santa Ana, CA 92711
Phone: (714)832-2950
Free: 888-731-1000
Owner: Trinity Broadcasting Network Inc., PO Box A, Santa Ana, CA 92711, Ph: (714)832-2950, Free: 888-731-1000.

18172 ■ KKBJ-AM - 1360
2115 Washington Ave. S
Bemidji, MN 56601
Phone: (218)751-7777
Format: Talk. **Owner:** R.P. Broadcasting Inc., 2115 Washington Ave. S, Bemidji, MN 56601, Ph: (218)751-7777, Fax: (218)759-0658. **Founded:** 1977. **Key Personnel:** Dan Voss, Gen. Mgr; Brian Schultz, Contact. **Wattage:** 5,000 Day; 2,500 Nig. **Ad Rates:** $4-$10 for 30 seconds; $6-$15 for 60 seconds. Combined advertising rates available with KKBJ-FM. **URL:** http://www.kkbjam.com.

18173 ■ KKBJ-FM
102 Lincoln Ave. S
Box 1360
Bemidji, MN 56601
Phone: (218)751-7777
Fax: (218)759-0658
Email: kkbjwbji@ncrthernnet.com
Format: Adult Contemporary. **Networks:** CNN Radio; Westwood One Radio. **Founded:** 1977. **Key Personnel:** Curt Peterson, Program Mgr. **Wattage:** 100,000 ERP. **Ad Rates:** $4-10 for 30 seconds; $6-15 for 60 seconds.

18174 ■ KKZY-FM - 95.5
502 Beltrami Ave. NW
Bemidji, MN 56601
Format: Adult Contemporary. **Owner:** Paul Bunyan Broadcasting Co., 502 Beltrami Ave. NW, Bemidji, MN 56601. **Wattage:** 100,000. **URL:** http://www.kzyfm955.com.

18175 ■ KNBJ-FM - 91.3
PO Box 578
Bemidji, MN 56619-0578
Phone: (218)751-8864
Fax: (218)751-8640
Format: News. **Founded:** 1994. **Key Personnel:** Tom Robertson, Reporter, trobertson@mpr.org; Barb Treat, Account Exec., btreat@mpr.org; Natalie Grosfield, Office Mgr., ngrosfield@mpr.org. **Wattage:** 60,000. **Ad Rates:** Noncommercial. **URL:** http://www.mpr.org.

18176 ■ KWRV-FM - 91.9
PO Box 578
Bemidji, MN 56619-0578
Phone: (218)751-8864
Fax: (218)751-8640
Free: 800-652-9700
Format: Classical. **Owner:** Minnesota Public Radio Inc., 480 Cedar St., Saint Paul, MN 55101, Ph: (651)290-

1500, Free: 800-228-7123. **Founded:** July 1993. **Key Personnel:** Kristi Booth, Regional Mgr., kbooth@mpr.org. **Wattage:** 100. **Ad Rates:** Noncommercial. **URL:** http://www.minnesota.publicradio.org.

18177 ■ Lakeland Public Television
108 Grant Ave. NE
Bemidji, MN 56601
Phone: (218)751-3407
Fax: (218)751-3142
Free: 800-292-0922
Format: Public TV. **Networks:** Public Broadcasting Service (PBS). **Founded:** 1980. **Key Personnel:** Dennis Weimann, News Dir., dweimann@lptv.org; Tom Lembrick, Engg. Mgr., tlembrick@lptv.org; Bill Sanford, Gen. Mgr., bsanford@lptv.org; Dan Hegstad, Station Mgr., dhegstad@lptv.org; Jeff Hanks, Production Mgr., jhanks@lptv.org. **Ad Rates:** Underwriting available. **URL:** http://www.lptv.org.

18178 ■ WBJI-FM - 98.3
2115 Washington Ave. S
Bemidji, MN 56601
Phone: (218)751-7777
Format: Country. **Founded:** 1206. **Key Personnel:** Marla Weckman, Bus. Mgr. **URL:** http://www.wbji.com.

BENSON

WC MN. Swift Co. 10 mi. N. of De Graff. Dairy.

18179 ■ Swift County Monitor-News
Swift County Monitor-News
101 12th St. S
Benson, MN 56215
Phone: (320)843-4111
Fax: (320)843-3246
Publisher's E-mail: ads@monitor-news.com
Community newspaper. **Freq:** Weekly (Wed.). **Cols./Page:** 6. **Col. Width:** 14 picas. **Col. Depth:** 21 1/2 inches. **Key Personnel:** Reed Anfinson, Publisher; Ronald Anfinson, Contact. **Subscription Rates:** $39 Individuals in Swift, Stevens, Chippewa, Kandiyohi & Pope counties; $51 Elsewhere in Michigan with the Peach & Canary ; $44 Elsewhere in Michigan without Peach & Canary ; $58 Out of state with the Peach & Canary; $51 Out of state without Peach & Canary. **URL:** http://swiftcountymonitor.com. **Mailing address:** PO Box 227, Benson, MN 56215. **Circ:** 3,200.

18180 ■ KBMO-AM - 1290
105 13th St. N
Benson, MN 56215
Phone: (320)843-3290
Email: info@kscr-kbmo.com
Founded: 1958. **Formerly**: KSCR-AM. **Key Personnel:** Paul Estenson, Gen. Mgr., pestenson@kscr-kbmo.com. **Wattage**: 033 Daytime; 024 Night. **Ad Rates:** Advertising accepted; rates available upon request. $11-13 for 30 seconds; $17-19.50 for 60 seconds. Combined advertising rates available with KSCR-FM. **URL:** http://www.kscr-kbmo.com.

18181 ■ KSCR-FM - 93.5
105 13th St. N
Benson, MN 56215
Phone: (320)843-3290
Email: info@kscr-kbmo.com
Format: News; Oldies; Sports. **Founded:** 1968. **Operating Hours**: 6:00 a.m. - 6:00 p.m. Monday - Friday; Continuous. Saturday; 6:00 a.m. - 11:00 p.m. **Key Personnel:** Paul Estenson, Gen. Mgr., Sales Mgr., Owner, pestenson@kscr-kbmo.com. **Wattage:** 25,000 ERP. **Ad Rates:** Advertising accepted; rates available upon request. $11-13 for 30 seconds; $17-19.50 for 60 seconds. Combined advertising rates available with KBMO-AM. **URL:** http://www.935kscr.com.

BIG LAKE

SEC MN. Sherburne Co. 7 mi W. of Elk River. Residential.

18182 ■ Clearwater Tribune
West Sherburne Tribune
PO Box 276
Big Lake, MN 55309
Phone: (763)263-3602
Fax: (763)263-8458
Community newspaper. **Founded:** 1986. **Freq:** Weekly (Fri.). **Key Personnel:** Gary W. Meyer, Publisher. **Subscription Rates:** $65 Individuals. **URL:** http://www.westsherburnetribune.com. **Circ:** ‡4972.

18183 ■ West Sherburne Tribune
West Sherburne Tribune
PO Box 276
Big Lake, MN 55309
Phone: (763)263-3602
Fax: (763)263-8458
Community interest newspaper. **Freq:** Weekly (Sat.). **Print Method:** Offset. **Cols./Page:** 6. **Col. Width:** 13.5 picas. **Col. Depth:** 224 agate lines. **Key Personnel:** Gary Meyer, Editor. **Subscription Rates:** $91 Individuals. **URL:** http://westsherburnetribune.com. **Ad Rates:** GLR $5.20; SAU $6.20; PCI $10.60. **Remarks:** Accepts advertising. **Circ:** ‡12,333.

18184 ■ KPXM-TV - 41
22601 176th St. NW
Big Lake, MN 55309
Phone: (763)263-8666
Fax: (763)263-6600
Key Personnel: Brandon Burgess, Chairman, CEO. **Ad Rates:** Advertising accepted; rates available upon request. **URL:** http://www.ionmedia.tv.

BIWABIK

NE MN. St. Louis Co. 64 mi. N. of Duluth. Iron mines.

18185 ■ Biwabik Times
Range Times
PO Box 169
Biwabik, MN 55708
Phone: (218)865-6265
Fax: (218)865-7007
Community newspaper. **Freq:** Weekly (Thurs.). **Print Method:** Letterpress. Uses mats. **Cols./Page:** 4. **Col. Width:** 28 nonpareils. **Col. Depth:** 210 agate lines. **Subscription Rates:** $14; $16 Out of area. **URL:** http://zenithcity.com/zenith-city-history-archives/minnesotas-arrowhead/history-of-biwabik-minnesota-including-merritt-and-mckinely-through-1922/. **Ad Rates:** GLR $.18; BW $180; PCI $3. **Remarks:** Accepts advertising. **Circ:** 1,512.

BLACKDUCK

NW MN. Beltrami Co. 25 mi. N. of Bemidji. Summer & winter resorts. Pulpwood & lumber products. Dairy & beef cattle.

18186 ■ Blackduck Cablevision Inc.
50 Margaret Ave. NE
Blackduck, MN 56630-0325
Phone: (218)835-4941
Owner: Blackduck Telephone Co., 50 Margaret Ave. NE, Blackduck, MN 56630, Ph: (218)835-4941, Fax: (218)835-3299, Free: 800-835-4941. **Founded:** 1983. **Cities Served:** subscribing households 400. **Mailing address:** PO Box 325, Blackduck, MN 56630-0325.

BLOOMING PRAIRIE

SE MN. Steele Co. 20 mi. SE of Owatonna.

18187 ■ Blooming Prairie Times
Blooming Prairie Times
411 E Main St.
Blooming Prairie, MN 55917
Phone: (507)583-4431
Fax: (507)583-4445
Publication E-mail: bptimes@frontiernet.net
Local newspaper. **Freq:** Weekly (Tues.). **Print Method:** Web offset. **Cols./Page:** 6. **Col. Width:** 2 1/16 inches. **Col. Depth:** 21 inches. **Subscription Rates:** $33 Individuals; $37 Out of area. **URL:** http://www.bloomingprairieonline.com. **Formerly:** Blooming Prairie News. **Mailing address:** PO Box 247, Blooming Prairie, MN 55917-0247. **Ad Rates:** BW $475; SAU $3.77. **Remarks:** Accepts advertising. **Circ:** ‡1,029.

BLOOMINGTON

SE MN. Hennepin Co. 25 mi. SW of Saint Paul. Residential.

18188 ■ Feedstuffs
Miller Publishing Co.
7900 International Dr., Ste. 650
Bloomington, MN 55439
Phone: (952)930-4344
Fax: (952)938-1832
Publisher's E-mail: comments@feedstuffs.com
Magazine serving the grain and feed industries and animal agriculture. **Freq:** Weekly. **Print Method:** Uses mats. Offset. **Trim Size:** 10 x 14 1/2. **Cols./Page:** 4. **Col. Width:** 26 nonpareils. **Col. Depth:** 193 agate lines. **Key Personnel:** Sarah Muirhead, Publisher, Editor, phone: (630)462-2466, fax: (630)462-2251. **ISSN:** 0014--9624 (print). **Subscription Rates:** $144 Individuals print & internet version; $230 Two years print & internet version. **URL:** http://feedstuffs.com. **Ad Rates:** BW $6995; 4C $8870. **Remarks:** Accepts advertising. **Circ:** (Not Reported).

BLUE EARTH

SC MN. Faribault Co. 40 mi. S. of Mankato. Manufactures monuments, electronics parts, running boards, truck boxes. Cannery. Grain, stock, poultry, dairy farms. Corn, oats, barley, soybeans.

18189 ■ Faribault County Register
Faribault County Register
125 N Main St.
Blue Earth, MN 56013
Phone: (507)526-7324
Community newspaper. **Freq:** Weekly. **Key Personnel:** Lori Nauman, General Manager, Publisher; Wanda Gieser, Office Manager; Chuck Hunt, Managing Editor. **Subscription Rates:** $45 Individuals /year (home delivery by carrier, in county); $55 Out of country /year by mail. **URL:** http://www.faribaultcountyregister.com. **Mailing address:** PO Box 98, Blue Earth, MN 56013. **Remarks:** Accepts advertising. **Circ:** (Not Reported).

18190 ■ KBEW-AM - 1560
PO Box 767
Winona, MN 55987-0767
Phone: (507)526-2181
Fax: (507)526-7468
Email: kbew@bevcomm.net
Format: Oldies; Information. **Networks:** ABC. **Founded:** 1963. **Operating Hours**: 12 hours Daily. **Key Personnel:** Kevin Benson, Gen. Mgr.; Randy Allen, Dir. of Programs. **Wattage**: 1,000. **Ad Rates:** Noncommercial.

18191 ■ KJLY-FM - 104.5
PO Box 72
Blue Earth, MN 56013
Phone: (507)526-3233
Fax: (507)526-3235
Email: kjly@newmail.kinshipradio.org
Format: Religious. **Networks:** Moody Broadcasting; USA Radio. **Owner:** Minnesota-Iowa Christian Broadcasting, 103 West Broadway, Eagle Grove, IA 50533, Ph: (515)448-4588, Fax: (515)448-3010, Free: 800-450-7729. **Founded:** 1983. **Operating Hours**: Continuous; 40% network, 60% local. **Key Personnel:** Matthew Dorfner, Exec. Dir.; Steve Ware, Dir. of Programs. **Local Programs**: *Wings of Worship*, Monday Tuesday Wednesday Thursday Friday 9:00 p.m. - 9:30 p.m. **Wattage**: 50,000. **Ad Rates:** Noncommercial. **URL:** http://www.kjly.com.

BRAINERD

C MN. Crow Wing Co. On Mississippi River, 53 mi. N. of Saint Cloud. Lake resort region. Pulp, paper, lumber mills. Dairy, poultry, grain farms.

18192 ■ Brainerd Daily Dispatch
The Brainerd Daily Dispatch
506 James St.
Brainerd, MN 56401
Phone: (218)829-4705
Fax: (218)829-7735
Free: 800-432-3703
Publication E-mail: dailyd@brainerd.net
General newspaper. **Founded:** 1881. **Freq:** Daily. **Print Method:** Offset. **Cols./Page:** 6. **Col. Width:** 11.2 picas. **Col. Depth:** 21.5 inches. **Key Personnel:** Tim Bogenschutz, Publisher, phone: (218)855-5844; Roy Miller, Editor, phone: (218)555-5855. **Subscription Rates:** $119 Individuals. **URL:** http://brainerddispatch.com. **Feature Editors:** Brian S. Peterson, *Features*, phone: (218)855-5864, brian.peterson@brainerddispatch.com. **Mailing address:** PO Box 974, Brainerd, MN 56401. **Remarks:** Accepts advertising. **Circ:** Mon.-Fri. 13,578, Sun. 18,576.

Circulation: ★ = AAM; △ or • = BPA; ♦ = CAC; ❑ = VAC; ⊕ = PO Statement; ‡ = Publisher's Report; Boldface figures = sworn; Light figures = estimated.

18193 ■ KAWB-TV - 22
422 NW 3rd St.
Brainerd, MN 56401
Phone: (218)855-0022
Fax: (218)855-0024
Free: 888-292-0922
Networks: Public Broadcasting Service (PBS). **Owner:** Lakeland Public Television, 108 Grant Ave. NE, Bemidji, MN 56601, Ph: (218)751-3407, Fax: (218)751-3142, Free: 800-292-0922. **Founded:** 1988. **Key Personnel:** Jeff Hanks, Program Mgr., jhanks@lakelandptv.org; Dan Hegstad, Station Mgr., dhegstad@lakelandptv.org. **URL:** http://www.lptv.org.

18194 ■ K204ES-FM - 88.7
PO Box 391
Twin Falls, ID 83303
Fax: (208)736-1958
Free: 800-357-4226
Format: Religious; Contemporary Christian. **Owner:** CSN International, PO Box 391, Twin Falls, ID 83303, Ph: (208)736-1958, Fax: (208)736-1958, Free: 800-357-4226. **Key Personnel:** Kelly Carlson, Dir. of Engg.; Ray Gorney, Asst. Dir.; Don Mills, Music Dir., Prog. Dir. **URL:** http://www.csnradio.com.

18195 ■ WWWI-AM - 1270
305 W Washington St.
Brainerd, MN 56401
Phone: (218)828-9994
Format: News; Talk. **Networks:** CBS. **Founded:** 1987. **Formerly:** WJJY-AM. **Operating Hours:** Continuous; 25: local, 7% network. **Key Personnel:** Tom Martin, News Dir.; Jim Pryor, Gen. Mgr., Owner, Sales Exe., jim@3wiradio.com; Mary Pryor, Office Mgr., Owner, marypryor@3wiradio.com; Mitch Pryor, Engineer, mitchp@3wiradio.com. **Local Programs:** *Big Wild Fishing/Hunting*. **Wattage:** 5,000. **Ad Rates:** $10-19 for 30 seconds; $19.20-30 for 60 seconds. **URL:** http://www.redrockradiobrainerd.com.

18196 ■ WWWI-FM - 95.9
305 W Washington St.
Brainerd, MN 56401
Phone: (218)828-9994
Format: News; Talk. **Key Personnel:** Tom Martin, Station Mgr.; Mary Pryor, VP, marypryor@3wiradio.com. **Ad Rates:** Advertising accepted; rates available upon request. **URL:** http://www.kkinradio.com.

BRICELYN

SC MN. Faribault Co. 30 mi. SE of Blue Earth.

18197 ■ Cannon Valley Cablevision Inc.
202 N 1st St.
Bricelyn, MN 56014
Phone: (507)653-4444
Free: 800-753-5113
Owner: Cannon Valley Communications, Inc. **Cities Served:** Bricelyn, Coates, Empire, Frost, Hampton, Hampton, Kiester, Marshan, Morristown, Nininger, Randolph, Ravenna, Stanton, Vermillion, Warsaw, Minnesota; Dakota County.; 52 channels. **Mailing address:** PO Box 337, Bricelyn, MN 56014.

BROOKLYN CENTER

Hennepin Co.

18198 ■ KPNP-AM - 1600
6500 Brooklyn Blvd., Ste. 206
Brooklyn Center, MN 55429
Phone: (763)585-1600
Email: peter@kpnp1600.com
Format: Ethnic. **Key Personnel:** Peter Phia Xiong, Mgr., peter@kpnp1600.com. **URL:** http://www.kpnp1600.com.

BUFFALO

SEC MN. Wright Co. On Buffalo Lake, 38 mi. NW of Minneapolis. Grain, livestock. Resort. Poultry, stock, dairy, grain farms.

18199 ■ The Drummer
Wright County Journal Press
108 Central Ave.
Buffalo, MN 55313
Phone: (763)682-1221
Fax: (763)682-5458
Free: 800-880-5047
Publisher's E-mail: business@thedrummer.com
Shopper. **Founded:** 1971. **Freq:** Weekly (Thurs.). **Print Method:** Offset. **Cols./Page:** 8. **Col. Width:** 21 nonpareils. **Col. Depth:** 301 agate lines. **Key Personnel:** James P. McDonnell, Jr., Publisher. **Subscription Rates:** $31 Individuals; $39 Out of state. **URL:** http://www.thedrummer.com. **Mailing address:** PO Box 159, Buffalo, MN 55313. **Circ:** ‡5600.

18200 ■ Wright County Journal-Press
Wright County Journal Press
108 Central Ave., Hwy. 25
Buffalo, MN 55313
Phone: (763)682-1221
Fax: (763)682-5458
Free: 800-880-5047
Publisher's E-mail: business@thedrummer.com
Newspaper. **Freq:** Weekly (Thurs.). **Print Method:** Offset. **Cols./Page:** 8. **Col. Width:** 21 nonpareils. **Col. Depth:** 301 agate lines. **Key Personnel:** James P. McDonnell, Jr., Editor. **Subscription Rates:** $10. **URL:** http://www.thedrummer.com. **Mailing address:** PO Box 159, Buffalo, MN 55313. **Ad Rates:** GLR $.176. **Remarks:** Accepts advertising. **Circ:** ‡5600.

18201 ■ KRWC-AM - 1360
PO Box 267
Buffalo, MN 55313
Phone: (763)682-4444
Fax: (763)682-3542
Free: 800-380-1360
Email: info@krwc1360.com
Format: News; Public Radio. **Networks:** CNN Radio; Minnesota News. **Owner:** Donnell Inc., 3264 Medlock Bridge Rd., Ste. 100, Norcross, GA 30092, Ph: (770)449-5798, Fax: (770)441-3790. **Founded:** 1971. **Operating Hours:** Continuous. **Key Personnel:** Joe Carlson, Station Mgr.; Tim Matthews, Operations Mgr. **Local Programs:** *Spotlight*, Monday Tuesday Wednesday Thursday Friday 10:07 a.m. **Wattage:** 500 Day; 027 Night. **Ad Rates:** $7.75-9.75 for 30 seconds; $9.75-11.75 for 60 seconds. **URL:** http://www.krwc1360.com.

BURNSVILLE

SE MN. Dakota Co. 12 mi. S. of Saint Paul. Residential.

18202 ■ Dakota County Tribune
Dakota County Tribune Inc.
12190 County Rd. 11
Burnsville, MN 55337
Phone: (952)894-1111
Community newspaper. **Freq:** Weekly (Thurs.). **Print Method:** Offset. **Cols./Page:** 5. **Col. Width:** 15 nonpareils. **Col. Depth:** 218 agate lines. **Subscription Rates:** $23 Individuals senior citizen; $16 Individuals college student; $24 Individuals. **URL:** http://sunthisweek.com/dakota-county-tribune; http://www.mnnews.com/newspapers/burnsvilletrib.html. **Ad Rates:** GLR $3.50; BW $1004.25; 4C $1454.25; PCI $13.39. **Remarks:** Accepts classified advertising. **Circ:** ‡1096.

CALEDONIA

SW MN. Houston Co. 23 mi. SW of LaCrosse, WI. Butter factory; lumber, grist mills; iron works. Hatcheries. Hardwood timber. Stock, dairy, poultry farms. Agricultural trade center.

18203 ■ Caledonia Argus
Caledonia Argus
314 W Lincoln St.
Caledonia, MN 55921
Phone: (507)724-3475
Community newspaper. **Freq:** Weekly (Wed.). **Print Method:** Offset. **Cols./Page:** 6. **Col. Width:** 12 picas. **Col. Depth:** 301 agate lines. **Key Personnel:** Jill Hahn, Office Manager; Charlie Warner, Editor; Julian Andersen, Publisher. **ISSN:** 2350-2600 (print). **USPS:** 082-960. **Subscription Rates:** $41 Individuals; $43 Out of area; $45 Out of state. **URL:** http://hometownargus.com. **Mailing address:** PO Box 227, Caledonia, MN 55921-0227. **Ad Rates:** BW $856.56; PCI $7.10. **Remarks:** Accepts display and classified advertising. **Circ:** Combined ‡2,715.

18204 ■ KCLH-FM
PO Box 99
La Crosse, WI 54601
Phone: (608)787-0947
Format: Adult Contemporary. **Wattage:** 2,100 ERP. **Ad Rates:** Noncommercial.

CAMBRIDGE

EC MN. Isanti Co. 40 mi. N. of Minneapolis. Creamery; woolen mill. Agriculture. Potatoes, oats, corn, soybeans.

18205 ■ Isanti County News
ECM Group
234 S Main St.
Cambridge, MN 55008
Phone: (763)689-1981
Fax: (763)689-4372
Community newspaper. **Freq:** Weekly (Wed.). **Print Method:** Offset. **Cols./Page:** 6. **Col. Depth:** 21 inches. **Key Personnel:** Rachel Kytonen, Editor; Jeff Andres, General Manager; Jerry Gloe, Manager, Sales. **ISSN:** 8750-2267 (print). **Subscription Rates:** $48 Individuals; $43 Individuals Senior. **Ad Rates:** BW $450; PCI $6. **Remarks:** Accepts classified advertising. **Circ:** Combined 13044.

18206 ■ Scotsman
ECM Group
234 Main St.
Cambridge, MN 55008
Phone: (763)689-1981
Fax: (763)689-4372
Shopper. **Freq:** Weekly (Sun.). **Print Method:** Offset. **Trim Size:** 11 1/2 x 16. **Cols./Page:** 6. **Col. Width:** 24 nonpareils. **Col. Depth:** 224 agate lines. **Key Personnel:** Julian L. Andersen, Publisher; Marge Winkelman, General Manager. **Subscription Rates:** $48 Individuals; $43 Individuals senior citizen. **URL:** http://www.hometownsource.com. **Ad Rates:** GLR $.83; BW $1,935; 4C $2,235; PCI $20. **Remarks:** Accepts advertising. **Circ:** Paid ‡100, Free ‡60000.

CANNON FALLS

SE MN. Goodhue Co. Goodhue Co. (SE). 22 m W of Red Wing. Manufactures stock feed, malt & barley products, farm products. Stock, dairy, poultry, grain farms.

18207 ■ Beacon
Beacon
120 S Fourth St.
Cannon Falls, MN 55009
Phone: (507)263-3991
Fax: (507)263-2300
Free: 800-263-3991
Newspaper with a Republican orientation. **Founded:** Aug. 04, 1876. **Freq:** Weekly (Thurs.). **Print Method:** Offset. **Cols./Page:** 6. **Col. Width:** 2 inches. **Col. Depth:** 21.5 picas. **Key Personnel:** Dick Dalton, Editor; Jen Rutter, Contact; Greg Hepola, Contact. **Subscription Rates:** $32 Individuals within 25 miles; $36 Elsewhere in Minnesota; $39 Out of state. **URL:** http://www.cannonfalls.com/. **Mailing address:** PO Box 366, Cannon Falls, MN 55009. **Ad Rates:** GLR $.20; PCI $5.40. **Remarks:** Accepts advertising. **Circ:** ‡4400.

18208 ■ Cannon Shopper
Beacon
120 S Fourth St.
Cannon Falls, MN 55009
Phone: (507)263-3991
Fax: (507)263-2300
Free: 800-263-3991
Publication E-mail: ccshopper@gmail.com
Shopper. **Freq:** Weekly (Mon.). **Print Method:** Offset. **Cols./Page:** 6. **Col. Width:** 27 nonpareils. **Col. Depth:** 294 agate lines. **Subscription Rates:** Free. **URL:** http://www.canonshopper.com. **Mailing address:** PO Box 366, Cannon Falls, MN 55009. **Ad Rates:** GLR $.24; PCI $7.55. **Remarks:** Accepts advertising. **Circ:** Free ‡9120.

CHASKA

SC MN. Carver Co. On Minnesota River, 20 mi. SW of Minneapolis. Manufactures beet sugar, sauerkraut, pickles, butter. Truck, dairy farms.

18209 ■ Chaska Herald
Southwest Suburban Publishing
123 W 2nd St.
Chaska, MN 55318
Phone: (952)448-2650
Fax: (952)448-3146
Publication E-mail: editor@chaskaherald.com
Community newspaper. **Freq:** Weekly (Thurs.). **Print**

Method: Offset. **Trim Size:** 13 x 21. **Cols./Page:** 6. **Col. Width:** 28 nonpareils. **Col. Depth:** 301 agate lines. **Subscription Rates:** $33 Individuals print and digital; residents of Chaska and Carver MN; 1 year; $37 Individuals print and digital; mailed in Carver or Scott MN counties; 1 year; $48 Individuals print and digital; mailed outside of Carver or Scott MN counties; 1 year; $68 Individuals print and online; mailed in Carver or Scott MN counties; 2 years; $88 Individuals print and online; mailed outside of Carver or Scott MN counties; 2 years. **URL:** http://www.swnewsmedia.com/chaska_herald/; http://www.mnnews.com/newspapers/chaska.html. **Formerly:** Carver County Herald. **Mailing address:** PO Box 113, Chaska, MN 55318. **Ad Rates:** BW $851; 4C $1141; PCI $6.60. **Remarks:** Accepts advertising. **Circ:** 4,994.

18210 ■ Quarterly Journal of the International Lilac Society
International Lilac Society
c/o Karen McCauley, Treasurer
325 W 82nd St.
Chaska, MN 55318
Publication E-mail: editor@internationallilacsociety.org
Freq: Quarterly. **ISSN:** 1046--9761 (print). **Subscription Rates:** Included in membership; $5 Single issue back issue. **URL:** http://www.internationallilacsociety.org/about-ils. **Remarks:** Advertising not accepted. **Circ:** (Not Reported).

CHISHOLM

NE MN. St. Louis Co. 8 mi. NW of Hibblings. Tourism. Manufactures outerware, tools, specialty meat products, noodles, spaghetti sauces. Iron mines; timber; trucks. Dairy farms. Agriculture. Potatoes, vegetables, hay.

18211 ■ The Chisholm Tribune-Press
The Chisholm Tribune-Press
327 West Lake St.
Chisholm, MN 55719
Phone: (218)254-4432
Fax: (218)254-7141
Publication E-mail: tribune@mx3.com
Community newspaper. **Founded:** 1901. **Freq:** Weekly (Wed.). **Print Method:** Letterpress and offset. **Cols./Page:** 6. **Col. Width:** 2 inches. **Col. Depth:** 21 inches. **Key Personnel:** Brian K. Anderson, Editor. **Subscription Rates:** $22 Individuals; $26 Out of area. **URL:** http://www.mnnews.com/newspapers/chisholm.html. **Formed by the merger of:** Tribune-Press; Free Press. **Ad Rates:** GLR $.40; BW $415.30; 4C $515.80; SAU $3.92; PCI $3.30. **Remarks:** Accepts advertising. **Circ:** ‡1,580.

CLARISSA

18212 ■ Independent News Herald
Independent News Herald
310 W Main St.
Clarissa, MN 56440
Phone: (218)756-2131
Fax: (218)756-2126
Publisher's E-mail: news@inhnews.com
Newspaper. **Freq:** Weekly. **Print Method:** Offset. **Cols./Page:** 6. **Col. Width:** 2 inches. **Col. Depth:** 301 agate lines. **Key Personnel:** Kathy Marquardt, Managing Editor; Ray Benning, Editor; Marlo Benning, Editor. **USPS:** 163-640. **Subscription Rates:** $28 Individuals local; $35 Out of area; $40 Out of state. **URL:** http://www.inhnews.com. **Mailing address:** PO Box 188, Clarissa, MN 56440. **Ad Rates:** BW $900. **Remarks:** Accepts classified advertising. **Circ:** Paid 2,450.

CLINTON

WC MN. Big Stone Co. 10 mi. N. of Ortonville. Farming community.

18213 ■ Northern Star
Northern Star
PO Box 368
Clinton, MN 56225-0368
Phone: (320)325-5152
Fax: (320)325-5280
Publication E-mail: northernstar@mchsi.com
Local newspaper serving the communities of Clinton, Graceville, and Beardsley, MN. **Founded:** May 01, 1965. **Freq:** Weekly (Thurs.). **Print Method:** Offset. **Cols./Page:** 6. **Col. Width:** 26 nonpareils. **Col. Depth:** 301 agate lines. **URL:** http://www.mnnews.com/newspapers/clinton.html. **Formerly:** Graceville Enterprise, Clinton Advocate. **Ad Rates:** PCI $4.85. **Remarks:** Accepts advertising. **Circ:** 1840.

CLOQUET

EC MN. Carlton Co. 18 mi. W. of Duluth. Manufactures paper, knitted garments, matches, insulation materials, building board, chemicals. Dairy, poultry farms.

18214 ■ Pine Journal
Cloquet Newspapers
122 Ave. C
Cloquet, MN 55720
Phone: (218)879-1950
Publisher's E-mail: news@pinejournal.com
Community newspaper. **Freq:** Semiweekly. **Print Method:** Web offset. **Cols./Page:** 6. **Col. Width:** 11 picas. **Col. Depth:** 21.5 inches. **Key Personnel:** Jana Peterson, Editor; Julie Schulz, Business Manager; Wendy Johnson, Publisher. **Subscription Rates:** $30 Individuals in Carlton County. **URL:** http://www.pinejournal.com. **Formed by the merger of:** Cloquet Journal; Cloquet Pine Knot. **Ad Rates:** BW $700; 4C $800; PCI $8. **Remarks:** Accepts advertising. **Circ:** Paid 2780, Non-paid 37.

18215 ■ Pine Journal
Pine Journal
122 Ave. C
Cloquet, MN 55720
Phone: (218)879-1950
Fax: (218)879-2078
Publisher's E-mail: news@pinejournal.com
Community newspaper. **Freq:** Semiweekly. **Print Method:** Web offset. **Cols./Page:** 6. **Col. Width:** 11 picas. **Col. Depth:** 21.5 inches. **Key Personnel:** Jana Peterson, Editor; Julie Schulz, Business Manager; Wendy Johnson, Publisher. **Subscription Rates:** $30 Individuals in Carlton County. **URL:** http://www.pinejournal.com. **Formed by the merger of:** Cloquet Journal; Cloquet Pine Knot. **Ad Rates:** BW $700; 4C $800; PCI $8. **Remarks:** Accepts advertising. **Circ:** Paid 2780, Non-paid 37.

18216 ■ WKLK-AM
807 Cloquet Ave.
Cloquet, MN 55720
Phone: (218)879-4534
Format: Oldies. **Networks:** Satellite Music Network. **Founded:** 1950. **Wattage:** 720. **Ad Rates:** $6-11 for 30 seconds; $8.50-15.50 for 60 seconds. **URL:** http://www.northwoodsradio.com/.

18217 ■ WKLK-FM
1720 Big Lake Rd.
Cloquet, MN 55720
Phone: (218)879-4534
Format: Oldies. **Networks:** Satellite Music Network. **Founded:** 1992. **Wattage:** 36,000 ERP. **Ad Rates:** $6-11 for 30 seconds; $8.50-15.50 for 60 seconds.

COLD SPRING

SE MN. Stearns Co. 15 mi. SW of Saint Cloud.

18218 ■ Cold Spring Record
Cold Spring Record Inc.
403 W Wind Ct.
Cold Spring, MN 56320
Phone: (320)685-8621
Fax: (320)685-8885
Publication E-mail: csrecord@midconetwork.com
Local newspaper. **Freq:** Weekly (Tues.). **Print Method:** Offset. **Trim Size:** 16 x 21. **Cols./Page:** 6. **Col. Width:** 28 nonpareils. **Col. Depth:** 301 agate lines. **USPS:** 121-020. **Subscription Rates:** $24 Individuals Cold Spring Trade area; $26 Elsewhere; $23 Individuals Cold Spring Trade Area - senior citizen; $22 Elsewhere senior citizen. **URL:** http://www.csrecord.net. **Mailing address:** PO Box 456, Cold Spring, MN 56320. **Ad Rates:** SAU $4.60. **Remarks:** Accepts advertising. **Circ:** Paid ‡8,300.

COLLEGEVILLE

C MN. Stearns Co. 12 mi. NW of Saint Cloud. St. John's University. Dairy farms.

18219 ■ Worship
Liturgical Press
31802 County Rd. 159
Collegeville, MN 56321-7500
Phone: (320)363-2213
Fax: (320)363-3299
Free: 800-858-5450
Liturgical studies magazine. **Freq:** 6/year published in January, March, May, July, September, and November. **Print Method:** Offset. **Trim Size:** 6 x 9 1/4. **Cols./Page:** 1. **Col. Width:** 52 nonpareils. **Col. Depth:** 98 agate lines. **Key Personnel:** Kevin R. Seasoltz, Editor; Allan Bouley, Associate Editor. **ISSN:** 0043-941X (print). **Subscription Rates:** $42 Individuals domestic; $77 Two years domestic; $63 Other countries foreign; $119 Two years foreign; $66.15 Canada; $124.95 Two years Canada; $70 Libraries; $133 Two years Libraries; $73.50 Canada Libraries; $139.65 Two years Libraries (Canada); 8.50 Single issue. **URL:** http://www.litpress.org/Subscriptions/Journals/worship.html; http://www.saintjohnsabbey.org/our-work/publishing/worship-magazine. **Mailing address:** PO Box 7500, Collegeville, MN 56321-7500. **Ad Rates:** BW $400. **Remarks:** Accepts advertising. **Circ:** 1652, ‡2300.

18220 ■ KBPN-FM - 88.3
PO Box 7011
Collegeville, MN 56321
Phone: (218)829-1072
Fax: (218)751-8640
Format: News. **Owner:** Minnesota Public Radio Inc., 480 Cedar St., Saint Paul, MN 55101, Ph: (651)290-1500, Free: 800-228-7123. **Founded:** 2003. **Operating Hours:** Continuous. **Wattage:** 34,000. **Ad Rates:** Noncommercial; underwriting available. **URL:** http://www.minnesota.publicradio.org/radio/stations/kbpnkbpr.

18221 ■ KBPR-FM - 90.7
PO Box 7011
Collegeville, MN 56321
Phone: (218)829-1072
Fax: (218)751-8640
Format: Classical. **Networks:** National Public Radio (NPR); American Public Radio (APR); Minnesota Public Radio. **Owner:** Minnesota Public Radio Inc., 480 Cedar St., Saint Paul, MN 55101, Ph: (651)290-1500, Free: 800-228-7123. **Founded:** 1988. **Operating Hours:** Continuous. **Key Personnel:** Kristi Booth, Reg. Dir., kbooth@mpr.org. **Wattage:** 34,000. **Ad Rates:** Noncommercial. **URL:** http://www.minnesota.publicradio.org.

18222 ■ KJNB-FM - 99.9
St. John's University
Collegeville, MN 56321
Phone: (320)363-3379
Email: kjnb@csbsju.edu
Format: Alternative/New Music/Progressive. **Owner:** St. John's University, 8000 Utopia Pkwy., Queens, NY 11439, Ph: (718)990-2000. **Founded:** 1977. **Formerly:** KSJU-FM. **Operating Hours:** Continuous. **Key Personnel:** James Darcy, Dir. of Programs; Ben Jacobson, Music Dir.; Sean Cannon, Dir. of Mktg. **Ad Rates:** Noncommercial. **Mailing address:** PO Box 2000, Collegeville, MN 56321. **URL:** http://www.kjnbradio.org.

18223 ■ KNCM-FM - 88.5
PO Box 7011
Collegeville, MN 56321
Phone: (320)363-7702
Format: News. **Owner:** Minnesota Public Radio Inc., 480 Cedar St., Saint Paul, MN 55101, Ph: (651)290-1500, Free: 800-228-7123. **Founded:** 1997. **Wattage:** 34,000. **Ad Rates:** Noncommercial. **URL:** http://www.minnesota.publicradio.org.

18224 ■ KNSR-FM - 88.9
PO Box 7011
Collegeville, MN 56321
Phone: (320)363-7702
Fax: (320)363-4948
Format: News. **Networks:** National Public Radio (NPR); American Public Radio (APR); Minnesota Public Radio. **Owner:** Minnesota Public Radio Inc., 480 Cedar St., Saint Paul, MN 55101, Ph: (651)290-1500, Free: 800-228-7123. **Founded:** 1988. **Operating Hours:** Continuous. **Key Personnel:** Nick Kereakos, Chief Tech. Ofc., VP of Operations, VP of Engg. **Wattage:** 100,000. **Ad Rates:** Noncommercial. **URL:** http://www.minnesota.

Circulation: ★ = AAM; △ or • = BPA; ♦ = CAC; ❑ = VAC; ⊕ = PO Statement; ‡ = Publisher's Report; Boldface figures = sworn; Light figures = estimated.

publicradio.org/radio/stations/knsrksjr.

18225 ■ KRSU-FM - 91.3
PO Box 7011
Collegeville, MN 56321
Phone: (320)363-7702
Format: Classical. **Owner:** Minnesota Public Radio Inc., 480 Cedar St., Saint Paul, MN 55101, Ph: (651)290-1500, Free: 800-228-7123. **Founded:** 1989. **Operating Hours**: Continuous. **Key Personnel:** Chris Cross, Regional Mgr., ccross@mpr.org. **Wattage**: 75,000. **Ad Rates:** Noncommercial; underwriting available. **URL:** http://www.minnesota.publicradio.org/radio/stations/kncmkrsu.

18226 ■ KSJR-FM - 90.1
PO Box 7011
Collegeville, MN 56321
Phone: (320)363-7702
Fax: (320)363-4948
Format: Classical. **Networks:** Minnesota Public Radio; American Public Radio (APR). **Owner:** Minnesota Public Radio Inc., 480 Cedar St., Saint Paul, MN 55101, Ph: (651)290-1500, Free: 800-228-7123. **Founded:** 1967. **Operating Hours**: Continuous. **Key Personnel:** Nick Kereakos, Chief Tech. Ofc., VP of Operations. **Wattage**: 100,000. **Ad Rates:** Noncommercial. **URL:** http://www.minnesota.publicradio.org/radio/stations/knsrksjr.

COMFREY

SC MN. Cottonwood Co. 25 mi. SW of New Ulm. Fertilizer plant. Livestock. Dairy, poultry, grain farm. Hay.

18227 ■ The Comfrey Times
Central Publications
PO Box 122
Comfrey, MN 56019
Phone: (507)877-2281
Fax: (507)897-2251
Publication E-mail: comfreytimes@frontiernet.net
Community newspaper weekly. **Freq:** Weekly (Thurs.). **Print Method:** Web. **Cols./Page:** 6. **Col. Width:** 24 nonpareils. **Col. Depth:** 280 agate lines. **Key Personnel:** John P. Andreasen, Editor. **USPS:** 105-060. **Subscription Rates:** $40 Individuals print & online; in counties; $43 Individuals print & online; in State of Minnesota; $45 Individuals print & online; outside State of Minnesota; $30 Individuals print; in counties; $33 Individuals print; in State of Minnesota; $35 Individuals print; outside State of Minnesota; $15 Individuals online. **URL:** http://www.mnnews.com/newspapers/comfrey.html. **Ad Rates:** GLR $3; BW $150; 4C $350; SAU $2; PCI $3. **Remarks:** Accepts advertising. **Circ:** 557.

COOK

NC MN. St. Louis Co. 25 mi. NNW of Virginia.

18228 ■ Cook News-Herald
Cook News-Herald Publishing, Inc.
PO Box 1179
Cook, MN 55723
Phone: (218)666-5944
Fax: (218)666-5609
Community newspaper. **Freq:** Weekly. **Print Method:** Offset. **Trim Size:** 11 x 15. **Cols./Page:** 4. **Col. Width:** 14 picas. **Subscription Rates:** $30 Individuals in country; $36 Individuals all other areas in Minnesota; $38 Individuals all other areas in U.S.; $26 Students in USA. **URL:** http://www.cooknewsherald.com. **Ad Rates:** PCI $4.68. **Remarks:** Accepts advertising. **Circ:** 3,652.

COON RAPIDS

SEC MN. Anoka Co. 11 mi. N of Minneapolis. Residential.

18229 ■ Anoka County Shopper
Anoka County Shopper
4101 Coon Rapids Blvd.
Coon Rapids, MN 55433
Phone: (763)421-4444
Fax: (763)421-4315
Shopper. **Freq:** Weekly (Wed.). **Print Method:** Offset. **Cols./Page:** 6. **Col. Width:** 26 nonpareils. **Col. Depth:** 308 agate lines. **Key Personnel:** Eric Olson, General Manager. **Subscription Rates:** Free. **URL:** http://abcnewspapers.com; http://ecmpublishers.com/publications. **Remarks:** Accepts advertising. **Circ:** Non-paid ‡50,381.

18230 ■ Anoka County Union
Anoka County Shopper
4101 Coon Rapids Blvd.
Coon Rapids, MN 55433
Phone: (763)421-4444
Fax: (763)421-4315
Local newspaper. **Freq:** Weekly (Fri.). **Print Method:** Offset. **Cols./Page:** 6. **Col. Width:** 26 nonpareils. **Col. Depth:** 308 agate lines. **Key Personnel:** Mandy Moran Froemming, Editor, phone: (762)712-3514; Brian Ploeger, Manager, Advertising, phone: (763)712-3523. **Subscription Rates:** $38 Individuals; $50 Out of area; $56 Two years; $68 Out of area Two years; $28 Individuals senior citizen; $40 Out of area senior citizen. **URL:** http://abcnewspapers.com; http://ecmpublishers.com/publications. **Remarks:** Accepts advertising. **Circ:** Paid ‡2948.

18231 ■ Blaine Spring Lake Park Life
Anoka County Shopper
4101 Coon Rapids Blvd.
Coon Rapids, MN 55433
Phone: (763)421-4444
Fax: (763)421-4315
Local newspaper. **Freq:** Weekly (Fri.). **Print Method:** Offset. **Cols./Page:** 6. **Col. Width:** 26 nonpareils. **Col. Depth:** 308 agate lines. **Key Personnel:** Tim Hennagir, Editor, phone: (763)712-3509; Jill Donahue, Business Manager. **Subscription Rates:** $38 Individuals; $50 Out of area; $56 Two years; $68 Out of area Two years; $28 Individuals senior citizen; $40 Out of area senior citizen; $42 Two years senior citizen; $54 Two years out of area; senior citizen. **URL:** http://abcnewspapers.com; http://ecmpublishers.com/publications. **Remarks:** Accepts advertising. **Circ:** Combined ‡17,028.

18232 ■ Coon Rapids Herald
Anoka County Shopper
4101 Coon Rapids Blvd.
Coon Rapids, MN 55433
Phone: (763)421-4444
Fax: (763)421-4315
Local newspaper. **Freq:** Weekly (Fri.). **Print Method:** Offset. **Cols./Page:** 6. **Col. Width:** 26 nonpareils. **Col. Depth:** 308 agate lines. **Key Personnel:** Peter Bodley, Managing Editor, phone: (763)712-3513; Mandy Moran Froemming, Editor, phone: (763)712-3514; Jason Olson, Editor, phone: (763)712-3507. **Subscription Rates:** $38 Individuals; $50 Out of area. **URL:** http://abcnewspapers.com. **Remarks:** Accepts advertising. **Circ:** Paid ‡2343.

18233 ■ Crystal Robbinsdale Sun Post
ECM Publishers Inc.
4095 Coon Rapids Blvd.
Coon Rapids, MN 55433
Phone: (763)712-2400
Community newspaper. **Freq:** Weekly (Thurs.). **Print Method:** Offset. **Cols./Page:** 8. **Col. Width:** 20 nonpareils. **Col. Depth:** 300 agate lines. **Key Personnel:** Peggy Bakken, Executive Editor. **Subscription Rates:** $87 By mail. **URL:** http://post.mnsun.com/tag/crystal. **Remarks:** Accepts advertising. **Circ:** Paid 707, Non-paid 10250, 23163.

18234 ■ Elk River Star News
ECM Publishing
4095 Coon Rapids Blvd.
Coon Rapids, MN 55433
Phone: (763)712-2400
Publication E-mail: editor.erstarnews@ecm-inc.com
Community newspaper. **Freq:** Weekly (Wed.). **Print Method:** Offset. **Cols./Page:** 6. **Col. Width:** 2 inches. **Col. Depth:** 21 inches. **Key Personnel:** Tom Murray, General Manager, phone: (763)441-3500; Jim Boyle, Editor, phone: (763)241-3670; Joni Astrup, Associate Editor, phone: (763)241-3668. **Subscription Rates:** $40 Individuals; $120 Other countries; $39 Individuals senior citizen; $119 Other countries senior citizen. **URL:** http://erstarnews.com. **Ad Rates:** BW $1,386; 4C $1,761; SAU $5.69; PCI $5.65. **Remarks:** Accepts advertising. **Circ:** Combined ‡20570.

18235 ■ Minnetonka Sun Sailor
ECM Publishers Inc.
4095 Coon Rapids Blvd.
Coon Rapids, MN 55433
Phone: (763)712-2400
Regional community newspaper. **Key Personnel:** Dennis Thomsen, Account Manager, phone: (952)392-6878; Sylvia Fitzsimmons, Manager, Circulation; Mike Erickson, Manager, Production, phone: (952)392-6830; Peggy Bakken, Executive Editor, phone: (952)392-6822; Paul Wahl, Managing Editor. **URL:** http://sailor.mnsun.com. **Remarks:** Accepts advertising. **Circ:** Combined ♦62620.

18236 ■ Morrison County Record
ECM Publishers Inc.
4095 Coon Rapids Blvd.
Coon Rapids, MN 55433
Phone: (763)712-2400
Publisher's E-mail: mcr@mcrecord.com
County newspaper (tabloid). **Freq:** Weekly (Sun.). **Print Method:** Offset. **Trim Size:** 10 x 15. **Cols./Page:** 5. **Col. Width:** 20 nonpareils. **Col. Depth:** 210 agate lines. **Key Personnel:** Faye Santala, Manager, Production; Carmen Meyer, Manager, Sales; Tom West, General Manager, Managing Editor. **Ad Rates:** BW $528.75; 4C $200; SAU $8.15; PCI $8.15. **Remarks:** Accepts advertising. **Circ:** Non-paid ♦19099.

18237 ■ New Hope/Golden Valley Sun-Post
ECM Publishers Inc.
4095 Coon Rapids Blvd.
Coon Rapids, MN 55433
Phone: (763)712-2400
Community newspaper (tabloid). **Freq:** Weekly. **Print Method:** Offset. **Col. Width:** 10 3/8 inches. **Col. Depth:** 12 1/2 inches. **Key Personnel:** Sylvia Fitzsimmons, Manager, Circulation; Mark Berriman, Director, Operations, phone: (651)796-1116; Mike Erickson, Manager, Production, phone: (952)392-6830; Peggy Bakken, Executive Editor. **Ad Rates:** BW $1860; 4C $1953. **Remarks:** Accepts advertising. **Circ:** Paid 1,106, Non-paid 10,092.

18238 ■ North Crow River News
ECM Publishers Inc.
4095 Coon Rapids Blvd.
Coon Rapids, MN 55433
Phone: (763)712-2400
Community newspaper. **Freq:** Weekly (Mon.). **Print Method:** Offset. **Cols./Page:** 6. **Col. Width:** 1.88 inches. **Col. Depth:** 294 agate lines. **Key Personnel:** Peggy Bakken, Executive Editor. **Subscription Rates:** $38 Individuals; $64 Two years; $25 Individuals 6 months. **URL:** http://www.ecm-inc.com/web-publications; http://pressnews.com. **Ad Rates:** GLR $.62; BW $1097; 4C $1391; PCI $17.20. **Remarks:** Accepts advertising. **Circ:** Thurs. ♦2,633.

18239 ■ North Minneapolis Sun-Post
ECM Publishers Inc.
4095 Coon Rapids Blvd.
Coon Rapids, MN 55433
Phone: (763)712-2400
Community newspaper (tabloid). **Freq:** Weekly (Wed.). **Print Method:** Offset. **Cols./Page:** 4. **Col. Width:** 2.5 inches. **Col. Depth:** 15 inches. **Subscription Rates:** Free; $87 U.S. **Remarks:** Accepts advertising. **Circ:** Free 9195.

18240 ■ Osseo-Maple Grove Press
ECM Publishers Inc.
4095 Coon Rapids Blvd.
Coon Rapids, MN 55433
Phone: (763)712-2400
Community newspaper. **Freq:** Weekly (Wed.). **Print Method:** Offset. **Cols./Page:** 6. **Col. Width:** 2 inches. **Col. Depth:** 301 agate lines. **Key Personnel:** Peggy Bakken, Executive Editor. **Subscription Rates:** $38 Individuals; $64 Two years; $25 Individuals 6 months. **URL:** http://pressnews.com; http://www.ecm-inc.com/publications. **Ad Rates:** GLR $.80; BW $1408; 4C $1702; PCI $19. **Remarks:** Advertising accepted; rates available upon request. **Circ:** (Not Reported).

18241 ■ Plymouth Sun Sailor
ECM Publishers Inc.
4095 Coon Rapids Blvd.
Coon Rapids, MN 55433
Phone: (763)712-2400
Regional community newspaper. **Key Personnel:** Peggy Bakken, Executive Editor, phone: (952)392-6822; Sylvia Fitzsimmons, Manager, Circulation, phone: (763)424-7370; Brian Rosemeyer, Editor. **Subscription Rates:** $87 By mail anywhere in the U.S. **URL:** http://sailor.mnsun.com/tag/plymouth. **Remarks:** Accepts advertising. **Circ:** (Not Reported).

18242 ■ St. Croix Valley Peach
ECM Publishers Inc.
4095 Coon Rapids Blvd.
Coon Rapids, MN 55433
Phone: (763)712-2400
Publication E-mail: jeff.andres@ecm-inc.com
Shopping guide. **Freq:** Weekly (Sun.). **Print Method:** Offset. **Cols./Page:** 6. **Col. Width:** 20 nonpareils. **Col. Depth:** 15 inches. **Key Personnel:** Jeff Andres, General Manager. **Subscription Rates:** Free. **URL:** http://forestlaketimes.com/st-croix-valley-peach. **Ad Rates:** GLR $8.75; BW $1,067; 4C $1,367; PCI $13.45. **Remarks:** Accepts advertising. **Circ:** Non-paid ‡27846.

18243 ■ Shorewood Sun Sailor
ECM Publishers Inc.
4095 Coon Rapids Blvd.
Coon Rapids, MN 55433
Phone: (763)712-2400
Regional community newspaper. **Key Personnel:** Jeremy Bradfield, Director, Advertising, phone: (952)392-6841. **Subscription Rates:** $87 By mail anywhere in the U.S. **URL:** http://sailor.mnsun.com. **Remarks:** Accepts display and classified advertising. **Circ:** (Not Reported).

18244 ■ Sun Current
ECM Publishers Inc.
4095 Coon Rapids Blvd.
Coon Rapids, MN 55433
Phone: (763)712-2400
Regional community newspaper. **Freq:** Weekly (Thurs.). **Key Personnel:** Jeremy Bradfield, Director, Advertising, phone: (952)392-6841. **URL:** http://current.mnsun.com. **Formerly**: Rosemount Sun Current. **Remarks:** Accepts display and classified advertising. **Circ:** ‡31379.

18245 ■ Sun ThisWeek
ECM Publishers Inc.
4095 Coon Rapids Blvd.
Coon Rapids, MN 55433
Phone: (763)712-2400
Regional community newspaper. **Key Personnel:** Jeff Coolman, Publisher, phone: (952)392-6807; Jeremy Bradfield, Director, Advertising, phone: (952)392-6841; Dennis Thomsen, Account Manager, phone: (952)392-6878; Pam Miller, Manager, Advertising, phone: (952)392-6862; Sylvia Fitzsimmons, Manager, Circulation; Mike Erickson, Manager, Production, phone: (952)392-6830; Peggy Bakken, Executive Editor, phone: (952)392-6822. **URL:** http://sunthisweek.com. **Formerly**: Lakeville Sun Current. **Remarks:** Accepts advertising. **Circ:** (Not Reported).

18246 ■ The Town and Country Shopper
ECM Publishers Inc.
4095 Coon Rapids Blvd.
Coon Rapids, MN 55433
Phone: (763)712-2400
Shopper. **Freq:** Weekly (Mon.) morning. **Print Method:** Offset. **Trim Size:** 11 1/2 x 17. **Cols./Page:** 6. **Col. Width:** 20 nonpareils. **Col. Depth:** 224 agate lines. **Subscription Rates:** Free; $25 By mail. **URL:** http://towncountrynews.com; http://ecmpublishers.com/publications. **Ad Rates:** BW $539.40; PCI $6.25. **Remarks:** Advertising accepted; rates available upon request. **Circ:** Free 25500.

18247 ■ Waconia Patriot
ECM Publishers Inc.
4095 Coon Rapids Blvd.
Coon Rapids, MN 55433
Phone: (763)712-2400
Newspaper. **Freq:** Weekly (Thurs.). **Print Method:** Offset. **Cols./Page:** 6. **Col. Width:** 24 nonpareils. **Col. Depth:** 301 agate lines. **Key Personnel:** Todd Moen, Editor. **Subscription Rates:** $31 Individuals. **URL:** http://sunpatriot.com/tag/waconia-patriot; http://www.ecm-inc.com/publications. **Ad Rates:** GLR $.25. **Remarks:** Accepts advertising. **Circ:** (Not Reported).

18248 ■ Wayzata/Orono/Long Lake Sun-Sailor
ECM Publishers Inc.
4095 Coon Rapids Blvd.
Coon Rapids, MN 55433
Phone: (763)712-2400
Community newspaper (tabloid). **Freq:** Weekly (Thurs.). **Print Method:** Offset. **Cols./Page:** 4. **Col. Width:** 2 1/2 inches. **Col. Depth:** 15 inches. **Key Personnel:** Peggy Bakken, Executive Editor, phone: (952)392-6822. **Subscription Rates:** $87 By mail. **URL:** http://sailor.mnsun.com. **Formerly**: Plymouth Post. **Ad Rates:** BW $1750. **Remarks:** Accepts advertising. **Circ:** (Not Reported).

COTTAGE GROVE

SE MN. Washington Co. 10 mi. SE of Saint Paul, on the Mississippi River. Residential. Manufactures chemicals, reflective & printing products. Dairy, poultry, truck farms.

18249 ■ South Washington County Bulletin
South Washington County Bulletin
7584 80th St. S
Cottage Grove, MN 55016
Phone: (651)319-4280
Fax: (651)459-9491
Publisher's E-mail: pressrelease@swcbulletin.com
Newspaper. **Freq:** Daily. **Print Method:** Offset. **Cols./Page:** 6. **Col. Width:** 24 nonpareils. **Col. Depth:** 294 agate lines. **Key Personnel:** Patricia Drey Busse, Editor; Jeff Patterson, General Manager. **Subscription Rates:** $40 Individuals local; $42 Two years local; $46 Individuals non-local; $85 Two years non-local. **URL:** http://www.swcbulletin.com. **Formerly**: Washington County Bulletin. **Remarks:** Accepts classified advertising. **Circ:** (Not Reported).

COTTONWOOD

NE MN. Lyon Co. 13 mi. NNE of Marshall.

18250 ■ Tri-County News
Tri-County News
74 W Main St.
Cottonwood, MN 56229
Phone: (507)423-6239
Fax: (507)423-6230
Publication E-mail: tcedit@mvtvwireless.com
Local newspaper. **Founded:** 1892. **Freq:** Weekly (Wed.). **Print Method:** Offset. **Trim Size:** 14 x 21. **Cols./Page:** 6. **Col. Width:** 2 1/8 inches. **Col. Depth:** 21 inches. **URL:** http://www.tricountynewsmn.net/; http://www.mnnews.com/newspapers/cottonwood.html. **Formerly**: Independent/Current/Enterprise News; Tri-County Advocate. **Mailing address:** PO Box 76, Cottonwood, MN 56229-0076. **Ad Rates:** BW $387; 4C $587; PCI $3.35. **Remarks:** Accepts advertising. **Circ:** 963.

CROOKSTON

NW MN. Polk Co. 25 mi. SE of Grand Forks, ND. Manufactures wind energy components, aluminum castings, custom drapes and quilts, agricultural fertilizers and chemicals, agricultural equipment, precast concrete items. Agriculture. Grain, sugar beets, sunflowers, potatoes, livestock, wheat.

18251 ■ Crookston Daily Times
Crookston Times Printing Co.
124 S Broadway St.
Crookston, MN 56716
Phone: (218)281-2730
General newspaper. **Founded:** 1885. **Freq:** Daily (eve.). **Print Method:** Offset. **Cols./Page:** 6. **Col. Width:** 2 1/16 inches. **Col. Depth:** 21 1/2 inches. **Key Personnel:** Randy Hultgren, Publisher; Mike Christopherson, Managing Editor; Calvin Anderson, Manager, Advertising. **Subscription Rates:** $30 By mail 3 months; $52 By mail 6 months; $90 By mail; $105 Individuals carrier. **URL:** http://www.crookstontimes.com. **Ad Rates:** GLR $1.08; BW $899.13; 4C $190; SAU $6.42. **Remarks:** Accepts advertising. **Circ:** (Not Reported).

18252 ■ KROX-AM - 1260
208 S Main St.
Crookston, MN 56716
Phone: (218)281-1140
Fax: (218)281-5036
Email: krox@rrv.net
Format: News; Sports; Information. **Networks:** NBC; Minnesota News; CNN Radio. **Founded:** 1948. **Operating Hours:** 5:30 a.m.-midnight; 10% network, 90% local. **Key Personnel:** Frank Fee, Sports Dir., Gen. Mgr., President, Sales Mgr., ffee@rrv.net; Chris Fee, Contact, chrisjfee@yahoo.com. **Wattage:** 1,000. **Ad Rates:** $6.50-10 for 30 seconds; $8.50-13.50 for 60 seconds. **URL:** http://www.kroxam.com.

CROSBY

C MN. Crow Wing Co. 15 mi. NW of Brainerd. Lake resort. Timber. Manufacturing.

18253 ■ Crosby-Ironton Courier
Crosby-Ironton Courier Inc.
12 E Main St.
Crosby, MN 56441-0067
Phone: (218)546-5029
Fax: (218)546-8352
Publication E-mail: courier@crosbyironton.net
Community newspaper. **Freq:** Weekly (Wed.). **Print Method:** Offset. **Cols./Page:** 6. **Col. Width:** 12 picas. **Col. Depth:** 21.5 inches. **Key Personnel:** Thomas M. Swensen, Publisher; Dina Richards, Editor; Krista Wynn, Advertising Representative; Lori LaBorde, Publisher. **USPS:** 138-480. **Subscription Rates:** $.75 Individuals. **URL:** http://cicourierinc.com/main.html. **Mailing address:** PO Box 67, Crosby, MN 56441-0067. **Ad Rates:** SAU $7; PCI $7. **Remarks:** Accepts advertising. **Circ:** 3728.

CROSSLAKE

18254 ■ Crosslake Communications
35910 County Road 66
Crosslake, MN 56442
Phone: (218)692-2777
Fax: (218)692-2410
Free: 800-992-8220
Email: webinfo@crosslake.net
Founded: 1960. **Formerly**: Crosslake Telephone Co. **Cities Served:** United States; 31 channels. **URL:** http://www.crosslake.net.

DAWSON

SW MN. Lac qui Parle Co. On Lac qui Parle River, 150 mi. W. of Minneapolis. Trucking. elevators; soybean-processing, feed plants. Milk and cheese processing. Ships livestock and grain. Stock, grain, poultry and dairy farms.

18255 ■ Dawson Sentinel
Sentinel
PO Box 1015
Dawson, MN 56232
Phone: (320)769-2497
Fax: (320)769-2459
Publication E-mail: dawsonsentinel@frontiernet.net
Newspaper with a Republican orientation. **Freq:** Weekly (Wed.). **Print Method:** Offset. **Cols./Page:** 6. **Col. Width:** 26 nonpareils. **Col. Depth:** 301 agate lines. **Key Personnel:** Dave C. Hickey, Managing Editor. **URL:** http://www.dawsonmn.com/business_listings/033/. **Ad Rates:** BW $325; PCI $4. **Remarks:** Accepts advertising. **Circ:** Paid ‡2,150, Free ‡15.

DEER RIVER

SC MN. Itasca Co. 14 mi. WNW of Grand Rapids.

18256 ■ Western Itasca Review
Deer River Publishing
15 First St. NE
Deer River, MN 56636
Phone: (218)246-8533
Publisher's E-mail: drpub@paulbunyan.net
Local newspaper. **Freq:** Weekly (Thurs.). **Print Method:** Tab. **Trim Size:** 10 1/4 x 16. **Cols./Page:** 6. **Col. Width:** 1 1/2 inches. **Col. Depth:** 16 inches. **Key Personnel:** Bob Barnacle, Editor. **Subscription Rates:** $3 Individuals 30 days; $15 Individuals 6 months; $25 Individuals 1 year. **URL:** http://westernitasca.com. **Formed by the merger of**: Deer River News; Itasca Progressive. **Mailing address:** PO Box 427, Deer River, MN 56636. **Ad Rates:** BW $343.68; 4C $493.68; SAU $4.64; PCI $5.56. **Remarks:** Accepts advertising. **Circ:** Combined 1,550.

DETROIT LAKES

WC MN. Becker Co. 50 mi. E. of Fargo, ND. Manufactures furnace fittings, silos, boats, sausage. Resort. Mink ranching; hatchery. Stock, dairy, truck, poultry farms. Potatoes.

18257 ■ Becker County Record
Forum Communications Co.
511 Washington Ave.

Circulation: ★ = AAM; △ or • = BPA; ♦ = CAC; ❑ = VAC; ⊕ = PO Statement; ‡ = Publisher's Report; Boldface figures = sworn; Light figures = estimated.

Detroit Lakes, MN 56501-3007
Phone: (218)847-3151
Fax: (218)847-9409
Publication E-mail: nbowe@dlnewspapers.com
Local newspaper. **Freq:** Weekly (Wed.). **Print Method:** Offset Uses mats. **Cols./Page:** 6. **Col. Width:** 25 nonpareils. **Col. Depth:** 301 agate lines. **Key Personnel:** Mary Brenk, Manager, Advertising; Nate Bowe, Editor; Viola Anderson, Manager, Circulation; Dennis Winskowski, Publisher. **URL:** http://www.dl-online.com; http://www.forumcomm.com/newspapers. **Ad Rates:** BW $1355; 4C $1680; SAU $10.50; PCI $10.50. **Remarks:** Accepts advertising. **Circ:** Free ■ **12,093**, Paid ■ **438**, Combined ■ **12,531**.

18258 ■ Detroit Lakes Tribune
Forum Communications Co.
511 Washington Ave.
Detroit Lakes, MN 56501-3007
Phone: (218)847-3151
Fax: (218)847-9409
Publication E-mail: nbowe@dlnewspapers.com
Local newspaper. **Freq:** Weekly (Sun.). **Print Method:** Offset Uses mats. **Cols./Page:** 6. **Col. Width:** 25 nonpareils. **Col. Depth:** 301 agate lines. **Key Personnel:** Nathan Bowe, Editor; Mary Brenk, Manager, Advertising; Kathy Bope, Business Manager; Viola Anderson, Manager, Circulation; Dennis Winskowski, Publisher. **Subscription Rates:** $54 Individuals Becker County; $47 Individuals 6 months; Becker County; $59 Individuals surrounding County; $47 Individuals 6 months; surrounding County; $81 Individuals inside Minnesota; $52 Individuals 6 months; inside Minnesota. **URL:** http://www.forumcomm.com/newspapers/; http://www.dl-online.com. **Ad Rates:** BW $1,355; 4C $1,680; SAU $10.50; PCI $10.50. **Remarks:** Accepts advertising. **Circ:** Paid ■ **4277**, Free ■ **10**, Combined ■ **4287**.

18259 ■ KBOT-FM - 104.1
1340 Richwood Rd.
Detroit Lakes, MN 56501
Phone: (218)847-5624
Free: 800-545-1041
Format: Adult Contemporary. **Networks:** Westwood One Radio. **Owner:** Leighton Broadcasting, 619 W St. Germain, Saint Cloud, MN 56301, Ph: (320)251-1450, Fax: (320)251-8952. **Operating Hours:** Continuous; 100% local. **Wattage:** 50,000. **Ad Rates:** $18 for 60 seconds. Combined advertising rates available with KDLM-AM. **URL:** http://www.catchthewave1041.com.

18260 ■ KDLM-AM - 1340
PO Box 746
Detroit Lakes, MN 56502
Phone: (218)847-5624
Fax: (218)847-7657
Format: Adult Contemporary; News; Information; Sports. **Networks:** CBS. **Owner:** Leighton Broadcasting, 619 W St. Germain, Saint Cloud, MN 56301, Ph: (320)251-1450, Fax: (320)251-8952. **Founded:** 1951. **Operating Hours:** Continuous; 5% network, 95% local. **ADI:** Fargo, ND. **Key Personnel:** Andy Lia, News Dir; Joel Swanson, Contact, jswansonkdlm@yahoo.com. **Wattage:** 1,000. **Ad Rates:** $12 for 30 seconds; $18 for 60 seconds. Combined advertising rates available with KBOT-FM. **URL:** http://www.1340kdlm.com.

DODGE CENTER

SE MN. Dodge Co. 20 mi. W. of Rochester. Manufactures cement trucks. Fishing tackle, corn, pea canning factories. Grain, dairy, truck farms.

18261 ■ Dodge Center Star-Record
Community News Corp.
40 W Main St.
Dodge Center, MN 55927
Phone: (507)374-6531
Fax: (507)374-9327
Publication E-mail: dcstar@kmtel.com
Newspaper with a Republican orientation. **Freq:** Weekly (Wed.). **Print Method:** Offset. **Cols./Page:** 6. **Col. Width:** 1.833 inches. **Col. Depth:** 21 inches. **Key Personnel:** Larry Dobson, Editor. **Subscription Rates:** $33 Individuals in Dodge County; $36 Individuals surrounding counties; $40 Elsewhere in Minnesota and Snowbird; $45 Elsewhere in USA; $53 Out of country. **URL:** http://www.communitynewscorp.com; http://www.mnnews.com/newspapers/dodgecenter.html. **Mailing address:** PO Box 279, Dodge Center, MN 55927. **Ad Rates:** BW $727.65; 4C $916.65; SAU $4.85; PCI $6.51. **Remarks:** Accepts advertising. **Circ:** Paid 1450, Free 50, 861.

DULUTH

NE MN. St. Louis Co. On N. end of Lake Superior, 5 mi. N. of Superior WI. University of Minnesota (at Duluth). College of Saint Scholastica. Manufacturing. Paper mill. Trade in iron ore, taconite, grain, and dairy products. Grain elevators, coal, stone, cement, and ore docks. Commercial and industrial center.

18262 ■ CSS Cable
College of St. Scholastica
1200 Kenwood Ave.
Duluth, MN 55811
Phone: (218)723-6000
Fax: (218)723-6290
Free: 800-447-5444
Publication E-mail: cable@css.edu
Collegiate magazine. **Freq:** Weekly (Fri.). **Print Method:** Offset. **Cols./Page:** 4. **Col. Width:** 24 nonpareils. **Col. Depth:** 182 agate lines. **Key Personnel:** Bailey Aro, Editor; Aaron Rose, Editor-in-Chief. **URL:** http://www.css.edu/About/The-Cable/The-Cable-News.html. **Ad Rates:** BW $260; PCI $7.50. **Remarks:** Accepts advertising. **Circ:** Controlled ‡1,000.

18263 ■ Duluth Budgeteer News
Duluth Budgeteer News
424 W 1st St.
Duluth, MN 55802
Phone: (218)723-5212
Fax: (218)727-7348
Publication E-mail: budgeteer@duluthbudgeteer.com
Local newspaper. **Freq:** Weekly (Sun.). **Print Method:** Offset. **Cols./Page:** 5. **Col. Width:** 11 picas. **Col. Depth:** 154 agate lines. **Key Personnel:** Jana Peterson, Editor; Kathleen Pennington, Manager, Sales. **Subscription Rates:** $213.20 Individuals. **URL:** http://www.duluthnewstribune.com; http://www.mnnews.com/newspapers/duluthbudg.html. **Formerly:** Budgeteer Press. **Ad Rates:** SAU $29.95. **Remarks:** Accepts display and classified advertising. **Circ:** Paid 260, Non-paid 49,500, 40,000.

18264 ■ Duluth News Tribune
Forum Communications Co.
424 W First St.
Duluth, MN 55802
Phone: (218)723-5281
Fax: (218)723-5295
Publisher's E-mail: cbursack@forumcomm.com
General newspaper. **Freq:** Daily. **Print Method:** Flexo. **Trim Size:** 13 3/4 x 22 3/4. **Cols./Page:** 6. **Col. Width:** 12 2/5 picas. **Col. Depth:** 21 inches. **Key Personnel:** Robin Washington, Editor; Ken Browall, Publisher. **USPS:** 162-180. **URL:** http://www.duluthnewstribune.com; http://www.forumcomm.com/newspapers. **Remarks:** Accepts advertising. **Circ:** Mon.-Sat. ■ **34,505**, Sun. ■ **52,757**.

18265 ■ The Duluthian
Duluth Area Chamber of Commerce
5 W 1st St., Ste. 101
Duluth, MN 55802
Phone: (218)722-5501
Fax: (218)722-3223
Publication E-mail: djohnson@duluthchamber.com
Chamber of Commerce magazine with business and community orientation. **Freq:** Bimonthly. **Print Method:** Letterpress and offset. **Trim Size:** 8 1/4 x 11. **Cols./Page:** 3. **Col. Width:** 26 nonpareils. **Col. Depth:** 140 agate lines. **ISSN:** 0012-7116 (print). **Subscription Rates:** $24 Individuals. **URL:** http://www.duluthchamber.com/publications/duluthian/. **Ad Rates:** BW $2800; 4C $1800. **Remarks:** Accepts advertising from members only. **Circ:** ‡1,800.

18266 ■ Journal of Great Lakes Research: Devoted to Research on Large Lakes of the World and Their Watersheds
International Association for Great Lakes Research
c/o Robert E. Hecky
University Minnesota Duluth Large Lakes Observatory
2005 E Fifth St.
Duluth, MN 55812-2401
Phone: (218)726-7926
Fax: (218)726-6979
Publication E-mail: editor@iaglr.org
Interdisciplinary, technical journal covering large lakes worldwide. **Freq:** Quarterly. **Print Method:** Offset. **Trim Size:** 8 1/2 x 11. **Cols./Page:** 2. **Col. Width:** 20 picas. **Col. Depth:** 53 picas. **Key Personnel:** Robert Hecky, Editor-in-Chief. **ISSN:** 0380--1330 (print). **Subscription Rates:** Included in membership; $564 Institutions online; $753 Institutions print. **Alt. Formats:** PDF. **URL:** http://iaglr.org/journal/; http://www.iaglr.org/journal/; http://www.journals.elsevier.com/journal-of-great-lakes-research. **Remarks:** Advertising not accepted. **Circ:** (Not Reported).

18267 ■ Labor World
Duluth AFL-CIO Central Labor Body
2002 London Rd.
Duluth, MN 55812
Phone: (218)728-4469
Publication E-mail: laborworld@qwestoffice.net
Labor newspaper. **Freq:** Biweekly. **Print Method:** Offset. **Trim Size:** 11 1/2 x 13 3/4. **Cols./Page:** 5. **Col. Depth:** 12 3/4 inches. **Key Personnel:** Larry Sillanpa, Editor, Manager. **ISSN:** 0023-6667 (print). **URL:** http://www.laborworld.org. **Ad Rates:** BW $511; PCI $8.70. **Remarks:** Accepts advertising. **Circ:** Paid ‡17,000.

18268 ■ Lake Superior Magazine
Lake Superior Port Cities Inc.
310 E Superior St., Ste. 125
Duluth, MN 55802-3134
Phone: (218)722-5002
Fax: (218)722-4096
Free: 888-244-5253
Consumer magazine featuring articles and photography about the Lake Superior region. **Freq:** Bimonthly. **Print Method:** Offset. **Trim Size:** 8 1/8 x 10 7/8. **Cols./Page:** 3. **Col. Width:** 13 picas. **Col. Depth:** 59 picas. **Key Personnel:** Cindy M. Hayden, Publisher; Paul Hayden, Publisher; Konnie LeMay, Editor. **ISSN:** 0890--3050 (print). **Subscription Rates:** $24.95 Individuals; $36.95 Canada; $54.95 Other countries; $4.95 Single issue. **URL:** http://www.lakesuperior.com. **Mailing address:** PO Box 16417, Duluth, MN 55802-3134. **Remarks:** Advertising accepted; rates available upon request. **Circ:** (Not Reported).

18269 ■ New Moon Girls
New Moon Girl Media, Inc.
PO Box 161287
Duluth, MN 55816
Phone: (218)878-9673
Free: 800-381-4743
Publisher's E-mail: newmoon@newmoon.com
Magazine edited by and directed toward girls aged 8-14. **Freq:** Bimonthly. **Key Personnel:** Nancy Gruver, Founder, Chief Executive Officer, Publisher; Celanie Polanick, Associate Publisher; Helen Cordes, Executive Editor; Megan Fischer-Prins, Editor. **ISSN:** 1943--488X (print); **EISSN:** 2161--914X (electronic). **Subscription Rates:** $40.95 Individuals one year; print only; $35.95 Individuals one year renewal; print only; C$44.95 Individuals one year; print only; $49.95 Other countries one year; print only; $55.99 Individuals one year; print + online; C$59.99 Individuals one year; print + online; $64.99 Other countries one year; print + online; $49.99 Individuals one year; e-magazine + online; $34.95 Individuals one year; e-magazine only; $25.99 Individuals one year; online only; $2.99 Individuals one year; adult membership. **URL:** http://newmoon.com/girls-world-magazine-new-moon-girls. **Formerly:** New Moon: The Magazine for Girls and Their Dreams. **Remarks:** Advertising not accepted. **Circ:** (Not Reported).

18270 ■ The Roaring Muse
University of Minnesota Duluth Literary Guild
410 Humanities Bldg.
10 University Dr.
Duluth, MN 55812
Magazine containing poetry, prose, short stories and artwork from students of the University of Minnesota. **Freq:** Annual. **Subscription Rates:** $3 Individuals. **Remarks:** Accepts advertising. **Circ:** (Not Reported).

18271 ■ TIMES
College of St. Scholastica Alumni Association
Tower Hall 1410
1200 Kenwood Ave.
Duluth, MN 55811-4199

Phone: (218)723-6071
Free: 866-935-3731
Publisher's E-mail: alumni@css.edu
Magazine featuring news about College of St. Scholastica, as well as programs, events, activities and accomplishments of St. Scholastica alumni. **Freq:** 3/year. **Subscription Rates:** Free. **Alt. Formats:** PDF. **Remarks:** Advertising not accepted. **Circ:** 15000.

18272 ■ UMD Statesman
University of Minnesota Duluth
1049 University Dr.
Duluth, MN 55812
Phone: (218)726-8000
Publisher's E-mail: kirby@d.umn.edu
Collegiate newspaper. **Freq:** Weekly during the academic year except for holidays and exam weeks. **Print Method:** Offset. **Cols./Page:** 5. **Col. Width:** 24 nonpareils. **Col. Depth:** 210 agate lines. **Key Personnel:** Manda Lillie, Editor-in-Chief; Brad Bedford, Business Manager; Aly Klein, Manager, Advertising. **USPS:** 647-340. **Subscription Rates:** $18 Individuals semester. **URL:** http://umdstatesman.wp.d.umn.edu. **Ad Rates:** BW $367.50; PCI $5. **Remarks:** Accepts advertising. **Circ:** 6,000.

18273 ■ KBJR-TV - 6
246 S Lake Ave.
Duluth, MN 55802
Phone: (218)720-9600
Fax: (218)720-9699
Format: Commercial TV. **Networks:** NBC. **Owner:** Granite Broadcasting Corp., 767 3rd Ave., 34th Fl., New York, NY 10017-2083, Ph: (212)826-2530, Fax: (212)826-2858. **Founded:** 1954. **Formerly:** WDSM-TV. **Operating Hours:** Continuous. **ADI:** Duluth, MN-Superior, WI. **Wattage:** 100,000 ERP. **Ad Rates:** Advertising accepted; rates available upon request. **URL:** http://www.northlandsnewscenter.com.

18274 ■ KBMX-FM - 107.7
14 E Central Entrance
Duluth, MN 55811
Phone: (218)727-4500
Format: Adult Contemporary. **Owner:** Gapwest Broadcasting, 4300 N Miller Rd., Ste. 116, Scottsdale, AZ 85251, Ph: (480)970-1360, Fax: (480)423-6966. **Key Personnel:** Dan Hanger, Contact, danhanger@gapbroadcasting.com. **Ad Rates:** Noncommercial. **URL:** http://mix108.com/.

18275 ■ KDAL-AM - 610
11 E Superior St., Ste. 380
Duluth, MN 55802
Phone: (218)722-4321
Fax: (218)722-5423
Email: streaming@kdal610.com
Format: News; Sports; Talk. **Owner:** Midwest Communications Inc., 904 Grand Ave., Wausau, WI 54403, Ph: (715)842-1437, Fax: (715)842-7061. **Operating Hours:** Continuous. **ADI:** Duluth, MN-Superior, WI. **Wattage:** 5,000. **Ad Rates:** Advertising accepted; rates available upon request. **URL:** http://www.kdal610.com.

18276 ■ KDAL-FM - 95.7
715 E Central Entrance
Duluth, MN 55811
Phone: (218)722-4321
Fax: (218)722-5423
Format: Album-Oriented Rock (AOR); Alternative/New Music/Progressive. **Networks:** Independent. **Owner:** Midwest Communications Inc., 904 Grand Ave., Wausau, WI 54403, Ph: (715)842-1437, Fax: (715)842-7061. **Founded:** 1989. **Operating Hours:** Continuous. **ADI:** Duluth, MN-Superior, WI. **Wattage:** 100,000. **Ad Rates:** Advertising accepted; rates available upon request. **URL:** http://www.my957.com.

18277 ■ KDLH-TV - 3
246 S Lake Ave.
Duluth, MN 55802
Phone: (218)720-9600
Fax: (218)720-9699
Format: Commercial TV. **Networks:** CBS. **Owner:** Granite Broadcasting Corp., 767 3rd Ave., 34th Fl., New York, NY 10017-2083, Ph: (212)826-2530, Fax: (212)826-2858. **Founded:** 1954. **Formerly:** KDAL-TV. **Operating Hours:** Continuous; 70% network, 30% local. **ADI:** Duluth, MN-Superior, WI. **Ad Rates:** Noncommercial. **URL:** http://www.northlandsnewscenter.com.

18278 ■ KDNI-FM - 90.5
1101 E Central Entrance
Duluth, MN 55811
Format: Religious. **Owner:** Northwestern College Radio. **Key Personnel:** Scott Michaels, Gen. Mgr. **Ad Rates:** Noncommercial. **URL:** http://www.radio.net.

18279 ■ KDNW-FM - 97.3
1101 E Central Entrance
Duluth, MN 55811
Phone: (218)722-6700
Fax: (218)722-1092
Free: 888-720-9730
Format: Contemporary Christian. **Networks:** AP. **Owner:** University of Northwestern - St. Paul, 3003 N Snelling Ave., Saint Paul, MN 55113-1598, Ph: (651)631-5100, Free: 800-692-4020. **Founded:** 1983. **Operating Hours:** Continuous; 5% network, 80% local, 15% syndicated. **ADI:** Duluth, MN-Superior, WI. **Wattage:** 72,000. **Ad Rates:** Noncommercial. **URL:** http://www.life973.com.

18280 ■ KDWZ-FM - 102.5
715 Central Entrance
Duluth, MN 55811
Phone: (218)723-2327
Fax: (218)722-5423
Format: Adult Contemporary; Contemporary Hit Radio (CHR); Classic Rock. **Owner:** Midwest Communications Inc., 904 Grand Ave., Wausau, WI 54403, Ph: (715)842-1437, Fax: (715)842-7061. **Founded:** 1979. **Formerly:** KRBR-FM; KZIO. **Operating Hours:** Continuous. **Key Personnel:** Duke Wright, CEO, President; Deb Messer, Gen. Mgr. **Wattage:** 100,000. **Ad Rates:** Advertising accepted; rates available upon request. **URL:** http://www.1025kdwz.com.

18281 ■ KKCB-FM - 105.1
14 E Central Entrance
Duluth, MN 55811
Phone: (218)727-4500
Format: Country. **Owner:** Townsquare Media Inc., 240 Greenwich Ave., Greenwich, CT 06830-6507, Ph: (203)861-0900. **ADI:** Duluth, MN-Superior, WI. **Wattage:** 100,000. **Ad Rates:** Advertising accepted; rates available upon request. **URL:** http://kkcb.com.

18282 ■ KLDJ-FM - 101.7
8480 E Orchard Rd., Ste. 1300
Greenwood Village, CO 80111
Phone: (303)773-9378
Fax: (303)221-4794
Format: Oldies. **Owner:** Gapwest Broadcasting, at above address. **ADI:** Duluth, MN-Superior, WI. **Wattage:** 18,500. **Ad Rates:** Noncommercial.

18283 ■ KQDS-FM - 94.9
2001 London Rd.
Duluth, MN 55812
Phone: (218)724-7625
Format: Classic Rock. **Founded:** 1976. **ADI:** Duluth, MN-Superior, WI. **Wattage:** 100,000 ERP. **Ad Rates:** Advertising accepted; rates available upon request. **URL:** http://www.95kqds.com/.

18284 ■ KQDS-TV - 21
2001 London Rd.
Duluth, MN 55812
Fax: (218)728-8932
Founded: 1994. **Key Personnel:** Greg Chandler, Sports Dir. **URL:** http://www.fox21online.com.

18285 ■ KTCO-FM - 98.9
715 E Central Entrance
Duluth, MN 55811
Phone: (218)722-4321
Fax: (218)722-5423
Format: Country. **ADI:** Duluth, MN-Superior, WI. **Wattage:** 100,000. **Ad Rates:** Noncommercial. **URL:** http://www.katcountry989.com.

18286 ■ KUMD-FM - 103.3
130 Humanities Bldg.
1201 Ordean Ct.
Duluth, MN 55812
Phone: (218)726-7181
Fax: (218)726-6571
Free: 800-566-KUMD
Email: kumd@kumd.org
Format: Public Radio; Eclectic. **Networks:** Public Radio International (PRI). **Owner:** Regents of the University of Minnesota, 100 Church St. SE, Minneapolis, MN 55455. **Founded:** 1956. **Operating Hours:** 5 am-3 am weekdays; 6 am-3 am Saturday and Sunday; 20% network, 80% local. **ADI:** Duluth, MN-Superior, WI. **Key Personnel:** Vicki Jacoba, Station Mgr., vjacoba@d.umn.edu; Christine Dean, Music Dir., cdean@d.umn.edu. **Wattage:** 95,000. **Ad Rates:** Noncommercial. **URL:** http://www.kumd.org.

18287 ■ WAKX-FM - 98.9
11 E Superior St., Ste. 380
Duluth, MN 55802
Phone: (218)722-4321
Fax: (218)722-5423
Format: Classic Rock; News; Sports. **Networks:** ABC; Fox; NBC. **Founded:** 1972. **Operating Hours:** Continuous. **ADI:** Duluth, MN-Superior, WI. **Key Personnel:** Rick Hencley, Contact; Lewis Latto, President; Mike Cushman, Operations Mgr; Rick Hencley, Contact. **Wattage:** 100,000 ERP. **Ad Rates:** $16-72 for 30 seconds; $20-90 for 60 seconds. **URL:** http://katcountry989.com.

18288 ■ WDIO-TV - 10
Ten Observation Rd.
Duluth, MN 55811
Phone: (218)727-6864
Fax: (218)727-4415
Free: 800-477-1013
Email: wdio_engineers@wdio.com
Format: Commercial TV. **Networks:** ABC. **Owner:** Hubbard Broadcasting Inc., 3415 University Ave., Saint Paul, MN 55114-2099, Ph: (651)646-5555, Fax: (651)642-4172. **Founded:** 1966. **Operating Hours:** 5 a.m.-1 a.m.; 80% network, 20% local. **ADI:** Duluth, MN-Superior, WI. **Wattage:** 316,000. **Ad Rates:** Advertising accepted; rates available upon request. **Mailing address:** PO Box 16897, Duluth, MN 55811. **URL:** http://www.wdio.com.

18289 ■ WDSE-TV - 8
632 Niagara Ct.
Duluth, MN 55811-3098
Phone: (218)788-2831
Fax: (218)788-2832
Free: 888-563-9373
Email: email@wdse.org
Format: Educational. **Networks:** Public Broadcasting Service (PBS). **Owner:** Duluth-Superior Educational Television Corp., at above address, Duluth, MN 55811. **Founded:** 1964. **Operating Hours:** Continuous. **Key Personnel:** Allen D. Harmon, Gen. Mgr. **Wattage:** 316,000. **Ad Rates:** Underwriting available. **URL:** http://www.wdse.org.

18290 ■ WDSM-AM - 710
11 E Superior St., Ste. 380
Duluth, MN 55802
Phone: (218)722-4321
Fax: (218)722-5423
Format: Talk. **Owner:** Midwest Communications Inc., 904 Grand Ave., Wausau, WI 54403, Ph: (715)842-1437, Fax: (715)842-7061. **Founded:** 1939. **Operating Hours:** Continuous. **Wattage:** 10,000 Day ; 5,000 N. **Ad Rates:** Advertising accepted; rates available upon request. **URL:** http://www.wdsm710.com.

18291 ■ WEBC-AM - 560
14 E Central Entrance
Duluth, MN 55811
Phone: (218)727-4500
Format: Sports. **Networks:** ABC; NBC; Talknet. **Owner:** Townsquare Media Inc., 240 Greenwich Ave., Greenwich, CT 06830-6507, Ph: (203)861-0900. **Founded:** 1924. **Operating Hours:** Continuous; 75% network, 25% local. **ADI:** Duluth, MN-Superior, WI. **Key Personnel:** Eric Larson, Dir. of Programs, ericlarson@townsquaremedia.com; Merry Wallin, Gen. Mgr., merrywallin@townsquaremedia.com. **Wattage:** 5,000. **Ad Rates:** Noncommercial. **URL:** http://webc560.com.

18292 ■ WGGL-FM - 91.1
207 W Superior St., Ste. 224
Duluth, MN 55802
Phone: (218)722-9411
Fax: (218)720-4900
Format: Classical; News. **Networks:** American Public Radio (APR); National Public Radio (NPR); Minnesota

Circulation: ★ = AAM; △ or • = BPA; ♦ = CAC; ❏ = VAC; ⊕ = PO Statement; ‡ = Publisher's Report; Boldface figures = sworn; Light figures = estimated.

Public Radio; Public Radio International (PRI). **Owner:** Minnesota Public Radio Inc., 480 Cedar St., Saint Paul, MN 55101, Ph: (651)290-1500, Free: 800-228-7123. **Founded:** Feb. 1982. **Operating Hours:** Continuous. **Key Personnel:** Patty Mester, Regional Mgr., pmester@mpr.org; Cathy Nevanen, Contact, cnevanen@mpr.org. **Wattage:** 100,000. **Ad Rates:** Noncommercial. **URL:** http://www.minnesota.publicradio.org.

18293 ■ WIRN-FM - 92.5
207 W Superior St., No. 224
Duluth, MN 55802
Phone: (218)722-9411
Fax: (218)720-4900
Format: News. **Owner:** Minnesota Public Radio Inc., 480 Cedar St., Saint Paul, MN 55101, Ph: (651)290-1500, Free: 800-228-7123. **Founded:** 1993. **Operating Hours:** Continuous. **Wattage:** 26,000. **Ad Rates:** Noncommercial; underwriting available. **URL:** http://www.minnesota.publicradio.org/radio/stations/wirnwirr.

18294 ■ WIRR-FM - 90.9
207 W Superior St. 224
Duluth, MN 55802
Phone: (218)722-9411
Format: Classical. **Networks:** Minnesota Public Radio. **Owner:** Minnesota Public Radio Inc., 480 Cedar St., Saint Paul, MN 55101, Ph: (651)290-1500, Free: 800-228-7123. **Founded:** 1985. **Operating Hours:** Continuous. **Key Personnel:** Peggy Mester, Regional Mgr., pmester@mpr.org; Bob Kelleher, Bur. Chief, bkelleher@mpr.org. **Wattage:** 21,000. **Ad Rates:** Noncommercial; underwriting available. **URL:** http://www.minnesota.publicradio.org/radio/stations/wirnwirr.

WIRT-TV - See Hibbing

18295 ■ WJRF-FM - 89.5
4604 Airpark Blvd.
Duluth, MN 55811
Phone: (218)722-2727
Email: info@refugeradio.com
Format: Contemporary Christian. **Owner:** Refuge Media Group, 6843 Washington Ave. S, Edina, MN 55439, Ph: (952)288-2886. **URL:** http://www.refugeradio.com.

18296 ■ WLSN-FM - 89.7
207 W Superior St., Ste. 224
Duluth, MN 55802
Phone: (218)722-9411
Fax: (218)720-4900
Email: pmester@mpr.org
Format: News; Talk. **Networks:** National Public Radio (NPR). **Owner:** Minnesota Public Radio Inc., 480 Cedar St., Saint Paul, MN 55101, Ph: (651)290-1500, Free: 800-228-7123. **Founded:** Sept. 2001. **Wattage:** 6,000. **URL:** http://www.mpr.org/listen/stations/wlsnwmls.

18297 ■ WMLS-FM - 88.7
207 W Superior St., No. 224
Duluth, MN 55802
Phone: (218)722-9411
Fax: (218)720-4900
Format: Classical. **Owner:** Minnesota Public Radio Inc., 480 Cedar St., Saint Paul, MN 55101, Ph: (651)290-1500, Free: 800-228-7123. **Operating Hours:** Continuous. **Wattage:** 6,000. **Ad Rates:** Noncommercial; underwriting available. **URL:** http://www.minnesota.publicradio.org/radio/stations/wlsnwmls.

18298 ■ WSCD-FM - 92.9
207 W Superior St., No. 224
Duluth, MN 55802
Phone: (218)722-9411
Fax: (218)720-4900
Format: Classical. **Networks:** Minnesota Public Radio. **Owner:** Minnesota Public Radio Inc., 480 Cedar St., Saint Paul, MN 55101, Ph: (651)290-1500, Free: 800-228-7123. **Founded:** 1975. **Operating Hours:** Continuous. **Wattage:** 70,000. **Ad Rates:** Noncommercial. **URL:** http://www.minnesota.publicradio.org.

18299 ■ WSCN-FM - 100.5
207 W Superior St., No. 224
Duluth, MN 55802
Phone: (218)722-9411
Fax: (218)720-4900
Format: News. **Owner:** Minnesota Public Radio Inc., 480 Cedar St., Saint Paul, MN 55101, Ph: (651)290-1500, Free: 800-228-7123. **Founded:** Nov. 1988. **Operating Hours:** Continuous. **Wattage:** 100,000. **Ad Rates:** Noncommercial; underwriting available. **URL:** http://www.minnesota.publicradio.org/radio/stations/wscnwscd.

18300 ■ WWAX-FM - 92.1
501 Lake Ave. S, Ste. 200
Duluth, MN 55802
Phone: (218)728-9500
Email: thebeat921@redrockradio.org
Format: Top 40. **Key Personnel:** Chris Postal, Promotions Dir., chris@921kissfm.com; Paul Jirovetz, Operations Mgr., paul@921kissfm.com; Michael Wilde, Music Dir., michael@921kissfm.com. **Wattage:** 5,400. **URL:** http://921thefan.com.

18301 ■ WWJC-AM - 850
1120 E McCuen St.
Duluth, MN 55808
Phone: (218)626-2738
Fax: (603)907-7881
Free: 877-626-2738
Format: Religious. **Networks:** USA Radio; International Broadcasting. **Owner:** WWJC Inc. **Founded:** 1963. **Operating Hours:** Sunrise-sunset. **ADI:** Duluth, MN-Superior, WI. **Key Personnel:** Ted Elm, Contact. **Wattage:** 10,000. **Ad Rates:** $3.25-6 for 30 seconds; $4.50-7.50 for 60 seconds.

DUNDAS

18302 ■ Dime Novel Roundup
Dime Novel Roundup
PO Box 226
Dundas, MN 55019-0226
Magazine devoted to the collecting, preservation and study of old-time dime and nickel novels, popular story papers, series books, and pulp magazines. **Founded:** Jan. 1931. **Freq:** Quarterly. **Print Method:** Offset. **Trim Size:** 5 1/2 x 8 1/2. **Cols./Page:** 1. **Col. Width:** 54 nonpareils. **Col. Depth:** 105 nonpareils. **Key Personnel:** J. Randolph Cox, Editor. **ISSN:** 0012-2874 (print). **Subscription Rates:** $20 Individuals; $4 Single issue; $35 Two years. **URL:** http://www.readseries.com/dnru.html. **Ad Rates:** BW $25; PCI $4. **Remarks:** Color advertising not accepted. **Circ:** ‡250.

EAGAN

Dakota Co.

18303 ■ Quirk's Marketing Research Review
Quirk Enterprises Inc.
4662 Slater Rd.
Eagan, MN 55122
Phone: (651)379-6200
Publisher's E-mail: info@quirks.com
Trade publication for the marketing research industry. **Freq:** Monthly. **Print Method:** Web. **Trim Size:** 8 x 10 7/8. **Cols./Page:** 2 and 3. **Col. Width:** 3 1/2 and 2 9/16 inches. **Col. Depth:** 10 inches. **Key Personnel:** Joseph Rydholm, Editor; Evan Tweed, Vice President, Sales; Steve Quirk, President, Publisher. **ISSN:** 0893-7451 (print). **URL:** http://www.quirks.com. **Ad Rates:** BW $2,535; 4C $3,460; PCI $125. **Remarks:** Accepts advertising. **Circ:** Non-paid 16000.

18304 ■ The Voice of Agriculture
Minnesota Farm Bureau Federation
3080 Eagandale Pl.
Eagan, MN 55121
Phone: (651)768-2100
Fax: (651)768-2159
Publisher's E-mail: info@fbmn.org
Publication reporting on Minnesota's agricultural industry. **Founded:** 1917. **Freq:** Bimonthly January, March, May, July, September and November. **Print Method:** Offset. **Trim Size:** 11 3/8 x 15. **Cols./Page:** 5. **Col. Width:** 2 1/2 inches. **Col. Depth:** 14 inches. **Key Personnel:** Kristin Harner, Editor, phone: (651)768-2100. **ISSN:** 1529-1669 (print). **USPS:** 668-410. **Subscription Rates:** Included in membership. **URL:** http://www.fbmn.org/pages/the-voice-of-agriculture. **Mailing address:** PO Box 64370, Saint Paul, MN 55164. **Ad Rates:** GLR $36.75; BW $2,848; 4C $3,498; PCI $50. **Circ:** Paid 30000.

18305 ■ KKMS-AM - 980
2110 Cliff Rd.
Eagan, MN 55122
Phone: (651)405-8800
Fax: (651)405-8222
Email: comments@kkms.com
Format: Religious; Talk. **Owner:** Salem Media Group Inc., 4880 Santa Rosa Rd., Camarillo, CA 93012, Ph: (805)987-0400, Fax: (805)384-4520. **Key Personnel:** Ross Brendel, Promotions Dir.; Laurie Krier, Bus. Mgr.; Smit Steve, Chief Engineer; Lee Michaels, Operations Mgr., leemichaels@salemtc.com; Nic Anderson, Gen. Sales Mgr. **Ad Rates:** Advertising accepted; rates available upon request. **URL:** http://www.kkms.com.

18306 ■ KYCR-AM - 1440
2110 Cliff Rd.
Eagan, MN 55122
Phone: (651)405-8800
Email: comments@business1570.com
Format: News; Sports; Talk. **Owner:** Salem Media Group Inc., 4880 Santa Rosa Rd., Camarillo, CA 93012, Ph: (805)987-0400, Fax: (805)384-4520. **Founded:** 1963. **Operating Hours:** Continuous. **Key Personnel:** Nic Anderson, Gen. Mgr.; Laurie Krier, Contact, lauriekrier@salemtc.com. **Wattage:** 5,000 Day 500 Night. **URL:** http://www.twincitiesbusinessradio.com.

18307 ■ WWTC-AM - 1280
2110 Cliff Rd.
Eagan, MN 55122
Phone: (651)405-8800
Fax: (651)405-8222
Email: comments@am1280thepatriot.com
Format: Talk. **Owner:** Salem Media Group Inc., 4880 Santa Rosa Rd., Camarillo, CA 93012, Ph: (805)987-0400, Fax: (805)384-4520. **Founded:** 1931. **Operating Hours:** Continuous. **ADI:** Minneapolis-St. Paul, MN. **Key Personnel:** Nic Anderson, Gen. Mgr., nicanderson@salemtc.com; Lee Michaels, Operations Mgr.; Ross Brendel, Div. Dir.; Laurie Krier, Bus. Mgr.; Mike Murphy, Sales Mgr. **Wattage:** 5,000. **Ad Rates:** Advertising accepted; rates available upon request. **URL:** http://www.am1280thepatriot.com.

EAST GRAND FORKS

NW MN. Polk Co. 80 mi. directly N. of Fargo, ND. Beet sugar refinery. Manufactures sugar, potato chips. Agriculture. Wheat, potatoes, barley.

18308 ■ Exponent
Exponent
406 Third St.
East Grand Forks, MN 56721
Phone: (218)773-2808
Fax: (218)773-9212
Publisher's E-mail: exponent@rrv.net
Community newspaper. **Founded:** July 11, 1979. **Freq:** Weekly (Wed.). **Print Method:** Offset. **Cols./Page:** 6. **Col. Width:** 12 picas. **Col. Depth:** 21.5 inches. **Key Personnel:** Missy Thompson, Office Manager; Jordan Meyer, Editor. **USPS:** 490-890. **Subscription Rates:** $33 Individuals print; in Polk County; $41 Individuals print; elsewhere in Minnesota or North Dakota; $42 Individuals print; elsewhere in USA; $43 Individuals print and online; in Polk County; $51 Individuals print and online; elsewhere in Minnesota or North Dakota; $52 Individuals print and online; elsewhere in USA; $22 Individuals online. **URL:** http://www.page1publications.com/v2/content.aspx?ID=20866&MemberID=1811. **Mailing address:** PO Box 285, East Grand Forks, MN 56721. **Ad Rates:** BW $378; SAU $4.75; PCI $4.75. **Remarks:** Accepts advertising. **Circ:** ‡2,300.

EDEN PRAIRIE

SEC MN ST MN. Hennepin Co Hennepin Co. SW of Minneapolis 15 mi. SW of Minneapolis. Residential.

18309 ■ ATEA Journal
American Technical Education Association
General Marketing Solutions GMS
7500 Golden Triangle
Eden Prairie, MN 55344
Publication E-mail: nrazek@udayton.edu
Magazine of the American Technical Education Association; includes book reviews and employment opportunities. **Freq:** Semiannual. **Key Personnel:** Nasser Razek, Editor; Sandra Krebsbach, Managing Editor. **ISSN:** 0889--6488 (print). **Subscription Rates:** Included in membership. **URL:** http://www.ateaonline.org/ATEAJournalGuidelines. **Remarks:** Accepts advertising. **Circ:** 2000.

18310 ■ Bloomington Sun Current
Minnesota Sun Publications
10917 Valley View Rd.
Eden Prairie, MN 55344
Phone: (952)829-0797
Fax: (952)392-6888
Community newspaper (tabloid). **Freq:** Weekly (Wed.). **Print Method:** Offset. **Cols./Page:** 4. **Col. Width:** 2 1/2 inches. **Col. Depth:** 15 inches. **Key Personnel:** Peggy Bakken, Executive Editor, phone: (763)424-7373; Dennis Thomsen, Account Manager, phone: (952)392-6878; Sylvia Fitzsimmons, Manager, Circulation, phone: (763)424-7370, fax: (763)424-7396; Pam Miller, Manager, Advertising, phone: (952)392-6862; Jeff Coolman, Publisher, phone: (952)392-6807; Gene Carr, Chief Executive Officer, phone: (952)392-6851. **URL:** http://current.mnsun.com. **Remarks:** Accepts advertising. **Circ:** ♦**24711**.

18311 ■ Brooklyn Center Sun-Post
Minnesota Sun Publications
10917 Valley View Rd.
Eden Prairie, MN 55344
Phone: (952)829-0797
Fax: (952)392-6888
Community newspaper. **Freq:** Weekly (Thurs.). **Print Method:** Offset. **Cols./Page:** 4. **Col. Width:** 2 1/2 inches. **Col. Depth:** 15 inches. **Key Personnel:** Dick Hendrickson, Chief Financial Officer, phone: (952)392-6854; Mike Erickson, Manager, Production, phone: (952)392-6830; Peggy Bakken, Executive Editor, phone: (763)424-7373; Jeff Coolman, Publisher, phone: (952)392-6807. **URL:** http://post.mnsun.com/tag/brooklyn-center; http://www.mnnews.com/newspapers/brooklyncenter.html. **Remarks:** Accepts advertising. **Circ:** ♦**26525**.

18312 ■ Brooklyn Park Sun-Post
Minnesota Sun Publications
10917 Valley View Rd.
Eden Prairie, MN 55344
Phone: (952)829-0797
Fax: (952)392-6888
Community newspaper (tabloid). **Freq:** Weekly. **Print Method:** Offset. **Cols./Page:** 4. **Col. Width:** 2 1/2 inches. **Col. Depth:** 15 inches. **Key Personnel:** Sylvia Fitzsimmons, Manager, Circulation; Dick Hendrickson, Chief Financial Officer, Chief Operating Officer, phone: (952)392-6854; Peggy Bakken, Executive Editor, phone: (952)392-6822. **Subscription Rates:** $87 By mail anywhere in the U.S. **Remarks:** Accepts advertising. **Circ:** Paid 513, Non-paid 19170.

18313 ■ Eden Prairie News
Southwest Suburban Publishing
PO Box 44220
Eden Prairie, MN 55344
Phone: (952)934-5045
Fax: (952)934-7960
Community newspaper. **Freq:** Weekly (Thurs.). **Print Method:** Offset. **Cols./Page:** 6. **Col. Width:** 2 inches. **Col. Depth:** 21 inches. **Key Personnel:** Mark Weber, Publisher. **Subscription Rates:** $37 Individuals print + online; $50 Out of area /year (print + online); $90 Out of area 2 years (print + online). **URL:** http://www.swnewsmedia.com/eden_prairie_news. **Remarks:** Advertising accepted; rates available upon request. **Circ:** (Not Reported).

18314 ■ Eden Prairie Sun Current
Minnesota Sun Publications
10917 Valley View Rd.
Eden Prairie, MN 55344
Phone: (952)829-0797
Fax: (952)392-6888
Community newspaper (tabloid). **Freq:** Weekly. **Print Method:** Offset. **Cols./Page:** 5. **Col. Width:** 1 15/16 INS. **Col. Depth:** 16 inches. **Key Personnel:** Pam Miller, Manager, Advertising, phone: (952)392-6862; Sylvia Fitzsimmons, Manager, Circulation, phone: (763)424-7370, fax: (763)424-7396; Peggy Bakken, Executive Editor, phone: (952)392-6822; Dick Hendrickson, Chief Financial Officer, Chief Operating Officer, phone: (952)392-6854. **Subscription Rates:** $87 By mail anywhere in the U.S. **URL:** http://current.mnsun.com/tag/eden-prairie/. **Formerly:** Sun Prarie Sailor. **Remarks:** Accepts advertising. **Circ:** Combined 14,461.

18315 ■ Edina Sun Current
Minnesota Sun Publications
10917 Valley View Rd.
Eden Prairie, MN 55344
Phone: (952)829-0797
Fax: (952)392-6888
Community newspaper (tabloid). **Freq:** Weekly (Thurs.). **Print Method:** Offset. **Cols./Page:** 4. **Col. Width:** 2 1/2 inches. **Col. Depth:** 15 inches. **Key Personnel:** Pam Miller, Manager, Advertising, phone: (952)392-6862; Jeff Coolman, Publisher, phone: (952)392-6807; Dennis Thomsen, Account Manager, phone: (952)392-6878; Mike Erickson, Manager, Production, phone: (952)392-6830; Dick Hendrickson, Chief Financial Officer, Chief Operating Officer, phone: (952)392-6854; Peggy Bakken, Executive Editor, phone: (952)392-6822. **Subscription Rates:** $87 By mail. **URL:** http://current.mnsun.com/tag/edina/. **Remarks:** Accepts advertising. **Circ:** Paid 16668, Non-paid 17301.

18316 ■ Excelsior/Shorewood/Chanhassen Sun-Sailor
Minnesota Sun Publications
10917 Valley View Rd.
Eden Prairie, MN 55344
Phone: (952)829-0797
Fax: (952)392-6888
Community newspaper (tabloid). **Freq:** Weekly (Thurs.). **Print Method:** Offset. **Cols./Page:** 4. **Col. Width:** 2 1/2 inches. **Col. Depth:** 15 inches. **Key Personnel:** Dick Hendrickson, Chief Financial Officer, Chief Operating Officer, phone: (952)392-6854; Peggy Bakken, Executive Editor, phone: (952)392-6822; Mike Erickson, Manager, Production, phone: (952)392-6830. **Subscription Rates:** $87 By mail anywhere in the U.S. **URL:** http://sailor.mnsun.com/tag/excelsior/. **Ad Rates:** PCI $11.50. **Remarks:** Accepts advertising. **Circ:** 5,990.

18317 ■ Hopkins/East Minnetonka Sailor-Sun
Minnesota Sun Publications
10917 Valley View Rd.
Eden Prairie, MN 55344
Phone: (952)829-0797
Fax: (952)392-6888
Community newspaper (tabloid). **Freq:** Weekly. **Print Method:** Offset. **Cols./Page:** 5. **Col. Width:** 1 15/16 inches. **Col. Depth:** 16 inches. **Key Personnel:** Peggy Bakken, Executive Editor, phone: (952)392-6822; Dick Hendrickson, Chief Financial Officer, Chief Operating Officer, phone: (952)392-6854. **Subscription Rates:** $87 By mail anywhere in the U.S. **URL:** http://sailor.mnsun.com/tag/hopkins; http://sailor.mnsun.com/tag/minnetonka. **Ad Rates:** PCI $20.50. **Remarks:** Accepts advertising. **Circ:** 17,556.

18318 ■ Let's Play Hockey
Let's Play Inc.
8925 Aztec Dr., Ste. 1
Eden Prairie, MN 55347
Publication E-mail: letsplay@letsplayhockey.com
Consumer publication covering all levels of hockey in the U.S. **Freq:** 29/yr, weekly during season and monthly off-season. **Print Method:** Cold Web offset. **Trim Size:** 10 7/8 x 16 1/2. **Cols./Page:** 4. **Col. Width:** 2 3/8 inches. **Col. Depth:** 16 inches. **Key Personnel:** Kevin Kurtt, Editor; Linda Johnson, Associate Publisher; Doug Johnson, Publisher. **ISSN:** 0889--4795 (print). **Subscription Rates:** $58 Individuals; $99 Two years; $105 Individuals first class; $105 Canada. **URL:** http://www.letsplayhockey.com. **Ad Rates:** BW $1152. **Remarks:** Accepts advertising. **Circ:** (Not Reported).

18319 ■ Richfield Sun Current
Minnesota Sun Publications
10917 Valley View Rd.
Eden Prairie, MN 55344
Phone: (952)829-0797
Fax: (952)392-6888
Community newspaper (tabloid). **Freq:** Weekly (Thurs.). **Print Method:** Offset. **Cols./Page:** 4. **Col. Width:** 2 1/2 inches. **Col. Depth:** 15 inches. **Key Personnel:** Sylvia Fitzsimmons, Manager, Circulation, phone: (763)424-7370; Dick Hendrickson, Chief Financial Officer, Chief Operating Officer, phone: (952)392-6854; Peggy Bakken, Executive Editor, phone: (763)424-7373. **Subscription Rates:** $87 By mail anywhere in the U.S. **URL:** http://current.mnsun.com/tag/richfield/. **Remarks:** Advertising accepted; rates available upon request. **Circ:** Combined ♦**9586**.

18320 ■ St. Louis Park Sun-Sailor
Minnesota Sun Publications
10917 Valley View Rd.
Eden Prairie, MN 55344
Phone: (952)829-0797
Fax: (952)392-6888
Community newspaper (tabloid). **Freq:** Weekly (Thurs.). **Print Method:** Offset. **Cols./Page:** 5. **Col. Width:** 1 15/16 INS. **Col. Depth:** 16 inches. **Key Personnel:** Jeff Coolman, Publisher, phone: (952)392-6807; Peggy Bakken, Executive Editor, phone: (952)392-6822; Jeremy Bradfield, Director, Advertising, phone: (952)392-6894. **Subscription Rates:** $87 By mail anywhere in the U.S.; $38.95 Individuals voluntary. **URL:** http://sailor.mnsun.com/tag/st-louis-park/. **Ad Rates:** PCI $15.50; 4C $1,633. **Remarks:** Accepts advertising. **Circ:** Combined ♦**11,228**.

18321 ■ Wayzata Sun-Sailor
Minnesota Sun Publications
10917 Valley View Rd.
Eden Prairie, MN 55344
Phone: (952)829-0797
Fax: (952)392-6888
Community newspaper (tabloid). **Freq:** Weekly (Thurs.). **Print Method:** Offset. **Cols./Page:** 5. **Col. Width:** 1 15/16 inches. **Col. Depth:** 16 inches. **Key Personnel:** Peggy Bakken, Executive Editor, phone: (952)392-6822; Dick Hendrickson, Chief Financial Officer, phone: (952)392-6854; Gene Carr, Chief Executive Officer, phone: (952)392-6851. **Subscription Rates:** $87 By mail anywhere in the U.S. **URL:** http://sailor.mnsun.com/tag/wayzata/. **Remarks:** Accepts advertising. **Circ:** 22,617.

18322 ■ KMSP-TV - 9
11358 Viking Dr.
Eden Prairie, MN 55344
Phone: (952)944-9999
Fax: (952)944-8296
Format: Commercial TV. **Networks:** United Paramount Network. **Founded:** 1955. **Operating Hours:** Continuous. **ADI:** Minneapolis-St. Paul, MN. **Key Personnel:** Chris Wright, President. **Ad Rates:** Noncommercial. **URL:** http://www.myfoxtwincities.com.

18323 ■ KTNF-AM - 950
11320 Valley View Rd.
Eden Prairie, MN 55344
Phone: (952)946-8885
Fax: (952)946-0888
Format: News; Talk. **Operating Hours:** Continuous. **Wattage:** 1,000. **Ad Rates:** Advertising accepted; rates available upon request.

EDINA

W MN. Hennepin Co. Adjoins Minneapolis on SW. Residential.

18324 ■ IPA Bulletin
IPA - Association of Graphic Solutions Providers
7200 France Ave. S, Ste. 223
Edina, MN 55435
Phone: (952)896-1908
Fax: (952)896-0181
Free: 800-255-8141
Publisher's E-mail: info@ipa.org
Freq: Bimonthly. **Subscription Rates:** Included in membership. **URL:** http://www.idealliance.org/about/our-resources/bulletin-magazine. **Remarks:** Accepts advertising. **Circ:** (Not Reported).

18325 ■ Minnesota Golfer: Official publication of the Minnesota Golf Association
Minnesota Golf Association
6550 York Ave. S, Ste. 211
Edina, MN 55435
Phone: (952)927-4643
Free: 800-642-4405
Publisher's E-mail: info@touchpointpublishing.com
Association magazine covering golf and golf related events throughout Minnesota. **Freq:** Quarterly. **Print Method:** Heat offset. **Trim Size:** 8 1/4 x 10 7/8. **Cols./Page:** 3. **Col. Width:** 2 1/4 inches. **Col. Depth:** 9 1/2 inches. **ISSN:** 1062--1105 (print). **Subscription Rates:** Included in membership. **URL:** http://www.mngolf.org/

Circulation: ★ = AAM; △ or • = BPA; ♦ = CAC; ❑ = VAC; ⊕ = PO Statement; ‡ = Publisher's Report; Boldface figures = sworn; Light figures = estimated.

Home. **Remarks:** Accepts advertising. **Circ:** (Not Reported).

ELY

NE MN. St. Louis Co. 48 mi. NE of Virginia. Lake resort. Fishing and canoe areas. Wood products.

18326 ■ Ely Echo
Milestones Inc.
15 E Chapman St.
Ely, MN 55731-1227
Phone: (218)365-3141
Fax: (218)365-3142
Free: 800-492-3555
Publication E-mail: elyecho@aol.com
Community newspaper. **Freq:** Weekly (Mon.). **Print Method:** Offset. **Trim Size:** 13 x 21 1/2. **Cols./Page:** 6. **Col. Width:** 25 nonpareils. **Col. Depth:** 298 agate lines. **Key Personnel:** Tom Coombe, Editor; Anne Swenson, Publisher; Nick Wognum, General Manager. **ISSN:** 0746-7087 (print). **Subscription Rates:** $37 Individuals; $69 Two years; $47 Out of area; $93 Two years out of area; $61 Out of country two years; $117 Two years out of country; $30 Individuals online. **URL:** http://www.elyecho.com. **Ad Rates:** BW $728.28; 4C $808.28; SAU $9.71; PCI $6. **Remarks:** Accepts advertising. **Circ:** 4,900.

18327 ■ WELY-AM - 1450
133 E Chapman
Ely, MN 55731
Phone: (218)365-4444
Fax: (218)365-3657
Format: Full Service. **Networks:** ABC; Mutual Broadcasting System; Minnesota News. **Owner:** Bois Forte Band of Chippewa, 5344 Lakeshore Dr., Nett Lake, MN 55772, Ph: (218)757-3261, Fax: (218)757-3312, Free: 800-221-8129. **Founded:** 1954. **Formerly:** WXLT-AM. **Operating Hours:** 30% network, 70% local. **Wattage:** 1,000. **Ad Rates:** $3.25-4 for 15 seconds; $5.25-6 for 30 seconds; $7.25-8.50 for 60 seconds. **URL:** http://www.wely.com.

18328 ■ WELY-FM - 94.5
133 E Chapman St.
Ely, MN 55731
Phone: (218)365-4444
Format: Talk; Full Service. **Owner:** EJL Broadcasting, at above address. **Founded:** 1992. **Wattage:** 6,000. **Ad Rates:** Noncommercial. **Mailing address:** PO Box 630, Ely, MN 55731. **URL:** http://www.wely.com.

ELYSIAN

SC MN. Waseca Co. 21 mi. E. of Mankato. Lake resort. Dairy, poultry, grain, stock farms.

18329 ■ The Elysian Enterprise
The Elysian Enterprise
PO Box 119
Elysian, MN 56028-0119
Phone: (507)267-4323
Fax: (507)362-4458
Publication E-mail: lrlife@frontiernet.net
Community newspaper. **Freq:** Weekly (Thurs.). **Print Method:** Offset. **Cols./Page:** 6. **Col. Width:** 30 nonpareils. **Col. Depth:** 301 agate lines. **Key Personnel:** Jay Schneider, Managing Editor; Chuck Wann, Owner, Publisher. **Subscription Rates:** $26 Individuals. **URL:** http://www.mnnews.com/newspapers/elysian.html. **Ad Rates:** GLR $.14; SAU $3.50. **Remarks:** Accepts advertising. **Circ:** 448.

EMILY

18330 ■ Emily Cooperative Telephone Co.
40040 State Highway 6
Emily, MN 56447
Phone: (218)763-3000
Fax: (218)763-2042
Free: 800-450-1036
Email: emilytel@emily.net
Founded: 1975. **Key Personnel:** Paul Hoges, Gen. Mgr., phoge@emily.net; Diane Andrews, Bus. Mgr., Contact; Diane Andrews, Contact. **Cities Served:** Emily, Fifty Lakes, Outing, Minnesota: subscribing households 940; United States; 23 channels; 2 community access channels. **Mailing address:** PO Box 100, Emily, MN 56447. **URL:** http://www.emily.net.

ERSKINE

NW MN. Polk Co. 58 mi. E. of Grand Forks, ND. Manufactures hay bale loaders and conveyors, snow plows, dairy products. Agriculture. Wheat, potatoes.

18331 ■ Erskine Echo
Erskine Echo
309 1st St.
Erskine, MN 56535
Phone: (218)687-3775
Fax: (218)687-3744
Publication E-mail: echonews@gvtel.com
Community newspaper. **Freq:** Weekly (Thurs.). **Print Method:** Offset. **Cols./Page:** 6. **Col. Width:** 24 nonpareils. **Col. Depth:** 301 agate lines. **Key Personnel:** Robert Hole, Editor. **USPS:** 178-580. **Subscription Rates:** $20 Individuals; $22 Out of state. **URL:** http://www.mnnews.com/newspapers/erskine.html. **Ad Rates:** SAU $3.75. **Remarks:** Accepts advertising. **Circ:** 964.

EVELETH

NE MN. St. Louis Co. 5 mi SW of Gilbert.

18332 ■ KRBT-AM - 1340
PO Box 650
Eveleth, MN 55734
Phone: (218)741-5922
Fax: (218)741-7302
Format: Talk. **Networks:** ABC. **Owner:** Lewis Latto Group, 5732 Eagle View Dr., Duluth, MN 55803. **Founded:** 1947. **Operating Hours:** Continuous. **ADI:** Duluth, MN-Superior, WI. **Wattage:** 1,000. **Ad Rates:** Advertising accepted; rates available upon request. Combined advertising rates available with WEVE-FM, KGPZ-FM. **URL:** http://radioredzone.com.

18333 ■ WEVE-FM - 97.9
PO Box 650
Eveleth, MN 55734
Phone: (218)741-5922
Format: Adult Contemporary. **Networks:** ABC. **Owner:** Lew Latto Group, Not Available. **Founded:** 1978. **Operating Hours:** Continuous. **ADI:** Duluth, MN-Superior, WI. **Key Personnel:** Dennis Jerrold, Gen. Mgr., VP, djerrold@wevefm.com; Steve Carlson, News Dir., steve@wevefm.com; Lew Latto, Owner, President. **Wattage:** 71,000. **Ad Rates:** Noncommercial. Combined advertising rates available with KRBT-AM, KGPZ-FM.

FAIRMONT

SC MN. Martin Co. 50 mi. SW of Mankato. Manfactures railway maintenance equipment, frozen and canned foods, ribbon, plastics, frozen gourmet foods, electronics, cement blocks, feed. Grain, dairy, poultry, stock farms. Lake resort.

18334 ■ Fairmont Photo Press
Fairmont Photo Press
112 E First St.
Fairmont, MN 56031
Phone: (507)238-9456
Fax: (507)238-9457
Publisher's E-mail: frontdesk@fairmontphotopress.com
Local shopper/newspaper. **Freq:** Weekly (Wed.). **Print Method:** Offset. **Trim Size:** 11 3/8 x 16. **Cols./Page:** 6. **Col. Width:** 20 nonpareils. **Col. Depth:** 213 agate lines. **Key Personnel:** Angie Jedlicka, Manager; Karen Luedtke Fisher, Chief Executive Officer, Publisher; Sherman L. Kumba, Editor. **Subscription Rates:** Free; $22.50 By mail. **URL:** http://www.fairmontphotopress.com. **Mailing address:** PO Box 973, Fairmont, MN 56031. **Ad Rates:** BW $388.88; PCI $4.25. **Remarks:** Accepts advertising. **Circ:** Free ‡11,900, 12,140.

18335 ■ Sentinel
Sentinel
64 Downtown Plz.
Fairmont, MN 56031
Phone: (507)235-3303
Fax: (507)235-3718
Free: 800-598-5597
Publication E-mail: news@fairmontsentinel.com
General newspaper. **Founded:** 1874. **Freq:** Mon.-Sat. (morn.). **Print Method:** Offset. **Cols./Page:** 6. **Col. Width:** 24 nonpareils. **Col. Depth:** 301 agate lines. **Subscription Rates:** $150.80 Individuals home delivery-carrier; Monday-Saturday; $156 Individuals home delivery-motor route; Monday-Saturday; $156 By mail Monday-Saturday; $202.80 Individuals beyond 50 mile radius. **URL:** http://www.fairmontsentinel.com/. **Mailing address:** PO Box 681, Fairmont, MN 56031. **Ad Rates:** GLR $.72; 4C $200; SAU $1,549.29; PCI $12.01. **Remarks:** Accepts advertising. **Circ:** Mon.-Sat. ★6525.

18336 ■ KFMC-FM - 106.5
1371 W Lair Rd.
Fairmont, MN 56031
Phone: (507)235-5595
Fax: (507)235-5973
Email: kfmcprod@kfmc.com
Format: News; Information; Sports. **Owner:** Woodward Broadcasting, Inc., at above address. **Founded:** 1979. **Operating Hours:** 6:35 a.m. - 5:10 p.m. **Key Personnel:** Mike Murphy, Contact. **Wattage:** 100,000. **Ad Rates:** Advertising accepted; rates available upon request. Combined advertising rates available with KSUM-AM. **URL:** http://www.kfmc.com.

18337 ■ KSUM-AM - 1370
1371 W Lair Rd.
Fairmont, MN 56031
Phone: (507)235-5595
Fax: (507)235-5973
Format: Agricultural; News; Sports; Contemporary Country; Information. **Networks:** CNN Radio. **Owner:** Woodward Broadcasting, Inc., at above address. **Founded:** 1948. **Operating Hours:** Continuous; 10% network, 90% local. **ADI:** Minneapolis-St. Paul, MN. **Key Personnel:** Rod Halverson, Sports Dir., News Dir. **Wattage:** 1,000. **Ad Rates:** $16-60 for 30 seconds; $20-70 for 60 seconds. Combined advertising rates available with KFMC-FM. **URL:** http://www.ksum.com.

FARIBAULT

SE MN. Rice Co. 53 mi. S. of Saint Paul. Resort area. Lakes. Manufactures floor trucks, ice cube making machines, air conditioners, concrete products, woolens, amusement park equipment, fabricated casings for computing machines, hoes, silos, lumber, plastic plumbing fixtures, tile, butter, blue cheese. Turkey processing and cannery plants. Foundry. Nurseries; hatchery. Stock, dairy, poultry farms.

18338 ■ News
Faribault Daily News
514 Central Ave.
Faribault, MN 55021
Phone: (507)333-3100
Fax: (507)333-3102
General newspaper. **Founded:** 1914. **Freq:** Daily (eve.). **Print Method:** Offset. **Cols./Page:** 6. **Col. Width:** 24 nonpareils. **Col. Depth:** 301 agate lines. **Subscription Rates:** $142.50 Individuals carrier; $156.50 Individuals motor route; $162.50 By mail in county. **URL:** http://www.faribault.com. **Mailing address:** PO Box 249, Faribault, MN 55021. **Ad Rates:** SAU $6.70. **Remarks:** Accepts advertising. **Circ:** (Not Reported).

18339 ■ Charter Communications
1400 Cannon Cir.
Faribault, MN 55021
Free: 888-438-2427
Founded: 1993. **Key Personnel:** Mary Jo Moehle, VP of Investor Rel. **Cities Served:** 129 channels. **URL:** http://www.charter.com.

18340 ■ KDHL-AM - 920
601 Central Ave.
Faribault, MN 55021
Phone: (507)334-0061
Format: Country; News; Sports. **Networks:** ABC; Minnesota News. **Owner:** Cumulus Media Inc., 3280 Peachtree Rd. NW, Ste. 2300, Atlanta, GA 30305-2455, Ph: (404)949-0700, Fax: (404)949-0740. **Founded:** 1948. **Operating Hours:** Continuous. **Key Personnel:** Paul Benzick, Bus. Mgr., paul.benzick@cumulus.com; Jerry Groskreutz, Farm Mgr., jerry.groskreutz@cumulus.com. **Local Programs:** *AM Minnesota*, Monday Tuesday Wednesday Thursday Friday 9:30 a.m. - 10:00 a.m. **Wattage:** 5,000. **Ad Rates:** Noncommercial. **URL:** http://www.kdhlradio.com.

18341 ■ KQCL-FM - 95.9
601 Central Ave.
Faribault, MN 55021
Phone: (507)334-0061
Email: missi.jensen@townsquaremedia.com
Format: Classic Rock. **Owner:** Cumulus Broadcasting

Inc., 3280 Peachtree Rd. NW, Ste. 2300, Atlanta, GA 30305-2447, Ph: (404)949-0700, Fax: (404)949-0740. **Key Personnel:** Shannon Knoepke, Mgr., shannon.knoepke@townsquaremedia.com; Mike Eiler, Dir. of Programs, mike.eiler@cumulus.com. **URL:** http://www.power96radio.com.

FARMINGTON

18342 ■ Farmington-Rosemount Independent Town Pages
Forum Communications Co.
312 Oak St.
Farmington, MN 55024
Publisher's E-mail: cbursack@forumcomm.com
Local newspaper serving Farmington and Rosemount area. **Freq:** Weekly (Thurs.). **Key Personnel:** Steve Messick, Publisher. **URL:** http://www.forumcomm.com/blog/portfolio_page/farmington-rosemount-independent-town-pages. **Remarks:** Accepts advertising. **Circ:** (Not Reported).

18343 ■ Forum
Westar Institute
PO Box 346
Farmington, MN 55024
Phone: (651)200-2372
Journal focusing on research on biblical and American traditions. **Founded:** 1981. **Freq:** Semiannual. **Trim Size:** 6 x 9. **ISSN:** 0883-4970 (print). **Subscription Rates:** $30 Individuals; $35 Other countries. **URL:** http://westarinstitute.org/Periodicals/periodicals.html. **Formerly:** Foundations & Facets Forum. **Remarks:** Advertising not accepted. **Circ:** Paid 805.

18344 ■ Fourth R
Westar Institute
PO Box 346
Farmington, MN 55024
Phone: (651)200-2372
Freq: Bimonthly. **ISSN:** 0893-1658 (print). **Subscription Rates:** included in membership dues; $30 U.S.; $35 Other countries. **URL:** http://www.westarinstitute.org/resources/more-about-the-fourth-r/. **Remarks:** Advertising not accepted. **Circ:** (Not Reported).

FERGUS FALLS

WC MN. Otter Tail Co. On Red River, 200 mi. E. of Duluth. Manufactures cabinets, dairy, bakery products, flour, farm machinery, fertilizer, protein meal. Summer resort. Dairy, livestock, grain farms.

18345 ■ Faith and Fellowship
The Church of the Lutheran Brethren
2010 W. Alcott Ave.
Fergus Falls, MN 56537
Publication E-mail: clb@clba.org
Lutheran magazine. **Freq:** Monthly. **Print Method:** Offset. **Trim Size:** 8 x 10 1/2. **Cols./Page:** 2. **Col. Width:** 40 nonpareils. **Col. Depth:** 125 agate lines. **USPS:** 184-600. **Subscription Rates:** $28 Individuals; $19 Other countries; $2 Single issue. **URL:** http://www.clba.org/magazine. **Remarks:** Advertising not accepted. **Circ:** (Not Reported).

18346 ■ Fergus Falls Daily Journal
Boone Newspaper
914 E Channing Ave.
Fergus Falls, MN 56537
Phone: (218)736-7511
Fax: (218)736-5919
Publisher's E-mail: newsroom@fergusfallsjournal.com
General newspaper. **Freq:** Mon-Fri. (eve.) & Sat. (morn.). **Print Method:** Offset. **Cols./Page:** 6. **Col. Width:** 24 nonpareils. **Col. Depth:** 301 agate lines. **Key Personnel:** David D. Churchill, President, Publisher, phone: (218)739-7012; Joel Myhre, General Manager, phone: (218)739-7023; Jeff Hage, Managing Editor, phone: (218)739-7026. **Subscription Rates:** $10.95 Individuals per month by local carrier; $14 Individuals per month by motor route; $14 By mail per month; in Minnesota; $14 Out of state per month via postal mail; $9.85 Individuals per month by local carrier - senior citizen; $12.70 Individuals per month by motor route - senior citizen; $12.70 By mail per month; in Minnesota - senior citizen; $12.70 Out of state per month via postal mail - senior citizen. **URL:** http://www.fergusfallsjournal.com. **Mailing address:** PO Box 506, Fergus Falls, MN 56537. **Ad Rates:** PCI $10.25. **Remarks:** Accepts classified advertising. **Circ:** Mon.-Sat. 6,200.

18347 ■ Smart Choices
Communicating for America
112 E Lincoln Ave.
Fergus Falls, MN 56537
Phone: (218)739-3241
Fax: (218)739-3832
Free: 800-432-3276
Magazine containing organizational achievements, healthy lifestyle tips and health care legislation. **Freq:** Quarterly. **URL:** http://www.communicatingforamerica.org/join-ca/. **Remarks:** Advertising not accepted. **Circ:** (Not Reported).

18348 ■ KBRF-AM - 1250
728 Western Ave., N
Fergus Falls, MN 56537
Phone: (218)736-7596
Email: contactus@lakesradio.net
Format: Talk; News. **Networks:** Mutual Broadcasting System; Minnesota News. **Owner:** Result Radio Group, 1355 N Dutton Ave., Ste. 225, Santa Rosa, CA 95401, Ph: (707)546-9185. **Founded:** 1926. **Formerly:** KGDE-AM. **Operating Hours:** Continuous; 12% network, 88% local. **ADI:** Fargo, ND. **Key Personnel:** Doug Gray, Gen. Mgr. **Wattage:** 5,000. **Ad Rates:** $6-12 for 30 seconds; $9.50-18 for 60 seconds. Combined advertising rates available with KZCR-FM, KJJK-AM & FM, KPRW-FM. **Mailing address:** PO Box 495, Fergus Falls, MN 56537. **URL:** http://www.lakesradio.net.

18349 ■ KJJK-AM - 1020
728 West Ave.
Fergus Falls, MN 56537
Phone: (218)736-7596
Fax: (218)736-2836
Format: News; Sports; Information. **Owner:** Result Radio, Inc., at above address. **Founded:** 1986. **Operating Hours:** Continuous. **Wattage:** 2,000 KW. **Ad Rates:** Advertising accepted; rates available upon request. $8-12 for 30 seconds; $12-18 for 60 seconds. Combined advertising rates available with KJJK-FM, KBRF-AM, KZCR-FM, KPRW-FM. **Mailing address:** PO Box 495, Fergus Falls, MN 56537. **URL:** http://www.lakesradio.net.

18350 ■ KJJK-FM - 96.5
728 Western Ave. N
Fergus Falls, MN 56537
Phone: (218)736-7596
Email: contactus@lakesradio.net
Format: Country. **Networks:** ABC. **Owner:** Result Radio Group, 1355 N Dutton Ave., Ste. 225, Santa Rosa, CA 95401, Ph: (707)546-9185. **Founded:** 1981. **Operating Hours:** Continuous. **Wattage:** 100,000. **Ad Rates:** $9-12 for 30 seconds; $13.50-18 for 60 seconds. Combined advertising rates available with KJJK-AM, KBRF-AM, KZCR-FM, KPRW-FM. **URL:** http://www.lakesradio.net.

18351 ■ K207DP-FM - 89.1
PO Box 391
Twin Falls, ID 83303
Phone: (202)719-7903
Format: Religious. **Owner:** CSN International, PO Box 391, Twin Falls, ID 83303, Ph: (208)736-1958, Fax: (208)736-1958, Free: 800-357-4226. **Key Personnel:** Mike Kestler, President; Don Mills, Music Dir., Prog. Dir.; Daniel Davidson, Dir. of Operations. **URL:** http://www.csnradio.com.

18352 ■ KZCR-FM - 103.3
728 Western Ave., N
Fergus Falls, MN 56538
Phone: (218)736-7596
Format: Album-Oriented Rock (AOR). **Owner:** Result Radio Group, 1355 N Dutton Ave., Ste. 225, Santa Rosa, CA 95401, Ph: (707)546-9185. **Founded:** 1968. **Formerly:** KBRF-FM. **Operating Hours:** Continuous; 100% local. **ADI:** Fargo, ND. **Key Personnel:** Doug Gray, Gen. Mgr.; Greg Brady, Operations Mgr. **Wattage:** 100,000. **Ad Rates:** $6-12 for 30 seconds; $9.15-18 for 60 seconds. Combined advertising rates available with KBRF-AM, KJJK-AM & FM, KPRW-FM. **URL:** http://www.lakesradio.net/Z103-3FM/10244720.

FOREST LAKE

SE MN. Washington Co. 25 mi. N. of Saint Paul. Summer resort. Manufactures tools, snow and lawn fences, protective helmets & gear, wood products, component electronic parts; feed, hammer mills. Creamery. Dairy, poultry, truck farms. Aluminum utensils, fixtures.

18353 ■ Forest Lake Times
ECM Publishers Inc.
880 15th St. SW
Forest Lake, MN 55025
Phone: (651)464-4601
Fax: (651)464-4605
Publication E-mail: editor.forestlaketimes@ecm-inc.com
Community newspaper. **Founded:** 1903. **Freq:** Weekly (Thurs.). **Print Method:** Offset. **Cols./Page:** 6. **Col. Width:** 77 picas. **Col. Depth:** 21 inches. **USPS:** 205-080. **Subscription Rates:** $48 Individuals; $43 Individuals senior; $36 Students. **URL:** http://forestlaketimes.com. **Formerly:** The Times. **Ad Rates:** GLR $8.75; BW $1,493.10; 4C $1,793.10; PCI $13.45. **Remarks:** Accepts advertising. **Circ:** 13500.

18354 ■ WLKX-FM - 95.9
15226 W Freeway Dr.
Forest Lake, MN 55025
Phone: (651)464-6796
Fax: (651)464-3638
Format: Talk; News; Sports; Country; Contemporary Christian. **Networks:** USA Radio. **Owner:** Lakes Broadcasting Co., Inc., at above address. **Founded:** 1978. **Operating Hours:** 6:00 a.m.-12:00 p.m Monday-Friday;9:00 a.m.-3:00 p.m Sunday. **Wattage:** 3,000. **Ad Rates:** Advertising accepted; rates available upon request. $7-16 for 30 seconds; $11.50-26.50 for 60 seconds. **URL:** http://www.spirit.fm.

FOSSTON

NW MN. Polk Co. 68 mi. E of Grand Forks, ND. Creamery. Dairy, stock, grain farms.

18355 ■ City of Fosston Cable TV
220 E 1st St.
Fosston, MN 56542
Phone: (218)435-1959
Fax: (218)435-1961
Founded: 1977. **Cities Served:** subscribing households 605. **URL:** http://www.fosston.com/index.asp?Type=B_BASIC&SEC=%7B358BA73D-61A6-4D28-A35C-3A8514809527%7D.

18356 ■ KKCQ-AM - 1480
PO Box 606
Fosston, MN 56542
Phone: (218)435-1919
Fax: (218)435-1480
Free: 855-436-5572
Format: Country. **Simulcasts:** KKCQ-FM. **Networks:** AP; ABC. **Owner:** Pine to Prairie Broadcasting, at above address. **Founded:** 1966. **Formerly:** KEHG-AM. **Operating Hours:** Continuous. **Key Personnel:** Phil Ehlke, Gen. Sales Mgr., brian@q107fm.com. **Wattage:** 5,000 Day; 090 Night. **Ad Rates:** Noncommercial. $5-6.50 for 30 seconds; $7.15-9.30 for 60 seconds. **URL:** http://rjbroadcasting.com/index.cfm?page=contact-us.

18357 ■ KKEQ-FM - 107.1
PO Box 180
Fosston, MN 56542
Phone: (218)435-1071
Fax: (218)435-1480
Free: 800-435-1071
Format: Religious. **Simulcasts:** K285BG. **Networks:** ABC; Satellite Music Network. **Owner:** Pine to Prairie Broadcasting, at above address. **Founded:** 1993. **Formerly:** KEHG-FM. **Operating Hours:** Continuous. **ADI:** Mobile, AL-Pensacola, FL. **Key Personnel:** Phil Ehlke, Gen. Mgr., phil@q107fm.com; Tom Lano, Sports Dir., tom@q107fm.com; Laura Hamilton, News Dir., laura@q107fm.com; Don Brinkman, Dir. of Traffic, don@q107fm.com; Jim Offerdahl, Chief Engineer, jim@q107fm.com; Jamie Nesvold, Dir. of Production, Music Dir., jamie@q107fm.com. **Wattage:** 50,000. **Ad Rates:** Advertising accepted; rates available upon request. Combined advertising rates available with KKCQ-FM; KKCQ-AM. **URL:** http://yourqfm.com.

FULDA

18358 ■ Fulda Free Press
Fulda Free Press

Circulation: ★ = AAM; △ or • = BPA; ♦ = CAC; ❑ = VAC; ⊕ = PO Statement; ‡ = Publisher's Report; Boldface figures = sworn; Light figures = estimated.

118 N St. Paul Ave.
Fulda, MN 56131
Phone: (507)425-2303
Publisher's E-mail: photo@fuldafreepress.net
Community newspaper. **Freq:** Weekly (Wed.). **Print Method:** Offset. **Cols./Page:** 8. **Col. Width:** 10.5 picas. **Col. Depth:** 21 1/2 inches. **Key Personnel:** Gerald Johnson, Editor. **USPS:** 211-500. **URL:** http://www.fuldafreepress.net. **Mailing address:** PO Box 439, Fulda, MN 56131. **Ad Rates:** BW $602; SAU $3.75; PCI $3.25. **Remarks:** Accepts advertising. **Circ:** ‡1,400.

GLENCOE

SC MN. McLeod Co. 45 mi. NW of Mankato. Creamery; cheese factory; corn and pea cannery. Dairy, cattle, poultry, grain farms. Sugar beets, peas, corn. Ships.

18359 ■ The Bulletin
McLeod Publishing Inc.
716 E Tenth St.
Glencoe, MN 55336
Phone: (320)864-5518
Publisher's E-mail: info@glencoenews.com
Community newspaper. **Founded:** Sept. 08, 1892. **Freq:** Weekly. **Print Method:** Offset. **Trim Size:** 21 1/2 x 32. **Cols./Page:** 7. **Col. Width:** 12 picas. **Col. Depth:** 21 1/2 inches. **Key Personnel:** Derek Blyth, Editor; Deborah Forsyth, Assistant Editor; Kathleen Cagney, Assistant Editor. **USPS:** 068-020. **Subscription Rates:** €85 Individuals Belgium; €145 Out of area air mail; €235 Out of state air mail; €150 Two years Belgium; €270 Two years EU air mail; €450 Two years outside EU air mail. **URL:** http://www.xpats.com. **Formerly**: Brownton Bulletin. **Ad Rates:** BW $376; SAU $3.35. **Remarks:** Accepts advertising. **Circ:** ‡1,026.

18360 ■ McLeod County Chronicle
McLeod Publishing Inc.
716 E Tenth St.
Glencoe, MN 55336
Phone: (320)864-5518
Publication E-mail: richg@glencoenews.com
advertising@glencoenews.com
Community newspaper. **Freq:** Weekly. **Print Method:** Web Offset. **Trim Size:** 13 x 21 1/2. **Cols./Page:** 6. **Col. Width:** 2 inches. **Col. Depth:** 21 1/2 inches. **Key Personnel:** Rich Glennie, Managing Editor; Sue Keenan, Manager, Advertising; Bill Ramige, Publisher. **Subscription Rates:** $39 Individuals in McLeod & New Auburn - 12 months; $69 Individuals in McLeod & New Auburn 24 months; $51 Individuals 12 months outside Minnesota; $93 Two years outside Minnesota; $135 Individuals 36 months outside Minnesota; $45 Individuals elsewhere in Minnesota 12 months; $81 Individuals elsewhere in Minnesota 24 months; $117 Individuals elsewhere in Minnesota 36 months; $3 Individuals snowbird 3rd class/months; $39 Students 9 months. **URL:** http://www.glencoenews.com. **Ad Rates:** GLR $6.35; BW $619; 4C $75; SAU $5; PCI $6. **Remarks:** Accepts advertising. **Circ:** Paid ‡3300, Free 56.

18361 ■ Charter Communications
2104 E 10th St.
Glencoe, MN 55336
Free: 888-438-2427
Owner: Charter Communications Inc., 400 Atlantic St., Stamford, CT 06901, Ph: (203)905-7801. **Founded:** Dec. 1983. **Formerly**: Bresnan Communications. **Key Personnel:** Neil Smit, CEO; Michael J. Lovett, COO; Marwan Fawaz, Chief Tech. Ofc. **Cities Served:** subscribing households 1,500. **URL:** http://www.bresnan.com.

GLENWOOD

WC MN. Pope Co. On Lake Minnewaska, 69 mi. NW of Saint Cloud. Summer resort. Museum (Indian artifacts). Fabricating and machine parts factories. Fish Hatchery. Dairy, stock, grain farms.

18362 ■ Pope County Tribune
Pope County Tribune
14 First Ave. SE
Glenwood, MN 56334
Phone: (320)634-4571
Fax: (320)634-5522
Publication E-mail: news@pctribune.com tdouglass@pctribune.com
Local newspaper. **Freq:** Weekly (Mon.). **Print Method:** Offset. **Cols./Page:** 6. **Col. Width:** 28 nonpareils. **Col. Depth:** 301 agate lines. **Key Personnel:** Tim Douglas, Publisher; Deb Mercier, Editor. **Subscription Rates:** $28 Individuals. **URL:** http://www.pctribune.com. **Ad Rates:** GLR $.25; SAU $5.30; PCI $5.36. **Remarks:** Accepts advertising. **Circ:** Paid ‡4000, Free ‡100.

18363 ■ Starbuck Times
Starbuck Times
14 1st Ave., SE
Glenwood, MN 56334
Phone: (320)634-4571
Fax: (320)634-5522
Publisher's E-mail: news@pctribune.com
Community newspaper. **Founded:** 1898. **Freq:** Weekly (Tues.). **Print Method:** Offset. **Cols./Page:** 6. **Col. Width:** 2 1/4 inches. **Col. Depth:** 21 1/2 inches. **Key Personnel:** Zach Anderson, Editor. **URL:** http://www.pctribune.com/main.asp?SectionID=22&TM=80051.11. **Formerly**: Times. **Ad Rates:** GLR $.14; BW $360; 4C $505.62; SAU $3.90; PCI $3.30. **Remarks:** Accepts advertising. **Circ:** Paid ‡1800, Free ‡25.

GLYNDON

18364 ■ Dakota Farmer
Farm Progress Companies Inc.
c/o Lon Tonneson, Ed.
6258 90th Ave. N
Glyndon, MN 56547
Phone: (218)236-8420
Fax: (218)236-1134
Publisher's E-mail: circhelp@farmprogress.com
Agricultural magazine. **Freq:** Monthly. **Print Method:** Offset. **Trim Size:** 8 x 10 3/4. **Cols./Page:** 3. **Key Personnel:** Lon Tonneson, Editor; Frank Holdmeyer, Executive Editor, phone: (515)278-7782, fax: (515)278-7796. **ISSN:** 1043--5775 (print). **Subscription Rates:** $26.95 Individuals. **URL:** http://farmprogress.com/dakota-farmer. **Remarks:** Accepts advertising. **Circ:** (Not Reported).

GOLDEN VALLEY

SE MN. Hennepin Co. 28 mi. NW of Bemidji. Residential.

18365 ■ KQSP-AM - 1530
919 Lilac DR N
Golden Valley, MN 55422
Phone: (763)230-7602
Fax: (763)230-7607
Email: info@lapicosa.us
Format: Hispanic. **Owner:** Broadcast One, Inc., at above address. **URL:** http://www.lapicosa.us.

18366 ■ WLOL-AM - 1330
7575 Golden Valley Rd., No. 310
Golden Valley, MN 55427
Phone: (612)643-4110
Fax: (763)546-4444
Format: Religious. **Owner:** Relevant Radio, 1496 Bellevue St., Ste. 202, Green Bay, WI 54311, Free: 888-577-5443. **Key Personnel:** Brian Acker, Gen. Mgr., backer@relevantradio.com; Paul Sadek, Operations Mgr., psadek@relevantradio.com.

GRAND MARAIS

NE MN. Cook Co. 112 mi. NE of Duluth. Summer & winter sports resort. Logging. Timber.

18367 ■ WTIP-FM - 90.7
PO Box 1005
Grand Marais, MN 55604
Phone: (218)387-1070
Fax: (218)387-1120
Free: 800-473-9847
Email: wtip@boreal.org
Format: Adult Contemporary. **Owner:** Cook County Community Radio Corp, at above address. **Founded:** 1998. **Operating Hours**: 5:00 a.m.-3:00 p.m. **Key Personnel:** BarbaraJean Meyers, Dir. Pub. Aff., News Dir., radionews@wtip.org. **Wattage**: 25,000. **Ad Rates:** Noncommercial. **URL:** http://www.wtip.org.

GRAND RAPIDS

NC MN. Itasca Co. On Mississippi River, 36 mi. SW of Hibbing. Resort. Industrial park. Light manufacturing. Manufactures paper and wood products. Iron Ore mining. Dairy, potato and beef cattle farming.

18368 ■ KAXE-FM - 91.7
260 NE 2nd St.
Grand Rapids, MN 55744
Phone: (218)326-1234
Fax: (218)326-1235
Format: Public Radio. **Networks:** National Public Radio (NPR); Public Radio International (PRI). **Owner:** Northern Community Radio Inc., 260 NE Second St., Grand Rapids, MN 55744, Ph: (218)326-1234, Fax: (218)326-1235, Free: 800-662-5799. **Founded:** 1976. **Operating Hours**: 5 a.m.-1 a.m.; 45% network, 55% local. **Wattage**: 100,000. **Ad Rates:** Noncommercial. **URL:** http://www.kaxe.org.

18369 ■ KGPZ-FM - 96.1
504 NW 1st Ave., Ste. 290
Grand Rapids, MN 55744
Format: Country. **Operating Hours**: Continuous. **Wattage**: 100,000. **Ad Rates:** Noncommercial. **URL:** http://www.kgpzfm.com.

18370 ■ KMFY-FM - 96.9
PO Box 597
Grand Rapids, MN 55744
Phone: (218)999-5669
Fax: (218)999-5609
Format: Adult Contemporary. **Networks:** ABC; Minnesota News; Satellite Music Network. **Owner:** Itasca Broadcasting Inc. **Formerly**: KNNS-FM. **Operating Hours**: Continuous. **Wattage**: 100,000. **Ad Rates:** $8.75-11.75 for 30 seconds; $10.75-13.75 for 60 seconds. Combined advertising rates available with KOZY-AM. **URL:** http://www.kmfyradio.com.

18371 ■ KOZY-AM - 1320
PO Box 597
Grand Rapids, MN 55744
Phone: (218)999-5669
Fax: (218)999-5609
Format: Oldies; News. **Networks:** ABC. **Owner:** Itasca Broadcasting Inc. **Founded:** 1948. **Operating Hours:** Continuous. **ADI:** Duluth, MN-Superior, WI. **Key Personnel:** Kathy Lynn, Traffic Mgr., kathy@kozyradio.com; Tim Edwards, Chief Engineer, tim@kozyradio.com; Jim Lamke, Prog. Dir., jimlamke@kozyradio.com. **Local Programs**: *The Morning Mess*, Monday Tuesday Wednesday Thursday Friday 6:00 a.m. 9:00 a.m. **Wattage**: 5,000. **Ad Rates:** $11.75-13.75 for 30 seconds; $11.75-13.75 for 60 seconds. Combined advertising rates available with KMFY-FM. **URL:** http://www.kozyradio.com.

18372 ■ K209DS-FM - 89.7
PO Box 391
Twin Falls, ID 83303
Fax: (208)736-1958
Free: 800-357-4226
Format: Religious; Contemporary Christian. **Owner:** CSN International, PO Box 391, Twin Falls, ID 83303, Ph: (208)736-1958, Fax: (208)736-1958, Free: 800-357-4226. **Key Personnel:** Don Mills, Prog. Dir., Div. Dir. **URL:** http://www.csnradio.com.

GRANITE FALLS

SW MN. Yellow Medicine Co. On Minnesota River, 123 mi. W. of Minneapolis. Manufactures oilers, hydraulic equipment; rock crushing plants. Dairy, stock, mink, grain farms. Corn, wheat, hogs.

18373 ■ The Advocate-Tribune
GateHouse Media Inc.
713 Prentice St.
Granite Falls, MN 56241
Phone: (320)564-2126
Community newspaper. **Founded:** 1902. **Freq:** Weekly (Thurs.). **Print Method:** Offset. **Cols./Page:** 6. **Col. Width:** 21 nonpareils. **Col. Depth:** 226 agate lines. **Key Personnel:** Scott Tedrick, Editor; Dave Smiglewski, Publisher; Betty Harguth, Manager, Production. **Subscription Rates:** $20 Individuals. **URL:** http://www.granitefallsnews.com. **Formerly**: Advocate; Tri-County Advocate; The Clarkfield Advocate; Granite Falls Tribune. **Ad Rates:** GLR $5.45; BW $450; 4C $500; PCI $4.25. **Remarks:** Accepts advertising. **Circ:** Paid ‡3,700, Free ‡100.

GRYGLA

NW MN. Marshall Co. 40 mi. NE of Thief River Falls. Hunters paradise. Center of Agricultural services.

18374 ■ The Grygla Eagle
PO Box 17
Grygla, MN 56727
Phone: (218)294-6220
Fax: (218)487-5251
Publication E-mail: richards@gvtel.com
Community newspaper. **Freq:** Weekly (Wed.). **Print Method:** Letterpress and offset. **Cols./Page:** 6. **Col. Width:** 20 nonpareils. **Col. Depth:** 224 agate lines. **Key Personnel:** Richard Richards, Publisher; Joy Nordby, Editor. **Subscription Rates:** $18 Individuals. **Ad Rates:** GLR $.33; BW $216; SAU $3.25; PCI $2.25. **Remarks:** Accepts advertising. **Circ:** ‡672.

HALLOCK

NW MN. Kittson Co. 60 mi. N. of Grand Forks, ND. Stock, dairy, poultry, grain farms. Wheat, sugar beets.

18375 ■ Kittson County Enterprise
Kittson County Enterprise Co.
118 2nd St. S
Hallock, MN 56728
Phone: (218)843-2868
Fax: (218)853-2888
Publication E-mail: kce@wiktel.com
Community newspaper. **Freq:** Weekly (Wed.). **Print Method:** Offset. **Cols./Page:** 6. **Col. Width:** 12 picas. **Col. Depth:** 21 1/4 inches. **Key Personnel:** Michael Moore, Publisher; Myrna Moore, Publisher. **Subscription Rates:** $33 Individuals print only; $39 Out of area print only; $47 Out of state print only; $29.95 Individuals online; $43 Individuals print and online; $56 Out of area print and online. **URL:** http://www.kittsonarea.com. **Formerly**: Northern Media. **Mailing address:** PO Box 730, Hallock, MN 56728. **Ad Rates:** SAU $4.75. **Remarks:** Accepts advertising. **Circ:** Paid ‡1500.

HANSKA

SC MN. Brown Co. 100 mi. SW of Minneapolis. Stock, dairy, poultry farms. Hogs, soybeans, corn.

18376 ■ The Hanska Herald
The Hanska Herald
PO Box 45
Hanska, MN 56041
Phone: (507)439-6214
Community newspaper. **Freq:** Weekly (Thurs.). **Print Method:** Offset. **Trim Size:** 16 x 22 1/2. **Cols./Page:** 7. **Col. Width:** 2 1/16 inches. **Col. Depth:** 21 inches. **Key Personnel:** Michael Koob, Publisher. **USPS:** 234-680. **Subscription Rates:** $23 Individuals print; $26 Out of state print; $20 Individuals online. **URL:** http://www.prairiepublishingmn.com/25902/1972/hanska-herald. **Ad Rates:** BW $382.20; SAU $2.60. **Remarks:** Accepts advertising. **Circ:** Paid ⊕**772**, Free ⊕**28**.

HARMONY

SE MN. Fillmore Co. 15 mi. S. of Preston.

18377 ■ Harmony Cable Inc.
35 1st Ave. N
Harmony, MN 55939
Founded: 1984. **Key Personnel:** Kenneth Halverson, Contact. **Cities Served:** subscribing households 385. **URL:** http://harmonytel.com/2015/wordpress/wp-content/uploads/2015/07/BCCW-Brochure-14.pdf;harmonytel.com/2015/wordpress/wp-content/uploads/2015/07/BCCW-Brochure-14.pdf.

HASTINGS

SE MN. Washington Co. On Mississippi River, 20 mi SE of Saint Paul. Manufactures flour, sprayers, dusters, filing equipment, wire specialties, scotch tape, reflective sheeting, petroleum products, ammonia, ready-to-mix concrete. Dairy, poultry, grain farms. Corn, wheat, rye. Paper, clay products.

18378 ■ Hastings Star Gazette
Hastings Star Gazette
745 Spiral Blvd.
Hastings, MN 55033
Phone: (651)437-6153
Fax: (651)437-5911
Publisher's E-mail: news@hastingsstargazette.com
Community newspaper. **Freq:** Weekly (Thurs.). **Print Method:** Offset. **Cols./Page:** 6. **Col. Width:** 30 nonpareils. **Col. Depth:** 294 agate lines. **Key Personnel:** Chad Richardson, General Manager, Editor. **Subscription Rates:** $51 Individuals local; $87 Two years local; $70 Other countries non-local; $129 Other countries non-local, 2 years. **URL:** http://www.hastingsstargazette.com. **Mailing address:** PO Box 277, Hastings, MN 55033. **Ad Rates:** GLR $.20. **Remarks:** Accepts advertising. **Circ:** ‡5547.

18379 ■ KDWA-AM - 1460
514 Vermillion St.
Hastings, MN 55033
Phone: (651)437-1460
Fax: (651)438-3042
Email: shop@kdwa.com
Format: News; Sports; Talk. **Simulcasts:** KDWA -FM. **Owner:** K and M Broadcasting Inc. **Founded:** 1963. **Key Personnel:** Dan Massman, Gen. Mgr., dan@kdwa.com. **Local Programs**: *Local Sports.* **Wattage**: 1,000 Day; 041 Night. **Ad Rates:** $10 for 30 seconds; $15 for 60 seconds. **URL:** http://kdwa.com.

HAWLEY

WC MN. Clay Co. 23 mi. E. of Fargo, ND. Agriculture equipment manufactured. Grain and dairy products.

18380 ■ Hawley Herald
Hawley Herald
608 Main St.
Hawley, MN 56549
Phone: (218)483-3306
Fax: (218)483-4457
Publication E-mail: ads@hawleyherald.net
Newspaper. **Freq:** Weekly (Mon.). **Print Method:** Offset. **Cols./Page:** 6. **Col. Width:** 21 nonpareils. **Col. Depth:** 301 agate lines. **Key Personnel:** James Martodam, Editor; Gene Prim, Publisher. **Subscription Rates:** $45 Individuals print and online - Clay and Becker Counties Only; $50 Out of area print and online; $55 Out of state print and online ; $35 Individuals print only - Clay and Becker Counties Only; $40 Out of area print only ; $42 Out of state print only; $35 Individuals online only. **URL:** http://www.hawleyherald.net/49337/2221/1/home. **Mailing address:** PO Box 709, Hawley, MN 56549. **Ad Rates:** SAU $4.75. **Remarks:** Accepts advertising. **Circ:** Paid ‡1891.

HECTOR

18381 ■ Bird Island Union
Hubin Publishing Company Inc.
PO Box 278
Hector, MN 55342
Phone: (320)365-3266
Publication E-mail: union@willmar.com
Community newspaper. **Freq:** Weekly (Wed.). **Cols./Page:** 6. **Col. Width:** 26 nonpareils. **Col. Depth:** 301 agate lines. **Subscription Rates:** $27 U.S.; $31 Out of country; $38 Out of state. **URL:** http://www.mnnews.com/newspapers/birdisland.html. **Ad Rates:** BW $300; PCI $4.05. **Remarks:** Accepts advertising. **Circ:** 795.

HERMAN

WC MN. Grant Co. 40 mi. S. of Fergus Falls. Stock, dairy, grain farms. Soybeans, corn, barley, sugarbeets.

18382 ■ Herman-Hoffman Tribune
Herman-Hoffman Tribune
408 Berlin Ave. S
Herman, MN 56248
Phone: (320)677-2229
Fax: (320)677-2229
Community newspaper. **Freq:** Weekly (Tues.). **Print Method:** Web. **Trim Size:** 8 x 11. **Cols./Page:** 5. **Col. Width:** 23 nonpareils. **Col. Depth:** 210 agate lines. **Key Personnel:** Kris Beuckens, Editor; Nick Ripperger, Owner, Publisher. **USPS:** 242-180. **Subscription Rates:** $22 Individuals Grant and adjoining counties; $28 Elsewhere; $40 Other countries; $0.50 Single issue. **URL:** http://www.hermanreview.com. **Formerly**: Herman Review. **Mailing address:** PO Box E, Herman, MN 56248. **Remarks:** Accepts advertising. **Circ:** ‡1275.

HERON LAKE

NW MN. Jackson Co. 21 mi. NW of Jackson.

18383 ■ Tri County News
Tri County News
931 2nd Ave.
Heron Lake, MN 56137
Phone: (507)793-2327
Fax: (507)793-2327
Publication E-mail: tcnews@mysmbs.com
Community newspaper. **Founded:** 1886. **Freq:** Weekly (Wed.). **Print Method:** Offset. **Cols./Page:** 8. **Col. Width:** 1 3/4 inches. **Col. Depth:** 21.5 inches. **ISSN:** 0273-5482 (print). **URL:** http://tricountynewsmn.net/. **Mailing address:** PO Box 227, Heron Lake, MN 56137. **Remarks:** Accepts classified advertising. **Circ:** Paid ‡877, Free ‡25.

HIBBING

NE MN. St. Louis Co. 78 mi. NW of Duluth. Hibbing Community College. National historic site. Taconite mining. Foundry, iron ore deposits.

18384 ■ Hibbing Daily Tribune
Daily Tribune
2142 First Ave.
Hibbing, MN 55746
Phone: (218)262-1011
Fax: (218)262-4318
Publication E-mail: tribune@hibbingmn.com
General newspaper. **Freq:** Daily and Sun. (eve.). **Print Method:** Offset. **Cols./Page:** 6. **Col. Width:** 24 nonpareils. **Col. Depth:** 301 agate lines. **Subscription Rates:** $200 Individuals carrier delivery, print & online; $75 Individuals online only; $200 Individuals carrier delivery, print only. **URL:** http://www.hibbingmn.com. **Ad Rates:** SAU $7.35. **Remarks:** Accepts advertising. **Circ:** Sun. 4973, Mon.-Sat. 4519.

18385 ■ KMFG-FM - 102.9
807 W 37 St.
Hibbing, MN 55746
Phone: (218)263-7531
Fax: (218)263-6112
Email: info@kmfgfm.com
Format: Classic Rock. **Networks:** Satellite Music Network. **Owner:** Midwest Communications Inc., 904 Grand Ave., Wausau, WI 54403, Ph: (715)842-1437, Fax: (715)842-7061. **Operating Hours**: Continuous. **Key Personnel:** Zach Martin, Contact. **Wattage:** 25,000. **Ad Rates:** Noncommercial.

18386 ■ WIRT-TV - 13
Ten Observation Rd.
Duluth, MN 55811
Phone: (218)727-6864
Fax: (218)727-4415
Free: 800-477-1013
Format: Commercial TV. **Simulcasts:** WDIO-TV Duluth, MN. **Networks:** ABC. **Owner:** Hubbard Broadcasting Inc., 3415 University Ave., Saint Paul, MN 55114-2099, Ph: (651)646-5555, Fax: (651)642-4172. **Founded:** 1966. **Operating Hours**: Continuous. **ADI**: Duluth, MN-Superior, WI. **Ad Rates:** Noncommercial. **Mailing address:** PO Box 16897, Duluth, MN 55816. **URL:** http://www.wdio.com.

18387 ■ WMFG-AM - 1240
807 W 37th St.
Hibbing, MN 55746
Phone: (218)263-7531
Fax: (218)263-6112
Format: Adult Contemporary. **Owner:** Midwest Radio Network L.L.C. **Founded:** 1935. **Operating Hours**: Continuous. **ADI**: Duluth, MN-Superior, WI. **Wattage**: 1,000. **Ad Rates:** $8-12 for 30 seconds; $10-16 for 60 seconds. Combined advertising rates available with WMFG-FM & KMFG-FM.

18388 ■ WMFG-FM - 106.3
807 W 37th St.
Hibbing, MN 55746
Phone: (218)263-7531
Fax: (218)263-6112
Format: Oldies. **Networks:** Satellite Music Network. **Owner:** Midwest Radio Network L.L.C. **Founded:** 1923. **Operating Hours**: Continuous. **Wattage:** 25,000. **Ad Rates:** Noncommercial. Combined advertising rates available with WMFG-AM & KMFG-FM. **URL:** http://mwcradio.com.

18389 ■ WNMT-AM - 650
807 W 37th St.
Hibbing, MN 55746

Circulation: ★ = AAM; △ or • = BPA; ♦ = CAC; ❑ = VAC; ⊕ = PO Statement; ‡ = Publisher's Report; Boldface figures = sworn; Light figures = estimated.

Phone: (218)263-7531
Fax: (218)263-6112
Format: News; Talk; Sports. **Networks:** ABC. **Owner:** Midwest Communications Inc., 904 Grand Ave., Wausau, WI 54403, Ph: (715)842-1437, Fax: (715)842-7061. **Founded:** 1975. **Formerly:** WKKQ-AM. **Operating Hours:** Continuous; 95% network, 5% local. **Wattage:** 10,000. **Ad Rates:** $12-22 for 30 seconds; $13-27 for 60 seconds. Combined advertising rates available with WTBX. **URL:** http://www.wnmtradio.com.

18390 ■ WTBX-FM - 93.9
93.9 WTBX 807 West 37th St.
Hibbing, MN 55746
Phone: (218)263-7531
Fax: (218)263-6112
Free: 866-720-5198
Format: Adult Contemporary. **Owner:** Midwest Communications Inc., 904 Grand Ave., Wausau, WI 54403, Ph: (715)842-1437, Fax: (715)842-7061. **URL:** http://www.wtbx.com.

18391 ■ WUSZ-FM - 99.9
807 W 37th St.
Hibbing, MN 55746
Phone: (218)263-7531
Fax: (218)263-6112
Free: 866-873-0965
Format: Country. **Owner:** Midwest Communications Inc., 904 Grand Ave., Wausau, WI 54403, Ph: (715)842-1437, Fax: (715)842-7061. **URL:** http://www.radiousa.com.

HINCKLEY

EC MN. Pine Co. 80 mi. SW of Duluth. Wood pallet & photo engineering plants. Dairy,

18392 ■ SCI Broadband
PO Box 810
Hinckley, MN 55037
Phone: (320)384-7442
Free: 800-222-9809
Founded: Sept. 07, 2006. **Cities Served:** 25 channels. **URL:** http://www.scibroadband.com.

18393 ■ WYSG-FM - 96.3
PO Box 79
Hinckley, MN 55037
Phone: (320)384-6167
Format: Religious. **Owner:** Hinckley Adventist Broadcasting Corp. **URL:** http://www.wysg.org/article.php?id=33&search=WYSG.

HOFFMAN

18394 ■ Runestone Cable TV
100 Runestone Dr.
Hoffman, MN 56339
Phone: (320)986-2013
Fax: (320)986-2050
Founded: 1950. **Key Personnel:** Paul Brutlag, Contact. **Cities Served:** 105 channels. **Mailing address:** PO Box 336, Hoffman, MN 56339. **URL:** http://www.runestone.net.

HOPKINS

SE MN. Hennepin Co. 6 mi. SW of Minneapolis. Manufactures farm machinery; berry crates. Greenhouses. Fruit truck farms. Raspberries, celery, vegetables.

18395 ■ Art of the West
Duerr and Tierney Ltd.
15612 Hwy. 7, Ste. 235
Hopkins, MN 55345-3599
Publication E-mail: aotw@.aotw.com
Magazine featuring art of the West, including cowboys, landscapes, and western wildlife. **Freq:** 7/year. **Print Method:** Web. **Trim Size:** 8 1/4 x 10 7/8. **Cols./Page:** 3. **Col. Width:** 13 picas. **Col. Depth:** 58 picas. **Key Personnel:** Vicki Stavig, Editor; Allan J Duerr, Publisher; Thomas F. Tierney, Publisher. **ISSN:** 1047--4994 (print). **Subscription Rates:** $25 Individuals; $45 Two years; $43 Other countries; $80 Two years. **URL:** http://www.aotw.com. **Ad Rates:** BW $2,290; 4C $2,530. **Remarks:** Accepts advertising. **Circ:** Paid ‡25000, Non-paid ‡5000.

18396 ■ Class Action Reporter
Beard Group Inc.
750 Second St. NE, Ste. 100
Hopkins, MN 55343
Phone: (952)930-0630
Fax: (952)930-0631
Publisher's E-mail: info@beardgroupinc.com
Professional magazine covering class action litigations throughout the United States. **Freq:** Daily. **Key Personnel:** Christopher Beard, Publisher, phone: (240)629-3300, fax: (240)629-3360. **ISSN:** 1525-2272 (print). **Subscription Rates:** $575 six months. **URL:** http://litigationdatadepot.com/classActionReporter.php. **Remarks:** Advertising not accepted. **Circ:** (Not Reported).

18397 ■ Plant Prospector: Business Cutbacks and Closings
Beard Group Inc.
750 Second St. NE, Ste. 100
Hopkins, MN 55343
Phone: (952)930-0630
Fax: (952)930-0631
Publisher's E-mail: info@beardgroupinc.com
Professional magazine covering businesses showing signs of financial strains. Delivered via email. **Freq:** Weekly. **Key Personnel:** Christopher Beard, Publisher, phone: (240)629-3300, fax: (240)629-3360. **ISSN:** 1083-5636 (print). **Subscription Rates:** $575 U.S. six months. **Alt. Formats:** PDF. **URL:** http://bankrupt.com/periodicals/pp.html. **Remarks:** Advertising not accepted. **Circ:** (Not Reported).

18398 ■ Troubled Company Reporter
Beard Group Inc.
750 Second St. NE, Ste. 100
Hopkins, MN 55343
Phone: (952)930-0630
Fax: (952)930-0631
Publisher's E-mail: info@beardgroupinc.com
Electronic magazine covering businesses showing financial strain. **Freq:** Daily. **ISSN:** 1520--9474 (print). **Subscription Rates:** $1350 Individuals. **URL:** http://bankrupt.com/periodicals/tcr/tcr.html. **Remarks:** Advertising not accepted. **Circ:** (Not Reported).

HOUSTON

SW MN. Houston Co. 20 mi. SW of La Crosse, WI. Residential.

18399 ■ AceLink Telecommunications Inc.
207 E Cedar St.
Houston, MN 55943
Fax: (507)896-2149
Free: 888-404-4940
Email: info@acegroup.cc
Founded: Sept. 08, 2006. **Cities Served:** 39 channels.

HUTCHINSON

SC MN. McLeod Co. 58 mi. W. of Minneapolis. Manufactures counters, fixtures, farm machinery, wood, concrete products, beverages, cellophane, electronic components, audio and video magnetic tape. Cold storage plant. Dairy, grain, stock, truck farms.

18400 ■ Hutchinson Leader
Hutchinson Leader Inc.
36 Washington Ave. W
Hutchinson, MN 55350
Phone: (320)587-5000
Fax: (320)587-6104
Community newspaper. **Freq:** Semiweekly (Wed. and Sun.). **Print Method:** Offset. **Cols./Page:** 6 and 6. **Col. Width:** 24 nonpareils and 13 inches. **Col. Depth:** 301 agate lines and 21 1/2 inches. **Key Personnel:** Doug Hanneman, Editor, phone: (320)234-4156. **USPS:** 254-800. **Subscription Rates:** $75 Individuals print and online - (McLeod, Meeker, Wright, Renville, Sibley, Carver); $85 Out of area print and online. **URL:** http://www.crowrivermedia.com/hutchinsonleader. **Remarks:** Accepts advertising. **Circ:** Paid ‡4907.

18401 ■ Leader Shopper
Hutchinson Leader Inc.
36 Washington Ave. W
Hutchinson, MN 55350
Phone: (320)587-5000
Fax: (320)587-6104
Shopping guide. **Freq:** Weekly (Sun.). **Key Personnel:** Matt McMillan, Publisher, phone: (320)234-4143; Tina McMillan, Director, Advertising, phone: (320)234-4141; Doug Hanneman, Editor, phone: (320)234-4156. **URL:** http://www.crowrivermedia.com/hutchinsonleader/. **Remarks:** Accepts advertising. **Circ:** Non-paid ♦28765.

18402 ■ KARP-FM - 106.9
20132 Hwy. 15 N
Hutchinson, MN 55350
Phone: (320)587-2140
Fax: (320)587-5158
Free: 800-955-6113
Email: info@kduz.com
Format: Country. **Key Personnel:** Dale Koktan, Gen. Mgr., dkoktan@kduz.com. **Ad Rates:** Advertising accepted; rates available upon request. **URL:** http://www.kduz.com/page/home.

18403 ■ KDUZ-AM - 1260
20132 Hwy. 15 N
Hutchinson, MN 55350
Phone: (320)587-2140
Fax: (320)587-5158
Free: 800-955-6113
Email: info@kduz.com
Format: News; Talk. **Networks:** ABC; Linder Farm. **Founded:** 1953. **Operating Hours:** Continuous; 10% network, 90% local. **Key Personnel:** Dale Koktan, Gen. Mgr., dkoktan@kduz.com. **Wattage:** 1,000. **Ad Rates:** $15.95-18.90 for 30 seconds; $18.35-22.60 for 60 seconds. $15.95-$18.90 for 30 seconds; $18.35-$22.60 for 60 seconds. Combined advertising rates available with KKJR-FM. **Mailing address:** PO Box 366, Hutchinson, MN 55350. **URL:** http://www.kduz.com.

INTERNATIONAL FALLS

NC MN. Koochiching Co. On Rainy River, 165 mi. NW of Duluth. Manufactures paper, lumber. Summer resort. Pine, spruce timber. Dairy, truck farms. Clover, alfalfa seed, potatoes, vegetables.

18404 ■ KADU-FM - 90.1
PO Box 433
International Falls, MN 56649
Phone: (218)285-7398
Format: Contemporary Christian; Religious. **Owner:** Heartland Christian Broadcasters, Inc., at above address. **Founded:** 1994. **Operating Hours:** Continuous. **Key Personnel:** Bruce Christopherson, Contact. **Local Programs:** *A Life That Matters.* **Ad Rates:** Noncommercial. **URL:** http://www.psalmfm.org.

18405 ■ KBHW-FM - 99.5
PO Box 433
International Falls, MN 56649
Phone: (218)285-7398
Email: email@psalmfm.org
Format: Religious. **Owner:** Heartland Christian Broadcasters, Inc., at above address. **Key Personnel:** Jeff Adams, Contact; Bruce Christopherson, Contact; Jeff Adams, Contact; Tim Nelson, Contact. **Wattage:** 100,000. **Ad Rates:** Noncommercial. **URL:** http://www.psalmfm.org.

18406 ■ KGHS-AM - 1230
519 3rd St.
International Falls, MN 56649
Phone: (218)283-3481
Fax: (218)283-3087
Free: 888-283-1041
Format: Oldies; News. **Networks:** Minnesota News; ABC. **Founded:** 1959. **Operating Hours:** Continuous; 20% network, 80% local. **ADI:** Duluth, MN-Superior, WI. **Wattage:** 500 Day; 250 Night. **Ad Rates:** $8-12 for 30 seconds; $12-18 for 60 seconds. $8.50-$12.50 for 60 seconds. Combined advertising rates available with KSDM-FM. **URL:** http://www.ksdmradio.com.

18407 ■ KICC-FM - 91.5
Hwy. 71 & 15th St.
1501 Hwy-71
International Falls, MN 56649
Format: Eclectic; Educational. **Owner:** Rainy River Community College, 1501 Highway 71, International Falls, MN 56649, Ph: (218)285-7722, Fax: (218)285-2239, Free: 800-456-3996. **Founded:** 1970. **Key Personnel:** Scott Crowe, Gen. Mgr.; Jim Rockstad, Chief Engineer. **Wattage:** 180.

18408 ■ KSDM-FM - 104.1
519 3rd St.
International Falls, MN 56649
Phone: (218)283-2622

Fax: (218)283-3087
Free: 888-283-1041
Email: production@ksdmradio.com
Format: Country. **Networks:** Minnesota News; ABC. **Founded:** 1979. **Operating Hours:** Continuous; 15% network, 85% local. **Wattage:** 8,500. **Ad Rates:** Noncommercial. $7.50-$10.50 for 30 seconds; $8.50-$12.50 for 60 seconds. Combined advertising rates available with KGHS-AM. **URL:** http://www.ksdmradio.com.

18409 ■ KXBR-FM - 91.9
PO Box 433
International Falls, MN 56649
Phone: (218)285-9190
Format: Alternative/New Music/Progressive. **Ad Rates:** Advertising accepted; rates available upon request.

ISLE

EC MN. Mille Lacs Co. 38 mi. E. of Brainerd. Manufactures wood products, fishing tackle, boats, metal plating. Resort. Granite quarries; timber. Dairy, stock, poultry farms.

18410 ■ Mille Lacs Messenger
MessAge Media Inc.
280 W Main St.
Isle, MN 56342
Phone: (320)676-3123
Fax: (320)676-8450
Free: 888-676-3123
Publisher's E-mail: news@millelacsmessenger.com
Community newspaper. **Freq:** Weekly (Wed.). **Print Method:** Offset. **Trim Size:** 9 3/4 x 15. **Cols./Page:** 5. **Col. Width:** 11 picas. **Col. Depth:** 15 inches. **Key Personnel:** Brett Larson, Editor; Kevin G. Anderson, Publisher; Jamie Root-Larsen, Manager, Advertising. **Subscription Rates:** $33 Individuals resident of Garrison, Hillman, or McGrath; $39 Individuals rest of Minnesota; $46 Individuals outside Minnesota. **URL:** http://www.messagemedia.co/millelacs. **Mailing address:** PO Box 26, Isle, MN 56342. **Remarks:** Accepts advertising. **Circ:** 5600.

IVANHOE

SW MN. Lincoln Co. 90 mi. NE of Sioux Falls, SD. Dairy, stock, poultry, grain farms. Corn, barley, oats, soybeans.

18411 ■ Ivanhoe Times
Ivanhoe Times
409 N Norman St.
Ivanhoe, MN 56142
Phone: (507)694-1246
Fax: (507)694-1246
Publication E-mail: luminamin@frontiernet.net
Newspaper with a Democratic orientation. **Freq:** Weekly (Thurs.). **Print Method:** Offset. **Cols./Page:** 6. **Col. Width:** 26 nonpareils. **Col. Depth:** 287 agate lines. **Key Personnel:** Ellen Beck, Publisher; Brent Beck, Editor. **Subscription Rates:** $25 Individuals. **URL:** http://ivanhoetimes.freeservers.com; http://ivanhoetimes-com.webs.com. **Ad Rates:** GLR $.145; BW $200; SAU $3; PCI $3.50. **Remarks:** Accepts advertising. **Circ:** Paid 1100, Non-paid 55.

JACKSON

SW MN. Jackson Co. On Des Moines River, 62 mi. SW of Mankato. Manufactures spraying equipment, electronic components. Agriculture. Hog, beef, dairy products, poultry. Grain. Corn, soybeans.

18412 ■ Jackson County Pilot
Livewire Printing Co.
310 Second St.
Jackson, MN 56143
Phone: (507)847-3771
Fax: (507)847-5822
Publisher's E-mail: info@livewireprinting.com
Community newspaper. **Freq:** Weekly (Thurs.). **Print Method:** Offset. **Trim Size:** 16 x 22 8/10. **Cols./Page:** 7. **Col. Width:** 21 nonpareils. **Col. Depth:** 301 agate lines. **Key Personnel:** Justin R. Lessman, Editor. **USPS:** 271-880. **Subscription Rates:** $46 Individuals local; $56 Individuals non-local; $43 Students for 9 months. **URL:** http://www.jacksoncountypilot.com. **Mailing address:** PO Box 208, Jackson, MN 56143. **Ad Rates:** PCI $10.65. **Remarks:** Accepts display and classified advertising. **Circ:** Paid ‡1850.

18413 ■ Livewire
Livewire Printing Co.
310 Second St.
Jackson, MN 56143
Phone: (507)847-3771
Fax: (507)847-5822
Publication E-mail: info@livewireprinting.com
Shopper. **Founded:** 1936. **Freq:** Weekly (Mon.). **Print Method:** Offset. **Trim Size:** 11 3/8 x 16. **Cols./Page:** 6. **Col. Width:** 1 1/2 inches. **Col. Depth:** 15 inches. **Key Personnel:** Justin R. Lessman, Publisher; Tom Murray, Manager, Sales. **Subscription Rates:** Free in Jackson County; $30 Elsewhere. **URL:** http://livewireprinting.com. **Formerly**: Jackson County Livewire. **Mailing address:** PO Box 208, Jackson, MN 56143. **Ad Rates:** PCI $11.90. **Remarks:** Accepts display and classified advertising. **Circ:** Free 10700.

18414 ■ Southern Minnesota Peach
Livewire Printing Co.
310 Second St.
Jackson, MN 56143
Phone: (507)847-3771
Fax: (507)847-5822
Publisher's E-mail: info@livewireprinting.com
Shopper. **Freq:** Weekly. **Print Method:** Offset. **Cols./Page:** 6. **Col. Width:** 10 inches. **Col. Depth:** 15 inches. **Key Personnel:** Justin R. Lessman, Publisher. **URL:** http://livewireprinting.com/publications. **Mailing address:** PO Box 208, Jackson, MN 56143. **Remarks:** Accepts advertising. **Circ:** (Not Reported).

18415 ■ KKOJ-AM - 1190
PO Box 29
Jackson, MN 56143
Phone: (507)847-5400
Fax: (507)847-5745
Free: 800-879-3113
Email: info@kkoj.com
Format: Contemporary Country. **Networks:** AP. **Owner:** Kleven Broadcasting Company of Minnesota, PO Box 29, Jackson, MN 56143. **Founded:** 1980. **Operating Hours:** Sunrise-sunset; 25% network, 75% local. **Wattage:** 5,000. **Ad Rates:** Advertising accepted; rates available upon request. KRAQ-FM. **URL:** http://www.kkoj.com.

18416 ■ KRAQ-FM - 105.7
PO Box 29
Jackson, MN 56143
Phone: (507)847-5400
Fax: (507)847-5745
Free: 800-879-3113
Email: info@kkoj.com
Format: Oldies. **Founded:** Apr. 25, 1994. **Ad Rates:** Advertising accepted; rates available upon request. **URL:** http://www.kkoj.com.

JORDAN

SE MN. Scott Co. 29 mi. Sw of Minneapolis. Manufactures wheelchairs. Sand and gravel pits. Dairy, stock, poultry, grain farms.

18417 ■ Jordan Independent
Southwest Suburban Publishing
109 Rice St. S
Jordan, MN 55352
Phone: (952)492-2224
Fax: (952)492-2231
Community newspaper. **Freq:** Weekly (Thurs.). **Print Method:** Offset. **Cols./Page:** 6. **Col. Width:** 2 1/8 inches. **Col. Depth:** 21 1/2 inches. **Key Personnel:** Mathias Baden, Editor, phone: (952)345-6571; Laurie Hartmann, Publisher, phone: (952)345-6878; Mark Weber, General Manager, phone: (952)345-6672; Brian Hall, Editor, phone: (952)345-6587; Brandon Otte, Contact, phone: (952)345-6570; Nancy Etzel, Advertising Representative, phone: (952)345-6572. **Subscription Rates:** $40 Individuals print and online; $50 Out of area print and online. **URL:** http://www.jordannews.com; http://www.minnesota-newspaper-subscriptions.com/jordan-independent.html; http://www.mnnews.com/newspapers/jordan.html. **Ad Rates:** BW $529; 4C $904; PCI $4.50. **Remarks:** Accepts advertising. **Circ:** 1949.

KENYON

SE MN. Goodhue Co. 14 mi. E. of Faribault. Mattresses and wood products manufactured; canned corn. Grain, dairy, stock, poultry farms. Corn, wheat, barley, soybeans.

18418 ■ The Kenyon Leader
The Kenyon Leader
638 Second St.
Kenyon, MN 55946
Phone: (507)789-6161
Publication E-mail: editor@thekenyonleader.com
Community newspaper. **Freq:** Weekly (Wed.). **Print Method:** Offset. **Cols./Page:** 6. **Col. Width:** 24 nonpareils. **Col. Depth:** 301 agate lines. **Key Personnel:** Terri Lenz, Publisher, Editor, phone: (507)333-3148; Kristy Jacobson, Editor; Jaci Smith, Managing Editor. **USPS:** 293-580. **Subscription Rates:** $70.20 Individuals access to all digital content ; $5.85 Individuals print and digital, monthly. **URL:** http://www.southernminn.com/the_kenyon_leader. **Ad Rates:** GLR $.286; BW $516; SAU $4. **Remarks:** Accepts advertising. **Circ:** (Not Reported).

KERKHOVEN

SW MN. Swift Co. 16 mi. SE of Benson.

18419 ■ The Kerkhoven Banner
The Kerkhoven Banner
PO Box 148
Kerkhoven, MN 56252
Phone: (320)264-3071
Fax: (320)264-3070
Local newspaper. **Freq:** Weekly (Thurs.). **Print Method:** Offset. **Cols./Page:** 6. **Col. Width:** 2 1/8 nonpareils. **Col. Depth:** 301 agate lines. **USPS:** 293-700. **Ad Rates:** GLR $.15; BW $270.90; SAU $3; PCI $3. **Remarks:** Advertising accepted; rates available upon request. **Circ:** 1500.

KIESTER

SC MN. Faribault Co. 25 mi SW of Albert Lea. Feed mill. Stock, dairy, poultry, grain farms. Corn, oats, barley, soybeans.

18420 ■ The Courier-Sentinel
The Courier-Sentinel
405 W Center St.
Kiester, MN 56051
Phone: (507)294-3400
Publisher's E-mail: coursent@smig.net
Community newspaper. **Freq:** Weekly (Thurs.). **Print Method:** Offset. **Trim Size:** 16 x 23. **Cols./Page:** 7. **Col. Width:** 21 nonpareils. **Col. Depth:** 294 agate lines. **Key Personnel:** Cynthia A. Matson, Editor. **URL:** http://www.mnnews.com/newspapers/kiester.html. **Mailing address:** PO Box 250, Kiester, MN 56051. **Ad Rates:** GLR $.15; SAU $2.92. **Remarks:** Accepts advertising. **Circ:** 1599.

KIMBALL

C MN. Stearns Co. 18 mi. SW of Saint Cloud. Lakes. Ski recreation area. Resort. Manufactures concrete products, truck and trailer equipment. Dairy, poultry farms.

18421 ■ Tri-County News
Tri-County News
70 Main St. S
Kimball, MN 55353
Phone: (320)398-5000
Fax: (320)398-5000
Publication E-mail: news@tricountynews.mn
Community newspaper. **Founded:** 1948. **Freq:** Weekly (Thurs.). **Print Method:** Offset. **Cols./Page:** 5. **Col. Width:** 22 nonpareils. **Col. Depth:** 210 agate lines. **Key Personnel:** Jean Doran Matua, Editor. **USPS:** 639-180. **Subscription Rates:** $31 Individuals 9 months; $21 Individuals 6 months; $12 Individuals 3 months; $36 Individuals inside Minnesota; $46 Out of state; $26 Individuals inside Minnesota; $36 Out of state with senior discount. **URL:** http://www.kimballarea.com. **Mailing address:** PO Box 220, Kimball, MN 55353-0220. **Ad Rates:** GLR $4; BW $4.50; 4C $400; PCI $4.50. **Remarks:** Accepts advertising. **Circ:** Paid 1375.

Circulation: ★ = AAM; △ or • = BPA; ♦ = CAC; ❑ = VAC; ⊕ = PO Statement; ‡ = Publisher's Report; Boldface figures = sworn; Light figures = estimated.

LA CRESCENT

SE MN. Houston Co. 3 mi. W. of La Crosse, WI, on Mississippi River. Recreation, sports area. Manufactures concrete. Apple orchards. Dairy farms.

18422 ■ WXOW-TV - 19
3705 County Highway 25
La Crescent, MN 55947
Phone: (507)895-9969
Fax: (507)895-8124
Email: aedesk@wxow.com
Format: Commercial TV. **Networks:** ABC. **Owner:** Quincy Newspapers Inc., 130 S 5th St., Quincy, IL 62306, Ph: (217)223-5100. **Founded:** 1970. **Operating Hours**: 19.5 hours Daily; 60% network, 40% local. **ADI:** La Crosse-Eau Claire, WI. **Key Personnel:** Deb Simonis, Div. Dir., dsimonis@wxow.com; Sean Dwyer, News Dir., sdwyer@wxow.com; David Booth, Gen. Mgr., dbooth@wxow.com. **Wattage**: 630,000 Visual 63,000. **Ad Rates:** Advertising accepted; rates available upon request. **URL:** http://www.wxow.com.

LAFAYETTE

SC MN. Nicollet Co. 36 mi. NW of Mankato. Manufactures cement blocks, tiles. Agriculture. Corn, oats, barley, wheat, soybeans.

18423 ■ Lafayette-Nicollet Ledger
Ledger Publishing Co.
631 Main Ave.
Lafayette, MN 56054
Phone: (507)228-8985
Publication E-mail: ledger@prairiepublishingmn.com
Community newspaper. **Founded:** 1904. **Freq:** Weekly (Thurs.). **Print Method:** Offset. **Cols./Page:** 7. **Col. Width:** 24 nonpareils. **Col. Depth:** 301 agate lines. **USPS:** 301-420. **Subscription Rates:** $35 Individuals; $40 Out of state; $30 Individuals online. **URL:** http://www.prairiepublishingmn.com/21001/1972/1/home. **Mailing address:** PO Box 212, Lafayette, MN 56054. **Ad Rates:** GLR $.50; SAU $4. **Remarks:** Accepts advertising. **Circ:** 1263.

LAKE CITY

SE MN. Wabasha Co. On Lake Pepin, 58 mi. SE of Saint Paul. Manufactures iron and aluminum pistons, flour, precision tools. Nurseries. Resort. Grain, dairy, stock, poultry farms.

18424 ■ Deer Farmer
North American Deer Farmers Association
1215 N Seventh St., No. 104
Lake City, MN 55041-1266
Phone: (651)345-5600
Fax: (651)345-5603
Publisher's E-mail: info@nadefa.org
Trade journal covering deer farming and ranching. **Freq:** Quarterly. **Trim Size:** 8 x 11. **Key Personnel:** Holly Johnson, Editor. **ISSN:** 1084--0583 (print). **Formerly:** The North American Deer Farmer: The Official Journal of the North American Deer Farmers Association. **Ad Rates:** BW $355; 4C $443. **Remarks:** Accepts advertising. **Circ:** Combined 1200.

18425 ■ Lake City Graphic
Lake City Graphic
118 S 8th St.
Lake City, MN 55041
Phone: (651)345-3316
Fax: (651)345-4200
Publisher's E-mail: graphic@rconnect.com
Community newspaper. **Founded:** 1861. **Freq:** Weekly (Thurs.). **Print Method:** Offset. **Trim Size:** 14 1/2 x 22 3/4. **Cols./Page:** 6. **Col. Width:** 12.5 picas. **Col. Depth:** 21.5 inches. **USPS:** 301-840. **Subscription Rates:** $25 Individuals; $30 Out of area. **URL:** http://www.mnnews.com/newspapers/lakecity.html. **Mailing address:** PO Box 469, Lake City, MN 55041. **Ad Rates:** GLR $.52; BW $941.70; SAU $7.30; PCI $7.30. **Remarks:** Advertising accepted; rates available upon request. **Circ:** ‡3,240.

18426 ■ KLCH-FM - 94.9
117 S Washington St.
Lake City, MN 55041
Phone: (651)388-7151
Fax: (651)388-7153
Format: Oldies. **Wattage**: 5,000. **URL:** http://www.lakehits95.com.

LAKEFIELD

SW MN. Jackson Co. 80 mi. SW of Mankato. Heat woodburning furnace production. Egg-packing plant. Dairy, stock, poultry, grain farms.

18427 ■ Lakefield Standard
Lakefield Standard
403 Main St.
Lakefield, MN 56150
Phone: (507)662-5555
Fax: (507)662-6770
Publication E-mail: info@livewireprinting.com
General newspaper. **Freq:** Weekly (Thurs.). **Print Method:** Offset. **Cols./Page:** 7. **Col. Width:** 1 7/8 inches. **Col. Depth:** 21 1/2 inches. **Key Personnel:** Justin Lessman, Publisher; Amy Durst, Manager, Circulation; Ryan Brinks, Editor. **USPS:** 302-980. **Subscription Rates:** $47 Individuals inside Jackson County; $57 Out of area; $44 Students nine months. **URL:** http://www.lakefieldstandard.com. **Mailing address:** PO Box 249, Lakefield, MN 56150. **Ad Rates:** GLR $.185; BW $406; 4C $600; SAU $3.90; PCI $5.30. **Remarks:** Accepts advertising. **Circ:** Paid ‡1150.

18428 ■ Speaking of Columbias
Columbia Sheep Breeders Association of America
PO Box 722
Lakefield, MN 56150
Phone: (507)360-2160
Fax: (507)662-6294
Freq: 3/year. **Subscription Rates:** $10 U.S.; $15 Canada; Included in membership. **URL:** http://columbiasheep.org/publication.htm. **Ad Rates:** BW $195; 4C $295. **Remarks:** Accepts advertising. **Circ:** (Not Reported).

LAKEVILLE

SE MN. Dakota Co. 22 mi S. of Saint Paul. Industrial area.

18429 ■ Farm Show
Farm Show Publishing Inc.
PO Box 1029
Lakeville, MN 55044-1029
Fax: (952)469-5575
Free: 800-834-9665
Publication E-mail: mark@farmshow.com
Magazine reporting on new products and product evaluations. **Founded:** Jan. 1977. **Freq:** Bimonthly. **Print Method:** Offset. **Cols./Page:** 4. **Col. Width:** 27 nonpareils. **Col. Depth:** 192 agate lines. **Key Personnel:** Mark Newhall, Editor; Bill Gergen, Associate Editor. **ISSN:** 0163-4518 (print). **Subscription Rates:** $23.95 Individuals; $44.95 Two years; $29.95 Canada; $56.95 Two years Canada; $53.95 Other countries; $104.95 Other countries 2 years. **URL:** http://www.farmshow.com. **Remarks:** Advertising not accepted. **Circ:** 185000.

18430 ■ FATE Magazine: True Reports of the Strange and Unknown
FATE Magazine
PO Box 460
Lakeville, MN 55044
Fax: (952)891-6091
Free: 800-728-2730
Publisher's E-mail: fate@fatemag.com
Paranormal magazine focusing on UFOs, hauntings, psychic phenomena, mystery animals, ancient mysteries, and personal mystical experiences. **Freq:** Monthly. **Print Method:** Web offset. **Trim Size:** 5 3/8 x 7 5/8. **Key Personnel:** Phyllis Galde, Editor-in-Chief; David Godwin, Managing Editor. **ISSN:** 0014-8776 (print). **Subscription Rates:** $9.95 Individuals e-Edition 6 months; $19.95 Individuals e-Edition 1 year; $36.95 Two years e-Edition; $14.95 Individuals Print - 6 months; $27.95 Individuals Print - 1 year; $53.95 Two years Print; $36.95 Individuals print & e-edition; $69.95 Two years print & e-edition. **URL:** http://www.fatemag.com. **Ad Rates:** GLR $1.25; BW $850; 4C $850. **Remarks:** Advertising accepted; rates available upon request. **Circ:** Paid 13,000, Free 300.

18431 ■ Journal of Sexual Medicine
International Society for the Study of Women's Sexual Health
PO Box 1233
Lakeville, MN 55044
Phone: (218)461-5115
Fax: (612)808-0491
Publisher's E-mail: info@isswsh.org
Freq: Monthly. **ISSN:** 1743--6095 (print); **EISSN:** 1743--6109 (electronic). **Subscription Rates:** Included in membership; $493 Individuals print and online. **URL:** http://www.isswsh.org/resources/jsm; http://onlinelibrary.wiley.com/journal/10.1111/(ISSN)1743-6109. **Remarks:** Advertising not accepted. **Circ:** (Not Reported).

18432 ■ WETT-AM - 1590
16233 Kenyon Ave., Ste. 220
Lakeville, MN 55044
Phone: (952)683-1111
Format: Talk. **Networks:** Mutual Broadcasting System; Talknet. **Founded:** 1958. **Operating Hours**: 6 a.m.-midnight; 100% local. **ADI**: Salisbury, MD. **Key Personnel:** Wayne Cannon, Operations Mgr.; Jack Gillen, Gen. Mgr. **Wattage**: 1,000. **Ad Rates:** $12-18 for 30 seconds; $16-22 for 60 seconds.

18433 ■ WXRD-FM
16233 Kenyon Ave.
Lakeville, MN 55044
Format: Classic Rock. **Wattage**: 1,350 ERP.

18434 ■ WZVN-FM
16233 Kenyon Ave.
Lakeville, MN 55044
Format: Adult Contemporary. **Wattage**: 2,650 ERP. **Ad Rates:** Noncommercial.

LAMBERTON

SW MN. Redwood Co. 75 mi. W. of Mankato. Grain, stock, dairy farms. Corn, soybeans.

18435 ■ Lamberton News
Lamberton News
218 Main St.
Lamberton, MN 56152
Phone: (507)752-7181
Fax: (507)752-7181
Publication E-mail: lambnews@centurylink.net
Community newspaper. **Freq:** Weekly (Wed.). **Print Method:** Offset. **Cols./Page:** 6. **Col. Width:** 24 nonpareils. **Col. Depth:** 301 agate lines. **Key Personnel:** Joseph G. Dietl, Editor. **USPS:** 303-640. **URL:** http://www.mnnews.com/newspapers/lamberton.html. **Mailing address:** PO Box 308, Lamberton, MN 56152-0308. **Ad Rates:** GLR $.15; BW $387; SAU $3; PCI $3. **Remarks:** Advertising accepted; rates available upon request. **Circ:** ‡1726.

LE CENTER

SC MN. Le Sueur Co. 26 mi. NE of Mankato. Manufactures formica counter tops, polyethelene liquid containers, electrical generators, dehydrated alfalfa products. Diversified farming. Dairying, corn, livestock, soybeans, wheat.

18436 ■ Le Center Leader
Minnesota Valley News Publishing L.L.C.
62 E Minnesota St.
Le Center, MN 56057
Phone: (507)357-2233
Fax: (507)357-6656
Community newspaper. **Freq:** Weekly (Wed.). **Print Method:** Offset. **Cols./Page:** 6. **Col. Width:** 13 picas. **Col. Depth:** 301 agate lines. **Key Personnel:** Terri McMillen, Editor. **Subscription Rates:** $49.40 Individuals 52 weeks. **URL:** http://www.southernminn.com/le_center_leader. **Ad Rates:** BW $774; SAU $6; PCI $6. **Remarks:** Accepts advertising. **Circ:** (Not Reported).

LE ROY

SE MN. Mower Co. 23 mi. SE of Austin. State Park. Manufactures plastic & nylon coating of metals, electrical assemblies, plaques. Creamery. Lumber. Dairy, beef, hog, grain farms. Soybeans, oats, corn.

18437 ■ Le Roy Independent: LeRoy Independent
Evans Printing & Publishing
135 E Main St.
Le Roy, MN 55951-0089
Phone: (507)324-5325
Fax: (507)324-5267

Publisher's E-mail: evans@frontiernet.net
Community newspaper. **Freq:** Weekly (Thurs.). **Print Method:** Offset. **Cols./Page:** 6. **Col. Width:** 2.16 inches. **Col. Depth:** 21 inches. **USPS:** 310-330. **URL:** http://www.leroyindependent.com. **Mailing address:** PO Box 89, Le Roy, MN 55951-0089. **Remarks:** Accepts advertising. **Circ:** ‡1238.

LE SUEUR

SC MN. Le Sueur Co. On Minnesota River, 50 mi. S. of Minneapolis. Cheese factory. Aluminum foundry. Food packing and canning.

18438 ■ Le Sueur News-Herald
Le Sueur Publishing
101 Bridge St.
Le Sueur, MN 56058
Phone: (507)665-3332
Local newspaper. **Freq:** Weekly (Tues.). **Print Method:** Offset. **Cols./Page:** 6. **Col. Width:** 28 nonpareils. **Col. Depth:** 301 agate lines. **Key Personnel:** Stephanie Hill, Editor. **Subscription Rates:** $49.40 Individuals. **URL:** http://www.southernminn.com/le_sueur_news_herald. **Ad Rates:** GLR $.61. **Remarks:** Accepts advertising. **Circ:** ‡1536.

LINDSTROM

EC MN. Chisago Co. 38 mi. NE of Saint Paul. Lake Resort. Plastic products. Fishing. Dairy, grain farms. Potatoes.

18439 ■ Chisago County Press
Chisago County Press
12615 Lake Blvd.
Hwy. 8, West End of Town
Lindstrom, MN 55045
Phone: (651)257-5115
Publication E-mail: chisago@citlink.net
Community newspaper. **Freq:** Weekly (Thurs.). **Print Method:** Offset. **Cols./Page:** 6. **Col. Width:** 28 nonpareils. **Col. Depth:** 294 agate lines. **Key Personnel:** Matt Silver, Publisher; Denise Martin, Managing Editor. **USPS:** 106-140. **Subscription Rates:** $47 Individuals; $49.50 Out of area. **URL:** http://www.chisagocountypress.com. **Mailing address:** PO Box 748, Lindstrom, MN 55045. **Ad Rates:** GLR $.50; BW $805.14; 4C $75; SAU $7.10; PCI $12.85. **Remarks:** Accepts advertising. **Circ:** Paid ‡3835, Free ‡30.

LITCHFIELD

18440 ■ Litchfield Independent-Review
Litchfield Independent-Review
217 N Sibley Ave.
Litchfield, MN 55355
Phone: (320)693-3266
Fax: (320)693-9177
Community newspaper. **Freq:** Weekly (Thurs.). **Print Method:** Web offset. **Cols./Page:** 8. **Col. Width:** 10 picas. **Col. Depth:** 21 1/2 inches. **Subscription Rates:** $27 Individuals print & online - 6-county area (Meeker, McLeod, Wright, Renville, Stearns, Kandiyohi) 6 months; $39 Individuals print & online - 6-county area (Meeker, McLeod, Wright, Renville, Stearns, Kandiyohi) 12 months; $66 Individuals print & online - 6-county area (Meeker, McLeod, Wright, Renville, Stearns, Kandiyohi) 24 months; $37 Individuals print & online - outside of 6 county area 6 months; $54 Individuals print & online -outside of 6 county area 12 months. **URL:** http://www.independentreview.net/. **Ad Rates:** SAU $6.40; PCI $5.17. **Remarks:** Accepts advertising. **Circ:** Thurs. ♦**5,444**.

18441 ■ Meeker County Advertiser
Litchfield Independent-Review
217 N Sibley Ave.
Litchfield, MN 55355
Phone: (320)693-3266
Fax: (320)693-9177
Shopping guide. **Freq:** Weekly (Sat.). **Key Personnel:** Matt McMillan, Publisher, phone: (320)234-4143; Brent Schacherer, Publisher, phone: (320)693-3266. **Subscription Rates:** $36 By mail. **URL:** http://www.crowrivermedia.com/independentreview/. **Remarks:** Accepts advertising. **Circ:** Non-paid ‡10696.

18442 ■ KLFD-AM - 1410
234 N Sibley Ave.
Litchfield, MN 55355
Phone: (320)693-3281
Fax: (320)693-3283
Email: register@klfd1410.com
Format: Sports. **Networks:** ABC; Fox; CBS; NBC. **Owner:** Mid Minnesota Media L.L.C., at above address. **Founded:** 1959. **Operating Hours**: Continuous. **ADI**: Minneapolis-St. Paul, MN. **Key Personnel:** Steve Gretsch, Gen. Mgr., steve@klfd1410.com; Tim Bergstrom, News Dir., tim@klfd1410.com. **Local Programs**: *Imagination Theatre*, Saturday Sunday 9:00 p.m. 6:00 p.m. **Wattage**: 500 Day; 045 Night. **Ad Rates:** Advertising accepted; rates available upon request. for 30 seconds; for 60 seconds. **URL:** http://www.klfd1410.com.

LITTLE FALLS

C MN. Morrison Co. On Mississippi River, 33 mi. NW of Saint Cloud. Resort. Manufactures plastic planting pots, pulp and newsprint, boats, snowplows, conveyors, food ingredients, monuments, furniture, bricks, cement blocks, Hatcheries. Dairy, stock, poultry, truck farms.

18443 ■ KFML-FM - 94.1
16405 Haven Rd.
Little Falls, MN 56345
Phone: (320)632-2992
Fax: (320)632-2571
Free: 800-568-7249
Format: Adult Contemporary. **Networks:** CNN Radio; Minnesota News. **Owner:** Little Falls Radio Corp., 16405 Haven Rd., Little Falls, MN 56345, Ph: (320)632-2992, Fax: (320)632-2571, Free: 800-568-7249. **Founded:** 1988. **Operating Hours**: Continuous. **Wattage**: 6,000. **Ad Rates:** Noncommercial. Combined advertising rates available with WYRQ-KLIF. **URL:** http://www.fallsradio.com.

18444 ■ KLTF-AM - 960
16405 Haven Rd.
Little Falls, MN 56345
Phone: (320)632-2992
Fax: (320)632-2571
Free: 800-568-7249
Format: News; Sports; Talk; Information. **Networks:** ABC; Minnesota News. **Owner:** Little Falls Radio Corp., 16405 Haven Rd., Little Falls, MN 56345, Ph: (320)632-2992, Fax: (320)632-2571, Free: 800-568-7249. **Founded:** 1950. **Operating Hours**: Continuous. **ADI**: Minneapolis-St. Paul, MN. **Key Personnel:** Chris Grams, Contact, chris@fallsradio.com; Rod Grams, Contact; Donna Hilmerson, Contact. **Local Programs**: *Party Line*, Monday Tuesday Wednesday Thursday Friday 10:00 a.m. - 11:00 a.m. **Wattage**: 5,000. **Ad Rates:** $15.50 for 30 seconds; $22 for 60 seconds. **URL:** http://www.fallsradio.com.

LONG PRAIRIE

SC MN. Todd Co. 23 mi. ENE of Alexandria.

18445 ■ Long Prairie Leader
Long Prairie Leader
21 Third St. S
Long Prairie, MN 56347
Phone: (320)732-2151
Fax: (320)732-2152
Publisher's E-mail: news@lpleader.com
County newspaper. **Freq:** Weekly. **Print Method:** Offset. **Cols./Page:** 6. **Col. Width:** 12.5 picas. **Col. Depth:** 21 agate lines. **Key Personnel:** Susan Farmer, Editor; Jason C. Brown, Editor. **Subscription Rates:** $35 Individuals Todd County - print; $40 Out of area print; $5 Individuals 1 month online. **URL:** http://www.lpleader.com. **Mailing address:** PO Box 479, Long Prairie, MN 56347. **Ad Rates:** BW $436.50; SAU $7; PCI $6.90. **Remarks:** Color advertising accepted; rates available upon request. **Circ:** 3300.

18446 ■ KEYL-AM - 1400
PO Box 187
Long Prairie, MN 56347
Phone: (612)732-2164
Fax: (612)732-2284
Free: 877-448-5935
Format: Country. **Networks:** ABC; Satellite Music Network; Minnesota News. **Owner:** Prairie Broadcasting Company Inc., 207 N Fifth St., Fargo, ND 58102, Ph: (701)241-6900, Fax: (701)239-7650, Free: 800-359-6900. **Founded:** 1959. **Operating Hours**: Controlled; 45% local, 55% network. **ADI**: Minneapolis-St. Paul, MN. **Key Personnel:** Gene Sullivan, Gen. Mgr.; Clif Cline, Dir. of Programs; Mary Stencel, Contact. **Wattage**: 1,000. **Ad Rates:** Noncommercial. Combined advertising rates available with KXDL-FM. **URL:** http://www.kxdlhotrodradio.com.

18447 ■ KXDL-FM - 99.7
221 Central Ave.
Long Prairie, MN 56347
Phone: (320)732-2164
Fax: (320)732-2284
Free: 877-448-5935
Format: Oldies. **Networks:** Satellite Music Network; ABC. **Owner:** Prairie Broadcasting Company Inc., 207 N Fifth St., Fargo, ND 58102, Ph: (701)241-6900, Fax: (701)239-7650, Free: 800-359-6900. **Founded:** 1992. **Operating Hours**: Continuous. **ADI**: Minneapolis-St. Paul, MN. **Key Personnel:** Todd Jensen, Sales Mgr. **Wattage**: 6,000. **Ad Rates:** Noncommercial. Combined advertising rates available with KEYL-AM. **Mailing address:** PO Box 187, Long Prairie, MN 56347. **URL:** http://www.kxdlhotrodradio.com.

LONGVILLE

18448 ■ Pine Cone Press-Citizen
Pine Cone Press-Citizen
166 Hardy Ln., Ste. 100
Longville, MN 56655-0401
Phone: (218)363-2002
Fax: (218)363-3043
Publisher's E-mail: presscit@eot.com
Community newspaper. **Freq:** Weekly (Tues.). **URL:** http://www.mnnews.com/newspapers/longville.html. **Formerly**: Pine Cone Press. **Mailing address:** PO Box 401, Longville, MN 56655-0401. **Remarks:** Accepts advertising. **Circ:** ‡6778.

LUVERNE

SW MN. Rock Co. 30 mi. E. of Sioux Falls, SD. Manufactures fire apparatus, butter, silos, automatic feeders, water softeners, ventilating equipment. Dairy, stock, poultry, grain farms, livestock.

18449 ■ Rock County Star Herald
Star-Herald.com
117 W Main St.
Luverne, MN 56156
Phone: (507)283-2333
Fax: (507)283-2335
Publisher's E-mail: sales@star-herald.com
Community newspaper. **Freq:** Weekly (Thurs.). **Print Method:** Offset. **Cols./Page:** 6. **Col. Width:** 24 nonpareils. **Col. Depth:** 294 agate lines. **Key Personnel:** Lori Ehde, Editor; John Rittenhouse, Editor; Rick Peterson, General Manager. **Subscription Rates:** $44 Individuals online; $72 Individuals in County - print; $89 Individuals out of County - print; $85 Individuals in County - print and online; $110 Individuals out of County - print and online. **URL:** http://www.star-herald.com. **Ad Rates:** GLR $.23. **Remarks:** Accepts advertising. **Circ:** 2566.

18450 ■ KLQL-FM - 101.1
1140 150th Ave.
Luverne, MN 56156
Phone: (507)283-4444
Format: Country; Agricultural. **Networks:** ABC. **Owner:** Three Eagles Communication, 3800 Cornhusker Hwy., Lincoln, NE 68504, Ph: (402)466-1234, Fax: (402)467-4095. **Founded:** 1983. **Operating Hours**: Continuous. **ADI**: Sioux Falls-Mitchell, SD. **Wattage**: 100,000. **Ad Rates:** $8-15 for 30 seconds; $10-17 for 60 seconds. **URL:** http://www.k101fm.net.

18451 ■ KQAD-AM - 800
1140 150th Ave.
Luverne, MN 56156
Phone: (507)283-4444
Format: Adult Contemporary. **Networks:** ABC; Westwood One Radio. **Founded:** 1971. **Operating Hours**: Continuous; 20% local, 80% network. **ADI**: Sioux Falls-Mitchell, SD. **Key Personnel:** Matt Crosby, News Dir., mcrosby@kqad.threeeagles.com. **Wattage**: 500. **Ad Rates:** $4-7 for 15 seconds; $6-9 for 30 seconds; $8-11 for 60 seconds.

Circulation: ★ = AAM; △ or • = BPA; ♦ = CAC; ❑ = VAC; ⊕ = PO Statement; ‡ = Publisher's Report; Boldface figures = sworn; Light figures = estimated.

MADELIA

SC MN. Watonwan Co. 24 mi. SW of Mankato. Cement tile, frozen foods, feed mills. Grain, stock, poultry, truck farms.

18452 ■ Times-Messenger
Madelia Times-Messenger
112 W Main St.
Madelia, MN 56062
Phone: (507)642-3636
Fax: (507)642-3535
Community newspaper. **Founded:** 1870. **Freq:** Weekly (Thurs.). **Print Method:** Offset. **Cols./Page:** 6. **Col. Width:** 24 nonpareils. **Col. Depth:** 21 1/2 inches. **Subscription Rates:** $35 Individuals; $42 Out of area; $50 Out of state; $30 Individuals online. **URL:** http://www.prairiepublishingmn.com/21001/1972/1/home. **Ad Rates:** GLR $3.50; BW $416; 4C $615; SAU $2.60; CNU $4.75; PCI $3.50. **Remarks:** Accepts advertising. **Circ:** Paid ‡1132.

MADISON

SW MN. Lac qui Parle Co. 90 mi. S. of Fergus Falls. Manufactures flour, fertilizer. Grain, dairy, poultry, stock farms. Corn, rye, wheat, oats, barley, soybeans.

18453 ■ Western Guard
Western Guard
216 6th Ave.
Madison, MN 56256
Phone: (320)598-7521
Fax: (320)598-7523
Publication E-mail: westerng@frontiernet.net
Community newspaper. **Freq:** Weekly (Wed.). **Print Method:** Offset. **Cols./Page:** 6. **Col. Width:** 26 nonpareils. **Col. Depth:** 301 agate lines. **URL:** http://www.mnnews.com/newspapers/madison.html. **Ad Rates:** GLR $.22; SAU $2.90. **Remarks:** Accepts advertising. **Circ:** 2115.

18454 ■ KLQP-FM - 92.1
623 W 3rd St.
Madison, MN 56256
Phone: (320)598-7301
Fax: (320)598-7955
Email: klqpfm@farmerstel.net
Format: Country; News. **Networks:** CNN Radio; Fox. **Owner:** Lac Qui Parle Broadcasting Co. Inc. **Founded:** 1983. **Operating Hours:** Continuous; 100% local. **Key Personnel:** Maynard Meyer, Gen. Mgr., News Dir.; Kris Kuechenmeister, Office Mgr. **Wattage:** 25,000. **Ad Rates:** $5 for 30 seconds; $7.50 for 60 seconds. **Mailing address:** PO Box 70, Madison, MN 56256. **URL:** http://www.klqpfm.com.

MADISON LAKE

SC MN. Blue Earth Co. 12 mi. E. of Mankato. Summer resort. Dairy, grain, stock farms.

18455 ■ Lake Region Times
Lake Region Times
513 Main St.
Madison Lake, MN 56063-0128
Phone: (507)243-3031
Fax: (507)243-3122
Publication E-mail: lrtimes@hickorytech.net
Community newspaper. **Freq:** Weekly (Wed.). **Print Method:** Letterpress and offset. **Cols./Page:** 6. **Col. Width:** 22 nonpareils. **Col. Depth:** 210 agate lines. **USPS:** 001-940. **URL:** http://www.mnnews.com/newspapers/madisonlake.html. **Mailing address:** PO Box 128, Madison Lake, MN 56063-0128. **Ad Rates:** GLR $4; BW $441; 4C $491; PCI $4.50. **Remarks:** Accepts advertising. **Circ:** 901.

MAHNOMEN

NW MN. Mahnomen Co. 58 mi. NE of Fargo. Manufactures butter, lumber. Timber. Dairy, grain farms.

18456 ■ KRJM-FM - 101.5
PO Box 420
Mahnomen, MN 56557
Format: Oldies. **Owner:** R&J Broadcasting Inc., 312 W Main St., Ada, MN 56510, Ph: (218)784-2844, Fax: (218)784-3749, Free: 800-569-4171. **Operating Hours:** Continuous. **Wattage:** 25,000. **Ad Rates:** $14 for 30 seconds; $28 for 60 seconds. @CRB KRJB-ADA. **URL:** http://krjmradio.com.

MAHTOMEDI

18457 ■ International Vocational Education and Training
International Vocational Education and Training Association
186 Wedgewood Dr.
Mahtomedi, MN 55115-2702
Phone: (651)770-6719
Publisher's E-mail: iveta@visi.com
Freq: Semiannual. **ISSN:** 1075--2455 (print). **URL:** http://www.iveta.org/journal. **Remarks:** Advertising not accepted. **Circ:** (Not Reported).

MANKATO

SC MN. Nicollet Co. On Minnesota and Blue Earth Rivers, 80 mi. SW of Minneapolis. Mankato State University, Bethany Lutheran College. Manufactures flour, cement, stone products, electronic components, tools, hydraulic equipment, soft drinks, paper boxes, power hammers, farm machinery, sashes, doors, incubators. Stone quarries. Agriculture. Livestock, dairy products, corn, barley. Building materials, oil refinery, breweries.

18458 ■ The Betsy-Tacy Society Journal
Betsy-Tacy Society
PO Box 94
Mankato, MN 56002-0094
Phone: (507)345-9777
Publisher's E-mail: BTSMankato@gmail.com
Journal presenting captivating stories of small town life, family traditions and enduring friendships. **Freq:** Periodic. **Subscription Rates:** $5 Individuals hardcover. **URL:** http://www.betsy-tacysociety.org/betsy-tacy-journal. **Remarks:** Advertising not accepted. **Circ:** (Not Reported).

18459 ■ Home Magazine
Home Magazine
1400 Madison Ave., Ste. 610
Mankato, MN 56001
Phone: (507)387-7953
Fax: (507)387-4775
Publisher's E-mail: homemag@homemagonline.com
Shopper. **Freq:** Weekly. **Print Method:** Offset. **Trim Size:** 11 x 16. **Cols./Page:** 6. **Col. Width:** 21 nonpareils. **Col. Depth:** 210 agate lines. **Key Personnel:** Kelly Hulke, General Manager; MaryKay Degrood, Manager, Advertising; Robin Stenzel, Manager, Circulation. **URL:** http://www.homemagonline.com. **Mailing address:** PO Box 4423, Mankato, MN 56002. **Ad Rates:** BW $1,125; 4C $1,320; PCI $13.90. **Remarks:** Accepts advertising. **Circ:** Combined 40136.

18460 ■ Mankato Free Press
Community Newspaper Holdings Inc.
418 S Second St.
Mankato, MN 56001
Publication E-mail: editor@mankatofreepress.com
Newspaper serving South Central Minnesota. **Freq:** Mon.-Sun. **Key Personnel:** Joe Spear, Managing Editor, phone: (507)344-6384; Jim Santori, Publisher, phone: (507)344-6310. **Subscription Rates:** $166 Individuals carrier delivery; $199 Individuals mail delivery. **URL:** http://www.mankatofreepress.com. **Remarks:** Accepts advertising. **Circ:** (Not Reported).

18461 ■ Reporter
Minnesota State University - Mankato
228 Wiecking Ctr.
Mankato, MN 56001-6062
Phone: (507)389-1866
Fax: (507)389-2227
Free: 800-722-0544
Publisher's E-mail: campushub@mnsu.edu
Collegiate newspaper. **Founded:** Mar. 26, 1926. **Freq:** Semiweekly (Tues. and Thurs. during the academic year). **Print Method:** Letterpress and offset. **Cols./Page:** 5. **Col. Width:** 1 3/4 inches. **Subscription Rates:** Free for visitor. **URL:** http://www.msureporter.com. **Ad Rates:** GLR $4.65; BW $296.25; 4C $556.25; PCI $3.95. **Remarks:** Advertising accepted; rates available upon request. **Circ:** Free 7500.

18462 ■ Charter Communications
1724 Madison Ave.
Mankato, MN 56001
Free: 888-438-2427
Key Personnel: Mary Jo Moehle, VP of Investor Rel. **Cities Served:** 126 channels. **URL:** http://www.charter.com.

18463 ■ KDOG-FM - 96.7
59346 Madison Ave.
Mankato, MN 56001
Phone: (507)345-5800
Format: Contemporary Hit Radio (CHR). **Networks:** ABC. **Founded:** 1985. **Operating Hours:** Continuous; 5% network, 95% local. **ADI:** Mankato, MN. **Key Personnel:** Jo Bailey, Gen. Mgr., Dir. of Sales, jobailey@radiomankato.com; Chris Painter, Contact, chrispainter@radiomankato.com; Deb Armstrong, Contact, debarmstrong@radiomankato.com; Chris Painter, Contact, chrispainter@radiomankato.com; Deb Armstrong, Contact, debarmstrong@radiomankato.com. **Wattage:** 4,000. **Ad Rates:** $10-14.50 for 30 seconds; $15-21 for 60 seconds. **URL:** http://www.hot967.fm.

18464 ■ KEEZ-FM - 99
1807 Lee Blvd. N
Mankato, MN 56003
Phone: (507)345-4646
Fax: (507)345-3299
Format: Adult Contemporary. **Networks:** Mutual Broadcasting System. **Owner:** Three Eagles Communications, 3800 Cornhusker Hwy., Lincoln, NE 68504, Ph: (402)466-1234, Fax: (402)467-4095. **Founded:** 1977. **Operating Hours:** Continuous; 10% network, 90% local. **ADI:** Mankato, MN. **Wattage:** 100,000. **Ad Rates:** $18-36 for 30 seconds; $21-42 for 60 seconds.

18465 ■ KEYC-TV - 12
1570 Lookout Dr.
Mankato, MN 56003
Phone: (507)625-7905
Fax: (507)625-5745
Email: keycnews@keyc.com
Format: Commercial TV. **Networks:** CBS. **Founded:** 1960. **Operating Hours:** 5 a.m.-1 a.m. **ADI:** Mankato, MN. **Key Personnel:** John Ginther, Contact, tvjohn@keyc.com. **Local Programs:** *Bandwagon, News 12,* Saturday 11:00 a.m. **Wattage:** 100,000. **Ad Rates:** $25-700 per unit. **URL:** http://www.keyc.com.

18466 ■ KMSK-FM - 91.3
228 Wiecking Ctr.
Mankato, MN 56001-6062
Phone: (507)389-5678
Fax: (507)389-1705
Free: 800-456-7810
Format: Public Radio; News; Jazz. **Owner:** Minnesota State University, 122 Taylor Ctr., Mankato, MN 56001, Ph: (507)389-1866, Free: 800-722-0544. **Operating Hours:** Continuous. **Key Personnel:** James Gullickson, Owner, james.gullickson@mnsu.edu; Karen Wright, Dir. of Operations, karen.wright@mnsu.edu; Shelley Pierce, Music Dir., shelley215@juno.com. **Ad Rates:** Noncommercial. **URL:** http://www.mnsu.edu/kmsufm.

18467 ■ KMSU-FM - 89.7
228 Wiecking Ctr.
Mankato, MN 56001
Phone: (507)389-5678
Fax: (507)389-1705
Free: 800-456-7810
Email: dars-questions@mnsu.edu
Format: Public Radio; Eclectic; Talk. **Networks:** National Public Radio (NPR). **Owner:** Minnesota State University, 122 Taylor Ctr., Mankato, MN 56001, Ph: (507)389-1866, Free: 800-722-0544. **Founded:** 1963. **Operating Hours:** Continuous; 70% network, 30% local. **ADI:** Mankato, MN. **Key Personnel:** James Gullickson, Gen. Mgr., james.gullickson@mnsu.edu; Karen Wright, Dir. of Operations; Shelley Pierce, Music Dir., shelley215@juno.com. **Wattage:** 20,000. **Ad Rates:** Noncommercial. **URL:** http://www.mnsu.edu.

18468 ■ KRBI-AM - 1310
1807 Lee Blvd. N
Mankato, MN 56003
Phone: (507)345-4646
Email: studio@myz99.com
Format: Talk; Oldies; News; Sports. **Networks:** ABC; Linder Farm; AP. **Owner:** Three Eagles Communications, 3800 Cornhusker Hwy., Lincoln, NE 68504, Ph: (402)466-1234, Fax: (402)467-4095. **Founded:** Oct. 1957. **Operating Hours:** Continuous; 50% local, 50% network. **ADI:** Minneapolis-St. Paul, MN. **Key Personnel:** Jen Jones, Dir. of Sales, jjones@krbi.threeeagles.

com. **Wattage:** 1,000. **Ad Rates:** Noncommercial. River 105-FM. **URL:** http://www.river105.com.

18469 ■ KRRW-FM - 101.5
59346 Madison Ave.
Mankato, MN 56001
Email: katoinfo@katoinfo.com
Format: Country. **Owner:** Radio Mankato, 59346 Madison Ave., Mankato, MN 56002, Ph: (507)345-4537, Fax: (507)345-5364. **Wattage:** 14,000. **URL:** http://www.katoinfo.com.

18470 ■ KTOE-AM - 1420
59346 Madison Ave.
Mankato, MN 56001
Phone: (507)345-4537
Fax: (507)345-5364
Email: news@ktoe.com
Format: Adult Contemporary; News; Talk. **Networks:** Talknet. **Founded:** 1950. **Operating Hours:** Continuous; 30% network; 70% local. **ADI:** Mankato, MN. **Key Personnel:** Don Linder, Founder. **Wattage:** 5,000. **Ad Rates:** $23 for 30 seconds; $34 for 60 seconds. **URL:** http://www.ktoe.com.

18471 ■ KXLP-FM - 94.1
59346 Madison Ave.
Mankato, MN 56001
Phone: (507)345-4537
Format: Classic Rock. **Networks:** Fox; CNN Radio; CBS; NBC; ESPN Radio; ABC. **Founded:** 1986. **Operating Hours:** Continuous. **Wattage:** 3,700 ERP. **Ad Rates:** Advertising accepted; rates available upon request. Combined advertising rates available with KYSM-AM; KYSM-FM. **URL:** http://www.94kxlp.com.

18472 ■ Radio Mankato
59346 Madison Ave.
Mankato, MN 56002
Phone: (507)345-4537
Fax: (507)345-5364
Format: Oldies; Country; Sports; Talk; Classic Rock; Top 40; Information. **ADI:** Mankato, MN. **Key Personnel:** Chris Painter, Dir. of Sales, chrispainter@radiomankato.com; Deb Armstrong, Sales Mgr., debarmstrong@radiomankato.com; Jo Bailey, VP, Gen. Mgr., jobailey@radiomankato.com. **Ad Rates:** Accepts Advertising. **URL:** http://www.radiomankato.com.

MAPLE GROVE

18473 ■ Antique Motorcycle
Antique Motorcycle Club of America
Cornerstone Registration Ltd.
PO Box 1715
Maple Grove, MN 55311-6715
Phone: (763)420-7829
Fax: (763)420-7849
Free: 866-427-7583
Publisher's E-mail: amca@cornerstonereg.com
Consumer magazine covering motorcycles. **Freq:** Quarterly. **Key Personnel:** Bill Wood, Editor. **Subscription Rates:** Included in membership. **URL:** http://www.antiquemotorcycle.org/index.php?page=sample-the-magazine. **Ad Rates:** BW $625; 4C $720. **Remarks:** Accepts advertising. **Circ:** (Not Reported).

18474 ■ Antique Studebaker Review
Antique Studebaker Club
PO Box 1715
Maple Grove, MN 55311-6715
Phone: (763)420-7829
Freq: Bimonthly. **URL:** http://www.theantiquestudebakerclub.com/reviewmag/reviewmagprimary.htm. **Remarks:** Accepts advertising. **Circ:** (Not Reported).

18475 ■ Automotive History Review
Society of Automotive Historians
PO Box 1715
Maple Grove, MN 55311-6715
Publisher's E-mail: sah@cornerstonereg.com
Magazine covering automotive history. **Freq:** Semiannual. **Key Personnel:** Thomas S. Jakups, Contact. **ISSN:** 1056-2729 (print). **Subscription Rates:** free for members. **URL:** http://www.autohistory.org/index.php/about. **Remarks:** Advertising not accepted. **Circ:** 1000, 1000.

18476 ■ The Cormorant Magazine
Packard Club
c/o Cornerstone Registration
PO Box 1715
Maple Grove, MN 55311-6715
Phone: (763)420-7829
Fax: (763)420-7849
Free: 866-427-7583
Publisher's E-mail: pacnatoffice@aol.com
Freq: Quarterly. **Key Personnel:** Stuart Blond, Editor. **Subscription Rates:** $8 /back issue. **URL:** http://www.packardclub.org/html/club.htm#anchor8. **Remarks:** Advertising not accepted. **Circ:** (Not Reported).

18477 ■ Journal of Investigative Surgery
Academy of Surgical Research
15490 101st Ave. N, Ste. 100
Maple Grove, MN 55369
Phone: (763)235-6464
Fax: (763)235-6461
Publisher's E-mail: healthcare.enquiries@informa.com
Biomedical research journal dealing with scientific articles for the advancement of surgery, to the ultimate benefit of patient care and rehabilitation. **Freq:** Bimonthly. **Print Method:** Offset. **Trim Size:** 7 x 10. **Key Personnel:** David E.R. Sutherland, Associate Editor; George Bock, Board Member; Eugen Faist, Associate Editor; William M. Kuzon, Board Member; Karl O. Bandlien, Board Member; Jorge Cervantes, Board Member; Roberto Anaya-Prado, Associate Editor; Luis H. Toledo-Pereyra, Editor-in-Chief; Peter A. Ward, Associate Editor. **ISSN:** 0894--1939 (print); **EISSN:** 1521--0553 (electronic). **Subscription Rates:** $1849 Institutions online; $1946 Institutions print and online. **URL:** http://www.tandfonline.com/toc/iivs20/current. **Remarks:** Accepts advertising. **Circ:** (Not Reported).

18478 ■ Lama Review
Laboratory Animal Management Association
15490 101st Ave. N, Ste. 100
Maple Grove, MN 55369
Phone: (763)235-6483
Fax: (763)235-6461
Freq: Quarterly. **Subscription Rates:** included in membership dues. **URL:** http://www.lama-online.org/lama-review/. **Remarks:** Accepts advertising. **Circ:** (Not Reported).

18479 ■ Lincoln & Continental Comments
Lincoln and Continental Owners Club
PO Box 1715
Maple Grove, MN 55311-6715
Phone: (763)420-7829
Fax: (763)420-7849
Publisher's E-mail: lcoc@cornerstonereg.com
Freq: Bimonthly. **Subscription Rates:** Included in membership. **URL:** http://www.lcoc.org/Comments.htm. **Formerly:** Continental Comments. **Remarks:** Accepts advertising. **Circ:** (Not Reported).

WQPM-AM - See Princeton, MD

MAPLE LAKE

SEC MN. Wright Co. 45 mi. W. of Minneapolis. Lake resort. Stock, dairy farms.

18480 ■ Maple Lake Messenger
Maple Lake Messenger
PO Box 817
Maple Lake, MN 55358
Phone: (320)963-3813
Fax: (320)963-6114
Publisher's E-mail: publisher@maplelakemessenger.com
Newspaper with unbiased orientation. **Freq:** Weekly (Wed.). **Print Method:** Offset. **Cols./Page:** 6. **Col. Width:** 28 nonpareils. **Col. Depth:** 301 agate lines. **Key Personnel:** Theresa Andrus, Editor; Kayla Erickson, Manager, Advertising. **ISSN:** 3285-6000 (print). **Subscription Rates:** $28 Individuals in Wright County; $31 Out of area; $53.50 Out of state; $26 Individuals E-edition only. **URL:** http://www.maplelakemessenger.com. **Remarks:** Accepts classified advertising. **Circ:** ‡1750.

MARSHALL

SW MN. Lyon Co. 30 mi. NW of Springfield. Southwest State University. Dairy products, diversified agriculture.

18481 ■ Marshall Independent
Marshall Independent
508 W Main St.
Marshall, MN 56258
Phone: (507)537-1551
Fax: (507)537-1557
Publication E-mail: news@marshallindependent.com
General newspaper. **Founded:** 1874. **Freq:** Daily. **Print Method:** Offset. **Cols./Page:** 6. **Col. Width:** 24 nonpareils. **Col. Depth:** 301 agate lines. **Key Personnel:** Tara Brandl, Manager, Advertising; Russ Labat, General Manager, Publisher; Per Peterson, Editor; Julie Dobrenski, Manager, Circulation. **Subscription Rates:** $166.40 Individuals Monday thru Saturday; home delivery + digital; $184.60 By mail Monday thru Saturday; home delivery + digital; $270.40 Out of state Monday thru Saturday; by mail + digital. **URL:** http://www.marshallindependent.com. **Formerly:** Marshall Messenger. **Ad Rates:** 4C $270; PCI $20.89. **Remarks:** Advertising accepted; rates available upon request. **Circ:** Mon.-Sat. ★**7498**, Sat. ★**7475**.

18482 ■ Yellow Medicine Review: A Journal of Indigenous Literature, Art & Thought
Yellow Medicine Review
c/o Judy Wilson, Ph.D. Department of English 1501 State St.
Dept. of English
Southwest Minnesota State University
1501 State St.
Marshall, MN 56258
Publisher's E-mail: editor@yellowmedicinereview.com
Journal featuring fiction, poetry, scholarly essays and art. **Freq:** 2/yr. **Key Personnel:** Judy Wilson, Contact. **ISSN:** 1939--4624 (print). **Subscription Rates:** $23.09 Individuals; $32.21 Other countries. **URL:** http://www.yellowmedicinereview.com. **Circ:** (Not Reported).

18483 ■ Charter Communications
1108 E College Dr.
Marshall, MN 56258
Free: 888-438-2427
Key Personnel: Neil Smit, CEO, President; Marwan Fawaz, Chief Tech. Ofc., Exec. VP; Michael J. Lovett, COO, Exec. VP. **Cities Served:** 131 channels. **URL:** http://www.charter.com.

18484 ■ KARL-FM - 105.1
1414 E College Dr.
Marshall, MN 56258
Phone: (507)532-2282
Format: Country. **Owner:** KMHL Broadcasting Corp., 1414 E College Dr., Marshall, MN 56258-2027, Ph: (507)532-2282, Fax: (507)532-3739. **Wattage:** 45,000. **Ad Rates:** Noncommercial. **URL:** http://1051karl.com.

18485 ■ KARZ-FM - 107.5
1414 E College Dr.
Marshall, MN 56258
Phone: (507)532-2282
Format: Classical; Classic Rock. **Owner:** KMHL Broadcasting Corp., 1414 E College Dr., Marshall, MN 56258-2027, Ph: (507)532-2282, Fax: (507)532-3739. **Founded:** 1986. **Formerly:** KBJJ-FM. **Operating Hours:** Continuous, 100% local. **ADI:** Sioux Falls-Mitchell, SD. **Wattage:** 18,000. **Ad Rates:** $8.25 for 15 seconds; $8.25-10.50 for 30 seconds; $9.25-13.50 for 60 seconds. Combined advertising rates available with KMHL-AM, KKCK-FM, KARL-FM.

18486 ■ KKCK-FM
PO Box 61
Marshall, MN 56258-1420
Phone: (507)532-2282
Email: info@marshallradio.net
Format: Contemporary Hit Radio (CHR); Top 40. **Networks:** ABC. **Owner:** KMHL Broadcasting Corp., 1414 E College Dr., Marshall, MN 56258-2027, Ph: (507)532-2282, Fax: (507)532-3739. **Founded:** 1967. **Wattage:** 100,000 ERP. **Ad Rates:** $9.75 for 15 seconds; $10-17.25 for 30 seconds; $12-23 for 60 seconds.

18487 ■ KMHL-AM - 1400
1414 E College Dr.
Marshall, MN 56258
Phone: (507)532-2282
Email: info@marshallradio.net
Format: News; Talk. **Simulcasts:** KARL-FM. **Networks:** ABC; Linder Farm. **Owner:** Linder Radio Group. **Operating Hours:** Continuous; 18% network, 82% local. **Key**

Circulation: ★ = AAM; △ or • = BPA; ♦ = CAC; ❑ = VAC; ⊕ = PO Statement; ‡ = Publisher's Report; Boldface figures = sworn; Light figures = estimated.

Personnel: Joyce Holm, Contact; Heath Radke, Contact. **Wattage:** 1,000. **Ad Rates:** $8.25 for 15 seconds; $11-21 for 30 seconds; $14-27 for 60 seconds. Combined advertising rates available with KKCK-FM, KARL-FM, KARZ-FM. **URL:** http://www.marshallradio.net.

18488 ■ KNSG-FM - 94.7
PO Box 61
Marshall, MN 56258
Phone: (507)723-5000
Fax: (507)723-5604
Free: 800-444-5685
Email: countryhog@clearchannel.com
Format: Classical. **Owner:** Clear Channel Communications Inc., at above address, Ph: (210)822-2828, Fax: (210)822-2299. **Founded:** July 1995. **Operating Hours:** Continuous. **Key Personnel:** Marj Frederickson, Gen. Mgr., marjfrederickson@clearchannel.com; Brian Filzer, Dir. of Programs. **Wattage:** 50,000. **Ad Rates:** $20-30 for 60 seconds.

MELROSE

C MN. Stearns Co. 30 mi. NW of Saint Cloud. Manufactures dairy products, monuments. Turkey processing plant. Lake resorts. Dairy, poultry, stock farms.

18489 ■ Melrose Beacon
Melrose Beacon
408 E Main St.
Melrose, MN 56352
Phone: (320)256-3240
Publisher's E-mail: melrosenews@acnpapers.com
Community newspaper. **Freq:** Weekly (Fri.). **Print Method:** Offset. **Cols./Page:** 7. **Col. Width:** 24 nonpareils. **Col. Depth:** 301 agate lines. **Key Personnel:** Dave Simpkins, Publisher; Carol Moorman, Editor. **URL:** http://www.melrosebeacon.com. **Mailing address:** PO Box 186, Melrose, MN 56352. **Remarks:** Accepts advertising. **Circ:** 1978.

MILACA

EC MN. Mille Lacs Co. 30 mi. NE of Saint Cloud. Manufactures butter, powdered milk, garments, plastic products. Dairy, poultry farms. Potatoes, oats.

18490 ■ Mille Lacs County Times
Mille Lacs County Times
225 2nd St. SW
Milaca, MN 56353
Phone: (320)983-6111
Fax: (320)983-6112
Publication E-mail: jeff.hage@ecm-inc.com
Newspaper. **Freq:** Weekly (Thurs.). **Print Method:** Offset. **Cols./Page:** 6. **Col. Width:** 35 nonpareils. **Col. Depth:** 294 agate lines. **Key Personnel:** Jeff Hage, Editor, phone: (320)983-6111. **Subscription Rates:** $38 Individuals; $43 Out of area; $53 Out of state; $30 Students nine months; $35 Individuals senior rate. **URL:** http://millelacscountytimes.com/. **Ad Rates:** GLR $.17. **Remarks:** Accepts advertising. **Circ:** Paid ♦**1911**.

MINNEAPOLIS

SE MN. Hennepin Co. On Mississippi River, adjacent to Saint Paul. Important grain and milling center. University of MinnesotaAugsburg College, Minneapolis College of Art and Design, North Central Bible College, Saint Mary's Junior College, Minneapolis Communit College. Financial Center. Medical Center. Manufactures food, dairy products, electronic computers, structural steel, thermostatic controls, conveyor equipment, medical electronics equipment, farm machinery, ball bearings, gears, electric portable tools, construction machinery, boilers, tanks, burglar alarm systems, bases and concentrates, textiles, packaging, garden tools, power lawn mowers, sprinklers.

18491 ■ ABA Journal of Labor and Employment Law
University of Minnesota Law School
University of Minnesota Law School
229 19th Ave. S
Minneapolis, MN 55455
Publisher's E-mail: lawcomm@umn.edu
Covers current developments in labor and employment law to meet the practical needs of attorneys, judges, administrators, and the public. **Freq:** 3/year winter, spring, fall. **Key Personnel:** Stephen F. Befort, Editor; Laura J. Cooper, Editor. **ISSN:** 8756--2995 (print). **Subscription Rates:** Included in membership; $45 Nonmembers $51 for Alaska, Hawaii, U.S. possessions, and foreign countries; $16.95 Single issue plus $3.95 handling. **URL:** http://www.americanbar.org/publications/aba_journal_of_labor_employment_law_home.html; http://www1.law.umn.edu/abajlel/index.html. **Formerly:** The Labor Lawyer. **Remarks:** Advertising not accepted. **Circ:** (Not Reported).

18492 ■ Aerosol Science and Technology
Taylor & Francis Group Journals
c/o Peter McMurry, Ed.-in-Ch.
University of Minnesota
Department of Mechanical Engineering
111 Church St. SE
Minneapolis, MN 55455-0111
Phone: (612)624-2817
Fax: (612)625-6069
Publisher's E-mail: customerservice@taylorandfrancis.com
Journal of the American Association for Aerosol Research. **Freq:** Monthly. **Key Personnel:** Peter McMurry, Editor-in-Chief; Chong S. Kim, Advisor; B.Y.H. Liu, Editor, Founder; David S. Ensor, Editor, Founder; Philip K. Hopke, Editor; David T. Shaw, Editor, Founder. **ISSN:** 0278--6826 (print); **EISSN:** 1521--7388 (electronic). **Subscription Rates:** $1391 Institutions print and online; $1321 Institutions online only. **URL:** http://www.tandfonline.com/toc/uast20/current. **Remarks:** Accepts advertising. **Circ:** (Not Reported).

18493 ■ American Craft
American Craft Council
1224 Marshall St. NE, Ste. 200
Minneapolis, MN 55413-1089
Phone: (612)206-3100
Fax: (612)355-2330
Free: 800-836-3470
Publisher's E-mail: council@craftcouncil.org
Journal covering contemporary crafts. **Freq:** Bimonthly. **Print Method:** Offset. **Trim Size:** 8.25 x 10.875. **Col. Width:** 3 1/2 inches. **Col. Depth:** 10 inches. **Key Personnel:** John Gourlay, Publisher; Monica Moses, Editor-in-Chief. **ISSN:** 0194-8008 (print). **Subscription Rates:** $29 Individuals 6 issues - 1 year; $40 Canada 6 issues - 1 year. **URL:** http://www.craftcouncil.org/magazine; http://craftcouncil.org/magazine/about. **Formerly:** Craft Horizons. **Ad Rates:** BW $3,100; 4C $4,420. **Remarks:** Accepts advertising. **Circ:** Paid 40,000, 43000.

18494 ■ American Jewish World
AJS Publishing Inc.
4820 Minnetonka Blvd., Ste. 104
Minneapolis, MN 55416
Phone: (952)259-5234
Fax: (952)920-6205
Publication E-mail: editor@ajwnews.com
Jewish interest newspaper. **Freq:** Weekly. **Cols./Page:** 5. **Col. Width:** 1 7/8 inches. **Col. Depth:** 16 inches. **Key Personnel:** Mordecai Specktor, Editor. **ISSN:** 0002--9084 (print). **Subscription Rates:** $45 Individuals /year; $80 Two years. **URL:** http://ajwnews.com. **Ad Rates:** BW $960; 4C $1360; PCI $15. **Remarks:** Advertising accepted; rates available upon request. **Circ:** ‡7000.

18495 ■ American Journal of Human Biology
Human Biology Association
c/o Ellen W. Demerath, Ph.D.
Division of Epidemiology and Community Health, School of Public Health
University of Minnesota
1300 S 2nd St., Ste. 300
Minneapolis, MN 55454
Freq: Bimonthly. **EISSN:** 1520-6300 (electronic). **Alt. Formats:** PDF. **URL:** http://humbio.org/publications. **Remarks:** Advertising not accepted. **Circ:** (Not Reported).

18496 ■ The Annals of Probability
Institute of Mathematical Statistics
c/o Ofer Zeitouni, Ed.
Dept. of Mathematics
University of Minnesota
206 Church St., SE
Minneapolis, MN 55455
Publisher's E-mail: ims@imstat.org
Journal dedicated to publishing the theory of probability and its applications. **Freq:** Bimonthly. **Key Personnel:** Patrick Kelly, Editor. **ISSN:** 0091--1798 (print). **Subscription Rates:** $74 Individuals. **URL:** http://www.imstat.org/aop. **Ad Rates:** BW $325. **Remarks:** Accepts advertising. **Circ:** ‡2700.

18497 ■ Architecture Minnesota: The Magazine of AIA Minnesota
AIA Minnesota
275 Market St., Ste. 54
Minneapolis, MN 55405
Phone: (612)338-6763
Fax: (612)338-7981
Publisher's E-mail: info@aia-mn.org
Regional design arts magazine. **Freq:** 6/year. **Print Method:** Webb. **Trim Size:** 8 1/4 x 11. **Cols./Page:** 3. **Col. Width:** 27 nonpareils. **Col. Depth:** 138 agate lines. **Key Personnel:** Christopher Hudson, Editor, phone: (612)338-6736. **ISSN:** 0149-9106 (print). **Subscription Rates:** $15 Individuals; $35 Individuals 3 years; $42 Individuals three years. **URL:** http://www.aia-mn.org/features/architecture-mn-magazine. **Ad Rates:** BW $1,185; 4C $1,635. **Remarks:** Accepts advertising. **Circ:** Paid ‡3000, Controlled ‡4000.

18498 ■ Arizona Bride
Tiger Oak Publications Inc.
900 S Third St.
Minneapolis, MN 55415-1209
Phone: (612)548-3180
Fax: (612)548-3181
Publisher's E-mail: service@tigeroak.com
Consumer magazine for brides and grooms. **Freq:** Semiannual. **Key Personnel:** R. Craig Bednar, Publisher. **URL:** http://arizonabridemag.com. **Remarks:** Advertising accepted; rates available upon request. **Circ:** (Not Reported).

18499 ■ AUA News
American Underground Construction Association
3001 Hennepin Ave. S, Ste. D202
Minneapolis, MN 55408
Phone: (212)465-5541
Publisher's E-mail: underground@auca.org
Freq: Quarterly. **Subscription Rates:** included in membership dues. **Remarks:** Accepts advertising. **Circ:** (Not Reported).

18500 ■ BEEF: The Business Publication of the Cattle Industry
Southwest Farm Press - Agribusiness Div.
7900 International Dr., Ste. 300
Minneapolis, MN 55425-1510
Phone: (952)851-4613
Fax: (952)851-4701
Trade magazine for beef producers. **Freq:** Monthly. **Print Method:** Offset. **Trim Size:** 7 7/8 x 10 3/4. **Cols./Page:** 3. **Col. Width:** 26 nonpareils. **Col. Depth:** 140 agate lines. **Key Personnel:** Wes Ishmael, Editor, phone: (817)249-4545; Joe Roybal, Editor, phone: (952)851-4669; Burt Rutherford, Senior Editor, phone: (806)353-8528. **ISSN:** 0005-7738 (print). **URL:** http://beefmagazine.com. **Ad Rates:** BW $12550; 4C $15099. **Remarks:** Accepts advertising. **Circ:** △**100,010**.

18501 ■ Bench & Bar of Minnesota
Minnesota State Bar Association
600 Nicollet Mall, Ste. 380
Minneapolis, MN 55402
Phone: (612)333-1183
Free: 800-882-6722
Publisher's E-mail: helpdesk@mnbar.org
Official magazine of Minnesota State Bar Association. Includes editorial on issues of law and law practice, and human interest material of interest to Minnesota lawyers. **Freq:** 11/year. **Print Method:** Web Offset. **Trim Size:** 8 3/8 x 10 7/8. **Cols./Page:** 3. **Col. Width:** 2 5/16 inches. **Col. Depth:** 10 inches. **Key Personnel:** Karol Engstrom Narum, Director, Publications; Judson Haverkamp, Editor, phone: (612)278-6333, fax: (612)333-4927. **ISSN:** 0276-1505 (print). **USPS:** 050-060. **URL:** http://mnbenchbar.com. **Ad Rates:** BW $951; 4C $1,276. **Remarks:** Accepts advertising. **Circ:** 17000.

18502 ■ Bible Editions and Versions
International Society of Bible Collectors
PO Box 26654
Minneapolis, MN 55426
Journal covering book reviews and news of old and current translations and translators of the Bible. **Freq:** Quarterly. **Key Personnel:** William E. Paul, Executive

Editor; Carl V. Johnson, President. **Subscription Rates:** $25 U.S. and Canada; $30 Other countries; $3 Single issue back issue; $27 Other countries two years; Included in membership. **URL:** http://www.biblecollectors.org/; http://www.biblecollectors.org/membership.htm. **Ad Rates:** BW $35. **Remarks:** Advertising accepted; rates available upon request. **Circ:** 275, 275.

18503 ■ The Bible Friend
Osterhus Publishing House Inc.
4500 W Broadway
Minneapolis, MN 55422
Phone: (763)537-9311
Fax: (763)537-9585
Free: 877-643-4229
Religious newspaper. **Freq:** 10/year. **Print Method:** Offset. **Trim Size:** 9 1/2 x 12. **Cols./Page:** 3. **Col. Width:** 32 nonpareils. **Col. Depth:** 154 agate lines. **Key Personnel:** Daniel Osterhus, Editor. **Subscription Rates:** $6 Individuals; $7 Canada. **URL:** http://www.osterhuspub.com/The-Bible-Friend-p/14.htm. **Remarks:** Advertising not accepted. **Circ:** Paid 8000, Non-paid 3000.

18504 ■ Biopreservation and Biobanking
Mary Ann Liebert Inc., Publishers
c/o Allison Hubel, PhD, Dep. Ed.
Department of Mechanical Engineering
University of Minnesota
111 Church St. SE
Minneapolis, MN 55455-0150
Publisher's E-mail: info@liebertpub.com
Peer-reviewed journal covering field of biospecimen procurement, processing, preservation and banking. **Freq:** Bimonthly. **Trim Size:** 8 1/2 x 11. **Cols./Page:** 2. **Col. Width:** 19 nonpareils. **Col. Depth:** 57.5 agate lines. **Key Personnel:** Jim Vaught, PhD, Editor-in-Chief; Barry Fuller, PhD, Board Member. **ISSN:** 1947-5535 (print). **Subscription Rates:** $714 Individuals print and online; $835 Other countries print and online; $660 Individuals online only; $1170 Institutions print and online; $1345 Institutions, other countries print and online; $1046 Institutions print only; $1203 Institutions, other countries print only; $1125 Institutions online only. **URL:** http://www.liebertpub.com/products/product.aspx?pid=110. **Formerly**: Cell Preservation Technology. **Ad Rates:** BW $1,060; 4C $1,810. **Remarks:** Advertising accepted; rates available upon request. **Circ:** (Not Reported).

18505 ■ Boating Industry
Ehlert Publishing Group Inc.
10405 6th Ave. N, Ste. 210
Minneapolis, MN 55441
Phone: (763)383-4400
Fax: (763)383-4499
Magazine covering marine market. **Freq:** 9/year. **Key Personnel:** Jonathan Sweet, Editor-in-Chief, phone: (763)383-4419. **Subscription Rates:** $149 Other countries. **URL:** http://www.boatingindustry.com. **Ad Rates:** BW $4930. **Remarks:** Accepts advertising. **Circ:** △**59925**.

18506 ■ Camping Life
Ehlert Publishing Group Inc.
3300 Fernbrook Lane N, Ste. 200
Minneapolis, MN 55447
Free: 800-848-6247
Magazine covering family camping information including vacation and weekend destinations, equipment reviews and buyers' guides for tent campers and owners of truck campers and pop-up trailers. **Freq:** Monthly. **Print Method:** Web offset. **Trim Size:** 7 3/4 x 10 1/2. **Cols./Page:** 3. **Col. Depth:** 133 agate lines. **Key Personnel:** Stuart Bourdon, Editor; Tom Kaiser, Managing Editor; Jill Anderson, Manager, Circulation. **ISSN:** 0046--0990 (print). **URL:** http://www.campinglife.com. **Remarks:** Accepts advertising. **Circ:** (Not Reported).

18507 ■ Classic Cookbooks
Pillsbury Co.
PO Box 9452
Minneapolis, MN 55440
Magazine containing new recipes. **Freq:** Monthly. **Print Method:** Web. **Trim Size:** 5 11/16 x 9. **Cols./Page:** 2. **ISSN:** 1089-0432 (print). **Subscription Rates:** $19.95 Individuals; $43.95 Canada; $67.95 Other countries. **URL:** http://www.pillsbury.com/magazines-cookbooks/. **Ad Rates:** 4C $10,000. **Remarks:** Accepts advertising. **Circ:** Paid 450000.

18508 ■ Collector: The Official Publication of the ACA International
ACA International
4040 W 70th St.
Minneapolis, MN 55435
Phone: (952)926-6547
Fax: (952)926-1624
Publisher's E-mail: aca@acainternational.org
Magazine on consumer credit and debt collection services. **Freq:** Monthly. **Print Method:** Offset. **Trim Size:** 8 1/2 x 11. **Cols./Page:** 3 and 2. **Col. Width:** 26 and 41 nonpareils. **Col. Depth:** 140 agate lines. **Key Personnel:** Patrick J. Morris, Chief Executive Officer; Anne Rosso, Editor. **Subscription Rates:** $70 U.S.; $90 Canada by airmail; $90 Other countries by airmail. **URL:** http://www.acainternational.org/collectormagazine.aspx. **Mailing address:** PO Box 390106, Minneapolis, MN 55439-0106. **Ad Rates:** BW $1,850; 4C $2,925. **Remarks:** Advertising accepted; rates available upon request. **Circ:** ‡6100.

18509 ■ Compliance Today
Health Care Compliance Association
6500 Barrie Rd., Ste. 250
Minneapolis, MN 55435-2358
Phone: (952)405-7900
Fax: (952)988-0146
Free: 888-580-8373
Publisher's E-mail: service@hcca-info.org
Freq: Monthly. **Subscription Rates:** Included in membership. **URL:** http://www.hcca-info.org/AdvertiseSponsor/Publications.aspx. **Remarks:** Accepts advertising. **Circ:** (Not Reported).

18510 ■ Corn + Soybean Digest
Penton
7900 International Dr., Ste. 300
Minneapolis, MN 55425
Phone: (952)851-9329
Fax: (952)851-4601
Publication E-mail: csd@csdigest.com
Magazine for the corn and soybean market, providing in-depth coverage to maximize production and marketing for profit. **Freq:** Monthly. **Key Personnel:** Kurt Lawton, Editor; Susan Winsor, Managing Editor; Jennifer Bennett, Editor. **Subscription Rates:** Free to qualified subscribers. **URL:** http://cornandsoybeandigest.com. **Remarks:** Accepts advertising. **Circ:** (Not Reported).

18511 ■ Crime and Justice: A Review of Research
University of Chicago Press Journals Division
c/o Michael Tonry, Ed.
University of Minnesota Law School
313 Walter F. Mondale Hall
229-19th Ave. S
Minneapolis, MN 55455
Phone: (612)624-4860
Publisher's E-mail: marketing@press.uchicago.edu
Peer-reviewed journal focusing on crime-related research subjects. **Freq:** Annual. **Key Personnel:** Michael Tonry, Editor. **ISSN:** 0192--3234 (print); **EISSN:** 2153--0416 (electronic). **Subscription Rates:** $65 Individuals online; $100 Individuals print and online; $33 Students online. **URL:** http://www.journals.uchicago.edu/toc/cj/current; http://press.uchicago.edu/ucp/books/series/CJ.html; http://www.journals.uchicago.edu/action/showPublications?&alphabetRange=C. **Remarks:** Accepts advertising. **Circ:** 92.

18512 ■ Cultural Critique
University of Minnesota Press
111 3rd Ave. S, Ste. 290
Minneapolis, MN 55401-2520
Phone: (612)627-1970
Fax: (612)627-1980
Free: 800-621-2736
Publisher's E-mail: ump@umn.edu
Scholarly journal covering issues in culture, theory and politics. **Freq:** 3/year spring, fall and winter. **Trim Size:** 6 x 9. **Key Personnel:** Nancy Armstrong, Member; Cesare Casarino, Editor; Simona Sawhney, Editor; Tim August, Editor; John Mowitt, Editor. **ISSN:** 0882--4371 (print). **Subscription Rates:** $30 Individuals domestic; $35 Individuals outside U.S.; $78 Institutions domestic; $83 Institutions, other countries. **URL:** http://upress.umn.edu/journal-division/Journals/cultural-critique. **Ad Rates:** BW $200, full page; BW $150, half page. **Remarks:** Accepts advertising. **Circ:** (Not Reported).

18513 ■ Current Cardiology Reviews
Bentham Science Publishers Ltd.
Dept. of Medicine/Cardiology
University of Minnesota Medical School
Minneapolis, MN 55455
Publisher's E-mail: subscriptions@benthamscience.org
Journal publishing frontier reviews on all the latest advances on the practical and clinical approach to the diagnosis and treatment of cardiovascular disease. **Freq:** Quarterly. **Key Personnel:** Dr. Jianyi Zhang, Board Member; Jian'an Wang, Editor-in-Chief. **ISSN:** 1573--403X (print); **EISSN:** 1875--6557 (electronic). **Subscription Rates:** $250 Individuals print; $290 print and online - academic; $540 print or online - academic; $1400 print and online - corporate; $1170 print or online - corporate. **URL:** http://benthamscience.com/journals/current-cardiology-reviews. **Ad Rates:** BW $600; 4C $800. **Remarks:** Accepts advertising. **Circ:** ‡400.

18514 ■ Delta Farm Press
Southwest Farm Press - Agribusiness Div.
7900 International Dr., Ste. 300
Minneapolis, MN 55425-1510
Phone: (952)851-4613
Fax: (952)851-4701
Publication E-mail: greg.frey@penton.com
Agriculture tabloid. **Founded:** 1942. **Freq:** Weekly (Fri.). **Print Method:** Offset. **Trim Size:** 11 x 14 1/2. **Cols./Page:** 4. **Col. Width:** 2 1/4 inches. **Col. Depth:** 13 1/2 inches. **Key Personnel:** Greg Frey, Vice President; Elton Robinson, Editor; Hembree Brandon, Director, Editorial. **ISSN:** 0011-8036 (print). **Subscription Rates:** Free Delta region. **URL:** http://deltafarmpress.com. **Ad Rates:** SAU $1195. **Remarks:** Accepts advertising. **Circ:** (Not Reported).

18515 ■ Downtown Journal
Minnesota Premier Publications Inc.
1115 Hennepin Ave.
Minneapolis, MN 55403
Phone: (612)825-9205
Fax: (612)436-4396
Publisher's E-mail: editor@mnparent.com
Local newspaper serving St. Paul and Minneapolis and south, west and southwest suburbs. **Freq:** Biweekly. **Print Method:** Offset. **Trim Size:** 11 x 13 1/2. **Cols./Page:** 6. **Col. Width:** 1 1/2 inches. **Col. Depth:** 196 agate lines. **Key Personnel:** Janis Hall, Owner, Publisher; Sarah McKenzie, Editor. **URL:** http://www.journalmpls.com. **Formerly**: Skyway News. **Ad Rates:** GLR $0.95; BW $2493; 4C $2843; PCI $39. **Circ:** ‡35000.

18516 ■ Edina Magazine
Tiger Oak Publications Inc.
900 S Third St.
Minneapolis, MN 55415-1209
Phone: (612)548-3180
Fax: (612)548-3181
Publisher's E-mail: service@tigeroak.com
Local magazine of Edina city. **Freq:** Monthly. **Key Personnel:** R. Craig Bednar, Publisher. **Subscription Rates:** $12 Individuals. **URL:** http://edinamag.com. **Remarks:** Advertising accepted; rates available upon request. **Circ:** Combined 30000.

18517 ■ Enterprise Minnesota Magazine
Enterprise Minnesota Inc.
310 - 4th Ave. S, Ste. 7050
Minneapolis, MN 55415
Phone: (612)373-2900
Free: 800-325-3073
Official undergraduate magazine of the University of Minnesota's Institute of Technology. **Freq:** Quarterly. **Print Method:** Offset. **Trim Size:** 8 1/2 x 11. **Cols./Page:** 3. **Key Personnel:** Tom Mason, Editor; Lynn Shelton, Publisher; Andrea Lahouze, Editor. **ISSN:** 0026--5691 (print). **Subscription Rates:** Free. **URL:** http://www.enterpriseminnesota.org/news-and-publications/magazine. **Formerly**: Minnesota Technology. **Remarks:** Advertising accepted; rates available upon request. **Circ:** Non-paid ‡14500.

18518 ■ Family Relations
National Council on Family Relations
1201 W River Pky., Ste. 200

Circulation: ★ = AAM; △ or • = BPA; ♦ = CAC; ❑ = VAC; ⊕ = PO Statement; ‡ = Publisher's Report; Boldface figures = sworn; Light figures = estimated.

Minneapolis, MN 55454-1115
Phone: (763)781-9331
Fax: (763)781-9348
Free: 888-781-9331
Publisher's E-mail: info@ncfr.org
Journal containing basic and applied articles that are original, innovative and interdisciplinary and that focus on diverse family forms and issues. **Freq:** 5/year. **Key Personnel:** Jason Hans. **ISSN:** 0197--6664 (print); **EISSN:** 1741--3729 (electronic). **Subscription Rates:** $161 Individuals print and online; £130 Other countries print and online; €194 Individuals print and online; $68 Students print and online; £65 Students, other countries print and online; €97 Students print and online. **URL:** http://onlinelibrary.wiley.com/journal/10.1111/(ISSN)1741-3729. **Remarks:** Accepts advertising. **Circ:** ‡5000.

18519 ■ Far Eastern Affairs
East View Information Services.
10601 Wayzata Blvd.
Minneapolis, MN 55305-1515
Phone: (952)252-1201
Fax: (952)252-1202
Free: 800-477-1005
Publisher's E-mail: info@eastview.com
Journal covering developments in China, Japan, and the Asia-Pacific region. **Freq:** Quarterly. **ISSN:** 0869--5636 (print). **Subscription Rates:** $510 Institutions print; $85 Individuals print; $140 Other countries print; $475 Institutions online; $80 U.S. online; $80 Other countries online; $550 Individuals print and online; $95 U.S. print and online; $160 Other countries print and online. **URL:** http://www.eastviewpress.com/Journals/FarEasternAffairs.aspx. **Ad Rates:** BW $380; 4C $1,800. **Remarks:** Accepts advertising. **Circ:** (Not Reported).

18520 ■ Farm Industry News
Southwest Farm Press - Agribusiness Div.
7900 International Dr., Ste. 300
Minneapolis, MN 55425-1510
Phone: (952)851-4613
Fax: (952)851-4701
Publication E-mail: fin@primediabusiness.com
Agriculture trade magazine covering new products and technology. **Founded:** 1967. **Freq:** 12/yr. **Print Method:** Offset. **Trim Size:** 8 1/2 x 11. **Cols./Page:** 3. **Key Personnel:** Karen McMahon, Editor-in-Chief; Jodie Wehrspann, Senior Editor. **URL:** http://www.farmindustrynews.com/. **Ad Rates:** BW $18,110; 4C $21,710; PCI $501. **Remarks:** Advertising accepted; rates available upon request. **Circ:** (Not Reported).

18521 ■ fedgazette
Federal Reserve Bank of Minneapolis
90 Hennepin Ave.
Minneapolis, MN 55401-1804
Phone: (612)204-5000
Fax: (612)204-5515
Regional business and economics newspaper. **Freq:** Quarterly. **Print Method:** Offset. **Trim Size:** 6 x 20 1/2. **Cols./Page:** 6. **Col. Depth:** 287 agate lines. **Key Personnel:** David Fettig, Senior Editor; Ronald A. Wirtz, Editor; Jenni C. Schoppers, Managing Editor; Tobias Madden, Economist; Rob Grunewald, Economist; Douglas Clement, Writer; Phil Davies, Writer; Joe Mahon, Writer; Phil Swenson, Art Director. **ISSN:** 1045-3334 (print). **URL:** http://www.minneapolisfed.org/publications_papers/fedgazette/index.cfm?; http://www.minneapolisfed.org/publications_papers/index.cfm. **Remarks:** Accepts advertising. **Circ:** (Not Reported).

18522 ■ Finance and Commerce
Finance & Commerce
United States Trust Bldg., Ste. 100, 730 Second Ave. S
730 2nd Ave.
Minneapolis, MN 55402
Phone: (612)333-4244
Business newspaper. **Freq:** Daily Tues.-Sat. **Print Method:** Offset. **Trim Size:** 16 1/2 x 22 3/4. **Cols./Page:** 6. **Col. Width:** 2 3/16 inches. **Col. Depth:** 21 3/16 inches. **Key Personnel:** Bill Gaier, Publisher. **USPS:** 190-580. **Subscription Rates:** $249 Individuals print & online 1 year; $249 Individuals online 1 year; $29 Individuals print & online 1 month. **URL:** http://finance-commerce.com. **Remarks:** Advertising accepted; rates available upon request. **Circ:** ‡1500.

18523 ■ Game Informer Magazine
Sunrise Publications Inc.
724 N First St., Fourth Fl.
Minneapolis, MN 55401
Phone: (612)486-6100
Fax: (612)486-6101
Publication E-mail: gifulfillment@gameinformer.com
Consumer magazine covering video and computer game information and reviews. **Freq:** Monthly. **Print Method:** Perfect Bound. **Trim Size:** 9 1/4 x 11. **Key Personnel:** Andy McNamara, Editor-in-Chief, phone: (952)946-7248; Cathy Preston, Publisher, phone: (952)946-7221; Andrew Reiner, Executive Editor. **ISSN:** 1067--6392 (print). **Subscription Rates:** $14.99 Individuals; $19.98 12 issues - print and digital; $24.98 21 issues - print. **Ad Rates:** BW $99,965; 4C $111,080. **Remarks:** Accepts advertising. **Circ:** ‡3498935.

18524 ■ Gather Magazine
Augsburg Fortress Publishers
100 S Fifth St., Ste. 600
Minneapolis, MN 55402
Phone: (612)330-3300
Fax: (612)330-3455
Free: 800-426-0115
Publisher's E-mail: info@augsburgfortress.org
Women of the Evangelical Lutheran Church Bible study magazine. **Founded:** 1908. **Freq:** 10/yr. **Print Method:** Offset. **Trim Size:** 8 1/8 x 10 1/2. **Cols./Page:** 2. **Col. Width:** 3 3/8 inches. **Col. Depth:** 9 inches. **ISSN:** 0896-209X (print). **Subscription Rates:** $12 Individuals online; $22 Two years; $33 Individuals three years. **URL:** http://www.elca.org/Growing-In-Faith/Ministry/Women-of-the-ELCA/Gather-maga zine/About-Us.aspx. **Formerly:** Scope; Lutheran Women; Lutheran Woman Today. **Mailing address:** PO Box 1209, Minneapolis, MN 55402. **Ad Rates:** BW $4,500. **Remarks:** Accepts advertising. **Circ:** Paid 150000.

18525 ■ Gilbert Magazine
American Chesterton Society
4117 Pebblebrook Cir.
Minneapolis, MN 55437
Phone: (952)831-3096
Fax: (952)831-0387
Free: 800-343-2425
Publisher's E-mail: info@chesterton.org
Freq: 8/year. **Key Personnel:** Sean P. Dailey, Editor-in-Chief. **Subscription Rates:** Included in membership. **URL:** http://www.chesterton.org/membership. **Remarks:** Accepts advertising. **Circ:** 2400.

18526 ■ Hay & Forage Grower
Southwest Farm Press - Agribusiness Div.
7900 International Dr., Ste. 300
Minneapolis, MN 55425-1510
Phone: (952)851-4613
Fax: (952)851-4701
Trade magazine for large-acreage producers of forage crops. **Founded:** 1986. **Freq:** 7/yr. **Print Method:** Offset. **Trim Size:** 8 1/2 x 11. **Key Personnel:** Neil Tietz, Editor; Fae Holin, Editor. **URL:** http://hayandforage.com/. **Ad Rates:** BW $9,440; 4C $11,370. **Remarks:** Accepts advertising. **Circ:** (Not Reported).

18527 ■ Homestore Home Plans
HomeStyles.com
901 N 3rd St., Ste. 216
Minneapolis, MN 55401-1001
Free: 888-447-1946
Publisher's E-mail: customize@homeplans.com
Featuring the best home plans available special issues focus on designs for move-up homes, homes with special attentives, homes for empty nesters and homes inspired by European design. Design styles include country, contemporary, Mediterranean, Southern, and Victorian. **Freq:** Quarterly. **Print Method:** Web offset. **Trim Size:** 8 x 10 3/4. **Cols./Page:** 3. **URL:** http://www.homeplans.com. **Remarks:** Accepts advertising. **Circ:** Non-paid 53000.

18528 ■ Illustrator
Art Instruction Schools
6465 Wayzata Blvd., Ste. 240
Minneapolis, MN 55426
Free: 800-278-4787
Trade magazine covering artwork and past graduates of Art Instruction Schools. **Freq:** Annual. **Print Method:** Litho. **Trim Size:** 8 1/4 x 10 7/8. **ISSN:** 0019-2465 (print). **Subscription Rates:** Free. **URL:** http://artinstructionschools.com/; http://www.ais-illustrator.com/. **Remarks:** Advertising not accepted. **Circ:** (Not Reported).

18529 ■ Industrial Fire World
International Rescue and Emergency Care Association
PO Box 431000
Minneapolis, MN 55443
Phone: (763)391-8519
Fax: (763)391-8501
Trade magazine covering industrial firefighting. **Freq:** Monthly. **Print Method:** Web press. **Trim Size:** 8 3/8 x 10 1/2. **Key Personnel:** David White, President, Publisher; Anton Riecher, Editor. **ISSN:** 0749--089X (print). **Subscription Rates:** $20 U.S. and Canada; $40 Other countries. **URL:** http://www.fireworld.com/NewStore/Magazine.aspx. **Ad Rates:** BW $2050; 4C $2825. **Remarks:** Accepts advertising. **Circ:** Paid 21600.

18530 ■ Insight News
Insight News Inc.
Marcus Garvey House
1815 Bryant Ave. N
Minneapolis, MN 55411
Phone: (612)588-1313
Fax: (612)588-2031
Publisher's E-mail: info@insightnews.com
Newspaper serving the African-American community in Minneapolis. **Freq:** Weekly (Mon.). **Print Method:** Photo offset. **Key Personnel:** Al McFarlane, Editor-in-Chief, President; Batala-Ra McFarlane, Publisher. **URL:** http://insightnews.com/. **Remarks:** Accepts advertising. **Circ:** Non-paid ♦**35000.**

18531 ■ Iterations: Interdisciplinary Journal of Software History
Charles Babbage Institute for the History of Information Technology
211 Andersen Library
222 21st Ave. S
Minneapolis, MN 55455
Phone: (612)624-5050
Fax: (612)625-8054
Publisher's E-mail: cbi@umn.edu
Freq: publishes continuously. **Subscription Rates:** free. **URL:** http://www.cbi.umn.edu/iterations/. **Remarks:** Advertising not accepted. **Circ:** (Not Reported).

18532 ■ Journal of Biological Inorganic Chemistry
Society of Biological Inorganic Chemistry
c/o Lawrence Que, Editor-in-Chief
University of Minnesota
Dept. of Chemical
207 Pleasant St. SE
Minneapolis, MN 55455-0431
Phone: (612)626-9405
Fax: (612)625-0078
Publisher's E-mail: info@sbichem.org
Journal providing a forum to understand the biological function at the molecular level. Publishes research articles relating to metal ions or other inorganic species and having biological significance. **Freq:** 8/year. **Key Personnel:** Lawrence Que, Editor-in-Chief. **ISSN:** 0949--8257 (print); **EISSN:** 1432--1327 (electronic). **Subscription Rates:** €63.02 Individuals print + online. **URL:** http://www.springer.com/life+sciences/biochemistry+%26+biophysics/journal/775; http://sbichem.org/Our-Journal-JBIC.aspx. **Remarks:** Advertising accepted; rates available upon request. **Circ:** (Not Reported).

18533 ■ Journal of College Orientation & Transition
National Orientation Directors Association
2829 University Ave., Ste. 415
Minneapolis, MN 55414
Phone: (612)301-6632
Fax: (612)624-2628
Free: 866-521-6632
Publisher's E-mail: noda@umn.edu
Professional journal covering issues for college orientation directors and administrators. **Freq:** Semiannual fall and spring. **Key Personnel:** Dr. Jeanine Ward-Roof, Associate Editor, Senior Editor, phone: (850)644-2428, fax: (850)644-0687. **ISSN:** 1534--2263 (print). **Subscription Rates:** $25 Individuals and libraries; $15 Single issue; Included in membership. **URL:** http://www.nodaweb.org/?page=JCOT. **Circ:** (Not Reported).

18534 ■ Journal of Marriage and Family
National Council on Family Relations
1201 W River Pky., Ste. 200
Minneapolis, MN 55454-1115
Phone: (763)781-9331
Fax: (763)781-9348
Free: 888-781-9331
Publisher's E-mail: info@ncfr.org
Publication in the family field featuring original research and theory, research interpretation, and critical discussion related to marriage and the family. **Freq:** 5/year February, May, August, November and December. **Print Method:** Offset. **Trim Size:** 6 x 9 1/2. **Cols./Page:** 2. **Col. Width:** 2 inches. **Col. Depth:** 112 agate lines. **Key Personnel:** David H. Demo, Board Member; Cheryl Buehler, Board Member; David R. Johnson, Board Member. **ISSN:** 0022-2445 (print); **EISSN:** 1741-3737 (electronic). **Subscription Rates:** $166 Individuals print + online; £141 Other countries print + online; $1532 Institutions print + online; $2288 Institutions, other countries print + online; Included in membership. **URL:** http://www.ncfr.org/jmf. **Ad Rates:** BW $900. **Remarks:** Accepts advertising. **Circ:** 6000, ‡6,200.

18535 ■ Journal of Pension Planning and Compliance
Wolters Kluwer Law and Business
c/o Bruce J. McNeil, Ed.-in-Ch.
Leonard, Street & Deinard
150 Fifth St., Ste. 2300
Minneapolis, MN 55402
Journal covering pension compliance and design issues for professionals. **Freq:** Quarterly. **Key Personnel:** Bruce J. McNeil, Editor-in-Chief. **ISSN:** 0148-2181 (print). **Subscription Rates:** $539 Individuals paperback. **URL:** http://www.wklawbusiness.com/store/products/journal-pension-planning-compliance-prod-ss01482181/paperback-item-1-ss01482181. **Circ:** (Not Reported).

18536 ■ Journal of the Viola da Gamba Society of America
Viola da Gamba Society of America
PO Box 582628
Minneapolis, MN 55458-2628
Free: 855-846-5415
Publisher's E-mail: post@vdgsa.org
Freq: Annual. **ISSN:** 0607- 0252 (print). **Subscription Rates:** Included in membership; $7 Individuals back issues. **URL:** http://vdgsa.org/pgs/toc.html. **Remarks:** Advertising not accepted. **Circ:** 1200.

18537 ■ Lake Minnetonka Magazine
Tiger Oak Publications Inc.
900 S Third St.
Minneapolis, MN 55415-1209
Phone: (612)548-3180
Fax: (612)548-3181
Publisher's E-mail: service@tigeroak.com
Local magazine of Lake Minnetonka. **Key Personnel:** Tamara Prato, Publisher. **Subscription Rates:** $12 Individuals. **URL:** http://lakeminnetonkamag.com. **Remarks:** Advertising accepted; rates available upon request. **Circ:** Combined 30000.

18538 ■ Lavender: Minnesota's Gay-Lesbian-Bisexual-Transgender Magazine
Lavender Media Inc.
3715 Chicago Ave. S
Minneapolis, MN 55407
Publication E-mail: info@lavendermagazine.com
Lifestyle magazine for the gay and lesbian community. **Freq:** Biweekly. **Trim Size:** 7 x 9.3. **Key Personnel:** Ethan Boatner, Editor, phone: (612)436-4670; George Holdgrafer, Associate Editor. **Subscription Rates:** $26 Individuals 26 issues, 3rd class mailing. **URL:** http://www.lavendermagazine.com. **Remarks:** Accepts advertising. **Circ:** (Not Reported).

18539 ■ Law and Inequality: A Journal of Theory and Practice
University of Minnesota Law School
Walter F. Mondale Hall
229 19th Ave. S
Minneapolis, MN 55455
Phone: (612)625-1000
Fax: (612)626-2011
Publisher's E-mail: lawcomm@umn.edu
Journal addressing issues of inequality in law and society. **Freq:** Semiannual. **Key Personnel:** Evan Gelles, Editor-in-Chief. **Subscription Rates:** $18 Individuals /year; $10 Single issue current volume; Free to prisoners. **URL:** http://www.law.umn.edu/lawineq/index.html. **Circ:** (Not Reported).

18540 ■ Let's Play Softball
Let's Play Inc.
2721 E 42nd St.
Minneapolis, MN 55406
Phone: (612)729-0023
Fax: (612)729-0259
Publication E-mail: letsplay@letsplaysoftball.com
Magazine about softball. **Freq:** Monthly. **Print Method:** Cold Web Offset. **Trim Size:** 10 7/8 x 16 1/2. **Cols./Page:** 4. **Col. Width:** 2 3/8 inches. **Col. Depth:** 16 inches. **Key Personnel:** Mike Thill, Photographer; Kevin Kurtt, Editor; Doug Johnson, Manager, Advertising, Publisher. **ISSN:** 0892--9440 (print). **Subscription Rates:** $12 Individuals. **Ad Rates:** BW $739.20. **Remarks:** Advertising accepted; rates available upon request. **Circ:** (Not Reported).

18541 ■ Maple Grove Magazine
Tiger Oak Publications Inc.
900 S Third St.
Minneapolis, MN 55415-1209
Phone: (612)548-3180
Fax: (612)548-3181
Publisher's E-mail: service@tigeroak.com
Local magazine of Maple Grove city. **Freq:** Monthly. **Key Personnel:** Tamara Prato, Publisher. **URL:** http://maplegrovemag.com. **Remarks:** Advertising accepted; rates available upon request. **Circ:** (Not Reported).

18542 ■ Midwest Home & Garden: A Supplement Magazine to Minnesota Monthly Magazine
Greenspring Media Group Inc.
706 2nd Ave S Ste 1000
Minneapolis, MN 55402-3003
Phone: (612)371-5800
Fax: (612)371-5801
Free: 800-933-4398
Publisher's E-mail: letters@mnmo.com
Supplement to Minnesota Monthly. **Freq:** 6/year. **Print Method:** Offset. **Trim Size:** 8 3/8 x 11. **Cols./Page:** 3. **Col. Width:** 2 1/4 inches. **Col. Depth:** 10 inches. **Key Personnel:** Jamie Flaws, Publisher, phone: (612)371-5847. **Subscription Rates:** $9.95 Individuals domestic; $17.95 Individuals 2 years, domestic; $24.95 Individuals 3 years, domestic. **URL:** http://midwesthomemag.com. **Ad Rates:** BW $5,730; 4C $4,400. **Remarks:** Accepts advertising. **Circ:** Paid ★**50000**.

18543 ■ Military Thought: A Russian Journal of Military Theory and Strategy
East View Information Services.
10601 Wayzata Blvd.
Minneapolis, MN 55305-1515
Phone: (952)252-1201
Fax: (952)252-1202
Free: 800-477-1005
Publisher's E-mail: info@eastview.com
Scholarly journal covering military policy in Russia. **Freq:** Quarterly. **Trim Size:** 8 x 5. **Key Personnel:** S.V. Rodikov, Editor-in-Chief; A. Alyoshin, Board Member; O. Burtsev, Board Member. **ISSN:** 0869--5636 (print). **Subscription Rates:** $1115 Institutions print; $245 Individuals print; $355 Other countries print, U.S; $1075 Institutions online; $240 Individuals online, U.S and other Countries; $1220 Institutions print and online; $295 Individuals print and online, U.S; $395 Other countries print and online. **URL:** http://www.eastviewpress.com/Journals/MilitaryThought.aspx. **Ad Rates:** BW $380. **Remarks:** Accepts advertising. **Circ:** 200.

18544 ■ Minneapolis Labor Review
MPLS Central Labor Union Council
312 Central Ave., Ste. 542
Minneapolis, MN 55414
Phone: (612)379-4206
Fax: (612)379-1307
Publication E-mail: laborreview@minneapolisunions.org
Labor newspaper. **Freq:** Monthly last Friday or second to last Friday of each month. Exception: November -- second Friday of the month. **Print Method:** Offset. **Cols./Page:** 6. **Col. Width:** 19 nonpareils. **Col. Depth:** 205 agate lines. **Key Personnel:** Steve Share, Editor. **ISSN:** 0274--9017 (print). **Subscription Rates:** $10 Individuals. **URL:** http://www.minneapolisunions.org/cluc_labor_review.php. **Remarks:** Advertising accepted; rates available upon request. **Circ:** (Not Reported).

18545 ■ Minneapolis/St. Paul Business Journal
American City Business Journals Inc.
333 S 7th St., Ste. 350
Minneapolis, MN 55402-2414
Phone: (612)288-2100
Fax: (612)288-2121
Local business newspaper. **Freq:** Weekly. **Key Personnel:** Mark Reilly, Managing Editor, phone: (612)288-2110; Tom Smith, Editor, phone: (612)288-2102; Kim Johnson, Assistant Managing Editor, phone: (612)288-2114; Katharine Grayson, Reporter, phone: (612)288-2106; John Vomhof, Jr., Reporter; Dirk DeYoung, Editor, phone: (612)288-2111; Carole Kroening, Director, Production, phone: (612)288-2145. **ISSN:** 0883--3044 (print). **Subscription Rates:** $91 Individuals print and digital issue; $4.99 Single issue PDF. **URL:** http://www.bizjournals.com/twincities. **Ad Rates:** BW $4,230, full page spread; BW $3,225, island spread; BW $2,810, 1/2 page spread; BW $2,475, full page; BW $1,790, 1/2 page; BW $1,355, 1/4 page. **Remarks:** Accepts advertising. **Circ:** (Not Reported).

18546 ■ Minnesota
University of Minnesota Alumni Association
McNamara Alumni Ctr.
200 Oak St. SE, Ste. 200
Minneapolis, MN 55455-2040
Phone: (612)624-2323
Fax: (612)626-8167
Free: 800-862-5867
Publisher's E-mail: umalumni@umn.edu
University alumni magazine. **Freq:** Quarterly. **Print Method:** Web offset. **Trim Size:** 8 1/4 x 10 13/16. **Cols./Page:** 3. **Col. Width:** 28 nonpareils. **Col. Depth:** 124 agate lines. **Key Personnel:** Cynthia Scott, Editor, phone: (612)624-8490. **ISSN:** 0164--9450 (print). **USPS:** 014-012. **Subscription Rates:** Included in membership. **URL:** http://www.minnesotaalumni.org/s/1118/content.aspx?sid=1118&gid=1&pgid=1891. **Ad Rates:** 4C $5395. **Remarks:** Accepts advertising. **Circ:** 50000.

18547 ■ Minnesota Bride
Tiger Oak Publications Inc.
900 S Third St.
Minneapolis, MN 55415-1209
Phone: (612)548-3180
Fax: (612)548-3181
Publisher's E-mail: service@tigeroak.com
Consumer magazine for brides and grooms. **Freq:** Semiannual. **Key Personnel:** R. Craig Bednar, Publisher; Mary O'Regan; Katie Roberts, CAM, Associate Publisher. **URL:** http://mnbride.com. **Remarks:** Advertising accepted; rates available upon request. **Circ:** (Not Reported).

18548 ■ Minnesota Business
Tiger Oak Publications Inc.
900 S Third St.
Minneapolis, MN 55415-1209
Phone: (612)548-3180
Fax: (612)548-3181
Publisher's E-mail: service@tigeroak.com
Business magazine. **Key Personnel:** Stefani Pennaz, Publisher; Sheri O'Meara, Editor-in-Chief. **URL:** http://www.minnesotabusiness.com. **Remarks:** Advertising accepted; rates available upon request. **Circ:** (Not Reported).

18549 ■ The Minnesota Daily
University of Minnesota - Twin Cities
2221 University Ave. SE Ste. 450
Minneapolis, MN 55414
Phone: (612)435-5700
Fax: (612)435-5772
Collegiate newspaper (tabloid). **Freq:** Mon.-Fri. **Print Method:** Offset. **Cols./Page:** 5. **Col. Width:** 1 7/8 inches. **Col. Depth:** 16 inches. **Key Personnel:** Dylan Scott, Editor-in-Chief. **USPS:** 351-480. **URL:** http://www.mndaily.com. **Ad Rates:** BW $799; 4C $1249; PCI $9.99. **Remarks:** Accepts advertising. **Circ:** Free ‡27000.

18550 ■ Minnesota Good Age
Minnesota Premier Publications Inc.
1115 Hennepin Ave.
Minneapolis, MN 55403

Circulation: ★ = AAM; △ or • = BPA; ♦ = CAC; ❑ = VAC; ⊕ = PO Statement; ‡ = Publisher's Report; Boldface figures = sworn; Light figures = estimated.

Phone: (612)825-9205
Fax: (612)436-4396
Publisher's E-mail: editor@mnparent.com
Magazine covering health, housing, finance and legal issues. **Freq:** Monthly. **Key Personnel:** Janis Hall, Publisher, Owner. **ISSN:** 2333--3197 (print). **Subscription Rates:** $12 Individuals. **URL:** http://mngoodage.com. **Remarks:** Accepts advertising. **Circ:** ‡72500.

18551 ■ Minnesota Journal of International Law
University of Minnesota Law School
Walter F. Mondale Hall
229 19th Ave. S
Minneapolis, MN 55455
Phone: (612)625-1000
Fax: (612)626-2011
Publisher's E-mail: lawcomm@umn.edu
Journal consisting of articles on a variety of topics within the field of international law. **Freq:** Semiannual. **Key Personnel:** Allyson Billeaud, Editor-in-Chief. **URL:** http://minnjil.org. **Circ:** (Not Reported).

18552 ■ Minnesota Journal of Law, Science and Technology
University of Minnesota Law School
Walter F. Mondale Hall
229 19th Ave. S
Minneapolis, MN 55455
Phone: (612)625-1000
Fax: (612)626-2011
Publisher's E-mail: lawcomm@umn.edu
Journal focusing on law, health, the sciences and bioethics. **Freq:** Semiannual. **Key Personnel:** Emily Harrison, Editor-in-Chief. **Subscription Rates:** $35 Individuals /volume. **URL:** http://mjlst.umn.edu. **Circ:** (Not Reported).

18553 ■ Minnesota Law & Politics
Key Professional Media Inc.
225 S Sixth St., Ste. 5200
Minneapolis, MN 55402
Professional magazine covering law and politics in Minnesota. **Freq:** Bimonthly. **Print Method:** Web offset. **Trim Size:** 9 1/8 x 10 7/8. **Key Personnel:** Bill White, Publisher, phone: (612)313-1761, fax: (612)335-8809; Steven Kaplan, Editor, phone: (612)313-1762; Seth Woehrle, Associate Editor, phone: (612)313-1765; Adam Wahlberg, Executive Editor, phone: (612)313-1760; Michael Maupin, Managing Editor, phone: (612)373-9626. **Subscription Rates:** Free. **URL:** http://lawandpolitics.com/minnesota/default.asp. **Formerly:** Minnesota's Journal of Law & Politics. **Ad Rates:** BW $4,075; 4C $4,650. **Remarks:** Accepts advertising. **Circ:** Controlled ‡17760, Paid ‡8633.

18554 ■ Minnesota Law Review
University of Minnesota Law School
Walter F. Mondale Hall
229 19th Ave. S
Minneapolis, MN 55455
Phone: (612)625-1000
Fax: (612)626-2011
Publication E-mail: mnlawrev@umn.edu
Legal journal. **Freq:** Bimonthly. **Print Method:** Letterpress. **Cols./Page:** 1. **Col. Width:** 54 nonpareils. **Col. Depth:** 112 agate lines. **Key Personnel:** Emily Scholtes, Editor-in-Chief. **ISSN:** 0026--5535 (print). **Subscription Rates:** $40 Individuals; $10 Single issue; $46 Other countries. **URL:** http://www.minnesotalawreview.org. **Remarks:** Accepts advertising. **Circ:** 1,345.

18555 ■ Minnesota Medicine: A Journal of Clinical and Health Affairs
Minnesota Medical Association
1300 Godward St. NE, Ste. 2500
Minneapolis, MN 55413
Phone: (612)378-1875
Fax: (612)378-3875
Free: 800-342-5662
Publisher's E-mail: mma@mnmed.org
Magazine on medical, socioeconomic, public health, medical-legal, and biomedical ethics issues of interest to physicians. **Freq:** Monthly. **Print Method:** Web. **Trim Size:** 8 1/8 x 10 7/8. **Cols./Page:** 2 and 3. **Col. Width:** 3 1/2 and 2 1/4 inches. **Col. Depth:** 9 5/8 inches. **Key Personnel:** Charles Meyer, MD, Editor-in-Chief; Kim Kiser, Editor, phone: (612)362-3758. **ISSN:** 0026--556X (print). **Subscription Rates:** $45 Individuals; $81 Two years; $10 Single issue. **URL:** http://www.mnmed.org/news-and-publications/mn-medicine-magazine. **Remarks:** Advertising accepted; rates available upon request. **Circ:** (Not Reported).

18556 ■ Minnesota Monthly
Greenspring Media Group Inc.
706 2nd Ave S Ste 1000
Minneapolis, MN 55402-3003
Phone: (612)371-5800
Fax: (612)371-5801
Free: 800-933-4398
Publisher's E-mail: letters@mnmo.com
Regional magazine. **Freq:** Monthly. **Print Method:** Offset. **Trim Size:** 8 x 10 7/8. **Cols./Page:** 3. **Col. Width:** 13.5 picas. **Col. Depth:** 60 picas. **Key Personnel:** Andrew Putz, Editor; Abbey Jensen, Manager, Traffic, phone: (612)371-5849; Tim Morgan, Manager, Circulation, phone: (612)371-5804; Kylie Engle, Account Executive, phone: (612)371-5807; Marta Simpson, Account Executive, phone: (612)371-5875; Kelly Fitzgerald, Editor; Joel Hoekstra, Editor; Dara Moskowitz Grumdahl, Senior Editor. **ISSN:** 0739--8700 (print). **Subscription Rates:** $19.95 Individuals 1 year. **URL:** http://www.minnesotamonthly.com; http://www.greenspring.com/publications. **Ad Rates:** BW $4,450; 4C $6,675. **Remarks:** Advertising accepted; rates available upon request. **Circ:** (Not Reported).

18557 ■ Minnesota Spokesman
Minnesota Spokesman-Recorder
3744 Fourth Ave. S
Minneapolis, MN 55409
Phone: (612)827-4021
Fax: (612)827-0577
Publication E-mail: display@spokesman-recorder.com
Black community newspaper. **Freq:** Weekly. **Print Method:** Offset. **Cols./Page:** 6. **Col. Width:** 21 nonpareils. **Col. Depth:** 218 agate lines. **Key Personnel:** Vicki Evans-Nash, Editor-in-Chief; Jerry Freeman, Senior Editor. **Subscription Rates:** $35 Individuals; $60 Two years; $40 Out of state; $70 Out of area 2 years. **URL:** http://www.spokesman-recorder.com. **Formerly:** Minneapolis Spokesman & St. Paul Recorder; Minneapolis Spokesman-Recorder. **Mailing address:** PO BOX 8558, Minneapolis, MN 55408-0558. **Remarks:** Advertising accepted; rates available upon request. **Circ:** Combined ‡5450.

18558 ■ Minnesota Spokesman-Recorder
St. Paul Recorder
3744-4th Ave. S
Minneapolis, MN 55409
Phone: (612)827-4021
Fax: (612)827-0577
Publication E-mail: vnash@spokesman-recorder.com
Black community newspaper. **Freq:** Weekly (Tues.). **Subscription Rates:** $35 Individuals; $60 Two years; $40 Individuals non-Minnesota residents; $70 Two years non-Minnesota residents. **URL:** http://www.spokesman-recorder.com. **Formerly:** St. Paul Recorder. **Ad Rates:** BW $6,806.52; 4C $536.47; PCI $54.02. **Circ:** ‡10100.

18559 ■ Minnesota Sports
Minnesota Premier Publications Inc.
1115 Hennepin Ave.
Minneapolis, MN 55403
Phone: (612)825-9205
Fax: (612)436-4396
Publisher's E-mail: editor@mnparent.com
Magazine about sports in Minnesota. **Freq:** 11/year. **Key Personnel:** Glenn R. Hansen, Editor; Shelly Fling, Managing Editor; Anna Bjorlin, Editor. **Subscription Rates:** $15. **URL:** http://www.minnesotaparent.com/topics/sports. **Remarks:** Advertising accepted; rates available upon request. **Circ:** (Not Reported).

18560 ■ MIS Quarterly
University of Minnesota Carlson School of Management
Management Information Systems Research Center
321 19th Ave. S, Ste. 4-173
Minneapolis, MN 55455
Phone: (612)625-0862
Fax: (612)626-1600
Publisher's E-mail: misrc@umn.edu
Refereed research journal for academics and practitioners in the management information systems field. **Founded:** Mar. 1977. **Freq:** Quarterly (March, June, September, and December). **Print Method:** Offset. **Trim Size:** 7 x 10. **Cols./Page:** 2. **Col. Width:** 16 picas. **Col. Depth:** 48 picas. **Key Personnel:** Arun Rai, Editor-in-Chief. **ISSN:** 0276-7783 (print). **Subscription Rates:** $100 Individuals online only; $1000 Institutions online only; $175 Individuals print only; $350 Institutions print only; $275 Individuals print and online; $1350 Institutions print and online; $150 Students print only; $175 Students, other countries print only. **URL:** http://www.misq.org. **Ad Rates:** BW $425, full page; BW $325, half page. **Remarks:** Accepts advertising. **Circ:** Paid 3,000, Non-paid 100.

18561 ■ The Moving Image
University of Minnesota Press
111 3rd Ave. S, Ste. 290
Minneapolis, MN 55401-2520
Phone: (612)627-1970
Fax: (612)627-1980
Free: 800-621-2736
Publisher's E-mail: ump@umn.edu
Peer-reviewed journal covering issues surrounding the preservation and restoration of film. **Freq:** Semiannual. **Key Personnel:** Michael Baskett, Editor; Liza Palmer, Managing Editor; Grover Crisp, Board Member. **ISSN:** 1532-3978 (print). **Subscription Rates:** $30 Individuals; $75 Institutions; $35 Individuals outside U.S.; $80 Institutions outside U.S. **Alt. Formats:** Electronic publishing. **URL:** http://www.upress.umn.edu/journal-division/Journals/the-moving-image. **Ad Rates:** BW $300. **Remarks:** Accepts advertising. **Circ:** (Not Reported).

18562 ■ Mpls.St.Paul Magazine: The Best of the Twin Cities
MSP Communications
220 S Sixth St., Ste. 500
Minneapolis, MN 55402
Phone: (612)339-7571
Fax: (612)339-5806
Free: 800-999-5589
Publisher's E-mail: outstandingnurses@mspmag.com
Metropolitan lifestyle magazine. **Freq:** Monthly. **Print Method:** Offset-Web. **Trim Size:** 8 x 10 7/8. **Cols./Page:** 3. **Col. Width:** 26 nonpareils. **Col. Depth:** 140 agate lines. **Key Personnel:** Deb Hopp, Publisher. **ISSN:** 0162--6655 (print). **USPS:** 132-510. **Subscription Rates:** $19.95 Individuals; $33.95 Two years; $43.95 Individuals 3 years. **URL:** http://mspmag.com. **Ad Rates:** BW $6955; 4C $9350. **Remarks:** Accepts advertising. **Circ:** Paid 60593.

18563 ■ National Hog Farmer
Southwest Farm Press - Agribusiness Div.
7900 International Dr., Ste. 300
Minneapolis, MN 55425-1510
Phone: (952)851-4613
Fax: (952)851-4701
Trade magazine for pork producers. **Founded:** 1956. **Freq:** Monthly. **Print Method:** Offset. **Trim Size:** 7 7/8 x 10 3/4. **Cols./Page:** 3. **Col. Width:** 2 1/8 inches. **Col. Depth:** 140 agate lines. **Key Personnel:** Joe Vansickle, Senior Editor, fax: (952)851-4670; Bret Kealy, Publisher; Dale Miller, Editor, phone: (952)851-4661; Eric Meester, Director, Production. **ISSN:** 0027-9447 (print). **URL:** http://nationalhogfarmer.com. **Ad Rates:** BW $9975; 4C $11945. **Remarks:** Accepts advertising. **Circ:** △**26,420**.

18564 ■ Neurocritical Care
Neurocritical Care Society
5841 Cedar Lake Rd., Ste. 204
Minneapolis, MN 55416
Phone: (952)646-2031
Fax: (952)545-6073
Publisher's E-mail: info@neurocriticalcare.org
Peer-reviewed scientific journal publishing new knowledge on all aspects of acute neurological care. **Freq:** Bimonthly. **Key Personnel:** Eelco F.M. Wijdicks, MD, Editor-in-Chief. **ISSN:** 1541--6933 (print); **EISSN:** 1556--0961 (electronic). **Subscription Rates:** €2401 Institutions print and electronic; €2881 Institutions print and enchanced access; Included in membership. **URL:** http://www.springer.com/medicine/internal/journal/12028; http://www.neurocriticalcare.org/publications/neurocritical-care-journal. **Ad Rates:** BW $1450; 4C $1300. **Remarks:** Accepts advertising. **Circ:** 1000.

18565 ■ Northeaster & Northnews
Northeaster
3207 Central Ave. NE, No. 11
Minneapolis, MN 55418
Phone: (612)788-9003
Fax: (612)788-3299

Publisher's E-mail: contact@nenorthnews.com
Community newspaper. **Freq:** Semimonthly. **Print Method:** Web offset. **Cols./Page:** 5. **Col. Width:** 11 picas. **Col. Depth:** 15 inches. **Key Personnel:** Margo Ashmore, Editor, Publisher. **Subscription Rates:** $18 Individuals. **URL:** http://www.nenorthnews.com/Home.asp. **Formerly:** Northeaster. **Remarks:** Advertising accepted; rates available upon request. **Circ:** ‡32500.

18566 ■ Northern Breezes Sailing Magazine
Northern Breezes Inc.
3949 Winnetka Ave. N
Minneapolis, MN 55427
Phone: (763)542-9707
Fax: (763)542-8998
Publication E-mail: info@sailingbreezes.com
Consumer magazine covering sailing in the Upper Midwest U.S. **Freq:** 5/year. **Print Method:** Web offset. **Trim Size:** 8 1/4 x 10 3/4. **Cols./Page:** 3. **Col. Width:** 2 1/4 inches. **Key Personnel:** Thom Burns, Publisher; Alan Kretzschmar, Managing Editor. **URL:** http://www.sailingbreezes.com. **Remarks:** Advertising accepted; rates available upon request. **Circ:** Paid ‡20300, Non-paid ‡17800.

18567 ■ Northwestern Financial Review
NFR Communications Inc.
7400 Metro Blvd., Ste. 217
Minneapolis, MN 55439
Phone: (952)835-2275
Fax: (952)835-2295
Publisher's E-mail: info@northwesternfinancialreview.com
Trade publication covering commercial banking. **Freq:** 24/yr. **Print Method:** Offset. **Trim Size:** 8 1/4 x 11. **Cols./Page:** 3. **Col. Width:** 12 picas. **Col. Depth:** 58 picas. **Key Personnel:** Tom Bengston, Editor, Publisher. **ISSN:** 1042-1254 (print). **Subscription Rates:** $99 Individuals. **URL:** http://www.northwesternfinancialreview.com. **Formerly:** Northwestern Banker; Commercial West. **Ad Rates:** BW $1,205; 4C $2,055. **Remarks:** Accepts display and classified advertising. **Circ:** Paid 8000.

18568 ■ Oregon Bride
Tiger Oak Publications Inc.
900 S Third St.
Minneapolis, MN 55415-1209
Phone: (612)548-3180
Fax: (612)548-3181
Publisher's E-mail: service@tigeroak.com
Consumer magazine for brides and grooms. **Freq:** Semiannual. **Key Personnel:** R. Craig Bednar, Publisher; Heather Matheny, Director, Advertising. **URL:** http://orbridemag.com. **Remarks:** Advertising accepted; rates available upon request. **Circ:** (Not Reported).

18569 ■ The Physician and Sportsmedicine
McGraw-Hill Healthcare Information Group
4530 W 77th St., 3rd Fl.
Minneapolis, MN 55435
A peer-reviewed journal on the medical aspects of sports, exercise, and fitness. **Freq:** Quarterly. **Print Method:** Web offset. **Trim Size:** 7 3/4 x 10 3/4. **Cols./Page:** 3 and 2. **Col. Width:** 16 and 12 picas. **Col. Depth:** 140 agate lines. **Key Personnel:** Nicholas A. Dinubile, MD, Executive Editor; Brian B. Adams, MD, Board Member; Jack Andrish, MD, Board Member. **ISSN:** 0091--3847 (print). **Subscription Rates:** $1559 Institutions online only; $1641 Institutions print and online; $217 Individuals print and online. **URL:** http://www.tandfonline.com/toc/ipsm20/current#.VdLadbLt2ko. **Ad Rates:** BW $5374; 4C $7184. **Remarks:** Accepts advertising. **Circ:** Paid 15000.

18570 ■ PLUS Journal
Professional Liability Underwriting Society
5353 Wayzata Blvd., Ste. 600
Minneapolis, MN 55416-1335
Phone: (952)746-2580
Fax: (952)746-2599
Free: 800-845-0778
Publisher's E-mail: info@plusweb.org
Journal containing topics and issues impacting the professional liability marketplace. **Freq:** Monthly. **Subscription Rates:** Included in membership. **URL:** http://stage.plusweb.org/Journal.aspx. **Remarks:** Advertising not accepted. **Circ:** (Not Reported).

18571 ■ Plymouth Magazine
Tiger Oak Publications Inc.
900 S Third St.
Minneapolis, MN 55415-1209
Phone: (612)548-3180
Fax: (612)548-3181
Publisher's E-mail: service@tigeroak.com
Local magazine of the city of Plymouth. **Freq:** Monthly. **Key Personnel:** Laura Haraldson, Managing Editor. **URL:** http://plymouthmag.com. **Remarks:** Advertising accepted; rates available upon request. **Circ:** (Not Reported).

18572 ■ Powersports Business
Ehlert Publishing Group Inc.
10405 6th Ave. N, Ste. 210
Minneapolis, MN 55441
Phone: (763)383-4400
Fax: (763)383-4499
Publication E-mail: dmcmahon@powersportsbusiness.com
Powersports trade magazine. **Freq:** 16/yr. **Print Method:** Web Offset. **Trim Size:** 10 7/8 x 15. **Cols./Page:** 4. **Col. Width:** 2 3/8 inches. **Col. Depth:** 13 7/8 inches. **Key Personnel:** Dave McMahon, Senior Editor; David Voll, Account Manager. **ISSN:** 0883--8259 (print). **URL:** http://www.powersportsbusiness.com. **Formerly:** Snow Goer Trade; Snowmobile Business; Watercraft Business. **Ad Rates:** BW $4360; 4C $5645. **Remarks:** Accepts advertising. **Circ:** (Not Reported).

18573 ■ Precision Manufacturing: Journal of the Minnesota Precision Manufacturing Association
Synergy Resource Group Inc.
5353 Wayzata Blvd., Ste. 350
Minneapolis, MN 55416
Phone: (952)564-3041
Fax: (952)952-8096
Publication E-mail: mpma@mpma.com
Trade magazine covering manufacturing in Minnesota. **Freq:** Bimonthly. **Print Method:** Sheet-Fed. **Trim Size:** 8 1/8 x 10 7/8. **Key Personnel:** Amy Slettum, Director, Publications, Editor; Tim Crooley, Manager, Sales; Jaime Nolan, Executive Director. **ISSN:** 0273--7523 (print). **Subscription Rates:** Free to any manufacturer in Minnesota. **URL:** http://pm-mn.com. **Formerly:** Minnesota Precision Manufacturing Association Journal. **Ad Rates:** BW $2150. **Remarks:** Accepts advertising. **Circ:** Non-paid 6535, Controlled ‡8200.

18574 ■ Profane Existence: A Source for Underground Music, Literature & culture since 1989
Profane Existence
PO Box 18051
Minneapolis, MN 55418
Consumer magazine covering punk music, radical politics, and alternative issues. **Freq:** Quarterly. **URL:** http://profaneexistence.storenvy.com. **Ad Rates:** BW $400. **Remarks:** Accepts advertising. **Circ:** Combined 20000.

18575 ■ Real Food: The magazine for the way we eat today
Greenspring Media Group Inc.
706 2nd Ave S Ste 1000
Minneapolis, MN 55402-3003
Phone: (612)371-5800
Fax: (612)371-5801
Free: 800-933-4398
Publisher's E-mail: letters@mnmo.com
Magazine featuring food choices. **Freq:** Quarterly. **Print Method:** Web offset. **Trim Size:** 8 x 10.5. **Key Personnel:** Mary Subialka, Contact, phone: (612)371-5823; Joel Schettler, Editor. **Subscription Rates:** $20 Individuals. **URL:** http://www.realfoodmag.com; http://www.greenspring.com/real-food. **Remarks:** Accepts advertising. **Circ:** (Not Reported).

18576 ■ The Region
Federal Reserve Bank of Minneapolis
90 Hennepin Ave.
Minneapolis, MN 55401-1804
Phone: (612)204-5000
Fax: (612)204-5515
Magazine covering banking and policy issues. **Freq:** Quarterly. **Key Personnel:** Jenni C. Schoppers, Managing Editor; David Fettig, Senior Editor; Douglas Clement, Editor. **ISSN:** 1045--3369 (print). **URL:** http://www.minneapolisfed.org/publications/the-region. **Remarks:** Advertising not accepted. **Circ:** (Not Reported).

18577 ■ Seattle Bride
Tiger Oak Publications Inc.
900 S Third St.
Minneapolis, MN 55415-1209
Phone: (612)548-3180
Fax: (612)548-3181
Publisher's E-mail: service@tigeroak.com
Consumer magazine for brides and grooms. **Freq:** Semiannual. **Key Personnel:** R. Craig Bednar, Publisher; Ali Brownrigg, Editor. **URL:** http://seattlebridemag.com. **Remarks:** Advertising accepted; rates available upon request. **Circ:** (Not Reported).

18578 ■ Shots Magazine
Shots
PO Box 27755
Minneapolis, MN 55427-0755
Publication E-mail: shotsmag@juno.com
Photography magazine. **Freq:** Quarterly. **Print Method:** Web offset. **Trim Size:** 8 x 11. **ISSN:** 1048-793X (print). **Subscription Rates:** $29 Individuals 1 year; $55 Individuals 2 years; $38 Canada 1 year; $74 Canada 2 years; $52 Other countries 1 year; $99 Other countries 2 years. **URL:** http://www.shotsmag.com/menu.htm. **Remarks:** Accepts advertising. **Circ:** Paid 900, Non-paid 1,500.

18579 ■ Sons of Norway Viking
Sons of Norway
1455 W Lake St.
Minneapolis, MN 55408-2666
Phone: (612)827-3611
Fax: (612)827-0658
Free: 800-945-8851
Publisher's E-mail: fraternal@sofn.com
Freq: Monthly. **ISSN:** 0038- 1462 (print). **Subscription Rates:** Included in membership. **Alt. Formats:** PDF. **URL:** http://www.sofn.com/norwegian_culture/viking_magazine. **Ad Rates:** 4C $2,458; BW $1,894. **Remarks:** Accepts advertising. **Circ:** (Not Reported).

18580 ■ Southeast Farm Press
Southwest Farm Press - Agribusiness Div.
7900 International Dr., Ste. 300
Minneapolis, MN 55425-1510
Phone: (952)851-4613
Fax: (952)851-4701
Publication covering agriculture in the southeastern U.S. for farmers. **Founded:** 1974. **Freq:** 28/yr. **Key Personnel:** Greg Frey, Vice President, Publisher; Hembree Brandon, Director, Editorial. **URL:** http://southeastfarmpress.com/. **Remarks:** Accepts advertising. **Circ:** Combined 53000.

18581 ■ Southwest Journal
Minnesota Premier Publications Inc.
1115 Hennepin Ave.
Minneapolis, MN 55403
Phone: (612)825-9205
Fax: (612)436-4396
Publisher's E-mail: editor@mnparent.com
Community newspaper. **Freq:** Biweekly. **Key Personnel:** Terry Gahan, Publisher; Janis Hall, Owner, Publisher. **Alt. Formats:** PDF. **URL:** http://www.southwestjournal.com. **Remarks:** Accepts advertising. **Circ:** (Not Reported).

18582 ■ Star Tribune: Newspaper of the Twin Cities
Star Tribune
425 Portland Ave.
Minneapolis, MN 55488
Phone: (612)673-4000
Fax: (612)673-7872
General newspaper. **Freq:** Daily. **Print Method:** Letterpress. **Cols./Page:** 6. **Col. Width:** 25 nonpareils. **Col. Depth:** 301 agate lines. **Key Personnel:** Michael J. Klingensmith, Publisher. **ISSN:** 0895--2825 (print). **Subscription Rates:** $12 Single issue Monday-Saturday; $4 Single issue Sunday. **URL:** http://www.startribune.com. **Formerly:** Minneapolis Star and Tribune. **Ad Rates:** BW $43185.24; 4C $45185.24; PCI $342.74. **Remarks:** Accepts advertising. **Circ:** Mon.-Sat. ★**172130**, Sun. ★**447150**.

Circulation: ★ = AAM; △ or • = BPA; ♦ = CAC; ❑ = VAC; ⊕ = PO Statement; ‡ = Publisher's Report; Boldface figures = sworn; Light figures = estimated.

18583 ■ Sweden and America
Swedish Council of America
3030 W River Pky.
Minneapolis, MN 55406
Phone: (612)871-0593
Publisher's E-mail: swedcoun@swedishcouncil.org
Magazine containing records and issues that reflect people, places, activities and events of Swedish-America. **Freq:** Quarterly. **Subscription Rates:** Included in membership. **URL:** http://www.swedishcouncil.org/magazine. **Remarks:** Advertising not accepted. **Circ:** (Not Reported).

18584 ■ Tack'n Togs Merchandising: The Monthly Business Magazine for Equine Retailers
Farm Progress Companies Inc.
5810 W 78th St.
Minneapolis, MN 55439
Publisher's E-mail: circhelp@farmprogress.com
International trade magazine for marketers of products for horse and rider. **Freq:** Monthly. **Print Method:** Web Offset Uses mats. **Trim Size:** 8 x 10 3/4. **Cols./Page:** 3. **Col. Width:** 40 nonpareils. **Col. Depth:** 140 agate lines. **Key Personnel:** Julie Golson Richards, Associate Editor; Trish Diedrich, Administrative Assistant, phone: (952)930-4357; Cindy Miller Johnson, Manager, Advertising and Sales; Sarah Muirhead, Editor, phone: (630)462-2466, fax: (630)462-2251. **ISSN:** 0149--3442 (print). **URL:** http://tackntogs.com. **Ad Rates:** BW $3758; 4C $4869; PCI $177. **Remarks:** Accepts advertising. **Circ:** (Not Reported).

18585 ■ Teradata Magazine
Teradata Corp.
c/o Kelly Carver
220 S 6th St., Ste. 500
Minneapolis, MN 55402
Phone: (612)336-9251
Journal covering all varieties of advertisement. **Freq:** Quarterly. **Key Personnel:** Kelly Carver, Contact. **URL:** http://www.teradatamagazine.com. **Ad Rates:** BW $2600. **Remarks:** Accepts advertising. **Circ:** (Not Reported).

18586 ■ Theoretical Chemistry Accounts
Springer-Verlag GmbH & Company KG
c/o Christopher J. Cramer, Editor
Dept. of Chemistry
University of Minnesota
207 Pleasant St. SE
Minneapolis, MN 55455-0240
Publisher's E-mail: customerservice@springer.com
Peer-reviewed journal dealing with theoretical chemistry, computational chemistry, and modeling. **Key Personnel:** Klaus Ruedenberg, Editor; Christopher J. Cramer, Editor; Donald G. Truhlar, Executive Editor, phone: (612)624-7555, fax: (612)626-7541. **ISSN:** 1432--881X (print); **EISSN:** 1432--2234 (electronic). **Subscription Rates:** €149 Institutions online. **URL:** http://www.springer.com/chemistry/journal/214. **Remarks:** Advertising accepted; rates available upon request. **Circ:** (Not Reported).

18587 ■ Theory and Research in Social Education
National Council for the Social Studies
c/o Patricia G. Avery, Ed.
University of Minnesota
168 Peik Hall
159 Pillsbury Dr. SE
Minneapolis, MN 55455
Phone: (612)625-5802
Fax: (612)624-8277
Publisher's E-mail: membership@ncss.org
Scholarly journal dealing with research in social studies education. **Freq:** Quarterly. **Print Method:** Offset. **Trim Size:** 6 x 9. **Cols./Page:** 1. **Key Personnel:** Patricia G. Avery, Editor; Dr. Carla L. Peck, Editor. **ISSN:** 0093-3104 (print); **EISSN:** 2163-1654 (electronic). **Subscription Rates:** $154 Institutions online only; $176 Institutions print and online; $93 Individuals print and online. **URL:** http://www.socialstudies.org/publications/theoryandresearch; http://www.tandfonline.com/toc/utrs20/current#.VHW8q9lwrlc. **Remarks:** Accepts advertising. **Circ:** 896, 1000.

18588 ■ Tunneling and Underground-Space Technology
American Underground Construction Association
3001 Hennepin Ave. S, Ste. D202
Minneapolis, MN 55408
Phone: (212)465-5541
Publisher's E-mail: underground@auca.org
Freq: Quarterly. **ISSN:** 0886--7798 (print). **Subscription Rates:** Individuals. **Remarks:** Advertising not accepted. **Circ:** (Not Reported).

18589 ■ University of St. Thomas Law Journal
University of St. Thomas School of Law
1000 LaSalle Ave.
Minneapolis, MN 55403
Phone: (651)962-4895
Fax: (651)962-4876
Free: 800-328-6819
Publisher's E-mail: lawschool@stthomas.edu
Journal promoting ethical actions, the integration of faith and reason and social justice. **Key Personnel:** Marc Spooner, Editor-in-Chief. **URL:** http://ir.stthomas.edu/ustlj. **Circ:** (Not Reported).

18590 ■ Viking
Sons of Norway
1455 W Lake St.
Minneapolis, MN 55408-2666
Phone: (612)827-3611
Fax: (612)827-0658
Free: 800-945-8851
Publisher's E-mail: fraternal@sofn.com
Official Sons of Norway magazine reporting on fraternal society's programs and activities. It also features Norwegian and Norwegian-American history and culture. **Founded:** 1904. **Freq:** Monthly. **Print Method:** Web offset. **Trim Size:** 7 1/4 x 9 3/4. **Cols./Page:** 3. **Col. Width:** 2 1/4 inches. **ISSN:** 0038-1462 (print). **Subscription Rates:** $30 Individuals. **URL:** http://www.sofn.com/norwegian_culture/viking_index.jsp. **Ad Rates:** BW $1,894; 4C $2,458. **Remarks:** Accepts advertising. **Circ:** ‡42000.

18591 ■ Western Farm Press
Southwest Farm Press - Agribusiness Div.
7900 International Dr., Ste. 300
Minneapolis, MN 55425-1510
Phone: (952)851-4613
Fax: (952)851-4701
Agricultural newspaper for large-scale farm operators in California and Arizona. **Founded:** 1979. **Freq:** Daily. **Key Personnel:** Dennis Miner, Manager, Sales; Greg Frey, Vice President, Publisher. **URL:** http://westernfarmpress.com/. **Ad Rates:** 4C $2,740. **Remarks:** Accepts advertising. **Circ:** Combined 32100.

18592 ■ Wisconsin Bride
Tiger Oak Publications Inc.
900 S Third St.
Minneapolis, MN 55415-1209
Phone: (612)548-3180
Fax: (612)548-3181
Publisher's E-mail: service@tigeroak.com
Consumer magazine for brides and grooms. **Freq:** Semiannual. **Key Personnel:** Sarah Baumann, Editor. **URL:** http://wibride.com. **Remarks:** Accepts advertising. **Circ:** (Not Reported).

18593 ■ Woodbury Magazine
Tiger Oak Publications Inc.
900 S Third St.
Minneapolis, MN 55415-1209
Phone: (612)548-3180
Fax: (612)548-3181
Publisher's E-mail: service@tigeroak.com
Local magazine of the city of Woodbury. **Freq:** Monthly. **Key Personnel:** Tamara Prato, Publisher. **URL:** http://woodburymag.com. **Remarks:** Advertising accepted; rates available upon request. **Circ:** (Not Reported).

18594 ■ KARE-TV - 11
8811 Olson Memorial Hwy.
Minneapolis, MN 55427
Phone: (763)546-1111
Email: news@kare11.com
Format: Full Service. **Networks:** NBC. **Owner:** Gannett Company Inc., 7950 Jones Branch Dr., McLean, VA 22107-0150, Ph: (703)854-6089. **Founded:** 1954. **ADI:** Minneapolis-St. Paul, MN. **Key Personnel:** Jerry Bodine, Contact, jbodine@kare11.com; Andrea Yoch, Contact, ayoch@kare11.com. **Local Programs:** *Days of Our Lives,* Monday Tuesday Wednesday Thursday Friday 12:00 p.m. **Wattage:** 30,800 ERP. **Ad Rates:** Advertising accepted; rates available upon request. **URL:** http://www.kare11.com.

18595 ■ KBEM-FM - 88.5
1555 James Ave. N
Minneapolis, MN 55411
Phone: (612)668-1735
Fax: (612)668-1766
Email: studio@jazz88fm.com
Format: Jazz. **Networks:** Public Radio International (PRI); AP. **Owner:** Minneapolis Public Schools, 1250 W Broadway Ave., Minneapolis, MN 55411-2533, Ph: (612)668-0000. **Founded:** 1972. **Operating Hours:** Continuous; 5% network, 95% local. **Key Personnel:** Kevin O'Connor, Music Dir.; Michele Jansen, Station Mgr.; Ted Allison, Promotions Dir.; Ed Jones, News Dir. **Wattage:** 2,150. **Ad Rates:** Noncommercial. **URL:** http://www.jazz88.mpls.k12.mn.us.

18596 ■ KCCO-TV - 7
90 S 11th St.
Minneapolis, MN 55403
Phone: (612)339-4444
Fax: (612)330-2767
Free: 800-444-9226
Format: Commercial TV. **Networks:** CBS. **Founded:** 1958. **Formerly:** KCMT-TV. **Operating Hours:** Continuous. **ADI:** Minneapolis-St. Paul, MN. **Wattage:** 316,000. **URL:** http://www.minnesota.cbslocal.com.

KCHK-FM - See New Prague, MN

18597 ■ KDIZ-AM - 1440
2000 SE Elm St.
Minneapolis, MN 55414
Phone: (612)676-8277
Format: Educational. **Networks:** ABC. **Owner:** Radio Disney, 500 S Buena Vista St. MC 7663, Burbank, CA 91521-7716. **Founded:** 1948. **Formerly:** KQRS-AM. **Operating Hours:** Continuous. **ADI:** Minneapolis-St. Paul, MN. **Wattage:** 5,000 Day; 500 Night. **Ad Rates:** $50-75 per unit.

18598 ■ KFAI-FM - 90.3
1808 Riverside Ave.
Minneapolis, MN 55454
Phone: (612)341-3144
Email: board@kfai.org
Format: Sports; Eclectic. **Networks:** Pacifica; CNN Radio; CBS; NBC; ESPN Radio; ABC. **Founded:** 1978. **Operating Hours:** Continuous. **ADI:** Minneapolis-St. Paul, MN. **Key Personnel:** Dale Connelly, News Dir., daleconnelly@kfai.org; Dan Zimmermann, Chief Engineer, engineer@kfai.org. **Wattage:** 900 ERP. **Ad Rates:** Noncommercial. Underwriting available. **URL:** http://www.kfai.org.

18599 ■ KFXN-AM - 690
1600 Utica Ave. S, Ste. 400
Minneapolis, MN 55416
Phone: (952)417-3000
Fax: (952)417-3001
Format: Sports; Talk. **ADI:** Minneapolis-St. Paul, MN. **Wattage:** 500. **Ad Rates:** Noncommercial.

18600 ■ KJZI-FM - 100.3
1600 Utica Ave. S, Ste. 400
Minneapolis, MN 55416
Format: Jazz; News; Sports; Information. **Founded:** Sept. 15, 2006. **Operating Hours:** Continuous. **ADI:** Minneapolis-St. Paul, MN. **Key Personnel:** Erik Christopherson, Gen. Sales Mgr., erikchristopherson@clearchannel.com. **Wattage:** 98,000. **Ad Rates:** Advertising accepted; rates available upon request. **URL:** http://kfan.iheart.com.

18601 ■ KKDQ-FM
PO Box 16683
Minneapolis, MN 55416-0683
Phone: (218)681-4900
Fax: (218)681-6311
Format: Country. **Networks:** Unistar. **Owner:** Olmstead Broadcasting, Inc., at above address. **Founded:** 1990. **Wattage:** 18,000 ERP. **Ad Rates:** $6.50 for 30 seconds; $9.50 for 60 seconds.

18602 ■ KMNB-FM - 102.9
625 2nd Ave. S
Minneapolis, MN 55402
Phone: (651)989-1029
Fax: (612)370-0683

Format: Adult Contemporary. **Owner:** CBS Radio Inc., 1271 Avenue of the Americas, 44th Fl., New York, NY 10020-1401, Ph: (212)649-9600. **Founded:** 1969. **Formerly:** WCCO-FM; WLTE-FM. **Operating Hours:** Continuous. **ADI:** Minneapolis-St. Paul, MN. **Key Personnel:** Chris Kalis, Dir. of Mktg., Promotions Dir., chris.kalis@cbsradio.com; Rob Berrell, Gen. Sales Mgr., rob.berrell@cbsradio.com; John Lassman, Dir. of Programs, john.lassman@cbsradio.com. **Wattage:** 100. **Ad Rates:** $300-550 for 60 seconds. Combined advertising rates available with WCCO-AM, WXPT-FM, KDOW-AM. **URL:** http://buzn1029.cbslocal.com.

18603 ■ KMNV-AM - 1400
1516 E Lake St., Ste. 200
Minneapolis, MN 55407
Phone: (612)729-5900
Format: Hispanic. **Owner:** Davidson Media Group, at above address. **Operating Hours:** Continuous. **ADI:** Minneapolis-St. Paul, MN. **Key Personnel:** Areli Cruz, Contact. **Wattage:** 1,000.

18604 ■ KMOJ-FM - 89.9
2123 W Broadway, Ste. 200,
Minneapolis, MN 55411
Phone: (612)377-0594
Owner: Center for Communications & Development, Not Available. **Founded:** 1973. **ADI:** Minneapolis-St. Paul, MN. **Key Personnel:** Walter Banks, Jr., Operations Mgr., qbear@kmojfm.com. **Wattage:** 6,200 ERP. **Ad Rates:** Advertising accepted; rates available upon request. **URL:** http://www.kmojfm.com.

18605 ■ KNOF-FM - 95.3
910 Elliot Ave.
Minneapolis, MN 55404
Phone: (612)343-4400
Fax: (612)343-4778
Free: 800-289-6222
Format: Contemporary Christian. **Networks:** Independent. **Founded:** 1960. **Operating Hours:** 5:55-10:00 pm Mon.-Sat.; 7:45 a.m.-9:00 a.m. Sunday. **ADI:** Minneapolis-St. Paul, MN. **Wattage:** 6,000. **URL:** http://www.northcentral.edu.

18606 ■ KQRS-FM - 92.5
2000 SE Elm St.
Minneapolis, MN 55414
Phone: (651)989-7625
Fax: (612)676-8292
Format: Classic Rock. **Networks:** ABC. **Founded:** Sept. 07, 2006. **Operating Hours:** Continuous. **ADI:** Minneapolis-St. Paul, MN. **Wattage:** 100,000. **Ad Rates:** Advertising accepted; rates available upon request. **URL:** http://www.92kqrs.com.

18607 ■ KTCZ-FM - 97.1
1600 Utica Ave. S, Ste. 500
1600 Utica Ave. S, Ste. 400
Minneapolis, MN 55416
Phone: (952)417-3000
Format: Adult Album Alternative. **Networks:** Independent. **Owner:** Clear Channel Radio, 200 E Basse Rd., San Antonio, TX 78209, Ph: (210)822-2828, Fax: (210)832-3428. **Operating Hours:** Continuous; (100% local). **ADI:** Minneapolis-St. Paul, MN. **Key Personnel:** Mike Crusham, Gen. Mgr. **Wattage:** 100,000. **Ad Rates:** Advertising accepted; rates available upon request. **URL:** http://www.cities97.com.

18608 ■ KTRF-AM
PO Box 16683
Minneapolis, MN 55416-0683
Phone: (218)681-1230
Fax: (218)681-3717
Format: Full Service. **Networks:** CBS; Minnesota News. **Owner:** Tom Ingstad Broadcasting Group., PO Box 1248, Hanover, MN 55341, Ph: (952)938-0575, Fax: (952)938-2297. **Founded:** 1947. **Key Personnel:** Todd McDonald, News Dir. **Wattage:** 1,000. **Ad Rates:** $10 for 30 seconds; $16 for 60 seconds.

18609 ■ KTTB-FM - 96.3
420 N 5th St., Ste. 150
Minneapolis, MN 55401
Phone: (612)659-4848
Format: Hip Hop; Folk; Classic Rock. **Key Personnel:** Steve Woodbury, Gen. Mgr., President; John McMonagle, Gen. Sales Mgr.; Sam Elliot, Dir. of Programs; Terry Henne, Bus. Mgr.; Shannan Paul, Promotions Dir.; Jon Bailey, Dir. of Production. **Wattage:** 19,000 ERP. **Ad Rates:** Advertising accepted; rates available upon request. **URL:** http://go963mn.com.

18610 ■ K25IA - 25
PO Box A
Santa Ana, CA 92711
Phone: (714)832-2950
Free: 888-731-1000
Owner: Trinity Broadcasting Network Inc., PO Box A, Santa Ana, CA 92711, Ph: (714)832-2950, Free: 888-731-1000. **URL:** http://www.tbn.org.

18611 ■ KUOM-AM - 770
610 Rarig Ctr.
330 21st Ave., S
Minneapolis, MN 55455-0415
Phone: (612)625-3500
Fax: (612)625-2112
Email: request@radiok.org
Format: Eclectic. **Simulcasts:** KUOM-FM. **Networks:** AP. **Founded:** 1922. **Operating Hours:** Sunrise-sunset. 100% local. **Key Personnel:** Caleigh Souhan, Prog. Dir.; Sara Miller, Div. Dir., stationmanager@radiok.org. **Wattage:** 5,000. **Ad Rates:** Noncommercial. **URL:** http://www.radiok.org.

18612 ■ KUOM-FM - 106.5
610 Rarig Ctr.
330 21st Ave. S
Minneapolis, MN 55455
Phone: (612)625-3500
Fax: (612)625-2112
Format: Eclectic. **Owner:** University of Minnesota, 3 Morrill Hall 100 Church St. SE, Minneapolis, MN 55455, Ph: (612)625-5000. **Operating Hours:** Continuous. **Key Personnel:** Ron Miller, News Dir.; Jake Knight, Dir. of Traffic. **Ad Rates:** Noncommercial; underwriting available. **URL:** http://www.radiok.org.

18613 ■ KXXR-FM - 93.7
2000 SE Elm St.
Minneapolis, MN 55414
Phone: (612)617-4000
Format: Album-Oriented Rock (AOR). **Networks:** ABC. **Owner:** Citadel Broadcasting Corp., 7201 W Lake Mead Blvd., Ste. 400, Las Vegas, NV 89128-8366, Ph: (702)804-5200, Fax: (702)804-8250. **Founded:** 1968. **Formerly:** KEGE-FM; KRXX-AM. **Operating Hours:** Continuous. **Key Personnel:** Shelly Malecha Wilkes, VP, Dept. Mgr., shelly.wilkes@citcomm.com. **Local Programs:** *Morning Show*. **Wattage:** 100,000. **Ad Rates:** Advertising accepted; rates available upon request. **URL:** http://www.93x.com.

18614 ■ KZJK-FM - 104.1
625 2nd Ave. S
Minneapolis, MN 55402
Phone: (612)370-0611
Format: Classic Rock; Easy Listening; Ethnic. **Operating Hours:** Continuous. **Key Personnel:** Chris Kalis, Promotions Dir., chris.kalis@cbsradio.com. **Ad Rates:** Advertising accepted; rates available upon request. **URL:** http://www.1041jackfm.cbslocal.com.

18615 ■ 105 The Vibe - 105.1
2000 SE Elm St.
Minneapolis, MN 55414
Phone: (612)617-4000
Fax: (612)676-8292
Format: Classical; Oldies. **Owner:** Citadel Broadcasting Corp., 7201 W Lake Mead Blvd., Ste. 400, Las Vegas, NV 89128-8366, Ph: (702)804-5200, Fax: (702)804-8250. **Operating Hours:** 5:00 a.m. - 11:00 p.m. Monday - Friday; 11:00 a.m. - 11:00 p.m. Saturday - Sunday. **Wattage:** 2,600 ERP. **Ad Rates:** Advertising accepted; rates available upon request. **URL:** http://www.105thevibe.com.

18616 ■ WCCO-AM - 830
625 2nd Ave. S
Minneapolis, MN 55402
Phone: (612)370-0611
Format: News; Talk. **Networks:** CBS. **Owner:** CBS Radio Stations Inc., 1515 Broadway, New York, NY 10036, Ph: (212)846-3939. **Founded:** 1924. **Operating Hours:** Continuous-Mon.-Fri. & Sat.; 5.30am-11pm -Sun. **Key Personnel:** Wendy Paulson, Dir. of Programs. **Wattage:** 50,000. **Ad Rates:** Noncommercial. **URL:** http://www.minnesota.cbslocal.com.

18617 ■ WCCO-TV - 4
90 S 11th St.
Minneapolis, MN 55403
Phone: (612)339-4444
Fax: (612)330-2767
Free: 800-444-9226
Email: newstips@wccoradio.com
Format: Commercial TV. **Networks:** CBS. **Owner:** CBS Corp., 51 W 52nd St., New York, NY 10019-6188, Ph: (212)975-4321, Fax: (212)975-4516, Free: 877-227-0787. **Founded:** 1949. **Operating Hours:** Continuous. **ADI:** Minneapolis-St. Paul, MN. **Key Personnel:** Scott Libin, News Dir. **Ad Rates:** Advertising accepted; rates available upon request. **URL:** http://www.minnesota.cbslocal.com.

18618 ■ WDGY-AM - 630
2619 E Lake St.
Minneapolis, MN 55406
Phone: (612)729-3776
Format: Oldies; Sports; Talk. **Networks:** Mutual Broadcasting System. **Owner:** iHeartMedia Inc., 200 E Basse Rd., San Antonio, TX 78209, Ph: (210)832-3314. **Founded:** 1949. **Operating Hours:** Continuous. **ADI:** Minneapolis-St. Paul, MN. **Key Personnel:** Guadalupe Gonzalez, President, radiorey630am@yahoo.com; Mike Castillo, Gen. Mgr., manuel@radiorey630am.com; Felicia Ortega, Acct. Mgr., felicia@radiorey630am.com. **Wattage:** 2,500. **Ad Rates:** Noncommercial. **URL:** http://www.radiorey630am.com.

18619 ■ WFTC-TV - 29
1701 Broadway St. NE
Minneapolis, MN 55413
Phone: (612)379-2929
Fax: (612)379-2900
Email: feedback@fox29.com
Format: Commercial TV. **Networks:** Fox. **Founded:** 1982. **Formerly:** KITN-TV. **Operating Hours:** Continuous. **Key Personnel:** Dave Huddleston, Contact, davehuddleston@fox29.com. **Ad Rates:** Advertising accepted; rates available upon request. **URL:** http://www.fox9.com.

18620 ■ WGVX-FM - 105.1
2000 SE Elm St.
Minneapolis, MN 55414
Phone: (612)617-4000
Email: info@105theticket.com
Format: Adult Contemporary. **Owner:** Citadel Broadcasting Corp., 7201 W Lake Mead Blvd., Ste. 400, Las Vegas, NV 89128-8366, Ph: (702)804-5200, Fax: (702)804-8250. **Operating Hours:** Continuous. **Key Personnel:** Dan McKeague, Sales Mgr. **Ad Rates:** Advertising accepted; rates available upon request. **URL:** http://www.105theticket.com.

18621 ■ WGVZ-FM - 105.7
2000 SE Elm St.
Minneapolis, MN 55414
Phone: (612)617-4000
Email: info@105TheTicket.com
Format: Adult Album Alternative. **Owner:** Citadel Broadcasting Corp., 7201 W Lake Mead Blvd., Ste. 400, Las Vegas, NV 89128-8366, Ph: (702)804-5200, Fax: (702)804-8250. **Operating Hours:** Continuous. **Ad Rates:** Advertising accepted; rates available upon request. **URL:** http://www.105theticket.com.

18622 ■ WUMN-TV - 17
250 Marquette Ave., Ste. 540
Minneapolis, MN 55401
Email: univisionmn@wumn13.com
Format: News; Sports. **Simulcasts:** WIPR. **Networks:** Univision. **Owner:** Equity Broadcasting Co., at above address. **ADI:** Minneapolis-St. Paul, MN. **Wattage:** 15,000 ERP. **Ad Rates:** Advertising accepted; rates available upon request. **URL:** http://www.prnewswire.com.

18623 ■ WXPT-FM - 104.1
625 2nd Ave. S
Minneapolis, MN 55402
Phone: (612)370-0611
Email: kmjz@usinternet.com
Format: Album-Oriented Rock (AOR). **Networks:** ABC. **Founded:** 1962. **Formerly:** KJJO-FM. **Key Personnel:** John Gehron, VP; Rolf Pepple, Gen. Mgr.; Dusty Hayes, Sales Mgr.; Dave Bestler, Gen. Sales Mgr. **Wattage:**

Circulation: ★ = AAM; △ or • = BPA; ♦ = CAC; ❑ = VAC; ⊕ = PO Statement; ‡ = Publisher's Report; Boldface figures = sworn; Light figures = estimated.

100,000 ERP. **Ad Rates:** Combined advertising rates available with KSGS-AM. **URL:** http://1041jackfm.cbslocal.com.

MINNEOTA

SW MN. Lyon Co. 15 mi NW of Marshall.

18624 ■ Minneota Mascot
Minneota Mascot
210 N Jefferson
Minneota, MN 56264
Phone: (507)872-6492
Fax: (507)872-6840
Publisher's E-mail: editor@minneotamascot.com
Community newspaper. **Freq:** Weekly (Wed.). **Cols./Page:** 6. **Col. Width:** 2 inches. **Col. Depth:** 21 inches. **Key Personnel:** Byron Higgin, Publisher, phone: (507)872-6492. **URL:** http://www.minneotamascot.com. **Mailing address:** PO Box 9, Minneota, MN 56264. **Circ:** 1,400.

MINNESOTA LAKE

SC MN. Faribault Co. 28 mi. SE of Mankato. Stock, poultry, grain farms. Corn, oats, soybeans.

18625 ■ Minnesota Lake Tribune
Tribune
PO Box 278
Minnesota Lake, MN 56068
Phone: (507)462-3321
Fax: (507)462-3321
Publication E-mail: mltrib@bevcomm.net
Community newspaper. **Freq:** Weekly (Wed.). **Print Method:** Offset. **Trim Size:** 11 1/2 x 16. **Cols./Page:** 5. **Col. Width:** 11 picas. **Col. Depth:** 15 inches. **Ad Rates:** GLR $.10. **Remarks:** Accepts advertising. **Circ:** ‡646.

MINNETONKA

SE MN. Hennepin Co. 5 mi. W. of Minneapolis. Residential.

18626 ■ Handy: Handyman Club of America Magazine
North American Media Group Inc.
12301 Whitewater Dr.
Minnetonka, MN 55343
Do-it-yourself home improvement magazine. **Freq:** Bimonthly. **Print Method:** Offset. **Trim Size:** 7 3/4 x 10 1/2. **Cols./Page:** 3. **Col. Width:** 2 1/4 inches. **Col. Depth:** 10 inches. **Key Personnel:** Newell Thompson, Publisher, phone: (212)502-0580, fax: (212)502-0584; Chris Dolan, Publisher. **ISSN:** 1071--3980 (print). **Subscription Rates:** $18 Individuals; $36 Two years; $49 Canada; $97 Canada two years. **Formerly:** American How-To; Handyman How-To. **Ad Rates:** BW $39,345; 4C $57,435. **Remarks:** Advertising accepted; rates available upon request. **Circ:** Combined ★**730185**.

18627 ■ North American Fisherman
North American Fishing Club
12301 Whitewater Dr.
Minnetonka, MN 55343
Free: 800-843-6232
Publisher's E-mail: memberservices@fishingclub.com
Freq: Bimonthly. **Subscription Rates:** Included in membership. **URL:** http://archive.fishing.scout.com/magazine/current-issue.aspx. **Remarks:** Accepts advertising. **Circ:** 425000.

KMGM-FM - See Montevideo, MN

MONTEVIDEO

SW MN. Chippewa Co. On Minnesota River, 133 mi. W. of Minneapolis. Manufactures electronic components, mobile homes, stock feed. Creameries. Stock, dairy, poultry, grain, hog & cattle farms.

18628 ■ Montevideo American-News
Montevideo Publishing Co.
PO BOX 99
Montevideo, MN 56265
Phone: (320)269-2156
Fax: (320)269-2159
Community newspaper. **Freq:** Weekly (Thurs.). **Print Method:** Web. **Cols./Page:** 6. **Col. Width:** 26 nonpareils. **Col. Depth:** 301 agate lines. **Key Personnel:** Dave Smiglewski, Publisher. **USPS:** 360-880. **Subscription Rates:** $47 Individuals; $56 Out of area; $62 Elsewhere; $37 Students. **URL:** http://www.montenews.com. **Ad Rates:** GLR $0.44; BW $806.25; 4C $981.25; SAU $6.25; PCI $6.25. **Remarks:** Accepts advertising. **Circ:** (Not Reported).

18629 ■ KBPG-FM - 89.5
PO Box 2440
Tupelo, MS 38803
Phone: (662)844-8888
Format: Religious. **Owner:** American Family Radio, at above address. **Founded:** Feb. 1991. **Key Personnel:** Rick Robertson, Contact; Rick Robertson, Contact. **Wattage**: 500. **Ad Rates:** Noncommercial. **URL:** http://www.afr.net.

18630 ■ KDMA-AM - 1460
PO Box 513
Montevideo, MN 56265
Phone: (320)269-8815
Fax: (320)269-8449
Email: kdma@info-link.net
Format: Country; Information; Full Service; Talk. **Networks:** ABC. **Owner:** KDMA-AM, Ph: (320)269-8815. **Founded:** 1951. **Key Personnel:** Dwight Mulder, Dir. of Programs. **Wattage:** 1,000 KW. **Ad Rates:** $12.50 for 30 seconds; $18.75 for 60 seconds. Combined advertising rates available with KMGM, KKRC. **URL:** http://www.kdmakmgmkkrc.com/.

18631 ■ KKRC-FM - 93.9
4454 Hwy. 212
Montevideo, MN 56265
Phone: (320)269-8815
Format: Oldies. **Operating Hours**: Continuous. **Wattage**: 6,000 ERP. **Ad Rates:** Advertising accepted; rates available upon request. **URL:** http://www.kdmanews.com.

18632 ■ KKRM-FM - 96.7
109 N 1st St.
Montevideo, MN 56265
Phone: (320)269-3696
Format: Adult Album Alternative. **Key Personnel:** Jacob Niemand, Contact. **Wattage**: 100. **Mailing address:** PO Box 332, Montevideo, MN 56265. **URL:** http://www.kram967.com.

18633 ■ KMGM-FM - 105.5
5038 Holiday Rd.
Minnetonka, MN 55345
Phone: (612)269-8815
Fax: (612)269-8449
Format: Eclectic. **Networks:** ABC. **Owner:** Iowa City Broadcasting Co., Not Available. **Founded:** 1982. **Operating Hours**: Continuous. **Wattage**: 3,000. **Ad Rates:** $10.25 for 30 seconds; $15.40 for 60 seconds.

MONTICELLO

SEC MN. Wright Co. On Mississippi River, 35 mi. NW of Minneapolis. Manufactures heaters, ballpoints, screwdrivers. Egg producing plant. Dairy, beef, grain & potato farms.

18634 ■ Monticello Shopper
Monticello Times Inc.
540 Walnunt St.
Monticello, MN 55362
Phone: (763)295-3131
Publisher's E-mail: monticellonews@acnpapers.com
Shopper. **Freq:** Weekly (Sun.). **Print Method:** Offset. **Cols./Page:** 6. **Col. Width:** 12.6 picas. **Col. Depth:** 301 nonpareils. **Key Personnel:** Jim Dickrell, Editor. **Subscription Rates:** $39 Individuals; $45 Out of area; $54 Out of state; $38 Individuals Senior Citizens; $74 Two years; $48 Individuals snowbirds. **URL:** http://www.monticellotimes.com. **Formerly:** Monticello Big Lake Shopper. **Mailing address:** PO Box 420, Monticello, MN 55362. **Ad Rates:** 4C $320; SAU $8.70; PCI $9.20. **Remarks:** Accepts advertising. **Circ:** (Not Reported).

18635 ■ Times
Monticello Times Inc.
540 Walnut St.
Monticello, MN 55362
Phone: (763)295-3131
Publisher's E-mail: monticellonews@acnpapers.com
Community newspaper. **Founded:** May 1857. **Freq:** Weekly (Thurs.). **Print Method:** Offset. **Cols./Page:** 6. **Col. Width:** 12.6 picas. **Col. Depth:** 21.5 inches. **USPS:** 361-660. **Subscription Rates:** $39 Individuals Wright & Sherburne counties; $45 Out of area Minnesota residents; $54 Out of state; $38 Individuals senior citizens (Wright & Sherburne counties); $74 Two years. **URL:** http://www.monticellotimes.com/. **Mailing address:** PO Box 420, Monticello, MN 55362. **Ad Rates:** PCI $7.40. **Remarks:** Accepts advertising. **Circ:** ‡3450.

MOORHEAD

WC MN. Clay Co. On REd River, adjacent to Fargo, ND. Concordia College; Moorhead State University. Trade center. Butter, sugar,cheese, boat factories; bottling, sheet metal works; elevator. Ships potatoes, grain. Agriculture. Grain, potatoes, sugar beets.

18636 ■ The Concordian: The student-run newspaper of Concordia College, Moorhead, Minnesota
Concordia College
901 8th St. S
Moorhead, MN 56562
Phone: (218)299-4000
Publisher's E-mail: info@cord.edu
Collegiate newspaper (tabloid). **Freq:** Weekly (Fri.) except during holidays & exam weeks. **Print Method:** Offset. **Trim Size:** 11 x 17. **Cols./Page:** 5. **Col. Width:** 1 7/8 inches. **Col. Depth:** 16 inches. **Key Personnel:** William Craft, Publisher. **Subscription Rates:** $25 Individuals; Free Students. **URL:** http://theconcordian.org. **Ad Rates:** BW $720. **Remarks:** Advertising accepted; rates available upon request. **Circ:** ‡1200.

18637 ■ Moorhead State University Advocate
Moorhead State University
1104 7th Ave. S
Moorhead, MN 56563
Free: 800-593-7246
Publisher's E-mail: webteam@mnstate.edu
Collegiate newspaper (tabloid). **Freq:** Weekly (Thurs.) during college sessions. **Print Method:** Offset. **Cols./Page:** 5. **Col. Width:** 24 nonpareils. **Col. Depth:** 196 agate lines. **Key Personnel:** Josie Gereszek, Editor-in-Chief. **URL:** http://msumadvocate.com. **Ad Rates:** PCI $5.50; BW $440. **Remarks:** Accepts advertising. **Circ:** Free ‡6000.

18638 ■ KCMF-FM - 89.7
3333 Hwy. 10 E
Moorhead, MN 56560
Phone: (218)299-3666
Fax: (218)287-5664
Format: Classical. **Owner:** Minnesota Public Radio Inc., 480 Cedar St., Saint Paul, MN 55101, Ph: (651)290-1500, Free: 800-228-7123. **Founded:** 2003. **Operating Hours**: Continuous. **Key Personnel:** Connie Peterson, Account Exec., Coord., cdpeterson@mpr.org; Dan Gunderson, Bur. Chief, dgunderson@mpr.org. **Wattage**: 2,100. **Ad Rates:** Noncommercial; underwriting available. **URL:** http://minnesota.publicradio.org.

18639 ■ KMSC-AM - 1500
Owens Hall
Moorhead, MN 56563
Phone: (218)477-2116
Email: kmsc1500am@yahoo.com
Format: News; Eclectic. **Owner:** Minnesota State University Moorhead, 1104 7th Ave. S, Moorhead, MN 56563, Ph: (218)477-2134, Fax: (218)477-2482. **Operating Hours**: Continuous. **Key Personnel:** Dustin Johnson, Dir. of Programs, johnsondu@mnstate.edu; Andrew Johnson, Advisor, drewman21@hotmail.com; Ross Peterson, Station Mgr., petersonro@mnstate.edu. **Ad Rates:** Advertising accepted; rates available upon request. **URL:** http://www.dragonradio.org.

18640 ■ KNTN-FM - 102.7
Concordia College
901 S 8th St.
Moorhead, MN 56562
Phone: (218)299-3666
Format: News. **Owner:** Minnesota Public Radio Inc., 480 Cedar St., Saint Paul, MN 55101, Ph: (651)290-1500, Free: 800-228-7123. **Founded:** 1991. **Operating Hours**: Continuous. **Key Personnel:** Nick Kereakos, Chief Tech. Ofc., VP of Technology Dev. **Wattage**: 100,000. **Ad Rates:** Noncommercial. **URL:** http://www.minnesota.publicradio.org.

18641 ■ KQMN-FM - 91.5
901 S 8th St.
Moorhead, MN 56562
Phone: (218)299-3666
Fax: (218)287-5664

Format: Classical. **Owner:** Minnesota Public Radio Inc., 480 Cedar St., Saint Paul, MN 55101, Ph: (651)290-1500, Free: 800-228-7123. **Founded:** 1990. **Operating Hours:** Continuous. **Key Personnel:** Jeff Jones, Producer; Michael Olson, Corr.; Mike Edgerly, Editor; Jeff Smith, Sr. VP; Derrick Stevens, Sr. VP; Jennifer Allen, Sr. VP, Gen. Counsel; Tim Roesler, Div. Dir.; Nick Kereakos, CEO. **Wattage:** 84,000. **Ad Rates:** Noncommercial. **URL:** http://minnesota.publicradio.org.

MOOSE LAKE

EC MN. Carlton Co. 43 mi. SW of Duluth. Resort. Butter, tile, fishing tackle, pottery, timber products manufactured. Dairy, poultry farms.

18642 ■ Moose Lake Star Gazette
Star-Gazette
308 Elm Ave.
Moose Lake, MN 55767
Phone: (218)485-4406
Fax: (218)485-0237
Free: 800-247-0882
Publisher's E-mail: evergreen@mlstargazette.com
Community newspaper. **Founded:** 1895. **Freq:** Weekly (Thurs.). **Print Method:** Offset. **Cols./Page:** 7. **Col. Width:** 28 nonpareils. **Col. Depth:** 301 agate lines. **Key Personnel:** Colette Stadin, Editor. **ISSN:** 0746-2980 (print). **Subscription Rates:** $28 Individuals; $32 Out of area senior. **URL:** http://www.mlstargazette.com. **Formerly:** Star-Gazette. **Ad Rates:** GLR $5.50; BW $285; SAU $4; PCI $5.50. **Remarks:** Accepts advertising. **Circ:** (Not Reported).

MORA

EC MN. Kanabec Co. 60 mi. N. of Minneapolis. Manufactures plastic products, precious metals fabrication, fiberglass pleasure cruisers, steel fabricating, poultry feeds, milk drying equipment. Stock, dairy, poultry farms. Small grains.

18643 ■ Kanabec County Times
Kanabec County Times
107 Park St. S
Mora, MN 55051
Phone: (320)679-2661
Publication E-mail: editor@moraminn.com
Community newspaper. **Freq:** Weekly (Thurs.). **Print Method:** Offset. **Cols./Page:** 5. **Col. Width:** 23 nonpareils. **Col. Depth:** 210 agate lines. **Key Personnel:** Annette Krist, Publisher, phone: (320)225-5124. **Subscription Rates:** $37 Individuals in Kanabec Country; $46 Out of area; $69 Two years in Kanabec County; $87 Out of area two years. **URL:** http://www.presspubs.com/kanabec/. **Remarks:** Advertising accepted; rates available upon request. **Circ:** Paid ‡3000, Free ‡11000.

18644 ■ KBEK-FM - 95.5
PO Box 136
Mora, MN 55051
Format: Oldies; News; Sports. **Wattage:** 25,000. **Ad Rates:** Advertising accepted; rates available upon request. **URL:** http://www.kbek.com/.

MORRIS

WC MN. Stevens Co. 80 mi. directly W. of Saint Cloud. University of Minnesota USDA Agricultural Research Regional Center. Manufactures butter, ice-cream. Agriculture. Livestock, corn, soybeans, small grains.

18645 ■ Morris Sun-Tribune
Morris Sun-Tribune
607 Pacific Ave.
Morris, MN 56267
Phone: (320)589-2525
Community newspaper. **Founded:** 1877. **Freq:** Semiweekly (Tuesday & Thursday). **Print Method:** Offset. **Cols./Page:** 6. **Col. Width:** 2.0625 inches. **Col. Depth:** 21.5 inches. **Key Personnel:** Sue Dieter, Publisher. **USPS:** 363-660. **Subscription Rates:** $46 Individuals local; $52 Out of area; $79 Two years local; $91 Out of area two years. **URL:** http://www.morrissuntribune.com. **Mailing address:** PO Box 470, Morris, MN 56267. **Ad Rates:** BW $664.35; 4C $904.35; SAU $5; PCI $5. **Remarks:** Accepts advertising. **Circ:** ‡3,840.

18646 ■ KKOK-FM - 95.7
PO Box 533
Morris, MN 56267
Phone: (320)589-3131
Fax: (320)589-2715
Format: Country. **Founded:** 1976. **Key Personnel:** Deborah Mattheis, Gen. Mgr.; Milissa Bjorge, Office Mgr., kmrskkok@fedtel.net. **Ad Rates:** Noncommercial. **URL:** http://www.kmrskkok.com.

18647 ■ KMRS-AM - 1230
PO Box 533
Morris, MN 56267
Phone: (320)589-3131
Fax: (320)589-2715
Format: News; Sports. **Networks:** ABC; Minnesota News. **Owner:** Ingstad Broadcasting, 317 N Minnesota St., New Ulm, MN 56073, Ph: (507)359-2921, Fax: (507)359-4520. **Founded:** 1956. **Operating Hours:** 18.5 hours Daily. **Key Personnel:** Deborah Driggins-Mattheis, Gen. Mgr.; Milissa Bjorge, Contact. **Wattage:** 1,000. **URL:** http://www.kmrskkok.com.

18648 ■ KUMM-FM - 89.7
600 E Fourth St.
Morris, MN 56267
Phone: (320)589-6355
Email: infoctr@morris.umn.edu
Format: Public Radio. **Owner:** University of Minnesota-Morris, 600 E 4th St., Morris, MN 56267, Ph: (320)589-6035, Free: 888-866-3382. **Founded:** 1972. **Operating Hours:** 7:00 a.m. - 2:00 a.m. **Wattage:** 700 ERP. **Ad Rates:** WCAL, KQAL, KMSU, KUSC, KSRQ, KAXE, KUMD, KUOM, KBEM, KFAI. **URL:** http://www.kumm.org.

MOUNTAIN LAKE

WC MN. Cottonwood Co. 50 mi. W. of Mankato. Farm & stock feeding equipment, hydraulic cylinders & pumps, dairy products manufactured. Stock, grain, poultry farms. Corn, oats, soybeans, flax.

18649 ■ Mountain Lake/Butterfield Observer/Advocate
Citizen Publishing Co.
237 11th St. N
Mountain Lake, MN 56159
Phone: (507)427-2725
Fax: (507)427-2724
Publisher's E-mail: citizen@windomnews.com
Community newspaper. **Freq:** Weekly (Wed.). **Print Method:** Offset. **Cols./Page:** 6. **Col. Width:** 28 nonpareils. **Col. Depth:** 301 agate lines. **Key Personnel:** Rahn Larson, Editor. **Subscription Rates:** $37 Students 9 month; print and online; $30 Individuals 1 year; online only; $52 Individuals 1 year; in-area; print and online; $42 Individuals 1 year; in-area; print only; $62 Out of area 1 year; print and online; $52 Out of area 1 year; print only. **URL:** http://www.mtlakenews.com. **Remarks:** Advertising accepted; rates available upon request. **Circ:** Free ‡1000.

NETT LAKE

18650 ■ Bois Forte Band of Chippewa
5344 Lakeshore Dr.
Nett Lake, MN 55772
Phone: (218)757-3261
Fax: (218)757-3312
Free: 800-221-8129
Email: office@boisforte-nsn.gov
Format: News; Sports. **Networks:** National Public Radio (NPR); ABC. **Founded:** 1866. **URL:** http://www.boisforte.com.

NEVIS

NC MN. Hubbard Co. 13 mi. NE of Park Rapids.

18651 ■ Northwoods Press
Northwoods Press
PO Box 28
Nevis, MN 56467-0028
Publication E-mail: nwpnews2@arvig.net
Community newspaper. **Freq:** Weekly (Thurs.). **Print Method:** Offset. **Cols./Page:** 6. **Col. Width:** 1 5/8 inches. **Col. Depth:** 16 inches. **USPS:** 580-180. **Subscription Rates:** $38 Individuals in Hubbard County; $44 Out of area; $48 Individuals print and online; $54 Out of area print and online; $36 Individuals online. **URL:** http://www.lakeandpine.com/46789/2205/subscribe-to-northwoods-press. **Formerly:** Hubbard County Independent. **Ad Rates:** BW $393.60; 4C $493.60; SAU $6; PCI $4. **Remarks:** Accepts advertising. **Circ:** 1590.

NEW PRAGUE

SC MN. Scott Co. 40 mi. SW of Minneapolis. Medical Center. Manufactures flour, butter, space and cryogenic equipment, printed paper products. Diversified farming. Dairy products, livestock, grain.

18652 ■ New Prague Times
New Prague Times
200 E Main St.
New Prague, MN 56071
Phone: (952)758-4435
Fax: (952)758-4135
Community newspaper. **Freq:** Weekly (Thurs.). **Cols./Page:** 6. **Col. Width:** 13 picas. **Col. Depth:** 21.5 picas. **Key Personnel:** Lois Suel Wann, Chairman, Editor; Charles Wann, President, Publisher; Chuck Kajer, Managing Editor. **Subscription Rates:** $42 Individuals LeSueur, Rice & Scott Counties; $51 Individuals Minnesota & snowbirds; $60 Individuals Outside Minnesota. **URL:** http://www.newpraguetimes.com; http://www.newpraguetimes.com/category/publication/new-prague-times. **Mailing address:** PO Box 25, New Prague, MN 56071. **Remarks:** Accepts advertising. **Circ:** 4,505.

18653 ■ KCHK-AM - 1350
PO Box 251
New Prague, MN 56071
Phone: (952)758-2571
Fax: (952)758-3170
Free: 888-758-2575
Format: Oldies; Full Service. **Networks:** ABC. **Owner:** Ingstad Brothers Broadcasting, LLC, at above address. **Founded:** 1969. **Formerly:** KTMF-AM. **Wattage:** 500 KW. **Ad Rates:** Advertising accepted; rates available upon request. $14 for 30 seconds; $15 for 60 seconds. **URL:** http://kchkradio.net/.

18654 ■ KCHK-FM - 95.5
207 Textile Bldg.
119 N 4th St.
Minneapolis, MN 55401
Format: Full Service. **Owner:** Ingstad Brothers Broadcasting, LLC, at above address. **Founded:** 1983. **Ad Rates:** Advertising accepted; rates available upon request. $28-50 for 60 seconds.

18655 ■ KCHK-FM - 95.5
25821 Langford Ave.
New Prague, MN 56071
Phone: (952)758-2571
Format: Oldies. **Networks:** ABC. **Founded:** 1989. **Operating Hours:** Continuous; 90% network, 10% local. **Key Personnel:** Dave Ernewein, Dir. of Programs; Ned Newberg, Gen. Mgr. **Wattage:** 3,000. **Ad Rates:** $14 for 30 seconds; $15 for 60 seconds. **Mailing address:** PO Box 251, New Prague, MN 56071. **URL:** http://www.kchkradio.net.

NEW ULM

SC MN. Brown Co. 75 mi. S. of Minneapolis. Dr. Martin Luther College. Manufactures cheese, dairy products, beer,- asbestos, plastic, micro film. Greenhouses. Diversified farming. Wheat, corn, barley, soybeans.

18656 ■ Prairie Catholic
Roman Catholic Diocese of New Ulm
1400 Sixth St. N
New Ulm, MN 56073
Phone: (507)359-2966
Publication E-mail: dnu@dnu.org
Official newspaper of the Diocese of New Ulm. **Freq:** Monthly. **Key Personnel:** Dan Rossini, Editor-in-Chief; Christine Clancy, Editor. **Remarks:** Advertising not accepted. **Circ:** Combined ⊕**26255**.

18657 ■ KNUJ-AM - 860
317 N Minnesota
New Ulm, MN 56073
Phone: (507)359-2921
Fax: (507)359-4520
Email: knuj@knuj.net
Format: Full Service; Country. **Networks:** NBC; Minnesota News. **Owner:** Ingstad Brothers Broadcasting,

Circulation: ⋆ = AAM; △ or • = BPA; ♦ = CAC; ❑ = VAC; ⊕ = PO Statement; ‡ = Publisher's Report; Boldface figures = sworn; Light figures = estimated.

LLC, at above address. **Founded:** 1949. **Operating Hours**: Continuous; 30% network, 70% local. **Key Personnel:** Denise Fischer, Contact, denise@knuj.net; Jim Bartels, Gen. Mgr. **Wattage**: 1,000. **Ad Rates:** $19-65 for 30 seconds; $24-75 for 60 seconds. **Mailing address:** PO Box 368, New Ulm, MN 56073. **URL:** http://www.knuj.net.

18658 ■ KNUJ-FM - 107.3
PO Box 368
New Ulm, MN 56073
Phone: (507)359-2921
Fax: (507)359-4520
Email: knuj@knuj.net
Format: Adult Contemporary. **Simulcasts:** KNUJ-AM 860. **Networks:** CBS; CNN Radio; NBC. **Founded:** 1949. **Wattage**: 4,000. **Ad Rates:** Advertising accepted; rates available upon request. **URL:** http://www.knuj.net.

NISSWA

18659 ■ The Boathouse
Bob Speltz Land-O-Lakes Chapter of the Antique and Classic Boat Society
c/o Lee Wangstad, Editor
1694 S., Agate Shore Dr. SW
Nisswa, MN 56468
Phone: (218)963-7782
Magazine containing articles and information on boat history, boat restoration, and Bob Speltz Land O' Lakes Chapter of the Antique and Classic Boat Society events. **Freq:** Quarterly in July, April, July, and October. **Key Personnel:** Lee Wangstad, Editor. **URL:** http://acbs-bslol.com/chapter-information/the-boathouse-quarterly-magazine. **Remarks:** Accepts advertising. **Circ:** (Not Reported).

18660 ■ Lakes Area Advertiser
Lakes Area Advertiser Inc.
P.O Box 136
Nisswa, MN 56468
Phone: (218)961-3111
Publication E-mail: laads@nisswa.net
Weekly Shopping Guide. **Freq:** Weekly (Wed.). **Subscription Rates:** Free. **URL:** http://www.lakesareaadvertiser.com. **Remarks:** Accepts classified advertising. **Circ:** Free ■ **229000**, Paid ■ **74**.

NORTH BRANCH

EC MN. Chisago Co. 45 mi. N. of Saint Paul.

18661 ■ ECM Post-Review
ECM Publishers Inc.-North Branch
6448 Main St., Ste. 13
North Branch, MN 55056
Phone: (651)674-7025
Publisher's E-mail: editor.postreview@ecm-inc.com
Community newspaper. **Freq:** Weekly (Wed.). **Print Method:** Offset. **Trim Size:** 11 3/8 x 16. **Cols./Page:** 6. **Col. Width:** 20 nonpareils. **Col. Depth:** 210 agate lines. **Key Personnel:** Mary Helen Swanson, Editor; Jeff Andres, General Manager, phone: (651)464-4601. **Subscription Rates:** $45 Individuals; $47 Out of area. **URL:** http://ecmpostreview.com. **Ad Rates:** BW $1184.40; PCI $9.40. **Remarks:** Accepts advertising. **Circ:** Paid ‡1765.

NORTH MANKATO

SC MN. Nicollet Co. 5 mi. N. of Skyline.

18662 ■ KQYK-FM - 95.7
1807 Lee Blvd.
North Mankato, MN 56003
Phone: (507)344-0957
Format: Album-Oriented Rock (AOR).

18663 ■ KRBI-FM - 105.5
1807 Lee Blvd.
North Mankato, MN 56003
Phone: (507)345-4646
Fax: (507)345-3299
Format: Classic Rock. **Networks:** ABC. **Owner:** Three Eagles Communications, 3800 Cornhusker Hwy., Lincoln, NE 68504, Ph: (402)466-1234, Fax: (402)467-4095. **Founded:** 1957. **Operating Hours**: Continuous. **ADI**: Minneapolis-St. Paul, MN. **Wattage**: 25,000. **Ad Rates:** $14-20 for 30 seconds; $18-24 for 60 seconds. Combined advertising rates available with KRBI-AM. **URL:** http://www.river105.com.

18664 ■ KYSM-AM - 1230
1807 Lee Blvd.
North Mankato, MN 56003
Phone: (507)388-2900
Fax: (507)345-4675
Format: Sports. **Networks:** CNN Radio. **Founded:** 1938. **Operating Hours**: Continuous. **Key Personnel:** Mike Crusham, Pres. of Mktg., mikecrusham@clearchannel.com. **Wattage**: 1,000. **Ad Rates:** $20 for 30 seconds; $28 for 60 seconds. Combined advertising rates available with KYSM-FM; KXLP-FM. **URL:** http://www.kfan.com/pages/fanradionetwork.html.

18665 ■ KYSM-FM - 103.5
1807 Lee Blvd.
North Mankato, MN 56003
Phone: (507)345-4646
Format: Country. **Founded:** 1948. **Operating Hours**: Continuous. **Wattage**: 100,000. **Ad Rates:** $35 for 30 seconds; $50 for 60 seconds. Combined advertising rates available with KXLP-FM & KYSM-AM. **URL:** http://www.country103.com.

NORTHFIELD

SE MN. Rice Co. 30 mi. S. of Minneapolis. Carleton College; St. Olaf College. Manufactures woodworking machinery, cereal, snack foods, spiral freezing, building products, plastic fabrication of industrial laminates & flexible circuitry, conveyor systems. Agricultural crop research. Dairy, stock, poultry, grain farms.

18666 ■ The Carletonian
Carleton College
1 N College St.
Northfield, MN 55057
Phone: (507)222-4000
Student newspaper. **Freq:** Weekly. **Cols./Page:** 6. **Col. Width:** 2 1/8 inches. **Col. Depth:** 21 inches. **Key Personnel:** Devin Daugherty, Editor-in-Chief; James McMenimen, Business Manager; Lily Vanderstaay, Editor; Matt Hart, Editor; Sally Morgridge, Executive Editor; Tim Wills, Manager, Advertising; Andreas Stoehr, Executive Editor; Sophie Bushwick, Editor; Kate Trenerry, Editor. **Subscription Rates:** $29.99 Individuals digital; $73.99 By mail. **URL:** http://apps.carleton.edu/carletonian. **Remarks:** Accepts advertising. **Circ:** Paid 500, Non-paid 2500.

18667 ■ German Studies Review
Carleton College
1 N College St.
Northfield, MN 55057
Phone: (507)222-4000
Scholarly journal covering research in German history, literature, politics, and related fields. **Freq:** 3/yr (February, May, October). **Trim Size:** 6 x 9. **Key Personnel:** Sabine Hake, Editor. **ISSN:** 0149--7952 (print). **Subscription Rates:** $73 Individuals print - 3 issues; $146 Two years print - 3 issues. **URL:** http://www.press.jhu.edu/journals/german_studies_review/index.html. **Ad Rates:** BW $140. **Remarks:** Accepts advertising. **Circ:** Combined 2000.

18668 ■ Journal of Geoscience Education
National Association of Geoscience Teachers
c/o Carleton College W-SERC
1 N College St.
Northfield, MN 55057
Phone: (507)222-7096
Fax: (507)222-5175
Professional journal covering issues for geoscience teachers. **Freq:** Quarterly February, May, August and November. **Key Personnel:** Kristen St. John, PhD, Editor-in-Chief, phone: (540)568-6675, fax: (540)568-8058. **ISSN:** 1089--9995 (print). **Subscription Rates:** $150 Institutions online only; $200 Institutions print and online; $220 Institutions, other countries print and online; $20 U.S. back issue; $25 Other countries back issue; Included in membership. **URL:** http://nagt-jge.org. **Remarks:** Advertising accepted; rates available upon request. **Circ:** (Not Reported).

18669 ■ Journal of Risk Management in Financial Institutions
Professional Risk Managers' International Association
400 Washington St.
Northfield, MN 55057
Phone: (612)605-5370
Fax: (212)898-9076
Freq: Quarterly. **ISSN:** 1752-8887 (print); **EISSN:** 1752-8895 (electronic). **Subscription Rates:** £340 Individuals; $495 Individuals; £355 Other countries. **URL:** http://www.prmia.org/risk-resources/outside-publications; http://www.henrystewartpublications.com/jrm. **Remarks:** Advertising not accepted. **Circ:** (Not Reported).

18670 ■ Manitou Messenger
St. Olaf College
1520 St. Olaf Ave.
Northfield, MN 55057-1098
Phone: (507)786-2222
Publication E-mail: mess-news@stolaf.edu
Collegiate newspaper. **Freq:** Weekly (Fri.). **Print Method:** Offset. Broadsheet. **Cols./Page:** 6. **Col. Depth:** 21 inches. **Key Personnel:** Amy Mihelich, Managing Editor. **Subscription Rates:** $75 Individuals. **URL:** http://manitoumessenger.com. **Ad Rates:** BW $400; PCI $4. **Remarks:** Accepts advertising. **Circ:** Free ‡3100.

18671 ■ Northfield News
Northfield News Publishing Co.
115 W 5th St.
Northfield, MN 55057-2007
Phone: (507)645-5615
Fax: (507)645-6005
Publication E-mail: sgett@northfieldnews.com
Community newspaper. **Founded:** 1876. **Freq:** Semiweekly. **Print Method:** Offset. **Trim Size:** 21 1/2 x 13. **Cols./Page:** 6. **Key Personnel:** Chad Hjellming, Publisher, Editor. **Subscription Rates:** $95 Individuals print and online. **URL:** http://www.southernminn.com/northfield_news/. **Mailing address:** PO Box 58, Northfield, MN 55057-0058. **Ad Rates:** BW $964; 4C $1264; SAU $7.48. **Remarks:** Advertising accepted; rates available upon request. **Circ:** Paid 5,105, Free 375.

18672 ■ Northfield Shopper
Northfield News Publishing Co.
115 W 5th St.
Northfield, MN 55057-2007
Phone: (507)645-5615
Fax: (507)645-6005
Shopper. **Freq:** Weekly (Sun.). **Print Method:** Offset. **Trim Size:** 21 1/2 x 13. **Cols./Page:** 6. **Col. Width:** 26 nonpareils. **Col. Depth:** 294 agate lines. **Key Personnel:** Chad Hjellming, Publisher. **Subscription Rates:** Free. **URL:** http://www.southernminn.com/eedition/northfieldshopper/. **Mailing address:** PO Box 58, Northfield, MN 55057-0058. **Ad Rates:** GLR $.29; BW $1000; 4C $1250; SAU $7.75. **Remarks:** Accepts advertising. **Circ:** Free 12,000.

18673 ■ KRLX-FM - 88.1
300 N College St.
Northfield, MN 55057-4000
Phone: (507)222-4102
Format: News; Eclectic. **Founded:** Sept. 07, 2006. **URL:** http://radio.krlx.org.

18674 ■ KYMN-AM - 1080
200 Division St. S, Ste. 260
Northfield, MN 55057
Phone: (507)645-5695
Fax: (507)645-9768
Format: News; Information. **Networks:** NBC; Westwood One Radio; Motor Racing; Linder Farm. **Founded:** 1968. **Operating Hours**: Sunrise-sunset. **Key Personnel:** Jeff Johnson, Contact; Jeff Johnson, Contact. **Local Programs:** *Raider Wrap*, Saturday 10:00 a.m.; *Wayne Eddy Affair*, Monday Tuesday Wednesday Thursday Friday 9:00 a.m. 9:30 a.m. **Wattage**: 1,000 (day); 011 (night). **Ad Rates:** $8-18 for 30 seconds; $11.50-22 for 60 seconds. **URL:** http://www.kymnradio.net.

OLIVIA

SW MN. Renville Co. 100 mi. W. of Minneapolis. Manufactures plastic binders, concrete products, sunflower seeds, fiberglass shower stalls, custom welding products. Hatcheries. Dairy, stock, poultry, grain farms. Corn, beets, flax, oats, soybeans.

18675 ■ Renville County Register
Renco Publishing Inc.
816 E Lincoln
Olivia, MN 56277
Phone: (320)523-2032
Fax: (320)523-2033
Publication E-mail: otj@rencopub.com

Newspaper. **Freq:** Weekly (Thurs.). **Print Method:** Offset. **Cols./Page:** 7. **Col. Width:** 2 inches. **Col. Depth:** 21 1/2 inches. **Key Personnel:** Rose Hettig, Publisher; Craig DeFrance, Editor. **Subscription Rates:** $28 Individuals. **Formerly**: Olivia Times-Journal. **Ad Rates:** BW $677.25; SAU $4.50; PCI $4.50. **Remarks:** Advertising accepted; rates available upon request. **Circ:** 2404.

ORTONVILLE

WC MN. Lac qui Parle Co. On Big Stone Lake, 124 mi. S. of Fargo, ND. Manufactures monuments, cheese, butter; canned corn. Summer resort. Granite quarries. Dairy, grain, stock farms.

18676 ■ The Ortonville Independent
Kaercher Publications
29 NW Second St.
Ortonville, MN 56278-0336
Phone: (320)839-6163
Fax: (320)839-3761
Publication E-mail: mail@ortonvilleindependent.com
Community newspaper. **Freq:** Weekly (Tues.). **Print Method:** Letterpress and offset. **Trim Size:** 13 3/4 x 21 1/2. **Cols./Page:** 6. **Col. Width:** 26 nonpareils. **Col. Depth:** 301 agate lines. **ISSN:** 4108--3226 (print). **USPS:** 9-. **URL:** http://www.ortonvilleindependent.com/Ortonville_Independent.html. **Ad Rates:** BW $400; 4C $800; SAU $5; PCI $5.50. **Remarks:** Accepts advertising. **Circ:** ‡3,650.

18677 ■ KCGN-FM - 101.5
402 Pike St. E
Osakis, MN 56360
Phone: (612)343-3500
Free: 800-658-2229
Email: mail@praisefm.org
Format: Religious; Contemporary Christian. **Networks:** Sun Radio; Moody Broadcasting. **Owner:** Christian Heritage Broadcasting, Inc. **Operating Hours:** Continuous; 20% network, 80% local. **Wattage:** 98,000. **Ad Rates:** Noncommercial. **Mailing address:** PO Box 247, Osakis, MN 56360. **URL:** http://www.praisefm.org.

OSAKIS

WC MN. Todd Co. 10 mi. SE of Alexandria.

18678 ■ Journal of Exercise Physiology
American Society of Exercise Physiologists
503 8th Ave. W
Osakis, MN 56360
Publisher's E-mail: info@asep.org
Freq: Bimonthly. **ISSN:** 1097- 9751 (print). **Subscription Rates:** free. **URL:** http://www.asep.org/asep/asep/fldr/fldr.htm. **Remarks:** Accepts advertising. **Circ:** (Not Reported).

18679 ■ KBHL-FM - 103.9
PO Box 247
Osakis, MN 56360
Phone: (612)343-3500
Free: 800-658-2229
Format: Religious. **Networks:** Moody Broadcasting; SkyLight Satellite. **Owner:** Christian Heritage Broadcasting, Inc. **Founded:** 1985. **Operating Hours**: Continuous; 40% network, 60% local. **Key Personnel:** Matt Brown, Contact; Jack Zitzmann, Dir. of Production, jackson@praisefm.org; David McIver, Exec. Dir., david@praisefm.org; Sherrie McIver, Exec. Dir. **Wattage**: 6,000. **Ad Rates:** Noncommercial. **URL:** http://www.praisefm.org.

KBHZ-FM - See Willmar

KCGN-FM - See Ortonville

OSSEO

SE MN. Hennepin Co. 25 mi. N. of Minnetonka. Agriculture, feed mill.

18680 ■ Champlin Dayton Press
Press and News in Osseo
33 2nd St. NE
Osseo, MN 55369-1252
Phone: (763)425-3323
Fax: (763)425-2945
Community newspaper. **Freq:** Weekly (Thurs.). **Print Method:** Offset. **Cols./Page:** 6. **Col. Width:** 1.88 inches. **Col. Depth:** 294 agate lines. **Key Personnel:** Peggy Bakken, Executive Editor. **Subscription Rates:** $34 Individuals; $49 Two years; $20 Individuals 6 months. **URL:** http://pressnews.com/tag/champlin. **Mailing address:** PO Box 280, Osseo, MN 55369-0280. **Ad Rates:** GLR $.65; BW $1,141; 4C $1,435; PCI $11. **Remarks:** Accepts advertising. **Circ:** Thurs. ♦**1618**.

18681 ■ The Delano Eagle
Minnesota Sun Publications
PO Box 280
Osseo, MN 55369
Phone: (763)425-3323
Fax: (763)425-2945
Publication E-mail: sunpressmail@acnpapers.com
Regional community newspaper. **Freq:** Weekly (Mon.). **Key Personnel:** Peggy Bakken, Executive Editor, phone: (952)392-6822. **URL:** http://mnnews.com/newspapers/deagle.html. **Remarks:** Color advertising accepted; rates available upon request. **Circ:** 946.

18682 ■ North Crow River News
Press and News in Osseo
33 2nd St. NE
Osseo, MN 55369-1252
Phone: (763)425-3323
Fax: (763)425-2945
Community newspaper. **Freq:** Weekly (Mon.). **Print Method:** Offset. **Cols./Page:** 6. **Col. Width:** 1.88 inches. **Col. Depth:** 294 agate lines. **Key Personnel:** Peggy Bakken, Executive Editor. **Subscription Rates:** $38 Individuals; $64 Two years; $25 Individuals 6 months. **URL:** http://www.ecm-inc.com/web-publications; http://pressnews.com. **Ad Rates:** GLR $.62; BW $1097; 4C $1391; PCI $17.20. **Remarks:** Accepts advertising. **Circ:** Thurs. ♦**2,633**.

18683 ■ Rockford Area News Leader
Press and News in Osseo
33 2nd St. NE
Osseo, MN 55369-1252
Phone: (763)425-3323
Fax: (763)425-2945
Community newspaper. **Freq:** Weekly (Mon.). **Print Method:** Offset. **Cols./Page:** 6. **Col. Width:** 1.88 inches. **Col. Depth:** 21 inches. **Subscription Rates:** $34 Individuals; $59 Two years; $20 Individuals 6 months. **URL:** http://www.pressnews.com. **Mailing address:** PO Box 280, Osseo, MN 55369-0280. **Ad Rates:** GLR $.53; BW $934; 4C $1,228; PCI $11.45. **Remarks:** Accepts advertising. **Circ:** (Not Reported).

18684 ■ South Crow River News
Press and News in Osseo
33 2nd St. NE
Osseo, MN 55369-1252
Phone: (763)425-3323
Fax: (763)425-2945
Community newspaper. **Freq:** Weekly (Mon.). **Cols./Page:** 6. **Col. Width:** 1.88 inches. **Col. Depth:** 21 inches. **Key Personnel:** Peggy Bakken, Executive Editor. **Subscription Rates:** $38 Individuals 1 year; $64 Two years; $25 Individuals 6 months. **URL:** http://www.pressnews.com. **Mailing address:** PO Box 280, Osseo, MN 55369-0280. **Ad Rates:** GLR $.53; BW $934; 4C $1,228; PCI $11.45. **Remarks:** Accepts advertising. **Circ:** Thurs. ♦**952**.

OWATONNA

SE MN. Steele Co. 15 mi. S. of Faribault. Pillsbury College. Manufactures jewelry, tools farm machinery, ventilating, testing forms, exerise equipment, butter, cement, tile, leather gloves, dried milk products, service tools for auto industry, beverages, band accessories, canned goods, tannery, glass lamination and tempering. Nurseries. Dairy. Agriculture, machinery, truck farms.

18685 ■ Faribault Area Shopper
Huckle Publishing
135 W Pearl
Owatonna, MN 55060
Phone: (507)333-3100
Shopping guide. **Freq:** Weekly (Sun.). **URL:** http://www.southernminn.com/eedition/faribaultshopper. **Circ:** (Not Reported).

18686 ■ Owatonna People's Press
Owatonna People's Press
135 W Pearl St.
Owatonna, MN 55060
Phone: (507)451-2840
Fax: (507)444-2382
General newspaper. **Freq:** Tues.-Sun. **Print Method:** Offset. **Cols./Page:** 6. **Col. Width:** 1.833 inches. **Col. Depth:** 21 1/2 inches. **Key Personnel:** Jeffrey Jackson, Managing Editor; Carol Harvey, Manager, Circulation. **ISSN:** 0890--2860 (print). **USPS:** 416-200. **Subscription Rates:** $184 Individuals 52 weeks. **URL:** http://www.southernminn.com/owatonna_peoples_press. **Ad Rates:** GLR $15; BW $1,935; 4C $2,270; SAU $15. **Remarks:** Advertising accepted; rates available upon request. **Circ:** Combined ‡7058, Combined ‡5974.

18687 ■ KOWZ-FM - 100.9
255 Cedardale
Owatonna, MN 55060
Phone: (507)444-9224
Fax: (507)444-9080
Email: kowz@kowzonline.com
Format: Contemporary Hit Radio (CHR); Adult Contemporary. **Wattage:** 100,000. **URL:** http://www.kowzfm.com.

18688 ■ KRFO-AM - 1390
245 18th St. SE
Owatonna, MN 55060
Phone: (507)451-2250
Format: Oldies; News; Information. **Key Personnel:** John Connor, Gen. Sales Mgr., john.connor@cumulus.com. **Wattage:** 500 Day time; 004 Nigh. **Ad Rates:** Advertising accepted; rates available upon request. **URL:** http://www.krforadio.com.

18689 ■ KRFO-FM - 104.9
245 18th St. SE
Owatonna, MN 55060
Phone: (507)451-2250
Format: News; Sports; Talk. **Owner:** Cumulus Media Inc., 3280 Peachtree Rd. NW, Ste. 2300, Atlanta, GA 30305-2455, Ph: (404)949-0700, Fax: (404)949-0740. **Wattage:** 4,700 ERP. **Ad Rates:** Advertising accepted; rates available upon request. **URL:** http://www.krforadio.com.

KRUE-FM - See Waseca, MN

18690 ■ Linder Farm Network
255 Cedardale Dr. SE
Owatonna, MN 55060
Phone: (507)444-9224
Fax: (507)444-9080
Key Personnel: Lynn Ketelsen, Exec. Dir., lynn@linderradio.com; Jeff Stewart, Contact, jeffstewart@linderradio.com. **Ad Rates:** Advertising accepted; rates available upon request. **URL:** http://www.linderfarmnetwork.com.

PARK RAPIDS

SW MN. Hubbard Co. 40 mi. S. of Bemidji. Dairy farms.

18691 ■ Park Rapids Enterprise
Park Rapids Enterprise
203 Henrietta Ave. N
Park Rapids, MN 56470
Phone: (218)732-3364
Fax: (218)732-8757
Community newspaper for Hubbard County. **Freq:** Semiweekly. **Print Method:** Offset. **Cols./Page:** 6. **Col. Width:** 13 3/4 inches. **Col. Depth:** 21 3/4 inches. **Key Personnel:** Candy Parks, Manager, Advertising; Kevin Cederstrom, Editor. **Subscription Rates:** $57.25 Individuals Hubbard and Adjoining Countries; $66.50 Out of area; $74.50 Out of state; $57.25 Students. **URL:** http://www.parkrapidsenterprise.com. **Mailing address:** PO Box 111, Park Rapids, MN 56470. **Remarks:** Advertising accepted; rates available upon request. **Circ:** (Not Reported).

18692 ■ KDKK-FM - 97.5
PO Box 49
Park Rapids, MN 56470
Phone: (218)732-3306
Fax: (218)732-3307
Email: kprmkdkk@unitelc.com
Format: Adult Contemporary. **Simulcasts:** KPRM-AM. **Networks:** Jones Satellite; NBC; Music of Your Life/Fairwest. **Owner:** DeLaHunt Broadcasting Group, at above address. **Founded:** 1967. **Formerly**: KPRM-FM. **Operating Hours**: 18.25 hours Daily; 80% network, 20% local. **Key Personnel:** Ed De La Hunt, Owner. **Wattage**:

Circulation: ★ = AAM; △ or • = BPA; ♦ = CAC; ❑ = VAC; ⊕ = PO Statement; ‡ = Publisher's Report; Boldface figures = sworn; Light figures = estimated.

100,000. **Ad Rates:** $6-8.25 for 15 seconds; $10-14 for 30 seconds; $12-16 for 60 seconds. Combined advertising rates available with KPRM-AM. **URL:** http://www.kkradionetwork.com.

18693 ■ KOPJ-FM - 89.3
200 S Main Ave.
Park Rapids, MN 56470
Phone: (218)237-4673
Format: Religious. **Owner:** LifeTalk Radio Network, 11291 Pierce St., Riverside, CA 92505, Ph: (615)469-5122, Free: 800-775-4673. **Mailing address:** PO Box 481, Park Rapids, MN 56470.

18694 ■ KPRM-AM
PO Box 49
Park Rapids, MN 56470
Phone: (218)732-3306
Fax: (218)732-3307
Format: Talk; News; Country; Contemporary Country; Religious; Agricultural. **Networks:** CBS. **Owner:** DeLa-Hunt Broadcasting Group, at above address. **Founded:** 1962. **Key Personnel:** Ed De La Hunt, Contact. **Wattage:** 50,000 Day; 1,000 Ni. **Ad Rates:** $5-7 for 15 seconds; $8-20 for 30 seconds; $9-20 for 60 seconds.

PARKERS PRAIRIE

18695 ■ The Independent
Parkers Prairie Independent
117 N Otter Ave.
Parkers Prairie, MN 56361
Phone: (218)338-2741
Fax: (218)338-2745
Publication E-mail: ppinews@me.com
Community newspaper. **Founded:** 1902. **Freq:** Weekly (Thurs.). **Print Method:** Offset. **Trim Size:** 16 x 22 3/4. **Cols./Page:** 6. **Col. Width:** 2 1/16 inches. **Col. Depth:** 21 1/2 inches. **USPS:** 260-760. **Subscription Rates:** $28 Individuals; $31 Out of area; $35 Out of state. **URL:** http://www.ppindependent.net/The_Parkers_Prairie_Independent,_LLC/Welcome.h tml. **Mailing address:** PO Box 42, Parkers Prairie, MN 56361-4996. **Ad Rates:** BW $376.25; SAU $6.50; PCI $2.50. **Remarks:** Accepts advertising. **Circ:** 1200.

PELICAN RAPIDS

WC MN. Otter Tail Co. On Pelican River, 40 mi. SE of Fargo, ND. Resort. Modular homes manufactured; turkey processing plants. Dairy, poultry, stock, grain farms.

18696 ■ Pelican Rapids Press
Pelican Rapids Press
29 W Mill
Pelican Rapids, MN 56572-0632
Phone: (218)863-1421
Fax: (218)863-1423
Publisher's E-mail: prpress@loretel.net
Local newspaper. **Freq:** Weekly (Wed.). **Print Method:** Offset. **Cols./Page:** 6. **Col. Width:** 27 nonpareils. **Col. Depth:** 301 agate lines. **Key Personnel:** Jeff Meyer, Editor. **USPS:** 424-960. **Subscription Rates:** $27 Individuals; $31 Out of area. **URL:** http://www.pelicanrapidspress.com. **Mailing address:** PO Box 632, Pelican Rapids, MN 56572-0632. **Ad Rates:** BW $645; 4C $720; PCI $7.49. **Remarks:** Accepts advertising. **Circ:** ‡2713.

PEQUOT LAKES

C MN. Crow Wing Co. 40 mi. NE of Wadena.

18697 ■ KCFB-FM - 91.5
PO Box 409
Pequot Lakes, MN 56472
Free: 866-568-4422
Format: Religious. **Networks:** Moody Broadcasting. **Owner:** Minnesota Christian Broadcasters Inc., PO Box 409, Pequot Lakes, MN 56472, Ph: (866)568-4422. **Founded:** 1986. **Operating Hours:** Continuous; 30% network, 70% local. **Key Personnel:** Chuck Heuberger, Contact. **Wattage:** 15,000. **Ad Rates:** Noncommercial. **URL:** http://www.theword.mn.

18698 ■ KTIG-FM - 102.7
PO Box 409
Pequot Lakes, MN 56472
Free: 866-568-4422
Format: Religious. **Networks:** Moody Broadcasting; Ambassador Inspirational Radio; Sun Radio. **Owner:** Minnesota Christian Broadcasters Inc., PO Box 409, Pequot Lakes, MN 56472, Ph: (866)568-4422. **Founded:** 1978. **Operating Hours:** Continuous; 33.5% network, 66.5% local. **Key Personnel:** Mike Heuberger, Contact; Chuck Heuberger, Contact. **Local Programs:** *Revive Our Hearts*, Monday Tuesday Wednesday Thursday Friday 11:30 a.m. - 12:00 p.m.; *Rise and Shine*, Monday Tuesday Wednesday Thursday Friday 6:00 a.m. - 8:55 a.m.; *Haven*, Monday Tuesday Wednesday Thursday Friday 11:00 a.m. - 11:30 a.m. **Wattage:** 50,000. **Ad Rates:** Noncommercial. **URL:** http://www.theword.mn.

PERHAM

WC MN. Otter Tail Co. 22 mi. NW of Wadena. Feed mills. Manufactures dog food, dried milk; poultry products processing plants. Creamery. Greenhouse. Resort. Stock, dairy, poultry farms. Potatoes, corn, small grains.

18699 ■ Contact
Contact
222 2nd Ave. SE
Perham, MN 56573
Phone: (218)346-5900
Shopper. **Freq:** Weekly (Sun.). **Print Method:** Offset. **Trim Size:** 15 1/4 x 21 1/2. **Cols./Page:** 7. **Col. Width:** 26 nonpareils. **Col. Depth:** 294 agate lines. **Key Personnel:** Patricia Mackie, Contact. **Subscription Rates:** $65 Canada; $130 Out of state. **URL:** http://www.thecontactnewspaper.cfbtrenton.com. **Mailing address:** PO Box 288, Perham, MN 56573. **Ad Rates:** GLR $.41; 4C $70; PCI $6.65. **Remarks:** Color advertising accepted; rates available upon request. **Circ:** Free 10000.

18700 ■ Perham Focus
Perham Enterprise Bulletin
222 Second Ave. SE
Perham, MN 56573
Publication E-mail: mswenson@eotfocus.com
Community newspaper. **Freq:** Weekly (Thurs.). **Print Method:** Offset. **Cols./Page:** 7. **Col. Width:** 26 nonpareils. **Col. Depth:** 294 agate lines. **Key Personnel:** Melissa Swenson, General Manager, phone: (218)346-5900; Kathy Bope, Business Manager. **Subscription Rates:** $23 Individuals in County; 6 months; $22 Individuals in County, senior citizen; $24 Out of country 6 months; $26 Out of state 6 months; $25 Individuals student in state; 9 months; $27 Students out of state; 9 months. **URL:** http://www.perhamfocus.com; http://www.forumcomm.com/newspapers. **Formerly:** Perham Enterprise Bulletin. **Ad Rates:** SAU $5.65. **Remarks:** Accepts advertising. **Circ:** 3200.

18701 ■ KPRW-FM - 99.5
235 W Main St.
Perham, MN 56573
Phone: (218)346-4800
Fax: (218)346-7595
Format: Adult Contemporary. **Networks:** CNN Radio. **Owner:** Result Radio, Inc., at above address. **Founded:** Aug. 1996. **Operating Hours:** Continuous. **Wattage:** 6,000. **Ad Rates:** Noncommercial. Combined advertising rates available with KBRF-AM, KZCR-FM, KJJK-AM, and KJJK-FM.

PINE CITY

EC MN. Pine Co. 65 mi. N. of Saint Paul. Manufactures computer components, wood stoves, soft drinks, recreational vehicles. Dairy, poultry, grain farms. Corn, hay, oats.

18702 ■ Pine City Pioneer
Pine City Pioneer
405 SE 2nd Ave.
Pine City, MN 55063
Phone: (320)629-6771
Publisher's E-mail: editor@pinecitymn.com
Community newspaper. **Founded:** 1885. **Freq:** Weekly (Thurs.). **Print Method:** Offset. **Cols./Page:** 6. **Col. Width:** 26 nonpareils. **Col. Depth:** 294 agate lines. **Subscription Rates:** $34 Individuals in county; $46 Out of area; $64 Two years in county; $83 Out of area two years. **URL:** http://www.pinecitymn.com. **Formerly:** Pioneer. **Ad Rates:** BW $395; SAU $6.51; PCI $6.51. **Remarks:** Advertising accepted; rates available upon request. **Circ:** ‡3532.

18703 ■ WCMP-AM - 1350
15429 Pokegema Lake Rd.
Pine City, MN 55063
Phone: (320)629-7575
Fax: (320)629-3933
Free: 888-629-7575
Format: Adult Contemporary. **Networks:** ABC. **Owner:** Red Rock Radio Corporation, 501 Lake Ave. S, Duluth, MN 55802, Ph: (218)728-9500, Free: 888-629-7575. **Founded:** 1957. **Operating Hours:** Continuous. **Key Personnel:** Jennifer Thorson, Gen. Mgr., jennifer@redrockonair.com; Tracy Fairbanks, Office Mgr. **Wattage:** 1,000. **Ad Rates:** Advertising accepted; rates available upon request. Combined advertising rates available with WCMP-FM.

18704 ■ WCMP-FM - 100.9
15429 Pokegema Lake Rd.
Pine City, MN 55063
Phone: (320)629-7575
Fax: (320)629-3933
Free: 888-629-7575
Format: Country. **Networks:** ABC. **Owner:** Red Rock Radio Corporation, 501 Lake Ave. S, Duluth, MN 55802, Ph: (218)728-9500, Free: 888-629-7575. **Founded:** 1978. **Operating Hours:** Continuous; 5% network, 95% local. **Key Personnel:** Jennifer Thorson, Gen. Mgr., jennifer@redrockonair.com. **Wattage:** 25,000. **Ad Rates:** $1-12 for 30 seconds; $1-24 for 60 seconds. Combined advertising rates available with WCMP-AM. **URL:** http://bringmethenews.com.

18705 ■ WXCX-FM - 105.7
15429 Pokegema Lake Rd.
Pine City, MN 55063
Phone: (320)629-7575
Free: 888-629-7575
Format: Oldies. **Owner:** Red Rock Radio Corporation, 501 Lake Ave. S, Duluth, MN 55802, Ph: (218)728-9500, Free: 888-629-7575. **Founded:** 1957. **Key Personnel:** Jennifer Schultz, Gen. Mgr., jennifer@redrockonair.com. **URL:** http://redrockonair.com.

PINE ISLAND

SE MN. Olmsted Co. 15 mi. NW of Rochester.

18706 ■ BEVCOMM
108 2nd St. SW
Pine Island, MN 55963
Phone: (507)356-8302
Fax: (320)848-2323
Free: 800-992-8857
Email: info@bevcomm.net
Founded: 1896. **Cities Served:** Oronoco, Pine Island, Minnesota: subscribing households 1,350; United States; 100 channels; 1 community access channel. **Mailing address:** PO Box 588, Pine Island, MN 55963. **URL:** http://www.bevcomm.net.

PIPESTONE

SW MN. Pipestone Co. 42 mi. NE of Sioux Falls SD. Light manufacturing. Stock, dairy, poultry, grain farms.

18707 ■ Jasper Journal
Pipestone Publishing Company, Inc.
115 2nd St. NE
Pipestone, MN 56164
Phone: (507)825-3333
Fax: (507)825-2168
Free: 800-325-6440
Publication E-mail: journal@pipestonestar.com
Community newspaper. **Freq:** Weekly (Mon.). **Print Method:** Offset. **Trim Size:** 10 3/4 x 15. **Cols./Page:** 5. **Col. Width:** 12 picas. **Col. Depth:** 15 inches. **Key Personnel:** Charles Draper, Publisher; Deloris Quissell, Manager, Advertising; James Coolahan, Editor. **ISSN:** 0744-3110 (print). **Subscription Rates:** $35 Individuals; $46 Out of area. **URL:** http://www.pipestonestar.com/Stories/Story.cfm?SID=10117. **Mailing address:** PO Box 277, Pipestone, MN 56164. **Ad Rates:** PCI $5.90, Local; PCI $7.40, National. **Remarks:** Advertising accepted; rates available upon request. **Circ:** ‡694.

18708 ■ KISD-FM - 98.7
PO Box 456
Pipestone, MN 56164

Phone: (507)825-4282
Fax: (507)825-3364
Email: kloh@klohradio.com
Format: Oldies. **Networks:** Satellite Music Network; ABC. **Owner:** Wallace Christensen Broadcasting, 2660 Broadway Ave., Slayton, MN 56172, Ph: (507)825-4282, Fax: (507)825-3364. **Founded:** 1969. **Operating Hours:** Continuous. **Key Personnel:** Carmen Christensen, Sales Mgr.; Mylan Ray, Music Dir. **Wattage:** 100,000. **Ad Rates:** $5-10 for 30 seconds; $8-18 for 60 seconds. **URL:** http://www.christensenbroadcasting.com.

18709 ■ KLOH-AM - 1050
PO Box 456
Pipestone, MN 56164
Phone: (507)825-4282
Email: kloh@klohradio.com
Format: Top 40; Country. **Networks:** ABC; Satellite Music Network; Linder Farm. **Owner:** Christensen Broadcasting, PO Box 456, Pipestone, MN 56164, Ph: (507)825-4282, Fax: (507)825-3364. **Founded:** 1955. **Operating Hours:** Continuous. **Key Personnel:** Carmen Christensen, Contact; Carmen Christensen, Contact. **Wattage:** 9,000. **Ad Rates:** $5-10 for 30 seconds; $8-18 for 60 seconds. **URL:** http://www.klohradio.com.

PLYMOUTH

SE MN. Hennepin Co. NW of Minneapolis.

18710 ■ Over the Front
League of World War I Aviation Historians
c/o Daniel Polglaze, Membership Secretary
16820 25th Ave. N
Plymouth, MN 55447-2228
Publisher's E-mail: OTF-president@overthefront.com
Historical journal of WWI aviation. **Freq:** Quarterly. **Print Method:** Web offset. **Trim Size:** 8 1/2 x 11. **Key Personnel:** Jack Herris, Editor; Richard L. Bennett, Editor; Jim Streckfuss, Editor. **ISSN:** 0888--272X (print). **Remarks:** Accepts advertising. **Circ:** (Not Reported).

18711 ■ Snow Goer
Ehlert Publishing Group Inc.
10405 6th Ave. N, Ste. 210
Plymouth, MN 55441
Phone: (763)383-4499
Sports magazine for snowmobilers. **Freq:** Quarterly. **Key Personnel:** John Prusak, Editor; Andy Swanson, Managing Editor. **Subscription Rates:** $16.97 U.S. /year; $23.97 Canada /year; $30.97 Other countries /year. **URL:** http://snowgoer.com. **Circ:** (Not Reported).

18712 ■ USA Hockey Magazine
Touchpoint Publishing
505 N Hwy. 169, Ste. 465
Plymouth, MN 55441
Phone: (763)595-0808
Free: 800-597-5656
Publisher's E-mail: info@touchpointpublishing.com
U.S.A. Hockey (sports association) magazine. **Freq:** 10/year. **Print Method:** Web Offset. **Trim Size:** 8 1/4 x 10 7/8. **Cols./Page:** 3. **Col. Width:** 26 nonpareils. **Col. Depth:** 140 agate lines. **Key Personnel:** Jim McEwen, President; Steve Farbman, Chief Executive Officer; Harry Thompson, Editor-in-Chief. **ISSN:** 1551--6741 (print). **Subscription Rates:** $15 Individuals /year. **URL:** http://www.usahockeymagazine.com. **Remarks:** Advertising accepted; rates available upon request. **Circ:** Paid **★410000**.

18713 ■ The World Wide Web Journal of Biology
Epress Inc.
130 Union Terrace Ln.
Plymouth, MN 55441
Publisher's E-mail: editor@epress.com
Journal on Bio-informatics. **Key Personnel:** Lester F. Harris, PhD, Editor-in-Chief. **Subscription Rates:** Free online. **Alt. Formats:** CD-ROM. **URL:** http://www.epress.com/w3jbio. **Circ:** (Not Reported).

18714 ■ WCTS-AM - 1030
900 Forestview Ln. N
Plymouth, MN 55441
Phone: (763)417-8270
Format: Religious. **Networks:** AP. **Owner:** Central Baptist Theological Seminary, 6601 Monticello Rd., Shawnee, KS 66226-3513. **Founded:** 1965. **Formerly:** WMIN-AM. **Operating Hours:** 5:30 a.m.-midnight. **ADI:** Minneapolis-St. Paul, MN. **Key Personnel:** Steve Davis, Contact, sdavis@centralseminary.edu; Steve Davis, Contact. **Local Programs:** *Christianity in a Changing Culture*, Monday Tuesday Wednesday Thursday Friday 8:30 a.m. - 7:00 p.m. **Wattage:** 50,000. **Ad Rates:** Noncommercial. **URL:** http://www.centralseminary.edu.

PRESTON

SE MN. Fillmore Co. 37 mi. SE of Rochester. Manufactures butter, flour. Poultry dressing plant. Ships livestock. Hardwood timber. Diversified farming. Hogs, cattle, corn. Dairy farms.

18715 ■ KFIL-AM - 1060
PO Box 370
Preston, MN 55965
Phone: (507)765-3856
Format: News; Country; Sports. **Owner:** Cumulus Media Inc., 3280 Peachtree Rd. NW, Ste. 2300, Atlanta, GA 30305-2455, Ph: (404)949-0700, Fax: (404)949-0740. **Founded:** 1966. **Operating Hours:** Sunrise - sunset. **Key Personnel:** Mike Sveen, Music Dir. **Wattage:** 1,000 Daytime. **Ad Rates:** Advertising accepted; rates available upon request. $6.50-8 for 30 seconds; $8.35-10.50 for 60 seconds. **URL:** http://kfilradio.com.

18716 ■ KFIL-FM - 103.1
300 St. Paul St. SW
Preston, MN 55965
Phone: (507)765-3344
Format: Country. **Networks:** Mutual Broadcasting System; Linder Farm. **Owner:** Cumulus Media Inc., 3280 Peachtree Rd. NW, Ste. 2300, Atlanta, GA 30305-2455, Ph: (404)949-0700, Fax: (404)949-0740. **Founded:** 1970. **Operating Hours:** Continuous. **Key Personnel:** Shannon Knoepke, Mgr., shannon.knoepke@townsquaremedia.com. **Wattage:** 9,000. **Ad Rates:** $6.50-8.50 for 30 seconds; $8.35-10.50 for 60 seconds. **URL:** http://www.kfilradio.com.

PRINCETON

EC MN. Sherburne Co. 50 mi. NW of Minneapolis. Manufactures school furniture, custom cabinets. Auto parts rebuilding. Dairy, poultry farms. Potatoes, corn, rye.

18717 ■ Princeton Union-Eagle
ECM Publishers Inc.
208 N Rum River Dr.
Princeton, MN 55371
Phone: (763)389-1222
Fax: (763)389-1728
Community newspaper. **Freq:** Weekly (Thurs.). **Print Method:** Offset. **Cols./Page:** 6. **Col. Width:** 28 nonpareils. **Col. Depth:** 294 agate lines. **Key Personnel:** Jeff Andres, General Manager; Jeffrey Hage, Editor. **USPS:** 445-060. **Subscription Rates:** $38 Individuals; $43 Out of area; $53 Out of state; $35 Individuals senior. **URL:** http://unioneagle.com. **Ad Rates:** BW $662; 4C $775; SAU $4; PCI $8.10. **Remarks:** Accepts advertising. **Circ:** Paid 3400.

PRIOR LAKE

SE MN. Scott Co. 7 mi. SE of Shakopee. Residential. Manufactures cabinets, machine parts, signs.

18718 ■ Prior Lake American
Southwest Suburban Publishing
14093 Commerce Ave. NE
Prior Lake, MN 55372
Phone: (952)447-6669
Fax: (952)447-6671
Local newspaper. **Freq:** Weekly (Sat.). **Print Method:** Offset. **Trim Size:** 13 x 21 1/2. **Cols./Page:** 6. **Col. Width:** 2 inches. **Col. Depth:** 21 1/2 inches. **Key Personnel:** Nancy Huddleston, Managing Editor; Laurie Hartmann, Publisher, phone: (952)345-6878. **Subscription Rates:** $35 Individuals in Prior Lake, Spring Lake and Credit River - print and digital; $39 By mail in Scott and Carver counties - print and digital; $50 By mail outside Scott and Carver counties - print and digital; $70 Two years print including Online Access - Mailed in Scott or Carver MN Counties; $90 Two years print including Online Access - 2 years - Mailed outside of Scott or Carver MN Counties. **URL:** http://www.swnewsmedia.com/prior_lake_american/. **Mailing address:** PO Box 538, Prior Lake, MN 55372. **Ad Rates:** BW $1070.70; 4C $1445.70; SAU $7.92; PCI $9.20. **Remarks:** Accepts advertising. **Circ:** 8,328.

PROCTOR

NE MN. St. Louis Co. 10 mi. W. of Duluth. Tourist attractions. Iron ore sorting yard. Dairy, truck farms.

18719 ■ Proctor Journal
Proctor Journal
215 Fifth St.
Proctor, MN 55810
Phone: (218)624-3344
Fax: (218)624-7037
Publication E-mail: journal@proctormn.com
Newspaper. **Freq:** Weekly (Thurs.). **Print Method:** Web offset. **Cols./Page:** 5. **Col. Width:** 22 nonpareils. **Col. Depth:** 210 agate lines. **USPS:** 445-800. **Subscription Rates:** $34 Individuals print and online, in 557 and 558 zip codes; $38 Individuals print and online, outside 557 and 558 zip codes; $43 Out of state print and online; $40.50 Individuals Snowbird Rate, print and online. **URL:** http://proctorjournal.com/v2/content.aspx?IsHome=1&MemberID=2008&ID=24807. **Ad Rates:** SAU $4; PCI $5.10. **Remarks:** Advertising accepted; rates available upon request. **Circ:** Paid 1950, Free 50.

RAMSEY

18720 ■ KLCI-FM - 106.1
14443 Armstrong Blvd. NW
Ramsey, MN 55303
Phone: (763)450-7777
Format: Country. **Key Personnel:** Neil Freeman, Station Mgr., neil@bobfm.us.

RAYMOND

SW MN. Kandiyohi Co. 85 mi. NW of Minneapolis. Residential.

18721 ■ The Raymond-Prinsburg News
The Raymond-Prinsburg News
PO Box 157
Raymond, MN 56282
Community newspaper. **Founded:** 1900. **Freq:** Weekly (Wed.). **Print Method:** Offset. **Trim Size:** 13 1/2 x 21 1/2. **Cols./Page:** 6. **Col. Width:** 2 1/8 inches. **Col. Depth:** 301 agate lines. **USPS:** 456-000. **Subscription Rates:** $24 Individuals; $28 Out of area; $30 Out of state. **URL:** http://www.raymondprinsburgnews.com/. **Formerly:** Raymond News. **Ad Rates:** SAU $4. **Remarks:** Advertising accepted; rates available upon request. **Circ:** ‡943.

RED WING

SE MN. Goodhue Co. On Mississippi River, 35 mi. SE of Saint Paul. Manufactures leather, rubber goods, footwear,marine engines, pottery, kitchen cabinets, nuclear power, shoes, malt, flour, soybean, linseed oil, trophies, ice & roller skates, rubber goods, insulation, concrete blocks, utility light poles, farm feed. Dairy, stock, grain farms.

18722 ■ Republican-Eagle
Republican Eagle
2760 N Service Dr.
Red Wing, MN 55066
Phone: (651)388-8235
Publisher's E-mail: contactus@republican-eagle.com
Community newspaper. **Freq:** Biweekly Wednesday and Saturday. **Print Method:** Offset. **Trim Size:** 14 x 22 3/4. **Cols./Page:** 6. **Col. Width:** 2 inches. **Col. Depth:** 21 1/2 inches. **Key Personnel:** Steve Messick, Publisher, phone: (651)301-7801; Anne Jacobson, Editor, phone: (651)301-7870. **USPS:** 145-760. **Subscription Rates:** $79 Individuals 52 weeks; $139 Two years local mail; $199 Individuals 3 years; local mail; $45 Individuals 6 months; $65 Individuals 6 months; $98 Individuals 52 weeks; non-local; $170 Two years non-local; $242 Individuals 3 years; non-local. **URL:** http://www.republican-eagle.com. **Mailing address:** PO Box 15, Red Wing, MN 55066. **Ad Rates:** GLR $0.82; BW $1,470.42; 4C $1,794.42; PCI $12.60. **Remarks:** Accepts advertising. **Circ:** (Not Reported).

Circulation: ★ = AAM; △ or • = BPA; ♦ = CAC; ❑ = VAC; ⊕ = PO Statement; ‡ = Publisher's Report; Boldface figures = sworn; Light figures = estimated.

18723 ■ KCUE-AM
474 Guernsey Ln.
Red Wing, MN 55066
Phone: (651)388-3511
Fax: (651)388-7153
Format: News; Talk; Country. **Networks:** ABC; Mutual Broadcasting System; Minnesota News; NBC; Business Radio. **Owner:** Sorenson Broadcasting Corp., 604 N Kiwanis, Sioux Falls, SD 57104, Ph: (605)334-1117, Fax: (605)338-0326. **Founded:** 1949. **Formerly**: KAAA-AM. **Key Personnel:** Frank Hanford, Gen. Mgr. **Wattage**: 1,000 Day; 110 Night. **Ad Rates:** $6.75-11.30 for 30 seconds; $10.15-16.95 for 60 seconds. **URL:** http://www.1250kcue.com/.

18724 ■ KWNG-FM - 105.9
474 Guernsey Ln.
Red Wing, MN 55066
Phone: (651)388-7151
Fax: (651)388-7153
Format: Oldies. **Key Personnel:** Jack Colwell, Sports Dir. **URL:** http://www.kwng.com.

REDWOOD FALLS

SW MN. Redwood Co. On Redwood River, 115 mi. SW of Minneapolis. Manufactures computer components, metal fabricating, mobile homes, rehabilitation equipment, concrete products. Stock, dairy, poultry, grain farms. Corn, soybeans. Diversified agriculture.

18725 ■ Redwood Falls Gazette
Redwood Gazette Inc.
219 South Washington
Redwood Falls, MN 56283
Phone: (507)637-2929
Publication E-mail: tkrause@redwoodfallsgazette.com
Community newspaper. **Freq:** Semiweekly Tues. and Thurs. **Print Method:** Offset. **Cols./Page:** 6. **Col. Width:** 28 nonpareils. **Col. Depth:** 301 agate lines. **Key Personnel:** Pat Schmidt, Publisher; Troy Krause, Editor; Sue Rima, Director, Sales. **URL:** http://www.redwoodfallsgazette.com. **Formerly**: Redwood Gazette. **Ad Rates:** GLR $.29; PCI $4.50. **Remarks:** Accepts advertising. **Circ:** ‡5100.

18726 ■ KLGR-AM - 1490
639 W Bridge
Redwood Falls, MN 56283
Phone: (507)637-2989
Fax: (507)637-5347
Email: klgr@mchsi.com
Format: News; Sports; Information. **Owner:** Three Eagles Communications, 3800 Cornhusker Hwy., Lincoln, NE 68504, Ph: (402)466-1234, Fax: (402)467-4095. **Founded:** 1954. **Operating Hours**: Continuous. **Wattage**: 1,000 KW. **Ad Rates:** Advertising accepted; rates available upon request. **Mailing address:** PO Box 65, Redwood Falls, MN 56283. **URL:** http://www.klgram.com.

18727 ■ KLGR-FM - 97.7
PO Box 65
Redwood Falls, MN 56283
Phone: (507)637-2989
Fax: (507)637-5347
Email: klgr@mchsi.com
Format: Adult Contemporary. **Networks:** Minnesota News. **Owner:** Three Eagles Communications, 3800 Cornhusker Hwy., Lincoln, NE 68504, Ph: (402)466-1234, Fax: (402)467-4095. **Founded:** 1974. **Operating Hours**: Continuous; 100% local. **Wattage**: 3,000. **Ad Rates:** Advertising accepted; rates available upon request. **URL:** http://www.myklgr.com.

REMER

18728 ■ Eagle Cable Vision
205 1st Ave. NE
Remer, MN 56672-0039
Cities Served: 14 channels. **URL:** http://www.jtc-companies.com/cable.html.

RICHFIELD

SE MN. Hennepin Co. 10 mi. S. of Minneapolis.

18729 ■ The Fort Mudge Most
Pogo Fan Club and Walt Kelly Society
Spring Hollow Books
6908 Wentworth Ave.
Richfield, MN 55423
Freq: Quarterly. **Subscription Rates:** $25 /year; $35 Other countries. **URL:** http://www.pogo-fan-club.org/fortmudgemost.html. **Remarks:** Accepts advertising. **Circ:** 450.

ROBBINSDALE

18730 ■ Robbinsdale Sun Post
Minnesota Sun Publications
4080 W Broadway, Ste. 113
Robbinsdale, MN 55422
Phone: (763)536-7500
Fax: (763)536-7519
Regional community newspaper. **Key Personnel:** Peggy Bakken, Executive Editor, phone: (952)392-6822; Mark Weber, General Manager. **Subscription Rates:** $87 By mail anywhere in the U.S. **URL:** http://post.mnsun.com/tag/robbinsdale. **Remarks:** Accepts advertising. **Circ:** (Not Reported).

ROCHESTER

SE MN. Olmsted Co. 75 mi. S. of Minneapolis. Rochester Community College. Mayo Clinic. Trade Center. Manufactures dairy products, phonographs, hospital supplies, home pasteurizers, silos, beverages, toilet preparation, computer equipment; canned vegetables. Dairy, grain, stock, poultry farms.

18731 ■ Agri News
Post-Bulletin
18 1st Ave. SE
Rochester, MN 55903-6118
Phone: (507)285-7600
Free: 800-562-1758
Publication E-mail: wilmes@agrinews.com
Farm newspaper distributed in Minnesota and northern Iowa. **Founded:** Aug. 04, 1976. **Freq:** Weekly (Thurs.). **Print Method:** Offset. **Trim Size:** 13 x 21. **Cols./Page:** 6. **Col. Width:** 26 nonpareils. **Col. Depth:** 294 agate lines. **Key Personnel:** Jean Caspers-Simmet, Writer, phone: (507)281-7418; Mychal Wilmes, Managing Editor, phone: (507)285-7659; Rosanne Allen, Manager, Advertising, Manager, Circulation, phone: (507)285-7674; Janet Kubat Willette, Writer, phone: (507)285-7790. **Subscription Rates:** $187.20 Individuals carrier; $205.40 Individuals motor route; $36.82 Members. **URL:** http://www.agrinews.com. **Mailing address:** PO Box 6118, Rochester, MN 55903-6118. **Remarks:** Advertising accepted; rates available upon request. **Circ:** Combined ♦**12040**.

18732 ■ Audubon
Zumbro Valley Audubon Society
PO Box 6244
Rochester, MN 55903-6244
Phone: (507)398-5390
Publication E-mail: editor@audubon.org
Freq: Bimonthly. **Key Personnel:** David Siedeman, Editor-in-Chief. **ISSN:** 0097--7136 (print). **Subscription Rates:** Included in membership; $20 Nonmembers. **URL:** http://www.audubonmagazine.org. **Ad Rates:** 4C $47,450, full page; 4C $28,470, half page; BW $28,700, full page; BW $17,220, half page. **Remarks:** Accepts advertising. **Circ:** (Not Reported).

18733 ■ Corporate Event: Corporate Event
Exhibitor Publications Inc.
206 S Broadway, Ste. 745
Rochester, MN 55904
Phone: (507)289-6556
Fax: (507)289-5253
Free: 888-235-6155
Magazine that covers case studies of business-to-business event marketing. **Freq:** Quarterly. **Key Personnel:** Lee Knight, Chief Executive Officer, Editor-in-Chief; Randal T. Acker, Chief Operating Officer; Mark Kuehl, Manager, Advertising. **Subscription Rates:** $78 Individuals; $108 Canada; $125 Individuals Mexico; $165 Other countries. **URL:** http://www.exhibitoronline.com. **Remarks:** Accepts advertising. **Circ:** (Not Reported).

18734 ■ Exhibitor Magazine
Exhibitor Publications Inc.
206 S Broadway, Ste. 745
Rochester, MN 55904
Phone: (507)289-6556
Fax: (507)289-5253
Free: 888-235-6155
Magazine covering educational and informational tools for trade show and event industry professionals in the U.S. and abroad. **Freq:** Monthly. **Print Method:** Offset. **Trim Size:** 8 1/2 x 11. **Cols./Page:** 3. **Col. Width:** 25 nonpareils. **Col. Depth:** 126 agate lines. **Key Personnel:** Sherry Flury, Advertising Representative; Teresa Blume, Coordinator; Mark Kuehl, Manager, Advertising. **ISSN:** 0360--4217 (print). **Subscription Rates:** $18 Individuals; $108 Canada; $125 Individuals Mexico; $165 Other countries; $36 Two years; $200 Two years Canada; $230 Two years Mexico; $300 Two years all other countries. **Alt. Formats:** Electronic publishing. **URL:** http://www.exhibitoronline.com/magazine. **Remarks:** Advertising accepted; rates available upon request. **Circ:** 30000.

18735 ■ Genetic Epidemiology
International Genetic Epidemiology Society
c/o Mariza de Andrade, PhD, Treasurer
Mayo Clinic
200 1st St. SW
Rochester, MN 55905-0002
Publisher's E-mail: iges@geneticepi.org
Freq: 8/year. **Key Personnel:** Sanjay Shete, PhD, Editor-in-Chief. **ISSN:** 0741--0395 (print); **EISSN:** 1098--2272 (electronic). **Subscription Rates:** Members online (free); $96 Members print; $4653 Institutions online only (U.S., Canada, Mexico, and rest of the world); £2377 Institutions online only; €3003 Institutions online only. **URL:** http://www.geneticepi.org/genetic-epidemiology-journal; http://onlinelibrary.wiley.com/journal/10.1002/(ISSN)1098-2272. **Remarks:** Advertising not accepted. **Circ:** (Not Reported).

18736 ■ Post-Bulletin
Post-Bulletin
LLC 18 1st Ave., SE
Rochester, MN 55903-6118
Phone: (507)285-7600
Publication E-mail: rchapman@postbulletin.com
General newspaper. **Freq:** Mon.-Sat. (eve.). **Print Method:** Offset. **Cols./Page:** 6. **Col. Width:** 27 nonpareils. **Col. Depth:** 301 agate lines. **Key Personnel:** Randy Chapman, Publisher, phone: (507)285-7602; Ron Hanson, Consultant, phone: (507)285-7741; Mary Kay Costello, Advertising Representative, phone: (507)285-7783; Sue Lovejoy, Manager, Sales, phone: (507)281-7492. **Subscription Rates:** $3.95 weekly rate. **URL:** http://www.postbulletin.com/. **Mailing address:** PO Box 6118, Rochester, MN 55903-6118. **Ad Rates:** BW $2,659; 4C $3,159; PCI $9. **Remarks:** Accepts advertising. **Circ:** Mon.-Fri. ♦**2610**, Sat. ♦**10695**.

18737 ■ Professional Skater
Professional Skaters Association
3006 Allegro Park SW
Rochester, MN 55902
Phone: (507)281-5122
Publisher's E-mail: office@skatepsa.com
Freq: Bimonthly. **ISSN:** 0273- 5571 (print). **Subscription Rates:** Included in membership; $19.95 U.S.; $29 Canada; $45 Other countries. **URL:** http://www.skatepsa.com/PS-Magazine.htm. **Remarks:** Accepts advertising. **Circ:** 6500.

18738 ■ Sleep Medicine
World Association of Sleep Medicine
3270 19th St. NW, Ste. 109
Rochester, MN 55901-2950
Phone: (507)316-0084
Free: 877-659-0760
Journal primarily focusing on the human aspects of sleep, integrating the various disciplines that are involved in sleep medicine: neurology, clinical neurophysiology, internal medicine (particularly pulmonology and cardiology), psychology, psychiatry, sleep technology, pediatrics, neurosurgery, otorhinolaryngology, and dentistry. **Freq:** Bimonthly. **Key Personnel:** S. Chokroverty, Editor-in-Chief; R.A. Ferber, Associate Editor; C. Bassetti, Associate Editor; J. Hedner, Associate Editor; A. Culebras, Associate Editor; T. Young, Associate Editor; M. Thorpy, Associate Editor; S. Katayama, Associate Editor. **ISSN:** 1389--9457 (print). **Subscription Rates:** $308 Individuals print and online; $262 Individuals online only; Included in membership. **URL:** http://www.sleep-journal.com; http://wasmonline.org/sleep-medicine-journal-2; http://www.journals.elsevier.com/

sleep-medicine. **Remarks:** Advertising not accepted. **Circ:** (Not Reported).

18739 ■ Vaccine
RELX Group P.L.C.
c/o G.A. Poland, Ed.-in-Chief
Mayo Clinic & Foundation
611C Guggenheim Bldg.
200 First St. SW
Rochester, MN 55905
Phone: (507)284-4968
Fax: (507)266-4716
Publisher's E-mail: amsterdam@relx.com
Journal covering vaccines and vaccination for academics, researchers, product developers, clinicians, workers, and others in the medical and veterinary fields. **Freq:** Weekly. **Key Personnel:** G.A. Poland, Editor-in-Chief; Valentina Sasselli, Managing Editor. **ISSN:** 0264-410X (print). **Subscription Rates:** $500 Individuals; $1959.20 Institutions online; $6397 Institutions print. **Circ:** (Not Reported).

18740 ■ Year Book of Orthopedics
Elsevier
c/o Bernard F. Morrey, MD, Ed.-in-Ch.
Mayo Medical School
Department of Orthopedics
Mayo Clinic
Rochester, MN 55905
Publisher's E-mail: t.reller@elsevier.com
Journal reporting developments in orthopedics, including trauma and amputation surgery, hip and knee replacement, sports medicine, and orthopedic oncology. **Founded:** Jan. 1966. **Freq:** Annual October. **Print Method:** Web. **Trim Size:** 11 1/2 x 17. **Cols./Page:** 4. **Col. Width:** 14 picas. **Col. Depth:** 16 inches. **Key Personnel:** Hamlet A. Peterson, MD, Board Member; Marc F. Swiontkowski, MD, Board Member; Bernard F. Morrey, MD, Editor-in-Chief; Christopher P. Beauchamp, MD, Board Member; Michael J. Yaszemski, MD, Board Member; Stephen D. Trigg, MD, Board Member. **ISSN:** 0276-1092 (print). **Subscription Rates:** $215 Other countries; $180 Individuals; $281 Institutions, other countries; $265 Institutions. **URL:** http://www.elsevier.com/journals/year-book-of-orthopedics/0276-1092. **Circ:** (Not Reported).

18741 ■ Zebrafish
Mary Ann Liebert Inc., Publishers
Department of Biochemistry & Molecular Biology
Guggenheim 1321A
200 1st St. S
203 Smith Hall
Rochester, MN 55905
Publisher's E-mail: info@liebertpub.com
Peer-reviewed journal focusing on the zebrafish, which is valuable in the study of vertebrate development. **Freq:** Quarterly. **Key Personnel:** Brant Weinstein, PhD, Board Member; Gerrit Begemann, PhD, Board Member; Peter Alestrom, PhD, Board Member; David Barnes, PhD, Board Member; Paul Collodi, PhD, Board Member; Stephen C. Ekker, PhD, Editor-in-Chief. **ISSN:** 1545--8547 (print); **EISSN:** 1557--8542 (electronic). **Subscription Rates:** $539 U.S. print and online; $647 Other countries print and online; $531 Individuals online only. **URL:** http://www.liebertpub.com/overview/zebrafish/122. **Remarks:** Accepts advertising. **Circ:** (Not Reported).

18742 ■ KFAN-AM - 1270
1530 Greenview Dr. SW, Ste. 200
Rochester, MN 55902
Phone: (507)288-3888
Fax: (507)288-7815
Format: News; Talk. **Networks:** Minnesota Ag (Magnet Farm); Minnesota News; CNN Radio. **Owner:** iHeartMedia Inc., 200 E Basse Rd., San Antonio, TX 78209, Ph: (210)832-3314. **Founded:** 1957. **Formerly**: KGHR-AM; KQAQ-AM; KWEB-AM. **Operating Hours**: Continuous. **ADI**: Rochester, MN-Mason City, IA-Austin, MN. **Key Personnel:** Mary Anne Nonn, Sales Mgr., maryannenonn@clearchannel.com; Greg Henn, Div. Dir., greghenn@iheartmedia.com; Craig Erpestad, Operations Mgr. **Wattage**: 5,000 Day; 1,000 Night. **Ad Rates:** Advertising accepted; rates available upon request. Combined advertising rates available with KRCH-AM: $29-$60 for 60 seconds. **URL:** http://www.fan1270.com/main.html.

18743 ■ K56HW - 56
PO Box A
Santa Ana, CA 92711
Phone: (714)832-2950
Free: 888-731-1000
Owner: Trinity Broadcasting Network Inc., PO Box A, Santa Ana, CA 92711, Ph: (714)832-2950, Free: 888-731-1000. **URL:** http://www.tbn.org.

18744 ■ KFSI-FM - 92.9
4016 28th St. SE
Rochester, MN 55904
Phone: (507)289-8585
Fax: (507)529-4017
Format: Religious. **Founded:** 1981. **ADI**: Rochester, MN-Mason City, IA-Austin, MN. **Key Personnel:** Paul Logan, Contact; Ray Logan, Contact; Mike Anderson, Contact. **Wattage**: 6,000. **Ad Rates:** Noncommercial. **URL:** http://www.kfsi.org.

18745 ■ KGAC-FM - 90.5
206 S Broadway, Ste. 735
Rochester, MN 55904
Phone: (507)282-0910
Fax: (507)282-2107
Format: Classical. **Networks:** National Public Radio (NPR); American Public Radio (APR). **Owner:** Minnesota Public Radio Inc., 480 Cedar St., Saint Paul, MN 55101, Ph: (651)290-1500, Free: 800-228-7123. **Founded:** Mar. 1985. **Operating Hours**: Continuous; 25% network, 75% local. **Key Personnel:** Chris Cross, Regional Mgr., ccross@mpr.org. **Wattage**: 75,000. **Ad Rates:** Noncommercial. **URL:** http://www.minnesota.publicradio.org/radio/stations/kngakgac.

18746 ■ KLCD-FM - 89.5
206 S Broadway, Ste. 735
Rochester, MN 55904
Phone: (507)282-0910
Fax: (507)282-2107
Format: Classical. **Owner:** Minnesota Public Radio Inc., 480 Cedar St., Saint Paul, MN 55101, Ph: (651)290-1500, Free: 800-228-7123. **Founded:** June 1977. **Operating Hours**: Continuous. **Key Personnel:** Chris Cross, Regional Mgr., ccross@mpr.org. **Wattage**: 100. **Ad Rates:** Noncommercial. **URL:** http://www.minnesota.publicradio.org.

18747 ■ KLCX-FM - 107.7
122 Fourth St. SW
Rochester, MN 55902
Phone: (507)286-1010
Format: Album-Oriented Rock (AOR). **Owner:** Cumulus Media Inc., 3280 Peachtree Rd. NW, Ste. 2300, Atlanta, GA 30305-2455, Ph: (404)949-0700, Fax: (404)949-0740. **Key Personnel:** Jeff Cecil, Dir. of Programs, jeff@zrock1077.com; Terry Lee, Sales Mgr., terry.lee@cumulus.com; Brent Ackerman, Operations Mgr., brent.ackerman@cumulus.com; Shannon Knoepke, Gen. Mgr., shannon.knoepke@cumulus.com. **Ad Rates:** Noncommercial.

18748 ■ KLNI-FM - 88.7
1530 Greenview Dr. SW, Ste. 215
Rochester, MN 55902
Phone: (507)292-8630
Fax: (507)292-2107
Format: News. **Owner:** Minnesota Public Radio Inc., 480 Cedar St., Saint Paul, MN 55101, Ph: (651)290-1500, Free: 800-228-7123. **Founded:** 1993. **Key Personnel:** Kerri Miller, Producer; Jeff Jones, Producer; Chris Cross, Regional Mgr., ccross@mpr.org; Derrick Stevens, Production Mgr.; Jennifer Allen, Music Dir.; Nick Kereakos, Chief Tech. Ofc., VP of Operations & Engg.; Tim Roesler, Sr. VP, Officer; Stephanie Curtis, Editor. **Wattage**: 100. **URL:** http://minnesota.publicradio.org/radio/stations/klniklcd.

18749 ■ KLSE-FM - 103.3
1530 Greenview Dr. SW, Ste. 215
Rochester, MN 55902
Phone: (507)292-8630
Fax: (507)282-2107
Format: Classical. **Owner:** Minnesota Public Radio Inc., 480 Cedar St., Saint Paul, MN 55101, Ph: (651)290-1500, Free: 800-228-7123. **Founded:** Dec. 1974. **Operating Hours**: Continuous. **Key Personnel:** Jeff Jones, Producer; Chris Cross, Regional Mgr., ccross@mpr.org; Sea Stachura, Reporter, sstachura@mpr.org; Michael Hofbauer, Account Exec., mhofbauer@mpr.org; Mary Stapek, Account Exec., mstapek@mpr.org; Stacy Davis, Associate, stdavis@mpr.org; Jennifer Allen, Music Dir.; Tim Roesler, Sr. VP, Officer; Stephanie Curtis, Editor; Nick Kereakos, Chief Tech. Ofc., VP of Operations, VP of Engg.; Jeff Smith, Corp. Dev. Ofc.; Mike Edgerly, News Dir.; Michael Olson, Editor. **Wattage**: 94,000. **Ad Rates:** Advertising accepted; rates available upon request; Noncommercial. **URL:** http://www.mpr.org/listen/stations/knseklse.

18750 ■ KMFX-AM - 1190
1530 Greenview Dr. SW, Ste. 200
Rochester, MN 55902
Phone: (507)288-3888
Fax: (507)288-7815
Format: Country. **Founded:** 1976. **Operating Hours**: 6 a.m.-sunset. **Key Personnel:** Craig Erpestad, Mgr., craigerpestad@iheartmedia.com; Bob Fox, Gen. Mgr. **Wattage**: 1,000. **Ad Rates:** $5-19 for 30 seconds; $8-22 for 60 seconds. **URL:** http://www.1025thefox.com.

18751 ■ KMFX-FM - 102.5
1530 Greenview Dr. SW, Ste. 200
Rochester, MN 55902
Phone: (507)288-3888
Format: Country. **Founded:** Sept. 15, 2006. **ADI**: Rochester, MN-Mason City, IA-Austin, MN. **Key Personnel:** Craig Erpestad, Operations Mgr., craigerpestad@clearchannel.com; Mary Ann Nonn, Sales Mgr., maryannnonn@clearchannel.com; Jessica Demsky, Contact, jessicademsky@clearchannel.com. **Wattage**: 9,400. **Ad Rates:** Noncommercial. **URL:** http://www.foxcountry.net.

18752 ■ KMSE-FM - 88.7
1530 Greenview Dr. SW
Rochester, MN 55904
Phone: (507)292-8630
Fax: (507)282-2107
Format: Contemporary Hit Radio (CHR). **Owner:** Minnesota Public Radio Inc., 480 Cedar St., Saint Paul, MN 55101, Ph: (651)290-1500, Free: 800-228-7123. **ADI**: Rochester, MN-Mason City, IA-Austin, MN. **Wattage**: 850. **URL:** http://minnesota.publicradio.org/radio/stations/kzsekIse.

18753 ■ KNGA-FM - 90.5
206 S Broadway, Ste. 735
Rochester, MN 55904
Phone: (507)282-0910
Fax: (507)282-2107
Format: Classical. **Key Personnel:** Chris Cross, Regional Mgr., ccross@mpr.org. **Ad Rates:** Noncommercial. **URL:** http://www.minnesota.publicradio.org.

18754 ■ KNXR-FM - 97.5
305 Alliance Pl. NE
220 S Broadway
Rochester, MN 55906
Phone: (507)285-5697
Format: Soft Rock; Full Service. **Networks:** ABC. **Owner:** Unoted Audio Corporation, at above address. **Founded:** 1965. **Operating Hours**: 6 a.m.-1 a.m.; 1% network, 99% local. **Key Personnel:** Thomas H. Jones, Contact. **Wattage**: 100,000. **URL:** http://www.mn975.com.

18755 ■ KOLM-AM - 1520
122 4th St. SW
Rochester, MN 55902
Phone: (507)286-1010
Format: Sports. **Networks:** CNN Radio; Westwood One Radio; ABC. **Owner:** Cumulus Media Inc., 3280 Peachtree Rd. NW, Ste. 2300, Atlanta, GA 30305-2455, Ph: (404)949-0700, Fax: (404)949-0740. **Operating Hours**: Continuous. **Key Personnel:** Brent Ackerman, Mgr., brent.ackerman@townsquaremedia.com; Shannon Knoepke, Gen. Mgr., shannon.knoepke@townsquaremedia.com. **Wattage**: 10,000 Day; 800 Night. **Ad Rates:** $6-11 for 30 seconds; $10-15 for 60 seconds. KWWK; KLCX. **URL:** http://www.1520theticket.com.

18756 ■ KRCH-FM - 101.7
1530 Greenview Dr. SW, Ste. 200
Rochester, MN 55902
Phone: (507)288-3888
Fax: (507)288-7815

Circulation: ★ = AAM; △ or • = BPA; ♦ = CAC; ❑ = VAC; ⊕ = PO Statement; ‡ = Publisher's Report; Boldface figures = sworn; Light figures = estimated.

Format: Classic Rock. **Founded:** 1968. **Operating Hours**: Continuous. **Wattage**: 39,000. **Ad Rates:** Noncommercial. Combined advertising rates available with KWEB-AM: $29-$60 for 60 seconds. **URL:** http://www.laser1017.net.

18757 ■ KROC-AM - 1340
122 4th St. SW
Rochester, MN 55902
Phone: (507)281-2400
Format: News; Talk. **Networks:** ABC; Westwood One Radio. **Owner:** Cumulus Broadcasting Inc., 3280 Peachtree Rd. NW, Ste. 2300, Atlanta, GA 30305-2447, Ph: (404)949-0700, Fax: (404)949-0740. **Operating Hours**: Continuous; 33% network, 67% local. **Key Personnel:** Terry Lee, Contact, terry.lee@cumulus.com; Brent Ackerman, Contact, brent@kroc.com; Terry Lee, Contact, terry.lee@cumulus.com; Brent Ackerman, Contact, brent@kroc.com. **Wattage**: 1,000. **Ad Rates:** $38.40-60.80 for 60 seconds. Combined advertising rates available with KROC-FM. **URL:** http://www.kroc.com.

18758 ■ KROC-FM - 106.9
122 4th St. SW
Rochester, MN 55902
Phone: (507)286-1010
Format: Contemporary Hit Radio (CHR). **Networks:** ABC; Mutual Broadcasting System. **Owner:** Cumulus Media Inc., 3280 Peachtree Rd. NW, Ste. 2300, Atlanta, GA 30305-2455, Ph: (404)949-0700, Fax: (404)949-0740. **Founded:** 1965. **Operating Hours**: Continuous; 5% network, 95% local. **ADI**: Rochester, MN-Mason City, IA-Austin, MN. **Key Personnel:** Terry Lee, Contact, terry.lee@cumulus.com; Brent Ackerman, Contact, brent@kroc.com; Terry Lee, Contact, terry.lee@cumulus.com; Brent Ackerman, Contact, brent@kroc.com. **Wattage**: 100,000. **Ad Rates:** Noncommercial. Combined advertising rates available with KROC-AM. **URL:** http://kroc.com.

18759 ■ KTTC-TV - 10
6301 Bandel Rd. NW
Rochester, MN 55901-8798
Phone: (507)288-4444
Fax: (507)288-6324
Email: news@kttc.com
Format: Public TV. **Networks:** NBC; Warner Brothers Studios. **Owner:** Quincy Newspapers Inc., 130 S 5th St., Quincy, IL 62306, Ph: (217)223-5100. **Founded:** July 1953. **Formerly**: KROC-TV. **Operating Hours**: Continuous; 77% network, 23% local. **Key Personnel:** Jerry Watson, Gen. Mgr., VP, jwatson@kttc.com; Liz Dahlen, Station Mgr., edahlen@kttc.com; Tim Morgan, Chief Engineer, tmorgan@kttc.com; Brendan Ford, Production Mgr., bford@kttc.com; Rita Duda, Promotions Mgr., rduda@kttc.com; Dave Osborn, Dir. of Creative Svcs., dosborn@kttc.com; Noel Sederstrom, News Dir., nsederstrom@kttc.com; Vickie Broughton, Traffic Mgr., Program Mgr., vbroughton@kttc.com. **Local Programs**: *NewsCenter*, Monday Tuesday Wednesday Thursday Friday Saturday Sunday 5:00 a.m.; 12:00 p.m.; 5:00 p.m.; 6:00 p.m.; 10:00 p.m. 6:00 p.m.; 10:00 p.m. 5:00 p.m.; 10:00 p.m. **Wattage**: 316,000. **Ad Rates:** Advertising accepted; rates available upon request. **URL:** http://www.kttc.com.

18760 ■ KVGO-FM - 104.3
122 4th St. SW
Rochester, MN 55902
Phone: (507)286-1010
Format: Oldies. **Owner:** Cumulus Broadcasting Inc., 3280 Peachtree Rd. NW, Ste. 2300, Atlanta, GA 30305-2447, Ph: (404)949-0700, Fax: (404)949-0740.

18761 ■ KWWK-FM - 96.5
122 Fourth St. SW
Rochester, MN 55902
Phone: (507)286-1010
Format: Contemporary Country. **Networks:** Westwood One Radio; Jones Satellite. **Owner:** Olmsted County Board Co. **Founded:** 1967. **Operating Hours**: Continuous. **Key Personnel:** Alan Reed, Contact; Shannon Knoepke, Dir. of Sales, shannon.knoepke@townsquaremedia.com; Alan Reed, Contact; Jas Caffrey, Contact. **Local Programs**: *Quick Country Morning Show*, Monday Tuesday Wednesday Thursday Friday 5:00 a.m - 10:00 a.m. **Wattage**: 50,000. **Ad Rates:** $16-35 for 30 seconds; $18-38 for 60 seconds. KOLM; KLCX. **URL:** http://www.quickcountry.com.

18762 ■ KXLC-FM - 91.1
206 S Broadway, Ste. 735
Rochester, MN 55904
Phone: (507)282-0910
Fax: (507)282-2107
Format: News. **Networks:** National Public Radio (NPR). **Owner:** Minnesota Public Radio Inc., 480 Cedar St., Saint Paul, MN 55101, Ph: (651)290-1500, Free: 800-228-7123. **Founded:** Jan. 1991. **Operating Hours**: Continuous. **Key Personnel:** Chris Cross, Regional Mgr., ccross@mpr.org. **Wattage**: 230. **Ad Rates:** Noncommercial. **URL:** http://www.minnesota.publicradio.org.

18763 ■ KXLT-TV - 47
6301 Bandel Rd. NW
Rochester, MN 55901
Phone: (507)252-4747
Fax: (507)252-5050
Email: promotions@myfox47.com
Format: Commercial TV. **Networks:** Fox. **Owner:** Sagamorehill Broadcasting, at above address. **Founded:** Jan. 19, 1998. **Operating Hours**: Continuous. **ADI**: Rochester, MN-Mason City, IA-Austin, MN. **Key Personnel:** Kristopher Lake, Sales Mgr., klake@fox47kxlt.com. **Wattage**: 1,500,000. **Ad Rates:** Noncommercial. **URL:** http://www.myfox47.com.

18764 ■ KYBA-FM - 105.3
122 4th St. SW
Rochester, MN 55902
Phone: (507)286-1010
Format: Soft Rock; Adult Contemporary. **Networks:** ABC. **Owner:** Cumulus Broadcasting Inc., 3280 Peachtree Rd. NW, Ste. 2300, Atlanta, GA 30305-2447, Ph: (404)949-0700, Fax: (404)949-0740. **Founded:** Feb. 01, 1993. **Operating Hours**: Continuous. **ADI**: Rochester, MN-Mason City, IA-Austin, MN. **Key Personnel:** Terry Lee, Sales Mgr., terry.lee@cumulus.com; Brent Ackerman, Operations Mgr., brent.ackerman@cumulus.com; Tom Garrett, Dir. of Programs, tom.garrett@cumulus.com; Shannon Knoepke, Gen. Mgr., shannon.knoepke@townsquaremedia.com. **Wattage**: 50,000. **Ad Rates:** $19-30 for 30 seconds. KROC AM/FM. **URL:** http://www.y105fm.com.

18765 ■ KZSE-FM - 90.7
206 S Broadway, Ste. 735
Rochester, MN 55904
Phone: (507)282-0910
Fax: (507)282-2107
Format: News. **Networks:** National Public Radio (NPR). **Owner:** Minnesota Public Radio Inc., 480 Cedar St., Saint Paul, MN 55101, Ph: (651)290-1500, Free: 800-228-7123. **Founded:** 1977. **Operating Hours**: Continuous. **Key Personnel:** Chris Cross, Regional Mgr., ccross@mpr.org. **Wattage**: 1,000. **Ad Rates:** Noncommercial. **URL:** http://www.minnesota.publicradio.org.

ROSEAU

NW MN. Roseau Co. 115 mi. NE of Grand Falls, ND. Butter, snowmobiles manufactured. Dairy, stock, beef, grass seed, poultry farms. Flax, small grain.

18766 ■ Roseau Times-Region
Roseau Times-Region
1307 3rd St., NE, Ste. 109
Roseau, MN 56751-0220
Phone: (218)463-1521
Fax: (218)463-1530
Publication E-mail: rtr@mncable.net
Community newspaper. **Freq:** Weekly (Sat.). **Print Method:** Offset. **Cols./Page:** 6. **Col. Width:** 2 inches. **Col. Depth:** 21.5 inches. **Key Personnel:** Jodi Driscoll, Publisher. **USPS:** 470-780. **Subscription Rates:** $35 in county; $50 Out of country; $25 online. **URL:** http://roseautimes-region.com/. **Mailing address:** PO Box 220, Roseau, MN 56751-0220. **Ad Rates:** PCI $4.25. **Remarks:** Accepts advertising. **Circ:** ‡3593, ‡3593.

18767 ■ KCAJ-FM - 102.1
107 Center St. W
Roseau, MN 56751
Phone: (218)463-3360
Fax: (218)463-1977
Email: info@wild102fm.com
Format: Full Service. **Networks:** NBC; Westwood One Radio; Minnesota News. **Owner:** North Country Media Inc., 203 2nd Ave. NE, Roseau, MN 56751, Ph: (218)463-0161, Fax: (888)202-4047, Free: 866-253-0436. **Founded:** June 1996. **Operating Hours**: Continuous. **Local Programs**: *Friend & Neighbors*. **Wattage**: 50,000. **Ad Rates:** Noncommercial. **URL:** http://www.wild102fm.com.

ROSEVILLE

SE MN. Ramsey Co. 11 mi. NW of Maplewood. Residential.

18768 ■ Fabric Architecture
TARP Association
1801 County Road B W
Roseville, MN 55113
Phone: (651)225-6926
Publisher's E-mail: generalinfo@ifai.com
Freq: Bimonthly. **ISSN:** 1045- 0483 (print). **Subscription Rates:** $39 Two years U.S; $49 Two years Canada; $69 Two years International. **URL:** http://www.ifai.com/product/fabric-architecture-magazine/. **Remarks:** Accepts advertising. **Circ:** 13915.

18769 ■ Fabric Architecture: The International Membrane Structure and Design Magazine
TARP Association
1801 County Road B W
Roseville, MN 55113
Phone: (651)225-6926
Publisher's E-mail: generalinfo@ifai.com
Magazine specializing in interior and exterior design ideas and technical information for architectural fabric applications in architecture and the landscape. **Freq:** Bimonthly. **Print Method:** Web Offset. **Trim Size:** 8 1/4 x 11. **Cols./Page:** 3 and 2. **Col. Width:** 13 and 20 picas. **Col. Depth:** 60 picas. **Key Personnel:** Mary Hennessy, President, Chief Executive Officer, phone: (651)225-6986; Susan Niemie, Publisher. **ISSN:** 1045-0483 (print). **Subscription Rates:** $39 Two years; $49 Two years Canada and Mexico; $69 Two years international. **URL:** http://www.ifai.com/product/fabric-architecture-magazine/. **Formerly**: Fabrics & Architecture. **Ad Rates:** 4C $4,695. **Remarks:** Accepts advertising. **Circ:** Controlled 10000.

18770 ■ Geosynthetics
TARP Association
1801 County Road B W
Roseville, MN 55113
Phone: (651)225-6926
Publisher's E-mail: generalinfo@ifai.com
Magazine containing information to promote and strengthen the use of geosynthetics. **Freq:** Bimonthly. **Print Method:** Offset. **Trim Size:** 8 1/4 x 10 7/8. **Cols./Page:** 3 and 2. **Col. Width:** 13 and 20 picas. **Col. Depth:** 60 picas. **Key Personnel:** Mary Hennessy, Publisher; Susan Niemi, Associate Publisher; Ron Bygness, Editor, phone: (651)225-6988. **ISSN:** 0882-4983 (print). **Subscription Rates:** $59 Two years United States; $69 Two years Canada; $99 Other countries 2 years. **URL:** http://geosyntheticsmagazine.com; http://www.ifai.com/product/geosynthetics-magazine/; http://www.ifai.com/publications/geo. **Formerly**: Geotechnical Fabrics Report. **Ad Rates:** BW $4755; 4C $4895. **Remarks:** Accepts advertising. **Circ:** 16,000, 16000.

18771 ■ InTents
TARP Association
1801 County Road B W
Roseville, MN 55113
Phone: (651)225-6926
Publisher's E-mail: generalinfo@ifai.com
Freq: Bimonthly. **Subscription Rates:** $7 Members back issues; $10 Nonmembers back issues. **URL:** http://www.ifai.com/inventory/intents-magazine-back-issues. **Remarks:** Accepts advertising. **Circ:** (Not Reported).

18772 ■ The International Journal OF Clinical Acupuncture
American Academy of Acupuncture and Oriental Medicine
1925 County Road B2 W
Roseville, MN 55113-2703
Phone: (651)631-0204
Fax: (651)631-0361
Freq: Quarterly. **Alt. Formats:** PDF. **URL:** http://www.aaaom.edu/selected-publications; http://www.allertonpress.com/cgi/journal.pl?jid=4. **Remarks:** Adver-

tising not accepted. **Circ:** (Not Reported).

18773 ■ Marine Fabricator
TARP Association
1801 County Road B W
Roseville, MN 55113
Phone: (651)225-6926
Publisher's E-mail: generalinfo@ifai.com
Magazine covering marine fabrication industry. **Freq:** Bimonthly. **Trim Size:** 8 1/4 X 10 7/8. **Key Personnel:** Susan Niemi, Publisher, phone: (651)225-6984; Chris Tschida, Director, Editorial, phone: (651)225-6970, fax: (651)225-6966. **ISSN:** 1079--8250 (print). **Subscription Rates:** $24 Members; $54 Nonmembers. **URL:** http://marinefabricatormag.com; http://www.ifai.com/publications/marinefab. **Ad Rates:** BW $4085. **Remarks:** Accepts advertising. **Circ:** 5,000.

18774 ■ Northern Gardener
Minnesota State Horticultural Society
2705 Lincoln Dr.
Roseville, MN 55113
Phone: (651)643-3601
Fax: (651)643-3638
Free: 800-676-6747
Publication E-mail: info@northerngardener.org
Gardening information magazine and horticulture. **Freq:** 9/year. **Print Method:** Sheet fed. **Trim Size:** 8 3/8 x 10 7/8. **Cols./Page:** 3. **Col. Width:** 26 nonpareils. **Col. Depth:** 129 agate lines. **Key Personnel:** Lynn M. Steiner, Editor; Terri Goodfellow-Heyer, Director, Contact. **ISSN:** 0026-5500 (print). **Subscription Rates:** $62 Individuals level 1 ; $114 Individuals level 2. **URL:** http://www.northerngardener.org. **Formerly:** Minnesota Horticulturist. **Ad Rates:** BW $790; 4C $1050; PCI $.65. **Remarks:** Accepts advertising. **Circ:** ‡60,000.

RUSHFORD

SE MN. Fillmore Co. 19 mi. S. of Winona. Residential. Farm marketing. Dairy, hogs, beef, corn, soybeans.

18775 ■ Tri-County Record
Tri-County Publishing Inc.
300 S Mill St.
Rushford, MN 55971
Phone: (507)864-7700
Fax: (507)864-2356
Publication E-mail: info@bluffcountrynews.com
Community newspaper. **Freq:** Weekly (Thurs.). **Print Method:** Offset. **Trim Size:** 14 x 22 1/2. **Cols./Page:** 6. **Col. Width:** 12.5 picas. **Col. Depth:** 301 agate lines. **Key Personnel:** Darlene J. Schober, Publisher; Myron J. Schober, Publisher. **USPS:** 639-340. **URL:** http://www.bluffcountrynews.com/Content/Default/Rushford-area-news/-3/556. **Ad Rates:** BW $537; SAU $5; PCI $4.35. **Remarks:** Accepts advertising. **Circ:** **1612**.

18776 ■ Tri-County Record Special Edition
Tri-County Publishing Inc.
300 S Mill St.
Rushford, MN 55971
Phone: (507)864-7700
Fax: (507)864-2356
Publisher's E-mail: tricopub@rushford.net
Shopper. **Freq:** Monthly. **Trim Size:** 14 x 22 1/2. **Cols./Page:** 6. **Col. Width:** 2 3/16 inches. **Col. Depth:** 21 1/2 inches. **Key Personnel:** Myron J. Schober, Publisher; Darlene J. Schober, Publisher. **Subscription Rates:** $32 Individuals; $36 Elsewhere in U.S. **URL:** http://bluffcountrynews.com/Content/Default/Rushford-area-news/-3/556. **Ad Rates:** SAU $6.24; PCI $5.65; BW $701.76. **Remarks:** Accepts advertising. **Circ:** Paid 1700.

SAINT ANTHONY

SE MN. Stearns Co. 15 mi. NW of Maplewood. Residential.

18777 ■ The St. Anthony Bulletin
Lillie Suburban Newspapers
2515 E 7th Ave. N
Saint Paul, MN 55109
Phone: (651)777-8800
Fax: (651)777-8288
Local newspaper. **Freq:** Weekly (Wed.). **Print Method:** Offset. Uses mats. **Trim Size:** Broadsheet. **Cols./Page:** 6. **Col. Width:** 21 nonpareils. **Col. Depth:** 294 agate lines. **Key Personnel:** Mary Lee Hagert, Executive Editor, phone: (651)748-7820; Holly Wenzel, Managing Editor, phone: (651)748-7811; Laurie Young, Manager, Circulation, phone: (651)777-8800. **Subscription Rates:** $34.95 Individuals; $29.95 Individuals senior citizen. **URL:** http://www.bulletin-news.com/articles/st-anthony-bulletin-news. **Ad Rates:** BW $2734.20; SAU $22.70; PCI $31.50. **Remarks:** Accepts advertising. **Circ:** Paid ‡10, Free ‡2,137, Combined ‡2,147.

SAINT CHARLES

SE MN. Winona Co. 28 mi. SW of Winona. Near Whitewater State Park. Stock, dairy, poultry, grain farms.

18778 ■ Press
St. Charles Press
924 Whitewater Ave.
Saint Charles, MN 55972
Phone: (507)932-3663
Fax: (507)932-5537
Publication E-mail: scpress@hbcsc.net
Newspaper. **Founded:** 1898. **Freq:** Weekly (Tues.). **Print Method:** Offset. **Cols./Page:** 6. **Col. Width:** 28 nonpareils. **Col. Depth:** 301 agate lines. **Key Personnel:** Tim Mack, Publisher; Susan Benedett, Editor. **Subscription Rates:** $20 Individuals. **Mailing address:** PO Box 617, Saint Charles, MN 55972. **Ad Rates:** GLR $.245; PCI $7.60. **Remarks:** Accepts advertising. **Circ:** 1511.

SAINT CLOUD

C MN. Stearns Co. On Mississippi River, 67 mi. NW of Minneapolis. St. Cloud State University. Corrugated boxes, auto specialties, truck bodies, boats, freezers, paper, wire products,tools, milling and ground feeds, meat, plastic, concrete, foundry products, sashes, doors, beverages, sporting goods, Granite quarries. Stock, dairy, poultry, grain farms. Metalworking, railroad shops.

18779 ■ Cybernetics & Human Knowing: A Journal of Second Order Cybernetics & Cyber-Semiotics
International Center for Information Ethics
720 4th Ave.
720 4th Ave. So.
St. Cloud State University
Saint Cloud, MN 56301
Peer-reviewed journal covering articles on semiotics (cybersemiotics). **Freq:** Quarterly. **Key Personnel:** Soren Brier, Editor-in-Chief, phone: (45)381 53246; Jeanette Bopry, Associate Editor. **ISSN:** 0907--0877 (print); **EISSN:** 1756--6177 (electronic). **Subscription Rates:** £69.30 Individuals per volume; £152.25 Institutions online only; per volume; £186.90 Institutions online and print; per volume. **URL:** http://www.imprint.co.uk/product/cybernetics-human-knowing. **Remarks:** Advertising not accepted. **Circ:** (Not Reported).

18780 ■ Electronic Journal on Information Systems in Developing Countries: Journal for practitioners, teachers, researchers and policy makers
International Center for Information Ethics
720 4th Ave.
720 4th Ave. So.
St. Cloud State University
Saint Cloud, MN 56301
Journal covering knowledge, experience, development, implementation, management, evaluation of information systems and technologies in developing countries. **Key Personnel:** Roger Harris, Editor-in-Chief; Sajda Qureshi, Advisor; Robert M. Davison, Editor-in-Chief. **ISSN:** 1681--4835 (print). **URL:** http://www.ejisdc.org/ojs2/index.php/ejisdc. **Remarks:** Advertising not accepted. **Circ:** (Not Reported).

18781 ■ International Review of Information Ethics
International Center for Information Ethics
720 4th Ave.
720 4th Ave. So.
St. Cloud State University
Saint Cloud, MN 56301
The International Journal of Information Ethics (IRIE) - formerly IJIE, renamed due to a name similarity with another information ethics journal - is the official journal of the International Center for Information Ethics (ICIE) and envisions an international as well as intercultural discussion focusing on the ethical impacts of information technology on human practices and thinking, social interaction, and other areas of science and research. **Freq:** Semiannual. **Key Personnel:** Prof. Rafael Capurro, Editor-in-Chief; Prof. Johannes, Britz, Advisor; Prof. Thomas Hausmanninger, Editor; Prof. Nakada Makoto, Editor; Dr. Felix Weil, Editor. **ISSN:** 1614--1687 (print). **Subscription Rates:** Free. **URL:** http://www.i-r-i-e.net. **Formerly:** International Journal of Information Ethics. **Circ:** (Not Reported).

18782 ■ Journal of the Society of Christian Ethics
Society of Christian Ethics
PO Box 5126
Saint Cloud, MN 56302-5126
Phone: (320)253-5407
Fax: (320)252-6984
Journal comprising of scholarly papers, book reviews, and advertisements regarding Christian ethics. **Freq:** Semiannual. **Key Personnel:** Kathryn Blanchard, Editor. **ISSN:** 1540--7942 (print). **Subscription Rates:** Included in membership. **URL:** http://scethics.org/journal. **Remarks:** Accepts advertising. **Circ:** (Not Reported).

18783 ■ St. Cloud Times
St. Cloud Newspapers Inc.
3000 N 7th St.
Saint Cloud, MN 56302-0768
Phone: (320)255-8776
Fax: (320)255-8775
Free: 877-424-4921
Publisher's E-mail: obits@stcloudtimes.com
General newspaper. **Founded:** 1861. **Freq:** Daily (morn.). **Print Method:** Offset. **Trim Size:** 22 3/4 x 13 5/8. **Cols./Page:** 6. **Col. Width:** 25 nonpareils. **Col. Depth:** 301 agate lines. **Key Personnel:** John Bodette, Executive Editor, phone: (320)255-8760; Sue Halena, Managing Editor, phone: (320)255-8777. **Subscription Rates:** $22 Individuals print, monday-sunday, per month; $16.50 Individuals print, thursday-sunday, per month; $14 Individuals print, saturday and sunday, per month; $12 Individuals digital only, per month. **URL:** http://www.sctimes.com. **Formerly:** St. Cloud Daily Times. **Mailing address:** PO Box 768, Saint Cloud, MN 56302-0768. **Ad Rates:** SAU $21.50; GLR $2; BW $6842.16; 4C $7391.26; PCI $53.04. **Remarks:** Accepts advertising. **Circ:** Mon.-Fri. ★**27,079**, Sun. ★**36,413**, Sat. ★**29,901**.

18784 ■ Surveillance & Society: The Fully Peer-Reviewed Transdisciplinary Online Surveillance Studies Journal
International Center for Information Ethics
720 4th Ave.
720 4th Ave. So.
St. Cloud State University
Saint Cloud, MN 56301
Journal covering surveillance studies. **Freq:** Quarterly. **Key Personnel:** Dr. David Murakami Wood, Editor-in-Chief. **ISSN:** 1477--7487 (print). **URL:** http://ojs.library.queensu.ca/index.php/surveillance-and-society/index. **Remarks:** Advertising not accepted. **Circ:** (Not Reported).

18785 ■ University Chronicle
St. Cloud State University
720 4th Ave. S
Saint Cloud, MN 56301-4498
Phone: (320)308-0121
Collegiate newspaper. **Freq:** Semiweekly weekly in summers/schedule exceptions during academic breaks. **Cols./Page:** 5. **Col. Width:** 22 nonpareils. **Col. Depth:** 210 agate lines. **Key Personnel:** Jun-Kai Teoh, Editor-in-Chief; Michael Runyon, Editor. **USPS:** 121-580. **Subscription Rates:** $12 Individuals fall semester; $12 Individuals spring semester; $12 Individuals summer semester; $25 Individuals fall, spring, and summer. **URL:** http://www.universitychronicle.net. **Formerly:** SCS Chronicle. **Ad Rates:** BW $640. **Remarks:** Accepts advertising. **Circ:** Free ‡7,000.

18786 ■ The Visitor
Diocese of Saint Cloud
305 7th Ave. N
Saint Cloud, MN 56302
Phone: (320)251-3022
Fax: (320)251-0424
Publication E-mail: editor@stcloudvisitor.org
Official newspaper (tabloid) of the Catholic Diocese of St. Cloud. **Founded:** 1938. **Freq:** Weekly. **Print Method:**

Circulation: ★ = AAM; △ or • = BPA; ♦ = CAC; ❑ = VAC; ⊕ = PO Statement; ‡ = Publisher's Report; Boldface figures = sworn; Light figures = estimated.

Offset. **Trim Size:** 11 x 15. **Cols./Page:** 5. **Col. Width:** 11 picas. **Col. Depth:** 210 agate lines. **Key Personnel:** Joe Towalski, Editor; Rose Kruger-Fuchs, Manager, Advertising. **Subscription Rates:** $18 Individuals. **URL:** http://visitor.stcdio.org. **Formerly**: St. Cloud Visitor. **Mailing address:** PO Box 1068, Saint Cloud, MN 56302. **Ad Rates:** BW $900; 4C $1,200; PCI $12. **Remarks:** Accepts advertising. **Circ:** ‡45500.

18787 ■ KCLD-FM - 104.7
619 W St. Germain
Saint Cloud, MN 56302
Phone: (320)251-1450
Fax: (320)251-8952
Email: studio@1047kcld.com
Format: Music of Your Life. **Owner:** Leighton Broadcasting, 619 W St. Germain, Saint Cloud, MN 56301, Ph: (320)251-1450, Fax: (320)251-8952. **Founded:** 1948. **Operating Hours**: Continuous. **ADI**: Minneapolis-St. Paul, MN. **Wattage**: 100,000. **Ad Rates:** Advertising accepted; rates available upon request. **URL:** http://www.1047kcld.com.

18788 ■ KCML-FM - 99.9
619 W St. Germain St.
Saint Cloud, MN 56301-3640
Phone: (320)251-1450
Format: Adult Contemporary; Alternative/New Music/Progressive. **Operating Hours**: Continuous. **Wattage**: 2,900 ERP. **Ad Rates:** Advertising accepted; rates available upon request. **URL:** http://www.999morefm.com.

18789 ■ KKSR-FM - 96.7
640 SE Lincoln Ave.
Saint Cloud, MN 56304
Phone: (320)251-4422
Format: Album-Oriented Rock (AOR). **Networks:** Unistar. **Owner:** Townsquare Media Inc., 2000 Fifth Third Ctr. 511 Walnut St., Cincinnati, OH 45202, Ph: (513)651-1190. **Founded:** 1988. **Operating Hours**: Continuous. **ADI**: Minneapolis-St. Paul, MN. **Key Personnel:** Joey Hoops, Contact. **Wattage**: 50,000. **Ad Rates:** Noncommercial. **URL:** http://www.rev967.com.

18790 ■ KLZZ-FM - 103.7
640 SE Lincoln Ave.
Saint Cloud, MN 56304
Phone: (320)251-4422
Format: Classic Rock. **Key Personnel:** David Engberg, Gen. Mgr., david.engberg@townsquaremedia.com; Pete Hanson, District Mgr., pete@1037theloon.com; Steve Lahr, Dir. of Sales, steve.lahr@townsquaremedia.com. **Ad Rates:** Noncommercial. **URL:** http://www.1037theloon.com.

18791 ■ KMXK-FM - 94.9
629 Lincoln Ave. NE
Saint Cloud, MN 56304
Phone: (320)251-5695
Format: Adult Contemporary. **Key Personnel:** David Engberg, Gen. Mgr., david.engberg@townsquaremedia.com; Steve Lahr, Dir. of Sales, steve.lahr@townsquaremedia.com. **Ad Rates:** Noncommercial. **URL:** http://www.mix949.com.

18792 ■ K19BG - 19
PO Box A
Santa Ana, CA 92711
Phone: (714)832-2950
Free: 888-731-1000
Owner: Trinity Broadcasting Network Inc., PO Box A, Santa Ana, CA 92711, Ph: (714)832-2950, Free: 888-731-1000. **URL:** http://www.tbn.org.

18793 ■ KNSI-AM - 1450
619 West St. Germain
Saint Cloud, MN 56301
Phone: (320)251-1450
Format: News; Talk. **Networks:** NBC; Mutual Broadcasting System. **Founded:** 1938. **Operating Hours**: Continuous. **ADI**: Minneapolis-St. Paul, MN. **Key Personnel:** Doug Rice, Gen. Sales Mgr. **Wattage**: 1,000. **URL:** http://knsiradio.com/contact/map-and-directions.

18794 ■ KVSC-FM - 88.1
720 4th Ave. S
27 Stewart Hall
Saint Cloud, MN 56301-4442
Phone: (320)308-5872
Fax: (320)308-5337
Email: info@kvsc.org
Format: Full Service. **Owner:** St. Cloud State University, 720 4th Ave. S, Saint Cloud, MN 56301-4498, Ph: (320)308-0121. **Founded:** May 1967. **Operating Hours**: Continuous. **Key Personnel:** Jo McMullen-Boyer, Station Mgr.; Jim Gray, Dir. of Operations, jim@kvsc.org. **Wattage:** 16,500 ERP V. **Ad Rates:** Advertising accepted; rates available upon request. **URL:** http://www.kvsc.org.

18795 ■ KXSS-AM - 1390
640 SE Lincoln Ave.
Saint Cloud, MN 56304
Phone: (320)257-7195
Format: Sports. **Owner:** Regent Broadcasting of St. Cloud, 640 SE Lincoln Ave, St Cloud, MN. **Ad Rates:** Noncommercial. **URL:** http://www.1390thefan.com.

18796 ■ KZPK-FM - 98.9
619 W St. Germain St.
Saint Cloud, MN 56302-1458
Phone: (320)251-1450
Fax: (320)251-8952
Format: Country. **Key Personnel:** Matt Senne, Prog. Dir. **Wattage:** 24,000. **Ad Rates:** Noncommercial. **URL:** http://www.wildcountry99.com.

18797 ■ WJON-AM - 1240
640 SE Lincoln Ave.
Saint Cloud, MN 56304
Phone: (320)251-4422
Format: News; Talk. **Networks:** ABC; Minnesota News. **Owner:** Townsquare Media Inc., 240 Greenwich Ave., Greenwich, CT 06830-6507, Ph: (203)861-0900. **Founded:** 1950. **Operating Hours**: Continuous. **ADI**: Minneapolis-St. Paul, MN. **Key Personnel:** Jim Maurice, News Dir.; David Engberg, Gen. Mgr., david.engberg@townsquaremedia.com; Steve Lahr, Dir. of Sales, steve.lahr@townsquaremedia.com. **Wattage**: 1,000. **Ad Rates:** $10-38 for 30 seconds. **URL:** http://www.wjon.com.

18798 ■ WWJO-FM - 98.1
640 SE Lincoln Ave.
Saint Cloud, MN 56304
Phone: (320)252-9897
Format: Country. **Networks:** ABC; Minnesota News. **Owner:** Townsquare Media Inc., 240 Greenwich Ave., Greenwich, CT 06830-6507, Ph: (203)861-0900. **Founded:** 1970. **Operating Hours**: Continuous. **ADI**: Minneapolis-St. Paul, MN. **Key Personnel:** David Engberg, Gen. Mgr.; Steve Lahr, Dir. of Sales; Jay Caldwell, Contact; Tim Lyon, Contact. **Wattage**: 100,000 ERP. **Ad Rates:** Noncommercial. $13-42 for 30 seconds. $6.80-$27 for 30 seconds. Combined advertising rates available with WJON-AM: $10.55-$38.05 for 30 seconds. **URL:** http://www.98country.com.

SAINT FRANCIS

18799 ■ WYRQ-FM - 92.1
25801 Nacre St. NW
Saint Francis, MN 55070
Phone: (612)632-2992
Format: Contemporary Country; Agricultural. **Networks:** NBC; Minnesota News. **Owner:** Jack Hansen, 2111 Cypress Rd., Saint Cloud, MN 56303, Ph: (612)632-2573. **Founded:** 1980. **Operating Hours**: Continuous. **Key Personnel:** Damian Dupre, Dir. of Programs; Pete Brondos, Sports Dir; Jack Hansen, Contact; Steve Van Slooten, Contact; Kim Spitzka, Contact. **Wattage**: 3,000. **Ad Rates:** $5.50-7 for 15 seconds; $7.50-9.75 for 30 seconds; $9.75-14.50 for 60 seconds.

SAINT JAMES

SC MN. Watonwan Co. 39 mi. SW of Mankato. Manufactures precision tools. Chrome plating, metal fabrication company, Frozen food processing, poultry packing plant. Diversified farming. Agriculture.

18800 ■ Plaindealer: St. James Plaindealer Serving Watonwan County, MN
GateHouse Media Inc.
604 1st Ave. S
Saint James, MN 56081
Phone: (507)375-3161
Community newspaper. **Freq:** Weekly (Thurs.). **Print Method:** Web. **Cols./Page:** 6. **Col. Width:** 12 picas. **Col. Depth:** 21 1/2 inches. **Key Personnel:** Duane Durheim, Publisher; Deb Melheim, Receptionist, Specialist, Circulation; Rhonda Miller, Bookkeeper, Office Manager; Kyle Nordhausen, Advertising Representative; Hal G. Senal, Writer. **Subscription Rates:** $57 Individuals Watonwan County & surrounding counties; $65 Out of area other Minnesota counties; $72 Elsewhere in the United States; $42.75 Students September-May, anywhere in the United States. **URL:** http://www.stjamesnews.com. **Mailing address:** PO Box 67, Saint James, MN 56081. **Ad Rates:** BW $877; 4C $1057; SAU $6.80; PCI $6.80. **Remarks:** Accepts advertising. **Circ:** ‡2,790.

SAINT LOUIS PARK

SEC MN. Hennepin Co. 6 mi. SW of Minneapolis.

18801 ■ EI Digest: Hazardous Waste Market Place
Environmental Information Ltd.
7515 Wayzata Blvd. Ste. 13
Saint Louis Park, MN 55426
Phone: (952)831-2473
Fax: (952)831-6550
Publisher's E-mail: digest@envirobiz.com
Journal covering issues on industrial and hazardous waste management. **Freq:** Weekly. **Print Method:** Online Access Only. **Key Personnel:** Cary L. Perket, Contact. **URL:** http://envirobiz.com/ei-digest-fyi-hazardous-universal-waste.html. **Mailing address:** PO Box 390266, Saint Louis Park, MN 55426. **Remarks:** Advertising not accepted. **Circ:** (Not Reported).

18802 ■ Family Times
Family Times Inc.
PO Box 16422
Saint Louis Park, MN 55416
Phone: (952)922-6186
Publisher's E-mail: info@familytimesinc.com
Parenting magazine. **Freq:** Semiannual. **Print Method:** Web press. **Trim Size:** 11 1/2 x 14. **Cols./Page:** 4. **Col. Width:** 2 3/8 inches. **Col. Depth:** 12 3/8 inches. **Key Personnel:** Felicia Schaefer, Associate Publisher, Director, Sales; Thomas Winninger, Publisher; Annie O'Brien, Editor. **Ad Rates:** BW $1,600; 4C $1,900. **Remarks:** Accepts advertising. **Circ:** 25000.

18803 ■ KDWB-FM - 101.3
1600 Utica Ave. S, Ste. 400
Saint Louis Park, MN 55416
Phone: (651)989-5392
Fax: (952)417-3001
Format: Contemporary Hit Radio (CHR). **Owner:** iHeartMedia Inc., 200 E Basse Rd., San Antonio, TX 78209, Ph: (210)832-3314. **Founded:** 1959. **Formerly**: WYOO-FM. **Operating Hours**: Continuous; 100% local. **Wattage**: 100,000. **Ad Rates:** Advertising accepted; rates available upon request. **URL:** http://www.kdwb.com.

18804 ■ KDXL-FM - 106.5
6425 W 33rd St.
Saint Louis Park, MN 55426
Phone: (952)928-6000
Fax: (952)928-6020
Email: info@slpschools.org
Format: Alternative/New Music/Progressive; Rap; Top 40. **Founded:** 1978. **Key Personnel:** Dick Johnson, Contact; Dick Johnson, Contact. **Wattage**: 010. **URL:** http://rschooltoday.com/html.

18805 ■ KEEY-FM - 102.1
1600 Utica Ave. S, Ste. 400
Saint Louis Park, MN 55416
Phone: (952)417-3000
Fax: (952)417-3001
Format: Country. **Owner:** iHeartMedia Inc., 200 E Basse Rd., San Antonio, TX 78209, Ph: (210)832-3314. **Founded:** 1983. **Operating Hours**: Continuous. **Key Personnel:** Gregg Swedberg, Dir. of Programs, greggswedberg@clearchannel.com. **Wattage**: 100,000. **Ad Rates:** Noncommercial. **URL:** http://www.k102.com//main.html.

18806 ■ KQQL-FM - 107.9
1600 Utica Ave. S, Ste. 400
Saint Louis Park, MN 55416
Phone: (651)989-2020
Format: Oldies. **Owner:** iHeartMedia Inc., 200 E Basse Rd., San Antonio, TX 78209, Ph: (210)832-3314. **Founded:** 1988. **Operating Hours**: Continuous. **ADI**: Minneapolis-St. Paul, MN. **Key Personnel:** Ken Brady, Gen. Sales Mgr. **Local Programs**: *Twin Cities Insight*,

Sunday 10:00 p.m. - 10:30 p.m. **Wattage**: 100,000. **Ad Rates:** Advertising accepted; rates available upon request. **URL:** http://www.kool108.com.

18807 ■ Twin Cities News Talk - 100.3
1600 Utica Ave. S, Ste. 500
Saint Louis Park, MN 55416
Phone: (952)417-3000
Fax: (952)417-3001
Format: News; Talk. **Owner:** iHeartMedia Inc., 200 E Basse Rd., San Antonio, TX 78209, Ph: (210)832-3314. **Operating Hours**: Continuous. **Ad Rates:** Advertising accepted; rates available upon request. **URL:** http://www.twincitiesnewstalk.com//main.html.

SAINT PAUL

SE MN. Ramsey Co. On Mississippi River, adjacent to Minneapolis. The State Capital. Printing and transportation center. Science Museum. Como Park. Educational center. University of Minnesota Agricultural College; Hamline University; Macalester College; bethel College, College of St. Thomas, Concordia College, Saint Paul Seminary, William Mitchell College of Law, College of St. Catherine, Saint Paul Bible College. Zoological Gardens. McKnight Omni-Theatre. Largest livestock market and meat-packing center in the country. Manufactures hoists and derricks, rugs. Computer, electronics & other specialized fields. Recreational activities area.

18808 ■ American Cake Decorating
Grace McNamara Inc.
2594 Rice St.
Saint Paul, MN 55113
Publisher's E-mail: info@wf-vision.com
Consumer magazine covering cake decoration. **Freq:** Bimonthly. **Print Method:** Web offset. **Trim Size:** 8.125 x 10.875. **Key Personnel:** Grace McNamara, Publisher. **ISSN:** 1094--8732 (print). **Subscription Rates:** $28 Individuals /year (print and online); $50 Two years print and online; $19.95 Individuals /year (online only). **URL:** http://www.americancakedecorating.com. **Ad Rates:** BW $1870; 4C $2340. **Remarks:** Accepts advertising. **Circ:** Paid 12000.

18809 ■ American Catholic Philosophical Quarterly
Philosophy Documentation Center
University of St. Thomas
2115 Summit Ave., JCR 241
Saint Paul, MN 55105-1096
Phone: (651)962-5000
Publication E-mail: acpq@stthomas.edu
Peer-reviewed journal featuring scholarly articles, topical discussions, and book reviews dealing with all philosophical areas and approaches. **Freq:** Quarterly plus supplement. **Print Method:** Letterpress. **Trim Size:** 6 x 9. **Cols./Page:** 1. **Col. Width:** 48 nonpareils. **Col. Depth:** 91 agate lines. **Key Personnel:** Christopher Toner, Associate Editor; David Clemenson, Editor; Ann M. Hale, Managing Editor. **ISSN:** 1051--3558 (print); **EISSN:** 2153--8441 (electronic). **Subscription Rates:** $80 Institutions print; $231 Institutions online; $277 Institutions print and online; $25 Individuals single print; $25 /issue for nonmembers. **URL:** http://www.pdcnet.org/acpq. **Formerly**: The New Scholastician. **Remarks:** Accepts advertising. **Circ:** ‡1800.

18810 ■ American Woodturner
American Association of Woodturners
222 Landmark Ctr.
75 5th St. W
Saint Paul, MN 55102-7704
Phone: (651)484-9094
Free: 877-595-9094
Freq: Bimonthly. **Subscription Rates:** Included in membership. **URL:** http://www.woodturner.org/?page=Journal. **Ad Rates:** 4C $1,823; BW $1,205. **Remarks:** Accepts advertising. **Circ:** 16500.

18811 ■ Biomaterials
Controlled Release Society
3340 Pilot Knob Rd.
Saint Paul, MN 55121
Phone: (651)454-7250
Fax: (651)454-0766
Publisher's E-mail: crs@scisoc.org
Peer-reviewed journal reporting on the science and application of biomaterials. **Freq:** 38/yr. **Key Personnel:** Prof. D.F. Williams, Editor-in-Chief; P. Ducheyne, Associate Editor. **ISSN:** 0142--9612 (print). **Subscription Rates:** $4557.60 Institutions online; €9114 Institutions print; $6836.40 Individuals online. **URL:** http://www.journals.elsevier.com/biomaterials; http://www.controlledreleasesociety.org/publications/Pages/Biomaterials.aspx; http://www.sciencedirect.com/science/journal/01429612. **Remarks:** Accepts advertising. **Circ:** (Not Reported).

18812 ■ Brewers Digest
Brewers Digest
PO Box 16545
Saint Paul, MN 55116-0545
Phone: (651)293-0937
Magazine serving the brewing industry. **Founded:** 1926. **Freq:** Monthly. **Print Method:** Offset. **Trim Size:** 8 1/4 x 11 1/4. **Cols./Page:** 3. **Col. Width:** 26 nonpareils. **Col. Depth:** 140 agate lines. **Key Personnel:** Tom Volke, Publisher; Mike Urseth, Editor-in-Chief, Publisher, Editor. **Subscription Rates:** $50 Individuals; $100 Two years. **URL:** http://www.brewersdigest.net; http://brewersdigest.net/. **Ad Rates:** 4C $1,266; BW $726. **Remarks:** Accepts advertising. **Circ:** Paid ‡2759, Non-paid ‡119.

18813 ■ The Catholic Spirit: News with a Catholic Heart
The Catholic Spirit Publishing Co.
244 Dayton Ave.
Saint Paul, MN 55102-9882
Phone: (651)291-4444
Fax: (651)251-7789
Publication E-mail: catholicspirit@archspm.org
Catholic publication. **Freq:** Biweekly Thursday. **Print Method:** Offset. **Cols./Page:** 4. **Col. Width:** 30 nonpareils. **Col. Depth:** 196 agate lines. **Key Personnel:** Rev. John C. Nienstedt, Publisher; Pat Norby, Editor; Bob Zyskowski, Associate Publisher; Joe Towalski, Editor, phone: (651)291-4455. **USPS:** 093-580. **Subscription Rates:** $29.95 Individuals; $24.95 Individuals senior. **URL:** http://thecatholicspirit.com. **Formerly**: Catholic Bulletin. **Ad Rates:** GLR $8. **Remarks:** Accepts classified advertising. **Circ:** Paid 87,000, ‡82,083.

18814 ■ Cereal Chemistry
AACC International
3340 Pilot Knob Rd.
Saint Paul, MN 55121-2055
Phone: (651)454-7250
Fax: (651)454-0766
Publisher's E-mail: aacc@scisoc.org
Journal focusing on cereal chemistry and research on raw materials, processes and products in the cereals area. **Freq:** Bimonthly. **Print Method:** Offset. **Trim Size:** 8 1/2 x 11. **Cols./Page:** 2. **Col. Width:** 21 picas. **Col. Depth:** 138 agate lines. **Key Personnel:** Jan A. Delcour, Senior Editor; Carl R. Hoseney, Editor-in-Chief. **ISSN:** 0009-0352 (print). **Subscription Rates:** $882 Individuals print; $922 Elsewhere. **URL:** http://cerealchemistry.aaccnet.org/journal/cchem. **Ad Rates:** BW $3,165, full page; BW $2,760, half page - island; BW $2,645, half page - horizontal or vertical. **Remarks:** Accepts advertising. **Circ:** Paid ‡3260, Controlled ‡26.

18815 ■ Cereal Foods World
AACC International
3340 Pilot Knob Rd.
Saint Paul, MN 55121-2055
Phone: (651)454-7250
Fax: (651)454-0766
Publisher's E-mail: aacc@scisoc.org
Journal for cereal foods industry focusing on the use, processing, and marketing of cereal grains and cereal-based foods. **Freq:** Bimonthly. **Print Method:** Letterpress and offset. **Trim Size:** 8 1/2 x 11. **Cols./Page:** 3 and 2. **Col. Width:** 26 and 40 nonpareils. **Col. Depth:** 140 agate lines. **Key Personnel:** Steven Nelson, Publisher; Jordana Anker, Managing Editor. **ISSN:** 0146-6283 (print). **Subscription Rates:** $465 U.S. /year; $549 Elsewhere /year. **URL:** http://www.aaccnet.org/publications/plexus/cfw/Pages/default.aspx. **Ad Rates:** BW $1,865; 4C $970; PCI $45. **Remarks:** Advertising accepted; rates available upon request. **Circ:** Paid ‡4231, Controlled ‡303.

18816 ■ Cycle Sport America
Time Inc.
2225 University Ave.
Saint Paul, MN 55114
Free: 888-329-2533
Publication E-mail: info@cyclesportmag.com
Magazine focusing on bicycling. **Freq:** 13/yr. **Key Personnel:** Keith Foster, Director, Publications. **Subscription Rates:** £48.99 Individuals print; £84.49 Two years print; £40.99 Individuals online. **URL:** http://www.cyclingweekly.co.uk/publication/cycle-sport. **Circ:** (Not Reported).

18817 ■ Dakota Collector
Dakota Postal History Society
PO Box 600039
Saint Paul, MN 55106
Journal covering postal history in the Dakotas. **Freq:** Quarterly. **Alt. Formats:** PDF. **URL:** http://dakotapostalhistorysociety.org/dakota_collector.html. **Ad Rates:** BW $20. **Remarks:** Accepts advertising. **Circ:** Combined 70.

18818 ■ East Side Review
Lillie Suburban Newspapers
2515 E 7th Ave. N
Saint Paul, MN 55109
Phone: (651)777-8800
Fax: (651)777-8288
Publication E-mail: eastside@lillienews.com
Community newspaper. **Freq:** Weekly (Mon.). **Print Method:** Offset. **Cols./Page:** 6. **Col. Width:** 21 nonpareils. **Col. Depth:** 294 agate lines. **Key Personnel:** Holly Wenzel, Managing Editor, phone: (651)748-7811; Mary Lee Hagert, Executive Editor, phone: (651)748-7820; Scott Nichols, Editor, phone: (651)748-7816. **Subscription Rates:** $34.95 Individuals; $29.95 Individuals senior citizen. **URL:** http://www.eastsidereviewnews.com; http://www.eastsidereviewnews.com/content/subscribe-east-side-review-print-edition. **Ad Rates:** BW $1,134; SAU $13.70; PCI $12.45. **Remarks:** Accepts advertising. **Circ:** Free ‡14119, Paid ‡28, Combined ‡14147.

18819 ■ Elysian Fields Quarterly: The Baseball Review
Knothole Publishing
PO Box 14385
Saint Paul, MN 55114-0385
Phone: (651)644-8558
Publisher's E-mail: info@efqreview.com
Journal which contains eclectic writings on baseball. Articles include opinion, history, fiction, poetry, scholarship, humor, trivia, art, illustrations, and book reviews. **Freq:** Quarterly. **Key Personnel:** Tom Goldstein, Publisher. **ISSN:** 1526--6346 (print). **Subscription Rates:** $25 U.S. /year; $32.50 Canada and Mexico /year; $48 Other countries /year; $47.50 Two years USA; $57.50 Canada and Mexico two years; $90 Other countries two years; $70 U.S. three years; $82.50 Canada and Mexico three years. **URL:** http://www.efqreview.com. **Formerly**: The Minneapolis Review of Baseball. **Ad Rates:** BW $295. **Remarks:** Accepts advertising. **Circ:** Paid ‡2000, Non-paid ‡150.

18820 ■ Experience Life: Being Healthy is a Revolutionary Act
Life Time Fitness Inc.
2145 Ford Pky., Ste. 105
Saint Paul, MN 55116
Phone: (952)947-0000
Fax: (651)690-2746
Magazine featuring health and fitness. **Freq:** 10/year. **Key Personnel:** David Schimke, Executive Editor; Pilar Gerasimo, Editor-in-Chief; Craig Cox, Managing Editor. **Subscription Rates:** $31.95 U.S. print, 2 years; $21.95 U.S. print, 1 year; $41.95 Canada print only, 2 years; $31.95 Canada print only, 1 year; $51.95 Other countries print only, 2 years; $41.95 Other countries print only, 1 year. **URL:** http://experiencelife.com. **Remarks:** Accepts advertising. **Circ:** (Not Reported).

18821 ■ Eyewitness
Contact Lens Society of America
2025 Woodlane Dr.
Saint Paul, MN 55125-2998
Phone: (703)437-5100
Fax: (703)437-0727
Free: 800-296-9776
Publisher's E-mail: clsa@clsa.info
Magazine covering developments in the contact lens industry. **Freq:** Quarterly. **Subscription Rates:** Included in membership. **URL:** http://www.clsa.info. **Remarks:**

Circulation: ★ = AAM; △ or • = BPA; ♦ = CAC; ❑ = VAC; ⊕ = PO Statement; ‡ = Publisher's Report; Boldface figures = sworn; Light figures = estimated.

Accepts advertising. **Circ:** (Not Reported).

18822 ■ International Journal of Pluralism and Economics Education
Inderscience Enterprises Ltd.
c/o Jack Reardon, Ed.-in-Ch.
Department of Management & Economics
School of Business, Hamline University
1536 Hewitt Ave., MS-A1740
Saint Paul, MN 55104
Publisher's E-mail: copyright@inderscience.com
Journal covering economics education and pluralism. **Freq:** Quarterly. **Key Personnel:** Jack Reardon, Editor-in-Chief. **ISSN:** 1757--5648 (print); **EISSN:** 1757--5656 (electronic). **Subscription Rates:** $685 Individuals print only - annual (includes surface mail); or online (for single user only); $928 Individuals print and online. **URL:** http://www.inderscience.com/jhome.php?jcode=ijpee. **Circ:** (Not Reported).

18823 ■ International Journal on World Peace
International Journal on World Peace
2700 University Ave. W
Saint Paul, MN 55114-1016
Phone: (612)644-2809
Fax: (612)644-0997
Academic journal on peace. **Freq:** Quarterly. **Key Personnel:** Gordon L. Anderson, Editor-in-Chief. **ISSN:** 0742--3640 (print). **Subscription Rates:** $40 Libraries annual; $30 Individuals annual; $25 Students, other countries annual, mail; $55 Other countries annual; $9 Single issue back issue. **Alt. Formats:** PDF. **URL:** http://www.ijwp.org. **Circ:** ‡10000.

18824 ■ Journal of the American Society of Brewing Chemists
American Society of Brewing Chemists
3340 Pilot Knob Rd.
Saint Paul, MN 55121-2097
Phone: (651)454-7250
Fax: (651)454-0766
Publisher's E-mail: asbc@scisoc.org
Freq: Quarterly. **Trim Size:** 8.5 x 11. **ISSN:** 0361--0470 (print). **Subscription Rates:** $344 Institutions print only; $361 Institutions, other countries print only. **Alt. Formats:** PDF. **URL:** http://www.asbcnet.org/publications/journal/Pages/default.aspx. **Ad Rates:** 4C $900. **Remarks:** Accepts advertising. **Circ:** (Not Reported).

18825 ■ Journal of Upland Conservation
Pheasants Forever
1783 Buerkle Cir.
Saint Paul, MN 55110
Phone: (651)773-2000
Fax: (651)773-5500
Free: 877-773-2070
Publisher's E-mail: contact@pheasantsforever.org
Journal featuring in-depth stories and top-notch photography of wildlife habitat, pheasants, pheasant hunting and bird dogs. **Remarks:** Advertising not accepted. **Circ:** (Not Reported).

18826 ■ Logos: A Journal of Catholic Thought and Culture
Philosophy Documentation Center
The University of St. Thomas
2115 Summit Ave., Mail No. 55-S
Saint Paul, MN 55105-1096
Publication E-mail: logos@stthomas.edu
Peer-reviewed interdisciplinary journal publishing articles about Christianity as it is rooted in and shaped by Catholicism. **Freq:** Quarterly. **Key Personnel:** Michael C. Jordan, Editor. **ISSN:** 1091--6687 (print); **EISSN:** 1533--791X (electronic). **Subscription Rates:** $42 Individuals print; $36 Students print; $64 Institutions print; $17 Institutions single issue; $11 Individuals single issue. **URL:** http://www.pdcnet.org/logos/Logos:-A-Journal-of-Catholic-Thought-and-Culture. **Circ:** (Not Reported).

18827 ■ The Mac Weekly: Macalester's Independent Student Newspaper Since 1914
Macalester College
1600 Grand Ave.
Saint Paul, MN 55105-1899
Phone: (651)696-6000
Free: 800-231-7974
Publisher's E-mail: webmaster@macalester.edu
Collegiate newspaper. **Freq:** Weekly (Thurs.). **Print Method:** Letterpress and offset. **Trim Size:** 11 x 16. **Cols./Page:** 5. **Col. Width:** 22 nonpareils. **Col. Depth:** 210 agate lines. **Key Personnel:** Sloane Peterson, Business Manager; Stef Steinbrenner, Managing Editor; Brian Griffin, Editor-in-Chief. **URL:** http://themacweekly.com. **Remarks:** Accepts advertising. **Circ:** ‡1,600, 2,000.

18828 ■ Maplewood Review
Lillie Suburban Newspapers
2515 E 7th Ave. N
Saint Paul, MN 55109
Phone: (651)777-8800
Fax: (651)777-8288
Local newspaper. **Freq:** Weekly (Wed.). **Print Method:** Offset. Uses mats. **Trim Size:** Broadsheet. **Cols./Page:** 6. **Col. Width:** 21 nonpareils. **Col. Depth:** 294 agate lines. **Key Personnel:** Mary Lee Hagert, Executive Editor, phone: (651)748-7820. **Subscription Rates:** $35.95 Individuals regular; $59.95 Two years regular; $70.95 Individuals three years, regular; $30.95 Individuals senior citizen; $55.95 Two years senior citizen; $64.95 Individuals three years, senior citizen. **URL:** http://www.review-news.com/. **Ad Rates:** SAU $22.70. **Remarks:** Accepts advertising. **Circ:** Free ‡7, Paid ‡579, Combined ‡586.

18829 ■ MBAA Technical Quarterly
Master Brewers Association of the Americas
3340 Pilot Knob Rd.
Saint Paul, MN 55121
Phone: (651)454-7250
Fax: (651)454-0766
Publisher's E-mail: mbaa@mbaa.com
Technical brewing magazine. **Freq:** Quarterly. **Print Method:** Offset. **Trim Size:** 8 1/2 x 11. **Cols./Page:** 2. **Col. Width:** 4 1/2 inches. **Col. Depth:** 10 1/2 inches. **Key Personnel:** Amy Hope, Publisher. **ISSN:** 0743--9407 (print). **Subscription Rates:** Included in membership. **Alt. Formats:** PDF; Print. **URL:** http://www.mbaa.com/publications/tq/Pages/default.aspx. **Remarks:** Accepts advertising. **Circ:** 3800.

18830 ■ Melpomene Journal
Melpomene Institute
550 Rice St., Ste. 104
Saint Paul, MN 55103
Publisher's E-mail: admin@melpomene.org
Freq: 3/year. **ISSN:** 1043--8734 (print). **Subscription Rates:** Included in membership. **Remarks:** Advertising not accepted. **Circ:** 2500.

18831 ■ Middle East Critique
Carfax Publishing
c/o Eric Hooglund, Ed.
Hamline University
Middle Eastern Studies, MB 211
1536 Hewitt Ave.
Saint Paul, MN 55104-1284
Publication E-mail: enquiry@tandf.co.uk
Promotes an academic and critical examination of the history and contemporary political, social, economic, and cultural aspects of Middle Eastern countries. **Freq:** 4/yr. **Key Personnel:** Eric Hooglund, Editor. **ISSN:** 1943-6149 (print). **Subscription Rates:** $693 Institutions print and online; $184 Individuals. **URL:** http://www.tandfonline.com/loi/ccri20#.VITh6dKUfIc. **Formerly:** Critique: Critical Middle Eastern Studies. **Remarks:** Advertising accepted; rates available upon request. **Circ:** (Not Reported).

18832 ■ Minnesota Conservation Volunteer
Department of Natural Resources
500 Lafayette Rd.
Saint Paul, MN 55155-4040
Phone: (651)296-6157
Free: 800-646-6367
Publication E-mail: lettertoeditor.mcv@state.mn.us
Government magazine covering conservation and the wise use of the natural resources in Minnesota. **Freq:** Bimonthly. **Print Method:** Web offset. **Trim Size:** 5 1/2 x 8. **Key Personnel:** Kathleen Weflen, Editor-in-Chief, phone: (651)259-5357; Susan Ryan, Manager, Circulation, phone: (651)259-5365; David Lent, Coordinator, phone: (651)259-5347. **USPS:** 129-880. **Subscription Rates:** Free. **URL:** http://www.dnr.state.mn.us/mcvmagazine/index.html. **Formerly:** The Minnesota Volunteer; The Conservation Volunteer. **Remarks:** Advertising not accepted. **Circ:** 135000.

18833 ■ Minnesota Grocer: Official Publication of the Minnesota Grocers Association
Minnesota Grocers Association
533 St. Clair Ave.
Saint Paul, MN 55102
Phone: (651)228-0973
Fax: (651)228-1949
Free: 800-966-8352
Publisher's E-mail: mga@mngrocers.com
Grocery trade magazine. **Freq:** Quarterly plus a directory. **Print Method:** Offset. **Trim Size:** 8 1/4 x 10 7/8. **Cols./Page:** 3 and 2. **Col. Width:** 26 and 40 nonpareils. **Col. Depth:** 140 agate lines. **Key Personnel:** Nancy Christensen, Editor; Jamie Pfuhl, President. **URL:** http://www.mngrocers.com/index.php/about/publications/. **Ad Rates:** BW $918; 4C $1395. **Remarks:** Advertising accepted; rates available upon request. **Circ:** ‡1,500.

18834 ■ Minnesota History
Minnesota Historical Society
345 W Kellogg Blvd.
Saint Paul, MN 55102
Phone: (651)259-3000
Fax: (651)296-9961
Free: 800-657-3773
Publisher's E-mail: collections@mnhs.org
Historical journal. **Freq:** Quarterly. **Key Personnel:** Anne R. Kaplan, Managing Editor, phone: (651)297-4462; Ann Regan, Director (Acting), Editor-in-Chief, phone: (651)259-3206. **ISSN:** 0026-5497 (print). **Subscription Rates:** $20 Individuals. **URL:** http://www.mnhs.org/market/mhspress/minnesotahistory/. **Remarks:** Advertising not accepted. **Circ:** ‡18,500.

18835 ■ Minnesota Legionnaire: Official Publication, Minnesota American Legion
Minnesota American Legion Publishing Co.
20 W 12th St., Rm. 300A
Saint Paul, MN 55155-2069
Phone: (651)291-1800
Fax: (651)291-1057
Publication E-mail: azdon@mnlegion.org
Membership newspaper. **Freq:** Monthly. **Print Method:** Offset. **Trim Size:** 11 1/2 x 15. **Cols./Page:** 6. **Col. Width:** 22 nonpareils. **Col. Depth:** 210 agate lines. **Key Personnel:** Tom Lannon, President; Jack Schulstad, Vice President; Al Zdon, Contact. **USPS:** 013-679. **Subscription Rates:** $10 Nonmembers. **Alt. Formats:** PDF. **URL:** http://www.mnlegion.org/html/legionnaire.html; http://www.mnnews.com/newspapers/legion.html. **Remarks:** Accepts advertising. **Circ:** ‡107,311.

18836 ■ Minnesota Women's Press
Minnesota Women's Press Inc.
970 Raymond Ave., Ste. 201
Saint Paul, MN 55114
Phone: (651)646-3968
Fax: (651)646-2186
Publisher's E-mail: women@womenspress.com
Feminist newspaper providing news coverage by and for women. **Freq:** Biweekly. **Trim Size:** 10 1/4 x 15. **Col. Width:** 1 7/8 inches. **Key Personnel:** Norma Smith Olson, Editor, Publisher; Kathy Magnuson, Editor, Publisher; Glenda Martin, Founder, Publisher; Mollie Hoben, Founder, Publisher. **Subscription Rates:** $28 Individuals; $53 Two years; $33 Canada and Mexico; $53 Other countries. **URL:** http://womenspress.com. **Ad Rates:** GLR $.95; BW $2,384; 4C $2,597; SAU $48.30; PCI $47.50. **Remarks:** Accepts advertising. **Circ:** 35000.

18837 ■ New Brighton-Mounds View Bulletin
Lillie Suburban Newspapers
2515 E 7th Ave. N
Saint Paul, MN 55109
Phone: (651)777-8800
Fax: (651)777-8288
Publication E-mail: review@lillienews.com
Local newspaper. **Freq:** Weekly (Wed.). **Print Method:** Letterpress and Offset Uses mats. **Trim Size:** Broadsheet. **Cols./Page:** 6. **Col. Width:** 21 nonpareils. **Col. Depth:** 294 agate lines. **Key Personnel:** Mary Lee Hagert, Executive Editor, phone: (651)748-7820. **Subscription Rates:** $34.95 Individuals; $29.95 Individuals senior citizen. **URL:** http://www.bulletin-news.com/articles/new-brighton-mounds-view-bulletin-news. **Formerly:** New Brighton Bulletin. **Ad Rates:** BW $2734; SAU $22.70; PCI $31.50. **Remarks:** Accepts advertising. **Circ:** (Not Reported).

18838 ■ The New Earth
The New Earth
244 Dayton Ave.
Saint Paul, MN 55102
Phone: (612)291-4453
Fax: (612)291-4460
Publication E-mail: news@fargodiocese.org
Catholic Diocese newspaper. **Freq:** Monthly 11/yr. **Print Method:** Offset. **Cols./Page:** 5. **Col. Width:** 24 nonpareils. **Col. Depth:** 182 agate lines. **Key Personnel:** Tanya Watterud, Editor; Samuel J. Aguila, Publisher. **Subscription Rates:** $9 Out of area. **URL:** http://www.fargodiocese.org/newearth2014. **Ad Rates:** BW $616; 4C $916; SAU $9.50; PCI $11. **Remarks:** Accepts advertising. **Circ:** 32000.

18839 ■ Oakdale-Lake Elmo Review
Lillie Suburban Newspapers
2515 E 7th Ave. N
Saint Paul, MN 55109
Phone: (651)777-8800
Fax: (651)777-8288
Local newspaper. **Freq:** Weekly (Wed.). **Print Method:** Offset Uses mats. **Trim Size:** Broadsheet. **Cols./Page:** 6. **Col. Width:** 21 nonpareils. **Col. Depth:** 294 agate lines. **Key Personnel:** Mary Lee Hagert, Executive Editor, phone: (651)748-7820. **Subscription Rates:** $35.95 Individuals; $59.95 Two years; $70.95 Individuals 3 years; $30.95 Individuals senior ceitizen; $55.95 Two years senior ceitizen; $64.95 Individuals 3 years; senior citizen. **URL:** http://www.lillienews.com/content/oakdale-lake-elmo-review-contacts. **Formerly**: Washington County Review. **Ad Rates:** SAU $22.70. **Remarks:** Accepts advertising. **Circ:** Free ‡7,686, Paid ‡191, Combined ‡7,877.

18840 ■ The Oracle
Hamline University
1536 Hewitt Ave.
Saint Paul, MN 55104-1284
Phone: (651)523-2800
Fax: (651)523-2458
Free: 800-753-9753
Publisher's E-mail: admission@hamline.edu
Collegiate newspaper. **Founded:** 1888. **Freq:** Weekly (Tues.) published on Tuesday. **Print Method:** Offset. **Trim Size:** Tabloid. **Cols./Page:** 5. **Key Personnel:** Eric Burgess, Editor-in-Chief; Anne Kuenzie, Managing Editor. **URL:** http://www.hamlineoracle.com; http://www.hamline.edu/offices/dean-of-students/student-media/oracle.html. **Remarks:** Accepts advertising. **Circ:** ‡1,600.

18841 ■ Outdoor America
Izaak Walton League of America Midwest Office
1619 Dayton Ave., Ste. 202
Saint Paul, MN 55104
Phone: (651)649-1446
Fax: (651)649-1494
Publication E-mail: oa@iwla.org
Freq: Quarterly. **Print Method:** Offset. **Trim Size:** 8 1/4 x 10 7/8. **Cols./Page:** 3. **Col. Width:** 27 nonpareils. **Col. Depth:** 135 agate lines. **Key Personnel:** David W. Hoskins, Executive Director. **ISSN:** 0021-3314 (print). **Subscription Rates:** Included in membership. **Alt. Formats:** PDF. **URL:** http://www.iwla.org/news-events/outdoor-america/about-outdoor-america; http://www.iwla.org/index.php?ht=display/ContentDetails/i/92581/pid/203; http://www.iwla.org/index.php?ht=d/Contents/contenttype_id/16/pid/203/order/crt#cat_id_2305. **Mailing address:** c/o Mr. Tracy Longenecker, Membership Officer1911 Scull St., Lebanon, PA 17046-2780. **Ad Rates:** BW $1150; 4C $1600. **Remarks:** Accepts advertising. **Circ:** 45000.

18842 ■ Pediatric Neurology
Mosby Inc.
University of Minnesota
Medical School
1821 University Ave. W, Ste. N-188
Saint Paul, MN 55104
Journal publishing peer-reviewed clinical and research articles covering all aspects of the developing nervous system. **Freq:** Monthly. **Key Personnel:** K.F. Swaiman, MD, Editor; J. Aicardi, Board Member; S. Ashwal, Associate Editor; C.S. Camfield, Board Member; G.N. Breningstall, Associate Editor; H.T. Chugani, Board Member; L.W. Brown, Board Member. **ISSN:** 0887--8994 (print). **Subscription Rates:** $682 Individuals; $1408.80 Institutions online; $1567 Institutions print. **URL:** http://www.journals.elsevier.com/pediatric-neurology. **Remarks:** Accepts advertising. **Circ:** (Not Reported).

18843 ■ Pheasants Forever Journal
Pheasants Forever
1783 Buerkle Cir.
Saint Paul, MN 55110
Phone: (651)773-2000
Fax: (651)773-5500
Free: 877-773-2070
Publisher's E-mail: contact@pheasantsforever.org
Journal for conservationist pheasant hunters. **Freq:** 5/year. **Print Method:** Web offset. **Trim Size:** 8 3/8 x 10 7/8. **Cols./Page:** 3. **Key Personnel:** Mark Herwig, Editor. **Subscription Rates:** Included in membership. **Ad Rates:** BW $3,310; 4C $5,110; PCI $135. **Remarks:** Accepts advertising. **Circ:** (Not Reported).

18844 ■ Phytopathology
American Phytopathological Society
3340 Pilot Knob Rd.
Saint Paul, MN 55121
Phone: (651)454-7250
Fax: (651)454-0766
Publisher's E-mail: aps@scisoc.org
Freq: Monthly. **Key Personnel:** Krishna Subbarao, Executive. **ISSN:** 0031- 949X (print). **Subscription Rates:** $895 Libraries & institutions; $1009 Elsewhere library and institutions. **URL:** http://www.apsnet.org/publications/phytopathology/Pages/default.aspx. **Remarks:** Advertising not accepted. **Circ:** (Not Reported).

18845 ■ The Posthorn: Journal of the Scandinavian Collectors Club
Scandinavian Collectors Club
PO Box 16213
Saint Paul, MN 55116-0213
Publication E-mail: palbright@wiche.edu
Journal covering philately, specifically Scandinavian stamps and postal history. **Freq:** Quarterly. **Trim Size:** 7 x 10. **Cols./Page:** 1. **Col. Width:** 6 inches. **Col. Depth:** 9 inches. **Key Personnel:** Paul Albright, Business Manager, Editor. **ISSN:** 0551--6897 (print). **Alt. Formats:** PDF. **URL:** http://www.scc-online.org/posthorn. **Remarks:** Advertising accepted; rates available upon request. **Circ:** (Not Reported).

18846 ■ Powder and Bulk Engineering
CSC Publishing Inc.
1155 Northland Dr.
Saint Paul, MN 55120
Phone: (651)287-5600
Fax: (651)287-5650
Journal serving chemical, food, plastics, pulp and paper, and electronic industries. **Freq:** Monthly. **Print Method:** Web. **Trim Size:** 8 1/8 x 10 7/8. **Key Personnel:** Kayla Carrigan, Associate Editor; Richard Cress, Publisher, phone: (651)287-5601, fax: (651)287-5650; Terry O'Neill, Editor; Katherine Davich, Senior Editor; Robert Harkin, Assistant Manager; Harry Myers, Assistant Manager. **ISSN:** 0897--6627 (print). **Subscription Rates:** Free. **URL:** http://www.powderbulk.com. **Ad Rates:** BW $5,350; 4C $7,250. **Remarks:** Accepts advertising. **Circ:** (Not Reported).

18847 ■ QRCA VIEWS
Qualitative Research Consultants Association
1000 Westgate Dr., Ste. 252
Saint Paul, MN 55114
Phone: (651)290-7491
Fax: (651)290-2266
Free: 888-674-7722
Publisher's E-mail: admin@qrca.org
Freq: Quarterly. **Subscription Rates:** Included in membership. **Alt. Formats:** Download; PDF. **URL:** http://www.qrca.org/?page=views_magazine. **Remarks:** Accepts advertising. **Circ:** (Not Reported).

18848 ■ Quail Forever Journal
Quail Forever
1783 Buerkle Cir.
Saint Paul, MN 55110
Phone: (651)773-2000
Free: 877-773-2070
Publisher's E-mail: contact@quailforever.org
Journal featuring cutting edge habitat improvement advice, exciting hunting features and coverage of conservation issues on state and national levels. **Freq:** Quarterly. **Key Personnel:** Mark Herwig, Editor. **Subscription Rates:** $35 Individuals per year. **Remarks:** Advertising not accepted. **Circ:** (Not Reported).

18849 ■ Qualelibet
International Society for Hildegard Von Bingen Studies
787 Iowa Ave. W
Saint Paul, MN 55117
Phone: (651)487-6357
Freq: Semiannual. **ISSN:** 1546--4520 (print). **Subscription Rates:** Included in membership. **URL:** http://www.hildegard-society.org/p/qualelibet.html. **Remarks:** Accepts advertising. **Circ:** (Not Reported).

18850 ■ Roseville Review
Lillie Suburban Newspapers
2515 E 7th Ave. N
Saint Paul, MN 55109
Phone: (651)777-8800
Fax: (651)777-8288
Local newspaper. **Freq:** Weekly (Tues.). **Print Method:** Offset Uses mats. **Trim Size:** Broadsheet. **Cols./Page:** 6. **Col. Width:** 21 nonpareils. **Col. Depth:** 294 agate lines. **Key Personnel:** Mary Lee Hagert, Executive Editor, phone: (651)748-7820. **Subscription Rates:** $34.95 Individuals; $29.95 Individuals senior citizen. **URL:** http://www.lillienews.com/content/roseville-little-canada-review-contacts. **Ad Rates:** SAU $14. **Remarks:** Accepts advertising. **Circ:** Free ‡14200, Paid ‡45, Combined ‡14245.

The St. Anthony Bulletin - See Saint Anthony

18851 ■ St. Paul Pioneer Press
Digital First Media
345 Cedar St.
Saint Paul, MN 55101
Phone: (651)222-1111
Free: 800-950-9080
Publication E-mail: infodesk@pioneerpress.com
General newspaper. **Freq:** Daily. **Print Method:** Offset. **Cols./Page:** 6. **Col. Width:** 26 nonpareils. **Col. Depth:** 294 agate lines. **Key Personnel:** Mike Burbac, Editor, phone: (651)228-5544; Mike Decaire, Editor, phone: (651)228-2125; Jen Westpfahl, Editor, phone: (651)228-5510. **Online:** Digital First Media Digital First Media. **Alt. Formats:** Handheld. **URL:** http://www.twincities.com. **Ad Rates:** BW $2,090; 4C $4,190. **Remarks:** Accepts advertising. **Circ:** Mon.-Fri. ★**193054**, Sun. ★**254010**, Sat. ★**163808**.

Shoreview-Arden Hills Bulletin - See Shoreview

18852 ■ South-West Review
Lillie Suburban Newspapers
2515 E 7th Ave. N
Saint Paul, MN 55109
Phone: (651)777-8800
Fax: (651)777-8288
Community newspaper. **Freq:** Weekly (Sun.). **Print Method:** Offset. **Trim Size:** Broadsheet. **Cols./Page:** 6. **Col. Width:** 21 nonpareils. **Col. Depth:** 294 agate lines. **Key Personnel:** Heather Edwards, Writer, phone: (651)748-7824; Derrick Knutson, Editor, phone: (651)748-7815; Holly Wenzel, Managing Editor, phone: (651)748-7811; Mary Lee Hagert, Executive Editor, phone: (651)748-7820. **ISSN:** 0038--4712 (print). **Subscription Rates:** $30 Individuals 1 year; $60 Individuals 2 years; $90 Individuals 3 years. **URL:** http://www.southwestreviewnews.com. **Ad Rates:** SAU $18. **Remarks:** Accepts advertising. **Circ:** Free ‡12316, Paid ‡34, Combined ‡12350.

18853 ■ SSP Journal of Sensory Studies
Society of Sensory Professionals
3340 Pilot Knob Rd.
Saint Paul, MN 55121
Phone: (651)454-7250
Fax: (651)454-0766
Publisher's E-mail: ssp@scisoc.org
Freq: Bimonthly. **Subscription Rates:** Included in membership. **URL:** http://sensorysociety.org/knowledge/Pages/Journal-Access.aspx. **Remarks:** Advertising not accepted. **Circ:** (Not Reported).

18854 ■ Tablets and Capsules
CSC Publishing Inc.
1155 Northland Dr.
Saint Paul, MN 55120
Phone: (651)287-5600

Circulation: ★ = AAM; △ or • = BPA; ♦ = CAC; ❑ = VAC; ⊕ = PO Statement; ‡ = Publisher's Report; Boldface figures = sworn; Light figures = estimated.

Fax: (651)287-5650
Magazine is a technical publication for pharmacists and related fields focusing on the tablet and capsule processing industries. **Freq:** Bimonthly. **Key Personnel:** Matthew Knopp, Editor; Maria Novak, Manager, Production; Richard R. Cress, Publisher, phone: (651)287-5601; Evan Hansen, Senior Editor. **ISSN:** 1549--9928 (print). **Subscription Rates:** Free to qualified subscribers. **URL:** http://www.tabletscapsules.com. **Remarks:** Accepts advertising. **Circ:** (Not Reported).

18855 ■ Villager
Villager Communications Inc.
757 Snelling Ave. S
Saint Paul, MN 55116-2296
Phone: (651)699-1462
Fax: (651)699-6501
Publication E-mail: news@myvillager.com
Local newspaper (tabloid). Free 110,000 readership. 2,000 census: Median Family income 4,090 greater than Twin City's average. Also publish Grand Gazette. **Founded:** Mar. 1953. **Freq:** Bimonthly. **Print Method:** Offset. **Cols./Page:** 6. **Col. Depth:** 210 agate lines. **Key Personnel:** John Rauch, General Manager; Michael J. Mischke, Publisher. **URL:** http://www.myvillager.com. **Formerly:** The Highland Villager. **Ad Rates:** PCI $30. **Remarks:** Accepts advertising. **Circ:** ‡60,000.

18856 ■ The Wanderer
The Wanderer Press
201 Ohio St.
Saint Paul, MN 55107
Phone: (651)224-5733
Fax: (651)224-9666
Publication E-mail: generalinfo@thewandererpress.com
Catholic newspaper (national). **Founded:** 1867. **Freq:** Weekly (Thurs.). **Print Method:** Offset. **Trim Size:** 15 x 22. **Cols./Page:** 7. **Col. Width:** 23 nonpareils. **Col. Depth:** 280 agate lines. **Key Personnel:** Joseph Matt, Editor; Alphonse Matt, Sr., Editor. **USPS:** 665-780. **Subscription Rates:** $75 Individuals print edition; $50 Individuals e-edition. **URL:** http://thewandererpress.com. **Ad Rates:** GLR $1; BW $1988; 4C $2788; PCI $14. **Remarks:** Accepts advertising. **Circ:** ‡35,000.

18857 ■ Woodbury-South Maplewood Review
Lillie Suburban Newspapers
2515 E 7th Ave. N
Saint Paul, MN 55109
Phone: (651)777-8800
Fax: (651)777-8288
Community newspaper. **Freq:** Weekly (Mon.). **Print Method:** Offset. **Trim Size:** Broadsheet. **Cols./Page:** 6. **Col. Width:** 21 nonpareils. **Col. Depth:** 294 agate lines. **Key Personnel:** Holly Wenzel, Managing Editor, fax: (651)748-7811; Mary Lee Hagert, Executive Editor, phone: (651)748-7820. **Subscription Rates:** $35.95 Individuals; $30.95 Individuals senior citizen; $59.95 Two years; $55.95 Two years senior citizen; $70.95 Individuals; $64.95 three years (senior citizen). **URL:** http://www.woodburyreviewnews.com. **Ad Rates:** SAU $8.80. **Remarks:** Accepts advertising. **Circ:** Free ‡10456, Paid ‡7, Combined ‡10463.

18858 ■ KCMP-FM - 89.3
480 Cedar St.
Saint Paul, MN 55101
Phone: (651)290-1500
Free: 800-228-7123
Format: Public Radio; Eclectic. **Owner:** Minnesota Public Radio Inc., 480 Cedar St., Saint Paul, MN 55101, Ph: (651)290-1500, Free: 800-228-7123. **Founded:** 2005. **Operating Hours**: Continuous. **Key Personnel:** Kerri Miller, Producer; Bob Collins, Producer; Jeff Jones, Producer; Tim Roesler, Sr. VP; Nick Kereakos, Chief Tech. Ofc., VP of Operations; Stephanie Curtis, Editor; Derrick Stevens, Production Mgr.; Jennifer Allen, Music Dir. **Ad Rates:** Noncommercial; underwriting available. **URL:** http://minnesota.publicradio.org/radio/stations/knowksjn.

18859 ■ KLIZ-AM - 1380
3415 University Ave.
Saint Paul, MN 55114
Phone: (651)642-4656
Fax: (651)647-2932
Format: Talk; News. **Networks:** USA Radio; Talknet; Westwood One Radio. **Owner:** Omni Broadcasting Co., 8275 South East Ave., Ste. 200, Las Vegas, NV 89123, Ph: (702)938-0467, Fax: (702)990-8681. **Founded:** 1945. **ADI**: Minneapolis-St. Paul, MN. **Key Personnel:** Jeff Hilborn, Contact, hilborn@brainerdonline.com. **Wattage:** 5,000 KW. **Ad Rates:** $6-8.50 for 30 seconds; $8-12 for 60 seconds. **URL:** http://www.kliz.com.

18860 ■ KMWB-TV - 23
1640 Como Ave.
Saint Paul, MN 55108
Phone: (651)646-2300
Fax: (651)646-1220
Format: Commercial TV. **Owner:** Sinclair Broadcast Group Inc., 631 Mainstream Dr., Nashville, TN 37228. **Founded:** Nov. 13, 1998. **Formerly**: KTMA-TV; KLGT. **Operating Hours**: Continuous. **ADI**: Minneapolis-St. Paul, MN. **Key Personnel:** Art Lanham, Gen. Mgr., alanham@kmwb.sbgnet.com. **Wattage**: 5,000,000. **Ad Rates:** Advertising accepted; rates available upon request. **URL:** http://thecw23.com.

18861 ■ KNOW-FM - 91.1
480 Cedar St.
Saint Paul, MN 55101
Phone: (651)290-1500
Free: 800-228-7123
Format: News; Talk. **Networks:** National Public Radio (NPR); Public Radio International (PRI). **Owner:** Minnesota Public Radio Inc., 480 Cedar St., Saint Paul, MN 55101, Ph: (651)290-1500, Free: 800-228-7123. **Founded:** Nov. 1979. **Operating Hours**: Continuous; 75% network, 25% local. **ADI**: Minneapolis-St. Paul, MN. **Key Personnel:** Tim Roesler, Sr. VP. **Wattage**: 100,000. **Ad Rates:** Noncommercial. **URL:** http://www.minnesota.publicradio.org.

18862 ■ KNWF-FM - 95.1
480 Cedar St.
Saint Paul, MN 55101
Phone: (651)290-1500
Format: News; Classical; Public Radio. **Owner:** Minnesota Public Radio Inc., 480 Cedar St., Saint Paul, MN 55101, Ph: (651)290-1500, Free: 800-228-7123. **Founded:** Apr. 2003. **Key Personnel:** Mike Edgerly, Producer; Jeff Jones, Editor; Tim Roesler, Dept. Mgr.; Nick Kereakos, VP; Derrick Stevens, Exec. VP; Michael Olson, Editor; Jennifer Allen, Music Dir. **URL:** http://minnesota.publicradio.org.

18863 ■ KSAX-TV - 42
3415 University Ave.
Saint Paul, MN 55114-2099
Phone: (320)763-5729
Format: Commercial TV. **Networks:** ABC. **Owner:** Hubbard Broadcasting Inc., 3415 University Ave., Saint Paul, MN 55114-2099, Ph: (651)646-5555, Fax: (651)642-4172. **Founded:** 1987. **Operating Hours**: Continuous; 50% network, 50% local. **ADI**: Minneapolis-St. Paul, MN. **Key Personnel:** Ed Smith, Station Mgr. **Wattage**: 2,700,000. **Ad Rates:** Noncommercial. **URL:** http://www.kstp.com.

18864 ■ KSJN-FM - 99.5
480 Cedar St.
Saint Paul, MN 55101
Phone: (651)290-1500
Free: 800-228-7123
Format: Classical. **Networks:** Public Radio International (PRI). **Owner:** Minnesota Public Radio Inc., 480 Cedar St., Saint Paul, MN 55101, Ph: (651)290-1500, Free: 800-228-7123. **Founded:** Apr. 1967. **Formerly**: WLOL-FM. **Operating Hours**: Continuous; 100% local. **Key Personnel:** Mike Edgerly, News Dir.; Nick Kereakos, Chief Tech. Ofc., VP of Operations, VP of Engg. **Wattage:** 100,000. **Ad Rates:** Noncommercial. **URL:** http://www.minnesota.publicradio.org.

18865 ■ KSTC-TV - 45
3415 University Ave.
Saint Paul, MN 55114
Phone: (651)645-4500
Email: tech@kstc45.com
Format: Sports. **Networks:** Independent. **Operating Hours:** Continuous. **Key Personnel:** Susan Wenz, Station Mgr., swenz@kstc45.com; Joe Johnston, Dir. of Mktg., Promotions Dir., jjohnston@kstc45.com. **Wattage:** 100,000 ERP H. **Ad Rates:** Advertising accepted; rates available upon request. **URL:** http://www.kstc45.com.

18866 ■ Kstp-Am L.L.C. - 1500
3415 University Ave.
Saint Paul, MN 55114
Phone: (651)646-8255
Free: 877-615-1500
Format: Talk; Sports. **Networks:** ABC. **Owner:** Hubbard Broadcasting Inc., 3415 University Ave., Saint Paul, MN 55114-2099, Ph: (651)646-5555, Fax: (651)642-4172. **Founded:** 1924. **Local Programs**: *Saturday Sports Talk*, Saturday. **URL:** http://www.1500espn.com.

18867 ■ KSTP-FM - 94.5
3415 University Ave.
Saint Paul, MN 55114
Phone: (651)642-4141
Fax: (651)647-2904
Format: Adult Contemporary. **Networks:** ABC. **Owner:** Hubbard Broadcasting Inc., 3415 University Ave., Saint Paul, MN 55114-2099, Ph: (651)646-5555, Fax: (651)642-4172. **Founded:** 1965. **Operating Hours**: Continuous. **ADI**: Minneapolis-St. Paul, MN. **Wattage**: 95,000. **Ad Rates:** Noncommercial. **URL:** http://www.ks95.com.

18868 ■ KSTP-TV - 5
3415 University Ave.
Saint Paul, MN 55114-2099
Phone: (651)646-5555
Fax: (651)642-4409
Format: Commercial TV. **Networks:** ABC. **Owner:** Hubbard Broadcasting Inc., 3415 University Ave., Saint Paul, MN 55114-2099, Ph: (651)646-5555, Fax: (651)642-4172. **Founded:** Apr. 27, 1948. **Operating Hours**: Continuous; 40% network, 60% local. **ADI**: Minneapolis-St. Paul, MN. **Ad Rates:** Noncommercial. **URL:** http://www.kstp.com.

18869 ■ KTIS-AM - 900
3003 N Snelling Ave.
Saint Paul, MN 55113-1598
Phone: (651)631-5000
Format: Contemporary Christian; Talk. **Networks:** SkyLight Satellite. **Owner:** Northwestern College, 101 7th Street SW, Orange City, IA 51041, Ph: (712)707-7000. **Founded:** 1949. **Operating Hours**: Continuous; 50% network, 50% local. **ADI**: Minneapolis-St. Paul, MN. **Wattage**: 25,000. **Ad Rates:** Noncommercial. **URL:** http://www.myfaithradio.com.

18870 ■ KTIS-FM - 98.5
3003 Snelling Ave. N
Saint Paul, MN 55113-1598
Phone: (651)631-5000
Format: Contemporary Christian. **Networks:** SkyLight Satellite. **Owner:** Northwestern College, 101 7th Street SW, Orange City, IA 51041, Ph: (712)707-7000. **Founded:** 1949. **Operating Hours**: Continuous; 50% network, 50% local. **ADI**: Minneapolis-St. Paul, MN. **Wattage**: 100,000. **Ad Rates:** Noncommercial. **URL:** http://www.myktis.com.

18871 ■ KULO-FM - 94.3
3415 University Ave., St. Paul
Saint Paul, MN 55114
Format: Oldies. **Key Personnel:** Dave Vagle, Gen. Mgr. **Wattage:** 12,000. **Ad Rates:** $20-35 for 60 seconds. **Mailing address:** PO Box 1024, Alexandria, MN 56308.

18872 ■ KVBR-AM - 1340
3415 University Ave.
Saint Paul, MN 55114
Phone: (651)642-4656
Fax: (651)647-2932
Format: News; Talk. **Founded:** 1964. **Formerly**: KQBR-AM. **ADI**: Minneapolis-St. Paul, MN. **Key Personnel:** Don Jahnke; Jeff Hilborn, Gen. Mgr.; Dave Torkelson, Dir. of Programs; Don Kelley, News Dir.; Sam Morriss, Sports Dir. **Wattage**: 1,000. **Ad Rates:** $7 for 30 seconds; $11 for 60 seconds. **URL:** http://www.kliz.com.

18873 ■ TPT 2-TV - 2
172 E 4th St.
Saint Paul, MN 55101
Phone: (651)222-1717
Free: 866-229-1300
Email: viewerservices@tpt.org
Format: Public TV. **Networks:** Public Broadcasting Service (PBS). **Owner:** Minnesota Public Television, 172 E 4th St., Saint Paul, MN 55101, Ph: (651)222-1717, Free: 866-229-1300. **Founded:** 1957. **Formerly**: KTCA-TV. **Operating Hours**: Continuous. **Ad Rates:**

Noncommercial. **URL:** http://www.tpt.org.

18874 ■ WFMP-FM - 107.1
3415 University Ave.
Saint Paul, MN 55114
Phone: (651)642-4107
Format: Country; News. **Simulcasts:** WIXK-AM. **Networks:** ABC. **Owner:** Hubbard Broadcasting Inc., 3415 University Ave., Saint Paul, MN 55114-2099, Ph: (651)646-5555, Fax: (651)642-4172. **Founded:** 1968. **Formerly:** WIXK-FM. **Operating Hours:** Continuous. **ADI:** Minneapolis-St. Paul, MN. **Wattage:** 18,000. **Ad Rates:** $16-23 for 30 seconds; $20-28.75 for 60 seconds.

WKCP-FM - See Miami, FL

18875 ■ WMCN-FM - 91.7
1600 Grand Ave.
Saint Paul, MN 55105
Phone: (651)696-6082
Email: wmcn@macalester.edu
Format: Eclectic. **Owner:** Macalester College, 1600 Grand Ave., Saint Paul, MN 55105-1899, Ph: (651)696-6000, Free: 800-231-7974. **Founded:** 1979. **Formerly:** KMAC-FM. **Operating Hours:** Continuous. **ADI:** Minneapolis-St. Paul, MN. **Wattage:** 010. **Ad Rates:** Noncommercial. **URL:** http://www.macalester.edu.

18876 ■ WMIN-AM - 740
PO Box 25130
Saint Paul, MN 55125
Phone: (651)436-4000
Fax: (651)436-5018
Networks: NBC. **Operating Hours:** Sunrise-sunset. **ADI:** Minneapolis-St. Paul, MN. **Key Personnel:** Tom Witschen, Dir. of Programs; Shelly Jarvis, Dir. of Operations; Greg Borgen, Gen. Mgr. **Wattage:** 1,000.

18877 ■ WNWC-AM - 1190
3003 Snelling Ave. N
Saint Paul, MN 55113
Phone: (651)631-5000
Fax: (608)271-1150
Free: 866-999-1025
Email: wnwc@nwc.edu
Format: Religious. **Owner:** University of Northwestern - St. Paul, 3003 N Snelling Ave., Saint Paul, MN 55113-1598, Ph: (651)631-5100, Free: 800-692-4020. **Founded:** 1982. **Formerly:** WERU-AM; WMAD-AM. **Operating Hours:** Continuous. **Key Personnel:** Greg Walters, Gen. Mgr., gawalters@nwc.edu. **Wattage:** 4,800 Day; 021 Night. **Ad Rates:** Advertising accepted; rates available upon request. Combined advertising rates available with WMAD-FM:. **URL:** http://myfaithradio.com.

18878 ■ WUCW-TV - 23
1640 Como Ave.
Saint Paul, MN 55108
Phone: (651)646-2300
Fax: (651)646-1220
Owner: Sinclair Broadcast Group Inc., 10706 Beaver Dam Rd., Hunt Valley, MD 21030, Ph: (410)568-1500, Fax: (410)568-1533. **Founded:** 1982. **URL:** http://www.thecw23.com.

SAINT PETER

SC MN. Nicollet Co. On Minnesota River, 12 mi. N. of Mankato. Gustavus Adolphus College. Manufactures electronic equipment, aluminum boats & canoes. Dairy, poultry, stock, grain farms. Corn, wheat, soybeans.

18879 ■ The Gustavian Weekly
Gustavus Adolphus College
800 W College Ave.
Saint Peter, MN 56082
Phone: (507)933-8000
Publication E-mail: weekly@gac.edu
Collegiate newspaper. **Freq:** Weekly (Fri.). **Print Method:** Offset. Uses mats. **Cols./Page:** 5. **Col. Width:** 22 nonpareils. **Col. Depth:** 210 agate lines. **Key Personnel:** Rebecca Hare, Editor-in-Chief; Vinny Bartella, Managing Editor; Ben Miller, Editor. **Subscription Rates:** $40 Individuals. **URL:** http://weekly.blog.gustavus.edu/. **Ad Rates:** PCI $7; BW $490. **Remarks:** display advertisements. **Circ:** Free ‡1,600.

SANDSTONE

EC MN. Pine Co. 65 mi. SW of Duluth. Starter, alternator rebuilding plant. Electronics assembly plant. Dairy, stock farms. Rutabagas, potatoes, corn.

18880 ■ Minnesota Flyer Magazine
Minnesota Flyer Magazine
PO Box 750
Sandstone, MN 55072-0750
Phone: (320)295-2111
Fax: (320)245-2438
Publication E-mail: mnflyer@pinenet.com
Midwest publication for aircraft owners/renters (pilots). **Freq:** Monthly. **ISSN:** 0889--4809 (print). **Subscription Rates:** $19 Individuals; $30 Two years; $67 Canada and Mexico; $126 Two years Canada and Mexico; $79 Other countries; $150 Two years other countries. **URL:** http://www.mnflyer.com/about. **Remarks:** Accepts advertising. **Circ:** (Not Reported).

SAUK CENTRE

C MN. Stearns Co. 45 mi. NW of Saint Cloud. Manufactures feeds. Dairy farms. Corn, hay.

18881 ■ Herald
Sauk Centre Publishers Inc.
522 Sinclair Lewis Ave.
Sauk Centre, MN 56378
Phone: (320)352-6577
Fax: (320)352-5647
Publisher's E-mail: jyeton@saukherald.com
Community newspaper. **Founded:** 1867. **Freq:** Weekly (Tues.). **Print Method:** Offset. **Trim Size:** 13 x 20. **Cols./Page:** 6. **Col. Width:** 14 picas. **Col. Depth:** 210 agate lines. **Subscription Rates:** $35 Individuals in Stearns, Todd, Douglas & Pope Counties; $42 Elsewhere news section only; $45 Elsewhere with Shopper or Canary; $45 Out of state news section only; $47 Out of state with Shopper or Canary. **URL:** http://www.saukherald.com. **Ad Rates:** GLR $.25; BW $548; 4C $773; SAU $5; PCI $2.90. **Remarks:** .25. **Circ:** 3500.

SAUK RAPIDS

SC MN. Benton Co. 20 mi. SW of Foley. Dairy products, granite quarries.

18882 ■ Sauk Rapids Herald
Sauk Centre Publishers Inc.
7 2nd Ave. S
Sauk Rapids, MN 56379
Phone: (320)251-1971
Fax: (320)251-1971
Publication E-mail: srherald1854@charterinternet.com
Community newspaper. **Freq:** Weekly (Wed.). **Cols./Page:** 7. **Col. Width:** 2 inches. **Col. Depth:** 21 1/2 inches. **Key Personnel:** Janell Westerman, Compositor; Jyeton Drayna, Receptionist; Dave Simpkins, Editor; , Writer; Pat Turner, Manager, Production; Andrea Borgerding, Writer; Bryan Zollman, Editor, News Director. **Subscription Rates:** $39 Individuals in Stearns, Todd, Douglas, Pope & Morrison counties; $46 Elsewhere in Minnesota; $49 Out of state; $25 Individuals E-Edition only - 1 year. **URL:** http://www.saukherald.com; http://www.mnnews.com/newspapers/saukrapids.html. **Feature Editors:** Carol Moorman, carol@saukherald.com. **Mailing address:** PO Box 8, Sauk Rapids, MN 56379. **Remarks:** Accepts advertising. **Circ:** 1,157.

18883 ■ KKJM-FM - 92.9
1310 Second St. N
Sauk Rapids, MN 56379
Email: friends@spirit929.com
Format: Contemporary Christian. **Networks:** AP. **Owner:** Gabriel Communications Co., at above address. **Operating Hours:** Continuous. **Key Personnel:** Deb Huschle, Gen. Mgr., deb@spirit929.com; Mike Moffett, Contact, mike@spirit929.com. **Wattage:** 25,000. **Ad Rates:** Advertising accepted; rates available upon request. **Mailing address:** PO Box 547, Sauk Rapids, MN 56379. **URL:** http://spirit929.com.

18884 ■ WBHR-AM - 660
1010 2nd St. N
Sauk Rapids, MN 56379
Phone: (320)257-6403
Email: mail@660wbhr.com
Format: Sports. **Networks:** ABC. **Owner:** Tri-Country Broadcasting Inc., 1010 2nd St. N, Sauk Rapids, MN 56379, Ph: (320)252-6200, Fax: (320)252-9367. **Founded:** 1963. **Formerly:** WVAL-AM. **Operating Hours:** Continuous. **Wattage:** 10,000 Day; 250 Night. **Ad Rates:** $10-13 for 30 seconds; $15-18 for 60 seconds. Combined advertising rates available with WVAL-AM. **URL:** http://www.660wbhr.com.

18885 ■ WHMH-FM - 101.7
1010 Second St. N
Sauk Rapids, MN 56379
Phone: (320)252-6200
Fax: (320)252-9367
Format: Album-Oriented Rock (AOR). **Owner:** Tri-County Broadcasting Inc., 1010 2nd St. N, Sauk Rapids, MN 56379, Ph: (320)252-6200, Fax: (320)252-9367. **Founded:** 1975. **Operating Hours:** Continuous. **Wattage:** 50,000. **Ad Rates:** Noncommercial. **Mailing address:** PO Box 366, Sauk Rapids, MN 56379. **URL:** http://www.tricountybroadcasting.com.

SAVAGE

18886 ■ Savage Pacer
Southwest Suburban Publishing
PO Box 376
Savage, MN 55378
Phone: (952)440-1234
Fax: (952)447-6671
Community newspaper. **Freq:** Weekly (Sat.). **Print Method:** Offset. **Key Personnel:** Laurie Hartmann, Director, Operations, phone: (952)345-6878. **Subscription Rates:** $37 Individuals Savage residents; $40 Individuals in Scott or Carver Counties and Burnsville; $50 Individuals outside of Scott or Carver Counties ; $72 Two years in Scott or Carver Counties and Burnsville; $90 Two years outside of Scott or Carver Counties. **URL:** http://www.swnewsmedia.com/savage_pacer. **Remarks:** Accepts advertising. **Circ:** 5569.

SEBEKA

WC MN. Wadena Co. 40 mi. E. of Detroit Lakes. Forest products manufactured. Resort. Agriculture.

18887 ■ Review-Messenger
Review-Messenger
PO Box 309
Sebeka, MN 56477
Publication E-mail: remess@wcta.net
Newspaper with a Republican orientation. **Freq:** Weekly (Wed.). **Print Method:** Offset. **Cols./Page:** 7. **Col. Width:** 24 nonpareils. **Col. Depth:** 301 agate lines. **Key Personnel:** Tim Bloomquist, Editor; Bernice Eckenrode, Manager, Advertising, phone: (218)837-5558. **USPS:** 487-840. **Subscription Rates:** $46 Individuals local, print and online; $53 Individuals elsewhere in Minnesota, print and online; $60 Individuals outside of Minnesota, print and online; $36 Individuals local, print only; $43 Individuals elsewhere in Minnesota, print only; $50 Individuals outside of Minnesota, print only; $36 Individuals online only, 12 months; $20 Individuals online only, 6 months; $12 Individuals online only, 3 months. **URL:** http://www.lakeandpine.com/46758/2205/1/home. **Ad Rates:** GLR $.35; BW $855; 4C $1055; SAU $5.70; CNU $5.70; PCI $8.25. **Remarks:** Accepts advertising. **Circ:** ‡3,421.

18888 ■ United Data-Vision
308 Frontage Rd.
Sebeka, MN 56477
Free: 800-945-2163
Owner: West Central Telephone Association, 308 Frontage Rd., Sebeka, MN 56477, Ph: (218)837-5151, Free: 800-945-2163. **Founded:** 1995. **Key Personnel:** Anthony V. Mayer, Gen. Mgr., tonym@wcta.net. **Cities Served:** Menahga, Sebeka, Minnesota: subscribing households 772; 200 channels; 1 community access channel; 24 hours per week community access programming. **Postal Areas Served:** 56477. **URL:** http://www.wcta.net.

SHAKOPEE

NE MN. Scott Co. 18 mi. SW of Minneapolis. Soft drinks, agriculture.

18889 ■ Edible Twin Cities
Edible Communities Inc.
327 Marschall Rd.
Shakopee, MN 55379
Phone: (952)445-3333
Publication E-mail: info@edibletwincities.net
Magazine covering the local food of Twin Cities area.

Circulation: ★ = AAM; △ or • = BPA; ♦ = CAC; ❑ = VAC; ⊕ = PO Statement; ‡ = Publisher's Report; Boldface figures = sworn; Light figures = estimated.

Freq: Bimonthly. **Subscription Rates:** $5 back issues. **URL:** http://edibletwincities.com. **Mailing address:** PO Box 8, Shakopee, MN 55379. **Ad Rates:** 4C $2500. **Remarks:** Accepts advertising. **Circ:** (Not Reported).

18890 ■ Shakopee Valley News
Southwest Suburban Publishing
327 S Marschall Rd.
Shakopee, MN 55379
Phone: (952)445-3333
Publication E-mail: editor@shakopeenews.com
Local newspaper. **Freq:** Weekly (Thurs.). **Print Method:** Offset. **Cols./Page:** 6. **Col. Width:** 2 inches. **Col. Depth:** 21 inches. **Key Personnel:** Craig Theis, Manager, Advertising, phone: (952)345-6477; Pat Minelli, Editor, phone: (952)345-6680; Laurie Hartman, Publisher, phone: (952)345-6878; Tess Lee, Advertising Representative; Shannon Fiecke, Writer, phone: (952)345-6679. **Subscription Rates:** $37 Individuals SVN Print and Online Editions - 1 year - Mailed in Scott or Carver MN Counties; $35 Individuals SVN Print Edition - 1 year - Mailed in Scott or Carver MN Counties; $48 Individuals SVN Print+Online Editions - 1 year - Mailed outside of Scott or Carver MN Counties; $46 Individuals SVN Print Edition - 1 year - Mailed outside of Scott or Carver MN Counties; $68 Individuals SVN Print+Online Editions - 2 years - Mailed in Scott or Carver MN Counties; $64 Individuals SVN Print Edition - 2 years - Mailed in Scott or Carver MN Counties; $88 Individuals SVN Print+Online Editions - 2 years - Mailed outside of Scott or Carver MN Counties; $84 Individuals SVN Print Edition - 2 years - Mailed outside of Scott or Carver MN Counties; $30 Individuals SVN Unlimited Online Edition - 1 year. **URL:** http://www.swnewsmedia.com/shakopee_valley_news/; http://www.mnnews.com/newspapers/shakopee.html. **Mailing address:** PO Box 8, Shakopee, MN 55379. **Remarks:** Accepts advertising. **Circ:** 5139.

SHOREVIEW

18891 ■ Contingent Workforce Strategies
Staffing Industry Analysts Inc.
1080 W County Rd. E
Shoreview, MN 55126
Magazine that provides information for business executives who currently use or are considering temporary or contract workers. **Freq:** Weekly. **Key Personnel:** Subadhra Sriram, Director, Editorial. **Subscription Rates:** $96 Individuals; $126 Canada; $146 Out of country. **URL:** http://www.staffingindustry.com/Research-Publications/Publications/CWS-3.0. **Remarks:** Accepts advertising. **Circ:** (Not Reported).

18892 ■ Shoreview-Arden Hills Bulletin
Lillie Suburban Newspapers
2515 E 7th Ave. N
Saint Paul, MN 55109
Phone: (651)777-8800
Fax: (651)777-8288
Local newspaper. **Freq:** Weekly (Wed.). **Print Method:** Offset. **Cols./Page:** 6. **Col. Width:** 21 nonpareils. **Col. Depth:** 294 agate lines. **Key Personnel:** Mary Lee Hagert, Executive Editor, phone: (651)748-7820. **Subscription Rates:** $34.95 Individuals; $29.95 Individuals senior citizen. **URL:** http://www.bulletin-news.com/articles/shoreview-arden-hills-bulletin-news. **Formerly:** Shoreview Bulletin. **Ad Rates:** BW $2734; SAU $22.70; PCI $31.50. **Remarks:** Accepts advertising. **Circ:** (Not Reported).

18893 ■ SI Review
Staffing Industry Analysts Inc.
1080 W County Rd. E
Shoreview, MN 55126
Online news publication covering news and developments in employment and staffing. **Freq:** 8/year. **Key Personnel:** Craig Johnson, Managing Editor. **Subscription Rates:** $129 Canada; $149 Other countries. **URL:** http://sireview.staffingindustry.com. **Remarks:** Accepts advertising. **Circ:** (Not Reported).

18894 ■ Staffing Industry Report
Staffing Industry Analysts Inc.
1080 W County Rd. E
Shoreview, MN 55126
Online news publication covering all sectors and segments of the staffing industry. **Freq:** Daily. **Key Personnel:** Craig Johnson, Managing Editor. **URL:** http://www2.staffingindustry.com/Research/Research-Topics-Reports. **Remarks:** Accepts advertising. **Circ:** (Not Reported).

SLAYTON

SW MN. Murray Co. 90 mi. w. of Mankato. Manufactures butter. Lake resort. Stock, grain farms. Corn, oats, barley.

18895 ■ Murray County Wheel/Herald
Wheel Beers
2734 Broadway St.
Slayton, MN 56172
Phone: (507)836-8726
Fax: (507)836-8942
Publication E-mail: wheelherald@iw.net
Shopper. **Freq:** Weekly (Mon.). **Print Method:** Offset. **Cols./Page:** 8. **Col. Width:** 20 nonpareils. **Col. Depth:** 21 1/2 inches. **Key Personnel:** Will Beers, Editor; Sherri Halbur, Business Manager. **Subscription Rates:** Free print, in county; $10 Individuals online edition, per year, in counyt; $38 Out of area print or online; $45 Out of area print and online. **URL:** http://www.mnnews.com/newspapers/slaytonwh.html; http://www.wheelherald.com. **Mailing address:** PO Box 263, Slayton, MN 56172. **Ad Rates:** BW $490; PCI $4.10. **Remarks:** Accepts advertising. **Circ:** ‡7295.

18896 ■ KJOE-FM - 106.1
2660 Broadway Ave.
Slayton, MN 56172
Phone: (507)836-6125
Email: kjoe@kjoeradio.com
Format: Country. **Owner:** Christensen Broadcasting, PO Box 456, Pipestone, MN 56164, Ph: (507)825-4282, Fax: (507)825-3364. **Founded:** 1993. **Operating Hours:** Continuous. **Wattage:** 10,000 ERP. **Ad Rates:** Advertising accepted; rates available upon request. **URL:** http://www.kjoeradio.com.

SLEEPY EYE

SC MN. Brown Co. 41 mi. W. of Mankato. Manufactures bleachers, picnic tables, cement step forms, calendars, dried milk; canned peas and corn. Hatcheries; poultry packing plant. Dairy, stock, poultry, grain farms. Corn, soybeans. Diversified agriculture.

18897 ■ Sleepy Eye Herald-Dispatch
Sleepy Eye Herald-Dispatch
119 Main St. E
Sleepy Eye, MN 56085
Phone: (507)794-3511
Publisher's E-mail: publisher@sleepyeyenews.com
Community newspaper. **Freq:** Weekly (Thurs.). **Print Method:** Offset. **Cols./Page:** 6. **Col. Width:** 24 nonpareils. **Col. Depth:** 301 agate lines. **Key Personnel:** Robin Havemeier, Manager, Production; Jenny Boettger, General Manager; Penny Mathiowetz, Manager, Circulation. **USPS:** 498-700. **URL:** http://www.sleepyeyenews.com. **Mailing address:** PO Box 499, Sleepy Eye, MN 56085. **Ad Rates:** GLR $8.75; BW $1057.80; 4C $1000; SAU $5.82; PCI $8.20. **Remarks:** Accepts advertising. **Circ:** Paid ‡3,600, Free ‡310.

SOUTH SAINT PAUL

18898 ■ Marriage Magazine: Celebrating Committed Couples
International Marriage Encounter Inc.
PO Box 387
South Saint Paul, MN 55075
Phone: (651)454-6434
Fax: (651)452-0466
Free: 800-627-7424
An abundantly rich resource that celebrates and nurtures marriages and relationships, inspiring insights, practical how-to's, intensity ideas, and couple's sharing success secrets on a different theme for each issue. **Freq:** Bimonthly. **Print Method:** Sheetfed offset. **Trim Size:** 8 1/2 x 11. **Cols./Page:** 2 and 3. **Col. Width:** 3 inches. **Col. Depth:** 8 1/2 inches. **Key Personnel:** Krysta Kavenaugh, Editor-in-Chief. **ISSN:** 1063-1054 (print). **Subscription Rates:** $19.95 Individuals; $24.95 Other countries; $37.95 Two years; $47.95 Other countries two years. **URL:** http://www.marriagemagazine.org/default.asp. **Formerly:** Agape; Marriage Encounter. **Ad Rates:** BW $500; 4C $1,080. **Remarks:** Accepts advertising. **Circ:** 11000.

18899 ■ The Septs
Irish Genealogical Society International
1185 Concord St. N, Ste. 218
South Saint Paul, MN 55075-1150
Publisher's E-mail: questions@irishgenealogical.org
Journal containing information about Irish genealogical research methods and examples of successful searches. **Freq:** Quarterly. **Subscription Rates:** Included in membership; $10 Single issue back issues from January 2011 onward; $7 Single issue back issues from January 2005 through December 2010; $5 Single issue back issues from January 1996 through October 2004; $1 Single issue back issues for October 1995 and prior. **URL:** http://irishgenealogical.org/page/septs. **Remarks:** Advertising not accepted. **Circ:** (Not Reported).

SPICER

Kandiyohi Co.

18900 ■ KGLH-FM - 96.9
7730 Northshore Dr.
Spicer, MN 56288
Email: info@kglh.org
Format: Religious; Contemporary Christian; Gospel. **Operating Hours**: Continuous. **Ad Rates:** Noncommercial.

SPRING GROVE

SE MN. Houston Co. 32 mi. W. of La Crosse, WI. Recreation Area. Lumber Industry. Soft drinks manufactured. Dairy, stock farms.

18901 ■ Herald
Herald
115 W Main St.
Spring Grove, MN 55974
Phone: (507)498-3868
Fax: (507)498-6397
Newspaper with a Republican orientation. **Founded:** 1891. **Freq:** Weekly (Wed.). **Print Method:** Offset. **Cols./Page:** 6. **Col. Width:** 26 nonpareils. **Col. Depth:** 287 agate lines. **URL:** http://www.springgroveherald.com/. **Mailing address:** PO Box 68, Spring Grove, MN 55974. **Ad Rates:** GLR $.30; BW $360; 4C $460; SAU $3; PCI $3. **Remarks:** Accepts advertising. **Circ:** Paid ‡1232.

SPRINGFIELD

SC MN. Brown Co. On Cottonwood River, 60 mi. W. of Mankato. Manufactures bricks, tile, flour, feed. Carding mill; nursery. Grain, stock, poultry, dairy farms.

18902 ■ Springfield Advance-Press
Springfield Advance-Press
13 S Marshall Ave.
Springfield, MN 56087
Phone: (507)723-4225
Fax: (507)723-4400
Publication E-mail: aps@newulmtel.net
Newspaper with a Republican orientation. **Freq:** Weekly (Wed.). **Print Method:** Offset. **Trim Size:** 14 x 22 1/2. **Cols./Page:** 6. **Col. Width:** 12.5 picas. **Col. Depth:** 301 agate lines. **Key Personnel:** Doris M. Weber, Editor; D.J. Hedstrom, Publisher; Peter C. Hedstrom, Publisher. **USPS:** 512-500. **Subscription Rates:** $34 Brown, Redwood, Cottonwood only; $37 Out of state Brown, Redwood, Cottonwood only. **URL:** http://www.mnnews.com/newspapers/springfield.html. **Mailing address:** PO Box 78, Springfield, MN 56087. **Ad Rates:** GLR $.61; BW $477.30; PCI $4.50. **Remarks:** Color advertising accepted; rates available upon request. **Circ:** Paid ‡1685.

STEPHEN

NW MN. Marshall Co. 52 mi. NE of Grand Forks, ND. State Parks. Manufacturing. Grain farms. Potatoes, sugar beets. Sunflowers.

18903 ■ The Messenger
The Messenger
586 Pacific Ave.
Stephen, MN 56757-0048
Phone: (218)478-2210
Fax: (218)478-2210
Publication E-mail: messenger@wiktel.com
Newspaper with a Democratic orientation. **Founded:** 1883. **Freq:** Weekly (Thurs.). **Print Method:** Offset. **Cols./Page:** 6. **Col. Width:** 2 1/8 inches. **Col. Depth:** 21 1/4 inches. **Key Personnel:** Earl L. Anderson, Editor.

Subscription Rates: $18 Out of country; $21 Other countries. **URL:** http://www.mnnews.com/newspapers/stephen.html; http://www.stephenmn.com/index.asp?Type=B_BASIC&SEC=%7BA88FD4F2-D110-419D-9B56-B21DECD3F488%7D. **Mailing address:** PO Box 48, Stephen, MN 56757-0048. **Ad Rates:** GLR $.17; SAU $3.72; PCI $3. **Circ:** 1,432.

STILLWATER

SE MN. Washington Co. On St. Croix River, 20 mi. NE of Saint Paul. Manufactures windows, doors, clothing, flour, boats, plastics, precision sheetmetal, tractors, road machinery, screen process printing, dried milk products, plastics, ventilation equipment. Dairy farms.

18904 ■ Stillwater Gazette
Minnesota Sun Publications
1931 Curve Crest Blvd.
Stillwater, MN 55082
Phone: (651)439-3130
Fax: (651)439-4713
Publication E-mail: stwgztte@acnpapers.com
Regional community newspaper. **Freq:** Daily. **Cols./Page:** 9. **Col. Width:** 1.181 INS. **Key Personnel:** Mark Berriman, Director, Operations, phone: (651)796-1116; Jonathan Young, Managing Editor. **Subscription Rates:** $87 By mail. **URL:** http://stillwatergazette.com. **Ad Rates:** GLR $8.25; PCI $16.72. **Remarks:** Accepts advertising. **Circ:** ‡2500.

18905 ■ KLBB-AM - 1220
104 N Main St.
Stillwater, MN 55082
Phone: (651)439-5006
Free: 877-646-1220
Format: Full Service; Music of Your Life. **Networks:** Westwood One Radio. **Operating Hours:** Continuous; 5% network, 95% local. **ADI:** Minneapolis-St. Paul, MN. **Wattage:** 1,000. **Ad Rates:** $34-60 per unit. **URL:** http://www.klbbradio.com/klbbhome.aspx.

THIEF RIVER FALLS

NW MN. Pennington Co. 40 mi. NE of Grand Forks, ND. Manufactures dairy products, poultry & animal feeds, soft drinks, front-end loaders, snow machines, seed cleaning, and recycling equipment. Dairy, poultry, grocery, fruit distributing center.

18906 ■ Northern Light
Northland Community and Technical College
1101 Highway 1 E
Thief River Falls, MN 56701
Phone: (218)683-8800
Fax: (218)683-8980
Free: 800-959-6282
Publisher's E-mail: admissions@northlandcollege.edu
Collegiate magazine. **Founded:** 1965. **Freq:** 3/yr. **Print Method:** Offset. **Trim Size:** 12 x 14. **Cols./Page:** 4. **Col. Width:** 11 picas. **Col. Depth:** 13 inches. **Key Personnel:** John Doppler, Editor, phone: (218)681-0741. **Subscription Rates:** Free. **URL:** http://www.northlandcollege.edu. **Ad Rates:** PCI $3. **Remarks:** Accepts advertising. **Circ:** Non-paid ‡1,500.

18907 ■ Northern Watch: Northwest Minnesota's Regional Newspaper
Thief River Falls Times Inc.
324 Main Ave. N
Thief River Falls, MN 56701-1906
Phone: (218)681-4450
Fax: (218)681-4455
Publisher's E-mail: trftimes@trftimes.com
Community newspaper. **Freq:** Weekly (Sat.). **Print Method:** Web Offset. **Trim Size:** 14 x 22 3/4. **Cols./Page:** 6. **Col. Width:** 2 1/8 inches. **Col. Depth:** 21 1/2 inches. **Key Personnel:** Randy Hultgren, Publisher; DeDe Coltom, Contact. **URL:** http://www.trftimes.com/northernwatch. **Mailing address:** PO Box 100, Thief River Falls, MN 56701-0100. **Remarks:** Accepts advertising. **Circ:** (Not Reported).

18908 ■ Thief River Falls Times
Thief River Falls Times Inc.
324 Main Ave. N
Thief River Falls, MN 56701-1906
Phone: (218)681-4450
Fax: (218)681-4455
Publisher's E-mail: trftimes@trftimes.com
Community newspaper. **Founded:** 1910. **Freq:** Weekly (Wed.). **Print Method:** Offset. **Trim Size:** 14 x 22 3/4. **Cols./Page:** 6. **Col. Width:** 12 1/4 picas. **Col. Depth:** 21 1/2 inches. **Key Personnel:** DeDe Coltom, Contact. **ISSN:** 8750-3883 (print). **Subscription Rates:** $22 Individuals 6 months; $36 Individuals; $2.99 Individuals trial. **URL:** http://www.trftimes.com. **Formerly:** The Times. **Mailing address:** PO Box 100, Thief River Falls, MN 56701-0100. **Ad Rates:** BW $793; 4C $1,093; SAU $6.15; PCI $6.15. **Remarks:** Advertising accepted; rates available upon request. **Circ:** ‡5043.

18909 ■ KBRR-TV - 10
4015 9th Ave. SW
Fargo, ND 58103
Phone: (701)277-1515
Fax: (701)277-1830
Format: Commercial TV. **Simulcasts:** KVRR-TV. **Networks:** Independent; Fox. **Owner:** Red River Broadcasting Corp., at above address. **Founded:** 1985. **ADI:** Fargo, ND.

18910 ■ KKAQ-AM
PO Box 40
Thief River Falls, MN 56701-0040
Phone: (218)681-4900
Fax: (218)681-3717
Format: Contemporary Country. **Networks:** ABC. **Founded:** 1979. **Wattage:** 2,500 Day; 150 Night. **Ad Rates:** $6.50 for 30 seconds; $9.50 for 60 seconds.

18911 ■ KSRQ-FM - 90.1
1101 Hwy. 1 E
Thief River Falls, MN 56701
Phone: (218)683-8800
Fax: (218)683-8980
Free: 800-959-6282
Format: Educational. **Networks:** CNN Radio. **Owner:** Northland Community and Technical College, 1101 Highway 1 E, Thief River Falls, MN 56701, Ph: (218)683-8800, Fax: (218)683-8980, Free: 800-959-6282. **Founded:** 1969. **Formerly:** KAVS-FM. **Operating Hours:** Continuous; 100% local. **Key Personnel:** Travis Ryder, Station Mgr.; Mark Johnson, Contact; Mark Johnson, Contact. **Wattage:** 24,000. **Ad Rates:** Noncommercial. Combined advertising rates available with KAXE; KBEM; KFAI; KMOJ; KMSU; KQAL; KUMD; KUMM; KUOM. **URL:** http://www.northlandcollege.edu.

18912 ■ Sjoberg's Cable TV Inc.
315 Main Ave. N
Thief River Falls, MN 56701
Email: sjobergs@mncable.net
Cities Served: 86 channels. **URL:** http://trf.mncable.net.

18913 ■ Sjoberg's Inc.
315 N Main Ave.
Thief River Falls, MN 56701
Phone: (218)681-3044
Free: 800-828-8808
Email: office1@mncable.net
Founded: 1962. **Cities Served:** 279 channels. **URL:** http://trf.mncable.net.

TOWER

NE MN. St. Louis Co. On Lake Vermillion, 25 mi. N. of Virginia. Summer resorts. Iron mines; timber.

18914 ■ The Timberjay
The Timberjay Inc.
414 Main St.
Tower, MN 55790
Phone: (218)365-3114
Fax: (218)753-2950
Community newspaper. **Freq:** Weekly (Mon.). **Print Method:** Offset. **Trim Size:** 9 3/4 x 15. **Cols./Page:** 4. **Col. Width:** 2 1/4 inches. **Col. Depth:** 15 inches. **Key Personnel:** Marshall Helmberger, Publisher. **URL:** http://www.timberjay.com. **Mailing address:** PO Box 636, Tower, MN 55790. **Ad Rates:** BW $360; SAU $5.66; PCI $6.10. **Remarks:** Accepts advertising. **Circ:** (Not Reported).

18915 ■ Tower News
News
510 Main St.
Tower, MN 55790
Phone: (218)753-7777
Fax: (218)753-7778
Publication E-mail: towernews1@accessmn.com
Newspaper. **Founded:** 1900. **Freq:** Weekly (Fri.). **Print Method:** Offset. **Cols./Page:** 5. **Col. Width:** 22 nonpareils. **Col. Depth:** 210 agate lines. **URL:** http://www.mnnews.com/newspapers/towernews.html. **Formerly:** News. **Mailing address:** PO Box 447, Tower, MN 55790. **Ad Rates:** GLR $.20; BW $262.50. **Remarks:** Accepts advertising. **Circ:** 1329.

TRACY

SW MN. Lyon Co. 80 mi. W. of Mankato. Manufactures butter, powdered buttermilk, soft drinks. Stock, dairy, grain farms.

18916 ■ Headlight Herald
Tracy Publishing Company Inc.
207 Fourth St.
Tracy, MN 56175
Phone: (507)629-4300
Fax: (507)629-4301
Newspaper with a Republican orientation. **Founded:** 1879. **Freq:** Weekly (Thurs.). **Print Method:** Offset. **Cols./Page:** 6. **Col. Width:** 28 nonpareils. **Col. Depth:** 297 agate lines. **Key Personnel:** Seth Schmidt, Editor; Lisa Sell, Manager, Advertising. **Subscription Rates:** $47 Individuals Lyon, Murray, Redwood or Cottonwood; $49 Elsewhere Minnesota; $56 Out of country. **URL:** http://www.headlightherald.com. **Remarks:** Accepts advertising. **Circ:** Controlled 1900.

TRUMAN

18917 ■ The Truman Tribune
The Truman Tribune
118 E Ciro St.
Truman, MN 56088
Phone: (507)776-2751
Fax: (507)776-2751
Publication E-mail: trutrib1@frontiernet.net
Community newspaper. **Freq:** Weekly (Wed.). **Print Method:** Offset. **Cols./Page:** 6. **Col. Width:** 12 picas. **Col. Depth:** 21 1/2 inches. **Key Personnel:** Vickie Greiner, Editor. **ISSN:** 0891--1401 (print). **Subscription Rates:** $30 Individuals within Martin County/Lewisville; $35 Individuals elsewhere in MN; $42 Individuals out of state. **URL:** http://www.thetrumantribune.com. **Mailing address:** PO Box 98, Truman, MN 56088. **Ad Rates:** SAU $3.75. **Remarks:** Accepts advertising. **Circ:** 822.

TWO HARBORS

NE MN. Lake Co. On Lake Superior, 25 mi. NE of Duluth. Residential. Resort. Truck and dairy farms.

18918 ■ Hibbing Manney Shopper
Manney's Shopper Inc.
626 1/2 2nd Ave.
Two Harbors, MN 55616
Shopper. **Freq:** Weekly (Sun.). **Print Method:** Offset. **Trim Size:** 12 x 21 3/4. **Cols./Page:** 6. **Col. Width:** 11 8/10 picas. **Col. Depth:** 301 agate lines. **Key Personnel:** Brian Polakangas, Contact, phone: (218)263-8357, fax: (218)263-9201. **Subscription Rates:** Free; $38 Out of area. **URL:** http://www.hibbingmn.com. **Ad Rates:** GLR $.57; BW $761.10; 4C $1,270.33; PCI $8.99. **Remarks:** Accepts advertising. **Circ:** Free ‡15973.

18919 ■ Lake County News-Chronicle
Forum Communications Co.
109 Waterfront Dr.
Two Harbors, MN 55616
Phone: (218)834-2141
Fax: (218)834-2144
Publication E-mail: chronicle@lcnewschronicle.com
Community newspaper. **Freq:** Weekly (Fri.). **Print Method:** Offset. **Cols./Page:** 6. **Col. Width:** 1.833 inches. **Col. Depth:** 21 inches. **Key Personnel:** Mike Creger, Editor; Tammy Francois, Editor, phone: (218)834-2141; David Lukkonen, Manager, Advertising. **Subscription Rates:** $37.44 Individuals in Lake County residents; $42.64 Individuals seasonal residents; $42.64 Individuals Minnesota residents; $50.96 Out of state. **URL:** http://www.twoharborsmn.com/. **Ad Rates:** GLR $6.95. **Remarks:** Accepts advertising. **Circ:** (Not Reported).

TYLER

SW MN. Lincoln Co. 80 mi. NE of Sioux Falls, SD. Manufactures cement blocks, tile, feed. Elevators. Dairy, poultry, grain farms.

Circulation: ★ = AAM; △ or • = BPA; ♦ = CAC; ❏ = VAC; ⊕ = PO Statement; ‡ = Publisher's Report; Boldface figures = sworn; Light figures = estimated.

18920 ■ The Tyler Tribute
The Tyler Tribute
151 N Tyler St.
Tyler, MN 56178-0466
Phone: (507)247-5502
Publisher's E-mail: tribute@tylertribute.com
Community newspaper. **Freq:** Weekly (Wed.). **Print Method:** Offset. **Cols./Page:** 6. **Col. Width:** 24 nonpareils. **Col. Depth:** 294 agate lines. **Key Personnel:** William Clark, Publisher; Robert Wolfington, Editor; Diane Clark, Publisher. **USPS:** 963-720. **Subscription Rates:** $35 Individuals Lincoln, Pipestone, and Lyon County; $40 Out of area; $45 Out of state. **URL:** http://www.tylertribute.com. **Ad Rates:** GLR $.32; BW $555; 4C $745; SAU $6.70; PCI $4.30. **Remarks:** Accepts advertising. **Circ:** ‡1,100.

VERNDALE

SW MN. Wadena Co. 40 mi. W. of Brainerd.

18921 ■ The Verndale Sun
The Verndale Sun
121 S Farwell, Office 3
Verndale, MN 56481
Phone: (218)445-6397
Fax: (218)445-6200
Publication E-mail: news@inhnews.com
Community newspaper (tabloid). **Freq:** Weekly (Thurs.). **Print Method:** Offset. **Trim Size:** 11 1/2 x 16. **Cols./Page:** 5. **Col. Width:** 11.5 picas. **Col. Depth:** 15 inches. **Key Personnel:** Aaron J. Kurt, Publisher. **USPS:** 658-100. **Subscription Rates:** $24 Individuals; $27 Out of area; $30 Out of state; $35 Individuals dual residence. **URL:** http://www.inhnews.com. **Mailing address:** PO Box E, Verndale, MN 56481. **Ad Rates:** GLR $3; BW $168.75; 4C $198.25; PCI $2. **Remarks:** Accepts advertising. **Circ:** ‡675.

VIRGINIA

NE MN. St. Louis Co. 26 mi. E. of Hibbing. Lake resort area. Voyageurs National Park. State Community College. Iron ore mines; taconite pellet. Lumber.

18922 ■ Mesabi Daily News
Superior Publishing
PO Box 956
Virginia, MN 55792
Phone: (218)741-5544
General newspaper. **Founded:** 1893. **Freq:** Daily (morn.). **Print Method:** Offset. **Cols./Page:** 6. **Col. Width:** 24 nonpareils. **Col. Depth:** 301 agate lines. **Key Personnel:** Bill Hanna, Editor; Chris Knight, General Manager. **Subscription Rates:** $188 Individuals Carrier delivery and online access; $65 Individuals online access. **URL:** http://www.virginiamn.com. **Ad Rates:** SAU $8.65. **Remarks:** Accepts advertising. **Circ:** Mon.-Sat. ♦**9,642**, Sun. ♦**11,173**.

WADENA

WC MN. Wadena Co. 80 mi. NW of Saint Cloud. Manufactures butter, woodwork, clothing, beverages. Dairy, poultry farms. Corn, hay, oats.

18923 ■ Intercom
Wadena Pioneer Journal
314 S Jefferson
Wadena, MN 56482
Phone: (218)631-2561
Fax: (218)631-1621
Publisher's E-mail: editorial@wadenapj.com
Community newspaper. **Freq:** Weekly (Sun.). **Subscription Rates:** Free. **URL:** http://www.wadenapj.com. **Mailing address:** PO Box 31, Wadena, MN 56482. **Remarks:** Accepts advertising. **Circ:** Free ‡8470.

18924 ■ Pioneer Journal
Wadena Pioneer Journal
314 S Jefferson
Wadena, MN 56482
Phone: (218)631-2561
Fax: (218)631-1621
Publisher's E-mail: editorial@wadenapj.com
Community newspaper. **Freq:** Weekly (Thurs.). **Print Method:** Offset. **Cols./Page:** 6. **Col. Width:** 28 nonpareils. **Col. Depth:** 301 agate lines. **Key Personnel:** Cordell Schott, Editor, General Manager. **Subscription Rates:** $39 Individuals; $50 Out of state; $31 Students 9 months; $38 Individuals senior. **URL:** http://www.wadenapj.com. **Mailing address:** PO Box 31, Wadena, MN 56482. **Ad Rates:** GLR $.53. **Remarks:** Accepts advertising. **Circ:** Paid ‡2,914.

18925 ■ KKWS-FM - 105.9
201 1/2 S Jefferson St.
Wadena, MN 56482
Phone: (218)631-1803
Format: Country. **Networks:** ABC. **Owner:** BL Broadcasting, Not Available. **Founded:** 1968. **Operating Hours:** Continuous; 60% network, 40% local. **Key Personnel:** Rick Youngbauer, Gen. Mgr., rick@kwadknsp.com. **Wattage:** 100,000. **Ad Rates:** $6-12 for 30 seconds. **Mailing address:** PO Box 551, Wadena, MN 56482. **URL:** http://www.superstationk106.com.

18926 ■ KNSP-AM - 1430
201 1/2 S Jefferson St.
Wadena, MN 56482
Phone: (218)631-1803
Format: Contemporary Country. **Networks:** Independent. **Owner:** BL Broadcasting, Not Available. **Founded:** 1982. **Operating Hours:** 5:45 a.m.-10 p.m. **Wattage:** 1,000. **Ad Rates:** Noncommercial. **Mailing address:** PO Box 551, Wadena, MN 56482. **URL:** http://www.superstationk106.com.

18927 ■ KWAD-AM - 920
201 1/2 S Jefferson St.
Wadena, MN 56482
Phone: (218)631-1803
Format: Contemporary Country. **Simulcasts:** KNSP. **Networks:** ABC; Minnesota News. **Owner:** BL Broadcasting, Not Available. **Founded:** 1948. **Operating Hours:** Continuous. **Wattage:** 1,000. **Ad Rates:** $5-9.50 for 30 seconds. Combined advertising rates available with KKWS. **Mailing address:** PO Box 551, Wadena, MN 56482. **URL:** http://www.superstationk106.com.

WAITE PARK

18928 ■ The Shopping News
Gannett Company Inc.
3000 4th Ave. NE
Waite Park, MN 56387
Phone: (320)259-3600
Fax: (320)252-1031
Publication E-mail: art@theshoppingnews.com
Shopper. **Founded:** 1957. **Freq:** Weekly (Mon.). **Print Method:** Offset. **Cols./Page:** 6. **Col. Width:** 12.5 picas. **Col. Depth:** 21.5 picas. **Key Personnel:** Gaye Kirchoff, Manager, Sales. **Subscription Rates:** $22 Individuals full access; mon.-sun. /month; $16.50 Individuals full access; thurs.-sun. /month; $14 Individuals full access; sat. & sun. /month; $12 Individuals digital only /month. **URL:** http://www.sctimes.com. **Ad Rates:** GLR $.50; BW $1,006; PCI $8.75. **Remarks:** Accepts advertising. **Circ:** Combined ‡50183.

WARROAD

NW MN. Roseau Co. On Lake of the Woods, 115 mi. of Grand Forks, ND. International Boundry Line. Resort. Fisheries; timber. Mink ranches. Manufactures wood windows, insulated glass, hockey sticks, lumber. Agriculture. Seed potatoes, hay, grass seed.

18929 ■ The Warroad Pioneer
Warroad Pioneer
501 Lake St. NE
Warroad, MN 56763
Phone: (218)386-3970
Fax: (218)386-3120
Publisher's E-mail: wpioneer@centurytel.net
Community newspaper. **Freq:** Weekly (Tues.). **Print Method:** Offset. **Cols./Page:** 6. **Col. Width:** 26 nonpareils. **Col. Depth:** 301 agate lines. **Key Personnel:** Rollin Bergman, Publisher; Julie M. Nordine, Publisher; Sybil Butler, Managing Editor; Bonnie Nordvall, Editor. **Subscription Rates:** $30 Individuals In Roseau County; $36 Out of area; $40 Out of state; $25 Individuals online. **URL:** http://www.warroadmnnews.com/34029/2095/1/online-edition; http://www.mnnews.com/newspapers/warroad.html. **Mailing address:** PO Box E, Warroad, MN 56763. **Ad Rates:** PCI $4.25; 4C $7. **Remarks:** Accepts advertising. **Circ:** 1,490.

18930 ■ KKWQ-FM - 92.5
Lake Street Ctr., Ste. 113A
Warroad, MN 56763
Phone: (218)386-3024
Format: Country. **Owner:** Border Broadcasting LP, 113A Lake Street Center, WARROAD, MN 56763, Ph: (218)386-3024, Fax: (218)386-3090. **Founded:** 1989. **Wattage:** 100,000. **Ad Rates:** Noncommercial. $9 for 30 seconds; $14 for 60 seconds. **Mailing address:** PO Box 69, Warroad, MN 56763.

18931 ■ KRWB-AM - 1410
Lake Street Ctr., Ste. 113 A
Warroad, MN 56763
Format: Classic Rock. **Networks:** ABC; Minnesota News. **Owner:** Border Broadcasting L.L.P., Lake Street Ctr, Ste. 113 A, Warroad, MN 56763. **Operating Hours:** 5:30 a.m.-midnight. **Key Personnel:** Mike Pederson, Contact, mp_pederson@hotmail.com; Mike Pederson, Contact, mp_pederson@hotmail.com. **Wattage:** 1,000. **Ad Rates:** $3.95-4.80 for 30 seconds; $5.65-6.85 for 60 seconds. **Mailing address:** PO Box 69, Warroad, MN 56763. **URL:** http://www.kq92.com.

WASECA

SC MN. Waseca Co. 25 mi. E. of Mankato. University of Minnesota Technical College at Waseca. Lake resort. Manufactures frozen foods, electronic equipment, steel products, truck bodies, modular homes, sporting goods. Hatcheries. Dairy, cattles, poultry, hog farms. Corn, soybeans, oats, flax, rye.

18932 ■ Arabian Horse Times
Arabian Horse Times
299 Johnson Ave., Ste. 150
Waseca, MN 56093
Fax: (507)835-5138
Free: 800-248-4637
Magazine featuring articles on the care and management of Arabian horses. **Freq:** Monthly. **Trim Size:** 8 x 10. **Key Personnel:** Lara Ames, Publisher. **ISSN:** 0279--8125 (print). **Subscription Rates:** $40 U.S. 1 year; $65 Canada 1 year; $95 Other countries 1 year; $65 U.S. 2 years; $125 Canada 2 years; $185 Other countries 2 years; $90 U.S. 3 years; $170 Canada 3 years; $280 Other countries 3 years; $25 Individuals online; 1 year; $45 Individuals online; 2 years; $60 Individuals online; 3 years. **URL:** http://www.ahtimes.com. **Remarks:** Advertising accepted; rates available upon request. **Circ:** Paid 22000.

18933 ■ Waseca County News
Waseca County News
213 Second St. NW
Waseca, MN 56093
Phone: (507)835-3380
Fax: (507)835-3435
Publisher's E-mail: classifieds@wasecacountynews.com
Community newspaper. **Freq:** Semiweekly (Tues. and Thurs.). **Print Method:** Offset. **Cols./Page:** 6. **Col. Width:** 26 nonpareils. **Col. Depth:** 301 agate lines. **Key Personnel:** Julie Frazier, Editor; Zack Hacker, Managing Editor. **USPS:** 664-350. **Subscription Rates:** $98.80 Individuals print and online; 1 year; $32.40 Individuals print and online; 6 months. **URL:** http://www.southernminn.com/waseca_county_news/. **Formed by the merger of:** Waseca Sun-Review. **Ad Rates:** GLR $.44; BW $689.82; 4C $960.08; SAU $6.21; PCI $6.21. **Remarks:** Accepts advertising. **Circ:** Paid ‡3,727.

18934 ■ KOWZ-AM - 1170
222 N State St.
Waseca, MN 56093-2931
Phone: (507)444-9224
Fax: (507)444-9080
Format: News; Sports; Information. **Owner:** Linder Radio Group. **Founded:** 1971. **Operating Hours:** 12:00 p.m. - 1:00 p.m. Monday - Friday, 8.45 a.m. - 4:00 p.m. Saturday, 7:00 a.m. - 4:00 p.m. Sunday. **Key Personnel:** DJ White, News Dir. **Wattage:** 2,500. **Ad Rates:** Advertising accepted; rates available upon request. $8 for 30 seconds; $12 for 60 seconds. Combined advertising rates available with KOWZ 100.9, KRUE 92.1, KTOE. **URL:** http://kowzam.com/.

18935 ■ KRUE-FM - 92.1
255 Cedardale Dr.
Owatonna, MN 55060
Phone: (507)444-9224
Fax: (507)444-9080
Email: booth@krue1170.com

Format: Oldies. **Networks:** ABC. **Founded:** 1972. **Operating Hours:** Continuous. **Key Personnel:** Matt Ketelsen, Sales Mgr., mattk@kowzonline.com. **Wattage:** 25,000. **Ad Rates:** $8 for 30 seconds; $12 for 60 seconds. **URL:** http://www.krue1170.com.

18936 ■ Mediacom Communications Corp.
1504 Second St. SE
Waseca, MN 56093
Email: closedcaption@mediacomcc.com
Founded: Sept. 06, 2006. **Key Personnel:** Mark E. Stephan, CFO, Exec. VP; Rocco B. Commisso, Chairman, CEO. **URL:** http://mediacomcable.com.

WATERTOWN

SC MN. Carver Co. 30 mi. W. of Minneapolis. Agriculture. Dairy, poultry, beef, grain, corn, wheat, soybeans.

18937 ■ Carver County News
Carver County News
130 Lewis Ave. S
Watertown, MN 55388
Phone: (952)955-1111
Fax: (952)955-2241
Publisher's E-mail: patriotgeneral@acnpapers.com
Newspaper with a Republican orientation. **Freq:** Weekly (Thurs.). **Print Method:** Offset. **Cols./Page:** 6. **Col. Width:** 24 nonpareils. **Col. Depth:** 301 agate lines. **Key Personnel:** James D. Berreth, Publisher; Todd Moen, Editor. **Subscription Rates:** $31 Individuals; $36 Individuals in state; $37 Out of state. **URL:** http://www.mnnews.com/newspapers/watertown.html; http://sunpatriot.com/tag/ccn. **Mailing address:** PO Box 188, Watertown, MN 55388. **Remarks:** Accepts advertising. **Circ:** ‡1837.

WELLS

SC MN. Faribault Co. 42 mi. SE of Mantako. Canneries, food processing. Manufactures tile, concrete. Hatchery. Dairy, poultry, stock, grain farms.

18938 ■ Wells Mirror
The Wells Mirror
40 W Franklin
Wells, MN 56097
Phone: (507)553-3131
Fax: (507)553-3132
Publication E-mail: wellsmir@bevcomm.net
Newspaper. **Freq:** Weekly (Thurs.). **Print Method:** Offset. **Cols./Page:** 6. **Col. Width:** 29 nonpareils. **Col. Depth:** 301 agate lines. **USPS:** 674-060. **URL:** http://www.mnnews.com/newspapers/wells.html. **Ad Rates:** PCI $3.50. **Remarks:** Advertising accepted; rates available upon request. **Circ:** 1568.

WESTBROOK

18939 ■ Westbrook Sentinel & Tribune
Westbrook Sentinel & Tribune
621 1st Ave.
Westbrook, MN 56183-0098
Phone: (507)274-6136
Fax: (507)274-6137
Publisher's E-mail: sentrib@prairie.lakes.com
Community newspaper. **Freq:** Weekly (Wed.). **Cols./Page:** 7. **Col. Width:** 12 3/10 picas. **Col. Depth:** 21 1/2 inches. **URL:** http://www.ncppub.com/pages/?cat=60. **Mailing address:** PO Box 98, Westbrook, MN 56183-0098. **Circ:** ‡1134.

WHEATON

18940 ■ Wheaton Gazette
Wheaton Gazette
1114 Broadway
Wheaton, MN 56296-1308
Phone: (320)563-8146
Fax: (320)563-8147
Publisher's E-mail: wgazette@frontiernet.net
Community newspaper. **Freq:** Weekly (Tues.). **Cols./Page:** 7. **Col. Width:** 12.5 picas. **Col. Depth:** 21 1/2 inches. **URL:** http://www.mna.org/mna/55-MNA.html. **Circ:** Tues. 1795.

WHITE BEAR LAKE

SE MN. Washington Co. On White Bear Lake, 12 mi. NE of Saint Paul. Lakewood Communuity College. Manufactures sport boats, airport carts, sound equipment, steel fabricators, Corrugated boxes, fishing sinkers.

18941 ■ Burnett County Sentinel
Press Publications
4779 Bloom Ave.
White Bear Lake, MN 55110
Phone: (651)407-1200
Fax: (651)429-1242
Publisher's E-mail: news@presspubs.com
Newspaper. **Freq:** Weekly (Wed.). **Print Method:** Offset. **Cols./Page:** 6. **Col. Width:** 24 nonpareils. **Col. Depth:** 294 agate lines. **Key Personnel:** Todd Beckmann, Editor; Stacy Coy, Manager, Production. **USPS:** 080-020. **Subscription Rates:** $37 Individuals; $43 Individuals; $29 Individuals online. **URL:** http://www.presspubs.com/burnett. **Ad Rates:** GLR $5.15; BW $450; PCI $4.75. **Remarks:** Advertising accepted; rates available upon request. **Circ:** Combined 3750.

18942 ■ Christian Magnifier
Lutheran Braille Evangelism Association
1740 Eugene St.
White Bear Lake, MN 55110-3312
Phone: (651)426-0469
Publisher's E-mail: mail@lbea.org
Freq: 11/year. **Subscription Rates:** $8 /year. **Alt. Formats:** PDF. **URL:** http://www.lbea.org/LargePrintCatalog.htm. **Remarks:** Advertising not accepted. **Circ:** (Not Reported).

18943 ■ Forest Lake Press
Press Publications
4779 Bloom Ave.
White Bear Lake, MN 55110
Phone: (651)407-1200
Fax: (651)429-1242
Publisher's E-mail: news@presspubs.com
Local newspaper. **Freq:** Weekly (Wed.). **Trim Size:** 14 x 22 3/4. **Cols./Page:** 6. **Col. Width:** 2 1/16 inches. **Col. Depth:** 21 inches. **Key Personnel:** Carter C. Johnson, Publisher; Michelle Miron, Managing Editor, phone: (651)407-1226. **Subscription Rates:** $18 Individuals 6 months; $30 Individuals 1 year; $49 Two years; $23 Individuals 6 months plus carrier tip; $40 Individuals 1 year plus carrier tip; $69 Two years plus carrier tip. **URL:** http://www.presspubs.com/forest_lake. **Formerly:** Little Canada Press. **Remarks:** Accepts advertising. **Circ:** (Not Reported).

18944 ■ Quad Community Press
Press Publications
4779 Bloom Ave.
White Bear Lake, MN 55110
Phone: (651)407-1200
Fax: (651)429-1242
Publisher's E-mail: news@presspubs.com
Community newspaper. **Freq:** Weekly (Tues.). **Print Method:** Offset. **Trim Size:** 14 x 21. **Cols./Page:** 6. **Col. Width:** 1 13/16 inches. **Col. Depth:** 21 inches. **Key Personnel:** Eugene D. Johnson, Publisher, phone: (651)407-1200; Wade Martin, Manager, Circulation, phone: (651)407-1241; Bruce Treichler, Director, Advertising, phone: (651)407-1208; Michelle Miron, Managing Editor, phone: (651)407-1226. **Subscription Rates:** $30 Individuals; $49 Two years; $40 Individuals one year subscription plus carrier tip; $69 Two years one year subscription plus carrier tip. **URL:** http://www.presspubs.com/quad/. **Ad Rates:** GLR $5.75; BW $1,474.20; 4C $1,669.20; SAU $11.70; CNU $11.70; PCI $11.70. **Remarks:** Accepts advertising. **Circ:** Free ‡6993, Paid ‡1093, Combined ‡8086.

18945 ■ St. Croix Valley Press
Press Publications
4779 Bloom Ave.
White Bear Lake, MN 55110
Phone: (651)407-1200
Fax: (651)429-1242
Publisher's E-mail: news@presspubs.com
Local newspaper. **Freq:** Weekly (Thurs.). **Print Method:** Offset. **Trim Size:** 9 9/16 x 15. **Cols./Page:** 5. **Col. Width:** 1 13/16 inches. **Col. Depth:** 15 inches. **Key Personnel:** Wade Martin, Manager, Circulation, phone: (651)407-1241; Eugene D. Johnson, Publisher, phone: (651)407-1200; Michelle Miron, Managing Editor, phone: (651)407-1226. **Subscription Rates:** $30 Individuals; $49 Two years; $40 Individuals one year subscription plus carrier tip; $69 Two years one year subscription plus carrier tip. **URL:** http://www.presspubs.com/st_croix/. **Ad Rates:** GLR $5.75; BW $934; 4C $1,129; SAU $14.39; CNU $14.39; PCI $14.39. **Remarks:** Accepts advertising. **Circ:** (Not Reported).

18946 ■ Shoreview Press
Press Publications
4779 Bloom Ave.
White Bear Lake, MN 55110
Phone: (651)407-1200
Fax: (651)429-1242
Publisher's E-mail: news@presspubs.com
Local newspaper. **Freq:** Weekly (Tues.). **Cols./Page:** 6. **Col. Width:** 1 13/16 inches. **Col. Depth:** 21 inches. **Key Personnel:** Carter C. Johnson, Publisher. **Subscription Rates:** $15 Individuals 6 months; $26 Individuals 1 year; $20 Individuals 6 months plus carrier tip; $36 Individuals 1 year plus carrier tip. **URL:** http://www.presspubs.com/shoreview. **Remarks:** Accepts advertising. **Circ:** (Not Reported).

18947 ■ Vadnais Heights Press
Press Publications
4779 Bloom Ave.
White Bear Lake, MN 55110
Phone: (651)407-1200
Fax: (651)429-1242
Publisher's E-mail: news@presspubs.com
Local newspaper. **Freq:** Weekly (Wed.). **Print Method:** Offset. **Trim Size:** 14 x 22 3/4. **Cols./Page:** 6. **Col. Width:** 1 13/16 inches. **Col. Depth:** 21 inches. **Key Personnel:** Michelle Miron, Managing Editor, phone: (651)407-1226; Wade Martin, Manager, Circulation, phone: (651)407-1241; Gene Johnson, Publisher, phone: (651)407-1200. **Subscription Rates:** $30 Individuals; $49 Two years; $40 Individuals one year subscription plus carrier tip; $69 Two years one year subscription plus carrier tip. **URL:** http://www.presspubs.com/vadnais/. **Ad Rates:** GLR $5.75; BW $901; 4C $1,081; SAU $9.72; CNU $9.72; PCI $9.72. **Remarks:** Accepts advertising. **Circ:** (Not Reported).

18948 ■ White Bear Press
Press Publications
4779 Bloom Ave.
White Bear Lake, MN 55110
Phone: (651)407-1200
Fax: (651)429-1242
Publisher's E-mail: news@presspubs.com
Local newspaper. **Freq:** Weekly (Wed.). **Print Method:** Offset. **Trim Size:** 14 x 22.75. **Cols./Page:** 6. **Col. Width:** 1 13/16 inches. **Col. Depth:** 21 inches. **Key Personnel:** Wade Martin, Manager, Circulation, phone: (651)407-1241; Bruce Treichler, Director, Advertising, phone: (651)407-1208; Michelle Miron, Managing Editor, phone: (651)407-1226; Gene Johnson, Publisher, phone: (651)407-1200. **Subscription Rates:** $30 Individuals; $49 Two years; $40 Individuals one year subscription plus carrier tip; $69 Two years one year subscription plus carrier tip. **URL:** http://www.presspubs.com/white_bear/. **Ad Rates:** GLR $5.75; BW $3049; 4C $3244; SAU $24.20; CNU $24.20; PCI $24.20. **Remarks:** Accepts advertising. **Circ:** Free ‡15,507, Paid ‡27,68, Combined ‡18,275.

WILLMAR

SWC MN. Kandiyohi Co. 92 mi. W. of Minneapolis. Willman Community College. Medical center. Tourist area. Farm equipment, sash and door, soft drink factories. Metal fabricating. Turkey processing. Agriculture. Dairying, turkeys.

18949 ■ West Central Tribune
West Central Tribune
2208 Trott Ave. SW
Willmar, MN 56201
Phone: (320)235-1150
Fax: (320)235-6769
Publication E-mail: online@wctrib.com
General newspaper. **Freq:** Mon.-Sat. (morn.). **Print Method:** Offset. **Cols./Page:** 6. **Col. Width:** 25 nonpareils. **Col. Depth:** 294 agate lines. **Key Personnel:** Dan Burdett, Editor; Susan Lunneborg, Editor; Gary Miller, Associate Editor; Ron Adams, Photographer; Steven Ammermann, Publisher; Kelly Boldan, Editor. **USPS:** 675-080. **Subscription Rates:** $162.45 Individuals carrier/motor route; $107.73 Individuals Friday-

Circulation: ★ = AAM; △ or • = BPA; ♦ = CAC; ❑ = VAC; ⊕ = PO Statement; ‡ = Publisher's Report; Boldface figures = sworn; Light figures = estimated.

Saturday (carrier/motor route); $173.85 By mail; $107.73 By mail Friday-Saturday; $180.12 Out of area by mail. **URL:** http://www.wctrib.com. **Feature Editors:** Sharon Bomstad, sharonb@wctrib.com. **Mailing address:** PO Box 839, Willmar, MN 56201. **Ad Rates:** GLR $4.70; BW $1,810; 4C $2,175; SAU $17.70; PCI $14.03. **Remarks:** 4.70. **Circ:** Free ■ **727**, Paid ■ **14793**, Combined ■ **15520**.

18950 ■ KBHZ-FM - 91.9
PO Box 247
Osakis, MN 56360
Free: 800-658-2229
Email: mail@praisefm.org
Format: Religious. **Key Personnel:** David McLiver, Exec. Dir., david@praisefm.org; Jack Zitzmann, Dir. of Production, News Dir., jackson@praisefm.org; Sherrie McIver, Music Dir., sherrie@praisefm.org; Steve Neprath, Contact, steve@praisefm.org. **Ad Rates:** Noncommercial. **URL:** http://www.praisefm.org.

18951 ■ KDJS-AM - 1590
730 NE Hwy. 71 Service Dr.
Willmar, MN 56201
Phone: (320)231-1600
Fax: (320)235-7010
Format: Oldies; Talk. **Networks:** Westwood One Radio. **Founded:** Mar. 17, 1981. **Operating Hours:** Continuous. **Key Personnel:** Doug Hanson, Gen. Mgr.; Jeremy Goulet, Traffic Mgr., Office Mgr.; Bev Ahlquist, News Dir., bahlquist@k-musicradio.com. **Wattage:** 1,000. **Ad Rates:** Noncommercial. Combined advertising rates available with KDJS-FM and KRVY-FM. **URL:** http://www.k-musicradio.com.

18952 ■ KDJS-FM - 95.3
730 NE Hwy. 71, Service Dr.
Willmar, MN 56201
Phone: (320)231-1600
Fax: (320)235-7010
Format: Hot Country. **Networks:** Westwood One Radio. **Founded:** 1993. **Operating Hours:** Continuous. **Key Personnel:** Bev Ahlquist, News Dir., bahlquist@k-musicradio.com; Jeremy Goulet, Office Mgr., jgoulet@yahoo.com. **Wattage:** 50,000. **Ad Rates:** $18 for 30 seconds; $24 for 60 seconds. Combined advertising rates available with KDJS-AM. **URL:** http://k-musicradio.com.

18953 ■ KKLN-FM - 94.1
1605 S 1st St.
Willmar, MN 56201
Phone: (320)235-1194
Fax: (320)235-6894
Format: Classic Rock; Album-Oriented Rock (AOR). **Key Personnel:** Justin Klinghagen, Owner, justin@kkln.com; John Jennings, Owner, john@kkln.com. **Ad Rates:** Advertising accepted; rates available upon request. **URL:** http://www.kkln.com.

18954 ■ KKLW-FM - 90.9
PO Box 779002
Rocklin, CA 95677-9972
Fax: (916)251-1901
Free: 800-525-5683
Format: Contemporary Christian. **Owner:** Educational Media Foundation, PO Box 2098, Omaha, NE 68103-2098, Free: 800-434-8400. **Key Personnel:** Mike Novak, President, CEO; Alan Mason, COO. **Wattage:** 400. **URL:** http://www.klove.com.

18955 ■ KQIC-FM - 102
PO Box 838
Willmar, MN 56201
Phone: (320)235-3535
Format: Adult Contemporary. **Founded:** 1999. **Ad Rates:** Noncommercial. **URL:** http://www.willmarradio.com.

18956 ■ KRVY-FM - 97.3
730 NE Hwy., 71 Service Dr.
Willmar, MN 56201
Phone: (320)231-1600
Fax: (320)235-7010
Format: Classic Rock; Contemporary Hit Radio (CHR). **Key Personnel:** Doug Hanson, Gen. Mgr.; Jeremy Goulet, Office Mgr.; Bev Ahlquist, News Dir., bahlquist@k-musicradio.com. **Wattage:** 50,000. **Ad Rates:** Advertising accepted; rates available upon request. **URL:** http://www.k-musicradio.com.

18957 ■ KWLM-AM - 1340
1340 N 7th St. NW
Willmar, MN 56201
Phone: (320)235-1340
Email: askus@kwlm.com
Format: News; Talk. **Networks:** ABC; Mutual Broadcasting System. **Owner:** Lakeland Broadcasting Co., 1340 7th St. NW, Willmar, MN 56201, Ph: (320)235-1342. **Operating Hours:** Continuous. **Wattage:** 1,000. **Ad Rates:** $9-23 for 30 seconds; $13-25 for 60 seconds. **Mailing address:** PO Box 838, Willmar, MN 56201. **URL:** http://www.kwlm.com.

WINDOM

SW MN. Cottonwood Co. 120 mi. SW of Saint Paul. Manufactures snowblowers, lawn mowers, farm equipment wood burning stoves. Beef packing plant. Elevator. Corn, soybeans, dairy products, honey and livestock.

18958 ■ Cottonwood County Citizen
Cottonwood County Citizen
260 Tenth St.
Windom, MN 56101
Phone: (507)831-3455
Fax: (507)831-3740
Free: 800-658-2510
Publication E-mail: citizen@windomnews.com
Community newspaper. **Freq:** Weekly (Wed.). **Print Method:** Offset. **Cols./Page:** 6. **Col. Width:** 28 nonpareils. **Col. Depth:** 301 agate lines. **Key Personnel:** Trevor Slette, Publisher; Rahn Larson, Editor. **Subscription Rates:** $37 Students 9 months; print and online; $22 Individuals online only; $70 Other countries print and online; 1 year; $60 Other countries print only; 1 year; $45 Individuals print only; 76 Two years print only. **URL:** http://www.windomnews.com. **Mailing address:** PO Box 309, Windom, MN 56101. **Ad Rates:** GLR $.42; BW $748; 4C $948; PCI $8.20. **Remarks:** Accepts advertising. **Circ:** ‡3,000.

18959 ■ Minnesota Educator
Education Minnesota
560 2nd Ave.
Windom, MN 56101
Phone: (507)831-5484
Fax: (507)831-0190
Free: 800-652-9073
Publication E-mail: educator@edmn.org
Educational newspaper. **Freq:** Monthly. **Print Method:** Offset. Uses mats. **Trim Size:** 16 1/2 x 11 1/2. **Cols./Page:** 5. **Col. Width:** 28 nonpareils. **Col. Depth:** 210 agate lines. **ISSN:** 1521-9062 (print). **Subscription Rates:** $25 Nonmembers; $2.50 Single issue. **URL:** http://www.educationminnesota.org/news/minnesota-educator/minnesota-educator. **Remarks:** Accepts advertising. **Circ:** ‡78,000.

18960 ■ KDOM-AM - 1580
1450 N Hwy. 60 & 71
Windom, MN 56101
Phone: (507)831-3908
Fax: (507)831-3913
Email: kdomnews@windomnet.com
Format: Full Service; Country. **Operating Hours:** Continuous. **Wattage:** 1,000. **Ad Rates:** Noncommercial. **Mailing address:** PO Box 218, Windom, MN 56101. **URL:** http://www.kdomradio.com.

18961 ■ KDOM-FM - 94.3
1450 N Hwy. 60 & 71
Windom, MN 56101
Phone: (507)831-3908
Fax: (507)831-3913
Email: kdomnews@windomnet.com
Format: News; Sports. **Wattage:** 6,000. **Ad Rates:** Noncommercial. **Mailing address:** PO Box 218, Windom, MN 56101. **URL:** http://www.kdomradio.com.

18962 ■ KQRB-FM - 89.9
PO Box 3206
Tupelo, MS 38803
Format: Religious. **Owner:** American Family Radio, at above address. **URL:** http://www.afa.net.

18963 ■ Windom Cable Communications
444 9th St.
Windom, MN 56101
Phone: (507)831-6129
Email: support@windomnet.com
Founded: Apr. 1984. **Key Personnel:** Steve Nasby, Administrator. **Cities Served:** subscribing households 1,600. **URL:** http://www.windomnet.com.

WINONA

SE MN. Winona Co. On Mississippi River, 30 mi. N. of La Crosse, WI. Barge connections. St. Mary's College; College of St. Teresa; Winona State College. Steamboat Museum. Manufactures flour, patent medicines, cosmetics, food, dairy products, auto chains, sweaters, metalware, gloves, mitts, candy, malt, feed, plastic compounds, wooden boxes, excavators, bricks, rock drills, iron benders, fertilizers. Nurseries. Agriculture.

18964 ■ The Courier
Roman Catholic Diocese of Winona
55 W Sanborn
Winona, MN 55987-0949
Phone: (507)454-4643
Fax: (507)454-8106
Publisher's E-mail: dioceseofwinona@dow.org
Catholic magazine. **Founded:** 1910. **Freq:** Monthly. **Print Method:** Offset. **Trim Size:** 11 1/2 x 16. **Cols./Page:** 4. **Col. Width:** 28 nonpareils. **Col. Depth:** 224 agate lines. **Subscription Rates:** $5 Individuals. **URL:** http://www.dow.org/courier.html. **Mailing address:** PO Box 949, Winona, MN 55987-0949. **Remarks:** Accepts advertising. **Circ:** Combined ‡42000.

18965 ■ International Journal on Computers and Their Applications
International Society for Computers and their Applications
64 White Oak Ct.
Winona, MN 55987
Phone: (507)458-4517
Publisher's E-mail: isca@ipass.net
Journal publishing research in the theory and design of computers as well as current innovative activities in the applications of computers. **Freq:** Quarterly. **Key Personnel:** Prof. Frederick C. Harris, Jr., Dr., Editor-in-Chief. **ISSN:** 1076-5204 (print). **Subscription Rates:** Included in membership; $275 Libraries; $35 Single issue. **URL:** http://www.isca-hq.org/journal.htm. **Remarks:** Advertising not accepted. **Circ:** (Not Reported).

18966 ■ Telicom
International Society for Philosophical Enquiry
Dr. Patrick M. O'Shea, Acting Comptroller
700 Terrace Heights, No. 60
Winona, MN 55987
Freq: Quarterly. **ISSN:** 1087- 6456 (print). **Subscription Rates:** included in membership dues. **URL:** http://www.thethousand.com/telicom. **Remarks:** Advertising not accepted. **Circ:** 500.

18967 ■ Winona Daily News
Lee Enterprises Inc.
902 E 2nd St., Ste. 110
Winona, MN 55987
Phone: (507)453-3500
Fax: (507)454-1440
General newspaper. **Freq:** Daily. **Print Method:** Offset. **Cols./Page:** 6. **Col. Width:** 24 nonpareils. **Col. Depth:** 301 agate lines. **Key Personnel:** Tess Thruman, Manager, Sales, phone: (608)791-8210; Tom Kelley, Manager, Advertising, phone: (507)453-3561; Jerome Christenson, Editor, phone: (507)453-3522. **Subscription Rates:** $46.15 Individuals 13 weeks; carrier delivery; $92.30 Individuals 26 weeks; carrier delivery; $184.60 Individuals 52 weeks; carrier delivery; $46.15 Individuals 13 weeks; motor route; $92.30 Individuals 26 weeks; motor route; $184.60 Individuals 52 weeks; motor route. **URL:** http://www.winonadailynews.com. **Ad Rates:** BW $1258; 4C $1483; PCI $9.75. **Remarks:** Accepts advertising. **Circ:** Mon.-Sat. ★**9,502**, Sun. ★**10,211**.

18968 ■ Winona Post
Winona Post
64 E Second St.
Winona, MN 55987
Phone: (507)452-1262
Fax: (507)454-6409
Free: 800-353-2126
Publication E-mail: winpost@winonapost.com
Community newspaper. **Freq:** Semiweekly. **Key Personnel:** John O. Edstrom, Publisher; Frances M. Edstrom, Editor-in-Chief; Patrick Marek, Manager, Sales. **Subscription Rates:** Free. **Formerly:** Winona Post and

Shopper. **Ad Rates:** BW $1,218.17; 4C $1,421.33; SAU $11.29. **Remarks:** Accepts advertising. **Circ:** ‡55987.

18969 ■ Winonan
Winona State University
175 West Mark St.
Winona, MN 55987
Phone: (507)457-5000
Free: 800-342-5978
Publisher's E-mail: webmaster@winona.edu
Collegiate newspaper. **Freq:** Weekly. **Print Method:** Offset. **Cols./Page:** 5. **Col. Width:** 2.05 inches. **Col. Depth:** 224 agate lines. **URL:** http://www.winona.edu/diversity/winonanarticles.asp. **Mailing address:** PO Box 5838, Winona, MN 55987. **Ad Rates:** PCI $7. **Remarks:** Accepts advertising. **Circ:** Free ‡5,000.

18970 ■ KAGE-AM - 1380
752 Bluffview Cir.
Winona, MN 55987
Phone: (507)452-4000
Format: Country. **Owner:** Kage, Inc., at above address. **Founded:** Feb. 19, 1957. **Operating Hours**: Sunrise-sunset. **Local Programs**: *Partyline*, Monday Tuesday Wednesday Thursday Friday 10:00 a.m.; *KG Country Cash Call.* **Wattage**: 4,000 Day; 052 Night. **Ad Rates:** Noncommercial. **Mailing address:** PO Box 767, Winona, MN 55987. **URL:** http://www.winonaradio.com.

18971 ■ KAGE-FM - 95.3
752 Bluffview Cir.
Winona, MN 55987
Phone: (507)452-4000
Fax: (507)452-9494
Free: 800-584-6782
Format: Adult Contemporary. **Networks:** AP. **Owner:** Winona Radio, at above address. **Founded:** 1971. **Operating Hours**: Continuous. **Wattage**: 11,000. **Ad Rates:** Noncommercial. **Mailing address:** PO Box 767, Winona, MN 55987-0767. **URL:** http://www.winonaradio.com.

KBEW-AM - See Blue Earth, MN

18972 ■ KBEW-FM - 98.1
PO Box 767
Winona, MN 55987-0767
Phone: (507)526-2181
Fax: (507)526-7468
Email: kbew@bevcomm.net
Format: Contemporary Country. **Networks:** Linder Farm. **Owner:** Kbew Inc., 752 Bluffview Cir., Winona, MN 55987. **Founded:** Aug. 1993. **Operating Hours**: Continuous. **Key Personnel:** Kevin Benson, Gen. Mgr., kbew@bevcomm.net. **Wattage:** 25,000 ERP. **Ad Rates:** $7.50-10.75 for 30 seconds. **URL:** http://www.kbew98country.com.

18973 ■ KQAL-FM - 89.5
PO Box 5838
Winona, MN 55987
Phone: (507)457-2222
Fax: (507)457-5226
Format: Educational. **Networks:** AP. **Owner:** Winona State University, 175 West Mark St., Winona, MN 55987, Ph: (507)457-5000, Free: 800-342-5978. **Founded:** 1975. **Operating Hours**: Continuous. **Key Personnel:** Doug Westerman, Gen. Mgr.; Mike Martin, Operations Mgr.; Terese Tenseth, Dir. of Programs. **Wattage:** 2,500 ERP. **Ad Rates:** Accepts Advertising. **URL:** http://www.kqal.org.

18974 ■ KWNO-FM - 99.3
752 Bluffview Cir.
Winona, MN 55987
Phone: (507)452-4000
Fax: (507)452-9494
Free: 800-584-6782
Format: Hot Country. **Networks:** AP. **Owner:** Winona Radio, at above address. **Founded:** 1991. **Operating Hours:** Continuous. **ADI:** La Crosse-Eau Claire, WI. **Key Personnel:** Daryl Smelser, Contact. **Wattage**: 25,000. **Ad Rates:** $14-20 for 30 seconds; $18-25 for 60 seconds. **Mailing address:** PO Box 767, Winona, MN 55987. **URL:** http://www.winonaradio.com.

WINSTED

SC MN. McLeod Co. 42 mi. W. of Minneapolis. Milk products, lighting standards manufactured. Dairy, stock, grain farms.

18975 ■ Enterprise Dispatch
Herald Journal Publishing
120 Sixth St. N
Winsted, MN 55395
Phone: (320)485-2535
Fax: (320)485-2878
Free: 800-567-8303
Publisher's E-mail: hj@heraldjournal.com
Community newspaper. **Freq:** Weekly. **Print Method:** Offset. **Cols./Page:** 6. **Col. Width:** 28 nonpareils. **Col. Depth:** 301 agate lines. **Key Personnel:** Chris Schultz, Manager, Advertising; Lynda Jensen, Editor, phone: (320)485-2535. **USPS:** 120-800. **Subscription Rates:** $38 Individuals local; $43 Out of area; $48 Out of state; $42 Individuals print and online; $47 Out of area print and online; $52 Out of state print and online. **URL:** http://www.dasselcokato.com. **Formerly**: Cokato Enterprise; Dassel Dispatch. **Mailing address:** PO Box 129, Winsted, MN 55395. **Ad Rates:** GLR $.06; BW $593; 4C $788; SAU $4.25; PCI $4.60. **Remarks:** alcoholic beverages. **Circ:** Paid 2700.

18976 ■ Herald Journal
Herald Journal Publishing
120 Sixth St. N
Winsted, MN 55395
Phone: (320)485-2535
Fax: (320)485-2878
Free: 800-567-8303
Publication E-mail: herald@herald-journal.com
Community newspaper. **Freq:** Weekly (Mon.). **Cols./Page:** 7. **Col. Width:** 2 inches. **Key Personnel:** Ivan Raconteur, Editor; Aaron Schultz, Editor; Ryan Gueningsman, Managing Editor, phone: (320)282-6530; Matt Kane, Writer, phone: (320)282-0669; Chris Schultz, Manager, Advertising; Dale Kovar, General Manager, fax: (320)282-6501. **Subscription Rates:** $37 Individuals print only; $42 Out of area print only; $47 Out of state print only; $4 Individuals online only; $41 Individuals print and online; $46 Out of area print and online; $51 Out of state print and online. **URL:** http://www.herald-journal.com. **Mailing address:** PO Box 129, Winsted, MN 55395. **Remarks:** Accepts advertising. **Circ:** Paid 3050.

18977 ■ Herald Journal Shopper
Herald Journal Publishing
120 Sixth St. N
Winsted, MN 55395
Phone: (320)485-2535
Fax: (320)485-2878
Free: 800-567-8303
Publisher's E-mail: hj@heraldjournal.com
Shopper. **Freq:** Weekly (Mon.). **Print Method:** Offset. **Cols./Page:** 7. **Col. Width:** 2 inches. **Col. Depth:** 21 1/2 inches. **Key Personnel:** Ivan Raconteur, Editor; Chris Schultz, Manager, Advertising; Dale Kovar, General Manager. **Subscription Rates:** Free in trade area only. **URL:** http://www.herald-journal.com. **Formerly**: Howard Laker; Laker Shopper. **Mailing address:** PO Box 129, Winsted, MN 55395. **Ad Rates:** BW $865; SAU $8. **Remarks:** Accepts advertising. **Circ:** Free ‡6600.

WOODBURY

EC MN. Washington Co. 30 mi. SW of Stillwater.

18978 ■ Llewellyn's New Worlds of Mind and Spirit
Llewellyn Worldwide Ltd.
2143 Wooddale Dr.
Woodbury, MN 55125
Phone: (651)291-1970
Fax: (651)291-1908
Free: 800-843-6666
Publication E-mail: nweditor@llewellyn.com
Consumer magazine for readers interested in practical applications of astrology, psychology, occult philosophy, and inner awareness techniques. Includes reviews, articles, and news for the New Age community. **Freq:** Bimonthly. **Print Method:** Offset. **Trim Size:** 8 1/4 x 10 3/4. **Cols./Page:** 3. **Col. Width:** 14 picas. **Col. Depth:** 60 picas. **Key Personnel:** Jerry Roers, Manager, Marketing; Carl Llewellyn Weschcke, Publisher. **ISSN:** 0893-1534 (print). **Subscription Rates:** Free. **URL:** http://www.llewellyn.com/newworlds.php. **Formerly**: Llewellyn New Times. **Remarks:** Advertising not accepted. **Circ:** Combined ‡80,000.

18979 ■ Woodbury Bulletin
Woodbury Bulletin
8420 City Centre Dr.
Woodbury, MN 55125
Phone: (651)319-4270
Fax: (651)702-0977
Publisher's E-mail: editor@woodburybulletin.com
Community newspaper. **Freq:** Weekly. **Key Personnel:** Jeff Patterson, Publisher; Bob Eighmy, Editor; Patrick Johnson, Editor. **URL:** http://www.woodburybulletin.com. **Remarks:** Accepts advertising. **Circ:** (Not Reported).

WORTHINGTON

SW MN. Nobles Co. 60 mi. E. of Sioux Falls, SD. Worthington Community College. Lake Resort. Industrial Center. Dairy, poultry, and grain farms.

18980 ■ KITN-FM - 93.5
28779 County Hwy. 35
Worthington, MN 56187
Phone: (507)376-6165
Fax: (507)376-5071
Email: contactus@935thebreeze.com
Format: Jazz; News; Sports. **Owner:** Three Eagle Communications, 3800 Cornhusker Hwy., Lincoln, NE 68504. **Key Personnel:** Joel Koetke, Gen. Mgr., sales@935thebreeze.com. **Ad Rates:** Advertising accepted; rates available upon request. **URL:** http://www.935thebreeze.com.

18981 ■ KNSW-FM - 91.7
1450 College Way
Worthington, MN 56187
Phone: (507)372-2904
Format: News. **Founded:** 1973. **Key Personnel:** Chris Cross, Regional Mgr., ccross@mpr.org. **Wattage**: 99,000. **Ad Rates:** Noncommercial. **URL:** http://www.minnesota.publicradio.org.

18982 ■ KRSD-FM - 88.1
1450 College Way
Worthington, MN 56187
Phone: (605)335-6666
Format: Classical. **Networks:** National Public Radio (NPR). **Founded:** 1985. **Operating Hours**: Continuous. **ADI**: Sioux Falls-Mitchell, SD. **Wattage**: 2,000. **Ad Rates:** Noncommercial. **URL:** http://www.access.minnesota.publicradio.org.

18983 ■ KRSW-FM - 89.3
1450 College Way
Worthington, MN 56187
Phone: (507)372-2904
Format: Classical. **Networks:** National Public Radio (NPR). **Founded:** Dec. 1994. **Operating Hours**: Continuous; 33% network, 67% local. **Key Personnel:** Nick Kereakos, Chief Tech. Ofc., VP of Operations, VP of Engg. **Wattage**: 100,000. **Ad Rates:** Noncommercial. **URL:** http://www.minnesota.publicradio.org.

18984 ■ KWOA-AM - 730
28779 County Hwy. 35
Worthington, MN 56187-6387
Phone: (507)376-6165
Email: info@myradioworks.net
Format: News; Talk; Information. **Networks:** CBS. **Owner:** Three Eagles Communications, 3800 Cornhusker Hwy., Lincoln, NE 68504, Ph: (402)466-1234, Fax: (402)467-4095. **Founded:** 1947. **Operating Hours**: Continuous; 10% network, 90% local. **ADI:** Sioux Falls-Mitchell, SD. **Key Personnel:** Jared Rademacher, Sports Dir., jrademacher@kwoa.threeeagles.com. **Wattage**: 1,000. **Ad Rates:** Noncommercial. Combined advertising rates available with KWOA-FM/KITN-FM. **URL:** http://www.kwoa.com.

18985 ■ KWOA-FM - 95.1
28779 County Hwy. 35
Worthington, MN 56187
Phone: (507)376-6165
Fax: (507)376-5071
Email: contactus@951theeagle.com
Format: Adult Contemporary. **Owner:** Three Eagles Communications, 3800 Cornhusker Hwy., Lincoln, NE 68504, Ph: (402)466-1234, Fax: (402)467-4095. **Key Personnel:** Todd Mejia, Gen. Mgr. **Ad Rates:** Advertising accepted; rates available upon request. **URL:** http://www.951theeagle.com.

Circulation: ★ = AAM; △ or • = BPA; ♦ = CAC; ❑ = VAC; ⊕ = PO Statement; ‡ = Publisher's Report; Boldface figures = sworn; Light figures = estimated.

ZUMBROTA

18986 ■ The News Record
Grimsrud Publishing Inc.
225 Main St.
Zumbrota, MN 55992
Phone: (507)732-7617
Fax: (507)732-7619
Publication E-mail: news@zumbrota.com
Community newspaper. **Founded:** 1995. **Freq:** Weekly (Wed.). **Cols./Page:** 6. **Col. Width:** 14 picas. **Col. Depth:** 21 1/2 inches. **Key Personnel:** Peter Grimsrud, Publisher; Matt Grimsrud, Editor. **Subscription Rates:** $29 Individuals Dodge, Goodhue, Olmsted and Wabasha Counties; $42 Elsewhere in Minnesota; $52 Out of state; $29 Individuals online; $65 Other countries. **URL:** http://www.mnnews.com/newspapers/zumbrota.html; http://www.zumbrota.com. **Mailing address:** PO Box 97, Zumbrota, MN 55992. **Ad Rates:** BW $451; PCI $3.52. **Remarks:** Accepts advertising. **Circ:** ‡3,219.

AMORY

NE MS. Monroe Co. On Tennessee - Tombigbee Waterway, 40 mi. N. of Columbus. Manufactures industrial valves, lumber, cotton, grain, dairy products. Gas wells. Diversified farming. Livestock.

18987 ■ WAFM-FM - 95.7
PO Box 458
Amory, MS 38821
Phone: (662)256-9726
Fax: (662)256-9725
Email: fm95@fm95radio.com

Format: Oldies. **Networks:** ABC; Jones Satellite. **Owner:** Stanford Communications Inc., 521 Highway 278 W, Amory, MS 38821-5008, Ph: (662)256-9725. **Founded:** 1974. **Operating Hours**: Continuous. **Key Personnel:** Ed Stanford, Contact; Ed Stanford, Contact; Ken Wardlaw, Contact. **Local Programs:** *Backseat Oldies.* **Wattage**: 6,000. **Ad Rates:** $7 for 30 seconds; $8 for 60 seconds. Combined advertising rates available with WAMY-AM, WWZQ-AM. **URL:** http://www.fm95radio.com.

18988 ■ WAMY-AM
PO Box 458
Amory, MS 38821
Phone: (662)256-9725
Email: wamywafm@traceroad.net

Owner: Stanford Communications Inc., 521 Highway 278 W, Amory, MS 38821-5008, Ph: (662)256-9725. **Founded:** 1955. **Ad Rates:** $4 for 30 seconds; $5 for 60 seconds.

18989 ■ WWZQ-AM - 1240
PO Box 458
Amory, MS 38821
Phone: (662)256-9726
Fax: (662)256-9725
Email: fm95@fm95radio.com

Format: Oldies. **Founded:** Sept. 07, 2006. **Ad Rates:** Advertising accepted; rates available upon request. **URL:** http://www.fm95radio.com.

ASHLAND

18990 ■ WBII-TV - 20
PO Box 8
Ashland, MS 38603
Phone: (662)224-3220
Fax: (662)224-8588

Owner: Mid-South Broadcasting Inc. **URL:** http://wbiitv.8m.com.

BATESVILLE

NW MS. Panola Co. 58 mi. S. of Memphis, TN. Cotton ginning. Agriculture. Cattle, cotton, corn.

18991 ■ The Panolian
Panolian Inc.
363 Hwy. 51 N
Batesville, MS 38606
Phone: (662)563-4591
Fax: (662)563-5610
Free: 800-310-4591
Publisher's E-mail: newsroom@panolian.com

Community newspaper. **Freq:** Biweekly Tues. & Fri. **Print Method:** Offset. **Trim Size:** 7 1/2 x 11. **Cols./Page:** 6. **Col. Width:** 24 nonpareils. **Col. Depth:** 301 agate lines. **Key Personnel:** Rupert K. Howell, Managing Editor; John H. Howell, Sr., Publisher; Rita W. Howell, Editor. **USPS:** 777-280. **Subscription Rates:** $59.95 Individuals print; in Mississippi; $74.95 Out of state print and online; $54.95 Individuals print; senior citizen; in Mississippi; $74.95 Out of state print and online; senior citizen; in Mississippi; $49.95 Individuals print; in Mississippi; $64.95 Out of state print; $27 Individuals online. **URL:** http://www.panolian.com. **Mailing address:** PO Box 1616, Batesville, MS 38606. **Ad Rates:** GLR $.39; BW $1161; 4C $1461; SAU $9; PCI $9. **Remarks:** Accepts advertising. **Circ:** ‡9,675.

18992 ■ WBLE-FM - 100.5
PO Box 1528
Batesville, MS 38606
Phone: (662)563-4664
Fax: (662)563-9002

Format: Country. **Owner:** Batesville Broadcasting Co., Inc., 1040 Hwy. 6 W, Batesville, MS 38606, Ph: (662)563-4664. **Founded:** 1953. **Operating Hours:** Continuous. **Wattage:** 50,000. **URL:** http://www.wble101.com.

18993 ■ WHKL-FM - 106.9
PO Box 1528
Batesville, MS 38606
Phone: (662)563-4664
Fax: (662)563-9002
Email: news@wble101.com

Format: Country. **Owner:** Batesville Broadcasting Co., Inc., 1040 Hwy. 6 W, Batesville, MS 38606, Ph: (662)563-4664. **Founded:** Feb. 02, 1996. **Operating Hours:** Sun-Fri 5a.m.-11p.m.; Sat 5a.m.- 4a.m. **Wattage:** 6,000. **URL:** http://www.gainbuzz.com.

BAY SAINT LOUIS

S MS. Hancock Co. On a bay of the Gulf of Mexico, 52 mi. NE of New Orleans, LA. Manufactures plastic, metal products, electrical appliances. Logging; seafood packing. Winter resort. Dairy and truck farms.

18994 ■ The Sea Coast Echo
Bay Saint Louis Newspapers Inc.
124 Ct. St.
Bay Saint Louis, MS 39520
Phone: (228)467-5473
Fax: (228)467-0333
Publisher's E-mail: rponder@seacoastecho.com

Community newspaper. **Freq:** Semiweekly (Wed. and Sun.). **Print Method:** Offset. **Cols./Page:** 6. **Col. Width:** 21 1/2 nonpareils. **Col. Depth:** 301 agate lines. **Key Personnel:** James R. Ponder, Editor, Publisher; Geoff Belcher, Editor. **Subscription Rates:** $45 Individuals; $30 Individuals 6 months; $20 Out of area 3 months; $70 Individuals within United States. **URL:** http://www.seacoastecho.com/. **Mailing address:** PO Box 2009, Bay Saint Louis, MS 39521. **Ad Rates:** GLR $.61; BW $1,354.50; 4C $1,594.50; SAU $10.25; PCI $8. **Remarks:** Accepts advertising. **Circ:** ‡6630.

BAY SPRINGS

E MS. Jasper Co. 21 mi. NW of Laurel. Saw mills. Manufactures hydraulic cylinders, farm equipment, cotton, lumber. Agriculture.

18995 ■ Smith County Reformer
Buckley Newspapers Inc.
3362 Hwy. 15 N
Bay Springs, MS 39422

Newspaper with a Democratic orientation. **Freq:** Weekly (Wed.). **Print Method:** Offset. **Trim Size:** 14 1/4 x 21 1/2. **Cols./Page:** 6. **Col. Width:** 2 inches. **Col. Depth:** 21 1/2 inches. **Key Personnel:** Ronnie L. Buckley, Publisher; Brenda Ingram, Manager, Sales; Blenda Singleton, Editor. **Subscription Rates:** $25 Individuals in county, 1 year; $40 Out of area 1 year; $45 Out of state 1 year. **URL:** http://www.impactads.com/pages/scr. **Ad Rates:** GLR $.20; BW $838.50; 4C $1113.50; PCI $6.50. **Remarks:** Advertising accepted; rates available upon request. **Circ:** (Not Reported).

18996 ■ TEC/Bay Springs Div.
2988 Hwy. 15
Bay Springs, MS 39422
Phone: (601)764-2121
Fax: (601)764-2051
Free: 800-898-2782

Founded: 1923. **Key Personnel:** Wes Jones, Mgr. **Cities Served:** United States; 250 channels. **URL:** http://www.tec.com.

18997 ■ WIZK-AM
PO Box 548
Bay Springs, MS 39422
Phone: (601)764-2499

Format: Country; Gospel. **Networks:** ABC. **Owner:** Jerome Hughey, at above address. **Founded:** 1971. **Formerly:** WHII-AM; WXIY-AM. **Key Personnel:** Mitchell Hughey, Contact. **Wattage**: 3,200 Day. **Ad Rates:** $6-10 for 30 seconds; $12-20 for 60 seconds.

BELZONI

W MS. Humphreys Co. 40 mi. SE of Greenville. Cotton ginning. Catfish, crawfish. Agriculture. Feed, cotton, corn, hay, soybeans, rice.

18998 ■ The Belzoni Banner
The Belzoni Banner
115 E Jackson St.
Belzoni, MS 39038
Phone: (662)247-3373
Fax: (662)247-3372

Community newspaper. **Freq:** Weekly (Wed.). **Print Method:** Offset. **Cols./Page:** 6. **Col. Width:** 2 1/16 inches. **Col. Depth:** 21 1/2 inches. **Subscription Rates:** $25 Individuals; $30 Out of area print and online; $30 Individuals online; $35 Out of area online. **URL:** http://www.thebelzonibanner.com. **Mailing address:** PO Box 610, Belzoni, MS 39038. **Ad Rates:** BW $645; 4C $770; PCI $5. **Remarks:** display Ads. **Circ:** ‡1,250.

18999 ■ Cable TV of Belzoni Inc.
102 S Hayden St.
Belzoni, MS 39038
Phone: (662)247-1834

Circulation: ★ = AAM; △ or • = BPA; ♦ = CAC; ❑ = VAC; ⊕ = PO Statement; ‡ = Publisher's Report; Boldface figures = sworn; Light figures = estimated.

Key Personnel: Les Vance, Contact, lvance@belzonicable.com; Del Lott, Contact. **Cities Served:** 97 channels. **URL:** http://www.belzonicable.com.

BILOXI

S MS. Harrison Co. On Gulf of Mexico, 12 mi. E. of Gulfport. Military and government installation. Summer and winter resort. Manufactures building products, tents, awnings , nets and trawls, wire, cable, cat food, electric harness, appliances, seafood packing; canning. Boat building and repairing.

19000 ■ Fun Times Guide
Mississippi Gulf Coast
2350 Beach Blvd. Ste. A
Biloxi, MS 39531
Phone: (228)896-6699
Fax: (228)280-3140
Free: 888-467-4853
Publisher's E-mail: tourism@gulfcoast.org
Magazine containing visitor information for Mississippi's Gulf Coast. **Freq:** Semiannual. **Key Personnel:** Janice Jones, Manager. **URL:** http://www.gulfcoast.org/about/request-a-visitors-guide. **Circ:** (Not Reported).

19001 ■ Gulf Pine Catholic
Gulf Pine Catholic
1790 Popps Ferry Rd.
Biloxi, MS 39532
Phone: (228)702-2126
Fax: (228)702-2128
Publication E-mail: gulfpine@ametro.net
Official newspaper (tabloid) of the Roman Catholic Diocese of Biloxi. **Freq:** Biweekly. **Print Method:** Offset. **Trim Size:** 11 1/2 X 12 3/4. **Cols./Page:** 6. **Col. Width:** 1 1/2 inches. **Key Personnel:** Deborah Mowrey, Contact; Rev. Thomas J. Rodi, Publisher, phone: (228)702-2100; Terry Dickson, Editor. **USPS:** 704-450. **Subscription Rates:** $12.50 Individuals per year. **URL:** http://biloxidiocese.org/gulf-pine-catholic; http://www.signatureflip.com/sf01/?i=48. **Ad Rates:** BW $690; 4C $690; PCI $7. **Remarks:** Advertising accepted; rates available upon request. **Circ:** ‡17700.

19002 ■ Jackpot! Magazine Online!: The South's Largest Guide to Gaming and Fun
Mississippi Gulf Coast
2350 Beach Blvd. Ste. A
Biloxi, MS 39531
Phone: (228)896-6699
Fax: (228)280-3140
Free: 888-467-4853
Publisher's E-mail: tourism@gulfcoast.org
Magazine providing in-depth news coverage of gaming. **Freq:** 26/yr. **Key Personnel:** Michael Sunderman, President, Publisher; Lori Beth Susman, Executive Editor, General Manager. **URL:** http://www.jackpotmagazine.com. **Remarks:** Accepts advertising. **Circ:** (Not Reported).

19003 ■ WAML-AM - 1340
336 Rodenberg Ave.
Biloxi, MS 39531
Phone: (601)425-4285
Format: Gospel. **Networks:** NBC; Mississippi. **Owner:** Walking by Faith Ministries, Inc., 3715 Argent Blvd., Ridgeland, SC 29936. **Founded:** 1932. **Operating Hours:** 6 a.m.-midnight. **ADI:** Laurel-Hattiesburg, MS. **Wattage:** 1,000. **Ad Rates:** $4-7 for 30 seconds; $7-8 for 60 seconds. $4-$7 for 30 seconds; $7-$8 for 60 seconds. Combined advertising rates available with WEEZ-FM.

19004 ■ WBUV-FM - 104.9
286 Debuys Rd.
Biloxi, MS 39531
Phone: (228)388-2323
Fax: (228)388-2362
Format: News; Talk. **ADI:** Biloxi-Gulfport-Pascagoula, MS. **Wattage:** 33,000. **Ad Rates:** Advertising accepted; rates available upon request. **URL:** http://www.newsradio1049fm.com.

19005 ■ WLOX-TV - 13
208 DeBuys Rd.
Biloxi, MS 39531
Phone: (228)896-1313
Email: wlox@wlox.com
Format: Commercial TV. **Networks:** ABC. **Owner:** Raycom Media Inc., 201 Monroe St., RSA Twr., 20th Fl., Montgomery, AL 36104-3731, Ph: (334)206-1400. **Founded:** 1962. **Operating Hours:** Continuous; 50% network, 50% local. **ADI:** Biloxi-Gulfport-Pascagoula, MS. **Key Personnel:** Rick Williams, Gen. Mgr.; Mary Graham, President; Leon Long, Contact. **Ad Rates:** Advertising accepted; rates available upon request. **URL:** http://www.wlox.com.

19006 ■ WMAH-FM - 90.3
3825 Ridgewood Rd.
Jackson, MS 39211
Phone: (601)432-6565
Fax: (601)432-6907
Email: events@mpbonline.org
Format: Classical; News; Information; Public Radio. **Networks:** National Public Radio (NPR); Public Radio International (PRI). **Owner:** Mississippi Public Broadcasting, 3825 Ridgewood Rd, Jackson, MS 39211. **Founded:** 1983. **Operating Hours:** Continuous. **ADI:** Biloxi-Gulfport-Pascagoula, MS. **Local Programs:** *Southern Remedy*, Monday Tuesday Wednesday Thursday Friday 11:00 a.m. - 12:00 p.m.; *Creature Comforts*, Thursday 9:00 a.m. **Wattage:** 100,000. **Ad Rates:** Noncommercial. **URL:** http://www.mpbonline.org.

19007 ■ WMAH-TV - 19
3825 Ridgewood Rd.
3825 Ridgewood Rd.
Jackson, MS 39211
Phone: (601)432-6565
Fax: (601)982-6746
Free: 800-472-2580
Format: Public TV. **Simulcasts:** WMPN-TV Jackson, MS. **Networks:** Public Broadcasting Service (PBS). **Owner:** Mississippi Authority for Educational TV, at above address. **Operating Hours:** 6:45 am-11:15 pm weekdays; noon-11:15 pm Sat.; noon-11 pm Sun. **ADI:** Biloxi-Gulfport-Pascagoula, MS. **Key Personnel:** A.J. Jaeger, Contact.

19008 ■ WMJY-FM - 93.7
286 DeBuys Rd.
Biloxi, MS 39531
Phone: (228)388-2323
Fax: (228)388-2362
Format: Adult Contemporary. **Owner:** Clear Channel Inc., 200 E Basse Rd., San Antonio, TX 78209, Ph: (612)336-9700, Fax: (612)336-9701. **Founded:** 1966. **Formerly:** WQID-FM. **Operating Hours:** Continuous. **Key Personnel:** Walter Brown, Contact, walterbrown@clearchannel.com; Katie Mitchell, Contact, katiemitchell@clearchannel.com. **Wattage:** 96,000. **Ad Rates:** Advertising accepted; rates available upon request. **URL:** http://www.magic937.com.

19009 ■ WQFX-AM
336 Rodenberg Ave.
Biloxi, MS 39531
Phone: (228)435-2456
Ad Rates: Advertising accepted; rates available upon request.

19010 ■ WQYZ-FM - 92.5
286 DeBuys Rd.
Biloxi, MS 39531
Phone: (228)388-2323
Fax: (228)388-2362
Format: Adult Contemporary; Urban Contemporary. **Formerly:** WXOR-FM. **Operating Hours:** Continuous. **Key Personnel:** Walter Brown, Dir. of Programs, walterbrown@clearchannel.com. **Wattage:** 6,000 ERP. **Ad Rates:** Noncommercial. **URL:** http://www.925fmthebeat.com.

19011 ■ W215BE-FM - 90.9
PO Box 391
Twin Falls, ID 83303
Fax: (208)736-1958
Free: 800-357-4226
Format: Religious; Contemporary Christian. **Owner:** CSN International, PO Box 391, Twin Falls, ID 83303, Ph: (208)736-1958, Fax: (208)736-1958, Free: 800-357-4226. **Key Personnel:** Kelly Carlson, Dir. of Engg.; Ray Gorney, Asst. Dir. **URL:** http://www.csnradio.com.

BOONEVILLE

NE MS. Prentiss Co. 75 mi. S. of Jackson, TN. Northeast Mississippi Community College. Manufactures furniture, clothing. Lumber mills; cotton ginning. Clay pits. Diversified farming. Cotton, corn, hay.

19012 ■ WBIP-AM
PO Box 356
Booneville, MS 38829-0356
Fax: (601)728-2572
Format: Sports. **Founded:** 1950. **Wattage:** 1,000. **Ad Rates:** $2-4 for 30 seconds; $2.50-5 for 60 seconds.

19013 ■ WBIP-FM - 99.3
PO Box 356
Booneville, MS 38829-0356
Fax: (601)728-2572
Format: Southern Gospel; Sports. **Networks:** Mississippi; USA Radio. **Founded:** 1976. **Operating Hours:** Continuous. **Key Personnel:** Larry Melton, President; Max Wilson, Dir. of Programs; Randy Brooks, Office Mgr.; Larry Hill, Gen. Mgr. **Wattage:** 6,000. **Ad Rates:** $4-6 for 30 seconds; $5-8 for 60 seconds. $5-$7 for 30 seconds; $5.50-$9 for 60 seconds. Combined advertising rates available with WBIP-AM.

19014 ■ WMAE-FM - 89.5
3825 Ridgewood Rd.
Jackson, MS 39211
Phone: (601)432-6565
Email: events@mpbonline.org
Format: News; Bluegrass; Classical; Information; Public Radio. **Networks:** National Public Radio (NPR); Public Radio International (PRI). **Owner:** Mississippi Public Broadcasting, 3825 Ridgewood Rd, Jackson, MS 39211. **Founded:** 1983. **Operating Hours:** Continuous. **ADI:** Jackson, MS. **Local Programs:** *Grass Roots*, Saturday 8:00 p.m.; *Friday Night Under The Lights*, Friday 10:00 p.m. - 12:30 a.m. **Wattage:** 85,000. **Ad Rates:** Noncommercial. **URL:** http://www.mpbonline.org.

BRANDON

SC MS. Rankin Co. 13 mi. E. of Jackson. Manufactures cement, textiles. Saw mills. Pine timber. Diversified farming. Cotton, corn, livestock.

19015 ■ Annals of Plastic Surgery
Lippincott Williams and Wilkins
c/o William C. Lineaweaver, MD, Ed.-in-Ch.
Joseph M. Still Burn & Reconstructive Center
Brandon, MS 39042
Publisher's E-mail: ronna.ekhouse@wolterskluwer.com
Medical journal for the plastic surgeon. **Freq:** Monthly. **Print Method:** Offset. **Trim Size:** 8 1/8 x 10 7/8. **Cols./Page:** 2. **Col. Width:** 3 3/8 nonpareils. **Col. Depth:** 10 inches. **Key Personnel:** William C. Lineaweaver, MD, Editor-in-Chief; Ali Gavendra, Publisher. **ISSN:** 0148--7043 (print); **EISSN:** 1536--3708 (electronic). **Subscription Rates:** $726 Individuals; $1452 Two years. **URL:** http://www.lww.com/product/?0148-7043; http://journals.lww.com/annalsplasticsurgery/pages/default.aspx. **Ad Rates:** BW $1,390; 4C $2,190. **Remarks:** Accepts advertising. **Circ:** 735.

19016 ■ Rankin County News
Rankin County News
207 E Government St.
Brandon, MS 39043
Phone: (601)825-8333
Fax: (601)825-8334
Publication E-mail: rankincn@aol.com
Community newspaper. **Freq:** Weekly (Wed.). **Print Method:** Offset. **Trim Size:** 14 1/4 x 21 1/2. **Cols./Page:** 6. **Col. Width:** 12 picas. **Col. Depth:** 21.5 inches. **Key Personnel:** Marcus Bowers, Publisher. **USPS:** 455-440. **Subscription Rates:** $20 Individuals; $23 Out of area; $26 Out of state. **URL:** http://www.rankincn.com; http://www.rankincn.com/475/1179/1/read-it-online. **Mailing address:** PO Box 107, Brandon, MS 39043. **Ad Rates:** BW $838.50; 4C $1138.50; SAU $6; PCI $6.50. **Remarks:** Accepts advertising. **Circ:** ‡8,000.

BROOKHAVEN

SW MS. Lincoln Co. 60 mi. S. of Jackson. Lumber mills. Manufactures garments, lawn mowers, wiring harnesses, thermometers, wire screen, bricks, electronics equipment, truck beds. Bottling works. Pine, hardwood timber. Farming. Dairying, truck crops, cattle.

19017 ■ WBKN-FM - 92.1
PO Box 30
Magnolia, MS 39652
Phone: (601)783-6600
Owner: Brookhaven Broadcasting Inc., PO Box 711, Brookhaven, MA 39602, Ph: (601)833-9210. **Founded:**

1976. **Wattage:** 3,400. **Ad Rates:** Noncommercial.

19018 ■ WCHJ-AM - 1470
PO Box 177
Brookhaven, MS 39602
Phone: (601)823-9006
Fax: (601)823-0503
Owner: Tillman Broadcasting Network, Inc., 983 Sawmill Ln NE, Brookhaven, MA 39601, Ph: (601)823-9006. **Founded:** 1956. **ADI:** Jackson, MS. **Wattage:** 1,000. **Ad Rates:** $4 for 30 seconds; $5 for 60 seconds.

19019 ■ WDXO-FM - 92.9
110 W Monticello St.
Brookhaven, MS 39601
Phone: (601)587-7652
Fax: (601)587-9401
Format: Adult Contemporary. **Key Personnel:** Heather Thurgood, heather@wrqo-q102.com; Chuck Ivey, chuck@wrqo-q102.com; Robert Byrd, robert@wdxo-dx929.com; Jim Richardson, jim@wrqo-q102.com. **Ad Rates:** Noncommercial. **URL:** http://myespn929.com.

BRUCE

NC MS. Calhoun Co. 65 mi. NW of Columbus. Manufactures mattresses, furniture parts, lumber, camper units. Cotton gins. Agriculture. Livestock. Cotton, soybeans.

19020 ■ Calhoun County Journal
Calhoun County Journal
PO Box 278
Bruce, MS 38915
Phone: (662)983-2570
Fax: (662)983-7667
Publisher's E-mail: calhouncountyjournal@gmail.com
Newspaper. **Freq:** Weekly (Thurs.). **Print Method:** Offset. **Cols./Page:** 6. **Col. Width:** 21 nonpareils. **Col. Depth:** 294 agate lines. **Key Personnel:** S. Gale Denley, Publisher; Lisa Denley McNeece, Associate Editor, Manager, Advertising; Celia Denley Hillhouse, Managing Editor. **Subscription Rates:** $30 Individuals. **URL:** http://www.calhouncountyjournal.com. **Ad Rates:** SAU $3.80; PCI $5.78. **Remarks:** Accepts advertising. **Circ:** Paid 4,771.

BUDE

Franklin Co.

19021 ■ WMAU-FM - 90.9
3825 Ridgewood Rd.
Jackson, MS 39211
Phone: (601)432-6565
Free: 800-922-9698
Format: Classical; News; Information; Public Radio. **Networks:** Public Radio International (PRI); National Public Radio (NPR). **Owner:** Mississippi Public Broadcasting, 3825 Ridgewood Rd, Jackson, MS 39211. **Founded:** 1983. **Operating Hours:** Continuous. **ADI:** Jackson, MS. **Key Personnel:** Jay Woods, Dep. Dir. **Wattage:** 100,000. **Ad Rates:** Noncommercial. **URL:** http://www.mpbonline.org.

CANTON

WC MS. Madison Co. 24 mi. NE of Jackson. Manufactures lumber, furniture, plant foods, fertilizer. Cotton ginning; compress; creamery. Poultry processing. Diversified farming. Livestock. Cotton, corn, soybeans.

19022 ■ WMGO-AM
PO Box 182
Canton, MS 39046
Phone: (601)859-2373
Fax: (601)859-2664
Format: Full Service. **Networks:** Mississippi. **Founded:** 1954. **Formerly:** WDOB-AM. **Key Personnel:** Jerry Lousteau, Gen. Mgr. **Wattage:** 1,000 Day; 028 Night. **Ad Rates:** $5.50-10.50 for 30 seconds; $7.00-12.50 for 60 seconds.

CARTHAGE

C MS. Leake Co. On Pearl River, 50 mi. NE of Jackson. Manufactures metal products, clothing. Lumber mills. Agriculture. Cotton, poultry, cattle.

19023 ■ Carthaginian
Carthaginian
122 W Franklin St.
Carthage, MS 39051
Phone: (601)267-4501
Fax: (601)267-5290
Publication E-mail: news@thecarthaginian.com
Newspaper with Democratic orientation. **Freq:** Weekly (Thurs.). **Print Method:** Offset. **Cols./Page:** 6. **Col. Width:** 20 nonpareils. **Col. Depth:** 301 agate lines. **Key Personnel:** Waid Prather, Publisher; John H. Keith, Owner; Jimmy Moore, Manager, Advertising. **USPS:** 092-260. **Subscription Rates:** $24 Individuals online; $28 Individuals in Leake County; $32 Out of area; $36 Out of state. **URL:** http://www.thecarthaginian.com/50926/1182/1/online-editionhome. **Ad Rates:** PCI $8.40. **Remarks:** Accepts advertising. **Circ:** ‡5,700.

19024 ■ WSSI-AM - 1080
PO Box 475
Carthage, MS 39051
Format: News; Talk. **Owner:** Michael D. Goodwin, at above address. **Founded:** 1968. **Formerly:** WECP-AM. **Operating Hours:** Sunrise-sunset. **ADI:** Jackson, MS. **Key Personnel:** Linda D. Goodwin, Office Mgr; Michael D. Goodwin, Contact. **Wattage:** 5,000. **Ad Rates:** $5-6 for 30 seconds; $7 for 60 seconds.

19025 ■ WSSI-FM - 98.3
PO Box 475
Carthage, MS 39051
Phone: (601)267-8361
Fax: (601)267-8363
Format: Country. **Owner:** Michael D. Goodwin, at above address. **Founded:** 1979. **Formerly:** WWYN-FM. **Operating Hours:** 5 a.m.-11 p.m. **ADI:** Jackson, MS. **Key Personnel:** Linda D. Goodwin, Office Mgr; Michael D. Goodwin, Contact. **Wattage:** 3,000. **Ad Rates:** $6-6 for 30 seconds; $8 for 60 seconds.

CENTREVILLE

19026 ■ KPAE-FM - 91.5
PO Box 1390
Centreville, MS 39631
Phone: (601)645-6515
Fax: (601)645-9122
Free: 800-324-1108
Format: Southern Gospel. **Simulcasts:** WPAE. **Networks:** Moody Broadcasting. **Owner:** Port Allen Educational Broadcasting Foundation, 13028 US Hwy., Port Allen, LA 70767. **Founded:** 1984. **Operating Hours:** Continuous; 60% network, 40% local. **Wattage:** 5,000. **Ad Rates:** Noncommercial. **URL:** http://www.soundradio.org.

19027 ■ WPAE-FM - 89.7
PO Box 1390
Centreville, MS 39631
Phone: (601)645-6515
Fax: (601)645-9122
Free: 800-324-1108
Email: wpaefm@telepak.net
Format: Religious. **Founded:** 1985. **Ad Rates:** Noncommercial. **URL:** http://www.soundradio.org.

CLARKSDALE

NW MS. Coahoma Co. 70 mi. S. of Memphis, TN. Coahoma Junior College. Manufactures cottonseed, soybean oil, uniforms, rubber products, burlap and textile bags. Cotton ginning. Timber. Agriculture. Corn, hay, cotton, rice, soybeans.

19028 ■ WROX-AM - 1450
PO Box 1176
Clarksdale, MS 38614
Phone: (662)627-1450
Fax: (662)621-1176
Email: wrox@deltaradio.net
Format: Gospel; News; Talk; Classic Rock; Information. **Owner:** Delta Radio, PO Box 905, Cleveland, MS 38732, Ph: (662)843-3392, Fax: (662)846-9002. **Founded:** 1944. **Operating Hours:** Continuous. **Wattage:** 1,000 KW. **Ad Rates:** Advertising accepted; rates available upon request. $3 for 30 seconds; $4 for 60 seconds. **URL:** http://www.wroxradio.com.

CLEVELAND

W MS. Bolivar Co. 35 mi. NE of Greenville. Delta State University. Bottling works. Manufactures tile, auto trim, nails and staples. Agriculture. Soybeans, cotton, rice.

19029 ■ Bolivar Commercial
Division of Cleveland Newspapers Inc.
821 N Chrisman Ave.
Cleveland, MS 38732-1050
General newspaper. **Freq:** Daily and Sun. (eve.). **Print Method:** Offset. **Cols./Page:** 6. **Col. Width:** 26 nonpareils. **Col. Depth:** 301 agate lines. **Key Personnel:** David Laster, Manager, Advertising; Mark Williams, Editor; Denise Strub, Managing Editor; Sharon Clinton, Manager; Curtis Peeples, Manager, Circulation. **Subscription Rates:** $78 Individuals by carrier; $78 By mail in Bolivar County; $90 Out of area by mail. **URL:** http://www.bolivarcommercial.com. **Remarks:** Accepts classified advertising. **Circ:** (Not Reported).

19030 ■ Delta Magazine
Coopwood Publishing Group Inc.
PO Box 117
Cleveland, MS 38732
Phone: (662)843-2700
Fax: (662)843-0505
Publisher's E-mail: scott@coopwoodpublishinggroup.com
Magazine offers travel, historical information and photographs about and of the Mississippi Delta. **Freq:** Bimonthly. **Print Method:** Web offset. **Trim Size:** 8 1/8 x 10 7/8. **Key Personnel:** Melissa Townsend, Editor. **ISSN:** 1557--6787 (print). **URL:** http://deltamagazine.com. **Remarks:** Advertising accepted; rates available upon request. **Circ:** (Not Reported).

19031 ■ Sketch Book
Kappa Pi International Art Honor Society
307 S 5th Ave.
Cleveland, MS 38732
Phone: (662)846-4729
Publisher's E-mail: nfo@kappapiart.com
Freq: Annual. **Alt. Formats:** Download. **URL:** http://www.kappapiart.org/sketchbook.html. **Remarks:** Advertising not accepted. **Circ:** 5000.

19032 ■ WAID-FM - 106.5
PO Box 780
Cleveland, MS 38732
Phone: (662)627-2281
Fax: (662)624-2900
Format: Urban Contemporary. **Owner:** Radio Cleveland, Inc., 112 Leflore Avenue, Clarksdale, MA 38614, Ph: (662)627-2281. **Founded:** 1977. **Operating Hours:** Continuous. **Wattage:** 50,000. **Ad Rates:** Advertising accepted; rates available upon request.

19033 ■ WCLD-AM - 1490
PO Box 780
Cleveland, MS 38732
Phone: (662)843-4091
Fax: (662)843-9805
Format: Sports. **Networks:** CNN Radio. **Owner:** Radio Cleveland, Inc., 112 Leflore Avenue, Clarksdale, MA 38614, Ph: (662)627-2281. **Founded:** 1949. **Operating Hours:** Continuous. **ADI:** Greenwood-Greenville, MS. **Wattage:** 1,000.

19034 ■ WCLD-FM - 103.9
PO Box 780
Cleveland, MS 38732
Phone: (662)843-4091
Fax: (662)843-9805
Format: Urban Contemporary. **Founded:** 1972. **Operating Hours:** Continuous. **ADI:** Greenwood-Greenville, MS. **Wattage:** 25,000. **Ad Rates:** Noncommercial.

19035 ■ WDFX-FM
Cleveland, MS
Format: Religious. **Key Personnel:** Fred Jackson, News Dir; Sherrie Black, Contact; Brad Bullock, Contact. **Wattage:** 25,000 ERP. **Ad Rates:** Noncommercial. **URL:** http://www.afr.net.

19036 ■ WDTL-FM - 92.9
PO Box 1438
Cleveland, MS 38732
Phone: (662)846-0929
Fax: (662)843-1410
Email: wdtl@deltaradio.net
Format: Country. **Simulcasts:** WZYQ-FM. **Networks:** ABC. **Owner:** Delta Radio Inc., at above address. **Founded:** 1971. **Formerly:** WQAZ. **Operating Hours:** Continuous. **ADI:** Greenwood-Greenville, MS. **Key Personnel:** Andy Hodges, Gen. Mgr.; Jim Gregory, Dir.

Circulation: ★ = AAM; △ or • = BPA; ♦ = CAC; ❏ = VAC; ⊕ = PO Statement; ‡ = Publisher's Report; Boldface figures = sworn; Light figures = estimated.

of Programs, jgregory@deltaradio.net. **Wattage**: 50,000. **Ad Rates:** $10.59-14.12 for 30 seconds; $12.94-16.47 for 60 seconds. Combined advertising rates available w/ WRKG-FM, WDSK-AM,. **URL:** http://www.kix921.com.

19037 ■ W56DY - 56
PO Box A
Santa Ana, CA 92711
Phone: (714)832-2950
Free: 888-731-1000
Email: comments@tbn.org
Owner: Trinity Broadcasting Network Inc., PO Box A, Santa Ana, CA 92711, Ph: (714)832-2950, Free: 888-731-1000. **URL:** http://www.tbn.org.

19038 ■ WMJW-FM
PO Box 780
Cleveland, MS 38732
Phone: (662)843-4091
Fax: (662)843-9805
Format: Adult Contemporary. **Owner:** Radio Cleveland, Inc., 112 Leflore Avenue, Clarksdale, MA 38614, Ph: (662)627-2281. **Key Personnel:** Clint Webster, Gen. Mgr.; Kevin Cox, Gen. Sales Mgr. **Wattage**: 25,000 ERP.

CLINTON

SWC MS. Hinds Co. 10 mi. NW of Jackson. Mississippi College. Residential.

19039 ■ WHJT-FM - 93.5
100 S Jefferson St.
Clinton, MS 39058
Phone: (601)925-3458
Fax: (601)924-4506
Email: whjt@nc.edu
Format: Adult Contemporary; Contemporary Christian; Religious. **Networks:** Independent; USA Radio; Sun Radio. **Owner:** Mississippi College, 200 South capitol S, Clinton, MS 39058, Ph: (601)925-3000. **Founded:** 1972. **Formerly**: WSLI-FM. **Operating Hours**: Continuous. **Key Personnel:** Josh Lee, Production Mgr. **Wattage**: 6,000. **Ad Rates:** Noncommercial. $12-15 for 30 seconds; $15-18 for 60 seconds. **Mailing address:** PO Box 4048, Clinton, MS 39058. **URL:** http://www.star93fm.com.

COLUMBIA

S MS. Marion Co. On Pearl River, 75 mi. SE of Jackson. Manufactures boxes, veneer, canned vegetables, hosiery, garments. Naval stores. Bottling works. Pine timber. Agriculture. Cotton, potatoes, truck crops.

19040 ■ WCJU-AM - 1450
PO Box 472
Columbia, MS 39429
Phone: (601)736-2616
Fax: (601)736-2617
Format: News; Talk; Gospel. **Networks:** ABC. **Founded:** 1946. **Operating Hours**: Continuous; 55% satelite, 45% local. **Wattage**: 1,000. **Ad Rates:** $3-6 for 30 seconds; $4.50-7.50 for 60 seconds.

19041 ■ WFFF-AM - 1360
PO Box 550
Columbia, MS 39429
Format: Country. **Simulcasts:** WFFF-FM. **Networks:** ABC; Mississippi. **Founded:** 1961. **Operating Hours**: Continuous. **ADI**: Laurel-Hattiesburg, MS. **Wattage**: 1,000 Day; 159 Night. **Ad Rates:** $6 for 30 seconds; $12 for 60 seconds. $10 for 30 seconds; $14 for 60 seconds. Combined advertising rates available with WFFF-FM.

19042 ■ WFFF-FM - 96.7
PO Box 550
Columbia, MS 39429
Phone: (601)736-1360
Fax: (601)736-1361
Format: Adult Contemporary. **Simulcasts:** WFFF-AM. **Networks:** ABC; Mississippi. **Founded:** 1966. **Operating Hours**: Continuous. **ADI**: Laurel-Hattiesburg, MS. **Wattage**: 6,000. **Ad Rates:** $6 for 30 seconds; $8 for 60 seconds. Combined advertising rates available with WFFF-AM: $10 for 30 seconds; $14 for 60 seconds.

COLUMBUS

E MS. Lowndes Co. On Tombigbee River, 130 mi. NE of Jackson. Mississippi University for Women. Columbus Air Force Base. Manufactures brick, monuments, electrical motors, prefab metal buildings, cement, vinyl wall covering, carpet underlay, chemicals, plastics, clothing. Timber. Diversified farming.

19043 ■ The Commercial Dispatch
The Commercial Dispatch Publishing Inc.
516 Main St.
Columbus, MS 39701-0511
Phone: (662)328-2424
Publication E-mail: news@cdispatch.com
Newspaper. **Founded:** Mar. 12, 1922. **Freq:** Daily (eve.). **Print Method:** Offset. **Trim Size:** 13 x 21 1/2. **Cols./Page:** 6. **Col. Width:** 2 1/16 inches. **Col. Depth:** 21 1/2 inches. **Key Personnel:** Birney Imes, III, Editor; Beth Proffitt, Director, Advertising. **Subscription Rates:** $11.50 Individuals home delivery and online; Sunday - Friday; /month; $7.50 Individuals sunday only; $11 Individuals print only; Sunday - Friday; $7 Individuals print only, sunday only; $7.95 Individuals online. **URL:** http://www.cdispatch.com. **Formed by the merger of**: The Dispatch; Commercial. **Ad Rates:** BW $1180.35; 4C $1580.35; SAU $10.60. **Remarks:** Accepts classified advertising. **Circ:** Mon.-Fri. ‡15,000.

19044 ■ WACR-FM - 103.9
1910 14th Ave. N
Columbus, MS 39701
Phone: (662)328-1050
Format: Urban Contemporary. **Owner:** T & W Communications, Inc., West Point, MS. **Operating Hours**: Continuous. **ADI**: Columbus-Tupelo (West Point), MS. **Key Personnel:** Danny Byrd, Gen. Mgr.; Sherwinn Prescott, Gen. Sales Mgr.; Jerold Jackson, Dir. of Programs. **Wattage**: 3,000. **Ad Rates:** $25 per unit. **URL:** http://wtwgam1050.com.

19045 ■ WCBI-TV - 4
201 Fifth St. S
Columbus, MS 39701
Phone: (662)327-4444
Fax: (662)329-1004
Email: news@wcbi.com
Format: Commercial TV. **Networks:** CBS. **Owner:** Morris Multimedia Inc., 27 Abercorn St., Savannah, GA 31401, Ph: (912)233-1281, Fax: (912)232-4639. **Founded:** July 13, 1956. **ADI**: Columbus-Tupelo (West Point), MS. **Key Personnel:** Derek Rogers, Gen. Mgr.; Robert Davidson, News Dir.; Bobby Berry, Gen. Mgr., berryb@wcbi.com. **Wattage**: 708,000 ERP H. **Ad Rates:** Advertising accepted; rates available upon request. **URL:** http://www.wcbi.com.

19046 ■ WCSO-FM - 90.5
PO Box 2440
Tupelo, MS 38803
Phone: (662)844-8888
Format: Religious. **Owner:** American Family Radio, at above address. **URL:** http://www.afa.net.

19047 ■ WKOR-FM - 94.9
200 6th St. N, Ste. 205
Columbus, MS 39702
Phone: (662)327-1183
Format: Country. **Owner:** Cumulus Broadcasting Inc., 3280 Peachtree Rd. NW, Ste. 2300, Atlanta, GA 30305-2447, Ph: (404)949-0700, Fax: (404)949-0740. **Key Personnel:** Greg Benefield, Dir. of Mktg., Mktg. Mgr., greg.benefield@cumulus.com; Brian Taylor, Dir. of Programs, brian.taylor@cumulus.com. **URL:** http://www.nashfm949.com.

19048 ■ WMUW-FM - 88.5
1100 College St.
Columbus, MS 39701
Phone: (662)329-4750
Free: 877-462-8439
Format: Hip Hop; News; Blues. **Owner:** Mississippi University for Women, 1100 College St., Columbus, MS 39701. **Key Personnel:** Eric Harlan, Contact. **Ad Rates:** Advertising accepted; rates available upon request. **URL:** http://www.muw.edu.

19049 ■ WMXU-FM - 106.1
PO Box 1076
Columbus, MS 39703
Fax: (601)328-1122
Format: Music of Your Life; News. **Owner:** Cumulus Media Inc., 3280 Peachtree Rd. NW, Ste. 2300, Atlanta, GA 30305-2455, Ph: (404)949-0700, Fax: (404)949-0740. **Founded:** 1964. **Formerly**: WSMU-FM; WKYJ-FM. **Wattage**: 40,000 ERP. **Ad Rates:** Advertising accepted; rates available upon request. $4.25-8.25 for 30 seconds. Combined advertising rates available with WMSU-FM, WSMS-FM, WKOR-FM, WKOR-AM, WSSO-AM.

19050 ■ WNMQ-FM - 103.1
105 5th St. N, Ste. 400
200 6th St. N
Columbus, MS 39701
Phone: (404)949-0700
Format: Contemporary Hit Radio (CHR). **Networks:** NBC; Mississippi. **Owner:** Cumulus Media Inc., 3280 Peachtree Rd. NW, Ste. 2300, Atlanta, GA 30305-2455, Ph: (404)949-0700, Fax: (404)949-0740. **Founded:** 1968. **Formerly**: WMBC-FM. **Operating Hours**: Continuous. **ADI**: Columbus-Tupelo (West Point), MS. **Wattage**: 50,000. **Ad Rates:** $12-22 for 30 seconds; $14-26 for 60 seconds. Combined advertising rates available with WAJV-FM, WJWF-AM. **URL:** http://www.1031theteam.com.

19051 ■ WSMS-FM - 99.9
200 6th St. N, Ste. 205
Columbus, MS 39701
Phone: (662)327-1183
Fax: (662)654-6510
Free: 866-999-WSMS
Format: Album-Oriented Rock (AOR). **Ad Rates:** Noncommercial. **URL:** http://www.999thefoxrocks.com.

19052 ■ WSSO-AM - 1230
200 6th St. N
Court Square Towers, Ste. 205
Columbus, MS 39701
Phone: (662)327-1183
Fax: (662)241-4821
Format: Sports. **Owner:** Cumulus Licensing L.L.C., 3280 Peachtree Rd. NW, Ste. 2300, Atlanta, GA 30305, Ph: (404)949-0700, Fax: (404)949-0740. **Founded:** 1948. **Operating Hours**: Continuous. **ADI**: Columbus-Tupelo (West Point), MS. **Key Personnel:** Lewis W. Dickey, Jr., Chairman, CEO, President. **Wattage**: 1,000. **Ad Rates:** Noncommercial.

19053 ■ W25AD - 25
PO Box A
Santa Ana, CA 92711
Phone: (714)832-2950
Free: 888-731-1000
Owner: Trinity Broadcasting Network Inc., PO Box A, Santa Ana, CA 92711, Ph: (714)832-2950, Free: 888-731-1000. **URL:** http://www.tbn.org.

CORINTH

NE MS. Alcorn Co. 89 mi. SE of Memphis, TN. Manufactures clothing, hosiery, furniture, cottonseed oil, dairy products, handles, sawmill machinery, motors, pulleys, hydraulic pumps, telephone equipment, organs. Agriculture. Cotton, corn, soybeans, poultry.

19054 ■ The Daily Corinthian
Paxton Media Group
1607 S Harper Rd.
Corinth, MS 38834
Phone: (662)287-6111
Publication E-mail: news@dailycorinthian.com
General newspaper. **Freq:** Daily (morn.). **Print Method:** Offset. **Cols./Page:** 6. **Col. Width:** 26 nonpareils. **Col. Depth:** 294 agate lines. **Key Personnel:** Reece Terry, Publisher; Beth Cossitt, Business Manager; Logan Mosby, Editor. **USPS:** 142-560. **Subscription Rates:** $139.85 Individuals print; home delivery; $198.90 By mail print; $165.85 Individuals print and online; home delivery; $224.90 By mail print and online. **URL:** http://dailycorinthian.com. **Mailing address:** PO Box 1800, Corinth, MS 38834. **Remarks:** Accepts advertising. **Circ:** (Not Reported).

19055 ■ WYDL-FM - 100.7
102 N Cass St., Ste. D
Corinth, MS 38834
Phone: (662)284-4611
Fax: (662)284-9609
Format: Top 40. **Key Personnel:** Mike Brandt, Gen. Mgr., mike@wydl.com; Heather Simmons, Sales Mgr., heather@wydl.com. **Ad Rates:** Advertising accepted; rates available upon request. **URL:** http://wydl-fm.tritondigitalmedia.com.

CRYSTAL SPRINGS

SW MS. Copiah Co. 25 mi. SW of Jackson. Gravel mining. Manufactures machine tools, plastic pellets, laboratory and pharmaceutical fixtures, electric transformers copper, brass and aluminum wire. Pine and hardwood timber. Poultry industry.

19056 ■ Meteor
Meteor Newspaper Inc.
201 E Georgetown St.
Crystal Springs, MS 39059-0353
Phone: (601)892-2581
Fax: (601)892-2249
Publication E-mail: themeteor@bellsouth.net
Community newspaper. **Freq:** Weekly (Wed.). **Print Method:** Offset. **Trim Size:** 15 x 22 1/2. **Cols./Page:** 6. **Col. Width:** 25 nonpareils. **Col. Depth:** 294 agate lines. **Key Personnel:** Henry Carney, Editor. **USPS:** 342-440. **Subscription Rates:** $24 Individuals in Copiah county; $32 Individuals outside Copiah county. **URL:** http://themeteor.com. **Ad Rates:** BW $938; SAU $6.30; PCI $6.20. **Remarks:** Accepts advertising. **Circ:** ‡5000.

DE KALB

E MS. Kemper Co. 30 mi. N. of Meridian. Saw mills; cotton ginning. Pine timber. Agriculture. Cotton, corn, potatoes.

19057 ■ Kemper County Messenger
Messenger
102 Main St.
De Kalb, MS 39328
Phone: (601)743-5760
Fax: (601)743-4430
Community newspaper. **Freq:** Weekly (Thurs.). **Print Method:** Offset. **Cols./Page:** 6. **Col. Width:** 2 1/8 inches. **Col. Depth:** 21 inches. **Key Personnel:** Jim Prince, Editor, phone: (601)656-4000; Patty Jowers, Office Manager. **Subscription Rates:** $30 Individuals /year; $34 Out of area /year; $37 Out of state /year. **URL:** http://kempercountymessenger.com. **Remarks:** Accepts advertising. **Circ:** (Not Reported).

DECATUR

19058 ■ WSQH-FM - 91.7
PO Box 2440
Tupelo, MS 38803
Phone: (662)844-8888
Format: Religious. **Owner:** American Family Radio, at above address. **URL:** http://www.afr.net.

DUCK HILL

19059 ■ WAUM-FM - 91.9
PO Box 2440
Tupelo, MS 38803
Phone: (662)844-8888
Format: Religious; Contemporary Christian. **Owner:** American Family Radio, at above address. **Ad Rates:** Noncommercial. **URL:** http://www.afr.net.

EUPORA

NC MS. Webster Co. 52 mi. E. of Greenwood. Sawmills; cotton ginning; glove factory. Pine, hardwood timber. Agriculture. Cotton, corn, potatoes, dairying.

19060 ■ Webster Progress-Times
Webster Progress
58 N Dunn
Eupora, MS 39744
Phone: (662)258-7532
Fax: (662)258-6474
Newspaper. **Freq:** Weekly (Wed.). **Print Method:** Offset. **Cols./Page:** 6. **Col. Width:** 12 ems. **Col. Depth:** 21 1/2 inches. **Key Personnel:** Joseph McCain, Editor. **Subscription Rates:** $26 Individuals all access. **URL:** http://websterprogresstimes.com. **Ad Rates:** BW $572; 4C $687; SAU $4.25; PCI $6.25. **Remarks:** Advertising accepted; rates available upon request. **Circ:** Paid ‡2700.

FAYETTE

SW MS. Jefferson Co. 9 mi. S. of Lorman. Manufactures lumber. Residential.

19061 ■ The Fayette Chronicle
The Fayette Chronicle
PO Box 536
Fayette, MS 39069-0536
Phone: (601)786-3661
Fax: (601)786-3661
Free: 800-449-3260
Publication E-mail: fayettenews@hotmail.com
General circulation newspaper. Authorized to publish government and legal notices. **Freq:** Weekly (Thurs.). **Print Method:** computer. **Trim Size:** 13 x 22. **Cols./Page:** 6. **Col. Width:** 12 picas. **Col. Depth:** 21.5 inches. **Key Personnel:** Charles Kwame Shepphard, Editor. **ISSN:** 0889--5171 (print). **URL:** http://www.members.tripod.com/~fayettenews. **Remarks:** Accepts advertising. **Circ:** (Not Reported).

FLORA

19062 ■ WYAB-FM - 103.9
740 US Hwy. 49 N, Ste. R
Flora, MS 39071
Phone: (601)879-0093
Fax: (601)427-0088
Format: Oldies; Talk; News. **Networks:** Mississippi. **Owner:** SSR Communications Inc., at above address. **Founded:** 1997. **Operating Hours:** Continuous. **Wattage:** 6,000. **Ad Rates:** Noncommercial. $8.50 for 30 seconds; $12.50 for 60 seconds; $12.50 for 60 seconds. **URL:** http://www.wyab.com.

FOREST

C MS. Scott Co. 45 mi. E. of Jackson. Bienville National Forest. Manufactures frozen desserts, knit clothing, steel flow control valves, military electronic hardware. Lumber. Log homes. Poultry processing. Hatcheries. Agriculture. Soybeans, corn, milo, feed.

19063 ■ Scott County Times
Scott Publishing Inc.
311 Smith St.
Forest, MS 39074
Phone: (601)469-2561
Fax: (601)469-2004
Publisher's E-mail: news@sctonline.net
Community newspaper. **Freq:** Weekly (Wed.). **Print Method:** Offset. **Cols./Page:** 6. **Col. Width:** 25 nonpareils. **Col. Depth:** 301 agate lines. **Key Personnel:** Tim Beeland, Publisher. **USPS:** 485-440. **Subscription Rates:** $30 Individuals /year (in county); $40 Individuals /year (out of area). **URL:** http://sctonline.net. **Mailing address:** PO Box 89, Forest, MS 39074. **Remarks:** Accepts advertising. **Circ:** Paid 4000.

19064 ■ Northland Cable
PO Box 1538
Forest, MS 39074
Phone: (601)469-3712
Fax: (601)469-4203
Owner: Northland Cable, 1201 3rd Ave., Ste. 3600, Seattle, WA 98101, Ph: (206)621-1351. **Key Personnel:** Wayne Robinson, Gen. Mgr. **Cities Served:** subscribing households 4,250.

FRENCH CAMP

19065 ■ WFCA-FM - 107.9
40 Mecklin Ave.
French Camp, MS 39745
Phone: (662)547-6414
Fax: (662)547-9451
Format: Gospel. **Key Personnel:** Chuck Carroll, Contact; Glen Barlow, Contact; Shawna Grice, Contact. **Wattage:** 100,000 ERP. **Ad Rates:** Advertising accepted; rates available upon request. **URL:** http://www.wfcafm108.com.

FULTON

NE MS. Itawamba Co. On Tombigbee River, 60 mi. N. of Columbus. Itawamba Community College. Manufactures wood, copper products, furniture, garments. Sawmill. Timber. Agriculture. Cotton, poultry, dairying.

19066 ■ Itawamba County Times
Itawamba County Times
106 W Main St.
Fulton, MS 38843-1143
Phone: (662)862-3141
Community newspaper. **Freq:** Weekly (Wed.). **Print Method:** Offset. **Cols./Page:** 6. **Col. Width:** 10.5 picas. **Col. Depth:** 21.5 inches. **URL:** http://djournal.com/itawamba. **Mailing address:** PO Box 909, Fulton, MS 38843-1143. **Circ:** (Not Reported).

19067 ■ Fulton TV Cable Co. Inc.
101 W Wiygul S
Fulton, MS 38843
Owner: GTR, Inc., PO Box 548, Shawneetown, IL 62984, Ph: (618)269-4411, Fax: (618)269-4414. **Key Personnel:** Dwight McGee, Gen. Mgr. **Cities Served:** Fulton, Mantachie, Tremont, Mississippi: subscribing households 4,000; 36 channels; 2 community access channels; 120 hours per week community access programming. **Mailing address:** PO Box 950, Dobson, NC 27017. **URL:** http://corp.sos.ms.gov/corp/portal/c/page/corpBusinessIdSearch/portal.aspx?#.

GREENVILLE

W MS. Washington Co. On Lake Ferguson, still water harbor, 132 mi. S. of Memphis, TN. Bridges across river. Boat connections. Manufactures carpeting, concrete products, boxes, lumber, cottonseed oil, wall board, plastics, auto parts, boilers, stoppers, screws, wire and saws. Bottling works; shipyard. Fisheries. Hardwood timber. Agriculture. Cotton, alfalfa, soybeans, rice, cattle.

19068 ■ Delta Democrat Times
Freedom Communications Inc.
988 N Broadway
Greenville, MS 38701
Phone: (662)335-1155
Fax: (662)335-2860
Publisher's E-mail: info@freedom.com
General newspaper. **Freq:** Daily and Sun. (morn.). **Print Method:** Offset. **Cols./Page:** 6. **Col. Depth:** 301 agate lines. **Key Personnel:** Kenneth Mister, Editor; Matt Guthrie, Publisher. **Subscription Rates:** $156 Individuals print edition; daily & Sunday; $126 Individuals print edition; by mail; $72 Individuals online. **URL:** http://www.ddtonline.com. **Mailing address:** PO Box 1618, Greenville, MS 38701. **Remarks:** Accepts classified advertising. **Circ:** (Not Reported).

19069 ■ WABG-AM - 960
849 Washington Ave.
Greenville, MS 38701
Phone: (662)332-0949
Fax: (662)344-1814
Free: 800-898-0968
Format: Country; Talk. **Operating Hours:** 6 a.m.-1 a.m. **ADI:** Greenwood-Greenville, MS. **Wattage:** 1,000 Day; 500 Night. **Ad Rates:** $8-12 for 30 seconds; $10-14 for 60 seconds. **Mailing address:** PO Box 1243, Greenville, MS 38701. **URL:** http://wabg.com.

19070 ■ WABG-TV - 6
849 Washington Ave.
Greenville, MS 38701
Free: 800-898-0968
Format: Commercial TV. **Networks:** ABC. **Founded:** 1959. **Operating Hours:** Continuous; 80% network, 20% local. **ADI:** Greenwood-Greenville, MS. **Wattage:** 100,000. **Ad Rates:** $25-450 for 30 seconds. **URL:** http://www.yourdeltanews.com.

19071 ■ WBAD-FM - 94.3
94 3 Fm Independently Owned & Operate D 4426
Wbad Fm
Greenville, MS 38704
Phone: (662)335-9265
Fax: (662)335-5538
Format: Urban Contemporary. **Networks:** American Urban Radio. **Owner:** Interchange Communications, Inc., at above address. **Founded:** 1973. **Operating Hours:** Continuous. Daily; 8% network, 92% local. **ADI:** Greenwood-Greenville, MS. **Key Personnel:** William D. Jackson, Contact; Stanley S. Sherman, Contact. **Wattage:** 50,000. **Ad Rates:** $14-18 for 30 seconds; $17.5-22 for 60 seconds. **URL:** http://www.wbadfm.com/advertising.html.

19072 ■ WDMS-FM - 100.7
1383 Pickett St.
Greenville, MS 38703
Phone: (662)332-1315
Format: Contemporary Country. **Owner:** WDMS, Inc., 1383 Pickett Street, Greenville, MS 38702, Ph: (662)334-4559. **Founded:** 1967. **Operating Hours:** Continuous. **ADI:** Greenwood-Greenville, MS. **Key Personnel:** Mi-

Circulation: ★ = AAM; △ or • = BPA; ♦ = CAC; ❑ = VAC; ⊕ = PO Statement; ‡ = Publisher's Report; Boldface figures = sworn; Light figures = estimated.

chelle Nicholson, Sales Mgr. **Wattage:** 100,000 ERP. **Ad Rates:** Advertising accepted; rates available upon request. Combined advertising rates available with WGVM-AM. **URL:** http://www.wdms.fm.

19073 ■ WESY-AM
7 Oaks Rd.
Greenville, MS 38704-5804
Phone: (662)378-9405
Fax: (662)335-5538
Format: Religious; Urban Contemporary. **Networks:** American Urban Radio. **Owner:** Interchange Communications, Inc., at above address. **Founded:** 1959. **Key Personnel:** Truman Ford, Music Dir; Stanley S. Sherman, Contact. **Wattage:** 1,000 Day; 048 Night. **Ad Rates:** $3-4 for 30 seconds; $4-5 for 60 seconds. **Mailing address:** PO Box 5804, Greenville, MS 38704-5804.

19074 ■ W42CY - 42
PO Box A
Santa Ana, CA 92711
Phone: (714)832-2950
Free: 888-731-1000
Email: comments@tbn.org
Owner: Trinity Broadcasting Network Inc., PO Box A, Santa Ana, CA 92711, Ph: (714)832-2950, Free: 888-731-1000. **URL:** http://www.tbn.org.

19075 ■ WGVM-AM - 1260
3130 Hwy. 82 E
Greenville, MS 38703
Phone: (662)378-3888
Email: wdms@tecinfo.com
Format: Sports; Talk. **Networks:** ESPN Radio. **Founded:** 1948. **Operating Hours:** 6:00 a.m. - 6:00 p.m. **ADI:** Greenwood-Greenville, MS. **Wattage:** 5,000 ERP Day. **Ad Rates:** Advertising accepted; rates available upon request. Combined advertising rates available with WDMS.

19076 ■ WIQQ-FM - 102.3
1399 E Reed Rd.
Greenville, MS 38703-7234
Phone: (662)378-2617
Email: info@deltaradio.net
Format: Contemporary Hit Radio (CHR). **Networks:** USA Radio; Jones Satellite. **Founded:** 1985. **Operating Hours:** Continuous; 55% network, 45% local. **ADI:** Greenwood-Greenville, MS. **Key Personnel:** Larry Fuss, President; Kevin Keith, Contact. **Wattage:** 3,000. **Ad Rates:** for 60 seconds. WNIX-AM, WBAQ-FM. **URL:** http://www.deltaradio.net.

19077 ■ WLRK-FM - 91.5
PO Box 2098
Omaha, NE 68103-2098
Free: 800-525-5683
Email: info@klove.com
Format: Contemporary Christian. **Owner:** Educational Media Foundation, 2351 Sunset Blvd., Ste. 170-218, Rocklin, CA 95677, Ph: (800)434-8400. **URL:** http://www.klove.com.

19078 ■ WLTM-FM - 97.9
1399 E Reed Rd.
Greenville, MS 38703
Phone: (662)378-2617
Email: info@deltaradio.net
Format: Easy Listening. **Networks:** ABC. **Owner:** Delta Radio L.L.C., 9408 Grand Gate St., Las Vegas, NV 89143, Ph: (702)898-4669, Fax: (208)567-6865. **Founded:** 1970. **Formerly:** WBAQ-FM. **Operating Hours:** 5:30 a.m.-midnight; 10% network; 90% local. **ADI:** Greenwood-Greenville, MS. **Wattage:** 50,000. **Ad Rates:** WIDQ/WNIX. **URL:** http://deltaradio.net.

19079 ■ WNIX-AM - 1330
1399 E Reed Rd.
Greenville, MS 38703
Phone: (662)378-2617
Fax: (662)378-8341
Email: info@deltaradio.net
Format: News; Talk. **Networks:** USA Radio; ABC. **Owner:** Delta Radio L.L.C., 9408 Grand Gate St., Las Vegas, NV 89143, Ph: (702)898-4669, Fax: (208)567-6865. **Founded:** 1939. **Formerly:** WJPR-AM. **Operating Hours:** Continuous. **ADI:** Greenwood-Greenville, MS. **Key Personnel:** Jim Gregory, Contact; Jim Gregory, Contact. **Wattage:** 1,000 Day; 500 Night. **Ad Rates:** for 60 seconds. WIQQ-FM, WBAQ-FM. **URL:** http://www.wnixradio.com.

19080 ■ WXVT-TV - 15
3015 E Reed Rd.
Greenville, MS 38703
Phone: (662)334-1500
Fax: (662)378-8122
Format: Public TV. **Networks:** CBS. **Owner:** Saga Communications Inc., 73 Kercheval Ave., Ste. 201, Grosse Pointe Farms, MI 48236, Ph: (313)886-7070, Fax: (313)886-7150. **Founded:** 1980. **Operating Hours:** Continuous; 75% network, 25% local. **ADI:** Greenwood-Greenville, MS. **Key Personnel:** Earl Phelps, News Dir., ephelps@wxvt.com; Larry Cazavan, Gen. Sales Mgr., Station Mgr., lcazavan@wxvt.com. **Ad Rates:** $20-250 for 10 seconds; $28-350 for 15 seconds; $40-500 for 30 seconds; $80-1000 for 60 seconds. **URL:** http://www.wxvt.com.

GREENWOOD

NWC MS. Leflore Co. On Yazoo River, 52 mi. NE of Greenville. Extensive buying of cotton. Manufactures cottonseed products, radio testing instruments, pianos, indexing equipment, seat belts, farm implements, picture frames, fishing gear, medicines, trailers. Bottling works. Cotton plantations.

19081 ■ Greenwood Commonwealth
Greenwood Commonwealth
PO Box 8050
Greenwood, MS 38935
Phone: (662)453-5312
Fax: (662)453-2908
Free: 800-898-0730
Publisher's E-mail: commonwealth@gwcommonwealth.com
General newspaper. **Freq:** Monday-Friday afternoons/ Sunday morning. **Print Method:** Offset. **Cols./Page:** 6. **Col. Width:** 26 nonpareils. **Col. Depth:** 301 agate lines. **URL:** http://www.gwcommonwealth.com. **Remarks:** Accepts classified advertising. **Circ:** (Not Reported).

19082 ■ Staplreview
Staplcotn Cooperative Association
214 W Market St.
Greenwood, MS 38930
Phone: (662)453-6231
Fax: (662)453-4622
Publisher's E-mail: sales@imvinfo.com
Magazine on cotton marketing, warehousing and financing. **Freq:** Quarterly. **Print Method:** Offset. **Trim Size:** 8 1/2 x 11. **Key Personnel:** Jean Blunden, Editor. **Alt. Formats:** PDF. **URL:** http://www.staplcotn.com/resources/staplreview. **Mailing address:** PO Box 547, Greenwood, MS 38935-0547. **Remarks:** Advertising not accepted. **Circ:** (Not Reported).

19083 ■ WGRM-AM
1110 Wright St.
Greenwood, MS 38930
Phone: (662)453-1240
Fax: (662)453-1241
Format: Gospel. **Networks:** NBC. **Owner:** Willis Broadcasting Corp., at above address. **Founded:** 1937. **Wattage:** 720. **Ad Rates:** $10-15 for 30 seconds.

19084 ■ WMAO-FM - 90.9
3825 Ridgewood Rd.
Jackson, MS 39211
Phone: (601)432-6565
Fax: (601)432-6907
Free: 800-922-9698
Email: events@mpbonline.org
Format: Classical; News; Information; Public Radio. **Networks:** National Public Radio (NPR); Public Radio International (PRI). **Owner:** Mississippi Public Broadcasting, 3825 Ridgewood Rd, Jackson, MS 39211. **Founded:** 1983. **Operating Hours:** Continuous. **ADI:** Greenwood-Greenville, MS. **Wattage:** 100,000. **Ad Rates:** Noncommercial. **URL:** http://www.mpbonline.org.

19085 ■ WMAO-TV - 23
3825 Ridgewood Rd.
Jackson, MS 39211
Phone: (601)432-6565
Free: 800-922-9698
Format: Public TV. **Simulcasts:** WMPN-TV Jackson, MS. **Networks:** Public Broadcasting Service (PBS). **Owner:** Mississippi Authority for Educational TV, at above address. **Founded:** 1972. **Operating Hours:** 6:45 am-11:15 pm weekdays; noon-11:15 pm Sat.; noon-11 pm Sun. **ADI:** Greenwood-Greenville, MS. **Key Personnel:** Maggie Gibson, Dep. Dir.; Jay Woods, Dep. Dir. **Ad Rates:** Noncommercial. **URL:** http://www.mpbonline.org.

GRENADA

19086 ■ W30BY - 30
PO Box A
Santa Ana, CA 92711
Phone: (714)832-2950
Free: 888-731-1000
Owner: Trinity Broadcasting Network Inc., PO Box A, Santa Ana, CA 92711, Ph: (714)832-2950, Free: 888-731-1000. **URL:** http://www.tbn.org.

GULFPORT

S MS. Harrison Co. On Gulf of Mexico, 11 mi. W. of Biloxi. Resort. Manufactures lumber, cotton. Seafood canneries.

19087 ■ The Sun Herald
McClatchy Newspapers Inc.
205 DeBuys Rd.
Gulfport, MS 39507
Publisher's E-mail: pensions@mcclatchy.com
General newspaper. **Founded:** 1965. **Freq:** Daily. **Print Method:** Offset. **Trim Size:** 12 3/4 x 21 1/2. **Cols./Page:** 6. **Col. Width:** 2 inches. **Col. Depth:** 21 1/2 inches. **Key Personnel:** Glen Nardi, President, Publisher; Stan Tiner, Executive Editor, phone: (228)896-2300; Kim Anderson, Contact, phone: (228)896-0545; Margaret Baker, Contact. **USPS:** 615-080. **Subscription Rates:** $4.45 Individuals weekly, print and online. **URL:** http://www.sunherald.com/. **Remarks:** Accepts advertising. **Circ:** Mon.-Fri. ★43963, Sun. ★49822.

19088 ■ WCPR-FM - 97.9
1909 E Pass Rd., Ste. D-11
Gulfport, MS 39507
Phone: (228)388-2001
Fax: (228)896-9114
Format: Alternative/New Music/Progressive; Album-Oriented Rock (AOR). **Key Personnel:** Kenny Vest, Dir. of Operations, kennyvest@cableone.net. **Wattage:** 50,000. **Ad Rates:** Noncommercial. **URL:** http://www.979cprrocks.com.

19089 ■ WGBL-FM - 96.7
1909 E Pass Rd., Ste. D-11
Gulfport, MS 39507
Phone: (228)388-2001
Format: Country. **ADI:** Biloxi-Gulfport-Pascagoula, MS. **Key Personnel:** Michelle Shortridge, Contact. **Wattage:** 4,300. **Ad Rates:** Advertising accepted; rates available upon request.

19090 ■ WGCM-FM
PO Box 2639
Gulfport, MS 39501-2639
Fax: (601)863-7516
Format: Oldies. **Networks:** Satellite Music Network. **Founded:** 1969. **Key Personnel:** Kelli Bell, Contact. **Wattage:** 50,000 ERP. **URL:** http://www.coast102.com.

19091 ■ WHGO-FM - 105.9
1909 E Pass Rd., Ste. D-11
Gulfport, MS 39507
Phone: (228)388-2001
Fax: (228)896-9114
Format: Classic Rock. **Owner:** Triad Broadcasting Company, LLC, 2511 Garden Rd., No. 104A, Monterey, CA 93940, Ph: (831)655-6350, Fax: (831)655-6355. **Ad Rates:** Noncommercial.

19092 ■ WJZD-FM - 94.5
PO Box 6216
Gulfport, MS 39506
Phone: (228)896-5307
Fax: (228)896-5703
Email: info@wjzd.com
Format: Urban Contemporary. **Key Personnel:** Tamara Wingerter, Gen. Sales Mgr., tamara@wjzd.com. **Ad Rates:** Advertising accepted; rates available upon request. **Mailing address:** PO Box 6216, Gulfport, MS 39506. **URL:** http://www.wjzd.com.

19093 ■ WLNF-FM - 95.3
PO Box 939
Gulfport, MS 39501

Phone: (228)867-9953
Fax: (228)868-0095
Free: 888-548-3953
Email: studio@live95fm.com
Format: Contemporary Hit Radio (CHR). **Owner:** Tralyn Broadcasting, Inc., at above address. **Founded:** July 1997. **Formerly**: WLUN-FM. **Operating Hours**: Continuous. **ADI**: Biloxi-Gulfport-Pascagoula, MS. **Key Personnel:** Darren Kies, Gen. Mgr., dkies@datasync.com; Scott Sands, Office Mgr., sands@datasync.com; Bill Brock, Gen. Sales Mgr.; Nickie Welch, Traffic Mgr. **Wattage**: 50,000. **Ad Rates:** $50 per unit. **URL:** http://www.live95fm.com.

19094 ■ WROA-AM
PO Box 2639
Gulfport, MS 39505-2639
Phone: (228)896-5500
Fax: (228)896-0458
Format: Middle-of-the-Road (MOR); News; Sports. **Networks:** Mississippi. **Founded:** 1955. **Wattage**: 5,000.

WRPM-AM - See Poplarville, MS

19095 ■ WTNI-AM - 1640
1909 E Pass Rd., Ste. D-11
Gulfport, MS 39506
Phone: (228)388-2001
Format: News; Talk. **Operating Hours**: Continuous. **Key Personnel:** Kenny Vest, Operations Mgr., kennyvest@cableone.net; Wayne Watkins, Dir. of Programs, kenallen@datasync.com; Bo Clark, Sales Mgr., boclark@cableone.net. **Ad Rates:** Advertising accepted; rates available upon request.

19096 ■ WXXV-TV - 25
14351 Hwy. 49 N
Gulfport, MS 39503
Phone: (228)832-2525
Fax: (228)832-4442
Email: promotions@wxxv25.com
Format: News; Sports; Information. **Networks:** Fox. **Owner:** Morris Multimedia Inc., 27 Abercorn St., Savannah, GA 31401, Ph: (912)233-1281, Fax: (912)232-4639. **ADI**: Biloxi-Gulfport-Pascagoula, MS. **Key Personnel:** Bobby Edwards, Gen. Mgr.; Donna Ingram, Bus. Mgr.; Scott Wilson, Gen. Sales Mgr. **Wattage**: 300,000 ERP. **Ad Rates:** Noncommercial. **URL:** http://www.wxxv25.com.

19097 ■ WXYK-FM - 107.1
1909 E Pass Rd., Ste. D-11
Gulfport, MS 39507
Phone: (228)388-2001
Fax: (228)896-9114
Format: Top 40. **Founded:** Sept. 12, 2006. **Key Personnel:** Kenny Vest, Operations Mgr., kenny.vest@alphamediausa.com; Michelle Shortridge, Bus. Mgr., michelle.shortridge@alphamediausa.com. **Ad Rates:** Noncommercial. **URL:** http://www.1071themonkey.net.

19098 ■ WZKX-FM - 107.9
PO Box 2639
Gulfport, MS 39503
Phone: (228)896-4530
Fax: (228)896-0458
Free: 888-343-4530
Format: Country; Contemporary Hit Radio (CHR); News. **Owner:** Coast Radio Group, 10250 Lorraine Rd., Gulfport, MS 39503-6005. **Founded:** 1964. **Operating Hours**: Continuous. **ADI**: Biloxi-Gulfport-Pascagoula, MS. **Key Personnel:** Steve Spillman, Gen. Sales Mgr., steve@kicker108.com. **Wattage**: 100,000 ERP. **Ad Rates:** Advertising accepted; rates available upon request. **URL:** http://www.kicker108.com.

HATTIESBURG

SE MS. Lamar Co. 70 mi. N. of Gulfport. University of Southern Mississippi and William Carey College. Manufactures lumber, lumber products, explosives, chemicals, textiles, concrete pipes, paints, turpentine, metal products. Meat, poultry processing plants; gas and oil fields, oil refinery, sand and gravel pits; naval stores. Agriculture. Cotton, corn, truck products.

19099 ■ Annual in Therapeutic Recreation: ATRA's Research Journal
American Therapeutic Recreation Association
629 N Main St.
Hattiesburg, MS 39401
Phone: (601)450-2872
Fax: (601)582-3354
Publisher's E-mail: national@atra-online.com
Journal published in conjunction with American Association for Leisure and Recreation covering rehabilitation issues. **Freq:** Annual. **Subscription Rates:** Included in membership. **URL:** http://www.atra-online.com/resources/publications. **Remarks:** Advertising not accepted. **Circ:** 3750.

19100 ■ Clinical Kinesiology
American Kinesiotherapy Association
118 College Dr., No. 5142
Hattiesburg, MS 39406
Free: 800-296-2582
Publisher's E-mail: info@akta.org
Journal of the American Kinesiotherapy Association containing news and research. **Freq:** Quarterly. **ISSN:** 0896--9620 (print). **Subscription Rates:** $30 Nonmembers; $75 Institutions libraries. **URL:** http://akta.org/resources/clinical-kinesiology; http://www.clinicalkinesiology.net. **Circ:** (Not Reported).

19101 ■ The Hattiesburg American
Gannett Company Inc.
825 N Main St.
Hattiesburg, MS 39401
Phone: (601)582-4321
Fax: (601)584-3075
General newspaper. **Freq:** Daily. **Print Method:** Offset. **Trim Size:** 13 3/4 x 22 3/4. **Cols./Page:** 6. **Col. Width:** 1.833 inches. **Col. Depth:** 21 1/2 inches. **Key Personnel:** Erin Kosnac, Managing Editor, phone: (601)584-3070; Tracie Fowler, General Manager, phone: (601)584-3000; Rosalind Cooley, Manager, Circulation, phone: (601)584-3056. **URL:** http://www.hattiesburgamerican.com. **Remarks:** Accepts advertising. **Circ:** (Not Reported).

19102 ■ Impact of Hattiesburg
Buckley Newspapers Inc.
219 S 40th Ave., Ste. E
Hattiesburg, MS 39402
Phone: (601)264-8181
Fax: (601)264-8398
Shopping guide. **Freq:** Weekly (Wed.). **Key Personnel:** Ryan Griffin, Manager. **Subscription Rates:** Free. **URL:** http://www.impactads.com; http://go.jbpageflip.com/Hattiesburg. **Circ:** Combined 179033.

19103 ■ International Journal of Comparative Psychology
International Society for Comparative Psychology
University of Southern Mississippi
Dept. of Psychology
118 College Dr., No. 5025
Hattiesburg, MS 39406
Publisher's E-mail: ijcpmail@gmail.com
Freq: Quarterly. **Key Personnel:** Lori Marino, Associate Editor; Joseph Call, Board Member; Dani Brunner, Editor-in-Chief. **ISSN:** 0889--3667 (print); **EISSN:** 2168--3344 (electronic). **URL:** http://escholarship.org/uc/uclapsych_ijcp. **Remarks:** Accepts advertising. **Circ:** (Not Reported).

19104 ■ Mississippi Review
University of Southern Mississippi
118 College Dr.
Hattiesburg, MS 39406-0001
Phone: (601)266-1000
Literary magazine covering poetry, fiction and interviews. **Freq:** Semiannual. **Trim Size:** 5 1/2 x 8 3/4. **Key Personnel:** Andrew Malan Milward, Editor-in-Chief. **ISSN:** 0047--7559 (print). **URL:** http://www.usm.edu/mississippi-review/index.html. **Remarks:** Accepts advertising. **Circ:** Combined 1500.

19105 ■ Southern Quarterly: A Journal of the Arts in the South
University of Southern Mississippi
118 College Dr.
Hattiesburg, MS 39406-0001
Phone: (601)266-1000
Journal of literary essays, reviews, and art portfolios. **Freq:** Quarterly fall, winter, summer and spring. **Print Method:** Offset. **Trim Size:** 7 x 10. **Cols./Page:** 1. **Key Personnel:** Diane DeCesare Ross, Managing Editor; Chester Bo Morgan, Associate Editor; Douglas Chamber, Editor. **ISSN:** 0038--4496 (print). **Subscription Rates:** $65 Institutions /year (online); $35 Individuals /year; $91 Institutions /year (print and online). **URL:** http://sites.usm.edu/southern-quarterly-literary-magazine. **Ad Rates:** BW $150; 4C $200. **Remarks:** Accepts advertising. **Circ:** (Not Reported).

19106 ■ The Talon
University of Southern Mississippi Alumni Association
118 College Dr., No. 5013
Hattiesburg, MS 39406-0001
Phone: (601)266-5013
Fax: (601)266-4214
Publication E-mail: jenny.boudreaux@usm.edu
Member magazine of the University Alumni Association. **Founded:** July 01, 1949. **Freq:** Quarterly. **Print Method:** Offset. **Trim Size:** 8 1/2 x 11. **Cols./Page:** 3. **Col. Width:** 28 nonpareils. **Col. Depth:** 140 agate lines. **Key Personnel:** Jennifer Payne, Associate Director, phone: (601)266-4095; Jenny Boudreaux, Assistant Director, phone: (601)266-5722; Jerry DeFatta, Executive Director. **URL:** http://www.southernmissalumni.com/s/995/internal.aspx?sid=995&gid=1&pgid=309. **Formerly**: USM Alumni News. **Ad Rates:** 4C $1,400. **Remarks:** Accepts advertising. **Circ:** ‡16500.

19107 ■ WAII-FM - 89.3
PO Box 2440
Tupelo, MS 38803
Free: 800-326-4543
Format: Religious. **Owner:** American Family Radio, at above address. **URL:** http://www.afa.net.

19108 ■ WDAM-TV - 7
PO Box 16269
Hattiesburg, MS 39404
Email: pics@wdam.com
Format: Commercial TV. **Networks:** NBC. **Owner:** Raycom Media Inc., 201 Monroe St., RSA Twr., 20th Fl., Montgomery, AL 36104-3731, Ph: (334)206-1400. **Founded:** 1956. **Operating Hours**: 5:30 a.m.-12:30 a.m. weekdays; 6:30 a.m.-1:30 Saturday and Sunday. **ADI**: Laurel-Hattiesburg, MS. **Key Personnel:** Randy Swan, News Dir., rswan@wdam.com; Mitchell Williams, Sports Dir., mwilliams@wdam.com; Joe Sciortino, Gen. Mgr., jcameron@wdam.com. **Ad Rates:** Advertising accepted; rates available upon request. **URL:** http://www.wdam.com.

19109 ■ WEEZ-AM - 890
106 Campbell Loop
Hattiesburg, MS 39401
Phone: (601)319-1211
Format: Gospel. **ADI**: Laurel-Hattiesburg, MS. **Key Personnel:** Mike Comfort, Gen. Mgr. **Wattage**: 10,000 ERP. **Ad Rates:** Noncommercial. **URL:** http://www.whjaradio.com.

19110 ■ WHLT-TV - 22
990 Hardy St.
Hattiesburg, MS 39403
Phone: (601)545-2077
Fax: (601)545-3589
Format: Commercial TV. **Networks:** CBS. **Owner:** Media General Broadcast Group, 333 E Franklin St., Richmond, VA 23219, Ph: (804)887-5000. **Founded:** 1987. **Operating Hours**: Continuous. **ADI**: Laurel-Hattiesburg, MS. **Key Personnel:** Larry Blackerby, Gen. Mgr. **Mailing address:** PO Box 232, Hattiesburg, MS 39403.

19111 ■ WHSY-AM - 950
PO Box 15276
Hattiesburg, MS 39401
Phone: (601)582-7078
Fax: (601)582-7122
Email: contact@whsy950.com
Format: Talk; Sports; News. **Networks:** ABC; CBS; Mutual Broadcasting System. **Owner:** Southern Communications Inc., at above address. **Founded:** 1948. **Operating Hours**: 6 a.m.-1 a.m.; 75% network, 25% local. **ADI**: Laurel-Hattiesburg, MS. **Wattage**: 5,000 Day; 064 Night. **Ad Rates:** $15-17.50 for 30 seconds; $20-25 for 60 seconds.

19112 ■ WJKX-FM - 102.5
6555 Hwy. 98 W, Ste. 8
Hattiesburg, MS 39402
Phone: (601)296-9800
Email: contact@102jkx.com
Format: Urban Contemporary; Blues. **Networks:** ABC. **Founded:** 1973. **Formerly**: WBSJ-FM. **Operating**

Circulation: ★ = AAM; △ or • = BPA; ♦ = CAC; ❑ = VAC; ⊕ = PO Statement; ‡ = Publisher's Report; Boldface figures = sworn; Light figures = estimated.

Hours: 80% network; 20% local. **Key Personnel:** Mike Comfort, Dir. of Mktg., Mktg. Mgr.; Michael Watkins, Account Mgr. **Wattage:** 50,000. **Ad Rates:** Noncommercial. **URL:** http://www.102jkx.com//main.html.

19113 ■ WJMG-FM
1204 Graveline S
Hattiesburg, MS 39401-1372
Phone: (601)544-1941
Fax: (601)544-1947
Format: Urban Contemporary; Adult Contemporary. **Networks:** American Urban Radio. **Founded:** 1982. **Key Personnel:** Vernon C. Floyd, CEO, Gen. Mgr. **Wattage:** 6,000 ERP.

19114 ■ WLVZ-FM - 107.1
PO Box 2098
Omaha, NE 68103-2098
Free: 800-525-5683
Format: Contemporary Christian. **Owner:** Educational Media Foundation, 2351 Sunset Blvd., Ste. 170-218, Rocklin, CA 95677, Ph: (800)434-8400. **URL:** http://www.klove.com.

19115 ■ WMFM-FM - 106.3
6555 Hwy. 98 W, Ste. 8
Hattiesburg, MS 39402
Phone: (601)545-1063
Fax: (601)583-8817
Email: lite106@aol.com
Format: Information; News. **Founded:** 1986. **Operating Hours:** Continuous. **ADI:** Laurel-Hattiesburg, MS. **Key Personnel:** Yancey Sanford, Operations Mgr; Bill Hickman, Contact. **Wattage:** 3,000 ERP. **Ad Rates:** $8-12 for 30 seconds; $10-13 for 60 seconds. **URL:** http://wild1063.iheart.com.

19116 ■ WNSL-FM - 100.3
6555 Hwy. 98 W, Ste. 8
Hattiesburg, MS 39402
Phone: (601)296-9800
Email: contact@sl100.com
Format: Top 40. **Key Personnel:** Mike Comfort, Mktg. Mgr. **Ad Rates:** Noncommercial. **URL:** http://www.sl100.com.

19117 ■ WORV-AM
1204 Graveline
Hattiesburg, MS 39401
Fax: (601)544-1947
Format: Urban Contemporary; Gospel; Blues. **Networks:** American Urban Radio; American Urban Radio. **Founded:** 1969. **Key Personnel:** Vernon Floyd, Gen. Mgr. **Wattage:** 1,000 Day; 088 Night.

19118 ■ WUSM-FM - 88.5
118 College Dr., No. 10045
Hattiesburg, MS 39406
Phone: (601)266-4287
Email: wusm@usm.edu
Format: Educational. **Owner:** University of Southern Mississippi, 118 College Dr., Hattiesburg, MS 39406-0001, Ph: (601)266-1000. **Founded:** 1973. **Formerly:** WMSU-FM. **Operating Hours:** 6 a.m.-2 a.m.; 5% network, 95% local. **Key Personnel:** Jeffrey Rassier, Gen. Mgr., jeffrey.rassier@usm.edu. **Wattage:** 3,000. **Ad Rates:** Noncommercial. **URL:** http://www.usm.edu.

19119 ■ WUSW-FM - 103.7
6555 Hwy. 98 W, Ste. 8
Hattiesburg, MS 39402
Phone: (601)544-1037
Email: contact@thefoxrocks1037.com
Format: Album-Oriented Rock (AOR). **Key Personnel:** Kahilla Hakimzadeh, Sales Mgr., kahillahakimzadeh@clearchannel.com; Mike Comfort, VP of Mktg., mikecomfort@clearchannel.com. **URL:** http://www.thefoxrocks1037.com.

19120 ■ WXRR-FM - 104
PO Box 16596
Hattiesburg, MS 39404
Phone: (601)544-0095
Fax: (601)545-8199
Email: rock104@rock104fm.com
Format: Classic Rock. **Ad Rates:** Noncommercial. **URL:** http://www.rock104fm.com.

19121 ■ WZLD-FM - 106.3
6555 Hwy. 98 W, Ste. 8
Hattiesburg, MS 39402
Phone: (601)545-1063
Format: Hip Hop; Urban Contemporary. **Ad Rates:** Advertising accepted; rates available upon request. **URL:** http://www.wild1063.com.

HAZLEHURST

SW MS. Copiah Co. 32 mi. S. of Jackson. Manufactures mops, brooms, metal culverts, electrical windings. Lumber mills; poultry process hatcheries. Diversified farming. Cattle.

19122 ■ Copiah County Courier
Courier
103 S Ragsdale Ave.
Hazlehurst, MS 39083
Phone: (601)894-3141
Fax: (601)894-3144
Community newspaper. **Freq:** Weekly (Wed.). **Print Method:** Offset. **Cols./Page:** 6. **Col. Width:** 13 picas. **Col. Depth:** 21 1/2 inches. **Key Personnel:** Joe B. Coates, Editor, Publisher. **Subscription Rates:** $24 Individuals online; $40 Out of area print; $30 Individuals print; $50 Individuals print & online; $55 Out of area print & online. **Formed by the merger of:** Courier Plus. **Mailing address:** PO Box 351, Hazlehurst, MS 39083. **Remarks:** Accepts advertising. **Circ:** (Not Reported).

HERNANDO

NW MS. DeSoto Co. 23 mi. S. of Memphis, TN.

19123 ■ DeSoto Times-Tribune
DeSoto Times-Tribune
2445 Hwy. 51 S
Hernando, MS 38632
Phone: (662)429-6397
Community newspaper. **Freq:** Biweekly Tuesday and Thursday. **Print Method:** Offset. **Cols./Page:** 6. **Col. Width:** 12 picas. **Col. Depth:** 21.5 picas. **Key Personnel:** Cynthia Bullion, Reporter; Charlotte Hopper, Specialist, Circulation; Cyndi Pittman, Publisher. **Subscription Rates:** $59 Individuals yearly; $6 Individuals monthly. **URL:** http://desototimes.com. **Formed by the merger of:** DeSoto County Tribune; DeSoto Times Today. **Ad Rates:** BW $1316; 4C $1721; SAU $10.20; PCI $10.20. **Remarks:** Accepts advertising. **Circ:** Paid ‡9,897, Free ‡8,100.

19124 ■ WVIM-FM - 95.3
PO Box 487
Hernando, MS 38632
Phone: (601)429-4465
Fax: (601)429-0704
Format: Contemporary Christian. **Networks:** Unistar. **Owner:** Talmadge Lane, at above address. **Founded:** 1976. **Operating Hours:** Continuous. **Key Personnel:** Andy Montgomery, Operations Mgr. **Wattage:** 3,000. **Ad Rates:** $7-14 for 30 seconds; $8-16 for 60 seconds.

HOLLY SPRINGS

N MS. Marshall Co. 42 mi. SE of Memphis, TN. Rust College. Mississippi Industrial College. Manufacturing brick, tile, piano, small appliances, windows, metal fabrication, foam equipment, plastics, ornamental metal. Diversified farming. Cotton, cattle, soybeans, dairying. Cotton ginning.

19125 ■ Pigeon Roost News
The South Reporter
PO Box 278
Holly Springs, MS 38635
Phone: (662)252-4261
Fax: (662)252-3388
Publisher's E-mail: south@dixie-net.com
Community newspaper. **Freq:** Weekly. **Print Method:** Offset. **Trim Size:** 13 x 21. **Cols./Page:** 5. **Col. Width:** 12 picas. **Col. Depth:** 13 inches. **URL:** http://www.southreporter.com. **Remarks:** Accepts advertising. **Circ:** (Not Reported).

19126 ■ The South Reporter
The South Reporter
PO Box 278
Holly Springs, MS 38635
Phone: (662)252-4261
Fax: (662)252-3388
Publisher's E-mail: south@dixie-net.com
Newspaper. **Freq:** Weekly (Thurs.). **Print Method:** Offset. **Cols./Page:** 6. **Col. Width:** 24 nonpareils. **Col. Depth:** 294 agate lines. **Key Personnel:** Barry Burleson, Editor. **USPS:** 504-320. **Subscription Rates:** $25 Individuals online only; $1 Individuals online only; 1 week; $13 Individuals online only; 6 months. **URL:** http://www.southreporter.com. **Remarks:** Accepts advertising. **Circ:** (Not Reported).

19127 ■ WKRA-AM - 1110
145 Memphis St.
Holly Springs, MS 38635
Phone: (662)252-1110
Fax: (662)252-2739
Format: Gospel; News; Talk. **Owner:** Billy Autry. **Founded:** 1966. **Operating Hours:** Sunrise-sunset. **ADI:** Memphis, TN. **Wattage:** 1,000. **Ad Rates:** $25 for 15 seconds; $45 for 30 seconds; $75 for 60 seconds. Combined advertising rates available with WKRA-FM.

19128 ■ WKRA-FM - 92.7
145 Memphis St.
Holly Springs, MS 38635
Phone: (662)252-6692
Fax: (662)252-2739
Email: wkraradio@vista-express.com
Format: Urban Contemporary. **Networks:** ABC. **Owner:** Billy R. Autry. **Founded:** 1976. **Operating Hours:** Continuous. **ADI:** Memphis, TN. **Key Personnel:** Rick Williams, Operations Mgr. **Wattage:** 3,000. **Ad Rates:** $12 for 30 seconds; $15 for 60 seconds. Combined advertising rates available with WKRA-AM.

HORN LAKE

19129 ■ Better Bridge
American Contract Bridge League
6575 Windchase Blvd.
Horn Lake, MS 38637-1523
Phone: (662)253-3100
Fax: (662)253-3187
Publisher's E-mail: service@acbl.org
Magazine covering bridge playing. **Freq:** Bimonthly. **Subscription Rates:** $29 Individuals. **URL:** http://www.betterbridge.com/products/Better-Bridge-Magazine-Annual-Subscription. **Circ:** (Not Reported).

19130 ■ The Bridge Bulletin
American Contract Bridge League
6575 Windchase Blvd.
Horn Lake, MS 38637-1523
Phone: (662)253-3100
Fax: (662)253-3187
Publisher's E-mail: service@acbl.org
Freq: Monthly. **Subscription Rates:** Included in membership. **URL:** http://www.acbl.org/join/the-bridge-bulletin. **Remarks:** Accepts advertising. **Circ:** (Not Reported).

HOUSTON

NW MS. Chickasaw Co. 10 mi. W. of Buena Vista. Dairying.

19131 ■ WCPC-AM - 940
1189 N Jackson St.
Houston, MS 38851
Phone: (601)456-3071
Free: 888-989-2299
Format: Contemporary Christian. **Networks:** USA Radio. **Owner:** Wilkins Communication Network Inc., 292 S Pine St., Spartanburg, SC 29302, Ph: (864)585-1885, Fax: (864)597-0687, Free: 888-989-2299. **Founded:** 1955. **Operating Hours:** 5 a.m.- 9 p.m.; 10% network, 90% local. **Key Personnel:** Chris Hester, Station Mgr. **Wattage:** 50,000. **Ad Rates:** Noncommercial. **URL:** http://www.wilkinsradio.com/pages.

INDIANOLA

NW MS. Sunflower Co. 85 mi. N. of Jackson. Manufactures cottonseed products, catfish feed, dogfood, power mowers, wheelbarrows, tricycles, wagons. Agriculture. Cotton, cattle, sheep, hogs, rice, soybeans. Farm raised catfish.

19132 ■ Catfish Journal
Catfish Farmers of America
1100 Highway 82 E, Ste. 202
Indianola, MS 38751
Freq: 6/year. **Subscription Rates:** Included in membership. **Remarks:** Accepts advertising. **Circ:** (Not Reported).

19133 ■ WNLA-AM - 1380
44 Hwy. 448
Indianola, MS 38751
Format: Gospel. **Networks:** ABC. **Founded:** 1954. **Operating Hours**: 6 a.m.-6 p.m. **Key Personnel:** Ricardo Thomas, Station Mgr., recardo.thomas@debutbroadcasting.com; Regina Hawkins, News Dir. **Wattage**: 500. **Ad Rates:** $5-8 for 30 seconds; $7-12 for 60 seconds.

19134 ■ WNLA-FM - 105.5
PO Box 667
Indianola, MS 38751
Phone: (662)887-1380
Fax: (888)704-4762
Founded: 1954. **Operating Hours**: Continuous. **Wattage**: 4,400. **Ad Rates:** $4-7 for 30 seconds; $5-9 for 60 seconds. **URL:** http://www.wnlaradio.com.

19135 ■ WYTF-FM - 88.7
PO Box 2440
Tupelo, MS 38803
Phone: (662)844-8888
Format: Religious. **Owner:** American Family Radio, at above address. **URL:** http://radio-locator.com.

IUKA

NE MS. Tishomingo Co. 115 mi. E. of Memphis, TN. Resort, mineral springs. Agriculture. Soybeans, corn, hay.

19136 ■ WADI-FM - 95.3
121 Front St.
Iuka, MS 38852
Phone: (662)287-3101
Fax: (662)287-9262
Format: Contemporary Country. **Operating Hours**: Continuous. **Key Personnel:** Joe Taylor Jobe, Contact; Joan Jobe, Contact. **Wattage**: 4,200. **Ad Rates:** $5 for 30 seconds; $5.5 for 60 seconds.

JACKSON

SWC MS. Rankin Co. On Pearl River, 42 mi. E. of Vicksburg. The State Capital. Belhaven College, Millsaps College, Mississippi College, University of Mississippi Dental and Medical School, University of Mississippi at Jackson, University of Southern Mississippi at Jackson, Jackson State University, Tougaloo College. Important cottonseed oil manufacturing and distributing center, also oil and natural gas center. Fertilizer and bottling works; meat packing plants; lumber mill. Manufactures valves, fittings, electrical switch gear, transformers, heating and plumbing materials, crates and boxes, textiles, furniture, flourescent lights, cooking utensils, bedding, steel fabrication, feed, auto parts, cement blocks, tile, hydraulic aircraft, missile parts.

19137 ■ Annals of Allergy, Asthma, & Immunology
American College of Allergy, Asthma and Immunology
2500 N State St., Ste. N416
Jackson, MS 39216
Phone: (601)815-4871
Fax: (601)815-4770
Publication E-mail: annallergy@medicine.umsmed.edu
Clinical journal for practicing allergists. **Freq:** Monthly. **Print Method:** Offset. **Trim Size:** 8 1/4 x 11. **Cols./Page:** 2. **Col. Depth:** 126 agate lines. **Key Personnel:** Gailen D. Marshall, MD, Editor-in-Chief; Kimberly K. Stamper, Managing Editor; Richard W. Weber, MD, Associate Editor. **ISSN:** 1081--1206 (print). **Subscription Rates:** $148 Individuals print and online; $204 Canada print and online; $192 Other countries print and online. **URL:** http://www.annallergy.org. **Formerly**: Annals of Allergy. **Remarks:** Accepts advertising. **Circ:** (Not Reported).

19138 ■ The Baptist Record: Journal of Mississippi Baptist Convention
Mississippi Baptist Convention
PO Box 530
Jackson, MS 39205-0530
Phone: (601)968-3800
Fax: (601)714-7419
Free: 800-748-1651
Baptist magazine (tabloid). **Freq:** Weekly. **Print Method:** Letterpress. **Trim Size:** 11 1/2 x 14 1/2. **Cols./Page:** 5. **Col. Width:** 12 picas. **Col. Depth:** 13 inches. **Key Personnel:** William H. Perkins, Editor; Brenda Quattlebaum, Manager, Circulation. **ISSN:** 0005--5778 (print). **Subscription Rates:** $11.99 Individuals /year. **URL:** http://www.mbcb.org/business-services/the-baptist-record/about-the-baptist-record. **Remarks:** Accepts advertising. **Circ:** (Not Reported).

19139 ■ The Clarion Ledger
Gannett Company Inc.
201 S Congress St.
Jackson, MS 39205-0040
General newspaper. **Freq:** Daily. **Print Method:** Offset. **Cols./Page:** 6. **Col. Width:** 1.833 inches. **Col. Depth:** 21 inches. **Key Personnel:** Joe Williams, Director, Finance, phone: (601)961-7202; Leslie Hurst, President, Publisher. **Subscription Rates:** $10 Individuals online only; monthly; $24 Individuals print and online; monthly; $16 Individuals Friday - Sunday; $14 Individuals Sunday - Thursday. **URL:** http://www.clarionledger.com. **Formed by the merger of:** Jackson Daily News. **Mailing address:** PO Box 40, Jackson, MS 39205-0040. **Remarks:** Accepts advertising. **Circ:** (Not Reported).

19140 ■ International Journal of Environmental Research and Public Health
Molecular Diversity Preservation International
Molecular Toxicology Research Laboratory
Jackson State University
Jackson, MS 39217
Phone: (601)979-3321
Fax: (601)979-2349
Publication E-mail: ijerph@mdpi.org
Peer-reviewed scientific journal publishing original articles, critical reviews, research notes, and short communications in the interdisciplinary area of environmental health sciences and public health. **Freq:** Monthly. **Key Personnel:** Dr. Paul B. Tchounwou, Editor-in-Chief. **ISSN:** 1661--7827 (print). **Subscription Rates:** Free online. **URL:** http://www.mdpi.com/journal/ijerph. **Remarks:** Accepts advertising. **Circ:** (Not Reported).

19141 ■ Jackson Advocate
Natchez Democrat Inc.
100 W Hamilton St.
Jackson, MS 39202
Phone: (601)948-4122
Fax: (601)948-4125
Publication E-mail: thejacksonadvocate@gmail.com
Black community newspaper. **Freq:** Weekly. **Print Method:** Offset. **Cols./Page:** 6. **Col. Width:** 2 1/8 inches. **Col. Depth:** 21 inches. **Key Personnel:** Alice Thomas-Tisdale, Publisher. **URL:** http://www.jacksonadvocateonline.com. **Remarks:** Accepts advertising. **Circ:** (Not Reported).

19142 ■ Jackson Free Press: The City's Smart Alternative
Jackson Free Press
125 S Congress St., Ste. 1324
Jackson, MS 39201
Phone: (601)362-6121
Fax: (601)510-9019
Publisher's E-mail: letters@jacksonfreepress.com
Newspaper covering news, politics, events, entertainment and dining in Jackson, Mississippi. **Freq:** Weekly. **Key Personnel:** Donna Ladd, Editor-in-Chief; Todd Stauffer, Publisher; Ronni Mott, Managing Editor. **URL:** http://www.jacksonfreepress.com. **Remarks:** Accepts classified advertising. **Circ:** ‡17000.

19143 ■ The Journal of Mississippi History
Mississippi Historical Society
PO Box 571
Jackson, MS 39205-0571
Phone: (601)576-6849
Publication E-mail: storemanager@mdah.state.ms.us
Scholarly journal covering the history of the lower Mississippi Valley Region and of the South in general. **Freq:** Quarterly latest issue: Volume 74, Number 1, Spring 2012. **Print Method:** Offset. **Trim Size:** 6 x 9. **Cols./Page:** 1. **Col. Width:** 60 nonpareils. **Col. Depth:** 95 agate lines. **Key Personnel:** Chris Goodwin, Managing Editor, phone: (601)576-6850, fax: (601)576-6975; Rev. Dennis Mitchell, Editor; H.T Holmes, Editor-in-Chief. **ISSN:** 0022--2771 (print). **Subscription Rates:** $25 Single issue /year. **URL:** http://www.mdah.ms.gov/new/interact/subscribe/journal-of-mississippi-history. **Remarks:** Accepts advertising. **Circ:** (Not Reported).

19144 ■ Microsurgery
John Wiley & Sons Inc.
c/o Feng Zhang, Phd., Ed.-in-Ch.
Division of Plastic Surgery
University of Mississippi Medical Center
Jackson, MS 39216-4505
Publisher's E-mail: info@wiley.com
Journal providing information on the use of the operating microscope in a variety of areas and on further applications of microsurgical methodologies and techniques. **Freq:** 8/year. **Trim Size:** 11 x 8 1/4. **Key Personnel:** Dr. William C. Lineaweaver, Editor; Feng Zhang, PhD, Editor-in-Chief; Michelle D. Gadsden, Managing Editor. **ISSN:** 0738--1085 (print); **EISSN:** 1098--2752 (electronic). **Subscription Rates:** $1417 Institutions online only - USA/Canada & Mexico/ROW; £724 Institutions online only - UK; €915 Institutions online only - Europe; $207 Individuals online only - USA/Canada and Mexico; $255 Other countries online only - UK/Europe/ROW. **URL:** http://onlinelibrary.wiley.com/journal/10.1002/(ISSN)1098-2752. **Ad Rates:** BW $772; 4C $1,009. **Remarks:** Accepts advertising. **Circ:** 6650.

19145 ■ The Mississippi Banker
Mississippi Bankers Association
640 N State St.
Jackson, MS 39202
Phone: (601)948-6366
Fax: (601)355-6461
Publication E-mail: magazine@msbankers.com
Magazine mailed to all banks in Mississippi, including bank directors and individual bank personnel, plus bank-related firms and other interested parties. **Freq:** Bimonthly. **Print Method:** Offset. **Trim Size:** 8 1/2 x 11. **Cols./Page:** 3. **Col. Width:** 26 nonpareils. **Col. Depth:** 139 agate lines. **ISSN:** 0026--6159 (print). **Subscription Rates:** $25 Individuals /year; $5 Single issue; $24.95 Individuals soft cover; $54.95 Individuals hard cover. **URL:** http://www.msbankers.com/themississippibanker. **Mailing address:** PO Box 37, Jackson, MS 39205-0037. **Ad Rates:** BW $750; 4C $500. **Remarks:** Accepts advertising. **Circ:** ‡1900.

19146 ■ Mississippi Business Journal
Venture Publications Inc.
200 N Congress St. Ste. 400
Jackson, MS 39201
Phone: (601)364-1000
Fax: (601)364-1006
Free: 800-283-4625
Publisher's E-mail: mbj@msbusiness.com
Magazine offering community business news. **Freq:** Weekly (Mon.). **Print Method:** Offset. **Trim Size:** 11 x 13 3/4. **Cols./Page:** 4. **Col. Width:** 14 picas. **Key Personnel:** Ross Reily, Editor, phone: (601)364-1018; Alan Turner, Publisher, phone: (601)364-1021. **ISSN:** 0195--0002 (print). **Subscription Rates:** $89 Individuals print and online (limited time only); $73 Two years online; $168 Two years print and online; $13 Individuals 13 weeks print and online. **URL:** http://msbusiness.com. **Remarks:** Accepts advertising. **Circ:** (Not Reported).

19147 ■ Mississippi Libraries
Mississippi Library Association
PO Box 13687
Jackson, MS 39236-3687
Phone: (601)981-4586
Fax: (601)981-4501
Publisher's E-mail: info@misslib.org
Journal on libraries. **Freq:** Quarterly. **Print Method:** Offset. **Trim Size:** 8 1/2 x 11. **Cols./Page:** 3. **Col. Width:** 27 nonpareils. **Col. Depth:** 140 agate lines. **Key Personnel:** Ann Branton, Editor. **ISSN:** 0194--388X (print). **URL:** http://www.misslib.org/publications. **Remarks:** Accepts advertising. **Circ:** (Not Reported).

19148 ■ Mississippi Magazine
Downhome Publications Inc.
PO Box 16445
Jackson, MS 39216
Phone: (601)982-8418
Mississippi homes, history, entertaining and lifestyles. **Freq:** Bimonthly. **Print Method:** Web offset. **Trim Size:** 8 1/8 x 10 7/8. **Cols./Page:** 3. **Col. Width:** 27 nonpareils. **Col. Depth:** 140 agate lines. **Key Personnel:** Melanie M. Ward, Editor; Patty Roper, Director, Editorial; Richard B. Roper, Publisher. **ISSN:** 0747-1602 (print). **Subscription Rates:** $25 Individuals print; $11.99 Individuals

Circulation: ★ = AAM; △ or • = BPA; ♦ = CAC; ❑ = VAC; ⊕ = PO Statement; ‡ = Publisher's Report; Boldface figures = sworn; Light figures = estimated.

online. **URL:** http://www.mississippimagazine.com. **Mailing address:** PO Box 16445, Jackson, MS 39216. **Ad Rates:** BW $1625; 4C $2455. **Remarks:** Accepts advertising. **Circ:** Paid ‡34,000, Non-paid ‡500.

19149 ■ TileLetter
National Tile Contractors Association
626 Lakeland East Dr.
Jackson, MS 39232
Phone: (601)939-2071
Fax: (601)932-6117
Journal covering North America's most comprehensive show for those who involved in the tile and stone industries. **Freq:** Monthly. **Subscription Rates:** Free. **URL:** http://www.tile-assn.com/?page=TileLetter. **Mailing address:** PO Box 13629, Jackson, MS 39236. **Ad Rates:** BW $650; 4C $2000. **Remarks:** Accepts advertising. **Circ:** Combined ‡14000.

19150 ■ Transgenics
Old City Publishing
c/o Julius M. Cruse
University of Mississippi Medical Ctr.
Dept. of Pathology, Immunopathology Section
2500 N State St.
Jackson, MS 39216
Publisher's E-mail: info@oldcitypublishing.com
Scientific journal that publishes original reports of biological analysis through DNA transfer in vivo and in vitro. **Freq:** Quarterly. **Trim Size:** 8 1/2 x 11. **Key Personnel:** Julius M. Cruse, Editor-in-Chief; Robert E. Lewis, Senior Editor; Alexander Kuklin, Associate Editor. **ISSN:** 1023--6171 (print); **EISSN:** 1607--8586 (electronic). **Subscription Rates:** $616 Institutions print and online; €559 Institutions print and online; ¥75770 Institutions print and online; $153 Individuals print only; €152 Individuals print only; ¥20610 Individuals print only. **URL:** http://www.oldcitypublishing.com/journals/transgenics-home. **Circ:** (Not Reported).

19151 ■ WDBD-TV - 40
One Great Pl.
Jackson, MS 39209
Phone: (601)922-1234
Format: Commercial TV. **Networks:** Fox. **Owner:** Jackson Television, LLC & Mississippi Television, LLC, at above address. **Founded:** 1984. **Operating Hours:** Continuous; 14% network, 86% local. **ADI:** Jackson, MS. **Ad Rates:** Noncommercial. **URL:** http://www.msnewsnow.com.

19152 ■ WDBT-FM - 95.5
1375 Beasley Rd.
Jackson, MS 39206
Phone: (601)982-1062
Fax: (601)362-1905
Format: Religious. **Key Personnel:** Doug Jones, Dir. of Sales. **Ad Rates:** Advertising accepted; rates available upon request. **URL:** http://www.hallelujah955.com.

19153 ■ WEEZ-FM - 99.3
6311 Ridgewood Rd.
Jackson, MS 39211
Phone: (601)957-1700
Fax: (601)425-4486
Free: 800-238-3942
Format: Gospel; Religious. **Networks:** USA Radio. **Owner:** Clear Channel Communications Inc., at above address, Ph: (210)822-2828, Fax: (210)822-2299. **Founded:** 1982. **Operating Hours:** Continuous. **ADI:** Laurel-Hattiesburg, MS. **Key Personnel:** Gerald Williams, Gen. Mgr.; Bobby Brignac, Operations Mgr.; Kathy McDonneall, Station Mgr. **Wattage:** 50,000 ERP. **Ad Rates:** $4-7 for 15 seconds; $7-10 for 30 seconds; $8-12 for 60 seconds. **URL:** http://www.supertalk.fm/stations/laurel-99-3.

19154 ■ WHER-FM - 99.3
6311 Ridgewood Rd.
Jackson, MS 39211
Fax: (888)808-8637
Format: Talk; News. **Founded:** 1966. **Operating Hours:** Continuous. **ADI:** Laurel-Hattiesburg, MS. **Key Personnel:** Mike Comfort, Gen. Mgr. **Wattage:** 50,000 ERP. **Ad Rates:** Advertising accepted; rates available upon request. **URL:** http://www.supertalk.fm/stations/laurel-99-3.

19155 ■ WHLH-FM - 95.5
1375 Beasley Rd.
Jackson, MS 39206
Phone: (601)982-1062
Fax: (601)362-1905
Format: Gospel. **Operating Hours:** Continuous. **ADI:** Jackson, MS. **Wattage:** 100,000 ERP. **URL:** http://www.hallelujah955.com.

19156 ■ WJDX-AM - 620
1375 Beasley Rd.
Jackson, MS 39206
Phone: (601)982-1062
Fax: (601)362-1905
Format: Sports. **Owner:** iHeartMedia Inc., 200 E Basse Rd., San Antonio, TX 78209, Ph: (210)832-3314. **Key Personnel:** Randy Bell, Dir. of Mktg., randybell@clearchannel.com; Kenny Windham, Gen. Mgr., Prog. Dir.; Doug Jones, Div. Dir.; Jan Michaels, Prog. Dir.; Rick Adams, Sr. VP; Todd Berry, Dir. of Sales. **Wattage:** 5,000 Day; 1,000 Night. **Ad Rates:** Noncommercial. **URL:** http://www.wjdx.com.

19157 ■ WJNT-AM - 1180
PO Box 9446
Jackson, MS 39286-9446
Phone: (601)957-1300
Fax: (601)956-0516
Email: contactus@wjnt.com
Format: News; Talk. **Simulcasts:** WJNT-FM. **Networks:** CBS; ABC; Westwood One Radio; CNN Radio. **Founded:** 1980. **Formerly:** WKKE-AM. **Operating Hours:** Continuous. **Local Programs:** *This Morning With Gordon Deal*, Monday Tuesday Wednesday Thursday Friday Saturday 4:00 a.m. - 8:00 a.m. 4:00 a.m. - 6:00 a.m. **Wattage:** 50,000 Day/ 500 Night. **Ad Rates:** $22-38 for 30 seconds; $28-65 for 60 seconds. **URL:** http://www.wjnt.com.

19158 ■ WJNT-FM - 103.3
PO Box 9446
Jackson, MS 39286-9446
Phone: (601)957-1300
Fax: (601)956-0516
Email: contactus@wjnt.com
Format: News; Talk. **Operating Hours:** Continuous. **Key Personnel:** Teresa Gerald, Bus. Mgr., tgerald@wjmi.com. **Wattage:** 50,000 day 10,000 critical 500 night. **Ad Rates:** Advertising accepted; rates available upon request. **URL:** http://www.wjnt.com.

19159 ■ WJSU-FM - 88.5
1230 Raymon Rd.
Jackson, MS 39204
Phone: (601)979-2285
Fax: (601)979-2878
Email: wjsufm@jsums.edu
Format: Jazz. **Founded:** June 01, 1976. **Key Personnel:** Dale Morris, Engineer, dale.m.morris@jsums.edu; Gina P. Carter-Simmers, Gen. Mgr., gina.p.carter-simmers@jsums.edu. **Wattage:** 24,500. **Ad Rates:** Noncommercial. **URL:** http://www.wjsu.org.

19160 ■ WJTV-TV - 12
1820 TV Rd.
Jackson, MS 39204
Phone: (601)372-6311
Fax: (601)372-8798
Email: wjtvnews@wjtv.com
Format: Commercial TV. **Networks:** CBS. **Owner:** Media General Communications Holdings L.L.C., 333 E Franklin St., Richmond, VA 23219, Ph: (804)649-6000. **Founded:** Jan. 20, 1953. **Operating Hours:** Continuous. **ADI:** Jackson, MS. **Key Personnel:** Jackie McDonald, Gen. Mgr., jmcdonald@wjtv.com. **Local Programs:** *Live Vipir Radar.* **Wattage:** 49,200 ERP H. **Ad Rates:** Advertising accepted; rates available upon request. **URL:** http://www.wjtv.com.

19161 ■ WJXN-FM - 100.9
PO Box 2098
Omaha, NE 68103
Free: 800-525-8400
Format: Contemporary Christian. **Owner:** Educational Media Foundation, 5700 W Oaks Blvd., CA 95765, Free: 800-800434-8400. **URL:** http://www.klove.com.

19162 ■ WKXG-AM - 1540
6311 Ridgewood Rd.
Jackson, MS 39211
Phone: (662)453-2174
Format: Urban Contemporary; Blues; Gospel. **Networks:** American Urban Radio. **Owner:** Telesouth Communications Inc., at above address. **Founded:** 1987. **Formerly:** WSWG-AM. **Operating Hours:** 6 a.m.-10 p.m.; 10% network, 90% local. **ADI:** Greenwood-Greenville, MS. **Wattage:** 1,000. **Ad Rates:** Noncommercial.

19163 ■ WLBT-TV - 3
715 S Jefferson St.
Jackson, MS 39201
Phone: (601)948-3333
Fax: (601)355-7830
Email: news@wlbt.com
Format: Commercial TV. **Networks:** NBC. **Founded:** 1953. **Operating Hours:** Continuous; 70% network, 30% local. **ADI:** Jackson, MS. **Key Personnel:** Dennis Smith, News Dir., dsmith@wlbt.com. **Ad Rates:** Advertising accepted; rates available upon request. **URL:** http://www.msnewsnow.com.

19164 ■ WLEZ-FM - 100.1
916 Foley St.
Jackson, MS 39202
Phone: (601)352-6691
Format: Adult Contemporary; Soft Rock. **Networks:** CNN Radio. **Founded:** Jan. 03, 1993. **Formerly:** WPFR-FM. **Operating Hours:** Continuous. **ADI:** Terre Haute, IN. **Key Personnel:** Edward Saint Pe, Founder, President, edward@weathervision.com; Jason McCleave, VP, jason@weathervision.com. **Wattage:** 50,000. **Ad Rates:** Noncommercial.

19165 ■ WLOO-TV - 41
1 Great Pl.
Jackson, MS 39209
Phone: (601)948-3333
Email: marketing@wlbt.net
Networks: Fox. **Owner:** Jackson Television L.L.C., 200 Clarendon St., 51st Fl., Boston, MA 02116, Ph: (617)262-7770. **Founded:** 2003. **URL:** http://www.msnewsnow.com.

19166 ■ WMAB-FM - 89.9
3825 Ridgewood Rd.
Jackson, MS 39211
Phone: (601)432-6565
Email: mpbinfo@mpbonline.org
Format: Classical; News; Information; Public Radio. **Networks:** National Public Radio (NPR); Public Radio International (PRI). **Owner:** Mississippi Public Broadcasting, 3825 Ridgewood Rd, Jackson, MS 39211. **Founded:** 1983. **Operating Hours:** Continuous. **ADI:** Jackson, MS. **Wattage:** 63,000. **Ad Rates:** Noncommercial. **URL:** http://www.mpbonline.org/programs/radio.

WMAE-FM - See Booneville

19167 ■ WMAE-TV - 12
3825 Ridgewood Dr.
Jackson, MS 39211
Phone: (601)432-6565
Fax: (601)432-6907
Free: 800-922-9698
Email: events@mpbonline.org
Format: Public TV. **Simulcasts:** WMPN-TV. **Networks:** Public Broadcasting Service (PBS). **Owner:** Mississippi Authority for Educational TV, at above address. **Founded:** 1974. **Operating Hours:** 6:45 am-11:15 pm weekdays; noon-11:15 pm Sat.; noon-11 pm Sun. **ADI:** Columbus-Tupelo (West Point), MS. **Key Personnel:** Maggie Gibson, Dep. Dir. **Ad Rates:** Noncommercial. **URL:** http://www.mpbonline.org.

WMAH-FM - See Biloxi

WMAH-TV - See Biloxi

WMAO-FM - See Greenwood

WMAO-TV - See Greenwood

WMAU-FM - See Bude

19168 ■ WMAU-TV - 17
3825 Ridgewood Rd.
Jackson, MS 39211
Phone: (601)982-6565
Format: Public TV. **Networks:** Public Broadcasting Service (PBS). **Owner:** Mississippi Authority for Educational TV, at above address. **Key Personnel:** A.J. Jaeger, Contact. **Wattage:** 682,000 ERP. **URL:** http://www.mpbonline.org/.

WMAV-FM - See Oxford

WMAV-TV - See Oxford

WMAW-FM - See Meridian

WMAW-TV - See Meridian

19169 ■ WMPN-FM - 91.3
3825 Ridgewood Rd.
Jackson, MS 39211
Phone: (601)432-6565
Email: events@mpbonline.org
Format: News; Information; Public Radio. **Networks:** National Public Radio (NPR); Public Radio International (PRI); AP. **Owner:** Mississippi Public Broadcasting, 3825 Ridgewood Rd, Jackson, MS 39211. **Founded:** 1983. **Formerly**: WMAA-FM. **Operating Hours**: Continuous. **ADI**: Jackson, MS. **Wattage**: 100,000. **Ad Rates:** Noncommercial. **URL:** http://www.mpbonline.org.

19170 ■ WMPN-TV - 29
3825 Ridgewood Rd.
Jackson, MS 39211
Phone: (601)432-6565
Fax: (601)432-6907
Free: 800-922-9698
Email: events@mpbonline.org
Format: Public TV. **Networks:** Public Broadcasting Service (PBS). **Owner:** Mississippi Authority for Educational TV, at above address. **Founded:** 1970. **Operating Hours**: 5 a.m.-11 p.m. **ADI**: Jackson, MS. **Key Personnel:** Maggie Gibson, Dep. Dir.; Cy Vance, Dep. Dir. **URL:** http://www.mpbonline.org.

19171 ■ WMPR-FM - 90.1
1018 Pecan Park Cir.
Jackson, MS 39209
Phone: (601)948-5835
Fax: (601)948-6162
Email: frontoffice@wmpr901.com
Format: Blues; Gospel. **Networks:** National Public Radio (NPR). **Founded:** 1983. **Operating Hours**: Continuous; 20% network; 80% local. **ADI**: Jackson, MS. **Key Personnel:** Charles Evers, Contact. **Wattage**: 100,000. **Ad Rates:** $15 for 60 seconds. **URL:** http://www.wmpr901.com.

19172 ■ WMSI-FM - 102.9
1375 Beasley Rd.
Jackson, MS 39206
Phone: (601)982-1062
Fax: (601)362-1905
Format: Country. **Networks:** ABC. **Owner:** iHeartMedia Inc., 200 E Basse Rd., San Antonio, TX 78209, Ph: (210)832-3314. **Founded:** 1948. **Operating Hours**: Continuous. **ADI**: Jackson, MS. **Key Personnel:** Kenny Windham, Gen. Mgr., VP; Rick Adams, Dir. of Programs, rickadams@clearchannel.com; Todd Berry, Operations Mgr.; Jan Michaels, Dir. of Mktg. **Wattage**: 100,000. **Ad Rates:** $40-90 for 30 seconds; $50-100 for 60 seconds. Combined advertising rates available with WJDX-AM. **URL:** http://www.miss103.com//main.html.

19173 ■ WOSM-FM - 103.1
6311 Ridgewood Rd.
Jackson, MS 39201
Phone: (228)875-9031
Fax: (228)875-6461
Format: Southern Gospel. **Networks:** AP. **Owner:** Charles H. Cooper, at above address. **Founded:** 1971. **Operating Hours**: Continuous. **ADI**: Biloxi-Gulfport-Pascagoula, MS. **Key Personnel:** Phil Moss; Margaret Cooper, Contact. **Wattage**: 50,000.

19174 ■ WPBQ-AM
129 Woodland Cir.
Jackson, MS 39216
Phone: (601)982-3210
Fax: (601)982-3220
Email: espn@espnradio1240.com
Format: Talk; Sports. **Wattage**: 880.

19175 ■ WQJQ-FM - 105.1
1375 Beasley Rd.
Jackson, MS 39206
Phone: (601)982-1062
Fax: (601)362-1905
Format: Oldies. **Founded:** Sept. 15, 2006. **Key Personnel:** Kenneth Windham, Gen. Mgr., VP; Jan Michaels, Dir. of Programs; Doug Jones, Dir. of Sales. **Wattage**: 100,000. **Ad Rates:** Noncommercial.

19176 ■ WQLJ-FM - 93.7
6311 Ridgewood Rd.
Jackson, MS 39211
Phone: (601)957-1700
Fax: (601)956-5228
Format: Adult Contemporary; Sports. **Networks:** Mississippi. **Owner:** Telesouth Communications, Inc., 6311 Ridgewood Rd., Jackson, MS 39211, Ph: (601)957-1700, Fax: (601)956-5228, Free: 888-808-8637. **Founded:** 1985. **Formerly**: WKLJ-FM. **Operating Hours**: Continuous. **ADI**: Jackson, MS. **Key Personnel:** Rick Mize, Gen. Mgr., q937@exceedtech.net. **Wattage**: 11,000 ERP. **Ad Rates:** $6.50-11 for 30 seconds; $11-18 for 60 seconds. Combined advertising rates available with WTNM. **Mailing address:** PO Box 1077, Oxford, MS 38655. **URL:** http://www.supertalk.fm.

19177 ■ WRBJ-FM - 97.7
745 N State St.
Jackson, MS 39202
Phone: (601)487-6614
Format: Talk; Folk; Full Service. **Owner:** Roberts Broadcasting Co., 901 Locust St., Saint Louis, MO 63101-1401, Ph: (314)367-4600, Fax: (314)367-0174. **Operating Hours**: 12:00 a.m. - 5:00 a.m. Sunday - Friday. **Wattage**: 6,000 ERP. **URL:** http://thebeatofthecapital.com.

19178 ■ WRJH-FM - 97.7
1985 Lakeland Dr.
Jackson, MS 39216
Phone: (601)713-0977
Format: Urban Contemporary. **Simulcasts:** WRKN-AM. **Owner:** On Top Communications, at above address. **Founded:** 1974. **Operating Hours**: 6 a.m.-midnight. **Key Personnel:** Stan Carter, Chief Engineer; Rita Wilbanks, Sales Mgr. **Wattage**: 6,000. **Ad Rates:** $4 for 30 seconds; $6 for 60 seconds.

19179 ■ WROB-AM - 1450
6311 Ridgewood Rd.
Jackson, MS 39211-2035
Phone: (601)957-1700
Fax: (662)494-9762
Format: Oldies. **Owner:** Telesouth Communications Inc., at above address. **Founded:** 1947. **Operating Hours**: Continuous. **Wattage**: 1,000.

19180 ■ WRXW-FM - 93.9
222 Beasley Rd.
Jackson, MS 39206
Ad Rates: Noncommercial.

19181 ■ WSTZ-FM - 106.7
1375 Beasley Rd.
Jackson, MS 39206
Phone: (601)982-1062
Fax: (601)362-1905
Format: Classic Rock. **Networks:** AP. **Owner:** iHeartMedia Inc., 200 E Basse Rd., San Antonio, TX 78209, Ph: (210)832-3314. **Founded:** 1968. **Operating Hours**: Continuous. **ADI**: Jackson, MS. **Key Personnel:** Steve Kelly, Operations Mgr., stevekelly2@clearchannel.com; Dave Spain, Dir. of Programs, spainman@clearchannel.com; Doug Jones, Dir. of Sales, dougjones@clearchannel.com; Jan Michaels, Dir. of Mktg.; Kenny Windham, VP, Gen. Mgr.; Rick Adams, Director; Todd Berry, Operations Mgr. **Wattage**: 100,000. **Ad Rates:** $40-52 for 30 seconds; $52-65 for 60 seconds. **URL:** http://www.z106.com//main.html.

19182 ■ WTWZ-AM - 1120
4611 Terry Rd.
Jackson, MS 39212-5646
Phone: (601)346-0074
Format: News; Bluegrass. **Networks:** USA Radio. **Owner:** Wood Broadcasting Co., 4611 Terry Rd, Jackson, MS 39212, Ph: (601)346-0074. **Founded:** 1981. **Operating Hours**: 7:00 a.m. - Midnight. **ADI**: Jackson, MS. **Wattage**: 10,000 Day. **Ad Rates:** $8 for 30 seconds; $10 for 60 seconds. **URL:** http://www.wtwzradio.com.

19183 ■ WWJK-FM - 107.3
222 Beasley Rd.
Jackson, MS 39206
Format: Adult Contemporary. **Owner:** Backyard Broadcasting Holdings L.L.C., 3948 Third St. S, Ste. 295, Jacksonville Beach, FL 32250-5847. **Operating Hours**: Continuous. **ADI**: Jackson, MS. **Wattage**: 98,000. **Ad Rates:** Advertising accepted; rates available upon request.

19184 ■ WYMX-FM - 99.1
6311 Ridgewood Rd.
Jackson, MS 39211
Phone: (601)453-2174
Fax: (601)455-5733
Format: Adult Contemporary. **Networks:** ABC. **Owner:** Telesouth Communications, Inc., 6311 Ridgewood Rd., Jackson, MS 39211, Ph: (601)957-1700, Fax: (601)956-5228, Free: 888-808-8637. **Founded:** 1986. **Formerly**: WSWG-FM. **Operating Hours**: Continuous; 10% network, 90% local. **ADI**: Greenwood-Greenville, MS. **Key Personnel:** Wes Sterling, Sales Mgr.; Rea Holmes, Office Mgr.; Kim Dillon, President, COO; Larry Tate, VP of Sales; Rick Mize, Gen. Mgr.; Robert Byrd, Gen. Mgr. **Wattage**: 100,000. **Ad Rates:** $10-18 for 30 seconds; $12-20 for 60 seconds. **URL:** http://www.telesouth.com.

19185 ■ WZRX-AM - 1590
1375 Beasley Rd.
Jackson, MS 39206
Phone: (601)982-1062
Fax: (601)362-8270
Format: News; Sports; Information. **Networks:** American Urban Radio. **Founded:** 1965. **Operating Hours**: Continuous. **ADI**: Jackson, MS. **Key Personnel:** Kenny Windham, Gen. Mgr., VP. **Wattage**: 5,000 Day; 1,000 Night. **Ad Rates:** Noncommercial. WRTM-FM/WRTM-AM.

KILN

19186 ■ WQRZ-FM - 103.5
PO Box 1145
Kiln, MS 39556-1145
Phone: (228)463-1035
Fax: (228)467-3366
Free: 877-818-WQRZ
Email: wqrznews@aol.com
Format: Eclectic. **Owner:** Hancock County Amateur Radio Assoc, Inc., at above address, Kiln, MS. **Key Personnel:** Brice L. Phillips, President. **URL:** http://www.katrinaradio.com.

KOSCIUSKO

C MS. Attala Co. 68 mi. NE of Jackson. Manufactures electric motors, dairy products, mobile homes, wood products, vent pipe & fittings, soft drinks, lamps, shades, corrugated containers, textiles, feed, plastic products. Pine, oak, hickory timber. Stock, dairy, poultry farms. Cotton, corn, hay.

19187 ■ The Star-Herald
Community Newspaper Holdings Inc.
207 N Madison St.
Kosciusko, MS 39090
Phone: (662)289-2251
Newspaper serving central Mississippi. **Freq:** Weekly (Thurs.). **Key Personnel:** Cindi Compton, General Manager. **Subscription Rates:** $35 Individuals; $50 Out of country. **URL:** http://starherald.net. **Remarks:** Accepts advertising. **Circ:** (Not Reported).

19188 ■ WJTA-FM - 91.7
PO Box 742
Kosciusko, MS 39090
Phone: (601)289-5703
Fax: (601)290-6080
Format: Southern Gospel. **Networks:** Bible Broadcasting. **Owner:** Dr. William G. Suratt, at above address. **Founded:** 1989. **Operating Hours**: Continuous; 10% network, 90% local. **Wattage**: 383. **Ad Rates:** $2.50-4.50 for 30 seconds; $3.35-5.50 for 60 seconds.

19189 ■ WKOZ-AM - 1340
PO Box 1700
Kosciusko, MS 39090
Phone: (662)289-1050
Format: Blues; Oldies. **Networks:** CNN Radio. **Owner:** Boswell Radio L.L.C., 1 Golf Course Rd., Kosciusko, MS 39090, Ph: (662)289-1050. **Founded:** 1947. **Operating Hours**: Continuous. **Key Personnel:** Johnny Boswell, President; Eric Matthews, Operations Mgr.; Lora Beckham, Bus. Mgr. **Wattage**: 1,000. **Ad Rates:** $3.75-4.50 for 30 seconds; $4-6 for 60 seconds. Combined advertising rates available with WBKJ-FM: $2.70-4.50 for 30 seconds; $3.60-6 for 60 seconds. **URL:** http://

Circulation: ★ = AAM; △ or • = BPA; ♦ = CAC; ❑ = VAC; ⊕ = PO Statement; ‡ = Publisher's Report; Boldface figures = sworn; Light figures = estimated.

www.boswellmedia.net/Wkoz.htm.

19190 ■ WLIN-FM - 101.1
PO Box 1700
Kosciusko, MS 39090
Phone: (662)289-1050
Fax: (662)289-7907
Email: breezy@kopower.com
Format: Adult Contemporary. **Networks:** USA Radio. **Owner:** Boswell Radio L.L.C., 1 Golf Course Rd., Kosciusko, MS 39090, Ph: (662)289-1050. **Founded:** 1973. **Formerly**: WEQZ-FM. **Operating Hours**: Continuous; 98% local. **ADI**: Jackson, MS. **Key Personnel:** Lora Beckham, Sales Mgr.; Johnny Boswell, Owner. **Wattage**: 25,000. **Ad Rates:** $9 for 30 seconds; $12 for 60 seconds. **URL:** http://www.breezynews.com.

LAKE

19191 ■ WMBU-FM - 89.1
PO Box 400
Lake, MS 39092
Phone: (601)775-3100
Fax: (601)775-8283
Free: 888-624-7234
Email: wmbu@moody.edu
Format: Religious. **Owner:** Moody Broadcasting Network, 820 N La Salle Blvd., Chicago, IL 60610, Ph: (312)329-4300, Fax: (312)329-4339, Free: 800-356-6639. **Founded:** 1990. **Key Personnel:** Rob Moore, Station Mgr. **Ad Rates:** Advertising accepted; rates available upon request.

LAUREL

SE MS. Jones Co. 55 mi. SW of Meridian. Southeastern Baptist College. Manufactures building board, wood products, distribution transformers, farm implements, forms, auto parts, machinery, garments, machine shop and foundry products, walk-in coolers and freezers, electric blankets, oil drilling products. Oil refinery; bottling works. Pine, hardwood timber. Agriculture.

19192 ■ Impact of Laurel
Buckley Newspapers Inc.
PO Box 4406
PO Box 4406
Laurel, MS 39440
Shopper. **Freq:** Semiweekly (Wed. and Sun.). **Print Method:** Offset. **Cols./Page:** 6. **Col. Width:** 19 nonpareils. **Col. Depth:** 196 agate lines. **Key Personnel:** Kevin Williamson, Manager. **Subscription Rates:** Free; $13 By mail. **URL:** http://impact360.ms. **Ad Rates:** GLR $.61; BW $1092; 4C $1342; PCI $13. **Remarks:** Accepts advertising. **Circ:** (Not Reported).

19193 ■ Laurel Leader Call
Laurel Leader Call
130 Beacon St.
Laurel, MS 39441-0728
General newspaper. **Freq:** Weekly Tuesday, Thursday and Saturday. **Print Method:** Offset. **Cols./Page:** 6. **Col. Width:** 25 nonpareils. **Col. Depth:** 301 agate lines. **Key Personnel:** Mark Thornton, Editor; Robin Bice, Manager, Advertising; Melissa Carter, Manager, Circulation. **Subscription Rates:** $65 Individuals; $95 Out of area; $50 Individuals online only. **URL:** http://leader-call.com. **Remarks:** Accepts classified advertising. **Circ:** Mon.-Sat. ★6892, Sun. ★6635.

19194 ■ WATP-FM - 90.9
PO Box 2440
Tupelo, MS 38803
Free: 800-326-4543
Format: Gospel. **Owner:** American Family Radio, at above address. **Ad Rates:** Noncommercial. **URL:** http://radio-locator.com.

19195 ■ WBBN-FM - 95.9
PO Box 6408
Laurel, MS 39441
Phone: (601)649-0095
Fax: (601)649-8199
Email: b95@b95country.com
Format: Country. **Networks:** ABC. **Founded:** 1985. **Operating Hours:** Continuous; 100% local. **ADI:** Laurel-Hattiesburg, MS. **Key Personnel:** Larry Blakeney, President, CEO, larry@b95country.com; Debbie Blakeney, Gen. Mgr., Sales Mgr., debbie@b95country.com. **Wattage:** 50,000. **Ad Rates:** $22-60 for 30 seconds; $26-64 for 60 seconds. WXRR-FM, WKZW-FM, WXHB-FM. **URL:** http://www.b95country.com.

19196 ■ WKZW-FM - 94.3
PO Box 6408
Laurel, MS 39441
Phone: (601)649-0095
Fax: (601)649-8199
Email: kz943@kz943.com
Format: Adult Contemporary. **Founded:** Sept. 12, 2006. **Key Personnel:** Debbie Blakeney, Gen. Mgr., Sales Mgr., debbie@kz943.com; Larry Blakeney, CEO, President, larry@kz943.com. **Wattage:** 50,000. **Ad Rates:** Advertising accepted; rates available upon request. **URL:** http://www.kz943.com.

LEAKESVILLE

SE MS. Greene Co. 30 mi. NW of Mobile, AL.

19197 ■ Greene County Herald
Greene County Herald
PO Box 220
Leakesville, MS 39451
Phone: (601)394-5070
Fax: (601)394-4389
Publisher's E-mail: herald@tds.net
Newspaper with a Democratic orientation. **Freq:** Weekly (Thurs.). **Print Method:** Offset. **Trim Size:** 13 x 21 1/2. **Cols./Page:** 6. **Col. Width:** 2 1/16 inches. **Col. Depth:** 21 inches. **Key Personnel:** George Turner, Editor; Joni Cooley McMillon, Director, Advertising. **USPS:** 228-600. **Subscription Rates:** $27 Individuals out of area, online only; $37 Out of area print and online. **URL:** http://www.greenecountyheraldonline.com. **Ad Rates:** GLR $.21; BW $370.44; 4C $590.44; SAU $2.94. **Remarks:** Accepts advertising. **Circ:** ‡3,150.

LEXINGTON

WC MS. Holmes Co. 58 mi. N. of Jackson. Saints College. Manufactures mobile homes. Sawmills; cotton ginning. Timber. Agriculture. Cotton, corn, truck crops.

19198 ■ Holmes County Herald
East Holmes Publishing Enterprises Inc.
308 Court Sq.
Lexington, MS 39095
Phone: (662)834-1151
Fax: (662)834-1074
Newspaper. **Freq:** Weekly (Thurs.). **Print Method:** Offset. **Cols./Page:** 6. **Col. Width:** 2 inches. **Col. Depth:** 21 1/2 inches. **Key Personnel:** Bruce Hill, Editor. **USPS:** 247-680. **Subscription Rates:** $35 Individuals in Holmes County; $40 Individuals in Missisippi; $50 Individuals outside Missisippi. **URL:** http://www.holmescountyherald.com. **Mailing address:** PO Box 60, Lexington, MS 39095. **Remarks:** Accepts advertising. **Circ:** (Not Reported).

19199 ■ WXTN-AM
100 Radio Rd.
Lexington, MS 39095
Fax: (662)834-2612
Format: Ethnic; Religious. **Networks:** Independent. **Owner:** Holmes County Broadcasting Co., at above address. **Founded:** 1959. **Wattage:** 5,000 Day.

LIBERTY

SW MS. Amite Co. 45 mi. SE of Natchez. Timber. Dairy, truck farms. Beef, cattle.

19200 ■ The Southern Herald
Southern Herald
262 Main St.
Liberty, MS 39645
Phone: (601)657-4818
Publisher's E-mail: southernherald@bellsouth.net
Community newspaper. **Freq:** Weekly (Thurs.). **Print Method:** Offset. **Cols./Page:** 6. **Col. Width:** 33 nonpareils. **Col. Depth:** 301 agate lines. **Key Personnel:** Rick Stratton, Publisher. **Subscription Rates:** $22 Individuals; $25 Out of state. **URL:** http://thesouthernherald.com; http://sth.stparchive.com. **Ad Rates:** GLR $.20; BW $516; 4C $666; SAU $4; PCI $4. **Remarks:** Accepts advertising. **Circ:** Paid ‡1300, Free ‡30.

LORMAN

19201 ■ WPRL-FM
1000 Asu Dr.
Lorman, MS 39096
Phone: (601)877-6613
Fax: (601)887-2213
Format: Big Band/Nostalgia; Jazz; Public Radio; News; Information; Gospel; Sports. **Networks:** ABC; AP; National Public Radio (NPR); Public Radio International (PRI). **Owner:** Alcorn State University, 1000 ASU Dr., Lorman, MS 39096-7500, Ph: (601)877-6100. **Founded:** 1922. **Formerly**: WWAZ-AM. **Key Personnel:** Dr. Shafiqur Rahman, Gen. Mgr., srahman@lorman.alcorn.edu. **Wattage**: 3,000 ERP. **Ad Rates:** Noncommercial; Advertising accepted; rates available upon request.

LOUISVILLE

EC MS. Winston Co. 60 mi. SW of Columbus. Manufactures auto accessories, car seats, gloves, material handling machinery, plywood, particleboard, bricks, chemicals, food processing equipment. Lumber mill. Dairy and poultry farms. Cotton, corn.

19202 ■ Choctaw Plaindealer
The Plaindealer Publishing Company Inc.
c/o Winston County Journal
119 N Court
Louisville, MS 39339
Phone: (662)773-6248
Fax: (662)285-6695
Publisher's E-mail: reporter@choctawplaindealer.com
Community newspaper. **Freq:** Weekly (Thurs.). **Print Method:** Offset. Uses mats. **Trim Size:** 14 1/2 x 22 1/2. **Cols./Page:** 6. **Col. Width:** 21 nonpareils. **Col. Depth:** 301 agate lines. **Key Personnel:** Joseph McCain, Editor; Amanda McBride, Editor. **Subscription Rates:** $26 Individuals print and online. **URL:** http://choctawplaindealer.com. **Ad Rates:** GLR $.25; BW $301; 4C $400; SAU $4.50; PCI $4. **Remarks:** Advertising accepted; rates available upon request. **Circ:** Paid ‡1,500.

19203 ■ WLSM-FM - 107.1
PO Box 279
Louisville, MS 39339
Phone: (601)773-3481
Fax: (601)773-3482
Format: Country. **Networks:** ABC; Mississippi. **Owner:** Harrison Communication, 9199 Reisterstown Rd., Ste. 212C, Owings Mills, MD 21117, Ph: (410)804-1728. **Founded:** 1953. **Operating Hours**: Continuous; 10% network, 90% local. **Wattage:** 25,000. **Ad Rates:** $4-6 for 30 seconds; $5-7 for 60 seconds.

MACON

E MS. Noxubee Co. 60 mi. N. of Meridian. Manufactures veneers, clay products, lumber, clothing, brick and tile. Pine timber. Dairy farms. Soybeans, cattle.

19204 ■ Macon Beacon
Macon Beacon
403 S Jefferson St.
Macon, MS 39341
Phone: (662)726-4747
Newspaper. **Freq:** Weekly (Thurs.). **Print Method:** Offset. **Trim Size:** 11 x 12 3/4. **Cols./Page:** 4. **Key Personnel:** R. Scott Boyd, Publisher; Donna J. Parker, Business Manager. **Subscription Rates:** $50 Individuals. **URL:** http://www.facebook.com/MaconBeacon. **Mailing address:** PO Box 32, Macon, MS 39341. **Ad Rates:** GLR $.55; BW $550; SAU $3; PCI $21. **Remarks:** Accepts advertising. **Circ:** 2845, 2845.

MADISON

WC MS. Madison Co. 15 mi. N. of Jackson.

19205 ■ WQVI-FM - 90.5
PO Box 2440
Tupelo, MS 38803
Phone: (662)844-8888
Format: Religious. **Owner:** American Family Radio, at above address. **Founded:** 1977. **URL:** http://www.afa.net.

MAGNOLIA

S MS. Pike Co. 6 mi. S. of McComb.

19206 ■ Magnolia Gazette
Magnolia Gazette
280 Magnolia St.
Magnolia, MS 39652
Phone: (601)783-2441
Community newspaper. **Freq:** Weekly. **Print Method:** Offset. **Cols./Page:** 6. **Col. Width:** 129 picas. **Col. Depth:** 21 1/2 inches. **Key Personnel:** Dr. Lucius Lampton, Contact; Nancy Morris, Contact. **Subscription Rates:** $19.95 Individuals + tax. **Formerly:** Osyka Eagle. **Ad Rates:** GLR $4; BW $550.83; 4C $850.83; SAU $4.39; PCI $2. **Remarks:** Accepts advertising. **Circ:** Paid ‡1100.

19207 ■ WAKH-FM - 105.7
PO Box 30
Magnolia, MS 39652
Phone: (601)684-4654
Fax: (601)684-4658
Format: Country. **Networks:** Mississippi. **Founded:** 1982. **Operating Hours:** Continuous. **ADI:** Jackson, MS. **Key Personnel:** Charles Dowdy, Gen. Mgr. **Wattage:** 100,000. **Ad Rates:** $16-28 for 30 seconds.

WBKN-FM - See Brookhaven, MS

MARKS

19208 ■ WQMA-AM - 1520
1820 W Marks Rd.
Marks, MS 38646
Phone: (662)902-0757
Fax: (831)604-3343
Format: Oldies. **Operating Hours:** Continuous. **URL:** http://Q1520radio.Com.

MATHISTON

NC MS. Webster Co. 12 mi. NW of Starkville.

19209 ■ The Breeze
Wood College
PO Box 289
Mathiston, MS 39752
Phone: (601)263-8128
Fax: (662)263-4964
Publication E-mail: breezeeditor@gmail.com
Collegiate newspaper. **Founded:** 1938. **Freq:** Semiweekly. **Print Method:** Offset. **Trim Size:** 10 x 12 1/2. **Cols./Page:** 5. **Col. Width:** 24 nonpareils. **Col. Depth:** 175 agate lines. **Key Personnel:** Torie Foster, Editor-in-Chief; Rachel Dozier, Managing Editor. **Subscription Rates:** Free. **URL:** http://www.breezejmu.org. **Ad Rates:** BW $87.75; PCI $1.50. **Remarks:** Accepts advertising. **Circ:** Free ‡9,500.

MCCOMB

S MS. Pike Co. 75 mi. S. of Jackson. Manufactures clothing, aluminum windows, lumber and wood products, wire-bound boxes, corrugated containers. Bottling plant. Dairy and truck farms. Beef, cattle, corn, soybeans.

19210 ■ Enterprise-Journal
J.O. Emmerich and Associates Inc.
112 Oliver Emmerich Dr.
McComb, MS 39648
Phone: (601)684-2421
Publication E-mail: publisher@enterprise-journal.com
General newspaper. **Founded:** 1889. **Freq:** Weekly. **Print Method:** Offset. **Trim Size:** 13 3/4 x 22 3/4. **Cols./Page:** 6. **Col. Width:** 12.5 picas. **Col. Depth:** 21.5 inches. **Key Personnel:** Jack Ryan, Editor, Publisher; Lauren Devereaux, Director, Advertising; Matt Williamson, Managing Editor. **USPS:** 335-580. **Subscription Rates:** $144 Individuals. **URL:** http://www.enterprise-journal.com/. **Remarks:** Accepts advertising. **Circ:** Mon.-Fri. ★**9,791**, Sun. ★**10,693**.

19211 ■ WAQL-FM - 90.5
PO Box 2440
Tupelo, MS 38803
Phone: (662)844-8888
Format: Religious. **Owner:** American Family Radio, at above address. **Ad Rates:** Advertising accepted; rates available upon request. **URL:** http://www.afa.net.

19212 ■ W36AC - 36
PO Box A
Santa Ana, CA 92711
Phone: (714)832-2950
Free: 888-731-1000
Owner: Trinity Broadcasting Network Inc., PO Box A, Santa Ana, CA 92711, Ph: (714)832-2950, Free: 888-731-1000. **URL:** http://www.tbn.org.

MEADVILLE

SW MS. Franklin Co. 30 mi. E. of Natchez. Manufactures rail cars and clothing. Pine and hardwood timber. Agriculture. Soybeans, livestock.

19213 ■ Wilk-Amite Record
Wilk-Amite Record
111 Main St.
Meadville, MS 39653
Phone: (601)384-2484
Fax: (601)384-2276
County newspaper. **Freq:** Weekly (Fri.). **Print Method:** Offset. **Cols./Page:** 7. **Col. Width:** 10.5 picas. **Col. Depth:** 21 1/2 inches. **USPS:** 684-140. **Subscription Rates:** $40 Individuals; $45 Out of state. **URL:** http://www.wilkamiterecord.com. **Ad Rates:** BW $792. **Remarks:** Accepts advertising. **Circ:** (Not Reported).

MERIDIAN

E MS. Lauderdale Co. 95 mi. E. of Jackson. Meridian Community College. Manufactures lumber products, sound systems, auto parts. Timber.

19214 ■ Meridian Star
Meridian Star Inc.
814 22nd Ave.
Meridian, MS 39301-5023
Phone: (601)693-1551
Fax: (601)485-1210
General newspaper. **Founded:** Mar. 03, 1879. **Freq:** Daily (morn.). **Print Method:** Offset. **Cols./Page:** 6. **Col. Width:** 25 nonpareils. **Col. Depth:** 301 agate lines. **Key Personnel:** Crystal Dupre, Publisher; Bill Gilmore, Director, Advertising. **Subscription Rates:** $168 Individuals; $11.99 Individuals /month; digital access. **URL:** http://www.meridianstar.com. **Mailing address:** PO Box 1591, Meridian, MS 39302-1591. **Ad Rates:** SAU $10. **Remarks:** Accepts advertising. **Circ:** Mon.-Sat. ★**14,805**, Sun. ★**16,167**.

19215 ■ 97OKK-FM - 97.1
3436 Hwy. 45N
Meridian, MS 39301
Phone: (601)693-3697
Fax: (601)483-0826
Format: Country. **Networks:** ABC. **Owner:** New South Communications, Inc., at above address. **Operating Hours:** Continuous. **Key Personnel:** Scott Stevens, Operations Mgr., Prog. Dir., scott.stevens@wokk.com. **Wattage:** 100,000. **Ad Rates:** Noncommercial. Combined advertising rates available with WMLV-FM, WMMZ-FM. **URL:** http://Wokk.Com.

19216 ■ WALT-AM - 910
PO Box 5797
Meridian, MS 39302
Format: Talk; News. **Networks:** ABC. **Owner:** New South Communications, Inc., at above address. **Founded:** 1964. **Operating Hours:** Continuous. **ADI:** Meridian, MS. **Wattage:** 5,000. **Ad Rates:** $8 for 30 seconds; $12 for 60 seconds. Combined advertising rates available with WOKK, WMMZ, WMLV. **URL:** http://www.radiopeople.com.

19217 ■ WFFX-AM - 1450
PO Box 1699
Meridian, MS 39302
Phone: (601)693-2661
Format: Sports; Talk. **Founded:** 2001. **Formerly:** WMPG-AM; WMDN-AM. **Operating Hours:** Continuous. **ADI:** Meridian, MS. **Key Personnel:** Kenny Windham, Gen. Mgr.; Leslie Hiatt, Promotions Mgr.; Lee Taylor, Dir. of Programs; Ron Harper, Dir. of Sales. **Wattage:** 1,000. **Ad Rates:** $5 for 30 seconds; $8 for 60 seconds.

19218 ■ WHTU-FM - 97.9
PO Box 5797
Meridian, MS 39301
Phone: (601)693-3434
Format: Oldies. **Key Personnel:** Mark Maharrey, Gen. Mgr.

19219 ■ WIIN-AM - 780
3436 Hwy. 45 N
Meridian, MS 39302
Phone: (601)956-0102
Fax: (601)978-3980
Ad Rates: Noncommercial.

19220 ■ WJDQ-FM - 95.1
4307 Hwy. 39 N
Meridian, MS 39301
Phone: (601)693-2381
Format: Adult Contemporary. **Founded:** 1965. **Formerly:** WDAL-FM. **Operating Hours:** Continuous. **ADI:** Meridian, MS. **Wattage:** 100,000. **Ad Rates:** $18-34 for 30 seconds; $24-45 for 60 seconds.

19221 ■ WKNN-FM - 99.1
286 Old Hwy. 45 N
Meridian, MS 39301
Phone: (601)693-2661
Fax: (601)483-0826
Format: Country. **Owner:** iHeartMedia Inc., 200 E Basse Rd., San Antonio, TX 78209, Ph: (210)832-3314. **Founded:** 1964. **Operating Hours:** Continuous; 1% network, 99% local. **ADI:** Biloxi-Gulfport-Pascagoula, MS. **Key Personnel:** Bill Black, Dir. of Programs. **Wattage:** 100,000. **Ad Rates:** $50-140 for 30 seconds; $50-140 for 60 seconds. **URL:** http://www.k99fm.com.

19222 ■ WKZB-FM - 106.9
3436 Hwy. 45 N
Meridian, MS 39301
Phone: (601)693-2661
Fax: (601)483-0826
Format: Oldies. **Networks:** ABC. **Founded:** 1978. **Formerly:** WQGL-FM. **Operating Hours:** Continuous. **ADI:** Meridian, MS. **Wattage:** 50,000. **Ad Rates:** Advertising accepted; rates available upon request. Combined advertising rates available with WPRN-AM-FM.

19223 ■ WMAW-FM - 88.1
3825 Ridgewood Rd.
Jackson, MS 39211
Phone: (601)432-6565
Email: mpbinfo@mpbonline.org
Format: Public Radio; News; Full Service; Information. **Networks:** National Public Radio (NPR); American Public Radio (APR). **Owner:** Mississippi Public Broadcasting, 3825 Ridgewood Rd, Jackson, MS 39211. **Founded:** 1983. **Operating Hours:** Continuous. **Key Personnel:** Maggie Gibson, Div. Dir. **Wattage:** 100,000. **Ad Rates:** Noncommercial. **URL:** http://www.mpbonline.org.

19224 ■ WMAW-TV - 14
3825 Ridgewood Rd.
Jackson, MS 39211
Phone: (601)432-6565
Fax: (601)432-6907
Free: 800-922-9698
Format: Public TV. **Simulcasts:** WMPN-TV. **Networks:** Public Broadcasting Service (PBS). **Owner:** Mississippi Authority for Educational TV, at above address. **Founded:** 1970. **Operating Hours:** 5:45 a.m.-2 a.m. Mon.-Sat.; 5:45 a.m.-midnight Sun. **ADI:** Meridian, MS. **Key Personnel:** Maggie Gibson, Dep. Dir., maggie.gibson@mpbonline.org. **Wattage:** 550,000. **Ad Rates:** Noncommercial. **URL:** http://www.mpbonline.org.

19225 ■ WMER-AM - 1390
404 AIRPORT ROAD
Meridian, MS 39307
Phone: (601)693-1414
Fax: (601)482-7887
Format: Religious. **Networks:** Sun Radio. **Owner:** New Life Outreach Ministries, PO Box 1414, Meridian, MS 39302. **Founded:** 1973. **Formerly:** WFEZ-AM. **Operating Hours:** 5 a.m.-12 a.m.; 20% network, 80% local. **ADI:** Meridian, MS. **Wattage:** 5,000. **Ad Rates:** $5 for 30 seconds; $13 for 60 seconds.

19226 ■ WMOX-AM - 1010
PO Box 5184
Meridian, MS 39301
Phone: (601)693-1891
Fax: (601)483-1010
Free: 800-513-8733
Email: wmox@wmox.net
Format: Talk; Sports; News. **Networks:** UPI; Mississippi. **Owner:** Magnolia State Broadcasting.

Circulation: ★ = AAM; △ or • = BPA; ♦ = CAC; ❑ = VAC; ⊕ = PO Statement; ‡ = Publisher's Report; Boldface figures = sworn; Light figures = estimated.

Founded: 1946. **Operating Hours:** 5 a.m.-midnight; 10% network, 90% local. **Key Personnel:** Eddie Smith, Owner; Ellie Massey, Contact. **Wattage:** 10,000. **Ad Rates:** $8-16 for 30 seconds; $10-20 for 60 seconds. **URL:** http://www.wmox.net.

19227 ■ WMSO-FM - 101.3
4307 Hwy. 39 N
Meridian, MS 39301
Phone: (601)693-2381
Fax: (601)485-2972
Format: Country. **Owner:** Clear Channel Communication, Inc., 200 E Basse Rd., San Antonio, TX 78209, Ph: (210)822-2828, Fax: (210)822-2828. **Key Personnel:** Mark Maharrey, Gen. Mgr. **Ad Rates:** Advertising accepted; rates available upon request. **URL:** http://www.clearchannel.com/Radio/StationSearch.aspx?RadioSearch=WMSO.

19228 ■ WNBN-AM - 1290
266-23rd St.
Meridian, MS 39301
Phone: (601)483-3401
Fax: (601)483-3411
Email: wnbn@onlineyp.net
Format: Religious; Gospel; Urban Contemporary. **Networks:** American Urban Radio. **Owner:** Mississippi Association Broadcasters, 855 S Pear Orchard Rd., Ste. 403, Ridgeland, MS 39157, Ph: (601)957-9121, Fax: (601)957-9175. **Founded:** 1988. **Operating Hours:** 6 a.m.-11:00 p.m. **ADI:** Meridian, MS. **Key Personnel:** Frank Rackley, Jr., Gen. Mgr. **Wattage:** 2,500. **Ad Rates:** Noncommercial.

19229 ■ WTOK-TV - 11
815 23rd Ave.
Meridian, MS 39301-5016
Phone: (601)693-1441
Fax: (601)483-3266
Email: wtok@wtok.com
Format: Commercial TV. **Networks:** ABC. **Founded:** 1953. **Operating Hours:** Continuous. **ADI:** Meridian, MS. **Key Personnel:** Tim Walker, Gen. Mgr., tim.walker@wtok.com. **Wattage:** 90,000 ERP. **Ad Rates:** Noncommercial; Advertising accepted; rates available upon request. **URL:** http://www.wtok.com.

19230 ■ W217AQ-FM - 91.3
PO Box 391
Twin Falls, ID 83303
Fax: (208)736-1958
Free: 800-357-4226
Format: Religious; Contemporary Christian. **Owner:** CSN International, PO Box 391, Twin Falls, ID 83303, Ph: (208)736-1958, Fax: (208)736-1958, Free: 800-357-4226. **Key Personnel:** Don Mills, Music Dir., Prog. Dir.; Ray Gorney, Dir. of Engg.; Kelly Carlson, Dir. of Engg. **URL:** http://www.csnradio.com.

19231 ■ WYHL-AM - 1450
4307 Hwy. 39 N
Meridian, MS 39301
Format: News; Talk.

19232 ■ WYYW-FM - 95.1
PO Box 5797
Meridian, MS 39301
Phone: (601)693-3434
Format: Country. **Founded:** 2001. **Formerly:** WZMP-FM; WQIC-FM. **Operating Hours:** Continuous. **ADI:** Meridian, MS. **Key Personnel:** Ron Harper, Gen. Mgr.; Jay King, Dir. of Programs; Leslie Hiatt, Promotions Dir.; Pam Gray, Gen. Sales Mgr. **Wattage:** 50,000. **Ad Rates:** Noncommercial.

19233 ■ WZKS-FM - 104.1
4307 Hwy. 39 N
Meridian, MS 39301
Phone: (601)693-2381
Fax: (601)485-2972
Format: Urban Contemporary; Southern Gospel.

MISSISSIPPI STATE

E MS. Oktibbeha Co. 22 mi. W. of Columbus. Tombigbee River Waterway nearby. Mississippi State University. Mississippi Research and Technology Park. Dairying center.

19234 ■ The Faulkner Journal
William Faulkner Society
c/o Ted Atkinson, President
PO Box 5272
Mississippi State, MS 39762
Freq: Semiannual. **ISSN:** 0884-2949 (print). **Subscription Rates:** $20 Individuals; $30 Institutions; $28 Other countries; $38 Institutions, other countries. **URL:** http://english.cah.ucf.edu/faulkner/; http://faulknersociety.com/resources.htm. **Remarks:** Advertising not accepted. **Circ:** (Not Reported).

19235 ■ The Mississippi Quarterly: The Journal of Southern Cultures
Mississippi State University College of Arts and Sciences
2nd Fl., Allen Hall
Drawer AS
Mississippi State, MS 39762
Phone: (662)325-2646
Fax: (662)325-8740
Publication E-mail: lew86@msstate.edu
Scholarly journal covering humanities and social sciences dealing with the Southern U.S. and its authors. **Freq:** Quarterly. **Print Method:** Offset and Docutech. **Trim Size:** 6 x 9. **Key Personnel:** Laura West, Managing Editor; Robert M. West, Associate Editor. **ISSN:** 0026--637X (print). **Subscription Rates:** $24 Individuals; $29 Other countries; $27 Canada and Mexico; $44 Two years; $49 Canada and Mexico two years; $53 Other countries two years. **URL:** http://www.missq.msstate.edu. **Ad Rates:** BW $100. **Remarks:** Accepts advertising. **Circ:** Combined 900.

19236 ■ Mississippi State Alumnus: For Mississippi State's Graduates and Former Students
Mississippi State Alumni Association
PO Box 5325
Mississippi State, MS 39762-5325
Phone: (662)325-3442
Fax: (662)325-7455
University alumni magazine. **Freq:** 3/yr. **Print Method:** Offset. **Trim Size:** 8 1/2 x 11. **Cols./Page:** 3. **Col. Width:** 28 nonpareils. **Col. Depth:** 133 agate lines. **Key Personnel:** Allen Snow, Editor. **USPS:** 354-520. **URL:** http://www.alumni.msstate.edu/s/811/index.aspx?pgid=743. **Remarks:** Accepts advertising. **Circ:** ‡22,600.

19237 ■ WMSV-FM - 91.1
Student Media Ctr.
Mississippi State, MS 39762-6210
Phone: (662)325-8034
Fax: (662)325-8037
Email: wmsv@msstate.edu
Format: Educational. **Founded:** Sept. 07, 2006. **Key Personnel:** Steve Ellis, Gen. Mgr.; Anthony Craven, Dir. Pub. Aff., News Dir. **Ad Rates:** Advertising accepted; rates available upon request. **Mailing address:** PO Box 6210, Mississippi State, MS 39762-6210. **URL:** http://www.wmsv.msstate.edu.

MONTICELLO

SC MS. Lawrence Co. 15 mi. SE of Nola. Manufactures clothing, veneer, cotton.

19238 ■ Lawrence County Press
Lawrence County Press
PO Box 549
Monticello, MS 39654
Phone: (601)587-2781
Fax: (601)587-2794
Publisher's E-mail: info@lawrencecountypress.com
Community newspaper. **Freq:** Weekly. **Print Method:** Offset. **Trim Size:** 7 3/4 x 11 1/2. **Cols./Page:** 6. **Col. Width:** 13 picas. **Col. Depth:** 21 inches. **Key Personnel:** John Carney, Editor; J.J. Carney, Associate Editor. **USPS:** 306-840. **Subscription Rates:** $29 Individuals in county, print, 12 months; $54 Individuals in county, print, 24 months; $42 Individuals out of county, print, 12 months; $79 Individuals out of county, print, 24 hours; $24 Individuals online only, 12 months; $45 Individuals online only, 24 months; $29 Individuals print and online, in county, 12 months; $54 Individuals print and online, in county, 24 months; $42 Individuals print and online, out of county, 12 months; $79 Individuals print and online, out of county, 24 months. **URL:** http://www.lawrencecountypress.com. **Ad Rates:** BW $1033.20; 4C $1383.20; SAU $7.60; PCI $8.20. **Remarks:** Accepts advertising. **Circ:** Paid ‡3,462.

19239 ■ Galaxy Cablevision
214 Main St., Ste. C
Monticello, MS 39654
Free: 800-365-6988
Owner: Galaxy Communications, PO Box 573, Barlow, KY 42024. **Cities Served:** subscribing households 1,025.

19240 ■ WMLC-AM
PO Box 444
Monticello, MS 39654-0444
Fax: (601)587-7524
Format: Talk; Sports. **Networks:** UPI. **Founded:** 1970. **Wattage:** 1,000 Day; 053 Night. **Ad Rates:** $5 for 30 seconds; $7 for 60 seconds.

19241 ■ WRQO-FM
PO Box 2016
Monticello, MS 39654
Phone: (601)587-9363
Format: Country. **Wattage:** 50,000 ERP. **Ad Rates:** Noncommercial. **URL:** http://www.wrqo-q102.com.

MORTON

19242 ■ WQST-AM - 850
36 2nd St.
Morton, MS 39117
Phone: (601)469-3701
Format: Gospel. **Networks:** AP. **Founded:** 1955. **Key Personnel:** Mark Damron, Contact. **URL:** http://www.850amwqst.com.

NATCHEZ

SW MS. Adams Co. On Mississippi River, 60 mi. S. of Vicksburg. Copiah Lincoln Community College. Natchez Junior College. Bridge to Vidalia, LA. Terminus of four boat lines. Manufactures culverts, storage tanks, boxes, beverages, tires, rayon, pulp. Lumber and cotton mills. Pine timber. Agriculture. Cattle, oil, cotton.

19243 ■ Miss-Lou Guide
Natchez Newspapers Inc.
PO Box 1447
Natchez, MS 39121
Phone: (601)442-9101
Fax: (601)442-7315
Publisher's E-mail: newsroom@natchezdemocrat.com
Shopper. **Freq:** Weekly (Wed.). **Print Method:** Offset. **Cols./Page:** 6. **Col. Width:** 25 nonpareils. **Col. Depth:** 301 agate lines. **Subscription Rates:** Free. **URL:** http://www.bninews.com. **Remarks:** Advertising accepted; rates available upon request. **Circ:** ‡10,500.

19244 ■ The Natchez Democrat
Natchez Newspapers Inc.
PO Box 1447
Natchez, MS 39121
Phone: (601)442-9101
Fax: (601)442-7315
Publication E-mail: newsroom@natchezdemocrat.com
General newspaper. **Freq:** Daily. **Print Method:** Offset. **Cols./Page:** 6. **Col. Width:** 2 1/16 inches. **Col. Depth:** 301 agate lines. **Key Personnel:** Johnnie Griffin, Manager, Production, phone: (601)445-3609; Kevin Cooper, Publisher, phone: (601)445-3539; Julie Cooper, Managing Editor, phone: (601)445-3551. **Subscription Rates:** $168 Individuals home delivery, 1 year; $85 Individuals home delivery, 6 months; $43 Individuals home delivery, 3 months; $15 Individuals home delivery, monthly; $233.60 Individuals by mail, 1 year; $116.80 Individuals by mail, 6 months; $58.25 Individuals by mail, 3 months; $20 Individuals by mail, monthly; $117 Individuals sunday only, 1 year; $58.50 Individuals sunday only, 6 months; $29.25 Individuals sunday only, 3 months; $9.75 Individuals sunday only, monthly. **URL:** http://www.natchezdemocrat.com; http://www.bninews.com/community/natchez.shtml. **Remarks:** Advertising accepted; rates available upon request. **Circ:** Mon.-Sat. ■ **8,651**, Sun. ■ **707**.

19245 ■ WASM-FM - 91.1
PO Box 2440
Tupelo, MS 38803
Phone: (662)844-8888
Format: Religious. **Owner:** American Family Radio, at above address. **URL:** http://www.afa.net.

19246 ■ WNAT-AM - 1450
Two O'Ferrall St.
Natchez, MS 39120
Phone: (601)442-4895
Fax: (601)446-8260
Format: News; Talk; Sports. **Owner:** First Natchez Radio Group, 2 Oferrall St , Natchez, MA 39120, Ph: (601)442-4895. **Wattage**: 1,000. **URL:** http://www.1450amwnat.com.

19247 ■ WQNZ-FM
PO Box 768
Natchez, MS 39121
Phone: (601)442-4895
Fax: (601)446-8260
Email: info@95country.com
Format: Contemporary Country. **Networks:** ABC. **Founded:** 1968. **Key Personnel:** Margaret Perkins, Gen. Mgr., margaret@95country.com. **Wattage:** 100,000 ERP. **Ad Rates:** Noncommercial.

19248 ■ W27CX - 27
PO Box A
Santa Ana, CA 92711
Phone: (714)832-2950
Free: 888-731-1000
Owner: Trinity Broadcasting Network Inc., PO Box A, Santa Ana, CA 92711, Ph: (714)832-2950, Free: 888-731-1000. **URL:** http://www.tbn.org.

NEW ALBANY

N MS. Union Co. 85 mi. SE of Memphis, TN. Manufactures lumber, cheese, upholstered furniture, electric carts, brake linings and pistons, batteries, refrigeration equipment, milk cartons. Cotton ginning; grist mills; hatcheries. Gum, poplar, oak timber. Dairy, poultry farms. Cotton, corn, sorghum cane, soybeans.

19249 ■ New Albany Gazette
New Albany Gazette
713 Carter Ave.
New Albany, MS 38652
Phone: (662)534-6321
Publisher's E-mail: news@newalbanygazette.com
Community newspaper. **Freq:** Semiweekly (Wed. and Fri.). **Print Method:** Offset. **Cols./Page:** 6. **Col. Width:** 27 nonpareils. **Col. Depth:** 301 agate lines. **Key Personnel:** David Johnson, Managing Editor; Mike Foster, Manager, Production; Ashley Andrews Reed, Manager, Circulation. **USPS:** 377-660. **Subscription Rates:** $20 Individuals online, 1 year; $41 Individuals home delivery, 1 year. **URL:** http://www.newalbanygazette.com. **Ad Rates:** BW $584.37; 4C $734.37; SAU $5.22; PCI $5.22. **Remarks:** Advertising accepted; rates available upon request. **Circ:** Paid ‡6,095, Free ‡12,112.

19250 ■ WNAU-AM - 1470
PO Box 808
New Albany, MS 38652
Phone: (601)534-8133
Format: Oldies; Sports. **Networks:** Mississippi; ABC. **Owner:** MPM Investment Group, 450 Kendall St., Cambridge, MA 02142, Ph: (617)425-9200. **Founded:** 1955. **Operating Hours:** Continuous; 8% network, 92% local. **ADI:** Memphis, TN. **Wattage:** 500. **Ad Rates:** $2.50-5 for 30 seconds; $5-7 for 60 seconds. **URL:** http://www.wnau.com.

OXFORD

N MS. Lafayette Co. 62 mi. SE of Memphis, TN. University of Mississippi. Manufactures electric motors, appliances, stoves, flakeboard. Pine and hardwood timber. Dairy and poultry farms. Cattle, cotton, beans.

19251 ■ The Oxford Eagle
The Oxford Eagle
916 Jackson Ave.
Oxford, MS 38655
Phone: (662)234-4331
Fax: (662)234-4351
Publisher's E-mail: online@oxfordeagle.com
Newspaper. **Freq:** Daily (eve.). **Print Method:** Offset. **Trim Size:** 10 13/16 x 21. **Cols./Page:** 6. **Col. Width:** 25 nonpareils. **Col. Depth:** 294 agate lines. **Key Personnel:** Lucy Schultze, Writer; John Davis, Editor; Brian Roy, Director, Advertising. **Subscription Rates:** $31.50 Individuals by carrier; 3 months; $50 Individuals by U.S. mail; 3 months; $120 Individuals by carrier, 1 year; $195 Individuals by U.S. mail, 1 year; $5 Individuals online, 1 month. **URL:** http://oxfordeagle.com. **Mailing address:** PO Box 866, Oxford, MS 38655. **Ad Rates:** 4C $210; SAU $5.90; CNU $743.40; PCI $8.6. **Remarks:** Accepts advertising. **Circ:** Paid ‡6000, Free ‡13,000, Free 11,000.

19252 ■ Y'All: The Magazine of Southern People
GRM L.L.C.
PO Box 1217
Oxford, MS 38655
Phone: (662)236-1928
Publication E-mail: mail@yall.com
Magazine covering Southern celebrities. **Freq:** Bimonthly. **Key Personnel:** Tabatha Hunter, Managing Editor. **ISSN:** 1557--2331 (print). **URL:** http://yall.com. **Remarks:** Accepts advertising. **Circ:** (Not Reported).

19253 ■ WAVI-FM - 91.5
PO Box 2440
Tupelo, MS 38803
Phone: (662)844-8888
Format: Religious. **Owner:** American Family Association, at above address. **URL:** http://www.afr.net.

19254 ■ WMAV-FM - 90.3
3825 Ridgewood Rd.
Jackson, MS 39211
Phone: (601)432-6565
Email: mpbinfo@mpbonline.org
Format: Information; News; Public Radio. **Networks:** National Public Radio (NPR); Public Radio International (PRI). **Owner:** Mississippi Public Broadcasting, 3825 Ridgewood Rd, Jackson, MS 39211. **Founded:** 1983. **Operating Hours**: Continuous. **ADI:** Columbus-Tupelo (West Point), MS. **Key Personnel:** Dr. Judy Lewis, Exec. Dir. **Wattage**: 100,000. **Ad Rates:** Noncommercial. **URL:** http://www.mpbonline.org/programs/radio/music-radio.

19255 ■ WMAV-TV - 18
c/o WMPN-TV
3825 Ridgewood Rd.
Jackson, MS 39211
Phone: (601)432-6565
Fax: (601)432-6311
Free: 800-850-4406
Format: Public TV. **Networks:** Public Broadcasting Service (PBS). **Owner:** Mississippi Authority for Educational TV, at above address. **Founded:** 1972. **Key Personnel:** A.J. Jaeger, Contact. **Wattage**: 272,500 ERP. **URL:** http://www.mpbonline.org/.

19256 ■ WOXD-FM - 95.5
302 Higway 7 S
Oxford, MS 38655
Founded: Sept. 12, 2006. **Wattage**: 6,000. **Ad Rates:** Advertising accepted; rates available upon request.

PASCAGOULA

SE MS. Jackson Co. On Pascagoula River and Gulf of Mexico, 21 mi. E. of Biloxi. Coastal resort and fishing center. Shipbuilding. Manufactures pet foods, fertilizers, petroleum products, chemicals.

19257 ■ W51CU - 51
PO Box A
Santa Ana, CA 92711
Phone: (714)832-2950
Free: 888-731-1000
Email: comments@tbn.org
Owner: Trinity Broadcasting Network Inc., PO Box A, Santa Ana, CA 92711, Ph: (714)832-2950, Free: 888-731-1000. **URL:** http://www.tbn.org.

19258 ■ WNSI-AM - 1000
PO Box 1369
Pascagoula, MS 39568
Phone: (228)762-5683
Email: wnsi@gulftel.com
Format: News; Information; Sports. **Owner:** Great American Radio Network, Inc., at above address. **Operating Hours:** Continuous. **Key Personnel:** Walter Bowen, President, walter@wnsiradio.com. **Ad Rates:** Underwriting available.

PHILADELPHIA

EC MS. Neshoba Co. 10 mi. S. of Burnside. Lumber. Diversified agriculture.

19259 ■ WWSL-FM - 102.3
PO Box 26
Philadelphia, MS 39350
Phone: (601)656-7102
Format: News; Sports; Information. **Owner:** WHOC, Inc., 1016 W Beacon St., Philadelphia, MS 39350, Ph: (601)656-1491. **Founded:** 1980. **Key Personnel:** Joe Vines, Contact. **Wattage:** 4,900 ERP. **Ad Rates:** $4 for 30 seconds; $6 for 60 seconds. **URL:** http://www.whocmedia.com.

PICAYUNE

SC MS. Pearl River Co. 35 mi. WNW of Gulfport. Manufactures lumber, clothing, oil, dairy products. Livestock.

19260 ■ Picayune Item
Community Newspaper Holdings Inc.
17 Richardson/Ozona Rd.
Picayune, MS 39466
Phone: (601)798-4766
Fax: (601)798-8602
Publication E-mail: picayuneitem@bellsouth.net
General newspaper. **Founded:** June 01, 1904. **Freq:** Tues. -Fri. (eve.); Sun. (morn.). **Print Method:** Offset. **Trim Size:** 13 x 21 1/2. **Cols./Page:** 6. **Key Personnel:** Linda Gilmore, Publisher; Will Sullivan, Managing Editor. **Subscription Rates:** $80 Individuals carrier delivery. **URL:** http://www.picayuneitem.com. **Mailing address:** PO Box 580, Picayune, MS 39466. **Ad Rates:** SAU $6.44. **Remarks:** Accepts classified advertising. **Circ:** Tues.-Fri. ★**4480**, Sun. ★**5575**.

19261 ■ The Swap Shop
The Swap Shop
PO Box 907
Picayune, MS 39466
Phone: (601)798-4835
Fax: (601)798-9755
Free: 800-284-5036
Free Shopper. **Freq:** Semimonthly 1st and 3rd week of the month. **Subscription Rates:** Free. **URL:** http://www.wrjwradio.com/swapshop.html. **Ad Rates:** BW $390; 4C $590. **Remarks:** Advertising accepted; rates available upon request. **Circ:** 20000.

19262 ■ WRJW-AM - 1320
PO Box 907
Picayune, MS 39466
Phone: (601)798-4835
Fax: (601)798-9755
Email: wrjwradio@bellsouth.net
Format: Country. **Networks:** ABC; Jones Satellite; Mississippi. **Owner:** Pearl River Communications Inc., 2438 HWY 43 S , Picayune, MS 39466-7486, Ph: (601)798-4835, Fax: (601)798-9755, Free: 800-284-5036. **Founded:** 1949. **Operating Hours**: 5:30 a.m.-9:00 p.m. **Wattage**: 1,000. **Ad Rates:** Advertising accepted; rates available upon request. Swap Shop Newspaper. **URL:** http://www.wrjwradio.com.

PONTOTOC

NE MS. Pontotoc Co. 60 mi. NW of Columbus. Manufactures furniture, orthopedic supplies, golf equipment, magnetic wire, metal mouldings and forgings. Lumber and planing mill; cotton ginning; industrial packaging. Agriculture. Dairying and poultry farms. Cotton, wheat, soybeans. Livestock.

19263 ■ WSEL-AM
Hwy. 6 E
Pontotoc, MS 38863
Phone: (601)489-1974
Format: Religious. **Networks:** USA Radio. **Owner:** Jim Powell, 124 Senate St., Pontotoc, MS 38863. **Key Personnel:** Jim Powell, Contact. **Wattage**: 1,000 Day; 066 Night. **Ad Rates:** $3.50 for 30 seconds; $7 for 60 seconds.

POPLARVILLE

SC MS. Pearl River Co. 10 mi. NE of Derby. Pearl River Junior College. Manufactures turpentine, lumber.

19264 ■ WRPM-AM - 1530
PO Box 2639
Gulfport, MS 39505-2639
Phone: (601)795-4900
Fax: (601)795-0277

Circulation: ★ = AAM; △ or • = BPA; ♦ = CAC; ❑ = VAC; ⊕ = PO Statement; ‡ = Publisher's Report; Boldface figures = sworn; Light figures = estimated.

Format: Southern Gospel. **Networks:** ABC. **Owner:** Dowdy and Dowdy Partnership. **Founded:** 1963. **Operating Hours**: Sunrise-sunset; 10% network, 90% local. **Wattage**: 10,000 dy ; 1,000 Night. **Ad Rates:** $2-5 for 30 seconds.

PORT GIBSON

SW MS. Claiborne Co. 25 mi. S. of Vicksburg. Manufactures lumber, textiles, cottonseed products. Agriculture. Cattle, hogs. Soybeans.

19265 ■ WATU-FM - 89.3
PO Box 2440
Tupelo, MS 38803
Free: 800-326-4543
Format: Religious. **Owner:** American Family Radio, at above address. **URL:** http://www.afr.net.

PRENTISS

S MS. Jefferson Davis Co. 40 mi. NW of Hattiesburg. Prentiss Normal and Industrial Institute. Manufactures kraft paper, pulpwood, cresote, garments. Agriculture. Corn, sorghum, pimento, peppers, wheat, oats.

19266 ■ WJDR-FM
PO Box 880
Prentiss, MS 39474
Phone: (601)792-2056
Fax: (601)792-2057
Format: Contemporary Country. **Networks:** Westwood One Radio. **Founded:** 1982. **Key Personnel:** Debbie Beets, Contact. **Wattage:** 6,000 ERP. **Ad Rates:** $6 for 30 seconds; $7.50 for 60 seconds.

RAYMOND

19267 ■ W219CV-FM - 91.9
PO Box 391
Twin Falls, ID 83303
Fax: (208)736-1958
Free: 800-357-4226
Format: Religious; Contemporary Christian. **Owner:** CSN International, PO Box 391, Twin Falls, ID 83303, Ph: (208)736-1958, Fax: (208)736-1958, Free: 800-357-4226. **Key Personnel:** Kelly Carlson, Dir. of Engg.; Ray Gorney, Asst. Dir. **URL:** http://www.csnradio.com.

RICHTON

SE MS. Perry Co. 22 mi. E. of Hattiesburg. Garment factory. Plywood, pole mills. Pine and hardwood timber. Agriculture. Corn, cotton, sweet potatoes.

19268 ■ The Richton Dispatch
The Richton Dispatch
110 Walnut St.
Richton, MS 39476-0429
Phone: (601)788-6031
Fax: (601)788-6031
Publication E-mail: richtondispatch@c-gate.net news@therichtondispatch.com
Newspaper with a Democratic orientation. **Freq:** Weekly (Thurs.). **Print Method:** Offset. **Trim Size:** 7 1/4 x 11 1/4. **Cols./Page:** 6. **Col. Width:** 11 picas. **Col. Depth:** 21 inches. **USPS:** 465-660. **Subscription Rates:** $18 Individuals; $19 Out of area; $23 Out of state. **URL:** http://therichtondispatch.com. **Mailing address:** PO Box 429, Richton, MS 39476-0429. **Ad Rates:** GLR $16; BW $384.30; 4C $584.30; SAU $3.85. **Remarks:** Accepts advertising. **Circ:** Mon.-Sat. ‡1,695.

RIDGELAND

19269 ■ Journal of the Mississippi State Medical Association
Mississippi State Medical Association
PO Box 2548
Ridgeland, MS 39158-2548
Phone: (601)853-6733
Fax: (601)853-6746
Free: 800-898-0251
Medical magazine, including scientific papers; Association news and policy reports; and national, state, and local medical news. **Freq:** Monthly. **Print Method:** Offset. **Trim Size:** 8 1/2 x 11. **Cols./Page:** 2. **Col. Width:** 40 nonpareils. **Col. Depth:** 140 agate lines. **Key Personnel:** Stanley D. Hartness, MD, Associate Editor, phone: (662)289-1800, fax: (662)289-1858; Lucius M. Lampton, MD, Editor, phone: (601)783-2374, fax: (601)783-5126. **ISSN:** 0026--6393 (print). **URL:** http://www.msmaonline.com/M/Public/Journal_MSMA/Editors/Public/Journal/Editors.aspx?hkey=c1487485-764b-4236-b83f-4ab077fb41b5. **Ad Rates:** 4C $1100. **Remarks:** Accepts advertising. **Circ:** Paid ‡4500.

19270 ■ The Madison Journal
The Madison Journal
PO Box 219
Ridgeland, MS 39158
Phone: (601)853-4222
Fax: (601)856-9419
Publication E-mail: publishers@madisonjournal.com
Community newspaper. **Freq:** Weekly (Thurs.). **Print Method:** Offset. **Cols./Page:** 6. **Col. Width:** 26 nonpareils. **Col. Depth:** 295 agate lines. **Key Personnel:** Price Rosson, Editor, phone: (601)853-4222, fax: (601)856-9419; James E. Prince, III, Editor, Publisher. **Subscription Rates:** $42 Individuals in Madison, Rankin & Hinds counties; $46 Individuals in-state; $52 Out of state; $67 Two years. **URL:** http://onlinemadison.com. **Ad Rates:** GLR $.25; BW $504; 4C $661; PCI $4.40. **Remarks:** Accepts advertising. **Circ:** ‡3400.

19271 ■ The Stockman Grass Farmer
Mississippi Valley Publishing Corp.
234 W School St.
Ridgeland, MS 39157
Phone: (601)853-1861
Magazine reporting on livestock intensive grazing and pasture management. **Freq:** Monthly. **Print Method:** Offset. **Trim Size:** 10 1/2 x 12. **Cols./Page:** 4. **Key Personnel:** Sally Imgrund, Director, Advertising, phone: (601)483-0633, fax: (601)483-9633. **ISSN:** 0899-1057 (print). **Subscription Rates:** $32 U.S.; $50 Canada and Mexico airmail; $90 Other countries airmail; $150 Two years airmail. **URL:** http://www.stockmangrassfarmer.com/index.php. **Formerly**: Stockman Farmer. **Ad Rates:** BW $2030; 4C $650; PCI $85. **Remarks:** Accepts advertising. **Circ:** Paid 10,961.

19272 ■ Today in Mississippi
Electric Power Associations of Mississippi
PO Box 3300
Ridgeland, MS 39158-3300
Phone: (601)605-8600
Publication E-mail: news@epaofms.com
Statewide magazine covering political, economic, and legislative rural electrification matters statewide for EPA member-owners. **Freq:** Monthly. **Print Method:** Offset. **Trim Size:** 13 7/8 x 11 1/8. **Cols./Page:** 4. **Col. Width:** 14 picas. **Col. Depth:** 76 picas. **Key Personnel:** Ron Stewart, Senior Vice President; Debbie Stringer, Editor. **ISSN:** 1052--2433 (print). **URL:** http://www.todayinmississippi.com. **Formerly**: Mississippi EPA News. **Remarks:** Advertising accepted; rates available upon request. **Circ:** (Not Reported).

19273 ■ WIIN-AM - 780
265 High Point Dr.
Ridgeland, MS 39157
Phone: (601)956-0102
Fax: (601)978-3980
Format: Classic Rock. **Networks:** Winners News (WNN). **Owner:** Eddie Holladay, at above address. **Operating Hours:** Daylight hours; 100% network. **ADI:** Jackson, MS. **Key Personnel:** Dick O'Neil, Gen. Mgr., Gen. Sales Mgr.; Roger Allen, Dir. of Creative Svcs. **Wattage:** 5,000. **Ad Rates:** $10-24 for 30 seconds.

19274 ■ WJKK-FM - 98.7
265 High Point Dr.
Ridgeland, MS 39157
Format: Adult Contemporary. **Ad Rates:** Noncommercial. **URL:** http://www.mix987.com.

19275 ■ WJMI-FM - 99.7
731 S Pear Orchard Rd., Ste. 27
Ridgeland, MS 39157
Phone: (601)957-1300
Format: Urban Contemporary. **Ad Rates:** Noncommercial. **URL:** http://www.wjmi.com.

19276 ■ WKXI-FM - 107.5
731 S Pear Orchard Rd., Ste. 27
Ridgeland, MS 39157
Phone: (601)957-1300
Email: contact@wkxi.com
Format: Urban Contemporary. **Simulcasts:** WKXI-FM. **Networks:** ABC. **Owner:** Inner City Broadcasting Corp., C O Access Comm, 333 7th Ave., 14th Fl., New York, NY 10001-5014. **Operating Hours**: Continuous. **Wattage:** 5,000. **Ad Rates:** $20-25 per unit. Combined advertising rates available with WKXI-FM. **URL:** http://www.wkxi.com.

19277 ■ WOAD-AM - 1300
731 S Pear Orchard Rd., Ste. 27
Ridgeland, MS 39157
Phone: (601)995-1059
Format: Gospel. **Networks:** NBC. **Owner:** Inner City Broadcasting of Mississippi. **Founded:** 1984. **Formerly**: WJQS-AM. **Operating Hours**: Continuous. **Key Personnel:** Percy Davis, Dir. of Programs. **Wattage**: 1,000. **Ad Rates:** Noncommercial. $4.20-$28 for 30 seconds; $5.25-$33.25 for 60 seconds. Combined advertising rates available with WJMI-FM. **URL:** http://www.woad.com.

19278 ■ WOAD-FM - 105.9
731 S Pear Orchard Rd., Ste. 27
Ridgeland, MS 39157
Phone: (601)995-1059
Format: Gospel. **Operating Hours**: 14 hours Daily. **Key Personnel:** Teresa Gerald, Bus. Mgr.; Bill Wilson, Dir. of Production; Stan Branson, Operations Mgr.; Percy Davis, Dir. of Programs. **Ad Rates:** Advertising accepted; rates available upon request. **URL:** http://www.woad.com.

19279 ■ WSFZ-AM - 930
571 Hwy. 51 N, Ste. H
Ridgeland, MS 39157
Phone: (601)605-6656
Fax: (601)605-6646
Format: Sports. **Operating Hours**: Continuous. **Ad Rates:** Advertising accepted; rates available upon request. **URL:** http://Supersport930.Com.

19280 ■ W245AH-FM - 96.9
PO Box 391
Twin Falls, ID 83303
Fax: (208)736-1958
Free: 800-357-4226
Format: Religious; Contemporary Christian. **Owner:** CSN International, PO Box 391, Twin Falls, ID 83303, Ph: (208)736-1958, Fax: (208)736-1958, Free: 800-357-4226. **URL:** http://www.csnradio.com.

19281 ■ WUSJ-FM - 96.3
265 Highpoint Dr.
Ridgeland, MS 39157
Phone: (601)995-9600
Fax: (601)978-3980
Format: Country. **Key Personnel:** Russ L. Williams, Dir. of Programs, russl@us963.com; Gwen Rakestraw, Sales Mgr.; Nancy Fletcher, Sales Mgr.; Fisher Alexander, Dir. of Production. **URL:** http://www.us963.com.

19282 ■ WYOY-FM - 101.7
265 Highpoint Dr.
Ridgeland, MS 39157
Phone: (601)956-0102
Fax: (601)991-3344
Format: Top 40. **Key Personnel:** Nate West, Music Dir., nate@y101.com; Gwen Rakestraw, Gen. Mgr., gwenr@radiopeople.net; Bill Rakestraw, Gen. Sales Mgr., billr@radiopeople.net; Nancy Fletcher, Sales Mgr., nancy@radiopeople.net. **Ad Rates:** Noncommercial. **URL:** http://www.y101.com.

RIPLEY

N MS. Tippah Co. 72 mi. SE of Memphis, TN. Manufactures lumber, furniture, staves, rubber products, clothing, shoes. Pine and hardwood timber. Farming. Cotton, corn, soybeans.

19283 ■ Ripley Video Cable Co.
115 N Main St.
Ripley, MS 38663
Phone: (662)837-4881
Owner: Leon M. Bailey, Jr., 115 North Main St., Ripley, MS. **Founded:** 1969. **Key Personnel:** Leon Bailey, Owner, leon@ripleycable.net; Diane E. Bailey, Owner, dbailey@ripleycable.net; Jody Steverson, Contact, jody@ripleycable.net. **Cities Served:** Blue Mountain, Falkner, Pine Grove, Mississippi: subscribing households 3,654; 98 channels; 1 community access channel; 108 hours per week community access programming. **Mailing address:** PO Box 368, Ripley, MS 38663. **URL:** http://www.ripleycable.net.

SARDIS

NW MS. Panola Co. 48 mi. S. of Memphis, TN. Manufactures clothes, lumber, luggage, hospital furniture. Cotton ginning. Cattle, stock, dairy, soybeans.

19284 ■ KBUD-FM - 102.1
627 E Lee St.
Sardis, MS 38666
Phone: (662)487-3503
Format: Contemporary Christian. **Owner:** Flinn Broadcasting Corporation, 6080 Mt. Moriah, Memphis, TN 38115, Ph: (901)375-9324, Fax: (901)375-5889. **Key Personnel:** Ederic Kerney, CEO, Gen. Mgr., ak1021fm@yahoo.com; Annette Kerney, Dir. of Programs, ak1021fm@yahoo.com.

SENATOBIA

NW MS. Tate Co. 34 mi. S. of Memphis, TN. Northwest Mississippi Community College. Manufactures chrome furniture, clothing. Sawmills, cotton ginning, printing plant. Dairy, stock, poultry farms. Cotton, corn, hay.

19285 ■ The Democrat
The Democrat
219 E Main St.
Senatobia, MS 38668
Phone: (662)562-4414
Community newspaper. **Founded:** Dec. 18, 1881. **Freq:** Weekly (Tues.). **Print Method:** Offset. **Trim Size:** 13 x 21 1/2. **Cols./Page:** 6. **Col. Width:** 12 picas. **Col. Depth:** 21.5 inches. **Key Personnel:** Melissa Turner, Editor; Faye Price, Office Manager. **USPS:** 534-040. **Subscription Rates:** $26 Individuals print, 1 year. **URL:** http://www.thedemocrat.com. **Formerly:** Tate County Democrat. **Remarks:** Accepts advertising. **Circ:** ‡5,200.

19286 ■ WKNA-FM - 98.3
1 Radio Ln.
Logan, OH 43138
Phone: (740)380-9546
Fax: (740)385-4022
Email: blazer@parfm.com
Format: Talk. **Founded:** 1973. **Operating Hours:** 8:30 a.m. - 5:00 p.m. Monday - Friday. **Key Personnel:** Scott Blazer, Gen. Mgr. **Wattage:** 6,000 ERP. **Ad Rates:** Advertising accepted; rates available upon request. **URL:** http://www.983samfm.com.

19287 ■ WSAO-AM
PO Box 190
Senatobia, MS 38668
Fax: (601)562-4445
Free: 888-550-2009
Format: Religious; Gospel. **Founded:** 1961. **Key Personnel:** Jesse Ross, Contact. **Wattage:** 5,000 Day. **Ad Rates:** $6 for 30 seconds; $8 for 60 seconds.

SOUTHAVEN

NW MS. DeSoto Co. 10 mi. S. of Memphis, TN.

19288 ■ WAVN-AM - 1240
6080 Mt. Moriah
Memphis, TN 38115
Phone: (901)375-9324
Fax: (901)375-5889
Format: Gospel; Hispanic. **Owner:** Flinn Broadcasting Corporation, at above address. **URL:** http://www.flinn.com.

STARKVILLE

E MS. Oktibbeha Co. 22 mi. W. of Columbus. Mississippi State University. Manufactures paper, cotton, felt, feed, apparel, clocks, motors, food and dairy products. Oak and pine timber. Dairy farming. Hay, soybeans.

19289 ■ The Starkville Daily News: Starkville Daily News
Chicago Newspaper Liquidation Corp.
304 Lampkin St.
PO Drawer 1068
Starkville, MS 39760-6586
Phone: (601)323-1642
Fax: (601)323-6586
Publisher's E-mail: news@starkvilledailynews.com
Newspaper. **Freq:** Daily (morn.). **Print Method:** Offset. **Cols./Page:** 6. **Col. Width:** 26 nonpareils. **Col. Depth:** 301 agate lines. **Key Personnel:** Don Norman, Publisher; Marcia B. Deaton, Business Manager; Leilani Salter, Managing Editor. **USPS:** 519-660. **Subscription Rates:** $106 Individuals carrier delivery; $168 By mail; $72 Individuals online. **URL:** http://www.starkvilledailynews.com. **Ad Rates:** GLR $.60; BW $1109.40; 4C $1334.40; SAU $8.60. **Remarks:** Accepts advertising. **Circ:** ‡6,500.

19290 ■ WACR-AM - 1050
608 Yellow Jacket Dr.
Starkville, MS 39759
Phone: (662)338-5424
Format: Religious; Urban Contemporary. **Owner:** T & W Communications, Inc., PO Box 312, West Point, MS 39773. **Founded:** 1953. **Operating Hours:** Sunrise-sunset; 5% network, 95% local. **ADI:** Columbus-Tupelo (West Point), MS. **Key Personnel:** Danny Byrd, Gen. Mgr. **Wattage:** 1,000. **Ad Rates:** $20 for 30 seconds; $25 for 60 seconds. **URL:** http://www.wacr1053.com/contact-us-2/.

19291 ■ WAJV-FM
608 Yellow Jacket Rd.
Starkville, MS 39759
Phone: (662)338-5424
Fax: (662)338-5436
Format: Religious; Southern Gospel. **Networks:** Mississippi. **Founded:** 1995. **Wattage:** 5,800 ERP. **Ad Rates:** $7-10 for 30 seconds; $9-12 for 60 seconds.

19292 ■ WLZA-FM - 96.1
PO Box 884
Starkville, MS 39760-0884
Phone: (662)324-9601
Fax: (662)324-7400
Email: newsnotes@961wlza.com
Format: Adult Contemporary. **Networks:** Satellite Radio. **Founded:** 1974. **Formerly:** WEXA-FM. **Operating Hours:** Continuous. **Wattage:** 50,000. **Ad Rates:** $9-10 for 30 seconds; $10-12 for 60 seconds. **URL:** http://www.961wlza.com.

TAYLOR

19293 ■ Life 101
Nautilus Publishing Co.
426 S Lamar Blvd., Ste. 16
Taylor, MS 38673
Phone: (662)513-0159
Magazine featuring leadership profiles, resume writing, college Q & A, independent living, money management, interview skills, and financial aid. **Key Personnel:** Neil White, Creative Director, Publisher. **Subscription Rates:** $5 Individuals. **URL:** http://www.nautiluspublishing.com/other001.html. **Circ:** (Not Reported).

19294 ■ Princeton Health
Nautilus Publishing Co.
426 S Lamar Blvd., Ste. 16
Taylor, MS 38673
Phone: (662)513-0159
Health magazine featuring the latest health-related news and information. **Freq:** Bimonthly. **Subscription Rates:** Free. **Alt. Formats:** PDF. **URL:** http://www.princetonhcs.org/phcs-home/who-we-serve/community/princeton-health.aspx. **Formerly:** Health Focus: The Latest in Health News & Information. **Circ:** (Not Reported).

TUNICA

19295 ■ The Tunica Times
Tunica Publishing Co.
986 Magnolia St.
Tunica, MS 38676
Phone: (662)363-1511
Community newspaper. **Freq:** Weekly (Thurs.). **Print Method:** Offset. **Cols./Page:** 6. **Col. Width:** 2 inches. **Col. Depth:** 21 1/2 inches. **Key Personnel:** Brooks Taylor, Publisher. **Subscription Rates:** $25 Individuals 6 months; $50 Individuals. **URL:** http://www.tunicatimes.com. **Formerly:** The Tunica Times-Democrat. **Mailing address:** PO Box 308, Tunica, MS 38676. **Ad Rates:** PCI $5.75. **Remarks:** Accepts advertising. **Circ:** Paid ‡3000.

19296 ■ WIVG-FM - 96.1
6080 Mt. Moriah
Memphis, TN 38115
Phone: (901)375-9324
Fax: (901)375-5889
Format: Hispanic. **Owner:** Flinn Broadcasting Corporation, at above address. **Formerly:** WYYL-FM. **URL:** http://www.flinn.com.

TUPELO

NE MS. Lee Co. 55 mi. N. of Columbus. Manufactures milk and dairy products, beverages, garments, fluorescent fixtures, tires, power tools, church and school furniture, fertilizer. Poultry processing plant. Cotton ginning; sawmills. Fish hatchery. Pine timber. Agriculture. Dairy. Livestock.

19297 ■ AFA Journal
American Family Association
PO Box 2440
Tupelo, MS 38803
Phone: (662)844-5036
Publisher's E-mail: faq@afa.net
Journal of the American Family Association. **Freq:** Monthly except July/August. **Key Personnel:** Angie May, Contact. **URL:** http://www.afajournal.org; http://www.afa.net/divisions/afa-journal. **Remarks:** Accepts advertising. **Circ:** 180,000.

19298 ■ Northeast Mississippi Daily Journal
Journal Inc.
1242 S Green St.
Tupelo, MS 38804-6301
General newspaper. **Freq:** Daily. **Print Method:** Offset. **Cols./Page:** 6. **Col. Width:** 26 nonpareils. **Col. Depth:** 301 agate lines. **Key Personnel:** Cindy Carr, Manager, Advertising, phone: (662)678-1534. **Subscription Rates:** $2.48 Individuals /week; print + online; $0.33 Individuals /day; online. **URL:** http://djournal.com. **Circ:** Sun. ★**36,647**, Mon.-Fri. ★**36,130**.

KAFH-FM - See Great Falls, MT

KAKA-FM - See Salina, KS

KAKO-FM - See Ada, OK

KANL-FM - See Baker City, OR

KANX-FM - See Sheridan, AR

KAOG-FM - See Jonesboro, AR

KAOW-FM - See Fort Smith, AR

KAPG-FM - See Bentonville, AR

KAPI-FM - See Ruston, LA

KAPK-FM - See Grants Pass, OR

KAPM-FM - See Alexandria, LA

KAQD-FM - See Abilene, TX

KAQF-FM - See Clovis, NM

KARG-FM - See Poteau, OK

KARH-FM - See Forrest City, AR

KASD-FM - See Rapid City, SD

KAUF-FM - See Kennett, MO

KAVK-FM - See Many, LA

KAVO-FM - See Borger, TX

KAVW-FM - See Amarillo, TX

KAXR-FM - See Arkansas City, KS

KAXV-FM - See Bastrop, LA

KAYA-FM - See Hubbard, NE

KAYB-FM - See Sunnyside, WA

KAYC-FM - See Durant, OK

KAYM-FM - See Weatherford, OK

19299 ■ KAYP-FM - 89.9
PO Box 2440
Tupelo, MS 38801-2440
Phone: (319)758-6911
Fax: (319)758-6922
Free: 866-493-5297
Email: kayp@mchsi.com

Circulation: ★ = AAM; △ or • = BPA; ♦ = CAC; ❑ = VAC; ⊕ = PO Statement; ‡ = Publisher's Report; Boldface figures = sworn; Light figures = estimated.

Format: Religious. **Owner:** American Family Radio, PO Box 3206, Tupelo, MS 38803, Ph: (662)844-5036, Fax: (662)842-7798. **Founded:** 2000. **Ad Rates:** Noncommercial.

KBAN-FM - See DeRidder, LA

KBCM-FM - See Blytheville, AR

KBDA-FM - See Great Bend, KS

KBDC-FM - See Mason City, IA

KBDO-FM - See Des Arc, AR

KBGM-FM - See Park Hills, MO

KBJQ-FM - See Bronson, KS

KBMH-FM - See Holbrook, AZ

KBMJ-FM - See Heber Springs, AR

KBNV-FM - See Fayetteville, AR

KBPG-FM - See Montevideo, MN

KBPW-FM - See Hampton, AR

KBQC-FM - See Independence, KS

19300 ■ KBUZ-FM
PO Box 2440
Tupelo, MS 38801-2440
Free: 800-326-4543
Format: Religious. **Owner:** American Family Radio, at above address. **Founded:** Sept. 13, 2006. **ADI:** Topeka, KS. **Wattage:** 11,000 ERP. **Ad Rates:** Noncommercial.

KDVI-FM - See Devils Lake, ND

19301 ■ KIA-FM - 93.9
PO Box 2440
Tupelo, MS 38801-2440
Phone: (641)423-1300
Fax: (641)423-2906
Free: 800-747-2346
Email: tamiramon@clearchannel.com
Format: Country. **Founded:** 1986. **Formerly:** KNIQ-FM. **Operating Hours:** Continuous. **Key Personnel:** Charlie Thomas, Gen. Mgr., charliethomas@clearchannel.com; Mary Nygren, Gen. Sales Mgr., marynygren@clearchannel.com. **Wattage:** 100,000. **Ad Rates:** $33 for 30 seconds; $33 for 60 seconds.

KIAD-FM - See Dubuque, IA

KMEO-FM - See Mertzon, TX

KMSL-FM - See Shreveport, LA

KNLL-FM - See Nashville, AR

KPAQ-FM - See Plaquemine, LA

KQPD-FM - See Ardmore, OK

KQRB-FM - See Windom, MN

KSFS-FM - See Sioux Falls, SD

KTXG-FM - See Greenville, TX

19302 ■ KVRS-FM - 90.3
PO Box 2440
Tupelo, MS 38803
Format: Religious. **Owner:** American Family Association, at above address. **ADI:** Wichita Falls, TX-Lawton, OK. **Key Personnel:** Judith Meriwether, Dir. of Dev., jmeriwether@krvs.org; James Hebert, Operations Mgr., jhebert@krvs.org. **Wattage:** 9,800. **Ad Rates:** Noncommercial. **URL:** http://krvs.org.

KWVI-FM - See Waverly, IA

KZFT-FM - See Beaumont, TX

WAAE-FM - See New Bern, NC

WAEF-FM - See Cordele, GA

19303 ■ WAFR-FM - 88.3
PO Box 2440
Tupelo, MS 38803
Phone: (662)844-8888
Format: Religious. **Owner:** American Family Radio, at above address. **Ad Rates:** Noncommercial. **URL:** http://www.afa.net.

WAII-FM - See Hattiesburg

19304 ■ WAJS-FM - 91.7
PO Box 2440
Tupelo, MS 38803
Phone: (662)844-8888
Format: Religious. **Owner:** American Family Radio, at above address. **Founded:** Feb. 1991. **Key Personnel:** Rick Robertson, Contact; Rick Robertson, Contact. **Ad Rates:** Noncommercial.

WAKD-FM - See Sheffield, AL

WALN-FM - See Carrollton, AL

WAMP-FM - See Jackson, TN

19305 ■ WAOY-FM - 91.7
PO Box 2440
Tupelo, MS 38801-2440
Phone: (228)831-3020
Fax: (228)831-4540
Email: waoy@waoy.com
Format: Religious. **Owner:** American Family Radio, PO Box 3206, Tupelo, MS 38803, Ph: (662)844-5036, Fax: (662)842-7798. **Key Personnel:** Ron Meyers, Station Mgr.; Emily Wallace, Office Mgr. **Ad Rates:** Noncommercial.

WAPD-FM - See Campbellsville, KY

WAPO-FM - See Mount Vernon, IL

19306 ■ WAQB-FM - 90.9
PO Box 2440
Tupelo, MS 38803
Free: 800-326-4543
Format: Gospel; Contemporary Christian. **Owner:** American Family Radio, at above address. **Founded:** 1977. **URL:** http://www.afr.net.

WAQG-FM - See Dothan, AL

WAQL-FM - See McComb

WAQU-FM - See Selma, AL

WARN-FM - See Culpeper, VA

WASM-FM - See Natchez

WASW-FM - See Waycross, GA

WATI-FM - See Vincennes, IN

WATP-FM - See Laurel

WATU-FM - See Port Gibson

WAUI-FM - See Shelby, OH

WAUM-FM - See Duck Hill

WAUO-FM - See Hohenwald, TN

WAUQ-FM - See Charles City, VA

WAUV-FM - See Ripley, TN

WAVI-FM - See Oxford

WAWH-FM - See Dublin, GA

WAWI-FM - See Lawrenceburg, TN

WAWJ-FM - See Marion, IL

WAWN-FM - See Franklin, PA

WAXG-FM - See Mount Sterling, KY

WAXR-FM - See Geneseo, IL

WAZD-FM - See Savannah, TN

WBFY-FM - See Pinehurst, NC

WBHZ-FM - See Elkins, WV

WBIA-FM - See Shelbyville, TN

WBIE-FM - See Delphos, OH

WBJY-FM - See Americus, GA

WBKG-FM - See Macon, GA

WBKU-FM - See Ahoskie, NC

WBMK-FM - See Morehead, KY

19307 ■ WBVV-FM - 99.3
PO Box 3300
Tupelo, MS 38803
Phone: (601)728-5301
Fax: (601)728-2572
Format: Gospel.

WCSO-FM - See Columbus

WDLL-FM - See Dillon, SC

WEFI-FM - See Effingham, IL

19308 ■ WELO-AM
PO Box 410
Tupelo, MS 38802
Phone: (662)842-7658
Fax: (662)842-0197
Format: Oldies; News; Talk. **Networks:** ABC; Unistar; Mississippi. **Owner:** San Dow Broadcasting, PO Box 1056, Oxford, MS 38655. **Founded:** 1944. **Formerly:** WWPR-AM. **Key Personnel:** Leslie Nabors, Gen. Sales Mgr; Sam H. Howard, Contact; Melissa Murff, Contact. **Wattage:** 770 Day; 095 Night.

19309 ■ WESE-FM - 92.5
5026 Cliff Gookin Blvd.
Tupelo, MS 38801
Phone: (662)842-1067
Format: Hip Hop; Blues. **Networks:** ABC; NBC. **Founded:** 1980. **Operating Hours:** Continuous. **ADI:** Columbus-Tupelo (West Point), MS. **Wattage:** 6,000. **Ad Rates:** Noncommercial. Combined advertising rates available with WWZD-FM, WTVP-AM, WNRX-AM. **URL:** http://www.power925jamz.com.

19310 ■ WFTA-FM - 101.9
PO Box 2116
Tupelo, MS 38803
Phone: (601)842-7625
Fax: (601)842-9568
Owner: Air South Radio Inc. **Wattage:** 50,000. **Ad Rates:** Noncommercial.

WJJE-FM - See Delaware, OH

WJKA-FM - See Jacksonville, NC

19311 ■ WJZB-FM - 88.7
PO Box 3206
Tupelo, MS 38803
Format: Religious. **Founded:** 1987. **Key Personnel:** Fred Jackson, News Dir. **Ad Rates:** Advertising accepted; rates available upon request. **URL:** http://afr.net.

19312 ■ WKMQ-AM
PO Box 3300
Tupelo, MS 38803
Phone: (662)842-1067
Fax: (662)842-0725
Format: Talk. **Wattage:** 960 Day; 012 Night. **Ad Rates:** Advertising accepted; rates available upon request. **URL:** http://www.wkmqonline.com/.

19313 ■ WLOV-TV - 27
PO Box 1732
Tupelo, MS 38802
Phone: (662)842-2227
Email: manager@wlov.com
Format: Commercial TV. **Networks:** Fox. **Owner:** Lingard Broadcasting Corp., at above address. **Founded:** 1983. **Formerly:** WVSB-TV. **Operating Hours:** 5 a.m.-2 a.m. **ADI:** Columbus-Tupelo (West Point), MS. **Key Personnel:** Jennifer Dennington, Gen. Mgr. **Ad Rates:** Noncommercial. **URL:** http://www.wlov.com.

WMSB-FM - See Memphis, TN

WPAS-FM - See Mobile, AL

WPWV-FM - See Princeton, WV

WQSG-FM - See Lafayette, IN

19314 ■ WQST-FM - 92.5
PO Box 2440
Tupelo, MS 38801-2440
Phone: (601)469-3701
Format: Country. **Founded:** 1962. **Operating Hours:** 5 a.m.-midnight. **Key Personnel:** Mark Damron, Gen. Mgr.; Ron Coulter, Music Dir. **Wattage:** 100,000. **Ad Rates:** $8.55-11.80 for 30 seconds; $13.25-16.20 for 60 seconds.

WQVI-FM - See Madison

WRAE-FM - See Raeford, NC

WRIH-FM - See Richmond, VA

WSLE-FM - See Salem, IL

WSQH-FM - See Decatur

WTLG-FM - See Starke, FL

19315 ■ WTUP-AM - 1490
PO Box 3300
Tupelo, MS 38803-3300
Phone: (662)842-1067
Fax: (601)842-0725
Owner: Clear Channel Communications Inc., at above address, Ph: (210)822-2828, Fax: (210)822-2299. **Founded:** 1953. **Formerly:** Tupelo Broadcasting Corporation. **ADI:** Columbus-Tupelo (West Point), MS. **Wattage:** 1,000. **Ad Rates:** $7-15 for 30 seconds; $9-17 for 60 seconds.

19316 ■ WTVA-TV - 9
PO Box 350
Tupelo, MS 38802
Phone: (662)842-7620

Fax: (662)844-7061
Format: Commercial TV. **Networks:** NBC. **Owner:** WTVA Inc., PO Box 320, Tupelo, MS 38802-0320, Ph: (662)842-7620. **Founded:** 1957. **Operating Hours:** Continuous. **ADI:** Columbus-Tupelo (West Point), MS. **Key Personnel:** Steve Rogers, News Dir.; Jeff Houston, Contact, jhouston@wtva.com; Phil Sullivan, CFO, Station Mgr., psullivan@wtva.com; Jon Ball, Dir. of Operations, jball@wtva.com; Dan Modisett, Gen. Mgr. **Ad Rates:** Noncommercial. **URL:** http://www.wtva.com.

19317 ■ WWKZ-FM - 103.5
PO Box 3300
Tupelo, MS 38803-3300
Phone: (662)842-1067
Email: request@kz103radio.com
Format: Contemporary Hit Radio (CHR); Top 40; Alternative/New Music/Progressive; Information. **Networks:** ABC; Westwood One Radio. **Founded:** 1966. **Operating Hours:** Continuous. **ADI:** Columbus-Tupelo (West Point), MS. **Key Personnel:** Rick Stevens, Contact; Rebecca Yarbrough, Contact, sales@kz103.com; Rick Stevens, Contact; Brian Phillips, Contact. **Wattage:** 50,000. **Ad Rates:** $15-45 for 30 seconds; $20-60 for 60 seconds.

19318 ■ WWMS-FM - 97.5
PO Box 410
Tupelo, MS 38802
Phone: (601)234-6881
Fax: (601)236-5014
Format: Contemporary Country; News; Agricultural. **Networks:** ABC. **Owner:** Mississippi Radio Group, 2214 S Gloster St., Tupelo, MS 38801, Ph: (662)842-7658, Fax: (662)842-0197. **Founded:** 1969. **Operating Hours:** Continuous. **ADI:** Columbus-Tupelo (West Point), MS. **Wattage:** 100,000 ERP. **URL:** http://www.miss98.net.

19319 ■ WWZD-FM - 106.7
5026 Cliff Gookin Blvd.
Tupelo, MS 38801
Phone: (662)844-9106
Fax: (662)842-0725
Format: Full Service. **Key Personnel:** Mark Maharrey, Contact, markmaharrey@urbanradio.fm. **Ad Rates:** Advertising accepted; rates available upon request. **URL:** http://www.wizard106.com.

WYAZ-FM - See Yazoo City

WYTF-FM - See Indianola

WZKM-FM - See Waynesboro

19320 ■ WZLQ-FM
PO Box 410
Tupelo, MS 38802
Phone: (662)842-7658
Fax: (662)842-0197
Format: Hot Country. **Networks:** ABC. **Owner:** San-Dow Bradcasting, PO Box 15056, Oxford, NJ. **Founded:** 1968. **Wattage:** 100,000 ERP. **URL:** http://www.z985.net/.

UNIVERSITY

N MS. Lafayette Co. Adjoins Oxford on North. University of Mississippi.

19321 ■ The Daily Mississippian
University of Mississippi Student Media Center
201 Bishop Hall
University, MS 38677
Phone: (662)915-5503
Fax: (662)915-5703
Publisher's E-mail: studentmedia@olemiss.edu
Collegiate newspaper. **Freq:** Daily. **Print Method:** Offset. **Cols./Page:** 5. **Col. Width:** 2 inches. **Col. Depth:** 16 inches. **Key Personnel:** Tyler Clemons, Editor-in-Chief; Nicole Spinuzzi, Managing Editor. **USPS:** 351-710. **URL:** http://thedmonline.com; http://smc.olemiss.edu/daily-mississippian. **Ad Rates:** PCI $9.05. **Remarks:** Accepts advertising. **Circ:** ‡13,000.

19322 ■ Global South
Indiana University Press
c/o Leigh Anne Duck, Ed.
University of Mississippi
PO Box 1848
University, MS 38677
Journal focusing on world literature and cultures. **Freq:** Semiannual. **Key Personnel:** Leigh Anne Duck, Editor. **ISSN:** 1932--8648 (print); **EISSN:** 1932--8656 (electronic). **Subscription Rates:** $37.50 Individuals online only; $70 Institutions online only. **URL:** http://www.jstor.org/journal/globalsouth. **Remarks:** Accepts advertising. **Circ:** (Not Reported).

19323 ■ Living Blues: The Magazine of the African-American Blues Tradition
University of Mississippi Center for the Study of Southern Culture
Sorority Row & Grove Loop
University, MS 38677
Phone: (662)915-5993
Fax: (662)915-5814
Publication E-mail: mark@livingblues.com
Magazine covering the African-American blues tradition. **Freq:** Bimonthly. **Print Method:** Offset. **Trim Size:** 8 1/2 x 11. **Cols./Page:** 3. **Col. Width:** 14 picas. **Col. Depth:** 60 picas. **Key Personnel:** Mark Camarigg, Director, Publications; Brett Bonner, Editor. **ISSN:** 0024-5232 (print). **Subscription Rates:** $29.95 Individuals; $35.95 Canada; $47.95 Other countries; $47.95 Two years; $59.95 Canada 2 years; $73.95 Other countries 2 years; $15 Individuals online only. **URL:** http://www.livingblues.com; http://southernstudies.olemiss.edu/publications/living-blues. **Mailing address:** PO Box 1848, University, MS 38677. **Ad Rates:** 4C $1,996; BW $1,464. **Remarks:** Accepts advertising. **Circ:** (Not Reported).

19324 ■ Mississippi Law Journal
Mississippi Law Journal
PO Box 849
University, MS 38677
Phone: (662)915-6870
Professional legal journal. **Freq:** 6/year September through August. **Key Personnel:** Michael Cowan, Editor-in-Chief; J.Lott Warren, Executive Editor. **Subscription Rates:** $35 Individuals /year; $40 Other countries /year; $15 Single issue. **URL:** http://mississippilawjournal.org. **Ad Rates:** BW $380. **Remarks:** Accepts advertising. **Circ:** Paid 900.

19325 ■ Ole Miss Alumni Review
University of Mississippi Alumni Association
Triplett Alumni Center, Rm. 172
651 Groove Loop
University, MS 38677
Phone: (662)915-7375
Fax: (662)915-7756
Publisher's E-mail: alumni@olemiss.edu
Alumni magazine. **Freq:** Quarterly. **Print Method:** Web offset. **Trim Size:** 8 1/8 x 10 7/8. **Cols./Page:** 4. **Col. Width:** 2 inches. **Col. Depth:** 9 11/16 inches. **Key Personnel:** Jim Urbanek, Assistant Director. **Subscription Rates:** Included in membership. **URL:** http://www.olemissalumni.com/alumnireview. **Mailing address:** PO Box 1848, University, MS 38677. **Ad Rates:** BW $1,260; 4C $1,890. **Remarks:** Accepts advertising. **Circ:** 25000.

19326 ■ WUMS-FM - 92.1
201 Bishop Hall
University, MS 38677
Phone: (662)915-6692
Format: Alternative/New Music/Progressive; Top 40. **Networks:** Westwood One Radio. **Owner:** University of Mississippi, University Ave., University, MS 38677, Ph: (662)915-7211, Free: 800-OLE-MISS. **Founded:** 1989. **Formerly:** WCBH-FM. **Operating Hours:** Continuous. **Wattage:** 2,900. **Ad Rates:** $6-12 for 30 seconds; $8-16 for 60 seconds. $4-$9.50 for 30 seconds; $5-$12 for 60 seconds.

VICKSBURG

W MS. Warren Co. On Mississippi River, 42 mi. W. of Jackson. Port of entry. Tourist center. Manufactures trailers, caskets, chemicals, small appliances, cement, lighting fixtures, packing boxes and crates, lumber, veneer, hardwood flooring, earth moving equipment, feed, fertilizers. Paper mill; bottlings works. U.S. Government machine shops. Boat building yards. Large waterways experimental station. Fisheries. Pine, oaks, cypress timber. Agriculture. Cotton, corn, peas, soybeans.

19327 ■ Dredging Research
United States Army Corps of Engineers - Engineer Research and Development Center
3909 Halls Ferry Rd.
Vicksburg, MS 39180-6199
Phone: (601)636-3111
Research publication covering dredging activities at the U.S. Army Engineer Research and Development Center. **Freq:** Quarterly. **Remarks:** Advertising not accepted. **Circ:** Non-paid 2200.

19328 ■ Vicksburg Post
Vicksburg Printing and Publishing Company Inc.
1601-F N Frontage Rd.
Vicksburg, MS 39182
Phone: (601)636-4545
Fax: (601)634-0897
General newspaper serving Vicksburg and surrounding communities. **Freq:** Daily. **Print Method:** Offset. **Cols./Page:** 6. **Col. Width:** 25 nonpareils. **Col. Depth:** 294 agate lines. **Key Personnel:** Karen Gamble, Managing Editor; Barney Partridge, Director, Advertising. **ISSN:** 0884-8912 (print). **Subscription Rates:** $15 Individuals per month; seven days; $12.25 Individuals per month; six days; $12.75 Individuals per month; Friday, Saturday, Sunday & Monday; $80.25 By mail 3 months; seven days; $50.25 By mail 3 months; Sunday only. **URL:** http://www.vicksburgpost.com/. **Mailing address:** PO Box 821668, Vicksburg, MS 39182. **Ad Rates:** BW $1,285.20; 4C $1,470.20; PCI $10.20. **Remarks:** Accepts advertising. **Circ:** Mon.-Sat. ■ **12169**, Sun. ■ **12858**.

19329 ■ Vicksburg Video
900 Hwy. 61 N
Vicksburg, MS 39183
Phone: (601)636-1351
Cities Served: 157 channels. **URL:** http://www.vicksburgvideo.com.

19330 ■ WBBV-FM - 101.3
900 Belmount St.
Vicksburg, MS 39180
Phone: (601)636-2340
Format: Country. **Networks:** Mississippi; ABC. **Founded:** 1989. **Operating Hours:** Continuous; 10% network, 90% local. **Key Personnel:** Tamra Miller, Contact, tamra.miller@debutbroadcasting.com. **Wattage:** 25,000. **Ad Rates:** $12 for 30 seconds; $16 for 60 seconds. **URL:** http://www.river101.com.

19331 ■ WQBC-AM - 1420
2560 Oakwood Ter.
Vicksburg, MS 39180
Phone: (601)636-1108
Fax: (601)636-1108
Free: 888-253-9254
Email: wqbc@wqbc.net
Format: Talk; Religious. **Key Personnel:** Mike Corley, Owner, mike@mikecorley.org. **Ad Rates:** Noncommercial.

19332 ■ WVBG-AM - 1490
1102 Newitt Vick Dr.
Vicksburg, MS 39183
Phone: (601)883-0848
Format: Information. **Owner:** Owensville Communications, LLC, at above address. **Key Personnel:** Mark Jones, Owner, mark@vicksburgv105.com; Dailon Huskey, Sports Dir., Operations Mgr., dailon@vicksburgv105.com. **URL:** http://www.newstalk1490.net.

WALNUT

19333 ■ WLRC-AM - 850
PO Box 37
Walnut, MS 38683
Phone: (662)223-4071
Fax: (662)223-4072
Format: Religious. **Founded:** June 21, 1982. **Wattage:** 1,000. **Ad Rates:** for 10 seconds; for 15 seconds; for 30 seconds; for 60 seconds. **URL:** http://www.wlrcradio.com.

WAYNESBORO

SE MS. Wayne Co. 52 mi. S. of Meridian. Oil. Pine and hardwood timber. Manufactures electrical appliances, wood products, gloves. Livestock.

19334 ■ W218BV-FM - 91.5
PO Box 391
Twin Falls, ID 83303
Fax: (208)736-1958
Free: 800-357-4226

Circulation: ★ = AAM; △ or • = BPA; ♦ = CAC; ❑ = VAC; ⊕ = PO Statement; ‡ = Publisher's Report; Boldface figures = sworn; Light figures = estimated.

Format: Religious; Contemporary Christian. **Owner:** CSN International, PO Box 391, Twin Falls, ID 83303, Ph: (208)736-1958, Fax: (208)736-1958, Free: 800-357-4226. **Key Personnel:** Kelly Carlson, Dir. of Engg.; Ray Gorney, Asst. Dir. **URL:** http://www.csnradio.com.

19335 ■ WZKM-FM - 89.7
PO Box 2440
Tupelo, MS 38803
Phone: (662)844-8888
Format: Religious. **Owner:** American Family Radio, at above address. **URL:** http://www.afa.net.

WESSON

SW MS. Copiah Co. 10 mi. S. of Hazelhurst. Copiah Lincoln Community College. Residential.

19336 ■ Wolf Tales
Copiah-Lincoln Community College
1028 JC Redd Dr.
Wesson, MS 39191
Phone: (601)643-8304
Fax: (601)643-8222
Collegiate newspaper. **Freq:** Bimonthly. **Print Method:** Offset. **Cols./Page:** 5. **Col. Width:** 1 3/4 inches. **Col. Depth:** 11 1/2 inches. **Key Personnel:** Natalie Davis, Advisor. **URL:** http://www.colin.edu/publications; http://www.colin.edu/student-life/clubs-and-organizations. **Mailing address:** PO Box 649, Wesson, MS 39191. **Remarks:** Accepts advertising. **Circ:** Free ‡2000.

WEST POINT

E MS. Clay Co. 20 mi. NW of Columbus. Manufactures aluminum boats, garments, steam boilers, toys, dairy products, steel fabrication, packing boxes. Meat packing plant. Hardwood. Diversified farming. Dairying.

19337 ■ Daily Times Leader
Daily Times Leader
221 E Main St.
West Point, MS 39773
Phone: (662)494-1422
Fax: (662)494-1414
Publisher's E-mail: editor@dailytimesleader.com
General newspaper. **Freq:** Mon.-Sun. (morn.). **Key Personnel:** Brandon Walker, Managing Editor; Don Norman, Publisher; Jeannetta Edwards, Editor. **Subscription Rates:** $84 Individuals carrier delivery - 1 year; $49.50 Individuals carrier delivery - 6 months; $115 By mail 1 year; $75 By mail 6 months; $29.50 Individuals carrier delivery - 3 months; $40 By mail 3 months. **URL:** http://www.dailytimesleader.com. **Ad Rates:** SAU $9.50. **Remarks:** Accepts advertising. **Circ:** (Not Reported).

WIGGINS

S MS. Stone Co. 35 mi. N. of Gulfport. Lumber mills. Agriculture.

19338 ■ Stone County Enterprise
Stone County Enterprise
143 S First St.
Wiggins, MS 39577
Phone: (601)928-4802
Fax: (601)928-2191
Publisher's E-mail: editor@stonecountyenterprise.com
Community newspaper. **Freq:** Weekly (Wed.). **Print Method:** Offset. **Cols./Page:** 6. **Col. Width:** 2 1/16 inches. **Col. Depth:** 21 1/2 inches. **Key Personnel:** Heather Freret, Editor, Publisher. **USPS:** 522-300. **Subscription Rates:** $30 Individuals; $40 Out of area; $50 Out of state. **URL:** http://www.stonecountyenterprise.com. **Mailing address:** PO Box 157, Wiggins, MS 39577. **Ad Rates:** GLR $5; BW $630; 4C $823.50; SAU $5.50; PCI $5. **Remarks:** Accepts advertising. **Circ:** 3500.

19339 ■ WLUN-FM - 95.3
PO Box 723
Wiggins, MS 39577
Format: Gospel; Country. **Networks:** Satellite Music Network. **Founded:** 1986. **Operating Hours:** Continuous. **Key Personnel:** George A. Cospelich, Station Mgr.; Barbara Naramore, Operations Mgr; A.R. Byrd, Contact; Gay Byrd, Contact. **Wattage:** 100,000. **Ad Rates:** $10 for 30 seconds; $15 for 60 seconds.

WINONA

NC MS. Montgomery Co. 90 mi. N. of Jackson. Manufactures cotton goods, cottonseed and dairy products, picture frames, auto parts and clothing. Pine, gum, oak timber. Dairy, stock, poultry farms.

19340 ■ The Fincastle Herald and Botetourt County News
Montgomery Publishing Inc.
401 Summit St.
Winona, MS 38967
Phone: (662)283-1131
Fax: (662)283-5374
Newspaper. **Freq:** Weekly (Wed.). **Print Method:** Offset. **Cols./Page:** 6. **Col. Width:** 25 nonpareils. **Col. Depth:** 294 agate lines. **Key Personnel:** Brian Hoffman, Editor. **USPS:** 190-680. **URL:** http://ourvalley.org/category/newspapers/the-fincastle-herald. **Remarks:** Accepts advertising. **Circ:** (Not Reported).

19341 ■ The Winona Times
Montgomery Publishing Inc.
401 Summit St.
Winona, MS 38967
Phone: (662)283-1131
Fax: (662)283-5374
Publisher's E-mail: publisher@winonatimes.com
Newspaper with a Democratic orientation. **Freq:** Weekly (Thurs.). **Print Method:** Offset. **Cols./Page:** 6. **Col. Width:** 12.5 picas. **Col. Depth:** 21 1/2 inches. **Key Personnel:** Amanda Sexton, Editor, Publisher; Frances Woods, Clerk; Racine Howard, Contact; Robin Nail, Contact. **Subscription Rates:** $30 Individuals; $40 Out of area; $40 Out of state; $15 Individuals online edition. **URL:** http://www.winonatimes.com. **Mailing address:** PO Box 151, Winona, MS 38967. **Ad Rates:** BW $812.70; 4C $1,037.70; PCI $6.30. **Remarks:** Accepts advertising. **Circ:** Paid ‡2979.

WOODVILLE

SW MS. Wilkinson Co. 35 mi. SE of Natchez. Sawmill. Pine and hardwood timber. Diversified farming. Beans, truck cropping, cattle.

19342 ■ The Woodville Republican
The Woodville Republican Inc.
425 Depot St.
Woodville, MS 39669
Phone: (601)888-4293
Fax: (601)888-6156
Publication E-mail: wrepublican@bellsouth.net
Community newspaper. **Freq:** Weekly (Thurs.). **Print Method:** Offset. **Trim Size:** 13 3/4 x 22 3/4. **Cols./Page:** 7. **Col. Width:** 9 picas. **Col. Depth:** 294 agate lines. **Key Personnel:** Andrew J. Lewis, Editor. **USPS:** 462-260. **Subscription Rates:** $21 Individuals; $23 Out of area; $25 Out of state. **URL:** http://woodville4.tripod.com/Woodvillerepub.htm. **Mailing address:** PO Box 696, Woodville, MS 39669-0696. **Ad Rates:** GLR $.429; BW $882; 4C $416; SAU $8.25; PCI $416. **Remarks:** Accepts advertising. **Circ:** (Not Reported).

YAZOO CITY

WC MS. Yazoo Co. On Yazoo River, 40 mi. NW of Jackson. Cotton market. Manufactures lumber, paper bags, wire harnessing, fertilizer, feed. Oil refinery. Fisheries. Corn, soybeans, cotton. Livestock.

19343 ■ WBYP-FM - 107.1
611 Center Park Ln.
Yazoo City, MS 39194
Phone: (662)746-7676
Fax: (662)746-1525
Format: Country; Eclectic. **Owner:** Zoobel Broadcasting Inc., at above address. **Mailing address:** PO Box 130, Yazoo City, MS 39194. **URL:** http://www.power107radio.com.

19344 ■ WELZ-AM - 1460
PO Box 130
Yazoo City, MS 39194
Phone: (662)746-7676
Fax: (662)746-1525
Format: Country. **Networks:** ABC. **Owner:** Zoobel Broadcasting Inc., at above address. **Founded:** 1986. **Operating Hours:** Continuous. **Wattage:** 3,000. **Ad Rates:** Advertising accepted; rates available upon request.

19345 ■ WJNS-FM - 92.1
1405 Enchanted Dr.
Yazoo City, MS 39194
Phone: (662)746-5921
Owner: Family Worship Center Church, Inc., PO Box 1122, Port Orchard, WA 98366, Ph: (360)874-0903, Fax: (360)616-4828. **Founded:** 1968. **Wattage:** 4,800 ERP. **Ad Rates:** Accepts Advertising. **URL:** http://www.msidia.com/radio_fm/wjns-fm.htm.

19346 ■ WYAZ-FM - 89.5
PO Box 2440
Tupelo, MS 38803
Phone: (662)844-8888
Format: Religious. **Owner:** American Family Radio, at above address. **URL:** http://www.afa.net.

ADRIAN

W MO. Bates Co. 50 mi. SE of Kansas City. Dairy farming. Agriculture. Corn, wheat, oats.

19347 ■ The Adrian Journal
Adrian Journal
39 E Main St.
Adrian, MO 64720
Phone: (816)297-2100
Newspaper with a Republican orientation. **Freq:** Weekly (Thurs.). **Print Method:** Web offset. **Cols./Page:** 6. **Col. Width:** 25 nonpareils. **Col. Depth:** 294 agate lines. **USPS:** 005-860. **Subscription Rates:** $30 Individuals; $36 Out of area; $41 Out of state. **Mailing address:** PO Box 128, Adrian, MO 64720. **Ad Rates:** BW $693; SAU $5.50. **Remarks:** Accepts advertising. **Circ:** ‡1500.

19348 ■ Drexel Star
Adrian Journal
39 E Main St.
Adrian, MO 64720
Phone: (816)297-2100
Community newspaper. **Freq:** Weekly (Thurs.). **Cols./Page:** 6. **Col. Width:** 12 1/5 picas. **Col. Depth:** 21 inches. **URL:** http://www.drexelstar.com; http://www.adrianjournal.com. **Mailing address:** PO Box 128, Adrian, MO 64720. **Ad Rates:** BW $737; SAU $5.85; PCI $3. **Remarks:** Accepts advertising. **Circ:** 700.

19349 ■ Star Lite Shoppers Guide
Adrian Journal
39 E Main St.
Adrian, MO 64720
Phone: (816)297-2100
Shopper. **Freq:** Weekly. **Cols./Page:** 6. **Col. Width:** 2 inches. **Col. Depth:** 21 inches. **Mailing address:** PO Box 128, Adrian, MO 64720. **Ad Rates:** 4C $1,014; SAU $4; BW $504. **Remarks:** Accepts advertising. **Circ:** Free ‡5500.

ARNOLD

E. MO. Jefferson Co. 10 mi. E. of House Springs. Residential.

19350 ■ KGNA-FM - 89.9
PO Box 187
Washington, MO 63090
Phone: (636)239-0400
Fax: (636)239-4448
Free: 877-385-3787
Email: info@goodnewsvoice.org
Format: Religious. **Simulcasts:** KGNV-FM, KGNN-FM. **Networks:** Moody Broadcasting. **Owner:** Missouri River Christian Broadcasting Inc., PO Box 187, Washington, MO 63090, Ph: (636)239-0400. **Founded:** 1999. **Formerly:** KCWA-FM. **Operating Hours:** Continuous; 90% network, 10% local. **Local Programs:** *Key Life,* Monday Tuesday Wednesday Thursday Friday 11:09 a.m. - 11:25 a.m.; 6:35 p.m. - 6:51 p.m. **Wattage:** 150. **Ad Rates:** Noncommercial. $4 for 15 seconds; $6 for 30 seconds; $8 for 60 seconds. **URL:** http://www.goodnewsvoice.org.

ASHLAND

SE MO. Boone Co. 14 mi. NNW of Jefferson City.

19351 ■ Boone County Journal
Boone County Journal
209 Johnson
Ashland, MO 65010
Phone: (573)657-2334
Fax: (573)657-2002
Publisher's E-mail: reporter@bocojo.com
County newspaper. **Freq:** Weekly (Wed.). **Print Method:** Web press. **Cols./Page:** 6. **Col. Width:** 2 inches. **Col. Depth:** 21 inches. **Key Personnel:** Bruce Wallace, Owner. **Subscription Rates:** $25 Individuals; $48 Two years; $33 Out of area; $35 Out of state. **URL:** http://www.bocojo.com. **Mailing address:** PO Box 197, Ashland, MO 65010. **Ad Rates:** GLR $1; BW $453.60; 4C $600; SAU $4; CNU $5; PCI $4. **Remarks:** Accepts advertising. **Circ:** ‡1750.

AVA

S. MO. Douglas Co. 60 mi. SE of Springfield. Sporting goods, lumber, staves, electric motors, feed, milk products manufactured. Mountain resort. Pine, oak timber. Hatchery. Beef, pork producers. Dairy, poultry, truck, fruit, grain farms.

19352 ■ Douglas County Herald
Herald Publishing Co.
302 E Washington
Ava, MO 65608
Phone: (417)683-4181
Fax: (417)683-4102
Publisher's E-mail: info@douglascountyherald.com
Newspaper with a Republican orientation. **Freq:** Weekly (Thurs.). **Print Method:** Offset. **Cols./Page:** 7. **Col. Width:** 12 picas. **Col. Depth:** 294 agate lines. **Key Personnel:** Keith Moore, Managing Editor; Jody Porter, Manager, Advertising. **USPS:** 160-320. **Subscription Rates:** $25.20 Individuals; $32.17 Elsewhere in Missouri; $33 Out of state. **URL:** http://www.douglascountyherald.com. **Mailing address:** PO Box 577, Ava, MO 65608. **Ad Rates:** GLR $.14; BW $294; SAU $3.90; PCI $2.10. **Remarks:** Advertising accepted; rates available upon request. **Circ:** (Not Reported).

19353 ■ KKOZ-AM - 1430
PO Box 386
Ava, MO 65608
Phone: (417)683-4191
Fax: (417)683-4192
Email: jcorum@kkoz.com
Format: News; Country; Agricultural; Sports; Talk; Religious. **Simulcasts:** KKOZ-FM. **Owner:** Corum Ind., Inc., 306 Se 2nd Ave, Ava, MO 65608, Ph: (417) 683-4191. **Founded:** 1967. **Operating Hours:** 6 a.m.-10 p.m. (15% network; 85% local). **Key Personnel:** Art Corum, Operations Mgr., acroum@kkoz.com; Jeanette Gooden, Office Mgr., jgooden@kkoz.com; Joe Corum, Gen. Mgr. **Wattage:** 6,000. **Ad Rates:** Noncommercial. $5.25 for 30 seconds; $8.50 for 60 seconds. **URL:** http://www.kkoz.com.

19354 ■ KKOZ-FM - 92.1
305 S E 2nd Ave.
Ava, MO 65608
Phone: (417)683-4191
Fax: (417)683-4192
Free: 800-683-4191
Email: sales@kkoz.com
Format: Country; Full Service; Agricultural; Talk. **Simulcasts:** KKOZ-AM. **Networks:** Missouri. **Founded:** 1967. **Formerly:** KSOA-AM. **Operating Hours:** 6 a.m.-10 p.m.; 15% network, 85% local. **Key Personnel:** Joe Corum, Gen. Mgr., jcorum@kkoz.com; Art Corum, Gen. Mgr., acorum@kkoz.com. **Wattage:** 6,000. **Ad Rates:** $5.25 for 30 seconds; $8.50 for 60 seconds. **URL:** http://www.kkoz.com.

BETHANY

NW MO. Harrison Co. 60 mi. NE of Saint Joseph. Limestone quarry, cheese factory. Diversified farming. Corn, oats, dairying.

19355 ■ Bethany Republican-Clipper
Bethany Printing Co.
PO Box 351
Bethany, MO 64424
Phone: (660)425-6325
Fax: (660)425-3441
Publication E-mail: rclipper@grm.net
Newspaper with a Republican orientation. **Freq:** Weekly (Wed.). **Print Method:** Offset. **Cols./Page:** 7. **Col. Width:** 12.5 picas. **Col. Depth:** 21 inches. **Key Personnel:** Philip G. Conger, Editor, phone: (660)425-6325; Kathy Conger, Designer, Manager, Advertising; Angela Ragan, Advertising Representative. **USPS:** 052-680. **Subscription Rates:** $28 Individuals for Harrison County and adjoining counties.; $46 Out of area; $52 Out of state; $28 Individuals e-edition. **URL:** http://www.bethanyclipper.com. **Ad Rates:** GLR $.32; BW $623; 4C $662; SAU $4.24; PCI $4.50. **Remarks:** Advertising accepted; rates available upon request. **Circ:** ‡3500.

19356 ■ KAAN-AM - 870
PO Box 447
Bethany, MO 64424
Phone: (660)425-6380
Fax: (660)425-8148
Format: Country; News; Information. **Simulcasts:** KAAN-FM. **Networks:** ABC. **Owner:** GoodRadio.TV. **Founded:** 1983. **Formerly:** KIRK-AM. **Operating Hours:** Sunrise-sunset; 15% network, 85% local. **ADI:** St. Joseph, MO. **Key Personnel:** Stuart Johnson, Sports Dir., stuartj@regionalradio.com; Doug Schmitz, Gen. Mgr., dschmitz@regionalradio.com; Mike Mattson, Sales Mgr., Station Mgr., mikem@regionalradio.com. **Wattage:** 1,000. **Ad Rates:** $10.50-15 for 30 seconds. **URL:** http://www.northwestmoinfo.com.

19357 ■ KAAN-FM - 95.5
PO Box 447
Bethany, MO 64424
Phone: (660)425-6380
Fax: (660)425-8148
Format: Country. **Simulcasts:** KAAN-AM. **Networks:** ABC. **Owner:** GoodRadio.TV. **Founded:** 1978. **Operating Hours:** 18 hours Daily; 15% network, 85% local. **ADI:** St. Joseph, MO. **Key Personnel:** Stuart Johnson, Prog. Dir., stuart.johnson@digity.me; Doug Schmitz, Gen. Mgr., dschmitz@regionalradio.com; Mike Mattson,

Circulation: ★ = AAM; △ or • = BPA; ♦ = CAC; ❑ = VAC; ⊕ = PO Statement; ‡ = Publisher's Report; Boldface figures = sworn; Light figures = estimated.

Station Mgr., mikem@regionalradio.com. **Wattage**: 50,000. **Ad Rates:** $10.50-15 for 30 seconds. **URL:** http://www.northwestmoinfo.com.

BIRCH TREE

SC MO. Shannon Co. 5 mi. E. of Teresita.

19358 ■ KBMV-FM - 107.1
PO Box 215
Birch Tree, MO 65438
Format: Contemporary Hit Radio (CHR). **Owner:** Scenic Rivers Broadcasting, at above address. **Founded:** 1982. **Operating Hours**: Continuous; 100% local. **ADI**: Springfield, MO. **Key Personnel:** DiAnna Riffle, Contact. **Wattage**: 25,000. **Ad Rates:** $5-7.50 for 30 seconds; $8-9.50 for 60 seconds. **URL:** http://www.klove.com/.

BLAND

EC MO. Osage Co. 40 mi. SE of Jefferson City. Shoe factory. Fire-clay pits. Lumber. Diversified farming. Cattle.

19359 ■ Mules and More
Mules and More Inc.
PO Box 460
Bland, MO 65014-0460
Phone: (573)646-3934
Fax: (573)646-3407
Consumer magazine for mule, wagon and harness enthusiasts. **Freq:** Monthly. **Key Personnel:** Sue Cole, Senior Editor; Cori Basham, Managing Editor. **USPS:** 008-589. **Subscription Rates:** $30 Individuals; $50 Canada; $100 Other countries; $30 /year. **URL:** http://www.mulesandmore.com/index.html. **Ad Rates:** BW $200; 4C $325. **Remarks:** Accepts advertising. **Circ:** (Not Reported).

BOLIVAR

SWC MO. Polk Co. 26 mi. NW of Springfield. Southwest Baptist University. Manufactures sewn specialty products, floral products; computer software. Agriculture. Dairy, beef, cattle.

19360 ■ Bolivar Herald-Free Press
Community Publishers Inc. -Missouri
335 S Springfield Ave.
Free Press Plz.
Bolivar, MO 65613-0330
Phone: (417)326-7636
Fax: (417)326-7643
Publisher's E-mail: news@bolivarmonews.com
Community newspaper. **Freq:** Semiweekly (Wed. and Fri.). **Print Method:** Offset. **Cols./Page:** 6. **Col. Width:** 1.79 inches. **Col. Depth:** 301 agate lines. **Key Personnel:** Dave Berry, Publisher; Charlotte Marsch, Editor; Deanna Moore, Manager, Sales. **USPS:** 060-080. **Subscription Rates:** $59.02 Individuals 104 issues; $34.05 Out of area 52 issues; $22.70 Out of area 26 issues; $82.86 Out of state 104 issues; $47.67 Out of state 52 issues; $30.11 Out of state 26 issues. **URL:** http://bolivarmonews.com. **Mailing address:** PO Box 330, Bolivar, MO 65613-0330. **Ad Rates:** $50-1289; $50-100. SAU $4C $. **Remarks:** Accepts classified advertising. **Circ:** ‡6000.

19361 ■ Omnibus
Southwest Baptist University
1600 University Ave.
Bolivar, MO 65613
Phone: (417)328-5281
Free: 800-526-5859
Publisher's E-mail: admissions@sbuniv.edu
Collegiate newspaper. **Founded:** 1961. **Freq:** Weekly. **Print Method:** Offset. **Trim Size:** 10 x 12. **Cols./Page:** 5. **Col. Width:** 27 nonpareils. **Col. Depth:** 182 agate lines. **URL:** http://www.omnibusonline.com. **Ad Rates:** BW $240; PCI $4. **Remarks:** Accepts advertising. **Circ:** Free ‡1400.

19362 ■ KYOO-AM - 1200
205 N Pike Ave.
Bolivar, MO 65613
Phone: (417)326-5257
Format: Country. **Networks:** ABC. **Owner:** KYOO Communication. **Founded:** 1961. **Formerly**: KLTB-AM; KBLR-AM. **Operating Hours**: Sunrise-sunset. **Wattage**: 1,000. **Ad Rates:** $3-15 for 30 seconds. KYOO-FM.

BOWLING GREEN

S. MO. Pike Co. 30 mi. SE of Hannibal. Manufactures wire rope, textiles. Hatchery. Rock quarries; limestone. Diversified farming. Wheat, corn, soybeans. Swine.

19363 ■ The Bowling Green Times
Lakeway Publishers Inc.
106 W Main St.
Bowling Green, MO 63334
Phone: (573)324-2222
Fax: (573)324-3991
Newspaper. **Freq:** Weekly (Wed.). **Print Method:** Offset. **Cols./Page:** 6. **Col. Width:** 24 3/4 nonpareils. **Col. Depth:** 301 agate lines. **Key Personnel:** Linda Luebrecht, Publisher. **Subscription Rates:** $28 Individuals 6 months; print + online; $37 Individuals /year; online. **URL:** http://www.bowlinggreentimes.com. **Ad Rates:** SAU $3.85. **Remarks:** Accepts advertising. **Circ:** 3352.

19364 ■ KBMX-FM - 101.9
PO Box 430
Bowling Green, MO 63334-0430
Email: kbmx@socket.net
Format: Easy Listening. **Networks:** ABC. **Owner:** Contemporary Media Inc., Bowling Green, MO. **Founded:** 1988. **Operating Hours**: Continuous. **Key Personnel:** Mike Rice, President; Mike Watson, Gen. Mgr.; Janet Cox, VP. **Wattage**: 6,000 ERP. **Ad Rates:** $10-27.50 for 60 seconds.

BRANSON

S. MO. Taney Co. 40 mi. S. of Springfield. Lake resort. Manufactures cedar novelties, garments, charcoal, furniture, stave bolts. Rock quarries. Cedar, oak timber. Diversified farming.

19365 ■ America's Flyways
United States Pilots Association
1652 Indian Point Rd.
Branson, MO 65616
Phone: (417)338-2225
Magazine covering issues for pilots in the U.S. **Freq:** Monthly. **Subscription Rates:** $16.95 Individuals. **Ad Rates:** BW $750; 4C $970. **Remarks:** Accepts advertising. **Circ:** 20000.

19366 ■ Branson Tri-Lakes News
Branson TriLakes Daily News
PO Box 1900
Branson, MO 65615
Phone: (417)334-3161
Fax: (417)334-1460
Publisher's E-mail: internet@bransondailynews.com
General newspaper. **Freq:** Bimonthly Wednesday and Saturday. **Print Method:** Offset. **Cols./Page:** 6. **Col. Width:** 21 nonpareils. **Col. Depth:** 294 agate lines. **Key Personnel:** Chad Hunter, Editor; Michael Shuver, Publisher; Shane Walton, Account Executive. **Subscription Rates:** $65 Individuals inside Taney or Stone County; $115 Out of area. **URL:** http://bransontrilakesnews.com. **Formerly:** Branson Daily News. **Ad Rates:** GLR $15; 4C $200; PCI $15. **Remarks:** Accepts classified advertising. **Circ:** (Not Reported).

19367 ■ KLFC-FM - 88.1
PO Box 2030
Branson, MO 65615
Phone: (417)334-5532
Fax: (417)335-2437
Email: 881fm@klfcradio.com
Format: Religious. **Networks:** SkyLight Satellite; USA Radio. **Owner:** Mountaintop Broadcasting Inc., at above address. **Founded:** Nov. 1994. **Operating Hours**: Continuous. **Key Personnel:** Herb Smith, Gen. Mgr. **Wattage**: 1,800. **Ad Rates:** Noncommercial. **URL:** http://www.klfcradio.com.

19368 ■ KOMC-AM - 1220
202 Courtney St.
Branson, MO 65616
Phone: (417)334-6003
Format: News. **Networks:** CBS. **Wattage**: 1,000 Day; 044 Night. **Ad Rates:** Advertising accepted; rates available upon request. **URL:** http://www.mykomc.com.

19369 ■ KOMC-FM - 100.1
202 Courtney St.
Branson, MO 65616
Phone: (417)334-6003
Format: Adult Contemporary. **Founded:** Oct. 1997. **Operating Hours**: Continuous Monday - Saturday; 6:00 a.m. - Midnight Sunday. **Wattage**: 36,000 ERP. **Ad Rates:** Accepts Advertising. **URL:** http://www.mykomc.com.

19370 ■ KRZK-FM - 106.3
202 Courtney St.
Branson, MO 65616
Phone: (417)334-6003
Fax: (417)334-7141
Free: 888-870-5035
Format: Country. **Networks:** ABC. **Operating Hours**: Continuous. **Wattage**: 27,000. **Ad Rates:** Noncommercial. **URL:** http://www.hometowndailynews.com.

BRECKENRIDGE

19371 ■ Green Hills Communications Inc.
7926 NE State Rte M
Breckenridge, MO 64625
Phone: (660)644-5411
Fax: (660)644-5464
Free: 800-846-3426
Founded: 1982. **Cities Served:** 47 channels. **Mailing address:** PO Box 227, Breckenridge, MO 64625. **URL:** http://www.greenhills.net.

BROOKFIELD

N. MO. Linn Co. 40 mi. NW of Moberly. Shoe and textile factories. Diversified farming. Corn, wheat, livestock.

19372 ■ Best Broadcast Group
107 S Main
Brookfield, MO 64628
Phone: (660)258-3383
Fax: (660)258-7307
Email: towers@bestbroadcastgroup.com
Format: Eclectic. **Key Personnel:** Dale A. Palmer, Gen. Mgr. **Ad Rates:** , $6.00 up to $35+ per ad. **URL:** http://www.bestbroadcastgroup.com/Contact-Us.html.

19373 ■ KZBK-FM - 96.9
107 S Main St.
Brookfield, MO 64628
Phone: (660)258-3383
Fax: (660)258-7307
Email: kzbk@shighway.com
Format: Adult Contemporary; Contemporary Hit Radio (CHR). **Owner:** Best Broadcast Group, 107 S Main, Brookfield, MO 64628, Ph: (660)258-3383, Fax: (660)258-7307. **Wattage**: 50,000. **Ad Rates:** Advertising accepted; rates available upon request. **URL:** http://www.kzbkradio.com/.

BROOKLINE

19374 ■ KADI-FM - 99.5
5431 W Sunshine
Brookline, MO 65619
Phone: (417)831-0995
Fax: (417)831-4026
Format: Adult Contemporary. **Founded:** 1990. **Key Personnel:** Mark Hill, Station Mgr., station.manager@kadi.com. **Ad Rates:** Noncommercial. **URL:** http://www.99hitfm.com.

BROOKLINE STATION

19375 ■ KADI-FM - 99.5
5431 W Sunshine
Brookline Station, MO 65619
Phone: (417)831-0995
Format: Religious; Contemporary Christian. **Networks:** USA Radio. **Owner:** Vision Communications, 1601 W Sunshine, Ste. H, Springfield, MO 65807. **Founded:** 1990. **Operating Hours**: Continuous. **Key Personnel:** R.C. Amer, Gen. Mgr. **Wattage**: 6,000. **Ad Rates:** $13-19 for 30 seconds; $16-22 for 60 seconds. **URL:** http://kadi.com.

BUCKLIN

19376 ■ Chariton Valley Cablevision
606 Oak St.
Bucklin, MO 64631
Phone: (660)395-9000
Fax: (660)695-3603
Free: 800-769-8731

Email: feedback@cvalley.net
Founded: Sept. 05, 2006. **Key Personnel:** Cheryl Long, President; Don Shawn, VP; Jim Simon, Gen. Mgr. **Cities Served:** 61 channels. **URL:** http://cvalley.net.

BUFFALO

SW MO. Dallas Co. 28 mi. N. of Springfield.

19377 ■ Buffalo Reflex
Buffalo Reflex
114 E Lincoln St.
Buffalo, MO 65622-0770
Phone: (417)345-2224
Publisher's E-mail: news@buffaloreflex.com
Community newspaper. **Freq:** Weekly (Wed.). **Print Method:** Offset. **Cols./Page:** 6. **Col. Width:** 24 nonpareils. **Col. Depth:** 21 1/2 inches. **Key Personnel:** Paul Campbell, Editor, General Manager; Joy Beamer, Office Manager. **USPS:** 069-600. **Subscription Rates:** $42.98 Individuals Dallas & adjoining counties (52 issues); $52.03 Out of area 52 issues; $60.90 Out of state 52 issues. **URL:** http://buffaloreflex.com. **Mailing address:** PO Box 770, Buffalo, MO 65622-0770. **Ad Rates:** BW $568; 4C $838; SAU $4.40; PCI $4.40. **Remarks:** Accepts advertising. **Circ:** ‡4700.

BUTLER

WC MO. Bates Co. 10 mi. S. of Passaic. Agriculture.

19378 ■ KMAM-AM - 1530
800 E Nursery St.
Butler, MO 64730-1771
Phone: (660)679-4191
Fax: (660)679-4193
Format: Country; Religious; News; Agricultural. **Simulcasts:** KMAM, KMOE-FM. **Networks:** ABC; Brownfield. **Owner:** Bates County Broadcasting Co., 800 E Nursery, Butler, MO 64730, Ph: (660)679-4191. **Founded:** 1962. **Operating Hours:** Daytime. **Key Personnel:** Bill Thornton, Owner, Gen. Mgr.; Melody Thornton, Gen. Mgr. **Local Programs:** *Brownfield Headline News*, Monday Tuesday Wednesday Thursday Friday 12:20 p.m. - 12:45 p.m. **Wattage:** 500. **Ad Rates:** $12 for 30 seconds; $14 for 60 seconds. Combined advertising rates available with KMOE-FM. **URL:** http://www.921kmoe.com.

19379 ■ KMOE-FM - 92.1
800 E Nursery
Butler, MO 64730
Phone: (660)679-4191
Fax: (660)679-4193
Email: fm92@embarqmail.com
Format: Country. **Simulcasts:** KMAM-AM. **Networks:** ABC. **Owner:** Bates County Broadcasting Co., 800 E Nursery, Butler, MO 64730, Ph: (660)679-4191. **Founded:** 1975. **Operating Hours:** 6 a.m.-10 p.m.; 5% network, 95% local. **Key Personnel:** Melody Thornton, Gen. Mgr. **Wattage:** 5,000. **Ad Rates:** $12 for 30 seconds; $14 for 60 seconds. Combined advertising rates available with KMAM-AM. **URL:** http://www.921kmoe.com.

CABOOL

19380 ■ The Cabool Enterprise
Cabool Enterprise Inc.
525 Main St.
Cabool, MO 65689-0040
Phone: (417)962-4411
Publication E-mail: news@thecaboolenterprise.com
Community newspaper. **Freq:** Weekly (Thurs.). **Cols./Page:** 6. **Col. Width:** 2 inches. **Col. Depth:** 21 inches. **Key Personnel:** Russell C. Wood, Publisher. **USPS:** 082-300. **Subscription Rates:** $29.50 Individuals print and online - Texas, Wright, Douglas & Howell Counties; $36.75 Elsewhere in Missouri; print and online; $44.50 Out of state print and online; $27 Individuals online only. **URL:** http://www.thecaboolenterprise.com. **Mailing address:** PO Box 40, Cabool, MO 65689-0040. **Ad Rates:** SAU $4.16. **Remarks:** Accepts advertising. **Circ:** 2,100.

CALIFORNIA

C. MO. Moniteau Co. 25 mi. W. of Jefferson City. Manufactures small engines, fiberglass wire markers, steel fabrications. Food processing plants. Woodworking. Stock, dairy, poultry farms.

19381 ■ California Democrat
California Democrat
319 S High St.
California, MO 65018
Phone: (573)796-2135
Publication E-mail: editor@californiademocrat.com
Newspaper. **Founded:** 1858. **Freq:** Weekly (Wed.). **Key Personnel:** Paula Earls, Editor, phone: (573)796-4220. **USPS:** 083-720. **Subscription Rates:** $30 Individuals carrier delivery and mail; weekly; $35 Out of area Mail; weekly; $40 Out of state Mail; weekly. **URL:** http://www.californiademocrat.com/. **Formerly:** Democrat. **Ad Rates:** GLR $5.15. **Remarks:** Accepts advertising. **Circ:** ‡4000.

CAMDENTON

S. MO. Camden Co. On Ozark Lake, 50 mi. SW of Jefferson City. Resort. Cedar products, auto products, sporting goods. Oak, pine timber. Diversified farming. Corn, molasses, wheat.

KCVJ-FM - See Osceola

19382 ■ KCVO-FM - 91.7
PO Box 800
Camdenton, MO 65020
Phone: (573)346-3200
Fax: (573)346-1010
Free: 800-336-0917
Format: Religious; Contemporary Christian. **Networks:** USA Radio. **Founded:** 1985. **Operating Hours:** 6 a.m.-midnight; 25% network, 75% local. **Key Personnel:** Dana Nichols, Owner; Jim McDermott, Contact. **Wattage:** 6,000. **Ad Rates:** Noncommercial. **URL:** http://www.spiritfm.org/about-spirit-fm/find-us-on-the-dial.

KCVQ-FM - See Knob Noster

19383 ■ KHGN-FM - 90.7
PO Box 800
Camdenton, MO 65020
Phone: (573)346-3200
Free: 800-336-0917
Email: khgn@kvmo.net
Format: Religious. **Key Personnel:** Dennis Phelps, President; Tom Lloyd, Chief Engineer, VP; Bill Riley, Bd. Member; Vicki Lloyd, Secretary. **Ad Rates:** Noncommercial. **URL:** http://www.spiritfm.org.

CAMERON

NW MO. DeKalb Co. 50 mi. N. of Independence. Residential.

19384 ■ Cameron Citizen Observer
Cameron Newspapers Inc.
BB Hwy.
Cameron, MO 64429
Phone: (816)632-6543
Fax: (816)632-4508
Publisher's E-mail: publisher@mycameronnews.com
Local newspaper. **Freq:** Weekly (Thurs.). **Print Method:** Offset. **Cols./Page:** 6. **Col. Width:** 18 nonpareils. **Col. Depth:** 224 agate lines. **Key Personnel:** Jamey Honeycutt, Publisher; D'Anna Balliett, General Manager; Jeff King, Director, Production; Andrew Bottrell, Editor; Debbie Wiedmaier, Office Manager; Helen Guffey, Specialist, Advertising and Sales. **Subscription Rates:** $35 Individuals print; $40 Out of area print; $52 Out of state print; $36 Individuals print and online; $40 Out of area print and online; $52 Out of state print and online; $36 Individuals online; $40 Out of area online; $52 Out of state online. **URL:** http://www.mycameronnews.com. **Mailing address:** PO Box 498, Cameron, MO 64429. **Ad Rates:** BW $180; SAU $3; PCI $7.50. **Remarks:** Accepts advertising. **Circ:** Paid ‡2000.

19385 ■ KKWK-FM - 100.1
PO Box 643
Cameron, MO 64429
Phone: (816)632-6661
Fax: (816)632-1334
Email: kkwk-tv@northwestmoinfo.com
Format: Oldies. **Key Personnel:** Doug Schmitz, Gen. Mgr., dschmitz@regionalradio.com. **URL:** http://www.northwestmoinfo.com.

19386 ■ KMRN-AM - 1360
607 E Platte Clay Way
Cameron, MO 64429
Phone: (816)632-6661
Free: 800-233-1001
Format: Talk; News. **Founded:** 1971. **Operating Hours:** 6:00 a.m. - 7:00 p.m.; 90% network, 10% local. **Key Personnel:** Doug Schmitz, Gen. Mgr., dschmitz@regionalradio.com; Chris Ward, Sports Dir., Prog. Dir., barryp@regionalradio.com; Chet Querry, Cust. Srv. Mgr., chetq@regionalradio.com. **Wattage:** 500. **Ad Rates:** $8-12 for 30 seconds; $16-24 for 60 seconds. Combined advertising rates available with KKWK-FM. **Mailing address:** PO Box 643, Cameron, MO 64429.

CANTON

NE MO. Lewis Co. On Mississippi River, 20 mi. NW of Quincy, IL. Culver Stockton College. Manufactures telephone service parts. Fisheries. Stock, poultry, grain farms.

19387 ■ Megaphone
Culver-Stockton College
1 College Hill
Canton, MO 63435
Phone: (573)288-6000
Free: 800-537-1883
Publisher's E-mail: admissions@culver.edu
Collegiate newspaper. **Freq:** Bimonthly. **Print Method:** Offset. **Trim Size:** 12 x 23. **Cols./Page:** 4. **Col. Width:** 22 nonpareils. **Col. Depth:** 224 agate lines. **URL:** http://www3.culver.edu/megaphone. **Ad Rates:** BW $240; PCI $5. **Remarks:** Accepts advertising. **Circ:** Free ‡1000.

CAPE GIRARDEAU

SE MO. Scott Co. On Mississippi River, 105 mi. SE of Saint Louis. Highway bridge over river. Boatyard. Southeast Missouri State University. Manufactures shoes, cement, lumber, dairy products, electric appliances, furniture, men's clothing, concrete, plastics, paper and meat products. Ships lumber, cement, shoes. Hardwood timber; stone quarries. Diversified farming. Corn, soybeans, wheat, cotton. Cattle, hogs.

19388 ■ The Arrow
Southeast Missouri State University
1 University Plz.
Cape Girardeau, MO 63701
Phone: (573)651-2000
Publisher's E-mail: contact@semo.edu
Collegiate tabloid. **Freq:** Biweekly Mondays and Thursday. **Print Method:** Offset. **Trim Size:** 11 x 17. **Cols./Page:** 5. **Col. Width:** 23 nonpareils. **Col. Depth:** 210 agate lines. **Key Personnel:** Zarah Laurence, Managing Editor; Jay Forness, Editor. **Subscription Rates:** Free. **URL:** http://www.southeastarrow.com. **Formerly:** The Capaha Arrow. **Remarks:** Accepts advertising. **Circ:** (Not Reported).

19389 ■ Monett Times
Rust Communications
301 Broadway St.
Cape Girardeau, MO 63701
Phone: (573)335-6611
Free: 800-879-1210
Newspaper with a Republican orientation. **Freq:** Daily (eve.). **Print Method:** Offset. **Trim Size:** 22 3/4 x 28. **Cols./Page:** 6. **Col. Width:** 2 1/16 inches. **Col. Depth:** 21 1/2 inches. **Key Personnel:** Jacob Brower, Publisher. **Subscription Rates:** $12.80 Individuals monthly; $10 Individuals digital (monthly). **URL:** http://www.monett-times.com. **Remarks:** Accepts advertising. **Circ:** (Not Reported).

19390 ■ Nevada Daily Mail
Rust Communications
301 Broadway St.
Cape Girardeau, MO 63701
Phone: (573)335-6611
Free: 800-879-1210
Newspaper with a Democratic orientation. **Freq:** Daily (eve.). **Print Method:** Offset. **Cols./Page:** 6. **Col. Width:** 24 nonpareils. **Col. Depth:** 301 agate lines. **Key Personnel:** Lorie Harter, Manager, Advertising; Floyd Jernigan, Jr., Publisher; Ralph Pokorny, Editor. **USPS:** 595-890. **Subscription Rates:** $92 Individuals; $84 Individuals EZ pay; $122 Out of area. **URL:** http://www.nevadadailymail.com. **Ad Rates:** 4C $8; PCI $8. **Remarks:** Accepts advertising. **Circ:** Mon.-Fri. 2600.

Circulation: ⋆ = AAM; △ or • = BPA; ♦ = CAC; ❑ = VAC; ⊕ = PO Statement; ‡ = Publisher's Report; Boldface figures = sworn; Light figures = estimated.

19391 ■ Southeast Missourian
Southeast Missourian Plus
301 Broadway
Cape Girardeau, MO 63702
Phone: (573)335-6611
Fax: (573)334-7288
Free: 800-879-1210
Publication E-mail: webmaster@semissourian.com
Community newspaper. **Freq:** Daily and Sun. **Print Method:** Offset. **Trim Size:** 12.5 x 21.5. **Cols./Page:** 6. **Col. Width:** 1.667 inches. **Col. Depth:** 20 1/2 inches. **Key Personnel:** Jon K. Rust, Publisher; Bob Miller, Editor, phone: (573)388-3625; Mark Kneer, General Manager; Donna Denson, Director, Advertising. **Subscription Rates:** $15.95 Individuals print and digital access (monthly); $11.95 Individuals monthly (online). **URL:** http://www.semissourian.com. **Mailing address:** PO Box 699, Cape Girardeau, MO 63702. **Ad Rates:** GLR $20; BW $2,952; 4C $3,352; SAU $24; PCI $24. **Remarks:** Accepts advertising. **Circ:** Mon.-Fri. ♦**12205**, Wed. ♦**27190**, Sun. ♦**25175**.

19392 ■ KAPE-AM - 1550
901 S Kingshighway St.
Cape Girardeau, MO 63703
Phone: (573)339-7000
Fax: (573)651-4100
Free: 800-467-1007
Email: news@withersradio.net
Format: News; Sports; Talk. **Networks:** Unistar; CNN Radio; NBC; Talknet. **Owner:** Withers Broadcasting Companies, 1822 N Court St., Marion, IL 62959, Ph: (303)242-5000. **Founded:** 1940. **Operating Hours:** Continuous; 100% network. **ADI:** Paducah,KY-Cape Girardeau,MO-Marion,IL. **Key Personnel:** Rick Lambert, Gen. Mgr. **Wattage:** 5,000. **Ad Rates:** Noncommercial. **URL:** http://www.kaperadio1550.com.

19393 ■ KBSI-TV - 23
806 Enterprise
Cape Girardeau, MO 63703
Phone: (573)334-1223
Format: Commercial TV. **Networks:** Fox. **Owner:** Sinclair Broadcast Group Inc., 10706 Beaver Dam Rd., Hunt Valley, MD 21030, Ph: (410)568-1500, Fax: (410)568-1533. **Founded:** 1983. **Operating Hours:** Continuous. **ADI:** Paducah,KY-Cape Girardeau,MO-Marion,IL. **Wattage:** 705,000 ERP H. **Ad Rates:** Combined advertising rates available with WDKA-TV and WB49. **URL:** http://www.kbsi23.com.

19394 ■ KCGQ-FM - 99.3
324 Broadway
Cape Girardeau, MO 63701
Phone: (573)335-8291
Fax: (573)335-4806
Free: 888-839-9936
Format: Album-Oriented Rock (AOR). **Networks:** Independent. **Owner:** Mississippi River Radio, at above address. **Founded:** 1978. **Formerly:** KJAQ-FM. **Operating Hours:** Continuous; 100% local. **ADI:** Paducah,KY-Cape Girardeau,MO-Marion,IL. **Key Personnel:** Stephen K., Dir. of Programs; Scott Richards, Gen. Mgr.; Erik Sean, Sports Dir. **Wattage:** 6,000. **Ad Rates:** Advertising accepted; rates available upon request. **URL:** http://www.realrock993.com.

19395 ■ KEZS-FM - 102.9
324 Broadway
Cape Girardeau, MO 63701
Phone: (573)651-3003
Fax: (573)335-4806
Free: 800-455-5103
Format: Country. **Networks:** ABC. **Owner:** Mississippi River Radio, at above address. **Founded:** 1969. **Operating Hours:** Continuous. **ADI:** Paducah,KY-Cape Girardeau,MO-Marion,IL. **Key Personnel:** Erik Sean, Sports Dir. **Wattage:** 100,000 ERP. **Ad Rates:** Noncommercial. **URL:** http://www.k103fm.com.

19396 ■ KFVS-TV - 12
310 Broadway
Cape Girardeau, MO 63701
Phone: (573)335-1212
Fax: (573)335-6303
Free: 800-455-5387
Email: news@kfvs12.com
Format: Commercial TV. **Networks:** CBS. **Owner:** Raycom Media Inc., 201 Monroe St., RSA Twr., 20th Fl., Montgomery, AL 36104-3731, Ph: (334)206-1400. **Founded:** 1954. **Operating Hours:** Continuous. **ADI:** Paducah,KY-Cape Girardeau,MO-Marion,IL. **Key Personnel:** Dave Thomason, VP, Gen. Mgr., dthomason@kfvs12.com; Scott Thomas, Dir. of Sales, scott.thomas@kfvs12.com; Arnold Killian, Engg. Mgr.; Kathy Cowan, Prog. Dir., kcowan@kfvs12.com; Paul Keener, Dir. of Mktg., pkeener@kfvs12.com. **Wattage:** 6,800 ERP. **Ad Rates:** Advertising accepted; rates available upon request. **Mailing address:** PO Box 100, Cape Girardeau, MO 63701. **URL:** http://www.kfvs12.com.

19397 ■ KGIR-AM - 1220
324 Broadway
Cape Girardeau, MO 63701
Phone: (573)334-1220
Owner: Mississippi River Radio, at above address. **Founded:** 1966. **ADI:** Paducah,KY-Cape Girardeau,MO-Marion,IL. **Key Personnel:** Scott Richards, Gen. Mgr.; Erik Sean, Sports Dir., Prog. Dir. **Wattage:** 250 Day; 137 Night K. **Ad Rates:** Noncommercial. **URL:** http://www.semoespn.com.

19398 ■ KGKS-FM - 93.9
324 Broadway
Cape Girardeau, MO 63701
Phone: (573)335-8291
Format: Adult Contemporary. **Operating Hours:** Continuous Monday - Friday. **Wattage:** 16,500 ERP. **URL:** http://www.939river.com.

19399 ■ KGMO-FM - 100.7
901 S Kings Hwy.
Cape Girardeau, MO 63703
Phone: (573)339-1007
Free: 800-467-1007
Format: Classic Rock. **Key Personnel:** Rick Lambert, Gen. Mgr., rlambert@withersradio.net; Kevin Casey, Prog. Dir. **Ad Rates:** Noncommercial. **URL:** http://www.kgmo.com.

19400 ■ KHIS-FM - 96.5
PO Box 358
Cape Girardeau, MO 63702
Phone: (805)327-0631
Fax: (805)327-0633
Founded: 1963. **ADI:** Bakersfield, CA. **Wattage:** 50,000. **Ad Rates:** $5-10 for 30 seconds; $8-12 for 60 seconds.

19401 ■ KJXX-AM - 1170
901 S Kings Hwy.
Cape Girardeau, MO 63703
Phone: (573)339-7000
Format: Contemporary Christian; Adult Contemporary. **Owner:** Withers Broadcasting of Missouri, 1822 N Court St., Marion, IL 62959. **Key Personnel:** Rick Lambert, Gen. Mgr., rlambert@withersradio.net; Steve Thomas, Operations Mgr., sthomas@withersradio.net; Josh Hanlon, Sales Mgr., jhanlon@withersradio.net. **URL:** http://www.1170kjxx.com.

19402 ■ KLSC-FM - 92.9
324 Broadway St.
Cape Girardeau, MO 63701
Phone: (573)335-8291
Fax: (573)335-4806
Free: 877-342-5929
Format: Oldies. **Owner:** Mississippi River Radio, at above address. **Key Personnel:** Nicole Arnzen, Promotions Mgr.; Scott Richards, Gen. Mgr.; Mike Renick, Dir. of Programs. **URL:** http://www.klscfm.com.

19403 ■ KMAL-FM - 92.9
324 Broadway
Cape Girardeau, MO 63701
Phone: (757)437-9800
Email: kmal@sheltonbbs.com
Format: Adult Contemporary; News; Sports; Sports. **Networks:** AP. **Owner:** BBC Inc., PO Box 1996, Malden, MO 63863. **Founded:** 1979. **Operating Hours:** Continuous 5% network; 95% local. **Key Personnel:** Dave Green, Gen. Mgr.; Chuck Sutton, News Dir.; Denise Evans, Dir. of Traffic; Sherry Barnes, Sales Mgr.; Steve Conner, Music Dir. **Wattage:** 25,000. **Ad Rates:** $8 for 15 seconds; $10 for 30 seconds; $12 for 60 seconds. **URL:** http://www.semoespn.com.

19404 ■ KRCU-FM - 90.9
1 University Plz.
Cape Girardeau, MO 63701
Phone: (573)651-5070
Free: 888-651-5070
Email: comments@krcu.org
Format: Public Radio; Full Service. **Networks:** National Public Radio (NPR); Public Radio International (PRI). **Owner:** Southeast Missouri State University, 1 University Plz., Cape Girardeau, MO 63701, Ph: (573)651-2000. **Founded:** 1975. **Operating Hours:** Continuous. **ADI:** Paducah,KY-Cape Girardeau,MO-Marion,IL. **Key Personnel:** Jeanette Lawson, Mgr., jlawson@semo.edu; Dan Woods, Gen. Mgr., djwoods@semo.edu; Allen Lane, Chief Engineer, aelane@semo.edu; Jason Brown, Dir. of Operations, jbrown@semo.edu. **Wattage:** 6,500. **Ad Rates:** Noncommercial. **URL:** http://www.krcu.org.

19405 ■ KREZ-FM - 104.7
901 S Kings Hwy.
Cape Girardeau, MO 63703
Phone: (573)339-7000
Fax: (573)651-4100
Format: Soft Rock. **Owner:** Withers Broadcasting Co., 19 S Kingshighway, Cape Girardeau, MO 63703, Ph: (573)339-7000, Fax: (573)339-1550. **Key Personnel:** Rick Lambert, Gen. Mgr.; Steve Thomas, Dir. of Programs. **Wattage:** 7,700. **Ad Rates:** Advertising accepted; rates available upon request; Accepts classified advertising. **URL:** http://www.1047krez.com.

19406 ■ KRHW-AM - 1520
901 S Kingshighway St.
Cape Girardeau, MO 63703
Phone: (573)339-7000
Fax: (573)339-1550
Format: Gospel. **Networks:** CNN Radio. **Owner:** Withers Broadcasting Co., Missouri, 1822 N Court St., Marion, IL 62959. **Founded:** 1966. **Operating Hours:** Continuous. **Key Personnel:** Rick Lambert, Gen. Mgr., rlambert@withersradio.net; Steve Thomas, Operations Mgr., sthomas@withersradio.net. **Wattage:** 5,000. **Ad Rates:** $10-18 for 60 seconds.

19407 ■ KSEF-FM - 88.9
1 University Plz., MS 0300
Cape Girardeau, MO 63701
Phone: (573)651-5070
Free: 888-651-5070
Email: comments@krcu.org
Format: Public Radio. **Owner:** Southeast Missouri State University, 1 University Plz., Cape Girardeau, MO 63701, Ph: (573)651-2000. **Key Personnel:** Dan Woods, Gen. Mgr., djwoods@semo.edu; Jason Brown, Dir. of Operations, jbrown@semo.edu; Allen Lane, Chief Engineer, aelane@semo.edu. **URL:** http://www.semo.edu/sepr.

19408 ■ KSIM-AM - 1400
324 Broadway
Cape Girardeau, MO 63701
Phone: (573)335-8291
Fax: (573)335-4806
Free: 800-825-5960
Format: News; Talk. **Networks:** ABC. **Founded:** 1948. **Operating Hours:** Continuous. **ADI:** Paducah,KY-Cape Girardeau,MO-Marion,IL. **Local Programs:** *Strength for Living*, Sunday 8:30 a.m. - 9:00 a.m. **Wattage:** 1,000. **Ad Rates:** Noncommercial. **URL:** http://www.1400ksim.com.

19409 ■ KZIM-AM - 960
324 Broadway
Cape Girardeau, MO 63701
Format: News; Sports; Agricultural; Talk. **Networks:** ABC. **Founded:** 1925. **Operating Hours:** Continuous. **ADI:** Paducah,KY-Cape Girardeau,MO-Marion,IL. **Wattage:** 5,000 Day; 500 Night. **Ad Rates:** Noncommercial. **URL:** http://www.960kzim.com.

19410 ■ WDKA-TV - 49
806 Enterprise St.
Cape Girardeau, MO 63703
Phone: (573)334-1223
Fax: (573)334-1208
Format: Commercial TV. **Networks:** Fox; CBS; NBC; Univision; ABC. **Operating Hours:** Continuous. **ADI:** Paducah,KY-Cape Girardeau,MO-Marion,IL. **Wattage:** 1,000,000 ERP H. **Ad Rates:** Accepts Advertising. **URL:** http://www.mywdka.com.

19411 ■ WKIB-FM - 96.5
901 S Kings Hwy.
Cape Girardeau, MO 63703
Phone: (573)339-7000
Fax: (256)428-1461

Format: Top 40; Contemporary Hit Radio (CHR). **Owner:** Withers Broadcasting Companies, 1822 N Court St., Marion, IL 62959, Ph: (303)242-5000. **Operating Hours:** Continuous. **Key Personnel:** Rick Lambert, Gen. Mgr., rlambert@withersradio.net; Steve Thomas, Dir. of Programs, sthomas@withersradio.net. **Wattage:** 50,000. **URL:** http://www.mix965.net.

19412 ■ WPTN-AM - 780
PO Box 1628
Cape Girardeau, MO 63702-1628
Phone: (573)651-0707
Fax: (931)528-8400
Format: Oldies; News; Talk. **Networks:** ABC. **Founded:** 1962. **Operating Hours:** Sunrise-sunset. **ADI:** Nashville (Cookeville), TN. **Key Personnel:** Bruce Welker, Gen. Mgr. **Wattage:** 1,000. **Ad Rates:** $6-10 per unit.

CARROLLTON

SC MO. Carroll Co. 30 mi. S. of Chillicothe. Dairy products.

19413 ■ KAOL-AM - 1430
102 N Mason
Carrollton, MO 64633
Phone: (660)542-0404
Fax: (660)542-0420
Free: 800-214-2173
Format: Country; Agricultural. **Networks:** NBC. **Owner:** Kanza Inc., 102 N Mason, Carrollton, MO 64633, Ph: (660)542-0404. **Founded:** 1959. **Operating Hours:** Continuous. **ADI:** Kansas City, MO (Lawrence, KS). **Wattage:** 500 Day; 027 Night. **Ad Rates:** $40-140 for 30 seconds; $50-165 for 60 seconds. **URL:** http://www.kmzu.com.

19414 ■ KMZU-FM - 100.7
102 N Mason
Carrollton, MO 64633
Phone: (660)542-0404
Fax: (660)542-0420
Free: 800-214-2173
Email: news@kmzu.com
Format: Agricultural; Country. **Simulcasts:** KAOL-AM. **Networks:** NBC; ABC. **Owner:** Kanza Inc., 102 N Mason, Carrollton, MO 64633, Ph: (660)542-0404. **Founded:** 1962. **Formerly:** KAOL-FM. **Operating Hours:** Continuous. **Local Programs:** *Fifth Quarter Show*, Friday 9:30 p.m. **Wattage:** 99,000 ERP. **Ad Rates:** Advertising accepted; rates available upon request. Combined advertising rates available with KAOL. **URL:** http://www.kmzu.com.

19415 ■ KRLI-FM - 103.9
102 N Mason St.
Carrollton, MO 64633
Phone: (660)542-0404
Format: Adult Contemporary. **Operating Hours:** Continuous. **Wattage:** 12,000. **Ad Rates:** $6-10 for 30 seconds; $8-12 for 60 seconds. **URL:** http://www.krlicountry.com.

CARTHAGE

SW MO. Jasper Co. 150 mi. S. of Kansas City. Manufactures men's textiles, bed springs, wire drawings, upholstry springs, fluorescent light fixtures, concrete, woodworking, tanks, powder explosives, auto accessories, sheet metal. Cheese processing and packaging, flour, feeds. Marble quarries; oak timber. Farming, wheat, cattle and other livestock.

19416 ■ The Carthage Press: Southwest Missouri's Oldest Daily Newspaper
The Carthage Press
800 W Central Ave.
Carthage, MO 64836
Phone: (417)358-2191
General newspaper. **Freq:** Daily. **Print Method:** Offset. **Cols./Page:** 6. **Col. Width:** 25 nonpareils. **Col. Depth:** 301 agate lines. **Key Personnel:** John Hacker, Managing Editor. **Subscription Rates:** $39 Individuals /year (e-edition). **URL:** http://www.carthagepress.com. **Mailing address:** PO Box 678, Carthage, MO 64836. **Ad Rates:** SAU $7.10. **Remarks:** Advertising accepted; rates available upon request. **Circ:** (Not Reported).

19417 ■ KDMO-AM - 1490
221 E 4th St.
Carthage, MO 64836
Phone: (417)358-6054
Fax: (417)358-1278
Format: Sports. **Owner:** Ronald L. Petersen, PO Box 426, Carthage, MO 64836. **Founded:** 1947. **Key Personnel:** Ronald L. Petersen, Gen. Mgr., President. **Wattage:** 1,000 KW. **Ad Rates:** $6.75-9 for 30 seconds; $8-10.50 for 60 seconds. **URL:** http://www.1490kdmo.com.

19418 ■ KMXL-FM - 95.1
221 E 4th St.
Carthage, MO 64836
Phone: (417)358-4881
Fax: (417)358-1278
Free: 800-249-5895
Format: Adult Contemporary. **Networks:** NBC. **Owner:** Carthage Broadcasting Company, at above address, Carthage, MO. **Formerly:** KRGK-FM. **Operating Hours:** Continuous. **Wattage:** 50,000. **Ad Rates:** $12-17 for 30 seconds; $14-19 for 60 seconds. **URL:** http://www.951mikefm.com.

CARUTHERSVILLE

SE MO. Pemiscot Co. On Mississippi River, 30 mi. N. of Blytheville, AR. Cotton ginning and compressing; metal fabricating; engine rebuilding; shoe, boat, veneer, and box factories; bottling, sand, and gravel works. Cottonwood, gum, oak timber. Agriculture. Cotton, milo, corn, rice, wheat.

19419 ■ The Democrat Argus
Pemi-scott Publishers
403 Ward Ave.
Caruthersville, MO 63830
Phone: (573)333-4336
Fax: (573)333-2307
Newspaper with a Democratic orientation. **Founded:** 1908. **Freq:** Weekly (Thurs.). **Print Method:** Offset. **Cols./Page:** 6. **Col. Width:** 24 nonpareils. **Col. Depth:** 294 agate lines. **Key Personnel:** Lisa Bryant, Manager, Advertising; Herb Smith, Editor; David Tennyson, Publisher. **URL:** http://www.democratargus.com/. **Formerly:** The Missouri Herald; The Friday Democrat Herald. **Mailing address:** PO Box 1059, Caruthersville, MO 63830. **Ad Rates:** GLR $.10; 4C $200. **Remarks:** Accepts advertising. **Circ:** Paid ‡2500.

CENTRALIA

C. MO. Boone Co. 25 mi. SE of Moberly. Panhandle Eastern Pipeline. Manufactures anchors, diversified plastics, electric switches, hot line tools, barrel staves, pole line hardware. Grain farms. Corn, soybeans, cattle.

19420 ■ KMFC-FM - 92.1
1249 E Hwy. 22
Centralia, MO 65240
Phone: (573)682-5525
Fax: (573)682-2744
Free: 800-769-5632
Format: Religious. **Networks:** Independent; USA Radio. **Owner:** The Clair Group, 1249 E Highway 22, Centralia, MO 65240, Ph: (573)682-5525. **Founded:** 1986. **Operating Hours:** Continuous. **Key Personnel:** Gerri Dollens, Contact, gerri@kmfc.com. **Wattage:** 3,900. **Ad Rates:** Noncommercial.

CHARLESTON

SE MO. Mississippi Co. 35 mi. S. of Cape Girardeau. Tourism. Historical site. Manufactures shoes, rubber auto hoses, modular homes. Pork, grain sorghum, soybeans, corn, potatoes, fruit. Cotton.

19421 ■ KCHR-AM
205 E Commercial
Charleston, MO 63834-0432
Phone: (573)683-6044
Format: Eclectic. **Networks:** Mutual Broadcasting System. **Founded:** 1953. **Wattage:** 1,000 Day; 079 Night. **Ad Rates:** $8.50 for 30 seconds; $10.50 for 60 seconds.

CHESTERFIELD

St. Louis Co.

19422 ■ American Christmas Tree Journal
National Christmas Tree Association
16020 Swingley Ridge Rd., Ste. 300
Chesterfield, MO 63017
Phone: (636)449-5070
Fax: (636)449-5051
Publisher's E-mail: info@realchristmastrees.org
Christmas tree industry trade magazine covering growing, harvesting, and retailing. **Freq:** 3/year winter/spring, summer and fall. **Print Method:** Offset. **Trim Size:** 8 1/2 x 11. **Cols./Page:** 3. **Col. Width:** 28 nonpareils. **Col. Depth:** 140 agate lines. **ISSN:** 0569-3845 (print). **Subscription Rates:** $58 U.S., Canada, and Mexico nonmembers; $94 Other countries; $37 Members /year. **URL:** http://www.christmastree.org/dnn/MemberCenter/Publications.aspx; http://www.realchristmastrees.org/dnn/MemberCenter/Publications.aspx. **Ad Rates:** BW $657; 4C $987; PCI $30. **Remarks:** Advertising accepted; rates available upon request. **Circ:** ‡1500.

19423 ■ Employment Marketplace
Employment Marketplace
PO Box 4334
Chesterfield, MO 63006
Phone: (314)560-2627
Fax: (636)458-4955
Publisher's E-mail: info@eminfo.com
Trade magazine for recruiting professionals. **Freq:** Monthly. **Subscription Rates:** $109 Individuals 1 year. **URL:** http://www.eminfo.com. **Remarks:** Accepts advertising. **Circ:** Controlled 18000.

19424 ■ The German Postal Specialist
Germany Philatelic Society
PO Box 6547
Chesterfield, MO 63006-6547
Publisher's E-mail: info@germanyphilatelicsocietyusa.org
Magazine devoted to German philately. **Freq:** Monthly. **Print Method:** Offset. **Trim Size:** 6 x 9. **Cols./Page:** 2. **Col. Width:** 40 nonpareils. **Col. Depth:** 133 agate lines. **ISSN:** 0116--8823 (print). **Alt. Formats:** CD-ROM. **URL:** http://www.germanyphilatelicsocietyusa.org. **Ad Rates:** BW $87.50. **Remarks:** Accepts advertising. **Circ:** Paid ‡1650, Controlled ‡30.

19425 ■ IN
Consortium for Graduate Study in Management
229 Chesterfield Business Pky.
Chesterfield, MO 63005
Phone: (636)681-5460
Fax: (636)681-5499
Publisher's E-mail: recruiting@cgsm.org
Freq: Monthly. **Remarks:** Accepts advertising. **Circ:** (Not Reported).

19426 ■ WNOO-AM - 1260
PO Box 4062
Chesterfield, MO 63006
Phone: (615)894-1023
Fax: (615)875-3066
Format: Blues; Gospel. **Networks:** American Urban Radio. **Founded:** 1951. **Formerly:** WMFS-AM. **Operating Hours:** Sunrise-sunset. **Key Personnel:** Frank St. James, Dir. of Programs; Diane Crane, Traffic Mgr; Fred Webb, Contact; Cherri McIntyre, Contact. **Wattage:** 5,000. **Ad Rates:** Advertising accepted; rates available upon request.

CHILLICOTHE

NW MO. Livingston Co. 74 mi. E. of Saint Joseph. Recreation area. Manufactures gloves, industrial air cleaners, machinery, automotive parts, bricks, tile, concrete. Meat packing. Dairy products. Livestock. Agriculture. Corn, wheat, soybeans, oats.

19427 ■ Chillicothe Constitution-Tribune
GateHouse Media Inc.
818 Washington St.
Chillicothe, MO 64601
Phone: (660)646-2411
Fax: (660)646-2028
General newspaper. **Freq:** Daily (eve.). **Print Method:** Offset. **Cols./Page:** 6. **Col. Width:** 25 nonpareils. **Col. Depth:** 301 agate lines. **Key Personnel:** Catherine Stortz Ripley, Editor; Rod Dixon, Publisher; Jenetta Cranmer, Manager, Circulation. **Subscription Rates:** $7.99 Individuals digital (monthly); $2.02 Individuals digital and print (weekly). **URL:** http://www.chillicothenews.com. **Ad Rates:** SAU $5. **Remarks:** Accepts advertising. **Circ:** (Not Reported).

Circulation: ⋆ = AAM; △ or • = BPA; ♦ = CAC; ❑ = VAC; ⊕ = PO Statement; ‡ = Publisher's Report; Boldface figures = sworn; Light figures = estimated.

19428 ■ KCHI-AM - 1010
421 Washington St.
Chillicothe, MO 64601
Phone: (660)646-4173
Fax: (660)646-2868
Email: kchi@greenhills.net
Format: Oldies; News; Information. **Simulcasts:** KCHI-FM. **Networks:** ABC. **Owner:** Leatherman Communications Inc., 421 Washington St , Chillicothe, MO 64601-2521, Ph: (660)646-4173. **Founded:** 1950. **Operating Hours:** 6 a.m.-midnight; 15% network, 85% local. **Key Personnel:** Dan Leatherman, Gen. Mgr., Owner; Tom Tingerthal, News Dir.; Randy Dean, Sports Dir. **Wattage**: 250. **Ad Rates:** Noncommercial. **URL:** http://www.kchi.com.

19429 ■ KCHI-FM - 98.5
421 Washington
Chillicothe, MO 64601
Phone: (660)646-4173
Fax: (660)646-2868
Email: kchi@greenhills.net
Format: Oldies. **Simulcasts:** KCHI-AM. **Networks:** ABC. **Owner:** Leatherman Communications Inc., 421 Washington St , Chillicothe, MO 64601-2521, Ph: (660)646-4173. **Founded:** 1976. **Operating Hours:** Continuous; 15% network, 85% local. **Key Personnel:** Dan Leatherman, Gen. Mgr., Owner; Tom Tingerthal, News Dir.; Randy Dean, Operations Mgr. **Wattage:** 4,100. **Ad Rates:** $10 for 30 seconds; $15-20 for 60 seconds. **URL:** http://www.kchi.com.

19430 ■ KULH-FM - 105.9
802 Calhoun St.
Chillicothe, MO 64601
Phone: (660)646-2255
Free: 877-639-1059
Format: Contemporary Christian. **Wattage**: 6,000. **Ad Rates:** Noncommercial. **URL:** http://www.1059thewave.com.

CLARENCE

NE MO. Shelby Co. 25 mi. NE of Moberly. Ships corn, wheat, oats and soybean. Stock, poultry, grain farms.

19431 ■ The Clarence Courier
The Clarence Courier
103 W Chestnut
Clarence, MO 63437
Fax: (660)699-2194
Publisher's E-mail: news@clarencecourier.com
Community newspaper. **Freq:** Weekly (Wed.). **Print Method:** Offset. **Cols./Page:** 5. **Col. Width:** 12 1/2 picas. **Col. Depth:** 13 inches. **Key Personnel:** Dennis W. Williams, Publisher, Owner. **USPS:** 115-230. **Subscription Rates:** $27 Individuals; $32 Out of area. **URL:** http://nemonews.net/shelby-county-news. **Ad Rates:** GLR $.20; BW $217.75; SAU $3; PCI $3.35. **Remarks:** Accepts advertising. **Circ:** (Not Reported).

CLARK

NC MO. Randolph Co. 30 mi. N. of Columbia. Residential.

19432 ■ Small Farm Today: The How-to Magazine of Alternative and Traditional Crops, Livestock and Direct Marketing and Rural Living
Missouri Farm Publishing Inc.
3903 W Ridge Trl. Rd.
Clark, MO 65243-9525
Fax: (573)687-3148
Free: 800-633-2535
Publication E-mail: smallfarm@socket.net
Magazine promoting and dealing with all aspects of small farming and rural living. **Freq:** Bimonthly. **Print Method:** Offset. **Trim Size:** 8 1/2 x 11. **Cols./Page:** 3. **Col. Width:** 14 picas. **Col. Depth:** 10 inches. **Key Personnel:** Ronald E. Macher, Publisher. **ISSN:** 1079--9729 (print). **URL:** http://www.smallfarmtoday.com. **Formerly**: Missouri Farm. **Ad Rates:** BW $915; 4C $1,270; PCI $40. **Remarks:** Accepts advertising. **Circ:** 7000.

CLAYTON

E. MO. St. Louis Co. 4 mi. W. of Saint Louis. Residential.

19433 ■ Arthuriana
International Arthurian Society - North American Branch
c/o Evelyn Meyer, Secretary/Treasurer
6637A San Bonita Ave.
Clayton, MO 63105-3121
Scholarly journal covering Arthurian Studies from beginnings to present. **Freq:** Quarterly January, April, September, December. **Trim Size:** 6 x 9. **Key Personnel:** Dorsey Armstrong, Editor; Bonnie Wheeler, Executive Editor. **ISSN:** 1078--6279 (print). **Subscription Rates:** $75 Individuals print only; $100 Other countries print only; $150 Institutions print only; $175 Institutions, other countries print only; $100 Individuals nonmembers. **URL:** http://www.arthuriana.org. **Formerly**: Quondamet Futurus; Arthurian Interpretations. **Ad Rates:** BW $125. **Remarks:** Accepts advertising. **Circ:** (Not Reported).

CLINTON

W. MO. Henry Co. 40 mi. SW of Sedalia. Tourism. Manufactures press punches, small appliances, textiles. Processes cheese; creamery. Hatcheries. Coal mines. Diversified farming. Corn, wheat, oats.

19434 ■ KDKD-AM - 1280
PO Box 448
Clinton, MO 64735
Phone: (660)885-6141
Fax: (660)885-4801
Free: 866-541-9595
Email: bob@kdkd.net
Format: Oldies. **Networks:** ABC. **Owner:** Legend Communications L.L.C., 324 Coffeen Ave., Sheridan, WY 82801, Fax: (307)672.1722. **Founded:** 1949. **Operating Hours:** Continuous; 85% network, 15% local. **Key Personnel:** David Lee, Sports Dir., News Dir., dlee@kdkd.net; Ken Dillon, Dir. of Programs, ken@kdkd.net. **Wattage**: 1,000. **Ad Rates:** Advertising accepted; rates available upon request. Combined advertising rates available with KDKD-FM. **URL:** http://www.kdkd.net.

19435 ■ KDKD-FM - 95.3
PO Box 448
Clinton, MO 64735-0448
Free: 866-541-9595
Format: Contemporary Country. **Networks:** ABC; Brownfield; Meadows Racing; Precision Racing. **Owner:** Legend Communications L.L.C., 324 Coffeen Ave., Sheridan, WY 82801, Fax: (307)672.1722. **Founded:** 1975. **Operating Hours**: Continuous; 33% network, 67% local. **Key Personnel:** Ken Dillon, Dir. of Programs, ken@kdkd.net; David Lee, Sports Dir., News Dir., dlee@kdkd.net; Bob May, Gen. Mgr., bob@kdkd.net. **Wattage**: 25,000. **Ad Rates:** $11-16 for 30 seconds; $13-18 for 60 seconds. Combined advertising rates available with KDKD-AM.

COLUMBIA

C. MO. Boone Co. 30 mi. N. of Jefferson City. Stephens College; Columbia College; University of Missouri. Manufactures air filters, visual electronic products, circuit breakers, industrial heating elements.Coal mines. Stone quarries. Farming. Corn, wheat, oats.

19436 ■ AgBioForum
AgBioForum
129 Mumford Hall
University of Missouri-Columbia
Columbia, MO 65211
Phone: (573)882-0143
Fax: (573)882-3958
Publisher's E-mail: admin@agbioforum.org
Journal publishing articles covering latest research on agricultural biotechnology and economics. **Key Personnel:** Nicholas Kalaitzandonakes, Editor; Carl E. Pray, Editor. **ISSN:** 1522-936X (print). **Subscription Rates:** Included in membership. **URL:** http://www.agbioforum.org. **Circ:** (Not Reported).

19437 ■ Archives of Insect Biochemistry and Physiology: Published in Collaboration with the Entomological Society of America
John Wiley & Sons Inc.
c/o David Stanley, Exec. Ed.
Biological Control of Insects Research Laboratory
1503 S Providence Rd.
Columbia, MO 65203
Phone: (573)875-5361
Fax: (573)875-5364
Publisher's E-mail: info@wiley.com
Research journal. **Freq:** Monthly. **Print Method:** Offset. **Trim Size:** 8 1/2 x 11 1/4. **Cols./Page:** 1. **Col. Width:** 48 nonpareils. **Col. Depth:** 133 agate lines. **Key Personnel:** David Stanley, Executive Editor; Terri Lynn Stanley, Managing Editor, phone: (573)446-8631; Xavier Belles, Board Member. **ISSN:** 0739--4462 (print); **EISSN:** 1520--6327 (electronic). **Subscription Rates:** $4324 Institutions U.S. and other countries - online only; £2208 Institutions U.K. - online only; €2791 Institutions Europe - online only; $117 Members online only. **URL:** http://onlinelibrary.wiley.com/journal/10.1002/(ISSN)1520-6327. **Ad Rates:** BW $757; 4C $1,009. **Remarks:** Accepts advertising. **Circ:** (Not Reported).

19438 ■ Calexico Chronicle
Tribune Publishing Co.
100 N Fourth St.
Columbia, MO 65201
Phone: (573)815-1680
Fax: (573)815-1698
Free: 800-333-6256
Publisher's E-mail: tburns@tribunepublishing.com
Newspaper. **Freq:** Weekly (Thurs.). **Print Method:** Offset. **Cols./Page:** 6. **Col. Width:** 9.5 picas. **Col. Depth:** 182 agate lines. **Key Personnel:** Steve Larson, Publisher; Rosa Nogueda, Office Manager; Brenda Torres, Business Manager, Manager, Advertising. **URL:** http://tribwekchron.com. **Mailing address:** PO Box 798 , Columbia, MO 65205. **Ad Rates:** BW $468. **Remarks:** Accepts advertising. **Circ:** (Not Reported).

19439 ■ Classical and Modern Literature
University of Missouri Department of Classical Studies
405 Strickland Hall
Columbia, MO 65211-4150
Phone: (573)882-0679
Fax: (573)884-6540
Literary journal. **Freq:** Quarterly. **Key Personnel:** Michael Barnes, Editor, phone: (573)882-7864. **ISSN:** 0197--2227 (print). **Subscription Rates:** $26 Individuals; $6 Single issue; $29 Institutions. **URL:** http://classics.missouri.edu/cml/index.html. **Remarks:** Advertising not accepted. **Circ:** 500.

19440 ■ Columbia Daily Tribune
Tribune Publishing Co.
100 N Fourth St.
Columbia, MO 65201
Phone: (573)815-1680
Fax: (573)815-1698
Free: 800-333-6256
Publication E-mail: editor@columbiatribune.com
General newspaper. **Freq:** Daily (eve.), Sat. and Sun. (morn.). **Print Method:** Offset. **Trim Size:** 10 7/8 x 13. **Cols./Page:** 6. **Col. Width:** 12 picas. **Col. Depth:** 21 inches. **Key Personnel:** Dirk Dunkle, Manager, Circulation, phone: (573)815-1608. **Subscription Rates:** $3.75 Individuals print online (weekly, home delivery for a year); $3.50 Individuals print and online (weekly, home delivery monthly auto pay); $3 Individuals online only (monthly auto pay). **URL:** http://www.columbiatribune.com. **Mailing address:** PO Box 798 , Columbia, MO 65205. **Ad Rates:** 4C $307.50; PCI $8.50. **Remarks:** Accepts classified advertising. **Circ:** 16200, 44500, 1700, 20000.

19441 ■ Columbia Missourian
Missourian Publishing Association Inc.
221 S 8th St.
Columbia, MO 65201
Phone: (573)882-5720
Publisher's E-mail: news@columbiamissourian.com
General newspaper. **Freq:** 5/week except the day after Christmas. **Print Method:** Offset. **Trim Size:** 13 x 21 1/2. **Cols./Page:** 6. **Col. Width:** 25 nonpareils. **Col. Depth:** 301 agate lines. **Key Personnel:** Daniel S. Potter, General Manager; Tom Warhover, Executive Editor, phone: (573)882-5734. **Subscription Rates:** $5.95 online (30 days); $7.95 print and online (30 days). **URL:** http://columbiamissourian.com. **Mailing address:** PO Box 917, Columbia, MO 65205. **Remarks:** Accepts advertising. **Circ:** ‡5986.

19442 ■ Holtville Tribune
Tribune Publishing Co.
100 N Fourth St.
Columbia, MO 65201
Phone: (573)815-1680
Fax: (573)815-1698
Free: 800-333-6256
Publisher's E-mail: tburns@tribunepublishing.com
Community newspaper (tabloid). **Freq:** Weekly (Thurs.). **Print Method:** Offset. **Trim Size:** 11 1/2 x 14. **Cols./**

Page: 6. **Col. Width:** 9.5 picas. **Col. Depth:** 13 inches. **Key Personnel:** Steve Larson, Publisher; Brenda Torres, Business Manager, Manager, Advertising. **ISSN:** 0164--9140 (print). **Alt. Formats:** PDF. **URL:** http://tribwekchron.com. **Mailing address:** PO Box 798 , Columbia, MO 65205. **Ad Rates:** BW $468. **Remarks:** Accepts advertising. **Circ:** (Not Reported).

19443 ■ Imperial Valley Weekly
Tribune Publishing Co.
100 N Fourth St.
Columbia, MO 65201
Phone: (573)815-1680
Fax: (573)815-1698
Free: 800-333-6256
Publisher's E-mail: tburns@tribunepublishing.com
Community newspaper (tabloid) serving Imperial County, CA. **Freq:** Weekly (Thurs.). **Print Method:** Offset. **Trim Size:** 11 1/2 x 14. **Cols./Page:** 6. **Col. Width:** 9.5 picas. **Col. Depth:** 13 inches. **Key Personnel:** Brenda Torres, Business Manager; Steve Larson, Editor; Rosa Nogueda, Office Manager; Sonia Torres, Contact. **ISSN:** 0016--9140 (print). **URL:** http://www.imperialvalleynews.com. **Mailing address:** PO Box 798 , Columbia, MO 65205. **Ad Rates:** BW $468. **Remarks:** Accepts advertising. **Circ:** (Not Reported).

19444 ■ IRE Journal
Investigative Reporters and Editors, Inc.
Missouri School of Journalism
141 Neff Annex
Columbia, MO 65211
Phone: (573)882-2042
Publisher's E-mail: info@ire.org
Freq: Quarterly. **ISSN:** 0164- 7016 (print). **Subscription Rates:** Members free; $70 Nonmembers. **URL:** http://www.ire.org/publications/ire-journal/. **Remarks:** Accepts advertising. **Circ:** 5000.

19445 ■ Journal of Aging Studies
Elsevier Inc.
c/o J.F. Gubrium, Editor
Department of Sociology
University of Missouri
Columbia, MO 65211
Publisher's E-mail: healthpermissions@elsevier.com
Journal of aging studies. **Freq:** Quarterly. **Print Method:** Offset. **Trim Size:** 6 7/8 x 10. **Cols./Page:** 1. **Key Personnel:** M. Ardelt, Board Member; S.M. Albert, Board Member; J.F. Gubrium, Editor. **ISSN:** 0890--4065 (print). **Subscription Rates:** $213 Individuals print; $370.40 Institutions online; $741 Institutions print. **URL:** http://www.journals.elsevier.com/journal-of-aging-studies. **Circ:** (Not Reported).

19446 ■ Journal of Dispute Resolution
University of Missouri at Columbia
230 Jesse Hall
Columbia, MO 65211
Phone: (573)882-2121
Fax: (573)884-4671
Publisher's E-mail: question@moreview.com
Law journal emphasizing alternative dispute resolution processes. **Freq:** Semiannual. **Key Personnel:** Rachel M. Hirshberg, Editor-in-Chief. **ISSN:** 1052-2859 (print). **Subscription Rates:** $35 Individuals. **URL:** http://law.missouri.edu/journal. **Formerly:** Missouri Journal of Dispute Resolution. **Circ:** Paid 450, Non-paid 14.

19447 ■ Journal of Dispute Resolution
University of Missouri, Columbia School of Law
203 Hulston Hall
Columbia, MO 65211
Phone: (573)882-6042
Fax: (573)882-9625
Free: 888-MUL-aw4U
Publisher's E-mail: MULawAdmissions@missouri.edu
Journal containing articles on a wide variety of topics in the rapidly developing field of dispute resolution. **Freq:** Semiannual January and June. **Key Personnel:** James R. Montgomery, Editor-in-Chief. **Subscription Rates:** $35 Individuals. **URL:** http://law.missouri.edu/journal. **Circ:** (Not Reported).

19448 ■ Journal of Environmental and Sustainability Law
University of Missouri, Columbia School of Law
203 Hulston Hall
Columbia, MO 65211
Phone: (573)882-6042
Fax: (573)882-9625
Free: 888-MUL-aw4U
Publisher's E-mail: MULawAdmissions@missouri.edu
Journal focusing on national environmental issues, while adding an emphasis on law and policy relevant to a sustainable world. **Freq:** Semiannual. **Key Personnel:** Scott Martin, Editor-in-Chief. **Subscription Rates:** $14 Individuals. **URL:** http://law.missouri.edu/jesl. **Circ:** (Not Reported).

19449 ■ Journal of Multinational Financial Management
The Haworth Press Inc.
c/o S.P. Ferris Ed.
University of Missouri
Department of Finance
Columbia, MO 65211
Publisher's E-mail: getinfo@haworthpress.com
Trade journal dealing with foreign risk management and business strategies. **Freq:** Quarterly 5/year. **Trim Size:** 6 x 8 3/8. **Key Personnel:** P.G. Szilagyi, Editor. **ISSN:** 1042--444X (print). **Subscription Rates:** $80 Individuals print only; $231.47 Institutions e-journal; $694 Institutions print only. **URL:** http://www.haworthpress.com; http://www.journals.elsevier.com/journal-of-multinational-financial-management. **Ad Rates:** BW $300. **Remarks:** Accepts advertising. **Circ:** 144.

19450 ■ Journal of Research in Music Education
National Association for Music Education
c/o Wendy L. Sims, Editor
University of Missouri - Columbia
140 Fine Arts Bldg.
Columbia, MO 65211-6120
Phone: (573)882-3238
Publisher's E-mail: memberservices@nafme2.org
Scholarly publication. **Freq:** Quarterly current issue: July 2016. **Print Method:** Offset. **Trim Size:** 6 x 9. **Cols./Page:** 1. **Col. Width:** 4 1/2 inches. **Key Personnel:** Wendy L. Sims, Editor; Ella Wilcox, Contact. **ISSN:** 0022--4294 (print); **EISSN:** 1945--0095 (electronic). **Subscription Rates:** $251 Institutions e-access; $273 Institutions print only; $279 Institutions print and online; $307 Institutions current volume print & all online content; $983 Institutions e-access (Content through 1998); $75 Institutions single issue. **URL:** http://jrm.sagepub.com; http://www.nafme.org/my-classroom/journals-magazines. **Remarks:** Advertising not accepted. **Circ:** (Not Reported).

19451 ■ Missouri Historical Review
State Historical Society of Missouri
1020 Lowry St.
Columbia, MO 65201
Phone: (573)882-1187
Fax: (573)884-4950
Free: 800-747-6366
Publication E-mail: shsofmo@umsystem.edu
Journal presenting scholarly articles on the history of Missouri. **Freq:** Quarterly. **Print Method:** Offset. **Trim Size:** 7 1/2 x 10 1/2. **Cols./Page:** 1. **Col. Width:** 29 picas. **Col. Depth:** 54 picas. **Key Personnel:** Dr. Gary R. Kremer, Executive Editor. **ISSN:** 0026--6582 (print). **URL:** http://shs.umsystem.edu/publications/mhr/index.shtml. **Remarks:** Advertising not accepted. **Circ:** ‡5700.

19452 ■ Missouri Law Review
University of Missouri, Columbia School of Law
203 Hulston Hall
Columbia, MO 65211
Phone: (573)882-6042
Fax: (573)882-9625
Free: 888-MUL-aw4U
Publication E-mail: umclawrev@missouri.edu
Law journal. **Freq:** Quarterly Winter, Spring, Summer, and Fall. **Key Personnel:** Bradley Craigmyle, Editor-in-Chief. **ISSN:** 0026--6604 (print). **URL:** http://law.missouri.edu/lawreview. **Remarks:** Advertising not accepted. **Circ:** (Not Reported).

19453 ■ Missouri Press News
Missouri Press Association
802 Locust St.
Columbia, MO 65201-4888
Phone: (573)449-4167
Fax: (573)874-5894
Free: 800-568-1927
Journalistic professional magazine. **Freq:** Monthly. **Print Method:** Offset. **Trim Size:** 8 1/2 x 11. **Cols./Page:** 3. **Col. Width:** 2 1/4 inches. **Col. Depth:** 10 inches. **Key Personnel:** Matthew Barba, Editor. **ISSN:** 0026--6671 (print). **Subscription Rates:** $15 Individuals. **URL:** http://www.mopress.com/magazine.php. **Ad Rates:** BW $180; PCI $6. **Remarks:** Accepts advertising. **Circ:** (Not Reported).

19454 ■ The Missouri Realtor
Missouri REALTORS
2601 Bernadette Pl.
Columbia, MO 65203
Phone: (573)445-8400
Fax: (573)445-7865
Free: 800-403-0101
Publication E-mail: missourirealtors@morealtor.com
News articles on real estate. **Freq:** Quarterly. **Print Method:** Offset. **Trim Size:** 8 1/2 x 11. **Cols./Page:** 3. **Col. Width:** 2 1/4 inches. **Col. Depth:** 8 1/2 inches. **Key Personnel:** John Sebree, Chief Executive Officer. **USPS:** 355-640. **URL:** http://www.missourirealtor.org/home. **Ad Rates:** 4C $50047. **Remarks:** Color advertising not accepted. **Circ:** ‡18000.

19455 ■ The Missouri Review: Discovering the Best in Fiction, Essays and Poetry
University of Missouri at Columbia
230 Jesse Hall
Columbia, MO 65211
Phone: (573)882-2121
Fax: (573)884-4671
Publication E-mail: question@moreview.com
Literary magazine publishing fiction, essays, poetry, interviews, reviews, and special features of literary interest. **Freq:** Triennial. **Key Personnel:** Evelyn Somers, Associate Editor; Michael Nye, Managing Editor; Speer Morgan, Editor. **ISSN:** 0191-1961 (print). **Subscription Rates:** $30 Individuals; $50 Two years; $24 Individuals online. **URL:** http://www.missourireview.com. **Ad Rates:** BW $500. **Remarks:** Accepts advertising. **Circ:** Paid 6800, Non-paid 200.

19456 ■ Missouri State Genealogical Association Journal
Missouri State Genealogical Association
PO Box 833
Columbia, MO 65205-0833
Publication E-mail: journal@mosga.org
Journal covering genealogy in Missouri. **Freq:** Quarterly. **Print Method:** Offset. **Key Personnel:** Carrie V. Tuck, Editor. **ISSN:** 0747--5667 (print). **Subscription Rates:** Included in membership. **URL:** http://mosga.org/cpage.php?pt=16. **Remarks:** Advertising not accepted. **Circ:** Paid 705.

19457 ■ MIZZOU Magazine
Mizzou Alumni Association
123 Reynolds Alumni Ctr.
Columbia, MO 65211
Phone: (573)882-6611
Fax: (573)882-5145
Free: 800-372-6822
Publication E-mail: mizzou@missouri.edu
University alumni magazine. **Freq:** Quarterly. **Print Method:** Offset. **Trim Size:** 8 3/8 x 10 7/8. **Cols./Page:** 3. **Col. Width:** 14 picas. **Col. Depth:** 55.6 picas. **Key Personnel:** Scott Reeter, Director, Advertising, phone: (573)882-7358; Dale Smith, Associate Editor, phone: (573)882-5916. **URL:** http://mizzoumag.missouri.edu. **Formerly:** Missouri Alumnus. **Ad Rates:** BW $4265; 4C $4,815. **Remarks:** Accepts advertising. **Circ:** ‡201688.

19458 ■ Molecular Plant-Microbe Interactions
American Phytopathological Society
c/o Gary Stacey, Ed.-in-Ch.
University of Missouri
Columbia, MO 65211
Phone: (573)884-4752
Fax: (573)884-9676
Publisher's E-mail: aps@scisoc.org
Peer-reviewed journal covering research on the molecular aspects of plant-microbe interactions. **Freq:** Monthly. **Print Method:** Sheet-fed offset. **Trim Size:** 8 1/2 x 11. **Cols./Page:** 2. **Col. Width:** 3 1/2 inches. **Col. Depth:** 10 inches. **Key Personnel:** John P. Carr, Senior Editor; Jane Glazebrook, Editor-in-Chief, phone: (612)624-5194, fax: (612)624-5194. **ISSN:** 0894-0282 (print). **Subscription Rates:** $994 U.S. institution & libraries; print; $1087 Elsewhere institution & libraries; print; $956

Circulation: ★ = AAM; △ or • = BPA; ♦ = CAC; ❑ = VAC; ⊕ = PO Statement; ‡ = Publisher's Report; Boldface figures = sworn; Light figures = estimated.

Institutions; $1045 Elsewhere libraries and institutions. **URL:** http://apsjournals.apsnet.org/loi/mpmi; http://www.apsnet.org/publications/mpmi/Pages/default.aspx. **Ad Rates:** BW $950; 4C $1,750. **Remarks:** Accepts advertising. **Circ:** 1000.

19459 ■ Morgan County Press
Vernon Publishing Inc.
409 Vandiver Drive, Building 3, Suite 100
Columbia, MO 65205
Free: 800-474-1111
Publication E-mail: press@vernonpublishing.com
Community newspaper. **Freq:** Weekly (Wed.). **Print Method:** Offset. **Cols./Page:** 6. **Col. Width:** 2 1/16 inches. **Col. Depth:** 21 inches. **Key Personnel:** Dane Vernon, Publisher, phone: (573)378-5441; Connie Viebrock, Editor, phone: (573)377-4616. **USPS:** 362-840. **Subscription Rates:** $31 Individuals print or online; $38 Elsewhere in Missouri; $43 Out of state. **URL:** http://www.vernonpublishing.com/Press/Main/. **Ad Rates:** BW $85; 4C $160, full color; PCI $13. **Remarks:** Accepts advertising. **Circ:** ‡1,500.

19460 ■ Muse: Annual of the museum of art and archaeology
University of Missouri at Columbia
230 Jesse Hall
Columbia, MO 65211
Phone: (573)882-2121
Fax: (573)884-4671
Publisher's E-mail: question@moreview.com
Peer-reviewed scholarly journal covering University of Missouri, Museum of Art and Archaeology collections research. **Freq:** Annual. **Print Method:** offset lithography. **Trim Size:** 7 x 9. **Cols./Page:** 1. **Col. Width:** 4 1/2 inches. **Col. Depth:** 6 3/4 inches. **ISSN:** 0077-2194 (print). **URL:** http://maa.missouri.edu/research/pubs.html. **Remarks:** Advertising not accepted. **Circ:** Controlled 543.

19461 ■ Oral Tradition
Slavica Publishers
Center for Studies in Oral Tradition
243 Walter Williams Hall
Columbia, MO 65211
Phone: (573)882-9720
Fax: (573)884-0291
Publication E-mail: journal@oraltradition.org
Magazine focusing on the study of oral traditions across the world. **Founded:** 1992. **Freq:** Semiannual. **Key Personnel:** Mark Amodio, Board Member. **ISSN:** 0883-5365 (print); **EISSN:** 1542-4308 (electronic). **URL:** http://journal.oraltradition.org. **Circ:** (Not Reported).

19462 ■ School and Community
Missouri State Teachers Association
407 S Sixth St.
Columbia, MO 65205
Phone: (573)442-3127
Free: 800-392-0532
Publisher's E-mail: msta@spsmail.org
Education magazine. **Freq:** Quarterly. **Print Method:** Offset. **Trim Size:** 8 3/8 x 10 7/8. **Cols./Page:** 3. **Col. Width:** 26 nonpareils. **Col. Depth:** 140 agate lines. **Key Personnel:** Sarah Kohnle, Managing Editor. **ISSN:** 0036-6447 (print). **Subscription Rates:** $15 Individuals /yr; $3.75 Single issue. **URL:** http://www.msta.org/member-benefits/publications/school-community. **Mailing address:** PO Box 458, Columbia, MO 65205. **Remarks:** Accepts advertising. **Circ:** ‡43000.

19463 ■ Seminars in Oncology Nursing
Mosby Inc.
University of Missouri
Columbia, MO 65211
Journal publishing materials to disseminate knowledge in the complex field of cancer nursing. **Freq:** Quarterly. **Trim Size:** 8 1/4 X 11. **Key Personnel:** Connie H. Yarbro, Editor; Patricia C. Buchsel, Board Member. **ISSN:** 0749--2081 (print). **Subscription Rates:** $131 U.S. online & print; $258 Canada online & print; $250 Other countries online & print; $111 Individuals online only; $131 Students online & print; $258 Students, Canada online & print; $250 Students, other countries online & print. **URL:** http://www.nursingoncology.com; http://www.journals.elsevier.com/seminars-in-oncology-nursing. **Ad Rates:** BW $1,260; 4C $1,510. **Remarks:** Accepts advertising. **Circ:** (Not Reported).

19464 ■ Stephens Life
Stephens College
1200 E Broadway
Columbia, MO 65215
Phone: (573)442-2211
Publisher's E-mail: info@stephens.edu
Collegiate magazine. **Freq:** Biweekly. **Print Method:** Offset. **Cols./Page:** 5. **Col. Width:** 25 nonpareils. **Col. Depth:** 208 agate lines. **Key Personnel:** Kathy Vogt, Business Manager. **USPS:** 521-280. **URL:** http://blog.stephens.edu/stephenslife. **Ad Rates:** BW $7; PCI $4. **Remarks:** Accepts advertising. **Circ:** Paid 250, Non-paid 2000.

19465 ■ Synthesis and Reactivity in Inorganic, Metal-Organic, and Nano-Metal Chemistry
Taylor and Francis Group PLC
c/o Kattesh V. Katti, Exec. Ed.
Dept. of Radiology & Physics
Rm. 106, Alton Bldg., 301 Business Loop 70 W
University of Missouri-Columbia
Columbia, MO 65212
Publisher's E-mail: enquiries@taylorandfrancis.com
Journal covering synthesis & reactivity in inorganic, bio-inorganic and metal-organic & Nano-metal chemistry. **Freq:** Monthly. **Print Method:** Offset. **Trim Size:** 8 1/4 x 10 7/8. **Key Personnel:** Kattesh V. Katti, Executive Editor; P.K. Das, Associate Editor; J.J. Vittal, Associate Editor; Dr. Kattesh V. Katti, Executive Editor; S. Liu, Board Member; M. Yamashita, Associate Editor; R. Alberto, Board Member; W. Linert, Associate Editor; Maria-Isabelle Baraton, Board Member. **ISSN:** 1553--3174 (print); **EISSN:** 1553--3182 (electronic). **Subscription Rates:** $957 Individuals print only; $3758 Institutions online only; $4295 Institutions print and online. **URL:** http://www.tandfonline.com/toc/lsrt20/current#.Vd7NNyWqqko. **Formerly:** Synthesis & Reactivity in Inorganic & Metal--Organic Chemistry. **Ad Rates:** BW $890; 4C $1,935. **Remarks:** Accepts advertising. **Circ:** 300.

19466 ■ Today's Farmer
MFA Inc.
201 Ray Young Dr.
Columbia, MO 65201
Phone: (417)345-2121
Agricultural magazine. **Freq:** 9/year. **Print Method:** Offset. **Trim Size:** 8 1/8 x 10 7/8. **Cols./Page:** 3. **Col. Width:** 27 nonpareils. **Col. Depth:** 111 agate lines. **Subscription Rates:** $15 Individuals. **URL:** http://todaysfarmermagazine.com. **Remarks:** Accepts advertising. **Circ:** (Not Reported).

19467 ■ Veterinary and Comparative Oncology
Veterinary Cancer Society
PO Box 30855
Columbia, MO 65205
Phone: (573)823-8497
Fax: (573)445-0353
Publisher's E-mail: vetcancersociety@yahoo.com
Peer-reviewed journal focusing on the clinical and scientific studies for all veterinary oncologists concerned with aetiology, diagnosis and clinical course of cancer in domestic animals and its prevention. **Freq:** Quarterly. **Key Personnel:** Prof. David Argyle, Editor; Paolo Buracco, Board Member; Mathew Breen, Board Member; Tim Scase, Board Member; Prof. David M. Vail, Board Member; Douglas Thamm, Editor; Marlene Hauck, Board Member. **ISSN:** 1476--5810 (print); **EISSN:** 1476--5829 (electronic). **Subscription Rates:** $944 Institutions print and online; £513 Institutions print and online; €651 Institutions print and online; $1109 Institutions, other countries print and online; $218 Individuals print and online; £120 Individuals print and online - UK and Europe (non-euro zone); €179 Individuals print and online; £131 Other countries print and online. **URL:** http://onlinelibrary.wiley.com/journal/10.1111/(ISSN)1476-5829. **Remarks:** Accepts advertising. **Circ:** (Not Reported).

19468 ■ KBIA-FM - 91.3
409 Jesse Hall
Columbia, MO 65211
Phone: (573)882-3431
Fax: (573)882-2636
Free: 800-292-9136
Email: kbia@kbia.org
Format: Public Radio; News; Classical. **Networks:** National Public Radio (NPR); Public Radio International (PRI). **Owner:** University of Missouri Board of Curators, 316 University Hall, Columbia, MO 65211, Ph: (573)882-2388, Fax: (573)882-0010. **Founded:** 1972. **Operating Hours:** Continuous; 40% network; 60% local. **ADI:** Columbia-Jefferson City, MO. **Key Personnel:** Mike Dunn, Gen. Mgr., dunnm@missouri.edu; Sally Jameson, Bus. Mgr., jamesonsm@missouri.edu; Janet Saidi, News Dir., saidij@missouri.edu. **Wattage:** 100,000. **Ad Rates:** Noncommercial; underwriting available. $20-45 for 15 seconds. **URL:** http://www.kbia.org.

19469 ■ KBXR-FM - 102.3
503 Old Hwy. 63 N
Columbia, MO 65201
Phone: (573)874-1023
Fax: (573)449-7770
Email: 1023bxr@gmail.com
Format: Alternative/New Music/Progressive; Adult Album Alternative. **Owner:** Cumulus Media Inc., 3280 Peachtree Rd. NW, Ste. 2300, Atlanta, GA 30305-2455, Ph: (404)949-0700, Fax: (404)949-0740. **Founded:** 1994. **Operating Hours:** Continuous. **Wattage:** 3,500. **Ad Rates:** Noncommercial. Combined advertising rates available with KFRU, KPLA, KOQL, KJCQ, KJMO, and KLIK. **URL:** http://www.bxr.com.

19470 ■ KCLR-FM - 99.3
3215 Lemone Industrial Blvd.
Columbia, MO 65201
Phone: (573)875-1099
Free: 800-449-5257
Format: Country. **Wattage:** 33,000. **Ad Rates:** Noncommercial. **URL:** http://www.clear99.com.

19471 ■ KCMQ-FM - 96.7
3215 Lemone Industrial Blvd., Ste. 200
Columbia, MO 65201
Phone: (573)875-1967
Free: 800-455-1967
Format: Classic Rock. **Networks:** Fox; ABC. **ADI:** Columbia-Jefferson City, MO. **Wattage:** 99,100 ERP. **Ad Rates:** Advertising accepted; rates available upon request. **URL:** http://kcmq.com.

19472 ■ KCOU-FM - 88.1
2500 MU Student Ctr.
Columbia, MO 65211
Phone: (573)882-7820
Format: Alternative/New Music/Progressive; Folk; Jazz; Top 40. **Owner:** Missouri Students Association, 2500 Student Ctr. University of Missouri, Columbia, MO 65201. **Founded:** 1961. **Formerly:** KCCS-FM; KEJJ. **Operating Hours:** Continuous. **ADI:** Columbia-Jefferson City, MO. **Wattage:** 430. **Ad Rates:** Noncommercial. **URL:** http://kcou.fm.

19473 ■ KFMZ-FM - 98.3
1101 E Walnut
Columbia, MO 65205
Phone: (573)874-3000
Fax: (573)443-1460
Email: kfmz@socketis.net
Format: Alternative/New Music/Progressive; Alternative/New Music/Progressive. **Networks:** ABC. **Owner:** Contemporary Broadcasting, Inc, at above address. **Founded:** 1971. **Operating Hours:** Continuous; 1% network, 99% local. **Key Personnel:** Robert Cox, Gen. Mgr.; Matt Brown, Dir. of Programs. **Wattage:** 23,500. **Ad Rates:** $18 for 30 seconds; $28 for 60 seconds. **Mailing address:** PO Box 1268, Columbia, MO 65205. **URL:** http://www.983thebuzz.com.

19474 ■ KFRU-AM - 1400
503 Old Hwy. 63 N
Columbia, MO 65201
Phone: (573)449-4141
Fax: (573)449-7770
Free: 866-229-5378
Format: News; Sports; Talk. **Networks:** ABC; Fox; NBC. **Founded:** 1925. **Operating Hours:** Continuous. **ADI:** Columbia-Jefferson City, MO. **Wattage:** 1,000. **Ad Rates:** Advertising accepted; rates available upon request. $20 for 30 seconds; $120 for 60 seconds. KPLA, KJMO, KLIK-AM, KBXR, KBBM, KOOL. **URL:** http://www.kfru.com.

19475 ■ KMIZ-TV - 17
501 Business Loop 70 E
Columbia, MO 65201
Phone: (573)449-0917
Fax: (573)875-7078

Format: News; Sports. **Networks:** ABC; Fox. **Owner:** JW Broadcasting L.L.C., at above address. **Founded:** 1971. **Formerly**: KCBJ-TV. **Operating Hours**: Continuous; 60% network, 40% local. **ADI**: Columbia-Jefferson City, MO. **Wattage**: 1,580,000. **Ad Rates:** Noncommercial. **URL:** http://www.abc17news.com.

19476 ■ KMOU-TV - 8
5550 Hwy. 63 S
Columbia, MO 65201
Phone: (573)884-6397
Fax: (573)884-8888
Founded: Dec. 21, 1953. **Key Personnel:** Sarah Hill, Contact; Sarah Hill, Contact. **Ad Rates:** Advertising accepted; rates available upon request. **URL:** http://www.komu.com/ssi/ba8c4979-c0a8-2f11-01ab-a6aaf4c5cdb8.page.

19477 ■ KOMU-TV - 8
5550 Hwy. 63 S
Columbia, MO 65201
Phone: (573)882-8888
Fax: (573)884-8888
Email: news@komu.com
Format: Commercial TV. **Networks:** NBC. **Owner:** University of Missouri-Columbia University Affairs, 407 Reynolds Alumni Ctr., Columbia, MO 65211, Ph: (573)882-4523, Fax: (573)884-4666. **Founded:** 1953. **Operating Hours:** Continuous. **ADI**: Columbia-Jefferson City, MO. **Key Personnel:** Tom Dugan, Contact; Matt Garrett, Contact, garrettm@missouri.edu; Stacey Woelfel, Contact, woelfels@missouri.edu; Chris Gervino, Contact. **Wattage**: 316,000. **Ad Rates:** Advertising accepted; rates available upon request. **URL:** http://www.komu.com.

19478 ■ KOPN-FM - 89.5
915 E Broadway
Columbia, MO 65201-4857
Phone: (573)874-1139
Fax: (573)499-1662
Free: 800-895-5676
Email: mail@kopn.org
Format: News; Talk; Eclectic. **Networks:** National Public Radio (NPR); Pacifica. **Owner:** New Wave Corp., 915 E Broadway, Columbia, MO 65201, Ph: (578)874-1139. **Founded:** Mar. 03, 1973. **Operating Hours**: Continuous. **Key Personnel:** David Owens, Gen. Mgr. **Local Programs**: *Evening Edition*, Tuesday 6:00 p.m. - 7:00 p.m.; *Rootin Tootin Radio*, Sunday 12:00 p.m. - 3:00 p.m.; *Anything Goes*, Tuesday 3:00 p.m. - 5:00 p.m. **Wattage**: 36,000. **Ad Rates:** Noncommercial; underwriting available. **URL:** http://www.kopn.org.

19479 ■ KOQL-FM - 106.1
503 Old Hwy. 63 N
Columbia, MO 65201
Phone: (573)449-1061
Free: 800-786-1061
Format: Top 40. **Owner:** Cumulus Media Inc., 3280 Peachtree Rd. NW, Ste. 2300, Atlanta, GA 30305-2455, Ph: (404)949-0700, Fax: (404)949-0740. **Founded:** 1993. **Operating Hours**: Continuous. **Wattage**: 69,000 ERP. **Ad Rates:** $20 for 30 seconds; $80 for 60 seconds. KJMO, KPLA, KFRU, KBXR, KLIK-AM, KLIK-FM. **URL:** http://www.q1061.com.

19480 ■ KPLA-FM - 101.5
503 Old Hwy. 63 N
Columbia, MO 65201
Phone: (573)442-1015
Free: 800-480-1015
Format: Adult Contemporary. **Founded:** 1983. **Operating Hours:** Continuous. **ADI**: Columbia-Jefferson City, MO. **Wattage**: 41,000 ERP. **Ad Rates:** Advertising accepted; rates available upon request. $35 for 30 seconds; $125 for 60 seconds. KBXR, KFRU, KOQL, KLIK-AM, KBSM, KJMO. **URL:** http://www.kpla.com.

19481 ■ KQFX-TV - 17
501 Business Loop 70 E
Columbia, MO 65201
Phone: (573)449-0917
Fax: (573)875-7078
Format: Commercial TV. **Networks:** Fox. **Owner:** JW Broadcasting L.L.C., at above address. **Operating Hours**: Continuous; 50% network, 40% local. **Key Personnel:** Curtis Varns, News Dir.; David Stockard, Sales Mgr.; Eric Jones, Chief Engineer; Jeff Page, Gen. Sales Mgr. **Wattage**: 150,000. **Ad Rates:** Noncommercial. **URL:** http://www.abc17news.com.

19482 ■ KSSZ-FM - 93.9
3215 Lemone Industrial Blvd., Ste. 200
Columbia, MO 65201
Phone: (573)875-1099
Free: 800-529-5572
Format: Talk. **Wattage**: 25,000. **Ad Rates:** Noncommercial. **URL:** http://theeagle939.com.

19483 ■ KTGR-AM - 1580
3215 Lemone Industrial Blvd., Ste. 200
Columbia, MO 65201
Phone: (573)875-1099
Format: Sports. **Networks:** ESPN Radio. **Owner:** Zimmer Radio of Mid-Missouri, Inc. **Founded:** 1954. **Operating Hours:** Continuous. **ADI**: Columbia-Jefferson City, MO. **Wattage**: 214 Day; 008 Night. **Ad Rates:** Advertising accepted; rates available upon request. **URL:** http://www.ktgr.com.

19484 ■ KTXY-FM - 106.9
3215 Lemone Industrial Blvd., Ste. 200
Columbia, MO 65201
Phone: (573)875-1099
Format: Top 40. **Ad Rates:** Noncommercial. **URL:** http://y107.com.

19485 ■ KWWC-FM - 90.5
1200 E Broadway
Columbia, MO 65215
Phone: (573)876-7207
Fax: (573)876-7237
Free: 800-876-7207
Email: inquiry@stephens.edu
Format: Jazz. **Owner:** Stephens College, 1200 E Broadway, Columbia, MO 65215, Ph: (573)442-2211. **Founded:** 1965. **Operating Hours**: Continuous. **ADI**: Columbia-Jefferson City, MO. **Key Personnel:** Jonna Wiseman, Gen. Mgr., jwiseman@stephens.edu. **Wattage**: 1,250. **Ad Rates:** Advertising accepted; rates available upon request. **URL:** http://www.stephens.edu.

19486 ■ Nash-FM - 100.1
503 Old Hwy. 63 N
Columbia, MO 65202
Format: Classic Rock. **Formerly**: KBBM-FM.

19487 ■ NEWS TALK 1400, KFRU - 1400
503 Old Highway 63 N
Columbia, MO 65201
Phone: (573)449-4141
Fax: (573)449-7770
Free: 866-229-5378
Format: News; Talk. **Owner:** Cumulus Broadcasting Inc., 3280 Peachtree Rd. NW, Ste. 2300, Atlanta, GA 30305-2447, Ph: (404)949-0700, Fax: (404)949-0740. **URL:** http://www.kfru.com.

CONCORDIA

W. MO. Lafayette Co. 50 mi. E. of Kansas City. Manufactures animal feeds, recreational vehicles, paper boxes, textiles. Beef, dairy, grain, hog farms. Wheat, corn, beans, grain sorghum.

19488 ■ The Concordian
The Concordian Inc.
714 S Main
Concordia, MO 64020-0999
Phone: (660)463-7522
Fax: (660)463-7942
Publisher's E-mail: concordian@galaxycable.net
Community newspaper. **Freq:** Weekly (Wed.). **Print Method:** Offset. **Trim Size:** 7 x 14 1/2. **Cols./Page:** 6. **Col. Width:** 12 picas. **Col. Depth:** 21 inches. **Key Personnel:** Jacques Gallant, Editor-in-Chief; Kamila Hinkson, Managing Editor. **USPS:** 128-060. **Subscription Rates:** $29 Individuals /year; $33 Individuals /year (Lafayette County, Emma, Sweet Springs, Blackburn, Knob Noster, Whiteman Air Force Base, and Warrensburg); $39 Out of area /year; $47 Out of state /year; $22 Individuals online. **URL:** http://www.theconcordianonline.com. **Mailing address:** PO Box 999, Concordia, MO 64020-0999. **Ad Rates:** GLR $.36; BW $630; 4C $780; PCI $5. **Remarks:** Accepts advertising. **Circ:** Paid ‡7000.

CREVE COEUR

19489 ■ KJSL-AM - 630
10845 Olive Blvd., Ste. 160
Creve Coeur, MO 63141
Phone: (314)878-3600
Fax: (314)656-3608
Email: events@crawfordbroadcasting.com
Format: Contemporary Christian. **Owner:** Crawford Broadcasting Co., 2821 S Parker Rd., Ste. 1205, Denver, CO 80014, Ph: (303)433-5500, Fax: (303)433-1555. **Ad Rates:** Advertising accepted; rates available upon request. **URL:** http://www.crawfordbroadcasting.com.

19490 ■ KSTL-AM - 690
10845 Olive Blvd., Ste. 160
Creve Coeur, MO 63141
Phone: (314)969-6900
Fax: (314)656-3608
Format: Talk; Contemporary Christian. **Networks:** Independent. **Owner:** Crawford Broadcasting Co., 2821 S Parker Rd., Ste. 1205, Denver, CO 80014, Ph: (303)433-5500, Fax: (303)433-1555. **Founded:** 1948. **Operating Hours**: Sunrise-sunset; 100% local. **ADI**: St. Louis, MO (Mt. Vernon, IL). **Key Personnel:** Deborah Holmes, Station Mgr., dholmes@crawfordbroadcasting.com. **Wattage**: 1,000. **Ad Rates:** $11.20 for 30 seconds; $14 for 60 seconds. **URL:** http://www.crawfordbroadcasting.com.

19491 ■ WIL-AM - 1430
6500 W Main St., Ste. 315
Belleville, IL 62223
Format: Country. **Owner:** Bonneville International Corp., 55 North 300 West, Salt Lake City, UT 84101-3502, Ph: (801)575-7500. **Operating Hours**: Continuous. **ADI**: St. Louis, MO (Mt. Vernon, IL). **Key Personnel:** Chris Redgrave, Gen. Mgr., VP. **Ad Rates:** Advertising accepted; rates available upon request.

DES PERES

19492 ■ KHZR-FM - 99.1
13358 Manchester Rd., Ste. 100
Des Peres, MO 63131
Phone: (314)969-4569
Fax: (314)835-9739
Free: 866-969-4569
Email: helpdesk@joyfmonline.org
Format: Contemporary Christian. **Key Personnel:** Jeremy Louis, Dept. Mgr.; Sandi Brown, Div. Dir., sandi@joyfmonline.org; Kim Underwood, Contact, kim@joyfmonline.org. **URL:** http://www.joyfmonline.org.

19493 ■ KLJY-FM - 99.1
13358 Manchester Rd., Ste. 100
Des Peres, MO 63131
Fax: (314)835-9739
Format: Contemporary Christian. **Owner:** Gateway Creative Broadcasting Inc. **Wattage**: 100,000. **URL:** http://www.joyfmonline.org.

DEXTER

SE MO. Stoddard Co. 45 mi. S. of Cape Girardeau. Manufactures textiles, automotive filters, exhaust systems, wood products. Cotton ginning. Food processing. Agriculture. Livestock. Diversified farming. Wheat,corn, cotton.

19494 ■ The Daily Statesman
Delta Publishing Co.
133 S Walnut
Dexter, MO 63841
Phone: (573)624-4545
Fax: (573)624-7449
General newspaper. **Freq:** Daily (eve.). **Print Method:** Offset. **Cols./Page:** 6. **Col. Width:** 24 nonpareils. **Col. Depth:** 301 agate lines. **Key Personnel:** Ron Kemp; Betty Watkins, Manager, Advertising; Noreen Hyslop, Managing Editor. **Subscription Rates:** $100 Individuals carrier or local mail delivery; $54 Individuals six months, carrier or local mail delivery; $28 Individuals three months, carrier or local mail delivery; $10 Individuals one month, carrier or local mail delivery; $107 Individuals regional mail delivery; $58 Individuals six months, regional mail delivery; $32 Individuals three months, regional mail delivery; $128 Out of area mail delivery; $70 Out of area six months, mail delivery; $38 Out of

Circulation: ★ = AAM; △ or • = BPA; ♦ = CAC; ❏ = VAC; ⊕ = PO Statement; ‡ = Publisher's Report; Boldface figures = sworn; Light figures = estimated.

area three months, mail delivery; $7 Individuals /month; online. **URL:** http://www.dailystatesman.com. **Mailing address:** PO Box 579, Dexter, MO 63841. **Remarks:** Accepts classified advertising. **Circ:** (Not Reported).

19495 ■ KDEX-AM - 1590
PO Box 249
Dexter, MO 63841-0249
Phone: (573)624-3591
Fax: (573)624-9926
Owner: Dexter Broadcasting Inc., at above address. **Founded:** 1956. **Key Personnel:** Walter F. Turner, Gen. Mgr., President. **Wattage:** 620 Daytime. **Ad Rates:** $10 for 30 seconds; $13 for 60 seconds. **URL:** http://www.kdexfm.com/.

19496 ■ KDEX-FM - 102.3
PO Box 249
Dexter, MO 63841
Phone: (573)624-3591
Format: Contemporary Country. **Simulcasts:** KDEX-AM. **Networks:** ABC. **Founded:** 1969. **Operating Hours**: Continuous. **ADI**: Paducah,KY-Cape Girardeau,MO-Marion,IL. **Key Personnel:** Tony James, Dir. of Programs, kdex1@sbcglobal.net. **Wattage:** 6,000. **Ad Rates:** $10 for 30 seconds; $13 for 60 seconds.

EAST PRAIRIE

SE MO. Mississippi Co. 10 mi. S. of Charleston. Residential.

19497 ■ The Enterprise-Courier
The Enterprise-Courier
319 Clay Morgan Rd.
East Prairie, MO 63845
Phone: (573)683-3351
Fax: (573)649-9530
Publisher's E-mail: news@enterprisecourier.com
Community newspaper. **Founded:** 1874. **Freq:** Weekly (Thurs.). **Print Method:** Offset. **Cols./Page:** 6. **Col. Width:** 2 inches. **Col. Depth:** 21 1/2 inches. **Key Personnel:** Liz Anderson, Contact. **Subscription Rates:** $26 Individuals print only; $35 Out of area print only; $31 Individuals print and online; $40 Out of country print and online; $20 Individuals online. **URL:** http://www.enterprisecourier.com/. **Ad Rates:** BW $469.56; 4C $569.56; PCI $3.64. **Remarks:** Accepts advertising. **Circ:** ‡3400.

EL DORADO SPRINGS

SW MO. Cedar Co. 18 mi. NW of Stockton. Residential.

19498 ■ El Dorado Springs Sun
El Dorado Springs Sun
125 N Main St.
El Dorado Springs, MO 64744
Phone: (417)876-3841
Fax: (417)876-3848
Community newspaper. **Freq:** Weekly (Thurs.). **Print Method:** Offset. **Cols./Page:** 6. **Col. Width:** 25 nonpareils. **Col. Depth:** 294 agate lines. **Subscription Rates:** $25 Individuals; $30 Out of area; $32 Individuals Kansas; $31 Out of state; $20 Individuals web access. **URL:** http://www.eldoradospringsmo.com. **Ad Rates:** 4C $240; SAU $3; PCI $3. **Remarks:** Accepts advertising. **Circ:** (Not Reported).

19499 ■ KESM-AM - 1580
200 Radio Ln.
El Dorado Springs, MO 64744-1957
Phone: (417)876-2741
Fax: (417)876-2743
Email: kesm@kesmradio.com
Format: Country; Adult Contemporary. **Networks:** NBC; CNN Radio. **Operating Hours**: Sunrise-sunset. **ADI**: Springfield, MO. **Wattage**: 500. **Ad Rates:** Noncommercial. **URL:** http://www.kesmradio.com.

19500 ■ KESM FM 105.5 - 105.5
200 Radio Ln.
El Dorado Springs, MO 64744
Phone: (417)876-2741
Fax: (417)876-2743
Email: kesm@kesmradio.com
Format: Country; Adult Contemporary. **Networks:** NBC; CNN Radio. **Owner:** Wildwood Communication Inc., 200 Radio Ln., El Dorado Springs, MO 64744. **Operating Hours**: 6 a.m.-midnight. **ADI**: Springfield, MO. **Wattage**: 6,000. **Ad Rates:** Noncommercial. **URL:** http://kesmradio.com.

ELDON

C. MO. Miller Co. 30 mi. SW of Jefferson City. Manufactures cheese, dairy products, textiles. Timber. Agriculture.

19501 ■ The Eldon Advertiser
Vernon Publishing Inc.
415 S Maple
Eldon, MO 65026
Phone: (573)392-5658
Publisher's E-mail: advertiser@vernonpublishing.com
Newspaper. **Founded:** 1894. **Freq:** Weekly (Thurs.). **Print Method:** Offset. **Cols./Page:** 6. **Col. Width:** 2 1/16 inches. **Col. Depth:** 21 inches. **Key Personnel:** Tim Flora, Editor; Trevor Vernon, Publisher. **USPS:** 171-200. **Subscription Rates:** $43 Individuals print + online; $49 Out of area print + online; $57 Out of state print + online; 43 Out of area web access. **URL:** http://www.vernonpublishing.com/Advertiser/Main/. **Formerly**: Advertiser. **Mailing address:** PO Box 315, Eldon, MO 65026. **Ad Rates:** BW $567; 4C $727; SAU $4.50; PCI $5.50. **Remarks:** Accepts advertising. **Circ:** ‡5000.

19502 ■ Miller County Autogram-Sentinel
Vernon Publishing Inc.
415 S Maple
Eldon, MO 65026
Phone: (573)392-5658
Publisher's E-mail: advertiser@vernonpublishing.com
Community newspaper. **Freq:** Weekly. **Print Method:** Offset. **Col. Width:** 1.83 inches. **Key Personnel:** Trevor Vernon, Publisher; Ginny Duffield, Editor. **USPS:** 349-680. **URL:** http://www.vernonpublishing.com/Autogram-Sentinel. **Mailing address:** PO Box 315, Eldon, MO 65026. **Ad Rates:** BW $410; 4C $570; SAU $3.25; PCI $3.50. **Remarks:** Accepts advertising. **Circ:** ‡1925.

ELSBERRY

NE MO. Lincoln Co. 30 mi. NNW of Saint Charles. Limestone quarries.

19503 ■ The Elsberry Democrat
Lakeway Publishers Inc.
106 N 3rd St. A
Elsberry, MO 63343
Phone: (573)898-2318
Fax: (573)898-2173
Newspaper with a Democratic orientation. **Founded:** 1900. **Freq:** Weekly (Wed.). **Print Method:** Offset. **Cols./Page:** 7. **Col. Width:** 26 nonpareils. **Col. Depth:** 301 agate lines. **Key Personnel:** Michael Short, General Manager. **Subscription Rates:** $19 Individuals 6 months; print + online; $22 Individuals /year; online. **URL:** http://www.elsberrydemocrat.com/news/index.asp. **Formerly**: Democrat. **Mailing address:** PO Box 105, Elsberry, MO 63343. **Ad Rates:** GLR $.135. **Remarks:** Accepts advertising. **Circ:** 1337.

EMINENCE

S MO. Shannon Co. 110 mi. E. of Springfield. Summer resort. Manufactures staves and lumber products. Copper mines; timber. Agriculture. Corn, wheat, hay.

19504 ■ The Current Wave
Current Wave Newspaper
PO Box 728
Eminence, MO 65466-9998
Phone: (573)226-5229
Fax: (573)226-3335
Publisher's E-mail: cwave128@gmail.com
Local newspaper. **Freq:** Weekly (Wed.). **Print Method:** Offset. **Cols./Page:** 6. **Col. Width:** 12 picas. **Col. Depth:** 21 inches. **Key Personnel:** Carol Dillon, General Manager; Roger Dillon, Editor, Publisher. **Subscription Rates:** $24 Individuals; $26 Out of area; $30 Elsewhere; $32 Out of state. **URL:** http://www.shannoncountycurrentwave.com. **Ad Rates:** SAU $4; PCI $4.25. **Remarks:** Advertising accepted; rates available upon request. **Circ:** (Not Reported).

EXCELSIOR SPRINGS

W. MO. Ray Co. 12 mi. NE of Kansas City. Health resort; mineral springs. Manufactures plastics. Diversified farming. Corn, oats, wheat.

19505 ■ The Excelsior Springs Standard
Excelsior Publishing Company Inc.
417 S Thompson Ave.
Excelsior Springs, MO 64024
Fax: (816)637-8411
General newspaper. **Freq:** Daily (eve.). **Print Method:** Offset. **Cols./Page:** 7. **Col. Width:** 10 3/5 picas. **Col. Depth:** 21 inches. **Key Personnel:** Eric Copeland, Managing Editor; Brian Rice, Editor, Publisher. **Subscription Rates:** $45 Individuals; $25 Individuals six months; $15 Individuals carrier, three months; $60 By mail; $35 By mail six months; $20 By mail three months; $45 Individuals e-edition. **URL:** http://www.excelsiorspringsstandard.com. **Ad Rates:** GLR $.42; BW $765; SAU $7.26; PCI $9.90. **Remarks:** Accepts advertising. **Circ:** (Not Reported).

19506 ■ Town & Country Leader
Excelsior Publishing Company Inc.
417 S Thompson Ave.
Excelsior Springs, MO 64024
Fax: (816)637-8411
Shopper. **Freq:** Weekly (Wed.). **Print Method:** Offset. **Cols./Page:** 6. **Col. Width:** 20 nonpareils. **Col. Depth:** 224 agate lines. **Key Personnel:** Eric Copeland, Managing Editor; Brian Rice, Editor, Publisher. **Subscription Rates:** $45 Individuals carrier; $25 Individuals six month, carrier; $60 By mail; $45 Individuals e-edition. **URL:** http://www.excelsiorspringsstandard.com. **Ad Rates:** GLR $.32; BW $427; SAU $7.26; PCI $9.90. **Remarks:** Accepts advertising. **Circ:** Paid ‡20735.

19507 ■ KNLM-FM - 91.9
201 N Industrial Park Rd.
Excelsior Springs, MO 64024
Format: Religious. **Operating Hours**: Continuous. **Wattage**: 1,750 ERP. **Ad Rates:** Noncommercial. Underwriting available. **URL:** http://www.thecatholicradionetwork.com.

19508 ■ KPIO-AM - 1570
201 N Industrial Park Rd.
Excelsior Springs, MO 64024
Format: Religious; Classical; Gospel. **Owner:** Catholic Radio Network, at above address. **Founded:** Sept. 23, 2008. **Formerly**: KSXT-AM. **Operating Hours**: Continuous. **Wattage**: 7,000 Daytime; 018 Nighttime. **URL:** http://www.thecatholicradionetwork.com.

FARMINGTON

SE MO. St. Francois Co. 9 mi. S. of Desloge. Residential. Lead deposits.

19509 ■ KPWB-FM - 104.9
900 E Karsch Blvd.
Farmington, MO 63640
Phone: (573)223-4218
Fax: (573)223-2351
Email: kpwb@showme.net
Format: Country. **Simulcasts:** KPWB-AM. **Networks:** Jones Satellite. **Founded:** 1966. **Operating Hours**: Continuous. **Ad Rates:** Noncommercial.

19510 ■ KREI-AM - 800
1401 Krei Blvd.
Farmington, MO 63640
Phone: (573)756-6476
Fax: (573)756-1110
Free: 800-842-2330
Format: Talk; News; Information; Sports. **Networks:** ABC; NBC. **Owner:** The Shepherd Group, at above address. **Founded:** 1947. **Operating Hours**: 12:00 a.m. - 9:00 p.m. Monday - Saturday; 12:00 a.m. - 10:00 p.m. Sunday. **Key Personnel:** Richard Womack, Gen. Mgr., dick_womack@yahoo.net; Becky Ward, Contact, beckyw@regionalradio.com. **Wattage**: 1,000 Daytime; 150 N. **Ad Rates:** Advertising accepted; rates available upon request. $3-15 for 30 seconds; $6-30 for 60 seconds. KTJJ-FM, KJFF-FM. **URL:** http://www.krei.com.

19511 ■ KTJJ-FM - 98.5
PO Box 461
Farmington, MO 63640
Phone: (573)756-6476
Fax: (573)756-1110
Format: Country. **Ad Rates:** Noncommercial. **URL:** http://www.j98.com.

19512 ■ KYLS-FM
900 E Karsch Blvd.
Farmington, MO 63640
Email: froggy96@socket.net

Format: Oldies. **Networks:** NBC. **Founded:** Mar. 1982. **Key Personnel:** Sheila Dockins, Contact. **Wattage:** 3,100 ERP. **Ad Rates:** Advertising accepted; rates available upon request. $14 for 30 seconds; $16 for 60 seconds.

19513 ■ WGRO-AM - 960
900 E Karch Blvd.
Farmington, MO 63640
Phone: (904)752-0960
Fax: (904)752-9861
Format: Country. **Founded:** 1958. **Operating Hours:** Continuous; 100% local. **Key Personnel:** Scott Berns, Operations Mgr.; Robert Hendrickson, Contact; Robert Hendrickson, Contact. **Wattage:** 500 day; 1,000 night. **Ad Rates:** $4.60 for 30 seconds; $9.50 for 60 seconds. **Mailing address:** PO Box 318, Lake City, FL 32055.

19514 ■ WNFK-FM - 105.5
900 E Karch Blvd.
Farmington, MO 63640
Phone: (904)584-2972
Fax: (904)584-4616
Format: Country. **Simulcasts:** WPRY-AM. **Networks:** NBC; Florida Radio. **Owner:** RAHU Broadcasting, Inc., Perry, FL. **Founded:** 1990. **Operating Hours:** 6 a.m.-midnight. **Key Personnel:** Don W. Hughes, Contact; Linda Thurman, Contact. **Wattage:** 3,000. **Ad Rates:** $3-6 for 15 seconds; $4-7 for 30 seconds; $5-9 for 60 seconds. **Mailing address:** PO Box 779, Perry, FL 32347.

FAYETTE

C. MO. Howard Co. 20 mi. NW of Columbia. Central Methodist College. Textile factory. Agriculture. Soybeans, corn, wheat, milo, cattle.

19515 ■ The Democrat-Leader
Wood Creek Media Inc.
202 E Morrison St.
Fayette, MO 65248
Phone: (660)248-2235
Fax: (660)248-1200
Publication E-mail: news@woodcreekmedia.com
Newspaper - general circulation. **Freq:** Weekly (Sat.). **Print Method:** Offset. **Trim Size:** 14 x 23. **Cols./Page:** 6. **Col. Width:** 24 nonpareils. **Col. Depth:** 294 agate lines. **Key Personnel:** Patrick Roll, Publisher; James H. Steele, Editor, Publisher. **USPS:** 153-200. **Subscription Rates:** $42 Individuals in Howard County, Rocheport, Harrisburg; $72 Two years in Howard County, Rocheport, Harrisburg; $49 Elsewhere Missouri; $54 Out of state; $40 Out of state online. **URL:** http://www.fayettenewspapers.com. **Mailing address:** PO Box 32, Fayette, MO 65248. **Ad Rates:** BW $411; SAU $3.26; PCI $3.26. **Remarks:** Accepts advertising. **Circ:** 2300.

19516 ■ The Fayette Advertiser
Wood Creek Media Inc.
202 E Morrison St.
Fayette, MO 65248
Phone: (660)248-2235
Fax: (660)248-1200
Publication E-mail: news@woodcreekmedia.com
Community newspaper. **Freq:** Weekly (Wed.). **Print Method:** Offset. **Trim Size:** 14 x 23. **Cols./Page:** 6 and 6. **Col. Width:** 24 nonpareils and 12 picas. **Col. Depth:** 294 agate lines and 21 inches. **Key Personnel:** Patrick Roll, Publisher; James H. Steele, Editor, Publisher. **USPS:** 188-300. **Subscription Rates:** $42 Individuals in Howard County, Harrisburg, Highbee or Rocheport; $72 Two years in Howard County, Harrisburg, Highbee or Rocheport; $49 Out of area; $54 Out of state; $40 Out of state online. **URL:** http://www.fayettenewspapers.com. **Mailing address:** PO Box 32, Fayette, MO 65248. **Ad Rates:** BW $411; SAU $3.26; PCI $3.26. **Remarks:** Accepts advertising. **Circ:** 2300.

FENTON

St. Louis Co.

19517 ■ Beer Cans & Brewery Collectibles Magazine
Brewery Collectibles Club of America
747 Merus Ct.
Fenton, MO 63026-2092
Phone: (636)343-6486
Publisher's E-mail: bcca@bcca.com
Freq: Bimonthly. **Subscription Rates:** Included in membership. **URL:** http://bcca.com/publications. **Circ:** (Not Reported).

19518 ■ Living Faith: Daily Catholic Devotions
Creative Communications for the Parish
1564 Fencorp Dr.
Fenton, MO 63026
Phone: (636)305-9777
Fax: (636)305-9333
Free: 800-325-9414
Publication E-mail: info@livingfaith.com
Devotional magazine. **Freq:** Quarterly. **Print Method:** Offset. **Trim Size:** 4 x 5 1/2. **Key Personnel:** Claire King, Contact; Joyce Rupp, Contact; Terri Mifek, Director; Julia DiSalvo, Assistant Editor; Kevin Perrotta, Editor; Mark Neilsen, Associate Editor; James E. Adams, Editor. **ISSN:** 0884-1330 (print). **Subscription Rates:** $12 Individuals pocket size book; $15 Canada pocket size book; $22 Two years pocket size book; $27 Canada two years (pocket size book); $32 Individuals three years (pocket size book); $14 Individuals large size book; $19 Canada large size book; $26 Individuals two years (large size book); $46 Canada two years (large size book). **URL:** http://www.livingfaith.com/. **Formerly:** Living Words. **Remarks:** Advertising not accepted. **Circ:** (Not Reported).

19519 ■ NAEDA Equipment Dealer
North American Equipment Dealers Association
1195 Smizer Mill Rd.
Fenton, MO 63026-3480
Phone: (636)349-5000
Fax: (636)349-5443
Publisher's E-mail: naeda@naeda.com
Magazine serving retailers of farm and industrial and outdoor power equipment, accessories, repair parts. **Freq:** Monthly. **Print Method:** Offset. **Trim Size:** 8 1/4 x 10 7/8. **Cols./Page:** 3. **Col. Width:** 26 nonpareils. **Col. Depth:** 140 agate lines. **Key Personnel:** Richard Lawhun, President, Chief Executive Officer. **ISSN:** 1074-5017 (print). **USPS:** 490-630. **Subscription Rates:** $45 Individuals ground delivery; $150 Other countries mail. **URL:** http://www.naeda.com/Publications/NAEDAEquipmentDealerMagazine.aspx. **Formerly:** Farm & Power Equipment Dealer. **Ad Rates:** BW $1,695; 4C $2,190; PCI $63. **Remarks:** Accepts advertising. **Circ:** (Not Reported).

FESTUS

E. MO. Jefferson Co. 30 mi. SW of Saint Louis. Manufactures tool & die, plate glass, fertilizer, cement, nuclear pellets, styrofoam, lead smelting, cans, industrial sound equipment. Agriculture.

19520 ■ KJFF-AM - 1400
PO Box 368
Festus, MO 63028
Phone: (636)937-7642
Fax: (636)937-3636
Free: 877-246-1400
Format: Talk; News. **Networks:** ABC. **Owner:** The Shepherd Group, 1800 Century Pk. E, Ste. 600, Los Angeles, CA 90067, Ph: (310)229-5969. **Founded:** 1951. **Formerly:** KJCF-AM. **Operating Hours:** Continuous; 20% network, 80% local. **ADI:** St. Louis, MO (Mt. Vernon, IL). **Key Personnel:** Kirk Mooney, Station Mgr.; Dick Womack, Gen. Mgr. **Local Programs:** *The Michael Medved Show*, Monday Tuesday Wednesday Thursday Friday 2:00 p.m. - 4:05 p.m.; *Sports Talk*, Monday Tuesday Wednesday Thursday Friday 4:15 p.m. - 5:05 p.m. **Wattage:** 1,000. **Ad Rates:** Noncommercial. Combined advertising rates available with KREI-AM, KJCF-AM. **URL:** http://www.kjff.com/.

19521 ■ KTBJ-FM - 89.3
PO Box 391
Twin Falls, ID 83303
Fax: (208)736-1958
Free: 800-357-4226
Format: Religious. **Owner:** CSN International, PO Box 391, Twin Falls, ID 83303, Ph: (208)736-1958, Fax: (208)736-1958, Free: 800-357-4226. **Founded:** Sept. 13, 2006. **Ad Rates:** Noncommercial. **URL:** http://www.csnradio.com.

FULTON

C. MO. Callaway Co. 26 mi. NE of Jefferson City. Westminster College. William Woods College. Missouri School for the Deaf. FultonState Hospital. Nuclear plant. Mineral springs. Manufactures shoes, textiles. Diversified farming. Corn, wheat, oats.

19522 ■ KFAL-AM - 900
1805 Westminister
Fulton, MO 65251
Free: 800-455-1099
Format: Contemporary Country; Sports. **Networks:** ABC; Missouri. **Owner:** Zimmer Radio Group, 3215 Lemone Industrial Blvd., Columbia, MO 65201, Fax: (573)875-2439, Free: 800-455-1099. **Founded:** 1950. **Operating Hours:** Continuous. **Local Programs:** *Jeremy in the Morning*, Monday Tuesday Wednesday Thursday Friday 11:00 a.m. - 1:00 p.m.; *Cowboy Corner*, Saturday Sunday 8:00 a.m. 9:00 a.m. **Wattage:** 1,000 Day; 135 Night. **Ad Rates:** $10-18 for 30 seconds; $13-23.40 for 60 seconds. KKCA-FM. **URL:** http://www.kfalthebig900.com.

GAINESVILLE

S. MO. Ozark Co. 65 mi. SE of Springfield. Resort. Manufactures cedar products, charcoal, plastic pipe, textiles, lumber. Farming. Cattle.

19523 ■ Ozark County Times
Ozark County Times
36 Court Sq.
Gainesville, MO 65655
Phone: (417)679-4641
Fax: (417)679-3423
Publisher's E-mail: editor@ozarkcountytimes.com
Community newspaper. **Freq:** Weekly (Wed.). **Print Method:** Offset. **Cols./Page:** 6. **Col. Width:** 24 nonpareils. **Col. Depth:** 294 agate lines. **Key Personnel:** Jessi Dreckman, Office Manager, Reporter; Sue Ann Jones, Editor; Jenny Yarger, Manager, Advertising; Norene Prososki, Publisher. **USPS:** 416-680. **Subscription Rates:** $28 Individuals Ozark and adjoining counties; $37 Out of area; $40 Out of state; $20 Individuals online. **URL:** http://www.ozarkcountytimes.com. **Mailing address:** PO Box 188, Gainesville, MO 65655. **Ad Rates:** BW $35; 4C $90; PCI $3.35. **Remarks:** Accepts advertising. **Circ:** Paid 3350.

GALLATIN

NW MO. Daviess Co. 54 mi. E. of Saint Joseph. Manufacturing. Corn, wheat, hay, soybeans.

19524 ■ North Missourian
Gallatin Publishing Co.
609B S Main St.
Gallatin, MO 64640
Phone: (660)663-2154
Fax: (660)663-2498
Publisher's E-mail: news@northwestmissouri.com
Newspaper with a Democratic orientation. **Freq:** Weekly (Wed.). **Print Method:** Offset. **Cols./Page:** 5. **Col. Width:** 11 picas. **Col. Depth:** 16 inches. **Key Personnel:** Darryl Wilkinson, Editor, Publisher. **USPS:** 213-200. **Subscription Rates:** $36 Individuals in Missouri; print + online; $45 Out of state print + online; $24 Individuals online. **URL:** http://www.gallatinnorthmissourian.com. **Mailing address:** PO Box 37, Gallatin, MO 64640. **Ad Rates:** GLR $.20; BW $378; SAU $3; PCI $6. **Remarks:** .20. **Circ:** Paid ‡1700.

GERALD

19525 ■ Fidelity Communications
727 W Springfield Ave.
Gerald, MO 63037
Phone: (573)764-2321
Fax: (573)764-5152
Free: 800-392-8070
Email: helpdesk@fidelitycommunications.com
Founded: 1940. **Key Personnel:** Mike Davis, COO; John Colbert, President. **Cities Served:** 283 community access channels. **URL:** http://www.fidelitycommunications.com.

GLASGOW

C. MO. Howard Co. On Missouri River, 20 mi. SW of Moberly. Sawmills. Manufactures asphalt, textiles. Ships

Circulation: ★ = AAM; △ or • = BPA; ♦ = CAC; ❑ = VAC; ⊕ = PO Statement; ‡ = Publisher's Report; Boldface figures = sworn; Light figures = estimated.

livestock, grain. Diversified farming.

19526 ■ The Glasgow Missourian
The Glasgow Missourian
109 Market St.
Glasgow, MO 65254-0248
Phone: (660)338-2195
Fax: (660)338-2494
Community Newspaper. **Freq:** Weekly (Thurs.). **Print Method:** Offset. **Cols./Page:** 6. **Col. Depth:** 21 1/2 inches. **Key Personnel:** Frank Mercer, Owner, Publisher; Michael Heying, Editor, General Manager. **USPS:** 219-240. **Subscription Rates:** $32.60 Individuals; $42.35 Individuals out of county; $45 Individuals out of state; $24.99 Individuals online. **Mailing address:** PO Box 248, Glasgow, MO 65254-0248. **Ad Rates:** BW $403.20; SAU $4; PCI $2.95. **Remarks:** Accepts display and classified advertising. **Circ:** ‡1600.

GRAIN VALLEY

NW MO. Jackson Co. 5 mi. E. of Independence. Residential.

19527 ■ Land Line
Owner-Operator Independent Drivers Association
1 NW OOIDA Dr.
Grain Valley, MO 64029-7903
Phone: (816)229-5791
Fax: (816)229-0518
Free: 800-444-5791
Publisher's E-mail: webmaster@ooida.com
Freq: 10/year. **ISSN:** 0279- 6503 (print). **Subscription Rates:** included in membership dues (only one subscription); $32 /year for individuals (9 issues). **Alt. Formats:** CD-ROM. **URL:** http://www.ooida.com/BenefitsServices/Services/LLM.asp. **Mailing address:** PO Box 100, Grain Valley, MO 64029-7903. **Remarks:** Accepts advertising. **Circ:** 204941.

19528 ■ Land Line: The Business Magazine for Professional Truckers
Owner-Operator Independent Drivers Association
1 NW OOIDA Dr.
Grain Valley, MO 64029-7903
Phone: (816)229-5791
Fax: (816)229-0518
Free: 800-444-5791
Publisher's E-mail: webmaster@ooida.com
Business magazine for professional truckers. **Freq:** Monthly. **Print Method:** Offset. **Trim Size:** 7 7/8 x 10 7/8. **Cols./Page:** 3. **Col. Width:** 27 nonpareils. **Col. Depth:** 136 agate lines. **Key Personnel:** Sandi Soendker, Editor-in-Chief; Jami Jones, Senior Editor; Todd Spencer, Executive Vice President. **ISSN:** 0279--6503 (print). **URL:** http://www.landlinemag.com. **Mailing address:** PO Box 100, Grain Valley, MO 64029-7903. **Ad Rates:** GLR $20; BW $7,200; 4C $9062; PCI $140. **Remarks:** Accepts advertising. **Circ:** 217000.

GRANDVIEW

19529 ■ Jackson County Advocate
Jackson County Advocate
1102 A Main St.
Grandview, MO 64030
Phone: (816)761-6200
Fax: (816)763-2979
Publisher's E-mail: newsdesk@jcadvocate.com
Legal local newspaper. **Freq:** Weekly (Thurs.). **Print Method:** Offset. **Cols./Page:** 6. **Col. Width:** 2 inches. **Col. Depth:** 21 1/2 inches. **Key Personnel:** David Weikel, Publisher. **Subscription Rates:** $30 Individuals inside Cass and Jackson counties; $35 Individuals Missouri resident (outside counties); $40 Out of state; $20 Individuals e-edition. **URL:** http://www.jcadvocate.com. **Ad Rates:** GLR $6; BW $600; PCI $7. **Remarks:** Accepts advertising. **Circ:** 6,200.

GRAVOIS MILLS

19530 ■ KCRL-FM - 90.3
30690 Gray Eagle Rd.
Gravois Mills, MO 65037
Free: 800-875-1903
Owner: Bott Radio Network, 10550 Barkley, Overland Park, KS 66212, Ph: (913)642-7770, Fax: (913)642-1319, Free: 800-345-2621. **Wattage:** 25,000. **Ad Rates:** Noncommercial; underwriting available.

GRAY SUMMIT

19531 ■ KGNV-FM - 89.9
PO Box 187
Washington, MO 63090
Phone: (636)239-0400
Fax: (636)239-4448
Free: 877-385-3787
Email: info@goodnewsvoice.org
Format: Religious. **Simulcasts:** KGNN-FM, KGNA-FM. **Networks:** Moody Broadcasting. **Owner:** Missouri River Christian Broadcasting Inc., PO Box 187, Washington, MO 63090, Ph: (636)239-0400. **Founded:** 1987. **Operating Hours:** Continuous; 90% network, 10% local. **Wattage:** 1,000. **Ad Rates:** Noncommercial. $4 for 15 seconds; $6 for 30 seconds; $8 for 60 seconds. **URL:** http://www.goodnewsvoice.org.

GREENWOOD

19532 ■ ABTA Quarterly Magazine
American Bridge Teachers' Association
PO Box 232
Greenwood, MO 64034-0232
Phone: (816)237-0519
Magazine of the American Bridge Teachers' Association. **Freq:** Quarterly. **Key Personnel:** Joyce Penn, President. **ISSN:** 0891-6462 (print). **Subscription Rates:** Included in membership. **Alt. Formats:** PDF. **URL:** http://www.abtahome.com/index.php?id=36. **Remarks:** Advertising accepted; rates available upon request. **Circ:** 1000.

HANNIBAL

NE MO. Ralls Co. On Mississippi River, 20 mi. S. of Quincy, IL. Bridge to Hull, IL. Tourism. Mark Twain Museum. Manufactures shoes, cement, steel, lumber products. Dairy, grain farms. Wheat, oats, corn.

19533 ■ U.S. Cable
647 Clinic Rd.
Hannibal, MO 63401-2404
Phone: (573)221-0060
Cities Served: Hannibal, Missouri: subscribing households 6,588; 41 channels. **URL:** http://www.uscable.com.

HARRISONVILLE

W. MO. Cass Co. 40 mi. SE of Kansas City. Manufactures wire and fiber optic cable, concrete cabinets. Stock, dairy, poultry, grain farms.

19534 ■ Cass County Shopper
Cass County Publishing Co.
206 E Mechanic St.
Harrisonville, MO 64701
Phone: (816)380-3228
Fax: (816)380-7650
Publisher's E-mail: classifieds@demo-mo.com
Shopping guide. **Freq:** Weekly (Fri.). **Print Method:** Web offset. **Cols./Page:** 6. **Col. Width:** 11 1/2 INS. **Col. Depth:** 21 INS. **Key Personnel:** Mark Maassen, Publisher; Kim Ford, Manager, Circulation. **URL:** http://www.demo-mo.com/about. **Ad Rates:** GLR $.46; BW $819; SAU $6; PCI $6.50. **Remarks:** Advertising accepted; rates available upon request. **Circ:** (Not Reported).

HIGGINSVILLE

W. MO. Lafayette Co. 40 mi. E. of Kansas City. Residential. Coal. Manufactures brick, tile, and incubators.

19535 ■ On Track!
International Machine Quilters Association, Inc.
PO Box 419
Higginsville, MO 64037-0419
Phone: (660)584-8171
Fax: (660)584-3841
Publisher's E-mail: Admin@IMQA.org
Freq: Quarterly. **Subscription Rates:** Included in membership. **URL:** http://www.imqa.org/on-track/. **Remarks:** Accepts advertising. **Circ:** (Not Reported).

HOUSTON

C. MO. Texas Co. 42 mi. N. of West Plains. Lumber.

19536 ■ Cable America Corp.
115 E Pine St.
Houston, MO 65483
Phone: (417)967-5571
Free: 800-338-1808
Email: helpdesk@cablemo.net
Founded: 1971. **Key Personnel:** William G. Jackson, President; Christopher A. Dyrek, Exec. VP; Alan C. Jackson, VP. **Cities Served:** subscribing households 50,000. **URL:** http://www.cableamerica.com.

19537 ■ KBTC-AM - 1250
PO Box 230
Houston, MO 65483
Phone: (417)967-3353
Free: 866-967-3353
Format: Country. **Networks:** Missouri. **Owner:** Media Professionals Inc., 1393 S Inca, Denver, CO 80223, Free: 888-876-2765. **Founded:** 1962. **Operating Hours:** 5 a.m.-midnight. **Wattage:** 1,000 Day; 051 Night. **Ad Rates:** $4 for 15 seconds; $6-8 for 30 seconds; $10 for 60 seconds. **Mailing address:** PO Box 230, Houston, MO 65483.

19538 ■ KUNQ-FM - 99.3
17647 Hwy. B
Houston, MO 65483
Phone: (417)967-3353
Free: 866-967-3353
Format: Country. **Networks:** ABC. **Founded:** 1960. **Operating Hours:** Continuous. **Key Personnel:** Amy Vermillion, Contact; Rocky Gilbert, Supervisor, rocky@bigcountry99.com; Alexis Neuroth, Contact, alexis@bigcountry9.com. **Local Programs:** *Tradio.* **Wattage:** 30,000. **Ad Rates:** Advertising accepted; rates available upon request. **Mailing address:** PO Box 230, Houston, MO 65483. **URL:** http://www.bigcountry99.com.

INDEPENDENCE

W. MO. Jackson Co. Adjoins Kansas City. Manufactures farm machinery, stoves and furnaces, cement, plastics, aluminum awnings, beds, mattresses, box springs. Diversified farming. Potatoes, corn, wheat, soybeans, apples, peaches.

19539 ■ Army Motors
Military Vehicle Preservation Association
3305 Blue Ridge Cutoff
Independence, MO 64055
Phone: (816)833-6872
Fax: (816)833-5115
Free: 800-365-5798
Publication E-mail: armymotors@shaw.ca
Freq: Quarterly. **Key Personnel:** Reg Hodgson, Editor. **ISSN:** 0195--5632 (print). **Subscription Rates:** $13.50 Nonmembers; Included in membership. **URL:** http://www.mvpa.org/publications/army-motors-supply-line. **Mailing address:** PO Box 520378, Independence, MO 64052. **Ad Rates:** BW $185. **Remarks:** Accepts advertising. **Circ:** Controlled 10000, 9000.

19540 ■ The Examiner
GateHouse Media Inc.
410 S Liberty St.
Independence, MO 64050
Phone: (816)254-8600
General newspaper serving Eastern Jackson County, Missouri. **Founded:** 1898. **Freq:** Daily (eve.) and Sat. (morn.). **Print Method:** Offset. **Cols./Page:** 6. **Col. Width:** 25 nonpareils. **Col. Depth:** 301 agate lines. **Key Personnel:** Stephen Wade, Publisher, phone: (816)350-6311; Karl Zinke, Managing Editor, phone: (816)350-6319; Sheila Davis, Executive Editor, phone: (816)350-6365. **Subscription Rates:** $13.25 Individuals monthly; $12 Individuals monthly - ez pay. **Alt. Formats:** Microfilm. **URL:** http://examiner.net; http://www.examiner.net/section/publications. **Remarks:** Accepts advertising. **Circ:** Mon.-Fri. ‡11460, Wed. ‡6888, Sat. ‡11890.

19541 ■ Herald Magazine
Herald House-Independence Press
1001 W Walnut St.
Independence, MO 64051-0390
Phone: (816)521-3015
Fax: (816)521-3066
Free: 800-767-8181
Publisher's E-mail: sales@heraldhouse.org
Religious family-oriented magazine for the Community of Christ. **Founded:** Jan. 1860. **Freq:** Monthly. **Print Method:** Offset. **Trim Size:** 8 1/2 x 11. **Cols./Page:** 3. **Col. Width:** 13.5 picas. **Col. Depth:** 56 picas. **ISSN:** 0036-3251 (print). **Subscription Rates:** $32 Individuals.

URL: http://www.heraldhouse.org/herald-magazine.htm. **Formerly**: Saints Herald; Herald. **Mailing address:** PO BOX 390, Independence, MO 64051- 0390. **Remarks:** Advertising not accepted. **Circ:** ‡25000.

19542 ■ Overland Journal
Oregon-California Trails Association
524 S Osage St.
Independence, MO 64051
Phone: (816)252-2276
Fax: (816)836-0989
Free: 888-811-6282
Magazine featuring scholarly articles and book reviews of the Oregon-California Trails. **Freq:** Quarterly. **Key Personnel:** Marlene Smith-Baranzini, Editor. **Subscription Rates:** Included in membership. **URL:** http://www.octa-trails.org/connect/publications. **Mailing address:** PO Box 1019, Independence, MO 64051. **Remarks:** Accepts advertising. **Circ:** (Not Reported).

19543 ■ Comcast Cable
4700 Little Blue Pkwy.
Independence, MO 64057
Key Personnel: Lawrence J. Salva, Chief Acct. Ofc., Exec. VP; Allan Singer, Sr. VP; Amy L. Banse, Sr. VP; David L. Cohen, Sr. Exec. VP; William E. Dordelman, Sr. VP; Brian L. Roberts, Chairman, CEO; Stephen B. Burke, Sr. VP; Douglas Gaston, Sr. VP, Gen. Counsel; Jeff Allen, Sr. VP; Mark Reilly, Sr. VP; Thomas Coughlin, Sr. VP; Michael Parker, Sr. VP; Marc A. Rockford, VP, Gen. Counsel; Arthur R. Block, Sr. VP, Gen. Counsel; Kevin M. Casey, Div. Pres.; William Connors, Dept. Head; Gregg M. Goldstein, VP of Corp. Dev.; Justin Smith, VP; David N. Watson, COO, Exec. VP; David A. Scott, Contact; Karen Dougherty Buchholz, Sr. VP of Admin.; Wayne Davis, Sr. VP of HR; Melissa Maxfield, Sr. VP; Ron Meyer, V. Chmn. of the Bd.; Robert S. Pick, Sr. VP; Neil Smit, President, CEO; Tim Collins, Sr. VP; John Crowley, Sr. VP; Amy Smith, Sr. VP; Leonard J. Gatti, VP. **Cities Served:** 200 channels. **URL:** http://www.comcast.com.

19544 ■ KCWJ-AM - 1030
18920 E Valley View Pkwy., Ste. C
Independence, MO 64055
Phone: (816)795-6826
Fax: (816)795-8565
Format: Contemporary Christian; Religious. **Ad Rates:** Noncommercial. **URL:** http://www.kcwj.com.

JACKSON

SE MO. Cape Girardeau Co. 10 mi. NW of Cape Girardeau. Manufactures shoes, bricks, lumber, flour, pottery, plastic parts. Hardwood timber. Diversified farming. Corn, wheat, hay. Livestock.

19545 ■ The Cash-Book Journal
The Cash-Book Journal
210 W Main St.
Jackson, MO 63755
Phone: (573)243-3515
Fax: (573)243-3517
Legal newspaper. **Freq:** Weekly (Wed.). **Print Method:** Offset. **Trim Size:** 7 x 11. **Cols./Page:** 6. **Col. Width:** 12 picas. **Col. Depth:** 301 agate lines. **Key Personnel:** David Bloom, Editor; Gina Rafferty, Publisher; Jim Salzman, Manager, Advertising. **USPS:** 272-080. **Subscription Rates:** $30 Individuals Cape Girardeau County; $32 Individuals in Perry, Scott, Bollinger County; $36 Individuals in state; $45 Out of state; $30 Individuals e-edition; $8 Individuals online; current paper. **URL:** http://www.thecash-book.com. **Feature Editors:** Elane Moonier, elane.moonier@thecash-book.com. **Mailing address:** PO Box 369, Jackson, MO 63755-0369. **Ad Rates:** GLR $.46; BW $720; 4C $960; SAU $7.50. **Remarks:** Accepts classified advertising. **Circ:** (Not Reported).

19546 ■ KUGT-AM - 1170
1301 Woodland Dr.
Jackson, MO 63755
Phone: (573)243-0649
Fax: (573)243-0640
Format: Religious; Contemporary Christian. **Networks:** Christian Broadcasting (CBN). **Owner:** W. Russell Withers, Jr., PO Box 1591, Mount Vernon, IL 62864, Ph: (618)242-3500. **Founded:** 1988. **Formerly**: KJAS-AM. **Operating Hours**: 6 a.m.-6 p.m. **Wattage:** 250. **Ad Rates:** $6.50-8 for 15 seconds; $8-9.50 for 30 seconds; $9.50-11 for 60 seconds. **URL:** http://www.jacksonmo.com/orgs/KUGT.html.

JEFFERSON CITY

C. MO. Cole Co. The State Capital. On the Missouri River, 30 mi. SE of Columbia. Lincoln University. Shoe, plate glass, and scholastic magazine distribution centers. Manufactures cosmetics, small electrical appliances, underground transformers; steel fabricating; printing and book binding. Poultry, fruit farms. Wheat, corn.

19547 ■ The Catholic Missourian
Diocese of Jefferson City
2207 W Main St.
Jefferson City, MO 65109-0914
Phone: (573)635-9127
Fax: (573)635-2286
Publisher's E-mail: info@diojeffcity.org
Official newspaper of the Diocese of Jefferson City. **Freq:** 44/yr. **Trim Size:** 10 1/2 x 14. **Cols./Page:** 5. **Col. Width:** 9.75 inches. **Col. Depth:** 12.5 inches. **Key Personnel:** Kelly Martin, Manager, Advertising; Chris Baker, Assistant Editor; Jay Nies, Editor. **USPS:** 556-940. **Subscription Rates:** $16 Individuals; $14 parish. **URL:** http://www.diojeffcity.org/index.php?option=com_k2&view=item&id=44:the-catholic-missourian&Itemid=444. **Mailing address:** PO Box 104900, Jefferson City, MO 65109-0914. **Ad Rates:** GLR $.65; PCI $10. **Remarks:** Accepts advertising. **Circ:** Paid ‡23200.

19548 ■ The Counseling Interviewer
Missouri School Counselor Association
3340 American Ave., Ste. F
Jefferson City, MO 65109
Phone: (573)635-9109
Fax: (573)635-2858
Publisher's E-mail: info@moschoolcounselor.org
Journal containing professional articles on counseling. **Freq:** Quarterly. **Subscription Rates:** included in membership dues. **Mailing address:** PO Box 684, Jefferson City, MO 65102. **Remarks:** Accepts advertising. **Circ:** (Not Reported).

19549 ■ Focus
Missouri Dental Association
3340 American Ave.
Jefferson City, MO 65109-1088
Phone: (573)634-3436
Fax: (573)635-0764
Publisher's E-mail: admin@modental.org
Dental journal. **Founded:** 1921. **Freq:** Bimonthly. **Print Method:** Offset. **Trim Size:** 10 x 15. **ISSN:** 0887-4646 (print). **Subscription Rates:** $100 Nonmembers and private business/company; $50 Institutions; $100 Other countries. **URL:** http://www.modental.org/mx/hm.asp?id=focus. **Formerly:** Missouri Dental Journal. **Ad Rates:** BW $578; 4C $867. **Remarks:** Advertising accepted; rates available upon request. **Circ:** ‡2200.

19550 ■ Jefferson City News Tribune
News Tribune Co.
210 Monroe St.
Jefferson City, MO 65101
Phone: (573)636-3131
Publisher's E-mail: nt@newstribune.com
General newspaper. **Freq:** Daily. **Key Personnel:** Rob Siebeneck, Manager, Circulation. **URL:** http://www.newstribune.com. **Remarks:** Accepts advertising. **Circ:** Sun. 22442, Mon.-Sat. 18266.

19551 ■ Journal of the Missouri Bar
Missouri Bar
326 Monroe
Jefferson City, MO 65102-0119
Phone: (573)635-4128
Fax: (573)635-2811
Publisher's E-mail: mobar@mobar.org
Freq: Bimonthly. **Print Method:** Offset. **Trim Size:** 8 1/2 x 11. **Cols./Page:** 3. **Key Personnel:** Gary Toohey, Director, Communications. **ISSN:** 0026--6485 (print). **URL:** http://www.mobar.org/publications/journal. **Mailing address:** PO Box 119, Jefferson City, MO 65102-0119. **Ad Rates:** BW $1193; BW $1,170, full page; BW $1,023, 2/3 page; BW $870, half page; BW $456, 1/3 page; BW $308, 1/6 page. **Remarks:** Accepts advertising. **Circ:** (Not Reported).

19552 ■ Missouri Architect
American Institute of Architects Missouri
PO Box 105938
Jefferson City, MO 65110
Phone: (573)635-8555
Fax: (573)636-5783
Magazine containing information regarding events in architecture and issues of interest beyond the legislative arena. **URL:** http://www.aiamo.org/architect.asp. **Remarks:** Advertising not accepted. **Circ:** (Not Reported).

19553 ■ Missouri Conservationist
Missouri Department of Conservation
2901 W Truman Blvd.
Jefferson City, MO 65109
Phone: (573)751-4115
Fax: (573)751-4467
Government magazine covering fish, forests, and wildlife. **Freq:** Monthly. **Key Personnel:** Tom Cwynar, Author, Editor; Ara Clark, Editor-in-Chief; Nichole LeClair, Managing Editor. **ISSN:** 0026--6515 (print). **Subscription Rates:** $10 Other countries; Free adult Missouri residents. **URL:** http://mdc.mo.gov/conmag. **Remarks:** Advertising not accepted. **Circ:** Combined 440000.

19554 ■ The Missouri Engineer
Missouri Society of Professional Engineers
200 E McCarty St., Ste. 200
Jefferson City, MO 65101-3113
Phone: (573)636-4861
Fax: (573)636-5475
Magazine for the engineering profession. **Freq:** every other month: February/March, April/May, June/July, August/September, October/November and December/January. **Print Method:** Offset. **Trim Size:** 10 x 13. **Cols./Page:** 4. **Col. Width:** 2 3/8 inches. **Col. Depth:** 13 inches. **Key Personnel:** Cherie L. Bishop, Editor, phone: (573)636-6949, fax: (573)636-5475; Bruce A. Wylie, Executive Director. **ISSN:** 0026--6558 (print). **URL:** http://mspe.org/news.php. **Ad Rates:** BW $780; PCI $60. **Remarks:** Accepts advertising. **Circ:** Paid 1750.

19555 ■ Missouri Medicine: State Medical Journal
Missouri State Medical Association
113 Madison St.
Jefferson City, MO 65102
Phone: (573)636-5151
Fax: (573)636-8552
Free: 800-869-6762
Peer-reviewed journal reporting on the interests of medical and public health professionals in Missouri. **Freq:** Bimonthly. **Print Method:** Offset. **Trim Size:** 8 1/4 x 11. **Cols./Page:** 3. **Col. Width:** 2 inches. **Col. Depth:** 98 agate lines. **Key Personnel:** John Hagan, III, Editor; Lizabeth Fleenor, Managing Editor. **ISSN:** 0026--6620 (print). **Subscription Rates:** $75 Individuals; $8 Members single issue; $12 Nonmembers single issue. **URL:** http://www.msma.org/mx/hm.asp?id=MissouriMedicine. **Mailing address:** PO Box 1028, Jefferson City, MO 65102. **Ad Rates:** BW $600; 4C $1,500. **Remarks:** Accepts advertising. **Circ:** ‡6500.

19556 ■ Missouri Municipal Review
Missouri Municipal League
1727 Southridge Dr.
Jefferson City, MO 65109
Phone: (573)635-9134
Fax: (573)635-9009
Publisher's E-mail: info@mocities.com
Magazine for local officials actively engaged in the procurement of products and services, policy-making, and local government administration. **Freq:** Bimonthly. **Print Method:** Offset. **Trim Size:** 8 1/2 x 11. **Cols./Page:** 3. **Col. Width:** 2 3/8 inches. **Col. Depth:** 10 inches. **Key Personnel:** Laura Holloway, Editor, phone: (573)635-9134. **ISSN:** 0026--6647 (print). **Subscription Rates:** $30 Nonmembers; Included in membership. **URL:** http://www.mocities.com/?page=ReviewMagazine. **Ad Rates:** BW $575. **Remarks:** Accepts advertising. **Circ:** (Not Reported).

19557 ■ The Missouri Nurse
Missouri Nurses Association
PO Box 105228
Jefferson City, MO 65110
Phone: (573)636-4623

Circulation: ★ = AAM; △ or • = BPA; ♦ = CAC; ❑ = VAC; ⊕ = PO Statement; ‡ = Publisher's Report; Boldface figures = sworn; Light figures = estimated.

Fax: (573)636-9576
Publisher's E-mail: info@missourinurses.org
Professional magazine covering nursing and activities of the Missouri Nurses Association. **Freq:** 2-3/yr. **Trim Size:** 8.5 x 11. **ISSN:** 0026--6655 (print). **Subscription Rates:** Free for members; $25 Nonmembers. **URL:** http://www.missourinurses.org/?page=124. **Ad Rates:** BW $500. **Remarks:** Accepts advertising. **Circ:** (Not Reported).

19558 ■ Missouri Pharmacist
Missouri Pharmacy Association
211 E Capitol Ave.
Jefferson City, MO 65101
Phone: (573)636-7522
Fax: (573)636-7485
Magazine serving licensed pharmacists (MPA members). **Freq:** Quarterly. **Print Method:** Offset. **Trim Size:** 8 1/2 x 11. **Cols./Page:** 3. **Col. Width:** 26 nonpareils. **Col. Depth:** 140 agate lines. **Subscription Rates:** Included in membership. **URL:** http://www.morx.com/publications#.Ve1S5tKqqkp. **Ad Rates:** BW $405; 4C $1,055. **Remarks:** Advertising accepted; rates available upon request. **Circ:** Paid 6500.

19559 ■ NASW Missouri Chapter Newspaper
National Association of Social Workers - Missouri Chapter
PO Box 2043
Jefferson City, MO 65102-2043
Phone: (573)635-6965
Fax: (573)635-6728
Publisher's E-mail: chapter@nasw-mo.org
Newspaper containing legislative, social issue news and employment bulletins of the National Association of Social Workers Missouri Chapter. **Freq:** Bimonthly. **Subscription Rates:** Included in membership. **URL:** http://nasw-heartland.site-ym.com/?page=MOHome. **Remarks:** Accepts advertising. **Circ:** (Not Reported).

19560 ■ Rural Missouri
Association of Missouri Electric Cooperatives
2722 E McCarty St.
Jefferson City, MO 65102
Phone: (573)635-6857
Magazine serving electric cooperative consumers. **Freq:** Monthly. **Print Method:** Offset. **Trim Size:** 10 3/8 x 14 1/2. **Cols./Page:** 4. **Col. Width:** 2 1/4 inches. **Col. Depth:** 13 1/2 inches. **Key Personnel:** Jim McCarty, Vice President, Communications; Jason Jenkins, Managing Editor; Heather Berry, Associate Editor. **ISSN:** 0164--8578 (print). **USPS:** 473-000. **Subscription Rates:** $10 Individuals; $22 Individuals three years. **URL:** http://www.ruralmissouri.org; http://www.amec.org/content/communications-printing. **Formerly:** Rural Electric Missourian. **Mailing address:** PO Box 1645, Jefferson City, MO 65102. **Ad Rates:** BW $10600. **Remarks:** Accepts advertising. **Circ:** ‡540000.

19561 ■ Show Me Missouri Farm Bureau News
Missouri Farm Bureau
701 S Country Club Dr.
Jefferson City, MO 65109
Phone: (573)893-1400
Free: 800-922-4632
Publisher's E-mail: momail@mofb.com
Agricultural magazine for members of the Missouri Farm Bureau. **Freq:** Bimonthly. **Print Method:** Letterpress. **Trim Size:** 8 3/8 X 10 3/4. **Cols./Page:** 3. **Col. Width:** 2 1/4 inches. **Col. Depth:** 10 inches. **Key Personnel:** Blake Hurst, President, phone: (573)893-1401. **USPS:** 015-398. **Subscription Rates:** $30 Individuals includes membership. **Formerly:** Missouri Farm Bureau News. **Mailing address:** PO Box 658, Jefferson City, MO 65109. **Ad Rates:** BW $1,397; 4C $1,907; PCI $54. **Remarks:** Accepts advertising. **Circ:** Controlled ‡91000.

19562 ■ Something Better
Missouri NEA
1810 E Elm St.
Jefferson City, MO 65101
Phone: (573)634-3202
Fax: (573)634-5646
Free: 800-392-0236
Publisher's E-mail: info@mnea.org
Education magazine. **Freq:** Quarterly. **Print Method:** Offset. Uses mats. **Trim Size:** 8 x 10 1/2. **Cols./Page:** 5. **Col. Width:** 8 picas. **Col. Depth:** 56.5 picas. **ISSN:** 1076--223X (print). **USPS:** 011-415. **Subscription Rates:** Included in membership. **URL:** http://www.mnea.org/Missouri/SomethingBetterOnline1.aspx. **Ad Rates:** BW $750; 4C $1050. **Remarks:** Accepts advertising. **Circ:** Paid ‡30000, Non-paid ‡1000.

19563 ■ Teen Times
Family, Career and Community Leaders of America - Missouri Chapter
Jefferson Bldg., 5th Fl.
205 Jefferson St.
Jefferson City, MO 65101
Phone: (573)751-7964
Fax: (573)526-4261
Publication E-mail: teentimes@fcclainc.org
Student association magazine reporting organization news and discussing issues of concern to teens. **Freq:** Quarterly September, November, January and March. **Print Method:** Web. **Trim Size:** 8 1/4 x 10 7/8. **Cols./Page:** 3. **Col. Width:** 2.25 inches. **ISSN:** 0735--6986 (print). **Subscription Rates:** $8 Individuals /year; $16 Two years. **URL:** http://fcclainc.org/news--media/teen-times.php; http://www.fcclainc.org/content/teen-times. **Ad Rates:** BW $3000. **Remarks:** Accepts advertising. **Circ:** ‡219000.

19564 ■ Teen Times
Family, Career and Community Leaders of America - Missouri Chapter
Jefferson Bldg., 5th Fl.
205 Jefferson St.
Jefferson City, MO 65101
Phone: (573)751-7964
Fax: (573)526-4261
Magazine containing articles and news for teens. **Freq:** Quarterly. **Subscription Rates:** $8 Individuals; $16 Two years. **URL:** http://www.fcclainc.org/content/teen-times/. **Mailing address:** PO Box 480, Jefferson City, MO 65102-0480. **Circ:** (Not Reported).

19565 ■ Word and Way
Word and Way
3236 Emerald Ln., Ste. 400
Jefferson City, MO 65109-3700
Publisher's E-mail: wordandway@wordandway.org
Religious magazine. **Freq:** Monthly. **Print Method:** Offset. **Trim Size:** 11 1/2 x 15. **Cols./Page:** 5. **Col. Width:** 11.5 picas. **Col. Depth:** 13.5 inches. **Key Personnel:** Jan Conley, Communications Specialist; Vicki Brown, Associate Editor; Bill Webb, Editor; Margene Neuhart, Bookkeeper; Ken Satterfield, Coordinator, Marketing. **ISSN:** 0049--7959 (print). **Subscription Rates:** $17.50 Individuals. **URL:** http://www.wordandway.org. **Ad Rates:** BW $1200. **Remarks:** Church related only. **Circ:** ‡17000.

19566 ■ KATI-FM - 94.3
3109 S Ten Mile Dr.
Jefferson City, MO 65109
Phone: (573)893-5696
Free: 800-700-5284
Format: Country. **Ad Rates:** Advertising accepted; rates available upon request.

19567 ■ KJLU-FM - 88.9
1004 E Dunklin St.
Jefferson City, MO 65101
Phone: (573)681-5301
Fax: (573)681-5299
Email: registrar@lincolnu.edu
Format: Jazz; Urban Contemporary. **Owner:** Lincoln University of Missouri, 820 Chestnut St., Jefferson City, MO 65101, Ph: (573)681-5342, Fax: (573)681-5998. **Founded:** Aug. 20, 1973. **Operating Hours:** 6:00 a.m. - Midnight Monday - Sunday. **Key Personnel:** Mike Downey, Gen. Mgr., downeym@lincolnu.edu; Leslie Cross, Contact. **Local Programs:** *Classic Soul Saturday*, Saturday 2:00 p.m. - 6:00 p.m.; *Smooth Jazz with The Hitman*, Monday Tuesday Wednesday Thursday Friday Monday Thursday 6:00 a.m. - 9:00 a.m. 3:00 p.m. - 8:00 p.m. **Wattage:** 29,500 ERP. **Ad Rates:** Noncommercial. Underwriting available. **Mailing address:** PO Box 29, Jefferson City, MO 65102-0029. **URL:** http://www.kjluradio.com.

19568 ■ KJMO-FM - 97.5
3605 Country Club Dr.
Jefferson City, MO 65109
Free: 800-264-5566
Format: Oldies. **Networks:** NBC; Westwood One Radio. **Owner:** Cumulus Broadcasting Inc., 3280 Peachtree Rd. NW, Ste. 2300, Atlanta, GA 30305-2447, Ph: (404)949-0700, Fax: (404)949-0740. **Founded:** 1974. **Operating Hours:** Continuous. **ADI:** Columbia-Jefferson City, MO. **Key Personnel:** Richard Matthews, Contact. **Wattage:** 6,000. **Ad Rates:** Noncommercial.

19569 ■ KLIK-AM - 1240
1002 Diamond Ridge, Ste. 400
Jefferson City, MO 65109-1070
Phone: (573)893-5100
Fax: (573)893-8330
Free: 866-632-1240
Format: News; Talk; Information. **Owner:** Cumulus Broadcasting Inc., 3280 Peachtree Rd. NW, Ste. 2300, Atlanta, GA 30305-2447, Ph: (404)949-0700, Fax: (404)949-0740. **Founded:** 1954. **Operating Hours:** Continuous. **ADI:** Columbia-Jefferson City, MO. **Wattage:** 1,000. **Ad Rates:** Advertising accepted; rates available upon request. **URL:** http://www.klik1240.com.

19570 ■ KNLJ-TV - 25
311 W Dunklin
Jefferson City, MO 65101
Phone: (573)896-5105
Format: Commercial TV; Religious. **Owner:** Christian Television Network Inc., 6922 142nd Ave, Largo, FL 33771, Ph: (727)535-5622, Fax: (727)531-2497. **Founded:** Sept. 15, 2007. **ADI:** Columbia-Jefferson City, MO. **Key Personnel:** Vickie Davenport, Gen. Mgr. **Ad Rates:** Noncommercial. **URL:** http://www.knlj.tv.

19571 ■ KWOS-AM - 950
3109 S 10 Mile Dr.
Jefferson City, MO 65109
Phone: (573)893-5696
Format: News. **Owner:** Zimmer Radio Group, 3215 Lemone Industrial Blvd., Columbia, MO 65201, Fax: (573)875-2439, Free: 800-455-1099. **Founded:** 1920. **Operating Hours:** Continuous. **Wattage:** 5,000 Day; 500 Night. **Ad Rates:** Advertising accepted; rates available upon request. **URL:** http://kwos.com.

19572 ■ KZJF-FM - 104.1
1002 Diamond Rdg., Ste. 400
Jefferson City, MO 65109
Phone: (573)893-5100
Fax: (573)893-8330
Format: Country. **Owner:** Cumulus Broadcasting Inc., 3280 Peachtree Rd. NW, Ste. 2300, Atlanta, GA 30305-2447, Ph: (404)949-0700, Fax: (404)949-0740. **Key Personnel:** Kevin Joyce, Dir. of Mktg., Mktg. Mgr., kevin.joyce@cumulus.com; Nick Snyder, Promotions Dir., nick.snyder@cumulus.com. **Ad Rates:** Advertising accepted; rates available upon request.

JOPLIN

SW MO. Newton Co. 75 mi. W. of Springfield. Missouri Southern State College; Ozark Bible College. Manufactures leather goods, engraving and typesetting equipment, store fixtures, furniture, insulation, explosives, hydraulic pumps, missiles, chemicals, alcohol, fertilizer, dog food, bearings.

19573 ■ Grassroots Editor
International Society of Weekly Newspaper Editors
Missouri Southern State University
3950 E Newman Rd.
Joplin, MO 64801-1595
Trade magazine devoted to professional journalism. **Freq:** Quarterly. **Print Method:** Offset. **Trim Size:** 8 1/2 x 11. **Cols./Page:** 3. **Col. Width:** 26 nonpareils. **Col. Depth:** 128 agate lines. **Key Personnel:** Chad Stebbins, Executive Director. **ISSN:** 0017--3541 (print). **Subscription Rates:** Included in membership. **URL:** http://www.iswne.org/grassroots_editor. **Remarks:** Advertising not accepted. **Circ:** (Not Reported).

19574 ■ The Joplin Globe
The Joplin Globe Publishing Co.
117 E 4th St.
Joplin, MO 64801
Phone: (417)623-3480
Free: 800-444-8514
Publication E-mail: news@joplinglobe.com
General newspaper. **Freq:** Mon.-Sun. (morn.). **Print Method:** Offset. **Cols./Page:** 6. **Col. Width:** 25 nonpareils. **Col. Depth:** 311 agate lines. **Key Personnel:** Carol Stark, Editor; Michael Beatty, Publisher; Tim Holder, Director, Advertising. **Subscription Rates:** $13.98 Individuals print and online - monthly; $13.98 Individuals online only - monthly. **URL:** http://www.joplinglobe.com. **Mailing address:** PO Box 7, Joplin,

MO 64801. **Remarks:** Advertising accepted; rates available upon request. **Circ:** (Not Reported).

19575 ■ American Media Investments Inc. - 105.3
2510 W 20th
Joplin, MO 64804
Phone: (417)781-1313
Format: News. **URL:** http://www.mynewliferadio.com.

19576 ■ KBTN-FM - 99.7
2510 W 20th St.
Joplin, MO 64804
Phone: (417)781-1313
Format: Country. **Founded:** 1995. **Wattage:** 16,500 ERP. **Ad Rates:** Accepts Advertising. **URL:** http://www.kbtnradio.com.

19577 ■ KCAR-FM - 104.3
2510 W 20th St.
Joplin, MO 64804
Format: Oldies. **ADI:** Joplin, MO-Pittsburg, KS. **Key Personnel:** Jennifer Isom, Bus. Mgr., jennisom@crjoplin.com. **Wattage:** 6,000. **Ad Rates:** Accepts Advertising. **URL:** http://www.cool1043.com/.

19578 ■ KGCS-TV - 22
Missouri Southern State University
3950 E Newman Rd.
Joplin, MO 64801
Phone: (417)625-9375
Fax: (417)625-9742
Email: info@mssu.edu
Key Personnel: Judy Stiles, Gen. Mgr. **URL:** http://www.mssu.edu.

19579 ■ KIXQ-FM - 102.5
2702 E 32nd St.
Joplin, MO 64804
Phone: (417)624-1025
Fax: (417)781-6842
Format: Country. **Networks:** Independent. **Owner:** Zimmer Broadcasting Co., Inc., at above address. **Founded:** 1974. **Formerly:** WMBH-FM; KJKT-FM. **Operating Hours:** Continuous. **Key Personnel:** Larry Boyd, Dir. of Mktg., Mktg. Mgr., lboyd@zrgmail.com; Chad Elliot, Dir. of Programs, Operations Mgr.; Mel Williams, Dir. of Engg., williams@zrgmail.com; Rob Meyer, Operations Mgr. **Wattage:** 100,000. **Ad Rates:** $40-50 for 30 seconds; $40-50 for 60 seconds. **URL:** http://www.kix1025.com.

19580 ■ KJMK-FM - 93.9
2702 E 32nd St.
Joplin, MO 64804
Phone: (417)624-1025
Fax: (417)781-6842
Format: Adult Contemporary. **Founded:** Sept. 13, 2006. **Key Personnel:** Larry Boyd, Dir. of Mktg., Mktg. Mgr., lboyd@zrgmail.com; Chad Elliot, Dir. of Programs, Operations Mgr., chade@zrgmail.com; Kyle Thomas, Dir. of Programs, kylet@zrgmail.com; Mel Williams, Dir. of Info. Technology, Engineer, williams@zrgmail.com. **Ad Rates:** Noncommercial. **URL:** http://www.939literock.com/.

19581 ■ KJPX-TV - 47
Joplin, MO
Wattage: 50,000 ERP. **URL:** http://www.ionline.tv.

19582 ■ KKLL-AM - 1100
PO Box 85
Joplin, MO 64802
Phone: (314)421-3020
Fax: (314)421-1702
Free: 800-334-3276
Email: kkll@clandjop.com
Format: Contemporary Christian. **Networks:** USA Radio. **Founded:** 1984. **Operating Hours:** Sunrise-sunset. **Key Personnel:** Don Stubblefield, Gen. Mgr., Owner, Contact; Art Rogers, Dir. of Programs; Jim Young, Sales Mgr.; Jim Taylor, News Dir; Don Stubblefield, Contact. **Wattage:** 5,000. **Ad Rates:** $5.75-6.75 for 30 seconds; $8.25-9.25 for 60 seconds. **URL:** http://hereshelpnet.org/public-inspection-files/kkll-am-1100-webb-city-mo/.

19583 ■ KMOQ-FM - 107.1
2510 W 20th St.
Joplin, MO 64804
Phone: (417)781-1313
Format: Oldies. **Networks:** Satellite Music Network. **Founded:** 1980. **Formerly:** KBLT-FM. **Operating Hours:** Continuous. **ADI:** Joplin, MO-Pittsburg, KS. **Key Personnel:** Bobby Landis, Gen. Mgr.; Patrick Golay, President, Contact, pgolay@lanogo.com; Patrick Golay, Contact. **Wattage:** 6,000. **Ad Rates:** $15 for 30 seconds; $18 for 60 seconds. Combined advertising rates available with WMBM-AM, KQYX-AM. **URL:** http://www.mynewliferadio.com.

19584 ■ KOBC-FM - 90.7
2711 Peace Church Rd.
Joplin, MO 64801
Phone: (417)781-6401
Fax: (417)782-1841
Free: 800-299-5622
Email: kobc@kobc.org
Format: Gospel; Religious. **Owner:** Ozark Christian College, 1111 N Main St., Joplin, MO 64801. **Founded:** 1974. **Operating Hours:** Continuous. **ADI:** Joplin, MO-Pittsburg, KS. **Key Personnel:** Rob Kime, Gen. Mgr., rkime@kobc.org; Lisa Davis, Music Dir., ldavis@kobc.org. **Wattage:** 60,000 ERP. **Ad Rates:** Underwriting available. **URL:** http://www.kobc.org/.

19585 ■ KODE-TV - 12
1502 S Cleveland Ave.
Joplin, MO 64802
Phone: (417)781-2345
Fax: (417)782-2417
Format: Commercial TV. **Networks:** ABC. **Owner:** Nexstar Broadcasting Group Inc., 545 E John Carpenter Fwy., Ste. 700, Irving, TX 75062, Ph: (972)373-8800. **Operating Hours:** Continuous. **ADI:** Joplin, MO-Pittsburg, KS. **Key Personnel:** John Hoffmann, Gen. Mgr., jhoffmann@ksn16.tv; Gary Hood, Sales Mgr., ghood@kode12.tv; Jeff Gamble, Dir. of Sales; Dean Edwards, Dir. of Creative Svcs., dean@kode12.tv; Shirley Morton, Station Mgr.; Pam Mounce, Sales Mgr., pmounce@ksn16.tv; Jeff Hadley, Engineer. **Ad Rates:** Noncommercial. **Mailing address:** PO Box 1393, Joplin, MO 64802. **URL:** http://www.fourstateshomepage.com.

19586 ■ KOZJ-TV - 26
408 Joplin St.
Joplin, MO 64801
Phone: (417)782-1226
Format: Public TV. **Networks:** Public Broadcasting Service (PBS). **Founded:** 1981. **Key Personnel:** Ray Meyer, Dir. of Programs. **Wattage:** 55,000 ERP.

19587 ■ KQYX-AM - 1450
2510 W 20th St.
Joplin, MO 64804
Phone: (417)781-1313
Fax: (417)781-1316
Format: News; Talk. **Networks:** ABC; CNN Radio; Business Radio; USA Radio. **Owner:** FFD Holdings, Inc., at above address. **Founded:** 1962. **Operating Hours:** 6 a.m.-two hours past sunset. **ADI:** Joplin, MO-Pittsburg, KS. **Key Personnel:** William B. Neal, Gen. Mgr.; Matt Krueger, News Dir. **Wattage:** 10,000. **URL:** http://www.1450thedove.com/.

19588 ■ KSNF-TV - 16
1502 S Cleveland Ave.
Joplin, MO 64802
Phone: (417)781-2345
Fax: (417)782-2417
Email: closedcaptioning@ksn16.tv
Format: Commercial TV. **Networks:** NBC. **Owner:** Nexstar Broadcasting Group Inc., 545 E John Carpenter Fwy., Ste. 700, Irving, TX 75062, Ph: (972)373-8800. **Operating Hours:** Continuous. **Key Personnel:** John Hoffmann, Gen. Mgr., jhoffmann@ksn16.tv; Pam Mounce, Sales Mgr., pmounce@ksn16.tv. **Ad Rates:** Advertising accepted; rates available upon request. **Mailing address:** PO Box 1393, Joplin, MO 64802. **URL:** http://www.fourstateshomepage.com.

19589 ■ KSYN-FM - 92.5
2702 E 32nd St.
Joplin, MO 64804
Phone: (417)624-1025
Fax: (417)781-6842
Format: Top 40. **Networks:** Independent. **Owner:** Zimmer Radio Group - Joplin, at above address. **Operating Hours:** Continuous. **ADI:** Joplin, MO-Pittsburg, KS. **Key Personnel:** Larry Boyd, Dir. of Mktg., Mktg. Mgr.; Chad Elliot, Dir. of Programs, Operations Mgr.; Mel Williams, Dir. of Engg., Dir. of Info. Technology. **Wattage:** 100,000. **Ad Rates:** $30-40 for 30 seconds; $30-40 for 60 seconds. **URL:** http://www.ksyn925.com.

19590 ■ K207BT-FM - 90.3
PO Box 391
Twin Falls, ID 83303
Fax: (208)736-1958
Free: 800-357-4226
Format: Religious; Contemporary Christian. **Owner:** CSN International, PO Box 391, Twin Falls, ID 83303, Ph: (208)736-1958, Fax: (208)736-1958, Free: 800-357-4226. **Key Personnel:** Mike Kestler, President; Don Mills, Music Dir., Prog. Dir. **URL:** http://www.csnradio.com.

19591 ■ KXDG-FM - 97.9
2702 E 32nd St.
Joplin, MO 64804
Phone: (417)624-1025
Fax: (417)781-6842
Format: Classic Rock. **Key Personnel:** Larry Boyd, Dir. of Sales; Chad Elliot, Dir. of Operations; Chris Hayes, Prog. Dir.; Mel Williams, Dir. of Info. Technology. **Ad Rates:** Noncommercial. **URL:** http://www.bigdog979.com.

19592 ■ KXMS-FM - 88.7
3950 E Newman Rd.
Joplin, MO 64801-1595
Phone: (417)625-9356
Email: info@mssu.edu
Format: Classical; Folk. **Networks:** Beethoven Satellite. **Founded:** 1986. **Operating Hours:** Continuous. **Key Personnel:** Judy Stiles, Contact; Robert Harris, Music Dir; Judy Stiles, Contact; Richard W. Masso, Contact. **Wattage:** 10,000. **Ad Rates:** Noncommercial. **URL:** http://www.mssu.edu/kxms.

19593 ■ KZYM AM1230 - 1230
2702 E 32nd St.
Joplin, MO 64804
Phone: (417)624-1025
Fax: (417)781-6842
Format: Sports. **Key Personnel:** Larry Boyd, Dir. of Mktg., Mktg. Mgr., lboyd@zrgmail.com; Chad Elliot, Dir. of Programs, Operations Mgr., chade@zrgmail.com. **Ad Rates:** Advertising accepted; rates available upon request. **URL:** http://www.1230thetalker.com.

KAHOKA

NE MO. Clark Co. 50 mi. N. of Hannibal.

19594 ■ Media
Media
PO Box 230
Kahoka, MO 63445
Phone: (660)727-3395
Publisher's E-mail: themedia@centurytel.net
Local newspaper. **Freq:** Weekly (Wed.). **Print Method:** Offset. **Cols./Page:** 6. **Col. Width:** 2 inches. **Col. Depth:** 21 inches. **Key Personnel:** Mike Scott, Editor. **USPS:** 289-380. **Subscription Rates:** $25.20 Individuals; $33.24 Out of area; $30 Single issue. **URL:** http://nemonews.net. **Formerly:** Gazette Herald; Clark Gazette; Clark County Courier. **Ad Rates:** GLR $.42; BW $555.66; 4C $855; PCI $4.24. **Remarks:** Accepts advertising. **Circ:** Paid ‡2,600.

KAISER

19595 ■ KLOZ-FM - 92.7
387 Hwy. 42
Kaiser, MO 65047
Phone: (573)348-1958
Format: Adult Contemporary. **Networks:** ABC. **Owner:** Benne Broadcasting L.L.C., at above address. **Formerly:** KLDN-FM. **Operating Hours:** Continuous; 2% network, 98% local. **Wattage:** 31,000. **Ad Rates:** Noncommercial. **URL:** http://www.mix927.com.

19596 ■ KQUL-FM - 102.7
160 Hwy. 42
Kaiser, MO 65047
Phone: (573)348-1958
Format: Oldies. **Owner:** Benne Broadcasting L.L.C., at above address. **Operating Hours:** Continuous. **Wattage:** 6,000. **URL:** http://www.cool1027.com.

Circulation: ★ = AAM; △ or • = BPA; ♦ = CAC; ❑ = VAC; ⊕ = PO Statement; ‡ = Publisher's Report; Boldface figures = sworn; Light figures = estimated.

KANSAS CITY

W. MO. Platte Co. On Missouri River, at mouth of Kansas (Kaw) River, 45 mi. S. of Saint Joseph. University of Missouri at Kansas City; 19 other colleges, universities, and theological schools. Largest city in Missouri. A strong diverse economic foundation. First in the nation in farm equipment distribution and hard winter wheat marketing. The Worlds's Food Capital. Leading national market in automobile and truck production, greeting card publishing. Frozen food storage and distribution center. Center of the midcontinent oil fields. Manufactures agriculture chemicals, airplane accessories, ammunition, paints, wire goods, textiles, trucks, electrical brick, beverages, malt syrup, furniture, caskets, mattresses, motor cars, stationery, drugs. Local culture centers.

19597 ■ Baking Buyer
Sosland Publishing Co.
4800 Main St., Ste. 100
Kansas City, MO 64112
Phone: (816)756-1000
Fax: (816)756-0494
Publisher's E-mail: nwages@sosland.com
Magazine for retail, in-store, foodservice, specialty, and wholesale bakers. **Freq:** Monthly. **Print Method:** Web offset. **Trim Size:** 8.75 x 10.75. **Key Personnel:** Jeff Gelski, Associate Editor; Ron Sterk, Assistant Editor; Laurie Gorton, Executive Editor; L. Joshua Sosland, Editor; Jay Sjerven, Senior Editor; Eric Schroeder, Managing Editor. **ISSN:** 1056-6007 (print). **Subscription Rates:** $25 Individuals; $19 Individuals discount rate. **URL:** http://www.bakemag.com. **Ad Rates:** BW $4,424, full page; BW $2,589, half page; 4C $5,627, full page; 4C $3,591, half page. **Remarks:** Accepts advertising. **Circ:** 20,106.

19598 ■ Baking & Snack
Sosland Publishing Co.
4800 Main St., Ste. 100
Kansas City, MO 64112
Phone: (816)756-1000
Fax: (816)756-0494
Publisher's E-mail: nwages@sosland.com
Equipment, engineering, production and formulating magazine for commercial manufacturers of baked and snack foods. **Freq:** Monthly (except January). **Print Method:** Offset. **Trim Size:** 8 x 10.75. **Cols./Page:** 3. **Col. Width:** 2 1/8 inches. **Col. Depth:** 10 inches. **Key Personnel:** Dan Malovany, Editor; Laurie Gorton, Executive Editor. **ISSN:** 1040--9254 (print). **URL:** http://www.bakingbusiness.com; http://www.sosland.com/wholesale-baking.html. **Ad Rates:** BW $7910. **Remarks:** Accepts advertising. **Circ:** ‡12119.

19599 ■ Biofuels Business
Sosland Publishing Co.
4800 Main St., Ste. 100
Kansas City, MO 64112
Phone: (816)756-1000
Fax: (816)756-0494
Publisher's E-mail: nwages@sosland.com
Magazine covering the ethanol and biodiesel industries. **Print Method:** Web offset. **Key Personnel:** Nola Hector, Publisher; Susan Reidy, Editor. **URL:** http://www.sosland.com. **Ad Rates:** BW $2,350. **Remarks:** Accepts advertising. **Circ:** (Not Reported).

19600 ■ The Call
Kansas City Call Inc.
1715 E 18th St.
Kansas City, MO 64108
Phone: (816)842-3804
Free: 877-842-4420
Black community newspaper. **Freq:** Weekly (Fri.). **Print Method:** Offset. **Cols./Page:** 8. **Col. Width:** 18 nonpareils. **Col. Depth:** 294 agate lines. **Key Personnel:** Barbara Way, Contact; Eric Wesson, Contact. **Subscription Rates:** $30 Individuals; $36 Out of area; $56 Out of state. **URL:** http://www.kccall.com. **Ad Rates:** GLR $.50. **Remarks:** Accepts advertising. **Circ:** (Not Reported).

19601 ■ Celebration: An Ecumenical Worship Resource
National Catholic Reporter Publishing Company Inc.
115 E Armour Blvd.
Kansas City, MO 64111-1203
Fax: (816)968-2268
Free: 800-333-7373
Magazine providing resources that assist Christian churches in planning and preparing Sunday and seasonal worship. **Freq:** Annual. **Print Method:** Offset. **Trim Size:** 8 1/2 x 11. **Cols./Page:** 3. **Col. Width:** 27 nonpareils. **Col. Depth:** 137 agate lines. **Key Personnel:** Patrick Marrin, Editor. **ISSN:** 0094--2421 (print). **Subscription Rates:** $69.95 Individuals; $87.95 Other countries; $124.95 Two years; $160.95 Two years other countries; $49.95 Individuals online only. **URL:** http://www.celebrationpublications.org. **Remarks:** Advertising accepted; rates available upon request. **Circ:** (Not Reported).

19602 ■ Charolais Journal
American-International Charolais Association
11700 NW Plaza Cir.
Kansas City, MO 64153
Phone: (816)464-5977
Fax: (816)464-5759
International magazine on Charolais cattle, including special interest articles, show/sale reports, and association news. **Freq:** Monthly. **Trim Size:** 8.5 x 11. **Key Personnel:** David Hobbs, Manager; Kori Conley, Editor; Neil J. Orth, President; Molly Mader, Coordinator, Advertising. **ISSN:** 0191-5444 (print). **Subscription Rates:** $75 Individuals U.S.; $100 Individuals U.S 1st class; $125 Other countries; $25 Members paid junior. **Alt. Formats:** PDF. **URL:** http://www.charolaisusa.com/journalhome.html. **Ad Rates:** BW $700; BW $510, 2/3 page; BW $395, half page - horizontal; BW $450, half page - vertical. **Remarks:** Accepts advertising. **Circ:** ‡6000.

19603 ■ China Clipper
China Stamp Society
c/o H. James Maxwell, President
1050 West Blue Ridge Blvd.
Kansas City, MO 64145-1216
Phone: (816)210-1234
Journal covering stamps and postal history of China. **Freq:** Bimonthly. **Key Personnel:** Paul H. Gault, Contact; Ralph Weil, Editor. **ISSN:** 0885--9779 (print). **Subscription Rates:** $21 Individuals complete volume number (six issues); $3.50 Single issue back issue. **URL:** http://www.chinastampsociety.org/china-clipper-magazine. **Ad Rates:** BW $100; 4C $350. **Remarks:** Accepts advertising. **Circ:** Controlled 850.

19604 ■ Collinsorum
Kansas Herpetological Society
c/o Eric Kessler, President
5624 Cherry St.
Kansas City, MO 64111
Phone: (816)444-4794
Publishes manuscripts and notes of interest dealing with the biology of herpetofauna. Contains information and reports of Society activities. **Freq:** Semiannual. **Key Personnel:** Curtis J. Schmidt, Editor, phone: (785)650-2447; Travis W. Taggart, Associate Editor, phone: (785)650-0865. **URL:** http://www.cnah.org/khs/publications.aspx. **Formerly**: Journal of Kansas Herpetology. **Circ:** (Not Reported).

19605 ■ Discover Mid-America
Discovery Publications Inc.
1501 Burlington, Ste. 207
Kansas City, MO 64116
Phone: (816)474-1516
Fax: (816)474-1427
Free: 800-899-9730
Publication E-mail: dispub@discoverypub.com
Trade magazine covering antiques, arts, crafts, regional history, and events. **Freq:** Monthly. **Print Method:** Web Offset. **Key Personnel:** Bruce Rodgers, Executive Editor, Publisher; Al Hedrick, Account Executive. **Alt. Formats:** PDF. **URL:** http://www.discoverypub.com. **Ad Rates:** BW $1,135; 4C $1,362. **Remarks:** Accepts advertising. **Circ:** Non-paid 25000.

19606 ■ Economic Review
Federal Reserve Bank of Kansas City
1 Memorial Dr.
Kansas City, MO 64108-4604
Phone: (816)881-2000
Fax: (816)881-2846
Free: 800-333-1010
Business, finance, and economics journal. **Founded:** 1916. **Freq:** Quarterly. **Print Method:** Offset. **Trim Size:** 7 1/2 x 9 1/2. **Cols./Page:** 2. **Col. Width:** 33 nonpareils. **Col. Depth:** 100 agate lines. **ISSN:** 0161-2387 (print). **URL:** http://www.kansascityfed.org/publications/research/er/er-2013.cfm. **Remarks:** Advertising not accepted. **Circ:** Free ‡26,000.

19607 ■ eKC
Discovery Publications Inc.
1501 Burlington, Ste. 207
Kansas City, MO 64116
Phone: (816)474-1516
Fax: (816)474-1427
Free: 800-899-9730
Publisher's E-mail: publisher@discoverypub.com
Consumer magazine covering local news and entertainment. **Freq:** Weekly. **Key Personnel:** Bruce Rodgers, Editor; Al Hedrick, Account Executive; Mark Rodgers, Managing Editor. **URL:** http://www.kcactive.com. **Formerly**: Explore Kansas City; Explore KC. **Ad Rates:** BW $955; 4C $1251. **Remarks:** Accepts advertising. **Circ:** Non-paid 10,000.

19608 ■ Fair and Equitable
International Association of Assessing Officers
314 W 10th St.
Kansas City, MO 64105
Phone: (816)701-8100
Fax: (816)701-8149
Free: 800-616-4226
Publisher's E-mail: info@iaao.org
Magazine publishing research on today's assessment issues, association news, educational course listings, events coverage, an events calendar and classified advertising. **Freq:** Monthly. **Subscription Rates:** $140 Nonmembers 12 issues; $10 Nonmembers single issue; Included in membership. **URL:** http://www.iaao.org/wmc/Resources_Content/Pubs/Fair_Equitable.aspx. **Remarks:** Accepts advertising. **Circ:** 7200.

19609 ■ FCA Magazine
Fellowship of Christian Athletes
8701 Leeds Rd.
Kansas City, MO 64129
Phone: (816)921-0909
Fax: (816)921-8755
Free: 800-289-0909
Publisher's E-mail: fca@fca.org
Freq: Monthly. **Subscription Rates:** $16.99 Individuals; $28.99 Two years. **URL:** http://www.fca.org/fca-magazine. **Formerly**: Sharing the Victory. **Remarks:** Accepts advertising. **Circ:** (Not Reported).

19610 ■ Forum
Kansas City Artists Coalition
201 Wyandotte
Kansas City, MO 64105
Phone: (816)421-5222
Fax: (816)421-0656
Publisher's E-mail: information@kansascityartistscoalition.org
Online art journal. **Founded:** 1975. **URL:** http://www.kansascityartistscoalition.org. **Remarks:** Advertising not accepted. **Circ:** Paid 600, Non-paid 10000.

19611 ■ Hereford World
Hereford Publications Inc.
PO Box 014059
Kansas City, MO 64101-0059
Phone: (816)842-3757
Fax: (816)842-6931
Publication E-mail: hworld@hereford.org
Magazine on Hereford cattle. **Founded:** 1910. **Freq:** Monthly. **Print Method:** Offset. **Trim Size:** 8 1/8 x 10 3/4. **Cols./Page:** 3. **Col. Width:** 26 nonpareils. **Col. Depth:** 140 agate lines. **Key Personnel:** Alison Marx, Advertising Representative; Angie Stump Denton, Editor; Caryn Vaught, Manager, Production; Sara Guglemeyer, Assistant Editor. **ISSN:** 1085-9896 (print). **Subscription Rates:** $35 Individuals; $70 Individuals first class; $60 Other countries; $110 Other countries first class. **URL:** http://www.hereford.org/node/268. **Formerly**: American Hereford Journal; Polled Hereford World. **Ad Rates:** BW $725; 4C $1150; PCI $30. **Remarks:** Accepts advertising. **Circ:** Combined ‡25,600.

19612 ■ Ingram's: Kansas City's Business Magazine
Show-Me Publishing Inc.
2049 Wyandotte
Kansas City, MO 64108
Phone: (816)842-9994

Fax: (816)474-1111
Publisher's E-mail: editorial@ingrams.com
Business and lifestyle magazine covering Lawrence, Topeka, Overland Park, KS, and Kansas City and St. Joseph, MO. **Founded:** 1974. **Freq:** Monthly. **Print Method:** Offset. **Trim Size:** 8 1/8 x 10 7/8. **Cols./Page:** 3. **Col. Width:** 2 1/8 inches. **Col. Depth:** 10 inches. **Key Personnel:** Jim Ryan, Controller; Joe Sweeney, Editor-in-Chief, Publisher; Jack Cashill, Executive Editor; Michelle Sweeney, Vice President. **ISSN:** 0273-9968 (print). **Subscription Rates:** $44.95 Individuals; $69.95 Two years; $99.95 Individuals three years. **URL:** http://www.ingrams.com. **Formerly**: Corporate Report; Corporate Report Kansas City. **Mailing address:** PO Box 411356, Kansas City, MO 64106. **Ad Rates:** BW $2760; 4C $3070. **Remarks:** Accepts advertising. **Circ:** Combined 24,944.

19613 ■ Instore Buyer
Sosland Publishing Co.
4800 Main St., Ste. 100
Kansas City, MO 64112
Phone: (816)756-1000
Fax: (816)756-0494
Publisher's E-mail: nwages@sosland.com
Magazine covering merchandising, product research, consumer attitudes and purchasing behavior, and labor and management issues for supermarket and club store bakery, deli and foodservice executives. **Freq:** Bimonthly. **Trim Size:** 8.75 x 10.75. **Key Personnel:** John Sonderegger, Publisher; John Unrein, Editor. **Subscription Rates:** Free to qualified subscribers U.S. and Canada; $80 Other countries / year. **URL:** http://www.bakemag.com/instore. **Ad Rates:** BW $3,913; 4C $4,976. **Remarks:** Accepts advertising. **Circ:** △**12250**.

19614 ■ Journal of the American Academy of Matrimonial Lawyers
University of Missouri, Kansas City School of Law
500 E 52nd St.
Kansas City, MO 64110
Phone: (816)235-1644
Fax: (816)235-5276
Publisher's E-mail: office@aaml.org
Journal featuring articles on a selected family-law theme. **Freq:** Semiannual. **Subscription Rates:** $100 Individuals. **URL:** http://law.umkc.edu/academics/journals/journal-of-the-american-academy-of-matrimonial-lawyers; http://www.aaml.org/library/journal-of-the-american-academy-of-matrimonial-lawyers. **Circ:** (Not Reported).

19615 ■ Journal of Electroneurodiagnostic Technology
American Society of Electroneurodiagnostic Technologists
402 E Bannister Rd., Ste. A
Kansas City, MO 64131-3019
Phone: (816)931-1120
Fax: (816)931-1145
Publisher's E-mail: info@aset.org
Freq: Quarterly. **ISSN:** 1086- 508X (print). **Subscription Rates:** Included in membership. **URL:** http://www.aset.org/i4a/pages/index.cfm?pageid=3314. **Remarks:** Accepts advertising. **Circ:** 3500.

19616 ■ Journal of Gastrointestinal Surgery
Americas Hepato-Pancreato-Biliary Association
PO Box 410454
Kansas City, MO 64141
Phone: (913)402-7102
Fax: (913)273-1140
Publisher's E-mail: info@detroitautoscene.com
Contains articles on the latest developments in gastrointestinal surgery. **Freq:** Monthly. **ISSN:** 1091--255X (print); **EISSN:** 1873--4626 (electronic). **Subscription Rates:** Included in membership; $636 Institutions print or online. **URL:** http://www.ssat.com/cgi-bin/Journal-of-GI-Surgery.cgi; http://www.ahpba.org/resources/links.phtml; http://www.springer.com/medicine/surgery/journal/11605. **Remarks:** Accepts advertising. **Circ:** (Not Reported).

19617 ■ Journal of Low Vision and Neuro-Optometric Rehabilitation
Trozzolo Creative Resources Inc.
802 Broadway St., Ste. 300
Kansas City, MO 64105-1528
Phone: (816)842-8111
Fax: (816)842-8111
Free: 800-243-5201
Publisher's E-mail: info@trozzolo.com
Journal for low vision theoreticians and practitioners. **Freq:** Quarterly. **Trim Size:** 8 1/2 x 11. **Key Personnel:** Elizabeth A. Cavanaugh, Contact; Randy Jose, Publisher. **ISSN:** 1041--0384 (print). **Subscription Rates:** $95; $105 Canada; $125 Other countries air mail; $110 Other countries surface; $170 Two years; $189 Two years; $225 Two years air mail; $198 Two years surface. **URL:** http://www.trozzolo.com. **Formerly**: Journal of Vision Rehabilitation. **Ad Rates:** BW $250. **Remarks:** Advertising accepted; rates available upon request. **Circ:** Paid 500.

19618 ■ Journal of Property Tax Assessment & Administration
International Association of Assessing Officers
314 W 10th St.
Kansas City, MO 64105
Phone: (816)701-8100
Fax: (816)701-8149
Free: 800-616-4226
Publisher's E-mail: info@iaao.org
Professional journal covering taxation. **Freq:** Quarterly. **ISSN:** 1357--1419 (print). **Subscription Rates:** Free to members. **URL:** http://www.iaao.org/wcm/Resources/Publications_access/JPTAA/wmc/Resources_Content/Pubs/Journal_of_Property_Tax_Assessment_Administration.aspx. **Formerly**: Assessment Journal. **Remarks:** Advertising accepted; rates available upon request. **Circ:** (Not Reported).

19619 ■ Kansas City Business Journal
Kansas City Business Journal
1100 Main St., Ste. 210
Kansas City, MO 64105-5123
Phone: (816)421-5900
Fax: (816)472-4010
Publisher's E-mail: kansascity@bizjournals.com
Local business newspaper. **Freq:** Weekly. **Print Method:** Offset. **Cols./Page:** 4. **Col. Width:** 28 nonpareils. **Col. Depth:** 189 agate lines. **Key Personnel:** Jonna Lorenz, Editor; Joyce Hayhow, Publisher; Chris Curry, Editor; James Dornbrook, Reporter; Brian Kaberline, Editor; Russell Gray, Managing Editor. **Subscription Rates:** $100 Individuals 52 weeks. **Online:** American City Business Journals Inc. American City Business Journals Inc. **URL:** http://www.bizjournals.com/kansascity. **Ad Rates:** BW $15,965, 2-page spread; 4C $9,170, full page; BW $8,340, 3/4 page; BW $7,830, island; BW $6,900, 1/2 page; BW $7,100; 4C $8,400. **Remarks:** Accepts advertising. **Circ:** Paid 10941.

19620 ■ Kansas City Hispanic News
Kansas City Hispanic News
2918 Southwest Blvd.
Kansas City, MO 64108
Phone: (816)472-5246
Fax: (816)931-6397
English and Spanish newspaper serving the five-county greater Kansas City area. **Freq:** Weekly. **Print Method:** Web offset. **Trim Size:** 13 1/2 x 22 1/2. **Cols./Page:** 5. **Col. Width:** 2.3 inches. **Col. Depth:** 21 inches. **Key Personnel:** Joe M. Arce, Publisher; Jose Faus, Editor. **Subscription Rates:** Free; $15 By mail. **URL:** http://www.kchispanicnews.com. **Ad Rates:** BW $1,200; 4C $1,500; PCI $15. **Remarks:** Accepts advertising. **Circ:** 10000.

19621 ■ The Kansas City Star
ProQuest L.L.C.
1729 Grand Blvd.
Kansas City, MO 64108
Phone: (816)234-4636
Publication E-mail: publiceditor@kcstar.com
General newspaper. **Freq:** Mon.-Sun. (morn.). **Print Method:** Offset. **Cols./Page:** 6. **Col. Width:** 26 nonpareils. **Col. Depth:** 311 agate lines. **Key Personnel:** Steve Shirk, Managing Editor; Mike Fannin, Editor; Mi-Ai Parrish, President, Publisher. **Online:** Dow Jones & Company Inc.; LexisNexis; Kansas City Star Co. Kansas City Star Co.; NewsBank Inc. **Alt. Formats:** Handheld. **URL:** http://www.kansascity.com. **Remarks:** Accepts advertising. **Circ:** (Not Reported).

19622 ■ Ladies Auxiliary VFW Magazine
Veterans of Foreign Wars of the United States, Ladies Auxiliary
406 W 34th St., 10th Fl.
Kansas City, MO 64111
Phone: (816)561-8655
Fax: (816)931-4753
Publisher's E-mail: info@ladiesauxvfw.org
Magazine containing information on the national programs, the National President's travels to every department, the newest member benefits and the candidates running for National Guard. **Freq:** 6/year. **URL:** http://vfwauxiliary.org/magazine. **Remarks:** Advertising not accepted. **Circ:** (Not Reported).

19623 ■ Meat & Poultry: The Business Journal of the Meat & Poultry Industry
Sosland Publishing Co.
4800 Main St., Ste. 100
Kansas City, MO 64112
Phone: (816)756-1000
Fax: (816)756-0494
Publisher's E-mail: nwages@sosland.com
Magazine serving the meat and poultry processing, distributing, and wholesaling industries in the U.S. and Canada. **Founded:** Jan. 1955. **Freq:** Monthly. **Print Method:** Offset. **Trim Size:** 8 x 10.75. **Cols./Page:** 3. **Col. Width:** 13 picas. **Col. Depth:** 140 agate lines. **Key Personnel:** Dave Crost, Publisher; Keith Nunes, Executive Editor; Dr. Temple Grandin, Editor; Steve Kay, Editor; Joel Crews, Editor. **ISSN:** 0892-6077 (print). **Subscription Rates:** $85 Other countries print; $165 Other countries print, airmail delivery. **URL:** http://www.meatpoultry.com. **Formerly**: Meat Industry. **Ad Rates:** BW $4,213; 4C $3,935. **Remarks:** Accepts advertising. **Circ:** Combined 22211.

19624 ■ Milling & Baking News
Sosland Publishing Co.
4800 Main St., Ste. 100
Kansas City, MO 64112
Phone: (816)756-1000
Fax: (816)756-0494
Publication E-mail: mbncirc@sosland.com?subject=mbn
Trade magazine covering the grain-based food industries. **Freq:** Weekly (Tues.). **Print Method:** Offset. **Trim Size:** 8 x 10 3/4. **Cols./Page:** 3. **Col. Width:** 26 nonpareils. **Col. Depth:** 140 agate lines. **Key Personnel:** Jay Sjerven, Senior Editor; Morton Sosland, Editor-in-Chief; Josh Sosland, Editor. **USPS:** 508-300. **Subscription Rates:** $135 U.S. and Canada; $210 U.S. and Canada 2 years; $290 U.S. and Canada 3 years; $190 Out of country; $320 Out of country 2 years; $455 Out of country 3 years. **URL:** http://www.bakingbusiness.com. **Ad Rates:** BW $3,490; 4C $5,090. **Remarks:** Accepts advertising. **Circ:** (Not Reported).

19625 ■ The National Catholic Reporter: The Independent Catholic Newsweekly
National Catholic Reporter Publishing Company Inc.
115 E Armour Blvd.
Kansas City, MO 64111-1203
Fax: (816)968-2268
Free: 800-333-7373
Catholic publication. **Freq:** 26/yr. **Print Method:** Offset. **Trim Size:** Tabloid. **Cols./Page:** 4. **Col. Width:** 2 7/16 inches. **Col. Depth:** 210 agate lines. **Key Personnel:** Tom Fox, Publisher; Thomas Roberts, Editor; Vicki Breashears, Specialist, Advertising and Sales; Wally Reiter, Business Manager, Chief Financial Officer. **Subscription Rates:** $49.95 Individuals; $87.95 Out of state; $94.95 Two years; $170.95 Two years Outside U.S. **URL:** http://ncronline.org. **Ad Rates:** BW $2630. **Remarks:** Accepts advertising. **Circ:** Paid ‡50000, 120000.

19626 ■ The Neurodiagnostic Journal
American Society of Electroneurodiagnostic Technologists
402 E Bannister Rd., Ste. A
Kansas City, MO 64131-3019
Phone: (816)931-1120
Fax: (816)931-1145
Publisher's E-mail: info@aset.org
Professional Journal. **Freq:** Quarterly. **Print Method:** Offset. **Trim Size:** 6 x 9. **Cols./Page:** 1. **Col. Width:** 4 5/9 inches. **Col. Depth:** 6 7/8 inches. **Key Personnel:** Anna M. Bonner, Managing Editor. **ISSN:** 2164--6821 (print); **EISSN:** 2375--8627 (electronic). **Subscription Rates:** $163 Individuals print only; $321 Institutions online only; $367 Institutions print and online. **URL:**

Circulation: ⋆ = AAM; △ or • = BPA; ♦ = CAC; ❑ = VAC; ⊕ = PO Statement; ‡ = Publisher's Report; Boldface figures = sworn; Light figures = estimated.

http://www.aset.org/i4a/pages/index.cfm?pageid=3314. **Formerly**: American Journal of EEG Technology; American Journal of Electroneurodiagnostic Technology: Journal of the American Society of Electroneurodiagnostic Technologists, Inc. **Ad Rates:** BW $475; 4C $1,200. **Remarks:** Advertising accepted; rates available upon request. **Circ:** 4000.

19627 ■ New Letters: A Magazine of Writing & Art
University of Missouri at Kansas City
5100 Rockhill Rd.
Kansas City, MO 64110
Phone: (816)235-1000
Publication E-mail: newletters@umkc.edu
Magazine containing poetry, fiction, essays, interviews, and art. **Freq:** Quarterly. **Print Method:** Offset. **Trim Size:** 6 x 9. **Cols./Page:** 1. **Col. Width:** 48 nonpareils. **Key Personnel:** Robert Stewart, Editor-in-Chief. **ISSN:** 0146--4930 (print). **Subscription Rates:** $28 Individuals; $40 Two years 2 years; $36 Institutions and libraries; 2 years; $58 Institutions and libraries; 2 years. **URL:** http://www.newletters.org. **Formerly**: University Review. **Ad Rates:** BW $450. **Remarks:** Color advertising not accepted. **Circ:** (Not Reported).

19628 ■ OfficePRO
International Association of Administrative Professionals
10502 N Ambassador Dr., Ste. 100
Kansas City, MO 64153
Phone: (816)891-6600
Fax: (816)891-9118
Magazine for administrative assistants, office managers, and secretaries featuring information on trends in business, technology, career development, and management. **Freq:** 7/year. **Print Method:** Web Offset. **Trim Size:** 8 1/4 x 10 7/8. **Cols./Page:** 3. **Col. Width:** 30 nonpareils. **Col. Depth:** 130 agate lines. **Key Personnel:** Emily Allen, Managing Editor. **ISSN:** 1096--5807 (print). **Subscription Rates:** $35 Individuals; $50 Two years; $42 Other countries; $65 Other countries two year; Included in membership. **URL:** http://www.iaap-hq.org/page/OfficeProMagazine. **Formerly**: The Secretary. **Ad Rates:** 4C $5165. **Remarks:** Accepts advertising. **Circ:** (Not Reported).

19629 ■ O'Lochlainn's Personal Journal of Irish Families
Irish Genealogical Foundation
PO Box 7575
Kansas City, MO 64116
Phone: (816)399-0905
Freq: Monthly. **Subscription Rates:** Included in membership. **Remarks:** Accepts advertising. **Circ:** (Not Reported).

19630 ■ Pearls and Rubies
FarmHouse Fraternity, Inc.
7306 NW Tiffany Spring Pky., Ste. 210
Kansas City, MO 64153
Phone: (816)891-9445
Fax: (816)891-0838
Publisher's E-mail: fhhq@farmhouse.org
Freq: Semiannual. **USPS:** 424- 540. **Alt. Formats:** PDF. **URL:** http://www.farmhouse.org/p&r.htm. **Remarks:** Advertising not accepted. **Circ:** (Not Reported).

19631 ■ The Pitch
Kansas City Pitch L.L.C.
1701 Main St.
Kansas City, MO 64108
Phone: (816)561-6061
Fax: (816)756-0502
Alternative weekly focusing on Kansas City's news and entertainment. **Founded:** 1980. **Freq:** Weekly. **Key Personnel:** Natalie Gallagher, Editor. **URL:** http://www.pitch.com. **Formerly**: PitchWeekly. **Remarks:** Accepts advertising. **Circ:** (Not Reported).

19632 ■ Progress in Pediatric Cardiology
Elsevier
Children's Mercy Hospital
2401 Gilliam Rd.
Kansas City, MO 64108
Publisher's E-mail: t.reller@elsevier.com
Journal presenting information and experienced opinion of importance in the understanding and management of cardiovascular diseases in children. **Freq:** Quarterly. **Key Personnel:** G.K. Lofland, Editor-in-Chief; S.W. Allen, Board Member; B.W. McCrindle, Associate Editor. **ISSN:** 1058--9813 (print). **Subscription Rates:** $338 Individuals online; $375 Individuals print and online. **URL:** http://www.ppc-journal.com. **Circ:** (Not Reported).

19633 ■ The Rockhurst Sentinel
Rockhurst University
1100 Rockhurst Rd.
Kansas City, MO 64110
Phone: (816)501-4000
Free: 800-842-6776
Publication E-mail: sentinel@rockhurst.edu
Collegiate daily newspaper. **Freq:** Biweekly. **Print Method:** Offset. **Trim Size:** 11 x 15. **Cols./Page:** 5. **Col. Width:** 2 inches. **Col. Depth:** 15 inches. **Key Personnel:** Brian Roewe, Editor-in-Chief; Dan James, Managing Editor. **Subscription Rates:** Free. **URL:** http://www.rockhurst.edu/academics/undergraduate/majors/communication-fine-arts/student-involvement/. **Formerly**: The Rockhurst Hawk. **Ad Rates:** GLR $15; BW $300; PCI $4. **Remarks:** Accepts advertising. **Circ:** (Not Reported).

19634 ■ Scaffold and Access
Scaffold and Access Industry Association
400 Admiral Blvd.
Kansas City, MO 64106
Phone: (816)595-4860
Fax: (816)472-7765
Publisher's E-mail: info@saiaonline.org
Trade magazine covering the scaffolding industry. **Freq:** Bimonthly. **Trim Size:** 8 1/2 x 11. **Subscription Rates:** $ Included in membership; $85 Nonmembers; $14.99 Single issue. **URL:** http://www.saiaonline.org/ScaffoldIndustryMagazine. **Formerly**: Scaffold Industry Association Magazine. **Remarks:** Accepts advertising. **Circ:** (Not Reported).

19635 ■ Sertoman
Sertoma Inc.
1912 E Meyer Blvd.
Kansas City, MO 64132
Phone: (816)333-8300
Fax: (816)333-4320
Publisher's E-mail: infosertoma@sertomahq.org
Freq: Quarterly. **ISSN:** 0744--2807 (print). **Subscription Rates:** Included in membership. **URL:** http://members.sertoma.org/sslpage.aspx?pid=357. **Remarks:** Accepts advertising. **Circ:** (Not Reported).

19636 ■ Shorthorn Country
American Shorthorn Association
7607 NW Prairie View Rd.
Kansas City, MO 64151
Phone: (816)599-7777
Fax: (816)599-7782
Publisher's E-mail: info@shorthorn.org
Magazine on Shorthorn cattle. **Freq:** 11/year. **Print Method:** Offset. **Trim Size:** 8 1/4 x 10 3/4. **Cols./Page:** 3. **Col. Width:** 26 nonpareils. **Col. Depth:** 140 agate lines. **Key Personnel:** Don Cagwin, Publisher; Tracy Duncan, Art Director, Editor. **ISSN:** 0149--9319 (print). **Subscription Rates:** $24 U.S.; $120 Other countries; $60 Canada; $38 Two years; $110 Canada 2 years; $220 Other countries 2 years. **URL:** http://www.shorthorncountry.net. **Ad Rates:** 4C $285. **Remarks:** Accepts advertising. **Circ:** Paid ‡3500, Non-paid ‡200.

19637 ■ Sickle & Sheaf: The Magazine of Alpha Gamma Rho Agriculture Fraternity
Alpha Gamma Rho
10101 NW Ambassador Dr.
Kansas City, MO 64153-1395
Phone: (816)891-9200
Fax: (816)891-9401
Publisher's E-mail: grant@alphagammarho.org
Agriculture fraternity magazine. **Freq:** Quarterly March, June, September, December. **Print Method:** Offset. **Trim Size:** 10 7/8 x 17. **Cols./Page:** 4. **Key Personnel:** Jason Gerke, Editor; Philip Josephson, Business Manager; Sarah Nadler, Contact. **ISSN:** 8750--6866 (print). **URL:** http://www.alphagammarho.org/sickle-and-sheaf. **Remarks:** Advertising not accepted. **Circ:** ‡40000.

19638 ■ Soccer Journal
National Soccer Coaches Association of America
30 W Pershing Rd., Ste. 350
Kansas City, MO 64108-2463
Phone: (816)471-1941
Fax: (816)474-7408
Publisher's E-mail: info@nscaa.com
Freq: 7/year. **ISSN:** 0560- 517X (print). **Subscription Rates:** Included in membership. **Alt. Formats:** PDF. **URL:** http://www.nscaa.com/education/resources/soccer-journal. **Remarks:** Accepts advertising. **Circ:** 17000.

19639 ■ Tangent
Tangent
4601 Wallace, No. 4
Kansas City, MO 64129
Magazine providing reviews on short stories. **Key Personnel:** Eric James Stone, Web Administrator; Dave Truesdale, Founder, Managing Editor. **URL:** http://www.tangentonline.com. **Remarks:** Advertising accepted; rates available upon request. **Circ:** (Not Reported).

19640 ■ University News
University of Missouri-Kansas City
5327 Holmes St.
Kansas City, MO 64110
Phone: (816)235-1393
Publisher's E-mail: ucenter@umkc.edu
Collegiate newspaper. **Founded:** 1933. **Freq:** Weekly (Mon.). **Print Method:** Offset. **Cols./Page:** 5. **Col. Width:** 24 nonpareils. **Col. Depth:** 228 agate lines. **Key Personnel:** Ashley Lane, Manager; Kynslie Otte, Editor-in-Chief; Leanna Bales, Advertising Executive. **Subscription Rates:** $25 Individuals; $1 Single issue. **URL:** http://info.umkc.edu/unews/. **Ad Rates:** BW $720; 4C $870; PCI $9. **Remarks:** Accepts advertising. **Circ:** Free 4,000.

19641 ■ Veterans' Voices
Vetarans Voices Writing Project
406 W 34th St., Ste. 103
Kansas City, MO 64111
Phone: (816)701-6844
Publisher's E-mail: volunteer@veteransvoices.org
Freq: 3/year. **ISSN:** 0504--0779 (print). **Subscription Rates:** $25 Individuals. **URL:** http://www.veteransvoices.com/subscribe. **Remarks:** Advertising not accepted. **Circ:** 7000.

19642 ■ VFW Magazine
VFW Magazine
406 W 34th St.
Kansas City, MO 64111
Phone: (816)756-3390
Fax: (816)968-1149
Publisher's E-mail: info@vfw.org
Magazine for the Veterans of Foreign Wars. **Freq:** Monthly. **Print Method:** Offset. **Trim Size:** 7 3/4 x 10 3/4. **Cols./Page:** 3. **Col. Width:** 2 1/4 inches. **Col. Depth:** 140 agate lines. **Key Personnel:** Richard K. Kolb, Director, Publications, Editor-in-Chief, Publisher; Janie Blankenship, Associate Editor; Robert Widener, Art Director. **ISSN:** 0161--8598 (print). **Subscription Rates:** Included in membership; $15 Nonmembers; 20 Out of country. **URL:** http://www.vfw.org/News-and-Events/Magazine. **Ad Rates:** BW $29830; 4C $37755. **Remarks:** Accepts advertising. **Circ:** Paid *1561257.

19643 ■ World Grain
Sosland Publishing Co.
4800 Main St., Ste. 100
Kansas City, MO 64112
Phone: (816)756-1000
Fax: (816)756-0494
Publisher's E-mail: nwages@sosland.com
International magazine for grain industry managers and related government officials. **Freq:** Monthly. **Print Method:** Offset. **Trim Size:** 8 x 10 3/4. **Cols./Page:** 3. **Col. Width:** 27 nonpareils. **Col. Depth:** 140 agate lines. **Key Personnel:** Meyer Sosland, Managing Editor, phone: (816)756-1000; Charles Sosland, President, Chief Executive Officer; Dan Flavin, Publisher, Director, Advertising and Sales; Arvin Donley, Editor. **ISSN:** 0745--8991 (print). **Subscription Rates:** Free to qualified subscribers. **URL:** http://www.world-grain.com. **Ad Rates:** BW $4450; 4C $6000. **Remarks:** Accepts advertising. **Circ:** 11288, ‡11195.

19644 ■ KBEQ-FM - 104.3
508 Westport Rd., Ste. 202
Kansas City, MO 64112
Phone: (816)753-4000
Fax: (816)753-4045
Format: Country. **Owner:** Wilks Broadcast Group L.L.C., 100 N Point Center E, Ste. 310, Alpharetta, GA 30022, Ph: (770)754-3211, Fax: (678)893-0123.

Founded: 1973. **Operating Hours**: Continuous. **Wattage:** 100,000. **Ad Rates:** Advertising accepted; rates available upon request. **URL:** http://www.q104kc.com.

19645 ■ KCKC-FM - 102.1
508 Westport Rd., Ste. 202
Kansas City, MO 64111
Phone: (816)576-7102
Fax: (816)753-4045
Format: Adult Contemporary; Contemporary Christian. **Owner:** Wilks Broadcast Group L.L.C., 100 N Point Center E, Ste. 310, Alpharetta, GA 30022, Ph: (770)754-3211, Fax: (678)893-0123. **Operating Hours**: Continuous. **Key Personnel:** Marc Harrell, Gen. Sales Mgr. **Ad Rates:** Advertising accepted; rates available upon request. **URL:** http://kc1021.com.

19646 ■ KCPT-TV - 19
125 E 31st St.
Kansas City, MO 64108
Phone: (816)756-3580
Free: 888-203-1747
Email: customer_service@kcpt.org
Format: Public TV. **Networks:** Public Broadcasting Service (PBS). **Owner:** Public Television 19 Inc., 125 E Thirty First St., Kansas City, MO 64108, Ph: (816)756-3580, Free: 888-203-1747. **Founded:** 1961. **Formerly**: KCSD-TV. **Operating Hours**: 6 a.m.-12:30 midnight. **ADI**: Kansas City, MO (Lawrence, KS). **Key Personnel:** Jeff Evans, Contact; Michael Murphy, Contact; Jeff Evans, Contact; Michael Zeller, Contact; Michael Murphy, Contact. **Local Programs**: *RUCKUS*, Sunday Thursday 11:30 a.m. - 12:00 p.m. 7:00 p.m. - 7:30 p.m.; *Kansas City Week in Review*, Saturday Sunday Friday 12:30 a.m. - 1:00 a.m. 11:00 a.m. - 11:30 a.m. 7:30 p.m. - 8:00 p.m.; *Rare Visions and Roadside Revelations*, Thursday 12:30 a.m. - 1:00 a.m. **Ad Rates:** Noncommercial. **URL:** http://www.kcpt.org.

19647 ■ KCUR-FM - 89.3
4825 Troost Ave., Ste. 202
Kansas City, MO 64110
Phone: (816)235-1551
Fax: (816)235-2864
Email: kcur@umkc.edu
Format: Public Radio; Talk; Jazz; News; Information. **Networks:** National Public Radio (NPR). **Owner:** University of Missouri, Columbia, MO 65211, Ph: (573)882-2121, Free: 800-225-6075. **Founded:** 1957. **Operating Hours**: Continuous. **ADI**: Kansas City, MO (Lawrence, KS). **Key Personnel:** Danny Baker, Dir. of Dev., danny@kcur.org; Robin Cross, Engg. Mgr., crossr@umkc.edu; Bill Anderson, Dir. of Programs, andersonw@umkc.edu. **Wattage**: 100,000 ERP. **Ad Rates:** Noncommercial. **URL:** http://www.kcur.org.

19648 ■ KCWE-TV - 29
6455 Winchester Ave.
Kansas City, MO 64133
Phone: (816)221-2900
Email: news@kmbc.com
Format: Commercial TV. **Networks:** United Paramount Network. **Owner:** KCWE-TV, Inc., at above address. **Founded:** Sept. 16, 2006. **ADI**: Kansas City, MO (Lawrence, KS). **Key Personnel:** Jason Ferguson, Sales Mgr., smhart@hearst.com. **Ad Rates:** Noncommercial. **URL:** http://www.kmbc.com/kcwetv.

19649 ■ KFKF-FM - 94.1
508 Westport Rd., Ste. 202
Kansas City, MO 64111
Phone: (816)753-4000
Fax: (816)753-4045
Format: Country. **Operating Hours**: 9:00 a.m. - 5:00 p.m. Monday - Thursday; 9:00 a.m. - 4:00 p.m. Friday. **ADI**: Kansas City, MO (Lawrence, KS). **Wattage**: 100,000 ERP. **Ad Rates:** Advertising accepted; rates available upon request. **URL:** http://www.kfkf.com.

19650 ■ KKFI-FM - 90.1
3901 Main St.
Kansas City, MO 64111
Phone: (816)931-3122
Fax: (816)931-7078
Format: Music of Your Life. **Owner:** Mid-Coast Radio Project, Inc., at above address. **Founded:** 1988. **Operating Hours**: Continuous. **ADI**: Kansas City, MO (Lawrence, KS). **Local Programs**: *Your Morning Buzz*, Monday Tuesday Wednesday Thursday Friday 6:00 a.m. - 8:00 a.m. **Wattage**: 100,000 ERP. **Ad Rates:** Noncommercial. Underwriting available. **URL:** http://www.kkfi.org.

19651 ■ KLJC-FM - 88.5
15800 Calvary Rd.
Kansas City, MO 64147
Phone: (816)331-8700
Fax: (816)331-3497
Format: Religious. **Networks:** USA Radio; Moody Broadcasting. **Owner:** Calvary Bible College, 15800 Calvary Rd., Kansas City, MO 64147, Ph: (816)322-0110. **Founded:** 1970. **Operating Hours**: Continuous; 15% network, 85% local. **Key Personnel:** T.J. Jackson, Promotions Dir; Michael Randall, Contact. **Wattage**: 100,000. **Ad Rates:** Noncommercial.

19652 ■ KLRQ-FM - 96.1
PO Box 779002
Rocklin, CA 95677-9972
Fax: (916)251-1901
Free: 800-525-5683
Format: Contemporary Christian. **Owner:** Educational Media Foundation, PO Box 2098, Omaha, NE 68103-2098, Free: 800-434-8400. **Key Personnel:** Mike Novak, President, CEO; Alan Mason, COO. **Wattage**: 100,000. **URL:** http://www.klove.com.

19653 ■ KMCI-TV
4720 Oak St.
Kansas City, MO 64112
Phone: (816)753-4141
Format: Sports; Contemporary Christian. **Networks:** Independent. **Owner:** Scripps TV Station Group, at above address. **Founded:** 1988. **Operating Hours**: Continuous. **ADI**: Kansas City, MO (Lawrence, KS). **Wattage**: 730,000 ERP. **Ad Rates:** $30-50 per unit. **URL:** http://www.38thespot.com.

19654 ■ KPRS-FM - 103.3
11131 Colorado Ave.
Kansas City, MO 64137-2546
Phone: (816)763-2040
Fax: (816)761-1495
Format: Urban Contemporary. **Networks:** American Urban Radio; ABC. **Owner:** Carter Broadcast Group Inc., 11131 Colorado Ave., Kansas City, MO 64137, Ph: (816)763-2040, Fax: (816)966-1055. **Founded:** 1969. **Operating Hours**: Continuous. **Key Personnel:** Beth Baker, Dir. of Traffic; Rich McCauley, Promotions Dir.; Jeff Charney, Dir. of Production; Andre Carson, Operations Mgr.; Myron Fears, Music Dir.; Mark Leaver, Chief Engineer. **Wattage**: 100,000 ERP. **Ad Rates:** Noncommercial. **URL:** http://www.kprs.com.

19655 ■ KPRT-AM - 1590
11131 Colorado Ave.
Kansas City, MO 64137
Phone: (816)763-2040
Fax: (816)966-1055
Format: Gospel; Talk. **Networks:** American Urban Radio; CNN Radio. **Owner:** Carter Broadcast Group Inc., 11131 Colorado Ave., Kansas City, MO 64137, Ph: (816)763-2040, Fax: (816)966-1055. **Founded:** 1950. **Formerly**: KPRS-AM. **Operating Hours**: Continuous. **ADI**: Kansas City, MO (Lawrence, KS). **Key Personnel:** Myron Fears, Dir. of Programs, myrond@kprs.com; Rich McCauley, Promotions Dir., richmc@kprs.com. **Wattage**: 1,000. **Ad Rates:** $25 for 30 seconds; $35 for 60 seconds. **URL:** http://www.kprs.com/KPRT.

19656 ■ KPXE-TV - 50
4220 Shawnee Mission Pkwy., Ste. 110 B
Fairway, KS 66205
Phone: (816)924-5050
Fax: (816)931-1818
Key Personnel: Brandon Burgess, Chairman, CEO. **Ad Rates:** Advertising accepted; rates available upon request. **URL:** http://www.ionmedia.tv.

19657 ■ KSHB-TV - 41
4720 Oak St.
Kansas City, MO 64112
Phone: (816)753-4141
Format: News. **Networks:** NBC. **Owner:** The E. W. Scripps Co., 312 Walnut St., Cincinnati, OH 45202, Ph: (513)977-3000. **Founded:** 1970. **Formerly**: KBMA-TV. **Operating Hours**: Continuous. **ADI**: Kansas City, MO (Lawrence, KS). **Key Personnel:** Jack Harry, Sports Dir., harry@nbcactionnews.com. **Wattage**: 3,980,000. **Ad Rates:** Advertising accepted; rates available upon request. **URL:** http://www.kshb.com.

19658 ■ WDAF-TV - 4
3030 Summit St.
Kansas City, MO 64108
Phone: (816)753-4567
Fax: (816)561-4181
Free: 866-369-4669
Format: Commercial TV. **Networks:** Fox. **Owner:** Local TV L.L.C., 1717 Dixie Hwy., Ste. 650, Fort Wright, KY 41011. **Founded:** Oct. 14, 1949. **Operating Hours**: Continuous. **ADI**: Kansas City, MO (Lawrence, KS). **Key Personnel:** Bryan McGruder, News Dir., bryan.mcgruder@wdaftv4.com. **Ad Rates:** Noncommercial. **URL:** http://www.fox4kc.com.

KENNETT

SE MO. Dunklin Co. 80 mi. S. of Cape Girardeau. Manufactures textiles, business forms, electrical equipment, industrial hose, ready mix concrete. Cotton gins and oil mill; cotton compresses. Agriculture. Cotton, soybeans, wheat, corn.

19659 ■ The Daily Dunklin Democrat
The Daily Dunklin Democrat
203 First St.
Kennett, MO 63857-2052
Phone: (573)888-4505
Fax: (573)888-5114
General newspaper. **Freq:** Triennial Tues.-Fri. (eve); Sun. (morn.). **Print Method:** Offset. **Cols./Page:** 6. **Col. Width:** 26 nonpareils. **Col. Depth:** 294 agate lines. **Key Personnel:** Shelia Rouse, Publisher; Debbie Wright, Office Manager. **Subscription Rates:** $84 Individuals e-z pay; $101.60 By mail; $133 By mail out of state. **URL:** http://www.dddnews.com. **Mailing address:** PO Box 669, Kennett, MO 63857-0669. **Ad Rates:** GLR $.32; BW $774; 4C $996; SAU $6.43; PCI $6.55. **Remarks:** Advertising accepted; rates available upon request. **Circ:** (Not Reported).

19660 ■ KAUF-FM - 89.9
PO Box 2440
Tupelo, MS 38803
Phone: (662)844-8888
Email: contact@afa.net
Format: Religious. **Owner:** American Family Radio, at above address.

19661 ■ KCRV-AM - 1370
1303 Southwest Dr.
Kennett, MO 63857-0509
Phone: (573)628-3300
Format: News; Sports; Information. **Simulcasts:** KCRV-FM. **Owner:** Pollack Broadcasting Co., 1303 Southwest Dr., Kennett, MO 63857. **Founded:** 1950. **Key Personnel:** Monte Lyons, Operations Mgr. **Wattage**: 1,000 Daytime; 063 Ni. **Ad Rates:** Advertising accepted; rates available upon request. $8 for 30 seconds; $15 for 60 seconds. **Mailing address:** PO Box 509, Kennett, MO 63857-0509. **URL:** http://www.kcrvradio.com/kcrv-am-1370.html.

19662 ■ KCRV-FM - 105.1
PO Box 509
Kennett, MO 63857
Phone: (573)888-4616
Fax: (573)888-4890
Free: 800-522-1055
Format: Oldies. **Owner:** Pollack Broadcasting, at above address, Memphis, TN. **Operating Hours**: Continuous. **Wattage**: 4,800. **Ad Rates:** $9 for 30 seconds; $15 for 60 seconds. **URL:** http://www.kcrvradio.com.

19663 ■ KMIS-AM - 1050
1303 Southwest Dr.
Kennett, MO 63857
Phone: (573)888-4616
Fax: (573)888-4890
Free: 800-552-1055
Format: Sports. **Networks:** Fox. **Owner:** Pollack Broadcasting Co., 1303 Southwest Dr., Kennett, MO 63857. **Founded:** 1960. **Key Personnel:** Ray Taylor, Dir. of Programs. **Wattage**: 600 ERP DAY. **Ad Rates:** $6-8 for 30 seconds; $9-11 for 60 seconds. **Mailing address:** PO Box 509, Kennett, MO 63857. **URL:** http://www.kmisradio.com.

Circulation: ★ = AAM; △ or • = BPA; ♦ = CAC; ❑ = VAC; ⊕ = PO Statement; ‡ = Publisher's Report; Boldface figures = sworn; Light figures = estimated.

19664 ■ Time Warner Cable
717 Hwy.
Kennett, MO 63857
Phone: (573)888-4686
Owner: Time Warner Inc., 1 Time Warner Ctr., New York, NY 10019-8016, Ph: (212)484-8000. **Founded:** 1963. **Formerly:** Kennett Cablevision. **Cities Served:** subscribing households 5,100. **URL:** http://www.timewarnercable.com.

KIDDER

19665 ■ Piedmontese Profile
Piedmontese Association of the United States
6134 NW Theil Dr.
Kidder, MO 64649
Phone: (816)786-3155
Magazine featuring beef production. **Freq:** Quarterly. **Subscription Rates:** $35 Individuals. **Remarks:** Accepts advertising. **Circ:** (Not Reported).

KING CITY

NW MO. Gentry Co. Gentry Co. Purebred cattle and hogs. Dairy, poultry farms. Corn, oats, soybeans.

19666 ■ Tri-County News
Pearl Publishing Co.
PO Box 428
King City, MO 64463
Phone: (816)535-4313
Free: 800-421-1765
Publication E-mail: tcn@ppc.com
Legal advertising newspaper. **Founded:** 1923. **Freq:** Weekly (Fri.). **Print Method:** Letterpress. Uses mats. **Trim Size:** 10 1/4 x 16. **Cols./Page:** 6 and 5. **Col. Width:** 24 nonpareils and 1 13/16 inches. **Col. Depth:** 224 agate lines and 16 inches. **Key Personnel:** Phil W. Cobb, Editor; Lisa J. Andrysiak, Contact; Cherie Jolly, Managing Editor. **USPS:** 638-520. **Subscription Rates:** $12 in St. Joseph County; $20 Two years in St. Joseph County; $17 Out of area; $30 Two years out of area; $22.25; $26.25; $35. **Ad Rates:** BW $260; 4C $350; SAU $4; PCI $4; GLR $.50; BW $514.50; PCI $5.50. **Remarks:** Accepts advertising. **Circ:** ‡1000, 1850.

KIRKSVILLE

N. MO. Adair Co. 90 mi. N. of Columbia. Northeast Missouri State University. Kirkville College of Osteopathy and Surgery. Manufactures shoes, business forms, hospital supplies. Dairy farming; meat processing. Corn, beans, cattle, hogs.

19667 ■ Journal of the American Osteopathic College of Dermatology
American Osteopathic College of Dermatology
2902 N Baltimore St.
Kirksville, MO 63501
Phone: (660)665-2184
Fax: (660)627-2623
Free: 800-449-2623
Subscription Rates: Included in membership. **Alt. Formats:** PDF. **URL:** http://www.aocd.org/?page=JAOCD. **Mailing address:** PO Box 7525, Kirksville, MO 63501. **Remarks:** Advertising not accepted. **Circ:** (Not Reported).

19668 ■ Kirksville Daily Express and News
Kirksville Daily Express
110 E McPherson St.
Kirksville, MO 63501
Phone: (660)665-2808
Publisher's E-mail: circulation@kirksvilledailyexpress.com
Newspaper. **Freq:** Daily. **Print Method:** Offset. **Cols./Page:** 6. **Col. Width:** 11 picas. **Col. Depth:** 21 inches. **Key Personnel:** Kathy Veatch, Manager, Production; Jason Hunsicker, Managing Editor; Larry Freels, Publisher; George Wriedt, General Manager. **USPS:** 296-060. **Subscription Rates:** $147 Individuals; $150 Out of state; $165 Individuals online. **URL:** http://www.kirksvilledailyexpress.com. **Ad Rates:** GLR $9.65; BW $1216; 4C $1376; SAU $6; PCI $10.92. **Remarks:** Accepts advertising. **Circ:** Mon.-Fri. ‡7,600, Sun. ‡8,000.

19669 ■ KIRX-AM - 1450
PO Box 130
Kirksville, MO 63501
Phone: (660)665-3781
Email: kirx@cableone.net
Format: Full Service; Oldies; Talk; News; Sports; Information. **Networks:** ABC; Brownfield; Missouri. **Owner:** KIRX Inc., PO Box 130, Kirksville, MO 63501, Ph: (660)665-9828. **Founded:** 1947. **Operating Hours:** Continuous. **ADI:** Ottumwa, IA-Kirksville, MO (Wapello, IA). **Key Personnel:** Steve Lloyd, Gen. Mgr.; Duncan Miller, Operations Mgr., duncanmiller@cableone.net. **Wattage:** 1,000. **Ad Rates:** $18.50 for 30 seconds; $18.50-27.50 for 60 seconds. KRXL and KTUF. **URL:** http://www.1450kirx.com.

19670 ■ KLTE-FM - 107.9
No. 3 Crown Dr., Ste. 100
Kirksville, MO 63501
Phone: (660)627-5583
Format: Religious. **Owner:** Bott Radio Network, 10550 Barkley, Overland Park, KS 66212, Ph: (913)642-7770, Fax: (913)642-1319, Free: 800-345-2621. **Operating Hours:** Continuous. **Wattage:** 100,000. **Ad Rates:** Noncommercial; underwriting available. **URL:** http://www.bottradionetwork.com.

19671 ■ KRXL-FM - 94.5
1308 N Baltimore
Kirksville, MO 63501
Phone: (660)665-9828
Format: Classic Rock. **Networks:** ABC. **Owner:** KIRX Inc., PO Box 130, Kirksville, MO 63501, Ph: (660)665-9828. **Founded:** 1967. **Operating Hours:** Continuous. **ADI:** Ottumwa, IA-Kirksville, MO (Wapello, IA). **Key Personnel:** Steve Lloyd, Gen. Mgr.; Duncan Miller, Dir. of Programs. **Wattage:** 100,000. **Ad Rates:** $19.50 for 30 seconds; $25.25-28.50 for 60 seconds. KTUF and KIRX. **Mailing address:** PO Box 130, Kirksville, MO 63501. **URL:** http://www.945thex.com.

19672 ■ KTRM-FM - 88.7
100 E Normal Ave.
Kirksville, MO 63501
Phone: (660)785-4506
Format: News; Information; Sports. **Owner:** Truman State University, 100 E Normal Ave., Kirksville, MO 63501, Ph: (660)785-4000. **Operating Hours:** Continuous. **URL:** http://www.truman.edu.

19673 ■ KTRM-TV
1400 S Franklin
Kirksville, MO 63501
Fax: (660)785-7601
Owner: Truman State University, 100 E Normal Ave., Kirksville, MO 63501, Ph: (660)785-4000.

19674 ■ KTUF-FM
1308 N Baltimore S
Kirksville, MO 63501-2509
Format: Country. **Founded:** 1206. **Wattage:** 50,000 ERP.

19675 ■ KTVO-TV - 3
15518 US Highway 63 N
Kirksville, MO 63501
Phone: (660)627-3333
Format: Commercial TV. **Networks:** ABC. **Owner:** Sinclair Broadcast Group Inc., 10706 Beaver Dam Rd., Hunt Valley, MD 21030, Ph: (410)568-1500, Fax: (410)568-1533. **Founded:** 1955. **Operating Hours:** Continuous; 60% network, 32% syndicated, 8% local. **ADI:** Ottumwa, IA-Kirksville, MO (Wapello, IA). **Key Personnel:** Crystal Amini-Rad, Bus. Mgr., camini-rad@ktvotv3.com; Merle Snyder, Sales Mgr., msnyder@ktvotv3.com. **Ad Rates:** $35-750 for 30 seconds. **Mailing address:** PO Box 949, Kirksville, MO 63501. **URL:** http://www.heartlandconnection.com.

KNOB NOSTER

W. MO. Johnson Co. 60 mi. E. of Kansas City. Knob Noster State Park. Whiteman AFB. Stock and grain farms.

19676 ■ KCVQ-FM
PO Box 800
Camdenton, MO 65020-0800
Phone: (573)346-3200
Fax: (573)346-1010
Free: 800-336-0917
Format: Contemporary Christian. **Owner:** Spirit FM Radio Network, PO Box 800, Camdenton, MO 65020. **Founded:** 1985. **Key Personnel:** Jim McDermott, Contact; Darren Alexander, Contact; Christy Pond, Contact; Kc Wright, Contact; Fred Young, Contact. **Wattage:** 7,700 ERP. **Ad Rates:** Noncommercial.

LA GRANGE

19677 ■ Press-News Journal: Serving the Lewis County, MO., Communities Since 1862
Press-News Journal
109 N 4th St.
La Grange, MO 63448
Phone: (573)288-5668
Fax: (573)288-0000
Publication E-mail: news@lewispnj.com
Newspaper with a Democratic orientation. **Freq:** Weekly (Thurs.). **Print Method:** Offset. **Trim Size:** 15 x 21. **Cols./Page:** 6. **Col. Width:** 1.75 inches. **Col. Depth:** 294 agate lines. **Key Personnel:** Daniel W. Steinbeck, Managing Editor, Publisher; Jennifer Pegler, Business Manager. **USPS:** 088-820. **Subscription Rates:** $29 Individuals print + online; $40 Out of area print + online; $48 Individuals print + online; $15 Individuals online. **URL:** http://lewispnj.com. **Mailing address:** PO Box 227, Canton, MO 63435. **Ad Rates:** GLR $3.50; BW $409.50; 4C $495; SAU $3.75; PCI $3.5. **Remarks:** Accepts advertising. **Circ:** ‡3500.

LAMAR

SW MO. Barton Co. 40 mi. NE of Joplin. Manufactures stereo equipment, office furniture, wire display racks. Diversified farming. Wheat, milo, corn, hay, soybeans. Cattle. Sheep, hogs.

19678 ■ Lamar Democrat
Lamar Democrat
900 N Gulf St.
Lamar, MO 64759
Phone: (417)682-5529
Fax: (417)682-5595
Publisher's E-mail: info@lamardemocrat.com
Community newspaper. **Founded:** 1870. **Freq:** Semiweekly (Wed. and Sat.). **Print Method:** Offset. **Cols./Page:** 6. **Col. Width:** 26 nonpareils. **Col. Depth:** 301 agate lines. **Key Personnel:** Rayma Davis, Editor. **ISSN:** 0745-9300 (print). **Subscription Rates:** $59.04 Individuals; $66.56 Out of state; $53.73 Individuals senior citizen; $15 Individuals new subscribers. **URL:** http://www.lamardemocrat.com. **Mailing address:** PO Box 458, Lamar, MO 64759. **Ad Rates:** BW $709.50; 4C $909.50; SAU $5.95. **Remarks:** Accepts advertising. **Circ:** Paid ‡3,850, Free ‡600.

LEBANON

SC MO. Laclede Co. 49 mi. NE of Springfield. Recreation. Trout fishing. Camping. Manufactures aluminum boats, campers, barrels, textiles, fishing lures, furniture, steel dies, tools, mufflers. Oak, walnut timber. Dairy, stock, poultry farms.

19679 ■ The Lebanon Daily Record
Lebanon Publishing Co.
100 E Commercial St.
Lebanon, MO 65536
Phone: (417)532-9131
Publisher's E-mail: editor@lebanondailyrecord.com
General newspaper. **Freq:** Daily and Sat. (morn.). **Print Method:** Offset. **Cols./Page:** 6. **Col. Width:** 25 nonpareils. **Col. Depth:** 294 agate lines. **Key Personnel:** Ken York, Editor. **Subscription Rates:** $9.65 Individuals 1 month (print); $9 Individuals 1 month (online). **URL:** http://lebanondailyrecord.com. **Formerly:** Rustic-Republican. **Ad Rates:** BW $877; 4C $1052; SAU $7.15; BW $1032; 4C $1207; SAU $8.40. **Remarks:** Accepts classified advertising. **Circ:** (Not Reported).

19680 ■ KBNN-AM - 750
PO Box 1112
Lebanon, MO 65536
Phone: (417)532-9111
Fax: (417)588-4191
Format: News. **Networks:** ABC; Missouri. **Founded:** 1972. **Operating Hours:** Sunrise-sunset. **ADI:** Springfield, MO. **Wattage:** 5,000. **Ad Rates:** $13.50 for 30 seconds; $27 for 60 seconds. **URL:** http://www.myozarksonline.com.

19681 ■ KCLQ-FM - 107.9
18785 Finch Rd.
Lebanon, MO 65536
Phone: (417)532-2962
Fax: (417)532-5184

Format: Country. **Founded:** 1993. **Formerly:** KLWT-FM. **Operating Hours:** Continuous. **Key Personnel:** Dan Caldwell, Gen. Mgr.; Kristopher Caldwell, Dir. of Programs. **Wattage:** 50,000. **Ad Rates:** Noncommercial. Combined advertising rates available with KLWT-AM. **URL:** http://www.1079thecoyote.com.

19682 ■ KJEL-FM - 103.7
18553 Gentry Rd.
Lebanon, MO 65536
Format: News; Sports. **Simulcasts:** KFBD-FM 97.9, KOZQ-FM 102.3, KBNN-AM 750, KJPW-AM 1390, KIIK-AM 127. **Owner:** Ozark Broadcasting Corp. **Key Personnel:** Mike Edwards, Gen. Mgr. **Wattage:** 100,000. **Mailing address:** PO Box 1112, Lebanon, MO 65536.

19683 ■ KLWT-AM - 1230
18785 Finch Rd.
Lebanon, MO 65536
Phone: (417)532-2962
Fax: (417)588-4092
Email: klwt@klwt1230.com
Owner: Pearson Broadcasting of Lebanon. **Founded:** 1948. **Key Personnel:** Dan Caldwell, Gen. Mgr; Brian Hanley, Contact. **Wattage:** 1,000. **Ad Rates:** Accepts Advertising. **URL:** http://klwt1230.com/.

19684 ■ KTTK-FM - 90.7
PO Box 1232
Lebanon, MO 65536
Phone: (417)588-1435
Fax: (417)532-3055
Format: Bluegrass; Contemporary Country. **Owner:** Lebanon Educational Broadcasting Foundation, PO BOX 1232, Lebanon, MO 65536-1232. **Founded:** 1986. **ADI:** Harrisburg-York-Lancaster-Lebanon, PA. **Wattage:** 11,000. **Ad Rates:** Underwriting available.

LEES SUMMIT

19685 ■ Lee's Summit Journal
Lee's Summit Journal Inc.
415 SE Douglas St.
Lees Summit, MO 64063-4246
Phone: (816)524-2345
Fax: (816)524-5136
Community newspaper. **Freq:** Semiweekly Wednesday and Friday. **Print Method:** Offset. **Cols./Page:** 6. **Col. Width:** 2 1/16 inches. **Col. Depth:** 21 inches. **Key Personnel:** John McCall, Manager, Circulation, phone: (816)282-7025; John Beaudoin, Publisher, phone: (816)282-7001; Ronda Moore, Business Manager. **Subscription Rates:** $48 Individuals. **URL:** http://www.lsjournal.com. **Formerly:** Lee's Summit Tribune. **Ad Rates:** GLR $.50; BW $882; 4C $1232; SAU $7. **Remarks:** .50. **Circ:** Combined ‡3744.

19686 ■ Lee's Summit Journal-Extra
Lee's Summit Journal Inc.
415 SE Douglas St.
Lees Summit, MO 64063-4246
Phone: (816)524-2345
Fax: (816)524-5136
Total-market coverage shopper. **Freq:** Weekly (Wed.). **Print Method:** Letterpress and offset. **Cols./Page:** 6. **Col. Width:** 2 1/16 inches. **Col. Depth:** 21 inches. **Key Personnel:** Ronda Moore, Business Manager, phone: (816)282-7002; John Beaudoin, Publisher, phone: (816)282-7001; John McCall, Manager, Circulation, phone: (816)282-7025. **Subscription Rates:** Free. **URL:** http://www.lsjournal.com. **Ad Rates:** GLR $.55; BW $793.80; 4C $1,333.80; SAU $7.70. **Remarks:** Accepts advertising. **Circ:** Free ‡5100.

19687 ■ NLGI Spokesman
National Lubricating Grease Institute
249 SW Noel St., Ste. 249
Lees Summit, MO 64063-2241
Phone: (816)524-2500
Fax: (816)524-2504
Publisher's E-mail: nlgi@nlgi.org
Freq: Bimonthly. **Print Method:** Offset. **Trim Size:** 8 3/8 x 11. **Cols./Page:** 3. **Col. Width:** 2 1/8 inches. **Col. Depth:** 9 1/8 inches. **Key Personnel:** Kimberly Bott, Executive Director; Kimberly Hartley, Executive Director. **ISSN:** 0027--6782 (print). **Subscription Rates:** $80 Canada non-members; $109 Other countries non-members; $7 Single issue; $147 Individuals airmail; non-members; $8 Canada single issue; $65 Members; $65 Nonmembers. **URL:** http://www.nlgi.org/products-page/nlgi-spokesman. **Ad Rates:** BW $385; 4C $450. **Remarks:** Accepts advertising. **Circ:** 3000, 3000.

LIBERTY

W. MO. Clay Co. 5 mi. N. of Kansas City. William Jewell College. Residential.

19688 ■ Liberty Tribune
News-Press and Gazette Co.
104 N Main St.
Liberty, MO 64068
Phone: (816)781-4941
Publication E-mail: libtrib@libertytribune.com
Community newspaper. **Freq:** Weekly (Wed.). **Print Method:** Offset. **Trim Size:** 11 x 21. **Cols./Page:** 6. **Col. Width:** 2 1/8 inches. **Col. Depth:** 21 inches. **Key Personnel:** Amy Neal, Managing Editor; Tony Luke, General Manager. **Subscription Rates:** $36 Individuals; $51.95 Out of area. **URL:** http://www.libertytribune.com. **Remarks:** Accepts advertising. **Circ:** 7000.

19689 ■ KCXL-AM - 1140
310 S La Frenz Rd.
Liberty, MO 64068
Phone: (816)792-1140
Fax: (816)792-8258
Email: kcxl@kc.rr.com
Format: Talk; Information. **Networks:** Jones Satellite. **Founded:** 1994. **Formerly:** KLDY-AM; KBIL-AM. **Operating Hours:** Continuous. **ADI:** Kansas City, MO (Lawrence, KS). **Key Personnel:** David Brewer, Station Mgr. **Local Programs:** *Junk in my Trunk*, Thursday Saturday 10:00 a.m. **Wattage:** 500 Day/006 Watts Night. **Ad Rates:** Noncommercial. **URL:** http://www.kcxl.com.

19690 ■ KWJC-FM - 91.9
William Jewell College
500 College Hill
Liberty, MO 64068
Phone: (816)781-7700
Fax: (816)415-5040
Free: 888-253-9355
Format: Adult Contemporary; Educational. **Owner:** William Jewell College, 500 College Hill, Liberty, MO 64068, Ph: (816)781-7700, Fax: (816)415-5040, Free: 888-253-9355. **Founded:** 1974. **Formerly:** KWPB-FM. **Operating Hours:** Continuous; 5% network, 95% local. **Key Personnel:** Todd Wirth, Gen. Mgr., wirtht@william.jewell.edu. **Wattage:** 250. **Ad Rates:** Noncommercial. **URL:** http://www.jewell.edu.

LICKING

19691 ■ Licking News
Salem Publishing
115 S Main St.
Licking, MO 65542
Phone: (573)674-2412
Fax: (573)674-4892
Publisher's E-mail: thenews@centurytel.net
Community newspaper. **Freq:** Weekly (Thurs.). **Print Method:** Offset. **Trim Size:** 13 1/2 x 11 1/4. **Cols./Page:** 6. **Col. Width:** 2 1/16 inches. **Col. Depth:** 21 inches. **Key Personnel:** Debbie Dakin, Office Manager; Donald Dodd, Publisher, phone: (573)729-4126; Angela Barnes, Managing Editor, phone: (573)674-2412. **USPS:** 312-020. **Subscription Rates:** $26 Individuals Texas and Adjoining Counties; $31 Individuals elsewhere in Missouri; $36 Out of state; $45 Two years Texas and Adjoining Counties; $54 Two years elsewhere in Missouri; $62 Out of state two years. **URL:** http://thelickingnews.com; http://www.salempublishing.com. **Mailing address:** PO Box 297, Licking, MO 65542. **Ad Rates:** BW $422.10; SAU $3.35; PCI $2.60. **Remarks:** Accepts advertising. **Circ:** ‡2,500.

LIGUORI

E. MO. Jefferson Co. 22 mi. S. of Saint Louis. Stock, poultry farms. Corn, wheat, oats.

19692 ■ Liguorian
Liguori Publications
One Liguori Dr.
Liguori, MO 63057-9999
Phone: (636)464-2500
Fax: (800)325-9526
Free: 800-325-9521
Publisher's E-mail: liguori@liguori.org
Catholic magazine. **Freq:** Monthly. **Print Method:** Offset. **Trim Size:** 8 x 10 5/8. **Cols./Page:** 2. **Col. Width:** 27 nonpareils. **Col. Depth:** 101 agate lines. **Key Personnel:** Mat Kessler, Publisher. **Subscription Rates:** $25 Individuals; $45 Two years. **URL:** http://www.liguorian.org. **Ad Rates:** 4C $3,325. **Remarks:** Accepts advertising. **Circ:** 82000.

LINN

C. MO. Osage Co. 20 mi. E. of Jefferson City. Diaspore and flint clay mines. Oak timber. Diversified farming. Corn, wheat, hay.

19693 ■ Mid Missouri Broadband & Cable
PO Box 524
Linn, MO 65051
Phone: (573)417-4004

LOUISIANA

E. MO. Pike Co. On Mississippi River, 25 mi. S. of Hannibal. Bridge to Quincy Junction and Pike, IL. Manufactures tube cement, plastics, chemicals, foundry products. Nursery. Diversified farming. Cattle, grain, apples.

19694 ■ KJFM-FM - 102.1
615 Georgia St.
Louisiana, MO 63353
Phone: (573)754-5102
Fax: (573)324-0304
Format: Contemporary Country. **Networks:** Missouri. **Owner:** Foxfire Communications, Inc., at above address. **Founded:** 1984. **ADI:** St. Louis, MO (Mt. Vernon, IL). **Key Personnel:** Thom T. Sanders, Contact. **Wattage:** 3,700 ERP. **Ad Rates:** $8-12 for 30 seconds; $12-18 for 60 seconds. **Mailing address:** PO Box 438, Louisiana, MO 63353. **URL:** http://www.kjfmeagle102.net.

MACKS CREEK

19695 ■ The American Dance Circle
Lloyd Shaw Foundation Inc.
186 Carnahan Rd.
Macks Creek, MO 65786
Phone: (573)363-5868
Fax: (573)363-5820
Magazine covering dance descriptions, dance history, and foundation activities. **Freq:** Quarterly March, June, September, and December. **Subscription Rates:** Included in membership. **Alt. Formats:** Download; PDF. **URL:** http://www.lloydshaw.org/american-dance-circle.html. **Remarks:** Advertising accepted; rates available upon request. **Circ:** (Not Reported).

MACON

N. MO. Macon Co. 65 mi. W. of Hannibal. Fishing and boating. Manufactures electrical products. Frozen food processing. Ships agriculture products, stock. Meat packing. Coal mines. Diversified farming.

19696 ■ KLTI-AM - 1560
PO Box 188
Macon, MO 63552-0452
Phone: (660)385-1560
Fax: (660)385-7090
Format: Oldies; Middle-of-the-Road (MOR). **Founded:** 1966. **Operating Hours:** Sunrise-sunset. **Key Personnel:** Steve Stewart, Contact; Steve Stewart, Contact; John Jameson, Contact. **Wattage:** 1,000. **URL:** http://www.kltiradio.com/Contact-Us.html.

MAITLAND

19697 ■ American Broadband
208 Ash St.
Maitland, MO 64466
Phone: (660)935-2211
Founded: 1941. **Cities Served:** United States; 36 channels. **Mailing address:** PO Box 112, Maitland, MO 64466. **URL:** http://www.abbmissouri.com.

MANSFIELD

S. MO. Wright Co. 46 mi. SE of Springfield. Shoe manufacturing; cheese plant; steel foundry & fabrication plant. Timber. Diversified farming. Dairying, poultry.

Circulation: ★ = AAM; △ or • = BPA; ♦ = CAC; ❑ = VAC; ⊕ = PO Statement; ‡ = Publisher's Report; Boldface figures = sworn; Light figures = estimated.

19698 ■ Mirror-Republican
Mansfield Mirror
300 E Commercial St.
Mansfield, MO 65704
Phone: (417)924-3226
Fax: (417)924-3227
Newspaper with a Republican orientation. **Freq:** Weekly (Thurs.). **Print Method:** Offset. **Cols./Page:** 6. **Col. Width:** 21 nonpareils. **Col. Depth:** 294 agate lines. **Key Personnel:** Larry Dennis, Publisher. **Subscription Rates:** $28 Individuals Wright; $32 Out of area Missouri; $38 Out of state. **Mailing address:** PO Box 197, Mansfield, MO 65704. **Ad Rates:** GLR $.12; SAU $2.45; PCI $1.90. **Remarks:** Accepts advertising. **Circ:** ‡2300.

19699 ■ KTRI-FM - 95.9
PO Box 88
Mansfield, MO 65704-0088
Wattage: 8,900. **URL:** http://www.pacersnetwork.com.

MARBLE HILL

SE MO. Bollinger Co. 30 mi. W. of Cape Girardeau. Manufactures wooden pallets, furniture, textiles. Oak timber. Agriculture. Beef and hogs.

19700 ■ The Banner-Press
The Banner-Press
103 Walnut St.
Marble Hill, MO 63764
Phone: (573)238-2821
Fax: (573)238-0020
Community newspaper. **Founded:** 1881. **Freq:** Weekly (Thurs.). **Print Method:** Offset. **Cols./Page:** 6. **Col. Width:** 2 inches. **Col. Depth:** 21 1/2 inches. **ISSN:** 0416-4000 (print). **URL:** http://columbustelegram.com/banner-press/. **Ad Rates:** BW $325; PCI $4.25. **Remarks:** Accepts advertising. **Circ:** (Not Reported).

19701 ■ KMHM-FM - 104.1
PO Box 266E, Rte. 1
Marble Hill, MO 63764
Phone: (573)238-1041
Fax: (573)238-0104
Email: kmhm@clas.net
Format: Full Service. **Owner:** Harold and Carlene Lawder, at above address. **Founded:** 1995. **Formerly:** KQUA-FM. **Operating Hours:** Continuous. **Wattage:** 6,000. **Ad Rates:** Noncommercial. **URL:** http://mysoutherngospel.net.

MARSHALL

NWC MO. Saline Co. 30 mi. N. of Sedalia. Missouri Valley College. Manufactures shoes, feed. Food processing. Diversified farming. Dairy products. Corn, wheat, soybeans.

19702 ■ The Marshall Democrat-News
The Marshall Democrat-News
121 N Lafayette St.
Marshall, MO 65340
Phone: (660)886-2233
Fax: (660)886-8544
General newspaper. **Freq:** Daily (eve.). **Print Method:** Offset. **Cols./Page:** 6. **Col. Width:** 24 nonpareils. **Col. Depth:** 301 agate lines. **Key Personnel:** Dave Phillips, Publisher; Sarah Reed, Editor; Pat Morrow, Business Manager. **Subscription Rates:** $114.50 Individuals 1 year; $124 By mail 1 year; $135 By mail 1 year (outside area); $128 Out of state 1 year; $69 Individuals 1 year (online only). **URL:** http://www.marshallnews.com. **Mailing address:** PO Box 100, Marshall, MO 65340. **Ad Rates:** BW $857.85; 4C $1073.85; SAU $6.65; PCI $5.50. **Remarks:** Accepts advertising. **Circ:** (Not Reported).

19703 ■ KMMO-AM - 1300
PO Box 128
Marshall, MO 65340
Phone: (660)886-7422
Fax: (660)886-6291
Free: 800-727-5666
Format: News; Sports; Contemporary Country; Agricultural. **Simulcasts:** KMMO-FM. **Networks:** CBS; Kansas Information; Brownfield. **Owner:** Missouri Valley Broadcasting Inc., 1190 N Lexington Ave., Hwy. 65 N, Marshall, MO 65340, Ph: (660)886-7422, Fax: (660)886-6291, Free: 800-727-5666. **Founded:** 1949. **Operating Hours:** Continuous; 10% network, 90% local. **Key Personnel:** John Wilson, Gen. Mgr. **Wattage:** 1,000. **Ad Rates:** $15 for 30 seconds; $22 for 60 seconds. **URL:** http://www.kmmo.com.

19704 ■ KMMO-FM - 102.9
1190 N Hwy. 65
Marshall, MO 65340
Phone: (660)886-7422
Fax: (660)886-6291
Free: 800-727-5666
Format: Country; Agricultural. **Simulcasts:** KMMO-AM. **Networks:** CBS; Brownfield; Missouri. **Owner:** Missouri Valley Broadcasting Inc., 1190 N Lexington Ave., Hwy. 65 N, Marshall, MO 65340, Ph: (660)886-7422, Fax: (660)886-6291, Free: 800-727-5666. **Founded:** 1969. **Operating Hours:** Continuous; 10% network, 90% local. **Key Personnel:** John Wilson, Gen. Mgr. **Wattage:** 100,000. **Ad Rates:** Noncommercial. **Mailing address:** PO Box 128, Marshall, MO 65340. **URL:** http://www.kmmo.com.

19705 ■ KMVC-FM
500 E College St.
Marshall, MO 65340
Format: Alternative/New Music/Progressive; Album-Oriented Rock (AOR); Urban Contemporary. **Networks:** Independent. **Owner:** Missouri Valley College, 500 East College, Marshall, MO 65340. **Founded:** 1969. **Formerly:** KNOS-FM. **Key Personnel:** Karl Bean, Contact. **Ad Rates:** Noncommercial.

MARSHFIELD

S. MO. Webster Co. 24 mi. NE of Springfield. Manufactures caskets, textiles, steel fabricated products. Walnut and oak timber. Diversified farming. Poultry, dairy, livestock.

19706 ■ The Marshfield Mail
The Marshfield Mail
225 N Clay St.
Marshfield, MO 65706
Phone: (417)859-2013
Fax: (417)859-7930
Publisher's E-mail: news@marshfieldmail.com
County newspaper. **Freq:** Weekly (Wed.). **Print Method:** Offset. **Cols./Page:** 6. **Col. Width:** 2 inches. **Col. Depth:** 21 inches. **Key Personnel:** Debbie Chapman, Advertising Representative; Roxane Shreck, Office Manager; Dave Berry, Publisher. **USPS:** 331-080. **Subscription Rates:** $43.12 Individuals all access; $3.15 Individuals digital only. **URL:** http://marshfieldmail.com. **Mailing address:** PO Box A, Marshfield, MO 65706. **Ad Rates:** BW $1298. **Remarks:** Accepts advertising. **Circ:** (Not Reported).

MARTHASVILLE

E. MO. Warren Co. On Missouri River, 30 mi. SW of Saint Charles. Lumber mill; hat factory. Timber. Stock, poultry, dairy, grain farms. Wheat, corn, oats, soybeans.

19707 ■ Missouri Ruralist
Farm Progress Companies Inc.
21680 Smith Creek Rd.
Marthasville, MO 63357
Phone: (636)932-4664
Publisher's E-mail: circhelp@farmprogress.com
Agriculture magazine. **Freq:** Monthly. **Print Method:** Offset. **Trim Size:** 8 x 10 7/8. **Cols./Page:** 3. **Col. Width:** 14 picas. **Col. Depth:** 140 agate lines. **Key Personnel:** Willie Vogt, Director, Editorial, phone: (651)454-6994, fax: (651)994-0661; Mindy Ward, Editor, phone: (636)932-4664. **ISSN:** 0026--668X (print). **Subscription Rates:** $29.95 Individuals; $48.95 Two years; $64.95 Individuals three years. **URL:** http://farmprogress.com/missouri-ruralist. **Ad Rates:** BW $2,780; 4C $4,170; PCI $110. **Remarks:** Accepts advertising. **Circ:** (Not Reported).

MARYLAND HEIGHTS

St. Louis Co.

19708 ■ Cytokine
International Cytokine Society
3251 Riverport Ln.
Maryland Heights, MO 63043
Phone: (314)447-8000
Fax: (314)447-8033
Publication E-mail: usinfo-ehelp@elsevier.com
Key Personnel: S.L. Gaffen, Associate Editor; Gordon W. Duff, Editor; S.K. Durum, Editor. **ISSN:** 1043--4666 (print). **Subscription Rates:** $342 Individuals print; $869.33 Institutions online; $2608 Institutions print. **URL:** http://www.journals.elsevier.com/cytokine; http://www.weizmann.ac.il/cytokine. **Remarks:** Accepts advertising. **Circ:** (Not Reported).

19709 ■ Journal of Cystic Fibrosis
Elsevier - Mosby Journal Div.
3251 Riverport Ln.
Maryland Heights, MO 63043
Phone: (314)447-8000
Fax: (314)447-8033
Publication E-mail: usinfo-ehelp@elsevier.com
Journal publishing articles on cystic fibrosis. **Freq:** 6/year. **Key Personnel:** D. Bilton, Board Member; G. Doring, Editor-in-Chief; J. Abbott, Board Member; Dr. H.G.M. Heijerman, Editor, Founder, Deputy. **ISSN:** 1569-1993 (print). **Subscription Rates:** $402 Individuals; $199.47 Institutions e-journal (access for 5 users and to 4 years of archives); $643 Institutions print; $483 Institutions e-journal. **URL:** http://www.cysticfibrosisjournal.com; http://www.journals.elsevier.com/journal-of-cystic-fibrosis; http://www.us.elsevierhealth.com/product.jsp?isbn=15691993; http://ecfs.eu/publications/the_journal_of_cystic_fibrosis; http://www.sciencedirect.com/jcf. **Remarks:** Advertising not accepted. **Circ:** (Not Reported).

19710 ■ Journal of Hand Therapy
American Society of Hand Therapists
3251 Riverport Ln.
Maryland Heights, MO 63043
Phone: (314)447-8000
Fax: (314)447-8033
Publication E-mail: usinfo-ehelp@elsevier.com
Freq: Quarterly. **ISSN:** 0894--1130 (print). **Subscription Rates:** Included in membership. **URL:** http://www.elsevier.com/journals/journal-of-hand-therapy/0894-1130; http://www.asht.org/research/research-resources/journal-hand-therapy. **Remarks:** Accepts advertising. **Circ:** (Not Reported).

19711 ■ Journal of Nutrition Education and Behavior
Society for Nutrition Education and Behavior
3251 Riverport Ln.
Maryland Heights, MO 63043
Phone: (314)447-8000
Fax: (314)447-8033
Publication E-mail: usinfo-ehelp@elsevier.com
Freq: Bimonthly. **ISSN:** 1499- 4046 (print). **Subscription Rates:** Included in membership; $279 Individuals /year; online only; US, Canada and other countries; $310 Individuals /year; online + print; US; $341 Individuals /year; online + print; Canada and other countries. **URL:** http://www.sneb.org/publications/jneb.html; http://www.jneb.org. **Remarks:** Accepts advertising. **Circ:** 4,500.

19712 ■ Ozanam News
National Council of the United States Society of St. Vincent de Paul
58 Progress Pky.
Maryland Heights, MO 63043-3706
Phone: (314)576-3993
Fax: (314)576-6755
Publisher's E-mail: usacouncil@svdpusa.org
Freq: Quarterly. **Subscription Rates:** free. **URL:** http://www.ssvpscotland.com/about-us/ozanam-news. **Remarks:** Advertising not accepted. **Circ:** 78,000.

MARYVILLE

NW MO. Nodaway Co. 45 mi. N. of Saint Joseph. Northwest Missouri State University. Manufactures lightning rods, paper products, auto chains, batteries, rivets, tools. Grain, dairy, stock, poultry farms. Corn, wheat, soybeans.

19713 ■ The Compass: Earth Science Journal of Sigma Gamma Epsilon
Sigma Gamma Epsilon
c/o Aaron Johnson, President
Dept. of Natural Sciences
Northwest Missouri State University
1335 Garret-Strong
800 College Park Dr.
Maryville, MO 64468
Phone: (660)562-1569
Fax: (660)562-1055

Freq: Quarterly. **Key Personnel:** Larry E. Davis, Editor. **ISSN:** 0894--802X (print). **URL:** http://digitalcommons.csbsju.edu/compass. **Circ:** (Not Reported).

19714 ■ The Laurel Review
GreenTower Press
c/o Eng Dept., NW Missouri State Univ., 800 University Dr.
800 Univ Dr.
Maryville, MO 64468-6001
Phone: (660)562-1739
Free: 800-633-1175
Publisher's E-mail: tlr@nwmissouri.edu
Literary magazine covering poetry, fiction and nonfiction. **Freq:** Semiannual. **Trim Size:** 5 1/2 x 10 1/2. **Cols./Page:** 1. **Key Personnel:** John Gallaher, Editor. **ISSN:** 0023--9003 (print). **Subscription Rates:** $10 Individuals; $18 Two years. **URL:** http://laurelreview.org. **Remarks:** Accepts advertising. **Circ:** Controlled 700.

19715 ■ Maryville Daily Forum
Maryville Daily Forum
111 E Jenkins
Maryville, MO 64468
Phone: (660)562-2424
Fax: (660)562-2823
Newspaper. **Founded:** 1869. **Freq:** Daily Monday - Friday. **Print Method:** Offset Uses mats. **Trim Size:** 6 x 21 1/2. **Key Personnel:** Deb Brown, Manager, Production; Lana Cobb, Business Manager; Rita Piveral, Office Manager. **USPS:** 332-360. **Subscription Rates:** $27 Individuals 6 months; $55 Individuals 1 year. **URL:** http://www.maryvilledailyforum.com. **Mailing address:** PO Box 188, Maryville, MO 64468. **Ad Rates:** BW $75; 4C $215; SAU $5.95; PCI $5.95. **Remarks:** Accepts advertising. **Circ:** ‡18,400.

19716 ■ Northwest Alumni Magazine
Northwest Missouri State University
800 University Dr.
Maryville, MO 64468
Phone: (660)562-1212
Free: 800-633-1175
Publisher's E-mail: comment@nwmissouri.edu
Alumni magazine for Northwest Missouri State University. **Freq:** Semiannual. **Subscription Rates:** Free to qualified subscribers. **URL:** http://www.nwmissouri.edu/ALUMNI/magazine/index.htm. **Remarks:** Advertising not accepted. **Circ:** (Not Reported).

19717 ■ Northwest Missourian
Northwest Missouri State University
800 University Dr.
Maryville, MO 64468
Phone: (660)562-1212
Free: 800-633-1175
Publication E-mail: northwestmissourian@hotmail.com
Newspaper covering the news, sports and events on campus and in the community. **Freq:** Weekly (Thurs.). **Print Method:** Offset. **Trim Size:** 13 x 21. **Cols./Page:** 6. **Col. Width:** 26 nonpareils. **Col. Depth:** 126 agate lines. **Subscription Rates:** Free. **URL:** http://www.nwmissourinews.com. **Ad Rates:** 4C $709.93; BW $604.93. **Remarks:** Accepts advertising. **Circ:** ‡4000.

19718 ■ KNIM-AM - 1580
1618 S Main
Maryville, MO 64468
Phone: (660)582-2151
Fax: (660)582-3211
Format: Oldies. **Key Personnel:** Jim Cronin, Dir. of Programs, jimcronin@knimmaryville.com; Joyce Cronin, Gen. Sales Mgr., joycec@knimmaryville.com. **Ad Rates:** Advertising accepted; rates available upon request. **Mailing address:** PO Box 278, Maryville, MO 64468.

19719 ■ KNIM-FM - 97.1
Not Available
Maryville, MO 64468
Format: Oldies. **Ad Rates:** Advertising accepted; rates available upon request. **Mailing address:** PO Box 278, Maryville, MO 64468. **URL:** http://www.nodawaybroadcasting.com.

19720 ■ KRNW-FM - 88.9
Wells Hall
800 University Dr.
Maryville, MO 64468
Phone: (660)562-1163
Fax: (660)562-1832
Email: kxcv@nwmissouri.edu
Format: Public Radio. **Key Personnel:** Rodney Harris, Gen. Mgr.; Patty Holley, Dir. of Programs; John Coffey, Producer, jcoffey@nwmissouri.edu; Darren Perkins, Chief Engineer, perkins@nwmissouri.edu. **URL:** http://www.kxcv.org.

19721 ■ KVVL-FM - 97.1
1618 S Main
Maryville, MO 64468
Phone: (660)582-2151
Fax: (660)582-3211
Format: Blues. **Owner:** Nodaway Broadcasting Corp., 1618 S Main, Maryville, MO 64468, Ph: (660)582-2151, Fax: (660)582-3211. **Key Personnel:** Joyce Cronin, Gen. Sales Mgr., joycec@knimmaryville.com; Jim Cronin, Dir. of Programs, jimcronin@knimmaryville.com.

19722 ■ KXCV-FM - 90.5
800 University Dr.
Maryville, MO 64468
Phone: (660)562-1163
Fax: (660)562-1832
Email: kxcv@nwmissouri.edu
Format: Public Radio; Jazz; News; Classical; Big Band/Nostalgia. **Networks:** Public Radio International (PRI); National Public Radio (NPR). **Owner:** Northwest Missouri State University, 800 University Dr., Maryville, MO 64468, Ph: (660)562-1212, Free: 800-633-1175. **Founded:** 1971. **Operating Hours**: Continuous; 51% network, 49% local. **Key Personnel:** Kirk Wayman, News Dir., kwayman@nwmissouri.edu; Rodney Harris, Gen. Mgr., rharris@nwmissouri.edu; Darren Perkins, Chief Engineer, perkins@nwmissouri.edu; Patty Holley, Prog. Dir., pholley@nwmissouri.edu. **Local Programs**: *You Bet Your Garden*, Friday 12:00 p.m. **Wattage**: 100,000. **Ad Rates:** Noncommercial. **URL:** http://www.kxcv.org.

19723 ■ KZLX-FM
640 College Ave.
Maryville, MO 64468
Format: Sports. **Founded:** 1206. **Wattage**: 042 ERP. **Ad Rates:** Noncommercial.

MEMPHIS

19724 ■ Memphis Democrat
Memphis Democrat
121 S Main St.
Memphis, MO 63555
Phone: (660)465-7016
Publisher's E-mail: memdemocrat@nemr.net
Community newspaper. **Freq:** Weekly (Wed.). **Subscription Rates:** $29.82 Individuals Scotland county and adjoining counties in Missouri; $28 Individuals Adjoining counties in Iowa; $39.41 Out of state Non-adjoining counties in Missouri; $37 Other countries. **URL:** http://memphisdemocrat.com/. **Ad Rates:** BW $472.50; SAU $3.75; PCI $3.75. **Remarks:** Accepts advertising. **Circ:** 2400.

19725 ■ KMEM-FM - 100.5
650 N Clay St.
Memphis, MO 63555
Phone: (660)465-7225
Fax: (660)465-2626
Free: 800-748-7875
Format: Country. **Networks:** ABC. **Owner:** Boyer Broadcasting Company Inc., at above address. **Founded:** Apr. 1982. **Key Personnel:** Mark Denney, Gen. Mgr., mdenney@kmemfm.com; Rick Fischer, Dir. of Programs, News Dir., rfischer@kmemfm.com; Donnie Middleton, Sports Dir. **Wattage**: 25,000 ERP. **URL:** http://www.kmemfm.com.

MEXICO

NEC MO. Audrain Co. 38 mi. E. of Moberly. Missouri Military Academy. Manufactures shoes, fire-clay products, bank and newspaper supplies, feed bags. Fire-clay pits. Agriculture. Corn, wheat, soybeans. Livestock.

19726 ■ The Mexico Ledger
GateHouse Media Inc.
300 N Washington St.
Mexico, MO 65265
Phone: (573)581-1111
Publication E-mail: news@mexicoledger.com
Newspaper with a Democratic orientation. **Founded:** 1855. **Freq:** Daily Monday through Friday. **Print Method:** Offset. **Cols./Page:** 6. **Col. Width:** 21 1/2 nonpareils. **Col. Depth:** 301 agate lines. **Key Personnel:** Jonathan Griffin, Editor. **Subscription Rates:** $3.50 Individuals digital and print (weekly); $5.99 Individuals digital (monthly). **URL:** http://mexicoledger.com/. **Ad Rates:** BW $1,355; 4C $1,620; SAU $10.50. **Remarks:** Accepts advertising. **Circ:** (Not Reported).

19727 ■ Top Producer: A Farm Journal Publication for Executive Farmers
Farm Journal Media Inc.
PO Box 958
Mexico, MO 65265
Phone: (573)581-9646
Publication E-mail: bthompson@farmjournal.com
Agricultural magazine published for executive farmers and ranchers. **Freq:** Monthly. **Print Method:** Offset. **Trim Size:** 8 x 10 1/2. **Cols./Page:** 3. **Col. Width:** 2 1/4 inches. **Col. Depth:** 140 agate lines. **Key Personnel:** Jeanne Bernick, Editor. **ISSN:** 1056--0831 (print). **Subscription Rates:** $40 Individuals. **URL:** http://www.agweb.com/topproducer. **Remarks:** Advertising accepted; rates available upon request. **Circ:** Non-paid ‡123,289.

19728 ■ KJAB-FM - 88.3
621 W Monroe St.
Mexico, MO 65265
Phone: (573)581-8606
Email: kjab@kjab.com
Format: Religious; Gospel; Southern Gospel; Talk. **Networks:** USA Radio. **Founded:** 1986. **Operating Hours**: Continuous; 8% network, 92% local. **Key Personnel:** Adam Weber, Gen. Mgr., adam@kjab.com; Dawn Weber, Music Dir., Office Mgr., dawn@kjab.com. **Local Programs:** *Sunrise Show*, Monday Tuesday Wednesday Thursday Friday 6:30 a.m. - 8:00 a.m. **Wattage**: 6,000. **Ad Rates:** Noncommercial. **URL:** http://www.kjab.com.

19729 ■ KWWR-FM - 95.7
PO Box 475
Mexico, MO 65265-0475
Phone: (573)581-5500
Free: 800-264-5997
Format: Country. **Owner:** KXEO Radio Inc., PO Box 475, Mexico, MO 65265, Fax: (573)581-1801. **Founded:** 1966. **Key Personnel:** Gary Leonard, Contact, gary@radiogetsresults.net; Greg Holman, Contact, greg@radiogetsresults.net; Chris Newbrough, Contact, news@radiogetsresults.net. **Wattage**: 91,000. **Ad Rates:** Advertising accepted; rates available upon request. **URL:** http://info.kwwr.com.

19730 ■ KXEO-AM - 1340
PO Box 475
Mexico, MO 65265-0475
Phone: (573)581-2340
Fax: (573)581-1801
Email: kxeo@radiogetsresults.net
Format: News; Sports; Agricultural; Soft Rock. **Networks:** CNN Radio; Westwood One Radio; Brownfield; Missouri. **Owner:** KXEO Radio Inc., PO Box 475, Mexico, MO 65265, Fax: (573)581-1801. **Founded:** 1948. **Operating Hours**: Continuous; 5% network, 95% local. **Wattage**: 1,000. **Ad Rates:** Noncommercial. Combined advertising rates available with KWWR. **URL:** http://www.kxeo.com.

MOBERLY

NC MO. Randolph Co. 36 mi. N. of Columbia. Moberly Junior College. Manufactures shoes, tools, sirups, cheese and other dairy products; hay presses. Coal mines. Diversified farming. Poultry.

19731 ■ Moberly Monitor-Index & Evening Democrat: Daily Newspaper
Moberly Monitor-Index and Evening Democrat
218 N Williams St.
Moberly, MO 65270
Phone: (660)263-4123
Publication E-mail: moberlymonitor@missvalley.com
General newspaper. **Freq:** Daily and Sun. (eve.). **Key Personnel:** Bob Cunningham, Publisher; Ruth Carr, Editor. **Subscription Rates:** $7.99 Individuals digital (montly); $2.65 Individuals digital and print (weekly). **URL:** http://www.moberlymonitor.com/. **Ad Rates:** BW $816.57; 4C $1,079.57; SAU $10.61; PCI $10.61. **Re-**

Circulation: ★ = AAM; △ or • = BPA; ♦ = CAC; ❑ = VAC; ⊕ = PO Statement; ‡ = Publisher's Report; Boldface figures = sworn; Light figures = estimated.

marks: Accepts advertising. **Circ:** Mon.-Fri. 6395, Sun. 6700.

19732 ■ KRES-FM - 104.7
300 W Reed St.
Moberly, MO 65270
Phone: (660)263-1600
Free: 800-892-2300
Format: Country. **Key Personnel:** Terry Strickland, Gen. Mgr., terrys@regionalradio.com; Brad Boyer, Sports Dir., News Dir., Prog. Dir., bradb@regionalradio.com; Stephanie Ross, Music Dir., stephanier@regionalradio.com. **URL:** http://www.regionalradio.com.

19733 ■ KWIX-AM - 1230
300 W Reed St.
Moberly, MO 65270
Phone: (660)263-1600
Fax: (660)269-8811
Free: 800-892-2300
Email: kresnews@regionalradio.com
Format: Full Service. **Networks:** CBS. **Owner:** Shepherd Group Moberly MO. **Founded:** 1950. **Formerly**: KNCM-AM. **Operating Hours**: Continuous; 60% network, 40% local. **Key Personnel:** Brad Boyer, Contact; Ken Kujawa, Contact; Brad Boyer, Contact. **Wattage**: 1,000. **Ad Rates:** $8-18 for 30 seconds. **URL:** http://centralmoinfo.com.

19734 ■ KZZT-FM - 105.5
Jct. of Hwy. 63 & Rte. Ee.
Moberly, MO 65270
Phone: (660)263-9390
Fax: (660)263-8800
Email: kzzt@mcmsys.com
Format: Classic Rock; News; Sports; Information. **Networks:** ABC. **Owner:** Best Broadcasting, Inc. **Founded:** 1987. **Operating Hours**: Continuous. **Key Personnel:** Dale Palmer, Gen. Mgr., kzbk@shighway.com. **Wattage**: 50,000 ERP. **Ad Rates:** Advertising accepted; rates available upon request. $5-18 for 30 seconds; $7.50-27 for 60 seconds. **Mailing address:** PO Box 128, Moberly, MO 65270. **URL:** http://www.kzztradio.com/.

MONETT

SW MO. Lawrence Co. 45 mi. Se of Joplin. Manufactures shoes, textiles, aluminum doors and windows, heavy conveyor equipment. Milk, cheese and poultry processing plants. Dairy, fruit & truck farms. Strawberries, apples, tomatoes.

19735 ■ KKBL-FM - 95.9
PO Box 109
Monett, MO 65708
Phone: (417)235-6041
Fax: (417)235-6388
Free: 800-928-5253
Format: Adult Contemporary. **Networks:** ABC; Missouri; Westwood One Radio. **Owner:** Eagle Broadcasting Inc., 126 South Jefferson, Aurora, MO 65605, Ph: (417)235-6041. **Founded:** 1977. **Operating Hours**: Continuous. **ADI**: Springfield, MO. **Key Personnel:** Dewayne Gandy, Contact. **Wattage**: 6,000. **Ad Rates:** $14-17 for 30 seconds. Combined advertising rates available with KRMO-AM.

19736 ■ KQMO-FM - 97.7
PO Box 109
Monett, MO 65708
Phone: (417)235-6041
Free: 800-928-5253
Format: Hispanic. **Owner:** Talcon Broadcasting, Inc., at above address; Eagle Broadcasting Inc., 126 South Jefferson, Aurora, MO 65605, Ph: (417)235-6041. **Ad Rates:** Advertising accepted; rates available upon request.

19737 ■ KRMO-AM - 990
PO Box 109
Monett, MO 65708
Phone: (417)235-6041
Fax: (417)235-6388
Free: 800-928-5253
Format: Country; News. **Networks:** ABC; Brownfield; Missouri. **Owner:** Eagle Broadcasting Inc., 126 South Jefferson, Aurora, MO 65605, Ph: (417)235-6041. **Founded:** 1950. **Operating Hours**: Continuous. **ADI**: Springfield, MO. **Wattage**: 2,500 Day; 047 Night. **Ad Rates:** Noncommercial. KKBL-FM.

19738 ■ KSWM-AM - 940
PO Box 109
Monett, MO 65708
Phone: (417)235-6041
Fax: (417)235-6388
Free: 800-928-5253
Format: Talk; News. **Owner:** Eagle Broadcasting Inc., 126 South Jefferson, Aurora, MO 65605, Ph: (417)235-6041. **Key Personnel:** Dewayne Gandy, Contact. **Ad Rates:** Advertising accepted; rates available upon request.

MONTGOMERY CITY

E. MO. Montgomery Co. 60 mi. NE of Saint Charles. Feed manufacturing. Fire clay mines. Foundry. Fertilizer plant. Dairy, stock, poultry, grain farms. Wheat, corn, oats, beans.

19739 ■ KMCR-FM - 103.9
405 E Norman
Montgomery City, MO 63361
Phone: (573)564-2275
Fax: (573)564-8026
Format: News; Sports; Information. **Owner:** Best Broadcasting, Inc., 107 S Main, Brookfield, MO 64628, Ph: (660)258-3383, Fax: (660)258-7307. **Founded:** 1977. **Formerly**: KVCM-FM; KOMC-FM. **Operating Hours**: Continuous. **Wattage**: 6,000 ERP. **Ad Rates:** Advertising accepted; rates available upon request. $7.50-18 for 30 seconds; $11.25-27 for 60 seconds. **Mailing address:** PO Box 128, Montgomery City, MO 63361. **URL:** http://www.kmcrradio.com.

MOSCOW MILLS

19740 ■ KPVR-FM - 94.1
30 Tower St.
Moscow Mills, MO 63362
Format: Talk; Sports; News; Information. **Owner:** Westplex Broadcasting L.L.C. **Wattage**: 7,500. **URL:** http://www.westplexnewstalk.com.

MOUNTAIN GROVE

S. MO. Wright Co. 60 mi. SE of Springfield. Manufactures lumber, shoes, and wood products. Missouri Fruit and Poultry Experiment Stations. Timber. Agriculture. Dairy products and poultry.

19741 ■ Mountain Grove News-Journal
Lebanon Publishing Co.
PO Box 530
Mountain Grove, MO 65711
Phone: (417)926-5148
Fax: (417)926-6648
Publication E-mail: mgnj@news-journal.net
Newspaper with a Republican orientation. **Freq:** Weekly. **Print Method:** Offset. **Cols./Page:** 6. **Col. Width:** 21 nonpareils. **Col. Depth:** 294 agate lines. **Key Personnel:** Doug Berger, Editor; Sandy Anderson, Publisher. **ISSN:** 0746--682X (print). **URL:** http://www.news-journal.net. **Remarks:** Accepts advertising. **Circ:** (Not Reported).

19742 ■ KELE-FM - 92.5
800 N Hubbard
Mountain Grove, MO 65711
Phone: (417)926-4650
Format: Full Service. **Simulcasts:** 1360 KELE-AM. **Founded:** 1958. **Formerly**: KRFI-FM; KLRS-FM; KCMG-FM. **Operating Hours**: Continuous; 60% network, 40% local. **Wattage**: 3,000. **Ad Rates:** Advertising accepted; rates available upon request. $4 for 30 seconds; $8 for 60 seconds.

NEOSHO

SW MO. Newton Co. 20 mi. SE of Joplin. Manufactures canned milk, footwear, trailers, concrete, metal products, butter, furniture, feed, industrial gases. Summer resort. Nurseries; fish hatcheries. Agriculture. Grain.

19743 ■ Neosho Daily News
GateHouse Media Inc.
1006 W Harmony
Neosho, MO 64850
Phone: (417)451-1520
Fax: (417)451-6408
Newspaper with an Independent orientation. **Founded:** Feb. 1905. **Freq:** Daily (eve.). **Print Method:** Offset. **Cols./Page:** 6. **Col. Width:** 25 nonpareils. **Col. Depth:** 301 agate lines. **Key Personnel:** Matt Guthrie, Publisher; Todd Nighswonger, Editor. **USPS:** 377-100. **Subscription Rates:** Free print; $39.99 Individuals online. **URL:** http://www.neoshodailynews.com; http://www.gatehousemedia.com/section/publications. **Ad Rates:** BW $1,012.65; 4C $1,162.65; PCI $7.85. **Remarks:** Accepts advertising. **Circ:** (Not Reported).

19744 ■ Seneca News-Dispatch
Seneca News-Dispatch
212 E Main St.
Neosho, MO 64850
Phone: (417)776-2236
Fax: (417)776-2204
Community newspaper. **Freq:** Weekly (Tues.). **Key Personnel:** Jimmy Sexton, Publisher. **Subscription Rates:** $22 Individuals in Newton County - print and online; $28 Out of state print and online; $17 Other countries online only. **URL:** http://thenewsdispatch.net. **Ad Rates:** SAU $4. **Remarks:** Accepts advertising. **Circ:** (Not Reported).

19745 ■ KBTN-AM - 1420
216 W Spring
Neosho, MO 64850
Phone: (417)781-1313
Email: kbtn@cebridge.net
Owner: American Media Investments, at above address. **Founded:** 1954. **Key Personnel:** Gail Johnson, Mgr. **Wattage**: 1,000 Daytime; 500 N. **Ad Rates:** $8.50-10.50 for 30 seconds; $14.55-16.50 for 60 seconds. Combined advertising rates available with KBIN-FM. **Mailing address:** PO Box K, Neosho, MO 64850. **URL:** http://www.kbtnradio.com.

19746 ■ KNEO-FM - 91.7
10827 Hwy. 86 E
Neosho, MO 64850
Phone: (417)451-5636
Format: Gospel; Religious. **Founded:** 1986. **Operating Hours**: Continuous. **Key Personnel:** Mark Taylor, Contact; Mark Taylor, Contact. **Wattage**: 14,000 ERP. **Ad Rates:** Accepts Advertising. **URL:** http://www.kneo.org.

NEVADA

W. MO. Vernon Co. 100 mi. S. of Kansas City. Manufactures plumbing supplies, air filters, adhesives, tents, sheet metal, farm machinery. Crude oil wells; asphalt, coal mines. Diversified farming. Corn, wheat, oats, soybeans. Milo, cattle, hogs.

19747 ■ Charter Communications
606 E Cherry St.
Nevada, MO 64772
Free: 888-438-2427
Owner: Tele-Communications Inc., 505 3rd Ave. E, Oneonta, AL 35121, Ph: (205)625-3591. **Formerly**: TCI Cablevision of Alabama. **Key Personnel:** Michael J. Lovett, CEO, President. **Cities Served:** 36 channels. **URL:** http://www.charter.com.

19748 ■ KNEM-AM - 1240
414 E Walnut
Nevada, MO 64772
Phone: (417)667-3113
Fax: (417)667-9797
Free: 800-934-4584
Format: Country. **Simulcasts:** KNMO-FM. **Networks:** ABC; Brownfield. **Owner:** Harbit Communications, Inc., 414 E Walnut Street, Nevada, MO 64772, Ph: (417)667-3113. **Founded:** 1949. **Operating Hours**: Continuous. **ADI**: Joplin, MO-Pittsburg, KS. **Key Personnel:** Chris Hacker, Promotions Dir., chacker@knemknmo.com; Mike Harbit, Gen. Mgr., President, mharbit@knemknmo.com; Russ Warren, Sports Dir., News Dir., news@knemknmo.com. **Wattage**: 500 ERP. **Ad Rates:** $7.26-9.96 for 30 seconds; $11.74-16.12 for 60 seconds. Combined advertising rates available with KNMO-FM. **Mailing address:** PO Box 447, Nevada, MO 64772. **URL:** http://www.knemknmo.com.

19749 ■ KNMO-FM - 97.5
414 E Walnut
Nevada, MO 64772
Phone: (417)667-3113
Fax: (417)667-9797
Free: 800-934-4584
Format: Country. **Simulcasts:** KNEM-AM. **Networks:** ABC; Brownfield. **Owner:** Harbit Communications, Inc.,

414 E Walnut Street, Nevada, MO 64772, Ph: (417)667-3113. **Founded:** 1983. **Operating Hours:** Continuous; 5% network, 95% local. **ADI:** Joplin, MO-Pittsburg, KS. **Key Personnel:** Mike Harbit, Gen. Mgr., President, mharbit@knemknmo.com; Chris Hacker, Dir. of Production, Operations Mgr. **Wattage:** 6,000 ERP. **Ad Rates:** $7.26-9.96 for 30 seconds; $11.74-16.12 for 60 seconds. Combined advertising rates available with KNEM-AM. **Mailing address:** PO Box 447, Nevada, MO 64772. **URL:** http://www.knemknmo.com.

19750 ■ K206CH-FM - 89.1
PO Box 391
Twin Falls, ID 83303
Free: 800-357-4226
Format: Religious; Contemporary Christian. **Owner:** CSN International, PO Box 391, Twin Falls, ID 83303, Ph: (208)736-1958, Fax: (208)736-1958, Free: 800-357-4226.

NEW BLOOMFIELD

19751 ■ KNLG-FM - 90.3
1411 Locust St.
New Bloomfield, MO 65063-2525
Phone: (314)421-3020
Fax: (314)421-1702
Free: 800-334-3276
Format: Religious. **Owner:** New Life Evangelistic Center, Inc., Saint Louis, MO, Ph: (314)421-3020. **Key Personnel:** Larry Rice, Gen. Mgr. **Mailing address:** PO Box 2525, New Bloomfield, MO 65063-2525. **URL:** http://hereshelpnet.org/.

19752 ■ KRCG-TV - 13
10188 Old Hwy. 54 N
New Bloomfield, MO 65063
Phone: (573)896-5144
Fax: (573)896-5193
Email: info@krcg.com
Format: News; Sports. **Networks:** CBS. **Owner:** Sinclair Broadcast Group Inc., 10706 Beaver Dam Rd., Hunt Valley, MD 21030, Ph: (410)568-1500, Fax: (410)568-1533. **Founded:** 1955. **Operating Hours:** 5 a.m.-1:30 a.m.; 70% network; 30% local. **ADI:** Columbia-Jefferson City, MO. **Key Personnel:** Betsy Farris, Gen. Mgr., bfarris@krcg.com; Jim Malone, Chief Engineer; Gregg Palermo, News Dir., gpalermo@krcg.com. **Local Programs:** *KRCG 13 Live at Sunrise*, Monday Tuesday Wednesday Thursday Friday 5:00 a.m. - 7:00 a.m. **Wattage:** 316,000. **Ad Rates:** Noncommercial. **URL:** http://www.connectmidmissouri.com.

NEW HAVEN

E. MO. Franklin Co. On Missouri River, 50 mi. E. of Jefferson City. Canvas product factories; feed mills. Nursery. Diversified farming. Wheat, corn, hay.

19753 ■ New Haven Leader
Spirit Newspapers of Missouri Inc.
403 Charles Cook Plz.
New Haven, MO 63068
Phone: (573)237-3222
Publication E-mail: leader@fidnet.com
Community newspaper. **Freq:** Weekly (Wed.). **Print Method:** Offset. **Trim Size:** 14 x 22 5/8. **Cols./Page:** 6. **Col. Width:** 24 nonpareils. **Col. Depth:** 301 agate lines. **Key Personnel:** Sue Blesi, Editor. **USPS:** 379-780. **Subscription Rates:** $22 Individuals 6 months; $22 Individuals 1 year (digital); $35 Individuals 1 year (archives). **URL:** http://www.newhavenleader.com/?page_id=32. **Ad Rates:** GLR $4.30; BW $554.70; 4C $779.70; SAU $4; PCI $4. **Remarks:** Accepts advertising. **Circ:** ‡1300.

NEW LONDON

NE MO. Ralls Co. 18 mi. S. of Palmyra. Residential.

19754 ■ Ralls County Herald-Enterprise
Ralls County Herald Enterprise
411 Main St.
New London, MO 63459
Community newspaper. **Freq:** Weekly (Thurs.). **Print Method:** Offset. **Cols./Page:** 6. **Col. Width:** 2 inches. **Col. Depth:** 21.5 inches. **Subscription Rates:** $35 Individuals print + online; $20 Individuals online; $27 Individuals in county (print and online). **URL:** http://www.rallshe.com. **Remarks:** Accepts advertising. **Circ:** (Not Reported).

NEW MADRID

SE MO. New Madrid Co. On Mississippi River, 50 mi. S. of Cape Girardeau. Manufactures concrete, feed, aluminium, textiles, modular homes. Oak, hickory, cottonwood timber. Stock, grain, cotton, beans, corn, wheat.

19755 ■ The Weekly Record
The Weekly Record
218 Main St.
New Madrid, MO 63869
Phone: (573)748-2120
Fax: (573)748-5435
Publisher's E-mail: ed@weeklyrecord.net
Newspaper with a Democratic orientation. **Founded:** 1866. **Freq:** Weekly (Fri.). **Print Method:** Offset. **Cols./Page:** 6. **Col. Width:** 1 13/16 inches. **Col. Depth:** 21 1/2 inches. **Key Personnel:** Ed Thomason, Editor; Linda Thomason, Publisher. **USPS:** 672-980. **Subscription Rates:** $30 Individuals New Madrid County; $40 Out of area; $30 Individuals online. **URL:** http://www.weeklyrecord.net/. **Ad Rates:** PCI $4. **Remarks:** Accepts advertising. **Circ:** ‡1150.

NIXA

SW MO. Christian Co. 15 mi. S. of Springfield. Manufactures vinegar, aluminum marine products, custom grinding. Agriculture. Hay, wheat, oats. Dairy. Beef, sheep.

19756 ■ Journal of Ophthalmic Photography
Ophthalmic Photographers' Society
1887 W Ranch Rd.
Nixa, MO 65714-8262
Phone: (417)725-0181
Fax: (417)724-8450
Free: 800-403-1677
Publisher's E-mail: ops@opsweb.org
Peer-reviewed journal covering ophthalmology. **Freq:** Semiannual. **Key Personnel:** Chris Barry, Editor. **ISSN:** 0198--6155 (print). **Alt. Formats:** PDF. **URL:** http://www.opsweb.org/?page=journal. **Remarks:** Advertising accepted; rates available upon request. **Circ:** (Not Reported).

ODESSA

W. MO. Lafayette Co. 25 mi. SE of Independence. Residential. Manufactures shoes. Livestock farms.

19757 ■ The Odessan
The Odessan
212 W Mason St.
Odessa, MO 64076
Phone: (816)230-5311
Fax: (816)633-8430
Community newspaper. **Freq:** Weekly (Thurs.). **Print Method:** Offset. **Cols./Page:** 6. **Col. Width:** 1.833 nonpareils. **Col. Depth:** 21.5 agate lines. **Key Personnel:** Kory Hales, Editor; Renee Spaar, Customer Service, Office Manager; John Spaar, Manager, Advertising, Publisher; Sharon Guevel, Manager, Circulation; Joe Spaar, Manager, Production, Publisher; Betty S. Spaar, Owner; Leanna Thompson, Bookkeeper. **Subscription Rates:** $40 Individuals Lafayette and Johnson counties; $45 Elsewhere in Missouri; $50 Out of state. **URL:** http://www.theodessan.net. **Mailing address:** PO Box 80, Odessa, MO 64076. **Ad Rates:** PCI $6.50; 4C $25. **Remarks:** Accepts classified advertising. **Circ:** Paid ‡3500.

OREGON

NW MO. Holt Co. 18 mi. W. of Savannah. Residential.

19758 ■ South Holt Cablevision Inc.
PO Box 227
118 East Nodaway
Oregon, MO 64473
Phone: (660)446-2900
Fax: (660)446-2800
Key Personnel: Robert Williams, President.

OSAGE BEACH

C. MO. Miller Co. 14 mi. NE of Candenton on Lake Ozark. Residential.

19759 ■ KRMS-AM - 1150
5715 Hwy. 54 W
Osage Beach, MO 65065
Phone: (573)348-2772
Fax: (573)348-2779
Email: info@krmsradio.com
Format: News; Talk. **Networks:** CBS. **Owner:** Viper Communications, 11A Commerce Way, Totowa, NJ 07512, Free: 800-494-1240. **Founded:** 1952. **Operating Hours:** Continuous. **Key Personnel:** Ken Kuenzie, Owner; Dennis Klautzer, Owner; Carolyn Warnebold, Bus. Mgr. **Local Programs:** *Ozarks this morning*, Monday Tuesday Wednesday Thursday Friday 6:00 a.m. - 9:00 a.m. **Wattage:** 1,000 Day; 055 Night. **Ad Rates:** Advertising accepted; rates available upon request. **Mailing address:** PO Box 225, Osage Beach, MO 65065. **URL:** http://www.krmsradio.com.

19760 ■ KZWV-FM - 101.9
1081 Osage Beach Rd.
Osage Beach, MO 65065
Phone: (573)746-7873
Fax: (573)746-7874
Format: Music of Your Life; Easy Listening. **Key Personnel:** Steve Richards, Dir. of Production, srichards@1019thewave.com. **Wattage:** 42,500. **URL:** http://www.1019thewave.com.

OSCEOLA

19761 ■ KCVJ-FM - 92.3
PO Box 800
Camdenton, MO 65020
Phone: (573)346-3200
Fax: (573)346-1010
Free: 800-336-0917
Format: Contemporary Christian. **Owner:** Spirit FM Radio Network, PO Box 800, Camdenton, MO 65020. **Key Personnel:** Christy Pond, Contact; Darren Alexander, Contact; Fred Young, Contact. **Ad Rates:** Noncommercial. **URL:** http://www.spiritfm.org.

OVERLAND

NW MO. St. Louis Co. 10 mi. WNW of Saint Louis.

19762 ■ KRHS-FM
2420 Woodson Rd.
Overland, MO 63114-4241
Phone: (314)429-7111
Fax: (314)429-6725
Format: Full Service. **Networks:** Independent. **Founded:** 1976. **Formerly:** KRSH-FM. **Key Personnel:** Alan Mitchell, Gen. Mgr.

OWENSVILLE

EC MO. Gasconade Co. 45 mi. SE of Jefferson City. Manufactures shoes, plastics, printing. Clay, flint, diaspore mines. Diversified farming. Corn, wheat.

19763 ■ Gasconade County Republican
Warden Publishing Co.
106 E Washington Ave.
Owensville, MO 65066
Phone: (314)437-2323
Fax: (314)437-3033
Publisher's E-mail: wardpub@fidnet.com
Newspaper. **Freq:** Weekly (Wed.). **Print Method:** Offset. **Trim Size:** 13 1/2 x 23. **Cols./Page:** 6. **Col. Width:** 11.5 picas. **Col. Depth:** 21 inches. **Key Personnel:** Dave Marner, Managing Editor; Dennis Warden, Manager, Advertising, Publisher; Kari Schweer, Office Manager. **USPS:** 021-460. **Subscription Rates:** $35 Individuals in Gasconade County; $40 Individuals in Missouri; $45 Out of state; $18 Individuals online. **URL:** http://www.gasconadecountyrepublican.com. **Mailing address:** PO Box 540, Owensville, MO 65066-0540. **Remarks:** Accepts advertising. **Circ:** (Not Reported).

OZARK

SW MO. Christian Co. 12 mi. S. of Springfield. Manufactures textiles, small electric motors, wood products, ceramics, cheese. Feed mill. Summer resort. Stock, dairy farms. Corn, wheat, oats.

Circulation: ★ = AAM; △ or • = BPA; ♦ = CAC; ❑ = VAC; ⊕ = PO Statement; ‡ = Publisher's Report; Boldface figures = sworn; Light figures = estimated.

19764 ■ Christian County Headliners News
Ozark Publications Inc.
116 N 2nd Ave.
Ozark, MO 65721
Phone: (417)581-3541
Fax: (417)581-3577
Publisher's E-mail: news@ccheadliner.com
Newspaper. **Freq:** Semiweekly (Wed. and Sat.). **Print Method:** Offset. **Cols./Page:** 6. **Col. Width:** 24 nonpareils. **Col. Depth:** 301 agate lines. **Key Personnel:** Donna Osborn, Editor; Kimberly Bruce, Office Manager; Greg White, General Manager. **Subscription Rates:** $36.28 Individuals local; $52.15 Elsewhere in Missouri; $56.70 Out of state; $25.20 Individuals online. **URL:** http://ccheadliner.com. **Formerly**: Ozark Headliner. **Mailing address:** PO Box 490, Ozark, MO 65721. **Ad Rates:** BW $1363. **Remarks:** Advertising accepted; rates available upon request. **Circ:** (Not Reported).

PALMYRA

NE MO. Marion Co. 11 mi. NW of Hannibal. Manufactures chemicals, fertilizer, lumber products. Diversified farming.

19765 ■ Palmyra Spectator
Palmyra Spectator
304 S Main St.
Palmyra, MO 63461
Phone: (573)769-3111
Fax: (573)769-3554
Publication E-mail: editorial@palmyra-spectator.com
Newspaper with a Democratic orientation. **Freq:** Weekly (Wed.). **Print Method:** Offset. **Cols./Page:** 6. **Col. Width:** 12 picas. **Col. Depth:** 280 agate lines. **Key Personnel:** Patty Cheffey, Publisher; Mark Cheffey, Publisher. **Subscription Rates:** $23 Individuals Marion county and adjoining counties; $21 Individuals senior; $30 Elsewhere; $0.50 Single issue. **URL:** http://www.palmyra-spectator.com. **Mailing address:** PO Box 391, Palmyra, MO 63461. **Remarks:** Accepts advertising. **Circ:** (Not Reported).

PARK HILLS

19766 ■ KBGM-FM - 91.1
PO Box 3206
Tupelo, MS 38803
Format: Contemporary Christian. **Owner:** American Family Association, at above address. **Wattage:** 8,000. **URL:** http://www.afr.net.

19767 ■ KFMO-AM - 1240
804 St. Joe Dr.
Park Hills, MO 63601
Phone: (573)431-1000
Format: Contemporary Country; Soft Rock. **Networks:** CBS; ESPN Radio. **Founded:** 1947. **Operating Hours:** Continuous; 20% network, 80% local. **Key Personnel:** Matt Sharp, Dir. of Programs; Kelly Valle, Sales Mgr., kv@b104fm.com; Larry D. Joseph, Gen. Mgr., VP, ldj@b104fm.com. **Wattage:** 1,000. **Ad Rates:** $6-9 for 30 seconds; $7.20-12 for 60 seconds. **URL:** http://www.b104fm.com.

PARKVILLE

NW MO. Platte Co. On Missouri River, 10 mi. NW of Kansas City. Park College. Diversified farming. Grain, tobacco.

19768 ■ Dive Training: The Monthly Magazine for New Divers and Their Instructors
Dive Training Ltd.
5215 Crooked Rd.
Parkville, MO 64152-3447
Phone: (816)741-5151
Fax: (816)741-6458
Publication E-mail: divetraining@spc-mag.com
Diving magazine promoting training, safety, and education. **Freq:** Monthly. **Print Method:** Offset. **Trim Size:** 7 7/8 x 10 1/2. **Cols./Page:** 3. **Key Personnel:** Mark Young, Publisher; Gene Gentrup, Managing Editor. **ISSN:** 1061--3323 (print). **Subscription Rates:** $21.95 Individuals /year (print and online); $17.95 Individuals /year (online). **URL:** http://dtmag.com. **Remarks:** Accepts advertising. **Circ:** (Not Reported).

19769 ■ Restaurant Startup & Growth: Good Restaurateurs Are Always Learning
Smooth Propeller Corp.
5215 NW Crooked Rd.
Parkville, MO 64152-3447
Publication E-mail: rsg@spc-mag.com
Magazine about starting and operating a restaurant business. **Freq:** Monthly. **Trim Size:** 8 x 10.75. **Subscription Rates:** Included in membership. **URL:** http://www.restaurantowner.com; http://www.rsgmag.com. **Ad Rates:** BW $6,090; 4C $8,560. **Remarks:** Accepts advertising. **Circ:** (Not Reported).

19770 ■ KGSP-FM - 90.5
8700 NW River Park Dr.
Parkville, MO 64152
Phone: (816)741-2000
Free: 800-745-7275
Format: Educational. **Owner:** Park University, 8700 NW River Park Dr., Parkville, MO 64152, Ph: (816)741-2000, Free: 800-745-7275. **Wattage**: 100. **URL:** http://kgsp.park.edu.

PERRYVILLE

SE MO. Perry Co. 38 mi. N. of Cape Girardeau. St. Mary's Seminary and College. Manufactures shoes, food products, automotive parts, foam products, jet engine refurbishing. Stock, grain farms.

19771 ■ The Perry County Republic-Monitor
Perryville Newspapers Inc.
10 West, Ste. Maries St.
Perryville, MO 63775
Phone: (573)547-4567
Publisher's E-mail: webeditor@perryvillenews.com
Community newspaper. **Freq:** Semiweekly every Tuesday and Thursday. **Print Method:** Offset. **Cols./Page:** 6. **Col. Width:** 1 7/8 inches. **Col. Depth:** 21 inches. **Key Personnel:** Angie Schuessler, Office Manager; Beth Chism, Publisher, Editor. **USPS:** 428-200. **Subscription Rates:** $46.22 Individuals; $41.50 Individuals seniors; $73.34 Out of state. **URL:** http://www.perryvillenews.com/. **Ad Rates:** BW $850.50; 4C $1,300.50; SAU $6.75. **Remarks:** Accepts advertising. **Circ:** (Not Reported).

19772 ■ The Republic-Monitor Shopping Guide
Perryville Newspapers Inc.
10 West, Ste. Maries St.
Perryville, MO 63775
Phone: (573)547-4567
Publisher's E-mail: webeditor@perryvillenews.com
Non-duplicating free distribution shopper. **Freq:** Weekly. **Print Method:** Offset. **Cols./Page:** 6. **Col. Width:** 1 7/8 inches. **Col. Depth:** 21 inches. **Key Personnel:** Kate Martin, Editor; Bev Fritsche, General Manager, phone: (573)547-4567. **Subscription Rates:** Free. **URL:** http://www.perryvillenews.com. **Formerly**: The Republic/Extra. **Ad Rates:** BW $850.50; 4C $1,300.50; SAU $6.75. **Remarks:** Accepts advertising. **Circ:** Free ‡8400.

PIEDMONT

SE MO. Wayne Co. 70 mi. W. of Cape Girardeau. Manufactures plastic bottles, wood pallets, shoes, hats, textiles. Lumber mills. Oak, pine timber. Stock, grain farms. Corn, wheat, oats.

19773 ■ Wayne County Journal-Banner
Ellinghouse Publishing Company Inc.
101 West Elm
Piedmont, MO 63957
Phone: (573)223-7122
Fax: (573)223-7871
Free: 800-923-7122
Community Newspaper. **Freq:** Weekly (Thurs.). **Print Method:** Offset. **Trim Size:** 6 1/4 x 11 1/2. **Cols./Page:** 6. **Col. Width:** 11 picas. **Col. Depth:** 21 1/2 inches. **Key Personnel:** Harold T. Ellinghouse, Editor; Brenda Ellinghouse, Business Manager, Editor. **USPS:** 670-400. **Subscription Rates:** $32 Individuals /year (print); $45 Elsewhere /year (print). **URL:** http://www.waynecojournalbanner.com. **Mailing address:** PO Box 97, Piedmont, MO 63957. **Remarks:** Advertising accepted; rates available upon request. **Circ:** (Not Reported).

PLATTE CITY

NW MO. Platte Co. 25 mi. W. of Kansas. Diversified farming. Wheat, corn, tobacco.

19774 ■ Platte County Citizen
Platte County Citizen
1110 Branch St.
Platte City, MO 64079
Phone: (816)858-5154
Publisher's E-mail: editor@plattecountycitizen.com
Community newspaper. **Freq:** Weekly. **Print Method:** Offset. **Trim Size:** 13 3/4 x 22 3/4. **Cols./Page:** 6. **Col. Width:** 24 nonpareils. **Col. Depth:** 301 agate lines. **Key Personnel:** Ross Martin, Editor; Pam Ulitschan, Manager, Advertising. **ISSN:** 0746--3596 (print). **Subscription Rates:** $30 Individuals /year; $55 Two years; $40 Out of state /year; $75 Out of state two years. **URL:** http://www.plattecountycitizen.com. **Mailing address:** PO Box 888, Platte City, MO 64079. **Ad Rates:** PCI $6; BW $700. **Remarks:** Accepts advertising. **Circ:** (Not Reported).

PLEASANT HILL

W. MO. Cass Co. 25 mi. SE of Kansas City. Manufactures horizontal earth augers, posthole diggers, textiles. Sawmills; hatchery. Diversified farming. Corn, milk.

19775 ■ Pleasant Hill Times
Pleasant Hill Times Inc.
126 First St.
Pleasant Hill, MO 64080
Phone: (816)540-3500
Fax: (816)987-5699
Publisher's E-mail: info@phtimes.net
Newspaper with a Democratic orientation. **Freq:** Weekly (Wed.). **Print Method:** Offset. **Cols./Page:** 6. **Col. Width:** 12 1/2 picas. **Col. Depth:** 21 inches. **Key Personnel:** F. Kirk Powell, Editor, Publisher; Cheryl Miller, Manager, Advertising; Betty Beason, Business Manager. **Subscription Rates:** $30 Individuals in Cass county; $35 Elsewhere in Missouri; $45 Out of state. **URL:** http://www.phtimes.net. **Mailing address:** PO Box 8, Pleasant Hill, MO 64080. **Ad Rates:** PCI $6.75. **Remarks:** Accepts advertising. **Circ:** Paid ‡2100.

POINT LOOKOUT

S. MO. Taney Co. 3 mi. S. of Branson. The School of the Ozarks. Museum.

19776 ■ The Outlook
College of the Ozarks
PO Box 17
Point Lookout, MO 65726-0017
Phone: (417)334-6411
Free: 800-222-0525
Collegiate newspaper. **Founded:** 1961. **Freq:** Weekly 32/yr. **Print Method:** Offset. **Cols./Page:** 5. **Col. Width:** 22 nonpareils. **Col. Depth:** 224 agate lines. **URL:** http://www.cofo.edu/. **Circ:** (Not Reported).

19777 ■ Teaching History: A Journal of Methods
Emporia State University
c/o Stephen Kneeshaw, Ed.
Department of History
College of the Ozarks
Point Lookout, MO 65726-0017
Phone: (417)690-3264
Fax: (417)335-3250
Publisher's E-mail: webmaster@emporia.edu
Professional publication covering teaching ideas for history teachers at all levels. **Freq:** Semiannual April and November. **Key Personnel:** Stephen Kneeshaw, Editor; Christopher Lovett, Director, Publications, fax: (620)341-5143; Calvin Allen, Board Member. **ISSN:** 0730--1383 (print). **Subscription Rates:** $12 Individuals; $12 Institutions; $30 Individuals 3 years; $30 Institutions 3 years. **URL:** http://www.emporia.edu/~teaching-history. **Circ:** (Not Reported).

19778 ■ KCOZ-FM - 91.7
PO Box 17
Point Lookout, MO 65726
Phone: (417)334-6411
Free: 800-222-0525
Email: webmaster@cofo.edu
Format: Contemporary Christian. **Owner:** College Of the Ozarks, at above address. **Founded:** 1962. **Formerly**: KSOZ-FM. **Operating Hours**: Continuous. **Key Personnel:** Colvin Hooser, Contact, hooser@cofo.edu. **Wattage**: 200 ERP. **Ad Rates:** Accepts Advertising. **URL:** http://www.cofo.edu/AcademicDept/masscomm.asp?page=3.

POPLAR BLUFF

SE MO. Butler Co. 160 mi. S. of Saint Louis. Three Rivers Community College. Manufactures Christmas tree stands, shoes, paperboxes, portable buildings, furniture, custom made drapes, concrete burial vaults, machine parts, satellite antennas, wood stoves, aluminum gas tanks for boats, timber. Agriculture. Livestock, cotton, corn, rice.

19779 ■ Daily American Republic
Butler County Publishing Co.
208 Poplar st.
Poplar Bluff, MO 63901
Free: 888-276-2242
Publisher's E-mail: news@darnews.com
General newspaper. **Freq:** Daily (eve.). **Print Method:** Offset. **Cols./Page:** 6. **Col. Width:** 24 nonpareils. **Col. Depth:** 301 agate lines. **USPS:** 141-290. **Subscription Rates:** $120 Individuals 1 year (carrier delivery rates); $130 By mail 1 year (in state); $166 Out of state 1 year (mail rates); $10 Individuals EZ pay - carrier delivery; $72 Individuals 1 year (online). **URL:** http://info.darnews.com/Daily_American_Republic/Home_Page.html. **Mailing address:** PO Box 7, Poplar Bluff, MO 63901. **Remarks:** Advertising accepted; rates available upon request. **Circ:** (Not Reported).

19780 ■ The Journal
Butler County Publishing Co.
208 Poplar st.
Poplar Bluff, MO 63901
Free: 888-276-2242
Publisher's E-mail: news@darnews.com
Local newspaper. **Founded:** 1980. **Freq:** Weekly (Wed.). **Print Method:** Offset. **Cols./Page:** 9. **Col. Width:** 19 nonpareils. **Col. Depth:** 301 agate lines. **Subscription Rates:** $78 Individuals Sunday Only; $104 Individuals Saturday & Sunday; $150 Individuals 7 days home delivery; $129.96 By mail Sunday Only; $150 By mail Saturday & Sunday; $189.96 By mail 7 days. **URL:** http://www.journal-news.net/. **Mailing address:** PO Box 7, Poplar Bluff, MO 63901. **Circ:** (Not Reported).

19781 ■ Boycom Cablevision Inc.
3467 Township Line Rd.
Poplar Bluff, MO 63901
Phone: (573)686-9101
Free: 888-207-0203
Email: customer_service@boycomonline.com
Cities Served: 58 channels. **URL:** http://www.boycom.com.

19782 ■ KDFN-AM - 1500
932 Country Rd. 448
Poplar Bluff, MO 63901
Phone: (573)686-3700
Format: Oldies. **Networks:** ABC. **Owner:** Fox Radio Network, 661 Little Britain Rd. , New Windsor, NY 12553, Ph: (845)561-2131, Fax: (845)561-2138, Free: 866-353-6903. **Founded:** 1963. **Operating Hours:** Sunrise-sunset. **Wattage:** 2,500. **Ad Rates:** $2-6 for 30 seconds; $1.75-8 for 60 seconds.

19783 ■ KFEB-FM - 107.5
932 Country Rd. 448
Poplar Bluff, MO 63901
Phone: (573)686-3700
Fax: (573)686-1713
Format: Alternative/New Music/Progressive. **Owner:** Fox Radio Network, 661 Little Britain Rd. , New Windsor, NY 12553, Ph: (845)561-2131, Fax: (845)561-2138, Free: 866-353-6903. **Founded:** 1952. **Wattage:** 17,500. **URL:** http://www.foxradionetwork.com.

19784 ■ KJEZ-FM - 95.5
1015 W Pine St.
Poplar Bluff, MO 63901
Phone: (573)785-0881
Format: Classic Rock; Album-Oriented Rock (AOR); Top 40. **Networks:** Unistar. **Owner:** Mississippi River Radio, at above address. **Founded:** 1977. **Operating Hours:** Continuous. **Wattage:** 100,000. **Ad Rates:** Advertising accepted; rates available upon request. **URL:** http://www.kjez.com.

19785 ■ KKLR-FM - 94.5
1015 W Pine
Poplar Bluff, MO 63901
Phone: (573)785-0881
Fax: (573)785-0646
Free: 800-455-5962
Format: Country. **Ad Rates:** Advertising accepted; rates available upon request. **URL:** http://www.kklr.com.

19786 ■ KLID-AM - 1340
Klid Bldg.
102 N 11th
Poplar Bluff, MO 63901
Phone: (573)686-1600
Format: Oldies; Full Service; Talk. **Owner:** Browning Skidmore Broadcasting, Inc., at above address, Fax: (573)785-9844. **Founded:** 1961. **Key Personnel:** Jerry Evans, News Dir; Sunny Skidmore, Contact. **Wattage:** 1,000. **Ad Rates:** $7-9 for 30 seconds; $9-11 for 60 seconds. **URL:** http://klidradio.com.

19787 ■ KLUE-FM - 103.5
PO Box 4165
Poplar Bluff, MO 63901
Phone: (573)778-6049
Fax: (573)686-6898
Free: 877-464-9944
Format: Adult Contemporary; Top 40. **Owner:** Stratemeyer Media, 6120 Waldo Church Rd., Metropolis, IL 62960, Ph: (618)564-9836, Fax: (618)564-3202. **Key Personnel:** Jim Borders, Gen. Mgr. **Wattage:** 50,000. **Ad Rates:** Advertising accepted; rates available upon request. **URL:** http://www.klue103.com.

19788 ■ KLUH-FM - 90.3
PO Box 1313
Poplar Bluff, MO 63902
Phone: (573)686-1663
Fax: (573)686-7703
Email: info@dcmliferadio.org
Format: Southern Gospel. **Owner:** David Craig Ministries, at above address, Sikeston, MO. **Founded:** 1988. **Operating Hours:** Continuous. **Key Personnel:** David Craig, Phd, Gen. Mgr. **Wattage:** 25,000. **Ad Rates:** Noncommercial. **URL:** http://www.unity903.org.

19789 ■ KOEA-FM - 97.5
932 Country Rd., 448
Poplar Bluff, MO 63901
Format: Country. **Networks:** ABC; Missouri; Brownfield. **Owner:** Fox Radio Network, 661 Little Britain Rd. , New Windsor, NY 12553, Ph: (845)561-2131, Fax: (845)561-2138, Free: 866-353-6903. **Founded:** 1975. **Operating Hours:** Continuous; 20% network, 80% local. **Wattage:** 40,000. **Ad Rates:** $2.90-6 for 30 seconds; $2.25-8 for 60 seconds. **URL:** http://www.foxradionetwork.com.

19790 ■ KOKS-FM - 89.5
2773 Barron Road in
Poplar Bluff, MO 63901
Phone: (573)686-5080
Format: Southern Gospel. **Owner:** Calvary Educational Broadcasting Network, Inc., at above address. **Founded:** 1988. **Operating Hours:** Continuous. **Wattage:** 100,000. **Ad Rates:** Noncommercial. **URL:** http://www.koksradio.org.

19791 ■ KPOB-TV - 476 - 482
c/o WSIL-TV
1416 Country Aire
Carterville, IL 62918
Phone: (618)985-2333
Fax: (618)985-3709
Format: Commercial TV. **Simulcasts:** WSIL-TV Carterville, IL. **Networks:** ABC. **Owner:** Melvin C. Wheeler L.L.C., at above address. **Operating Hours:** Continuous. **Wattage:** 34,500. **Ad Rates:** Advertising accepted; rates available upon request.

19792 ■ KWOC-AM - 930
1015 W Pine St.
Poplar Bluff, MO 63901
Phone: (573)785-0881
Format: News; Talk; Sports. **Wattage:** 5,000. **Ad Rates:** Advertising accepted; rates available upon request. **URL:** http://www.kwoc.com.

19793 ■ KXOQ-FM - 104.3
932 Country Rd. 448
Poplar Bluff, MO 63901
Phone: (573)686-3700
Fax: (573)686-1713
Format: Classic Rock. **Owner:** Fox Radio Network, 661 Little Britain Rd. , New Windsor, NY 12553, Ph: (845)561-2131, Fax: (845)561-2138, Free: 866-353-6903. **Wattage:** 6,000. **URL:** http://www.foxradionetwork.com.

19794 ■ KYHO-FM - 106.9
PO Box 1018
Laguna Beach, CA 92652
Fax: (469)241-6795
Free: 800-639-5433
Format: Religious. **Owner:** New Life Ministries, 330 Wellington Ave., Rochester, NY 14619. **Key Personnel:** Stephen Arterburn, Chairman, Founder. **URL:** http://www.newlife.com.

19795 ■ KZMA-FM - 99.9
6120 Waldo Church Rd.
Metropolis, IL 62960
Phone: (618)564-9836
Fax: (618)564-3202
Email: info@stratemeyermedia.com
Format: Contemporary Hit Radio (CHR). **Owner:** Stratemeyer Media, 5101 Hinkleville Rd., Ste. 375, Paducah, KY 42001, Ph: (270)442-0098. **Key Personnel:** Jim Borders, Gen. Mgr., jhborders@yahoo.com. **Wattage:** 6,000. **Ad Rates:** Advertising accepted; rates available upon request.

POTOSI

E. MO. Washington Co. 60 mi. SW of Saint Louis. Manufactures barrel staves, lumber products, shoes. Lead, zinc, iron, barytes, lumber, limestone industries. Agriculture.

19796 ■ KYRO-AM - 1280
Hwy. 21
Potosi, MO 63664
Phone: (573)438-2136
Fax: (573)438-3108
Email: kyro@kyro.com
Format: Country. **Networks:** ABC. **Owner:** Savoy Broadcasting Co., at above address. **Founded:** 1959. **Operating Hours:** Continuous. **Key Personnel:** Debbie Porter, President, debbie@kyro.com; Jeremy Porter, News Dir., Prog. Dir., jeremy@kyro.com; Chris Knight, Gen. Mgr. **Wattage:** 500. **Ad Rates:** $9.50 for 30 seconds; $14 for 60 seconds. **Mailing address:** PO Box 280, Potosi, MO 63664. **URL:** http://westplexnewstalk1280.com.

RAYTOWN

W. MO. Jackson Co. 10 mi. SE of downtown Kansas City. Industry. Residential.

19797 ■ Stained Glass Quarterly
Stained Glass Association of America
9313 E 63rd St.
Raytown, MO 64133
Phone: (816)737-2090
Fax: (816)737-2801
Free: 800-438-9581
Publication E-mail: quarterly@sgaaonline.com
Magazine on architectural stained and decorative art glass. **Founded:** 1906. **Freq:** Quarterly. **Print Method:** Web. **Trim Size:** 8 1/4 x 11. **Cols./Page:** 3. **Col. Width:** 27 nonpareils. **Col. Depth:** 130 agate lines. **Key Personnel:** Richard Gross, Editor. **ISSN:** 0895-7002 (print). **Subscription Rates:** $29 Individuals; $47 Canada and Mexico; $59 Other countries. **URL:** http://stainedglassquarterly.com/. **Formerly:** Stained Glass; Stained Glass Magazine. **Remarks:** Accepts advertising. **Circ:** Paid ‡9000, Non-paid ‡140.

RICHMOND

NW MO. Ray Co. 35 mi. NE of Kansas City. Manufactures meal and feed, plastics, lawn and garden furniture, automotive supplies, storm doors, windows. Agriculture. Meat processing. Livestock. Cattle. Corn, wheat, oats.

19798 ■ Reflections
Ray County Genealogical Association
c/o Lisa Smalley
901 W Royle St.
Richmond, MO 64085-1545
Phone: (816)776-2305
Publisher's E-mail: morcga@yahoo.com
Journal containing historical Ray County records, 1889 newspaper articles, obituaries, births, and marriages. **Freq:** Quarterly. **Subscription Rates:** $3.50 Individuals back issue. **URL:** http://www.rootsweb.ancestry.com/~

Circulation: ★ = AAM; △ or • = BPA; ♦ = CAC; ❑ = VAC; ⊕ = PO Statement; ‡ = Publisher's Report; Boldface figures = sworn; Light figures = estimated.

morcga/toc.html. **Circ:** (Not Reported).

19799 ■ Richmond Daily News
The Daily News
204 W Main St.
Richmond, MO 64085
Phone: (816)776-5454
Fax: (816)470-6397
General newspaper. **Freq:** Daily (eve.). **Print Method:** Offset. **Trim Size:** 13 1/2 x 22 3/4. **Cols./Page:** 7. **Col. Width:** 1 5/8 inches. **Col. Depth:** 21 inches. **Key Personnel:** JoEllen Black, Publisher; David Knopf, Editor. **USPS:** 465-560. **Subscription Rates:** $55 Individuals e-edition or print; $50 Individuals e-edition or print (seniors); $75 Out of area print. **URL:** http://www.richmond-dailynews.com. **Mailing address:** PO Box 100, Richmond, MO 64085. **Ad Rates:** 4C $100; PCI $5.50. **Remarks:** Accepts advertising. **Circ:** ‡3936.

19800 ■ KAYX-FM - 92.5
111 W Main St.
Richmond, MO 64085
Phone: (816)470-9925
Owner: Bott Communications, Inc., 10550 Barkley, Overland Park, KS 66212, Ph: (913)642-7770, Fax: (913)642-1319. **Founded:** Nov. 28, 1994. **Wattage:** 2,350. **Ad Rates:** Noncommercial.

19801 ■ KLEX-AM - 1570
111 W Main St.
Richmond, MO 64085
Phone: (816)470-9925
Fax: (816)470-8925
Owner: Bott Communications, Inc., 10550 Barkley, Overland Park, KS 66212, Ph: (913)642-7770, Fax: (913)642-1319. **Founded:** 1956. **Ad Rates:** $4-8 for 30 seconds; $6-12 for 60 seconds.

ROCK PORT

NW MO. Atchison Co. 80 mi. NW of Saint Joseph. Diversified farming. Corn, wheat, livestock.

19802 ■ Rock Port Telephone Co.
PO Box 147
Rock Port, MO 64482
Phone: (660)744-5311
Free: 877-202-1764
Email: rptel@rpt.coop
Founded: 1965. **Cities Served:** United States. **URL:** http://www.rptel.net.

ROGERSVILLE

19803 ■ K204DT-FM - 88.7
PO Box 391
Twin Falls, ID 83303
Fax: (208)736-1958
Free: 800-357-4226
Format: Religious; Contemporary Christian. **Owner:** CSN International, PO Box 391, Twin Falls, ID 83303, Ph: (208)736-1958, Fax: (208)736-1958, Free: 800-357-4226. **Key Personnel:** Don Mills, Music Dir., Prog. Dir.; Kelly Carlson, Dir. of Engg.; Ray Gorney, Asst. Dir. **URL:** http://www.csnradio.com.

ROLLA

SEC MO. Phelps Co. 100 mi. SW of Saint Louis. Phelps Co. (SEC). 100 m SW of St. Louis. University of Missouri at Rolla. Missouri School of Mines and Metallurgy. Mark Twain National Forest. Manufactures plastic pipe, fan blades, wooden tresses. Pyrite mines; clay pits. Timber. Stock, dairy, poultry, fruit farms. Grapes, apples, melons.

19804 ■ Global Journal of Pure and Applied Mathematics
Howard University Press
c/o M. Bohner, Assoc. Ed.
University of Missouri at Rolla
Department of Mathematics
106 Rolla Bldg.
Rolla, MO 65409-0020
Publisher's E-mail: howardupress@howard.edu
Journal publishing research articles from pure and applied mathematics. Covers pure and applied aspects of all sub-disciplines of mathematical analysis. **Freq:** 6/year. **Key Personnel:** M. Bohner, Board Member; Prof. Taekyun Kim, Editor-in-Chief; S. Mathur, Associate Editor. **ISSN:** 0973--1768 (print); **EISSN:** 0973--9750 (electronic). **Subscription Rates:** $390 Individuals print; Rs 3000 Individuals print; $820 Libraries and institutions; print + online; $780 Libraries and institution; print only; $760 Libraries and institution; online only. **URL:** http://www.ripublication.com/gjpam.htm. **Circ:** (Not Reported).

19805 ■ International Journal of Difference Equations
Research India Publications
c/o Dr. Martin Bohner, Ed.-in-Ch.
Department of Mathematics & Statistics
Missouri University of Science & Technology
106 Rolla Bldg.
Rolla, MO 65409-0020
Publisher's E-mail: info@ripublication.com
Journal covering areas related to difference equations and dynamical systems. **Freq:** Semiannual. **Key Personnel:** Martin Bohner, Editor-in-Chief. **ISSN:** 0973--6069 (print). **Subscription Rates:** $320 Institutions print; $300 Institutions online only; $360 Institutions print + online; $160 Individuals online only; Rs 3500 Individuals. **URL:** http://www.ripublication.com/ijde.htm; http://campus.mst.edu/ijde. **Circ:** (Not Reported).

19806 ■ Phelps County Genealogical Society Quarterly
Phelps County Genealogical Society
PO Box 571
Rolla, MO 65402-0571
Phone: (573)364-9597
Publisher's E-mail: pcgs@rollanet.org
Genealogical magazine. **Freq:** Quarterly. **ISSN:** 0884--2140 (print). **URL:** http://pcgsrolla.weebly.com/quarterlies.html; http://www.rollanet.org. **Remarks:** Advertising not accepted. **Circ:** Paid 190.

19807 ■ Rolla Daily News
GateHouse Media Inc.
101 W 7th.
Rolla, MO 65401
Phone: (573)364-2468
General newspaper. **Freq:** Daily and Sun. (eve.). **Print Method:** Offset. **Key Personnel:** Paul Hackbarth, Editor; Marcia Burns, Manager, Advertising. **URL:** http://www.therolladailynews.com. **Remarks:** Accepts advertising. **Circ:** (Not Reported).

19808 ■ Fidelity Communications
1304 Hwy. 72 E
Rolla, MO 65401
Phone: (573)426-5000
Fax: (573)364-0620
Email: helpdesk@fidelitycommunications.com
Founded: 1992. **Key Personnel:** John Colbert, President. **Cities Served:** 276 channels. **URL:** http://www.fidelitycommunications.com.

19809 ■ KKID-FM - 92.9
1415 Forum Dr.
Rolla, MO 65401
Phone: (573)364-4433
Free: 888-263-9002
Format: Classic Rock. **Key Personnel:** Rae McKenzie, Dir. of Production. **Ad Rates:** Advertising accepted; rates available upon request.

19810 ■ KMCV-FM - 106.3
1701 N Bishop Ave., Ste. 15
Rolla, MO 65401
Phone: (573)647-6285
Fax: (573)426-4450
Email: kmcv@bottradionetwork.com
Format: Religious. **Owner:** Bott Radio Network, 10550 Barkley, Overland Park, KS 66212, Ph: (913)642-7770, Fax: (913)642-1319, Free: 800-345-2621. **Operating Hours:** Continuous. **Key Personnel:** Sue Stoltz, Mgr., sstoltz@bottradionetwork.com. **Wattage:** 18,000. **URL:** http://www.bottradionetwork.com.

19811 ■ KMNR-FM - 89.7
218 Havener Ctr.
1346 N Bishop Ave.
Rolla, MO 65409-1440
Phone: (573)341-4272
Format: Eclectic. **Owner:** Missouri University of Science and Technology, 1870 Miner Cir., Rolla, MO 65409, Ph: (573)341-4111, Free: 800-522-0938. **Founded:** 1964. **Formerly:** KMSM-FM. **Operating Hours:** Continuous. **Wattage:** 450. **Ad Rates:** Noncommercial; underwriting available. **URL:** http://kmnr.org.

19812 ■ KMST-FM - 88.5
400 W 14th St., G-6 Library
Rolla, MO 65409-0130
Phone: (573)341-4386
Free: 888-776-5678
Email: kmst@mst.edu
Format: Public Radio; Eclectic. **Simulcasts:** 96.3. **Networks:** National Public Radio (NPR); Public Radio International (PRI). **Founded:** 1973. **Formerly:** KUMR-FM. **Operating Hours:** Continuous; 60% network. **Key Personnel:** Wayne Bledsoe, Gen. Mgr., wbledsoe@mst.edu; John Francis, Dir. of Programs, jfrancis@mst.edu; Chuck Knapp, Chief Engineer, cknapp@mst.edu; Norm Movitz, Producer, movitz@mst.edu; Joel Goodridge, Mktg. Mgr. **Local Programs:** *Bluegrass for a Saturday Night*, Saturday 7:00 p.m.; *Sunday Morning Sounds*, Sunday 7:00 a.m.; *Sounds Eclectic*, Monday Tuesday Wednesday Thursday Friday 12:00 p.m. - 1:00 p.m. **Wattage:** 100,000. **Ad Rates:** Noncommercial. **URL:** http://www.kmst.org.

RUTLEDGE

19813 ■ Communities: Life in Cooperative Culture
Fellowship for Intentional Community
PO Box 156
Rutledge, MO 63563-9720
Free: 800-462-8240
Contains information, issues, stories, and ideas about intentional communities in North America, from urban co-ops to co-housing groups to ecovillages to rural communes. **Freq:** Quarterly. **ISSN:** 0199--9346 (print). **Subscription Rates:** $25 U.S. per year. **URL:** http://www.ic.org/communities-magazine-home; http://www.ic.org/community-bookstore/category/communities-magazine. **Remarks:** Accepts advertising. **Circ:** 3,000.

SAINT CHARLES

E. MO. St. Charles Co. On Missouri River, 22 mi. NW of Saint Louis. St. Charles Co. (E). On Missouri River, 22 m NW of St. Louis. Lindenwood College. Missouri's First State Capitol. National historical landmark. Manufactures railroad cars, steel dies,foundry products. Sand, gravel, coal deposits. Diversified farming. Wheat, corn, oats.

19814 ■ TPA Travelers Magazine
Travelers Protective Association of America
2041 Exchange Dr.
Saint Charles, MO 63303
Fax: (636)724-2457
Free: 877-872-2638
Publisher's E-mail: support@tpahq.org
Magazine featuring stories, news, programs, activities, events and accomplishments of Travelers Protective Association (TPA) and its members. **Freq:** Quarterly. **ISSN:** 0039--8454 (print). **Subscription Rates:** Included in membership. **Alt. Formats:** Download; PDF. **URL:** http://www.tpahq.org/publications. **Remarks:** Advertising not accepted. **Circ:** (Not Reported).

19815 ■ KCLC-FM - 89.1
209 S Kingshighway
Saint Charles, MO 63301
Phone: (636)949-4891
Email: fm891@lindenwood.edu
Format: Full Service; Adult Contemporary; Bluegrass; Religious; Public Radio. **Networks:** ABC. **Owner:** Lindenwood University, 209 S Kingshighway St., Saint Charles, MO 63301, Ph: (636)949-2000. **Founded:** 1968. **Operating Hours:** 5:30 a.m.-2.00 a.m.; 3% network, 97% local. **ADI:** St. Louis, MO (Mt. Vernon, IL). **Key Personnel:** Mike Wall, Contact, mwall@lindenwood.edu. **Wattage:** 25,500. **Ad Rates:** Noncommercial. **URL:** http://www.891thewood.com.

19816 ■ KHOJ-AM - 1460
2130 Wade Hampton Blvd.
Greenville, SC 29615
Format: Religious. **Owner:** Family Life Center International, 2130 Wade Hampton Blvd., Greenville, SC 29615-1039. **URL:** http://dads.org.

SAINT JOSEPH

NW MO. Buchanan Co. On Missouri River, 40 mi. N. of Kansas City. Missouri Western College. Agricultural center. Manufactures flour, feed, cereal, packing house products, stationery, serum, office fixtures, paper and wood boxes, textiles, disinfectants, agricultural chemicals, candy, chemicals, structural steel, wood products, automotive parts, batteries, motor boats, steel castings, wire rope. Leather tanneries. Meat packing; flour milling. Grain, tobacco, livestock.

19817 ■ Angus Beef Bulletin
Angus Productions Inc.
3201 Frederick Ave.
Saint Joseph, MO 64506-2997
Free: 800-821-5478
Publisher's E-mail: journal@angusjournal.com
Tabloid for beef cattle producers. **Freq:** 5/year (Jan., Feb, Mar., Sept., Oct.). **Print Method:** Offset. **Trim Size:** 10 1/2 x 12 1/2. **Cols./Page:** 4. **Col. Width:** 11.5 picas. **Col. Depth:** 69 picas. **Key Personnel:** Mary Black, Artist, phone: (816)383-5218; Barb Baylor Anderson, Editor, phone: (618)656-0870; Linda Robbins, Assistant Editor, phone: (816)383-5245; Shauna Rose Hermel, Editor, phone: (816)383-5270; Craig Simmons, Artist, phone: (816)383-5231; Michael Bush, Artist, phone: (816)383-5210. **ISSN:** 1524-8488 (print). **Subscription Rates:** Free. **URL:** http://www.angusbeefbulletin.com. **Ad Rates:** BW $1,295. **Remarks:** Accepts advertising. **Circ:** Non-paid ‡70000.

19818 ■ Angus Journal
American Angus Association
3201 Frederick Ave.
Saint Joseph, MO 64506-2997
Fax: (816)233-6575
Free: 800-821-5478
Publication E-mail: journal@angusjournal.com
Livestock breed magazine. **Freq:** Monthly. **Print Method:** Offset. **Cols./Page:** 3. **Col. Width:** 13.5 picas. **Col. Depth:** 59.5 picas. **Key Personnel:** Shauna Rose Hermel, Editor, phone: (816)383-5270, fax: (816)233-6575; Terry Cotton, Contact; Eric Grant, General Manager. **ISSN:** 0194--9543 (print). **Subscription Rates:** $50 Individuals; $110 Individuals first class; $80 Canada; $130 Canada first class; $125 Other countries. **URL:** http://www.angusjournal.com. **Ad Rates:** BW $875; 4C $300. **Remarks:** Accepts advertising. **Circ:** 14000.

19819 ■ The Griffon News
Missouri Western State University
4525 Downs Dr.
Saint Joseph, MO 64507
Phone: (816)271-4200
Fax: (816)271-5833
Free: 800-662-7041
Publication E-mail: griffy@griffon.mwsc.edu
Collegiate newspaper. **Freq:** Weekly. **Print Method:** Offset. **Trim Size:** 12 x 23. **Cols./Page:** 6. **Col. Width:** 25 nonpareils. **Col. Depth:** 294 agate lines. **Key Personnel:** Mika Cummins, Editor-in-Chief. **Subscription Rates:** Free. **URL:** http://www.thegriffonnews.com. **Remarks:** Accepts advertising. **Circ:** (Not Reported).

19820 ■ St. Joseph News-Press
News-Press and Gazette Co.
825 Edmond St.
Saint Joseph, MO 64501
Phone: (816)271-8600
General newspaper. **Freq:** Mon.-Sun. (morn.). **Print Method:** Offset. **Cols./Page:** 6. **Col. Depth:** 301 agate lines. **Subscription Rates:** $239.88 Individuals all access; $215.88 Individuals daily home delivery; $128.88 Individuals weekend home delivery; $76.56 Individuals Sunday only; $156.96 Individuals all digital access. **URL:** http://www.newspressnow.com. **Mailing address:** PO Box 29, Saint Joseph, MO 64502-0029. **Ad Rates:** BW $57.19; 4C $505. **Remarks:** Advertising accepted; rates available upon request. **Circ:** Mon.-Fri. ★**24240**, Sun. ★**27673**.

19821 ■ KESJ-AM - 1550
4104 Country Ln.
Saint Joseph, MO 64506
Phone: (816)233-8881
Format: Sports. **Owner:** Eagle Communications Inc., 2703 Hall St., Ste. 15, Hays, KS 67601, Ph: (785)625-4000, Fax: (785)625-8030. **Key Personnel:** Dave Riggert, Sports Dir. **URL:** http://www.1550espn.com.

19822 ■ KFEQ-AM - 680
4104 Country Ln.
Saint Joseph, MO 64506
Phone: (816)233-8881
Format: News; Talk; Sports. **Key Personnel:** Gary Exline, Dir. of Programs, Div. Dir., Gen. Mgr., gregg.lynn@eagleradio.net. **Ad Rates:** Advertising accepted; rates available upon request. **URL:** http://www.680kfeq.com.

19823 ■ KGNM-AM - 1270
2414 S Leonard Rd.
Saint Joseph, MO 64503-1899
Phone: (816)233-2577
Fax: (816)233-2374
Owner: Good News Ministries, Inc., at above address, Indianapolis, IN 46206-1871. **Founded:** 1980. **ADI:** St. Joseph, MO. **Wattage:** 1,000. **Ad Rates:** $9 for 30 seconds; $12 for 60 seconds.

19824 ■ KKJO-FM - 105.5
4104 Country Ln.
Saint Joseph, MO 64506
Phone: (816)233-8881
Format: Adult Contemporary; Contemporary Hit Radio (CHR). **Founded:** 1975. **Formerly:** KSFT-FM. **Ad Rates:** $25-50 for 30 seconds; $30-55 for 60 seconds. **URL:** http://www.kjo1055.com.

19825 ■ KQTV-TV - 2
40th & Faraon St.
Saint Joseph, MO 64506
Format: Commercial TV. **Networks:** ABC. **Owner:** Nexstar Broadcasting Group Inc., 545 E John Carpenter Fwy., Ste. 700, Irving, TX 75062, Ph: (972)373-8800. **Founded:** 1953. **Formerly:** KFEQ-TV. **Operating Hours:** 5 a.m.-1 a.m. **ADI:** St. Joseph, MO. **Key Personnel:** Heather Shearin, Gen. Mgr., hshearin@kq2.com. **Ad Rates:** Advertising accepted; rates available upon request. **URL:** http://www.stjoechannel.com.

19826 ■ KSJQ-FM - 92.7
4104 Country Ln.
Saint Joseph, MO 64508
Phone: (816)233-8881
Format: Country. **Owner:** Eagle Communication, Inc., 2703 Hall St., Ste. 15, Hays, KS 67601, Ph: (785)625-4000, Fax: (785)625-8030. **Wattage:** 50,000. **URL:** http://www.myqcountry.com.

19827 ■ KSRD-FM - 91.9
1212 Faraon St.
Saint Joseph, MO 64501
Email: info@ksrdradio.com
Format: Religious. **Owner:** Horizon Broadcast Network, at above address. **Wattage:** 100,000 ERP. **URL:** http://www.ksrdradio.com/.

19828 ■ KTAJ-TV - 16
4410 S 40th, St., Ste.8
Saint Joseph, MO 64503
Phone: (816)364-1616
Fax: (816)364-6729
Email: ktaj@xc.org
Owner: All American TV, 3000 W McArthur, Ste. 530, Santa Ana, CA 92704, Ph: (714)957-9699, Fax: (714)957-9690. **Founded:** 1986. **Operating Hours:** Continuous. **ADI:** St. Joseph, MO. **Key Personnel:** Jeff Landers, Chief Engineer, landers@tbn.org; Julie Cluck, Station Mgr., Contact, jcluck@tbn.org; Julie Cluck, Contact. **Wattage:** 1,000,000. **Ad Rates:** $20-50 for 30 seconds; $29-70 for 60 seconds. **URL:** http://tbn.org.

19829 ■ St. Joseph Cablevision
102 N Woodbine
Saint Joseph, MO 64508
Owner: News-Press and Gazette Co., 825 Edmond St., Saint Joseph, MO 64501, Ph: (816)271-8600. **Founded:** 1965. **Key Personnel:** Hank Bradley, President. **Cities Served:** subscribing households 29,000. **URL:** http://bsd.sos.mo.gov/BusinessEntity/BusinessEntityDetail.aspx?page=beSearch&ID=958591.

SAINT LOUIS

EC MO. St. Louis city St. Louis city. 10 mi. NE of Granite City On Mississippi River, 20 mi. below the mouth of the Missouri River. Independent City. Immense river traffic. Center of Great Lakes to the Gulf Waterway. St. Louis University (Cath.), Washington Univ., University of Missouri - St. Louis, professional and technological institutions. National historical landmark. Museum. Clay, limestone quarries. Primary market for agricultural products, cattle, hogs, horses, mules, grain. Insurance & banking centers. Manufactures meat, bread, beer, flour, grain products, malt, liquors, chemicals, drugs, paints and varnish, machinery, refrigerators, textiles, iron and steel, street and railroad cars, shoes, paper products, hardware, electrical motors and equipment, automobile accessories and automobiles and trucks, auto parts, petroleum and coal, non-ferrous metals, stone, clay and glass, furniture, aircraft, aerospace equipment.

19830 ■ ACM Transactions on Sensor Networks
Association for Computing Machinery
Prof. Chenyang Lu, Ed.-in-Ch.
Washington University in St. Louis
School of Engineering & Applied Sciences
One Brookings Dr.
Saint Louis, MO 63130
Publisher's E-mail: acmhelp@acm.org
Publication of the Association for Computing Machinery. **Freq:** Quarterly. **Key Personnel:** Prof. Tarek F. Abdelzaher, Associate Editor; Prof. Chenyang Lu, Editor-in-Chief. **ISSN:** 1550-4859 (print); **EISSN:** 1550-4867 (electronic). **Subscription Rates:** $175 Nonmembers print only; $136 Nonmembers online only; $204 Nonmembers online & print; Members included in membership dues. **URL:** http://sites.google.com/site/acmtosn. **Circ:** (Not Reported).

19831 ■ American Journal of Botany
Botanical Society of America
4475 Castleman Ave.
Saint Louis, MO 63110
Phone: (314)577-5112
Fax: (314)577-9515
Publication E-mail: ajb@botany.org
Magazine containing botanical research papers. **Freq:** Monthly. **Print Method:** Offset. **Trim Size:** 8 1/2 x 11. **Cols./Page:** 2. **Key Personnel:** Judy Jernstedt, Editor-in-Chief; Amy McPherson, Managing Editor. **ISSN:** 0002--9122 (print); **EISSN:** 1537--2197 (electronic). **Subscription Rates:** $825 U.S. print and online; $775 U.S. online only; $860 Canada and Mexico print and online; $775 Canada and Mexico online only; $920 Other countries print and online; $775 Other countries print and online. **URL:** http://www.amjbot.org. **Ad Rates:** BW $550; 4C $1075. **Remarks:** Accepts advertising. **Circ:** ‡4,693, ‡1,020, 5000.

19832 ■ American Optometric Association News
American Optometric Association
243 N Lindbergh Blvd., 1st Fl.
Saint Louis, MO 63141-7881
Phone: (314)991-4100
Fax: (314)991-4101
Free: 800-365-2219
Publisher's E-mail: ilamo@aoa.org
Journal covering the profession of eye and vision care. **Freq:** 12/yr. **Key Personnel:** Bob Foster, Editor-in-Chief. **ISSN:** 0094--9620 (print). **Subscription Rates:** $159 Individuals print or online. **URL:** http://www.aoa.org/news?sso=y. **Circ:** (Not Reported).

19833 ■ American Philosophical Quarterly
University of Illinois Press
c/o John Greco, Editor
Department of Philosophy
Saint Louis University
3800 Lindell Blvd.
Saint Louis, MO 63108
Publisher's E-mail: uipress@uillinois.edu
Scholarly journal covering philosophy. **Freq:** Quarterly. **Key Personnel:** Nicholas Rescher, Executive Editor; Dorothy Henle, Manager, Operations. **ISSN:** 0003--0481 (print); **EISSN:** 2152--1123 (electronic). **Subscription Rates:** $60 Individuals print only; $336 Institutions print or online; $377 Institutions print + online; $40 Individuals single issues; $90 Institutions single issues. **URL:** http://www.press.uillinois.edu/journals/apq.html. **Ad Rates:** BW $250. **Remarks:** Accepts advertising. **Circ:** 1100.

19834 ■ Analytical and Quantitative Cytology and Histology
Science Printers and Publishers Inc.
8342 Olive Blvd.
Saint Louis, MO 63132-2814
Phone: (314)991-4440

Circulation: ★ = AAM; △ or • = BPA; ♦ = CAC; ❑ = VAC; ⊕ = PO Statement; ‡ = Publisher's Report; Boldface figures = sworn; Light figures = estimated.

Publication E-mail: editor@aqch.com
Journal covering analytical and quantitative cytology and histology. **Freq:** Bimonthly. **Print Method:** Offset. **Trim Size:** 8 x 10 3/4. **Cols./Page:** 2. **Col. Width:** 3 3/8 inches. **Col. Depth:** 10 inches. **Key Personnel:** Peter H. Bartels, Editor-in-Chief; David G. Bostwick, Editor; Liang Cheng, Editor. **ISSN:** 0884--6812 (print). **Subscription Rates:** $570 Individuals online; $920 Institutions online. **URL:** http://www.aqch.com. **Remarks:** Accepts advertising. **Circ:** (Not Reported).

19835 ■ Animal Reproduction Science
Elsevier - Mosby Journal Div.
3251 Riverport Ln.
Saint Louis, MO 63146-3318
Phone: (314)872-8370
Fax: (314)432-1380
Free: 800-325-4177
Publisher's E-mail: info@elsevier.com
Journal for research workers in animal and human reproduction and animal health workers. **Freq:** Monthly. **Key Personnel:** A.C.O. Evans, Editor-in-Chief; J.E. Kinder, Editor-in-Chief. **ISSN:** 0378-4320 (print). **Subscription Rates:** $4325 Institutions print; $1327.73 Institutions e-journal (access for 5 users and to 4 years of archives). **URL:** http://www.journals.elsevier.com/animal-reproduction-science. **Mailing address:** PO Box 46908, Saint Louis, MO 63146-3318. **Remarks:** Accepts advertising. **Circ:** (Not Reported).

19836 ■ AOA News
American Optometric Association
243 N Lindbergh Blvd., 1st Fl.
Saint Louis, MO 63141-7881
Phone: (314)991-4100
Fax: (314)991-4101
Free: 800-365-2219
Publisher's E-mail: ilamo@aoa.org
Magazine of news and events for the American Optometric Association. **Freq:** 18/yr. **Print Method:** Offset. **Trim Size:** 10 3/8 x 15. **Cols./Page:** 4. **Col. Width:** 2 1/4 inches. **Col. Depth:** 14 1/4 inches. **ISSN:** 0094--9620 (print). **USPS:** 908-120. **URL:** http://www.aoa.org. **Ad Rates:** BW $3,920; 4C $5,600; PCI $94. **Remarks:** Accepts advertising. **Circ:** (Not Reported).

19837 ■ AOSA Foresight: Optometry Looking Forward
American Optometric Student Association
243 N Lindbergh, Ste. 311
Saint Louis, MO 63141
Phone: (314)983-4231
Freq: Semiannual. **Subscription Rates:** Included in membership. **URL:** http://www.theaosa.org/aosa-exclusives/351-2. **Ad Rates:** $100-1200, for display advertising; $1050-1250, for full page/bleed. **Remarks:** Accepts display advertising. **Circ:** (Not Reported).

19838 ■ Atherosclerosis
European Atherosclerosis Society
11830 Westline Industrial Dr.
Saint Louis, MO 63146
Phone: (314)453-7076
Fax: (314)523-5153
Free: 877-839-7126
Publication E-mail: usinfo-ehelp@elsevier.com
Freq: Monthly. **Key Personnel:** S. Humphries, Editor-in-Chief; M. Law, Board Member; K. Kajinami, Board Member; R. Asmis, Associate Editor. **ISSN:** 0021-9150 (print). **Subscription Rates:** $392 Individuals print; $7816 Institutions print; $2427 Institutions e-journal (access for 5 users and to 4 years of archives). **URL:** http://www.journals.elsevier.com/atherosclerosis. **Remarks:** Accepts advertising. **Circ:** (Not Reported).

19839 ■ Auto Mag
National Automatic Pistol Collectors Association
PO Box 15738
Saint Louis, MO 63163-0738
Publisher's E-mail: info@napca.net
Journal containing articles, reference works, and featured collections and collectors of semi-automatic pistols. **Freq:** Monthly. **Subscription Rates:** Included in membership. **URL:** http://www.napca.net/automag/. **Remarks:** Advertising not accepted. **Circ:** (Not Reported).

19840 ■ Automatic
National Automatic Pistol Collectors Association
PO Box 15738
Saint Louis, MO 63163-0738
Publisher's E-mail: info@napca.net
Consumer magazine covering automatic pistol collecting. **Founded:** Apr. 01, 1968. **Freq:** Monthly. **Subscription Rates:** Included in membership. **URL:** http://www.napca.net/automag/. **Circ:** (Not Reported).

19841 ■ BREAST DISEASES: A YEAR BOOK QUARTERLY
Mosby Inc.
11830 Westline Industrial Dr.
Saint Louis, MO 63146-3313
Phone: (314)872-8370
Fax: (314)432-1380
Journal on the latest developments in the diagnosis, treatment, screening, and prevention of breast diseases. **Freq:** Quarterly. **Key Personnel:** Thomas A. Buchholz, MD, Editor-in-Chief; Debu Tripathy, MD, Editor; Carlos A. Perez, MD, Editor; Craig I. Henderson, MD, Editor; Gerald D. Dodd, MD, Editor; Charles M. Balch, MD, Editor, Founder. **ISSN:** 1043-321X (print). **Subscription Rates:** $280 Individuals print; $113.07 Institutions e-journal (access for 5 users and to 4 years of archives); $436 Institutions print; $280 Other countries online & print; $230 Individuals online & print; $100 Students online & print; $140 Students, other countries online & print. **URL:** http://www.elsevier.com/journals/breast-diseases-a-year-book-quarterly/1043-321X; http://www.breastdiseasesquarterly.com. **Remarks:** Accepts advertising. **Circ:** (Not Reported).

19842 ■ Calcified Tissue International
Springer Science + Business Media LLC
Division of Bone & Mineral Diseases
Washington University School of Medicine
660 S Euclid Ave.
Box 8301
Saint Louis, MO 63110
Phone: (314)454-8906
Fax: (314)454-5325
Publisher's E-mail: service-ny@springer.com
Journal dealing with the structure and function of bone and other mineralized systems in living organisms. **Founded:** 1967. **Freq:** Monthly. **Print Method:** Offset. **Trim Size:** 8 1/4 x 11. **Cols./Page:** 2. **Col. Width:** 38 nonpareils. **Col. Depth:** 128 agate lines. **Key Personnel:** Robert Civitelli, MD, Editor; Stuart H. Ralston, MD, Editor, phone: (44)131 6511037, fax: (44)131 6511085. **ISSN:** 0171-967X (print). **Subscription Rates:** €2120 Institutions print or online; €2544 Institutions print & enchanced access. **URL:** http://link.springer.com/journal/223. **Remarks:** Accepts advertising. **Circ:** Combined 300.

19843 ■ Catholic Health World
Catholic Health Association of the United States
4455 Woodson Rd.
Saint Louis, MO 63134-3701
Phone: (314)427-2500
Fax: (314)427-0029
Publisher's E-mail: webteam@chausa.org
Tabloid containing national and regional news stories, human interest items, healthcare legislation articles, and photos of interest to administrators of U.S. Catholic hospitals, medical centers, and long-term care facilities. **Freq:** Semimonthly on the 1st and 15th except monthly in January and July. **Print Method:** Offset. **Trim Size:** 10 x 15 1/2. **Cols./Page:** 4. **Col. Width:** 2 1/3 inches. **Key Personnel:** Donna Grace Troy, Coordinator. **ISSN:** 8756--4068 (print). **Subscription Rates:** $45 Members; $50 Nonmembers; $50 Other countries. **URL:** http://www.chausa.org/publications/catholic-health-world/current-issue. **Ad Rates:** $1680-2030, for Tabloid spread(8 columns wide); $1470-1780, for full page(4 columns wide); $745-900, for Jr. page(3 columns wide). BW $, for Tabloid spread(8 columns wide)BW $, for full page(4 columns wide)BW $, for Jr. page(3 columns wide)BW $1400; PCI $30. **Remarks:** Accepts display advertising; Color advertising accepted; rates available upon request. **Circ:** (Not Reported).

19844 ■ Cherry Diamond
Missouri Athletic Club
405 Washington Ave.
Saint Louis, MO 63102
Phone: (314)231-7220
Fax: (314)231-2327
Missouri Athletic Club affairs magazine. **Freq:** Monthly. **Print Method:** Offset. **Trim Size:** 8 1/2 x 11. **Cols./Page:** 3 and 2. **Col. Width:** 28 and 42 nonpareils. **Col. Depth:** 140 agate lines. **Subscription Rates:** Free. **URL:** http://www.mac-stl.org/Default.aspx?p=dynamicmodule&pageid=25&ssid=10042&vnf=1. **Ad Rates:** BW $715; 4C $936. **Remarks:** Accepts advertising. **Circ:** (Not Reported).

19845 ■ Chest Diseases, Thoracic Surgery and Tuberculosis
Elsevier
11830 Westline Industrial Dr.
Saint Louis, MO 63146
Phone: (314)453-7076
Fax: (314)523-5153
Free: 877-839-7126
Publication E-mail: usinfo-ehelp@elsevier.com
Journal covering lung and respiratory tract diseases, thoracic surgery and tuberculosis. **Freq:** 16/yr. **Print Method:** Offset. **Trim Size:** 8 1/8 x 10 7/8. **Cols./Page:** 2. **Col. Width:** 26 nonpareils. **Col. Depth:** 138 agate lines. **ISSN:** 0014--4193 (print). **Subscription Rates:** $5928 Institutions print. **URL:** http://www.elsevier.com/journals/chest-diseases-thoracic-surgery-and-tuberculosis-section-15-embase/0014-4193. **Circ:** (Not Reported).

19846 ■ Clinical Nutrition
Elsevier - Mosby Journal Div.
3251 Riverport Ln.
Saint Louis, MO 63146-3318
Phone: (314)872-8370
Fax: (314)432-1380
Free: 800-325-4177
Publisher's E-mail: info@elsevier.com
Journal providing essential scientific information on nutritional and metabolic care and the relationship between nutrition and disease both in the setting of basic science and clinical practice. **Freq:** Bimonthly. **Key Personnel:** N.E.P. Deutz, Editor. **ISSN:** 0261-5614 (print). **Subscription Rates:** $492 Individuals print ; $1794 Institutions print; $569.33 Institutions e-journal (access for 5 users and to 4 years of archives). **URL:** http://www.clinicalnutritionjournal.org; http://www.journals.elsevier.com/clinical-nutrition. **Mailing address:** PO Box 46908, Saint Louis, MO 63146-3318. **Remarks:** Accepts advertising. **Circ:** (Not Reported).

19847 ■ Collinsville Herald-Journal
St. Louis Post-Dispatch L.L.C.
900 N Tucker Blvd.
Saint Louis, MO 63101
Phone: (314)340-8000
Fax: (314)340-3050
Free: 800-365-0820
Publisher's E-mail: service@stltoday.com
Community newspaper. **Freq:** Semiweekly. **Print Method:** Offset. **Cols./Page:** 6. **Col. Width:** 26 nonpareils. **Col. Depth:** 308 agate lines. **Key Personnel:** Lee Bachlet, Manager, Advertising. **Subscription Rates:** Free. **Remarks:** Accepts advertising. **Circ:** (Not Reported).

19848 ■ The Credit Professional
Credit Professionals International
10726 Manchester Rd., Ste. 210
Saint Louis, MO 63122
Phone: (314)821-9393
Fax: (314)821-7171
Publisher's E-mail: creditpro@creditprofessionals.org
Magazine containing articles, reviews, and practical strategies of improving professional ethics in the field of credit or collection departments of business firms or professional offices. **Freq:** Semiannual. **Subscription Rates:** $10 Members; $15 Nonmembers. **Remarks:** Advertising not accepted. **Circ:** (Not Reported).

19849 ■ Current Diagnostic Pathology
Elsevier - Mosby Journal Div.
3251 Riverport Ln.
Saint Louis, MO 63146-3318
Phone: (314)872-8370
Fax: (314)432-1380
Free: 800-325-4177
Publisher's E-mail: info@elsevier.com
Journal for diagnostic pathologists. **Freq:** Bimonthly. **ISSN:** 0968-6053 (print). **Subscription Rates:** ¥64500 Institutions; €597 Institutions European Countries; $532 Institutions for all Countries except Europe and Japan; ¥16200 Students; €149 Students European Countries; $134 Students for all Countries except Europe and Japan; ¥16200 Individuals; €149 Individuals European

Countries; $134 Individuals for all Countries except Europe and Japan; ¥30600 Individuals. **URL:** http://www.elsevier.com/journals/current-diagnostic-pathology/0968-6053. **Mailing address:** PO Box 46908, Saint Louis, MO 63146-3318. **Circ:** (Not Reported).

19850 ■ DECOR: The Art & Framing Business Resource
Pfingsten Publishing Company L.L.C.
1801 Pk., 270 Dr.
Saint Louis, MO 63146
Trade magazine covering information, education and marketing services for art and framing retailers, distributors, and wholesalers. **Founded:** 1880. **Freq:** Monthly. **Key Personnel:** Meg Glasgow. **Subscription Rates:** $40 Canada and Mexico; $60 Canada and Mexico two years; $60 Out of country; $100 Out of country two years. **URL:** http://decormagazine.com. **Ad Rates:** BW $2,160; 4C $3,210. **Remarks:** Accepts advertising. **Circ:** (Not Reported).

19851 ■ Drug Facts and Comparisons
Wolters Kluwer Health
77 Westport Plz., Ste. 450
Saint Louis, MO 63146-3125
Phone: (314)392-0000
Free: 800-223-0554
Publisher's E-mail: service@fandc.com
Drug information organized by therapeutic category. **Founded:** 1945. **Freq:** Monthly. **Print Method:** CD-ROM. **Key Personnel:** Robert Brown, Director, Marketing. **ISSN:** 0014-6617 (print). **Subscription Rates:** $299.95 Individuals 2015 book; $77 Individuals 2009 pocket version. **URL:** http://www.factsandcomparisons.com; http://www.factsandcomparisons.com/drug-facts-and-comparisons-bound. **Remarks:** Advertising not accepted. **Circ:** (Not Reported).

19852 ■ Early Human Development
Elsevier - Mosby Journal Div.
3251 Riverport Ln.
Saint Louis, MO 63146-3318
Phone: (314)872-8370
Fax: (314)432-1380
Free: 800-325-4177
Publisher's E-mail: info@elsevier.com
Journal for researchers and clinicians. **Freq:** Monthly. **Key Personnel:** E.F. Maalouf, Editor-in-Chief. **ISSN:** 0378-3782 (print). **Subscription Rates:** $3205 Institutions print; $303 Individuals print; $988 Institutions e-journal (access for 5 users and to 4 years of archives). **URL:** http://www.earlyhumandevelopment.com; http://www.journals.elsevier.com/early-human-development. **Mailing address:** PO Box 46908, Saint Louis, MO 63146-3318. **Circ:** (Not Reported).

19853 ■ The Electrical Distributor
National Association of Electrical Distributors
1181 Corporate Lake Dr.
Saint Louis, MO 63132-1716
Phone: (314)991-9000
Fax: (314)991-3060
Free: 888-791-2512
Publisher's E-mail: memberservices@naed.org
Freq: Monthly. **ISSN:** 0422--8707 (print). **Subscription Rates:** Members free; $40 Nonmembers. **URL:** http://www.tedmagazine-digital.com/tedmagazine/april_2015#pg1. **Remarks:** Accepts advertising. **Circ:** 28000.

19854 ■ Engineering Structures
RELX Group P.L.C.
c/o P.L. Gould, Ed.-in-Ch.
Department of Mechanical Engineering & Aerospace
Washington University
Saint Louis, MO 63130
Phone: (314)935-6303
Fax: (314)935-4338
Publisher's E-mail: amsterdam@relx.com
Journal covering applications of structural engineering principles and theories in all areas of technology. **Freq:** 24/yr. **Key Personnel:** P.L. Gould, Editor-in-Chief; D.A. Nethercot, Editor. **ISSN:** 0141--0296 (print). **Subscription Rates:** $312.80 Individuals print; $3930 Institutions print; $3929.60 online. **URL:** http://www.journals.elsevier.com/engineering-structures/ion. **Circ:** (Not Reported).

19855 ■ European Urology
Elsevier - Mosby Journal Div.
3251 Riverport Ln.
Saint Louis, MO 63146-3318
Phone: (314)872-8370
Fax: (314)432-1380
Free: 800-325-4177
Publisher's E-mail: info@elsevier.com
Journal publishing peer-reviewed original articles and topical reviews on a wide range of urological problems. **Freq:** Monthly. **Key Personnel:** Francesco Montorsi, Editor; Anders Bjartell, Editor, Consultant; Christian Stief, Editor, Consultant. **ISSN:** 0302-2838 (print). **Subscription Rates:** $1851 Individuals print; $5263 Institutions print; $1720 Institutions e-journal (access for 5 users and to 4 years of archives); Free members. **URL:** http://www.journals.elsevier.com/european-urology; http://www.uroweb.org/publications/european-urology; http://www.europeanurology.com/news-item/82/2013-impact-factor-12-480. **Mailing address:** PO Box 46908, Saint Louis, MO 63146-3318. **Remarks:** Accepts advertising. **Circ:** (Not Reported).

19856 ■ Forum for Social Economics
St. Louis University Department of Economics
John Cook School of Business
3674 Lindell Blvd.
Saint Louis, MO 63108
Phone: (314)977-3848
Fax: (314)977-1478
Publisher's E-mail: econbiz@slu.edu
Scholarly journal covering economics. **Freq:** Semiannual. **Cols./Page:** 1. **ISSN:** 0736--0932 (print). **URL:** http://www.slu.edu/readstory/more/5922. **Formerly:** Forum for School Economics. **Remarks:** Advertising not accepted. **Circ:** Controlled 450.

19857 ■ Gateway Journalism Review
Gateway Journalism Review
PO Box 12474
Saint Louis, MO 63132
Publication E-mail: gatewayjr@siu.edu
Magazine evaluating journalism, print and broadcast media, advertising and public relations. Notes issues not covered by the mass media. **Freq:** Quarterly. **Print Method:** Offset. **Trim Size:** 7 x 9 1/2. **Cols./Page:** 3. **Col. Width:** 2.233 inches. **Col. Depth:** 9 1/2 inches. **Key Personnel:** William A. Babcock, Editor. **ISSN:** 0036--2972 (print). **URL:** http://gatewayjr.org. **Formerly:** The St. Louis Journalism Review: A critique of metropolitan media and events. **Ad Rates:** BW $900; 4C $1,350. **Remarks:** Accepts advertising. **Circ:** (Not Reported).

19858 ■ Global Aquaculture Advocate
Global Aquaculture Alliance
4111 Telegraph Rd., Ste. 302
Saint Louis, MO 63129
Phone: (314)293-5500
Magazine covering farmed seafood production, innovative technology, the marketplace and aquaculture advocacy. **Freq:** Bimonthly. **Subscription Rates:** Included in membership. **URL:** http://advocate.gaalliance.org. **Remarks:** Accepts advertising. **Circ:** (Not Reported).

19859 ■ Happy Times
Concordia Publishing House
3558 S Jefferson Ave.
Saint Louis, MO 63118-3910
Phone: (314)268-1000
Fax: (800)490-9889
Free: 800-325-3040
Publisher's E-mail: order@cph.org
Story magazine for preschoolers. **Freq:** Bimonthly. **Print Method:** Letterpress and offset. **Trim Size:** 8 x 8 1/4. **Cols./Page:** 2. **Col. Width:** 27 nonpareils. **Col. Depth:** 133 agate lines. **USPS:** 234-880. **Subscription Rates:** $16 Individuals; $30 Two years. **URL:** http://www.cph.org/t-magazines-happy.aspx. **Remarks:** Advertising not accepted. **Circ:** (Not Reported).

19860 ■ Hauntworld Magazine
Hauntworld Inc.
1525 S 8th St.
Saint Louis, MO 63104
Phone: (314)241-3456
Fax: (314)621-3728
Magazine featuring the haunted house industry. **Freq:** Quarterly. **Key Personnel:** Larry Kirchner, Contact; Jim Kelly, Contact; Patti Ludwinski, Manager, Sales. **Subscription Rates:** $45.95 U.S.; $55.95 Canada; $65.95 Other countries. **URL:** http://www.hauntedhousemagazine.com. **Ad Rates:** 4C $1,000. **Remarks:** Accepts advertising. **Circ:** (Not Reported).

19861 ■ Health Policy
Elsevier - Mosby Journal Div.
3251 Riverport Ln.
Saint Louis, MO 63146-3318
Phone: (314)872-8370
Fax: (314)432-1380
Free: 800-325-4177
Publisher's E-mail: info@elsevier.com
Journal serving as a vehicle for the exploration and discussion of health policy issues and is aimed in particular at enhancing communication between health policy researchers, legislators, decision-makers, and professionals concerned with developing, implementing, and analyzing health policy. **Freq:** Monthly. **Key Personnel:** Prof. Reinhard Busse, Editor-in-Chief. **ISSN:** 0168-8510 (print). **Subscription Rates:** $531 Individuals print; $1173.87 Institutions e-journal (access for 5 users and to 4 years of archives); $3788 Institutions print. **URL:** http://www.journals.elsevier.com/health-policy. **Mailing address:** PO Box 46908, Saint Louis, MO 63146-3318. **Circ:** (Not Reported).

19862 ■ Health Progress
Catholic Health Association of the United States
4455 Woodson Rd.
Saint Louis, MO 63134-3701
Phone: (314)427-2500
Fax: (314)427-0029
Publisher's E-mail: webteam@chausa.org
Freq: 6/year. **ISSN:** 0882--1577 (print); **EISSN:** 1943--3417 (electronic). **Subscription Rates:** $65 Nonmembers; $55 Members; $65 Canada and other Countries; Single issue Free to members; $10 Single issue nonmembers. **URL:** http://www.chausa.org/publications/health-progress/current-issue. **Ad Rates:** $990-1200, for full page; $810-975, for 2/3 page vertical; $660-800, for 1/2 page horizontal; $470-570, for 1/3 page vertical. BW $, for full pageBW $, for 2/3 page verticalBW $, for 1/2 page horizontalBW $, for 1/3 page vertical. **Remarks:** Accepts advertising. **Circ:** (Not Reported).

19863 ■ Health Progress: Official Journal of the Catholic Health Association of the United States
Catholic Health Association of the United States
4455 Woodson Rd.
Saint Louis, MO 63134-3701
Phone: (314)427-2500
Fax: (314)427-0029
Publisher's E-mail: webteam@chausa.org
Magazine for administrative-level and other managerial personnel in Catholic healthcare and related organizations. Featured are articles on management concepts, legislative and regulatory trends, and theological, sociological, ethical, legal, and technical issues. **Freq:** Bimonthly. **Print Method:** Web offset. **Trim Size:** 8 1/8 x 10 7/8. **Cols./Page:** 3 and 2. **Col. Width:** 26 and 39 nonpareils. **Col. Depth:** 140 agate lines. **Key Personnel:** Pamela Schaeffer, Editor. **ISSN:** 0882--1577 (print); **EISSN:** 1943--3417 (electronic). **Subscription Rates:** $55 Members; $65 Nonmembers; $65 Other countries. **URL:** http://www.chausa.org/publications/health-progress. **Formerly:** Hospital Progress. **Ad Rates:** BW $990. **Remarks:** Accepts advertising. **Circ:** (Not Reported).

19864 ■ Heart Failure Clinics
Elsevier - Mosby Journal Div.
3251 Riverport Ln.
Saint Louis, MO 63146-3318
Phone: (314)872-8370
Fax: (314)432-1380
Free: 800-325-4177
Publisher's E-mail: info@elsevier.com
Journal that provides basic science, clinical management, investigational modalities, and detailed discussions by experts in the field of heart failure. **Freq:** Quarterly. **Key Personnel:** Ragavendra R. Baliga, MD, Editor; James B. Young, MD, Editor. **ISSN:** 1551--7136 (print). **Subscription Rates:** $300 Individuals; $499 Institutions. **URL:** http://www.elsevier.com/journals/heart-failure-clinics/1551-7136. **Mailing address:** PO

Circulation: ★ = AAM; △ or • = BPA; ♦ = CAC; ❑ = VAC; ⊕ = PO Statement; ‡ = Publisher's Report; Boldface figures = sworn; Light figures = estimated.

Box 46908, Saint Louis, MO 63146-3318. **Remarks:** Accepts advertising. **Circ:** (Not Reported).

19865 ■ HIV Clinical Trials
Thomas Land Publishers Inc.
255 Jefferson Rd.
Saint Louis, MO 63119-3627
Phone: (314)963-7445
Fax: (314)963-9345
Publisher's E-mail: publisher@thomasland.com
Journal covering developments and techniques in HIV/AIDS therapeutics. **Freq:** 6/year. **Print Method:** offset. **Trim Size:** 8 1/8 x 10 7/8. **Key Personnel:** Prof. Milos Opravil, MD, Board Member; Judith A. Aberg, MD, Editor; Prof. Caroline A. Sabin, PhD, Editor; Alain Lafeuillade, MD, Editor. **ISSN:** 1528--4336 (print); **EISSN:** 1945--5771 (electronic). **Subscription Rates:** $423 Institutions print and online; $183 Individuals print and online; $372 Institutions online only. **URL:** http://www.tandfonline.com/loi/yhct20. **Remarks:** Accepts advertising. **Circ:** (Not Reported).

19866 ■ Hospital Pharmacy
Wolters Kluwer Health
77 Westport Plz., Ste. 450
Saint Louis, MO 63146-3125
Phone: (314)392-0000
Free: 800-223-0554
Publisher's E-mail: service@fandc.com
Peer-reviewed journal for pharmacists in hospitals and organized health systems, promoting safe medication and prevention of medical errors. **Freq:** Monthly. **Print Method:** Web offset. **Trim Size:** 8 1/8 x 10 7/8. **Cols./Page:** 2. **Col. Width:** 39 nonpareils. **Col. Depth:** 140 agate lines. **Key Personnel:** Michael R. Cohen, Assistant Editor; Joyce A. Generali, Editor-in-Chief; Dennis J. Cada, PhD, Editor. **ISSN:** 0018--5787 (print). **Subscription Rates:** $75 Individuals online; worldwide; $217 Institutions print and online; single site; $145 U.S. and Canada print and online; $289 U.S. and Canada print and online, single site license. **URL:** http://www.thomasland.com/hospitalpharmacy.html. **Ad Rates:** GLR $13; BW $4140; 4C $2165. **Remarks:** Accepts advertising. **Circ:** Controlled ‡33900.

19867 ■ Insight into Diversity: The EEO Recruitment Publication
INSIGHT Into Diversity
c/o Potomac Publishing, Inc.
225 Meramec Ave., Ste. 400
Saint Louis, MO 63105
Phone: (314)863-2900
Fax: (314)863-2905
Free: 800-537-0655
Publisher's E-mail: aareeo@concentric.net
Journal for business, academia, non-profit organizations and the government to use in recruiting females, Native Americans, minorities, veterans, and persons with disabilities. **Freq:** Monthly. **Print Method:** Offset. **Trim Size:** 8 1/2 x 11. **Cols./Page:** 3 and 2. **Col. Width:** 2 1/4 and 3 1/2 inches. **Col. Depth:** 9 3/4 inches. **Key Personnel:** Lenore Pearlstein, Publisher, phone: (301)219-6464. **ISSN:** 0146--2113 (print). **Subscription Rates:** $12.95 Individuals. **URL:** http://www.insightintodiversity.com. **Formerly:** Affirmative Action Register. **Ad Rates:** BW $2895; 4C $3620. **Remarks:** Advertising accepted; rates available upon request. **Circ:** (Not Reported).

19868 ■ Integrite: A Faith and Learning Journal
Missouri Baptist University
1 College Park Dr.
Saint Louis, MO 63141-8698
Phone: (314)434-1115
Free: 877-434-1115
Journal that examines the philosophical, theological, and pedagogical issues related to the integration of Christian faith and higher learning. **Freq:** Semiannual. **Key Personnel:** John J. Han, Editor. **ISSN:** 1547--0873 (print). **URL:** http://www.mobap.edu/about-mbu/publications/integrite. **Circ:** (Not Reported).

19869 ■ International Dredging Review
International Dredging Review
319 N Fourth St., Ste. 650
Saint Louis, MO 63102
Phone: (314)241-4314
Fax: (314)241-4207
Publisher's E-mail: sales@dredgemag.com
Magazine covering the dredging industry. **Freq:** Bimonthly. **Print Method:** Offset. Uses mats. **Trim Size:** 8 1/2 x 11. **Cols./Page:** 3 and 2. **Col. Width:** 26 and 40 nonpareils. **Col. Depth:** 140 agate lines. **Key Personnel:** Anna Townshend, Editor. **ISSN:** 0737--8181 (print). **Subscription Rates:** $45 Individuals; $80 Two years; $85 Other countries. **URL:** http://www.dredgemag.com. **Remarks:** Accepts advertising. **Circ:** Paid 1500, Controlled 1450.

19870 ■ Jesuit Bulletin
The Jesuits of the Missouri Province
4511 W Pine Blvd.
Saint Louis, MO 63108-2109
Magazine publicizing the spirituality and works of Missouri Province Jesuits. **Freq:** 3/year. **Print Method:** Offset. **Trim Size:** @eig. **Key Personnel:** Robert Burns, Executive Editor. **ISSN:** 1524-1815 (print). **Subscription Rates:** Free. **URL:** http://www.jesuitsmissouri.org/publications. **Remarks:** Advertising not accepted. **Circ:** Non-paid 20000.

19871 ■ The Journal
Webster University
470 E Lockwood Ave.
Saint Louis, MO 63119-3194
Free: 800-981-9801
Publication E-mail: wujournal@gmail.com
Collegiate newspaper. **Founded:** 1924. **Freq:** Weekly (Thurs.). **Print Method:** Offset. **Trim Size:** 13 x 22.5. **Cols./Page:** 6. **Col. Width:** 2.17 inches. **Col. Depth:** 22.5 inches. **Subscription Rates:** Free. **URL:** http://www.webujournal.com. **Ad Rates:** BW $700; 4C $1,200; PCI $11. **Remarks:** Accepts advertising. **Circ:** Free ‡3000.

19872 ■ Journal of Affective Disorders
Elsevier - Mosby Journal Div.
3251 Riverport Ln.
Saint Louis, MO 63146-3318
Phone: (314)872-8370
Fax: (314)432-1380
Free: 800-325-4177
Publication E-mail: journalaffdis@googlemail.com
Journal publishing papers concerned with affective disorders. **Freq:** 18/yr. **Key Personnel:** H.S. Akiskal, Editor; C. Katona, Editor; C. Altamura, Board Member. **ISSN:** 0165-0327 (print). **Subscription Rates:** $721 Individuals print; $1941.33 Institutions e-journal (access for 5 users and to 4 years of archives); $6310 Institutions print. **URL:** http://www.jad-journal.com; http://www.journals.elsevier.com/journal-of-affective-disorders. **Mailing address:** PO Box 46908, Saint Louis, MO 63146-3318. **Remarks:** Accepts advertising. **Circ:** (Not Reported).

19873 ■ Journal of the American Medical Directors Association: Long-term Care: Management, Applied Research and Clinical Issues
Elsevier Inc.
c/o John E. Morley MD, Ed.-in-Ch.
St. Louis University Medical Center
Division of Geriatric Medical
1402 S Grand Blvd., Rm. M238
Saint Louis, MO 63104
Phone: (314)977-8462
Fax: (314)771-8575
Publisher's E-mail: healthpermissions@elsevier.com
Official journal of the American Medical Directors Association for medical and nursing professionals providing long-term elder care. **Freq:** Monthly. **Print Method:** Web offset. **Trim Size:** 8 1/8 x 10 7/8. **Key Personnel:** Valerie Tanner, Managing Editor; John E. Morley, MD, Editor-in-Chief. **ISSN:** 1525--8610 (print). **Subscription Rates:** $312 Individuals print and online; $384 Canada print and online; $134 Students print and online; $189 Students, Canada print and online; $246 Individuals online only; $105 Students online only. **URL:** http://www.jamda.com; http://store.elsevier.com/product.jsp?issn=15258610. **Ad Rates:** BW $2,985; 4C $1,625. **Remarks:** Advertising accepted; rates available upon request. **Circ:** ‡5325.

19874 ■ Journal of Dermatological Science
Elsevier - Mosby Journal Div.
3251 Riverport Ln.
Saint Louis, MO 63146-3318
Phone: (314)872-8370
Fax: (314)432-1380
Free: 800-325-4177
Publisher's E-mail: info@elsevier.com
Journal publishing manuscripts on a wide range of topics related to dermatology. **Freq:** Monthly. **Key Personnel:** Yoshiki Tokura, Editor-in-Chief. **ISSN:** 0923-1811 (print). **Subscription Rates:** $352 Individuals print; $807.73 Institutions e-journal (access for 5 users and to 4 years of archives); $2570 Institutions print. **URL:** http://www.jdsjournal.com; http://www.journals.elsevier.com/journal-of-dermatological-science. **Mailing address:** PO Box 46908, Saint Louis, MO 63146-3318. **Circ:** (Not Reported).

19875 ■ Journal of Financial Stability
Elsevier - Mosby Journal Div.
3251 Riverport Ln.
Saint Louis, MO 63146-3318
Phone: (314)872-8370
Fax: (314)432-1380
Free: 800-325-4177
Publisher's E-mail: info@elsevier.com
Journal that provides a forum for theoretical and empirical macro and micro economic and financial analysis of the causes, management, resolution and preventions of financial crises, including banking, securities market, payments and currency crises. **Freq:** 6/year. **Key Personnel:** G.G. Kaufman, Editor; W.C. Hunter, Editor; I. Hasan, Managing Editor. **ISSN:** 1572--3089 (print). **Subscription Rates:** $85 Individuals print; $406 Institutions online, access for 5 users and access to 4 years of archives; $487 Institutions print. **URL:** http://www.journals.elsevier.com/journal-of-financial-stability. **Mailing address:** PO Box 46908, Saint Louis, MO 63146-3318. **Remarks:** Accepts advertising. **Circ:** (Not Reported).

19876 ■ The Journal of Health Law and Policy
Saint Louis University School of Law
100 N Tucker Blvd.
Saint Louis, MO 63101
Phone: (314)977-2800
Fax: (314)977-1464
Publisher's E-mail: admissions@law.slu.edu
Journal featuring articles that provide in-depth analysis of topical and developing issues in health law and policy. **Freq:** Semiannual. **URL:** http://law.slu.edu/journals; http://law.slu.edu/academics/journals/journal-health-law-policy. **Circ:** (Not Reported).

19877 ■ Journal of Hospital Infection
Elsevier - Mosby Journal Div.
3251 Riverport Ln.
Saint Louis, MO 63146-3318
Phone: (314)872-8370
Fax: (314)432-1380
Free: 800-325-4177
Publication E-mail: jhi@his.org.uk
Journal publishing articles in the field of hospital-acquired infection and related subjects. **Freq:** Monthly. **Key Personnel:** J. Child, Editor, phone: (44)20 77130273. **ISSN:** 0195-6701 (print). **Subscription Rates:** $426 Individuals print; $537.60 Institutions e-journal (access for 5 users and to 4 years of archives); $1694 Institutions print; Included in membership. **URL:** http://www.journalofhospitalinfection.com; http://www.his.org.uk/journal; http://www.journals.elsevier.com/journal-of-hospital-infection. **Mailing address:** PO Box 46908, Saint Louis, MO 63146-3318. **Remarks:** Accepts advertising. **Circ:** (Not Reported).

19878 ■ Journal of Infection
Elsevier - Mosby Journal Div.
3251 Riverport Ln.
Saint Louis, MO 63146-3318
Phone: (314)872-8370
Fax: (314)432-1380
Free: 800-325-4177
Publisher's E-mail: info@elsevier.com
Journal publishing papers on all aspects of infection - clinical, microbiological, epidemiological and molecular. **Freq:** Monthly. **Key Personnel:** R. Read, Editor-in-Chief, phone: (44)114 2724072, fax: (44)114 2739926. **ISSN:** 0163-4453 (print). **Subscription Rates:** $379 Individuals print; $460.53 Institutions e-journal (access for 5 users and to 4 years of archives); $1463 Institutions print. **URL:** http://www.journalofinfection.com; http://www.journals.elsevier.com/journal-of-infection; http://www.britishinfection.org/news/journal-infection. **Mailing address:** PO Box 46908, Saint Louis, MO 63146-3318. **Remarks:** Advertising accepted; rates available upon request. **Circ:** (Not Reported).

19879 ■ The Journal of Reproductive Medicine: For the Obstetrician and Gynecologist
Science Printers and Publishers Inc.
8342 Olive Blvd.
Saint Louis, MO 63132-2814
Phone: (314)991-4440
Publisher's E-mail: editor@reproductivemedicine.com
Journal of obstetrics, gynecology and reproductive endocrinology containing clinical articles, reviews, and case reports. **Freq:** Bimonthly. **Print Method:** Offset. **Trim Size:** 8 x 10 3/4. **Cols./Page:** 2. **Col. Width:** 40 nonpareils. **Col. Depth:** 152 agate lines. **Key Personnel:** Donna Kessel, Managing Editor; Lawrence D. Devoe, MD, Editor-in-Chief. **ISSN:** 0024--7758 (print). **Subscription Rates:** $495 Individuals online; $910 Institutions online. **URL:** http://www.reproductivemedicine.com. **Remarks:** Accepts advertising. **Circ:** (Not Reported).

19880 ■ Ladue News: The Place To Be
Suburban Journals
8811 Ladue Rd., Ste. D
Saint Louis, MO 63124
Phone: (314)863-3737
Fax: (314)863-4445
Publisher's E-mail: bwalsh@yourjournal.com
Community newspaper. **Freq:** Weekly (Fri.). **Key Personnel:** Justin Nangle, Publisher; Lisa Watson, Associate Editor; Trish Muyco-Tobin, Editor-in-Chief. **Subscription Rates:** $45 Individuals. **URL:** http://www.laduenews.com. **Remarks:** Accepts advertising. **Circ:** Paid ♦**134**.

19881 ■ Lumberyard
The Firecracker Press
2838 Cherokee St.
Saint Louis, MO 63118
Phone: (314)776-7271
Literary magazine. **Freq:** Semiannual. **Key Personnel:** Jen Woods, Contact. **Subscription Rates:** $20 Individuals. **URL:** http://typecastpublishing.com/lumberyard. **Circ:** (Not Reported).

19882 ■ Lutheran Witness
Board for Communication Services/The Lutheran Church - Missouri Synod
1333 S Kirkwood Rd.
Saint Louis, MO 63122-7295
Phone: (314)965-9000
Fax: (314)996-1016
Free: 888-843-5267
Lutheran magazine. **Freq:** Monthly. **Print Method:** Offset. **Trim Size:** 8 1/8 x 10 5/8. **Cols./Page:** 3. **Col. Width:** 28 nonpareils. **Col. Depth:** 133 agate lines. **ISSN:** 0024--757X (print). **Subscription Rates:** $19.99 Individuals print and online. **URL:** http://blogs.lcms.org/category/lutheran-witness. **Ad Rates:** BW $9980. **Remarks:** Accepts advertising. **Circ:** (Not Reported).

19883 ■ MBU Magazine: A Publication of Missouri Baptist University
Missouri Baptist University
1 College Park Dr.
Saint Louis, MO 63141-8698
Phone: (314)434-1115
Free: 877-434-1115
Magazine focusing on the activities of Missouri Baptist university constituents and issues affecting higher education. **Freq:** Semiannual. **Print Method:** Offset. **Trim Size:** 11 x 15. **Cols./Page:** 4. **Col. Width:** 14 picas. **Key Personnel:** Dr. Alton R. Lacey, President, phone: (314)392-2355; Bryce Chapman, Editor. **ISSN:** 0362--3696 (print). **URL:** http://www.mobap.edu/about-mbu/publications/mbu-magazine. **Remarks:** Advertising not accepted. **Circ:** (Not Reported).

19884 ■ Midwest Traveler
AAA Auto Club of Missouri
12901 N 40 Dr.
Saint Louis, MO 63141
Phone: (314)523-7350
Fax: (314)523-6982
Motor club magazine with an emphasis on travel. **Freq:** Bimonthly. **Print Method:** Offset. **Trim Size:** 7 7/8 x 10 13/16. **Cols./Page:** 3. **Col. Width:** 32 nonpareils. **Col. Depth:** 133 agate lines. **ISSN:** 0026--3435 (print). **USPS:** 348-280. **Formerly:** The Midwest Motorist. **Ad Rates:** 4C $16545. **Remarks:** Accepts advertising. **Circ:** Combined ‡589887.

19885 ■ Missouri Botanical Garden Annals
Missouri Botanical Garden Press
PO Box 299
Saint Louis, MO 63166-0299
Phone: (314)577-9594
Fax: (314)577-9594
Publisher's E-mail: bob.magill@mobot.org
Trade magazine covering original research in botany. **Freq:** Quarterly. **Trim Size:** 7 x 10. **Key Personnel:** Allison Brock, Associate Editor; Victoria C. Hollowell, Editor; Beth Parada, Managing Editor. **ISSN:** 0026--6493 (print). **Subscription Rates:** $20 Single issue. **URL:** http://www.mbgpress.info/index.php?task=title. **Remarks:** Advertising not accepted. **Circ:** (Not Reported).

19886 ■ Missouri Courier
Missouri Credit Union Association
2055 Craigshire Rd.
Saint Louis, MO 63146-4009
Phone: (314)542-0555
Fax: (314)542-1320
Free: 800-392-3074
Freq: Quarterly. **Alt. Formats:** PDF. **Remarks:** Advertising not accepted. **Circ:** 4000.

19887 ■ Nanomedicine: Nanotechnology, Biology and Medicine
Elsevier - Mosby Journal Div.
3251 Riverport Ln.
Saint Louis, MO 63146-3318
Phone: (314)872-8370
Fax: (314)432-1380
Free: 800-325-4177
Publisher's E-mail: info@elsevier.com
Journal that publishes basic, clinical, and engineering research in the field of nanomedicine. **Freq:** 8/year. **Key Personnel:** Lajos P. Balogh, PhD, Editor-in-Chief; Mansoor Amiji, PhD, Associate Editor. **ISSN:** 1549--9634 (print). **Subscription Rates:** $99 Individuals print; $1676 Institutions print; $1628.80 Institutions online. **URL:** http://www.journals.elsevier.com/nanomedicine-nanotechnology-biology-and-medicine. **Mailing address:** PO Box 46908, Saint Louis, MO 63146-3318. **Remarks:** Accepts advertising. **Circ:** (Not Reported).

19888 ■ The National Gardener: A Whole World of Wonders
National Garden Clubs
c/o Susan Davidson, Editor
102 Elm Ave.
Saint Louis, MO 63119
Phone: (314)968-1664
Publisher's E-mail: headquarters@gardenclub.org
Club magazine covering gardening, environmental issues, conservation, landscaping, flower arranging, and gardening for youths, senior citizens, and the handicapped. **Freq:** Quarterly. **Print Method:** Offset. **Trim Size:** 6 x 9. **Cols./Page:** 2. **Col. Width:** 14 picas. **Col. Depth:** 105 agate lines. **Key Personnel:** Susan Davidson, Editor. **ISSN:** 0027--9331 (print). **Subscription Rates:** $18 Other countries; $36 Other countries including air mail. **URL:** http://www.gardenclub.org/about-us/publications/the-national-gardener.aspx. **Ad Rates:** BW $380; PCI $45. **Remarks:** Accepts advertising. **Circ:** (Not Reported).

19889 ■ Neuromuscular Disorders
Elsevier - Mosby Journal Div.
3251 Riverport Ln.
Saint Louis, MO 63146-3318
Phone: (314)872-8370
Fax: (314)432-1380
Free: 800-325-4177
Journal covering all aspects of neuromuscular disorders in childhood and adult life (including the muscular dystrophies, spinal muscular atrophies, hereditary neuropathies, congenital myopathies, myasthenias, myotonic syndromes, metabolic myopathies and inflammatory myopathies). **Freq:** Monthly. **Key Personnel:** V. Dubowitz, Editor-in-Chief. **ISSN:** 0960-8966 (print). **Subscription Rates:** $2076 Institutions print; $641.60 Institutions e-journal (access for 5 users and to 4 years of archives); $918 Individuals print and online; $780 Individuals online only. **URL:** http://www.nmd-journal.com; http://www.journals.elsevier.com/neuromuscular-disorders; http://www.worldmusclesociety.org/home/journal. **Remarks:** Accepts advertising. **Circ:** (Not Reported).

19890 ■ Novon: A Journal of Botanical Nomenclature
Missouri Botanical Garden Press
PO Box 299
Saint Louis, MO 63166-0299
Phone: (314)577-9594
Fax: (314)577-9594
Publisher's E-mail: bob.magill@mobot.org
Trade magazine covering botany. **Freq:** Quarterly. **Trim Size:** 7 x 10. **Key Personnel:** Beth Parada, Managing Editor, phone: (314)577-9473, fax: (314)577-9594; Victoria C. Hollowell, Editor. **ISSN:** 1055--3177 (print). **Subscription Rates:** $20 Single issue. **URL:** http://mbgpress.info. **Remarks:** Advertising not accepted. **Circ:** (Not Reported).

19891 ■ Nurse Leader
Elsevier Inc.
11830 Westline Industrial Dr.
Saint Louis, MO 63146
Phone: (314)453-7041
Fax: (800)225-6030
Free: 800-654-2452
Publisher's E-mail: support@elsevier.com
Journal publishing articles on the vision, skills, and tools needed by nurses currently aspiring to leadership positions. **Freq:** Bimonthly. **Print Method:** Sheetfed. **Trim Size:** 8 1/8 x 10 7/8. **Key Personnel:** Roxane B. Spitzer, PhD, Editor-in-Chief; Mary C. Tonges, Board Member; Frank Shaffer, Board Member; Katherine Vestal, Board Member; Rhonda Anderson, Board Member; Jim Cato, Board Member; Lisa Johnson, Manager. **ISSN:** 1541--4612 (print). **Subscription Rates:** $102 Individuals online and print; $164 Canada online and print; $152 Other countries online and print; $85 Individuals online only. **URL:** http://www.nurseleader.com; http://www.journals.elsevier.com/nurse-leader. **Ad Rates:** BW $1,505; 4C $1,620. **Remarks:** Advertising accepted; rates available upon request. **Circ:** ‡7595, 8700.

19892 ■ The Optimist Magazine
Optimist International
4494 Lindell Blvd.
Saint Louis, MO 63108-2404
Phone: (314)371-6000
Fax: (314)735-4100
Free: 800-500-8130
Publisher's E-mail: marketing@optimist.org
Official publication of Optimist International. **Freq:** Quarterly October 1, January 15, April 1 and June 1. **Print Method:** Offset. **Trim Size:** 8 3/8 x 10 7/8. **Cols./Page:** 3. **Col. Width:** 26 nonpareils. **Col. Depth:** 139 agate lines. **ISSN:** 0744--4672 (print). **URL:** http://www.optimist.org/e/member/magazine.cfm. **Ad Rates:** BW $1,900; 4C $2,400. **Remarks:** Advertising accepted; rates available upon request. **Circ:** (Not Reported).

19893 ■ Optometry: Journal of the American Optometric Association
American Optometric Association
243 N Lindbergh Blvd., 1st Fl.
Saint Louis, MO 63141-7881
Phone: (314)991-4100
Fax: (314)991-4101
Free: 800-365-2219
Publisher's E-mail: ilamo@aoa.org
Peer-reviewed clinical journal for members of the American Optometric Association. **Freq:** Monthly. **Print Method:** Offset. **Trim Size:** 8 x 10 7/8. **Cols./Page:** 3. **Col. Width:** 3 1/8 inches. **Col. Depth:** 9 inches. **Key Personnel:** J. Luebbert, Editor; D. Maino, Board Member; B. Coffey, Board Member; Dr. Paul Freeman, Editor-in-Chief. **ISSN:** 1529--1839 (print). **URL:** http://www.aoa.org/journal. **Ad Rates:** BW $4,040; 4C $5,770. **Remarks:** Accepts advertising. **Circ:** Paid ‡28230.

19894 ■ Portals of Prayer
Concordia Publishing House
3558 S Jefferson Ave.
Saint Louis, MO 63118-3910
Phone: (314)268-1000
Fax: (800)490-9889
Free: 800-325-3040
Publisher's E-mail: order@cph.org

Circulation: ★ = AAM; △ or • = BPA; ♦ = CAC; ❑ = VAC; ⊕ = PO Statement; ‡ = Publisher's Report; Boldface figures = sworn; Light figures = estimated.

Religion and theology magazine (English, German and large print). **Freq:** Quarterly. **Print Method:** Offset. **Trim Size:** 4 1/8" x 5 3/4". **Cols./Page:** 1. **Col. Width:** 38 nonpareils. **Col. Depth:** 66 agate lines. **ISSN:** 0032--4884 (print). **Subscription Rates:** $15 Individuals pocket size; $16 Individuals digest-print; $17 Individuals large size; $15 Individuals online. **Alt. Formats:** Large print. **URL:** http://www.cph.org/portals. **Remarks:** Advertising not accepted. **Circ:** (Not Reported).

19895 ■ Pure and Applied Geophysics
Springer-VDI-Verlag
c/o Brian Mitchell, Ed.-in-Ch.
Dept. of Earth & Atmospheric Sciences
St. Louis University
3624 Lindell Blvd.
Saint Louis, MO 63108
Publisher's E-mail: leserservice@technikwissen.de
Journal publishing scientific papers in the areas of solid earth and atmospheric sciences, and oceanic sciences. **Freq:** 12/yr. **Key Personnel:** Prof. Carla F. Braitenberg, Editor-in-Chief; Brian Mitchell, Editor. **ISSN:** 0033--4553 (print); **EISSN:** 1420--9136 (electronic). **Subscription Rates:** €3221 Institutions print including free access or e-only; €3865 Institutions print plus enhanced access. **Alt. Formats:** Electronic publishing. **URL:** http://www.springer.com/birkhauser/geo+science/journal/24. **Remarks:** Advertising accepted; rates available upon request. **Circ:** (Not Reported).

19896 ■ The Quarterly Journal Index
Personal Freedom Outreach
PO Box 26062
Saint Louis, MO 63136-0062
Phone: (314)921-9800
Journal containing articles, side articles, editorials, news updates and book reviews that have been published in The Quarterly Journal newsletter. **Freq:** Quarterly. **URL:** http://www.pfo.org/OnlineIndex.html. **Remarks:** Advertising not accepted. **Circ:** (Not Reported).

19897 ■ Res Philosophica
St. Louis University
1 N Grand
Saint Louis, MO 63103
Phone: (314)977-8505
Fax: (314)977-8513
Free: 800-758-3678
Publisher's E-mail: admissions@slu.edu
Journal promoting historical research and critical analysis of philosophy. **Freq:** Quarterly. **Trim Size:** 6 x 9. **Key Personnel:** William Charron, Editor. **ISSN:** 0026-8402 (print). **Subscription Rates:** $40 Individuals print or online; $60 Individuals print and online; $60 Institutions; $210 Institutions online; $250 Institutions print and online. **URL:** http://www.slu.edu/department-of-philosophy/res-philosophica. **Formerly:** The Modern Schoolman: A Quarterly of Philosophy. **Remarks:** Accepts advertising. **Circ:** Paid ‡600, Non-paid ‡50.

19898 ■ Review for Religious: A Journal of Catholic Spirituality
Review for Religious
3601 Lindell Blvd.
Saint Louis, MO 63108
Phone: (314)633-4610
Fax: (314)633-4611
Journal of theological and spiritual information and reflection about religious life. **Freq:** Quarterly. **Print Method:** Offset. **Trim Size:** 5 5/8 x 8 5/8. **Cols./Page:** 1. **Col. Width:** 27.5 picas. **Col. Depth:** 44 picas. **Key Personnel:** Michael G. Harter, Editor; Rosemary Jermann, Editor. **ISSN:** 0034--639X (print). **URL:** http://www.relipress.org/review-for-religious. **Remarks:** Advertising not accepted. **Circ:** Paid ‡5500, Non-paid ‡242.

19899 ■ River Styx
Big River
3547 Olive St., Ste. 107
Saint Louis, MO 63103-1024
Publisher's E-mail: BigRiver@riverstyx.org
Literary magazine covering poetry, fiction, essays, interviews, and art. **Freq:** 3/year. **Key Personnel:** Richard Newman, Editor; Catherine Tufariello, Associate Editor; Adrian Matejka, Editor; Benjamin Moeller-Gaa, Editor. **ISSN:** 0149--8851 (print). **URL:** http://www.riverstyx.org. **Remarks:** Accepts advertising. **Circ:** (Not Reported).

19900 ■ Riverfront Times: The Weekly Newspaper of St. Louis
Riverfront Times L.L.C.
6358 Delmar Blvd., Ste. 200
Saint Louis, MO 63130-4719
Phone: (314)754-5966
Publisher's E-mail: feedback@riverfronttimes.com
Alternative newspaper (tabloid) with political articles, in-depth features, entertainment, and classified and personal ads. **Freq:** Weekly. **Print Method:** Offset. **Trim Size:** 10 3/4 x 13 3/4. **Cols./Page:** 4. **Col. Width:** 28 nonpareils. **Col. Depth:** 196 agate lines. **Key Personnel:** Tom Finkel, Editor; Sarah Fenske, Managing Editor; Brady Rehm, Director, Advertising. **URL:** http://www.riverfronttimes.com. **Remarks:** Accepts advertising. **Circ:** ‡55000.

19901 ■ Saddle & Bridle: Oldest Name In Show Horse Magazines
Saddle & Bridle Inc.
375 Jackson Ave.
Saint Louis, MO 63130-4243
Phone: (314)725-9115
Fax: (314)725-6440
Publisher's E-mail: saddlebr@saddleandbridle.com
Publication for owners, trainers, breeders, and horse show managers of English show horses. **Freq:** Monthly. **Print Method:** Offset. **Trim Size:** 8 5/8 x 10 7/8. **Cols./Page:** 3. **Col. Width:** 27 nonpareils. **Col. Depth:** 135 agate lines. **Key Personnel:** Mary G. Bernhardt, Managing Editor; Jeffrey Thompson, Editor; Christopher Thompson, Manager, Advertising. **ISSN:** 0036--2271 (print). **Subscription Rates:** $75 Individuals 1 year (online); $92 Individuals 1 year (print); $167 Other countries 1 year (print); $142 Individuals 1 year (print & online); $217 Other countries 1 year (print & online). **URL:** http://www.saddleandbridle.com. **Ad Rates:** BW $595; 4C $1,085. **Remarks:** Advertising accepted; rates available upon request. **Circ:** (Not Reported).

19902 ■ St. Art Museum Bulletin
Saint Louis Art Museum
1 Fine Arts Dr.
Forest Park
Saint Louis, MO 63110-1380
Phone: (314)721-0072
Fax: (314)721-6172
Trade magazine covering historical art research. **Freq:** Annual. **Subscription Rates:** Members. **Alt. Formats:** PDF. **URL:** http://stlouis.art.museum. **Remarks:** Advertising not accepted. **Circ:** (Not Reported).

19903 ■ St. Charles Journal
St. Louis Post-Dispatch L.L.C.
900 N Tucker Blvd.
Saint Louis, MO 63101
Phone: (314)340-8000
Fax: (314)340-3050
Free: 800-365-0820
Publisher's E-mail: service@stltoday.com
Community newspaper. **Freq:** 3/week. **Print Method:** Offset. **Cols./Page:** 6. **Col. Width:** 26 nonpareils. **Col. Depth:** 308 agate lines. **Key Personnel:** Erin Schultz, Managing Editor, phone: (636)946-6111; Tammy Mortensen, Manager, Advertising; Bob Williams, Publisher. **Subscription Rates:** Free. **URL:** http://www.stltoday.com/suburban-journals/stcharles. **Circ:** (Not Reported).

19904 ■ St. Louis Bar Journal
Bar Association of Metropolitan St. Louis
555 Washington Ave., Ste. 100
Saint Louis, MO 63101-1249
Phone: (314)421-4134
Fax: (314)421-0013
Official magazine of Purchasing Association Kansas City. **Freq:** Quarterly. **Print Method:** Offset. **Trim Size:** 8 1/2 x 11. **Cols./Page:** 3. **Col. Width:** 26 nonpareils. **Col. Depth:** 140 agate lines. **Key Personnel:** Charles A. White, Editor. **ISSN:** 0581--3344 (print). **Subscription Rates:** Included in membership. **URL:** http://www.bamsl.org/?106. **Remarks:** Accepts advertising. **Circ:** (Not Reported).

19905 ■ St. Louis Business Journal
American City Business Journals Inc.
815 Olive St., Ste. 100
Saint Louis, MO 63101
Phone: (314)421-6200
Fax: (314)621-5031
Publication E-mail: stlouis@bizjournals.com
Business newspaper. **Freq:** Weekly. **Print Method:** Offset. **Trim Size:** 29. **Cols./Page:** 4. **Col. Width:** 28 nonpareils. **Col. Depth:** 189 agate lines. **Key Personnel:** Ellen Sherberg, Publisher; Joe Dwyer, III, Managing Editor, phone: (314)421-8324; Patricia Miller, Editor, phone: (314)421-8326. **ISSN:** 0271--6453 (print). **Subscription Rates:** $97 Individuals print or online. **Online:** American City Business Journals Inc. American City Business Journals Inc. **URL:** http://www.bizjournals.com/stlouis. **Ad Rates:** BW $4185. **Remarks:** Accepts advertising. **Circ:** (Not Reported).

19906 ■ St. Louis Commerce
St. Louis Regional Chamber
1 Metropolitan Sq., Ste. 1300
211 N Broadway
Saint Louis, MO 63102
Phone: (314)231-5555
Fax: (314)206-3222
Community business and economic development magazine. **Freq:** Monthly. **Print Method:** Offset. **Trim Size:** 8 3/8 x 10 7/8. **Cols./Page:** 3. **Col. Width:** 27 nonpareils. **Col. Depth:** 140 agate lines. **Key Personnel:** John Bilhorn, Advertising Representative, phone: (314)444-1161; Dick Fleming, Publisher; Joe Reagan, Publisher; Mary Perez, Contact, phone: (314)444-1181. **Ad Rates:** BW $2,290; 4C $2,770. **Remarks:** Accepts advertising. **Circ:** 9700.

19907 ■ St. Louis Homes & Lifestyles
Network Communications Inc.
1878 Craigshire Rd.
Saint Louis, MO 63146
Phone: (314)542-6000
Magazine featuring articles about homes, gardens, entertainment, dining, and cultural events in St. Louis, Southern Illinois, and Eastern Missouri. **Freq:** 9/year. **Key Personnel:** Vicki Pickle, Editor-in-Chief; Suzie Osterloh, Publisher, phone: (314)542-6000. **Subscription Rates:** $20 Individuals print; $34 Two years print. **URL:** http://www.stlouishomesmag.com. **Remarks:** Accepts advertising. **Circ:** 23000.

19908 ■ St. Louis Jewish Light
St. Louis Jewish Light
6 Millstone Campus Dr., Ste. 3010
Saint Louis, MO 63146-5776
Phone: (314)743-3600
Fax: (314)743-3690
Jewish newspaper (tabloid). **Freq:** Weekly. **Print Method:** Offset. Uses mats. **Trim Size:** 11 1/4 x 17 1/4. **Cols./Page:** 6 and 1. **Col. Width:** 20 nonpareils and 1 5/8 inches. **Col. Depth:** 224 agate lines and 16 inches. **Key Personnel:** Larry Levin, Chief Executive Officer, Publisher, phone: (314)743-3672; Ellen Futterman, Editor. **ISSN:** 0036--2964 (print). **Subscription Rates:** $45 Individuals; $75 Two years. **URL:** http://www.stljewishlight.com. **Ad Rates:** BW $2,400; 4C $2,800; PCI $24. **Remarks:** Accepts advertising. **Circ:** 9000.

19909 ■ St. Louis Lawyer
Bar Association of Metropolitan St. Louis
555 Washington Ave., Ste. 100
Saint Louis, MO 63101-1249
Phone: (314)421-4134
Fax: (314)421-0013
Legal journal of The Bar Association of Metropolitan St. Louis. **Freq:** Monthly. **Print Method:** Offset. **Trim Size:** 8 1/2 x 11. **Cols./Page:** 3. **Col. Width:** 26 nonpareils. **Col. Depth:** 140 agate lines. **Key Personnel:** Zoe Lyle, Executive Director; Susan Welch, Editor; Tony Nolan, Publisher; Paul Adrignola, Manager, Advertising; Chuck Ramsay, Managing Editor. **ISSN:** 0893--5971 (print). **USPS:** 002-031. **Subscription Rates:** $24 Nonmembers; Included in membership. **Alt. Formats:** PDF. **URL:** http://www.bamsl.org. **Ad Rates:** BW $955; 4C $1,355. **Remarks:** Advertising not accepted. **Circ:** ‡5660.

19910 ■ The St. Louis Metro Evening Whirl
Thomas Publication Company Inc.
PO Box 8055
Saint Louis, MO 63156-8055
Black and general community newspaper. **Freq:** Weekly (Tues.). **Print Method:** Offset. **Trim Size:** 75 x 129 picas. **Cols./Page:** 7. **Col. Width:** 9 picas. **Col. Depth:** 301 agate lines. **Key Personnel:** Barry R. Thomas, Publisher; Anthony L. Sanders, Editor-in-Chief. **USPS:** 466-530. **Subscription Rates:** $65 Individuals 1 year; $50 Individuals 6 months; $30 Individuals 3 months.

URL: http://www.thewhirlonline.com. **Formerly**: The Evening Whirl Examiner; The Evening Whirl. **Ad Rates:** BW $2,709; 4C $750; SAU $18; PCI $18. **Remarks:** Advertising accepted; rates available upon request. **Circ:** (Not Reported).

19911 ■ St. Louis Metropolitan Medicine
St. Louis Metropolitan Medical Society
680 Craig Rd., Ste. 308
Saint Louis, MO 63141-7120
Phone: (314)989-1014
Fax: (314)989-0560
Medical association business magazine. **Freq:** 6/year. **Print Method:** Offset. **Trim Size:** 8 1/2 x 11. **Cols./Page:** 2. **Col. Width:** 3 5/8 inches. **Col. Depth:** 9 1/4 inches. **Key Personnel:** James Braibish, Managing Editor; David M. Nowak, Executive Vice President. **ISSN:** 0892--1334 (print). **USPS:** 006-522. **URL:** http://www.slmms.org/index.php/magazine. **Formerly**: St. Louis Medicine. **Ad Rates:** BW $724; 4C $941. **Remarks:** Accepts advertising. **Circ:** 1600.

19912 ■ St. Louis Post-Dispatch
Lee Enterprises Inc.
900 N Tucker Blvd.
Saint Louis, MO 63101
Phone: (314)340-8000
General newspaper. **Founded:** 1878. **Freq:** Mon.-Sun. (morn.). **Print Method:** Offset. Uses mats. **Cols./Page:** 6. **Col. Width:** 25 nonpareils. **Col. Depth:** 315 agate lines. **Key Personnel:** Amy Bertrand, Editor; Jane Henderson, Editor. **USPS:** 476-480. **Subscription Rates:** $13.50 Individuals print or online. **URL:** http://www.stltoday.com; http://www.lee.net. **Remarks:** Accepts advertising. **Circ:** Sun. ⋆**360450**, Mon. ⋆**196232**.

19913 ■ St. Louis Review
St. Louis Review
20 Archbishop May Dr.
Saint Louis, MO 63119-5738
Phone: (314)792-7500
Fax: (314)792-7534
Publisher's E-mail: advertising@stlouisreview.com
Catholic newspaper. **Freq:** Weekly (Fri.). **Print Method:** Offset. **Trim Size:** 11 5/8 x 20 15/16. **Cols./Page:** 6. **Col. Width:** 11 picas. **Col. Depth:** 124 picas. **Key Personnel:** Teak Phillips, Editor, phone: (314)792-7500. **ISSN:** 0036--3022 (print). **URL:** http://www.stlouisreview.com. **Ad Rates:** GLR $1.63; BW $2,489.76; 4C $2,989.76; PCI $22.88. **Remarks:** Accepts advertising. **Circ:** (Not Reported).

19914 ■ St. Louis/Southern Illinois Labor Tribune
St. Louis/Southern Illinois Tribune
505 S Ewing Ave.
Saint Louis, MO 63103
Phone: (314)535-9660
Fax: (314)531-6131
Publisher's E-mail: info@labortribune.com
Labor newspaper (AFL-CIO). **Freq:** Weekly (Thurs.). **Print Method:** Offset. **Trim Size:** 11 3/8 x 14 1/2. **Cols./Page:** 6. **Col. Width:** 1 5/8 inches. **Col. Depth:** 13 inches. **ISSN:** 0885--6869 (print). **Subscription Rates:** $75 Individuals; $150 Institutions. **URL:** http://www.labortribune.com. **Ad Rates:** GLR $2.28; BW $2,496; 4C $2,996; PCI $38.41. **Remarks:** Accepts advertising. **Circ:** Paid ‡60000.

19915 ■ Saint Louis University Law Journal
Saint Louis University School of Law
100 N Tucker Blvd.
Saint Louis, MO 63101
Phone: (314)977-2800
Fax: (314)977-1464
Publisher's E-mail: admissions@law.slu.edu
Journal covering articles related to legal topics. **Freq:** Quarterly. **Key Personnel:** Emily D. Roman, Editor-in-Chief. **URL:** http://www.slu.edu/colleges/law/journal. **Circ:** (Not Reported).

19916 ■ Sauce Magazine
Bent Mind Creative Group L.L.C.
1820 Chouteau Ave.
Saint Louis, MO 63103
Phone: (314)772-8004
Fax: (314)241-8004
Free: 877-772-8004
Publisher's E-mail: sales@saucemagazine.com
Magazine focusing on dining and entertainment in St. Louis. **Freq:** Monthly. **Key Personnel:** Stacy Schultz, Writer; Allyson Mace, Founder, Publisher. **URL:** http://www.saucemagazine.com/issues.php. **Remarks:** Advertising accepted; rates available upon request. **Circ:** 84000.

19917 ■ Schutzhund USA: The Official Publication of the United Schutzhund Clubs of America
United Schutzhund Clubs of America
4407 Meramec Bottom Rd., Ste. J
Saint Louis, MO 63129
Phone: (314)638-9686
Fax: (314)638-0609
Publication E-mail: usaoffice@germanshepherddog.com
Club breed and sport publication for German shepherd dog enthusiasts. **Freq:** Bimonthly. **Print Method:** Sheetfed offset. **Trim Size:** 8 1/2 x 10 3/8. **Cols./Page:** 2. **Col. Depth:** 7 inches. **ISSN:** 0194--5033 (print). **URL:** http://www.leerburg.com/schusa.htm. **Remarks:** Advertising accepted; rates available upon request. **Circ:** (Not Reported).

19918 ■ Somatosensory and Motor Research
Informa Healthcare
Dept. of Neurology & Neurological Surgery
Washington University School of Medicine
CB 8213
4566 Scott Ave.
Saint Louis, MO 63110
Fax: (314)362-8359
Publisher's E-mail: healthcare.enquiries@informa.com
Journal featuring somatic, motor, and neural research. **Freq:** Quarterly. **Print Method:** Offset. **Trim Size:** 209mm x 200mm. **Cols./Page:** 2. **Col. Width:** 80 nonpareils. **Col. Depth:** 250 agate lines. **Key Personnel:** Thomas A. Woolsey, Editor-in-Chief; Eberhard E. Fetz, Associate Editor; Barry E. Stein, Associate Editor. **ISSN:** 0899--0220 (print); **EISSN:** 1369--1651 (electronic). **Subscription Rates:** $1389 Institutions online only; $1462 Institutions print and online. **URL:** http://www.tandfonline.com/toc/ismr20/current. **Formerly**: Somatosensory Research. **Remarks:** Advertising accepted; rates available upon request. **Circ:** Paid 250.

19919 ■ South County Journal
St. Louis Post-Dispatch L.L.C.
4210 Chippewa
Saint Louis, MO 63116
Phone: (314)664-2700
Fax: (314)664-8533
Publisher's E-mail: service@stltoday.com
Community newspaper. **Founded:** 1960. **Freq:** 3/week Sun., Wed., and Fri. **Print Method:** Offset. **Cols./Page:** 6. **Col. Width:** 26 nonpareils. **Col. Depth:** 308 agate lines. **Subscription Rates:** $19.99 Individuals. **URL:** http://www.stltoday.com/suburban-journals/. **Remarks:** Accepts advertising. **Circ:** ‡300.

19920 ■ South County Times
Webster-Kirkwood Times Inc.
122 W Lockwood Ave., 2nd Fl.
Saint Louis, MO 63119
Phone: (314)968-2699
Fax: (314)968-2961
Community newspaper. **Founded:** Apr. 04, 1986. **Freq:** Weekly (Fri.). **Print Method:** Offset. **Trim Size:** 11 x 17 1/2. **Cols./Page:** 4. **Col. Width:** 26 nonpareils. **Col. Depth:** 224 agate lines. **Key Personnel:** Terry Cassidy, Contact; Marianne Furhmann, Contact; Cathy Joyner, Contact; Dwight Bitikofer, General Manager, Publisher; Kevin Murphy, Managing Editor; Don Corrigan, Editor-in-Chief; Dennie O'Dowd, Contact; Poly Brackman, Contact. **Subscription Rates:** $35 Out of area 3 months; $66 Out of area 6 months; $99 Out of area 1 year. **URL:** http://www.southcountytimes.com/1homebody.lasso. **Formerly**: Gravois Watson Times; South St. Louis County News; South County News-Times. **Ad Rates:** BW $2,399; PCI $55. **Remarks:** Accepts advertising. **Circ:** Combined ‡76715.

19921 ■ Southwest County Journal
St. Louis Post-Dispatch L.L.C.
900 N Tucker Blvd.
Saint Louis, MO 63101
Phone: (314)340-8000
Fax: (314)340-3050
Free: 800-365-0820
Publisher's E-mail: service@stltoday.com
Community newspaper. **Freq:** Semiweekly (Wed. and Sun.). **Print Method:** Offset. **Cols./Page:** 6. **Col. Width:** 26 nonpareils. **Col. Depth:** 308 agate lines. **Subscription Rates:** Free carrier. **URL:** http://www.stltoday.com. **Formerly**: Fenton Journal. **Circ:** ‡29576.

19922 ■ Steamshovel Press: All conspiracy, no theory
Steamshovel Press
PO Box 210553
Saint Louis, MO 63121
Fax: (815)253-6300
Free: 800-718-4514
Alternative political publication. **Freq:** Quarterly. **Trim Size:** 8 x 10. **Key Personnel:** Kenn Thomas, Editor. **ISSN:** 0602--3795 (print). **Subscription Rates:** $11.95 Single issue kindle; $17.21 Single issue paperback. **URL:** http://www.steamshovel.press. **Ad Rates:** BW $110; 4C $650. **Remarks:** Accepts advertising. **Circ:** (Not Reported).

19923 ■ Student Life
Washington University in St. Louis
1 Brookings Dr.
Saint Louis, MO 63130
Phone: (314)935-5000
Fax: (314)935-4290
Free: 800-638-0700
Publisher's E-mail: admissions@wustl.edu
Collegiate newspaper. **Freq:** Biweekly Monday and Thursday (during academic year). **Print Method:** Offset. **Trim Size:** 13 x 21. **Cols./Page:** 6. **Col. Width:** 2 1/16 inches. **Col. Depth:** 294 agate lines. **Key Personnel:** Michelle Merlin, Editor-in-Chief; Alex Dropkin, Associate Editor. **URL:** http://www.studlife.com. **Ad Rates:** BW $1,512; 4C $1,862; PCI $12. **Remarks:** Accepts advertising. **Circ:** Paid ‡6000.

19924 ■ TED The Electrical Distributor Magazine: Official Publication of the National Association of Electrical Distributors (NAED)
National Association of Electrical Distributors
1181 Corporate Lake Dr.
Saint Louis, MO 63132-1716
Phone: (314)991-9000
Fax: (314)991-3060
Free: 888-791-2512
Publisher's E-mail: memberservices@naed.org
Magazine for electrical distributors. **Freq:** Monthly. **Print Method:** Offset. **Trim Size:** 8 1/8 x 10 7/8. **Cols./Page:** 3. **Col. Width:** 26 nonpareils. **Col. Depth:** 140 agate lines. **Key Personnel:** Misty Byers, Editor; Scott Costa, Publisher. **ISSN:** 1067--3806 (print). **Subscription Rates:** $40 U.S. and Canada; $50 Other countries plus postage. **URL:** http://www.tedmag.com. **Ad Rates:** BW $8,035; 4C $10,605. **Remarks:** Accepts advertising. **Circ:** △**27836**.

19925 ■ Topical Time
American Topical Association
c/o Wayne Youngblood, Editor
PO Box 4601
Saint Louis, MO 63108-4601
Publisher's E-mail: americantopical@msn.com
Freq: Bimonthly. **Print Method:** Offset. **Trim Size:** 6 x 9. **Cols./Page:** 2. **Col. Width:** 29 nonpareils. **Col. Depth:** 105 agate lines. **Key Personnel:** Wayne Youngblood, Editor; Robert Sazama, Manager, Advertising. **ISSN:** 0040-9332 (print). **Subscription Rates:** Included in membership; $5 Single issue back issue. **URL:** http://www.americantopicalassn.org; http://www.americantopicalassn.org/topicaltime.shtml. **Ad Rates:** BW $225. **Remarks:** Accepts display advertising. **Circ:** ‡4000.

19926 ■ Topics in Spinal Cord Injury Rehabilitation
Thomas Land Publishers Inc.
255 Jefferson Rd.
Saint Louis, MO 63119-3627
Phone: (314)963-7445
Fax: (314)963-9345
Publisher's E-mail: publisher@thomasland.com
Journal covering field of spinal cord injury rehabilitation. **Freq:** Quarterly. **ISSN:** 1082--0744 (print). **Subscription Rates:** $317 Institutions print and online, single site; $679 Institutions print and online, multi site; $177 Individuals print and online; $277 Institutions online only,

Circulation: ⋆ = AAM; △ or • = BPA; ♦ = CAC; ❑ = VAC; ⊕ = PO Statement; ‡ = Publisher's Report; Boldface figures = sworn; Light figures = estimated.

single site; $579 Institutions online only, multi site; $87 Individuals online only. **URL:** http://thomasland.com/about-spinalrehab.html. **Circ:** (Not Reported).

19927 ■ Topics in Stroke Rehabilitation
Thomas Land Publishers Inc.
255 Jefferson Rd.
Saint Louis, MO 63119-3627
Phone: (314)963-7445
Fax: (314)963-9345
Publisher's E-mail: publisher@thomasland.com
Professional medical journal covering stroke rehabilitation.Contains reviews and reports clinical practices, state-of-the-art concepts, and new developments in stroke patient care and research. Both primary research papers and comprehensive reviews of existing literature are included. **Freq:** Bimonthly. **Key Personnel:** Elliot J. Roth, MD, Editor. **ISSN:** 1074-9357 (print); **EISSN:** 1945--5119 (electronic). **Subscription Rates:** $235 Individuals print and online; $495 Institutions print and online; $170 Individuals online only; $448 Institutions online only. **URL:** http://www.maneyonline.com/loi/tsr. **Remarks:** Accepts advertising. **Circ:** (Not Reported).

19928 ■ Ultrasound in Medicine & Biology
Elsevier - Mosby Journal Div.
3251 Riverport Ln.
Saint Louis, MO 63146-3318
Phone: (314)872-8370
Fax: (314)432-1380
Free: 800-325-4177
Publisher's E-mail: t.reller@elsevier.com
Journal publishing original contributions on significant advances in clinical diagnostic, interventional and therapeutic applications, new and improved clinical techniques, the physics, engineering and technology of ultrasound in medicine and biology, and the interactions between ultrasound and biological materials, including bioeffects. **Freq:** Monthly. **Key Personnel:** Christy K. Holland, Editor-in-Chief; Denis N. White, Editor, Founder; Rose M. Randolph, Managing Editor. **ISSN:** 0301-5629 (print). **Subscription Rates:** $523 Individuals print and online; $554 Students Canada and other Countries (print and online; $508 Individuals; $2272 Institutions; $538 Other countries; $2389 Institutions, other countries; $2389 Institutions, Canada. **URL:** http://www.umbjournal.org; http://www.journals.elsevier.com/ultrasound-in-medicine-and-biology. **Mailing address:** PO Box 945, New York, NY 10159-0945. **Remarks:** Accepts advertising. **Circ:** (Not Reported).

19929 ■ University News: A Student Voice of Saint Louis University Since 1921
University News
20 N Grand Blvd.
Saint Louis, MO 63103
Phone: (314)977-2812
Publication E-mail: newsroom@unewsonline.com
University newspaper. **Freq:** Weekly (Thurs.). **Print Method:** Offset. **Cols./Page:** 6. **Col. Width:** 2 1/16 inches. **Col. Depth:** 21 1/2 inches. **Key Personnel:** Brianna Radici, Editor-in-Chief. **URL:** http://www.unewsonline.com/category/news. **Ad Rates:** BW $790. **Remarks:** Accepts advertising. **Circ:** Paid 250.

19930 ■ Voices
Women for Faith and Family
PO Box 300411
Saint Louis, MO 63130
Phone: (314)863-8385
Fax: (314)863-5858
Publisher's E-mail: wf-f@wf-f.org
Journal of the Women for Faith & Family organization. **Founded:** 1985. **Freq:** Quarterly. **Key Personnel:** Helen Hull Hitchcock, Editor. **ISSN:** 1066-8136 (print). **Subscription Rates:** Included in membership. **URL:** http://www.wf-f.org/Voices.html. **Remarks:** Advertising not accepted. **Circ:** Non-paid 10000.

19931 ■ The Washington University Global Studies Law Review
Washington University - School of Law - Law Library
1 Brookings Dr., CB 1120
Saint Louis, MO 63130-4899
Phone: (314)935-6400
Fax: (314)935-7125
Publisher's E-mail: applylaw@wustl.edu
Publication covering issues of international, comparative and foreign law for legal scholars and practitioners worldwide. **Freq:** Quarterly. **Key Personnel:** Susannah Lake, Editor-in-Chief. **Subscription Rates:** $37.50 Individuals; $45 Out of country; $12.50 Single issue; $15 Single issue foreign. **Alt. Formats:** PDF. **URL:** http://openscholarship.wustl.edu/law_globalstudies. **Circ:** (Not Reported).

19932 ■ The Washington University Global Studies Law Review
Washington University School of Law
Anheuser-Busch Hall
1 Brookings Dr.
Saint Louis, MO 63130-4899
Phone: (314)935-6400
Publisher's E-mail: applylaw@wustl.edu
Publication covering issues of international, comparative and foreign law for legal scholars and practitioners worldwide. **Freq:** Quarterly. **Key Personnel:** Susannah Lake, Editor-in-Chief. **Subscription Rates:** $37.50 Individuals; $45 Out of country; $12.50 Single issue; $15 Single issue foreign. **Alt. Formats:** PDF. **URL:** http://openscholarship.wustl.edu/law_globalstudies. **Circ:** (Not Reported).

19933 ■ Washington University Journal of Law and Policy
Washington University - Journal of Law and Policy
1 Brookings Dr.
Saint Louis, MO 63130-4899
Phone: (314)935-6498
Fax: (314)935-4480
Journal covering city planning and redevelopment law. **Freq:** Annual. **Key Personnel:** Claire Botnick, Editor-in-Chief. **ISSN:** 1533--4686 (print); **EISSN:** 1943--0000 (electronic). **Subscription Rates:** $30 Individuals including shipping and handling; $10 Single issue back volumes. **URL:** http://openscholarship.wustl.edu/law_journal_law_policy. **Formerly:** Journal of Urban and Contemporary Law. **Mailing address:** PO Box 1120, Saint Louis, MO 63130-4899. **Circ:** (Not Reported).

19934 ■ Washington University Journal of Law and Policy
Washington University School of Law
Anheuser-Busch Hall
1 Brookings Dr.
Saint Louis, MO 63130-4899
Phone: (314)935-6400
Journal covering city planning and redevelopment law. **Freq:** Annual. **Key Personnel:** Claire Botnick, Editor-in-Chief. **ISSN:** 1533--4686 (print); **EISSN:** 1943--0000 (electronic). **Subscription Rates:** $30 Individuals including shipping and handling; $10 Single issue back volumes. **URL:** http://openscholarship.wustl.edu/law_journal_law_policy. **Formerly:** Journal of Urban and Contemporary Law. **Mailing address:** PO Box 1120, Saint Louis, MO 63130-4899. **Circ:** (Not Reported).

19935 ■ The Waterways Journal
Waterways Journal Inc.
319 N Fourth St., Ste. 650
Saint Louis, MO 63102
Phone: (314)241-7354
Fax: (314)241-4207
Publisher's E-mail: info@waterwaysjournal.net
Marine commercial traffic magazine. **Freq:** Weekly (Mon.). **Print Method:** Offset. **Trim Size:** 10 1/4 x 13 1/2. **Cols./Page:** 4. **Col. Width:** 26 nonpareils. **Col. Depth:** 161 agate lines. **Key Personnel:** Nelson H. Spencer, Publisher; David Murray, Writer; John Shoulberg, Associate Publisher, Editor. **ISSN:** 0043--1524 (print). **URL:** http://www.waterwaysjournal.net. **Ad Rates:** BW $1,585; 4C $400; PCI $70. **Remarks:** Accepts advertising. **Circ:** (Not Reported).

19936 ■ Webster-Kirkwood Times
Webster-Kirkwood Times Inc.
122 W Lockwood Ave., 2nd Fl.
Saint Louis, MO 63119
Phone: (314)968-2699
Fax: (314)968-2961
Community newspaper. **Freq:** Weekly (Fri.). **Print Method:** Offset. **Trim Size:** 11 x 17 1/2. **Cols./Page:** 4. **Col. Width:** 26 nonpareils. **Col. Depth:** 224 agate lines. **Key Personnel:** Terry Cassidy, Contact; Polly Brackman, Contact; Marty Harris, Associate Editor; Mary Chambers, Manager, Administration, Manager, Sales; Fran Mannino, Editor; Dwight Bitikofer, General Manager, Publisher; Don Corrigan, Editor-in-Chief; Kevin Murphy, Managing Editor. **URL:** http://www.websterkirkwoodtimes.com/1homebody.lasso. **Ad Rates:** BW $2,399; PCI $17.50. **Remarks:** Accepts advertising. **Circ:** (Not Reported).

19937 ■ West County Journal
St. Louis Post-Dispatch L.L.C.
900 N Tucker Blvd.
Saint Louis, MO 63101
Phone: (314)340-8000
Fax: (314)340-3050
Free: 800-365-0820
Publisher's E-mail: service@stltoday.com
Community newspaper. **Freq:** Semiweekly (Wed. and Sun.). **Print Method:** Offset. **Cols./Page:** 6. **Col. Width:** 26 nonpareils. **Col. Depth:** 308 agate lines. **Key Personnel:** Carolyn Marty, Managing Editor. **Subscription Rates:** Free. **URL:** http://www.stltoday.com/suburban-journals. **Ad Rates:** PCI $11.85. **Remarks:** Accepts advertising. **Circ:** (Not Reported).

19938 ■ West End Word
Webster Kirkwood Times Inc.
122 W Lockwood Ave. Fl. 2
Saint Louis, MO 63119
Phone: (314)968-4637
Fax: (314)968-2961
Community newspaper. **Freq:** Weekly. **Print Method:** Web. **Trim Size:** 10 x 15 3/4. **Key Personnel:** Don Corrigan, Editor-in-Chief; Dwight Bitikofer, General Manager, Publisher. **Subscription Rates:** $60 Individuals. **URL:** http://www.westendword.com. **Formerly:** West End-Clayton Word. **Ad Rates:** BW $1300; 4C $1710; PCI $30. **Remarks:** Accepts advertising. **Circ:** Non-paid 20000.

19939 ■ WHERE St. Louis
Miller Publishing Group L.L.C.
1750 S Brentwood Blvd., Ste. 511
Saint Louis, MO 63144
Phone: (314)968-4940
Fax: (314)968-0813
Consumer magazine for visitors to St. Louis, Missouri. **Freq:** Monthly. **Print Method:** Offset. **Trim Size:** 8 x 10 7/8. **Key Personnel:** Ethan Woods, Publisher. **URL:** http://www.wheretraveler.com/st-louis; http://www.wheretraveler.com/st-louis/tp#. **Remarks:** Accepts advertising. **Circ:** Controlled ‡34000.

19940 ■ WomenArts Quarterly Journal
Vivace Press
265 Gerneral Services Bldg.
1 University Blvd.
Saint Louis, MO 63121
Phone: (314)516-4990
Fax: (314)516-4992
Publisher's E-mail: vivacepress@umsl.edu
Journal featuring the work of women writers, composers, performers and artists in all disciplines of art. **Freq:** Quarterly. **Key Personnel:** Lindsay Shadwell, Managing Editor; Dr. Barbara Harbach, Senior Editor. **Subscription Rates:** $45 Institutions; $30 Individuals; $60 Other countries; $90 Institutions, other countries. **URL:** http://www.vivacepress.com/waq. **Circ:** (Not Reported).

19941 ■ Birach Broadcasting Corp. - 770
21700 Northwestern Hwy.
Tower 14, Ste. 1190
Southfield, MI 48075
Phone: (248)557-3500
Fax: (248)557-2950
Format: Ethnic. **Owner:** Birach Broadcasting Corp., at above address. **Key Personnel:** Sima Birach, Operations Mgr., sima@birach.com. **Wattage:** 13,000. **URL:** http://www.birach.com.

19942 ■ Falcon Capital Cable
450 N Lindbergh, Ste. 101
Saint Louis, MO 63141
Owner: Charter Communications Inc., 400 Atlantic St., Stamford, CT 06901, Ph: (203)905-7801. **Key Personnel:** Bobby Williams, Mgr. **URL:** http://bsd.sos.mo.gov/BusinessEntity/BusinessEntityDetail.aspx?page=beSearch&ID=721387.

19943 ■ Falcon/Capital Cable Partners L.P.
450 N Lindbergh, Ste. 101
Saint Louis, MO 63141
Owner: Falcon/Capital Cable Partners L.P., at above address. **Founded:** 1988. **Key Personnel:** Scott Widham, President, scott@widham.com; Mary Meier, Contact, mmcap@meysinet.net; Ed Trower, Contact, eddie@capitalcabletv.com; Miriam Monroy, Contact. **Cit-**

ies Served: Communities throughout Iowa, Kansas, Missouri, Indiana, Illi nois and Kentucky. **Mailing address:** PO Box 207, Coon Rapids, IA 50058. **URL:** http://bsd.sos.mo.gov/BusinessEntity/BusinessEntityDetail.aspx?page=beSearch&ID=721387.

19944 ■ KATZ-AM - 1600
1001 Highlands Plaza Dr. W, Ste. 100
Saint Louis, MO 63110
Phone: (314)333-8000
Format: Gospel. **Networks:** Satellite Music Network; ABC; American Urban Radio. **Founded:** 1955. **Operating Hours**: Continuous. **Key Personnel:** Dennis Lamme, Gen. Mgr.; Arika Parr, Promotions Dir., arikaparr@clearchannel.com. **Wattage**: 5,000. **Ad Rates:** Advertising accepted; rates available upon request. **URL:** http://www.hallelujah1600.com.

19945 ■ KAUL-FM - 106.7
1411 Locust St.
Saint Louis, MO 63166
Phone: (314)421-3020
Format: Religious. **Owner:** New Life Evangelistic Center Inc., 1411 Locust St., Saint Louis, MO 63103, Ph: (314)421-3020, Fax: (314)421-1702, Free: 800-334-3276. **Ad Rates:** Noncommercial. **URL:** http://www.hereshelpnet.org/.

19946 ■ KBDY-FM - 89.9
PO Box 4728
Saint Louis, MO 63108
Format: Public Radio; Jazz. **Networks:** American Public Radio (APR). **Founded:** 1973. **Key Personnel:** Hank Thompson, Gen. Mgr.; Mashon Nielson, Gen. Sales Mgr. **Wattage**: 1,000. **Ad Rates:** Noncommercial.

19947 ■ KBIY-FM - 91.3
1411 Locust St.
Saint Louis, MO 63103
Phone: (314)421-3020
Email: larryr@hereshelpnet.org
Format: Religious. **Owner:** New Life Evangelistic Center Inc., 1411 Locust St., Saint Louis, MO 63103, Ph: (314)421-3020, Fax: (314)421-1702, Free: 800-334-3276. **Key Personnel:** Larry Rice, Director. **Ad Rates:** Noncommercial. **URL:** http://hereshelpnet.org.

19948 ■ KCFV-FM - 89.5
3400 Pershall Rd.
Saint Louis, MO 63135-1499
Phone: (314)513-4472
Fax: (314)513-4217
Email: kcfvmusic@stlcc.edu
Format: Educational. **Owner:** St. Louis Community College, 2645 Generations Dr., Wildwood, MO 63040, Ph: (636)422-2000, Fax: (636)422-2020. **Founded:** Apr. 17, 1972. **Operating Hours**: Monday - Friday 8 a.m. - midnight, Saturday - Sunday 8 a.m. - midnight. **Key Personnel:** Tim Gorry, Gen. Mgr., tgorry@stlcc.edu; Jeff Siler, Dir. of Programs, kcfvmusic@stlcc.edu. **Wattage**: 100. **Ad Rates:** Noncommercial. **URL:** http://www.stlcc.edu/FV/KCFV/Index.html.

19949 ■ KDHX-FM - 88.1
3504 Magnolia Ave.
Saint Louis, MO 63118
Phone: (314)664-3955
Email: volunteer@kdhx.org
Format: Eclectic. **Founded:** 1987. **Operating Hours**: Continuous; 100% local. **ADI**: St. Louis, MO (Mt. Vernon, IL). **Key Personnel:** Jeff Corbin, Contact. **Wattage**: 42,000 ERP. **Ad Rates:** Accepts Advertising. **URL:** http://kdhx.org.

19950 ■ KDNL-TV - 30
1215 Cole St.
Saint Louis, MO 63106
Phone: (314)436-3030
Format: Commercial TV. **Networks:** ABC. **Owner:** Sinclair Broadcast Group Inc., 10706 Beaver Dam Rd., Hunt Valley, MD 21030, Ph: (410)568-1500, Fax: (410)568-1533. **Founded:** 1969. **Operating Hours**: Continuous. **ADI**: St. Louis, MO (Mt. Vernon, IL). **Wattage**: 2,290,000. **Ad Rates:** $25-4000 for 30 seconds. **URL:** http://www.abcstlouis.com.

19951 ■ KETC-TV - 9
3655 Olive St.
Saint Louis, MO 63108-6915
Phone: (314)512-9000
Fax: (314)512-9005
Email: tgates@ketc.org
Format: Public TV. **Networks:** Public Broadcasting Service (PBS). **Owner:** St. Louis Regional Educational and Public Television Commission, at above address. **Founded:** 1952. **Operating Hours**: Continuous. **ADI**: St. Louis, MO (Mt. Vernon, IL). **Key Personnel:** Patricia Kistler, VP; Patrick Murphy, VP of Production; Chrys Marlow, VP of Operations & Engg.; Amy Shaw, VP of Comm. & Public Affairs; Dick Skalski, CFO, COO, Sr. VP. **Wattage**: 316,000. **Ad Rates:** Advertising accepted; rates available upon request. **URL:** http://www.ninenet.org.

19952 ■ KEZK-FM - 102.5
3100 Market St.
Saint Louis, MO 63103
Phone: (314)531-0000
Fax: (314)962-7576
Free: 866-326-0590
Format: Soft Rock; Talk; Sports. **Networks:** Independent; ESPN Radio. **Owner:** Big League Broadcasting, ; CBS Radio Inc., at above address. **Founded:** 1968. **Formerly**: WKLL-AM. **Operating Hours**: Continuous. **ADI**: St. Louis, MO (Mt. Vernon, IL). **Key Personnel:** John Sheehan, Sr. VP. **Wattage**: 100,000. **Ad Rates:** Noncommercial. $250-400 for 60 seconds. **URL:** http://www.fresh1025.cbslocal.com.

19953 ■ KFTK-FM - 97.1
800 St. Louis Union Sta.
The Powerhouse
Saint Louis, MO 63103
Phone: (314)231-9710
Fax: (314)621-3000
Free: 866-455-9797
Format: Talk; News. **Key Personnel:** John Beck, Sr. VP, john@stl.emmis.com; Jeff Allen, Prog. Dir., jaallen@stl.emmis.com; Jim Modglin, Sales Mgr., jmodglin@stl.emmis.com; Karen Kelly, Sales Mgr., kkelly@stl.emmis.com; Tony Colombo, Dir. of Mktg., tcolombo@stl.emmis.com. **Ad Rates:** Noncommercial. **URL:** http://www.971talk.com.

19954 ■ KFUO-AM - 850
1335 S Kirkwood Rd.
Saint Louis, MO 63122
Phone: (314)821-0850
Format: Religious. **Networks:** AP. **Owner:** The Lutheran Church - Missouri Synod, 1333 S Kirkwood Rd., Saint Louis, MO 63122-7226, Ph: (314)996-9000, Free: 888-843-5267. **Founded:** 1924. **Operating Hours:** Sunrise-sunset; 10% network, 90% local. **Key Personnel:** Jenny Williams, Contact, jennyw@kfuo.org; Paul Clayton, Contact, pclayton@kfuo.org. **Local Programs**: *Issues, Etc.*, Monday Tuesday Wednesday Thursday Friday 3:04 p.m. - 5:04 p.m.; *The Word Today*, Sunday Saturday 7:45 a.m. - 8:00 a.m. 7:45 a.m. - 8:05 a.m. **Wattage**: 5,000. **Ad Rates:** Noncommercial. **URL:** http://www.kfuo.org.

19955 ■ KFUO-FM - 99.1
85 Founders Ln.
Saint Louis, MO 63105
Phone: (314)725-0099
Fax: (314)725-3801
Free: 800-844-0524
Format: Classical; Religious. **Networks:** CNN Radio; Wall Street Journal Radio. **Owner:** The Lutheran Church - Missouri Synod, 1333 S Kirkwood Rd., Saint Louis, MO 63122-7226, Ph: (314)996-9000, Free: 888-843-5267. **Founded:** 1948. **Operating Hours**: Continuous. **Key Personnel:** Ron Klemm, Mgr.; Dennis Stortz, Director. **Wattage**: 100,000. **Ad Rates:** Noncommercial. $75 per unit. **URL:** http://www.classic99.com.

19956 ■ KIHT-FM - 104.7
800 St. Louis Union Sta.
The Powerhouse
Saint Louis, MO 63103
Format: Classic Rock. **Owner:** Emmis Radio Corp., 1 EMMIS Plz., 40 Monument Cir., Ste. 700, Indianapolis, IN 46204-3011, Ph: (317)266-0100, Fax: (317)631-3750. **Wattage**: 760. **Ad Rates:** Noncommercial. **URL:** http://www.k-hits.com.

19957 ■ KLOU-FM - 103.3
1001 Highlands Plaza Dr. W, Ste. 100
Saint Louis, MO 63110
Phone: (314)333-8000
Fax: (314)533-2103
Free: 800-877-1033
Format: Oldies. **Networks:** AP. **Owner:** American Radio Systems, at above address, Ph: (617)375-7500. **Operating Hours**: Continuous. **ADI**: St. Louis, MO (Mt. Vernon, IL). **Key Personnel:** Mark Anderson, Dir. of Programs; Aaron Hyland, Dir. of Sales; Paul Arca, Dir. of Production; David Dunkin, Dir. of Programs; Sean Luce, Gen. Sales Mgr.; Beth Davis, Mktg. Mgr., VP. **Wattage**: 100,000. **Ad Rates:** Advertising accepted; rates available upon request. $175 for 60 seconds. **URL:** http://www.1033klou.com.

19958 ■ KMJM-FM - 104.9
1001 Highlands Plaza Dr. W, Ste. 100
Saint Louis, MO 63110
Phone: (314)333-8000
Format: Urban Contemporary. **Networks:** Independent. **Founded:** 1972. **Operating Hours**: Continuous. **ADI**: St. Louis, MO (Mt. Vernon, IL). **Wattage**: 8,000. **Ad Rates:** Advertising accepted; rates available upon request. **URL:** http://www.kmjm.com.

19959 ■ KMOV-TV - 4
One Memorial Dr.
Saint Louis, MO 63102
Phone: (314)621-4444
Fax: (314)621-3367
Email: website@kmov.com
Format: Commercial TV. **Networks:** CBS. **Owner:** Belo Corp., 400 S Record St., Dallas, TX 75202-4841, Ph: (214)977-6606, Fax: (214)977-6603. **Founded:** July 08, 1954. **Formerly**: KMOX-TV. **Operating Hours**: Continuous. **ADI**: St. Louis, MO (Mt. Vernon, IL). **Key Personnel:** Liz Mullen, Contact, lmullen@kmov.com. **Ad Rates:** Advertising accepted; rates available upon request. **URL:** http://www.kmov.com.

19960 ■ KMOX-AM - 1120
1220 Olive St., 3rd Fl.
Saint Louis, MO 63103
Phone: (314)621-2345
Fax: (314)444-3230
Email: kmoxnews@kmox.com
Format: News; Talk; Sports. **Networks:** CBS. **Owner:** CBS Radio Inc., 1271 Avenue of the Americas, 44th Fl., New York, NY 10020-1401, Ph: (212)649-9600. **Founded:** 1925. **Operating Hours**: Continuous. **Key Personnel:** Steve Moore, Dir. of Operations, Prog. Dir., swmoore@cbs.com; John Butler, News Dir., jmbutler@cbs.com; Stacie Gentry, Dir. of Mktg., slgentry@cbs.com; Ron Jacober, Contact, rdjacober@cbs.com. **Wattage**: 50,000. **Ad Rates:** $50-1000 for 60 seconds. Combined advertising rates available with KYKY, KEZK. **URL:** http://www.stlouis.cbslocal.com.

19961 ■ KMRF-AM - 1510
1411 Locust St.
Saint Louis, MO 63103
Phone: (314)421-3020
Fax: (314)421-1702
Free: 800-334-3276
Format: Religious. **Networks:** Missouri; Brownfield; USA Radio. **Owner:** New Life Evangelistic Center Inc., 1411 Locust St., Saint Louis, MO 63103, Ph: (314)421-3020, Fax: (314)421-1702, Free: 800-334-3276. **Founded:** 1969. **Formerly**: KOSC-AM; KEMM-AM. **Operating Hours**: Sunrise-sunset; 100% local. **Wattage**: 250. **Ad Rates:** Noncommercial. **URL:** http://www.hereshelpnet.org.

19962 ■ KNLC-TV - 24
PO Box 924
Saint Louis, MO 63188
Phone: (314)436-2424
Fax: (314)436-2434
Format: Religious. **Networks:** Independent. **Owner:** New Life Evangelistic Center Inc., 1411 Locust St., Saint Louis, MO 63103, Ph: (314)421-3020, Fax: (314)421-1702, Free: 800-334-3276. **Founded:** 1982. **Operating Hours**: Continuous. **ADI**: St. Louis, MO (Mt. Vernon, IL). **Key Personnel:** Victor Anderson, Dir. of Programs, victor@knlc.tv. **Wattage**: 3,090,000. **Ad Rates:** Noncommercial. **URL:** http://www.knlc.tv.

19963 ■ KNLN-FM - 90.9
1411 Locust St.
Saint Louis, MO 63103
Phone: (314)421-3020

Circulation: ★ = AAM; △ or • = BPA; ♦ = CAC; ❑ = VAC; ⊕ = PO Statement; ‡ = Publisher's Report; Boldface figures = sworn; Light figures = estimated.

Fax: (314)421-1702
Format: Religious. **Ad Rates:** Noncommercial. **URL:** http://hereshelpnet.org.

19964 ■ KPLR-TV - 11
2250 Ball Dr.
Saint Louis, MO 63146
Phone: (314)213-7831
Format: News; Sports; Talk. **Networks:** Independent. **Owner:** Edward "Ted" Koplar, at above address. **Founded:** 1959. **Operating Hours**: Continuous. **ADI**: St. Louis, MO (Mt. Vernon, IL). **Key Personnel:** Spencer Koch, Gen. Mgr. **Wattage**: 1,000,000 ERP. **Ad Rates:** Advertising accepted; rates available upon request. **URL:** http://kplr11.com.

19965 ■ KPNT-FM - 105.7
800 Union Sta.
Saint Louis, MO 63103
Phone: (314)969-3833
Fax: (314)621-3000
Format: Alternative/New Music/Progressive. **Owner:** Emmis Communications Corp., One Emmis Plz., 40 Monument Cir., Ste. 700, Indianapolis, IN 46204-3011, Ph: (317)266-0100. **Operating Hours**: Continuous. **ADI**: St. Louis, MO (Mt. Vernon, IL). **Key Personnel**: Tommy Mattern, Dir. of Programs; Matthew Chambers, Dir. of Mktg.; Becky Duncan, Sales Mgr.; Drew Patterson, Creative Dir. **Ad Rates:** Advertising accepted; rates available upon request. **URL:** http://www.1057thepoint.com.

19966 ■ KRJY-FM - 96.3
401 S 18th St., Ste. 100
Saint Louis, MO 63103
Phone: (314)621-4106
Fax: (314)621-3000
Format: Oldies. **ADI**: St. Louis, MO (Mt. Vernon, IL). **Key Personnel:** Richard Miller, Gen. Mgr. **URL:** http://www.now963.com.

19967 ■ KSD-FM - 93.7
1001 Highlands Plaza Dr. W, Ste. 100
Saint Louis, MO 63110
Phone: (314)241-0937
Format: Country. **Networks:** Independent. **Founded:** 1954. **Operating Hours:** Continuous. **Key Personnel:** Dennis Lamme, Gen. Mgr.; Mark Anderson, Dir. of Programs. **Wattage**: 100,000. **Ad Rates:** Advertising accepted; rates available upon request. **URL:** http://www.937thebull.com.

19968 ■ KSDK-TV - 5
1000 Market St.
Saint Louis, MO 63101
Phone: (314)421-5055
Format: Commercial TV. **Networks:** NBC. **Owner:** Gannett Broadcasting, 7950 Jones Branch Dr., McLean, VA 22107-0150, Ph: (703)854-6000. **Founded:** 1947. **Formerly**: KSD-TV. **Operating Hours**: Continuous. **ADI**: St. Louis, MO (Mt. Vernon, IL). **Local Programs**: *Show Me St. Louis*, Monday Tuesday Wednesday Thursday Friday 10:00 a.m. - 10:30 a.m. **Ad Rates:** Advertising accepted; rates available upon request. **URL:** http://www.ksdk.com.

19969 ■ KSHE-FM - 95
800 St. Louis Union Sta.
The Powerhouse
Saint Louis, MO 63103
Phone: (314)621-0095
Free: 800-842-5743
Email: feedback@kshe95.com
Format: Album-Oriented Rock (AOR). **Owner:** Emmis Communications Corp., One Emmis Plz., 40 Monument Cir., Ste. 700, Indianapolis, IN 46204-3011, Ph: (317)266-0100. **Founded:** 1961. **Operating Hours:** Continuous. **ADI**: St. Louis, MO (Mt. Vernon, IL). **Key Personnel:** John Beck, Gen. Mgr. **Wattage**: 100,000. **Ad Rates:** Noncommercial. **URL:** http://www.kshe95.com.

19970 ■ KSIV-FM - 91.5
1750 S Brentwood Blvd., Ste. 811
Saint Louis, MO 63144
Phone: (314)961-1320
Email: comments@bottradionetwork.com
Format: Religious. **Operating Hours:** Continuous. **Key Personnel:** Dale Smith, Office Mgr., dsmith@bottradionetwork.com. **Wattage:** 100,000. **Ad Rates:** Noncommercial. **URL:** http://www.bottradionetwork.com.

19971 ■ KSLZ-FM - 107.7
1001 Highlands Plaza Dr. W
Saint Louis, MO 63110
Phone: (314)333-8000
Format: Contemporary Hit Radio (CHR). **ADI**: St. Louis, MO (Mt. Vernon, IL). **Wattage:** 100,000. **Ad Rates:** Advertising accepted; rates available upon request. **URL:** http://www.z1077.com.

19972 ■ KTRS-AM - 550
638 W Port Plz.
Saint Louis, MO 63146
Phone: (314)453-5500
Fax: (314)453-9704
Free: 888-550-5877
Email: communications@ktrs.com
Format: News; Talk; Sports. **Networks:** ABC. **Owner:** KSD-AM, LLC, at above address. **Operating Hours**: Continuous. **Wattage**: 5,000. **Ad Rates:** Noncommercial. **URL:** http://www.ktrs.com.

19973 ■ KTVI-TV - 2
2250 Ball Dr.
Saint Louis, MO 63146
Phone: (314)213-7831
Email: ktvinews@tvstl.com
Format: Commercial TV; News; Information. **Networks:** Fox. **Founded:** 1953. **Formerly**: WTVI-TV. **Operating Hours**: Continuous. **ADI**: St. Louis, MO (Mt. Vernon, IL). **Key Personnel:** Cindy Solomon, Sales Mgr. **Ad Rates:** Noncommercial. **URL:** http://www.fox2now.com.

19974 ■ K220HT-FM - 91.9
PO Box 391
Twin Falls, ID 83303
Fax: (208)736-1958
Free: 800-357-4226
Format: Religious; Contemporary Christian. **Owner:** CSN International, PO Box 391, Twin Falls, ID 83303, Ph: (208)736-1958, Fax: (208)736-1958, Free: 800-357-4226. **Key Personnel:** Mike Kestler, Contact; Don Mills, Music Dir., Prog. Dir. **URL:** http://www.csnradio.com.

19975 ■ KWMU-FM - 90.7
3651 Olive St.
Saint Louis, MO 63108
Phone: (314)516-5968
Format: Talk; News. **Networks:** National Public Radio (NPR); Public Radio International (PRI). **Owner:** University of Missouri-St. Louis, One University Blvd., Saint Louis, MO 63121-4400, Ph: (314)516-5000, Free: 888-GO-2-UMSL. **Founded:** 1972. **Operating Hours**: Continuous; 73% network, 27% local. **ADI**: St. Louis, MO (Mt. Vernon, IL). **Key Personnel:** Bill Raack, News Dir.; Tim Eby, Gen. Mgr.; Shelley Kerley, Dir. of Dev.; Mike Schrand, Program Mgr. **Local Programs**: *Cityscape*, Friday 12:00 p.m. - 1:00 p.m.; *St. Louis on the Air*, Monday Tuesday Wednesday Thursday 12:00 p.m.; 10:00 p.m. **Wattage**: 100,000. **Ad Rates:** Noncommercial. **URL:** http://news.stlpublicradio.org.

19976 ■ KWUR-FM - 90.3
One Brookings Dr.
One Brookings Dr.
Saint Louis, MO 63130
Phone: (314)935-5952
Fax: (314)935-8833
Format: Alternative/New Music/Progressive; News; Sports. **Owner:** Washington University in St. Louis, 1 Brookings Dr., Saint Louis, MO 63130, Ph: (314)935-5000, Fax: (314)935-4290, Free: 800-638-0700. **Founded:** 1976. **Operating Hours:** Continuous; 100% local. **Key Personnel:** Kenny Hofmeister, Gen. Mgr. **Wattage**: 100. **Ad Rates:** Noncommercial. **URL:** http://www.kwur.com.

19977 ■ KXEN-AM - 1010
5615 Pershing Ave., Ste. 12
Saint Louis, MO 63112
Phone: (314)454-0400
Email: info@kxen1010am.com
Format: Contemporary Christian. **Wattage**: 50,000. **Ad Rates:** Advertising accepted; rates available upon request. **URL:** http://www.kxen1010am.com.

19978 ■ KYKY-FM - 98.1
3100 Market St.
Saint Louis, MO 63103
Phone: (314)531-0000
Fax: (314)531-9855
Format: Adult Contemporary. **Networks:** Independent. **Owner:** CBS Radio Inc., 1271 Avenue of the Americas, 44th Fl., New York, NY 10020-1401, Ph: (212)649-9600. **Founded:** 1972. **Formerly**: KSLQ-FM. **Operating Hours**: Continuous; 100% local. **Key Personnel:** John Sheehan, Sr. VP. **Wattage**: 90,000. **Ad Rates:** Advertising accepted; rates available upon request. **URL:** http://y98.cbslocal.com.

19979 ■ Suddenlink Communications
12444 Powerscourt Dr.
Saint Louis, MO 63131-3660
Phone: (479)264-1854
Free: 800-490-9604
Email: dlsdl-allcarrierrelations@suddenlink.com
Owner: Cebridge Connections, at above address. **Founded:** 2003. **Formerly**: Cebridge Connections Inc. **Key Personnel:** Jerald L. Kent, CEO. **Cities Served:** Forest Cove, Kingwood, Texas; 372 channels. **Postal Areas Served:** 77339. **URL:** http://www.suddenlink.com.

19980 ■ TALK-FM - 97.1
Union Station Powerhouse
800 St. Louis
Saint Louis, MO 63103
Phone: (314)231-9710
Fax: (314)621-3000
Free: 866-455-9797
Format: Talk; News. **Operating Hours**: Continuous. **Key Personnel:** Jim Modglin, Prog. Dir.; Karen Kelly, Gen. Mgr.; John Beck, Sr. VP, john@stl.emmis.com; Jeff Allen, Dir. of Programs, jaallen@stl.emmis.com; Tony Colombo, Promotions Dir., tcolombo@stl.emmis.com. **Ad Rates:** Advertising accepted; rates available upon request. **URL:** http://www.971talk.com.

19981 ■ WARH-FM - 106.5
11647 Olive Blvd.
Saint Louis, MO 63141
Phone: (314)983-6000
Email: kkraus@1065thearch.com
Format: Eclectic. **Owner:** Bonneville International Corp., 55 North 300 West, Salt Lake City, UT 84101-3502, Ph: (801)575-7500. **URL:** http://www.1065thearch.com.

19982 ■ WEW-AM - 770
2740 Hampton Ave.
Saint Louis, MO 63139
Phone: (314)781-9397
Fax: (314)781-8545
Format: Big Band/Nostalgia; Music of Your Life; News; Information. **Owner:** Birach Broadcasting Corp., at above address. **Founded:** 1921. **Operating Hours**: 6 a.m.-8:30 p.m. **ADI**: St. Louis, MO (Mt. Vernon, IL). **Wattage**: 1,000. **Ad Rates:** $34-48 for 60 seconds. **URL:** http://wewradio.com.

19983 ■ WFUN-FM - 95.5
9666 Olive Blvd., Ste. 610
Saint Louis, MO 63132
Phone: (314)989-9550
Fax: (314)989-9551
Format: Urban Contemporary. **Owner:** Radio One Inc., 1010 Wayne Ave., 14th Fl., Silver Spring, MD 20910, Ph: (301)306-1111, Fax: (302)636-5454. **Operating Hours**: Continuous. **ADI**: St. Louis, MO (Mt. Vernon, IL). **Key Personnel:** Gary Benett, Chief Engineer. **URL:** http://www.oldschool955.com.

19984 ■ WHHL-FM - 104.1
9666 Olive Blvd., Ste. 610
Saint Louis, MO 63132
Phone: (314)989-9550
Fax: (314)989-9551
Format: Urban Contemporary; Hip Hop. **Owner:** Radio One Inc., 1010 Wayne Ave., 14th Fl., Silver Spring, MD 20910, Ph: (301)306-1111, Fax: (302)636-5454. **Operating Hours**: Continuous. **Key Personnel:** Darla Harper, Bus. Mgr.; Gary T. Bennett, Chief Engineer. **Ad Rates:** Advertising accepted; rates available upon request. **URL:** http://www.hot1041stl.com.

19985 ■ WHOJ-FM - 91.9
4424 Hampton Ave.
Saint Louis, MO 63109
Phone: (314)752-7000
Free: 877-305-1234
Format: Religious. **Owner:** Covenant Network, 3210 Michigan Ave., Ste. 300, Kansas City, MO 64109. **Local Programs**: *Mornings with Mother*, Monday Tuesday

Wednesday Thursday Friday 1:30 a.m. - 2:30 a.m. **URL:** http://www.covenantnet.net.

19986 ■ WIHM-AM - 1410
4424 Hampton Ave.
Saint Louis, MO 63109
Phone: (314)752-7000
Free: 877-305-1234
Format: Religious. **Owner:** Eternal Word Television Network, 5817 Old Leeds Rd., Irondale, AL 35210-2164, Ph: (205)271-2900, Fax: (205)271-2925. **URL:** http://www.ewtn.com.

19987 ■ WIJR-AM - 880
13063 Winu Dr.
Highland, IL 62249
Phone: (618)654-5615
Email: sima@birach.com
Format: Public Radio; Hispanic. **Owner:** Birach Broadcasting Corp., 21700 Northwestern Hwy. Tower 14, Ste. 1190, Southfield, MI 48075, Ph: (248)557-3500, Fax: (248)557-2950. **Key Personnel:** Sima Birach, CEO, President, sima@birach.com. **URL:** http://www.birach.com/wijr.htm.

19988 ■ WIL-FM - 92.3
11647 Olive Blvd.
Saint Louis, MO 63141
Phone: (314)983-6000
Email: keith.kraus@wil92.com
Format: Country. **Owner:** Hubbard Broadcasting Inc., 3415 University Ave., Saint Paul, MN 55114-2099, Ph: (651)646-5555, Fax: (651)642-4172. **ADI:** St. Louis, MO (Mt. Vernon, IL). **Ad Rates:** Advertising accepted; rates available upon request. $325 for 60 seconds. **URL:** http://www.wil92.com.

19989 ■ WKBQ-FM - 104.1
800 St. Louis Union Sta.
Saint Louis, MO 63103-2257
Fax: (314)878-1564
Free: 800-455-1040
Format: Top 40. **Networks:** Independent. **Owner:** Zimmer Broadcasting, PO Box 1617, Cape Girardeau, MO 63702, Ph: (573)335-8291, Fax: (573)335-4809. **Founded:** 1965. **Operating Hours:** Continuous. **ADI:** St. Joseph, MO. **Key Personnel:** John Beck, Gen. Mgr. **Wattage:** 39,000.

19990 ■ WKKX-FM - 106.5
800 St. Louis Union Sta.
Saint Louis, MO 63103-2257
Phone: (314)621-0400
Format: Contemporary Country. **Networks:** Independent. **Owner:** RCK 1 Group, LLC, at above address. **Founded:** 1958. **Formerly:** WJBM-FM. **Operating Hours:** Continuous; 100% local. **Wattage:** 90,000. **Ad Rates:** Advertising accepted; rates available upon request.

19991 ■ WRBU-TV - 46
1408 N Kings Hwy., Ste. 300
Saint Louis, MO 63113
Owner: Roberts Broadcasting Co., 901 Locust St., Saint Louis, MO 63101-1401, Ph: (314)367-4600, Fax: (314)367-0174. **Wattage:** 109,400.

19992 ■ WRYT-AM - 1080
4424 Hampton Ave.
Saint Louis, MO 63139
Phone: (314)752-7000
Free: 877-305-1234
Format: Religious. **Networks:** Eternal Word TV. **Owner:** Covenant Network, 3210 Michigan Ave., Ste. 300, Kansas City, MO 64109. **Founded:** 1980. **Operating Hours:** Sunrise-sunset. **ADI:** St. Louis, MO (Mt. Vernon, IL). **Local Programs:** *Life on the Rock*, Friday 7:00 p.m. **Wattage:** 500. **Ad Rates:** Noncommercial. **URL:** http://www.covenantnet.net.

19993 ■ WSDD-FM - 104.9
1001 Highlands Plaza Dr. W, Ste. 200
Saint Louis, MO 63110
Phone: (314)333-8000
Format: Adult Contemporary. **Networks:** Independent; ABC. **Founded:** 1961. **Formerly:** KATZ-FM. **Operating Hours:** Continuous. **ADI:** St. Louis, MO (Mt. Vernon, IL). **Wattage:** 50,000. **Ad Rates:** Noncommercial. **URL:** http://www.wild1049stl.com.

19994 ■ WSDZ-AM - 1260
638 Westport Plz.
Saint Louis, MO 63146
Phone: (314)682-1269
Format: Eclectic. **Networks:** Satellite Radio; ABC. **Owner:** ABC Entertainment Group, 500 S Buena Vista St., Burbank, CA 91521-4588. **Founded:** 1947. **Formerly:** WIBV-AM. **Operating Hours:** Continuous. **Wattage:** 20,000 Day; 5,000 Night. **Ad Rates:** Advertising accepted; rates available upon request.

19995 ■ WSSM-FM - 97.7
11647 Olive Blvd.
Saint Louis, MO 63141
Phone: (314)983-6000
Format: Eighties; News. **Simulcasts:** WSMM-FM 102.3. **Operating Hours:** Continuous. **Wattage:** 2,900. **Ad Rates:** Advertising accepted; rates available upon request.

19996 ■ WTPC-FM - 105.3
Principia College
13201 Clayton Rd.
Saint Louis, MO 63131
Phone: (314)434-2100
Format: Educational. **Owner:** Principia Communications Corp., at above address. **Founded:** 1970. **Operating Hours:** 4:00 p.m.-2:00 a.m. **Key Personnel:** George Cooke, Contact. **Wattage:** 017 ERP. **Ad Rates:** Noncommercial. **URL:** http://www.community.principia.edu.

19997 ■ WVRV-FM - 101.1
11647 Olive Blvd.
Saint Louis, MO 63141
Phone: (651)642-4334
Format: Sports; News. **Networks:** NBC; CBS; ESPN Radio; ABC. **Owner:** Bonneville International Corp., 55 North 300 West, Salt Lake City, UT 84101-3502, Ph: (801)575-7500. **Founded:** 1963. **Formerly:** WSNL-FM; WMRY-FM; WFXB-FM. **Operating Hours:** Continuous. **ADI:** St. Louis, MO (Mt. Vernon, IL). **Key Personnel:** Chris Redgrave, Gen. Mgr., VP. **Wattage:** 100,000 ERP. **Ad Rates:** Advertising accepted; rates available upon request. **URL:** http://www.101sports.com.

19998 ■ WXOS-FM - 101.1
11647 Olive Blvd.
Saint Louis, MO 63141
Phone: (314)969-0101
Format: Sports. **Owner:** Bonneville International Corp., 55 North 300 West, Salt Lake City, UT 84101-3502, Ph: (801)575-7500. **Operating Hours:** Continuous. **Ad Rates:** Advertising accepted; rates available upon request. **URL:** http://www.101sports.com.

SAINT PETERS

19999 ■ Paint & Decorating Retailer
Paint and Decorating Retailers Association
1401 Triad Center Dr.
Saint Peters, MO 63376-7353
Phone: (636)326-2636
Publisher's E-mail: info@pdra.org
Magazine serving retailers of paint and decorating products. **Freq:** Monthly. **Print Method:** Offset. **Trim Size:** 8 1/8 x 10 7/8. **Cols./Page:** 3. **Col. Width:** 42 nonpareils. **Col. Depth:** 140 agate lines. **Key Personnel:** Dan Simon, Contact. **ISSN:** 1096--6927 (print); **EISSN:** 0011--7404 (electronic). **Subscription Rates:** Included in membership. **URL:** http://www.pdra.org/magazine. **Formerly:** Decorating Retailer. **Remarks:** Accepts advertising. **Circ:** (Not Reported).

20000 ■ PDRA Paint and Decorating Retailer
Paint and Decorating Retailers Association
1401 Triad Center Dr.
Saint Peters, MO 63376-7353
Phone: (636)326-2636
Publisher's E-mail: info@pdra.org
Freq: Monthly. **ISSN:** 0011--7404 (print). **Subscription Rates:** Free. **URL:** http://www.pdra.org/magazine/about-pdr-magazine. **Remarks:** Accepts advertising. **Circ:** 27000.

20001 ■ KNSX-FM - 93.3
PO Box 93
Saint Peters, MO 63376
Phone: (314)921-9330
Format: Adult Album Alternative. **Key Personnel:** Ruth Choate, Gen. Sales Mgr., Prog. Dir., ruth@knsx.com.

SAINT ROBERT

20002 ■ KFLW-FM - 98.9
555 Marshall Dr.
Saint Robert, MO 65584
Phone: (573)336-5359
Format: Classic Rock. **Key Personnel:** Tracy O'Quinn, Gen. Mgr. **Ad Rates:** Noncommercial. **URL:** http://www.kflw989.com.

SAINTE GENEVIEVE

SE MO. Ste. Genevieve Co. 10 mi. E. of Bloomsdale. Marbles quarry, agriculture.

20003 ■ Ste. Genevieve Herald
Ste. Genevieve Newspapers Inc.
330 Market St.
Sainte Genevieve, MO 63670
Phone: (573)883-2222
Fax: (573)883-2833
Publisher's E-mail: news@stegenherald.com
Community newspaper. **Freq:** Weekly (Wed.). **Print Method:** Web offset. **Trim Size:** 11 1/2 x 12 1/2. **Cols./Page:** 6. **Col. Width:** 10.5 picas. **Col. Depth:** 21 inches. **Key Personnel:** Toby Carrig, Editor; Robert J. Burr, Publisher; Tammy Miller, Business Manager; Janet A. Mace, General Manager; Jill Gettinger, Manager, Advertising. **USPS:** 240-760. **Subscription Rates:** $26 Individuals In Ste. Genevieve County; $35 Elsewhere in Missouri; $40 Out of area; $0.75 Single issue; $30 Individuals e-edition. **URL:** http://www.stegenherald.com. **Mailing address:** PO Box 447, Sainte Genevieve, MO 63670. **Ad Rates:** BW $667.80; 4C $867.80; SAU $6.30; PCI $6.30. **Remarks:** Accepts advertising. **Circ:** ‡4,700.

20004 ■ KBDZ-FM - 93.1
PO Box 428
Sainte Genevieve, MO 63670-0428
Phone: (573)547-8005
Fax: (573)883-2866
Format: Country; News. **Networks:** Unistar. **Owner:** Donze Communication, Inc., at above address. **Founded:** 1991. **Operating Hours:** Continuous. **Wattage:** 6,000. **Ad Rates:** Advertising accepted; rates available upon request. **URL:** http://classicrock931.com.

20005 ■ KSGM-AM - 980
PO Box 428
Sainte Genevieve, MO 63670
Phone: (573)883-2980
Format: Country; Talk. **Owner:** Donze Communications Inc., 122D Perry Plz., Perryville, MO 63775-4203, Ph: (573)547-8005. **Founded:** July 05, 1947. **Wattage:** 1,000. **URL:** http://ksgm980.com.

SALEM

SEC MO. Dent Co. 96 mi. S. of Jefferson City. Manufactures textiles, lumber, charcoal briquets. Wholesale food distributor. Oak and pine timber. Diversified farming. Feeder pigs and calves.

20006 ■ The Salem News: Online Edition
The Salem News
500 N. Washington St.
Salem, MO 65560-0798
Phone: (573)729-4126
Fax: (573)729-4920
Publisher's E-mail: salemnews@thesalemnewsonline.com
Online. **Freq:** Semiweekly. **Print Method:** Offset. **Trim Size:** 13 1/2 x 22 3/4. **Cols./Page:** 6. **Col. Width:** 20 nonpareils. **Col. Depth:** 294 agate lines. **URL:** http://www.thesalemnewsonline.com. **Mailing address:** PO Box 798, Salem, MO 65560-0798. **Ad Rates:** BW $780.45; 4C $950.45; SAU $4.89. **Remarks:** Accepts advertising. **Circ:** (Not Reported).

20007 ■ KGNN-FM - 94.9; 104.9; 90.3
PO Box 187
Washington, MO 63090
Phone: (636)239-0400
Fax: (636)239-4448
Free: 877-385-3787
Email: info@goodnewsvoice.org

Circulation: ★ = AAM; △ or • = BPA; ♦ = CAC; ❑ = VAC; ⊕ = PO Statement; ‡ = Publisher's Report; Boldface figures = sworn; Light figures = estimated.

Format: Religious. **Simulcasts:** KGNV-FM, KGNA-FM. **Networks:** Moody Broadcasting. **Owner:** Missouri River Christian Broadcasting Inc., PO Box 187, Washington, MO 63090, Ph: (636)239-0400. **Founded:** 1988. **Formerly:** KBCC-AM; KGNN-AM. **Operating Hours:** Continuous; 90% network, 10% local. **Wattage:** 6,300. **Ad Rates:** Advertising accepted; rates available upon request. **URL:** http://www.goodnewsvoice.org.

20008 ■ KSMO-AM - 1340
800 S Main St.
Salem, MO 65560
Phone: (573)729-6117
Fax: (573)729-7337
Email: info@ksmoradio.com

Format: Sports. **Owner:** KSMO Enterprises, at above address. **Founded:** 1953. **Key Personnel:** Stan Stevens, Sports Dir., News Dir.; Melba Headrick, Sales Mgr. **Local Programs:** *Open Market*, Monday Tuesday Wednesday Thursday Friday 1:00 p.m. **Wattage:** 1,000. **Ad Rates:** Advertising accepted; rates available upon request. **URL:** http://www.ksmoradio.com.

SEDALIA

WC MO. Pettis Co. 62 mi. W. of Jefferson City. State Fair Community College. Manufactures disinfectants, aluminum cable, conductors, commercial kitchen appliances, tables, gadgets, glass blocks, steel fabrication, textiles, shoes, truck trailers and beds, brooms. Planing mill. Limestonequarries. Diversified farming. Corn, wheat, oats.

20009 ■ KDRO-AM - 1490
301 E Ohio St.
Sedalia, MO 65301
Phone: (660)826-5005
Fax: (660)826-5557
Free: 877-310-9700

Format: Country. **Networks:** CBS. **Founded:** 1939. **Operating Hours:** Continuous; 10% network, 90% local. **Key Personnel:** Stu Steinmetz, Station Mgr., ssteinmetz@bennemedia.com. **Wattage:** 780. **Ad Rates:** $13.50 for 30 seconds; $18 for 60 seconds. **URL:** http://www.kdro.com.

20010 ■ KPOW-FM - 97.7
301 S Ohio St.
Sedalia, MO 65301
Free: 877-310-9700
Email: sales@bennemedia.com

Format: Classic Rock. **Ad Rates:** Noncommercial. **URL:** http://www.power977.com.

20011 ■ KSIS-AM - 1050
2209 S Limit
Sedalia, MO 65301
Phone: (660)826-1050
Fax: (660)827-5072
Free: 800-748-8354

Format: News; Talk; Sports. **Owner:** Double O Radio, at above address. **Founded:** 1986. **Operating Hours:** 5:00 a.m. - 12:00 a.m. Sunday - Friday; 6:00 a.m. - 12:00 a.m. Saturday. **Key Personnel:** Mike Jenkins, Gen. Mgr.; Dennis Polk, Gen. Mgr.; Doug Sokolowski, Dir. of Sales, doug.allen@townsquaremedia.com. **Wattage:** 1,000 Day; 086 Night. **Ad Rates:** Advertising accepted; rates available upon request. **URL:** http://www.ksisradio.com.

20012 ■ KXKX-FM - 105.7
2209 S Limit Ave.
Sedalia, MO 65301
Phone: (660)826-1050

Format: Country. **Key Personnel:** Mike Jenkins, Gen. Mgr. **Wattage:** 40,000. **Ad Rates:** Advertising accepted; rates available upon request. **URL:** http://kxkx.com.

20013 ■ pectrum Reach
210 W 7th St.
Sedalia, MO 65301
Phone: (844)566-4548
Free: 888-438-2427

Owner: Charter Communications Inc., 400 Atlantic St., Stamford, CT 06901, Ph: (203)905-7801. **Cities Served:** subscribing households 1,121. **URL:** http://www.chartermedia.com.

SEYMOUR

20014 ■ Webster County Citizen
Webster County Citizen
221 S Commercial St.
Seymour, MO 65746
Phone: (417)935-2257
Publisher's E-mail: citizen@webstercountycitizen.com

Community newspaper. **Freq:** Weekly. **Key Personnel:** Dan Wehmer, Editor; Beverly Hannum, Director, Production; Anna Sturdefant, Office Manager. **Subscription Rates:** $28 Individuals in Webster County; $32 Elsewhere in Missouri; $40 Out of state; $28 Individuals 6 months; $15 Individuals in-office pick up; $20 Individuals E-edition only. **URL:** http://www.webstercountycitizen.com. **Ad Rates:** SAU $4. **Remarks:** Accepts advertising. **Circ:** Controlled 2408.

SIKESTON

SE MO. Scott Co. 35 mi. S. of Cape Girardeau. Manufactures hardware, paper and wood products, copper wire and cable, animal feed, seed corn, wholesale grocery supplies. Diversified farming. Soybeans, cotton, corn, wheat, milo.

20015 ■ Sikeston Standard Democrat
Standard Democrat
205 S New Madrid St.
Sikeston, MO 63801
Phone: (573)471-1137
Fax: (573)471-6981
Free: 800-675-6980

Newspaper with a Democratic orientation. **Freq:** Sunday - Friday. **Print Method:** Offset. **Cols./Page:** 6. **Col. Width:** 24 nonpareils. **Col. Depth:** 304 agate lines. **Key Personnel:** Michael Jensen, Publisher; DeAnna Nelson, Manager, Advertising; Don Culberston, General Manager; Merlin Hagy, Manager, Circulation. **Subscription Rates:** $93.50 Individuals 1 year (carrier); $82 Individuals 1 year (senior citizen); $46.25 Individuals 1 year (web only). **URL:** http://www.standard-democrat.com. **Formerly:** The Standard Democrat. **Ad Rates:** PCI $6.60. **Remarks:** Accepts advertising. **Circ:** (Not Reported).

20016 ■ KBXB-FM - 97.9
125 S Kingshighway
Sikeston, MO 63801
Phone: (573)471-2000

Format: Country. **Key Personnel:** Joe Bill Davis, Contact, jbdavis@withersradio.net. **Wattage:** 50,000. **Ad Rates:** Advertising accepted; rates available upon request. **URL:** http://www.b979.net.

20017 ■ Newwave Communications
1 Montgomery Plz., 4th Fl.
Sikeston, MO 63801
Fax: (573)472-9502
Free: 888-863-9928
Email: info@newwavecom.com

Key Personnel: Jerry Smith, Gen. Mgr.; Mark Clark, VP, Gen. Mgr. **Cities Served:** 62 channels. **URL:** http://www.newwavecom.com.

20018 ■ SEMO Communications Corp.
107 Semo Ln.
Sikeston, MO 63801
Phone: (573)471-6599
Fax: (573)471-6878
Free: 800-635-8230
Email: semosupport@cablerocket.com

Founded: 1976. **Cities Served:** Midwest and Southeast Missouri region; 62 channels. **Mailing address:** PO Box C, Sikeston, MO 63801. **URL:** http://www.semocommunications.com.

SPRINGFIELD

SW MO. Greene Co. 184 mi. SE of Kansas City; 225 mi. SW of Saint Louis. Drury College; Southwest Missouri State University; Baptist College; Central Bible Institute; Evangel College. Light manufacturing, agriculture and tourism. Shipping center for poultry eggs, milk. Flour mill; meat packing plants; manufactures clothing, paper products, furniture, plastics, trucks and trailers, railroad and refrigerator iron and steel, concrete products, feed, fertilizers, typewriters, electrical equipment, chemicals, machine tools, firearms, matches.

20019 ■ Advances in Mathematics of Communications
American Institute of Mathematical Sciences
PO Box 2604
Springfield, MO 65801
Phone: (417)886-0559
Fax: (417)886-0559
Publisher's E-mail: general@aimsciences.org

Journal covering scholarly research papers in all areas of mathematics and computer science which are relevant to applications in communications technology. **Freq:** Quarterly. **Key Personnel:** Marcus Greferath, Editor-in-Chief. **ISSN:** 1930--5346 (print); **EISSN:** 1930--5338 (electronic). **Subscription Rates:** $755 Individuals online. **URL:** http://aimsciences.org/journals/home.jsp?journalID=10. **Circ:** (Not Reported).

20020 ■ Annals of the American Psychotherapy Association
American Psychotherapy Association
2750 E Sunshine St.
Springfield, MO 65804
Phone: (417)823-0173
Free: 800-205-9165
Publisher's E-mail: info@americanpsychotherapy.com

Freq: Monthly. **ISSN:** 1535--4075 (print). **Subscription Rates:** Included in membership. **URL:** http://www.americanpsychotherapy.com/annals. **Remarks:** Accepts advertising. **Circ:** (Not Reported).

20021 ■ Annals of Psychotherapy & Integrative Health
American Association of Integrative Medicine
2750 E Sunshine St.
Springfield, MO 65804-2047
Phone: (417)881-9995
Fax: (417)823-9959
Free: 877-718-3053

Journal containing research, news and commentary on integrative medicine and mental health. **Freq:** Monthly. **Subscription Rates:** $29.95 Individuals electronic for 2 years; $53.95 Individuals electronic for 4 years. **URL:** http://www.annalsofpsychotherapy.com; http://www.aaimedicine.com/jaaim. **Formerly:** JAAIM-Online. **Remarks:** Advertising accepted; rates available upon request. **Circ:** (Not Reported).

20022 ■ Big Data and Information Analytics
American Institute of Mathematical Sciences
PO Box 2604
Springfield, MO 65801
Phone: (417)886-0559
Fax: (417)886-0559
Publisher's E-mail: general@aimsciences.org

Journal promoting cutting-edge research, technology transfer and knowledge translation about complex data and information processing. **Freq:** Quarterly. **Key Personnel:** Nick Cercone, Editor-in-Chief. **ISSN:** 2380--6966 (print); **EISSN:** 2380--6974 (electronic). **Subscription Rates:** $700 Individuals print and online; $600 Individuals online. **Alt. Formats:** Print. **URL:** http://aimsciences.org/journals/BDIA.jsp?journalID=27. **Circ:** (Not Reported).

20023 ■ Communications on Pure and Applied Analysis
American Institute of Mathematical Sciences
PO Box 2604
Springfield, MO 65801
Phone: (417)886-0559
Fax: (417)886-0559
Publisher's E-mail: general@aimsciences.org

Journal covering scholarly research in all the major areas of analysis and its applications with a central theme on theoretical and numeric differential equations. **Freq:** Bimonthly. **Key Personnel:** Shouchuan Hu, Editor-in-Chief. **ISSN:** 1534--0392 (print); **EISSN:** 1553--5258 (electronic). **Subscription Rates:** $1275 Individuals online; $1425 Other countries. **URL:** http://aimsciences.org/journals/home.jsp?journalID=3. **Circ:** (Not Reported).

20024 ■ Discrete and Continuous Dynamical Systems - Series A
American Institute of Mathematical Sciences
PO Box 2604
Springfield, MO 65801
Phone: (417)886-0559
Fax: (417)886-0559
Publisher's E-mail: general@aimsciences.org

Journal containing peer-reviewed original papers and invited expository papers on the theory and methods of analysis, differential equations and dynamical systems. **Freq:** Monthly. **Key Personnel:** Shouchuan Hu, Editor-in-Chief. **ISSN:** 1078--0947 (print); **EISSN:** 1553--5231 (electronic). **URL:** http://aimsciences.org/journals/home.jsp?journalID=1. **Circ:** (Not Reported).

20025 ■ Discrete and Continuous Dynamical Systems, Series B: A Journal Bridging Mathematics and Sciences
American Institute of Mathematical Sciences
PO Box 2604
Springfield, MO 65801
Phone: (417)886-0559
Fax: (417)886-0559
Publisher's E-mail: general@aimsciences.org
Journal publishing research papers focusing on the interdisciplinary interactions between mathematical modeling, analysis and scientific computations. **Freq:** 10/year. **Key Personnel:** Peter E. Kloeden, Editor-in-Chief; Xin Lu, Managing Editor; Patricia Bauman, Board Member. **ISSN:** 1531--3492 (print); **EISSN:** 1553--524X (electronic). **URL:** http://www.aimsciences.org/journals/home.jsp?journalID=2. **Remarks:** Advertising not accepted. **Circ:** (Not Reported).

20026 ■ Discrete and Continuous Dynamical Systems - Series S
American Institute of Mathematical Sciences
PO Box 2604
Springfield, MO 65801
Phone: (417)886-0559
Fax: (417)886-0559
Publisher's E-mail: general@aimsciences.org
Journal covering each issue devoted to a specific area of the mathematical, physical and engineering sciences. **Freq:** Bimonthly. **Key Personnel:** Xin Lu, Editor-in-Chief. **ISSN:** 1937--1632 (print); **EISSN:** 1937--1179 (electronic). **URL:** http://aimsciences.org/journals/home.jsp?journalID=15. **Circ:** (Not Reported).

20027 ■ The Drury Mirror: The Official Student Newspaper of Drury University
Drury University
900 N Benton Ave.
Springfield, MO 65802
Free: 800-922-2274
Publisher's E-mail: drury@drury.edu
Collegiate newspaper. **Freq:** Weekly. **Print Method:** Offset. **Trim Size:** 11 x 17. **Cols./Page:** 4. **Col. Width:** 2 1/4 nonpareils. **Col. Depth:** 16 1/2 agate lines. **Key Personnel:** Lillian Stone, Editor-in-Chief; Cory Bledsoe, Managing Editor. **URL:** http://www.drurymirror.org. **Ad Rates:** GLR $5; BW $300; PCI $6.25. **Remarks:** Accepts advertising. **Circ:** (Not Reported).

20028 ■ Enrichment Journal: Journal for Pentecostal Ministry
General Council of the Assemblies of God
1445 Boonville Ave.
Springfield, MO 65802-1894
Phone: (417)862-2781
Free: 877-840-4800
Publication E-mail: enrichment@ag.org
Leadership journal for Assemblies of God ministers. **Freq:** Quarterly. **Print Method:** Offset. **Trim Size:** 8 x 10.75. **Cols./Page:** 3. **Col. Width:** 27 nonpareils. **Col. Depth:** 130 agate lines. **ISSN:** 1082-1791 (print). **Subscription Rates:** $24 Individuals; $42 Two years; $54 Other countries; $102 Two years other countries. **URL:** http://enrichmentjournal.ag.org/. **Formerly:** Advance. **Remarks:** Accepts advertising. **Circ:** ‡32000.

20029 ■ Fairs and Expos
International Association of Fairs and Expositions
3043 E Cairo St.
Springfield, MO 65802-6204
Phone: (417)862-5771
Free: 800-516-0313
Publisher's E-mail: iafe@fairsandexpos.com
Magazine containing information on fair trends, innovative ideas and association activities. **Freq:** Bimonthly. **Trim Size:** 7.5 x 10. **Key Personnel:** Rebekah Lee, Editor. **Subscription Rates:** $18 Members; $30 Nonmembers; Included in membership. **URL:** http://www.fairsandexpos.com/eweb/DynamicPage.aspx?Site=iafe&WebCode=Magazine. **Remarks:** Accepts advertising. **Circ:** (Not Reported).

20030 ■ International Journal of Knowledge and Web Intelligence
Inderscience Publishers
Glass Hall 387
Computer Information Systems
Missouri State University
901 S National Ave.
Springfield, MO 65897
Publisher's E-mail: editor@inderscience.com
Peer-reviewed journal focusing on knowledge engineering and web intelligence. **Freq:** Quarterly. **Key Personnel:** Dr. Toyohide Watanabe, Editor-in-Chief; Prof. Lakhmi C. Jain, Editor. **ISSN:** 1755--8255 (print); **EISSN:** 1755--8263 (electronic). **Subscription Rates:** $685 Individuals print only - annual (includes surface mail); or online (for single user only); $928 Individuals print and online. **URL:** http://www.inderscience.com/jhome.php?jcode=ijkwi. **Circ:** (Not Reported).

20031 ■ Inverse Problems and Imaging
American Institute of Mathematical Sciences
PO Box 2604
Springfield, MO 65801
Phone: (417)886-0559
Fax: (417)886-0559
Publisher's E-mail: general@aimsciences.org
Journal covering scholarly research articles that employ innovative mathematical and modeling techniques to study inverse and imaging problems arising in engineering and other sciences. **Freq:** Quarterly. **Key Personnel:** Gunther Uhlmann, Editor-in-Chief. **ISSN:** 1930--8337 (print); **EISSN:** 1930--8345 (electronic). **Subscription Rates:** $1105 Other countries; $985 Individuals online. **URL:** http://aimsciences.org/journals/home.jsp?journalID=11. **Circ:** (Not Reported).

20032 ■ Journal of Computational Dynamics
American Institute of Mathematical Sciences
PO Box 2604
Springfield, MO 65801
Phone: (417)886-0559
Fax: (417)886-0559
Publisher's E-mail: general@aimsciences.org
Journal containing papers that explore new computational methods for analyzing dynamic problems or use novel dynamical methods to improve computation. **Freq:** Semiannual. **Key Personnel:** Michael Dellnitz, Editor-in-Chief. **ISSN:** 2158--2491 (print); **EISSN:** 2158--2505 (electronic). **Subscription Rates:** $550 Individuals online. **URL:** http://aimsciences.org/journals/home.jsp?journalID=24. **Circ:** (Not Reported).

20033 ■ Journal of Dynamics and Games
American Institute of Mathematical Sciences
PO Box 2604
Springfield, MO 65801
Phone: (417)886-0559
Fax: (417)886-0559
Publisher's E-mail: general@aimsciences.org
Journal containing peer-review and expository papers at the interface of Dynamical Systems (discrete, continuous, deterministic, or stochastic) and Game Theory. **Freq:** Quarterly. **Key Personnel:** Michel Benaim, Editor-in-Chief. **ISSN:** 2164--6066 (print); **EISSN:** 2164--6074 (electronic). **Subscription Rates:** $525 Individuals online. **URL:** http://aimsciences.org/journals/home.jsp?journalID=26. **Circ:** (Not Reported).

20034 ■ Journal of Geometric Mechanics
American Institute of Mathematical Sciences
PO Box 2604
Springfield, MO 65801
Phone: (417)886-0559
Fax: (417)886-0559
Publisher's E-mail: general@aimsciences.org
Journal containing research articles devoted to geometric methods in mechanics and control theory, and intends to facilitate interaction between theory and applications. **Freq:** Quarterly. **Key Personnel:** Manuel de Leon, Editor-in-Chief. **ISSN:** 1941--4889 (print); **EISSN:** 1941--4897 (electronic). **Subscription Rates:** $955 Individuals print and online; $885 Individuals online. **URL:** http://aimsciences.org/journals/home.jsp?journalID=17. **Circ:** (Not Reported).

20035 ■ Journal of Industrial and Management Optimization
American Institute of Mathematical Sciences
PO Box 2604
Springfield, MO 65801
Phone: (417)886-0559
Fax: (417)886-0559
Publisher's E-mail: general@aimsciences.org
Journal containing peer-reviewed, original papers on the non-trivial interplay between numerical optimization methods and practically significant problems in industry or management so as to achieve superior design, planning and/or operation. **Freq:** Quarterly. **Key Personnel:** Hongye Su, Editor-in-Chief. **ISSN:** 1547--5816 (print); **EISSN:** 1553--166X (electronic). **Subscription Rates:** $1115 Other countries print and online; $1035 Individuals online. **URL:** http://aimsciences.org/journals/home.jsp?journalID=5. **Circ:** (Not Reported).

20036 ■ Journal of Modern Dynamics
American Institute of Mathematical Sciences
PO Box 2604
Springfield, MO 65801
Phone: (417)886-0559
Fax: (417)886-0559
Publisher's E-mail: general@aimsciences.org
Journal publishing research articles on the theory of dynamical systems with particular emphasis on the mutual interaction between dynamics and other major areas of mathematical research. **Freq:** Quarterly. **Key Personnel:** Anatole Katok, Editor-in-Chief. **ISSN:** 1930--5311 (print); **EISSN:** 1930--532X (electronic). **Subscription Rates:** $985 Individuals print and online; $865 Individuals online. **URL:** http://jmdmath.s3-website-us-east-1.amazonaws.com. **Circ:** (Not Reported).

20037 ■ Kinetic and Related Models
American Institute of Mathematical Sciences
PO Box 2604
Springfield, MO 65801
Phone: (417)886-0559
Fax: (417)886-0559
Publisher's E-mail: general@aimsciences.org
Journal covering research papers in the areas of kinetic equations spanning from mathematical theory to numerical analysis, simulations and modeling. **Freq:** Quarterly. **Key Personnel:** Kazuo Aoki, Editor-in-Chief. **ISSN:** 1937--5093 (print); **EISSN:** 1937--5077 (electronic). **Subscription Rates:** $865 Individuals online. **URL:** http://aimsciences.org/journals/home.jsp?journalID=16. **Circ:** (Not Reported).

20038 ■ The Lance: The Student Voice of Evangel College
Evangel University
1111 N Glenstone Ave.
Springfield, MO 65802
Phone: (417)865-2815
Fax: (417)865-9599
Free: 800-382-6435
Collegiate newspaper. **Freq:** Weekly. **Print Method:** Offset. **Trim Size:** 11 1/4 x 17 1/2. **Cols./Page:** 5. **Col. Width:** 1 15/16 inches. **Col. Depth:** 15 1/2 inches. **Key Personnel:** Melinda Booze, Advisor. **URL:** http://www.evangel.edu/departments/communication/more-information/the-lance-newspaper. **Ad Rates:** PCI $4.50. **Remarks:** Accepts advertising. **Circ:** (Not Reported).

20039 ■ Mathematical Control and Related Fields
American Institute of Mathematical Sciences
PO Box 2604
Springfield, MO 65801
Phone: (417)886-0559
Fax: (417)886-0559
Publisher's E-mail: general@aimsciences.org
Journal containing original research as well as expository papers on mathematical control theory and related fields. **Freq:** Quarterly. **Key Personnel:** Jean-Michel Coron, Editor-in-Chief. **ISSN:** 2156--8472 (print); **EISSN:** 2156--8499 (electronic). **Subscription Rates:** $695 Individuals online. **URL:** http://aimsciences.org/journals/home.jsp?journalID=23. **Circ:** (Not Reported).

20040 ■ The Mirror
Diocese of Springfield-Cape Girardeau
601 S Jefferson Ave.
Springfield, MO 65806-3143
Catholic Diocesan newspaper (tabloid). **Founded:** 1965.

Circulation: ★ = AAM; △ or • = BPA; ♦ = CAC; ❑ = VAC; ⊕ = PO Statement; ‡ = Publisher's Report; Boldface figures = sworn; Light figures = estimated.

Freq: Weekly. **Print Method:** Offset. **Trim Size:** 11 3/8 x 14. **Cols./Page:** 4. **Col. Width:** 29 nonpareils. **Col. Depth:** 227 agate lines. **USPS:** 117-330. **URL:** http://www.the-mirror.org. **Ad Rates:** BW $675; 4C $1,075; PCI $13.50. **Circ:** ‡17500.

20041 ■ Missouri Archaeologist
Missouri Archaeological Society
901 S National Ave.
Springfield, MO 65897
Phone: (417)836-3773
Fax: (417)836-6335
Publisher's E-mail: lhaney@missouristate.edu
Journal on archaeology and related topics. **Freq:** Annual. **Trim Size:** 6 x 9. **Cols./Page:** 1. **Col. Width:** 4 3/4 inches. **Col. Depth:** 7 1/4 inches. **Key Personnel:** W. Raymond Wood, Editor; Melody Galen, Associate Editor, Manager, Production. **ISSN:** 0076--9576 (print). **Subscription Rates:** $30 Members; $35 Institutions. **URL:** http://associations.missouristate.edu/mas/journals.html. **Remarks:** Advertising not accepted. **Circ:** Paid 825.

20042 ■ Missouri Grocer
Missouri Grocers Association
315 N Ken Ave.
Springfield, MO 65802
Phone: (417)831-6667
Fax: (417)831-3907
Retail grocery trade newsletter. **Freq:** Monthly. **Print Method:** Offset. **Trim Size:** 8 1/2 x 11. **Cols./Page:** 2. **Col. Width:** 14 picas. **Col. Depth:** 133 agate lines. **Key Personnel:** Janelle Haik, Communications Specialist. **ISSN:** 1522--1008 (print). **URL:** http://www.missourigrocers.com/page.php?id=7. **Ad Rates:** BW $275. **Remarks:** Accepts advertising. **Circ:** (Not Reported).

20043 ■ Numerical Algebra, Control and Optimization
American Institute of Mathematical Sciences
PO Box 2604
Springfield, MO 65801
Phone: (417)886-0559
Fax: (417)886-0559
Publisher's E-mail: general@aimsciences.org
Journal publishing peer-refereed original papers on any non-trivial interplay between numerical linear algebra, control and optimization. **Freq:** Quarterly. **Key Personnel:** Yongzhong Song, Editor-in-Chief. **ISSN:** 2155--3289 (print); **EISSN:** 2155--3297 (electronic). **Subscription Rates:** $815 Individuals print and online; $735 Individuals online. **URL:** http://aimsciences.org/journals/home.jsp?journalID=22. **Circ:** (Not Reported).

20044 ■ Pentecostal Evangel
General Council of the Assemblies of God
1445 Boonville Ave.
Springfield, MO 65802-1894
Phone: (417)862-2781
Free: 877-840-4800
Publisher's E-mail: info@ag.org
Assemblies of God official magazine. **Freq:** Weekly. **Print Method:** Offset. **Trim Size:** 8 x 10 3/4. **Cols./Page:** 4 and 3. **Col. Width:** 20.6 and 27 nonpareils. **Col. Depth:** 130 agate lines. **Key Personnel:** Jodi Harmon, Coordinator, Advertising; Efraim Espinoza, Coordinator; Marc McBride, Art Director; John W. Kennedy, Editor; Scott Harrup, Managing Editor. **ISSN:** 0031--4897 (print). **URL:** http://pentecostalevangel.ag.org. **Formerly**: Today's Pentecostal Evangel. **Ad Rates:** 4C $3,400. **Remarks:** Advertising accepted; rates available upon request. **Circ:** (Not Reported).

20045 ■ Springfield Business Journal: Serving Southwest Missouri
Springfield Business Journal
313 Park Central W
Springfield, MO 65806-1244
Phone: (417)831-3238
Fax: (417)864-4901
Business newspaper. **Freq:** Weekly. **Print Method:** Offset. **Cols./Page:** 4. **Col. Width:** 3 7/16 inches. **Col. Depth:** 13 inches. **Key Personnel:** Dianne Elizabeth Osis, President, Chairperson, phone: (417)831-4461; Jennifer Jackson, Publisher; Eric Olson, Director, Editorial, phone: (417)616-5850. **Subscription Rates:** $89 Individuals; $163 Two years; $229 Individuals 3 years. **Ad Rates:** BW $1,648; 4C $2,023. **Remarks:** Advertising accepted; rates available upon request. **Circ:** Non-paid 800.

20046 ■ The Standard
Missouri State University
901 S National Ave.
Springfield, MO 65897
Phone: (417)836-5000
Fax: (417)836-6334
Free: 800-492-7900
Publisher's E-mail: info@missouristate.edu
Collegiate newspaper. **Founded:** 1912. **Freq:** Semi-weekly Every Tuesday and Friday. **Print Method:** Offset. **Trim Size:** 13 x 22. **Cols./Page:** 6. **Col. Width:** 25 nonpareils. **Col. Depth:** 294 agate lines. **Key Personnel:** Eli Wohlenhaus, Editor-in-Chief. **URL:** http://www.the-standard.org. **Ad Rates:** BW $1,230; PCI $12. **Remarks:** Accepts advertising. **Circ:** Free ‡7000.

20047 ■ Tame Pet: For Urban Pets and their Families
Hudson-Bryce L.L.C.
219 W Commercial St., Ste. 104
Springfield, MO 65803
Magazine focusing on the lives of pets and pet owners. **Freq:** Quarterly. **Key Personnel:** Brooke Kempker, Associate Editor; Connie Rhoades, Editor-in-Chief, Founder; Stephanie Ponder, Director, Editorial, Founder. **URL:** http://tamepetmagswmo.com. **Remarks:** Accepts advertising. **Circ:** (Not Reported).

20048 ■ Transmission Digest: The Automotive Powertrain Industry Journal
MD Publications Inc.
PO Box 2210
Springfield, MO 65801-3917
Phone: (417)866-3917
Fax: (417)866-2781
Free: 800-274-7890
Automotive transmission industry news. **Freq:** Monthly. **Print Method:** Web offset. **Trim Size:** 8 1/8 x 10 7/8. **Cols./Page:** 3. **Col. Width:** 2 1/4 inches. **Col. Depth:** 137 agate lines. **Key Personnel:** Gary Sifford, Editor; Bobby Mace, Publisher. **ISSN:** 0277--8300 (print). **URL:** http://www.transmissiondigest.com. **Ad Rates:** BW $2,975; 4C $4,035. **Remarks:** Accepts advertising. **Circ:** (Not Reported).

20049 ■ Undercar Digest
MD Publications Inc.
PO Box 2210
Springfield, MO 65801-3917
Phone: (417)866-3917
Fax: (417)866-2781
Free: 800-274-7890
Magazine for the undercar service and supply industry. **Freq:** Monthly. **Print Method:** Web Offset. **Trim Size:** 8 1/8 x 10 7/8. **Cols./Page:** 3. **Col. Width:** 2 1/4 inches. **Col. Depth:** 140 agate lines. **Key Personnel:** Jim Wilder, Editor; Gary Sifford, Editor. **ISSN:** 0893--6943 (print). **URL:** http://www.undercardigest.com. **Formerly**: Muffler Digest. **Ad Rates:** BW $3,390; 4C $4,450. **Remarks:** Accepts advertising. **Circ:** (Not Reported).

20050 ■ KBFL-AM - 1060
3000 E Chestnut Expy.
Springfield, MO 65802
Phone: (417)862-3751
Fax: (417)869-7675
Email: websales@radiospringfield.com
Format: Big Band/Nostalgia. **Owner:** Meyer Communications, 3000 E Chestnut Expy., Springfield, MO 65802, Ph: (417)862-3751, Fax: (417)869-7675. **URL:** http://www.radiospringfield.com.

20051 ■ KBFL-FM - 99.9
3000 E Chestnut Expy.
Springfield, MO 65802
Format: Music of Your Life. **Networks:** CBS; Missouri. **Owner:** Meyer Communications, 3000 E Chestnut Expy., Springfield, MO 65802, Ph: (417)862-3751, Fax: (417)869-7675. **Operating Hours**: 6 a.m.-10 p.m. **Wattage**: 3,100. **Ad Rates:** $8-12 for 30 seconds; $16-24 for 60 seconds. **URL:** http://kbflfm.com.

20052 ■ KDEB-TV - 27
2650 E Division St.
Springfield, MO 65803
Phone: (972)373-8800
Email: feedback@fox27.com
Format: Commercial TV. **Networks:** Fox. **Owner:** Quorum Broadcasting of MO., Inc., at above address. **Founded:** 1968. **Formerly**: KMTC-TV. **Operating Hours**: Continuous. **Key Personnel:** Kemp Nichol, Gen. Mgr., VP, kemp@fox27.com; Jim Prestwood, Gen. Sales Mgr., jim@fox27.com; Jack McGee, Operations Mgr.; Polly Van Doren Orr, Sales Mgr., News Dir., dave@fox27.com; Georgetta Lowery, Traffic Mgr., georgetta@fox27.com; Mark Hodorowski, Promotions Mgr., mark@fox27.com; Nancy Bingaman, Dir. of Programs, nancy@fox27.com. **Wattage**: 5,000 ERP. **Ad Rates:** Advertising accepted; rates available upon request. **URL:** http://www.ozarksfirst.com.

20053 ■ KGBX-FM - 105.9
1856 S Glenstone
Springfield, MO 65804
Phone: (417)890-5555
Fax: (417)869-1000
Format: Adult Contemporary. **Operating Hours**: Continuous. **ADI**: Springfield, MO. **Key Personnel:** John Borders, President; Donna Baker, VP. **Wattage**: 50,000. **URL:** http://kgbx.iheart.com.

20054 ■ KGMY-AM - 1400
1856 S Glenstone Ave.
Springfield, MO 65804
Phone: (417)890-5555
Fax: (417)890-5050
Format: Sports. **Founded:** Sept. 18, 2006. **Operating Hours**: Continuous. **ADI**: Springfield, MO. **Key Personnel:** Paul Windisch, Gen. Mgr. **Wattage**: 1,000. **Ad Rates:** Noncommercial.

20055 ■ KKLH-FM - 104.7
2453 E Elm St.
Springfield, MO 65802
Phone: (417)577-7104
Format: Classic Rock. **Owner:** Mid-West Family Broadcasting Group, 201 State St., La Crosse, WI 54602, Ph: (608)782-1230. **Founded:** July 1996. **Operating Hours**: Continuous. **Key Personnel:** John Kimmons, Music Dir., Prog. Dir., johnkimmons@1047thecave.com; Malcolm Hukriede, Dir. of Sales, mhukriede@mwfmarketing.fm. **Wattage**: 34,000. **Ad Rates:** Noncommercial. KOSP, KOMG. **URL:** http://www.1047thecave.com.

20056 ■ KLFJ-AM - 1550
601A E Battlefield St.
PMB 253
Springfield, MO 65807-4865
Phone: (417)831-5535
Fax: (417)831-5544
Email: klfj@dialus.com
Owner: He N' Me Broadcasting, Inc., at above address. **Founded:** 1974. **ADI**: Springfield, MO. **Key Personnel:** Alan Smith, Contact. **Wattage**: 5,000 Daytime; 028 Ni. **Ad Rates:** $12 for 30 seconds; $18 for 60 seconds. **URL:** http://www.talk1550.com.

20057 ■ KOLR-TV - 10
2650 E Division
Springfield, MO 65803
Phone: (417)862-1010
Fax: (417)862-6439
Format: News. **Networks:** CBS. **Owner:** Nexstar Broadcasting Group Inc., 545 E John Carpenter Fwy., Ste. 700, Irving, TX 75062, Ph: (972)373-8800. **Founded:** 1953. **Formerly**: KTTS-TV. **Operating Hours**: Continuous. **ADI**: Springfield, MO. **Key Personnel:** Dean Wasson, Station Mgr. **Wattage**: 360,000 ERP. **Ad Rates:** Noncommercial. **URL:** http://www.ozarksfirst.com.

20058 ■ KOMG-FM - 105.1
319-B E Battlefield
Springfield, MO 65807
Phone: (417)886-5677
Format: Country. **Key Personnel:** Malcolm Hukriede, Dir. of Sales; Keith Abercrombie, Sales Mgr., kabercrombie@mwfmarketing.fm. **URL:** http://www.1051bob.fm.

20059 ■ KOSP-FM
2453 E ELM St.
Springfield, MO 65802
Phone: (417)886-5677
Format: Oldies. **Owner:** Mid-West Family Broadcast Group, 730 Rayovac Dr., Madison, WI 53711, Ph: (608)273-1000, Fax: (608)271-0400. **Founded:** Aug. 1992. **Key Personnel:** Chris Cannon, Contact, chriscannon@star1051.fm; Chris Cannon, Contact, chriscannon@star1051.fm; Summer Stevens, Contact, mikeandsummer@star1051.fm. **Wattage**: 50,000 ERP. **Ad Rates:** Noncommercial.

20060 ■ KOZK-TV - 21
901 S National Ave.
Springfield, MO 65897
Phone: (417)836-3500
Free: 866-684-5695
Email: mail@optv.org
Format: Public TV. **Networks:** Public Broadcasting Service (PBS). **Founded:** 1974. **Operating Hours:** Continuous. **ADI:** Springfield, MO. **Key Personnel:** Rachel Ferguson, Project Mgr.; Tom Carter, Mgr.; Barb McMeekin, Mgr.; Brent Moore, Chief Engineer. **Wattage:** 60,000. **Ad Rates:** Underwriting available. **URL:** http://www.optv.org.

20061 ■ KQRA-FM - 102.1
319 E Battlefield St., Ste. B
Springfield, MO 65807
Format: Alternative/New Music/Progressive. **Owner:** Mid-West Family Broadcasting Group, 730 Rayovac Dr., Madison, WI 53711, Ph: (608)273-1000. **Wattage:** 4,900. **URL:** http://www.q1021.fm.

20062 ■ KSCV-FM - 90.1
1111 S Glenstone Ave., Ste. 3-102
Springfield, MO 65804
Phone: (417)864-0901
Fax: (417)862-7263
Format: Religious. **Owner:** Bott Radio Network, 10550 Barkley, Overland Park, KS 66212, Ph: (913)642-7770, Fax: (913)642-1319, Free: 800-345-2621. **Key Personnel:** Monna Stafford, Regional Mgr., mstafford@bottradionetwork.com; Paul Schneider, Operations Mgr., pschneider@bottradionetwork.com. **URL:** http://www.bottradionetwork.com.

20063 ■ KSFX-TV - 27
2650 E Division St.
Springfield, MO 65801
Owner: Nexstar Broadcasting Group Inc., 545 E John Carpenter Fwy., Ste. 700, Irving, TX 75062, Ph: (972)373-8800. **Key Personnel:** Mark Gordon, Gen. Mgr.; Dave Thomason, Gen. Sales Mgr.; Polly Van Doren, News Dir. **URL:** http://www.nexstar.tv.

20064 ■ KSGF-AM - 1260
2330 W Grand St
Springfield, MO 65802
Phone: (417)447-1837
Fax: (417)865-9643
Format: Talk; News. **Founded:** Sept. 13, 2006. **Key Personnel:** Vince Jericho, Dir. of Programs, vjericho@ksgf.com; Kortni Williams, Producer, kwilliams@ksgf.com; Bill Cantrell, Reporter, bcantrell@ksgf.com. **Ad Rates:** Noncommercial. **URL:** http://advertisingspringfieldradio.com.

20065 ■ KSGF-FM - 104.1
2330 N Grand St.
Springfield, MO 65802
Format: News; Talk. **Key Personnel:** Vince Jericho, Dir. of Programs, vjericho@ksgf.com; Kortni Williams, Producer, kwilliams@ksgf.com. **URL:** http://www.ksgf.com.

20066 ■ KSMU-FM - 91.1; 90.5
901 S National Ave.
Springfield, MO 65897
Phone: (417)836-5878
Fax: (417)836-5889
Free: 800-767-5768
Email: ksmu@missouristate.edu
Format: Public Radio. **Networks:** National Public Radio (NPR); Public Radio International (PRI); BBC World Service. **Owner:** Missouri State University, 901 S National Ave., Springfield, MO 65897, Ph: (417)836-5000, Fax: (417)836-6334, Free: 800-492-7900. **Founded:** 1974. **Formerly:** KSMS-FM. **Operating Hours:** Continuous. **ADI:** Springfield, MO. **Key Personnel:** Tammy Wiley, Gen. Mgr.; Barb McMeekin, Mgr.; Doug Waugh, Chief Engineer; Missy Shelton, News Dir. **Wattage:** 40,000. **Ad Rates:** $12-20 per unit. **URL:** http://www.ksmu.org.

20067 ■ KSPR-TV - 33
999 W Sunshine St.
Springfield, MO 65807
Phone: (417)831-1333
Fax: (417)831-9358
Format: Commercial TV. **Networks:** ABC. **Founded:** 1983. **Operating Hours:** Continuous. **ADI:** Springfield, MO. **Key Personnel:** Angela Moyle, Bus. Mgr.; Mike Scott, News Dir., Div. Dir. **Wattage:** 5,000 KW Visual; 500 KW Aural. **Ad Rates:** Advertising accepted; rates available upon request. **URL:** http://www.kspr.com.

20068 ■ KSPW-FM - 96.5
2330 W Grand St.
Springfield, MO 65802
Phone: (417)865-6614
Fax: (417)865-9643
Format: Contemporary Hit Radio (CHR). **Owner:** Journal Broadcast Corp., 333 W State St., Milwaukee, WI 53203, Ph: (414)332-9611, Fax: (414)967-5400. **Key Personnel:** Rex Hansen, Gen. Mgr., rhansen@journalbroadcastgroup.com; Valorie Knight, Operations Mgr., Prog. Dir., vknight@journalbroadcastgroup.com; Janelle Carter, Sales Mgr., jcarter@journalbroadcastgroup.com. **Ad Rates:** Advertising accepted; rates available upon request. **URL:** http://www.power965.com.

20069 ■ KSWF-FM - 100.5
1856 S Glenstone Ave.
Springfield, MO 65804
Phone: (417)890-5555
Fax: (417)890-5050
Free: 888-633 5452
Format: Country. **Ad Rates:** Advertising accepted; rates available upon request. **URL:** http://www.1005thewolf.com.

20070 ■ KTOZ-FM - 95.5
1856 S Glenstone Ave.
Springfield, MO 65804
Phone: (417)890-5555
Format: Eclectic. **Owner:** Clear Channel Communication, Inc., 200 E Basse Rd., San Antonio, TX 78209, Ph: (210)822-2828, Fax: (210)822-2828. **Founded:** 1984. **Operating Hours:** Continuous. **ADI:** Springfield, MO. **Key Personnel:** Sarah Green, Promotions Dir., sarahgreen@clearchannel.com; Kelli Presley, Sales Mgr. **Wattage:** 50,000. **Ad Rates:** $23-40 for 30 seconds; $28-45 for 60 seconds. **URL:** http://www.alice955.com.

20071 ■ KTTS-FM - 94.7
2330 W Grand
Springfield, MO 65802
Phone: (417)577-7000
Fax: (417)865-9643
Email: icontribute@ktts.com
Format: News. **Owner:** Journal Broadcast Group Inc., 333 W State St., Milwaukee, WI 53203-1305, Ph: (414)332-9611, Fax: (414)967-5400. **Founded:** 1948. **ADI:** Springfield, MO. **Key Personnel:** Curly Clark, Contact, cclark@ktts.com. **Wattage:** 98,000 ERP. **Ad Rates:** Advertising accepted; rates available upon request. Combined advertising rates available with KTTF-AM and KSPW-FM. **URL:** http://www.ktts.com.

20072 ■ KTXR-FM - 101.3
3000 E Chestnut Expy.
Springfield, MO 65802
Phone: (417)862-3751
Fax: (417)869-7675
Email: manager@radiospringfield.com
Format: Adult Contemporary; Full Service. **Networks:** NBC. **Owner:** Meyer Communications, 3000 E Chestnut Expy., Springfield, MO 65802, Ph: (417)862-3751, Fax: (417)869-7675. **Founded:** 1962. **Operating Hours:** Continuous. **Wattage:** 100,000. **Ad Rates:** $20-24 for 30 seconds; $30-32 for 60 seconds. **URL:** http://www.ktxrfm.com.

20073 ■ KWFC-FM - 89.1
PO Box 8900
Springfield, MO 65801-8900
Phone: (417)869-0891
Fax: (417)866-7525
Free: 800-658-0353
Email: info@kwfc.org
Format: Southern Gospel; News. **Networks:** USA Radio. **Owner:** Baptist Bible College Inc., 538 Venard Rd., Clarks Summit, PA 18411. **Founded:** Apr. 09, 1969. **Operating Hours:** Continuous. **ADI:** Springfield, MO. **Wattage:** 98,000. **Ad Rates:** Noncommercial. **URL:** http://www.kwfc.org.

20074 ■ KWND-FM - 88.3
2550 S Campbell Ave., Ste. 100
Springfield, MO 65807
Phone: (417)889-0883
Fax: (417)886-8656
Format: Contemporary Christian. **Key Personnel:** Kathleen Birdsong, Office Mgr.; Chalmer Harper, Station Mgr. **Ad Rates:** Noncommercial. **URL:** http://88.3thewind.com.

20075 ■ KWTO-AM - 560
3000 E Chestnut Expy.
Springfield, MO 65802
Phone: (417)862-3751
Fax: (417)869-7675
Format: Talk; News. **Networks:** ABC. **Owner:** Meyer Communications, 3000 E Chestnut Expy., Springfield, MO 65802, Ph: (417)862-3751, Fax: (417)869-7675. **Founded:** 1933. **Operating Hours:** Continuous. **ADI:** Springfield, MO. **Local Programs:** *Ask the Professionals*, Monday Tuesday Wednesday Thursday Friday 10:00 a.m. - 11:00 a.m.; 2:00 p.m. - 4:00 p.m.; *MorningLine Weekends*, Monday Tuesday Wednesday Thursday Friday 7:00 a.m. - 9:00 a.m. **Wattage:** 5,000. **Ad Rates:** Advertising accepted; rates available upon request. **URL:** http://www.newstalk560.com.

20076 ■ KWTO-FM - 98.7
3000 E Chestnut Expy.
Springfield, MO 65802
Phone: (417)862-3751
Fax: (417)869-7675
Format: Sports. **Networks:** Mutual Broadcasting System. **Owner:** Meyer Communications, 3000 E Chestnut Expy., Springfield, MO 65802, Ph: (417)862-3751, Fax: (417)869-7675. **Operating Hours:** Continuous. **ADI:** Springfield, MO. **Wattage:** 96,000. **Ad Rates:** Noncommercial. **URL:** http://jock987.com.

20077 ■ KXUS-FM - 97.3
1856 S Glenstone Ave.
Springfield, MO 65804
Phone: (417)890-5555
Format: Classic Rock. **ADI:** Springfield, MO. **Key Personnel:** Kelli Presley, Contact, kellipresley@iheartmedia.com. **Wattage:** 100,000. **Ad Rates:** Advertising accepted; rates available upon request. **URL:** http://www.us97.com.

20078 ■ KYTV-TV - 3
999 W Sunshine St.
Springfield, MO 65807
Phone: (417)268-3000
Fax: (417)268-3100
Format: Commercial TV. **Networks:** NBC. **Owner:** Schurz Communications Inc., 1301 E Douglas Rd., Mishawaka, IN 46545, Ph: (574)247-7237. **Founded:** 1953. **Operating Hours:** Continuous; 75% network, 25% local. **ADI:** Springfield, MO. **Key Personnel:** Brian McDonough, Gen. Mgr.; Kevin McNally, Operations Mgr.; Angela Moyle, Bus. Mgr.; Scott Brady, News Dir.; Dan McGrane, Dir. of Mktg. **Local Programs:** *Ozarks Today.* **Ad Rates:** Advertising accepted; rates available upon request. **URL:** http://www.ky3.com.

20079 ■ Mediacom
1533 S Enterprise
Springfield, MO 65804
Owner: Mediacom, One Mediacom Way, Mediacom Park, NY 10918. **Founded:** 1979. **Formerly:** AT&T Broadband. **Key Personnel:** Arnold Cool, Gen. Mgr., acool@mediacomcc.com; Carl Dyson, Tech. Mgr., cdyson@mediacomcc.com; Steve Davis, Producer, sdavis@mediacomcc.com; Darryl Chaney, Mktg. Mgr., dchaney@mediacomcc.com. **Cities Served:** Battlefield, Greene County, Springfield, Missouri: subscribing households 54,000; 241 channels; 8 community access channels; 80 hours per week community access programming. **URL:** http://mediacomcable.com.

ST. LOUIS

20080 ■ Current Analytical Chemistry
Bentham Science Publishers Ltd.
c/o Samuel Achilefu, Ed.-in-Ch.
Washington University
4525 Scott Avenue
St. Louis, MO 63110-1030
Publisher's E-mail: subscriptions@benthamscience.org

Circulation: ★ = AAM; △ or • = BPA; ♦ = CAC; ❑ = VAC; ⊕ = PO Statement; ‡ = Publisher's Report; Boldface figures = sworn; Light figures = estimated.

Journal publishing authoritative reviews, written by experts in the field on all the most recent advances in analytical chemistry. **Freq:** Quarterly. **Key Personnel:** S. Achilefu, Board Member. **ISSN:** 1573-4110 (print); **EISSN:** 1875-6727 (electronic). **Subscription Rates:** $1680 Institutions corporate; print or online; $780 Institutions academic; print or online; $2020 Institutions corporate; print and online; $860 Institutions academic; print and online; $360 Individuals print. **URL:** http://benthamscience.com/journal/index.php?journalID=cac. **Remarks:** Accepts advertising. **Circ:** (Not Reported).

STEELVILLE

SEC MO. Crawford Co. 80 mi. SW of Saint Louis. Manufactures charcoal, shoes. Oak timber; iron mines. Agriculture. Fruits; fruit farms.

20081 ■ Steelville Star/Crawford Mirror
Steelville Star/Crawford Mirror
106 S 1st St.
Steelville, MO 65565
Phone: (573)775-5454
Fax: (573)775-2668
Publisher's E-mail: stvlstar@misn.com
Newspaper with a Republican orientation. **Freq:** Weekly. **Print Method:** Offset. **Trim Size:** 11 1/4 x 13 1/2. **Cols./Page:** 5. **Col. Width:** 26 nonpareils. **Col. Depth:** 182 agate lines. **Key Personnel:** Chris Case, Editor; Rob Viehman, Publisher. **URL:** http://www.threeriverspublishing.com/TRP3/index.php?option=com_contact&view=contact&id=10:steelville-star-crawford-mirror&catid=12&Itemid=3. **Mailing address:** PO Box BG, Steelville, MO 65565. **Remarks:** Accepts advertising. **Circ:** Paid ‡2074.

STOCKTON

SW MO. Cedar Co. 50 mi. NW of Springfield. Manufactures gearboxes, textiles. Black walnut processing plant. Stock, dairy, poultry, grain farms.

20082 ■ Cedar County Republican
Cedar County Republican
No. 26 Public Sq.
Stockton, MO 65785
Phone: (417)276-4211
Fax: (417)276-5760
Publisher's E-mail: news@cedarrepublican.com
Newspaper. **Freq:** Weekly (Wed.). **Print Method:** Offset. **Cols./Page:** 6. **Col. Width:** 1.83 inches. **Col. Depth:** 294 agate lines. **Key Personnel:** Robert Jackson, Editor; Marilyn Ellis, Manager, Advertising, General Manager; Becky Jones, Office Manager. **Subscription Rates:** $38.55 Individuals print and online; $2.65 Individuals /month - online only. **URL:** http://www.cedarrepublican.com. **Mailing address:** PO Box 1018, Stockton, MO 65785. **Ad Rates:** BW $1246. **Remarks:** Accepts advertising. **Circ:** (Not Reported).

20083 ■ KRWP-FM - 107.7
1225 S St., Ste. B
Stockton, MO 65785
Phone: (417)276-5253
Format: Country; Sports. **Owner:** Cumulus Media Inc., 3280 Peachtree Rd. NW, Ste. 2300, Atlanta, GA 30305-2455, Ph: (404)949-0700, Fax: (404)949-0740. **Founded:** Jan. 25, 1999. **Wattage:** 11,700 ERP. **Ad Rates:** Advertising accepted; rates available upon request. **URL:** http://www.krwp1077.com.

SULLIVAN

E. MO. Franklin Co. 68 mi. SW of Saint Louis. Manufactures shoes, piston rings, lumber products, precision metal parts, tool, tool dies. Timber. Iron mining. Diversified farming. Wheat, corn, dairying.

20084 ■ The Sullivan Independent News
Sullivan Independent News
411 Scottsdale
Sullivan, MO 63080-1307
Newspaper. **Freq:** Weekly (Wed.). **Print Method:** Offset. **Trim Size:** 8 1/2 x 11. **Cols./Page:** 5. **Col. Width:** 24 nonpareils. **Col. Depth:** 224 agate lines. **USPS:** 525-240. **Subscription Rates:** $34 Individuals in Franklin, Crawford and Washington Counties; $40 Individuals other Missouri Counties; $49 Out of state. **URL:** http://www.mysullivannews.com. **Ad Rates:** BW $380; 4C $560; PCI $6. **Remarks:** Advertising accepted; rates available upon request. **Circ:** Combined ‡6200.

20085 ■ Fidelity Communications Co.
64 N Clark St.
Sullivan, MO 63080
Phone: (573)364-5206
Fax: (573)364-0620
Free: 800-392-8070
Email: helpdesk@fidelitycommunications.com
Founded: 1940. **Key Personnel:** Andrew Davis, Gen. Mgr.; Mike Davis, COO, Sr. VP; John Davis, President; John Colbert, Sr. VP; John Bell, CFO, VP of Fin. **Cities Served:** Gerald, New Haven, Owensville, Rolla, Salem, Missouri; 276 channels. **URL:** http://www.fidelitycommunications.com.

20086 ■ KTUI-AM - 1560
64 N Clark St.
Sullivan, MO 63080
Fax: (573)468-5440
Free: 800-392-8070
Email: custserv@fidelitycommunications.com
Format: News; Talk. **Networks:** People's Network; UPI; Missouri. **Owner:** Fidelity Communication Co., 64 N Clark St., Sullivan, MO 63080, Fax: (573)468-5440, Free: 800-392-8070. **Founded:** 1966. **Operating Hours:** Sunrise-sunset. **ADI:** St. Louis, MO (Mt. Vernon, IL). **Key Personnel:** John Colbert, President; John C. Rice, Sports Dir., Gen. Mgr.; Sam Scott, Dir. of Programs; Perry Allen, Music Dir. **Wattage:** 1,000. **Ad Rates:** $9-11 for 30 seconds; $14-17 for 60 seconds. **URL:** http://www.fidelitycommunications.com.

20087 ■ KTUI-FM - 102.1
64 N Clark St.
Sullivan, MO 63080
Phone: (573)468-8081
Fax: (573)468-5440
Free: 800-392-8070
Email: helpdesk@fidelitycommunications.com
Format: Country; Sports. **Networks:** St. Louis Cardinals; UPI; Missouri. **Owner:** Fidelity Communication Co., 64 N Clark St., Sullivan, MO 63080, Fax: (573)468-5440, Free: 800-392-8070. **Founded:** 1981. **Operating Hours:** Continuous. **ADI:** St. Louis, MO (Mt. Vernon, IL). **Key Personnel:** John C. Rice, Sports Dir., Gen. Mgr.; Perry Allen, Music Dir.; Sam Scott, Dir. of Programs. **Wattage:** 3,000. **Ad Rates:** $11-15 for 30 seconds; $17-21 for 60 seconds. **URL:** http://www.fidelitycommunications.com.

SWEET SPRINGS

20088 ■ Cass County Cable Inc.
PO Box 293
Sweet Springs, MO 65351
Fax: (800)533-3079
Founded: Aug. 01, 1990. **Key Personnel:** Daryl Granzella, Mgr. **Cities Served:** Belton, Hume, Newtown, Missouri.

TARKIO

NW MO. Atchison Co. 55 mi. N. of Saint Joseph. Residential.

20089 ■ KRSS-FM - 93.5
23979 Hwy. 136
Tarkio, MO 64491
Phone: (660)736-4321
Fax: (660)736-5789
Free: 866-500-5447
Format: Religious. **Operating Hours:** Continuous. **Ad Rates:** Noncommercial.

THAYER

S. MO. Oregon Co. 130 mi. SE of Springfield. Manufactures feed, fertilizer. Timber. Diversified farming. Grain, fruits. Livestock.

20090 ■ KALM-AM - 1290
PO Box 15
Thayer, MO 65791
Phone: (417)264-7211
Fax: (417)264-7212
Email: news@kkountry.com
Format: Agricultural; Information; Sports. **Simulcasts:** KWPM, KUKU. **Networks:** ABC. **Owner:** Ozark Radio Network Inc., 11 Court Sq., West Plains, MO 65775, Ph: (417)256-2147, Fax: (417)256-1531. **Founded:** 1953. **Operating Hours:** Sunrise-sunset. **Key Personnel:** Bob Eckman, Contact, eckman@centurytel.net; Lynn Hobbs, Contact, lhobbs@centurytel.net. **Wattage:** 1,000 Day; 056 Night. **Ad Rates:** $3.70-15 for 30 seconds; $6.95-21.35 for 60 seconds. Combined advertising rates available with KAMS-FM; $5.70-6.65 for 30 seconds; $6.95-8.60 for 60 seconds. **URL:** http://www.kkountry.com.

20091 ■ KAMS-FM - 95.1
PO Box 15
Thayer, MO 65791
Phone: (417)264-7211
Fax: (417)264-7212
Email: news@kkountry.com
Format: Country. **Networks:** ABC. **Owner:** E-Communication, LLC, at above address. **Operating Hours:** Continuous. **Key Personnel:** Peggy Underwood, Contact, peggy@kkountry.com. **Wattage:** 100,000. **Ad Rates:** Noncommercial. **URL:** http://www.kkountry.com.

TIPTON

C. MO. Moniteau Co. 27 mi. E. of Sedalia. Manufactures textiles, shoes, metal fabricators, furniture. Agriculture. Livestock. Wheat, oats, soybeans, corn.

20092 ■ Leader-Statesman
Vernon Publishing Inc.
113 E Morgan St.
Tipton, MO 65081
Phone: (660)433-5721
Local newspaper. **Freq:** Weekly (Thurs.). **Print Method:** Offset. **Cols./Page:** 6. **Col. Width:** 2 1/16 inches. **Col. Depth:** 21 inches. **Key Personnel:** Bryan Jones, Managing Editor; Dane Vernon, Publisher. **USPS:** 307-700. **Mailing address:** PO Box U, Tipton, MO 65081. **Ad Rates:** GLR $0.30; BW $441; 4C $591; SAU $3.50. **Remarks:** Accepts advertising. **Circ:** ‡3200.

20093 ■ The Tipton Times
Vernon Publishing Inc.
113 E Morgan St.
Tipton, MO 65081
Phone: (660)433-5721
Newspaper with a Democratic orientation. **Freq:** Weekly (Thurs.). **Print Method:** Offset. **Cols./Page:** 6. **Col. Width:** 2 1/16 inches. **Col. Depth:** 21 inches. **Key Personnel:** Becky Holloway, Editor, phone: (660)433-5721; Dane Vernon, Publisher, phone: (573)378-0418. **USPS:** 631-580. **Subscription Rates:** $34 Individuals in County; $42 Elsewhere in Missouri; $45 Out of state; $34 Out of state website access only. **URL:** http://www.vernonpublishing.com/Times/News. **Mailing address:** PO Box U, Tipton, MO 65081. **Ad Rates:** GLR $.30; BW $441; 4C $591; SAU $3.50; PCI $4.25. **Remarks:** Accepts advertising. **Circ:** Combined 11375.

TRENTON

N. MO. Grundy Co. 85 mi. NE of Kansas City. Trenton Junior College. Rock quarries. Manufactures concrete products, chemical fertilizers, radiators, windows. Sawmill. Cannery. Stock, dairy, poultry, grain farms.

20094 ■ Trenton Republican-Times
W.B. Rogers Printing Company Inc.
122 E 8th St.
Trenton, MO 64683-0548
Phone: (660)359-2212
Fax: (660)359-4414
Publisher's E-mail: rtimes@lyn.net
General newspaper. **Freq:** Monday - Friday. **Print Method:** Offset. **Cols./Page:** 6. **Col. Width:** 25 nonpareils. **Col. Depth:** 294 agate lines. **Key Personnel:** Diane Lowrey, Editor, phone: (660)359-2212. **Subscription Rates:** $64.64 Individuals in Grundy and surrounding counties; $59.25 Individuals local senior citizen; $73.79 Individuals state senior citizen; $90 Out of state 1 year. **URL:** http://republican-times.com/subscribe/#.V1eZbzV94dU. **Ad Rates:** BW $567; 4C $777; SAU $4.50; PCI $4.50. **Remarks:** Accepts advertising. **Circ:** (Not Reported).

20095 ■ KGOZ-FM - 101.7
804 Main
Trenton, MO 64683
Phone: (660)359-2261
Fax: (660)359-4126
Email: anniversary@kttn.com
Format: Hot Country. **Networks:** Jones Satellite. **Owner:** Par Broadcasting Group. **Founded:** 1954. **Operating Hours:** Continuous. **ADI:** Kansas City, MO (Lawrence, KS). **Key Personnel:** John Anthony, Gen.

Mgr; Jeanette Houck, Contact. **Wattage:** 15,000. **Ad Rates:** $8.50-15 for 30 seconds. Combined advertising rates available with KTTN-FM/KTTN-AM. **Mailing address:** PO Box 307, Trenton, MO 64683. **URL:** http://www.kttn.com.

20096 ■ KTTN-AM - 1600
804 Main
Trenton, MO 64683
Fax: (660)359-4126
Free: 888-FOR-KTTN
Email: kttnamfm@grm.net
Format: Soft Rock. **Simulcasts:** 7-8am. **Networks:** AP. **Owner:** Luehrs Broadcasting Inc., at above address. **Founded:** 1955. **Operating Hours**: Continuous. **ADI**: Kansas City, MO (Lawrence, KS). **Key Personnel:** John Anthony, Owner. **Ad Rates:** $3.75-15 for 30 seconds; $8.75-20 for 60 seconds. KTTN-FM. **URL:** http://www.kttn.com.

20097 ■ KTTN-FM - 92.3
804 Main St.
Trenton, MO 64683
Phone: (660)359-2261
Fax: (660)359-4126
Free: 888-367-5886
Email: kttnamfm@grm.net
Format: Classical. **Networks:** Jones Satellite; Brownfield; Missouri. **Owner:** Par Broadcasting Group. **Founded:** 1978. **Operating Hours**: Continuous. **ADI**: Kansas City, MO (Lawrence, KS). **Key Personnel:** John Anthony, Owner. **Local Programs**: *Open Line.* **Wattage**: 25,000. **Ad Rates:** $9.50-15 for 30 seconds; $14.50-20 for 60 seconds. Combined advertising rates available with KTTN-AM, KGOZ-FM. **URL:** http://tunein.com.

TROY

20098 ■ Lincoln County Journal
Lakeway Publishers Inc.
20 Business Park Dr.
Troy, MO 63379
Phone: (636)528-9550
Publication E-mail: lcjpub@lcs.net
Community newspaper. **Freq:** Weekly (Thurs.). **Print Method:** Offset. **Trim Size:** 10 x 16. **Cols./Page:** 5. **Col. Width:** 11.5 picas. **Col. Depth:** 16 inches. **USPS:** 313-420. **Subscription Rates:** $65 Out of area full access (print and digital); $40 Individuals /year full digital access. **URL:** http://www.lincolncountyjournal.com. **Remarks:** Accepts advertising. **Circ:** (Not Reported).

20099 ■ Troy Free Press
Troy Free Press
20 Business Park Dr.
Troy, MO 63379
Fax: (636)528-9550
Community newspaper. **Freq:** Weekly. **Print Method:** Offset; accept mats. **Cols./Page:** 6. **Col. Depth:** 21 1/2 INS. **Subscription Rates:** $29.50 Individuals full access. **URL:** http://www.troyfreepress.com/wp-content/themes/citizentribune/index.html. **Ad Rates:** BW $348.30; PCI $2.70. **Remarks:** Color advertising accepted; rates available upon request. **Circ:** (Not Reported).

UNITY VILLAGE

20100 ■ Daily Word
Unity School of Christianity
1901 NW Blue Pkwy.
Unity Village, MO 64065-0001
Phone: (816)524-3550
Fax: (816)251-3554
Publisher's E-mail: unity@unityonline.org
Religious magazine. Prints edition in Spanish, La Palabra Diaria; also prints edition in large type. **Freq:** Bimonthly. **Print Method:** Letterpress and offset. **Trim Size:** 4 1/8 x 5 1/2. **Cols./Page:** 1. **Col. Width:** 38 nonpareils. **Col. Depth:** 66 agate lines. **ISSN:** 0011--5525 (print). **Subscription Rates:** $20.95 Individuals digital and print; $9.95 Individuals digital; $15.95 Individuals print. **URL:** http://www.dailyword.com. **Remarks:** Accepts advertising. **Circ:** (Not Reported).

UNIVERSITY CITY

20101 ■ The 2River View
Sister 2River Street Irregular Press
7474 Drexel Dr.
University City, MO 63130
Phone: (314)721-7393
Publisher's E-mail: long@2river.org
Literary magazine containing poetry, art, and theory, including only 10 authors each issue. **Freq:** Quarterly. **Key Personnel:** Richard Long, Publisher, Editor. **ISSN:** 1536-2086 (print). **URL:** http://www.2river.org. **Circ:** (Not Reported).

VANDALIA

NEC MO. Ralls Co. 30 mi. S. of Hannibal. Manufactures refractories, fire-clay products, textiles. Clay pits. Stock, poultry, fruit, grain farms.

20102 ■ Vandalia Leader-Press
The Vandalia Leader
PO Box 239
Vandalia, MO 63382
Phone: (573)594-2222
Fax: (573)594-6741
Publisher's E-mail: vandalialeader@lcs.net
Newspaper with a Democratic orientation. **Freq:** Weekly (Wed.). **Print Method:** Offset. **Cols./Page:** 6. **Col. Width:** 24 nonpareils. **Col. Depth:** 129 agate lines. **Key Personnel:** Ron Schott, General Manager. **Subscription Rates:** $32 Individuals print and online. **URL:** http://www.vandalialeader.com. **Ad Rates:** GLR $3.25; BW $419.25; 4C $519.25; SAU $3; PCI $3.25. **Remarks:** Advertising accepted; rates available upon request. **Circ:** (Not Reported).

20103 ■ KKAC-FM - 104.3
400 S Lindell
Vandalia, MO 63382
Format: Country. **Key Personnel:** Randy Wachter, Engineer, randy@knsx.com. **Ad Rates:** Noncommercial. **URL:** http://www.actioncountry.com.

VERSAILLES

C. MO. Morgan Co. 47 mi. SE of Sedalia. Trout fisheries; coal mines; timber. Diversified farming.

20104 ■ KTKS-FM - 95.1
PO Box 409
Versailles, MO 65084
Phone: (573)378-5669
Fax: (573)378-6640
Format: Country. **Networks:** CNN Radio. **Owner:** Twin Lakes Communications Inc., 201 W Gore Ave., Gainesboro, TN 38562, Ph: (931)476-2151. **Founded:** Feb. 1988. **Formerly**: KLGS-FM. **Operating Hours**: Continuous. **Key Personnel:** Jay Fisher, Gen. Mgr.; Sheryl Lerman, Gen. Sales Mgr.; J.T. Gerlt, Dir. of Programs, jt@lakeradio.net. **Wattage**: 12,500. **Ad Rates:** Noncommercial. **URL:** http://www.lakeradio.com.

WARRENSBURG

W. MO. Johnson Co. 52 mi. E. of Kansas City. Central Missouri State University. Manufactures textiles, chemicals, machinery, lawnmowers. Hatcheries; coal mines. Stock, dairy, poultry, grain farms.

20105 ■ Journal of Institute of Justice and International Studies
University of Central Missouri James C. Kirkpatrick Library Special Collections
Dept. of Criminal Justice
Humphreys 300
Warrensburg, MO 64093
Phone: (660)543-8913
Fax: (660)543-8306
Publication E-mail: cjinst@ucmo.edu
Journal that publishes reports on international crime including corrections, media coverage, public policy, counter terrorism, and civil liberties. **Freq:** Annual. **ISSN:** 1538--7909 (print). **Subscription Rates:** Free to qualified subscribers. **URL:** http://www.ucmo.edu/cjinst/Journal.html. **Remarks:** Advertising not accepted. **Circ:** (Not Reported).

20106 ■ Muleskinner
University of Central Missouri James C. Kirkpatrick Library Special Collections
PO Box 800
Warrensburg, MO 64093
Phone: (660)543-4111
Fax: (660)543-8517
Free: 877-729-8266
Publication E-mail: muleskinner@ucmo.edu
Collegiate newspaper, weekly. **Freq:** Weekly during the academic yr. **Print Method:** Offset. **Cols./Page:** 6. **Col. Width:** 21 nonpareils. **Col. Depth:** 126 agate lines. **Key Personnel:** Leah Wankum, Managing Editor; James Watson, Business Manager. **URL:** http://muleskinner.net. **Remarks:** Accepts advertising. **Circ:** 6000.

20107 ■ The Pentagon: A Mathematics Magazine for Students
Kappa Mu Epsilon
c/o Dr. Rhonda McKee, President
Dept. of Mathematics and Computer Science
University of Central Missouri
Warrensburg, MO 64093
Phone: (660)543-8929
Fax: (417)865-9599
Journal covering mathematics for undergraduates. **Freq:** Semiannual December & May. **Key Personnel:** Don Tosh, Business Manager. **ISSN:** 0031--4870 (print). **URL:** http://www.kappamuepsilon.org/pages/a/pentagon.php. **Remarks:** Advertising not accepted. **Circ:** (Not Reported).

20108 ■ World Safety Journal
World Safety Organization
PO Box 518
Warrensburg, MO 64093
Phone: (660)747-3132
Fax: (660)747-2647
Publisher's E-mail: info@worldsafety.org
Journal discussing practice skills, arts, and technologies of safety and accident prevention. **Freq:** Semiannual. **ISSN:** 1015- 5589 (print). **Subscription Rates:** Included in membership. **URL:** http://worldsafety.org/wso-world-safety-journal/. **Remarks:** Accepts advertising. **Circ:** (Not Reported).

20109 ■ KAYQ-FM - 97.1
712 Chaucer Ln.
Warrensburg, MO 64093
Phone: (660)438-7343
Fax: (660)438-7159
Format: Country. **Networks:** Jones Satellite; AP. **Owner:** Valkyrie Broadcasting Inc., at above address. **Founded:** Mar. 10, 1980. **Operating Hours:** Continuous. **ADI:** Springfield, MO. **Key Personnel:** Joey Anderson, Gen. Mgr.; Glenna Thrasher, Sales Mgr. **Wattage**: 6,000. **Ad Rates:** Noncommercial.

20110 ■ KMOS-TV - 6
University of Central Missouri
Warrensburg, MO 64093
Phone: (660)543-4155
Email: kmos@kmos.org
Format: Public TV. **Networks:** Public Broadcasting Service (PBS). **Owner:** University of Central Missouri, 108 West South St., Warrensburg, MO 64093. **Founded:** 1979. **Operating Hours**: 6:00 a.m.-midnight. **ADI**: Columbia-Jefferson City, MO. **Wattage:** 100,000. **Ad Rates:** Noncommercial. **Mailing address:** PO Box 800, Warrensburg, MO 64093. **URL:** http://www.kmos.org.

20111 ■ KOKO-AM - 1450
PO Box 398
Warrensburg, MO 64093
Phone: (660)747-9191
Fax: (660)747-5611
Format: Oldies. **Simulcasts:** Some local sports. **Networks:** ABC; Brownfield. **Owner:** D & H Media LLC, at above address. **Operating Hours:** Continuous. **Wattage**: 1,000. **Ad Rates:** $5.50-13.47 for 30 seconds; $8.25-19.06 for 60 seconds. KWKJ-FM. **URL:** http://www.warrensburgradio.com.

20112 ■ KTBG-FM - 90.9
Wood 11
Warrensburg, MO 64093
Fax: (660)543-8863
Free: 866-909-2743
Format: Eclectic; News. **Networks:** National Public Radio (NPR). **Owner:** Board of Governors, Central Missouri State University. **Founded:** 1962. **Operating Hours**: Continuous%; 55% network, 45% local. **Key Personnel:** Jon Hart, Contact, Music Dir., VP; Jon Hart,

Circulation: ★ = AAM; △ or • = BPA; ♦ = CAC; ❏ = VAC; ⊕ = PO Statement; ‡ = Publisher's Report; Boldface figures = sworn; Light figures = estimated.

Contact. **Wattage:** 100,000. **Ad Rates:** Noncommercial. **URL:** http://bridge909.org.

20113 ■ KWKJ-FM - 98.5
800 PCA Rd.
Warrensburg, MO 64093
Phone: (660)747-9191
Format: Country. **Wattage:** 10,000. **Ad Rates:** Advertising accepted; rates available upon request. **Mailing address:** PO Box 398, Warrensburg, MO 64093. **URL:** http://warrensburgradio.com.

WARRENTON

E. MO. Warren Co. 55 mi. W. of Saint Louis. Limestone. Copper wire bars, glass tempering, sheet metal plant. Coal mines; fire clay pits. Agriculture. Grain.

20114 ■ KFAV-FM - 99.9
PO Box 220
Warrenton, MO 63383
Phone: (636)377-2300
Free: 877-259-7373
Format: Country. **Networks:** USA Radio. **Owner:** Kaspar Broadcasting Co., PO Box 220, Warrenton, MO 63383, Ph: (636)377-2300, Free: 877-259-7373. **Founded:** Dec. 06, 1991. **Operating Hours**: Continuous. **Key Personnel:** Mike Thomas, Contact; Mike Thomas, Contact; Steve Kaspar, Contact, skaspar999@yahoo.com. **Wattage:** 10,500. **Ad Rates:** $36 for 60 seconds. **URL:** http://www.kfavradio.com.

20115 ■ KWRE-AM - 730
PO Box 220
Warrenton, MO 63383
Phone: (636)377-2300
Fax: (636)456-8767
Free: 877-259-7373
Format: Country. **Networks:** USA Radio. **Owner:** Kaspar Broadcasting Company of Missouri Inc., PO Box 220, Warrenton, MO 63383-1330, Ph: (636)377-2300, Fax: (636)456-8767, Free: 877-259-7373. **Founded:** 1949. **Operating Hours**: 5 a.m.-11 p.m. Mon.-Sat.; 7 a.m.-8 p.m. Sun. **ADI**: St. Louis, MO (Mt. Vernon, IL). **Key Personnel:** Mark Becker, Sales Mgr. **Local Programs**: *Country Store*, Monday Tuesday Wednesday Thursday Friday Saturday 12:30 p.m. - 1:30 p.m. 9:10 a.m. - 10:00 a.m.; *World News*, Monday Tuesday Wednesday Thursday Friday Saturday Sunday 5:00 a.m. - 5:55 a.m. 5:00 a.m. - 6:00 a.m.; 2:00 p.m. - 3:00 p.m.; 6:00 p.m. 3:00 p.m. - 4:35 p.m.; 5:00 p.m. - 6:00 p.m.; *Live Wire*, Monday Tuesday Wednesday Thursday Friday 9:10 a.m. - 10:00 a.m. **Wattage**: 1,000 Day ; 120 Night. **Ad Rates:** Advertising accepted; rates available upon request. **URL:** http://www.kwre.com.

WARSAW

WC MO. Benton Co. 33 mi. S. of Sedalia. Vacation center.

20116 ■ Benton County Enterprise
Benton County Enterprise Inc.
PO Box 128
Warsaw, MO 65355
Phone: (660)438-6312
Fax: (660)438-3464
Local newspaper. **Freq:** Weekly. **Print Method:** 13 x 21 1/2. Offset. **Trim Size:** 13 3/4 x 22 3/4. **Cols./Page:** 6. **Col. Width:** 2 inches. **Key Personnel:** James Mahlon White, Publisher. **Subscription Rates:** $28 Individuals Benton and surrounding counties; $38 Out of area. **URL:** http://www.bentoncountyenterprise.com. **Ad Rates:** BW $485; 4C $685; SAU $3.85; PCI $5. **Remarks:** Accepts advertising. **Circ:** (Not Reported).

WASHINGTON

E. MO. Franklin Co. On Missouri River, 50 mi. W. of Saint Louis. Manufactures vinyl products, piston rings, transformers, metal and plastic fabrication, aircraft and automobile parts, footwear, plastics. Diversified farming. Dairy products. Corn, wheat, soybeans. Livestock.

20117 ■ Washington Missourian
Missourian Publishing Co.
14 W Main St.
Washington, MO 63090
Phone: (636)239-7701
Fax: (636)239-0915
Free: 888-239-7701
Publication E-mail: washnews@emissourian.com
Newspaper with a Democratic orientation. **Freq:** Semiweekly (Wed. and on the weekend). **Print Method:** Offset. **Cols./Page:** 6. **Col. Width:** 21 nonpareils. **Col. Depth:** 294 agate lines. **Key Personnel:** Bill Miller, Editor; Bill Battle, Editor; Ed Pruneau, Managing Editor. **USPS:** 667-820. **Subscription Rates:** $50 Individuals Franklin County; $85 Out of area; $106 Out of state non-local. **URL:** http://www.emissourian.com. **Mailing address:** PO Box 336, Washington, MO 63090. **Ad Rates:** BW $999.75; 4C $1,239.75; SAU $7.75. **Remarks:** Accepts advertising. **Circ:** (Not Reported).

KGNA-FM - See Arnold

KGNN-FM - See Salem

KGNV-FM - See Gray Summit

20118 ■ KLPW-AM - 1220
PO Box 623
Washington, MO 63090
Phone: (636)583-5155
Fax: (636)583-1644
Format: Talk. **Networks:** ABC. **Founded:** 1954. **Operating Hours**: Continuous; 33% local; 66% network. **Key Personnel:** Jeff Hill, Sales Mgr., jeff@klpw.com. **Wattage**: 1,000 Day; 126 Night. **Ad Rates:** $15 for 30 seconds; $19 for 60 seconds. Combined advertising rates available with KLPW-FM. **URL:** http://www.klpw.com.

20119 ■ KSLQ-FM - 104.5
511 W Fifth St.
Washington, MO 63090
Phone: (636)239-6800
Format: Country. **ADI**: Greenville-New Bern-Washington, NC. **Wattage:** 3,000. **Ad Rates:** Advertising accepted; rates available upon request. **URL:** http://www.kslq.co.

20120 ■ KWMO-AM
511 W Fifth St.
Washington, MO 63090
URL: http://www.sportskrap.com/.

20121 ■ KYMC-FM - 89.7
PO Box 187
Washington, MO 63090
Phone: (314)367-4646
Format: Full Service; Alternative/New Music/Progressive; Religious. **Owner:** West County YMCA, 16464 Burkhardt Pl., Chesterfield, MO 63017, Ph: (636)532-6515. **Founded:** 1977. **Operating Hours:** Continuous. **Key Personnel:** Natalie Hall, Prog. Dir., Station Mgr., nhall@ymcastlouis.org. **Wattage:** 120. **Ad Rates:** Underwriting available. **URL:** http://www.goodnewsvoice.org.

WAYNESVILLE

SC MO. Pulaski Co. 70 mi. NE of Springfield. Residential.

20122 ■ KJPW-AM - 1390
PO Box D
Waynesville, MO 65583
Phone: (573)336-4913
Fax: (573)336-2222
Email: kjpw@regionalradio.com
Format: Country. **Simulcasts:** KJPW-FM. **Networks:** NBC; Missouri. **Founded:** 1962. **Operating Hours:** 5 a.m.-midnight. **Key Personnel:** Mike Edwards, Gen. Mgr. **Wattage**: 5,000 Day; 067 Night. **Ad Rates:** Noncommercial. KJPW-FM. **URL:** http://www.myozarksonline.com.

20123 ■ KJPW-FM - 102.3
PO Box D
Waynesville, MO 65583
Phone: (573)336-4913
Fax: (573)336-2222
Email: kjpw@regionalradio.com
Format: Country. **Simulcasts:** KJPW-AM. **Networks:** NBC. **Founded:** 1968. **Operating Hours:** 5 a.m.-midnight. **Key Personnel:** Mike Edwards, Gen. Mgr. **Wattage:** 1,000. **Ad Rates:** Noncommercial. KJPW-AM. **URL:** http://www.myozarksonline.com.

20124 ■ KOZQ-AM - 1270
PO Box D
Waynesville, MO 65583
Phone: (573)336-4913
Fax: (573)336-2222
Format: News; Talk. **Key Personnel:** Mike Edwards, Gen. Mgr., medwards@regionalradio.com; Marcy Todd, Bus. Mgr., mtodd@regionalradio.com. **URL:** http://www.myozarksonline.com.

WEBB CITY

SW MO. Jasper Co. 6 mi. NE of Joplin. Manufactures furniture, scales, machine tools, fertilizer, plastics, textles, caskets. Sand and gravel pits. Dairy, grain farms.

20125 ■ Webb City Sentinel
Webb City Sentinel Inc.
8 S Main St.
Webb City, MO 64870
Phone: (417)673-2421
Community newspaper. **Freq:** Weekly (Fri.). **Print Method:** Offset. **Cols./Page:** 6. **Col. Width:** 1.83 inches. **Col. Depth:** 69.9 picas. **Available online. URL:** http://www.webbcity.net. **Mailing address:** PO Box 150, Webb City, MO 64870. **Ad Rates:** GLR $4.50; SAU $5.89. **Remarks:** Accepts advertising. **Circ:** 11000.

WEST PLAINS

S. MO. Howell Co. 90 mi. SE of Springfield. Manufactures chairs, motors, wood pallets, steel truck bodies, electronic products, shoes, feed. Livestock market. Pine and hardwood timber. Diversified farming. Blackberries, walnuts, poultry. Grape vineyards. Dairy products.

20126 ■ West Plains Daily Quill
West Plains Daily Quill
PO Box 110
West Plains, MO 65775
Phone: (417)256-9191
Publication E-mail: wpqnews@centurytel.net
Newspaper with a Democratic orientation. **Freq:** Daily (eve.). **Print Method:** Offset. **Trim Size:** 14 x 22 1/2. **Cols./Page:** 6. **Col. Width:** 26 nonpareils. **Col. Depth:** 294 agate lines. **Key Personnel:** Jim Perry, Publisher; Vicki Johnson, Manager, Advertising; Judy Collins, Business Manager; Jerry Womack, General Manager, Managing Editor. **USPS:** 675-740. **Subscription Rates:** $85.73 Individuals West Plains - home delivery & full digital access; $91.09 Individuals adjoining counties - home delivery & full digital access; $105.02 Out of area home delivery & full digital access; $120 Out of state home delivery & full digital access; $50 Individuals digital only. **URL:** http://www.westplainsdailyquill.net. **Ad Rates:** GLR $.25; BW $1,323; 4C $1,523; SAU $10.50; PCI $10.50. **Remarks:** Accepts advertising. **Circ:** (Not Reported).

20127 ■ KKDY-FM - 102.5
983 US Hwy. E 160
West Plains, MO 65775
Phone: (417)256-2208
Format: Country. **Networks:** CNN Radio; AP. **Owner:** Tom Marhefka, at above address. **Operating Hours**: Continuous. **Wattage**: 50,000. **Ad Rates:** Noncommercial. Combined advertising rates available with Ozarek Radio Network. **URL:** http://www.kkdy.com.

20128 ■ KSPQ-FM
983 US Hwy. 160 E
West Plains, MO 65775
Format: Classic Rock. **Wattage:** 100,000 ERP. **Ad Rates:** Advertising accepted; rates available upon request.

20129 ■ KUKU-FM - 100.3
983 E US Hwy. 160
West Plains, MO 65775
Phone: (417)255-1682
Format: Oldies. **Key Personnel:** Gary Lee, Dir. of Programs, garylee@kuku.com.

20130 ■ KUPH-FM - 96.9
983 E US Hwy. 160
West Plains, MO 65775
Phone: (417)934-1000
Fax: (417)934-2565
Format: Contemporary Hit Radio (CHR); Oldies. **Key Personnel:** Gary Lee, Dir. of Programs, garylee@kuku.com; Dustin Miller, Contact; Rebecca Santo, Contact, rsanto@ozarkradionetwork.com.

20131 ■ KWPM-AM - 1450
983 E US Hwy. 160
West Plains, MO 65775
Phone: (417)256-3131
Format: Talk; News. **Owner:** Ozark Radio Network Inc., 11 Court Sq., West Plains, MO 65775, Ph: (417)256-2147, Fax: (417)256-1531. **Founded:** July 15, 1947.

WINDYVILLE

20132 ■ Thresholds
Interfaith Church of Metaphysics
163 Moon Valley Rd.
Windyville, MO 65783
Phone: (417)345-8411
Publisher's E-mail: som@som.org
Journal educating and inspiring with Universal Truth. **Freq:** Quarterly. **ISSN:** 1073- 7421 (print). **Subscription Rates:** Included in membership. **URL:** http://www.som.org/10global/thresholds.htm. **Remarks:** Accepts advertising. **Circ:** (Not Reported).

Circulation: ★ = AAM; △ or • = BPA; ♦ = CAC; ❑ = VAC; ⊕ = PO Statement; ‡ = Publisher's Report; Boldface figures = sworn; Light figures = estimated.

BAKER

Fallon Co. Fallon Co. (EC).

20133 ■ Fallon County Times
Fallon County Times
115 S Main St.
Baker, MT 59313
County seat legal newspaper. **Freq:** Weekly (Fri.). **Cols./Page:** 6. **Col. Width:** 2 1/8 INS. **Col. Depth:** 129 1/2 INS. **Key Personnel:** Darlene Hornung, Publisher. **Subscription Rates:** $39 Individuals; $44 Out of area; $54 Out of state. **URL:** http://www.fallóncountyextra.com. **Ad Rates:** BW $480; 4C $654.75; SAU $5; PCI $7.10. **Remarks:** Accepts advertising. **Circ:** (Not Reported).

20134 ■ KFLN-AM - 960
PO Box 790
Baker, MT 59313
Phone: (406)778-3371
Format: Country; News. **Owner:** Newell Broadcasting Corporation, at above address. **Key Personnel:** Devon Banister, Sales Mgr.; Russ Newell, Gen. Mgr., Owner. **Wattage:** 5,000.

20135 ■ KJJM-FM - 100.5
PO Box 790
Baker, MT 59313
Format: Classic Rock.

BELGRADE

S MS. Gallatin Co. 4 mi. W. of Bozeman. Recreational. Agriculture.

20136 ■ KCMM-FM - 99.1
201 W Madison, Ste. 100
Belgrade, MT 59714
Phone: (406)813-8364
Fax: (406)813-8368
Format: Contemporary Christian. **Founded:** 1999. **Key Personnel:** Mark Brashear, Sales Mgr., mark@kcmmtheone.com; Bob Sloane, Dir. of Programs, bob@kcmmtheone.com. **Ad Rates:** Noncommercial. **URL:** http://www.kcmmtheone.org.

20137 ■ KGVW-AM - 640
PO Box 167
Belgrade, MT 59714
Phone: (406)388-4281
Fax: (406)388-1700
Format: Religious; Gospel; Talk; Agricultural; Sports; News. **Networks:** USA Radio; Ambassador Inspirational Radio; Moody Broadcasting; Montana News. **Owner:** Gallatin Vally Witness Inc., at above address. **Founded:** 1959. **Operating Hours:** Continuous. **ADI:** Helena, MT. **Key Personnel:** Bob Sloane, Dir. of Programs, bob@kcmmtheone.com; Wendy Jorgenson, Office Mgr., wendy@kcmmtheone.com; Mark Brashear, Gen. Mgr.; C.J. Swoboda, Dir. of Programs; Dale Heidner, Chief Engineer; Joyce Brashear, Office Mgr. **Wattage:** 10,000 day; 1,000 night. **Ad Rates:** Noncommercial. $6-6 for 30 seconds; $7.50-7.50 for 60 seconds.

BIGFORK

NW MS. Flathead Co. 15 mi. SE of Kalispell.

20138 ■ Bigfork Eagle
Bigfork Eagle
PO Box 406
Bigfork, MT 59911
Phone: (406)837-5131
Fax: (406)837-1132
Publisher's E-mail: editor@bigforkeagle.com
Newspaper. **Founded:** 1977. **Freq:** Weekly (Wed.). **Print Method:** Offset. **Cols./Page:** 6. **Col. Width:** 26 nonpareils. **Col. Depth:** 294 agate lines. **Key Personnel:** David Reese, Managing Editor; Rick Weaver, Publisher. **USPS:** 533-001. **Subscription Rates:** $21.50 Individuals; $24.50 Out of area; $31.50 Out of state; $21.50 Individuals eEdition only. **URL:** http://www.flatheadnewsgroup.com/bigforkeagle/. **Remarks:** Accepts advertising. **Circ:** Paid ‡1600, Free ‡4500.

BILLINGS

Yellowstone Co. Yellowstone Co. (SEC). 225 m SE of Helena. Eastern Montana College; Rocky Mountain College. Important distribution center. Manufactures sugar, flour, farm machinery, electric signs, furniture, paint, metal ornaments, cereal, creamery and meat products, canned vegetables, concrete. Oil refineries. Diversified farming. Sugar beets, wheat, beans, livestock.

20139 ■ The Billings Gazette
The Billings Gazette
PO Box 36300
Billings, MT 59107-6300
Phone: (406)657-1200
Fax: (406)657-1409
Free: 800-543-2505
General newspaper. **Freq:** Daily. **Print Method:** Offset. **Cols./Page:** 6. **Col. Width:** 25 nonpareils. **Col. Depth:** 21 1/2 inches. **Key Personnel:** Mike Gulledge, Publisher, phone: (406)657-1225; Allen Wilson, Manager, Circulation, phone: (406)657-1471; Steve Prosinski, Editor, phone: (406)657-1289. **Subscription Rates:** $28 Individuals /month (7-day with digital); $16.20 Individuals /month (Saturday-Sunday with digital); $13.25 Individuals /month (Sunday only with digital); $13.25 Individuals /month (digital only). **URL:** http://billingsgazette.com. **Feature Editors:** Christine Rubich, phone: (406)657-1301, crubich@billingsgazette.com. **Remarks:** Accepts advertising. **Circ:** (Not Reported).

20140 ■ The Billings Outpost
Billings Outpost
1833 Grand Ave.
Billings, MT 59102
Phone: (406)248-1616
Fax: (406)248-2414
Publisher's E-mail: outpost@billingsnews.com
Community newspaper. **Freq:** Weekly. **Print Method:** web. **Trim Size:** 10 x 16. **Key Personnel:** David Crisp, Editor; Jim Larson, Manager, Sales; Paula Close, Manager, Production. **Subscription Rates:** $35 By mail; $60 Two years; $85 By mail three years. **Online:** MontehInternet Service Providers. **Ad Rates:** BW $725, full page; BW $347, half page. **Remarks:** Accepts advertising. **Circ:** Free ‡10000.

20141 ■ The Billings Times
The Billings Times
2919 Montana Ave.
Billings, MT 59101
Phone: (406)245-4994
Fax: (406)245-5115
Publisher's E-mail: mail@billingstimes.net
Community newspaper. **Freq:** Weekly (Thurs.). **Print Method:** Offset. **Trim Size:** 11 1/2 x 15 1/2. **Cols./Page:** 4. **Col. Width:** 14 picas. **Col. Depth:** 14 inches. **Key Personnel:** William R. Turner, Editor. **USPS:** 056-260. **Subscription Rates:** $38 By mail; $41 Out of area; $75 Single issue. **URL:** http://www.billingstimes.net/. **Ad Rates:** SAU $5; PCI $4. **Remarks:** Color advertising not accepted. **Circ:** Paid ‡1700, Free ‡50.

20142 ■ The Retort
Associated Students of Montana State University Billings
Student Union Bldg., Rm. 213
1500 University Dr.
Billings, MT 59101-0298
Phone: (406)657-2011
Free: 800-565-6782
Publisher's E-mail: webmaster@msubillings.edu
Collegiate newspaper. **Founded:** 1927. **Freq:** Weekly. **Print Method:** Offset. **Trim Size:** 11 x 14. **Cols./Page:** 4. **Col. Width:** 2 inches. **Col. Depth:** 16 inches. **Key Personnel:** Miranda Zugg, Editor, phone: (406)657-2195. **URL:** http://www.msubillings.edu. **Ad Rates:** BW $11.50, for National Advertising Rates. **Remarks:** Accepts advertising. **Circ:** Free 2000.

20143 ■ KBBB-FM - 103.7
27 N 27th St., 23rd Fl., Crowne Plz.
Billings, MT 59101
Phone: (203)861-0900
Format: Adult Contemporary. **Networks:** Independent. **Owner:** GAP West Broadcasting L.L.C., 4300 N Miller Rd., Ste. 116, Scottsdale, AZ 85251, Ph: (480)970-1360, Fax: (480)423-6966. **Operating Hours:** Continuous. **Wattage:** 100,000. **Ad Rates:** Advertising accepted; rates available upon request. **URL:** http://kmhk.com.

20144 ■ KBLG-AM - 910
2075 Central Ave.
Billings, MT 59102
Phone: (406)652-5254
Format: Talk; Sports; News. **Networks:** Fox. **Owner:** Connoisseur Media L.L.C., 180 Post Rd., E, Ste. 201, Westport, CT 06880, Ph: (203)227-1978. **Operating Hours:** Continuous. **Wattage:** 1,000. **Ad Rates:** Noncommercial. KYYA-FM. **URL:** http://www.kblg910.com.

20145 ■ KBLW-FM - 90.1
317 First St.
Havre, MT 59501
Free: 800-442-9222
Email: info@ynop.org
Format: Religious; Contemporary Christian. **Operating Hours:** Continuous. **Key Personnel:** Brenda Boyum, Station Mgr.; Ron Huckeby, Chief Engineer; David Brown, Prog. Dir.; Roger Lonnquist, Gen. Mgr. **Ad Rates:** Noncommercial. **Mailing address:** PO Box

Circulation: ★ = AAM; △ or • = BPA; ♦ = CAC; ❑ = VAC; ⊕ = PO Statement; ‡ = Publisher's Report; Boldface figures = sworn; Light figures = estimated.

2426, Havre, MT 59501. **URL:** http://www.ynop.org.

KBMC-FM - See Bozeman

20146 ■ KBUL-AM - 970
27 N 27th St.
Billings, MT 59101
Phone: (406)248-7827
Format: News; Talk. **Networks:** ABC. **Owner:** Gapwest Broadcasting, 4300 N Miller Rd., Ste. 116, Scottsdale, AZ 85251, Ph: (480)970-1360, Fax: (480)423-6966. **Formerly**: KCTR-AM; KDWG-AM. **Operating Hours**: Continuous. **ADI**: Billings-Hardin, MT. **Wattage**: 5,000. **Ad Rates:** Advertising accepted; rates available upon request. **URL:** http://newstalk955.com/.

20147 ■ KCHH-FM - 95.5
27 N 27th St.
Billings, MT 59101
Phone: (406)248-7827
Format: Eighties. **Owner:** Townsquare Media Inc., 240 Greenwich Ave., Greenwich, CT 06830-6507, Ph: (203)861-0900. **URL:** http://www.newstalk955.com.

20148 ■ KCTR-FM - 102.9
2376 Main St.
Billings, MT 59101
Phone: (406)248-7827
Email: online@catcountry1029.com
Format: Contemporary Country. **Networks:** ABC. **Owner:** Townsquare Media Inc., 240 Greenwich Ave., Greenwich, CT 06830-6507, Ph: (203)861-0900. **Founded:** 1976. **Operating Hours**: Continuous. **ADI**: Billings-Hardin, MT. **Wattage**: 100,000. **Ad Rates:** Noncommercial. **URL:** http://www.catcountry1029.com.

20149 ■ KECC-FM - 90.7
1500 University Dr.
Billings, MT 59101
Phone: (406)657-2941
Fax: (406)657-2977
Free: 800-441-2941
Format: Public Radio; News; Talk; Jazz. **Founded:** Sept. 1406. **Operating Hours**: Continuous. **Wattage**: 500. **Ad Rates:** Noncommercial. Underwriting available. **URL:** http://ypradio.org/#stream/0.

20150 ■ KGHL-AM
PO Box 1742
Billings, MT 59103-1742
Phone: (406)656-1410
Fax: (406)656-0110
Free: 800-735-1187
Format: Country. **Networks:** CBS. **Founded:** 1935. **Key Personnel:** Patrick Gorman, Gen. Mgr., Sales Mgr.; Nick Tyler, Music Dir. **Wattage:** 5,000 Day; 1,800 Nig.

20151 ■ KHMT-TV - 22
445 S 24th St. W
Billings, MT 59102
Phone: (406)652-4743
Fax: (406)652-6963
Networks: Fox. **Owner:** Mission Broadcasting Inc., 7650 Chippewa Rd., Ste. 305, Brecksville, OH 44141, Ph: (440)526-2227, Fax: (440)546-1903. **Founded:** 1980. **Key Personnel:** Tim White, Sales Mgr., TWhite@ksvi.com; Sandra Zoldowski, Gen. Mgr., szoldowski@ksvi.com; Bill Burckhard, Station Mgr. **URL:** http://yourbigsky.com.

20152 ■ KIDX-FM - 98.5
222 N 32nd St., 10th Fl.
Billings, MT 59101-1911
Phone: (406)656-1410
Fax: (406)656-0110
Free: 800-735-1187
Format: Hot Country. **Networks:** CBS. **Founded:** 1979. **Formerly**: KBSR-FM; KGHL-FM. **Operating Hours**: Continuous. **ADI**: Billings-Hardin, MT. **Key Personnel:** Patrick Gorman, Gen. Mgr; Shelly Morast, Contact. **Wattage:** 85,000. **Ad Rates:** Combined advertising rates available with KGML-AM. **URL:** http://985thewolf.com/.

20153 ■ KJCR-AM - 1240
PO Box 31035
Billings, MT 59107
Phone: (406)245-3121
Fax: (406)245-0822
Format: Contemporary Christian. **Formerly**: KMZK-AM. **Ad Rates:** Noncommercial. **URL:** http://kurlradio.com.

20154 ■ KLMT-FM - 89.3
PO Box 21888
Carson City, NV 89721
Phone: (775)883-5647
Free: 800-541-5647
Email: info@pilgrimradio.com
Format: Contemporary Christian; Religious. **Owner:** Pilgrim Radio, PO Box 21888, Carson City, NV 89721, Ph: (775)883-5647, Free: 800-541-5647. **URL:** http://www.pilgrimradio.com.

20155 ■ KLRV-FM - 90.9
PO Box 779002
Rocklin, CA 95677-9972
Fax: (916)251-1901
Free: 800-525-5683
Format: Contemporary Christian. **Owner:** Educational Media Foundation, PO Box 2098, Omaha, NE 68103-2098, Free: 800-434-8400. **Key Personnel:** Alan Mason, COO; Mike Novak, President, CEO. **Wattage:** 7,500. **URL:** http://www.klove.com.

20156 ■ KMHK-FM - 103.7
27 N 27th St.
Billings, MT 59101
Phone: (406)294-1037
Format: Classic Rock. **Owner:** GAP West Broadcasting L.L.C., 4300 N Miller Rd., Ste. 116, Scottsdale, AZ 85251, Ph: (480)970-1360, Fax: (480)423-6966. **ADI:** Billings-Hardin, MT. **Wattage**: 100,000. **Ad Rates:** Advertising accepted; rates available upon request. **URL:** http://www.kmhk.com.

20157 ■ KPBR-FM - 105.9
101 Grand Ave.
Billings, MT 59101
Phone: (406)248-7777
Format: Classic Rock. **Owner:** Connoisseur Media L.L.C., 180 Post Rd., E, Ste. 201, Westport, CT 06880, Ph: (203)227-1978. **Operating Hours**: Continuous. **Ad Rates:** Advertising accepted; rates available upon request.

20158 ■ KPLN-FM - 106.7
2075 Central Ave.
Billings, MT 59102
Phone: (406)248-7777
Fax: (406)248-8577
Format: Adult Contemporary. **Networks:** Independent. **Owner:** Connoisseur Media L.L.C., 180 Post Rd., E, Ste. 201, Westport, CT 06880, Ph: (203)227-1978. **Formerly**: KOZN-FM; KMKX-FM; KJQY-FM. **Operating Hours**: Continuous. **Wattage:** 100,000. **Ad Rates:** Advertising accepted; rates available upon request. Combined advertising rates available with KYXY-FM. **URL:** http://www.planet1067.com.

20159 ■ KPRQ-FM
KEMC - FM
Billings, MT 59101
Fax: (801)637-8191
Format: Oldies. **Networks:** Global Satellite. **Owner:** Halloran Broadcasting Co., 163 E 100 N Price, Utah, UT 84501-2501. **Founded:** 1985. **Key Personnel:** Mike Halloran, Contact. **Wattage:** 450 ERP. **Ad Rates:** $10-16 for 30 seconds; $15-25 for 60 seconds.

20160 ■ KRKX-FM - 94.1
2075 Central Ave.
Billings, MT 59102
Phone: (406)652-8400
Fax: (406)652-4899
Format: Classic Rock. **Networks:** NBC. **Founded:** 1989. **Operating Hours**: Continuous. **ADI**: Billings-Hardin, MT. **Key Personnel:** Sammy Talkington, Contact. **Wattage:** 100,000. **Ad Rates:** $15-23 for 30 seconds; $18-26 for 60 seconds. **URL:** http://www.941ksky.com.

20161 ■ KRSQ-FM - 101.9
222 N 32nd St., Tenth Fl.
Billings, MT 59101
Phone: (406)238-1000
Email: admin@hot1019.com
Format: Top 40; Contemporary Hit Radio (CHR). **Key Personnel:** Kyle McCoy, Dir. of Programs, kyle.mccoy@benedettimedia.com. **Ad Rates:** Advertising accepted; rates available upon request. **URL:** http://www.hot1019.com.

20162 ■ KRZN-FM - 96.3
2075 Central Ave.
Billings, MT 59102
Phone: (406)655-9696
Format: Alternative/New Music/Progressive. **Founded:** Sept. 07, 2006. **Ad Rates:** Noncommercial. **URL:** http://www.963thezone.com.

20163 ■ KSVI-TV - 6
445 S 24th St. W
Billings, MT 59102
Phone: (406)652-4743
Fax: (406)652-6963
Format: Commercial TV. **Networks:** ABC. **Founded:** 1980. **Formerly**: KOUS-TV. **Operating Hours**: Continuous. **ADI**: Billings-Hardin, MT. **Key Personnel:** Sandra Zoldowski, Gen. Mgr., szoldowski@ksvi.com; Scott Smith, Info. Technology Mgr., ssmith@ksvi.com; Ed Connors, Production Mgr., econnors@ksvi.com; Brian Jones, Exec. VP, COO. **Wattage**: 100,000 ERP. **Ad Rates:** Noncommercial. **URL:** http://yourbigsky.com.

20164 ■ KTVQ-TV - 2
3203 3rd Ave. N
Billings, MT 59101
Phone: (406)252-5611
Fax: (406)252-9938
Email: phofferber@ktvq.com
Format: Commercial TV. **Networks:** CBS. **Owner:** Evening Post Industries Inc., 134 Columbus St., Charleston, SC 29403, Ph: (843)577-7111. **Operating Hours**: Continuous. **ADI**: Billings-Hardin, MT. **Wattage**: 26,100 ERP. **Ad Rates:** Advertising accepted; rates available upon request. $10-350 for 30 seconds. **URL:** http://www.ktvq.com.

20165 ■ K217EM-FM - 91.3
PO Box 391
Twin Falls, ID 83303
Fax: (208)736-1958
Free: 800-357-4226
Format: Religious; Contemporary Christian. **Owner:** CSN International, PO Box 391, Twin Falls, ID 83303, Ph: (208)736-1958, Fax: (208)736-1958, Free: 800-357-4226. **Key Personnel:** Don Mills, Music Dir., Prog. Dir.; Kelly Carlson, Dir. of Engg.; Ray Gorney, Asst. Dir. **URL:** http://www.csnradio.com.

20166 ■ KULR-TV - 8
2045 Overland Ave.
Billings, MT 59102
Phone: (406)656-8000
Email: news@kulr.com
Format: Commercial TV. **Networks:** NBC. **Founded:** 1957. **Formerly**: KGHL-TV. **Operating Hours**: Continuous. **ADI**: Billings-Hardin, MT. **Key Personnel:** Chris Byers, Sports Dir., cbyers@kulr.com. **Ad Rates:** Noncommercial. **URL:** http://www.kulr8.com.

20167 ■ KURL-AM - 730
PO Box 30315
Billings, MT 59107
Phone: (406)245-3121
Fax: (406)245-0822
Email: genmgr@kurlradio.com
Format: Religious. **Networks:** SkyLight Satellite; USA Radio; Ambassador Inspirational Radio. **Owner:** Elenbaas Media, Inc., at above address. **Founded:** 1962. **Operating Hours**: Continuous. **Wattage**: 100,000. **Ad Rates:** Advertising accepted; rates available upon request. KMZK. **URL:** http://www.kurlradio.com.

20168 ■ KWMY-FM - 105.9
101 Grand Ave.
Billings, MT 59101
Phone: (406)248-7777
Format: Oldies. **Key Personnel:** Cam Maxwell, Gen. Mgr. **URL:** http://www.my1059.com.

20169 ■ KYYA-FM - 93.3
PO Box 30315
Billings, MT 59107
Phone: (406)245-3121
Format: Adult Contemporary; Full Service; Talk. **Networks:** Westwood One Radio. **Owner:** Cherry Creek Radio LLC, 501 S Cherry St., Ste. 480, Denver, CO 80246, Ph: (303)468-6500, Fax: (303)468-6555. **Founded:** 1975. **Formerly**: KOYN-FM. **Operating Hours**: Continuous Monday - Friday, 7:00 a.m. - 6:00 p.m. Saturday, 7:00 a.m. - 6:30 p.m. Sunday. **ADI**: Billings-Hardin, MT. **Wattage**: 60,000 ERP. **Ad Rates:**

$14-21 for 30 seconds; $19-35 for 60 seconds. Combined advertising rates available with KRKY-FM & KBLG-AM. **URL:** http://www.kurlradio.com.

20170 ■ 97.1 Kiss FM - 97.1
27 N 27th St., 23rd Fl.
Billings, MT 59103
Phone: (406)245-9700
Format: Oldies. **Formerly**: KKBR-FM. **Ad Rates:** Noncommercial. **URL:** http://popcrush971.com.

BLACK EAGLE

20171 ■ KFBB-TV - 5
3200 Old Havre Hwy.
Black Eagle, MT 59414
Phone: (406)453-4377
Format: Commercial TV. **Networks:** ABC. **Owner:** Max Media Montana, 2200 Stephens Ave., Missoula, MT 59801, Ph: (406)542-8900, Fax: (406)728-4800. **Founded:** 1954. **Operating Hours**: Continuous Sun. - Thur.; 6 a.m. to 2:05 a.m. Fri. & Sat. **ADI**: Great Falls, MT. **Ad Rates:** Noncommercial. **URL:** http://www.kfbb.com.

20172 ■ KFRW-FM - 91.9
290 Hegenberger Rd.
Oakland, CA 94621
Free: 800-543-1495
Email: info@familyradio.org
Format: Religious. **Owner:** Family Stations Inc., 290 Hegenberger Rd., Oakland, CA 94621, Free: 800-543-1495. **ADI**: Great Falls, MT. **Wattage**: 50,000. **URL:** http://www.familyradio.org.

BOULDER

20173 ■ Boulder Monitor
Boulder Monitor Inc.
104 W Centennial
Boulder, MT 59632
Phone: (406)225-3821
Publisher's E-mail: janderson@jeffersoncountycourier.com
Community newspaper. **Freq:** Weekly (Wed.). **Print Method:** Offset. **Cols./Page:** 5. **Col. Width:** 11.6 picas. **Col. Depth:** 16 inches. **Key Personnel:** Jan Anderson, Editor. **USPS:** 061-680. **Subscription Rates:** $26 Individuals in Jefferson county - print; $28 Individuals elsewhere in Jefferson county - print; $31 Individuals U.S. address outside Montana - print; $2 Single issue print; $26 Individuals online. **URL:** http://www.jeffersoncountycourier.com. **Mailing address:** PO Box 66, Boulder, MT 59632. **Ad Rates:** GLR $5.50; BW $337.50; 4C $382.50; PCI $4.50. **Remarks:** Accepts advertising. **Circ:** ‡790.

BOZEMAN

Gallatin Co. Gallatin Co. (S). 80 m E of Butte. Montana State University. Residential. Museum of The Rockies. Major ski areas.

20174 ■ Backpacking Light Magazine: The Magazine of Lightweight Hiking and Backcountry Travel
Beartooth Mountain Press
1627 W Main St., Ste. 310
Bozeman, MT 59715-4011
Magazine offering an insightful technical articles and in-depth features about hiking. **Freq:** Quarterly. **Key Personnel:** Alan Dixon, Managing Editor; Ryan Jordan, Editor. **ISSN:** 1550--4417 (print). **Subscription Rates:** $24.99 Individuals; $4.99 Single issue. **URL:** http://backpackinglight.com/. **Circ:** (Not Reported).

20175 ■ Journal of Community Informatics
Journal of School Counseling
305 Herrick Hall
Dept. of Counselor Education
Montana State University
Bozeman, MT 59717
Publication E-mail: editor@ci-journal.net
Peer-reviewed journal that publishes articles related to community improvement via communications technologies and overcoming digital divides. **Freq:** 3/year. **Key Personnel:** Lareen Ann Newman, Associate Editor; Peter Day, Board Member; Michael Gurstein, PhD, Editor-in-Chief. **ISSN:** 1712--4441 (print). **Subscription Rates:** Free online. **URL:** http://ci-journal.net/index.php/ciej. **Remarks:** Accepts advertising. **Circ:** (Not Reported).

20176 ■ Journal of School Counseling
Journal of School Counseling
305 Herrick Hall
Dept. of Counselor Education
Montana State University
Bozeman, MT 59717
Peer-reviewed online journal that publishes articles with the aim of promoting effective school counseling. **Freq:** Continuous. **Key Personnel:** Mark D. Nelson, EdD, Editor; Rebecca Koltz, PhD, Editor. **Subscription Rates:** Free online. **URL:** http://jsc.montana.edu/index.html. **Remarks:** Accepts advertising. **Circ:** (Not Reported).

20177 ■ Montana Farm Bureau Spokesman
Montana Farm Bureau Federation
502 S 19th Ave., Ste. 104
Bozeman, MT 59718
Phone: (406)587-3153
Fax: (406)587-0319
Publisher's E-mail: info@mfbf.org
Freq: Quarterly. **Print Method:** Offset. Uses mats. **Trim Size:** 8 1/2 x 11. **Cols./Page:** 2. **Col. Width:** 17 nonpareils. **Col. Depth:** 154 agate lines. **Key Personnel:** John Youngberg, Publisher; Rebecca Colnar, Editor. **ISSN:** 0886--3075 (print). **Subscription Rates:** Included in membership; $25 Nonmembers /year. **URL:** http://mfbf.org/newsroom/the-spokesman. **Formerly**: Montana Agriculture. **Remarks:** Accepts advertising. **Circ:** 8500.

20178 ■ Sim Talk
American Simmental Association
1 Genetics Way
Bozeman, MT 59718
Phone: (406)587-4531
Fax: (406)587-9301
Subscription Rates: free. **URL:** http://www.simmental.org/site/index.php/simtalk/subscribe-to-simtalk-free. **Remarks:** Accepts advertising. **Circ:** (Not Reported).

20179 ■ The Winchester Collector
Winchester Arms Collectors Association
PO Box 10427
Bozeman, MT 59719
Phone: (541)526-5929
Fax: (971)285-9046
Magazine containing related products, great articles and photographs of outstanding Winchester arms. **Freq:** Quarterly. **Subscription Rates:** Included in membership. **URL:** http://winchestercollector.org/magazine. **Remarks:** Advertising not accepted. **Circ:** (Not Reported).

20180 ■ KBMC-FM - 102.1
1500 University Dr.
Billings, MT 59101-0298
Phone: (406)657-2941
Fax: (406)657-2977
Free: 800-441-2941
Format: Public Radio. **Founded:** 1972. **Key Personnel:** Ken Siebert, Director, Gen. Mgr. **Wattage**: 100,000 Watts. **Ad Rates:** Noncommercial. **URL:** http://www.yellowstonepublicradio.org.

20181 ■ KBOZ-AM
PO Box 519
Bozeman, MT 59771
Phone: (406)587-9999
Email: reier@littleappletech.com
Format: Country; Full Service. **Networks:** ABC. **Founded:** 1975. **Key Personnel:** William Reier, Gen. Mgr. **Wattage**: 5,000.

20182 ■ KBOZ-FM
PO Box 20
Box 20
Bozeman, MT 59718-2041
Fax: (406)587-8201
Format: Soft Rock. **Networks:** ABC; Unistar; Westwood One Radio. **Founded:** 1977. **Formerly**: KATH-FM; KYBS-FM. **Wattage:** 19,000 ERP. **Ad Rates:** Advertising accepted; rates available upon request.

20183 ■ KBZK-TV - 7
90 Television Way
Bozeman, MT 59718
Phone: (406)922-2400
Fax: (406)586-4135
Email: z7tips@kbzk.com
Format: Commercial TV. **Networks:** CBS. **Owner:** Evening Post Industries Inc., 134 Columbus St., Charleston, SC 29403, Ph: (843)577-7111. **Founded:** Dec. 01, 1993. **Operating Hours**: 5:30 a.m.-1:35 a.m. **ADI**: Butte, MT. **Ad Rates:** Noncommercial. **URL:** http://www.kbzk.com.

20184 ■ KBZM-FM - 104.7
8274 Huffine Ln.
Bozeman, MT 59718-8118
Phone: (406)582-1045
Fax: (406)582-0388
Format: Classic Rock. **Key Personnel:** Susan Balding, Gen. Sales Mgr., sbalding@kbzm.com; Jeff Balding, Gen. Mgr., jbalding@kbzm.com. **Ad Rates:** Advertising accepted; rates available upon request. **URL:** http://www.montanassuperstation.com.

20185 ■ KGLT-FM - 91.9
PO Box 174240
Bozeman, MT 59717-4240
Phone: (406)994-3001
Fax: (406)994-1987
Format: Adult Contemporary. **Owner:** Montana University System Board of Regents, at above address, Helena, MT. **Founded:** 1967. **Operating Hours**: Continuous. **Key Personnel:** Ellen King-Rodgers, Gen. Mgr.; Jim Kehoe, Music Dir. **Wattage**: 2,000. **Ad Rates:** Noncommercial. **URL:** http://www.kglt.net.

20186 ■ KMMS-AM - 1450
125 W Mendenhall
Bozeman, MT 59715
Phone: (406)586-2343
Fax: (406)587-2202
Format: Talk; News. **Owner:** Gapwest Broadcasting, 4300 N Miller Rd., Ste. 116, Scottsdale, AZ 85251, Ph: (480)970-1360, Fax: (480)423-6966. **Founded:** 2002. **Wattage**: 1,000. **URL:** http://www.kmmsam.com.

20187 ■ KMMS-FM - 95.1
125 W Mendenhall, Ste. 1
Bozeman, MT 59715
Phone: (406)586-2343
Fax: (406)587-2202
Format: Album-Oriented Rock (AOR). **Owner:** Gap West Broadcasting, at above address. **Wattage:** 94,000. **Ad Rates:** Noncommercial. **URL:** http://www.mooseradio.com.

20188 ■ KPRK-AM - 1340
125 W Mendenhall
Bozeman, MT 59715
Phone: (406)586-2352
Format: Talk; News. **Networks:** ABC. **Owner:** Townsquare Media Inc., 240 Greenwich Ave., Greenwich, CT 06830-6507, Ph: (203)861-0900. **Founded:** 1947. **Operating Hours**: 5:30 a.m.-12:01 a.m. **ADI**: Billings-Hardin, MT. **Key Personnel:** Bill Wilson, Exec. VP; Erik Hellum, Exec. VP. **Wattage**: 1,000. **Ad Rates:** Noncommercial. **URL:** http://www.townsquaremedia.com/markets/montana.

20189 ■ KSCY-FM - 96.7
8170 Gooch Hill Rd.
Bozeman, MT 59718
Phone: (406)582-1045
Ad Rates: Accepts Advertising.

20190 ■ K218DN-FM - 91.5
PO Box 391
Twin Falls, ID 83303
Fax: (208)736-1958
Free: 800-357-4226
Format: Religious; Contemporary Christian. **Owner:** CSN International, PO Box 391, Twin Falls, ID 83303, Ph: (208)736-1958, Fax: (208)736-1958, Free: 800-357-4226. **Key Personnel:** Don Mills, Music Dir., Prog. Dir.; Kelly Carlson, Dir. of Engg.; Ray Gorney, Asst. Dir. **URL:** http://www.csnradio.com.

20191 ■ K268AS-FM - 101.5
PO Box 391
Twin Falls, ID 83303
Fax: (208)736-1958
Free: 800-357-4226
Format: Religious; Contemporary Christian. **Owner:** CSN International, PO Box 391, Twin Falls, ID 83303, Ph: (208)736-1958, Fax: (208)736-1958, Free: 800-357-4226. **Key Personnel:** Mike Kestler, President; Don Mills, Music Dir., Prog. Dir. **URL:** http://www.csnradio.com.

Circulation: ★ = AAM; △ or • = BPA; ♦ = CAC; ❑ = VAC; ⊕ = PO Statement; ‡ = Publisher's Report; Boldface figures = sworn; Light figures = estimated.

20192 ■ KUSM-TV - 9
Montana State University
Visual Communications Bldg., Rm. 183
Bozeman, MT 59717
Phone: (406)994-3437
Fax: (406)994-6545
Email: feedback@montanapbs.org
Format: Public TV. **Networks:** Public Broadcasting Service (PBS). **Owner:** Montana PBS, Visual Communications Bldg. 183, Montana State University, Bozeman, MT 59717, Ph: (406)994-3437, Fax: (406)994-6545, Free: 866-832-0829. **Founded:** 1984. **Operating Hours:** Continuous. **ADI:** Billings-Hardin, MT. **Key Personnel:** Gus Chambers, Producer; Lisa Titus, Dir. of Dev.; Aaron Pruitt, Director; Dean Lawver, Tech. Dir.; Eric Hyyppa, Gen. Mgr.; William Marcus, Director; Linda Talbott, Assoc. Dir.; Daniel Dauterive, Dir. of Operations. **Ad Rates:** Advertising accepted; rates available upon request. **URL:** http://www.montanapbs.org.

20193 ■ KXLB-FM - 100.7
125 W Mendenhall St.
Bozeman, MT 59715
Phone: (406)586-2343
Format: Country. **Owner:** Townsquare Media Inc., 240 Greenwich Ave., Greenwich, CT 06830-6507, Ph: (203)861-0900. **Wattage:** 94,000. **Ad Rates:** Advertising accepted; rates available upon request. **URL:** http://www.xlcountry.com.

20194 ■ KZMY-FM - 103.5
125 W Mendenhall
Bozeman, MT 59715
Phone: (406)556-0123
Fax: (406)587-2202
Format: Adult Contemporary. **Owner:** Townsquare Media Inc., 240 Greenwich Ave., Greenwich, CT 06830-6507, Ph: (203)861-0900. **URL:** http://my1035.com.

BROWNING

Glacier Co. Glacier Co. (N). 110 m NW of Great Falls. Recreation. Trading center for Blackfeet Indian Reservation. Ships hay, pencils, livestock. Oil wells. Lumber. Stock, hay.

20195 ■ Glacier Reporter
Glacier Reporter
PO Box 349
Browning, MT 59417
Phone: (406)338-2090
Fax: (406)338-2410
Community newspaper. **Freq:** Weekly (Thurs.). **Print Method:** Offset. **Trim Size:** 13 3/4 x 22 1/2. **Cols./Page:** 6. **Col. Width:** 24 nonpareils. **Col. Depth:** 294 agate lines. **Key Personnel:** Marlene Augare, Representative, Advertising and Sales; Brian Kavanagh, Owner, Publisher; John McGill, Editor. **USPS:** 885-100. **Subscription Rates:** $40 Individuals in Glacier County; $45 Out of area; $50 Out of state; $35 Individuals e-edition. **URL:** http://cutbankpioneerpress.com/glacier_reporter/?cal=default. **Remarks:** Accepts advertising. **Circ:** 2,549.

BUTTE

Silver Bow Co. (SW). 66 m SW of Helena. One of the most important United States copper mining centers. Gold, silver, lead, zinc, manganese mines. Montana College of Mineral Science and Technology. Manufactures motors; dairy, food products, compressed and liquefied gases, beverages, optical goods, chemicals, steel fabrication. Livestock auction yards, phosphate products, wood preserving; commercial printing plants.

20196 ■ The Technocrat
Montana Tech of the University of Montana
1300 W Park St.
Butte, MT 59701
Phone: (406)496-4241
Fax: (406)496-4702
Free: 800-445-8324
Publication E-mail: technocrat@mtech.edu
Collegiate newspaper. **Freq:** Weekly (Wed.). **Print Method:** Offset. **Trim Size:** 11 x 17. **Cols./Page:** 5. **Col. Width:** 1 3/4 inches. **Col. Depth:** 14 3/4 inches. **Key Personnel:** Aaron Briggs, Editor. **URL:** http://montanatechnocrat.blogspot.com. **Remarks:** Accepts advertising. **Circ:** (Not Reported).

20197 ■ KAAR-FM - 92.5
Butte, MT
Phone: (406)494-1030
Free: 800-905-8020
Format: Country. **Founded:** Sept. 07, 2006. **URL:** http://www.925kaar.com/.

20198 ■ KFRD-FM - 88.9
290 Hegenberger Rd.
Oakland, CA 94621
Free: 800-543-1495
Email: international@familyradio.org
Format: Religious. **Owner:** Family Stations Inc., 290 Hegenberger Rd., Oakland, CA 94621, Free: 800-543-1495. **Founded:** 1981. **URL:** http://www.familyradio.org.

20199 ■ KMBR-FM - 95.5
750 Dewey Blvd., Ste. 1
Butte, MT 59701
Phone: (406)494-1030
Fax: (406)494-6020
Format: Classic Rock; Album-Oriented Rock (AOR). **Owner:** Cherry Creek Radio LLC, 501 S Cherry St., Ste. 480, Denver, CO 80246, Ph: (303)468-6500, Fax: (303)468-6555. **Founded:** 1979. **Operating Hours:** Continuous. **ADI:** Butte, MT. **Key Personnel:** Chris Ackerman, Gen. Mgr., cackerman@cherrycreekradio.com; Jeff Gray, Dir. of Programs, jeffgray@cherrycreekradio.com. **Wattage:** 50,000. **Ad Rates:** Noncommercial. Combined advertising rates available with KXTL-AM, KAAR-FM. **URL:** http://www.955kmbr.com.

20200 ■ KMSM-FM - 103.9
1300 W Park St.
Butte, MT 59701
Fax: (406)496-4802
Free: 800-445-TECH
Format: Educational. **Owner:** Montana Tech, 1300 W Park St., Butte, MT 59701, Fax: (406)496-4334, Free: 800-445-8324. **ADI:** Butte, MT. **Wattage:** 740. **URL:** http://www.mtech.edu/kmsm.

20201 ■ KOPR-FM - 94.1
660 Dewey Blvd.
Butte, MT 59701
Phone: (406)494-7777
Fax: (406)494-5534
Format: Adult Contemporary. **Networks:** ABC; InterMountain. **Owner:** Butte Broadcasting Inc., 660 Dewey Blvd., Butte, MT 59701, Ph: (406)494-7777. **Founded:** 1972. **Operating Hours:** Continuous. **ADI:** Butte, MT. **Key Personnel:** Ron Davis, Gen. Mgr. **Wattage:** 65,000. **Ad Rates:** Noncommercial.

20202 ■ KQLR-FM - 89.7
PO Box 779002
Rocklin, CA 95677-9972
Free: 800-525-LOVE
Format: Contemporary Christian. **Owner:** Educational Media Foundation, PO Box 2098, Omaha, NE 68103-2098, Free: 800-434-8400. **URL:** http://www.klove.com.

20203 ■ KTVM-TV - 6
750 Dewey Blvd.
Butte, MT 59701
Phone: (406)494-7603
Fax: (406)494-2572
Email: sales@ktvm.com
Format: Commercial TV. **Networks:** NBC. **Owner:** Bonten Media Group Inc., Empire State Bldg., 350 Fifth Ave., Ste. 5340, New York, NY 10118, Ph: (212)710-7771, Fax: (212)949-0909. **Founded:** 1971. **Operating Hours:** Continuous. **ADI:** Butte, MT. **Key Personnel:** Jean Zosel, Station Mgr., jrzosel@keci.com. **Ad Rates:** $35-350 per unit. **Mailing address:** PO Box 3118, Butte, MT 59701. **URL:** http://www.nbcmontana.com.

20204 ■ KXLF-TV - 4
1003 S Montana St.
Butte, MT 59701
Phone: (406)496-8400
Fax: (406)782-8906
Format: Commercial TV. **Networks:** CBS. **Owner:** Evening Post Industries Inc., 134 Columbus St., Charleston, SC 29403, Ph: (843)577-7111. **Founded:** 1953. **Operating Hours:** Continuous. **ADI:** Butte, MT. **Wattage:** 10,000 ERP H. **Ad Rates:** Advertising accepted; rates available upon request. **URL:** http://www.kxlf.com.

20205 ■ KXTL-AM - 1370
750 Dewey Blvd., Ste. 1
Butte, MT 59701
Phone: (406)494-1030
Fax: (406)494-6020
Format: Oldies; Talk. **Owner:** Cherry Creek Radio LLC, 501 S Cherry St., Ste. 480, Denver, CO 80246, Ph: (303)468-6500, Fax: (303)468-6555. **ADI:** Butte, MT. **Wattage:** 5,000. **Ad Rates:** Accepts Advertising. **URL:** http://www.kxtl.com.

CASCADE

Cascade Co. Cascade Co. (NC). 20 m SW of Great Falls. Residential.

20206 ■ Cascade Courier
Cascade Courier
338 2nd St. N
Cascade, MT 59421
Phone: (406)468-9231
Community newspaper. **Freq:** Weekly (Thurs.). **Print Method:** Offset. **Cols./Page:** 5. **Col. Width:** 11.5 picas. **Col. Depth:** 12 inches. **Key Personnel:** Felicia O'Brien, Publisher. **USPS:** 092-400. **Subscription Rates:** $30 Individuals in Cascade; Lewis & Clark Counties; $35 Out of area; $40 Out of state. **URL:** http://www.cascademontana.com/courier.htm. **Mailing address:** PO Box 309, Cascade, MT 59421. **Remarks:** Accepts advertising. **Circ:** (Not Reported).

CHESTER

Liberty Co. Liberty Co. (N). 90 m NE of Great Falls. Oil and gas wells. Grain farms. Wheat.

20207 ■ Liberty County Times
Liberty County Times
46 First St. E
Chester, MT 59522
Phone: (406)759-5355
Publication E-mail: lctimes@itstriangle.com
Newspaper. **Freq:** Weekly (Thurs.). **Print Method:** Offset. **Cols./Page:** 6. **Col. Width:** 25 nonpareils. **Col. Depth:** 264 agate lines. **Key Personnel:** Paul Overlie, Editor. **URL:** http://www.libertycountytimes.net. **Mailing address:** PO Box 689, Chester, MT 59522. **Remarks:** Accepts advertising. **Circ:** (Not Reported).

CHINOOK

Blaine Co. Blaine Co. (NC). 10 m W of Zurich.

20208 ■ Blaine County Journal
The Blaine County Journal News Opinion
217 Indiana St.
Chinook, MT 59523-0279
Phone: (406)357-3573
Fax: (406)357-3736
Publisher's E-mail: info@chinookmontana.com
Community newspaper. **Freq:** Weekly (Wed.). **Print Method:** Offset. **Trim Size:** 11.75. **Cols./Page:** 6. **Col. Width:** 2 inches. **Col. Depth:** 21.5 picas. **Key Personnel:** Keith Hanson, Editor; Keri Hanson, Editor; Paula Reynolds, Manager, Advertising. **USPS:** 106-040. **Subscription Rates:** $38 Individuals local; $40 Out of area; $45.50 Out of state. **URL:** http://www.chinookmontana.com. **Formerly:** The Chinook Opinion. **Mailing address:** PO Box 279, Chinook, MT 59523-0279. **Ad Rates:** BW $341.85; PCI $2.65. **Remarks:** Accepts advertising. **Circ:** Controlled ‡2,210.

CHOTEAU

Teton Co. Teton Co. (N). 45 m NW of Great Falls. Recreation. Oil. Dairy, stock, grain farms. Wheat, oats, barley.

20209 ■ Choteau Acantha
Choteau Acantha
216 1st Ave. NW
Choteau, MT 59422
Phone: (406)466-2403
Publication E-mail: acantha@3rivers.net
Community newspaper. **Freq:** Weekly. **Print Method:** Offset. **Trim Size:** 14 x 23. **Cols./Page:** 6. **Col. Width:** 2 1/16 inches. **Col. Depth:** 21 inches. **Key Personnel:** Jeff Martinsen, Manager, Advertising, Publisher; Melody Martinsen, Editor. **USPS:** 106-360. **Subscription Rates:** $34 Individuals in Teton County; $40 Out of area print; $48 Out of state print; $34 Individuals for online only subscriptions. **URL:** http://www.choteauacantha.com. **Mailing address:** PO Box 320, Choteau, MT 59422. **Ad Rates:** 4C $100. **Remarks:** Accepts advertising. **Circ:** 1825.

CIRCLE

McCone Co. McCone Co. (NE). 175 m NE of Billings. Oil, coal. Ships wheat and livestock. Stock, grain farms. Livestock.

20210 ■ Mid-Rivers Telephone Cooperative Inc.
904 C Ave.
Circle, MT 59215
Phone: (406)485-3301
Fax: (406)485-2924
Free: 800-452-2288
Email: airport@midrivers.com
Founded: 1952. **Cities Served:** United States; 51 channels. **Mailing address:** PO Box 280, Circle, MT 59215-0280. **URL:** http://www.midrivers.com.

COLUMBUS

Stillwater Co. Stillwater Co. (C).

20211 ■ Carbon County News
News Montana Inc.
PO Box 659
Columbus, MT 59019
Phone: (406)322-5212
Fax: (406)322-5391
Free: 800-823-7426
Publication E-mail: news@carboncountynews.com
Community newspaper. **Freq:** Weekly (Thurs.). **Print Method:** Offset. **Cols./Page:** 6. **Col. Width:** 24 nonpareils. **Col. Depth:** 294 agate lines. **Key Personnel:** Frank Perea, II, Publisher; Alastair Baker, Editor. **USPS:** 090-100. **Subscription Rates:** $11.75 Individuals 3 months; $23.50 Individuals 6 months; $40 Individuals; $71.00 Two years; $99 Individuals 3 years; $17 Out of country 3 months; $34 Out of country 6 months; $57.50 Out of country; $100 Two years out of County; $135 Out of country 3 years. **URL:** http://www.carboncountynews.com. **Remarks:** Accepts advertising. **Circ:** 3000.

20212 ■ Stillwater County News
News Montana Inc.
PO Box 659
Columbus, MT 59019
Phone: (406)322-5212
Fax: (406)322-5391
Free: 800-823-7426
Publication E-mail: publisher@newsmontana.com
County newspaper. **Freq:** Weekly. **Print Method:** Offset. **Trim Size:** 23 1/2 x 14. **Cols./Page:** 6. **Col. Width:** 2 inches. **Col. Depth:** 21 inches. **Key Personnel:** John Cribb, Publisher. **URL:** http://www.stillwatercountynews.com. **Formerly:** The Stillwater Sun. **Remarks:** Accepts advertising. **Circ:** (Not Reported).

CONRAD

Pondera Co. Pondera Co. (N). 55 m N of Great Falls. Creamery. Oil wells. Ships wheat, barley and other small grain. Poultry, grain farms.

20213 ■ KTZZ-FM - 93.7
PO Box 1239
Great Falls, MT 59403
Phone: (406)761-1310
Fax: (406)454-3775
Format: Classic Rock. **Networks:** Westwood One Radio. **Owner:** Munson Radio Inc., at above address. **Founded:** July 01, 1997. **Formerly:** KEIN-FM. **Operating Hours:** Continuous. **Key Personnel:** Steven Dow, President. **Wattage:** 100,000. **Ad Rates:** Noncommercial.

CULBERTSON

Roosevelt Co. Roosevelt Co. (NE). 178 m S of Regina, Sask, Canada. Safflower processing plant. Agriculture. Wheat, cattle, sheep, hogs, safflower.

20214 ■ The Searchlight
Interactive Media Ltd.
PO Box 152
Kingstown, Saint Vincent and the Grenadines
Phone: (784)456-1558
Fax: (784)457-2250
Publication E-mail: editor@searchlight.vc
Community newspaper. **Founded:** 1902. **Freq:** Semiweekly. **Print Method:** Offset. **Cols./Page:** 5. **Col. Width:** 24 nonpareils. **Col. Depth:** 217 agate lines. **Subscription Rates:** $25 Individuals. **URL:** http://searchlight.vc/index1.htm. **Ad Rates:** GLR $.11; PCI $3. **Remarks:** Accepts advertising. **Circ:** (Not Reported).

20215 ■ K201FG-FM - 88.1
PO Box 391
Twin Falls, ID 83303
Fax: (208)736-1958
Free: 800-357-4226
Format: Religious; Contemporary Christian. **Owner:** CSN International, PO Box 391, Twin Falls, ID 83303, Ph: (208)736-1958, Fax: (208)736-1958, Free: 800-357-4226. **Key Personnel:** Don Mills, Music Dir., Prog. Dir.; Kelly Carlson, Dir. of Engg.; Ray Gorney, Asst. Dir. **URL:** http://www.csnradio.com.

DILLON

Beaverhead Co. Beaverhead Co. (SW). 65 m S of Butte. Western Montana College. Tourism. Gold, Silver, lead, copper mines. Timber. Agriculture.

20216 ■ Dillon Tribune
Dillon Tribune
22 S Montana St.
Dillon, MT 59725-0911
Phone: (406)683-2331
Fax: (406)683-2332
Free: 800-386-3156
Publisher's E-mail: news@dillontribune.com
Community newspaper. **Freq:** Weekly (Wed.). **Print Method:** Offset. **Cols./Page:** 6. **Col. Width:** 12 picas. **Col. Depth:** 294 agate lines. **Key Personnel:** Jennifer Engstrom, Account Representative, Specialist, Circulation; Dick Crockford, Publisher; J.P. Plutt, Editor. **Subscription Rates:** $39 Individuals Beaverhead County; $52 Out of area; $58 Out of state. **URL:** http://www.dillontribune.com. **Formerly:** Dillon Tribune-Examiner. **Mailing address:** PO Box 911, Dillon, MT 59725-0911. **Remarks:** Accepts advertising. **Circ:** (Not Reported).

20217 ■ KDBM-AM - 1490
610 N Montana St.
Dillon, MT 59725
Phone: (406)683-2800
Fax: (406)683-9480
Format: Country; Album-Oriented Rock (AOR); Adult Contemporary. **Networks:** ABC; Northern Agricultural. **Owner:** Beaverhead Madison Broadcasting Inc., at above address; Dead Air Broadcasting Company Inc., at above address. **Founded:** 1956. **Operating Hours:** Continuous. **Key Personnel:** Joann Juliano, Owner; John Schuyler, VP; Kasey Briggs, Sales Mgr., Contact; Larry Chaffin, Contact; Wally Feldt, Contact; Kasey Briggs, Contact. **Wattage:** 1,000. **Ad Rates:** Advertising accepted; rates available upon request. $8.25; $2.40-3.90 for 30 seconds; $3.20-4.70 for 60 seconds. Combined advertising rates available with KBEV-FM. **URL:** http://www.kdbm-kbev.com.

20218 ■ KDWG-FM - 90.9
710 S Atlantic St.
Dillon, MT 59725
Phone: (406)683-7331
Free: 877-683-7331
Email: kdwg@umwestern.edu
Format: Alternative/New Music/Progressive; Educational. **Owner:** The University of Montana Western, 710 S Atlantic St., Dillon 59725. **Founded:** 2001. **URL:** http://www.my.umwestern.edu.

20219 ■ K219CS-FM - 91.7
Broadcast Media Ctr.
University of Montana
Missoula, MT 59812
Phone: (406)243-4931
Fax: (406)243-3299
Free: 800-325-1565
Email: contact@mtpr.org
Format: Eclectic. **Owner:** Montana Public Radio, 32 Campus Dr., Missoula, MT 59812, Ph: (406)243-4931, Fax: (406)243-3299, Free: 800-325-1565. **Founded:** 1965. **Key Personnel:** Sally Mauk, Director; Michael Marsolek, Dir. of Programs. **URL:** http://www.mtpr.org.

EUREKA

Lincoln Co. Lincoln Co. (NW). 50 m NW of Whitefish. Logging; sawmills; machine parts manufactured. Cattle raising. Recreation, tourism.

20220 ■ Tobacco Valley News
Ten Lakes Publishing
520 Dewey Ave.
Eureka, MT 59917
Phone: (406)297-2514
Fax: (406)297-7807
Publisher's E-mail: eurekaeditor@gmail.com
Community newspaper. **Freq:** Weekly (Thurs.). **Print Method:** Offset. **Cols./Page:** 6. **Col. Width:** 29 nonpareils. **Key Personnel:** Krista Tincher; Robin Newman, Manager, Advertising; Steve Newman, Editor, Publisher. **Subscription Rates:** $40 Individuals in Lincoln County; $45 Out of area; $49 Out of state; $40 Individuals online; $127 Other countries. **URL:** http://tobaccovalleynews.com. **Mailing address:** PO Box 307, Eureka, MT 59917. **Remarks:** Accepts advertising. **Circ:** (Not Reported).

FAIRFIELD

Teton Co. Teton Co. (N). 30 m NW of Great Falls. Flour mills. Agriculture. Wheat, alfalfa, dairying, livestock.

20221 ■ Fairfield Sun Times
Times Publishing L.L.C.
PO Box 578
Fairfield, MT 59436
Phone: (406)467-2334
Fax: (406)467-3354
Community newspaper. **Founded:** 1912. **Freq:** Weekly (Thurs.). **Print Method:** Offset. Uses mats. **Cols./Page:** 6. **Col. Width:** 24 nonpareils. **Col. Depth:** 294 agate lines. **Key Personnel:** Darryl L. Flowers, Publisher; Laura Brown, Office Manager. **Subscription Rates:** $30 Individuals local; $35 Individuals other Montana areas; $40 Elsewhere in United States. **URL:** http://www.fairfieldsuntimes.com/. **Formerly:** Fairfield Times-Wheat Center News; Fairfield Times; Sun Times. **Ad Rates:** BW $389; PCI $4.25. **Remarks:** Accepts advertising. **Circ:** Paid 1150, Free 20.

GLASGOW

Valley Co. Valley Co. (NE). 45 m NW of Wolf Point. Residential.

20222 ■ The Glasgow Courier
The Glasgow Courier
341 3rd Ave. S
Glasgow, MT 59230
Phone: (406)228-9301
Publication E-mail: courier@nemontel.net
Community newspaper. **Freq:** Weekly (Wed.). **Print Method:** Offset. **Trim Size:** 11 1/4 x 14. **Cols./Page:** 6. **Col. Width:** 24 nonpareils. **Col. Depth:** 294 agate lines. **Key Personnel:** Samar Fay, Editor; Jim Orr, Publisher. **USPS:** 219-220. **Subscription Rates:** $36 By mail in Valley County; $41 Out of area; $51 Out of state; $25 Students for College studentss, nine months; $35 Individuals online only. **URL:** http://www.glasgowcourier.com. **Remarks:** Accepts advertising. **Circ:** 2653.

20223 ■ KLAN-FM - 93.5
504 2nd Ave. S
Glasgow, MT 59230
Phone: (406)228-9336
Fax: (406)228-9338
Format: Adult Contemporary. **Key Personnel:** Shirley Trang, Gen. Mgr.; Annette Vegge, Office Mgr.; Tim Phillips, Dir. of Programs; Lori Mason, Music Dir.; Gwen Page, Traffic Mgr. **Ad Rates:** Advertising accepted; rates available upon request. **Mailing address:** PO Box 671, Glasgow, MT 59230. **URL:** http://www.kltz.com.

20224 ■ KLTZ-AM - 1240
504 2nd Ave. S
Glasgow, MT 59230
Phone: (406)228-9336
Fax: (406)228-9338
Email: kltz@kltz.com
Format: Country; News; Sports. **Owner:** Glasgow Broadcasting Co., 504 2nd Ave South, Glasgow, MT 59230, Ph: (406)228-9336, Fax: (406)228-9338. **Key Personnel:** Stan Ozark, Sports Dir., News Dir.; Shirley Trang, Gen. Mgr.; Tim Phillips, Prog. Dir. **Wattage:** 1,000. **Ad Rates:** Noncommercial. **Mailing address:** PO Box 671, Glasgow, MT 59230. **URL:** http://www.kltz.com.

Circulation: ★ = AAM; △ or • = BPA; ♦ = CAC; ❑ = VAC; ⊕ = PO Statement; ‡ = Publisher's Report; Boldface figures = sworn; Light figures = estimated.

GLENDIVE

Dawson Co. Dawson Co. (NE). On Yellowstone River, head of navigation, 80 m NE of Miles City. Makoshika State Park. Dawson College. Coal mines, gas and oil wells. Stock, poultry, grain farms. Wheat, flax, oats.

20225 ■ Glendive Ranger-Review
Livingston Enterprise
119 W Bell St.
Glendive, MT 59330
Phone: (406)377-3303
Fax: (406)377-5435
Publication E-mail: rrads@rangerreview.com
Community newspaper. **Freq:** Semiweekly Sun. and Thurs. **Print Method:** Offset. **Cols./Page:** 6. **Col. Width:** 26 nonpareils. **Col. Depth:** 301 agate lines. **Key Personnel:** Jamie Ausk Crisafulli, Publisher; Justin Joiner, Managing Editor. **Subscription Rates:** $45 Individuals; $72 By mail in county; $84 By mail out of state; $45 Individuals online only. **URL:** http://www.rangerreview.com. **Mailing address:** PO Box 61, Glendive, MT 59330. **Remarks:** Color advertising accepted; rates available upon request. **Circ:** 3200.

20226 ■ KDSR-FM - 101.1
210 S Douglas
Glendive, MT 59330
Phone: (406)377-3377
Format: Adult Contemporary. **Networks:** CNN Radio. **Owner:** Marks Radio Group, at above address. **Founded:** 1985. **Operating Hours**: Controlled. **Wattage**: 100,000 ERP. **Ad Rates:** $5.51-7.96 for 30 seconds; $7.35-13 for 60 seconds.

20227 ■ KDZN-FM - 96.5
210 S Douglas
Glendive, MT 59330
Phone: (406)377-3377
Fax: (406)365-2181
Email: webmaster@glendivebroadcasting.com
Format: Country. **Key Personnel:** Paul Sturlaugson, Gen. Mgr.; Steve Marks, Owner; Loretta Taggart, Office Mgr. **Wattage**: 90,000. **Ad Rates:** Advertising accepted; rates available upon request. **URL:** http://www.kxgn.com.

20228 ■ KGLE-AM - 590
86 Seven Mile Dr.
Glendive, MT 59330
Phone: (406)377-3331
Fax: (406)377-3332
Free: 800-568-6935
Email: kgle@midrivers.com
Format: Gospel. **Owner:** Friends of Christian Radio, Inc., at above address, Elkhart, IN. **Operating Hours:** Continuous. **ADI**: Minot-Bismarck-Dickinson, ND-Glendive, MT. **Key Personnel:** Cody Ross, Contact. **Wattage**: 1,000. **Mailing address:** PO Box 931, Glendive, MT 59330. **URL:** http://www.kgle.org.

20229 ■ K215CW-FM - 90.9
PO Box 391
Twin Falls, ID 83303
Fax: (208)736-1958
Free: 800-357-4226
Format: Religious; Contemporary Christian. **Owner:** CSN International, PO Box 391, Twin Falls, ID 83303, Ph: (208)736-1958, Fax: (208)736-1958, Free: 800-357-4226. **Key Personnel:** Don Mills, Prog. Dir., Div. Dir. **URL:** http://www.csnradio.com.

20230 ■ KXGN-AM
210 S Douglas
Glendive, MT 59330
Format: Oldies; Adult Contemporary. **Wattage**: 1,000. **Ad Rates:** Advertising accepted; rates available upon request.

20231 ■ KXGN-TV - 5
210 S Douglas
Glendive, MT 59330
Phone: (406)377-3377
Fax: (406)365-2181
Email: kxgnkdzn@midrivers.com
Format: Commercial TV. **Networks:** CBS; NBC. **Owner:** Glendive Broadcasting Corp., at above address. **Founded:** 1957. **Operating Hours**: Continuous. **ADI**: Minot-Bismarck-Dickinson, ND-Glendive, MT. **Key Personnel:** Ed Agre, News Dir; Dan Frenzel, Contact. **Wattage**: 1,000 ERP Horizontal. **Ad Rates:** $110 for 30 seconds. **URL:** http://www.kxgn.com/?page=tv.

GREAT FALLS

Cascade Co. Cascade Co. (NC). 167 m NE of Butte. College of Great Falls. Malmstrom Air Force Base. State School for the Deaf & Blind. Manufactures flour, feed, furs, electric signs, concrete blocks, solar equipment, woolen goods. Meat packing plant. Oil refinery. Grain elevators. State fish hatchery.

20232 ■ Consumers Press: Wheels, Deals, Steals
Lee Publications
401 9th St. S
Great Falls, MT 59403
Shopping guide. **Freq:** Weekly (Thurs.). **Subscription Rates:** Free. **Ad Rates:** BW $965; 4C $200; PCI $8. **Remarks:** Accepts advertising. **Circ:** Combined 23000.

20233 ■ Great Falls Tribune
Gannett Company Inc.
205 River Dr. S
Great Falls, MT 59405
Phone: (406)791-1444
General newspaper. **Founded:** 1885. **Freq:** Daily and Sun. (morn.). **Print Method:** Offset. **Col. Width:** 26 nonpareils. **Col. Depth:** 301 agate lines. **Key Personnel:** Jim Strauss, Editor, Publisher. **Subscription Rates:** $23 Individuals print and online, monthly; $10 Individuals digital access. **URL:** http://www.gannett.com; http://www.greatfallstribune.com. **Ad Rates:** BW $3,806; 4C $4,275; SAU $23.16; PCI $3.95; BW $4,999; 4C $5,469; SAU $23.16; PCI $4.40. **Remarks:** Advertising accepted; rates available upon request. **Circ:** Mon.-Fri. ***28383**, Sun. ***30213**, Sat. ***27383**.

20234 ■ We Proceeded On
Lewis and Clark Trail Heritage Foundation
4201 Giant Springs Rd.
Great Falls, MT 59405
Phone: (406)454-1234
Free: 888-701-3434
Publisher's E-mail: york@lewisandclark.org
Freq: Quarterly. **ISSN:** 0275- 6706 (print). **Subscription Rates:** included in membership dues. **URL:** http://www.lewisandclark.org/wpo/index.html. **Mailing address:** PO Box 3434, Great Falls, MT 59403. **Remarks:** Advertising not accepted. **Circ:** 3500.

20235 ■ KAAK-FM - 98.9
PO Box 3309
Great Falls, MT 59403
Phone: (406)761-7600
Fax: (406)761-5511
Wattage: 100,000. **Ad Rates:** Noncommercial.

20236 ■ KAFH-FM - 91.5
PO Box 3206
Tupelo, MS 38803
Format: Religious. **Owner:** American Family Radio, at above address. **ADI**: Great Falls, MT. **Wattage**: 1,000. **URL:** http://www.afa.net.

20237 ■ KAWZ 89.9 FM - 88.1
PO Box 391
Twin Falls, ID 83303
Fax: (208)736-1958
Free: 800-357-4226
Format: Religious; Contemporary Christian. **Owner:** CSN International, PO Box 391, Twin Falls, ID 83303, Ph: (208)736-1958, Fax: (208)736-1958, Free: 800-357-4226. **Key Personnel:** Mike Kestler, Contact; Don Mills, Music Dir.; Kelly Carlson, Asst. Dir.; Ray Gorney, Asst. Dir. **URL:** http://www.csnradio.com.

20238 ■ KBGF-TV - 6
13 6th St. S
Great Falls, MT 59401
Phone: (406)771-1666
Owner: KRTV Communications, LLC, 100 W Lyndale Ave., Ste. A, Helena, MT 59601, Ph: (406)457-1212, Free: 866-544-7194.

20239 ■ KEIN-AM - 1310
PO Box 139
Great Falls, MT 59403
Phone: (406)761-1310
Fax: (406)454-3775
Format: Middle-of-the-Road (MOR); Adult Contemporary. **Networks:** ABC. **Owner:** Munson Radio Inc., at above address. **Founded:** 1922. **Operating Hours**: Continuous. **Wattage**: 5,000. **Ad Rates:** Advertising accepted; rates available upon request.

20240 ■ KGFC-FM - 88.9
317 First St.
Havre, MT 59501
Free: 800-442-9222
Email: info@ynop.org
Format: Religious. **Key Personnel:** Roger Lonnquist, Gen. Mgr. **Ad Rates:** Noncommercial. **Mailing address:** PO Box 2426, Havre, MT 59501. **URL:** http://www.ynop.org.

20241 ■ KGPR-FM - 89.9
2100 16th Ave. S, Rm. G118
Great Falls, MT 59405
Phone: (406)268-3739
Fax: (406)268-3736
Email: info@kgpr.org
Format: Public Radio. **Operating Hours**: Continuous. **ADI**: Great Falls, MT. **Wattage**: 9,500 ERP. **Mailing address:** PO Box 3343, Great Falls, MT 59403-3343. **URL:** http://www.kgpr.org.

20242 ■ KINX-FM - 107.3
1300 Central Ave.
Great Falls, MT 59404
Phone: (406)761-2800
Email: troyboy@sam1073.com
Format: Eclectic. **Owner:** Fisher Radio Regional Group, 1300 Central Ave. W, Great Falls, MT 59404, Ph: (406)761-2800, Fax: (406)727-7218. **Key Personnel:** Terry Strickland, Gen. Mgr., terry@q106rocks.com; Dave France, Operations Mgr., dave@q106rocks.com; Anna Palagi, Sales Mgr., apalagi@q106rocks.com. **Wattage**: 100,000. **Ad Rates:** Advertising accepted; rates available upon request. **URL:** http://www.kinx1027.com/station-info.html.

20243 ■ KLSK-FM - 100.3
6080 Mount Moriah
Memphis, TN 38115
Phone: (901)375-9324
Fax: (901)375-5889
Email: mail@flinn.com
Format: Contemporary Christian. **Owner:** Flinn Broadcasting Corporation, at above address. **Founded:** 1983. **Operating Hours**: Continuous. **Key Personnel:** George Flinn, President. **Wattage**: 100,000. **Ad Rates:** Advertising accepted; rates available upon request. **URL:** http://www.flinn.com.

20244 ■ KMON-AM - 560
20 3rd St. N, Ste. 231
Great Falls, MT 59401
Phone: (406)761-7600
Format: Country; News. **Networks:** ABC. **Operating Hours**: Continuous. **Wattage**: 5,000. **Ad Rates:** $15.50-25 for 30 seconds; $21.75-37.50 for 60 seconds. **URL:** http://www.kmonam.com.

20245 ■ KQDI-AM - 1450
1300 Central Ave. W
Great Falls, MT 59404
Phone: (406)761-2800
Format: News; Talk. **Owner:** Fisher Communications Inc., 140 4th Ave. N, Ste. 500, Seattle, WA 98109-4940, Ph: (206)404-7000, Fax: (206)404-6037. **Operating Hours**: Continuous. **Wattage**: 1,000. **Ad Rates:** Noncommercial. **URL:** http://newstalk1450.com.

20246 ■ KRTV-TV - 3
PO Box 2989
Great Falls, MT 59403
Phone: (406)791-5400
Format: Commercial TV. **Networks:** CBS. **Owner:** Evening Post Industries Inc., 134 Columbus St., Charleston, SC 29403, Ph: (843)577-7111. **Founded:** 1958. **Operating Hours**: Continuous. **ADI**: Great Falls, MT. **Local Programs**: *KRTV News*, Monday Tuesday Wednesday Thursday Saturday Sunday 12:00 p.m.; 5:30 p.m.; 10:00 p.m. 5:30 p.m.; 10:00 p.m 10:00 p.m. **Ad Rates:** Advertising accepted; rates available upon request. **URL:** http://www.krtv.com.

20247 ■ KTGF-TV - 16
118 Sixth St. S
Great Falls, MT 59401-3688
Phone: (406)761-8816
Fax: (406)454-3484
Format: Commercial TV. **Networks:** NBC. **Founded:** 1986. **Operating Hours**: Continuous. **ADI**: Great Falls,

MT. **Key Personnel:** Roger Lonnquist, Gen. Mgr. **Wattage:** 2,040,000. **Ad Rates:** Advertising accepted; rates available upon request.

KTZZ-FM - See Conrad, MT

20248 ■ KVVR-FM - 97.9
PO Box 3309
Great Falls, MT 59401
Phone: (406)761-7600
Fax: (406)761-5511
Founded: Sept. 07, 2006. **Wattage:** 100,000.

HAMILTON

Ravalli Co. Ravalli Co. (W). 48 m S of Missoula. Lumber mills; creameries. Pine timber. Diversified farming. Dairy products, livestock.

20249 ■ Ravalli Republic
Ravalli Republic
232 W Main St.
Hamilton, MT 59840
Phone: (406)363-3300
Fax: (406)363-1767
Publication E-mail: editor@ravallinews.com
General newspaper. **Freq:** Daily (morn.). **Print Method:** Offset. **Trim Size:** 12 x 21 1/2. **Cols./Page:** 6. **Col. Width:** 3.756 inches. **Col. Depth:** 21.5 agate lines. **Key Personnel:** Sherry Devlin, Managing Editor; Clint Burson, Editor; Perry Backus, Reporter; Mark Heintzelman, Publisher. **USPS:** 145-080. **Subscription Rates:** $10 Individuals digital only; $13 Individuals full access. **URL:** http://ravallirepublic.com. **Remarks:** Accepts advertising. **Circ:** 5995, 7396.

20250 ■ KLYQ-AM - 1240
3250 S Reserve St., No. 200
Missoula, MT 59806
Email: support@townsquaremedia.com
Format: News. **Networks:** ABC. **Owner:** Townsquare Media Inc., 240 Greenwich Ave., Greenwich, CT 06830-6507, Ph: (203)861-0900. **Operating Hours:** Continuous. **Wattage:** 1,000. **Ad Rates:** $9-12 for 30 seconds; $13.50-18 for 60 seconds. **URL:** http://www.townsquaremedia.com/markets/montana.

20251 ■ KMZO-FM - 90.7
2201 S 6th St.
Las Vegas, NV 89104
Phone: (702)731-5452
Fax: (702)731-1992
Free: 800-804-5452
Format: Contemporary Christian. **Owner:** SOS Radio Network, 2201 S 6th St., Las Vegas, NV 89104, Ph: (702)731-5452, Fax: (702)731-1992, Free: 800-804-5452. **Wattage:** 5,000. **URL:** http://www.sosradio.net.

20252 ■ K204CX-FM - 88.7
PO Box 391
Twin Falls, ID 83303
Fax: (208)736-1958
Free: 800-357-4226
Format: Religious; Contemporary Christian. **Owner:** CSN International, PO Box 391, Twin Falls, ID 83303, Ph: (208)736-1958, Fax: (208)736-1958, Free: 800-357-4226. **Key Personnel:** Don Mills, Music Dir., Prog. Dir. **URL:** http://www.csnradio.com.

20253 ■ KUFN-FM - 91.9
629 6th E
Missoula, MT 59812-8064
Phone: (406)243-4931
Fax: (406)243-3299
Free: 800-325-1565
Email: contact@mtpr.org
Format: Public Radio. **Owner:** Montana Public Radio, 32 Campus Dr., Missoula, MT 59812, Ph: (406)243-4931, Fax: (406)243-3299, Free: 800-325-1565. **Key Personnel:** Sally Mauk, News Dir.; Michael Marsolek, Div. Dir.; Eric Whitney, News Dir.; Linda Talbott, Assoc. Dir., linda.talbott@mtpr.org. **URL:** http://mtpr.org/listen.

HARDIN

Big Horn Co. Big Horn Co. (S). 50 m E of Billings. Coal mining; gas wells. Ships cattle. Diversified farming. Wheat, sugar beets, alfalfa.

20254 ■ Big Horn County News
Big Horn County News
240 N Center Ave.
Hardin, MT 59034
Publication E-mail: ads@bighorncountynews.com
Community newspaper. **Freq:** Weekly (Wed.). **Print Method:** Offset. **Cols./Page:** 6. **Col. Width:** 26 nonpareils. **Col. Depth:** 294 agate lines. **Key Personnel:** Jim Eshleman, General Manager. **Subscription Rates:** $39 Individuals print & e-edition; $55.75 Out of area print & e-edition; $60 Out of state print & e-edition. **URL:** http://www.bighorncountynews.com. **Formerly:** Hardin Tribune; Hardin Tribune Herald. **Mailing address:** PO Box 926, Hardin, MT 59034. **Remarks:** Accepts classified advertising. **Circ:** (Not Reported).

20255 ■ Greasy Grass
Custer Battlefield Historical and Museum Association
PO Box 902
Hardin, MT 59034-0902
Freq: Annual. **Subscription Rates:** Included in membership. **URL:** http://www.custerbattlefield.org/publications.shtml. **Remarks:** Advertising not accepted. **Circ:** (Not Reported).

HARLEM

Blaine Co. Blaine Co. (N). 140 m NE of Great Falls. Rock quarries. Diversified farming. Wheat, livestock.

20256 ■ KGVA-FM - 88.1
PO Box 159
Harlem, MT 59526
Format: Educational; Public Radio. **Owner:** Aaniiih Nakoda College, at above address. **Founded:** 1996. **Key Personnel:** Gerald J. Stiffarm, Station Mgr. **URL:** http://www.kgvafm.org.

HAVRE

Hill Co. Hill Co. (NC). 20 m E of Fresno.

20257 ■ Havre Daily News
Havre Daily News
119 Second St.
Havre, MT 59501
Phone: (406)265-6795
Fax: (406)265-6798
Free: 800-993-2459
Publisher's E-mail: news@havredailynews.com
Daily newspaper. **Freq:** Daily. **Key Personnel:** Martin Cody, Publisher; John Kelleher, Managing Editor; Stacy Mantle, Director, Advertising. **ISSN:** 0745-7782 (print). **Subscription Rates:** $78 Individuals carrier delivery - 6 months; $156 Individuals carrier delivery - 13 months; $90 Individuals motor delivery - 6 months; $180 Individuals motor delivery - 13 months; $96 Individuals mail hill county - 6 months; $192 Individuals mail hill county - 13 months; $108 Individuals mail Montana - 6 months; $216 Individuals mail Montana - 13 months; $120 Out of state mail - 6 months; $240 Out of state mail - 13 months; $36 Individuals mail Friday - 6 months; $72 Individuals mail Friday - 13 months. **URL:** http://www.havredailynews.com/. **Mailing address:** PO Box 431, Havre, MT 59501. **Ad Rates:** SAU $6.60; PCI $6.60. **Remarks:** Advertising accepted; rates available upon request. **Circ:** Paid ⊕**4000**.

KAXG-FM - See Gillette, WY

20258 ■ KBBJ-TV - 9
2 Cowan Dr., Rm. 213B
Havre, MT 59501
Free: 866-544-7194
Owner: KRTV Communications, LLC, 100 W Lyndale Ave., Ste. A, Helena, MT 59601, Ph: (406)457-1212, Free: 866-544-7194.

KBLW-FM - See Billings

KGFC-FM - See Great Falls

KMCJ-FM - See Miles City

20259 ■ KNMC-FM - 90.1
PO Box 7751
Havre, MT 59501
Phone: (406)265-3709
Email: knmcradio@msun.edu
Format: Eclectic; Information. **Networks:** Independent. **Owner:** Montana State University-Northern, PO Box 7751, Havre, MT 59501, Ph: (406)265-3704. **Formerly:** KNOG-FM. **Operating Hours:** midnight. **Wattage:** 500. **Ad Rates:** Noncommercial. **URL:** http://msun.edu/future.

20260 ■ KOJM-AM - 610
2210 31st St. N
Havre, MT 59501
Phone: (406)265-7841
Fax: (406)265-8855
Email: nmb@nmbi.com
Format: Classic Rock. **Networks:** ABC. **Owner:** New Media Broadcasters Inc., at above address. **Operating Hours:** 5 a.m.-midnight, Mon.-Fri.; 6 a.m.-midnight, Sat.-Sun. **Local Programs:** *Montana Road Report*; *Tradio*. **Wattage:** 1,000. **Ad Rates:** Noncommercial. Combined advertising rates available with KPQX-FM, KRYK-FM. **URL:** http://www.kojm.com.

KPLG-FM - See Plains

20261 ■ KPQ-FM
Attn: C. David Leeds
Havre, MT 59501-8003
Phone: (509)665-6565
Fax: (509)663-1150
Format: Adult Contemporary. **Owner:** Wescoast Broadcasting Co., at above address. **Founded:** 1967. **Wattage:** 96,000 ERP. **Ad Rates:** Noncommercial.

20262 ■ KPQX-FM - 92.5
2210 31st St. N
Havre, MT 59501
Phone: (406)265-7841
Fax: (406)265-8855
Email: nmb@nmbi.com
Format: Country. **Owner:** New Media Broadcasters Inc., at above address. **Founded:** 1975. **Operating Hours:** Continuous. **Key Personnel:** John Mosher, Contact; David Leeds, Contact. **Wattage:** 96,000 ERP. **Ad Rates:** Noncommercial. Combined advertising rates available with KOJM-AM & KRUK-FM. **URL:** http://www.kpqx.com.

20263 ■ KRYK-FM - 101.3
2210 31st St.
Havre, MT 59501
Phone: (406)265-7841
Fax: (406)265-8855
Format: Full Service. **Owner:** New Media Broadcasters Inc., at above address. **Wattage:** 100,000 ERP. **Ad Rates:** $5-5.90 for 30 seconds; $6-6.90 for 60 seconds. **URL:** http://www.kryk.com.

KVCM-FM - See Helena

20264 ■ KXEI-FM - 95.1
317 First St.
Havre, MT 59501
Phone: (406)949-4308
Email: info@ynop.org
Format: Religious. **Networks:** Moody Broadcasting; SkyLight Satellite. **Owner:** Your Network of Praise, 317 First St, Havre, MT 59501, Free: 866-752-5257. **Founded:** 1983. **Operating Hours:** Continuous; 50% network, 50% local. **Key Personnel:** Roger Lonnquist, Gen. Mgr.; Brenda Boyum, Station Mgr. **Wattage:** 100,000. **Ad Rates:** Noncommercial. **URL:** http://www.ynop.org.

HELENA

Lewis and Clark Co. Lewis and Clark Co. (WC). The State Capital. 60 m NE of Butte, and midway between Glacier and Yellowstone National Parks. Carroll College. Lime and concrete, paints, machine parts, ceramics manufactured. Trade center. Gold mines. Cattle and sheep. Diversified farming. Hay, grain, potatoes. Resort.

20265 ■ AERO Sun-Times
Alternative Energy Resources Organization
PO Box 1558
Helena, MT 59624
Phone: (406)443-7272
Fax: (406)442-9120
Publisher's E-mail: aero@aeromt.org
Magazine covering resource conservation, sustainable agriculture, smart community growth, and local food systems. **Freq:** Quarterly. **Print Method:** Tabloid-newsprint. **ISSN:** 1046- 0993 (print). **Subscription Rates:** $15 /year. **URL:** http://www.aeromt.org/category/aerosuntimes. **Remarks:** Accepts advertising. **Circ:** Paid 630, Controlled 50.

Circulation: ★ = AAM; △ or • = BPA; ♦ = CAC; ❑ = VAC; ⊕ = PO Statement; ‡ = Publisher's Report; Boldface figures = sworn; Light figures = estimated.

20266 ■ Helena Independent Record
Independent Record
317 Cruse Ave.
Helena, MT 59601
Phone: (406)447-4000
General newspaper. **Freq:** Mon.-Sun. (morn.). **Print Method:** Offset. **Cols./Page:** 8. **Col. Width:** 18 nonpareils. **Col. Depth:** 301 agate lines. **Key Personnel:** Greg Lemon, Editor; Tyler Miller, Publisher, phone: (406)447-4002. **Subscription Rates:** $11 Individuals print and online. **URL:** http://helenair.com. **Mailing address:** PO Box 4249, Helena, MT 59601-5003. **Ad Rates:** 4C $279. **Remarks:** Accepts advertising. **Circ:** 13200, 13700.

20267 ■ The Montana Catholic
Roman Catholic Diocese of Helena
515 N Ewing
Helena, MT 59624-1729
Phone: (406)442-5820
Fax: (406)442-5191
Catholic newspaper (tabloid). **Freq:** Monthly. **Print Method:** Offset. **Trim Size:** 11 1/2 x 13 1/4. **Cols./Page:** 4. **Col. Width:** 14.5 picas. **Col. Depth:** 12 inches. **Key Personnel:** Renee St. Martin Wizeman, Editor; George Leo Thomas, Publisher. **ISSN:** 0883-7899 (print). **Subscription Rates:** $14 Individuals within Montana; $18 Out of state; $32 Other countries. **URL:** http://www.diocesehelena.org. **Formerly:** WestMont Word. **Mailing address:** PO Box 1729, Helena, MT 59624-1729. **Remarks:** alcoholic beverages, tobacco products, and political causes. **Circ:** ‡9200.

20268 ■ Montana: The Magazine of Western History
Montana Historical Society
225 N Roberts St.
Helena, MT 59620
Phone: (406)444-2694
Fax: (406)444-2696
History magazine. **Freq:** Quarterly. **Print Method:** Offset. **Trim Size:** 7 3/4 x 10 3/4. **Cols./Page:** 2. **Col. Width:** 36 nonpareils. **Col. Depth:** 126 agate lines. **Key Personnel:** Tammy L. Ryan, Business Manager, phone: (406)444-4708; Molly Holz, Director, Publications, Editor, phone: (406)444-0090. **ISSN:** 0026--9891 (print). **USPS:** 594-320. **Subscription Rates:** $35 Individuals. **URL:** http://mhs.mt.gov/pubs/magazine. **Mailing address:** PO Box 201201, Helena, MT 59620-1201. **Remarks:** Accepts advertising. **Circ:** (Not Reported).

20269 ■ Parliamentary Debate
National Parliamentary Debate Association
Carroll College
1601 N Benton Ave.
Helena, MT 59625-0001
Phone: (503)768-7729
Fax: (503)768-7620
Journal publishing information for National Parliamentary Debate Association members. **Freq:** Semiannual. **ISSN:** 2381--4616 (print). **Subscription Rates:** Included in membership. **URL:** http://www.parlidebate.org/parliamentary-debate/parliamentary-debate-about-the-journal/. **Remarks:** Advertising not accepted. **Circ:** (Not Reported).

20270 ■ Trial Trends
Montana Trial Lawyers Association
32 S Ewing, Ste. 312
Helena, MT 59601
Phone: (406)443-3124
Fax: (406)530-6050
Publisher's E-mail: mtla@mt.net
Trade magazine covering law for the Montana Trial Lawyers Association. **Freq:** Quarterly. **Key Personnel:** Syd McKenna, President; Craig Daue, Vice President. **Subscription Rates:** $300 Individuals. **URL:** http://www.monttla.com/mt/index.cfm?event=showAppPage&pg=store&action=ViewDetails&ItemID=8710&Category=401. **Mailing address:** PO Box 838, Helena, MT 59624. **Remarks:** Accepts advertising. **Circ:** (Not Reported).

20271 ■ KBLL-AM - 1240
PO Box 4111
Helena, MT 59604
Format: News; Talk. **Networks:** ABC; CNN Radio; Westwood One Radio. **Owner:** Cherry Creek Radio LLC, 501 S Cherry St., Ste. 480, Denver, CO 80246, Ph: (303)468-6500, Fax: (303)468-6555. **Formerly:** KXLJ-AM; KPFA-AM. **Operating Hours:** Continuous; 85% network, 15% local. **ADI:** Helena, MT. **Key Personnel:** Jay Scott, Contact; Jay Scott, Contact. **Wattage:** 1,000. **Ad Rates:** $6-8.50 for 30 seconds; $7.50-10 for 60 seconds. **URL:** http://www.kbllradio.com.

20272 ■ KBLL-FM - 99.5
110 Broadway
Helena, MT 59601
Phone: (406)442-4490
Fax: (406)442-7356
Format: Hot Country. **Networks:** ABC. **Owner:** Cherry Creek Radio LLC, 501 S Cherry St., Ste. 480, Denver, CO 80246, Ph: (303)468-6500, Fax: (303)468-6555. **Operating Hours:** Continuous; 10% network; 90% local. **ADI:** Helena, MT. **Key Personnel:** Travis L. Cronen, VP, Dir. of Operations, tcronen@cherrycreekradio.com; Joe Schwartz, President, CEO, jschwartz@cherrycreekradio.com. **Wattage:** 12,000. **Ad Rates:** $8-14 for 30 seconds; $12-21 for 60 seconds. **Mailing address:** PO Box 4111, Helena, MT 59601. **URL:** http://www.cherrycreekradio.com.

20273 ■ KCAP-AM - 1340
501 S Cherry St., Ste. 480
Denver, CO 80246
Phone: (303)468-6500
Format: Talk; Sports; News. **Networks:** CBS. **Owner:** Cherry Creek Radio LLC, 501 S Cherry St., Ste. 480, Denver, CO 80246, Ph: (303)468-6500, Fax: (303)468-6555. **Founded:** 1949. **Operating Hours:** Continuous. **Key Personnel:** Dewey Bruce, Gen. Mgr., dbruce@cwealthradio.com; Stan Evans, Dir. of Programs, sevans@cwealthradio.com; Chris McCarthy, Sales Mgr., cmccarthy@cwealthradio.com; Travis L. Cronen, Bus. Mgr., tcronen@cwealthradio.com; Ken Eklund, Engineer, alasken@alaska.com; Michele McAlister, Traffic Mgr., mmcalister@cwealthradio.com. **Wattage:** 1,000. **Ad Rates:** Noncommercial.

20274 ■ KHKR-FM - 104.1
PO Box 4111
Helena, MT 59604
Phone: (406)442-4490
Fax: (406)442-7356
Format: Country. **Networks:** AP. **Owner:** Cherry Creek Radio LLC, 501 S Cherry St., Ste. 480, Denver, CO 80246, Ph: (303)468-6500, Fax: (303)468-6555. **Founded:** 1988. **Operating Hours:** Continuous. **ADI:** Helena, MT. **Key Personnel:** Dewey Bruce, Gen. Mgr., dbruce@cherrycreekradio.com. **Wattage:** 5,000. **Ad Rates:** $8 for 30 seconds. Combined advertising rates available with KCAP; KZMT. **URL:** http://www.cherrycreekradio.com.

20275 ■ KHLV-FM - 90.1
PO Box 779002
Rocklin, CA 95677-9972
Fax: (916)251-1901
Free: 800-525-5683
Format: Contemporary Christian. **Owner:** Educational Media Foundation, PO Box 2098, Omaha, NE 68103-2098, Free: 800-434-8400. **ADI:** Helena, MT. **Key Personnel:** Mike Novak, President, CEO; Alan Mason, COO. **Wattage:** 001 H;3,500 V. **URL:** http://www.klove.com.

20276 ■ KMTF-TV - 10
100 W Lyndale Ave., Ste. B
Helena, MT 59601
Phone: (406)457-1010
Fax: (406)457-2758
Email: cw10@surewest.net
Key Personnel: Paul Albertson, Contact, palbertson@surewest.net; Carmen Sharp, Sales Mgr., csharp@beartoothnbc.com. **URL:** http://yourcwtv.com/partners/helena.

20277 ■ KMTX-FM - 105.3
516 Fuller Ave.
Helena, MT 59624
Phone: (406)442-0400
Fax: (406)442-0491
Email: sales@kmtxradio.com
Format: Adult Contemporary. **Networks:** ABC. **Founded:** 1985. **Operating Hours:** Continuous. **ADI:** Helena, MT. **Wattage:** 100,000 ERP. **Ad Rates:** Advertising accepted; rates available upon request.

20278 ■ KTVH-TV - 12
100 W Lyndale Ave.
Helena, MT 59601
Phone: (406)457-1212
Fax: (406)442-5106
Format: Commercial TV. **Networks:** NBC. **Owner:** KRTV Communications, LLC, 100 W Lyndale Ave., Ste. A, Helena, MT 59601, Ph: (406)457-1212, Free: 866-544-7194. **Founded:** 1959. **Operating Hours:** Continuous. **ADI:** Helena, MT. **Key Personnel:** Debbie Schmidt, Mktg. Coord.; Kathy Ernst, Gen. Mgr., kaernst@ktvh.com. **Wattage:** 120,000. **Ad Rates:** $20-350 for 30 seconds. **URL:** http://www.ktvh.com.

20279 ■ K215CG-FM - 90.9
PO Box 391
Twin Falls, ID 83303
Fax: (208)736-1958
Free: 800-357-4226
Format: Religious; Contemporary Christian. **Owner:** CSN International, PO Box 391, Twin Falls, ID 83303, Ph: (208)736-1958, Fax: (208)736-1958, Free: 800-357-4226. **Key Personnel:** Mike Kestler, Contact; Don Mills, Music Dir.; Ray Gorney, Dir. of Engg.; Kelly Carlson, Dir. of Engg. **URL:** http://www.csnradio.com.

20280 ■ KUHM-FM - 91.7
629 S 6th E
Missoula, MT 59812-8064
Phone: (406)243-4931
Fax: (406)243-3299
Free: 800-325-1565
Email: contact@mtpr.org
Format: Public Radio. **Owner:** Montana Public Radio, 32 Campus Dr., Missoula, MT 59812, Ph: (406)243-4931, Fax: (406)243-3299, Free: 800-325-1565. **ADI:** Helena, MT. **Key Personnel:** Sally Mauk, News Dir.; Michael Marsolek, Div. Dir.; Linda Talbott, Assoc. Dir., linda.talbott@mtpr.org; Eric Whitney, News Dir. **URL:** http://mtpr.org/listen.

20281 ■ KVCM-FM - 103.1
317 1st St.
Havre, MT 59501
Phone: (406)265-5845
Fax: (406)265-8860
Free: 800-442-9222
Email: info@ynop.org
Format: Religious. **Owner:** Your Network of Praise, 317 First St, Havre, MT 59501, Free: 866-752-5257. **ADI:** Helena, MT. **Key Personnel:** Roger Lonnquist, Gen. Mgr.; David Brown, Dir. of Programs; Brenda Boyum, Station Mgr.; Ron Huckeby, Chief Engineer. **Mailing address:** PO Box 2426, Havre, MT 59501. **URL:** http://www.ynop.org/stationlist.html.

20282 ■ KXLH-TV
100 W Lyndale
Helena, MT 59601
Phone: (406)422-1018
Email: news@kxlh.com
Format: News; Sports. **Owner:** Evening Post Industries Inc., 134 Columbus St., Charleston, SC 29403, Ph: (843)577-7111. **Founded:** 1958. **Key Personnel:** Tim McGonigal, Producer. **Ad Rates:** Advertising accepted; rates available upon request. **Mailing address:** PO Box 7479, Helena, MT 59604. **URL:** http://www.kxlh.com.

20283 ■ KZMT-FM - 101.1
501 S Cherry St., Ste. 480
Denver, CO 80246
Phone: (303)377-6910
Format: Classic Rock. **Networks:** CBS. **Owner:** Cherry Creek Radio LLC, 501 S Cherry St., Ste. 480, Denver, CO 80246, Ph: (303)468-6500, Fax: (303)468-6555. **Founded:** 1975. **Operating Hours:** Continuous. **ADI:** Helena, MT. **Key Personnel:** Dewey Bruce, Gen. Mgr., dbruce@cwealthradio.com; Stan Evans, Dir. of Programs, sevans@cwealthradio.com; Chris McCarthy, Sales Mgr., cmccarthy@cwealthradio.com; Travis L. Cronen, Bus. Mgr., tcronen@cwealthradio.com; Michele McAlister, Traffic Mgr., mmcalister@cwealthradio.com; Ken Eklund, Engineer, alasken@alaska.com. **Wattage:** 100,000. **Ad Rates:** Noncommercial.

KALISPELL

Flathead Co. Flathead Co. (NW). On Flathead River, 30 m W of Glacier National Park, 10 m N of Flathead Lake. Resort area. Lumber and Planning mills; aluminum plant; pulpwood products factory. Trade center. Pine, fir timber. Agriculture. Cherry orchards, wheat, oats, rye. Christmas trees.

20284 ■ The Daily Inter Lake
Inter Lake Publishing Co.
727 E Idaho
Kalispell, MT 59901
Phone: (406)755-7000
Fax: (406)752-6114
Publisher's E-mail: newsed@dailyinterlake.com
General newspaper. **Freq:** Daily (morn.). **Print Method:** Offset. **Cols./Page:** 6. **Col. Width:** 25 nonpareils. **Col. Depth:** 21 inches. **Key Personnel:** Dale Piedalue, Supervisor, phone: (406)758-4480; Brant Horn, Manager, Circulation, phone: (406)758-4490; Cindy Sease, Director, Advertising, phone: (406)758-4410; Rick Weaver, Publisher, phone: (406)755-7000; Dorothy Glencross, Business Manager, phone: (406)755-7000; Frank Miele, Managing Editor, phone: (406)758-4447. **Subscription Rates:** $20.84 Individuals full access; $12.30 Individuals for digital. **URL:** http://www.dailyinterlake.com. **Ad Rates:** GLR $13; BW $1,638; 4C $2028; PCI $15.13. **Remarks:** Accepts advertising. **Circ:** Mon.-Sat. ♦**15285**, Sun. ♦**16291**.

20285 ■ Montana English Journal
Montana Association of Teachers of English Language Arts
c/o Dana Haring, Treasurer
620 1st. Ave. W
Kalispell, MT 59901
Journal containing publications of literature, learning, and comments relevant to Montana Association of Teachers of English Language Arts members. **Freq:** Annual. **Subscription Rates:** included in membership dues. **Remarks:** Advertising not accepted. **Circ:** (Not Reported).

20286 ■ KAJ-TV - 18
301 First Ave. E
Kalispell, MT 59901
Phone: (406)756-5888
Fax: (406)756-5889
Format: News; Commercial TV. **Simulcasts:** KPAX-TV. **Networks:** CBS. **Owner:** KPAX Communications, Inc., at above address. **Founded:** 1988. **Operating Hours:** Continuous. **ADI:** Missoula, MT. **Key Personnel:** Bob Hermes, Gen. Mgr., bob@kpax.com. **Ad Rates:** Advertising accepted; rates available upon request. KPAX-TV. **URL:** http://www.kaj18.com.

20287 ■ KALS-FM - 97.1
106 Cooperative Way, Ste. 102
Kalispell, MT 59901
Format: Contemporary Christian; Religious. **Networks:** Sun Radio; AP. **Owner:** Kalispell Christian Radio Fellowship Inc., at above address. **Founded:** 1974. **Operating Hours:** Continuous. **Key Personnel:** David Brown, Dir. of Programs. **Wattage:** 26,500. **Ad Rates:** $8.50-11.50 for 30 seconds; $12.50-16.50 for 60 seconds. **URL:** http://www.kals.com.

20288 ■ KBBZ-FM - 98.5
2432 US Highway 2 E
Kalispell, MT 59901
Phone: (406)755-7625
Format: Classic Rock. **Owner:** Bee Broadcasting Radio Network, 2432 Hwy. 2 E, Kalispell, MT 59903, Ph: (406)755-8700. **Operating Hours:** Continuous. **Wattage:** 61,000 Horizontal ER. **Ad Rates:** Advertising accepted; rates available upon request. **URL:** http://www.kbbz.com.

20289 ■ KCFW-TV - 9
401 1st Ave. E
Kalispell, MT 59901
Phone: (406)755-5239
Fax: (406)752-8002
Email: news@kcfw.com
Format: Commercial TV. **Networks:** NBC. **Owner:** Bonten Media Group Inc., Empire State Bldg., 350 Fifth Ave., Ste. 5340, New York, NY 10118, Ph: (212)710-7771, Fax: (212)949-0909. **Founded:** 1968. **Operating Hours:** Continuous. **ADI:** Missoula, MT. **Local Programs:** *News At Six*, Monday Tuesday Wednesday Thursday Friday 6:00 p.m. **Ad Rates:** Noncommercial. **URL:** http://www.nbcmontana.com/kcfw/news.

20290 ■ KDBR-FM - 106.3
PO Box 5409
Kalispell, MT 59903
Phone: (406)257-5327
Format: Country. **Owner:** Bee Broadcasting Radio Network, 2432 Hwy. 2 E, Kalispell, MT 59903, Ph: (406)755-8700. **Ad Rates:** Noncommercial. **URL:** http://www.kdbr.com.

20291 ■ KGEZ-AM
PO Box 958
Kalispell, MT 59903
Phone: (406)752-2600
Fax: (406)257-0459
Email: info@z600.com
Format: News; Talk; Sports. **Networks:** Fox. **Owner:** Z600 Inc., at above address. **Founded:** 1927. **Key Personnel:** Pam Stokes, Contact, stokes@z600.com. **Wattage:** 5,000 Day; 1,000 Nig. **Ad Rates:** $10-18 for 30 seconds; $20-30 for 60 seconds.

20292 ■ KHNK-FM - 95.9
2432 Hwy. 2 E
Kalispell, MT 59901-2310
Phone: (406)755-8700
Email: hank@myhank.com
Format: Country. **Wattage:** 55,000 H;5,600 V. **Ad Rates:** Advertising accepted; rates available upon request. **URL:** http://www.myhank.com.

20293 ■ KJJR-AM - 880
2432 Hwy. 2 E
Kalispell, MT 59901
Phone: (406)755-8700
Format: News; Talk. **Networks:** Fox. **Operating Hours:** Continuous Monday - Saturday; 6:00 a.m. - Noon Sunday. **Wattage:** 10,000 Day; 500 Nigh. **Ad Rates:** Advertising accepted; rates available upon request. **URL:** http://www.kjjr.com.

20294 ■ KOFI-AM - 1180
317 1st Ave. E
Kalispell, MT 59901
Phone: (406)755-6690
Email: kofi@kofiradio.com
Format: News; Talk; Oldies. **Networks:** ABC. **Owner:** KOFI Inc., 317 1st Ave. E, Kalispell, MT 59901, Ph: (406)755-6690. **Founded:** 1955. **Operating Hours:** Continuous; 30% network, 70% local. **Wattage:** 50,000. **Ad Rates:** $16.90-18.75 for 30 seconds; $21.50-25.50 for 60 seconds. 5% discount for combo rates. **URL:** http://www.kofiradio.com.

20295 ■ K201EY-FM - 88.1
PO Box 391
Twin Falls, ID 83303
Fax: (208)736-1958
Free: 800-357-4226
Format: Religious; Contemporary Christian. **Owner:** CSN International, PO Box 391, Twin Falls, ID 83303, Ph: (208)736-1958, Fax: (208)736-1958, Free: 800-357-4226. **Key Personnel:** Mike Kestler, Contact; Don Mills, Music Dir., Prog. Dir. **URL:** http://www.csnradio.com.

20296 ■ KUKL-FM - 90.1
629 S 6th E
Missoula, MT 59812-8064
Phone: (406)243-4931
Fax: (406)243-3299
Free: 800-325-1565
Email: contact@mtpr.org
Format: Public Radio. **Owner:** Montana Public Radio, 32 Campus Dr., Missoula, MT 59812, Ph: (406)243-4931, Fax: (406)243-3299, Free: 800-325-1565. **Key Personnel:** Michael Marsolek, Prog. Dir., michael.marsolek@mtpr.org; Linda Talbott, Div. Dir., linda.talbott@mtpr.org; Sally Mauk, News Dir., sally.mauk@mtpr.org. **URL:** http://mtpr.org/listen.

KWOL-FM - See Whitefish

20297 ■ KZMN-FM - 103.9
317 First Ave., E
Kalispell, MT 59901
Phone: (406)755-6690
Format: Classic Rock. **Networks:** CNN Radio. **Owner:** KOFI Inc., 317 1st Ave. E, Kalispell, MT 59901, Ph: (406)755-6690. **Formerly:** KOFI-FM. **Operating Hours:** Continuous; 100% local. **Key Personnel:** Dave Rae, Contact, dave@monster1039.com; Dave Rae, Contact, dave@monster1039.com. **Wattage:** 100,000 H;43,000 V. **Ad Rates:** $16.90-18.75 for 30 seconds; $21.50-25.50 for 60 seconds. Combined advertising rates available with KOFI-AM. **URL:** http://www.monster1039.com.

LAUREL

Yellowstone Co. Yellowstone Co. (SC). 20m SW of Billings. Residential.

20298 ■ Laurel Outlook
Outlook Publishing Inc.
415 E Main
Laurel, MT 59044
Phone: (406)628-4412
Fax: (406)628-8260
Free: 800-295-4412
Community newspaper. **Freq:** Weekly (Thurs.). **Print Method:** Offset. **Cols./Page:** 6. **Col. Width:** 12 picas. **Col. Depth:** 21 1/2 inches. **Key Personnel:** Milton Wester, Editor; Gloria Wester, Publisher; Jennifer Ries, Managing Editor. **Subscription Rates:** $31 Individuals in Laurel, delivered by carrier; $33 Out of area in Yellowstone, Carbon and Stillwater counties; $36 Elsewhere by mail; $31 Individuals military personnel; $31 Students 9 months; $30 Individuals senior. **URL:** http://www.laureloutlook.com. **Mailing address:** PO Box 278, Laurel, MT 59044. **Remarks:** Accepts advertising. **Circ:** Paid ‡3587, Free ‡55.

20299 ■ Cable Montana
222 W 1st St.
Laurel, MT 59044
Cities Served: 53 channels. **URL:** http://usacommunications.tv.

20300 ■ KBSR-AM - 1490
PO Box 248
Laurel, MT 59044-0216
Phone: (406)628-8271
Fax: (406)665-2131
Owner: Big Sky Radio, Hardin, MT. **Founded:** 1979. **Key Personnel:** David Berg, Sales Rep. **Wattage:** 1,000 ERP. **URL:** http://www.bigskyradio.net.

LEWISTOWN

Fergus Co. Fergus Co. (C). 107 m SE of Great Falls. Lumber mills. Gold mines. Stockyards. Stock, grain farms. Sheep, cattle, wheat.

20301 ■ Lewistown News-Argus
Lewistown News-Argus
521 W Main St.
Lewistown, MT 59457
Publication E-mail: newsstaff@lewistownnews.com
Community newspaper. **Freq:** Semiweekly (Wed. and Sat.). **Print Method:** Offset. **Trim Size:** 12 1/2 x 22 3/4. **Cols./Page:** 6. **Col. Width:** 1.819 inches. **Col. Depth:** 21.5 inches. **Key Personnel:** Oron Jacobs, Publisher; Jacques Rutten, Editor. **Subscription Rates:** $65 Individuals online only; $70 Individuals in county; $82 Out of area print and online; $98 Out of state print and online. **URL:** http://www.lewistownnews.com. **Mailing address:** PO Box 900, Lewistown, MT 59457-0900. **Ad Rates:** GLR $.58; BW $795.06; SAU $7.17. **Remarks:** Accepts advertising. **Circ:** ‡4200.

20302 ■ KBAO-TV - 13
620 NE Main St.
Lewistown, MT 59457
Free: 866-544-7195
Owner: KRTV Communications, LLC, 100 W Lyndale Ave., Ste. A, Helena, MT 59601, Ph: (406)457-1212, Free: 866-544-7194.

20303 ■ KLCM-FM - 95.9
620 NE Main St.
Lewistown, MT 59457
Phone: (406)535-3441
Email: traffic@kxlo-klcm.com
Format: Adult Contemporary; News. **Simulcasts:** KXLO-FM. **Networks:** ABC; CBS; Westwood One Radio. **Owner:** Montana Broadcast Communications Inc., at above address. **Founded:** 1975. **Key Personnel:** Fred Lark, President, lark@kxlo-klcm.com; Phyllis Hall, Station Mgr. **Wattage:** 3,000 ERP. **Ad Rates:** Advertising accepted; rates available upon request. **URL:** http://www.kxlo-klcm.com.

20304 ■ KXLO-AM - 1230
620 NE Main St.
Lewistown, MT 59457
Phone: (406)535-3441
Email: traffic@kxlo-klcm.com

Circulation: ★ = AAM; △ or • = BPA; ♦ = CAC; ❑ = VAC; ⊕ = PO Statement; ‡ = Publisher's Report; Boldface figures = sworn; Light figures = estimated.

Format: Country. **Simulcasts:** KLCM-FM. **Owner:** KXLO Broadcast Inc., at above address, Lewistown, MT 59457. **Founded:** 1947. **Key Personnel:** Fred Lark, Owner, President; Phyllis Hall, Mgr. **Wattage:** 1,000. **Ad Rates:** Advertising accepted; rates available upon request. **URL:** http://www.kxlo-klcm.com.

20305 ■ Mid-Rivers Communications
223 W Janeaux St.
Lewistown, MT 59457
Phone: (406)535-3336
Fax: (406)535-5193
Free: 800-452-2288
Founded: 1952. **Cities Served:** 85 channels. **URL:** http://www.midrivers.com.

LIBBY

Lincoln Co. Lincoln Co. (NW). 215 m NW of Missoula. Heritage museum. Hiking, skiing, fishing and hunting. Manufactures lumber and vermiculite. Lead, silver, gold, mines; pine, fir, larch timber.

20306 ■ Western News
Western News
PO Box 1377
Libby, MT 59923
Phone: (406)293-4124
Fax: (406)293-7187
Community newspaper. **Founded:** 1902. **Freq:** Semi-weekly Tuesday anf Friday. **Print Method:** Offset. **Cols./Page:** 8. **Col. Width:** 21 nonpareils. **Col. Depth:** 127 agate lines. **Key Personnel:** Matt Bunk, Publisher, phone: (406)293-4124. **Subscription Rates:** $47 Individuals print or online. **URL:** http://www.thewesternnews.com. **Ad Rates:** GLR $.28; BW $810.50; 4C $1,000. **Remarks:** Accepts advertising. **Circ:** 4200.

20307 ■ KLCB-AM - 1230
PO Box 730
Libby, MT 59923
Phone: (406)293-6234
Format: Country; News; Sports; Contemporary Country. **Networks:** ABC. **Owner:** Lincoln County Broadcasters, Inc., Libby, MT. **Founded:** 1950. **Operating Hours:** 6.30 a.m. - 5.30 p.m. Monday - Friday. **Wattage:** 1,000 KW. **Ad Rates:** Advertising accepted; rates available upon request. **URL:** http://www.klcb-ktny.com.

20308 ■ KTNY-FM - 101.7
251 W Cedar St.
Libby, MT 59923
Phone: (406)293-6234
Format: Easy Listening; News; Oldies; Talk. **Networks:** ABC. **Owner:** Lincoln County Broadcasters, Inc., Libby, MT. **Founded:** 1986. **Wattage:** 3,000 ERP. **Ad Rates:** Advertising accepted; rates available upon request. **URL:** http://www.klcb-ktny.com.

LIVINGSTON

Park Co. Park Co. (S). On Yellowstone River, 100 m W of Billings. Lumbering, marble and granite works; feed and flour mill. Travertine. Dairy, stock, grain farms. Cattle, sheep, wheat. Tourist center.

20309 ■ Atlantis Rising: Ancient Mysteries, Unexplained Anomalies, Future Science
Atlantis Rising
PO Box 441
Livingston, MT 59047
Fax: (406)222-3078
Free: 800-228-8381
Magazine featuring unexplained anomalies, future science, and ancient mysteries. **Freq:** Bimonthly. **Key Personnel:** J. Douglas Kenyon, Editor. **ISSN:** 1541--5031 (print). **Subscription Rates:** $29.95 U.S. new subscription; $50 Two years new subscription; $25 U.S. renewal; $39.95 Two years renewal. **URL:** http://www.atlantisrising.com/index.shtml. **Remarks:** Accepts advertising. **Circ:** (Not Reported).

20310 ■ The Flyfisher
Federation of Fly Fishers
5237 US Highway 89 S, Ste. 11
Livingston, MT 59047
Phone: (406)222-9369
Freq: Semiannual Quarterly. **Key Personnel:** Chris Bessler, Publisher. **Subscription Rates:** Included in membership. **URL:** http://flyfishermagazine.com; http://www.fedflyfishers.org/About/Flyfisher.aspx. **Remarks:** Accepts advertising. **Circ:** 13000.

20311 ■ Livingston Enterprise
Livingston Enterprise
401 S Main St.
Livingston, MT 59047
Phone: (406)222-2000
Fax: (406)222-8580
Free: 800-345-8412
Publisher's E-mail: enterprise@livent.net
General newspaper. **Founded:** June 04, 1883. **Freq:** Daily (eve.). **Print Method:** Offset. **Trim Size:** 12 1/2 x 23 3/4. **Cols./Page:** 6. **Col. Width:** 21 nonpareils. **Col. Depth:** 301 agate lines. **Key Personnel:** Dwight Harriman, Editor; John Sullivan, Editor, Publisher. **Subscription Rates:** $120 Individuals carrier delivery; in Livingston; $132 Individuals motor route delivery; $165 By mail in Park County; $215 By mail; $440 Other countries. **URL:** http://livingstonenterprise.com. **Mailing address:** PO Box 2000, Livingston, MT 59047. **Ad Rates:** BW $703.05; 4C $753.05; SAU $5.90; PCI $6.50. **Remarks:** Accepts advertising. **Circ:** ‡3500.

MALTA

Phillips Co. Phillips Co. (N). 170 m NE of Great Falls. Gas wells. Cattle, sheep, dairy, grain farms. Alfalfa seed.

20312 ■ KMMR-FM - 100.1
155 1/2 S 1st Ave.
Malta, MT 59538
Phone: (406)654-2472
Owner: KMMR Radio, Inc., at above address. **Founded:** 1980. **Key Personnel:** Claudette Kielb, Contact. **Wattage:** 2,250 ERP. **Ad Rates:** $5-7 for 30 seconds; $7-9 for 60 seconds. **Mailing address:** PO Box 1073, Malta, MT 59538. **URL:** http://www.kmmrfm.com.

MARYSVILLE

20313 ■ K296BI-FM - 107.1
Broadcast Media Ctr.
University of Montana
Missoula, MT 59812
Phone: (406)243-4931
Fax: (406)243-3299
Free: 800-325-1565
Format: Eclectic. **Owner:** Montana Public Radio, 32 Campus Dr., Missoula, MT 59812, Ph: (406)243-4931, Fax: (406)243-3299, Free: 800-325-1565. **Key Personnel:** Sally Mauk, News Dir. **URL:** http://www.archive.mtpr.net.

MILES CITY

Custer Co. Custer Co. (SE). On Yellowstone River, 152 m E of Billings. U.S. Livestock Range Experiment Station, 57,000 acres. Shipping and trade center of the horse, cattle, wool district of Eastern Montana. Manufactures saddles, harnesses, creamery products, flour. Gas wells. Agriculture. Sugar beets, alfalfa, wheat, corn.

20314 ■ Miles City Star
Star Printing and Supply Co.
818 Main St.
Miles City, MT 59301
Phone: (406)234-0450
Fax: (406)234-6687
Free: 800-323-6505
Publication E-mail: mceditor@midrivers.com
General newspaper. **Freq:** Daily. **Print Method:** Offset. **Cols./Page:** 6. **Col. Width:** 25 nonpareils. **Col. Depth:** 301 agate lines. **Key Personnel:** Marla Prell, Managing Editor; Dan Killoy, Publisher; Jeff Virag, Manager, Circulation, phone: (406)234-0450. **Subscription Rates:** $136.80 Individuals carrier delivery; $218.88 By mail in Custer county; $159.60 Individuals motor route delivery; $236.55 Out of area by mail. **URL:** http://www.milescitystar.com. **Ad Rates:** SAU $5.46. **Remarks:** Accepts advertising. **Circ:** Mon.-Fri. ‡4000.

20315 ■ KATL-AM - 770
818 Main St.
Miles City, MT 59301
Phone: (406)234-7700
Free: 800-473-5285
Email: katlradio@katlradio.com
Format: Adult Contemporary. **Networks:** ABC; Westwood One Radio; Northern Agricultural. **Owner:** Star Print Mail Inc., West Ghosen Business Pk., 1075 Andrew Dr., West Chester, PA 19380, Ph: (610)439-1111, Fax: (610)436-1155. **Formerly:** KRJF-AM. **Operating Hours:** Continuous; 65% network, 35% local. **ADI:** Billings-Hardin, MT. **Wattage:** 10,000 Day; 1,000 Night. **Ad Rates:** $6.25-7.90 for 30 seconds; $10.80-13.15 for 60 seconds. **Mailing address:** PO Box 700, Miles City, MT 59301. **URL:** http://www.katlradio.com.

20316 ■ KMCJ-FM - 99.5
317 First St.
Havre, MT 59501
Phone: (406)949-4308
Free: 800-442-9222
Email: ynop@ynop.org
Format: Religious. **Owner:** Your Network of Praise, 317 First St, Havre, MT 59501, Free: 866-752-5257. **Key Personnel:** Brenda Boyum, Station Mgr.; David Brown, Prog. Dir.; Roger Lonnquist, Gen. Mgr.; Ron Huckeby, Chief Engineer. **Wattage:** 100,000. **Mailing address:** PO Box 2426, Havre, MT 59501. **URL:** http://www.ynop.org/stationlist.html.

20317 ■ KMTA-AM
508 Main St.
Box 1426
Miles City, MT 59301
Phone: (406)232-5626
Fax: (406)232-7000
Networks: CNN Radio. **Owner:** Senger Broadcasting Corporation, at above address. **Founded:** 1986. **Wattage:** 10,000 Day; 136 Nigh. **Ad Rates:** $5 for 30 seconds. **URL:** http://www.kyuskmta.com/.

20318 ■ KYUS-FM - 92.3
508 Main St.
Miles City, MT 59301
Phone: (406)234-5626
Format: Adult Contemporary; Hot Country. **Owner:** Marks Radio Group, at above address. **Operating Hours:** Continuous. **Key Personnel:** Terry Virag, Gen. Mgr.; Charice Virag, Office Mgr. **Wattage:** 100,000. **URL:** http://www.kyuskmta.com.

MISSOULA

Missoula Co. Missoula Co. (W). 120 m NW of Helena. University of Montana. U.S. Forest Service. Resort area. Dairy and meat products plants; plywood, pulp, lumber manufactured. - Diversified farming. Dairying, beef cattle.

20319 ■ Adventure Cyclist
Adventure Cycling Association
150 E Pine St.
Missoula, MT 59807
Phone: (406)721-1776
Fax: (406)721-8754
Free: 800-755-2453
Magazine covering bicycle travel and adventure. **Freq:** 9/year. **Trim Size:** 8.5 x 11.125. **Key Personnel:** John Schubert, Contact; Michael Deme, Editor; Aaron Teasdale, Editor. **Subscription Rates:** Included in membership. **URL:** http://www.adventurecycling.org/adventure-cyclist. **Mailing address:** PO Box 8308, Missoula, MT 59807. **Ad Rates:** BW $2915; 4C $4100. **Remarks:** Accepts advertising. **Circ:** Paid ‡42100, 40000.

20320 ■ College Music Symposium
College Music Society
312 E Pine St.
Missoula, MT 59802
Phone: (406)721-9616
Fax: (406)721-9419
Publisher's E-mail: cms@music.org
Periodical devoted to musicology. **Freq:** Annual. **Trim Size:** 5 x 8. **Key Personnel:** Janna Saslaw, Contact; Arthur Houle, Board Member; Louis Bergonzi, Board Member; Steven J. Cahn, Board Member. **ISSN:** 0069--5696 (print). **Subscription Rates:** $25 latest issues; $10 back issues. **URL:** http://www.music.org/index.php?option=com_hikashop&view=product&layout=listing&Itemid=892. **Ad Rates:** BW $200. **Remarks:** Accepts advertising. **Circ:** 2,000.

20321 ■ Fair Chase
Boone and Crockett Club
250 Station Dr.
Missoula, MT 59801
Phone: (406)542-1888
Fax: (406)542-0784
Free: 888-840-4868

Publisher's E-mail: bcclub@boone-crockett.org
Magazine publishing articles about hunting adventures and conservation of North American big game. **Freq:** Quarterly. **Subscription Rates:** $25 web only. **URL:** http://www.boone-crockett.org/join/associates_magazine.asp?area=join. **Remarks:** Accepts advertising. **Circ:** (Not Reported).

20322 ■ Folk Harp Journal
International Society of Folk Harpers and Craftsmen
Alice Williams, Secretary
1614 Pittman Dr.
Missoula, MT 59803
Phone: (406)542-1976
Freq: Quarterly. **ISSN:** 0094--8934 (print). **Subscription Rates:** included in membership dues; $9 Single issue; $5 Individuals back issue. **Remarks:** Accepts advertising. **Circ:** (Not Reported).

20323 ■ Missoula Independent
Independent Publishing Inc.
317 S Orange St.
Missoula, MT 59801
Phone: (406)543-6609
Fax: (406)543-4367
Community newspaper. **Freq:** Weekly (Thurs.). **Key Personnel:** Lynne Foland, Publisher. **URL:** http://missoulanews.bigskypress.com. **Ad Rates:** GLR $15; BW $1,070; 4C $1,370. **Remarks:** Accepts advertising. **Circ:** Combined ■ **2200**.

20324 ■ Missoulian
Missoulian
500 S Higgins
Missoula, MT 59807
Phone: (406)523-5200
Fax: (406)523-5221
Free: 800-366-7102
Publisher's E-mail: newsdesk@missoulian.com
General newspaper. **Freq:** Mon.-Sun. (morn.). **Print Method:** Offset. **Trim Size:** 27. **Cols./Page:** 6. **Col. Width:** 25 nonpareils. **Col. Depth:** 301 agate lines. **Key Personnel:** Sherry Devlin, Editor, phone: (406)523-5250. **Subscription Rates:** $55.75 Individuals home delivery; 7 days; 12 weeks; $33.75 Individuals home delivery; Saturday & Sunday; 12 weeks; $28.20 Individuals home delivery; Sunday; 12 weeks; $89.25 Out of state mail delivery; 7 days; 12 weeks; $52.80 Out of state mail delivery; Sunday; 12 weeks; $76.50 By mail 12 weeks. **URL:** http://missoulian.com. **Mailing address:** PO Box 8029, Missoula, MT 59807. **Remarks:** Accepts advertising. **Circ:** Mon.-Fri. ★**27955**, Sat. ★**28596**, Sun. ★**32480**.

20325 ■ The Montana Business Quarterly
University of Montana Bureau of Business and Economic Research
Gallagher Business Bldg.
32 Campus Dr., Rm. 6840
Missoula, MT 59812-6840
Phone: (406)243-5113
Fax: (406)248-2086
Regional economics journal for decision-makers. **Founded:** 1962. **Freq:** Quarterly. **Print Method:** Offset. **Trim Size:** 8 1/2 x 11. **Cols./Page:** 3. **Col. Width:** 2 3/8 inches. **Col. Depth:** 8 3/4 inches. **Key Personnel:** Shannon Furniss, Director. **Subscription Rates:** $35 Individuals; $65 Two years; $90 Individuals tree years. **URL:** http://www.bber.umt.edu/MBQ/MBQ.asp. **Remarks:** Advertising not accepted. **Circ:** Paid ‡1300, Non-paid ‡200.

20326 ■ Montana Journalism Review
The University of Montana School of Journalism
Don Anderson Hall
32 Campus Drive
Missoula, MT 59812
Phone: (406)243-4001
Publisher's E-mail: journalism@selway.umt.edu
Journalism review publication. **Freq:** Annual. **Print Method:** Offset. **Trim Size:** 8 1/2 x 11. **Cols./Page:** 3. **Col. Width:** 14 picas. **Col. Depth:** 60 picas. **Key Personnel:** Clemens P. Work, Editor. **URL:** http://mjr.jour.umt.edu. **Remarks:** Accepts advertising. **Circ:** (Not Reported).

20327 ■ Montana Kaimin
University of Montana
32 Campus Dr.
Missoula, MT 59801
Phone: (406)243-4310
Collegiate newspaper. **Freq:** Daily (morn.) Tues.-Fri. **Print Method:** Offset. **Trim Size:** 9 1/2 x 12 1/2. **Cols./Page:** 5. **Col. Width:** 19 nonpareils. **Col. Depth:** 175 agate lines. **Key Personnel:** Ric Sanchez, Editor-in-Chief. **URL:** http://www.umt.edu; http://www.montanakaimin.com. **Remarks:** Advertising accepted; rates available upon request. **Circ:** Free 6000.

20328 ■ Montana Magazine
Montana Magazine
PO Box 8689
Missoula, MT 59807
Free: 888-666-8624
Regional interest magazine. **Founded:** May 01, 1970. **Freq:** Bimonthly. **Print Method:** Web offset. **Trim Size:** 8 x 10 7/8. **Cols./Page:** 3. **Col. Width:** 13 picas. **Col. Depth:** 135 agate lines. **Key Personnel:** Jenna Cederberg, Editor. **ISSN:** 0274-9955 (print). **Subscription Rates:** $25 Individuals; $60 Individuals 3 years; $44 Two years; $47 Canada; $67 Other countries. **URL:** http://montanamagazine.com. **Ad Rates:** BW $1,590; 4C $2,216. **Remarks:** Accepts advertising. **Circ:** Paid ‡27895.

20329 ■ Montanan: The Magazine of the University of Montana
University of Montana
32 Campus Dr.
Missoula, MT 59812
Phone: (406)243-0211
Publication E-mail: themontanan@umontana.edu
University magazine. **Freq:** 3/year. **Print Method:** Web offset. **Trim Size:** 50 x 65.6. **Cols./Page:** 3. **Col. Width:** 14 picas. **Col. Depth:** 59 picas. **Key Personnel:** John Heaney, Editor-in-Chief; Todd Goodrich, Editor; Eric Elander, Advertising Representative, phone: (406)360-3321; Denise Dowling, Advisor, Board Member; Eileen Chontos, Designer. **Alt. Formats:** PDF. **URL:** http://montanan.umt.edu/issues/spring-2015/default.php. **Remarks:** Accepts advertising. **Circ:** (Not Reported).

20330 ■ Perceptual and Motor Skills
Ammons Scientific Ltd.
1917 S Higgins Ave.
Missoula, MT 59801
Phone: (406)728-1710
Publisher's E-mail: submissions@ammonsscientific.com
Technical journal featuring experimental and theoretical articles on perception or motor skills, especially as affected by experience; includes articles on general methodology. **Freq:** Bimonthly. **Print Method:** Offset. **Trim Size:** 6 1/8 x 9 1/8. **Cols./Page:** 1. **Col. Width:** 4 1/2 inches. **Col. Depth:** 7 1/4 inches. **Key Personnel:** C.H. Ammons, Senior Editor. **ISSN:** 0031--5125 (print). **Subscription Rates:** £112 Individuals print and online. **URL:** http://www.amsciepub.com/loi/pms. **Mailing address:** PO Box 9229, Missoula, MT 59807-9229. **Remarks:** Advertising not accepted. **Circ:** ‡2000.

20331 ■ Psychological Reports
Ammons Scientific Ltd.
1917 S Higgins Ave.
Missoula, MT 59801
Phone: (406)728-1710
Publisher's E-mail: submissions@ammonsscientific.com
Technical journal in psychology featuring experimental, theoretical, and speculative articles. **Freq:** Bimonthly. **Print Method:** Offset. **Trim Size:** 6 1/8 x 9 1/2. **Cols./Page:** 1. **Col. Width:** 4 1/2 inches. **Col. Depth:** 7 1/4 inches. **Key Personnel:** C.H. Ammons, Senior Editor; Doug Ammons, Editor; R.B. Ammons, Senior Editor. **ISSN:** 0332--2941 (print). **Subscription Rates:** $480 Individuals plus postage. **URL:** http://www.amsciepub.com/loi/pr0. **Mailing address:** PO Box 9229, Missoula, MT 59807-9229. **Remarks:** Advertising not accepted. **Circ:** ‡2000.

20332 ■ Your National Forests
National Forest Foundation
Bldg. 27, Ste. 3
Fort Missoula Rd.
Missoula, MT 59804-7212
Phone: (406)542-2805
Fax: (406)542-2810
Freq: Semiannual. **Subscription Rates:** free. **URL:** http://www.nationalforests.org/our-forests/your-national-forests-magazine/pushing-the-boundaries. **Remarks:** Advertising not accepted. **Circ:** (Not Reported).

20333 ■ KBAZ-FM - 96.3
3250 S Reserve St., Ste. 200
Missoula, MT 59801
Phone: (406)829-9630
Email: angel@963theblaze.com
Format: Alternative/New Music/Progressive. **URL:** http://www.963theblaze.com.

20334 ■ KBGA-FM - 89.9
University of Montana
University Center
Missoula, MT 59812
Phone: (406)243-6758
Fax: (406)243-6428
Email: news@kbga.org
Format: News; Educational. **Owner:** University of Montana, at above address. **Founded:** Aug. 23, 1996. **Operating Hours:** Continuous. **Key Personnel:** Clark Grant, Gen. Mgr., gm@kbga.org; Chris Justice, Dir. of Programs. **Wattage:** 1,000. **Ad Rates:** Noncommercial. **URL:** http://www.kbga.org.

20335 ■ KDTR-FM - 103.3
2425 W Central Ave., Ste. 203
Missoula, MT 59801
Format: Adult Album Alternative. **Wattage:** 1,840. **URL:** http://www.trail1033.com.

20336 ■ KECI-TV - 13
340 W Main
Missoula, MT 59802
Phone: (406)721-2063
Email: sales@keci.com
Format: Commercial TV. **Simulcasts:** KCFW-TV and KTVM-TV. **Networks:** NBC. **Founded:** 1954. **Formerly:** KMSO-TV; KGVO-TV. **Operating Hours:** Continuous. **ADI:** Missoula, MT. **Key Personnel:** Gavin Maliska, News Dir. **Ad Rates:** Noncommercial. **URL:** http://www.nbcmontana.com/keci/news.

20337 ■ KENR-FM - 107.5
3250 S Reserve
Missoula, MT 59801
Phone: (406)728-9300
Format: Contemporary Hit Radio (CHR). **Owner:** Townsquare Media Inc., 240 Greenwich Ave., Greenwich, CT 06830-6507, Ph: (203)861-0900. **Key Personnel:** Greg Baird, Managing Ed., greg.baird@townsquaremedia.com. **URL:** http://1075zoofm.com.

20338 ■ KGGL-FM - 93.3
1600 N Ave.
Missoula, MT 59801
Phone: (406)728-5000
Fax: (406)721-3020
Format: Country. **Owner:** Cherry Creek Radio LLC, 501 S Cherry St., Ste. 480, Denver, CO 80246, Ph: (303)468-6500, Fax: (303)468-6555. **Founded:** 1972. **Operating Hours:** Continuous; 100% local. **Key Personnel:** Joe Schwartz, President, jschwartz@cherrycreekradio.com. **Wattage:** 43,000. **Ad Rates:** Advertising accepted; rates available upon request. **URL:** http://www.cherrycreekradio.com.

20339 ■ KGRZ-AM - 1450
501 S Cherry St., Ste. 480
Denver, CO 80246
Phone: (303)468-6500
Fax: (303)468-6555
Format: Sports; Talk. **Networks:** ESPN Radio. **Owner:** Fisher Radio Regional Group Inc., Not Available. **Operating Hours:** 100% satellite. **ADI:** Missoula, MT. **Key Personnel:** Travis L. Cronen, VP, Dir. of Operations, tcronen@cherrycreekradio.com; Joe Schwartz, President, CEO, jschwartz@cherrycreekradio.com. **Wattage:** 1,000. **Ad Rates:** Noncommercial. **URL:** http://www.cherrycreekradio.com.

20340 ■ KGVO-AM - 1290
3250 S Reserve, Ste. 200
Missoula, MT 59801
Phone: (406)728-9300
Email: kgvonewsroom@townsquaremedia.com
Format: Talk; News. **Owner:** Gap West Broadcasting, at above address. **ADI:** Missoula, MT. **Wattage:** 5,000. **Ad Rates:** Advertising accepted; rates available upon request. **URL:** http://www.newstalkkgvo.com.

20341 ■ KHDV-FM - 107.9
725 Strand Ave.
Missoula, MT 59801

Circulation: ★ = AAM; △ or • = BPA; ♦ = CAC; ❑ = VAC; ⊕ = PO Statement; ‡ = Publisher's Report; Boldface figures = sworn; Light figures = estimated.

Phone: (406)542-1025
Fax: (406)721-1036
Email: info@mtnbdc.com
Format: Country. **Owner:** Mountain Broadcasting, 725 Strand Ave., Missoula, MT 59801, Ph: (406)542-1025, Fax: (406)721-1036. **Key Personnel:** Sheila Callahan, Gen. Mgr., sheila@mtnbdc.com; Kris Hardy, Dir. of Traffic, kris.hardy@mtnbdc.com. **URL:** http://www.mountain1025.com.

20342 ■ KJFT-FM - 90.3
PO Box 391
Twin Falls, ID 83303
Fax: (208)736-1958
Free: 800-357-4226
Format: Religious. **Owner:** CSN International, PO Box 391, Twin Falls, ID 83303, Ph: (208)736-1958, Fax: (208)736-1958, Free: 800-357-4226. **Key Personnel:** Mike Kestler, President. **URL:** http://www.csnradio.com.

20343 ■ KKVU-FM - 104.5
2425 W Central Ave., Ste. 203
Missoula, MT 59801
Format: Adult Contemporary. **Owner:** Montana Radio Company L.L.C., 100 W Lyndale Ave., Ste. B, Helena, MT 59601, Ph: (406)442-6645, Fax: (406)422-0639. **Wattage**: 12,500. **URL:** http://www.fresh1045.com.

KLYQ-AM - See Hamilton

20344 ■ KMPT-AM - 930
3250 S Reserve St., Ste. 200
Missoula, MT 59802
Phone: (406)728-9300
Format: Talk; News. **Networks:** ABC. **Owner:** Townsquare Media Inc., 240 Greenwich Ave., Greenwich, CT 06830-6507, Ph: (203)861-0900. **Founded:** 1959. **Formerly**: KLCY-AM. **Operating Hours**: Continuous; 90% network, 10% local. **ADI**: Missoula, MT. **Local Programs**: *Midnight Radio*, Monday Monday Tuesday Wednesday Thursday Friday Saturday Sunday 12:00 a.m. - 4:00 a.m. 11:00 p.m. - 4:00 a.m. 11:00 p.m. - 12:00 a.m. **Wattage**: 5,000. **Ad Rates:** $8-30 for 30 seconds; $12-45 for 60 seconds. Combined advertising rates available with KYSS, KGVO, KBAZ.

20345 ■ KMSO-FM - 102.5
725 Strand Ave.
Missoula, MT 59801
Phone: (406)542-1025
Fax: (406)721-1036
Format: Adult Contemporary; News. **Owner:** Mountain Broadcasting, 725 Strand Ave., Missoula, MT 59801, Ph: (406)542-1025, Fax: (406)721-1036. **Founded:** 1985. **Formerly**: KUEZ-FM. **Operating Hours**: Continuous. **ADI**: Missoula, MT. **Key Personnel:** Sheila Callahan, Gen. Mgr., sheila@mtnbdc.com. **Wattage**: 14,000. **Ad Rates:** $13-16 for 30 seconds; $17-20 for 60 seconds. **URL:** http://mountain1077.com/1025.

20346 ■ KMZL-FM - 91.1
2201 S 6th St.
Las Vegas, NV 89104
Phone: (702)731-5452
Fax: (702)731-1992
Free: 800-804-5452
Format: Contemporary Christian. **Owner:** SOS Radio Network, 2201 S 6th St., Las Vegas, NV 89104, Ph: (702)731-5452, Fax: (702)731-1992, Free: 800-804-5452. **Key Personnel:** Chris Staley, VP. **URL:** http://www.sosradio.net.

20347 ■ KPAX-TV - 8
1049 W Central Ave.
Missoula, MT 59801
Phone: (406)542-4400
Fax: (406)543-7111
Format: Commercial TV. **Networks:** CBS. **Owner:** Evening Post Industries Inc., 134 Columbus St., Charleston, SC 29403, Ph: (843)577-7111. **Founded:** 1977. **Operating Hours**: Continuous. **ADI**: Missoula, MT. **Key Personnel:** Bob Hermes, Gen. Mgr., bob@kpax.com. **Wattage**: 22,500 ERP H. **Ad Rates:** Advertising accepted; rates available upon request. **URL:** http://www.kpax.com.

20348 ■ KTMF-TV - 23
2200 Stephens Ave.
Missoula, MT 59801
Phone: (406)542-8900
Fax: (406)652-8507
Format: Commercial TV. **Networks:** ABC. **Founded:** 1990. **Operating Hours**: Continuous. **Wattage**: 1,800,000. **Ad Rates:** Noncommercial. **URL:** http://www.abcfoxmontana.com.

20349 ■ K218AI-FM - 91.5
629 S 6th E
University of Montana
Missoula, MT 59812
Phone: (406)243-4931
Fax: (406)243-3299
Free: 800-325-1565
Format: Eclectic. **Owner:** Montana Public Radio, 32 Campus Dr., Missoula, MT 59812, Ph: (406)243-4931, Fax: (406)243-3299, Free: 800-325-1565. **Key Personnel:** Michael Marsolek, Prog. Dir.; Sally Mauk, Div. Dir., sally.mauk@mtpr.org; William Marcus, Station Mgr.; Linda Talbott, Assoc. Dir.; Eric Whitney, News Dir., eric.whitney@mtpr.org. **Wattage**: 250. **URL:** http://www.mtpr.org.

K252AD-FM - See White Sulphur Springs

20350 ■ K204EV-FM - 88.7
PO Box 391
Twin Falls, ID 83303
Fax: (208)736-1958
Free: 800-357-4226
Format: Religious; Contemporary Christian. **Owner:** CSN International, PO Box 391, Twin Falls, ID 83303, Ph: (208)736-1958, Fax: (208)736-1958, Free: 800-357-4226. **Key Personnel:** Don Mills, Prog. Dir., Div. Dir. **URL:** http://www.csnradio.com.

K219BN-FM - See Whitefish

K219CS-FM - See Dillon

K296BI-FM - See Marysville

K216BE-FM - See Swan Lake

20351 ■ KUFM-FM - 89.1
University of Montana
Missoula, MT 59812-8064
Phone: (406)243-4931
Fax: (406)243-3299
Free: 800-325-1565
Email: contact@mtpr.org
Format: Public Radio. **Owner:** Montana Public Radio, 32 Campus Dr., Missoula, MT 59812, Ph: (406)243-4931, Fax: (406)243-3299, Free: 800-325-1565. **Operating Hours**: Continuous. **Key Personnel:** John Myers, Dept. Mgr.; Sally Mauk, News Dir.; Michael Marsolek, Tech. Dir.; Linda Talbott, Bus. Mgr; Joe Korona, Contact. **Ad Rates:** Noncommercial; underwriting available. **URL:** http://mtpr.org.

20352 ■ KUFM-TV - 11
University of Montana
32 Campus Dr.
Missoula, MT 59812
Phone: (406)243-4101
Fax: (406)243-3299
Email: kufm@montanapbs.org
Key Personnel: Daniel Dauterive, Dir. of Operations; Gus Chambers, Producer. **URL:** http://www.montanapbs.org.

KUFN-FM - See Hamilton

KUHM-FM - See Helena

KUKL-FM - See Kalispell

20353 ■ KVWE-FM - 101.5
3250 S Reserve, Ste. 200
Missoula, MT 59802
Phone: (406)728-9300
Format: Soft Rock. **Owner:** Gapwest Broadcasting, 4300 N Miller Rd., Ste. 116, Scottsdale, AZ 85251, Ph: (480)970-1360, Fax: (480)423-6966. **Formerly**: KXGZ-FM. **Key Personnel:** Shawna Batt, Contact, shawnabatt@townsquaremedia.com. **URL:** http://newstalkkgvo.com.

20354 ■ KYJK-FM - 105.9
2425 W Central Ave., Ste. 203
Missoula, MT 59806
Format: Adult Contemporary. **Owner:** Montana Radio Company L.L.C., 100 W Lyndale Ave., Ste. B, Helena, MT 59601, Ph: (406)442-6645, Fax: (406)422-0639. **ADI**: Missoula, MT. **Wattage**: 1,840. **URL:** http://www.jackfmmissoula.com/main.

20355 ■ KYLT-AM - 1340
1600 N Ave.
Missoula, MT 59801
Phone: (406)728-5000
Fax: (406)721-3020
Format: Talk. **Networks:** Westwood One Radio. **Owner:** Cherry Creek Radio LLC, 501 S Cherry St., Ste. 480, Denver, CO 80246, Ph: (303)468-6500, Fax: (303)468-6555. **Operating Hours**: Continuous. **ADI**: Missoula, MT. **Key Personnel:** Joe Schwartz, President, CEO, jschwartz@cherrycreekradio.com; Travis L. Cronen, VP, Dir. of Operations, tcronen@cherrycreekradio.com. **Wattage**: 1,000. **Ad Rates:** Advertising accepted; rates available upon request. Combined advertising rates available with KZOQ-FM, KGRZ-AM, KGGL-FM, KXDR-FM. **URL:** http://www.cherrycreekradio.com.

20356 ■ KYSS-FM - 94.9
3250 S Reserve St.
Missoula, MT 59808
Phone: (406)728-9300
Format: Country. **Networks:** ABC. **Founded:** 1969. **Operating Hours**: Continuous. **ADI**: Missoula, MT. **Key Personnel:** Shawna Batt, Contact, shawnabatt@townsquaremedia.com. **Local Programs**: *Denny Bedard*, Monday Tuesday Wednesday Thursday Friday Saturday 3:00 p.m. - 7:00 p.m. 10:00 a.m. - 3:00 p.m. **Wattage**: 63,000 ERP. **Ad Rates:** Advertising accepted; rates available upon request. **URL:** http://kyssfm.com.

20357 ■ KZOQ-FM - 100.1
1600 N Ave.
Missoula, MT 59801
Phone: (406)728-5000
Email: bbreck@cherrycreekradio.com
Format: Classic Rock. **Owner:** Cherry Creek Radio LLC, 501 S Cherry St., Ste. 480, Denver, CO 80246, Ph: (303)468-6500, Fax: (303)468-6555. **Operating Hours**: Continuous. **ADI**: Missoula, MT. **Wattage**: 13,500. **Ad Rates:** Noncommercial. Combined advertising rates available with KYLT-AM, KGGL-FM, KGRZ-AM, KXDR-FM. **URL:** http://www.z100missoula.com.

PABLO

20358 ■ Char-Koosta News: The Official News Publication Of The Flathead Indian Nation
Confederated Salish and Kootenai Tribes of the Flathead Reservation
PO Box 278
Pablo, MT 59855
Phone: (406)675-2700
Fax: (406)675-2806
Free: 888-835-8766
Publisher's E-mail: info@cskt.org
Native American newspaper for the tribes of the Flathead Indian Nation. **Freq:** Weekly (Thurs.). **Key Personnel:** Sam Sandoval, Publisher, Editor; Leslie Camel, Assistant Editor. **ISSN:** 0893--8970 (print). **Subscription Rates:** $25 Individuals /year within the reservation; $30 Individuals /year within Montana; $40 Out of state /year; $75 Out of country /year; $15 Students /year. **Remarks:** Advertising accepted; rates available upon request. **Circ:** (Not Reported).

KSKC-TV - See Saint Ignatius

PLAINS

Sanders Co. Sanders Co. (NW). 30 m SW of Hot Springs.

20359 ■ Valley Press
Valley Press
105 W Lynch St.
Plains, MT 59859
Phone: (406)826-3402
Fax: (406)826-5577
Free: 800-440-3402
Community newspaper. **Founded:** 1899. **Freq:** Weekly (Wed.). **Trim Size:** 11 1/4 x 17. **Cols./Page:** 5. **Col. Width:** 2 1/16 inches. **Col. Depth:** 16 inches. **Key Personnel:** Dan Drewry, Publisher; Cheri Minemyer, Office Manager. **ISSN:** 1041-1437 (print). **Subscription Rates:** $27 Individuals In County - Print; $28 Individuals Out of County - Print; $38 Out of state Print; $2.25 Individuals eEdition only. **URL:** http://www.vp-mi.com. **Formerly**: Plainsman Edition; Camas Record Edition. **Mailing address:** PO Box 667, Plains, MT 59859. **Ad**

Rates: BW $204; SAU $3.15. **Remarks:** Accepts advertising. **Circ:** 1800.

20360 ■ KPLG-FM - 91.5
317 First St.
Havre, MT 59501
Phone: (406)265-5845
Fax: (406)265-8860
Free: 800-442-9222
Email: ynop@ynop.org
Format: Religious. **Owner:** Your Network of Praise, 317 First St, Havre, MT 59501, Free: 866-752-5257. **Operating Hours:** Continuous. **Key Personnel:** Roger Lonnquist, Gen. Mgr.; David Brown, Dir. of Programs; Ron Huckeby, Chief Engineer. **URL:** http://www.ynop.org/stationlist.html.

20361 ■ Plains Cable TV
PO Box 249
Plains, MT 59859
Phone: (406)826-3081
Founded: 1982. **Key Personnel:** Verdie McCallum, Contact; George McCallum, Contact.

PLENTYWOOD

Sheridan Co. Sheridan Co. (NE). 120 m S of Regina, Sask, Canada. Ships wheat. Coal mines; oil wells. Stock, poultry, grain farms. Flax, corn.

20362 ■ The Greeter
The Greeter
108 N Main St.
Plentywood, MT 59254-1816
Phone: (406)765-1733
Fax: (406)765-2106
Publisher's E-mail: publisher@mygreeter.com
Community newspaper. **Freq:** Weekly (Tues.). **Print Method:** Web offset. **Cols./Page:** 5. **Col. Width:** 2 1/16 inches. **Col. Depth:** 13 inches. **Key Personnel:** Richard Rice, Publisher. **Subscription Rates:** Free. **URL:** http://www.mygreeter.com/The_Greeter/Welcome.html. **Ad Rates:** BW $350; SAU $5; PCI $8. **Remarks:** Accepts advertising. **Circ:** Free ‡3000.

20363 ■ KATQ-AM - 1070
112 3rd Ave., E
Plentywood, MT 59254
Phone: (406)765-1480
Fax: (406)765-2357
Email: katq@nemont.net
Format: Country. **Simulcasts:** KATQ-FM. **Networks:** ABC; Northern Agricultural. **Founded:** 1976. **Operating Hours:** 6 a.m.-6 p.m.; 50% network, 50% local. **Wattage:** 5,000. **Ad Rates:** $6.25-7.50 for 30 seconds; $8.50-9.50 for 60 seconds.

20364 ■ KATQ-FM - 100.1
112 Third Ave. E
Plentywood, MT 59254
Phone: (406)765-1480
Email: katq@nemont.net
Format: Country. **Simulcasts:** KATQ-AM. **Networks:** ABC; Northern Agricultural. **Owner:** Radio International-KATQ Inc., at above address. **Founded:** 1963. **Formerly:** KPWD-FM. **Operating Hours:** Continuous; 50% network, 50% local. **Wattage:** 3,000. **Ad Rates:** $6.25-7.5 for 30 seconds; $8.5-9.50 for 60 seconds. **URL:** http://www.katqradio.com.

POLSON

Lake Co. Lake Co. (NW). On Flathead Lake, 69 m N of Missoula. Sawmills. Timber. Dairy, stock farms. Wheat, hay, cherries. Resort.

20365 ■ Lake County Leader
Flathead Publishing Group
PO Box 1090
Polson, MT 59860
Phone: (406)883-4343
Fax: (406)883-4349
Community newspaper. **Freq:** Weekly (Wed.). **Print Method:** Offset. **Cols./Page:** 6. **Col. Width:** 12 picas. **Col. Depth:** 21 inches. **Key Personnel:** David Reese, Editor; Laurie Ramos, General Manager, Director, Advertising. **URL:** http://www.leaderadvertiser.com; http://www.flatheadnewsgroup.com. **Formed by the merger of:** Ronan Pioneer/Mission Valley News; Flathead Courier. **Ad Rates:** GLR $.85; BW $441; 4C $691; PCI $5.10. **Remarks:** Accepts advertising. **Circ:** (Not Reported).

Anderson Radio Broadcasting Co. - See Ronan

20366 ■ KERR-AM - 750
36581 N Reservoir Rd.
Polson, MT 59860
Phone: (406)883-5255
Fax: (406)883-4441
Format: Country. **Networks:** ABC. **Owner:** Anderson Radio Broadcasting Co., 36581 N Reservior Rd., Polson, MT 59860, Ph: (406)883-5255, Fax: (406)883-4441. **Operating Hours:** Continuous; 5% network, 95% local. **ADI:** Missoula, MT. **Key Personnel:** Gary Meili, Contact. **Wattage:** 50,000. **Ad Rates:** $4-8.75 for 30 seconds; $6.40-14 for 60 seconds. **URL:** http://www.750kerr.com.

20367 ■ KIBG-FM - 100.7
36581 N Reservoir Rd.
Polson, MT 59860
Phone: (406)883-5255
Fax: (406)883-4441
Format: Adult Contemporary. **Owner:** Anderson Radio Broadcasting Co., 36581 N Reservior Rd., Polson, MT 59860, Ph: (406)883-5255, Fax: (406)883-4441. **Wattage:** 85,000. **Ad Rates:** Advertising accepted; rates available upon request. **URL:** http://www.thebig100.com.

20368 ■ KKMT-FM - 92.3
36581 N Reservoir Rd.
Polson, MT 59860
Format: Adult Contemporary. **Owner:** Anderson Radio Broadcasting Co., 36581 N Reservior Rd., Polson, MT 59860, Ph: (406)883-5255, Fax: (406)883-4441. **Wattage:** 60,000. **URL:** http://www.star99hits.com/.

KQRK-FM - See Ronan

PRYOR

20369 ■ KPGB-FM - 88.3
PO Box 24
Pryor, MT 59066
Format: Religious; Gospel. **Owner:** Fundamental Broadcasting Network, 520 Roberts Rd., Newport, NC 28570, Ph: (252)223-4600, Fax: (800)245-9685, Free: 800-245-9685. **Operating Hours:** Continuous. **Wattage:** 100. **Ad Rates:** Noncommercial. **URL:** http://www.fbnradio.com.

RED LODGE

Carbon Co. Carbon Co. (S). 60 m SW of Billings. Gateway to Beartooth Mountain and Yellowstone Park. Creamery. Agriculture. Livestock, sugar beets. Resort.

20370 ■ KMXE-FM
PO Box 1678
Red Lodge, MT 59068
Phone: (406)446-1199
Fax: (406)446-1199
Free: 800-649-9964
Format: Adult Contemporary. **Networks:** Independent. **Owner:** Burt Oliphant, Brent Oliphant & Jeffrey Oliphant, at above address. **Founded:** 1994. **Wattage:** 30,000 ERP. **Ad Rates:** $5-8 per unit.

RONAN

Lake Co. Lake Co. (NW). 55 m N of Missoula. Access to Mission Mountains and Flathead Lake. Timber. Agriculture. Dairying, grain, potatoes, alfalfa.

20371 ■ Anderson Radio Broadcasting Co.
36581 N Reservior Rd.
Polson, MT 59860
Phone: (406)883-5255
Fax: (406)883-4441
Format: Contemporary Hit Radio (CHR); Country; Soft Rock. **URL:** http://www.andersonbroadcasting.com.

20372 ■ KQRK-FM - 92.3
36581 N Reservoir Rd.
Polson, MT 59860
Phone: (406)883-5255
Fax: (406)883-4441
Format: Album-Oriented Rock (AOR). **Owner:** Anderson Radio Broadcasting Co., 36581 N Reservior Rd., Polson, MT 59860, Ph: (406)883-5255, Fax: (406)883-4441.

SAINT IGNATIUS

Lake Co. Lake County. South of Ronan, Agriculture, cattle, mining.

20373 ■ KSKC-TV - 28
PO Box 70
Pablo, MT 59855
Phone: (406)275-4800
Owner: Salish Kootenai College, 58138 US Hwy 93, Pablo, MT 59855. **Founded:** 1988. **Key Personnel:** Roy Bigcrane, Dir. of Programs, roy_bigcrane@skc.edu. **URL:** http://kskctv.skc.edu.

SCOBEY

Daniels Co. Daniels Co. (NE). 40 m W of Plentywood. Coal mines and oil wells. Stock, grain farms. Wheat, flax, barley.

20374 ■ Daniels County Leader
Daniels County Leader
PO Box 850
Scobey, MT 59263
Phone: (406)487-5303
Fax: (406)487-5304
Publisher's E-mail: 2leader@nemont.net
Newspaper. **Freq:** Weekly (Thurs.). **Print Method:** Letterpress and offset. **Trim Size:** 11 x 17. **Cols./Page:** 6. **Col. Width:** 22 nonpareils. **Col. Depth:** 224 agate lines. **Key Personnel:** Milton Gunderson, Editor; Burley R. Bowler, Publisher. **URL:** http://www.northeastmontananews.com. **Ad Rates:** SAU $5.22. **Remarks:** Accepts advertising. **Circ:** (Not Reported).

20375 ■ KCGM-FM - 95.7
20 Main St.
Scobey, MT 59263
Phone: (406)487-2293
Format: Country; Contemporary Country; Agricultural. **Networks:** AP; USA Radio; Montana News; Northern Agricultural. **Owner:** Prairie Communications Inc., at above address. **Founded:** 1971. **Operating Hours:** 6 a.m.-10 p.m.; 10% network, 90% local. **Wattage:** 52,000. **Ad Rates:** $4.48 for 15 seconds; $6.72 for 30 seconds; $8.96 for 60 seconds. **Mailing address:** PO Box 220, Scobey, MT 59263.

SEELEY LAKE

20376 ■ The Seeley Swan Pathfinder
The Seeley Swan Pathfinder
PO Box 702
Seeley Lake, MT 59868
Phone: (406)677-2022
Publication E-mail: pathfinder@montana.com
Community newspaper. **Freq:** Weekly. **Key Personnel:** Dwight Jenkins, Publisher, phone: (406)677-2022. **ISSN:** 0894--2994 (print). **Subscription Rates:** $39 Individuals; $75 Two years; $110 Individuals 3 years. **URL:** http://www.seeleyswanpathfinder.com. **Ad Rates:** BW $315; 4C $515; PCI $5. **Remarks:** Accepts advertising. **Circ:** Paid ⊕**1300**.

SHELBY

Toole Co. Toole Co. (N). 88 m NW of Great Falls. Oil and gas wells. Dairy, stock, poultry, grain farms. Wheat, oats, hay.

20377 ■ Shelby Promoter
The Shelby Promoter
PO Box 610
Shelby, MT 59474
Phone: (406)434-5171
Fax: (406)434-5955
Publisher's E-mail: promoter@3rivers.net
Community newspaper. **Freq:** Weekly (Wed.). **Print Method:** Offset. **Cols./Page:** 6. **Col. Width:** 26 nonpareils. **Col. Depth:** 301 agate lines. **Key Personnel:** Brian Kavanagh, Publisher; LeAnne Kavanagh, Publisher, Owner. **Subscription Rates:** $40 Individuals 1 year; $34 Students 1 year; $45 Out of area 1 year; $50 Out of state 1 year; $38 Out of state students; $140 Canada 1 year; $35 Individuals e-edition. **URL:** http://cutbankpioneerpress.com/shelby_promoter/?cal=shelbypromoter. **Ad Rates:** GLR $.32; BW $553.41; 4C $753.41; SAU $4.50; PCI $5. **Remarks:** Accepts advertising. **Circ:** ‡1900.

20378 ■ KSEN-AM - 1150
830 Oilfield Ave.
Shelby, MT 59474
Phone: (406)434-5241
Format: Oldies. **Networks:** ABC; CBS; CNN Radio;

Circulation: ★ = AAM; △ or • = BPA; ♦ = CAC; ❑ = VAC; ⊕ = PO Statement; ‡ = Publisher's Report; Boldface figures = sworn; Light figures = estimated.

NBC; ESPN Radio. **Owner:** Townsquare Media Inc., 240 Greenwich Ave., Greenwich, CT 06830-6507, Ph: (203)861-0900. **Key Personnel:** Bill Wilson, Exec. VP. **Wattage:** 10,000 Day; 5,000 Ni. **Ad Rates:** Noncommercial. **URL:** http://ksenam.com.

20379 ■ KZIN-FM - 96.7
830 Oilfield Ave.
Shelby, MT 59474
Phone: (406)434-5241
Format: Country. **Networks:** ABC; Northern Agricultural. **Owner:** Townsquare Media Inc., 240 Greenwich Ave., Greenwich, CT 06830-6507, Ph: (203)861-0900. **Founded:** 1978. **Operating Hours:** Continuous. **Wattage:** 100,000. **Ad Rates:** Noncommercial. **URL:** http://www.k96fm.com.

SIDNEY

Richland Co. Richland Co. (NE). On Yellowstone River, 120 m NE of Miles City. Beet sugar factory. Coal and oil development. Ships livestock. Stock, dairy, grain farms. Sugar beets, wheat, corn.

20380 ■ Sidney Herald
Wick Communications
310 2nd Ave. NE
Sidney, MT 59270
Phone: (406)433-2403
Fax: (406)433-7802
Community newspaper. **Freq:** Semiweekly (Wed. and Sun.). **Print Method:** Offset. **Trim Size:** 13 x 21. **Cols./Page:** 6. **Col. Width:** 25 nonpareils. **Col. Depth:** 294 agate lines. **Key Personnel:** Bill Vander Weele, Managing Editor; Ellen Wznick, Manager; Deb Crossland, Manager, Advertising; Libby Berndt, Editor; Dawn Steinbeisser, Manager, Circulation. **USPS:** 495-760. **Subscription Rates:** $55 By mail 1 year (carrier & Richland County); $62 By mail 1 year (out of area); $70 Individuals 1 year (out of trade); $35 Individuals online. **URL:** http://www.sidneyherald.com. **Formerly:** The Sidney Herald-Leader. **Ad Rates:** GLR $.40; BW $680; 4C $821; SAU $6; PCI $6. **Remarks:** Accepts classified advertising. **Circ:** Paid ‡3100.

STANFORD

20381 ■ Judith Basin Press
Judith Basin Press
117 Central Ave.
Stanford, MT 59479
Phone: (406)566-2471
Publication E-mail: press@itstriangle.com
Community newspaper. **Freq:** Weekly (Thurs.). **Cols./Page:** 5. **Col. Width:** 10.5 picas. **Col. Depth:** 15 inches. **Key Personnel:** Doreen Heintz, Editor; Jacques Rutten, Publisher; Jane Hughs, Manager, Advertising. **Subscription Rates:** $32.50 Individuals 6 months; $44 Individuals 1 year; $34.10 Out of state 6 months; $47.85 Out of state 1 year; $105.60 Individuals 3 years; $114.84 Out of state 3 years. **URL:** http://www.russellcountry.com/judith-basin-press.html. **Ad Rates:** PCI $4.95. **Remarks:** Accepts advertising. **Circ:** 825.

SWAN LAKE

20382 ■ K216BE-FM - 91.1
Broadcast Media Ctr.
University of Montana
Missoula, MT 59812
Fax: (406)243-3299
Format: Eclectic. **Owner:** Montana Public Radio, 32 Campus Dr., Missoula, MT 59812, Ph: (406)243-4931, Fax: (406)243-3299, Free: 800-325-1565. **Key Personnel:** Sally Mauk, News Dir., sally.mauk@mtpr.org; Michael Marsolek, Prog. Dir.; William Marcus, Station Mgr.; Eric Whitney, News Dir. **URL:** http://mtpr.org.

TERRY

Prairie Co. Prairie Co. (E). On Yellowstone River, 190 m E of Billings. Tourism. Ships livestock, grain. Diversified farming. Irrigated & Dryland. Mineral Development.

20383 ■ Terry Tribune
Yellowstone Newspapers
204 Logan Ave.
Terry, MT 59349
Phone: (406)635-5513
Publication E-mail: tribune@midrivers.com
Community newspaper. **Freq:** Weekly (Wed.). **Print Method:** Offset. **Cols./Page:** 5. **Col. Width:** 26 nonpareils. **Col. Depth:** 210 agate lines. **Key Personnel:** Dan Killoy, Publisher; Kay Braddock, Editor. **Subscription Rates:** $35 Individuals 1 year; $40.25 Out of area 1 year. **URL:** http://terrytribune.com. **Mailing address:** PO Box 127, Terry, MT 59349. **Ad Rates:** GLR $.175; BW $220; 4C $90; SAU $4.05; CNU $405. **Remarks:** Accepts display and classified advertising. **Circ:** ‡850.

THOMPSON FALLS

Sanders Co. Sanders Co. (NW). 103 m NW of Missoula. Antimony mine; pine, tamarack, fir, spruce timber. Agriculture. Hay, cattle. Tourism.

20384 ■ Sanders County Ledger
Sanders County Ledger
603 Main
Thompson Falls, MT 59873
Phone: (406)827-3421
Fax: (406)827-4375
Publication E-mail: ledger@blackfoot.net
Community newspaper. **Freq:** Weekly (Thurs.). **Print Method:** Offset. **Cols./Page:** 6. **Col. Width:** 24 nonpareils. **Col. Depth:** 294 agate lines. **Key Personnel:** Tom Eggensperger, Editor, Publisher; Bina Eggensperger, Business Manager, Publisher. **Subscription Rates:** $36 Individuals; $50 Out of area; $51 Out of state; $30 Students 9 months; $43.50 Individuals snowbird. **URL:** http://www.scledger.net. **Mailing address:** PO Box 219, Thompson Falls, MT 59873. **Ad Rates:** GLR $4.50; BW $4.50; 4C $599; SAU $3.60; PCI $3.50. **Remarks:** Accepts advertising. **Circ:** Paid ‡2650.

TOWNSEND

Broadwater Co. Broadwater Co. (C). On Missouri River, 33 m SE of Helena. Creamery; sawmills. Gold mines; pine, fir timber. Agriculture. Livestock, beets, potatoes.

20385 ■ The Townsend Star
The Townsend Star
314 Broadway
Townsend, MT 59644
Phone: (406)266-3333
Fax: (406)266-5440
Community newspaper. **Freq:** Weekly (Thurs.). **Print Method:** Offset. **Cols./Page:** 6. **Col. Width:** 24 nonpareils. **Col. Depth:** 294 agate lines. **USPS:** 635-560. **Subscription Rates:** $39 Individuals in Broadwater County; $30 Out of area; $36 Out of state; $.75 Single issue. **Mailing address:** PO Box 1011, Townsend, MT 59644. **Remarks:** Accepts advertising. **Circ:** ‡1600.

WEST YELLOWSTONE

20386 ■ KWYS-AM - 920
15 Madison Ave.
West Yellowstone, MT 59758
Phone: (406)646-7361
Email: kwys@yellowstone.com
Format: Classic Rock. **Owner:** Chaparral Broadcasting, 645 South Cache, Jackson, WY. **Founded:** 1967. **Operating Hours:** Continuous. **Wattage:** 1,000. **Ad Rates:** Advertising accepted; rates available upon request. Combined advertising rates available with KECH, KYZK, KEZQ-FM. **Mailing address:** PO Box 9, West Yellowstone, MT 59758. **URL:** http://kwys920.com.

WHITE SULPHUR SPRINGS

Meagher Co. Meagher Co. (WC). 80 m E of Helena. Health resort. Gold, silver mines. Stock, grain farms. Hay.

20387 ■ The Meagher County News
Meagher County News
PO Box 349
White Sulphur Springs, MT 59645-0349
Phone: (406)547-3831
Publication E-mail: mcnews@mtintouch.net
Community newspaper (tabloid). **Freq:** Weekly (Thurs.). **Print Method:** Offset. **Trim Size:** 11 3/8 x 14. **Cols./Page:** 5. **Col. Width:** 24 nonpareils. **Col. Depth:** 189 agate lines. **Key Personnel:** Verle L. Rademacher, Editor; Patricia M. Rademacher, Publisher. **USPS:** 336-620. **Subscription Rates:** $33 Individuals; $38 Out of area; $42 Out of state. **URL:** http://www.meagher-county-news.com. **Remarks:** Color advertising accepted; rates available upon request. **Circ:** ‡1200.

20388 ■ Our Toxic Times
Chemical Injury Information Network
PO Box 301
White Sulphur Springs, MT 59645
Phone: (406)547-2255
Publisher's E-mail: chemicalinjury@ciin.org
Magazine covering a wide range of pertinent information for those concerned about multiple chemical sensitivity, from technical to practical. **Freq:** Monthly. **Key Personnel:** Cynthia Wilson, Editor-in-Chief; John Wilson, Managing Editor. **Subscription Rates:** Included in membership; $6 Canada and Mexico per copy; $7 Other countries per copy. **URL:** http://www.ciin.org/news_ott.html. **Ad Rates:** BW $388; PCI $10. **Remarks:** Accepts advertising. **Circ:** (Not Reported).

20389 ■ K252AD-FM - 98.3
Broadcast Media Ctr.
University of Montana
Missoula, MT 59812
Phone: (406)243-4931
Fax: (406)243-3299
Free: 800-325-1565
Email: contact@mtpr.org
Format: Eclectic. **Owner:** Montana Public Radio, 32 Campus Dr., Missoula, MT 59812, Ph: (406)243-4931, Fax: (406)243-3299, Free: 800-325-1565. **Founded:** 1965. **Key Personnel:** Sally Mauk, Director; Michael Marsolek, Dir. of Programs. **URL:** http://www.mtpr.org.

WHITEFISH

Flathead Co. Flathead Co. (NW). 110 m N of Missoula. Saw and planing mills. Timber. Agriculture. Summer & winter resort.

20390 ■ Montana Living
Montana Living Magazine
309 Wisconsin
Whitefish, MT 59937
Phone: (406)862-6489
Fax: (406)862-6487
Consumer magazine covering local lifestyle and travel. **Freq:** Quarterly. **Print Method:** Web. **Trim Size:** 8.375 x 10.875. **Key Personnel:** David M. Reese, Editor; Therese Wood, Director, Advertising. **ISSN:** 1094--6187 (print). **Remarks:** Accepts advertising. **Circ:** (Not Reported).

20391 ■ K258AP-FM - 99.5
PO Box 391
Twin Falls, ID 83303
Fax: (208)736-1958
Free: 800-357-4226
Format: Religious; Contemporary Christian. **Owner:** CSN International, PO Box 391, Twin Falls, ID 83303, Ph: (208)736-1958, Fax: (208)736-1958, Free: 800-357-4226. **Key Personnel:** Mike Kestler, President; Don Mills, Music Dir., Prog. Dir.; Kelly Carlson, Dir. of Engg.; Ray Gorney, Dir. of Engg. **URL:** http://www.csnradio.com.

20392 ■ K219BN-FM - 91.7
Broadcast Media Ctr.
University of Montana
Missoula, MT 59812
Phone: (406)243-4931
Fax: (406)243-3299
Free: 800-325-1565
Email: contact@mtpr.org
Format: Eclectic. **Owner:** Montana Public Radio, 32 Campus Dr., Missoula, MT 59812, Ph: (406)243-4931, Fax: (406)243-3299, Free: 800-325-1565. **Key Personnel:** Sally Mauk, News Dir.; Michael Marsolek, Dir. of Programs; Linda Talbott, Assoc. Dir.; Eric Whitney, News Dir. **URL:** http://www.mtpr.org.

20393 ■ KWOL-FM - 103.7
2432 Hwy. 2 E
Kalispell, MT 59901
Phone: (406)257-5665
Email: info@1051cool.com
Format: Oldies. **Owner:** Bee Broadcasting Network, PO Box 5409, Kalispell, MT 59903, Ph: (406)755-8700. **Operating Hours:** Continuous. **Wattage:** 100. **Ad Rates:** Advertising accepted; rates available upon request. **URL:** http://www.1051cool.com.

WOLF POINT

Roosevelt Co. Roosevelt Co. (NE). On Missouri River, 200 m S of Regina, Sask, Canada. Oil wells. Ships large quantities of wheat. Diversified farming. Ranching.

20394 ■ Herald-News
Herald-News
408 Main St.
Wolf Point, MT 59201
Phone: (406)653-2222
Fax: (406)653-2221
Publisher's E-mail: herald@nemont.net

Newspaper. **Founded:** 1913. **Freq:** Weekly (Thurs.). **Print Method:** Offset. **Cols./Page:** 6. **Col. Width:** 12 picas. **Col. Depth:** 294 agate lines. **Key Personnel:** John Plestina, Editor; Darla Shumway, Publisher. **Subscription Rates:** $30 Individuals local. **URL:** http://www.wolfpointherald.com. **Formerly**: Herald Publications. **Mailing address:** PO Box 639, Wolf Point, MT 59201. **Ad Rates:** GLR $6.75; BW $585.90; SAU $4.65; CNU $4.65; PCI $4.65. **Remarks:** Accepts advertising. **Circ:** 2200.

20395 ■ KVCK-FM - 92.7
324 Main St.
Wolf Point, MT 59201

Format: Country. **Wattage**: 11,500. **URL:** http://www.wolfpoint.com.

Circulation: ★ = AAM; △ or • = BPA; ♦ = CAC; ❑ = VAC; ⊕ = PO Statement; ‡ = Publisher's Report; Boldface figures = sworn; Light figures = estimated.

AINSWORTH

Brown Co. Brown Co. (N). 140 m NW of Grand Island. Feed, hay machinery. Trade center for cattle and farm products. Dairy, stock, poultry, grain farms. Hay, corn.

20396 ■ KBRB-AM - 1400
PO Box 285
Ainsworth, NE 69210
Phone: (402)387-1400
Fax: (402)387-2624
Email: kbrb@sscg.net
Format: News; Information; Agricultural. **Networks:** ABC. **Owner:** K.B.R. Broadcasting Co., Inc., PO Box 285, Ainsworth, NE 69210, Ph: (402)387-1400, Fax: (402)387-2624. **Founded:** 1968. **Operating Hours**: Continuous; 5% network, 95% local. **Key Personnel:** Larry Rice, Founder; Angie Vonheeder, Sales Mgr., angiekbrb@sscg.net. **Wattage**: 1,000. **Ad Rates:** Noncommercial. Combined advertising rates available with KBRB-FM. **URL:** http://www.kbrbradio.com.

20397 ■ KBRB-FM - 92.7
PO Box 285
Ainsworth, NE 69210
Phone: (402)387-1400
Fax: (402)387-2624
Email: kbrb@sscg.net
Format: Adult Contemporary. **Networks:** ABC. **Owner:** K.B.R. Broadcasting Co., Inc., PO Box 285, Ainsworth, NE 69210, Ph: (402)387-1400, Fax: (402)387-2624. **Founded:** 1968. **Operating Hours:** Continuous. **Key Personnel:** Cody Goochey, Dir. of Programs; Graig Kinzie, Gen. Mgr.; Randy Brudigan, Engineer, Sales Mgr; Connie Dillon, Contact. **Wattage**: 26,000. **Ad Rates:** $6-9 for 30 seconds; $8.25-12.38 for 60 seconds. **URL:** http://www.kbrbradio.com.

ALBION

Boone Co. Boone Co. (EC). 55 m NE of Grand Island. Manufactures electronics; meat packing. Stock, grain, dairy, poultry farms. Alfalfa, corn, livestock.

20398 ■ Albion News
Albion News
328 W Church St.
Albion, NE 68620
Community newspaper. **Founded:** 1879. **Freq:** Weekly (Wed.). **Print Method:** Offset. **Cols./Page:** 6. **Col. Width:** 11 nonpareils. **Col. Depth:** 21 inches. **USPS:** 012-640. **Subscription Rates:** $30 Individuals online only; $30 Individuals Boone county and Newman Grove ans Spalding NE; print + online; $37 Elsewhere in Nebraska; print + online; $47 Out of state print + online. **URL:** http://www.albionnewsonline.com/. **Mailing address:** PO Box 431, Albion, NE 68620. **Ad Rates:** GLR $0.46; BW $441; SAU $3.50; PCI $3. **Remarks:** Accepts advertising. **Circ:** ‡3200.

ALLIANCE

Box Butte Co. Box Butte Co. (NW). 45 m NE of Scottsbluff. Manufactures car trailers, electric hose, transistors, beverages, sleeping bags, down-filled garments. Stock, poultry, grain farms. Wheat, rye, barley, potatoes, beans, sugarbeets.

20399 ■ Alliance Times-Herald
Alliance Times-Herald
114 E Fourth St.
Alliance, NE 69301
General newspaper. **Freq:** Daily (eve.) and Sat. (morn.). **Print Method:** Offset. **Cols./Page:** 6. **Col. Width:** 26 nonpareils. **Col. Depth:** 301 agate lines. **Key Personnel:** Steve Stackenwalt, Director, Sales and Marketing; John Weare, Managing Editor; Fred Kuhlman, Publisher. **USPS:** 014-020. **Subscription Rates:** $52 Individuals; $26 Students; Free military subscription. **URL:** http://www.alliancetimes.com. **Mailing address:** PO Box G, Alliance, NE 69301. **Ad Rates:** BW $1,096.50; 4C $1,291.50. **Remarks:** Accepts advertising. **Circ:** (Not Reported).

20400 ■ KAAQ-FM - 105.9
1210 W 10th St.
Alliance, NE 69301
Phone: (308)762-1400
Fax: (308)762-7804
Format: Country. **Simulcasts:** KQSK-FM. **Networks:** ABC; Satellite Music Network. **Owner:** Eagle Communications Inc., 2703 Hall St., Ste. 15, Hays, KS 67601, Ph: (785)625-4000, Fax: (785)625-8030. **Founded:** 1985. **Operating Hours**: 95% network, 5% local. **ADI:** Cheyenne, WY-Scottsbluff, NE (Sterling, CO). **Key Personnel:** Kevin Horn, Contact, kevin.horn@eagleradio.net. **Wattage:** 100,000. **Ad Rates:** for 30 seconds; for 60 seconds. Combined advertising rates available with KQSK-FM. **Mailing address:** PO Box 600, Alliance, NE 69301. **URL:** http://www.panhandlepost.com.

20401 ■ KCOW-AM - 1400
1210 W 10th St.
Alliance, NE 69301
Phone: (308)762-1400
Fax: (308)762-7804
Email: kcow@bbc.net
Format: Adult Contemporary. **Networks:** ABC; Satellite Music Network. **Owner:** Eagle Communications, Inc., at above address. **Founded:** 1949. **Operating Hours**: Continuous; 65% network, 35% local. **Key Personnel:** Kevin Horn, Contact. **Local Programs**: *AgriTalk*. **Wattage:** 1,000. **Ad Rates:** Noncommercial. **Mailing address:** PO Box 600, Alliance, NE 69301. **URL:** http://www.panhandlepost.com.

20402 ■ KTNE-FM - 91.1
1800 N 33rd St.
Lincoln, NE 68503
Phone: (402)472-6141
Fax: (402)472-2403
Free: 888-638-7346
Format: Public Radio. **Simulcasts:** K208CB. **Networks:** National Public Radio (NPR); Public Radio International (PRI). **Owner:** Net Radio, 1800 N 33rd St., Lincoln, NE 68503. **Founded:** 1990. **Operating Hours**: 6 a.m.-1 a.m. **Key Personnel:** Nancy Finken, Contact; Martin Wells, News Dir; Nancy Finken, Contact. **Local Programs**: *Afternoon Concert*, Monday Tuesday Wednesday Thursday Friday 12:00 p.m. - 4:00 p.m. 12:00 p.m. - 1:00 p.m.; *Morning Concert*, Monday Tuesday Wednesday Thursday Friday 9:03 a.m. - 12:00 p.m. 10:03 a.m. - 12:00 p.m.; *All Things Considered*, Monday Tuesday Wednesday Thursday Friday Saturday Sunday 4:00 p.m. - 6:30 p.m. 4:00 p.m. - 5:00 p.m. **Wattage**: 92,000. **Ad Rates:** Noncommercial; underwriting available. **URL:** http://www.netnebraska.org.

ARAPAHOE

Furnas Co. Furnas Co. (S). 80 m SW of Hastings. Dairy, stock, poultry, grain farms. Corn, wheat, alfalfa.

20403 ■ Arapahoe Public Mirror
Arapahoe Public Mirror
420 Nebraska Ave.
Arapahoe, NE 68922-0660
Phone: (308)962-7261
Community newspaper. **Freq:** Weekly (Wed.). **Print Method:** Offset. **Cols./Page:** 6. **Col. Width:** 24 nonpareils. **Col. Depth:** 301 agate lines. **Key Personnel:** T.M. Gill, Owner, Publisher; Gayle Schutz, Owner, Publisher. **Subscription Rates:** $30 Individuals; $31 Out of area; $35 Out of state; $28 Individuals e-edition. **URL:** http://www.arapahoemirror.com. **Mailing address:** PO Box 660, Arapahoe, NE 68922-0660. **Ad Rates:** GLR $.41; SAU $3; PCI $2.45. **Remarks:** Accepts advertising. **Circ:** (Not Reported).

20404 ■ Elwood Bulletin
Elwood Bulletin
PO Box 660
Arapahoe, NE 68922
Phone: (308)962-7261
Community newspaper. **Freq:** Weekly (Wed.). **Cols./Page:** 6. **Col. Width:** 2 inches. **Col. Depth:** 21 1/2 inches. **Key Personnel:** Gayle Schutz, Publisher, phone: (308)962-7261, fax: (308)962-7865. **USPS:** 174-620. **Subscription Rates:** $18 Individuals; $23.50 Out of state. **URL:** http://arapahoemirror.com. **Ad Rates:** GLR $.50. **Remarks:** .50. **Circ:** 850.

ARLINGTON

Washington Co. Washington Co. (E). 25 m NE of Omaha. Nurseries. Farm implement manufacturing. Alfalfa dehydrating plant. Diversified farming. Wheat, corn, cattle.

20405 ■ Arlington Citizen
Enterprise Publishing Company Inc.
PO Box 460
Arlington, NE 68002-0460
Phone: (402)426-2121
Fax: (402)426-2227
Publisher's E-mail: online@enterprisepub.com
Community newspaper. **Freq:** Weekly (Thurs.). **Print Method:** Offset. **Trim Size:** 16 x 23. **Cols./Page:** 6. **Col. Width:** 12 picas. **Col. Depth:** 301 agate lines. **Key Personnel:** Mark Rhoades, Publisher; Melissa G. Rice, Assistant Editor; Doug Barber, Editor, General Manager. **ISSN:** 0319--4000 (print). **Subscription Rates:** $19 Individuals 6 months; in county; $22 Out of country 6 months; $25 Out of state 6 months; $29 Individuals 1 year; in county; $37 Individuals 1 year; out of county; $41 Out of state 1 year. **URL:** http://www.enterprisepub.

Circulation: ★ = AAM; △ or • = BPA; ♦ = CAC; ❑ = VAC; ⊕ = PO Statement; ‡ = Publisher's Report; Boldface figures = sworn; Light figures = estimated.

com/arlingtoncitizen. **Ad Rates:** GLR $5; BW $662; 4C $857; PCI $5.25. **Remarks:** Accepts advertising. **Circ:** Paid ‡700.

ASHLAND

Saunders Co. Saunders Co. (E). 24 m NE of Lincoln. Sand and gravel pits. Rock quarries. Grain farms. Wheat, corn, milo, soybeans.

20406 ■ The Ashland Gazette
The Gazette
1518 Silver St.
Ashland, NE 68003
Phone: (402)944-3397
Fax: (402)944-3398
Free: 877-556-7898
Publisher's E-mail: suzi.nelson@ashland-gazette.com
Newspaper. **Freq:** Weekly (Thurs.). **Print Method:** Offset. **Cols./Page:** 6. **Col. Width:** 25 nonpareils. **Col. Depth:** 301 agate lines. **Key Personnel:** Teresa Livers, Office Manager; Shon Barenklau, Publisher, phone: (402)277-5500; Suzi Nelson, Editor, phone: (402)944-3397. **Subscription Rates:** $58 Individuals inside Nebraska; $84 Out of area. **URL:** http://www.wahoo-ashland-waverly.com/ashland. **Ad Rates:** BW $6.50; 4C $225; SAU $4.50. **Remarks:** Advertising accepted; rates available upon request. **Circ:** ⊕**1870**.

ATKINSON

Holt Co. Holt Co. (N). 200 m NW of Omaha. Hunting and fishing. Center pivot irrigator manufacturer. Irrigated farming. Cattle, swine. Dairy.

20407 ■ The Atkinson Graphic
The Atkinson Graphic
PO Box 159
Atkinson, NE 68713-0159
Phone: (402)925-5411
Publisher's E-mail: news@atkinsongraphic.com
Newspaper with a Republican orientation. **Freq:** Weekly (Thurs.). **Print Method:** Offset. **Cols./Page:** 7. **Col. Width:** 25 nonpareils. **Col. Depth:** 298 agate lines. **Key Personnel:** Brook D. Curtiss, Editor, General Manager, Publisher. **Subscription Rates:** $25 Individuals; $32 Out of area; $20 Individuals e-edition. **URL:** http://www.atkinsongraphic.com. **Ad Rates:** GLR $.222; BW $300; SAU $3.10; PCI $3.10. **Remarks:** Accepts advertising. **Circ:** (Not Reported).

AUBURN

Nemaha Co. Nemaha Co. (SE). 70 m SE of Lincoln. Manufactures wood cabinets, bronze bushings, grounds maintenance and light construction equipment, garments. Diversified farming. Corn, wheat.

20408 ■ Nemaha County Herald
Auburn Newspapers
PO Box 250
Auburn, NE 68305
Phone: (402)274-3185
Fax: (402)274-3273
Publisher's E-mail: kendall@newspaper.net
Community newspaper. **Founded:** Jan. 1888. **Freq:** Weekly (Thurs.). **Print Method:** Offset. **Cols./Page:** 7. **Col. Width:** 2 1/16 inches. **Col. Depth:** 21 1/2 inches. **Key Personnel:** Kendall Neiman, Publisher; Darrell Wellman, Managing Editor. **USPS:** 376-940. **Subscription Rates:** $44 Individuals e-edition only; $44 Individuals print and e-edition; $48 Out of area print and e-edition; $54 Out of state print and e-edition. **URL:** http://www.anewspaper.net/. **Formed by the merger of:** Auburn Press-Tribune. **Ad Rates:** GLR $0.24; BW $5; SAU $4.60; PCI $6. **Remarks:** Accepts advertising. **Circ:** Paid ‡3275, Free ‡87.

20409 ■ Time Warner Cable
1304 Courthouse Ave.
Auburn, NE 68305
Phone: (402)421-0330
Fax: (402)421-0305
Owner: Time Warner Inc., 1 Time Warner Ctr., New York, NY 10019-8016, Ph: (212)484-8000. **Founded:** Apr. 1966. **Formerly:** Auburn Cablevision. **Key Personnel:** Valerie Kramer, Gen. Mgr. **Cities Served:** Auburn, Humboldt, Nebraska City, Pawnee City, Table Rock, Tecumseh, Nebraska: subscribing households 5,482. **URL:** http://www.timewarnercable.com/en/about-us/press/time_warner_cablebigtennetworkinvitehuskerfanstoshowtheirpride.html.

AURORA

Hamilton Co. Hamilton Co. (SEC). 20 m E of Grand Island. Manufactures butter and flour, electronic components, steel, mobile homes. Stock, grain, dairy farms. Corn, wheat, sugar beets. Live stock feeding.

20410 ■ KMMJ-AM - 750
PO Box 8
Aurora, NE 68818
Free: 888-920-5665
Format: Religious. **Networks:** AP. **Operating Hours:** Sunrise-sunset; 60% network, 40% local. **ADI:** Lincoln-Hastings-Kearney, NE. **Wattage:** 10,000. **Ad Rates:** $10-11.50 for 30 seconds; $15-17.25 for 60 seconds. **URL:** http://www.praisenetwork.info.

20411 ■ Mid-State Community TV
1001 12th St.
Aurora, NE 68818
Phone: (402)694-4401
Fax: (402)694-2848
Email: midstate@midstatetv.com
URL: http://www.midstatetv.com.

BEATRICE

Gage Co. Gage Co. (SE). 40 m S of Lincoln. Manufactures store fixtures, farm machinery, steel, aluminum, containers, hardware specialties, windmills, fertilizer (dry & liquid). Livestock, dairy farms. Wheat corn, soybeans, milo.

20412 ■ Beatrice Daily Sun
Beatrice Daily Sun
200 N 7th St.
Beatrice, NE 68310-0847
Phone: (402)223-5233
Fax: (402)228-3571
Free: 800-666-5233
Publisher's E-mail: beatrice.news@lee.net
Community newspaper. **Founded:** June 1902. **Freq:** Daily (eve.) and Sat. (morn.). **Print Method:** Offset. **Cols./Page:** 6. **Col. Width:** 26 nonpareils. **Col. Depth:** 301 agate lines. **Key Personnel:** Patrick Ethridge, Editor, Publisher; Jim Ristow, Publisher; Tara Seible, Director, Advertising. **USPS:** 047-060. **Subscription Rates:** $138.95 Individuals foot carrier route; $163.60 By mail mail in Gage County; $201 By mail mail outside of Gage County; $5.95 Individuals digital. **URL:** http://www.beatricedailysun.com. **Ad Rates:** BW $999.75; 4C $1,322.75; PCI $7.75. **Remarks:** Advertising accepted; rates available upon request. **Circ:** Sat. ★**16350**.

20413 ■ KWBE-AM - 1450
200 Sherman St.
Beatrice, NE 68310
Phone: (402)228-5923
Fax: (402)228-3704
Email: kuttbrad@diodecom.net
Format: News; Sports; Agricultural. **Networks:** ABC. **Owner:** Triad Broadcasting Company, LLC, 2511 Garden Rd., No. 104A, Monterey, CA 93940, Ph: (831)655-6350, Fax: (831)655-6355. **Founded:** 1949. **Operating Hours:** Continuous; 40% network, 60% local. **Local Programs:** *Sports Shot Extra*, Monday Tuesday Wednesday Thursday Friday 5:34 p.m. **Wattage:** 1,000. **Ad Rates:** Noncommercial. **URL:** http://www.kwbe.com.

BEE

20414 ■ Classic Farm and Tractor
Green Magazine
2652 Davey Rd.
Bee, NE 68314
Phone: (402)643-6269
Fax: (402)643-3912
Publication E-mail: info@tractorshop.com
Magazine featuring tractors built from 1960 to 1990. **Freq:** Bimonthly. **Subscription Rates:** $29 U.S.; $42 Canada; $63 Other countries; $5 U.S. single issue; $7 Single issue, Canada; $11 Other countries single issue. **URL:** http://www.classicfarmandtractor.com. **Formerly:** Tractor Shop. **Ad Rates:** BW $100. **Remarks:** Accepts advertising. **Circ:** (Not Reported).

20415 ■ Little Green
Green Magazine
2652 Davey Rd.
Bee, NE 68314
Phone: (402)643-6269
Fax: (402)643-3912
Publisher's E-mail: info@greenmagazine.com
Magazine featuring farm tractor for children. **Freq:** Bimonthly. **Subscription Rates:** $16 U.S.; $22 Canada; $34 Other countries. **URL:** http://www.greenmagazine.com/shop.asp?cat=2&id=1. **Circ:** (Not Reported).

BELLEVUE

Sarpy Co. Sarpy Co. (E) 9 m S of Omaha. Offutt AFB. Chemicals, textile, high tech defense contractors.

20416 ■ Bellevue Leader
Bellevue Leader
604 Fort Crook Rd. N
Bellevue, NE 68005
Phone: (402)733-7300
Publisher's E-mail: news@bellevueleader.com
Community newspaper. **Freq:** Weekly. **Print Method:** Offset. **Cols./Page:** 8. **Col. Width:** 9 picas. **Col. Depth:** 21.5 inches. **Key Personnel:** Paul Swanson, Manager, Advertising, phone: (402)505-3602; Melissa Vanek, Manager, Circulation, phone: (402)505-3603; Shon Barenklau, Publisher, phone: (402)505-3600; Ron Petak, Executive Editor, phone: (402)505-3620. **Subscription Rates:** $42 Individuals 52 weeks (home delivery); $51.50 By mail 52 weeks (in Sarpy, Douglas & Cass Counties); $62 By mail 52 weeks (out of area). **URL:** http://www.omaha.com/sarpy/bellevue. **Mailing address:** PO Box 1219, Bellevue, NE 68005. **Ad Rates:** GLR $.95; BW $2,858; 4C $635; PCI $16.62. **Remarks:** Accepts advertising. **Circ:** (Not Reported).

20417 ■ Bellevue Visitor's Guide
Greater Bellevue Area Chamber of Commerce
1102 Galvin Rd. S
Bellevue, NE 68005
Phone: (402)898-3000
Fax: (402)291-8729
Magazine containing visitor information about Bellevue, NE area; including a business and community guide. **Freq:** Annual. **Subscription Rates:** Included in membership. **Circ:** (Not Reported).

20418 ■ The Nebraska Bird Review: A Magazine of the Nebraska Region
Nebraska Ornithologists' Union Inc.
c/o Betty Grenon, Treas.
1409 Childs Rd. E.
Bellevue, NE 68005
Phone: (402)731-2383
A quarterly journal with reports and articles on bird observations in Nebraska; occasional reviews of books on birds. **Freq:** Quarterly. **Print Method:** Letterpress and offset. **Trim Size:** 6 x 9. **Cols./Page:** 1. **Col. Width:** 54 nonpareils. **Col. Depth:** 102 agate lines. **Key Personnel:** Anita Breckbill, Contact; Betty Allen, President. **ISSN:** 0028--1816 (print). **Subscription Rates:** $15 Individuals in the United States; $18 Individuals in Canada ; $30 Out of country; $4 Single issue; $8 Elsewhere Single copies; $5 Single issue in Canada. **URL:** http://www.noubirds.org/Publications/NBR.aspx. **Remarks:** Advertising not accepted. **Circ:** Paid ‡263, Non-paid ‡20.

BENKELMAN

Dundy Co. Dundy Co. (SW). 90 m SW of North Platte. State fish hatcheries. Stock, grain, dairy, poultry farms. Corn.

20419 ■ BWTelcom
607 Chief St.
Benkelman, NE 69021
Phone: (308)423-2000
Fax: (308)423-5618
Email: bwtelcom@bwtelcom.net
Founded: 1944. **Cities Served:** United States; 61 channels. **Mailing address:** PO Box 645, Benkelman, NE 69021-0645. **URL:** http://www.bwtelcom.net.

BERTRAND

20420 ■ The Bertrand Herald
The Bertrand Herald
PO Box 425
Bertrand, NE 68927
Phone: (308)472-3217

Fax: (308)472-5165
Weekly newspaper. **Freq:** Weekly 52 issues/year. **Print Method:** Offset. **Trim Size:** 14 x 22 3/4. **Cols./Page:** 6. **Col. Width:** 12.5 picas. **Col. Depth:** 21 1/2 inches. **Key Personnel:** Kay Lavene, Editor. **Subscription Rates:** $30 Individuals in-state; $36 Individuals out-of-state; $22 Individuals in-state college. **URL:** http://thebertrandherald.webs.com. **Ad Rates:** GLR $4; BW $516; 4C $566; SAU $4; PCI $4.50, black and white; PCI $6, color. **Remarks:** Accepts advertising. **Circ:** Paid ‡600.

BLAIR

Washington Co. Washington Co. (E). 18 m NW of Omaha. Dana College. Manufactures grain elevators, farm machinery, fertilizers, limestone, heavy road equipment. Silage storage bagging machines, ethanol.

20421 ■ Blair Enterprise
Enterprise Publishing Company Inc.
138 N 16th St.
Blair, NE 68008
Phone: (402)426-2121
Fax: (402)426-2227
Publisher's E-mail: online@enterprisepub.com
Community newspaper. **Freq:** Semiweekly. **Print Method:** Offset. **Trim Size:** 11.5 x 21.5. **Cols./Page:** 6. **Col. Width:** 1.83 inches. **Col. Depth:** 301 agate lines. **Subscription Rates:** $48 Individuals 12 months; $61 Out of area 12 months; $68 Out of state 12 months. **Mailing address:** PO Box 328, Blair, NE 68008. **Ad Rates:** GLR $8; BW $1,008; 4C $1,203; PCI $8. **Remarks:** Accepts advertising. **Circ:** (Not Reported).

20422 ■ The Bridge: Journal of the Danish American Heritage Society
Danish American Heritage Society
1717 Grant St.
Blair, NE 68008
Phone: (402)426-9610
Freq: Semiannual. **Key Personnel:** Julie Allen, Editor. **ISSN:** 0741--1200 (print). **URL:** http://www.danishamericanheritagesociety.org/AboutTheBridge.html. **Remarks:** Advertising not accepted. **Circ:** (Not Reported).

20423 ■ Great Plains Cable TV Inc.
1635 Front St.
Box 500
Blair, NE 68008
Phone: (402)426-9511
Fax: (402)456-6550
Free: 855-853-1483
Owner: Great Plains Communications Telephone Co., 1635 Front St., Blair, NE 68008. **Founded:** 1985. **Key Personnel:** LeAnn Quist, Contact. **Cities Served:** subscribing households 1,500. **URL:** http://www.gpcom.com/contact.

20424 ■ HunTel Cablevision
1605 Washington St.
Blair, NE 68008
Phone: (402)426-6200
Fax: (402)533-6300
Free: 888-262-2661
Email: contact@abbnebraska.com
Founded: 1980. **Key Personnel:** Mike Jacobson, President, mjacobson@huntelworld.com. **Cities Served:** 54 channels. **URL:** http://www.abbnebraska.com.

20425 ■ KDCV-FM - 91.1
2848 Dana College Dr.
Blair, NE 68008
Format: Eclectic. **Owner:** Dana College, 2848 College Dr., Blair, NV 68008, Free: 800-444-3262. **Founded:** 1972. **Operating Hours**: Continuous. **Wattage**: 010. **Ad Rates:** Noncommercial.

BLUE HILL

Webster Co. Webster Co. (S). 20 m S of Hastings. Livestock. Sorghum, corn, wheat.

20426 ■ Glenwood Telecommunications
510 W Gage St.
Box 357
Blue Hill, NE 68930
Phone: (402)756-3131
Fax: (402)756-3134
Free: 866-756-4746
Founded: Jan. 1985. **Key Personnel:** Stanley Rouse, Gen. Mgr; C. McKinney, Contact. **Cities Served:** Bladen, Blue Hill, Campbell, Funk, Guide Rock, Holstein, Lawrence, Lochland/Hastings, Roseland, Roseland, Upland, Nebraska: subscribing households 1,200; Hastings AFB. **URL:** http://shopglenwood.net.

BRIDGEPORT

20427 ■ Bridgeport News-Blade
The Blade
801 Main St.
Bridgeport, NE 69336-0400
Phone: (308)262-0675
Fax: (308)262-0675
Publication E-mail: newsblade@hamilton.net
Community newspaper. **Freq:** Weekly (Wed.). **Print Method:** Offset. **Cols./Page:** 6. **Col. Width:** 2 inches. **Col. Depth:** 21 inches. **Key Personnel:** John Erickson. **Subscription Rates:** $20 Individuals online; $39 Two years online; $30 Individuals print & online in Panhandle Counties - Morrill, Garden, Cheyenne, Scotts Bluff, Banner, Kimball, Dawes, Box Butte, Sioux, Deuel, and Sheridan; $59 Two years print & online in Panhandle Counties - Morrill, Garden, Cheyenne, Scotts Bluff, Banner, Kimball, Dawes, Box Butte, Sioux, Deuel, and Sheridan; $35.50 Individuals print & online other Nebraska counties; $70 Two years print & online other Nebraska counties; $43 Individuals print & online outside Nebraska; 85 Two years print & online outside Nebraska. **URL:** http://www.newsblade.com; http://newsblade.net. **Mailing address:** PO Box 400, Bridgeport, NE 69336-0400. **Ad Rates:** PCI $4.50. **Remarks:** Accepts advertising. **Circ:** 1650.

BROKEN BOW

Custer Co. Custer Co. (C). In center of State, 75 m NE of North Platte. Surgical supplies, pipe and water turbine pumps manufactured. Agriculture. Especially grain and livestock. Corn, soybeans.

20428 ■ Custer County Chief
Custer County Chief
305 S 10th Ave.
Broken Bow, NE 68822
Phone: (308)872-2471
Fax: (308)872-2415
Publication E-mail: chiefnews@custercountychief.com
Community newspaper. **Freq:** Weekly (Thurs.). **Print Method:** Offset. **Cols./Page:** 6. **Col. Width:** 26 nonpareils. **Col. Depth:** 301 agate lines. **Key Personnel:** Bill Parsons, Publisher; Mary Coffman, Advertising Representative; Mona Weatherly, Editor. **USPS:** 140-980. **Subscription Rates:** $32 Individuals; $38 Out of area; $48 Out of state; $60 Two years; $72 Two years out of area; $88 Two years out of state. **URL:** http://www.custercountychief.com. **Mailing address:** PO Box 190, Broken Bow, NE 68822. **Ad Rates:** GLR $.36; PCI $6.25. **Remarks:** Accepts advertising. **Circ:** (Not Reported).

20429 ■ KBBN-FM - 95.3
PO Box 409
Broken Bow, NE 68822
Phone: (308)872-5881
Format: Sports; Classic Rock. **Networks:** NBC. **Owner:** Custer County Broadcasting Co., PO Box 409, Broken Bow, NE 68822, Ph: (308)872-5881. **Founded:** 1982. **Operating Hours**: 6 a.m.- 12 p.m. **Key Personnel:** Jeff Bailey, Prog. Dir; David Birnie, Contact; Bob Bowles, Contact; Larry Cotnoir, Contact. **Wattage**: 3,400. **Ad Rates:** Noncommercial. **URL:** http://www.kbbn.com.

20430 ■ KCNI-AM - 1280
PO Box 409
Broken Bow, NE 68822
Phone: (308)872-2801
Format: Full Service; Contemporary Country; Agricultural. **Networks:** NBC. **Founded:** 1949. **Operating Hours:** 6 a.m.-7 p.m. **Key Personnel:** Dave Birnie, Station Mgr.; Jeff Bailey, Dir. of Programs. **Wattage:** 1,000. **Ad Rates:** Noncommercial.

BURWELL

Garfield Co. Garfield Co. (C). 70 m NW of Grand Island. Residential.

20431 ■ Burwell Tribune
Burwell Tribune Newspapers
PO Box 547
Burwell, NE 68823
Phone: (308)346-4504
Publication E-mail: bwtrib@tribune2000.com
Local newspaper. **Freq:** Weekly (Wed.). **Print Method:** Offset. **Cols./Page:** 8. **Col. Width:** 10.5 nonpareils. **Col. Depth:** 976 agate lines. **Subscription Rates:** $32 Individuals local area; $34 Out of area; $36 Out of state. **URL:** http://www.burwelltribune.com/burwelltrib/TRIBUNESITE/tribuneindex.cfm. **Ad Rates:** GLR $3. **Remarks:** Advertising accepted; rates available upon request. **Circ:** (Not Reported).

20432 ■ Wheeler County Independent
Burwell Tribune Newspapers
PO Box 547
Burwell, NE 68823
Phone: (308)346-4504
Publisher's E-mail: bwtrib@tribune2000.com
Local newspaper. **Freq:** Weekly. **Print Method:** Offset. **Cols./Page:** 8. **Col. Width:** 10.5 picas. **Col. Depth:** 210 agate lines. **Key Personnel:** Byron Neiman, Publisher. **Subscription Rates:** $17; $19 Out of state. **Ad Rates:** GLR $.35; PCI $4.98. **Remarks:** Accepts advertising. **Circ:** 325.

BUTTE

Boyd Co. Boyd Co. (N). 130 m NW of Sioux City, Iowa. Grain, stock, poultry farms. Hay, corn, rye.

20433 ■ The Butte Gazette
The Butte Gazette
627 Thayer St.
Butte, NE 68722
Phone: (402)775-2431
Community newspaper. **Freq:** Weekly (Wed.). **Print Method:** Offset. **Cols./Page:** 7. **Col. Width:** 21 nonpareils. **Col. Depth:** 297 agate lines. **Key Personnel:** Leon Wells, Editor. **USPS:** 081-200. **Subscription Rates:** $23 Individuals; $28 Elsewhere; $33 Out of state. **Ad Rates:** GLR $.24; BW $170; SAU $2.80; PCI $2.80. **Remarks:** Accepts advertising. **Circ:** (Not Reported).

CALLAWAY

Custer Co. Custer Co (C). 45 m. NE of North Platte. Museum and park area. Hunting and fishing. Fertilizer plants. Farming.

20434 ■ The Callaway Courier
The Callaway Courier
PO Box 69
Callaway, NE 68825-0331
Phone: (308)836-2200
Publisher's E-mail: ccourier@gpcom.net
Community newspaper. **Freq:** Weekly (Wed.). **Print Method:** Offset. **Cols./Page:** 6. **Col. Width:** 23 nonpareils. **Col. Depth:** 182 agate lines. **Key Personnel:** Michael Wendorff, Publisher; Suzanne Wendorff, Publisher. **Subscription Rates:** $25 Individuals in Nebraska; $27 Out of state. **URL:** http://www.thecallawaycourier.zenfolio.com. **Ad Rates:** GLR $2.50; BW $145; SAU $2.50; PCI $2.20. **Remarks:** Accepts advertising. **Circ:** Paid ‡850, Free ‡18.

20435 ■ KKCS-FM - 104.7
PO Box 356
Callaway, NE 68825
Phone: (308)836-2277
Owner: Callaway Village Radio Inc., at above address. **Founded:** 1975. **Formerly**: KSTX-FM; KRLN-FM; KSTY-FM. **Wattage**: 1,550.

CAMBRIDGE

Furnas Co. Furnas Co. (S). 75 m SE of North Platte. Manufacturers steel, farm equipment. Diversified farming. Corn, wheat, alfalfa.

20436 ■ Pinpoint Cable TV
611 Patterson St.
Cambridge, NE 69022
Phone: (308)697-7678
Fax: (308)697-3631
Free: 800-793-2788
Email: info@pnpt.com

Circulation: ★ = AAM; △ or • = BPA; ♦ = CAC; ❑ = VAC; ⊕ = PO Statement; ‡ = Publisher's Report; Boldface figures = sworn; Light figures = estimated.

Founded: Sept. 06, 2006. **Cities Served:** 25 channels. **Mailing address:** PO Box 490, Cambridge, NE 69022. **URL:** http://www.pnpt.com.

CENTRAL CITY

Merrick Co. Merrick Co. (EC). On Platte River, 22 m NE of Grand Island. Concrete products, wood pallets, mobile homes manufactured. Popcorn processing plant. Diversified farming. Corn, wheat, alfalfa.

20437 ■ Central City Republican Nonpareil
Republican Nonpareil
802 C Ave.
Central City, NE 68826
Phone: (308)946-3081
Community newspaper. **Freq:** Weekly (Thurs.). **Print Method:** Offset. **Cols./Page:** 4. **Col. Width:** 24 nonpareils. **Col. Depth:** 196 agate lines. **Key Personnel:** Robert M. Jensen, Editor; Penelope A. Jensen, Publisher. **Subscription Rates:** $20 Individuals; $27 Out of state. **URL:** http://republicannonpareil.com. **Formerly:** Republican Nonpareil. **Mailing address:** PO Box 26, Central City, NE 68826. **Ad Rates:** BW $597.24; SAU $4; PCI $6.74. **Remarks:** Advertising accepted; rates available upon request. **Circ:** (Not Reported).

20438 ■ Cable Nebraska
1604 16th St.
Central City, NE 68826
Cities Served: 114 channels. **URL:** http://usacommunications.tv.

CHADRON

Dawes Co. Dawes Co. (NW). 30 m NW of Rushville. Residential.

20439 ■ Chadron Record
Chadron Record
248 W Second St.
Chadron, NE 69337
Phone: (308)432-5511
Fax: (308)432-2385
Publication E-mail: cdrrecord@bbc.net
Newspaper. **Founded:** 1884. **Freq:** Weekly (Wed.). **Print Method:** Offset. **Cols./Page:** 5. **Col. Width:** 24 nonpareils. **Col. Depth:** 294 agate lines. **Key Personnel:** George Ledbetter, Editor; Linda Teahon, Manager, Advertising; RaeLynn Nuno, Office Manager. **Subscription Rates:** $20 Individuals; $36 Individuals. **URL:** http://www.thechadronnews.com/. **Ad Rates:** GLR $.49; BW $400; 4C $590; SAU $6.80; PCI $8.65. **Remarks:** Accepts advertising. **Circ:** Paid ‡2100, Free ‡7700.

20440 ■ Museum of the Fur Trade Quarterly
Museum of the Fur Trade
6321 Highway 20
Chadron, NE 69337
Phone: (308)432-3843
Fax: (308)432-5963
Publisher's E-mail: museum@furtrade.org
Freq: Quarterly. **ISSN:** 0027- 4135 (print). **Subscription Rates:** $550 complete set. **URL:** http://www.furtrade.org/publications/museum-quarterly. **Remarks:** Advertising not accepted. **Circ:** 3000.

20441 ■ KCSR-AM - 610
226 Bordeaux St.
Chadron, NE 69337
Phone: (308)432-5545
Fax: (308)432-5601
Free: 800-266-4682
Email: kcsr@chadrad.com
Format: Country. **Networks:** ABC; Mid-America Ag. **Owner:** Chadrad Communications Inc., at above address. **Founded:** 1953. **Operating Hours:** Continuous. **ADI:** Denver (Steamboat Springs), CO. **Key Personnel:** Dennis Brown, Owner, dennis@chadrad.com; Kathi Brown, Owner, kathi@chadrad.com; Sara Taylor, Bus. Mgr., accounting@chadrad.com. **Local Programs:** *Sound Off*, Monday Tuesday Wednesday Thursday Friday 8:17 a.m.; *Mid-America Ag Network*, Saturday; *Swap Shop*, Monday Tuesday Wednesday Thursday Friday 9:00 a.m. **Wattage:** 1,000. **Ad Rates:** Advertising accepted; rates available upon request. **URL:** http://www.chadrad.com.

20442 ■ KQSK-FM - 97.5
331 Main St., Ste. C
Chadron, NE 69337-1117
Phone: (308)432-2060
Fax: (308)432-2059
Email: kcow@bbc.net
Format: Country. **Simulcasts:** KAAQ-FM. **Networks:** ABC. **Owner:** Eagle Radio of Hays, 2300 Hall St., Hays, KS 67601, Ph: (785)625-2578, Fax: (785)625-3632. **Founded:** 1979. **Operating Hours:** 5:30-1 a.m.; 80% network, 20% local. **Key Personnel:** John Axtell, Sports Dir., News Dir.; John Jones, Sales Mgr. **Wattage:** 200,000. **Ad Rates:** $8-20 for 30 seconds; $10-25 for 60 seconds. **Mailing address:** PO Box 1117, Chadron, NE 69337-1117. **URL:** http://www.doubleqcountry.com.

COLERIDGE

20443 ■ Coleridge Blade
Coleridge Blade
107 W Broadway
Coleridge, NE 68727
Phone: (402)283-4267
Fax: (402)283-4267
Publisher's E-mail: coleridgeblade@nntc.net
Community newspaper. **Freq:** Weekly (Wed.). **Cols./Page:** 5. **Col. Width:** 11 picas. **Col. Depth:** 15 1/2 inches. **Key Personnel:** Betty Foxhoven, Contact; Alecia Heimes, Office Manager; Rob Dump, Editor. **Subscription Rates:** $15 Individuals; $17 Out of area; $19 Out of state. **Mailing address:** PO Box 8, Coleridge, NE 68727. **Ad Rates:** GLR $3.60; SAU $2.60. **Remarks:** Advertising accepted; rates available upon request. **Circ:** 909.

COLUMBUS

Platte Co. Platte Co. (E). 75 m NW of Lincoln. Trade center. Manufactures surgical supplies, cement products; steel processing and agricultural equipment. Electronics plants; planing and feed mills; machine shop. Stock, poultry, grain farms. Corn, wheat, cattle.

20444 ■ Columbus Telegram
Lee Enterprises Inc.
1254 27th Ave.
Columbus, NE 68601
Fax: (402)563-7500
Free: 877-680-6397
General newspaper. **Freq:** Weekly (Mon.) six-day newspaper (Mon.-Fri. afternoon, & Sunday morning). **Print Method:** Offset. **Cols./Page:** 6. **Col. Width:** 12 picas. **Col. Depth:** 21.5 inches. **Key Personnel:** John DiMambro, Publisher; Tyler Ellyson, Editor; Tiffany Wehr, Manager, Circulation. **USPS:** 124-500. **Subscription Rates:** $165.75 Individuals carrier route-city; $175.50 Individuals motor route; $269.10 By mail; $5.95 Individuals digital. **URL:** http://www.columbustelegram.com. **Remarks:** Accepts advertising. **Circ:** Mon.-Fri. 11000.

20445 ■ KJSK-AM - 900
1418 25th St.
Columbus, NE 68601
Format: News; Talk. **Owner:** Three Eagles Communications, 3800 Cornhusker Hwy., Lincoln, NE 68504, Ph: (402)466-1234, Fax: (402)467-4095. **Ad Rates:** Advertising accepted; rates available upon request. **URL:** http://threeeagles.com.

20446 ■ KKOT-FM - 93.5
1418 25th St.
Columbus, NE 68601
Phone: (402)564-2866
Free: 800-651-5568
Format: Classic Rock. **Networks:** ABC. **Owner:** Three Eagles Communications, 3800 Cornhusker Hwy., Lincoln, NE 68504, Ph: (402)466-1234, Fax: (402)467-4095. **Founded:** 1969. **Formerly:** KWMG-FM; KTTT-FM. **Operating Hours:** Sunrise-sunset. **Wattage:** 100,000. **Ad Rates:** Advertising accepted; rates available upon request. **URL:** http://www.mycentralnebraska.com.

20447 ■ KLIR-FM - 101.1
1418 25th St.
Columbus, NE 68601
Format: Adult Contemporary. **Owner:** Three Eagles Communications, 3800 Cornhusker Hwy., Lincoln, NE 68504, Ph: (402)466-1234, Fax: (402)467-4095. **Wattage:** 100,000. **Ad Rates:** Noncommercial. **URL:** http://threeeagles.com.

20448 ■ KTLX-FM - 91.3
2200 25th St.
Columbus, NE 68601
Format: Religious. **Networks:** Independent. **Operating Hours:** 15% local, 85% other. **Wattage:** 250. **Ad Rates:** Noncommercial. **URL:** http://www.ktlx.org.

COZAD

Dawson Co. Dawson Co. (SC). On Platte River, 45 m SE of North Platte. Manufactures and ships alfalfa products, auto equipment, cooperage, feed mill. Stock, poultry, grain farms. Alfalfa, corn, wheat.

20449 ■ Tri-City Trib
Tri-City Trib
320 West 8th St.
Cozad, NE 69130-0006
Phone: (308)784-3644
Fax: (308)784-3647
Publication E-mail: news@tricitytrib.com
Community newspaper. **Freq:** Weekly. **Print Method:** Offset. **Cols./Page:** 6. **Col. Width:** 2 nonpareils. **Col. Depth:** 224 agate lines. **Subscription Rates:** $31.50 Individuals /year (Dawson County); $41.50 Elsewhere /year; $.75 Single issue; $3 By mail single issue. **URL:** http://www.tricitytrib.com. **Mailing address:** PO Box 6, Cozad, NE 69130-0006. **Ad Rates:** GLR $.30; BW $300; 4C $320; SAU $6.75. **Remarks:** Accepts advertising. **Circ:** (Not Reported).

CRAWFORD

Dawes Co. Dawes Co. (NW). 25 m SW of Chadron. Residential.

20450 ■ Rare Breeds Journal: The Digest of the Alternative Livestock Industry
Rare Breeds Journal
PO Box 66
Crawford, NE 69339
Phone: (308)665-1431
Fax: (308)665-3919
Publication E-mail: rarebreed@bbc.net
Journal covering rare breeds. **Freq:** Bimonthly. **Print Method:** Web press. **Trim Size:** 8 1/2 x 11. **Cols./Page:** 4. **Col. Width:** 11 picas. **Col. Depth:** 58 picas. **Key Personnel:** Maureen Neidhardt, Editor, phone: (308)665-1431. **ISSN:** 1048--986X (print). **Remarks:** Accepts advertising. **Circ:** (Not Reported).

CRETE

Saline Co. Saline Co. (SE). 20 m SW of Lincoln. Doane College. Manufactures voting equipment. Flour mills; pet foods, pork processing. Stock, grain, dairy, poultry farms. Corn, wheat, hay.

20451 ■ The Crete News
The Crete News Inc.
1201 Linden Ave.
Crete, NE 68333
Phone: (402)826-2147
Fax: (402)826-5072
Publisher's E-mail: officemgr@cretenews.net
Community newspaper. **Freq:** Weekly (Wed.). **Print Method:** Offset. **Trim Size:** 16 x 22 1/2. **Cols./Page:** 7. **Col. Width:** 25 nonpareils. **Col. Depth:** 301 agate lines. **Key Personnel:** John Reeves, General Manager, Publisher; Andy McCallister, Editor; Jenn Lampila, Managing Editor. **USPS:** 137-860. **URL:** http://cretenews.net. **Mailing address:** PO Box 40, Crete, NE 68333. **Ad Rates:** GLR $.25; BW $528.50; SAU $3.50. **Remarks:** Accepts advertising. **Circ:** ‡3252.

20452 ■ Doane Owl
Doane College
1014 Boswell Ave.
Crete, NE 68333
Fax: (402)826-2161
Free: 800-333-6263
Publication E-mail: doaneline@doane.edu
Collegiate newspaper. **Freq:** Weekly Weekly (Thurs.) print online. **Print Method:** Offset. **Cols./Page:** 12. **Col. Width:** 7 picas. **Col. Depth:** 21.5 inches. **Key Personnel:** David Swartzlander, Advisor, phone: (402)826-8269; Alyssa Bouc, Managing Editor; Erin Bell, Editor-in-Chief. **URL:** http://www.doaneline.com; http://www.doane.edu/facstaff/media/owl. **Ad Rates:** 4C $250; PCI $4.70. **Remarks:** Accepts advertising. **Circ:** (Not Reported).

20453 ■ KDNE-FM - 91.9
1014 Boswell Ave.
Crete, NE 68333
Phone: (402)826-8677
Email: kdne@doane.edu
Format: Alternative/New Music/Progressive. **Owner:** Doane College Board of Trustees, 1014 Boswell Ave., Crete, NE 68333, Ph: (402)826-2161, Fax: (402)826-8600, Free: 800-333-6263. **Founded:** Sept. 14, 2006. **Key Personnel:** John Thayer, Sports Dir. **Ad Rates:** Noncommercial. **URL:** http://www.doane.edu/facstaff/media/kdne.

DILLER

20454 ■ Diode Communication
PO Box 236
Diller, NE 68342
Phone: (402)793-5125
Free: 800-203-1524
Email: customerservice@diodecom.net
Cities Served: 24 channels. **URL:** http://diodecom.net.

DONIPHAN

Hall Co. Hall Co. (SE). 10 m S of Grand Island.

20455 ■ The Doniphan Herald
The Doniphan Herald
PO Box 211
Doniphan, NE 68832
Phone: (402)756-2077
Community newspaper. **Freq:** Weekly. **Print Method:** Web press. **Trim Size:** 9 1/4 x 13. **Cols./Page:** 5. **Col. Width:** 1 7/8 inches. **Col. Depth:** 13 inches. **USPS:** 914-680. **Subscription Rates:** $20 Individuals online; $24.50 Individuals print only; $26.50 Out of state print only. **URL:** http://www.doniphanherald.com. **Ad Rates:** BW $204; SAU $3.20; PCI $5. **Remarks:** Accepts advertising. **Circ:** (Not Reported).

FAIRBURY

Jefferson Co. Jefferson Co. (SE). 57 m SW of Lincoln. Trade center. Manufactures stone, concrete, brick, fertilizer, men's & boy's jackets. Stock, grain, poultry, dairy farms. Corn, wheat, hogs. Livestock feeding.

20456 ■ Fairbury Journal-News
Fairbury Journal-News
516 5th St.
Fairbury, NE 68352
Community newspaper. **Freq:** Weekly (Wed.). **Print Method:** Offset. **Cols./Page:** 6. **Col. Width:** 21 nonpareils. **Col. Depth:** 294 agate lines. **Key Personnel:** Fred A. Arnold, Jr., Publisher; Susan Bartels, Director, Advertising. **USPS:** 184-000. **Subscription Rates:** $75 Individuals 1 year (print + online); $78 Out of area 1 year (print + online); $85 Elsewhere 1 year (print + online); $40 Individuals 1 year (online). **URL:** http://fairburyjournalnews.com. **Mailing address:** PO Box 415, Fairbury, NE 68352. **Ad Rates:** 4C $380; PCI $8.60. **Remarks:** Accepts advertising. **Circ:** ‡4500.

20457 ■ KGMT-AM - 1310
414 4th St.
Fairbury, NE 68352
Phone: (402)729-3382
Fax: (402)729-3446
Email: kutt@diodecom.net
Format: Oldies. **Networks:** ABC. **Owner:** Rick Siebert, Not Available. **Operating Hours:** 12 hours Daily; 10% network, 90% local. **ADI:** Lincoln-Hastings-Kearney, NE. **Key Personnel:** Randy Bauer, Dir. of Programs, kuttpd@diodecom.net; Stan Smith, News Dir.; Nichole Scholl, Promotions Dir. **Wattage:** 500. **Ad Rates:** $7-17 for 30 seconds. Combined advertising rates available with KUTT-FM. **URL:** http://www.kutt995.com.

20458 ■ KUTT-FM - 99.5
414 Fourth St.
Fairbury, NE 68352
Phone: (402)729-3382
Fax: (402)729-3446
Free: 800-457-6647
Format: Country. **Networks:** Satellite Music Network. **Owner:** Siebert Communications, at above address. **Founded:** Oct. 01, 1994. **Operating Hours:** Continuous; 80% network, 20% local. **ADI:** Lincoln-Hastings-Kearney, NE. **Key Personnel:** Randy Bauer, Prog. Dir., kuttpd@diodecom.net; Stan Smith, News Dir., kuttnews@diodecom.net; Nicole Scholl, Promotions Dir., kuttcopy@diodecom.net; Rick Siebert, Station Mgr., rlsiebert@diodecom.net. **Wattage:** 100,000. **Ad Rates:** $11-15 for 30 seconds; $15-18 for 60 seconds. Combined advertising rates available with KGMT. **URL:** http://www.kutt995.com.

FALLS CITY

Richardson Co. Richardson Co. (SE). 75 m SE of Lincoln. Grain bins, agricultural fans, sledge-hammer heads, burial vaults, business forms manufactured. Meat processing plant. Ships cattle, hogs and grain. Diversified farming. Corn, wheat, hogs, soybeans.

20459 ■ KLZA-FM - 101.3
1602 Stone
Falls City, NE 68355
Phone: (402)245-6010
Fax: (402)245-6040
Email: sunny1013fm@hotmail.com
Format: Adult Contemporary. **Founded:** July 07, 1998. **Operating Hours:** Continuous. **Wattage:** 25,000. **Ad Rates:** Advertising accepted; rates available upon request. **URL:** http://www.sunny1013.com.

20460 ■ KTNC-AM - 1230
1602 Stone St.
Hiawatha, KS 66434
Phone: (785)547-3461
Fax: (402)245-6040
Free: 800-414-3867
Email: ktnc@sentco.net
Format: Oldies; News; Sports. **Networks:** ABC; Brownfield. **Owner:** C.R. Communications Inc., at above address. **Founded:** 1957. **Operating Hours:** Continuous; 10% network, 90% local. **ADI:** Omaha, NE. **Key Personnel:** Jackie Johnson, Dir. of Traffic. **Local Programs:** *20/20 Weather*, Monday Tuesday Wednesday Thursday Friday 6:30 a.m.; 7:20 a.m.; 12:20 p.m.; 5:20 p.m. **Wattage:** 500 Day; 1,000 Night. **Ad Rates:** $3.10-3.60 for 10 seconds; $7.30-8.80 for 30 seconds; $13.60-16.60 for 60 seconds. **URL:** http://www.ktncradio.com.

FRANKLIN

Franklin Co. Franklin Co. (S). 62 m SW of Hastings. Stock, grain, dairy, poultry, truck farms.

20461 ■ K220HX-FM - 91.9
PO Box 391
Twin Falls, ID 83303
Fax: (208)736-1958
Free: 800-357-4226
Format: Religious; Contemporary Christian. **Owner:** CSN International, PO Box 391, Twin Falls, ID 83303, Ph: (208)736-1958, Fax: (208)736-1958, Free: 800-357-4226. **Key Personnel:** Mike Kestler, President; Don Mills, Music Dir., Prog. Dir.; Ray Gorney, Asst. Dir.; Kelly Carlson, Dir. of Engg. **URL:** http://www.csnradio.com.

FREMONT

Dodge Co. Dodge Co. (E). On Platte River, 35 m NW of Omaha. Midland College. Trade and sales center. Manufactures flour and feed, boxes, metal & steel, cement and tile products, hydraulic equipment, bearings, ladies garments, chemicals, canvas. Grain, stock, dairy, poultry, fruit farms. Corn, wheat, alfalfa.

20462 ■ Fremont Area Shopper
Fremont-Tribune Newspapers Inc.
135 N Main St.
Fremont, NE 68025
Phone: (402)721-5000
Fax: (402)721-8047
Buyer's guide. **Freq:** Weekly (Tues.). **Cols./Page:** 6. **Col. Width:** 1 9/16 inches. **Col. Depth:** 12 3/4 inches. **URL:** http://fremonttribune.com/app/shopper. **Formerly:** The Fremonter; HomeFront Buyer's Guide. **Remarks:** Advertising accepted; rates available upon request. **Circ:** (Not Reported).

20463 ■ Fremont Tribune
Fremont-Tribune Newspapers Inc.
135 N Main St.
Fremont, NE 68025
Phone: (402)721-5000
Fax: (402)721-8047
General newspaper. **Freq:** Daily (eve.). **Print Method:** Offset. **Cols./Page:** 6. **Col. Width:** 25 nonpareils. **Col. Depth:** 305 agate lines. **Key Personnel:** Tammy McKeighan, Editor; Tracy Buffington, Editor, phone: (402)941-1436. **Subscription Rates:** $172.75 Individuals /year (print; walking carrier route); $181.35 Individuals /year (print; motor route); $269.10 By mail /year (print); $5.95 Individuals /month; digital only. **URL:** http://fremonttribune.com. **Ad Rates:** GLR $10.37; BW $1,353.37; 4C $1,673.29; SAU $10.37. **Remarks:** Accepts classified advertising. **Circ:** 5000.

20464 ■ KFMT-FM - 105.5
118 E 5th St.
Fremont, NE 68025
Phone: (402)721-1340
Fax: (402)721-5023
Format: Classic Rock. **Owner:** KHUB/KFMT NRG Media L.L.C., at above address. **Founded:** 1939. **Operating Hours:** Continuous. **Key Personnel:** Del Meyer, Gen. Mgr.; Barry Reker, Promotions Mgr., Sales Mgr; Chris Walz, Contact, cwalz@nrgmedia.com. **Wattage:** 3,000. **Ad Rates:** Noncommercial. $15.90-$19.25 for 30 seconds; $20.10-$23.45 for 60 seconds. Combined advertising rates available with KHUB-AM. **URL:** http://www.myfremontradio.com.

20465 ■ KHUB-AM - 1340
118 E 5th St.
Fremont, NE 68025
Phone: (402)721-1340
Fax: (402)721-5023
Format: News; Talk. **Networks:** ABC. **Owner:** NRG Media, 2875 Mount Vernon Rd. SE, Cedar Rapids, IA 52403, Ph: (319)862-0300, Fax: (319)286-9383. **Founded:** 1939. **Operating Hours:** Continuous. **Key Personnel:** Del Meyer, Gen. Mgr., dmeyer1@nrgmedia.com; Virginia Marshall, Bus. Mgr., Dir. of Traffic, vmarshall@nrgmedia.com; Chris Walz, Contact, cwalz@nrgmedia.com. **Wattage:** 500 Day; 1,000 Night. **Ad Rates:** $11.20-13.55 for 30 seconds; $14.15-16.50 for 60 seconds. $15.90- $19.25; $20.10-$23.45 for 60 seconds. Combined advertising rates available with KFMT-FM.

GENEVA

Fillmore Co. Fillmore Co. (SE). 65 m SW of Lincoln. Manufactures flour and feed. Stock, dairy, poultry, grain farms. Wheat, corn, milo.

20466 ■ The Nebraska Signal
The Nebraska Signal
131 N 9th
Geneva, NE 68361-0233
Phone: (402)759-3117
Fax: (402)759-4214
Community newspaper. **Freq:** Weekly (Wed.). **Print Method:** Offset. **Cols./Page:** 6. **Col. Width:** 2 inches. **Col. Depth:** 294 agate lines. **Subscription Rates:** $34 By mail /year; $39 By mail /year (out of area); $20 Individuals e-edition; $49 By mail e-edition. **URL:** http://thenebraskasignal.com. **Ad Rates:** BW $913.50. **Remarks:** Accepts advertising. **Circ:** Paid ‡2450.

GERING

Scotts Bluff Co. Scotts Bluff Co. (W). On Platte River, 3 m S of Scottsbluff. Scotts Bluff National Monument. Manufactures bean and beet irrigation systems, machinery. Oil fields. Dairy, stock, poultry, grain farms. Sugar beets, wheat, corn.

20467 ■ Gering Courier
Gering Courier
1405 Broadway
Gering, NE 69341
Phone: (308)436-2222
Fax: (308)436-7127
Newspaper with a Republican orientation. **Freq:** Weekly (Thurs.). **Print Method:** Offset. **Cols./Page:** 6. **Col. Width:** 25 nonpareils. **Col. Depth:** 294 agate lines. **Key Personnel:** Brad Staman, Editor. **Subscription Rates:** $25 Out of area; $27 Out of state. **URL:** http://www.starherald.com/marketplace/gering-courier/business_39046776.html; http://www.starherald.com/gering. **Mailing address:** PO Box 1709, Gering, NE 69341. **Ad Rates:** GLR $.19; SAU $4. **Remarks:** Accepts classified advertising. **Circ:** (Not Reported).

Circulation: ★ = AAM; △ or • = BPA; ♦ = CAC; ❑ = VAC; ⊕ = PO Statement; ‡ = Publisher's Report; Boldface figures = sworn; Light figures = estimated.

20468 ■ WinDBreak Cable
1140 10th St.
Gering, NE 69341
Free: 800-282-4650
Owner: William D. Bauer, at above address, Fax: (308)436-4779. **Founded:** 1988. **Key Personnel:** William D. Baver, Contact, bill@intertech.net. **Cities Served:** subscribing households 120. **URL:** http://www.windbreak.com.

GIBBON

Buffalo Co. Buffalo Co. (SC). 33 m SW of Grand Island. Turkey processing, packing plants. Farming. Potatoes, hay, wheat.

20469 ■ The Gibbon Reporter
The Gibbon Reporter
817 Front St.
Gibbon, NE 68840
Publication E-mail: info@clipperpubco.com
Community Newspaper. **Founded:** 1891. **Freq:** Weekly (Wed.). **Print Method:** Offset. **Trim Size:** 13 3/4 x 22. **Cols./Page:** 6. **Col. Width:** 12.5 picas. **Col. Depth:** 20.5 inches. **Subscription Rates:** $37 Individuals. **URL:** http://www.clipperpubco.com/index.php?option=com_content&view=article&id=8. **Formerly:** Reporter. **Mailing address:** PO Box 820, Gibbon, NE 68840. **Ad Rates:** BW $275.91; PCI $3.50. **Remarks:** Color advertising not accepted. **Circ:** Paid ‡1121, Free ‡13.

GORDON

Sheridan Co. Sheridan Co. (NW). 30 m NE of Rushville.

20470 ■ KSDZ-FM - 95.5
PO Box 390
Gordon, NE 69343
Phone: (308)282-2500
Email: thetwister@ksdzfm.com
Format: Hot Country; Oldies. **Networks:** ABC. **Owner:** DJ Broadcasting, Inc., at above address, Altavista, VA. **Operating Hours**: Continuous. **Wattage**: 60,000. **Ad Rates:** $23.50 for 30 seconds; $28 for 60 seconds. **URL:** http://www.ksdzfm.com.

GOTHENBURG

Dawson Co. Dawson Co. (SC). 35 m SE of North Platte. Original pony express station. Alfalfa dehydrating plants. Stock, grain farms. Corn, alfalfa, wheat, sugar beets.

20471 ■ The Gothenburg Times
The Gothenburg Times
406 10th St.
Gothenburg, NE 69138-0385
Phone: (308)537-3636
Fax: (308)537-7554
Free: 888-537-3636
Publication E-mail: ads@gothenburgtimes.com
Newspaper. **Freq:** Weekly (Wed.). **Print Method:** Offset. **Cols./Page:** 6. **Col. Width:** 11 picas. **Col. Depth:** 294 agate lines. **Key Personnel:** Greg Viergutz, Publisher; Elizabeth Barrett, Editor. **USPS:** 223-900. **Subscription Rates:** $31.95 Individuals in Dawson, Brady & Arnold County; $19.75 Individuals 6 months, in Dawson, Brady & Arnold County; $35 Individuals remainder of Nebraska; $21.60 Individuals 6 months, remainder of Nebraska; $41 Out of state; $25.35 Out of state 6 months; $25 Individuals e-subscription (52 weeks). **URL:** http://www.gothenburgtimes.com. **Mailing address:** PO Box 385, Gothenburg, NE 69138-0385. **Ad Rates:** GLR $.36; BW $636.30; 4C $811.30; SAU $5.05; PCI $5.05. **Remarks:** Accepts classified advertising. **Circ:** (Not Reported).

GRAND ISLAND

Hall Co. Hall Co. (C). On Platte River, 90 m W of Lincoln. Museum. Park area. Manufacturing, wholesaling and retail center. Livestock and grain marketing center. Manufactures farm equipment, livestock feeds, irrigation equipment, plastic products, metal buildings and construction components and ammunition; food processing plants. Agriculture. Corn, soybeans, milo, alfalfa, wheat and cattle.

20472 ■ Grand Island Independent
Grand Island Independent
422 W 1st St.
Grand Island, NE 68802
Phone: (308)382-1000
Free: 800-658-3160
Publisher's E-mail: newsdesk@theindependent.com
Newspaper. **Freq:** Mon.-Sun. (morn.) except Christmas day. **Print Method:** Offset. **Cols./Page:** 6. **Col. Width:** 12.4 picas. **Col. Depth:** 21.5 inches. **Key Personnel:** Don Smith, Publisher, phone: (308)381-9410; Jim Faddis, Managing Editor, phone: (308)381-9413. **URL:** http://www.theindependent.com. **Ad Rates:** GLR $0.75; BW $1,598.31; 4C $1,898.31; SAU $12.39; PCI $12.39. **Remarks:** Accepts classified advertising. **Circ:** (Not Reported).

20473 ■ West Nebraska Register
West Nebraska Register
2708 Old Fair Rd.
Grand Island, NE 68802
Phone: (308)382-6565
Fax: (308)382-6569
Free: 800-652-0004
Publisher's E-mail: wnr@charterinternet.com
Official newspaper of the Catholic Diocese of Grand Island. **Freq:** Semimonthly. **Print Method:** Offset. **Cols./Page:** 5. **Col. Width:** 1 7/8 INS. **Col. Depth:** 168 agate lines. **Key Personnel:** Mary Parlin, Editor; Bishop William J. Dendinger, Publisher; Colleen Gallion, Associate Editor. **Subscription Rates:** $20 Individuals. **URL:** http://register.gidiocese.org. **Mailing address:** PO Box 608, Grand Island, NE 68802. **Ad Rates:** BW $1,078.56. **Remarks:** Accepts advertising. **Circ:** (Not Reported).

20474 ■ KGIN-TV - 11
123 N Locust
Grand Island, NE 68801
Phone: (308)563-2200
Fax: (308)382-3216
Format: Commercial TV. **Networks:** CBS. **Owner:** Busse Corp., PO Box 1069, WI. **Key Personnel:** Frank Jonas, Gen. Mgr. **Wattage:** 25,000 ERP.

20475 ■ KKJK-FM - 103.1
3205 W North Front St.
Grand Island, NE 68802
Phone: (308)381-1430
Free: 888-505-1031
Format: Album-Oriented Rock (AOR); Classic Rock. **Wattage:** 100,000 ERP. **URL:** http://www.2dayfm1031.com.

20476 ■ KLNB-FM - 88.3
PO Box 779002
Rocklin, CA 95677-9972
Fax: (916)251-1901
Free: 800-525-5683
Format: Contemporary Christian. **Owner:** Educational Media Foundation, PO Box 2098, Omaha, NE 68103-2098, Free: 800-434-8400. **Key Personnel:** Mike Novak, President, CEO; Alan Mason, COO. **Wattage:** 1,700. **URL:** http://www.klove.com.

20477 ■ KRGI-AM - 1430
3205 W N Front St.
Grand Island, NE 68803
Phone: (308)381-1430
Fax: (308)382-6701
Email: info@hometownfamilyradio.com
Format: News; Sports; Talk. **Networks:** ABC; Westwood One Radio; Mutual Broadcasting System. **Owner:** GI Family Radio, 3205 W N Front St. , Grand Island, NE 68803-4024, Ph: (308)381-1430, Fax: (308)382-6701. **Founded:** Apr. 01, 1953. **Operating Hours**: Continuous; 30% network, 70% local. **Key Personnel:** Brad Fossberg, Sports Dir., News Dir. **Wattage:** 5,000 Day; 1,000 Night. **Ad Rates:** $22-44 for 30 seconds; $27-53 for 60 seconds. $22-$44 for 30 seconds; $27-$53 for 60 seconds. Combined advertising rates available with KRGI-FM, KIRB-FM, KMMJ-AM. **URL:** http://www.newsacrossnebraska.com.

20478 ■ KRGI-FM - 96.5
3205 W N Front St.
Grand Island, NE 68803
Format: Country. **Networks:** ABC. **Owner:** GI Family Radio, 3205 W N Front St. , Grand Island, NE 68803-4024, Ph: (308)381-1430, Fax: (308)382-6701. **Operating Hours:** Continuous. **Key Personnel:** Chris Loghry, Contact. **Wattage:** 100,000. **Ad Rates:** $22-44 for 30 seconds; $27-53 for 60 seconds. $22-$44 for 30 seconds; $27-$53 for 60 seconds. Combined advertising rates available with KRGI-AM. **URL:** http://gifamilyradio.com.

20479 ■ KRGY-FM - 97.3
3205 W N Front St.
Grand Island, NE 68803
Phone: (308)398-0973
Fax: (308)382-6701
Format: Classic Rock. **Owner:** Legacy Communications L.L.C., at above address.

20480 ■ KROR-FM - 101.5
3532 W Capital Ave.
Grand Island, NE 68803
Phone: (308)381-1077
Fax: (308)384-8900
Format: Classic Rock. **Founded:** Sept. 07, 2006. **Ad Rates:** Advertising accepted; rates available upon request. **URL:** http://www.rock1015.com.

20481 ■ KSYZ-FM - 107.7
3532 W Capital Ave.
Grand Island, NE 68803
Phone: (308)381-1077
Fax: (308)384-8900
Format: Adult Contemporary. **Owner:** NRG Media, 2875 Mount Vernon Rd. SE, Cedar Rapids, IA 52403, Ph: (319)862-0300, Fax: (319)286-9383. **Founded:** 1982. **Operating Hours**: Continuous. **Wattage**: 100,000. **Ad Rates:** Noncommercial. **URL:** http://www.ksyz.com.

GRANT

Perkins Co. Perkins Co. (W). 60 m SW of North Platte. Grain, stock, dairy, poultry farms. Wheat, corn, alfalfa.

20482 ■ Grant Tribune Sentinel
Johnson Publications Inc.
327 Central Ave.
Grant, NE 69140
Phone: (308)352-4311
Fax: (308)352-4101
Publication E-mail: grantrib@gpcom.net
Community newspaper. **Freq:** Weekly. **Print Method:** Offset. **Key Personnel:** Jan Rahn, Managing Editor. **Subscription Rates:** $29 Individuals print and online. **URL:** http://www.granttribune.com. **Mailing address:** PO Box 67, Grant, NE 69140. **Remarks:** Accepts advertising. **Circ:** (Not Reported).

GRETNA

Sarpy Co. Sarpy Co. (E). 25 m SW of Omaha. Grain elevators. State fish hatchery. Stock, grain, dairy farms. Wheat, corn, oats.

20483 ■ Gretna Guide & News
Gretna Guide & News
PO Box 240
Gretna, NE 68028
Phone: (402)332-3232
Fax: (402)332-4733
Publisher's E-mail: frontdesk@gretnaguide.com
Community newspaper. **Freq:** Weekly (Wed.). **Print Method:** Offset. **Cols./Page:** 7. **Col. Width:** 24 nonpareils. **Col. Depth:** 301 agate lines. **Key Personnel:** Mike Overmann, Publisher; Mike Fischer, Editor. **Subscription Rates:** $20 Individuals print; $20 Individuals electronic; $16 Students; $3 Single issue; $27 Individuals all Nebraska counties outside Sarpy county; $32 Individuals outside Nebraska. **URL:** http://www.dcpostgazette.com/gretnaguide. **Mailing address:** 620 N Hwy. 6, Gretna, NE 68028. **Ad Rates:** GLR $7; BW $110; 4C $295; SAU $5.50; CNU $5; PCI $5.25. **Remarks:** Accepts advertising. **Circ:** ‡4,470.

HARTINGTON

Cedar Co. Cedar Co (NE). 40 m N of Norfolk. Cheese processing plant. Corn, oats, hogs, cattle.

20484 ■ Osmond Republican
Northeast Nebraska News Co.
102 W Main St.
Hartington, NE 68739-0977
Local newspaper. **Freq:** Weekly (Wed.). **Print Method:** Offset. **Cols./Page:** 6. **Col. Width:** 25 nonpareils. **Col. Depth:** 294 agate lines. **Key Personnel:** Peggy Year, Publisher; Alecia Heimes, Office Manager; Rob Dump, Editor. **USPS:** 412-960. **Subscription Rates:** $29.50 Individuals; $37 Out of area; $31 Individuals online; $49 Individuals zone 7 and 8. **Ad Rates:** GLR $.186; BW $655.20; SAU $5.20; PCI $2.60. **Remarks:** Accepts advertising. **Circ:** ‡925.

20485 ■ CedarVision Inc.
103 W Centre St.
Hartington, NE 68739
Phone: (402)254-3901
Fax: (402)254-2453
Key Personnel: Bill Dendinger, Gen. Mgr. **Cities Served:** 49 channels. **Mailing address:** PO Box 157, Hartington, NE 68739. **URL:** http://www.hartel.net.

HASTINGS

Adams Co. Adams Co. (SE). 90 m W of Lincoln. Hastings College. Wholesale and distributing center. Animal research center. Manufactures butter, cheese, automobile accessories, hardware, plastic, wheat, flour and corn products, land rollers, pumps, air conditioners, metal grain bins, farm tools, irrigation equipment. Beef, cattle, sheep. Agriculture. Corn, wheat, hogs, cattle.

20486 ■ Hastings Tribune
Seaton Publications
908 W 2nd St.
Hastings, NE 68901
Phone: (402)462-2131
Fax: (402)461-4657
Free: 800-742-6397
General newspaper. **Freq:** Daily (eve.). **Print Method:** Offset. **Trim Size:** 12 1/2 x 22 3/4. **Cols./Page:** 6 and 5. **Col. Width:** 10.8 and 10.8 picas. **Col. Depth:** 21 and 11.50 inches. **Key Personnel:** Darran Fowler, Publisher; Angie Duering, Office Manager. **Subscription Rates:** $105 Individuals 1 year (Adams, Clay, Nuckolls, Webster, Doniphan, Giltner Counties); $112 Individuals 1 year (Fillmore, Franklin, Kearney, Thayer Counties); $145 Individuals 1 year; $145 Individuals 1 year (Smith, Jewell Counties); $155 Out of area 1 year; $195 Out of state 1 year. **URL:** http://www.hastingstribune.com. **Mailing address:** PO Box 788, Hastings, NE 68901. **Ad Rates:** GLR $1,146.60; BW $1,196.37; 4C $315; SAU $10.72; CNU $863; PCI $1562.73. **Remarks:** Accepts classified advertising. **Circ:** (Not Reported).

20487 ■ HC Today
Hastings College
710 N Turner Ave.
Hastings, NE 68901
Free: 800-532-7642
Publisher's E-mail: djackson@hastings.edu
Collegiate magazine. **Freq:** Semiannual. **Print Method:** Web. **Trim Size:** 8 3/8 x 10 7/8. **Key Personnel:** Camille Kirchhoff, Graphic Designer, Publisher; Amber Medina, Editor, Writer. **Subscription Rates:** Free. **URL:** http://www.hastings.edu. **Formerly:** Hastings Today. **Remarks:** Advertising not accepted. **Circ:** Non-paid ‡31000.

20488 ■ KCNT-FM - 88.1
550 S Technical Blvd.
Hastings, NE 68902-1024
Phone: (402)463-9811
Fax: (402)461-2454
Format: Contemporary Hit Radio (CHR); Educational. **Owner:** Central Community College, 4500 63rd St., Columbus, NE 68602-1027, Ph: (402)564-7132, Fax: (402)562-1201, Free: 877-CCC-0780. **Founded:** 1971. **Operating Hours**: Continuous. **ADI**: Lincoln-Hastings-Kearney, NE. **Key Personnel:** John Brooks, Contact, jbrooks@cccneb.edu; Carole Meyer, Contact, cmeyer@cccneb.edu. **Wattage:** 2,000. **Ad Rates:** Noncommercial. **Mailing address:** PO Box 1024, Hastings, NE 68902-1024. **URL:** http://www.cccneb.edu.

20489 ■ KFKX-FM - 90.1
710 N Turner Ave.
Hastings, NE 68901
Email: kfkx@hastings.edu
Format: Sports; News. **Owner:** Hastings College, at above address. **Key Personnel:** Sharon Brooks, Gen. Mgr., sbrooks@hastings.edu; Bart Jones, Chief Engineer, bjones@hastings.edu. **URL:** http://www.kfkx.org.

20490 ■ KHAS-AM - 1230
500 E J St.
Hastings, NE 68902
Phone: (402)462-2511
Fax: (402)461-3866
Email: khaskics@khasradio.com
Format: News; Information; Sports. **Networks:** CBS; Brownfield; Mid-America Ag. **Owner:** Platte River Radio Inc., 1460 N Grand Island Ave., Grand Island, NE 68803. **Founded:** 1940. **Operating Hours**: Continuous; more than 90% local. **ADI**: Lincoln-Hastings-Kearney, NE. **Key Personnel:** Craig Eckert, Gen. Mgr. **Local Programs**: *Party Line*, Monday Tuesday Wednesday Thursday Friday Saturday 9:06 a.m. - 10:00 a.m.; *Sunrise 60*, Monday Tuesday Wednesday Thursday Friday 7:00 a.m. - 8:00 a.m. **Wattage:** 1,000. **Ad Rates:** $7.65-17.65 for 60 seconds. Combined advertising rates available with KICS-AM. **Mailing address:** PO Box 726, Hastings, NE 68902. **URL:** http://hastingslink.com.

20491 ■ KHNE-FM - 89.1
1800 N 33rd St.
Lincoln, NE 68503
Phone: (402)472-6141
Fax: (402)472-2403
Free: 888-638-7346
Email: radio@netnebraska.org
Format: Public Radio; Classical; News; Jazz. **Networks:** Public Broadcasting Service (PBS); Public Radio International (PRI). **Owner:** Nebraska Educational Telecommunications Commission, at above address. **Founded:** 1990. **Operating Hours**: Continuous. **Key Personnel:** David Feingold, Contact. **Local Programs**: *Afternoon Concert*, Monday Tuesday Wednesday Thursday Friday 12:00 p.m. - 4:00 p.m. 12:00 p.m. - 1:00 p.m.; *Morning Concert*, Monday Tuesday Wednesday Thursday Friday 9:03 a.m. - 12:00 p.m. 10:03 a.m. - 12:00 p.m. **Wattage**: 068. **Ad Rates:** Noncommercial. **URL:** http://www.netnebraska.org.

20492 ■ KICS-AM - 1550
PO Box 726
Hastings, NE 68902
Phone: (402)462-5101
Free: 888-445-3776
Email: generalmanager@espnsuperstation.com
Format: Sports. **Owner:** Platte River Radio Inc., PO Box 130, Kearney, NE 68848-0130, Ph: (308)236-9900, Fax: (308)234-6781. **Ad Rates:** Advertising accepted; rates available upon request. **URL:** http://www.espnsuperstation.com.

20493 ■ KLIQ-FM - 94.5
PO Box 726
Hastings, NE 68901
Phone: (402)461-4922
Fax: (402)461-3866
Free: 800-832-0208
Email: thebreeze@kliqfm.com
Format: Adult Contemporary. **Key Personnel:** Craig Eckert, Gen. Mgr., generalmanager@kliqfm.com. **URL:** http://www.kliqfm.com.

HAYES CENTER

Hayes Co. Hayes Co. (SW). 50 m S of North Platte. Stock, grain, dairy, poultry farms.

20494 ■ KWNB-TV - 6
c/o KHGI-TV
Kearney, NE 68848
Phone: (308)743-2494
Fax: (308)743-2644
Email: news@nebraska.tv
Format: Commercial TV. **Networks:** ABC. **Owner:** Pappas Telecasting Company of Central Nebraska, 500 S Chinowth Rd., Visalia, CA 93277, Ph: (559)733-7800, Fax: (559)733-7878. **Founded:** 1955. **Operating Hours**: Continuous. **ADI**: Lincoln-Hastings-Kearney, NE. **Key Personnel:** Scott Swenson, Sales Mgr.; Vincent F. Barresi, Gen. Mgr.; Cheryl Alkire, Promotions Mgr.; Anita Wragge, Traffic Mgr. **Wattage:** 100. **Ad Rates:** Noncommercial. **URL:** http://www.nebraska.tv.

HEBRON

20495 ■ Hebron Journal Register
Hebron Journal Register
318 Lincoln Ave.
Hebron, NE 68370
Phone: (402)768-6602
Fax: (402)768-7354
Publisher's E-mail: hebronjr@windstream.net
Community newspaper. **Freq:** Weekly (Wed.). **Cols./Page:** 6. **Col. Width:** 14 picas. **Col. Depth:** 21 inches. **Key Personnel:** Mike Edgecombe, Publisher. **ISSN:** 0740--0997 (print). **Subscription Rates:** $34 Individuals; $39 Out of state; $23 Individuals e-edition. **Circ:** 3400.

HENDERSON

York Co. York Co. (SEC). 60 m W of Lincoln. Machinery, concrete and irrigation products manufactured. Printing. Stock, dairy farms. Corn, soybeans, oats.

20496 ■ Mainstay Cable TV
1000 N Main St.
Henderson, NE 68371
Phone: (402)723-4448
Fax: (402)723-4451
Free: 800-868-4848
Email: mainstay@mainstaycomm.net
Key Personnel: Matt Friesen, Mgr. **Cities Served:** 35 channels. **Mailing address:** PO Box 487, Henderson, NE 68371. **URL:** http://www.mainstaycomm.net.

HOLDREGE

Phelps Co. Phelps Co. (S). 55 m SW of Hastings. Manufactures mobil lighting, lighted directional signs, church pew cushions, cultivation equipment. Cattle feeding. Agriculture. Corn, milo, wheat, alfalfa, soybeans.

20497 ■ KMTY-FM - 97.7
PO Box 465
Holdrege, NE 68949
Format: Alternative/New Music/Progressive. **Networks:** ABC. **Owner:** Legacy Communications L.L.C., at above address. **Operating Hours**: Continuous. **Key Personnel:** Bryan Loker, Contact, bryan@highplainsradio.net; Bryan Loker, Contact, bryan@highplainsradio.net. **Wattage:** 50,000. **Ad Rates:** Advertising accepted; rates available upon request. **URL:** http://www.kmtyfm.com/.

20498 ■ KUVR-AM - 1380
PO Box 465
Holdrege, NE 68949
Phone: (308)995-4020
Fax: (308)995-2202
Format: Oldies. **Networks:** ABC. **Owner:** Armada Media Inc., at above address. **Founded:** 1956. **Operating Hours**: 6 a.m.- sunset. **Wattage:** 500. **Ad Rates:** Noncommercial.

HUBBARD

20499 ■ KAYA-FM - 91.3
PO Box 2440
Tupelo, MS 38803
Phone: (662)844-8888
Email: contact@afa.net
Format: Religious. **Owner:** American Family Radio, at above address.

IMPERIAL

Chase Co. Chase Co. (SW). 90 m SW of North Platte. Grain, stock, poultry farms. Alfalfa, corn, wheat, potatoes, beets, beans.

20500 ■ The Imperial Republican
Johnson Publications Inc.
622 Broadway
Imperial, NE 69033
Phone: (308)882-4453
Fax: (308)882-5167
Community newspaper. **Freq:** Weekly (Thurs.). **Print Method:** Offset. **Cols./Page:** 6. **Col. Width:** 12.2 picas. **Col. Depth:** 21 1/2 inches. **Key Personnel:** Russ Pankonin, Publisher; Lori Pankonin, Publisher. **USPS:** 259-980. **Subscription Rates:** $42 Individuals Print and e-Edition(Imperial/Enders/Wauneta/ Champion/Lamar)/ year; $48 Out of area Print and e-Edition(Nebraska and Phillips Co. Colo.)/year ; $57 Out of state Print and e-Edition/year; 30 Individuals /year (online). **URL:** http://www.imperialrepublican.com. **Mailing address:** PO Box 727, Imperial, NE 69033. **Ad Rates:** GLR $4.40; BW $568; SAU $4.40. **Remarks:** Accepts advertising. **Circ:** (Not Reported).

KEARNEY

Buffalo Co. Buffalo Co. (SC). 43 m W of Grand Island. Kearney State College. Shipping and wholesale trade center. Alfalfa meal mills; foundry and machine shops; manufactures creamery products, hosiery, pumps, radios, cement block. Diversified farming. Corn, alfalfa,

Circulation: ★ = AAM; △ or • = BPA; ♦ = CAC; ❑ = VAC; ⊕ = PO Statement; ‡ = Publisher's Report; Boldface figures = sworn; Light figures = estimated.

sugar beets, potatoes, cattle.

20501 ■ Antelope Newspaper
University of Nebraska at Kearney
905 W 25th St.
Kearney, NE 68845-4238
Phone: (308)865-8441
Collegiate newspaper. **Freq:** Weekly (Thurs.). **Print Method:** Offset. **Trim Size:** 13 x 21 1/2. **Cols./Page:** 6. **Col. Width:** 23 nonpareils. **Col. Depth:** 301 agate lines. **Key Personnel:** Allison Buchli, Editor-in-Chief. **URL:** http://www.unkantelope.com. **Ad Rates:** 4C $250; PCI $10. **Remarks:** Accepts advertising. **Circ:** ‡2300.

20502 ■ Kearney Hub
Kearney Hub Publishing Co.
13 E 22 St.
Kearney, NE 68848
Phone: (308)237-2152
Fax: (308)233-9736
Free: 800-950-6113
Publisher's E-mail: news@kearneyhub.com
General newspaper. **Freq:** Mon.-Sat. **Print Method:** Offset. **Trim Size:** 13 1/2 x 22 3/4. **Cols./Page:** 6. **Col. Width:** 25 nonpareils. **Col. Depth:** 294 agate lines. **Key Personnel:** Mike Konz, Managing Editor. **Subscription Rates:** $150.80 Individuals 1 year - carrier delivery; $189.90 Individuals 1 year - motor delivery; $189.80 Individuals 1 year - by mail (regional); $226.20 Individuals 1 year - by mail (non-regional). **URL:** http://www.kearneyhub.com. **Formerly**: Kearney Daily Hub. **Mailing address:** PO Box 1988, Kearney, NE 68848. **Remarks:** Accepts advertising. **Circ:** (Not Reported).

20503 ■ Platte Valley Review
University of Nebraska at Kearney
905 W 25th St.
Kearney, NE 68845-4238
Phone: (308)865-8441
Publication E-mail: pvr@unk.edu
Multi-genre interdisciplinary journal covering Midwestern and Plains subjects, with contributions from scholars and creative writers from the US and Canada. **Freq:** Semiannual. **Print Method:** Offset. **Key Personnel:** Allison Adelle Hedge Coke, Editor. **ISSN:** 0092--4318 (print). **URL:** http://www.plattevalleyreview.org/Webpages/2011%20start/PVR%20Main%20Web%20Pages/; http://www.plattevalleyreview.org. **Remarks:** Advertising not accepted. **Circ:** Combined 1000.

20504 ■ Cable Nebraska
2123 Central Ave., Ste. 200
Kearney, NE 68847
Free: 877-234-0102
Cities Served: 115 channels. **URL:** http://www.cablene.com/.

20505 ■ Cable USA
2123 Central Ave., Ste. 200
Kearney, NE 68847
Free: 877-234-0102
Owner: Cable USA, Inc., at above address. **Formerly**: Tele-Cable Service Corp. **Cities Served:** Bombay Beach, Borrego Springs, Calipatria, Desert Shores, Julian, Mecca, Niland, Ocotillo, Ocotillo, Salton City, Salton Sea, Thermal, California; 71 channels. **URL:** http://www.cableusa.com.

20506 ■ KFXL-TV - 51
PO Box 220
Kearney, NE 68848
Phone: (308)743-2494
Fax: (308)743-2644
Networks: Fox. **Owner:** Omaha World-Herald Company Inc., Omaha World-Herald Bldg. 1334 Dodge St., Omaha, NE 68102-1138, Ph: (402)444-1000, Free: 800-284-6397. **Founded:** 2006. **Formerly**: KCWL-TV. **Key Personnel:** Vincent F. Barresi, Contact; Cheryl Alkire, Bus. Mgr.; Marcie Ryan, Station Mgr.; Anita Wragge, Div. Mgr., awragge@nebraska.tv. **URL:** http://www.foxnebraska.com.

20507 ■ KGFW-AM - 1340
PO Box 669
Kearney, NE 68848
Phone: (308)698-2100
Fax: (308)237-0312
Format: Talk; News. **Networks:** CBS. **Owner:** NRG Media, 2875 Mount Vernon Rd. SE, Cedar Rapids, IA 52403, Ph: (319)862-0300, Fax: (319)286-9383. **Founded:** 1927. **Operating Hours**: Continuous. **ADI**: Lincoln-Hastings-Kearney, NE. **Key Personnel:** Steve Altmaier, News Dir., saltmaier@nrgmedia.com; Mark Reid, Operations Mgr., mreid@nrgmedia.com; Sharon White, Director, swhite@nrgmedia.com. **Local Programs**: *KGFW Headlines*; *Breakfast Flakes*, Monday Tuesday Wednesday Thursday Friday 7:00 a.m. - 8:00 a.m. **Wattage**: 1,000 Watts. **Ad Rates:** Advertising accepted; rates available upon request. Combined advertising rates available with Waitt Radio Stations. **URL:** http://www.kgfw.com.

20508 ■ KKPR-FM - 98.9
PO Box 130
Kearney, NE 68848-0130
Phone: (308)236-9900
Fax: (308)234-6781
Free: 800-237-5577
Email: generalmanager@kkpr.com
Format: Oldies. **Networks:** Satellite Music Network. **Owner:** Platte River Radio Inc., 1460 N Grand Island Ave., Grand Island, NE 68803. **Founded:** 1962. **Operating Hours**: Continuous. **ADI**: Lincoln-Hastings-Kearney, NE. **Wattage**: 100,000. **Ad Rates:** Advertising accepted; rates available upon request. Combined advertising rates available with KXPN-AM. **URL:** http://www.kkpr.com.

20509 ■ KLPR-FM
University of Nebraska at Kearney
Kearney, NE 68849-1340
Phone: (308)234-8250
Format: Jazz; Blues; Alternative/New Music/Progressive. **Owner:** University of Nebraska at Kearney, 905 W 25th St., Kearney, NE 68845-4238, Ph: (308)865-8441. **Founded:** 1968. **Formerly**: KOVF-FM; KSCV-FM. **Wattage**: 3,800 ERP. **Ad Rates:** Noncommercial.

20510 ■ KQKY-FM - 105.9
PO Box 669
Kearney, NE 68848
Phone: (308)698-2100
Fax: (308)237-0312
Email: support@marketron.com
Format: Top 40. **Founded:** 1979. **Operating Hours**: Continuous. **ADI**: Lincoln-Hastings-Kearney, NE. **Key Personnel:** Sharon White, Station Mgr.; Mark Reid, Operations Mgr.; Jason Murphy, Dir. of Programs. **Wattage**: 100,000 ERP. **Ad Rates:** Noncommercial. Waitt Radio Stations. **URL:** http://www.kqky.com.

20511 ■ KRNY-FM - 102.3
PO Box 669
Kearney, NE 68848
Phone: (308)698-2100
Fax: (308)237-0312
Format: Country. **Key Personnel:** Mark Reid, Operations Mgr., mreid@nrgmedia.com; Sharon White, Dir. of Sales, swhite@nrgmedia.com; Scott O'Rourke, Dir. of Programs, scotty0@krny.com. **Ad Rates:** Advertising accepted; rates available upon request. **URL:** http://www.krny.com.

20512 ■ KSNB-TV - 4
PO Box 220
Kearney, NE 68848
Phone: (308)743-2494
Fax: (308)743-2644
Networks: Fox; United Paramount Network. **Owner:** Pappas Telecasting Co. of Central Nebraska, at above address. **Founded:** 1964. **Key Personnel:** Tim Freeburg, Gen. Mgr., tfreeburg@nebraska.tv. **Wattage**: 23,500 ERP Horizonta. **URL:** http://www.kfxl.tv/.

KWNB-TV - See Hayes Center

20513 ■ KXPN-AM - 1460
PO Box 130
Kearney, NE 68848-0130
Phone: (308)236-9900
Fax: (308)234-6781
Email: generalmanager@espnsuperstation.com
Format: Sports. **Networks:** ESPN Radio. **Founded:** 1956. **Formerly**: KKPR-AM. **Operating Hours**: Continuous. **ADI**: Lincoln-Hastings-Kearney, NE. **Wattage**: 5,000 Day; 056 Night. **Ad Rates:** Noncommercial. Combined advertising rates available with KKPR-FM. **URL:** http://www.espnsuperstation.com.

KIMBALL

Kimball Co. Kimball Co. (W). 45 m S of Scottsbluff. Manufactures electronics and farm machinery. Ships wheat, potatoes, beans, cattle.

20514 ■ Western Nebraska Observer
Western Nebraska Observer
118 E Second St.
Kimball, NE 69145
Phone: (308)235-3631
Publisher's E-mail: editor@westernnebraskaobserver.net
Community newspaper. **Freq:** Weekly (Thurs.). **Print Method:** Offset. **Trim Size:** 11.625 x 21 1/2. **Cols./Page:** 6. **Col. Width:** 11 picas. **Col. Depth:** 301 agate lines. **Key Personnel:** Dave Faries, Editor. **USPS:** 678-940. **Subscription Rates:** $39 Individuals print; $46 Out of area print; $37 Individuals online; $78 Individuals print/2 years; $92 Out of area print/2 years; $75 Individuals online/2 years. **URL:** http://www.westernnebraskaobserver.net. **Ad Rates:** GLR $4.6; BW $502; PCI $6.75. **Remarks:** Accepts advertising. **Circ:** 2000.

LEXINGTON

Dawson Co. Dawson Co. (SC). 20 m NW of Overton.

20515 ■ Clipper-Herald
Midlands Newspapers
114 W 5th St.
Lexington, NE 68850
Phone: (308)324-5511
Publisher's E-mail: lexch@lexch.com
Community newspaper. **Freq:** Semiweekly (Wed. and Sat.). **Print Method:** Offset. **Trim Size:** 13 x 21 3/4. **Cols./Page:** 6. **Col. Width:** 12 picas. **Col. Depth:** 21 1/2 inches. **USPS:** 311-240. **Subscription Rates:** $62 Individuals Lexington and rural Lexington, Elwood, Overton, Cozad, Gothenburg, Eddyville, Oconto, Sumner, Smithfield, Bertrand and Elm Creek; $72 Out of area. **URL:** http://lexch.com. **Formed by the merger of:** Lexington Clipper; Dawson County Herald. **Remarks:** Accepts advertising. **Circ:** ‡3000.

20516 ■ KLNE-FM - 88.7
1800 N 33rd St.
Lincoln, NE 68583
Phone: (402)472-7722
Free: 888-638-7346
Email: radio@netnebraska.org
Format: Public Radio. **Networks:** National Public Radio (NPR); Public Radio International (PRI). **Owner:** Nebraska Educational Telecommunications Commission, at above address. **Founded:** 1990. **Operating Hours:** 5 a.m.- 1 a.m. **Key Personnel:** Randy Hansen, Asst. Gen. Mgr. of Sales/Mktg., rhansen@netnebraska.org. **Wattage**: 60,000. **Ad Rates:** Noncommercial. **URL:** http://www.netnebraska.org/radio/about.htm.

20517 ■ KRVN-AM - 880
PO Box 880
Lexington, NE 68850-0880
Phone: (308)324-2371
Format: Country; Agricultural; News; Sports. **Networks:** ABC. **Owner:** Nebraska Rural Radio Association, 1007 Plum Creek Pky., Lexington, NE 68850. **Founded:** 1951. **Operating Hours**: Continuous. **ADI**: Lincoln-Hastings-Kearney, NE. **Key Personnel:** Tim Marshall, Station Mgr.; Don Norman, Sales Mgr.; Bob Brogan, Editor; Rod Zeigler, Dir. of Engg., rzeigler@krvn.com; Jayson Jorgensen, Sports Dir., jjorgensen@krvn.com; Eric Brown, Gen. Mgr.; Dirk Christensen, Prog. Dir.; Beth Rogers, Promotions Dir. **Local Programs**: *Adam in the Afternoon*. **Wattage**: 50,000. **Ad Rates:** Advertising accepted; rates available upon request. KTIC-KWPN, KRVN-FM, KNEB AM/FM. **URL:** http://www.krvn.com.

20518 ■ KRVN-FM - 93.1
1007 Plum Creek Pkwy.
Lexington, NE 68850-0880
Phone: (308)324-2371
Format: Full Service; Adult Contemporary. **Networks:** NBC. **Owner:** Nebraska Rural Radio Association, 1007 Plum Creek Pky., Lexington, NE 68850. **Founded:** 1962. **Operating Hours**: Continuous. **ADI**: Lincoln-Hastings-Kearney, NE. **Key Personnel:** Beth Rogers, Promotions Dir.; Eric Brown, Gen. Mgr.; Rod Zeigler, Dir. of Engg.; Jayson Jorgensen, Sports Dir.; Don Norman, Sales Mgr.; Dirk Christensen, Prog. Dir.; Tim Marshall, Station Mgr.; Bob Brogan, Sports Dir. **Local Programs**: *Pam Snyder in the Evening*. **Wattage**: 100,000 ERP. **Ad Rates:**

Noncommercial. KRVN/AM, KNEB AM/FM, KTIC/KWPN. **URL:** http://www.krvn.com.

LINCOLN

Lancaster Co. Lancaster Co. (SE). The State Capital, 55 m SW of Omaha. University of Nebraska, other colleges and institutions. Trade and grain marketing center. Cold storage plant; flour and feed mill; meat packing plant. Manufacturing biological, creamery products, farm machinery, farm belts, radiator hose, telephone equipment, pharmaceutical, plumbing supplies, pumps, motor scooters, wax, filing equipment and office supplies; printing, lithographic, engraving, metal, stone, concrete products.

20519 ■ Alpacas Magazine
Alpaca Owners Association, Inc.
8300 Cody Dr., Ste. A
Lincoln, NE 68512
Phone: (402)437-8484
Fax: (402)437-8488
Journal covering latest research of Alpaca Owners and Breeders Association. **Freq:** 3/year. **Subscription Rates:** $75 international; $30 /year for nonmembers. **URL:** http://www.alpacainfo.com/magazine. **Ad Rates:** $1025-1140; $640-735. 4C $BW $. **Remarks:** Accepts advertising. **Circ:** (Not Reported).

20520 ■ The Children's Friend
Christian Record Services for the Blind
4444 S 52nd St.
Lincoln, NE 68516-1302
Phone: (402)488-0981
Fax: (402)488-7582
Publisher's E-mail: info@christianrecord.org
Christian Magazine for blind children. **Freq:** Quarterly. **Print Method:** Braille. **Trim Size:** 11 x 12. **Key Personnel:** Larry Pitcher, President. **URL:** http://www.christianrecord.org. **Mailing address:** PO Box 6097, Lincoln, NE 68506-0097. **Remarks:** Advertising not accepted. **Circ:** Non-paid ‡1300.

20521 ■ Christian Record
Christian Record Services for the Blind
4444 S 52nd St.
Lincoln, NE 68516-1302
Phone: (402)488-0981
Fax: (402)488-7582
Publisher's E-mail: info@christianrecord.org
Magazine for the blind. **Freq:** Quarterly. **Print Method:** Braille. **Trim Size:** 11 x 12. **URL:** http://services.christianrecord.org/periodicals/media.php?sid=1b83d3c4391a45c35433ba026bb85d45&a=20. **Mailing address:** PO Box 6097, Lincoln, NE 68506-0097. **Remarks:** Advertising not accepted. **Circ:** Non-paid ‡2900.

20522 ■ Christian Record Services Encounter
Christian Record Services for the Blind
4444 S 52nd St.
Lincoln, NE 68516-1302
Phone: (402)488-0981
Fax: (402)488-7582
Publisher's E-mail: info@christianrecord.org
Freq: Quarterly. **URL:** http://services.christianrecord.org/audio/media.php?a=3. **Mailing address:** PO Box 6097, Lincoln, NE 68506-0097. **Remarks:** Advertising not accepted. **Circ:** (Not Reported).

20523 ■ Cognitive Technology
Society for Applied Research in Memory and Cognition
University of Alaska
223 Burnett Hall
Lincoln, NE 68588-0308
Journal addressing the dynamic intersection of cognition and technology. Containing theories and methods pertaining to human cognition. **Subscription Rates:** $200 Institutions; $80 Individuals print only; $25 Individuals online only. **URL:** http://www.cognitivetechnologyjournal.com. **Remarks:** Advertising not accepted. **Circ:** (Not Reported).

20524 ■ Computer Power User
Sandhills Publishing Co.
120 W Harvest Dr.
Lincoln, NE 68521
Fax: (402)479-2104
Publication E-mail: editor@computerpoweruser.com
Magazine covering new computer hardware and software. **Freq:** Monthly. **ISSN:** 1536--7568 (print). **URL:** http://computerpoweruser.com. **Remarks:** Accepts advertising. **Circ:** (Not Reported).

20525 ■ Confident Living
Good News Broadcasting Association Inc.
6400 Cornhusker Hwy.
Lincoln, NE 68507-3123
Phone: (402)464-7200
Fax: (402)464-7474
Free: 800-811-2397
Publisher's E-mail: info@backtothebible.org
Religious magazine. **Freq:** Monthly (July/August issues combined). **Print Method:** Web offset. **Trim Size:** 8 x 10 3/4. **Key Personnel:** Jan Reeser, Managing Editor. **ISSN:** 0890--457X (print). **Mailing address:** PO Box 82808, Lincoln, NE 68501-2808. **Circ:** ‡60000.

20526 ■ Controller: The Marketplace for Piston Aircraft
Sandhills Publishing Co.
120 W Harvest Dr.
Lincoln, NE 68521
Phone: (402)479-2181
Fax: (402)479-2195
Free: 800-331-1978
Publication E-mail: feedback@controller.com
Aircraft for-sale publication. **Freq:** Weekly. **Print Method:** Offset Web. **Trim Size:** 10 7/16 x 15 7/8. **Cols./Page:** 6. **Col. Width:** 1 5/8 inches. **Col. Depth:** 16 inches. **Subscription Rates:** $59 Individuals 3rd class mail weekly; $24 Individuals 3rd class mail monthly; $38 Individuals 3rd class mail bi-weekly. **URL:** http://www.controller.com/info/mediakit.aspx. **Mailing address:** PO Box 82545, Lincoln, NE 68501-5310. **Remarks:** Advertising accepted; rates available upon request. **Circ:** (Not Reported).

20527 ■ Current HIV Research
Bentham Science Publishers Ltd.
University of Nebraska
School of Biological Sciences
Rm. 102C, Morrison Ctr.
4240 Fair St.
Lincoln, NE 68583-0900
Publisher's E-mail: subscriptions@benthamscience.org
Journal covering all the latest and outstanding developments of HIV Research. **Freq:** 6/year. **Key Personnel:** Charles Wood, PhD, Editor-in-Chief. **ISSN:** 1570--162X (print); **EISSN:** 1873--4251 (electronic). **Subscription Rates:** $240 Individuals print; $1010 print and online - academic; $920 print or online - academic; $1980 print and online - corporate; $1650 print or online - corporate. **URL:** http://benthamscience.com/journals/current-hiv-research. **Ad Rates:** BW $700; 4C $900. **Remarks:** Accepts advertising. **Circ:** ‡900.

20528 ■ Daily Nebraskan
University of Nebraska at Lincoln
1400 R St.
Lincoln, NE 68588
Phone: (402)472-7211
Publication E-mail: dn@unl.edu
Collegiate newspaper (tabloid). **Freq:** Daily (morn.). **Print Method:** Offset. **Trim Size:** 12 x 21. **Cols./Page:** 6. **Col. Width:** 1 13/16 inches. **Col. Depth:** 21 inches. **Key Personnel:** Hailey Konnath, Editor-in-Chief. **ISSN:** 1090--4085 (print). **Subscription Rates:** $75 Individuals. **URL:** http://www.dailynebraskan.com. **Ad Rates:** BW $1,764; 4C $2,014; SAU $14; PCI $14. **Remarks:** Accepts advertising. **Circ:** (Not Reported).

20529 ■ Executive Controller: The Marketplace for Turbine Aircraft
Sandhills Publishing Co.
PO Box 85310
Lincoln, NE 68501-5310
Phone: (402)479-2143
Fax: (402)479-2135
Free: 800-247-4890
Publisher's E-mail: feedback@sandhills.com
Magazine for sellers and buyers of turboprop and jet aircraft. **Freq:** Monthly every four weeks. **Trim Size:** 10.5 x 15.917. **URL:** http://www.controller.com/info/mediakit.aspx?guid=002B253B30A44309BD4FEDFF9%20CC1BF61#aboutexec. **Remarks:** Accepts advertising. **Circ:** (Not Reported).

20530 ■ Feminist Economics
International Association for Feminist Economics
371 CBA
Dept. of Economics
College of Business Administration
University of Nebraska-Lincoln
Lincoln, NE 68588-0479
Phone: (402)472-3372
Fax: (866)257-8304
Publisher's E-mail: info@iaffe-europe.org
Peer-reviewed journal publishing forum about feminist economic perspectives. **Freq:** Quarterly. **ISSN:** 1354-5701 (print); **EISSN:** 1466-4372 (electronic). **Subscription Rates:** Included in membership; $607 Institutions print + online. **URL:** http://www.feministeconomics.org. **Remarks:** Accepts advertising. **Circ:** (Not Reported).

20531 ■ Frontiers: A Journal of Women Studies
University of Nebraska Press
1111 Lincoln Mall
Lincoln, NE 68588-0630
Phone: (402)472-3581
Fax: (402)472-6214
Free: 800-848-6224
Publisher's E-mail: pressmail@unl.edu
Peer-reviewed scholarly journal covering women studies. **Freq:** Triennial. **Print Method:** Offset. **Trim Size:** 11 1/2 x 17 1/2. **Cols./Page:** 10. **Col. Width:** 21 nonpareils. **Col. Depth:** 290 agate lines. **Key Personnel:** Guisela Latorre, Editor. **ISSN:** 0160--9009 (print). **USPS:** 458-020. **URL:** http://www.nebraskapress.unl.edu/product/Frontiers,673226.aspx; http://frontiers.osu.edu. **Ad Rates:** BW $265. **Remarks:** Accepts advertising. **Circ:** (Not Reported).

20532 ■ The Gettysburg Magazine: Historical Articles of Lasting Interest
University of Nebraska Press
1111 Lincoln Mall
Lincoln, NE 68588-0630
Phone: (402)472-3581
Fax: (402)472-6214
Free: 800-848-6224
Publisher's E-mail: pressmail@unl.edu
Journal covering the Battle of Gettysburg. **Freq:** Semiannual. **Print Method:** Offset. **Trim Size:** 8 1/2 X 11. **Key Personnel:** James S. Pula, Editor. **ISSN:** 2372--6059 (print). **Subscription Rates:** $27 U.S. 1 year; $39 Other countries 1 year; $63 Institutions 1 year; $75 Institutions, other countries 1 year. **URL:** http://www.nebraskapress.unl.edu/product/The-Gettysburg-Magazine,675907.aspx. **Remarks:** Advertising not accepted. **Circ:** (Not Reported).

20533 ■ Great Plains Research: A Journal of Natural and Social Sciences
University of Nebraska at Lincoln Center for Great Plains Studies
Hewit Pl.
1155 Q St.
Lincoln, NE 68588-0214
Phone: (402)472-0602
Fax: (402)472-0463
Publication E-mail: gpr@unl.edu
Scholarly, multidisciplinary journal covering natural and social sciences dealing with issues of the Great Plains environment. **Freq:** Semiannual Spring and Fall. **Trim Size:** 8 1/2 x 11. **Key Personnel:** Peter Longo, Editor. **ISSN:** 1052--5165 (print). **Subscription Rates:** $40 Individuals; $73 Institutions; $52 Other countries; $85 Institutions, other countries. **URL:** http://www.unl.edu/plains/publications/GPR/gpr.shtml. **Mailing address:** PO Box 880214, Lincoln, NE 68588-0214. **Ad Rates:** BW $150. **Remarks:** Accepts advertising. **Circ:** 500.

20534 ■ Histories of Anthropology Annual
University of Nebraska Press
1111 Lincoln Mall
Lincoln, NE 68588-0630
Phone: (402)472-3581
Fax: (402)472-6214
Free: 800-848-6224
Publisher's E-mail: pressmail@unl.edu
Journal covering historical approaches in teaching, learning, and applying anthropology. **Key Personnel:** Frederic W. Gleach, Editor; Regna Darnell, Editor. **ISSN:** 1557--637X (print). **Subscription Rates:** $40 Individuals paperback. **URL:** http://www.nebraskapress.unl.edu/Catalog/ProductSearch.aspx?ExtendedSearch=false&SearchOnLoad=true&rhl=Histories+of+Anthropology+Annual&sj=746&rhdcid=746.

Circulation: ★ = AAM; △ or • = BPA; ♦ = CAC; ❑ = VAC; ⊕ = PO Statement; ‡ = Publisher's Report; Boldface figures = sworn; Light figures = estimated.

Remarks: Accepts advertising. **Circ:** (Not Reported).

20535 ■ International Journal of Public Opinion Research
World Association for Public Opinion Research
201 N 13th St.
Lincoln, NE 68588-0242
Phone: (402)472-7720
Fax: (402)472-7727
Publication covering sociology and social work. **Freq:** Quarterly. **Key Personnel:** Lilach Nir, Editor-in-Chief; Michael W. Traugott, Advisor; Albert C. Gunther, Board Member; Ottar Hellevik, Board Member; Marta Lagos, Board Member. **ISSN:** 0954--2892 (print); **EISSN:** 1471--6909 (electronic). **Subscription Rates:** £366 Institutions print and online; $710 Institutions print and online; €549 Institutions print and online; £288 Institutions online only; $559 Institutions online only; €432 Institutions online only; £337 Institutions print only; $654 Institutions print only; €505 Institutions print only; £127 Members print only; $241 Members print only; €190 Members print only. **URL:** http://ijpor.oxfordjournals.org; http://wapor.org/journal. **Remarks:** Accepts advertising. **Circ:** (Not Reported).

20536 ■ Journal of Air Law and Commerce
Joe Christensen Inc.
1540 Adams St.
Lincoln, NE 68521-1898
Fax: (402)476-3094
Free: 800-228-5030
Journal covering legal issues affecting aviation and commerce. **Freq:** Quarterly. **Print Method:** Offset. **Trim Size:** 6 x 9. **Cols./Page:** 1. **Col. Width:** 55 nonpareils. **Col. Depth:** 112 agate lines. **Key Personnel:** Jacqui Bogucki, Editor-in-Chief; Andria Minyard, Editor-in-Chief, phone: (214)768-1804; Emily Leezer Landeros, Managing Editor, phone: (214)768-1802; Lisa Browning, Office Manager, phone: (214)768-2570. **ISSN:** 0021-8642 (print). **Subscription Rates:** $43 Individuals; $50 Other countries; $16 Single issue. **URL:** http://www.smu.edu/lra/Journals/JALC/Overview.asp. **Ad Rates:** GLR $140; GLR $140. **Remarks:** Accepts advertising. **Circ:** ‡2,300.

20537 ■ Journal of the American Historical Society of Germans from Russia
American Historical Society of Germans From Russia
631 D St.
Lincoln, NE 68502-1199
Phone: (402)474-3363
Fax: (402)474-7229
Publisher's E-mail: ahsgr@ahsgr.org
Journal covering history. **Freq:** Quarterly. **ISSN:** 0162--8283 (print). **Formerly**: Work Papers. **Remarks:** Advertising not accepted. **Circ:** 5500.

20538 ■ Journal of Database Management
IGI Global
Dept. of Management, 209 CBA
University of Nebraska-Lincoln
Lincoln, NE 68588-0491
Publisher's E-mail: cust@igi-global.com
Journal covering the research of database administrators and managers. **Freq:** Quarterly. **Trim Size:** 8 1/2 x 11. **Cols./Page:** 2. **Key Personnel:** Dinesh Batra, Associate Editor; Hock Chan, Associate Editor; Richard Baskerville, Associate Editor; Roger Chiang, Associate Editor; Juhani Iivari, Associate Editor; Guy Fitzgerald, Associate Editor; Mark Gillenson, Associate Editor; Keng Siau, Editor-in-Chief; Shirley Becker, Associate Editor. **ISSN:** 1063--8016 (print); **EISSN:** 1533--8010 (electronic). **Subscription Rates:** $584 Institutions print + free e-access + free print copy; $208 Institutions print + free e-access or e-access + free print copy. **URL:** http://www.igi-global.com/journal/journal-database-management-jdm/1072. **Formerly**: Journal of Database Administration. **Remarks:** Advertising accepted; rates available upon request. **Circ:** Controlled 300.

20539 ■ Journal of Sports Media
University of Nebraska Press
1111 Lincoln Mall
Lincoln, NE 68588-0630
Phone: (402)472-3581
Fax: (402)472-6214
Free: 800-848-6224
Publisher's E-mail: pressmail@unl.edu
Journal featuring information on sports media. **Freq:** Semiannual. **Key Personnel:** Howard Schlossberg, Editor; Brad Schultz, Editor, Founder. **ISSN:** 1558--4313 (print). **Subscription Rates:** $55 Individuals; $81 Institutions; $67 Other countries; $93 Institutions, other countries; $36 Institutions online. **URL:** http://www.nebraskapress.unl.edu/product/Journal-of-Sports-Media,673232.aspx. **Ad Rates:** BW $75. **Remarks:** Accepts advertising. **Circ:** (Not Reported).

20540 ■ Legacy: A Journal of American Women Writers
University of Nebraska Press
1111 Lincoln Mall
Lincoln, NE 68588-0630
Phone: (402)472-3581
Fax: (402)472-6214
Free: 800-848-6224
Publisher's E-mail: pressmail@unl.edu
Publication covering women and literature. **Freq:** Semiannual. **Key Personnel:** Nicole Tonkovich, Editor; Jennifer S. Tuttle, Editor. **ISSN:** 0748-4321 (print). **Subscription Rates:** $40 Individuals US; $52 Other countries; $94 Institutions; $102 Institutions, other countries; $30 Students. **URL:** http://legacywomenwriters.org; http://www.nebraskapress.unl.edu/product/Legacy,673233.aspx. **Ad Rates:** BW $265, full page; BW $182.50, half page; BW $315, back cover. **Remarks:** Accepts advertising. **Circ:** (Not Reported).

20541 ■ Lincoln Journal Star
Lee Enterprises Inc.
926 P St.
Lincoln, NE 68508
Phone: (402)475-4200
General newspaper. **Freq:** Mon.-Sun. **Key Personnel:** Julie Bechtel, Publisher, phone: (402)473-7410; Dave Bundy, Editor, phone: (402)473-7334. **Subscription Rates:** $585.52 Individuals 7 days; $358.80 Individuals six days; $254.80 Individuals Sunday only. **URL:** http://www.journalstar.com. **Remarks:** Accepts advertising. **Circ:** Mon.-Fri. ★**70253**, Sun. ★**72252**.

20542 ■ Machinery Trader Central Edition
Sandhills Publishing Co.
120 W Harvest Dr.
Lincoln, NE 68521
Phone: (402)479-2181
Fax: (402)479-2195
Free: 800-331-1978
Publisher's E-mail: feedback@sandhills.com
Magazine on heavy construction equipment. **Freq:** Weekly. **Print Method:** Web Offset. **Trim Size:** 10 1/2 x 15 7/8. **Cols./Page:** 6. **Col. Width:** 20 nonpareils. **Col. Depth:** 224 agate lines. **Subscription Rates:** $59 Individuals weekly; $38 Individuals bi-weekly; $24 Individuals monthly. **URL:** http://www.machinerytrader.com. **Mailing address:** PO Box 82545, Lincoln, NE 68501-5310. **Remarks:** Color advertising accepted; rates available upon request. **Circ:** (Not Reported).

20543 ■ Machinery Trader Eastern Edition
Sandhills Publishing Co.
120 W Harvest Dr.
Lincoln, NE 68521
Phone: (402)479-2181
Fax: (402)479-2195
Free: 800-331-1978
Publisher's E-mail: feedback@sandhills.com
Magazine on heavy construction equipment. **Freq:** Weekly. **Print Method:** Web Offset. **Trim Size:** 10 1/2 x 15 7/8. **Cols./Page:** 6. **Col. Width:** 20 nonpareils. **Col. Depth:** 224 agate lines. **Subscription Rates:** $59 Individuals 3rd class mail weekly; $38 Individuals 3rd class mail bi-weekly; $24 Individuals 3rd class mail monthly. **URL:** http://www.machinerytrader.com. **Mailing address:** PO Box 82545, Lincoln, NE 68501-5310. **Remarks:** Color advertising accepted; rates available upon request. **Circ:** (Not Reported).

20544 ■ Machinery Trader Western Edition
Sandhills Publishing Co.
120 W Harvest Dr.
Lincoln, NE 68521
Phone: (402)479-2181
Fax: (402)479-2195
Free: 800-331-1978
Publication E-mail: feedback@machinerytrader.com
Magazine on heavy construction equipment. **Freq:** Weekly. **Print Method:** Web Offset. **Trim Size:** 10 1/2 x 15 7/8. **Cols./Page:** 6. **Col. Width:** 20 nonpareils. **Col. Depth:** 224 agate lines. **Subscription Rates:** $59 Individuals 3rd class mail weekly; $38 Individuals 3rd class mail bi-weekly; $24 Individuals 3rd class mail monthly. **URL:** http://www.machinerytrader.com. **Mailing address:** PO Box 82545, Lincoln, NE 68501-5310. **Remarks:** Color advertising accepted; rates available upon request. **Circ:** (Not Reported).

20545 ■ The National Hair & Skin
National Hair Society
1672 Van Dorn St.
Lincoln, NE 68502
Phone: (402)302-0822
Freq: Quarterly. **Alt. Formats:** CD-ROM. **URL:** http://probeauty.org/press/portfolio/the-national-hair-skin-journal. **Remarks:** Accepts advertising. **Circ:** (Not Reported).

20546 ■ Native South
University of Nebraska Press
1111 Lincoln Mall
Lincoln, NE 68588-0630
Phone: (402)472-3581
Fax: (402)472-6214
Free: 800-848-6224
Publisher's E-mail: pressmail@unl.edu
Journal focusing on the investigation of Southeastern Indian history. **Freq:** Annual. **Key Personnel:** Robbie Ethridge, Editor; James T. Carson, Editor; Greg O'Brien, Editor. **ISSN:** 1943--2569 (print). **Subscription Rates:** $42 Individuals; $86 Institutions; $48 Other countries; $92 Institutions, other countries; $36 Individuals online. **URL:** http://www.nebraskapress.unl.edu/product/Native-South,673964.aspx. **Ad Rates:** BW $150. **Remarks:** Accepts advertising. **Circ:** (Not Reported).

20547 ■ Nebraska
Alumni Association of the University of Nebraska
1520 R St.
Lincoln, NE 68508
Phone: (402)472-2841
Free: 888-353-1874
Publisher's E-mail: alumni@huskeralum.org
University alumni magazine. **Freq:** Quarterly. **Print Method:** Offset. **Trim Size:** 8 3/8 x 10 7/8. **Cols./Page:** 3. **Col. Width:** 28 nonpareils. **Col. Depth:** 126 agate lines. **URL:** http://www.huskeralum.org/s/1620/social.aspx?sid=1620&gid=1&pgid=448. **Formerly**: Nebraska Alumnus. **Ad Rates:** BW $1,900. **Remarks:** Accepts advertising. **Circ:** ‡24000.

20548 ■ Nebraska Cattleman
Nebraska Cattlemen
1010 Lincoln Mall, Ste. 101
Lincoln, NE 68508-2833
Phone: (402)475-2333
Fax: (402)475-0822
Publisher's E-mail: nc@necattlemen.org
Magazine for the cattle industry in Nebraska. **Freq:** 10/year the first of every month (except May and July). **Print Method:** Offset. **Trim Size:** 8 3/8 x 10 7/8. **Cols./Page:** 3. **Col. Width:** 28 nonpareils. **Col. Depth:** 138 agate lines. **Key Personnel:** Mike Fitzgerald, Editor, phone: (402)475-2333. **USPS:** 375-880. **URL:** http://www.nebraskacattlemen.org/magazine.aspx. **Ad Rates:** BW $645; 4C $1,105; PCI $22. **Remarks:** Advertising accepted; rates available upon request. **Circ:** ‡151500.

20549 ■ Nebraska Farm Bureau News
Nebraska Farm Bureau
5225 S 16th St.
Lincoln, NE 68512
Phone: (402)421-4400
Fax: (402)421-4439
Free: 800-742-4016
Publisher's E-mail: information@nefb.org
Nebraska Farm Bureau newspaper emphasizing legislation, policies, and regulations affecting agriculture. **Freq:** Monthly except July. **Print Method:** Offset. **Trim Size:** 11 1/2 x 18 3/4. **Cols./Page:** 4. **Col. Width:** 14.5 picas. **Col. Depth:** 16.5 picas. **Key Personnel:** Tina Henderson, Editor, fax: (402)421-4446. **ISSN:** 0745--6522 (print). **URL:** http://www.nefb.org. **Formerly**: Nebraska Agriculture. **Mailing address:** PO Box 80299, Lincoln, NE 68501-0299. **Ad Rates:** BW $4.50; PCI $9. **Circ:** Paid ‡45000, Non-paid ‡500.

20550 ■ Nebraska Farmer
Farm Progress Companies Inc.
5625 O St., Ste. 5
Lincoln, NE 68510-2133

Phone: (402)489-9331
Fax: (402)489-9335
Publication E-mail: dmccabe@farmprogress.com
Agricultural magazine. **Founded:** 1859. **Freq:** Monthly. **Print Method:** Offset. **Trim Size:** 8 x 10 7/8. **Cols./Page:** 3. **Col. Width:** 13 picas. **Col. Depth:** 59 picas. **Key Personnel:** Alan Newport, Editor, phone: (580)362-3483, fax: (580)362-3483; Willie Vogt, Director, Editorial, phone: (651)454-6994, fax: (651)994-0661; John Otte, Editor, phone: (515)278-7785, fax: (515)278-7797; Don McCabe, Editor; Frank Holdmeyer, Executive Editor, phone: (515)278-7782, fax: (515)278-7796. **USPS:** 376-020. **Subscription Rates:** $26.95 Individuals; $45 Two years; $59.95 Individuals three years. **URL:** http://farmprogress.com/nebraska-farmer. **Remarks:** Accepts advertising. **Circ:** (Not Reported).

20551 ■ Nebraska History
Nebraska State Historical Society
1500 R St.
Lincoln, NE 68501
Phone: (402)471-3272
Publication E-mail: publish@nebraskahistory.org
History journal. **Founded:** 1918. **Freq:** Quarterly. **Print Method:** Offset. **Trim Size:** 8 1/2 x 11. **Cols./Page:** 3. **Col. Width:** 28 picas. **Col. Depth:** 54 picas. **Key Personnel:** Donald Cunningham, Editor, phone: (402)471-4748. **ISSN:** 0028-1859 (print). **Subscription Rates:** $29 Members; $40 Individuals. **URL:** http://www.nebraskahistory.org/magazine/. **Mailing address:** PO Box 82554, Lincoln, NE 68501. **Remarks:** Advertising not accepted. **Circ:** ‡3800.

20552 ■ Nebraska Humanities
Nebraska Humanities Council
215 Centennial Mall S, Ste. 330
Lincoln, NE 68508-1836
Phone: (402)474-2131
Fax: (402)474-4852
Publisher's E-mail: info@humanitiesnebraska.org
Magazine of the Nebraska Humanities Council. **Freq:** Annual. **Key Personnel:** Dayle Wallien, Executive Director. **ISSN:** 1064--3516 (print). **URL:** http://humanitiesnebraska.org. **Remarks:** Advertising not accepted. **Circ:** (Not Reported).

20553 ■ The Nebraska Lawyer
Nebraska State Bar Association
635 S 14th St., Ste. 200
Lincoln, NE 68501
Phone: (402)475-7091
Fax: (402)475-7098
Free: 800-927-0117
Professional magazine covering law. **Freq:** 6/year. **Trim Size:** 9 x 12. **Key Personnel:** Liz Neeley, PhD, Executive Director, phone: (402)475-7091; Kathryn A. Bellman, Director. **Subscription Rates:** $28 Free to qualified subscribers; $28 Individuals. **URL:** http://www.nebar.com/?TNLMagazine. **Formerly**: NSBA Newsletter. **Mailing address:** PO Box 81809, Lincoln, NE 68508. **Ad Rates:** BW $800, full page; BW $650, 2/3 page vertical or horizontal; BW $550, half page; BW $450, 1/3 page vertical or horizontal; BW 400 Dh, quarter page; BW $350, 1/6 page vertical or horizontal; BW $185, business card; BW $1,050, inside front cover (full page); BW $1,150, inside back (full page); BW 950, inside back cover (full page). **Remarks:** Accepts advertising. **Circ:** Combined 8700.

20554 ■ Nebraska Mortar and Pestle
Nebraska Pharmacists Association
6221 S 58th St., Ste. A
Lincoln, NE 68516
Phone: (402)420-1500
Fax: (402)420-1406
Publisher's E-mail: info@npharm.org
Freq: Bimonthly 6/year Feb., Apr., June, Aug., Oct., and Dec. **Print Method:** Offset. **Trim Size:** 8 1/2 x 11. **Cols./Page:** 2. **Col. Width:** 42 nonpareils. **Col. Depth:** 136 agate lines. **ISSN:** 0028--1891 (print). **Subscription Rates:** for members only. **URL:** http://www.npharm.org; http://www.npharm.org/content.asp?contentid=35. **Ad Rates:** BW $375; 4C $855. **Remarks:** Accepts advertising. **Circ:** Paid 1300, Non-paid 950, 1450.

20555 ■ Nebraska Municipal Review
League of Nebraska Municipalities
1335 L St.
Lincoln, NE 68508
Phone: (402)476-2829
Fax: (402)476-7052
Freq: Monthly. **Print Method:** Offset. **Trim Size:** 8 1/4 x 11 1/4. **Cols./Page:** 3. **Col. Width:** 27 nonpareils. **Col. Depth:** 140 agate lines. **ISSN:** 0028--1905 (print). **Subscription Rates:** $50 Individuals /year; $5 Single issue. **URL:** http://www.lonm.org; http://www.lonm.org/index.php/publications. **Ad Rates:** BW $530. **Remarks:** Accepts advertising. **Circ:** 3500, 3400.

20556 ■ Nebraska Music Educator
Nebraska Music Educators Association
PO Box 85362
Lincoln, NE 68501
Phone: (402)937-3359
Fax: (402)975-6003
Professional journal for music teachers. **Freq:** Quarterly. **Print Method:** Offset. **Trim Size:** 8 1/2 x 11. **Key Personnel:** Joyce Patch, Editor. **ISSN:** 0732--1503 (print). **Subscription Rates:** $10 Individuals. **URL:** http://www.nmeanebraska.org/music-educator-magazine. **Ad Rates:** BW $208; 4C $683. **Remarks:** Accepts advertising. **Circ:** Paid 1650.

20557 ■ Nebraska School Law Reporter
Nebraska Council of School Attorneys
1311 Stockwell St.
Lincoln, NE 68502
Phone: (402)423-4951
Free: 800-422-4572
Journal summarizing Nebraska legal decisions which affect education. **Freq:** Quarterly. **Key Personnel:** Sandy Janssen, Contact. **Subscription Rates:** $80 Individuals. **URL:** http://members.nasbonline.org/servicesandprograms/Services/Legal/NCOSA/SitePages/Publications.aspx. **Remarks:** Advertising not accepted. **Circ:** (Not Reported).

20558 ■ Nebraska Trucker
Truck Services Inc.
PO Box 81010
Lincoln, NE 68501
Phone: (402)476-8504
Fax: (402)476-8570
Magazine for commercial truckers and shippers. **Freq:** Bimonthly. **Print Method:** Offset. **Trim Size:** 8 1/2 x 11. **Cols./Page:** 3. **Col. Width:** 26 nonpareils. **Col. Depth:** 140 agate lines. **Key Personnel:** Larry Johnson, Executive Editor; Sue Wilson, Contact; Michelle Drahota, Contact. **Subscription Rates:** $24; $3 Single issue. **URL:** http://www.nebtrucking.com. **Ad Rates:** GLR $18.20; BW $290; 4C $920; PCI $175. **Remarks:** Accepts advertising. **Circ:** ‡1725.

20559 ■ NEBRASKAland
Nebraska Game and Parks Commission
2200 N 33rd St.
Lincoln, NE 68503
Phone: (402)471-0641
Fax: (402)471-5528
Magazine on outdoor recreation and conservation in Nebraska. **Freq:** 10/year. **Print Method:** Offset. **Trim Size:** 8 1/4 x 10 7/8. **Cols./Page:** 3. **Col. Width:** 13.5 picas. **Col. Depth:** 8 3/8 inches. **Key Personnel:** Jeff Kurrus, Editor; Tim Reigert, Art Director. **ISSN:** 0028--1964 (print). **Subscription Rates:** $18 Individuals; $33 Two years; $44 Individuals three years. **Formerly**: Nebraskaland Magazine. **Ad Rates:** $400-1000. GLR $. **Remarks:** Accepts classified advertising. **Circ:** Paid ‡35000, Non-paid ‡4100.

20560 ■ Nine: A Journal of Baseball History and Culture
University of Nebraska Press
1111 Lincoln Mall
Lincoln, NE 68588-0630
Phone: (402)472-3581
Fax: (402)472-6214
Free: 800-848-6224
Publisher's E-mail: pressmail@unl.edu
Publication covering sports, fitness and history. **Freq:** Semiannual. **Key Personnel:** Trey Strecker, Editor. **ISSN:** 1188--9330 (print). **Subscription Rates:** $55 Individuals; $67 Other countries; $105 Institutions; $117 Institutions, other countries. **URL:** http://nine.iweb.bsu.edu; http://www.nebraskapress.unl.edu/product/NINE,673173.aspx. **Ad Rates:** BW $150, full page; BW $100, half page; BW $225, back cover. **Remarks:** Accepts advertising. **Circ:** (Not Reported).

20561 ■ Nineteenth Century French Studies
University of Nebraska Press
1111 Lincoln Mall
Lincoln, NE 68588-0630
Phone: (402)472-3581
Fax: (402)472-6214
Free: 800-848-6224
Publisher's E-mail: pressmail@unl.edu
Scholarly journal covering 19th-century French literature and related fields. **Freq:** Semiannual. **Print Method:** Offset. **Trim Size:** 6 x 9. **Key Personnel:** Marshall C. Olds, Editor. **ISSN:** 0146--7891 (print); **EISSN:** 1536--0172 (electronic). **Subscription Rates:** $128 Institutions online only; $179.20 Institutions print & online. **URL:** http://ncfs.unl.edu; http://muse.jhu.edu/journals/nineteenth_century_french_studies. **Ad Rates:** BW $265. **Remarks:** Accepts advertising. **Circ:** Combined 800.

20562 ■ NSEA Voice
Nebraska State Education Association
605 S 14th St., Ste. 200
Lincoln, NE 68508
Phone: (402)475-7611
Fax: (402)475-2630
Free: 800-742-0047
Education newspaper (tabloid). **Freq:** Monthly. **Key Personnel:** Nancy Fulton, President; Julie Wolf, Administrative Assistant; Craig R. Christiansen, Executive Director; Karen Kilgarin, Director, Public Affairs; Al Koontz, Assistant Director. **ISSN:** 1085--0783 (print). **USPS:** 000-369. **Subscription Rates:** Free online. **URL:** http://www.nsea.org/voice. **Formerly**: ED News. **Remarks:** Accepts advertising. **Circ:** (Not Reported).

20563 ■ Prairie Schooner
University of Nebraska
3835 Holdrege St.
Lincoln, NE 68583
Phone: (402)472-2111
Fax: (402)472-1237
Publication E-mail: prairieschooner@unl.edu
Magazine of poems, short stories, essays, translations, and book reviews. **Freq:** Quarterly. **Print Method:** Letterpress and offset. **Trim Size:** 6 x 9. **Cols./Page:** 1. **Col. Width:** 58 nonpareils. **Col. Depth:** 105 agate lines. **Key Personnel:** Hilda Raz, Editor-in-Chief; Marianne Kunkel, Manager, Production. **ISSN:** 0032--6682 (print). **Subscription Rates:** $28 Individuals; $45 Two years; $65 Individuals 3 years. **URL:** http://prairieschooner.unl.edu. **Ad Rates:** BW $200. **Remarks:** Accepts advertising. **Circ:** Paid ‡2800, Non-paid ‡300.

20564 ■ Processor: The Marketplace for Computer Equipment
Sandhills Publishing Co.
120 W Harvest Dr.
Lincoln, NE 68521
Phone: (402)479-2181
Fax: (402)479-2195
Free: 800-331-1978
Publication E-mail: editor@processor.com
Computer sales magazine. **Freq:** Biweekly. **Print Method:** Offset. **Trim Size:** 10 7/16 x 15 7/8. **Cols./Page:** 6. **Col. Width:** 1 5/8 inches. **Col. Depth:** 16 inches. **Subscription Rates:** Free for qualified subscribers. **URL:** http://www.processor.com. **Mailing address:** PO Box 82545, Lincoln, NE 68501-5310. **Remarks:** Accepts advertising. **Circ:** (Not Reported).

20565 ■ Qui Parle: Critical Humanities and Social Sciences
University of Nebraska Press
1111 Lincoln Mall
Lincoln, NE 68588-0630
Phone: (402)472-3581
Fax: (402)472-6214
Free: 800-848-6224
Publisher's E-mail: pressmail@unl.edu
Journal covering theoretical and critical work in humanities and social sciences. **Freq:** Semiannual. **Key Personnel:** Marta Figlerowicz, Editor; Simon Porzak, Editor. **ISSN:** 1041--8385 (print). **Subscription Rates:** $42 Individuals; $87 Institutions; $54 Other countries; $99 Institutions, other countries. **URL:** http://www.nebraskapress.unl.edu/product/Qui-Parle,674052.aspx. **Ad Rates:** BW $150. **Remarks:** Accepts advertising. **Circ:** (Not Reported).

Circulation: ⋆ = AAM; △ or • = BPA; ♦ = CAC; ❑ = VAC; ⊕ = PO Statement; ‡ = Publisher's Report; Boldface figures = sworn; Light figures = estimated.

20566 ■ Rural Electric Nebraskan
Nebraska Rural Electric Association
PO Box 82048
Lincoln, NE 68501-2048
Phone: (402)475-4988
Fax: (402)475-0835
Rural farm and ranch magazine. **Freq:** Monthly. **Print Method:** Offset. **Trim Size:** 8 1/2 x 11. **Cols./Page:** 3. **Col. Width:** 28 nonpareils. **Col. Depth:** 133 agate lines. **Key Personnel:** Wayne Price, Editor. **Subscription Rates:** $10 Individuals; $15 Two years; $20 Individuals 3 years. **URL:** http://www.nrea.org. **Ad Rates:** BW $1,114; 4C $1,614; PCI $59. **Remarks:** Accepts advertising. **Circ:** (Not Reported).

20567 ■ Southern Nebraska Register
Southern Nebraska Register
PO Box 80328
Lincoln, NE 68501
Phone: (402)488-0090
Fax: (402)488-3569
Publication E-mail: snr@inebraska.com
Official newspaper of the Catholic Diocese of Lincoln, NE. **Freq:** Weekly. **Print Method:** Tabloid. **Trim Size:** 17 x 13 1/2. **Col. Width:** 12.5 picas. **Col. Depth:** 17 inches. **Key Personnel:** Fr. Kenneth Borowiak, Editor; Favian Bruskewitz, President; Kimberly Breitfield, Contact. **Subscription Rates:** $20 Out of area; $13 Individuals. **Ad Rates:** BW $900; PCI $12. **Remarks:** Accepts advertising. **Circ:** ‡21500.

20568 ■ Storyworlds: A Journal of Narrative Studies
University of Nebraska Press
1111 Lincoln Mall
Lincoln, NE 68588-0630
Phone: (402)472-3581
Fax: (402)472-6214
Free: 800-848-6224
Publisher's E-mail: pressmail@unl.edu
Journal publishing state-of-the-art research in the field of interdisciplinary narrative theory. **Freq:** Annual. **Key Personnel:** David Herman, Editor. **ISSN:** 1946--2204 (print). **Subscription Rates:** $42 Individuals; $91 Institutions; $54 Other countries; $103 Institutions, other countries; $36 Individuals online. **URL:** http://www.nebraskapress.unl.edu/product/Storyworlds,674134.aspx. **Ad Rates:** BW $150. **Remarks:** Accepts advertising. **Circ:** (Not Reported).

20569 ■ The Student
Christian Record Services for the Blind
4444 S 52nd St.
Lincoln, NE 68516-1302
Phone: (402)488-0981
Fax: (402)488-7582
Publisher's E-mail: info@christianrecord.org
Magazine for blind Bible students produced in Braille & on cassette. **Freq:** Monthly. **Print Method:** Braille and audiocassette. **Trim Size:** 11 x 12. **Key Personnel:** Larry Pitcher, President. **Subscription Rates:** Free to blind and visually impaired people. **URL:** http://www.christianrecord.org. **Mailing address:** PO Box 6097, Lincoln, NE 68506-0097. **Remarks:** Advertising not accepted. **Circ:** (Not Reported).

20570 ■ Studies in American Indian Literatures
University of Nebraska Press
1111 Lincoln Mall
Lincoln, NE 68588-0630
Phone: (402)472-3581
Fax: (402)472-6214
Free: 800-848-6224
Publisher's E-mail: pressmail@unl.edu
Journal presenting literature created by Native Americans. **Freq:** Quarterly. **Key Personnel:** Chadwick Allen, Editor. **ISSN:** 0730--3238 (print). **Subscription Rates:** $50 Individuals 1 year - U.S; $74 Individuals 1 year - foreign; $38 Individuals 1 year - online; $141 Institutions 1 year - U.S; $165 Institutions, other countries 1 year - online; $38 /year for individuals; $95 /year for institutions. **Alt. Formats:** PDF. **URL:** http://www.nebraskapress.unl.edu/product/Studies-in-American-Indian-Literat%20ures,673235.aspx. **Ad Rates:** BW $265. **Remarks:** Accepts advertising. **Circ:** (Not Reported).

20571 ■ Studies in American Naturalism
University of Nebraska Press
1111 Lincoln Mall
Lincoln, NE 68588-0630
Phone: (402)472-3581
Fax: (402)472-6214
Free: 800-848-6224
Publisher's E-mail: pressmail@unl.edu
Journal publishing critical essays, documents, notes, bibliographies and reviews concerning American literary naturalism. **Freq:** 2/yr. **Key Personnel:** Keith Newlin, Editor; Stephen Brennan, Editor. **ISSN:** 1931-2555 (print). **Subscription Rates:** $78 Institutions; $40 Individuals; $27.50 Individuals electronic. **URL:** http://www.uncw.edu/san/. **Remarks:** Accepts advertising. **Circ:** (Not Reported).

20572 ■ Symploke
University of Nebraska Press
1111 Lincoln Mall
Lincoln, NE 68588-0630
Phone: (402)472-3581
Fax: (402)472-6214
Free: 800-848-6224
Publication E-mail: editor@symploke.org
Scholarly journal covering comparative literature and theory. **Freq:** Semiannual. **Trim Size:** 6 x 9. **Key Personnel:** Ronald Bogue, Advisor, Board Member; Edward Casey, Advisor, Board Member; Christian Moraru, Advisor, Board Member; Stanley Corngold, Advisor, Board Member; Jeffrey R. Di Leo, Editor-in-Chief; Charles Altieri, Advisor, Board Member. **ISSN:** 1069-0697 (print). **Subscription Rates:** $83 Institutions and libraries; $40 Individuals; $27 Individuals e-subscribers. **URL:** http://www.symploke.org; http://www.nebraskapress.unl.edu/product/symploke,673237.aspx. **Ad Rates:** BW $265, full page; BW $182.50, half page. **Remarks:** Advertising accepted; rates available upon request. **Circ:** (Not Reported).

20573 ■ Truck Paper
Sandhills Publishing Co.
120 W Harvest Dr.
Lincoln, NE 68501-5010
Phone: (402)479-2140
Fax: (402)479-2134
Publisher's E-mail: feedback@sandhills.com
Tabloid featuring trucks, trailers, and parts for sale. **Freq:** Weekly. **Print Method:** Offset. **Trim Size:** 10 1/2 x 15 7/8. **Cols./Page:** 6. **Col. Width:** 20 nonpareils. **Col. Depth:** 224 agate lines. **ISSN:** 1040--6484 (print). **USPS:** 002-755. **Subscription Rates:** $59 Individuals 3rd class mail weekly; $38 Individuals 3rd class mail bi-weekly; $24 Individuals 3rd class mail monthly. **URL:** http://www.truckpaper.com. **Mailing address:** PO Box 85010, Lincoln, NE 68501-5010. **Ad Rates:** 4C $950. **Circ:** Controlled ‡445186, Paid ‡28577.

20574 ■ Uncoverings
American Quilt Study Group
1610 L St.
Lincoln, NE 68508-2509
Phone: (402)477-1181
Fax: (402)477-1181
Publisher's E-mail: aqsg2@americanquiltstudygroup.org
Scholarly journal covering quilts, textiles and quilt makers. **Freq:** Annual. **Key Personnel:** Laurel Horton, Editor; Judy Brott Buss, PhD, Executive Director. **ISSN:** 0227-0628 (print). **Subscription Rates:** $10 Single issue; Included in membership; $20 Nonmembers. **URL:** http://www.americanquiltstudygroup.org/publications.asp. **Ad Rates:** BW $250. **Remarks:** Accepts advertising. **Circ:** Paid 1,500.

20575 ■ U.S. Roller Skating
U.S.A. Roller Sports
4730 South St.
Lincoln, NE 68506
Phone: (402)483-7551
Fax: (402)483-1465
Freq: Monthly Bimonthly. **Key Personnel:** Ricci Porter, Editor. **ISSN:** 1044--0801 (print). **Subscription Rates:** $12 Individuals 1 year - 4 issues; $20 Other countries. **URL:** http://www.teamusa.org/USA-Roller-Sports/Resources/The-Magazine. **Ad Rates:** BW $960, full page; 4C $1500, full page; 4C $900, half page; BW $620, half page. **Remarks:** Accepts advertising. **Circ:** Paid 15000, 7000.

20576 ■ The Voice
Nebraska Grocery Industry Association
5935 S 56th St., Ste. B
Lincoln, NE 68516
Phone: (402)423-5533
Fax: (402)423-8686
Magazine for food industry. **Founded:** 1903. **Freq:** Bimonthly. **Print Method:** Offset. **Trim Size:** 7 7/8 x 10 7/8. **Cols./Page:** 2. **Col. Width:** 38 nonpareils. **Col. Depth:** 140 agate lines. **Subscription Rates:** $75 Members. **URL:** http://www.nebgrocery.com. **Formerly:** The Nebraska Retailer. **Ad Rates:** BW $405; 4C $325. **Remarks:** Accepts advertising. **Circ:** ‡1200.

20577 ■ Women in German Yearbook
University of Nebraska Press
1111 Lincoln Mall
Lincoln, NE 68588-0630
Phone: (402)472-3581
Fax: (402)472-6214
Free: 800-848-6224
Publisher's E-mail: pressmail@unl.edu
Peer-reviewed journal featuring feminist approaches to all aspects of German literature, culture and language, including pedagogy. **Freq:** Annual. **Key Personnel:** Margarete Lamb-Faffelberger, Editor; Elizabeth Ametsbichler, Editor. **ISSN:** 1058--7446 (print). **Subscription Rates:** $43 Individuals; $86 Institutions; $49 Other countries; $92 Institutions, other countries; $40 Individuals online. **URL:** http://www.nebraskapress.unl.edu/product/Women-in-German-Yearbook,673912.aspx. **Ad Rates:** BW $200. **Remarks:** Accepts advertising. **Circ:** (Not Reported).

20578 ■ Women and Music
University of Nebraska Press
1111 Lincoln Mall
Lincoln, NE 68588-0630
Phone: (402)472-3581
Fax: (402)472-6214
Free: 800-848-6224
Publisher's E-mail: pressmail@unl.edu
Publication covering music and women. **Freq:** Annual. **Key Personnel:** Suzanne G. Cusick, Board Member. **ISSN:** 1090--7505 (print). **Subscription Rates:** $43 Individuals; $49 Other countries; $86 Institutions; $92 Institutions, other countries; $40 Individuals online only. **URL:** http://www.nebraskapress.unl.edu/product/Women-and-Music,673171.aspx. **Ad Rates:** BW $150, full page; BW $100, half page. **Remarks:** Accepts advertising. **Circ:** (Not Reported).

20579 ■ Consolidated Cable Inc.
PO Box 6147
Lincoln, NE 68506-0147
Phone: (402)489-2728
Fax: (402)489-9034
Free: 800-742-7464
Email: support@nebnet.net
Founded: Sept. 06, 2006. **Cities Served:** 15 channels. **URL:** http://www.nebnet.net.

20580 ■ KAMI-AM - 1580
233 S 13th St., Ste. 1520
Lincoln, NE 68508
Phone: (402)465-8850
Fax: (402)465-8852
Format: Talk. **Owner:** Bott Radio Network, 10550 Barkley, Overland Park, KS 66212, Ph: (913)642-7770, Fax: (913)642-1319, Free: 800-345-2621. **Founded:** 1965. **Operating Hours:** 8 a.m.-5 p.m. **ADI:** Lincoln-Hastings-Kearney, NE. **Key Personnel:** Richard Rich Bott, II, CEO, President, rbott@bottradionetwork.com; Richard Dick Bott, Sr., Chairman, Founder, dbott@bottradionetwork.com. **Wattage:** 1,000. **Ad Rates:** Noncommercial. Combined advertising rates available with KAMI-FM. **URL:** http://www.bottradionetwork.com.

20581 ■ KBBK-FM - 107.3
4343 O St.
Lincoln, NE 68510
Phone: (402)475-4567
Format: Adult Contemporary. **Networks:** Westwood One Radio. **Owner:** Nebraska Broadcasting, 11414 W Center Rd., Omaha, NE 68144. **Founded:** 1968. **Operating Hours:** Continuous. **ADI:** Lincoln-Hastings-Kearney, NE. **Key Personnel:** Steve Albertsen, Account Mgr., salbertsen@broadcasthouse.com; Ami Graham, Sales Mgr., amig@broadcasthouse.com. **Wattage:** 100,000 ERP. **Ad Rates:** Noncommercial. **URL:** http://www.b1073.com.

20582 ■ KCNE-FM - 91.9
1800 N 33rd St.
Lincoln, NE 68503
Phone: (402)472-7722
Free: 888-638-7346
Email: radio@netnebraska.org
Format: Public Radio. **Networks:** National Public Radio (NPR). **Owner:** Nebraska Educational Telecommunications Commission, at above address. **Founded:** 1989. **Operating Hours:** 6:00 a.m.-1:00 a.m. **Key Personnel:** Randy Hansen, Asst. Gen. Mgr. of Sales/Mktg., rhansen@netnebraska.org. **Wattage:** 8,400. **Ad Rates:** Noncommercial. **URL:** http://www.netnebraska.org/radio/about.htm.

20583 ■ KFGE-FM - 98.1
4343 O St.
Lincoln, NE 68510
Phone: (402)474-3764
Format: Hot Country. **Owner:** TRIAD, 6525 Busch Blvd., Columbus, OH 43229, Ph: (614)846-8761, Fax: (614)846-8763, Free: 800-288-7423. **Founded:** 1992. **Operating Hours:** Continuous. **ADI:** Lincoln-Hastings-Kearney, NE. **Wattage:** 100,000. **URL:** http://www.froggy981.com.

20584 ■ KFOR-AM - 1240
3800 Cornhusker Hwy.
Lincoln, NE 68504
Phone: (402)466-1234
Format: News; Talk; Adult Contemporary. **Networks:** ABC. **Owner:** Three Eagles Communications, 3800 Cornhusker Hwy., Lincoln, NE 68504, Ph: (402)466-1234, Fax: (402)467-4095. **Founded:** Mar. 1924. **Operating Hours:** Continuous. **ADI:** Lincoln-Hastings-Kearney, NE. **Key Personnel:** Jeffrey Gold, Chancellor. **Local Programs:** *The Judy a la carte Show*; *Lincoln Live*, Monday Tuesday Wednesday Thursday Friday 12:30 p.m. - 1:00 p.m. **Wattage:** 1,000. **Ad Rates:** $24-56 for 30 seconds; $30-70 for 60 seconds. Combined advertising rates available with KFRX, KRKR, KLMS. **URL:** http://www.kfor1240.com.

20585 ■ KFRX-FM - 106.3
3800 Cornhusker Hwy.
Lincoln, NE 68504
Phone: (402)466-1234
Fax: (402)467-4095
Email: lindsey@kfrxfm.com
Format: Top 40. **Owner:** Three Eagles Communications, 3800 Cornhusker Hwy., Lincoln, NE 68504, Ph: (402)466-1234, Fax: (402)467-4095. **Founded:** 1965. **Operating Hours:** Continuous. **Key Personnel:** Matt Mckay, Dir. of Programs, matt@kfrxfm.com. **Wattage:** 100,000 ERP. **Ad Rates:** $14-28 for 30 seconds; $17-35 for 60 seconds. **URL:** http://www.kfrxfm.com.

KHNE-FM - See Hastings

KIAQ-FM - See Fort Dodge, IA

20586 ■ KIBZ-FM - 104.1
3800 Cornhusker Hwy.
Lincoln, NE 68504
Phone: (402)466-1234
Format: Album-Oriented Rock (AOR). **Owner:** Three Eagles Communication, 3800 Cornhusker Hwy., Lincoln, NE 68504, Ph: (402)466-1234, Fax: (402)467-4095. **ADI:** Lincoln-Hastings-Kearney, NE. **Key Personnel:** Lester St. James, Operations Mgr. **Wattage:** 50,000. **Ad Rates:** Advertising accepted; rates available upon request. **URL:** http://www.kibz.com.

KKEZ-FM - See Fort Dodge, IA

20587 ■ KLCV-FM - 88.5
233 S 13th St., Ste. 1520
Lincoln, NE 68508
Phone: (402)465-8850
Fax: (402)465-8852
Email: comments@bottradionetwork.com
Format: Religious; News; Talk. **Networks:** Business Radio; Sun Radio. **Owner:** Bott Communications, Inc., 10550 Barkley, Overland Park, KS 66212, Ph: (913)642-7770, Fax: (913)642-1319. **Founded:** July 15, 1996. **Operating Hours:** Continuous. **ADI:** Lincoln-Hastings-Kearney, NE. **Key Personnel:** Tom Millett, Mgr., tmillett@bottradionetwork.com. **Wattage:** 100,000. **Ad Rates:** Noncommercial. **URL:** http://www.bottradionetwork.com.

20588 ■ KLDZ-FM - 95.1
1230 O St., Ste. 311
Lincoln, NE 68508
Phone: (402)476-3222
Fax: (402)476-1300
Owner: Radio One Broadcasting, Inc., at above address. **Founded:** 1975. **Operating Hours:** Continuous. **ADI:** Lincoln-Hastings-Kearney, NE. **Key Personnel:** Wayne Walker, Gen. Mgr., President; Dallas Michaels, Operations Mgr. **Wattage:** 50,000 ERP. **Ad Rates:** $12-34 for 30 seconds; $15-38 for 60 seconds.

20589 ■ KLIN-AM - 1400
4343 O St.
Lincoln, NE 68510
Phone: (402)475-4567
Fax: (402)479-1411
Email: news@klin.com
Format: News; Talk. **Networks:** CBS. **Owner:** Nebraska Broadcasting, 11414 W Center Rd., Omaha, NE 68144. **Founded:** 1947. **Operating Hours:** Continuous. **ADI:** Lincoln-Hastings-Kearney, NE. **Wattage:** 1,000 Day; 1,000 night. **Ad Rates:** Noncommercial. **URL:** http://www.klin.com.

20590 ■ KLKN-TV - 8
3240 S Tenth St.
Lincoln, NE 68502
Phone: (402)434-8000
Format: Commercial TV. **Networks:** ABC. **Owner:** Citadel Broadcasting Corp., 7201 W Lake Mead Blvd., Ste. 400, Las Vegas, NV 89128-8366, Ph: (702)804-5200, Fax: (702)804-8250. **Founded:** 1995. **Operating Hours:** 5 a.m.-1 a.m. **ADI:** Lincoln-Hastings-Kearney, NE. **Key Personnel:** Jeff Swanson, Program Mgr., jswanson@klkntv.com; Roger Moody, Gen. Mgr., rmoody@klkntv.com; Kay Wunderlich, Sales Mgr., kwunderlich@klkntv.com. **Wattage:** 353,000 ERP. **Ad Rates:** Advertising accepted; rates available upon request. **URL:** http://www.klkntv.com.

20591 ■ KLMS-AM - 1480
3800 Cornhusker Hwy.
Lincoln, NE 68504
Phone: (402)466-1234
Fax: (402)467-4095
Format: Sports. **Owner:** Three Eagles Broadcasting. **Founded:** 1949. **Ad Rates:** Noncommercial. **URL:** http://www.threeeagles.com.

20592 ■ KLMY-FM - 106.3
3800 Cornhusker Hwy.
Lincoln, NE 68504
Phone: (402)466-1234
Fax: (402)486-1063
Format: Contemporary Hit Radio (CHR). **Operating Hours:** Continuous. **ADI:** Lincoln-Hastings-Kearney, NE. **Wattage:** 100,000. **Ad Rates:** Noncommercial; Advertising accepted; rates available upon request. **URL:** http://www.kfrxfm.com/contact.

KLNE-FM - See Lexington

20593 ■ KMNE-FM - 90.3
1800 N 33rd St.
Lincoln, NE 68503
Free: 888-638-7346
Email: radio@netnebraska.org
Format: Public Radio. **Networks:** National Public Radio (NPR). **Owner:** Nebraska Educational Telecommunications Commission, at above address. **Founded:** 1989. **Operating Hours:** 6:00 a.m.-1:00 a.m. **Wattage:** 94,600. **Ad Rates:** Noncommercial. **URL:** http://netnebraska.org/radio/about.htm#.

20594 ■ KOLN-TV - 10
840 N 40th St.
Lincoln, NE 68503
Phone: (402)467-4321
Free: 800-475-1011
Email: info@kolnkgin.com
Format: Commercial TV. **Networks:** CBS. **Owner:** Gray Television Inc., 4370 Peachtree Rd. NE, No. 400, Atlanta, GA 30319-3054, Ph: (404)266-8333. **Founded:** 1953. **Operating Hours:** Continuous. **ADI:** Lincoln-Hastings-Kearney, NE. **Key Personnel:** Troy Frankforter, Operations Mgr. **URL:** http://www.1011now.com.

20595 ■ KPNE-FM - 91.7
1800 N 33rd St.
Lincoln, NE 68503
Phone: (402)472-7722
Free: 888-638-7346
Email: news@netnebraska.org
Format: Public Radio. **Networks:** National Public Radio (NPR). **Owner:** Nebraska Educational Telecommunications Commission, at above address. **Founded:** July 02, 1991. **Operating Hours:** 6:00 a.m.-1:00 a.m. **ADI:** North Platte, NE. **Wattage:** 16,000 H;78,000 V. **Ad Rates:** Noncommercial. **URL:** http://www.netnebraska.org/radio.

KPNE-TV - See North Platte

20596 ■ KPNY-FM - 102.1
PO Box 30345
Lincoln, NE 68503
Free: 888-627-1020
Email: info@kpnyfm.com
Format: Adult Contemporary; Sports. **Networks:** Satellite Music Network. **Owner:** Mission Nebraska, Inc., at above address. **Founded:** 1978. **Formerly:** KFAH-FM. **Operating Hours:** Continuous. **Wattage:** 100,000. **Ad Rates:** $7.30-11.90 for 30 seconds; $9.15-15.35 for 60 seconds. **URL:** http://www.mybridgeradio.net.

20597 ■ KQIQ-FM - 89.3
8800 O St.
Lincoln, NE 68520
Phone: (301)230-3510
Format: Educational. **Owner:** Southeast Community College, at above address. **Key Personnel:** Robin Moore, Dir. of Admin., rmoore@southeast.edu. **URL:** http://www.southeast.edu.

20598 ■ KRKR-FM
PO Box 30345
Lincoln, NE 68503
Phone: (402)466-1234
Fax: (402)467-4095
Format: Classic Rock. **Wattage:** 50,000 ERP. **Ad Rates:** Advertising accepted; rates available upon request.

20599 ■ KRNE-FM - 91.5
1800 N 33rd St.
Lincoln, NE 68503
Phone: (402)472-7722
Free: 888-638-7346
Email: radio@netnebraska.org
Format: Public Radio. **Networks:** National Public Radio (NPR). **Owner:** Nebraska Educational Telecommunications Commission, at above address. **Founded:** 1989. **Operating Hours:** 6:00 a.m.-1:00 a.m. **Key Personnel:** Randy Hansen, Asst. Gen. Mgr. of Sales/Mktg., rhansen@netnebraska.org. **Wattage:** 92,000. **Ad Rates:** Noncommercial. **URL:** http://www.netnebraska.org/radio/about.htm.

20600 ■ KRNU-FM - 90.3
147 Andersen Hall
Lincoln, NE 68588-0466
Format: Alternative/New Music/Progressive. **Networks:** ABC. **Owner:** University of Nebraska Board of Regents, 3835 Holdrege St., Lincoln, NE 68583, Ph: (402)472-3906. **Founded:** 1970. **Operating Hours:** 8 a.m.-1 a.m. Mon.-Sat., 10 a.m.-midnight Sun. **Key Personnel:** Rick Alloway, Gen. Mgr. **Wattage:** 100. **Ad Rates:** Noncommercial. **Mailing address:** PO Box 880466, Lincoln, NE 68588-0466. **URL:** http://krnu.unl.edu.

20601 ■ KROA-FM - 95.7
PO Box 30345
Lincoln, NE 68503
Free: 888-627-1020
Email: email@mybridgeradio.net
Format: Religious. **Networks:** AP; Moody Broadcasting. **Owner:** Mission Nebraska, Inc., at above address. **Operating Hours:** Continuous; 30% network, 70% local. **Key Personnel:** Gordon Wheeler, Contact; Taryn Julane, Contact. **Wattage:** 100,000. **Ad Rates:** Noncommercial. **URL:** http://www.mybridgeradio.net.

20602 ■ KSLI-FM - 104.1
3800 Cornhusker Hwy.
Lincoln, NE 68504
Phone: (503)517-6200
Format: Top 40. **Owner:** Triathlon Broadcasting, Inc., at above address. **Founded:** 1976. **Operating Hours:** Continuous Monday - Friday, 5:00 a.m. - 12:00 a.m. **ADI:** Lincoln-Hastings-Kearney, NE. **Key Personnel:** Julie Gade, Gen. Mgr.; Julie Broman, Dir. of Sales; Julie

Circulation: ★ = AAM; △ or • = BPA; ♦ = CAC; ❑ = VAC; ⊕ = PO Statement; ‡ = Publisher's Report; Boldface figures = sworn; Light figures = estimated.

Wolfe, Bus. Mgr., Contact; Julie Wolfe, Contact. **Wattage:** 31,000 ERP. **Ad Rates:** Advertising accepted; rates available upon request. **URL:** http://www.kibz.com.

20603 ■ KTGL-FM - 92.9
3800 Cornhusker Hwy.
Lincoln, NE 68504
Phone: (402)466-1234
Fax: (402)467-4095
Format: Classic Rock. **Owner:** Three Eagles Communications, 3800 Cornhusker Hwy., Lincoln, NE 68504, Ph: (402)466-1234, Fax: (402)467-4095. **Founded:** 1987. **Formerly:** KMAZ-FM. **Operating Hours:** Continuous. **Wattage:** 100,000. **Ad Rates:** $32-36 for 30 seconds; $35-43 for 60 seconds. **URL:** http://www.ktgl.com.

KTLB-FM - See Fort Dodge, IA

KTNE-FM - See Alliance

20604 ■ KTTT-AM - 1510
3800 Cornhusker Hwy.
Lincoln, NE 68504
Phone: (402)466-1234
Format: Talk; Polka. **Networks:** ABC. **Owner:** Three Eagles Communications, 3800 Cornhusker Hwy., Lincoln, NE 68504, Ph: (402)466-1234, Fax: (402)467-4095. **Founded:** 1962. **Operating Hours:** Sunrise-sunset. **Wattage:** 500. **Ad Rates:** Noncommercial. **URL:** http://www.mycentralnebraska.com.

20605 ■ K29GL - 29
PO Box A
Santa Ana, CA 92711
Phone: (714)832-2950
Free: 888-731-1000
Owner: Trinity Broadcasting Network Inc., PO Box A, Santa Ana, CA 92711, Ph: (714)832-2950, Free: 888-731-1000. **URL:** http://www.tbn.org.

20606 ■ KUCV-FM - 91.1
1800 N 33rd St.
Lincoln, NE 68503
Phone: (402)472-6141
Free: 888-638-7346
Email: radio@netnebraska.org
Format: Public Radio. **Networks:** National Public Radio (NPR); Public Radio International (PRI). **Owner:** Nebraska Educational Telecommunications Commission, at above address. **Founded:** 1968. **Operating Hours:** 5 a.m.-1 a.m. **ADI:** Lincoln-Hastings-Kearney, NE. **Wattage:** 19,500 H;100,000 V. **Ad Rates:** Noncommercial. Combined advertising rates available with KTNE, KMNE, KCNE, KHNE, KLNE, KRNE, KXNE, KPNE. **URL:** http://netnebraska.org.

20607 ■ KUON-TV - 12
1800 N 33rd St.
Lincoln, NE 68503
Free: 800-868-1868
Email: customerservice@netnebraska.org
Format: Public TV. **Networks:** Public Broadcasting Service (PBS). **Owner:** Nebraska Educational Telecommunications, at above address. **Founded:** 1954. **Operating Hours:** 6:30 a.m.-11:00 p.m.; 90% network, 10% local. **ADI:** Lincoln-Hastings-Kearney, NE. **Key Personnel:** Rod Bates, Gen. Mgr. **Wattage:** 316,000. **Ad Rates:** Noncommercial. **URL:** http://www.netnebraska.org.

KVFD-AM - See Fort Dodge, IA

KWMT-AM - See Fort Dodge, IA

20608 ■ KXNE-FM - 89.3
1800 N 33rd St.
Lincoln, NE 68503
Phone: (402)472-7722
Free: 888-638-7346
Email: news@netnebraska.org
Format: Public Radio; Classical; News; Jazz. **Networks:** National Public Radio (NPR); Public Radio International (PRI). **Owner:** Nebraska Educational Telecommunications, at above address. **Founded:** 1990. **Operating Hours:** Continuous. **ADI:** Lincoln-Hastings-Kearney, NE. **Key Personnel:** Dennis Kellogg, News Dir., dkellogg@netnebraska.org; Nancy Finken, Mgr., nfinken@netnebraska.org. **Wattage:** 4,230. **Ad Rates:** Noncommercial. **URL:** http://www.netnebraska.org.

KXNE-TV - See Norfolk

KYNE-TV - See Omaha

20609 ■ KZEN-FM - 100.3
3800 Cornhusker Hwy.
Lincoln, NE 68504
Phone: (402)466-1234
Format: Country; News. **Networks:** ABC. **Owner:** Three Eagles Communications, 3800 Cornhusker Hwy., Lincoln, NE 68504, Ph: (402)466-1234, Fax: (402)467-4095. **Operating Hours:** Continuous. **Wattage:** 100,000. **Ad Rates:** $90 for 30 seconds; $110 for 60 seconds. **URL:** http://www.threeeagles.com.

20610 ■ KZKX-FM - 96.9
3800 Cornhusker Hwy.
Lincoln, NE 68504
Phone: (402)466-1234
Format: Country. **Networks:** AP. **Owner:** Three Eagles Communication, 3800 Cornhusker Hwy., Lincoln, NE 68504, Ph: (402)466-1234, Fax: (402)467-4095. **Operating Hours:** Continuous; 5% network, 95% local. **Wattage:** 100,000. **Ad Rates:** $20-50 per unit. **URL:** http://www.threeeagles.com.

20611 ■ KZUM-FM - 89.3
3534 S 48th St., Ste. 6
Lincoln, NE 68506
Phone: (402)474-5086
Email: development@kzum.org
Format: Eclectic. **Networks:** Corporation for Public Broadcasting. **Owner:** Sunrise Communications Inc., at above address. **Founded:** 1978. **Operating Hours:** Continuous. **ADI:** Lincoln-Hastings-Kearney, NE. **Wattage:** 1,500 ERP. **Ad Rates:** Noncommercial. Underwriting available. **URL:** http://www.kzum.org.

MCCOOK

Red Willow Co. Red Willow Co. (SW). 65 m S of North Platte. Hose, garden & appliances, capacitors, foot appliance, stock product, bottling industry. Stock, grain farms. Corn, wheat, livestock.

20612 ■ KBRL-AM - 1300
1811 W O St.
McCook, NE 69001
Phone: (308)345-5400
Fax: (308)345-4720
Format: Oldies. **Networks:** ABC. **Owner:** McCook Radio Group L.L.C., at above address. **Founded:** Sept. 20, 2006. **Operating Hours:** Continuous. **Wattage:** 5,000. **Ad Rates:** Noncommercial. Combined advertising rates available with KICX-FM.

20613 ■ KICX-FM - 96.1
1811 W O St.
McCook, NE 69001
Phone: (308)345-5400
Fax: (308)345-4720
Format: Adult Contemporary. **Networks:** ABC; Satellite Music Network. **Owner:** McCook Radio Group L.L.C., at above address. **Founded:** 1979. **Operating Hours:** Continuous. **Wattage:** 55,000. **Ad Rates:** Noncommercial. Combined advertising rates available with KBRL-AM.

20614 ■ KIOD-FM - 105.3
106 W Eighth St.
McCook, NE 69001-0939
Phone: (308)345-1981
Format: Country. **Founded:** 1981. **Wattage:** 100,000 ERP. **Ad Rates:** Advertising accepted; rates available upon request. **Mailing address:** PO Box 939, McCook, NE 69001-0939. **URL:** http://www.coyote105.com.

20615 ■ KNGN-AM - 1360
38005 Rd. 717
McCook, NE 69001-7217
Phone: (308)345-2006
Fax: (308)345-2052
Free: 800-710-1360
Email: adam@kngn.org
Format: Contemporary Christian. **Networks:** SkyLight Satellite; Ambassador Inspirational Radio. **Owner:** Kansas Nebraska Good News Broadcasting Corp., at above address. **Founded:** Apr. 1990. **Operating Hours:** 6 a.m. to 9.10 p.m. **Key Personnel:** Adam Spanier, Mgr. **Wattage:** 1,000. **Ad Rates:** Noncommercial. **URL:** http://www.kngn.org.

20616 ■ KRKU-FM
1811 W O St.
McCook, NE 69001
Phone: (308)345-5400
Fax: (308)345-4720
Owner: McCook Radio Group L.L.C., at above address. **Founded:** 2000. **Ad Rates:** $8-11 for 30 seconds; $13-16 for 60 seconds. **Mailing address:** PO Box 333, McCook, NE 69001.

20617 ■ KSWN-FM - 93.9
PO Box 939
McCook, NE 69001
Phone: (308)345-1981
Fax: (308)345-7202
Format: Talk; News. **Networks:** Fox; ESPN Radio. **Founded:** 1998. **Operating Hours:** Continuous. **ADI:** Lincoln-Hastings-Kearney, NE. **Wattage:** 50,000. **Ad Rates:** Noncommercial.

MILFORD

Seward Co. Seward Co. (S.E.). On Big Blue River, 15 m SW of Lincoln. Dairy, poultry, grain farms. Corn, wheat, alfalfa, livestock.

20618 ■ The Nebraska Sheriff
Nebraska Sheriffs' Association
521 1st St.
Milford, NE 68405
Phone: (402)761-2216
Magazine featuring law enforcement stories from 93 counties of Nebraska. **Freq:** Semiannual. **Alt. Formats:** PDF. **URL:** http://www.nesheriffsassoc.org/magzines/magazines.php. **Mailing address:** PO Box 10, Lincoln, NE 68501. **Remarks:** Accepts advertising. **Circ:** (Not Reported).

NEBRASKA CITY

Otoe Co. Otoe Co. (SE). On Missouri River, 45 m S of Omaha. State school for visually handicapped. Historic. Manufactures garments, plastic pipes, gas meters, fence posts, concrete pipes. Food processing plants. Dairy, stock, fruit, grain farms.

20619 ■ Nebraska City News-Press
GateHouse Media Inc.
823 Central Ave.
Nebraska City, NE 68410
Publication E-mail: publisher@midnews.com
Newspaper. **Founded:** 1854. **Freq:** Daily (eve.) Monday - Friday. **Print Method:** Offset. **Trim Size:** 13 x 22. **Cols./Page:** 6. **Col. Width:** 11.5 picas. **Col. Depth:** 301 agate lines. **Key Personnel:** Tammy Pearson, Editor, phone: (402)873-3334; Kathy Kaufman, Manager, Advertising. **USPS:** 375-960. **Subscription Rates:** $86 Individuals. **URL:** http://www.ncnewspress.com/. **Mailing address:** PO Box 757, Nebraska City, NE 68410. **Ad Rates:** BW $995.40; 4C $155; SAU $6.95; PCI $7.90. **Remarks:** Accepts advertising. **Circ:** Mon.-Fri. ‡2100.

20620 ■ Penny Press 1
Nebraska City News Press Inc.
823 Central Ave.
Nebraska City, NE 68410
Phone: (402)873-3334
Shopper (tabloid). **Founded:** 1975. **Freq:** Weekly (Mon.). **Print Method:** Offset. **Trim Size:** 11 1/2 x 17. **Cols./Page:** 6. **Col. Width:** 11.5 picas. **Col. Depth:** 15 1/2 inches. **Subscription Rates:** Free. **URL:** http://www.ncnewspress.com. **Mailing address:** PO Box 757, Nebraska City, NE 68410. **Ad Rates:** BW $800; 4C $955; PCI $12.55. **Remarks:** Accepts advertising. **Circ:** Free ‡20,850.

20621 ■ KNCY-AM - 1600
814 Central Ave.
Nebraska City, NE 68410
Phone: (402)873-3348
Fax: (402)873-7882
Free: 866-873-3584
Format: Country. **Key Personnel:** Mike Flood, Owner, mike@us92.com; Dave Brock, Gen. Mgr. **Ad Rates:** Advertising accepted; rates available upon request. **URL:** http://www.bigappleradio.am.

20622 ■ KNCY-FM - 103.1
814 Central Ave.
Nebraska City, NE 68410

Format: Full Service. **Simulcasts:** 1600 AM. **Wattage:** 500. **Ad Rates:** Advertising accepted; rates available upon request.

NELIGH

Antelope Co. Antelope Co. (NEC). 35 m NW of Norfolk. Mobile homes; farm machinery, plastic flag manufactured. Agriculture. Corn, rye, oats.

20623 ■ Neligh News and Leader
News Publishing Co.
PO Box 46
Neligh, NE 68756
Phone: (402)887-4840
Fax: (402)887-4711
Community newspaper. **Freq:** Weekly (Wed.). **Print Method:** Offset. **Cols./Page:** 7. **Col. Width:** 21 nonpareils. **Col. Depth:** 294 agate lines. **Key Personnel:** Joan Wright, Editor, Publisher. **Subscription Rates:** $40 Individuals Antelope County; $45 Out of area; $50 Out of state; $55 Individuals delivery service in Neligh, print subscription; $40 Individuals e-edition; $13.95 Individuals print & e-edition. **URL:** http://www.nelighnews.com. **Ad Rates:** BW $396.90; SAU $3.10. **Remarks:** Accepts advertising. **Circ:** ‡2564, ‡2564.

NORFOLK

Madison Co. Madison Co. (NE). 75 m SW of Sioux City, Iowa. Manufactures farm machinery, electronic resistors, precast concrete items, electrical products, steel, disposable hypodermic syringes, steel joists and girders, milk and milk products, dehydrated eggs and meat, dried milk products, beef carcasses and processed beef products, livestock and poultry feeds, soft drinks, processed pork products. Livestock, poultry, cattle, hogs farms. Corn, oats, sorghum grains, soybeans, rye, barley.

20624 ■ KEXL-FM - 97.5
309 Braasch Ave.
Norfolk, NE 68702
Phone: (402)371-0780
Fax: (402)371-6303
Free: 800-284-2750
Format: Adult Contemporary; News; Sports. **Networks:** Jones Satellite. **Owner:** WJAG Inc., 309 Braasch Ave., Norfolk, NE 68702, Ph: (402)371-0780. **Founded:** 1971. **Operating Hours**: Continuous. **ADI**: Sioux City, IA. **Key Personnel:** Bradley Hughes, Gen. Mgr., VP, bhughes@wjag.com; Sally Lewis, Account Mgr., slewis@wjag.com; Denise Reikofski, Station Mgr.; Marci Pierce, Owner, President. **Local Programs**: *Voice of the People*; *Auction Block*, Monday Tuesday Wednesday Thursday Friday 8:55 a.m. **Wattage**: 100,000 ERP. **Ad Rates:** Advertising accepted; rates available upon request. Combined advertising rates available with WJAG-AM. **Mailing address:** PO Box 789, Norfolk, NE 68702. **URL:** http://www.literock97.com.

20625 ■ KNEN-FM - 94.7
PO Box 747
Norfolk, NE 68701
Phone: (402)371-0100
Fax: (402)371-0050
Format: Top 40; Sports. **Ad Rates:** Noncommercial. **URL:** http://www.94rock.fm.

20626 ■ KPNO-FM - 90.9
109 S 2nd St.
Norfolk, NE 68701
Phone: (402)379-3677
Fax: (402)379-3662
Email: kpno@newsnet.com
Format: Contemporary Christian; Religious. **Networks:** Moody Broadcasting. **Owner:** The Praise Network, Inc., PO Box 8, Aurora, NE 68818-0008, Ph: (308)946-2656. **Founded:** Sept. 23, 1992. **Operating Hours**: Continuous. **Key Personnel:** Brian Gall, Station Mgr.; Stacy Glandt, Office Mgr.; Bill Taylor, Music Dir.; Gene Henes, Mgr. **Wattage**: 100,000. **Ad Rates:** Noncommercial.

20627 ■ K21HS - 21
PO Box A
Santa Ana, CA 92711
Phone: (714)832-2950
Free: 888-731-1000
Owner: Trinity Broadcasting Network Inc., PO Box A, Santa Ana, CA 92711, Ph: (714)832-2950, Free: 888-731-1000. **URL:** http://www.tbn.org.

20628 ■ K219DW-FM - 91.7
PO Box 391
Twin Falls, ID 83303
Format: Religious; Contemporary Christian; Music of Your Life; News. **Owner:** CSN International, PO Box 391, Twin Falls, ID 83303, Ph: (208)736-1958, Fax: (208)736-1958, Free: 800-357-4226. **Key Personnel:** Mike Kestler, President; Don Mills, Music Dir., Prog. Dir.; Daniel Davidson, Dir. of Operations. **URL:** http://www.csnradio.com.

20629 ■ KUSO-FM - 92.7
214 N Seventh St., Ste. 1
Norfolk, NE 68701
Phone: (402)371-8792
Free: 866-371-8792
Format: Country. **Key Personnel:** Mike Flood, Owner, mike@us92.com; Angie Stenger, Gen. Mgr., angie@us92.com. **Mailing address:** PO Box 747, Norfolk, NE 68701. **URL:** http://www.us92.com.

20630 ■ KXNE-TV - 19
1800 N 33rd St.
Lincoln, NE 68503
Phone: (402)472-3611
Free: 800-868-1868
Email: tv@netnebraska.org
Format: Public TV; Full Service; Talk. **Networks:** Public Broadcasting Service (PBS). **Owner:** Nebraska Educational Telecommunications, at above address. **Founded:** 1965. **Operating Hours**: Continuous. **Key Personnel:** Rod Bates, Gen. Mgr., rbates1@unl.edu. **Wattage:** 475,000 ERP Horizon. **Ad Rates:** Accepts Advertising. **URL:** http://www.netnebraska.org/about/services.html.

20631 ■ WJAG Inc.
309 Braasch Ave.
Norfolk, NE 68702
Phone: (402)371-0780
Format: News; Talk. **Operating Hours:** Continuous. **Ad Rates:** Advertising accepted; rates available upon request. **Mailing address:** PO Box 789, Norfolk, NE 68702. **URL:** http://www.newstalkradio.net.

NORTH BEND

Dodge Co. Dodge Co. (E). 50 m NW of Omaha. Stock, poultry, grain farms. Wheat, corn.

20632 ■ North Bend Eagle
North Bend Eagle
721 Main St.
North Bend, NE 68649
Phone: (402)652-8312
Publication E-mail: nbeagle@gmail.com
Community newspaper. **Freq:** Weekly (Wed.). **Print Method:** Offset. **Cols./Page:** 4. **Col. Width:** 28 nonpareils. **Col. Depth:** 182 agate lines. **Key Personnel:** Nathan Arneal, Editor, Owner, Publisher; Mary Le Arneal, Office Manager. **Subscription Rates:** $29 Individuals Nebraska; $32 Out of state; $23 Students Nebraska Aug-May; $27 Out of state students Aug-May; $146 Other countries; $27 Individuals online e-subscription. **URL:** http://www.northbendeagle.com. **Mailing address:** PO Box 100, North Bend, NE 68649. **Ad Rates:** GLR $.25; BW $193.44; SAU $3.72. **Circ:** ‡1500.

NORTH PLATTE

Lincoln Co. Lincoln Co. (SW). On Platte River, 130 m W of Grand Island. ""Buffalo Bill" Cody's ranch. Railroad classification yard Light manufacturing; processing agricultured products. Diversified farming. Cattle raising. Corn, wheat, alfalfa and hay.

20633 ■ The Dish
Homer Laughlin China Collectors Association
PO Box 721
North Platte, NE 69103-0721
Fax: (308)534-7015
Publisher's E-mail: info@hlcca.org
Freq: Quarterly. **Subscription Rates:** Included in membership. **URL:** http://www.hlcca.org/Publications.aspx. **Remarks:** Advertising not accepted. **Circ:** (Not Reported).

20634 ■ North Platte Telegraph
Midlands Newspapers
621 N Chestnut
North Platte, NE 69101
Phone: (308)532-6000
Fax: (308)532-9268
Publisher's E-mail: lexch@lexch.com
General newspaper. **Freq:** Tues.-Sun. **Print Method:** Offset. **Cols./Page:** 6. **Col. Width:** 25 nonpareils. **Col. Depth:** 304 agate lines. **Key Personnel:** Holli Synder, Business Manager; Peter Rogers, Publisher; Dee D. Klein, Director, Sales. **Subscription Rates:** $161.20 Individuals local delivery; $130 Individuals 6 months; $70 Individuals 3 months; $175.80 Individuals online access. **URL:** http://www.nptelegraph.com. **Mailing address:** PO Box 370, North Platte, NE 69101. **Ad Rates:** BW $1,164.06; 4C $1,329.06; SAU $8.92; PCI $9.87. **Remarks:** Accepts advertising. **Circ:** Mon.-Sat. ★**12851**, Sun. ★**12942**.

20635 ■ KELN-FM - 97.1
1301 E Fourth St.
North Platte, NE 69101
Phone: (308)532-1120
Free: 877-532-1120
Format: Adult Contemporary. **Networks:** ABC; Satellite Music Network. **Owner:** Eagle Communications of Nebraska, 2703 Hall St., Ste. 13, Hays, KS 67601, Ph: (785)625-4000, Free: 877-613-2453. **Founded:** 1979. **Operating Hours**: Continuous. **ADI**: North Platte, NE. **Key Personnel:** David Fudge, Operations Mgr., david.fudge@eagleradio.net. **Local Programs**: *Sports*. **Wattage**: 100,000 ERP. **Ad Rates:** $8-20 for 30 seconds; for 30 seconds; $12-25 for 60 seconds; for 60 seconds. Combined advertising rates available with KOOQ-AM. **URL:** http://www.eaglecom.net.

20636 ■ KJLT-AM - 970
PO Box 709
North Platte, NE 69103-0709
Phone: (308)532-5515
Email: kjlt@kjlt.org
Format: Classic Rock; Album-Oriented Rock (AOR). **Owner:** Tri-State Broadcasting Assoc. Inc., at above address. **Operating Hours**: Sunrise-sunset. **Key Personnel:** John Townsend, Station Mgr., jlt@kjlt.org; Gary Hofer, Asst. Mgr., Chief Engineer, ghofer@kjlt.org. **Wattage**: 5,000 Day; 055 Night. **Ad Rates:** Noncommercial. **URL:** http://kjlt.org.

20637 ■ KJLT-FM - 94.9
PO Box 709
North Platte, NE 69103-0709
Phone: (308)532-5515
Email: kjlt@kjlt.org
Format: Album-Oriented Rock (AOR); Classic Rock. **Networks:** Moody Broadcasting; SkyLight Satellite. **Owner:** Tri-State Broadcasting Assoc. Inc., at above address. **Founded:** Sept. 18, 2006. **Operating Hours**: Continuous. **Key Personnel:** John Townsend, Station Mgr., jlt@kjlt.org; Gary Hofer, Asst. Mgr., ghofer@kjlt.org. **Wattage**: 100,000. **Ad Rates:** Noncommercial. **URL:** http://kjlt.org.

20638 ■ KNOP-TV - 2
8020 N Hwy. 83
North Platte, NE 69101
Phone: (308)532-2222
Fax: (308)532-9579
Email: knop@knoptv.com
Format: Commercial TV. **Networks:** NBC. **Owner:** Hoak Media Corp., 500 Crescent Ct., Ste. 220, Dallas, TX 75201, Ph: (972)960-4848, Fax: (972)960-4899. **Founded:** Dec. 1958. **Operating Hours**: 6:30 a.m.-12:30 a.m. **ADI**: North Platte, NE. **Key Personnel:** Larry Brown, Producer; Jacque Harms, Producer. **URL:** http://www.knopnews2.com.

20639 ■ KODY-AM - 1240
Box 1085
North Platte, NE 69101
Phone: (308)532-3344
Fax: (308)534-6651
Format: Talk; News. **Networks:** Talknet. **Founded:** 1930. **Operating Hours**: Continuous. **ADI**: North Platte, NE. **Key Personnel:** Rob Mandeville, Gen. Mgr., rmandeville@nrgmedia.com. **Wattage**: 1,000. **Ad Rates:** $7-16 for 30 seconds. **URL:** http://www.huskeradio.com.

Circulation: ★ = AAM; △ or • = BPA; ♦ = CAC; ❑ = VAC; ⊕ = PO Statement; ‡ = Publisher's Report; Boldface figures = sworn; Light figures = estimated.

20640 ■ KOOQ-AM - 1410
1301 E 4th St.
North Platte, NE 69101
Phone: (308)532-1120
Fax: (308)532-0458
Free: 877-532-1120
Format: Sports. **Networks:** ABC; Satellite Music Network. **Owner:** Eagle Communications of Nebraska, 2703 Hall St., Ste. 13, Hays, KS 67601, Ph: (785)625-4000, Free: 877-613-2453. **Founded:** 1966. **Operating Hours**: Continuous. **ADI**: North Platte, NE. **Key Personnel:** Jerome Gilg, Gen. Mgr., jerome.gilg@eagleradio.net. **Local Programs:** *News*; *Sports*. **Wattage:** 5,000 Day; 500 Night. **Ad Rates:** $8-20 for 30 seconds; $11-25 for 60 seconds. Combined advertising rates available with KELN-FM. **URL:** http://business.nparea.com.

20641 ■ KPNE-TV - 9
1800 N 33rd St.
Lincoln, NE 68503
Phone: (402)472-3611
Free: 800-868-1868
Format: Public TV. **Simulcasts:** KUON-TV. **Networks:** Public Broadcasting Service (PBS). **Owner:** Nebraska Educational Telecommunications, at above address. **Founded:** 1966. **Operating Hours**: 6:30 a.m. - 11:30 pm; 90% network, 10% local. **ADI**: North Platte, NE. **Key Personnel:** Rod Bates, Gen. Mgr. **Wattage**: 316. **Ad Rates:** Noncommercial. **URL:** http://netnebraska.org.

20642 ■ KXNP-FM - 103.5
305 E Fourth St.
North Platte, NE 69101
Phone: (308)532-3344
Fax: (308)534-6651
Format: Country. **Owner:** Armada Media Inc., at above address. **ADI**: North Platte, NE. **Key Personnel:** Tony Lama, Contact, tlama@huskeradio.com. **Wattage**: 100,000 ERP. **Ad Rates:** Noncommercial; Advertising accepted; rates available upon request. **Mailing address:** PO Box 1085, North Platte, NE 69101. **URL:** http://www.tlama.com.

O'NEILL

Holt Co. Holt Co. (N). 75 m NW of Norfolk. Manufactures cheese. Cattle ranching. Ships hogs. Farming. Corn, rye, oats, hay.

20643 ■ KBRX-AM - 1350
251 N Jefferson
O'Neill, NE 68763
Phone: (402)336-1612
Fax: (402)336-3585
Email: live@kbrx.com
Format: Oldies. **Networks:** ABC. **Owner:** Ranchland Broadcast Co., Inc., at above address. **Founded:** 1955. **Operating Hours**: Continuous. **Key Personnel:** Scott Poese, Gen. Mgr., scott@kbrx.com. **Wattage:** 1,000. **Ad Rates:** $12 for 30 seconds; $15 for 60 seconds. **Mailing address:** PO Box 150, O'Neill, NE 68763. **URL:** http://www.kbrx.com.

20644 ■ KBRX-FM - 102.9
251 N Jefferson
O'Neill, NE 68763
Phone: (402)336-1612
Format: Country. **Networks:** ABC. **Owner:** Ranchland Broadcast Co., Inc., at above address. **Founded:** 1973. **Operating Hours**: Continuous. **Key Personnel:** Sharon Lang, Contact. **Local Programs:** *Party Line*. **Wattage:** 100,000. **Ad Rates:** Noncommercial. **Mailing address:** PO Box 150, O'Neill, NE 68763. **URL:** http://www.kbrx.com.

20645 ■ KGRD-FM - 105.3
128 S 4th St.
O'Neill, NE 68763
Phone: (402)336-3886
Fax: (402)336-3833
Free: 800-842-1053
Email: email@goodnewsgreatmusic.org
Format: Religious. **Networks:** Moody Broadcasting; SkyLight Satellite; Ambassador Inspirational Radio. **Owner:** The Praise Network, Inc., PO Box 8, Aurora, NE 68818-0008, Ph: (308)946-2656. **Founded:** 1987. **Operating Hours**: Continuous. **Key Personnel:** Todd Gennarson, Station Mgr.; Bill Taylor, Music Dir. **Wattage**: 100,000. **Ad Rates:** Noncommercial. **URL:** http://www.goodnewsgreatmusic.org.

OGALLALA

Keith Co. Keith Co. (WC). 15 m W of Roscoe.

20646 ■ KMCX-FM - 106.5
113 W Fourth St.
Ogallala, NE 69153
Phone: (308)284-3633
Format: Country. **Networks:** ABC. **Founded:** 1975. **Formerly**: KIBC-FM. **Operating Hours**: Continuous. **Wattage**: 100,000. **Ad Rates:** $11-17 for 30 seconds; $17-25 for 60 seconds. **URL:** http://www.kmcx.com.

20647 ■ KOGA-AM - 930
113 W Fourth St.
Ogallala, NE 69153
Phone: (308)284-3633
Fax: (308)284-3517
Format: Big Band/Nostalgia. **Networks:** ABC. **Founded:** 1956. **Operating Hours**: Continuous. **Key Personnel:** Katrina Twomey, Gen. Mgr. **Wattage**: 5,000. **Ad Rates:** Noncommercial. **URL:** http://www.930koga.com.

20648 ■ KOGA-FM - 99.7
113 W 4th St.
Ogallala, NE 69153
Phone: (308)284-3633
Format: Adult Contemporary. **Networks:** ABC. **Founded:** 1978. **Operating Hours**: Continuous. **Key Personnel:** Katrina Twomey, Gen. Mgr. **Wattage**: 100,000. **Ad Rates:** $11-17 for 30 seconds; $17-25 for 60 seconds. **URL:** http://www.997thelake.com.

20649 ■ K26CV - 26
PO Box A
Santa Ana, CA 92711
Phone: (714)832-2950
Free: 888-731-1000
Owner: Trinity Broadcasting Network Inc., PO Box A, Santa Ana, CA 92711, Ph: (714)832-2950, Free: 888-731-1000. **URL:** http://www.tbn.org.

OMAHA

Douglas Co. Douglas Co. (E). On Missouri River. Bridge to Council Bluffs, Iowa. Creighton University; University of Nebraska Medical School; University of Nebraska at Omaha; Metropolitan Technical Community College. Manufacturing, distribution & service center. Important livestock, dairy products and grain market. Manufactures feed, farm machinery, paint and varnish, paper boxes, electrical signs, garden tools, ball bearings; flour & cereal mills; slaughter and meat packing plants. Smelters.

20650 ■ Absolute Advantage
Wellness Council of America
17002 Marcy St., Ste. 140
Omaha, NE 68118-2933
Phone: (402)827-3590
Fax: (402)827-3594
Publisher's E-mail: wellworkplace@welcoa.org
Freq: 10/year. **Subscription Rates:** $89 /year. **Remarks:** Advertising not accepted. **Circ:** (Not Reported).

20651 ■ Creighton International and Comparative Law Journal
Creighton University School of Law
2500 California Plz.
Omaha, NE 68178
Phone: (402)280-2586
Publication E-mail: lawreview@creighton.edu
Journal containing topics regarding international law in legal practice and academia. **URL:** http://law.creighton.edu/current-students/student-resources/international-comparative-law-journal. **Circ:** (Not Reported).

20652 ■ Creighton University Magazine
Creighton University Public Relations and Information
2500 California Plz.
Omaha, NE 68178
Phone: (402)280-2700
University magazine. **Freq:** Quarterly February, May, August and November,. **Key Personnel:** Sheila Swanson, Associate Editor, phone: (402)280-2069; Rick Davis, Editor, phone: (402)280-1785. **URL:** http://www.creighton.edu/creightonmagazine. **Formerly**: Window. **Feature Editors:** Pam Vaughn, phone: (402)551-9856, pamvaughn@creighton.edu. **Remarks:** Advertising not accepted. **Circ:** (Not Reported).

20653 ■ Creightonian
Creighton University
601 N 38 St.
Omaha, NE 68144
Phone: (402)280-4854
Publisher's E-mail: webmaster@creighton.edu
Collegiate newspaper. **Freq:** Weekly (Fri.). **Print Method:** Offset. **Trim Size:** 11 1/2 x 16 1/2. **Cols./Page:** 4. **Col. Width:** 28 nonpareils. **Col. Depth:** 210 agate lines. **Key Personnel:** Madeline Zukowski, Editor-in-Chief. **USPS:** 137-460. **URL:** http://www.creightonian.com. **Ad Rates:** BW $380; 4C $890; PCI $7.50. **Remarks:** Accepts advertising. **Circ:** Paid ‡4600, Free ‡200.

20654 ■ The Gateway
University of Nebraska at Omaha
6001 Dodge St.
Omaha, NE 68182
Phone: (402)554-6281
Fax: (402)554-3990
Publication E-mail: news@unogateway.com
Collegiate newspaper. **Founded:** 1913. **Freq:** Semi-weekly Tuesdays and Fridays during fall and spring semesters. **Print Method:** Web Offset. **Trim Size:** 10 3/8 x 15 1/2. **Cols./Page:** 6. **Col. Width:** 1.625 inches. **Col. Depth:** 15 1/2 inches. **Key Personnel:** Rachel Ruwe, Manager, Advertising; Kelsey Jochum, Editor-in-Chief; Christine Dunn, Manager, Advertising. **Subscription Rates:** Free. **URL:** http://unothegateway.com. **Ad Rates:** BW $613.80; 4C $300; PCI $6.60. **Remarks:** Accepts advertising. **Circ:** Free 6000.

20655 ■ Grace Tidings
Grace University
1311 S 9th St.
Omaha, NE 68108-3629
Phone: (402)449-2800
Fax: (402)341-9587
Publication E-mail: tidings@graceu.edu
Magazine containing inspirational articles and college activities information. **Freq:** Semiannual. **Print Method:** Letterpress. **Trim Size:** 8 1/2 x 11. **Cols./Page:** 3. **Col. Width:** 26 nonpareils. **Col. Depth:** 136 agate lines. **USPS:** 224-960. **URL:** http://graceuniversity.edu/news/grace-universitys-masterworks-chorus-2. **Remarks:** Advertising not accepted. **Circ:** Non-paid 24000.

20656 ■ Grief Digest: Hope, Information, Support
Centering Corp.
7230 Maple St.
Omaha, NE 68134
Phone: (402)553-1200
Free: 866-218-0101
Magazine featuring articles on coping and dealing with grief, help for the caregiver, and the usual quality and support from family. **Freq:** Quarterly. **Key Personnel:** Andrea Gambill, Editor. **Subscription Rates:** $30 Individuals. **URL:** http://griefdigestmagazine.com. **Circ:** (Not Reported).

20657 ■ Home & Away
H&A Media Group
10703 J St., Ste. 100
Omaha, NE 68127
Phone: (402)592-5000
Publication E-mail: editorial@homeandawaymagazine.com
American Automobile Association travel magazine. **Founded:** July 1986. **Freq:** Bimonthly. **Print Method:** Web offset. **Trim Size:** 7 7/8 x 10 7/8. **Cols./Page:** 3. **Key Personnel:** Gary Peterson, Editor; Terry Ausenbaugh, Director, Advertising, Publisher, phone: (402)592-5000; Randy Achee, Chief Executive Officer, President. **ISSN:** 0889-4078 (print). **URL:** http://www.homeandawaymagazine.com. **Formerly**: The Traveler. **Ad Rates:** BW $15760; 4C $20472. **Remarks:** Accepts advertising. **Circ:** (Not Reported).

20658 ■ Home & Away: Mid-America's Leisure and Lifestyle Magazine
Home and Away Inc.
PO Box 3535
Omaha, NE 68103
Phone: (402)592-5000
Fax: (402)331-5194
Publisher's E-mail: editorial@homeandawaymagazine.com

Travel and recreation magazine published for American Automobile Association members in the Midwest. **Freq:** Bimonthly. **Print Method:** Offset. **Trim Size:** 7 7/8 x 10 7/8. **Cols./Page:** 3. **Col. Width:** 26 nonpareils. **Col. Depth:** 138 agate lines. **Key Personnel:** Terry Ausenbaugh, President, Chief Executive Officer; Gary Peterson, Editor-in-Chief. **ISSN:** 0199--7009 (print). **URL:** http://www.homeandawaymagazine.com/ZipGate. **Ad Rates:** BW $58,488; 4C $69,216. **Remarks:** Advertising accepted; rates available upon request. **Circ:** Paid 3355000.

20659 ■ IAATC Travel Guide
International Association of Air Travel Couriers
PO Box 31279
Omaha, NE 68131
Phone: (402)218-1982
Publisher's E-mail: inforeq@iaatc.org
Freq: Monthly. **ISSN:** 1082--3859 (print). **Subscription Rates:** $48 /year. **Remarks:** Accepts advertising. **Circ:** (Not Reported).

20660 ■ Information Technology for Development
Routledge
c/o Sajda Qureshi, Ed.-in-Ch.
College of Information Science & Technology
University of Nebraska at Omaha
6001 Dodge St.
Omaha, NE 68182-0116
Publisher's E-mail: book.orders@tandf.co.uk
Journal focusing on the relationship between IT and development by proposing theories or frameworks, best practices, and/or tools and techniques. **Freq:** Quarterly. **Trim Size:** 6 7/8 x 10. **Key Personnel:** Eric Monteiro, Associate Editor; Anthony Ming, Managing Editor, phone: (44)20 77476359; Sajda Qureshi, Editor-in-Chief; Erran Carmel, Associate Editor. **ISSN:** 0268--1102 (print); **EISSN:** 1554--0170 (electronic). **Subscription Rates:** $528 Individuals print; $659 Institutions online; $754 Institutions print and online. **URL:** http://www.tandfonline.com/toc/titd20/current#.Uvr1EmlyIrg. **Ad Rates:** BW $1,217; 4C $1,545. **Remarks:** Accepts classified advertising. **Circ:** (Not Reported).

20661 ■ Jewish Press
Jewish Federation of Omaha
333 S 132nd St.
Omaha, NE 68154
Phone: (402)334-8200
Fax: (402)333-5497
Publication E-mail: jpress@jewishomaha.org
Jewish community newspaper. **Freq:** Weekly (Fri.). **Print Method:** Offset. **Trim Size:** 11 x 16. **Cols./Page:** 6. **Col. Width:** 9.5 picas. **Col. Depth:** 224 agate lines. **Key Personnel:** Annette van de Kamp-Wright, Editor. **USPS:** 275-620. **Subscription Rates:** $40 Individuals; $72 Other countries. **URL:** http://www.jewishomaha.org/jewish-press. **Ad Rates:** GLR $1.15; BW $960; 4C $1,089.20; PCI $11.25. **Remarks:** Color advertising accepted; rates available upon request. **Circ:** 3800.

20662 ■ Journal of Child Neurology: An Interdisciplinary Forum for Child Neurology and Development/Behavioral Pediatrics
SAGE Publications Inc.
c/o Roger A. Brumback, MD, Ed.
Creighton University Medical Center
Omaha, NE 68131
Publisher's E-mail: sales@pfp.sagepub.com
Peer-reviewed journal covering all aspects of nervous system disorders in children, including medical, surgical, psychological, and genetic perspectives. The Journal features topics of interest to clinical and research pediatric neurologists, pediatric neuropathologists, neuroradiologists, and behavioral pediatricians.Focuses on the special needs of neurologic patients from birth to age 18 years. Offers highly-cited cutting edge articles and case reports written by leading international specialists. **Freq:** 14/yr. **Print Method:** Offset. **Trim Size:** 8 1/8 x 10 7/8. **Cols./Page:** 2. **Col. Width:** 20 picas. **Col. Depth:** 56 picas. **Key Personnel:** Roger A. Brumback, MD, Editor, Founder. **ISSN:** 0883--0738 (print); **EISSN:** 1708--8283 (electronic). **Subscription Rates:** $462 Individuals print and e-access; $1034 Institutions e-access; $1126 Institutions print only; $1149 Institutions print and e-access; $43 Individuals single print ; $88 Institutions single print. **URL:** http://jcn.sagepub.com. **Ad Rates:** BW $1,740, Display Ad.; BW $1,130, Classified Ad. **Remarks:** Accepts advertising. **Circ:** ‡600.

20663 ■ Journal of Leadership Education
Association of Leadership Educators, Inc.
c/o Jennifer Moss Breen, President
2500 California Plz.
Omaha, NE 68178
Phone: (402)280-3952
Peer-reviewed journal covering forum for development of the knowledge base and practice of leadership education. **ISSN:** 1552--9045 (print). **Alt. Formats:** PDF. **URL:** http://www.journalofleadershiped.org; http://www.leadershipeducators.org/page-1014283. **Remarks:** Advertising not accepted. **Circ:** (Not Reported).

20664 ■ Journal of Religion and Film
University of Nebraska - Omaha Department of Philosophy and Religion
Art and Sciences Hall, Rm. 205
6001 Dodge St.
Omaha, NE 68182-0265
Phone: (402)554-2628
Publisher's E-mail: unophilosophy@unomaha.edu
Journal covering the description, review, and embodiment of religion in film. **Key Personnel:** Michele Desmarais, Board Member, phone: (402)554-2679; William L. Blizek, Editor, Founder, phone: (402)554-3347; Paul Allen Williams, Board Member, phone: (402)554-6016. **ISSN:** 1092--1311 (print). **Alt. Formats:** PDF. **URL:** http://digitalcommons.unomaha.edu/jrf. **Circ:** (Not Reported).

20665 ■ Journal of Religion & Society
Creighton University Public Relations and Information
2500 California Plz.
Omaha, NE 68178
Phone: (402)280-2700
Publication E-mail: rsmkns@creighton.edu
Journal devoted to the scholarly research in religion and its diverse social dimensions. **Freq:** Annual. **Key Personnel:** Ronald A. Simkins, Editor; John C.M. Calvert, Board Member; Wendy M. Wright, Board Member; Christina Clark, Board Member; Naser Alsharif, Board Member; Gregory S. Bucher, Board Member; Susan A. Calef, Board Member. **ISSN:** 1522--5658 (print). **Subscription Rates:** Free. **URL:** http://moses.creighton.edu/JRS/. **Circ:** (Not Reported).

20666 ■ The Ledger
Bh Media Group Holdings Inc.
Omaha World Herald Bldg. 1
Omaha, NE 68102
Phone: (402)444-1000
Publication E-mail: ledger@bbc.net
Community newspaper. **Founded:** July 1906. **Freq:** Weekly (Thurs.). **Print Method:** Offset. **Cols./Page:** 6. **Col. Width:** 26 nonpareils. **Col. Depth:** 304 agate lines. **Key Personnel:** Amber Ningen, Publisher. **Subscription Rates:** $29 Individuals within Hemingford region; $31 Out of area. **URL:** http://www.ledgeronline.com. **Formerly:** The Journal. **Remarks:** Accepts advertising. **Circ:** Paid ‡1214, Free ‡31.

20667 ■ The Lincoln Business Journal
Midlands Business Journal Publications
1324 S 119th St.
Omaha, NE 68144
Phone: (402)330-1760
Fax: (402)758-9315
Business publication covering regional business and government issues in Lincoln, Nebraska. **Freq:** Weekly. **Print Method:** Offset. **Trim Size:** 10 1/4 x 12 1/2. **Key Personnel:** Jeff Hookie, Vice President, Production; Jill Micek, Editor, Vice President, Assistant Publisher; Jim Brazda, Writer; Robert Hoig, Publisher, Founder. **Subscription Rates:** $53.50 Individuals /year; $96.30 Two years; $139.10 Individuals 3 years. **URL:** http://www.mbj.com/Papers/LBJ.html. **Ad Rates:** BW $575. **Remarks:** Accepts advertising. **Circ:** (Not Reported).

20668 ■ The Midlands Business Journal
Midlands Business Journal Publications
1324 S 119th St.
Omaha, NE 68144
Phone: (402)330-1760
Fax: (402)758-9315
Trade journal covering local business. **Freq:** Weekly. **Print Method:** Offset. **Key Personnel:** Robert Hoig, Publisher, Founder; Jill Micek, Editor, Vice President, Assistant Publisher. **Subscription Rates:** $75 Individuals 1 year; $135 Two years; $190 Individuals 3 years. **Ad Rates:** BW $940. **Remarks:** Accepts advertising. **Circ:** (Not Reported).

20669 ■ The Omaha Business Journal
Midlands Business Journal Publications
1324 S 119th St.
Omaha, NE 68144
Phone: (402)330-1760
Fax: (402)758-9315
Business publication covering local start-ups and entrepreneurs. **Freq:** Monthly. **Print Method:** Offset. **Trim Size:** 10 1/4 x 12 1/2. **URL:** http://www.mbj.com/Papers/OBJP.html. **Remarks:** Advertising not accepted. **Circ:** (Not Reported).

20670 ■ Omaha World-Herald
ProQuest L.L.C.
Omaha World-Herald Bldg.
1314 Douglas St., Ste. 900
Omaha, NE 68102-1138
Phone: (402)444-1000
Free: 800-284-6397
Publication E-mail: webmaster@omaha.com
General newspaper. **Freq:** Daily (eve.), Sat. and Sun. (morn.). **Print Method:** Letterpress. **Cols./Page:** 6. **Col. Width:** 24 nonpareils. **Col. Depth:** 301 agate lines. **Key Personnel:** Melissa Matczak, Managing Editor; Joanne Stewart, Assistant Managing Editor; Kristy Gerry, Director, Production, phone: (402)444-3129; Mike Reilly, Executive Editor, phone: (404)444-1277; Terry Kroeger, President, Publisher, phone: (402)444-1179. **USPS:** 408-280. **Subscription Rates:** $4.45 Individuals 7 day subscription; weekly; print only; $57.85 Individuals 7 day subscription; 13 weeks; print only; $115.70 Individuals 7 day subscription; 26 weeks; print only; $231.40 Individuals 7 day subscription; 52 weeks; print only; $2.20 Individuals 6 day subscription; weekly; print only; $28.60 Individuals 6 day subscription; 13 weeks; print only; $57.20 Individuals 6 day subscription; 26 weeks; print only; $114.40 Individuals 6 day subscription; 52 weeks; print only; $1.75 Individuals weekday subscription; weekly; print only; $22.75 Individuals weekday subscription; 13 weeks; print only; $45.50 Individuals weekday subscription; 26 weeks; print only; $91 Individuals weekday subscription; 52 weeks; print only; $3.05 Individuals Fri.-Sun. subscription; weekly; print only; $39.65 Individuals Fri.-Sun. subscription; 13 weeks; print only; $79.30 Individuals Fri.-Sun. subscription; 26 weeks; print only; $158.60 Individuals Fri.-Sun. subscription; 52 weeks; print only; $2.25 Individuals Sun. subscription; weekly; print only; $29.25 Individuals Sun. subscription; 13 weeks; print only; $58.50 Individuals Sun. subscription; 26 weeks; print only; $117 Individuals Sun. subscription; 52 weeks; print only; $1 Single issue Mon.-Sat.; print only; $2.50 Single issue Sun.; print only; $25 Individuals /mo.; Mon.-Sun.; digital only. **Online:** ProQuest L.L.C. ProQuest L.L.C.; Omaha World-Herald Company Inc. Omaha World-Herald Company Inc. **Alt. Formats:** Handheld. **URL:** http://www.omaha.com; http://www.owh.com. **Ad Rates:** BW $8,154.09; 4C $9,131.09; SAU $67.50; PCI $74. **Remarks:** Accepts advertising. **Circ:** Mon.-Fri. ★**185039**, Sat. ★**181256**, Sun. ★**235185**.

20671 ■ An Sionnach
Creighton University
601 N 38 St.
Omaha, NE 68144
Phone: (402)280-4854
Publisher's E-mail: webmaster@creighton.edu
Magazine that covers creative writing, literature, and culture for the United States, England, and Ireland. **Freq:** Semiannual. **Key Personnel:** Dr. David Gardiner, Editor. **ISSN:** 1554--8953 (print). **Subscription Rates:** $15 Single issue. **URL:** http://www.creighton.edu/cupress; http://www.an-sionnach.com. **Remarks:** Advertising not accepted. **Circ:** (Not Reported).

20672 ■ Wfm: Woodmen of the World Fraternal Magazine
Woodmen of the World/Omaha Woodmen Life Insurance Society
1700 Farnam St.
Omaha, NE 68102-2025
Free: 800-225-3108
Publisher's E-mail: wow@woodmen.org

Circulation: ★ = AAM; △ or • = BPA; ♦ = CAC; ❑ = VAC; ⊕ = PO Statement; ‡ = Publisher's Report; Boldface figures = sworn; Light figures = estimated.

Fraternal magazine for organization's members and their families. **Freq:** Bimonthly. **Print Method:** Offset. **Trim Size:** 8 x 10 1/2. **Cols./Page:** 3. **ISSN:** 1069--1790 (print). **Subscription Rates:** $2 Individuals. **URL:** http://www.woodmen.org. **Formerly**: Woodmen of the World Magazine; WOODMEN Magazine. **Mailing address:** PO Box 2962, Omaha, NE 68103-2962. **Remarks:** Advertising not accepted. **Circ:** ‡485000.

20673 ■ WoodmenLife
Woodmen of the World/Omaha Woodmen Life Insurance Society
1700 Farnam St.
Omaha, NE 68102-2025
Free: 800-225-3108
Publisher's E-mail: wow@woodmen.org
Freq: 3/year. **Subscription Rates:** $3 /year. **Alt. Formats:** PDF. **URL:** http://www.woodmen.org/about/magazine.cfm. **Mailing address:** PO Box 2962, Omaha, NE 68103-2962. **Remarks:** Advertising not accepted. **Circ:** (Not Reported).

20674 ■ Cox Communications, Omaha L.L.C.
11501 W Dodge St.
Omaha, NE 68154
Phone: (402)933-3000
Owner: Cox Cable Communications, at above address, Ph: (404)843-5000, Fax: (401)828-3835. **Founded:** 1981. **Cities Served:** subscribing households 91,000. **URL:** http://www.cox.com/support/omaha/contact/locations.asp.

KAIK-FM - See Tillamook, OR
KAIP-FM - See Davenport, IA
KAIW-FM - See Laramie, WY
KAIX-FM - See Cheyenne, WY
KAKL-FM - See Anchorage, AK
KARA-FM - See Sacramento

20675 ■ Karban TV Systems Inc.
PO Box 2016
Omaha, NE 68103-2016
Free: 800-236-0233
Email: sales@ktvs.net
Founded: 1984. **Cities Served:** Boulder Junction, Land O'Lakes, Mercer, Three Lakes; 42 channels. **URL:** http://www.ktvs.net.

KARO-FM - See Boise, ID

20676 ■ KCMT-FM - 98.9
PO Box 2098
Omaha, NE 68103-2098
Phone: (916)251-1600
Email: kcmt@psln.com
Format: Adult Contemporary; Classical. **Networks:** CNN Radio. **Owner:** John Samuels, at above address. **Founded:** 1989. **Formerly:** KCFM-FM. **Operating Hours**: Continuous. **Key Personnel:** John Samuels, Owner; Laurie Wann, Gen. Mgr. **Wattage**: 25,000. **Ad Rates:** $8-9 for 30 seconds; $9.75-11 for 60 seconds. $8-$9 for 30 seconds; $9.75-$11 for 60 seconds. Combined advertising rates available with KPCO-AM. **URL:** http://www.klove.com.

20677 ■ KCRO-AM - 660
11717 Burt St., Ste. 202
Omaha, NE 68154
Phone: (402)422-1600
Email: info@ambassador4me.com
Format: Religious. **Networks:** Sun Radio. **Owner:** Salem Media Group Inc., 4880 Santa Rosa Rd., Camarillo, CA 93012, Ph: (805)987-0400, Fax: (805)384-4520. **Founded:** 1922. **Operating Hours**: Continuous; 20% network, 80% local. **ADI**: Omaha, NE. **Key Personnel:** Greg Vogt, Gen. Mgr., gvogt@salemomaha.com; Nick Buras, Asst. Mgr., nburas@salemomaha.com; Jim Leedham, Chief Engineer; Mike Shane, Operations Mgr.; Sue Garrett, Sales Mgr., sgarrett@salemomaha.com. **Local Programs**: *Search the Scriptures*, Monday Tuesday Wednesday Thursday Friday 10:00 a.m.; 5:30 p.m.; 10:30 p.m. **Wattage**: 1,000. **Ad Rates:** Noncommercial. KGBI-FM, KOTI-AM. **URL:** http://www.kcro.com.

KDKL-FM - See King City, CA

20678 ■ KETV-TV - 7
2665 Douglas St.
Omaha, NE 68131-2699
Phone: (402)345-7777
Fax: (402)978-8931
Format: Commercial TV. **Networks:** ABC. **Owner:** Hearts Television Inc., 300 W 57th St., New York, NY 10019-3789, Ph: (212)887-6800, Fax: (212)887-6855. **Founded:** 1957. **Operating Hours**: Continuous. **ADI**: Omaha, NE. **Ad Rates:** Advertising accepted; rates available upon request. **URL:** http://www.ketv.com.

20679 ■ KEZO-FM - 92.3
5030 N 72nd St.
Omaha, NE 68134
Phone: (402)592-5300
Free: 800-955-9230
Format: Album-Oriented Rock (AOR). **Owner:** Journal Broadcast Group Inc., 333 W State St., Milwaukee, WI 53203-1305, Ph: (414)332-9611, Fax: (414)967-5400. **Founded:** 1942. **Operating Hours**: Continuous; 100% local. **Key Personnel:** Jim Spector, Dir. of Programs, jspector@journalbroadcastgroup.com; Andy Gassman, Contact, agassman@journalbroadcastgroup.com. **Wattage:** 1,000,000. **Ad Rates:** $100 per unit. **URL:** http://www.z92.com.

20680 ■ KFAB-AM - 1110
5010 Underwood Ave.
Omaha, NE 68132
Phone: (402)561-2000
Format: News; Talk. **Networks:** CBS. **Owner:** iHeartMedia Inc., 200 E Basse Rd., San Antonio, TX 78209, Ph: (210)832-3314. **Founded:** 1924. **Operating Hours**: Continuous. **ADI**: Omaha, NE. **Key Personnel:** Taylor Walet, Gen. Mgr. **Local Programs**: *Grow Omaha*, Saturday 9:00 a.m. - 10:00 a.m.; *Talkers Radio Countdown*, Saturday 6:00 p.m. - 8:00 p.m. **Wattage**: 50,000. **Ad Rates:** $45-250 per unit. Combined advertising rates available with KRQC-FM, KXKT-FM, KGOR-FM. **URL:** http://www.kfab.com.

20681 ■ KFFF-FM - 93.3
5010 Underwood Ave.
Omaha, NE 68132
Phone: (402)561-2000
Fax: (402)556-8937
Format: Album-Oriented Rock (AOR). **Owner:** iHeartMedia Inc., 200 E Basse Rd., San Antonio, TX 78209, Ph: (210)832-3314. **Formerly**: KHUS-FM. **ADI**: Omaha, NE. **Key Personnel:** Heath Hedstrom, Dir. of HR; Erik Johnson, Prog. Dir., Music Dir.; Marnie Simpson, Gen. Sales Mgr.; Kevin Simonson, Promotions Dir. **Wattage**: 3,600. **Ad Rates:** Noncommercial. **URL:** http://www.thedamstation.com/main.html.

20682 ■ KGBI-FM - 100.7
11717 Burt St., Ste. 202
Omaha, NE 68154-1500
Phone: (402)422-1600
Format: Religious. **Networks:** SkyLight Satellite. **Owner:** Salem Media Group Inc., 4880 Santa Rosa Rd., Camarillo, CA 93012, Ph: (805)987-0400, Fax: (805)384-4520. **Founded:** 1966. **Operating Hours**: Continuous. **Key Personnel:** Greg Moyer, Contact. **Wattage**: 100,000. **Ad Rates:** Noncommercial. **URL:** http://www.kgbifm.com.

20683 ■ KGOR-FM - 99.9
5010 Underwood Ave.
Omaha, NE 68132
Phone: (402)561-2000
Format: Contemporary Hit Radio (CHR); Top 40. **Owner:** IHeartCommunications Inc., 200 E Base Rd., San Antonio, TX 78209, Ph: (210)822-2828. **Founded:** 1959. **Operating Hours**: Midnight - 7:00 p.m. **Wattage**: 110,000 ERP. **Ad Rates:** Advertising accepted; rates available upon request. Combined advertising rates available with KXKT-FM, KRQC-FM, KFAB-AM. **URL:** http://www.kgor.com.

KIKL-FM - See Lafayette, LA
KILV-FM - See Sioux City, IA

20684 ■ KIOS-FM - 91.5
3230 Burt St.
Omaha, NE 68131
Phone: (402)557-2777
Email: listener@kios.org
Format: Public Radio; News; Information; Jazz. **Networks:** National Public Radio (NPR); Public Radio International (PRI); American Public Radio (APR). **Owner:** Omaha Public Schools, at above address. **Founded:** 1969. **ADI**: Omaha, NE. **Key Personnel:** Ken Dudzik, Station Mgr., manager@kios.org; Bob Coate, Prog. Dir.; Mike Jacobs, Music Dir. **Wattage**: 55,000 ERP. **Ad Rates:** Noncommercial. Underwriting available. **URL:** http://www.kios.org.

20685 ■ KKAR-AM - 1290
5011 Capital Ave.
Omaha, NE 68132
Format: News; Talk. **Networks:** CNN Radio. **Owner:** NRG Media, 2875 Mount Vernon Rd. SE, Cedar Rapids, IA 52403, Ph: (319)862-0300, Fax: (319)286-9383. **Operating Hours**: Continuous. **Wattage**: 5,000. **Ad Rates:** for 30 seconds; for 60 seconds. **URL:** http://www.1290kkar.com/.

20686 ■ KKCD-FM - 105.9
5030 N 72nd St.
Omaha, NE 68134-2363
Phone: (402)592-5300
Fax: (402)598-6605
Free: 800-955-9230
Format: Music of Your Life. **Owner:** Journal Broadcasting Group, Inc., 720 East Capitol Dr., Milwaukee, WI 53212, Ph: (414)332-9611. **Founded:** 1964. **ADI**: Omaha, NE. **Wattage**: 50,000 ERP. **Ad Rates:** Advertising accepted; rates available upon request. **URL:** http://www.cd1059.com/.

KLKA-FM - See Globe, AZ
KLMK-FM - See Marvell, AR
KLOF-FM - See Gillette, WY
KLOP-FM - See Ocean Park, WA
KLOV-FM - See Roseburg, OR
KLRD-FM - See Yucaipa
KLRM-FM - See Mountain Home, AR
KLUW-FM - See Wenatchee, WA
KLVA-FM - See Phoenix, AZ
KLVG-FM - See Eureka, CA
KLVN-FM - See Modesto, CA
KLVW-FM - See Odessa, TX
KLWC-FM - See Casper, WY
KLWV-FM - See Cheyenne, WY

20687 ■ KMLV-FM - 88.1
PO Box 2098
Omaha, NE 68103
Free: 800-525-5683
Format: Religious. **Owner:** Educational Media Foundation, 2351 Sunset Blvd., Ste. 170-218, Rocklin, CA 95677, Ph: (800)434-8400. **Ad Rates:** Noncommercial. **URL:** http://www.klove.com.

20688 ■ KMTV-TV - 3
10714 Mockingbird Dr.
Omaha, NE 68127
Phone: (402)592-3333
Format: Full Service. **Networks:** CBS. **Owner:** Emmis Communications Corp., One Emmis Plz., 40 Monument Cir., Ste. 700, Indianapolis, IN 46204-3011, Ph: (317)266-0100. **Founded:** 1949. **Operating Hours**: Continuous. **ADI**: Omaha, NE. **Wattage**: 1,000,000 ERP Horizo. **Ad Rates:** $35-1000 per unit. **URL:** http://www.kmtv.com/.

KNAR-FM - See San Angelo, TX
KNKL-FM - See Ogden, UT

20689 ■ KNKN-FM - 106.9
PO Box 2098
Omaha, NE 68103-2098
Phone: (916)251-1600
Format: Hispanic. **Owner:** Metropolitan Radio Group Inc., 2010 S Stewart Ave., Springfield, MO 65804, Ph: (417)862-0852, Fax: (417)862-9079, Free: 800-481-7677. **Founded:** 1994. **Formerly**: KIKN-FM. **Operating Hours**: Continuous. **ADI**: Colorado Springs-Pueblo, CO. **Key Personnel:** Mark Acker, President. **Wattage**: 27,500. **Ad Rates:** $10-20 for 30 seconds. Combined advertising rates available with KRMX-AM. **URL:** http://www.klove.com.

20690 ■ KOCY-FM - 105.3
PO Box 2098
Omaha, NE 68102
Phone: (800)525-5683
Format: Adult Contemporary. **Networks:** Ambassador Inspirational Radio. **Owner:** Mindy R. Worlow, at above address. **Founded:** Jan. 01, 1996. **Formerly**: KHOX-FM. **Operating Hours**: Continuous. **Wattage**: 25,000. **Ad Rates:** $10 for 30 seconds; $15 for 60 seconds.

URL: http://www.klove.com/contact.

20691 ■ KOIL-AM - 1020
5011 Capitol Ave.
Omaha, NE 68132-2921
Phone: (402)342-2000
Founded: 1925. **Operating Hours:** Continuous. **ADI:** Omaha, NE. **Wattage:** 50,000. **Ad Rates:** Noncommercial. **URL:** http://www.newstalk1290koil.com.

KOKF-FM - See Oklahoma City, OK

20692 ■ KOOO-FM - 101.9
Omaha, NE 68132
Wattage: 96,000. **Ad Rates:** Noncommercial; Accepts classified advertising.

20693 ■ KOTK-AM - 1420
11717 Burt St., Ste. 202
Omaha, NE 68154
Format: Hispanic. **Owner:** Salem Media Group Inc., 4880 Santa Rosa Rd., Camarillo, CA 93012, Ph: (805)987-0400, Fax: (805)384-4520. **Formerly:** KHLP-AM. **URL:** http://www.1420kotk.com.

20694 ■ KOZN-AM - 1620
5011 Capitol Ave.
Omaha, NE 68132
Phone: (402)342-2000
Fax: (402)342-6146
Email: usc@1620thezone.com
Format: Sports. **Networks:** ESPN Radio. **Owner:** NRG Media, 2875 Mount Vernon Rd. SE, Cedar Rapids, IA 52403, Ph: (319)862-0300, Fax: (319)286-9383. **Operating Hours:** Continuous. **ADI:** Omaha, NE. **Wattage:** 10,000. **Ad Rates:** Noncommercial. **URL:** http://www.1620thezone.com.

20695 ■ KPTM-TV - 42
4625 Farnam St.
Omaha, NE 68132
Phone: (402)558-4200
Fax: (402)554-4290
Email: contact42@kptm.com
Format: Commercial TV. **Networks:** Fox. **Founded:** 1986. **Operating Hours:** Continuous Mon.-Sat.; 6 a.m.-1 a.m. Sun. **ADI:** Omaha, NE. **Key Personnel:** John King, Contact; John King, Contact. **Wattage:** 5,000,000. **Ad Rates:** Advertising accepted; rates available upon request. **URL:** http://www.fox42kptm.com.

20696 ■ KQBW-FM - 96.1
5010 Underwood Ave.
Omaha, NE 68132
Phone: (918)664-4581
Format: Classic Rock; Album-Oriented Rock (AOR). **Owner:** Clear Channel Communication, Inc., 200 E Basse Rd., San Antonio, TX 78209, Ph: (210)822-2828, Fax: (210)822-2828. **Operating Hours:** Continuous. **Key Personnel:** Meg Delone, Sales Mgr., megdelone@clearchannel.com; Jean James, Gen. Sales Mgr., jeanstjames@clearchannel.com; Michelle Matthews, Operations Mgr., Music Dir., Program Mgr., michelle@961thebrew.com; Greg Gade, Chief Engineer, greggade@clearchannel.com; Tom Stanton, News Dir., tomstanton@clearchannel.com; Heath Hedstrom, Promotions Dir., heathhedstrom@clearchannel.com. **Ad Rates:** Advertising accepted; rates available upon request. **URL:** http://961kissonline.iheart.com.

20697 ■ KQCH-FM - 94.1
5030 N 72nd St.
Omaha, NE 68134
Phone: (402)938-9400
Format: Top 40. **Key Personnel:** Stephanie Chandler, Promotions Mgr., schandler@journalbroadcastgroup.com; Kris Christiansen, Program Mgr., kchristiansen@journalbroadcastgroup.com; Mark Todd, Program Mgr., mtodd@journalbroadcastgroup.com. **Ad Rates:** Noncommercial. **URL:** http://www.channel941.com.

20698 ■ KQKQ-FM - 98.5
5011 Capitol Ave.
Omaha, NE 68132
Phone: (402)342-2000
Format: Adult Contemporary. **Networks:** Independent. **Owner:** Waitt Radio, Inc., at above address. **Founded:** 1974. **Operating Hours:** Continuous; 100% local. **Wattage:** 100,000. **Ad Rates:** for 30 seconds; for 60 seconds. **URL:** http://www.q985fm.com.

KQRI-FM - See Albuquerque, NM

KRKL-FM - See Tri-Cities, WA

20699 ■ KSJY-FM - 90.9
PO Box 2098
Omaha, NE 68103-2098
Phone: (916)251-1600
Format: Adult Contemporary; Gospel. **Founded:** 1988. **Operating Hours:** Continuous; 100% Local. **ADI:** Lafayette, LA. **Key Personnel:** Wendy Christian, Gen. Mgr. **Wattage:** 6,000. **Ad Rates:** Noncommercial. **URL:** http://www.klove.com.

20700 ■ KSRZ-FM - 104.5
10714 Mockingbird Dr.
Omaha, NE 68127
Phone: (402)951-1045
Free: 888-633-5452
Format: Adult Contemporary. **Simulcasts:** KBBX-FM. **Founded:** 1972. **Operating Hours:** Continuous. **ADI:** Omaha, NE. **Key Personnel:** Kurt Owens, Dir. of Programs, kurt@104star.com; Kris Christiansen, Sales Mgr., kchristiansen@journalbroadcastgroup.com. **Wattage:** 100,000. **Ad Rates:** $65 for 60 seconds. Combined advertising rates available with KBBX-AM; KEZO-FM; KKCD-FM; KQCH-FM; KOSR-AM; KOMJ-AM. **URL:** http://www.104star.com.

KVKL-FM - See Las Vegas, NV

KVLB-FM - See Bend, OR

KVLW-FM - See Waco, TX

20701 ■ KVNO-FM - 90.7
6001 Dodge St.
CB 200
Omaha, NE 68182-0315
Phone: (402)554-2358
Fax: (402)554-3541
Format: Classical. **Networks:** Public Radio International (PRI). **Owner:** University of Nebraska Board of Regents, 3835 Holdrege St., Lincoln, NE 68583, Ph: (402)472-3906. **Founded:** 1972. **Operating Hours:** Continuous; 99% local. **Key Personnel:** Ben Rasmussen, Music Dir., brasmussen@unomaha.edu. **Wattage:** 8,900. **Ad Rates:** Noncommercial; underwriting available. **URL:** http://www.nebraska.edu.

KVRA-FM - See Bend, OR

20702 ■ KVSS-FM - 88.9
13326 A St.
Omaha, NE 68144
Phone: (402)571-0200
Fax: (402)571-0833
Free: 855-571-0200
Email: kvss@kvss.com
Format: Religious. **Owner:** VSS Catholic Communications, 13326 A St., Omaha, NE 68144. **Founded:** 1999. **Key Personnel:** Jim Carroll, Gen. Mgr., jimc@kvss.com; Bruce McGregor, Dir. of Programs, bruce@kvss.com. **Ad Rates:** Noncommercial. **URL:** http://www.spiritcatholicradio.com.

KWBX-FM - See Salem, OR

20703 ■ KXKT-FM - 103.7
5010 Underwood Ave.
Omaha, NE 68132
Phone: (402)561-2000
Fax: (402)556-8937
Format: Country. **Networks:** AP. **Owner:** Clear Channel Communication, Inc., 200 E Basse Rd., San Antonio, TX 78209, Ph: (210)822-2828, Fax: (210)822-2828. **Founded:** 1966. **ADI:** Omaha, NE. **Wattage:** 100,000. **Ad Rates:** Noncommercial. **URL:** http://www.clearchannel.com.

KXRI-FM - See Amarillo, TX

20704 ■ KXSP-AM - 590
10714 Mockingbird Dr.
Omaha, NE 68127
Phone: (402)573-0590
Free: 877-244-0590
Format: Sports. **Owner:** Journal Broadcast Corp., 333 W State St., Milwaukee, WI 53203, Ph: (414)332-9611, Fax: (414)967-5400. **Key Personnel:** Kurt Owens, Prog. Dir. **URL:** http://www.bigsports590.com.

20705 ■ KXVO-TV - 15
4625 Farnam St.
Omaha, NE 68132
Phone: (402)554-1500
Fax: (402)554-4290
Email: contact15@kxvo.com
Format: Commercial TV. **Owner:** Pappas Telecasting of the Midlands, 4625 Farnam St., Omaha, NE 68132, Ph: (402)554-1500. **Founded:** Sept. 1992. **Operating Hours:** Continuous. **ADI:** Omaha, NE. **Key Personnel:** Patrick Kelly, Operations Mgr.; Kathi Blaha, Acct. Mgr., Personnel Mgr.; Mike Wallace, Production Mgr.; Jeff Miller, Gen. Mgr.; Shannon McIntosh, Traffic Mgr.; Vicki White, Sales Mgr.; Tim Moan, Sales Mgr. **URL:** http://www.cw15kxvo.com.

KYIX-FM - See Chico, CA

KYLU-FM - See Bakersfield, CA

20706 ■ KYNE-TV - 26
1800 N 33rd St.
Lincoln, NE 68503
Phone: (402)472-6141
Free: 888-638-7346
Format: Public TV. **Networks:** Public Broadcasting Service (PBS). **Owner:** Nebraska Educational Telecommunications, at above address. **Founded:** 1965. **Operating Hours:** Continuous. **ADI:** Omaha, NE. **Key Personnel:** Rod Bates, Gen. Mgr. **Wattage:** 520,000. **Ad Rates:** Noncommercial. **URL:** http://netnebraska.org.

KZKL-FM - See Wichita Falls, TX

KZLO-FM - See Tyler, TX

KZLV-FM - See San Antonio, TX

WBKL-FM - See Baton Rouge, LA

WCKU-FM - See Clarksburg, WV

WCVJ-FM - See Jefferson, OH

WDKL-FM - See Clarksburg, WV

WDKV-FM - See Fond du Lac, WI

WGCK-FM - See Coeburn, VA

WIKV-FM - See Plymouth, IN

WJLR-FM - See Seymour, IN

WJXN-FM - See Jackson, MS

WKVB-FM - See State College, PA

WKVC-FM - See Myrtle Beach, SC

WKVH-FM - See Tallahassee, FL

WKVJ-FM - See Plattsburgh, NY

WKVP-FM - See Cherry Hill, NJ

WKVU-FM - See Utica, NY

WKVW-FM - See Charleston, WV

WKVY-FM - See Somerset, KY

WKWR-FM - See Key West, FL

WKWV-FM - See Watertown, NY

WLAI-FM - See Wilmore, KY

WLKH-FM - See Somerset, PA

WLKJ-FM - See Johnstown, PA

WLKP-FM - See Parkersburg, WV

WLKU-FM - See Quad Cities, IL

WLKV-FM - See Ripley, WV

WLRK-FM - See Greenville, MS

20707 ■ WLTK-FM - 103.3
PO Box 2098
Omaha, NE 68103
Free: 800-525-5683
Format: Religious; Contemporary Christian. **Simulcasts:** WBTX-AM. **Networks:** USA Radio. **Owner:** Massanutten Broadcasting Company Inc., at above address. **Founded:** 1989. **Operating Hours:** 24/7. **ADI:** Harrisonburg, VA. **Wattage:** 2,200. **Ad Rates:** $15-22 for 30 seconds; $18-25 for 60 seconds. Combined advertising rates available with WBTX-AM, WNLR-AM. **URL:** http://www.klove.com.

Circulation: ★ = AAM; △ or • = BPA; ♦ = CAC; ❑ = VAC; ⊕ = PO Statement; ‡ = Publisher's Report; Boldface figures = sworn; Light figures = estimated.

WLVZ-FM - See Hattiesburg, MS

WLXP-FM - See Savannah, GA

WNKL-FM - See Toledo, OH

WNKV-FM - See New Orleans, LA

WOAR-FM - See South Vienna, OH

WOKL-FM - See Dayton, OH

20708 ■ WOWT-TV - 6
3501 Farnam St.
Omaha, NE 68131
Phone: (402)346-6666
Email: sixonline@wowt.com
Format: Commercial TV. **Networks:** NBC. **Owner:** Gray Television Inc., 4370 Peachtree Rd. NE, No. 400, Atlanta, GA 30319-3054, Ph: (404)266-8333. **Key Personnel:** John Clark, News Dir. **Ad Rates:** Advertising accepted; rates available upon request. **URL:** http://www.wowt.com.

WQKV-FM - See Rochester, IN

WRCK-FM - See Utica, NY

WTKL-FM - See New Bedford, MA

WVDA-FM - See Valdosta, GA

WWLT-FM - See London, KY

WXKY-FM - See Danville, KY

WYKV-FM - See Albany, NY

20709 ■ WYLV-FM - 89.1
PO Box 2118
Omaha, NE 68103-2118
Free: 888-937-2471
Email: info@air1.com
Format: Contemporary Christian. **Key Personnel:** Mike Novak, CEO, President. **Ad Rates:** Noncommercial. **URL:** http://www.air1.com.

20710 ■ WZKT-FM - 98.3
PO Box 2098
Omaha, NE 68103-2098
Phone: (918)664-4581
Email: z98@dp.net
Format: Top 40. **Networks:** ABC. **Owner:** Farr Communications, at above address. **Founded:** 1967. **Formerly:** WESA-FM. **Operating Hours:** Continuous; 10% network, 90% local. **ADI:** Pittsburgh, PA. **Key Personnel:** Larry Resick, Operations Mgr., News Dir.; Scott Tavares, Music Dir. **Wattage:** 6,000. **Ad Rates:** $5-33 per unit.

WZRI-FM - See Fayetteville, NC

ORD

Valley Co. Valley Co. (C). 55 m NW of Grand Island. Alfalfa mill. Popcorn marketing center. Stock, dairy, poultry, grain farms.

20711 ■ KNLV-AM - 1060
205 S 16th St.
Ord, NE 68862
Format: Oldies. **Simulcasts:** Oldies. **Networks:** ABC. **Owner:** KNLV Inc., PO Box 98, Ericson, NE 68637. **Founded:** 1965. **Operating Hours:** Continuous. **Key Personnel:** Mark Jensen, Contact. **Wattage:** 1,000. **Ad Rates:** $4.95 for 15 seconds; $7.10 for 30 seconds; $10 for 60 seconds. **URL:** http://www.knlvradio.com.

20712 ■ KNLV-FM - 103.9
205 S 16th St.
Ord, NE 68862
Format: Country. **Simulcasts:** KNLV-AM. **Networks:** ABC. **Owner:** KNLV Radio, 205 S 16th St., Ord, NE 68862, Ph: (308)728-3263. **Founded:** 1981. **Operating Hours:** Continuous. **Key Personnel:** Mark Jensen, Contact. **Wattage:** 30,000. **Ad Rates:** $4.95 for 15 seconds; $7.10 for 30 seconds; $9.70 for 60 seconds. **URL:** http://www.knlvradio.com.

20713 ■ KNLV Radio - 103.9
205 S 16th St.
Ord, NE 68862
Phone: (308)728-3263
Format: Oldies; Eighties; Country; Contemporary Christian. **Operating Hours:** Continuous. **Wattage:** 30,000 ERP. **URL:** http://www.knlvradio.com.

OSHKOSH

Garden Co. Garden Co. (W). 85 m NW of North Platte. Pressure gauges, grain, golf cart tops. Dairy farms. Stock, grain, wheat, corn, turkeys, honey.

20714 ■ Garden County News
Oshkosh
PO Box 290
Oshkosh, NE 69154
Phone: (308)772-3555
Fax: (308)772-4475
Publisher's E-mail: gcnews@embarqmail.com
Community newspaper. **Freq:** Weekly (Thurs.). **Print Method:** Offset. Uses mats. **Cols./Page:** 6. **Col. Width:** 25 nonpareils. **Col. Depth:** 294 agate lines. **Key Personnel:** Buddy Paulsen, Owner, Publisher; Kelly Rece, Owner, Publisher. **Subscription Rates:** $30 Individuals in state; $35 Out of state. **URL:** http://www.gardencountynews.com. **Ad Rates:** GLR $.14; BW $304.92; PCI $2.72. **Remarks:** Accepts advertising. **Circ:** 1884.

PAPILLION

Sarpy Co. Sarpy Co. (E). 10 m S. of Omaha. Suburban residential.

20715 ■ The Ralston Recorder
Times Publishing
1413 Washington St.
Papillion, NE 68046
Publication E-mail: news@ralstonrecorder.com
Community newspaper. **Freq:** Weekly (Wed.). **Print Method:** Offset. **Trim Size:** 13 3/4 x 22 1/2. **Cols./Page:** 6. **Col. Width:** 2 1/16 inches. **Col. Depth:** 21 1/2 inches. **Key Personnel:** Shon Barenklau, Publisher; Melissa Vanek, Manager, Circulation; Ron Petak, Executive Editor. **Subscription Rates:** $4.54 By mail EZ Pay out of county; $29.75 By mail 26 weeks out of county; $54 By mail 52 weeks out of county; $99 By mail 104 weeks out of county. **URL:** http://www.omaha.com/sarpy/ralston. **Ad Rates:** BW $516; 4C $783; SAU $4. **Remarks:** Accepts advertising. **Circ:** 1850.

PAWNEE CITY

Pawnee Co. Pawnee Co. (EC). 35 m ESE of Beatrice. Ships livestock.

20716 ■ The Pawnee Republican
The Pawnee Republican
PO Box 111
Pawnee City, NE 68420
Phone: (402)852-2575
Community newspaper. **Freq:** Weekly. **Print Method:** Web press. **Cols./Page:** 5. **Col. Width:** 12 picas. **Col. Depth:** 15 inches. **Key Personnel:** Beverly J. Puhalla, Owner, Publisher; Ronald J. Puhalla, Owner, Publisher. **Subscription Rates:** $35 Individuals in Pawnee County and surrounding counties, print and e-Edition; $36 Individuals in Nebraska, print and e-Edition; $44 Out of state print and e-Edition; $30 Individuals e-Edition. **URL:** http://pawneerepublican.com. **Ad Rates:** SAU $6.70; PCI $6.95. **Remarks:** Color advertising not accepted. **Circ:** Paid 1834, Free 52.

PLAINVIEW

Pierce Co. Pierce Co. (NE). 32 m NW of Norfolk. Stock, grain, poultry farms. Wheat, corn.

20717 ■ Plainview News
Stump Publishing Co.
PO Box 9
Plainview, NE 68769
Phone: (402)582-4921
Fax: (402)582-4922
Community newspaper. **Freq:** Weekly (Tues.). **Print Method:** Offset. **Cols./Page:** 6. **Col. Width:** 28 nonpareils. **Col. Depth:** 301 agate lines. **Key Personnel:** Lee Warneke, Editor, Consultant; Brook D. Curtiss, Editor, General Manager, Publisher. **Subscription Rates:** $30 Individuals Pierce county; $37 Out of area inside Nebraska; $45 Out of state. **URL:** http://www.theplainviewnews.com/. **Ad Rates:** GLR $.23. **Remarks:** Accepts advertising. **Circ:** 3380.

PONCA

Dixon Co. Dixon Co. (NE). 22 m NW of Sioux City, Iowa. Stock, grain farms. Corn.

20718 ■ Nebraska Journal-Leader
Nebraska Journal Leader
110 East St.
Ponca, NE 68770-0545
Phone: (402)755-2203
Newspaper. **Freq:** Weekly (Thurs.). **Print Method:** Offset. **Cols./Page:** 6. **Col. Width:** 20 nonpareils. **Col. Depth:** 217 agate lines. **Key Personnel:** Richard D. Volkman, Editor. **Subscription Rates:** $26.50 Individuals mail delivery; $41 Other countries mail delivery. **URL:** http://www.nebnjl.com. **Ad Rates:** GLR $.135. **Remarks:** Accepts advertising. **Circ:** 1300.

SACRAMENTO

20719 ■ KARA-FM - 99.1
PO Box 2118
Omaha, NE 68103-2118
Free: 888-937-2471
Format: Contemporary Christian. **Networks:** Independent. **Owner:** Educational Media Foundation, 5700 W Oaks Blvd., CA 95765, Free: 800-800434-8400. **Founded:** 1964. **Operating Hours:** Continuous. **Key Personnel:** Mike Novak, President, CEO. **Wattage:** 550. **URL:** http://www.air1.com.

SAINT COLUMBANS

Sarpy Co. (E). 10 m S of Omaha.

20720 ■ Columban Mission
Missionary Society of St. Columban
PO Box 10
Saint Columbans, NE 68056
Phone: (402)291-1920
Fax: (402)291-4984
Free: 877-299-1920
Publisher's E-mail: mission@columban.org
Freq: 8/year. **Print Method:** Offset. **Trim Size:** A4. **Cols./Page:** 3 and 2. **Col. Width:** 26 and 42 nonpareils. **Col. Depth:** 140 agate lines. **Key Personnel:** Señor Jeanne Jansen, Editor; Kate Kenny, Managing Editor; Fr. Cyril Lovett, Editor; Robert Fraass, Managing Editor; Fr. Arturo Aguilar, Director, Publisher. **ISSN:** 0095--4438 (print). **Subscription Rates:** $10 Individuals promoter; €15 By mail. **URL:** http://columban.org/columban-mission-magazine; http://columban.org/category/magazine. **Formerly:** The Far East. **Remarks:** Advertising not accepted. **Circ:** Controlled ‡120000.

SCOTTSBLUFF

Scotts Bluff Co. Scotts Bluff Co. (W). 160 m NW of North Platte. Tourist. Hunting and fishing. Trade Center. Manufactures mobile homes, farm equipment, irrigation sprinkler systems, electronic equipment; sugar refining; meat packing plant. Agriculture. Grain, beets, corn, beans, potatoes.

20721 ■ Business Farmer-Stockman
Business Farmer Inc.
22 W 17th St.
Scottsbluff, NE 69361
Phone: (308)635-3110
Fax: (308)635-7435
Agricultural newspaper. **Freq:** Weekly (Fri.). **Print Method:** Offset. **Cols./Page:** 6. **Col. Width:** 9 picas. **Key Personnel:** Jeff Robertson, Publisher, phone: (307)532-2184; Andrew Cummins, Editor, phone: (308)635-3110. **Subscription Rates:** $34.95 Individuals auto pay; $37.95 Individuals manual pay; $44.95 Out of area auto pay; $48.95 Out of area manual pay. **URL:** http://www.thebusinessfarmer.com. **Ad Rates:** BW $409.50; 4C $534.50; PCI $5.25. **Remarks:** Accepts advertising. **Circ:** (Not Reported).

20722 ■ Star-Herald: Pride in the Panhandle
Star-Herald
1405 Broadway
Scottsbluff, NE 69361
Phone: (308)632-9000
Fax: (308)632-9001
Free: 800-846-6102
Publisher's E-mail: news@starherald.com
General newspaper. **Freq:** Daily (morn.) Tues.-Sun. **Print Method:** Offset. **Trim Size:** 11.625 x 21 3/4. **Cols./Page:** 6. **Col. Width:** 11 picas. **Col. Depth:** 301 agate lines. **Key Personnel:** Jim Holland, Publisher; Steve Frederick, Editor; Doug Southard, Director, Advertising; Jim Mortimore, Manager, Production; Roger Tollefson, Manager, Circulation. **USPS:** 485-960. **Subscription Rates:** $16 Individuals within the Star-Herald region, 1

month; $32 Individuals within the Star-Herald region, 2 months; $45 Individuals within the Star-Herald region, 3 months; $84 Individuals within the Star-Herald region, 6 months; $117 Individuals within the Star-Herald region, 9 months; $149 Individuals within the Star-Herald region, 1 year; $18 Individuals outside Star-Herald region, 1 month; $35.50 Individuals outside Star-Herald region, 2 months; $51.50 Individuals outside Star-Herald region, 3 months; $98.50 Individuals outside Star-Herald region, 6 months; $144.00 Individuals outside Star-Herald region, 9 months; $168.50 Individuals outside Star-Herald region, 1 year. **URL:** http://www.starherald.com. **Ad Rates:** BW $1,976; 4C $2,286; PCI $14.15. **Remarks:** Accepts advertising. **Circ:** 16000.

20723 ■ Charter Communications, Inc.
1601 E 27th St.
Scottsbluff, NE 69361
Phone: (308)635-3163
Fax: (308)635-1721
Owner: Charter Communications Inc., 400 Atlantic St., Stamford, CT 06901, Ph: (203)905-7801. **Founded:** 1968. **Cities Served:** Bayard, Bridgeport, Gering, Kimball, Melbeta, Minatare, Mitchell, Mitchell, Morrill, Scottsbluff, Terrytown, Nebraska: subscribing households 12,000; 180 channels; 7 community access channels. **URL:** http://www.charter.com.

20724 ■ KCMI-FM - 97.1
209 E 15th St.
Scottsbluff, NE 69361
Phone: (308)632-5264
Email: contact@kcmifm.com
Format: Contemporary Christian. **Owner:** Christian Media Inc., 209 E 15th St., Scottsbluff, NE 69361-3176. **Operating Hours**: Continuous. **ADI**: Cheyenne, WY-Scottsbluff, NE (Sterling, CO). **Key Personnel:** Russ Garrett, Contact. **Wattage**: 100,000 ERP. **Ad Rates:** Advertising accepted; rates available upon request. **URL:** http://www.kcmifm.org.

20725 ■ KDUH-TV - 4
1523 1st Ave.
Scottsbluff, NE 69361
Phone: (308)632-3071
Fax: (308)632-3596
Format: Commercial TV. **Networks:** ABC. **Owner:** Duhamel Broadcasting, at above address. **Founded:** 1956. **Operating Hours**: Continuous. **ADI**: Cheyenne, WY-Scottsbluff, NE (Sterling, CO). **Key Personnel:** John Petersen, Dept. Mgr.; Doug Loos, Dir. of Production; Lia Green, News Dir. **Wattage:** 100,000. **Ad Rates:** $35-250 for 30 seconds; $70-500 for 60 seconds. **URL:** http://www.kotatv.com/news/nebraska-news.

20726 ■ KLJV-FM - 88.3
PO Box 779002
Rocklin, CA 95677-9972
Fax: (916)251-1901
Free: 800-525-5683
Format: Contemporary Christian. **Owner:** Educational Media Foundation, PO Box 2098, Omaha, NE 68103-2098, Free: 800-434-8400. **ADI**: Cheyenne, WY-Scottsbluff, NE (Sterling, CO). **Key Personnel:** Mike Novak, President, CEO; Alan Mason, COO. **Wattage**: 390. **URL:** http://www.klove.com.

20727 ■ KMOR-FM - 93.3
2002 Char Ave.
Scottsbluff, NE 69361
Phone: (308)632-5667
Fax: (308)635-1905
Format: Classic Rock. **Networks:** AP. **Owner:** Tracy Broadcasting Corp., 731 E 38Th St., Scottsbluff, NE 69361. **Founded:** 1978. **Operating Hours**: Continuous; 5% network, 95% local. **Wattage**: 100,000. **Ad Rates:** Noncommercial. Combined advertising rates available with KOAQ-AM, KOLT-AM, KOLT-FM, KBFZ-FM.

20728 ■ KNEB-AM - 960
PO Box 239
Scottsbluff, NE 69363
Phone: (308)632-7121
Fax: (308)635-1079
Format: News; Talk; Information. **Networks:** ABC; Mutual Broadcasting System. **Founded:** 1947. **Operating Hours:** 5 a.m.-1 a.m. Mon.-Sat.; 5 a.m.-midnight Sun. **ADI**: Cheyenne, WY-Scottsbluff, NE (Sterling, CO). **Key Personnel:** Craig Larson, Station Mgr., clarson@kneb.com. **Wattage**: 5,000 Day; 500 Night. **Ad Rates:** $11.70-50 for 30 seconds; $17.50-75 for 60 seconds; $70 per unit. $17.50-$75 for 30 seconds; $26.50-$85 for 60 seconds. Combined advertising rates available with KNEB-FM. **URL:** http://www.kneb.com.

20729 ■ KNEB-FM - 94.1
1928 E Portal Pl.
Scottsbluff, NE 69361
Phone: (308)632-7121
Fax: (308)635-1079
Email: feedback@kneb.com
Format: Contemporary Country; Agricultural. **Networks:** ABC. **Owner:** Nebraska Rural Radio Association, 1007 Plum Creek Pky., Lexington, NE 68850. **Founded:** 1961. **Operating Hours:** 5 a.m.-1 a.m.; 10% network, 90% local. **ADI**: Cheyenne, WY-Scottsbluff, NE (Sterling, CO). **Key Personnel:** Craig Larson, Station Mgr., clarson@kneb.com; Kendra Feather, Sales Mgr., kfeather@kneb.com; Kevin Mooney, News Dir., kmooney@kneb.com. **Wattage:** 100,000. **Ad Rates:** $11.70-50 for 30 seconds; $17.50-75 for 60 seconds. Combined advertising rates available with KNEB-AM: $17.50-$75 for 30 seconds; $26.50-$85 for 60 seconds. **URL:** http://www.kneb.com.

20730 ■ KOAQ-AM - 690
2002 Char Ave.
Scottsbluff, NE 69361
Phone: (308)632-5667
Fax: (308)635-1905
Format: Oldies. **Networks:** AP. **Owner:** Hometown Family Radio, 3205 W N Front St., Grand Island, NE 68803-4024. **Founded:** 1961. **Operating Hours**: Continuous; 10% network, 90% local. **Wattage**: 1,000 Day; 065 Night. **Ad Rates:** Advertising accepted; rates available upon request. Combined advertising rates available with KMOR-FM, KOLT-AM, KOLT-FM, KBFZ-FM.

20731 ■ KOLT-AM - 1320
PO Box 1263
Scottsbluff, NE 69363
Phone: (308)632-5667
Format: News; Talk; Sports. **Networks:** ESPN Radio. **Founded:** 1930. **Operating Hours**: Continuous. **Wattage:** 5,000 Day; 1,000 Night. **Ad Rates:** Advertising accepted; rates available upon request. Combined advertising rates available with KOLT-FM, KBFZ-FM, KOAQ-AM, KMOR-FM.

20732 ■ KOZY-FM - 101.3
2002 Char Ave.
Scottsbluff, NE 69361
Phone: (308)632-5667
Fax: (308)635-1905
Format: Adult Contemporary. **Founded:** 1996. **Operating Hours**: Continuous; 10% network, 90% local. **Wattage:** 7,000. **Ad Rates:** $10 for 30 seconds; $15 for 60 seconds. Combined advertising rates available with KNEA-AM, KJBR-FM, KKEY-FM.

20733 ■ K212EJ-FM - 90.3
PO Box 391
Twin Falls, ID 83303
Fax: (208)736-1958
Free: 800-357-4226
Format: Religious; Contemporary Christian. **Owner:** CSN International, PO Box 391, Twin Falls, ID 83303, Ph: (208)736-1958, Fax: (208)736-1958, Free: 800-357-4226. **Key Personnel:** Mike Kestler, Contact; Don Mills, Music Dir., Prog. Dir. **URL:** http://www.csnradio.com.

SEWARD

Seward Co. Seward Co. (SE). 25 m W of Lincoln. Concordia Teachers College. Manufactures electrical transmission equipment, fiber glass plant. Fertilizers, feed, animal products, china, cement. Agriculture.

20734 ■ The Connection
The Connection
129 S Sixth St.
Seward, NE 68434
Phone: (402)643-3676
Community newspaper. **Founded:** 1992. **Freq:** Weekly (Thurs.). **Print Method:** Photo offset. **Cols./Page:** 6. **Col. Width:** 26 12.2 nonpareils picas. **Col. Depth:** 294 21.25 agate lines inches. **Key Personnel:** Marcia Goff, General Manager; Mark Rhoades, Publisher; Lynn Dance, Manager, Advertising; Joe Arena, Editor; William P. Dole, Publisher; Don Morse, Manager, Advertising; Robert G. Edgar, Publisher, phone: (313)343-5588. **Subscription Rates:** $18 local annual; Free in county; $19 Out of area. **Mailing address:** PO Box 449, Seward, NE 68434. **Ad Rates:** GLR $8.55; BW $1,077.30; 4C $1,477.30; SAU $12.50; BW $873.38; 4C $1,123.88; PCI $9.80. **Remarks:** Accepts advertising. **Circ:** Combined 5000, Free ‡32000.

20735 ■ Seward County Independent
Seward County Independent
129 S Sixth St.
Seward, NE 68434
Phone: (402)643-3676
Fax: (402)643-6774
Publisher's E-mail: scinews@sewardindependent.com
Community newspaper. **Freq:** Monthly. **Print Method:** Offset. Uses mats. **Cols./Page:** 6. **Col. Width:** 12.2 picas. **Col. Depth:** 21 1/4 inches. **Key Personnel:** Kevin L. Zadina, Publisher; Jill Martin, Editor. **Subscription Rates:** $40 Individuals in Seward County; $30 Individuals 6 months in Seward County; $42 Individuals in Lancaster, York, Saline, Butler, and Saunders; $32 Elsewhere 6 months; $57 Out of state; $38 Out of state 6 months; $81 Out of state. **URL:** http://www.sewardindependent.com. **Mailing address:** PO Box 449, Seward, NE 68434. **Ad Rates:** 4C $1,123.38; PCI $6.85. **Remarks:** Accepts advertising. **Circ:** Free 107.

SHELTON

Buffalo Co. Buffalo Co. (SC). 23 m SW of Grand Island. Ships potatoes, grain, livestock, sugar beets. Diversified farming. Alfalfa, corn, wheat.

20736 ■ The Shelton Clipper
Clipper Publishing Inc.
113 C St.
Shelton, NE 68876
Phone: (308)647-5158
Fax: (308)647-6953
Publisher's E-mail: info@clipperpubco.com
Local newspaper. **Founded:** 1884. **Freq:** Weekly (Wed.). **Print Method:** Offset. **Trim Size:** 13 3/4 x 22. **Cols./Page:** 6. **Col. Width:** 12.5 picas. **Col. Depth:** 20.5 inches. **USPS:** 492-780. **Subscription Rates:** $30 Individuals in Buffalo, Hall, Adams & Kearney; $37 Out of area. **URL:** http://www.clipperpubco.com/index.php?option=com_content&view=article&id=9. **Formerly**: Clipper. **Mailing address:** PO Box 640, Shelton, NE 68876. **Ad Rates:** BW $275.91; PCI $3.50. **Remarks:** Accepts advertising. **Circ:** Paid ‡1006, Free ‡10.

20737 ■ The Wood River Sunbeam
Clipper Publishing Inc.
113 C St.
Shelton, NE 68876
Phone: (308)647-5158
Fax: (308)647-6953
Publisher's E-mail: info@clipperpubco.com
Newspaper with a Republican orientation. **Freq:** Weekly (Wed.). **Print Method:** Offset. **Trim Size:** 10 1/2 x 12 1/2. **Cols./Page:** 5. **Col. Width:** 11 1/2 picas. **Col. Depth:** 12 inches. **Key Personnel:** Steve Glenn, Owner, Publisher. **USPS:** 690-240. **Subscription Rates:** $35 Individuals Hall, Howard, Adams and Buffalo Counties; $42 Out of country. **URL:** http://www.clipperpubco.com/index.php?option=com_content&view=article&id=10. **Mailing address:** PO Box 640, Shelton, NE 68876. **Ad Rates:** GLR $4; BW $378; 4C $347.50; SAU $3.30; PCI $7.75. **Remarks:** alcoholic beverages and tobacco products. **Circ:** Paid ‡495.

SIDNEY

Cheyenne Co. Cheyenne Co. (W). 120 m W of North Platte. Manufactures farm machinery, heavy equipment, wire and cable. Hops and food processing; ethanol production. Stock, grain farms. Wheat, sugar beets, corn, sunflowers, milo, millet, potatoes.

20738 ■ Sidney Sun Telegraph
Robert D. Van Vleet, Sr.
817 12th Ave.
Sidney, NE 69162
Phone: (308)254-2818
Fax: (308)254-3925
Publisher's E-mail: ads@suntelegraph.com
Community newspaper. **Founded:** Sept. 1997. **Freq:** Daily Tues. through Sat. **Print Method:** Web offset.

Circulation: ★ = AAM; △ or • = BPA; ♦ = CAC; ❑ = VAC; ⊕ = PO Statement; ‡ = Publisher's Report; Boldface figures = sworn; Light figures = estimated.

Cols./Page: 6. **Col. Width:** 2 picas. **Col. Depth:** 21 inches. **Key Personnel:** Sue Mizell, Publisher; Kim Bruns, Manager, Circulation. **Subscription Rates:** $108 Individuals; $128 Out of country; $97 for seniors; $115.75 Out of country for seniors. **URL:** http://www.suntelegraph.com. **Formed by the merger of:** Sidney Daily Sun; Sidney Telegraph. **Mailing address:** PO Box 193, Sidney, NE 69162-0193. **Ad Rates:** GLR $1; PCI $7.10. **Remarks:** 1. **Circ:** Paid ‡2518.

20739 ■ KSID-AM - 1340
2306 Legion Park Rd.
Sidney, NE 69162
Phone: (308)254-5803
Fax: (308)254-5901
Free: 800-322-5743
Format: Contemporary Country; News; Agricultural; Sports. **Networks:** ABC; Brownfield. **Founded:** 1952. **Operating Hours:** Continuous. **Key Personnel:** Elizabeth Young, President, ibsyoung@hamilton.net; Susan Ernest, Gen. Sales Mgr., Gen. Mgr. **Wattage:** 1,000. **URL:** http://www.ksidradio.com/pages/index.cfm?id=1277.

SUPERIOR

Nuckolls Co. Nuckolls Co. (S). 90 m SW of Lincoln. Manufactures cement and cheese, products. Alfalfa dehydrating plant. Diversified farming. Grain, alfalfa, cattle.

20740 ■ Jewell County News: The Superior Express
Superior Publishing Company Inc.
148 E Third St.
Superior, NE 68978-1705
Phone: (402)879-3291
Fax: (402)879-3463
Publisher's E-mail: tse@superiorne.com
Community newspaper. **Founded:** Jan. 1900. **Freq:** Weekly (Thurs.). **Print Method:** Offset. **Trim Size:** 16 x 22 3/4. **Cols./Page:** 7. **Col. Width:** 12 picas. **Col. Depth:** 294 agate lines. **Subscription Rates:** $24 Individuals in Nebraska; $25.50 Individuals in Kansas; $35 Elsewhere. **URL:** http://www.superiorne.com. **Also known as:** The Superior Express. **Mailing address:** PO Box 408, Superior, NE 68978-1705. **Ad Rates:** GLR $.18; BW $423; SAU $4. **Remarks:** Accepts advertising. **Circ:** (Not Reported).

20741 ■ Jewell County Record
Superior Publishing Company Inc.
148 E Third St.
Superior, NE 68978-1705
Phone: (402)879-3291
Fax: (402)879-3463
Publisher's E-mail: tse@superiorne.com
Community newspaper. **Freq:** Weekly (Wed.). **Print Method:** Offset. **Trim Size:** 16 x 22 3/4. **Cols./Page:** 7. **Col. Width:** 12 picas. **Col. Depth:** 21 inches. **Subscription Rates:** $27.50 Individuals Kansas. **URL:** http://superiorne.com/jcfrntpg.htm. **Formerly:** Jewell County Post. **Mailing address:** PO Box 408, Superior, NE 68978-1705. **Remarks:** Advertising accepted; rates available upon request. **Circ:** (Not Reported).

20742 ■ The Superior Express
The Superior Express
148 E 3rt St.
Superior, NE 68978
Phone: (402)879-3291
Free: 800-359-2120
Publisher's E-mail: tse@superiorne.com
Community newspaper. **Founded:** Jan. 1900. **Freq:** Weekly (Thurs.). **Print Method:** Offset. **Trim Size:** 16 x 22 3/4. **Key Personnel:** Bill Blauvelt, Editor. **ISSN:** 0740-0969 (print). **Subscription Rates:** $26 Individuals in Nebraska; $27.50 Individuals in Kansas; $37 Elsewhere; $70 Individuals in Nebraska, 3 years suscription; $75 Individuals in Kansas, 3 years suscription; $99 Elsewhere 3 years suscription. **URL:** http://superiorne.com/sefrntpg.htm; http://superiorne.com/. **Mailing address:** PO Box 408, Superior, NE 68978. **Ad Rates:** SAU $4; PCI $4. **Remarks:** Accepts advertising. **Circ:** (Not Reported).

20743 ■ KRFS-AM - 1600
RR 2, PO Box 149
Superior, NE 68978-9802
Phone: (402)879-4741
Fax: (402)879-4741
Format: Country; Adult Contemporary; News; Sports; Information. **Owner:** CK Broadcastin Inc., at above address, Ph: (402)879-3370. **Founded:** 1959. **Operating Hours:** Continuous. **Key Personnel:** Cory Kopsa, Gen. Mgr., Gen. Mgr., Owner. **Wattage:** 500 KW. **Ad Rates:** $4.50 for 30 seconds; $7.50 for 60 seconds. **URL:** http://krfsfm.com.

20744 ■ KRFS-FM - 103.9
RR 2, PO Box 149
Superior, NE 68978-9802
Phone: (402)879-4741
Fax: (402)879-4741
Format: Contemporary Country; News; Sports. **Networks:** ABC; Brownfield. **Owner:** Herb Hoeflicker, Rte. 1, Box 149, Superior, NE 68978, Ph: (402)879-3370. **Founded:** 1977. **Key Personnel:** Cory Kopsa, Contact; Cory Kopsa, Contact. **Wattage:** 12,000 ERP. **Ad Rates:** $4.50 for 30 seconds; $7.50 for 60 seconds. **URL:** http://krfsfm.com/.

SUTTON

Clay Co. Clay Co. (S). 30 m E of Hastings. Agriculture. Stock. Corn, soybeans, wheat, milo.

20745 ■ Clay County News
Clay County News
PO Box 405
Sutton, NE 68979-0405
Phone: (402)773-5576
Newspaper with a Republican orientation. **Freq:** Weekly (Wed.). **Print Method:** Offset. **Cols./Page:** 6. **Col. Width:** 26 nonpareils. **Col. Depth:** 294 agate lines. **USPS:** 116-700. **Subscription Rates:** $29 Individuals e-edition; $45 Individuals print & e-edition (Clay, Nuckolls, Adams and Fillmore); $49 Out of area print & e-edition; $29 Individuals print (Clay, Nuckolls, Adams and Fillmore); $33 Out of area print. **URL:** http://www.theclaycountynews.com. **Ad Rates:** GLR $.23; BW $544; SAU $5.06; PCI $8.25. **Remarks:** Accepts advertising. **Circ:** Paid 2,500.

VALENTINE

Cherry Co. Cherry Co. (NW). 120 m N of North Platte. Valentine National Waterfowl Refuge. State fish hatchery. Canoeing, fishing. Fur and metal processing. Cattle ranches. Stock, dairy, grain farms.

20746 ■ KVSH-AM - 940
126 W 3rd St.
Valentine, NE 69201
Phone: (402)376-2400
Format: Middle-of-the-Road (MOR). **Networks:** ABC. **Owner:** Heart City Radio Co., 126 W 3rd st., Valentine, NE 69201-1826, Ph: (800)658-4442. **Founded:** 1961. **Operating Hours:** 6 a.m.-10 p.m. **Wattage:** 5,000. **Ad Rates:** $4.85 for 10 seconds; $6.65 for 30 seconds; $7.90 for 60 seconds. **URL:** http://www.kvsh.com.

VERDIGRE

20747 ■ Verdigre Eagle
Verdigre Eagle
202 Main St.
Verdigre, NE 68783-5110
Phone: (402)668-2242
Fax: (402)668-2242
Community newspaper. **Freq:** Weekly (Thurs.). **Print Method:** Offset. **Cols./Page:** 7. **Col. Width:** 2 inches. **Col. Depth:** 21 inches. **Subscription Rates:** $30 Individuals In Knox, Antelope, Holt, and Boyd counties - 1 year; $37 Elsewhere in Nebraska - 1 year; $42 Out of state 1 year; $47 Individuals Hawaii, Alaska; $.75 Individuals single copy at Newsstand; $3.50 By mail single copy; $27 Students Entire College term only; $32 Students Entire College term only - out of state. **Ad Rates:** PCI $4.75, Black and white; PCI $5.25, color. **Remarks:** Accepts advertising. **Circ:** ‡1500.

WAHOO

Saunders Co. Saunders Co. (E). 35 m W of Omaha. Manufactures railroad parts, culverts, pre-cut houses, block cement, hog houses. Grain, dairy, poultry farms. Wheat, corn.

20748 ■ Wahoo Newspaper
Bh Media Group Inc.
564 N Broadway
Wahoo, NE 68066
Phone: (402)443-4162
Community newspaper. **Freq:** Weekly (Thurs.). **Print Method:** Offset. **Trim Size:** 13 3/4 x 22 3/4. **Cols./Page:** 6. **Col. Width:** 12.5 picas. **Col. Depth:** 21.5 inches. **Key Personnel:** Shon Barenklau, Publisher; Dave Shaw, Manager, Production; Lisa Brichacek, Editor. **USPS:** 664-460. **Subscription Rates:** $43 Individuals local; $51.50 Out of state. **URL:** http://www.wahoo-ashland-waverly.com. **Ad Rates:** BW $544.38; 4C $260; SAU $7.20. **Remarks:** Accepts advertising. **Circ:** (Not Reported).

WAUNETA

Chase Co. Chase Co. (SW). 100 m SW of North Platte. Diversified farming. Wheat, corn, barley, alfalfa, cattle.

20749 ■ Wauneta Breeze
Johnson Publications Inc.
324 N Tecumseh
Wauneta, NE 69045
Phone: (308)394-5398
Fax: (308)394-5931
Community newspaper. **Freq:** Weekly (Thurs.). **Print Method:** Offset. **Trim Size:** 14 3/4 x 22 3/4. **Cols./Page:** 6. **Col. Width:** 12.2 picas. **Col. Depth:** 21 1/2 inches. **Key Personnel:** Tina Kitt, Editor. **USPS:** 669-800. **URL:** http://www.waunetanebraska.com. **Mailing address:** PO Box 337, Wauneta, NE 69045. **Ad Rates:** GLR $15.50; BW $567.60; SAU $4.40. **Remarks:** Accepts advertising. **Circ:** (Not Reported).

WAUSA

Knox Co. Knox Co. (NE). 35 m N of Norfolk. Recreational. Hunting. Grain, stock, dairy, poultry farms. Corn, soybeans, oats, alfalfa, barley.

20750 ■ The Wausa Gazette
The Wausa Gazette
510 E Broadway St.
Wausa, NE 68786-8786
Phone: (402)586-2661
Publisher's E-mail: wausagazette@gpcom.net
Community newspaper. **Freq:** Weekly (Wed.). **Print Method:** Offset. **Cols./Page:** 6. **Col. Width:** 12 1/2 picas. **Col. Depth:** 301 agate lines. **USPS:** 215-160. **Subscription Rates:** $29.50 Individuals Pierce/Knox/Cedar; $37 Out of area; $49 Individuals zones 7 & 8; $31 Individuals online. **URL:** http://www.northeastnebraskanews.us. **Mailing address:** PO Box G, Wausa, NE 68786-8786. **Ad Rates:** GLR $.22; SAU $3.35. **Remarks:** Advertising accepted; rates available upon request. **Circ:** ‡1012.

WAVERLY

Lancaster Co. Lancaster Co. (NE). 12 m NE of Lincoln.

20751 ■ Grouse Partnership News
North American Grouse Partnership
10630 North 135th St.
Waverly, NE 68462-1256
Fax: (402)786-5547
Publisher's E-mail: TGP@GrousePartners.org
Magazine publishing articles on grouse conservation. **Freq:** Annual. **URL:** http://www.grousepartners.org/grouse-partners-news. **Remarks:** Advertising not accepted. **Circ:** (Not Reported).

WAYNE

Wayne Co. Wayne Co. (NE). 31 m NE of Norfolk. Wayne State College. Manufactures waterbed mattresses, modular homes, steel combination windows, semi-truck trailers. Livestock, grain, dairy farms.

20752 ■ Wayne Stater
Wayne State College
1111 Main St.
Wayne, NE 68787
Phone: (402)375-7000
Free: 866-WSC-CATS
Publication E-mail: wstater@wsc.edu
Provides a learning laboratory for journalism students as well as a local news source for the college and larger community. **Freq:** Weekly (Tues.) during the academic year. **Print Method:** Offset. **Cols./Page:** 5. **Col. Width:** 11 picas. **Col. Depth:** 301 agate lines. **Key Personnel:**

Richard Rhoden, Editor. **URL:** http://thewaynestater.com. **Ad Rates:** BW $330; PCI $3.40. **Remarks:** Accepts advertising. **Circ:** (Not Reported).

20753 ■ KCTY-FM - 104.9
PO Box 413
Wayne, NE 68787
Phone: (402)375-3700
Format: Adult Album Alternative; Adult Contemporary. **Owner:** Wayne Radio Works, LLC, at above address. **Founded:** July 1993. **Formerly**: KOTD-FM. **Operating Hours**: Continuous. **Key Personnel:** Dave Kelly, Gen. Mgr.; Alison Steele, Dir. of Programs. **Wattage**: 25,000. **Ad Rates:** $18-55 for 30 seconds; $18-55 for 60 seconds. **URL:** http://waynedailynews.com.

20754 ■ KTCH-AM - 1590
PO Box 413
Wayne, NE 68787
Phone: (402)375-3700
Fax: (402)375-5402
Email: ktch@ktch.com
Format: Country. **Simulcasts:** With KTCH-FM, 7A-1P (M-F). **Networks:** ABC; Brownfield. **Owner:** Wayne Radio Works, LLC, at above address. **Founded:** 1968. **Operating Hours**: Continuous; 60% network, 40% local. **ADI:** Sioux City, IA. **Key Personnel:** Dan Baddorf, Dir. of Programs, danbaddorf@ktch.com; Dave Kelly, Gen. Mgr., Owner. **Wattage**: 2,500 Daytime. **Ad Rates:** $7 for 30 seconds; $9 for 60 seconds. Combined advertising rates available with KNEN-FM, KTCH-FM, KZSR-FM. **URL:** http://www.ktch.com.

20755 ■ KTCH-FM - 104.9
PO Box 413
Wayne, NE 68787
Phone: (402)375-3700
Fax: (402)375-5402
Email: ktch@ktch.com
Simulcasts: KCTY. **Networks:** ABC; Mid-America Ag; Brownfield. **Owner:** Wayne Radio Works, LLC, at above address. **Founded:** 1975. **Key Personnel:** Dan Baddorf, Dir. of Programs. **Wattage**: 25,000. **Ad Rates:** Advertising accepted; rates available upon request. $9 for 30 seconds; $11 for 60 seconds. Combined advertising rates available with KTCH-AM, KNEN-FM, KZSR-FM. **URL:** http://www.ktch.com/.

20756 ■ KWSC-FM - 91.9
Wayne State College
1111 Main St.
Wayne, NE 68787
Phone: (402)375-7561
Format: Album-Oriented Rock (AOR). **Owner:** Wayne State College, 1111 Main St., Wayne, NE 68787, Ph: (402)375-7000, Free: 866-WSC-CATS. **Founded:** 1971. **Operating Hours**: Continuous; 100% local. **Key Personnel:** Mark Vrbicky, Gen. Mgr.; Riley VanLeeuwen, Dir. of Programs. **Wattage**: 350. **Ad Rates:** Noncommercial. **URL:** https://ecampus.wsc.edu.

WEST POINT

Cuming Co. Cuming Co. (NE). 60 m NW of Omaha. Meat processing plants. Diversified farming. Corn, wheat, oats, soybeans, alfalfa, cattle, hogs.

20757 ■ Elkhorn Valley Shopper
West Point News
134 E Grove St.
West Point, NE 68788
Phone: (402)372-2461
Fax: (402)372-3530
Free: 800-372-2461
Publisher's E-mail: editor@wpnews.com
Shopper. **Freq:** Weekly (Wed.). **Print Method:** Offset. **Trim Size:** 11 3/8 x 14. **Cols./Page:** 6. **Col. Width:** 19 nonpareils. **Col. Depth:** 189 agate lines. **Key Personnel:** Mike O'Brien, Editor; Tom Kelly, Publisher; Willis Mahannah, Editor. **Subscription Rates:** Free to area households. **URL:** http://www.wpnews.com. **Ad Rates:** BW $639; SAU $7.90. **Remarks:** Color advertising not accepted. **Circ:** Free ‡10115.

20758 ■ West Point News
West Point News
134 E Grove St.
West Point, NE 68788
Phone: (402)372-2461
Fax: (402)372-3530
Free: 800-372-2461
Publisher's E-mail: editor@wpnews.com
Community newspaper. **Freq:** Weekly (Thurs.). **Print Method:** Offset. **Trim Size:** 14 x 22 3/4. **Cols./Page:** 6. **Col. Width:** 24 nonpareils. **Col. Depth:** 301 agate lines. **Key Personnel:** Willis Mahannah, Editor; Tom Kelly, Publisher. **USPS:** 675-780. **Subscription Rates:** $43.50 Individuals; $58.50 Elsewhere in Nebraska; $73.50 Out of state. **URL:** http://www.wpnews.com/main.asp?SectionID=1. **Ad Rates:** BW $995; SAU $7.90; PCI $7.90. **Remarks:** Accepts advertising. **Circ:** (Not Reported).

20759 ■ KTIC-AM - 840
1011 N Lincoln St.
West Point, NE 68788
Phone: (402)372-5423
Fax: (402)372-5425
Format: Country; Agricultural. **Networks:** ABC. **Owner:** Nebraska Rural Radio Association, 1007 Plum Creek Pky., Lexington, NE 68850. **Founded:** 1985. **Formerly**: KWPN-AM. **Operating Hours**: Daily. **ADI**: Omaha, NE. **Key Personnel:** Dwight Lane, Station Mgr., dlane@kticradio.com; Judy Mauch, Sales Mgr., jmauch@kticradio.com; Chad Moyer, Farm Mgr., cmoyer@kticradio.com. **Wattage**: 5,000. **Ad Rates:** Noncommercial. Combined advertising rates available with KWPN-FM. **Mailing address:** PO Box 84, West Point, NE 68788. **URL:** http://kticradio.com.

20760 ■ KTIC-FM - 107.9
1011 N Lincoln St.
West Point, NE 68788-0084
Phone: (402)372-5423
Fax: (402)372-5425
Format: Country. **Networks:** ABC. **Owner:** Nebraska Rural Radio Association, 1007 Plum Creek Pky., Lexington, NE 68850. **Founded:** 1988. **Operating Hours**: Daily. **ADI**: Omaha, NE. **Key Personnel:** Dwight Lane, Contact, dlane@kticradio.com; Judy Mauch, Contact, jmauch@kticradio.com; Tom McMahon, Sports Dir., tmcmahon@kticradio.com. **Wattage**: 50,000. **Ad Rates:** $40 for 30 seconds. Combined advertising rates available with KTIL-AM, KTIC-AM. **Mailing address:** PO Box 840, West Point, NE 68788-0084. **URL:** http://kticradio.com.

WOOD RIVER

Hall Co. Hall Co. (C). 15 m SW of Grand Island. Residential.

20761 ■ The Wood River Sunbeam
The Wood River Sunbeam
PO Box 356
Wood River, NE 68883-0356
Phone: (308)647-5158
Fax: (308)647-6953
Free: 888-966-6870
Publisher's E-mail: info@clipperpubco.com
Newspaper with a Republican orientation. **Freq:** Weekly (Wed.). **Print Method:** Offset. **Trim Size:** 10 1/2 x 12 1/2. **Cols./Page:** 5. **Col. Width:** 11 1/2 picas. **Col. Depth:** 12 inches. **Key Personnel:** Steve Glenn, Owner, Publisher. **USPS:** 690-240. **Subscription Rates:** $35 Individuals Hall, Howard, Adams and Buffalo Counties; $42 Out of country. **URL:** http://www.clipperpubco.com/index.php?option=com_content&view=article&id=10. **Mailing address:** PO Box 640, Shelton, NE 68876. **Ad Rates:** GLR $4; BW $378; 4C $347.50; SAU $3.30; PCI $7.75. **Remarks:** alcoholic beverages and tobacco products. **Circ:** Paid ‡495.

WYMORE

20762 ■ Wymore Arbor State
Wymore Arbor State
204 S Seventh St.
Wymore, NE 68466
Phone: (402)645-3344
Fax: (402)645-3345
Publisher's E-mail: arborstate@diodecom.net
Community newspaper. **Freq:** Weekly (Wed.). **Subscription Rates:** $40 Individuals Gage county - 1 year; $45 Out of area 1 year; $20 By mail 1 year. **URL:** http://www.wymorearborstate.com. **Ad Rates:** PCI $5.50. **Remarks:** Accepts advertising. **Circ:** 1700.

YORK

York Co. York Co. (SEC). 50 m W of Lincoln. York College. Manufactures irrigation equipment, mobile homes, concrete products, electronics, aerospace components. Nursery; hatcheries. Agriculture. Corn, oats, alfalfa, milo, cattle, hogs.

20763 ■ York News-Times
York News-Times
327 Platte Ave.
York, NE 68467
Phone: (402)362-4478
Fax: (402)362-6748
Free: 800-334-4530
General newspaper. **Freq:** Daily (eve.) and Sat. (morn.). **Print Method:** Offset. **Cols./Page:** 6. **Col. Width:** 25 nonpareils. **Col. Depth:** 294 agate lines. **Key Personnel:** Kathy Larson, Manager, Advertising; Steve Baker, Publisher. **USPS:** 686-100. **URL:** http://www.yorknewstimes.com. **Remarks:** Accepts advertising. **Circ:** (Not Reported).

20764 ■ KAWL-AM - 1370
1515 Harre Ln.
York, NE 68467-9804
Phone: (402)362-4361
Email: kawl@alltel.net
Format: Oldies; Full Service. **Networks:** ABC. **Founded:** 1954. **Operating Hours**: Continuous. **ADI**: Lincoln-Hastings-Kearney, NE. **Key Personnel:** Mark G. Jensen, Gen. Mgr. **Wattage**: 500. **Ad Rates:** $14 for 30 seconds; $20 for 60 seconds.

20765 ■ KTMX-FM - 104.9
1309 Rd. 11
York, NE 68467
Phone: (402)362-4433
Fax: (402)362-6501
Format: Adult Contemporary. **Networks:** ABC. **Founded:** 1971. **Formerly**: KAWL-FM. **Operating Hours**: Continuous. **ADI**: Lincoln-Hastings-Kearney, NE. **Key Personnel:** Brad Leggett, Mgr., bleggett@ruralradio.com. **Wattage**: 13,000. **Ad Rates:** $14 for 30 seconds; $20 for 60 seconds. **URL:** http://1049maxcountry.com.

YUCAIPA

20766 ■ KLRD-FM - 90.1
PO Box 2118
Omaha, NE 68103-2118
Free: 888-937-2471
Format: Religious; Contemporary Hit Radio (CHR). **Networks:** USA Radio. **Owner:** Educational Media Foundation, 2351 Sunset Blvd., Ste. 170-218, Rocklin, CA 95677, Ph: (800)434-8400. **Founded:** 1983. **Operating Hours**: Continuous; 5% network, 95% local. **ADI**: Los Angeles (Corona & San Bernardino), CA. **Key Personnel:** Mike Novak, President, CEO; Alan Mason, COO. **Wattage**: 300. **URL:** http://www.air1.com/Music/StationList.aspx.

Circulation: ⋆ = AAM; △ or • = BPA; ♦ = CAC; ❑ = VAC; ⊕ = PO Statement; ‡ = Publisher's Report; Boldface figures = sworn; Light figures = estimated.

CALIENTE

Lincoln Co. Lincoln Co. (SE). 155 m NE of Las Vegas. State park. Mining. Agriculture.

20767 ■ Lincoln County Record
Battle Born Media
PO Box 150820
Ely, NV 89315
Phone: (775)289-4491
Community newspaper. **Freq:** Weekly (Thurs.). **Print Method:** Offset. Uses mats. **Cols./Page:** 5. **Col. Width:** 26 nonpareils. **Col. Depth:** 182 agate lines. **Key Personnel:** Ben Rowley, Managing Editor. **USPS:** 587-120. **Subscription Rates:** $30 Individuals; $36 Out of country. **URL:** http://www.lccentral.com. **Formerly**: Pioche Record Publishing Co., Inc. **Ad Rates:** GLR $.33; BW $330; SAU $5; PCI $9.50. **Remarks:** Advertising accepted; rates available upon request. **Circ:** ⊕**1,700**.

CARSON CITY

Carson City Co. (W). The State Capital, 30 m S of Reno. Western Nevada Community College. Park areas. Historical sites and museums. Hunting and fishing. Bolt and screws, reinforced plastics factories.

20768 ■ Lahontan Valley News
Swift Communications Inc.
580 Mallory Way
Carson City, NV 89701-5360
Phone: (775)283-5500
Fax: (775)283-5577
Publisher's E-mail: info@swiftcom.com
General newspaper. **Freq:** Weekly (Wed.). **Print Method:** Offset. **Cols./Page:** 6. **Col. Width:** 2 1/16 inches. **Col. Depth:** 21 1/2 inches. **Key Personnel:** Steve Ranson, Editor; Keith Sampson, Manager, Circulation. **USPS:** 925-960. **Subscription Rates:** $2.10 Individuals /week - print and digital ; $1.65 Individuals digital only; $2 Individuals 24 hour access. **URL:** http://www.nevadaappeal.com/News/LahontanValley. **Ad Rates:** BW $1057.80; 4C $1317.80; SAU $8.20. **Remarks:** Accepts advertising. **Circ:** (Not Reported).

20769 ■ Nevada
Nevada
401 N Carson St.
Carson City, NV 89701
Phone: (775)687-5416
Fax: (775)687-6159
Publication E-mail: editor@nevadamagazine.com
Travel magazine. **Founded:** 1936. **Freq:** Bimonthly. **Print Method:** Offset. **Trim Size:** 8 3/8 x 10 7/8. **Cols./Page:** 3. **Col. Width:** 27 nonpareils. **Col. Depth:** 134 agate lines. **ISSN:** 0199-1248 (print). **Subscription Rates:** $19.95 Individuals; $29.95 Out of country; $29.95 Canada. **URL:** http://www.nevadamagazine.com. **Remarks:** Accepts advertising. **Circ:** Paid ‡10000, Non-paid ‡10000.

20770 ■ Nevada Appeal
Swift Communications Inc.
580 Mallory Way
Carson City, NV 89701-5360
Phone: (775)283-5500
Fax: (775)283-5577
Publisher's E-mail: info@swiftcom.com
General newspaper. **Freq:** Tues.-Sun. (morning). **Print Method:** Offset. **Cols./Page:** 6. **Col. Width:** 25 nonpareils. **Col. Depth:** 301 agate lines. **Key Personnel:** Brooke Warner, General Manager; Adam Trumble, Editor; Mick Raher, Director, Sales. **URL:** http://www.swiftcom.com/publications/nevada-appeal. **Ad Rates:** BW $1915.65; 4C $2287.65; SAU $14.85. **Remarks:** Accepts advertising. **Circ:** Paid 25000, Paid 35.

20771 ■ Nevada Events and Shows: Section of Nevada Magazine
Nevada Magazine
401 N Carson St., Ste. 100
Carson City, NV 89701
Phone: (775)687-0605
Fax: (775)687-6159
Publisher's E-mail: editor@nevadamagazine.com
Travel magazine. **Freq:** Bimonthly. **Print Method:** Web Offset. **Trim Size:** 8 3/8 x 10 7/8. **Cols./Page:** 3. **Col. Width:** 27 nonpareils. **Col. Depth:** 134 agate lines. **Key Personnel:** Janet M. Geary, Publisher, phone: (775)687-0603. **ISSN:** 0896--2588 (print). **Subscription Rates:** $19.95 Individuals; $62.85 Other countries. **URL:** http://www.nevadamagazine.com. **Ad Rates:** BW $4000; 4C $5750; PCI $175. **Remarks:** Accepts advertising. **Circ:** Paid ‡189800, Non-paid ‡11000.

20772 ■ Range Magazine: The Cowboy Spirit on America's Outback
Range Magazine
106 E Adams, Ste. 201
Carson City, NV 89706
Phone: (775)884-2200
Fax: (775)884-2213
Free: 800-RAN-GE4U
Publisher's E-mail: info@rangemagazine.com
Consumer magazine covering cowboys, sheepherders, and other people who work on and enjoy the land in the Western U.S. **Freq:** Quarterly. **Print Method:** Web press. **Trim Size:** 8 1/2 x 11. **Key Personnel:** C.J. Hadley, Editor. **ISSN:** 1093--3670 (print). **Subscription Rates:** $19.95 Individuals; $28 Canada and Mexico; $49.95 Other countries; $15.95 Individuals web special. **URL:** http://www.rangemagazine.com. **Remarks:** Advertising accepted; rates available upon request. **Circ:** 150000.

20773 ■ The Record-Courier
Swift Communications Inc.
580 Mallory Way
Carson City, NV 89701-5360
Phone: (775)283-5500
Fax: (775)283-5577
Publisher's E-mail: info@swiftcom.com
Community newspaper. **Founded:** 1904. **Freq:** Daily. **Key Personnel:** Pat Bridges, Publisher; Tony King, Manager, Circulation; Kurt Hildebrand, Editor, phone: (775)782-5121. **Subscription Rates:** $6.95 Individuals print and online per month; $3.95 Individuals online per month; $1 Single issue online. **URL:** http://www.recordcourier.com. **Remarks:** Accepts advertising. **Circ:** Sun. ♦**4859**, Wed. ♦**4507**, Fri. ♦**4507**.

20774 ■ The Union
Swift Communications Inc.
580 Mallory Way
Carson City, NV 89701-5360
Phone: (775)283-5500
Fax: (775)283-5577
General newspaper. **Founded:** 1864. **Freq:** Mon.-Sat. (eve.). **Print Method:** Offset. **Trim Size:** 13 1/8 x 27 3/4. **Cols./Page:** 6. **Col. Width:** 24 nonpareils. **Col. Depth:** 301 agate lines. **Key Personnel:** Brian Hamilton, Editor. **Subscription Rates:** $11.95 Individuals all access, monthly (online and print); $10.50 Individuals unlimited web pass, monthly (online); $2.00 Individuals single day pass (online). **Alt. Formats:** Electronic publishing. **URL:** http://www.theunion.com. **Ad Rates:** PCI $19.50. **Remarks:** Accepts advertising. **Circ:** Mon.-Sat. ♦**13553**.

20775 ■ KCMY-AM - 1300
1960 Idaho St.
Carson City, NV 89701
Format: Country. **Owner:** Evans Broadcast Co., at above address.

20776 ■ KCSP-FM - 90.3
PO Box 21888
Carson City, NV 89721
Phone: (307)265-5414
Format: Contemporary Christian; Talk. **Networks:** AP. **Owner:** Western Inspirational Broadcasters Inc., 6363 Hwy. 50 E, Carson City, NV 89701, Ph: (702)883-5647. **Founded:** 1990. **Operating Hours**: Continuous. **ADI:** Casper-Riverton, WY. **Wattage**: 100,000 ERP. **URL:** http://pilgrimradio.com.

KDNR-FM - See Cheyenne, WY

KLMT-FM - See Billings, MT

20777 ■ KNIS-FM - 91.3
PO Box 21888
Carson City, NV 89721
Phone: (775)883-5647
Free: 800-541-5647
Email: info@pilgrimradio.com
Format: Religious; Contemporary Christian. **Networks:** AP. **Owner:** Western Inspirational Broadcasters Inc., 6363 Hwy. 50 E, Carson City, NV 89701, Ph: (702)883-5647. **Founded:** 1970. **Operating Hours**: Continuous; 10% network, 90% local. **ADI:** Reno, NV. **Wattage**: 67,000. **Ad Rates:** Noncommercial. **URL:** http://www.pilgrimradio.com.

20778 ■ KPTL-AM - 1300
1960 Idaho St.
Carson City, NV 89701
Phone: (775)884-8000
Format: Oldies; Talk. **Networks:** CBS. **Owner:** Jerry Evans, at above address. **Founded:** 1955. **Operating Hours:** Continuous. **Key Personnel:** Ron Harrison, Gen. Mgr; Scott Gahagen, Contact. **Wattage:** 5,000. **Ad Rates:** $25 per unit.

20779 ■ K259AK-FM - 99.7
PO Box 391
Twin Falls, ID 83303
Fax: (208)736-1958

Circulation: ★ = AAM; △ or • = BPA; ♦ = CAC; ❑ = VAC; ⊕ = PO Statement; ‡ = Publisher's Report; Boldface figures = sworn; Light figures = estimated.

Free: 800-357-4226
Format: Religious; Contemporary Christian. **Owner:** CSN International, PO Box 391, Twin Falls, ID 83303, Ph: (208)736-1958, Fax: (208)736-1958, Free: 800-357-4226. **Key Personnel:** Mike Kestler, President; Don Mills, Music Dir., Prog. Dir. **URL:** http://www.csnradio.com.

CRESCENT VALLEY

20780 ■ Welara Journal
American Welara Pony Society
471 4th St., Nevelco Unit 1
Crescent Valley, NV 89821
Publisher's E-mail: info@welararegistry.com
Freq: Semiannual. **Subscription Rates:** included in membership dues; $5 /year for nonmembers in U.S.; $6 /year for nonmembers outside U.S.; $1.50 single copy. **Alt. Formats:** CD-ROM. **URL:** http://www.welararegistry.com/P1.html#1.0. **Remarks:** Accepts advertising. **Circ:** (Not Reported).

ELKO

Elko Co. Elko Co. (NE). 290 m E of Reno. Tourism.

20781 ■ KEBG-FM - 103.9
1750 Manzanita Dr., Ste. 1
Elko, NV 89801
Phone: (775)777-1196
Fax: (775)777-9587
Email: sales@rubyradio.fm
Format: Country. **Owner:** Ruby Radio Corporation, 1750 Manzanita Dr., Elko, NV 89801. **URL:** http://www.bigcountry.fm.

20782 ■ KELK-AM - 1240
1800 Idaho St.
Elko, NV 89801
Phone: (775)738-1240
Fax: (775)753-5556
Email: elkoradio@elkoradio.com
Format: Adult Contemporary. **Networks:** ABC. **Owner:** Elko Broadcasting Co., at above address. **Founded:** 1947. **Operating Hours:** Continuous; 2% network, 98% local. **ADI:** Salt Lake City (Cedar City), UT. **Wattage:** 1,000. **Ad Rates:** $13 for 30 seconds; $17.50 for 60 seconds. **URL:** http://www.elkoradio.com.

20783 ■ KENV-TV - 10
1025 Chilton Cir.
Elko, NV 89801
Phone: (775)777-8500
Fax: (775)777-7758
Format: News. **Networks:** NBC. **Owner:** Sunbelt Communications Co., 1500 Foremaster Ln., Las Vegas, NV 89101, Ph: (702)642-3333, Fax: (702)657-3423. **Founded:** Jan. 01, 1996. **Operating Hours:** 12:00 a.m. - 3:30 a.m. **Key Personnel:** Jim Elliott, Station Mgr., jim@kenv.com. **Wattage:** 1,500 ERP H. **Ad Rates:** Advertising accepted; rates available upon request. **URL:** http://kenvtv.com.

20784 ■ KHIX-FM - 96.7
1750 Manzanita Dr., Ste. 1
Elko, NV 89801
Phone: (775)777-1196
Format: Adult Contemporary. **Key Personnel:** Ken Sutherland, President, ken@rubyradio.fm; Alene Sutherland, VP, alene@rubyradio.fm. **Ad Rates:** Noncommercial. **URL:** http://www.bigcountry.fm.

20785 ■ KLKO-FM - 93.7
1800 Idaho St.
Elko, NV 89801
Phone: (775)738-1240
Fax: (775)753-5556
Email: elkoradio@elkoradio.com
Format: Eclectic. **Owner:** Elko Broadcasting Co., at above address. **Founded:** 1982. **Operating Hours:** 100% local. **ADI:** Salt Lake City (Cedar City), UT. **Key Personnel:** Lori Gilbert, News Dir. **Wattage:** 050 k. **Ad Rates:** $13 for 30 seconds; $17.50 for 60 seconds. $9-$10 for 30 seconds; $12-$14 for 60 seconds. Combined advertising rates available with KELK-AM. **URL:** http://www.elkoradio.com.

20786 ■ KNCC-FM - 91.5
Mail Stop 0294
Reno, NV 89557
Phone: (775)327-5867
Fax: (775)327-5386
Format: Public Radio. **Owner:** University of Nevada, 1664 N Virginia St., Reno, NV 89557, Ph: (775)784-1110. **Key Personnel:** David Stipech, Gen. Mgr., dstipech@kunr.org. **URL:** http://www.kunr.org.

20787 ■ KRJC-FM - 95.3
1250 Lamoille Hwy., No. 1045
Elko, NV 89801
Phone: (775)738-9895
Fax: (775)753-8085
Format: Country. **Owner:** Holiday Broadcasting, Not Available. **Founded:** 1982. **Operating Hours:** Continuous. **Key Personnel:** Stacey Sawyer, Gen. Mgr. **Wattage:** 25,000. **Ad Rates:** Advertising accepted; rates available upon request. **URL:** http://www.krjc.com.

20788 ■ KTSN-AM - 1340
1250 Lamoile Hwy., Ste. 1045
Elko, NV 89801
Phone: (775)738-9895
Fax: (775)753-8085
Format: Talk; Sports; News. **Ad Rates:** Noncommercial.

20789 ■ K220HG-FM - 91.9
PO Box 391
Twin Falls, ID 83303
Free: 800-357-4226
Format: Religious; Contemporary Christian. **Owner:** CSN International, PO Box 391, Twin Falls, ID 83303, Ph: (208)736-1958, Fax: (208)736-1958, Free: 800-357-4226. **Key Personnel:** Don Mills, Prog. Dir., Div. Dir. **URL:** http://www.csnradio.com.

20790 ■ KZBI-FM - 94.5
1750 Manzanita Dr., Ste. 1
Elko, NV 89801
Phone: (775)777-1196
Fax: (775)777-9587
Format: News; Talk. **Owner:** Ruby Radio Corporation, 1750 Manzanita Dr., Elko, NV 89801. **Key Personnel:** Ken Sutherland, President, ken@rubyradio.fm; Alene Sutherland, Chmn. of the Bd., alene@rubyradio.fm. **URL:** http://www.bigcountry.fm.

ELY

White Pine Co. White Pine Co. (E). 260 m E of Reno. Gold, silver mines. Dairy, stock farms. Sheep.

20791 ■ The Ely Times
Battle Born Media
515 Murry St.
Ely, NV 89315
Phone: (775)289-4491
Fax: (775)289-4566
General newspaper. **Freq:** Daily. **Print Method:** Offset. **Trim Size:** 13 x 21 1/2. **Cols./Page:** 6. **Col. Width:** 26 nonpareils. **Col. Depth:** 301 agate lines. **Key Personnel:** Gary Cook, Publisher, Director; Shari Gilson, Manager. **USPS:** 174-660. **URL:** http://www.elynews.com. **Formerly:** Ely Daily Times. **Mailing address:** PO Box 150820, Ely, NV 89315. **Ad Rates:** BW $1154; PCI $8.95. **Remarks:** Accepts advertising. **Circ:** (Not Reported).

20792 ■ KDSS-FM - 92.7
501 Aultman St.
Ely, NV 89301
Phone: (775)289-6474
Fax: (775)289-6531
Email: kdssfm@sbcglobal.net
Format: Country. **Networks:** Jones Satellite. **Owner:** Coates Broadcasting, Inc., at above address. **Founded:** 1984. **Formerly:** KBXS-FM. **Operating Hours:** Continuous. **Key Personnel:** Patrick Coates, Gen. Mgr., President; Samantha Coates, Sales Mgr., VP. **Wattage:** 100,000. **Ad Rates:** $15 for 30 seconds; $17 for 60 seconds.

20793 ■ KELY-AM - 1230
PO Box 151465
Ely, NV 89315
Phone: (775)289-2077
Format: Talk; News. **Networks:** CNN Radio; Jones Satellite. **Owner:** Ely Radio, LLC, at above address. **Founded:** 1950. **Operating Hours:** Continuous; 75% network, 25% local. **Key Personnel:** Fred Weinberg, Owner. **Wattage:** 1,000. **Ad Rates:** $6-13.50 per unit.

20794 ■ K217DN-FM - 91.3
PO Box 391
Twin Falls, ID 83303
Fax: (208)736-1958
Free: 800-357-4226
Format: Religious; Contemporary Christian. **Owner:** CSN International, PO Box 391, Twin Falls, ID 83303, Ph: (208)736-1958, Fax: (208)736-1958, Free: 800-357-4226. **Key Personnel:** Don Mills, Prog. Dir., Div. Dir. **URL:** http://www.csnradio.com.

FALLON

Churchill Co. Churchill Co. (WC).60 m E of Reno. Manufactures butter, alfalfa meal, ice cream. Ore refining; barite, tungsten, silver mines. Agriculture. Alfalfa, wheat and garden produce.

20795 ■ KVLV-AM - 980
562 N Maine St.
Fallon, NV 89406
Phone: (775)423-6041
Fax: (775)423-0474
Format: News; Sports; Information. **Simulcasts:** KOWL. **Networks:** ABC. **Owner:** Lahontan Valley Broadcasting Company L.L.C., at above address. **Founded:** 1957. **Key Personnel:** Steve Ranson, Editor, sranson@lahontanvalleynews.com; Larry Barker, Editor, lbarker@lahontanvalleynews.com. **Wattage:** 5,000 KW. **Ad Rates:** Advertising accepted; rates available upon request. $15 for 30 seconds; $20 for 60 seconds. Combined advertising rates available with KVLV-FM. **URL:** http://www.lahontanvalleynews.com/.

20796 ■ KVLV-FM - 99.3
1155 Gummow Dr.
Fallon, NV 89406
Format: Adult Contemporary. **Networks:** AP; Jones Satellite. **Owner:** Lahontan Valley Broadcasting Company L.L.C., at above address. **Founded:** 1966. **Operating Hours:** 6 a.m.-MID; 1% network, 99% local. **Key Personnel:** Steve Ranson, Editor, sranson@lahontanvalleynews.com; Pete Copeland, Publisher, pcopeland@lahontanvalleynews.com; Larry Barker, Editor, lbarker@lahontanvalleynews.com. **Wattage:** 3,700. **Ad Rates:** $15 for 30 seconds; $20 for 60 seconds. Combined advertising rates available with KVLV-AM.

20797 ■ KWHG-AM
1050 W Williams
Fallon, NV 89406
Phone: (775)423-5494
Fax: (775)428-1765
Owner: Media Enterprises L.L.C.

GARDNERVILLE

Douglas Co. (W). 47 m S of Reno. Grain warehouse; creamery. Gold, silver, tungsten, barium mines. Agriculture. Cattle. Hay, grain, sheep.

20798 ■ The Record-Courier
The Record-Courier
1503 Hwy. 395 N, Ste. G
Gardnerville, NV 89410
Phone: (775)782-5121
Fax: (775)782-6152
Publisher's E-mail: info@swiftcom.com
Community newspaper. **Founded:** 1904. **Freq:** Daily. **Key Personnel:** Pat Bridges, Publisher; Tony King, Manager, Circulation; Kurt Hildebrand, Editor, phone: (775)782-5121. **Subscription Rates:** $6.95 Individuals print and online per month; $3.95 Individuals online per month; $1 Single issue online. **URL:** http://www.recordcourier.com. **Remarks:** Accepts advertising. **Circ:** Sun. ♦**4859**, Wed. ♦**4507**, Fri. ♦**4507**.

HENDERSON

Clark Co. Clark Co. (SE). 12 m SE of Las Vegas. Summer and winter recreation. Warehouse distribution. Titanium plant. Manufactures chemicals, electronics.

20799 ■ Casino Connection
Global Gaming Business L.L.C.
921 American Pacific Dr., Ste. 304
Henderson, NV 89014
Publication E-mail: casinoconnectionac@gmail.com
Magazine that highlights positive contributions of the gaming industry for Atlantic City's casino employees. **Freq:** Monthly. **Key Personnel:** Daryl Bulthuis, Contact; Roger Gros, Publisher. **Subscription Rates:** Free. **URL:**

http://www.casinoconnectionac.com. **Remarks:** Accepts advertising. **Circ:** (Not Reported).

20800 ■ Global Gaming Business
Global Gaming Business L.L.C.
921 American Pacific Dr., Ste. 304
Henderson, NV 89014
Publication E-mail: info@globalgamingbusiness.com
Magazine that aims to serve the communications needs of the international casino industry. **Freq:** Monthly. **Trim Size:** 8.375 x 10.875. **Key Personnel:** Roger Gros, Publisher; Frank Legato, Editor; Becky Kingman-Gros, Director, Operations. **ISSN:** 1555--922X (print). **Subscription Rates:** $99 Individuals; $129 Elsewhere; $159 Two years; $209 Elsewhere 2 years. **URL:** http://ggbmagazine.com. **Ad Rates:** 4C $4175. **Remarks:** Accepts advertising. **Circ:** (Not Reported).

20801 ■ Las Vegas Weekly
Radiant City Publications L.L.C.
2360 Corporate Circle Dr., 4th Fl.
Henderson, NV 89074
Phone: (702)990-2400
Community arts and culture newspaper. **Founded:** 1991. **Freq:** Weekly (Thurs.). **URL:** http://www.lasvegasweekly.com. **Formerly:** Scope. **Remarks:** Advertising accepted; rates available upon request. **Circ:** (Not Reported).

20802 ■ Nevada Business Journal: The Decision Maker's Magazine
Division of Business Link L.L.C.
375 N Stephanie St., Bldg. 23
Henderson, NV 89014
Phone: (702)735-7003
Fax: (702)733-5953
Publisher's E-mail: info@nbj.com
Magazine spotlighting and promoting business in Nevada. **Freq:** Bimonthly. **Print Method:** Offset. **Trim Size:** 8.375 x 10.875. **Cols./Page:** 3. **Col. Width:** 2.5 picas. **Col. Depth:** 9 5/8 inches. **Key Personnel:** Lyle E. Brennan, Publisher; Connie Brennan, Chief Executive Officer, Publisher. **Subscription Rates:** $44 Individuals /year - 12 issues; $79 Individuals 3 years. **URL:** http://www.nevadabusiness.com. **Ad Rates:** BW $4000; 4C $5500. **Remarks:** Accepts advertising. **Circ:** (Not Reported).

20803 ■ Vegas
Greenspun Media Group
2360 Corporate Cir., 3rd Fl.
Henderson, NV 89074
Phone: (702)990-2550
Publication E-mail: vegas@pubservice.com
Magazine that covers shopping, restaurants, casinos, celebrities, and clubs in Las Vegas. **Freq:** 8/year. **Key Personnel:** Joseph Vann, Publisher; John Kushnir, Chief Financial Officer; Kate Bennett, Editor-in-Chief. **ISSN:** 1549--8506 (print). **Subscription Rates:** $42 U.S. **URL:** http://www.vegasmagazine.com. **Remarks:** Advertising accepted; rates available upon request. **Circ:** △**65000**.

20804 ■ KVVU-TV - 5
25 TV-5 Dr.
Henderson, NV 89014
Phone: (702)435-5555
Fax: (702)451-4220
Free: 888-369-4762
Email: askfox@fox.com
Format: Commercial TV. **Networks:** Fox. **Owner:** Meredith Corp., 1716 Locust St., Des Moines, IA 50309-3038, Ph: (515)284-3000. **Founded:** Sept. 1967. **Formerly:** KHBV-TV. **Operating Hours:** Continuous. **ADI:** Las Vegas, NV. **Ad Rates:** Advertising accepted; rates available upon request. **URL:** http://www.fox5vegas.com.

INCLINE VILLAGE

Washoe Co.

20805 ■ North Lake Tahoe Bonanza
North Lake Tahoe Bonanza
925 Tahoe Blvd., Ste. 206
Incline Village, NV 89452
Phone: (775)831-4666
Community newspaper. **Freq:** Weekly (Thurs.). **Key Personnel:** Kevin MacMillan, Managing Editor, phone: (775)831-4666; Sylas Wright, Editor. **URL:** http://www.sierrasun.com. **Remarks:** Accepts advertising. **Circ:** Non-paid ♦**3022**.

LAS VEGAS

Clark Co. Clark Co. (SE). 180 m NE of San Bernardino, Calif. Tourist resort.

20806 ■ AGS Spectra
American Gem Society
8881 W Sahara Ave.
Las Vegas, NV 89117
Publisher's E-mail: rbatson@ags.org
Magazine publishing information for American Gem Society members with an informative and entertaining resource for member, organization, and industry news. **Freq:** Quarterly. **Subscription Rates:** Included in membership. **URL:** http://www.americangemsociety.org/spectra-guidelines. **Remarks:** Accepts advertising. **Circ:** 4400.

20807 ■ Ames Tribune
Stephens Media L.L.C.
1111 W Bonanza Rd.
Las Vegas, NV 89106
Phone: (702)383-0211
Fax: (702)383-4676
Publisher's E-mail: sfrederick@stephensmedia.com
Newspaper covering local news, community events, entertainment, sports, business, real estate and classified ads. **Key Personnel:** Paul Heidbreder, Publisher. **URL:** http://amestrib.com. **Mailing address:** PO Box 70, Las Vegas, NV 89125-0070. **Circ:** (Not Reported).

20808 ■ Cocktails Magazine
Destiny Productions for Print, Radio and Cable Promotions
3395 S Jones Blvd., No. 217
Las Vegas, NV 89146-6729
Phone: (702)438-1470
Publication E-mail: cocktailsm@aol.com
Trade magazine for the alcohol service industry. **Freq:** Monthly. **Trim Size:** 8 1/2 x 11. **URL:** http://www.cocktail.com/. **Remarks:** Accepts advertising. **Circ:** Paid 25000.

20809 ■ EdgeScience
Society for Scientific Exploration
c/o Stephen E. Braude, Ph.D.
University of Maryland - Baltimore County
8022 S Rainbow Blvd., Ste. 236
Las Vegas, NV 89139
Freq: Quarterly. **Key Personnel:** Patrick Huyghe, Editor. **Subscription Rates:** $4.95 Single issue; Included in membership. **Alt. Formats:** PDF. **URL:** http://www.scientificexploration.org/edgescience. **Circ:** (Not Reported).

20810 ■ eJuggle: The Official Magazine of the International Jugglers Association
Stagewrite Publishing Inc.
3315 E Russell Rd., A4-203
Las Vegas, NV 89120
Fax: (702)248-2550
Publication E-mail: editor@jugglemagazine.com
Magazine of interest to jugglers and other independent variety entertainers. **Freq:** Bimonthly. **Print Method:** Offset. **Trim Size:** 8 1/2 x 10 7/8. **Cols./Page:** 3. **Col. Width:** 42 nonpareils. **Col. Depth:** 196 agate lines. **Key Personnel:** Alan Howard, Editor, phone: (702)798-0099. **ISSN:** 1520--7471 (print). **URL:** http://www.juggle.org; http://ezine.juggle.org. **Formerly:** Juggle: The Official Magazine of the International Jugglers Association. **Remarks:** Accepts advertising. **Circ:** 3000.

20811 ■ El Tiempo
Las Vegas Review-Journal
PO Box 70
Las Vegas, NV 89125
Phone: (702)383-0211
Fax: (702)383-4676
Publisher's E-mail: rhofliger@eltiempolibre.com
Community newspaper (Spanish) for the Las Vegas area. **Freq:** Weekly (Thurs.). **Print Method:** Offset. **Subscription Rates:** Free. **URL:** http://www.eltiempolv.com/. **Ad Rates:** PCI $9. **Remarks:** Advertising accepted; rates available upon request. **Circ:** Free ♦**46500**.

20812 ■ FOH
Timeless Communications
6000 S Eastern Ave., Ste. 14-J
Las Vegas, NV 89119
Phone: (702)932-5585
Fax: (702)932-5584
Magazine covering professional audio equipment for concert performances. **Key Personnel:** Bill Evans, Editor; Breanne George, Managing Editor; Geri Jeter, Associate Editor. **Subscription Rates:** Free to members. **URL:** http://www.fohonline.com. **Also known as:** Front of House. **Remarks:** Accepts advertising. **Circ:** (Not Reported).

20813 ■ In Light Times: Concepts for Conscious Living
In Light Times
PO Box 12063
Las Vegas, NV 89112
Phone: (702)259-6843
Magazine featuring stories on holistic and spiritual ways of living. **Freq:** Monthly. **Key Personnel:** Michelene K. Bell, Editor, Founder, Publisher; Eugenia Martini-Jarrett, Associate Editor. **Subscription Rates:** $31.50 Individuals; $39.90 Canada; $68.50 Other countries. **URL:** http://www.inlightimes.com. **Remarks:** Accepts advertising. **Circ:** 10,000.

20814 ■ International Journal of Integrated Supply Management
Inderscience Publishers
c/o Dr. Joel D. Wisner, Founding Ed.
University of Nevada, Las Vegas
College of Business, Department of Management
Las Vegas, NV 89154-6009
Publication E-mail: info@inderscience.com
Journal aiming to attract and publish empirical and theoretical manuscripts from academics in all disciplines and professionals regarding a wide range of supply management issues, including purchasing and other incoming supply issues, internal materials management, information systems and quality issues, and outbound supply, logistics, and customer service issues. **Freq:** Quarterly. **Key Personnel:** Dr. Joel D. Wisner, Editor; Dr. Ajay Das, Editor-in-Chief. **ISSN:** 1477--5360 (print); **EISSN:** 1741--8097 (electronic). **Subscription Rates:** €685 Individuals print or online for 1 user; €1164.50 Individuals online only for 2-3 users; €928 Individuals print and online; €1712.50 Individuals online only for 4-5 users; €2226.25 Individuals online only for 6-7 users; €2705.75 Individuals online only for 8-9 users; €3151 Individuals online only for 10-14 users; €3596.25 Individuals online only for 15-19 users; €4247 Individuals online only for 20+ users. **URL:** http://www.inderscience.com/jhome.php?jcode=ijism. **Circ:** (Not Reported).

20815 ■ Jeffers Studies
Robinson Jeffers Association
c/o Charles Rodewald, Treasurer
5140 Cutty Way
Las Vegas, NV 89130
Publisher's E-mail: president@robinsonjeffersassociation.org
Freq: Semiannual. **ISSN:** 1096--5076 (print). **Alt. Formats:** PDF. **URL:** http://www.robinsonjeffersassociation.org/jeffers-studies. **Remarks:** Advertising not accepted. **Circ:** 250.

20816 ■ Journal of Scientific Exploration
Society for Scientific Exploration
c/o Stephen E. Braude, Ph.D.
University of Maryland - Baltimore County
8022 S Rainbow Blvd., Ste. 236
Las Vegas, NV 89139
Freq: Quarterly. **Key Personnel:** Stephen E. Braude, PhD, Editor-in-Chief. **ISSN:** 0892--3310 (print). **URL:** http://www.scientificexploration.org/journal. **Circ:** (Not Reported).

20817 ■ Las Vegas Business Press
Stephens Media L.L.C.
1111 W Bonanza Rd.
Las Vegas, NV 89106
Phone: (702)383-0211
Fax: (702)383-4676
Publisher's E-mail: sfrederick@stephensmedia.com
Local business newspaper. **Founded:** 1985. **Freq:** Weekly. **Print Method:** Offset. **Trim Size:** 10 1/4 x 12 1/2. **Cols./Page:** 4. **Col. Width:** 2 3/8 inches. **Col. Depth:** 12 1/2 inches. **Key Personnel:** Jennifer Land, Managing Editor; James Wright, Editor; Michelle Stewart, Manager, Advertising and Sales. **Subscription Rates:** $52 Individuals. **URL:** http://www.reviewjournal.com/business/business-press. **Mailing address:** PO

Circulation: ★ = AAM; △ or • = BPA; ♦ = CAC; ❑ = VAC; ⊕ = PO Statement; ‡ = Publisher's Report; Boldface figures = sworn; Light figures = estimated.

Box 70, Las Vegas, NV 89125-0070. **Ad Rates:** BW $1,739; 4C $2,239. **Remarks:** Accepts advertising. **Circ:** (Not Reported).

20818 ■ Las Vegas CityLife
Las Vegas Review-Journal
PO Box 70
Las Vegas, NV 89125
Phone: (702)383-0211
Fax: (702)383-4676
Publisher's E-mail: rhofliger@eltiempolibre.com
Community newspaper. (Tabloid). **Freq:** Weekly (Thurs.). **Key Personnel:** Scott Dickensheets, Editor; Andrew Kiraly, Managing Editor; Geoff Schumacher, Publisher. **Ad Rates:** BW $2000; 4C $2500. **Remarks:** Advertising accepted; rates available upon request. **Circ:** Free ■ **40000.**

20819 ■ Las Vegas Review-Journal
GateHouse Media Inc.
1111 W Bonanza Rd.
Las Vegas, NV 89125
Phone: (702)383-0211
General newspaper. **Freq:** Daily. **Print Method:** Offset. **Cols./Page:** 6. **Col. Width:** 26 nonpareils. **Col. Depth:** 301 agate lines. **Key Personnel:** Jason Taylor, Publisher; Michael Hengel, Editor, phone: (702)387-2906; Graydon Johns, Director, phone: (702)383-0274. **Subscription Rates:** $16.77 Individuals /mo.; print + online; $12.99 Individuals /mo.; print only; $9.99 Individuals /mo.; online only. **Online:** GateHouse Media Inc. GateHouse Media Inc.; ProQuest L.L.C. **URL:** http://www.reviewjournal.com. **Mailing address:** PO Box 70, Las Vegas, NV 89125. **Ad Rates:** BW $17997; 4C $20351; PCI $142.83. **Remarks:** Accepts classified advertising. **Circ:** (Not Reported).

20820 ■ Las Vegas Sentinel-Voice
Griot Communications Group Inc.
900 E Charleston Blvd.
Las Vegas, NV 89104
Phone: (702)380-8100
Fax: (702)380-8102
Publication E-mail: lvsentinelvoice@yahoo.com
Black community newspaper. **Freq:** Weekly (Thurs.). **Cols./Page:** 6. **Col. Width:** 1 5/8 inches. **Col. Depth:** 14 inches. **Key Personnel:** Ramon Savoy, Editor. **Subscription Rates:** $25 Individuals. **URL:** http://lasvegastribune.net. **Ad Rates:** GLR $0.75; BW $924; 4C $1500; PCI $11. **Remarks:** Accepts advertising. **Circ:** 5,000.

20821 ■ Las Vegas Sports
Love Media Group Inc.
PO Box 31734
Las Vegas, NV 89173-1734
Magazine featuring sports in Las Vegas. **Freq:** Monthly. **Key Personnel:** Thomas J. Love, Editor-in-Chief, Publisher; Isaac Kuhlman, Editor-in-Chief. **URL:** http://lvsportsmagazine.com/lmg/. **Circ:** (Not Reported).

20822 ■ Magic: The Independent Magazine for Magicians
Stagewrite Publishing Inc.
6220 Stevenson Way
Las Vegas, NV 89120-2722
Phone: (702)798-0099
Fax: (702)798-0220
Publication E-mail: editor@magicmagazine.com
Trade journal for magicians and magic enthusiasts. **Freq:** Monthly. **Print Method:** Web Offset. **Trim Size:** 8 1/2 x 10 7/8. **Cols./Page:** 3. **Key Personnel:** Stan Allen, Editor, Founder. **ISSN:** 1062--2845 (print). **Subscription Rates:** $4 U.S. and Canada month-to-month digital; $36 U.S. and Canada one year digital; $58 U.S. one year print + Digital; $111 U.S. 2 year print + digital; $79 Canada One year print + Digital; $4 Other countries month-to-month digital; $36 Other countries one year digital; $96 Other countries one year - digital (air mail); $136 Other countries one year - digital (express mail). **Remarks:** Accepts advertising. **Circ:** Controlled 10500.

20823 ■ McDonald County Press
Stephens Media L.L.C.
1111 W Bonanza Rd.
Las Vegas, NV 89106
Phone: (702)383-0211
Fax: (702)383-4676
Publisher's E-mail: sfrederick@stephensmedia.com
Newspaper with a Democratic orientation. **Freq:** Weekly (Wed.). **Print Method:** Offset. **Cols./Page:** 6. **Col. Width:** 2 1/16 inches. **Col. Depth:** 21 inches. **Key Personnel:** Rick Peck, Editor; Tom Stallbaumer, Publisher, phone: (479)872-5001. **Subscription Rates:** $49 Individuals /year (print and online); $3.99 Individuals /month (online). **URL:** http://mdcp.nwaonline.com. **Mailing address:** PO Box 70, Las Vegas, NV 89125-0070. **Ad Rates:** BW $700. **Remarks:** Accepts advertising. **Circ:** (Not Reported).

20824 ■ Nevada Law Journal
University of Nevada - Las Vegas William S. Boyd School of Law
4505 Maryland Pky.
Box 451003
Las Vegas, NV 89154-1003
Phone: (702)895-2440
Fax: (702)895-2414
Publisher's E-mail: request@law.unlv.edu
Journal discussing the law and policy implications of significant case law, legislation, administrative regulations and important legal events. **Subscription Rates:** $30 Individuals domestic; $35 Other countries; $15 Single issue back issue. **URL:** http://law.unlv.edu/nevada-law-journal. **Circ:** (Not Reported).

20825 ■ Nevada Lawyer
State Bar of Nevada
3100 W Charleston Blvd., Ste. 100
Las Vegas, NV 89102
Phone: (702)382-2200
Publication E-mail: nvlawyer@nvbar.org
Professional magazine of the State Bar of Nevada covering the practice of law. **Freq:** Monthly. **Key Personnel:** Jenni Smith, Director, Publications. **ISSN:** 1068--882X (print). **Subscription Rates:** $60 Individuals; $50 Individuals bar applicant; $25 Students law school; $6 Single issue. **URL:** http://nvbar.org/articles. **Formerly**: Inter Alia. **Ad Rates:** BW $761; 4C $936. **Remarks:** Accepts advertising. **Circ:** Controlled 5900.

20826 ■ Nevada Senior
Love Media Group Inc.
PO Box 31734
Las Vegas, NV 89173-1734
Magazine covering all that is important for local seniors. **Freq:** Bimonthly. **Key Personnel:** Thomas J. Love, President. **URL:** http://lvsportsmagazine.com/lmg/. **Circ:** (Not Reported).

20827 ■ Nifty Nickel
Las Vegas Review-Journal
PO Box 70
Las Vegas, NV 89125
Phone: (702)383-0211
Fax: (702)383-4676
Publisher's E-mail: rhofliger@eltiempolibre.com
Shopper. **Founded:** 1964. **Freq:** Weekly (Fri.). **Print Method:** Web press offset. **Trim Size:** 11 1/4 x 17. **Cols./Page:** 7. **Col. Width:** 1 5/16 inches. **Col. Depth:** 16 inches. **Subscription Rates:** Free. **URL:** http://adportal.reviewjournal.com/print/niche-publications/nifty-nickel. **Ad Rates:** BW $1,344; 4C $1,644; PCI $12. **Remarks:** Accepts advertising. **Circ:** Free ‡60612.

20828 ■ Recharger Magazine
Recharger Magazine
1050 E Flamingo Rd., Ste. N237
Las Vegas, NV 89119
Phone: (702)438-5557
Fax: (702)873-9671
Publication E-mail: info@rechargermag.com
Magazine serving the office products recycling industry. **Freq:** Monthly. **Key Personnel:** Patricia Ames, Publisher; Katie Fernelius, Associate Editor. **ISSN:** 1053--7503 (print). **Subscription Rates:** $45 U.S. and Canada domestic; $105 Other countries. **URL:** http://www.irecyclingtimes.com. **Ad Rates:** BW $570; 4C $1,085. **Remarks:** Accepts advertising. **Circ:** (Not Reported).

20829 ■ Roxanne
Warren Williams Media L.L.C.
2300 W Sahara Ave., Ste. 800
Las Vegas, NV 89102
Phone: (702)664-0035
Magazine showcasing women's lifestyle and fashion. **Freq:** Bimonthly. **Trim Size:** 11 x 14.5. **Key Personnel:** Roxanne Diana, Executive Editor. **URL:** http://roxannemagazine.com. **Remarks:** Accepts advertising. **Circ:** Controlled 40000.

20830 ■ Stage Directions: The Hands-On Magazine for People Involved in Community, Regional, Church, and Academic Theater
Timeless Communications
6000 S Eastern Ave., Ste. 14-J
Las Vegas, NV 89119
Phone: (702)932-5585
Fax: (702)932-5584
Publication for and about people who participate in live theater. **Freq:** Monthly. **Print Method:** Offset. **Trim Size:** 8 x 10 7/8. **Cols./Page:** 3. **Key Personnel:** Jacob Coakley, Editor; Terry Lowe, Publisher, phone: (702)932-5585; William Vanyo, General Manager. **ISSN:** 1047--1901 (print). **Subscription Rates:** Free. **Alt. Formats:** PDF. **URL:** http://www.stage-directions.com. **Ad Rates:** BW $2,720; 4C $3,843. **Remarks:** Accepts advertising. **Circ:** Paid ‡20401, Non-paid ‡20378.

20831 ■ Today in Las Vegas
Key Magazines Inc.
6268 S Rainbow Blvd., Ste. 100
Las Vegas, NV 89118
Phone: (702)385-2737
Fax: (702)733-9103
Publisher's E-mail: info@keymilwaukee.com
Visitor's guide publication featuring coverage of events, dining, shopping, and more. **Freq:** Weekly. **Trim Size:** 6 x 9 7/8. **Key Personnel:** Lisa Armijo, Chief Financial Officer, Publisher. **URL:** http://www.keymagazine.com/lasvegas/index.html. **Formerly**: Key Magazine Las Vegas. **Remarks:** Accepts advertising. **Circ:** Combined ‡83500.

20832 ■ UNLV Gaming Law Journal
University of Nevada - Las Vegas William S. Boyd School of Law
4505 Maryland Pky.
Box 451003
Las Vegas, NV 89154-1003
Phone: (702)895-2440
Fax: (702)895-2414
Publisher's E-mail: request@law.unlv.edu
Journal covering the law and policy implications of gaming case law, legislation, administrative regulations, and important gaming legal events. **Key Personnel:** Stephanie Getler, Editor-in-Chief. **Subscription Rates:** $40 Individuals /year; $50 Other countries /year. **URL:** http://scholars.law.unlv.edu/glj; http://law.unlv.edu/unlv-gaming-law-journal. **Circ:** (Not Reported).

20833 ■ What's On! The Las Vegas Guide: The Las Vegas Guide
What's On Magazines
101 Convention Ctr. Dr., Ste. P119
Las Vegas, NV 89109
Phone: (702)684-5800
Fax: (702)737-7833
Guide for the attractions of the city of Las Vegas. **Freq:** Biweekly. **Print Method:** Heatset offset/digital. **Trim Size:** 8 1/8 x 9 7/8. **Key Personnel:** Megan Riggs, Managing Editor; Jim Mcglasson, Publisher. **ISSN:** 1081-5945 (print). **Subscription Rates:** $5.95 Single issue; $6.95 Single issue Canada; $11.95 Single issue other countries; $45 Individuals digital; 26 issues. **URL:** http://whats-on.com. **Formerly**: What's On in Las Vegas Magazine; What's On Magazine. **Ad Rates:** BW $3,637; 4C $4,237. **Remarks:** Advertising accepted; rates available upon request. **Circ:** 200000.

20834 ■ Witness
University of Nevada Department of English
Flora Dungan Humanities Bldg.
4505 Maryland Pky., 6th Fl.
Las Vegas, NV 89154-5011
Phone: (702)895-3533
Fax: (702)895-4801
Publication E-mail: witness@unlv.edu
Magazine blending the features of a literary and issue-oriented publication. **Founded:** 1987. **Freq:** Semiannual. **Key Personnel:** Peter Stine, Editor, Founder; Juan Martinez, Associate Editor; Sidney Lutz, Founder, Publisher. **ISSN:** 0891-1371 (print). **Subscription Rates:** $10 Individuals; $18 Two years; $14 Other countries 2 years; $22 Other countries 2 years. **URL:** http://witness.blackmountaininstitute.org. **Mailing address:** PO Box 455011, Las Vegas, NV 89154-5011. **Ad Rates:** BW $100. **Remarks:** Accepts advertising. **Circ:** Paid ‡1500, Controlled ‡1500.

20835 ■ Women in Sport and Physical Activity Journal
University of North Carolina at Greensboro
1400 Spring Garden St.
Greensboro, NC 27412
Phone: (336)334-5000
Peer-reviewed scholarly journal covering women in sports. **Freq:** Semiannual. **Trim Size:** 6 x 9. **Key Personnel:** Lynda Ransdell, Editor; Ann Boyce, Editor. **ISSN:** 1063-6161 (print). **Subscription Rates:** $30 Nonmembers; $25 Members; $50 Libraries. **URL:** http://womenofdiversity.org; http://uncg.edu. **Mailing address:** PO Box 26170, Greensboro, NC 27402-6170. **Remarks:** Advertising not accepted. **Circ:** Paid 250.

20836 ■ Women in Sport and Physical Activity Journal
Women of Diversity Productions Inc.
5790 Park St.
Las Vegas, NV 89149-2304
Phone: (702)341-9807
Fax: (702)341-9828
Peer-reviewed scholarly journal covering women in sports. **Freq:** Semiannual. **Trim Size:** 6 x 9. **Key Personnel:** Lynda Ransdell, Editor; Ann Boyce, Editor. **ISSN:** 1063-6161 (print). **Subscription Rates:** $30 Nonmembers; $25 Members; $50 Libraries. **URL:** http://womenofdiversity.org; http://uncg.edu. **Mailing address:** PO Box 26170, Greensboro, NC 27402-6170. **Remarks:** Advertising not accepted. **Circ:** Paid 250.

20837 ■ KBAD-AM - 920
8755 W Flamingo Rd.
Las Vegas, NV 89147
Phone: (702)876-1460
Format: Sports. **Networks:** ABC; ESPN Radio. **Owner:** Lotus Communications, at above address. **Founded:** 1953. **Formerly**: KORK-AM. **Operating Hours**: Continuous. **ADI**: Las Vegas, NV. **Wattage**: 5,000 Day/ 500 Night. **Ad Rates:** Noncommercial.

20838 ■ KCEP-FM - 88.1
Summer Revival, 1221 N "J" St.
Las Vegas, NV 89106-3327
Phone: (702)648-0104
Fax: (702)647-0803
Email: power88@power88lv.com
Format: Blues; Hip Hop; Urban Contemporary; Gospel. **Networks:** American Urban Radio. **Founded:** 1973. **Operating Hours**: 100% local. **ADI**: Las Vegas, NV. **Wattage**: 10,000. **Ad Rates:** Underwriting available. $25 for 30 seconds. **URL:** http://www.power88lv.com.

20839 ■ KCNV-FM - 89.7
1289 S Torrey Pines Dr.
Las Vegas, NV 89146
Phone: (702)258-9895
Fax: (702)258-5646
Free: 866-895-5677
Format: Classical; Public Radio. **Owner:** Nevada Public Radio Corp., 1289 S Torrey Pines Dr., Las Vegas, NV 89146. **Key Personnel:** Florence Rogers, Gen. Mgr., President, flo@knpr.org; Dave Becker, Dir. of Programs, davebecker@knpr.org; Melanie Cannon, Dir. of Dev., melanie@knpr.org. **Ad Rates:** Noncommercial. **URL:** http://www.classical897.org.

20840 ■ KCYE-FM - 102.7
1455 E Tropicana, Ste. 800
Las Vegas, NV 89119
Phone: (702)730-0300
Fax: (702)736-8447
Format: Country. **Owner:** Beasley Broadcast Group Inc., 3033 Riviera Dr., Ste. 200, Naples, FL 34103-2750, Ph: (239)263-5000, Fax: (239)263-8191. **Key Personnel:** Steve Rutherford, Chief Engineer, stephen.rutherford@bbgilv.com; Cory Cuddeback, Dir. of Sales, tricia.gallenbeck@atsbbgilv.com; Justin Chase, Dir. of Programs, justin.chase@bbgilv.com. **Ad Rates:** Advertising accepted; rates available upon request. **URL:** http://1027thecoyote.com.

20841 ■ KDOX-AM - 1280
PO Box 42788
Las Vegas, NV 89116
Phone: (702)258-0285
Format: News; Talk. **Networks:** Fox. **Owner:** Summit Media Inc., 120 Main St., Sutton, WV 26601. **Founded:** 1956. **Operating Hours**: Continuous. **ADI**: Las Vegas, NV. **Wattage**: 5,000 Day; 500 post sunset; 050 Night. **Ad Rates:** Advertising accepted; rates available upon request.

20842 ■ KEKL-FM - 88.5
PO Box 779002
Rocklin, CA 95677-9972
Fax: (916)251-1901
Free: 800-525-5683
Format: Contemporary Christian. **Owner:** Educational Media Foundation, PO Box 2098, Omaha, NE 68103-2098, Free: 800-434-8400. **Key Personnel:** Mike Novak, President, CEO; Alan Mason, COO. **Wattage**: 20,500. **URL:** http://www.klove.com.

20843 ■ KILA-FM - 90.5
2201 S Sixth St.
Las Vegas, NV 89104
Phone: (702)731-5452
Fax: (702)731-1992
Email: info@sosradio.net
Format: Contemporary Christian; Religious. **Networks:** SOS Radio. **Owner:** Faith Communications Corp., 2201 S 6th St., Las Vegas, NV 89104, Ph: (702)731-5452, Free: 800-804-5452. **Founded:** 1972. **Operating Hours**: Continuous; 5% network, 95% local. **ADI**: Las Vegas, NV. **Key Personnel:** Brad Staley, Gen. Mgr.; Jack French, Gen. Mgr.; Chris Staley, Dir. of Programs. **Wattage**: 100,000. **Ad Rates:** Noncommercial.

20844 ■ KINC-TV - 15
500 Pilot Rd., Ste. D
Las Vegas, NV 89119
Phone: (702)434-0015
Fax: (702)434-0527
Owner: Entravision Communications Corporation, 2425 Olympic Blvd., Ste. 6000 W, Santa Monica, CA 90404-4030, Ph: (310)447-3870, Fax: (310)447-3899. **Key Personnel:** Walter F. Ulloa, Founder, Exec. Chmn. of the Bd., CEO; David Candelaria, Exec. VP of Mktg.; Karl Meyer, Exec. VP; Chris Moncayo, Exec. VP; Jeff Apodaca, Exec. VP of Mktg. **URL:** http://www.entravision.com.

20845 ■ KISF-FM
6767 W Tropicana Ave., Ste. 102
Las Vegas, NV 89103
Phone: (702)284-6400
Fax: (702)284-6475
Format: Hispanic. **Founded:** 1991. **Formerly**: KMMK-FM; KEDC-FM. **ADI**: Las Vegas, NV. **Wattage**: 100,000 ERP. **Ad Rates:** Noncommercial. **URL:** http://www.univision.net/corp/en/radio_directory.jsp.

20846 ■ KJUL-FM - 104.7
150 Spectrum Blvd.
Las Vegas, NV 89101
Phone: (702)258-0285
Format: News. **Networks:** Fox. **Owner:** Summit Media Inc., 120 Main St., Sutton, WV 26601. **Founded:** 1986. **Operating Hours**: Continuous. **ADI**: Las Vegas, NV. **Key Personnel:** Scott Gentry, Gen. Mgr., scott@smiradio.com. **Wattage**: 100,000 ERP. **URL:** http://www.kjul1047.com.

20847 ■ KKLZ-FM - 96.3
3950 S Las Vegas Blvd.
Las Vegas, NV 89119
Phone: (702)730-0300
Fax: (702)736-8447
Free: 888-9-297-849
Format: Classic Rock. **Networks:** Independent. **Owner:** Beasley Broadcast Group Inc., 3033 Riviera Dr., Ste. 200, Naples, FL 34103-2750, Ph: (239)263-5000, Fax: (239)263-8191. **Founded:** 1984. **Operating Hours**: Continuous. **ADI**: Las Vegas, NV. **Key Personnel:** Cory Cuddeback, Dir. of Sales, Sales Mgr.; Justin Chase, Prog. Dir., justin.chase@bbgilv.com; Tom Humm, Gen. Mgr., tom.humm@bbgilv.com; Courtney Smith, Dir. of Mktg.; Sandy Ellis, Div. Dir. **Wattage**: 100,000. **Ad Rates:** Noncommercial. **URL:** http://www.963kklz.com.

20848 ■ KKVV-AM - 1060
3185 S Highland Dr., Ste. 13
Las Vegas, NV 89109
Phone: (702)731-5588
Format: Contemporary Christian; Talk. **Networks:** Sun Radio. **Owner:** Las Vegas Broadcasters, at above address, Las Vegas, NV 89109. **Founded:** 1990. **Operating Hours**: Continuous. **ADI**: Las Vegas, NV. **Key Personnel:** Fred Hodges, Station Mgr. **Local Programs**: *The Narrow Path*, Monday Tuesday Wednesday Thursday Friday 2:00 p.m. - 3:00 p.m. **Wattage**: 5,000. **Ad Rates:** Advertising accepted; rates available upon request. **URL:** http://www.kkvv.com.

20849 ■ KLAS-TV - 8
3228 Channel 8 Dr.
Las Vegas, NV 89109
Phone: (702)792-8888
Fax: (702)792-9034
Email: cbleakley@klastv.com
Format: Commercial TV. **Networks:** CBS. **Owner:** Landmark Communications Inc., 11300 Atlantis Pl., Alpharetta, GA 30022, Ph: (770)813-1000. **Founded:** July 1953. **Operating Hours**: Continuous. **ADI**: Las Vegas, NV. **Key Personnel:** Misty Morgan, Sales Mgr.; Kathy Kramer, Dir. of Programs, Prog. Dir., kkramer@klastv.com; Linda Bonnici, VP of Sales, Sales Mgr.; Dan Schwarz, Sales Mgr.; Emily Neilson, Gen. Mgr., President; Emily Neilson, President & General Manager; Linda Bonnici, Sales Manager. **Ad Rates:** Noncommercial. **Mailing address:** PO Box 15047, Las Vegas, NV 89114-5047. **URL:** http://www.8newsnow.com.

20850 ■ KLAV-AM
2000 S Las Vegas Blvd.
Las Vegas, NV 89104
Phone: (702)796-1230
Fax: (702)385-2261
Format: Full Service; Ethnic. **Networks:** CNN Radio. **ADI**: Las Vegas, NV. **Wattage**: 1,000.

KLNR-FM - See Panaca

20851 ■ KLSQ-AM - 870
6767 W Tropicana Ave., Ste. 102
Las Vegas, NV 89103
Phone: (702)284-6400
Fax: (702)284-6403
Format: Hispanic. **Owner:** Univision Radio Inc., 3102 Oak Lawn Ave., Ste. 215, Dallas, TX 75219-4259, Ph: (214)525-7700, Fax: (214)525-7750. **Operating Hours**: 8:30 a.m.-5:30 p.m. Mon.-Fri. **Ad Rates:** Noncommercial.

20852 ■ KLVX-TV - 10
4210 Channel 10 Dr.
Las Vegas, NV 89119
Phone: (702)799-1010
Format: Public TV; Educational; News. **Networks:** BBC World Service. **Owner:** Clark County School District, 5100 W Sahara Ave., Las Vegas, NV 89146, Ph: (702)799-2273. **Founded:** Mar. 1968. **Operating Hours**: Continuous. **ADI**: Las Vegas, NV. **Key Personnel:** Tom Axtell, Gen. Mgr., taxtell@vegaspbs.org. **Local Programs**: *Nevada Week in Review*, Saturday Sunday Friday 12:30 a.m. 6:30 a.m. 7:30 p.m. **Wattage**: 105,000. **Ad Rates:** Accepts Advertising. **URL:** http://www.vegaspbs.org.

20853 ■ KMXB-FM - 94.1
CBS Radio Las Vegas
6655 W Sahara Ave., Ste. D-110
Las Vegas, NV 89146
Phone: (702)364-9400
Fax: (702)257-2936
Format: Contemporary Hit Radio (CHR). **Key Personnel:** Tom Humm, Gen. Mgr., tomhumm@mix941.fm; Brandon Bell, Music Dir., brandon.bell@cbsradio.com. **Ad Rates:** Advertising accepted; rates available upon request. **URL:** http://www.mix941fm.cbslocal.com.

KMZL-FM - See Missoula, MT

KMZO-FM - See Hamilton, MT

20854 ■ KNPR-FM - 88.9
1289 S Torrey Pines Dr.
Las Vegas, NV 89146
Phone: (702)258-9895
Fax: (702)258-5646
Free: 888-258-9895
Format: Public Radio; News. **Networks:** National Public Radio (NPR). **Owner:** Nevada Public Radio Corp., 1289 S Torrey Pines Dr., Las Vegas, NV 89146. **Founded:** 1980. **Operating Hours**: Continuous; 20% network, 80% local. **ADI**: Las Vegas, NV. **Key Personnel:** Dave Becker, Div. Dir., davebecker@nevadapublicradio.org; Melanie Cannon, Dir. of Dev., melanie@nevadapublicradio.org; Florence Rogers, Gen. Mgr., President, flo@knpr.org; Phillip Burger, Dir. of Opera-

Circulation: ★ = AAM; △ or • = BPA; ♦ = CAC; ❑ = VAC; ⊕ = PO Statement; ‡ = Publisher's Report; Boldface figures = sworn; Light figures = estimated.

tions; Chris Smith, Art Dir., chris@desertcompanion.com. **Local Programs**: *As It Happens*; *Vinyl Cafe*, Saturday 8:00 p.m. - 9:00 p.m. **Wattage**: 100,000. **Ad Rates:** Noncommercial. **URL:** http://www.knpr.org.

20855 ■ KNUU-AM - 970
1455 E Tropicana Ave., Ste. 550
Las Vegas, NV 89119
Phone: (702)735-8644
Fax: (702)734-4755
Format: Talk; News. **Networks:** ABC; CNN Radio; AP. **Founded:** July 05, 1977. **Operating Hours**: Continuous; 20% network, 80% local. **ADI**: Las Vegas, NV. **Key Personnel:** Andy Vierra, Program Mgr., andy.vierra@970knuu.com. **Wattage**: 5,000 Day; 500 Night. **Ad Rates:** $40 for 30 seconds; $43 for 60 seconds.

20856 ■ KOAS-FM - 105.7
1455 E Tropicana, Ste. 800
Las Vegas, NV 89119
Phone: (702)730-0300
Fax: (702)736-8447
Free: 855-566-0300
Format: Jazz. **Ad Rates:** Noncommercial. **URL:** http://www.oldschool1057.com.

20857 ■ KOMP-FM - 92.3
8755 W Flamingo Rd.
Las Vegas, NV 89147-8667
Phone: (702)876-3692
Format: Album-Oriented Rock (AOR). **Owner:** Lotus Communication Corp., 3301 Barham Blvd., Ste. 200, Los Angeles, CA 90068, Ph: (323)512-2225, Fax: (323)512-2224. **Founded:** 1966. **Ad Rates:** Noncommercial; Advertising accepted; rates available upon request. **URL:** http://www.komp.com.

20858 ■ KPLV-FM - 93.1
2880 Meade Ave., Ste. 250, 2nd Fl.
Las Vegas, NV 89102
Phone: (702)238-7300
Fax: (702)732-4890
Format: Adult Contemporary. **Owner:** iHeartMedia Inc., 200 E Basse Rd., San Antonio, TX 78209, Ph: (210)832-3314. **Key Personnel:** Amy Fewox, Dir. of Mktg., Dir. of Public Rel., amyfewox@clearchannel.com. **Ad Rates:** Advertising accepted; rates available upon request. **URL:** http://www.my931.com.

20859 ■ KQRT-FM - 105.1
500 Pilot Rd., Ste. D
Las Vegas, NV 89119
Phone: (702)597-3070
Fax: (702)507-1084
Format: Hispanic. **Owner:** Entravision Communications Corporation, 2425 Olympic Blvd., Ste. 6000 W, Santa Monica, CA 90404-4030, Ph: (310)447-3870, Fax: (310)447-3899. **ADI**: Las Vegas, NV. **Key Personnel:** Chris Roman, Gen. Mgr. **URL:** http://www.entravision.com.

20860 ■ KRGT-FM - 99.3
6767 W Tropicana Ave., Ste. 102
Las Vegas, NV 89103
Phone: (702)284-6400
Fax: (702)284-6475
Format: Hispanic. **Owner:** Univision Communications Inc., 3102 Oak Lawn Ave., Ste. 215, Dallas, TX 75219, Ph: (214)525-7700, Fax: (214)525-7750. **Key Personnel:** Rafael Miramontes, Dir. of Programs. **URL:** http://993lasvegas.univision.com.

20861 ■ KRRN-FM - 92.7
500 Pilot Rd., Ste. D
Las Vegas, NV 89119
Phone: (702)597-3070
Fax: (702)896-3599
Format: Hispanic. **Owner:** Entravision Communications Corporation, 2425 Olympic Blvd., Ste. 6000 W, Santa Monica, CA 90404-4030, Ph: (310)447-3870, Fax: (310)447-3899. **ADI**: Las Vegas, NV. **Key Personnel:** Chris Roman, Gen. Mgr. **URL:** http://www.entravision.com.

20862 ■ KSGU-FM - 90.3
1289 S Torrey Pines Dr.
Las Vegas, NV 89146
Phone: (702)258-9895
Fax: (702)258-5646
Free: 888-258-9895
Format: Public Radio; News. **Founded:** 1975. **Operating Hours**: Continuous. **Key Personnel:** Florence Rogers, Gen. Mgr., President, flo@knpr.org; Dave Becker, Dir. of Programs, davebecker@knpr.org; Melanie Cannon, Dir. of Dev., melanie@knpr.org; Phil Burger, Director, phil@knpr.org; Lou Ann Boone, Traffic Mgr., louann@nevadapublicradio.org; Jay Bartos, Mgr., jayb@knpr.org. **Wattage**: 2,000. **Ad Rates:** Noncommercial; underwriting available.

20863 ■ KSHP-AM - 1400
2400 S Jones Blvd., No. 3
Las Vegas, NV 89146
Phone: (702)221-1200
Format: News; Talk. **Owner:** Las Vegas Radio Company Inc., 2400 S Jones Blvd., Ste. 3, Las Vegas, NV 89146, Ph: (702)221-1200. **Founded:** 1996. **Operating Hours**: Continuous. **Wattage**: 1,000. **Ad Rates:** Noncommercial. **URL:** http://www.kshp.com.

20864 ■ KSNE-FM - 106.5
2880 Meade Ave., Ste. 250
Las Vegas, NV 89102
Phone: (702)238-7300
Fax: (702)734-1065
Format: Adult Contemporary. **Networks:** Independent. **Founded:** 1987. **Operating Hours**: Continuous; 100% local. **Key Personnel:** Tom Chase, Operations Mgr., Program Mgr., tomchase@clearchannel.com. **Wattage**: 100,000. **Ad Rates:** Advertising accepted; rates available upon request. **URL:** http://www.sunny1065.com//main.html.

20865 ■ KSNV-TV - 3
1500 Foremaster Ln.
Las Vegas, NV 89101
Phone: (702)642-3333
Email: comments@mynews3.com
Networks: NBC. **Owner:** Intermountain West Communications Co. **Founded:** 1955. **Formerly**: KVBC Las Vegas. **Key Personnel:** Lisa Howfield, Gen. Mgr., VP, lhowfield@kvbc.com. **URL:** http://www.mynews3.com.

20866 ■ KSTJ-FM - 104.3
6725 Via Austi Pky., 2nd Fl.
Las Vegas, NV 89119
Phone: (702)730-0300
Fax: (702)736-8447
Format: Eighties; Hip Hop; Top 40. **ADI**: Las Vegas, NV. **Key Personnel:** Tom Davis, Gen. Mgr., tom.davis@bbgilv.com; Don Hallett, Dir. of Programs, don.hallett@bbgilv.com; Patti Mills, Gen. Sales Mgr., patti.mills@bbgilv.com; Courtney Smith, Dir. of Mktg., Promotions Dir., courtney.smith@bbgilv.com; Ray Fodge, Chief Engineer, ray.fodge@bbgilv.com. **Wattage**: 24,500 ERP. **Ad Rates:** Advertising accepted; rates available upon request. **URL:** http://1043now.com.

20867 ■ KTNV-TV - 13
3355 S Valley View Blvd.
Las Vegas, NV 89102
Phone: (702)876-1313
Fax: (702)876-2237
Format: Commercial TV. **Networks:** ABC. **Owner:** Journal Broadcast Corp., 333 W State St., Milwaukee, WI 53203, Ph: (414)332-9611, Fax: (414)967-5400. **Formerly**: KSHO-TV. **Operating Hours**: Continuous. **ADI**: Las Vegas, NV. **Key Personnel:** Jim Prather, Gen. Mgr., VP, jprather@ktnv.com; Thomas Porterfield, Gen. Sales Mgr., Station Mgr., tporterfield@ktnv.com; Karin Movesian, News Dir., kmovesian@ktnv.com; Greg Rogers, Contact, grogers@ktnv.com. **Ad Rates:** Advertising accepted; rates available upon request. **URL:** http://www.ktnv.com.

20868 ■ KTPH-FM - 91.7
1289 S Torrey Pines Dr.
Las Vegas, NV 89146
Phone: (702)258-9895
Fax: (702)258-5646
Free: 888-258-9895
Format: Public Radio. **Networks:** National Public Radio (NPR). **Owner:** Nevada Public Radio Corp., 1289 S Torrey Pines Dr., Las Vegas, NV 89146. **Founded:** 1988. **Operating Hours**: Continuous. **ADI**: Las Vegas, NV. **Key Personnel:** Susan Brennan, Partner; Lamar Marchese, Gen. Mgr.; Andrew Kiraly, Dept. Mgr.; Phil Burger, Mktg. Mgr.; Dave Becker, Div. Dir.; Chris Smith, Art Dir.; Megan Jones, Chmn. of the Bd.; Melanie Cannon, Bus. Mgr. **Wattage**: 100. **Ad Rates:** Noncommercial. **URL:** http://www.knpr.org.

20869 ■ KTUD-TV
6760 Surrey St.
Las Vegas, NV 89119
Phone: (702)222-2225
URL: http://www.ilovevegastv.com/home.html.

20870 ■ K211DC-FM - 90.1
PO Box 391
Twin Falls, ID 83303
Fax: (208)736-1958
Free: 800-357-4226
Format: Religious; Contemporary Christian. **Owner:** CSN International, PO Box 391, Twin Falls, ID 83303, Ph: (208)736-1958, Fax: (208)736-1958, Free: 800-357-4226. **Key Personnel:** Kelly Carlson, Dir. of Engg.; Ray Gorney, Asst. Dir.; Don Mills, Music Dir., Prog. Dir. **URL:** http://www.csnradio.com.

20871 ■ K234AI-FM - 94.7
1665 Briargate Blvd., Ste. 100
Colorado Springs, CO 80920-3400
Fax: (208)736-1958
Free: 800-357-4226
Format: Religious; Contemporary Christian. **Owner:** CSN International, PO Box 391, Twin Falls, ID 83303, Ph: (208)736-1958, Fax: (208)736-1958, Free: 800-357-4226. **Key Personnel:** Mike Kestler, President; Don Mills, Music Dir., Prog. Dir.; Daniel Davidson, Dir. of Operations. **URL:** http://www.csnradio.com.

KUDA-FM - See Pahrump

20872 ■ KUNV-FM - 91.5
4505 S Maryland Pkwy.
Las Vegas, NV 89154-2010
Phone: (702)895-5868
Fax: (702)895-0068
Format: Jazz. **Networks:** National Public Radio (NPR). **Founded:** 1981. **Operating Hours**: Continuous. **ADI**: Las Vegas, NV. **Key Personnel:** Frank Mueller, Gen. Mgr.; Gretchen Rexroad, Bus. Mgr., gretchen.rexroad@unlv.edu; Kim Linzy, Music Dir., kim.linzy@unlv.edu. **Wattage**: 15,000. **Ad Rates:** Noncommercial; underwriting available. **Mailing address:** PO Box 452010, Las Vegas, NV 89154. **URL:** http://www.kunv.org.

20873 ■ KVCW-TV - 33
3830 S Jones Blvd.
Las Vegas, NV 89103
Phone: (702)382-2121
Fax: (702)952-4676
Email: closedcaptioning@thecwlasvegas.tv
Format: Commercial TV. **Owner:** Sinclair Broadcasting Group Inc., 10706 Beaver Dam Rd., Cockeysville, MD 21030. **Formerly**: KUPN-TV; KFBT-TV. **Operating Hours**: Continuous. **ADI**: Las Vegas, NV. **Ad Rates:** Noncommercial. **URL:** http://www.thecwlasvegas.tv.

20874 ■ KVEG-FM - 97.5
3999 S Las Vegas Blvd., Ste. K
Las Vegas, NV 89119
Phone: (702)736-6161
Fax: (702)736-2986
Format: Hip Hop. **Wattage**: 100,000. **Ad Rates:** Noncommercial. **URL:** http://www.kvegas.com.

20875 ■ KVGS-FM - 107.9
1455 E Torpicana, Ste. 800
Las Vegas, NV 89119
Phone: (702)730-0300
Fax: (702)736-8447
Format: Alternative/New Music/Progressive. **Owner:** Riviera Broadcast Group, at above address. **Key Personnel:** Tom Humm, Gen. Mgr., tom.humm@bbgilv.com; Sean Lynch, Dir. of Programs, sean.lynch@bbgilv.com. **Ad Rates:** Advertising accepted; rates available upon request. **URL:** http://www.1079thealternative.com.

20876 ■ KVKL-FM - 91.1
PO Box 2098
Omaha, NE 68103
Free: 800-525-LOVE
Format: Contemporary Christian. **Owner:** Educational Media Foundation, 5700 W Oaks Blvd., CA 95765, Free: 800-800434-8400. **URL:** http://www.klove.com.

20877 ■ KVMY-TV - 21
3830 S Jones Blvd.
Las Vegas, NV 89103
Phone: (702)382-2121
Fax: (702)952-4676

Owner: Sinclair Broadcast Group Inc., 10706 Beaver Dam Rd., Hunt Valley, MD 21030, Ph: (410)568-1500, Fax: (410)568-1533. **Formerly**: KVWB-TV. **URL:** http://www.mylvtv.com.

20878 ■ KWID-FM - 101.9
2880-B Meade Ave., Ste. 250
Las Vegas, NV 89102
Phone: (702)238-7300
Fax: (702)732-4890
Format: Hispanic. **ADI**: Las Vegas, NV. **Key Personnel:** Brandy Newman, Gen. Mgr. **Wattage**: 100,000. **Ad Rates:** Noncommercial.

20879 ■ KWNR-FM - 95.5
2880 Meade Ave., Ste. 250
Las Vegas, NV 89102
Phone: (702)238-7300
Fax: (702)732-4890
Format: Contemporary Country. **Networks:** Independent. **Owner:** Clear Channel Communications Inc., at above address, Ph: (210)822-2828, Fax: (210)822-2299. **Founded:** 1988. **Operating Hours:** Continuous. **ADI**: Las Vegas, NV. **Key Personnel:** Sean Cassidy, Sales Mgr., seancassidy@clearchannel.com; Rik McNeil, Prog. Dir., rikmcneil@clearchannel.com; J.C. Simon, Contact, jcsimon@clearchannel.com. **Wattage**: 100,000. **Ad Rates:** $160 per unit. **URL:** http://www.955thebull.com.

20880 ■ KWWN-AM - 1100
8755 W Flamingo Rd.
Las Vegas, NV 89147
Phone: (702)876-1460
Fax: (702)876-6685
Format: Sports; Talk. **Owner:** Lotus Communications Corp., 3301 Barham Blvd., Ste. 200, Los Angeles, CA 90068, Ph: (323)512-2225, Fax: (323)512-2224. **Key Personnel:** Howard A. Kalmenson, President, CEO; John Paley, VP of Corp. Rel.; William H. Shriftman, Sr. VP. **URL:** http://www.lotuscorp.com.

20881 ■ KXNT-AM - 840
7255 S Tenaya Way, Ste. 100
Las Vegas, NV 89113
Phone: (702)889-7300
Format: News; Talk. **Networks:** ABC. **Owner:** CBS Radio Inc., 1271 Avenue of the Americas, 44th Fl., New York, NY 10020-1401, Ph: (212)649-9600. **Founded:** 1988. **Operating Hours**: Mon. - Fri. & Sun. - Continuous; 6am - 1 am - Sat. **Key Personnel:** Cat Thomas, Dir. of Programs; Corey Olson, News Dir., cpolson@cbs.com. **Wattage**: 50,000 Day 25,000 Night. **Ad Rates:** Advertising accepted; rates available upon request. Combined advertising rates available with KSFN-AM. **URL:** http://www.lasvegas.cbslocal.com.

20882 ■ KXPT-FM - 97.1
8755 W Flamingo Rd.
Las Vegas, NV 89147
Phone: (702)876-1460
Format: Classic Rock. **Networks:** Independent. **Owner:** Lotus Communications Corp., 3301 Barham Blvd., Ste. 200, Los Angeles, CA 90068, Ph: (323)512-2225, Fax: (323)512-2224. **Formerly**: KYRK-FM. **Operating Hours**: Continuous. **ADI**: Las Vegas, NV. **Key Personnel:** Howard A. Kalmenson, President, CEO; John Paley, VP of Corp. Rel.; William H. Shriftman, Sr. VP. **Wattage:** 25,000. **Ad Rates:** $105-160 per unit. **URL:** http://lotuscorp.com.

20883 ■ KXTE-FM - 107.5
6655 W Sahara Ave.
Las Vegas, NV 89146-0851
Phone: (702)257-1075
Format: Alternative/New Music/Progressive. **Owner:** CBS Radio Inc., 1271 Avenue of the Americas, 44th Fl., New York, NY 10020-1401, Ph: (212)649-9600. **Key Personnel:** Cat Thomas, Dir. of Programs. **Ad Rates:** Noncommercial.

20884 ■ 98.5 KLUC-FM - 98.5
7255 S Tenaya Way, Ste. 100
Las Vegas, NV 89113
Phone: (702)253-9800
Fax: (702)889-7373
Format: Top 40. **Key Personnel:** Cat Thomas, Dir. of Programs, cat@kluc.com; John James, Dir. of Production, jj@kluc.com. **URL:** http://kluc.cbslocal.com.

20885 ■ 720 AM KDWN - 720
2920 S Durango Dr.
Las Vegas, NV 89117
Phone: (702)730-0300
Format: Talk; News. **Networks:** AP. **Owner:** Beasley Broadcast Group Inc., 3033 Riviera Dr., Ste. 200, Naples, FL 34103-2750, Ph: (239)263-5000, Fax: (239)263-8191. **Founded:** 1975. **Operating Hours**: Continuous; 10% network, 90% local. **ADI**: Las Vegas, NV. **Key Personnel:** Tom Humm, Dir. of Mktg., Mktg. Mgr.; John Shaffer, Dir. of Programs; Bill Davis, Dir. of Sales. **Wattage:** 50,000. **Ad Rates:** $18-28 for 30 seconds; $22-38 for 60 seconds. **URL:** http://www.kdwn.com.

LAUGHLIN

Clark Co.

20886 ■ KLBC-TV - 2
3100 S Needles Hwy., Ste. 1700
Laughlin, NV 89029
Phone: (702)298-2222
Fax: (702)298-0011
Key Personnel: Bruce Clark, Gen. Mgr., rbc@tv2klbc.com. **URL:** http://www.tv2klbc.com.

LOVELOCK

Pershing Co. Pershing Co. (S). Tungsten and Copper mines.

20887 ■ K204FR-FM - 88.7
PO Box 391
Twin Falls, ID 83303
Fax: (208)736-1958
Free: 800-357-4226
Format: Religious; Contemporary Christian. **Owner:** CSN International, PO Box 391, Twin Falls, ID 83303, Ph: (208)736-1958, Fax: (208)736-1958, Free: 800-357-4226. **Key Personnel:** Don Mills, Prog. Dir., Div. Dir. **URL:** http://www.csnradio.com.

NORTH LAS VEGAS

20888 ■ Red Rock Review
College of Southern Nevada
c/o Dr. Richard Logsdon, Editor
CSN Department of English, J2A
3200 E Cheyenne Ave.
North Las Vegas, NV 89030
Phone: (702)651-4094
Journal featuring fiction, creative non-fiction and poetry. **Freq:** Semiannual. **Key Personnel:** Dr. Richard Logsdon, Editor; Todd Moffett, Senior Editor. **ISSN:** 1086--4342 (print). **Subscription Rates:** $6.50 Single issue. **Alt. Formats:** Electronic publishing. **URL:** http://sites.csn.edu/english/redrockreview. **Circ:** (Not Reported).

20889 ■ K295AJ-FM
PO Box 391
Twin Falls, ID 83303
Fax: (208)736-1958
Free: 800-357-4226
Owner: CSN International, PO Box 391, Twin Falls, ID 83303, Ph: (208)736-1958, Fax: (208)736-1958, Free: 800-357-4226. **URL:** http://www.csnradio.com.

PAHRUMP

20890 ■ Pahrump Valley Times
Stephens Media L.L.C.
1570 E Highway 372
Pahrump, NV 89048-4638
Phone: (775)727-5102
Fax: (775)727-5309
Publication E-mail: mward@pvtimes.com
Community newspaper. **Freq:** Semiweekly (Wed. and Fri.). **Key Personnel:** Marie Wujek, Publisher; Chuck King, Manager, Production. **Subscription Rates:** $45 Individuals /year (home delivery, print); $110 By mail /year (print); $25 Individuals 6 months (home delivery, print); $80 By mail 6 months (print). **URL:** http://pvtimes.com. **Ad Rates:** PCI $1-13/16; PCI $7.15. **Remarks:** Accepts advertising. **Circ:** 34000.

20891 ■ KNYE-FM - 95.1
1230 Dutch Ford St.
Pahrump, NV 89048
Email: knye@knye.com
Format: Contemporary Hit Radio (CHR); Oldies. **Founded:** Sept. 13, 2006. **Ad Rates:** Noncommercial. **URL:** http://www.knye.com.

20892 ■ KUDA-FM - 107.5
7255 S Tenaya Way, Ste. 100
Las Vegas, NV 89113
Phone: (702)257-1075
Fax: (702)889-7555
Format: Music of Your Life; News. **Founded:** 1989. **ADI**: Las Vegas, NV. **Key Personnel:** Julie Cannon, News Dir.; Joe Sands, Chief Engineer; Scott Seidenstricker, Contact; Scott Seidenstricker, Contact; Bill Tod, Contact. **Wattage**: 24,500 ERP. **Ad Rates:** Accepts Advertising. **URL:** http://x1075lasvegas.cbslocal.com.

PANACA

20893 ■ KLNR-FM
1289 S Torrey Pines Dr.
Las Vegas, NV 89146-1004
Email: knpr@accessnv.com
Format: Classical; News. **Networks:** National Public Radio (NPR). **Owner:** Nevada Public Radio Corp., 1289 S Torrey Pines Dr., Las Vegas, NV 89146. **Founded:** 1989. **Wattage**: 1,000 ERP.

RENO

Washoe Co. Washoe Co. (W). 140 m NE of Sacramento, Calif. University of Nevada-Reno. Tourist resort, legalized gambling, recreation & winter skiing. Western warehousing and distribution center. Manufactures cement, labeling devices, suntan lotion, valves, dairy and food products, gaming, pet food, microwave, electronic equipment. Livestock, agricultural produce. Alfalfa seed, grain.

20894 ■ Bay and Delta Yachtsman
Recreation Publications Inc.
4090 S McCarran Blvd., Ste. E
Reno, NV 89502
Phone: (775)353-5100
Fax: (775)353-5111
Free: 800-878-7886
Magazine for boating and yachting enthusiasts. **Freq:** Monthly. **Print Method:** Offset. **Trim Size:** 7.25 x 10. **Cols./Page:** 3. **Col. Width:** 2 1/4 inches. **Col. Depth:** 130 agate lines. **Key Personnel:** Ty Mellott, Publisher. **ISSN:** 0191--4731 (print). **URL:** http://www.yachtsmanmagazine.com. **Ad Rates:** BW $1,365. **Remarks:** Accepts advertising. **Circ:** ‡30000.

20895 ■ Case in Point
National Judicial College
Judicial College Bldg., MS 358
Reno, NV 89557
Phone: (775)784-6747
Fax: (775)784-1253
Free: 800-255-8343
Publisher's E-mail: info@judges.org
Freq: Periodic. **Subscription Rates:** Free. **Alt. Formats:** PDF. **Remarks:** Advertising not accepted. **Circ:** (Not Reported).

20896 ■ Computers in the Schools: The Interdisciplinary Journal of Practice, Theory, and Applied Research
Routledge Journals Taylor & Francis Group
c/o LaMont D. Johnson, PhD, Ed.
Dept. of Educational Counseling & Educational Psychology
College of Education
University of Nevada-Reno
Reno, NV 89557
Interdisciplinary journal of practice, theory, and applied research relating to the use of computers in education. **Freq:** Quarterly. **Trim Size:** 6 x 8 3/8. **Cols./Page:** 1. **Col. Width:** 4 1/2 inches. **Col. Depth:** 7 1/4 inches. **Key Personnel:** Jerry Willis, Board Member; Cleborne Maddux, Associate Editor; LaMont D. Johnson, PhD, Editor; Mary L. Johnson, Managing Editor; Scott W. Brown, Board Member; Rhoda Cummings, Board Member. **ISSN:** 0738-0569 (print); **EISSN:** 1528-7033 (electronic). **Subscription Rates:** $797 Institutions online only; $148 Individuals online only; $911 Institutions print + online; $160 Individuals print + online. **URL:** http://www.tandfonline.com/toc/wcis20/current#.VGv9izQwpM4. **Ad Rates:** BW $315; 4C $550. **Remarks:** Accepts advertising. **Circ:** Paid 542.

Circulation: ★ = AAM; △ or • = BPA; ♦ = CAC; ❑ = VAC; ⊕ = PO Statement; ‡ = Publisher's Report; Boldface figures = sworn; Light figures = estimated.

20897 ■ Democracy and Security
Routledge
c/o Leonard Weinberg, Editor-in-Chief
Dept. of Political Science
University of Nevada
Mail Stop 302
Reno, NV 89557
Publisher's E-mail: book.orders@tandf.co.uk
Academic journal that publishes articles about democracy and security. **Freq:** Quarterly. **Key Personnel:** Jerrold Post, Board Member; Giovanni Capoccia, Board Member; Arie Perliger, Editor-in-Chief; Rogelio Alonso, Board Member; Leonardo Morlino, Board Member. **ISSN:** 1741--9166 (print); **EISSN:** 1555--5860 (electronic). **Subscription Rates:** $569 Institutions print and online; $498 Institutions online only; $139 Individuals print only. **URL:** http://www.tandfonline.com/toc/fdas20/current#.VH5GNdlwrlc. **Remarks:** Accepts advertising. **Circ:** (Not Reported).

20898 ■ Juvenile and Family Court Journal
National Council of Juvenile and Family Court Judges
PO Box 8970
Reno, NV 89507
Phone: (775)507-4777
Fax: (775)507-4855
Publisher's E-mail: contactus@ncjfcj.org
Peer-reviewed journal covering juvenile and family law. **Freq:** Quarterly. **Trim Size:** 8 1/2 x 11. **Cols./Page:** 2. **Col. Width:** 3 1/2 inches. **Col. Depth:** 9 inches. **Key Personnel:** Maurice Portley, Editor; Prof. Douglas E. Abrams, Associate Editor. **ISSN:** 0161--7109 (print); **EISSN:** 1755--6988 (electronic). **Subscription Rates:** included in membership dues; $350 /year for institutions in America and rest of the world, online only; £178 /year for institutions in UK, online only; €227 /year for institutions in Europe, online only; $350 /year for institutions in America and rest of the world, print and online; £214 /year for institutions in UK, print and online; €273 /year for institutions in Europe, print and online. **URL:** http://www.blackwellpublishing.com/journal.asp?ref=0161-7109. **Remarks:** Advertising not accepted. **Circ:** Combined ⊕**2300**.

20899 ■ The Meadow
Truckee Meadows Community College
7000 Dandini Blvd.
Reno, NV 89512
Phone: (775)673-7000
Fax: (775)673-7028
Publisher's E-mail: tmoore@tmcc.edu
Journal featuring arts and literature. **Freq:** Annual. **Key Personnel:** Lindsay Wilson, Editor-in-Chief. **ISSN:** 0886--8654 (print). **URL:** http://www.tmcc.edu/meadow. **Circ:** (Not Reported).

20900 ■ The Nevada Sagebrush
University of Nevada, Reno
1664 N Virginia St.
Reno, NV 89557
Phone: (702)784-1110
Publication E-mail: editor@nevadasagebrush.com
Collegiate newspaper covering all aspects of campus life. **Freq:** Weekly (Tues.) during Fall & Spring semesters. **Print Method:** Offset. Uses mats. **Cols./Page:** 6. **Col. Width:** 147 INS. **Col. Depth:** 21 inches. **URL:** http://nevadasagebrush.com. **Formerly:** Sagebrush. **Ad Rates:** GLR $7.90; SAU $7.90. **Remarks:** 7.90. **Circ:** 3500.

20901 ■ PetFolio
Animal Fanfare Publishing Inc.
PO Box 8997
Reno, NV 89507
Phone: (775)722-9914
Publisher's E-mail: events@petfoliomagazine.com
Magazine for animal lovers. **Freq:** Bimonthly. **Key Personnel:** Bruce Witmer, MD, Publisher; Michelle McHarty, Managing Editor; Landess Legier Witmer, Executive Editor. **Subscription Rates:** $20 Individuals. **URL:** http://www.petfoliomagazine.com/. **Circ:** (Not Reported).

20902 ■ The Reno Gazette-Journal
Gannett Company Inc.
955 Kuenzli St.
Reno, NV 89502-2000
Phone: (775)788-6200
General newspaper. **Freq:** Mon.-Sun. (morn.). **Print Method:** Letterpress and Offset. **Trim Size:** 13 x 21 1/2. **Cols./Page:** 6. **Col. Width:** 26 nonpareils. **Col. Depth:** 301 agate lines. **Key Personnel:** John Maher, President, Publisher; Kelly Ann Scott, Executive Editor. **Subscription Rates:** $7 Individuals Sunday - online and print; $9 Individuals /month (online and print, Wednesday - Sunday); $12 Individuals /month (print and online only-Monday and Sunday); $9.99 Individuals online only. **URL:** http://www.rgj.com. **Formerly:** Nevada State Journal and Reno Evening Gazette. **Remarks:** Accepts advertising. **Circ:** (Not Reported).

20903 ■ Western Roofing/Insulation/Siding
Dodson Publications Inc.
546 Court St.
Reno, NV 89501
Phone: (775)333-1080
Fax: (775)333-1081
Publication E-mail: info@westernroofing.net
Roofing, siding, and insulation magazine published for the western roofing industry in affiliation with the Western Roofing Contractors Association. **Freq:** Bimonthly. **Print Method:** Offset. **Trim Size:** 8 3/8 x 10 7/8. **Cols./Page:** 3. **Col. Width:** 27 nonpareils. **Col. Depth:** 137 agate lines. **Key Personnel:** Marc Dodson, Editor; Marcus Dodson, Publisher. **ISSN:** 0273--5687 (print). **Subscription Rates:** $12 Individuals; $28 Individuals 3 years; $60 Other countries. **URL:** http://www.westernroofing.net/Home.html. **Ad Rates:** BW $2,025; 4C $4,675. **Remarks:** Accepts advertising. **Circ:** Paid ‡3973, Controlled ‡20410.

20904 ■ KAME-TV - 21
4920 Brookside Ct.
Reno, NV 89502
Phone: (775)856-1100
Format: Commercial TV. **Networks:** Fox; Independent. **Founded:** 1981. **Operating Hours:** Continuous. **ADI:** Reno, NV. **Key Personnel:** Ray Stofer, Chief Engineer, ray.stofer@coxinc.com; Steve Cummings, Gen. Mgr., VP, steve.cummings@ccoxinc.com; Amie Chapman, Gen. Sales Mgr., amie.chapman@coxinc.com. **Ad Rates:** Advertising accepted; rates available upon request. **URL:** http://www.foxreno.com.

20905 ■ KBDB-AM - 1400
6080 Mt. Moriah
Memphis, TN 38115
Phone: (901)375-9324
Fax: (901)375-5889
Email: mail@flinn.com
Format: Hispanic. **Owner:** Flinn Broadcasting Corporation, at above address. **ADI:** Reno, NV. **URL:** http://www.flinn.com.

20906 ■ KBUL-FM - 98.1
595 E Plumb Ln.
Reno, NV 89502
Phone: (775)789-6700
Fax: (775)789-6767
Format: Country. **Owner:** Citadel Broadcasting Corp., 7201 W Lake Mead Blvd., Ste. 400, Las Vegas, NV 89128-8366, Ph: (702)804-5200, Fax: (702)804-8250. **Founded:** 1984. **Operating Hours:** Continuous. **Key Personnel:** Jennifer Odom, Sales Mgr.; Derek Gunn, Promotions Dir.; Brad Hansen, Dir. of Programs. **Wattage:** 76,000. **Ad Rates:** Noncommercial. Combined advertising rates available with KNEV-FM and KROW-AM. **URL:** http://www.kbul.com.

20907 ■ KBZZ-AM - 1270
961 Matley Ln., Ste. 120
Reno, NV 89502
Phone: (775)829-1964
Format: Talk.

20908 ■ KDOT-FM - 104.5
2900 Sutro St.
Reno, NV 89512
Phone: (775)329-9261
Fax: (775)323-1450
Format: Album-Oriented Rock (AOR). **Owner:** Lotus Communications Corp., 3301 Barham Blvd., Ste. 200, Los Angeles, CA 90068, Ph: (323)512-2225, Fax: (323)512-2224. **Founded:** 1966. **Formerly:** KIIQ-FM; KHIT-FM. **Operating Hours:** Continuous. **ADI:** Reno, NV. **Key Personnel:** Dane Wilt, Gen. Mgr., dane@lotusradio.com; Dee Kane, Sales Mgr., dee@lotusradio.com; Jave Patterson, Operations Mgr., javepatt@gmail.com. **Wattage:** 25,000. **Ad Rates:** Advertising accepted; rates available upon request. **URL:** http://www.kdot.com.

20909 ■ KGVN-FM - 93.7
595 E Plumb Ln.
Reno, NV 89503
Phone: (775)789-6700
Fax: (775)789-6767
Format: Oldies. **Owner:** Citadel Broadcasting Corp., 7201 W Lake Mead Blvd., Ste. 400, Las Vegas, NV 89128-8366, Ph: (702)804-5200, Fax: (702)804-8250. **ADI:** Reno, NV. **Wattage:** 3,600.

20910 ■ KIHM-AM
3256 Penryn Rd., Ste. 100
Loomis, CA 95650-8052
Free: 866-774-3278
Format: Religious. **Owner:** Immaculate Heart Radio, 3256 Penryn Rd., Ste. 100, Loomis, CA 95650-8052. **ADI:** Reno, NV. **Wattage:** 4,800 Day; 850 Night. **Ad Rates:** Noncommercial.

20911 ■ KJZS-FM - 92.1
300 E 2nd St., 14th Fl.
Reno, NV 89501
Phone: (775)333-0123
Fax: (775)322-7361
Format: Jazz. **Founded:** Sept. 14, 2006. **Ad Rates:** Advertising accepted; rates available upon request.

20912 ■ KKOH-AM - 780
595 E Plumb Ln.
Reno, NV 89502
Phone: (775)789-6700
Fax: (775)789-6767
Email: weekendmagazine@kkoh.com
Format: News; Talk. **Simulcasts:** KBUL-FM. **Networks:** ABC. **Owner:** Cumulus Media Inc., 3280 Peachtree Rd. NW, Ste. 2300, Atlanta, GA 30305-2455, Ph: (404)949-0700, Fax: (404)949-0740. **Founded:** 1970. **Operating Hours:** Continuous. **ADI:** Reno, NV. **Local Programs:** *Nevada Newsmakers*, Sunday 7:00 a.m. - 9:00 a.m.; *Nevada Outlook*, Sunday 6:00 p.m. - 7:00 p.m. **Wattage:** 50,000. **Ad Rates:** Combined advertising rates available with KNEV-FM. **URL:** http://www.kkoh.com.

20913 ■ KLCA-FM - 96.5
961 Matley Ln., Ste. 120
Reno, NV 89502
Phone: (775)829-1964
Fax: (775)825-3183
Format: Alternative/New Music/Progressive. **URL:** http://www.alice965.com.

20914 ■ KLRH-FM - 92.9
PO Box 779002
Rocklin, CA 95677-9972
Fax: (916)251-1901
Free: 800-525-5683
Format: Contemporary Christian. **Owner:** Educational Media Foundation, PO Box 2098, Omaha, NE 68103-2098, Free: 800-434-8400. **ADI:** Reno, NV. **Key Personnel:** Mike Novak, President, CEO; Alan Mason, COO. **Wattage:** 48,000. **URL:** http://www.klove.com.

KNCC-FM - See Elko, NV

20915 ■ KNEV-FM - 95.5
595 E Plumb Ln.
Reno, NV 89502
Phone: (775)789-6700
Fax: (775)789-6767
Format: Adult Contemporary. **Networks:** ABC. **Owner:** Citadel Broadcasting Corp., 7201 W Lake Mead Blvd., Ste. 400, Las Vegas, NV 89128-8366, Ph: (702)804-5200, Fax: (702)804-8250. **Founded:** 1953. **Operating Hours:** Continuous. **Wattage:** 64,000. **Ad Rates:** Advertising accepted; rates available upon request. Advertising accepted; contact publisher for rates. Combined advertising rates available with KROW-AM and KBUL-FM. **URL:** http://www.magic95.com.

20916 ■ KNHK-FM - 92.9
595 E Plumb Ln.
Reno, NV 89502
Phone: (800)525-5683
Format: Classic Rock. **Owner:** Citadel Broadcasting Corp., 7201 W Lake Mead Blvd., Ste. 400, Las Vegas, NV 89128-8366, Ph: (702)804-5200, Fax: (702)804-8250. **Key Personnel:** Kevin Godwin, Gen. Mgr., jeff.clark@citcomm.com. **Wattage:** 45,000. **URL:** http://www.klove.com/music/radio-stations.

20917 ■ KNPB-TV - 5
1670 N Virginia St.
Reno, NV 89503
Phone: (775)784-4555
Fax: (775)784-1438
Email: programming@knpb.org
Networks: Public Broadcasting Service (PBS). **Key Personnel:** Don Alexander, Producer; Tony Manfredi, VP, tony@knpb.org; Patricia Miller, VP, patm@knpb.org; Fred Ihlow, Operations Mgr., fred@knpb.org; Loree Daniels, Dir. of Fin. & Admin.; Barbara Harmon, Dept. Mgr.; Dave Santina, Div. Dir. **Wattage**: 160. **URL:** http://www.knpb.org.

KODS-FM - See Carnelian Bay, CA

20918 ■ KOH-AM - 780
595 E Plumb Ln.
Reno, NV 89502
Phone: (775)789-6700
Fax: (775)789-6767
Free: 800-564-5564
Format: News; Talk. **Key Personnel:** Bill Manders, Contact, billmanders@kkoh.com; Jon Sanchez, Contact, jon@sanchezwealthmanagement.com. **Ad Rates:** Advertising accepted; rates available upon request. **URL:** http://www.kkoh.com.

20919 ■ KOLO-TV - 8
4850 Ampere Dr.
Reno, NV 89502
Phone: (775)858-8888
Fax: (775)858-8855
Email: news@kolotv.com
Format: Commercial TV. **Networks:** ABC. **ADI**: Reno, NV. **Key Personnel:** Matt Eldredge, President, Gen. Mgr., matt.eldredge@kolotv.com. **Wattage**: 15,600 ERP. **Ad Rates:** Noncommercial; Advertising accepted; rates available upon request. **URL:** http://www.kolotv.com.

20920 ■ KOZZ-FM - 105.7
2900 Sutro St.
Reno, NV 89512
Phone: (775)793-1057
Fax: (775)323-1450
Format: Classic Rock. **Operating Hours**: Continuous. **ADI**: Reno, NV. **Key Personnel:** Dane Wilt, Contact, dane@lotusradio.com; Max Volume, Music Dir., max@lotusradio.com; Dee Kane, Sales Mgr., dee@lotusradio.com. **Wattage**: 25,000 ERP. **Ad Rates:** Noncommercial; Advertising accepted; rates available upon request. **URL:** http://www.kozzradio.com.

20921 ■ KPLY-AM - 1230
3301 Barham Blvd., Ste. 200
Los Angeles, CA 90068
Phone: (323)512-2225
Fax: (323)512-2224
Email: hq@lotuscorp.com
Owner: Lotus Communication Corp., 3301 Barham Blvd., Ste. 200, CA 90068. **ADI**: Reno, NV. **Key Personnel:** Howard A. Kalmenson, CEO, President. **Wattage**: 820. **Ad Rates:** $16 per unit.

20922 ■ KPTT-AM - 630
2900 Sutro St.
Reno, NV 89512
Phone: (702)329-9261
Fax: (702)323-1450
Format: Sports; Talk; News. **Networks:** Westwood One Radio. **Owner:** Lotus Communications Corp., 6777 Hollywood Blvd., Hollywood, CA 90028, Ph: (213)461-8225. **Founded:** 1967. **Formerly**: KONE-AM; KOZZ-AM. **Operating Hours**: Continuous. **ADI**: Reno, NV. **Key Personnel:** Dane Wilt, Gen. Mgr. **Wattage**: 5,000. **URL:** http://en.wikipedia.org/wiki/KPTT#KPTT-HD2.

20923 ■ KREN-TV - 27
5166 Meadowood Mall Cir.
Reno, NV 89502
Phone: (775)333-2727
Fax: (775)327-6862
Email: yourstation@kren.com
Owner: Pappas Telecasting of NV., 500 S Chinewth Rd., Visalia, CA 93277, Ph: (559)733-7800, Fax: (559)733-7878. **Founded:** 1986. **ADI**: Reno, NV. **Wattage**: 1,000,000 ERP. **Ad Rates:** Accepts Advertising. **URL:** http://www.kren.com.

20924 ■ KRNO-FM - 106.9
961 Matley Ln., Ste. 120
Reno, NV 89502
Phone: (775)793-1069
Fax: (775)825-3183
Email: info@1069morefm.com
Format: Soft Rock. **Owner:** Americom Broadcasting L.L.C., 961 Matley Ln., Reno, NV 89502, Ph: (775)829-1964, Fax: (775)825-3183. **Founded:** 1974. **Operating Hours**: Continuous; 100% local. **ADI**: Reno, NV. **Wattage**: 37,000. **Ad Rates:** Noncommercial. **URL:** http://www.1069morefm.com.

20925 ■ KRNV-TV - 4
1790 Vassar St.
Reno, NV 89502
Phone: (775)322-4444
Format: Commercial TV. **Networks:** NBC. **Founded:** 1962. **Operating Hours**: Continuous. **ADI**: Reno, NV. **Key Personnel:** Mary Beth Farrell, Station Mgr., mfarrell@krnv.com; John Finkbohner, Operations Mgr., jfinkbohner@krnv.com; Mark Murakami, Sales Mgr., mmurakami@krnv.com. **Ad Rates:** Advertising accepted; rates available upon request. **URL:** http://www.mynews4.com.

20926 ■ KRXI-TV - 11
4920 Brookside Ct.
Reno, NV 89502
Phone: (775)856-1100
URL: http://www.foxreno.com/station.

20927 ■ KRZQ-FM - 100.9
300 E 2nd St., Ste. 1400
Truckee River Office Tower, 14th Fl.
Reno, NV 89503
Phone: (775)333-0123
Fax: (775)322-7361
Format: Adult Album Alternative; Alternative/New Music/Progressive. **Networks:** Independent. **Owner:** Wilks Broadcasting Group, LLC, 6470 E Johns Crossing, Ste. 450, Duluth, GA 30097, Ph: (678)240-8976, Fax: (678)240-8989. **Founded:** 1987. **Operating Hours**: Continuous; 100% local. **ADI**: Reno, NV. **Ad Rates:** Advertising accepted; rates available upon request. **URL:** http://www.krzqfm.com.

20928 ■ KTVN-TV - 2
4925 Energy Way
Reno, NV 89502
Phone: (775)858-2222
Fax: (775)861-4298
Format: Commercial TV. **Networks:** CBS. **Founded:** 1967. **Operating Hours**: Continuous. **ADI**: Reno, NV. **Key Personnel:** John Richardson, Gen. Sales Mgr. **Ad Rates:** Advertising accepted; rates available upon request. **URL:** http://www.ktvn.com.

20929 ■ K291BN-FM
PO Box 391
Twin Falls, ID 83303
Fax: (208)736-1958
Free: 800-357-4226
Owner: CSN International, PO Box 391, Twin Falls, ID 83303, Ph: (208)736-1958, Fax: (208)736-1958, Free: 800-357-4226.

20930 ■ KUNR-FM - 88.7
PO Box 294
Reno, NV 89557
Phone: (775)327-5867
Fax: (775)327-5386
Free: 866-723-5867
Email: feedback@kunr.org
Format: Public Radio. **Networks:** National Public Radio (NPR); Public Radio International (PRI). **Founded:** 1963. **Operating Hours**: Continuous. **Key Personnel:** David Stipech, President, dstipech@kunr.org. **Local Programs**: *Club 88*, Sunday 6:00 p.m. - 7:00 p.m. **Wattage**: 20,000. **Ad Rates:** Noncommercial. **URL:** http://www.kunr.org.

20931 ■ KURK-FM - 100.9
300 E Second St., Ste. 1400
Reno, NV 89501
Phone: (775)333-0123
Format: Classic Rock. **Owner:** Wilks Broadcast Group L.L.C., 6470 E Johns Crossing, Ste. 450, Duluth, GA 30097, Ph: (678)240-8976, Fax: (678)240-8989. **Wattage**: 6,000. **URL:** http://www.renosbestrock.com.

20932 ■ KUUB-FM - 94.5
2900 Sutro St.
Reno, NV 89512
Phone: (775)329-9261
Fax: (775)323-1450
Format: Country. **Formerly**: KHXR-FM. **Key Personnel:** Dane Wilt, Gen. Mgr., dane@lotusradio.com; Chip Cooper, Gen. Sales Mgr., chip@lotusradio.com; Dee Kane, Sales Mgr., dee@lotusradio.com. **URL:** http://www.espn945.com.

20933 ■ KWNZ-FM - 93.7
6080 Mt. Moriah
Memphis, TN 38115
Phone: (901)375-9324
Format: Top 40. **Networks:** Independent. **Owner:** Flinn Broadcasting Corporation, at above address. **Founded:** 1985. **Operating Hours**: Continuous; 100% local. **ADI**: Reno, NV. **Wattage**: 87,100. **Ad Rates:** Advertising accepted; rates available upon request. **URL:** http://www.flinn.com.

20934 ■ KWYL-FM - 102.9
595 E Plumb Ln.
Reno, NV 89502
Format: Top 40; Contemporary Hit Radio (CHR). **Owner:** Citadel Broadcasting Corp., 7201 W Lake Mead Blvd., Ste. 400, Las Vegas, NV 89128-8366, Ph: (702)804-5200, Fax: (702)804-8250. **Operating Hours**: Continuous. **Key Personnel:** John W. Dickey, Exec. VP; Paul Agase, VP of Sales; Jeff Brown, VP; Peter Bolger, Operations Mgr., Prog. Dir; Andrew Perini, Contact, andrew.perini@citcomm.com. **Wattage**: 39,000. **Ad Rates:** Advertising accepted; rates available upon request. **URL:** http://www.citadelbroadcasting.com.

20935 ■ KXTO-AM - 1550
615 Margrave Dr.
Reno, NV 89509
Phone: (775)284-1000
Format: Hispanic. **Key Personnel:** Miguel Mena, Contact, mena@exitosam.com.

20936 ■ KZTQ-FM - 97.3
961 Matley Ln., Ste. 120
Reno, NV 89502
Phone: (775)829-1964
Fax: (775)825-3183
Format: Eighties; Music of Your Life. **Owner:** Americom Broadcasting L.L.C., 961 Matley Ln., Reno, NV 89502, Ph: (775)829-1964, Fax: (775)825-3183. **Key Personnel:** Carrie Carano, Gen. Sales Mgr., carriecarano@mightyreno.com. **URL:** http://www.cbelmira.com.

20937 ■ WFSS-FM - 91.9
1055 Moana Ln.
Reno, NV 89509
Phone: (910)672-2650
Fax: (910)672-1964
Format: Public Radio; Jazz; News. **Networks:** National Public Radio (NPR); Public Radio International (PRI). **Owner:** Fayetteville State University, 1200 Murchison Rd., Fayetteville, NC 28301, Ph: (910)672-1111. **Founded:** 1977. **Operating Hours**: Continuous. **Key Personnel:** Joe Ross, Gen. Mgr., jross@uncfsu.edu; Janet Wright, Dir. of Programs, jwright@uncfsu.edu; Jimmy Miller, Music Dir., jmiller@uncfsc.edu; Kathy Klaus, News Dir., kklaus@uncfsu.edu. **Wattage**: 100,000. **Ad Rates:** Noncommercial; underwriting available. **URL:** http://www.wfss.org.

ROUND MOUNTAIN

20938 ■ K215DX-FM - 90.9
PO Box 391
Twin Falls, ID 83303
Fax: (208)736-1958
Free: 800-357-4226
Format: Religious; Contemporary Christian. **Owner:** CSN International, PO Box 391, Twin Falls, ID 83303, Ph: (208)736-1958, Fax: (208)736-1958, Free: 800-357-4226. **Key Personnel:** Kelly Carlson, Dir. of Engg.; Ray Gorney, Asst. Dir.; Don Mills, Music Dir., Prog. Dir. **URL:** http://www.csnradio.com.

SPARKS

Washoe Co. Washoe Co. (W). 3 m E of Reno. Gaming. Industrial.

Circulation: ★ = AAM; △ or • = BPA; ♦ = CAC; ❑ = VAC; ⊕ = PO Statement; ‡ = Publisher's Report; Boldface figures = sworn; Light figures = estimated.

20939 ■ Sparks Tribune
Daily Sparks Tribune
1002 C St.
Sparks, NV 89431
Phone: (775)358-8061
Fax: (775)359-3837
Free: 800-669-1338
Publisher's E-mail: tribunenews@dailysparkstribune.com
General newspaper. **Freq:** Weekly (Tues.). **Print Method:** Offset. **Cols./Page:** 5. **Col. Width:** 2 1/16 inches. **Col. Depth:** 21 1/2 inches. **Key Personnel:** Kent Lauer, Publisher, Editor. **URL:** http://www.dailysparkstribune.com. **Ad Rates:** 4C $300; PCI $13. **Remarks:** Accepts advertising. **Circ:** ‡5000.

SUN VALLEY

20940 ■ K200AA-FM - 87.9
PO Box 391
Twin Falls, ID 83303
Fax: (208)736-1958
Free: 800-357-4226
Format: Religious; Contemporary Christian. **Owner:** CSN International, PO Box 391, Twin Falls, ID 83303, Ph: (208)736-1958, Fax: (208)736-1958, Free: 800-357-4226. **Key Personnel:** Ray Gorney, Asst. Dir.; Don Mills, Prog. Dir., Music Dir.; Kelly Carlson, Dir. of Engg. **Wattage**: 028. **URL:** http://www.csnradio.com.

TONOPAH

Nye Co. (SC). 170 m SE of Reno. Space testing. Gold, silver mines. Agriculture. Livestock, hay, grain.

20941 ■ K211EL-FM - 89.5
PO Box 391
Twin Falls, ID 83303
Phone: (208)733-3133
Format: Religious; Contemporary Christian; Music of Your Life; News. **Owner:** CSN International, PO Box 391, Twin Falls, ID 83303, Ph: (208)736-1958, Fax: (208)736-1958, Free: 800-357-4226. **Key Personnel:** Mike Kestler, President; Don Mills, Music Dir., Prog. Dir.; Daniel Davidson, Dir. of Operations. **URL:** http://www.csnradio.com.

WADSWORTH

20942 ■ KRNG-FM - 101.3
PO Box 490
Wadsworth, NV 89442
Phone: (775)575-7777
Free: 888-899-8990
Email: email@renegaderadio.org
Format: Contemporary Christian. **Wattage:** 1,650. **Ad Rates:** Noncommercial. **URL:** http://www.renegaderadio.org.

WELLS

Elko Co. Elko Co. (NE). 120 m S of Twin Falls, Idaho. Tourism. Barite mining. Oil exploration. Stock, grain farms. Hay.

20943 ■ K223AM-FM - 92.5
PO Box 391
Twin Falls, ID 83303
Fax: (208)736-1958
Free: 800-357-4226
Format: Religious; Contemporary Christian. **Owner:** CSN International, PO Box 391, Twin Falls, ID 83303, Ph: (208)736-1958, Fax: (208)736-1958, Free: 800-357-4226. **Key Personnel:** Mike Kestler, President; Don Mills, Music Dir., Prog. Dir. **URL:** http://www.csnradio.com.

WENDOVER

20944 ■ The Wendover Times: Wendover's Source For News, Events, & Gaming
The Wendover Times
PO Box 2716
Wendover, NV 89883
Phone: (435)665-2563
Fax: (435)665-7966
Publication E-mail: news@wendovertimes.com
Newspaper covering news and events in Elko County, Nevada, and Tooele County in Utah. **Freq:** Weekly (Fri.). **Key Personnel:** Deeanna Croasmun, Editor, phone: (775)408-0011. **ISSN:** 2152--9124 (print). **Subscription Rates:** $60 Individuals; $30 Individuals 6 months. **URL:** http://www.wendovertimes.com. **Remarks:** Accepts advertising. **Circ:** (Not Reported).

WINNEMUCCA

Humboldt Co. Humboldt Co. (NW). 80 m NE of Reno. Residential.

20945 ■ The Humboldt Sun
Winnemucca Publishing
1022 S Grass Valley Rd.
Winnemucca, NV 89445
Phone: (775)623-5011
Fax: (775)623-5243
Community newspaper. **Freq:** every Tues. & Fri. **Print Method:** Offset. **Cols./Page:** 6. **Col. Width:** 12 picas. **Col. Depth:** 21.5 picas. **Key Personnel:** Jen Anderson, Editor. **URL:** http://insidenorthernnevada.com. **Ad Rates:** BW $767.55; 4C $1,067.55; SAU $6.25. **Remarks:** Advertising accepted; rates available upon request. **Circ:** ‡4900.

20946 ■ Jones Spacelink Ltd.
PO Box 650
Winnemucca, NV 89445-0650
Fax: (702)623-5246
Owner: Jones Intercable Inc., 9697 E Mineral Ave., Englewood, CO 80112-3446, Ph: (303)792-3111, Fax: (303)790-0533. **Founded:** 1982. **Formerly**: Intermountain Cable. **Key Personnel:** Debbie Kontz, Gen. Mgr. **Cities Served:** subscribing households 2,250.

20947 ■ KKTT-FM - 97.9
PO Box 790
Winnemucca, NV 89446
Phone: (775)623-2785
Format: Religious. **Key Personnel:** Florence Guest, Station Mgr., floguest39@yahoo.com. **URL:** http://www.lifetalk.net.

20948 ■ K201FF-FM - 88.1
PO Box 391
Twin Falls, ID 83303
Fax: (208)736-1958
Free: 800-357-4226
Format: Religious; Contemporary Christian. **Owner:** CSN International, PO Box 391, Twin Falls, ID 83303, Ph: (208)736-1958, Fax: (208)736-1958, Free: 800-357-4226. **Key Personnel:** Mike Kestler, Contact; Don Mills, Music Dir., Prog. Dir. **URL:** http://www.csnradio.com.

20949 ■ KWNA-FM - 92.7
335 W Fourth St.
Winnemucca, NV 89445
Phone: (775)623-5203
Fax: (775)625-1011
Format: Country. **Founded:** 1982. **Wattage:** 060. **Ad Rates:** Advertising accepted; rates available upon request. **URL:** http://www.buckarooradio.com.

YERINGTON

Lyon Co. Lyon Co. (W). 80 m SE of Reno. Ships beef, hay, onions, potatoes. Silver mines. Stock, dairy farms.

20950 ■ Fernley Leader-Courier: The Voice of North and Central Lyon County
Mason Valley News
2 Main St.
Yerington, NV 89447
Community newspaper. **Founded:** 1979. **Freq:** Weekly (Wed.). **Print Method:** Offset. **Cols./Page:** 6. **Col. Width:** 12 picas. **Col. Depth:** 21.5 INS. **Subscription Rates:** $21.50 Individuals; $14.50 Individuals 6 months. **URL:** http://archive.rgj.com/section/MVN04/Leader-Courier-News. **Formerly**: Tri-Town Times. **Ad Rates:** BW $632.10; SAU $6; PCI $5. **Remarks:** Accepts advertising. **Circ:** Paid 3,100.

ZEPHYR COVE

20951 ■ KOWL-AM - 1490
PO Box 11101
Zephyr Cove, NV 89448
Phone: (775)586-8255
Free: 877-229-9703
Format: Talk; News. **Simulcasts:** KRLT-FM. **Networks:** ABC. **Owner:** D&H Broadcasting LLC, PO Box 11101, Zephyr Cove, NV 89448, Ph: (775)580-7130. **Founded:** 1956. **Operating Hours**: Continuous. **Wattage:** 1,000. **Ad Rates:** Advertising accepted; rates available upon request. Combined advertising rates available with KRLT-FM. **URL:** http://www.krltfm.com.

20952 ■ KRLT-FM - 93.9
PO Box 11101
Zephyr Cove, NV 89448
Phone: (775)586-8255
Free: 877-229-9703
Format: Adult Contemporary. **Simulcasts:** KOWL-AM. **Networks:** ABC. **Founded:** 1976. **Operating Hours**: Continuous. **Key Personnel:** Tony Driskill, Gen. Mgr., tdriskill@cherrycreekradio.com. **Wattage:** 3,000. **Ad Rates:** Advertising accepted; rates available upon request. **URL:** http://www.krltfm.com.

AMHERST

S. NH. Hillsborough Co. 10 mi. NW of Nashua.

20953 ■ Controlled Environments
Vicon Business Media Inc.
199 Rte. 101, Bldg. 7
Amherst, NH 03031
Phone: (973)920-7000
Magazine devoted to professionals engaged in sterile environments applicable to Life Sciences, Microelectronics, and other advanced applications. **Freq:** 11/year. **Trim Size:** 8 x 10 3/4. **Key Personnel:** Elizabeth Vickers, Publisher, phone: (631)241-6161. **URL:** http://www.cemag.us. **Mailing address:** PO Box 779, Amherst, NH 03031. **Ad Rates:** BW $6195; 4C $7090. **Remarks:** Accepts advertising. **Circ:** ‡20000.

20954 ■ Forensic Magazine
Vicon Business Media Inc.
199 Rte. 101, Bldg. 7
Amherst, NH 03031
Phone: (973)920-7000
Magazine for forensic professionals. **Freq:** Bimonthly. **Key Personnel:** Rebecca Waters, Editor-in-Chief; Liz Vickers, Publisher, phone: (631)241-6161. **URL:** http://www.forensicmag.com. **Mailing address:** PO Box 779, Amherst, NH 03031. **Remarks:** Advertising accepted; rates available upon request. **Circ:** △**10000.**

BEDFORD

20955 ■ WKDR-AM - 1390
288 S River Rd.
Bedford, NH 03110
Email: wkdr@together.net
Format: Talk; News. **Networks:** ABC. **Owner:** Hometown Broadcasting L.L.C., 156 W Huron St., Berlin, WI 54923, Ph: (920)361-3551, Fax: (866)594-4698. **Formerly**: WDOT-AM. **ADI**: Burlington-Hartford, VT-Plattsburgh, NY. **Key Personnel:** Mark Johnson, Gen. Mgr.; Jim Condon, News Dir.; Louie Manno, Dir. of Programs. **Wattage**: 5,000. **Ad Rates:** $7.50 for 15 seconds; $15 for 30 seconds; $20 for 60 seconds. **URL:** http://www.wcat98.com.

BELMONT

20956 ■ MetroCast Cablevision
Nine Apple Rd.
Belmont, NH 03220
Phone: (601)656-5050
Fax: (601)656-3223
Free: 800-457-5351
Formerly: Northland Cable Television. **Cities Served:** 36 channels. **URL:** http://www.metrocast.com.

20957 ■ MetroCast Cablevision of New Hampshire L.L.C.
9 Apple Rd.
Belmont, NH 03220-3251
Phone: (603)524-4425
Fax: (603)524-5190
Free: 800-608-6480
Founded: 1990. **Cities Served:** 92 channels. **URL:** http://www.metrocastcablevision.com.

BERLIN

Coos Co. N. NH. Coos Co. On Androscoggin River, 19 mi. E. of Lancaster. Manufactures paper, pulp products. Agriculture.

20958 ■ WEVC-FM - 107.1
Two Pillsbury St., 6th Fl.
Concord, NH 03301
Phone: (603)228-8910
Fax: (603)224-6052
Free: 800-639-4131
Format: Public Radio. **Owner:** New Hampshire Public Radio, 2 Pillsbury St., 6th Fl., Concord, NH 03301, Ph: (603)228-8910, Fax: (603)224-6052, Free: 800-639-4131. **Ad Rates:** Noncommercial. **URL:** http://www.nhpr.org.

20959 ■ WXLQ-FM - 107.1
PO Box 489
38 Glen Ave.
Berlin, NH 03570
Phone: (603)752-1230
Fax: (603)752-3117
Format: Country. **Networks:** CNN Radio. **Founded:** 1997. **Wattage:** 6,000. **Ad Rates:** Combined advertising rates available with WMOU-AM.

BOW

20960 ■ WTPL-FM - 107.7
501 S St., 3rd Fl.
Bow, NH 03304
Phone: (603)545-0777
Fax: (603)545-0781
Format: News; Talk; Sports. **Networks:** CBS. **Founded:** 1972. **Operating Hours:** 5:00 a.m. - 6:30 p.m. Monday - Friday; 8:00 a.m. - Noon Saturday; 7:00 a.m. - Noon Sunday. **Key Personnel:** Bob Lipman, Prog. Dir., blipman@greateasternradio.com; Jim Whedon, Sales Mgr., jwhedon@comcast.net. **Local Programs:** *Sports Center*, Monday Tuesday Wednesday Thursday Friday 12:00 a.m. - 5:00 a.m.; *New Hampshire Wake-Up Show*, Monday Tuesday Wednesday Thursday Friday 6:00 a.m. - 9:00 a.m. **Wattage:** 1,250 ERP H; 1,220 E. **URL:** http://www.wtplfm.com.

CLAREMONT

Sullivan Co. SW NH. Sullivan Co. On the Sugar River, 42 mi. NW of Concord. Manufactures mining machinery, shoes. Nurseries; pine timber; dairy farms. Summer resort.

20961 ■ Eagle Times
Eagle Publications Inc.
401 River Rd.
Claremont, NH 03743
General newspaper. **Freq:** Daily Morning - Sunday through Friday. **Print Method:** Offset. **Cols./Page:** 6. **Col. Width:** 25 nonpareils. **Col. Depth:** 301 agate lines. **Key Personnel:** Jim Freeland, Publisher. **USPS:** 115-200. **Subscription Rates:** $12 Individuals online only, 1 month; $28 Individuals online only, 3 months; $52 Individuals online only, 6 months; $72 Individuals online only, 12 months; $14 Individuals print and online - 13 weeks; $36.40 Individuals print and online - 26 weeks; $135.20 Individuals print and online - 1 year. **Mailing address:** PO Box 888, Claremont, NH 03743. **Ad Rates:** SAU $7.65; PCI $11.55; PCI $10.40. **Remarks:** Accepts advertising. **Circ:** Mon.-Fri. ★**8,711**, Sun. ★**9,100**.

COLEBROOK

N. NH. Coos Co. On Connecticut River, 33 mi. NW of Berlin. Summer resort. Timber; agriculture.

20962 ■ The News and Sentinel
The News and Sentinel
6 Bridge St.
Colebrook, NH 03576
Phone: (603)237-5501
Fax: (603)237-5060
Small country newspaper covering local affairs and area interests. **Freq:** Weekly (Wed.). **Trim Size:** 11 1/2 x 16 1/2. **Cols./Page:** 5. **Col. Width:** 11.4 picas. **Col. Depth:** 210 agate lines. **Key Personnel:** Karen H. Ladd, Publisher, Editor; Butch Ladd, Manager, Sales. **Subscription Rates:** $30 Individuals 1 year, online; $15 Individuals 6 months, online; $30 Individuals in New Hampshire, Vermont and Maine, 1 year, print; $26 Individuals for active-duty military, print; $20 Individuals for one-half year and for students, print; $35 Individuals Canada, print. **Mailing address:** PO Box 39, Colebrook, NH 03576. **Ad Rates:** 4C $100; SAU $5; PCI $6.50. **Remarks:** Accepts classified advertising. **Circ:** ⊕**5,000.**

20963 ■ White Mountain Cablevision
PO Box 66
Colebrook, NH 03576
Phone: (603)237-5573
Fax: (603)237-8256
Founded: 1954. **Key Personnel:** William Hinton, Gen. Mgr.; Sheryl Collins, Office Mgr. **Cities Served:** Beecher Falls, Canaan, Lemington, Vermont: subscribing households 1,584; 29 channels; 1 community access channel.

CONCORD

Merrimack Co. SC NH. Merrimack Co. State Capital. On the Merrimack River, 15 mi. N. of Manchester. New Hampshire Technical Institute. Manufactures leather, machinery, electronics. Granite finishing.

20964 ■ Concord Monitor
Concord Monitor
1 Monitor Dr.
Concord, NH 03302-1177
Phone: (603)224-5301
Fax: (603)224-6949
Publisher's E-mail: customerservice@cmonitor.com
General newspaper. **Freq:** Daily. **Print Method:** Offset. **Cols./Page:** 6. **Col. Width:** 24 nonpareils. **Col. Depth:** 301 agate lines. **Key Personnel:** Dana Wormald, Editor. **Subscription Rates:** $10.99 Individuals 1 month - online only; $109 Individuals 52 weeks - online only; $1 Individuals 1 day - online digital pass. **Mailing address:** PO Box 1177, Concord, NH 03302-1177. **Ad Rates:** BW $1020; 4C $1470; PCI $5. **Remarks:** Accepts advertising. **Circ:** Paid ‡14,480, Paid ‡16,134.

Circulation: ★ = AAM; △ or • = BPA; ♦ = CAC; ❑ = VAC; ⊕ = PO Statement; ‡ = Publisher's Report; Boldface figures = sworn; Light figures = estimated.

20965 ■ Forest Notes
Society for the Protection of New Hampshire Forests
54 Portsmouth St.
Concord, NH 03301
Phone: (603)224-9945
Fax: (603)228-0423
Publisher's E-mail: info@forestsociety.org
Journal on forestry and conservation. **Founded:** 1937. **Freq:** Quarterly. **Print Method:** Offset. **Trim Size:** 7 5/8 x 10 7/8. **Cols./Page:** 2. **Col. Width:** 20 picas. **Col. Depth:** 56 picas. **Key Personnel:** Jack Savage, Executive Editor; Jane A. Difley, President. **ISSN:** 0015-7457 (print). **URL:** http://www.forestsociety.org/news/forest-notes.asp. **Ad Rates:** 4C $1000. **Remarks:** Accepts advertising. **Circ:** Paid ‡12,000, Controlled ‡400.

20966 ■ IDEA: The Intellectual Property Law Review
University of New Hampshire School of Law
2 White St.
Concord, NH 03301
Phone: (603)513-5300
Fax: (603)513-5234
Publication E-mail: idea@law.unh.edu
Journal covering intellectual property practice and scholarship. **Freq:** 3/year. **Key Personnel:** Samuel A. McMahon, Editor-in-Chief. **ISSN:** 0019--1272 (print). **Subscription Rates:** $68 Individuals; $79 Other countries. **URL:** http://law.unh.edu/about/unh-law-publications/idea-journal-franklin-pierce-center-intellectual-property. **Remarks:** Accepts advertising. **Circ:** (Not Reported).

20967 ■ Infinite Energy: The Magazine of New Energy Science and Technology
New Energy Foundation Inc.
PO Box 2816
Concord, NH 03302-2816
Phone: (603)485-4700
Fax: (603)485-4710
Magazine featuring articles, technical reviews and the latest news on new energy science and technology. **Freq:** Bimonthly. **Key Personnel:** Eugene Mallove, Editor, Founder. **Subscription Rates:** $29.95 Individuals North America; $49.95 Other countries; $59.90 Two years North America; $99.90 Two years outside North America. **URL:** http://www.infinite-energy.com. **Remarks:** Accepts advertising. **Circ:** 5000.

20968 ■ The Inspector
American Society of Home Inspectors - New England Chapter
53 Regional Dr., Ste. 1
Concord, NH 03301-8500
Phone: (603)228-1231
Free: 800-248-2744
Magazine publishing articles related to home inspectors. **Freq:** Monthly. **Subscription Rates:** Included in membership. **URL:** http://www.nachi.org/bbsystem/viewtopic.php?t=4242&PHPSESSID=5093079eb32b966f5ed272940ebb8972. **Remarks:** Accepts advertising. **Circ:** Free ‡50000, 200.

20969 ■ Journal
New Hampshire Dental Society
23 S State St.
Concord, NH 03301
Phone: (603)225-5961
Fax: (603)226-4880
Free: 800-244-5961
Journal containing articles of dental interest. **Freq:** Biennial. **URL:** http://www.nhds.org. **Circ:** (Not Reported).

20970 ■ New Hampshire Bar Journal
New Hampshire Bar Association
2 Pillsbury St., Ste. 300
Concord, NH 03301-3549
Phone: (603)224-6942
Fax: (603)224-2910
Publisher's E-mail: nhbainfo@nhbar.org
Law journal. **Freq:** Quarterly. **Key Personnel:** Donna J. Parker, Coordinator, Advertising; Jeannine L. McCoy, Executive Director. **ISSN:** 0548-4928 (print). **Subscription Rates:** $10 Single issue. **URL:** http://www.nhbar.org. **Ad Rates:** BW $1,100; 4C $1,424. **Remarks:** Accepts advertising. **Circ:** (Not Reported).

20971 ■ New Hampshire Highways
New Hampshire Good Roads Association
261 Sheep Davis Rd., Ste. 5
Concord, NH 03301
Phone: (603)224-1823
Fax: (603)224-9399
Free: 800-552-7904
Publisher's E-mail: nhroads@aol.com
Provide information on the road and bridge construction and maintenance industry in the state. **Freq:** Quarterly. **Print Method:** Offset. **Cols./Page:** 2. **Col. Width:** 39 nonpareils. **Col. Depth:** 140 agate lines. **Key Personnel:** Brenda J. Clemons, Editor. **URL:** http://www.nhgoodroads.org/Publications. **Ad Rates:** BW $348, member; BW 654, non-member. **Remarks:** Accepts advertising. **Circ:** ‡1,600.

WEVC-FM - See Berlin

WEVH-FM - See Hanover

WEVJ-FM - See Jackson

20972 ■ WEVO-FM - 89.1
Two Pillsbury St., 6th Fl.
Concord, NH 03301-5003
Phone: (603)228-8910
Fax: (603)224-6052
Free: 800-639-4131
Email: news@nhpr.org
Format: News; Talk. **Networks:** National Public Radio (NPR); Public Radio International (PRI). **Owner:** New Hampshire Public Radio, 2 Pillsbury St., 6th Fl., Concord, NH 03301, Ph: (603)228-8910, Fax: (603)224-6052, Free: 800-639-4131. **Founded:** 1981. **Operating Hours:** Continuous; 50% network, 50% local. **Key Personnel:** Steve Donnell, Engineer; Betsy Gardella, CEO, President; Scott McPherson, Contact; Scott McPherson, Contact. **Wattage:** 50,000. **Ad Rates:** Noncommercial. **URL:** http://www.nhpr.org.

20973 ■ WEVS-FM - 92.7; 88.3
207 N Main St.
Concord, NH 03301
Phone: (603)228-8910
Fax: (603)224-6052
Free: 800-639-4131
Email: folkshow@nhpr.org
Format: Classic Rock; Oldies; Classic Rock; Classic Rock; Public Radio. **Networks:** Westwood One Radio; ABC; National Public Radio (NPR); Public Radio International (PRI); BBC World Service. **Owner:** New Hampshire Public Radio, 2 Pillsbury St., 6th Fl., Concord, NH 03301, Ph: (603)228-8910, Fax: (603)224-6052, Free: 800-639-4131. **Founded:** 1987. **Operating Hours:** Continuous. **Key Personnel:** Dale Ray, Dir. of Programs; Shannon Lowe, News Dir. **Wattage:** 3,300 ERP. **Ad Rates:** Advertising accepted; rates available upon request. $9-16 for 30 seconds. **URL:** http://www.nhpr.org.

20974 ■ WJYY-FM - 105.5
NH1 Media Ctr., 4 Church St.
Concord, NH 03301
Phone: (603)225-1160
Fax: (603)224-7280
Free: 888-817-1055
Format: Top 40. **Networks:** AP. **Owner:** Nassau Broadcasting, 619 Alexander Rd., 3rd Fl., Princeton, NJ 08540. **Founded:** 1983. **Operating Hours:** Continuous. **Key Personnel:** AJ Dukette, Dir. of Programs, adukette@nassaubroadcasting.com; Rob Fulmer, Regional Mgr., rfulmer@nassaubroadcasting.com; Shirley Clark, Sales Mgr., sclark@nassaubroadcasting.com; Zack Derby, Promotions Dir., zderby@nassaubroadcasting.com. **Wattage:** 1,550. **Ad Rates:** $28-44 per unit. WNHI, WOTX, WKXL AM/FM. **URL:** http://wjyy.nh1media.com.

20975 ■ WKXL-AM - 1450
37 Redington Rd.
Concord, NH 03301
Phone: (603)225-5521
Fax: (603)224-6404
Format: Full Service. **Founded:** 1946. **Formerly:** WRCI-Hillsboro; WKXL-FM. **Operating Hours:** 12:00 a.m. - 5:59 a.m. **Key Personnel:** Tom Gauthier, Contact. **Local Programs:** *AM NH*, Monday Tuesday Wednesday Thursday Friday 6:00 a.m. - 9:00 a.m. **Wattage:** 1,000 KW. **Ad Rates:** Advertising accepted; rates available upon request. $21-38 for 30 seconds; $23-40 for 60 seconds. **URL:** http://www.wkxl1450.com/dynamickxl/.

WLNH-FM - See Laconia

20976 ■ WSPS-FM - 90.5
325 Pleasant St.
Concord, NH 03301
Phone: (603)230-5810
Email: wsps@sps.edu
Format: Eclectic. **Owner:** St. Paul's School, 325 Pleasant St., Concord, NH 03301-2591, Ph: (603)229-4600. **Founded:** 1974. **Operating Hours:** Continuous. **Key Personnel:** Dr. Glenn Reider, Station Mgr. **Wattage:** 200. **Ad Rates:** Noncommercial. **URL:** http://www.wsps.sps.edu/pages/home.html.

20977 ■ WVNH-FM - 91.1
37 Redington Rd.
Concord, NH 03301
Phone: (603)227-0911
Format: Religious. **Owner:** New Hampshire Gospel Radio Inc., at above address. **Founded:** Sept. 07, 2006. **Key Personnel:** Peter J. Stohrer, President, Station Mgr.; John Loker, VP. **URL:** http://www.nhgr.org.

CONWAY

EC NH. Carroll Co. On Saco River, 5 mi. S. of North Conway.

20978 ■ WBNC-AM - 104.5
PO Box 2008
Conway, NH 03818
Phone: (603)356-8870
Fax: (603)356-8875
Format: Information. **Owner:** Mt. Washington Radio & Gramophone, LLC, at above address, North Conway, NH. **Founded:** 1955. **Operating Hours:** Continuous. **Wattage:** 1,000 Day; 063 Night. **Ad Rates:** Advertising accepted; rates available upon request. Combined advertising rates available with WVMJ-FM, WMWV-FM. **URL:** http://www.conwaymagic.com.

20979 ■ WMWV-FM - 93.5
PO Box 2008
Conway, NH 03818
Phone: (603)356-8870
Fax: (603)356-8875
Email: office@wmwv.com
Format: Adult Album Alternative. **Networks:** AP. **Owner:** Mt. Washington Radio & Gramophone, LLC, at above address, North Conway, NH. **Founded:** 1967. **Operating Hours:** Continuous. **Key Personnel:** Mark Johnson, Dir. of Programs, mark@wmwv.com. **Wattage:** 3,000. **Ad Rates:** Noncommercial. **URL:** http://www.wmwv.com.

20980 ■ WVMJ-FM - 104.5
PO Box 2008
Conway, NH 03818
Phone: (603)356-8870
Fax: (603)356-8875
Format: Adult Contemporary; Hot Country. **Owner:** Mt. Washington Radio & Gramophone, LLC, at above address, North Conway, NH. **Founded:** 1995. **Formerly:** WBNC-FM, 1995-2001. **Operating Hours:** Continuous. **Key Personnel:** Lucia Seavey, Contact, office@wmwv.com; Chris McNevitch, Contact, greg@wmwv.com. **Wattage:** 3,000. **Ad Rates:** Noncommercial. Combined advertising rates available with WMWV-FM, WBNC-AM. **URL:** http://www.conwaymagic.com.

DERRY

SE NH. Rockingham Co. On Beaver Brook, 10 mi. SE of Manchester. Manufactures shoes, circuit boards and electronics, novelties. Summer resort.

20981 ■ B&M Bulletin
Boston & Maine Railroad Historical Society
PO Box 469
Derry, NH 03038-0469
Phone: (978)454-3600
Publisher's E-mail: bmrrhs@gmail.com
Magazine containing articles, data, and photos describing the history of the Boston & Maine Railroad and its predecessor lines, equipment, and people. **Freq:** Quarterly. **Print Method:** Offset. **Trim Size:** 8 1/2 x 11. **Cols./Page:** 2. **Col. Width:** 21 picas. **Col. Depth:** 140 agate lines. **Key Personnel:** John Alan Roderick, Art Director; Andrew Wilson, Editor. **ISSN:** 0362--2711 (print). **URL:** http://www.bmrrhs.org/bm-bulletin. **Remarks:** Advertising not accepted. **Circ:** ‡2200.

20982 ■ Derry News
Derry Publishing Co.
46 W Broadway, Rte. 102
Derry, NH 03038
Phone: (603)437-7000
Fax: (603)432-4510
Community newspaper. **Freq:** Weekly. **Print Method:** Offset. **Cols./Page:** 6. **Col. Width:** 2 1/16 inches. **Col. Depth:** 21 inches. **Key Personnel:** Ken Johnson, Editor; Bruce Slichko, Manager, Circulation, phone: (603)421-3835. **USPS:** 154-700. **Subscription Rates:** $52 Individuals 52 weeks. **Mailing address:** PO Box 307, Derry, NH 03038. **Ad Rates:** 4C $395; SAU $14.90. **Remarks:** Accepts advertising. **Circ:** ‡11,000.

20983 ■ WBIN-TV - 50
11 A St.
Derry, NH 03038
Phone: (603)845-1000
Format: Commercial TV; Religious. **Founded:** 1983. **Operating Hours:** Continuous. **ADI:** Boston-Worcester,MA-Derry-Manchester,NH. **Wattage:** 7,300 ERP H. **Ad Rates:** Advertising accepted; rates available upon request. **URL:** http://www.wbintv.com.

20984 ■ WDER-AM - 1320
8 Lawrence Rd.
Derry, NH 03038
Phone: (603)437-9337
Format: Religious. **Owner:** Blount Communications Group, 8 Lawrence Rd., Derry, NH 03038, Ph: (603)437-9337, Fax: (603)434-1035. **Operating Hours:** 6 a.m.-10 p.m.; 7% network, 93% local. **Wattage:** 10,000. **Ad Rates:** Noncommercial. **Mailing address:** PO Box 465, Derry, NH 03038. **URL:** http://lifechangingradio.com.

20985 ■ WFEX-FM - 92.1
8 Lawrence Rd.
Derry, NH 03038
Phone: (603)437-9337
Email: wfnx@wfnx.com
Format: Alternative/New Music/Progressive; Contemporary Christian. **Operating Hours:** Continuous. **Wattage:** 1,700. **Ad Rates:** Noncommercial; Advertising accepted; rates available upon request. **Mailing address:** PO Box 465, Derry, NH 03038. **URL:** http://lifechangingradio.com.

20986 ■ WNHQ-FM - 92.1
8 Lawrence Rd
Derry, NH 03038
Fax: (603)434-1035
Format: News. **Founded:** 1971. **Formerly:** WMDK-FM. **Operating Hours:** Continuous. **ADI:** Boston-Worcester,MA-Derry-Manchester,NH. **Wattage:** 170 ERP. **Ad Rates:** Accepts Advertising. **Mailing address:** PO Box 465, Derry, NH 03038. **URL:** http://lifechangingradio.com/wder.

DOVER

Strafford Co. SE NH. Strafford Co. On Cocheco River, 12 mi. NW of Portsmouth. Park areas and recreation centers. Major retail, wholesale and service centers; diversified manufacturing. Greenhouses; agriculture.

20987 ■ Foster's Democrat
Foster's Democrat
150 Venture Dr.
Dover, NH 03820
Phone: (603)742-4455
Free: 800-660-8310
General newspaper. **Freq:** Mon.-Sat. **Print Method:** Offset. **Cols./Page:** 6. **Col. Width:** 25 nonpareils. **Col. Depth:** 301 agate lines. **Key Personnel:** Therese D. Foster, Editor; Rodney G. Doherty, Executive Editor. **Subscription Rates:** $137.80 Individuals 52 weeks (7 days per week); $93.60 Individuals 52 weeks (everything but sunday); $104 Individuals 52 weeks (Saturday and Sunday only); $83.20 Individuals 52 weeks (Sunday only). **Ad Rates:** BW $2254.92; 4C $2689.92; PCI $20.50. **Remarks:** Accepts advertising. **Circ:** Mon.-Sat. ♦**13,120**, Sun. ♦**14,423**.

20988 ■ Foster's Sunday Citizen
George J. Foster Co.
150 Venture Dr.
Dover, NH 03820-5913
Publisher's E-mail: weddings@fosters.com
Community newspaper. **Freq:** Weekly (Sun.). **Key Personnel:** Tom Caldwell, Editor. **Subscription Rates:** $104.00 Individuals 1 year. **URL:** http://www.fosters.com. **Remarks:** Accepts advertising. **Circ:** Combined ♦**14513**.

20989 ■ The Sanford News
George J. Foster Co.
150 Venture Dr.
Dover, NH 03820-5913
Publisher's E-mail: weddings@fosters.com
Local newspaper serving Southern Maine. **Freq:** Weekly. **Key Personnel:** Robert H. Foster, Publisher; Therese Foster, Editor; Mary Pat Rowland, Managing Editor. **Subscription Rates:** $10 Individuals. **URL:** http://www.fosters.com/sanford-news. **Ad Rates:** BW $1487.37; SAU $11.88; CNU $7.52. **Remarks:** Accepts advertising. **Circ:** (Not Reported).

20990 ■ WBYY-FM - 98.7
101 Back Rd.
Dover, NH 03821-0400
Phone: (603)742-0987
Fax: (603)742-0448
Free: 888-441-9876
Format: Soft Rock. **Owner:** Garrison City Broadcasting Inc., NH. **Founded:** 1995. **Operating Hours:** Continuous. **ADI:** Boston-Worcester,MA-Derry-Manchester,NH. **Key Personnel:** Carole Lanctot, Bus. Mgr., carole@987thebay.com; Dan Lunnie, Contact, dan@987thebay.com; Dan Lunnie, Contact, dan@987thebay.com; Pat Kelly, Contact, pat@987thebay.com. **Wattage:** 6,000. **Ad Rates:** $30-60 for 60 seconds. Combined advertising rates available with WTSN-AM. **URL:** http://www.987thebay.com.

20991 ■ WOKQ-FM - 97.5
292 Middle Rd.
Dover, NH 03821-0576
Phone: (603)749-9750
Free: 877-975-1037
Email: news@wokq.com
Format: Country. **Simulcasts:** WPKQ-FM. **Networks:** Independent. **Owner:** Citadel Broadcasting Corp., 7201 W Lake Mead Blvd., Ste. 400, Las Vegas, NV 89128-8366, Ph: (702)804-5200, Fax: (702)804-8250. **Founded:** 1970. **Formerly:** WDNH-FM. **Operating Hours:** Continuous; 100% local. **ADI:** Boston-Worcester,MA-Derry-Manchester,NH. **Key Personnel:** Paul Kelley, Mgr., Dir. of Sales, brian.lang@townsquaremedia.com; Don Briand, News Dir., don@morningwakingcrew.com; Mark Jennings, Dir. of Programs; Mark Ericson, Operations Mgr., mark@morningwakingcrew.com. **Wattage:** 50,000. **Ad Rates:** $65-195 for 30 seconds; $70-200 for 60 seconds. Combined advertising rates available with WPKQ-FM, WXBB-FM, WXBP-FM. **Mailing address:** PO Box 576, Dover, NH 03821-0576. **URL:** http://www.wokq.com.

20992 ■ WPHX-FM - 92.1
1 Washington St., Ste. 204
Dover, NH 03820
Phone: (603)749-5900
Format: Alternative/New Music/Progressive. **Key Personnel:** Peter Lawley, Gen. Sales Mgr., plawley@fnxradio.com.

20993 ■ WPKQ-FM - 103.7
PO Box 576
Dover, NH 03821
Phone: (603)749-9750
Email: news@wokq.com
Format: Country. **Simulcasts:** WOKQ-FM. **Owner:** Citadel Broadcasting Corp., 7201 W Lake Mead Blvd., Ste. 400, Las Vegas, NV 89128-8366, Ph: (702)804-5200, Fax: (702)804-8250. **Key Personnel:** Mark Jennings, Mgr., mark.jennings@townsquaremedia.com; Brian Lang, Gen. Mgr., brian.lang@townsquaremedia.com; Paul Kelley, Dir. of Sales. **Wattage:** 21,500 H ERP; 16,500 V ERP. **Ad Rates:** Noncommercial. **URL:** http://www.wokq.com.

20994 ■ WSAK-FM - 102.1
292 Middle Rd.
Dover, NH 03820-4901
Phone: (603)749-9750
Free: 877-457-4275
Email: advertising@shark1053.com
Format: Classic Rock. **Simulcasts:** WSHK-FM. **Owner:** Citadel Broadcasting Corp., 7201 W Lake Mead Blvd., Ste. 400, Las Vegas, NV 89128-8366, Ph: (702)804-5200, Fax: (702)804-8250. **Key Personnel:** Brian Lang, Gen. Mgr., brian.lang@townsquaremedia.com; Paul Kelley, Dir. of Sales. **Wattage:** 3,000. **Ad Rates:** Noncommercial. **Mailing address:** PO Box 576, Dover, NH 03821-0576. **URL:** http://www.shark1053.com.

20995 ■ WSHK-FM - 105.3
292 Middle Rd.
Dover, NH 03820-4901
Phone: (603)749-9750
Email: advertising@shark1053.com
Format: Classic Rock. **Owner:** Citadel Broadcasting Corp., 7201 W Lake Mead Blvd., Ste. 400, Las Vegas, NV 89128-8366, Ph: (702)804-5200, Fax: (702)804-8250. **Key Personnel:** Brian Lang, Gen. Mgr., brian.lang@townsquaremedia.com; Paul Kelley, Dir. of Sales; Jonathan Smith, Dir. of Programs. **Ad Rates:** Noncommercial. **URL:** http://www.shark1053.com.

20996 ■ WTSN-AM - 1270
PO Box 400
Dover, NH 03821
Phone: (603)742-1270
Fax: (603)742-0448
Free: 888-441-9876
Format: Talk; News; Sports. **Networks:** ABC. **Owner:** Garrison City Broadcasting Inc., NH. **Founded:** Aug. 1950. **Operating Hours:** 5 a.m. - midnight; 50% network, 50% local. **Key Personnel:** Carole Lanctot, Bus. Mgr., carole@987thebay.com. **Local Programs:** *Open Mic*, Monday Tuesday Wednesday Thursday Friday 9:00 a.m. - 10:00 a.m. **Wattage:** 5,000. **Ad Rates:** $23-45 for 60 seconds. Combined advertising rates available with WBYY. **URL:** http://www.wtsnam1270.com.

20997 ■ WWNH-AM - 1340
PO Box 69
Dover, NH 03821
Phone: (603)742-8575
Fax: (603)743-6444
Owner: Harvest Broadcasting Co., at above address. **Founded:** May 14, 1989. **Key Personnel:** Mike Novak, President, CEO; Alan Mason, COO. **Wattage:** 250. **Ad Rates:** Advertising accepted; rates available upon request.

DUBLIN

SW NH. Cheshire Co. 11 mi. ESE of Keene. Resort.

20998 ■ Desktop Engineering: Technology for Design Engineering
Desktop Engineering
1283 Main St.
Dublin, NH 03444
Phone: (603)563-1631
Fax: (603)563-8192
Publication E-mail: den@omeda.com
Magazine featuring computers and peripherals and other related fields on desktop engineering. **Freq:** Monthly. **Key Personnel:** Steve Robbins, Executive Editor; Anthony J. Lockwood, Editor; Tom Conlon, Publisher. **Subscription Rates:** Free to qualified subscribers. **URL:** http://www.deskeng.com/de/. **Mailing address:** PO Box 1039, Dublin, NH 03444. **Remarks:** Accepts advertising. **Circ:** (Not Reported).

20999 ■ Yankee Homes
Yankee Publishing Inc.
PO Box 520
Dublin, NH 03444
Phone: (603)563-8111
Magazine concerned with homes, architecture, and life in New England, particlarly with historic and unusual homes for sale. **Freq:** Monthly. **Print Method:** Offset. **Trim Size:** 11 x 13. **Cols./Page:** 4. **Col. Width:** 14 picas. **Col. Depth:** 80 picas. **Key Personnel:** Jim Collins, Editor; Rob Trowbridge, Publisher. **ISSN:** 8756-0259 (print). **Ad Rates:** BW $1,500. **Remarks:** Accepts advertising. **Circ:** ‡35000.

21000 ■ Yankee Magazine
Yankee Publishing Inc.
PO Box 520
Dublin, NH 03444
Phone: (603)563-8111

Circulation: ★ = AAM; △ or • = BPA; ♦ = CAC; ❑ = VAC; ⊕ = PO Statement; ‡ = Publisher's Report; Boldface figures = sworn; Light figures = estimated.

Features stories on New England life, including food, home, and travel. **Freq:** Bimonthly. **Subscription Rates:** $19.97 Individuals. **URL:** http://www.yankeemagazine.com. **Circ:** (Not Reported).

DURHAM

SE NH. Strafford Co. 5 mi. SW of Dover. University of New Hampshire.

21001 ■ Journal of Applied Communications
Association for Communication Excellence in Agriculture, Natural Resources, and Life and Human Sciences
Taylor Hall
59 College Rd.
Durham, NH 03824
Phone: (603)862-1564
Fax: (603)862-1585
Free: 855-657-9544
Publisher's E-mail: ace.info@unh.edu
Journal dealing with all aspects of applied communications. **Freq:** 3/year. **Key Personnel:** Dwayne Cartmell, Executive Editor, phone: (405)744-0461. **ISSN:** 1051--0834 (print). **Subscription Rates:** $116 Individuals print only; $394 Institutions online; $450 Institutions. **URL:** http://journalofappliedcommunications.org/. **Remarks:** Advertising not accepted. **Circ:** (Not Reported).

WEKW-TV - See Keene

21002 ■ WENH-TV - 11
268 Mast Rd.
Durham, NH 03824
Phone: (603)868-1100
Fax: (603)868-7552
Email: themailbox@nhptv.org
Format: Public TV. **Simulcasts:** WLED-TV, WEKW-TV. **Networks:** Public Broadcasting Service (PBS). **Owner:** New Hampshire Public Television, 268 Mast Rd., Durham, NH 03824, Ph: (603)868-1100. **Founded:** 1959. **Operating Hours:** Continuous. **ADI:** Boston-Worcester,MA-Derry-Manchester,NH. **Key Personnel:** Jeffrey Gilbert, Chairman. **Local Programs:** *NH Outlook.* **Ad Rates:** Noncommercial. **URL:** http://www.nhptv.org.

WLED-TV - See Littleton

21003 ■ WUNH-FM - 91.3
University of New Hampshire
Durham, NH 03824
Phone: (603)862-2541
Email: music@wunh.org
Format: Alternative/New Music/Progressive. **Owner:** University of New Hampshire, Durham, NH 03824, Ph: (603)862-1234, Fax: (603)862-0077. **Founded:** 1971. **Operating Hours:** Continuous. **Key Personnel:** Lily Townsend, Dir. of Production, prodo@wunh.org. **Wattage:** 6,000. **Ad Rates:** Noncommercial; underwriting available. **URL:** http://www.wunh.org.

EXETER

SE NH. Rockingham Co. 13 mi. SW of Portsmouth. Phillips Exeter Academy. Diversified manufacturing. Granite finishing. Nurseries.

21004 ■ Crosswinds
Exeter Area Chamber of Commerce
24 Front St., Ste. 101
Exeter, NH 03833-0278
Phone: (603)772-2411
Fax: (603)772-9965
Publisher's E-mail: info@exeterarea.org
Magazine containing information about the Exeter, NH area; includes demographics and business directory. **Freq:** Annual. **Subscription Rates:** Free members. **URL:** http://www.exeterarea.org. **Mailing address:** PO Box 278, Exeter, NH 03833-0278. **Circ:** (Not Reported).

21005 ■ FANA Journal
Fan Association of North America
2 Sterling Hill Ln., No. 228
Exeter, NH 03833
Publisher's E-mail: FANAPresident@fanassociation.org
Freq: Semiannual. **Subscription Rates:** Included in membership. **Remarks:** Accepts advertising. **Circ:** 250.

21006 ■ WMYF-AM - 1540
PO Box 1540
Box 1540
Exeter, NH 03833-1540
Phone: (603)583-4767
Format: Classic Rock. **Owner:** Precision Media Ltd. Partnership, at above address. **Key Personnel:** Judy Figliulo, Sales Mgr.; Al Perry, VP; Jack O'Brien, Operations Mgr.; Wendy Larson, Gen. Sales Mgr.; Dan Alexander, News Dir. **Wattage:** 5,000 KW. **Ad Rates:** Combined advertising rates available with WERZ-FM. **URL:** http://www.wxexradio.com.

21007 ■ WPEA-FM - 90.5
Phillips Exeter Academy
20 Main St.
Exeter, NH 03833-2460
Phone: (603)772-4311
Fax: (603)777-4384
Email: wpea@exeter.edu
Format: Eclectic. **Owner:** Trustees of Phillips Exeter Academy, 20 Main St., Exeter, NH 03833-2460, Ph: (603)772-4311, Fax: (603)777-4384. **Founded:** 1964. **Operating Hours:** Noon-10 p.m. **Wattage:** 100. **Ad Rates:** Noncommercial. **URL:** http://www.exeter.edu.

21008 ■ WXEX Radio - 1540
PO Box 1540
Exeter, NH 03833
Phone: (207)324-1183
Email: info@wxexradio.com
Format: News; Talk; Sports. **Wattage:** 5,000 Day; 2,500 Night. **Ad Rates:** Advertising accepted; rates available upon request. **URL:** http://www.wxexradio.com.

FARMINGTON

21009 ■ WNHI-FM - 106.5
19 Boas Ln.
Wilton, CT 06897
Free: 888-937-2471
Format: Educational; Contemporary Christian. **Owner:** Education Media Foundation, 2351 Sunset Blvd., Ste. 170-218, Rocklin, CA 95765, Ph: (916)251-1600, Free: 800-434-8400. **Formerly:** WMEX-FM. **Operating Hours:** Continuous. **Wattage:** 2,900 ERP. **Ad Rates:** Advertising accepted; rates available upon request. **URL:** http://www.air1.com.

FRANKLIN

Merrimack Co. C. NH. Merrimack Co. At junction of Pemigewasset and Winnepesaukee Rivers, 18 mi. N. of Concord. Diversified manufacturing.

21010 ■ WFTN-AM
Babbit Rd.
Franklin, NH 03235
Phone: (603)934-2500
Fax: (603)934-2933
Format: Country. **Networks:** Satellite Music Network; ABC. **Owner:** Northeast Communications Corp., Babbitt Rd., Franklin, NH 03235. **Founded:** 1967. **Key Personnel:** Jeff Fisher, Contact; Kurt Muhlfelder, Contact; Jeff Fisher, Contact; Fred Caruso, Contact; Cathy Keyser, Contact. **Wattage:** 1,000.

21011 ■ WFTN-FM - 94.1
PO Box 941
Franklin, NH 03235
Phone: (603)934-2500
Format: Adult Contemporary. **Networks:** Major Market Radio. **Owner:** Northeast Communications Corp., Babbitt Rd., Franklin, NH 03235. **Founded:** 1987. **Operating Hours:** Continuous; 45% network, 55% local. **Key Personnel:** Jeff Fisher, Gen. Mgr., President, jefff@mix941fm.com; Fred Caruso, Dir. of Programs, fred@mix941fm.com; Jeff Levitan, VP, jefflevitan@metrocast.net. **Wattage:** 6,000. **Ad Rates:** Noncommercial. Combined advertising rates available with WFTN-AM: $15-$22 for 30 seconds; $18-$25 for 60 seconds. **URL:** http://www.mix941fm.com.

21012 ■ WSCY 106.9 FM - 106.9
PO Box 99
Franklin, NH 03235
Free: 888-941-1069
Format: Country. **Key Personnel:** Joyce Danas, Dir. of Programs; Jeff Fisher, Gen. Mgr.; Jeff Lavitan, Gen. Sales Mgr., VP. **Ad Rates:** Advertising accepted; rates available upon request. **URL:** http://www.wscy.com.

GILFORD

C. NH. Belknap Co. 3 mi. ENE of Laconia.

21013 ■ The Firearms Instructor
International Association of Law Enforcement Firearms Instructors
25 Country Club Rd., Ste. 707
Gilford, NH 03249
Phone: (603)524-8787
Fax: (603)524-8856
Publisher's E-mail: info@ialefi.com
Magazine publishing features articles, training tips, reports and news of interest to the professional firearms instructor. **Freq:** Quarterly. **Subscription Rates:** Included in membership. **URL:** http://www.ialefi.com. **Remarks:** Advertising not accepted. **Circ:** (Not Reported).

21014 ■ WLKZ-FM - 104.9
25 Country Club Rd.
Gilford, NH 03249
Phone: (603)524-1323
Format: Oldies. **Networks:** Unistar. **Owner:** Nassau Broadcasting, 619 Alexander Rd., 3rd Fl., Princeton, NJ 08540. **Founded:** 1985. **Operating Hours:** 5AM - 12 midnight. **Key Personnel:** Zack Derby, Dir. of Programs, zack@thehawkrocks.com; Jim Adams, Gen. Mgr., jadams@nassaubroadcasting.com. **Wattage:** 3,000. **Ad Rates:** $12.50-23.50 for 30 seconds; $15-25 for 60 seconds.

GILMANTON

21015 ■ Journal of the Print World: Works of Art on Paper
Journal of the Print World Inc.
PO Box 369
Gilmanton, NH 03237
Phone: (603)267-7349
Publication E-mail: jprintworld@metrocast.net
Advertisements and articles from USA, Europe and Japan concerning museums, libraries, galleries, and individuals in all media of original works of art on paper. **Freq:** Quarterly. **Print Method:** Offset litho. **Trim Size:** 11.375 x 17.5. **Cols./Page:** 6. **Col. Width:** 1 9/16 INS. **Col. Depth:** 16 INS. **Key Personnel:** Rebecca Ronstadt, Publisher. **ISSN:** 0737-7436 (print). **Subscription Rates:** $35 Individuals; $44 Canada; $80 Other countries; $18 Students. **URL:** http://www.journaloftheprintworld.com. **Ad Rates:** BW $2,950. **Remarks:** Advertising accepted; rates available upon request. **Circ:** 10000.

GRANTHAM

21016 ■ Kearsarge Magazine
Kearsarge Magazine
PO Box 1482
Grantham, NH 03753
Phone: (603)863-7048
Publication E-mail: info@kearsargemagazine.com
Magazine covering events, arts, and history in Sunapee, New London, Grantham, Andover, Warner, Sutton, Newbury, Wilmot, Bradford and Springfield, New Hampshire. **Freq:** Quarterly. **Print Method:** Web offset. **Trim Size:** 8.125 x 10.875. **Key Personnel:** Laura Jean Whitcomb, Editor. **Subscription Rates:** $15 Individuals; $8 Individuals digital. **URL:** http://www.kearsargemagazine.com. **Ad Rates:** 4C $1,100. **Remarks:** Accepts advertising. **Circ:** ‡20000.

HANOVER

WC NH. Grafton Co. On Connectucut River, 5 mi. NNW of Lebanon. Dartmouth College.

21017 ■ Analecta Husserliana: The Yearbook of Phenomenological Research
World Phenomenology Institute
1 Ivy Pointe Way
Hanover, NH 03755
Phone: (802)295-3487
Fax: (802)295-5963
Publisher's E-mail: office@phenomenology.org
Freq: 3-5/year. **Key Personnel:** William S. Smith, Editor-in-Chief; Anna-Teresa Tymieniecka, Editor. **Subscription Rates:** €101.14 Individuals eBook; €149.99 Individuals hardcover; €119.95 Individuals softcover. **URL:** http://www.phenomenology.org/index.php/academic-journals; http://www.springer.com/series/5621; http://www.springer.com/gp/book/9789027701718. **Also known as:** Analecta Husserliana. **Mailing address:** PO

Box 5158, Hanover, NH 03755. **Remarks:** Advertising not accepted. **Circ:** 800.

21018 ■ The Dartmouth
Dartmouth
6175 Robinson Hall
Hanover, NH 03755
Phone: (603)646-2600
Fax: (603)646-3443
Collegiate newspaper (tabloid). **Freq:** Weekly Mon. to Fri. **Print Method:** Offset. **Cols./Page:** 5. **Col. Width:** 9 7/8 nonpareils. **Col. Depth:** 12 1/2 inches. **Key Personnel:** Katie McKay, Editor-in-Chief. **ISSN:** 0199-9931 (print). **Subscription Rates:** $149 Individuals. **Ad Rates:** PCI $15. **Remarks:** Accepts advertising. **Circ:** ‡3,000.

21019 ■ Dartmouth Alumni Magazine
Dartmouth College Library
7 Allen St., Ste. 201
Hanover, NH 03755-2065
Phone: (603)646-2256
Fax: (603)646-1209
Publication E-mail: alumni.magazine@dartmouth.edu
College alumni magazine. **Freq:** 9/yr (during the academic year). **Print Method:** Offset. **Trim Size:** 8 1/8 x 10 7/8. **Cols./Page:** 3. **Col. Width:** 13 picas. **Col. Depth:** 10 inches. **Key Personnel:** Sean Plottner, Editor. **USPS:** 148-560. **Subscription Rates:** $26 Individuals /year. **URL:** http://dartmouthalumnimagazine.com. **Ad Rates:** BW $2040; 4C $3042. **Remarks:** Accepts advertising. **Circ:** Paid ‡41,251, Non-paid ‡2,727.

21020 ■ Dartmouth Medicine
Dartmouth Medical School
1 Rope Ferry Rd.
Hanover, NH 03755-1404
Phone: (603)650-1200
Fax: (603)650-1202
Free: 877-DMS-1797
Publisher's E-mail: dms.administration@dartmouth.edu
A magazine for Alumni and Friends of Dartmouth Medical School and Dartmouth-Hitchcock Medical Center. **Freq:** Quarterly. **Print Method:** Web offset. **Trim Size:** 8 1/2 x 10 7/8. **Key Personnel:** Amos Esty, Writer. **URL:** http://dartmed.dartmouth.edu. **Formerly:** Dartmouth Medical School Alumni Magazine. **Ad Rates:** BW $1,110; 4C $1,050. **Remarks:** Accepts advertising. **Circ:** Non-paid 28000.

21021 ■ Early China
Society for the Study of Early China
Dartmouth College
HB 6191
Hanover, NH 03755
Free: 800-872-7423
Publisher's E-mail: ccs@berkeley.edu
Scholarly journal covering prehistoric China history. **Freq:** Annual. **Trim Size:** 6 x 9. **Cols./Page:** 1. **Col. Width:** 26 picas. **Key Personnel:** Katherine Lawn Chouta, Managing Editor, phone: (510)643-3378. **ISSN:** 0362--5028 (print); **EISSN:** 2325--2324 (electronic). **Subscription Rates:** $50 Individuals volume 35-36 (2012-2013) - current; $40 Individuals volume 33-34 or 32; $30 Individuals volume 30 or 31. **URL:** http://ieas.berkeley.edu/publications/early_china.html; http://www.dartmouth.edu/~earlychina/publications/early_china_journal/index.html; http://journals.cambridge.org/action/displayJournal?jid=EAC. **Remarks:** Advertising not accepted. **Circ:** Controlled 350, 400.

21022 ■ Ecological Economics
Elsevier
c/o Richard B. Howarth, Editor-in-Chief
Dartmouth College
Environmental Studies Program
113 Steele Hall
Hanover, NH 03755
Publisher's E-mail: t.reller@elsevier.com
Journal concerned with extending and integrating the study and management of ecology and economics. **Freq:** Monthly. **Key Personnel:** Paula Antunes, Associate Editor; David Stern, Associate Editor; B. Davidsdottir, Editor; R. Costanza, Editor, Founder; Anne Aitken, Managing Editor; R.U. Ayres, Board Member; D. Bromley, Board Member; K. Chopra, Board Member; Richard B. Howarth, Editor-in-Chief. **ISSN:** 0921--8009 (print). **Subscription Rates:** $1129.87 Institutions online; $3391 Institutions print. **URL:** http://www.journals.elsevier.com/ecological-economics; http://www.isecoeco.org/the-isee-journal. **Circ:** (Not Reported).

21023 ■ Linguistic Discovery
Dartmouth College Library
6086 Reed
Darmouth College
Hanover, NH 03755
Journal that covers the description and analysis of primary linguistic data. **Freq:** Semiannual. **Key Personnel:** Gerrit J. Dimmendaal, Board Member; Doris L. Payne, Board Member; Maria Polinsky, Board Member; Pamela Munro, Board Member; Stephen A. Marlett, Board Member; Anthony C. Woodbury, Board Member; Lindsay J. Whaley, Editor; Lyle Campbell, Board Member. **ISSN:** 1537--0852 (print). **Subscription Rates:** Free. **URL:** http://journals.dartmouth.edu/ljournal/about.html. **Remarks:** Advertising not accepted. **Circ:** (Not Reported).

21024 ■ Microscopy Research and Technique
John Wiley & Sons Inc.
Dept. of Biology
Dartmouth College
Hanover, NH 03755
Phone: (603)448-1726
Fax: (603)448-0174
Publisher's E-mail: info@wiley.com
Journal covering the application of and research on advanced microscopy. **Freq:** Monthly. **Trim Size:** 8 1/4 x 11. **Key Personnel:** George Ruben, Editor; Paul Munroe, Board Member; Sara E. Miller, Board Member. **ISSN:** 1059--910X (print); **EISSN:** 1097--0029 (electronic). **Subscription Rates:** $10782 Institutions online or print - USA online only - Canada & Mexico/ROW; $12939 Institutions, Canada and Mexico print & online; $13140 Institutions, Canada and Mexico print & online; $10950 Institutions, Canada and Mexico print only; £5502 Institutions online only - UK; £6758 Institutions print & online - UK; £5631 Institutions print only - UK; €6956 Institutions online only - Europe; €8543 Institutions print & online - Europe; €7119 Institutions print only - Europe; $13241 Institutions, other countries print & online; $11034 Institutions, other countries print only. **URL:** http://onlinelibrary.wiley.com/journal/10.1002/(ISSN)1097-0029. **Ad Rates:** BW $757; 4C $1,009. **Remarks:** Accepts advertising. **Circ:** 5600.

21025 ■ Phenomenological Inquiry: A Review of Philosophical Ideas and Trends
World Phenomenology Institute
1 Ivy Pointe Way
Hanover, NH 03755
Phone: (802)295-3487
Fax: (802)295-5963
Publisher's E-mail: office@phenomenology.org
Freq: Annual. **Key Personnel:** William S. Smith, Editor-in-Chief; Jadwiga S. Smith, Editor-in-Chief. **ISSN:** 0885--3886 (print). **Subscription Rates:** $65 Individuals /year; $72 Institutions /year; Included in membership. **URL:** http://www.phenomenology.org/index.php/academic-journals. **Formerly:** Phenomenology Information Bulletin. **Mailing address:** PO Box 5158, Hanover, NH 03755. **Ad Rates:** BW $300. **Remarks:** Accepts advertising. **Circ:** Paid 400, Non-paid 200.

21026 ■ WDCR-AM - 1340
6176 Robinson Hall
Hanover, NH 03755-3507
Phone: (603)646-3313
Fax: (603)643-7655
Format: Alternative/New Music/Progressive. **Networks:** Independent. **Owner:** Dartmouth Broadcasting, at above address. **Founded:** 1958. **Operating Hours:** Continuous. **Key Personnel:** Heath Cole, Operations Mgr. **Wattage:** 3,400. **Ad Rates:** Noncommercial. $6-$17.50 for 30 seconds; $8-$19.50 for 60 seconds. Combined advertising rates available with WFRD-FM: $12-$35 for 30 seconds. **URL:** http://www.webdcr.com.

21027 ■ WEVH-FM - 91.3
Two Pillsbury St., Ste. 600
Concord, NH 03301-5003
Phone: (603)228-8910
Fax: (603)224-6052
Free: 800-639-4131
Format: Public Radio. **Ad Rates:** Noncommercial. **URL:** http://www.nhpr.org.

21028 ■ WFRD-FM - 99.3
6176 Robinson Hall
Hanover, NH 03755
Phone: (603)646-3313
Fax: (603)643-7655
Format: Album-Oriented Rock (AOR). **Networks:** Independent. **Owner:** Dartmouth Broadcasting, at above address. **Founded:** 1976. **Operating Hours:** 21 hours Daily, 100% local. **Key Personnel:** Heath Cole, Operations Mgr., heath.cole@dartmouth.edu. **Wattage:** 3,400. **Ad Rates:** Noncommercial. Combined advertising rates available with WDCR-AM: $12-$35 for 30 seconds; $16-$39 for 60 seconds. **URL:** http://www.wfrd.com.

21029 ■ WMXR-FM
35 S Main St., Ste. 300
Hanover, NH 03755
Phone: (603)643-4007
Fax: (603)448-1755
Owner: Great Eastern Radio, LLC, at above address. **Founded:** 1989. **Ad Rates:** Noncommercial.

HENNIKER

SC NH. Merrimack Co. On Contoocook River, 14 mi. W. of Concord.

21030 ■ The New Englander
New England College
98 Bridge St.
Henniker, NH 03242
Phone: (603)428-2000
Publication E-mail: thenewenglander@nec.edu
Collegiate newspaper. **Freq:** Biweekly. **Print Method:** Offset. **Trim Size:** 11 x 16. **Cols./Page:** 4. **Col. Width:** 2 1/4 inches. **Col. Depth:** 16 inches. **Key Personnel:** Mel Mower, Editor-in-Chief; William Homestead, Contact. **URL:** http://www.nec.edu/students-faculty-staff/newspaper-new-englander. **Ad Rates:** BW $204; PCI $4.75. **Remarks:** Color advertising not accepted. **Circ:** Free ‡1,500.

21031 ■ WNEC-FM - 91.7
98 Bridge St.
Henniker, NH 03242
Phone: (603)428-2000
Email: helpdesk@nec.edu
Format: Alternative/New Music/Progressive. **Owner:** New England College, 98 Bridge St., Henniker, NH 03242, Ph: (603)428-2000. **Founded:** 1971. **Formerly:** WWEC-FM. **Operating Hours:** 9 a.m. - midnight. **Wattage:** 120. **Ad Rates:** Noncommercial. **URL:** http://www.nec.edu.

HOOKSETT

21032 ■ WFNQ-FM - 106.3
11 Kimball Dr., Ste. 114
Hooksett, NH 03106
Phone: (603)889-1063
Fax: (603)882-0688
Free: 877-370-1063
Format: Talk; Music of Your Life. **Owner:** Nassau Broadcasting Partners L.P., 619 Alexander Rd., 3rd Fl., Princeton, NJ 08540-6000, Ph: (609)452-9696, Fax: (609)452-6017. **Operating Hours:** 12:00 a.m. - 5:30 a.m. Monday - Sunday. **Wattage:** 950 ERP. **Ad Rates:** Advertising accepted; rates available upon request. **URL:** http://www.1063frankfm.com/.

21033 ■ WNHI-FM - 93.3
11 Kimball Dr., Unit 114
Hooksett, NH 03106
Phone: (603)228-4493
Fax: (603)224-7280
Free: 800-430-4493
Email: wnhi@aol.com
Format: Classic Rock. **Networks:** Westwood One Radio. **Owner:** Vox Radio Group Co., Inc., at above address. **Founded:** May 1989. **Operating Hours:** Continuous. **Key Personnel:** Brit Johnson, Gen. Mgr., britfm@aol.com; Harry Kozlowski, Dir. of Programs, promorobot@wjyy.com; Dawn Osborne, Sales Mgr., dawn@wjyy.com. **Wattage:** 3,000. **Ad Rates:** $22-41 for 60 seconds. WJYY, WOTX, WKXL AM/FM.

HUDSON

S. NH. Hillsboro Co. On Merrimack River, 3 mi. E. of Nashua.

Circulation: ★ = AAM; △ or • = BPA; ♦ = CAC; ❑ = VAC; ⊕ = PO Statement; ‡ = Publisher's Report; Boldface figures = sworn; Light figures = estimated.

21034 ■ Hudson Litchfield News
Area News Group
17 Executive Dr., Ste. 1
Hudson, NH 03051
Phone: (603)880-1516
Fax: (603)879-9707
Publisher's E-mail: news@areanewsgroup.com
Community newspaper. **Freq:** Weekly. **Key Personnel:** Len Lathrop, Editor-in-Chief; Robin Rodgers, Editor; Jeffrey Rodgers, Manager, Production. **Subscription Rates:** Free. **URL:** http://www.areanewsgroup.com. **Formerly:** Hudson News. **Ad Rates:** GLR $11.15; BW $1,438.92; PCI $11.42. **Remarks:** Accepts advertising. **Circ:** Free ‡24000.

21035 ■ The Telegraph
The Telegraph
17 Executive Dr.
Hudson, NH 03051
Phone: (603)882-2741
Fax: (603)882-2681
Publication E-mail: webeditor@telegraph-nh.com
Community newspaper. **Founded:** 1832. **Freq:** Daily and Sun. **Key Personnel:** Alan Greenwood, Editor, phone: (603)594-6427. **Subscription Rates:** $45.50 Individuals Home delivery; $19.50 Individuals Sunday only, home delivery. **URL:** http://www.nashuatelegraph.com. **Remarks:** Accepts advertising. **Circ:** Mon.-Fri. ★**26293**, Sun. ★**31972**, Sat. ★**26015**.

JACKSON

21036 ■ WEVJ-FM - 99.5
Two Pillsbury St., 6th Fl.
Concord, NH 03301-5003
Phone: (603)228-8910
Fax: (603)224-6052
Free: 800-639-4131
Format: Public Radio. **Owner:** New Hampshire Public Radio, 2 Pillsbury St., 6th Fl., Concord, NH 03301, Ph: (603)228-8910, Fax: (603)224-6052, Free: 800-639-4131. **Key Personnel:** Betsy Gardella, CEO; Donna Hiltz, Traffic Mgr. **URL:** http://www.nhpr.org.

KEENE

Cheshire Co. SW NH. Cheshire Co. On Ashuelot River, 15 mi. ENE of Brattleboro, VT. Keene State College. Summer resort. Major industrial and commercial center. Quarries, lumber, nurseries, agriculture.

21037 ■ Canoe News
United States Canoe Association
c/o Peter Heed, President
581 West St.
Keene, NH 03431
Phone: (603)209-2299
Freq: Quarterly. **Subscription Rates:** Included in membership. **URL:** http://www.uscanoe.com/About_Canoe_News_W1.cfm. **Remarks:** Accepts advertising. **Circ:** (Not Reported).

21038 ■ ISLE: Interdisciplinary Studies in Literature and the Environment
Association for the Study of Literature and Environment
PO Box 502
Keene, NH 03431-0502
Phone: (603)357-7411
Fax: (603)357-7411
Publisher's E-mail: info@asle.org
Freq: Quarterly. **ISSN:** 1076- 0962 (print); **EISSN:** 1759-1090 (electronic). **Subscription Rates:** £60 Individuals; $91 Individuals; €79 Individuals. **URL:** http://www.asle.org/research-write/isle-journal/. **Remarks:** Accepts advertising. **Circ:** 1200.

21039 ■ The Keene Sentinel
Keene Publishing Corp.
60 W St.
Keene, NH 03431
Phone: (603)352-1234
Fax: (603)352-0437
Free: 800-765-9994
Publication E-mail: news@keenesentinel.com
General newspaper. **Freq:** Daily (morn.) and Saturday and Sunday mornings. **Print Method:** Offset. **Cols./Page:** 6. **Col. Width:** 1.83 inches. **Col. Depth:** 301 agate lines. **Key Personnel:** Michael Breshears, Director, Advertising; Thomas M. Ewing, Publisher. **USPS:** 291-800. **Subscription Rates:** $99.84 Individuals online; $218.90 Individuals print and online. **URL:** http://www.sentinelsource.com. **Mailing address:** PO Box 546, Keene, NH 03431-0546. **Ad Rates:** BW $2342.64; 4C $2627.64; PCI $21. **Remarks:** Accepts advertising. **Circ:** Mon.-Sat. ★**12,602**, Sun. ★**12,419**.

21040 ■ WEKW-TV - 49
268 Mast Rd.
Durham, NH 03824
Phone: (603)868-1100
Email: themailbox@nhptv.org
Simulcasts: WENH-TV Durham, NH. **Networks:** Public Broadcasting Service (PBS). **Owner:** New Hampshire Public Television, 268 Mast Rd., Durham, NH 03824, Ph: (603)868-1100. **Founded:** 1959. **Operating Hours:** 6 a.m.-1:05 p.m. **ADI:** Boston-Worcester,MA-Derry-Manchester,NH. **Key Personnel:** Jeffrey Gilbert, Chairman. **Local Programs:** *Granite State Challenge*, Saturday Sunday Friday 6:00 p.m. 10:00 a.m.; 5:00 p.m. 3:00 p.m.; *New Hampshire Crossroads*; *Nature Works*. **Ad Rates:** Noncommercial. **URL:** http://www.nhptv.org.

21041 ■ WINQ-FM - 98.7
69 Stanhope Ave.
Keene, NH 03431
Phone: (603)352-9230
Fax: (603)357-3926
Free: 888-354-9465
Format: Country. **Owner:** Saga Communication Inc., 73 Kercheval Ave., Ste. 201, Grosse Pointe, MI 48236, Ph: (313)886-7070, Fax: (313)886-7150. **Founded:** 1983. **Key Personnel:** Edward K. Christian, Chairman, CEO, President; Bob Cox, Gen. Mgr., bcox@monadnockradiogroup.com; Susan Wells, Gen. Sales Mgr., swells@monadnockradiogroup.com. **Ad Rates:** Advertising accepted; rates available upon request. $20-30 per unit. **URL:** http://987wink.com.

WKBK-AM - See Winchester

21042 ■ WKNE-AM - 1290
69 Stanhope Ave.
Keene, NH 03431
Phone: (603)352-9230
Fax: (603)357-3926
Format: News; Talk. **Networks:** CBS. **Owner:** LB New Hampshire, Inc., at above address. **Founded:** 1927. **Operating Hours:** Continuous; 5% network, 95% local. **Wattage:** 5,000. **Ad Rates:** $53 for 60 seconds. Combined advertising rates available with WKNE-FM.

21043 ■ WKNE-FM - 103.7
69 Stanhope Ave.
Keene, NH 03431
Phone: (603)352-9230
Fax: (603)357-3926
Free: 800-445-1037
Format: Eclectic. **Networks:** Independent. **Founded:** 1958. **Operating Hours:** Continuous; 100% local. **Key Personnel:** Susan Wells, Operations Mgr., swells@monadnockradiogroup.com; Bob Cox, Gen. Mgr., bcox@monadnockradiogroup.com; Steve Hamel, Operations Mgr., shamel@monadnockradiogroup.com. **Wattage:** 12,000. **Ad Rates:** Noncommercial. Combined advertising rates available with WKNE-AM. **URL:** http://www.wkne.com.

21044 ■ WKNH-FM - 91.3
229 Main St.
Keene, NH 03435
Fax: (603)358-2419
Format: Eclectic. **Owner:** Keene State College, 229 Main St., Keene, NH 03431, Ph: (603)358-2276. **Founded:** 1975. **Formerly:** WKSC-FM. **Operating Hours:** 7 a.m.-1 a.m. **Key Personnel:** Alex Dubberly, Contact. **Wattage:** 300. **Ad Rates:** Noncommercial. **URL:** http://www.wknh.org.

21045 ■ WSNI-FM - 97.7
69 Stanhope Ave.
Keene, NH 03431
Phone: (603)352-9230
Fax: (603)357-3926
Free: 800-445-1037
Format: Oldies. **Owner:** Saga Communications Inc., 73 Kercheval Ave., Ste. 201, Grosse Pointe Farms, MI 48236, Ph: (313)886-7070, Fax: (313)886-7150. **Formerly:** Monadnock Radio Group; WOQL-FM. **Key Personnel:** Box Cox, Gen. Mgr., bcox@monadnockradiogroup.com. **URL:** http://www.sagacom.com.

WXOD-FM - See Winchester

21046 ■ WZBK-AM - 1220
69 Stanhope Ave.
Keene, NH 03431
Phone: (603)352-9230
Fax: (603)357-3926
Format: News; Talk. **Owner:** Saga Communications Inc., 73 Kercheval Ave., Ste. 201, Grosse Pointe Farms, MI 48236, Ph: (313)886-7070, Fax: (313)886-7150. **Key Personnel:** Edward Christian, CEO, President. **URL:** http://www.espnkeene.com.

LACONIA

Belknap Co. C. NH. Belknap Co. Near Lakes Winnisquam, Pangus, and Opechee, 22 mi. N. of Concord. White Mountain National Forest headquarters. Summer and winter resort. Diversified manufacturing, including knitting machines, wood products. Timber; farming.

21047 ■ The Citizen of Laconia
George J. Foster Co.
171 Fair St.
Laconia, NH 03246
Phone: (603)524-3800
Fax: (603)527-3593
Publisher's E-mail: weddings@fosters.com
Community newspaper. **Freq:** Mon.-Sat. **Key Personnel:** Tom Caldwell, Editor; Timothy Brady, Director, Advertising. **URL:** http://www.fosters.com/apps/pbcs.dll/section?category=CITNEWS. **Remarks:** Accepts advertising. **Circ:** Paid ♦**6293**.

21048 ■ Hearth & Home Magazine: The Voice of the Hearth, Barbecue and Patio Industries
PO Box 1288
Laconia, NH 03247
Free: 888-873-3610
Trade journal for manufacturers and retailers of hearth products, casual furniture and barbecue grills. **Freq:** Monthly. **Print Method:** Offset. **Trim Size:** 8 1/8 x 10 7/8. **Cols./Page:** 3. **Col. Width:** 27 nonpareils. **Col. Depth:** 152 agate lines. **Key Personnel:** Richard Wright, Editor; Jackie Avignone, Director, Advertising; Sheila Kufert, Contact. **ISSN:** 0273--5695 (print). **Subscription Rates:** $36 Individuals domestic; $60 Canada; $120 Other countries. **URL:** http://www.hearthandhome.com. **Formerly:** Wood 'n Energy. **Remarks:** Advertising accepted; rates available upon request. **Circ:** (Not Reported).

21049 ■ WEMJ-AM - 1490
PO Box 7326
Laconia, NH 03247
Phone: (603)524-1323
Fax: (603)528-5185
Format: Talk; News. **Networks:** Westwood One Radio; ABC; Mutual Broadcasting System; CBS. **Owner:** Nassau Broadcasting, 619 Alexander Rd., 3rd Fl., Princeton, NJ 08540. **Founded:** 1961. **Operating Hours:** 12 a.m.-12 p.m. **Key Personnel:** Pat Kelley, Contact, pkelly@nassaubroadcasting.com; Pat Kelley, Contact, pkelly@nassaubroadcasting.com. **Wattage:** 1,000. **Ad Rates:** Advertising accepted; rates available upon request.

21050 ■ WEZS-AM - 1350
277 Union Ave., Ste. 205
Laconia, NH 03246
Phone: (603)524-6288
Email: staff@wezs.com
Format: Easy Listening. **Networks:** USA Radio. **Owner:** WEZS Radio, 277 Union Ave., Ste. 205, Laconia, NH 03246, Ph: (603)524-6288. **Founded:** 1922. **Operating Hours:** 5:30 a.m. - 12 midnight. **Key Personnel:** Gary Hammond, Gen. Mgr. **Wattage:** 5,000. **Ad Rates:** $8-15 for 60 seconds. **URL:** http://www.wezs.com.

21051 ■ WEZS Radio - 1350
277 Union Ave., Ste. 205
Laconia, NH 03246
Phone: (603)524-6288
Format: Talk. **Networks:** Fox. **Operating Hours:** Continuous. **Key Personnel:** Gary Hammond, Gen. Mgr. **Wattage:** 5,000 Day; 112 Night. **URL:** http://www.wezs.com.

21052 ■ WLNH-FM - 98.3
NH1 Media Ctr., 4 Church St.
Concord, NH 03301
Phone: (603)524-3698

Fax: (603)528-5185
Free: 877-611-9564
Format: Adult Contemporary. **Owner:** Nassau Broadcasting, 619 Alexander Rd., 3rd Fl., Princeton, NJ 08540. **Operating Hours**: Continuous. **Key Personnel:** Scott Laudani, Dir. of Programs, Prog. Dir., mking@nassaubroadcasting.com. **Wattage**: 700 ERP. **Ad Rates:** Noncommercial; Advertising accepted; rates available upon request. **Mailing address:** PO Box 7326, Gilford, NH 03249. **URL:** http://wlnh.nh1media.com.

21053 ■ WWSS-FM - 101.5
PO Box 577
Laconia, NH 03247-0577
Phone: (603)279-4500
Fax: (603)279-3318
Format: Adult Contemporary; Soft Rock; News. **Networks:** CNN Radio. **Founded:** 1988. **Formerly**: WMRQ-FM. **Operating Hours**: Continuous. **Key Personnel:** Gary Howard, Gen. Mgr.; Keith Murray, Dir. of Programs; Mike Gagnon, News Dir; Constance Fortney, Contact. **Wattage**: 3,000 ERP. **Ad Rates:** $6.40-17.60 for 30 seconds; $8-22 for 60 seconds.

LANCASTER

NW NH. Coos Co. Near Connecticut and Israel Rivers, 19 mi. W. of Berlin. Summer resort. Trading center for surrounding agriculture. Pulpwood timber.

21054 ■ Berlin Reporter
Salmon Press
79 Main St.
Lancaster, NH 03584
Phone: (603)788-4939
Publication E-mail: democrat@salmonpress.com
Newspaper. **Freq:** Weekly (Wed.). **Print Method:** Offset. **Trim Size:** 10 x 15. **Cols./Page:** 9. **Col. Width:** 16 nonpareils. **Col. Depth:** 294 agate lines. **Key Personnel:** Bruce Pelletier, Advertising Representative. **Subscription Rates:** free for members. **URL:** http://www.newhampshirelakesandmountains.com. **Formerly**: The Daily Berlin Reporter. **Ad Rates:** BW $292.50; 4C $692.50; PCI $3. **Remarks:** Accepts advertising. **Circ:** 5012.

21055 ■ Coos County Democrat
Salmon Press
79 Main St.
Lancaster, NH 03584
Phone: (603)788-4939
Fax: (603)788-3022
Publisher's E-mail: info@tiltontrailer.com
Community newspaper. **Freq:** Weekly (Wed.). **Print Method:** Letterpress and offset. **Cols./Page:** 8. **Col. Width:** 11 nonpareils. **Col. Depth:** 21 agate lines. **Key Personnel:** Frank Chilinski, President, Publisher, phone: (603)279-4516. **USPS:** 222-580. **URL:** http://www.newhampshirelakesandmountains.com/118968.113119body.lasso?publication=LAN. **Ad Rates:** GLR $6; BW $1008; PCI $6. **Remarks:** Advertising accepted; rates available upon request. **Circ:** ‡6,500, ‡4,952.

WLTN-AM - See Littleton, NH

21056 ■ WMOU-AM - 1230
195 Main St.
Lancaster, NH 03584-3035
Phone: (603)788-3636
Simulcasts: WXLQ-PN. **Owner:** Barry P. Lunderville, LLC, at above address. **Founded:** 1947. **Wattage**: 1,000.

LEBANON

Grafton Co. WC NH. Grafton Co. 5 mi. SSE of Hanover. Resort. Diversified manufacturing.

21057 ■ Stereotactic and Functional Neurosurgery
S. Karger Publishers Inc.
c/o David W. Roberts, Ed.
Section of Neurosurgery
Dartmouth Medical Center
1 Medical Center Dr.
Lebanon, NH 03756-0001
Phone: (603)650-8734
Fax: (603)650-7911
Publisher's E-mail: karger@snet.net
Scientific medical journal. **Founded:** 1938. **Freq:** 6/year Bimonthly. **Print Method:** Offset. **Trim Size:** 210 x 280 mm. **Cols./Page:** 1. **Col. Width:** 84 nonpareils. **Col. Depth:** 141 agate lines. **Key Personnel:** David W. Roberts, Editor. **ISSN:** 1011-6125 (print); **EISSN:** 1423-0372 (electronic). **Subscription Rates:** 1990 FR Institutions print or online; €1658 Institutions in Germany; print or online; $2031 Institutions print or online; 1990 FR Institutions combined print and online; €1658 Institutions in Germany; combined print and online; $2031 Institutions combined print and online; 995 FR Individuals print and online; €829 Individuals print and online; $1016 Individuals print and online. **URL:** http://www.karger.com/Journal/Home/224132; http://www.assfn.org/. **Formerly**: Confinia Neurologica; Applied Neurophysiology. **Ad Rates:** BW $2,094; BW $1,555. **Remarks:** Accepts advertising. **Circ:** 900.

21058 ■ WGXL-FM - 92.3
31 Hanover St., Ste. 4
Lebanon, NH 03766
Phone: (603)448-1400
Format: Adult Contemporary. **Owner:** Great Eastern Radio, LLC, at above address. **Operating Hours**: Continuous. **ADI**: Boston-Worcester,MA-Derry-Manchester,NH. **Key Personnel:** Wally Caswell, Gen. Mgr., wcaswell@uppervalleyradio.com; Nichole Romano, Sales Mgr., nromano@uppervalleyradio.com; Justin Tyler, Operations Mgr., tmcduffie@uppervalleyradio.com. **Wattage**: 6,000 ERP. **Ad Rates:** Noncommercial.

21059 ■ WTSL-AM
PO Box 1400
Lebanon, NH 03766
Phone: (603)727-0262
Format: Talk; Sports; News; Sports. **Networks:** CBS; ABC. **Founded:** 1950. **Key Personnel:** Scott Roberts, Owner, Owner; Frank Kelly, Dir. of Programs. **Wattage**: 1,000. **Ad Rates:** $8-24 for 30 seconds; $12-28 for 60 seconds. **URL:** http://945espn.com.

21060 ■ WTSL-FM - 92.3
The Mall
Box 526
Lebanon, NH 03766
Phone: (603)448-1400
Fax: (603)448-1755
Format: Soft Rock. **Networks:** Independent. **Founded:** 1987. **Operating Hours**: Continuous; 100% local. **Key Personnel:** Bob Sherman, Sales Mgr; Darrel Clark, Contact. **Wattage**: 3,000. **Ad Rates:** $28-48 for 30 seconds; $35-55 for 60 seconds.

21061 ■ WVRR-FM - 101.7
31 Hanover St., No. 4
Lebanon, NH 03766
Phone: (603)448-1400
Fax: (603)448-1755
Format: Classic Rock; Country. **Networks:** CNN Radio; Westwood One Radio. **Founded:** Mar. 1997. **Formerly**: WXXK-FM; WCNL-FM. **Operating Hours**: Continuous. **Key Personnel:** Traci McDuffie, Dir. of Programs, tmcduffie@uppervalleyradio.com; Wally Caswell, Gen. Mgr., wcaswell@uppervalleyradio.com. **Wattage**: 3,000. **Ad Rates:** Advertising accepted; rates available upon request. $17-30 per unit. **URL:** http://www.wvrrfm.com.

LITTLETON

WC NH. Grafton Co. On Ammonoosuc River, 31 mi. SW of Berlin. Mountain resort. Manufactures shoes, wood products. Lumber, dairy farms.

21062 ■ Littleton Courier
Salmon Press
16 Mill St.
Littleton, NH 03561
Phone: (603)444-3927
Fax: (603)444-3920
Publisher's E-mail: info@tiltontrailer.com
Community newspaper. **Freq:** Weekly (Wed.). **Print Method:** Offset. **Cols./Page:** 6. **Col. Width:** 10.5 picas. **Col. Depth:** 21 inches. **URL:** http://www.newhampshirelakesandmountains.com. **Ad Rates:** 4C $100. **Remarks:** Accepts advertising. **Circ:** (Not Reported).

21063 ■ WLED-TV - 48
268 Mast Rd.
Durham, NH 03824
Phone: (603)868-1100
Email: themailbox@nhptv.org
Format: Public TV. **Simulcasts:** WENH-TV. **Networks:** Public Broadcasting Service (PBS). **Owner:** New Hampshire Public Television, 268 Mast Rd., Durham, NH 03824, Ph: (603)868-1100. **Founded:** 1959. **Operating Hours:** 6 a.m.-1:05 a.m. **ADI**: Burlington-Hartford, VT-Plattsburgh, NY. **Key Personnel:** Jeffrey Gilbert, Chairman. **Local Programs:** *Granite State Challenge*, Saturday 6:00 p.m.; *New Hampshire Crossroads*; *Roundtable*, Friday Sunday Monday Tuesday 6:00 p.m. 9:30 a.m. 5:30 a.m.; 6:00 p.m. 1:00 a.m. **Ad Rates:** Noncommercial. **URL:** http://www.nhptv.org.

21064 ■ WLTN-AM - 1400
195 Main St.
Lancaster, NH 03584-3035
Phone: (603)444-3911
Fax: (603)444-7186
Owner: Barry P. Lunderville, LLC, at above address. **Founded:** 1963. **Wattage:** 1,000. **Ad Rates:** $6.70-8.70 for 30 seconds; $9-11.70 for 60 seconds. Combined advertising rates available with WLTN-FM: $5-$13 for 30 seconds; $6.75-$17.50. **URL:** http://www.wltnradio.com.

21065 ■ WLTN-FM - 96.7
15 Main St.
Littleton, NH 03561
Phone: (603)444-3911
Fax: (603)444-7186
Email: bright967@landmarknet.net
Format: Adult Contemporary. **Networks:** Westwood One Radio. **Founded:** 1991. **Operating Hours**: Continuous. **Wattage**: 6,000. **Ad Rates:** Advertising accepted; rates available upon request. $6.70-$8.70 for 30 seconds; $9-$11.70 for 60 seconds; Combined advertising rates available with WLTN-AM.

21066 ■ WMTK-FM - 106.3
PO Box 106
Littleton, NH 03561
Phone: (603)444-5106
Fax: (603)444-1205
Format: Classic Rock. **Networks:** ABC; Satellite Music Network. **Owner:** Vermont Broadcast Associates Inc., 10 Church St., Lyndonville, VT 05851, Ph: (802)626-9800. **Founded:** 1985. **Operating Hours**: Continuous. **Wattage**: 390. **Ad Rates:** Advertising accepted; rates available upon request. **URL:** http://www.notchfm.com.

LONDONDERRY

21067 ■ Tree Care Industry Magazine
Tree Care Industry Association
136 Harvey Rd., Ste. 101
Londonderry, NH 03053
Phone: (603)314-5380
Fax: (603)314-5386
Free: 800-733-2622
Publisher's E-mail: garvin@tcia.org
Trade journal for the commercial tree care industry. **Freq:** Monthly. **Print Method:** Web offset. **Trim Size:** 8 1/8 x 10 7/8. **Cols./Page:** 3. **Col. Width:** 2 1/3 inches. **Col. Depth:** 10 inches. **Key Personnel:** Don Staruk, Editor; Mark Garvin, Publisher. **ISSN:** 1059--0528 (print). **Subscription Rates:** $40 Individuals 1 year, U.S.; $60 Individuals 1 year, other countries; $70 Individuals 2 years, U.S.; $105 Individuals 2 years, other countries. **URL:** http://www.tcia.org/publications/tci-magazine; http://tcia.org/publications/tci-magazine/archives. **Ad Rates:** BW $2599; 4C $3708. **Remarks:** Accepts advertising. **Circ:** ‡24000.

21068 ■ WLLO-FM - 102.9
268-C Mammoth Rd.
Londonderry, NH 03053
Phone: (603)432-6920
Fax: (603)425-1049
Format: Educational; Big Band/Nostalgia. **Owner:** Londonderry School District, 268C Mammoth Rd, Londonderry, NH 03053, Ph: (603)432-6920, Fax: (603)425-1049. **Founded:** 1990. **URL:** http://www.londonderry.org.

MANCHESTER

Hillsborough Co. S. NH. Hillsboro Co. On Merrimack River, 15 mi. N. of Nashua. New Hampshire College, Saint Anselm College, Notre Dame College, University of New Hampshire at Manchester. Largest city in NH; major manufacturing center. Products include electron-

Circulation: ★ = AAM; △ or • = BPA; ♦ = CAC; ❑ = VAC; ⊕ = PO Statement; ‡ = Publisher's Report; Boldface figures = sworn; Light figures = estimated.

ics, shoes, textiles, rubber, auto parts. Lumber; dairy farms.

21069 ■ New Hampshire Business Review
Business Publications Inc.
150 Dow St.
Manchester, NH 03101
Phone: (603)624-1442
Regional business newspaper. **Founded:** 1978. **Freq:** Biweekly. **Print Method:** Web offset. **Key Personnel:** Shirley Meyers, Business Manager; Jeff Feingold, Editor; Sharron McCarthy, President; Jodie Hall, Manager, Production; Shannon Spiliotis, Manager, Circulation. **ISSN:** 0164-8152 (print). **Subscription Rates:** $32 Individuals 1 year; $55 Two years; $80 Individuals 3 years. **URL:** http://www.nhbr.com/. **Ad Rates:** BW $2,025. **Remarks:** Accepts advertising. **Circ:** 15000.

21070 ■ New Hampshire Magazine
New Hampshire Magazine
150 Dow St.
Manchester, NH 03103
Phone: (603)624-1442
Publisher's E-mail: editor@nhmagazine.com
Consumer magazine covering business and lifestyle. **Freq:** Monthly. **Print Method:** Web offset. **Trim Size:** 8 1/8 x 10 7/8. **Subscription Rates:** $19.97 Individuals. **Formerly:** Manchester; Concord North; Hampshire East; Nashua; New Hampshire Editions. **Ad Rates:** BW $3,325; 4C $3,825. **Remarks:** Accepts advertising. **Circ:** Combined 123000.

21071 ■ Salem Observer
Salem Observer
100 William Loeb Dr.
Manchester, NH 03109
Publisher's E-mail: sales@salemobserver.com
Community newspaper. **Freq:** Weekly (Thurs.). **Print Method:** Offset. **Trim Size:** 7 x 10.61. **Cols./Page:** 6. **Col. Width:** 1.83 inches. **Col. Depth:** 301 agate lines. **Key Personnel:** Christine Heiser, Executive Editor, phone: (603)206-7811; Joe McQuaid, Publisher. **URL:** http://www.newhampshire.com/section/newhampshire1411. **Ad Rates:** PCI $11.90. **Remarks:** Accepts advertising. **Circ:** ‡8,000.

21072 ■ The Union Leader
Union Leader Corp.
100 William Loeb Dr.
Manchester, NH 03108-9555
Publisher's E-mail: letters@unionleader.com
General newspaper. **Founded:** 1863. **Freq:** Mon.-Sun. (morn.) Weekly (Thurs.). **Print Method:** Flexography. **Trim Size:** 21 1/4 x 13. **Cols./Page:** 6. **Col. Width:** 1.833 25 inches nonpareils. **Col. Depth:** 11.50 294 inches agate lines. **Key Personnel:** Joe McQuaid, Publisher. **Subscription Rates:** $202.80 Individuals home delivery, Mon. to Sun.; $138.84 Individuals home delivery, Thu. to Sun.; $74.88 Individuals home delivery, Sunday; $127.92 Individuals home delivery, Mon. to Sat.; $96.20 Individuals home delivery, Sat. and Sun.; $248.56 By mail Mon. to Sun.; $265.20 By mail Mon. to Sat.; $130 By mail Sunday; $20 Individuals 7 day home delivery; $18.20 Individuals 6 day home delivery; $9.30 Individuals sunday only; $9.95 Individuals digital only. **URL:** http://www.unionleader.com. **Mailing address:** PO Box 9555, Manchester, NH 03108-9555. **Ad Rates:** GLR $2.75; BW $4908.75; 4C $3600; PCI $38.42; SAU $18; PCI $15.75. **Remarks:** Accepts classified advertising. **Circ:** Mon.-Sat. **★52,549**, Sun. **★68,535**, Paid ‡8,000.

21073 ■ WFEA-AM - 1370
500 Commercial St.
Manchester, NH 03101
Phone: (603)669-5777
Fax: (603)669-4641
Format: Music of Your Life. **Networks:** CBS. **Owner:** Saga Communications Inc., 73 Kercheval Ave., Ste. 201, Grosse Pointe Farms, MI 48236, Ph: (313)886-7070, Fax: (313)886-7150. **Founded:** Mar. 01, 1932. **Operating Hours**: Continuous. **ADI**: Boston-Worcester,MA-Derry-Manchester,NH. **Key Personnel:** Pat Mckay, Operations Mgr., Gen. Mgr., pat@wzid.com. **Local Programs**: *Prime Of Life @ 9*, Wednesday Thursday Friday 9:00 a.m. - 10:00 a.m. **Wattage**: 5,000. **Ad Rates:** $50 per unit; $40 per unit. Combined advertising rates available with WZID-FM, WMLL-FM. **URL:** http://www.wfea1370.com.

21074 ■ WGIR-AM - 610
195 McGregor St., Ste. 810
Manchester, NH 03102
Phone: (603)625-6915
Fax: (603)625-9255
Format: News; Sports; Talk; Information. **Founded:** 1941. **Operating Hours**: Continuous. **Key Personnel:** Angela Comtois, Contact, angelacomtois@clearchannel.com. **Local Programs**: *Wine Crush*, Thursday 10:00 p.m. **Wattage**: 5,000 KW. **Ad Rates:** Advertising accepted; rates available upon request. **URL:** http://wgiram.iheart.com.

21075 ■ WGIR-FM - 101.1
195 McGregor St., Ste. 810
Manchester, NH 03102
Phone: (603)625-6915
Fax: (603)625-9255
Free: 888-556-7625
Format: Album-Oriented Rock (AOR). **Owner:** iHeartMedia and Entertainment Inc. , 200 E Basse Rd., San Antonio, TX 78209, Ph: (210)822-2828. **Founded:** 1963. **Operating Hours**: Continuous. **Wattage**: 9,600. **Ad Rates:** Noncommercial. **URL:** http://www.rock101fm.com.

21076 ■ WMLL-FM - 96.5
500 Commercial St.
Manchester, NH 03101
Phone: (603)669-9650
Fax: (603)669-4641
Free: 800-666-0957
Format: Classic Rock. **Founded:** Sept. 13, 2006. **Key Personnel:** Andy Orcutt, Dir. of Sales; Peter Stohrer, Dir. of Engg., pstohrer@comcast.net; Ray Garon, Gen. Mgr., President, raydionh@wzid.com. **Ad Rates:** Noncommercial. **URL:** http://www.965themill.com.

21077 ■ WMUR-TV - 9
100 S Commercial St.
Manchester, NH 03101
Phone: (603)669-9999
Fax: (603)641-9005
Format: Commercial TV. **Networks:** ABC. **Owner:** Hearst Television Inc., 300 W 57th St., New York, NY 10019-3741, Ph: (212)887-6800, Fax: (212)887-6855. **Operating Hours**: 5:30 a.m.-1:30 a.m. weekdays; 6:30-1:30 a.m. Saturday and Sunday. **ADI**: Boston-Worcester,MA-Derry-Manchester,NH. **Key Personnel:** Gerry McGavick, Contact. **Wattage**: 282 KW ERP. **Ad Rates:** Noncommercial. **URL:** http://www.wmur.com.

21078 ■ WZID-FM - 95.7
500 Commercial St.
Manchester, NH 03101
Phone: (603)669-5777
Fax: (603)669-4641
Free: 800-666-0957
Format: News. **Owner:** Saga Communications of NE Inc., 73 Kercheval Ave., Ste. 201, Grosse Pointe Farms, MI 48236, Ph: (313)886-7070. **ADI**: Boston-Worcester,MA-Derry-Manchester,NH. **Key Personnel:** Peter Stohrer, Dir. of Engg., pstohrer@manchesterrg.com; Andy Orcutt, Dir. of Sales, aorcutt@manchesterrg.com. **Wattage**: 14,500 ERP. **Ad Rates:** Advertising accepted; rates available upon request. $100-250 for 60 seconds. **URL:** http://www.wzid.com.

MEREDITH

C NH. Belknap Co. On Lake Winnipesaukee, 11 mi. N. of Laconia. Resort. Lumber; dairy farms.

21079 ■ The Meredith News
Salmon Press
Five Water St.
Meredith, NH 03253
Phone: (603)279-4516
Fax: (603)279-3331
Free: 877-766-6891
Publisher's E-mail: info@tiltontrailer.com
Community newspaper. **Freq:** Weekly (Wed.). **Print Method:** Offset. **Trim Size:** 11 1/2 x 16 1/2. **Cols./Page:** 5. **Col. Width:** 12 1/4 picas. **Col. Depth:** 16 inches. **Key Personnel:** Erin Plummer, Editor. **USPS:** 339-860. **URL:** http://www.newhampshirelakesandmountains.com/118968.113119body.lasso?publication=MER. **Mailing address:** PO Box 729, Meredith, NH 03253. **Ad Rates:** BW $590; SAU $7.38; PCI $7.38. **Remarks:** Accepts advertising. **Circ:** Combined 3,485.

21080 ■ The Record Enterprise
Salmon Press
5 Water St.
Meredith, NH 03253
Phone: (603)536-1311
Fax: (603)536-8940
Free: 800-491-4612
Publisher's E-mail: info@tiltontrailer.com
Newspaper with a Republican orientation. **Founded:** 1887. **Freq:** Weekly (Wed.). **Print Method:** Offset. **Trim Size:** 11 1/2 x 16 1/2. **Cols./Page:** 5. **Col. Width:** 2 1/16 inches. **Col. Depth:** 15 inches. **Key Personnel:** Frank Chilinski, Publisher; Brendan Berube, Editor, phone: (603)536-1311. **Subscription Rates:** $36 Individuals online/print; $49 Out of country online/print; $36 Individuals on-line; $24 Individuals 6 months, on-line/print; $31 Individuals 6 months, on-line/print; $24 Individuals 6 months, on-line. **URL:** http://www.newhampshirelakesandmountains.com/118968.113119body.lasso?publication=PLY. **Formerly**: Record Citizen; The Enterprise. **Ad Rates:** GLR $4; BW $326; 4C $726; SAU $4.35; PCI $4.90. **Remarks:** Accepts advertising. **Circ:** Combined ‡4,613.

MERRIMACK

SC NH. Hillsborough Co. On Merrimack River, 8 mi. N. of Nashua.

21081 ■ The Journal of Hypnotism
National Guild of Hypnotists
PO Box 308
Merrimack, NH 03054-0308
Phone: (603)429-9438
Fax: (603)424-8066
Publisher's E-mail: ngh@ngh.net
Journal containing studies on the field of hypnotism. **Freq:** Quarterly. **Subscription Rates:** Included in membership. **URL:** http://ngh.net/ngh-archives. **Remarks:** Accepts advertising. **Circ:** (Not Reported).

MILFORD

S. NH. Hillsboro Co. On Souhegan River, 11 mi. WNW of Nashua. Manufactures monuments, building granite, lumber, concrete. Diversified farming.

21082 ■ Bedford Journal
The Cabinet Press Inc.
54 School St.
Milford, NH 03055-0180
Phone: (603)673-3100
Fax: (603)673-8250
Publisher's E-mail: cabnews@cabinet.com
Community newspaper. **Freq:** Weekly (Fri.). **Print Method:** Web Offset. **Trim Size:** 12 3/4 x 22 1/4. **Key Personnel:** Phil Kincade, Managing Editor, phone: (603)594-6532. **Subscription Rates:** $51 Individuals in state; $59 Out of state; $98 Two years in state. **URL:** http://www.cabinet.com/cp/bedfordjournal. **Mailing address:** PO Box 180, Milford, NH 03055-0180. **Ad Rates:** 4C $125; PCI $19.15. **Remarks:** Accepts advertising. **Circ:** Combined ‡10700.

21083 ■ The Cabinet
The Cabinet Press Inc.
54 School St.
Milford, NH 03055-0180
Phone: (603)673-3100
Fax: (603)673-8250
Publisher's E-mail: cabnews@cabinet.com
Newspaper. **Freq:** Weekly (Thurs.). **Print Method:** Offset. **Trim Size:** 11.625 x 20.5. **Cols./Page:** 6. **Col. Width:** 26 nonpareils. **Col. Depth:** 294 agate lines. **Key Personnel:** Beth Eisenberg, Editor. **USPS:** 348-840. **Subscription Rates:** $51 Individuals in state, 1year; $59 Out of state 1 year; $98 Two years in state. **URL:** http://www.cabinet.com/cp/cabinet. **Formerly**: The Milford Cabinet & Wilton Journal. **Mailing address:** PO Box 180, Milford, NH 03055-0180. **Ad Rates:** PCI $19.15. **Remarks:** Accepts classified advertising. **Circ:** Paid ‡7,250.

21084 ■ Hollis Brookline Journal
The Cabinet Press Inc.
54 School St.
Milford, NH 03055-0180
Phone: (603)673-3100
Fax: (603)673-8250
Publisher's E-mail: cabnews@cabinet.com

Community newspaper. **Freq:** Weekly (Fri.). **Print Method:** Offset. **Trim Size:** 12 1/2 x 22 1/4. **Key Personnel:** Hatie Bernstein, Contact, phone: (603)673-3100; Phil Kincade, Managing Editor, phone: (603)594-6532. **Subscription Rates:** $51 Individuals 1 year - in state; $59 Out of state 1 year. **URL:** http://www.cabinet.com/cp/hollisbrooklinejournal. **Mailing address:** PO Box 180, Milford, NH 03055-0180. **Ad Rates:** BW $45; 4C $75. **Remarks:** Accepts advertising. **Circ:** ‡4700.

21085 ■ Merrimack Journal
The Cabinet Press Inc.
54 School St.
Milford, NH 03055-0180
Phone: (603)673-3100
Fax: (603)673-8250
Publisher's E-mail: cabnews@cabinet.com
Community newspaper. **Freq:** Weekly (Fri.). **Print Method:** Offset. **Key Personnel:** Phil Kincade, Executive Editor, phone: (603)594-6532. **Subscription Rates:** $51 Individuals 1 year; $59 Out of state 1 year. **URL:** http://www.cabinet.com/cp/merrimackjournal/. **Mailing address:** PO Box 180, Milford, NH 03055-0180. **Ad Rates:** PCI $18.25. **Remarks:** Accepts advertising. **Circ:** ‡9500.

NASHUA

Hillsborough Co. S. NH. Hillsboro Co. At junction of Nashua and Merrimack Rivers, near Massachusetts border, 22 mi. SW of Portsmouth. Rivier College, New Hampshire Vocational Technical College, Daniel Webster College, New England Aeronautical Institute. Manufactures lumber, wood and paper products, plastics, electronics, memorial tablets and grave markers, steel cabinets, rubber goods, chemicals, shoes. Shipping center.

21086 ■ Advanced Packaging
PennWell Corp., Advanced Technology Div.
98 Spit Brook Rd.
Nashua, NH 03062-5737
Phone: (603)891-0123
Fax: (603)891-9294
Free: 800-225-0556
Trade journal serving designers, fabricators, assemblers and suppliers in leading-edge electronic packaging technologies. **Freq:** Monthly. **Print Method:** Web Offset. **Trim Size:** 8 x 10 3/4. **Cols./Page:** 3. **Col. Width:** 2 1/8 inches. **Col. Depth:** 10 inches. **Key Personnel:** Peter Singer, Editor-in-Chief, Associate Publisher. **ISSN:** 1065-0555 (print). **Subscription Rates:** $258 Individuals; $360 Canada; $434 Other countries. **URL:** http://www.electroiq.com/index/packaging.html; http://www.pennwell.com/articles/2006/01/atd-organizational-changes.html. **Ad Rates:** BW $6950. **Remarks:** Accepts advertising. **Circ:** Controlled △**22,000**.

21087 ■ Cabling Installation & Maintenance: Solutions for Premises and Campus Communications Systems
PennWell Corp., Advanced Technology Div.
Publication E-mail: cim@halldata.com
Professional magazine focusing on copper-wire and fiber-optic cable systems. **Freq:** Monthly. **Print Method:** Web Offset. **Trim Size:** 8 x 10 3/4. **Cols./Page:** 2 and 3. **Col. Width:** 13 and 20 picas. **Col. Depth:** 57 picas. **Key Personnel:** Matt Vincent, Senior Editor, phone: (603)891-9262; Patrick McLaughlin, Editor-in-Chief, phone: (603)891-9222; Steven Smith, Executive Editor, phone: (603)891-9139. **ISSN:** 0741--5834 (print). **Subscription Rates:** $72 U.S. print; $84 Canada print; $104 Other countries print. **URL:** http://www.cablinginstall.com/index.html. **Remarks:** Accepts advertising. **Circ:** (Not Reported).

21088 ■ The Clubhouse
Boys & Girls Club of Greater Nashua
47 Grand Ave.
Nashua, NH 03060
Phone: (603)883-0523
Fax: (603)883-1074
Newspaper for the local Boys & Girls Club. **Freq:** Quarterly. **URL:** http://www.girlsandsports.com/clubhouse.php. **Remarks:** Accepts advertising. **Circ:** (Not Reported).

21089 ■ Industrial Laser Solutions
PennWell Corp., Advanced Technology Div.
98 Spit Brook Rd.
Nashua, NH 03062-5737
Phone: (603)891-0123
Fax: (603)891-9294
Free: 800-225-0556
Magazine reporting information on industrial laser solutions for manufacturing. **Freq:** Monthly. **Print Method:** Offset. **Trim Size:** 8 1/2 x 10 3/4. **Cols./Page:** 2. **Col. Width:** 42 nonpareils. **Col. Depth:** 152 agate lines. **Key Personnel:** David A. Belforte, Editor-in-Chief, Publisher, phone: (508)347-9324, fax: (508)347-7737. **ISSN:** 0888--935X (print). **Subscription Rates:** Free. **URL:** http://www.industrial-lasers.com/index.html. **Formerly**: Industrial Laser Review. **Ad Rates:** BW $6,345; 4C $7,445. **Remarks:** Accepts advertising. **Circ:** Paid 14296.

21090 ■ InfoStor
PennWell Corp., Advanced Technology Div.
98 Spit Brook Rd.
Nashua, NH 03062-5737
Phone: (603)891-0123
Fax: (603)891-9294
Free: 800-225-0556
Trade magazine covering storage products and technology for storage professionals. **Founded:** Oct. 1997. **Freq:** Monthly. **Trim Size:** tabloid. **Key Personnel:** David Simpson, Editor-in-Chief, phone: (949)715-9646, fax: (949)715-9761; James Maguire, Editor. **Subscription Rates:** $126 Individuals; $163 Canada; $200 Other countries; $152 Two years; $203 Canada 2 years; $252 Other countries 2 years; $215 Individuals 3 years; $284 Canada 3 years; $357 Other countries 3 years; $63 Individuals digital distribution. **URL:** http://www.infostor.com/. **Ad Rates:** 4C $3,000. **Remarks:** Accepts advertising. **Circ:** (Not Reported).

21091 ■ InfoStor Europe
PennWell Corp., Advanced Technology Div.
98 Spit Brook Rd.
Nashua, NH 03062-5737
Phone: (603)891-0123
Fax: (603)891-9294
Free: 800-225-0556
Publication covering information storage solutions in Europe. **Freq:** Quarterly. **Trim Size:** 20.75 x 12.625. **Key Personnel:** Kevin Komiega, Senior Editor, phone: (978)255-1510; David Simpson, Editor-in-Chief, phone: (818)484-5645. **URL:** http://www.infostor.com. **Remarks:** Accepts advertising. **Circ:** (Not Reported).

21092 ■ Laser Focus World: The Magazine for the Photonics and Optoelectronics Industry
PennWell Corp., Advanced Technology Div.
98 Spit Brook Rd.
Nashua, NH 03062-5737
Phone: (603)891-0123
Fax: (603)891-9294
Free: 800-225-0556
Magazine covering advances and applications in optoelectronics and photonics. **Freq:** Monthly. **Print Method:** Offset. **Trim Size:** 8 x 10 3/4. **Cols./Page:** 2. **Col. Width:** 30 nonpareils. **Col. Depth:** 140 agate lines. **Key Personnel:** Conard Holton, Associate Publisher, Editor-in-Chief; John Wallace, Senior Editor. **ISSN:** 0740--2511 (print). **Subscription Rates:** $162 Individuals; $216 Canada; $60 Individuals digital distribution; $270 Other countries. **URL:** http://www.laserfocusworld.com/index.html. **Formerly**: LASER FOCUS, The Magazine of Electro-optics Technology; PennWell Publishing Co. **Ad Rates:** BW $13,450; 4C $12,810. **Remarks:** Accepts advertising. **Circ:** △**70002**.

21093 ■ Lightwave: Fibre Optics Technology and Applications Worldwide
PennWell Corp., Advanced Technology Div.
98 Spit Brook Rd.
Nashua, NH 03062-5737
Phone: (603)891-0123
Fax: (603)891-9294
Free: 800-225-0556
An international publication covering fiber-optic communication technology and applications worldwide. **Freq:** Monthly. **Print Method:** Offset. **Trim Size:** 9 1/2 x 11 7/8. **Cols./Page:** 4. **Col. Width:** 2 3/4 inches. **Col. Depth:** 14 inches. **Key Personnel:** Carrie Meadows, Managing Editor, phone: (603)891-9382, fax: (603)891-0587; Stephen M. Hardy, Associate Publisher, Director, Editorial, phone: (603)891-9454; Meghan Fuller, Senior Editor, phone: (603)891-9327. **ISSN:** 0741--5834 (print). **URL:** http://www.lightwaveonline.com/index.html. **Ad Rates:** BW $1,960; 4C $2,650. **Remarks:** Accepts advertising. **Circ:** 37000.

21094 ■ Military & Aerospace Electronics: The Engineering Newspaper for the Worldwide Mil/Aero Electronics Industry
PennWell Corp., Advanced Technology Div.
98 Spit Brook Rd.
Nashua, NH 03062-5737
Phone: (603)891-0123
Fax: (603)891-9294
Free: 800-225-0556
Publication E-mail: ernestob@pennwell.com
Technical magazine. **Freq:** Monthly. **Print Method:** Web Offset. **Trim Size:** 10 3/4 x 13 15/16. **Key Personnel:** John Keller, Editor-in-Chief, phone: (603)891-9117, fax: (603)891-9146; Courtney E. Howard, Publisher, phone: (509)587-3344, fax: (509)587-3344. **Subscription Rates:** $175 U.S.; $270 Canada and Mexico; $325 Individuals; $465 Canada and Mexico 2 years; $620 Other countries 2 years; $440 Individuals 3 years; $600 Canada and Mexico 3 years; $810 Other countries 3 years. **URL:** http://www.militaryaerospace.com/index.html. **Ad Rates:** BW $9,185; 4C $14,700. **Remarks:** Accepts advertising. **Circ:** Combined △**37006**.

21095 ■ The Reiki Times
International Association of Reiki Professionals
PO Box 6182
Nashua, NH 03063-6182
Phone: (603)881-8838
Fax: (603)882-9088
Publisher's E-mail: info@iarp.org
Magazine featuring articles on Reiki. **Freq:** Quarterly. **Subscription Rates:** Included in membership. **URL:** http://www.iarpreiki.org/The_Reiki_Times_Magazine. **Remarks:** Advertising not accepted. **Circ:** (Not Reported).

21096 ■ Surface Mount Technology
PennWell Corp., Advanced Technology Div.
98 Spit Brook Rd.
Nashua, NH 03062-5737
Phone: (603)891-0123
Fax: (603)891-9294
Free: 800-225-0556
Periodical covering surface mount technology used in printed circuit board assembly. **Freq:** Monthly. **Key Personnel:** Lisa Lucke, Managing Editor; Meredith Courtemanche, Managing Editor, phone: (603)891-9176, fax: (603)891-9328; Gail Flower, Editor-in-Chief, phone: (603)203-0543, fax: (603)891-9328. **Subscription Rates:** $115 Canada; $215 Other countries. **URL:** http://www.ems007.com/pages/ems007.cgi. **Remarks:** Accepts advertising. **Circ:** (Not Reported).

21097 ■ Vision Systems Design
PennWell Corp., Advanced Technology Div.
98 Spit Brook Rd.
Nashua, NH 03062-5737
Phone: (603)891-0123
Fax: (603)891-9294
Free: 800-225-0556
Professional magazine for engineers, engineering managers, and corporate managers working for manufacturers and system integrators of vision and imaging systems. **Freq:** Monthly. **Key Personnel:** Andy Wilson, Editor-in-Chief, phone: (603)891-9115; David Wilson, Senior Editor. **Subscription Rates:** $130 Individuals; $148 Canada; $160 Out of country; $190 Two years; $217 Canada 2 years; $235 Other countries 2 years; $305 Other countries 3 years; $280 Canada 3 years; $244 Individuals 3 years; $66 Individuals digital distribution. **URL:** http://www.vision-systems.com. **Formerly**: Image Processing Europe. **Ad Rates:** BW $9,905; 4C $11,170. **Remarks:** Accepts advertising. **Circ:** △**32005**.

21098 ■ Woman Dentist Journal
PennWell Corp., Advanced Technology Div.
98 Spit Brook Rd.
Nashua, NH 03062-5737
Phone: (603)891-0123
Fax: (603)891-9294
Free: 800-225-0556

Circulation: ★ = AAM; △ or • = BPA; ♦ = CAC; ❑ = VAC; ⊕ = PO Statement; ‡ = Publisher's Report; Boldface figures = sworn; Light figures = estimated.

Magazine of the American Association of Women Dentists. **Key Personnel:** Sheri Doniger, Editor. **URL:** http://www.dentistryiq.com/articles/de/2003/02/pennwell-announces-new-magazine-woman-dentist-journal.html. **Remarks:** Accepts advertising. **Circ:** (Not Reported).

21099 ■ Woman Dentist Journal
PennWell Corp., Advanced Technology Div.
98 Spit Brook Rd.
Nashua, NH 03062-5737
Phone: (603)891-0123
Fax: (603)891-9294
Free: 800-225-0556
Magazine of the American Association of Women Dentists. **Key Personnel:** Sheri Doniger, Editor. **URL:** http://www.wdjournal.com/index.html. **Remarks:** Accepts advertising. **Circ:** (Not Reported).

21100 ■ Mangosoft Inc. - 90.7
15 Pine St.
Nashua, NH 03060
Format: Religious. **Owner:** American Family Radio, PO Box 3206, Tupelo, MS 38803, Ph: (662)844-5036, Fax: (662)842-7798. **Operating Hours:** Continuous. **URL:** http://www.mangosoft.com.

21101 ■ Vision Systems
98 Spit Brook Rd.
Nashua, NH 03062
Email: info@visionsystems.tv
Cities Served: 61 channels. **URL:** http://www.visionsystems.com.

21102 ■ WHOB-FM - 106.3
55 Lake St.
Nashua, NH 03060
Phone: (603)889-1063
Fax: (603)882-0688
Email: whob@xtdl.com
Format: Alternative/New Music/Progressive. **Networks:** Independent. **Owner:** Gateway Broadcasting, Inc., at above address. **Founded:** 1987. **Formerly:** WOTW-FM. **Operating Hours:** Continuous; 100% local. **Key Personnel:** Stephen Roberts, Gen. Mgr., steve@whob.com. **Wattage:** 3,000. **Ad Rates:** $35-70 per unit.

21103 ■ WSMN-AM - 1590
141 MAIN St.
Nashua, NH 03060
Phone: (603)880-9001
Fax: (603)577-8682
Format: Talk; News. **Owner:** Absolute Broadcasting, at above address. **Founded:** 1958. **Operating Hours:** Continuous; 50% local, 50% network. **Wattage:** 5,000. **Ad Rates:** $7-16 for 10 seconds; $9-24 for 30 seconds; $12-30 for 60 seconds. **URL:** http://www.wsmnradio.com.

21104 ■ WYCN-TV - 13
20 Industrial Park Dr.
Box 85
Nashua, NH 03060
Phone: (603)883-7435
Email: info@tv13nashua.com
Key Personnel: Carolyn Choate, Program Mgr. **URL:** http://www.tv13nashua.com.

NEW DURHAM

WSEW-FM - See Sanford, ME

NEW LONDON

21105 ■ WNTK-AM - 1020
PO Box 2295
New London, NH 03257
Phone: (603)448-0500
Fax: (603)448-6601
Email: info@wntk.com
Format: Talk. **Simulcasts:** WNTK-FM 99.7. **Networks:** ABC; Mutual Broadcasting System; Major Market Radio. **Owner:** KOOR Communications, PO Box 2295, New London, NH 03257. **Founded:** 1960. **Operating Hours:** 5 a.m.- 9 p.m. **Ad Rates:** $14-25 for 60 seconds. **URL:** http://www.wntk.com/contact.php.

21106 ■ WNTK-FM - 99.7
PO Box 2295
New London, NH 03257
Phone: (603)448-0500
Email: info@wntk.com
Format: Talk; Classical. **Simulcasts:** WNTK-AM. **Networks:** Mutual Broadcasting System; ABC; Major Market Radio. **Owner:** Sheila E. Vinikoor, 297 Beaver Meadow Rd., Norwich, VT 05055-9456. **Founded:** 1992. **Operating Hours:** Continuous. **Local Programs:** *Twin State Journal*, Saturday 8:00 a.m. - 9:00 a.m.; *Steve Malzberg Show*, Saturday Sunday 10:00 p.m. - 12:00 a.m. 9:00 p.m. - 10:00 p.m. **Wattage:** 3,000 ERP. **Ad Rates:** Noncommercial. $14-25 for 60 seconds. **URL:** http://www.wntk.com.

21107 ■ WSCS-FM - 90.9
541 Main St.
New London, NH 03257
Phone: (603)526-3000
Email: helpdesk@colby-sawyer.edu
Format: Educational. **Networks:** AP. **Owner:** Colby-Sawyer College, 541 Main St., New London, NH 03257, Ph: (603)526-3000. **Founded:** 1996. **Operating Hours:** 8:00 a.m.-1:00 a.m. **ADI:** Hartford-New Haven (New London), CT. **Wattage:** 250. **Ad Rates:** Noncommercial. **URL:** http://www.colby-sawyer.edu/wscs.

NEWMARKET

21108 ■ Lotus Realm
Triratna Buddhist Community
Aryaloka Buddhist Ctre.
14 Heartwood Cir.
Newmarket, NH 03857
Phone: (603)659-5456
Free: 800-630-3610
Publisher's E-mail: info@thebuddhistcentre.com
Freq: Quarterly. **Subscription Rates:** $15 /year. **Remarks:** Advertising not accepted. **Circ:** (Not Reported).

NORTH CONWAY

E. NH. Carroll Co. On Saco River, 29 mi. S. of Berlin. Mountain resort. Lumber; crafts.

21109 ■ The Conway Daily Sun
The Conway Daily Sun
PO Box 1940
North Conway, NH 03860
Phone: (603)356-3456
Fax: (603)356-8774
Publisher's E-mail: news@conwaydailysun.com
General newspaper. **Freq:** Daily. **Trim Size:** 10.25 x 13.5. **Cols./Page:** 6. **Col. Width:** 13.5 inches. **Col. Depth:** 13 1/2 inches. **Key Personnel:** Adam Hirshan, Founder; Mark Guerringue, Publisher; Bart Bachman, Editor. **URL:** http://www.conwaydailysun.com. **Ad Rates:** PCI $7. **Remarks:** Accepts advertising. **Circ:** 16100.

PETERBOROUGH

S. NH. Hillsboro Co. 28 mi. WNW of Nashua. MacDowell Artists Colony. Apple orchards.

21110 ■ Appleseeds
Cobblestone Publishing Co.
30 Grove St., Ste. C
Peterborough, NH 03458-1453
Publisher's E-mail: customerservice@caruspub.com
Educational, consumer magazine for children ages 7-9. **Freq:** 9/year. **Trim Size:** 7 x 19. **Key Personnel:** Steve O'Meara, Editor. **URL:** http://shop.cricketmedia.com/appleseeds.html. **Remarks:** Advertising not accepted. **Circ:** (Not Reported).

21111 ■ Ask: Arts and Sciences for Kids
Carus Publishing
30 Grove St., Ste. C
Peterborough, NH 03458
Phone: (603)924-7209
Free: 800-821-0115
Publisher's E-mail: customerservice@caruspub.com
Magazine contains articles for children ages 7-10 with features on science, history, technology, and the arts. **Freq:** 9/year. **ISSN:** 1535--4105 (print). **Subscription Rates:** $33.95 Individuals print; $9.99 Individuals digital; $39.95 Individuals print & digital. **URL:** http://shop.cricketmedia.com/magazines/ASK-Magazine-for-Kids.html?_ga=1.43441185.508296603.1470360174. **Remarks:** Accepts advertising. **Circ:** (Not Reported).

21112 ■ Babybug
The Cricket Magazine Group
30 Grove St., Ste. C
Peterborough, NH 03458
Free: 800-821-0115
Publisher's E-mail: donations@cricketmedia.com
Magazine featuring children's literature. **Freq:** 9/yr. **Trim Size:** 6 1/4 x 7. **Key Personnel:** Marianne Carus, Editor-in-Chief. **ISSN:** 1077--1131 (print). **Subscription Rates:** $33.95 Individuals; $17.99 Individuals digital; $39.95 Individuals print and digital. **URL:** http://www.cricketmag.com/BBB-BABYBUG-Magazine-for-Babies-6mo-3yrs. **Remarks:** Advertising not accepted. **Circ:** (Not Reported).

21113 ■ Babybug
Cricket Media, Inc.
13625A Dulles Technology Dr.
Herndon, VA 20171
Phone: (703)885-3400
Publisher's E-mail: donations@cricketmedia.com
Magazine featuring children's literature. **Freq:** 9/yr. **Trim Size:** 6 1/4 x 7. **Key Personnel:** Marianne Carus, Editor-in-Chief. **ISSN:** 1077--1131 (print). **Subscription Rates:** $33.95 Individuals; $17.99 Individuals digital; $39.95 Individuals print and digital. **URL:** http://www.cricketmag.com/BBB-BABYBUG-Magazine-for-Babies-6mo-3yrs. **Remarks:** Advertising not accepted. **Circ:** (Not Reported).

21114 ■ Cobblestone: Discover American History
Cobblestone Publishing Co.
30 Grove St., Ste. C
Peterborough, NH 03458-1453
Publisher's E-mail: donations@cricketmedia.com
Magazine on American history for ages 8-14. **Freq:** 9/year. **Print Method:** Offset. **Trim Size:** 7 x 9. **Cols./Page:** 2. **Key Personnel:** Meg Chorlian, Editor. **ISSN:** 0199--5197 (print). **Subscription Rates:** $43.95 Individuals 1 year print + 10 web-based; $58.95 Single issue 1 year print + 25 web-based. **Remarks:** Advertising not accepted. **Circ:** (Not Reported).

21115 ■ Cricket Magazine
Carus Publishing
30 Grove St., Ste. C
Peterborough, NH 03458
Phone: (603)924-7209
Free: 800-821-0115
Publisher's E-mail: customerservice@caruspub.com
Literary magazine for children, ages 9-14. **Freq:** 9/year. **Print Method:** Offset. **Trim Size:** 8 x 10. **Key Personnel:** Marianne Carus, Editor-in-Chief; Lonnie Plecha, Editor. **ISSN:** 0090--6034 (print). **Subscription Rates:** $33.95 Individuals print; $17.99 Individuals digital; $51.90 Individuals print and digital; $9.99 Individuals. **URL:** http://www.cricketmag.com. **Formerly:** Cricket, the Magazine for Children. **Remarks:** Advertising not accepted. **Circ:** Paid ‡75000.

21116 ■ Ladybug: The Magazine for Young Children
The Cricket Magazine Group
30 Grove St., Ste. C
Peterborough, NH 03458
Free: 800-821-0115
Publisher's E-mail: customerservice@caruspub.com
Magazine of ideas, adventures and activities for children ages 2 to 6. **Freq:** 9/yr. **Print Method:** Offset. **Trim Size:** 8 x 10. **Key Personnel:** Jason Patenaude, Chief Financial Officer. **ISSN:** 1051-4961 (print). **Subscription Rates:** $33.95 Individuals print; $17.99 Individuals online; $51.90 Individuals print and online. **URL:** http://www.cricketmag.com/LYB-LADYBUG-Magazine-for-Kids-ages-3-6. **Remarks:** Advertising not accepted. **Circ:** Paid ‡130000.

21117 ■ The Monadnock Ledger-Transcript
The Monadnock Ledger
20 Grove St.
Peterborough, NH 03458
Phone: (603)924-7172
Fax: (603)924-3681
Free: 800-621-9152
Publisher's E-mail: news@ledgertranscript.com
Community newspaper. **Freq:** Weekly. **Key Personnel:** Heather McKernan, Publisher; Steve Leone, Editor; Jonathan Gourlay, Editor. **USPS:** 358-540. **Subscription Rates:** $69 Individuals 104 issues - 1 year; $99 Out of state 104 issues - 1 year; $59 Individuals digital only. **URL:** http://www.ledgertranscript.com. **Formerly:** The Monadnock Ledger. **Mailing address:** PO Box 36, Peterborough, NH 03458. **Ad Rates:** GLR $2.25; BW

$945; 4C $1120; SAU $8.50; PCI $9.75. **Remarks:** Accepts advertising. **Circ:** (Not Reported).

21118 ■ Odyssey: Adventures in Science
Cobblestone Publishing Co.
30 Grove St., Ste. C
Peterborough, NH 03458-1453
Publication E-mail: blindstrom@caruspub.com
Magazine on science and technology for children ages 10-16. **Print Method:** Offset. **Trim Size:** 7 x 9. **Cols./Page:** 3 and 2. **Col. Width:** 13 and 20 picas. **Col. Depth:** 9 3/4 inches. **Key Personnel:** Beth Lindstrom, Senior Editor. **ISSN:** 0163--0946 (print). **Subscription Rates:** $17.99 Individuals digital /year; $33.95 Individuals print /year; $51.90 Individuals print and digital /year. **URL:** http://www.odysseymagazine.com. **Remarks:** Advertising not accepted. **Circ:** 28000.

21119 ■ Spider: The Magazine for Children
Carus Publishing
30 Grove St., Ste. C
Peterborough, NH 03458
Phone: (603)924-7209
Free: 800-821-0115
Publisher's E-mail: customerservice@caruspub.com
Magazine of stories, games, and projects for children ages 6 to 9. **Freq:** 9/year. **Trim Size:** 8 x 10. **Key Personnel:** Marianne Carus, Editor-in-Chief. **ISSN:** 1070-2911 (print). **Subscription Rates:** $33.95 Individuals print only; $9.99 Individuals digital only; $39.95 Individuals print and digital; $59.95 Two years print only. **URL:** http://shop.cricketmedia.com/magazines/SPIDER-Magazine-for-Kids.html. **Remarks:** Accepts advertising. **Circ:** Paid 80000.

PLYMOUTH

WC NH. Grafton Co. On Pemigewasset River, 30 mi. E. of Hanover. Plymouth State College. Resort. Manufactures textiles, wood products, electronics. Fruit, poultry, dairy farms.

21120 ■ Hawk Migration Studies
Hawk Migration Association of North America
PO Box 721
Plymouth, NH 03264
Publisher's E-mail: info@hmana.org
Journal publishing regional reports on the migration from across North America as well as articles on hawks, hawk identification, hawk watching and more. **Freq:** Semiannual. **URL:** http://www.hmana.org/hawk-migration-studies. **Remarks:** Advertising not accepted. **Circ:** 500.

21121 ■ The Penny Saver
The Pennysaver Inc.
607 Tenney Mountain Hwy.
Village Sq., Ste. 137
Plymouth, NH 03264
Publisher's E-mail: classifieds@pennysavernh.com
Shopper. **Founded:** Dec. 15, 1971. **Freq:** Weekly (Tues.). **Print Method:** Offset. **Cols./Page:** 6. **Col. Width:** 18 nonpareils. **Col. Depth:** 224 agate lines. **Subscription Rates:** Free. **URL:** http://www.pennysavernh.com. **Ad Rates:** PCI $6.40. **Remarks:** Accepts classified advertising. **Circ:** Free 18,000.

21122 ■ WPCR-FM - 91.7
17 High St.
Plymouth State College
Plymouth, NH 03264
Phone: (603)535-3030
Owner: Plymouth State College, 17 High St., Plymouth, NH. **Founded:** 1968. **Operating Hours:** Continuous. **Wattage:** 215 ERP. **Ad Rates:** Accepts Advertising. **URL:** http://www.wpcr.org.

PORTSMOUTH

Rockingham Co. SE NH. Rockingham Co. On Piscataqua River, 3 mi. from Atlantic Ocean. Bridge to Kittery, ME. Only commercial seaport of the state. Summer resort. Manufactures machine tools, electronic components, plastics, buttons, gypsum products. Lobster fisheries. U.S. Navy Yard on nearby Seavy's Island; Pease Air Force Base 2 mi. W.

21123 ■ Clinical and Applied Immunology Reviews
Association of Medical Laboratory Immunologists
40 Prospect St.
Portsmouth, NH 03801
Phone: (603)610-7766
Fax: (603)610-7288
Freq: Bimonthly. **ISSN:** 1529--1049 (print). **URL:** http://www.amli.org/about_history.php; http://www.elsevier.com/journals/clinical-and-applied-immunology-reviews/1529-1049. **Remarks:** Advertising not accepted. **Circ:** (Not Reported).

21124 ■ Exeter News-Letter
Seacoast Newspapers Inc.
111 New Hampshire Ave.
Portsmouth, NH 03801
Phone: (603)436-1800
Fax: (603)433-5760
Free: 800-439-0303
Publisher's E-mail: newsletter@seacoastonline.com
Community newspaper. **Freq:** every Tues., Fri., Sunday. **Print Method:** Offset. **Trim Size:** 15 3/16 x 21. **Cols./Page:** 6. **Col. Width:** 21.5 picas. **Key Personnel:** John Tabor, Publisher; Kelvin Parker, Director, Operations, Manager, Circulation; Howard Altschiller, Executive Editor. **ISSN:** 0886-3962 (print). **USPS:** 182-600. **Subscription Rates:** $116.09 Individuals; $61.10 Individuals 26 weeks; $30.55 Individuals 13 weeks; $8.95 Individuals per month. **URL:** http://www.seacoastonline.com/ExeterNewsLetter. **Remarks:** Accepts advertising. **Circ:** ‡5,875.

21125 ■ The Hampton Union
Seacoast Newspapers Inc.
111 New Hampshire Ave.
Portsmouth, NH 03801
Phone: (603)436-1800
Fax: (603)433-5760
Free: 800-439-0303
Publisher's E-mail: newsletter@seacoastonline.com
Community newspaper. **Freq:** Semiweekly Tues. and Fri. **Print Method:** Offset. **Trim Size:** 15 3/16 x 21. **Cols./Page:** 6. **Col. Width:** 2 1/16 ems. **Col. Depth:** 21 inches. **Key Personnel:** Howard Altschiller, Executive Editor; John Tabor, President, Publisher; Kelvin Parker, Manager, Circulation. **USPS:** 234-120. **Subscription Rates:** $116.09 Individuals; $61.10 Individuals 26 weeks; $30.50 Individuals 13 weeks; $8.95 Individuals per month. **URL:** http://www.seacoastonline.com/HamptonUnion. **Ad Rates:** GLR $.90; BW $1418; 4C $1763; SAU $11.25; PCI $11.25. **Remarks:** Accepts advertising. **Circ:** ‡4,915.

21126 ■ Portsmouth Herald
Portsmouth Herald
111 New Hampshire Ave.
Portsmouth, NH 03801
Fax: (603)433-5760
Free: 800-439-0303
Publisher's E-mail: news@seacoastonline.com
General newspaper. **Freq:** Daily. **Print Method:** Offset. **Trim Size:** 14 3/4 x 22 3/4. **Cols./Page:** 6. **Col. Width:** 2 1/16 inches. **Col. Depth:** 301 agate lines. **Key Personnel:** Howard Altschiller, Executive Editor, phone: (603)570-2202; John Tabor, Publisher, President, phone: (603)570-2100. **ISSN:** 0746--6218 (print). **Subscription Rates:** $238.95 Individuals 7 days (EZ pay); $192.15 Individuals 6 days (EZ pay); $212.95 Individuals Thursday to Sunday; $108.95 Individuals Sunday only. **URL:** http://www.seacoastonline.com/portsmouthherald. **Ad Rates:** PCI $20.20. **Remarks:** Accepts advertising. **Circ:** Mon.-Sat. ★**15,001**.

21127 ■ WERZ-FM - 107.1
815 Layfayette Rd.
Portsmouth, NH 03801
Phone: (603)436-7300
Fax: (603)430-9415
Free: 888-666-1071
Format: Contemporary Hit Radio (CHR). **Networks:** Independent. **Owner:** iHeartMedia and Entertainment Inc. , 200 E Basse Rd., San Antonio, TX 78209, Ph: (210)822-2828. **Operating Hours:** Continuous. **ADI:** Boston-Worcester,MA-Derry-Manchester,NH. **Wattage:** 6,000. **Ad Rates:** Advertising accepted; rates available upon request. Combined advertising rates available with WMYF-AM. **URL:** http://www.z107fm.com.

21128 ■ WGIN-AM - 930
815 LaFayette Rd.
Portsmouth, NH 03801
Phone: (603)436-7300
Fax: (603)430-9415
Format: News; Talk. **Owner:** iHeartMedia Inc., 200 E Basse Rd., San Antonio, TX 78209, Ph: (210)832-3314. **Operating Hours:** Continuous. **Wattage:** 5,000. **Ad Rates:** Noncommercial. **URL:** http://www.wmyf.com.

21129 ■ WHEB-FM - 100.3
815 Lafayette Rd.
Portsmouth, NH 03801
Phone: (603)436-7300
Fax: (603)430-9415
Format: Album-Oriented Rock (AOR). **Networks:** Independent. **Founded:** 1959. **Operating Hours:** Continuous; 100% local. **Wattage:** 50,000. **Ad Rates:** Noncommercial. **URL:** http://www.wheb.com.

21130 ■ WMYF-AM - 1380
815 Layfayette Rd.
Portsmouth, NH 03801
Phone: (603)436-7300
Fax: (603)430-9415
Format: Big Band/Nostalgia. **URL:** http://www.wmyf.com.

21131 ■ WQSO-FM - 96.7
815 Layfayette Rd.
Portsmouth, NH 03801
Phone: (603)436-7300
Fax: (603)430-9415
Free: 866-967-9283
Email: jefferypierce@clearchannel.com
Format: Oldies. **URL:** http://www.newsradio967.com.

21132 ■ WSKX-FM - 95.3
815 Layfayette Rd.
Portsmouth, NH 03801
Phone: (603)436-7300
Fax: (603)430-9415
Format: Top 40. **Key Personnel:** Jeff Pierce, Dir. of Programs, jefferypierce@clearchannel.com; Elizabeth Tretter, Promotions Dir., elizabethtretter@clearchannel.com. **URL:** http://www.z107fm.com.

21133 ■ WTMN-AM - 1380
PO Box 150
Portsmouth, NH 03802
Phone: (603)430-9500
Fax: (603)430-9501
Format: Sports. **Owner:** Knight Quality Stations, at above address. **Founded:** 1963. **Formerly:** WBBX-AM; WAVI-AM; WQMI-AM. **Operating Hours:** Continuous; 100% network. **ADI:** Boston-Worcester,MA-Derry-Manchester,NH. **Key Personnel:** Robert A. Knight, Gen. Mgr.; Glenn Stewart, Dir. of Programs; Shari Soffen, Sales Mgr. **Wattage:** 1,000.

WXHT-FM - See York Center, ME

RAYMOND

21134 ■ Slope
Slope Publishing Inc.
Five State, Rte. 27
Raymond, NH 03077
Publisher's E-mail: info@slope.org
Journal dedicated to poetry. **Key Personnel:** Ethan Paquin, Editor, Founder; Lucas Farrell, Editor. **ISSN:** 1536-0164 (print). **URL:** http://www.slope.org/. **Circ:** (Not Reported).

RINDGE

21135 ■ WFPR-AM - 640
Franklin Pierce College, 40 University Dr.
College Rd.
Rindge, NH 03461-0060
Phone: (603)899-4000
Fax: (603)899-4394
Format: Alternative/New Music/Progressive. **Key Personnel:** Mike Waterbury, Music Dir. **Ad Rates:** Noncommercial. **URL:** http://www.franklinpierce.edu.

ROCHESTER

Strafford Co. SE NH. Strafford Co. On Cocheco River, 18 mi. NW of Portsmouth. Manufactures paper, wooden boxes, fiber board, textiles. Dairy, poultry, fruit farms. Apples.

Circulation: ★ = AAM; △ or • = BPA; ♦ = CAC; ❑ = VAC; ⊕ = PO Statement; ‡ = Publisher's Report; Boldface figures = sworn; Light figures = estimated.

21136 ■ MetroCast Cablevision
21 Jarvis Ave.
Rochester, NH 03868
Phone: (603)332-5466
Fax: (603)335-4106
Free: 800-952-1001
Email: marketing@metrocast.com
Founded: 1998. **Cities Served:** 96 channels. **URL:** http://www.metrocast.com.

21137 ■ WSRI-FM - 96.7
PO Box 130
Rochester, NH 03866
Phone: (603)332-0930
Fax: (603)332-0800
Free: 800-649-9670
Email: radio967wnh@ultranet.com
Format: Alternative/New Music/Progressive. **Networks:** ABC; Westwood One Radio. **Founded:** 1949. **Formerly**: WKOS-FM. **Operating Hours:** Continuous. **Key Personnel:** Al Perry, Gen. Mgr., VP; Teresa Robles, Gen. Sales Mgr.; Chip Davis, Asst. Dir.; Jack O'Brien, Contact; Jack O'Brien, Contact. **Wattage**: 3,000.

SALEM

SE NH. Rockingham Co. Near Massachusetts border, 12 mi. E. of Nashua.

21138 ■ WNNW-AM - 1110
PO Box 1110
Salem, NH 03079
Phone: (603)894-1110
Format: Hispanic. **Networks:** CNN Radio; UPI. **Founded:** 1977. **Formerly**: WVNH-AM. **Operating Hours**: Sunrise-sunset. **Key Personnel:** Pat Costa, Gen. Mgr.; Luis Pena, News Dir.; Bob Perry, Chief Engineer. **Wattage**: 5,000.

WEST LEBANON

21139 ■ WHDQ-FM - 106.1
106 N Main
West Lebanon, NH 03784
Free: 800-639-1061
Format: Classic Rock. **Owner:** Nassau Broadcasting, 619 Alexander Rd., 3rd Fl., Princeton, NJ 08540. **Founded:** 1948. **Formerly**: WECM-FM. **Operating Hours**: Continuous. **ADI**: Boston-Worcester,MA-Derry-Manchester,NH. **Wattage**: 50,000. **Ad Rates:** Noncommercial. **URL:** http://www.theqrocks.com.

21140 ■ WWOD-FM - 104.3
106 N Main St.
West Lebanon, NH 03784
Phone: (603)298-7444
Fax: (603)727-0134
Format: Oldies. **Owner:** Nassau Broadcasting, 619 Alexander Rd., 3rd Fl., Princeton, NJ 08540. **Key Personnel:** Matt Houseman, Dir. of Programs, mhouseman@nassaubroadcasting.com; Ken Webbley, Contact, kwebbley@nassaubroadcasting.com. **URL:** http://www.nassaubroadcasting.com.

21141 ■ WXLF-FM - 107.1
106 N Main
West Lebanon, NH 03784
Format: Country. **Key Personnel:** Massimo Rosati, Gen. Mgr.; Scott Laudani, Operations Mgr.; Mike Trombly, Gen. Mgr., mtrombly@nassaubroadcasting.com. **URL:** http://www.953thewolf.com.

21142 ■ WZLF-FM - 95.3
106 N Main
West Lebanon, NH 03784
Phone: (603)298-0332
Fax: (603)727-0134
Format: Country. **Key Personnel:** Mike Trombly, Gen. Mgr., mtrombly@nassaubroadcasting.com.

WINCHESTER

21143 ■ WKBK-AM - 1290
69 Stanhope Ave.
Keene, NH 03431
Phone: (603)352-9230
Fax: (603)357-3926
Format: News; Talk. **Networks:** Canadian Broadcasting Corporation (CBC)/Societe Radio-Canada (SRC). **Owner:** Roberts Communications Inc., 64 Commercial St., Rochester, NY 14614. **Founded:** 1959. **ADI:** Boston-Worcester,MA-Derry-Manchester,NH. **Key Personnel:** Dan Mitchell, Dir. of Programs; Brent Myers, Sales Mgr. **Wattage**: 5,000. **Ad Rates:** $20-25 for 60 seconds. $9-$18 for 30 seconds; $11-$22 for 60 seconds. Combined advertising rates available with WOQL-FM. **URL:** http://wkbkradio.com/contact.

21144 ■ WXOD-FM - 98.7
69 Stanhope Ave.
Keene, NH 03431
Phone: (603)352-0037
Fax: (603)357-3926
Email: info@wkbkwxod.com
Format: Oldies. **Owner:** Roberts Communications Inc., 64 Commercial St., Rochester, NY 14614. **Founded:** 1991. **Formerly**: WKBK-FM. **Operating Hours**: Continuous. **Key Personnel:** Scott Roberts, President; Ira Wilner, Chief Engineer; Brent Myers, Gen. Mgr.; Jim Gold, Asst. Mgr., Gen. Mgr; A.J. Ca, Contact; A.J. Ca, Contact. **Wattage**: 6,000. **Ad Rates:** $25-30 for 60 seconds. $11-$23 for 30 seconds; $14-$29 for 60 seconds. Combined advertising rates available with WKBK-AM. **URL:** http://987wink.com.

21145 ■ WYRY-FM - 104.9
30 Warwick Rd., Ste. 10
Winchester, NH 03470
Phone: (603)239-8200
Fax: (603)239-6203
Free: 800-905-8020
Format: Contemporary Country. **Networks:** Independent. **Owner:** Tri Valley Broadcasting Corp., 95 Market St., Manchester, NH 03101-1933. **Founded:** 1987. **Operating Hours**: Continuous; 100% local. **Wattage**: 3,000. **Ad Rates:** Advertising accepted; rates available upon request. **URL:** http://www.wyry.com.

WOLFEBORO

EC NH. Carroll Co. On Lake Winnipesaukee, 37 mi. NW of Concord. Resort area. Lake port.

21146 ■ WASR-AM - 1420
PO Box 900
Wolfeboro, NH 03894-0900
Phone: (603)569-1420
Fax: (603)569-1900
Email: mail@wasr.net
Format: News; Middle-of-the-Road (MOR). **Networks:** ABC; AP. **Owner:** Winnepasaukee Network Inc., at above address. **Founded:** 1970. **Operating Hours**: 5:05 a.m. - 6:05 p.m.; 10% network, 90% local. **Wattage**: 5,000. **Ad Rates:** $9.60-25.60 for 30 seconds; $12-32 for 60 seconds. **URL:** http://www.wasr.net.

WOLFEBORO FALLS

21147 ■ Granite State News
Salmon Press
Clarke Plz.
Wolfeboro Falls, NH 03896
Publisher's E-mail: info@tiltontrailer.com
Newspaper. **Founded:** 1859. **Freq:** Weekly (Thurs.). **Print Method:** Offset. **Cols./Page:** 6. **Col. Width:** 26 nonpareils. **Col. Depth:** 294 agate lines. **Key Personnel:** Frank Chilinski, Publisher; Thomas Beeler, Editor, phone: (603)569-3126. **Subscription Rates:** $36 Individuals in county; $49 Individuals out of county. **URL:** http://www.newhampshirelakesandmountains.com/CallPage-8014.113119-Contact-Us.html. **Circ:** Combined ‡4,650.